A BARNES & NOBLE BOOK

TV Guide® and TV Guide & Design®
are registered trademarks of
TV Guide Magazine Group, Inc. and used with permission.
©2005 TV Guide Magazine Group, Inc.

ISBN 0-7607-7395-5

Cover design: Tom McKeveny
Cover image: Digital Vision/Punchstock
Typesetting: Scribe, Inc. (www.scribenet.com)

Printed in the U.S.A.

1 3 5 7 9 10 8 6 4 2

CONTENTS

CONTENTS

PREFACE

Welcome to the fourth edition of the *TV Guide Film and Video Companion*!

Perhaps you're wondering why you need another film guide. What makes us special is that we don't include every movie ever released—the good, the bad, and the just plain crappy—because you probably don't want to *see* every movie ever released. We've chosen movies we think matter, nearly 3,500 films we consider outstanding achievements of world cinema, important examples of a particular genre or movies with some special cultural or historical significance. We've also included a bunch of films we love because they're just plain fun. And since we've narrowed our focus, we can include much more information than other film guides: Our plot synopses are longer, our critiques go deeper, and each entry lists up to 10 actors with the names of their characters and extensive cast and crew credits.

As we do every year, we've added the most noteworthy films released since the previous volume, from foreign treasures like *Bad Education* to such Hollywood blockbusters as *Spider-Man II* and *Star Wars III: Revenge of the Sith*. We've also updated our comprehensive actors index, so you can search for movies by your favorite star, as well as our directors index, which features filmographies for notable directors whose films are included in this edition. Want to know which titles we consider to be the best (or the worst)? Check our star rating index, which lists titles according to our zero-to-five star scale.

These reviews were selected and condensed from the nearly 42,000 entries in CineBooks' landmark movie database, now available as a fully searchable Internet resource on TVGuide.com (http://www.tvguide.com/movies). If you're really into movies—and if you're reading this, we suspect you are—please explore the rest of our movie features. Get our daily recommendations on what to see in theaters or what to watch on TV, or Ask FlickChick (a.k.a. Maitland) your movie-related questions. You'll also find the latest DVD releases, weekly box-office grosses, and what's coming up in theaters.

Thanks for picking up the *Companion*. We value your input, and hope you'll send comments and suggestions to:

www.tvguide.com/services/feedback/online/contactus.asp, or:
TVGuide.com
1211 Avenue of the Americas, 4th Floor
New York, NY 10036

Sincerely,

Ken Fox and Maitland McDonagh
New York City
July 2005

HOW TO USE THIS BOOK

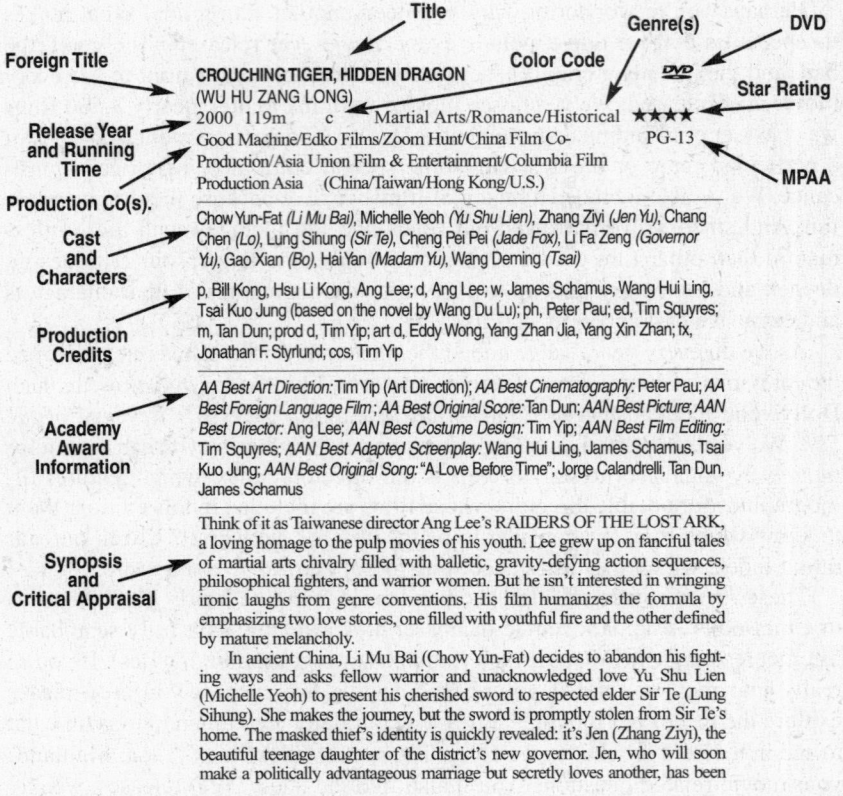

Title

Genre(s)

DVD

Foreign Title

Color Code

Star Rating

Release Year and Running Time

Production Co(s).

MPAA

Cast and Characters

Production Credits

Academy Award Information

Synopsis and Critical Appraisal

CROUCHING TIGER, HIDDEN DRAGON
(WU HU ZANG LONG)
2000 119m   c   Martial Arts/Romance/Historical ★★★★
Good Machine/Edko Films/Zoom Hunt/China Film Co-   PG-13
Production/Asia Union Film & Entertainment/Columbia Film
Production Asia   (China/Taiwan/Hong Kong/U.S.)

Chow Yun-Fat *(Li Mu Bai)*, Michelle Yeoh *(Yu Shu Lien)*, Zhang Ziyi *(Jen Yu)*, Chang Chen *(Lo)*, Lung Sihung *(Sir Te)*, Cheng Pei Pei *(Jade Fox)*, Li Fa Zeng *(Governor Yu)*, Gao Xian *(Bo)*, Hai Yan *(Madam Yu)*, Wang Deming *(Tsai)*

p, Bill Kong, Hsu Li Kong, Ang Lee; d, Ang Lee; w, James Schamus, Wang Hui Ling, Tsai Kuo Jung (based on the novel by Wang Du Lu); ph, Peter Pau; ed, Tim Squyres; m, Tan Dun; prod d, Tim Yip; art d, Eddy Wong, Yang Zhan Jia, Yang Xin Zhan; fx, Jonathan F. Styrlund; cos, Tim Yip

AA Best Art Direction: Tim Yip (Art Direction); *AA Best Cinematography:* Peter Pau; *AA Best Foreign Language Film* ; *AA Best Original Score:* Tan Dun; *AAN Best Picture; AAN Best Director:* Ang Lee; *AAN Best Costume Design:* Tim Yip; *AAN Best Film Editing:* Tim Squyres; *AAN Best Adapted Screenplay:* Wang Hui Ling, James Schamus, Tsai Kuo Jung; *AAN Best Original Song:* "A Love Before Time"; Jorge Calandrelli, Tan Dun, James Schamus

Think of it as Taiwanese director Ang Lee's RAIDERS OF THE LOST ARK, a loving homage to the pulp movies of his youth. Lee grew up on fanciful tales of martial arts chivalry filled with balletic, gravity-defying action sequences, philosophical fighters, and warrior women. But he isn't interested in wringing ironic laughs from genre conventions. His film humanizes the formula by emphasizing two love stories, one filled with youthful fire and the other defined by mature melancholy.

In ancient China, Li Mu Bai (Chow Yun-Fat) decides to abandon his fighting ways and asks fellow warrior and unacknowledged love Yu Shu Lien (Michelle Yeoh) to present his cherished sword to respected elder Sir Te (Lung Sihung). She makes the journey, but the sword is promptly stolen from Sir Te's home. The masked thief's identity is quickly revealed: it's Jen (Zhang Ziyi), the beautiful teenage daughter of the district's new governor. Jen, who will soon make a politically advantageous marriage but secretly loves another, has been

Films are listed alphabetically according to the title by which they were first released in the U.S. Films are rated according to the following scale: five stars = masterpiece; four stars = excellent; three stars = good; two stars = fair; one star = without merit. Half stars are also awarded. Key creative and technical personnel are abbreviated as follows: p (producer); d (director); w (writer); ph (cinematographer); ed (editor); m (music composer); prod d (production designer); art d (art director); fx (special effects); chor (choreographer); cos (costume designer); anim (animator).

The Motion Picture Association of America (MPAA) currently grades films according to the following codes: **G** (GENERAL AUDIENCES—All ages admitted); **PG** (PARENTAL GUIDANCE SUGGESTED—Some material may not be suitable for children); **PG-13** (PARENTS STRONGLY CAUTIONED—Some material may be inappropriate for children under 13); **R** (RESTRICTED—Under 17 requires accompanying parent or adult guardian); and **NC-17** (NO CHILDREN UNDER 17 ADMITTED). This book also contains ratings issued while earlier systems were in effect, as follows: **GP** (May be considered the equivalent of PG); **M** (Mature audiences, parental guidance suggested); and **X** (No one under 17 admitted).

A

A NOS AMOURS
1984   102m   c   Drama   ★★½
Livradois/FR3/Gaumont   (France)   R

Sandrine Bonnaire *(Suzanne)*, Dominique Besnehard *(Robert)*, Maurice Pialat *(The Father)*, Evelyne Ker *(The Mother)*, Anne-Sophie Maille *(Anne)*, Christophe Odent *(Michel)*, Cyr Boitard *(Luc)*, Maite Maille *(Martine)*, Pierre-Loup Rajot *(Bernard)*, Cyril Collard *(Jean-Pierre)*

p, Maurice Pialat; d, Maurice Pialat; w, Maurice Pialat, Arlette Langmann; ph, Jacques Loiseleux; ed, Yann Dedet, Sophie Coussein, Valerie Condroyer, Corinne Lazare, Jean Gargonne, Nathalie Letrosne, Catherine Legault; m, Klaus Nomy; art d, Jean-Paul Carnail; cos, Valerie Schlumberger, Martha de Villalonga

The story of 15-year-old Suzanne (Sandrine Bonnaire, in her first role), who is in a hopeless situation—she inspires love but cannot feel it herself. Since she is only happy when she is a guy, she sleeps with everyone who shows interest, except Luc (Cyr Boitard), the one boy who truly feels for her. Her behavior causes problems at home, where things are bad enough already: Her father is moving out, giving free rein to her decidedly unappetizing brother, and her mother is becoming increasingly neurotic. Hardly an uplifting story, but Bonnaire turns Suzanne into a truly compelling figure. Pialat does a fine job of telling the story from Suzanne's point of view, and himself turns in a good performance as her father, the one person with whom she has a genuine understanding.

A NOUS LA LIBERTE

1931   104m   bw   Comedy/Political   ★★★★★
SDFS   (France)

Henri Marchand *(Emile)*, Raymond Cordy *(Louis)*, Rolla France *(Jeanne)*, Paul Olivier *(Paul Imaque)*, Jacques Shelly *(Paul)*, Andre Michaud *(Foreman)*, Germaine Aussey *(Maud)*, Alex D'Arcy *(Gigolo)*, William Burke *(Old Convict)*, Vincent Hyspa *(Old Orator)*

d, Rene Clair; w, Rene Clair; ph, Georges Perinal; ed, Rene Clair, Rene Le Henaff; m, Georges Auric

AAN Best Interior Decoration: Lazare Meerson

This classic satire on the dehumanization of industrial workers is one of Rene Clair's greatest achievements, preceding Chaplin's indictment of the industrial revolution, MODERN TIMES, by five years. Clair's fast-paced and wickedly funny entertainment centers on the friendship between two prison inmates—Louis (Raymond Cordy), who escapes and becomes a phonograph company tycoon, and Emile (Henri Marchand), who, after he too escapes, is hired at his friend's factory. Filming without a script and giving his actors freedom to improvise, Clair structured his film like an operetta. Georges Auric wrote the music, to which the movements of the assembly lines of actors are choreographed. Clair's message is an angry one—"a bitter pill," as he described it, which "would be more easily swallowed when coated with diverting music." The film earned an Academy Award nomination for Best Interior Decoration.

ABBOTT AND COSTELLO MEET FRANKENSTEIN
1948   83m   bw   Comedy   ★★★★
Universal   (U.S.)

Bud Abbott *(Chick Young)*, Lou Costello *(Wilbur Grey)*, Lon Chaney Jr. *(Lawrence Talbot/The Wolf Man)*, Bela Lugosi *(Dracula)*, Glenn Strange *(The Monster)*, Lenore Aubert *(Sandra Mornay)*, Jane Randolph *(Joan Raymond)*, Frank Ferguson *(McDougal)*, Charles Bradstreet *(Dr. Stevens)*, Howard Negley *(Harris)*

p, Robert Arthur; d, Charles Barton; w, Robert Lees, Frederic I. Rinaldo, John Grant (based on the novel *Frankenstein* by Mary Shelley); ph, Charles Van Enger; ed, Frank Gross; m, Frank Skinner; fx, David S. Horsley

Hilarious spoof of the classic Universal horror films of the 1930s and early '40s, with Abbott and Costello playing railway porters who unwittingly deliver the "undead" bodies of Frankenstein's monster (Glenn Strange) and Dracula (Bela Lugosi) to a wax museum, where the bodies are revived. Thus awakened, Dracula becomes intent on replacing the catatonic Monster's brain with dim-witted Costello's, because it would make the beast easier to control. Lawrence Talbot (Lon Chaney, Jr.) attempts to help the boys, but he's got problems of his own: he turns into a wolfman whenever there's a full moon. Horror buffs will note that Chaney, Jr., who had played the Monster in THE GHOST OF FRANKENSTEIN, fills in for Strange in the shot where the Monster tosses actress Lenore Aubert out a window. Strange had broken his foot in an accident and, rather than lose three days of shooting, Chaney volunteered to don the makeup once again. After this film's considerable success at the box office, Abbott and Costello made seven more pictures in which they "met" Hollywood monsters, but none were as lively and entertaining as this one.

ABE LINCOLN IN ILLINOIS
1940   110m   bw   Biography   ★★★
RKO   (U.S.)

Raymond Massey *(Abraham Lincoln)*, Gene Lockhart *(Stephen Douglas)*, Ruth Gordon *(Mary Todd Lincoln)*, Mary Howard *(Ann Rutledge)*, Dorothy Tree *(Elizabeth Edwards)*, Harvey Stephens *(Ninian Edwards)*, Minor Watson *(Joshua Speed)*, Alan Baxter *(Billy Herndon)*, Howard da Silva *(Jack Armstrong)*, Maurice Murphy *(John McNeil)*

p, Max Gordon; d, John Cromwell; w, Grover Jones, Robert E. Sherwood (based on his play); ph, James Wong Howe; ed, George Hively; m, Roy Webb

AAN Best Actor: Raymond Massey; *AAN Best B/W Cinematography:* James Wong Howe

In adapting Robert E. Sherwood's popular play about the early years of Abraham Lincoln, the filmmakers wisely chose Raymond Massey, who played the title role on stage, to reprise his portrayal in the film. Massey heads an impressive cast in a picture spanning thirty years of Lincoln's life, following his career from his beginnings as a woodsman and shopkeeper to his entry into law and politics and culminating with his election as the 16th president of the United States. The film includes some memorable scenes of Lincoln's debates with his longtime political rival, Stephen Douglas (Gene Lockhart), and offers a vivid account of 19th-century life in the Midwest, with particular attention paid to the political processes of the day. Massey's excellent performance earned an Oscar nomination (he lost to James Stewart in THE PHILADELPHIA STORY) and the film was also nominated for Best Cinematography.

ABOMINABLE DR. PHIBES, THE

DVD

1971 93m c Horror ★★★

AIP (U.S./U.K.) PG

Vincent Price *(Dr. Anton Phibes)*, Joseph Cotten *(Dr. Vesalius)*, Hugh Griffith *(Rabbi)*, Terry-Thomas *(Dr. Longstreet)*, Virginia North *(Vulnavia)*, Aubrey Woods *(Goldsmith)*, Susan Travers *(Nurse Allan)*, Alex Scott *(Dr. Hargreaves)*, Peter Gilmore *(Dr. Kitaj)*, Edward Burnham *(Dr. Dunwoody)*

p, Louis M. Heyward, Ronald S. Dunas; d, Robert Fuest; w, James Whiton, William Goldstein; ph, Norman Warwick; ed, Tristam Cones; m, Basil Kirchin; art d, Bernard Reeves; cos, Elsa Fennell

A delightfully goofy horror film set in England circa 1929, THE ABOMINABLE DR. PHIBES stars Vincent Price as Dr. Anton Phibes, a horribly disfigured madman who enacts an insidious revenge on the team of physicians who failed to save the life of his dear, departed wife (Caroline Munro, seen mostly in photos). His face and voice destroyed in an auto accident, Phibes reconstructs his mutilated visage over the bones that remained, and recovers his lost voice by plugging a cord extended from his neck into a Victrola! The gruesome ends he devises for the doctors are patterned after the plagues brought down on Ramses in ancient Egypt (killer locusts, blood-sucking bats, rabid rats, etc.). Kept at a snappy pace by "Avengers" director Robert Fuest and given a bizarre art deco look by art director Bernard Reeves and set designer Brian Eatwell, this movie is a kitschy homage to the sillier horror pictures of the 1930s and well worth a look. An equally entertaining sequel, DR. PHIBES RISES AGAIN, was released in 1972.

ABOUT A BOY

DVD

2002 112m c Comedy ★★★

Tribeca Films/Studio Canal/Working Title PG-13
Productions/Kalima Productions
(U.K./U.S./France/Germany)

Hugh Grant *(Will)*, Toni Collette *(Fiona)*, Rachel Weisz *(Rachel)*, Nicholas Hoult *(Marcus)*, Sharon Small *(Christine)*, Madison Cook *(Imogen)*, Jordan Cook *(Imogen)*, Nicholas Hutchinson *(John)*, Ryan Speechley *(Barney)*, Joseph Speechley *(Barney)*

p, Tim Bevan, Robert De Niro, Brad Epstein, Eric Fellner, Jane Rosenthal; d, Paul Weitz, Chris Weitz; w, Peter Hedges, Chris Weitz, Paul Weitz (based on the novel by Nick Hornby); ph, Remi Adefarasin; ed, Nick Moore; m, Badly Drawn Boy; prod d, Jim Clay; art d, Gary Freeman; cos, Joanna Johnston

AAN Best Adapted Screenplay: Peter Hedges, Chris Weitz, Paul Weitz

If sibling directors Paul and Chris Weitz, best known for the slapstick teen comedy AMERICAN PIE, were looking to establish themselves as more mature filmmakers, they succeeded handily with this adaptation of UK author Nick Hornby's 1998 novel. Working from their own excellent screenplay, co-written with Peter Hedges, they chronicle the belated coming-of-age of a very immature man who learns some important life lessons from a troubled young boy.

Stylish, independently wealthy Londoner Will Freeman (Hugh Grant) has the financial security to do nothing but date indiscriminately, and discovers that dating insecure single mothers is a good way to ease quickly in and out of relationships unscathed by drama. And where better to meet unmarried moms than at a single-parents group? Needless to say, one of the children he meets, Marcus (Nicholas Hoult), gets under Will's skin with a combination of boyish charm and an undeniable need to be loved. The film takes these two unlikely friends through experiences that are both hilarious and heart-breaking. Marcus's wreck of a mother, Fiona (Toni Collette), lonely and suicidal, doesn't quite know what to make of this oddball friendship.

Bursting with (but not overburdened by) the pop culture references that are the trademark of both Hornby's fiction and the Weitz brothers' films, this wickedly funny and surprisingly sweet film may be the perfect star vehicle for Grant. He's full of piss and vinegar and has at long last set aside the wobbly, stammering persona best left at FOUR WEDDINGS AND A FUNERAL.

ABOUT SCHMIDT

DVD

2002 125m c Comedy/Drama ★★★½

Avery Pix/New Line (U.S.) R

Jack Nicholson *(Warren Schmidt)*, Kathy Bates *(Roberta Hertzel)*, Hope Davis *(Jeannie Schmidt)*, Dermot Mulroney *(Randall Hertzel)*, June Squibb *(Helen Schmidt)*, Howard Hesseman *(Larry Hertzel)*, Len Cariou *(Ray Nichols)*, Harry Groener *(John Rusk)*, Connie Ray *(Vicki Rusk)*, Mark Venhuizen *(Duncan Hertzel)*

p, Michael Besman, Harry Gittes; d, Alexander Payne; w, Alexander Payne, Jim Taylor (based on the novel by Louis Begley and the screenplay *The Coward* by Alexander Payne); ph, James Glennon; ed, Kevin Tent; m, Rolfe Kent; prod d, Jane Ann Stewart; art d, Tim Kirkpatrick; fx, Erik Henry; cos, Wendy Chuck

AAN Best Actor: Jack Nicholson; AAN Best Supporting Actress: Kathy Bates

Writer-director Alexander Payne and co-writer Jim Taylor completely rework Louis Begley's acclaimed novel into an odd, picaresque odyssey in which a retired 66-year-old insurance actuary takes to the road in a 35-foot Winnebago. It's not exactly a journey of self-discovery: Warren Schmidt (beautifully played by Jack Nicholson) is far too deluded to even know he's lost.

After years of faithful service to Omaha's Woodmen of the World Insurance Company, Schmidt is calling it a day. With nothing ahead but the dull prospect of touring the country in an enormous Winnebago with Helen (June Squibb), the wife of 42 years whom he can barely tolerate, Schmidt has to wonder what meaning, if any, his life holds. One afternoon, Schmidt sees an infomercial for a children's relief organization, and with one impulsive phone call becomes the proud sponsor of a six-year-old Tanzanian boy. The agency encourages sponsors to include a personal note with their monthly payment, so with each $22 check he writes, Schmidt obliges with a long letter brimming with petty bitterness, disappointment with himself and his daughter, Jeannie (Hope Davis), and disgust over her impending marriage to good-natured waterbed salesman Randall (Dermot Mulroney). Schmidt's neat world is turned completely upside down the day he returns home to find Helen dead on the kitchen floor. Ever the actuary, Schmidt calculates that he himself has a 75 percent chance of dying within the next nine years, and he's determined to make every new day count. So he hops in the Winnebago and sets out to do something meaningful: put a stop to Jeannie's wedding.

The film dares to ask you to care a fig about a completely ordinary and not terribly likeable old man, and perhaps one of the great accomplishments of Nicholson's career is that you do—at least a little. Typical of earlier Payne and Taylor collaborations (CITIZEN RUTH, ELECTION), the writing is sharp and often blithely cynical, though not above using a shooting star to prompt a lump in the throat. The tone, however, is uncertain. Once Schmidt arrives in Denver and finds himself in the bosom of Randall's kooky family—headed by a hilarious but larger-than-life Kathy Bates—it exudes the slight but unmistakable whiff of condescension.

ABSENCE OF MALICE
1981 116m c Drama ★★½
Columbia (U.S.) PG

Paul Newman *(Gallagher)*, Sally Field *(Megan)*, Bob Balaban *(Rosen)*, Melinda Dillon *(Teresa)*, Luther Adler *(Malderone)*, Barry Primus *(Waddell)*, Josef Sommer *(McAdam)*, John Harkins *(Davidek)*, Don Hood *(Quinn)*, Wilford Brimley *(Wells)*

p, Sydney Pollack; d, Sydney Pollack; w, Kurt Luedtke; ph, Owen Roizman; ed, Sheldon Kahn; m, Dave Grusin; prod d, Terence Marsh; cos, Bernie Pollack

AAN Best Actor: Paul Newman; *AAN Best Supporting Actress:* Melinda Dillon; *AAN Best Original Screenplay:* Kurt Luedtke

Gallagher (Paul Newman), the son of a dead mobster, runs a legitimate business in Miami, with his uncle (Luther Adler) his only connection to organized crime. A federal investigator (Bob Balaban) thinks Gallagher knows the details of a labor leader's disappearance, and leaks information to Megan (Sally Field), a reporter who writes a story implicating Gallagher. The story's publication brings tragic results, and Gallagher plots to get revenge. Sydney Pollack's film is a solid, absorbing drama that, in profiling the damage that can result from investigative reporting, presents a counterpoint to ALL THE PRESI-DENT'S MEN. Newman, Dillon, and Luedtke received Oscar nominations.

ABSENT-MINDED PROFESSOR, THE
1961 97m bw Comedy/Fantasy ★★★
Walt Disney Productions (U.S.) G

Fred MacMurray *(Prof. Ned Brainard)*, Nancy Olson *(Betsy Carlisle)*, Keenan Wynn *(Alonzo Hawk)*, Tommy Kirk *(Bill Hawk)*, Leon Ames *(Rufus Daggett)*, Elliott Reid *(Shelby Ashton)*, Edward Andrews *(Defense Secretary)*, Wally Brown *(Coach Elkins)*, Forrest Lewis *(Officer Kelly)*, James Westerfield *(Officer Hanson)*

p, Walt Disney; d, Robert Stevenson; w, Bill Walsh (based on the story by Samuel W. Taylor); ph, Edward Colman; ed, Cotton Warburton; m, George Bruns; art d, Carroll Clark; fx, Peter Ellenshaw, Eustace Lycett, Robert A. Mattey

AAN Best B/W Cinematography: Edward Colman; *AAN Best Art Direction-Set Decoration (B/W):* Carroll Clark (Art Direction), Emile Kuri (Set Decoration), Hal Gausman (Set Decoration); *AAN Best Special Effects:* Robert A. Mattey (Visual), Eustace Lycett (Visual)

A wacky comedy in which college professor Ned Brainard (Fred MacMurray) invents flying rubber, which he dubs "flubber." The substance has gravity-defying properties and, when applied to the soles of shoes, allows the wearer to leap to incredible heights. A variety of suitably screwy situations ensue, as the evil Alonzo Hawk (Keenan Wynn) plots to steal the formula for his own personal gain. This is a zanily inventive piece of work, with delightful special effects, which set the style for a long series of live-action Disney films. It earned Oscar nominations for Best Cinematography, Best Art Direction, and Best Special Effects. A 1964 sequel, THE SON OF FLUBBER, was less successful.

ABSOLUTE BEGINNERS
1986 107m c Musical ★★★
Palace/Virgin/Goldcrest (U.K.) PG-13

Eddie O'Connell *(Colin)*, Patsy Kensit *(Crepe Suzette)*, David Bowie *(Vendice Partners)*, James Fox *(Henley of Mayfair)*, Ray Davies *(Arthur)*, Mandy Rice-Davies *(Mum)*, Eve Ferret *(Big Jill)*, Tony Hippolyte *(Mr. Cool)*, Graham Fletcher-Cook *(Wizard)*, Joe McKenna *(Fabulous Hoplite)*

p, Stephen Woolley, Chris Brown; d, Julien Temple; w, Christopher Wicking, Richard Burridge, Don MacPherson (based on the novel by Colin MacInnes); ph, Oliver Stapleton (Super Techniscope, Rank Color); ed, Michael Bradsell, Gerry Hambling, Richard Bedford, Russell Lloyd; m, Gil Evans; prod d, John Beard; art d, Stuart Rose, Ken Wheatley; chor, David Toguri; cos, Sue Blane, David Perry

A visually inventive and energetic pop musical adapted from Colin MacInnes' 1958 cult novel of the same name. ABSOLUTE BEGINNERS is a tale of two swinging English teens, Colin (Eddie O'Connell) and Crepe Suzette (Patsy Kensit), set against the backdrop of emerging youth culture and racial tension in late 1950s London. As Suzette becomes a success in the fashion business and looks set to leave her street roots behind, Colin is torn between his youthful idealism and his desire to do whatever is necessary to lure her back. Though the characterization and plot waver on the transparent, ABSOLUTE BEGINNERS has no shortage of color, movement, and infectious music—it's a perfect example of a music video sensibility applied to a feature-length film. Highlights include songs by jazzman Slim Gaillard ("Selling Out") and The Style Council ("Have You Ever Had It Blue?") and a bravura, one-take opening sequence a la TOUCH OF EVIL.

ABYSS, THE
1989 140m c Science Fiction ★★½
Fox (U.S.) PG-13

Ed Harris *(Bud Brigman)*, Mary Elizabeth Mastrantonio *(Lindsey Brigman)*, Michael Biehn *(Lt. Coffey)*, George Robert Klek *(Wilhite)*, John Bedford Lloyd *("Jammer" Willis)*, Christopher Murphy *(Seal Schoenick)*, Adam Nelson *(Ensign Monk)*, J.C. Quinn *("Sonny" Dawson)*, Kimberly Scott *(Lisa "One Night" Standing)*, Capt. Kidd Brewer Jr. *(Lew Finler)*

p, Gale Anne Hurd; d, James Cameron; w, James Cameron; ph, Mikael Salomon, Dennis Skotak (DuArt Color); ed, Joel Goodman; m, Alan Silvestri; prod d, Leslie Dilley; art d, Peter Childs; cos, Deborah Everton

AAN Best Cinematography: Mikael Salomon; *AAN Best Art Direction-Set Decoration:* Leslie Dilley, Anne Kuljian; *AAN Best Sound:* Don Bassman, Kevin F. Cleary, Richard Overton, Lee Orloff; *AA Best Visual Effects:* John Bruno, Dennis Muren, Hoyt Yeatman, Dennis Skotak

Picture the opening scene of JAWS, except that, in THE ABYSS, it's not a great white shark but an underwater UFO that propels the movie into action. Spotted on sonar by a U.S. nuclear submarine, the "thing" is eerily tracked below deck, where it creates a disaster because of the crew's ensuing panic. The sub sinks onto the ledge of an abyss, and a team of oil riggers, led by foreman Bud Brigman (Ed Harris), is pressed into a rescue mission. The civilian crew is joined by engineer Lindsey Brigman (Mary Elizabeth Mastrantonio), who happens to be Bud's soon-to-be ex-wife, and a group of navy underwater experts headed by Lt. Coffey (Michael Biehn), whose top-secret priority is the 150 nuclear warheads located on the sub. The rescue takes on a new character when the extra-terrestrial force makes its presence known. Despite the fact that most of the action occurs below sea level, THE ABYSS simply recycles elements of the stellar blockbusters it tries so hard to emulate (CLOSE ENCOUNTERS, E.T., and director James Cameron's own ALIENS among them). Unfortunately, it lacks the emotional impact and suspense of its predecessors and is spoiled by a disappointingly inane ending. What ultimately saves the film are its extraordinary sets and phenomenal Oscar-winning visual effects.

ACCATTONE!
DVD
1961   120m   bw   Drama   ★★★
Arco   (Italy)

Franco Citti *(Vittorio Accattone)*, Franca Pasut *(Stella)*, Silvana Corsini *(Maddalena)*, Paolo Guidi *(Ascenza)*, Adriana Asti *(Amore)*, Renato Capogna *(Renato)*, Roberto Scaringella *(Cartagine)*, Mario Cipriani *(Balilla)*, Piero Morgia *(Pio)*, Umberto Bevilacqua *(Salvatore)*

p, Alfredo Bini; d, Pier Paolo Pasolini; w, Pier Paolo Pasolini; ph, Tonino Delli Colli; ed, Nino Baragli; m, Johann Sebastian Bach

Pasolini's first feature is a classic neorealist study of the Roman underworld of poverty and petty thievery. Accattone (Citti), a street youth who hates work, falls in love with Stella (Pasut) and attempts to find a job, but ultimately turns to crime. The film is based on Pasolini's own novel and supposedly mirrors his own experiences. The director uses nonprofessional actors to create a vivid portrait of an unremittingly grim environment.

ACCIDENT
DVD
1967   105m   c   Drama   ★★★★
Royal Avenue Chelsea   (U.K.)

Dirk Bogarde *(Stephen)*, Stanley Baker *(Charley)*, Jacqueline Sassard *(Anna)*, Michael York *(William)*, Vivien Merchant *(Rosalind)*, Delphine Seyrig *(Francesca)*, Alexander Knox *(Provost)*, Ann Firbank *(Laura)*, Brian Phelan *(Police Sergeant)*, Terence Rigby *(Plain Clothed Policeman)*

p, Joseph Losey, Norman Priggen; d, Joseph Losey; w, Harold Pinter (based on the novel by Nicholas Mosley); ph, Gerry Fisher (Eastmancolor); ed, Reginald Beck; m, John Dankworth; art d, Carmen Dillon; cos, Beatrice Dawson, De Luca of Rome

Dirk Bogarde gives a brilliant performance in this psychologically dense and compelling study, scripted by Harold Pinter, of an Oxford don and his infatuation with a beautiful student.

While typing late one night in his country home, Stephen (Dirk Bogarde), an Oxford philosophy professor, hears a crash and runs outside to find two of his pupils trapped inside a smashed car. William (Michael York) is dead, and Anna (Jacqueline Sassard) is in shock, but uninjured. Stephen remembers when he and the aristocratic William first met the Austrian Anna at school; in particular, he recalls a leisurely Sunday lunch spent at his own house. Charley (Stanley Baker), a brash colleague of Stephen's, had been having an affair with Anna, and it had eventually fallen to Stephen to deny the gravity of the situation to Charley's wife.

ACCIDENT is arguably director Joseph Losey's best film, equaling the superb THE SERVANT. There is something about Pinter's obliquely penetrating dialogue that brings out the best in Losey, raising the director's customary cerebral pessimism to new levels of insight. As Stephen, Bogarde brilliantly captures the mentality of his character—a civilized man who has sublimated his sexuality and now finds his fantasies taking over during a mid-life crisis. The rest of the cast is equally excellent, but Stanley Baker stands out as the amoral, but quite likable, Charley. Losey cleverly scrambles the time scheme of the plot, à la Alain Resnais, most notably in the complex structure of the long Sunday lunch sequence. Like the repressed characters, the visual style of the film is deceptively simple, with the beautiful colors of the serene British countryside used to mask the languorous sensuality and emotional devastation that lies beneath the surface.

ACCIDENTAL TOURIST, THE
DVD
1988   121m   c   Comedy   ★★★★
Warner Bros.   (U.S.)   PG

William Hurt *(Macon Leary)*, Kathleen Turner *(Sarah Leary)*, Geena Davis *(Muriel Pritchett)*, Amy Wright *(Rose)*, Bill Pullman *(Julian)*, Robert Gorman *(Alexander Pritchett)*, David Ogden Stiers *(Porter Leary)*, Ed Begley Jr. *(Charles Leary)*, Bradley Mott *(Mr. Loomis)*, Seth Granger *(Ethan)*

p, Lawrence Kasdan, Charles Okun, Michael Grillo; d, Lawrence Kasdan; w, Frank Galati, Lawrence Kasdan (based on the novel by Anne Tyler); ph, John Bailey (Technicolor); ed, Carol Littleton; m, John Williams; prod d, Bo Welch; cos, Ruth Myers

AAN Best Picture; AA Best Supporting Actress: Geena Davis; *AAN Best Adapted Screenplay:* Frank Galati, Lawrence Kasdan; *AAN Best Original Score:* John Williams

Writer-director Kasdan's fine adaptation of Tyler's novel hinges on Hurt's understated performance as a writer of travel guides for businessmen who hate to travel. Shortly after his wife, (who starred opposite Hurt in Kasdan's BODY HEAT), leaves him, he breaks a leg and moves in with his oddball middle-aged sister and brothers (Wright, Begley, and Stiers). Because his dead son's Welsh corgi has become a disciplinary problem, Hurt calls upon the dog-training services of Davis, a vibrant divorcee. They begin an awkward relationship that is further complicated when Turner wants to patch things up. Kasdan has remained true to the spirit of Tyler's award-winning novel, preserving much of her wonderful dialogue and humor. Hurt's performance is remarkably assured, and Davis beautifully captures her character's insouciance. Less than perfect is Turner, whose capable performance presents a figure somewhat hollow at the center. Although some may find the film slow-moving, its rich characterizations alone makes it well worth watching. Davis won the Best Supporting Actress Oscar. The film was nominated for Best Picture, Best Adapted Screenplay, and Best Original Score.

ACCUSED, THE
DVD
1988   110m   c   Drama   ★★½
Paramount   (U.S.)   R

Kelly McGillis *(Kathryn Murphy)*, Jodie Foster *(Sarah Tobias)*, Bernie Coulson *(Kenneth Joyce)*, Ann Hearn *(Sally Frazer)*, Steve Antin *(Bob Joiner)*, Tom O'Brien *(Larry)*, Allan Lysell *(Al Massi)*, Leo Rossi *(Cliff Albrecht)*, Carmen Argenziano *(Paul Rudolph)*, Terry David Mulligan *(Det. Duncan)*

p, Stanley R. Jaffe, Sherry Lansing; d, Jonathan Kaplan; w, Tom Topor; ph, Ralf D. Bode (Alpha Cine Services Color); ed, Jerry Greenberg, O. Nicholas Brown; m, Brad Fiedel; prod d, Richard Kent Wilcox

AA Best Actress: Jodie Foster

Only a riveting performance by Jodie Foster lifts THE ACCUSED above the level of a television movie. The story, which bears some resemblance to a much-publicized 1983 incident in Massachusetts, centers on the case of Foster, a tough, sexy young woman who is gang-raped in a neighborhood bar before a crowd of cheering onlookers. District attorney McGillis takes the case. She agrees to a plea bargain in which the rapists admit to reckless endangerment, because she fears her client's sordid past will destroy her credibility in court. After Foster castigates McGillis for selling her out, McGillis devises a new strategy—to put the crowd of onlookers on trial for "criminal solicitation."

Director Jonathan Kaplan and screenwriter Tom Topor purposely paint Foster as a slut in order to strengthen their argument—for no matter how provocatively she was dressed or how erotically she danced, no one can believe that Foster wanted to be gang-raped. Although the filmmakers are well-intentioned, THE ACCUSED is a predictable picture that lacks emotional insight; it works only because of the onscreen bond between Foster, who won a much-deserved Oscar for her performance, and McGillis. Foster charges forward into the frame with explosive energy, carrying the film and proving she has far too much talent to let mediocre material bring her down.

ACE VENTURA: PET DETECTIVE   *DVD*
1994 85m c   Comedy   ★★★
Ace Productions/Morgan Creek   (U.S.)   PG-13

Jim Carrey (*Ace Ventura*), Courteney Cox (*Melissa*), Sean Young (*Lieutenant Lois Einhorn*), Tone Loc (*Emilio*), Dan Marino (*Himself*), Noble Willingham (*Riddle*), Troy Evans (*Podacter*), Raynor Scheine (*Woodstock*), Udo Kier (*Camp*), Frank Adonis (*Vinnie*)

p, James G. Robinson; d, Tom Shadyac; w, Jack Bernstein, Tom Shadyac, Jim Carrey (from a story by Jack Bernstein); ph, Julio Macat; ed, Don Zimmerman; m, Ira Newborn; prod d, William A. Elliott; art d, Alan E. Muraoka; fx, Michael N. Arbogast, Matte World Digital; cos, Bobbie Read

ACE VENTURA: PET DETECTIVE marks the ascendance of a new star in film farce, as Jim Carrey elevates this stupid, suprisingly shoddy picture into the comedy stratosphere, mainly thanks to his Gumby-like ability to contort his face and body in the most amazing ways.

Ace Ventura (Jim Carrey) is an alarmingly eccentric private eye who specializes in cases involving animals. He cares far more for wildlife than he does for social niceties, and women and varmints love him right back. Ventura's the perfect man for the job when the aquatic mascot of the Miami Dolphins is kidnapped, but the plot thickens when star quarterback Dan Marino vanishes as well. Only Ace can get back the mammals, win the girl (team employee Melissa, played by Courteney Cox), and evade the strangely obstructive cop Lt. Einhorn (Sean Young).

One of the funniest films to emerge from Hollywood in the '90s, ACE VENTURA claimed huge audiences, despite dismissive reviews. Critics noted that every gag is carried much too far, as if daring the viewer not to laugh, but failed to account for the devoted following Carrey had cultivated with his sometimes grotesque clowning on TV's "In Living Color." Interestingly, Ace is not the typical movie goofball, smart aleck, or idiot savant; he's a genuine weirdo who happens to be stunningly competent at his job. The same can be said for the film's justly popular leading man.

ACROSS 110TH STREET   *DVD*
1972 102m c   Crime/Drama   ★★★½
UA   (U.S.)   R

Anthony Quinn (*Capt. Frank Mattelli*), Yaphet Kotto (*Det. Lt. Pope*), Anthony Franciosa (*Nick D'Salvio*), Paul Benjamin (*Jim Harris*), Ed Bernard (*Joe Logart*), Richard Ward (*Doc Johnson*), Norma Donaldson (*Gloria Roberts*), Antonio Fargas (*Henry Jackson*), Gilbert Lewis (*Shevvy*), Marlene Warfield (*Mrs. Jackson*)

p, Ralph Serpe, Fouad Said; d, Barry Shear; w, Luther Davis (based on the novel by Wally Ferris); ph, Jack Priestley; ed, Byron "Buzz" Brandt, Carl Pingitore; m, J.J. Johnson; art d, Perry Watkins; fx, Joe Lombardi Enterprises; cos, Joe Fretwell

Fast-paced, brutal actioner has three black hoods stealing a fortune from a Mafia-controlled Harlem numbers bank. They are tracked down by crooked cop Quinn, who walks a thin line between his duties as a policeman and his obligations to the Mafia. It's a race to see who gets the thieves first, the Mafia hoods or Quinn and his black partner, Kotto. Smartly edited with terrific location work in New York City. The dependable Kotto is a standout.

ACROSS THE PACIFIC
1942 97m   bw Spy   ★★★½
Warner Bros. (U.S.)

Humphrey Bogart (*Richard Lomas Leland*), Mary Astor (*Alberta Marlow*), Sydney Greenstreet (*Dr. Lorenz*), Charles Halton (*A.V. Smith*), Victor Sen Yung (*Joe Totsuiko*), Roland Got (*Sugi*), Lee Tung-Foo (*Sam Wing On*), Frank Wilcox (*Capt. Morrison*), Paul Stanton (*Col. Hart*), Lester Matthews (*Canadian Major*)

p, Jerry Wald, Jack Saper; d, John Huston (uncredited); w, Richard Macaulay (based on the *Saturday Evening Post* serial "Aloha Means Goodbye" by Robert Carson); ph, Arthur Edeson; ed, Frank Magee; m, Adolph Deutsch; art d, Robert Haas, Hugh Reticker; fx, Byron Haskin, Willard Van Enger; cos, Milo Anderson

With the success of THE MALTESE FALCON under his belt, young director John Huston took on this first-rate espionage adventure, using three principals from his previous film, Bogart, Astor, and Greenstreet. Bogart is introduced as a disgraced ex-Army man who has been court-martialed for selling military secrets, and who boards a Japanese ship bound for the Pacific via the Panama Canal. On board he meets Astor, a fashion designer going to the Canal Zone to visit her father; Greenstreet, a mysterious sociologist returning to his professorial post in Manila, a man who praises the Japanese to excess; and Tong, a silent Japanese passenger who identity is assumed by a replacement when the ship docks in New York. Here the viewer is allowed to see that Bogart is not a callous creature willing to sell his services to the highest bidder, but that his traitorous posture is only a cover for his true role of undercover agent; he has been planted on board to establish a liaison with Japanese agent Greenstreet and to discover what he can about Astor. As in THE MALTESE FALCON, Bogart takes a terrible beating, again at the orders of the sadistic Greenstreet. Yet he goes on to overcome all the odds in a wonderfully impossible ending which brazenly spoofs the spy genre. Good quality fun.

ADAM SANDLER'S EIGHT CRAZY NIGHTS   *DVD*
2002 89m   c   Animated/Comedy/Musical   ★★★
Happy Madison/Meatball Animated   (U.S.)   PG-13

VOICES OF: Adam Sandler (*Whitey Duvall/Davey Stone/Eleanor Duvall/Deer*), Jackie Titone (*Jennifer*), Austin Stout (*Benjamin*), Kevin Nealon (*Mayor*), Rob Schneider (*Chinese Waiter/Narrator*), Norm Crosby (*Judge*), Jon Lovitz (*Tom Baltezor*), Tyra Banks (*Victoria's Secret Gown*), Cole Sprouse (*K-B Toy Soldier*), Dylan Sprouse (*K-B Toy Soldier*)

p, Allen Covert, Jack Giarraputo, Adam Sandler; d, Seth Kearsley; w, Brooks Arthur, Allen Covert, Brad Isaacs, Adam Sandler; ed, Amy Budden; m, Teddy Castellucci, Marc Ellis, Ray Ellis; prod d, Perry Andelin Blake; art d, Philip Cruden; John Bermudes; anim, Fil Barlow, Steve Cunningham, Chris Dozois, Ralph Fernan, Stephan Franck, Holger Leihe, Melinda Sydney Padua, Chris Tsirgiotis

The anti-holiday sentiment of HOW THE GRINCH STOLE CHRISTMAS meets Adam Sandler's distinctive comic style in this offbeat, sometimes gross, and surprisingly appealing animated musical feature about the true meaning of the holidays.

Thirty-three-year-old delinquent Davey Stone (voice of Adam Sandler) lives in small-town Dukesberry, where people just love celebrating holidays. Davey's general ill-will toward men hits an all-time high on the first night of Hanukkah, when he gets busted for destroying the town's entire holiday display; were it not for diminutive basketball referee Whitey (also Sandler), Davey would face a 10-year stretch in the pokey. Whitey volunteers to take Davey under his wing, even though Davey is rude and plays mean-spirited pranks on the elfin oldster. Unflaggingly generous, Whitey reintroduces

Davey to his high-school crush, Jennifer (Jackie Titone), who's recently returned to town with her son, Benjamin (Austin Stout), and offers Davey a place to stay after his trailer burns down. Whitey's paranoid twin, Eleanor (Sandler yet again), however, is understandably skeptical about her kind-hearted brother's rowdy stray.

Sandler hams it up even more than usual as an animated holiday hater, but manages not to bury the movie's uplifting message—that the spirit of the holidays can reform the hardest heart—under his trademark scatological and politically incorrect gags. Given that this is the first feature-length film dedicated to Hanukkah, it's a little disappointing that history gets the brush-off and the Festival of Lights is relegated to serving as a backdrop for the movie's madcap mayhem.

ADAM'S RIB
1949 101m bw Comedy   ★★★½
MGM   (U.S.)

Spencer Tracy *(Adam Bonner)*, Katharine Hepburn *(Amanda Bonner)*, Judy Holliday *(Doris Attinger)*, Tom Ewell *(Warren Attinger)*, David Wayne *(Kip Lurie)*, Jean Hagen *(Beryl Caighn)*, Hope Emerson *(Olympia La Pere)*, Eve March *(Grace)*, Clarence Kolb *(Judge Reiser)*, Emerson Treacy *(Jules Frikke)*

p, Lawrence Weingarten; d, George Cukor; w, Ruth Gordon, Garson Kanin; ph, George Folsey; ed, George Boemler; m, Miklos Rozsa; art d, Cedric Gibbons, William Ferrari; fx, A. Arnold Gillespie; cos, Walter Plunkett

AAN Best Story and Screenplay: Ruth Gordon, Garson Kanin

Delightful, sophisticated comedy sparked by the famous chemistry between Katharine Hepburn and Spencer Tracy. When Tracy, an unyielding DA, prosecutes the client of his lawyer-wife, Hepburn, in an attempted murder case, it unleashes a battle of the sexes that almost wrecks their happy marriage. The defendant is Holliday (in an outstanding debut which led to her getting the "dumb blonde" lead in BORN YESTERDAY) who attempted to shoot a woman who was trysting with Holliday's slippery husband (Ewell, very funny here). Hepburn, an advocate of women's rights, is determined to prove that the prosecution's case is a reflection of sexist double standards, and that Holliday's husband would never be tried for the same actions. This rankles the conservative Tracy, and matters are further complicated when foppish David Wayne begins to move in on Hepburn. Throughout the trial, Tracy and Hepburn's marriage seems headed for the rocks, their courtroom resentments surfacing at home. Eventually, Hepburn wins an acquittal for Holliday through a case based on sexual equality, but admits, as does a petulant Tracy, that there are basic differences between men and women. "*Vive le différence!*" Tracy exclaims, and the marriage and the battle between the sexes go on. A thoroughly witty, sharply directed, fun film from Cukor, with a sprightly, Oscar-nominated script from Gordon and Kanin, ADAM'S RIB succeeds brilliantly through a combination of top talents, especially those of Hepburn and Tracy.

ADAPTATION
2002 114m c   Comedy/Drama   ★★★★
Magnet/Intermedia Films/Clinica   (U.S.)   R
Estetico/Columbia

Nicolas Cage *(Charlie Kaufman/Donald Kaufman)*, Meryl Streep *(Susan Orlean)*, Chris Cooper *(John Laroche)*, Tilda Swinton *(Valerie)*, Cara Seymour *(Amelia)*, Brian Cox *(Robert McKee)*, Judy Greer *(Alice the Waitress)*, Maggie Gyllenhaal *(Caroline)*, Ron Livingston *(Marty)*, Jay Tavare *(Matthew Osceola)*

p, Jonathan Demme, Vincent Landay, Edward Saxon; d, Spike Jonze; w, Charlie Kaufman, Donald Kaufman (based on the book *The Orchid Thief* by Susan Orlean); ph, Lance Acord; ed, Eric Zumbrunnen; m, Carter Burwell; prod d, K.K. Barrett; art d, Peter Andrus; fx, Gary D'Amico; cos, Casey Storm

AA Best Supporting Actor: Chris Cooper; *AAN Best Actor:* Nicolas Cage; *AAN Best Supporting Actress:* Meryl Streep; *AAN Best Adapted Screenplay:* Charlie Kaufman, Donald Kaufman

Impressed by his screenplay for BEING JOHN MALKOVICH, Sony Pictures hired writer Charlie Kaufman to turn Susan Orlean's nonfiction best-seller *The Orchid Thief* into a feature film. The book is a fascinating account of an unusual theft. In 1994, 36-year-old John Laroche was arrested for poaching rare ghost orchids from Florida's Fakahatchee Strand. But aside from Laroche's less-than-sensational crime, there really isn't much "story" in *The Orchid Thief*. Its substance lies in numerous digressions, which cover everything from obsessive orchid collecting to Orlean's personal quest for passion. Kaufman felt a responsibility to remain true to Orlean's book—no contrived romances, no guns, no life lessons—but after months of false starts, he couldn't find a way into the material. At his wit's end, Kaufman threw caution and, potentially, his career) to the wind and wrote a script about his inability to find the movie in Orlean's book. The end result, directed with amazing inventiveness by Spike Jonze, is one of the best movies Hollywood has ever made about itself, an extraordinary meta-narrative that continually questions its own ability to capture all the disappointment and loneliness of human experience.

Nicolas Cage, in a brilliant dual performance, plays Charlie Kaufman—balding, overweight, and racked by self-doubt—as well as Kaufman's fictitious foil, his twin brother, Donald. Thanks to script guru Robert McKee (Brian Cox), Donald is having much better luck with his ludicrous, formulaic serial-killer screenplay. Meryl Streep plays Orlean, and a superb Chris Cooper is Laroche, the thieving autodidact with no front teeth but a poetic streak. It's hilariously funny, but that deliberately ridiculous third act, which delivers everything Kaufman promised the film wouldn't, suggests something deeply depressing and gives the title its true meaning: the organisms that survive are the ones that learn to adapt to their environment, be it the Fakahatchee Strand or Hollywood.

ADDAMS FAMILY, THE
1991 99m c   Comedy/Horror   ★★½
Orion   (U.S.)   PG-13

Anjelica Huston *(Morticia Addams)*, Raul Julia *(Gomez Addams)*, Christopher Lloyd *(Uncle Fester Addams/Gordon Craven)*, Dan Hedaya *(Tully Alford)*, Elizabeth Wilson *(Abigail Craven)*, Judith Malina *(Granny)*, Carel Struycken *(Lurch)*, Dana Ivey *(Margaret Alford)*, Paul Benedict *(Judge Womack)*, Christina Ricci *(Wednesday Addams)*

p, Scott Rudin; d, Barry Sonnenfeld; w, Caroline Thompson, Larry Wilson (from the characters created by Charles Addams); ph, Owen Roizman; ed, Dede Allen, Jim Miller; m, Marc Shaiman; prod d, Richard MacDonald; art d, Marjorie Stone McShirley; fx, Alan Munro, Chuck Comiskey, Chuck Gaspar; chor, Peter Anastos; cos, Ruth Myers

AAN Best Costume Design: Ruth Myers

This meticulously composed homage owes far more to Charles Addams's original *New Yorker* cartoons than to the short-lived '60s TV series. Unfortunately, the filmmakers were so intent on creating the right look and attitude that they neglected to think about the plot; the result is a series of one-note jokes that no amount of visual style can redeem.

The Addamses are a ghoulish clan delighting in the macabre—the devilish opposite of a rosy, wholesome American family. The debonair Gomez Addams (Raul Julia)

and his morbidly elegant wife Morticia (Anjelica Huston) preside over an eccentric household that includes Wednesday (Christina Ricci) and Pugsley (Jimmy Workman), their precociously diabolical offspring; Lurch (Carel Struycken), their aptly named manservant; and Thing (Christopher Hart), a disembodied hand that serves as the family pet. Into this grim but happy bunch come Abigail Craven (Elizabeth Wilson) and her son Gordon (Christopher Lloyd), a con artist duo who, in conspiracy with Tully Alford (Dan Hedaya), the Addams's crooked lawyer, plan to make off with the Addams fortune. The plan revolves around the uncanny resemblance between Gordon and Gomez's long-lost brother, Fester (also played by Lloyd).

Cinematographer-turned-director Barry Sonnenfeld and screenwriters Larry Wilson and Caroline Thompson haven't solved the problem of how to construct a film around a one-joke concept, though the production design is a triumph of post-modern Gothic and there are some effective one-liners (Morticia to a depressed Gomez: "Don't torture yourself, Gomez. That's *my* job.").

ADDAMS FAMILY VALUES   DVD
1993 94m c   Comedy/Horror   ★★★
Paramount   (U.S.)   PG-13

Anjelica Huston *(Morticia Addams)*, Raul Julia *(Gomez Addams)*, Christopher Lloyd *(Uncle Fester Addams)*, Joan Cusack *(Debbie Jellinsky)*, Christina Ricci *(Wednesday Addams)*, Carol Kane *(Granny Addams)*, Jimmy Workman *(Pugsley Addams)*, Kaitlyn Hooper *(Pubert Addams)*, Kristin Hooper *(Pubert Addams)*, Carel Struycken *(Lurch the Butler)*

p, Scott Rudin; d, Barry Sonnenfeld; w, Paul Rudnick (from the characters created by Charles Addams); ph, Donald Peterman; ed, Arthur Schmidt, Jim Miller; m, Marc Shaiman; prod d, Ken Adam; fx, Alan Munro; chor, Peter Anastos; cos, Theoni V. Aldredge

AAN Best Art Direction-Set Decoration: Ken Adam, Marvin March

Like the first ADDAMS FAMILY, this continuation of the macabre clan's misadventures is really just a string of sight gags and one-liners. The good news is that the one-liners are much funnier than the first time, mainly thanks to the increased input of screenwriter Paul Rudnick.

The other major change *chez* Addams is that young Wednesday (Christina Ricci) has entered that "difficult" stage of growing up—boys are starting to pique her interest almost as much as ritual sacrifice. To complicate matters further, the family is upended by the arrival of a new baby of indeterminate gender ("Is it a boy? Is it a girl?"—"It's an Addams!" goes the post-birth exchange, though the infant does sport a Gomez-style mustache). Wednesday and Pugsley (Jimmy Workman) react with unconcealed venom toward their new, rival sibling, showing a keenness to play, not with him, but with his head. Meanwhile, a bogus nanny (Joan Cusack) is scheming to get her hands on Uncle Fester's (Christopher Lloyd) fortune. Her plan involves sending the older children off to an exclusive summer camp, where there are plenty of opportunities to poke fun at the rich, self-obsessed children of rich, self-obsessed parents.

When forced by the camp leader to take part in a cheesy Thanksgiving pageant he has "conceived," Wednesday complains that his work is lacking in both character definition and dramatic structure. The same could be said of ADDAMS FAMILY VALUES but, frankly, we don't give a damn.

ADVENTURES OF BARON MUNCHAUSEN, THE   DVD
1989 126m c   Science Fiction/Fantasy   ★★★
Prominent/Laura/Allied Film Makers   PG
(U.K./West Germany)

John Neville *(Baron Munchausen)*, Eric Idle *(Desmond/Berthold)*, Sarah Polley *(Sally Salt)*, Oliver Reed *(Vulcan)*, Charles McKeown

(Rupert/Adolphus), Winston Dennis *(Bill Albrecht)*, Jack Purvis *(Jeremy/Gustavus)*, Valentina Cortese *(Queen Ariadne/Violet)*, Jonathan Pryce *(Horatio Jackson)*, Bill Paterson *(Henry Salt)*

p, Thomas Schuhly, Ray Cooper; d, Terry Gilliam; w, Charles McKeown, Terry Gilliam (based on the stories by Rudolph Erich Raspe); ph, Giuseppe Rotunno (Eastmancolor); ed, Peter Hollywood; m, Michael Kamen; prod d, Dante Ferretti; art d, Massimo Razzi, Maria Teresa Barbasso; chor, Pino Penesse, Giorgio Rossi; cos, Gabriella Pescucci

AAN Best Art Direction-Set Decoration: Dante Ferretti (Art Direction), Francesca Lo Schiavo (Set Decoration); *AAN Best Costume Design:* Gabriella Pescucci; *AAN Best Visual Effects:* Richard Conway, Kent Houston; *AAN Best Makeup:* Maggie Weston, Fabrizio Sforza

Director Terry Gilliam's THE ADVENTURES OF BARON MUNCHAUSEN adapts the tall tales and fables associated with the real-life Karl Friedrich Hieronymous von Munchausen (1720-97), a German soldier and nobleman. The film begins in a walled city whose denizens suffer under a siege by the army of the Ottoman Empire, and under the government of their evil leader Horatio Jackson (Jonathan Pryce). Within the town, a theater troupe is staging a rendition of the Munchausen saga when an aged man in the audience (John Neville) announces that he's the *real* Baron, and that only he can save them from the siege. He then departs in a makeshift balloon to round up his former cohorts, the superhumanly gifted aides who will help him in his struggle. The narrative is highly episodic and only intermittently engaging, but Gilliam's wildly inventive *mise en scene*, ably assisted by production designer Dante Ferretti, is extraordinary.

ADVENTURES OF BUCKAROO BANZAI: ACROSS THE 8TH DIMENSION, THE   DVD
1984 103m c   Comedy/Science Fiction ★★½
Sherwood   (U.S.)   PG

Peter Weller *(Buckaroo Banzai)*, John Lithgow *(Dr. Emilio Lizardo/Lord John Whorfin)*, Ellen Barkin *(Penny Priddy)*, Jeff Goldblum *(New Jersey)*, Christopher Lloyd *(John Bigboote)*, Lewis Smith *(Perfect Tommy)*, Rosalind Cash *(John Emdall)*, Robert Ito *(Prof. Hikita)*, Pepe Serna *(Reno Nevada)*, Ronald Lacey *(President Widmark)*

p, Neil Canton, W.D. Richter; d, W.D. Richter; w, Earl Mac Rauch; ph, Fred Koenekamp (Panavision, Metrocolor); ed, Richard Marks, George Bowers; m, Michael Boddicker; prod d, J. Michael Riva; art d, Richard Carter, Stephen Dane; fx, Michael Fink; cos, Aggie Guerard Rodgers

Clearly designed as a cult film, this messy trifle is not without its charms. These include the affably weird Goldblum, Lithgow's deliriously overstated mad scientist, and a band of alien invaders who are not emissaries of a vastly superior race, but beer-swilling mediocrities in Hawaiian shirts. Nevertheless, this strange film tries to do too much in too short a time. The title character (Weller) is a nuclear physicist, brain surgeon, and rock-'n'-roll singer who saves the world from the Red Lectroids, aliens from a distant galaxy. As the film opens, Weller is trying to drive his superpowered car through a mountain in an attempt to test the "oscillation overthruster" he has invented. The device is highly coveted by the aliens, who need it in order to return to their own world. Dr. Emilio Lizardo (Lithgow), who conducted the same research decades earlier, escapes from a mental institution and sets up shop again, making plans for world domination in league with the Red Lectroids. Few films appear so obviously to have dropped footage on the cutting-room floor. Punch lines appear without set-ups and set-ups without punch lines. Characters come and go with such bewildering speed that it is virtually impossible to keep track of the story, which jumps around enough to induce motion sickness. BUCKAROO BANZAI has nevertheless earned a loyal cult following among those who are willing to invest time in the roller-coaster ride.

ADVENTURES OF ICHABOD AND MR. TOAD, THE   DVD
1949 68m   c   Animated   ★★★★
Walt Disney Productions   (U.S.)

VOICES OF: Bing Crosby (Narrator), Basil Rathbone, Eric Blore, Pat O'Malley, John Floyardt, Colin Campbell, Campbell Grant, Claud Allister, The Rhythmaires

p, Walt Disney; d, Jack Kinney, Clyde Geronimi, James Algar; w, Erdman Penner, Winston Hibler, Joe Rinaldi, Ted Sears, Homer Brightman, Harry Reeves (based on the story "The Legend of Sleepy Hollow" by Washington Irving and the book *The Wind in the Willows* by Kenneth Grahame)

Split into two sequences, this feature-length cartoon is one of Disney's finest efforts, with attention paid to every animated detail. The first sequence deals with the madcap, aristocratic Mr. Toad of Kenneth Grahame's British classic *The Wind in the Willows*, a haughty amphibian who thinks himself too good for such fellows as Mr. Pig and stuffy Mr. Rat. Toad, who is obsessed with planes and autos, lands through his own recklessness in trouble, debt, and jail, and his friends must rally to get him out and defeat the band of thieving weasels that framed him. The second segment, concerning the emaciated Ichabod Crane of Washington Irving's "The Legend of Sleepy Hollow," is delightfully narrated by Bing Crosby, who also croons some eerie tunes with the Rhythmaires. Ichabod, the new schoolmaster in a small New England village, has a memorable Halloween night when he is chased by the legendary Headless Horseman. For pure imaginative animation, this pell-mell race through forests and glens is still unequaled. ADVENTURE is superb family entertainment, though very young children may find the climactic sequence of the "Sleepy Hollow" portion too frightening. The two segments have been released separately on videocassette.

ADVENTURES OF MARK TWAIN, THE
1944 130m   bw   Biography   ★★★
Warner Bros. (U.S.)

Fredric March (Samuel Clemens), Alexis Smith (Olivia Langdon), Donald Crisp (J. B. Pond), Alan Hale (Steve Gillis), C. Aubrey Smith (Oxford Chancellor), John Carradine (Bret Harte), William Henry (Charles Langdon), Robert Barrat (Horace E. Bixby), Walter Hampden (Jervis Langdon), Joyce Reynolds (Clara Clemens)

p, Jesse L. Lasky; d, Irving Rapper; w, Alan LeMay, Harry Chandlee (based on an adaptation by Alan LeMay and Harold M. Sherman of biographical material owned by the Mark Twain Co.); ph, Sol Polito, Laurence Butler, Eddie Linden, Don Siegel, James Leicester; ed, Ralph Dawson; m, Max Steiner; art d, John Hughes; fx, Paul Detlefsen, John Crous

AAN Best Score (Drama or Comedy): Max Steiner; AAN Best Interior Decoration (B/W): John J Hughes (Art Direction), Fred MacLean (Interior Decoration); AAN Best Special Effects: Paul Detlefsen (Photographic), John Crous (Photographic), Nathan Levinson (Sound)

Cliched but engaging film biography, with a solid performance by Fredric March as the young adventurer who left Hannibal, Missouri, to learn the Mississippi River's tricky ways as a navigator. In one scene, the young navigator is attempting to steer a riverboat through fogbound waters when he hears a deckhand, after throwing out a weight to determine the water's depth, shout: "Mark the twain [twine—the rope tied about the weight] 15 [feet]." Thus the *nom de plume* of one of America's finest writers and humorists. Sharp dialogue sparks the predictable story line as Twain moves from the Mississippi to the West as a newspaper editor, then on to Gold Rush California, where he writes the short story "The Celebrated Jumping Frog of Calaveras County," the success of which launches his literary career. The episodic film chronicles Twain's meetings with the greats of his day (U.S. Grant, Bret Harte, Oliver Wendell Holmes, Ralph Waldo Emerson, etc.), as well as his courtship of and marriage to Olivia Langdon (Alexis Smith), as it follows Twain from young manhood to old age. March imbues his character with quiet nobility, projecting the forceful, courageous soul of the immortal Twain. What's missing is the vinegary, difficult side of Twain that made him as unforgettable a man as he was a writer.

ADVENTURES OF MILO AND OTIS, THE   DVD
(KONEKO MONOGATARI)
1989 76m   c   Children's   ★★★
Fuji Television   (Japan)   G

Dudley Moore (Narrator)

p, Masaru Kakutani, Satoru Ogata; d, Masanori Hata; w, Mark Saltzman (based on a story by Masanori Hata); ph, Hideo Fujii, Shinji Tomita; ed, Chizuko Osada; m, Michael Boddicker

Of all the buddy movies ever made, MILO AND OTIS features one of the most unlikely pairs of friends—a cat and dog that befriend each other on a farm and eventually wander out into the not-so-friendly world. Not a single human being appears onscreen in this delightful live-action entry from Japan. It all starts when the kitten, Milo, decides to take a trip down the river in a box, with his faithful canine chum, Otis, following behind. But soon Otis loses track of his friend, who gets into many adventures. Based on a charming screenplay by Mark Saltzman, this clever children's film contains beautiful nature photography and moments of humor along with many impressive animal stunts. Surely it was no small feat to get bears and dogs, chickens and cats, pigs and cows to work together harmoniously. Shot from the animals' point of view and narrated by Dudley Moore, MILO AND OTIS contains some important messages about the responsibilites of friendship. Slow in spots, but a treat nevertheless.

ADVENTURES OF PRISCILLA, QUEEN OF   DVD
THE DESERT, THE
1994 102m   c   Musical/Drama/Comedy   ★★★
Latent Image/Specific Films   (Australia)   R

Terence Stamp (Bernadette), Hugo Weaving (Tick/Mitzi), Guy Pearce (Adam/Felicia), Bill Hunter (Bob), Sarah Chadwick (Marion), Mark Holmes (Benji), Julia Cortez (Cynthia), Ken Radley (Frank), Alan Dargin (Aboriginal Man), Rebel Russell (Logowoman)

p, Al Clark, Michael Hamlyn; d, Stephan Elliott; w, Stephan Elliott; ph, Brian Breheny; ed, Sue Blainey; m, Guy Gross; prod d, Owen Patterson; art d, Colin Gibson; chor, Mark White; cos, Lizzy Gardiner, Tim Chappel

AA Best Costume Design: Lizzy Gardiner, Tim Chappel

This offbeat Australian road movie about a busload of female impersonators became a surprise hit in the U.S., heralding a wave of cinematic interest in cross-dressing that would embrace everything from WIGSTOCK, a documentary about New York's much-loved open air drag festival, to the star-studded mainstream production, TO WONG FOO, THANKS FOR EVERYTHING, JULIE NEWMAR.

Drag performer Tick/Mitzi (Hugo Weaving) invites recently bereaved transsexual Bernadette (Terence Stamp)

to join him and Adam/Felicia (Guy Pearce) on a journey to the outback town of Alice Springs, where they've been invited to put on a show at a casino run by an ex-partner of Tick's. The Priscilla of the title is the dilapidated bus Adam buys for the trip.

PRISCILLA is less concerned with "normalizing" gay lifestyles than earlier cross-dressing comedies such as LA CAGE AUX FOLLES and VICTOR/VICTORIA. The script is spiked with cheeky, occasionally hilarious encounters, like the trio's stroll through a lazy Outback town in flamboyant space-age drag, or Bernadette's deliciously unprintable riposte to a hostile woman in a bar. But the film tends toward pat, sitcom-style resolutions to its potentially interesting conflicts, and cannot sustain the manic, farcical pace of its best moments.

Things truly come alive during the drag performances and rehearsals, boosted by an irrepressible disco soundtrack. The Oscar-winning costumes by Lizzy Gardiner and Tim Chappel are wildly inspired, and the filmmakers indulge themselves—and us—with extended shots of the outrageously attired performers set against the spectacularly barren landscape. The true heart of the movie, though, is Terence Stamp. He may be a little stiff in the show routines but, offstage, he's a revelation, giving a performance of near-perfect restraint and dignity.

ADVENTURES OF ROBIN HOOD, THE   **DVD**
1938   102m   c   Adventure   ★★★★★
Warner Bros. (U.S.)

Errol Flynn *(Sir Robin of Locksley/Robin Hood)*, Olivia de Havilland *(Maid Marian)*, Basil Rathbone *(Sir Guy of Gisbourne)*, Claude Rains *(Prince John)*, Patric Knowles *(Will Scarlett)*, Eugene Pallette *(Friar Tuck)*, Alan Hale *(Little John)*, Melville Cooper *(High Sheriff of Nottingham)*, Ian Hunter *(King Richard the Lion-Hearted)*, Una O'Connor *(Bess)*

p, Henry Blanke; d, Michael Curtiz, William Keighley; w, Norman Reilly Raine, Seton I. Miller (based on the novel *Ivanhoe* by Sir Walter Scott and the opera *Robin Hood* by De Koven-Smith); ph, Sol Polito, Tony Gaudio (Technicolor); ed, Ralph Dawson; m, Erich Wolfgang Korngold; art d, Carl Jules Weyl; cos, Milo Anderson

AAN Best Picture; AA Best Film Editing: Ralph Dawson; *AA Best Score:* Erich Wolfgang Korngold; *AA Best Interior Decoration:* Carl J. Weyl

When King Richard the Lion-Hearted (Ian Hunter) is captured by Austrians and held for ransom, evil Prince John (Claude Rains) declares himself ruler of England and makes no attempt to secure Richard's safe return. Though John has all the nobles and their armies on his side, it doesn't sway a lone knight, Robin Hood (Errol Flynn), who swears his allegiance to Richard and sets out to raise the ransom money by stealing from the caravans of the rich that cross through Sherwood Forest. Robin is aided by his lady love, Maid Marian (Olivia de Havilland), and his band of merry men, including Little John (Alan Hale) and Friar Tuck (Eugene Pallette), as he battles the false monarch and the villainous Sheriff of Nottingham (Melville Cooper) in his effort to return the throne to its rightful owner. This is one of the truly great adventure films of all time, and features a terrific performance by the perfectly cast Flynn. Handsome, dashing, and athletic, Flynn is everything that Robin Hood should be, with a wicked sense of humor to boot. His adversaries are all memorable villains, particularly Basil Rathbone as the conniving Sir Guy of Gisbourne. Rathbone spent many hours with a fencing instructor to prepare for his climactic duel with Flynn, one of the most exciting battles ever put on film. Only a spirited and extravagant production could do justice to the Robin Hood legend; this film is more than equal to the

task. Korngold's score won a well-deserved Oscar, as did the editing and art direction.

ADVENTURES OF ROBINSON CRUSOE, THE   **DVD**
1952   90m   c   Adventure   ★★★½
UA   (Mexico)

Dan O'Herlihy *(Robinson Crusoe)*, Jaime Fernandez *(Friday)*, Felipe de Alba *(Capt. Oberzo)*, Chel Lopez *(Bos'n)*, Jose Chavez, Emilio Garibay *(Leaders of the Mutiny)*

p, Oscar Dancigers, Henry Ehrlich; d, Luis Bunuel; w, Hugo Butler, Luis Bunuel (based on the novel *The Life and Strange Surprising Adventures of Robinson Crusoe* by Daniel Defoe); ph, Alex Phillips (Pathecolor); ed, Carlos Savage, Alberto Valenzuela; m, Anthony Collins

AAN Best Actor: Dan O'Herlihy

A fairly faithful adaptation of Daniel Defoe's classic *The Life and Strange Surprising Adventures of Robinson Crusoe,* directed by Bunuel in Mexico. Shipwrecked in a storm, sailor Robinson Crusoe (Dan O'Herlihy) finds himself washed up on the shore of a desert island. All other hands have been killed in the storm, but Crusoe is able to salvage a cat, a dog, and some weapons and provisions from the wreckage. He takes up residence in a cave and begins living as his prehistoric ancestors must have done, all the while striving to overcome his oppressive loneliness. After going 18 years without seeing another human being, he is shocked when a small band of natives visits the island one day. They are about to kill and eat one of their party when Crusoe intervenes, saves the intended victim, and chases off the others. The two develop a strong relationship as they spend another ten years on the island, after which Crusoe is finally returned to civilization by the crew of a ship that anchors offshore.

Bunuel's adaptation is particularly effective in evoking the loneliness of the stranded survivor and in depicting the changes that gradually occur within him as his memories of civilization begin to fade. O'Herlihy earned an Academy Award nomination for his performance, but lost to Marlon Brando for ON THE WATERFRONT.

ADVENTURES OF SHERLOCK HOLMES, THE   **DVD**
1939   85m   bw   Mystery   ★★★★
Fox   (U.S.)

Basil Rathbone *(Sherlock Holmes)*, Nigel Bruce *(Dr. Watson)*, Ida Lupino *(Ann Brandon)*, Alan Marshal *(Jerrold Hunter)*, Terry Kilburn *(Billy)*, George Zucco *(Prof. Moriarty)*, Henry Stephenson *(Sir Ronald Ramsgate)*, E.E. Clive *(Inspector Bristol)*, Arthur Hohl *(Bassick)*, May Beatty *(Mrs. Jameson)*

p, Gene Markey; d, Alfred Werker; w, Edwin Blum, William A. Drake (based on the play by William Gillette and the works of Arthur Conan Doyle); ph, Leon Shamroy; ed, Robert Bischoff

A taut script and sharp, witty dialogue make this, the second of the Basil Rathbone/Nigel Bruce Sherlock Holmes vehicles, one of the finest crime adventures ever made. Arch-villain Professor Moriarty (Zucco, in the first of many appearances as Holmes's chief nemesis) plots a grand theft by sidetracking Holmes (Rathbone) with two foul murders, one involving Ann Brandon (Lupino). As Holmes investigates the murders, Moriarty begins work on his real goal, stealing the crown jewels from the Tower of London.

ADVENTURES was released a mere six months after THE HOUND OF THE BASKERVILLES and is generally considered superior to its predecessor, thanks to Alfred Werker's direction. Although both films were box office hits, Fox executives thought of the Holmes films as expensive "B" pictures and declined to continue the series at the outbreak of

WWII, assuming the public would be uninterested in the 19th century British sleuth. In 1942 Universal reunited Rathbone and Bruce, updated the scenarios to reflect contemporary themes (i.e., Nazi spies), scaled down the production costs and turned out 11 successful, if inferior, installments.

ADVENTURES OF TOM SAWYER, THE
1938 93m c Adventure ★★★½
Selznick (U.S.)

Tommy Kelly *(Tom Sawyer)*, Jackie Moran *(Huckleberry Finn)*, Ann Gillis *(Becky Thatcher)*, May Robson *(Aunt Polly)*, Walter Brennan *(Muff Potter)*, Victor Jory *(Injun Joe)*, David Holt *(Sid Sawyer)*, Victor Kilian *(Sheriff)*, Nana Bryant *(Mrs. Thatcher)*, Olin Howlin *(Schoolmaster)*

p, David O. Selznick, William H. Wright; d, Norman Taurog; w, John V.A. Weaver (based on the novel by Mark Twain); ph, James Wong Howe, Wilfrid M. Cline (Technicolor); ed, Margaret Clancy

AAN Best Interior Decoration: Lyle Wheeler (Art Direction)

Mark Twain's beloved Tom Sawyer comes to life in this excellent Selznick production, with Tommy Kelly portraying the brave, mischievous boy. He is caught between the manners of his very proper home, ruled by tough but loving Aunt Polly (May Robson), and the wild, roaming, trouble-seeking nature of his friend Huckleberry Finn, ably portrayed by Jackie Moran. The great Sawyer adventures are faithfully re-created—the conning of the two boys into whitewashing his aunt's fence, a wild ride down the Mississippi on a raft, the witnessing of Injun Joe's crimes and his pursuit of Tom and the terrified Becky Sharp (Ann Gillis) into the giant cave. The incorrigible boys even witness their own funeral ceremony before informing the grieving townsfolk that they are still among the living. A lively production featuring a quick pace, a chilling climax, and a surprising amount of wit.

ADVENTURESS, THE
1946 111m bw Spy 📀 ★★★★
Individual (U.K.)

Deborah Kerr *(Bridie Quilty)*, Trevor Howard *(Lt. David Bayne)*, Raymond Huntley *(Miller)*, Michael Howard *(Hawkins)*, Norman Shelley *(Man in Straw Hat)*, Liam Redmond *(Timothy)*, Brefni O'Rorke *(Michael O'Callaghan)*, James Harcourt *(Grandfather)*, W.G. O'Gorman *(Danny Quilty)*, George Woodbridge *(Steve)*

p, Sidney Gilliat; d, Frank Launder; w, Sidney Gilliat, Frank Launder, Wolfgang Wilhelm; ph, Wilkie Cooper; ed, Thelma Myers; m, William Alwyn

An expertly crafted suspense film that is too often overlooked. Deborah Kerr, making her fifth feature at age 24, appears as an Irish spitfire who has been weaned on her grandfather's tales of British cruelty to the Irish; she leaves her small village of Ballygarry, spouting anti-British venom to a stranger, Huntley, on board a train to Dublin, where the IRA rejects her. But Huntley, a Nazi agent, uses her as a pawn, telling her that he represents another branch of the movement and involving her in the rescue of "one of the lads" imprisoned in a British jail—in reality, another Nazi spy. Howard, as a British intelligence agent, tracks her down and falls in love with her, staying a step behind through one perilous adventure after another, both to protect her and to uncover the Nazi spy ring. This is a highly suspenseful, atmospheric film in the Hitchcock tradition with a sophisticated script by Launder and Gilliat, who authored THE LADY VANISHES. The acting, particularly by Kerr (who won the 1947 New York Film Critics Award for this role and her appearance in BLACK NARCISSUS), Howard, and Huntley, is outstanding.

ADVISE AND CONSENT
1962 140m bw Political 📀 ★★★½
Columbia (U.S.)

Henry Fonda *(Robert Leffingwell)*, Charles Laughton *(Sen. Seabright "Seb" Cooley)*, Don Murray *(Sen. Brigham Anderson)*, Walter Pidgeon *(Sen. Bob Munson)*, Peter Lawford *(Sen. Lafe Smith)*, George Grizzard *(Sen. Fred Van Ackerman)*, Gene Tierney *(Dolly Harrison)*, Franchot Tone *(The President)*, Lew Ayres *(The Vice-President)*, Burgess Meredith *(Herbert Gelman)*

p, Otto Preminger; d, Otto Preminger; w, Wendell Mayes (based on the novel by Allen Drury); ph, Sam Leavitt; ed, Louis Loeffler; m, Jerry Fielding; prod d, Lyle Wheeler; cos, Hope Bryce

Incisive, sometimes brutal, study of American high politics, based on Allen Drury's best-selling novel, featuring outstanding performances from the leads and a great collection of character actors.

Fonda has been appointed Secretary of State, and the film revolves around his appointment's confirmation by the U.S. Senate. Pidgeon and his cohorts are trying to push the appointment through, past such ancient pelicans as Laughton, in a marvelous portrayal of a crusty old Dixiecrat. Murray, a freshman senator whose vote in support of the nomination is vital, will not commit to his party leader, Pidgeon. This leads Grizzard, a ruthless, power-hungry colleague, to attempt to blackmail Murray into siding with his voting block. He digs up Murray's former homosexual activities and threatens to expose him unless he votes "the right way," with unexpectedly tragic results.

In an all-star cast, Laughton shines in his last role, but the subdued work by Tone and Ayres shows how underplaying can sometimes work best before the camera. Though the film sensationalizes politics, Preminger's touch is more precise and cautious than usual; this is a more realistic if less human portrait of the Senate than Capra's MR. SMITH GOES TO WASHINGTON. Both films proved to be unpopular with their role models, who refused to comment on them.

AFFLICTION
1998 114m c Drama 📀 ★★★
Kingsgate Films (U.S.) R

Nick Nolte *(Wade Whitehouse)*, Sissy Spacek *(Margie Fogg)*, James Coburn *(Glen Whitehouse)*, Willem Dafoe *(Rolfe Whitehouse)*, Mary Beth Hurt *(Lillian)*, Jim True *(Jack Hewitt)*, Marian Seldes *(Alma Pittman)*, Holmes Osborne *(Gordon LaRiviere)*, Brigid Tierney *(Jill)*, Sean McCann *(Evan Twombley)*

p, Linda Reisman; d, Paul Schrader; w, Paul Schrader (based on the novel by Russell Banks); ph, Paul Sarossy; ed, Jay Rabinowitz; m, Michael Brook; prod d, Anne Pritchard; cos, Francois Laplante

AAN Best Actor: Nick Nolte; *AA Best Supporting Actor:* James Coburn

A desolate look at the poisonous legacy of violence, this adaptation of Russell Banks's novel (Banks also penned *The Sweet Hereafter*) is as icy and lacerating as its title suggests.

Wade Whitehouse (Nick Nolte) is a hard-drinking, quick-fisted cop in a Vermont town so small and virtually crime-free that he works a second job plowing snow to fill the time and make ends meet. He's dating local waitress Margie Fogg (Sissy Spacek) and trying to patch up his relationship with Jill (Brigid Tierney), his daughter by a first marriage that flew apart under the pressure of his boozing and explosive temper. The key to Wade's seething anger lies in his embittered relationship with his snarling, junkyard dog of a father (James Coburn), next to whom the average bad dad is a candidate for beatification. But Wade isn't much for deep thinking: that's for his brother, Rolfe (Willem Dafoe), who wisely got out the first minute he could. Wade's burning need to prove himself drives him to investigate obsessively the death of a vacationing union bigwig in what appears to be a hunting accident: a passing remark during a late-night phone conversation with Rolfe makes Wade suspect a conspiracy involving corrupt entrepreneurs, a local land grab, and maybe even organized crime. It's not long before even Oliver Stone would have to ask himself whether there truly is anything untoward going on, or whether battered Wade's mind is slowly slipping its greasy hinges.

Surrounded by pitch-perfect performances, Coburn is the show-stealer: he spews a near-constant stream of invective so corrosive it appears to have eaten away his gums and exposed his teeth clean up to the roots. Caustic and despairing, Paul Shrader's film lacks the delicate beauty of Atom Agoyan's SWEET HEREAFTER, but has just as much bitter power.

AFRICAN QUEEN, THE

1951 105m c   Adventure/Romance/War   ★★★★★
Horizon/Romulus   (U.S./U.K.)

Humphrey Bogart *(Charlie Allnut)*, Katharine Hepburn *(Rose Sayer)*, Robert Morley *(Rev. Samuel Sayer)*, Peter Bull *(Captain)*, Theodore Bikel *(1st Officer)*, Walter Gotell *(2nd Officer)*, Gerald Onn *(Petty Officer)*, Peter Swanwick, Richard Marner *(Officers at Shona)*

p, Sam Spiegel; d, John Huston; w, James Agee, John Huston (based on the novel by C.S. Forester); ph, Jack Cardiff (Technicolor); ed, Ralph Kemplen; m, Allan Gray

AA Best Actor: Humphrey Bogart; *AAN Best Actress:* Katharine Hepburn; *AAN Best Director:* John Huston; *AAN Best Screenplay:* James Agee, John Huston

---

John Huston's THE AFRICAN QUEEN is a film that has everything—adventure, humor, spectacular photography and superb performances.

In his only Oscar-winning performance, Bogart stars as Charlie Allnut, a reprobate who uses his little battered steamer, *The African Queen*, to run supplies to small villages in East Africa at the onset of WWI. At one stop he meets Rose (Katharine Hepburn), the devoted spinster sister of Rev. Samuel Sayer (Robert Morley). When Charlie returns to the village later, he finds that German troops have invaded and Sayer is dead, and he offers to take the distraught Rose back to civilization. Thus begins a perilous and unforgettable journey as Charlie and Rose decide to do their part in the war effort against the Germans.

THE AFRICAN QUEEN's marvelous screenplay was written as a straight drama by James Agee, but director John Huston and his stars give it a lyrical tongue-in-cheek treatment that fills the screen with hilarious humanity. Magnificently filmed on location in Africa by Jack Cardiff, THE AFRICAN QUEEN is Hollywood filmmaking of the highest order.

AFTER DARK, MY SWEET

1990 114m c   Crime   *DVD*
Avenue   (U.S.)   ★★★½   R

Jason Patric *(Collie)*, Rachel Ward *(Fay)*, Bruce Dern *(Uncle Bud)*, George Dickerson *(Doc Goldman)*, James Cotton *(Charlie)*, Corey Carrier *(Jack)*, Rocky Giordani *(Bert)*, Jeanie Moore *(Nanny)*, Tom Wagner *(Counterman)*, Burke Byrnes *(Cop)*

p, Ric Kidney, Robert Redlin; d, James Foley; w, James Foley, Robert Redlin (based on the novel by Jim Thompson); ph, Mark Plummer; ed, Howard Smith; m, Maurice Jarre; art d, Kenneth A. Hardy; fx, Ken Diaz

---

A latter-day film noir involving the intertwined destinies of three boozy lowlifes. Collie (Jason Patric) is a near-psychopathic ex-boxer who left the ring after killing a competitor. He becomes involved with Fay (Rachel Ward), a seductive, alcoholic widow, and Uncle Bud (Bruce Dern), a sleazy former lawman, and is drawn into their scheme to get rich quick by kidnapping the young scion of a wealthy local family.

AFTER DARK, MY SWEET is based on a 1955 novel by prolific tough-guy novelist Jim Thompson, who worked on the screenplays of THE KILLING and PATHS OF GLORY for Stanley Kubrick, and whose *The Grifters* and *The Kill-Off* were also turned into 1990 releases. Director James Foley (RECKLESS, AT CLOSE RANGE) and cinematographer Mark Plummer deftly conjure the sense of stifling containment that drives these characters to drink or sin, but Robert Redlin's screenplay fails to fully animate their personalities. Patric gives a tremendous, smoldering performance, but Ward fails to convey the mysterious radiance of a convincing femme fatale. Dern rounds out the unappetizing triangle with an unpleasant performance, proving himself a worthy contender in the Dennis Hopper/Harry Dean Stanton creepstakes.

AFTER HOURS

                             DVD
1985 96m c   Comedy   ★★★★
Double Play/Geffen   (U.S.)   R

Griffin Dunne *(Paul Hackett)*, Rosanna Arquette *(Marcy)*, Verna Bloom *(June)*, Tommy Chong *(Pepe)*, Linda Fiorentino *(Kiki)*, Teri Garr *(Julie)*, John Heard *(Tom, the Bartender)*, Richard "Cheech" Marin *(Neil)*, Catherine O'Hara *(Gail)*, Dick Miller *(Waiter)*

p, Amy Robinson, Griffin Dunne, Robert F. Colesberry; d, Martin Scorsese; w, Joseph Minion; ph, Michael Ballhaus (Duart Color); ed, Thelma Schoonmaker; m, Howard Shore; prod d, Jeffrey Townsend; art d, Stephen J. Lineweaver; cos, Rita Ryack

---

A wickedly funny black comedy that follows the increasingly bizarre series of events that befall hapless word-processer Griffin Dunne after he ventures out of his apartment on the Upper East Side of Manhattan and goes downtown in search of carnal pleasures. On a wild cab trip to SoHo, Dunne loses the only folding money he has on him. When he goes to the loft of the sexy but quirky Rosanna Arquette, he discovers only Linda Fiorentino, working on a papier-mache sculpture. Eventually Arquette shows up, but she's such a hyperactive mass of contradictions that Dunne leaves. However, when he plunks down the 90 cents he has to his name at the subway station, the attendant tells him the fare has gone up to $1.50 this very midnight. He's trapped in SoHo, and things only get worse as the night wears on.

Scorsese is in total command of his visual style in AFTER HOURS, a tightly constructed film that races from scene to scene. The story sprang from the mind of screenwriter Joseph Minion, a Columbia University film student who had written the script for a class. Dunne turns in a superb performance, and we share his mounting frustration, fear, shame, and guilt. Scorsese ordered Dunne to abstain from sex and sleep during filming to increase his anxiety level, and filmed this small gem on location for the small budget of $3.5 million.

AFTER THE THIN MAN

1936 107m bw   Comedy/Mystery   ★★★½
MGM   (U.S.)

William Powell *(Nick Charles)*, Myrna Loy *(Nora Charles)*, James Stewart *(David Graham)*, Joseph Calleia *(Dancer)*, Elissa Landi *(Selma Landis)*, Jessie Ralph *(Aunt Katherine Forrest)*, Alan Marshal *(Robert Landis)*, Sam Levene *(Lt. Abrams)*, Teddy Hart *(Floyd Casper)*, Penny Singleton, billed as Dorothy McNulty *(Polly Byrnes)*

p, Hunt Stromberg; d, W.S. Van Dyke II; w, Frances Goodrich, Albert Hackett (based on a story by Dashiell Hammett); ph,

Oliver T. Marsh; ed, Robert J. Kern; m, Herbert Stothart; art d, Cedric Gibbons

AAN Best Screenplay: Frances Goodrich, Albert Hackett

In this breezy sequel to THE THIN MAN, William Powell and Myrna Loy are up to their ears in three quick murders after Elissa Landi asks Powell to find her vanished husband. It seems that hubby has been trysting with nightclub song-bird Penny Singleton (later of BLONDIE fame), and is also blackmailing big shot Joseph Calleia. Powell learns that James Stewart, who also has a yen for Singleton, has paid the husband to "disappear" a former girl friend. The investi-gation proves to be the only distraction in the lives of Powell and Loy. (She's idle and rich; he drinks incessantly except when working, so of course she wants him working to curb the booze.) The missing husband, Alan Marshal, turns up murdered, so Powell rounds up the suspects and names the killer (an unlikely casting candidate).

The script is tight, the direction is swift and arresting, and the cast is tops—MGM surrounded its two quipping stars with the best character actors on the lot. Dashiell Hammett's snappy banter and cynical worldview were kept intact by Frances Goodrich and Albert Hackett, making this production all the more delectable.

AFTERGLOW

1997 113m c Romance/Drama ★★★★
Rain City/Gallery Motion Pictures (U.S./Canada) R

Julie Christie *(Phyllis Mann)*, Nick Nolte *(Lucky Mann)*, Lara Flynn Boyle *(Marianne Byron)*, Jonny Lee Miller *(Jeffrey Byron)*, Jay Underwood *(Donald Duncan)*, Domini Blythe *(Helene Pelletier)*, Yves Corbeil *(Bernard Ornay)*, Alan Fawcett *(Count Falco/Jack Dana)*, Genevieve Bissonnette *(Cassie)*, Michele-Barbara Pelletier *(Isabel Marino)*

p, Robert Altman; d, Alan Rudolph; w, Alan Rudolph; ph, Toyomichi Kurita; ed, Suzy Elmiger; m, Mark Isham; prod d, Francois Seguin; art d, Collin Niemi; cos, Francois Barbeau

AAN Best Actress: Julie Christie

Alan Rudolph returns to the subject of urban romance with a film that recalls the moods and textures of his 1984 hit CHOOSE ME. The four leads all give first-rate performances as people dealing with faded romance.

In Montreal, the marriages of two displaced couples are foundering. Contractor Lucky Mann (Nick Nolte) and his wife, Phyllis (Julie Christie), a former actress in B-budget hor-ror films, haven't been intimate since their daughter ran away from home eight years earlier. Jeffrey Byron (Jonny Lee Miller) is a successful young business executive whose wife, Marianne (Lara Flynn Boyle), wants to have a baby, although Jeffrey has been avoiding having sex with her. Marianne hires Lucky to do some repairs on their apartment, and begins to seduce him. Meanwhile, Jeffrey encounters Phyllis at a hotel bar and invites her to go away with him for the weekend. The two cheating couples discover their entanglements when all end up at the same hotel.

Like David Lynch, Alan Rudolph understands the way that film appeals to the unconscious and therefore uses dream-logic to structure his work. But while Lynch is fascinated by the dark undercurrents, Rudolph is an obsessive romantic. The fact that the plot of AFTERGLOW, like many of Rudolph's films, relies heavily on coincidence should be seen not as a defect in realism but as reinforcement that the film should be viewed on an emotional rather than rational level. The film maintains a consistent mood via the usual Rudolph trade-marks of strong performances, sensual camera work, and moodily erotic jazz score (by longtime Rudolph collaborator Mark Isham). AFTERGLOW may not win this underrecog-

nized filmmaker any new fans, but it will certainly delight those he already has.

AGE OF INNOCENCE, THE

1993 133m c Drama/Historical/Romance ★★★★
Columbia/Cappa/De Fina Productions (U.S.) PG

Daniel Day-Lewis *(Newland Archer)*, Michelle Pfeiffer *(Countess Ellen Olenska)*, Winona Ryder *(May Welland)*, Alexis Smith *(Louisa Van Der Luyden)*, Geraldine Chaplin *(Mrs. Welland)*, Mary Beth Hurt *(Regina Beaufort)*, Alec McCowen *(Sillerton Jackson)*, Richard E. Grant *(Larry Lefferts)*, Miriam Margolyes *(Mrs. Mingott)*, Robert Sean Leonard *(Ted Archer)*

p, Barbara De Fina; d, Martin Scorsese; w, Jay Cocks, Martin Scorsese (from the novel by Edith Wharton); ph, Michael Ballhaus; ed, Thelma Schoonmaker; m, Elmer Bernstein; prod d, Dante Ferretti; art d, Speed Hopkins, Jean-Michel Hugon; fx, John Ottesen, Illusion Arts; cos, Gabriella Pescucci, Tirelli Costumi Roma, Barbara Matera Ltd.

AAN Best Adapted Screenplay: Jay Cocks, Martin Scorsese; *AAN Best Supporting Actress:* Winona Ryder; *AAN Best Art Direction-Set Decoration:* Dante Ferretti, Robert J. Franco; *AA Best Costume Design:* Gabriella Pescucci; *AAN Best Original Score:* Elmer Bernstein

Rendered with sumptuous, almost painful accuracy, THE AGE OF INNOCENCE, adapted from the novel by Edith Wharton, seems at first glance an unlikely venture for relent-lessly contemporary New Yorker Martin Scorsese. But its lov-ing exploration of the arcane workings of a closed society, that of wealthy, well-bred New Yorkers of the 1870s, has more in common than one might expect with Scorsese's earlier work, from MEAN STREETS through GOODFELLAS. Perhaps the film's most remarkable aspect is how alien its underlying assumptions are to a society saturated with "Just Do It!" mes-sages. Beneath the delineation of manners and mannerisms, the examination of lushly appointed decor and clothing, the evocation of a time and a place lost to the forward rush of his-tory, THE AGE OF INNOCENCE rests on a moral struggle all but impossible to imagine in a modern-day setting.

Newland Archer (Daniel Day-Lewis), a respectable but vaguely discontented young lawyer, is engaged to marry the vapid and eminently proper May Welland (Winona Ryder). Their well-ordered lives are disrupted by the return of May's cousin, Ellen Olenska (Michelle Pfeiffer), a countess by virtue of her marriage to a Polish aristocrat. Intelligent, sophisticated, and just a bit too continental after her years abroad, Ellen is at first shunned by New York society, then tolerated after the Archers and the Wellands band together to draw her back into the fold. The film charts the painfully hesitant progress of Ellen and Newland's forbidden romance, no less passionate for being doomed.

THE AGE OF INNOCENCE is a feast for the eyes, and Scorsese brings to stuffy New York society the same keen regard for the rules of social games that characterize his ear-lier films.

AGNES OF GOD

1985 98m c Mystery ★★★
Columbia (U.S.) PG-13

Jane Fonda *(Dr. Martha Livingston)*, Anne Bancroft *(Sister Miriam Ruth)*, Meg Tilly *(Sister Agnes)*, Anne Pitoniak *(Dr. Livingston's Mother)*, Winston Rekert *(Detective Langevin)*, Gratien Gelinas *(Father Martineau)*, Guy Hoffman *(Justice Joseph Leveau)*, Gabriel Arcand *(Monsignor)*, Francoise Faucher *(Eve LeClaire)*, Jacques Tourangeau *(Eugene Lyon)*

p, Patrick Palmer, Norman Jewison; d, Norman Jewison; w, John Pielmeier (based on his play); ph, Sven Nykvist (Metrocolor); ed,

Antony Gibbs; m, Georges Delerue; prod d, Ken Adam; art d, Carol Spier; cos, Renee April

AAN Best Actress: Anne Bancroft; *AAN Best Supporting Actress:* Meg Tilly; *AAN Best Original Score:* Georges Delerue

Set in a Quebec convent, this well-made mystery raises theological and philosophical questions as it unfolds its tale of the murder of a baby born to a young nun who has no recollection of the infant's conception or delivery. Jane Fonda, a chain-smoking court-appointed psychiatrist, is given the task of determining whether Meg Tilly, a beatific young nun, is sane, sainted, mad, or a murderer. But Anne Bancroft, the convent's mother superior, questions whether the answer to the mystery lies in psychology, setting up a faith-versus-reason confrontation that is the real focus of the film. John Pielmeier's award-winning 1982 play is adapted for the screen here by director Norman Jewison, and though the plot has some annoying holes, the dialogue and the performances are excellent. Both Tilly and Bancroft received Oscar nominations for their work, along with Georges Delerue for his original music score.

AGUIRRE, THE WRATH OF GOD

(AGUIRRE, DER ZORN GOTTES)
1972   90m   c   Historical
(West Germany)

★★★★★

Klaus Kinski *(Don Lope de Aguirre)*, Ruy Guerra *(Don Pedro de Ursua)*, Del Negro *(Brother Gaspar de Carvajal)*, Helena Rojo *(Inez)*, Cecilia Rivera *(Flores)*, Peter Berling *(Don Fernando de Guzman)*, Alejandro Repulles *(Gonzalez Pizarro)*, Daniel Ades *(Perucho)*, Armando Polanha *(Armando)*, Edward Roland *(Okello)*

p, Werner Herzog; d, Werner Herzog; w, Werner Herzog; ph, Thomas Mauch (Eastmancolor); ed, Beate Mainka-Jellinghaus; m, Popol Vuh; fx, Juvenal Herrera, Miguel Vasquez

A stunning, terrifying exploration of human obsession descending into madness. Herzog's most powerful fiction film chronicles the Peruvian expedition led by Gonzalez Pizarro (half-brother of the brutal conqueror of the Incas) in search of the legendary city of gold, El Dorado. The film opens in 1560 when Pizarro (Repulles), his men exhausted from their excruciating journey through the dense jungles, decides to send a small party ahead to determine if exploration should continue. Though Don Pedro de Ursua (Guerra) is put in charge, he is challenged by the maniacally ambitious Aguirre (Kinski), who insists against increasingly overwhelming odds that the journey continue, with devastating consequences. The film is based on a journal written by Gaspar de Carvajal, who was one of an army of Spaniards who accompanied the real Gonzalez Pizarro.

Kinski's intensity makes him a remarkable Aguirre; indeed, it is difficult to recall a more intensely driven character in film. His madness is portrayed against an almost hallucinatory environment enhanced by Thomas Mauch's brilliant cinematography and Popol Vuh's spare score. Herzog's cast and crew suffered incredible hardships filming in unexplored regions of South America but as a result the director captured a hostile, mysterious jungle world in such a way as to trivialize complaints that traditional story elements and character development are missing. Just as Aguirre is able to overwhelm the people around him, so the watcher can count on a staggering cinematic experience that assaults the senses.

AH, WILDERNESS!

1935 101m bw Comedy
MGM   (U.S.)

★★★★

Wallace Beery *(Sid Davis)*, Lionel Barrymore *(Nat Miller)*, Aline MacMahon *(Lily Davis)*, Eric Linden *(Richard Miller)*, Cecilia

Parker *(Muriel McComber)*, Spring Byington *(Essie Miller)*, Mickey Rooney *(Tommy Miller)*, Charley Grapewin *(Mr. McComber)*, Frank Albertson *(Arthur Miller)*, Eddie Nugent *(Wint Selby)*

p, Hunt Stromberg; d, Clarence Brown; w, Albert Hackett, Frances Goodrich (based on the play by Eugene O'Neill); ph, Clyde De Vinna; ed, Frank E. Hull; m, Herbert Stothart; art d, Cedric Gibbons, William A. Horning

Eugene O'Neill's only comedy, written in five weeks, is a dream of the sweet, unaffected boyhood he never had, culminating in one long summer during which adolescence struggles into manhood. Eric Linden plays Richard Miller, a young man of sincerity and some charming stupidity. His mother busies herself with household problems, his mischievous brother and unruly sister vex him, his father nervously avoids instructing him in the ways of the world, and his often-inebriated uncle teaches him about life. It's a marvelous slice of Americana, filled with funny and tender scenes as young Richard strives to understand himself and those around him. Mickey Rooney, here playing the younger brother, played the lead role thirteen years later in the musical remake, SUMMER HOLIDAY.

A.I.: ARTIFICIAL INTELLIGENCE

2001 140m c   Science Fiction/Fantasy/Drama   ★★★
DreamWorks SKG/Warner Bros./Amblin/   PG-13
Stanley Kubrick   (U.S.)

Haley Joel Osment *(David)*, Jude Law *(Gigolo Joe)*, Sam Robards *(Henry Swinton)*, Frances O'Connor *(Monica Swinton)*, Jake Thomas *(Martin Swinton)*, Brendan Gleeson *(Lord Johnson-Johnson)*, William Hurt *(Professor Hobby)*, Jack Angel *(Voice of Teddy)*, Ben Kingsley *(Narrator)*, Robin Williams *(Voice of Dr. Know)*

p, Bonnie Curtis, Kathleen Kennedy, Steven Spielberg; d, Steven Spielberg; w, Steven Spielberg (based on a screen story by Ian Watson and the short story "Super-Toys Last All Summer Long" by Brian Aldiss); ph, Janusz Kaminski; ed, Michael Kahn; m, John Williams; prod d, Rick Carter; art d, Richard Johnson, Jim Teegarden, Thomas Valentine; fx, Chris Cunningham, Scott Farrar, Industrial Light & Magic, Michael Lantieri, Dennis Muren, Stan Winston (makeup); chor, Francesca Jaynes; cos, Bob Ringwood

AAN Best Original Score: John Williams; *AAN Best Visual Effects:* Dennis Muren, Scott Farrar, Stan Winston, Michael Lantieri

Steven Spielberg inherited this project from Stanley Kubrick, but it could be an offshoot of BLADE RUNNER. It's driven by the same fundamental question: How perfectly can we replicate ourselves in synthetic beings before we must ask ourselves what makes us human and them not?

In an ecologically devastated future, childbearing is strictly controlled and robotic "mechas" cater to the needs of the prosperous few. In the yearnings of childless couples, Professor Hobby (William Hurt) sees an opportunity: artificial children, programmed to love like the real thing. Hobby's prototype, David (Haley Joel Osment), is given to Henry and Monica Swinton (Sam Robards, Frances O'Connor), for testing; their own terminally ill son, Martin (Jake Thomas), lies in cryogenic deep-freeze awaiting a cure. David is built to love Monica, and she begins to love him back. Then, unexpectedly, Martin is cured and returns home, and his intense jealousy dictates that David must go. Rather than return him to the manufacturer for destruction, Monica lets David loose in the woods. David, tearful and uncomprehending, turns to the tale of "Pinocchio" to make sense of his abandonment: If he can somehow become a real boy, Monica will let him come home. David finds a reluctant protector in Gigolo Joe (Jude Law, who jolts the film to life), a sexbot on the run from the law, and begins to seek his place in the world.

It's pointless to wonder what Kubrick would have made of this evocative material. He had his chance and apparently felt the story was more up Spielberg's alley than his own, by which he presumably meant that it lent itself to sentiment and spectacle. Surprisingly, it's one of Spielberg's grimmest films. Shot through with haunting poetry, this dark, slickly crafted fable resonates with an emotional violence that's genuinely disturbing.

AIR FORCE

1943 124m bw War   ★★★½
Warner Bros.   (U.S.)

John Ridgely *(Capt. Mike Quincannon)*, Gig Young *(Lt. Bill Williams)*, Arthur Kennedy *(Lt. Tommy McMartin)*, Charles Drake *(Lt. Munchauser)*, Harry Carey *(Sgt. Robby White)*, George Tobias *(Cpl. Weinberg)*, Ward Wood *(Cpl. Peterson)*, Ray Montgomery *(Pvt. Chester)*, John Garfield *(Sgt. Joe Winocki)*, James Brown *(Lt. Tex Rader)*

p, Hal B. Wallis; d, Howard Hawks; w, Dudley Nichols; ph, James Wong Howe, Elmer Dyer; ed, George Amy; m, Franz Waxman; art d, John Hughes; fx, Roy Davidson, Rex Wimpy, H.F. Koenekamp

AAN Best Original Screenplay: Dudley Nichols; *AAN Best B/W Cinematography:* James Wong Howe, Elmer Dyer, Charles Marshall; *AA Best Film Editing:* George Amy; *AAN Best Special Effects:* Hans Koenekamp (Photographic), Rex Wimpy (Photographic), Nathan Levinson (Sound)

One of the finest American propaganda films produced during WWII, AIR FORCE fits perfectly into the canon of its director, Howard Hawks. A filmmaker who excels at portraying group action, Hawks tells the story of the "Mary Ann," a B-17 bomber, and its crew. While there is much here the viewer may find offensive (notably the predictable anti-"Jap" rhetoric), Hawks's mesmerizing direction and the assured and emotional performances of the cast, especially Garfield and Carey, draw the viewer in. Though by now beginning to date, Nichols's screenplay is powerful, with dialogue that is both meaningful and believable. The film earned Academy Award nominations for its script and cinematography and won Oscars for editing and special effects. A real fortress, later lost in the Pacific, was used for much of the filming, with interiors photographed inside a $40,000 model. Hawks was a veteran of the Air Corps of WWI, and his own experience and reverence for the service shows in every scene.

AIRPLANE!   *DVD*

1980 88m c Comedy   ★★½
Paramount   (U.S.)   PG

Robert Hays *(Ted Striker)*, Julie Hagerty *(Elaine)*, Kareem Abdul-Jabbar *(Murdock)*, Lloyd Bridges *(McCroskey)*, Peter Graves *(Capt. Oveur)*, Leslie Nielsen *(Dr. Rumack)*, Lorna Patterson *(Randy)*, Robert Stack *(Kramer)*, Stephen Stucker *(Johnny)*, Barbara Billingsley *(Jive Lady)*

p, Jon Davison; d, Jim Abrahams, David Zucker, Jerry Zucker; w, Jim Abrahams, David Zucker, Jerry Zucker; ph, Joseph Biroc (Metrocolor); ed, Patrick Kennedy; m, Elmer Bernstein; fx, Bruce Logan; chor, Tom Mahoney; cos, Rosanna Norton

Loaded with slapstick silliness and schoolboy wordplay, featuring tongue-in-cheek performances by familiar television personalities, and mostly just plain goofy, this inventive comedy from the Zucker-Abrahams-Zucker writing-directing team (THE KENTUCKY FRIED MOVIE, THE NAKED GUN) lampoons crisis-in-the-air films like THE CROWDED SKY and ZERO HOUR.

Ted Striker (Robert Hayes), a failed fighter pilot, is forced to take the controls of a commercial jet liner after the captain (Peter Graves) and co-pilot (basketball legend Kareem Abdul-Jabbar) become ill. Encouraged by his stewardess girlfriend (Julie Haggerty) and zany Dr. Rumack (Leslie Nielsen), and receiving ground support from the even zanier Kramer (Robert Stack), Striker does his best to follow the incomprehensible instructions he is given. Meanwhile, passengers become daffy, berserk, sex-crazed, and generally impossible. The onslaught of one-liners and sight gags in AIRPLANE! is so relentless that even the most dour viewer is ultimately won over—or exhausted.

AIRPORT   *DVD*

1970 137m c Disaster   ★★
Universal   (U.S.)   G

Burt Lancaster *(Mel Bakersfeld)*, Dean Martin *(Vernon Demerest)*, Jean Seberg *(Tanya Livingston)*, Jacqueline Bisset *(Gwen Meighen)*, George Kennedy *(Joe Patroni)*, Helen Hayes *(Ada Quonsett)*, Van Heflin *(D.O. Guerrero)*, Maureen Stapleton *(Inez Guerrero)*, Barry Nelson *(Lt. Anson Harris)*, Dana Wynter *(Mrs. Cindy Bakersfeld)*

p, Ross Hunter; d, George Seaton, Henry Hathaway (additional sequences); w, George Seaton (based on the novel by Arthur Hailey); ph, Ernest Laszlo (Todd-AO, Technicolor); ed, Stuart Gilmore; m, Alfred Newman; art d, Preston Ames, Alexander Golitzen; cos, Edith Head

AAN Best Picture; AA Best Supporting Actress: Helen Hayes; *AAN Best Supporting Actress:* Maureen Stapleton; *AAN Best Adapted Screenplay:* George Seaton; *AAN Best Cinematography:* Ernest Laszlo; *AAN Best Film Editing:* Stuart Gilmore; *AAN Best Original Score:* Alfred Newman; *AAN Best Art Direction-Set Decoration:* Alexander Golitzen, E. Preston Ames, Jack D. Moore, Mickey S. Michaels; *AAN Best Costume Design:* Edith Head; *AAN Best Sound:* Ronald Pierce, David Moriarty

An empty reshaping of GRAND HOTEL, held together by disaster in the sky.

Heflin smuggles a bomb on board, then blows himself out of an airborne jet, which limps along for more than two hours looking for a place to land while a score of passengers' lives are capsulized. Frantic ground people sweat over microphones and runway equipment, desperately trying to move a stalled plane on the only runway available (during a blizzard!) while ground crew chief Kennedy blathers heroically.

The film cost more than $10 million, and Universal chiefs held their breath. They need not have worried; the production soared beyond a $45 million gross and spawned three, progressively inferior, sequels. Nominated for ten Academy Awards including Best Picture. Both Stapleton and Hayes were nominated for Best Supporting Actress, and Hayes won, proving sentiment and cloying cuteness can conquer any mediocre script. AIRPORT will be remembered as the trailbler of the disaster epic, one of the most trivial genres in the history of motion pictures.

AKIRA   *DVD*

1988 124m c Animated/Action   ★★½
Akira Committee   (Japan)

VOICES OF: Mitsuo Iwara, Nozomu Sasaki, Mami Koyama, Taro Ishida

p, Ryohei Susuki, Shunzo Kato; d, Katsuhiro Otomo; w, Katsuhiro Otomo, Izo Hashimoto (from the graphic novel by Otomo); ph, Katsuji Misawa; m, Shoji Yamashiro; art d, Toshiharu Mizutani; anim, Takashi Nakamura

With this animated epic—adapted from the famous manga series by Katsuhiro Otomo—"Japanimation" jumped from cult to mainstream, just as comic books have graduated from children's entertainment to sophisticated graphic novels. AKIRA, likewise, sets out to use the animated format in a bold, adult way.

The time is 2019, 31 years after WWIII, during which Tokyo was destroyed by an atomic bomb. The rebuilt Neo Tokyo is an urban hell whose denizens live like rats at the foot of towering skyscrapers. The heroes of the movie are a group of teenage biker punks who terrorize the city with their violent gang wars. There is also a group of revolutionaries who are trying to overthrow the oppressive government. The government, meanwhile, is performing strange experiments with a mysterious invention called "Akira." It is part bomb, part god, and potentially destructive: when part of it is injected into a human being, that person is endowed with apocalyptic strength.

The animation shows off the kind of hyperactive filmmaking that would cost millions to produce in a live-action format. The opening sequence finds the biker gang burning down the freeways of Neo Tokyo at maximum speed, presenting the characters and the cityscape from every possible angle. The powerful movement of the movie is exhilarating, but it's all action with little characterization or plot. There is a moral here about mankind's lust for power, but it never clearly emerges from the spectacle of destruction and violence. Ultimately, AKIRA is really all about the animation.

ALADDIN
DVD
1992 90m c Animated/Comedy/Musical ★★★★
Walt Disney Productions (U.S.) G

VOICES OF: Scott Weinger (Aladdin), Robin Williams (Genie), Linda Larkin (Jasmine), Jonathan Freeman (Jafar), Frank Welker (Abu/Narrator), Gilbert Gottfried (Iago), Douglas Seale (Sultan), Lea Salonga (Singing Jasmine), Charlie Adler, Jack Angel

p, John Musker, Ron Clements; d, John Musker, Ron Clements; w, Ron Clements, John Musker, Ted Elliot, Terry Rossio; ed, H. Lee Peterson; m, Alan Menken; art d, Bill Perkins; anim, Ed Gombert, Rasoul Azadani, Kathy Altieri, Vera Lanpher, Don Paul, Steve Goldberg

AA Best Original Score: Alan Menken; AA Best Original Song: "Whole New World"; Alan Menken (Music), Tim Rice (Lyrics); AAN Best Original Song: "Friend Like Me"; Alan Menken (Music), Howard Ashman (Lyrics); AAN Best Sound: Terry Porter, Mel Metcalfe, David J. Hudson, Doc Kane; AAN Best Sound Effects Editing: Mark Mangini

A surprisingly hip outing for the Walt Disney company, which catapulted the classic fable into the 1990s, largely thanks to the input of Robin Williams as the voice of the mercurial, motor-mouthed Genie. ALADDIN is a fairy tale with an edge—a popular children's story that will have even the most media-savvy parents straining to keep up with Williams's machine-gun delivery of quips, allusions and imitations.

Animation, it turns out, is an ideal medium for Williams's talents. As he launches into his trademark free-associative riffs, impersonating everyone from Arnold Schwarzenegger to William Buckley to a bevy of harem women, the corresponding images spring to life with breathtaking speed and ingenuity; it would take several viewings to capture all the nuances of these comic cartoon jags.

This is not to say that the Genie-free segments of ALADDIN serve only as down time. The story moves at a brisk pace and is punctuated by some virtuoso sequences, in particular a dizzying magic carpet ride through the cave where the lamp is found. Though the lead characters are, as usual, bland, they're compensated for by a cheeky, entertaining supporting cast. Special mention should go to the mute but expressive magic carpet, and to Iago, hench-parrot of the principal villain, Jafar. Iago's cackling voice was provided by anarchic New York comedian Gilbert Gottfried, and Jafar's evil face was partially modeled, according to the animators, on that of former First Lady Nancy Reagan.

ALAMO, THE
DVD
1960 192m c War ★★★
Batjac (U.S.)

John Wayne (Col. David Crockett), Richard Widmark (Col. James Bowie), Laurence Harvey (Col. William Travis), Frankie Avalon (Smitty), Patrick Wayne (Capt. James Butler Bonham), Linda Cristal (Flaca), Joan O'Brien (Mrs. Dickinson), Chill Wills (Beekeeper), Joseph Calleia (Juan Sequin), Ken Curtis (Capt. Almeron Dickinson)

p, John Wayne; d, John Wayne; w, James Edward Grant; ph, William Clothier (Todd-AO, Technicolor); ed, Stuart Gilmore; m, Dimitri Tiomkin; art d, Alfred Ybarra; fx, Lee Zavitz

AAN Best Picture; AAN Best Supporting Actor: Chill Wills; AAN Best Color Cinematography: William H. Clothier; AAN Best Film Editing: Stuart Gilmore; AAN Best Score (Drama or Comedy): Dimitri Tiomkin; AAN Best Song: "The Green Leaves of Summer"; Dimitri Tiomkin (Music), Paul Francis Webster (Lyrics); AA Best Sound: Gordon E. Sawyer, Fred Hynes

Sprawling, ponderous history lesson that re-creates the defense of the Alamo in 1836 Texas, when 187 Americans and Texicans held off Santa Anna's army of 7,000 men for 13 days. The major focus is on Colonels William Travis (Laurence Harvey), Davy Crockett (John Wayne), and Jim Bowie (Richard Widmark). Wayne, whose Batjac Productions spent some $15 million mounting THE ALAMO (shot in 91 days, with $1.5 million spent re-creating the fort), produced, starred, and directed, with uncredited second-unit assistance from good friend John Ford. The result is an old-fashioned patriotic movie and a rousing epic that performed poorly at the box office, perhaps because it chronicled one of America's most famous military losses. All the pontificating about the joys of freedom becomes irritating, but James Edward Grant's dialogue occasionally crackles with enough humorous wit to hold an audience untill the gripping finale. Originally released at 192 minutes, it was later edited down to 140 minutes, with much of the Ford-directed footage reportedly cut out. The videocassette runs 161 minutes, but fails to recapture the sumptuous Todd-AO wide-screen photography.

ALAMO, THE
DVD
2004 137m c Historical/War/Drama ★★½
Texia Productions/Imagine Entertainment/ PG-13
Touchstone Pictures (U.S.)

Dennis Quaid (Sam Houston), Billy Bob Thornton (Davy Crockett), Jason Patric (Jim Bowie), Patrick Wilson (Colonel William Travis), Emilio Echevarria (General Antonio Lopez de Santa Anna), Jordi Molla (Juan Seguin), Leon Rippy (Sergeant William Ward), Tom Davidson (Colonel Green Jameson), Marc Blucas (James Butler Bonham), Robert Prentiss (Albert Grimes)

p, Ron Howard, Mark Johnson; d, John Lee Hancock; w, Leslie Bohem, Stephen Gaghan, John Lee Hancock; ph, Dean Semler; ed, Eric L. Beason; m, Carter Burwell; prod d, Michael Corenblith; art d, Dan Webster; fx, Larz Anderson, Craig Barron; cos, Daniel Orlandi

A shapeless, truncated epic, this painfully careful account of the siege and defeat of the ragtag forces defending a fortified San Antonio mission complex tries to be all things to all people and winds up a tedious muddle.

1836: Anglo settlers and longtime Tejano residents of the Texas territory are loosely united by shared dislike of the centralized Mexican government under military hero Antonio Lopez de Santa Anna (Emilio Echevarria). Hard-drinking, former Tennessee governor Sam Houston (Dennis Quaid) commands a small revolutionary army but opposes rash declarations of independence from Mexico. Lt. Col. William Travis (Patrick Wilson) is dispatched to the Alamo mission complex in San Antonio to lead the military troops stationed there, but immediately butts heads with ailing adventurer Jim Bowie (Jason Patric), who commands the rowdy civilian militiamen. Unbeknownst to any of them, Santa Anna's army is advancing steadily on San Antonio, and by the time backwoodsman-turned-congressman Davy Crockett (Billy Bob Thornton) has joined the ragtag crew gathered at the Alamo, the Mexican army is at the gates.

It took three screenwriters to wrestle this sprawling story into incoherence and conclude that war is hell and everyone suffers. A troubled production built on a contentious piece of American history (it's hard to make rousing entertainment out of failure), the project was repeatedly reconceived, then recut after completion, which no doubt accounts in part for the lamentable pacing. It's so slack it feels interminable, but it's too short to flesh out the complicated set of historical and individual circumstances that converged at the Alamo. Some fine performances are lost in the mire; only Thornton's vigorous, demythologizing turn as Crockett truly stands out.

ALEXANDER

2004 173m c Historical/War/Biography ★★
Intermedia Films/IMF/Moritz Borman Productions/ R
Warner Bros. (U.S./U.K./Netherlands/Germany)

Colin Farrell *(Alexander the Great)*, Angelina Jolie *(Olympias)*, Val Kilmer *(Philip)*, Anthony Hopkins *(Old Ptolemy)*, Rosario Dawson *(Roxane)*, Jared Leto *(Hephaistion)*, Jonathan Rhys Meyers *(Cassander)*, Christopher Plummer *(Aristotle)*, David Bedella *(Scribe)*, Jessie Kamm *(Child Alexander)*

p, Oliver Stone, Moritz Borman, Jon Kilik, Tomas Schuhly, Iain Smith; d, Oliver Stone; w, Laeta Kalogridis, Christopher Kyle, Oliver Stone; ph, Rodrigo Prieto; ed, Yann Herve, Alex Marquez, Tom Nordberg; m, Vangelis; prod d, Jan Roelfs; art d, Jonathan McKinstry; fx, John Scheele, Trevor Wood; chor, Piers Gielgud; cos, Jenny Beavan

Clocking in at just under three hours, Oliver Stone's epic biography of Alexander the Great is a $150 million-plus toga party that's nearly as megalomaniacally overreaching as its subject. While it's never boring, the film's entertainment value lies in all the wrong places: ridiculously staged grand tragedy, overblown acting, and a lot of inadvertently campy humor.

Alexandria, 363 BC: 40 years after Alexander's death at the age of 32, his faithful general Ptolemy (Anthony Hopkins) recounts the life of the Macedonian king who, by the age of 25, had conquered most of the known world. Born to the witchy Olympias (Angelina Jolie) and one-eyed King Philip II (Val Kilmer) and tutored alongside his lifelong beloved companion, Hephaistion (Jared Leto), by Aristotle (Christopher Plummer) himself, the young Alexander (a bottle-blond Colin Farrell) is clearly bound for greatness. After Philip is assassinated, presumably by envoys of the Persian king, Alexander is declared king. Vowing to avenge his father's murder and fulfill the Greek dream of an Eastern empire, Alexander marches his vast army across Asia on an eight-year expedition that would net him a vast empire, a Persian wife (Rosario Dawson)—despite the king's obviously carnal love for Hephaistion—and the enmity of his men. Alexander is able to quash an incipient mutiny, but no one can save Alexander from himself.

This is history as souped-up, sexed-over Hollywood spectacle, a series of increasingly elaborate and homoerotic orientalist fantasias that have as much in common with pre-Christian history as Stone's JFK had with the Kennedy assassination. There are two stunning battle sequences, but nothing, however, can dim the memory of Alexander hissing at a snarling Roxane on their wedding night, or Hephaistion's deathbed scene, a terrible miscalculation that Mel Brooks himself couldn't have staged for bigger laughs.

ALEXANDER NEVSKY

1938 107m bw Historical/War ★★★★
Mosfilm (U.S.S.R.)

Nikolai Cherkassov *(Prince Alexander Yaroslavich Nevsky)*, Nikolai Okhlopkov *(Vassily Buslai)*, Andrei Abrikosov, billed as A.L. Abrikossov *(Gavrilo Olexich)*, D.N. Orlov *(Ignat. Master Armourer)*, V. Novikov *(Pavsha, Governor of Pskov)*, N.N. Arski *(Domash, Nobleman of Novgorod)*, V.O. Massalitinova *(Amefa Timofeyevna, Mother of Buslai)*, V.S. Ivasbeva *(Olga, a Novgorod Girl)*, A.S. Danilova *(Vassilissa)*, V.L. Ersbov *(Master of the Teutonic Order)*

d, Sergei Eisenstein, D.I. Vassillev; w, Sergei Eisenstein, Peter Pavlenko; ph, Edward Tisse; m, Sergei Prokofiev

Sergei Eisenstein's classic tale of 13th-century Russia is as magnificent today as it must have been in 1938. A formidable achievement of Soviet cinema, this epic concerns the trying period when Russia was invaded by Teutonic knights on one front and Tartars on the other. As a result, the motherland is plundered, and the morale of the people crumbles. Finally, the moody, volatile Prince Nevsky (Nikolai Cherkassov) is summoned to lead his people in their struggle against the oppressors. A valiant and intelligent nobleman, Nevsky forms his army (an undertaking that consumes half the film), then wins a decisive battle at frozen Lake Peipus in 1242.

Eisenstein had the Russian army at his disposal, and the battle scenes, populated with thousands of men, are overwhelming. Wearing terrifying helmets fashioned after gargoyles, ogres, and fierce animals, the Teutonic knights engage the Russian army of peasants and nobles, hacking with sword, spear, and axe until the armor-burdened invaders fall victim to the lake's cracking ice. Eisenstein's attention to detail is meticulous down to the last horse blanket and homemade shoe, and the mounting of his monument to Russia's ancient hero is superb. His career on the verge of collapse, Eisenstein was rewarded for his work (an undeniably propagandist piece with the heroic Nevsky as Stalin and the savage Teutons as the Nazis) by being named head of Mosfilm Studios. The film represents a stylistic departure for Eisenstein, whose was beginning to abandon dialectical montage (e.g., THE BATTLESHIP POTEMKIN) for more conventional narrative methods. Prokofiev's vigorous score has become a concert piece in its own right.

ALEXANDER'S RAGTIME BAND

1938 105m bw Musical ★★★½
Fox (U.S.)

Tyrone Power *(Roger Grant)*, Alice Faye *(Stella Kirby)*, Don Ameche *(Charlie Dwyer)*, Ethel Merman *(Jerry Allen)*, Jack Haley *(Davey Lane)*, Jean Hersholt *(Prof. Heinrich)*, Helen Westley *(Aunt Sophie)*, John Carradine *(Taxi Driver)*, Paul Hurst *(Bill)*, Wally Vernon *(Himself)*

p, Harry Joe Brown; d, Henry King; w, Kathryn Scola, Lamar Trotti, Michael Sherman; ph, Peverell Marley; ed, Barbara McLean; art d, Bernard Herzbrun, Boris Leven; chor, Seymour Felix; cos, Gwen Wakeling

AAN Best Picture; AAN Best Original Story: Irving Berlin; *AAN Best Film Editing:* Barbara McLean; *AA Best Score:* Alfred Newman; *AAN Best Song:* "Now It Can Be Told"; Irving Berlin (Music & Lyrics); *AAN Best Interior Decoration:* Bernard Herzbrun, Boris Leven

Twenty-eight of Irving Berlin's greatest songs make this energetic, handsomely mounted production a must-see for musical fans. Spanning the years 1915 through 1938, the film follows the fortunes of Roger Grant (Tyrone Power), a Nob Hill San Franciscan who gives up his classical musical training in favor of playing ragtime. Grant starts his own "Alexander's Ragtime Band" (named for the song) and hires Stella Kirby (Alice Faye) as his singer. He falls in love with Kirby, but has a romantic rival in the shape of Charlie Dwyer (Don Ameche). Berlin was particularly pleased with Faye, of whom he said "I'd rather have Alice Faye introduce my songs than any other singer I know." With her limpid, bovine eyes and her throbbing contralto, Faye is the film's outstanding feature (best moment: her first outing with the band), but fans of the musical will also be interested in seeing young Ethel Merman strut her vintage stuff.

ALFIE   DVD
1966   114m   c   Drama   ★★★½
Lewis Gilbert/Sheldrake   (U.K.)

Michael Caine *(Alfie)*, Shelley Winters *(Ruby)*, Millicent Martin *(Siddie)*, Julia Foster *(Gilda)*, Jane Asher *(Annie)*, Shirley Ann Field *(Carla)*, Vivien Merchant *(Lily)*, Eleanor Bron *(The Doctor)*, Denholm Elliott *(Abortionist)*, Alfie Bass *(Harry)*

p, Lewis Gilbert; d, Lewis Gilbert; w, Bill Naughton (based on his play); ph, Otto Heller (Technicolor); ed, Thelma Connell; m, Sonny Rollins

AAN Best Picture; AAN Best Actor: Michael Caine; *AAN Best Supporting Actress:* Vivien Merchant; *AAN Best Adapted Screenplay:* Bill Naughton; *AAN Best Song:* "Alfie"; Burt Bacharach (Music), Hal David (Lyrics)

ALFIE is a surprisingly successful exercise in dramatic irony: the title character, a charming mediocrity who fancies himself a ladykiller, delivers a running commentary on his tawdry sexual conquests and penny-ante criminal ambitions, cheerfully oblivious to an audience that knows more about him than he will ever know himself. Screenwriter Bill Naughton had already employed this rather stagy strategy in a play and novel of the same title; that Alfie's extended asides work so well on screen is due to the disarming appearance of naivete with which Michael Caine is able to address the camera.

Alfie uses women shamelessly and without malice; when they demand commitment or emotional engagement from him, he's perplexed. Among a series of lovers, the most shabbily treated are Gilda (Julia Foster), his pregnant common-law wife, and Lily (Vivien Merchant), a married woman who looks for passion but finds pregnancy and abortion, both arranged by Alfie. In its time, the film was praised for its sexual frankness and persuasive rendering of Swinging London; both seem quaint by contemporary standards. Caine's Cockney Don Juan, however, is *sui generis.*

ALFIE   DVD
2004   106m   c   Comedy/Drama/Romance   ★★★
Charles Shyer/Patalex Productions/Paramount   R
(U.S./U.K.)

Jude Law *(Alfie)*, Jane Krakowski *(Dorie)*, Marisa Tomei *(Julie)*, Omar Epps *(Marlon)*, Susan Sarandon *(Liz)*, Sienna Miller *(Nikki)*, Nia Long *(Lonette)*, Gedde Watanabe *(Wing)*, Dick Latessa *(Joe)*, Renee Taylor *(Lu Schnitman)*

p, Elaine Pope, Charles Shyer; d, Charles Shyer; w, Charles Shyer, Elaine Pope (based on the screenplay by Bill Naughton); ph, Ashley Rowe; ed, Padraic McKinley; m, Mick Jagger, John Powell, David A. Stewart; prod d, Sophie Becher; art d, Ricky Eyres; fx, Ricky Farns, Sue Rowe; chor, Litza Bixler; cos, Beatrix Aruna Pasztor

Charles Shyer's modern update of the 1966 Michael Caine film can't match the original's shock factor, but Law's performance as archetypal Brit-cad Alfie Elkins is immensely enjoyable.

London transplant Alfie works as a chauffeur for a New York City limousine company, but he and his best pal, Marlon (Omar Epps), have a dream: starting their own high-end car service. In the meantime, metrosexual Alfie devotes his free time to his appearance and the constant pursuit of women. Alfie doesn't believe in love, but happily cavorts in the backseat of a limo with unhappily married Dorie (Jane Krakowski), turns to the soft comforts of loyal single-mom Julie (Marisa Tomei), and entangles himself in an erotic game of pool with Marlon's sultry ex, Lonette (Nia Long). Alfie's gift: the ability to make each feel truly desireable. Alfie tires of Dorie, Julie gets fed up with playing second fiddle, and his one-night tryst with Lonette leaves her pregnant, but instead of changing his ways, Alfie moves on to fresh-faced party girl Nikki (Sienna Miller) and worldly Liz (Susan Sarandon), a wealthy older woman who gives him a run for his money. It takes a health scare and some disturbing intimations of what the future holds for aging playboys to convince the confirmed bachelor that he might be missing out on something by rejecting love.

Feminists may bemoan the fact that the film's female characters still hurl themselves at this shameless womanizer, but these 21st-century foxes have a bit more spine and self-respect that the original film's morose hausfraus and fluttering dolly birds. Long and Miller are especially well-cast members of a generally strong ensemble; only Tomei is bland in what should be a pivotal part.

ALGIERS   DVD
1938   95m   bw   Crime   ★★★★
UA   (U.S.)

Charles Boyer *(Pepe Le Moko)*, Sigrid Gurie *(Ines)*, Hedy Lamarr *(Gaby)*, Joseph Calleia *(Slimane)*, Gene Lockhart *(Regis)*, Johnny Downs *(Pierrot)*, Alan Hale *(Grandpere)*, Nina Koshetz *(Tania)*, Joan Woodbury *(Aicha)*, Claudia Dell *(Marie)*

p, Walter Wanger; d, John Cromwell; w, John Howard Lawson, James M. Cain (based on the novel *Pepe Le Moko* by Roger D'Ashelbe); ph, James Wong Howe; ed, Otho Lovering, William Reynolds; m, Vincent Scotto, Muhammed Ygner Buchen; art d, Alexander Toluboff; cos, Omar Kiam, Irene

AAN Best Actor: Charles Boyer; *AAN Best Supporting Actor:* Gene Lockhart; *AAN Best Cinematography:* James Wong Howe; *AAN Best Interior Decoration:* Alexander Toluboff (Art Direction)

Down along the shadowy, labyrinthine alleyways of the Casbah, a notorious bastion in French Algiers that harbors criminals, the viewer is introduced to a remarkable thief and lover, Pepe Le Moko (the charismatic Boyer, a reigning screen sex symbol in 1938). Wanted for stealing jewels, Boyer has fled pursuing Parisian police and taken refuge in the Casbah. Calleia is the crafty French detective who plays a waiting game, watching for the moment the wanted man will step from the Casbah into the arms of his officers. Boyer grows restless, longing for the grand life of Paris, resenting the mooning woman who is devoted to him (Gurie). Lamarr, a dazzling Parisian tourist slumming among criminals, walks into his life and, even though she is engaged, invents excuses to slip back into the Casbah to meet Boyer. The film follows Boyer's and Lamarr's involvement to its fatalistic conclusion, and their love scenes are definitive examples of smoldering continental passion.

Lamarr's role made her an international star, though she subsequently failed to live up to the promise of her debut. Strong supporting performances are contributed by Calleia and Lockhart, the latter's portrayal of an informer garnering him an Oscar nomination for Best Supporting Actor. Director Cromwell reshot this movie almost scene-for-scene from the earlier French version, PEPE LE MOKO, directed by Julien Duvivier and starring Jean Gabin. The film was remade in 1948 as CASBAH with Tony Martin and Yvonne De Carlo. Oddly enough, the expression "Come wiz me to the Casbah" was never uttered onscreen in ALGIERS.

ALI

2001   158m   c/bw   Biography/Sports   ★★★

Peters Entertainment/Initial Entertainment Group/ Forward Pass Productions/Lee Caplin/Picture Entertainment Corporation/Overbrook Films   (U.S.)   R

Will Smith *(Cassius Clay/Muhammad Ali)*, Jamie Foxx *(Drew "Bundini" Brown)*, Jon Voight *(Howard Cosell)*, Mario Van Peebles *(Malcolm X)*, Ron Silver *(Angelo Dundee)*, Jeffrey Wright *(Howard Bingham)*, Mykelti Williamson *(Don King)*, Jada Pinkett Smith *(Sonji)*, Michael Bentt *(Sonny Liston)*, James N. Toney *(Joe Frazier)*

p, Paul Ardaji, A. Kitman Ho, James Lassiter, Michael Mann, Jon Peters; d, Michael Mann; w, Stephen J. Rivele, Eric Roth, Christopher Wilkinson, Michael Mann (based on a story by Gregory Allen Howard); ph, Emmanuel Lubezki; ed, William Goldenberg, Lynzee Klingman, Stephen Rivkin; m, Pieter Bourke, Lisa Gerrard; prod d, John Myhre; art d, Bill Rea, Tomas Voth; fx, Michael J. McAlister, David H. Watkins; cos, Marlene Stewart

AAN Best Actor: Will Smith; *AAN Best Supporting Actor:* Jon Voight

Three-time world heavyweight champion, African-American hero, American icon. For many Americans unsettled by the turbulence of the 1960s, Muhammad Ali was also something else: a threat. Director Michael Mann's reverential biopic attempts to resurrect this other, controversial Ali by focusing on the decade between the boxer's first heavyweight title victory and 1974's "Rumble in the Jungle," when Ali wrested the title back from George Foreman.

Miami, 1964: Twenty-two-year-old Cassius Clay Jr. (Will Smith) faces a hulking Sonny Liston (Michael Bentt) and walks away after six rounds with the heavyweight title. Declaring himself the "Greatest Boxer in the World," Ali renounces his "slave name" and becomes Muhammad Ali. The film then gets personal: Mann explores Ali's deep devotion to Islam, which leads him to turn his back on both his friend Malcolm X (Mario Van Peebles) and flashy first wife (Jada Pinkett Smith). Convicted of draft evasion in 1967, Ali is forbidden to fight in the U.S. and faces a five-year prison sentence. Ali turns to good friend Howard Cosell (Jon Voight, unrecognizable under makeup and hairpiece) and, surprisingly, Joe Frazier (James N. Toney), to help engineer the comeback that would lead to the "Rumble" in Zaire, one of the most widely publicized bouts in boxing history.

The film's fight sequences are straightforward and effective, and with an additional 35 pounds of muscle, Smith certainly makes an impression; his own megawatt charisma helps give a pretty good idea of what made Ali such a compelling personality. It's a brilliant impersonation—Smith gets Ali's Louisville accent exactly right, and facial prosthetics complete the transformation—but the film never quite finds the man under the enormous image. Those quintessential Mann moments, during which Ali is left alone to brood, remain surprisingly blank.

ALI, FEAR EATS THE SOUL

(ANGST ESSEN SEELE AUF)

1974   89m   c   Drama/Romance   ★★★★

Tango Film/Autorn   (West Germany)

Brigitte Mira *(Emmi)*, El Hedi Ben Salem *(Ali)*, Barbara Valentin *(Barbara)*, Irm Hermann *(Krista)*, Peter Gauhe *(Bruno)*, Rainer Werner Fassbinder *(Eugen)*, Karl Scheydt *(Albert)*, Elma Karlowa *(Mrs. Kargus)*, Anita Bucher *(Mrs. Ellis)*, Walter Sedlmayr *(Grocer)*

d, Rainer Werner Fassbinder; w, Rainer Werner Fassbinder; ph, Jurgen Jurges; ed, Thea Eymesz; prod d, Rainer Werner Fassbinder

ALI, FEAR EATS THE SOUL is one of Rainer Werner Fassbinder's finest films, a mordant satire that's also a touching romance and a powerful indictment of prejudice.

60-year-old German charwoman Emmi (Brigitte Mira) goes into a Munich bar frequented by Arab immigrants and dances with a 40-year-old Moroccan named Ali (El Hedi Ben Salem). Ali walks her home and spends the night at her apartment, then moves in with her, much to the chagrin of her neighbors and grown children. Emmi is shunned by her fellow cleaning-women and quarrels with her grocer (Walter Sedlmayr) after he refuses to serve Ali. Ali and Emmi decide to take a vacation, and when they return, suddenly everyone is nice to them. The problem: the lovers themselves begin to have their own reservations about the relationship.

Taking Douglas Sirk's classic 1955 melodrama ALL THAT HEAVEN ALLOWS as a starting point, Fassbinder expands on its theme of social prejudice by making his protagonists different races as well. In Fassbinder's hands, however, ALI, FEAR EATS THE SOUL is not simply an anti-racism polemic. The suffering that Emmi and Ali go through is symptomatic of the pain that all people inflict upon each other. From the first scene—a *tableau vivant* of the patrons in the Arab bar contemptuously staring at Emmi—the characters are all depicted as alienated outsiders, trapped in their own private hells.

Influenced by Sirk's cinematic style, Fassbinder uses saturated colors to create split compositions, and constantly shoots through doorways, windows, and staircases to create frames-within-frames which isolate his characters. Despite Fassbinder's emotional detachment, the film contains a large degree of deadpan humor and some incredibly poignant moments, including the bittersweet finale.

ALICE

(NECO Z ALENKY)

1988   85m   c   Fantasy   ★★★½

Film Four/Condor/SRG/Hessisches Rudfunk (Switzerland/U.K./West Germany)

Kristyna Kohoutova *(Alice)*, Camilla Power *(Voice of Alice)*

p, Peter-Christian Fueter; d, Jan Svankmajer; w, Jan Svankmajer (based on *Alice's Adventures in Wonderland* by Lewis Carroll); ph, Svatopluk Maly (Eastmancolor); ed, Marie Zemanova; anim, Bedrich Glaser

This is a dark, surrealist interpretation of Lewis Carroll's *Alice's Adventures in Wonderland* by the brilliant Czech animator Jan Svankmajer. The director combines live action and puppet animation to create a disturbing vision of Alice's world, filled with images of death and violence. Although all the action takes place within a dream, Svankmajer, in true surrealist spirit, keeps the line between dream and reality ambiguous. Alice is the only live creature in the film, and it is she who supplies the voices of her (often grotesque) animated companions. In one scene typical of Svankmajer's command of dream logic, the girl becomes her own doll. ALICE is macabre, haunting, and very true to the spirit of Carroll's book, exploring the marvels and fears of a child's imagination.

ALICE ADAMS

1935   99m   bw   Comedy/Drama   ★★★★
RKO   (U.S.)

Katharine Hepburn (*Alice Adams*), Fred MacMurray (*Arthur Russell*), Fred Stone (*Mr. Adams*), Evelyn Venable (*Mildred Palmer*), Frank Albertson (*Walter Adams*), Ann Shoemaker (*Mrs. Adams*), Charley Grapewin (*Mr. Lamb*), Grady Sutton (*Frank Dowling*), Hedda Hopper (*Mrs. Palmer*), Jonathan Hale (*Mr. Palmer*)

p, Pandro S. Berman; d, George Stevens; w, Dorothy Yost, Mortimer Offner (based on the novel by Booth Tarkington); ph, Robert de Grasse; ed, Jane Loring; m, Max Steiner; art d, Van Nest Polglase; cos, Walter Plunkett

AAN Best Picture; AAN Best Actress: Katharine Hepburn

The pathetic, social-climbing heroine of Booth Tarkington's novel was never better played than by Hepburn, who brought a fierce determination, clutching coyness, and tragic optimism to the part. She plays Alice Adams, who lives only a block or two from the wrong side of the tracks, but who pretends that she and her family enjoy the status of their wealthy peer group—a pretense that grows into a dangerous conviction. Her family of hopeless clods drags her down to grim reality at every turn, yet she tries to escape through rich acquaintances who are really nothing more than chic snobs. They merely tolerate her as a source of amusement, frivolously inviting her to an exclusive party where she meets the man of her dreams: rich, handsome, gracious MacMurray, who plays his part with unexpected sensitivity. He is attracted to her and is conned into believing that her folks are well-to-do. Hepburn inflates their importance and then risks all by inviting her hero to dinner at her home. George Stevens's dinner-party scene is a classically choreographed symphony of tragicomedy that remains with the viewer long after the tacked-on happy ending. Fred Stone, Ann Shoemaker and, young Frank Albertson, as Alice's grasping family, stand out in a capable ensemble cast, but supporting honors are stolen by Hattie McDaniel, in a slovenly turn as a hostess's worst nightmare. The painful yearning behind Alice's character speaks to audiences in a universal way, and the film proved an important stepping stone for 30-year-old director George Stevens, with his first major film, and Hepburn, who won a second Academy Award nomination for the part, after MORNING GLORY in 1933.

ALICE DOESN'T LIVE HERE ANYMORE

1974   112m   c   Drama   ★★★
Warner Bros. (U.S.)   PG

Ellen Burstyn (*Alice Hyatt*), Kris Kristofferson (*David*), Alfred Lutter (*Tommy Hyatt*), Billy "Green" Bush (*Donald Hyatt*), Diane Ladd (*Flo*), Lelia Goldoni (*Neighbor Bea*), Harvey Keitel (*Ben Everhart*), Lane Bradbury (*Ben's Wife*), Vic Tayback (*Mel*), Jodie Foster (*Audrey*)

p, David Susskind, Audrey Maas; d, Martin Scorsese; w, Robert Getchell; ph, Kent Wakeford (Technicolor); ed, Marcia Lucas; m, Richard LaSalle; prod d, Toby Rafelson

AA Best Actress: Ellen Burstyn; *AAN Best Supporting Actress:* Diane Ladd; *AAN Best Original Screenplay:* Robert Getchell

After achieving some success with the brilliant, independently made MEAN STREETS, Martin Scorsese was given a chance to direct a mainstream Hollywood film. The result is this effective but uneven work, which chronicles a woman's search for self.

Burstyn stars as an unhappy housewife living in New Mexico with her cruel husband (Bush) and their precocious, somewhat spoiled son (Lutter). When Bush dies, Burstyn and son pack up their belongings and head for Monterey, California, where she hopes to begin the singing career she has always dreamed about. Along the way she has a brief fling with the frightening Keitel, but must take flight when his violent temper erupts. When her car breaks down, she takes a job at an Arizona diner run by crusty Tayback and becomes best pals with salty Diane Ladd. Kristofferson is a rancher who frequents the restaurant, and he and Burstyn soon begin an awkward courtship. Burstyn won a well-deserved Oscar for her performance, and she is matched in expertise by Ladd and Tayback, but the acting cannot conceal the storyline's shortcomings. The film was the inspiration for the television series "Alice" starring Linda Lavin, with Tayback reprising his role as the owner of Mel's Diner. Also receiving Oscar nominations were Ladd for Supporting Actress and Getchell for his screenplay.

ALICE IN THE CITIES
(ALICE IN DEN STADTEN)
1974   110m   bw   Drama   ★★★
Bauer   (West Germany)

Rudiger Vogler (*Phillip*), Yella Rottlander (*Alice*), Elisabeth Kreuzer (*Lisa*), Edda Kochi (*Edda*), Didi Petrikat (*The Girl*), Ernest Bohm (*The Agent*), Sam Presti (*The Car Salesman*), Lois Moran (*Girl at Ticket Counter*), Hans Hirschmuller, Sybille Baier

p, Peter Genee; d, Wim Wenders; w, Wim Wenders, Veith der Furstenberg; ph, Robby Muller, Martin Schafer; ed, Peter Przygodda, Barbara von Weitershausen

An ancestor of director Wenders's 1984 film PARIS, TEXAS, this low-budget West German picture follows Vogler, a German journalist traveling across the U.S. East Coast in search of a story. He considers Polaroid snapshots a better way to capture America's landscapes, buildings, and signs than writing about them. While trying to return to Germany, Vogler meets Kreuzer and her nine-year-old daughter, Rottlander, who are also trying to arrange a flight home. Kreuzer mysteriously disappears, leaving Rottlander in Vogler's care, setting up the premise of this hypnotic odyssey, the beginning of a loosely connected Wenders road-movie trilogy (it was followed in 1975 by WRONG MOVE and, one year later, KINGS OF THE ROAD—all three starring Vogler). Like Vogler, Wenders is a documentarian who fills his frame with images of American culture (a hot dog stand, a used car lot, Shea Stadium) and strains of American music ("Under the Boardwalk," Canned Heat, Chuck Berry) to tell his story.

ALICE IN WONDERLAND

1951   74m   c   Animated/Children's/Fantasy   ★★★½
Walt Disney Productions   (U.S.)

VOICES OF: Kathryn Beaumont (*Alice*), Ed Wynn (*Mad Hatter*), Richard Haydn (*Caterpillar*), Sterling Holloway (*Cheshire Cat*), Jerry Colonna (*March Hare*), Verna Felton (*Queen of Hearts*), Pat O'Malley (*Walrus/Carpenter/Tweedledee/Tweedledum*), Bill Thompson (*White Rabbit/Dodo*), Heather Angel (*Alice's Sister*), Joseph Kearns (*Doorknob*)

p, Walt Disney; d, Clyde Geronimi, Hamilton Luske, Wilfred Jackson; w, Winston Hibler, Bill Peet, Joe Rinaldi, William Cottrell, Joe Grant, Del Connell, Ted Sears, Erdman Penner, Milt Banta, Dick Kelsey, Dick Huemer, Tom Oreb, John Walbridge (based on the stories of Lewis Carroll); m, Oliver Wallace; anim, Milt Kahl, Ward Kimball, Franklin Thomas, Eric Larson, John Lounsbery, Oliver M. Johnston, Wolfgang Reitherman, Marc Davis, Les Clark, Norman Ferguson, Josh Meador, Dan MacManus, George Rowley, Blaine Gibson

AAN Best Score (Musical): Oliver Wallace

Disney's beautifully animated but slightly chilly rendering of Alice's tale, aimed at a children's market for which Disney eschewed intellectual interpretations of Carroll's story, instead playing it straight as a storybook dream/nightmare. All of Alice's adventures are in place, including her tea party with the Mad Hatter and friends, her meeting with the bewildering Cheshire Cat, and her strange game of croquet with the temperamental Queen of Hearts. The film is dazzling in its use of color and odd shapes and is enhanced by the distinctive voices of Ed Wynn as the Mad Hatter, Sterling Holloway as the Cheshire Cat, Jerry Colonna as the March Hare, and Verna Felton as the Queen of Hearts.

ALICE'S RESTAURANT 📀

1969 111m c Drama ★★★
UA (U.S.) R

Arlo Guthrie *(Arlo)*, Pat Quinn *(Alice)*, James Broderick *(Ray)*, Michael McClanathan *(Shelly)*, Geoff Outlaw *(Roger)*, Tina Chen *(Marichan)*, Kathleen Dabney *(Karin)*, William Obanhein *(Officer Obie)*, Seth Allan *(Evangelist)*, Monroe Arnold *(Bluegrass)*

p, Hillard Elkins, Joe Manduke; d, Arthur Penn; w, Venable Herndon, Arthur Penn (based on the song "The Alice's Restaurant Massacre" by Arlo Guthrie); ph, Michael Nebbia (DeLuxe Color); ed, Dede Allen; m, Arlo Guthrie

AAN Best Director: Arthur Penn

Arlo Guthrie, son of folk-singing immortal Woody Guthrie, achieved some celebrity in the 1960s with his 18-minute song "The Alice's Restaurant Massacre," in which he tells the tale of his arrest and trial for littering, which led to his being rejected for the draft during the Vietnam War. Director Arthur Penn used a lengthy and bitterly amusing re-creation of the events depicted in the song as the centerpiece for this exploration of the '60s counterculture. Ray Brock (James Broderick) is an aging hippie who buys a church in Stockbridge, Massachusetts, and with his wife, Alice (Pat Quinn), shares the good life with a variety of societal drop-outs. Guthrie drops in long enough to run afoul of the local cop, Obie (William Obanheim, playing himself) and pays a visit to a New York hospital to see his father who is dying from Hodgkin's disease. To his credit, Penn refused to romanticize his subjects, and the film stands as a fairly accurate chronicle of the times. The real Alice Brock has a small role as one of the hippies.

ALIEN 📀

1979 124m c Horror/Science Fiction ★★★★
Brandywine/Shusett (U.S.) R

Tom Skerritt *(Dallas)*, Sigourney Weaver *(Ripley)*, Veronica Cartwright *(Lambert)*, Harry Dean Stanton *(Brett)*, John Hurt *(Kane)*, Ian Holm *(Ash)*, Yaphet Kotto *(Parker)*

p, Gordon Carroll, David Giler, Walter Hill; d, Ridley Scott; w, Dan O'Bannon (based on a story by O'Bannon and Ronald Shusett); ph, Derek Vanlint; ed, Terry Rawlings, Peter Weatherley; m, Jerry Goldsmith; prod d, Michael Seymour; fx, Carlo Rambaldi, Bernard Lodge; cos, John Mollo, H.R. Giger, Roger Dicken

AAN Best Art Direction-Set Decoration: Michael Seymour, Les Dilley, Roger Christian, Ian Whittaker; *AA Best Visual Effects:* H.R. Giger, Carlo Rambaldi, Brian Johnson, Nick Allder, Denys Ayling

A seminal work of late '70s science fiction, ALIEN remains notable for its influence as well as its excellence.

The crew of the industrial spaceship *Nostromo* lands on the surface of a mysterious planet and discovers a crashed spacecraft. Inside, a strange egg disgorges a multilegged lifeform that latches onto the face of crewman Kane (John Hurt), who, unconscious, is brought back to the *Nostromo*. There,

the creature resists all attempts to dislodge it. Soon, however, it disappears, only to turn up dead later as Kane revives, apparently none the worse for wear. The *Nostromo* takes off, and while the crew is having dinner, a snakelike creature erupts from Kane's stomach and vanishes into the bowels of the ship. After jettisoning Kane's body, the crew sets out in search of the alien. Other crew members are soon killed, and warrant officer Ripley (Sigourney Weaver) spearheads the battle against the seemingly indestructible creature.

ALIEN has been described as "a haunted house movie in space," and therein lies its appeal. There's nothing terribly complex or original about the movie, but it is distinguished by its clever and innovative use of B-movie staples in a hitech setting. Coming into his own as a director on his second feature, Ridley Scott wrings every possible ounce of suspense and atmosphere out of the proceedings. Swiss artist-designer H.R. Giger supplied the distinctive "bio-mechanical" concepts for the film, which help make the alien one of cinema's scariest creations: a nightmare synthesis of humanoid form, insect-like appendages, and mechanized structure that is all the more effective for not being seen too clearly for most of the film.

The non-star cast acquits itself well, bringing an appealing quality to their characters. One of them, Weaver's Ripley, would develop into one of the genre's most memorable heroines through the subsequent sequels. Perhaps because of its closed-in setting, the movie was an easy target for imitation. Several dozen low-budget copies have appeared since its initial release.

ALIENS 📀

1986 137m c Science Fiction ★★★
Brandywine (U.S.) R

Sigourney Weaver *(Ripley)*, Carrie Henn *(Newt)*, Michael Biehn *(Cpl. Hicks)*, Paul Reiser *(Burke)*, Lance Henriksen *(Bishop)*, Bill Paxton *(Pvt. Hudson)*, William Hope *(Lt. Gorman)*, Jenette Goldstein *(Pvt. Vasquez)*, Al Matthews *(Sgt. Apone)*, Mark Rolston *(Pvt. Drake)*

p, Gale Anne Hurd; d, James Cameron; w, James Cameron (based on a story by Cameron, David Giler, and Walter Hill and on characters created by Dan O'Bannon and Ronald Shusett); ph, Adrian Biddle (Eastmancolor); ed, Ray Lovejoy; m, James Horner; prod d, Peter Lamont; art d, Bert Davey, Fred Hole, Michael Lamont, Ken Court; fx, Stan Winston, L.A. Effects Group, John Richardson, Norman Baillie; cos, Emma Porteous

AAN Best Actress: Sigourney Weaver; *AAN Best Film Editing:* Ray Lovejoy; *AAN Best Original Score:* James Horner; *AAN Best Art Direction-Set Decoration:* Peter Lamont, Crispian Sallis; *AAN Best Sound:* Graham V. Hartstone, Nicolas LeMessurier, Michael A. Carter, Roy Charman; *AA Best Visual Effects:* Robert Skotak, Stan Winston, John Richardson, Suzanne Benson; *AA Best Sound Effects Editing:* Don Sharpe

The long-awaited sequel to the successful ALIEN is a nonstop, high-tech, souped-up war movie, with gung ho marines blasting special-effects creatures, and a genuinely convincing, exciting action heroine. Ripley (Sigourney Weaver) is found in deep space by a salvage ship and brought back to a space station, where Burke (Paul Reiser), a representative of The Company, tells her that she has been unconscious for 57 years. To her horror, Ripley also learns that the planet on which she and her crew found the creature in ALIEN has been colonized. It isn't long, however, until Burke tells her that they've lost contact with the colony and asks her to accompany a platoon of colonial marines to the planet as an adviser. Weaver is superb—tough, smart, and the best fighter, male or female, in the movie. The rest of the small cast also performs well, and director James Cameron handles the action superbly. The cutting is quick, the suspense unrelenting, and the monsters thoroughly frightening. Weaver returned for two further, less successful sequels—David Fincher's gloomy ALIEN3 (1992) and Jean-Pierre Jeunet's baroque ALIEN RESURRECTION (1997).

ALIEN³   DVD

1992 135m c   Science Fiction/Action/Horror   ★★½
Fox/Brandywine Productions   (U.S.)   R

Sigourney Weaver *(Ripley)*, Charles S. Dutton *(Dillon)*, Charles Dance *(Clemens)*, Paul McGann *(Golic)*, Brian Glover *(Andrews)*, Ralph Brown *(Aaron)*, Danny Webb *(Morse)*, Christopher John Fields *(Rains)*, Holt McCallany *(Junior)*, Lance Henriksen *(Bishop)*

p, Gordon Carroll, Walter Hill, David Giler; d, David Fincher; w, David Giler, Walter Hill, Larry Ferguson (from a story by Vincent Ward, based on characters created by Dan O'Bannon and Ronald Shusett); ph, Alex Thomson; ed, Terry Rawlings; m, Elliot Goldenthal; prod d, Norman Reynolds; art d, James Morahan, Fred Hole; fx, George Gibbs, Richard Edlund, Tom Woodruff Jr., Alec Gillis; cos, Bob Ringwood, David Perry

AAN Best Visual Effects: Richard Edlund, Alec Gillis, Tom Woodruff, Jr., George Gibbs

Cruising through space on the way back from her last battle with the ALIENS, Ripley (Sigourney Weaver) crash-lands on what is possibly the least desirable piece of real-estate in the Galaxy—a run-down, low-tech penal colony inhabited by a bunch of serial killers who have developed their own brand of fundamentalist religion. Ripley—her head shaved as a precaution against lice—holds her own among this unsavory bunch, even getting friendly with the colony's doctor (Charles Dance), a charming Englishman with a mysterious past. Before long, though, it's Ripley's past that comes back to haunt her, as it becomes increasingly clear that her old, double-jawed, acid-blooded friends are back.

ALIEN³ is a would-be blockbuster that is marred by an overlong, clumsily choreographed final chase scene, as the prisoners lure the alien through a seemingly endless series of tunnels in an attempt to trap it. Nevertheless, the absence of high-tech gadgetry, and the almost medieval atmosphere of the colony, put an intriguing, Gothic spin on what could easily have been a tired re-run. Director David Fincher, a 28-year-old music video whiz-kid who would go on to direct SE7EN and FIGHT CLUB, has done an impressive job with the visuals, which are artfully composed without drawing undue attention to themselves. Through it all, the incomparable Ms. Weaver does her patented feminist action-hero thing, projecting intelligence, resilience and grim humor.

ALIEN RESURRECTION   DVD

1997 108m c   Horror/Science Fiction/Action   ★★½
Brandywine (U.S.)   R

Sigourney Weaver *(Ripley)*, Winona Ryder *(Annalee Call)*, Dominique Pinon *(Vriess)*, Ron Perlman *(Johner)*, Michael Wincott *(Elgyn)*, Dan Hedaya *(General Perez)*, J.E. Freeman *(Dr. Wren)*, Brad Dourif *(Gediman)*, Gary Dourdan *(Christie)*, Raymond Cruz *(Distephano)*

p, Bill Badalato, Walter Hill, David Giler, Gordon Carroll; d, Jean-Pierre Jeunet; w, Joss Whedon (based on characters created by Dan O'Bannon and Ronald Shusett); ph, Darius Khondji; ed, Herve Schneid; m, John Frizzell; prod d, Nigel Phelps; art d, Andrew Neskoromny; fx, Bruce Devan, Eric Allard, Erik Henry, Pitof, Tom Woodruff Jr., Alec Gillis; cos, Bob Ringwood

"Been there, done that" hangs over the experience of ALIEN RESURRECTION like a blase pall. The third sequel to ALIEN is simply an effort to continue a flourishing franchise.

Two hundred years after Ellen Ripley (Sigourney Weaver) suicidally dove into a pit of molten metal to kill the alien spawn inside her, Ripley lives again. Scientists on the military research vessel *Auriga* have cloned Ripley in order to extract the alien queen from her body. The pirate freighter *Betty* docks on *The Auriga* to deliver hijacked "cargo"—colonists in stasis, whose bodies will be used to incubate the alien queen's eggs. Among the *Betty*'s crew is Call (Winona Ryder), who is secretly part of a resistance movement that aims to murder Ripley before the alien is removed. But she is too late, as she discovers when the creatures escape captivity and start a killing spree.

With its mixture of movie stars, moody visuals, nasty creatures, humor, and horror, ALIEN RESURRECTION manages to be entertaining. But the meat of the movie—a ragtag group trying to escape the aliens—merely rehashes ALIENS (1986). State-of-the-art computer effects do, however, make for faster moving, more grotesque monsters this time around. The work of French director Jean-Pierre Jeunet (who codirected 1991's DELICATESSEN) is appropriately stylish, a hallmark of the ALIEN series. But the movie lacks even a generic depth of characterization and emotion. The pairing of Weaver and Ryder is merely gimmickry, and sadly hollow in comparison to Weaver's previous iconic stature. The script by Joss Whedon is wiseacre witty, and contributes some good science-fiction ideas (amoral humans, humane robots, spiritual computers, clever aliens) that deserved fuller exploration.

ALIEN VS. PREDATOR   DVD

2004 90m c   Science Fiction/Horror/Action   ★★
Davis Entertainment/Lonlink Productions/   PG-13
Impact Pictures/Stillking Films/Kut Films/
Babelsberg Film (U.S./Canada/Czech Republic/Germany)

Sanaa Lathan *(Alexa Woods)*, Raoul Bova *(Sebastian de Rosa)*, Lance Henriksen *(Charles Bishop Weyland)*, Ewen Bremner *(Graeme Miller)*, Colin Salmon *(Maxwell Stafford)*, Tommy Flanagan *(Mark Verheiden)*, Joseph Rye *(Joe Connors)*, Agathe De La Boulaye *(Adele Rousseau)*, Carsten Norgaard *(Rusten Quinn)*, Sam Troughton *(Thomas Parks)*

p, Gordon Carroll, John Davis, David Giler, Walter Hill; d, Paul W.S. Anderson; w, Paul W.S. Anderson (from a story by Paul W.S. Anderson, based on characters created by Dan O'Bannon, Ronald Shusett, Jim Thomas, and John Thomas); ph, David Johnson; ed, Alexander Berner; m, Harald Kloser; prod d, Richard Bridgland; art d, Milena Koubkova, Adam O'Neil, Justin Warburton-Brown; fx, John Bruno, Gerd Feuchter; cos, Magali Guidasci

Two lethal alien species, three ancient civilizations, and references to genre touchstones from CUBE to "The X-Files" can't keep this combination ALIEN/PREDATOR sequel from being a reductive spook show in which a bunch of puny humans get chased around by scary monsters.

According to information relayed back to the Weyland Corporation by its own satellite, there's an undiscovered pyramid of incalculable age buried 2000 feet beneath the Antarctic ice. Billionaire Charles Bishop Weyland (Lance Henriksen) quickly assembles a team of experts, including a chemical engineer (Ewen Bremner), an archeologist (Raoul Bova), and Alexa "Lex" Woods (Sanaa Lathan), who specializes in leading scientific teams over ice-covered terrain. Their first surprise is waiting at base camp, an abandoned whaling station whose inhabitants all vanished mysteriously in 1904: someone has already drilled a shaft directly to the pyramid. Puzzled, Lex takes a team below ground and into the structure, where they discover artifacts depicting strange monsters, a chamber filled with skeletons whose ribs appear to have been shattered from the inside, and a sarcophagus containing some mysterious objects. The next surprise is that the pyramid is actually a giant maze that reconfigures itself. Surprise number three is that they aren't alone. Writer-director Paul W.S. Anderson clearly knows the worlds of the previous ALIEN and PREDATOR films well, and though some of his ideas echo those explored in the popular "Alien vs. Predator" comic book series and novels, the elaborate "Chariots of the Predators" alternate history of human development is all his. Unfortunately, it weighs down the movie with more epic backstory than any intergalactic smackdown really needs. Once the running and screaming starts, the proceedings degenerate into a morass of claustrophobic sprints through dark corridors, punctuated by boogie beasts springing out of the shadows.

ALL ABOUT EVE

1950 138m bw Drama ★★★★★
Fox (U.S.)

Bette Davis *(Margo Channing)*, Anne Baxter *(Eve Harrington)*, George Sanders *(Addison De Witt)*, Celeste Holm *(Karen Richards)*, Gary Merrill *(Bill Simpson)*, Hugh Marlowe *(Lloyd Richards)*, Thelma Ritter *(Birdie Coonan)*, Marilyn Monroe *(Miss Casswell)*, Gregory Ratoff *(Max Fabian)*, Barbara Bates *(Phoebe)*

p, Darryl F. Zanuck; d, Joseph L. Mankiewicz; w, Joseph L. Mankiewicz (based on the story "The Wisdom of Eve" by Mary Orr); ph, Milton Krasner; ed, Barbara McLean; m, Alfred Newman; art d, Lyle Wheeler, George W. Davis; fx, Fred Sersen; cos, Edith Head

AA Best Picture; AAN Best Actress: Anne Baxter; AAN Best Actress: Bette Davis; AA Best Supporting Actor: George Sanders; AAN Best Supporting Actress: Celeste Holm; AAN Best Supporting Actress: Thelma Ritter; AA Best Director: Joseph L. Mankiewicz; AA Best Screenplay: Joseph L. Mankiewicz; AAN Best B/W Cinematography: Milton Krasner; AAN Best Film Editing: Barbara McLean; AA Best Score (Drama or Comedy): Alfred Newman; AAN Best Art Direction-Set Decoration (B/W): Lyle Wheeler, George W. Davis, Thomas Little, Walter M. Scott; AA Best Costume Design (B/W): Edith Head, Charles LeMaire; AA Best Sound Recording: 20th Century Fox Sound Department

ALL ABOUT EVE is the consummate backstage story, a film that holds a magnifying glass up to theatrical environs and exposes all the egos, tempers, conspiracies and backstage back-biting that make up the world of make-believe on Broadway. The screenplay, written by Joseph L. Mankiewicz, who also directed, may be the most biting example of hard-boiled wit ever to come out of Hollywood, and it is stylishly performed at a breakneck pace by a uniformly expert cast.

The story, based on Mary Orr's "The Wisdom of Eve," concerns an aging star who befriends a seemingly innocent fan, who wants to take over and inhabit the star's life. Bette Davis won the part of vain, temperamental Margo Channing by default when Claudette Colbert broke her back, and single-handedly revived her career after having been dumped by Warner Bros. Though Mankiewicz and Davis always claimed the character was based on Austrian actress Elisabeth Bergner, Davis enacted her role as a mirror twin of then-fabled Broadway rival Tallulah Bankhead, thus fanning the flames of an already existing feud. EVE was the peak of Anne Baxter's star years and she almost matches Davis in her silky, dangerous portrayal of Eve. These two are supported by a who's who of matchless portraits, including Gary Merrill (whom Davis would fall in love with during filming and later marry), George Sanders (as a poisonous critic), the biting Thelma Ritter, Celeste Holm, and a young Marilyn Monroe as a cynical, dreamy starlet.

EVE won six Oscars: Best Picture, Director, Screenplay, Supporting Actor (Sanders), Costume Design (Edith Head),

and Sound Recording. It also was nominated for Cinematography, Art Direction, Score, Editing, and Supporting Actress (Holm and Ritter). Bette Davis was doomed to lose for Best Actress, canceled out by Baxter's shared nomination, and by rival old pro Gloria Swanson for SUNSET BOULEVARD (all lost to rookie Judy Holliday for BORN YESTERDAY). The musical *Applause*, a Broadway success with Lauren Bacall, and later Anne Baxter, was based on EVE.

ALL ABOUT MY MOTHER

(TODO SOBRE MI MADRE)
1999 101m c Drama ★★★½
El Deseo SA/Renn Productions/France 2 Cinema R
(Spain)

Cecilia Roth *(Manuela)*, Marisa Paredes *(Huma Rojo)*, Candela Pena *(Nina)*, Antonia San Juan *(Agrado)*, Penelope Cruz *(Sister Rosa)*, Rosa Maria Sarda *(Rosa's Mother)*, Fernando Fernan Gomez *(Rosa's Father)*, Toni Canto *(Lola)*, Eloy Azorin *(Esteban)*, Carlos Lozano *(Mario)*

d, Pedro Almodovar; w, Pedro Almodovar; ph, Affonso Beato; ed, Jose Salcedo; m, Alberto Iglesias; art d, Antxon Gomez; cos, Jose Maria de Cossio, Sabine Daigeler, Cornejo

AA Best Foreign Film

Classic melodrama given a thoroughly modern, utterly Almodovarian face-lift: gender-bending liaisons, outrageous turns of fortune and theatrical contrivances abound, all art directed to a candy-colored fare-thee-well.

The story revolves around the twin themes of performing and mothering and provides a quartet of actresses with the roles of a lifetime. Having lost her beloved son, Esteban (Eloy Azorin), in an accident, grieving Manuela (Cecilia Roth) impulsively decides to return to Barcelona where she abandoned Esteban's father 18 years earlier after he reinvented himself as a promiscuous transvestite named Lola (Toni Canto); Manuela feels obligated to tell Lola about the death of the son he never knew. She hunts down their old friend Agrado (Antonia San Juan), a sweet-natured, transgendered prostitute, who in turn introduces Manuela to angelic Sister Rosa (Penelope Cruz), who ministers to streetwalkers and is the last person to have seen Lola. In fact, Sister Rosa is pregnant by Lola, which makes the whole situation just that little bit more complicated. Manuela also insinuates herself into the life of aging actress Huma Rojo (Marisa Paredes), who's appearing with her much younger lover Nina (Candela Pena) in the touring production of *A Streetcar Named Desire* that Manuela and Esteban saw the night he died.

Like all of writer-director Pedro Almodovar's films, this wild mix of farce, fabulous fashions, and heartache is a visual tour de force, but beneath the flourishes lies a deep well of genuine feeling. The title echoes classic bitchfest ALL ABOUT EVE, but Almodovar's deep-rooted love of women produces an entirely different coloration; his film is a celebration of friendship, family, and resilience that's touching without ever being cloying.

ALL MY SONS

1948 93m bw Drama ★★★½
Universal (U.S.)

Edward G. Robinson *(Joe Keller)*, Burt Lancaster *(Chris Keller)*, Mady Christians *(Kate Keller)*, Louisa Horton *(Ann Deever)*, Howard Duff *(George Deever)*, Frank Conroy *(Herbert Deever)*, Lloyd Gough *(Jim Bayliss)*, Arlene Francis *(Sue Bayliss)*, Henry Morgan *(Frank Lubey)*, Elisabeth Fraser *(Lydia Lubey)* p, Chester Erskine; d, Irving Reis; w, Chester Erskine (based on the play by Arthur Miller); ph, Russell Metty; ed, Ralph Dawson; m, Leith Stevens; art d, Bernard Herzbrun, Hilyard Brown; fx, David S. Horsley; cos, Grace Houston

Arthur Miller's powerful drama tells the story of a family being ripped apart by the discovery of the father's corrupt business ethics during WWII (purposefully shipping defective military parts that resulted in the death of 21 men). The windy treatment is beginning to show its age, but is somewhat compensated for by acting of a high order. Robinson provides one of his best performances, showing the human frailty of his character in all its naked fury and shame, a role matched only by Lancaster's tense, taut presence as an embittered war veteran.

ALL OF ME
1984 93m c Comedy ★★½
Kings Road (U.S.) PG

Steve Martin *(Roger Cobb)*, Lily Tomlin *(Edwina Cutwater)*, Victoria Tennant *(Terry Hoskins)*, Madolyn Smith *(Peggy Schuyler)*, Richard Libertini *(Prahka Lasa)*, Dana Elcar *(Burton Schuyler)*, Jason Bernard *(Tyrone Wattell)*, Selma Diamond *(Margo)*, Eric Christmas *(Fred Hoskins)*, Gailard Sartain *(Fulton Norris)*

p, Stephen Friedman; d, Carl Reiner; w, Phil Alden Robinson, Henry Olek (based on the novel *Me Too* by Ed Davis); ph, Richard H. Kline (Technicolor); ed, Bud Molin; m, Patrick Williams; prod d, Edward Carfagno; fx, Bruce Steinheimer; cos, Ray Summers

Roger Cobb (Steve Martin) is a guitar-playing attorney semi-engaged to the daughter of his boss at a large law firm, whose most important client is the very rich, very ill Edwina Cutwater (Lily Tomlin). Through her personal guru, Cutwater is planning a mind/body switch with a beautiful young woman (Victoria Tennant) and needs some help reworking her will. When Cobb is assigned to the case, the transfer goes awry, and the lawyer winds up battling with Cutwater for control of *his* body. Martin does some of his best acting in this film and steals the movie from Tomlin, whose character is, at best, a one-note creation. If you're a Martin fan, you'll love ALL OF ME; if you aren't, there's still enough fun in spots to make it worth your time.

ALL QUIET ON THE WESTERN FRONT
1930 140m bw War ★★★★★
Universal (U.S.)

Louis Wolheim *(Katczinsky)*, Lew Ayres *(Paul Baumer)*, John Wray *(Himmelstoss)*, Slim Summerville *(Tjaden)*, Russell Gleason *(Muller)*, William Bakewell *(Albert)*, Scott Kolk *(Leer)*, Walter Rogers *(Behm)*, Ben Alexander *(Kemmerick)*, Owen Davis Jr. *(Peter)*

p, Carl Laemmle Jr.; d, Lewis Milestone; w, Del Andrews, Maxwell Anderson, Lewis Milestone (uncredited), George Abbott (based on the novel by Erich Maria Remarque); ph, Karl Freund (uncredited), Arthur Edeson; ed, Edgar Adams, Milton Carruth; m, David Broekman; art d, Charles D. Hall, William R. Schmidt; fx, Frank H. Booth

AA Outstanding Production: ; *AA Best Director:* Lewis Milestone; *AAN Best Writing Achievement:* George Abbott, Maxwell Anderson, Del Andrews; *AAN Best Cinematography:* Arthur Edeson

A remarkably faithful adaptation of Erich Maria Remarque's classic pacifist novel, ALL QUIET ON THE WESTERN FRONT is perhaps the greatest antiwar film ever made, holding considerable power even now due to Lewis Milestone's inventive direction.

Set during WWI and told from the German point of view, the story centers on Paul Baumer (Lew Ayres). A sensitive youth, Baumer is recruited by a war-mongering profes-

sor (Arnold Lucy) advocating "glory for the Fatherland." Paul and his friends enlist and are trained by Himmelstoss (John Wray), a kindly postmaster turned brutal corporal, then sent to the front lines to taste battle, blood, and death. Paul comes under the protective wing of an old veteran, Katczinsky (Louis Wolheim), who teaches him how to survive the horrors of war.

The film is emotionally draining, and so realistic that it will be forever etched in the mind of any viewer. Milestone's direction is frequently inspired, most notably during the battle scenes. In one such scene, the camera serves as a kind of machine gun, shooting down the oncoming troops as it glides along the trenches. Universal spared no expense during production, converting more than 20 acres of a large California ranch into battlefields occupied by more than 2,000 ex-servicemen extras. After its initial release, some foreign countries refused to run the film. Poland banned it for being pro-German, while the Nazis labeled it anti-German. Joseph Goebbels, later propaganda minister, publicly denounced the film.

ALL QUIET ON THE WESTERN FRONT received an Academy Award as Best Picture and Milestone was honored as Best Director. Originally released with a running time of 140 minutes, the film has suffered many cuts over the years with some prints running as short as 90 minutes. The most recent videotape release restores the film to 130 minutes of running time. An interesting, but now-forgotten, sequel titled THE ROAD BACK, directed by James Whale (THE BRIDE OF FRANKENSTEIN), was made in 1937. The original was remade as a television movie in 1979, with Richard Thomas unsuccessfully trying to match the timeless power of Ayres's performance.

ALL THAT HEAVEN ALLOWS
1955 89m c Drama ★★★★
Universal (U.S.)

Jane Wyman *(Cary Scott)*, Rock Hudson *(Ron Kirby)*, Agnes Moorehead *(Sara Warren)*, Conrad Nagel *(Harvey)*, Virginia Grey *(Alida Anderson)*, Gloria Talbott *(Kay Scott)*, William Reynolds *(Ned Scott)*, Jacqueline de Wit *(Mona Plash)*, Charles Drake *(Mick Anderson)*, Hayden Roarke *(Dr. Hennessy)*

p, Ross Hunter; d, Douglas Sirk; w, Peg Fenwick (based on a story by Edna L. Lee and Harry Lee); ph, Russell Metty (Technicolor); ed, Frank Gross, Fred Baratta; m, Frank Skinner, Joseph Gershenson; art d, Alexander Golitzen, Eric Orbom; cos, Bill Thomas

ALL THAT HEAVEN ALLOWS is a classic Douglas Sirk melodrama with Jane Wyman and Rock Hudson, that was the inspiration for Rainer Werner Fassbinder's ALI, FEAR EATS THE SOUL (1973).

After the death of her husband, New Englander Cary Scott (Jane Wyman) settles into the role of being a lonely, middle-aged widow, and her friend Sara (Agnes Moorehead) tries to get her back into the social scene. Harvey (Conrad Nagel), an elderly family friend, proposes to her, but she turns him down. Cary becomes friendly with her young gardener Ron Kirby (Rock Hudson), and despite their age difference, they fall in love and Ron asks her to marry him. Cary's grown children, Ned (William Reynolds) and Kay (Gloria Talbott), come home for a visit, and they're shocked to learn that she's planning to marry Ron, since he's much younger and from a different social class, and that she intends to move out of the family home. Cary takes Ron to a party to introduce him to her friends, but they're subjected to insults and mockery.

In the 1950s, Douglas Sirk was Universal's house director, turning out a succession of slick, commercially successful soap operas with producer Ross Hunter. On the surface, like most of Sirk's Universal tearjerkers, ALL THAT HEAVEN ALLOWS is a combination of "kitsch, craziness, and trashiness," to use the director's own words, yet, as always, he transforms the wish-fulfillment fantasy cliches into a poignant love story and incisive social critique through his masterful handling of actors and his transcendent mise-en-scene. Sirk draws a superb performance from Wyman, using composition and expressionistic colors to trap her in private, middle-classic prison, framed behind picturesque snow-covered windows, her sad image reflected in objects such as mirrors, furniture, and a television set, creating a pathetic imitation of life. Russell Metty's cinematography brilliantly serves Sirk's style of long takes, reframing the characters through subtle camera movements, and splitting the frame into sections while bathing the foreground and background of a shot with different colors to suggest the emotional state of the characters. A particularly stunning example is when Kay comes home in hysterics after her friends were teasing her about her mother getting married, and the multi-hued glass of a circular window throws a rainbow-pattern across her face as she's crying. With its touching story and stylized treatment, ALL THAT HEAVEN ALLOWS is one of Sirk's finest films.

ALL THAT JAZZ
1979 123m c   Musical
Columbia   (U.S.)

DVD
★★★
R

Roy Scheider *(Joe Gideon)*, Jessica Lange *(Angelique)*, Ann Reinking *(Kate Jagger)*, Leland Palmer *(Audrey Paris)*, Cliff Gorman *(David Newman)*, Ben Vereen *(O'Connor Flood)*, Erzebet Foldi *(Michelle)*, Michael Tolan *(Dr. Ballinger)*, Max Wright *(Joshua Benn)*, William La Messena *(Jonesy Hecht)*

p, Robert Alan Aurthur; d, Bob Fosse; ph, Giuseppe Rotunno (Technicolor); ed, Alan Heim; m, Ralph Burns; chor, Bob Fosse; cos, Albert Wolsky

AAN Best Picture; AAN Best Actor: Roy Scheider; *AAN Best Director:* Bob Fosse; *AAN Best Original Screenplay:* Robert Alan Aurthur, Bob Fosse; *AAN Best Cinematography:* Giuseppe Rotunno; *AA Best Film Editing:* Alan Heim; *AA Best Song Score:* Ralph Burns; *AA Best Art Direction-Set Decoration:* Philip Rosenberg, Tony Walton, Edward Stewart, Gary Brink; *AA Best Costume Design:* Albert Wolsky

With the possible exception of 2001: A SPACE ODYSSEY (1968), this Fellini-influenced tragicomic musical was probably the most outre work to date when it was nominated for a Best Picture Oscar.

Joe Gideon (Roy Scheider) is a famous New York choreographer who plays as hard as he works. He pops pills, drinks, smokes, and maniacally drives his dancers and himself in preparation for a new musical, while simultaneously editing a movie he directed and trying to keep his daughter, ex-wife, longtime lover, Broadway investors—and his own rampant libido—satisfied. The chores exhaust him; as a result he has a heart attack and cardiac surgery, and begins to hallucinate wild musical numbers archly metaphoric of his own life.

The dancing is frenzied, the dialogue piercing, the photography superb, and the acting first-rate, with non-showman Scheider an illustrious example of casting against type. Parallels between Fosse's own life and that of his onscreen alter ego are clear: Fosse was editing his film LENNY while rehearsing a show, then he suffered a heart attack, recovered, and after more stage success, made this movie. He cast his former lover Ann Reinking as Joe Gideon's fading flame, and basically dissected the life of a flip, doomed, dysfunctional antihero who alternately evokes sympathy, then repulses with his sexual addiction and constant need for ego-gratification. ALL THAT JAZZ is great-looking but not easy to watch; Fosse's indulgent vision at times approaches sour self-loathing, and nothing like the explicit open-heart surgery had been seen on mainstream American screens, let alone the morbid song-and-dance routines in an operating theater.

ALL THE KING'S MEN
1949 109m bw Political
Columbia   (U.S.)

DVD
★★★★★

Broderick Crawford *(Willie Stark)*, Joanne Dru *(Anne Stanton)*, John Ireland *(Jack Burden)*, John Derek *(Tom Stark)*, Mercedes McCambridge *(Sadie Burke)*, Shepperd Strudwick *(Adam Stanton)*, Ralph Dumke *(Tiny Duffy)*, Anne Seymour *(Lucy Stark)*, Katherine Warren *(Mrs. Burden)*, Raymond Greenleaf *(Judge Stanton)*

p, Robert Rossen; d, Robert Rossen; w, Robert Rossen (based on the novel by Robert Penn Warren); ph, Burnett Guffey; ed, Al Clark; m, Louis Gruenberg

AA Best Picture; AA Best Actor: Broderick Crawford; *AAN Best Supporting Actor:* John Ireland; *AA Best Supporting Actress:* Mercedes McCambridge; *AAN Best Director:* Robert Rossen; *AAN Best Screenplay:* Robert Rossen; *AAN Best Film Editing:* Robert Parrish, Al Clark

Academy Award-winning rise and fall of a rotten politician, based on the Pulitzer Prize-winning novel by Robert Penn Warren. This scathing, grimly realistic film, long a pet project for producer-director-writer Robert Rossen, served as a breakthrough for Broderick Crawford, who had previously been confined to B films. As Willie Stark, Crawford let loose a fierce and awesome acting *tour de force* he never again equaled (and won an Academy Award for his work). The character of Willie Stark himself was most certainly inspired by Louisiana's Huey Pierce Long, the controversial "Kingfish" who ruled the state as governor (and later senator) with an iron hand and an enduring populist appeal, soaking the wealthy and enhancing his personal power unscrupulously. Long's demagoguery, so accurately profiled in this film, ended with his assassination in 1935 by Dr. Carl Austin Weiss, a 29-year-old Baton Rouge physician whose sister may or may not have been raped by Long.

Rossen's film chronicles this life of raw power with compelling scenes, and Crawford's performance is well-supported by the rest of the cast—especially McCambridge, in her film debut, as a conniving political aide. Rossen shot the film in Stockton, California, a working-class town, and enlisted the aid of hundreds of citizens as extras and bit players, adding an edge of authenticity to the production of this hallmark political film.

ALL THE PRESIDENT'S MEN
1976 138m c   Political
Warner Bros.   (U.S.)

DVD
★★★★
PG

Dustin Hoffman *(Carl Bernstein)*, Robert Redford *(Bob Woodward)*, Jack Warden *(Harry Rosenfeld)*, Martin Balsam *(Howard Simons)*, Hal Holbrook *(Deep Throat)*, Jason Robards Jr. *(Ben Bradlee)*, Jane Alexander *(Bookkeeper)*, Meredith Baxter Birney *(Debbie Sloan)*, Ned Beatty *(Dardis)*, Stephen Collins *(Hugh Sloan, Jr.)*

p, Walter Coblenz; d, Alan J. Pakula; w, William Goldman (based on the book by Carl Bernstein and Bob Woodward); ph, Gordon Willis (Panavision, Technicolor); ed, Robert Wolfe; m, David Shire; prod d, George Jenkins

AAN Best Picture; AA Best Supporting Actor: Jason Robards; *AAN Best Supporting Actress:* Jane Alexander; *AAN Best Director:* Alan J. Pakula; *AA Best Adapted Screenplay:* William Goldman; *AAN Best Film Editing:* Robert L. Wolfe; *AA Best Art Direction-Set Decoration:* George Jenkins, George Gaines; *AA Best Sound:* Arthur Piantadosi, Les Fresholtz, Dick Alexander, Jim Webb

Landmark movie which combines elements of the political thriller, buddy picture-star vehicle, detective story, 1930s newspaper reporter programmer, and biopic. The two stars play the real-life *Washington Post* reporters who kicked off the Watergate investigation, with Hoffman as the Jewish, street-smart Carl Bernstein and Redford as the WASPy Bob Woodward. Robards, beginning his spate of crusty-ole-codger supporting roles, won an Oscar, as did screenwriter William Goldman. The film features a host of fine character portrayals and a compelling climax that compensates for its length.

ALL THE PRETTY HORSES

2000 117m c Western/Romance ★★★
Icarus/Columbia/Miramax (U.S.) R

Matt Damon *(John Grady Cole)*, Henry Thomas *(Lacey Rawlins)*, Penelope Cruz *(Alejandra)*, Lucas Black *(Jimmy Blevins)*, Ruben Blades *(Rocha)*, Miriam Colon *(Dona Alfonsa)*, Bruce Dern *(Judge)*, Robert Patrick *(Cole)*, Sam Shepard *(J.C. Franklin)*, Elizabeth Ibarra *(Maria)*

p, Billy Bob Thornton, Robert Salerno; d, Billy Bob Thornton; w, Ted Tally (based on the novel by Cormac McCarthy); ph, Barry Markowitz; ed, Sally Menke; m, Marty Stuart; prod d, Clark Hunter; art d, Richard Johnson, Max Biscoe; fx, Margaret Johnson, Randy Moore; cos, Doug Hall

Director Billy Bob Thornton holds these truths to be self-evident: A sweeping Western landscape is worth a thousand words; horses are just about God's finest creations; and Cormac McCarthy's spare narrative, set in the post-war American West, can survive separation from his evocative prose.

After his estranged mother sells off the family's West Texas spread, young John Grady Cole (Matt Damon) and his childhood pal, Lacey Rawlins (Henry Thomas), saddle up and head for Mexico, where they've heard there are still vast cattle ranches waiting to be worked by eager cowboys. The friends ride part of the way with an underage, hard-luck runaway named Blevins (Lucas Black), and part company with him under circumstances that come back to haunt them. They find work in Mexico, and Cole's gumption impresses *el jefe* Rocha (Ruben Blades), but he makes the mistake of falling for Rocha's headstrong daughter, Alejandra (Penelope Cruz). The consequences of Cole's impetuosity test both his love for Alejandra and his friendship with Rawlins.

Thornton's devotion to Western conventions is evident, as is his love of McCarthy's lengthy book; it must have pained him to pare away so much of its resonant detail. His determination to cast authentically is also laudable: Thornton rejected several bankable actresses for the role of Alejandra with a terse, "She ain't Mexican" (strictly speaking, neither is Cruz). But Damon is stiff and colorless, and the leads are older than their characters were originally written, robbing a certain poignance from their crash course in life's brutal unfairness. The movie's greatest liability, though, is the familiarity of the material, much parodied since the glory days of John Ford. Even Thornton's love for its iconography can't quite bring it to life.

ALL THIS AND HEAVEN TOO

1940 140m bw Romance ★★★★
Warner Bros. (U.S.)

Bette Davis *(Henriette Deluzy Desportes)*, Charles Boyer *(Duke De Praslin)*, Jeffrey Lynn *(Reverend Henry Field)*, Barbara O'Neil *(Duchesse De Praslin)*, Virginia Weidler *(Louise)*, Walter Hampden *(Pasquier)*, Harry Davenport *(Pierre)*, Fritz Leiber *(Abbe Gallard)*, Helen Westley *(Mme. Le Maire)*, Sibyl Harris *(Mlle. Maillard)*

p, David Lewis; d, Anatole Litvak; w, Casey Robinson (based on the novel by Rachel Lyman Field); ph, Ernest Haller; ed, Warren Low; m, Max Steiner; art d, Carl Jules Weyl; cos, Orry-Kelly

AAN Best Picture; AAN Best Supporting Actress: Barbara O'Neil; *AAN Best B/W Cinematography:* Ernest Haller

A classic of unrequited love, based on the best-selling Rachel Field novel set in 19th-century France. Governess Davis falls in love with nobleman Boyer who has engaged her to care for his children. Litvak's smooth, understated treatment produces restrained, ageless performances from both stars. Oscar nominee Barbara O'Neil (best remembered as Scarlett O'Hara's mother in GWTW) almost steals the picture in a serpentine portrayal of Boyer's possessive, neurotic wife. This moody, elaborate production, greatly enhanced by its Steiner score, is a deft example of the "women's picture."

ALMOST FAMOUS

2000 122m c Drama ★★★★
DreamWorks SKG/Vinyl·Films (U.S.) R

Billy Crudup *(Russell Hammond)*, Frances McDormand *(Elaine Miller)*, Kate Hudson *(Penny Lane)*, Jason Lee *(Jeff Bebe)*, Patrick Fugit *(William Miller)*, Zooey Deschanel *(Anita Miller)*, Michael Angarano *(Young William)*, Noah Taylor *(Dick Roswell)*, John Fedevich *(Ed Vallencourt)*, Mark Kozelek *(Larry Fellows)*

p, Cameron Crowe, Ian Bryce; d, Cameron Crowe; w, Cameron Crowe; ph, John Toll; ed, Joe Hutshing, Saar Klein; m, Nancy Wilson; art d, Clay A. Griffith, Clayton R. Hartley, Virginia Randolph-Weaver; fx, John Frazier, Jim Schwalm, Ed Jones; cos, Betsy Heimann

AA Best Original Screenplay: Cameron Crowe; *AAN Best Supporting Actress:* Kate Hudson; *AAN Best Supporting Actress:* Frances McDormand; *AAN Best Film Editing:* Joe Hutshing, Saar Klein

Woven from the early life experiences of writer-director Cameron Crowe, this quasi-autobiographical cinematic tapestry is a wonderfully evocative paean to the music that helped shape and define a generation.

It's 1973, and 15-year-old William Miller (Patrick Fugit), a gifted aspiring music journalist, has snagged an unbelievably plum assignment: a lengthy piece for the fledgling *Rolling Stone* profiling the talented but not-yet-famous Stillwater, fronted by Jeff Bebe (Jason Lee) and the charismatic Russell Hammond (Billy Crudup), whom William met while they were opening for Black Sabbath. In order to get the interviews and background material he needs, William first needs the consent of his overly protective mother (Frances McDormand), who worries about the sex and drugs she knows go hand-in-hand with rock and roll. William then joins the band and their barely legal "band aids" (groupies to the rest of us) on their ill-conceived "Almost Famous" bus tour of various U.S. cities. Despite the warnings of rock critic Lester Bangs (a brilliant Philip Seymour Hoffman) against ever befriending the band you're writing about, William does just that (what fan wouldn't?) and compounds his transgression by falling in love with Russell's personal band aid, Penny Lane (Kate Hudson).

Sharply observed, bittersweet, and suffused with the kind of detail that only someone who lived—and loved—through the era could summon up, Crowe's script is funny, heartfelt, and very cool. His ensemble cast—especially Fugit, Crudup, Hoffman, McDormand and the sensational Hudson—reward him with performances as vivid as a black light poster.

ALPHAVILLE

(ALPHAVILLE, UNE ETRANGE AVENTURE DE LEMMY CAUTION)
1965 99m bw Science Fiction ★★★★½
Athos/Chaumaine/Filmstudio (France/Italy)

Eddie Constantine *(Lemmy Caution)*, Anna Karina *(Natasha Von Braun)*, Akim Tamiroff *(Henri Dickson)*, Laszlo Szabo *(Chief*

Engineer), Howard Vernon *(Professor Von Braun—aka Leonard Nosferatu)*, Michel Delahaye *(Von Braun's Assistant)*, Jean-Andre Fieschi *(Professor Heckell)*, Jean-Louis Comolli *(Professor Jeckell)*, Jean-Pierre Leaud *(Bellhop)*

p, Andre Michelin; d, Jean-Luc Godard; w, Jean-Luc Godard; ph, Raoul Coutard; ed, Agnes Guillemot; m, Paul Misraki

Jean-Luc Godard's ALPHAVILLE is a poetic, funny, and visually inspired blend of sci-fi, detective-film satire, and political allegory.

Secret agent Lemmy Caution (Eddie Constantine) enters Alphaville in search of his predecessor Henri Dickson (Akim Tamiroff) and Professor Von Braun (Howard Vernon), the inventor of a death ray. Pretending to be a reporter, Lemmy discovers that Alphaville is a cold and loveless automated society that's run by a computer invented by Von Braun called Alpha 60. He meets Von Braun's daughter Natasha (Anna Karina) and finds Dickson at a hotel where dissidents are kept until they commit suicide. After seeing Dickson die, Natasha takes Lemmy to see her father. Von Braun's guards capture Lemmy and he's interrogated by Alpha 60, then given a tour of the computer's control center. There he learns that Von Braun intends to declare war on the Outlands.

ALPHAVILLE is a brilliant satire of an alienated society that has been robbed of its poetry and emotion by science and technology. The film's central conceit—and joke—is that this dystopian futuristic society is actually contemporary France, and the pod-like, conformist mindset of its people already exists. All of the interiors were filmed in dehumanizing glass and concrete office buildings and hotels, filled with sterile corridors and fluorescent computer rooms. All of the exteriors take place in a nocturnal Paris illuminated only by car lights and flashing neon. The casting of Eddie Constantine was inspired, as he had established the character of the hard-boiled dick Lemmy Caution in a series of French movies based on Peter Cheyney's novels. With his trench-coat, fedora, cigarette, and craggy face, Constantine recalls a poor-man's Humphrey Bogart, nonchalantly shooting everything in sight. Raoul Coutard's superbly mobile camerawork and Paul Misraki's excellent score all contribute to a movie that proves that you need neither a huge budget or computer effects to make a classic sci-fi movie, but only imagination.

AMADEUS *DVD*
1984 158m c Biography/Musical ★★★★★
Orion (U.S.) PG

F. Murray Abraham *(Antonio Salieri)*, Tom Hulce *(Wolfgang Amadeus Mozart)*, Elizabeth Berridge *(Constanze Mozart)*, Simon Callow *(Emanuel Schikaneder)*, Roy Dotrice *(Leopold Mozart)*, Christine Ebersole *(Katerina Cavalieri)*, Jeffrey Jones *(Emperor Joseph II)*, Charles Kay *(Count Orsini-Rosenberg)*, Kenny Baker *(Parody Commendatore)*, Lisbeth Bartlett *(Papagena)*

p, Saul Zaentz; d, Milos Forman; w, Peter Shaffer (based on his play); ph, Miroslav Ondricek (Panavision, Technicolor); ed, Nena Danevic, Michael Chandler; m, Wolfgang Amadeus Mozart, Antonio Salieri, Giovanni Battista Pergolesi; prod d, Patrizia von Brandenstein; art d, Karel Cerny, Francesco Chianese, Josef Svoboda; fx, Dick Smith; chor, Twyla Tharp; cos, Theodor Pistek

AA Best Picture; AA Best Actor: F. Murray Abraham; *AAN Best Actor:* Tom Hulce; *AA Best Director:* Milos Forman; *AA Best Adapted Screenplay:* Peter Shaffer; *AAN Best Cinematography:* Miroslav Ondricek; *AAN Best Film Editing:* Nena Danevic, Michael Chandler; *AA Best Art Direction-Set Decoration:* Patrizia Von Brandenstein, Karel Cerny; *AA Best Costume Design:* Theodor Pistek; *AA Best Sound:* Mark Berger, Tom Scott, Todd Boekelheide, Chris Newman; *AA Best Makeup:* Paul LeBlanc, Dick Smith

Milos Forman's brilliant, Oscar-winning adaptation of Peter Shaffer's hit play, AMADEUS is a fictionalized retelling of the final days of Antonio Salieri.

Salieri (F. Murray Abraham, who won the Best Actor Oscar for his portrayal), a famous composer in Mozart's day but now incarcerated in an insane asylum, begins his final confession to a young cleric. He tells the story of his relationship with Mozart (Tom Hulce), in a 30-year flashback to when he first met the 26-year-old prodigy. Furious that this boor can produce such beautiful music, Salieri determines to keep Mozart's talent from continued recognition.

The discerning but less talented Salieri has great influence in Vienna, being court composer to Joseph II of Austria (Jeffrey Jones), who realizes he knows little about music and therefore allows Salieri to decide what he should hear and whom he should be patron to. After Mozart manages to get the Emperor's ear, his career is launched, and we see him writing and conducting several of his best pieces. Then his friends, health, and resources waste away. He works most feverishly on his "Requiem," commissioned by a masked stranger who is actually Salieri. The effort proves the final stroke against the greater composer's weakened constitution, and he is buried in a pauper's grave.

Milos Forman's direction is flawless, Neville Marriner's musical direction is superb, and the film is a feast for the eyes and ears. Although Forman concentrates on Mozart's more popular works, the prodigious output of Mozart's short life is clearly conveyed. AMADEUS is a must for any music lover, any film lover, or anyone who reveres excellence.

AMARCORD *DVD*
1973 124m c Comedy ★★★★½
F.C./PECF (Italy/France) R

Magali Noel *(Gradisca)*, Bruno Zanin *(Titta Biondi)*, Pupella Maggio *(Miranda Biondi—Titta's Mother)*, Armando Brancia *(Aurelio Biondi—Titta's Father)*, Giuseppe Ianigro *(Titta's Grandfather)*, Nando Orfei *(Pataca)*, Ciccio Ingrassia *(Uncle Teo)*, Luigi Rossi *(Lawyer)*, Gennaro Ombra *(Bisein)*, Josiane Tanzilli *(Volpina)*

p, Franco Cristaldi; d, Federico Fellini; w, Federico Fellini, Tonino Guerra; ph, Giuseppe Rotunno (Technicolor); ed, Ruggero Mastroianni; m, Nino Rota; prod d, Danilo Donati; cos, Danilo Donati

AAN Best Director: Federico Fellini; *AAN Best Original Screenplay:* Federico Fellini, Tonino Guerra; *AA Best Foreign Language Film*

A pictorial weaving of the bizarre fragments of Fellini's imagination and memory, AMARCORD is set in a seaside village (very similar to Fellini's boyhood town of Rimini) in the 1930s. Through the eyes of the impressionable young Zanin, Fellini takes a penetrating look at family life, religion, love, sex, education, and politics. Among the characters are Zanin's constantly battling mother and father, and a priest who listens to confession only to spark his own deviant imagination. Although Italy is under the control of the Fascists, the regime's oppressiveness remains obscure to the naive villagers, who worship an immense, daunting banner of Il Duce's face. There is hardly a character in AMARCORD left unscathed by Fellini's biting wit, yet the director manages to present them lovingly. Unique personality traits, revelations of personal weakness (and thus humanness), are valued for the color and variety they add to the world. AMARCORD won the Academy Award for Best Foreign Film in 1974.

AMATEUR *DVD*
1994 105m c Drama/Thriller/Crime ★★★
Union Generale du Cinematographique/True R
Fiction Pictures/Zenith Productions/American

Playhouse/Theatrical Films/Channel Four Films/
La Sept   (U.S./U.K./France)

Isabelle Huppert *(Isabelle)*, Martin Donovan *(Thomas)*, Elina Lowensohn *(Sofia)*, Damian Young *(Edward)*, Chuck Montgomery *(Jan)*, David Simonds *(Kurt)*, Pamela Stewart *(Officer Melville)*, Erica Gimpel *(Irate Woman)*, Jan Leslie Harding *(Waitress)*, Terry Alexander *(Frank the Cook)*

p, Ted Hope, Hal Hartley; d, Hal Hartley; w, Hal Hartley; ph, Michael Spiller; ed, Steve Hamilton; m, Jeff Taylor; prod d, Steve Rosenzweig; art d, Ginger Tougas; fx, Drew Jiritano; cos, Alexander Welker

AMATEUR wears its themes on its sleeve, and questions of identity are always on the character's minds; everyone wants to change, to be redeemed, but nobody seems to know how.

Handsome, sharply dressed Thomas (Martin Donovan) wakes up in New York's trendy SoHo, unable to remember who he is or how he came to be lying face down on the cobblestone pavement. He stumbles into the fragile arms of Isabelle (Isabelle Huppert), an enigmatic beauty who tends to his head wound and assists him in his search for the secret of his identity. But the more Thomas learns about the man he used to be, the more he wants to emulate Isabelle, a former nun who's remaking herself as a literary pornographer.

A brittle comedy of manners for an ill-mannered age, AMATEUR sounds more engaging than it actually is. This elegantly photographed film features blackmail, attempted murder, amnesia, a stylish European porno star (Elina Lowensohn), and a hair-raising episode of torture—but it's more tedious than piquant. Though fans of Hartley's distinctive blend of coolly arch dialogue and preposterous happenstance won't be disappointed, AMATEUR is exasperatingly clever and ultimately superficial. Surprisingly, the film's last scene abandons the hip detachment that is director Hal Hartley's trademark and lends the film a genuinely poignant punch.

AMELIE   DVD
(LE FABULEUX DESTIN D'AMELIE POULAIN)
2001 117m c/bw Romance/Fantasy   ★★★
Filmstiftung Nordrhein-Westfalen/France   R
3 Cinema/La Sofica Sofinergie 5/Le Studio Canal/
MMC Independent GmbH/Tapioca Films/Victoires
Productions   (France/Germany)

Audrey Tautou *(Amelie)*, Mathieu Kassovitz *(Nino Quicampoix)*, Rufus *(Raphael Poulain—Amelie's Father)*, Yolande Moreau *(Madeleine Wallace—Concierge)*, Arthus De Penguern *(Hipolito—The Writer)*, Urbain Cancelier *(Collignon—The Grocer)*, Dominique Pinon *(Joseph)*, Isabelle Nanty *(Georgette)*, Serge Merlin *(Dufayel)*, Maurice Benichou *(Bretodeau—The Box Man)*

p, Claude Ossard, Jean-March Deschamps; d, Jean-Pierre Jeunet; w, Jean-Pierre Jeunet, Guillaume Laurant; ph, Bruno Delbonnel; ed, Herve Schneid; m, Yann Tiersen; prod d, Aline Bonetto; art d, Volker Schaefer; fx, Alain Carsoux, Yves Domenjoud; cos, Madeline Fontaine, Emma Lebail

AAN Best Foreign Language Film ; AAN Best Art Direction: Aline Bonetto, Marie-Laure Valla; AAN Best Cinematography: Bruno Delbonnel; AAN Best Sound: Vincent Arnardi, Guillaume Leriche, Jean Umansky; AAN Best Original Screenplay: Guillaume Laurant, Jean-Pierre Jeunet

An eccentric Parisian wallflower finds her soul mate in Jean-Pierre Jeunet's aggressively sunny romance.

Disappointed by her first forays into the world of dating, shy, young waitress Amelie (Audrey Tautou) devotes herself to cultivating life's small pleasures—cracking the glaze on a creme caramel, observing inconsequential details in the backgrounds of old movies—as she waits for her life's purpose to be revealed. Her destiny announces itself in the form of an old tin box filled with children's toys, which she finds behind a wall in her apartment. Amelie resolves to locate its owner and return the toys, and when that mission goes well, she starts meddling in the lives of her coworkers, family, and neighbors. Amelie launches a whimsical plan to persuade her father (Rufus) to resurrect his dormant dream of traveling, she fixes up two neurotic acquaintances (Dominique Pinon, Isabelle Nanty), and she befriends a reclusive, elderly painter (Serge Merlin). It's he who suggests that perhaps Amelie should work her magic on her own life, and so Amelie pursues Nino Quicampoix (Mathieu Kassovitz), a fellow every bit as odd as she.

Some may find this frenetic valentine to oddballs everywhere intolerably sugary, but it does have a bizarre edge. Jeunet's lifelong love of animation is evident throughout, and by digitally tweaking virtually every image, he creates a world as fantastic as those of the far less cheery DELICATESSEN or THE CITY OF LOST CHILDREN. It's unfortunate that Amelie and Nino are more aggregations of quirky character traits than characters, but the lanky, wide-eyed Tautou is so charming her smile could sweeten vinegar. That Kassovitz is less winning hardly matters; Tautou's charisma conquers all.

AMERICAN BEAUTY   DVD
1999 118m c   Comedy/Drama   ★★★★
Jinks/Cohen Company   (U.S.)   R

Kevin Spacey *(Lester Burnham)*, Annette Bening *(Carolyn Burnham)*, Thora Birch *(Jane Burnham)*, Wes Bentley *(Ricky Fitts)*, Mena Suvari *(Angela Hayes)*, Peter Gallagher *(Buddy Kane)*, Allison Janney *(Barbara Fitts)*, Chris Cooper *(Colonel Fitts)*, Scott Bakula *(Jim #1)*, Sam Robards *(Jim #2)*

p, Bruce Cohen, Dan Jinks; d, Sam Mendes; w, Alan Ball; ph, Conrad L. Hall; ed, Tariq Anwar, Chris Greenbury; m, Thomas Newman; prod d, Naomi Shohan; art d, David S. Lazan; fx, John C. Hartigan; chor, Paula Abdul; cos, Julie Weiss

AA Best Picture; AA Best Actor: Kevin Spacey; AA Best Original Screenplay: Alan Ball; AA Best Director: Sam Mendes; AA Best Cinematography: Conrad L. Hall; AAN Best Actress: Annette Bening; AAN Best Film Editing: Tariq Anwar; AAN Best Original Score: Thomas Newman

Black comedy of the deepest, richest darkness. First-time movie director Sam Mendes and screenwriter Alan Ball layer wicked satire over an aching meditation on dreams not so much deferred as unformed, unarticulated, and lost in the shuffle. This chronicle of suburban families imploding in slow motion contains genuine laughs, but they escape through clenched teeth.

Lester Burnham (Kevin Spacey) is having a mid-life meltdown. He's about to be fired in a cynical corporate downsizing, and his teenage daughter, Jane (Thora Birch), holds him in the furious contempt only judgmental teens can work up. Wife Carolyn (Annette Bening) has metamorphosed into a mad housewife, '90s style: Realtor, mother, homemaker, and student of self-empowerment, she's a perfectly coiffed bundle of crackling nerves. The Burnhams' friends and neighbors include new kid-next-door Ricky Fitts (Wes Bentley), a drug dealer who videotapes everything, particularly Jane; Ricky's dad, a marine hard-ass (Chris Cooper); and the Jims (Scott Bakula, Sam Robards), a pair of cheerful, gay urban professionals. And then there's Angela (Mena Suvari), Jane's seductive, underaged cheerleader pal who becomes the unwitting embodiment of Lester's longing for the glory days of heedless partying. Not a noble desire, but it spurs Lester to change his life and throw everyone else's into chaos.

Lester's opening voice-over announces that he'll be dead before his next birthday; the *what* is never in question, but the *how* keeps you spellbound. Mendes, a British theater verteran, elicits subtle and complex performances from the first-rate cast. Ball, whose background includes sitcoms and theater, pulls off his satirical jibes with pitch-perfect aplomb, weaving them into a plot that oozes menace. He's not pining for Pleasantville or blaming the American suburbs for the surfeit of brittle unhappiness, guns, and reasons for people to flip out. His subject is the hollowness of lives like American Beauty roses—richly colored, uniform, and scentless.

AMERICAN FRIEND, THE   📀
(DER AMERIKANISCHE FREUND)
1977   126m   c   Mystery/Thriller   ★★★★
Road Movies/Wim Wenders Produktion/
Westdeutschen Rundfunk/Films du Losange
(West Germany/France)

Bruno Ganz *(Jonathan Zimmermann)*, Dennis Hopper *(Tom Ripley)*, Gerard Blain *(Raoul Minot)*, Lisa Kreuzer *(Marianne Zimmermann)*, Nicholas Ray *(Prokasch, aka Derwatt)*, Samuel Fuller *(The American)*, Peter Lilienthal *(Marcangelo)*, Daniel Schmid *(Ingraham)*, Sandy Whitelaw *(Doctor in Paris)*, Jean Eustache *(Friendly Man)*

d, Wim Wenders; w, Wim Wenders (based on the novel *Ripley's Game* by Patricia Highsmith); ph, Robby Muller; ed, Peter Przygodda; m, Jurgen Knieper; prod d, Sickerts; art d, Heidi Ludi, Toni Ludi; fx, Theo Nischwitz; cos, Isolde Nist

Dennis Hopper and Bruno Ganz are superb in Wim Wenders's THE AMERICAN FRIEND, a gripping Hitchockian thriller based on a novel by Patricia Highsmith.

Jonathan Zimmermann (Bruno Ganz), a Hamburg picture-framer and painting-restorer who's suffering from an incurable blood disease, meets Tom Ripley (Dennis Hopper), an American who sells forged paintings in Germany and knows about Jonathan's illness. Because of a perceived slight when the two were introduced, Ripley spreads a rumor that Jonathan's death is imminent, and suggests his name to a criminal associate named Minot (Gerard Blain) who's looking for a non-professional hitman to dispose of his rivals. Jonathan refuses, but changes his mind as his anxiety over his condition increases; he carries out Minot's assignment, shooting a man in the Paris subway. Back in Germany, Minot pays him only half of the proposed fee, telling him he will give him the rest after he performs another killing.

THE AMERICAN FRIEND is a moody and riveting thriller-cum-existential character study that pays homage to the American cinema, not only by its casting of Wenders's two directorial cult-heroes, Nicholas Ray and Samuel Fuller, but also through direct stylistic and thematic references to the work of Alfred Hitchcock, who had made one of his best films, STRANGERS ON A TRAIN (1951) from a Highsmith novel.

Wenders handles the thriller aspects of the plot expertly, making it possibly his most accessible film. He also treats the story as an ironic commentary on the influence of American culture on Germany and the uneasy relationship between the two countries, as well as a personal meditation on the acts of looking and seeing. Hopper gives one of the best performances of his career as the devilish Ripley, driving around spouting philosophy into a tape-recorder. Ganz is equally superb as the tortured Jonathan, and both actors brilliantly play off the other's differing acting style. Wenders has categorized THE AMERICAN FRIEND as simply an "entertainment film," but it's a richly textured and deeply rewarding one.

AMERICAN GIGOLO   📀
1980   117m   c   Drama/Crime   ★★★½
Paramount   (U.S.)   R

Richard Gere *(Julian Kay)*, Lauren Hutton *(Michelle)*, Hector Elizondo *(Sunday)*, Nina Van Pallandt *(Anne)*, Bill Duke *(Leon Jaimes)*, Brian Davies *(Charles Stratton)*, K. Callan *(Lisa Williams)*, Tom Stewart *(Mr. Rheiman)*, Patti Carr *(Judy Rheiman)*, David Cryer *(Lt. Curtis)*

p, Jerry Bruckheimer; d, Paul Schrader; w, Paul Schrader; ph, John Bailey (Metrocolor); ed, Richard Halsey; m, Giorgio Moroder; prod d, Ferdinando Scarfiotti; art d, Ed Richardson; cos, Alice Rush

Richard Gere's supremely smug and narcissistic performance as an L.A. hustler propelled him to stardom in Paul Schrader's AMERICAN GIGOLO, a stylishly sleazy look at moral rot and redemption. The story becomes increasingly implausible as its thriller elements kick in, but the moving last shot (which owes much to Robert Bresson's PICKPOCKET) achieves a sense of spiritual transcendence and grace rare in American movies.

Handsome Julian Kay (Richard Gere) is a high-class male prostitute working for Scandinavian procurer Anne (Nina Van Pallandt); most of his clientele is made up of wealthy, older women. As a favor to a pimp named Leon (Bill Duke), Julian agrees to do a Palm Springs trick with a couple, the Rheimans. But they're heavily into S&M, and Julian leaves before the session is over, later meeting a woman named Michelle (Lauren Hutton) with whom he begins an intense relationship. Julian's carefully ordered life suddenly takes a nose-dive: Mrs. Rheiman is found dead and he's suspected of her murder; Leon refuses to help manufacture an alibi and Anne won't give Julian the time of day because he betrayed her by working for Leon; and Michelle turns out to be married to a local politician.

Abandoning the gritty realism of his first two films, BLUE COLLAR and HARDCORE, screenwriter-turned-director Schrader here adopted a sleek and stylish approach. The result was one of his most satisfying attempts to mesh a European sensibility and his own obsession with moral drift and emotional alienation. The film can be seen as the flip side of TAXI DRIVER (which Schrader wrote); it's also a virtual compendium of '80s music, fashion, and pop-culture symbols, as well as a vivid portrait of the era's rich Hollywood decadence, starting with Giorgio Moroder's throbbing synthesizer score and Blondie singing "Call Me" as Julian cruises L.A. in his Mercedes convertible.

AMERICAN GRAFFITI   📀
1973   110m   c   Comedy   ★★★★½
Universal   (U.S.)   PG

Richard Dreyfuss *(Curt)*, Ron Howard *(Steve)*, Paul LeMat *(John)*, Charles Martin Smith *(Terry)*, Cindy Williams *(Laurie)*, Candy Clark *(Debbie)*, Mackenzie Phillips *(Carol)*, Wolfman Jack *(Himself)*, Harrison Ford *(Falfa)*, Bo Hopkins *(Joe)*

p, Francis Ford Coppola, Gary Kurtz; d, George Lucas; w, George Lucas, Gloria Katz, Willard Huyck; ph, Ron Eveslage, Jan D'Alquen (Technicolor); ed, Verna Fields, Marcia Lucas; art d, Dennis Clark; cos, Aggie Guerard Rodgers

AAN Best Picture; AAN Best Supporting Actress: Candy Clark; *AAN Best Director:* George Lucas; *AAN Best Original Story and Screenplay:* George Lucas, Gloria Katz, Willard Huyck; *AAN Best Film Editing:* Verna Fields, Marcia Lucas

A hallmark film of the 1970s. In a series of touching and telling vignettes, AMERICAN GRAFFITI follows a memorable crew of small-town teenagers through one momentous night in 1962. Director Lucas' modest, near-verite approach contrasts strikingly with his glitzy following film, STAR WARS.

Steve (Ron Howard), a clean-cut youth, is to leave for college the next day; Curt (Richard Dreyfuss), the class intellectual, is also slated for college but has doubts about his future; Laurie (Cindy Williams), Curt's sister and Steve's girlfriend, is upset by the latter's impending departure; Terry (Charles Martin Smith) is a hopeless nerd who desperately yearns to be "cool"; John (Paul LeMat), who's very cool indeed, drives "the fastest car in the valley" and is constantly being forced to prove that boast. After the school dance, everyone goes cruising. John picks up loquacious 13-year-old Carol (Mackenzie Phillips), thinking she's much older until she climbs aboard his 1932 Ford Deuce Coupe. Steve and Laurie, driving about in his 1958 Impala, clash over their ambitions; he's full of hope for the future, while she's afraid her life is over at 17. Curt goes off in search of the elusive Girl in the White T-Bird, while Terry has an adventure with a reputedly "experienced" older girl (Candy Clark).

Based on George Lucas' own teenage hot-rodding days in Modesto, California, the appeal of AMERICAN GRAFFITI is in its fragmentary scenes; the nervous camera jumps from character to character to present a powerful collage of American youth on the brink of maturity and the complex experiences of the coming decade. The enormous financial and critical success of GRAFFITI—it grossed over $100 million domestically—allowed Lucas the freedom to finance one of the most beloved and highest-grossing films of all time—STAR WARS—and spawned numerous imitations, even inspiring the long-running TV sitcom "Happy Days." The film boosted the careers of a host of young performers including Dreyfuss, Howard, Williams, LeMat, Smith, Clark, Phillips, Harrison Ford, Kathleen Quinlan, and Suzanne Somers.

AMERICAN HISTORY X   ⟦DVD⟧
1998 118m c/bw Drama   ★★★½
The Turman/Morrissey Co./The Steve Tisch Co./   R
New Line (U.S.)

Edward Norton (Derek Vinyard), Edward Furlong (Danny Vinyard), Fairuza Balk (Stacey), Stacy Keach (Cameron Alexander), Avery Brooks (Bob Sweeney), Beverly D'Angelo (Doris Vinyard), Jennifer Lien (Davin), Ethan Suplee (Seth), Elliott Gould (Murray), Joe Cortese (Rasmussen)

p, John Morrissey; d, Tony Kaye; w, David McKenna; ph, Tony Kaye; ed, Gary Greenberg, Alan Heim; m, Anne Dudley; prod d, Jon Gary Steele; art d, Dan Olexiewicz, James Kyler Black; fx, Thomas Bellissimo; cos, Douglas Hall

AAN Best Actor: Edward Norton

Though it opened amid a flurry of hype and controversy, director Tony Kaye's social drama—set among members of California's White Power underground—is a powerful piece of filmmaking.

Derek Vinyard (Edward Norton), the leader of a violent, Venice Beach-based Neo-Nazi gang, is sent to prison for the brutal murder of a black man. Three years later, Derek leaves the penitentiary a changed man, eager to put all the racial hatred and senseless violence behind him. But he finds it's not so easy: his younger brother Danny (Edward Furlong) has been fully indoctrinated into the White Power movement. The film flashes back from the day of Derek's release to the defining moments of his past, including the murder of

his father, a fireman gunned down while trying to put out a crack-house fire.

The incendiary subject matter was only one reason Kaye's film garnered so much pre-release attention. The other was Kaye's own bizarre antics: he deemed the film's final cut so awful he petitioned to have his name removed and replaced with "Humpty Dumpty," and at one point marched into a production executive's office accompanied by a priest, a rabbi, and a Buddhist monk, presumably to bolster the moral weight of his grievances. Kaye, whose previous directing experience was in commercials and music video, needn't have made such a fuss: the film as released is a grim, uncompromising piece of work, intelligently written by David McKenna and dramatically shot—mostly in black and white—by Kaye himself. But it's Norton who makes the film such an enlightening experience. With the same spellbinding eloquence he brought to THE PEOPLE VS. LARRY FLYNT, Norton nails the charisma essential to his character and dares to make Derek dangerously attractive; it's hard to tell exactly where rationality breaks down and the ugly hate-speak begins, and the seduction of disenfranchised white teenagers becomes frighteningly comprehensible.

AMERICAN IN PARIS, AN   ⟦DVD⟧
1951 113m c Musical   ★★★★★
MGM (U.S.)

Gene Kelly (Jerry Mulligan), Leslie Caron (Lise Bouvier), Oscar Levant (Adam Cook), Georges Guetary (Henri Baurel), Nina Foch (Milo Roberts), Eugene Borden (George Mattieu), Martha Barnattre (Mathilde Mattieu), Mary Jones (Old Lady Dancer), Ann Codee (Therese), George Davis (Francois)

p, Arthur Freed; d, Vincente Minnelli; w, Alan Jay Lerner; ph, Alfred Gilks, John Alton (Technicolor); ed, Adrienne Fazan; art d, Cedric Gibbons, Preston Ames; fx, Warren Newcombe; chor, Gene Kelly; cos, Walter Plunkett (Beaux-Arts), Irene Sharaff (Ballet)

AA Best Picture; AAN Best Director: Vincente Minnelli; *AA Best Story and Screenplay:* Alan Jay Lerner; *AA Best Color Cinematography:* Alfred Gilks, John Alton; *AAN Best Film Editing:* Adrienne Fazan; *AA Best Score (Musical):* Johnny Green, Saul Chaplin; *AA Best Art Direction-Set Decoration (Color):* Cedric Gibbons, Preston Ames, Edwin B. Willis, Keogh Gleason; *AA Best Costume Design (Color):* Orry-Kelly, Walter Plunkett, Irene Sharaff

A classic film featuring the timeless music of George and Ira Gershwin, AN AMERICAN IN PARIS has a freshness and charm rare in the musical genre, and it was the film that forever identified MGM as *the* studio for musicals.

Jerry Mulligan (Gene Kelly) is an ex-GI and struggling artist in postwar Paris. His friend Adam Cook (Oscar Levant) is a piano player in a nearby cafe, a sarcastic and morose individual who offers nothing but discouragement to Jerry. However, another friend, Henri Baurel (Georges Guetary), a successful revue singer, is more encouraging. Henri informs his pal that he's going to marry a wonderful girl, an 18-year-old dancer whom he rescued from the Nazis during the war. Jerry, meanwhile, is discovered by Milo Roberts (Nina Foch), a wealthy patroness who purchases his paintings and encourages her friends to do the same. Innocently enjoying his newfound success, Jerry visits a nightclub and meets Lise (newcomer Leslie Caron, discovered by Kelly in the Ballets des Champs Elysees), falling for her immediately. She fends off his advances but laters agrees to a date, then informs him that she's engaged to Henri. Though they are in love, Jerry and Lise do the noble thing and decide not to meet again.

The plot was showing signs of age far earlier than 1951, but everything else about AN AMERICAN IN PARIS more than compensates: the songs are all Gershwin Brothers standards; Kelly's choreography is breathtaking; the original screenplay by playwright Alan Jay Lerner is alternately witty and touching; and Minnelli's direction feels buoyantly assured. The 17-minute Dufy-inspired ballet (art directors Cedric Gibbons and Preston Ames, along with costume designer Irene Sharaff, also contributed brilliantly to this sequence) is the showstopper here but an underrated standout is "I'll Build a Stairway to Paradise," performed with marvelous elan by Guetary. Although the setting is Paris, very little of the film was actually shot on location; the spectacular scenes were mostly sets built on the lot. AN AMERICAN IN PARIS received a total of seven Academy Awards, plus a special Oscar to Kelly.

AMERICAN MADNESS

1932 75m bw Drama ★★★
Columbia (U.S.)

Walter Huston *(Dickson)*, Pat O'Brien *(Matt)*, Kay Johnson *(Mrs. Dickson)*, Constance Cummings *(Helen)*, Gavin Gordon *(Cluett)*, Robert Ellis *(Dude Finlay)*, Jeanne Sorel *(Cluett's Secretary)*, Walter Walker *(Schultz)*, Berton Churchill *(O'Brien)*, Arthur Hoyt *(Ives)*

d, Frank Capra; w, Robert Riskin; ph, Joseph Walker; ed, Maurice Wright

Rare Capra work, and one of the few films to properly utilize the genius of the astonishing Walter Huston. Central theme of stressed-out bank president Huston as idealistic individual against the cruelty of the faceless crowd, struck a blow against Hooverism and for FDR's New Deal.

Like the single-set interiors of GRAND HOTEL, Capra filmed AMERICAN MADNESS totally within an enormous bank set, all the action taking place inside board rooms and vaults and behind tellers' cages, moving his camera with fluid truck and dolly shots, boom shots, and quick cuts that keep up the already established frenetic pace. To further create this sense of urgency, Capra cut out all dissolves (a device used to indicate the passing of time). He overlapped speeches and then had his actors hurry through their actions and dialogue.

AMERICAN MADNESS captured authentically the hysteria of the Great Depression; nor does the gratuitous romantic subplot mar its otherwise noble intentions.

AMERICAN PIE *DVD*

1999 100m c Comedy ★★★½
Zide-Perry Films/Zide Entertainment/
Universal Pictures (U.S.) R

Jason Biggs *(Jim)*, Mena Suvari *(Heather)*, Shannon Elizabeth *(Nadia)*, Alyson Hannigan *(Michelle)*, Chris Klein *(Oz)*, Tara Reid *(Vicky)*, Eugene Levy *(Jim's Dad)*, Eddie Kaye Thomas *(Finch)*, Natasha Lyonne *(Jessica)*, Thomas Ian Nicholas *(Kevin)*

p, Chris Weitz, Warren Zide, Craig Perry, Chris Moore; d, Paul Weitz; w, Adam Herz; ph, Richard Crudo; ed, Priscilla Nedd-Friendly; m, David Lawrence; prod d, Paul Peters; art d, Paul Peters; fx, Ron Trost; cos, Leesa Evans

If John Hughes had directed PORKY'S, the result would be something like this alternately sweet and raucous comedy about four graduating high school seniors determined not to enter college as virgins.

Kevin (Thomas Ian Nicholas) is the only one of his friends who's gotten as far as finding a steady girlfriend, Vicky (Tara Reid), and it's he who proposes a pact: lose it by prom night or forever hang your head in shame. Computer savvy Jim (Jason Biggs) has a hopeless crush on a leggy foreign exchange student, while his clueless, concerned dad (Eugene Levy) is eager to dispense fatherly advice about porno magazines, self-abuse, and why sexual congress with baked goods is a losing proposition. Lacrosse jock Oz (Chris Klein) joins the school chorus in hopes of scoring with some desperate goodie-goodie girl like Heather (Mena Suvari), only to find that he likes singing and likes Heather even

more. And budding sophisticate Finch (Eddie Kaye Thomas) winds up singing the praises of older women. In between, there are the requisite toilet jokes, locker room talk about body parts, high school humiliations, and bodily fluids in places they don't belong.

Is it stupid? Yeah. Is it often pretty funny? Well, yeah. The young cast members are generally engaging, and Klein is a standout among the leads. In supporting roles, Natasha Lyonne shines as a no-nonsense classmate, and Alyson Hannigan, essentially reprising her role as bookworm Willow from TV's "Buffy the Vampire Slayer," delivers what may be the movie's most unexpected line.

AMERICAN PSYCHO *DVD*

2000 101m c Thriller ★★★
Edward R. Pressman/Lions Gate/Muse/Single R
Cell/Quadra/Warner Bros. (U.S./Canada)

Christian Bale *(Patrick Bateman)*, Willem Dafoe *(Donald Kimball)*, Jared Leto *(Paul Allen)*, Josh Lucas *(Craig McDermott)*, Samantha Mathis *(Courtney Rawlinson)*, Matt Ross *(Luis Carruthers)*, Reese Witherspoon *(Evelyn Williams)*, Chloe Sevigny *(Jean)*, Cara Seymour *(Christie)*, Justin Theroux *(Timothy Bryce)*

p, Edward R. Pressman, Chris Hanley, Christian Halsey Solomon; d, Mary Harron; w, Mary Harron, Roberta Hanley, Guinevere Turner (based on the novel by Bret Easton Ellis); ph, Andrzej Sekula; ed, Andrew Marcus; m, John Cale; prod d, Gideon Ponte; art d, Andrew Stearn; fx, Michael Kavanagh; cos, Isis Mussenden

Director Mary Harron takes Bret Easton Ellis's notorious 1991 novel about empty sex and violent death among New York City's yuppie scum for what the book's apologists always claimed it was: a blood-soaked satire skewering the image-obsessed '80s, a morally bankrupt decade epitomized by corporate cannibalism, rampant cruelty, and greed. It's not a great film, but considering the source, this is as good as it was ever going to get.

Patrick Bateman (Christian Bale) is just one of many immaculately tailored and completely interchangeable vice presidents at a typical Wall Street firm, but he's the only one likely to quip "I'm in murders and executions" rather than "mergers and acquisitions" and mean it. At the end of a long day that starts with a rigorous beauty regimen involving pricey products pour l'homme, and a few hours at the office trying to get dinner reservations at the city's trendiest restaurants, Bateman makes time for the occasional brutal murder: one of the city's homeless, perhaps, or a young lady friend. Or maybe even an envied fellow VP.

Taking their cue from the outrage that greeted Ellis's novel, Harron and co-writers Guinevere Turner and Roberta Hanley cagily cover themselves on the misogyny and excessive violence fronts; the film's women are the only characters granted a modicum of humanity, and nearly all the notoriously gory set pieces have been cut or occur offscreen. Bale, pumped to underwear-model perfection, is a truly terrifying spectacle of artificiality, and Gideon Ponte's production design is perfect to the last gleaming detail. And if the film feels empty, Harron's covered herself there as well: gleaming details and emptiness is what it's all about.

AMERICAN SPLENDOR *DVD*

2003 101m c Biography/Drama ★★★½
HBO Films/Good Machine (U.S.) R

Paul Giamatti *(Harvey Pekar)*, Hope Davis *(Joyce Brabner)*, Judah Friedlander *(Toby Radloff)*, James Urbaniak *(Robert Crumb)*, Earl Billings *(Mr. Boats)*, Madylin Sweeten *(Danielle)*, Harvey Pekar *(Real Harvey)*, Joyce Brabner *(Real Joyce)*, Toby Radloff *(Real Toby)*, Danielle Batone *(Real Danielle)* p, Ted Hope; d, Robert Pulcini, Shari Springer Berman; w, Robert Pulcini, Shari Springer Berman (based on the comic book series *American Splendor* and Harvey Pekar and *Our Cancer Year* by Harvey Pekar and Joyce Brabner); ph, Terry Stacey; ed, Robert Pulcini; m, Mark Suozzo; prod d, Therese DePrez; fx, Twinkle; cos, Michael Wilkinson; anim, John Kuramoto, Gary Leib, Twinkle

---

AAN Best Adapted Screenplay: Robert Pulcini, Shari Springer Berman

---

Comic book stories aren't all superhero fantasies, and comic-book movies don't have to be special effects-heavy junk, as this bittersweet adaptation of Harvey Pekar's *American Splendor* proves. Pekar's autobiographical chronicle of day-to-day banality is a rich, if dingy, tapestry of ordinary life, which filmmakers Shari Springer Berman and Robert Pulcini bring to uniquely eccentric life.

Their stroke of genius was to allow real life, cartoon images, and straightforward realistic filmmaking to bleed together from scene to scene and shot to shot. The real Pekar comments on the film's multiple "Pekars"—not just actor Paul Giamatti's version, but also the disparate images created by various *American Splendor* illustrators —while the movie's Pekar shuffles dyspeptically through a world that regularly dissolves into artist's renderings of itself. It's a risky strategy that pays off brilliantly. Pekar's peculiar path to cult celebrity begins in his native Cleveland in the 1970s. He's suffocating in a dead-end job filing medical records at a local hospital, and his voice has constricted into a strangled squeak he's sure presages throat cancer. Pekar channels his frustrated creative energies into collecting old jazz 78s, which leads him to friendship with soon-to-be underground comic-book legend Robert Crumb (James Urbaniak). Crumb inspires Pekar to turn his bitterly articulated rants about mundane experiences into stories, and with Crumb's support, Pekar's slices of workaday life are transformed into *American Splendor*. The books confer cult immortality on the writer and his friends, including fan Joyce Brabner (Hope Davis), who becomes Pekar's wife and his lifeline when he really does get cancer.

From Pekar's brief and unlikely success on "The David Letterman Show" to the semblance of nuclear family happiness he eventually achieves, his story is, ultimately, truly splendid in its union of the singular and the prosaic.

AMERICAN WEREWOLF IN LONDON, AN   *DVD*

1981 97m c   Comedy/Science Fiction/Horror ★★★
Universal   (U.S.)   R

David Naughton *(David Kessler)*, Jenny Agutter *(Alex Price)*, Griffin Dunne *(Jack Goodman)*, John Woodvine *(Dr. Hirsch)*, Brian Glover *(Chess Player)*, David Schofield *(Dart Player)*, Lila Kaye *(Barmaid)*, Paul Kember *(Sgt. McManus)*, Don McKillop *(Inspector Villiers)*, Frank Oz *(Mr. Collins)*

p, George Folsey Jr.; d, John Landis; w, John Landis; ph, Robert Paynter (Technicolor); ed, Malcolm Campbell; m, Elmer Bernstein; art d, Leslie Dilley; fx, Rick Baker; cos, Deborah Nadoolman

---

AA Best Makeup: Rick Baker

A trendsetter in terms of special makeup effects, John Landis's film is an entertaining but uneven mix of horror and humor.

While hiking though the English moors, American college student David Kessler (David Naughton) and his friend Jack (Griffin Dunne) happen across an isolated pub. The inhabitants' eccentric behavior unnerves them, and they depart into the night. Soon, they are attacked by a wolflike beast that kills Jack and wounds David before being killed by the pub's patrons. Recovering in a London hospital, David is befriended by an attractive nurse named Alex (Jenny Agutter)—and visited by the undead Jack. He tells David that, having been

bitten by a werewolf, he is fated to become one himself at the next full moon. David ignores the warning, and when he leaves the hospital, he begins an affair with Alex. The night of the full moon arrives, and David becomes a monstrous wolf that savages several Londoners. He wakes up naked in a zoo with no memory of what happened, but undead Jack appears to him, along with the specters of his recent victims, to impel him to kill himself and end the curse.

AN AMERICAN WEREWOLF IN LONDON was a longtime pet project of Landis's; he was finally able to realize it following the box-office success of NATIONAL LAMPOON'S ANIMAL HOUSE (1978) and THE BLUES BROTHERS (1980). The writer-director goes for broke with both the horror and comedy content, and combines them best in the first 20 minutes, making viewers shiver and giggle with anticipation before shocking them out of their seats with the first werewolf attack. As the film goes on, though, Landis's hand becomes unsteady. Unlike THE HOWLING, 1981's earlier werewolf film, LONDON doesn't blend the chills and laughs so much as vacillate between them, so that the jokiness of the comic scenes comes to undercut the gruesome horror sequences and vice versa. And nowhere does the direction seem more uncertain than in the famed transformation scene. While Rick Baker's special effects work is remarkable (and won the first competitive Oscar for makeup), Landis seems content to simply showcase it, shooting it in close-ups and bright lighting without any attempt to build any emotion into the sequence.

Nevertheless, AMERICAN WEREWOLF IN LONDON undeniably delivers a good share of scares and dark laughs. And for all its lack of discipline, it's a model of directorial clarity when compared with Landis's subsequent work, which inexorably descended into indulgence and foolishness. A box-office success in 1981, the film built an enduring popularity that led to a sequel, AN AMERICAN WEREWOLF IN PARIS, 16 years later.

AMISTAD   *DVD*

1997 152m c   Historical/Drama   ★★★
HBO Pictures/DreamWorks Pictures   (U.S.)   R

Morgan Freeman *(Theodore Joadson)*, Nigel Hawthorne *(Martin Van Buren)*, Anthony Hopkins *(John Quincy Adams)*, Djimon Hounsou *("Cinque"—Sengbe)*, Matthew McConaughey *(Roger Baldwin)*, David Paymer *(U.S. Secretary of State Forsyth)*, Pete Postlethwaite *(Holabird)*, Stellan Skarsgard *(Lewis Tappan)*, Razaaq Adoti *(Yamba)*, Abu Bakaar Fofanah *(Fala)*

p, Steven Spielberg, Debbie Allen, Colin Wilson; d, Steven Spielberg; w, David Franzoni, Steve Zaillian; ph, Janusz Kaminski; ed, Michael Kahn; m, John Williams; prod d, Rick Carter; art d, Chris Burian-Mohr, Jim Teegarden, Tony Fanning; fx, Tom Ryba, Scott Farrar, Denise Eleanor Ream, Industrial Light & Magic; cos, Ruth E. Carter

---

AAN Best Supporting Actor: Anthony Hopkins; *AAN Best Cinematography:* Janusz Kaminski; *AAN Best Original Dramatic Score:* John Williams; *AAN Best Costume Design:* Ruth E. Carter

---

AMISTAD recounts the virtually forgotten, but historically significant, story of a slave ship uprising that led to a group of Africans battling through the U.S. court system to regain their freedom. While Steven Spielberg fails to deliver the SCHINDLER'S LIST (1993) of American slavery, this is a good film worthy of respect.

1839. In the hold of the Spanish slave ship *Amistad*, Cinque (Djimon Hounsou) breaks his chains, frees the 52 other prisoners, and then leads them in revolt against their captors. Two spared slave-traders promise to navigate the ship back to Africa, but surreptitiously steer north. Six weeks later, the tattered *Amistad* lands at New York's Long

Island, and the Africans are imprisoned again. Their case becomes a *cause celebre* for abolitionists, and runs risk of becoming a flash point in the developing conflict between North and South.

A strident affirmation of slavery's utter immorality would be a reassuringly cathartic experience, but AMISTAD aims for the head more than the heart. Spielberg's genius for using images to manipulate an audience's emotions is relatively subdued in this film, much of which is surprisingly clinical. Spielberg explicates the mind-set of a freedom-loving society that accepted "the peculiar institution" (how one person could look at another and not see a person, but an object), and how the *Amistad* incident contributed to changing that mind-set, leading to civil war only 20 years later. Ironically, the task of voicing the highest ideals of the United States is awarded to Brit Hopkins. In a masterful performance, Hopkins closes AMISTAD with a stirring oration affirming the absolute right of any man, of any color, to take up arms against his oppressors, and by so doing, make himself free.

AMITYVILLE HORROR, THE

1979 126m c Horror ★½
INT/American International Pictures (U.S.) R

James Brolin *(George Lutz)*, Margot Kidder *(Kathleen Lutz)*, Rod Steiger *(Fr. Delaney)*, Don Stroud *(Fr. Bolen)*, Natasha Ryan *(Amy)*, K.C. Martel *(Greg)*, Meeno Peluce *(Matt)*, Michael Sacks *(Jeff)*, Helen Shaver *(Carolyn)*, Val Avery *(Sgt. Gionfriddo)*

p, Ronald Saland, Elliot Geisinger; d, Stuart Rosenberg; w, Sandor Stern (based on the book by Jay Anson); ph, Fred Koenekamp; ed, Robert Brown; m, Lalo Schifrin; art d, Kim Swados; fx, Dell Rheaume

AAN Best Original Score: Lalo Schifrin

Based on Jay Anson's slimy best-seller, THE AMITYVILLE HORROR reaped a fortune for its studio, American International, just before it went out of business. The film chronicles the trials and tribulations of the hapless Lutz family (headed by Brolin and Kidder) as they discover that the new house they've purchased for a steal in Amityville, NY, is plagued by evil demons that manifest themselves in a variety of disgusting ways (flies, black gook, Rod Steiger overacting as a priest). Schifrin's score received an Oscar nomination. A TV prequel and three dreadful sequels (one in 3-D) followed.

AMORES PERROS DVD

2000 153m c Drama ★★★
Altavista Films/Zeta Films (Mexico) R

Emilio Echevarria *(El Chivo, "The Goat")*, Gael Garcia Bernal *(Octavio)*, Goya Toledo *(Valeria)*, Alvaro Guerrero *(Daniel)*, Vanessa Bauche *(Susana)*, Jorge Salinas *(Luis)*, Marco Perez *(Ramiro)*, Rodrigo Murray *(Gustavo)*, Humberto Busto *(Jorge)*, Gerardo Campbell *(Mauricio)*

p, Alejandro Gonzalez Inarritu; d, Alejandro Gonzalez Inarritu; w, Guillermo Arriaga; ph, Rodrigo Prieto; ed, Alejandro Gonzalez Inarritu, Luis Carballar, Fernando Perez Unda; m, Gustavo Santaolalla; prod d, Brigitte Broch; art d, Melo Hinojosa; fx, Alejandro Vazquez; cos, Gabriela Diaque

With a complex, three-part story structure that recalls the interwoven plots of PULP FICTION, Mexican director Alejandro Gonzalez Inarritu's thrilling, if brutal, debut chronicles the travails of three strangers whose lives are forever changed by a devastating car crash.

The film opens with a breathlessly edited car chase through the crowded streets of Mexico City. The driver making his getaway is Octavio (Gael Garcia Bernal), a good-natured young man who is desperately in love with Susana

(Vanessa Bauche), the wife of his abusive brother, Ramiro (Marco Perez). Hoping to raise enough money to run away with Susana, Ocatavio entered Ramiro's dog, Cofi, into the barbaric arena of dog fighting, but is now running for his own life. Valeria (Goya Toledo), meanwhile, is a successful fashion model whose career is cut short when Octavio crashes into her car. Confined to a wheelchair and cared for by her married lover (Alvaro Guerrero), Valeria begins to unravel; a further turn of the screw comes when her little dog disappears under the floorboards of her apartment. A witness to the car accident turns out to be a man known only as El Chivo (Emilio Echevarria)—"The Goat"—an assassin who lives like a beggar with his pack of stray dogs. El Chivo rescues the wounded Cofi from the backseat of Octavio's car and nurses him back to health, an act of kindness he'll soon regret.

Shot on grainy film stock under harsh light, the film has all the visual appeal of a bruise. But while the tripartite structure is cleverly constructed, the film delivers a series of painful rabbit punches instead of the TKO the filmmaker's evident talent promises. "Amores perros" translates roughly as "love's a bitch," which is as good a title as any for this unremittingly bleak film.

ANALYZE THAT DVD

2002 95m c Comedy ★
Baltimore Spring Creek Pictures/Face/Tribeca R
Productions/Village Roadshow/NPV Entertainment
(U.S./Australia)

Robert De Niro *(Paul Vitti)*, Billy Crystal *(Ben Sobel)*, Lisa Kudrow *(Laura Sobel)*, Joe Viterelli *(Jelly)*, Cathy Moriarty-Gentile *(Patty LoPresti)*, John Finn *(Richard Chapin)*, Kyle Sabihy *(Michael Sobel)*, Callie Thorne *(Agent Cerrone)*, Anthony LaPaglia *("Nick Caesar"—uncredited)*, Vincent Pastore *("Little Caesar" Mobster—uncredited)*

p, Jane Rosenthal, Paula Weinstein; d, Harold Ramis; w, Harold Ramis, Peter Steinfeld, Peter Tolan (based on characters created by Kenneth Lonergan and Peter Tolan); ph, Ellen Kuras; ed, Andrew Mondshein; m, David Holmes; prod d, Wynn Thomas; art d, Adam Matthew Scher; fx, Steve Kirshoff, Randall Balsmeyer; cos, Aude Bronson-Howard

ANALZYE THIS was an amusing comedy with a certain sitcom appeal; ANALZYE THAT is a dull retread that should sleep with the fishes.

Imprisoned Mafia capo Paul Vitti (Robert De Niro) has become the target of assassination attempts and is angling for an early release by feigning mental illness. The FBI calls in Vitti's psychiatrist, Ben Sobel (Billy Crystal), to assess the don's sanity, and Sobel agrees to take Vitti into his home for a month so that Vitti can get cleaned up and employed before his parole hearing. Through improbable leaps of logic, things get progressively more disjointed and more difficult to swallow, as if the filmmakers couldn't decide if this should be an odd-couple comedy, a fish-out-of-water story (Vitti unconvincingly works a series of odd jobs, including a stint as car salesman), a caper (there's a lazily plotted heist), or a satire (Anthony LaPaglia, Vincent Pastore, and others appear in a *Sopranos*-like series called "Little Caesar").

Throughout this *miseria*, De Niro does manage to make his character scary and authoritative. Cathy Moriarty-Gentile, in a neat reunion with her RAGING BULL costar, does a nice job playing a rival mob boss, and Lisa Kudrow, who was sadly wasted in ANALYZE THIS as Sobel's fiancée, is given a little more to do here as his wife. But otherwise, the movie is bewildering and bland. Reg Rogers, who plays "Little Caesar" creator Raoul Berman, delivers his lines like a stoned Pee-wee Herman, and the scene in which Sobel mutters and drools in a restaurant is just disturbing for anyone who has admired Crystal's past work.

ANALYZE THIS
DVD
1999 106m c   Comedy
★★★
Village Roadshow Pictures/NPV Entertainment/
R
Face Productions/Tribeca Productions/Baltimore/
Spring Creek Pictures   (U.S.)

Robert De Niro *(Paul Vitti)*, Billy Crystal *(Ben Sobol)*, Lisa Kudrow *(Laura MacNamara)*, Kyle Sahiby *(Michael Sobol)*, Joseph Viterelli *(Jelly)*, Chazz Palminteri *(Sindone)*, Bill Macy *(Ben's Father)*, Molly Shannon *(Patient)*, Leo Rossi *(Carlo Mangano)*, Jimmie Ray Weeks *(FBI Agent)*

p, Paula Weinstein, Jane Rosenthal; d, Harold Ramis; w, Peter Tolan, Harold Ramis, Kenneth Lonergan; ph, Stuart Dryburgh; ed, Christopher Tellefsen; m, Howard Shore; prod d, Wynn P. Thomas; art d, Jeff Sage; cos, Aude Bronson-Howard

THE FRESHMAN meets early Woody Allen in this canny send-up of both gangsters and therapy in the movies. As Paul Vitti, head of a powerful mob family, Robert De Niro capitalizes on years of playing mob heavies to hugely entertaining effect.

Vitti narrowly escapes a rubout only to find himself tormented by debilitating anxiety attacks. Neurotic therapist Ben Sobol (Billy Crystal)—who has an uneasy relationship with his famous father (Bill Macy), a media-hungry psychiatrist—prefers ordinary patients but finds he has little choice when he rear-ends Vitti's bodyguard, Jelly (Joseph Viterelli). Jelly recruits the only head doctor he's ever met to treat his agitated boss, who needs to learn to keep his cool in time for an upcoming summit of mafioso dons, which will include Vitti's murderous rival, Sindone (Chazz Palminteri).

Granted, the plot's progression isn't terrifically imaginative: after each mini-crisis, Vitti kidnaps Ben and forces him to "analyze" his problems. Nor is the movie's depiction of psychoanalysis very complex. But the screenwriters get to poke fun at some familiar conventions of therapy, including the inattentive, apparently indifferent therapists and their self-absorbed, oblivious patients. Crystal gets his chance to shine when Sobol tries to pass him off as Vitti's new *consigliere* at the Mafia summit. Though De Niro's recent ubiquity has somewhat dulled the thrill of his presence, he seems here to be having fun on screen for the first time in years, and it's infectious.

ANASTASIA
DVD
1956 105m c   Drama
★★★★
Fox   (U.S.)

Ingrid Bergman *(Anastasia)*, Yul Brynner *(Bounine)*, Helen Hayes *(Empress)*, Akim Tamiroff *(Chernov)*, Martita Hunt *(Baroness von Livenbaum)*, Felix Aylmer *(Russian Chamberlain)*, Sacha Pitoeff *(Petrovin)*, Ivan Desny *(Prince Paul)*, Natalie Schafer *(Lissenskaia)*, Gregoire Gromoff *(Stepan)*

p, Buddy Adler; d, Anatole Litvak; w, Arthur Laurents (based on Guy Bolton's adaptation of Marcelle Maurette's play); ph, Jack Hildyard (CinemaScope, DeLuxeColor); ed, Bert Bates; m, Alfred Newman; art d, Andre Andrejew, Bill Andrews; cos, Rene Hubert

AA Best Actress: Ingrid Bergman; *AAN Best Score (Drama or Comedy):* Alfred Newman

The peak of Ingrid bergman's triumphant career. Cheap impostor or grand duchess of Russia and daughter of the last czar? There was no doubt in the mind of any viewer after watching Bergman's sublime performance that Anastasia was the lost and unhappy Romanoff princess. This was Bergman's comeback to American screens after the Rosellini scandal and she played her part with such intense feeling that it won over audiences worldwide and earned her an Academy Award. Climax is Bergman's confrontation with Empress Hayes, the latter's best screen work. The Laurents screenplay is faithful to the Marcelle Maurette play. A grand entry in Hollywood history.

ANASTASIA
DVD
1997 92m c   Children's/Animated/Musical
★★½
Fox Family Films/Don Bluth/Gary Goldman
(U.S.)
G

VOICES OF: Meg Ryan *(Anya/Anastasia)*, John Cusack *(Dimitri)*, Angela Lansbury *(Grand Duchess Marie)*, Christopher Lloyd *(Rasputin)*, Hank Azaria *(Bartok—the Bat)*, Kelsey Grammer *(Vladimir)*, Bernadette Peters *(Sophie)*, Kirsten Dunst *(Young Anastasia)*, Liz Callaway *(Singing Voice of Anastasia)*, Lacey Chabert *(Singing Voice of Young Anastasia)*

p, Don Bluth, Gary Goldman; d, Don Bluth, Gary Goldman; w, Eric Tuchman (animation adaptation), Susan Gauthier, Bruce Graham, Bob Tzudiker, Noni White, Carrie Fisher; ed, Fiona Trayler; m, David Newman; fx, Peter Matheson (special effects animation supervisor); anim, Fernando Moro, Sandro Clevzo, Paul Newberry, Troy Saliba, Len Simon, John Hill

AAN Best Original Musical or Comedy Score: Stephen Flaherty, Lynn Ahrens, David Newman; *AAN Best Original Song:* "Journey To the Past"; Stephen Flaherty, Lynn Ahrens

That Anastasia Romanov, the six-year-old Russian grand duchess, survived the bloody 1918 massacre of her father, Tsar Nicholas, and the rest of the Romanov family at the hands of Bolshevik revolutionaries has been one of this century's more enduring rumors. All things considered, it's probably for the best that veteran animators Don Bluth and Gary Goldman have little use for history.

It seems it wasn't any silly revolution that took down Tsarist Russia, but an evil curse cast by the vengeful Rasputin (voiced by Christopher Lloyd). According to the film, "Anya" (Meg Ryan) escaped the ensuing carnage and grew up an amnesiac in a wretched Soviet orphanage. When she leaves as a teenager, Anya feels strangely compelled to visit Paris—now the home of her grandmother, the Dowager Empress (Angela Lansbury)—but must first obtain a bogus exit visa from con men Dmitri (John Cusack) and Vladimir (Kelsey Grammer), who just happen to be conspiring to present a false Anastasia to the rich and, they hope, deeply grateful empress. They talk Anya into playing the part—after all, she *could* be the young duchess. But when Rasputin, who has been literally rotting in limbo, hears of her existence, he vows to wipe the last living Romanov from the face of the Earth....

Sound confusing? Well, it is, and the fact that much of the story is set up in the song lyrics will only send the plot even further over the little ones' heads. But despite the creepy sight of the decaying Rasputin and the film's even creepier historical revisionism, there is much for tots to enjoy: decent songs, an amusing script, and some surprisingly imaginative animation. And when was the last time anyone shouted "Long live the Romanovs!" and the audience actually cheered?

ANATOMY OF A MURDER
DVD
1959 160m bw Drama
★★★★½
Columbia   (U.S.)

James Stewart *(Paul Biegler)*, Lee Remick *(Laura Manion)*, Ben Gazzara *(Lt. Frederick Manion)*, Arthur O'Connell *(Parnell McCarthy)*, Eve Arden *(Maida)*, Kathryn Grant *(Mary Pilant)*, Joseph N. Welch *(Judge Weaver)*, Brooks West *(Mitch*

Lodwick), George C. Scott *(Claude Dancer)*, Murray Hamilton *(Alphonse Paquette)*

p, Otto Preminger; d, Otto Preminger; w, Wendell Mayes; ph, Sam Leavitt; ed, Louis Loeffler; m, Duke Ellington

---

AAN Best Picture; AAN Best Actor: James Stewart; *AAN Best Supporting Actor:* Arthur O'Connell; *AAN Best Supporting Actor:* George C Scott; *AAN Best Adapted Screenplay:* Wendell Mayes; *AAN Best B/W Cinematography:* Sam Leavitt; *AAN Best Film Editing:* Louis R Loeffler

---

Courtroom histrionics given sizzle and sex by Otto Preminger and Duke Ellington's jazz. Stewart shocked 1950s audiences with his gritty, quirky performance as a confirmed bachelor defense attorney speaking directly about contraceptives, pink panties and rape. Old pros Arden and O'Connell flawlessly support the star performance in a talky tennis game. Gazzarra as a brutal army stud and Remick as his duplicitous, sluttish wife received well-deserved career boosts for their efforts.

The casting of Remick was Preminger's major concern after Lana Turner left the project (actress reportedly slapped director who slapped her back) and Jayne Mansfield backed off from the script. Joseph Welch, who plays the judge, was the famed Army-McCarthy hearings lawyer who would go on to become a real life judge. Even today, when these issues seem tame, the long drama crackles along. The film was nominated for Best Picture and Best Actor (the year BEN-HUR swept the competition) as well as Best Supporting Actor (both O'Connell and George C. Scott), Best Screenplay, Best Cinematography, and Best Film Editing.

ANCHORMAN: THE LEGEND OF RON BURGUNDY 📀
2004 91m c Comedy ★★★
Apatow Productions/DreamWorks (U.S.) PG-13

Will Ferrell *(Ron Burgundy)*, Christina Applegate *(Veronica Corningstone)*, Paul Rudd *(Brian Fantana)*, Steve Carell *(Brick Tamland)*, David Koechner *(Champ Kind)*, Fred Willard *(Ed Harken)*, Chris Parnell *(Garth Holliday)*, Kathryn Hahn *(Helen)*, Fred Armisen *(Tino)*, Vince Vaughn *(Wes Mantooth—uncredited)*

p, Judd Apatow; d, Adam McKay; w, Will Ferrell, Adam McKay; ph, Thomas Ackerman; ed, Brent White; m, Alex Wurman; prod d, Clayton R. Hartley; art d, Virginia Randolph-Weaver; fx, Richard R. Hoover, Raymond McIntyre Jr., Reid Paul; cos, Debra McGuire

---

This just in: Will Ferrell and director Adam McKay's clever send-up of chauvinistic attitudes in the dark days before sexual-harassment lawsuits is wickedly funny and a first-rate showcase for Ferrell. Stay tuned for further details.

San Diego's own Ron Burgundy (Ferrell) heads up Channel 4's top-rated news team, which includes sportscaster Champ Kind (David Koechner), weatherman Brick Tamland (Steve Carell), and man-on-the-street Brian Fantana (Paul Rudd). Burgundy's team reports hard and parties even harder, boozing and objectifying every woman who crosses their path, none of which stops viewers from tuning in to Ron's broadcasts. The only person who doesn't like Ron is Wes Mantooth (Vince Vaughn), head anchor at the city's second-ranked station. Ron's happy work environment is disrupted when station boss Ed Harken (Fred Willard) announces that beautiful, ambitious reporter Veronica Corningstone (Christina Applegate) will be joining the boys' club. Ron and his fellow misogynists are appalled, and rather than welcome her they make comments about her "assets" and call her crude names when she rebuffs their caveman advances. When she finally agrees to a date with Ron, she's surprised to find herself falling for him,

but their vicious newsroom competition threatens their budding relationship.

This relaxed comedy's numerous cameos are unusually well-timed, and some of its funniest moments come courtesy of "Daily Show" alumnus Carell's dope of a weatherman, who actually looks up to the boorish Brian and Ron with truly dimwitted devotion. It also offers a riotous gang war, an adorable kitty-cat costume show (one of many humiliating assignments handed to Veronica), a barrage of '70s fashion and hair disasters, and plenty of unexpected and off-the-cuff witticisms. And that's the news for now.

ANCHORS AWEIGH 📀
1945 143m c Musical ★★½
MGM (U.S.)

Frank Sinatra *(Clarence Doolittle)*, Gene Kelly *(Joseph Brady)*, Kathryn Grayson *(Susan Abbott)*, Jose Iturbi *(Himself)*, Dean Stockwell *(Donald Martin)*, Carlos Ramirez *(Carlos)*, Henry O'Neill *(Adm. Hammond)*, Leon Ames *(Commander)*, Rags Ragland *(Police Sergeant)*, Edgar Kennedy *(Police Captain)*

p, Joe Pasternak; d, George Sidney; w, Isobel Lennart (based on a story by Natalie Marcin); ph, Robert Planck, Charles P. Boyle (Technicolor); ed, Adrienne Fazan; m, George Stoll; art d, Cedric Gibbons, Randall Duell; chor, Gene Kelly; cos, Irene, Kay Dean

---

AAN Best Picture; AAN Best Actor: Gene Kelly; *AAN Best Color Cinematography:* Robert Planck, Charles Boyle; *AA Best Score (Musical):* Georgie Stoll; *AAN Best Song:* "I Fall in Love Too Easily"; Jule Styne (Music), Sammy Cahn (Lyrics)

This amiable musical of gobs on shore leave in Hollywood lacks the snap of ON THE TOWN but holds up when young Sinatra croons "I Fall in Love Too Easily" and when Kelly gets the chance to dance with animated mouse Jerry of "Tom & Jerry" fame. The technique of live action mixed with cartoons has been done often since then, most notably in 1988's WHO FRAMED ROGER RABBIT, but it has never been done to better advantage than in this film. Pamela Britton's comic relief Brooklyn girl feels more authentic than the sticky sentiments of Pekinese Grayson. A pleasant, mindless diversion.

AND GOD CREATED WOMAN 📀
(ET DIEU CREA LA FEMME)
1956 92m c Drama/Erotic ★★
Iena/UCIL/Cocinor (France)

Brigitte Bardot *(Juliette)*, Curt Jurgens *(Eric)*, Jean-Louis Trintignant *(Michel)*, Christian Marquand *(Antoine)*, Georges Poujouly *(Christian)*, Jean Tissier *(M. Vigier-Lefranc)*, Jeanne Marken *(Mme. Morin)*, Marie Glory *(Mme. Tardieu)*, Isabelle Corey *(Lucienne)*, Jean Lefebvre *(Rene)*

p, Raoul J. Levy; d, Roger Vadim; w, Roger Vadim, Raoul Levy; ph, Armand Thirard (CinemaScope, Eastmancolor); ed, Victoria Mercanton; m, Paul Misraki; art d, Jean Andre

---

… but Roger Vadim created Brigitte Bardot. This is the film that made Bardot a household name and liberated French cinema by putting it in the hands of the young and the beautiful. And it managed to do all these things without being very good. The story is a simple one: sexy orphan Juliette (Bardot) marries Michel (Jean-Louis Trintignant), is pursued by the wealthy Eric (Curt Jurgens), and sleeps with Antoine (Christian Marquand), Michel's brother. Nonetheless, Michel fights for Juliette and manages to lure her back. Slight on story, AND GOD CREATED WOMAN is strong on energy, all of it coming from Bardot's brilliant screen presence. Her pouty lips, accentuated breasts, skimpy clothing, and wildly erotic mambo routine late in the film helped whip audiences into a frenzy. They couldn't get enough of her in France, nor could they in America. While her effect on the American film scene was dubious (more and more soft-porn titillation was imported), her effect on the French film industry can be seen in the rise of the *Nouvelle Vague* directors, who were given greater opportunities in light of Vadim's commercial success. Vadim would continue along this same path with diminishing impact on the film world and then try to create "Woman" again in an unsuccessful 1988 remake (in title only) starring Rebecca DeMornay. Bardot went on to enjoy continued success without him, making one wonder if, perhaps, Bardot created Vadim.

AND NOW FOR SOMETHING COMPLETELY DIFFERENT
DVD

1971 88m c Comedy ★★★
Columbia (U.K.) PG

Graham Chapman, John Cleese, Eric Idle, Terry Jones, Michael Palin, Terry Gilliam, Carol Cleveland, Connie Booth

p, Patricia Casey; d, Ian MacNaughton; w, Graham Chapman, John Cleese, Terry Gilliam, Eric Idle, Terry Jones, Michael Palin; ph, David Muir; ed, Thom Noble; art d, Colin Grimes; anim, Terry Gilliam

Some of the best of the BBC TV's "Monty Python's Flying Circus" sketches reshot for feature film release. Although the cast is brilliant and the material generally funny, the film fails to take advantage of the big-screen format. The gang from Python did much better with the follow-up film, MONTY PYTHON AND THE HOLY GRAIL.

AND THE SHIP SAILS ON
DVD

(E LA NAVE VA)
1983 132m c Comedy ★★★
RAI-TV (Italy/France)

Freddie Jones *(Orlando)*, Barbara Jefford *(Ildebranda Cuffari)*, Victor Poletti *(Fuciletto)*, Peter Cellier *(Sir Reginald)*, Elisa Marinardi *(Teresa Valegnani)*, Norma West *(Sir Reginald's Wife)*, Paolo Paolini *(Orchestra Conductor)*, Sarah Jane Varley *(Dorothy)*, Fiorenzo Serra *(Grand Duke of Harzock)*, Pina Bausch *(Princess Lheremia)*

p, Franco Cristaldi; d, Federico Fellini; w, Federico Fellini, Tonino Guerra; ph, Giuseppe Rotunno; ed, Ruggero Mastroianni; m, Gianfranco Plenizio; art d, Dante Ferretti

A minor, eccentric offering from Fellini, involving an odd assortment of passengers who set sail in 1914 for the small island of Cleo. The purpose of their voyage ("the voyage of life?" one character queries) is to scatter the ashes of their friend, a famous opera diva. While the first-class cabins contain businessmen, opera colleagues, comedians, royalty, and various patrons of the arts, the steerage contains a slew of Serbo-Croatian freedom fighters on the run after assassinating Archduke Ferdinand—the catalysts of WWI. If that isn't enough variety, there is also a rhinoceros on board. Tensions rise when an Austro-Hungarian battleship arrives and demands that the revolutionaries be turned over to their custody.

With a line of logic that is as scattered as the diva's ashes, AND THE SHIP SAILS ON is a frustrating film which never quite comes together, and which has little basis in either psychological or physical reality (it was photographed entirely on Cinecitta sets, which Fellini shows us). The picture is worth watching, if only for the scenes with the rhino and the lengthy opening sequence, which begins as a scratchy, sepia-toned silent film that gradually but gloriously develops into a colorful sound picture.

AND THEN THERE WERE NONE
DVD

1945 97m bw Mystery ★★★★
Fox (U.S.)

Barry Fitzgerald *(Judge Quincannon)*, Walter Huston *(Dr. Armstrong)*, Louis Hayward *(Philip Lombard)*, Roland Young *(Blore)*, June Duprez *(Vera Claythorne)*, C. Aubrey Smith *(Gen. Mandrake)*, Judith Anderson *(Emily Brent)*, Mischa Auer *(Prince Starloff)*, Richard Haydn *(Rogers)*, Queenie Leonard *(Mrs. Rogers)*

p, Harry M. Popkin; d, Rene Clair; w, Dudley Nichols (based on the story "Ten Little Niggers" by Agatha Christie); ph, Lucien Andriot; ed, Harvey Manger; art d, Ernst Fegte

This classic Agatha Christie whodunit takes place on a desolate island off the English coast where ten strangers—all with criminal pasts—meet. All have been invited to spend an evening in a sprawling, eerie mansion as guests of maniacal Judge Quincannon (Fitzgerald). Among the colorful characters are the sinister Dr. Armstrong (Huston), the dictatorial General Mandrake (Smith), phony Prince Starloff (Auer), and lovers Philip (Hayward) and Vera (Duprez). It gradually dawns on the terrified guests that they have been marooned on the island for only one purpose—to be murdered one by one in retribution for their transgressions, as per the nursery rhyme "Ten Little Indians."

French director Clair took his time with this production, using his cameras to play cat-and-mouse with each victim and adopting the perfect pace for the story as originally conceived by Christie and tightly adapted by Nichols. The ending of this adaptation differs from Christie's original; the 1965 remake, TEN LITTLE INDIANS, restored the original finale, while the 1974 version, again titled TEN LITTLE INDIANS, used the Clair/Nichols ending.

ANDERSON TAPES, THE

1971 98m c Crime ★★★
Columbia (U.S.) GP

Sean Connery *(Anderson)*, Dyan Cannon *(Ingrid)*, Martin Balsam *(Haskins)*, Ralph Meeker *(Delaney)*, Alan King *(Angelo)*, Christopher Walken *(The Kid)*, Val Avery *(Parelli)*, Dick Williams *(Spencer)*, Garrett Morris *(Everson)*, Stan Gottlieb *(Pop)*

p, Robert M. Weitman; d, Sidney Lumet; w, Frank Pierson (based on the novel by Lawrence Sanders); ph, Arthur J. Ornitz (Technicolor); ed, Joanne Burke; m, Quincy Jones; art d, Philip Rosenberg

A solid, precise, well-made Lumet film, with tough ex-convict Connery, an habitual criminal, looking for a big score immediately upon leaving prison. He goes to the syndicate to seek funds to back a massive robbery, intending to ransack a posh East Side New York apartment building. Rounding up a gang of top-flight thieves, Connery proceeds to plan and carry out his caper, unaware that he is being taped at every turn by various government agencies to discover his links with organized crime. He and his men break into each apartment that is unoccupied—he has determined in advance what tenants are present—and carries out the systematic looting of each place. There are so many lawmen listening in that it seems the whole world is bugged. A good example of the now-neglected caper genre.

ANDREW LLOYD WEBBER'S THE PHANTOM OF THE OPERA
DVD

2004 141m c Musical/Horror/Romance ★★½
Really Useful Films/Scion Films production/ PG-13
Odyssey Entertainment/Warner Bros. (U.S./U.K.)

Gerard Butler *(The Phantom)*, Emmy Rossum *(Christine)*, Patrick Wilson *(Vicomte Raoul de Chagny)*, Miranda Richardson *(Madame Giry)*, Simon Callow *(Gilles Andre)*, Ciaran Hinds

(Richard Firmin), Kevin McNally *(Buquet),* Minnie Driver *(Carlotta),* Maragaret Preece *(Singing Voice of Carlotta),* Victor McGuire *(Piangi)*

p, Andrew Lloyd Webber; d, Joel Schumacher; w, Joel Schumacher, Andrew Lloyd Webber (based on the novel *Le Fantome de l'Opera* by Gaston Leroux and the stage musical by Andrew Lloyd Webber); ph, John Mathieson; ed, Terry Rawlings; m, Andrew Lloyd Webber; prod d, Anthony Pratt; art d, John Fenner, Paul Kirby; fx, Peter Hutchinson, Nathan McGuinness; chor, Peter Darling; cos, Alexandra Byrne

AAN Best Art Direction: Anthony Pratt (art direction); Celia Bobak (set decoration); *AAN Best Cinematography:* John Mathieson; *AAN Best Original Song:* "Learn to Be Lonely"; Andrew Lloyd Webber (music), Charles Hart (lyrics)

Director Joel Schumacher treats Andrew Lloyd Webber's monumental *coup de theatre,* whose lavish design and crashing chandelier helped distract theatergoers from the banality of the score, as though it were the jewel in the crown of contemporary musical theater. Beneath the bombast, however, it's pure paste and tinsel.

Paris, 1870: Orphaned, impoverished Christine Daae (17-year-old Emmy Rossum), who's lived at the lavish Opera Populaire since her father's death, has been receiving voice lessons from a mysterious voice she naively believes is her father's spirit. Christine's mentor is actually the mysterious "Opera Ghost" (Gerard Butler) who haunts the theater. Only ballet mistress Madame Giry (Miranda Richardson) knows that the "ghost" is a brilliant but disfigured composer who was hidden in the theater's recesses as a child and has grown into a lonely, tormented man. The Phantom launches a campaign to scare off vain, talentless diva La Carlotta (Minnie Driver) so Christine can take her place in the limelight, but his protege's betrayal—a tentative romance with the Opera's new patron, Raoul (Patrick Wilson)—sends the lovesick Phantom into a lethal rage.

The film's costumes and production design are gorgeous, but the casting is surprisingly weak. Schumacher deliberately cast actors who could sing but, ironically, the least-accomplished vocalist among the leads—Butler—has the most magnetism. Talented ingenue Rossum is as blandly dewy as a cake-topper swaddled in froufrou, and Wilson's stage charisma is nowhere in evidence. Driver's shrill Carlotta speaks with a community-theater accent and sings with another actress's voice (Margaret Preece). Nuanced supporting performances by Simon Callow, Ciaran Hinds and, especially, Richardson, can't compensate for the vacuum at the top.

ANDY WARHOL'S DRACULA   *DVD*
(DRACULA CERCA SANGUE DI VERGINE E... MORI DI SETE)
1974 90m   c   Horror   ★★★
CC Champion & 1/Carlo Ponti-Jean   R
Yanne-Jean-Pierre Rassam   (France/Italy)

Joe Dallesandro *(Mario),* Udo Kier *(Dracula),* Arno Juerging *(Anton),* Maxime McKendry *(Lady Difiore),* Vittorio De Sica *(Lord Difiore),* Dominique Darel *(Rubinia),* Stefania Cassini *(Saphiria),* Roman Polanski *(Man in Inn),* Gil Cagne *(Townsman),* Milena Vukotic *(Esmeralda)*

p, Carlo Ponti, Andrew Braunsberg, Jean-Pierre Rassam, Jean Yanne; d, Paul Morrissey, Antonio Margheriti; w, Paul Morrissey; ph, Luigi Kuveiller (Eastmancolor); ed, Jed Johnson, Franca Silvi; m, Carlo Gizzi; prod d, Enrico Job; art d, Gianni Giovagnoni; fx, Carlo Rambaldi, Roberto Arcangeli

Shot immediately after ANDY WARHOL'S FRANKENSTEIN with much of the same cast and crew, DRACULA is definitely the better of the two. More like a drug addict than a monster, Dracula (Kier) needs "virgin" blood to survive, and

virgins in his native Romania are in short supply. With his assistant, Juerging, and his sister (in a coffin), Dracula travels to Roman Catholic Italy, where virgins should be more prevalent, and winds up at the crumbling estate of a destitute marquis and his four unmarried daughters. Eager to marry one of his daughters off to the rich Romanian count, the marquis gives Dracula a warm welcome. Unbeknownst to the vampire, however, the two middle daughters have already lost their virginity to a hunky socialist handyman (Dallesandro).

Not so outright disgusting as Warhol's FRANKENSTEIN, DRACULA is stylishly directed, atmospheric, funny, and intense enough to please gorehounds—especially at the climax. Kier makes a wonderful Dracula with his thick accent and goofy mannerisms, but De Sica (director of such neorealist classics as SHOESHINE and THE BICYCLE THIEF) nearly steals the show as the eccentric marquis. Once again Morrissey's distinctive stamp is on the script, but many European sources credit Margheriti as the director. Look for Roman Polanski in a cameo as a goofy villager. Originally rated X by the MPAA, the rating was later changed to an R.

ANGEL AT MY TABLE, AN
1990 156m   c   Biography/Drama   ★★★★
Hibiscus Films/Sharmill Films   (New Zealand)   R

Kerry Fox *(Janet Frame),* Karen Fergusson *(Janet Frame—as a Teenager),* Alexia Keogh *(Janet Frame—as a Child),* Iris Churn *(Mum),* K.J. Wilson *(Dad),* Melina Bernecker *(Myrtle Frame),* Glynis Angell *(Isabel Frame),* Samantha Townsley *(Isabel Frame—as a Teenager),* Katherine Murray-Cowper *(Isabel Frame—as a Child),* Sarah Smuts-Kennedy *(June Frame)*

p, Bridget Ikin; d, Jane Campion; w, Laura Jones (from the autobiographies *To the Is-Land, An Angel at My Table* and *The Envoy from Mirror City* by Janet Frame); ph, Stuart Dryburgh; ed, Veronica Haussler; m, Don McGlashan; prod d, Grant Major; art d, Jackie Gilmore; cos, Glenys Jackson

Lushly photographed and beautifully acted, AN ANGEL AT MY TABLE was the second feature directed by New Zealander Jane Campion, who would win a world-wide reputation with her following film, THE PIANO.

Adapted from the autobiography of novelist and poet Janet Frame (Kerry Fox), the film tells the story of a stubborn, plain, introverted redhead whose thirst for knowledge and determination to be a writer set her apart in her isolated rural community. She's shy as a child; in college, she finds herself increasingly alienated from her fellow students. She feels awkward and ugly, and when her lively, self-confident sister (Glynis Angell) arrives, Janet only looks worse by comparison. She retreats into a life of fantasy and isolation, and eventually has a nervous breakdown. Committed to an institution, Janet is diagnosed—incorrectly, it later turns out—as an incurable schizophrenic. Leaving the hospital, Janet meets Frank Sargeson (Martyn Sanderson), an eccentric writer, who encourages her to broaden her perspectives by traveling. Slowly Janet emerges from her shell, and by the time she returns to New Zealand, some peace (if not exactly happiness) has become possible for her.

Jane Campion has established a reputation for making slightly off-center films in which regular folks get glimpses of the darkness that lurks beneath the surfaces of their lives. An admirer of Frame's novels since she was a teenager, Campion builds her film around a heroine who defies Hollywood conventions; she's not beautiful or sexy or sophisticated, and her adventures are mostly intellectual. Originally shot on 16mm and one-inch videotape as a three-part miniseries for Australian TV, then re-edited for 35mm theatrical release, the film doesn't look like a TV movie, except perhaps in the intimacy of its subject.

ANGELA'S ASHES

DVD

1999 145m c Drama ★★★

Dirty Hands Productions/Scott Rudin R
Productions/David Brown Productions/
Manhattan Project/ Universal (U.S.)

Emily Watson *(Angela McCourt)*, Robert Carlyle *(Malachy McCourt)*, Joe Breen *(Young Frank)*, Ciaran Owens *(Middle Frank)*, Michael Legge *(Older Frank)*, Ronnie Masterson *(Grandma Sheehan)*, Pauline McLynn *(Aunt Aggie)*, Liam Carney *(Uncle Pa Keating)*, Eanna MacLiam *(Uncle Pat)*, Andrew Bennett *(Narrator)*

p, David Brown, Scott Rudin, Alan Parker; d, Alan Parker; w, Laura Jones, Alan Parker (based on the book *Angela's Ashes: A Memoir* by Frank McCourt); ph, Michael Seresin; ed, Gerry Hambling; prod d, Geoffrey Kirkland; art d, Jonathan McKinstry; fx, Andrew Wilson, Jim Brady, Kent Houston; cos, Consolata Boyle

AAN Best Original Score: John Williams

That Frank McCourt's memoir of growing up wretchedly poor in Ireland was a best-seller owes much to his tone: wry, witty, self-deprecating, and remarkably free of self-pity, given that he and his brothers spent much of their childhoods hungry, cold, sick, and humiliated by spiteful children and feckless adults. Alan Parker's adaptation is meticulous, unsentimental, beautifully acted, and uses narration to evoke McCourt's distinctive voice, but nearly two and a half hours worth of dying babies, rain-spattered streets, ragged children, and filthy, bug-infested rooms is a bit oppressive.

Born in Brooklyn in 1930, Frank (played by Joe Breen as a child, Ciaran Owens as an adolescent, and Michael Legge as a teenager) was the oldest child of Angela (Emily Watson) and Malachy (Robert Carlyle) McCourt. His parents fled impoverished, class-conscious Ireland individually, hoping to find fortune in the U.S.; they returned home together, poorer than ever, after the death of their fifth child drove Angela to a nervous collapse. Malachy's alcoholism and stubborn pride (he continually refused work that was "beneath his dignity") insured that the family remained destitute and desperate; Malachy eventually decamped for good, leaving Angela and the children (she bore seven; four lived) to scrape by on welfare and church charity.

That the film isn't sheer misery is largely a credit to the cast. Watson nurtures a small spark in Angela, but never falls back on uplifting Hollywood cliches about smiling through the tears; her Angela is, ultimately, defeated by the burdens life piles on her shoulders. The subtle Carlyle breathes surprising warmth into the thankless role of Malachy, and Parker elicits excellent performances from the young actors.

ANGELS AND INSECTS

DVD

1995 116m c Drama/Romance/Historical ★★★½

Playhouse International Pictures (U.K./U.S.) R

Mark Rylance *(William Adamson)*, Patsy Kensit *(Eugenia Alabaster)*, Kristin Scott Thomas *(Matty Crompton)*, Jeremy Kemp *(Sir Harald Alabaster)*, Douglas Henshall *(Edgar Alabaster)*, Saskia Wickham *(Rowena Alabaster)*, Chris Larkin *(Robin Swinnerton)*, Annette Badland *(Lady Alabaster)*, Lindsay Thomas *(Lady Alabaster's Maid)*, Michelle Sylvester *(Margaret Alabaster)*

p, Joyce Herlihy, Belinda Haas; d, Philip Haas; w, Belinda Haas, Philip Haas (based on the novella *Morpho Eugenia* by A.S. Byatt); ph, Bernard Zitzermann; ed, Belinda Haas; m, Alexander Balanescu; prod d, Jennifer Kernke; art d, Alison Riva; chor, Kim Brandstrup; cos, Paul Brown

AAN Best Costume Design: Paul Brown

Director Philip Haas (THE MUSIC OF CHANCE) has taken a A.S. Byatt's novella *Morpho Eugenia* and turned it into one of the most intelligent costume films ever made.

Naturalist Will Adamson (Mark Rylance), survivor of a shipwreck off the coast of South America, comes to stay at the country estate of the Alabaster family in England. He is to help Lord Alabaster (Jeremy Kemp) catalogue his vast collection of scientific specimens, but soon falls in love with the Lord's oldest daughter, the beautiful Eugenia (Patsy Kensit). Eugenia, despondent over the suicide of her fiance, accepts Will's proposal of marriage over the objections of her snobby brother, Edgar (Douglas Henshall). As Will busies himself on the estate, accompanied by Matty (Kristin Scott Thomas), a poor relation of the Alabasters with a scientific bent of her own, Eugenia gives birth to a series of children who bear little resemblance to her husband. Something untoward is going on here, and Will may be the only one who doesn't know the Alabaster's dark secret.

Beautifully adapted by Haas and his wife Belinda, Byatt's story unfolds at a deliberate pace, but it's anything but a dull costumer: there are heaving passions and febrile minds under those crinolines and waistcoats. The disclosure of the family secret *is* a shocker, and it's staged as such, with Bernard Zitzermann's adroit photography and Alexander Balanescu's potent music as additional boons. While Kensit is a bit out of her depth as Eugenia, Rylance makes an appealing sobersides—you believe in Will's natural, simple goodness. But it's Scott Thomas who really makes the film worth seeing: perfectly in period, she resembles an Ingres painting come to life, and invests Matty with a fierce, clear-eyed intelligence.

ANGELS IN THE OUTFIELD

DVD

1951 99m bw Comedy/Sports ★★★½

MGM (U.S.)

Paul Douglas *(Guffy McGovern)*, Janet Leigh *(Jennifer Paige)*, Keenan Wynn *(Fred Bayles)*, Donna Corcoran *(Bridget White)*, Lewis Stone *(Arnold P. Hapgood)*, Spring Byington *(Sr. Edwitha)*, Bruce Bennett *(Saul Hellman)*, Marvin Kaplan *(Timothy Durney)*, Ellen Corby *(Sr. Veronica)*, Jeff Richards *(Dave Rothberg)*

p, Clarence Brown; d, Clarence Brown; w, Dorothy Kingsley, George Wells (based on a story by Richard Conlin); ph, Paul C. Vogel; ed, Robert J. Kern; m, Daniele Amfitheatrof

This delightful baseball comedy stars Paul Douglas as Guffy McGovern, the irascible manager of the Pittsburgh Pirates, who are firmly entrenched in the basement of the National League until the prayers of a little girl (Donna Corcoran) prompt the angel Gabriel to intervene. When Guffy sees the divine light and turns over a new leaf, more angels—baseball greats of the past—lend a helping glove, and the Pirates start winning ball games, shooting to the top of the standings. Reporter Jennifer Paige (Janet Leigh) suspects the Pirates are receiving help from above and begins an investigation into the matter. Great performances by all make this a little gem of a film. Dwight Eisenhower, interviewed during his presidency, named this his favorite movie. Note the fleeting presence of Hall of Famers Ty Cobb and Joe DiMaggio.

ANGELS OVER BROADWAY

DVD

1940 78m bw Drama ★★★★

Columbia (U.S.)

Douglas Fairbanks Jr. *(Bill O'Brien)*, Rita Hayworth *(Nina Barona)*, Thomas Mitchell *(Gene Gibbons)*, John Qualen *(Charles Engle)*, George Watts *(Hopper)*, Ralph Theodore *(Dutch Enright)*, Eddie Foster *(Louie Artino)*, Jack Roper *(Eddie Burns)*, Constance Worth *(Sylvia Marbe)*, Richard Bond *(Sylvia's Escort)* p, Ben Hecht; d, Ben Hecht, Lee Garmes; w, Ben Hecht; ph, Lee Garmes; ed, Gene Havlick; m, George Antheil; art d, Lionel Banks; cos, Ray Howell

---

AAN Best Original Screenplay: Ben Hecht

One of the more underappreciated films to come out of Hollywood, this marvelous Ben Hecht production annoyed the critics of the day for not pandering to its audience. Four leads and a host of supporting players make a single Broadway night come to life with zip and wit. Mitchell, as a silver-tongued, alcoholic playwright, saves Qualen, who is about to commit suicide after embezzling several thousand dollars. "Dismiss your hearse," Mitchell urges him. "Live, little man, and suffer!" The zany playwright proposes a surefire scheme to dupe some big-time card sharps in a battle royal, using Qualen's stolen loot to build a fortune. Enter slick Fairbanks, who shills for a top-drawer poker game, and his devoted but equally sharp girlfriend Hayworth. Fairbanks spots Qualen as an easy mark and intends to suck him into the game and take him for everything. Nothing, of course, goes according to anyone's plans as Hecht's clever script twists and turns its way to a startling and delightful conclusion.

The performances, particularly by Mitchell and Fairbanks, are captivating, and the dialogue sparkles with Hecht's poetic irony: "This town's a giant dice game—come on seven!" Because the film featured Rita Hayworth, who had been hand-picked for stardom by Columbia's boss Harry Cohn, Hecht was given a relatively free reign on this production, and went unhampered by interfering studio bureaucrats to create an unpredictable Broadway saga. Hecht earned an Academy Award nomination for his original screenplay, but lost to Preston Sturges for THE GREAT MCGINTY.

ANGELS WITH DIRTY FACES   **DVD**
1938   97m   bw   Crime   ★★★★
Warner Bros.   (U.S.)

James Cagney *(Rocky Sullivan)*, Pat O'Brien *(Jerry Connelly)*, Humphrey Bogart *(James Frazier)*, Ann Sheridan *(Laury Ferguson)*, George Bancroft *(Mac Keefer)*, Billy Halop *(Soapy)*, Bobby Jordan *(Swing)*, Leo Gorcey *(Bim)*, Bernard Punsley *(Hunky)*, Gabriel Dell *(Pasty)*

p, Samuel Bischoff; d, Michael Curtiz; w, John Wexley, Warren Duff (based on a story by Rowland Brown); ph, Sol Polito; ed, Owen Marks; m, Max Steiner; art d, Robert Haas

---

AAN Best Actor: James Cagney; *AAN Best Director:* Michael Curtiz; *AAN Best Original Story:* Rowland Brown

---

One of the most stirring, colorful and memorable gangster films of its day, and a perfect summary of Cagney's tough but soft-hearted screen image. As youths, Rocky Sullivan and his pal Jerry Connelly are caught in the act of breaking into a railroad car. Jerry escapes, but Rocky is caught and sent to reform school. The film then jumps ahead several years, with Rocky (now played by Cagney) a hardened criminal, and Jerry (Pat O'Brien) a priest in the neighborhood where the boys grew up. Rocky, recently released from jail, returns to the neighborhood, where a battle begins between the criminal and the priest for the hearts and minds of some tough kids in the neighborhood. Rocky also tries to get his double-crossing ex-partner (Humphrey Bogart) to come up with the $100,000 he owes him.

With Cagney, O'Brien, and Bogart plus the young actors known as the Dead End Kids, the film offers a host of terrific characters, crisp dialogue, and a generous portion of humor. (Particularly funny is the scene in which Rocky gives the young toughs a lesson in how to play basketball.) Films about boyhood friends who go down different paths in life were popular in the 1930s, but the tale was never more effectively told than in this fast-paced drama.

ANGER MANAGEMENT   **DVD**
2003   100m   c   Comedy   ★½
Happy Madison/Jack Giarraputo Productions   PG-13
(U.S.)

Adam Sandler *(Dave Buznik)*, Jack Nicholson *(Dr. Buddy Rydell)*, Marisa Tomei *(Linda)*, Luis Guzman *(Lou)*, Lynne Thigpen *(Judge Daniels)*, Woody Harrelson *(Galaxia)*, John Turturro *(Chuck)*, Heather Graham *(Kendra)*, John C. Reilly *(Arnie Shankman)*, Nancy Walls *(Flight Attendant)*

p, Barry Bernardi, Derek Dauchy, Todd Garner, Jack Giarraputo, John Jacobs, Joe Roth; d, Peter Segal; w, David Dorfman; ph, Donald M. McAlpine; ed, Jeff Gourson; m, Teddy Castellucci; prod d, Alan Au; art d, Domenic Silvestri; fx, John S. Baker, Sheena Duggal, Jonathan Rothbart; cos, Ellen Lutter

---

This Adam Sandler/Jack Nicholson vehicle spends a *long* 105 minutes spinning a witless sitcom variation of THE GAME.

Meek, desperately non-confrontational Dave Buznik (Sandler) toils for an abusive boss at a company that manufactures fashion accessories for overweight cats and dogs. On a plane to New York, Buznik makes the mistake of asking the flight attendant (Nancy Walls) for a pair of headphones; the next thing he knows, he's charged with air rage. Judge Daniels (Lynne Thigpen) orders Buznik to attend an anger-management class run by trendy celebrity shrink Buddy Rydell (Nicholson), whose therapy group features the usual assortment of mildly offensive stereotypes, including requisite screamingly gay Latino Lou (Luiz Guzman). Things go from bad to worse when Buznik, trying to extricate another member of the group from a bar fight, winds up clocking a blind man (an unbilled Harry Dean Stanton). Buznik finds himself back before Judge Daniels, who orders him to step up his therapy or do a year in jail. Buznik accepts, not realizing that Rydell is going to move into his apartment and insert himself into every area of Buznik's private life, including his relationship with girlfriend Linda (Marisa Tomei).

David Dorfman's contrived screenplay manages a couple of good throwaway jokes, including the non sequitur "I think Eskimos are smug," and a reference to a Carpenters CD as "songs of madness and obsession." There are some moderately amusing celebrity cameos (ex-NYC mayor Rudy Giuliani, pitcher Roger Clemens) and Sandler and Nicholson do what they can with the thin material—in fact, both *underplay* rather deftly. But by the time the big, not-so-surprise ending rolls around, most viewers will have long since stopped caring.

ANIMAL CRACKERS   **DVD**
1930   97m   bw   Comedy   ★★★½
Paramount   (U.S.)

Groucho Marx *(Captain Jeffrey Spaulding)*, Harpo Marx *(The Professor)*, Chico Marx *(Signor Emanuel Ravelli)*, Zeppo Marx *(Horatio Jamison)*, Lillian Roth *(Arabella Rittenhouse)*, Margaret Dumont *(Mrs. Rittenhouse)*, Louis Sorin *(Roscoe W. Chandler)*, Hal Thompson *(John Parker)*, Margaret Irving *(Mrs. Whitehead)*, Kathryn Reece *(Grace Carpenter)*

d, Victor Heerman; w, Morrie Ryskind (based on the musical play by Morrie Ryskind, George S. Kaufman, Bert Kalmar, and Harry Ruby); ph, George Folsey; art d, Ernst Fegte

---

The second Marx Brothers film is a riotous version of their stage hit.

Mrs. Rittenhouse (Margaret Dumont), a wealthy Long Island matron, throws a lavish party at her mansion, at which the noted African explorer Captain Spaulding (Groucho Marx) is the guest of honor. Mrs. Whitehead, a society rival of Mrs. Rittenhouse's, decides to sabotage the party by substituting a copy of a noted painting that will be unveiled that evening. Meanwhile, Mrs. Rittenhouse's daughter Arabella (Lillian Roth) plans to switch the painting with a copy done by her artist boyfriend John (Hal Thompson), in order to impress art impresario Roscoe W. Chandler (Louis Sorin), whom musicans Ravelli and The Professor (Chico and Harpo Marx) recognize as actually being a former fish peddler named Abie.

ANIMAL CRACKERS is exceedingly stagy and theatrical, even by 1930's standards, but is nevertheless very funny and highly enjoyable. Some of its classic bits include the "Hooray for Captain Spaulding" production number, featuring the melody that Groucho would later adopt as the theme song for his radio and television hit "You Bet Your Life"; the hilarious parody of Eugene O'Neill's *Strange Interlude,* with Spaulding stepping forward and vocalizing his internal thoughts in the middle of a scene; and the usual quota of bad puns. ANIMAL CRACKERS was also the hardest Marx Brothers film to see for many years, having been withheld from circulation from 1958 to 1974 due to a copyright dispute. When it was re-released to theaters in 1974, a whole new generation of Marx Brothers fans were born, and happily, Groucho was still alive to bask in the triumph.

ANNA AND THE KING OF SIAM   DVD
1946 128m bw Drama   ★★★★
Fox (U.S.)

Irene Dunne *(Anna),* Rex Harrison *(the King),* Linda Darnell *(Tuptin),* Lee J. Cobb *(Kralahome),* Gale Sondergaard *(Lady Thiang),* Mikhail Rasumny *(Alak),* Dennis Hoey *(Sir Edward),* Tito Renaldo *(Prince as a Man),* Richard Lyon *(Louis Owens),* William Edmunds *(Monshee)*

p, Louis D. Lighton; d, John Cromwell; w, Talbot Jennings, Sally Benson (based on the book by Margaret Landon); ph, Arthur Miller; m, Bernard Wheeler, William Darling; fx, Fred Sersen

AAN Best Supporting Actress; Gale Sondergaard; *AAN Best Screenplay:* Sally Benson, Talbot Jennings; *AA Best B/W Cinematography:* Arthur Miller; *AAN Best Score (Drama or Comedy):* Bernard Herrmann; *AA Best Interior Decoration (B/W):* Lyle Wheeler, William Darling, Thomas Little, Frank E. Hughes

An entertaining, touching tale of an English tutor who travels to Siam in 1862 with her young son. She is hired to educate the harem and 67 children of the rather savage king, who covets Western culture but insists upon maintaining Siam's customs and some particularly barbaric traditions. The story is drawn from the real life of 33-year-old Mrs. Anna Leonowens, brilliantly played by Dunne, who is at first repelled by and later attracted to Harrison, the king (in his first American film), and his different Eastern ways. She also meets and befriends the king's first wife (Sondergaard), long relegated to the back rooms of the imperial palace, and a lovely young addition to the harem (Darnell) who falls tragically in love with another. The supporting cast is uniformly excellent, including Cobb in the role of the king's chief minister. Director Cromwell keeps the well lighted and photographed story brisk and less sentimental than the musical remake, THE KING AND I. Dunne is the perfect British governess, and the theoretically miscast Harrison is simply majestic as the king who gropes toward both sensitivity and Western ideas, battling his authoritarian instincts all the way. It's a wonder that this production, richly costumed and boasting lavish sets, was not done in color.

ANNA CHRISTIE   DVD
1930 86m bw Drama   ★★★
MGM (U.S.)

Greta Garbo *(Anna Christie),* Charles Bickford *(Matt Burke),* George F. Marion Sr. *(Chris Christopherson),* Marie Dressler *(Marthy Owen),* James T. Mack *(Johnny the Harp),* Lee Phelps *(Larry)*

d, Clarence Brown; w, Frances Marion (based on the play by Eugene O'Neill); ph, William Daniels; ed, Hugh Wynn; art d, Cedric Gibbons; cos, Adrian

AAN Best Actress: Greta Garbo; *AAN Best Director:* Clarence Brown; *AAN Best Cinematography:* William H Daniels

Garbo talks. A fascinating cast and a convincingly murky atmosphere help overcome the primitive sound techniques that plague this stagy, somewhat preciously presented adaptation of Eugene O'Neill's famous if overrated play (first filmed in 1923 with Blanche Sweet and William Russell). Garbo, the cinema's great silent sphinx, who first spoke in this film, plays the title role, a woman who flees the mean-spirited farm family her sailor father left her with and ends up a prostitute. Renouncing her profession, Garbo returns to her father (George F. Marion Sr.), living on a broken-down barge as the film opens. During a storm Garbo and Marion rescue an Irish sailor (Bickford) from drowning, and though Bickford soon falls for Garbo and proposes, she angrily exorcises all her past pain by revealing her background as a whore. Although Bickford abandons her at first, genuine love eventually reconciles the pair.

The public fascination with the mysterious Garbo heightened ANNA CHRISTIE's popularity. Although critics and public alike were justifiably captivated by her husky, accented voice and famous delivery of her opening lines: "Gimme a viskey, ginger ale on the side … and don't be stingy, baby!" parts of her performance are exaggerated, reminiscent more of off-key silent-screen posturing than the equally intense but refined technique she would soon master. The sometimes mugging Dressler, on the other hand, in the star-making role of the aging wharf rat who commiserates with Garbo throughout the film, steals every scene she appears in and manages to convey both touching pathos and a rich humanity. Much of the film's creakiness is due to the cumbersome sound equipment that prevented director Clarence Brown from using his noise-making cameras freely. Nominated for an Academy Award for Best Actress for this film and ROMANCE, Garbo remade the film in German with Jacques Feyder (director of THE KISS, Garbo's last silent) and, reportedly, she liked Feyder's version better than Brown's, of which she said, "Isn't it terrible? Who ever saw Swedes act like that?"

ANNA KARENINA   DVD
1935 85m bw Drama   ★★★★
MGM (U.S.)

Greta Garbo *(Anna Karenina),* Fredric March *(Vronsky),* Freddie Bartholomew *(Sergei),* Maureen O'Sullivan *(Kitty),* May Robson *(Countess Vronsky),* Basil Rathbone *(Karenin),* Reginald Owen *(Stiva),* Reginald Denny *(Yashvin),* Phoebe Foster *(Dolly),* Gyles Isham *(Levin)*

p, David O. Selznick; d, Clarence Brown; w, Clemence Dane, Salka Viertel, S.N. Behrman (based on the novel by Leo Tolstoy); ph, William Daniels; ed, Robert J. Kern; m, Herbert Stothart; chor, Marguerite Wallmann, Chester Hale

A remake of the John Gilbert-Greta Garbo silent movie LOVE, this often splendid, moody Garbo vehicle under Clarence Brown's direction tells the tragic Tolstoy tale with great sensitivity. As the immortal Anna of 19th-century St. Petersburg, Garbo plays the pampered wife of Karenin

(Rathbone, in fine form), a rich but icy government official. After pleading with her straying married brother (Owen) not to jeopardize his marriage, she ironically meets and falls in love the dashing Captain Vronsky (March). When she asks her husband for a divorce, she is told that if she makes such an unheard-of move, she will be deprived of her son (Bartholomew). Remorseful but consumed by love, Anna runs off with Vronsky, who resigns his commission. Though happy at first, he soon longs for his carefree army days, and she is pained by her thwarted attempts to spend time with her son. The star-crossed lovers finally argue and separate and when Anna, rushing to the train station upon learning that Vronsky is leaving, sees him saying goodbye to another woman, she throws herself in front of the departing train.

Director Brown, in one of the best of his seven films with Garbo, and ace cinematographer William Daniels, Garbo's favorite, bathe their beloved actress in soft light that caresses her classic features. Adorned in luxurious but subdued gowns appropriate to both her own passionate but understated style and Anna's profound sadness, Garbo is unforgettable as a woman who only briefly experiences carefree happiness, whose desires are crushed by a rigid and unfeeling society. Especially memorable is the finale, as light flashes from the oncoming train alternately reveal and hide Anna's conflicting emotions. Meticulously and sumptuously mounted by producer David O. Selznick, the film carefully pares down Tolstoy's sprawling classic to center almost entirely upon its heroine, but the end result is highly satisfying nonetheless.

ANNA KARENINA 💿

1947 139m bw Drama ★★★½
Korda/London Films (U.K.)

Vivien Leigh (Anna Karenina), Ralph Richardson (Alexei Karenin), Kieron Moore (Count Vronsky), Sally Ann Howes (Kitty Scherbatsky), Niall MacGinnis (Levin), Martita Hunt (Princess Betty Tversky), Marie Lohr (Princess Scherbatsky), Michael Gough (Nicholai), Hugh Dempster (Stefan Oblonsky), Mary Kerridge (Dolly Oblonsky)

p, Alexander Korda; d, Julien Duvivier; w, Jean Anouilh, Guy Morgan, Julien Duvivier (based on the novel by Leo Tolstoy); ph, Henri Alekan; ed, Russell Lloyd; m, Constant Lambert; prod d, Andre Andrejew; fx, W. Percy Day; cos, Cecil Beaton

---

This remake of the Garbo classic has different values and approaches that enhance Vivien Leigh's magnetic performance as the ill-starred Anna, who leaves her stuffy bureaucrat husband, Karenin (Richardson), for an adventurous army officer, Vronsky (Moore), only to be discarded and sent to suicide in front of an onrushing train when husband, child, and lover are lost to her. Unlike the 1935 version, which also downplayed the novel's subplots far more, the psychological elements of this tragedy are underscored and registered with powerful impact through Leigh, whose raw emotions distort and finally destroy a once orderly, though predictably dull, life. Leigh is positively riveting, and Richardson as the priggish, pompous government official is properly vengeful and vexing. Only the very handsome Moore, in the admittedly colorless role as the self-centered lover, is a letdown, delivering a sometimes bland performance. Korda's production, though perhaps overlong, is truly spectacular, with a great supporting cast, countless extras, and authentic 19th-century sets that are mouth-openers. Duvivier's direction is moody and fast-paced, highlighted by sometimes frightening effects, with angles and cuts that reflect the image of a woman slipping deeper and deeper into her own destruction.

ANNE OF THE THOUSAND DAYS

1969 145m c Historical ★★★★
Universal (U.K.) M

Richard Burton (King Henry VIII), Genevieve Bujold (Anne Boleyn), Irene Papas (Queen Katherine), Anthony Quayle (Wolsey), John Colicos (Cromwell), Michael Hordern (Thomas Boleyn), Katherine Blake (Elizabeth), Peter Jeffrey (Norfolk), Joseph O'Conor (Fisher), William Squire (Thomas More)

p, Hal B. Wallis; d, Charles Jarrott; w, Bridget Boland, John Hale (adapted by Richard Sokolove, based on the play by Maxwell Anderson); ph, Arthur Ibbetson (Panavision, Technicolor); ed, Richard Marden; m, Georges Delerue; prod d, Maurice Carter; art d, Lionel Couch; chor, Mary Skeaping; cos, Margaret Furse

---

AAN Best Picture; AAN Best Actor: Richard Burton; AAN Best Actress: Genevieve Bujold; AAN Best Supporting Actor: Anthony Quayle; AAN Best Adapted Screenplay: John Hale, Bridget Boland, Richard Sokolove; AAN Best Cinematography: Arthur Ibbetson; AAN Best Original Score (Not a Musical): Georges Delerue; AAN Best Art Direction-Set Decoration: Maurice Carter, Lionel Couch, Patrick McLoughlin; AA Best Costume Design: Margaret Furse; AAN Best Sound: John Alfred

---

A superbly acted costume drama, ANNE OF THE THOUSAND DAYS recounts the story of Henry VIII (Richard Burton), who, in 1526, discards his wife, Katherine of Aragon (Irene Papas), in favor of the younger, prettier Anne Boleyn (Genevieve Bujold), who soon proves to be as crafty and ruthless as her sovereign. Resisting Henry's incessant advances, insisting that any child born to them must be decreed legitimate, Anne plays her cat-and-mouse game for six years, while Cardinal Wolsey (Quayle) collapses into ineffectual senility when he fails to have Anne's marriage to another annulled. Only the Iago-like Cromwell (John Colicos) solves the king's dilemma by precipitating a break with the Vatican, naming Henry head of the Church of England, and dispensing any religious controls over his or Anne's marital status. Although the union produces a daughter, Henry later seizes upon the birth of a stillborn son as an excuse to abandon his queen and and woo the attractive Jane Seymour (Lesley Paterson). After that Anne's days are numbered—one thousand, to be exact.

Based on the 1948 Maxwell Anderson play (a star vehicle for Rex Harrison on Broadway), ANNE OF THE THOUSAND DAYS has a touch of soap opera which helps explain its then-substantial gross of $7 million. But it also boasts lavish sets and handsome photography, an arresting performance by Burton—the epitome of the royal fox and oaf—and well-judged work from Bujold, Papas, and Quayle, all of which make for a rousing, bawdy, and often enlightening historical film. A successful entry in a series of such features made during the '60s, including BECKET (also produced by Wallis), A MAN FOR ALL SEASONS, and THE LION IN WINTER, the film received an Academy Award nomination for Best Picture but lost to John Schlesinger's gritty, contemporary MIDNIGHT COWBOY.

ANNIE GET YOUR GUN 💿

1950 107m c Musical/Western ★★★½
MGM (U.S.)

Betty Hutton (Annie Oakley), Howard Keel (Frank Butler), Louis Calhern (Buffalo Bill), J. Carrol Naish (Chief Sitting Bull), Edward Arnold (Pawnee Bill), Keenan Wynn (Charlie Davenport), Benay Venuta (Dolly Tate), Clinton Sundberg (Foster Wilson), James Harrison (Mac), Brad Mora (Little Jake)

p, Arthur Freed; d, George Sidney; w, Sidney Sheldon (based on the musical play, book by Herbert Fields and Dorothy Fields); ph, Charles Rosher (Technicolor); ed, James E. Newcom; m, Irving

Berlin; art d, Cedric Gibbons, Paul Groesse; fx, A. Arnold Gillespie, Warren Newcombe; chor, Robert Alton

AAN Best Color Cinematography: Charles Rosher; *AAN Best Film Editing:* James E. Newcom; *AA Best Score (Musical):* Adolph Deutsch, Roger Edens; *AAN Best Art Direction-Set Decoration (Color):* Cedric Gibbons, Paul Groesse, Edwin B. Willis, Richard A. Pefferle

Sprightly songfest that, surprisingly, captivated audiences wanting musicals with dancing. There is little dancing throughout, but the tunes became instant standards and the large sets, armies of extras, and Wild West motif offset the missing choreography. In a glove-fitting role, Hutton blasts her way on and off screen as the sharpshooting Annie Oakley Mozie (1860-1926), a homely girl from the Ozarks who becomes queen of Buffalo Bill's renowned Wild West Show, pitting her talents against marksman Frank Butler (Keel). She loves Keel, but her ability to best him keeps driving him away. Finally Sitting Bull (Naish) gives her worthwhile advice before she faces off against Keel one more time. "You miss, you win," the Indian chief tells her, and he's right.

Keel is excellent as the smug star of the show; Naish is likewise top-notch as a shrewd Sitting Bull; Calhern superb as a noble but slippery Buffalo Bill; Arnold solid as his show biz rival; and Wynn his usual truculent self. Standout numbers include "Doin' What Comes Natur'lly" sung by Hutton and siblings, "My Defenses Are Down" boomed by Keel, "I'm an Indian Too" with Hutton and a horde of leaping, lunging Indians, and the fantastic finale with hundreds of cowboys and Indians, "There's No Business Like Show Business."

MGM execs struggled to find the perfect Annie Oakley, first considering Judy Canova, Betty Garrett, and Doris Day before opting for Judy Garland, who was reportedly fired because of incessant tantrums. Hutton was finally brought in to save the day, which she did with typically unbridled enthusiasm, giving one of her most suitable performances, even though she proved to be no Ethel Merman, who originated the role in the smash Broadway production, when it came to singing the finale. Although the choice of director was similarly muddled by MGM moguls, passing from Busby Berkeley to Charles Walters and finally to George Sidney, the extremely lavish result went on to win the Oscar for Best Score in a Musical, as well as nominations for cinematography, art direction and editing.

ANNIE HALL [DVD]

1977 93m   c   Comedy   ★★★★
UA   (U.S.)   PG

Woody Allen *(Alvy Singer)*, Diane Keaton *(Annie Hall)*, Tony Roberts *(Rob)*, Carol Kane *(Allison)*, Paul Simon *(Tony Lacey)*, Colleen Dewhurst *(Mom Hall)*, Janet Margolin *(Robin)*, Shelley Duvall *(Pam)*, Christopher Walken *(Duane Hall)*, Donald Symington *(Dad Hall)*

p, Charles H. Joffe; d, Woody Allen; w, Woody Allen, Marshall Brickman; ph, Gordon Willis; ed, Ralph Rosenblum, Wendy Greene Bricmont; art d, Mel Bourne; cos, Ruth Morley, George Newman, Marilyn Putnam, Ralph Lauren, Nancy McArdle

AA Best Picture; AAN Best Actor: Woody Allen; *AA Best Actress:* Diane Keaton; *AA Best Director:* Woody Allen; *AA Best Original Screenplay:* Woody Allen, Marshall Brickman

Seminal, hilarious look at contemporary relationships, with Woody Allen playing Alvy Singer, a neurotic, insecure comedy writer (Allen began his own career as a gag writer for the "Tonight Show") who falls madly in love with Annie Hall (Diane Keaton), an aspiring singer. They fumble about in the early stages of their relationship like two teenagers groping toward sex and self-identity, mouthing cliches twisted in the Allen style to the wry, the incisive, and the sublimely ridiculous. They move in together, but he soon becomes so insecure about their affair that he pounces on her every move, interpreting these acts as rejection and disaffection. Eventually their own mutual uncertainty splits them apart and they are left to their careers and to trying again with other partners.

The simplicity of the seemingly impromptu story, set largely in Allen's beloved New York City, is part of ANNIE HALL's undeniable charm, along with Allen's flashbacks to childhood (with side-splitting Jonathan Munk as a young Woody) and constant asides to the camera, a device that sometimes has to carry the laughs. Allen moves freely through the flashbacks as a grown man, commenting on various scenes in a technique borrowed from Bergman's WILD STRAWBERRIES. The quip quotient is high (observing that Keaton habitually smokes a joint before they make love, Allen cracks, "Why don't you take sodium pentothal? Then you could sleep through the whole thing!") and Roberts is highly effective as the crass, materialistic sidekick.

ANOTHER DAY IN PARADISE [DVD]

1998 101m   c   Drama/Crime/Action   ★★★½
Chinese Bookie Pictures/Larry Clark Film   (U.S.)   R

James Woods *(Mel)*, Melanie Griffith *(Sid)*, Vincent Kartheiser *(Bobbie)*, Natasha Gregson Wagner *(Rosie)*, James Otis *(Reverend)*, Branden Williams *(Danny)*, Brent Briscoe *(Clem)*, Peter Sarsgaard *(Ty)*, Paul Hipp *(Richard Johnson)*, Kim Flowers *(Bonnie Johnson)*

p, Stephen Chin, Larry Clark, James Woods; d, Larry Clark; w, Christopher Landon, Stephen Chin (based on the book by Eddie Little); ph, Eric Edwards; ed, Luis Colina; prod d, Aaron Osborne; art d, Erin Cochran; fx, Darryl Pritchett; cos, Kathryn Morrison

Sex, drugs, and funky '70s rock 'n' roll drive this brutally beguiling walk on the wild side, directed by photographer turned director Larry Clark (KIDS) and based on a novel by ex-con Eddie Little.

Seductive guttersnipes Bobbie and Rosie (Vincent Kartheiser, Natasha Gregson Wagner) live for each other and heroin; they support the serious habits they're developing through inept petty thievery. Stylish Mel and Sid (James Woods, Melanie Griffith) are lifelong junkies and professional operators: stealing, selling dope, running scams... you name it, they've gotten away with it. Fate brings the couples together into a makeshift, dysfunctional family: Bobbie and Rosie, the products of violent, fractured homes, secretly long for benevolent parents. Sid sees in them the children she can't have, and Mel seems willing to play papa for her sake. The quartet tools around in Mel's big-ass Cadillac El Dorado, doping and stealing and sneering at the jerks working for chump change, until the bubble bursts in the inevitable bloody debacle.

There's more than a little DRUGSTORE COWBOY vibe here, but what makes Clark's picture more than just another exploitative slice of sleaze is his phenomenal cast. The youngsters are compelling, though a lot of that is sheer youth and physical vulnerability. But Griffith and Woods are mesmerizing as the older couple, all outlaw glamour and lowlife sophistication: you can see right through to the physical and moral rot underneath, but at the same time you can see how two kids who aren't as street-smart as they think they are would be dazzled. The same pornographic prurience that permeates Clark's KIDS (and his photography) is sporadically in evidence here, but the strength of Griffith and Woods' performances shifts the focus off the youngsters onto the complex web of relationships that bind the quartet together. The film's focus is small and mean, but it's dazzling nonetheless.

ANOTHER WOMAN
1988 84m c Drama ★★★½
Jack Rollins-Charles H. Joffe (U.S.) PG

Gena Rowlands *(Marion Post)*, Mia Farrow *(Hope)*, Ian Holm *(Ken Post)*, Blythe Danner *(Lydia)*, Gene Hackman *(Larry)*, Betty Buckley *(Kathy)*, Martha Plimpton *(Laura Post)*, John Houseman *(Marion's Dad)*, Sandy Dennis *(Claire)*, David Ogden Stiers *(Young Marion's Dad)*

p, Robert Greenhut; d, Woody Allen; w, Woody Allen; ph, Sven Nykvist (Duart color); ed, Susan E. Morse; prod d, Santo Loquasto; cos, Jeffrey Kurland

ANOTHER WOMAN stars Gena Rowlands as an aging professor who realizes she has led an unemotional life and must look into the past in order to prepare herself for the future. She is married to a physician (Holm), has a close relationship with her stepdaughter (Plimpton), avoids her brother (Yulin), and fears the loss of her ailing father (Houseman). When she overhears a pregnant psychiatric patient's therapy session, Marion becomes obsessed with knowing all about the woman (Farrow), who reminds her of her younger self.

Full of the hand-wringing and self-consciously intellectual exchanges that characterize Allen's Bergmanesque outings, ANOTHER WOMAN benefits from a superb ensemble cast. An especially endearing final performance comes from the frail and obviously ailing Houseman, who was to die very shortly after the film's release. Nykvist's photography is impeccable, as is Loquasto's spare production design.

ANTHONY ADVERSE
1936 139m bw Historical/Romance ★★
Warner Bros. (U.S.)

Fredric March *(Anthony Adverse)*, Olivia de Havilland *(Angela Guessippi)*, Edmund Gwenn *(John Bonnyfeather)*, Claude Rains *(Don Luis)*, Anita Louise *(Maria)*, Louis Hayward *(Denis Moore)*, Gale Sondergaard *(Faith Paleologus)*, Steffi Duna *(Neleta)*, Henry O'Neill *(Father Xavier)*, Billy Mauch *(Anthony as a Child)*

p, Henry Blanke; d, Mervyn LeRoy; w, Sheridan Gibney (based on the novel by Hervey Allen); ph, Tony Gaudio; ed, Ralph Dawson; m, Erich Wolfgang Korngold; art d, Anton Grot; cos, Milo Anderson

AAN Best Picture; AA Best Supporting Actress: Gale Sondergaard; *AA Best Cinematography:* Gaetano Gaudio; *AA Best Film Editing:* Ralph Dawson; *AA Best Score:* Warner Bros Studio Music Department, Leo Forbstein (Dept. Head); *AAN Best Interior Decoration:* Anton Grot (Art Direction); *AAN Best Assistant Director:* William Cannon

This lavish but overlong film remains true to the 1200-page bestseller on which it is based, though judging the result one wonders to what extent this is admirable. Popular and acclaimed in its day, and technically highly skilled, ANTHONY ADVERSE substitutes historical pageantry for drama and melodramatic flourish for characterization whenever it gets the chance.

March plays the title role, an illegitimate child whose father (Hayward) is killed in a duel and who is raised in a convent by a gentle priest (O'Neill). Adopted by a kindly Scottish trader (Gwenn), the growing boy soon finds romance with a girl (de Havilland) who aspires to sing grand opera. Although they marry, the couple are separated when a crucial note is blown away by a gust of wind. Anthony goes crazy with despair and jungle fever for several years while managing his stepfather's questionable African interests, and when he returns to Europe he finds his stepfather dead, his wife a diva linked romantically to Napoleon (Rollo Lloyd), and his inheritance jeopardized by the wicked Don Luis (Rains), who killed his real father back when. The wrap-up includes chicanery, a duel, and a surprise from de Havilland.

This massive but choppy historical soaper, aiming to both jerk tears and swash buckles, now seems inferior to other similar but more modest films. March has his moments, but seems more concerned with appearing young and stalwart than with giving the role the tongue-in-cheek dash it so desperately needs. De Havilland is mere decoration, and it is up to several of the supporting players, particularly Rains and Sondergaard (as a scheming, ambitious housekeeper), to serve as energetic foils to the film's rampant displays of virtue. Grot's sets and Gaudio's cinematography add definite sweep, and Korngold's score is both majestic and melancholic, befitting the romantic tragedy of star-crossed lovers this film would dearly like to be.

ANTONIA'S LINE
(ANTONIA)
1995 104m c Drama/Fantasy ★★
Antonia's Line International/Bergen Film/
Prime Time/Bard Entertainment/NPS Televisie
(Netherlands/Belgium/U.K.)

Willeke van Ammelrooy *(Antonia)*, Els Dottermans *(Danielle)*, Dora van der Groen *(Allegonde)*, Veerle van Overloop *(Therese)*, Jan Decleir *(Bas)*, Mil Seghers *(Crooked Finger)*, Marina de Graaf *(DeeDee)*, Jakob Beks *(Farmer Daan)*, Elsie de Brauw *(Lara)*, Thyrza Ravesteijn *(Sarah)*

p, Hans de Weers; d, Marleen Gorris; w, Marleen Gorris; ph, Willy Stassen; ed, Michiel Reichwein, Wim Louwrier; m, Ilona Sekacz; art d, Harry Ammerlaan; fx, Steven van Couwelaar, Olivier de Laveleye; cos, Jany Temime

AA Best Foreign Language Film

ANTONIA'S LINE is a multigenerational chronicle that won the 1996 Academy Award for Best Foreign Language Film.

Elderly Antonia (Willeke van Ammelrooy) decides one morning that this will be the day of her death, and surveys her life. After WW II, she returns to her rural hometown with her young daughter Danielle (Els Dottermans) to take over the family farm. As time goes by, Antonia's farm shelters assorted misfits and outcasts, including two refugees from a neighboring farm run by the ignorant bully Daan (Jakob Beks) and his sons. Antonia has a better relationship with another neighbor, Farmer Bas (Jan Decleir), though she rejects his proposal of marriage. Danielle goes to art school, then returns to the farm to paint. She decides that she wants a child, though not a husband, and gives birth to a daughter, Therese (Veerle van Overloop). Therese is educated at home by the misanthropic genius Crooked Finger (Mil Seghers), and subsequently goes to college. Following some unhappy relationships, she returns to the farm and has a child. On the day of Antonia's death, Therese's daughter, Sarah (Thyrza Ravesteijn), has a vision of a banquet shared by all the past and present residents of the farm.

A succession of events does not a plot make, as ANTONIA'S LINE proves. The film plays like the heavily edited highlights of an eight-hour miniseries, with any gaps filled in by portentous and occasionally inane narration. Characters drift in and out of the film with nothing more substantial than a funny name and a peculiar personality trait. Writer-director Marlene Gorris is less strident here than in her controversial A QUESTION OF SILENCE (1982), although her feminist philosophy at times seems simplistic.

ANTONIO DAS MORTES
(O DRAGAO DA MALADE CONTRA O SANTO GUERREIRO)
1969 100m c Action ★★★½
Grove (Brazil)

Mauricio do Valle *(Antonio das Mortes)*, Odete Lara *(Laura)*, Othon Bastos *(Teacher)*, Hugo Carvana *(Police Chief)*, Jofre Soares *(Colonel)*, Rosa Maria Penna *(Saint)*

p, Claude-Antoine Mapa; d, Glauber Rocha; w, Glauber Rocha; ph, Affonso Beato (Eastmancolor); m, Marlos Nobre

Powerful political film, with mercenary do Valle tracking down insurgents, killing all the members of one band and dispatching the leader in hand-to-hand combat in a wild bullet-ridden finale, only to discover his real sympathies are with the rebels. Clearly indebted to the directors of France's New Wave, Rocha would make greater films; nevertheless, ANTONIO DAS MORTES survives as a landmark in Brazil's emergent *Cinema Novo* by one of its finest filmmakers. Brazil's lush vegetation, mountains, and plains are beautifully photographed in this polemic, which lionizes the likes of revolutionary Che Guevara while indicting the cruel and impersonal landlords of a South American dictatorship.

ANTWONE FISHER 📀
2002 117m c Drama/Biography ★★★
Mundy Lane Productions/Todd Black Productions PG-13 (U.S.)

Derek Luke (*Antwone Fisher*), Joy Bryant (*Cheryl*), Denzel Washington (*Jerome Davenport*), Salli Richardson (*Berta*), Earl Billings (*James*), Kevin Connolly (*Slim*), Viola Davis (*Eva*), Rainoldo Gooding (*Grayson*), Novella Nelson (*Mrs. Tate*), James Brolin (*Captain*)

p, Todd Black, Randa Haines, Denzel Washington; d, Denzel Washington; w, Antwone Fisher; ph, Philippe Rousselot; ed, Conrad Buff; m, Mychael Danna; prod d, Nelson Coates; art d, David Lazan; fx, Marvin Felton, David Poole; cos, Sharen Davis

Doesn't the phrase "inspired by a true story" seem rather awkward when applied to a movie written by the person whose true story it is? If Erin Brockovich had scripted the movie version of her life, would *she* have called it "Erin Brockovich"? It's hard not to wonder such things while watching Denzel Washington's directing debut—a film of the kind routinely described as "inspirational"—which was indeed written by the titular Antwone Fisher and drawn directly from his personal experiences.

San Diego-based Navy seaman Fisher (well played by newcomer Derek Luke) is a 25-year-old swabbie with an anger management problem that's dramatized in a brief and highly effective explosion of unmotivated violence. Since this isn't the first time the intelligent, artistic Fisher has flown off the handle in a frightening way, would-be compassionate captain (James Brolin) sends him to base psychiatrist Jerome Davenport (Washington). After the obligatory sparring, Fisher gets in touch with the roots of his anger, which lie in a hellish, inner-city childhood in foster care for which the word "Dickensian" is barely adequate. Fisher is eventually reunited with the family he never knew, falls in love with beautiful Navy brat Cheryl (Joy Bryant), and inspires Dr. Davenport to reexamine empty areas in his own life.

On a purely technical level, the film is unimpeachable. The performances are uniformly excellent, and first-time director Washington keeps things moving with admirable efficiency. But there's a vaguely self-congratulatory tone to the screenplay that's a bit off-putting. Two separate speeches about what a great guy Fisher turned out to be despite the odds seem excessive, and there are several other instances of manipulative sentimentality that a more objective screenwriter would almost certainly have deep-sixed.

ANTZ 📀
1998 83m c Animated/Children's/Fantasy ★★★
Pacific Data Images/DreamWorks Pictures (U.S.) PG

VOICES OF: Woody Allen (*Z-4195*), Dan Aykroyd (*Chip*), Anne Bancroft (*Queen*), Jane Curtin (*Muffy*), Danny Glover (*Barbatus*), Gene Hackman (*General Mandible*), Jennifer Lopez (*Azteca*), Sylvester Stallone (*Weaver*), Christopher Walken (*Cutter*), John Mahoney (*Drunk Scout*)

p, Brad Lewis, Aron Warner, Patty Wooton; d, Eric Darnell, Tim Johnson; w, Todd Alcott, Chris Weitz, Paul Weitz; ed, Stan Webb; m, Harry Gregson-Williams, John Powell; prod d, John Bell; art d, Kendal Cronkhite; fx, Ken Bielenberg; anim, Rex Grignon, Raman Hui

And you thought ants liked being bustling little collectivists.

Not six-legged schlemiel Z (voiced by Woody Allen), a worker ant who dreams of bigger things, even as his shrink counsels him to revel in his natural insignificance. Z's life changes the night haughty Princess Bala (Sharon Stone) sneaks into the worker ants' bar to have some fun, and finds that nonconformist Z cuts quite a rug. In hopes of seeing her again, Z switches places with childhood pal Weaver (Sylvester Stallone), a soldier ant, thinking to catch Bala's attention as she reviews the ant troops. Imagine Z's surprise when instead he finds himself shipped off to battle against a termite colony, and his greater surprise when, after happenstance leaves him the sole survivor of the brutal rout, he's suddenly hailed as a war hero. More wacky happenstance later, Z accidentally kidnaps Bala and stumbles onto an evil plot by General Mandible (Gene Hackman) to betray the Queen (Anne Bancroft), kill the "weak" worker ants, and start a new colony under his own rule.

By any standard, the film is a remarkable technical achievement. The foam-rubbery, computer-generated ants are kind of creepy, which should be no deterrent to kids who live for worms 'n' dirt desserts and goop. The high-profile voice cast—which includes Jennifer Lopez, Danny Glover, Dan Aykroyd, Jane Curtin, John Mahoney, and Christopher Walken—is clearly a sop to the adults who find themselves doing kid-flick duty. Adults are also more likely to snicker at jokes about drunken wasps and to recognize the Objectivist screed (the will of a great man—even such unlikely a great man as Woody Allen-the-ant—can elevate the masses) lurking beneath the friendly surface.

ANY GIVEN SUNDAY 📀
1999 165m c Sports/Drama ★★★½
Illusion Entertainment Group/Ixtlan/ R
Donner's Company (U.S.)

Al Pacino (*Tony D'Amato*), Dennis Quaid (*Jack "Cap" Rooney*), Cameron Diaz (*Christina Pagniacci*), Jamie Foxx (*Willie Beamen*), Lawrence Taylor (*Luther "Shark" Lavay*), Lauren Holly (*Cindy Rooney*), James Woods (*Dr. Harvey Mandrake*), Charlton Heston (*Commissioner*), Jim Brown (*Montezuma Monroe*), Elizabeth Berkley (*Mandy*)

p, Lauren Shuler Donner, Clayton Townsend, Dan Halsted; d, Oliver Stone; w, John Logan, Oliver Stone; ph, Salvatore Totino; ed, Thomas J. Nordberg, Michael Mees, Keith Salmon; prod d, Victor Kempster; art d, Stella Vaccaro; cos, Mary Zophres

An extremely loud, often brutally realistic meditation on the power of money and testosterone in pre-millenial America. Oliver Stone looks at contemporary pro football with all the cynicism of NORTH DALLAS FORTY, plus the technical effects he pioneered in NATURAL BORN KILLERS: mismatched film stocks, faster-than-the-eye cutting, pulverizing sound and music. Stone isn't grinding an axe as loudly as usual here, but he remains one of our least subtle filmmakers. As entertaining as much of the movie undeniably is, the story is slight for its length—most astute viewers will have predicted the ROCKY-esque fate of Stone's fictional Miami Sharks before the appearance of the Warner Brothers logo—and, as usual, Stone's characters are somewhere between archetypes and cliches. Fortunately, by way of compensation, Stone handles his huge ensemble cast extremely well, getting terrific old-fashioned movie star turns from Al Pacino as a burnt-out head coach, Jim Brown as his philosophical assistant, Cameron Diaz as the ruthlessly bottom-line-oriented team owner, Ann-Margret as her alcoholic mother, Jamie Foxx as a quarterback who hits the big time too fast, and Matthew Modine and James Woods as team doctors with radically different medical ethics. Stone also gets some great work around the edges from Lauren Holly, who's amazing as a sports wife from hell, and from SHOWGIRLS laugh riot Elizabeth Berkely, who's charming (and all but unrecognizable) as a hooker/groupie. Former New York Giants star Lawrence Taylor, however, nearly steals the picture in the small but pivotal role of a blocker putting his life, literally, on the line.

ANYTHING ELSE

2003 96m c Romance/Comedy *DVD* ★★½
Gravier Productions/Perdido Productions/ R
Canal +/DreamWorks SKG/
Granada Film Productions
(U.S./France/U.K./Netherlands)

Jason Biggs *(Jerry Falk)*, Christina Ricci *(Amanda)*, Woody Allen *(David Dobel)*, Danny DeVito *(Harvey)*, Stockard Channing *(Paula)*, Fisher Stevens *(Manager)*, David Conrad *(Dr. Reed)*, Jimmy Fallon *(Bob)*, Kadee Strickland *(Brooke)*, Adrian Grenier *(Ray Polito)*

p, Letty Aronson; d, Woody Allen; w, Woody Allen; ph, Darius Khondji; ed, Alisa Lepselter; prod d, Santo Loquasto; art d, Tom Warren; fx, John Ottesen, Ronald Ottesen; cos, Laura Jean Shannon

Though strikingly similar to ANNIE HALL, Woody Allen's tale of a young man hobbled by neuroses has its share of funny moments, and once again Allen shows off New York City to great advantage.

Divorced 21-year-old comedy writer Jerry Falk (Jason Biggs) has spent his brief adult life in and out of therapy, trying to cope with his fear of sleeping alone and his inability to say goodbye; the latter explains why he's his manager's (Danny DeVito) only client and tolerates his aspiring-actress girlfriend Amanda's (Christina Ricci) insufferable behavior. At first, their affair was torrid, but now that they're living together their mutual passion has dwindled; they haven't had sex in six months and she hyperventilates at his touch. Amanda's eccentric mother (Stockard Channing), a cabaret singer with food issues, has moved in with them and encourages Jerry to sleep with other women. Jerry escapes by taking long walks in Central Park with fellow comedy writer David Dobel (Allen), during which the older man rants on a range of pet topics. Despite his own patent neuroses, David does his best to steer Jerry in the direction of self-sufficiency.

DeVito, whose performance verges on painful caricature, nearly sinks the picture, but Ricci is adorable and delivers Allen's sharp dialogue with real flair. Biggs—best-known primarily for his recurring role in the AMERICAN PIE trilogy—shows unexpected intelligence in the kind of role that Allen used to write for himself; Allen in turn deserves credit for not casting himself as Ricci's love interest. In the end, however, the most original thing about the film was its marketing campaign, which aggressively downplayed Allen's name in a bid to attract a younger audience.

APACHE

1954 91m c Western *DVD* ★★★
Hecht/Lancaster (U.S.)

Burt Lancaster *(Massai)*, Jean Peters *(Nalinle)*, John McIntire *(Al Sieber)*, Charles Bronson, billed as Charles Buchinsky *(Hondo)*,

John Dehner *(Weddle)*, Paul Guilfoyle *(Santos)*, Ian MacDonald *(Glagg)*, Walter Sande *(Lt. Col. Beck)*, Morris Ankrum *(Dawson)*, Monte Blue *(Geronimo)*

p, Harold Hecht; d, Robert Aldrich; w, James R. Webb (based on the novel *Bronco Apache* by Paul I. Wellman); ph, Ernest Laszlo (Technicolor); ed, Alan Crosland Jr.; m, David Raksin; art d, Nicolai Remisoff

A brutal western in which the acrobatic Lancaster, as one of Geronimo's chiefs, refuses to surrender, conducting a one-man war against the cavalry with knife, arrow, and gun. Swarms of troopers attempt to kill him, led by white scout McIntire, who is sympathetic to the plight of the Native Americans. Lancaster, who co-produced, is in his typically over-earnest mode here, all flashing, gnashing teeth and sweaty armpits. The perspective is notable for its links to several 1950s Westerns beginning with BROKEN ARROW (1950), which revived the social concern for the American Indian which late silent film had explored. Peters is a sensuous and attractive if somewhat glamourized mate for Lancaster, daughter of an Indian (Guilfoyle) who sells out the renegade. Silent screen matinee idol Blue also appears, but is not entirely convincing as Geronimo. UA compelled Lancaster to change the ending of this film; he wanted his hero to be shot to death by troopers after he had made peace and settled down to farm the land. Instead, he is exonerated, despite slaying a dozen men, because he has conducted a legitimate war and is therefore entitled to the provisions of peace settlements accorded warring nations. The end result is suitably lively but compromised cinema.

APARAJITO

1956 113m bw Drama *DVD* ★★★★
Epic (India)

Pinaki Sen Gupta *(Apu as a boy)*, Smaran Ghosal *(Apu as an adolescent)*, Karuna Banerji *(Mother)*, Kanu Banerji *(Father)*, Ramani Sen Gupta *(Old Uncle)*, Charu Ghosh *(Nanda Babu)*, Subodh Ganguly *(Headmaster)*, Kali Charan Ray *(Press Proprietor)*, Santi Gupta *(Landlord's Wife)*, K.S. Pandey *(Pandey)*

p, Satyajit Ray; d, Satyajit Ray; w, Satyajit Ray (based on the novel *Pather Panchali* by Bibhutibhusan Bandapadhaya); ph, Subrata Mitra; ed, Dulal Dutta; m, Ravi Shankar; art d, Bansi Chandragupta

The young Apu (Gupta) and his newly widowed mother (Banerji) struggle for existence in a small Indian town. Resisting a life in the priesthood, the boy persuades his mother to send him to school. Having done well in his studies over the years, as a young adult (now played by Ghosal) Apu wins a scholarship to the university in Calcutta. Engulfed in city life and the demands of his schoolwork, Apu gradually forgets about his mother. APARAJITO is the second chapter in THE APU TRILOGY (preceded by PATHER PANCHALI and followed by THE WORLD OF APU), among the finest and certainly the most famous group of films to come out of India, in which director Satyajit Ray, a painter and commercial artist, devoted his time, money, and passion to a personal project that many considered impossible, the cinematic adaptation of the popular Bengali novel *Pather Panchali*. Although very slow-moving and not as involving as the first and third episodes of Apu's fortunes, APARAJITO similarly shows the influence of Italian neorealism and remains a thoughtful, colorful, and poetic story of life in India. The beautiful black-and-white photography is accented by Shankar's traditional sitar score. Winner of the Golden Lion at the 1957 Venice Film Festival.

APARTMENT, THE

1960 125m bw Comedy/Drama   **DVD**   ★★★★★
UA   (U.S.)

Jack Lemmon *(C.C. Baxter)*, Shirley MacLaine *(Fran Kubelik)*, Fred MacMurray *(J.D. Sheldrake)*, Ray Walston *(Mr. Dobisch)*, David Lewis *(Mr. Kirkeby)*, Jack Kruschen *(Dr. Dreyfuss)*, Joan Shawlee *(Sylvia)*, Edie Adams *(Miss Olsen)*, Hope Holiday *(Margie MacDougall)*, Johnny Seven *(Karl Matuschka)*

p, Billy Wilder; d, Billy Wilder; w, Billy Wilder, I.A.L. Diamond; ph, Joseph La Shelle (Panavision); ed, Daniel Mandell; m, Adolph Deutsch; art d, Alexander Trauner

AA Best Picture; AAN Best Actor: Jack Lemmon; *AAN Best Actress:* Shirley MacLaine; *AAN Best Supporting Actor:* Jack Kruschen; *AAN Best Director:* Billy Wilder; *AA Best Original Story and Screenplay:* Billy Wilder, I.A.L. Diamond; *AAN Best B/W Cinematography:* Joseph LaShelle; *AA Best Film Editing:* Daniel Mandell; *AA Best Art Direction-Set Decoration (B/W):* Alexander Trauner, Edward G. Boyle; *AAN Best Sound:* Gordon E. Sawyer

Classic Billy Wilder comedy-drama about a put-upon insurance clerk (Lemmon) who rises through the ranks by loaning out his apartment as a trysting-place for his philandering superiors. When one of them (Fred MacMurray) callously casts off his elevator girl-mistress (Shirley MacLaine), causing her to attempt suicide, the clerk lovingly nurses her back to health.

A barbed and occasionally brutal comedy with few illusions about personal or corporate ethics, THE APARTMENT captured one of the singular images of early '60s America; the immense office (designed by Alexander Trauner) in which the human workers, seated behind endless, perfectly aligned rows of identical desks, appear completely subordinate to the dehumanizing mechanisms of conformity and efficiency.

Wilder had promised Lemmon "a plum" in exchange for committing to a drag role in SOME LIKE IT HOT, and this was undeniably it. The actor gives one of the finest performances of his career and is perfectly paired with MacLaine, whose "small business" as the forlorn, neurotic elevator operator is a joy to behold. MacMurray made a great heel, but his fan mail was so opposed to these kinds of portrayals that he comfortably stayed in the Disney camp. Fans of Wilder's character repertory will recognize mainstay Joan Shawlee as the office amazon, hilariously dancing on top of a desk at the Christmas party. Wilder shot the film right up to its finish without knowing the ending, handing his stars wet mimeographed script pages about 20 minutes before the final scenes. Quick readers, Lemmon and MacLaine then nailed it in one take. This film was later adapted into the smash Broadway musical *Promises, Promises*.

APOCALYPSE NOW

1979 153m c War   **DVD**   ★★★★
Zoetrope Studios   (U.S.)   R

Marlon Brando *(Col. Kurtz)*, Robert Duvall *(Lt. Col. Kilgore)*, Martin Sheen *(Capt. Willard)*, Frederic Forrest *(Chef)*, Albert Hall *(Chief)*, Sam Bottoms *(Lance)*, Laurence Fishburne, billed as Larry Fishburne *(Clean)*, Dennis Hopper *(Photojournalist)*, Harrison Ford *(Colonel)*, Scott Glenn *(Civilian)*

p, Francis Ford Coppola; d, Francis Ford Coppola; w, Michael Herr (narration), John Milius, Francis Ford Coppola; ph, Vittorio Storaro (Technovision, Technicolor); ed, Richard Marks; m, Carmine Coppola, Francis Ford Coppola; prod d, Dean Tavoularis; art d, Angelo Graham; fx, Joseph Lombardi, A.D. Flowers; chor, John Calvert (Playmate Show); cos, Charles James

AAN Best Picture; AAN Best Supporting Actor: Robert Duvall; *AAN Best Director:* Francis Coppola; *AAN Best Adapted Screenplay:* John Milius, Francis Coppola; *AA Best Cinematography:* Vittorio Storaro; *AAN Best Film Editing:* Richard Marks, Walter Murch, Gerald B. Greenberg, Lisa Fruchtman; *AAN Best Art Direction-Set Decoration:* Dean Tavoularis, Angelo Graham, George R. Nelson; *AA Best Sound:* Walter Murch, Mark Berger, Richard Beggs, Nat Boxer

Francis Ford Coppola's notorious and controversial contribution to the Vietnam movie subgenre remains, despite its flaws, one of the most complex and unforgettable war movies ever made. With a plot structure inspired by Joseph Conrad's *Heart of Darkness*, APOCALYPSE NOW follows Willard (Martin Sheen), a cold and amoral Army captain, as he journeys upriver into Cambodia to assassinate Col. Kurtz (Marlon Brando), a renegade Green Beret who has broken from the American military and set himself up as a god among a tribe of Montagnard warriors, using them to wage his own private war. What follows is a hallucinatory look at the madness of the American involvement in Vietnam.

More than five years in the making, APOCALYPSE NOW became a cause celebre even before it opened. As documented by numerous press accounts and the book *Notes*, a collection of journal entries written by Coppola's wife, Eleanor, the filming in the Philippines was hellish, disaster-plagued, and decadent, beginning with a $12 million budget and going over $31 million before the 238-day shooting schedule ended, with Coppola's own money making up the difference. Eleanor Coppola later used her journals, together with documentary footage shot during the production, as the basis of 1991's HEARTS OF DARKNESS, a fascinating account of the making of the film.

APOCALYPSE NOW REDUX

2001 202m c War   **DVD**   ★★★★
Zoetrope Studios   (U.S.)   R

Marlon Brando *(Col. Watler E. Kurtz)*, Robert Duvall *(Lt. Col. Bill Kilgore)*, Martin Sheen *(Capt. Benjamin L. Willard)*, Frederic Forrest *(Chef Hicks)*, Albert Hall *(Chief Phillips)*, Sam Bottoms *(Lance B. Johnson)*, Laurence Fishburne, billed as Larry Fishburne *(Clean)*, Dennis Hopper *(Photojournalist)*, Harrison Ford *(Colonel Lucas)*, Scott Glenn *(Captain Richard Colby)*

p, Kim Aubry; d, Francis Ford Coppola; w, Francis Ford Coppola, John Milius, Michael Herr (narration); ph, Vittorio Storaro; ed, Richard Marks (supervisor), Lisa Fruchtman, Gerald B. Greenberg, Walter Murch, Umberto Tosi; m, Carmine Coppola, Francis Ford Coppola; prod d, Dean Tavoularis; art d, Angelo Graham; fx, A.D. Flowers, Joseph Lombardi; chor, John Calvert (Playboy show); cos, Charles James

Some 20 years after Francis Ford Coppola's vision of the Vietnam War as Hell's Disneyland was first unveiled at the Cannes Film Festival as a "work in progress," the director found himself watching it on television and was startled to realize that the film now looked positively conventional. In March 2001, Coppola and editor/sound designer Walter Murch went back to the original dailies and spent six months remaking APOCALYPSE NOW in the editing room. They added entire sequences, lengthened others (adding 49 minutes to the 139-minute running time), and scrounged up unused music composed by Coppola's late father. More than a conventional re-release, REDUX is a rethinking of Coppola's hallucinatory masterpiece. And it's a mixed blessing, in some ways even richer and more atmospheric than the original version, in others attenuated and logy. Coppola retrieved a second sequence involving the Playboy Bunnies (Colleen Camp, Linda Eastman), more footage of Kurtz's (Marlon Brando) ramblings, and a sequence near the beginning of the trip in which Willard steals Lt. Colonel Kilgore's (Robert Duval) surfboard for Lance (Sam Bottoms). All this material adds depth without making the film feel longer. Ironically, the new version's greatest liability is the legendary sequence in which the crew encounter the inhabitants of a ghostly French plantation. As the war rages around them, the DeMarais family continues to play out a bizarre pantomime of civilized French country life in the middle of the burning, corpse-littered jungle. On the one hand, the sequence is a haunting respite from the carnage and strengthens some of the movie's themes. But it stops the journey into the heart of darkness in its tracks, and the music is unfortunately reminiscent of the synthesized tinkling common to soft-core European sex pictures.

APOLLO 13   DVD
1995 140m c   Drama/Historical   ★★★½
Imagine Entertainment   (U.S.)   PG

Tom Hanks (*Jim Lovell*), Bill Paxton (*Fred W. Haise*), Kevin Bacon (*John L. Swigart*), Gary Sinise (*Ken Mattingly*), Ed Harris (*Gene Kranz*), Kathleen Quinlan (*Marylin Lovell*), Mary Kate Schellhardt (*Barbara Lovell*), Emily Ann Lloyd (*Susan Lovell*), Miko Hughes (*Jeffrey Lovell*), Max Elliott Slade (*Jay Lovell*)

p, Brian Grazer; d, Ron Howard; w, William Broyles Jr., John Sayles (uncredited), Al Reinert (based on the book *Lost Moon* by James A. Lovell Jr. and Jeffrey Kluger); ph, Dean Cundey; ed, Dan Hanley, Michael Hill; m, James Horner; prod d, Michael Corenblith; art d, David J. Bomba, Bruce Allan Miller; fx, Matt Sweeney, Robert Legato, Digital Domain; cos, Rita Ryack

AAN Best Picture; AAN Best Supporting Actor: Ed Harris; *AAN Best Supporting Actress:* Kathleen Quinlan; *AAN Best Adapted Screenplay:* William Broyles Jr., Al Reinert; *AAN Best Art Direction-Set Decoration:* Michael Corenblith, Merideth Boswell; *AA Best Film Editing:* Mike Hill, Dan Hanley; *AAN Best Dramatic Score:* James Horner; *AA Best Sound:* Rick Dior, Steve Pederson, Scott Millan, David MacMillan; *AAN Best Visual Effects:* Robert Legato, Michael Kanfer, Leslie Ekker, Matt Sweeney

A boy's space adventure with an all-star cast, this blockbuster hit trades heavily on nostalgia for the glory years of the American space program. Paradoxically, it tells the story of 1970's ill-fated Apollo 13 mission, a failure by most standards. It was to be the third moon landing, but the ship malfunctioned in deep space, briefly recapturing the attention of a jaded public. For the better part of a tense week, it seemed that the crew of three— James A. Lovell, Jr. (Tom Hanks), Fred Haise, Jr. (Bill Paxton), and last-minute replacement John L. Swigert, Jr. (Kevin Bacon)—might not be coming back.

Viewers who have seen the eerily prescient MAROONED (1969) may get a sense of *deja vu*. But APOLLO 13 has all the advantages: top-notch special effects, including sequences filmed in a real zero-gravity simulator; attention to every detail, from the epic outer space vistas to the minutiae of life on board the crippled space vehicle; a cast that goes from really good to even better, including Gary Sinise as the unfortunate Ken Mattingly—who was bumped from the Apollo 13 crew at the 11th hour—and Ed Harris as flight director Gene Kranz, who headed up the massive effort to bring the boys home. Still, there's something oddly flat about the film. There's no hint of political or social context (unlike the flawed but fascinating THE RIGHT STUFF); it's all *Life* magazine cover shots, and director Ron Howard never digs beyond the surface. Like the real Apollo 13, it gets to the stars, but misses the moon.

APOSTLE, THE   DVD
1997 148m c   Drama   ★★★
Butchers Run Films/Good Machine   (U.S.)   PG-13

Robert Duvall (*Euliss "Sonny" Dewey—The Apostle E.F.*), Farrah Fawcett (*Jessie Dewey*), Miranda Richardson (*Toosie*), Billy Bob

Thornton (*Troublemaker*), June Carter Cash (*Mrs. Dewey Sr.*), Billy Joe Shaver (*Joe*), John Beasley (*Brother Blackwell*), Todd Allen (*Horace*), Walt Goggins, billed as Walter Goggins (*Sam*), Rick Dial (*Elmo*)

p, Rob Carliner; d, Robert Duvall; w, Robert Duvall; ph, Barry Markowitz; ed, Steve Mack; m, David Mansfield; prod d, Linda Burton; art d, Irfan Akdag; cos, Douglas Hall

AAN Best Actor: Robert Duvall

Robert Duvall wrote himself a great part, as an evangelical preacher, in THE APOSTLE, a heartfelt religious drama the actor also produced and directed. Despite imperfections, the film holds together well.

In New Boston, a rural town of Texas, "Sonny" Dewey (Duvall), a devout Pentecostal preacher, attacks the young minister, Horace (Todd Allen), who's been sleeping with Sonny's wife, Jessie (Farrah Fawcett), and has taken over his church. Sonny's act—braining Horace with a baseball bat—sends Horace into a coma and forces Sonny to leave town, change his name, and start a new life. Sonny heads for Louisiana, where, as E.F., he baptizes himself "the Apostle" to God. After preaching from town to town in small tent shows, E.F. requests to take charge of a congregation in Bayou Boutte. E.F. inspires the town by renovating a run-down church, with the help of a local radio station owner, Elmo (Rick Dial), and an admiring, though married, secretary, Toosie (Miranda Richardson).

It took Robert Duvall 13 years to bring THE APOSTLE to the screen, and his devotion shows in his work. With loving care, Duvall directs his own material with measured pacing and steady sensitivity. The excessive length of the film does not pose a problem, because Duvall uses every scene to develop the characters and situations. The most interesting character, of course, is Sonny, and it is Duvall's performance as this unusual minister that provides the highlight of the film (Duvall also gets excellent work from the others in the cast, including Farrah Fawcett, Miranda Richardson, and June Carter Cash). His attempt to understand—without cynically satirizing—the grassroots "holiness" church movement, the mass devotion to charismatic preachers, and the role of religion in society is more than admirable. For the most part, THE APOSTLE does justice portraying a major but often neglected area of American life.

APPLAUSE   DVD
1929 80m   bw Drama   ★★★★★
Paramount   (U.S.)

Helen Morgan (*Kitty Darling*), Joan Peers (*April Darling*), Fuller Mellish Jr. (*Hitch Nelson*), Jack Cameron (*Joe King*), Henry Wadsworth (*Tony*), Dorothy Cumming (*Mother Superior*)

p, Monta Bell; d, Rouben Mamoulian; w, Garrett Fort (based on the novel by Beth Brown); ph, George Folsey; ed, John Bassler

Morgan, the rage of Broadway musicals and nightclubs during the 1920s, is a fading burlesque singing star—she is shown to age on the stage as her born-in-a-trunk daughter grows up in a convent. The pathetic Morgan is being two-timed by a slippery boy friend. Moreover, she attempts to save her grown-up child from the clutches of fakes and ne'er-do-wells. Poignant though dated, this early talkie is rich in old burlesque backstage atmosphere and has many innovative techniques introduced by Mamoulian in his directorial debut. Then there is Morgan's singing, which is captivating and distinctive. She made her screen debut in this picture and would die of cirrhosis of the liver in 1941 at age 41.

APPRENTICESHIP OF DUDDY KRAVITZ, THE

1974 121m c   Comedy/Drama   ★★★★
International Cinemedia Centre   (Canada)   PG

Richard Dreyfuss *(Duddy)*, Micheline Lanctot *(Yvette)*, Jack Warden *(Max)*, Randy Quaid *(Virgil)*, Joseph Wiseman *(Uncle Benjy)*, Denholm Elliott *(Friar)*, Henry Ramer *(Dingleman)*, Joe Silver *(Farber)*, Zvee Scooler *(Grandfather)*, Robert Goodier *(Calder)*

p, John Kemeny; d, Ted Kotcheff; w, Mordecai Richler (based on his novel); ph, Brian West (Panavision, Bellevue-Pathe Color); ed, Thom Noble; m, Stanley Meyers; prod d, Anne Pritchard

AAN Best Adapted Screenplay: Mordecai Richler (Screenplay), Lionel Chetwynd (Adaptation)

Dreyfuss, a zealous Jewish boy determined to become rich in the world, loses all personal contact with women, friends, and family in his desperate business transactions. A strong, often very funny film that points out the potential emotional loss in the pressure to succeed put on the young by families. Not anti-Semitic, the film means to point out the corruption of youth and the power of greed in all young people, not the Jews alone, although the film did receive many negative reactions from Jewish groups, as did the book it is based on. Dreyfuss, who later went on to become one of the better-known faces of the 1970s, turns in an early great performance, making Duddy simultaneously loathsome, funny, and vulnerable. British actor Elliott masterfully portrays the washed-up British director Dreyfuss hires to make Bar Mitzvah movies for his relatives. In the most hilarious scene in the film, Dreyfuss's relatives are stunned to see that "artsy" filmmaker Elliott has juxtaposed Bar Mitzvah scenes with footage detailing African tribal dances celebrating the circumcision rights of the young warriors. Although there are quite a few holes in the script and Dreyfuss is undeniably grating, THE APPRENTICESHIP OF DUDDY KRAVITZ is a sad, funny, memorable film.

APT PUPIL   *DVD*
(UN ELEVE DOUE)
1998 111m c   Thriller/Drama   ★★★
Bad Hat Harry Productions/Phoenix Pictures   R
(U.S./France)

Ian McKellen *(Kurt Dussander)*, Brad Renfro *(Todd Bowden)*, Bruce Davison *(Richard Bowden)*, Elias Koteas *(Archie)*, David Schwimmer *(Edward French)*, Joshua Jackson *(Joey)*, Mickey Cottrell *(Sociology Teacher)*, Michael Reid MacKay *(Nightmare Victim)*, Ann Dowd *(Monica Bowden)*, James Karen *(Victor Bowden)*

p, Jane Hamsher, Don Murphy, Bryan Singer; d, Bryan Singer; w, Brandon Boyce (from the novella by Stephen King); ph, Newton Thomas Sigel; ed, John Ottman; m, John Ottman; prod d, Richard Hoover; art d, Kathleen M. McKernin; cos, Louise Mingenbach

A somber and deeply creepy adaptation of the Stephen King novella (from the 1982 *Different Seasons* collection, which also produced the source material for STAND BY ME and THE SHAWSHANK REDEMPTION) about an alienated teenager and the Nazi war criminal whose atrocity stories feed his twisted imagination.

Todd Bowden (Brad Renfro) discovers former concentration camp commander Kurt Dussander (Ian McKellen) living in his sleepy California home town under an assumed name. Morbidly fascinated by the Holocaust—its horror speaks to some deep-seated need for intense emotional experience beyond the pale of his cosseted suburban existence—Todd quietly assembles enough evidence to denounce the old man to Israeli war crimes investigators, then uses the threat of exposure as leverage to get what he really wants: Dussander's

firsthand account of his crimes against humanity. At first reluctant to disturb the demons of the past, Dussander slowly falls under the spell of his own worst nature. And so does Todd: Dussander and Todd are permanently, dangerously, bound together by their secret life.

Though the film is genuinely disquieting, it's undermined by the fact that neither Renfro nor the filmmakers seem to have any idea what's behind Todd's latent sociopathy: maybe this is a movie about the banality of evil, or maybe it's about the banality of the popular imagination. And the only hint of psychological subtext is a really disturbing one; Todd's relationship with Dussander is played out like a deeply pathological homoerotic seduction, with Todd in the role of an aggressive young hustler and Dussander playing the part of an apparently passive older man who's far more dangerous than he seems. Do director Bryan Singer and screenwriter Brandon Boyce really mean to suggest that the roots of genocide lie in homosexual desire?

ARIZONA DREAM

1991 142m c   Comedy/Drama   ★★★½
Union Generale Cinematographique/
Constellation/Hachette Premiere/
Arrowtooth Productions   (U.S.)

Johnny Depp *(Axel Blackmar)*, Jerry Lewis *(Leo Sweetie)*, Faye Dunaway *(Elaine Stalker)*, Lili Taylor *(Grace Stalker)*, Paulina Porizkova *(Millie)*, Vincent Gallo *(Paul Blackmar)*, Michael J. Pollard *(Fabian)*, Candyce Mason *(Blanche)*, Alexia Rena *(Angie)*, Polly Noonan *(Betty)*

p, Claudie Ossard, Cedomir Kolar, Yves Marmion; d, Emir Kusturica; w, Emir Kusturica, David Atkins; ph, Vilko Filac; ed, Andrlja Zasranovic; m, Goran Bregovic; prod d, Miljen Kljakovic; art d, Jan Pascale; fx, Gregory C. Landerer, Ken Estes, Max W. Anderson; cos, Jill M. Ohanneson

An offbeat and whimsical fantasy, ARIZONA DREAM is a lovingly crafted film with yet another quietly intense performance by Johnny Depp.

Axel (Depp) is a young man who works for the Department of Fish and Game, tagging fish in New York harbor while waxing philosophical about the honesty of fish and the importance of dreams. His reveries are disrupted when Cousin Paul (Vincent Gallo) is sent by Axel's Uncle Leo (Jerry Lewis), an incredibly wealthy Arizona car dealer, to bring Axel home for Leo's wedding to Millie (Paulina Porizkova), a woman half his age and subject to crying jags. Back in Arizona, Axel meets suicidal copper heiress Grace (Lili Taylor) and her flirty, flaky stepmother Elaine (Faye Dunaway). Axel becomes involved with Elaine and builds man-powered flying machines for her, but someone keeps smashing them. Accordion-wielding, turtle-nurturing Grace is his prime suspect, but it might be that giant halibut swimming in the Arizona breeze.

This independently produced 1992 film—the first in English by Bosnian-born director Emir Kusturica (TIME OF THE GYPSIES, UNDERGROUND)—has a dreamy, dazzling texture and non-linear story that often slides gracefully into surreal images. While the rambling plot and quirky dialogue sag in places, the richly detailed sets and deeply layered visuals are constantly entertaining; every moment is filled to bursting with things to look at and listen to. Characters and events often wobble unsteadily between parody and self-parody—a recurring Kusturica problem—but the actors embrace their roles with energy and intelligence. Lewis is only slightly awful, and he and Depp have a nice rapport; Dunaway gives a particularly juicy performance; and Taylor is simply amazing, seemingly able to transform herself physically for every role she plays.

ARMAGEDDON
1998 150m c Science Fiction/Action/Disaster ★★★½
Touchstone (U.S.) PG-13

Bruce Willis *(Harry S. Stamper)*, Billy Bob Thornton *(Dan Truman)*, Ben Affleck *(A.J. Frost)*, Liv Tyler *(Grace Stamper)*, Keith David *(General Kimsey)*, Chris Ellis *(Walter Clark)*, Jason Isaacs *(Ronald Quincy)*, Will Patton *(Charles "Chick" Chapple)*, Steve Buscemi *(Rockhound)*, Ken Campbell *(Max Lennert)*

p, Jerry Bruckheimer, Gale Anne Hurd, Michael Bay; d, Michael Bay; w, J.J. Abrams, Jonathan Hensleigh (adapted by Tony Gilroy and Shane Salerno from a story by Jonathan Hensleigh and Robert Pool); ph, John Schwartzman; ed, Mark Goldblatt, Chris Lebenzon, Glen Scantlebury; m, Trevor Rabin; prod d, Michael White; art d, Geoff Hubbard; fx, Pat McClung, Richard R. Hoover, John Frazier, Dream Quest Images, Richard Stutsman; cos, Michael Kaplan, Magali Guidasci

AAN Best Original Song: "I Don't Want to Miss a Thing"; Diane Warren; *AAN Best Sound:* Kevin O'Connell, Greg P. Russell, Keith A. Wester; *AAN Best Sound Effects Editing:* George Watters II; *AAN Best Visual Effects:* Richard R. Hoover, Pat McClung, John Frazier

Move over, science weenies and military wonks: saving the world from space junk is a job for Joe Six-Pack! We're informed by the voice of Moses (sorry, Charlton Heston), that 65,000,000 years ago an asteroid killed the dinosaurs, and *it could happen again.* Cut to the present: NASA engineer Dan Truman (Billy Bob Thornton) discovers that 18 days hence, the world's Filofaxes will be filled with "prepare to meet maker" reminders unless someone comes up with a viable asteroid-busting plan. His strategy—familiar to anyone who saw the identically themed DEEP IMPACT, which beat ARMAGEDDON into theaters by a matter of months—involves sending a crew to nuke the space invader, and he bullies third-generation wildcat oil driller Harry Stamper (Bruce Willis) into helping drill a hole into which to drop the nuclear device. Stamper, of course, will only work with his own motley crew of grungy, authority-hating misfits, including hunky rig-rat A.J. (Ben Affleck), the surrogate son who precipitated an Oedipal crisis by romancing Stamper's daughter Grace (Liv Tyler).

Sure, it's a glossy, supremely calculated, faux-populist thrill machine—you even get a sight-gag at Godzilla's expense for your ticket-buying dollars. Yes, it's a testosterone cocktail, but at least it doesn't leave you feeling as though you've been tumbled around in a gem polisher for two-and-a-half hours. Director Michael Bay has tamed the epileptic seizure-producing editing style that made THE ROCK such an eyeball-rattler. And if Bay makes the spectacle of crowds around the world preparing for their doom look like a series of epic Kodak moments, he also concocts a love scene built around A.J. slipping animal crackers into Grace's panties. "I wonder how many people are doing this same thing right now?" she muses sweetly. Now that's a question to get your teeth into.

AROUND THE WORLD IN 80 DAYS
1956 175m c Adventure ★★★★
Michael Todd (U.S.)

David Niven *(Phileas Fogg)*, Cantinflas *(Passepartout)*, Shirley MacLaine *(Princess Aouda)*, Robert Newton *(Inspector Fix)*, Charles Boyer *(Monsieur Casse)*, Joe E. Brown *(Station Master)*, Martine Carol *(Tourist)*, John Carradine *(Col. Proctor Stamp)*, Charles Coburn *(Clerk)*, Ronald Colman *(Railway Official)*

p, Michael Todd; d, Michael Anderson; w, S.J. Perelman, John Farrow, James Poe (based on the novel by Jules Verne); ph, Lionel Lindon (Todd-AO, Eastmancolor); ed, Gene Ruggiero, Paul Weatherwax; m, Victor Young; art d, James Sullivan, Ken Adam; fx, Lee Zavitz; chor, Paul Godkin; cos, Miles White

AA Best Picture; AAN Best Director: Michael Anderson; *AA Best Adapted Screenplay:* James Poe, John Farrow, S.J. Perelman; *AA Best Color Cinematography:* Lionel Lindon; *AA Best Film Editing:* Gene Ruggiero, Paul Weatherwax; *AA Best Score (Drama or Comedy):* Victor Young; *AAN Best Art Direction-Set Decoration (Color):* James W. Sullivan, Ken Adams, Ross J. Dowd; *AAN Best Costume Design (Color):* Miles White

David Niven is the punctual Phileas Fogg of the famous Jules Verne novel, who makes a bet with his fellow club members in London that he can encircle the globe within 80 days—this in 1872, when travel proceeded at a snail's pace. Fogg is accompanied by his bumbling valet (the great Mexican mimic Cantinflas) and along the way picks up a wandering princess (Shirley MacLaine), while being pursued by a London detective (Robert Newton) who believes the globetrotter has somehow robbed the Bank of England. Around these leads an army of 46 famous personalities of the day appear in bit parts. (This was the film that began the trend of stars appearing in cameo roles.) The star-spotting is fun, but so is the adventure, as Fogg journeys by train, ship, hot-air balloon, and elephant across Europe, India, Japan, the Pacific, the U.S., and the Atlantic in a race to win his bet. The film was shot in more than 100 natural settings and on 140 special sets. Everything about this big, beautiful movie smacks of authenticity, excitement, and massive showmanship. Winner of five Oscars: Best Picture, Best Screenplay, Best Cinematography, Best Score and Best Film Editing.

ARROWSMITH
1931 108m bw Drama ★★½
Goldwyn (U.S.)

Ronald Colman *(Dr. Martin Arrowsmith)*, Helen Hayes *(Leora)*, A.E. Anson *(Prof. Gottlieb)*, Richard Bennett *(Sondelius)*, Claude King *(Dr. Tubbs)*, Beulah Bondi *(Mrs. Tozer)*, Myrna Loy *(Joyce Lanyon)*, Russell Hopton *(Terry Wickett)*, DeWitt Jennings *(Mr. Tozer)*, John Qualen *(Henry Novak)*

p, Samuel Goldwyn; d, John Ford; w, Sidney Howard (based on the novel by Sinclair Lewis); ph, Ray June; ed, Hugh Bennett; m, Alfred Newman

AAN Best Picture; AAN Best Writing (Adaptation): Sidney Howard; *AAN Best Cinematography:* Ray June; *AAN Best Interior Decoration:* Richard Day (Art Direction)

Idealistic doctor Ronald Colman is obsessed with finding a cure for bubonic plague and wrestling with his moral conscience in this uneven Sidney Howard adaptation of Sinclair Lewis's novel. Hayes gets the big death scene, Loy gets the sexy seduction bits, John Ford gets the blame. Immensely popular with audiences and listed as one of the year's best films by *The New York Times*, ARROWSMITH was nominated as Best Picture but thankfully lost out to GRAND HOTEL.

ARSENIC AND OLD LACE
1944 118m bw Comedy ★★★½
Warner Bros. (U.S.)

Cary Grant *(Mortimer Brewster)*, Raymond Massey *(Jonathan Brewster)*, Priscilla Lane *(Elaine Harper)*, Josephine Hull *(Abby Brewster)*, Jean Adair *(Martha Brewster)*, Jack Carson *(O'Hara)*, Edward Everett Horton *(Mr. Witherspoon)*, Peter Lorre *(Dr. Einstein)*, James Gleason *(Lt. Rooney)*, John Alexander *("Teddy Roosevelt" Brewster)*

p, Frank Capra; d, Frank Capra; w, Julius J. Epstein, Philip G. Epstein (based on the play by Joseph Kesselring); ph, Sol Polito; ed, Daniel Mandell; m, Max Steiner; art d, Max Parker; fx, Byron Haskin, Robert Burks

Riotously funny film adaptation of the smash Broadway comedy (which ran for almost four years), coddled and coaxed into hilarious existence by master director Capra. The lovable Brewster sisters are spinster pillars of Brooklyn society, except for their secret penchant for poisoning old male callers with their homemade elderberry wine, to end the men's loneliness! Grant plays their frantic nephew who discovers their serial murders. The punch line that ended the play was cut by censors; the line in occurs after Grant learns he is free of hereditary insanity, and yells elatedly to his fiance: "Elaine! Did you hear? Do you understand? I'm a bastard!" Additional comedic lunacy results from macabre team of Lorre and Massey (the latter in a part made famous on Broadway by Boris Karloff) and Alexander as an eccentric uncle who believes he's Teddy Roosevelt.

ARSENIC was Capra's pet from beginning to end. He saw the play in New York and rushed backstage to buy the property, only to be told that Warner Brothers (his studio was Columbia) had optioned the film rights. He immediately went to the WB studio and had Jack Warner's own people prepare a modest budget, $400,000, for a hectic four-week shooting schedule ($100,000 for the star salary Grant demanded). Capra used only one interior set, that of the spooky old house belonging to the aunts, and an exterior set of the house next to an ancient cemetery. The lighting was low-keyed, from dusk to night, in keeping with the eerie atmosphere. Capra came in on schedule as usual and produced a romping, ripsnorting comedy classic.

ARTHUR   DVD
1981 117m c   Comedy   ★★★
Orion   (U.S.)   PG

Dudley Moore *(Arthur Bach)*, Liza Minnelli *(Linda Marolla)*, John Gielgud *(Hobson)*, Geraldine Fitzgerald *(Martha Bach)*, Jill Eikenberry *(Susan Johnson)*, Stephen Elliott *(Burt Johnson)*, Ted Ross *(Bitterman)*, Barney Martin *(Ralph Marolla)*, Thomas Barbour *(Stanford Bach)*, Anne DeSalvo *(Gloria)*

p, Robert Greenhut; d, Steve Gordon; w, Steve Gordon; ph, Fred Schuler (Technicolor); ed, Susan E. Morse; m, Burt Bacharach; prod d, Stephen Hendrickson; cos, Jane Greenwood

AAN Best Actor: Dudley Moore; *AA Best Supporting Actor:* John Gielgud; *AAN Best Original Screenplay:* Steve Gordon; *AA Best Original Song:* "Arthur's Theme (The Best That You Can Do)"; Burt Bacharach, Carole Bayer Sager, Christopher Cross, Peter Allen

Dudley Moore plays Arthur Bach, a dissolute playboy who would rather be drunk than face the reality of his great wealth and engagement to WASP witch Susan Johnson (Jill Eikenberry). Arthur, who is looked after by his kindly valet, Hobson (John Gielgud), soon falls for working girl Linda Marolla (Liza Minnelli), whom he prefers to his socialite fiancee. Susan, however, refuses to be shunned, and Arthur's father and grandmother threaten to cut off his inheritance if he continues to see working-class Linda. Moore is predictable as the spoiled scion of wealth, Minnelli is terrific as his candid sweetheart, but Gielgud's loyal yet sarcastic servant steals the film (he was rewarded with a supporting actor Oscar). The highly polished production is well paced and imaginatively directed, although the happy union of prince and pauper is harder to swallow in 1981 than it would have been in 1931, when cinematic escapism brought relief to depression-era audiences. A flat sequel, ARTHUR 2 ON THE ROCKS, was released in 1988.

AS GOOD AS IT GETS   DVD
1997 138m c   Romance/Comedy/Drama   ★★
Gracie Films   (U.S.)   PG-13

Jack Nicholson *(Melvin Udall)*, Helen Hunt *(Carol Connelly)*, Greg Kinnear *(Simon Bishop)*, Cuba Gooding Jr. *(Frank Sachs)*, Skeet

Ulrich *(Vincent)*, Shirley Knight *(Beverly)*, Jesse James *(Spencer Connelly)*, Yeardley Smith *(Jackie)*, Lupe Ontiveros *(Nora)*, Bibi Osterwald *(Neighbor Woman)*

p, James L. Brooks, Kristi Zea, Bridget Johnson; d, James L. Brooks; w, James L. Brooks, Mark Andrus (based on a story by Mark Andrus); ph, John Bailey; ed, Richard Marks; m, Hans Zimmer; prod d, Bill Brzeski; art d, Philip Toolin; fx, William Doane; cos, Molly Maginnis

AA Best Actor: Jack Nicholson; *AA Best Actress:* Helen Hunt; *AAN Best Picture; AAN Best Supporting Actor:* Greg Kinnear; *AAN Best Original Screenplay:* Mark Andrus, James L. Brooks; *AAN Best Original Musical or Comedy Score:* Hans Zimmer; *AAN Best Film Editing:* Richard Marks

This romantic comedy is impaired by generally uninspired jokes and a highly unlikely romance between mismatched leads.

Melvin (Jack Nicholson) is a superstitious bigot who writes romance novels for a living. He frequents a neighborhood cafe where he is served by Carol (Helen Hunt), an unmarried waitress with a sickly son (Jesse James). When he learns that Carol has quit her job to care for her little boy, Melvin pays for the child's medical care, ostensibly to get the mother back in the cafe waiting on him. Drafted to drive his neighbor, Simon (Greg Kinnear), a young homosexual artist, to Baltimore, where Simon intends to ask his parents for money, Melvin recruits Carol to accompany them. Despite having told Melvin earlier that she would never sleep with him, Carol agrees to a date with the jaded writer when the trio arrive in Baltimore. Their bumpy relationship goes from bad to worse due to Melvin's unabashed sarcasm.

In AS GOOD AS IT GETS, Helen Hunt registers as a visually lovely performer—the only thing that keeps her from becoming a major actress is a shortage of bite to complement the warmth and decency she conveys so well. Nicholson does as much as any actor could with a character who, in the real world, simply does not occur on the social level depicted here. Kinnear does the most he can—quite a lot—with his third-wheel character (one who probably belongs in a different movie).

The film's central problem: there is so little connective tissue between Melvin and Carol that viewers of AS GOOD AS IT GETS may find themselves startled, if not downright baffled, by the improbable romance that ultimately develops between them. Throughout, filmmaker James L. Brooks dotes on the psychological underpinnings of his characters. Inescapable conclusion: what '90s romantic comedy needs is a little less "unloading" and a little more Lubitsch.

ACE IN THE HOLE
1951 111m bw Drama   ★★★★
Paramount   (U.S.)

Kirk Douglas *(Charles Tatum—Chuck)*, Jan Sterling *(Lorraine Minosa)*, Robert Arthur *(Herbie Cook)*, Porter Hall *(Jacob Q. Boot)*, Frank Cady *(Mr. Federber)*, Richard Benedict *(Leo Minosa)*, Ray Teal *(Sheriff Gus Kretzer)*, Lewis Martin *(McCardle)*, John Berks *(Papa Minosa)*, Frances Dominguez *(Mama Minosa)*

p, Billy Wilder; d, Billy Wilder; w, Billy Wilder, Lesser Samuels, Walter Newman (from a story by Billy Wilder, Lesser Samuels, and Walter Newman); ph, Charles B. Lang Jr.; ed, Doane Harrison, Arthur Schmidt; m, Hugo Friedhofer; art d, Hal Pereira, Earl Hedrick; fx, Farciot Edouart; cos, Edith Head

AAN Best Story and Screenplay: Lesser Samuels, Walter Newman

Inspired by the real-life Floyd Collins cave-in disaster of the 1920s, ACE IN THE HOLE is a searing example of writer-director Billy Wilder at his most brilliantly misanthropic. An uncompromising portrait of human nature at its worst, the film was so far ahead of its time in its depiction of a media circus and the public's appetite for tragedy that it was a commercial disaster when first released, but now stands as one of the great American films of the 1950s.

After being fired from a number of big city newspapers, alcoholic reporter Chuck Tatum (Kirk Douglas) takes a job working for a paper in Albuquerque, New Mexico. On the way to cover a rattlesnake hunt, Tatum encounters a woman named Lorraine (Jan Sterling), who tells him that her husband Leo Minosa (Richard Benedict) got trapped in a mine cave-in while searching for some Indian treasure. Smelling a big story that will take him back to New York, Tatum goes into the cave and befriends Leo, then makes a deal with the corrupt local sheriff (Ray Teal) to boost his upcoming re-election campaign in exchange for exclusive rights to the story. Tatum and the sheriff coerce the contractor into prolonging the rescue operation to a week rather than 16 hours by drilling down from the top of the mountain instead of shoring up the walls and going in through the front. After a few days, a carnival atmosphere presides as TV, newsreel, and radio crews arrive, while thousands of tourists set up camp and trucks bring in amusement park rides.

The word used most often to describe Wilder in general, and ACE IN THE HOLE in particular, is "cynical," but a closer analysis reveals that this is really a misnomer. Wilder is actually a satirical moralist and a disillusioned romantic who knows that the world is an imperfect place and that everyone has the potential to be corrupt. The fact that the film was a box-office bomb is not surprising since the public was obviously not flattered by its depiction of them as gullible sensation-seekers who morbidly gather around a disaster for some all-American fun. Even today, the scenes of Tatum talking with the entombed Leo as dirt pours down on his face are harrowing to watch, primarily because Wilder broke his cardinal rule of sugar-coating messages with comic elements as an audience escape-valve. As a result, the film is as grim and pitiless as the relentless drill that pounds away at the mountain top.

ASHES AND DIAMONDS
(POPIOL I DIAMENT)
1958 105m bw Drama/War   ★★★
(Poland)

Zbigniew Cybulski *(Maciek)*, Ewa Krzyzewski *(Krystyna)*, Adam Pawlikowski *(Andrzej)*, Waclaw Zastrzezynski *(Szczuka)*, Bogumil Kobiela *(Drewnowski)*, Jan Ciecierski *(Porter)*, Stanislaw Milski *(Pienionzek)*, Artur Mlodnicki *(Kotowicz)*, Halina Kwiatkoska *(Mrs. Staniewicz)*, Ignacy Machowski *(Waga)*

d, Andrzej Wajda; w, Andrzej Wajda, Jerzy Andrzejewski (based on the novel by Jerzy Andrzejewski); ph, Jerzy Wojcik; ed, Halina Nawrocka; m, Aroclaw Radio Quintet; art d, Roman Mann; cos, Katarzyna Chodorowicz

After making A GENERATION (1954) and KANAL (1957), Andrzej Wajda completed his loose trilogy of WWII Polish Resistance films with the prize-winning ASHES AND DIAMONDS. Set at the beginning of the transitional period between occupation and socialization, when Communists and old-line partisans were unofficially at war, the movie tells the story of a young Polish veteran who is torn between the habit of violence and his better instincts.

ASHES AND DIAMONDS is not a movie that travels well. To Poles, it provided a rich and provocative portrait of their nation at a crucial and divisive turning point in its history, the transition from war, occupation, resistance, and victory to a new socialist order. Those moviegoers distanced by time and space may find the film a somewhat elusive and esoteric work. The movie's least parochial element is the lead character, Maciek (Zbigniew Cybulski), a moody and capri-

cious lad who more closely resembles young people of the mid-1950s, when the film was made, than the mid-'40s character he is meant to embody. In a single sequence, Maciek provides his girlfriend and the film s audience with a virtual catalogue of '50s youth attitudes: "Oh, God, how beautiful life could be!" (youthful yearning); "I don't know what is sad and what isn't" (youthful confusion); "I'd like to change certain things" (youthful idealism); "to lead a different life" (youthful frustration); "it's difficult to speak about it" (youthful inarticulateness).

Cybulski was dubbed "the Polish James Dean." He did indeed resemble Dean and spoke some of the same body language, but his performance as Maciek was little more extroverted than any of his American counterpart's screen portrayals. Cybulski was reputed to be, like Maciek, a hard drinker, womanizer, and gadfly, and like Dean, he died young.

Richly composed and photographed, with atmosphere aplenty, ASHES AND DIAMONDS suffers somewhat from an excess of loose plot ends and of underdeveloped characters, perhaps a consequence of having been based on a prestigious novel. Similar in some ways to the contemporaneous films of Carol Reed, it does not match them in lucidity, intrigue, or power.

ASPHALT JUNGLE, THE   *DVD*
1950 112m bw Crime   ★★★★½
MGM   (U.S.)

Sterling Hayden *(Dix Handley)*, Louis Calhern *(Alonzo D. Emmerich)*, Jean Hagen *(Doll Conovan)*, James Whitmore *(Gus Ninissi)*, Sam Jaffe *(Doc Erwin Riedenschneider)*, John McIntire *(Police Commissioner Hardy)*, Marc Lawrence *(Cobby)*, Barry Kelley *(Lt. Ditrich)*, Anthony Caruso *(Louis Ciavelli)*, Teresa Celli *(Maria Ciavelli)*

p, Arthur Hornblow Jr.; d, John Huston; w, Ben Maddow, John Huston (based on the novel by W.R. Burnett); ph, Harold Rosson; ed, George Boemler; m, Miklos Rozsa; art d, Cedric Gibbons, Randall Duell

AAN Best Supporting Actor: Sam Jaffe; *AAN Best Director:* John Huston; *AAN Best Screenplay:* Ben Maddow, John Huston; *AAN Best B/W Cinematography:* Harold Rosson

Adapted by director John Huston and co-screenwriter Ben Maddow from the novel by W.R. Burnett, this classic, often copied but never equaled, focuses on the robbery of a swank jewelry firm, meticulously planned by master criminal "Doc" Erwin Riedenschneider (Sam Jaffe) while imprisoned. Alonzo D. Emmerich (Louis Calhern) is a sleazy lawyer who'll fence the stolen jewels, giving "Doc" and his cohorts $1 million for their labors. The assembled gang includes Dix Handley (Sterling Hayden), a somewhat dumb but standup fellow who has dreams of buying back his father's Kentucky horse ranch; Gus Ninissi (James Whitmore), a tough-as-nails, cat-loving hunchback who runs a diner; and Louis Ciavelli (Anthony Caruso), a professional thief who's enlisted to blow the safe under Riedenschneider's supervision. After carefully drilling the gang members, "Doc" leads the men on the robbery attempt. The safe is blown and the gems secured, but his "perfect" crime immediately unravels.

Huston directed this superb production with tremendous assurance, developing his characters incisively but not at the expense of the rapidly developing plot. Indeed, THE ASPHALT JUNGLE boasts a rogues' gallery of definitive portrayals, led by creepy mastermind Jaffe, whose voyeuristic pursuit of Lolitas finally frames him. Calhern figures nicely as the crooked lawyer who keeps Monroe, in an outstanding cameo that foretold her future stardom. Jean Hagen's moll is a rare lead female performance, poignant and subtly shaded, that is totally devoid of studio-era vanity. Rosson's moody photography and Rozsa's moving score further enhance this *film noir* masterpiece.

ASSAULT, THE   *DVD*
1986   155m   c   Drama/War   ★★★★
Cannon   (Netherlands)   PG

Derek De Lint *(Anton Steenwijk)*, Marc van Uchelen *(Anton as a Boy)*, Monique Van de Ven *(Truus Coster/Saskia de Graaff)*, John Kraaykamp *(Cor Takes)*, Huub van der Lubbe *(Fake Ploeg/His Father)*, Elly Weller *(Mrs. Beumer)*, Ina van der Molen *(Karin Korteweg)*, Frans Vorstman *(Father Steenwijk)*, Edda Barends *(Mother Steenwijk)*, Caspar De Boer *(Peter Steenwijk)*

p, Fons Rademakers; d, Fons Rademakers; w, Gerard Soeteman (based on the novel by Harry Mulisch); ph, Theo Van de Sande (Fujicolor); ed, Kees Linthorst; m, Jurriaan Andriessen; art d, Dorus van der Linden; fx, Harry Wiessenhaan; cos, Anne-Marie van Beverwijk

AA Best Foreign Language Film

A powerful motion picture that poses more questions than it answers, THE ASSAULT will haunt anyone who understands the tragic psychological effects of emotional repression. Spanning a 40-year period, it begins in Holland as the war is waning and the Germans realize they will be beaten. One night while dining by candlelight during curfew, a Dutch family sees a local collaborator killed by a sniper. Fearing that they will be blamed, the family watches in horror as their neighbors drag the body in front of their home. Soon Germans are everywhere, the family is arrested and shot, their house is burned, and the son, Anton (Marc van Uchelen), is taken away to prison. Years later, he becomes a physician, marries, and has his own family, but the memory of that bleak night continues to haunt him.

Winner of the 1986 Academy Award for Best Foreign Film, THE ASSAULT is a powerful indictment of the Nazi horror, although it seldom editorializes. Much more than the war picture it begins as, this documentary-like Dutch film explores lives that have been torn apart by German occupation.

ASSAULT ON PRECINCT 13   *DVD*
1976   91m   c   Action   ★★★½
Turtle   (U.S.)   R

Austin Stoker *(Bishop)*, Darwin Joston *(Wilson)*, Laurie Zimmer *(Leigh)*, Martin West *(Lawson)*, Tony Burton *(Wells)*, Charles Cyphers *(Starker)*, Nancy Loomis *(Julie)*, Peter Bruni *(Ice Cream Man)*, John J. Fox *(Warden)*, Kim Richards *(Kathy)*

p, J.S. Kaplan; d, John Carpenter; w, John Carpenter; ph, Douglas Knapp (Metrocolor); ed, John T. Chance; m, John Carpenter; art d, Tommy Wallace; cos, Louise Kyes

Not really a horror film, but one that often comes up during discussions of George Romero's NIGHT OF THE LIVING DEAD (1968), this early Carpenter movie still holds up as one of the director's best works.

A low-budget and taut update of the classic Howard Hawks western RIO BRAVO, set in modern-day Los Angeles, the story concerns a lengthy siege by a multiracial street gang on a soon-to-be-closed police station. The gang has murdered a young girl, whose father has run to the station for help. He's is in shock and cannot speak to the lone cop (Stoker) or to the two secretaries (Zimmer and Loomis) waiting for the moving vans to take what's left of the station's file cabinets. Unexpectedly, three death-row prisoners en route to the penitentiary are forced to stop at the precinct. One of the prisoners is sick, and the three inmates are put in holding cells until authorities can contact a doctor. As night falls, the gang

attacks in full force, peppering the station with bullets shot from guns with silencers. The gang cuts the electricity and phone lines, rendering the station helpless in the center of the neighborhood. The inmates demand to be let loose so that they can defend themselves and prove to be honorable men.

The shadowy photography, great editing, snappy dialogue, and a moody synthesizer score by Carpenter himself make this one of the most successful homages to the Hawks brand of filmmaking—and a very impressive film in its own right. The parallels with Romero's film are obvious (the street gang is reminiscent of Romero's zombies), and Carpenter, who often borrows character names and situations from films and filmmakers he admires, may well have intended it that way.

ASSAULT ON PRECINCT 13   *DVD*
2005   109m   c   Action/Thriller   ★★★
Liaisons Films/Why Not Productions/   R
Focus Features/Rogue Pictures   (U.S./France)

Ethan Hawke *(Jake Roenick)*, Laurence Fishburne *(Marion Bishop)*, John Leguizamo *(Beck)*, Maria Bello *(Alex Sabian)*, Jeffrey Atkins, billed as Ja Rule *(Smiley)*, Drea de Matteo *(Iris Ferry)*, Matt Craven *(Capra)*, Aisha Hinds *(Anna)*, Brian Dennehy *(Jasper O'Shea)*, Gabriel Byrne *(Marcus Duvall)*

p, Pascal Caucheteux, Jeffrey Silver, Stephane Sperry; d, Jean-Francois Richet; w, James DeMonaco (based on the film written by John Carpenter); ph, Robert Gantz; ed, Bill Pankow; m, Graeme Revell; prod d, Paul Denham Austerberry; art d, Nigel Churcher; fx, Dennis Berardi, Jason Board, John MacGillivary; cos, Vicki Graef, Georgina Yarhi

Jean-Francois Richet's remake of John Carpenter's unabashed reworking of the classic western RIO BRAVO is a slicked up, perfectly watchable update of a movie that was already just about perfect on its own bleakly seedy terms.

Ever since an undercover drug bust went horribly wrong, Detroit cop Jake Roenick (Ethan Hawke) has become a high-strung booze hound. Now it's New Year's Eve and Jake is on desk duty at Precinct 13, a small, rundown stationhouse in a desolate industrial area. Come midnight, Precinct 13 will lock its doors for good. The computers are gone, emergency calls are already being automatically rerouted, and all the skeleton staff of three—Jake, veteran cop Jasper O'Shea (Brian Dennehy), and slutty secretary Iris Ferry (Drea DeMatteo)—need to do is shut off the lights on their way out. Shortly after Jake's department-ordered shrink (Maria Bello) stops by for a quick session, a prison bus carrying two guards and four prisoners—paranoid junkie Beck (John Leguizamo), dealer Smiley (Ja Rule), accused gang-banger Anna (Aisha Hinds), and crime lord Marion Bishop (Laurence Fishburne), who just killed a dirty undercover cop—pulls up to wait out the oncoming blizzard. Then a heavily-armed SWAT team comes gunning for Bishop, whose testimony could besmirch corrupt squad chief Marcus Duvall (Gabriel Byrne) and his crew. Naturally, everyone else in the forlorn jailhouse will have to die as well, but Jake gambles that by arming Bishop and the other prisoners they just might survive the night.

Screenwriter James DeMonaco and Richet keep the story moving and spread around the character bits so everyone gets a moment in the spotlight. The result is still formulaic, but it's never dull, and delivers one moment as unrepentently vicious as the original's casual murder of an adorable little girl buying an ice cream.

AT CLOSE RANGE   *DVD*
1986   111m   c   Crime   ★★★½
Hemdale   (U.S.)   R

Sean Penn *(Brad Whitewood, Jr.)*, Christopher Walken *(Brad Whitewood, Sr.)*, Mary Stuart Masterson *(Terry)*, Christopher

Penn *(Tommy Whitewood)*, Millie Perkins *(Julie Whitewood)*, Eileen Ryan *(Grandmother)*, Alan Autry *(Ernie)*, Candy Clark *(Mary Sue)*, R.D. Call *(Dickie Whitewood)*, Tracey Walter *(Patch)*

p, Elliott Lewitt, Don Guest; d, James Foley; w, Nicholas Kazan (based on a story by Lewitt and Kazan); ph, Juan Ruiz-Anchia (Panavision, CFI Color); ed, Howard Smith; m, Patrick Leonard; prod d, Peter Jamison; fx, Burt Dalton, Adams Calvert; cos, Hilary Rosenfeld

A chilling and realistic crime film, AT CLOSE RANGE features strong performances by Christopher Walken and Sean Penn. The film follows fresh-out-of-high-school Brad Whitewood, Jr. (Penn), as he struggles against the boredom of his rural existence. Living in a run-down house with his half-brother, Tommy (Christopher Penn, Sean's brother), his grandmother (Eileen Ryan, the Penn boys' mother), and his mother (Millie Perkins), Brad coasts along until two events change his life forever: he falls in love with Terry (Mary Stuart Masterson), and his wayward father (Walken) wanders back on the scene.

Relentlessly grim, AT CLOSE RANGE offers a frightening glimpse at the dark side of American life and poses disturbing questions about family ties. Unfortunately, although director James Foley handles the performances with skill, he also indulges in too many flashy directorial pyrotechnics, muting the emotional impact. Writer Nicholas Kazan (son of director Elia) based his script on the Johnston family murders in Pennsylvania in 1978.

ATLANTIC CITY
1981 104m c Crime/Romance ★★★½
Paramount (U.S./Canada) R

Burt Lancaster *(Lou)*, Susan Sarandon *(Sally)*, Kate Reid *(Grace)*, Michel Piccoli *(Joseph)*, Hollis McLaren *(Chrissie)*, Robert Joy *(Dave)*, Al Waxman *(Alfie)*, Robert Goulet *(Singer)*, Moses Znaimer *(Felix)*, Angus MacInnes *(Vinnie)*

p, Denis Heroux; d, Louis Malle; w, John Guare; ph, Richard Ciupka; ed, Suzanne Baron; m, Michel Legrand; prod d, Anne Pritchard; cos, Francois Barbeau

AAN Best Picture; AAN Best Actor: Burt Lancaster; *AAN Best Actress:* Susan Sarandon; *AAN Best Director:* Louis Malle; *AAN Best Original Screenplay:* John Guare (Screenplay)

Richly sad portraits of wasted American lives, filtered through a European sensibility. Burt Lancaster, in a masterful performance, plays Lou, an aging small-time criminal who hangs around Atlantic City doing odd jobs and taking care of the broken-down moll (Kate Reid) of the deceased gangster for whom Lou was a gofer. Living in an invented past, Lou identifies with yesteryear's notorious gangsters and gets involved with sexy would-be croupier, Sally (Susan Sarandon), and her drug-dealing estranged husband (Robert Joy).

Aided by a superb script from playwright John Guare, director Louis Malle (PRETTY BABY, AU REVOIR LES ENFANTS) pulls off a minor coup here, celebrating his wounded characters even as he mercilessly reveals their dreams for the hopeless illusions they really are. He is exceptionally well served by his cast and his location—a gone-to-seed resort town supported, like the principal characters, by memories of glories past.

ATTACK!
1956 107m bw War ★★★
UA (U.S.)

Jack Palance *(Lt. Costa)*, Eddie Albert *(Capt. Cooney)*, Lee Marvin *(Col. Bartlett)*, Robert Strauss *(Pvt. Bernstein)*, Richard Jaeckel *(Pvt. Snowden)*, Buddy Ebsen *(Sgt. Tolliver)*,

William Smithers *(Lt. Woodruff)*, Jon Shepodd *(Cpl. Jackson)*, James Goodwin *(Pvt. Ricks)*, Steven Geray *(Short German)*

p, Robert Aldrich; d, Robert Aldrich; w, James Poe (based on the play "The Fragile Fox" by Norman Brooks); ph, Joseph Biroc; ed, Michael Luciano; m, Frank DeVol

No sensibilities are spared in this brutal portrait of infantry warfare, featuring a powerful performance by Palance. In 1944 Belgium, Albert is a coward who has achieved the rank of captain only because of his father's political power. Because Marvin's political ambitions can be served by Albert's family, he overlooks Albert's incompetence. But Palance and his platoon (Ebsen, Jaeckel, Strauss) feel victimized, particularly Palance who becomes an almost supernatural force of vengeance. A cynical and grim account of war, ATTACK! features excellent performances from the entire cast and is one of director Aldrich's best films.

ATTACK OF THE KILLER TOMATOES
1978 87m c Comedy/Horror ★
NAI (U.S.) PG

David Miller *(Mason Dixon)*, George Wilson *(Jim Richardson)*, Sharon Taylor *(Lois Fairchild)*, Jack Riley *(Agriculture Official)*, Rock Peace *(Wilbur Finletter)*, Eric Christmas *(Senator Polk)*, Al Sklar *(Ted Swan)*, Ernie Meyers *(President)*, Jerry Anderson *(Major Mills)*, Ron Shapiro *(Newspaper Editor)*

p, J. Stephen Peace, John De Bello; d, John De Bello; w, Costa Dillon, J. Stephen Peace, John De Bello; ph, John K. Culley; m, Gordon Goodwin, Paul Sundfur

In a cynical bid for cult success, ATTACK OF THE KILLER TOMATOES employs calculatedly bad acting, ridiculous special effects, and inane dialog. Though it succeeded to some degree in achieving its goal, it's a thoroughly dull, unfunny effort. The film tries too hard at being ridiculous, and though the idea of savage vegetables rolling around the city splattering innocent bystanders sounds funny, actually sitting through nearly 90 minutes of it is enough to make anyone long for ATTACK OF THE 50 FOOT WOMAN. There are some funny song parodies, but that's about it.

AU HASARD, BALTHAZAR
1966 95m c Drama ★★★★★
New Line (France)

Anne Wiazemsky *(Marie)*, Francois Lafarge *(Gerard)*, Philippe Asselin *(Marie's Father)*, Nathalie Joyaut *(Marie's Mother)*, Walter Green *(Jacques)*, Jean-Claude Guilbert *(Arnold)*, Pierre Klossowski *(Merchant)*, Francois Sullerot *(Baker)*, M.C. Fremont *(Baker's Wife)*, Jean Remignard *(Notary)*

p, Mag Bodard; d, Robert Bresson; w, Robert Bresson; ph, Ghislain Cloquet; ed, Raymond Lamy; m, Jean Wiener; art d, Pierre Charbonnier

This poignant film is a powerful portrait of humanity seen through the life of a donkey. The animal is first the loving plaything of small children in rural France, then a working beast of burden named by a sullen child. As the girl grows up, the donkey's fortunes worsen with the young woman's when she is gang-raped and dies. Her sadistic lover, a leader of a motorcycle gang, tortures the donkey by setting its tail on fire. The donkey's life intersects with the lives of many of its other owners, as well. A brutal farmer owns the animal and beats it, but is finished off in grim irony. Then the donkey has a respite in becoming a momentary circus star, but then again returns to tilling the soil. It ends its days with a simple-minded but loving old man who considers the animal a saint. This great film, made with uncompromising honesty and devastating reality, is, according to Jean-Luc Godard, "the world in an hour and a half." Music includes Franz Schubert's "Piano Sonata No. 20."

AU REVOIR, LES ENFANTS

1987 104m c Drama/War ★★★★½
Nouvelle Editions de Films/MK2/Stella PG
(France)

Gaspard Manesse *(Julien Quentin)*, Ràphael Fejto *(Jean Bonnet)*, Francine Racette *(Mme. Quentin)*, Stanislas Carre de Malberg *(Francois Quentin)*, Philippe Morier-Genoud *(Father Jean)*, Francois Berleand *(Father Michel)*, Francois Negret *(Joseph)*, Peter Fitz *(Muller)*, Pascal Rivet *(Boulanger)*, Benoit Henriet *(Ciron)*

p, Louis Malle; d, Louis Malle; w, Louis Malle; ph, Renato Berta (Eastmancolor); ed, Emmanuelle Castro; m, Franz Schubert, Camille Saint-Saens; cos, Corinne Jorry

AAN Best Foreign Language Film ; AAN Best Original Screenplay: Louis Malle

A delicately rendered and exceptionally moving reminiscence of a boyhood friendship cut short by war. Louis Malle's semi-autobiographical film is set in January, 1944, during the German Occupation of France. Julien (Gaspard Manesse) is a privileged, precocious 12-year old with a doting mother and a superior attitude. Sent away to a provincial Catholic boarding school, he easily outclasses his loutish schoolmates until the arrival of Bonnet (Raphael Fejto), who is cultivated, literate, and oddly circumspect about revealing his background. At first, Julien hopes to expose and humiliate his rival, but their common interests lead to an uneasy alliance and finally friendship. Then Bonnet's secret is revealed: he is a Jew being hidden from the Gestapo by schoolmaster Fr. Jean (Philippe Morier-Genoud).

One of director-producer-writer Malle's most personal projects, AU REVOIR LES ENFANTS can be seen as the completion of a trilogy that began with MURMUR OF THE HEART (1971), a sunny comedy of evolving postwar manners, and continued with a darkly-hued portrait of a teenaged collaborator, LACOMBE LUCIEN (1974). All three films are about maturation during a decade of political upheaval, and each is concerned with choices thrust upon children—choices inevitably compromised by social and familial pressures beyond a child's control. Like the earlier films, AU REVOIR rejects any notion of youthful innocence, making it a bracingly welcome exception to the post-E.T. slew of films romanticizing childhood. Malle is adept at eliciting mature performances from children, and Manesse and Fejto are excellent even by adult standards.

AUDITION

(ODISHON) DVD
1999 115m c Thriller ★★★★
Omega Project/Creators Company Connection/ R
AFDF Korea/Body Sonic/Filmface
(Japan/South Korea)

Ryo Ishibashi *(Shigeharu Aoyama)*, Eihi Shiina *(Asami Yamazaki)*, Tetsu Sawaki *(Shigehiko Aoyama)*, Jun Kunimura *(Yasuhisa Yoshikawa)*, Renji Ishibashi *(Old Man in Wheelchair)*, Miyuki Matsuda *(Ryoko Aoyama)*, Tohsie Negishi *(Rie)*, Ren Osugi *(Shibata)*, Shigeru Saiki *(Toastmaster)*, Ken Teruishi *(Director)*

p, Satoshi Fukushima, Akemi Suyama; d, Takashi Miike; w, Daisuke Tengan (based on a story by Ryu Murakami); ph, Hideo Yamamoto; ed, Yasushi Shimamura; m, Koji Endo; prod d, Tatsuo Ozeki; fx, Yzichi Matsui; cos, Tomoe Kumagai

Somewhere far beyond the extremes of FATAL ATTRACTION and IN THE COMPANY OF MEN festers this elegantly composed, outrageously violent psycho-thriller from the wickedly perverse mind of Japanese director Takashi Miike.

Seven years after the death of his beloved Yoko, middle-aged Shigeharu Aoyama (Ryo Ishibashi) decides it's time to shop around for a new wife. But not just any wife: disgusted by all the loud, vulgar women who gather in cocktail lounges, Shigeharu wants a "nice" girl. Shigeharu's friend Yasuhisa (Jun Kunimura), a movie producer, comes up with a plan. He'll put out a casting call for an upcoming "production" and Shigeharu can sit in on the auditions and take his pick. Shigeharu knows it's cruel and deceptive, but he agrees. Out of the 30 naive hopefuls who undergo the humiliating audition process, Shigeharu chooses Asami (Eihi Shiina), a demure, angelic-looking woman half his age. Shigeharu asks her out in spite of his friend's warnings; something about Asami makes Yasuhisa uneasy. After the first blissful date, love-struck Shigeharu is ready to propose marriage; during a romantic weekend getaway, Asami makes him promise to love only her… and she means it.

Unlike Miike's gut-wrenching yakuza thrillers DEAD OR ALIVE and FUDOH: THE NEXT GENERATION, this exceedingly disturbing tale builds slowly, delivering a few strong warning shocks before exploding in a maelstrom of sadism in which extreme pain is the order of the day. Miike toys with points of view, and it's hard to say which side of the nightmare the film leaves you on, whether the final 20 minutes is the dark fantasy of a guilty conscience or playtime for a seriously disturbed young woman. One thing, however, is certain: you've never seen anything quite like it.

AUNTIE MAME

1958 143m c Comedy DVD ★★★★
Warner Bros. (U.S.)

Rosalind Russell *(Mame Dennis)*, Forrest Tucker *(Beauregard Burnside)*, Coral Browne *(Vera Charles)*, Fred Clark *(Mr. Babcock)*, Roger Smith *(Patrick Dennis)*, Patric Knowles *(Lindsay Woolsey)*, Peggy Cass *(Agnes Gooch)*, Jan Handzlik *(Patrick Dennis as a Child)*, Joanna Barnes *(Gloria Upson)*, Pippa Scott *(Pegeen Ryan)*

d, Morton Da Costa; w, Betty Comden, Adolph Green (based on the novel *Mame* by Patrick Dennis and the play by Jerome Lawrence, Robert E. Lee); ph, Harry Stradling (Technirama, Technicolor); ed, William Ziegler; m, Bronislau Kaper; art d, Malcolm Bert; cos, Orry-Kelly

AAN Best Picture; AAN Best Actress: Rosalind Russell; *AAN Best Supporting Actress:* Peggy Cass; *AAN Best Color Cinematography:* Harry Stradling Sr; *AAN Best Film Editing:* William Ziegler; *AAN Best Art Direction-Set Decoration:* Malcolm Bert (Art Direction), George James Hopkins (Set Decoration)

A showcase for the spectacular talents of Russell, who made the play a Broadway hit. Eccentric, colorful Mame Dennis adopts an orphan boy, exposing him to all manner of extravagant and bizarre characters in the 1920s and 1930s. The film is a trifle overlong and episodic, but Russell is supported in high style by a talented cast. Look for many amusing 1950s art direction and costume touches that are unusual. For once Hollywood agreed that Broadway's casting couldn't be improved; Russell's way with words, her rhythms, speed, and timing are irreplacably, impeccably right.

AUSTIN POWERS IN GOLDMEMBER

2002 94m c Comedy/Spy DVD ★★½
Gratitude International/Team Todd/ PG-13
Moving Pictures/New Line (U.S.)

Mike Myers *(Austin Powers/Dr. Evil/Fat Bastard/Goldmember)*, Beyoncè Knowles *(Foxxy Cleopatra)*, Michael Caine *(Nigel Powers)*, Seth Green *(Scott Evil)*, Michael York *(Basil Exposition)*,

Robert Wagner *(Number Two)*, Mindy Sterling *(Frau Farbissina)*, Verne J. Troyer *(Mini Me)*, Fred Savage *(Number Three)*, Nobu Matsuhisa *(Mr. Roboto)*

p, John Lyons, Eric McLeod, Demi Moore, Mike Myers, Suzanne Todd, Jennifer Todd; d, Jay Roach; w, Michael McCullers, Mike Myers (based on characters created by Mike Myers); ph, Peter Deming; ed, Greg Hayden, John Poll; m, George S. Clinton; prod d, Rusty Smith; art d, Mark Worthington; fx, David D. Johnson, Mike Meinardus; chor, Marguerite Derricks; cos, Deena Appel

As the third installment in this hugely popular series proves, Austin Powers (Mike Myers) may be a super-suave international man of mystery, but at heart he's just a neglected lad with unresolved issues. Austin's quest to win paternal respect is complicated by the fact that his father is Nigel Powers (Michael Caine), the most revered and sublimely shagadelic British spy of all time.

The movie opens in the present, as Hollywood is making a major motion picture—"Austinpussy"—about Austin's exploits, and the Queen is about to knight him for his selfless service to the empire. Surely, dad will now give Austin the recognition he craves! But no. Bad dad blows off the royal ceremony, triggering painful memories of Austin's lonely graduation from the British Intelligence Academy. Austin soon learns that his father has been kidnapped by super-villain Goldmember (Myers) and spirited back to the year 1975. Austin must rescue dad and return to the present to stop Dr. Evil (Myers) from destroying the world. Austin's '70s sidekick, disco diva Foxxy Cleopatra (Beyoncé Knowles, of pop trio Destiny's Child), comes along for the ride.

Once again, the movie's sense of humor is poised between juvenile toilet gags and snarky snickers at the expense of '60s and '70s fashions, popular culture, and attitudes; for every laugh, there's an equal and opposite groan of disgust. But casting Caine as Austin's father is a stroke of pure genius; even more than Sean Connery's James Bond, Caine's bespectacled spy Harry Palmer (THE IPCRESS FILE, FUNERAL IN BERLIN, BILLION DOLLAR BRAIN) is the model for Austin's geeky studliness. First-timer Knowles is no Pam Grier, but she turns in a surprisingly confident performance and gets to sing an inspired K.C. and the Sunshine Band medley.

AUSTIN POWERS: INTERNATIONAL MAN OF MYSTERY
DVD

1997 87m   c   Comedy ★★★
Eric's Boy Productions/Moving PG-13
Pictures/New Line   (U.S.)

Mike Myers *(Austin Powers/Dr. Evil)*, Elizabeth Hurley *(Vanessa Kensington)*, Michael York *(Basil Exposition)*, Mimi Rogers *(Mrs. Kensington)*, Robert Wagner *(Number Two)*, Seth Green *(Scott Evil)*, Fabiana Udenio *(Alotta Fagina)*, Mindy Sterling *(Frau Farbissina)*, Paul Dillon *(Patty O'Brien)*, Charles Napier *(Commander Gilmour)*

p, Suzanne Todd, Demi Moore, Jennifer Todd, Mike Myers; d, Jay Roach; w, Mike Myers; ph, Peter Deming; ed, Debra Neil-Fisher; m, George S. Clinton; prod d, Cynthia Charette; art d, Daniel Olexiewicz; fx, Rich Ratliff, Dave Johnson (visual effects); cos, Deena Appel

Mike Myers wrote and plays a dual role in AUSTIN POWERS: INTERNATIONAL MAN OF MYSTERY, a silly, but generally funny, spoof about a secret agent and his arch-nemesis who are both frozen in the swinging '60s, then thawed out in the politically correct '90s.

After being defrosted in 1997, Britain's top secret-agent, Austin Powers (Mike Myers) is able to resume his pursuit of the nefarious Dr. Evil (also played by Myers). Powers is teamed with Vanessa Kensington (Elizabeth Hurley), the prim-and-proper daughter of his former partner, who resists Powers's

charms at first, but finally succumbs. When Dr. Evil hijacks nuclear weapons and demands $100 billion not to use them, Powers and Vanessa go to Las Vegas to foil his plans. There, they are captured and tied up, and must use their wits (and the horrifying sight of Powers dancing) to combat the enemy.

AUSTIN POWERS is an enjoyably campy grab bag of 1960s movie, music, and pop-culture references, simultaneously spoofing and paying tribute to such British icons as Swinging London, James Bond, and The Beatles. Unlike the lame SPY HARD (1996) and scores of other genre spoofs, which perfunctorily present a checklist of scenes and dialogue from other movies and pass it off as parody, AUSTIN POWERS is not only imaginative, but ultimately succeeds because of the obvious affection for, and knowledge of, its subject. From the stylishly tacky art direction, costume design, and psychedelic musical transitions, to the little nuances like Austin's hilariously dated hipster jargon, every detail is evocative of its period. Although the film runs out of steam before the end, it sustains a fairly high level of comedic invention for much longer than most films of its type. Two hugely successful sequels, AUSTIN POWERS: THE SPY WHO SHAGGED ME (1999) and AUSTIN POWERS IN GOLD-MEMBER (2002), followed.

AUSTIN POWERS: THE SPY WHO SHAGGED ME
DVD

1999 95m   c   Comedy ★★
Eric's Boy/Moving Pictures/Team Todd/ PG-13
New Line   (U.S.)

Mike Myers *(Austin Powers/Doctor Evil/Fat Bastard)*, Heather Graham *(Felicity Shagwell)*, Michael York *(Basil Exposition)*, Robert Wagner *(Number Two)*, Rob Lowe *(Young Number Two)*, Seth Green *(Scott Evil)*, Mindy Sterling *(Frau Farbissina)*, Verne J. Troyer *(Mini-Me)*, Elizabeth Hurley *(Vanessa)*, Gia Carides *(Robin Swallows)*

p, Michael Myers, John S. Lyons, Suzanne Todd, Jennifer Todd, Demi Moore, Eric McLeod; d, Jay Roach; w, Mike Myers, Michael McCullers; ph, Ueli Steiger; ed, Jon Poll, Debra Neil-Fisher; m, George S. Clinton; prod d, Rusty Smith; art d, Alexander Hammond; fx, Mike Meinardus, Lauren Ritchie; chor, Marguerite Derricks; cos, Deena Appel

AAN Best Makeup: Michele Burke, Mike Smithson

How funny is the sight of Mike Myers, mangy mat of fake chest hair stuck to his pudgy flesh, capering naked through a posh hotel, his private areas mercifully obscured by a series of phallic props?

Let your answer be your guide when it comes to this sequel to the surprise hit AUSTIN POWERS: INTERNATIONAL MAN OF MYSTERY, in which swinging '60s super spy Powers was revived from cryogenic sleep to defeat the effete Dr. Evil (Myers), and found his shagadelic attitudes out of sync with the '90s. Here Austin gets sent back where he belongs via the wonder of time travel. Dr. Evil returns to 1969 with a nefarious plan to cripple Austin by stealing his studly "mojo," then bring the world to its knees with a giant laser—how *funny* that it resembles a big penis! Unmanned but unbowed, Austin joins forces with randy CIA cutie Felicity Shagwell (Heather Graham) and unleashes a steady stream of bodily function jokes and lame double entendres upon audiences who can only claim to be unsuspecting if they've been hiding out in a cryogenic freezer tube themselves.

There are plusses: Rob Lowe, who plays the younger version of Dr. Evil's suave sidekick, Number 2 (Robert Wagner), does a dead-on imitation of the older actor; Evil's pint-sized clone, Mini-Me (Verne J. Troyer), is an amusing conceit; Seth Green makes hay with the role of Evil's sullen son, Scott; and Graham looks absolutely fabulous in her Carnaby Street duds. But the elaborate, show-stopping set piece that relies on overlapping scenes of people spotting a suggestively shaped rocket, bridged by slang terms for penis (which the filmmakers found so hilarious they did it twice) would be too long even if it were twice as funny. And that about sums up the rest of the movie.

AUTO FOCUS
2002 104m c Biography/Crime *DVD* ★★★½
Propaganda Films/Focus Puller/Good Machine (U.S.) R

Greg Kinnear (*Bob Crane*), Willem Dafoe (*John Carpenter*), Rita Wilson (*Anne Crane*), Maria Bello (*Patricia Crane*), Ron Leibman (*Lenny*), Bruce Solomon (*Feldman—Hogan's Producer*), Michael Rodgers (*Richard Dawson*), Kurt Fuller (*Werner Klemperer/Klink*), Christopher Neiman (*Robert Clary/LeBeau*), Lyle Kanouse (*John Banner/Schultz*)

p, Scott Alexander, Alicia Allain, Pat Dollard, Larry Karaszewski, Todd Rosken; d, Paul Schrader; w, Michael Gerbosi (based on the book *The Murder of Bob Crane*, by Robert Graysmith); ph, Fred Murphy; ed, Kristina Boden; m, Angelo Badalamenti; prod d, James Chinlund; art d, Seth Reed; fx, John Hartigan; cos, Julie Weiss

In the early morning hours of June 29, 1978, someone broke into former "Hogan's Heroes" star Bob Crane's Arizona motel room and beat him to death with a camera stand. Crane was touring the dinner-theater circuit, but his life was really dedicated to his twin hobbies: casual sex and amateur porn. It's hard not to read his sad, sordid story as yet another Hollywood fable about public personas and private obsessions, and like SUNSET BLVD., director Paul Schrader's own cautionary tale is narrated by a dead man—the affable Crane himself, played to perfection by Greg Kinnear.

Los Angeles, 1964: Crane is a popular disc jockey who dreams of becoming the next Jack Lemmon. He's appalled when his agent (Ron Leibman) suggests doing a television series—a comedy set in a Nazi POW camp, no less—but Crane's wife, Anne (Rita Wilson), helps talk him into it. "Hogan's Heroes" turns out to be the number-one new show of the 1965 season, and Crane becomes an instantly recognizable face. On the set, he meets John Carpenter (Willem Dafoe), an audiovisual equipment salesman who introduces Crane to the brave new worlds of swinging sex and videotape recording, and Crane is soon documenting his countless conquests with smutty Polaroids and reels of XXX videotape. All this liberation, however, comes at a price: Anne files for divorce, and once "Hogan's Heroes" is cancelled, Crane can't find work. Crane's relationship with Carpenter, meanwhile, grows increasingly co-dependent and, the film flatly suggests, deadly.

The screenplay is based on Robert Graysmith's true-crime book *The Murder of Bob Crane*, but this ultra-stylish film is far more interested in exploring its own central metaphor—the camera—than forensic minutiae. It serves up a warning against the power of images to both enchant and enslave; entranced by his own pornographic likeness, Crane becomes a kinky Narcissus whose "real" life fades into sad insignificance.

AUTUMN LEAVES
1956 107m bw Drama ★★★
Columbia (U.S.)

Joan Crawford (*Milly*), Cliff Robertson (*Burt Hanson*), Vera Miles (*Virginia*), Lorne Greene (*Mr. Hanson*), Ruth Donnelly (*Liz*), Shepperd Strudwick (*Dr. Couzzens*), Selmer Jackson (*Mr. Wetherby*), Maxine Cooper (*Nurse Evans*), Marjorie Bennett (*Waitress*), Frank Gerstle (*Mr. Ramsey*)

p, William Goetz; d, Robert Aldrich; w, Jean Rouveral, Hugo Butler, Lewis Meltzer, Robert Blees; ph, Charles Lang; ed, Michael Luciano; m, H.J. Salter

Butch-bobbed, bug-eyed career gal spinster Crawford meets shy Cliff Robertson and grabs for love, gets a schizo. Released a year after the nihilist film noir classic KISS ME DEADLY, the film recaptured the twisted qualities of the human mind. Labeled a "woman's picture," AUTUMN LEAVES is an intense melodrama about loneliness, despair, and mental illness. Taking a pleasant romantic tale and plunging it into a whirlwind of schizophrenic violence has the same effect as seeing a hammer shatter a shiny piece of glass. Almost like a nightmare going on in Crawford's mind, the film's visual style gets more and more distorted and the lighting very harsh as Robertson's schizophrenia builds. Joan's performance is on the money and the Crawford cult will enjoy her "reading" Lorne Greene and Vera Miles as she chases them down the street ("And you, ya slut!"). The lady later said Robert Aldrich "likes evil things, twisted things." The title song, penned by Joseph Kosma, Jacques Prevert, and Johnny Mercer, was a big hit for Nat King Cole.

AUTUMN SONATA
1978 97m c Drama *DVD* ★★½
ITC (Sweden) PG

Ingrid Bergman (*Charlotte*), Liv Ullmann (*Eva*), Lena Nyman (*Helena*), Halvar Bjork (*Viktor*), Georg Lokkeberg (*Leonardo*), Knut Wigert (*Professor*), Eva von Hanno (*Nurse*), Erland Josephson (*Josef*), Linn Ullmann (*Eva as a Child*), Arne Bang-Hansen (*Uncle Otto*)

p, Lew Grade, Martin Starger; d, Ingmar Bergman; w, Ingmar Bergman; ph, Sven Nykvist (Eastmancolor); ed, Sylvia Ingemarsson; prod d, Anna Asp; cos, Inger Pehrsson

AAN Best Actress: Ingrid Bergman; *AAN Best Original Screenplay:* Ingmar Bergman (Story)

The meeting of the Bergmans is reason alone to see AUTUMN SONATA, the director's exploration of mother-daughter conflict, but whatever cohesion the film projects is a result of Ingrid Bergman, as magnetic as ever in her final film performance. Photographed beautifully by Sven Nykvist, this painful film compels audiences finally to turn away. There is too much talk, talk, talk about feelings and not enough demonstration of them, but like cream, Ingrid keeps rising to the top of the chatter.

AVALON
1990 126m c Drama *DVD* ★★★
Baltimore Pictures (U.S.) PG

Armin Mueller-Stahl (*Sam Krichinsky*), Joan Plowright (*Eva Krichinsky*), Aidan Quinn (*Jules Kaye*), Elizabeth Perkins (*Ann Kaye*), Kevin Pollak (*Izzy Kirk*), Israel Rubinek (*Nathan Krichinsky*), Leo Fuchs (*Hymie Krichinsky*), Eve Gordon (*Dottie Kirk*), Lou Jacobi (*Gabriel Krichinsky*), Elijah Wood (*Michael Kaye*)

p, Mark Johnson, Barry Levinson; d, Barry Levinson; w, Barry Levinson; ph, Allen Daviau (Technicolor); ed, Stu Linder; m, Randy Newman; prod d, Norman Reynolds; art d, Fred Hole, Edward Richardson; fx, Allen L. Hall, Thomas R. Burman, Bari Dreiband-Burman; cos, Gloria Gresham

AAN Best Original Screenplay: Barry Levinson; *AAN Best Cinematography:* Allen Daviau; *AAN Best Original Score:* Randy Newman; *AAN Best Costume Design:* Gloria Gresham

Completing writer-director Barry Levinson's "Baltimore trilogy," which began with the acclaimed DINER and continued with TIN MEN, the autobiographical AVALON is a lyrical, melancholy account of an immigrant family's rise and gradual disintegration.

Immigrating to Baltimore in 1914, Sam Krichinsky (Armin Mueller-Stahl) is reunited with his brothers—Gabriel (Lou Jacobi), Hymie (Leo Fuchs) and Nathan (Israel Rubinek)—and drawn into the "family circle," whose members pool their resources to bring relatives over from the old country. Wallpaper hangers during the week, the brothers are musicians during the weekends, and it is during one of their gigs that Sam meets Eva (Joan Plowright), his future wife. Their son, Jules (Aidan Quinn) does not follow in his father's footsteps as a manual laborer. Instead he becomes a door-to-door salesman, sometimes taking along his young son, Michael (Elijah Wood). During one of these outings, Michael watches in terror as his father is stabbed by a mugger. While recuperating, Jules is given a television set by his family. The only "program" at that time is a nonstop test pattern; nevertheless, Jules glimpses a future in the new invention.

AVALON is concerned with the perils of sacrificing humanity for material success, a sort of '90s cinematic hangover from the "go for it" excesses of the '80s. Allen Daviau's photography is exceptional; Quinn, Mueller-Stahl, and Plowright give commendable performances. Ultimately, though, Levinson's very personal project never acquires a personality of its own.

AVIATOR, THE   DVD
2004 166m c   Biography   ★★★
Miramax/Forward Pass/Initial Entertainment   PG-13
Group/Warner Bros.   (U.S.)

Leonardo DiCaprio (Howard Hughes), Cate Blanchett (Katharine Hepburn), Kate Beckinsale (Ava Gardner), John C. Reilly (Noah Dietrich), Alec Baldwin (Juan Trippe), Alan Alda (Sen. Ralph Owen Brewster), Ian Holm (Professor Fitz), Kelli Garner (Faith Domergue), Gwen Stefani (Jean Harlow), Jude Law (Errol Flynn)

p, Sandy Climan, Charles Evans Jr., Graham King, Michael Mann; d, Martin Scorsese; w, John Logan; ph, Robert Richardson; ed, Thelma Schoonmaker; m, Howard Shore; prod d, Dante Ferretti; art d, Robert Guerra; fx, Tami Goldsmith, Robert Legato, R. Bruce Steinheimer, Richard L. Thompson, Peter G. Travers; cos, Sandy Powell

AA Best Supporting Actress: Cate Blanchett; AA Best Art Direction: Dante Ferretti (art direction), Francesca LoSchiavo (set decoration); AA Best Cinematography: Robert Richardson; AA Best Costume Design: Sandy Powell; AA Best Film Editing: Thelma Schoonmaker; AAN Best Picture; AAN Best Actor: Leonardo DiCaprio; AAN Best Supporting Actor: Alan Alda; AAN Best Director: Martin Scorsese; AAN Best Sound Mixing: Tom Fleischman, Petur Hliddal; AAN Best Original Screenplay: John Logan

Brisk, glossy, and gloriously art-directed, Martin Scorsese's lavish biopic of the mercurial Howard Hughes is a pop trifle, engaging but not compelling.

After a brief prologue locating Hughes's lifelong neuroses in his mother's suffocating attentions, the film focuses on the 20 years preceding his 1947 trial by the Senate War Investigating Committee. The heir to an enormous drill-bit fortune, young Hughes (Leonardo DiCaprio) goes west to silent-era Hollywood, where he merges his interests in flying and moviemaking into HELL'S ANGELS, which sucked up three years and $3.8 million, including a near-total reshoot to accommodate the hot new technology on the lot—sound. At the same time, he launches a research program to break aviation speed records and, ultimately, make flying a commercially viable commodity. Hughes structures the airline that became TWA and battles Pan Am executive Juan Trippe (a splendidly oily Alec Baldwin) for transatlantic routes. Between visionary super-projects, Hughes romances movie stars Katharine Hepburn (Cate Blanchett) and Ava Gardner (Kate Beckinsale), and dallies with other beauties, including starstruck teen Faith Domergue (Kelli Garner). During WWII,

his engineers begin the grandest project of them all: a massive wooden troop- and equipment-transport plane they call the Hercules, later derisively dubbed the "Spruce Goose."

The film suffers the usual biopic flaws, including long stretches of uninspired recitation, and Scorsese seems stymied by the problem of dramatizing the inner turmoil of Hughes' disintegrating mind—the very thing he did so masterfully in TAXI DRIVER. DiCaprio is part of the problem—the baby-faced actor doesn't produce a compellingly weighted performance—and Blanchett's audacious turn as Hepburn is more impersonation than performance. The film's many glittering cameos include Jude Law as Errol Flynn and pop-tart Gwen Stefani as Jean Harlow.

AWAKENINGS   DVD
1990 121m c   Drama   ★★½
Columbia   (U.S.)   PG-13

Robert De Niro (Leonard Lowe), Robin Williams (Dr. Malcolm Sayer), Julie Kavner (Eleanor Costello), Ruth Nelson (Mrs. Lowe), John Heard (Dr. Kaufman), Penelope Ann Miller (Paula), Alice Drummond (Lucy), Judith Malina (Rose), Barton Heyman (Bert), George Martin (Frank)

p, Walter F. Parkes, Lawrence Lasker; d, Penny Marshall; w, Steve Zaillian (based on the novel by Oliver Sacks); ph, Miroslav Ondricek; ed, Jerry Greenberg, Battle Davis, Jere Huggins; m, Randy Newman; prod d, Anton Furst; art d, Bill Groom; cos, Cynthia Flynt

AAN Best Picture; AAN Best Actor: Robert De Niro; AAN Best Adapted Screenplay: Steven Zaillian

Over-earnest, slushy attempt by director Penny Marshall (A LEAGUE OF THEIR OWN) and screenwriter Steve Zaillian (SCHINDLER'S LIST) to create screen entertainment from the life and work of neurologist Oliver Sacks, whose name is changed to Dr. Malcolm Sayer for the film, set in 1969. Robin Williams plays the overwhelmingly shy research doctor who is engaged by the chronic care ward of a Bronx hospital and, despite resistance from the authorities, uses the new drug L-DOPA to bring long-abandoned catatonic cases back to (temporary) life. Williams gives one of his winsome "please like me, I'm working very hard" performances that makes you want to cry with impatience and De Niro, as one of his wards, brings new meaning to the word mannered. (Marshall's direction reveals little more than a sense of awe in the face of her high-powered cast and subject matter.) The script pushes all the expected buttons at all the expected moments, leaving you wondering what could have been achieved with a more rigorous, unsentimental approach.

AWFUL TRUTH, THE   DVD
1937 90m bw Comedy   ★★★★★
Columbia   (U.S.)

Irene Dunne (Lucy Warriner), Cary Grant (Jerry Warriner), Ralph Bellamy (Daniel Leeson), Alex D'Arcy (Armand Duvalle), Cecil Cunningham (Aunt Patsy), Molly Lamont (Barbara Vance), Esther Dale (Mrs. Leeson), Joyce Compton (Dixie Belle Lee/Toots Binswanger), Robert Allen (Frank Randall), Robert Warwick (Mr. Vance)

p, Leo McCarey; d, Leo McCarey; w, Vina Delmar (based on the play by Arthur Richman); ph, Joseph Walker; ed, Al Clark; art d, Stephen Goosson, Lionel Banks; cos, Robert Kalloch

AAN Best Picture; AAN Best Actress: Irene Dunne; AAN Best Supporting Actor: Ralph Bellamy; AA Best Director: Leo McCarey; AAN Best Screenplay: Vina Delmar; AAN Best Film Editing: Al Clark

A superbly lighthearted production, and the epitome of 1930s screwball comedies. Grant tells wife Dunne that he is going on a short Florida vacation, but then spends his time playing poker with the boys, establishing an alibi by burning himself under a sunlamp. When he returns home he finds his wife absent; then she appears with D'Arcy, a dashing voice teacher. Both Grant and Dunne assume that the other has been unfaithful and, after a rousing round of accusations, they decide to accept a 90-day interlocutory divorce. Their main courtroom battle focuses on their pet dog, Mr. Smith (Asta of the "Thin Man" series). As the legal wrangling moves into full swing, Dunne not only continues to see D'Arcy, but befriends Oklahoman oil baron Bellamy. Meanwhile, Grant looks up an old flame, Compton, a sexy nightclub singer. Dunne and Grant go their separate ways, but are still drawn to each other. When Grant begins to fall for socialite Lamont, Dunne invades a party at her mansion, pretending to be drunk and carrying on wildly until Grant escorts her home. She convinces him to drive her to their mountain retreat, where they play a cat-and-mouse game, finally acknowledging that they still love each other.

This classic comedy began life as a 1922 stage hit and had been filmed twice previously—in 1925 as a silent with Agnes Ayres and Warner Baxter, and again in 1929 with Henry Daniell and Ina Claire. Director Leo McCarey maintained the basic premise of the play but improved it greatly, adding sophisticated dialogue and encouraging his actors to improvise around anything they thought funny. THE AWFUL TRUTH was in the can in six weeks, and was such a success that Grant and Dunne were teamed again in another splendid comedy, MY FAVORITE WIFE, and in a touching tearjerker, PENNY SERENADE. The film was nominated for an Academy Award for Best Picture and disappointingly remade in 1953 as LET'S DO IT AGAIN with Jane Wyman and Ray Milland.

B

BABE   `DVD`
1995 94m c   Fantasy/Children's/Comedy   ★★★½
Kennedy Miller Productions   (Australia)   G

Christine Cavanaugh *(Voice of Babe)*, James Cromwell *(Arthur Hoggett)*, Miriam Margolyes *(Voice of Fly)*, Hugo Weaving *(Voice of Rex)*, Danny Mann *(Voice of Ferdinand)*, Miriam Flynn *(Voice of Maa)*, Evelyn Krape *(Voice of Old Ewe)*, Russie Taylor *(Voice of Cat)*, Michael Edward-Stevens *(Voice of Horse)*, Charles Bartlett *(Voice of Cow)*

p, George Miller, Doug Mitchell, Bill Miller; d, Chris Noonan; w, George Miller, Chris Noonan (based on the novel *The Sheep-Pig* by Dick King-Smith); ph, Andrew Lesnie; ed, Marcus D'Arcy, Jay Friedkin; m, Nigel Westlake; prod d, Roger Ford; art d, Colin Gibson; fx, Dave Roberts, Charles Gibson, John Stephenson, Jim Henson's Creature Shop, Rhythm & Hues Studios; cos, Roger Ford; anim, Rhythm & Hues

AAN Best Picture; AAN Best Supporting Actor: James Cromwell; *AAN Best Director:* Chris Noonan; *AAN Best Adapted Screenplay:* George Miller, Chris Noonan; *AAN Best Art Direction-Set Decoration:* Roger Ford (art direction), Kerrie Brown (set decoration); *AAN Best Film Editing:* Marcus D'Arcy; *AA Best Visual Effects:* Scott E. Anderson, Charles Gibson, Neal Scanlan, John Cox

---

The kind of movie that slyly seduces even the most unregenerate cynic, BABE is a clever family picture that brings surprising freshness to the timeworn premise of talking barnyard animals.

The title character (voice of Christine Cavanaugh) is a piglet raised for slaughter in a terrifying assembly-line breeding pen. Trucked to a county fair, Babe is won and taken home by taciturn but kind-hearted Farmer Hoggett (James Cromwell). Lonely and ignorant of the barnyard's social hierarchy, the piglet unconditionally befriends all beasts, from the sheepdog bitch Fly (voice of Miriam Margolyes), who becomes Babe's surrogate mother, to the aged ewe Maa (voice of Miriam Flynn). Gradually, Babe is accepted by his fellow animals, but the humans still plan to butcher him for Christmas dinner. In an attempt to make himself useful and save his bacon, Babe learns to herd the farm's unruly gang of sheep. Ultimately, his survival will depend on his performance as the sole "sheep-pig" in a prestigious sheepdog contest.

"A humorous look at the limitations and lunacy of a preordained society," was Universal's drily accurate press-kit summation of BABE, which treads a careful path between G-rated fun and didacticism. True, there's a heavy animal-rights undertone in early scenes of Babe's harsh babe-hood, and a soapy subplot about Rex, a dysfunctional dog with a dark secret, is almost too much. But a sense of whimsy prevails, the tone set by an irresistible chorus of Muppet mice who shrilly announce the story's successive chapters. The voice-over cast, refreshingly devoid of big-name Hollywood stars, is perfect, and the animatronics, done by the Jim Henson Creature Factory (plus an Aussie outfit specializing in robot sheep!), blends neatly with about 500 separate live animal performers.

BABES IN ARMS
1939 93m   bw   Musical   ★★★
MGM   (U.S.)

Mickey Rooney *(Mickey Moran)*, Judy Garland *(Patsy Barton)*, Charles Winninger *(Joe Moran)*, Guy Kibbee *(Judge Black)*, June Preisser *(Rosalie Essex)*, Grace Hayes *(Florrie Moran)*, Betty Jaynes *(Molly Moran)*, Douglas McPhail *(Don Brice)*, Rand Brooks *(Jeff Steele)*, Leni Lynn *(Dody Martini)*

p, Arthur Freed; d, Busby Berkeley; w, Jack McGowan, Kay Van Riper (based on the musical play by Richard Rodgers and Lorenz Hart); ph, Ray June; ed, Frank Sullivan; m, Roger Edens, George E. Stoll; art d, Cedric Gibbons, Merrill Pye; cos, Dolly Tree

AAN Best Actor: Mickey Rooney; *AAN Best Score:* Roger Edens, George Stoll

---

Based on the Rodgers and Hart play of the same name, BABES IN ARMS was the first Rooney/Garland vehicle helmed by Busby Berkeley, and its success set the tone for STRIKE UP THE BAND and BABES ON BROADWAY, their subsequent collaborations. (Garland later teamed with Berkeley and hoofer Gene Kelly for 1942's FOR ME AND MY GAL.)

Joe and Florrie Moran (Charles Winninger and Grace Hayes) are old vaudevillians who begin a touring show featuring many of their senior pals. Their children, Mickey (Rooney) and Molly (Betty Jaynes), want to tag along, but the old folks refuse so, at Patsy Barton's (Garland) urging, Mickey writes a show that he will star in as well as direct. The determined youngsters must also prove that, contrary to the demands of Martha Steele (Margaret Hamilton), they don't belong in a state-administered trade school.

Only "Where or When" remains from the original score, trampled by the unsubtle Berkeley (whom Garland would grow to loathe). This was the first of the Mickey/Judy "let's put on a show" extravaganzas but it's saved by Rooney's brash nerve and especially by the triple-threat charm of Garland, an performer unequaled in the annals of show business. The storyline here has been reduced to vaudeville corn, but watch Garland's ability to transcend cliché, transforming formulaic dross into critical and box-office gold.

BABES IN TOYLAND
DVD

1934 77m bw Fantasy/Musical ★★★
MGM (U.S.)

Stan Laurel (*Stanley Dum*), Oliver Hardy (*Oliver Dee*), Charlotte Henry (*Bo-Peep*), Felix Knight (*Tom-Tom*), Henry Brandon, billed as Henry Kleinbach (*Barnaby*), Florence Roberts (*Widow Peep*), Ferdinand Munier (*Santa Claus*), William Burress (*Toymaker*), Virginia Karns (*Mother Goose*), Johnny Downs (*Little Boy Blue*)

p, Hal Roach; d, Gus Meins, Charles Rogers; w, Nick Grinde, Frank Butler (based on the musical comedy by Victor Herbert); ph, Art Lloyd, Francis Corby; ed, William Terhune, Bert Jordan

---

Victor Herbert operetta presented as vehicle for comedic genius of Laurel and Hardy. As Stanley Dum and Oliver Dee, L&H become the unsung heroes of Toyland when they avert the marriage of Bo Peep and the evil Barnaby, save the widow's abode (a multilevel shoe), rescue Tom-Tom from his exile to Bogeyland (the highlight), and ultimately rid Toyland of the evil Barnaby forever. A beautiful example of family entertainment, with the "March of the Toys" number offering five minutes of raucous action that ends the film on a high note. BABES was remade, with increasingly diminished returns, by Disney in 1961 with Tommy Sands and Annette Funicello and in 1986 with Keanu Reeves and Drew Barrymore.

BABES ON BROADWAY

1941 121m bw Musical ★★★½
MGM (U.S.)

Mickey Rooney (*Tommy Williams*), Judy Garland (*Penny Morris*), Fay Bainter (*Miss Jones*), Virginia Weidler (*Barbara Jo*), Ray McDonald (*Ray Lambert*), Richard Quine (*Morton Hammond*), Donald Meek (*Mr. Stone*), Alexander Woollcott (*Himself*), Luis Alberni (*Nick*), James Gleason (*Thornton Reed*)

p, Arthur Freed; d, Busby Berkeley; w, Fred Finklehoffe, Elaine Ryan (based on a story by Burton Lane); ph, Lester White; ed, Frederick Y. Smith; cos, Robert Kalloch

---

AAN Best Song: "How About You?"; Burton Lane (Music), Ralph Freed (Lyrics)

This sequel to BABES IN ARMS is slightly superior, serving up Rooney and Garland in everything from soup to nuts. BROADWAY presents Rooney at his enthusiastic peak, especially when he impersonates Carmen Miranda, but he's still eclipsed by Garland when she sings "F.D.R. Jones." Minstrel finale, and tributes to past theatrical performers are dynamite moments. Trivia fans should watch for Joe Yule, Rooney's father, as Mason, and for the debut of Margaret O'Brien. Burton Lane and Ralph Freed's "How About You?" earned an Oscar nomination.

BABETTE'S FEAST
DVD

(BABETTE'S GASTEBUD)
1987 102m c Drama ★★★½
Panorama/Nordisk/Danish Film Institute (Denmark) G

Ghita Norby (*Narrator*), Stephane Audran (*Babette Hersant*), Jean-Philippe Lafont (*Achille Papin*), Gudmar Wivesson (*Lorenz Lowenhielm as a Young Man*), Jarl Kulle (*Lorenz Lowenhielm as an Old Man*), Bibi Andersson (*Swedish Court Lady-in-Waiting*), Hanne Stensgaard (*Young Philippa*), Bodil Kjer (*Old Philippa*), Vibeke Hastrup (*Young Martina*), Birgitte Federspiel (*Old Martina*)

p, Just Betzer, Bo Christensen; d, Gabriel Axel; w, Gabriel Axel (based on the short story by Isak Dinesen [Karen Blixen]); ph, Henning Kristiansen (Eastmancolor); ed, Finn Henriksen; m, Per Norgard, Wolfgang Amadeus Mozart; fx, Henning Bahs; cos, Annelise Hauberg, Pia Myrdal, Karl Lagerfeld

---

AA Best Foreign Language Film

Winner of the Oscar for Best Foreign-Language Film of 1987, this quiet Danish film seemed an unlikely candidate for international success; instead of sex, violence, or nudity, it offers sermons and hymns, a dozen or so elderly Danes, and a feast to end all feasts. An expository flashback opens the film, delving into the frustrated love lives of Hastrup and Stensgaard, the daughters of a prophetic minister in a small town on Denmark's rugged Jutland peninsula. The story then shifts to 1871, as the title character (Audran), whose husband and son were killed by the Paris Communards, arrives from France and enters the employ of the sisters, who are carrying on their now-dead father's ministry. After 14 years of service with the sisters, Babette wins 10,000 francs in the French lottery and uses it to prepare a sumptuous banquet in honor of the minister's 100th birthday. At first, the stoic townspeople are reluctant to participate fully in this "pagan" feast; but ultimately they joyously indulge in Babette's masterwork, and it is revealed that she was once the chef de cuisine at the famous Cafe Anglais in Paris.

A gentle film that metaphorically examines the artist's relationship to her art, BABETTE'S FEAST is the sort of story that one cannot help but find uplifting. The performances—by such art-house favorites as Audran, Federspiel (ORDET), Lafont (BIZET'S CARMEN), and Bergman veterans Kulle and Andersson—are uniformly wonderful. The story on which the film is based was the product of a bet between its author, Karen Blixen (aka Isak Dinesen, whom Meryl Streep portrayed in OUT OF AFRICA), and a friend who suggested that the best way to crack the American market was to write about food.

BABY DOLL

1956 114m bw Drama ★★★★
Warner Bros. (U.S.)

Karl Malden (*Archie*), Carroll Baker (*Baby Doll*), Eli Wallach (*Silva Vacarro*), Mildred Dunnock (*Aunt Rose Comfort*), Lonny Chapman (*Rock*), Eades Hogue (*Town Marshal*), Noah Williamson (*Deputy*)

p, Elia Kazan; d, Elia Kazan; w, Tennessee Williams (based on his play); ph, Boris Kaufman; ed, Gene Milford; m, Kenyon Hopkins; cos, Anna Hill Johnstone

---

AAN Best Actress: Carroll Baker; AAN Best Supporting Actress: Mildred Dunnock; AAN Best Adapted Screenplay: Tennessee Williams; AAN Best B/W Cinematography: Boris Kaufman

---

An explosive, provocative black comedy from Tennessee Williams and Elia Kazan. Williams reworked his one-act play, *27 Wagonloads of Cotton*, into a highly controversial screenplay that *Time* magazine called "possibly the dirtiest American picture ever legally exhibited."

Although BABY DOLL feels tame today, the cinematography and appropriately sleazy setting still have a sizzling effect, especially in a notorious porch-swing tryst between stars Carroll Baker and Eli Wallach. All the performances are masterful, amusing and archtypal in the Williams manner: Karl Malden's yokel, Baker's hothouse virgin, Mildred Dunnock's vague octogenarian (especially hilarious) and Wallach's wily Sicilian all score strongly, though the latter lacks the physical size and power to be a believably threatening stud. Arguably, Kazan has no peer at directing Williams: you can almost feel the moss growing, so authentic is this treatment.

This was Baker's first major role, following her film debut in 1953's EASY TO LOVE, and despite all the moral outrage, she deservedly received an Oscar nomination (she lost to Ingrid Bergman for ANASTASIA), as did the script, Dunnock, and Kaufman's starkly handsome black-and-white photography. At the other end of the spectrum, the Catholic Legion of Decency broadly condemned the film, stating that it "dwells upon carnal suggestiveness." Half the town of Benoit, Mississippi, where the film was shot on location, turned out as extras for this sexual potboiler, presumably from erotic curiosity.

BACHELOR AND THE BOBBY-SOXER, THE 📀
1947 95m bw Comedy ★★★
RKO (U.S.)

Cary Grant (Dick), Myrna Loy (Margaret), Shirley Temple (Susan), Rudy Vallee (Tommy), Ray Collins (Beemish), Harry Davenport (Thaddeus), Johnny Sands (Jerry), Don Beddoe (Tony), Lillian Randolph (Bessie), Veda Ann Borg (Agnes Prescott)

p, Dore Schary; d, Irving Reis; w, Sidney Sheldon; ph, Robert de Grasse, Nicholas Musuraca; ed, Frederic Knudtson; m, Leigh Harline; art d, Albert S. D'Agostino, Carroll Clark; fx, Russell A. Cully; cos, Edward Stevenson

AA Best Original Screenplay: Sidney Sheldon

Judge Loy, impatient with cocky playboy Grant after he has appeared before her because of a nightclub fracas, orders him to indulge Temple's schoolgirl crush until it plays itself out. Silly premise allows sophisticated Grant to explode into side-splitting antics, aping the teenaged set. If you adore Grant, you'll enjoy this farce, but Loy's breezy charm is wasted and Temple has reached that age where her preciousness can be irritating to behold. This was Dore Schary's last personal production before taking over the reins of RKO.

BACHELOR MOTHER
1939 80m bw Comedy ★★★★½
RKO (U.S.)

Ginger Rogers (Polly Parrish), David Niven (David Merlin), Charles Coburn (J. B. Merlin), Frank Albertson (Freddie Miller), E.E. Clive (Butler), Elbert Coplen Jr. (Johnnie), Ferike Boros (Mrs. Weiss), Ernest Truex (Investigator), Leonard Penn (Jerome Weiss), Paul Stanton (Hargraves)

p, B.G. DeSylva, Pandro S. Berman; d, Garson Kanin; w, Norman Krasna (based on a story by Felix Jackson); ph, Robert de Grasse; ed, Henry Berman, Robert Wise; m, Roy Webb; art d, Van Nest Polglase, Carroll Clark; fx, Vernon L. Walker; cos, Irene

AAN Best Original Story: Felix Jackson

Although Rogers had starred in four hit films sans Fred Astaire during the mid-1930s, it was really with BACHELOR MOTHER, her first solo effort after the team's separation and RKO's biggest hit of 1939, that she really confirmed that she didn't need to sing or dance to appeal to mass audiences. Notable as an example of the slight relaxation during the late 1930s of Hollywood's self-enforced Production Code, the slightly risque story features Rogers as a single saleswoman for a large Macy's-like department store who finds a baby on her doorstep, whereupon everyone assumes that she's its mother.

Many of the witty lines apparently went right over the heads of the censors. Niven, delightful in his first major romantic comedy lead, portrays the playboy son of store owner Coburn, falling for Rogers even though he too assumes that she is the child's mother. Director Kanin, here enjoying one of his earliest successes, shapes the material as though he had had decades of experience. The supporting cast is uniformly excellent, especially Albertson and the hilariously befuddled, scene-stealing Coburn ("I don't care who's the father... I'm the

grandfather!"). Originally made in Hungary in 1935, the film easily outpaces its wet-blanket remake with Debbie Reynolds and Eddie Fisher, BUNDLE OF JOY (1956).

BACK STREET
1941 89m bw Drama ★★★★
Universal (U.S.)

Charles Boyer (Walter Saxel), Margaret Sullavan (Ray Smith), Richard Carlson (Curt Stanton), Frank McHugh (Ed Porter), Tim Holt (Richard Saxel), Frank Jenks (Harry Niles), Esther Dale (Mrs. Smith), Samuel S. Hinds (Felix Darren), Peggy Stewart (Freda Smith), Nell O'Day (Elizabeth Saxel)

p, Frank Shaw; d, Robert Stevenson; w, Bruce Manning, Felix Jackson (based on the novel by Fannie Hurst); ph, William Daniels; ed, Ted J. Kent; m, Frank Skinner; art d, Seward Webb

AAN Best Score (Drama): Frank Skinner

This restrained, luminous version of Fannie Hurst's oft-filmed saga is easily the best. BACK STREET's success is largely due to the tragic nobility Boyer and Sullavan invest this story of a woman who remains devoted to a married man. In real life, both actors' fates had the same elements of sad inevitibility: Boyer and Sullavan died from barbiturate overdoses which were self-inflicted; Boyer in a depression after his wife passed away and Sullavan as a result of her frustration with increasing deafness. Her complicated nature and tempestuous life was chronicled by her daughter in the book *Haywire*. Sullavan's first three husbands were Henry Fonda, William Wyler, and Leland Hayward.

BACK TO BATAAN 📀
1945 97m bw War ★★★½
RKO (U.S.)

John Wayne (Col. Joe Madden), Anthony Quinn (Capt. Andres Bonifacio), Beulah Bondi (Miss Bertha Barnes), Fely Franquelli (Dalisay Delgado), Richard Loo (Maj. Hasko), Philip Ahn (Col. Kuroki), J. Alex Havier (Sgt. Biernesa), Ducky Louie (Maximo), Lawrence Tierney (Lt. Cmdr. Waite), Leonard Strong (Gen. Homma)

p, Theron Warth; d, Edward Dmytryk; w, Ben Barzman, Richard Landau (based on a story by Aeneas MacKenzie, William Gordon); ph, Nicholas Musuraca; ed, Marston Fay; m, Roy Webb; art d, Albert S. D'Agostino, Ralph Berger; fx, Vernon L. Walker

Rousing, square-jawed, flag waving WWII drama with Filipino guerrillas following John Wayne to victory in the Pacific. Interesting subplot has Franquelli as Quinn's sweetheart and a suspected Tokyo Rose/Axis Sally broadcaster. This is the only film in which Dmytryk and Wayne were both involved—a none-too-surprising fact considering Wayne's strong right-wing stance and Dmytryk's left-wing leanings.

BACK TO SCHOOL 📀
1986 96m c Comedy ★★★
Paper Clip (U.S.) PG-13

Rodney Dangerfield (Thornton Melon), Sally Kellerman (Diane), Burt Young (Lou), Keith Gordon (Jason Melon), Robert Downey Jr. (Derek), Paxton Whitehead (Philip Barbay), Terry Farrell (Valerie), M. Emmet Walsh (Coach Turnbull), Adrienne Barbeau (Vanessa), William Zabka (Chas)

p, Chuck Russell; d, Alan Metter; w, Steven Kampmann, Will Aldis, Peter Torokvei, Harold Ramis (based on a story by Dangerfield, Greg Fields, Dennis Snee); ph, Thomas Ackerman (DeLuxe Color); ed, David Rawlins; m, Danny Elfman; prod d, David L. Snyder; fx, Michael Lantieri; cos, Durinda Wood

Broad, crude comedy hit has Rodney Dangerfield as Thornton Melon, the immensely wealthy owner of a chain of "Big Men's" clothing stores. His son Jason (Keith Gordon), a student at Grand Lakes University, has lied and told his father that he is a "big man on campus" and a champion diver. In truth, the boy is a nerdy towel attendant for the diving team and has only one friend, Derek (Robert Downey, Jr.), a self-styled revolutionary. Thornton decides to enroll in the school so that he will be closer to his son and can help him through his current problems, but finds the task more difficult than he anticipated—money helps, however. The plot is suitably slight, allowing plenty of room for the barrage of jokes that roll off Dangerfield's tongue. The result is unsophisticated, unilluminating, unambitious, and hilarious.

BACK TO THE FUTURE
1985   116m   c   Science Fiction/Comedy   ★★★
Amblin/Universal   (U.S.)   PG

Michael J. Fox (Marty McFly), Christopher Lloyd (Dr. Emmett Brown), Lea Thompson (Lorraine Baines), Crispin Glover (George McFly), Thomas F. Wilson (Biff Tannen), Claudia Wells (Jennifer Parker), Marc McClure (Dave McFly), Wendie Jo Sperber (Linda McFly), George DiCenzo (Sam Baines), James Tolkan (Mr. Strickland)

p, Bob Gale, Neil Canton; d, Robert Zemeckis; w, Robert Zemeckis, Bob Gale; ph, Dean Cundey (Panavision, Technicolor); ed, Arthur Schmidt, Harry Keramidas; m, Alan Silvestri; prod d, Lawrence G. Paull; art d, Todd Hallowell; fx, Kevin Pike; chor, Brad Jeffries; cos, Deborah L. Scott

AA Best Sound Effects Editing: Charles L. Campbell, Robert Rutledge AAN; AAN Best Original Song: "Power of Love"; Chris Hayes (Music), Johnny Colla (Music), Huey Lewis (Lyrics); AAN Best Sound: Bill Varney, Tennyson Sebastian II, Robert Thirtwell, William B. Kaplan

Marty McFly (Michael J. Fox) is a decent teenager who plays an electric guitar, sails about on a skateboard, and courts pretty Claudia Wells. But all is not well in Fox's little world. His father (Crispin Glover) is a milquetoast, his mother (Lea Thompson) is an alcoholic, and his brother and sister (Marc McClure and Wendie Jo Sperber) are decidedly weird. Marty's friend, the positively manic Christopher Lloyd, has been working on a device for time travel. Marty activates the device and finds that he has traveled back to 1955, where he encounters his own parents as teenagers. If that isn't troublesome enough, he also discovers that he doesn't have enough special plutonium fuel to return to the future. All this makes for a snappy, happy, and wonderfully nostalgic outing, with ample time-traveling twists and turns. The laughs are plentiful and the acting by Fox, Thompson, and Glover is superb. Robert Zemeckis's direction, like the technical contributions, is first-rate, and after an ambling start takes off into frenetic, non-stop fun.

BACKBEAT
1994   100m   c   Musical/Drama/Biography   ★★★
Polygram/Scala Productions   (United Kingdom)   R

Sheryl Lee (Astrid Kircherr), Stephen Dorff (Stuart Sutcliffe), Ian Hart (John Lennon), Gary Bakewell (Paul McCartney), Chris O'Neill (George Harrison), Scot Williams (Pete Best), Kai Wiesinger (Klaus Voormann), Jennifer Ehle (Cynthia Powell), Wolf Kahler (Bert Kaempfert), James Doherty (Tony Sheridan)

p, Finola Dwyer, Stephen Woolley; d, Iain Softley; w, Stephen Ward, Iain Softley, Michael Thomas; ph, Ian Wilson; ed, Martin Walsh; prod d, Joseph Bennett, Petra Borghoff; art d, Michael Carlin, Joseph Plagge; cos, Sheena Napier

Set amid the neon tawdriness of Hamburg and the working-class grime of Liverpool, BACKBEAT is about two friends, their band, and the woman who comes between them. The story is a cliché, but the band is the Beatles, and the friends are John Lennon and Stuart Sutcliffe—the real "fifth Beatle" who left the group before they became famous and then died of a brain hemorrhage in 1962.

We first meet Lennon (Ian Hart) and his longtime friend and bandmate Sutcliffe (Stephen Dorff) in a tough Liverpool nightclub, then follow them to Hamburg, where—with Paul (Gary Bakewell), George (Chris O'Neill), and drummer Pete Best (Scot Williams)—they play sleazy clubs and live the low life. Stu falls for Astrid Kirchherr (Sheryl Lee), a German art student and world-class bohemian, and the stage is set for a clash between love and friendship, high continental bohemianism and raucous pop culture.

Those expecting an "early days of the Beatles" saga may be disappointed by BACKBEAT, but those willing to entertain the story of Stu Sutcliffe and his famous friends should enjoy it—though it evokes a time and place better than it establishes characters. Noted producer Don Was (of Was Not Was) assembled a group of indie/grunge music stars, including Thurston Moore, Mike Mills, and Dave Pirner (of Sonic Youth, R.E.M., and Soul Asylum, respectively) as the off-camera band (doing contemporary rock and roll covers, not Beatles songs), and first-time director Iain Softley makes the film more visually distinctive than most music bios.

BACKDRAFT
1991   135m   c   Action/Thriller/Drama   ★★★
Imagine Films Entertainment/Trilogy   R
Entertainment Group/Raffaella Productions   (U.S.)

Kurt Russell (Stephen McCaffrey), William Baldwin (Brian McCaffrey), Robert De Niro (Donald Rimgale), Donald Sutherland (Ronald Bartel), Jennifer Jason Leigh (Jennifer Vaitkus), Scott Glenn (John Adcox), Rebecca De Mornay (Helen McCaffrey), Jason Gedrick (Tim Krizminski), J.T. Walsh (Martin Swayzak), Tony Mockus Sr. (Chief John Fitzgerald)

p, Richard B. Lewis, John Watson, Pen Densham; d, Ron Howard; w, Gregory Widen; ph, Mikael Salomon; ed, Dan Hanley, Michael Hill; m, Hans Zimmer; prod d, Albert Brenner; art d, Carol Winstead Wood; fx, Allen Hall; chor, Monica Devereux; cos, Jodie Tillen

AAN Best Sound: Gary Summers, Randy Thom, Gary Rydstrom, Glenn Williams; AAN Best Visual Effects: Mikael Salomon, Allen Hall, Clay Pinney, Scott Farrar; AAN Best Sound Effects Editing: Gary Rydstrom, Richard Hymns

Directed by Ron Howard from a screenplay by former fireman Gregory Widen, BACKDRAFT offers an insider's look at a profession seldom featured in movies. Unfortunately, the film drags when the fire is offscreen, only springing to life when it's the main attraction.

The McCaffrey brothers, Stephen (Kurt Russell) and Brian (William Baldwin), are driven by an intense rivalry that started when they were children. When Brian decides to follow Stephen—who in turn followed their late father—into the fire department, tempers flare. Their antagonistic relationship forces Brian's transfer to another assignment: he's made assistant to Donald Rimgale (Robert De Niro), a fire department investigator who specializes in cases of arson. Rimgale is working on a series of fires involving a "backdraft," in which a smoldering fire, exposed to oxygen, suddenly explodes in a literal fireball. Brian meets Rimgale's nemesis, Ronald Bartel (Donald Sutherland), a compulsive fire starter who dreams of seeing the entire world in flames. The investigation points to a corrupt city alderman (J.T. Walsh), but after consulting with Bartel, Brian begins to suspect his brother.

Despite the novelty of the setting, the family drama that forms BACKDRAFT's core is predictable. What makes

BACKDRAFT enthralling is the fire itself. Much—in fact, too much—is made dialogue-wise of the fire being a living thing, a kind of beast that slinks in the shadows and preys on the careless, the unsuspecting and the overconfident. But BACKDRAFT's fire more than lives up to expectations. It's spectacular, yes, but that's not all. Not only do the firefighting scenes evoke a feeling of gritty authenticity, but the fire itself really does seem to be alive. A scene in which a door warps ever-so-slightly, almost imperceptibly outward because a smoldering fire lurks behind it, waiting for the blast of oxygen that will bring it to roaring life, would work just as well in a finely crafted horror movie; the sentience, the subtle and cruel intelligence of the fire seems beyond dispute.

BAD AND THE BEAUTIFUL, THE
1952 116m bw Drama ★★★★★
MGM (U.S.)

Lana Turner *(Georgia Lorrison)*, Kirk Douglas *(Jonathan Shields)*, Walter Pidgeon *(Harry Pebbel)*, Dick Powell *(James Lee Bartlow)*, Barry Sullivan *(Fred Amiel)*, Gloria Grahame *(Rosemary Bartlow)*, Gilbert Roland *(Victor "Gaucho" Ribera)*, Leo G. Carroll *(Henry Whitfield)*, Vanessa Brown *(Kay Amiel)*, Paul Stewart *(Syd Murphy)*

p, John Houseman; d, Vincente Minnelli; w, Charles Schnee (based on a story by George Bradshaw); ph, Robert Surtees; ed, Conrad A. Nervig; m, David Raksin; art d, Cedric Gibbons, Edward Carfagno; fx, A. Arnold Gillespie, Warren Newcombe; cos, Helen Rose

AAN Best Actor: Kirk Douglas; *AA Best Supporting Actress:* Gloria Grahame; *AA Best Screenplay:* Charles Schnee; *AA Best B/W Cinematography:* Robert Surtees; *AA Best Art Direction-Set Decoration (B/W):* Cedric Gibbons, Edward C. Carfagno, Edwin B. Willis, Keogh Gleason; *AA Best Costume Design (B/W):* Helen Rose

The rise, fall and resurgence of a loutish Hollywood producer, as told through the eyes of three people he made then alienated. This quintessential movie on movies is an engrossing, seductive Minnelli epic, graced with superb performances.

The three separate stories, revolving around Douglas, a ruthless producer whose cunning ways allow him to climb to the top of the Hollywood heap, are told by star Turner, director Sullivan and writer Powell. Some film buffs believe that Douglas's role model was Val Lewton, the extravagant, driven producer of the 1940s, since Lewton made CAT PEOPLE and Douglas produces "The Cat Men" in the film. However, the character is more likely based on mogul David O. Selznick, particularly his beginnings as a B-film producer, his grooming of future wife Jennifer Jones and his making of a colossal Civil War film which, of course, was GONE WITH THE WIND.

Pidgeon's part is most certainly based upon the cost-conscious B-production chief at MGM, Harry Rapf, for whom Selznick first went to work. Schnee's sharp script, which acutely profiles every type of Hollywood character, from the grubbing agent to the mighty mogul, enables one easily to identify Turner's character with that of Diana Barrymore, the tragedy-struck daughter of the Great Profile, John Barrymore. The Powell role, an excellently understated profile, is best associated with writer F. Scott Fitzgerald, whose romance with Hollywood turned sour and who was married to southern belle Zelda Sayre Fitzgerald.

Cost-conscious MGM used many sets from its previous productions for this film, showing them in their naked construction, such as the sweeping staircase used earlier in Turner's MERRY WIDOW. More "inside" ploys were used in the production; Turner's own makeup man and hairdresser, Del Armstrong and Helen Young, appear in the film in their real-life roles, as does Alyce My, Turner's regular stand-in. Raksin's stirring, moody score is superb. The sets by Edwin

B. Willis and Keogh Gleason, especially in the roomy, dust-laden mansions, the movie lots, the sets, and the studio offices, totally reflect the Hollywood that is no more but which is forever preserved in this always-fascinating classic.

BAD BLOOD
(MAUVAIS SANG)
1986 128m c Crime/Romance ★★★
Plain Chant/Soprofilms/FR3/CNC/Sofima (France)

Denis Lavant *(Alex)*, Juliette Binoche *(Anna)*, Michel Piccoli *(Marc)*, Hans Meyer *(Hans)*, Julie Delpy *(Lise)*, Carroll Brooks *(The American Woman)*, Hugo Pratt *(Boris)*, Serge Reggiani *(Charlie)*, Mireille Perrier *(The Young Mother)*, Jerome Zucca *(Thomas)*

p, Philippe Diaz; d, Leos Carax; w, Leos Carax; ph, Jean-Yves Escoffier (Fujicolor); ed, Nelly Quettier; m, Benjamin Britten, Serge Prokofiev, Charles Chaplin; art d, Michel Vandestien, Thomas Peckre, Jack Dubus; fx, Guy Trielli; chor, Christine Burgos; cos, Robert Nardone, Dominique Gregogna, Martine Metert

Artsy, occasionally inspired piece by French *wunderkind* Leos Carax, who clearly wants us to know how much he owes to Cocteau and Godard. The pulp-novel plot, which takes a backseat to Carax's moody, romantic visuals, concerns a fictional AIDS-like plague called STBO which one contracts by "making love without love." The majority of those infected are adolescents whose lovemaking had previously been without consequence. The only known serum is locked away at the top of a skyscraper, with a lot of different people trying to get their hands on it. Though the storyline moves in unconvincing fits and starts, Carax gets good performances from his hip young stars—including Denis Lavant, Juliette Binoche and Julie Delpy—and pulls off some bravura set pieces. Worth a look.

BAD COMPANY
1972 93m c Western ★★★★
Paramount (U.S.) PG

Jeff Bridges *(Jake Rumsey)*, Barry Brown *(Drew Dixon)*, Jim Davis *(Marshal)*, David Huddleston *(Big Joe)*, John Savage *(Loney)*, Jerry Houser *(Arthur Simms)*, Damon Cofer *(Jim Bob Logan)*, Joshua Hill Lewis *(Boog Bookin)*, Charles Tyner *(Farmer)*, Geoffrey Lewis

p, Stanley R. Jaffe; d, Robert Benton; w, David Newman, Robert Benton; ph, Gordon Willis (Technicolor); ed, Ralph Rosenblum; m, Harvey Schmidt; art d, Robert Gundlach

A highly engaging sleeper. Draft dodging is evidently an old American custom, according to this screenplay by Benton and Newman, the duo who scripted BONNIE AND CLYDE. Marking Benton's directorial debut, BAD COMPANY is a comedy-drama about the Civil War equivalent of the Viet Nam protesters. Instead of going north to Canada, these young men wend their ways west. Bridges, Brown, Houser, Cofer, Savage, and Lewis are a bunch of young Easterners who drift out beyond the Mississippi and encounter several adventures. A segmented movie, BAD COMPANY manages to sustain interest through deft direction and an intelligent screenplay. The movie shows the down side of the Old West: deprivation, the cold, the murders, and very little of the dime-novel glamour that young men read about in their gaslit Manhattan rooms. It's a mixture of comedy and drama—and when it's funny, it's terrific.

BAD DAY AT BLACK ROCK
1955 81m c Drama ★★★★
MGM (U.S.)

Spencer Tracy *(John J. MacReedy)*, Robert Ryan *(Reno Smith)*, Anne Francis *(Liz Wirth)*, Dean Jagger *(Tim Horn)*, Walter

Brennan *(Doc Velie)*, John Ericson *(Pete Wirth)*, Lee Marvin *(Hector David)*, Ernest Borgnine *(Coley Trimble)*, Russell Collins *(Mr. Hastings)*, Walter Sande *(Sam)*

p, Dore Schary; d, John Sturges; w, Don McGuire, Millard Kaufman (based on a story by Howard Breslin); ph, William Mellor (CinemaScope, Eastmancolor); ed, Newell P. Kimlin; m, Andre Previn; art d, Cedric Gibbons, Malcolm Brown

AAN Best Actor: Spencer Tracy; *AAN Best Director:* John Sturges; *AAN Best Screenplay:* Millard Kaufman

In this powerful, lightning-paced film, Tracy plays a one-armed stranger who uncovers a dangerous skeleton in a western hick town's closet, with harrowing results. Tracy is at his subdued, thoughtful best, while Ryan perfectly conveys the ignorance behind racial prejudice and Borgnine and Marvin are memorable heavies. Sturges's direction is superbly timed, and Kaufman's script was so memorable that many of its lines quickly passed into public use.

BAD EDUCATION ***DVD***
(LA MALA EDUCACION)
2004 109m c   Thriller   ★★★★
Canal + Espana/El Deseo/Television Espanola   NC-17
(Spain)

Gael Garcia Bernal *(Angel/Juan/Zahara)*, Fele Martinez *(Enrique Goded)*, Javier Camara *(Paquito)*, Daniel Gimenez Cacho *(Father Manolo)*, Lluis Homar *(Mr. Berenguer)*, Francisco Boira *(Ignacio)*, Juan Fernandez *(Martin)*, Alberto Ferreiro *(Enrique Serrano in "The Visit")*, Francisco Maestre *(Father Jose)*, Raul Garcia Forneiro *(Young Enrique)*

p, Agustin Almodovar, Pedro Almodovar; d, Pedro Almodovar; w, Pedro Almodovar; ph, Jose Luis Alcaine; ed, Jose Salcedo; m, Alberto Iglesias; art d, Antxon Gomez; fx, Jorge Calvo; cos, Paco Delgado, Jean-Paul Gaultier

Pedro Almodovar's bold, Hitchcockian thriller in the VERTIGO vein makes provocative entertainment from material most filmmakers approach with solemn gravity.

The nesting-box narrative unfolds in three time periods—1980, 1977, and 1964—and refracts the same events through several levels of reality. Madrid, 1980: Up-and-coming filmmaker Enrique Goded (Fele Martinez) is visited by Ignacio (Gael Garcia Bernal), who attended a Catholic boarding school for boys with Enrique 16 years earlier and has matured into an exceptionally beautiful young man who calls himself Angel. Ignacio/Angel comes bearing "The Visit," a story inspired by their childhood, but he's really angling for a part in Enrique's next film. Enrique gives Ignacio/Angel the brush-off but is so enthralled by "The Visit" that it seems to unfold before his eyes. 1977: Transvestite junkie Zahara (Bernal) picks up drunken admirer Enrique Serrano (Alberto Ferreiro), who turns out to be her childhood sweetheart. As 10-year-old schoolmates in the mid-'60s, Zahara—then Ignacio (Nacho Perez)—and Enrique (played as a boy by Raul Garcia Froneiro) exchanged furtive affections at a movie theater. They were separated by pedophile priest Father Manolo (Daniel Gimenez Cacho), who expelled Enrique so he could have Ignacio to himself. Fired up by angry memories, Zahara decides to blackmail Father Manolo. In the present, Enrique realizes he's found his next project, though he has his own ideas about the ending. Angel is determined to play Zahara, Enrique resists and the conflict rekindles their youthful attraction. And just when the intersection of reality and fantasy seems as tangled as it can get, Father Manolo, who's left the clergy and reclaimed his old name, Berenguer (Lluis Homar), shows up to add some additional twists to the snarl of secrets and lies.

By turns enthralling, seductive, and deeply disturbing, Almodovar's tragic fable is steeped in a swooning sense of passion's power to inspire, pervert, and destroy that draws the fractured narrative into a satisfying whole.

BAD INFLUENCE ***DVD***
1990 99m   c   Mystery/Thriller   ★★★
Epic   (U.S.)   R

Rob Lowe *(Alex)*, James Spader *(Michael Boll)*, Lisa Zane *(Claire)*, Christian Clemenson *(Pismo Boll)*, Kathleen Wilhoite *(Leslie)*, Tony Maggio *(Patterson)*, Marcia Cross *(Ruth Fielding)*

p, Steve Tisch; d, Curtis Hanson; w, David Koepp; ph, Robert Elswit; ed, Bonnie Koehler; m, Trevor Jones; prod d, Ron Foreman; art d, William S. Combs

Slick thriller that capitalized on Lowe's bad boy publicity. Spader befriends Lowe after the latter comes to his aid in a barroom, and soon finds the creep controlling his life; to describe any of the twists would ruin the surprises in the story. Hanson keeps the film moving along at a quick pace and makes the most of the shifting point of view and weird morality of David Koepp's screenplay.

A curious mixture of styles, BAD INFLUENCE is a Hitchcockian homage (particularly its second half) that's also reminiscent of more recent films including AT CLOSE RANGE and the Koepp-scripted APARTMENT ZERO. Spader is most effective here, and Lowe has finally found his niche as a junior league Richard Gere. The tension between the two is well handled and yet never quite explained, which adds to the mysterious "feel" of the movie and gives the characters a sexually ambiguous edge.

BAD LIEUTENANT ***DVD***
1992 96m   c   Crime/Thriller   ★★★½
Lt. Productions/Edward R. Pressman   NC-17
Film Corporation   (U.S.)

Harvey Keitel *(The Lieutenant)*, Victor Argo *(Bet Cop)*, Paul Calderon *(Cop One)*, Leonard Thomas *(Cop Two)*, Robin Burrows *(Ariane)*, Frankie Thorn *(Nun)*, Zoe Lund, billed as Zoe Tamarlaine Lund *(Zoe)*, Victoria Bastel *(Bowtay)*, Paul Hipp *(Jesus)*, Brian McElroy *(Lt.'s Son)*

p, Edward R. Pressman, Mary Kane; d, Abel Ferrara; w, Zoe Tamarlaine Lund, Abel Ferrara; ph, Ken Kelsch; ed, Anthony Redman; m, Joe Delia; prod d, Charles Lagola; cos, David Sawaryn

The Lieutenant (Harvey Keitel) is a New York City cop who's juggling two lives. At home, he's a family man who just wants the best for his wife and extended flock of relatives. On the job, he's a rogue agent heading for disaster. He drinks too much and has a coke problem; he abuses suspects and extorts sexual favors from prostitutes and drug addicts, including his strung-out mistress (Zoe Tamarlaine Lund, who co-wrote the screenplay and starred in Ferrara's early cult hit, MS. 45); and he's a compulsive gambler deep in hock to the Mafia.

All that changes when a young nun (Frankie Thorn) is brutally raped during a robbery at a convent in Spanish Harlem. The Lieutenant quickly launches his own investigation, figuring that he can use the reward money to pay off his debts. More importantly, his search takes on the aspect of a spiritual quest for redemption, even as he simultaneously indulges in a suicidal gambling spree that increases his indebtedness to an exasperated mob bookie.

The director of such stylish thrillers as CHINA GIRL and KING OF NEW YORK, Abel Ferrara has made his reputation by balancing lurid narratives and lush, seductive visuals. BAD LIEUTENANT is actually an aesthetic throwback to Ferrara's earliest work, 1979's DRILLER KILLER; it is harsh, gritty and utterly uncompromising. The photography has the bleak, documentary look of THE FRENCH CONNECTION, heavy on the hand-held camera; the editing is rough and jarring. One can empathize with the characters, but it's hard to imagine liking any of them. Harvey Keitel gives an astonishing performance here, playing a tortured soul who simultaneously revels in self-loathing and yearns for absolution. Excellent supporting performances, including Lund's turn as a philosophizing junkie, round out the picture. Though hardly a film for all sensibilities, BAD LIEUTENANT has the courage of its own convictions, and follows them to the bitter end.

BAD NEWS BEARS, THE

1976 102m c   Comedy   ***DVD***
Paramount   (U.S.)   ★★★   PG

Walter Matthau *(Coach Buttermaker)*, Tatum O'Neal *(Manda Whurlizer)*, Vic Morrow *(Roy Turner)*, Joyce Van Patten *(Cleveland)*, Ben Piazza *(Councilman Whitewood)*, Jackie Earle Haley *(Kelly Leak)*, Alfred Lutter *(Ogilvie)*, Brandon Cruz *(Joey Turner)*, Shari Summers *(Mrs. Turner)*, Joe Brooks *(Umpire)*

p, Stanley R. Jaffe; d, Michael Ritchie; w, Bill Lancaster; ph, John A. Alonzo (Movielab Color); ed, Richard A. Harris; m, Jerry Fielding; prod d, Polly Platt

As amusing for adults as it is for children, this charming, funny film takes a gentle poke at Little League baseball and the American obsession with winning. Morris Buttermaker (Walter Matthau), in a strong comic turn, a one-time minor leaguer, becomes the manager of the Bears, a team of multiracial Little League rejects in southern California. With Morris's help this hapless, foul-mouthed bunch, led by its star female hurler, Manda Whurlizer (Tatum O'Neal), begins improving and winning ball games. Director Michael Ritchie (DOWNHILL RACER, SMILE), working from a script by Burt Lancaster's son, Bill, provides a nice twist on the expected outcome. Although the film could have been preachy, Ritchie handles the story and theme with deftness. So popular was the film that it produced two sequels—THE BAD NEWS BEARS IN BREAKING TRAINING (1977) and THE BAD NEWS BEARS GO TO JAPAN (1978)—and at least one imitation, HERE COME THE TIGERS (1978), plus a TV series.

BAD SANTA

2003 95m c   Comedy   ★½
Dimension/Triptych Pictures   (U.S.)   R

Billy Bob Thornton *(Willie T. Stokes)*, Tony Cox *(Marcus)*, Brett Kelly *(The Kid)*, Lauren Graham *(Sue)*, Lauren Tom *(Sue)*, Bernie Mac *(Gin Slagel)*, John Ritter *(Bob Chipeska)*, Cloris Leachman *(Grandmother)*, Ajay Naidu *(Hindustani Troublemaker)*, Lorna Scott *(Milwaukee Mother)*

p, Sarah Aubrey, John Cameron, Bob Weinstein; d, Terry Zwigoff; w, Glenn Ficarra, John Requa; ph, Jamie Anderson; ed, Robert Hoffman; m, David Kitay; prod d, Sharon Seymour; art d, Peter Borck; fx, Scott Blackwell, Chris Brenczewski; cos, Wendy Chuck

Bad is right, unless the sight of a soused department-store Santa wetting himself in front of a gaggle of tiny tots, eyes all aglow, is your idea of holiday cheer.

Willie T. Stokes (Billy Bob Thornton) may be a gin-soaked draft dodger with a prison record nearly as long as his list of ex-wives, but Willie can crack a safe like nobody's business. He's not exactly department-store-Santa material, but Willie doesn't do it for the kids; once a year he and his partner, a pint-size Marcus (Tony Cox), hire themselves out to an unsuspecting store as a Santa-and-elf team. When

Christmas Eve rolls around, they help themselves to the contents of the store's safe. So far they've cleaned out seven stores in seven years, but this year's gig at Chamberlain's department store in sunny Phoenix, Ariz., might be a problem. Willie's drinking has gotten out of control, the mall's uptight general manager (John Ritter) suspects something isn't quite right, and the in-store dick (Bernie Mac) knows exactly what Willie and Marcus are up to and wants a cut. Complicating matters further is the sudden appearance of a strange, chubby kid (Brett Kelly) who seems to think Willie really is Santa Claus.

Quite a bit of talent went into this holiday turkey, which was produced by Joel and Ethan Coen and directed by Terry Zwigoff. The cast is actually very good; Lauren Graham is kind of cute as an alcoholic bartender with a Santa fetish. But the screenplay just isn't funny, and Zwigoff's deadpan pacing—perfect for the wry, sophisticated humor of GHOST WORLD—leaves too much time for viewers to realize just how sad and disturbing it all is.

BAD SLEEP WELL, THE

(WARUI YATSU HODO YOKU NEMURU)   ***DVD***
1960 135m bw   Drama
Tanaka-Kurosawa   (Japan)   ★★★

Toshiro Mifune *(Koichi Nishi)*, Takeshi Kato *(Itakura)*, Masayuki Mori *(Iwabuchi)*, Takashi Shimura *(Moriyama)*, Akira Nishimura *(Shirai)*, Kamatari Fujiwara *(Wada)*, Gen Shimizu *(Miura)*, Kyoko Kagawa *(Keiko)*, Tatsuya Mihashi *(Tatsuo)*, Kyu Sazanka *(Kaneko)*

p, Tomoyuki Tanaka, Akira Kurosawa; d, Akira Kurosawa; w, Akira Kurosawa, Shinobu Hashimoto, Hideo Oguni, Ryuzu Kikushima, Eijiro Hisaita; ph, Yuruzu Aizawa; ed, Akira Kurosawa; m, Masaru Sato

Samurai capitalism. One of Akira Kurosawa's most obviously political films, THE BAD SLEEP WELL is a prophetic indictment of Japan's cutthroat, feudalistic approach to business. Nishi (Toshiro Mifune) is a fast-rising young executive about to further his acquisition of power through marriage to Keiko (Kyoko Kagawa), the daughter of the firm's president, Iwabuchi (Masayuki Mori). Nishi, however, is something of a modern-day samurai—a heroic figure who has adopted a new identity in order to avenge the death of his father, a corporate vice president whose death can be traced to Iwabuchi. Nishi's method of revenge is to become part of the family and destroy Iwabuchi from within. But Nishi eventually discovers that there is no room for the noble hero in the ruthless world of high-powered executives and politicians. One of Kurosawa's finest achievements, THE BAD SLEEP WELL becomes even more interesting when viewed as a predecessor to HIGH AND LOW (1963), an equally jaundiced look at Japanese mores.

BADLANDS

1973 94m c   Crime/Drama   ***DVD***
Pressman Williams/Jill Jakes   (U.S.)   ★★★★★   PG

Martin Sheen *(Kit)*, Sissy Spacek *(Holly)*, Warren Oates *(Father)*, Ramon Bieri *(Cato)*, Alan Vint *(Deputy)*, Gary Littlejohn *(Sheriff)*, John Carter *(Rich Man)*, Bryan Montgomery *(Boy)*, Gail Threlkeld *(Girl)*, Charles Fitzpatrick *(Clerk)*

p, Terrence Malick; d, Terrence Malick; w, Terrence Malick; ph, Brian Probyn, Tak Fujimoto, Stevan Larner (Consolidated Color); ed, Robert Estrin; m, George Tipton, James Taylor; art d, Jack Fisk; cos, Dona Baldwin

Stark, brutal story obviously based on the Charles Starkweather-Carol Fugate murder spree through Nebraska and surrounding states in 1958, with Sheen playing the killer lashing out against a society that ignores his existence and Spacek as his misguided teenage consort. Sheen is forceful and properly weird as the mass murderer, killing Oates, Spacek's disapproving father, when he forbids his daughter to date him. He then goes on the run, Spacek in tow, randomly killing innocents who cross his path. (Starkweather and Fugate, although she later denied killing anyone, were responsible for the deaths of ten people.) The locale in the movie is changed to South Dakota but almost all the characteristics of the real culprits are intact, the strutting Sheen pretending to be James Dean in REBEL WITHOUT A CAUSE, while Spacek doesn't quite understand what he's all about, but goes along anyway.

Director Malick neither romanticizes nor condemns his subjects, maintaining a low-key approach to the story that results in a fascinating character study. Perhaps Starkweather himself provided the best insight into the character when he stated: "The more I looked at people the more I hated them, because I knew there wasn't any place for me with the kind of people I knew." The film did scant box office business, but it remains one of the most impressive directorial debuts ever. While Malick would continue to show promise in the equally impressive DAYS OF HEAVEN, by the end of the 1980s these two films would represent his entire oeuvre.

BAGDAD CAFE *DVD*
1987 91m c Comedy ★★★½
Pelemele/BR-HR/Project (West Germany) PG

Marianne Sagebrecht (*Jasmin Munchgstettner*), CCH Pounder (*Brenda*), Jack Palance (*Rudi Cox*), Christine Kaufmann (*Debbie*), Monica Calhoun (*Phyllis*), Darron Flagg (*Sal Junior*), George Aquilar (*Cahuenga*), G. Smokey Campbell (*Sal*), Hans Stadlbauer (*Munchgstettner*), Apesanahkwat (*Sheriff Arnie*)

p, Percy Adlon, Eleonore Adlon; d, Percy Adlon; w, Percy Adlon, Eleonore Adlon, Christopher Doherty (based on a story by Percy Adlon); ph, Bernd Heinl (Eastmancolor); ed, Norbert Herzner; m, Bob Telson, Johann Sebastian Bach; cos, Elizabeth Warner, Regina Batz

AAN Best Original Song: "Calling You"; Bob Telson (Music & Lyrics)

An adorable oddity. Director Percy Adlon's first English-language film is set in a run-down motel in the middle of the Mojave Desert and, like his earlier art-house hit SUGARBABY, stars the uniquely talented Marianne Sagebrecht. Jasmin Munchgstettner (Sagebrecht), a German *hausfrau*, is abandoned in the desert after an argument with her husband. After wandering for some time under the scorching sun, Jasmin checks into a dusty motel run by Brenda (C.C.H. Pounder), a tough-talking, no-nonsense woman who treats her new boarder like some sort of space alien. With time, however, the pair become the best of friends, turning the decrepit diner into the most exciting place west of Las Vegas, and Jasmin becomes one of the most popular entertainers for miles around—especially catching the fancy of Rudi Cox (Jack Palance), a cosmic romantic who desperately wants to paint her portrait. BAGDAD CAFE is a visually exhilarating and consciously modern film, more concerned with projecting an atmosphere or spirit than with telling a story. It's hard not to fall in love with this comic fable about the magic that develops at the meeting of two cultures.

BAISE-MOI *DVD*
2000 77m c Crime/Erotic ★★★
Pan Europeenne Production/Take One/Cine Valse/Toute Premiere Fois/Studio Canal + (France)

Raffaela Anderson (*Manu*), Karen Lancaume, billed as Karen Bach (*Nadine*), Delphine McCarty (*Severine*), Lisa Marshall (*Karla*), Estelle Isaac (*Alice*), Herve P. Gustave, billed as H.P.G.

(*Martin*), Marc Rioufol (*Architect*), Ouassini Embarek (*Radouan*), Adama Niane (*Boy with Billiards*), Tewfik Saad (*Server*)

p, Philippe Godeau; d, Virginie Despentes, Coralie Trinh Thi; w, Virginie Despentes, Coralie Trinh Thi (based on the novel by Virginie Despentes); ph, Benoit Chamaillard; ed, Ailo Auguste-Judith, Francine Lemaitre, Veronique Rosa; m, Varou Jan; art d, Paul Fayard, Irene Galitzine, Christophe Mureau, Claude Veyset; fx, Guillaume Castagne, Christophe Chabenet, Pierre-Paul Jayne, Frederic Laine, Perrine Poirier; cos, Magali Baret, Isabelle Frayesse

A brutal variation on THELMA & LOUISE that bares its nihilistic heart from the get-go; there's never a chance that this rubber-burning road trip will takes these anti-heroines anywhere good.

The embittered Manu (Raffaella Anderson) cadges money from her brother and picks up extra cash appearing in porno movies. Call girl Nadine (Karen Lancaume) lies around smoking dope and watching smutty movies. They're both sleepwalking through life, trapped by poverty and deeply ingrained attitudes towards women they're neither savvy nor motivated enough to challenge. But just beneath the surface of their torpor lies a reservoir of seething anger, waiting for something to set it off. For Manu, the trigger is a brutal sexual assault. For Nadine, the last straw is her prissy roommate's vilification of Nadine's best friend, an amiable junkie. Nadine lashes out, and when she comes to her senses, her roommate is dead. Nadine and Manu cross paths by chance and join forces to pay back a world that's dealt them nothing but dirt.

Clearly determined to *epater les bourgeois*, co-writers and -directors Virginie Despentes and Coralie Trinh Thi cast porn stars in the leads and push several of the film's sex scenes squarely into hardcore territory. But though it comes wrapped in a stylish French mantle of feminist rage and sexual empowerment, the picture ultimately belongs squarely in the tradition of rape revenge pictures, with I SPIT ON YOUR GRAVE representing the low end of the form and Abel Ferrara's MS. 45 its apotheosis. The difference is that Despentes and Trinh Thi have their polemical bona fides in impeccable order, the better to ward off accusations that they're exploiting the very images of sexualized violence they purport to condemn.

BAKER'S WIFE, THE
(LA FEMME DU BOULANGER)
1938 130m bw Comedy ★★★★
Marcel Pagnol (France)

Raimu (*Aimable, The Baker*), Ginette Leclerc (*Aurelie, The Baker's Wife*), Charles Moulin (*Dominique, The Shepherd*), Robert Vattier (*The Priest*), Robert Bassac (*The School Teacher*), Fernand Charpin (*The Marquis*), Maximilienne

p, Robert Hakim, Raymond Hakim; d, Marcel Pagnol; w, Marcel Pagnol (based on Jean Giono's novel *Jean Le Bleu*); ph, R. Lendruz, N. Daries; ed, Suzanne de Troeye; m, Vincent Scotto

Raimu, the star of Marcel Pagnol's Marseilles trilogy, here teams again with Pagnol as the baker Aimable, a new addition to a French village that has lacked a quality baker for some time. The tasting of Aimable's first loaves of bread is an event eagerly awaited by all the locals, giving the villagers a chance to take time away from their daily complaints and neighborly disagreements. Aimable takes great pride in his bread—a pride equalled only by his affection for his coquettish wife Aurelie (Ginette Leclerc). The villagers agree that if their new baker's bread is as lovely as his wife, all will be content. Unfortunately for Aimable, however, the handsome shepherd Dominique (Charles Moulin) prefers Aurelie to a brioche, and she prefers his affection to slaving over a hot stove. When they run off together, Aimable is no longer able to continue his baking. Rather than risk losing another baker, the villagers band together in an effort to bring Aurelie back home. A touching comedy that borders on the tragic, THE BAKER'S WIFE is brilliantly acted and directed, and proved one of the most popular French films of all time in the U.S.

BALL OF FIRE   DVD
1941 111m bw Comedy   ★★★★★
Goldwyn   (U.S.)

Gary Cooper *(Prof. Bertram Potts)*, Barbara Stanwyck *(Sugarpuss O'Shea)*, Oscar Homolka *(Prof. Gurkakoff)*, Henry Travers *(Prof. Jerome)*, S.Z. Sakall *(Prof. Magenbruch)*, Tully Marshall *(Prof. Robinson)*, Leonid Kinskey *(Prof. Quintana)*, Richard Haydn *(Prof. Oddly)*, Aubrey Mather *(Prof. Peagram)*, Allen Jenkins *(Garbage Man)*

p, Samuel Goldwyn; d, Howard Hawks; w, Charles Brackett, Billy Wilder (based on the story "From A to Z" by Thomas Monroe, Billy Wilder); ph, Gregg Toland; ed, Daniel Mandell; m, Alfred Newman; art d, Perry Ferguson

AAN Best Actress: Barbara Stanwyck; *AAN Best Original Story:* Thomas Monroe, Billy Wilder; *AAN Best Score (Drama):* Alfred Newman; *AAN Best Sound Recording:* Thomas Moulton

Skewed variation on "Snow White and the Seven Dwarfs," courtesy of Howard Hawks and a zany Wilder-Brackett screenplay. Cooper is a stodgy linguist researching slang for a new encyclopedia. In order to get closer to it, he recruits Stanwyck, as a stripper who knows exactly what color the cat's pajamas should be and why it's 23, not 24 or 22 Skiddoo. Cooper lives in a huge house with seven other longhairs and Stanwyck goes on the lam and moves in. There's a veritable corps de comedy in the character actors here; one look at the cast list will convince anyone that scene-stealing would have been rampant without the firm Hawks hand. Terrific, crackling dialogue, especially in the slangy, machine-gun mouth of La Stanwyck. Remade as A SONG IS BORN, again by Hawks.

BALLAD OF A SOLDIER   DVD
1959 89m bw Drama/War   ★★★★★
Mosfilm   (U.S.S.R.)

Vladimir Ivashov *(Alyosha)*, Zhanna Prokhorenko *(Shura)*, Antonina Maximova *(Alyosha's Mother)*, Nikolai Kruchkov *(General)*, Yevgeniy Urbanskiy *(Invalid)*

d, Grigori Chukhrai; w, Valentin Yezhov, Grigori Chukhrai; m, Michael Siv

AAN Best Original Story and Screenplay: Valentin Yoshov, Grigori Chukhrai

A young soldier (Ivashov) fighting on the front during WWII heroically disables two German tanks and is rewarded with a six-day leave. As he makes the long journey home to see his mother (Maximova) he meets a variety of people, both friendly and antagonistic, who need his help. Though he finally makes it to his mother's door, he never gets to spend his leave quite as he intended before having to return to almost certain death at the front.

This startlingly realistic and lovingly detailed picture transcends its dramatic premise to embody on several levels the tale of all the Soviet people. An episodic and visually haunting film with modest but never overdone touches of comedy, romance, and sentimentality, BALLAD OF A SOLDIER is a fine example of the Soviet realist tradition—a style of filmmaking paralleled by the more cinematically innovative techniques of such Soviet directors as Sergei Paradzhanov (SHADOWS OF FORGOTTEN ANCESTORS) and Andrei Tarkovsky (MY NAME IS IVAN). Although the film is nationalistic, this and several of Chukrai's other films (e.g.

THE FORTY-FIRST) nevertheless contain a palpable critique of Stalinism and its "cult of the hero," suggesting that humanity is more important than heroism.

BALLAD OF CABLE HOGUE, THE
1970 121m c Western   ★★★½
Warner Bros.   (U.S.)   R

Jason Robards Jr. *(Cable Hogue)*, Stella Stevens *(Hildy)*, David Warner *(Joshua)*, Strother Martin *(Bowen)*, Slim Pickens *(Ben)*, L.Q. Jones *(Taggart)*, Peter Whitney *(Cushing)*, R.G. Armstrong *(Quittner)*, Gene Evans *(Clete)*, William Mims *(Jensen)*

p, Phil Feldman, Sam Peckinpah, William Faralla; d, Sam Peckinpah; w, John Crawford, Edmund Penney; ph, Lucien Ballard (Technicolor); ed, Frank Santillo, Lou Lombardo; m, Jerry Goldsmith; art d, Leroy Coleman; cos, Robert Fletcher

Peckinpah demonstrated a sense of humor in THE BALLAD OF CABLE HOGUE that had not been seen since his early TV days when he ran one of the best and most overlooked cowboy shows ever, "The Westerner," starring Brian Keith. CABLE HOGUE is at its best when chronicling how the Old West passed and mercantilism spread across the Great Plains.

Robards is a prospector abandoned in the desert and left to die by Martin and Jones. (They worked together again that same year in THE BROTHERHOOD OF SATAN.) Instead of dying, he finds water in a previously arid spot, opens a rest stop for thirsty travelers, and prospers. Stevens is a whore determined to sleep her way to riches, and after a brief fling with Robards, she decides to move on to greener sheets, fleeing to San Francisco. (This is Stevens's best role and underlines the terrible waste of her career—she's terrific.) Warner pops in and out as a preacher who can't decide whether he should save souls or live a life of dedicated hedonism. Hedonism wins. If you're expecting blood and guts and slow-motion death forget it. Peckinpah decided to make a different movie here, and different it is. Not a hit at the box office, it remains one of his finest efforts, funny, touching and never mawkishly sentimental.

BALLAD OF NARAYAMA, THE
(NARAYAMA BUSHIKO)
1983 130m c Drama   ★★★★½
Toei   (Japan)

Ken Ogata *(Tatsuhei)*, Sumiko Sakamoto *(Orin, His Mother)*, Takejo Aki *(Tamayan, His Wife)*, Tonpei Hidari *(Risuke, His Brother)*, Shoichi Ozawa *(Katsuzo)*, Seiji Kurasaki *(Kesakichi, Older Son)*, Kaoru Shimamori *(Tomekichi, Younger Son)*, Ryutaro Tatsumi *(Matayan)*, Junko Takada *(Matsu)*, Nijiko Kiyokawa *(Old Widow Okane)*

p, Goro Kusakabe, Jiro Tomoda; d, Shohei Imamura; w, Shohei Imamura (based on the stories "Narayama Bushi-ko" and "Tohoku No Zunmatachi" by Scichiro Fakazawa); ph, Masao Tochizawa; ed, Hajime Okayasu; m, Shinichiro Ikebe; art d, Nobutaka Yoshino

A remarkable picture based on the award-winning stories by Fakazawa and previously filmed in 1958 under the same title. The story takes place in a 19th century Japanese village plagued by famine. In order to ration food, the village has ritualized the killing of redundant members of the community: newborn males are murdered, while the elderly are carried by their children to the top of Mount Narayama and left to die. Orin (Sakamoto) is a 69-year-old woman thus scheduled for extinction; her son (Ogata) is reluctant to carry out the ritual, but the mother, bound to tradition, is adamant. After finding wives for her children, she begins the arduous journey up the mountain, strapped to her son's back.

In deliberate contrast to the dreamy original, this remake is joltingly realistic. Director Imamura (THE PORNOGRAPHERS), who began as an assistant to Yasujiro Ozu, has a well-known flair for urban low-life; here, he turns to rural brutishness with equally striking results. The film revels in the indecorous (dead babies and a ritual gang-bang are highlights), but everything is rendered with a visual beauty that is probably intentionally incongruous. Winner of the Golden Palm at the 1983 Cannes festival.

BALSEROS

2004 120m c Documentary ★★★★
Bausan Films/TV3/Buenavida Producciones (Spain)

Mericys Gonzalez, Oscar Del Valle, Rafael Cano, Miriam Hernandez, Guillermo Armas, Juan Carlos, Misclaida

p, Loris Omedes; d, Carles Bosch, Josep M. Domenech; w, Carles Bosch, David Trueba; ph, Josep M. Domenech; ed, Ernest Blasi; m, Lucrecia

AAN Best Documentary Feature

Originally conceived as a half-hour, Spanish public television program, this absorbing documentary follows seven *balseros*—men and women who, desperate to escape the economic shambles of post-USSR Cuba, set sail for the U.S. on makeshift rafts—through seven tumultuous years of their lives.

Shortly after Castro opened the Cuban coasts in August 1994, a crew from TV3's "Trenta Minuts" arrived in Havana and began filming a group of *balseros* as they scrambled to assemble their rafts and set off for what they hoped would be a better life in the United States. Most returned to Cuba within days. Bad weather forced Mericys Gonzalez to turn her raft around, while Guillermo Armas, Oscar Del Valle, Rafael Cano, Miriam Hernandez, Mericys's sister Misclaida, and her common-law husband, Juan Carlos, were all intercepted by the U.S. Coast Guard. Nevertheless, TV3 reporter Carles Bosch and cameraman Josep M. Domenech continued to follow their stories; two years later, after most had entered the U.S. legally, the filmmakers produced an update. Their subjects were now living in cities as diverse as Miami, New York, and San Antonio, and facing radically different circumstances. Five years later, Bosch and Domenech once again tracked down their seven subjects for a third and final report, and their situations are often as surprising as they are poignant.

Brilliantly edited from well over 100 hours of tape, the final two-hour film recalls Michael Apted's *7 UP* series, whose seven-year updates on one group of English schoolchildren raise important questions about society and the individual. Once viewers get to know the *balseros* as individuals, rather than by a label thrust upon them by desperate circumstances, it's interesting to see how close to—or far from—their dreams the American experience takes them.

BAMBI 💿

1942 70m c Animated/Children's ★★★★★
Walt Disney Productions (U.S.) G

VOICES OF: Bobby Stewart *(Bambi)*, Peter Behn *(Thumper)*, Paula Winslowe *(Bambi's Mother)*, Stan Alexander *(Flower)*, Cammie King *(Faline)*, Donnie Dunagan, Hardie Albright, John Sutherland, Tim Davis, Sam Edwards

p, Walt Disney; d, David D. Hand; w, Perce Pearce, Larry Morey (based on the story by Felix Salten); m, Frank Churchill, Edward H. Plumb; art d, Tom Codrick, Robert Cormack, Al Zinnen, McLaren Stewart, Lloyd Harting, David Hilberman, John Hubley, Dick Kelsey; anim, Milt Kahl, Eric Larson, Franklin Thomas, Oliver M. Johnston Jr.

AAN Best Score (Drama or Comedy): Frank Churchill, Edward H. Plumb; *AAN Best Song:* "Love Is a Song"; Frank Churchill (Music), Larry Morey (Lyrics); *AAN Best Sound Recording:* Sam Slyfield

Said to be Walt Disney's own personal favorite of all his films, BAMBI is a brilliantly animated, heart-tugging parable about the cycles of life as reflected in the story of the growth of a young deer.

A fawn named Bambi learns to walk and talk with the help of his friends, a bunny named Thumper and a skunk named Flower. Bambi's mother teaches him about the joys of nature but warns him to stay away from the deadly creature named "Man." One spring day during a visit to a meadow, Bambi's mother is killed by a hunter. Years pass, and Bambi experiences the first pangs of romantic love when he becomes interested in a female deer named Faline. After winning a fight with another male for her affection, he further proves his heroism during a raging forest fire that nearly claims the lives of his friends and Faline.

Originally planned to follow Disney's first animated feature, SNOW WHITE AND THE SEVEN DWARFS (1937), BAMBI wound up taking five years to make. In contrast to the clean lines and bright colors of most Disney cartoons, the drawings in BAMBI have a soft, lush, and almost hazy quality to them, in keeping with the gentleness of the characters. The bittersweet fable is actually geared toward older kids and even adults, dealing with such traumatic subjects as the loss of childhood innocence and the death of a parent; the heartwrenching scene where Bambi's mother is killed has inspired countless nightmares among those who saw it at a very early age. This honest, non-sugar-coated approach to the hard truths of life, however, is what gives BAMBI its lasting emotional power, and makes it stand apart, not only from Disney's cartoons, but from virtually all others as well.

BANANAS 💿

1971 82m c Comedy/War ★★★
UA (U.S.)

Woody Allen *(Fielding Mellish)*, Louise Lasser *(Nancy)*, Carlos Montalban *(Gen. Vargas)*, Natividad Abascal *(Yolanda)*, Jacobo Morales *(Esposito)*, Miguel Suarez *(Luis)*, David Ortiz *(Sanchez)*, Rene Enriquez *(Diaz)*, Jack Axelrod *(Arroyo)*, Howard Cosell *(Himself)*

p, Charles H. Joffe, Jack Grossberg; d, Woody Allen; w, Woody Allen, Mickey Rose; ph, Andrew Costikyan (Deluxe Color); ed, Ron Kalish; m, Marvin Hamlisch; prod d, Ed Wittstein; cos, Gene Coffin

Woody Allen is Fielding Mellish, a neurotic New Yorker who's enamored of a political activist, Nancy (Louise Lasser, Allen's wife at the time), who'll have nothing to do with him because she's totally immersed in the revolution taking place in the banana republic of San Marcos. Wearing Castro-like fatigues and a false red beard, Allen accidentally winds up as president of San Marcos. He returns to the U.S., is unmasked as a fraud, tried for subversion, and winds up marrying Nancy. Although some of the humor falls flat in this early Allen comedy, his satire of revolutions and revolutionaries is perpetually topical; subsequent events in Central America have only enhanced the film's appeal.

BAND OF ANGELS

1957 125m c Drama ★★★★
Warner Bros. (U.S.)

Clark Gable *(Hamish Bond)*, Yvonne De Carlo *(Amantha Starr)*, Sidney Poitier *(Rau-Ru)*, Efrem Zimbalist Jr. *(Ethan Sears)*, Rex Reason *(Seth Parton)*, Patric Knowles *(Charles de Marigny)*, Torin

Thatcher *(Capt. Canavan)*, Andrea King *(Miss Idell)*, Ray Teal *(Mr. Calloway)*, Russell Evans *(Jimmee)*

d, Raoul Walsh; w, John Twist, Ivan Goff, Ben Roberts (based on the novel by Robert Penn Warren); ph, Lucien Ballard (Warner Color); ed, Folmar Blangsted; m, Max Steiner; art d, Franz Bachelin; cos, Marjorie Best

An entertainingly full-blown melodrama brimming with lust, notable for its similarities to GONE WITH THE WIND and for dealing with miscegenation and racial tensions. Forced to leave school when left penniless after her father's death, De Carlo learns that she is partially black and is promptly taken to be sold on the block. Before any mean-minded plantation owner can unbutton her bodice, however, powerful landowner Gable buys her and ensconces her inside his lavish mansion, where she soon becomes his loving and grateful mistress. The Civil War breaks out, and the Yankees capture New Orleans, recruiting ex-slaves to the colors. Poitier, Gable's overseer (in a soft profile of the legendary black leader Bras Coupe), deserts his master to join the Union Army, hating the patronizing Gable and his mulatto mistress. Risking execution by disobeying Yankee orders, Gable burns his crops and retreats to one of his remote plantations. Poitier follows in pursuit and the stage is set for several climactic confrontations.

Almost the entire cast is in top form, even sultry De Carlo, who had an occasional penchant for overacting. Gable almost does a reprise of his magnificent Rhett Butler from GONE WITH THE WIND. Outlandishly memorable is the scene on his patio where he drunkenly confesses his past as a slave trader while a summer storm rages overhead. Poitier, in an unsympathetic part, does what he can with a surly, graceless character. Walsh's direction is at its finest in a lively adaptation of the Warren novel. Steiner's score thunders, hums and calls plaintively where needed, while Ballard's photography shows the Old South in all its glories and gluttonies.

BAND OF OUTSIDERS   DVD
1964   95m   bw   Crime   ★★★
Anouchka/Orsay   (France)

Anna Karina *(Odile)*, Claude Brasseur *(Arthur)*, Sami Frey *(Franz)*, Louisa Colpeyn *(Mme. Victoria)*, Daniele Girard *(English Teacher)*, Ernest Menzer *(Arthur's Uncle)*, Chantal Darget *(Arthur's Aunt)*, Michele Seghers *(Pupil)*, Claude Makovski *(Pupil)*, Georges Staquet *(Legionnaire)*

d, Jean-Luc Godard; w, Jean-Luc Godard (based on the novel *Fool's Gold* by Dolores Hitchens); ph, Raoul Coutard; ed, Agnes Guillemot, Francoise Collin; m, Michel Legrand

Several years after the success of his debut feature, BREATHLESS, Godard returned to the crime genre and his fascination with American pop culture. Outsiders less by choice than by societal pressures, Odile (Karina), Arthur (Brasseur), and Franz (Frey) meet in an English language class and become fast friends. Odile tells Franz that she lives in a house where a large cache of loot is hidden, and soon he and Arthur, under the influence of the countless Hollywood films and pulp novels they've consumed, decide to burglarize the house. Odile, attracted to both men, completes the criminal triangle.

As anyone who has seen a Godard film might guess, there is very little concern for plot—the attraction of BAND OF OUTSIDERS lies not so much in its actual story as in Godard's telling of it. His voice-over narration is confrontational; his characters talk to the screen; there exists a strange, somewhat uneasy relationship between comedy and violence; and the frame is filled with various allusions to film, literature, and Godard himself. This was his seventh film in only five years and, as in Truffaut's SHOOT THE PIANO PLAYER, it attempts to find a new truth by retelling a familiar story in a

new way. Particularly memorable is the trio's nine-second tour of the Louvre.

If this film is less engaged with social and political realities than most of Godard's other work from this period and seems like nothing more than a playful attempt to re-create an old Hollywood genre, one must remember that even a lesser Godard is likely to be much more stimulating than another director's better films. At the height of his impish self-awareness, the filmmaker credits himself here as Jean-Luc Cinema Godard.

BAND WAGON, THE   DVD
1953   111m   c   Musical   ★★★★½
MGM   (U.S.)

Fred Astaire *(Tony Hunter)*, Cyd Charisse *(Gaby Gerard)*, Oscar Levant *(Lester Marton)*, Nanette Fabray *(Lily Marton)*, Jack Buchanan *(Jeffrey Cordova)*, James Mitchell *(Paul Byrd)*, Robert Gist *(Hal Benton)*, Thurston Hall *(Col. Tripp)*, Ava Gardner *(The Movie Star)*, LeRoy Daniels *(Shoeshine Boy)*

p, Arthur Freed; d, Vincente Minnelli; w, Betty Comden, Adolph Green; ph, Harry Jackson (Technicolor); ed, Albert Akst; chor, Michael Kidd, Oliver Smith

AAN Best Story and Screenplay: Betty Comden, Adolph Green; *AAN Best Score (Musical):* Adolph Deutsch; *AAN Best Costume Design (Color):* Mary Ann Nyberg

Seamlessly directed by Vincente Minnelli, THE BAND WAGON is one of the finest musicals ever made. Playing its hackneyed story with tongue firmly in cheek, it simultaneously reflects upon the musical genre, satirizes its conventions and delivers marvelous entertainment. Hollywood dancer Tony Hunter (Astaire) having fallen from favor with the moviegoing public, attempts a comeback on Broadway in a musical written by Lester and Lily Marton (Levant and Fabray, essentially playing the screenwriting team of Comden and Green). The play's arty director, Jeffrey Cordova (Buchanan), makes some misguided staging decisions, while Tony's lead, ballerina Gaby Gerard (Charisse), is less than enamored of him, setting up the problems the players must resolve.

Along the way, we are treated to a tart look at life behind the scenes and a host of highly engaging performances. Astaire has rarely been more appealing—or moving—in a thinly disguised autobiographical role. Fabray and Levant provide the sugar and vinegar in generous doses, Charisse's acting is quite satisfactory and her subdued, earthy sensuality makes her a surprisingly apt dance partner for Astaire, and Buchanan all but steals the film as the hilariously Faust-obsessed, maddeningly brilliant impresario. A low-key highlight is his delightful softshoe with Astaire to "I Guess I'll Have to Change My Plans," but the musical pleasures are many and varied, including "A Shine on Your Shoes," Astaire's romp in a 42nd Street penny arcade; "Dancing in the Dark," Astaire and Charisse's dreamy *pas de deux*; the legendary "Triplets," featuring a swaddled Buchanan, Astaire, and Fabray; the striking and sexy "Girl Hunt Ballet," a spoof of *film noir* and hardboiled detectives; and of course the witty showbiz anthem, "That's Entertainment."

BANDIT QUEEN   DVD
1995   129m   c   Drama/Biography/Political   ★★★½
Film Four International/Kaleidoscope   (India/U.K.)

Seema Biswas *(Phoolan Devi)*, Nirmal Pandey *(Vikram Mallah)*, Manoj Bajpai *(Man Singh)*, Rajesh Vivek *(Mustaquim)*, Raghuvir Yadav *(Madho)*, Govind Namdeo *(Sriram)*, Saurabh Shukla *(Kailash)*, Aditya Srivastava *(Puttilal)*, Agesh Markam *(Mad Woman)*, Anirudh Agarwal *(Babu Gujjar)*

p, Sundeep Singh Bedi; d, Shekhar Kapur; w, Mala Sen; ph, Ashok Mehta; ed, Renu Saluja; m, Nusrat Fateh Ali Khan; prod d, Eve Mavrakis; art d, Ashok Bhagat; cos, Dolly Ahluwalia

BANDIT QUEEN, a masterful Indian epic based on the life of a latterday woman warrior, makes few concessions to art-house taste, and viewers whose notions of India have been shaped by decorous Merchant/Ivory productions may shrink from its confrontational style.

This harrowing, wilfully controversial film tells the story of Phoolan Devi (Seema Biswas), the near-legendary leader of a band of *dacoits*—brigands—who conducted daring raids on landowners in north central India during the late 1970s and early '80s, often distributing the proceeds among lower-caste tenant farmers. Married at the age of 11 and abandoned by her husband after she resisted his sexual demands, Devi became a social outcast, defenseless against the depredations of rural India's exceptionally brutal patriarchy. In a particularly grue-some episode, Devi was gang-raped by most of the upper-caste men in the village of Behmai, Uttar Pradesh; she later took revenge by organizing a massacre that left 20 villagers dead. By the time of her arrest in 1983, Devi was a folk hero.

As electrically portrayed by Biswas, Devi is a furious embodiment of *shakti*—feminine power—and a figure of affronted womanhood that inevitably recalls the abundant rape-revenge subgenre of Indian commercial melodrama (it's no accident that examples of the colossal hoardings used to promote Bollywood movies are prominently visible during the Behmai massacre sequence). Production values are first-rate throughout, notably the mournful score by Nusrat Fateh Ali Khan and cinematographer Ashok Mehta's dazzling use of the unearthly ravine country of Chambral Valley.

BANG THE DRUM SLOWLY

1973 96m c Sports 📀
Paramount (U.S.) ★★★½

Robert De Niro (Bruce Pearson), Michael Moriarty (Henry Wiggen), Vincent Gardenia (Dutch Schnell), Phil Foster (Joe Jaros), Ann Wedgeworth (Katie), Pat McVey (Pearson's Father), Heather MacRae (Holly Wiggen), Selma Diamond (Tootsie), Barbara Babcock, Maurice Rosenfield (Team Owners)

p, Maurice Rosenfield, Lois Rosenfield; d, John Hancock; w, Mark Harris (based on his novel); ph, Richard Shore (Movielab Color); ed, Richard Marks; m, Stephen Lawrence; prod d, Robert Gundlach

AAN Best Supporting Actor: Vincent Gardenia

A well-done if depressing film, BANG THE DRUM SLOWLY is a sort of baseball version of "Brian's Song," the TV movie that told the story of the extraordinary friendship between the Chicago Bears' Gale Sayers and Brian Piccolo, who died of cancer. In this film, De Niro is the dying athlete, a journeyman big-league catcher who has contracted Hodgkin's disease. Moriarty, the team's star pitcher, becomes dedicated to his batterymate when he learns of De Niro's fatal illness and prevents him from being sent to the minors. When their teammates find out, they too belatedly make De Niro feel like one of the boys, and, surprisingly, his playing even improves. Alas, it's all a little too late.

One of De Niro's earliest roles—the quintessential bumpkin who wears a smiley-face T-shirt under his sports jacket—it's poles apart from the enigmatic loners that later became his specialty. To prepare for the part, De Niro not only practiced with the Cincinnati Reds, but also traveled to Georgia to perfect his accent. His hard work resulted in a wholly believable performance. Moriarty is also very effective as Henry Wiggen, the central character in a num-ber of baseball novels by Harris, who adapted one of them for this film. Previously done on TV with Paul Newman

and Albert Salmi, this version, under Hancock's fine direc-tion, became one of the best baseball movies ever. Vincent Gardenia received an Academy Award nomination for his supporting work as the team's manager, and Foster is won-derful as a coach.

BANK DICK, THE

1940 69m bw Comedy 📀
Universal (U.S.) ★★★★½

W.C. Fields (Egbert Souse), Cora Witherspoon (Agatha Souse), Una Merkel (Myrtle Souse), Evelyn Del Rio (Elsie Mae Adele Brunch Souse), Jessie Ralph (Mrs. Hermisillo Brunch), Franklin Pangborn (J. Pinkerton Snoopington), Shemp Howard (Joe Guelpe), Dick Purcell (Mackley Q. Greene), Grady Sutton (Og Oggilby), Russell Hicks (J. Frothingham Waterbury)

d, Edward F. Cline; w, W.C. Fields; ph, Milton Krasner; ed, Arthur Hilton; art d, Jack Otterson

Along with IT'S A GIFT, one of the definitive W.C. Fields films. THE BANK DICK is, as with all the best of Fields, appropriately thin on plot and heavy with hilarious set-pieces which allow "The Great Man" his full comic scope. The cynical, eccentric, bottle-hitting comedian plays an unemployed, henpecked (as usual) family man none-too-eagerly seeking work who accidentally captures a bank rob-ber and is rewarded with a job as guard inside the bank. When not busy bothering customers (as when he appre-hends a patron's son brandishing a toy gun), he runs between his deliciously horrid family and The Black Pussy Cat Cafe, where the proprietor (a Three Stooges-less Howard) spends most of his time pouring the guard, his only customer, a series of stiff ones.

The movie is filled with a marvelous series of Fields-patented comic bits, including an especially zany car chase, reminiscent of the best Mack Sennett, where "hostage" Fields once again inadvertently saves the day. Fields, who wrote the script under the typically improbable pseudonym of Mahatma Kane Jeeves, plays a character named Souse, which he pro-nounces, in the French manner, as "Sou-say"; the rest of the cast, as might be expected, merely follows the word's English pronunciation. With wonderful supporting work from Witherspoon, Ralph, Pangborn, Sutton, Jack Norton, Pierre Watkin, and many others.

BARBARIAN INVASIONS, THE

2003 95m c Comedy/Drama 📀
Astral Films/Production Barbares/CNC/ ★★★
Cinemaginaire/Studio Canal +/Pyramide R
Productions/Societe Radio Canada/SODEC/
Harold Greenberg Fund/Telefilm Canada
(Canada/France)

Remy Girard (Remy), Stephane Rousseau (Sebastien), Dorothee Berryman (Louise), Louise Portal (Diane), Dominique Michel (Dominique), Yves Jacques (Claude), Pierre Curzi (Pierre), Marie-Josee Croze (Nathalie), Marina Hands (Gaelle), Toni Cecchinato (Alessandro)

p, Daniel Louis, Denise Robert; d, Denys Arcand; w, Denys Arcand; ph, Guy Dufaux; ed, Isabelle Dedieu; m, Pierre Aviat; prod d, Francois Seguin; art d, Caroline Alder; cos, Denis Sperdouklis

AAN Best Original Screenplay: Denys Arcand; AA Best Foreign Language Film

Seventeen years after Denys Arcand arrived on the interna-tional scene with his BIG CHILL-esque drama, THE DECLINE OF THE AMERICAN EMPIRE, the

Quebecois auteur reunited much of the original cast for a belated sequel.

It's been 15 years since the marriage between history professor Remy (Remy Girard) and Louise (Dorothee Berryman) collapsed under the weight of his continual adultery, but surprisingly, Louise is once again at his side: Remy is now seriously ill, and the prognosis isn't good. Louise contacts their son, Sebastien (Stephane Rousseau), a hugely successful market operator in London, but Sebastien is somewhat reluctant to rush to his father's bedside. Sebastien blames his father for destroying his family, while Remy, an old socialist, decries his son's all-around lack of culture and slavish devotion to capitalism. But when Sebastien arrives in Quebec with his fiancee, Gaelle (Marina Hands), and sees the overcrowded conditions at his father's hospital, he agrees first to find Remy a private room, then to gather together all his old friends: Pierre (Pierre Curzi), Claude (Yves Jacques), Diane (Louise Portal), and Dominique (Dominique Michel). Also on hand is Nathalie (Marie-Josee Croze), Diane's estranged, drug-addicted daughter, who agrees to supply Remy with the one thing that, besides his friends, can ease his pain: heroin.

Many Cannes watchers were surprised when the 2003 jury awarded Arcand the festival's coveted best screenplay award (Croze was the film's other big winner, picking up the prize for best actress). But if the banter lacks the erudite sparkle of its predecessor, the acting is still first-rate, and the film will be best enjoyed by fans eager to spend another 90 minutes with a group of old friends.

BARBERSHOP
DVD
2002 102m c Comedy ★★★
State Street Pictures/Cube Vision/MGM (U.S.) PG-13

Ice Cube *(Calvin Palmer)*, Anthony Anderson *(JD)*, Cedric the Entertainer *(Eddie)*, Sean Patrick Thomas *(Jimmy James)*, Eve *(Terri Jones)*, Troy Garity *(Isaac Rosenberg)*, Michael Ealy *(Ricky Nash)*, Keith David *(Lester)*, Parvesh Cheena *(Samir)*, Lahmard Tate *(Billy)*

p, Mark Brown, Robert Teitel, George Tillman Jr.; d, Tim Story; w, Mark Brown, Don D. Scott, Marshall Todd (from a story by Mark Brown); ph, Tom Priestley; ed, John Carter; m, Terence Blanchard; prod d, Roger Fortune; art d, Gary Baugh; fx, Guy Clayton; cos, Devon P.F. Patterson

CAR WASH transplanted to an old-fashioned, South Chicago barbershop.

Ambitious Calvin (Ice Cube) inherited his father's barbershop two years ago, and he wants out. His newest moneymaking scheme involves setting up a recording studio in his basement, but he needs seed money, and the bank's already threatening foreclosure unless he pays back his earlier loans. So Calvin makes a deal with the devil, buttervoiced neighborhood sharpie Lester Williams (Keith David), who plans to turn the place into a strip joint with a barbershop theme. Meanwhile, the owner of the convenience shop next door (Parvesh Cheena) arrives to find his brand-new ATM gone. Dumb-and-dumber duo JD (Anthony Anderson) and Billy (Lahmard Tate) are busy dragging the stolen machine all over the hood, looking for a place to crack it, and the theft becomes one of many topics *du jour* at the barbershop. The motormouths include èminence grise Eddie (Cedric the Entertainer); volatile Terri Jones (rapper Eve, making a fine acting debut); know-it-all Jimmy James (Sean Patrick Thomas); white boy Isaac (Troy Garity), who wants to be black; and two-time loser Ricky Nash (Michael Ealy), who's trying to stay clean even though the police suspect him of everything—including the ATM heist.

Like CAR WASH, this loosely structured comedy is less about plot than it is about character, and its characters are

carefully drawn and flawlessly played; even spotlight-hoggers like Cedric the Entertainer work as part of the ensemble, and Ice Cube reiterates the lesson of the FRIDAY films: he's a world-class straight man. And unlike many directors with music video backgrounds, Tim Story keeps the flashy cutting to a minimum and lets the story unfold at its own unhurried pace.

BARCELONA
DVD
1994 101m c Comedy/Romance/Political ★★★
Film Barcelona/Castle Rock/Westerly Films (U.S.) PG-13

Taylor Nichols *(Ted Boynton)*, Chris Eigeman *(Fred Mason)*, Tushka Bergen *(Montserrat)*, Mira Sorvino *(Marta Ferrer)*, Pep Munne *(Ramon)*, Nuria Badia *(Aurora)*, Hellena Schmied *(Greta)*, Francis Creighton *(Frank)*, Thomas Gibson *(Dickie Taylor)*, Jack Gilpin *(The Consul)*

p, Whit Stillman; d, Whit Stillman; w, Whit Stillman; ph, John Thomas; ed, Chris Tellefsen; m, Mark Suozzo; prod d, Jose Maria Botines; cos, Edi Giguere

Among stale Hollywood romances like I.Q., SPEECHLESS, and LOVE AFFAIR, Whit Stillman's BARCELONA is the real McCoy, a gossamer blend of *chagrin d'amour*, musical beds, and translation errors in the language of love.

In Spain during the last years of the Cold War, Ted (Taylor Nichols), an American salesman, reluctantly plays host to his cousin, naval officer Fred (Christopher Eigeman). Bumming money or embroidering stories about Ted's sexual proclivities, Fred is a tactless but oddly charming loose cannon, and the two become social successes among the young women who work as hostesses for the Spanish Trade Fair. While Ted pursues Montserrat (Tushka Bergen), Fred sleeps with Marta (Mira Sorvino), a pretty but heedless party girl; meanwhile, a rising turmoil of anti-American sentiment threatens their idyll.

Writer-director Stillman (METROPOLITAN) showcases scenic Barcelona as a moonlit love-field where courtship is as likely to be interrupted by a USO bombing as by a lover's betrayal. Political innocents abroad, the cousins also lack the Spaniards' nonchalance in affairs of the heart; despite Fred's obnoxiousness and Ted's uptight theorizing, their genuine guilelessness never fails to shine through. BARCELONA represents a cinematic advance over the tighter but visually drab METROPOLITAN, but Stillman sacrifices pacing here: he has a lot to say and doesn't always have the editorial flair to nail down his sentiments as neatly as he might.

BAREFOOT IN THE PARK
DVD
1967 104m c Comedy ★★★½
Paramount (U.S.)

Robert Redford *(Paul Bratter)*, Jane Fonda *(Corie Bratter)*, Charles Boyer *(Victor Velasco)*, Mildred Natwick *(Mrs. Ethel Banks)*, Herb Edelman *(Telephone Man)*, James F. Stone *(Delivery Man)*, Ted Hartley *(Frank)*, Mabel Albertson *(Aunt Harriet)*, Fritz Feld *(Restaurant Proprietor)*

p, Hal B. Wallis; d, Gene Saks; w, Neil Simon (based on his play); ph, Joseph La Shelle (Technicolor); ed, William Lyon; m, Neal Hefti; cos, Edith Head

AAN Best Supporting Actress: Mildred Natwick

Laughs galore in early first screenplay by Simon, based on his Broadway success. Saks makes a fine impression in his first directorial stint, which features Redford and Fonda living in a small fifth-floor apartment in Greenwich Village. She thinks their place is lovely, but he, ever the conservative attorney, hates it. Boyer plays the slightly zany, womanizing upstairs neighbor who must go through their apartment to reach his. Ever a romantic, Fonda adores the old reprobate and fixes him up with her stodgy mother (Natwick). A series of comic and romantic complications ensues, some of which center around Redford's inability to let himself go—like the night he refused Fonda's entreaties to go barefoot in Central Park on a night when it was 17 degrees out and raining to boot. Love of course finds a way, and Redford finds a way to romp in a manner befitting the film's title. Redford and the Oscar-nominated Natwick, fresh from their Broadway triumph in the play, perform with the ease familiarity brings, and Fonda and Boyer also display the appropriate lightness of touch.

BARFLY   DVD
1987 100m c   Comedy/Romance   ★★★★
Francis Ford Coppola/Golan-Globus   (U.S.)   R

Mickey Rourke *(Henry Chinaski)*, Faye Dunaway *(Wanda Wilcox)*, Alice Krige *(Tully Sorenson)*, Jack Nance *(Detective)*, J.C. Quinn *(Jim)*, Frank Stallone *(Eddie)*, Gloria LeRoy *(Grandma Moses)*, Sandy Martin *(Janice)*, Roberta Bassin *(Lilly)*, Joe Unger *(Ben)*

p, Barbet Schroeder, Fred Roos, Tom Luddy; d, Barbet Schroeder; w, Charles Bukowski; ph, Robby Muller (TVC color); ed, Eva Gardos; prod d, Bob Ziembicki; cos, Milena Canonero

Not a film for everyone, but the unrelieved squalor of BARFLY offers its own peculiar fascinations. Director Barbet Schroeder (REVERSAL OF FORTUNE) positions the grungy world of cult writer Charles Bukowski under a cinematic microscope, affording titillating glimpses of lowlife.

Rourke plays Henry Chinaski, a slovenly, hard-drinking, fistfighting scribe who's taken with Wanda Wilcox (Dunaway), a haggard but attractive drunk he meets in a bar. Chinaski's work is admired by wealthy, pretty, self-assured publisher Tully Sorenson (Krige), and that provides the film with a romantic triangle as Wanda and Tully battle for Henry's attentions. Rourke, who turns in the finest performance of his career to date, takes a character who could be seen as pathetic and despicable and makes him, if not a likable hero, at least an understandable one. Dunaway gives an exceptional performance, and Krige is perfect in her role.

The making of BARFLY was nearly as extreme as anything in the film. Producer-director Schroeder had originally commissioned Bukowski to write a screenplay for $20,000, then struggled for years to get the project filmed. Finally, he entered the office of Cannon president Menahem Golan and threatened to cut off a finger unless Cannon made the film. After initially refusing, Golan realized Schroeder's obsession with BARFLY and eventually gave the project the go-ahead. The kind of film people are likely to disagree about strongly.

BARKLEYS OF BROADWAY, THE
1949 109m c   Musical   ★★★½
MGM   (U.S.)

Fred Astaire *(Josh Barkley)*, Ginger Rogers *(Dinah Barkley)*, Oscar Levant *(Ezra Miller)*, Billie Burke *(Mrs. Belney)*, Gale Robbins *(Shirlene May)*, Jacques Francois *(Jacques Barredout)*, George Zucco *(The Judge)*, Clinton Sundberg *(Bert Felsher)*, Inez Cooper *(Pamela Driscoll)*, Carol Brewster *(Gloria Amboy)*

p, Arthur Freed; d, Charles Walters; w, Betty Comden, Adolph Green; ph, Harry Stradling (Technicolor); ed, Albert Akst; m, Lennie Hayton; art d, Cedric Gibbons, Edward Carfagno; chor, Hermes Pan, Robert Alton; cos, Irene; anim, Irving G. Reis

AAN Best Color Cinematography: Harry Stradling

A very enjoyable if somewhat disappointing reunion for the unbeatable team of Astaire and Rogers. Handsomely produced, THE BARKLEYS OF BROADWAY retells with

some but not quite enough wit a thinly disguised version of what was perceived as the duo's actual working relationship. Astaire and Rogers play Josh and Dinah Barkley, an affectionate and highly successful, if sometimes contentious, married musical comedy team. Trouble comes when Dinah's dramatic ambitions and Josh's jealousy over the attention paid to his wife by a handsome French playwright (Francois) encourage the pair to split both professionally and personally. Although each enjoys considerable solo success, they finally realize they belong together doing musical comedy.

The team's first pairing in ten years, which came about after Astaire's costar in the previous year's highly successful EASTER PARADE, Judy Garland, suffered one of her many breakdowns, it would also prove to be their last together. THE BARKLEYS OF BROADWAY shows neither the screen duo nor screenwriters Comden and Green at their best, despite the sharp support from Levant, Burke, and others. The film's chief weakness is the score by Harry Warren and Ira Gershwin, though Fred and Ginger also reprise George and Ira Gershwin's decade-old classic, "They Can't Take That Away from Me." Oddly enough, the legendary pair most closely approximates their earlier magic during the warm comic and romantic interludes, though their delightful and spirited tap duet to "Bouncin' the Blues" does bring some of their patented incandescence onto the dance floor.

BARRETTS OF WIMPOLE STREET, THE
1934 110m bw Romance/Biography   ★★★½
MGM   (U.S.)

Fredric March *(Robert Browning)*, Norma Shearer *(Elizabeth Barrett)*, Charles Laughton *(Edward Moulton Barrett)*, Maureen O'Sullivan *(Henrietta Barrett)*, Katherine Alexander *(Arabel Barrett)*, Una O'Connor *(Wilson)*, Ian Wolfe *(Harry Bevan)*, Marion Clayton *(Bella Hedley)*, Ralph Forbes *(Capt. Surtees Cook)*, Vernon Downing *(Octavius Barrett)*

p, Irving Thalberg; d, Sidney Franklin; w, Ernest Vajda, Claudine West, Donald Ogden Stewart (based on the play by Rudolph Besier); ph, William Daniels; ed, Margaret Booth; art d, Cedric Gibbons; cos, Adrian

AAN Best Picture; AAN Best Actress: Norma Shearer

One of the better-known and more typical of MGM's adaptations of famous stage plays, THE BARRETTS OF WIMPOLE STREET is slightly strangled by its own sense of prestige, but proves worthy drama nonetheless. This historical romance tells how the near-invalid Elizabeth Barrett (Shearer) finds happiness and renewed vitality through the love of fellow poet Robert Browning (March), despite the efforts of her dictatorial and overly protective father (played exquisitely by Laughton). Confined to her room with little but her dog and her love of poetry for comfort, Elizabeth cannot even reach out to her brothers and sisters, also under the thumb of their father's tyranny. The battle between father and lover, seemingly simplistic, takes on increasing depth as the drama unfolds.

Though much of the acting is somewhat theatrical, it is also effective on its own terms in this rarefied atmosphere. The climactic moment as Elizabeth struggles out of her father's grasp, realizing that his smothering love for her isn't simply of a paternal nature, is extremely well handled by both Shearer and Laughton. Although the latter's villainy dominates the film, the supporting performances are generally good, particularly those of O'Sullivan as Elizabeth's hapless younger sister and O'Connor as a loyal servant. Not as good as contemporary reviews suggest, but nostalgically charming.

BARRETTS OF WIMPOLE STREET, THE
1956 105m c   Romance/Biography   ★★★★
MGM   (U.K.)

Jennifer Jones *(Elizabeth)*, John Gielgud *(Barrett)*, Bill Travers *(Robert Browning)*, Virginia McKenna *(Henrietta)*, Susan Stephen *(Bella)*, Vernon Gray *(Capt. Surtees Cook)*, Jean Anderson *(Wilson)*, Maxine Audley *(Arabel)*, Leslie Phillips *(Harry Bevan)*, Laurence Naismith *(Dr. Chambers)*

p, Sam Zimbalist; d, Sidney Franklin; w, John Dighton (based on the play by Rudolph Besier); ph, Freddie Young; ed, Frank Clark; m, Bronislau Kaper; art d, Alfred Junge; cos, Elizabeth Haffenden

Sidney Franklin directed both versions of this well-known biopic, originally filmed in 1934. Jones plays poet and near-invalid Elizabeth Barrett, whose father's (Gielgud) almost incestuous adoration for her all but confines her to his London house. She is understandably lonely and depressed; her only companions are her books, her servants, her dog, and her horde of brothers (all wonderfully played by bright young men of the period). Enter Robert Browning (Travers), a fellow poet rich in love and warmth, who sweeps Elizabeth off the couch and into bloom like a morning glory at dawn. Gielgud, in a magnificent performance imbued with understated menace, attempts to smash the relationship before it attains fruition, and the struggle for the young woman's happiness is on. A subtle, lovingly rendered if sometimes leisurely film with fine acting all around and a technical skill which surpasses its worthy 1934 predecessor, THE BARRETTS OF WIMPOLE STREET is very effective drama.

BARRY LYNDON
1975 184m c   Historical   ★★★★
Hawk/Peregrine   (U.K.)   PG

Ryan O'Neal *(Barry Lyndon)*, Marisa Berenson *(Lady Lyndon)*, Patrick Magee *(The Chevalier)*, Hardy Kruger *(Capt. Potzdorf)*, Steven Berkoff *(Lord Ludd)*, Gay Hamilton *(Nora)*, Leonard Rossiter *(Capt. Quin)*, Godfrey Quigley *(Capt. Grogan)*, Arthur O'Sullivan *(Highwayman)*, Diana Koerner *(German Girl)*

p, Stanley Kubrick; d, Stanley Kubrick; w, Stanley Kubrick (based on the novel by William Makepeace Thackeray); ph, John Alcott (Metrocolor); ed, Tony Lawson; m, Leonard Rosenman; prod d, Ken Adam; art d, Roy Walker

AAN Best Picture; AAN Best Director: Stanley Kubrick; *AAN Best Adapted Screenplay:* Stanley Kubrick; *AA Best Cinematography:* John Alcott; *AA Best Song Score:* Leonard Rosenman; *AA Best Art Direction-Set Decoration:* Roy Walker, Ken Adam, Vernon Dixon; *AA Best Costume Design:* Ulla-Britt Soderlund, Milena Canonero

Grave, painterly, and bitterly satirical, BARRY LYNDON baffled viewers who expected picaresque breeziness along the lines of TOM JONES. Kubrick's translation of the Thackeray novel downplays its frivolity and foregrounds its acerbic social critique. With an actor only slightly more expressive than Ryan O'Neal in the lead, this sombre costume epic might have reached the level of tragedy; as it is, the film is langorous to a fault, but so visually delightful and keenly observed that its excesses demand forgiveness.

The title character (Ryan O'Neal) is a rustic Irish boy who falls in love with a local lass (Gay Hamilton). When he threatens to disrupt her financially desirable match with an English officer (Leonard Rossiter), her family tricks him into leaving town. Barry's subsequent adventures encompass triumph and disaster: among other things, he is impressed into (and deserts from) two warring armies, becomes assistant to an itinerant society card sharp, and woos a widowed aristocrat (Marisa Berenson). His decision to marry her—dictated solely by his desire to acquire social standing—is a tragic

misstep; thenceforward, Barry's life describes an inexorable downward trajectory.

BARRY LYNDON received mixed notices, but even its detractors had to concede that it was one of the most visually beautiful movies ever shot: Kubrick lavished on his film a kind of attention to period detail that remained unmatched until the release of Scorsese's THE AGE OF INNOCENCE nearly 20 years later. In an effort to recreate the look of 18th-century canvasses, the director resolved to shoot the film wholly without artificial lighting; with cinematographer John Alcott, he pioneered the indoor use of ultra-high-speed color film—some scenes are lit only by candles! Music, as always with Kubrick, is integral to the project; Irish folk tunes by The Chieftains and Schubert's E-minor Trio (which has since become something of a movie cliché) are particularly well used.

BARTON FINK
1991 116m c   Comedy/Drama   ★★★½
Circle Films/Barton Circle Productions   (U.S.)   R

John Turturro *(Barton Fink)*, John Goodman *(Charlie Meadows)*, Judy Davis *(Audrey Taylor)*, Michael Lerner *(Jack Lipnick)*, John Mahoney *(W.P. Mayhew)*, Tony Shalhoub *(Ben Geisler)*, Jon Polito *(Lou Breeze)*, Steve Buscemi *(Chet)*, David Warrilow *(Garland Stanford)*, Richard Portnow *(Detective Mastrionotti)*

p, Ethan Coen; d, Joel Coen; w, Ethan Coen, Joel Coen; ph, Roger Deakins; ed, Roderick Jaynes; m, Carter Burwell; prod d, Dennis Gassner; art d, Leslie McDonald, Bob Goldstein; fx, Robert Spurlock, Laurel Schneider; cos, Richard Hornung

AAN Best Supporting Actor: Michael Lerner; *AAN Best Art Direction-Set Decoration:* Dennis Gassner (Art Direction), Nancy Haigh (Set Decoration); *AAN Best Costume Design:* Richard Hornung

The grand-prize winner at the 1991 Cannes festival, BARTON FINK is the fourth installment in the Coen Brothers' series of highly stylized homages to classical Hollywood. But like their earlier films, BARTON FINK is a *tour de force* of cinematic technique that encases a quirky narrative of little depth.

Barton Fink (John Turturro) is an earnest young New York playwright who hits it big with a Depression-era proletarian drama before being reluctantly seduced by a lucrative offer to go to Hollywood and write for the movies. Despite assurances that he will be given free reign by studio boss Jack Lipnick (Michael Lerner), Barton is asked to write a wrestling picture for Wallace Beery. Pent up in a surreal hotel room, Barton suffers acute and hallucinatory writer's block.

Unlike the Coen's previous works (the film noir BLOOD SIMPLE, the screwball comedy RAISING ARIZONA and the gangster film MILLER'S CROSSING), BARTON FINK is not a revisionist take on a classical genre but a bizarre, comic portrayal of the Hollywood studio system of the 1930s and '40s. The principal characters are clearly drawn from actual people in that system: Fink is a thinly veiled version of Clifford Odets, the leftist playwright who departed the socially committed Group Theatre in New York to write screenplays in Hollywood during WWII. And the dipsomaniac writer W.P. Mayhew (John Mahoney) is, of course, William Faulkner.

But the scene-stealer is Jack Lipnick, the larger-than-life movie mogul who is a composite of MGM's Louis B. Mayer and other studio heads. Michael Lerner's portrayal of Lipnick overwhelms even the fine acting of the leading players, not the least of which is Goodman's transformation from a lonely salesman into a psychotic killer. As Barton, John Turturro (DO THE RIGHT THING, MILLER'S CROSSING) can only deadpan his way amid these caricatures while careening from one baffling encounter to the next.

The film's period decor, mood lighting and artful camerawork are beautiful, at times thrilling, to look at. The surrealistic writer's block scenes, in which Barton silently watches wallpaper peel and its paste ooze, are particularly memorable—imagine ERASERHEAD in color. Ultimately, however, the look, sound and feel of this macabre comedy fail to support any coherent theme. The bombastic Philistines of Hollywood, the idealistic artists of the theater and the "common man" are all rather cruelly skewered in the film's finely polished characterizations. Much is denigrated, but little affirmed.

BASIC INSTINCT   **DVD**
1992 122m c   Erotic/Thriller   ★★½
Carolco/Canal Plus/Basic Inst Inc   (U.S.)   R

Michael Douglas *(Detective Nick Curran)*, Sharon Stone *(Catherine Tramell)*, George Dzundza *(Gus)*, Jeanne Tripplehorn *(Dr. Beth Gardner)*, Denis Arndt *(Lieutenant Walker)*, Leilani Sarelle *(Roxy)*, Bruce A. Young *(Andrews)*, Chelcie Ross *(Captain Talcott)*, Dorothy Malone *(Hazel Dobkins)*, Wayne Knight *(John Correli)*

p, Alan Marshall; d, Paul Verhoeven; w, Joe Eszterhas; ph, Jan De Bont; ed, Frank J. Urioste; m, Jerry Goldsmith; prod d, Terence Marsh; cos, Ellen Mirojnick

AAN Best Film Editing: Frank J. Urioste; *AAN Best Original Score:* Jerry Goldsmith

Directed by Paul Verhoeven (SPETTERS, ROBOCOP), BASIC INSTINCT is a psychological thriller with a liberal helping of soft porn thrown in for good measure.

At first glance, Catherine Tramell (Sharon Stone) seems like a dream date. A successful novelist with a classy psychology degree, Tramell is beautiful, rich, brilliant, and oversexed. There's only one problem. Anyone who has ever been close to Tramell has died in mysterious circumstances—circumstances which have been either recreated or predicted in her novels. Is she an evil genius who tests her brilliance by destroying those around her? Or is she being set up by a diabolical rival? This is what San Francisco cop Nick Curran (Michael Douglas) must determine after he is called in to investigate the murder of Tramell's boyfriend, a former rock star stabbed to death with an ice pick while engaging in that favorite pastime of rock stars, kinky sex.

Screenwriter Joe Eszterhas's story does generate a degree of suspense, particularly in the scenes where Tramell turns the tables on Curran; she is now writing a book based on *his* life, and rakes up some unpleasant details from the past concerning his "accidental" killing of two innocent tourists. But the screenplay also displays a flaw you would hope not to find in a $3 million script: it makes no logical sense.

The worst things about BASIC INSTINCT, though, are the explicit "love" scenes. They're supposed to contribute to a heady equation in which sex, violence and psychology are fused; instead, they're gratuitous, exploitative, and entirely unerotic.

BASKET CASE   **DVD**
1982 90m   c   Horror   ★★★★
Analysis   (U.S.)

Kevin Van Hentenryck *(Duane Bradley)*, Terri Susan Smith *(Sharon)*, Beverly Bonner *(Casey)*, Lloyd Pace *(Dr. Harold Needleman)*, Diana Browne *(Dr. Judith Kutter)*, Robert Vogel *(Hotel Manager)*, Bill Freeman *(Dr. Julius Lifflander)*, Joe Clarke *(Brian "Mickey" O'Donovan)*, Dorothy Strongin *(Josephine)*, Ruth Neuman *(Aunt)*

p, Edgar Levins; d, Frank Henenlotter; w, Frank Henenlotter; ph, Bruce Torbet; ed, Frank Henenlotter; m, Gus Russo; fx, Kevin Haney, John Caglione

This ultra-low-budget production was shot over the course of six months on location in the streets, apartments, and flophouses of New York City. It became a hit on the midnight-show circuit and is arguably one of the best horror films of the 1980s. Directed by Frank Henenlotter with as much style as is possible on a miniscule budget, the film centers on Duane (Van Hentenryck), a young man from Glens Falls, New York, who checks into a fleabag hotel on 42nd Street carrying a wicker basket. Inside the basket is his small, horribly misshapen Siamese twin, Belial. Communicating with Duane telepathically, Belial is determined to wreak vengeance on the physicians that separated him from his twin. Meanwhile, however, Duane has met a nice girl (Smith) and begun to make a life of his own, one that doesn't include Belial.

Disturbing, grotesque, and very funny at times, BASKET CASE is a unique work in which imagination triumphs over the limitations of budget. Blown up to 35mm from the 16mm original, the film's grainy, cheap look only enhances the seediness of Henenlotter's milieu, while, in Belial, Henenlotter has come up with one of the most memorable and sympathetic screen monsters since KING KONG. A rather cheap-looking puppet created by Kevin Haney and John Caglione, Belial has a certain shabby charm that has endeared him to horror fans throughout the world. In a film that contains many unforgettable images, perhaps the most startling—and most moving—is a flashback to Belial's childhood, in which the monster's kindly aunt lets the mutant child sit on her lap while reading aloud to him.

BATAAN   **DVD**
1943 113m   bw   War   ★★★★
MGM   (U.S.)

Robert Taylor *(Sgt. Bill Dane)*, George Murphy *(Lt. Steve Bentley)*, Thomas Mitchell *(Cpl. Jake Feingold)*, Lloyd Nolan *(Cpl. Barney Todd/Danny Burns)*, Lee Bowman *(Capt. Henry Lassiter)*, Robert Walker *(Leonard Purckett)*, Desi Arnaz *(Felix Ramirez)*, Barry Nelson *(F.X. Matowski)*, Phillip Terry *(Matthew Hardy)*, Roque Espiritu *(Cpl. Juan Katigbak)*

p, Irving Starr; d, Tay Garnett; w, Robert D. Andrews (based partly on the 1934 film THE LOST PATROL); ph, Sidney Wagner; ed, George White; m, Bronislau Kaper; art d, Cedric Gibbons; fx, A. Arnold Gillespie, Warren Newcombe

This tough, uncompromising film, extremely well handled by director Garnett, tells the story of a group of determined soldiers fighting on Bataan, knowing that they face certain death as they attempt to delay the advancing Japanese troops. Based on the heroic defense of the Philippines in early 1942, the film shows soldiers from all parts of America, as well as Filipinos fighting for their own soil. Taylor gives a rugged and inspiring performance as the grim but kind-hearted Sergeant Dane, who commands the small group in a rearguard action, protecting MacArthur's ragged army as it limps away down the narrow peninsula, where it would make its stand for three harrowing months. One by one, the soldiers are brutally picked off (not unlike the forlorn members of John Ford's 1934 film THE LOST PATROL) until only a handful are left. Although the film was clearly shot within the confines of a studio set, the use of miniatures is effective and the hand-to-hand combat scenes are startling and brutal. One of MGM's better war films.

BATMAN   **DVD**
1989 126m c   Science Fiction/Fantasy/Crime   ★★★★
Warner Bros. (U.S.)   PG-13

Michael Keaton *(Batman/Bruce Wayne)*, Jack Nicholson *(Joker/Jack Napier)*, Kim Basinger *(Vicki Vale)*, Robert Wuhl

(Alexander Knox), Pat Hingle *(Commissioner Gordon)*, Billy Dee Williams *(District Attorney Harvey Dent)*, Michael Gough *(Alfred)*, Jack Palance *(Carl Grissom)*, Jerry Hall *(Alicia)*, Lee Wallace *(Mayor)*

p, Jon Peters, Peter Guber, Chris Kenny; d, Tim Burton; w, Sam Hamm, Warren Skaaren (based on a story by Sam Hamm and characters created by Bob Kane); ph, Roger Pratt (Eastmancolor); ed, Ray Lovejoy; m, Danny Elfman; prod d, Anton Furst; art d, Leslie Tomkins, Terry Ackland-Snow, Nigel Phelps; cos, Bob Ringwood, Linda Henrikson

AA Best Art Direction-Set Decoration: Anton Furst (Art Direction), Peter Young (Set Decoration)

Gotham City, a crime-ridden, debris-strewn, sunless, architecturally incoherent metropolis, is desperately in need of a savior, for the city is in the corrupting grip of crime boss Carl Grissom (Palance). Ace photographer Vicki Vale (Basinger) has been intrigued by the sightings of a mysterious, giant vigilante bat. She meets enigmatic millionaire Bruce Wayne (Keaton), not suspecting that he's Batman. Wayne is quite taken with the lovely Vicki but is distracted by the wicked ways of Grissom's top henchman, Jack Napier (Nicholson), alias the Joker.

Perhaps it was inevitable, considering all the hype preceding and surrounding its release, that BATMAN would fall a bit flat once it finally reached the screen. Despite its interesting, grim tone and undeniably striking visuals from director Burton and production designer Furst, the film fails to synthesize its strengths into a compelling whole. Its obvious intention to parallel the Joker and Batman as two psychotics, one promoting good and the other evil, doesn't come through with as much impact as it should. The Joker seems maniacal, all right, but hardly as sinister as the silent Batman. In terms of acting, too, Nicholson's campy, full-blown rendering of the Joker (his best moment occurs as he pulls a ridiculously long pistol out of his pants) overshadows the miscast Keaton, whose attempt to be moody and macho gives him all the appeal of plywood.

BATMAN is dark, stylish, and full of "postmodern" touches—but wants to be more so. Given all its potential, it's a shame BATMAN wasn't more. It was, however, easily the biggest box-office hit of 1989, and one of the highest grossing films in history, a testament more to its massive marketing campaign than to its quality.

BATMAN FOREVER   📀
1995 121m c   Adventure/Action   ★★½
Warner Bros. (U.S.)   PG-13

Val Kilmer *(Batman/Bruce Wayne)*, Tommy Lee Jones *(Harvey Two-Face/Harvey Dent)*, Jim Carrey *(The Riddler/Edward Nygma)*, Nicole Kidman *(Dr. Chase Meridian)*, Chris O'Donnell *(Robin/Dick Grayson)*, Michael Gough *(Alfred Pennyworth)*, Pat Hingle *(Police Commissioner James Gordon)*, Debi Mazar *(Spice)*, Drew Barrymore *(Sugar)*, Ed Begley Jr. *(Fred Stickley)*

p, Tim Burton, Peter MacGregor-Scott; d, Joel Schumacher; w, Lee Batchler, Janet Scott Batchler, Akiva Goldsman (from a story by Lee Batchler and Janet Scott Batchler based on characters created by Bob Kane); ph, Stephen Goldblatt; ed, Dennis Virkler; m, Elliot Goldenthal; prod d, Barbara Ling; art d, Christopher Burian-Mohr, Joseph P. Lucky; fx, Tommy L. Fisher, John Dykstra, Illusion Arts; cos, Bob Ringwood, Ingrid Ferrin

AAN Best Cinematography: Stephen Goldblatt; AAN Best Sound: Donald O. Mitchell, Frank A. Montano, Michael Herbick, Petur Hliddal; AAN Best Sound Effects Editing: John Leveque, Bruce Stambler

The third entry in the wildly popular BATMAN cycle boasts a new Batman, new costumes, a revamped Batmobile, and

several new characters—including a Robin for the '90s, two super-villains, and yet another blonde love interest. Holy overkill!

It's not easy being the Batman (Val Kilmer). Old enemies, like the visually and psychologically bifurcated Two-Face (Tommy Lee Jones), desire revenge. Beautiful criminal psychologist Dr. Chase Meridian (Nicole Kidman) has designs on his mind and his body. A brilliant but crazed employee of Wayne Enterprises, Edward Nygma (Jim Carrey), is transformed into the Riddler, a fiendishly clever villain who joins forces with Two-Face in a scheme to brainwash the denizens of Gotham City. The emotionally conflicted hero meets the challenge with the help of his faithful butler Alfred (Michael Gough) and his new ward, Dick Grayson (Chris O'Donnell), a vengeance-driven circus acrobat who joins the fight in the heroic persona of Robin.

Warner Bros. brass deemed Tim Burton's BATMAN RETURNS too dark for kiddies, so they hired Joel Schumacher (THE CLIENT) to reimagine the series in ways more friendly to marketing tie-ins. He obliged by serving up "Batman Lite," a product made irresistible by its campy, colorful packaging, but less filling—and less satisfying—than previous incarnations. While Schumacher brings a distinctive sensibility to the project (reminiscent of the 1960s TV show), he lacks an organizing intelligence capable of accommodating so much new material. BATMAN FOREVER is a noisy riot of color with cramped, chaotic, and confusing action sequences. Carrey's stylized clowning is perfect for the Riddler, but most of the other talent is wasted or underutilized. At best, it's mildly diverting, brainless fun that feels like a long trailer for a better film.

BATTLE OF ALGIERS, THE   📀
(MAARAKAT ALGER)
1965 120m bw War   ★★★★
Magna   (Italy/Algeria)

Yacef Saadi *(Kader)*, Jean Martin *(Colonel)*, Brahim Haggiag *(Ali La Pointe)*, Tommaso Neri *(Captain)*, Samia Kerbash *(One of the Girls)*, Fawzia el Kader *(Halima)*, Michele Kerbash *(Fathia)*, Mohamed Ben Kassen *(Petit Omar)*

p, Antonio Musu, Yacef Saadi; d, Gillo Pontecorvo; w, Gillo Pontecorvo, Franco Solinas; ph, Marcello Gatti; ed, Mario Serandrei, Mario Morra; m, Gillo Pontecorvo, Ennio Morricone

AAN Best Foreign Language Film ; AAN Best Director: Gillo Pontecorvo; AAN Best Original Story and Screenplay: Franco Solinas, Gillo Pontecorvo

A powerful battle cry for Marxist revolutionaries, THE BATTLE OF ALGIERS details the struggle for Algerian independence from France. The film opens in 1957, as a tortured Arab prisoner informs against Ali la Pointe (Haggiag), the last surviving member of the FLN (Algerian Liberation Front). As French soldiers surround Ali's apartment, Colonel Mathieu (Martin) issues a final warning to Ali and his family: surrender or be blown to pieces. With the sides clearly laid out—revolutionary vs. colonial authority—the film shifts to 1954, as the Algerian conflict first develops.

Photographed in grainy black and white to suggest the style of documentaries and TV news reports, THE BATTLE OF ALGIERS most closely resembles the neorealism of Roberto Rossellini and the revolutionary editing techniques of Sergei Eisenstein. Like Eisenstein, director Pontecorvo took his camera to the actual locations of the revolution, re-created certain events, and cast local nonprofessionals. Only Martin is a professional actor, while Saadi, the film's coproducer, plays an FLN leader—a character based on his real-life role as the organizer of the resistance and the military commander of the FLN.

The content of the film has been attacked as being too inflammatory; it was reportedly used as a terrorist primer in the late 1960s. Yet it's entirely frank about its politics, something that can't be said of most Hollywood films. What makes the movie's power creditable is Pontecorvo's ability to present combatants on both sides as multidimensional, nonheroic human beings, even though it's obvious where the director's own sentiments lie. The film received the Golden Lion at Venice in 1966.

BATTLE OF BRITAIN

DVD

1969 133m c War ★★★½
Spitfire (U.K.) G

Harry Andrews *(Senior Civil Servant)*, Michael Caine *(Squadron Leader Canfield)*, Trevor Howard *(Air Vice Marshal Keith Park)*, Curt Jurgens *(Baron von Richter)*, Ian McShane *(Sgt. Pilot Andy)*, Kenneth More *(Group Capt. Baker)*, Laurence Olivier *(Air Chief Marshal Sir Hugh Dowding)*, Nigel Patrick *(Group Capt. Hope)*, Christopher Plummer *(Squadron Leader Harvey)*, Michael Redgrave *(Air Vice Marshal Evill)*

p, Harry Saltzman, S. Benjamin Fisz; d, Guy Hamilton; w, James Kennaway, Wilfred Greatorex; ph, Freddie Young, Bob Huke (Panavision, Technicolor); ed, Bert Bates; m, William Walton, Ron Goodwin; prod d, Sydney Streeter; art d, Maurice Carter, Bert Davey, Jack Maxsted, William Hutchinson, Gil Parrondo; fx, Cliff Richardson, Glen Robinson

This stirring if slightly overlong saga of England's WWII defense of its homeland features a staggering, star-studded cast, who abet the film's docudrama style with excellent portrayals down the line, despite the restrictions of their roles. Caine, Plummer, and More have the meatier parts, with Susannah York providing the obligatory love interest as Plummer's WAAF wife who hates the war and craves affection. Olivier is in fine form as Sir Hugh Dowding, whose crafty tactics with his limited fighter command induced the Luftwaffe to make fatal errors that led to its destruction, and Robert Shaw is superb as an exhausted but relentlessly tough fighter commander who orders his men again and again into the air.

While the film is a fitting paean to the noble RAF in its "Finest Hour," nodding recognition is also given to the Czech and Polish flyers who fought alongside their British comrades. Except for Jurgens, however, the German actors are mere caricatures of the Nazi high command, with Rolf Stiefel especially ludicrous as a berserk Hitler. The aerial photography of the German bombing and the dogfights between the British and German fighters are spectacular and fascinating; it was the high production value of these segments which cost the producers the bulk of their $12 million investment. Adolf Galland, one of the sharpest German aces to vex the British during WWII, was employed as a technical advisor on the film.

BATTLEGROUND

DVD

1949 118m bw War ★★★★
MGM (U.S.)

Van Johnson *(Holley)*, John Hodiak *(Jarvess)*, Ricardo Montalban *(Roderigues)*, George Murphy *(Pop Stazak)*, Marshall Thompson *(Jim Layton)*, Jerome Courtland *(Abner Spudler)*, Don Taylor *(Standiferd)*, Bruce Cowling *(Wolowicz)*, James Whitmore *(Kinnie)*, Douglas Fowley *(Kipp Kippton)*

p, Dore Schary; d, William A. Wellman; w, Robert Pirosh; ph, Paul C. Vogel; ed, John Dunning; m, Lennie Hayton; art d, Cedric Gibbons, Hans Peters; fx, Peter Ballbusch

AAN Best Picture; AAN Best Supporting Actor: James Whitmore; *AAN Best Director:* William A. Wellman; *AA Best Story and Screenplay:* Robert Pirosh; *AA Best B/W Cinematography:* Paul C. Vogel; *AAN Best Film Editing:* John Dunning

An excellent film, BATTLEGROUND tells the story of a squad of American foot soldiers trapped by the Germans in

Bastogne in 1944. A wide assortment of MGM actors—none of them overreaching the prosaic dimensions of his character—play this cross-section of citizens, including Johnson, a wisecracking, girl-chasing GI "inconvenienced" by the war; and Hodiak, a conscientious small-time newspaperman turned soldier. (At one point, when food is running out in the besieged town, Johnson and Hodiak see an old woman picking through a garbage can. "I don't see that," Johnson says in disgust, turning away. "Well, I see it," retorts Hodiak. "I'll always see it and I never want anyone to forget it!") Whitmore is terrific as the tobacco-chomping, frozen-footed sergeant, as tough as a whole Panzer division, and Montalban was never better than here, as a Mexican-American from southern California who delights in his first snowfall, frolicking in the flakes like a child.

Director Wellman expertly conveys the life of soldiers at war—a life screenwriter Pirosh knew well, since he had served at Bastogne. BATTLEGROUND was a special project for Schary, who brought it from RKO to MGM after he was named MGM production chief (it was his first production credit there). Initially nixed by mogul Louis B. Mayer on the grounds that the public was not ready to relive WWII, the film proved extremely popular and received six Academy Award nominations including Best Picture. Quite apart from the film's merit, BATTLEGROUND is also notable for initiating the rift between Mayer and Schary that eventually led to Mayer's ouster.

BEACH BLANKET BINGO

DVD

1965 100m c Musical/Comedy ★★½
AIP (U.S.)

Frankie Avalon *(Frankie)*, Annette Funicello *(Dee Dee)*, Deborah Walley *(Bonnie Graham)*, Harvey Lembeck *(Eric Von Zipper)*, John Ashley *(Steve Gordon)*, Jody McCrea *(Bonehead)*, Donna Loren *(Donna)*, Marta Kristen *(Lorelei)*, Linda Evans *(Sugar Kane)*, Timothy Carey *(South Dakota Slim)*

p, James H. Nicholson, Samuel Z. Arkoff; d, William Asher; w, William Asher, Leo Townsend; ph, Floyd Crosby (Panavision, Pathecolor); ed, Fred R. Feitshans Jr., Eve Newman; m, Les Baxter; art d, Howard Campbell

Probably the best known of the spate of "beach party" films of the 1960s, BEACH BLANKET BINGO provides 100 minutes of silly, mildly amusing entertainment if you're in the right mood. There's trouble in teen paradise when Frankie (Avalon) and Dee Dee (Funicello) clash over his infatuation with singer Sugar Kane (Evans). Meanwhile, a mermaid falls in love with nitwit surfer Bonehead (McCrea), and the nefarious Eric Von Zipper (Lembeck) and his Rat Pack kidnap Sugar. Don Rickles, Buster Keaton, Paul Lynde and others are also on hand, sandwiching their shtick between the musical numbers from Frankie, Annette, and their scantily clad pals.

BEACH, THE

DVD

2000 118m c Adventure/Thriller ★★½
Figment Films (U.K.) R

Leonardo DiCaprio *(Richard)*, Tilda Swinton *(Sal)*, Virginie Ledoyen *(Francoise)*, Guillaume Canet *(Etienne)*, Robert Carlyle *(Daffy)*, Paterson Joseph *(Keaty)*, Lars Arentz Hansen *(Bugs)*, Daniel York *(Hustler)*, Patcharawan Patarakijjanon *(Hotel Receptionist)*, Somboon Phutaroth *(Cleaning Woman)*

p, Andrew Macdonald; d, Danny Boyle; w, John Hodge (based on the novel *The Beach* by Alex Garland); ph, Darius Khondji; ed, Masahiro Hirakubo; m, Angelo Badalamenti; prod d, Andrew McAlpine; art d, Rod McLean; fx, Clive Beard, Computer Film Company; cos, Rachael Fleming

Danny Boyle's slick adaptation of Alex Garland's best-selling novel never decides whether it wants to be an exotic, titillating episode of MTV's "The Real World" or a Gen-X *Lord of the Flies.*

Richard (Leonardo DiCaprio), a disaffected member of the virtual generation, flees to Thailand in search of authentic experience, only to find himself stuck in a thoroughly commercialized, mall-style Asia, one packaged for youthful tourists like himself. The promise of something different is held out by a dope-addled waste case (Robert Carlyle) who calls himself Daffy Duck and commits bloody suicide after a single enigmatic conversation with Richard. Daffy leaves behind a hand-drawn map to an unspoiled corner of heaven on earth. Richard and an attractive French couple, Etienne and Francoise (Guillaume Canet, Virginie Ledoyen), make their way to the fabled beach and discover an idyllic commune led by the imperious Sal (Tilda Swinton). But Richard's affair with Francoise disrupts the hippie haven, and soon paradise is as rotten as an overripe mango.

Boyle and screenwriter John Hodge jettison much of the novel's telling details and so simplify the characters' ethical dilemmas that it's hard to care what they do. Stripped of the book's careful grounding in Richard's obsession with Vietnam War movies, the picture's obvious allusions to APOCALYPSE NOW and THE DEER HUNTER seem capricious, and the whole film moves with the shambling rhythm of a shaggy dog story. It's a canny move for DiCaprio, whose morally compromised Richard is light-years removed from TITANIC's Jack, but the movie is a disappointment overall. It could have been a seductive fable with a concealed sting; instead, it's just a lazy moral tale.

BEACHES

DVD

1988 123m c Drama ★★
Touchstone/Silver Screen Partners IV/ PG-13
Bruckheimer South-All Girl (U.S.)

Bette Midler *(C.C. Bloom)*, Barbara Hershey *(Hillary Whitney Essex)*, John Heard *(John Pierce)*, Spalding Gray *(Dr. Richard Milstein)*, Lainie Kazan *(Leona Bloom)*, James Read *(Michael Essex)*, Grace Johnston *(Victoria Essex)*, Mayim Bialik *(C.C., Age 11)*, Marcie Leeds *(Hillary, Age 11)*

p, Bonnie Bruckheimer-Martell, Bette Midler, Margaret Jennings South; d, Garry Marshall; w, Mary Agnes Donoghue (based on the novel by Iris Rainer Dart); ph, Dante Spinotti (Metrocolor); ed, Richard Halsey; m, Georges Delerue; prod d, Albert Brenner; cos, Robert de Mora

AAN Best Art Direction-Set Decoration: Albert Brenner (Art Direction), Garrett Lewis (Set Decoration)

This interminable melodrama purports to be a warm, humorous, and moving look at the relationship of two women over the course of 30 years. In reality BEACHES is a trite, maudlin, and terribly superficial effort of the sub-made-for-TV quality, an insult to anyone who has ever befriended another human being. The film depicts the unlikely friendship of a brassy, Jewish, Bronx-bred singer (Midler) and an icy, WASP-ish, San Francisco-bred socialite (Hershey) from their meeting in Atlantic City until the day the latter is buried, a victim of the kind of disease that seems only to afflict characters in movies like this.

An ego trip for star-executive producer Midler, the film tells its story mostly in flashback and entirely from her character's point of view, while the successful songstress drives a rented car from L.A. to San Francisco to be with the dying Hershey. Director Marshall fails to bring anything remotely resembling inspiration or spontaneity to screenwriter Donoghue's terribly mundane disease-of-the-week script, leaving the viewer wondering why these two women would even speak to each other, let alone commit

themselves to an apparently deeply emotional relationship. The problems they face are wholly synthetic, dealt with in a flash, and forgotten until the next minicrisis comes along. There is no sense of real joy, pain, or struggle here—merely a TV version that is only tangentially related to actual human experience.

BEAR, THE

DVD

1989 93m c Adventure ★★★½
Price/Renn (France) PG

Jack Wallace *(Bill)*, Tcheky Karyo *(Tom)*, Andre Lacombe *(The Dog Handler)*, Bart the Bear *(Kaar)*, Douce the Bear *(Youk)*

p, Claude Berri; d, Jean-Jacques Annaud; w, Gerard Brach (based on the novel *The Grizzly King* by James Oliver Curwood); ph, Philippe Rousselot; ed, Noelle Boisson; m, Philippe Sarde; prod d, Toni Ludi; art d, Heidi Ludi, Antony Greengrow, George Dietz; cos, Corinne Jorry, Francoise Disle; anim, Bretislav Pojar

AAN Best Film Editing: Noelle Boisson

This deceptively simple wilderness tale began production in 1982 with a four-line synopsis—"A big solitary bear. An orphan bear cub. Two hunters in the forest. The animals' point of view"—and went on to take in more than $100 million *before* its U.S. release. The plot, practically nonexistent at first, unfolds in British Columbia in 1885, detailing the idyllic daily routine of a bear cub. After the cub's mother is killed in a rockslide, however, the youngster must attempt to bond with a 2000-pound Kodiak male being pursued by a pair of hunters—Bill (Wallace), a calm, calculating veteran, and his young, overeager friend Tom (Karyo).

A far cry from the sweet nature adventures that Disney popularized, THE BEAR is a sublime, graceful tale of human nature told, somewhat paradoxically, through the eyes of an animal. Director Annaud tells his story almost exclusively through visuals, using a bare minimum of dialogue and an elegantly constructed soundtrack composed from the "language" of the bears. Though the film borrows from the sophisticated techniques of such masters of silent film as D.W. Griffith and Robert Flaherty, it gives the feel of having been captured effortlessly by the cameras.

BEAT THE DEVIL

DVD

1953 100m bw Comedy/Drama ★★★★
Romulus/Santana (U.S.)

Humphrey Bogart *(Billy Dannreuther)*, Gina Lollobrigida *(Maria Dannreuther)*, Jennifer Jones *(Gwendolyn Chelm)*, Robert Morley *(Peterson)*, Peter Lorre *(O'Hara)*, Edward Underdown *(Harry Chelm)*, Ivor Barnard *(Major Ross)*, Marco Tulli *(Ravello)*, Marion Perroni *(Purser)*, Alex Pochet *(Hotel Manager)*

d, John Huston; w, John Huston, Truman Capote (based on the novel by James Helvick); ph, Oswald Morris; ed, Ralph Kemplen; m, Franco Mannino; art d, Wilfred Shingleton

A screwball, wacky comedy that is played as straight as any film noir and is even funnier as a result. Five desperate and disparate men (Bogart, Lorre, Morley, Barnard, and Tulli) are out to garner control over East African land which they believe contains a rich uranium ore lode. Their scuzzy steamer is in port in Italy. Bogart is married to Gina (an odd choice for the role but she proves to be more than adept at the straightfaced comedy). The other four are their "business associates." Bogart and Gina meet another couple, Jones and Underdown. She's in a blonde wig and off-the-wall; he's a prig-and-a-half at first glance but in reality, he's a phony peer. Jones rattles on about her hubby's uranium holdings, all lies. The "associates" think they are being gulled by Bogart when it appears that Bogie is after Jones and Gina is hot for Underdown.

The boat leaves for Africa, then blows up. Seven survivors make it to shore and are taken in by a hostile group of Arabs. Their lives are saved when Bogart manages to charm the evil Arab police chief by promising the man an opportunity to meet his idol, Rita Hayworth. Underdown is supposed to have drowned and this causes Jones, a pathological liar, to tell the truth. The four villains are taken in by the Italian police, then Jones gets a telegram from her still-alive husband and is delighted to learn that Underdown made it to Africa and acquired the uranium-rich land the others yearned for.

If all the aforementioned sounds like a hodge-podge, you're right. But it is such wonderful nonsense—there isn't a moment when the picture doesn't take a left turn when you expect it to turn right. Director Huston, working from a quirky, literate script by Capote, manages to parody a number of his earlier films, including THE MALTESE FALCON, THE TREASURE OF THE SIERRA MADRE, and KEY LARGO. Bogart, who, of course, was in all those films, seems to be having a marvelous time skewering them and gives a memorable performance. The film's humor is not readily apparent, and the movie was quickly rejected by the public upon its release. But today it has achieved something of a cult following and is a sheer delight.

BEAU GESTE   DVD

1939 114m bw Adventure/War   ★★★½
Paramount   (U.S.)

Gary Cooper *(Michael "Beau" Geste)*, Ray Milland *(John Geste)*, Robert Preston *(Digby Geste)*, Brian Donlevy *(Sgt. Markoff)*, Susan Hayward *(Isobel Rivers)*, J. Carrol Naish *(Rasinoff)*, Albert Dekker *(Schwartz)*, Broderick Crawford *(Hank Miller)*, Charles Barton *(Buddy McMonigal)*, James Stephenson *(Maj. Henri de Beaujolais)*

p, William A. Wellman; d, William A. Wellman; w, Robert Carson (based on the novel by Percival Christopher Wren); ph, Theodor Sparkuhl, Archie Stout; ed, Thomas Scott; m, Alfred Newman; art d, Hans Dreier, Robert Odell

AAN Best Supporting Actor: Brian Donlevy; *AAN Best Interior Decoration:* Hans Dreier (Art Direction), Robert Odell (Art Direction)

Gary Cooper enacts the title role with quiet magnificence in this superb adventure tale loaded with drama, action, and mystery. The film opens with a relief column of Legionnaires crossing the desert dunes to Fort Zinderneuf. The fort seems strangely silent and a bugler is sent to investigate. He finds all inside the fort dead, and notices a sergeant on the parapet in whose hand is a note confessing to the theft of a fabulous gem called "the Blue Water." When the column enters the fort, the body of the sergeant is gone. Next the troops hear shots outside the fort and pursue what they think are tribal invaders. The fort suddenly erupts into flames, setting off the arsenal which destroys Zinderneuf.

In a flashback to 15 years earlier, we see three boys, the Geste brothers, at a great English mansion. The boys are cared for by kindly Thatcher, an impoverished blueblood who is so desperate to give the orphaned brothers and another child, Gillis, a good home that she secretly sells the treasured family jewel, the Blue Water, to raise the necessary funds. O'Connor secretly witnesses the transaction and watches Thatcher replace the gem with a fake. Years later, with O'Connor grown into Cooper, his brothers grown into Milland and Preston, and Gillis bloomed into Hayward, the lord of the manor, Huntley, appears seeking the great sapphire. To prevent Thatcher from having to admit her secret transaction, Cooper steals the phony gem, leaves a note for his brothers admitting the theft, and joins the Foreign Legion.

Cooper's great performance is given solid support by Ray Milland and Robert Preston, but Susan Hayward appears only briefly as the love interest and her performance is unmemo-

rable. Brian Donlevy almost steals every scene he's in with a snarling performance that will scare the blazes out of any viewer, and J. Carrol Naish's hyena-like Rasinoff is unforgettable. Great support also comes from veteran heavies Albert Dekker, Harry Woods, and Harold Huber, enacting the mutinous Legionnaires. Broderick Crawford and Charles Barton provide the comic relief as the Gestes' sidekicks.

When director William Wellman was brought in to remake the silent 1926 version of P.C. Wren's captivating story, he was instructed to follow the original almost to the letter, which he did, even using the same location, the spreading desert dunes of Yuma, Arizona, where a new Fort Zinderneuf was completely rebuilt. Paramount executives thought it would be impressive to run the first reel of the silent version before showing the 1939 remake to reviewers, to show what sound could do to improve a classic. It was a scheme that almost blew up in their faces; some reviewers still preferred the silent version, but most felt that the remake was superior.

BEAUTIFUL MIND, A   DVD

2001 130m c Biography/Drama   ★★★
DreamWorks Pictures/Imagine Entertainment/   PG-13
Brian Grazer Productions   (U.S.)

Russell Crowe *(John Nash)*, Ed Harris *(Parcher)*, Jennifer Connelly *(Alicia Nash)*, Christopher Plummer *(Dr. Rosen)*, Paul Bettany *(Charles)*, Adam Goldberg *(Sol)*, Josh Lucas *(Hansen)*, Vivien Cardone *(Marcee)*, Anthony Rapp *(Bender)*, Jason Gray-Stanford *(Ainsley)*

p, Ron Howard, Brian Grazer; d, Ron Howard; w, Akiva Goldsman (based on the book by Sylvia Nasar); ph, Roger Deakins; ed, Dan Hanley; m, James Horner; prod d, Wynn Thomas; art d, Robert Guerra; fx, Will Caban, Digital Domain, Kevin Mack, Matthew Butler (digital); cos, Rita Ryack

AA Best Picture; AA Best Director: Ron Howard; *AA Best Supporting Actress:* Jennifer Connelly; *AA Best Adapted Screenplay:* Akiva Goldsman; *AAN Best Actor:* Russell Crowe; *AAN Best Film Editing:* Mike Hill, Dan Hanley; *AAN Best Makeup:* Greg Cannom, Colleen Callaghan; *AAN Best Original Score:* James Horner

Inspired by the tumultuous life of mathematician John Forbes Nash Jr., who in 1994 won a Nobel Prize after a lifetime of battling schizophrenic delusions, this film at its core is a vivid evocation of the ravages of chronic mental illness.

Handsome, arrogant, but socially awkward, Nash (Russell Crowe) enters Princeton University's graduate mathematics department in 1948, when the discipline carried a whiff of post-war glamour: mathematicians filled the ranks of WWII code breakers and helped win the war. Within a span of 10 years, Nash produces a pioneering paper on game theory; forms a lifelong friendship with his roommate, Charles (Paul Bettany); accepts a prestigious position at MIT; is recruited for a top-secret cryptology project by the U.S. government; and marries Alicia (Jennifer Connelly), a physics student. Just when Nash is about to become a father, his mind comes crashing down in a shower of schizophrenic delusions.

Not all of this actually happens, but director Ron Howard presents Nash's elaborate delusions in an absolutely straightforward manner, obscuring the precise moment at which his perception of the world diverges from objective reality. When we finally realize just how extensive these delusions are, it's a genuine shock. The success of this effect, which helps elevate the movie above a classy disease-of-the-week saga, rests firmly on Crowe's performance, and it's a strikingly good one. But though based on Sylvia Nasar's biography of the same name, the movie shouldn't be taken for Nash's life story. Screenwriter Akiva Goldsman cheerfully admits that "most of the things that happen in the movie didn't happen in John's life," while many things that happened in Nash's life aren't in the movie.

BEAUTY AND THE BEAST
DVD
(LA BELLE ET LA BETE)
1946 90m   bw Fantasy   ★★★★★
Discina   (France)

Jean Marais *(Avenant/The Beast/The Prince)*, Josette Day *(Beauty)*, Marcel Andre *(The Merchant)*, Mila Parely *(Adelaide)*, Nane Germon *(Felice)*, Michel Auclair *(Ludovic)*

p, Andre Paulve; d, Jean Cocteau; w, Jean Cocteau (based on the fairy tale by Mme. Leprince de Beaumont); ph, Henri Alekan; ed, Claude Iberia; m, Georges Auric; art d, Christian Berard

A masterpiece. The great Jean Cocteau has written that in order for a myth to live it must continually be told and retold, and this is just what Cocteau does in BEAUTY AND THE BEAST—bringing Mme. Marie Leprince de Beaumont's 1757 fairy tale to the screen. Beauty (Josette Day) and the Beast (Jean Marais) are given a new life in the cinema thanks to Cocteau's poetry, Henri Alekan's cinematography, Georges Auric's music, and Christian Berard's art direction. The legend is familiar: a merchant's beautiful daughter saves her father's life by agreeing to visit the diabolical Beast, a fearsome creature with magical powers. Beauty faints with horror upon their first meeting, but gradually grows to love the Beast, finding the soul that exists beneath his gruesome exterior.

While the narrative is basic and familiar, the film's visuals are not. A magical white horse blazes across the screen; the Beast's hands smoke after a kill; the hanging white laundry of Beauty's family billows in the breeze; the Beast's fantastical candelabras are human arms that extend from the walls and emerge from the dinner table. It is a credit to Cocteau's genius (and to that of his collaborators) that he has taken the unreal world of a fairy tale and made it as real as the world around us.

BEAUTY AND THE BEAST
DVD
1991 84m c Animated/Musical/Romance   ★★★★½
Walt Disney Productions/Silver Screen   G
Partners IV   (U.S.)

VOICES OF: Paige O'Hara *(Belle)*, Robby Benson *(Beast)*, Rex Everhart *(Maurice)*, Richard White *(Gaston)*, Jesse Corti *(Le Fou)*, Angela Lansbury *(Mrs. Potts)*, Jerry Orbach *(Lumiere)*, David Ogden Stiers *(Cogsworth/Narrator)*, Bradley Michael Pierce *(Chip)*, Hal Smith *(Philippe)*

p, Don Hahn; d, Kirk Wise, Gary Trousdale; w, Linda Woolverton (from a story by Kelly Asbury, Brenda Chapman, Tom Ellery, Kevin Harkey, Robert Lence, Burny Mattinson, Brian Pimental, Joe Ranft, Christopher Sanders and Bruce Woodside); ed, John Carnochan; m, Alan Menken; art d, Brian McEntee; anim, Roger Allers, Ed Ghertner, Lisa Keene, Vera Lanpher, Randy Fullmer, Jim Hillin

AA Best Original Score: Alan Menken; *AA Best Original Song:* "Beauty and the Beast"; Alan Menken (Music), Howard Ashman (Lyrics); *AAN Best Original Song:* "Belle"; Alan Menken (Music), Howard Ashman (Lyrics); *AAN Best Original Song:* "Be Our Guest"; Alan Menken (Music), Howard Ashman (Lyrics); *AAN Best Picture; AAN Best Sound:* Terry Porter, Mel Metcalfe, David J. Hudson, Doc Kane

BEAUTY AND THE BEAST is a nostalgic feast, drawing shamelessly on the best traditions of screen animation and American musical theater and film. Thoroughly derivative but thoroughly charming.

Belle (Paige O'Hara) is a beautiful young woman in a small French town who dreams of escape, fending off advances from the handsome, but arrogant and chauvinistic Gaston (Richard White). Belle's father is lost in a dark wood and seeks refuge in an enchanted castle, lorded over by the Beast (Robby Benson), a spoiled young prince transformed by an enchantress into a hideous monster. The spell has transformed his castle into a dank, gloomy lair and his servants into household bric-a-brac. Enraged that Maurice has violated the castle grounds, the Beast locks him in a dungeon. When her father's horse returns home without him, Belle sets off in pursuit and finds her way to the castle, where the Beast agrees to let her father leave if she will remain in his stead—forever.

The familiar narrative is strengthened by the independent, self-assured character of Belle. Unlike Disney heroines from Snow White through Ariel, Belle is smart, knows what she wants, and doesn't spend her time pining away for the love of a handsome prince. Howard Ashman and Alan Menken propel the plot and character development along with their tuneful, witty and textured songs. As they enrich the palette of the narrative, they also invite comparison with some of the past glories of the American musical theater—from the opening numbers of *Fiddler on the Roof* and *She Loves Me* (the teeming "Belle" opener), the love soliloquies from *South Pacific* (the touching "Something There" soliloquies of Belle and the Beast), the "Shall We Dance?" waltz from *The King and I* (the soaring "Beauty and the Beast" waltz), to crowd-pleasing production numbers from Jerry Herman's *Hello Dolly* and *Mame* (the boisterous "Be Our Guest").

All this, though, would mean nothing if the animation were not of a standard to compare with the rest of the elements. It is. Using computer wizardry to simulate live-action film techniques like dollies, tracks and pans, the animation succeeds in creating an uncannily realistic world. The filmmakers have used considerable depth of field, permitting action to occur on many levels of the frame, from background to foreground, and to move, not only horizontally, but also back and forth from the camera eye. The camera sweeps above forests and down into castle chambers, and races around characters in 360 degree tracks. This is catnip for the kids, and should keep even the most jaded adults awake for the film's blessedly crisp 84 minutes.

BECKET
DVD
1964 148m c Historical   ★★★★
Paramount   (U.K.)

Richard Burton *(Thomas Becket)*, Peter O'Toole *(King Henry II)*, Donald Wolfit *(Bishop Folliot)*, John Gielgud *(King Louis VII)*, Martita Hunt *(Queen Matilda)*, Pamela Brown *(Queen Eleanor)*, Sian Phillips *(Gwendolyn)*, Paolo Stoppa *(Pope Alexander III)*, Gino Cervi *(Cardinal Zambelli)*, David Weston *(Brother John)*

p, Hal B. Wallis; d, Peter Glenville; w, Edward Anhalt (based on the play by Jean Anouilh); ph, Geoffrey Unsworth (Technicolor); ed, Anne V. Coates; m, Laurence Rosenthal; prod d, John Bryan; art d, Maurice Carter; cos, Margaret Furse

AAN Best Picture; AAN Best Actor: Richard Burton; *AAN Best Actor:* Peter O'Toole; *AAN Best Supporting Actor:* John Gielgud; *AAN Best Director:* Peter Glenvile; *AA Best Adapted Screenplay:* Edward Anhalt; *AAN Best Color Cinematography:* Geoffrey Unsworth; *AAN Best Film Editing:* Anne Coates; *AAN Best Original Score:* Laurence Rosenthal; *AAN Best Art Direction-Set Decoration (Color):* John Bryan, Maurice Carter, Patrick McLoughlin, Robert Cartwright; *AAN Best Costume Design (Color):* Margaret Furse; *AAN Best Sound:* John Cox

This notable improvement over the stage-bound Anouilh play recounts the story of two great friends turned unintentional foes, Becket (Richard Burton) and Henry II (Peter O'Toole).

Becket is Henry's chancellor until consecrated Archbishop of Canterbury, almost in jest, by Henry. Becket takes the job seriously and defends the church from royal onslaught. The two men drift further apart as Becket goes deeper into his ecclesiastical role, and the king realizes that his former friend must be killed after the two men meet for an attempted reconciliation in a wonderful scene on horseback at a British beach.

Ostensibly a story regarding the separation of church and state, Anouilh and Anhalt followed history closely and added their own undercurrent of homoerotic tension between the men, although this is so subtle that it was lost on many viewers. All technical credits are excellent and so are the performances. Many wonderful touches abound, including the scene wherein forks are introduced to the court. Wallis, whose career spanned six decades (everything from LITTLE CAESAR, CASABLANCA, and GUNFIGHT AT THE O.K. CORRAL to various Elvis Presley films) established himself in the pantheon of producers with this film.

BECKY SHARP
1935 83m c Drama **DVD**
Pioneer (U.S.) ★★½

Miriam Hopkins (*Becky Sharp*), Frances Dee (*Amelia Sedley*), Cedric Hardwicke (*Marquis of Steyne*), Billie Burke (*Lady Bareacres*), Alison Skipworth (*Miss Crawley*), Nigel Bruce (*Joseph Sedley*), Alan Mowbray (*Rawdon Crawley*), Colin Tapley (*William Dobbin*), G.P. Huntley Jr. (*George Osborne*), William Stack (*Pitt Crawley*)

p, Kenneth MacGowan; d, Rouben Mamoulian; w, Francis Edwards Faragoh (based on a play by Langdon Mitchell and *Vanity Fair* by William Makepeace Thackeray); ph, Ray Rennahan (Technicolor); ed, Archie Marshek; m, Roy Webb; prod d, Robert Jones; chor, Russell Lewis

AAN Best Actress: Miriam Hopkins

Landmark technicolor, but otherwise very flat indeed. Third version of *Vanity Fair* was a troubled production with original director Lowell Sherman dying, Mamoulian starting over. Hopkins always excelled at predatory roles, but unless flawlessly scripted and sat on by a director, her characterizations invariably went over the top. Watch if you want to see her play to the second balcony, otherwise be on the lookout for rare 1932 version with Myrna Loy. BECKY SHARP wasn't fine enough to make everyone race to film in color; it would take four more years with three mammoth MGM successes—GONE WITH THE WIND and THE WIZARD OF OZ among them—before it started to *really* take off.

BED SITTING ROOM, THE
1969 80m c Comedy
UA (U.K.) ★★★

Rita Tushingham (*Penelope*), Ralph Richardson (*Lord Fortnum*), Peter Cook (*Inspector*), Dudley Moore (*Sergeant*), Spike Milligan (*Mate*), Michael Hordern (*Blues Martin*), Roy Kinnear (*Plastic Mac Man*), Richard Warwick (*Allan*), Arthur Lowe (*Father*), Mona Washbourne (*Mother*)

p, Richard Lester; d, Richard Lester; w, John Antrobus, Charles Wood (based on a play by Antrobus and Spike Milligan); ph, David Watkin; ed, John Victor Smith; m, Ken Horne

A field day for funny collection of Brits. Weird picture originated in a well-known weird place, the mind of "Goon Show" alumnus Spike Milligan. An offbeat look at London after the bombs have been dropped, this episodic film follows several Blitz survivors (many of them played by British TV stars) as they make their way through the ruins of their great city. Lowe turns into a parrot, Washbourne becomes a chest of drawers, Tushingham announces that she's 17 months pregnant, and

Richardson metamorphoses into a bed sitting room! Although the basic situation may not be the funniest set-up imaginable, the players manage to keep the laughs flying thick and fast. Former Goons Cook and Moore are side-splittingly funny as government bureaucrats; Marty Feldman makes his debut.

BEDAZZLED
1967 104m c Comedy
Fox (U.K.) ★★★½

Peter Cook (*George Spiggot*), Dudley Moore (*Stanley Moon*), Eleanor Bron (*Margaret*), Raquel Welch (*Lillian Lust*), Alba (*Vanity*), Robert Russell (*Anger*), Barry Humphries (*Envy*), Parnell McGarry (*Gluttony*), Daniele Noel (*Avarice*), Howard Goorney (*Sloth*)

p, Stanley Donen; d, Stanley Donen; w, Peter Cook (based on a story by Cook, Dudley Moore); ph, Austin Dempster (Panavision, Deluxe Color); ed, Richard Marden; m, Dudley Moore

No one and nothing is safe from Cook and Moore's barbed screenplay. They take shots at nuns, priests, the upper classes of England, Lyndon Johnson, Julie Andrews, the Prime Minister and, eventually, God. It's a devilish plot with Moore as a short short-order cook in love with Bron, a waitress with sex exuding from every pore. Cook is the devil who grants him several wishes. Naturally, all of them go awry, and Moore winds up in a nun's habit as one of the Order of Leaping Berelians, sisters who do their penance on trampolines. Cook and Moore brilliantly shift from character to character with just a change of voice (not unlike Peter Sellers), and the movie never flags. Raquel Welch is at her sexiest as Lust, but Bron is the standout female as the recalcitrant waitress. She appeared with the Monty Python group on stage in London and is best recalled for her wonderful work as Bill Daniels' wife in TWO FOR THE ROAD (1966), also directed by Donen.

BEDKNOBS AND BROOMSTICKS
1971 117m c Fantasy **DVD**
Walt Disney Productions (U.S.) ★★★
G

Angela Lansbury (*Eglantine Price*), David Tomlinson (*Emelius Browne*), Roddy McDowall (*Mr. Jelk*), Sam Jaffe (*Bookman*), John Ericson (*Col. Heller*), Bruce Forsyth (*Swinburne*), Reginald Owen (*Gen. Teagler*), Tessie O'Shea (*Mrs. Hobday*), Arthur Gould-Porter (*Capt. Greer*), Ben Wrigley (*Street Sweeper*)

p, Bill Walsh; d, Robert Stevenson; w, Bill Walsh, Don DaGradi (based on the book by Mary Norton); ph, Frank Phillips (Technicolor); ed, Cotton Warburton; art d, Peter Ellenshaw, John B. Mansbridge; fx, Danny Lee, Eustace Lycett, Alan Maley; cos, Bill Thomas; anim, Ward Kimball

AAN Best Song Score: Richard M. Sherman, Robert B. Sherman, Irwin Kostal; *AAN Best Original Song:* "The Age of Not Believing"; Richard M. Sherman (Music & Lyrics), Robert B. Sherman (Music & Lyrics); *AAN Best Art Direction-Set Decoration:* John B. Mansbridge, Peter Ellenshaw, Emile Kuri, Hal Gausman; *AAN Best Costume Design:* Bill Thomas; *AA Best Special Visual Effects:* Alan Maley, Eustace Lycett, Danny Lee

Similar in many ways to MARY POPPINS, BEDKNOBS AND BROOMSTICKS is filled with unique special effects and delightful music. Angela Lansbury stars as Eglantine Price, the owner of a seaside house in England who has three children foisted on her during WWII. At first, the children aren't thrilled about being relocated. Then they learn that Eglantine is studying witchcraft by mail and has much mischief planned for the Nazis if they ever land in England. With a bedstead as their magic carpet, Eglantine takes the kids on a wonderful ride into several fantastic worlds. Animation is neatly mixed with live action, and Lansbury, engaging as ever, heads a capable cast.

BEDTIME FOR BONZO

DVD
1951 83m bw Comedy ★★½
Universal (U.S.)

Ronald Reagan *(Prof. Peter Boyd)*, Diana Lynn *(Jane)*, Walter Slezak *(Prof. Hans Neumann)*, Lucille Barkley *(Valerie Tillinghast)*, Jesse White *(Babcock)*, Herbert Heyes *(Dean Tillinghast)*, Herb Vigran *(Lt. Daggett)*, Harry Tyler *(Knicksy)*, Edward Clark *(Fosdick)*, Edward Gargan *(Policeman)*

p, Michel Kraike; d, Frederick de Cordova; w, Val Burton, Lou Breslow (based on a story by Raphael Blau, Ted Berkman); ph, Carl Guthrie; ed, Ted J. Kent; m, Frank Skinner

Cult comeuppance. For once Reagan is in synch with his costar, but Bonzo the chimp proved the more able farceur. Animal fans will be saddened to know Bonzo and four stand-ins died tragically in a trailer fire. The first assignment for Freddie de Cordova, longtime producer of the "Tonight Show." We all gotta start somewhere. A sequel followed—BONZO GOES TO COLLEGE—sans Reagan, who apparently couldn't handle the academic overload.

BEEFCAKE

DVD
1999 93m c/bw Docudrama ★★★½
Telefilm Canada/Alliance Atlantis/Nova Scotia
Film Development Corporation/Emotion Pictures/
Odeon Films/La Sept Arte/Channel Four Television
Corporation/Mikado Films/Telefilm Canada
(Canada/U.K./France)

Daniel MacIvor *(Bob Mizer)*, Josh Peace *(Neil O'Hara)*, Carroll Godsman *(Mrs. Mizer)*, Jonathan Torrens *(David)*, Jack Griffin Mazeika *(Red)*, Jack LaLanne *(Himself)*, Joe Dallesandro *(Himself)*, Russ Warner *(Himself)*, Dave Martin *(Himself)*, Jim Lassiter *(Himself)*

p, Shandi Mitchell, Thom Fitzgerald; d, Thom Fitzgerald; w, Thom Fitzgerald (inspired by the book by F. Valentine Hooven III); ph, Thomas M. Harting; ed, Susan Shanks, Michael Weir; m, John Roby, Michael Diabo, John Wesley Chisholm; prod d, D'Arcy Poultney; art d, Jennifer Stewart; cos, James A. Worthen

Long before undeniably homoerotic imagery infiltrated mainstream culture, there was Bob Mizer, amateur photographer, Super-8 filmmaker, and the subject of this fanciful and highly entertaining docudrama.

Mizer was one of a handful of post-WWII photographers who specialized in frankly erotic photos of muscular young men wearing little more than baby oil and posing straps; ostensibly physical-culture pictorials, their pictures were popular with gay men who had little to choose from in the way of erotica. In 1948, Mizer founded the Athletic Model Guild, intending to promote his models to other artists and physique photographers; it failed as an agency, but succeeded as a studio in its own right. The photographs became its *raison d'etre*, and Mizer began publishing his own magazine, *Physique Pictorial*. But as the Guild grew (Mizer's home, which he shared with his mother, became a bustling menagerie of naked men, animals, and tacky Greco-Roman props) A.M.G. ran afoul of California's harsh obscenity laws.

Director Thom Fitzgerald (THE HANGING GARDEN) tears into this fascinating slice of gay Americana like a kid at Christmas, using everything at his disposal to bring his personal vision of Mizer's world (naughty but essentially innocent, nude but never lewd) to life in all its kitsch glory. Still images and Super-8 reels from the A.M.G. archives are wittily woven into the fictional story of Neil O'Hara (Josh Peace), a handsome innocent from Pugwash, Nova Scotia (Fitzgerald's homeland), who meets Bob Mizer (Daniel MacIvor) and becomes a popular AMG model. Fitzgerald also interviews real-life physique pho-

tographers (Mizer himself died in 1993) and even a few models, including "Little Joe" Dallesandro and ever spry fitness guru Jack LaLanne.

BEETLEJUICE

DVD
1988 92m c Comedy/Horror ★★★½
Geffen (U.S.) PG

Alec Baldwin *(Adam Maitland)*, Geena Davis *(Barbara Maitland)*, Michael Keaton *(Betelgeuse)*, Catherine O'Hara *(Delia Deetz)*, Glenn Shadix *(Otho)*, Winona Ryder *(Lydia Deetz)*, Jeffrey Jones *(Charles Deetz)*, Sylvia Sidney *(Juno)*, Patrice Martinez *(Receptionist)*, Robert Goulet *(Maxie Dean)*

p, Richard Hashimoto, Larry Wilson, Michael Bender; d, Tim Burton; w, Michael McDowell, Warren Skaaren (based on a story by McDowell, Larry Wilson); ph, Thomas Ackerman (Technicolor); ed, Jane Kurson; m, Danny Elfman; prod d, Bo Welch; fx, Chuck Gaspar, Robert Short; chor, Chrissy Bocchino; cos, Aggie Guerard Rodgers

AA Best Makeup: Ve Neill, Steve LaPorte, Robert Short

A surreal, demented delight. The long-awaited second film from wunderkind director Tim Burton is a wildly inventive, unique horror comedy that plays like a twisted, surrealistic, cartoon remake of TOPPER (1937). Keaton is in rare form leading the haunt, rivaled by virtuoso Sidney as overloaded other side caseworker. Film won a much deserved Oscar for Best Achievement in Makeup.

BEFORE NIGHT FALLS

DVD
2000 126m c Biography ★★★★
Grandview Pictures/El Mar Pictures (U.S.) R

Javier Bardem *(Reinaldo Arenas)*, Olivier Martinez *(Lazaro Gomez Carriles)*, Andrea Di Stefano *(Pepe Malas)*, Johnny Depp *(Lieutenant Victor/Bon Bon)*, Sean Penn *(Cuco Sanchez)*, Michael Wincott *(Heberto Zorilla Ochoa)*, Olatz Lopez Garmendia *(Reinaldo's Mother)*, Hector Babenco *(Virgilio Pinera)*, Vito Maria Schnabel *(Teenage Reinaldo)*, Najwa Nimri *(Fina Zorilla Ochoa)*

p, Jon Kilik; d, Julian Schnabel; w, Cunningham O'Keefe, Lazaro Gomez Carriles, Julian Schnabel (based on the memoirs of Reinaldo Arenas); ph, Xavier Perez Grobet, Guillermo Rosas; ed, Michael Berenbaum; m, Carter Burwell, Lou Reed, Laurie Anderson; prod d, Salvador Parra; art d, Antonio Muno-Hierro; cos, Mariestela Fernandez

AAN Best Actor: Javier Bardem

Julian Schnabel has taken some liberties with Reinaldo Arenas's *Before Night Falls*, the fiery memoir published shortly before the Cuban writer's AIDS-related death in 1990. Schnabel has toned down the bilious, anti-Castro tone, invented characters, and trimmed most of the book's graphic sex scenes. Yet the defiant figure of Arenas still springs full-blown from this powerful film, thanks largely to the canny use of Arenas's own writing and an incredible performance from Javier Bardem.

Arenas is born dirt poor to a beautiful mother (Olatz Lopez Garmendia) and a wayward father who disappeared without even bothering to marry her. Growing up on his grandparents' farm, Arenas discovers his three great passions: writing, water, and beautiful men. As a teenager, Arenas (Bardem) takes advantage of the revolutionary fervor sweeping Cuba and leaves home to join Castro's rebels. He winds up in Havana, where he has his first novel published and is initiated into the city's booming gay underground through his bisexual friend Pepe (Andrea Di Stefano). But the sexual revolution that accompanied Castro's rise is short-lived, and life for a gay, anti-Castro writer soon becomes extremely dangerous under a regime with little tolerance for homosexuality, dissent, or counterrevolutionary artists.

This is potent stuff, and as Arenas endures the nightmare of a Cuban concentration camp and, later, exile and terminal illness, Bardem's performance is shattering. The film has the grainy look of sun-bleached color snapshots, and it's peppered with great cameos. Johnny Depp does double duty as a prison drag queen and a Cuban lieutenant, Sean Penn is nearly unrecognizable as a Cuban peasant, and Brazilian director Hector Babenco appears briefly as Arenas's literary mentor, Virgilio Pinera.

BEFORE SUNRISE   DVD

1995 101m c   Romance/Comedy/Drama   ★★★½
Detour Film/Filmhaus/Castle Rock Entertainment   R
(U.S.)

Ethan Hawke *(Jesse)*, Julie Delpy *(Celine)*, Andrea Eckert *(Wife on Train)*, Hanno Poschl *(Husband on Train)*, Karl Bruckschwaiger *(Guy on Bridge)*, Tex Rubinowitz *(Guy on Bridge)*, Erni Mangold *(Palm Reader)*, Dominik Castell *(Street Poet)*, Haymon Maria Buttinger *(Bartender)*, Harold Waiglein *(Guitarist in Club)*

p, Anne Walker-McBay; d, Richard Linklater; w, Richard Linklater, Kim Krizan; ph, Lee Daniel; ed, Sandra Adair; prod d, Florian Reichmann; cos, Florentina Welley

Director Richard Linklater's third feature is a wry, winning portrait of a brief encounter between two young people who meet on a train, spend the night in Vienna, and then part, defying Hollywood conventions of character and story development to charming effect.

The film has little plot in the mainstream sense of that term. Jesse (Ethan Hawke), a young American man, meets Celine (Julie Delpy), a French college student, on a train heading to Austria. The two begin to talk, and do little else for the next 101 minutes. Richard Linklater surprised many viewers by making an unapologetically romantic movie after the less conventionally sentimental SLACKER and DAZED AND CONFUSED. But BEFORE SUNRISE is a logical extension of Linklater's interests, particularly intertextual cultural references and rambling philosophical prattle. It feels like an American Eric Rohmer movie (imagine both the best and the worst that implies), defined by intimate yet heated conversations about life, art, love, religion, sex, and politics.

BEFORE SUNRISE leans heavily on the appeal of its leads, who are in virtually every shot and helped develop the dialogue during the improvisational rehearsal period. Ethan Hawke rises to the occasion, delivering a relaxed, engaging performance as Jesse. Julie Delpy (of KILLING ZOE and THREE COLORS: WHITE) is a revelation as Celine. The film's only real flaw is its failure to address the viewer's nagging feeling that in real life, the sweetly grave Celine would quickly tire of the rather callow Jessie. Still, it's encouraging to see a major Hollywood studio release a film that allows these characters to take center stage and keep it.

BEFORE SUNSET   DVD

2004 80m   c   Drama/Romance   ★★★½
Castle Rock Entertainment/Detour Filmproductions   R
(U.S.)

Ethan Hawke *(Jesse)*, Julie Delpy *(Celine)*, Veron Dobtcheff *(Bookstore Manager)*, Louise Lemonie Torres *(Journalist #1)*, Rodolphe Pauly *(Journalist #2)*, Mariane Plasteig *(Waitress)*, Diabolo *(Philippe)*, Denis Evrard *(Boat Attendant)*, Albert Delpy *(Man at Grill)*, Marie Pillet *(Woman in Courtyard)*

p, Anne Walker-McBay; d, Richard Linklater; w, Richard Linklater, Julie Delpy, Ethan Hawke (from a story by Richard Linklater and Kim Krizan, based on characters created by Richard Linklater and Kim Krizan); ph, Lee Daniel; ed, Sandra Adair; prod d, Baptiste Glaymann; cos, Thierry Delettre

AAN Best Adapted Screenplay: Richard Linklater, Julie Delpy, Ethan Hawke

Richard Linklater's enjoyable sequel to BEFORE SUNRISE picks up nine years after the first film left off. Time constraints again dictate the way the story, written collaboratively by Linklater and his stars, Julie Delpy and Ethan Hawke, unfolds. But instead of the protagonists sharing a too-short 14 hours, they now have just over one hour, which unfolds in real time.

Nine years ago, strangers Celine (Delpy) and Jesse (Hawke) met and spent one magical night roaming the streets of Vienna, only to separate at a train platform the following morning without exchanging any personal information but vowing to meet six months later at that same spot. Nearly a decade later, Jesse is a successful author whose European book tour has landed him in Paris. His novel, an idealized recounting of the events of that night, is being scrutinized by a press corps burning with the desire to know: Did the young lovers meet again? As Jesse struggles to evade the question, he spots Celine in the crowd. They arrange to meet outside and he leaves the bookstore with instructions from the manager to return soon. Celine and Jesse discuss their lives, world politics, and their divergent takes on what happened between them that fateful night. But beneath the comfortable chatter, the question lingers. Did either return to the train platform and, if so, what happened?

This sweet film is a genuine treat, even if there's little plot, no antic mayhem, and its 90-minute running time is mostly consumed by nonstop, sometimes pretentious dialogue. It requires more effort than the typical American romantic comedy, but Delpy and Hawke, who played a similar couple in Linklater's dreamy, animated WAKING LIFE, are thoroughly charming and slip effortlessly into their by now comfortable roles.

BEFORE THE RAIN

(PO DEZJU)
1994 115m   c   Drama/War/Political   ★★★★
Vardar Film/Aim Productions/Noe Productions
(Macedonia/U.K./France)

Katrin Cartlidge *(Anne)*, Rade Serbedzija *(Aleksandar)*, Gregoire Colin *(Kiril)*, Labina Mitevska *(Zamira)*, Jay Villiers *(Nick)*, Silvija Stojanovska *(Hana)*, Phyllida Law *(Anne's Mother)*, Josif Josifovski *(Father Marko)*, Boris Delcevski *(Petre)*, Dejan Velkov *(Mate)*

p, Judy Counihan, Cedomir Kolar, Sam Taylor, Cat Villiers; d, Milcho Manchevski; w, Milcho Manchevski; ed, Nicolas Gaster; m, Anastasia; prod d, Sharon Lamofsky, David Munns; fx, Valentin Lozey, John Fontana, Vasil Dikov; cos, Caroline Harris, Sue Yelland

AAN Best Foreign Language Film

Billed as the first feature made in the newly declared republic of Macedonia, formerly a region of Yugoslavia, Milcho Manchevski's film is a glossy, mystical, ultimately pessimistic take on the worldwide ripples caused by the Balkan genocide.

In Manchevski's elliptical three-part narrative, a young monk (Gregoire Colin) shelters a Muslim girl (Labina Mitevska); a trendy Londoner (Katrin Cartlidge, NAKED) struggles with some unanticipated personal consequences of war; a Macedonian photographer (Rade Serbedzija) returns to the village of his childhood and finds it changed beyond recognition. BEFORE THE RAIN won the Golden Lion (Best Picture) award at the 1994 Venice Film Festival and was nominated for that year's best foreign-language film Oscar. Released theatrically in the U.S. in 1995, it enjoyed wide critical acclaim and was sometimes compared to another Oscar nominee, PULP FICTION, which employed a similarly unconventional structure. Though the two films are completely divergent in theme and subject matter, both tell their stories out of chronological order. The circular structure of BEFORE THE RAIN adds to its impact. Near the end of the third segment, the viewer realizes that the three seemingly separate stories are interconnected, and that events are racing toward an inevitable, tragic conclusion.

Technically superior in every department, BEFORE THE RAIN features achingly beautiful Macedonian landscapes, lovingly exploited by cinematographer Manuel Teran. The visually stunning, vibrantly colorful Macedonian segments stand in stark contrast to the harsh, gray London settings. This disparity reiterates one of the film's messages: war in one region affects another, no matter how far removed geographically or culturally.

BEFORE THE REVOLUTION
(PRIMA DELLA RIVOLUZIONE)
1964   112m   bw   Drama   ★★★
Cineriz/Iride Cinematografica   (Italy)

Adriana Asti *(Gina)*, Francesco Barilli *(Fabrizio)*, Allen Midgette *(Agostino)*, Morando Morandini *(Cesare—Teacher)*, Domenico Alpi *(Fabrizio's Father)*, Giuseppe Maghenzani *(Fabrizio's Brother)*, Cecrope Barilli *(Puck)*, Cristina Pariset *(Clelia)*, Emilia Borghi *(Fabrizio's Mother)*, Iole unardi *(Fabrizio's Grandmother)*

d, Bernardo Bertolucci; w, Bernardo Bertolucci, Gianni Amico; ph, Aldo Scavardo; ed, Roberto Perpignani; m, Gino Paoli, Ennio Morricone

Bernardo Bertolucci's second film is a dense semi-autobiographical coming-of-age tale about a 20-year-old named Fabrizio (Francesco Barilli) who's struggling between Marxist ideology and a more comfortable bourgeois life. Fabrizio rejects his middle-class background and his shallow fiancee Clelia to pursue a Marxist lifestyle under the guidance of his communist schoolteacher friend Cesare, and also has a brief affair with his attractive young aunt, but eventually becomes politically disillusioned and leaves the communist party, then settles for a "normal" life with Clelia.

Made when Bertolucci was 22, (who, like Fabrizio, is also from Parma) the film already shows the key themes which would dominate his later work, specifically the concepts of an idealistic young dilettante and his spiritual and intellectual mentor, and the ultimate rejection of radicalism in favor of a safe, but stifling, bourgeois life (both of which are echoed in THE CONFORMIST among others). The film is much more abstract in its structure than Bertolucci's later works, with the "plot" merely alluded to in a series of moody and atmospheric vignettes in which music is prominently featured. Time and again, Bertolucci uses poetic sounds and images to try to communicate emotions and ideas, rather than plot, such as in the disturbing final scene where Fabrizio and Clelia's wedding is intercut with Cesare reading "Moby Dick" to a class of youngsters, as a tearful Gina hugs and kisses Fabrizio's much younger brother, indicating that the cycle is bound to repeat itself all over again. Cinematically, the film is technically accomplished, but shows Bertolucci still developing his distinctive style, assimilating the long, sensuous tracking shots of Alain Resnais, the whispered voice-overs and jagged jump-cuts of Jean-Luc Godard, the architectural compositions of Michelangelo Antonioni, the romantic realism of Robert Rossellini, and the social and political concerns of Pier Paolo Pasolini.

BEGGAR'S OPERA, THE
1952   94m   c   Musical   ★★★
Imperadio   (U.K.)

Laurence Olivier *(Capt. MacHeath)*, Stanley Holloway *(Lockit)*, George Devine *(Peachum)*, Mary Clare *(Mrs. Peachum)*, Athene Seyler *(Mrs. Trapes)*, Dorothy Tutin *(Polly Peachum)*, Daphne Anderson *(Lucy Lockit)*, Hugh Griffith *(The Beggar)*, Margot Grahame *(The Actress)*, Denis Cannan *(The Footman)*

p, Laurence Olivier, Herbert Wilcox; d, Peter Brook; w, Denis Cannan, Christopher Fry (based on the comic opera by John Gay); ph, Guy Green (Technicolor); ed, Reginald Beck; m, Arthur Bliss

Eclectic, thoughtful, but not an unmitigated smash. The esteemed Brook made his film directing debut with THE BEGGAR'S OPERA, an attempt at re-creating John Gay's original play on film. (It was also done as *The Threepenny Opera* with a score by Bertolt Brecht and Kurt Weill.) The music in this version is by Sir Arthur Bliss, with lyrics by Christopher Fry *(The Lady's Not For Burning)* as well as some additional dialogue for the Cannan screenplay. Olivier stars as MacHeath, with Holloway as Lockit, Griffith as the Beggar, and the wonderful Seyler (who gave one of the funniest performances in *any* comedy in MAKE MINE MINK and for years specialized in classical stage work) as Mrs. Trapes. Olivier provides a play-within-a-play as a prisoner in Newgate who creates an opera based on his own life.

It's all very complex and may have been better done in MAN OF LA MANCHA. This is an ambitious project that never quite comes off. Olivier and Holloway did their own singing, but the others were dubbed. Olivier is no Howard Keel and lacks the inherent sexiness to play MacHeath; he did well to stay out of musicals, unless doing character singing like THE ENTERTAINER. Bold attempt failed at the box office, but, for film enthusiasts, it remains an interesting curiosity.

BEING JOHN MALKOVICH   *DVD*
1999   112m   c   Comedy   ★★★½
Single Cell Pictures/Gramercy Pictures/   R
Propaganda Films   (U.S.)

John Cusack *(Craig Schwartz)*, Cameron Diaz *(Lotte Schwartz)*, Catherine Keener *(Maxine)*, Orson Bean *(Dr. Lester)*, Mary Kay Place *(Floris)*, John Malkovich *(John Horatio Malkovich)*, Ned Bellamy *(Derek Mantini)*, K.K. Dodds *(Wendy)*, Reggie Hayes *(Don)*, Byrne Piven *(Captain Mertin)*

p, Michael Stipe, Sandy Stern, Steve Golin, Vincent Landay; d, Spike Jonze; w, Charlie Kaufman; ph, Lance Acord; ed, Eric Zumbrunnen; m, Carter Burwell; prod d, K.K. Barrett; art d, Peter Andrus; fx, John Gray, Daniel Radford, Gray Marshall, Gray Matter FX; cos, Casey Storm

AAN Best Supporting Actress: Catherine Keener; *AAN Best Director:* Spike Jonze; *AAN Best Original Screenplay:* Charlie Kaufman

A puppeteer filled with existential despair, a mysterious filing firm on floor 7 1/2 of a downtown office building, a meek wife caught in a whirlpool of gender confusion and, of course, John Malkovich. Swirl them together and you get this utterly original and truly indescribable comedy.

Craig Schwartz (John Cusack) is a puppeteer who's passionately devoted to his art and dead broke because of it. His wife, Lotte (a frighteningly drabbed-down Cameron Diaz), starts hinting that maybe Craig should get some kind of job, so he signs on at the Lester Corporation. It's a strange place: Mr. Lester (Orson Bean) is a geriatric oddball, employees walk doubled over because of the low ceilings, and you have to pry the elevator doors open with a crowbar. But Chuck finds two reasons to love his job: Maxine (Catherine Keener), the no-nonsense man-eater who sets his loins afire, and the "portal," a muddy passageway hidden behind some filing cabinets that leads directly into the brain of John Malkovich (playing himself with considerable good humor). You can only stay in his head for 15 minutes before being ejected onto a swampy spot alongside the Jersey Turnpike, but it's a bizarre, voyeuristic thrill nonetheless, even when Malkovich is simply ordering towels from a mail-order catalogue operator.

Video director Spike Jonze's first feature is deeply peculiar and weirdly funny—emphasis on the weird. By the time Malkovich barges through the portal into his own head (where absolutely everyone is John Malkovich, from restaurant waiters to vampy cabaret chanteuses) you marvel at how well Jonze and screenwriter Charles Kaufman keep the whole thing from strangling on its own eccentricity. You just have to see it for yourself.

BEING JULIA
2004 105m c Drama ★★★½
Serendipity Point Films/First Choice Films/ R
Astral Media/Telefilm Canada/Corus Entertainment/
Myriad Pictures/ISL Films/Hogarth Productions/
Sony Pictures Classics (U.S./Canada/Hungary/U.K.)

Annette Bening *(Julia Lambert)*, Jeremy Irons *(Michael Gosselyn)*, Bruce Greenwood *(Lord Charles)*, Michael Gambon *(Jimmie Langton)*, Miriam Margolyes *(Dolly de Vries)*, Juliet Stevenson *(Evie)*, Shaun Evans *(Tom Fennel)*, Tom Sturridge *(Roger Gosselyn)*, Lucy Punch *(Avice Crichton)*, Maury Chaykin *(Walter Gibbs)*

p, Robert Lantos; d, Istvan Szabo; w, Ronald Harwood (based on the novel *Theatre* by W. Somerset Maugham); ph, Lajos Koltai; ed, Susan Shipton; m, Mychael Danna; prod d, Luciana Arrighi; art d, Paul Ghirardani, Lorand Javor; fx, Ferenc Ormos; cos, John Bloomfield

AAN Best Actress: Annette Bening

Vivid, sharp-tongued, and gloriously synthetic from crown to toenail, this rich slab of top-of-the-line theatrical cheese, adapted by playwright Ronald Harwood from W. Somerset Maugham's sublimely melodramatic *Theatre*, is ripe to perfection and perfectly served up by Annette Bening.

London, 1938: Acclaimed, adored, and still radiantly beautiful in the right light, Julia Lambert (Bening) is surrounded by fans and flatterers, but painfully aware that her days as the toast of the West End are numbered. Julia has few friends besides her sharp-tongued dresser (Juliet Stevenson) and her long-dead mentor, regional-theater hambone Jimmie Langton (Michael Gambon), who now wisps around the wings of her life, dispensing acerbic advice from the afterworld. Julia's serious-minded son (Tom Sturridge) has started college, her equally vain husband and manager, Michael Gosselyn (Jeremy Irons), has a roving eye, and, worst of all, Julia's life in the theater has begun to lose its shimmer. Enter the juvenile distraction, penniless, starstruck American Tom Fennel (Shaun Evans), whose ruthless pragmatism shines through the stars in his eyes. Julia's affair with the fresh-faced Fennel rekindles her joie de vivre—until she discovers that he hopes to use his influence to further the career of disingenuous ingenue Avice Crichton (Lucy Punch). Julia, however, is more than a match for any Eve Harrington, and patiently plots her vengeance.

Sumptuously costumed and luxuriously designed, Hungarian director Istvan Szabo's unabashed valentine to tubthumping melodrama rests on Bening's creamy shoulders, and it's a burden she bears as lightly as a perfectly pleated Fortuny gown. Sweeping through a series of splendidly appointed tableaux with an imperious shrug and an inscrutable smile, Bening's Julia is a surprisingly subtle creation; her studied,

utterly artificial mannerisms reveal more emotional nuance than many more superficially naturalistic performances.

BEING THERE *DVD*
1979 130m c Comedy ★★★★
Lorimar (U.S.) PG

Peter Sellers *(Chance)*, Shirley MacLaine *(Eve Rand)*, Melvyn Douglas *(Benjamin Rand)*, Jack Warden *(President Bobby)*, Richard Dysart *(Dr. Robert Allenby)*, Richard Basehart *(Vladmir Skrapinov)*, Ruth Attaway *(Louise)*, David Clennon *(Thomas Franklin)*, Fran Brill *(Sally Hayes)*, Denise DuBarry *(Johanna Franklin)*

p, Andrew Braunsberg; d, Hal Ashby; w, Jerzy Kosinski (based on his novel); ph, Caleb Deschanel (Technicolor); ed, Don Zimmerman; m, Johnny Mandel; art d, James Schoppe

AAN Best Actor: Peter Sellers; *AA Best Supporting Actor:* Melvyn Douglas

Deft tale of innocence's wisdom. Jerzy Kosinski's modern fable gets a terrific translation to the screen due to his tight screenplay, capable direction by Ashby, and a marvelous performance by Sellers, one unlike any other in his career. Simpleton becomes wealthy and famous, but flimsy idea goes on too long. MacLaine is funny as the sex-starved wife who at first is amusedly captivated by Sellers then falls in love with him. Deschanel's stunning cinematography also deserves praise, as does Mandel's very appropriate score. Sellers was nominated for a Best Actor Oscar but lost to Dustin Hoffman for KRAMER VS. KRAMER, while Douglas won his second Academy Award for Best Supporting Actor (his first came for HUD in 1963). Filmed in Washington, D.C.; Los Angeles; and at the Biltmore, the Vanderbilts' North Carolina mansion.

BELLE DE JOUR *DVD*
1967 100m c Drama/Comedy ★★★★★
Paris Film Production/Five Films Rome (France/Italy) R

Catherine Deneuve *(Severine Serizy)*, Jean Sorel *(Pierre Serizy)*, Michel Piccoli *(Henri Husson)*, Genevieve Page *(Madame Anais)*, Pierre Clementi *(Marcel)*, Francisco Rabal *(Hippolyte)*, Francis Blanche *(Monsieur Adolphe)*, Francoise Fabian *(Charlotte)*, Maria Latour *(Mathilde)*, Georges Marchal *(The Duke)*

p, Robert Hakim, Raymond Hakim; d, Luis Bunuel; w, Luis Bunuel, Jean-Claude Carriere (based on the novel by Joseph Kessel); ph, Sacha Vierny (Eastmancolor); ed, Walter Spohr; art d, Robert Clavel; cos, Helene Noury, Yves Saint Laurent

A delightful puzzle, and Deneuve's finest hour-and-a-half. She plays a happily married middle-class woman who genuinely loves, but is unable to feel passionate toward, her husband, a successful surgeon. She eventually finds fulfilment of a kind by pursing a career as a high-class, afternoons-only (hence "Belle de Jour") prostitute.

As the film opens, a handsome young 19th-century couple (Jean Sorel, Catherine Deneuve) whisper sweet nothings to each other during a carriage ride through a beautiful country estate. Suddenly and inexplicably angered, the man orders his partner out of the carriage, and has the two drivers drag her to a nearby tree, to which she is tied and subjected to a brutal whipping. The man then casually tells the drivers to rape her. Cut to the young woman lounging in bed in a modern-day Paris bedroom, where she has fantasized the entire sequence. Or has she?

Nothing else in BELLE DE JOUR quite lives up to the exquisite jolt of that first shift from fantasy to reality, or vice versa. Throughout, Bunuel juggles scenes that may be "real" with others that seem like dreams or wish-fulfilments. But, by the end, the technique seems more like a means of toying with the audience than a genuine correlative for the protagonist's conflicted state of mind. The result is almost, but not quite, a great movie—as opaque as its central character, it teases and intrigues, but falls short of delivering emotional satisfaction. Essential viewing, though, if only for Deneuve's signature performance; Pierre Clementi also shines in the role of a brutal young hood who develops an obsession with "Belle." Having been withdrawn from circulation by its producers at the end of the 1970s, BELLE DE JOUR was re-released theatrically (and billed as "presented by Martin Scorsese") in 1995 by Miramax Zoe, a new division of the independent juggernaut devoted to "rescuing" lost French classics.

BELLE EPOQUE

1992 108m c   Comedy/Historical/Romance   ★★★
Fernando Trueba PC/Lola Films/Anematorgrafo/   R
French Productions   (Spain/France/Portugal)

Fernando Fernan Gomez (Manolo), Jorge Sanz (Fernando), Maribel Verdu (Rocio), Ariadna Gil (Violetta), Miriam Diaz-Aroca (Clara), Penelope Cruz (Luz), Mary Carmen Ramirez (Amalia—Manolo's Wife), Michel Galabru (Danglard—Amalia's Manager), Gabino Diego (Juanito—Rocio's Suitor), Chus Lampreave (Dona Asun—Juanito's Mother)

p, Andres Vicente Gomez; d, Fernando Trueba; w, Rafael Azcona (from a story by Azcona, Jose Louis Garcia Sanchez and Fernando Trueba); ph, Jose Luis Alcaine; ed, Carmen Frias; m, Antoine Duhamel; art d, Juan Botella

AA Best Foreign Language Film

A deftly orchestrated romantic comedy that treats a turbulent historical period lightheartedly, yet without completely avoiding political realities; the film's infectious good spirits spring from an engaging story, well-developed characters, and adroit casting.

"Somewhere in Spain, in 1931." Fernando (Jorge Sanz), a young ex-seminarian defecting from the Army after the King's abdication, befriends Manolo (Fernando Fernan-Gomez), a free-thinking, self-proclaimed "heathen, rebel, and libertine" who invites Fernando to his home. Manolo later takes Fernando to the train station so he can flee to Madrid, but a look at the older man's four daughters compels Fernando to "miss" his train and lodge in Manolo's house. All the daughters—proper young widow Clara (Miriam Diaz-Aroca), frivolous, strong-willed Rocio (Maribel Verdu), aggressive, self-assertive Violeta (Ariadna Gil), and sweet, romantic Luz (Penelope Cruz)—subtly but surely pursue and seduce him, and shy Fernando is confused as to which of the ladies he loves.

Though the plot sounds like a salacious "farmer's daughters" joke, the four sisters are richly enough written to evade stereotypes. BELLE EPOQUE's one miscalculation comes at the denouement, when a tragedy shatters the otherwise merry atmosphere. Clearly meant to bring home the tensions and uncertainty of the time, and as a premonition of the civil war to come, it is an abrupt, unexpected turn, discordant in an otherwise lyrical, lightweight entertainment.

BELLES OF ST. TRINIAN'S, THE

1954 91m   bw   Comedy   ★★★
London Films   (U.K.)

Alastair Sim (Millicent Fritton/ Clarence Fritton), Joyce Grenfell (Sgt. Ruby Gates), George Cole (Flash Harry), Vivienne Martin (Arabella), Eric Pohlmann (Sultan of Makyad), Lorna Henderson (Princess Fatima), Hermione Baddeley (Miss Drownder), Betty Ann Davies (Miss Waters), Renee Houston (Miss Brimmer), Beryl Reid (Miss Dawn)

p, Frank Launder, Sidney Gilliat; d, Frank Launder; w, Frank Launder, Sidney Gilliat, Val Valentine; ph, Stanley Pavey; ed, Thelma Connell; m, Malcolm Arnold

Monstrously fun. This is a very funny comedy based on Ronald Searles's cartoons of a horrid girls' school known as St. Trinian's. The plot has to do with the horsenapping of a famous steed that is foiled by some of the school's pupils. Among the girls' antics is using the school's science lab to make gin, which is then sold by the crooked Flash Harry (George Cole). Alastair Sim is brilliant in two roles, playing the headmistress as well as her ne'er-do-well brother. Joyce Grenfell is also quite amusing as a police spy. This one was a winner, spawning less successful sequels BLUE MURDER AT ST. TRINIAN'S, THE PURE HELL OF ST. TRINIAN'S, and THE GREAT ST. TRINIAN'S TRAIN ROBBERY.

BELLS ARE RINGING

1960 126m c   Musical/Comedy   ★★★½
MGM   (U.S.)

Judy Holliday (Ella Peterson), Dean Martin (Jeffrey Moss), Fred Clark (Larry Hastings), Eddie Foy Jr. (J. Otto Prantz), Jean Stapleton (Sue), Ruth Storey (Gwynne), Dort Clark (Inspector Barnes), Frank Gorshin (Blake Barton), Ralph Roberts (Francis), Valerie Allen (Olga)

p, Arthur Freed; d, Vincente Minnelli; w, Betty Comden, Adolph Green (based on the musical play by Betty Comden, Adolph Green and Jule Styne); ph, Milton Krasner (CinemaScope Eastmancolor); ed, Adrienne Fazan; m, Jule Styne, Betty Comden, Adolph Green; art d, George W. Davis, Preston Ames; chor, Charles O'Curran; cos, Walter Plunkett

AAN Best Score (Musical): Andre Previn

The last performance of a much-loved star. Judy Holliday reprises her Broadway success in this adaptation of the hit Comden-Green-Jules Styne musical, playing Ella Peterson, who works at a telephone answering service and gets passionately involved in her clients' lives. Hapless playwright Jeffrey Moss (a miscast Dean Martin) is her love interest. In supporting roles, Jean Stapleton scores in one of her earliest appearances, as do Frank Gorshin in the role of a beatnik who wants to be a serious actor and Eddie Foy, Jr., as a bookie; jazz fans will recognize saxophone great Gerry Mulligan, married to Holliday at the time, as Ella's blind date. Vincente Minnelli's film might have benefited from less emphasis on dialogue and more on the musical numbers ("Just in Time" and "The Party's Over" among them), but Holliday is adorable and effortlessly "real" in one of the best roles of her sadly abbreviated career.

BELLS OF ST. MARY'S, THE

1945 126m bw   Drama   ★★★★
Rainbow   (U.S.)

Bing Crosby (Father Chuck O'Malley), Ingrid Bergman (Sister Benedict), Henry Travers (Mr. Bogardus), Ruth Donnelly (Sister Michael), Joan Carroll (Patsy), Martha Sleeper (Patsy's Mother), William Gargan (Joe Gallagher), Rhys Williams (Dr. McKay), Dick Tyler (Eddie), Una O'Connor (Mrs. Breen)

p, Leo McCarey; d, Leo McCarey; w, Dudley Nichols (based on a story by Leo McCarey); ph, George Barnes; ed, Harry Marker; m, Robert Emmett Dolan; art d, William Flannery; cos, Edith Head

AAN Best Picture; AAN Best Actor: Bing Crosby; *AAN Best Actress:* Ingrid Bergman; *AAN Best Director:* Leo McCarey; *AAN Best Film Editing:* Harry Marker; *AAN Best Score (Drama or Comedy):* Robert Emmett Dolan; *AAN Best Song:* "Aren't You Glad You're You"; James Van Heusen (Music), Johnny Burke (Lyrics); *AA Best Sound Recording:* Stephen Dunn

Touchingly sentimental, but strong in all the right places. The sequel to GOING MY WAY is nearly as good as its predecessor. Bing Crosby is trouble-shooting priest Father Chuck O'Malley, who's sent to the financially ailing St. Mary's. There he runs smack into charming, clever Sister Benedict (Ingrid Bergman), a mother superior who rules her students with a gentle but decisive hand. She is too rigid for Father O'Malley and he's too permissive for her, setting up a confrontation of styles that's a joy to behold. It's a gentle, uplifting story, and features some fine songs by Crosby, including "Adeste Fidelis," "In the Land of Beginning Again," and the sprightly "Aren't You Glad You're You." The two leads are seamless all the way home.

BELLY OF AN ARCHITECT, THE   *DVD*

1987 108m c   Drama   ★★★
Callender   (U.K./Italy)

Brian Dennehy *(Stourley Kracklite)*, Chloe Webb *(Louisa Kracklite)*, Lambert Wilson *(Caspasian Speckler)*, Vanni Corbellini *(Frederico)*, Sergio Fantoni *(Io Speckler)*, Stefania Casini *(Flavia Speckler)*, Alfredo Varelli *(Julio Ficcone)*, Geoffrey Copleston *(Caspetti)*, Francesco Carnelutti *(Pastarri)*, Marino Mase *(Trettorio)*

p, Colin Callender, Walter Donohue; d, Peter Greenaway; w, Peter Greenaway; ph, Sacha Vierny (Technicolor); ed, John Wilson; m, Wim Mertens, Glenn Branca; art d, Luciana Vedovelli; cos, Maurizio Millenotti

A film to either love or loathe. Exquisitely composed film about obsession reaffirms director Peter Greenaway's reputation as a meticulous visual artist. Stourley Kracklite (Brian Dennehy), a corpulent Chicago architect of some renown, travels to Rome with his considerably younger wife Louisa (Chloe Webb) to oversee an exhibition commemorating the work of Etienne Louis Boullee, a little-known but visionary 18th-century French architect. A handsome young Italian architect, Caspasian Speckler (Lambert Wilson), is in charge of the project's finances, and he covets both Kracklite's control of the exhibition and his wife. Kracklite's world begins to crumble as he becomes obsessed with the chronic abdominal pains from which he suffers, making him oblivious to Speckler's machinations. Dennehy's extraordinary performance buoys the film, and Wilson is entirely convincing as the rival architect, but Webb is badly miscast. The main attractions here are Greenaway's densely textured compositions, each one a triumph of symmetry and design.

BELOVED   *DVD*

1998 174m c   Historical/Drama   ★★★
Harpo Films/Clinica Estetico/Touchstone Pictures   R
(U.S.)

Oprah Winfrey *(Sethe)*, Danny Glover *(Paul D)*, Thandie Newton *(Beloved)*, Kimberly Elise *(Denver)*, Beah Richards *(Baby Suggs)*, Lisa Gay Hamilton *(Younger Sethe)*, Albert Hall *(Stamp Paid)*, Irma P. Hall *(Ella)*, Carol Jean Lewis *(Janey Wagon)*, Kessia Kordelle *(Amy Denver)*

p, Oprah Winfrey, Jonathan Demme, Edward Saxon, Kate Forte, Gary Goetzman; d, Jonathan Demme; w, Akosua Busia, Richard LaGravenese, Adam Brooks (based on the novel by Toni Morrison); ph, Tak Fujimoto; ed, Carol Littleton, Andy Keir; m, Rachel Portman; prod d, Kristi Zea; art d, Tim Galvin; fx, Tom Ward, John Ottesen; chor, Dianne McIntyre; cos, Colleen Atwood

AAN Best Costume Design: Colleen Atwood

A searing story of slavery's perpetual chains, Jonathan Demme's thoroughly respectable adaptation of Toni Morrison's Pulitzer Prize-winning novel will probably disappoint the book's admirers, even though it's nothing if not faithful.

Ohio, 1873. A former slave named Sethe (Oprah Winfrey) and her teenage daughter Denver (Kimberly Elise)

are haunted by the spirit of a murdered child. Sethe's adolescent sons have long since fled, terrified of the angry force that thrashes around in their home; gone, too, is Sethe's beneficent mother-in-law, Baby Suggs (Beah Richards), a self-styled preacher who exhorted her flock of former slaves, "Love your flesh, for out there they do not love your flesh." The arrival of Paul D (Danny Glover), another survivor of the farm where Sethe, Baby Suggs, and Sethe's husband Halle were once slaves, coincides with the mysterious appearance of Beloved (Thandie Newton), a strange young woman who wanders into Sethe's yard and sets off a chain of events that will disinter the scarcely buried past in all its pain and bitterness.

There are many love stories here, and ghosts and dark unspoken desires, but Demme's film conveys little of the novel's sense of sublime terror in the face of overwhelming history and an awful secret. Several scenes verge on evoking the novel's uncanny atmosphere, but by and large the film remains stubbornly earthbound. In trying to make the movie conform to conventional rules of storytelling, the rich reflections on memory, desire, and history that Morrison weaves subtly into the characters' thoughts are largely discarded in favor of external reality. How incongruous to complain that Demme and his cast reject easy, Spielbergian emotional button-pushing: after 10 years spent trying to bring the novel to the screen, they've achieved something that's genuinely extraordinary. But they've also taken material with the power to insinuate itself directly into the reader's imagination and rendered it strangely inert and lifeless.

BEND IT LIKE BECKHAM   *DVD*

2002 112m c   Comedy/Drama/Sports   ★★★
Kintop Pictures/Bend It Films/   PG-13
Roc Media/Road Movies   (U.K./Germany)

Parminder Nagra *(Jess Bhamra)*, Keira Knightley *(Jules Paxton)*, Jonathan Rhys Meyers *(Joe)*, Anupam Kher *(Mr. Bhamra)*, Archie Panjabi *(Pinky Bhamra)*, Shaznay Lewis *(Mel)*, Frank Harper *(Alan Paxton)*, Juliet Stevenson *(Paula Paxton)*, Shaheen Khan *(Mrs. Bhamra)*, Ameet Chana *(Tony)*

p, Gurinder Chadha, Deepak Nayar; d, Gurinder Chadha; w, Paul Mayeda Berges, Guljit Bindra, Gurinder Chadha; ph, Jong Lin; ed, Justin Krish; m, Craig Pruess; prod d, Nick Ellis; art d, Mark Scruton; fx, Scott Billups; chor, Simon Clifford; cos, Ralph Holes

Lightweight, thoroughly charming fluff about the gulf between immigrant parents and their assimilated children, and the family ties that bridge the divide.

London tomboy Jasminder "Jess" Bhamra (Parminder Nagra) will be the death of her tradition-minded Sikh parents (Anupam Kher, Shaheen Khan), who emigrated from India so their children could have better lives. They're thrilled that Jess's older sister, sharp-tongued stewardess Pinky (Archie Panjabi), is engaged to a successful Indian boy from a good family, but Mrs. Bhamra frets about her younger daughter's future. Jess is smart and studious, but she lives for football; her favorite player is Manchester United's David Beckham. Her dream of actually playing on a team comes when Jules Paxton (Keira Knightley) introduces Jess to the Hounslow Harriers, an amateur girls' team with uniforms, a practice field, and an actual coach (Jonathan Rhys Meyers). Jules hopes to win an athletic scholarship to a U.S. college, where women's sports are taken seriously, and while her tarty mum (Juliet Stevenson) never stops trying to get sporty Jules into frillies, her dad (Frank Harper) is thoroughly supportive. Jules gets Jess onto the team, but when Jess begins sneaking off to soccer matches behind her parents' backs, clouds begin to gather.

Screenwriters Guljit Bindra, Paul Mayeda Berges and Gurinder Chadha, who also directed, juggle a large cast of characters with enviable skill, and the uniformly fine performances carry the day. Panjabi's snippiness and Stevenson's blowsy dithering are perfect counterpoints to the fresh-faced enthusiasm of stars Nagra and Knightley. And while the delicate Rhys Meyers may be the least likely soccer coach ever, he's a flawlessly dreamy object of desire for two slightly sheltered teenage girls.

BEN-HUR
DVD

1959 212m c Historical/Religious ★★★★½
MGM (U.S.)

Charlton Heston (Judah Ben Hur), Jack Hawkins (Quintus Arrius), Stephen Boyd (Messala), Haya Harareet (Esther), Hugh Griffith (Sheik Ilderim), Martha Scott (Miriam), Sam Jaffe (Simonides), Cathy O'Donnell (Tirzah), Finlay Currie (Balthasar), Frank Thring (Pontius Pilate)

p, Sam Zimbalist; d, William Wyler; w, Karl Tunberg (based on the novel by Lew Wallace); ph, Robert Surtees (Camera 65, Panavision, Technicolor); ed, Ralph E. Winters, John Dunning; m, Miklos Rozsa; art d, William A. Horning, Edward Carfagno; fx, A. Arnold Gillespie, Robert MacDonald; cos, Elizabeth Haffenden

AA Best Picture; AA Best Actor: Charlton Heston; AA Best Supporting Actor: Hugh Griffith; AA Best Director: William Wyler; AAN Best Adapted Screenplay: Karl Tunberg; AA Best Color Cinematography: Robert L. Surtees; AA Best Film Editing: Ralph E. Winters, John D. Dunning; AA Best Score (Drama or Comedy): Miklos Rozsa; AA Best Art Direction-Set Decoration (Color): William A. Horning, Edward C. Carfagno, Hugh Hunt; AA Best Costume Design (Color): Elizabeth Haffenden; AA Best Sound: Franklin E. Milton; AA Best Special Effects: A. Arnold Gillespie (Visual), Robert MacDonald (Visual), Milo Lory (Audible)

Predictable but magnificent and satisfying. In remaking the silent 1927 classic, which starred Ramon Novarro and Francis X. Bushman, quality-conscious director Wyler shines the old chestnut up. Highlights include the galley ship and climatic chariot race with Heston—in a *tour de force* performance—besieged by the sexy but evil Boyd. (This sequence was actually helmed by action expert Andrew Marton.) Even with the western overtones, the actors make stunning rivals. Majesty is in almost every frame of this film thanks to Wyler, who tells the story in human, understated terms.

Everything about BEN HUR was enormous; more than 300 sets were employed, covering more than 340 acres. The arena housing the chariot race consumed 18 acres, the largest single set in film history. The four-story stands were packed with 8,000 extras, and 40,000 tons of sand were taken from beaches to make the track. Scores of Yugoslavian horses were imported for the spectacular 20-minute race, which took three months to shoot. More than 1000 workers labored for a year to build the colossal arena. Rome's Cinecitta Studios were gutted of more than a million props, and sculptors made more than 200 giant statues. Also unique were the wide-screen cameras employed, 65 millimeters wide, to achieve sharp, deep focus. MGM lavished about $12,500,000 on this stupendous production, which brought them near bankruptcy, but the returns were staggering: a gross of $40 million.

BENJI
DVD

1974 85m c Children's ★★★
Mulberry Square (U.S.) G

Higgins the Dog (Benji), Patsy Garrett (Mary), Allen Fiuzat (Paul), Cynthia Smith (Cindy), Peter Breck (Dr. Chapman), Frances Bavier (Lady with Cat), Terry Carter (Officer Tuttle), Edgar Buchanan (Bill), Tom Lester (Riley), Christopher Connelly (Henry)

p, Joe Camp; d, Joe Camp; w, Joe Camp; ph, Don Reddy; ed, Leon Seith; m, Euel Box; prod d, Harland Wright

AAN Best Song: "Benji's Theme (I Feel Love)"; Euel Box (Music), Betty Box (Lyrics)

A lovable mutt thwarts kidnappers. A-h-h-h-h-h. Much of the film is shot from a dog's-eye view, and this technique works perfectly. The human actors are okay but not as cool as the canine star, a veteran of TV's "Petticoat Junction" series. The title song was nominated for an Oscar! Sequel: FOR THE LOVE OF BENJI.

BENNY & JOON
DVD

1993 98m c Comedy/Drama ★★½
MGM (U.S.) PG

Johnny Depp (Sam), Mary Stuart Masterson (Joon), Aidan Quinn (Benny), Julianne Moore (Ruthie), Oliver Platt (Eric), CCH Pounder (Dr. Garvey), Dan Hedaya (Thomas), Joe Grifasi (Mike), William H. Macy (Randy Burch), Liane Alexandra Curtis (Claudia)

p, Susan Arnold, Donna Roth; d, Jeremiah Chechik; w, Barry Berman (from a story by Berman and Leslie McNeil); ph, John Schwartzman; ed, Carol Littleton; m, Rachel Portman; prod d, Neil Spisak; art d, Pat Tagliaferro; fx, J.D. Streett IV; cos, Aggie Guerard Rodgers

A gentle comedy about two misfits—a schizophrenic girl and a boy whom earlier generations would have called an odd duck—who find love, BENNY & JOON means well but overdoses on whimsy.

Benny Pearl (Aidan Quinn) is a smart, handsome mechanic who has dedicated his life to caring for his sister Joon (Mary Stuart Masterson), a creative free spirit with a dangerous penchant for setting fires. Sam (Johnny Depp) is a lovable misfit who does a fine Buster Keaton imitation but is functionally illiterate and a trial to his family. Sam and Joon complement one another, allowing Benny to date and enjoy a taste of freedom, but when he realizes they've fallen in love, the stage is set for a family crisis.

BENNY & JOON is one in a long line of films in which mental illness is conceived as making people more creative, honest, perceptive, and loving—in a word, *better*—than sane people. The script appears several times on the verge of testing dangerous waters—there's a hint of incestuous closeness in the siblings' relationship—but always retreats in favor of focusing on how cute Sam and Joon are as they bring a fresh perspective to such mundane activities as cooking: she whips up peanut butter and cereal milkshakes, he mashes potatoes with a tennis racket, and together they make grilled cheese with an iron.

If the performances were as cute and sweet as the characters, the film would need a warning label. But Depp's Sam is delicately touching, a maladjusted waif with both soul and grit, and Masterson resists the temptation to soften Joon.

BERLIN ALEXANDERPLATZ

1979 896m c Drama ★★★★
Bavaria Atelier/RAI/Westdeutscher Rundfunk (West Germany)

Gunter Lamprecht (Franz Biberkopf), Gottfried John (Reinhold), Barbara Sukowa (Mieze), Hanna Schygulla (Eva), Franz Buchrieser (Meck), Claus Holm (Wirt), Hark Bohm (Luders), Brigitte Mira (Mrs. Bast), Roger Fritz (Herbert), Werner Asam (Fritz)

p, Peter Marthesheimer; d, Rainer Werner Fassbinder; w, Rainer Werner Fassbinder (based on the novel by Alfred Doblin); ph, Xaver Schwarzenberger; ed, Juliane Lorenz, Rainer Werner Fassbinder; m, Peer Raben; art d, Helmut Gassner, Werner Achmann, Jurgen Henze; fx, Theo Nischwitz; cos, Barbara Baum

An astonishing, monumental work. Over the short span of 17 years—from 1965, when he directed his first 10-minute film, up to his death on June 10, 1982—Rainer Werner Fassbinder directed some 90 hours of film and television. BERLIN ALEXANDERPLATZ, an adaptation of Alfred Doblin's massive novel made for German television, runs approximately 15 hours, and makes up one-seventh of Fassbinder's total output. Comprised of 13 episodes and an epilogue, the film stars Gunter Lamprecht as the pimp Franz Biberkopf, released from prison after serving time for murdering a prostitute. Now that he has a certain freedom, he takes to the streets of Berlin in the late 1920s in search of his identity.

Simply recounting the plot does no justice to Fassbinder or the film. What Doblin tried to do in his novel (written from 1927 to 1929) was to put into print the atmosphere of Berlin life. Acknowledging his debt to Doblin, Fassbinder has said, "I had quite simply, without realizing it, made Doblin's fantasy into my life." In that sense, BERLIN ALEXANDER-PLATZ is not the story of Berlin, but the story of Fassbinder—and in these 15 hours the two are inseparable.

BEST IN SHOW 📀
2000 80m c Comedy ★★★★
Castle Rock Entertainment (U.S.) PG

Christopher Guest (Harlan Pepper), Parker Posey (Meg Swan), Michael Hitchcock (Hamilton Swan), Eugene Levy (Gerry Fleck), Catherine O'Hara (Cookie Fleck), John Michael Higgins (Scott Donlan), Michael McKean (Stefan Vanderhoof), Patrick Cranshaw (Leslie Cabot), Jennifer Coolidge (Sherri Ann Ward Cabot), Fred Willard (Buck Laughlin)

p, Karen Murphy; d, Christopher Guest; w, Christopher Guest, Eugene Levy; ph, Roberto Schaefer; ed, Robert Leighton; prod d, Joseph T. Garrity; art d, Gary Myers; fx, Gord Davis

Writer-director Christopher Guest proves once again just how skilled he is at ferreting out offbeat subjects—fading metal morons in the classic THIS IS SPINAL TAP, small-town theater productions in WAITING FOR GUFFMAN—and exploiting their satirical possibilities. This time, Guest uses the mockumentary form to sniff around the insular world of professional dog show competitions, and the result is a winner.

Through faux verite interviews, we're given the inside scoop and the backstage poop on eight big dog owners and their five top-notch pooches, all of whom have their eyes on the top prize at Philadelphia's annual (and entirely fictional) Mayflower Dog Show. The anxious and hopelessly devoted owners are all played with deft, nuanced comic flair: nerdy salesman Gerry Fleck and his tarty wife, Cookie (SCTV vets Eugene Levy, who co-scripted, and Catherine O'Hara), who have a Norwich terrier; uptight yuppie lawyers Meg and Hamilton Swan (Parker Posey, Michael Hitchcock), whose weimaraner suffers from chronic depression; hair salon owner Stefan Vanderhoof and his lover Scott Donlan (Michael McKean, John Michael Higgins), who dote on shih tzus Miss Agnes and Tyrone; buxom trophy wife Sherri Ann Cabot (Jennifer Coolidge), who's showing a teased-to-the-roots standard poodle named Rhapsody in White; and long-faced bloodhound owner Harlan Pepper (Guest). Fred Willard, meanwhile, delivers a hilariously scary turn as Buck Laughlin, the crass half of the dog show's color commentators.

Guest begins with a bare script outline and encourages his cast to build their performances around improvised scenes and dialogue. Happily, there's not a losing performance among them—and that goes for the pups, too.

BEST YEARS OF OUR LIVES, THE 📀
1946 172m bw Drama/War ★★★★★
Goldwyn (U.S.)

Myrna Loy (Milly Stephenson), Fredric March (Al Stephenson), Dana Andrews (Fred Derry), Teresa Wright (Peggy Stephenson), Virginia Mayo (Marie Derry), Cathy O'Donnell (Wilma Cameron), Hoagy Carmichael (Butch Engle), Harold Russell (Homer Parrish), Gladys George (Hortense Derry), Roman Bohnen (Pat Derry)

p, Samuel Goldwyn; d, William Wyler; w, Robert E. Sherwood (based on the blank-verse novella Glory for Me by MacKinlay Kantor); ph, Gregg Toland; ed, Daniel Mandell; m, Hugo Friedhofer; art d, George Jenkins, Perry Ferguson; cos, Irene Sharaff

AA Best Picture; AA Best Actor: Fredric March; AA Best Supporting Actor: Harold Russell; AA Best Director: William Wyler; AA Best Screenplay: Robert E. Sherwood; AA Best Film Editing: Daniel Mandell; AA Best Score (Drama or Comedy): Hugo Friedhofer; AAN Best Sound Recording: Gordon Sawyer

The best coming home movie ever made. "I don't care if it doesn't make a nickel," Sam Goldwyn reportedly said of THE BEST YEARS, "I just want every man, woman, and child in America to see it." The colorful producer got the idea for the film after reading a *Life* article about WWII veterans and their difficulties in adjusting to civilian life. With a brilliant script by Robert E. Sherwood, effective direction by William Wyler, masterful photography by Gregg Toland and excellent performances by the entire cast, this film about returning American servicemen is justifiably considered a classic.

Three servicemen—Al Stephenson (Fredric March), Fred Derry (Dana Andrews), and Homer Parrish (Harold Russell)—are shown returning to their hometown, plagued by memories of war and doubts about their future in a country they have difficulty remembering. After sharing space on board the bomber that flies them home, the three take a cab to their separate addresses. The sailor Homer comes home to his girl with a pair of hooks where his hands once were (Russell, the only nonprofessional in the cast, lost his hands in a training accident while in the service); middle-aged Al returns to his loving wife (Myrna Loy), children, and old job as a banker; Fred finds a spouse who has more or less abandoned him, and no prospects for a job.

Although everyone in Hollywood thought Goldwyn would lose his shirt on THE BEST YEARS OF OUR LIVES, it was a massive hit. Russell won a special Oscar for bringing hope to servicemen.

BETRAYAL
1982 95m c Drama ★★★½
Fox (U.K.) R

Jeremy Irons (Jerry), Patricia Hodge (Emma), Ben Kingsley (Robert)

p, Sam Spiegel; d, David Jones; w, Harold Pinter (based on his play); ph, Mike Fash; ed, John Bloom; m, Dominic Muldowney; prod d, Eileen Diss; cos, Jane Robinson, Jean Muir

AAN Best Adapted Screenplay: Harold Pinter (Screenplay)

Harold Pinter's screenplay for BETRAYAL begins at the end of its story and flashes back to the beginning, permitting the audience full awareness of the outcome as the events unfold, and thus giving those events a weight and structure that linear chronology would not endow on them. Robert (Ben Kingsley) is a book publisher whose wife, Emma (Patricia Hodge), is having an affair with Jerry (Jeremy Irons), a literary agent. The film begins after the affair is over and ends as Jerry and Emma meet. The immensely talented Kingsley is the fulcrum which moves the story backward (or forward, as the case may be). Uttering only a few words, his Robert knows exactly what is going on and conveys a subtle sense of menace. Director David Jones fashions a brisk film, despite having to deal with Pinter's lengthy silences. Hodge, who should have been the center of attraction, comes across as a mite cool—it's hard to see how she inspires passion in these two very different men. Once you've grasped the reverse chronology, the events peel away in layers that produce unexpected insights along the way.

BETTY BLUE *DVD*
(37.2 LE MATIN)
1986 120m c   Drama/Erotic   ★★★
Constellation/Cargo   (France)   R

Beatrice Dalle *(Betty)*, Jean-Hugues Anglade *(Zorg)*, Consuelo de Haviland *(Lisa)*, Gerard Darmon *(Eddy)*, Clementine Celarie *(Annie)*, Jacques Mathou *(Bob)*, Claude Confortes *(Owner)*, Philippe Laudenbach *(Gyneco Publisher)*, Vincent Lindon *(Policeman Richard)*, Raoul Billeray *(Old Policeman)*

p, Claudie Ossard, Jean-Jacques Beineix; d, Jean-Jacques Beineix; w, Jean-Jacques Beineix (based on the novel *37.2 Le Matin* by Philippe Djian); ph, Jean-Francois Robin (Fujicolor); ed, Monique Prim; m, Gabriel Yared; art d, Carlos Conti; fx, Jean-Francois Cousson, Georges Demetreau; cos, Elisabeth Tavernier

AAN Best Foreign Language Film

Jean-Jacques Beineix's attempt to combine the energetic high-gloss finish of his debut feature, DIVA, with the raw poetic intensity of MOON IN THE GUTTER, ends up as an inconsistent and unsatisfying tale of *amour fou* and literary ambition. Dalle embarks on a personal crusade to get her lover's (Anglade) novel published, but has a pretty hard time dealing with rejection notices. Eventually she starts hearing voices, and is finally driven to poke out her own eye. Anglade, best known in the U.S. as the "roller" in SUBWAY, is perfectly cast here, although the best thing about the film is the pouty, 21-year-old Dalle. While not a box-office smash in the U.S., BETTY BLUE did garner an Oscar nomination as Best Foreign Language Film. In 1991 Beineix released his original director's cut, at an expanded running time of 182 minutes, in France.

BEVERLY HILLS COP *DVD*
1984 105m c   Comedy/Crime   ★★★
Paramount   (U.S.)   R

Eddie Murphy *(Axel Foley)*, Judge Reinhold *(Detective Billy Rosewood)*, John Ashton *(Sgt. Taggart)*, Lisa Eilbacher *(Jenny Summers)*, Ronny Cox *(Lt. Bogomil)*, Steven Berkoff *(Victor Maitland)*, James Russo *(Mikey Tandino)*, Jonathan Banks *(Zack)*, Stephen Elliott *(Chief Hubbard)*, Gil Hill *(Inspector Todd)*

p, Don Simpson, Jerry Bruckheimer; d, Martin Brest; w, Daniel Petrie Jr. (based on a story by Daniel Petrie Jr. and Danilo Bach); ph, Bruce Surtees (Technicolor); ed, Billy Weber, Arthur Coburn; m, Harold Faltermeyer; prod d, Angelo Graham; art d, James J. Murakami; fx, Ken Pepiot; cos, Tom Bronson

AAN Best Original Screenplay: Daniel Petrie Jr (Screenplay), Danilo Bach (Story)

Brash, crude and very funny. Murphy's third film was phenomenally successful at the box office, aided substantially by a hit-filled soundtrack. BEVERLY HILLS COP is an entertaining, if empty-headed, cop film in which street-smart Detroit detective Murphy sets out to avenge the murder of a friend. Basically a star vehicle designed to show off the talents of Murphy—it succeeds admirably. The comedy is deftly balanced with the stunningly staged action scenes. Surprisingly, most of the laughs are given to Reinhold and Ashton. Acting honors go to Bronson Pinchot in a brief but career-making turn.

BEYOND THE VALLEY OF THE DOLLS
1970 109m c   Erotic/Drama   ★★★
20th Century Fox   (U.S.)   NC-17

Dolly Read *(Kelly MacNamara)*, Cynthia Myers *(Casey Anderson)*, Marcia McBroom *(Petronella Danforth)*, John LaZar *(Ronnie "Z-Man" Barzell)*, Michael Blodgett *(Lance Rocke)*, David Gurian *(Harris Allsworth)*, Edy Williams *(Ashley St. Ives)*, Erica Gavin *(Roxanne)*, Phyllis Davis *(Susan Lake)*, Harrison Page *(Emerson Thorne)*

p, Russ Meyer; d, Russ Meyer; w, Roger Ebert (based on a story by Russ Meyer and Roger Ebert); ph, Fred J. Koenekamp; ed, Dann Cahn, Dick Wormel; m, Stu Phillips; art d, Jack Martin Smith, Arthur Lonergan; fx, Jack Harmon; cos, David Hayes

Russ Meyer's BEYOND THE VALLEY OF THE DOLLS is an outrageously entertaining cult classic, and probably one of the most bizarre movies ever produced by a major Hollywood studio.

Eager to break into the big time, an all-girl rock band composed of Kelly (Dolly Read), Casey (Cynthia Myers) and Pet (Marcia McBroom) heads for Los Angeles, accompanied by their manager Harris (David Gurian), who's also Kelly's lover. Kelly's aunt introduces the girls to record producer Ronnie "Z-Man" Barzell (John LaZar), who turns the group into stars. As they become successful, Kelly abandons Harris for playboy Lance Rocke (Michael Blodgett), Harris is seduced by a porn star, and Pet falls in love with a law student. Casey, who gets hooked on pills and alcohol, is attracted to Kelly's aunt's lesbian employee. Things reach a head when Lance and the band members attend a party at Barzell's house; "Z-Man" freaks out and attacks his guests one by one in the guise of a superheroine named "Superwoman."

After losing a fortune on epic flops like DOCTOR DOOLITTLE (1967), Twentieth Century Fox enlisted Russ Meyer—who had earned millions with low-budget skin-flicks—to make a film for them. The result was a film that outraged the industry but turned a huge profit on a $1.2 million budget, despite Fox's trepidation in promoting it. Technically, Meyer's films were always topnotch, and in this, his first widescreen movie, he and cinematographer Fred Koenekamp create some stylish comic-book compositions, splashed with Day-Glo colors.

In addition to a cast of former-*Playboy* models and other non-actors delivering film critic Roger Ebert's mind-boggling dialogue ("You will drink the black sperm of my vengeance"), there are wild orgies, drug parties, Nazi butlers, and a gruesome Manson-like massacre that reaches a manic pitch of surreal hysteria. BEYOND is often repellent and demented—which is to say it's typical Meyer—but it's also a funny, psychedelic time-capsule.

BHAJI ON THE BEACH *DVD*
1994 100m c   Comedy/Drama   ★★★
Channel Four/Umbi Films   (United Kingdom)

Kim Vithana *(Ginder)*, Jimmi Harkishin *(Ranjit)*, Sarita Khajuria *(Hashida)*, Mo Sesay *(Oliver)*, Lalita Ahmed *(Asha)*, Surendra Kochar *(Bina)*, Shaheen Khan *(Simi)*, Zohra Segal *(Pushpa)*, Nisha Nayar *(Ladhu)*, Renu Kochar *(Madhu)*

p, Nadine Marsh-Edwards; d, Gurinder Chadha; w, Meera Syal (based on a story by Meera Syal and Gurinder Chadha); ph, John Kenway; ed, Oral Norrie Ottley; m, John Altman, Craig Preuss; prod d, Derek Brown; art d, Helen Raynor; cos, Annie Symons

First-time feature director Gurinder Chadha has called Ken Loach her most important influence, and BHAJI ON THE BEACH, a charming comic drama about women of Punjabi heritage living in urban England, is comparable to the best of Loach's realist comedies.

In a middle-class, mostly Indian neighborhood of Birmingham, housewife Ginder (Kim Vithana) has fled her abusive husband Ranjit (Jimmi Harkishin); she's persuaded by social worker Simi (Shaheen Khan) to join a group of Asian women on a day-trip to the nearby resort town of Blackpool. Along for the ride are Hashida (Sarita Khajuria), a pre-med student who has just discovered she's pregnant; Asha (Lalita Ahmed), a middle-aged newsagent; elderly gossips Pushpa (Zohra Segal) and Bina (Surendra Kochar); and a pair of giggly, assimilated teenagers, Ladhu (Nisha Nayar) and Madhu (Renu Kochar). Ranjit, however, discovers their destination and is soon in hot pursuit.

With remarkable assurance, BHAJI ON THE BEACH sketches a large number of characters who are both universally recognizable and plausible as the product of a particular subculture. Chadha sees herself as primarily a British (as opposed to Indian or female) filmmaker, and BHAJI, like her 1989 short subject I'M BRITISH BUT…, is deeply concerned with expanding popular notions of what it means to be British. The film is punctuated with delightful parodies of the Bombay commercial pictures that serve as a cultural umbilicus to Indians across the globe. Asha's consultation with a fearsome statue of Rama quotes the classic costume picture BAIJU BAWRA (1952); scenes of a sluttish Hashida insulting her elders refer to PURAB AUR PASCHIM/EAST AND WEST (1970), a melodrama decrying the insidious influence of Western culture on Indian youth.

BICYCLE THIEF, THE   ^{DVD}

(LADRI DI BICICLETTE)
1948   89m   bw   Drama   ★★★★★
Produzioni De Sica/Mayer/Burstyn   (Italy)

Lamberto Maggiorani *(Antonio Ricci)*, Lianella Carell *(Maria Ricci)*, Enzo Staiola *(Bruno Ricci)*, Elena Altieri *(The Fortune Teller)*, Vittorio Antonucci *(The Thief)*, Gino Saltamerenda *(Baiocco)*, Giulio Chiari *(The Doctor)*, Fausto Guerzoni *(Amateur Actor)*, Carlo Jachino, Michele Sakara

p, Vittorio De Sica; d, Vittorio De Sica; w, Cesare Zavattini, Vittorio De Sica, Oreste Biancoli, Suso D'Amico, Adolfo Franci, Gherardo Gherardi, Gerardo Guerrieri (from a story by Cesare Zavattini, based on the novel by Luigi Bartolini); ph, Carlo Montuori; ed, Eraldo Da Roma; m, Alesandro Cicognini; art d, Antonio Traverso

AAN Best Screenplay: Cesare Zavattini

The most famous, and arguably the greatest, of all the Italian neorealist films, Vittorio De Sica's THE BICYCLE THIEF is an extremely moving tale of a man's desperate search for his stolen bicycle.

Antonio (Lamberto Maggiorani), an unemployed laborer, is offered a job putting up movie posters in Rome, which requires the use of his bicycle. On his first day on the job, however, Antonio's bike is stolen, and he chases the thief, but can't catch him. He sets out with his young son Bruno (Enzo Staiola) to find the thief and his cherished bike.

Winner of an Oscar for Best Foreign Film, THE BICYCLE THIEF is often hailed as the epitome of the neorealist movement—which utilized authentic locations, largely nonprofessional casts, and a quasi-documentary technique to depict realistic slices of everyday life—but it's actually very professionally made in every respect. Although the two leads were amateurs, they both deliver superbly restrained performances. The lyrical, mournful music and poetic photography create an indelible sense of alienation and despair as the pair wander through the gloomy city, while the tightly structured script ingeniously combines the overriding pathos with irony, some unexpected humor, and even mysticism (via the fortune-teller motif). While the story's main focus is on Antonio's quest, it's also the story of his search for dignity and self-respect in the eyes of his son, and the terrible things that poverty does to children, a concern that De Sica dealt with in his other collaborations with writer Cesare Zavattini, including the haunting SHOESHINE (1946), and the delightful fantasy MIRACLE IN MILAN (1950). By the end, when Antonio and Bruno tearfully walk away and disappear into the crowd,

the problems of these "ordinary little people" have attained the force and universality of a Greek tragedy.

BIG   ^{DVD}

1988   104m   c   Comedy   ★★★½
Fox   (U.S.)   PG

Tom Hanks *(Josh Baskin)*, Elizabeth Perkins *(Susan Lawrence)*, Robert Loggia *("Mac" MacMillan)*, John Heard *(Paul Davenport)*, Jared Rushton *(Billy Kopeche)*, David Moscow *(Young Josh)*, Jon Lovitz *(Scotty Brennen)*, Mercedes Ruehl *(Mrs. Baskin)*, Josh Clark *(Mr. Baskin)*, Kimberlee M. Davis *(Cynthia Benson)*

p, James L. Brooks, Robert Greenhut; d, Penny Marshall; w, Gary Ross, Anne Spielberg; ph, Barry Sonnenfeld (DuArt Color); ed, Barry Malkin; m, Howard Shore; prod d, Santo Loquasto; chor, Patricia Birch; cos, Judianna Makovsky

AAN Best Actor: Tom Hanks; *AAN Best Original Screenplay:* Gary Ross, Anne Spielberg

The best of the spate of body-switching films in the late '80s. BIG features a brilliant, unforced performance by Tom Hanks as a New Jersey Little Leaguer, who after wishing he were older, suddenly finds himself walking around in a 35-year-old body. Hiding in Manhattan until his friend Rushton can track down the carny fortune-telling machine that granted the wish, Hanks gets a job with a toy manufacturing firm and rises quickly up the corporate ladder thanks to his unique kid's insight. BIG is a winning, charming film, primarily because Hanks makes it work. He is extraordinarily convincing as an adolescent who suddenly finds himself dealing with a new, adult body, responsibilities, and a romantic relationship, while simultaneously trying to survive vicious corporate infighting.

BIG CHILL, THE   ^{DVD}

1983   103m   c   Comedy/Drama   ★★½
Columbia/Carson Productions Group/   R
Delphi   (U.S.)

Glenn Close *(Sarah)*, Tom Berenger *(Sam)*, William Hurt *(Nick)*, Jeff Goldblum *(Michael)*, Mary Kay Place *(Meg)*, Kevin Kline *(Harold)*, Meg Tilly *(Chloe)*, Don Galloway *(Richard)*, JoBeth Williams *(Karen)*, James Gillis *(Minister)*

p, Michael Shamberg; d, Lawrence Kasdan; w, Lawrence Kasdan, Barbara Benedek; ph, John Bailey (Metrocolor); ed, Carol Littleton; prod d, Ida Random; cos, April Ferry

AAN Best Picture; AAN Best Supporting Actress: Glenn Close; *AAN Best Original Screenplay:* Lawrence Kasdan (Screenplay), Barbara Benedek (Screenplay)

THE BIG CHILL is a glib, seriocomic look at a 1980s reunion of a group of old college friends who were radicals during the 1960s, and how their lives have changed since that time. Strong acting and a string of classic rock and soul tunes make up for a superficial script.

A group of former college friends are reunited for a funeral after learning of the suicide of another friend who had been staying at the house of running shoe mogul Harold (Kevin Kline) and his physician wife Sarah (Glenn Close). After the funeral, the group gathers at Harold and Sarah's house for the weekend. As the friends get reacquainted while eating, drinking, flirting, getting stoned and dancing, corporate attorney Meg (Mary Kay Place) announces that she wants to have a baby and begins asking the men in the house if they will do the honors. Sarah encourages Harold to sleep with Meg, and he does so. In the meantime, suburban housewife Karen (JoBeth Williams) pursues TV star Sam (Tom Berenger), whom she's had a crush on since college, and magazine writer

Michael (Jeff Goldblum) tries to exploit the whole weekend into an article about the "lost hope" of the '60s generation.

THE BIG CHILL is the ultimate 1980s baby-boomer movie, presenting the definitive portrayal of the emerging yuppie archetype and all its traits: from running shoes, jogging, camcorders, and Motown, to baby-fever, self-analytical narcissism, and guilt-ridden upwardly mobile lifestyles. It is consistently entertaining and wonderfully acted, yet is finally undone by its refusal to deal honestly with the serious issues it raises; director/co-writer Lawrence Kasdan chooses instead to end virtually every scene with a cheap punchline. In the final analysis, the film doesn't amount to much, except to provide a good opportunity for the fine ensemble cast to show off their talents. One interesting cast note is that the character of Alex, who is never seen alive, but whose corpse is shown under the opening credits as it's being dressed for the funeral, was played by a then unknown Kevin Costner.

BIG CLOCK, THE
1948 95m   bw   Crime   ★★★½
Paramount   (U.S.)

Ray Milland (*George Stroud*), Charles Laughton (*Earl Janoth*), Maureen O'Sullivan (*Georgette Stroud*), George Macready (*Steven Hagen*), Rita Johnson (*Pauline York*), Elsa Lanchester (*Louise Patterson*), Harold Vermilyea (*Don Klausmeyer*), Dan Tobin (*Ray Cordette*), Henry Morgan (*Bill Womack*), Richard Webb (*Nat Sperling*)

p, Richard Maibaum; d, John Farrow; w, Jonathan Latimer (based on the novel by Kenneth Fearing); ph, John Seitz; ed, Gene Ruggiero; m, Victor Young; art d, Hans Dreier, Roland Anderson, Albert Nozaki; fx, Gordon Jennings; cos, Edith Head

Steady film noir production fraught with suspense, twisting its unique plot and characters to a clever and frightening conclusion. Milland is the shrewd editor of *Crimeways* magazine which is published by Laughton, a megalomaniacal media tycoon who kills his mistress. Milland tries to solve murder, but all clues point back at him! Almost stolen by the eccentric as usual Elsa Lanchester. In 1987, the film was remade with a military setting in NO WAY OUT, starring Kevin Costner and Gene Hackman.

BIG DEAL ON MADONNA STREET
(I SOLTI IGNOTI)
1958 91m   bw   Comedy/Crime   ★★★½
Lux   (Italy)

Vittorio Gassman (*Peppe*), Renato Salvatori (*Mario*), Rossana Rory (*Norma*), Carla Gravina (*Nicoletta*), Claudia Cardinale (*Carmelina*), Carlo Pisacane (*Capannelle*), Tiberio Murgia (*Ferribotte*), Memmo Carotenuto (*Cosimo*), Marcello Mastroianni (*Tiberio*), Toto (*Dante*)

p, Franco Cristaldi; d, Mario Monicelli; w, Suso Cecchi D'Amico, Agenore Incrocci, Furio Scarpelli, Mario Monicelli

AAN Best Foreign Language Film

A classic Italian spoof. Vittorio Gassman stars as Peppe, a bungling petty thief who leads a group of incompetent burglars in a plan to loot a jewelry store on Madonna Street. One of the finest examples of Italian comedy to reach American shores (it was nominated for a Best Foriegn Film Oscar in 1958), BIG DEAL ON MADONNA STREET satirizes all those procedural caper films that Hollywood turned out and the foreign homages that followed (such as RIFIFI and BOB LE FLAMBEUR). The entire burglarizing procedure, as directed by Mario Monicelli, is hilarious, thanks to the fine acting and the steady stream of sight gags that recall the classic comedies of silent days. CRACKERS, an unfunny remake from Louis Malle, appeared in 1984, and BIG DEAL ON

MADONNA STREET—20 YEARS LATER surfaced in 1985. The film was also unsuccessfully adapted for a broadway musical.

BIG EASY, THE   *DVD*
1987 108m   c   Crime/Thriller   ★★★
Kings Road   (U.S.)   R

Dennis Quaid (*Remy McSwain*), Ellen Barkin (*Anne Osborne*), Ned Beatty (*Jack Kellom*), Ebbe Roe Smith (*Detective Dodge*), John Goodman (*Detective DeSoto*), Lisa Jane Persky (*Detective McCabe*), Charles Ludlam (*Lamar*), Thomas O'Brien (*Bobby*), James Garrison (*Judge Noland*), Carol Sutton (*Judge Raskov*)

p, Stephen Friedman; d, Jim McBride; w, Daniel Petrie Jr., Jack Baran; ph, Affonso Beato (Deluxe Color); ed, Mia Goldman; m, Brad Fiedel; prod d, Jeannine Claudia Oppewall; fx, Bill Purcell; cos, Tracy Tynan

Colorful Cajun *noir*, spicy, romantic, efficient. Hot Noo Ahluns police detective (Dennis Quaid) clashes with assistant district attorney (Ellen Barkin) over cop corruption. The best scenes are the romantic ones; McBride effectively captures the Big Easy, a city that is almost a character in itself, but the ending is contrived. That's the late and beloved New York Ridiculous Theatre impressario Charles Ludlam, out of his corset, as Lamar.

BIG FISH   *DVD*
2003 110m   c   Drama/Fantasy   ★★★½
Jinks/Cohen Company/Zanuck Company/   PG-13
Columbia   (U.S.)

Ewan McGregor (*Young Ed Bloom*), Albert Finney (*Senior Ed Bloom*), Billy Crudup (*Will Bloom*), Jessica Lange (*Senior Sandra Bloom*), Alison Lohman (*Young Sandra Bloom*), Helena Bonham Carter (*Jenny/The Witch*), Robert Guillaume (*Senior Dr. Bennett*), Marion Cotillard (*Josephine Bloom*), Matthew McGrory (*Karl*), Danny DeVito (*Amos Calloway*)

p, Bruce Cohen, Dan Jinks, Richard D. Zanuck; d, Tim Burton; w, John August (based on the novel by Daniel Wallace); ph, Philippe Rousselot; ed, Chris Lebenzon; m, Danny Elfman; prod d, Dennis Gassner; art d, Richard Johnson; fx, Richard L. Hill, Kevin Mack, Hans Metz, Stan Parks, Sony Pictures Imageworks; cos, Colleen Atwood

AAN Best Original Score: Danny Elfman

Tim Burton's tall tale, in which a peevish son tries to let the air out of the whoppers his dying father has told him since childhood, is a deft blend of fantastic noodling and astute psychological drama.

Journalist William Bloom (Billy Crudup) has been estranged from his voluble father, Edward (Albert Finney), since Edward monopolized William's wedding with the umpteenth telling of a fabulous yarn about catching the biggest, wiliest catfish that ever trolled the bottom of a muddy river. When William's long-suffering mother, Sandra (Jessica Lange), calls with the news that Edward is dying, William makes the pilgrimage home with one goal in mind: he just wants to hear the plain, unvarnished truth about his father's life. But Edward can no more tell a straightforward story than he can send the grim reaper packing. Young Edward's (Ewan McGregor) spooky encounter with a swamp witch sets the tone for a series of picaresque remembrances that include rescuing his hometown from a misunderstood giant named Karl (Matthew McGrory); finding and escaping a rustic Shangri-La buried deep in some spooky woods just off a lost highway; joining the circus of Amos Calloway (Danny DeVito); and wooing his one true love, young Sandra (Alison Lohman), away from her bullying fiance.

Though Burton's prodigious gift for visual invention has always been apparent, his sense of narrative is less than rock solid; spectacular images trump story logic in many of his films. Daniel Wallace's *Big Fish: A Novel of Mythic Proportions* gives Burton a sturdy framework on which to hang the dark, whimsical images for which he's famous. Burton's fanciful visual inventions, in turn, keep Wallace's homespun messages in check, and the story's fundamental sweetness never becomes cloying.

BIG HEAT, THE

1953 89m bw Crime ★★★★
Columbia (U.S.)

Glenn Ford (*Dave Bannion*), Gloria Grahame (*Debby Marsh*), Jocelyn Brando (*Katie Bannion*), Alexander Scourby (*Mike Lagana*), Lee Marvin (*Vince Stone*), Jeanette Nolan (*Bertha Duncan*), Peter Whitney (*Tierney*), Willis Bouchey (*Lt. Wilkes*), Robert Burton (*Gus Burke*), Adam Williams (*Larry Gordon*)

p, Robert Arthur; d, Fritz Lang; w, Sydney Boehm (based on the serial in the *Saturday Evening Post* by William P. McGivern); ph, Charles Lang; ed, Charles Nelson; m, Daniele Amfitheatrof; art d, Robert Peterson; cos, Jean Louis

---

A scalding face-full of harsh reality, courtesy Fritz Lang. Starkly photographed and without a continuous score, the absence of which underlines the hard-hitting dialogue and the sound of smacking fists and thudding bullets, this film is as brutal as Lang's *M* was frightening. Ford, an ex-cop out to avenge the mob murder of his wife, gets upstaged by two performances of incredible power: Grahame and Marvin. Grahame plays a moll who squeals and pays; her performance defines the film noir anti-heroine, and in a world of comedic 1950s sex, she was the real thing, either coming along too late or too soon. Marvin moved his career up a definite notch as the sadistic killer.

This film, along with a spate of others, was spawned by the 1950 U.S. Senate crime investigations conducted via TV, which pinpointed widespread corruption by organized crime throughout America. Fritz Lang's THE BIG HEAT, meaning the heat brought down by the police, is one of the best expose films dealing with the national crime cartel, including HOODLUM EMPIRE, Robert Wise's startling CAPTIVE CITY, and Phil Karlson's hard-hitting KANSAS CITY CONFIDENTIAL. Lang's ferocious gangster film is directed with immaculate care, showing not so much violence on film as the reaction to violence, while examining the victims. A terse script by Boehm and sharp photography by Charles Lang in keeping with the theme contribute to this startling film noir.

BIG HOUSE, THE

1930 84m bw Prison ★★★★½
MGM (U.S.)

Chester Morris (*John Morgan*), Wallace Beery (*Machine Gun Butch Schmidt*), Lewis Stone (*Warden James Adams*), Robert Montgomery (*Kent Marlowe*), Leila Hyams (*Anne Marlowe*), George F. Marion Sr. (*Pop Reicher*), J.C. Nugent (*Mr. Marlowe*), Karl Dane (*Olsen*), DeWitt Jennings (*Capt. Wallace*), Matthew Betz (*Gopher*)

d, George Hill; w, Frances Marion, Joe Farnham, Martin Flavin; ph, Harold Wenstrom; ed, Blanche Sewell; art d, Cedric Gibbons; cos, David Cox

---

AAN Outstanding Production: ; *AAN Best Actor:* Wallace Beery; *AA Best Writing Achievement:* Frances Marion; *AA Best Sound Recording:* Douglas Shearer

---

The granddaddy of 'em all. Inspired by a particularly bloody riot that occurred in an Auburn, New York, prison in 1929,

THE BIG HOUSE spawned a host of movies like 20,000 YEARS IN SING SING and I AM A FUGITIVE FROM A CHAIN GANG. Grimly realistic and often brutal, it exposes the inhuman conditions and paranoia that deepen criminal resolve among inmates. George Hill's uncompromising direction captures all the ugliness and futility of prison life, and Beery (in a role originally intended for Lon Chaney Sr.) is the perfect goonish ringleader of the convicts—part clown, part thug, softhearted and softheaded, but with a killer instinct. Morris gives one of his best performances as the intelligent member of the threesome; Montgomery, at the beginning of his film career, is uncharacteristically spineless but wholly believable as a wretched, despicable cringer; and Stone, as always, contributes a solid portrayal of the establishment stalwart.

BIG KNIFE, THE

1955 111m bw Drama ★★★½
UA (U.S.)

Jack Palance (*Charles Castle*), Ida Lupino (*Marion Castle*), Shelley Winters (*Dixie Evans*), Wendell Corey (*Smiley Coy*), Jean Hagen (*Connie Bliss*), Rod Steiger (*Stanley Hoff*), Ilka Chase (*Patty Benedict*), Everett Sloane (*Nat Danziger*), Wesley Addy (*Hank Teagle*), Paul Langton (*Buddy Bliss*)

p, Robert Aldrich; d, Robert Aldrich; w, James Poe (based on the play by Clifford Odets); ph, Ernest Laszlo; ed, Michael Luciano; m, Frank DeVol; art d, William Glasgow

---

Hollywood sterotypes based on Odets but compelling and viciously done with a *tour de force* for Palance, as a tinseltown hunk with a dark, dishonest secret, supported by an amazing cast. Director Aldrich's unflinching use of a candid, almost documentary style results in a devastating mirror image of Hollywood at its most ruthless. Grim, lacking compassion and uncompromising, irrespective of the name-dropping of real personalities (Kazan, Wilder, Wyler, etc.) to authenticate the atmosphere. The script blares the philosophy that it is not only windy at the top but also lethal.

BIG LEBOWSKI, THE

1998 117m c Comedy/Mystery ★½
Bitter Creek Productions/Working Title Films/ R
PolyGram (U.S.)

Jeff Bridges (*Jeff Lebowski—the Dude*), John Goodman (*Walter Sobchak*), Julianne Moore (*Maude Lebowski*), Steve Buscemi (*Donny*), David Huddleston (*The Big Lebowski*), John Turturro (*Jesus Quintana*), Peter Stormare (*Uli—Nihilist*), Sam Elliott (*The Stranger*), David Thewlis (*Knox Harrington*), Ben Gazzara (*Jackie Treehorn*)

p, Ethan Coen; d, Joel Coen; w, Joel Coen, Ethan Coen; ph, Roger Deakins; ed, Roderick Jaynes, Tricia Cooke; m, Carter Burwell; prod d, Rick Heinrichs; art d, John Dexter; fx, Janek Sirrs, Janet Yale, The Computer Film Company; cos, Mary Zophres

---

What a strange reversal of fortune: two years after FARGO, the film that will probably stand as Joel and Ethan Coen's finest moment, they followed up with what is, without question, their worst.

This time out, the Coens turn their jaundiced eyes to L.A.—not the Hollywood they so recklessly skewered in BARTON FINK, but La-La Land as a state of mind. The plot, in a nutshell: Bunny Lebowski (Tara Reid) is missing, and Jeff "The Dude" Lebowski (Jeff Bridges), a burnt-out '70s leftover who has the bad luck to share the same first and last name as Mrs. Lebowski's millionaire husband, is in a heap of trouble. After a pair of thugs treat The Dude to a rather vicious swirlie, then pee on his carpet, wheelchair-bound Jeff "The Big" Lebowski (David Huddleston)—the intended target of the assault—offers the Dude a tidy sum of money to help get his wife back. Mixed up in all this is Maude (Julianne Moore), the Big Lebowski's wayward daughter (she's a "feminist artist"—honest); Walter (John Goodman), The Dude's paranoid Vietnam vet bowling partner; and a host of quirky cameos from the likes of John Turturro, David Thewlis, and Ben Gazzara. If any of this sounds at all like THE BIG SLEEP, then you've gotten the one—and only—joke.

Repopulating Raymond Chandler's L.A. with a cast of latter-day freaks, floozies, and failures has been done before—brilliantly, in fact, by Robert Altman. But where Chandler's tales of the City of Angels were convoluted to great effect, the Coens' vision of L.A.'s kooky underbelly is simply convoluted, and desperately so. Reworking the old "down these mean streets" formula, they've only replaced noir cliches with even thinner—and often blithely offensive—cliches of their own. The only real moments of inspiration come during The Dude's periodic bouts of unconsciousness, during which he dreams elaborate Busby Berkeley-style dance numbers. But if it's all supposed to be in fun, why does it feel so much like an insult?

BIG PARADE, THE
(DA YUE BING)
1985 102m c Drama   ★★★
Guangxi (China)

Huang Xueqi, Sun Chun, Lu Lei, Wu Ruofu

d, Chen Kaige; w, Gao Lili; ph, Zhang Yimou (Widescreen); ed, Zhou Xinxia; m, Qu Xiaosong, Zhao Liping; prod d, He Qun

Chinese director Chen Kaige's long-awaited second feature, following the critically acclaimed YELLOW EARTH, was a somewhat uneven effort, hampered by a cliched narrative that fails to live up to the brilliance of the imagery.

Set in modern-day China, the film follows a single airborne unit as it undergoes a grueling training session in preparation for the prestigious parade in Beijing celebrating the 35th anniversary of the revolution. Led by a tough drill sergeant who is a veteran of a China-Vietnam conflict, the undisciplined young men are slowly whipped into shape until they becomes a flawless unit capable of marching in perfect order.

In THE BIG PARADE director Kaige strives for something more than what some critics have called the "Chinese FULL METAL JACKET." The film illustrates the conflict between the group and the individual in today's China. This somewhat subversive theme may have been the reason Chinese officials prevented the film's release for two years (it was filmed in 1985). Unfortunately, to Western eyes used to countless war films, the exploration of this theme may be a bit too banal. Although the characters and situations are standard basic training fare, Kaige filled his film with frequently breathtaking visuals.

From the opening helicopter shot which shows miles and miles of troops training on the tarmac to the final slow-motion shots of various units, Kaige continually comes up with beautiful and fascinating images of men in motion. Most remarkable, however, is the sequence where the men are not in motion—the arduous drill where the soldiers must stand still in the blazing sun. The wide-screen shimmers with the brutal heat, and the sweat pours from beneath the soldiers' helmets, presenting a brilliant, unforgettable image of individual human endurance and mass stupidity.

BIG RED ONE, THE
           DVD
1980 113m c War   ★★★★
Lorimar (U.S.)   PG

Lee Marvin (Sergeant), Mark Hamill (Griff), Robert Carradine (Zab), Bobby Di Cicco (Vinci), Kelly Ward (Johnson), Siegfried

Rauch (Schroeder), Stephane Audran (Walloon), Serge Marquand (Ransonnet), Charles Macaulay (General/Captain), Alain Doutey (Broban)

p, Gene Corman; d, Samuel Fuller; w, Samuel Fuller; ph, Adam Greenberg (Metrocolor); ed, David Bretherton, Morton Tubor; m, Dana Kaproff; art d, Peter Jamison; fx, Kit West, Peter Dawson, Jeff Clifford

Samuel Fuller's episodic THE BIG RED ONE is a powerful, humorous, and touching autobiographical film that's the last of the great WWII movies.

In 1942, a Sergeant (Lee Marvin) leads a group of raw recruits in the First Infantry Division (nicknamed "the Big Red One"), including a quartet dubbed "The Four Horsemen"—Griff (Mark Hamill), a sharpshooter; Zab (Robert Carradine), an aspiring novelist; Vinci (Bobby Di Cicco), an Italian-American; and Johnson (Kelly Ward), a farmboy. In 1943 Sicily, with the help of a boy whose mother has been killed, they manage to destroy a huge German gun that's concealed at the top of a mountain. On D-Day in 1944, they take part in the Normandy invasion, but get trapped on Omaha Beach. Griff proves himself by eluding enemy gunfire and blowing up a fence, enabling them to escape. The squad then goes to Belgium and recaptures an insane asylum that's being used by the Nazis as their headquarters. In 1945, they experience the worst horror of their wartime careers when they're sent to liberate a concentration camp in Czechoslovakia.

Based in his own WWII experiences, THE BIG RED ONE was a dream project for Samuel Fuller, who had tried to get the film made for decades. Despite the film's limited budget, which necessitated that most of the location shooting be done in Israel, and the continuity lapses due to post-production tinkering, Fuller manages to create one of the most poignant war films ever made. Fuller demonstrates his philosophy that "the only glory in war is surviving," by focusing on the Four Horsemen and through a series of searing scenes filled with unforgettable images (a Nazi hiding behind a giant crucifix in the middle of a battlefield; the terrified eyes of concentration camp prisoners). Real-life ex-Marine Lee Marvin is perfect as the taciturn yet compassionate Sarge, and Robert Carradine is amusing as Zab, the cigar-chomping, pulp-novelist Fuller-surrogate, while the character of Griff is solemnly played by Mark Hamill. Vehemently antimilitaristic, the film celebrates camaraderie and brotherhood and eloquently demonstrates the ultimate futility of war.

BIG SKY, THE
1952 140m bw Western   ★★★½
Winchester (U.S.)

Kirk Douglas (Deakins), Dewey Martin (Boone), Elizabeth Threatt (Teal Eye), Arthur Hunnicutt (Zeb), Buddy Baer (Romaine), Steven Geray (Jourdonnais), Hank Worden (Poordevil), Jim Davis (Streak), Henri Letondal (Ladadie), Robert Hunter (Chouquette)

p, Howard Hawks; d, Howard Hawks; w, Dudley Nichols (based on the novel by A.B. Guthrie, Jr.); ph, Russell Harlan; ed, Christian Nyby; m, Dimitri Tiomkin; art d, Albert S. D'Agostino, Perry Ferguson; fx, Don Steward; cos, Dorothy Jeakins

AAN Best Supporting Actor: Arthur Hunnicutt; AAN Best B/W Cinematography: Russell Harlan

Up the Missouri, male bonding and will bending. Well-directed by Hawks, but nothing new under the sun (excepting an oddly prominent castration motif). Shot on location in the Grand Teton National Park and enhanced by lyrical, haunting Tiomkin score (he had recently won two Oscars for score and song for HIGH NOON). Aside from the fascinating upriver struggle where the men must pull the boat by rope while hostile Indians lurk nearby, the most interesting aspect of the film is the wizened Hunnicutt as the old trapper; he manages to steal almost every scene.

BIG SLEEP, THE
DVD
1946 118m bw Mystery/Crime
Warner Bros. (U.S.)
★★★★★

Humphrey Bogart *(Philip Marlowe)*, Lauren Bacall *(Vivian)*, John Ridgely *(Eddie Mars)*, Louis Jean Heydt *(Joe Brody)*, Elisha Cook Jr. *(Jones)*, Regis Toomey *(Bernie Ohls)*, Sonia Darrin *(Agnes)*, Bob Steele *(Canino)*, Martha Vickers *(Carmen)*, Tom Rafferty *(Carol Lundgren)*

p, Howard Hawks; d, Howard Hawks; w, William Faulkner, Jules Furthman, Leigh Brackett (based on the novel by Raymond Chandler); ph, Sid Hickox; ed, Christian Nyby; m, Max Steiner; art d, Carl Jules Weyl; fx, Roy Davidson; cos, Leah Rhodes

The most convoluted of the great noir films, based on the first yarn written by Raymond Chandler. THE BIG SLEEP comes magically alive through Hawks's careful direction and Bogart's persona, which is twin to his character of Philip Marlowe.

Summoned to the lavish mansion of General Sternwood (Charles Waldron), Marlowe is hired to investigate black-mailer Geiger (Theodore Von Eltz), a Hollywood smut book dealer who has compromising photos of the general's daughter Carmen (Vickers). The general's real aim, however, is to have Bogart locate his missing confidante Shawn Regan. Marlowe follows his clues to Geiger's home, finding the smut peddler dead and Carmen drugged. Before police arrive, Marlowe secrets Carmen back home and strikes up a romance with the general's other daughter, Vivian (Bacall). With Vivian at the gumshoe's side, Marlowe sinks deeper and deeper into a labyrinthine plot of gambling, blackmail, and murder.

One of the greatest detective films to come out of Hollywood, THE BIG SLEEP is perhaps most notorious for its famous unsolved murder—that of the Sternwood chauffeur. The unwieldy plot, scripted by William Faulkner, kept Hawks busy trying to figure out the puzzle. When Hawks called Chandler to ask the killer's identity, the writer reportedly stated: "How should I know? You figure it out," and hung up. It was on the set of THE BIG SLEEP that the Bogart and Bacall love-team image was cemented, although their first sizzling union on screen was in TO HAVE AND HAVE NOT. Their dazzling star personas, combined with the poetry of both Chandler's and Faulkner's words and Howard Hawks's direction, give THE BIG SLEEP some of the most sexually electric dialogue ever to hit the screen.

BIG TRAIL, THE
DVD
1930 125m c/bw Western
Fox (U.S.)
★★★

John Wayne *(Breck Coleman)*, Marguerite Churchill *(Ruth Cameron)*, El Brendel *(Gussie)*, Tully Marshall *(Zeke)*, Tyrone Power Sr. *(Red Flack)*, David Rollins *(Dave Cameron)*, Frederick Burton *(Pa Bascom)*, Charles Stevens *(Lopez)*, Russ Powell *(Windy Bill)*, Helen Parrish *(Honey Girl)*

d, Raoul Walsh; w, Jack Peabody, Marie Boyle, Florence Postal, Fred Sersen (based on a story by Hal Evarts and Raoul Walsh); ph, Lucien Andriot, Arthur Edeson (Grandeur); ed, Jack Dennis; m, Arthur Kay; art d, Harold Miles, Fred Sersen

Creaking, but sentimentally grand. Wayne was working as a property man, a kid just out of college, when director John Ford noticed him. When colleague Raoul Walsh was searching for the male lead for his latest project, Ford recommended Wayne, telling Walsh, who appeared in Griffith's THE BIRTH OF A NATION in 1915, and who would go on to

become one of the best action directors (OBJECTIVE BURMA, THEY DIED WITH THEIR BOOTS ON) that he "liked the looks of this new kid with a funny walk, like he owned the world."

The film deals with the first covered wagon train to cross the rugged Oregon Trail. There is the traditional Indian attack with pioneers beating off the redskins from their circle of wagons, a spectacular buffalo hunt, and a devastating scene where the entire cast was almost drowned when fording a river during a fierce rainstorm (Walsh always kept the cameras rolling). There is little plot other than the great trek west through the wilderness of Nebraska and Wyoming where the film was shot, with Wayne vying for Churchill's attentions with Tully Marshall and others.

Walsh's direction is superb as he captures the thrilling outdoor action in this epic which cost Fox $2 million to produce, a fortune in those days. Further, the film was one of the first to be made in Grandeur, a 55mm wide-screen color process so impressive that the premiere audience jumped to its feet and cheered at the conclusion. Most viewers, however, only saw the film on the standard 35mm black-and-white screen, and this took away from the film's impact.

Wayne seems uneasy, and it can't have helped that Fox producers insisted that Lumsden Hare, the studio voice coach, teach Wayne to sound like an Englishman in buckskin so that each preciously recorded word could be understood. Wayne next drifted into the oblivion of "poverty row" studios that would have him making sagebrush grinders for nine years until Ford once again came to the rescue by giving him the lead in his classic STAGECOACH.

BILL & TED'S EXCELLENT ADVENTURE
DVD
1989 90m c Science Fiction/Comedy
Nelson/Interscope/Nelson-Murphey (U.S.)
★★½
PG

Keanu Reeves *(Ted "Theodore" Logan)*, Alex Winter *(Bill S. Preston)*, George Carlin *(Rufus)*, Terry Camilleri *(Napoleon)*, Dan Shor *(Billy the Kid)*, Tony Steedman *(Socrates)*, Rod Loomis *(Sigmund Freud)*, Al Leong *(Genghis Khan)*, Jane Wiedlin *(Joan of Arc)*, Robert V. Barron *(Abraham Lincoln)*

p, Scott Kroopf, Michael S. Murphey, Joel Soisson; d, Stephen Herek; w, Chris Matheson, Ed Solomon; ph, Tim Suhrstedt (Technicolor); ed, Larry Bock, Patrick Rand; m, David Newman; prod d, Roy Forge Smith; art d, Gordon White; chor, Brad Jeffries; cos, Jill Ohanneson

Radical! Pair of rock 'n' roll airheads can't graduate unless they pass history exam. Along comes Carlin from the future to enable dudes to experience history for themselves. Dudes take off without film. Still, BILL & TED has an intangibly charming goofiness about it that is somehow endearing: here is a movie about teenagers that contains no excessive profanity, no drug references, and no explicit sexual activity.

BILL OF DIVORCEMENT, A
1932 70m bw Drama
Selznick (U.S.)
★★★★

John Barrymore *(Hillary Fairfield)*, Billie Burke *(Margaret Fairfield)*, Katharine Hepburn *(Sydney Fairfield)*, David Manners *(Kit Humphrey)*, Henry Stephenson *(Doctor Alliot)*, Paul Cavanagh *(Gray Meredith)*, Elizabeth Patterson *(Aunt Hester)*, Gayle Evers *(Bassett)*, Julie Haydon *(Party Guest)*

p, David O. Selznick; d, George Cukor; w, Howard Estabrook, Harry Wagstaff Gribble (based on the play by Clemence Dane); ph, Sid Hickox; ed, Arthur Roberts; m, Max Steiner; art d, Carroll Clark; cos, Josette De Lima

This was the second, definitive version of three filmings of the Clemence Dane play. (The first was a British silent of 1922, and RKO made a second worthy sound version with Adolphe Menjou and Maureen O'Hara in 1940.) John Barrymore was at the top of his profession with this performance, and a radiant Katharine Hepburn made her screen debut. Barrymore plays a man who has been living in a mental hospital for many years and who escapes on the day his wife (Burke) is divorcing him. His daughter's (Hepburn) rediscovery of her father, her reaction to the taint of hereditary mental illness in the family, and the wife's desire to remarry make for a compact and compelling drama.

Barrymore is simply superb, director George Cukor eliciting a lost, sensitive and caring man from beneath the occasional bravado. Hepburn, who was to work with Cukor nine more times in films and TV, was only 24 at the time. Her appearance was electric and sent critics reaching for new superlatives.

BILLY ELLIOT
DVD
2000 111m c Drama ★★★★
Working Title Films/BBC Films/Tiger Aspect R
Pictures/Studio Canal/Arts Council of England
(U.K.)

Julie Walters (Mrs. Wilkinson), Jamie Bell (Billy), Jamie Draven (Tony), Gary Lewis (Dad), Jean Heywood (Grandma), Stuart Wells (Michael), Mike Elliot (George Watson), Janine Birkett (Billy's Mum), Nicola Blackwell (Debbie), Billy Fane (Mr. Braithwaite)

p, Greg Brenman, Jon Finn; d, Stephen Daldry; w, Lee Hall; ph, Brian Tufano; ed, John Wilson; prod d, Maria Djukovic; art d, Adam O'Neill; fx, Stuart Murdoch, Double Negative; chor, Peter Darling; cos, Stewart Meachem

AAN Best Supporting Actress: Julie Walters; AAN Best Director: Stephen Daldry; AAN Best Original Screenplay: Lee Hall

It could easily have become mired in treacle, but director Stephen Daldry transforms this hard-knocks, coming-of-age tale into an exhilarating feel-good story that quietly undermines the notion of gain without loss.

Adolescent Billy Elliot (Jamie Bell) is the son of one striking coal miner (Gary Lewis) and the brother of another (Jamie Draven); his mother is dead, and his loving grandma (Jean Heywood) is slowly sliding into senility. Billy is loved, but adrift. Dad scrapes together the money for Billy's weekly boxing lessons, but the dreary northern English town offers few real options beyond mining. Imagine Billy's shock when the boxing gym is invaded by a flock of little girls in snowy tutus. It's middle-class Mrs. Wilkinson's (Julie Walters) displaced ballet class, and they'll be sharing space with punching bags and medicine balls. More shocking still, Billy finds himself at the barre, first on a dare from one of the fluttering girls, then because the formidable Mrs. Wilkinson invites him to stay. Billy's eventual confession that he wants to study ballet seriously doesn't go down well at home for a slew of interconnected reasons—class resentment, fear of homosexuality, and the very real worry that dance will take Billy away from them.

Nothing in this wonderful film is as black-and-white as it would be in a lesser movie; a shot of Billy's older brother dancing in his room to T. Rex speaks eloquently about dancing's natural allure, stripped of cultural preconceptions. Young Bell makes a phenomenal debut: Billy's reaction to his big chance to escape grinding but familiar poverty is a pitch-perfect mix of excitement and fear.

BILLY LIAR
DVD
1963 98m bw Drama ★★★★
Vic Films Ltd. (U.K.)

Tom Courtenay (Billy Fisher), Julie Christie (Liz), Wilfred Pickles (Geoffrey Fisher), Mona Washbourne (Alice Fisher), Ethel Griffies

(Florence), Finlay Currie (Duxbury), Rodney Bewes (Arthur Crabtree), Helen Fraser (Barbara), George Innes (Eric Stamp), Leonard Rossiter (Shadrack)

p, Joseph Janni; d, John Schlesinger; w, Keith Waterhouse, Willis Hall (based on their play); ph, Denys Coop; ed, Roger Cherrill; m, Richard Rodney Bennett; art d, Ray Simon

One of the seminal British working-class films of the 1960s, BILLY LIAR is a first-rate comedy-fantasy that features Tom Courtenay in a role which Albert Finney had played in the stage version by Waterhouse and Hall.

No one will argue the plot's derivation—James Thurber's classic short story "The Secret Life of Walter Mitty," with Courtenay as Billy Fisher, a dreamer who works for a funeral director, but who retreats into a fantasy world. Billy is also a pathological liar who, as Oscar Wilde once said, doesn't lie for gain, just for the sheer joy of lying. Billy is involved with three young women, two of whom share an engagement ring. Christie, in one of her earliest roles, is terrific as a adventurous young woman willing to overlook anything the charming Billy tosses at her.

All the secondary roles are sharply etched and wonderfully acted under the sure hand of John Schlesinger in his third feature. Although his two earlier films, TERMINUS and A KIND OF LOVING, were superb, it was really with this film that Schlesinger garnered widespread attention. A later stage musical and TV series were based on the same story.

BILOXI BLUES
DVD
1988 107m c Comedy/War ★★★½
Rastar (U.S.) PG-13

Matthew Broderick (Eugene Morris Jerome), Christopher Walken (Sgt. Merwin J. Toomey), Matt Mulhern (Joseph Wykowski), Corey Parker (Arnold Epstein), Markus Flanagan (Roy Selridge), Casey Siemaszko (Donald Carney), Michael Dolan (James J. Hennessey), Penelope Ann Miller (Daisy Hannigan), Park Overall (Rowena), Alan Pottinger (Peek)

p, Ray Stark; d, Mike Nichols; w, Neil Simon (based on his play); ph, Bill Butler; ed, Sam O'Steen; m, Georges Delerue; prod d, Paul Sylbert; cos, Ann Roth

BILOXI BLUES works better than the script alone would suggest, thanks to the skillful direction of Nichols and excellent performances from Broderick and Walken.

An adaptation of Simon's autobiographical play, the film follows New Yorker Broderick through his Army basic training in Biloxi, Mississippi, in the last days of WWII. The Biloxi heat gets him down, as does his strange drill sergeant, Walken, whose sadism works in quiet, mysterious ways, sowing dissent among his troops. Weeks of bad food, long marches, and humiliation are somewhat relieved when Broderick falls in love with Miller while on weekend leave. When his buddies find Broderick's notes and read his hurtful remarks about them—including his musings about whether Parker is homosexual—the aspiring writer discovers just how powerful words can be.

Successfully opening up Simon's popular play, Nichols avoids presenting the jokes in the sitcom formula typical of Simon, as set-ups to big punchlines. Broderick brings appealing nuances to the role he created onstage, and Walken makes his sergeant a quietly chilling, ambiguous character. An intelligent, tightly constructed film which manages to satirize both the military and the process of growing up.

BIRD

1988 161m c Biography **DVD** ★★★★
Malpaso (U.S.) R

Forest Whitaker *(Charlie "Yardbird" Parker)*, Diane Venora *(Chan Richardson Parker)*, Michael Zelniker *(Red Rodney)*, Samuel E. Wright *(Dizzy Gillespie)*, Keith David *(Buster Franklin)*, Michael McGuire *(Brewster)*, James Handy *(Esteves)*, Damon Whitaker *(Young Bird)*, Morgan Nagler *(Kim)*, Arlen Dean Snyder *(Dr. Heath)*

p, Clint Eastwood; d, Clint Eastwood; w, Joel Oliansky; ph, Jack N. Green (Technicolor); ed, Joel Cox; m, Lennie Niehaus; fx, Joe Day

AA Best Sound: Les Fresholtz, Dick Alexander, Vern Poore, Willie D. Burton

A tribute to the life and genius of saxophonist Charlie Parker, BIRD is a collage of passages from Parker's remarkable life, from his childhood in Kansas City, through his tumultuous interracial relationship with Chan Richardson, to his tragic death at the age of 34.

Derived mostly from Chan Parker's unpublished memoir, *Life in E-Flat*, the story is told through an intricate structure that jumps backward and forward in an ambitious attempt to create a narrative and visual equivalent to Parker's complicated music. In a remarkable directorial effort, Eastwood shows a great flair for atmosphere and composition and presents a nuanced, complex, humane portrait of Parker's talents, obstacles, virtues and failings. Whitaker gives a towering performance as the tortured musical genius, and Venora is equally impressive as the independent, compassionate Chan.

Wisely opting to use Parker's actual solos on the soundtrack instead of having a modern musician re-create them, Eastwood and musical director Lennie Niehaus took several previously unreleased recordings of Parker and digitally stripped away his accompanists (mostly because of poor recording techniques that featured Bird at the expense of the others), replacing them with modern musicians.

BIRD WITH THE CRYSTAL PLUMAGE, THE

DVD
(L'UCELLO DALLE PLUME DI CRISTALLO)
1969 98m c Horror ★★★★
Glazier (Italy/West Germany) PG

Tony Musante *(Sam Dalmas)*, Suzy Kendall *(Julia)*, Eva Renzi *(Monica)*, Enrico Maria Salerno *(Morosini)*, Mario Adorf *(Berto)*, Renato Romano *(Dover)*, Umberto Raho *(Ranieri)*

p, Salvatore Argento; d, Dario Argento; w, Dario Argento; ph, Vittorio Storaro (Eastmancolor); m, Ennio Morricone

A heart-stopping horror melodrama with excellent acting from all involved. Director Argento, here essaying his first film, uses humor, much like Hitchcock, to complement the suspense, but you never feel the master is being ripped off.

Walking home one night, Musante, a Yank scribe in Rome, sees Renzi being murdered in an art gallery. He can't make out the killer's face, but the police decide to garnish his passport, as this is but one of several murders of lone women. Musante cooperates with the police but also conducts his own investigation, which takes him into the underbelly of the Eternal City.

Memorable characters abound and Storaro's sensational camera work and Morricone's score highlight their seedy milieu aptly. Several terrifying sequences come one after another, but none are gratuitous and the film never wallows in its violence. With a different title and better marketing, this compelling film, which had considerable influence on what would become known as the "slasher" genre in the 1980s, would have been a smash.

BIRDCAGE, THE

1996 118m c Comedy **DVD** ★★
Icarus Productions/United Artists (U.S.) R

Robin Williams *(Armand Goldman)*, Gene Hackman *(Senator Keeley)*, Nathan Lane *(Albert)*, Dianne Wiest *(Louise Keeley)*, Dan Futterman *(Val Goldman)*, Calista Flockhart *(Barbara Keeley)*, Hank Azaria *(Agador)*, Christine Baranski *(Katharine)*, Tom McGowan *(Harry Radman)*, Grant Heslov *(Photographer)*

p, Mike Nichols; d, Mike Nichols; w, Elaine May (based on the screenplay *La Cage Aux Folles* by Jean Poiret, Francis Veber, Edouard Molinaro, and Marcello Danon, adapted from the stage play by Jean Poiret); ph, Emmanuel Lubezki; ed, Arthur Schmidt; prod d, Bo Welch; art d, Tom Duffield; fx, Stan Parks, Syd Dutton, Bill Taylor, Illusion Arts; chor, Vincent Paterson; cos, Ann Roth

AAN Best Art Direction: Bo Welch, Cheryl Carasik

In this flaccid remake of LA CAGE AUX FOLLES, Robin Williams and Nathan Lane play Armand and Albert, a middle-aged couple whose life together would be a model of bourgeois domesticity if they weren't both men. Armand owns a flashy Florida drag club called the Birdcage, and Albert is the unconvincing star attraction—it's not really clear who's clamoring to see this tubby, wholesome clown in a frock, but never mind. They're thrown into a tizz when their son (Dan Futterman)—he's actually Armand's kid by his ex-wife (Christine Baranski), but Albert might as well be his mother—announces his engagement to the daughter of a right-wing senator (Gene Hackman) who champions "family values." The Ozzie and Harriet of the drag set agree to play it straight for a night with the prospective in-laws, and tediously predictable complications ensue.

Unsurprisingly, the film rests on grotesque stereotypes of gay men (though it tries to have it both ways by flogging a simplistic plea for tolerance). What might be a surprise, given the talents involved, is how relentlessly unfunny it is. But this is drag comedy aimed squarely at middle America, where cuddly, sexless queens who sing show tunes, wear silly clothes, and cook delightful meals are good for an indulgent laugh. The biggest chuckles come courtesy of the couple's swishy Latin houseboy (Hank Azaria), who not only talks funny and executes a classic pratfall with the best of them, but also looks adorable in a Carmen Miranda-inspired halter top.

BIRDMAN OF ALCATRAZ

1962 147m bw Prison/Biography **DVD** ★★★½
UA (U.S.)

Burt Lancaster *(Robert Stroud)*, Karl Malden *(Harvey Shoemaker)*, Thelma Ritter *(Elizabeth Stroud)*, Betty Field *(Stella Johnson)*, Neville Brand *(Bull Ransom)*, Edmond O'Brien *(Tom Gaddis)*, Hugh Marlowe *(Roy Comstock)*, Telly Savalas *(Feto Gomez)*, Crahan Denton *(Kramer)*, James Westerfield *(Jess Younger)*

p, Stuart Millar, Guy Trosper; d, John Frankenheimer; w, Guy Trosper (based on the book by Thomas E. Gaddis); ph, Burnett Guffey; ed, Edward Mann; m, Elmer Bernstein

AAN Best Actor: Burt Lancaster; *AAN Best Supporting Actor:* Telly Savalas; *AAN Best Supporting Actress:* Thelma Ritter; *AAN Best B/W Cinematography:* Burnett Guffey

In a story based on fact, Lancaster plays surly, withdrawn inmate Robert Stroud, sentenced to life in prison, who cures a sick bird which flies into his cell one day, and later becomes an internationally recognized ornithologist. Fighting against an overly protective mother (Ritter) and a truculent warden (Malden), Stroud is nonetheless able to continue his research even when sent to Alcatraz, the notorious "Rock" in San Francisco Bay, home to only the most incorrigible prisoners. Finally, though, after an abortive romance (Field) and a prison riot which he helps quell, Stroud is able to tell his remarkable story to writer Tom Gaddis (O'Brien, playing the author of the film's source biography), who brings it to the world.

THE BIRDMAN OF ALCATRAZ has great production values, moving if sometimes plodding, overly deliberate scripting, and efficient direction from black-and-white specialist Frankenheimer which strives mightily to overcome the essentially static nature of the storyline. Lancaster's star turn in the title role, typically bravura yet more restrained than usual, plays a vital role in holding this lengthy movie together while staving off sentimentality in the process. Nominated for Best Actor, Lancaster lost to Gregory Peck for his role in TO KILL A MOCKINGBIRD. Malden is typically Malden, but Savalas, as one of Stroud's fellow inmates, and the reliable Ritter make the most of their roles and received supporting Oscar nominations, as did Guffey's skillful cinematography.

BIRDS, THE 📀
1963 120m c Horror ★★★★
Universal (U.S.)

Rod Taylor *(Mitch Brenner)*, Tippi Hedren *(Melanie Daniels)*, Jessica Tandy *(Lydia Brenner)*, Suzanne Pleshette *(Annie Hayworth)*, Veronica Cartwright *(Cathy Brenner)*, Ethel Griffies *(Mrs. Bundy)*, Charles McGraw *(Sebastian Sholes)*, Ruth McDevitt *(Mrs. MacGruder)*, Joe Mantell *(Salesman)*, Doodles Weaver *(Fisherman)*

p, Alfred Hitchcock; d, Alfred Hitchcock; w, Evan Hunter (based on the story by Daphne du Maurier); ph, Robert Burks (Technicolor); ed, George Tomasini; m, Bernard Herrmann; prod d, Robert Boyle; fx, Ub Iwerks; cos, Edith Head

AAN Best Special Visual Effects: Ub Iwerks

Hitchcock's follow-up to PSYCHO (1960) was yet another ground-breaking addition to the horror genre and further revealed the master director's darker obsessions.

Loosely based on a Daphne du Maurier short story, the action is set in Bodega Bay and follows bored, spoiled socialite Melanie Daniels (Hedren) as she romantically pursues dashing lawyer Mitch Brenner (Taylor). Tension soon develops among Melanie, schoolteacher Annie Hayworth, Mitch's former flame (Pleshette), and Mitch's domineering mother (Tandy). The emotional interplay is interrupted (and reflected) by the sudden and unexplained attack of thousands of birds on the area.

Hailed as one of Hitchcock's masterpieces by some and despised by others, THE BIRDS is certainly among the director's more complex and fascinating works. Volumes have been written about the film, with each writer picking it apart scene by scene in order to prove his or her particular critical theory—mostly of the psychoanalytic variety. Be that as it may, even those who grow impatient with the slow build-up or occasional dramatic lapses cannot deny the terrifying power of many of the film's haunting images: the bird point-of-view shot of Bodega Bay, the birds slowly gathering on the playground monkey bars, the attack on the children's birthday party, Melanie trapped in the attic, and the final ambiguous shot of the defeated humans leaving Bodega Bay while the thousands of triumphant birds gathered on the ground watch them go.

BIRDY 📀
1984 120m c Drama/War ★★★★½
Malton (U.S.) R

Matthew Modine *(Birdy)*, Nicolas Cage *(Al Columbato)*, John Harkins *(Dr. Weiss)*, Sandy Baron *(Mr. Columbato)*, Karen Young *(Hannah Rourke)*, Bruno Kirby *(Renaldi)*, Nancy Fish *(Mrs. Prevost)*, George Buck *(Birdy's Father)*, Delores Sage *(Birdy's Mother)*, Robert L. Ryan *(Joe Sagessa)*

p, Alan Marshall; d, Alan Parker; w, Sandy Kroopf, Jack Behr (based on the novel by William Wharton); ph, Michael Seresin (Metrocolor); ed, Gerry Hambling; m, Peter Gabriel; prod d, Geoffrey Kirkland; art d, Armin Ganz, Stewart Campbell; cos, Kristi Zea

BIRDY is one of those rare movies that successfully brings a psychological novel to the screen without sacrificing its saliency or complexity.

Although the book by William Wharton is set in the days after WWII, the film has been updated to the post-Vietnam era to tell the story of the deep friendship between Birdy (Modine) and Al Columbato (Cage), a pair of young men whose lives have been scarred by the war experience. Birdy has had an obsessive affinity for birds since childhood (scenes of which are shown in flashback), but in the period after his wartime service he believes he has actually been transformed into a bird. As a result he is confined to a military mental hospital. His best friend, Al (who was physically wounded in Vietnam), is determined to bring Birdy back to the real world.

One of the most bizarre accounts of postwar trauma, BIRDY succeeds because of an excellent, nuanced screenplay, supple direction by Parker, and the outstanding performances of both Cage and Modine. Modine's sensitive portrayal of the young man who transcends species boundaries is spellbinding; Cage is at once affable, concerned, and frustrated. Full of moments which will linger in the memory (such as the flashbacks showing Birdy's attempts to fly or the film's final scene), the film is at once stark, compassionate and hilarious. A fresh and welcome alternative to such "realistic" postwar films as COMING HOME, WHO'LL STOP THE RAIN, and ROLLING THUNDER. Winner of the 1985 Special Grand Jury Prize at Cannes.

BIRTH 📀
2004 100m c Drama/Mystery ★★★
Lou Yi Productions/Academy Productions/ R
Fine Line (U.S.)

Nicole Kidman *(Anna)*, Cameron Bright *(Young Sean)*, Danny Huston *(Joseph)*, Lauren Bacall *(Eleanor)*, Alison Elliott *(Laura)*, Michael Desautels *(Sean)*, Anne Heche *(Clara)*, Peter Stormare *(Clifford)*, Ted Levine *(Mr. Conte)*, Cara Seymour *(Mrs. Conte)*

p, Lizie Gower, Nick Morris, Jean-Louis Piel; d, Jonathan Glazer; w, Milo Addica, Jean-Claude Carriere, Jonathan Glazer; ph, Harris Savides; ed, Sam Sneade, Claus Wehlisch; m, Alexandre Desplat; prod d, Kevin Thompson; art d, Jonathan Arkin; fx, Tom Debenham, John M. Ottesen, Ronald Ottesen; cos, John Dunn

Terrific acting and fearless direction transform what might have been a silly exercise in the slightly spooky into a somber and deeply romantic mystery.

Ten years after the death of her beloved husband, Sean, Anna (Nicole Kidman) has decided to finally move on and marry Joseph (Danny Huston). No sooner does she set a date for the wedding, however, than a strange encounter with a 10-year-old boy gives Anna a discomfiting emotional jolt. The child wanders into an intimate birthday dinner for Anna's mother, Eleanor (Lauren Bacall), thrown at the family's sprawling Upper East Side Manhattan apartment, interrupting the festivities to announce that he is in fact Anna's dead husband and warns her against marrying Joseph. He also tells her that he still loves her. Anna tries to laugh the whole thing off as a rather painful prank, but she can't help but wonder how the kid knows so much about her and her life with Sean—a life that ended the year he was born. Anna claims she only wants to put the past behind her and build a new life with Joseph, but she finds herself falling in love with "Sean" all over again.

As absurd as Anna's dilemma may sound, it plays surprisingly well on screen. The screenplay, which flirts with intergenerational romance without ever seeming perverse, was originally conceived by director Jonathan Glazer and Jean-Claude Carriere, who wrote a number of Luis Bunuel's most daring films, including DIARY OF A CHAMBERMAID and BELLE DE JOUR. Not every scene works, but the elegant production design and powerful performances gloss over the glitches; Kidman, in particular, achieves an astonishing level of subtlety.

BIRTHDAY GIRL   🅳🆅🅳

2002   93m   c   Romance/Thriller   ★★★
FilmFour/HAL Films/Mirage Enterprises/   R
Birthday Girl Productions/Portobello Pictures
(U.K./U.S.)

Nicole Kidman *(Nadia/Sophia)*, Ben Chaplin *(John Buckingham)*, Vincent Cassel *(Alexei)*, Mathieu Kassovitz *(Yuri)*, Kate Evans *(Clare)*, Stephen Mangan *(Bank Manager)*, Xander Armstrong *(Robert Moseley)*, Sally Phillips *(Karen)*, Jo McInnes *(Waitress)*, Ben Miller *(Concierge)*

p, Steve Butterworth, Diana Phillips; d, Jez Butterworth; w, Tom Butterworth, Jez Butterworth; ph, Oliver Stapleton; ed, Christopher Tellefsen; m, Stephen Warbeck; prod d, Hugo Luczyc-Wyhowski; art d, Rebecca Holmes; fx, Graham Longhurst, Val Wardlow; cos, Phoebe De Gaye

A lonely bachelor finds that his Russian mail-order bride isn't what he expected in this romantic comedy that abruptly turns into a thriller.

Quiet bank clerk John Buckingham (Ben Chaplin) hasn't had much luck in love, and the pickings are slim in the London commuter suburb where he lives. So John turns to "From Russia With Love," a website that features marriage-minded Russian women looking to correspond with foreigners, and there he meets Nadia. John agrees to bring her to England, but the Nadia (Nicole Kidman) who arrives at the airport is rather different from the girl with whom he's been exchanging letters. She's certainly beautiful, but she chain smokes and doesn't speak a word of English. John wants to send her back, but the eminently pragmatic Nadia knows the way to a man's heart (hint: it's not through his stomach). Just as the film's uneasy take on modern romance is settling into its groove, two additional Russians—coarse Alexei (Vincent Cassel) and wise guy Yuri (Mathieu Kassovitz)—suddenly appear at John's door. They say they're here to surprise Nadia on her birthday, but they introduce a disruptive, vaguely menacing vibe into the mix. The next thing you know, this romance has mutated into a surprise-filled thriller.

The Butterworth brothers—director-co-writer Jez, co-writer Tom, and producer Steve—seem to have been inspired by Jonathan Demme's equally fractured SOMETHING WILD, and while they finesse the sudden shift in tone less smoothly, it's still a deft balancing job. Kidman accomplishes a remarkable feat of transformation, adopting not only an accent, but a slightly seedy, faintly feral demeanor that almost makes you forget her icy good looks and fashion model's figure.

BISHOP'S WIFE, THE   🅳🆅🅳

1947   105m   bw   Comedy/Drama/Fantasy   ★★★
RKO   (U.S.)

Cary Grant *(Dudley)*, David Niven *(Henry Brougham)*, Loretta Young *(Julia Brougham)*, Monty Woolley *(Prof. Wutheridge)*, James Gleason *(Sylvester)*, Gladys Cooper *(Mrs. Hamilton)*, Elsa Lanchester *(Matilda)*, Sara Haden *(Mildred Cassaway)*, Karolyn Grimes *(Debby Brougham)*, Tito Vuolo *(Maggenti)*

p, Samuel Goldwyn; d, Henry Koster; w, Robert E. Sherwood, Leonardo Bercovici (based on a novel by Robert Nathan); ph, Gregg Toland; ed, Monica Collingwood; m, Hugo Friedhofer; art d, Charles Henderson; cos, Irene Sharaff

AAN Best Picture; AAN Best Director: Henry Koster; *AAN Best Film Editing:* Monica Collingwood; *AAN Best Score (Drama or Comedy):* Hugo Friedhofer; *AA Best Sound Recording:* Goldwyn Sound Department

A warm, sentimental comedy-fantasy, a follow-up to the similar but superior IT'S A WONDERFUL LIFE.

Niven plays an Episcopalian bishop praying for money to build a new church. His marriage is apparently over and his faith is quivering when Grant, an angel who uses his powers so sparingly that he might have been from the Welcome Wagon, arrives on the scene. Young, as Niven's wife, never learns Cary is from Up There as he unobtrusively helps her and Niven achieve some peace on earth and goodwill toward each other.

Under Koster's typically smooth direction, everyone seems to be having a good time, enjoying the script without mocking its blandness. The picture runs on a bit long and it does pale by comparison to the book, but it was a welcome smile in 1947 and has the same effect today. Popular and acclaimed in its day, the film was rather surprisingly nominated for Best Picture of the year.

BLACK AND WHITE IN COLOR   🅳🆅🅳
(LA VICTOIRE EN CHANTANT)
1976   100m   c   Drama/War   ★★★
Allied Artists   (France)   PG

Jean Carmet *(Sgt. Bosselet)*, Jacques Dufilho *(Paul Rechampot)*, Catherine Rouvel *(Marinette)*, Jacques Spiesser *(Hubert Fresnoy)*, Dora Doll *(Maryvonne)*, Maurice Barrier *(Caprice)*, Claude Legros *(Jacques Rechampot)*, Jacques Monnet *(Pere Simon)*, Peter Berling *(Pere Jean De La Croix)*, Marius Beugre Boignan *(Barthelemy)*

p, Arthur Cohn, Jacques Perrin, Giorgio Silagni; d, Jean-Jacques Annaud; w, Jean-Jacques Annaud, Georges Conchon; ph, Claude Agostini (Eastmancolor); ed, Francoise Bonnot; m, Pierre Bachelet; art d, Max Douy

AA Best Foreign Language Film

The winner of the 1976 Oscar for Best Foreign Film, this first feature from Annaud (THE NAME OF THE ROSE) is set in a French colonial outpost in 1915.

When Spiesser, a conscientious young geologist, writes home to Paris to lament the "dangers" of Africa (chief among which is boredom), he begs for newspapers and books from home. Some time later the papers arrive, bringing the news—six months late—that France is at war with Germany. This poses a bit of a problem at the outpost for a number of reasons: the colonists are friendly with a group of neighboring Germans; their commander, Carmet, has never been in battle; and they have no trained army. Rising to the challenge, Carmet conscripts all the healthy male natives who live near the outpost and teaches them to speak French, operate bayonets, wear shoes, and sing "La Marseillaise." Ultimately, the natives are even honored with French names.

A biting satire on war, colonialism, and French patriotism which sometimes does not escape the character types it aims to parody, BLACK AND WHITE IN COLOR juxtaposes scenes of gaiety and humor with the brutalities of racism and war. The result is something of a combination of Philippe de Broca's cult antiwar satire, KING OF HEARTS, and Jamie Uys's THE GODS MUST BE CRAZY. Deserving of special mention is the playful score by Bachelet.

BLACK CAT, THE

1934　70m　bw　Horror　　　★★★★½
Universal　　(U.S.)

Boris Karloff *(Hjalmar Poelzig)*, Bela Lugosi *(Dr. Vitus Verdegast)*, David Manners *(Peter Allison)*, Julie Bishop, billed as Jacqueline Wells *(Joan Allison)*, Lucille Lund *(Karen)*, Egon Brecher *(Majordomo)*, Henry Armetta *(Sergeant)*, Albert Conti *(Lieutenant)*, Anna Duncan *(Maid)*, Herman Bing *(Car Steward)*

p, Carl Laemmle Jr.; d, Edgar G. Ulmer; w, Edgar G. Ulmer, Peter Ruric (based on the story by Edgar Allan Poe); ph, John Mescall; ed, Ray Curtiss; art d, Charles D. Hall

The first and best teaming of horror stars Karloff and Lugosi was this bizarre, haunting, and hypnotic film by director Ulmer.

Not an adaptation of Poe but rather a strikingly effective evocation of the twisted world of his literature, the story concerns a young couple, Peter (Manners) and Joan (Wells), who meet mysterious scientist Dr. Vitus Verdegast (Lugosi) while on their honeymoon in Budapest. The trio wind up at the home of Verdegast's old "friend" Hjalmar Poelzig (Karloff), an architect living atop a mountain in a modernistic, Art Deco mansion.

As it turns out, Poelzig is the leader of a satanic cult who, as a commander during WWI, caused the capture of Verdegast and the deaths of thousands of their countrymen in a bloody battle. While Verdegast rotted in prison, the architect stole his wife, who later died (he keeps her corpse in a glass case), then married Verdegast's daughter. Verdegast has now come for revenge, and Peter and Joan find themselves caught in a deadly game of cat and mouse.

A remarkable study of evil containing some unusually brutal scenes in its frenzied climax, THE BLACK CAT is still one of the most affecting horrors the genre has ever produced. With supreme directorial skill, Ulmer infuses the film with an overwhelming sense of unease, eroticism, and dread that remains powerful to this day. The literate script, magnificent set design, superbly fluid camerawork, and stunning performances by Karloff (whose character was inspired by occult hedonist Aleister Crowley) and Lugosi lend the film a timeless quality. Ulmer would go on to direct such low-budget classics as DETOUR (1945), but this is his masterpiece.

BLACK CAT, WHITE CAT

(CRNA MACKA, BELI MACOR)
1998　129m　c　Comedy　　　★★★½
CIBY 2000/Pandora/Komuna/U Saranji Sa　　R
(France/Germany)

Bajram Severdzan *(Matko Destanov)*, Doctor Kolja *(Matko Destanov)*, Florijan Ajdini *(Zare Destanov)*, Jas'ar Destani *(Grga Major)*, Adnan Bekir *(Little Grga)*, Zabit Mehmedovski *(Zarije Destinov)*, Sabri Sulejmani *(Grga Pitic)*, Srdan Todorovic *(Dadan)*, Salija Ibraimova *(Afrodita)*, Stojan Sotirov *(Bugarski Carinik)*

p, Karl Baumgartner; d, Emir Kusturica; w, Gordan Mihic, Emir Kusturica; ph, Thierry Arbogast; ed, Svetolik Mica Zajc; m, Dr. Nelle Karajlic', Voja Aralica, Dejan Sparavalo, Emir Kusturica; prod d, Milenko Jeremic'; cos, Nebojs'a Lipanovic'

Two years after the bitter controversy surrounding his 1996 masterpiece, UNDERGROUND, made Bosnian-born director Emir Kusturica swear off filmmaking, he changed his mind. For his welcome return, Kusturica reunited with screenwriter Gordan Mihic and revisited the world of their picaresque 1991 epic, TIME OF THE GYPSIES.

In the small Yugoslavian town of Surduk, on the banks of the Danube, ne'er-do-well Matko Destanov (Bajram

Severdzan) hatches a crazy plan to steal an entire trainload of petrol and turns to Dadan (Srdan Todorovic) for help. Bad move: Dadan is a sleazy, gold-plated gangster and alleged war criminal who's only looking out for his own cocaine-pumped self and three homely sisters. Unbeknownst to Matko, Dadan steals the train right out from under him, then demands that the now destitute Matko either return the pay off money Dadan invested in the scheme or agree to marry off his 17-year-old son (Florijan Ajdini) to Dadan's 23-year-old sister, a grouchy midget named Afrodita (Salija Ibraimova).

What follows very nearly verges on chaos: a wild, endlessly inventive romp set in a post-war world so full of machine guns and hand grenades that people barely flinch when one or the other goes off; where corruption is so pervasive that an honest swindler like Matko can hardly make a living. But it's also a joyful place where entertainment means a hefty singer with a crescent-shaped hairdo pulling nails from a board of wood with her buttocks, and there's a surprising warmth and even a little optimism behind Kusturica's gallows humor. Like the happy-marriage ending and the fornicating cats—one black, one white—that prowl the film, there's even hope for the end of murderous divisiveness.

BLACK CAULDRON, THE　▮DVD▮

1985　82m　c　Animated　　　★★★½
Walt Disney Productions/Silver Screen Partners II　　PG
(U.S.)

VOICES OF: Grant Bardsley *(Taran)*, Susan Sheridan *(Eilonwy)*, Freddie Jones *(Dallben)*, Nigel Hawthorne *(Fflewddur)*, Arthur Malet *(King Eidilleg)*, John Byner *(Gurgi/Doli)*, Lindsay Rich, Brandon Call, Gregory Levinson *(Fairfolk)*, Eda Reiss Merin *(Orddu)*

p, Joe Hale; d, Ted Berman, Richard Rich; w, David Jonas, Vance Gerry, Ted Berman, Richard Rich, Joe Hale, Al Wilson, Roy Morita, Peter Young, Art Stevens, Rosemary Anne Sisson, Roy Edward Disney (based on the five novels of the series *The Chronicles of Prydain* by Lloyd Alexander); ed, Jim Melton, Jim Koford, Armetta Jackson; m, Elmer Bernstein; anim, Walt Stanchfield

A glorious return to the days at Disney when animation was full and detail was everything, THE BLACK CAULDRON is betrayed by a routine storyline which fails to grip the imagination in the same way that such classics as PINOCCHIO or DUMBO do, but it's a remarkable achievement nonetheless.

A familiar sword-and-sorcery yarn, the story tells of Taran, an aspiring warrior, and his battle supreme with the villainous Horned King, who wants to gain possession of the Black Cauldron, a source of supernatural power. Taran knows that if the Horned King gets the Cauldron, civilization will cease. Taran is joined in his struggle by Eilonwy, a princess; a psychic pig named Hen Wen; Gurgi, a sycophantic creature; and a bevy of minifairies.

Only the second animated feature to be shot in 70mm (the first such widescreen extravaganza being 1959's SLEEPING BEAUTY), THE BLACK CAULDRON used more than 2.5 million drawings to bring its tale vividly to life. Every leaf has been patiently drawn, the depth of field is remarkable, the angles are chosen with care, and the result is a state-of-the-art cartoon that should be seen by anyone who loves the craft. Despite its drawbacks as entertainment, it remains one of the best technical cartoon features ever produced by Disney.

BLACK HAWK DOWN　▮DVD▮

2001　150m　c　War　　　★★★
Revolution Studios/Jerry Bruckheimer Films/　　R
Scott Free Productions　　(U.S.)

Josh Hartnett *(Eversmann)*, Ewan McGregor *(Grimes)*, Tom Sizemore *(McKnight)*, Eric Bana *(Hoot)*, William Fichtner

(Sanderson), Ewen Bremner *(Nelson)*, Sam Shepard *(Garrison)*, Gabriel Casseus *(Kurth)*, Kim Coates *(Wex)*, Hugh Dancy *(Schmid)*

p, Jerry Bruckheimer, Ridley Scott; d, Ridley Scott; w, Ken Nolan (based on the book by Mark Bowden); ph, Slawomir Idziak; ed, Pietro Scalia; m, Hans Zimmer; prod d, Arthur Max; art d, Pier Luigi Basile, Gianni Giovagnoni, Ivica Husnjak, Keith Pain, Cliff Robinson, Marco Trentini; fx, Neil Corbould, Tim Burke (visual), David M.V. Jones (visual), Nathan McGuiness (visual); cos, Sammy Howarth-Sheldon, David Murphy

AA Best Film Editing: Pietro Scalia; *AA Best Sound:* Mike Minkler, Myron Nettinga, Chris Munro; *AAN Best Cinematography:* Slawomir Idziak; *AAN Best Director:* Ridley Scott

What should have been a piece of cake wound up being the longest sustained firefight involving U.S. troops since the end of the Vietnam War. On October 3, 1993, an elite team of Delta Force operatives were dropped onto the streets of Mogadishu, Somalia. The target: a two-story building said to contain two high-ranking lieutenants of Mohamed Farah Aidid, the ruthless Somali warlord. Securing the perimeter around the building were some 75 U.S. Rangers, lowered onto the streets from the bellies of four Black Hawk helicopters. Waiting a few blocks away was a 12-vehicle convoy that was supposed to hustle everybody out once the grab was made. But no sooner did the Rangers touch ground than the streets erupted in a blizzard of bullets, the ground convoy became hopelessly lost and, at the height of the confusion, the unthinkable happened: Two of the circling Black Hawks—imposing symbols of U.S. military might—were downed by rocket-propelled grenades. Over 100 U.S. soldiers suddenly found themselves trapped in the middle of a rapidly escalating nightmare.

Black Hawk Down: A Story of Modern War, Mark Bowden's pulse-pounding account of the incident, was both a tribute to the extraordinary courage of the troops and a cautionary tale about U.S. involvement in other nations' civil wars. But director Ridley Scott cannily justifies the operation from the start, opening his film with haunting images of starving Somalis, and is careful not to depict too much so-called "collateral damage." More than 500 Somalis, many of them unarmed women and children, were killed during the engagement, but we see only ferocious-looking militiamen dying on the streets of "Mog."

BLACK NARCISSUS 📀

1946 100m c   Drama   ★★★★★
Archer   (U.K.)

Deborah Kerr *(Sister Clodagh)*, Sabu *(Dilip Rai)*, David Farrar *(Mr. Dean)*, Flora Robson *(Sister Philippa)*, Jean Simmons *(Kanchi)*, Esmond Knight *(Gen. Toda Rai)*, Kathleen Byron *(Sister Ruth)*, Jenny Laird *(Sister Honey)*, Judith Furse *(Sister Briony)*, May Hallatt *(Angu Ayah)*

p, Michael Powell, Emeric Pressburger; d, Michael Powell, Emeric Pressburger; w, Michael Powell, Emeric Pressburger (based on the novel by Rumer Godden); ph, Jack Cardiff (Technicolor); ed, Reginald Mills; m, Brian Easdale; prod d, Alfred Junge; fx, W. Percy Day (process shots); cos, Hein Heckroth

AA Best Color Cinematography: Jack Cardiff; *AA Best Art Direction-Set Decoration (Color):* Alfred Junge (Art Direction)

A stunner from one of the great collaborative teams in the history of cinema and an anomaly in British film of the 1940s. Powell and Pressburger continued their string of daring, idiosyncratic films (LIFE AND DEATH OF COLONEL BLIMP, A MATTER OF LIFE AND DEATH, THE RED SHOES) with this full-blown melodrama concerning a group of Anglican nuns who attempt to establish a

school and hospital at an ancient ruler's castle-cum-bordello high in the Himalayas.

Kerr is highly effective as the young, ambitious Sister Clodagh, given her first taste of authority but bedeviled by the climate, the natives, the cynical but sexy British government agent Mr. Dean (Farrar) and her own and her colleagues' emotional weaknesses. Indian-born juvenile actor Sabu, in his last major role, plays a rich, bejeweled young general (who wears Black Narcissus perfume) bewitched by a seductive native girl (Simmons, in an odd but highly effective bit of casting). The turbulent chain of events reaches its climax when Sister Ruth (Byron, superb in a performance which should have insured her career) becomes unhinged over her desires for Mr. Dean and her jealousy of Sister Clodagh.

An odd, unsettling film which suggests the dangers of both emotional restraint and unchecked passion, BLACK NARCISSUS is also one of the most visually beautiful films ever made in color. The acting of the leads excels, and they are splendidly abetted by Robson, Furst, and Laird as the other nuns and by Knight and Hallatt as, respectively, a paternal ruler and a hilariously cynical housekeeper.

Full of hysteria (especially at the cathartic climax, where Byron's makeup antedates that of THE EXORCIST) and continuing Powell and Pressburger's implicit critique of British stiff-upper-lip attitudes, BLACK NARCISSUS was ahead of its time, prefiguring the later melodramas of everyone from Sirk to Fassbinder to Ken Russell. The scenes where Sister Clodagh recalls her happy, romantic days before entering the convent were at first cut by censors. The film deservedly won the Oscars for color cinematography and art direction.

BLACK ORPHEUS 📀

(ORFEU NEGRO)
1959 100m c   Drama   ★★★½
Lopert   (France/Italy/Brazil)

Breno Mello *(Orfeo)*, Marpessa Dawn *(Eurydice)*, Lourdes de Oliveira *(Mira)*, Lea Garcia *(Serafina)*, Adhemar da Silva *(Death)*, Alexandro Constantino *(Hermes)*, Waldetar de Souza *(Chico)*, Jorge dos Santos *(Benedito)*, Aurino Cassanio *(Zeca)*

p, Sacha Gordine; d, Marcel Camus; w, Jacques Viot, Marcel Camus (based on the play "Orfeu da Conceicao" by Vinicius de Moraes); ph, Jean Bourgoin (CinemaScope, Eastmancolor); ed, Andree Feix; m, Antonio Carlos Jobim, Luiz Bonfa

AA Best Foreign Language Film

The Orpheus myth is transplanted onto the soil of Rio de Janeiro during Carnival—the one time of the year that calls for unrestrained celebration, music, dance, and costumes.

Orfeo (Mello) is a streetcar conductor and guitarist engaged to Mira (de Oliveira), an exotic and vivacious woman who lives as if every day were Carnival. However, anyone familiar with the legend of Orpheus (as the man in Rio's marriage office is) knows that he is destined to love Eurydice (Dawn—oddly enough, a dancer born in Pittsburgh), personified here as a newcomer to Rio who arrives in town to visit her cousin Serafina (Garcia). Eurydice has fled her hometown because she was being followed by a mysterious stranger, one who has followed her to Rio and has disguised himself as Death for Carnival. In order to save Eurydice, Orfeo must travel into the Underworld and bring her back to the world of the living.

From the opening shot, in which two Brazilian musicians literally burst through the frame, one can sense the explosiveness of BLACK ORPHEUS. Like Carnival, the film frame dances, the soundtrack sings, and the costumes swirl in an explosion of color and light. Besides its exhilarating style, however, the well-acted film works as an effective translation of the classic Greek myth into a Brazilian romance.

More successful as a travelogue of Brazilian scenery than an exploration of the country's folk culture, BLACK ORPHEUS was the second film from Camus, a Frenchman who traveled to Brazil to make this picture and would never again repeat its success. BLACK ORPHEUS received instant international acclaim and was honored with the Golden Palm at Cannes and the Academy Award for Best Foreign Film.

BLACK RAIN   *DVD*
(KUROI AME)
1989 123m bw Drama   ★★★½
Imamura/Hayashibara/Tohokushinsha   (Japan)

Yoshiko Tanaka *(Yasuko)*, Kazuo Kitamura *(Shigematsu)*, Etsuko Ichihara *(Shigako)*, Shoichi Ozawa *(Shokichi)*, Norihei Miki *(Kotaro)*, Keisuke Ishida *(Yuichi)*

p, Hisa Iino; d, Shohei Imamura; w, Shohei Imamura, Toshiro Ishido (based on a novel by Masuji Ibuse); ph, Takashi Kawamata; ed, Hajime Okayasu; m, Toru Takemitsu; art d, Hisao Inagaki

A potent if flawed study of the dropping of the atomic bomb on Hiroshima and its aftereffects, focusing on the dark destiny of one family caught in the holocaust.

The film opens with the bombing, showing the blinding flash of light, the shock wave that disintegrates people and buildings, and the black rain falling on young Yasuko (Tanaka), her aunt Shigako (Ichihara) and her uncle Shigematsu (Kitamura), which exposes them all to radiation poisoning. Five years pass, and the family's main problem is now the difficulty of finding a husband for Yasuko, whose contamination leaves her a pariah in the community. The locals have become used to funeral processions and to the taking of various home remedies; the desperate Shigako even turns to a noisy charlatan of a faith healer. Yasuko gradually becomes involved with Yuichi (Ishida), whose nerves have been shattered by the war, but the couple's time together is fatefully limited.

Imamura films his story in stark, elegant black and white, creating both haunting imagery (e.g. the escaping townspeople looking back at the mushroom cloud forming behind them) and a distance from the story's drama. Similar distancing is evoked by the soap opera treatment of the story and the bewildered resignation of the protagonists, never once expressing either real rage or sorrow at their plight. What is less clear is the critical perspective Imamura (or the audience) can take via such distancing. The problems of traditional Japanese formality are highlighted, as are the prejudices held by the Japanese against the bomb's victims (*hibakusha* in Japanese) and the horrors of warfare which bring about such conditions, but no single critique is fully fleshed out.

The film is full of touching moments, but at times the emotional resonance is characteristic of second-rate Hollywood, as when Yuichi's phobia of the sounds of moving vehicles vanishes during an ambulance ride at the film's end. In short, the film is powerfully grim but does not capture the horror of the bomb's blast, it is full of cool observation yet cannot resist idealizing the central family unit.

BLACK ROBE   *DVD*
1991 100m c Adventure/Drama/Historical   ★★★½
Alliance Entertainment/Samson Productions/   R
Cinegramme V   (Canada/Australia)

Lothaire Bluteau *(Father Laforgue)*, Aden Young *(Daniel)*, Sandrine Holt *(Annuka)*, August Schellenberg *(Chomina)*, Tantoo Cardinal *(Chomina's Wife)*, Billy Two Rivers *(Ougebmat)*, Lawrence Bayne *(Neehatin)*, Harrison Liu *(Awondoie)*, Wesley Cote *(Oujita)*, Frank Wilson *(Father Jerome)*

p, Robert Lantos, Stephane Reichel, Sue Milliken; d, Bruce Beresford; w, Brian Moore (from novel *Black Robe* by Brian Moore); ph, Peter James; ed, Tim Wellburn; m, Georges Delerue; prod d, Herbert Pinter; art d, Gavin Mitchell; fx, Louis Craig, Francois Dagenais, Darren Perks; cos, Renee April, John Hay

Despite an occasionally plodding screenplay, this white-man-in-the-wilderness drama goes DANCES WITH WOLVES one better by showing more genuine respect for its subject. Directed by Bruce Beresford, BLACK ROBE was adapted by Brian Moore from his own novel, which, in turn, was based on letters and journals written by Jesuit missionaries, whom the Indians dubbed "black robes," in the New World during the 17th century.

The story revolves around Father Laforgue (JESUS OF MONTREAL's Lothaire Bluteau) who is sent by Champlain (Jean Brousseau), the founder and governor of Quebec, 1,500 miles north to a frontier Jesuit mission to assist in the conversion of the Huron tribe to Catholicism in 1634. Pledging to guide and protect Laforgue, Algonquin leader Chomina (August Schellenberg) brings his wife, young son and beautiful teenage daughter Annuka (Sandrine Holt), as well as a small party of braves and their families. Driven as much by his passion for Annuka as his aspirations to the priesthood, young French settler Daniel (Aden Young) also volunteers to accompany Laforgue on what turns into a grueling journey.

Returning to the theme of his first international hit, BREAKER MORANT, as well as the more recent MISTER JOHNSON, Beresford's emphasis in BLACK ROBE is on European presumption in forcing native peoples to adopt Western culture. Nevertheless, BLACK ROBE tries to distinguish itself by pretending to a basic, at times brutal, "honesty" in its depiction of native culture. The Indians in BLACK ROBE aren't the starry-eyed noble savages that strain credibility in DANCES WITH WOLVES. Far from it: there are scenes of Indian brutishness that rival anything in overtly racist Hollywood films. These are balanced by a sympathetic portrayal of Laforgue's Indian companions, who appear as relatively complex human beings. Their spiritual beliefs ultimately impress Laforgue, though it happens too late to be of much help to anyone.

BLACK ROSE, THE   *DVD*
1950 120m c Adventure   ★★★★
Fox   (U.S.)

Tyrone Power *(Walter of Gurnie)*, Orson Welles *(Bayan)*, Cecile Aubry *(Maryam)*, Jack Hawkins *(Tristram Griffin)*, Michael Rennie *(King Edward)*, Finlay Currie *(Alfgar)*, Herbert Lom *(Anthemus)*, Mary Clare *(Countess Eleanor of Lessford)*, Robert Blake, billed as Bobby Blake *(Mahmoud)*, Alfonso Bedoya *(Lu Chung)*

p, Louis D. Lighton; d, Henry Hathaway; w, Talbot Jennings (based on the novel by Thomas B. Costain); ph, Jack Cardiff (Technicolor); ed, Manuel Del Campo; m, Richard Addinsell; art d, Paul Sheriff, William C. Andrews; fx, W. Percy Day; cos, Michael Whittaker

AAN Best Costume Design (Color): Michael Whittaker

This sweeping, well-made, if somewhat derivative adventure epic stars Power as a nobleman in 13th-century England ostracized for leading a revolt against King Edward (Rennie) a Norman whom Power, a Saxon, refuses to serve.

Traveling as wanted men, Power and his archer companion (Hawkins) are picked up in Antioch by a powerful warlord (Welles), and accompany him to the court of Kublai Khan. One of the gifts Welles is taking to Khan is a Eurasian beauty (Aubry), who falls in love with Power. Once in the Chinese court, Power realizes that, though they are treated graciously, he and Hawkins cannot leave the palace. A daring escape through ancient underground tunnels, a dramatic separation, and a key reconciliation occur before love emerges triumphant.

A beautifully photographed (in England and North Africa) film whose chief merits are its exciting action sequences and lavish production (courtesy of five million dollars worth of Fox assets frozen in England), THE BLACK ROSE borrows liberally from such earlier efforts as THE ADVENTURES OF ROBIN HOOD and THE ADVENTURES OF MARCO POLO, but benefits considerably from the well-cast players. Power was losing the vigor and mobile features of his youth, but he is still an eminently suitable swashbuckler. Hawkins and Welles play their standardized roles with tongues firmly in cheek and Aubrey is very appealing as the heroine. Perhaps the only exception is the arresting Bedoya, whose telltale Mexican accent unfortunately belies his Asian characterization.

BLACK STALLION, THE   DVD

1979   118m   c   Adventure   ★★★★
UA   (U.S.)   G

Kelly Reno (*Alec Ramsey*), Mickey Rooney (*Henry Dailey*), Teri Garr (*Alec's Mother*), Clarence Muse (*Snoe*), Hoyt Axton (*Alec's Father*), Michael Higgins (*Neville*), Ed McNamara (*Jake*), Doghmi Larbi (*The Arab*), John Burton, John Buchanan (*Jockeys*)

p, Tom Sternberg, Fred Roos; d, Carroll Ballard; w, Melissa Mathison, Jeanne Rosenberg, William D. Wittliff (based on the novel by Walter Farley); ph, Caleb Deschanel; ed, Robert Dalva; m, Carmine Coppola

AAN Best Supporting Actor: Mickey Rooney; *AAN Best Film Editing:* Robert Dalva; *AA Special Achievement Award—Sound Editing:* Alan Splet

This touching and beautifully photographed, if slightly overlong, tale of a boy and his horse follows the escapades of young Alec Ramsey (Reno), who is traveling across the ocean with his father.

The ship sinks, and Alec is saved by Black, a handsome Arabian stallion the boy had befriended earlier in the journey. After being shipwrecked on a deserted island, Alec and Black are rescued and returned to their small-town home. Eventually, Black is cared for by former horse trainer Henry Dailey (Rooney), who later takes Kelly under his wing to be trained as a jockey. Naturally, it all leads up to the big race—a stunningly photographed sequence brimming with tension.

A simple film, sentimental but not mawkish, as enjoyable for adults as it is for children, THE BLACK STALLION is one of the finest movies about children and horses since Elizabeth Taylor was seen in NATIONAL VELVET. It's also a pleasure to see Rooney back in the saddle again, so to speak, and his lively character turn won him a much-deserved Oscar nomination for Best Supporting Actor. A sequel, THE BLACK STALLION RETURNS (1983), is more a Saharan adventure than a sports picture.

BLACK SUNDAY   DVD

(LA MASCHERA DEL DEMONIO)
1960   83m   bw   Horror   ★★★★½
(Italy)

Barbara Steele (*Witch Princess Katia*), John Richardson (*Dr. Gorobec*), Ivo Garrani (*Prince*), Andrea Cecchi (*Dr. Choma*), Arturo Dominici (*Javutich*), Enrico Olivieri (*Constantin*), Antonio Pierfederici (*the Pope*), Clara Bindi (*Innkeeper*), Germana Dominici (*His Daughter*), Mario Passante (*Nikita*)

p, Massimo De Rita; d, Mario Bava; w, Ennio De Concini, Mario Serandrei (based on a story by Nikolai Gogol); ph, Mario Bava, Ubaldo Terzano; ed, Mario Serandrei; m, Les Baxter; art d, Giorgio Giovannini

In 1630, a beautiful witch princess, Asa (Barbara Steele), who is a vampire, and her lover, Juvato (Arturo Dominici), are put to death by her vengeful brother. He has iron masks with spikes on the inside placed on both of their faces and then sledgehammered home. Two hundred years later, blood is accidentally spilled on Asa's face and she rises from the dead along with Juvato to wreak revenge on the descendants of those who executed her—including her look-alike, Katia (also played by Steele).

Beautifully photographed in black and white by Bava himself, BLACK SUNDAY is hypnotic and compelling. From the brutal opening to the resurrection of the vampires and the horrors that follow, Bava's camera effortlessly glides through the fogbound sets, presenting one incredible image after another. Bava exhibits a comparable command of sound and music—or the lack thereof—with some sequences played out in virtual silence. Steele is magnificent in her dual role as vengeful devil and vestal virgin. As the resurrected Asa, her beautiful face is both seductive and horrifying, bearing the terrible holes punched by the iron mask. The role catapulted her to horror-movie stardom. Unfortunately, when released in the U.S. by American International Pictures, BLACK SUNDAY was badly dubbed and a bombastic Les Baxter score was imposed over the original by Roberto Nicolosi.

BLACK SUNDAY   DVD

1977   143m   c   Action   ★★★★
Paramount   (U.S.)   R

Robert Shaw (*Kabakov*), Bruce Dern (*Lander*), Marthe Keller (*Dahlia*), Fritz Weaver (*Corley*), Steven Keats (*Moshevsky*), Bekim Fehmiu (*Fasil*), Michael V. Gazzo (*Muzi*), William Daniels (*Pugh*), Walter Gotell (*Col. Riaf*), Victor Campos (*Nageeb*)

p, Robert Evans; d, John Frankenheimer; w, Ernest Lehman, Ivan Moffat, Kenneth Ross; ph, John A. Alonzo (Movielab Color); ed, Tom Rolf; m, John Williams

One of the best of the disaster films of the 1970s, the genuinely disturbing BLACK SUNDAY is likely to cause nightmares long after you've seen it. Keller and Fehmiu portray "Black September" agents (in a takeoff on the killers who terrorized the 1972 Olympics) who plan to hijack the Goodyear Blimp and send it into the teeming Super Bowl crowd firing thousands of steel darts. Dern, in typical and fine form as a deranged Vietnam veteran, is hired to pilot the killer blimp. Shaw, as an Israeli major, and Weaver, playing a heroic FBI agent, smoothly represent law and order. The scene where the blimp comes over the top of Miami's Orange Bowl is guaranteed to have you squirming in your seat. Far superior to the similar TWO MINUTE WARNING (1976), BLACK SUNDAY benefits from its technical skill, drawn-out suspense and developed characterizations, though the film could have been even more effectively tight with a shorter running time.

BLACK SWAN, THE

1942   85m   c   Adventure   ★★★★½
Fox   (U.S.)

Tyrone Power (*James Waring*), Maureen O'Hara (*Margaret Denby*), Laird Cregar (*Capt. Henry Morgan*), Thomas Mitchell (*Tommy Blue*), George Sanders (*Capt. Billy Leech*), Anthony Quinn (*Wogan*), George Zucco (*Lord Denby*), Edward Ashley (*Roger Ingram*), Fortunio Bonanova (*Don Miguel*), Stuart Robertson (*Capt. Graham*) p, Robert Bassler; d, Henry King; w, Ben Hecht, Seton I. Miller (based on the novel by Rafael Sabatini); ph, Leon Shamroy (Technicolor); ed, Barbara McLean; m, Alfred Newman; art d, Richard Day, James Basevi; cos, Earl Luick

---

AA Best Color Cinematography: Leon Shamroy; AAN Best Score (Drama or Comedy): Alfred Newman; AAN Best Special Effects: Fred Sersen, Roger Heman, George Leverett

---

Along with THE MARK OF ZORRO, the peak of Tyrone Power's career as a swashbuckler.

A sweeping pirate epic with Power as an aide to notorious buccaneer Henry Morgan (Cregar), the film opens with Morgan pardoned from the gallows and sent to Jamaica as its new governor. Trying to prevent his former associates from continuing their villainous activities, Morgan encounters resistance from two renegades (Sanders and Quinn). Power, meanwhile, falls for the daughter (O'Hara) of the former governor, but she spurns his brazen advances. Although kidnapping her and taking her along on his warship doesn't initially help matters, things change when Sanders and Quinn overpower his ship, forcing Power to fight for the woman he loves.

The story and dialogue smack of the Errol Flynn adventure CAPTAIN BLOOD, but the film employs its cliches with such overwhelming vigor and good humor that they seem like old friends. Even though his physique isn't quite up to the more beefcake aspects of the hardsell by the producers, Power is full of marvelous dash and derring-do. Cregar, all hearty bravado, is equally wonderful, his enormous body bedecked in wigs and finery, and the practically unrecognizable Sanders, sporting a thick red wig and beard, is quite effective as a less civilized type of villain than those he usually played. The ravishing, flame-haired, underrated O'Hara, too, is in her element as the feisty heroine and the result of all this happy casting is lavish Hollywoodiana at its sporting best.

BLACKBOARD JUNGLE   *DVD*
1955 100m bw Drama   ★★★½
MGM   (U.S.)

Glenn Ford *(Richard Dadier)*, Anne Francis *(Anne Dadier)*, Louis Calhern *(Jim Murdock)*, Margaret Hayes *(Lois Judby Hammond)*, John Hoyt *(Mr. Warneke)*, Richard Kiley *(Joshua Y. Edwards)*, Emile Meyer *(Mr. Halloran)*, Warner Anderson *(Dr. Bradley)*, Basil Ruysdael *(Prof. A.R. Kraal)*, Sidney Poitier *(Gregory W. Miller)*

p, Pandro S. Berman; d, Richard Brooks; w, Richard Brooks (based on the novel by Evan Hunter); ph, Russell Harlan; ed, Ferris Webster; m, Charles Wolcott; art d, Cedric Gibbons, Randall Duell

---

AAN Best Screenplay: Richard Brooks; AAN Best B/W Cinematography: Russell Harlan; AAN Best Film Editing: Ferris Webster; AAN Best Art Direction-Set Decoration (B/W): Cedric Gibbons (Art Direction), Randall Duell (Art Direction), Edwin B Willis (Set Decoration), Henry Grace (Set Decoration)

This searing if somewhat overrated condemnation of juvenile delinquency brought attention to some of the problems afflicting urban high schools and is notable as a reflection of certain 1950s social mores. Rendered in effectively grainy black and white and using violence with considerable impact, the dutifully sincere screenplay by director Brooks unfortunately substitutes a more upbeat ending for Evan Hunter's original.

Ford, in a typically edgy but likable, effective performance, is a newly returned veteran who takes his first teaching job in an inner-city school. He soons runs afoul of some of his tougher students, who are only hanging around until they are old enough to get jobs. Several story lines run through the film: Ford's wife (Francis, failing to transcend an ill-conceived part), tries to convince him to find another job; another teacher (Kiley) thinks he can reason with the kids but soon finds out

how wrong he is; an aging teacher (Calhern) just wants to survive until he can retire; and a pretty young teacher (Hayes) is frightened by her new assignment.

Vic Morrow is excellent as the leader of a gang of thugs, as is Poitier in a star-making performance, though at age 31 he unfortunately doesn't convince as a high school student. Future director Paul Mazursky and Jamie Farr (then Jameel Farah) play other students. BLACKBOARD JUNGLE also brought rock'n'roll to movie audiences with a bang, courtesy of Bill Haley and the Comets, who sing "Rock Around the Clock."

BLACKMAIL   *DVD*
1929 75m bw Mystery   ★★★★
Elstree/Wardour/British Intl.   (U.K.)

Anny Ondra *(Alice White)*, John Longden *(Frank Webber)*, Donald Calthrop *(Tracy)*, Cyril Ritchard *(The Artist)*, Sara Allgood *(Mrs. White)*, Charles Paton *(Mr. White)*, Harvey Braban *(Inspector)*, Phyllis Monkman *(Gossip)*, Hannah Jones *(Landlady)*, Percy Parsons *(Crook)*

p, John Maxwell; d, Alfred Hitchcock; w, Alfred Hitchcock, Benn W. Levy, Charles Bennett (based on the play by Charles Bennett); ph, Jack Cox; ed, Emile De Ruelle; m, John Hubert Bath, Henry Stafford, John Reynders

---

The first all-talkie for both Great Britain and Alfred Hitchcock, this adaptation of a 1928 play stars Ondra as Alice White, a young British woman who is to be married to Scotland Yard detective Frank Webber (Longdon). Alice, however, is drawn to a handsome artist (Ritchard), whom she ends up stabbing when he tries to force her to model nude. Of course, she soon falls prey to the crime of the title and of course her boyfriend heads up the murder investigation.

Although BLACKMAIL was completed and released as a silent film, Hitchcock was ordered by the studio to add some dialogue sequences for a "talkie" release in some specially equipped theaters. The main problem was Ondra's heavy Polish accent. Rather than reshoot all of her scenes, though, actress Joan Barry was brought in to dub the star's voice. This procedure was crude in those historic early sound days: Barry had to be positioned off camera next to Ondra and speak the lines as the leading lady mouthed them, and to some extent the effort shows in Ondra's somewhat strained performance. The film, though, was a great success, artistically and technically. Even though the film contains scenes obviously shot silent to which one telling sound was later added, the exploration of the medium's new capabilities is downright palpable. Moodily filmed in an effectively Germanic style, with a neat supporting turn by Calthrop and fine set pieces such as the chase through the British Museum, BLACKMAIL still plays well, and is a suitable precursor to the master director's later work. In one of his earliest cameos, Hitchcock appears as a subway rider annoyed by a pesky boy while trying to read a book.

BLACULA   *DVD*
1972 92m c Horror   ★★★
AIP   (U.S.)   PG

William Marshall *(Blacula)*, Vonetta McGee *(Tina)*, Denise Nicholas *(Michelle)*, Thalmus Rasulala *(Gordon Thomas)*, Gordon Pinsent *(Lt. Peters)*, Charles McCauley *(Dracula)*, Emily Yancy *(Nancy)*, Lance Taylor Sr. *(Swenson)*, Ted Harris *(Bobby)*, Rick Metzler *(Billy)*

p, Joseph T. Naar; d, William Crain; w, Joan Torres, Raymond Koenig; ph, John Stevens (Movielab Color); ed, Allan Jacobs; m, Gene Page; art d, Walter Scott Herndon

---

If BLACKENSTEIN was one of the worst blaxploitation films ever made, BLACULA is easily one of the best. Respected stage actor Marshall is outstanding in this subtle tongue-in-cheek version of the vampire legend. Action begins in the 18th century, when an African prince (Marshall) is visiting Transylvania There he is attacked by Count Dracula (McCauley), who makes him into one of the undead and renames him Blacula. Two hundred years later the story picks up in Los Angeles. A couple of fey interior designers have bought the contents of the Castle Dracula, including Blacula's coffin. Soon Blacula is romping around L.A. biting necks and chasing after the beautiful Tina (McGee), whom he believes is his reincarnated wife. Enter police pathologist Rasulala (Thomas) who thinks he has a vampire on his hands and is determined to end Blacula's reign of terror. Although BLACULA is surprisingly conventional (given the concept's potential) and painfully low-budget, the hammy performance by Marshall makes it enjoyable. A sequel—SCREAM, BLACULA, SCREAM—followed in 1973.

BLADE 📀

1998 110m c Horror/Action ★★
Amen Ra Films/Imaginary Forces/New Line R
(U.S.)

Wesley Snipes *(Blade)*, Stephen Dorff *(Deacon Frost)*, Kris Kristofferson *(Abraham Whistler)*, Kevin Patrick Walls *(Krieger)*, N'Bushe Wright *(Karen)*, Donal Logue *(Quinn)*, Arly Jover *(Mercury)*, Udo Kier *(Dragonetti)*, Traci Lords *(Racquel)*, Eric Edwards *(Pearl)*

p, Peter Frankfurt, Wesley Snipes, Robert Engelman; d, Stephen Norrington; w, David S. Goyer (based on characters created for Marvel Comics by Marv Wolfman and Gene Colan); ph, Theo Van de Sande; ed, Paul Rubell; m, Mark Isham; prod d, Kirk M. Petruccelli; art d, Barry Chusid; fx, Lou Carlucci; cos, Sanja Milkovic Hays

A vampire slayer flick that's better left buried. Hailed as one of the first African-American comic-book superheroes, Blade first appeared as a Marvel Comics character in 1973, so there should be plenty of material for the filmmakers to drawn on. But instead of plot, we're given a lot of breathlessly delivered back story, overdesigned sets, and Stephen Norrington's flat, suspense-defying direction.

Whether you knew it or not, vampires and humans have coexisted in relative harmony for thousands of years. An ancient race of "true blood" undead (those who were born vampires), led by the aristocratic Dragonetti (Udo Kier), has quietly infiltrated the human political and financial infrastructure, using the lazy centuries at their disposal to amass real estate and cash that they carefully stow in offshore accounts. But all that's about to change: Deacon Frost (Stephen Dorff)—a young "impure" vampire (born human, but "turned" as a child)—is determined to destroy the old vampire society and, by awakening an all-powerful blood god, turn Earth into the planet of the vampires. Enter Blade (Wesley Snipes), fearless vampire killer extraordinaire. Blade's human mother was bitten by a vampire shortly before giving birth, empowering her son with all the vampire strengths and none of their weaknesses, save one: Blade craves human blood, and must feed unless he's regularly dosed with a special serum. Equipped with a wicked titanium sword, a fanny-pack full of anti-vampire devices, a crusty sidekick (Kris Kristofferson) and a feisty gal-pal hematologist (N'Bushe Wright) who's looking to cure her own incipient vampirism, Blade sets out to save the world from the coming vampire apocalypse.

Oh, that anxious and complicated subtext! Throughout the film, vampirism is equated with the power elite, sexually transmitted viruses and, strangely enough, black identity: in the film's most uncomfortable moment, Frost accuses Blade, who passes for human, of playing Uncle Tom. Not that the film would be much fun without the undercurrents,

however contradictory: the few good lines go to Kristofferson and the ever-amusing Kier, and Snipes's considerable energy is buried under an affectless, Terminator-style demeanor. Though the sneering, snarling Dorff seems ready to rumble, there's precious little for him to, er, sink his teeth into. An endless parade of fight sequences entitled BLADE 2 appeared in 2002.

BLADE RUNNER 📀

1982 114m c Science Fiction ★★★★
The Ladd Company/Sir Run Run Shaw (U.S.) R

Harrison Ford *(Rick Deckard)*, Rutger Hauer *(Roy Batty)*, Sean Young *(Rachael)*, Edward James Olmos *(Gaff)*, M. Emmet Walsh *(Bryant)*, Daryl Hannah *(Pris)*, William Sanderson *(J.F. Sebastian)*, Brion James *(Leon)*, Joseph Turkel *(Tyrell)*, Joanna Cassidy *(Zhora)*

p, Michael Deeley; d, Ridley Scott; w, Hampton Fancher, David Peoples (based on the novel *Do Androids Dream of Electric Sheep?* by Philip K. Dick); ph, Jordan Cronenweth (Panavision, Technicolor); ed, Terry Rawlings; m, Vangelis; art d, David L. Snyder; fx, Douglas Trumbull, Richard Yuricich, David Dryer; cos, Charles Knode, Michael Kaplan

AAN Best Art Direction-Set Decoration: Lawrence G. Paull (Art Direction), David L. Snyder (Art Direction), Linda DeScenna (Set Decoration); *AAN Best Visual Effects:* Douglas Trumbull, Richard Yuricich, David Dryer

One of the most visually influential science fiction films ever made, BLADE RUNNER has a history as labyrinthine as any of its futuristic film noir sets. A fascinatingly contemplative detective story about a world-weary android-killer and his renegade prey, it has attracted a sizeable cult audience and retains a unique place in cinema.

Los Angeles, year 2019. Cynical ex-cop Deckard (Harrison Ford) is a retired assassin of rogue androids (called "replicants"). His former boss, Bryant (M. Emmet Walsh), presses him into service: he is to kill a group of physically superior replicants that are on the loose after escaping from an "off-world" colony. Deckard visits the Tyrell Corporation, where he encounters mogul Eldon Tyrell (Joseph Turkel) and his assistant, Rachael (Sean Young). Tyrell informs Deckard that Rachael is a new breed of replicant—implanted with memories, she believes herself to be human. Bent on speaking to Tyrell in order to find out what their "termination dates" are, two of the replicants—Roy Batty (Rutger Hauer) and Pris (Daryl Hannah)—insinuate themselves into the home of geneticist J.F. Sebastian (William Sanderson), who created the replicant design for Tyrell. In the meantime, two more of the replicants have been disposed of and Deckard has become romantically obsessed with Rachael.

A critical and commercial flop in its initial, 116-minute domestic release, BLADE RUNNER has been shown in numerous versions in the years since. Most notable are the original theatrical cut, an "unrated version" (featuring additional violent footage) prepared for home-video release, and director Ridley Scott's official "director's cut," which offered some key variations on the original theatrical version of the film. Whatever the version, and for all its stylistic achievements and excesses, this "future noir" contains performances as stunning as its look: Ford's pained, taciturn Deckard; Hauer's doomed, dangerous, tragic Batty; Sanderson's naive yet knowing Sebastian; and Young's icily cool yet terrified Rachael. The moody musical score evokes classic noir without sinking into caricature, and the pre-computer-animation special effects seem more lifelike than their sometimes sterile-looking counterparts in films made a decade later.

BLADE RUNNER stands as a tough, idiosyncratic, and highly original vision of the future that asks meaningful questions about the nature of being human. Despite its imperfections and occasionally muddy plot points, BLADE RUNNER successfully combines and transcends the sci-fi and detective genres to forge a serious drama, that stands head and shoulders above the cartoonlike approach of many of its popular genre brethren.

BLAIR WITCH PROJECT, THE
1999 87m   c/bw   Horror   ★★★★
Haxan Films   (U.S.)   R

Heather Donahue, Michael Williams, Joshua Leonard, Bob Griffith, Jim King, Sandra Sanchez, Ed Swanson, Patricia Decou

p, Gregg Hale, Robin Cowie; d, Eduardo Sanchez, Daniel Myrick; w, Eduardo Sanchez, Daniel Myrick; ph, Neal Fredericks; ed, Eduardo Sanchez, Daniel Myrick; m, Tony Cora; prod d, Ben Rock; art d, Ricardo R. Moreno

When was the last time a movie crawled under your skin and died there? Depending on your age, it may have been NIGHT OF THE LIVING DEAD or THE TEXAS CHAINSAW MASSACRE or THE EVIL DEAD. Like those films, Dan Myrick and Eduardo Sanchez's debut inspires an unpleasant mix of creeping dread and festering anxiety. That may not sound so nice, but many filmmakers try their whole careers without getting a real rise out of real horror fans.

The set-up is simplicity itself: a title card announces that in October of 1994, three student filmmakers disappeared near Burkittsville, MD. A year later, their footage was found. What follows looks quite convincingly as though it was edited together from video and black-and-white, 16mm amateur footage. We see Montgomery College students Heather Donahue, Joshua Leonard, and Michael Williams (the actors all use their real names) hike into the Black Hills forest outside Burkittville—formerly Blair—to make a documentary for anthropology class about a local campfire story. Since the 18th century, the Blair witch has been blamed for a string of spooky apparitions, mysterious disappearances, and mutilation murders. It all starts out in the spirit of fun, with Heather doing corny stand-ups on various nondescript rocks and river banks associated with the legend. But that's before they get lost in the woods and find themselves terrorized by something in the dark, something they never see, but that scrapes their nerves—and ours—to the bone.

Forget the self-referential scares of SCREAM: Myrick and Sanchez—who wrote, directed, and edited together—admit the influence of pop-culture detritus like '70s *In Search Of...* "documentaries," but their film is no schlock-fest. It's as chilling as Algernon Blackwood's elegantly unnerving short story "The Willows," played absolutely, unsettlingly straight. Gorehounds and smirking fans of the nudge-nudge, wink-wink school of self-referential horror may be disappointed, but that's their loss.

BLAZING SADDLES
1974 93m   c   Comedy/Western   ★★½
Warner Bros.   (U.S.)   R

Cleavon Little (Bart), Gene Wilder (Jim), Slim Pickens (Taggart), David Huddleston (Olson Johnson), Liam Dunn (Reverend Johnson), Alex Karras (Mongo), John Hillerman (Howard Johnson), George Furth (Van Johnson), Mel Brooks (Governor Lepetomane/Indian Chief), Harvey Korman (Hedley Lamarr)

p, Michael Hertzberg; d, Mel Brooks; w, Mel Brooks, Norman Steinberg, Andrew Bergman, Richard Pryor, Alan Uger (based on a story by Andrew Bergman); ph, Joseph Biroc (Technicolor); ed, John C. Howard, Danford B. Greene; m, John Morris; prod d, Peter Wooley; chor, Alan Johnson; cos, Vittorio Nino Novarese

AAN Best Film Editing: John C. Howard, Danford Greene; AAN Best Supporting Actress: Madeline Kahn; AAN Best Film Editing:

John C Howard, Danford Greene; AAN Best Song: "Blazing Saddles"; John Morris (Music), Mel Brooks (Lyrics)

A lewd spoof of westerns and racial prejudice; enough laughs to cover the fact that it is, essentially, a stupid movie. Little is terrific as a black sheriff who has been hired so that the citizens of the town will panic and sell their land out cheap to speculators who plan to run a railroad through town. When the village turns on Little, he must call on the jail's only con, Wilder, who was at one time the fastest gun in the West. Last fifteen minutes of the movie are an obvious cop-out and the humor is often toilet level, but in addition to Little, Kahn scores big (in a takeoff of Marlene Dietrich's saloon belles), as do Karras and Korman. What really lessens SADDLES is that its intentions aren't clear. Its humor provoked no thinking; insensitive moviegoers assumed the racial put-downs and cowboy crudeness were deliberate. The public loved the film—it stands as the highest grossing western in history—$45 million plus! But they loved it for all the wrong reasons.

BLIND SWORDSMAN: ZATOICHI, THE
2003 116m   c   Action/Historical/Comedy   ★★★½
Bandai Visual/Tokyo FM/Dentsu/TV Asahi/   R
Saito Entertainment/Office Kitano   (Japan)

Takeshi Kitano, billed as "Beat" Takeshi (Ichi), Michiyo Ohgusu (Aunt O-Ume), Guadalcanal Taka (Shinkichi), Daigoro Tachibana (Geisha O-Sei), Yuko Daike (Geisha O-Kinu), Tadanobu Asano (Gennosuke Hattori), Yui Natsukawa (O-Shino, Hattori's Wife), Saburo Ishikura (Boss Ogi), Koji Koike (Boss Funahachi), Ittoku Kishibe (Ginzo)

p, Masayuki Mori, Tsunehisa Saito; d, Takeshi Kitano; w, Takeshi Kitano (based on a short story by Kan Shimozawa); ph, Katsumi Yanagijima; ed, Takeshi Kitano; m, Keiichi Suzuki; prod d, Norihiro Isoda; art d, Shigeyuki Kondo; fx, Tomoo Haraguchi, Mitsuaki Hashimoto, Atsuo Inamura, Taro Kogaku, Yoji Miki, Takaaki Ohnishi, Okifumi Taira; chor, Toyotaka Azuma (Japanese dancing), Tatsumi Nikamoto (swordplay), The Stripes (Tap sequence); cos, Kazuko Kurosawa

One-man band Takeshi Kitano's first period film is a quirky take on the popular Edo-period Japanese character Zatoichi, a sightless swordsman who always seems three steps behind the bad guys until he abruptly reduces a mob of truculent samurai to fish food.

Itinerant masseur Zatoichi (Kitano) helps middle-aged O-Ume (Michiyo Ookusu) carry her vegetables from the market, and in return she offers him a place to stay. O-Ume confides that for the last decade the town has been run by the warring gangs of Boss Funahachi (Koji Koike) and Boss Ogi (Saburo Ishikura), but in recent months their increasing demands have pushed the villagers to the brink of despair. O-Ume also frets over her feckless nephew, Shinkichi (Guadalcanal Taka), who pours his time and money into gambling. Zatoichi helps Shinkichi win at dice and Shinkichi suggests they celebrate by hiring glamorous geisha sisters O-Kinu (Yuko Daike) and O-Sei Naruto (Daigoro Tachibana). Zatoichi immediately senses what no one else has noticed—O-Sei is actually a man—and O-Kinu explains that she and her brother are pursuing their parents' murderers. By the time Zatoichi moves on, everyone's wrongs have been righted and gallons of blood have been spilled. Created by writer Kan Shimozawa, Zatoichi appeared in 26 movies between 1962 and 1989, all starring Shintaro Katsu; the blind swordsman was also the star of a five-year Japanese TV series. Kitano retains all Zatoichi's familiar characteristics, from his love of gambling to the cane that conceals a samurai sword, as well as the series' familiar blend of humor and action. The subversive implications of O-sei's gender masquerade, however, are new, and quasi-musical sequences bring the film to a bravura tap-dancing finale as exhilarating as it is bizarre.

BLITHE SPIRIT *DVD*

1945   96m   c   Fantasy   ★★★★
Cineguild   (U.K.)

Rex Harrison *(Charles Condomine)*, Constance Cummings *(Ruth Condomine)*, Kay Hammond *(Elvira)*, Margaret Rutherford *(Madame Arcati)*, Hugh Wakefield *(Dr. Bradman)*, Joyce Carey *(Mrs. Bradman)*, Jacqueline Clark *(Edith)*

p, Noel Coward; d, David Lean; w, Noel Coward, David Lean, Anthony Havelock-Allan (based on the play by Noel Coward); ph, Ronald Neame (Technicolor); ed, Jack Harris; m, Richard Addinsell; art d, C.P. Norman

AA Best Special Effects: Thomas Howard (Visual)

A quicksilver cocktail. Novelist conjures up late first wife who can't resist causing trouble in his second marriage. Dry, but hilarious, Noel Coward romp, delivered seamlessly by David Lean. And stolen by Rutherford, the most inept, adorable medium ever. But the cinematography leaves something to be desired and only the Coward wit keeps this from not being a TOPPER rehash.

BLOB, THE *DVD*

1958   85m   c   Science Fiction   ★½
Paramount   (U.S.)

Steve McQueen *(Steve)*, Aneta Corseaut *(Judy)*, Earl Rowe *(Police Lieutenant)*, Olin Howlin *(Old Man)*, Stephen Chase, John Benson, Vincent Barbi, Tom Ogen, Julie Cousins, Ralph Roseman

p, Jack H. Harris; d, Irvin S. Yeaworth Jr.; w, Theodore Simonson, Kate Phillips (based on an idea by Irvine H. Millgate); ph, Thomas E. Spalding (Deluxe Color); ed, Alfred Hillman; m, Jean Yeaworth

Jack H. Harris, the cheapie producer who went on to make the forgettable MOTHER GOOSE A GO-GO, struck it rich with this silly picture that gave McQueen his first starring role after a few supporting jobs in SOMEBODY UP THERE LIKES ME and NEVER LOVE A STRANGER. It's a teenage horror tale as McQueen and Corseaut tell their tiny Pennsylvania town that they've seen this purple goop that's eating people up. Naturally, no one believes them.

A sequel was made called BEWARE THE BLOB, also known as SON OF BLOB. The title was what brought the people in to see this otherwise undistinguished movie. McQueen plays his role with believability, as he did almost everything in his brief career. The oddest thing about the movie is the title song by Hal David and a 29-year-old composer named Burt Bacharach. It's not a bad tune.

BLONDE VENUS

1932   92m   bw   Drama   ★★★★
Paramount   (U.S.)

Marlene Dietrich *(Helen Faraday)*, Herbert Marshall *(Edward Faraday)*, Cary Grant *(Nick Townsend)*, Dickie Moore *(Johnny Faraday)*, Francis Sayles *(Charlie Blaine)*, Robert Emmett O'Connor *(Dan O'Connor)*, Gene Morgan *(Ben Smith)*, Rita La Roy *(Taxi Belle Hooper)*, Sidney Toler *(Detective Wilson)*, Morgan Wallace *(Dr. Pierce)*

d, Josef von Sternberg; w, Jules Furthman, S.K. Lauren (based on a story by von Sternberg); ph, Bert Glennon; m, Oscar Potekar; art d, Wiard Ihnen; cos, Travis Banton

Dietrich suffers, for once; Von Sternberg's paen to the pain of love in all its variations is so lovingly rendered that the shoestring story looks almost seamless. No one ever looked lovelier after sinking to the gutter than Dietrich—even her tatters are photographed to maximum effect. Dickie Moore was perhaps the most beautiful little boy ever in movies and the two male stars are there to bask in all that is Dietrich. She also

appears in her hallmark top hat, white tie and tails singing "You Little So and So" but the sequence that lives on and on is the gorilla surprise and "Hot Voodoo," a highpoint of expressionistic eroticism, replete with blonde afro. Lensed two years before the code; hopefully your copy won't have the skinny-dipping opening deleted.

BLOOD AND SAND

1941   123m   c   Drama   ★★★★
Fox   (U.S.)

Tyrone Power *(Juan Gallardo)*, Linda Darnell *(Carmen Espinosa)*, Rita Hayworth *(Dona Sol des Muire)*, Anthony Quinn *(Manolo de Palma)*, Alla Nazimova *(Senora Augustias)*, J. Carrol Naish *(Garabato)*, John Carradine *(Nacional)*, Laird Cregar *(Natalio Curro)*, Lynn Bari *(Encarnacion)*, Vincente Gomez *(Guitarist)*

p, Robert T. Kane; d, Rouben Mamoulian; w, Jo Swerling (based on the novel *Sangre y Arena* by Vicente Blasco Ibanez); ph, Ernest Palmer, Ray Rennahan (Technicolor); ed, Robert Bischoff; m, Alfred Newman; art d, Richard Day, Joseph C. Wright; chor, Hermes Pan, Budd Boetticher; cos, Travis Banton

AA Best Color Cinematography: Ernest Palmer, Ray Rennahan; *AAN Best Interior Decoration (Color):* Richard Day, Joseph C. Wright, Thomas Little

Lavish, tragic mural that owes its pizazz to Mamoulian's use of color and composition; BLOOD AND SAND is like watching the great Spanish Masters do animation. Remake of the great Valentino triumph seems a little flat, mainly because Power lacks the magnetism and danger of his predecessor.

Students of sex symbolism should have fun comparing Darnell and Hayworth, although both ladies are still a light year away from possessing the full extent of their erotic powers. Hayworth, who won Donna Sol over Maria Montez and because Carole Landis refused to dye her hair red, became a contender for pin-up queen as a result of the film. As usual, she lacks the fatality of the greatest seductresses and looks unhappy, but all flaws go out the window when the lady starts to flamenco. The best performances are delivered by the compelling Nazimova and young Anthony Quinn. Ernest Palmer and Ray Rennahan won Oscars for the lush cinematography.

BLOOD SIMPLE *DVD*

1984   97m   c   Crime/Thriller   ★★★★
River Road   (U.S.)   R

John Getz *(Ray)*, Frances McDormand *(Abby)*, Dan Hedaya *(Julian Marty)*, M. Emmet Walsh *(Private Detective Visser)*, Samm-Art Williams *(Maurice)*, Deborah Neumann *(Debra)*, Raquel Gavia *(Landlady)*, Van Brooks *(Man from Lubbock)*, Senor Marco *(Mr. Garcia)*, William Creamer *(Old Cracker)*

p, Ethan Coen; d, Joel Coen; w, Ethan Coen, Joel Coen; ph, Barry Sonnenfeld (DuArt Color); ed, Roderick Jaynes, Don Wiegmann, Peggy Connolly; m, Carter Burwell; prod d, Jane Musky; fx, Loren Bivens; cos, Sara Medina-Pape

Stylish shoestring noir; an admirable filmmaking debut for the brothers Coen—Ethan (producer) and Joel (director).

Walsh is a sleazy private eye hired by Texas strip bar owner Hedaya to kill his wife McDormand and her lover Getz. Instead, Walsh fakes the double hit by doctoring photographs and then fills Hedaya with lead. When Getz discovers Hedaya in a pool of blood, he goes "simple"—foolishly cleaning up after the murder on the assumption that McDormand committed it. His actions distorted by his blinding passion, Getz then takes the body to an empty field to bury it, only to find that he, by a brutal twist of fate, is being buried.

Drawing from the crime novels of James M. Cain, BLOOD SIMPLE's characters have none of the Cain complexities one might hope for, existing simply as chess pieces to further flashy stylistics. The Coens' concern isn't emotional intensity but bravura camera moves and chic lighting of cinematographer Sonnenfeld.

McDormand is wonderfully naturalistic as the not-too-bright girl with a homey sensuality, and Hedaya somehow manages to be vile yet sympathetic. Hailed by some as the best American independent film, BLOOD SIMPLE was completed on an astonishingly small budget of less than $1.5 million and looks as if it cost ten times as much.

BLOW   DVD

2001 119m c   Crime/Drama   ★★★½
Apostle Pictures/Spanky Pictures/Avery Pix   R
New Line   (U.S.)

Johnny Depp *(George Jung)*, Penelope Cruz *(Mirtha)*, Jordi Molla *(Diego Delgado)*, Franka Potente *(Barbara)*, Rachel Griffiths *(Ermine Jung)*, Ray Liotta *(Fred Jung)*, Ethan Suplee *(Tuna)*, Paul Reubens *(Derek Foreal)*, Jesse James *(Young George)*, Max Perlich *(Kevin Dulli)*

p, Ted Demme, Georgia Kacandes, Denis Leary, Joel Stillerman; d, Ted Demme; w, Nick Cassavetes, David McKenna (based on the book by Bruce Porter); ph, Ellen Kuras; ed, Kevin Tent; m, Graeme Revell; prod d, Michael Hanan; art d, David Ensley, Bernardo Trujillo; cos, Mark Bridges

Seductive, whip-smart, and ultimately tragic, this fact-based movie about a genial pot dealer who wound up almost single-handedly blanketing the United States with Colombian snow is electrified by Johnny Depp's best work since DONNIE BRASCO.

After his working-class father (Ray Liotta) is forced to declare bankruptcy, little George Jung (Jesse James) discovers his inner Scarlett O'Hara and vows that he'll never be poor again. Flash forward: armed with little more than a high school diploma, Jung (Depp) winds up on Venice Beach at the tail-end of the hedonistic '60s where he finds a foxy girlfriend (Franka Potente) and a calling: funneling the grade-A pot to East-coast college students. A born salesman with a flair for smuggling, Jung inevitably lands in jail, where he makes the connection that changes his life forever. Car thief Diego Delgado (Jordi Molla) has friends in the fledgling Colombian cocaine trade who are looking for an entree into the U.S. market, and he later introduces them to Jung. From there it's one short step to pulling in $60 million and marrying a Colombian bombshell (Penelope Cruz), then pissing it all away.

The trajectory is familiar and the moral might as well be spelled out in neon, but director Ted Demme avoids the sanctimonious tone that undermines most cautionary tales. Jung ruins his life—and the lives of others—but you never wonder why he does what he does; it's all there in Depp's subtle, slippery performance. He evokes a complicated tangle of emotions and motivations that makes you empathize with Jung, even if you deplore his actions. And the ending is a heartbreaker, pure and simple.

BLOW OUT   DVD

1981 108m c   Mystery   ★★★★
Filmways   (U.S.)   R

John Travolta *(Jack)*, Nancy Allen *(Sally)*, John Lithgow *(Burke)*, Dennis Franz *(Karp)*, Peter Boyden *(Sam)*, Curt May *(Frank)*, Ernest McClure *(Jim)*, Dave Roberts *(Anchorman)*, Maurice Copeland *(Jack)*, Claire Carter *(Anchorwoman)*

p, George Litto; d, Brian De Palma; w, Brian De Palma; ph, Vilmos Zsigmond (Technicolor); ed, Paul Hirsch; m, Pino Donaggio; prod d, Paul Sylbert; cos, Vicki Sanchez

An homage to BLOW UP that far outstrips the original in emotional immediacy, political sophistication, and visual style. Jack Terry (John Travolta) is a sound-effects recorder who specializes in sounds for trashy porn-slasher films. While out recording one night, he hears a tire blow out and sees a car swerve off a bridge and into the water. He jumps in and saves Sally (Nancy Allen), a prostitute who was with a now-drowned politician. The media and the dead man's associates are all convinced it was an accident, but Jack hears something on his tape recording—a gunshot that precedes the blow out. Using Sally as bait, Jack begins a cat-and-mouse game to find the killer.

Like most of De Palma's films, BLOW OUT is replete with cinematic quotes and inside jokes; this time, however, there's real substance behind the flashy attitudinizing. De Palma, in a grim mood of post-Watergate disillusionment, is here concerned with the role of violence in American history: shades of Chappaquiddick and the Kennedy assassinations are everywhere; a psychotic CIA agent (chillingly played by John Lithgow) stands in for American idealism gone murderously wrong; the bloody climax is played out amidst a surreally rendered Bicentennial celebration. Travolta gives a sensitive performance, as does Nancy Allen, who was married to De Palma at the time. The film's emphasis on the role of sound technology in movie-making is unusual and instructive.

BLOW UP   DVD

1966 111m c   Drama/Mystery   ★★★½
Bridge Films   (U.K./Italy)

David Hemmings *(Thomas)*, Vanessa Redgrave *(Jane)*, Sarah Miles *(Patricia)*, Jane Birkin *(Teenager #1)*, Gillian Hills *(Teenager #2)*, Peter Bowles *(Ron)*, Henry Hutchinson *(Shopkeeper)*, John Castle *(Patricia's Artist Husband)*, Susan Broderick *(Antique Shop Owner)*, Mary Khal *(Fashion Editor)*

p, Carlo Ponti; d, Michelangelo Antonioni; w, Michelangelo Antonioni, Tonino Guerra, Edward Bond (based on the short story, "Final del Juego," by Julio Cortazar); ph, Carlo di Palma (Metrocolor); ed, Frank Clarke; m, Herbie Hancock, The Yardbirds; art d, Assheton Gorton; cos, Jocelyn Richards

AAN Best Director: Michelangelo Antonioni; *AAN Best Original Story and Screenplay:* Michelangelo Antonioni (Screenplay), Tonino Guerra (Screenplay), Edward Bond (Screenplay)

Pop-culture icon that has become a cult classic. Antonioni's adaptation of Cortazar's short story is an engrossing study of imagery and one's perception of the image. Set against the backdrop of 1960s London, BLOW UP follows fashionable young photographer Hemmings as he passively snaps his way through a world of drugs, models and parties. While wandering through a quiet park, he begins taking photos of two lovers embracing. One of them, Redgrave, chases after him and demands that he return the negatives. Later, after developing the photos, Hemmings thinks he sees something in the background—a man with a gun aimed at the back of Redgrave's partner. Returning that evening to the park, Hemmings finds the man's corpse. But the following morning, when he revisits the scene, the corpse has vanished . . .

In its time one of the most financially successful art films ever made, BLOW UP marked Antonioni's leap into the commercial arena, after an early career largely confined to film festivals. From the perspective of the '90s, though, it's hard to see what all the fuss was about. The "swinging '60s" stuff looks as dated as the Herbie Hancock score sounds,

Hemmings is a difficult actor to care about, and the neo-surrealist touches are downright irritating. There are moments of humor, though it's hard to gauge how many of them are intentional. Jane Birkin makes her screen debut, as one of the two giggling teenagers who "wrestle" with Hemmings.

BLUE   *DVD*
(TROIS COULEURS: BLEU)
1993 97m c Drama   ★★★
Marin Karmitz Productions/Tor Film Studios/   R
CAB Productions   (France/Poland/Switzerland)

Juliette Binoche (Julie), Benoit Regent (Olivier), Florence Pernel (Sandrine), Charlotte Very (Lucille), Emmanuelle Riva (The Mother), Helene Vincent (Journalist), Philippe Volter (Estate Agent), Hugues Quester (Patrice), Florence Vignon (Copyist), Yann Tregouet (Antoine)

p, Marin Karmitz; d, Krzysztof Kieslowski; w, Krzysztof Kieslowski, Krzysztof Piesiewicz; ph, Slawomir Idziak; ed, Jacques Witta; m, Zbigniew Preisner; prod d, Claude Lenoir; cos, Virginie Viard

In this first section of his THREE COLORS trilogy, director Krzysztof Kieslowski's noted visual style is amply on display: images are transformed from the familiar into the unearthly, with a sense of dislocation permeating the whole.

When Julie (Juliette Binoche) survives a car crash that claims the lives of her classical composer husband Patrice (Hugues Quester) and young child, she attempts suicide. After her convalescence, she instructs her lawyers to dispose of the family estate and all her belongings, and disappears, moving into an apartment in an unfamiliar new neighborhood. Julie hears that a composer friend and former lover, Olivier (Benoit Regent), has been asked to complete a piece that her husband had been working on for an important series of concerts. With Olivier's help, she confronts the facts of her husband's past and reckons with the mysteries surrounding his music.

While BLUE might at first be seen as a kind of elegy to genius, as Julie seems to have dedicated her life to upholding the myth of her husband's brilliance, it gradually turns into an examination of things that aren't what they seem to be. Juliette Binoche is almost always on screen and Kieslowski and his camera seem enchanted by her, perpetually finding new ways to photograph her coolly beautiful face. The music, by Zbigniew Preisner, is heard mostly in short snippets, but swells to a full-length finale at the end, revealing itself as rather kitschy and bland.

BLUE ANGEL, THE   *DVD*
(DER BLAUE ENGEL)
1930 99m bw Drama   ★★★★★
UFA   (Germany)

Emil Jannings (Prof. Immanuel Rath), Marlene Dietrich (Lola Frohlich), Kurt Gerron (Kiepert, a Magician), Rosa Valetti (Guste, his Wife), Hans Albers (Mazeppa), Eduard von Winterstein (Principal of the School), Reinhold Bernt (The Clown), Hans Roth (Beadle), Rolf Muller (Angst, a Student), Robert Klein-Lork (Goldstaub, a Student)

p, Erich Pommer; d, Josef von Sternberg; w, Robert Liebmann, Karl Vollmoeller, Carl Zuckmayer (based on the novel Professor Unrat by Heinrich Mann); ph, Gunther Rittau, Hans Schneeberger; ed, S.K. Winston; m, Friedrick Hollander

The one and only; an unqualified masterpiece and milestone. Grim, ritualistic rise and fall of a respectable man at the hands of a heartless tramp is still one of the most horrifying studies of human degradation ever made. THE BLUE ANGEL's international success can be attributed to any number of elements: The immortal Jannings, UFA's greatest actor and a victim of the transition from silents to sound, is astounding in an essentially silent performance; Dietrich is wholly captivating in her first role with Sternberg—a creative union from which arose the Dietrich persona that would become internationally recognizable. It is, however, the genius of Sternberg to which THE BLUE ANGEL owes its greatness. His use of lighting, composition and of silence as sound, his overall creation of a world that can seduce and destroy even its most upstanding citizen, attest to this filmmaker's greatness and to the stature of THE BLUE ANGEL. Filmed simultaneously in German and English, the film is available in two, slightly differing, videotape versions—in German with English subtitles, and in English, the former preferable to the latter.

BLUE COLLAR   *DVD*
1978 110m c Drama   ★★★½
T.A.T.   (U.S.)   R

Richard Pryor (Zeke Brown), Harvey Keitel (Jerry Bartkowski), Yaphet Kotto (Smokey), Ed Begley Jr. (Bobby Joe), Harry Bellaver (Eddie Johnson), George Memmoli (Jenkins), Lucy Saroyan (Arlene Bartowski), Lane Smith (Clarence Hill), Cliff De Young (John Burrows), Borah Silver (Miller)

p, Don Guest; d, Paul Schrader; w, Paul Schrader, Leonard Schrader (based on materials by Sidney A. Glass); ph, Bobby Byrne (Technicolor); ed, Tom Rolf; m, Jack Nitzsche, Ry Cooder; cos, Ron Dawson, Alice Rush

Unionism, corruption, and betrayal in a Detroit auto plant. The directorial debut of Paul Schrader, who wrote TAXI DRIVER for Martin Scorsese, is one of surprisingly few films concerned with the pressures and politics of the workplace, where, after all, most adults spend nearly half their waking hours. Co-workers Pryor and Keitel have learned the hard way that union jobs no longer guarantee middle-class comfort; their friend, cynical ex-con Kotto, suggests that they rob a safe in the office of their union local. The break-in yields little cash, but they find an incriminating ledger with which they hope to blackmail the union leadership. The union, unresponsive and complacent when it comes to worker complaints, reacts with deadly efficiency when its power is threatened.

A key film for an era of diminishing expectations, BLUE COLLAR depicts big business and big labor as collaborators, expertly manipulating class resentment and racial tension so as to keep the work force divided. The precipitous decline of American unionism since the film's release may blunt the film's impact, however: many viewers will now have cause to reflect that a corrupt union is better than no union at all. The three leads—particularly Pryor, in an essentially non-comedic role—are remarkable.

BLUE DAHLIA, THE
1946 96m bw Mystery   ★★★½
Paramount   (U.S.)

Alan Ladd (Johnny Morrison), Veronica Lake (Joyce Harwood), William Bendix (Buzz Wanchek), Howard da Silva (Eddie Harwood), Doris Dowling (Helen Morrison), Tom Powers (Capt. Hendrickson), Hugh Beaumont (George Copeland), Howard Freeman (Corelli), Don Costello (Leo), Will Wright ("Dad" Newell)

p, John Houseman; d, George Marshall; w, Raymond Chandler (based on his story); ph, Lionel Lindon; ed, Arthur Schmidt; m, Victor Young; art d, Hans Dreier, Walter Tyler; cos, Edith Head

AAN Best Original Screenplay: Raymond Chandler

Tidy *film noir*, although we prefer Ladd and Lake in THIS GUN FOR HIRE. This is the only film script Raymond Chandler did directly for the screen, and the script reflects his hard-boiled, grim wit. Ladd returns from the service, and his wife has become a tramp. When she's murdered, he has to clear himself. Taut film still plays like house afire.

BLUE SKY
1994 101m c   Drama   ★★★
Prairie Films/Heathrow Productions/Orion (U.S.) PG-13

Jessica Lange *(Carly Marshall)*, Tommy Lee Jones *(Captain Hank Marshall)*, Powers Boothe *(Vince Johnson)*, Carrie Snodgress *(Vera Johnson)*, Amy Locane *(Alex Marshall)*, Chris O'Donnell *(Glenn Johnson)*, Mitchell Ryan *(Ray Stevens)*, Dale Dye *(Colonel Mike Anwalt)*, Tim Scott *(Ned Owens)*, Annie Ross *(Lydia)*

p, Robert H. Solo; d, Tony Richardson; w, Rama Laurie Stagner, Jerry Leichtling, Arlene Sarner (from a story by Rama Laurie Stagner); ph, Steve Yaconelli; ed, Robert K. Lambert; m, Jack Nitzsche; prod d, Timian Alsaker; art d, Gary John Constable; cos, Jane Robinson

AA Best Actress: Jessica Lange

The late Tony Richardson's BLUE SKY was the last of Orion's pre-bankruptcy films to see the light of day, and seems a more fitting swan song for Arthur Krim's widely respected company than, say, CLIFFORD. But despite the director's pedigree (TOM JONES, THE LONELINESS OF THE LONG-DISTANCE RUNNER), this picture feels somehow enervated, perhaps reflecting Richardson's struggles with AIDS during its 1991 filming.

At the dawn of the 1960s, Major Hank Marshall (Tommy Lee Jones), a U.S. Army nuclear engineer, favors underground nuclear testing, despite the preference of army brass for open-air detonations. His wife Carly (Jessica Lange), a Barbie-doll bourgeoise, is slowly being suffocated by domestic torpor and encroaching age.

Jones is excellent here, as always, but the selling point is clearly Lange's seductive, damaged, mercurial Carly. She is both an American version of BETTY BLUE, allowed the full dramatic range of hysteria, and a more corrosive update of Auntie Mame or Jean Brodie—a charismatic kook whose eccentricities, in the end, aren't so charming once it becomes clear that she's seriously ill. And despite the implausible quality of some of the melodrama—it's a comparatively muted throwback to the glossy melos of the 1950s—BLUE SKY is a welcome alternative view of domesticity in a field increasingly devoted to half-baked "family values."

BLUE STEEL
1990 102m c   Thriller   ★★★
Lightning/Precision/Mack-Taylor (U.S.)   R

Jamie Lee Curtis *(Megan Turner)*, Ron Silver *(Eugene Hunt)*, Clancy Brown *(Nick Mann)*, Elizabeth Pena *(Tracy Perez)*, Louise Fletcher *(Shirley Turner)*, Philip Bosco *(Frank Turner)*, Kevin Dunn *(Assistant Chief Stanley Hoyt)*, Richard Jenkins *(Attorney Mel Dawson)*, Markus Flannagan *(Husband)*, Mary Mara *(Wife)*

p, Edward R. Pressman, Oliver Stone, Michael Rauch; d, Kathryn Bigelow; w, Kathryn Bigelow, Eric Red; ph, Amir Mokri (Technicolor); ed, Lee Percy; m, Brad Fiedel; prod d, Toby Corbett; fx, Steve Kirshoff; cos, Richard Shissler

Suspenseful and relentlessly stylish, BLUE STEEL is a slick, crypto-feminist thriller from Kathryn Bigelow (NEAR DARK, POINT BREAK), a gifted action director with a feel for the eroticism of violence.

During her first night on the job, rookie cop Megan Turner (Jamie Lee Curtis) breaks up a supermarket robbery and kills the gunman, whose pistol ends up in the hands of customer Eugene Hunt (Ron Silver). Hunt, a deranged Wall Street broker, takes the gun home and inscribes Megan's name on the bullets; obsessed with Megan, he begins a killing spree. Meanwhile, Megan has problems of her own: her mother (Louise Fletcher) is being abused by her father (Philip Bosco); she hasn't had a date in months. Enter Hunt, who

sweeps the unsuspecting Megan off her feet with fancy dinners and thrilling helicopter rides. But Hunt has more than romance on his mind: he's grooming Megan for a role in his murderous fantasies.

BLUE STEEL's greatest pleasure is its smashing cinematography, courtesy of Amir Mokri (who has given several Wayne Wang films a distinctive look), but also owing much to Bigelow's distinctive pop aesthetics. The dependable Curtis adds depth to what might have been a stock character; Silver is convincingly vicious and seductive. Lest we fail to take the film seriously, the screenplay (written by Bigelow with longtime collaborator Eric Red) drops some unobtrusive hints about violence as a tool of patriarchy.

BLUE VELVET
1986 120m c   Mystery   ★★★
DEG (U.S.)   R

Kyle MacLachlan *(Jeffrey Beaumont)*, Isabella Rossellini *(Dorothy Vallens)*, Dennis Hopper *(Frank Booth)*, Laura Dern *(Sandy Williams)*, Hope Lange *(Mrs. Williams)*, Dean Stockwell *(Ben)*, George Dickerson *(Detective Williams)*, Priscilla Pointer *(Mrs. Beaumont)*, Frances Bay *(Aunt Barbara)*, Jack Harvey *(Mr. Beaumont)*

p, Fred Caruso; d, David Lynch; w, David Lynch; ph, Frederick Elmes (Joe Dunton Camera Widescreen); ed, Duwayne Dunham; m, Angelo Badalamenti; prod d, Patricia Norris; fx, Greg Hull, George Hill; cos, Gloria Laughride

AAN Best Director: David Lynch

Weirdness, big time. The seamy side of small town Americana from——who else?—David Lynch. When archetypal college student Jeffrey Beaumont (MacLachlan) finds a severed human ear in a deserted field, he enlists the help of innocent high-schooler Sandy (Dern) in finding the body to which it once belonged. The key to the mystery is nightclub chanteuse Dorothy Vallens (Rossellini), whose husband and child are being held hostage by the demoniacal Frank Booth (Hopper), who sexually torments the singer in exchange for the safety of her loved ones. Eventually Jeffrey probes so deeply into this dark and troubling mystery that he comes face to face with Booth, the very embodiment of evil. As if to demonstrate the film's premise that people would prefer to avoid the dark side of life—the sadism, perversions, fetishism, drug addiction, and violence—many critics complained that BLUE VELVET was "dangerous" in its exploration of these traits, contending that these taboos were better left in the closet. Director David Lynch addresses that belief here—Hopper, the voice of evil, demands that people not look at him, while MacLachlan, the voice of good, not only looks but fights back. All of this revolves around the film's mystery elements, which are on a par with the innocent whodunit mentality of a Hardy Boys-Nancy Drew episode, although the rest of the film is deeply disquieting and sexually aggressive, not to be seen by those easily repulsed. There are certain similarities between this film and Alfred Hitchcock's 1943 classic SHADOW OF A DOUBT, in which Joseph Cotten's "Uncle Charlie" is a demented murderer whose diseased presence threatens a quiet California town. Surprisingly, for a picture as steeped in controversy as it was, BLUE VELVET *did* earn Lynch a Best Director Oscar nomination. In addition to the Bobby Vinton title tune, the film prominently features the Roy Orbison tune "In Dreams," and a lush score by Angelo Badalamenti. Depending on your point of view, either dark-sidedly brilliant or garbage heaped on top of whipped cream.

BLUES BROTHERS, THE   _DVD_
1980 133m c Comedy   ★★½
Universal   (U.S.)   R

John Belushi _(Joliet Jake)_, Dan Aykroyd _(Elwood)_, James Brown _(Rev. Cleophus James)_, Cab Calloway _(Curtis)_, Ray Charles _(Ray)_, Carrie Fisher _(Mystery Woman)_, Aretha Franklin _(Soul Food Cafe Owner)_, Henry Gibson _(Nazi Leader)_, John Candy _(Burton Mercer)_, Murphy Dunne _(Murph)_

p, Robert K. Weiss; d, John Landis; w, John Landis, Dan Aykroyd; ph, Stephen Katz (Technicolor); ed, George Folsey Jr.; m, Ira Newborn; cos, Deborah Nadoolman

THE BLUES BROTHERS is a monument to waste, noise and misplaced cool, but it does have its engagingly nutty moments. The premise for this $30 million flick is that blue-eyed soul brothers Jake and Elwood (John Belushi and Dan Aykroyd) need to raise $5,000 for their old orphanage. With no other motivation, they systematically destroy the city of Chicago. One of the most self-indulgent films of the 1980s, THE BLUES BROTHERS shows the dangers of giving untold sums of money to brash young directors. The highlights are few, but telling—all of the black performers score in their brief roles, especially Franklin and Calloway. Unfortunately, these performers's legitimate "soul" underlines the Blues Brothers's assumed soul. Henry Gibson is funny as a George Rockwell-type Nazi, and Frank Oz of Muppet fame makes a rare on-screen appearance as a corrections officer. This film has one pace—breakneck—and doesn't allow the audience to breathe, rest, or care about anyone or anything. It's worth noting that its big budget exceeded the amount Chaplin, Keaton, Laurel and Hardy, Charlie Chase, Harry Langdon, and Ben Turpin used to make _all_ their films.

BLUME IN LOVE
1973 115m c Comedy   ★★★
Warner Bros.   (U.S.)   R

George Segal _(Blume)_, Susan Anspach _(Nina Blume)_, Kris Kristofferson _(Elmo)_, Marsha Mason _(Arlene)_, Shelley Winters _(Mrs. Cramer)_, Donald Muhich _(Analyst)_, Paul Mazursky _(Blume's Partner)_

p, Paul Mazursky; d, Paul Mazursky; w, Paul Mazursky; ph, Bruce Surtees (Technicolor); ed, Donn Cambern; prod d, Pato Guzman

Sympathetic but self-indulgent masculine version of Mazursky's AN UNMARRIED WOMAN, a few years later. Segal is splendid as the lovesick lawyer who lusts after his ex, Anspach, who has taken up with Kristofferson. Mason is formidable as a woman waiting for divorced men. Mazursky, working without Larry Tucker for the first time, lets the picture get away from him a few times and does not edit with as tight an eye as for his previous films. His jaundiced look at love in California allows him to have some fun satirizing early 1970s types like Gottlieb (the bass player in the Limelighters group) as a guru and Denison as a Yoga leader. Winters is hysterical in a small role as a wife trying to decide whether or not to divorce her lecherous husband. Mazursky gave himself a role as Segal's partner which may explan moments when film feels unfocused.

BOB & CAROL & TED & ALICE   _DVD_
1969 104m c Comedy   ★★★
Columbia   (U.S.)   R

Natalie Wood _(Carol)_, Robert Culp _(Bob)_, Elliott Gould _(Ted)_, Dyan Cannon _(Alice)_, Horst Ebersberg _(Horst)_, Lee Bergere _(Emelio)_, Donald Muhich _(Psychiatrist)_, Noble Lee Holderread Jr. _(Sean)_, K.T. Stevens _(Phyllis)_, Celeste Yarnall _(Susan)_

p, Larry Tucker; d, Paul Mazursky; w, Paul Mazursky, Larry Tucker; ph, Charles Lang (Technicolor); m, Quincy Jones; chor, Miriam Nelson; cos, Moss Mabry

AAN Best Supporting Actor: Elliott Gould; _AAN Best Supporting Actress:_ Dyan Cannon; _AAN Best Original Story and Screenplay:_ Paul Mazursky, Larry Tucker; _AAN Best Cinematography:_ Charles B Lang

Written by Mazursky and Tucker, this very funny movie about mate-swapping spoke to the condition of moviegoers in 1969, but it has quickly become dated. Bob (Culp) and Carol (Wood) and Ted (Gould) and Alice (Cannon) are best friends. Culp and Wood visit a psycho-babble retreat in California and come home spouting all sorts of funny "Love Generation" dogma. Wood has an affair with a tennis pro, and Culp, living up to his new standards, congratulates her. Cannon is the most conservative of the group, but when Gould admits that he had an affair, she suggests the four have an orgy during their trip to Las Vegas. Culp and Wood and Gould and Cannon do indeed end up in bed together, but none of them knows where to start. The funniest scene in the picture is one in which Gould is wildly turned on and Cannon is anything but. The dialog is wonderful, but at times director Mazursky sacrifices the human element of his story to indulgent camerawork. Andre Phillipe plays Oscar here; if you look hard in most of Mazursky's films, you'll see him in some small role. Gould and Cannon were nominated for Academy Awards, as was the story and cinematography.

BOB LE FLAMBEUR   _DVD_
1955 98m bw Crime   ★★★★
Studios Jenner/OGC/La Cyme/Play Art   (France)

Isabelle Corey _(Anne)_, Daniel Cauchy _(Paolo)_, Roger Duchesne _(Bob Montagne)_, Guy Decomble _(Inspector Ledru)_, Andre Garret _(Roger)_, Gerard Buhr _(Marc)_, Claude Cerval _(Jean)_, Colette Fleury _(Suzanne—Jean's Wife)_, Simone Paris _(Yvonne)_, Howard Vernon _(McKimmie)_

p, Jean-Pierre Melville; d, Jean-Pierre Melville; w, Jean-Pierre Melville, Auguste le Breton; ph, Henri Decae; ed, Monique Bonnot; m, Eddie Barclay, Jo Boyer; art d, Claude Bouxin, Jean-Pierre Melville

The lightest movie of Jean-Pierre Melville's career, BOB LE FLAMBEUR is the story of an aging gambler and his attempt to end a lifelong streak of bad luck by pulling off the ultimate heist. Considered an important precursor of the French New Wave, this low-budget film was described by its creator as "not a pure _policier_, but a comedy of manners" and also as "a love-letter to Paris."

  Bob the Gambler (Roger Duchesne), a 50-year-old ex-thief who is down on his luck, is seated in a cafe with Paulo (Daniel Cauchy), an admiring young protege, when in walks Anne (Isabelle Corey), a sexy teenager, accompanied by Marc (Gerard Buhr), a pimp. Bob scares Marc off and then treats Anne to dinner, lectures her, and stakes her to a hotel bed while Paulo flirts with her. Days later, Bob puts Anne up in his apartment, no strings attached; he soon finds that Paulo and she have become romantically involved. Bob and his friend, Roger (Andre Garret), visit the Deauville Casino, where Roger bumps into Jean (Claude Cerval), an old pal and now a croupier. Jean tells Roger that the casino safe contains hundreds of millions of francs. Roger relays the information to Bob, who decides to hold the place up.

  Melville wrote the initial draft of BOB LE FLAMBEUR before he had seen THE ASPHALT JUNGLE (1950). Realizing that he couldn't match the grim power of the John Huston caper classic, he turned his own scenario into something of a comedy. In the title role of Bob, he cast Duchesne, who had been a major French star before WWII but had since drifted into shadier areas of employment. The director discovered 15-year-old Corey on a Paris street and cast her as Anne.

Alarmingly closer to "fille" fatale than a femme fatale, the seductively insouciant Anne became, in Corey's hands, one of the screen's great erotic figures of the 1950s.

At once a charming entertainment, a resonant character study, an ironic morality tale, and a bittersweet celebration of Montmartre, BOB LE FLAMBEUR reinforces Melville's reputation as one of history's premier filmmakers in the same way that Shakespeare's comedies enhance his reputation as a major tragedian. In foregrounding the wit and drollery that lurk beneath the surface of such weighty masterpieces as LES ENFANTS TERRIBLES (1949) and LE SAMOURAI (1967), BOB LE FLAMBEUR rounds out Melville's resume and secures him a berth in the cinema's pantheon.

BOB ROBERTS

DVD

1992 105m c Comedy/Political ★★½
The Bob Roberts Co./Working Title/Polygram R
(U.S./U.K.)

Tim Robbins *(Bob Roberts)*, Giancarlo Esposito *(Bugs Raplin)*, Ray Wise *(Chet MacGregor)*, Alan Rickman *(Lukas Hart, III)*, Gore Vidal *(Senator Brickley Paiste)*, James Spader *(News Anchor Chuck Marin)*, Helen Hunt *(Reporter Rose Pondell)*, Peter Gallagher *(News Anchor Dan Riley)*, Susan Sarandon *(News Anchor Tawna Titan)*, Fred Ward *(News Anchor Chip Daley)*

p, Forrest Murray; d, Tim Robbins; w, Tim Robbins; ph, Jean Lepine; ed, Lisa Churgin; m, David Robbins; prod d, Richard Hoover; art d, Gary Kosko; cos, Bridget Kelly

BOB ROBERTS is a smart, funny pseudo-documentary about a conservative folk-singer who campaigns to become U.S. Senator for Pennsylvania, cloaking his extreme right-wing views in the radical rhetoric of the 1960s.

Directed and written by its star, Tim Robbins, the film began life as a sketch for "Saturday Night Live" in 1985. Much of it feels like an extended "SNL" gag (one of the funniest sequences has the would-be Senator appearing on a thinly disguised version of the show called "Cutting Edge Live"), but Robbins has also clearly learned a lot from his work with Robert Altman on THE PLAYER.

Like Altman's best films, BOB ROBERTS builds a free-wheeling, multi-layered portrait of its characters' world where what happens in the background of a scene is often as entertaining—and revealing—as what we're "supposed" to be looking at. And like THE PLAYER, Robbins's film is peppered with cameos by celebrities including Susan Sarandon, Peter Gallagher and Fred Ward. Gore Vidal plays Roberts's opponent, an articulate, old-style Democrat whose campaign is tainted by allegations of an extra-marital affair.

Onto this hybrid of NASHVILLE and SPINAL TAP Robbins has layered a sub-plot worthy of J.F.K., featuring an investigative reporter played by Giancarlo Esposito. He claims to have evidence linking Robbins's right-hand man Lukas Hart, III (Alan Rickman), to S&L-financed drug-running, but pays dearly for his discovery.

Although the conspiracy theory helps keep BOB ROBERTS moving, the real joy of the film is in the incidental details: songs such as "Wall Street Rap," the video for which features pin-striped financiers celebrating the joys of wealth; the recurrent Bob Dylan pastiches, including a Roberts album titled "Bob on Bob"; and hilariously on-the-mark cameos from the likes of James Spader, as a vacuous local newscaster, and Bob Balaban, as the spineless producer of "Cutting Edge Live."

BOCCACCIO '70

DVD

1962 150m c Fantasy/Comedy ★★½
TCF (France/Italy)

THE RAFFLE: Sophia Loren *(Zoe)*, Luigi Gillianni *(Gaetano)*, Alfio Vita *(Cuspet)*, THE JOB: Romy Schneider *(Pupe)*, Tomas Milian

(The Count), Romolo Valli, Paolo Stoppa, THE TEMPTATION OF DR. ANTONIO: Anita Ekberg *(Anita)*, Peppino de Filippo *(Dr. Antonio)*, Dante Maggio

p, Carlo Ponti, Antonio Cervi; d, Federico Fellini, Vittorio De Sica, Luchino Visconti; w, Federico Fellini, Ennio Flaiano, Tullio Pinelli, Suso Cecchi D'Amico, Luchino Visconti, Cesare Zavattini; ph, Giuseppe Rotunno, Otello Marelli; m, Nino Rota, Armando Trovajoli

Three unconnected episodes dealing with modern stories the producers would have you think Boccaccio might have written if alive; from the lack of content and characterization, Boccaccio would have used a pseudonym for these turgid tales. The film is only an excuse to parade the Amazonian attributes of Ekberg and Loren, with Schneider thrown in for dramatic license. In one story, Ekberg is a billboard image that comes to life in a dream conjured by a middle-aged lecher. In "The Raffle," Loren plays a woman who operates a shooting gallery and is the sex prize of a Saturday night raffle. To accommodate a country bumpkin who begs to win the raffle, she fixes the drawing but does not deliver the goods; to show she is a noble slattern, however, Loren spreads the word that she has dallied with the clod so he will become a hero to his crowd. Schneider's segment is almost lost between these two stories; she plays a secretary in love with the boss and sacrificing her personal life for the ungrateful wretch. Contrived and spotty.

BODY AND SOUL

DVD

1947 104m bw Sports ★★★★½
Enterprise (U.S.)

John Garfield *(Charlie Davis)*, Lilli Palmer *(Peg Born)*, Hazel Brooks *(Alice)*, Anne Revere *(Anna Davis)*, William Conrad *(Quinn)*, Joseph Pevney *(Shorty Polaski)*, Canada Lee *(Ben)*, Lloyd Goff *(Roberts)*, Art Smith *(David Davis)*, James Burke *(Arnold)*

p, Bob Roberts; d, Robert Rossen; w, Abraham Polonsky; ph, James Wong Howe; ed, Robert Parrish; m, Hugo Friedhofer; art d, Nathan Juran; cos, Marion Herwood Keyes

AAN Best Actor: John Garfield; *AAN Best Original Screenplay:* Abraham Polonsky; *AA Best Film Editing:* Francis Lyon, Robert Parrish

The fight film to which all others are compared. John Garfield portrays Charlie Davis, a Jewish prizefighter whose parents want him to hang up the gloves and get an education. When his father is killed in a bomb explosion, however, the proud Charlie prevents his mother (Anne Revere) from accepting government relief, turns pro, and by hook and crook, rises quickly to the top, winning the championship from Ben (one-time welterweight Canada Lee), who is left with a life-threatening blood clot in his brain. As the champ, Charlie slides into a dissipated lifestyle and throws over his artist girlfriend, Peg Born (Lilli Palmer), for a floozy (Hazel Brooks), falling deeper into the clutches of the gangster who owns him (Lloyd Goff) in the process. Garfield's riveting, Oscar-nominated performance lifts BODY AND SOUL to the masterpiece level, as do Robert Rossen's superb direction, the marvelous photography of James Wong Howe and the Oscar-winning editing. The fight sequences, in particular, brought a kind of realism to the genre that had never before existed (Howe wore skates and rolled around the ring shooting the fight scenes with a hand-held camera). A knockout on all levels.

BODY HEAT

DVD

1981 113m c Crime/Erotic ★★★½
Ladd (U.S.) R

William Hurt *(Ned Racine)*, Kathleen Turner *(Matty Walker)*, Richard Crenna *(Edmund Walker)*, Ted Danson *(Peter*

Lowenstein), J.A. Preston (Oscar Grace), Mickey Rourke (Teddy Lewis), Kim Zimmer (Mary Ann), Jane Hallaren (Stella), Lanna Saunders (Roz Kraft), Michael Ryan (Miles Hardin)

p, Fred T. Gallo; d, Lawrence Kasdan; w, Lawrence Kasdan; ph, Richard H. Kline (Technicolor); ed, Carol Littleton; m, John Barry; cos, Renie Conley

An excellent crime drama in the style of Raymond Chandler, James M. Cain, and Dashiell Hammett. Director-writer Lawrence Kasdan borrows liberally in style from 1940s *film noir* and incorporates a plot reminiscent of DOUBLE INDEMNITY, but he adds a steamy sexuality more in keeping with contemporary films. Set in Florida, the movie follows the ill-fated course of Ned Racine (William Hurt), a rather dim-witted attorney who gets deeply involved with sultry Matty Walker (Kathleen Turner), a woman who wants her husband dead. Hurt gives a superior performance—we can actually see him thinking, rather painfully—while Turner makes a fine *femme fatale* after the model of Lauren Bacall. Ted Danson is also excellent as a slightly nerdy lawyer-friend of Ned's; Mickey Rourke, in one of his early screen appearances, shows the promise of things to come; and the other supporting roles are likewise well handled.

BODYGUARD, THE   DVD

1992 114m c   Romance/Thriller   ★★
TIG Productions/Kasdan Pictures   (U.S.)   R

Kevin Costner (Frank Farmer), Whitney Houston (Rachel Marron), Gary Kemp (Sy Spector), Bill Cobbs (Devaney), Ralph Waite (Herb Farmer), Tomas Arana (Portman), Michele Lamar Richards (Nicki), Mike Starr (Tony), Christopher Birt (Henry), DeVaughn Nixon (Fletcher)

p, Lawrence Kasdan, Jim Wilson, Kevin Costner; d, Mick Jackson; w, Lawrence Kasdan (from his story); ph, Andrew Dunn; ed, Richard A. Harris, Donn Cambern; m, Alan Silvestri; prod d, Jeffrey Beecroft; art d, William Ladd Skinner; cos, Susan Nininger

AAN Best Original Song: "I Have Nothing"; David Foster (Music), Linda Thompson (Lyrics); AAN Best Original Song: "Run to You"; Jud Friedman (Music), Allan Rich (Lyrics)

Based on a screenplay by Lawrence Kasdan, THE BODY-GUARD is a dreary, turgid melodrama featuring the much ballyhooed debut of pop diva Whitney Houston.

Frank Farmer (Kevin Costner) is an ex-secret serviceman who, racked with guilt because he was off duty the day President Reagan was shot, is now a bodyguard for hire. His latest client is Rachel Marron (Whitney Houston), a pop singer and Academy Award nominee who has recently begun receiving death threats. After a budding romance between the two is quashed by Farmer as a matter of professional protocol, it turns out the threats have been emanating from Rachel's jealous sister Nicki (Michele Lamar Richards), who has hired an assassin to kill Rachel. After accidentally doing away with Nicki, the killer makes a second attempt at the climactic Academy Awards ceremony, during which Rachel takes a very long, slow walk to the podium.

THE BODYGUARD should have remained in Kasdan's drawer. It echoes the worst aspects of previous flops like THE FAN and THE OSCAR without any attempt at reworking the lame plots and weak characters of those films. Instead, director Mick Jackson glosses over the shoddiness with a cheap-jack MTV burnish that ultimately serves to highlight the shortcomings of the narrative. As an actress, Whitney Houston is competent but bland; someone must have liked her forgettable songs, however, since the soundtrack album was a best seller.

BOMBSHELL

1933 90m bw Comedy   ★★★★
MGM   (U.S.)

Jean Harlow (Lola), Lee Tracy (Space), Frank Morgan (Pops), Franchot Tone (Gifford Middleton), Pat O'Brien (Brogan), Una Merkel (Mac), Ted Healy (Junior), Ivan Lebedeff (Marquis), Mary Forbes (Mrs. Middleton), C. Aubrey Smith (Mr. Middleton)

d, Victor Fleming; w, Jules Furthman, John Lee Mahin (based on a play by Caroline Francke, Mack Crane); ph, Chester Lyons, Harold Rosson; ed, Margaret Booth

One of the best films to satirize the movie industry, this is a trenchant, witty, fast-moving send-up of 1930s Hollywood lifestyles. Harlow plays a ditzy screen sexpot who gets involved in a series of madcap escapades. She becomes engaged to a "marquis" who is arrested as an illegal alien; tries to escape the clutches of an amorous director; unsuccessfully attempts to adopt a baby (her family gets in the way); and goes on retreat to Palm Springs, where she falls for an upper-crust beau but is finally forced to decide where her heart belongs. This early precursor to SUNSET BOULEVARD and THE BAD AND THE BEAUTIFUL was so inside that many people outside the movie business didn't catch the nuances, and it still packs a considerable comic punch.

BONNIE AND CLYDE   DVD

1967 111m c   Crime   ★★★★½
Tatira-Hill Productions/Warner Bros.   (U.S.)

Warren Beatty (Clyde Barrow), Faye Dunaway (Bonnie Parker), Michael J. Pollard (C.W. Moss), Gene Hackman (Buck Barrow), Estelle Parsons (Blanche), Denver Pyle (Frank Hamer), Dub Taylor (Ivan Moss), Evans Evans (Velma Davis), Gene Wilder (Eugene Grizzard), James Stiver (Grocery Store Owner)

p, Warren Beatty; d, Arthur Penn; w, David Newman, Robert Benton; ph, Burnett Guffey (Technicolor); ed, Dede Allen; m, Charles Strouse; art d, Dean Tavoularis; fx, Danny Lee; cos, Theadora Van Runkle

AAN Best Picture; AAN Best Actor: Warren Beatty; AAN Best Actress: Faye Dunaway; AAN Best Supporting Actor: Gene Hackman; AAN Best Supporting Actor: Michael J. Pollard; AA Best Supporting Actress: Estelle Parsons; AAN Best Director: Arthur Penn; AAN Best Original Story and Screenplay: David Newman, Robert Benton; AA Best Cinematography: Burnett Guffey; AAN Best Costume Design: Theadora Van Runkle

Landmark gangster film that made a huge commercial and cultural splash. The seminal script by David Newman and Robert Benton struck a nerve with the 1967 youth culture as it reimagined the two rural Depression-era outlaws as largely sympathetic nonconformists. The film set new standards for screen violence but it alternated its scenes of mayhem with lyrical interludes and jaunty slapstick sequences accompanied by spirited banjo music. While unusual for a Hollywood feature, such jarring shifts in tone were typical of the genre-bending works of French New Wave directors Francois Truffaut and Jean-Luc Godard, both of whom were slated to direct the feature at various points in its genesis.

Producer/star Beatty cajoled Warner Brothers into financing the production and selected Arthur Penn to direct. Penn initially aimed at realism, constructing scenes based on Walker Evans photographs and NRA posters, but a competing nostalgic impulse won out. The Oscar-winning cinematography of Burnett Guffey served up the Dust Bowl on a sumptuous Technicolor platter, and historical accuracy was jettisoned in favor of glossy romanticization. In the process, the story took on the quality of a folk ballad.

As portrayed by Beatty and Dunaway, Clyde Barrow and Bonnie Parker were just plain folks who liked to pose for photographs and rob banks. As one ad campaign proclaimed, "They are young, they are in love, they kill people." The rest of the Barrow gang is portrayed by a powerhouse group of supporting players: Gene Hackman, Estelle Parsons (who won the Oscar for Best Supporting Actress), and Michael J. Pollard. Gene Wilder also makes his screen debut as a nervous mortician.

BONNIE AND CLYDE grossed $23 million and became Warner's second best box-office attraction up to that time, after MY FAIR LADY. Despite its controversial nature, the film was nominated for nine Oscars (it only won two).

BOOGIE NIGHTS   DVD
1997 156m c   Drama   ★★★★
Lawrence Gordon Productions/Ghoulardi (U.S.)   R

Mark Wahlberg *(Eddie Adams/Dirk Diggler)*, Burt Reynolds *(Jack Horner)*, John C. Reilly *(Reed Rothchild)*, Julianne Moore *(Amber Waves)*, Heather Graham *(Rollergirl)*, Nicole Parker, billed as Nicole Ari Parker *(Becky Barnett)*, Philip Seymour Hoffman *(Scotty J.)*, Don Cheadle *(Buck Swope)*, Ricky Jay *(Kurt Longjohn)*, William H. Macy *(Little Bill)*

p, Paul Thomas Anderson, Lloyd Levin, John Lyons, Joanne Sellar; d, Paul Thomas Anderson; w, Paul Thomas Anderson; ph, Robert Elswit; ed, Dylan Tichenor; m, Michael Penn; prod d, Bob Ziembicki; art d, Ted Berner; fx, Lou Carlucci (supervisor); cos, Mark Bridges

AAN Best Supporting Actor: Burt Reynolds; *AAN Best Supporting Actress:* Julianne Moore; *AAN Best Original Screenplay:* Paul Thomas Anderson

Tongues back in mouths, please. This sprawling melodrama, set against the backdrop of the porno film industry during the pivotal period from 1977 to 1984, bares lots of flesh but isn't exactly what you'd call a turn-on.

The story's center is the, um, rise and fall of aimless but amiable Eddie Adams (Mark Wahlberg), who parlays his prodigious endowment into an adult-movie career under the *nom de smut* Dirk Diggler. But the supporting characters just about steal the show: porn director Jack Horner (Burt Reynolds), whose pretensions to art almost ruin his dirty movie career; adult-movie stars Amber Waves (Julianne Moore) and Rollergirl (Heather Graham), always juggling the sense of liberation and family they get from the industry with the personal price they pay; screen stud and amateur magician Reed Rothchild (John C. Reilly), who's always up to go where the day takes him; Buck Swope (John Cheadle), an African-American porn star in search of an image, nursing a secret dream to own his own stereo store; sad-sack assistant director Little Bill (William H. Macy), constantly cuckolded by his relentlessly promiscuous wife (real-life porn star Nina Hartley); hangers-on Scotty J. (Philip Seymour Hoffman), who nurses a secret crush on Dirk, and Maurice TT Rodriguez (Luis Guzman); businessman Floyd Gondolli (Philip Baker Hall), who sees that the future of porn is video, not film; vengeful ex-husband Thomas (John Doe), who uses Amber's involvement in porn to keep her from her child.

You have to give writer-director Paul Thomas Anderson (of HARD EIGHT, not the Paul Anderson of MORTAL KOMBAT and EVENT HORIZON) credit for both ambition and accomplishment: sure, the movie's a little long and the relentless bombardment by hideous '70s fashions and music becomes a bit tough to take, but on the whole he manages to guide his cast of characters through an epic story of self-delusion with a skill and grace that many more experienced filmmakers would be hard put to match.

BOOMERANG
1947 88m   bw Mystery   ★★★★
Fox   (U.S.)

Dana Andrews *(Henry L. Harvey)*, Jane Wyatt *(Mrs. Harvey)*, Lee J. Cobb *(Chief Robinson)*, Cara Williams *(Irene Nelson)*, Arthur Kennedy *(John Waldron)*, Sam Levene *(Woods)*, Taylor Holmes *(Wade)*, Robert Keith *(McCreery)*, Ed Begley *(Harris)*, Philip Coolidge *(Crossman)*

p, Louis de Rochemont; d, Elia Kazan; w, Richard Murphy (based on the *Reader's Digest* article "The Perfect Case" by Anthony Abbott); ph, Norbert Brodine; ed, Harmon Jones; m, David Buttolph

AAN Best Screenplay: Richard Murphy

A chilling *film noir* about the murder of a priest, the subsequent arrest and trial of a jobless drifter, and the efforts of a young state's attorney to uncover the truth. Closely based on the actual 1924 murder (still unsolved) of Fr. Hubert Dahme in Bridgeport, Connecticut, the film was directed by the young Elia Kazan in a highly effective, semi-documentary style. Kazan shot most of the film on location, using high-contrast cinematography and an extremely mobile camera to create a palpable sense of urgency. Producer Louis de Rochemont had earlier been responsible for the "March of Time" newsreel series, as well as the naturalistic features THE HOUSE ON 92ND STREET and 13 RUE MADELEINE.

BORN INTO BROTHELS
2004 85m   c/bw Documentary   ★★★★
(U.S.)   R

Avijit, Gour, Puja, Kochi, Manik, Shanti, Suchitra, Tapasi

p, Zana Briski, Ross Kauffman; d, Zana Briski, Ross Kauffman; ph, Zana Briski, Ross Kauffman; ed, Nancy Baker, Ross Kauffman; m, John McDowell

AA Best Documentary Feature

In a rare and inspiring example of how art can both reflect and alleviate human suffering, photojournalist Zana Briski's wrenching documentary chronicles her valiant use of photography to help children trapped in one of the most wretched places on earth.

Briski first came to northern Calcutta hoping to capture the lives of the illegal sex workers of the city's squalid red-light district. Knowing she would never gain access to this hermetic world as an outsider, Briski boldly took up residence in the polluted, labyrinthine neighborhood and began photographing not just the women, but the many children born into the brothels where their mothers worked, youngsters whose futures are entirely predetermined by their sordid, dangerous environment. After growing close to a group of these doomed children, Briski came up with a novel idea: she gave each a point-and-click camera and began teaching them the basics of photography. As the kids began photographing their surroundings and each other, Briski videotaped them.

The resulting documentary, shot with the help of cameraman Ross Kauffman, is a remarkable testament to the boundless creativity of children and the fortitude of one woman who tried to make a difference in their lives. Watching these adorable kids living amid rat-infested garbage, serving their mother's drunken clients, and facing verbal abuse from other prostitutes is tough going by any standard, but the film is surprisingly uplifting. Even in the face of the far-too-few happy endings, Briski's story—and the stories of the few children who do escape the brothels thanks to her efforts—is a major cause for celebration.

BORN ON THE FOURTH OF JULY

1989 140m c Drama/War
Fourth of July (U.S.)

DVD
★★★
R

Tom Cruise *(Ron Kovic)*, Bryan Larkin *(Young Ron)*, Raymond J. Barry *(Mr. Kovic)*, Caroline Kava *(Mrs. Kovic)*, Josh Evans *(Tommy Kovic)*, Seth Allen *(Young Tommy)*, Jamie Talisman *(Jimmy Kovic)*, Sean Stone *(Young Jimmy)*, Anne Bobby *(Susanne Kovic)*, Jenna von Oy *(Young Susanne)*

p, A. Kitman Ho, Oliver Stone; d, Oliver Stone; w, Oliver Stone, Ron Kovic (based on his autobiography); ph, Robert Richardson (Deluxe Color); ed, David Brenner, Joe Hutshing; m, John Williams; prod d, Bruno Rubeo; art d, Victor Kempster, Richard L. Johnson; cos, Judy Ruskin

AAN Best Picture; AAN Best Actor: Tom Cruise; *AA Best Director:* Oliver Stone; *AAN Best Adapted Screenplay:* Oliver Stone, Ron Kovic; *AAN Best Cinematography:* Robert Richardson; *AA Best Film Editing:* David Brenner, Joe Hutshing; *AAN Best Original Score:* John Williams; *AAN Best Sound:* Michael Minkler, Gregory H. Watkins, Wylie Stateman, Tod A. Maitland

Oliver Stone (PLATOON) returns to the Vietnam War era but here the focus is primarily on the homefront and the aftershocks of war. Ambitious matinee idol Tom Cruise stars in a showy change-of-pace characterization as Ron Kovic in the autobiographical story of a gung ho young man who went proudly off to Vietnam, came back home in a wheelchair, and, after a traumatic interval, became a high profile antiwar activist.

The film begins with a depiction of Kovic's youth in Massapequa, New York, where he is raised to be a deeply patriotic, God-fearing, macho all-American athelete. As such, he eagerly enlists in the Marines and ships off to Vietnam, convinced of the justness of the American cause. He becomes increasingly confused and disoriented after he accidentally kills one of his own men in a firefight. He later receives a bullet wound that leaves him paralyzed from the waist down. Back in the home of his family which no longer understands him, he degenerates into a drunken, self-pitying dropout. After a dissolute sequence in Mexico, he somehow gets a grip on himself, confronts his changed feelings about his life and his country, and becomes an antiwar activist, thereby regaining his self-respect.

Stone's film is undeniably emotionally powerful but problematic because it lingers on the pathos of Kovic's condition while skirting the less visually dramatic aspects of the character. Kovic clearly undergoes a political conversion but it is never dealt with directly—he changes during a fadeout. The effect is as unintentionally jarring as if a reel of the film were missing. The critique of masculinity is far more thoughtful and compelling than the vague ruminations about war. Nonetheless Cruise's impassioned performance as Kovic is an impressive accomplishment.

BORN YESTERDAY

1950 103m bw Comedy
Columbia (U.S.)

DVD
★★★★

Judy Holliday *(Billie Dawn)*, Broderick Crawford *(Harry Brock)*, William Holden *(Paul Verrall)*, Howard St. John *(Jim Devery)*, Frank Otto *(Eddie)*, Larry Oliver *(Norval Hedges)*, Barbara Brown *(Mrs. Hedges)*, Grandon Rhodes *(Sanborn)*, Claire Carleton *(Helen)*, Smoki Whitfield *(Bootblack)*

p, S. Sylvan Simon; d, George Cukor; w, Albert Mannheimer (based on the play by Garson Kanin); ph, Joseph Walker; ed, Charles Nelson; m, Frederick Hollander; cos, Jean Louis

AAN Best Picture; AA Best Actress: Judy Holliday; *AAN Best Director:* George Cukor; *AAN Best Screenplay:* Albert Mannheimer; *AAN Best Costume Design (B/W):* Jean Louis

The highlight of this lively Garson Kanin Broadway comedy is the most delightful "dumb blonde" to ever grace the screen, Holliday, in a role she originated on stage and nearly did not get to re-create on screen. As the malaprop-tossing mistress of scrap metal tycoon Crawford, she is unknowingly put in nominal charge of his shady empire so that he can cover his tracks. Though no paragon of high culture himself, Crawford is embarrassed by his paramour's lack of social refinement. He hires her a tutor, Holden, who actually plans to write a series of articles exposing Crawford's slippery operations. The PYGMALION-like process of changing the tasteless yet street-savvy Holliday into a cultured lady is loaded with laughs and inoffensive sexual innuendoes. The situation gets more complicated as Holliday and Holden fall in love.

Crawford is frightening yet funny as the tycoon and Holden is effective in his appealing if low-key role. But Holliday is the film's most enduring treasure. Indeed, she was so effective as a dumb blonde that she was typecast in most of her subsequent films. Holliday's priceless characterization earned her an Oscar for Best Actress (one of BORN YESTERDAY's five nominations including: Best Picture, Best Direction, Best Screenplay, and Best Costume Design), a considerable achievement in light of her stellar competition that year: Gloria Swanson in SUNSET BOULEVARD and Bette Davis in ALL ABOUT EVE. A sheer delight, even if one only remembers the classic gin rummy scene.

BOUDU SAVED FROM DROWNING

1932 84m bw Comedy
Pathe (France)

★★★½

Michel Simon *(Boudu)*, Charles Granval *(Monsieur Lestingois)*, Marcelle Hainia *(Madama Lestingois)*, Severine Lerczynska *(Anne-Marie)*, Jean Daste *(Student)*, Max Dalban *(Godin)*, Jean Gehret *(Vigour)*, Jacques Becker *(Poet on a Bench)*, Jane Pierson *(Rose, the Neighbor's Maid)*, George Darnoux *(Marriage Guest)*

p, Michel Simon, Jean Gehret; d, Jean Renoir; w, Jean Renoir (based on a play by Rene Fauchois); ph, Jean-Paul Alphen; ed, Marguerite Renoir; m, Leo Danideff, Johann Strauss; art d, Hugues Laurent, Jean Castanier

This social comedy is another masterpiece from Renoir. Made in 1932 but lost, then finally released in 1967 in the U.S., this film is a timeless satire on middle-class values centering on Boudu (Michel Simon), an archetypal tramp about to commit suicide in grief, apparently, over the loss of his dog. He leaps into the Seine from the Pont des Arts, but is saved by bourgeois bookseller Lestingois (Charles Granval), who takes Boudu home and tries to start him on the road to a productive, responsible life. Boudu, however, is a protohippie—a long-haired, bearded believer in freedom and anarchy. During his stay in Lestingois' very proper household, he turns the place into a shambles, seduces Lestingois' wife (Marcelle Hainia), and, after he strikes it rich in the lottery, marries the family's gold-digging maid (Severine Lerczynska). He is then faced with the choice of living as a socially responsible adult in a tuxedo or reasserting his own independence. Told in Renoir's characteristically liberating realist humanist manner and exquisitely photographed, the story is immeasurably enhanced by Simon's extraordinary portrayal of Boudu. As Renoir has written: "Everything that an actor can be in a film, Michel Simon is in BOUDU. Everything!" Crudely remade in 1986 as DOWN AND OUT IN BEVERLY HILLS, starring Nick Nolte.

BOUND

1996 107m c Crime/Thriller ★★★½

Dino De Laurentiis Communications/ R

Spelling Films (U.S.)

Jennifer Tilly *(Violet)*, Gina Gershon *(Corky)*, Joe Pantoliano *(Caesar)*, John P. Ryan *(Mickey Malnato)*, Christopher Meloni *(Johnnie Marzzone)*, Richard Sarafian *(Gino Marzzone)*, Barry Kivel *(Shelly)*, Mary Mara *(Bartender)*, Peter Spellos *(Lou)*, Susie Bright *(Jesse)*

p, Andrew Lazar, Stuart Boros; d, Larry Wachowski, Andy Wachowski; w, Larry Wachowski, Andy Wachowski; ph, Bill Pope; ed, Zach Staenberg; m, Don Davis; prod d, Eve Cauley; art d, Robert Goldstein, Andrea Dopaso; fx, Lou Carlucci; cos, Lizzy Gardiner

With its fast-paced dialogue, slick characterizations, and brash cinematography, BOUND is a clever, exceptionally stylish twist on the edge-of-the-seat thriller.

Soon after she starts renovating her Chicago high-rise apartment, ex-con Corky (Gina Gershon) meets neighbor Violet (Jennifer Tilly), who lives with mobster Caesar (Joe Pantoliano). Sick of Caesar and attracted to her new friend, Violet becomes romantically involved with Corky. Violet and Corky scheme to steal $2 million that Caesar is supposed to present to a Mafia boss. Their carefully thought-out plan starts to go awry when Caesar decides not to run for his life but to stay and prove a rival mobster guilty of stealing the cash.

It is to the credit of first-time writers-directors Andy and Larry Wachowski that BOUND remains suspenseful without stretching the plot's plausibility beyond the breaking point. The lesbian twist on the "young lovers dupe the rich boyfriend-husband" plot heightens the suspense,but it's not just a gimmick: the relationship is sexy, tender, and believable. But in this truly American film, the women are eventually brought into crisis situations due to emotional frailty and lack of physical strength. Is using traditional "feminine" traits as a plot device sexist? Probably, but the dynamic set up here between Violet and Corky is genuine and exciting, and the audience is set up to root for them.

Gershon is a wonder as Corky. While publicity was given to the fact that a "lesbian expert" was consulted for the script, Gershon's method of preparing for her role by studying how classic male actors played their love scenes is what makes her performance unique and powerful. Pantoliano's Caesar is also a terrific creation. He's smarter than he looks, tougher than people expect, and likable enough to keep the conflict honest.

BOUND FOR GLORY

1976 147m c Biography ★★★★

UA (U.S.) PG

David Carradine *(Woody Guthrie)*, Ronny Cox *(Ozark Bule)*, Melinda Dillon *(Mary Guthrie)*, Gail Strickland *(Pauline)*, John Lehne *(Locke)*, Ji-Tu Cumbuka *(Slim Snedeger)*, Randy Quaid *(Luther Johnson)*, Elizabeth Macey *(Liz Johnson)*, Allan Miller *(Agent)*

p, Robert F. Blumofe, Harold Leventhal; d, Hal Ashby; w, Robert Getchell (based on the autobiography of Woody Guthrie); ph, Haskell Wexler (DeLuxe Color); ed, Robert C. Jones, Pembroke J. Herring

AAN Best Picture; AAN Best Adapted Screenplay: Robert Getchell; AA Best Cinematography: Haskell Wexler; AAN Best Film Editing: Robert Jones, Pembroke J. Herring; AA Best Song Score: Leonard Rosenman; AAN Best Costume Design: William Theiss

A moving, brilliantly photographed picture that portrays the legendary eccentric folksinger Woody Guthrie in a trip across Depression-era America. Carradine is memorable as the penniless Okie who rides a train to California but is stopped at the border because the state is having difficulty providing for those that have arrived already. Carradine sneaks across the border and meets Quaid, and the two team up to look for work. Cox is an Ozark folk singer who periodically visits the labor camps to lighten the load of these poor men's lives. At one of the meetings, Carradine joins in the singing and Cox is so impressed that he gets him a job on the radio. Success is almost immediate, but Guthrie's social conscience compels him to use the radio as a political organ for recounting the travails of the farm workers he knows so intimately. He is told to cut out the politicking or leave. He chooses to be fired. Later he gets offered a chance to play the big time at Hollywood's Coconut Grove provided that he'll commercialize his work. No surprises here. He hits the road, hoping to bring the message of his music to people he meets along the way.

This is a superior biopic. Viewers get to see Guthrie warts and all. That easily half the audience is too young to know who he was should not matter. This is the story of an artist with deeply held political principles, a remarkable quality in any age. At 147 minutes, this film could lose a quarter of an hour or more with no loss to the drama.

Haskell Wexler proves again that he is a master of evocative cinematography as he uses the camera to its best advantage in every frame of this Hal Ashby directed film. Robert Getchell adapted Guthrie's autobiography for the screenplay but Ashby and his editor made extensive contributions.

BOURNE IDENTITY, THE

2002 113m c Thriller ★★★

Kennedy/Marshall Company/Hypnotic/ PG-13

Stillking/Universal (U.S./Czech Republic)

Matt Damon *(Jason Bourne)*, Franka Potente *(Marie)*, Chris Cooper *(Conklin)*, Clive Owen *(The Professor)*, Brian Cox *(Ward Abbott)*, Adewale Akinnuoye-Agbaje *(Wombosi)*, Gabriel Mann *(Zorn)*, Julia Stiles *(Nicolette)*, Orso Maria-Guerrini *(Giancarlo)*, Walton Goggins *(Research Tech)*

p, Patrick Crowley, Richard N. Gladstein, Doug Liman; d, Doug Liman; w, Tony Gilroy, W. Blake Herron (based on the novel by Robert Ludlum); ph, Oliver Wood; ed, Saar Klein; m, John Powell; prod d, Dan Weil; art d, Laurent Piron, Bettina von den Steinen; fx, Peter Donen, Philippe Hubin, Jean-Christophe Magnaud; cos, Pierre-Yves Gayraud

This savvy adaptation of Robert Ludlum's action-clogged 1980 bestseller benefits greatly from the fact that the filmmakers were smart enough to throw out most of the book's preposterous spills and thrills and concentrate instead on its intriguing central character.

Sixty miles off the coast of Marseilles, the body of a young man (Matt Damon) is pulled out of the stormy Mediterranean by the crew of a French fishing boat. He's alive, but the ordeal has left him with total amnesia. The only clue to his identity are the numbers of a Swiss bank account that have been implanted under his skin. By the time the boat reaches port, the stranger has recovered his health but not his memory. By the time he reaches Zurich, however, he's learned a few unsettling things about himself: He's fluent in several foreign languages; he can take out a number of men at once with his bare hands; and he can wriggle his way out of deadly situations with unnerving sangfroid. The contents of the Swiss safe-deposit box reveal his name and address: Jason Bourne, Paris. The guns, fake passports and wads of foreign currency strongly suggest that Bourne's game is international espionage.

Director Doug Liman (SWINGERS, GO) seems to know exactly what's gone stale and what still works in espionage thrillers. He dispenses with the glitz and complicated plotting and relies instead on great stunt work, a winning leading man/leading lady combo (RUN LOLA RUN's Franke Potente costars as the woman who agrees to help Bourne return to Paris—for a price) and an equally offbeat supporting cast that includes Chris Cooper, Clive Owen, Brian Cox and Julia Stiles.

BOURNE SUPREMACY, THE

DVD

2004 120m c Action/Thriller ★★★
MP Theta Productions/Kennedy/Marshall PG-13
Productions/Ludlum Entertainment/Universal/
Studio Babelsberg (U.S.)

Matt Damon *(Jason Bourne)*, Franka Potente *(Marie Kreutz)*, Brian Cox *(Ward Abbott)*, Julia Stiles *(Nicolette)*, Karl Urban *(Kirill)*, Gabriel Mann *(Danny Zorn)*, Joan Allen *(Pamela Landy)*, Marton Csokas *(Jarda)*, Tom Gallop *(Tom Cronin)*, Karel Roden *(Gretkov)*

p, Patrick Crowley, Frank Marshall, Paul L. Sandberg; d, Paul Greengrass; w, Tony Gilroy (based on the novel by Robert Ludlum); ph, Oliver Wood; ed, Richard Pearson, Christopher Rouse; m, John Powell; prod d, Dominic Watkins; art d, Peter Wenham; fx, Uli Nefzer, Kit West; cos, Dinah Collin

A refreshing alternative to the hypertrophied spy thrillers with more exaggerated action sequences, over-the-top villainy, and high-tech gadgetry than character and plot.

Amnesiac assassin Jason Bourne (Matt Damon) and his girlfriend, Marie (Franka Potente), have been in hiding since Bourne press-ganged her into helping him piece together a series of fragmentary clues about his very scary past. Still uncertain who he really is and tormented by nightmares, Bourne has used his covert skills to keep them both off the radar just in case his former colleagues decide to come calling. But their current idyll in Goa comes to a violent end when Bourne spots a stranger (Karl Urban) whose demeanor fairly screams "contract killer." In the ensuing melee, Bourne loses Marie and resolves to find out who ordered the hit and make them pay. Meanwhile, in Berlin, a covert operation managed by veteran CIA agent Pamela Landy (Joan Allen) goes very wrong, leaving two agents dead and several million in U.S. government funds missing. The single fingerprint found at the scene is Bourne's, and soon an international game of cat and mouse is on. Landy recruits Bourne's old contact, Nicolette (Julia Stiles), and former intelligence bigwig Ward Abbott (Brian Cox) to help her trap Bourne, who's after both the mysterious assassin and whoever's responsible for framing him.

Tony Gilroy's screenplay bears scant resemblance to Robert Ludlum's 1986 novel, the second installment in his *Bourne* trilogy, which involves a plot to plunge China into calamitous civil war. Paul Greengrass, taking over for BOURNE IDENTITY director Doug Liman, keeps the action believable and the tone briskly paranoid—the Cold War may be over, but espionage is still a chilly business.

BOWLING FOR COLUMBINE

DVD

2002 119m c/bw Documentary ★★★½
Salter Street Films/VIF 2/Dog Eat Dog Films/ R
Alliance Atlantis/UA (U.S./Canada/Germany)

Michael Moore, Charlton Heston, Marilyn Manson, Dick Clark, James Nichols, Matt Stone, Barry Glassner, Richard Castaldo

p, Charles Bishop, Jim Czarnecki, Michael Donovan, Kathleen Glynn, Tia Lessen, Michael Moore; d, Michael Moore; w, Michael Moore; ph, Brian Danitz, Michael McDonough; ed, Kurt Engfehr; m, Jeff Gibbs; anim, Harold Moss

AA Best Documentary Feature

Filmmaker and social critic Michael Moore takes aim at America's love of firearms and hits a much wider target: the culture of fear that he feels keeps gun owners on edge and their weapons locked and loaded.

The title is a wry reference to the report that teenage shooters Eric Harris and Dylan Klebold went bowling shortly before they entered Columbine High School and systematically gunned down 15 people. Columbine has become a rallying point for gun control advocates around the country, but in the media's rush to lay blame, Moore wonders impishly why bowling wasn't cited as a pernicious influence on our nation's youth. Riotously funny and deadly serious, Moore probes the received wisdom that the prevalence of guns is solely responsible for the staggering number of gun-related deaths in the United States. Looking for answers, Moore turns to Barry Glassner, author of *The Culture of Fear: Why Americans Are Afraid of the Wrong Things*, who argues that the news media creates an atmosphere of generalized terror and keeps a nervous—and armed—public scared of everything from "Africanized" killer bees to African Americans.

It's an interesting theory, but Moore knows it can't explain why Harris and Klebold took their weapons to school that day; his general point becomes somewhat muddled amid all the speculation. And while you might not cotton to Moore's guerrilla approach of ambushing interview subjects with a mike and camera (in a real coup, Moore bags NRA president Charlton Heston), it does get Kmart to pull handgun and assault ammunition from their shelves after two Columbine survivors show up at corporate headquarters with Moore's camera crew in tow and Kmart bullets still embedded in their bodies.

BOY FRIEND, THE

1971 108m c Musical ★★★½
MGM (U.K.) G

Twiggy *(Polly Browne)*, Christopher Gable *(Tony Brockhurst)*, Moyra Fraser *(Madame Dubonnet)*, Max Adrian *(Max)*, Bryan Pringle *(Percy)*, Catherine Wilmer *(Lady Brockhurst)*, Murray Melvin *(Alphonse)*, Georgina Hale *(Fay)*, Sally Bryant *(Nancy)*, Vladek Sheybal *(De Thrill)*

p, Ken Russell; d, Ken Russell; w, Ken Russell (based on a play by Sandy Wilson); ph, David Watkin (Metrocolor); ed, Michael Bradsell; art d, Simon Holland; chor, Christopher Gable, Terry Gilbert, Gillian Gregory; cos, Shirley Russell

AAN Best Song Score: Peter Maxwell Davies (Adaptation), Peter Greenwell (Adaptation)

Ken Russell's dizzy, affectionate homage to 1930s musicals and Busby Berkeley is for many his best film. Twiggy is the assistant stage manager who gets her big chance when star Glenda Jackson hurts her ankle. "Come back a star," the director tells her, and that's just what she does. (The same line was spoken by Warner Baxter to Ruby Keeler in 42ND STREET.) Russell's bombastic direction has never looked so right. Musical numbers (the film's song score received an Oscar nomination) are uniformly well done; included are renditions of old standards like "I Could Be Happy," "All I Do Is Dream Of You," and "You Are My Lucky Star."

THE BOY FRIEND is a sincere celebration of the musical from a camp point of view. And let it be said Russell discovered Tommy Tune many years before Broadway did.

BOYS DON'T CRY

DVD

1999 114m c Docudrama ★★★½
Killer Films/Hart-Sharp Entertainment/ R
Independent Film Channel (U.S.)

Hilary Swank *(Brandon Teena)*, Chloe Sevigny *(Lana)*, Peter Sarsgaard *(John)*, Brendan Sexton III *(Tom)*, Alison Folland *(Kate)*, Alicia Goranson *(Candace)*, Matt McGrath *(Lonny)*, Rob Campbell *(Brian)*, Jeannetta Arnette *(Lana's Mom)*

p, Jeffrey Sharp, John Hart, Eva Kolodner, Christine Vachon; d, Kimberly Peirce; w, Kimberly Peirce, Andy Bienen; ph, Jim Denault; ed, Lee Percy, Tracy Granger; m, Nathan Larsen; prod d, Michael Shaw; cos, Victoria Farrell

AA Best Actress: Hilary Swank; AAN Best Supporting Actress:
Chloe Sevigny

A harrowing dramatization of the final days of 21-year-old
Nebraskan Brandon Teena, whose short life ended in brutal
rape and murder.

Shortly before his 21st birthday, Brandon Teena
(Hilary Swank) blows into nowhere town Falls City, NE,
with little more than a rap sheet and a way with the ladies.
Brandon falls in with a rough crowd: volatile ex-con John
(Peter Sarsgaard), his buddy Tom (Brendan Sexton III),
and troubled friend Lana (Chloe Sevigny). Kicks in Grand
Falls are scarce—getting high, "bumper-skiing" (clinging
by a rope to the bumper of a reeling pick-up truck) and
hanging out—but Brandon is smitten with Lana, who in
turn falls hard for the tender, considerate Brandon. But
there's something Lana doesn't realize, even after they
have sex; Brandon Teena, born Teena Brandon, is a
woman. Once the truth is known, Brandon's dream world
comes to a sudden, savage end.

Teena, who died in 1993, has become a flash point for
academics and was the subject of the perceptive 1997 documentary THE BRANDON TEENA STORY, which offers
keen insight into the culture in which Brandon died. Director
Kimberly Peirce is more interested in emotional drama, the
rush of an audacious, often reckless life lived on the edge.
Swank's nuanced performance is remarkable, and it's a powerful film. But Peirce's quest for some truth underlying this
bewildering tale of lies, dissociation, and deception leads her
to fabricate a version of events that distorts what's known
about the case. The result is a flawed but compelling cinematic corollary to Norman Mailer's *The Executioner's Song* or
Truman Capote's *In Cold Blood*: non-fiction fiction, but
with an emphasis on the latter.

BOYS FROM BRAZIL, THE   *DVD*
1978 123m c   Thriller/War   ★★★½
Fox   (U.S./U.K.)   R

Gregory Peck *(Josef Mengele)*, Laurence Olivier *(Ezra Lieberman)*,
James Mason *(Eduard Seibert)*, Lilli Palmer *(Esther Lieberman)*,
Uta Hagen *(Frieda Maloney)*, Rosemary Harris *(Mrs. Doring)*, John
Dehner *(Henry Wheelock)*, John Rubinstein *(David Bennett)*, Anne
Meara *(Mrs. Curry)*, Steve Guttenberg *(Barry Kohler)*

p, Martin Richards, Stanley O'Toole; d, Franklin J. Schaffner; w,
Heywood Gould (based on the novel by Ira Levin); ph, Henri
Decae (Deluxe Color); ed, Robert Swink; m, Jerry Goldsmith; cos,
Anthony Mendleson

*AAN Best Actor: Laurence Olivier; AAN Best Film Editing: Robert
E. Swink; AAN Best Original Score: Jerry Goldsmith*

This fast-moving picture features a battle of wits between
the "Angel of Death," Nazi war criminal Josef Mengele
(Gregory Peck), and fictional Nazi hunter Ezra Lieberman
(Laurence Olivier, his character seemingly based on real-
life Nazi hunter Simon Wiesenthal), in a farfetched plot
having to do with the cloning of Hitler. Mengele's plan is
to harvest hundreds of young men (all of whom have been
raised in environments nearly identical to the one that
Hitler grew up in) in an attempt to replicate the Fuhrer's
upbringing as well as his genetic structure. The picture
barrels along for about 115 minutes, but then falls apart in
a wildly ludicrous finale. The cast is great—including
Peck, Olivier, James Mason, Denholm Elliott, and even
Steve Guttenberg (in one of his first roles). The film is
compelling, albeit pretty silly in its elaborate "what if?"
plot mechanications.

BOYS OF ST. VINCENT, THE   *DVD*
1993 210m c   Drama   ★★★★½
Les Productions Tele-Action/National
Film Board of Canada   (Canada)

Henry Czerny *(Peter Lavin)*, Johnny Morina *(Kevin Reevey—age
10)*, Sebastian Spence *(Kevin Reevey—age 25)*, Brian Dodd
(Steven Lunny—age 10), David Hewlett *(Steven Lunny—age 25)*,
Jonathan Lewis *(Eddie Linnane)*, Jeremy Keefe *(Mike Sproule)*,
Philip Dinn *(Mike Finn)*, Brian Dooley *(Detective Noseworthy)*,
Greg Thorney *(Brother Glackin)*

p, Sam Grana; d, John N. Smith; w, Des Walsh, John N. Smith,
Sam Grana; ph, Pierre Letarte; ed, Werner Nold, Andre
Corriveau; m, Neil Smolar; prod d, Real Ouellette

This two-part made-for-TV Canadian movie proved one of
the most emotionally devastating films released in the U.S.
in 1994. THE BOYS OF ST. VINCENT was inspired by a
notorious case involving the alleged sexual abuse of
dozens of children by Christian Brothers in a Catholic-
administered orphanage.

Part One is set in 1975 Newfoundland at St. Vincent, a
nightmarish institution where the authoritarian Brother Peter
Lavin (Henry Czerny) extorts sexual favors from young boys.
Part Two opens 15 years later in Montreal, Quebec, with the
arrest of Lavin, now married and the father of two pre-teen
sons. THE BOYS OF ST. VINCENT doesn't flinch from
depicting the physical and emotional horrors endured by the
boys but, despite the sensational subject-matter, its approach
is restrained and non-exploitative. The film is neither an anti-
Catholic nor homophobic diatribe but, rather, a dark and
impressively complex critique of the abuse of power. Henry
Czerny gives a terrifying but exquisitely modulated performance, roaming the corridors under his command with a crucifix jammed in his belt like a six-gun. Watching this martinet
try to "mother" a small child is genuinely unnerving. Perhaps
one of the greatest achievements of BOYS, though, is the
emergence of Lavin as more understandably human in the
second half. The verdict on Lavin is not disclosed, but it hardly matters; when the survivors on both sides are left so damaged, the idea of legal justice being served is small
consolation.

BOYS TOWN
1938 96m bw Drama   ★★★
MGM   (U.S.)

Spencer Tracy *(Father Edward Flanagan)*, Mickey Rooney *(Whitey
Marsh)*, Henry Hull *(Dave Morris)*, Leslie Fenton *(Dan Farrow)*,
Addison Richards *(The Judge)*, Edward Norris *(Joe Marsh)*, Gene
Reynolds *(Tony Ponessa)*, Minor Watson *(The Bishop)*, Jonathan
Hale *(John Hargraves)*, Bobs Watson *(Pee Wee)*

p, John W. Considine Jr.; d, Norman Taurog; w, John Meehan,
Dore Schary (based on a story by Dore Schary, Eleanore Griffin);
ph, Sidney Wagner; ed, Elmo Veron; m, Edward Ward; art d,
Cedric Gibbons, Urie McCleary; fx, Slavko Vorkapich

*AAN Best Picture; AA Best Actor: Spencer Tracy; AAN Best
Director: Norman Taurog; AA Best Original Story: Eleanore Griffin,
Dore Schary; AAN Best Screenplay: John Meehan, Dore Schary*

One of the more overrated films of its era. Not surprisingly one
of MGM tyrant Louis B. Mayer's favorite films, this sentimental wallow dramatizes the real-life story of Father Edward
Flanagan, founder of the famous Boys Town for errant youths.
What sounds like ideal "truth is stranger than fiction" material, with inspiration to boot, comes across as stilted, overly
sanctimonious moralizing. Father Flanagan's efforts against
incredible obstacles vanish with a magic flourish of the

scriptwriter's pen, and the generally reliable Tracy, one of the most talented and engaging actors of his day, compounds these errors with a performance dripping with piety. Tracy always claimed that his Oscar for Best Actor here belonged to Flanagan (he even sent the priest his statuette); the Academy should have bypassed the actor entirely and simply donated the crockery to Flanagan for his humanitarian activities. The soft-focus closeups of the film's star weren't needed to soften Tracy's likably craggy features; they were there to canonize the film's hero with a phony cinematic halo. Director Taurog, a competent but unimaginative contract man, was chosen for this epic because of his past success with child actors. Credit the electrifying 18-year-old Mickey Rooney with lending some edge to a picture that is soft, soft, soft. Also highly effective is the genuinely sweet child actor Bobs Watson, able to turn on the tears without batting an eyelid. Too respectful of its subject matter, BOYS TOWN is well-crafted and smoothly paced, probably most entertaining for those who can down maple syrup without benefit of pancakes. Nominated for Best Picture and Best Director, the film won an Oscar for Best Original Story.

BOYZ N THE HOOD

1991 107m c Drama ★★★★
Both Inc./Columbia (U.S.) R

Laurence Fishburne, billed as Larry Fishburne (*Furious Styles*), Ice Cube (*Doughboy Baker*), Cuba Gooding Jr. (*Tre Styles*), Nia Long (*Brandi*), Morris Chestnut (*Ricky Baker*), Tyra Ferrell (*Mrs. Baker*), Angela Bassett (*Reva Styles*), Meta King (*Brandi's Mom*), Whitman Mayo (*The Old Man*), Hudhail Al-Amir (*SAT Man*)

p, Steve Nicolaides; d, John Singleton; w, John Singleton; ph, Charles Mills; ed, Bruce Cannon; m, Stanley Clarke; art d, Bruce Bellamy

AAN Best Director: John Singleton; *AAN Best Original Screenplay:* John Singleton

John Singleton's debut feature is a low-key morality drama about the strained bonds of family and friendship in the midst of social disorder.

The film begins in South Central Los Angeles, circa 1984, where ten-year-old Tre Styles (Desi Arnez Hines II) is confronted with the violence of everyday life in the streets of his ghettoized, African-American neighborhood. After being entrusted by his divorced mother Reva (Angela Bassett) to her ex-husband Furious (Larry Fishburne), Tre receives moral guidance from his loving but disciplinarian father. Growing up he befriends the brothers who live across the street, bad-assed Doughboy and shy Ricky, who dreams of playing professional football. After Doughboy spends seven years in prison for juvenile crimes, the three are reunited during their last year of high school.

Tre (Cuba Gooding, Jr.) and Ricky (Morris Chestnut) are the inseparable good kids, while Doughboy (Ice Cube) leads the crew of bitter and combative boys in the 'hood. USC recruiters offer Ricky an athletic scholarship, while Tre and his girlfriend Brandi (Nia Long) discuss the possibility of getting married—after completing their college educations. But chaotic forces overwhelm even these best and brightest in their efforts to escape the terrors of their neighborhood.

"Increase the peace." The words which appear at the conclusion of BOYZ N THE HOOD ring out as a simple, intelligent, and urgent plea, befitting Singleton's powerful, unpretentious dramatization of life in a modern L.A. ghetto. Like fellow black filmmaker Spike Lee, Singleton fills his work with references to the particulars of black life: from little Tre's precocious lecture on Afrocentric history, to Furious's lessons about racial genocide and culturally biased IQ tests, to

Brandi and Tre's destinations at historically black colleges Spelman and Morehouse. The ensemble cast makes good on Singleton's true-to-life script, with particularly strong work performances by rap star-turned-actor Ice Cube as Doughboy and the understated Larry Fishburne as Furious Styles. Positive figures—Furious, Tre, Brandi—are rendered perhaps too virtuous, and Singleton becomes a bit preachy in the closing scenes, but an overt "message" movie may be the only appropriate response to the ongoing social crisis addressed by BOYZ N THE HOOD.

BRAINSTORM

1965 105m bw Thriller ★★★
Warner Bros. (U.S.)

Jeffrey Hunter (*Jim Grayam*), Anne Francis (*Lorrie Benson*), Dana Andrews (*Cort Benson*), Viveca Lindfors (*Dr. E. Larstadt*), Stacy Harris (*Josh Reynolds*), Kathie Browne (*Angie DeWitt*), Phillip Pine (*Dr. Ames*), Michael Pate (*Dr. Mills*), Robert McQueeney (*Sgt. Dawes*), Strother Martin (*Mr. Clyde*)

p, William Conrad; d, William Conrad; w, Mann Rubin (based on a story by Larry Marcus); ph, Sam Leavitt (Panavision); ed, William Ziegler; m, George Duning

Creepy yet contrived suspense film stars Hunter as a young scientist who saves distraught Francis from committing suicide. The pair fall in love, but Francis' rotten husband Andrews (who drove her to the brink of suicide in the first place) digs up the file on Hunter's earlier mental instability. He exacts his revenge by framing the scientist for obscene phone calls and other misdeeds so as to create the impression that he's cracking up again. Hunter and Francis retaliate with a plot to murder Andrews. Hunter expects to get a light sentence with an insanity defense since everyone is convinced he's crazy anyway. Hunter figures that he will be placed in a cushy mental institution, recover after a decent interval, and walk off scot-free into the waiting arms of Francis. Of course things don't work out as they plan....

Fine cast directed by actor Conrad, TV's "Cannon," in a clever and taut visual style. Good, spare musical score by George Duning.

BRAM STOKER'S DRACULA

1992 130m c Horror/Romance/Fantasy ★★★½
Columbia/American Zoetrope/Osiris Films (U.S.) R

Gary Oldman (*Count Vlad Dracul/Dracula*), Winona Ryder (*Mina Murray/Elisabeta*), Anthony Hopkins (*Professor Abraham Van Helsing*), Keanu Reeves (*Jonathan Harker*), Richard E. Grant (*Dr. Jack Seward*), Cary Elwes (*Lord Arthur Holmwood*), Bill Campbell (*Quincey P. Morris*), Sadie Frost (*Lucy Westenra*), Tom Waits (*R.M. Renfield*), Monica Bellucci (*Dracula's Bride*)

p, Francis Ford Coppola, Fred Fuchs, Charles Mulvehill; d, Francis Ford Coppola; w, James V. Hart (from the novel *Dracula* by Bram Stoker); ph, Michael Ballhaus; ed, Nicholas C. Smith, Glen Scantlebury, Anne Goursaud; m, Wojciech Kilar; prod d, Thomas Sanders; art d, Andrew Precht; cos, Eiko Ishioka

AA Best Costume Design: Eiko Ishioka; *AA Best Makeup:* Greg Cannom, Michele Burke, Matthew W. Mungle; *AA Best Sound Effects Editing:* Tom C. McCarthy, David E. Stone; *AAN Best Art Direction-Set Decoration:* Thomas Sanders, Garrett Lewis

Francis Ford Coppola's lavish new version of Bram Stoker's classic novel is a visual cornucopia, overstuffed with images of both beauty and grotesque horror.

Coppola has assembled a virtual Who's Who of young screen heartthrobs, all of whom—from Winona Ryder to Gary Oldman to Keanu Reeves to Cary Elwes—do their stuff against a range of brilliantly realized settings. Count Dracula's

Transylvanian lair has a deliberately tongue-in-cheek, mythological aura, and Victorian England is brought to life through meticulous, and humorous, production design.

DRACULA also boasts some impressive special effects, and Coppola clearly enjoys recreating the cutting-edge technology of the late 19th century, from a primitive blood-transfusion apparatus to the earliest moving pictures. The problem is that the visual pyrotechnics and period detail tend to blunt the dramatic impact of a narrative that's pretty bloodless to begin with. James V. Hart's screenplay sticks fairly close to Stoker's novel but loses steam after about 20 minutes, when continual cutting between different storylines creates more confusion than tension.

It's also hard to gauge the tone of this adaptation. Hart sets up an archly romantic relationship between the Count (Oldman) and a beautiful young woman (Ryder) who's a dead ringer for the love he lost centuries earlier. The couple's "love conquers all" scenes can't be taken seriously, but it's not entirely clear how ironic DRACULA is intended to be. Not, that is, until the late arrival of Anthony Hopkins as Professor Van Helsing. Hopkins clearly recognizes this big, overblown, theme park ride for what it is, and wisely decides to inject some campy humor into the proceedings. The resulting combination is fun—but not as much fun as BUFFY THE VAMPIRE SLAYER.

BRAVEHEART
1995 177m c Historical/Drama/Adventure ★★★
Icon Productions/The Ladd Co./Marquis Film/ R
Paramount (U.S.)

Mel Gibson *(William Wallace)*, Sophie Marceau *(Princess Isabelle)*, Patrick McGoohan *(Longshanks—King Edward I)*, Catherine McCormack *(Murron)*, Brendan Gleeson *(Hamish)*, James Cosmo *(Campbell)*, David O'Hara *(Stephen)*, Angus MacFadyen *(Robert the Bruce)*, Ian Bannen *(The Leper)*, Peter Hanly *(Prince Edward)*

p, Mel Gibson, Alan Ladd Jr., Bruce Davey; d, Mel Gibson; w, Randall Wallace; ph, John Toll; ed, Steven Rosenblum; m, James Horner; prod d, Thomas Sanders; art d, Dan Dorrance; fx, Nick Allder; cos, Charles Knode

AA Best Picture; AA Best Director: Mel Gibson; *AAN Best Original Screenplay:* Randall Wallace; *AA Best Cinematography:* John Toll; *AAN Best Costume Design:* Charles Knode; *AAN Best Film Editing:* Steven Rosenblum; *AA Best Makeup:* Peter Frampton, Paul Pattison, Lois Burwell; *AAN Best Dramatic Score:* James Horner; *AAN Best Sound:* Andy Nelson, Scott Millan, Anna Behlmer, Brian Simmons; *AA Best Sound Effects Editing:* Lon Bender, Per Hallberg

A massive, sweaty, sloppy and extremely heavy-handed epic, BRAVEHEART won Mel Gibson a Best Directing Oscar and delivers enough visceral excitement to make it an ideal rainy afternoon matinee.

As a boy, Scottish hero-to-be Sir William Wallace (Mel Gibson) witnesses the vicious treachery of King Edward I (Patrick McGoohan) when he slaughters a group of unarmed landowners. Educated abroad, Wallace returns as an adult to the tiny hamlet of Ellerslie to raise crops and children. After defending his wife from English rapists, he's forced to flee and begins enlisting locals in a bloody revolt. Wallace leads his army against the superior English forces at Stirling, beating them through cunning and bravery, and is declared "Guardian of Scotland." He takes his army into England, capturing the city of York. Sparks fly when he encounters comely Princess Isabelle (Sophie Marceau), but her husband, Prince Edward (Peter Hanly, in a performance that amounts to a homophobic caricature), schemes to destroy Wallace, who is soon betrayed by Robert the Bruce and Scottish aristocrats.

Although BRAVEHEART's scale is impressive, Gibson's attempt to create an old fashioned epic *a la* EL CID or SPARTACUS is not entirely successful. The pace is uneven and Gibson's abuse of slow motion reduces many dramatic scenes to tedium, though John Toll's gorgeous cinematography and Thomas Sanders's detailed, thoroughly authentic production design help overcome the film's sluggishness. And the fight sequences are truly outstanding: bloody, amazingly brutal, and efficiently edited, they create a compelling sense of the way it must have felt to be in the thick of brutal battle.

BRAZIL
1985 131m c Fantasy/Science Fiction ★★★½
Terry Gilliam (U.K.) R

Jonathan Pryce *(Sam Lowry)*, Robert De Niro *(Tuttle)*, Katherine Helmond *(Ida Lowry)*, Ian Holm *(Kurtzmann)*, Bob Hoskins *(Spoor)*, Michael Palin *(Jack Lint)*, Ian Richardson *(Warrenn)*, Peter Vaughan *(Helpmann)*, Kim Greist *(Jill Layton)*, Jim Broadbent *(Dr. Jaffe)*

p, Arnon Milchan; d, Terry Gilliam; w, Terry Gilliam, Tom Stoppard, Charles McKeown; ph, Roger Pratt (Technicolor); ed, Julian Doyle; m, Michael Kamen; prod d, Norman Garwood; art d, John Beard, Keith Pain; fx, George Gibbs, Richard Conway; cos, James Acheson

AAN Best Original Screenplay: Terry Gilliam (Screenplay), Tom Stoppard (Screenplay), Charles McKeown (Screenplay); *AAN Best Art Direction-Set Decoration:* Norman Garwood (Art Direction), Maggie Gray (Set Decoration)

Black humor dons its darkest robes in BRAZIL. Blindingly obtuse, excessively morose, the film is nevertheless dazzling in its inventive and massive sets and spectacular in its techniques. The theme is latter-day Orwell, well beyond 1984. The place could be anywhere in the future, where citizens of the regime live subterranean existences. One of these punctilious moles is Sam Lowry (Jonathan Pryce), a mundane statistician working in the Ministry of Information. He and millions of others work and live in a world crowded with a huge snake-like ductwork that heats, cools, and generally keeps the community going, when it works. A disaster, of sorts, is set off when a bug in the computer system causes everything to go haywire by altering the arrest record for a terrorist named Tuttle (Robert De Niro) to read Buttle. Lowry investigates the mistaken identity and discovers the girl of his fantasies, Jill Layton (Kim Greist). But in doing so he brings the scrutiny of superiors upon himself. The art direction (which earned the film an Academy Award nomination, as did the screenplay) and the special effects are nothing less than stunning. The storyline is a bit confusing—fragmented through interjected scenes and dizzying cross-cutting—so that some viewers may not grasp the sense of it all until it's almost over, and perhaps that's the point. Perhaps not. The plot's weaknesses become painfully apparent about halfway through the film. Still, BRAZIL is a powerful work that is both bleakly funny and breathtakingly assured. Following TIME BANDITS with this film, Gilliam firmly established himself as a director possessing true vision and remarkable style; few fantasy-film directors can compare with him. Haunting, lyrical and trendsetting, BRAZIL—a black comedy that remains ahead of its time—is one of the most audacious fantasies ever made.

BREAKER MORANT
1980 107m c Drama/War ★★★
South Australian Film (Australia)

Edward Woodward *(Lt. Harry Morant)*, Jack Thompson *(Maj. J.F. Thomas)*, John Waters *(Capt. Alfred Taylor)*, Bryan Brown *(Lt. Peter Handcock)*, Rod Mullinar *(Maj. Charles Bolton)*, Lewis Fitz-Gerald *(Lt. George Witton)*, Charles Tingwell *(Lt. Col. Denny)*,

Vincent Ball *(Lt. Ian (Johnny) Hamilton)*, Frank Wilson *(Dr. Johnson)*, Terence Donovan *(Capt. Simon Hunt)*

p, Matt Carroll; d, Bruce Beresford; w, Bruce Beresford, Jonathan Hardy, David Stevens (based on a play by Kenneth Ross); ph, Don McAlpine (Panavision, Eastmancolor); ed, William Anderson; m, Phil Cunneen; cos, Anna Senior

AAN Best Adapted Screenplay: Jonathan Hardy (Screenplay), David Stevens (Screenplay), Bruce Beresford (Screenplay)

A good court-martial drama in the old-fashioned style. Set during the Boer War—fought in South Africa between the descendants of Dutch colonists (the Boers) and the British during the years 1899-1902—BREAKER MORANT chronicles an obscure incident in 1901 when three Australian soldiers stationed in South Africa to assist the British were court martialed for executing enemy prisoners. Fighting what was, in essence, a guerrilla war, Lt. Harry "Breaker" Morant (Edward Woodward) ordered the executions acting under the orders of the British command. One of these prisoners turns out to have been a German citizen fighting alongside the Boers. Eager to maintain a good relationship with Germany, the British decide to make scapegoats of the Australians. Capably directed by Australian Bruce Beresford and well acted, BREAKER MORANT is a fascinating and satisfying experience. Unfolding his film in flashback during testimony at the trial, Beresford skillfully translates Kenneth Ross' play to the screen with an eye for historical accuracy.

BREAKFAST AT TIFFANY'S 📀
1961 115m c Drama ★★★★½
Paramount (U.S.)

Audrey Hepburn *(Holly Golightly)*, George Peppard *(Paul Varjak)*, Patricia Neal *(2-E)*, Buddy Ebsen *(Doc Golightly)*, Martin Balsam *(O.J. Berman)*, Mickey Rooney *(Mr. Yunioshi)*, Jose-Luis de Vilallonga *(Jose da Silva Perriera)*, John McGiver *(Tiffany's Clerk)*, Dorothy Whitney *(Mag Wildwood)*, Stanley Adams *(Rusty Trawler)*

p, Martin Jurow, Richard Shepherd; d, Blake Edwards; w, George Axelrod (based on the novella by Truman Capote); ph, Franz Planer (Technicolor); ed, Howard Smith; m, Henry Mancini; cos, Edith Head

AAN Best Actress: Audrey Hepburn; *AAN Best Adapted Screenplay:* George Axelrod; *AA Best Score (Drama or Comedy):* Henry Mancini; *AA Best Song:* "Moon River"; Henry Mancini, Johnny Mercer; *AAN Best Art Direction-Set Decoration (Color):* Hal Pereira, Roland Anderson, Sam Comer, Ray Moyer

Capote's novella comes to glorious if slightly sentimentalized onscreen life with Hepburn gamboling through the film as the fey, ever-charming Holly Golightly. Peppard, never again quite so appealing, is Paul, the upstairs neighbor both intrigued and puzzled by Holly's erratic behavior: throwing all-night bashes for dozens of friends one moment, a lonely neurotic the next. Also mysterious are her visits to an imprisoned ganglord (Alan Reed) and to nightclub powder rooms, from which she emerges with $50 in cash each time. Paul, too, has a puzzling relationship with a wealthy woman (Neal) which prevents his growing love for Holly from flowering. Finally, though, answers come in the form of Doc (Ebsen), a visitor from rural Texas who reveals some of the truth behind Holly's surface sophistication.

The film is well cast, with the exception of Rooney as a Japanese neighbor—a racist grotesque—driven to frenzy by Holly's noisy soirees. Balsam, as Holly's agent, offers a significant insight into his client's personality midway through the film when he notes: "She's a phony, all right, but a *real* phony." Amusingly helmed by director Edwards, romantic to the *n*th degree, and likely to disappoint only those devoted to Capote's novel, BREAKFAST AT TIFFANY'S is one of the

great New York films, swathing the city in a layers of dewy love and glossy chic. The song, "Moon River," memorably crooned by Hepburn, won an Oscar and went on to become a popular favorite.

BREAKFAST CLUB, THE 📀
1985 97m c Drama ★★★
A&M (U.S.) R

Emilio Estevez *(Andrew Clark)*, Paul Gleason *(Richard Vernon)*, Anthony Michael Hall *(Brian Johnson)*, John Kapelos *(Carl)*, Judd Nelson *(John Bender)*, Molly Ringwald *(Claire Standish)*, Ally Sheedy *(Allison Reynolds)*, Perry Crawford *(Allison's Father)*, Mary Christian *(Brian's Sister)*, Ron Dean *(Andy's Father)*

p, Ned Tanen, John Hughes; d, John Hughes; w, John Hughes; ph, Thomas Del Ruth (Panavision, Technicolor); ed, Dede Allen; m, Keith Forsey, Gary Chang; prod d, John W. Corso; fx, Bill Schirmer; chor, Dorain Grusman; cos, Marilyn Vance, Christian Zamiata

Of the plethora of teen-based films released in 1985, THE BREAKFAST CLUB stands as one of the best, but it's still not exactly a shining example of the genre. Set in suburban Chicago, the film features five high school students from different social backgrounds who must spend a Saturday sitting in the school library as punishment for various infractions. Estevez, a star wrestler, is the jock; Ringwald portrays a rich, spoiled "princess"; Hall is a nerdy "brain"; Sheedy plays an introverted loner; and Nelson is a rebellious punk. Nelson fixes the library doors so they will remain closed, giving the students a little privacy. Confronting their values head on, with an articulate and sarcastic verbal assault, Nelson works on the others until they slowly begin talking with one another. THE BREAKFAST CLUB, paradoxically, is one of the few teen-oriented films that truly addresses the troubles of its characters, yet it falters in dealing with the issues raised. Director-writer Hughes, though he gives the material a sense of fun and achieves several moments of genuine warmth, too often resorts to obvious cliches, stereotypes, and easy answers, and throws in the near-obligatory rock video as well. His cast, on the other hand, is a fine ensemble that infuses the material with the sense of reality that Hughes's script often misses.

BREAKING AWAY 📀
1979 100m c Comedy/Sports ★★★★
Fox (U.S.) PG

Dennis Christopher *(Dave Stohler)*, Dennis Quaid *(Mike)*, Daniel Stern *(Cyril)*, Jackie Earle Haley *(Moocher)*, Barbara Barrie *(Mrs. Stohler)*, Paul Dooley *(Mr. Stohler)*, Robyn Douglass *(Katherine)*, Hart Bochner *(Rod)*, Amy Wright *(Nancy)*, Peter Maloney *(Doctor)*

p, Peter Yates; d, Peter Yates; w, Steve Tesich; ph, Matthew F. Leonetti (Deluxe Color); ed, Cynthia Scheider; m, Patrick Williams; cos, Betsy Cox

AAN Best Picture; AAN Best Supporting Actress: Barbara Barrie; *AAN Best Director:* Peter Yates; *AA Best Original Screenplay:* Steve Tesich; *AAN Best Song Score:* Patrick Williams

A delightful sleeper. Set in Bloomington, Indiana, and nominated for an Oscar for Best Picture (it lost to KRAMER VS. KRAMER), BREAKING AWAY is a very funny and touching story about love, growing up, bicycle racing, and class consciousness. Dave Stohler (Christopher) and three of his friends (Quaid, Stern, and Haley) are recent high-school graduates. More importantly, in the eyes of nearby Indiana University students, they are "cutters"—declasse Bloomington townies, so named because many of the locals earn their living cutting rock in limestone quarries. For a time, Stohler, an avid bicycle racer, immerses himself in an alternative identity, pretends to be Italian, and does his best to woo a college coed. After a team of real Italian bicycle racers comes to town and treats Stohler horribly, he discards his false identity but not his desire to prove himself the equal of the college students. He and his cutter buddies (who barely know one end of a racing bicycle from another) enter the university's "Little 500" bicycle race with suspenseful but not-so-surprising results at the film's uplifting finish. Tesich won an Oscar for his amusing screenplay; Barrie, as Christopher's mother, was nominated for Best Supporting Actress; composer Williams and director Yates also received nominations from the Academy. The four young leads all deliver excellent performances, as does Dooley (unjustly overlooked by the Academy) as Dave's father. Cyclists of the world, unite. You have nothing to lose but your chains!

BREAKING THE WAVES   _DVD_

1996 156m c Drama   ★★★
Zentropa Entertainment/Trust Films/Liberator   R
Productions/Argus/Northern Lights/La Sept/Swedish
Television Drama/Media Investment Club/Nordic
Film & Television Fund/VPRO Television
(Denmark/Sweden/Norway/Netherlands/Finland/
France/U.S./Iceland)

Emily Watson *(Bess)*, Stellan Skarsgard *(Jan)*, Katrin Cartlidge *(Dodo)*, Jean-Marc Barr *(Terry)*, Udo Kier *(Man on the Trawler)*, Adrian Rawlins *(Doctor Richardson)*, Jonathan Hackett *(The Minister)*, Sandra Voe *(Bess' Mother)*, Mikkel Gaup *(Pits)*, Roef Ragas *(Pim)*

p, Vibeke Windelov, Peter Aalbaek Jensen; d, Lars Von Trier; w, Lars Von Trier, Peter Asmussen; ph, Robby Muller; ed, Anders Refn; m, Joachim Holbek; art d, Karl Juliusson; fx, Morten Jacobsen, Lars Andersen; cos, Manon Rasmussen

AAN Best Actress: Emily Watson

Lars Von Trier's BREAKING THE WAVES is a twisted fable about the miraculous powers of faith, sacrifice, and unconditional love. Despite moments of undeniable brilliance, the film is occasionally sabotaged by an unsettling cinematic technique.

In a tiny, severely puritanical Presbyterian fishing village in 1970s Scotland, Bess (Emily Watson), a seemingly unstable young woman, marries an earthy oil-rigger named Jan (Stellan Skarsgard). Bess is blissfully happy with her husband, but she panics whenever Jan reminds her that he must eventually return to work on the rig, which he soon does. Disconsolate, Bess begs God for his return; after an accident on the rig sends Jan home paralyzed from the neck down, Bess is convinced that God has answered her prayers. When Jan later suggests that she have sleazy sex with other men so she can pleasure him with the details, she agrees, and begins a degrading descent that ultimately ends in tragedy.

Von Trier has admitted that in the past he "had an almost fetishistic attraction to film technology," and this is certainly true here, where the chosen technique is employed so relentlessly that the film is often literally hard to watch. Celebrated cinematographer Robby Muller intentionally filmed with a shaky hand-held camera, then transferred to video, and then transferred back to film, and then finally into the Super 35 widescreen format. Unfortunately, the result is extremely off-putting and distancing. That said, there is much to admire in BREAKING THE WAVES, particularly Emily Watson's fearless and star-making performance. The ending is impressive and memorable, although it's a bit surprising to see the enfant terrible Von Trier aspiring to achieve a Carl Dreyer-like spiritual epiphany.

BREATHLESS   _DVD_

(A BOUT DE SOUFFLE)
1959 89m bw Crime   ★★★★★
Imperia/Societe nouvelle de cinema/
Film Georges DeBeauregard   (France)

Jean-Paul Belmondo *(Michel Poiccard/Laszlo Kovacs)*, Jean Seberg *(Patricia Franchini)*, Daniel Boulanger *(Police Inspector)*, Jean-Pierre Melville *(Parvulesco)*, Liliane Robin *(Minouche)*, Henri-Jacques Huet *(Antonio Berrutti)*, Van Doude *(Journalist)*, Claude Mansard *(Claudius Mansard)*, Michel Fabre *(Plainclothesman)*, Jean-Luc Godard *(Informer)*

p, Georges de Beauregard; d, Jean-Luc Godard; w, Jean-Luc Godard (based on an idea by Francois Truffaut); ph, Raoul Coutard; ed, Cecile Decugis, Lila Herman; m, Martial Solal; art d, Claude Chabrol

What Stravinsky's "La Sacre du Printemps" is to 20th-century music or Joyce's *Ulysses* is to the 20th-century novel, Godard's first feature, BREATHLESS, is to film. It stands apart from all that came before and has revolutionized all that followed.

Dedicated to the B-movies of Hollywood's Monogram Pictures, the film's structure begins with the conventions of the gangster film and film noir and proceeds to fragment them in a manner which greatly influenced the style of subsequent filmic narration. Michel Poiccard, alias Laszlo Kovacs (Belmondo, not conventionally attractive but giving a very sexy and appealing performance), is an amoral, dangerously careless petty criminal who models himself after Bogart and becomes the subject of a police dragnet when he senselessly guns down a traffic cop. He tries every avenue possible to cash a check endorsed "for deposit only" and hides out in the apartment of young American student Patricia Franchini (Seberg, whose imperfect French and limited acting skills lend something impossibly right to her enigmatic charcter). The couple, especially Michel, seem to be falling fatefully in love, but Godard is not content to merely develop character. During an extended, remarkable bedroom scene, this classic existential pair discusses art and philosophy in a way which prefigures Godard's lengthier and more profound ruminations in later films. Resuming the story, Godard ends his film with several ambiguous twists and an unforgettable closeup of Seberg.

Rather than tell his tale in a conventional manner, Godard uses nostalgia, humor, and brutality alike to create the cinematic equivalent of contemporary alienation. Quoting Hollywood affectionately, Godard is nevertheless more concerned with destroying previous film language and employing his own. He "jump cuts" with little concern for continuity and then dollies the camera for long, fluid takes. Some scenes have a documentary feel, while others are pure pulp fiction. As the title implies, Godard's philosophy is to leave the viewer breathless so that he may breathe new life into them. (Look for his cameo as an informer.)

BREWSTER'S MILLIONS   _DVD_

1945 79m bw Comedy   ★★★★
UA   (U.S.)

Dennis O'Keefe *(Monty Brewster)*, Helen Walker *(Peggy Gray)*, Eddie "Rochester" Anderson *(Jackson)*, June Havoc *(Trixie Summers)*, Gail Patrick *(Barbara Drew)*, Mischa Auer *(Michael Michaelovich)*, Joe Sawyer *(Hacky Smith)*, Nana Bryant *(Mrs. Gray)*, John Litel *(Swearengen Jones)*, Herbert Rudley *(Nopper Harrison)*

p, Edward Small; d, Allan Dwan; w, Sig Herzig, Charles Rogers, Wilkie Mahoney (based on the novel by George Barr McCutcheon and the play by Winchell Smith and Byron Ongley); ph, Charles Lawton Jr.; ed, Richard Heermance

AAN Best Score (Drama or Comedy): Lou Forbes

Probably the best of the many filmings of the popular novel and stage play. O'Keefe portrays Monty Brewster, the young, handsome, happy-go-lucky soldier returning from the war to his girlfriend Peggy Gray (Walker). Upon arriving home, he is stunned to find that he has inherited an estate worth $8,000,000, with one catch, however: he must spend $1,000,000 in the span of two months or he gets nothing. Brewster promptly embarks on a whirlwind of spending, racing around town in an effort to divest himself of the money by investing in a flop musical show, a bankrupt banker, the stock market, the racetrack, and a jewel-loving society woman. He soon finds out that spending money isn't as easy as it seems. BREWSTER'S MILLIONS is a broad farce and comes across as such, providing laughs throughout. While the opening is somewhat slow and deliberate, once the plot is established this modestly budgeted production rockets along with one climax topping another. The always reliable and appealing Walker and Anderson provide sturdy support, and O'Keefe gives one of his best performances. Previously filmed in 1921 with Fatty Arbuckle, and in a 1935 British production with Jack Buchanan and Lili Damita, the story was resurrected as THREE ON A SPREE with Jack Watling in 1961 and in an abysmal 1985 effort starring Richard Pryor and John Candy under the original title, with Walter Hill directing. In that version Brewster had to spend $30 million in 30 days to collect $300 million. Talk about inflation!

BRIDE OF CHUCKY
1998 88m c Horror/Comedy ★★½
David Kirschner Productions/Universal (U.S.) R

Jennifer Tilly (Tiffany), Brad Dourif (Voice of Chucky), Katherine Heigl (Jade), Nick Stabile (Jesse), Alexis Arquette (Damien), Gordon Michael Woolvett (David), John Ritter (Chief Warren Kincaid), Lawrence Dane (Lt. Preston), Michael Johnson (Norton), James Gallanders (Russ)

p, David Kirschner, Grace Gilroy; d, Ronny Yu; w, Don Mancini (based on characters created by Don Mancini); ph, Peter Pau; ed, David Wu, Randolph K. Bricker; m, Graeme Revell; prod d, Alicia Keywan; art d, James McAteer; fx, Colin Chilvers; cos, Lynne Mackay

God bless Jennifer Tilly, who attacks her role in this third sequel to 1988's killer-doll picture CHILD'S PLAY with incomparable slutty brio. Cooing and flirting and wielding her womanly curves like lethal weapons, Tilly's Tiffany is every bit the equal of murderous "Good Guy" doll Chucky, who houses the soul of Tiffany's late, unlamented boyfriend, serial murderer Charles Lee Ray (voiced by series regular Brad Dourif). Directed by Hong Kong cult favorite Ronny Yu, this newest installment in the Chucky chronicles has a campy edge that goes a long way to ameliorating the conventional stalk and slash stuff.

Tiffany has been searching for the plastic remains of her man for 10 years, and locates them in a police-evidence repository in some secluded corner of hell, alongside the Michael Myers and Jason masks. She patches up the battered doll and performs a voodoo rite that summons up Charles Lee Ray's nasty spirit just in time for him to do a number on her new suitor, pretentious Goth-boy Damien Blaylock (Alexis Arquette). But Tiffany and Chucky have a lover's spat: he murders her in her bath (electrocuted while watching the BRIDE OF FRANKENSTEIN; what a way to go!) and imprisons her soul in a tatty bride doll. Hoping to trade up to fresh, young human bodies, the two nasty dollies insinuate themselves into the complicated lives of Jesse and Jade (Nick Stabile, Katherine Heigl).

There's a peculiar subtext involving Jesse and Jade's sex life interruptus—if it isn't her creepy guardian (John Ritter) or the killer dolls making trouble, it's pervy grifters or their gay friend (Gordon Michael Woolvett) tagging along on the honeymoon—but mostly the movie's appeal lies in wisecracks and wet work, and there are plenty of both.

BRIDE OF FRANKENSTEIN
1935 75m bw Horror ★★★★★
Universal (U.S.)

Boris Karloff, billed as Karloff (The Monster), Colin Clive (Baron Henry Frankenstein), Valerie Hobson (Elizabeth), Ernest Thesiger (Dr. Septimus Pretorius), Elsa Lanchester (Mary Wollstonecraft Shelley/The Monster's Mate [billed as "?"]), Gavin Gordon (Lord Byron), Douglas Walton (Percy Bysshe Shelley), Una O'Connor (Minnie), E.E. Clive (Burgomaster), Lucien Prival (Albert, the Butler)

p, Carl Laemmle Jr.; d, James Whale; w, William Hurlbut, John Balderston (suggested by the novel Frankenstein by Mary Wollstonecraft Shelley); ph, John Mescall; ed, Ted Kent; m, Franz Waxman; art d, Charles D. Hall; fx, John P. Fulton

AAN Best Sound Recording: Gilbert Kurland

One of the seminal achievements of Hollywood cinema, this brilliant sequel to the original FRANKENSTEIN is one of the greatest films of its genre and remains a lasting tribute to the unique genius of director Whale.

Asked to continue the tale of the monster and its maker, Mary Shelley (Lanchester) picks up approximately where FRANKENSTEIN left off, with the injured Dr. Frankenstein (Clive) being taken back to his castle to recover, while the monster (Karloff), also alive, wanders the countryside, wreaking havoc in its search for friendship. Enter the eccentric Dr. Pretorius (Thesiger), an alchemist who has also created artificial life. (An utterly delightful scene ensues when he shows off his miniatures.) Pretorius blackmails the reluctant Frankenstein to aid him in creating a bride for the monster, which, in an incredible scene, they do.

A splendid combination of gothic horror and impish wit, BRIDE OF FRANKENSTEIN is a Whale masterpiece. The film is an unforgettable visual experience with its expressionistic sets, costumes and makeup; striking special effects; chiaroscuro lighting and bold camerawork. Waxman's magnificent score adds greatly to the overall effect, from the villagers' march to the mock-love theme attending the monstrous couple's "courtship" to the wedding bells pealing as the bride is presented. The performances are equally superb, with Clive again striking just the right note of nervous hysteria, Karloff beautifully injecting a sense of touching humanity into the confused and angry monster, and charcter actors Una O'Connor, O.P. Heggie, Dwight Frye and E.E. Clive lending ace support. Lanchester is quite amazing as both the deceptively demure Mary Shelley and her marvelously appropriate manifestation in her story, the bride. Thesiger, though, really steals the film with his pithy, menacing and hilarious portrait of the waspish Dr. Pretorius. A film whose black humor and sense of self-parody made Mel Brooks's delightful send-up YOUNG FRANKENSTEIN quite unnecessary, BRIDE OF FRANKENSTEIN transcends even the excesses allowed by its genre to become one of the oddest and most memorable films ever made in America.

BRIDGE ON THE RIVER KWAI, THE
1957 161m c War ★★★★½
Columbia (U.S.)

William Holden (Shears), Alec Guinness (Col. Nicholson), Jack Hawkins (Maj. Warden), Sessue Hayakawa (Col. Saito), James Donald (Maj. Clipton), Geoffrey Horne (Lt. Joyce), Andre Morell (Col. Green), Peter Williams (Capt. Reeves), John Boxer (Maj. Hughes), Percy Herbert (Grogan)

p, Sam Spiegel; d, David Lean; w, Carl Foreman (uncredited), Michael Wilson (uncredited, based on the novel by Pierre Boulle); ph, Jack Hildyard (CinemaScope, Technicolor); ed, Peter Taylor; m, Malcolm Arnold

AA Best Picture; AA Best Actor: Alec Guinness; *AAN Best Supporting Actor:* Sessue Hayakawa; *AA Best Director:* David Lean; *AA Best Adapted Screenplay:* Pierre Boulle, Michael Wilson, Carl Foreman; *AA Best Cinematography:* Jack Hildyard; *AA Best Film Editing:* Peter Taylor; *AA Best Score:* Malcolm Arnold

This intelligent and exciting WWII tale, masterfully helmed by Lean (at the start of his "epic" period), features a splendid performance from Guinness as Col. Nicholson, a British officer who has surrendered with his regiment to the Japanese in Burma in 1943. Martinet Nicholson insists that his men conduct themselves by the book and flatly refuses to cooperate with the equally dutiful Japanese commander, Col. Saito (Hayakawa, in an equally marvelous performance). When Saito insists that the British prisoners construct an elaborate bridge over the gorge of the River Kwai, Nicholson refuses to permit his officers to work side-by-side with the enlisted men, citing the Geneva Convention. After a series of incidents including torture and negotiations, Nicholson suddenly becomes determined to build the best bridge possible, thereby restoring his men's morale *and* providing a shining example of British rectitude. Meanwhile, Shears (Holden), an American, escapes from the prison camp and makes his way to Australia, where he impersonates an officer to obtain the privileges of rank. Major Warden (Hawkins), the British officer in charge of guerrilla operations, uncovers Shears' duplicity and sends him back to the jungle prison to destroy the bridge Nicholson and his men are so frantically attempting to complete.

Lean aptly juxtaposes action sequences with a psychological examination of the folly of war, emphasizing its many ironies (brought home most forcefully at the explosive finale). Screenwriters Carl Foreman and Michael Wilson retained Pierre Boulle's terse, tough dialogue, which finds its greatest expression in Holden's cowardly wise-guy character. Foreman and Wilson were denied credit on the film due to blacklisting problems; in 1996, the Writer's Guild of America officially restored their names. Based on fact, the film stands as one of the finest war films ever. Stunningly photographed and featuring a theme guaranteed to keep you whistling, THE BRIDGE ON THE RIVER KWAI won seven Oscars, including Best Picture, Actor (Guinness), and Director, as well as awards for writing, editing, cinematography, and music.

BRIDGE TOO FAR, A

1977 176m c War
UA (U.K.) PG

Dirk Bogarde *(Lt. Gen. Browning)*, James Caan *(Sgt. Dohun)*, Michael Caine *(Lt. Col. Vandeleur)*, Sean Connery *(Maj. Gen. Urquhart)*, Edward Fox *(Lt. Gen. Horrocks)*, Elliott Gould *(Col. Stout)*, Gene Hackman *(Maj. Gen. Sosabowski)*, Anthony Hopkins *(Lt. Col. John Frost)*, Hardy Kruger *(Gen. Ludwig)*, Laurence Olivier *(Dr. Spaander)*

p, Joseph E. Levine, Richard Levine, Michael Stanley-Evans; d, Richard Attenborough; w, William Goldman (based on the book by Cornelius Ryan); ph, Geoffrey Unsworth (Panavision, Technicolor); ed, Anthony Gibbs; m, John Addison; cos, Anthony Mendleson

A movie too long. A BRIDGE TOO FAR tells the true story of a WWII military blunder that cost many lives and, in the end, meant little to the war effort. Field Marshal Montgomery and General Eisenhower planned to drop 35,000 Allied troops into Holland to secure the six bridges leading to Germany, after which a British force was to speed

through Belgium to the last bridge at Arnhem. From there, the two groups were to smash into the Ruhr area and crush the already damaged factories of the German war effort. Murphy's Law acted up on a massive scale: foul weather, poor judgment, panic, and bad luck all took their toll, and the operation (code-named "Market Garden") was a total disaster. A BRIDGE TOO FAR is not a *total* disaster, but it does suggest that the curses hanging over certain historical debacles should perhaps be heeded by Hollywood filmmakers. Running three squirming hours and casting a dozen top stars in what are in some cases little more than cameos prove effective as sure ways to annoy an audience. (Gould's performance, for instance, comprises little more than his uttering "Shit!" as a bridge is blown up before his eyes.) A thoroughly disappointing and overproduced picture, A BRIDGE TOO FAR is nevertheless technically impressive and its sheer scope may interest hardcore warmongers. Screenwriter Goldman has also injected a handful of character touches which lend an occasional burst of humanity and intimacy to this otherwise overly indulgent behemoth.

BRIDGES AT TOKO-RI, THE

1954 102m c War
Paramount (U.S.)

William Holden *(Lt. Harry Brubaker, USNR)*, Fredric March *(Rear Adm. George Tarrant)*, Grace Kelly *(Nancy Brubaker)*, Mickey Rooney *(Mike Forney)*, Robert Strauss *(Beer Barrel)*, Charles McGraw *(Cmdr. Wayne Lee)*, Keiko Awaji *(Kimiko)*, Earl Holliman *(Nestor Gamidge)*, Richard Shannon *(Lt. Olds)*, Willis Bouchey *(Capt. Evans)*

p, William Perlberg; d, Mark Robson; w, Valentine Davies (based on a novel by James Michener); ph, Loyal Griggs; ed, Alma Macrorie; m, Lyn Murray; art d, Hal Pereira, Henry Bumstead; cos, Edith Head

AAN Best Film Editing: Alma Macrorie; *AA Best Special Effects*

A gripping psychological study of war's effects, starring Holden as Lt. Harry Brubaker, a family man called back to active duty who feels he has already done enough for his country in WW II and resents the Korean War's intrusion on his life with wife Nancy (Kelly) and their kids. Still a military man, however, Brubaker heeds the requests of his admiral (March) and doggedly goes about his duty as a pilot, spending long idle stretches aboard a battleship. The narrative drives toward the climactic bombing of the five bridges of Toko-ri, which span a strategic pass in Korea's interior. Along the way Holden and Kelly share some effective and intimate scenes together, and several enjoyable lighter moments occur in buddy scenes with fellow pilots Mike Forney (Rooney) and Nestor Gamidge (Holliman). Based on the novel by James Michener, this exciting and thoughtful film features excellent acting all around and is visually quite compelling thanks to Oscar-winning special effects in the aerial scenes. Also nominated for Best Film Editing.

BRIDGES OF MADISON COUNTY, THE

1995 135m c Romance/Drama
Amblin/Malpaso Productions (U.S.) PG-13

Clint Eastwood *(Robert Kincaid)*, Meryl Streep *(Francesca Johnson)*, Annie Corley *(Carolyn Johnson)*, Victor Slezak *(Michael Johnson)*, Jim Haynie *(Richard Johnson)*, Sarah Kathryn Schmitt *(Young Carolyn)*, Christopher Kroon *(Young Michael)*, Phyllis Lyons *(Betty)*, Michelle Benes *(Lucy Redfield)*, Alison Wiegert *(Child)*

p, Clint Eastwood, Kathleen Kennedy; d, Clint Eastwood; w, Richard LaGravenese (based on the novel by Robert James Waller); ph, Jack N. Green; ed, Joel Cox; m, Lennie Niehaus; prod d, Jeannine Oppewall; art d, William Arnold; fx, Steve Riley, John Frazier; cos, Colleen Kelsall

AAN Best Actress: Meryl Streep

Adapted from the best-selling and much-mocked novel, THE BRIDGES OF MADISON COUNTY is a tearjerker, pure and simple, but its warmth, humor, and charm make it an immensely satisfying one. Aptly exploiting the formidable screen presence of leads Clint Eastwood and Meryl Streep, it's a rare mainstream American romance in which two mature adults move from attraction and flirtation to love and passion.

Iowa, 1965. Francesca Johnson (Streep), an Italian woman married to a Midwesterner, looks forward to a week of splendid solitude with her family off at the State Fair. Her plans change when intriguing stranger Robert Kincaid (Eastwood) pulls into her driveway. He's a *National Geographic* photographer on assignment to shoot some of Madison County's historic covered bridges, and he's lost. The attraction between them is immediate. She's enthralled by his romantic style and tales of adventures in far-off places. The next night, she invites him over again, and they make love. Will Francesca abandon home and hearth for this charismatic drifter?

Robert Waller's *The Bridges of Madison County* was an American publishing phenomenon, a best-selling brew of naive poetry, fuzzy philosophizing, and over-ripe prose that was absolutely impervious to critical brickbats. To his credit, director and star Clint Eastwood has manufactured a cinematic silk purse from a literary sow's ear. Telling the story from Francesca's point of view is a smart change: her womanly wisdom—even in intrusive voice-over—is far more appealing than Kincaid's slippery New Age nonsense.

Eastwood brings an air of easy, romantic charm to Kincaid, but BRIDGES is Streep's film. She completely inhabits Francesca, bringing to life both the character's superficial frumpiness and a grace and natural elegance she has almost forgotten she has.

BRIDGET JONES: THE EDGE OF REASON *DVD*
2004 108m c Comedy/Romance ★★
StudioCanal/Working Title Productions/Universal/ R
Miramax/Atlantic Television/Little Bird
(U.K./France/Germany/Ireland/U.S.)

Renee Zellweger *(Bridget Jones)*, Colin Firth *(Mark Darcy)*, Hugh Grant *(Daniel Cleaver)*, Jacinda Barrett *(Rebecca)*, Jim Broadbent *(Bridget's Dad)*, Gemma Jones *(Bridget's Mum)*, Sally Phillips *(Shazzer)*, James Callis *(Tom)*, Shirley Henderson *(Jude)*, James Faulkner *(Uncle Geoffrey)*

p, Tim Bevan, Jonathan Cavendish; d, Beeban Kidron; w, Richard Curtis, Andrew Davies, Helen Fielding, Adam Brooks (based on the novel by Helen Fielding); ph, Adrian Biddle; ed, Greg Hayden; m, Harry Gregson-Williams; prod d, Gemma Jackson; art d, Dave Warren; fx, Stuart Brisdon; cos, Jany Temime

The genius of novelist Helen Fielding's silly and compulsively readable *Bridget Jones's Diary* was Bridget herself. A neurotic charmer who eats, smokes, and drinks to excess, dates dreadful men, and then castigates herself in her diary, Bridget struck a chord with a generation of women convinced by self-help gurus that all their problems are the product of their own inadequacies. Sadly, in both Fielding's sequel and Beeban Kidron's fat-joke-filled follow-up to BRIDGET JONES'S DIARY, all Bridget's problems *are* her own fault.

Now united with upper-crust human-rights lawyer Mark Darcy (Colin Firth), the intrepid Bridget is first seen skydiving bottom-first into a pigpen in the name of television journalism—the first of many cheap jokes at Bridget's expense. On the hopelessly bad advice of friends Shazzer (Sally Phillips), Jude (Shirley Henderson), and Tom (James Callis), Bridget eventually picks a relationship-souring fight over Mark's leggy associate (Jacinda Barrett) and soon after finds herself in

Bangkok filming a segment of "The Smooth Report," a boorish travelogue hosted by sleazy ex-flame Daniel Cleaver (Hugh Grant). Bridget gets arrested for smuggling cocaine and tossed into a hellish Thai prison, where she teaches her battered, drug-addicted cellmates to sing "Like a Virgin" and brings some sunshine into their lives with gifts of fancy bras, chocolate bars, and copies of *Men Are from Mars, Women Are from Venus*.

There's more—much more—and it's all equally labored and dispiriting. Bridget has degenerated into a clingy, obsessive, lumpen caricature of her former sparkling self, so witless and galling that Lucy Ricardo seems a steady, self-confident font of common sense by comparison. Readers who fell in love with the original Bridget laughed along with her mishaps, but like the oily Daniel, Kidron's film is merely laughing at her.

BRIDGET JONES'S DIARY *DVD*
2001 94m c Comedy/Romance ★★½
Universal/Studio Canal/Working Title/Miramax R
(U.S./U.K.)

Renee Zellweger *(Bridget Jones)*, Colin Firth *(Mark Darcy)*, Hugh Grant *(Daniel Cleaver)*, Jim Broadbent *(Bridget's Dad)*, Gemma Jones *(Bridget's Mum)*, Sally Phillips *(Sharon—"Shazza")*, Shirley Henderson *(Jude)*, James Callis *(Tom)*, Embeth Davidtz *(Natasha)*, Celia Imrie *(Una Alconbury)*

p, Tim Bevan, Jonathan Cavendish, Eric Fellner; d, Sharon Maguire; w, Helen Fielding, Andrew Davies, Richard Curtis (based on the novel by Helen Fielding); ph, Stuart Dryburgh; ed, Martin Walsh; m, Patrick Doyle; prod d, Gemma Jackson; art d, David Warren; fx, Frazer K. Churchill, Double Negative, David Harris; cos, Rachael Fleming

AAN Best Actress: Renee Zellweger

Anyone whose response to the casting of Texan Renee Zellweger as the irreducibly British heroine of Helen Fielding's enormously popular *Bridget Jones's Diary* was a groan followed by a list of actresses who *should* have had the role owes Miss Zellweger an apology. Armed with a flawless accent and 20 extra pounds, Zellweger simply *is* Bridget, the irrepressible, slightly zaftig, thirtysomething "singleton" with a ticking biological clock and a terrible fear that if she doesn't drop the weight and land a boyfriend soon, she'll die alone and be devoured by ravenous dogs. So with that crucial bit of casting so triumphantly in the bag, why is the movie such a let-down? Maybe because the real pleasure of *Bridget Jones* is purely a literary one: the naughty fun of paging through a stranger's diary, punctuated by horrifying but hilarious moments of self-recognition. The film tries to hold on to the diary conceit, delivering the action in bite-sized chunks spiced with Bridget's own hard-won wisdom in voiceover, but the plot soon dwindles down to little more than a flimsy, Austen-esque comedy of circumstance: marriage-minded heroine must choose between dashing bounder (Hugh Grant) and rich but stiff barrister (Colin Firth)—named Mr. Darcy, no less—who appears not to care for said heroine, but is secretly mad about her. The film marks the directing debut of TV producer Sharon Maguire, a friend of Fielding's, but she does little with the juicy material and relies too heavily on a trite soundtrack for emotional uplift. ("Ain't No Mountain High Enough"? Please.) A never-ending brawl between Darcy and Grant's character is a terrible idea, and surely Bridget herself would sniff at the film's soppy sentimentality.

BRIEF ENCOUNTER *DVD*
1945 86m bw Romance ★★★★★
Cineguild/Eagle-Lion (U.K.)

Celia Johnson *(Laura Jesson)*, Trevor Howard *(Alec Harvey)*, Cyril Raymond *(Fred Jesson)*, Stanley Holloway *(Albert Godby)*, Joyce

Carey *(Myrtle Bagot)*, Everley Gregg *(Dolly Messiter)*, Margaret Barton *(Beryl Waters)*, Dennis Harkin *(Stanley)*, Valentine Dyall *(Stephen Lynn)*, Marjorie Mars *(Mary Norton)*

p, Noel Coward; d, David Lean; w, Noel Coward, David Lean, Anthony Havelock-Allan (based on Noel Coward's play "Still Life"); ph, Robert Krasker; ed, Jack Harris; m, Sergei Rachmaninoff (Second Piano Concerto)

AAN Best Actress: Celia Johnson; *AAN Best Director:* David Lean; *AAN Best Screenplay:* Anthony Havelock-Allan, David Lean, Ronald Neame

A touching, exquisitely handled film dealing with two ordinary people who accidentally fall in love. BRIEF ENCOUNTER is a unique and sometimes misunderstood film whose very British restraint has not endeared it to all comers, but which if anything makes the film more passionate as a result. The famous use of Rachmaninoff for the musical score, which would seem ridiculous and cliched in later screen romances, is quite perfect here, as overpowering emotions threaten the reliable dullness the leading couple relies upon every day to get by. Krasker's gleaming black-and-white cinematography, at once delicately stylized and the peak of low-key realism, enhances the story of Alec (Howard) and Laura (Johnson), a doctor and housewife respectively, both happily married to others, who journey into town each Thursday on routine business. Alec's removing a cinder from Laura's eye at the train station one week initiates a casual friendship which rapidly grows into something far stronger than either could have expected. The couple share moments of tenderness, gentle confidences and even wry humor (e.g. while watching shlock cinema, surely writer Noel Coward's sly dig at pablum for the masses). Proof positive that director Lean was far better in his small-scale first half-dozen films than in his later overblown epics, BRIEF ENCOUNTER brings Coward's lovingly detailed and observant script to glowing life. The cast is uniformly faultless, from the sharp comic counterpont of Carey, Holloway, and Gregg to the wonderful gentility Raymond brings to the role of Laura's husband. Center stage, though, properly belongs to the leading couple. In two screen creations to cherish, dashing newcomer Howard gives a brilliantly nuanced, ardent and touching performance, while the ordinary-looking, carefully mannered Johnson achieves a heartbreaking performance whose beauty ranks with Garbo's CAMILLE.

BRIGADOON
1954 108m c Musical **DVD ★★**
MGM (U.S.)

Gene Kelly *(Tommy Albright)*, Van Johnson *(Jeff Douglas)*, Cyd Charisse *(Fiona Campbell)*, Elaine Stewart *(Jane Ashton)*, Barry Jones *(Mr. Lundie)*, Hugh Laing *(Harry Beaton)*, Albert Sharpe *(Andrew Campbell)*, Virginia Bosier *(Jean Campbell)*, Jimmie Thompson *(Charlie Crisholm Dalrymple)*, Tudor Owen *(Archie Beaton)*

p, Arthur Freed; d, Vincente Minnelli; w, Alan Jay Lerner (based on the musical play by Alan Jay Lerner and Frederick Loewe); ph, Joseph Ruttenberg (CinemaScope, Ansco Color); ed, Albert Akst; art d, Cedric Gibbons, Preston Ames; chor, Gene Kelly

AAN Best Art Direction-Set Decoration (Color): Cedric Gibbons (Art Direction), Preston Ames (Art Direction), Edwin B Willis (Set Decoration), Keogh Gleason (Set Decoration); *AAN Best Costume Design (Color):* Irene Sharaff; *AAN Best Sound Recording:* Wesley C Miller (Sound Director)

Possibly Minnelli's worst screen musical. Confined to an MGM soundstage, this adaptation of the Lerner and Loewe Broadway hit desperately needs air, creatively stifled as it is in practically every department. New Yorkers Jeff and Tommy (Johnson and Kelly) get lost in the Scottish highlands and stumble onto the village of Brigadoon on the one day every 100 years that it appears from out of the mists. The villagers, who sport the garb and manners of antiquity, are in a merry mood, and the Americans happily join in their dancing and festivities. Tommy is particularly enchanted when he falls for bonnie lass Fiona (Charisse). He then must decide whether to return to New York or remain with his love in the land of long ago. Tommy and Jeff do go back to their urban existence, but eventually Tommy returns to Scotland, and such is the power of his love that the village materializes long enough for him to join Fiona in fantasyland forever.

One would like to see more dancing in BRIGADOON, though what's there is generally fine (especially a spirited routine to "I'll Go Home with Bonnie Jean"). Praise should also go to Johnson for doing a good job with his cynical, wise-cracking role. Other than that, though, the pleasures of BRIGADOON are as fleeting as the village's centennial appearances. The sense of whimsy crucially needed to make this thing fly is nowhere to be found, and Minnelli seems to enjoy the stylized scenes of an obnoxious Manhattan more than the heather of the highlands. Kelly's patented good cheer is meagerly doled out and his exuberant energy seems to vanish into the Scottish ether. The somber, remote Charisse dances exquisitely but otherwise has all the appeal of plywood. Even the legendary score sounds a little flat. Nominated for three Academy Awards: Best Sound Recording, Best Costume Design and, inexplicably, Best Art Direction/Set Decoration.

BRIGHT VICTORY
1951 96m bw Drama **★★★★**
Universal (U.S.)

Arthur Kennedy *(Larry Nevins)*, Peggy Dow *(Judy Greene)*, Julie Adams *(Chris Paterson)*, James Edwards *(Joe Morgan)*, Will Geer *(Mr. Nevins)*, Minor Watson *(Mr. Paterson)*, Jim Backus *(Bill Grayson)*, Joan Banks *(Janet Grayson)*, Nana Bryant *(Mrs. Nevins)*, Marjorie Crossland *(Mrs. Paterson)*

p, Robert Buckner; d, Mark Robson; w, Robert Buckner (based on the novel *Lights Out* by Baynard Kendrick); ph, William Daniels; ed, Russell Schoengarth; m, Frank Skinner; art d, Bernard Herzbrun, Nathan Juran

AAN Best Actor: Arthur Kennedy; *AAN Best Sound Recording:* Leslie I. Carey (Sound Director)

Kennedy is absolutely riveting in one of the most brilliant performances of his distinguished career. He plays Larry Nevins, a blinded WWII veteran who returns home and begins the arduous process of adapting both to civilian life and his new affliction. At first reluctant to leave the military hospital where he is recuperating, and later resisting the involved and tedious training necessary to equip himself for normal civilian life, the bitter veteran meets a patient nurse (the radiant Dow) who helps him overcome his fear of returning home. Once there, however, his next-door girlfriend (Adams) is embarrassed by his disability, and his parents (Geer and Bryant) feel helpless and inadequate around their son. In one devastating scene, a welcome-home party goes bust when Larry puts out a cigarette in a dish of food. After undergoing a great deal of agony and self-examination, Kennedy winds up with Dow, facing the future with no illusions. It's a bravura performance by Kennedy, one that justly garnered him an Oscar nomination for Best Actor (an Oscar that went to Humphrey Bogart for THE AFRICAN QUEEN), and it should not be missed. Look for Rock Hudson in a small role as an enlisted man. The picture was also nominated for Best Sound.

BRIGHTNESS

DVD

(YEELEN)
1987 106m c Fantasy ★★★★
Cisse/Government of Mali/CNC-UTA/WDR/Fuji
(Mali)

Issiaka Kane *(Nianankoro)*, Aoua Sangare *(Attu)*, Niamanto Sanogo *(Soma)*, Balla Moussa Keita *(Peul King)*, Soumba Traore *(Nianankoro's Mother)*, Ismaila Sarr *(Djigui)*, Youssouf Tenin Cisse *(Attu's Son)*, Koke Sangare *(Komo Chief)*, Brehima Doumbia, Seyba M'Baye

p, Souleymane Cisse; d, Souleymane Cisse; w, Souleymane Cisse; ph, Jean-Noel Ferragut; ed, Dounamba Coulibaly, Andre Davanture, Marie-Catherine Miqueau, Jenny Frenck, Seipati N'Xumalo; m, Michel Portal, Salif Keita *(Djigui)*; fx, Frederic Duru, Nicos Metelopoulos; cos, Kossa Mody Keita

BRIGHTNESS is very likely the most highly praised African film made to date—a reflection both of the film's merit and of the West's lack of critical attention to Third World films. Boosted by a Special Jury Prize at the 1987 Cannes Film Festival and favorable receptions at the Berlin and New York Festivals, BRIGHTNESS fast became *the* film to see in 1988. Whatever artistic merit the film does or doesn't have (and some critics doubt that it is as great as many claim), it found an audience—an audience that, for the most part, left the film completely baffled and profoundly moved. Like the main character, the audience became involved in a search for knowledge and the hope of enlightment.

The film opens with a complicated written description of various mystical symbols and rituals of the Bambara tribe and a nutshell introduction to *Komo*—a science of the gods based on the elements of "nature" and key to understanding the greater thrust of the film. The story of a man's (Kane) search for his evil, all-powerful shaman father (Sanogo), the seemingly simple, episodic saga takes on elements of fantasy as its young hero acquires talismans which give him increasingly great magical powers. In a classic showdown we see not only the powers of good and evil finally confront each other, but also the inevitable conflict between father and son enacted on a mythic scale. We also see the embodiment of future generations as a young boy (played by producer-director-writer Cisse's son) literally discovers remnants of the conflict and figuratively acquires the knowledge of his ancestors. Marvelously photographed (the image of Kane and Sangare bathing under the waterfall is unforgettable) and perfectly acted by a cast of nonprofessionals (Sanogo, for example, was a real-life shaman), the production of BRIGHTNESS represents both a triumph over incredible odds (bad weather, financial woes, the death of actor Sarr) and a provocative, creative use by Cisse of indigenous folk mythology.

BRIGHTON ROCK

1947 92m bw Crime ★★★½
Boulting Bros. (U.K.)

Richard Attenborough *(Pinkie Brown)*, Hermione Baddeley *(Ida Arnold)*, William Hartnell *(Dallow)*, Carol Marsh *(Rose Brown)*, Nigel Stock *(Cubitt)*, Wylie Watson *(Spicer)*, Harcourt Williams *(Prewitt)*, Alan Wheatley *(Fred Hale)*, George Carney *(Phil Corkery)*, Charles Goldner *(Colleoni)*

p, Roy Boulting; d, John Boulting; w, Graham Greene, Terence Rattigan (based on the novel by Graham Greene); ph, Harry Waxman; ed, Frank McNally; m, Hans May

A brutal look at the British underworld—as seen through the amoral eyes of teenaged thug Pinkie Brown, played brilliantly by the 24 year-old Attenborough. In this adaptation of the popular Graham Greene novel, Pinkie heads a race track gang and commits a murder, using a pretty waitress (Marsh) as an alibi. Worried that she still might betray him, he marries the young woman, planning to kill her by driving her to suicide. His scheme eventually backfires in an ending which, though softened somewhat from Greene's original, still drips with cynical irony. A moody, well-acted film (Hartnell and Baddeley are particularly good), notable for bringing a new viciousness to British cinema (e.g. razor blade slashing). Striking handled by the Boulting brothers and still worth a look for its almost palpable sense of dread, the film can't quite recapture the impact it had upon its initial release.

BRIMSTONE AND TREACLE

DVD

1982 87m c Thriller ★★★
Namara Films/Pennies From Heaven Ltd. (U.K.) R

Sting *(Martin Taylor)*, Denholm Elliott *(Thomas Bates)*, Joan Plowright *(Norma Bates)*, Suzanna Hamilton *(Patricia Bates)*, Mary McLeod *(Valerie Holdsworth)*, Benjamin Whitrow *(Businessman)*, Dudley Sutton *(Stroller)*, Tim Preece *(Clergyman)*

p, Kenith Trodd; d, Richard Loncraine; w, Dennis Potter; ph, Peter Hannan (Technicolor); ed, Paul Green; m, Sting

This quirky, disturbing thriller is chiefly of interest as the work of Dennis Potter, author of PENNIES FROM HEAVEN and TV's "The Singing Detective." Pop star Sting stars as Martin Taylor, a con man so charming he can convince almost anyone that he's met them before. Thomas Bates (Elliott) sees through this ploy but falls victim to Taylor's larger schemes involving Bates's disabled daughter (Hamilton). Relying on psychological effect rather than violence, the picture is excruciatingly suspenseful, alternating goose bumps with nervous laughter in the tradition of Hitchcockian horror.

BRING IT ON

DVD

2000 105m c Comedy ★★★½
Beacon Pictures (U.S.) PG-13

Kirsten Dunst *(Torrance Shipman)*, Eliza Dushku *(Missy Pantone)*, Jesse Bradford *(Cliff Pantone)*, Gabrielle Union *(Isis)*, Clare Kramer *(Courtney)*, Nicole Bilderback *(Whitney)*, Tsianina Joelson *(Darcy)*, Rini Bell *(Kasey)*, Nathan West *(Jan)*, Huntley Ritter *(Les)*

p, Marc Abraham, Thomas A. Bliss, John Ketcham; d, Peyton Reed; w, Jessica Bendinger; ph, Shawn Maurer; ed, Larry Bock; m, Christophe Beck; prod d, Sharon Lomofsky; art d, Timothy Whidbee; chor, Anne Fletcher, Ray Jasper; cos, Mary Jane Fort

A movie about high school cheerleading must be either a joke or a jigglefest for lechers, right? Wrong. This high-spirited tale of back-stabbing on the competitive cheerleading circuit is fresh, clever, and thoroughly charming.

Perky, popular Torrance Shipman (Kirsten Dunst) has just assumed the mantle of squad leader for San Diego's nationally acclaimed Rancho Carne Toros squad, and to her horror, *nothing* is going right. On her first day in charge, Torrance loses a cheerleader to a broken leg, and the audition for a replacement is very grim indeed. Torrance is on the verge of rubber-stamping a hair-tossing, lip-glossed squad member's annoying younger sister when in swaggers recent transfer student Missy Pantone (Eliza Dushku). Cute name notwithstanding, the black-clad Missy is no starry-eyed pom-pom pusher; she wouldn't even be trying out if Rancho Carne High had a gymnastics team. Torrance takes Missy anyway, only to have the new recruit announce that the team's current routine, the one they were planning to take to the regional finals, was stolen from the East Compton Clovers, an inner-city L.A. squad. And it gets worse. For the first time ever, the Clovers, led by the ambitious Isis (Gabrielle Union), are competing professionally and plan to kick the Toros' lily-white butts.

Like CLUELESS, this sparkling trifle touches lightly on weighty matters—notably race/class privilege—without trivializing them. It showcases a trio of talented young actresses, captures the exuberant athleticism of competitive cheerleading, and positively exudes good-hearted charisma. Who could resist?

BRING ME THE HEAD OF ALFREDO GARCIA 📀

1974 112m c Crime ★★★★
UA (U.S.) R

Warren Oates *(Bennie)*, Isela Vega *(Elita)*, Gig Young *(Quill)*, Robert Webber *(Sappensly)*, Helmut Dantine *(Max)*, Emilio Fernandez *(El Jefe)*, Kris Kristofferson *(Paco)*, Chano Urueta *(One-armed Bartender)*, Jorge Russek *(Cueto)*

p, Martin Baum; d, Sam Peckinpah; w, Gordon Dawson, Sam Peckinpah (based on a story by Frank Kowalski); ph, Alex Phillips Jr.; ed, Garth Craven, Robbe Roberts, Sergio Ortega, Dennis Dolan; m, Jerry Fielding

When El Jefe (Fernandez), the head of a prominent Mexican family, learns the identity of the bounder responsible for his daughter's pregnancy, he offers a million dollars to the man who can bring him the head of the culprit, Alfredo Garcia. Two homosexual hit men (Young and Webber) working for Jefe enlist the aid of Bennie (Oates), a sleazy but good-natured bar owner, who convinces the pair that he can find Garcia. Learning from his hooker girlfriend Elita (Vega) that her former client Garcia is already dead, she and Bennie travel to the cemetery where Garcia is supposedly buried to cut off the corpse's head. Bennie successfully kills two motorcycle rapists along the way, but a rival Mexican gang appears and kills Elita, knocks Bennie out and steals the head. In a bloody confrontation Bennie massacres his rivals and then turns on his two gay partners and wipes them out too. All that remains is to turn in the prized head, though Bennie's final encounter with El Jefe also goes bloodily awry.

One of the cinema's more perversely intriguing experiences, the film is either appreciated as a bizarre minor classic or denounced as a piece of trash. In the only film over which the director says he had complete control, Peckinpah creates a haunting vision of a loser's quest for love and meaning in a harsh, brutal world. Although his "philosophy" and methods do not appeal to everyone and are certainly open to criticism, Peckinpah attempts to use explicit violence as a means for exploring the brutality he sees as inherent in all men. A nihilistic depiction of an existential quest, the film benefits from the presence of Oates in the leading role of a man driven obsessively in suicidal pursuit of self-respect and importance. The macabre scenes in the car where Bennie converses with the head as flies buzz around it are funny and telling. BRING ME THE HEAD OF ALFREDO GARCIA does have some sloppy photography, a few unintentionally humorous scenes, and an excess of Peckinpah's signature slow-motion violence, but it stands as one of Peckinpah's more daring films.

BRINGING DOWN THE HOUSE 📀

2003 105m c Comedy ★★½
Bungalow 78 Productions/Hyde Park PG-13
Entertainment/Kushner-Locke Company/
Meespierson Film CV/WMG Film/Touchstone (U.S.)

Steve Martin *(Peter Sanderson)*, Queen Latifah *(Charlene Morton)*, Eugene Levy *(Howie Rottman)*, Joan Plowright *(Mrs. Arness)*, Jean Smart *(Kate)*, Kimberly J. Brown *(Sarah Sanderson)*, Angus T. Jones *(Georgey Sanderson)*, Missi Pyle *(Ashley)*, Michael Rosenbaum *(Todd Gendler)*, Betty White *(Mrs. Kline)*

p, Ashok Amritraj, David Hoberman; d, Adam Shankman; w, Jason Filardi; ph, Julio Macat; ed, Jerry Greenberg; m, Lalo

Schifrin; prod d, Linda Descenna; art d, Jim Nedza; fx, Alan E. Lorimer; chor, Anne Fletcher; cos, Pamela Withers

This amusing comedy of modern manners manages to walk the thin line between poking fun at racial stereotypes and reinforcing them.

Divorced, workaholic tax lawyer Peter (Steve Martin) is trying to land an account with a wealthy and high-maintenance coffee heiress, Mrs. Arness (Joan Plowright), while improving his social life by planning a blind date with a female attorney he met on the Internet. But the buttoned-down blonde barrister with whom he thinks he's been chatting turns out to be Charlene (Queen Latifah), a brassy—and black—escaped convict who really wants Peter to help with her appeal. Charlene, who doesn't know the meaning of the word "no," turns Peter's meticulously organized life upside down despite his repeated attempts to get rid of her. Peter finally agrees to help Charlene with her case, and she reluctantly consents to play nanny to his kids so he's free to woo the uptight and deeply bigoted Mrs. Arness. Predictably, these opposites attract despite their differences. Charlene tries to make Peter hip and offers tips on what women really want, while Peter tries to prove her innocence and convince Charlene that she doesn't have to use slang in order to communicate.

Martin and Latifah have great chemistry, which is one reason his scenes without her seem generic; the other is that they are. Choreographer-turned-director Adam Shankman (THE WEDDING PLANNER) relies heavily on the terrific supporting cast for laughs, and he should be eternally grateful. Extra props to Eugene Levy as Peter's friend Howie, who's fascinated by Charlene's plus-size curves and tries to impress her with his mastery of slang; Betty White, who plays a nosy racist neighbor; and grande dame Plowright, whose Mrs. Arness finds her narrow-minded views broadened considerably after a few tokes from a joint.

BRINGING OUT THE DEAD 📀

1999 123m c Drama ★★
Touchstone (U.S.) R

Nicolas Cage *(Frank Pierce)*, Patricia Arquette *(Mary Burke)*, John Goodman *(Larry)*, Ving Rhames *(Marcus)*, Tom Sizemore *(Tom Wolls)*, Marc Anthony *(Noel)*, Mary Beth Hurt *(Nurse Constance)*, Cliff Curtis *(Cy Coates)*, Nestor Serrano *(Dr. Hazmat)*, Aida Turturro *(Nurse Crupp)*

p, Scott Rudin, Barbara De Fina; d, Martin Scorsese; w, Paul Schrader (based on the novel by Joe Connelly); ph, Robert Richardson; ed, Thelma Schoonmaker; m, Elmer Bernstein; prod d, Dante Ferretti; art d, Robert Guerra; fx, Michael Owens, Industrial Light & Magic, John M. Ottesen, Susan Greenhow, David Lambert; cos, Rita Ryack

Touted as the successor to TAXI DRIVER and based on the acclaimed first novel by former NYC paramedic Joe Connelly, Martin Scorsese's nightmarish vision of New York as the city of the walking dead falls far short of its grim potential.

Emergency medical technician Frank Pierce (Nicolas Cage) has been riding the nighttime streets for too long. He's emotionally numbed by dealing with overcrowded emergency rooms and harried, heedless doctors; sick of all the self-destructive drunks and junkies; and haunted by the people he failed to save. Over the course of three dismal shifts, Frank is teamed with three different partners—stolid Larry (John Goodman), mellow ladies' man Marcus (Ving Rhames), and sociopathic Tom (Tom Sizemore)—but the routine remains the same. Frank is drowning in the dead and the dying, praying he'll save someone and break what feels like a cosmic losing streak.

There's a little bit of plot—Frank falls tentatively in love with the ex-junkie daughter (Patricia Arquette) of a heart attack victim and crosses paths with homeless lunatic Noel (Marc Anthony)—but the movie is essentially one long howl of despair that starts in the gutter and never really goes anywhere, up or down. Maybe it's Cage, baring his teeth like a cornered rat from the first shot; maybe it's the supporting players who treat their roles like audition monologues; or maybe it's just the monotonous sameness of Frank's jaundiced, desperate experiences. Hard though it is to imagine, given Scorsese's vision and affinity for mean streets, first-time filmmaker Scott Ziehl actually examines very similar material more effectively in his low-budget BROKEN VESSELS.

BRINGING UP BABY
1938 102m bw Comedy ★★★★★
RKO (U.S.)

Katharine Hepburn (Susan Vance), Cary Grant (David Huxley), Charlie Ruggles (Maj. Horace Applegate), May Robson (Aunt Elizabeth), Barry Fitzgerald (Mr. Gogarty), Walter Catlett (Constable Slocum), Fritz Feld (Dr. Fritz Lehman), Leona Roberts (Hannah Gogarty), George Irving (Alexander Peabody), Virginia Walker (Alice Swallow)

p, Howard Hawks; d, Howard Hawks; w, Dudley Nichols, Hagar Wilde (based on a story by Hagar Wilde); ph, Russell Metty; ed, George Hively; m, Roy Webb; art d, Van Nest Polglase, Perry Ferguson; fx, Vernon L. Walker; cos, Howard Greer

A delightful piece of absurdity and one of director Hawks' most inspired lampoons of the battle between the sexes.

Hepburn and Grant are superb in this breathlessly funny screwball comedy with a plot that could have been hatched in a mental institution. She plays Susan Vance, an eccentric heiress whose dog (Asta of the "Thin Man" series) steals a bone from absentminded paleontologist David Huxley (Grant), the last he needs to complete his reconstruction of a dinosaur. David follows Susan to her Connecticut farm in search of the relic and runs smack into the authorities, the possible donor of $1 million to his museum, and a leopard named Baby who enjoys being serenaded with "I Can't Give You Anything but Love." Memorable moments abound throughout: Susan insistently playing David's ball at a golf game, which leads him further and further from his playing companion ("I'll be with you in a minute, Mr. Peabody!"); Susan's tricks with olives; Baby's encounter with a chicken coop; David facing Susan's elderly aunt (Robson) while wearing a frilly negligee ("I just decided to go gay all of a sudden!"); David caught in Susan's butterfly net (surely *not* the best way to catch a runaway leopard); Susan's aunt and cowardly big game hunter Maj. Applegate (Ruggles) deciding they need some exercise ("Shall we run?" "Yes, let's!"); Susan's imitation of a gangster's moll ("Hey flatfoot!")—the list could go on and on.

Though Hepburn fans might not be used to seeing her essay such an atypically scatterbrained role, her marvelous timing and zany comic elan are wonderfully engaging. Grant, meanwhile, manages the near-impossible feat of being goofy, suave, dimwitted and sexy all at once. Among a brilliant supporting cast, Robson, Ruggles, Catlett, Feld and Fitzgerald are standouts, and the pace never flags for an instant. A barbed satire of masculinity, romance, wealth, psychiatry and authority, BRINGING UP BABY was, not too surprisingly, a box-office flop in its day, probably because it poked fun at the very conventions it employed. Enormously influential on later comedy writing, it is a milestone of film merriment.

BROADCAST NEWS
1987 131m c Comedy/Romance ★★★½
Fox (U.S.) R

William Hurt (Tom Grunick), Albert Brooks (Aaron Altman), Holly Hunter (Jane Craig), Robert Prosky (Ernie Merriman), Lois Chiles (Jennifer Mack), Joan Cusack (Blair Litton), Peter Hackes (Paul Moore), Jack Nicholson (Bill Rorich, News Anchor), Christian Clemenson (Bobby), Robert Katims (Martin Klein)

p, James L. Brooks, Penney Finkelman Cox; d, James L. Brooks; w, James L. Brooks; ph, Michael Ballhaus (Deluxe Color); ed, Richard Marks; m, Bill Conti; prod d, Charles Rosen; art d, Kristi Zea; cos, Molly Maginnis

AAN Best Picture; AAN Best Actor: William Hurt; AAN Best Actress: Holly Hunter; AAN Best Supporting Actor: Albert Brooks; AAN Best Original Screenplay: James L Brooks; AAN Best Cinematography: Michael Ballhaus; AAN Best Film Editing: Richard Marks

Blessed with a good script, BROADCAST NEWS examines the ethics of modern-day electronic journalism and the often frazzled emotions of a tightly knit group of workaholics who find that their personal and professional lives have become one and the same. Network news producer Jane Craig (Hunter) and her best pal, veteran correspondent Aaron Altman (Brooks), share not only the same high ethical standards, but a warm and goofy sense of humor. Although Jane considers Aaron her best friend, he pines for a more romantic relationship. Enter Tom Grunick (Hurt), a handsome, affable, but somewhat dim newscaster to whom Jane is attracted.

Often touching, biting, and funny, BROADCAST NEWS is an entertaining film hoisted by the performances of its three leads. Hurt, in a rather odd change of pace, and newcomer Hunter display verve and skill and overcome the limitations of the somewhat annoying characters they play. In the seemingly lesser role of the one who stands by and suffers, however, Brooks provides the film's soul and many of its laughs to boot. Nicholson contributes a highly potent performance in a matter of moments as a smug, self-important New York anchorman and the rest of the supporting cast is uniformly fine. A more skillful director of actors than the camera, Brooks gives the script its full head and makes crystal clear the satirical point that appearances count for a great deal in the mass media. A film whose "TV movie" feel is at once incredibly appropriate and a notable drawback, BROADCAST NEWS is nevertheless worthy adult entertainment.

BROADWAY DANNY ROSE
1984 86m bw Comedy/Romance ★★★½
Rollins-Joffe (U.S.) PG

Woody Allen (Danny Rose), Mia Farrow (Tina Vitale), Nick Apollo Forte (Lou Canova), Sandy Baron, Corbett Monica, Jackie Gayle, Morty Gunty, Will Jordan, Howard Storm, Jack Rollins

p, Robert Greenhut; d, Woody Allen; w, Woody Allen; ph, Gordon Willis; ed, Susan E. Morse; prod d, Mel Bourne; cos, Jeffrey Kurland

AAN Best Director: Woody Allen; AAN Best Original Screenplay: Woody Allen (Screenplay)

After making several more ambitious films, writer-director Allen returned to *terra firma* with BROADWAY DANNY ROSE, a charming comedy shot in black and white that mixes several varieties of the New Yorkers that Allen loves so well. The film begins with a group of Broadway types sitting at the Carnegie Delicatessen reminiscing about the career of Danny Rose (Allen), a two-bit agent who specializes in offbeat acts that no other agent will handle. His one regular client is Lou Canova (Forte), a lounge singer who drinks too much, weighs too much, and uses Rose to cover for him when he's off cheating on his wife with girlfriend Tina (an unusually animated performance by Farrow). When Canova gets a chance to perform at a better place than the dives where he's been working, Rose has to pretend to be Tina's boyfriend, a move which gets him into a lot of trouble. Tina is supposedly engaged to a gangland figure, and the other mobsters, thinking that their pal has been cuckolded, begin chasing poor Danny all around the city. Although the film contains many of the great verbal jokes that are Allen's forte, the visual wit and the sentimental drama fall a bit short.

BROKEN ARROW

1996 108m c Action/Adventure
20th Century Fox/Mark Gordon Company/
Metropolis Entertainment (U.S.)

DVD
★★★
R

John Travolta *(Vic Deakins)*, Christian Slater *(Riley Hale)*, Samantha Mathis *(Terry Carmichael)*, Delroy Lindo *(Colonel Max Wilkins)*, Bob Gunton *(Pritchett)*, Frank Whaley *(Giles Prentice)*, Howie Long *(Kelly)*, Vondie Curtis-Hall, billed as Vondie Curtis-Hall *(Lt. Colonel Sam Rhodes)*, Jack Thompson *(Chairman, Joint Chief of Staff)*, Vyto Ruginis *(Johnson)*

p, Mark Gordon, Bill Badalato, Terence Chang; d, John Woo; w, Graham Yost; ph, Peter Levy; ed, John Wright, Steve Mirkovich, Joe Hutshing; m, Hans Zimmer; prod d, Holger Gross; art d, William O'Brien; fx, Richard Thompson, Peter Crosman, Don Baker, Jacques Stroweis, Elliot Markman; cos, Mary Malin

BROKEN ARROW's by-the-book mayhem is proof positive that Hong Kong *auteur* John Woo can make a solid, formulaic Hollywood action picture—he could probably make one standing on his head—but why should we want him to? Woo's Hong Kong pictures—which include THE KILLER, HARD BOILED and BULLET IN THE HEAD—are rapturous fusions of eroticized violence and operatic sentiment, enthralling precisely because they do things that mainstream American action pictures can't (or won't) do. BROKEN ARROW, however, is '90s Hollywood through-and-through: expertly constructed, reasonably entertaining, morally unambiguous, and thoroughly trivial.

John Travolta, blue eyes a-glint, plays gleefully against type as a turncoat pilot planning to blackmail the U.S. government with stolen nuclear weapons—"broken arrow," we learn, is the military code for a lost warhead. Christian Slater, his staunchly upright ex-buddy, is out to stop him, and Samantha Mathis plays the feisty young park ranger who gets stuck in the middle. Woo has never done well by female characters, and Mathis's plucky but colorless character is no exception—but that's not necessarily a liability, especially in a picture as insistently homoerotic as this one is. What matters is Travolta and Slater, who clamber all over an impressive array of military hardware, trading bullets, punches, and meaningful glances as a bass guitar vibrates portentously. The vestiges of Woo's achingly romantic style play badly in this can-do context, while the mayhem is never more—and occasionally less—than competent.

BRONX TALE, A

1993 122m c Drama
Bronx Tale Inc./Tribeca Productions/Gatien
Productions/Price Entertainment (U.S.)

DVD
★★★
R

Robert De Niro *(Lorenzo Anello)*, Chazz Palminteri *(Sonny)*, Lillo Brancato *(Calogero Anello—Age 17)*, Francis Capra *(Calogero Anello—Age Nine)*, Joe Pesci *(Carmine)*, Taral Hicks *(Jane)*, Kathrine Narducci *(Rosina Anello)*, Clem Caserta *(Jimmy*

Whispers), Robert D'Andrea *(Tony Toupee)*, Eddie Montanaro *(Eddie Mush)*

p, Robert De Niro, Jane Rosenthal, Jon Kilik; d, Robert De Niro; w, Chazz Palminteri (from his play); ph, Reynaldo Villablobos; ed, David Ray, R.Q. Lovett; m, Butch Barbella; prod d, Wynn Thomas; art d, Chris Shriver; fx, Steve Kirschoff; cos, Rita Ryack

Actor Robert De Niro's directing debut is a nostalgic memoir of growing up in New York in the 1960s, and covers much of the same ground as Martin Scorsese's GOODFELLAS. Developed from a one-man show written by and starring Chazz Palminteri, A BRONX TALE is at its best in the details: the swaggering hoods and the local girls with sky-high hair, skinny heels, and tight dresses; the cars and social clubs; the suave jukebox crooners... it's all evoked with a reverent clarity and precision that open a window onto one man's memories of the past, as it was and as he'd like it to have been.

Nine-year-old Calogero (Francis Capra) hangs out on his stoop with his friends, watching Sonny (Palminteri) and his henchmen make deals and issue orders. Calogero sees Sonny kill a man but, true to the code of the neighborhood—practiced even by Calogero's hardworking, law-abiding father Lorenzo (De Niro)—he tells the police he saw nothing, and Sonny goes free. Thus begins a relationship that becomes increasingly close as the boy grows older. Despite his father's objections, the teenage Calogero (Lillo Brancato)—or C, as he now prefers to be called—becomes first Sonny's mascot, then his errand boy, as Sonny and Lorenzo battle for C's love and respect.

A BRONX TALE tries to cover too much ground; racial conflict, family drama, first love, the lure of the gangster life, and the joys and tribulation of coming of age in a kinder, gentler New York are all crammed into the slight story. It all feels too familiar to sustain the viewer's interest, but Palminteri's and De Niro's equally compelling performances help give it life.

BROOD, THE

1979 91m c Horror
New World (Canada)

DVD
★★★½
R

Oliver Reed *(Dr. Raglan)*, Samantha Eggar *(Nola)*, Art Hindle *(Frank)*, Cindy Hinds *(Candice)*, Nuala Fitzgerald *(Julianna)*, Henry Beckman *(Barton Kelly)*, Susan Hogan *(Ruth)*, Michael McGhee *(Inspector Mrazek)*, Gary McKeehan *(Mike Trellan)*, Bob Silverman *(Jan)*

p, Claude Heroux; d, David Cronenberg; w, David Cronenberg; ph, Mark Irwin; ed, Alan Collins

Powerful and disturbing on both a physical and mental level, THE BROOD is the first Cronenberg film to use "name" actors, and marked a significant progression in the director's exploration of "biological horror."

Controversial psychotherapist Dr. Raglan (Oliver Reed) teaches mental patients to manifest their subconscious anger physically, as boils and welts on their bodies. One of his patients, Nola (Samantha Eggar), has actually begun giving birth to a small army of mutant babies—the ultimate projection of her hostilities. She houses her brood in a nearby cabin from which, dressed in their colorful Dr. Dentons, the murderous little creatures venture out and kill the objects of their mother's rage. Eggar's bitter ex-husband, who is trying to discredit Reed's treatments so he can gain custody of their daughter, uncovers the horrible truth.

More personal than earlier Cronenberg films (the director had just gone through a painful divorce at the time of shooting), THE BROOD is a mature, controlled work that finds horror not only in such institutions as hospitals and schools but, more specifically, in the family unit itself. While his previous efforts (THEY CAME FROM WITHIN, RABID) had been rather clinical exercises, Cronenberg presents more complex and genuinely sympathetic characters here, giving the film added resonance. THE BROOD also marks his growing confidence as a visual stylist, with some memorable—if highly gory—realizations of his pet themes.

BROTHER FROM ANOTHER PLANET, THE [DVD]

1984 110m c Fantasy/Science Fiction ★★★½
A Train (U.S.)

Joe Morton (The Brother), Daryl Edwards (Fly), Steve James (Odell), Leonard Jackson (Smokey), Bill Cobbs (Walter), Maggie Renzi (Noreen), Tom Wright (Sam), Ren Woods (Bernice), Reggie Rock Bythewood (Rickey), David Strathairn

p, Peggy Rajski, Maggie Renzi; d, John Sayles; w, John Sayles; ph, Ernest Dickerson (Movielab Color); ed, John Sayles; m, Mason Daring; prod d, Nora Chavooshian; art d, Stephen J. Lineweaver; cos, Karen Perry

Still John Sayles's most provocative work, THE BROTHER FROM ANOTHER PLANET blends a stock satirical premise—a look at the world through the eyes of an alien—with a runaway slave narrative, rendering a loosely constructed but keenly observed allegory of race and class in America. The Brother (Joe Morton) is an escaped slave from an unnamed planet who crash-lands his space capsule off Ellis Island. Unable to speak, and marked by his ragged clothing and dark complexion, he's taken for a homeless black man; New Yorkers treat him accordingly, with reactions ranging from pity to contempt. After some dispiriting encounters with white people, he makes his way to Harlem and ends up in a local bar. The regular patrons find him odd, to say the least, but set him up with a social worker after they discover that he can repair video games with just a touch of his hand. Hot on the black man's trail are a pair of white aliens (David Strathairn and John Sayles) dressed in black, who aim to recapture the escapee.

Buoyed by Morton's sensitive performance, the film proceeds as a series of vignettes, some of them unforgettable. In a sequence shot on the subway, a child offers to do a magic trick for the Brother: he'll make the white riders disappear. As the train pulls into the 96th Street Station, the whites file out and are replaced by uniformly black passengers headed uptown. It's a remarkable image of de facto racial segregation in urban America.

BROTHERHOOD OF THE WOLF [DVD]

(LE PACTE DES LOUPS)
2001 142m c Action/Horror/Historical ★★★½
Davis Film/Le Studio Canal/Eskwad (France) R

Samuel Le Bihan (Gregoire de Fronsac), Vincent Cassel (Jean Francois de Morangias), Emilie Dequenne (Marianne de Morangias), Monica Bellucci (Sylvia), Jeremie Renier (Thomas d'Apcher), Mark Dacascos (Mani), Jean Yanne (Comte de Morangias), Jean-Francois Stevenin (Sardis), Jacques Perrin (Old Thomas d'Apcher), Edith Scob (Mme de Morangias)

p, Richard Grandpierre, Samuel Hadida; d, Christophe Gans; w, Stephane Cabel, Christophe Gans; ph, Dan Lautsten; ed, Xavier Loutreuil, Sebastien Prangere, David Wu; m, Joseph Lo Duca; prod d, Guy-Claude Francois; art d, Francois Decaux, Thierry Francois; fx, Val Wardlaw, Hal Bertram, Seb Caudron, Georges Demetrau, Jim Henson's Creatures Shop; chor, Philip Kwok; cos, Dominique Borg

A rip-snorting, no-holds-barred mix of multinational and multigenre conventions that borrows liberally from classic American monster movies, high-octane Hong Kong martial arts pictures, and melodramatic French costume epics.

1864: The Gevaudan region of Southern France is under siege. Men, women, and children are being brutally killed as they herd their animals, tend their farms or simply venture outside their houses. Wolves are blamed, but slaughtering them doesn't stop the rampage. Enter noted naturalist Chevalier Gregoire de Fronsac (Samuel Le Bihan) and Iroquois shaman and martial artist Mani (Mark Dacascos), whom de Fronsac befriended while traveling in the New World colonies. Hot-headed, one-armed nobleman Jean Francois de Morangias (Vincent Cassel) resents having to listen to some fancy consultant from Paris, but de Fronsac is determined to stay. For one thing, he's there on orders of the king, whose advisors worry that the longer this "Beast of Gevaudon" business goes on, the more likely it is to undermine the regime's authority. For another, he's taken a shine to de Morangias's forthright sister, Marianne (Emilie Dequenne), and has found a sympathetic sidekick in openminded aristocrat Thomas d'Apcher (Hans Meyer), who agrees that there's more to the Gevaudon situation than meets the eye.

This is only the second feature outing for CRYING FREEMAN director Christophe Gans, and it's a remarkably assured accomplishment. Some viewers will absolutely hate this combination of costume drama, monster movie cliches, and MATRIX-style martial arts action, but if you have the right temperament for it, it's absolutely exhilarating.

BROTHERS KARAMAZOV, THE

1958 149m c Drama ★★½
MGM (U.S.)

Yul Brynner (Dmitri Karamazov), Maria Schell (Grushenka), Claire Bloom (Katya), Lee J. Cobb (Fyodor Karamazov), Richard Basehart (Ivan Karamozov), Albert Salmi (Smerdyakov), William Shatner (Alexey Karamazov), Judith Evelyn (Mme. Anna Hohlakov), Edgar Stehli (Grigory), Harry Townes (Ippoli Kirillov)

p, Pandro S. Berman; d, Richard Brooks; w, Richard Brooks (based on an adaptation by Julius J. and Philip G. Epstein of the novel by Feodor Dostoyevsky); ph, John Alton (Metrocolor); ed, John Dunning; m, Bronislau Kaper; cos, Walter Plunkett

AAN Best Supporting Actor: Lee J. Cobb

Marilyn Monroe campaigned desperately for Grushenka, the part played by Maria Schell in this film, and it's one of those casting tragedies that she didn't get her way. For while Schell is okay, the problem here is similar to Glenn Close in DANGEROUS LIASONS—no sex appeal—and typical of the film as a whole—lots of steam, but no heat. Richard Brooks directs like a traffic cop, without sweep or dramatic gesture. As a result, the film feels like "Classics Comics" instead of a classic.

BROWNING VERSION, THE [DVD]

1951 90m bw Drama ★★★★½
Javelin (U.K.)

Michael Redgrave (Andrew Crocker-Harris), Jean Kent (Millie Crocker-Harris), Nigel Patrick (Frank Hunter), Wilfrid Hyde-White (Frobisher), Brian Smith (Taplow), Bill Travers (Fletcher), Ronald Howard (Gilbert), Paul Medland (Wilson), Ivan Samson (Lord Baxter), Josephine Middleton (Mrs. Frobisher)

p, Teddy Baird; d, Anthony Asquith; w, Terence Rattigan (based on his play); ph, Desmond Dickinson; ed, John D. Guthridge

Good show! Rattigan adapted his own play for the screen, and it's lovingly directed by Asquith and acted within an inch of the viewer's life by Redgrave and a magnificent small ensemble. Story explores the tragic restriction of a headmaster's retirement and his wretched, unfaithful wife.

Redgrave won the Best Actor award and Terence Rattigan the writing prize at the 1951 Cannes Film Festival for this film. Absolutely not to be missed.

BRUCE ALMIGHTY   *DVD*

2003 94m c Comedy   ★½
Shady Acres Productions/Pit Bull   PG-13
Productions/Spyglass Entertainment (U.S.)

Jim Carrey (*Bruce Nolan*), Morgan Freeman (*God*), Jennifer Aniston (*Grace Connelly*), Philip Baker Hall (*Jack Baylor*), Catherine Bell (*Susan Ortega*), Lisa Ann Walker (*Debbie*), Steve Carell (*Evan Baxter*), Nora Dunn (*Ally Loman*), Eddie Jemison (*Bobby*), Paul Satterfield (*Dallas Coleman*)

p, Michael Bostick, James D. Brubaker, Jim Carrey, Steve Koren, Mark O'Keefe, Tom Shadyac; d, Tom Shadyac; w, Steve Koren, Mark O'Keefe, Steve Oedekerk (based on a story by Steve Koren and Mark O'Keefe); ph, Dean Semler; ed, Scott Hill; m, John Debney; prod d, Linda Descenna; art d, Jim Nedza; fx, Dave Kelsey; cos, Judy Ruskin

Jim Carrey plays a man granted omnipotence by a Supreme Being who's grown tired of his constant whining. It may at first seem a heavenly career choice for the endlessly inventive Carrey, but his performance is revealing: the mega-star has apparently fallen into the same trap that has snared so many other hugely successful comedians who now believe that everything they do or say is funny.

Bruce Nolan (Carrey) is a disgruntled reporter for Buffalo's WKBW Eyewitness News who's so unprofessional at his job and so insensitive to his live-in girlfriend, Grace (Jennifer Aniston), that it's hard to see how he holds on to either. Incensed after a smug colleague (Steve Carell) is chosen for the co-anchor position Nolan coveted, he goes ballistic during a live report and is summarily fired. Nolan blames the Almighty for his troubles, leading Him to teach Nolan a lesson: God (Morgan Freeman) bequeaths His power to Nolan; the job, divine perks and all, are now his.

It's a classic fantasy scenario overflowing with creative possibilities, but Carrey's Nolan isn't charmingly misguided or comically loathsome enough to deserve the lesson; he's just a big, inconsequential crybaby. Unfortunately, so much potential is wasted here in what amounts to a sour celebration of mean-spiritedness with an unconvincing moment of redemption tacked on to the end.

BRUTE FORCE   *DVD*

1947 94m bw Prison   ★★★★
Universal (U.S.)

Burt Lancaster (*Joe Collins*), Hume Cronyn (*Capt. Munsey*), Charles Bickford (*Gallagher*), Yvonne De Carlo (*Gina*), Ann Blyth (*Ruth*), Ella Raines (*Cora*), Anita Colby (*Flossie*), Sam Levene (*Louis*), Howard Duff (*Soldier*), Art Smith (*Dr. Walters*)

p, Mark Hellinger; d, Jules Dassin; w, Richard Brooks (based on a story by Robert Patterson); ph, William Daniels; ed, Edward Curtiss; m, Miklos Rozsa; art d, Bernard Herzbrun, John DeCuir; fx, David S. Horsley; cos, Rosemary Odell

Classic prison melo, BRUTE FORCE followed THE KILLERS, for Burt Lancaster, establishing him as a dangerously sexy lug in the most interesting period of his career. The predictable premise was directed with innovation by Jules Dassin and also featured the debut of Howard Duff, among a stellar cast. Flashbacks lead to actresses as well, and there's an interesting, untypical job by Hume Cronyn. Rozsa's pounding score and a savage climax make BRUTE FORCE first rate all the way.

BUDDY HOLLY STORY, THE   *DVD*

1978 113m c Biography   ★★★½
Columbia (U.S.)   PG

Gary Busey (*Buddy Holly*), Don Stroud (*Jesse*), Charles Martin Smith (*Ray Bob*), Bill Jordan (*Riley Randolph*), Maria Richwine (*Maria Elena Holly*), Conrad Janis (*Ross Turner*), Albert Popwell (*Eddie Foster*), Amy Johnston (*Jenny Lou*), James Beach (*Mr. Wilson*), John Goff (*T.J.*)

p, Fred Bauer; d, Steve Rash; w, Robert Gittler (based on the book by Don Coldrosen); ph, Stevan Larner; ed, David Blewitt; prod d, Joel Schiller; fx, Robby Knott; chor, Maggie Rush; cos, Michael Butler

AAN Best Actor: Gary Busey; *AA Best Song Score:* Joe Renzetti; *AAN Best Sound:* Tex Rudloff, Joel Fein, Curly Thirlwell, Willie Burton

Buddy Holly didn't live very long. His life ended in a snowstorm with The Big Bopper and Richie Valens in 1959. Their plane went down, and the event was later eulogized in Don McLean's song "American Pie." How much of a movie could be made about a young man who never survived his early twenties? The answer is … a whole lot! Busey is perfect as Holly, and all the small roles are well cast. The story only spans a few years, from Holly's youth in Lubbock to his death. Lubbock is one of those quiet and conservative towns, and Holly was chastised for his descent into rock and roll. The music was too "black" for the community's white sensibilities. Holly paid them no mind, started writing and recording, and was a star before he had to shave more than three times a week. If you are old enough to remember Buddy and The Crickets and their string of hits, you'll love this film. Busey did all his own singing and playing, as did Martin and Stroud as The Crickets, providing a welcome sense of realism. Busey's performance is terrific. It won him an Oscar nomination for Best Actor, although he lost to Jon Voight for COMING HOME. The film did win an Academy Award for best scoring, and was also nominated for Best Sound. Songs include "That'll Be the Day," "Peggy Sue," "Every Day," "Oh Boy"—all written by Holly and sung by Busey.

BUENA VISTA SOCIAL CLUB, THE   *DVD*

1999 105m c Musical/Documentary   ★★★½
Road Movies/Kintop Pictures/Arte/Instituto Cubano
del Arte y Industria Cinematograficos (Germany/U.S.)

Ry Cooder, Joachim Cooder, Ibrahim Ferrer, Ruben Gonzales, Eliades Ochoa, Omara Portuondo, Compay Segundo, Lopez Orlando "Cachaito", Amadito Valdes, Manuel "Guajiro" Mirabal

p, Ry Cooper; d, Wim Wenders; ph, Jorg Widmer; ed, Brian Johnson

AAN Best Documentary Feature

Guitarist and longtime Wim Wenders collaborator Ry Cooder struck gold when he helped organize "The Buena Vista Social Club," an enormously popular compilation of Cuban ballads released in 1997. Two years later, Cooder returned to record the solo album of singer and *Social Club* member Ibrahim Ferrer, and this time Wenders and crew were in tow. The resulting "musicumentary" cleverly mixes footage from various recording sessions and interviews with live performances in Amsterdam and New York City's Carnegie Hall. There's not a lot of insight into the collaborative process between the extremely reserved Cooder and the outgoing Cubans (Ferrer, pianist Ruben Gonzalez and songstress Omara Portuondo are singled out for special attention), but many of the gifted musicians freely offer personal stories as well their own thoughts on contemporary Cuba. Many of them continue to live in extremely humble surroundings—72-year-old Ferrer worked as a shoeshine before the album's success—and Wenders' camera captures Havana's crumbling architecture and battered '50s-era American cars. But the music and emotion behind the decay are transcendent, and one wonders whether this could be linked to the fact that for nearly 40 years, these musicians have lived in isolation from the world at large, immersed in their art and far from capitalism. Save for a stray shot of pro-Revolution grafitti, Wenders refrains from any political commentary, and a bemused Cooder pauses only to speculate on how you never know what's going to please the public.

BUFFALO '66
1998 101m c   Drama/Comedy   ★★
Cinepix Film/Muse Productions/Lions Gate Films   R
(Canada/U.S.)

Vincent Gallo (Billy Brown), Anjelica Huston (Janet "Jan" Brown), Christina Ricci (Layla), Ben Gazzara (Jimmy Brown), Rosanna Arquette (Wendy Balsam), Mickey Rourke (Bookie), Kevin Corrigan (Goon), Jan-Michael Vincent (Sonny), Kevin Pollak (TV Sportscaster), Alex Karras (TV Sportscaster)

p, Chris Hanley; d, Vincent Gallo; w, Vincent Gallo (from his screen story); ph, Lance Acord; ed, Curtiss Clayton; m, Vincent Gallo; prod d, Gideon Ponte; art d, James Chinlund; fx, Paul Murphy; cos, Beatrix Aruna Pasztor

Inexplicable indie idol Vincent Gallo makes his directing debut with this pretentious fairy-tale romance between a tortured ex-con and a tap-dancing teen.

Fresh out of prison and without a place to pee, lonely loser Billy Brown (Gallo) is an oozing sore of self-loathing and explosive rage whose troubles finding a toilet lead him to a store-front dance studio. Billy is under a lot of pressure, and not just from his bladder: he's told his parents (Anjelica Huston and Ben Gazzara) that he's married and has a lucrative government job. Hoping to make this series of whoppers credible, he kidnaps Layla (Christina Ricci), a pouty little tap student, and alternately bullies and cajoles her into coming to his parents' place for dinner and pretending she's his adoring wife. Unfortunately, mom's a hypocritical harridan obsessed with football and dad's a pervy former lounge singer who strangled Billy's childhood puppy and never misses an opportunity to put the nasty grab on Layla: both are oblivious to their son's emotional distress.

For all its art-movie pretensions, which include picture-within-picture flashbacks and a variety of self-conscious lighting and framing effects, Gallo's film is at heart a freak show. The lowlife itinerary includes the obligatory bowling alley, chain restaurant, back streets, bus station, hot sheets hotel, and downscale strip joint (this one owned by a washed-up football player who cavorts half-naked with a hard-faced bevy of topless tarts). The tour is populated by the likes of Billy's retarded pal, Goon (Kevin Corrigan); a sleazy bookie (Mickey Rourke); giggling floozy Wendy (Rosanna Arquette), who was Billy's grade-school crush; brain-damaged bowling alley manager Sonny (Jan-Michael Vincent); and, of course, Billy's parents. Gallo's "poor, poor pitiful me" routine wears very thin, very fast, but Ricci is incandescent, a softly-glowing dumpling of a dream-girl in powder-blue fishnet tights and sparkly tap shoes. She's the diamond in the dirt.

BUG'S LIFE, A
1998 94m   c   Animated/Children's   ★★★
PIXAR Animation Studios/Walt Disney   (U.S.)   G

VOICES OF: Dave Foley (Flik), Kevin Spacey (Hopper), Julia Louis-Dreyfus (Pricess Atta), Hayden Panettiere (Dot), Phyllis Diller (Queen), Richard Kind (Molt), David Hyde Pierce (Slim), Joe Ranft (Heimlich), Denis Leary (Francis), Jonathan Harris (Manny)

p, Kevin Reher, Darla K. Anderson; d, John Lasseter, Andrew Stanton; w, Andrew Stanton, Donald McEnery, Bob Shaw; ph, Sharon Calahan; ed, Lee Unkrich; m, Randy Newman; prod d, William Cone; art d, Tia W. Kratter, Bob Pauley; anim, Glenn McQueen, Rich Quade, Ewan Johnson

AAN Best Original Musical or Comedy Score: Randy Newman

It would be a shame if families who've already seen ANTZ skipped this technically astounding and unwaveringly bright film—bright both visually and thematically. Pixar (the team behind TOY STORY) has done some knockout work, full of movement and natural wonder.

As in ANTZ, the protagonist is an outcast insect, a nonconformist ant named Flik (voiced by Dave Foley). Flik and his fellow ants are forced to gather food for a swarm of marauding grasshoppers, led by the ruthless Hopper (Kevin Spacey, in an impressive vocal performance). After Flik's bumbling destroys the colony's offering and puts the entire colony at risk of annihilation, Flik hatches a plan to recruit bigger and nastier bugs to fight off the hopping horde. The Queen (Phyllis Diller) and her Queen-in-training daughter Atta (Julia Louis-Dreyfus), exasperated with Flik's incompetence, happily agree to let him strike out on his own. Out in the exciting insect city (really a garbage dump), Flik meets a troupe of feisty former flea circus performers—Francis (Denis Leary), a male ladybug; Manny (Jonathan Harris), an aging praying mantis; and Heimlich (Joe Ranft), a fey caterpillar—and, mistaking them for insect warriors, returns to the colony ready to fight Hopper and his gang of bullying bugs.

This motley crew of lively showbiz characters adds considerable verve to an already colorful story: the laudably industrious ants, sad to say, are a bit dull. The saucy repartee, however, will amuse adults, while the climactic showdowns—and there are more than one—are gripping entertainment for the whole family.

BUGSY
1991 135m   c   Crime/Historical/Romance   ★★★½
Baltimore Pictures/Mulholland Productions/   R
Desert Vision Productions   (U.S.)

Warren Beatty (Benjamin "Bugsy" Siegel), Annette Bening (Virginia Hill), Harvey Keitel (Mickey Cohen), Ben Kingsley (Meyer Lansky), Elliott Gould (Harry Greenberg), Joe Mantegna (George Raft), Richard Sarafian (Jack Dragna), Bebe Neuwirth (Countess di Frasso), Giancarlo Scandiuzzi (Count di Frasso), Wendy Phillips (Esta Siegel)

p, Mark Johnson, Barry Levinson, Warren Beatty; d, Barry Levinson; w, James Toback (from the book We Only Kill Each Other: The Life and Bad Times of Bugsy Siegel by Dean Jennings); ph, Allen Daviau; ed, Stu Linder; m, Ennio Morricone; prod d, Dennis Gassner; art d, Leslie McDonald; fx, Clay Pinney, Rob Bottin; cos, Albert Wolsky

AAN Best Picture; AAN Best Actor: Warren Beatty; AAN Best Supporting Actor: Harvey Keitel; AAN Best Supporting Actor: Ben Kingsley; AAN Best Director: Barry Levinson; AAN Best Original Screenplay: James Toback; AAN Best Cinematography: Allen Daviau; AAN Best Original Score: Ennio Morricone; AA Best Art Direction-Set Decoration: Dennis Gassner, Nancy Haigh; AA Best Costume Design: Albert Wolsky

BUGSY is an elegant, knowing, but ultimately heartless homage to the bygone glamour of Hollywood and Vegas. Director-star Beatty portrays gangster legend Benjamin "Bugsy" Siegel as both a romantic visionary and a psychopathic killer—a raw mass of contradictory impulses.

Bugsy Siegel (Beatty) arrives in California, charged with taking over the various L.A. rackets. Seduced by Hollywood's tacky glamour, he is soon romancing starlet Virginia Hill (Bening) and concocting a plan to build a luxury hotel and casino on an unpopulated expanse of Nevada desert—the roots of modern-day Las Vegas. As the cost of building the Flamingo soars to $6 million—six times the budget originally approved by his partners—Bugsy runs into increasing conflict with his superiors, particularly his mentor, Meyer Lansky (Kingsley).

Levinson's direction is brisk and, for a film largely about the allure of glamour, suitably flashy. Toback's script, if hardly profound, occasionally manages a colorful incident and some spiky dialogue. An impressive array of actors, meanwhile, help out with crisp performances. As opposed to the well-played if little-seen supporting characters, however, Siegel, who is everywhere, comes across as a two-dimensional, almost cartoon-like figure—someone it's impossible to really care about. By the time this rambling film finally chunters to its conclusion, the only point Levinson, Toback, and Beatty can make is that Bugsy was right that Las Vegas was a money-making proposition.

BUGSY MALONE

1976	93m	c	Children's/Musical	★★½
Paramount	(U.K.)			PG

Scott Baio *(Bugsy Malone)*, Jodie Foster *(Tallulah)*, Florrie Dugger *(Blousey)*, John Cassisi *(Fat Sam)*, Paul Murphy *(Leroy)*, Albin Jenkins *(Fizzy)*, Martin Lev *(Dandy Dan)*, Davidson Knight *(Knuckles)*, Paul Chirelstein *(Smolsky)*, Paul Besterman *(Yonkers)*

p, Alan Marshall; d, Alan Parker; w, Alan Parker; ph, Michael Seresin, Peter Biziou (Eastmancolor); ed, Gerry Hambling; m, Paul Williams; chor, Gillian Gregory; cos, Monica Howe

AAN Best Song Score: Paul Williams

Charming, delightful, all the things a G-rated picture should be, BUGSY MALONE is a spoof of the 1920s gangster era replete with all of the cliché characters except that this is a musical and everyone in the film is teenaged or younger. Hardly any of the boys' voices have changed, so the songs are all in keys for altos or sopranos. Williams has written a lovely Oscar-nominated score and Parker a lovely script. You've seen every single one of these characters played by Robinson or Cagney or Bogart or Steiger or Brando, but they come to life again when those tried-and-true lines ("I thought I tol' ya ta stay outta da Sout' side, Blackie") come out of the mouths of babes. The movie was not the hit it might have been, so Williams later took it to London as a live musical—where, again, it was not the hit it should have been. Many of the juveniles are British, but the few Americans have since gone on to some success: Baio in several TV shows and Foster in films. When the picture comes around on TV—or even in a revival house theater—make sure you see this one. And if you don't have any children of your own, rent a few and take them so that you can watch their faces as they enjoy BUGSY MALONE.

BULL DURHAM

DVD

1988	108m	c	Comedy	★★★½
Mount	(U.S.)			R

Kevin Costner *(Crash Davis)*, Susan Sarandon *(Annie Savoy)*, Tim Robbins *(Ebby Calvin "Nuke" LaLoosh)*, Trey Wilson *(Joe "Skip" Riggins)*, Robert Wuhl *(Larry Hockett)*, Jenny Robertson *(Millie)*, Max Patkin *(Himself)*, William O'Leary *(Jimmy)*, David Neidorf *(Bobby)*, Danny Gans *(Deke)*

p, Thom Mount, Mark Burg; d, Ron Shelton; w, Ron Shelton; ph, Bobby Byrne (Deluxe Color); ed, Robert Leighton, Adam Weiss; m, Michael Convertino; prod d, Armin Ganz; cos, Louise Frogley

AAN Best Original Screenplay: Ron Shelton

Smutty, terrific fun. Featuring outstanding lead performances by Kevin Costner, Susan Sarandon, and Tim Robbins; a witty, literate script; and an insider's familiarity with life around minor league baseball—BULL DURHAM is both one of the best films ever made about the national pastime and a charming romantic comedy. As smart as she is sexy, Annie Savoy (Sarandon), the No. 1 fan of the Class A Durham Bulls, chooses one player a year for her student in the art of lovemaking as well as in metaphysics and literature. This summer two players vie for her attentions: Nuke Laloosh (Robbins), a bonus-baby pitcher "with a million-dollar arm and five-cent head" and Crash Davis (Costner), the power-hitting longtime minor-league catcher brought to the club to prepare Nuke for the big leagues. First-time director Ron Shelton (who spent five years in the Baltimore Orioles farm system) suffuses his film with carefully realized bush-league details and evokes laugh after rich laugh. Costner (a former high school shortstop) is wholly convincing as a pro ballplayer, delivering perhaps his best performance to date. Sarandon sizzles, and BULL DURHAM is an extremely sexy movie that uses bared souls rather than bared bodies to turn up the heat. The diamond action was shot at El Toro Field, home of the real Durham Bulls. Max Patkin, "the Clown Prince of Baseball," also appears.

BULLDOG DRUMMOND STRIKES BACK

1934	83m	bw	Mystery	★★★★
UA	(U.S.)			

Ronald Colman *(Hugh Drummond)*, Loretta Young *(Lola Field)*, C. Aubrey Smith *(Inspector Nielsen)*, Charles Butterworth *(Algy Longworth)*, Una Merkel *(Gwen)*, Warner Oland *(Prince Achmed)*, George Regas *(Singh)*, Mischa Auer *(Hassan)*, Kathleen Burke *(Jane Sothern)*, Arthur Hohl *(Dr. Sothern)*

p, Joseph M. Schenck; d, Roy Del Ruth; w, Henry Lehrman, Nunnally Johnson (based on the novel by H.C. "Sapper" McNeile); ph, Peverell Marley; ed, Allen McNeil; art d, Richard Day; cos, Gwen Wakeling

Colman repeats his 1929 success in the first film he made after refusing to work for Samuel Goldwyn ever again. Fast-moving, smartly produced, laugh-studded melodrama is as incredible as it is engrossing. Drummond tries to convince Scotland Yard of the existence of a kidnapping ring in London, but every time he discovers a witness to prove the point, the witness mysteriously disappears. Colman was delighted to repeat his Drummond role because the improvement in sound and other technical refinements made it possible to portray the character with more polish and bite than the primitive 1929 version had permitted, even though he had received an Academy Award nomination for the earlier performance. Charles Butterworth's portrayal as Drummond's sidekick Algy was also a major factor in the film's success. This movie never lags and has all the plausibility of a well-written mystery novel read in the middle of the night.

BULLETS OVER BROADWAY

DVD

1994	99m	c	Comedy	★★★½
Sweetheart Productions/Sweetland Films		(U.S.)		R

John Cusack *(David Shayne)*, Jack Warden *(Julian Marx)*, Chazz Palminteri *(Cheech)*, Joe Viterelli *(Nick Valenti)*, Jennifer Tilly *(Olive Neal)*, Rob Reiner *(Sheldon Flender)*, Mary-Louise Parker *(Ellen)*, Dianne Wiest *(Helen Sinclair)*, Harvey Fierstein *(Sid Loomis)*, Jim Broadbent *(Warner Purcell)*

p, Robert Greenhut; d, Woody Allen; w, Woody Allen, Douglas McGrath; ph, Carlo Di Palma; ed, Susan E. Morse; prod d, Santo Loquasto; art d, Tom Warren; cos, Jeffrey Kurland

AA Best Supporting Actress: Dianne Wiest; *AAN Best Supporting Actor:* Chazz Palminteri; *AAN Best Supporting Actress:* Jennifer

Tilly; *AAN Best Director:* Woody Allen; *AAN Best Original Screenplay:* Woody Allen, Douglas McGrath; *AAN Best Art Direction-Set Decoration:* Santo Loquasto, Susan Bode; *AAN Best Costume Design:* Jeffrey Kurland

In a welcome return to straightforward comedy, erratic auteur Woody Allen laid off the arty melodramas in 1994, directing both an amusing made-for-TV film of his Broadway play, *Don't Drink the Water*, and this deft period farce, his most enjoyable movie in years.

At the height of the Roaring Twenties, Broadway playwright David Shayne (John Cusack) is an honest artist among the Philistines—until his backer, mobster Nicky Valenti (Joe Viterelli), sees Shayne's play as a vehicle for his ditzy showgirl mistress, Olive (Jennifer Tilly). Further concessions are called for by grande dame of the thea-tuh Helen Sinclair (Diane Wiest). But Shayne's most effective critic is dese-anddose hitman Cheech (Chazz Palminteri), who turns out to be a distinctly dangerous dramaturg.

Arguably, Allen continues his Great Masters series here, on the heels of the Fritz Lang chiaroscuro of SHADOWS AND FOG and the overripe Cassavetes stylings of HUSBANDS AND WIVES. Here he tips his hat to the Algonquin Round Table types he once emulated in his magazine prose—George S. Kaufman, Moss Hart, Thurber, Perelman, even the Marx Brothers' backstage high jinks in A NIGHT AT THE OPERA. After his brush with the tabloids, Allen appears to be making good on his frequent claim that what he desires most from an adoring public is his privacy. This is the first Woody Allen film in which neither he nor one of his romantic partners appears, and he's pruned back the autobiographical excess of several previous films. Moreover, everyone seems to be enjoying themselves, maybe for the first time since ANNIE HALL.

BULLITT

1968 113m c Crime   ★★★★
Warner Bros. (U.S.)

Steve McQueen *(Bullitt),* Robert Vaughn *(Chalmers),* Jacqueline Bisset *(Cathy),* Don Gordon *(Delgetti),* Robert Duvall *(Weissberg),* Simon Oakland *(Capt. Bennett),* Norman Fell *(Baker),* Georg Stanford Brown *(Dr. Willard),* Justin Tarr *(Eddy),* Carl Reindel *(Stanton)*

p, Philip D'Antoni; d, Peter Yates; w, Alan R. Trustman, Harry Kleiner (based on the novel *Mute Witness* by Robert L. Pike); ph, William A. Fraker (Technicolor); ed, Frank P. Keller; m, Lalo Schifrin; art d, Albert Brenner; cos, Theadora Van Runkle

AA Best Film Editing: Frank P Keller; *AAN Best Sound:* Seven Arts Studio Sound Department

Expert chase film, breathless and modern, that sent McQueen to the top of the box office heap. He plays the title character, a colorful and unorthodox police lieutenant assigned to protect a government witness scheduled to inform on the national crime syndicate. Climax has McQueen spotting hoodlums and following in one of the most spectacular car chases ever filmed, up and down the hills of San Francisco while handheld cameras record the perilous pursuit as each car narrowly misses intersecting autos, barriers, and buildings as they squeal, slide, and lurch along the narrow streets.

BULLITT was a return to the old, tough crime movies so expertly played by Bogart and Robinson, but made modern here by great technical advances and McQueen's taciturn, antihero stance. Yates's superb direction presents a fluid, always moving camera. All the performers are top-notch, from sour-faced Norman Fell to a curious bit part played by Robert Duvall as a cab driver who is seen almost entirely through a rear-view mirror. Aside from THE SAND PEB-

BLES, this fine production stands as McQueen's top achievement in a lamentably short career. The film won an Oscar for Best Film Editing and was nominated for Best Sound.

BULWORTH   *DVD*

1998 108m c   Political/Comedy   ★★★★
20th Century Fox   (U.S.)   R

Warren Beatty *(Sen. Jay Billington Bulworth),* Halle Berry *(Nina),* Oliver Platt *(Murphy),* Don Cheadle *(L.D.),* Paul Sorvino *(Graham Crockett),* Jack Warden *(Davers),* Christine Baranski *(Constance Bulworth),* Joshua Malina *(Bill Feldman),* Richard Sarafian *(Vinnie),* Isaiah Washington *(Darnell)*

p, Warren Beatty, Pieter Jan Brugge, Lauren Shuler-Donner; d, Warren Beatty; w, Warren Beatty, Jeremy Pikser; ph, Vittorio Storaro; ed, Robert C. Jones, Billy Weber; m, Ennio Morricone; prod d, Dean Tavoularis; art d, William F. O'Brien; fx, Pacific Title Digital; cos, Milena Canonero

AAN Best Original Screenplay: Warren Beatty, Jeremy Pikser

Bold, merciless, and frequently very funny, BULWORTH is Warren Beatty's contribution to the ranks of American political satire.

Sixties idealist turned telegenic sound-bite spitter Jay Billington Bulworth (Beatty) is the ghost of American politics present, an incumbent senator whose values and principles have long since been spun into ideological cotton candy. He has just enough integrity left to know he's sold out, and that shred of self-knowledge has driven him to a full-blown breakdown. Bulworth hasn't eaten or slept in three days. He's made a corrupt deal with an insurance lobbyist (Paul Sorvino) for a lucrative personal policy, and hired a hit man to assassinate him. Nature abhors a vacuum, like the one left by Bulworth's departing career savvy and sense of self-preservation. But what flows in to fill it is sheer political lunacy: Bulworth adopts the street style and attitude of a ghetto gangbanger and starts saying—no, make that *rapping*—what he really thinks, no matter how offensive.

Beatty's politics seem clear—through Bulworth, he espouses a liberal, anti-big business line—but he stages a preemptive strike against accusations of propaganda by seeding the film with nagging questions about Bulworth's conversion on the road to Washington. How valid *is* an agenda appropriated from disenfranchised African Americans by a privileged white man? Has he seen the light or simply succumbed to middle-age jungle fever, embodied in the beautiful, whipsmart Nina (Halle Berry), whom he spots at a campaign stop? His rhyming may be more Dr. Seuss than Dr. Dre, but Bulworth's scathing, vitriol-laced riffs on race relations, incestuous media/corporate monopolies, the distribution of wealth, and—of course—Hollywood are as provocative as they are profane.

BURNT MONEY   *DVD*

(PLATA QUEMADA)
2000 125m c   Crime   ★★★½
Mandarin Films/Tornasol Films/Taxi Films   R
(Uruguay/France/Argentina/Spain)

Eduardo Noriega *(Angel),* Leonardo Sbaraglia *(Nene),* Pablo Echarri *(Cuervo),* Leticia Bredice *(Giselle),* Ricardo Bartis *(Fontana),* Dolores Fonzi *(Vivi),* Carlos Roffe *(Nando),* Daniel Valenzuela *(Tabare),* Hector Alterio *(Losardo),* Claudio Rissi *(Realtor)*

p, Oscar Kramer; d, Marcelo Pineyro; w, Marcel Fugueras, Marcelo Pineyro (based on the novel *Plata Quemada* by Ricardo Piglia); ph, Alfredo Mayo; ed, Juan Carlos Macias; m, Osvaldo Montes; prod d, Belen Bernuy, Margarita Gomez, Noemi Nemirovsky; art d, Jorge Ferrari, Juan Mario Roust; fx, Tom Cundom

"They're young. They're in love. They kill people." BON-NIE & CLYDE's famous tagline could just as easily describe this violent yet oddly romantic true-crime drama set in mid-'60s Argentina.

Nene (Leonardo Sbaraglia) and Angel (Eduardo Noriega) are darkly handsome roughnecks who meet while cruising a public restroom in Buenos Aires. Nene is filled to brimming with self-loathing; Angel hears voices and is probably schizophrenic. Together, they make an ideal couple and soon become known in criminal circles as "the Twins." Fontana (Ricardo Bartis), a professional crook with a mug like something out of Dick Tracy, recruits the Twins and a coked-up playboy named Cuervo (Pablo Echarri) to rob a pay truck. The heist goes down and quickly goes bad: the two policemen in the truck are killed, Angel is seriously wounded, and the gang is wanted by every cop in the city. Angel, Nene, Fontana, and Cuervo slip into neighboring Uruguay, where they hole up in a ratty apartment until fake passports can be arranged. Things start to unravel: Angel's already fragile emotional state deteriorates even further, and a frustrated Nene starts cruising the midway of a nearby amusement park. He meets Giselle (Leticia Bredice), a prostitute who offers him a way out, but for a price.

Sex, drugs, gunplay, countless exploding squibs, poetry, the twist—you name it, director Marcelo Pineyro has found room for it, and the whole thing climaxes in a cataclysmic police standoff to end all police standoffs. But the most affecting parts of this film are its quieter, character-driven moments, and it's beautifully acted; if there is indeed an "Argentinean New Wave" afoot, Bredice might be its Anna Karina.

BUS STOP *DVD*
1956 94m c Comedy ★★★½
Fox (U.S.)

Marilyn Monroe (Cherie), Don Murray (Bo), Arthur O'Connell (Virgil), Betty Field (Grace), Eileen Heckart (Vera), Robert Bray (Carl), Hope Lange (Elma), Hans Conried (Life Photographer), Max Showalter, billed as Casey Adams (Life Reporter), Henry Slate (Manager of Night Club)

p, Buddy Adler; d, Joshua Logan; w, George Axelrod (based on the play by William Inge); ph, Milton Krasner (CinemaScope, DeLuxe Color); m, Alfred Newman, Cyril J. Mockridge

AAN Best Supporting Actor: Don Murray

Few Marilyn Monroe fans can listen to "That Old Black Magic" without recalling Monroe's tinny, off-key, magically poignant rendition of the standard in BUS STOP. In her energetic and warm portrayal of Cherie, whose dream of Hollywood and Vine is interrupted by the reality of a layover in Phoenix, Monroe exposes her vulnerability without sacrificing any of her radiance—for many viewers, this was the film that proved she could act.

In the Blue Dragon Cafe in Phoenix we meet Bo (Don Murray in his first screen role), a rambunctious cowboy who is in town to take part in a rodeo. He bullies the noisy patrons into a respectful silence during Cherie's big song and is rewarded with an innocent kiss of appreciation. From that moment on, he's determined to make her his wife, in spite of her protestations and the dismay of his loyal sidekick Virgil (Arthur O'Connell). Cherie boards a bus headed out of town to escape him, but Bo follows. The bus is stranded in a snowstorm and the passengers are forced to spend the night in a diner, where a fight involving the bus driver, protecting his passenger, and the cowboy, claiming his woman, leaves Bo defeated and humiliated. By the time the road is cleared the next day, a chastened Bo has begun to realize that he'll get nowhere acting like a brute.

During her year-long absence from the screen, Monroe had diligently pursued her craft under the firm hand of theater legend Lee Strasberg, and it shows. William Inge's rowdy play was adapted by George Axelrod (LORD LOVE A DUCK) with delightful results. The play, which unfolded on a single diner set, is skillfully opened out to include a ranch, a dance hall, a rodeo, and scenes of the countryside. The film is further enhanced by some action-packed rodeo sequences.

BUTCH CASSIDY AND THE SUNDANCE KID *DVD*
1969 112m c Western ★★★½
Campanile Productions/Newman-Foreman PG
Productions/20th Century Fox (U.S.)

Paul Newman (Butch Cassidy), Robert Redford (Sundance Kid), Katharine Ross (Etta Place), Strother Martin (Percy Garris), Henry Jones (Bike Salesman), Jeff Corey (Sheriff Bledsoe), George Furth (Woodcock), Cloris Leachman (Agnes), Ted Cassidy (Harvey Logan), Kenneth Mars (Marshal)

p, Paul Monash, John Foreman; d, George Roy Hill; w, William Goldman; ph, Conrad Hall (DeLuxe Color); ed, John C. Howard, Richard C. Meyer; m, Burt Bacharach; art d, Jack Martin Smith, Philip Jefferies; fx, L.B. Abbott, Art Cruickshank; cos, Edith Head

AAN Best Picture; AAN Best Director: George Roy Hill; AA Best Original Story and Screenplay: William Goldman; AA Best Cinematography: Conrad Hall; AA Best Original Score (Not a Musical): Burt Bacharach; AA Best Original Song: "Raindrops Keep Fallin' on My Head"; Burt Bacharach (Music), Hal David (Lyrics); AAN Best Sound: William Edmundson, David Dockendorf

Although much of its freshness has faded, this still-amusing film reinvented the Western for a new generation.

Newman and Redford reimagine the two famous train robbers as a pair of urbane businessmen who go about their work with the easy nonchalance of seasoned professionals. Threatened by determined Pinkertons and rapidly advancing technology, they reconsider their careers, returning to The Kid's native New York City for a brief vacation. But, succumbing to the desire to return to the work they know and love, they strike out for South America to start over. At first successful (despite not speaking a word of Spanish), they soon find the Bolivian government less tolerant and more aggressive than Pinkerton men, and die in a blaze of glory in a gunfight, unaware how seriously outnumbered they are.

BUTCH CASSIDY's winking awareness of its own cinematic nature (from the opening "silent movie" train robbery to the famous closing freeze frame) and witty banter give the story a degree of charm and exuberance, but otherwise it's trapped in its own context, most notably apparent in the (Oscar-winning) Bacharach score that now feels silly and dated. Ross' stiff performance as the Kid's paramour, Etta Place (a character who later spawned a terrible sequel) is more than offset by the wonderful supporting cast and, especially, the chemistry between the stars. This film revived Newman's flagging career and officially catapulted Redford to stardom (giving him the industry clout to make such personal projects as DOWNHILL RACER, THE CANDIDATE and JEREMIAH JOHNSON).

BUTCHER BOY, THE
1997 106m c Drama ★★★½
Butcher Boy Film Productions/Geffen Pictures (Ireland) R

Stephen Rea (Benny Brady—"Da"), Fiona Shaw (Mrs. Nugent), Eamonn Owens (Francie Brady), Alan Boyle (Joe Purcell), Niall Buggy (Father Dom), Brendan Gleeson (Father Bubbles), Peter Gowen (Leddy), Stuart Graham (Priest at College), Ian Hart (Uncle Alo), Tom Hickey (Gardener)

p, Redmond Morris, Stephen Woolley; d, Neil Jordan; w, Neil Jordan, Patrick McCabe (based on the novel by Patrick McCabe); ph, Adrian Biddle; ed, Tony Lawson; m, Elliot Goldenthal; prod d,

Anthony Pratt; art d, Anna Rackard; fx, Joss Williams, Steve Lloyd; cos, Sandy Powell

The comic-strip panels that fill the screen during the opening credits set the tone: Neil Jordan's adaptation of Patrick McCabe's award-winning novel is brash, broadly drawn, and awash in color. But just below the deliriously hyper-real surface is a wrenching and ultimately horrifying tale of adolescent isolation.

It's 1962, and as the Cuban Missile Crisis escalates to a nail-biting climax, a different kind of explosion is set to blow in a small Irish village. Francie Brady (Eamonn Owens) is a precocious 12-year-old hellion whose freckle-faced, manically cheerful exterior masks an ever-deepening emotional disturbance. Francie lives in a fantasy world of comic book heroes and TV, and with good reason: his mother (Aisling O'Sullivan) is chronically depressed, his father (Stephen Rea) is known as the best drinker in town, and Francie's archenemy—the Brady's evil neighbor Mrs. Nugent (Fiona Shaw)—repeatedly reminds the boy that he and his family are no better than pigs. So a pig is what Francie is determined to become, particularly after his mother commits suicide and his father lays the blame squarely on Francie's shoulders. As every childish nightmare of abandonment comes true and Francie is failed by every person he ever loved, his uncontrollable rage leads him to a moment of appalling—and appallingly understandable—violence.

Jordan and cowriter McCabe have done a masterful job adapting the novel for the screen, turning Francie's ranting interior monologue into a vivid vision of the world through the eyes of a disturbed child. Owens' remarkable, high-pitched performance and Jordan's lush, visionary style are perfectly suited to the material: Jordan fills Francie's head and the screen with extraordinary, often fantastic images—not the least of which is an amusing cameo by Sinead O'Connor as none other than the Virgin Mary.

BUTTERFIELD 8 *DVD*
1960 109m c Drama ★★★
MGM (U.S.)

Elizabeth Taylor *(Gloria Wandrous)*, Laurence Harvey *(Weston Liggett)*, Eddie Fisher *(Steve Carpenter)*, Dina Merrill *(Emily Liggett)*, Mildred Dunnock *(Mrs. Wandrous)*, Betty Field *(Mrs. Fanny Thurber)*, Jeffrey Lynn *(Bingham Smith)*, Kay Medford *(Happy)*, Susan Oliver *(Norma)*, George Voskovec *(Dr. Tredman)*

p, Pandro S. Berman; d, Daniel Mann; w, Charles Schnee, John Michael Hayes (based on the novel by John O'Hara); ph, Joseph Ruttenberg; ed, Ralph E. Winters; m, Bronislau Kaper; art d, George W. Davis, Urie McCleary; cos, Helen Rose

AA Best Actress: Elizabeth Taylor; *AAN Best Color Cinematography:* Joseph Ruttenberg, Charles Harten

Glossy trash with the star at full throttle, it's the quintessential La Liz movie. Loosely based on John O'Hara's novel, loose Gloria Wandrous encompasses the legendary wanton Taylor persona; indeed, Hollywood was so pleased by the cementing of Hurricane Liz's public image they rewarded her with an Oscar. As for Taylor's critical response, when she watched it the first time in a screening room, she threw a high heel at the screen, fled to a john, and promptly threw up. All the more reason to tune in...

Liz reluctantly plays Gloria (the very idea—casting Liz in something tawdry and commercial), a "model" searching for understanding, who, like Liz, cannot breathe if she is not in love. Enter married rake, ultimate héel Laurence Harvey, who fancies Liz in a sort of violent bedroom way and we're off to the races. Our fave scenes: that opening, which chronicles a

typical La Liz good morning, and the barside "disagreement" she shares with Harvey.

Miss Taylor gives quite a star performance and she's buoyed by a talented supporting cast with two eyesores: the bland Dina Merrill and the blank Eddie Fisher (his appearance was a consolation prize to soothe the star). This was the height of the "I stole Debbie's husband; so what?" scandal, so the public turned out in droves to snoop their chemistry (there was none) and hate Liz en masse. Hate turned to public sympathy when Taylor caught pneumonia in London and nearly died, surviving only when an emergency tracheotomy was performed (and guaranteed Liz a lot of Oscar sympathy votes). This was an important chapter in the Taylor Roadshow and she would next land CLEOPATRA, and celebrate by dumping Fisher. Meanwhile, enjoy BUTTERFIELD 8. It's a rave!

BUTTERFLY EFFECT, THE *DVD*
2004 113m c Fantasy/Thriller ★★½
Benderspink Productions/FilmEngine Productions/ R
Katalyst (U.S.)

Ashton Kutcher *(Evan Treborn)*, Amy Smart *(Kayleigh Miller)*, Melora Walters *(Andrea Treborn)*, Elden Henson *(Lenny Kagan)*, William Lee Scott *(Tommy Miller)*, John Patrick Amedori *(Evan at 13)*, Irene Gorovaia *(Kayleigh at 13)*, Kevin G. Schmidt *(Lenny at 13)*, Jesse James *(Tommy at 13)*, Logan Lerman *(Evan at 7)*

p, Chris Bender, A.J. Dix, Anthony Rhulen, J.C. Spink; d, Eric Bress, J. Mackye Gruber; w, Eric Bress, J. Mackye Gruber; ph, Matthew F. Leonetti; ed, Peter Amundson; m, Michael Suby; prod d, Douglas Higgins; art d, Shannon Grover, Jeremy Stanbridge; fx, Chad Malbon; cos, Carla Hetland

A somber fable about the far-reaching and unforeseen consequences that ripple outwards from every act, screenwriters Eric Bress and J. Mackye Gruber's joint directing debut falters under its weighty dramatic burdens.

Seven-year-old Evan Treborn (Logan Lerman) lives with his hardworking mother (Melora Walters), pines for his institutionalized dad (Callum Keith Rennie), and pals around with sensitive Lenny (Jake Kaese) and pretty Kayleigh Miller (Sarah Widdows). Kayleigh lives with her divorced father (Eric Stoltz) and delinquent brother, Tommy (Cameron Bright). Evan is subject to blackouts that frighten his mother and leave holes in his memory. As 13-year-olds, Tommy (Jesse James) instigates a prank that goes so horribly wrong that Lenny (Kevin G. Schmidt) is permanently traumatized, but Evan can't remember what happened. Later, when Evan (John Patrick Amedori) and Kayleigh (Irene Gorovaia) kiss for the first time, Tommy exacts a terrible revenge. Evan can't remember it, either. In the present day, brilliant psychology major Evan (Ashton Kutcher) is reading one of the journals he's kept since childhood when he's catapulted into a vivid waking dream of the past. He tracks down Kayleigh (Amy Smart) to compare memories, and finds her working in a diner. Their awkward encounter drives her to suicide and, convinced that what he experienced wasn't a dream, Evan tries to re-enter key traumatic junctures in his past in hopes of filling in the holes in his memory and fixing the things that went so terribly wrong.

Bress and Gruber's attempt to make a serious, spooky moral tale is ambitious, but their deeply disturbing material mixes uncomfortably with the film's time-travel conceit, which requires some serious suspension of disbelief. Kutcher's lightweight presence makes surrendering to that suspension doubly difficult.

BYE-BYE BRAZIL

1980 100m c Drama ★★★
Carnaval Unifilm (Brazil)

Jose Wilker *(Lord Gypsy)*, Betty Faria *(Salome)*, Fabio Junior *(Cico)*, Zaira Zambelli *(Dasdo)*, Principe Nabor *(Swallow)*, Jofre Soares *(Ze da Luz)*, Marcus Vinicius *(Gent)*, Jose Maria Lima *(Assistant)*, Emanuel Cavalcanti *(Mayor)*, Jose Marcio Reis *(Smuggler)*

p, Lucy Barreto; d, Carlos Diegues; w, Carlos Diegues; ph, Lauro Escorel Filho; ed, Anisio Medeiros

BYE BYE BRAZIL is a colorful, exotic collection of vignettes about modern Brazil. The film follows a carnival troupe as they travel throughout the country, wandering deep into the Amazonian jungles, in search of new places where they can put on a show. The eccentric group consists of Lord Cigano (Jose Wilker), a magician who organized the troupe; Salome (Betty Faria), his mistress and the show's exotic dancer/prostitute; Cico (Fabio Junior), a young accordionist infatuated with Salome; Dasdo (Zaira Zambelli), Cico's pregnant wife; and Swallow (Principe Nabor), a black, deaf-mute strongman. An insightful and humorous look at two Brazils in conflict—the traditional Brazil versus the progressive Brazil, with its infusions of North American culture.

C

CABARET

1972 124m c Musical/War ★★★★½
Allied Artists (U.S.) PG

Liza Minnelli *(Sally Bowles)*, Michael York *(Brian Roberts)*, Helmut Griem *(Maximilian von Heune)*, Joel Grey *(Master of Ceremonies)*, Fritz Wepper *(Fritz Wendel)*, Marisa Berenson *(Natalia Landauer)*, Elisabeth Neumann-Viertel *(Fraulein Schneider)*, Sigrid von Richthofen *(Fraulei+n Maur)*, Helen Vita *(Fraulein Kost)*, Gerd Vespermann *(Bobby)*

p, Cy Feuer; d, Bob Fosse; w, Jay Presson Allen (based on the stage play by Joe Masteroff, the stage play I Am a Camera by John Van Druten, and the writings of Christopher Isherwood); ph, Geoffrey Unsworth (Technicolor); ed, David Bretherton; m, Ralph Burns; art d, Jurgen Kiebach, Rolf Zehetbauer; chor, Bob Fosse; cos, Charlotte Flemming

AA Best Actress: Liza Minnelli; *AA Best Supporting Actor:* Joel Grey; *AA Best Director:* Bob Fosse; *AA Best Cinematography:* Geoffrey Unsworth; *AA Best Film Editing:* David Bretherton; *AA Best Song Score:* Ralph Burns; *AA Best Art Direction-Set Decoration:* Rolf Zehetbauer, Jurgen Kiebach, Herbert Strabel; *AA Best Sound:* Robert Knudson, David Hildyard; *AAN Best Picture*; *AAN Best Adapted Screenplay:* Jay Presson Allen

Chilling Fosse vision of Weimar Berlin, stylishly directed and choreographed, featuring a show-stopping musical performance by Minnelli, Grey's unforgettable emcee and thoughtful acting from Michael York. The screenplay utilizes much of the Broadway musical's book, but also is influenced by both play and screen versions of I AM A CAMERA. Englishman Brian Roberts (York) arrives in Berlin, takes a small flat, and meets a promiscuous, eccentric American, Sally Bowles (Minnelli), who earns her living singing in the seedy Kit Kat Club. Brian, a bisexual, becomes involved with both Sally and a wealthy

German playboy (Griem); meanwhile, Nazism is ever more evidently on the rise.

Minnelli's knockout musical delivery tends to obscure the film's finer points, and, because Liza literally becomes a star before our eyes, her enactment of Sally Bowles's tragic mediocrity isn't plausible. Fosse wisely scrapped several weak songs from the original score and songwriters Kander and Ebb added some fine new ones. Everyone raves about "Money," the Grey-Minnelli duet, but the film's real show-stoppers are "Mein Herr," where Liza rivals Dietrich in evoking Weimar-era decadence, and "Tomorrow Belongs to Me," in which a freshfaced German youth is gradually revealed as a Nazi. The final fadeout is extraordinary.

CABIN IN THE SKY

1943 98m bw Musical ★★★★
MGM (U.S.)

Ethel Waters *(Petunia Jackson)*, Eddie "Rochester" Anderson *(Little Joe)*, Lena Horne *(Georgia Brown)*, Louis Armstrong *(The Trumpeter)*, Rex Ingram *(Lucius/Lucifer, Jr.)*, Kenneth Spencer *(Rev. Green, The General)*, John "Bubbles" Sublett *(Domino)*, Oscar Polk *(The Deacon/Flatfoot)*, Mantan Moreland *(First Idea Man)*, Willie Best *(Second Idea Man)*

p, Arthur Freed; d, Vincente Minnelli; w, Joseph Schrank (based on the play by Lynn Root, John Latouche, Vernon Duke); ph, Sidney Wagner; ed, Harold F. Kress; m, Roger Edens

AAN Best Song: "Happiness is a Thing Called Joe"; Harold Arlen (Music), E.Y. Harburg (Lyrics)

Vincente Minnelli's debut as a Hollywood director was the first all-black musical since GREEN PASTURES in 1936 and a monument to Ethel Waters in all her glory. Though the film perpetuates racial stereotypes—hardly surprising, given the period in which it was made—it's a fresh, inventive take on the original Broadway production which showcases a number of prodigious talents.

The story focuses on Little Joe (Eddie "Rochester" Anderson), a gambler who is nearly killed in a bar-room brawl and whose soul then becomes the site of a battle (fought in dream sequences) between God's General (Kenneth Spencer) and Lucifer Jr. (Rex Ingram). This tug-of-war is reflected in another, real-life struggle, for Joe's heart, between his devoted wife (Waters) and the alluring Georgia Brown (Lena Horne).

Though shot in sepia, CABIN IN THE SKY offers ample proof of Minnelli's visual flair in several scenes, particularly an early sequence of a church service and a night-club dance routine (to "Shine") performed by Domino (John "Bubbles" Sublett). The cast is quite exceptional. Anderson makes an engaging, sympathetic rascal, whose moral dilemma is understandable given the siren call of the ravishing Lena Horne. Ethel Waters steals the show, blazing through the picture with sincerity and compassion and handling her songs with unparalleled assurance—"Taking a Chance on Love" and the Oscar-nominated "Happiness is a Thing Called Joe" are standouts.

CABIN was far from plain sailing for Minnelli and MGM. The director was supposedly romancing Horne, leading to tensions between her, Minnelli and Waters which came to a head over the "Honey in the Honeycomb" number. The number was originally slated to be sung by Waters but, during production, plans were changed to accommodate two versions, one to be performed by Waters as a ballad, one as a dance number led by Horne and featuring John "Bubbles" Sublett. Horne, however, broke her ankle during production, and the two numbers had to be reversed, with Horne singing the ballad (a highlight of the film) and Waters displaying surprising talent as a dancer.

The Duke Ellington Orchestra lends musical pizazz and Louis Armstrong can be seen as one of Lucifer Jr.'s hilarious henchmen—his joyous face almost steals every scene he's in. Only three of the songs and three principals—Minnelli, Waters and Ingram—came from the original Broadway show.

CABLE GUY, THE

DVD

| 1996 | 91m | c | Comedy/Thriller | ★★½ |

Bernie Brillstein/Brad Grey/Licht/Mueller Film Corp.   (U.S.) — PG-13

Jim Carrey *(Cable Guy)*, Matthew Broderick *(Steven)*, Leslie Mann *(Robin)*, Jack Black *(Rick)*, George Segal *(Steven's Father)*, Diane Baker *(Steven's Mother)*, Ben Stiller *(Sam Sweet)*, Eric Roberts *(Himself)*, Janeane Garofalo *(Medieval Waitress)*, Misa Koprova *(Heather)*

p, Andrew Licht, Jeffrey A. Mueller, Judd Apatow; d, Ben Stiller; w, Lou Holtz Jr.; ph, Robert Brinkmann; ed, Steven Weisberg; m, John Ottman; prod d, Sharon Seymour; art d, Jeff Knipp; fx, Matt Sweeney, Sony Pictures Imageworks; cos, Erica Edell Phillips

Much of this dark farce, about the chaos that erupts when a buttoned-down milksop (Matthew Broderick) slips the Cable Guy (Jim Carrey) 50 bucks for free premium service, verges on the unwatchable. It's an uneasy hybrid of vulgar slapstick and nightmarish comedy-of-mortification, and its modest ambitions are entirely subordinate to Carrey's manic mugging and capering. But it soars above the plebian rudeness of DUMB AND DUMBER by virtue of a few moments of excoriating brilliance.

Carrey's Cable Guy, his personality formed entirely by TV, is the neediest nerd of all time, and his dismantling of Broderick's ordered life is in the classic tradition of anarchic comedy, complete with undercurrents of class-based hostility and homoerotic menace. A cruel clown, Carrey puts the belligerent libido back in the sexless spazz character perfected by Jerry Lewis, and exploits teasing as the socially condoned form of torture it is. In all, about a third of the film is audaciously funny and genuinely disturbing. The rest will sorely test the devotion of Carrey's fans.

Although first-time writer Lou Holtz Jr.'s awkward script could easily have been played for light laughs, director Ben Stiller (REALITY BITES) consistently brings out its darkest implications. One keenly edited sequence intercuts Carrey's vigorously lewd karaoke rendering of Jefferson Airplane's "Somebody to Love" with Broderick's seduction by a wanton young woman (Misa Koprova). At once amusing and appropriately discomfiting, the scene is a perfectly balanced construct that could be toppled by a single false cut, and isn't. Though less unnerving, the sequence involving hokey theme restaurant "Medieval Times"—which features wry comedienne Janeane Garofalo as a sulky serving wench—is also a tour de force.

CADDYSHACK

DVD

| 1980 | 99m | c | Comedy | ★★½ |

Orion   (U.S.) — R

Rodney Dangerfield *(Al)*, Ted Knight *(Judge)*, Michael O'Keefe *(Danny)*, Bill Murray *(Carl)*, Sarah Holcomb *(Maggie)*, Scott Colomby *(Tony)*, Cindy Morgan *(Lacey)*, Dan Resin *(Dr. Beeper)*, Henry Wilcoxon *(Bishop)*, Albert Salmi *(Noonan)*

p, Douglas Kenney; d, Harold Ramis; w, Brian Doyle-Murray, Harold Ramis, Douglas Kenney; ph, Stevan Larner (Technicolor); ed, William Carruth; m, Johnny Mandel; prod d, Stan Jolly; art d, George Szeptycki

A slapstick comedy featuring a host of great clowns, CADDYSHACK boosted the career of "Saturday Night Live" alum Bill Murray and revived the sagging fortunes of the wonderful Rodney Dangerfield, whose opening scenes are some of the funniest on film.

Adorned in garish garb and throwing his money around, the newly wealthy Dangerfield offends the stuffed-shirt members of the swanky country club he has just joined. No one is more put off by Dangerfield than Knight, who considers the club his private fiefdom. Chase is a dissipated but tremendously talented golfer; O'Keefe is a clean-cut caddie trying to make good and snag a college scholarship by winning a tournament; and Murray is the grubby groundskeeper who spends much of his time devising methods to rid the course of a pesky gopher.

Too much time is spent on the forced romance between O'Keefe and Holcomb, an attractive waitress, however, and the slapstick becomes utterly mindless toward the end (as if the producer said, "Okay, it's time for this film to really get out of control!"). Still, the laughs keep coming. Even the film's absurd stereotypes provoke guilty titters. There is a marvelous moment when Wilcoxon, portraying a golf-loving clergyman, begins to play a perfect game in a raging rainstorm. Dropping one hole-in-one after another, laughing hysterically, thanking the Almighty for the greatest game of his life, he lifts his club heavenward and is struck by lightning while a crescendo from the score of THE TEN COMMANDMENTS (in which Wilcoxon played pharoah's general) blares on the soundtrack.

CAESAR AND CLEOPATRA

DVD

| 1945 | 138m | c | Biography/Historical | ★★★★ |

Two Cities   (U.K.)

Vivien Leigh *(Cleopatra)*, Claude Rains *(Caesar)*, Stewart Granger *(Apollodorus)*, Flora Robson *(Ftatateeta)*, Francis L. Sullivan *(Pothinus)*, Basil Sydney *(Rufio)*, Cecil Parker *(Britannus)*, Raymond Lovell *(Lucius Septimus)*, Anthony Eustrel *(Achillas)*, Ernest Thesiger *(Theodotus)*

p, Gabriel Pascal, J. Arthur Rank; d, Gabriel Pascal; w, George Bernard Shaw, Marjorie Deans (based on the play by George Bernard Shaw); ph, Freddie Young, Robert Krasker, Jack Hildyard, Jack Cardiff (Technicolor); ed, Frederick Wilson; m, Georges Auric; cos, Oliver Messel

AAN Best Interior Decoration (Color): John Bryan (Art Direction)

Don't be misled. Don't try to convince yourself this is wonderful entertainment, don't second guess your basic instinct. Yes, it's Shaw's acerbic and uncinematic play, but Pascal has slowed it down to a lumbering crawl and puffed it up to VIP dinosaur status. Two finer stars being saddled hopelessly we cannot recall, but this occasion frankly finds Rains dishing up ham too readily, and Leigh sorely lacking in the siren department (the arrival of handsome Stewart Granger barely rates a glance). Indeed, this doom laden production was far more interesting behind the cameras than it was in front of them.

Irascible Shaw became so fond of Leigh that he broke precedent and actually wrote an entirely new scene for her, although he adamantly refused to introduce "a little love interest" into the script as politely requested by producer J. Arthur Rank. Producer-director Pascal went at CAESAR AND CLEOPATRA with a vengeance, intent on proving that the British film industry could rival in scope anything Hollywood could create, particularly in the belt-tightening years of WWII. The result was the most extravagantly expensive film Britain produced up to that time, so opulent that when Shaw first viewed it he expressed annoyance at the lavish sets, the hordes of extras, and spendthrift feel of the overall production.

American distribution was promoted by Rank and United Artists with an enormous budget that initially caused U.S. audiences to flock to see favorites Leigh and Rains; but disappointment soon set in when viewers emerged bored, and the Rank organization sustained staggering losses—some $3 million—that brought it to the very brink of bankruptcy. But from the ranks of the film's over 100 bit players emerged many a star, including Michael Rennie, who plays a Centurion, Kay Kendall, a slave girl, and Jean Simmons, a harpist.

CAINE MUTINY, THE　　　DVD
1954　123m　c　Drama　★★★★
Columbia　(U.S.)

Humphrey Bogart (Capt. Philip Francis Queeg), Jose Ferrer (Lt. Barney Greenwald), Van Johnson (Lt. Steve Maryk), Fred MacMurray (Lt. Tom Keefer), Robert Francis (Ens. Willie Keith), May Wynn (May Wynn), Tom Tully (Capt. DeVriess), E.G. Marshall (Lt. Cmdr. Challee), Arthur Franz (Lt. Paynter), Lee Marvin (Meatball)

p, Stanley Kramer; d, Edward Dmytryk; w, Stanley Roberts, Michael Blankfort (based on the play and novel by Herman Wouk); ph, Franz Planer (Technicolor); ed, William Lyon, Henry Batista; m, Max Steiner; prod d, Rudolph Sternad; art d, Cary Odell; fx, Lawrence Butler; cos, Jean Louis

AAN Best Picture; AAN Best Actor: Humphrey Bogart; AAN Best Supporting Actor: Tom Tully; AAN Best Screenplay: Stanley Roberts; AAN Best Film Editing: William Lyon, Henry Batista; AAN Best Score (Drama or Comedy): Max Steiner; AAN Best Sound Recording: John P Livadary (Sound Director)

Complex, atypical Bogie performance is keynote for strong drama from Pulitzer-winning novel and Broadway show. Francis, Johnson, and MacMurray are shipmates early in WWII aboard a destroyer-cum-minesweeper. Bogart, in one of his greatest performances, boards the ship as her new captain and immediately establishes both his power over the men and his neurosis. When he clashes with Johnson, the latter is court-martialed, and Ferrer must defend him.

The scenes with Bogart disintegrating on the witness stand have become part of American film folklore, as he delineates the layers of perfectionism and obsessiveness overlaying an inferiority complex. This is a don't-miss picture, unnecessarily beefed up with a gratuitous, concocted love story between Wynn (using her own name in the film) and Francis. Bogart was later asked how he managed to totally capture the paranoid personality of Queeg. "Simple," growled Bogie, "everybody knows I'm nuts, anyway."

CALIFORNIA SUITE　　　DVD
1978　103m　c　Comedy　★★★½
Columbia　(U.S.)　　　PG

Alan Alda (Bill Warren), Michael Caine (Sidney Cochran), Bill Cosby (Dr. Willis Panama), Jane Fonda (Hannah Warren), Walter Matthau (Marvin Michaels), Elaine May (Millie Michaels), Richard Pryor (Dr. Chauncy Gump), Maggie Smith (Diana Barrie), Gloria Gifford (Lola Gump), Sheila Frazier (Bettina Panama)

p, Ray Stark; d, Herbert Ross; w, Neil Simon (based on his play); ph, David M. Walsh; ed, Michael A. Stevenson; m, Claude Bolling; cos, Ann Roth, Patricia Norris

AA Best Supporting Actress: Maggie Smith; AAN Best Adapted Screenplay: Neil Simon; AAN Best Art Direction: Albert Brenner, Marvin March

An all-star bitch fest, slickly served, but finally monotonous. The quartet of stories are weaved together more or less, with the Caine/Smith segment the most successful because the actors realize the value of comedic understatement—this kind of wordplay requires enough assurance to make it look as though you're not working. The Fonda/Alda sketch is interesting only because Fonda's character is such a welcome relief from her usual gung-ho over-achiever. Matthau and May are an acquired taste—your move. And the Cosby/Pryor sketch is so vile, you can't believe it even made it past an editor. Smith won an Oscar for her deft portrayal of an Academy Award nominee. Truly, a mixed bag.

CALL NORTHSIDE 777　　　DVD
1948　111m　bw　Biography/Crime　★★★★
Fox　(U.S.)

James Stewart (McNeal), Richard Conte (Frank Wiecek), Lee J. Cobb (Brian Kelly), Helen Walker (Laura McNeal), Betty Garde (Wanda Skutnik), Kasia Orzazewski (Tillie Wiecek), Joanna De Bergh (Helen Wiecek-Rayska), Howard Smith (Palmer), Moroni Olsen (Parole Board Chairman), John McIntire (Sam Faxon)

p, Otto Lang; d, Henry Hathaway; w, Jerry Cady, Jay Dratler (adapted by Leonard Hoffman and Quentin Reynolds from articles by James P. McGuire appearing in the Chicago Times); ph, Joseph MacDonald; ed, J. Watson Webb; m, Alfred Newman; art d, Lyle Wheeler, Mark-Lee Kirk; fx, Dick Smith, Fred Sersen; cos, Kay Nelson

One of the most impressive semi-documentary noir thrillers, CALL NORTHSIDE 777 was shot on location in Chicago in striking black-and-white by cinematographer Joe MacDonald. Renowned movie nice guy Jimmy Stewart stars in a change-of-pace characterization as a hard-boiled newspaper reporter who evolves from a sceptical news hound to a dedicated crusader when he investigates a decade-old cop killing based on the actual case of Joe Majczek of Chicago who was imprisoned for a crime he did not commit.

Stewart is handed an assignment by editor Cobb: follow up a small ad that appeared in his newspaper offering a $5,000 reward for information leading to the arrest and conviction of the man responsible for killing a policeman years earlier. Stewart learns that the ad was placed by a cleaning woman (Orzazewski) who has slaved for years to earn reward money for anyone able to clear her son of the murder. The cynical Stewart initially believes the convicted Conte is guilty but opts to write a human interest story about the loving mother. When the public reaction proves to be overwhelming, Cobb encourages Stewart to back up his original story with some more digging. As he investigates, Stewart unearths evidence that there was some police coverup in the case and that certain evidence is missing. His interest is piqued.

Stewart effectively plays the part of Jim McGuire, the Chicago Times reporter who won the Pulitzer Prize for his investigative efforts, and the rest of the cast turn in fine, realistic performances. For Stewart, this film was a departure from the genial roles (though sometimes dark-tinged) for which he had become famous (IT'S A WONDERFUL LIFE, THE PHILADELPHIA STORY, MAGIC TOWN); this performance paved the way for his more morally ambiguous and gritty characterizations for directors such as Hitchcock and Anthony Mann in the 1950s. Director Hathaway had recently had a resounding success with the Ben Hecht story, KISS OF DEATH, also shot in a grim realistic style. Newman's moody score adds depth and feeling to the emotionally charged story.

CALL OF THE WILD
1935　89m　c　Adventure　★★★
20th Century　(U.S.)

Clark Gable (Jack Thornton), Loretta Young (Claire Blake), Jack Oakie (Shorty Hoolihan), Frank Conroy (John Blake), Reginald Owen (Smith), Sidney Toler (Groggin), Katherine DeMille (Marie), Lalo Encinas (Kali), Charles Stevens (Francois), James Burke (Ole)

p, Darryl F. Zanuck; d, William A. Wellman; w, Gene Fowler, Leonard Praskins (based on the novel by Jack London); ph, Charles Rosher; ed, H.T. Fritch; m, Alfred Newman

This epic Alaskan adventure story features Clark Gable as prospector Jack Thornton. After losing his money gambling, Thornton acquires a huge dog, Buck, which is considered too vicious to be a sled dog. Thornton patiently trains the animal, then sets out with his friend Shorty Hoolihan (Jack Oakie) for the wilderness in search of gold. Thereafter they must battle the weather, the wilds, and crooks in their attempts to make their fortunes, and Thornton finds a love interest in the wife of a missing prospector. This hearty film was shot on the snowy slopes of Washington's Mount Baker, at 5,000 feet, where the harsh winter snows forced cast and crew to use snowplows to get to their daily locations. Through the hardships, they created a stirring adventure, loosely based on the writings of Jack London.

CALLE 54   DVD
2000 105m c Musical/Documentary   ★★★★
Arte France Cinema/Fandango/Fernando Trueba/   G
Producciones Cinematograficas/Studio Canal Plus/
MTM Cineteve/SGAE/Television Espanola/Tequila
Gang/Via Digital   (Spain/France)

Paquito D'Rivera, Eliane Elias, Chano Dominguez, Jerry Gonzalez and the Fort Apache Band, Gato Barbieri, Tito Puente, Chucho Valdes, Chico O'Farrill, Israel Lopez, Orlando Rios

p, Cristina Huete, Fabienne Servan Schreiber; d, Fernando Trueba; ph, Jose Luis Lopez-Linares; ed, Carmen Frias

Let's not mince words. Director Fernando Trueba's tribute to Latin jazz is right up there with THE LAST WALTZ and STOP MAKING SENSE as one of the best contemporary music documentaries ever made.

The format is simple: concert footage shot in the intimate confines of a small soundstage, interspersed with brief and usually amusing documentary snippets that put the music and performers in cultural and artistic context. The performances themselves are a succession of small miracles, from Chano Dominguez's electrifying fusion of Thelonius Monk and flamenco, to the late Tito Puente gleefully mugging his way through the rhythmic complexities of an irrepressible instrumental suite with the energy of a man one-quarter his age. Trueba's direction also verges on miraculous; despite the physical limitations imposed by his studio locations, he gives each segment a distinct visual identity through camera movement, costuming, lighting, editing, or a combination of the four. Yet his technique never calls attention to itself; it's always at the service of the music. If you had to single out a special sequence, the nod would probably go to the one featuring Chico O'Farrill's big band. When their harmonically inventive homage to Charlie Parker suddenly pops off the screen in drop-dead-gorgeous B&W (the rest of the film is in color), the effect is so startling, it's almost chemical. Unfortunately, the performances that follow feel a little anticlimactic in comparison. Still, that's pretty minor as complaints go. This is one of the most infectiously joyous celebrations of music making ever committed to film. See it and feel ennobled.

CAMILLE
1937 108m bw Romance   ★★★★★
MGM   (U.S.)

Greta Garbo (Marguerite), Robert Taylor (Armand), Lionel Barrymore (Duval), Elizabeth Allan (Nichette), Jessie Ralph (Nanine), Henry Daniell (Baron de Varville), Lenore Ulric (Olympe), Laura Hope Crews (Prudence), Rex O'Malley (Gaston), Russell Hardie (Gustave)

p, Bernard Hyman; d, George Cukor; w, Zoe Akins, Frances Marion, James Hilton (based on the novel and play La Dame aux Camelias by Alexander Dumas fils); ph, William Daniels; ed, Margaret Booth; m, Herbert Stothart

AAN Best Actress: Greta Garbo

The great Garbo at her radiant peak, and certainly among the top five most romantic movies ever made. Cukor's renowned "rapport" with actresses is unfailing here. MGM's glamour

shows unmistakable care—if it's not the same as style, the luxuriance befits the story of a courtesan. It's a puzzle why Garbo's Marguerite is a whore—she seems too intelligent, too yearning, too serious to have ever considered the demimonde life, yet her acting is so generous, so overcome with the warmth of true love, so tinged with the irony of the character's circumstances, that she sweeps you away. Her final scene is among the finest ever committed to film, as she signals death with her eyes in a lingering close-up.

Robert Taylor is so beautiful, you can forgive his lack of skill. His earnestness seems consistent with the rash actions of young love, and his ardent awe of Garbo imparts a worshipful aura that is touching. The fact that he looks younger makes the whore component of Garbo's character more believable; it justifies Armand's not immediately grasping his love's circumstances.

This is Daniell's most interesting performance, subtle in his control and villainy. Laura Hope Crews finally is able to utilize her vocal vulgarity; she is by far a better old strumpet than she was as an old maid busybody in so many films. Tempestuous Lenore Ulric is a curiosity that works. This former Belasco stage star embodies a disappointed envy of Garbo that Cukor uses to great advantage. Lionel Barrymore, all growling propriety, is the jarring note in the ensemble.

The screenplay was adapted from the Dumas play by Frances Marion, James Hilton, and Zoe Akins. And Adrian's costumes, usually white, for Miss Garbo, contribute to her divination of literature's most beloved dying swan. This was Irving Thalberg's last production; he died while it was being made and it was completed by Bernard Hyman.

CAMILLE CLAUDEL   DVD
1988 149m c Biography   ★★½
Christian Fechner/Lilith/Gaumont/A2/D.D.   R
(France)

Isabelle Adjani (Camille Claudel), Gerard Depardieu (Auguste Rodin), Laurent Grevill (Paul Claudel), Alain Cuny (Louis-Prosper Claudel), Madeleine Robinson (Louise-Athanaise Claudel), Katrine Boorman (Jessie Lipscomb), Daniele Lebrun (Rose Beuret), Aurelle Doazan (Louise Claudel), Madeleine Marie (Victoire), Maxime Leroux (Claude Debussy)

p, Christian Fechner; d, Bruno Nuytten; w, Bruno Nuytten, Marilyn Goldin (based on the biography by Reine-Marie Paris); ph, Pierre Lhomme (Eastmancolor, Fujicolor); ed, Joelle Hache, Jeanne Kef; m, Gabriel Yared; art d, Bernard Vezat; cos, Dominique Borg

AAN Best Actress: Isabelle Adjani; AAN Best Foreign Language Film

This film about the tragic life of French artist Camille Claudel is as dark and unwieldy as one of Claudel's own sculptures. Born in 1864, Claudel (played by Oscar-nominated Isabelle Adjani, who also coproduced) demonstrated talent early. At 20, she met sculptor Auguste Rodin (Gerard Depardieu), who became her mentor and lover. Their 12-year liaison was an artistically fertile time for Claudel, but the affair's disastrous outcome caused the already high-strung Claudel to deteriorate further emotionally to the point of becoming an impoverished recluse, and in 1913 she was forcibly committed to a psychiatric hospital.

Adjani and director Bruno Nuytten's film is an admiring but emotionally ininvolving and sketchy account of a woman about whom little is actually known. Faced with gaps in the record, they have imagined a life of towering romantic passion and destruction for Claudel, but the plot motivation becomes murky, leaving Adjani to indulge in protracted emotional fireworks that damage her portrayal. On the other hand, Depardieu is amazingly successful in his tricky role as the great Rodin, and ex-cinematographer Nuytten fills his film with memorable images.

His inexperience as a first-time director shows, however, in the film's uncertain pacing and lack of dramatic cohesiveness (the inadequate script is no help). In addition to Adjani's Oscar nomination, the film was also up for Best Foreign Film, but lost to CINEMA PARADISO.

CANDIDATE, THE   _DVD_
1972   109m   c   Political   ★★★½
Warner Bros.   (U.S.)

Robert Redford (*Bill McKay*), Peter Boyle (*Luck*), Don Porter (*Sen. Crocker Jarmon*), Allen Garfield (*Howard Klein*), Melvyn Douglas (*John J. McKay*), Quinn Redeker (*Rich Jenkin*), Michael Lerner (*Paul Corliss*), Karen Carlson (*Nancy McKay*), Morgan Upton (*Henderson*), Kenneth Tobey (*Starkey*)

p, Walter Coblenz; d, Michael Ritchie; w, Jeremy Larner; ph, Victor J. Kemper, John Korty (Technicolor); ed, Richard A. Harris, Robert Estrin; m, John Rubinstein; cos, Patricia Norris

AA Best Original Story and Screenplay: Jeremy Larner; *AAN Best Sound:* Richard Portman, Gene Cantamessa

Handlers, spin-doctors, and the good man they lead astray. Jeremy Larner's Academy Award-winning screenplay provides a voyage into the sea of politics; the result is a fascinating film that sometimes feels like a documentary. Despite minor glitches, this is a prophetic glimpse of politics in the age of TV.

Redford plays an altruistic attorney whose father (Douglas) was California's governor. Having seen all the dirt as a young man, Redford has no interest in politics. Porter is the typical big-state senator—bluff, hearty, and full of bull—there doesn't seem to be anyone who can come close to defeating him in the next election. Boyle asks Redford to run for office. After some soul-searching, Redford agrees—with the proviso that his father be kept out of the campaign and that he, Redford, be allowed to say what he feels with no political tracts being pushed upon him by the party. His candor appeals to the public, and he begins to climb in the opinion polls. With popularity behind him, will he sell out? This, ironically enough, is the film that inspired Dan Quayle to enter politics.

CANDY MOUNTAIN
1987   91m   c   Drama   ★★★½
Xanadu/Plain-Chant/Vision 4   R
(Switzerland/Canada/France)

Kevin J. O'Connor (*Julius Book*), Harris Yulin (*Elmore Silk*), Tom Waits (*Al Silk*), Bulle Ogier (*Cornelia*), Roberts Blossom (*Archie*), Leon Redbone (*Huey*), Dr. John (*Henry*), Rita MacNeil (*Winnie*), Joe Strummer (*Mario*), Laurie Metcalf (*Alice*)

p, Ruth Waldburger; d, Robert Frank, Rudy Wurlitzer; w, Rudy Wurlitzer; ph, Pio Corradi; ed, Jennifer Auge; m, Max Rebennack "Dr. John," David Johansen, Leon Redbone, Rita MacNeil, Tom Waits; fx, Jacques Godbout; cos, Carol Wood

Failed rock 'n' roll musician Julius Book (Kevin J. O'Connor) embarks on a mission to find guitar-maker Elmore Silk (Harris Yulin), a legendary craftsman who, 20 years before, at the height of his fame, dropped out of sight. Elmore's guitars are now worth $20,000 apiece, and Julius is hired by some music-industry big shots to find him. Desperately looking for a way to carve out a career for himself in the music business, Julius, who has never even heard of Elmore, takes the job and learns the hard way that "life ain't no candy mountain."

The product of a reportedly uneasy collaboration between photographer and filmmaker Robert Frank (PULL

MY DAISY) and screenwriter Rudy Wurlitzer (TWO LANE BLACKTOP, WALKER), CANDY MOUNTAIN is an excellent road movie detailing the enlightenment of a callow young musician who mistakenly believes that simply pulling off a scam will somehow make him a successful artist. Filled with beautiful imagery, poetic dialogue, sly humor, savvy cameos, and excellent music, the film travels straight north from New York City to "the last town on the last street in North America."

O'Connor is superb as the would-be rock star whose romantic notions persist despite the fact that he is an empty vessel with absolutely nothing to say, and this odd, offbeat film richly deserves the audience it failed to find during its theatrical run.

CANDYMAN   _DVD_
1992   101m   c   Horror   ★★★½
Propaganda Films   (U.S.)   R

Virginia Madsen (*Helen Lyle*), Tony Todd (*Candyman*), Xander Berkeley (*Trevor Lyle*), Kasi Lemmons (*Bernadette Walsh*), Vanessa Williams (*Anne-Marie McCoy*), DeJuan Guy (*Jake*), Marianna Eliott (*Clara*), Ted Raimi (*Billy*), Ria Pavia (*Monica*), Mark Daniels (*Student*)

p, Alan Poul, Sigurjon Sighvatsson, Steve Golin; d, Bernard Rose; w, Bernard Rose (from the short story "The Forbidden" by Clive Barker); ph, Anthony B. Richmond; ed, Dan Rae; m, Philip Glass; prod d, Jane Ann Stewart; art d, David Lazan; fx, Bob Keen; cos, Leonard Pollack

Serious, straightforward cinematic terror is hard to come by these days, but this literate shocker is the scariest film since THE SILENCE OF THE LAMBS, and joins BRAM STOKER'S DRACULA as one of the best supernatural movies in years.

A Chicago-based doctoral student named Helen Lyle (Virginia Madsen), is working on a paper about urban legends. One of the myths she's focusing on concerns a spirit called "Candyman," who supposedly appears before anyone who says his name five times into a mirror—then slaughters them with a hook. When Helen learns that a murder in the nearby Cabrini Green housing projects has been attributed by the residents to Candyman, she investigates. Local legend has it that Candyman was originally the son of a slave who had won fame as a painter in the 1800s, before an affair with a white woman lead to his gruesome murder by a white mob. Helen is skeptical, and comes to believe that he's just a bogeyman used by local drug dealers to cover their crimes and keep the residents in line. That is until Candyman himself (Tony Todd) appears before her, angrily intoning that he now must shed innocent blood to prove his existence.

It's one of the many strengths of CANDYMAN that its story is actually about something. Derived from Clive Barker's short story "The Forbidden," writer-director Bernard Rose turns his gruesome material into a dark meditation on the nature of urban legends. The way the Cabrini Green residents cling to the myth as a way to rationalize the violence of their daily lives is intriguing, and the film is notable for the way in which it manages to utilize ghetto realities without condescending to its black characters. The acting here is first-rate, with Madsen turning in a forceful performance as the confused but resilient heroine. And special mention must be made of Philip Glass's superlative score, which combines synthesizers, piano, and chorus to haunting effect.

CAPE FEAR   _DVD_
1962   105m   bw   Thriller   ★★★★
Melville/Talbot   (U.S.)

Gregory Peck (*Sam Bowden*), Robert Mitchum (*Max Cady*), Polly Bergen (*Peggy Bowden*), Lori Martin (*Nancy Bowden*), Martin

Balsam *(Mark Dutton)*, Jack Kruschen *(Dave Grafton)*, Telly Savalas *(Charles Sievers)*, Barrie Chase *(Diane Taylor)*, Paul Comi *(Garner)*, Edward Platt *(Judge)*

p, Sy Bartlett (Melville-Talbot); d, J. Lee Thompson; w, James R. Webb (based on the novel *The Executioners* by John D. MacDonald); ph, Sam Leavitt; ed, George Tomasini; m, Bernard Herrmann; art d, Alexander Golitzen, Robert Boyle; cos, Mary Wills

---

Unforgettable villainy. Suspenseful and very frightening, thanks to Robert Mitchum's lethally threatening performance and the frightened reactions of a pro cast.

Sexual deviate and lethal psychopath Mitchum is released from prison after serving a six-year term for rape and assault. He is bent on revenge against Peck, the witness whose testimony put him there, who is a family man and a lawyer with a private practice in Florida. When Peck learns Mitchum is in town, he goes to Balsam, the sheriff, who tries to make life miserable for Mitchum until a lawyer threatens to file suit on charges of harassment. Peck's dog is poisoned, then Mitchum takes to the phone, calling Bergen, the lawyer's wife, plaguing her with obscene remarks. Though he makes no overt threats, he intimates a dire fate for the family, including their teenage daughter, Martin. Because the police are helpless to jail the lunatic and the calls and oblique threats continue, Peck decides to handle matters himself.

J. Lee Thompson directs at a clip, until the crawl toward the bayou climax, where the minutes feel like hours, and your heart sits in your throat. Peck is careful not to act the fear; he's an interesting foe for Mitchum. Bergen's performance reminds one that she should have been a bigger star, given her beauty and undeniable talent, and Martin recalls an era when teenagers really were innocent. Balsam, Savalas, and Chase contribute effective cameos. The musical score by Bernard Herrmann is a nerve-beater.

CAPE FEAR
DVD
1991 128m c Thriller ★★★½
Universal/Cape Fear Inc./Amblin/Cappa Films/ R
Tribeca Productions (U.S.)

Robert De Niro *(Max Cady)*, Nick Nolte *(Sam Bowden)*, Jessica Lange *(Leigh Bowden)*, Juliette Lewis *(Danielle Bowden)*, Joe Don Baker *(Claude Kersek)*, Robert Mitchum *(Lieutenant Elgart)*, Gregory Peck *(Lee Heller)*, Martin Balsam *(Judge)*, Illeana Douglas *(Lori Davis)*, Fred Dalton Thompson *(Tom Broadbent)*

p, Barbara De Fina; d, Martin Scorsese; w, Wesley Strick (based on the 1962 screenplay by James R. Webb, from the novel *The Executioners* by John D. MacDonald); ph, Freddie Francis; ed, Thelma Schoonmaker; m, Bernard Herrmann; prod d, Henry Burnstead; art d, Jack G. Taylor Jr.; fx, J.B. Jones, Derek Meddings, Neal Martz, Stephan Dupuis; cos, Rita Ryack

---

AAN Best Actor: Robert DeNiro; *AAN Best Supporting Actress:* Juliette Lewis

---

Martin Scorsese's loose remake of J. Lee Thompson's 1962 thriller is an exercise in audience manipulation, with every frame designed to stagger the senses. During quiet scenes, the camera is in constant, unsettling motion. During big scenes, shock cuts to weird, menacing angles and reality-bending, high-tech optics accompany dark images of eroticism and violence.

In a telling twist on the original film, Nick Nolte plays lawyer Sam Bowden as a mean-spirited womanizer who has cheated on his burnt-out, embittered wife Leigh, played by Jessica Lange. (In the 1962 version, the Bowdens were morally pristine, impossibly upright citizens.) Leigh broods at home, venting her bile on teenage daughter Dani (Juliette

Lewis), who stumbles through the film pathetically shell-shocked and alone.

One of Sam's past professional betrayals comes home to roost. As a public defender, he railroaded client Max Cady (Robert DeNiro) into a 14-year prison sentence for sexual assault by burying a court report attesting to his victim's promiscuity. Now Cady is out and hungry for revenge, having spent his sentence remaking himself into a wily lawyer and con-man psychologist. Cady's plan is to destroy Max's career and family from within. He poisons the family dog, beats up and mutilates Bowden's employee Lori (Illeana Douglas), and comes close to twisting Dani's adolescent frustrations into sympathy with his cause, successfully goading Sam into violence.

There are no heroes in CAPE FEAR, only victims and their tormentors. De Niro rolls through the film like a demented descendant of Popeye the Sailor, his sinewy body awash with jailhouse tattoos (giving Mitchum the film's best line: "I don't know whether to look at him or read him"). Nolte winces, cowers and sweats; even normal activities like brushing his teeth are filmed in extreme close-ups that make him look subhuman. Lange looks pinched and drawn throughout, with the 17-year-old Lewis giving the movie's most impressive performance.

Scorsese's contempt for his characters extends to his handling of the scenario, credited to Wesley Strick (TRUE BELIEVER). The death of the Bowden's dog is treated with more genuine gravity than the notably gruesome crime against Lori. Though Scorsese throws in the occasional touch of humor, CAPE FEAR remains an overblown assault on the senses that leaves the viewer feeling physically—and morally—drained.

CAPTAIN BLOOD
DVD
1935 119m bw Adventure/Historical ★★★★
Warner Bros. (U.S.)

Errol Flynn *(Dr. Peter Blood)*, Olivia de Havilland *(Arabella Bishop)*, Lionel Atwill *(Col. Bishop)*, Basil Rathbone *(Capt. Levasseur)*, Ross Alexander *(Jeremy Pitt)*, Guy Kibbee *(Hagthorpe)*, Henry Stephenson *(Lord Willoughby)*, George Hassell *(Gov. Steed)*, Forrester Harvey *(Honesty Nuttall)*, Frank McGlynn Sr. *(Rev. Ogle)*

p, Harry Joe Brown; d, Michael Curtiz; w, Casey Robinson (based on the novel by Rafael Sabatini); ph, Hal Mohr, Ernest Haller; ed, George Amy; m, Erich Wolfgang Korngold; art d, Anton Grot; fx, Fred Jackman; cos, Milo Anderson

---

AAN Best Picture; AAN Best Sound Recording: Nathan Levinson

Flynn's star-making swashbuckler is right on target. Based on the novel by Rafael Sabatini, CAPTAIN BLOOD concerns the adventures of a young Brit surgeon who turns buccaneer after unjust persecution. The film had been originally earmarked for Robert Donat whose recurrent asthma convinced Jack Warner to gamble on Flynn. The unknown de Havilland also scored as love interest, and despite a tight budget, Curtiz contributed a lush production. Highlight is the trademark duel between Flynn and Rathbone.

Mindful that his two novice stars might bomb, wily Jack Warner decided not to build full-scale sailing ships for the many action scenes. To represent the bombardments, naval battles, and sinking of ships, technicians built several model ships 18 feet long, with 16-foot masts, and the battles were fought in a studio tank. Even the town of Port Royal was built in miniature. Clips from silent films (First National's 1924 SEA HAWK and Vitagraph's 1923 CAPTAIN BLOOD) were used to show full-scale ships in battle. The main decks of two ships were constructed on a soundstage for the life-size action, and on-location scenes were made along the California coastline.

Almost from the day of CAPTAIN BLOOD's release, Flynn was a Hollywood star, a favorite with a public that would forever see him as the great swashbuckler, a perception that he lived up to in one adventure film after another. BLOOD not only served to introduce Flynn as a stellar lead, but brought critical acclaim as well to lovely 19-year-old de Havilland, who carries off her part with great maturity and sophistication. She and the dashing Flynn eventually appeared together in eight films. Curtiz, the master of adventure films who shot every scene as if it were a cavalry charge, directed a total of nine Flynn epics, and Erich Wolfgang Korngold, whose rich and resonant scores set the musical standard for such spectacular films, composed seven scores for Flynn epics.

CAPTAIN FROM CASTLE
1947 140m c Adventure/Historical ★★★★
Fox (U.S.)

Tyrone Power *(Pedro De Vargas)*, Jean Peters *(Catana Perez)*, Cesar Romero *(Hernando Cortez)*, Lee J. Cobb *(Juan Garcia)*, John Sutton *(Diego De Silva)*, Antonio Moreno *(Don Francisco)*, Thomas Gomez *(Fr. Bartolome Romero)*, Alan Mowbray *(Prof. Botello)*, Barbara Lawrence *(Luisa De Caravajal)*, George Zucco *(Marquis De Caravajal)*

p, Lamar Trotti; d, Henry King; w, Lamar Trotti (based on the novel by Samuel Shellabarger); ph, Charles Clarke, Arthur E. Arling (Technicolor); ed, Barbara McLean; m, Alfred Newman; art d, Richard Day, James Basevi; fx, Fred Sersen; cos, Charles LeMaire

AAN Best Score (Drama or Comedy): Alfred Newman

A sweeping, majestic spectacle, neatly divided into a double feature: Spanish inquisition and the expedition of Cortez into Mexico. CAPTAIN FROM CASTLE was a major star vehicle for Power, and he's supported in style by Peters (in her film debut; she was discovered as a 20-year-old Ohio State coed), Cobb, Sutton, and especially Romero, as Cortez.

Although the script sometimes stretches credibility, King's panorama is distracting enough to sweep away your suspicions. CASTILE was a return to the old and glorious pageantry of yesteryear Hollywood, a huge $4.5 million production with one of the most memorable and stirring scores ever composed by Newman. The film was a pet project for Zanuck, who bought Princeton professor Samuel Shellabarger's unpublished novel for $100,000 when it was serialized in *Cosmopolitan* magazine.

Henry King, Fox's top action director, loved to scout locations in his small private plane. He had flown over Morales, a province of southern Mexico, as early as 1933 and selected this remote and rugged area as the site for this project. The trek deep into Mexico was similar to Cortez's own march, except that this one involved eight railroad cars packed with dozens of actors and technicians, including a dry cleaning unit for the expensive costumes and a refrigerated car in which the Technicolor film was kept.

Power, a pilot himself, flew 50 cast members down in a large chartered plane. A smoldering volcano near the location constantly threatened to erupt, delaying the shooting schedule which stretched on for almost four months while the budget doubled and Zanuck fumed. The film lost money but it remains as one of Fox's great epics.

CAPTAIN HORATIO HORNBLOWER
1951 116m c Adventure ★★★½
Warner Bros. (U.K.)

Gregory Peck *(Horatio Hornblower)*, Virginia Mayo *(Lady Barbara Wellesley)*, Robert Beatty *(Lt. William Bush)*, James Robertson

Justice *(Quist)*, Denis O'Dea *(Adm. Leighton)*, Terence Morgan *(Lt. Gerard)*, Richard Hearne *(Polwheal)*, James Kenney *(Midshipman Longley)*, Moultrie Kelsall *(Lt. Crystal)*, Michael Dolan *(Gundarson)*

p, Gerry Mitchell; d, Raoul Walsh; w, Ivan Goff, Ben Roberts, Aeneas MacKenzie (based on the novel by C.S. Forester); ph, Guy Green (Technicolor); ed, Jack Harris; m, Robert Farnon

Full of valiant guff. Peck took over for dissipated Errol Flynn, playing title role of 19th-century English hero who outwits the French and Spanish during the Napoleonic wars. Alas, Peck's a touch sober for a credible swashbuckler. In another instance of offbeat casting, Mayo plays Lady Barbara, the Duke of Wellington's sister, and she has a bad fever! Despite miscasting, Walsh's direction has no time to linger. Guy Green's camerawork and Robert Farnon's jolly score are helpful. In the small role of Polwheal is Richard Hearne, who may be remembered as Britain's comic "Mr. Pastry!"—an acrobatic, often hilarious silent comedian whom Ed Sullivan loved.

CAPTAINS COURAGEOUS
1937 115m bw Adventure ★★★★★
MGM (U.S.)

Freddie Bartholomew *(Harvey)*, Spencer Tracy *(Manuel)*, Lionel Barrymore *(Disko)*, Melvyn Douglas *(Mr. Cheyne)*, Charley Grapewin *(Uncle Salters)*, Mickey Rooney *(Dan)*, John Carradine *("Long Jack")*, Oscar O'Shea *(Cushman)*, Jack LaRue *(Priest)*, Walter Kingsford *(Dr. FinFley)*

p, Louis D. Lighton; d, Victor Fleming; w, John Lee Mahin, Marc Connelly, Dale Van Every (based on the novel by Rudyard Kipling); ph, Harold Rosson; ed, Elmo Veron; m, Franz Waxman; art d, Cedric Gibbons

AAN Best Picture; AA Best Actor: Spencer Tracy; *AAN Best Screenplay:* Marc Connelly, John Lee Mahin, Dale Van Every; *AAN Best Film Editing:* Elmo Veron

For once, a script perfectly suited to its director and star and one of the most lyrical children's classics ever made. Ignore the typical MGM "prestige picture" touches and enjoy the spirited cast performing under man's man director Fleming, who is reverential to the Kipling story. Young Harvey (Freddie Bartholomew), the spoiled-rotten son of a business tycoon, believes he can lie, cheat, and whine his way through life. On a trip to Europe with his father, the young man falls off a posh ocean liner into the sea and is rescued by a boat filled with Portuguese fishermen. One of the sailors is Manuel (Spencer Tracy), a big-hearted veteran of the seas who has a lot to teach the selfish Harvey about life.

CAPTAINS COURAGEOUS is a wonderful sea adventure with a heartwarming drama at its core. Tracy is excellent as the gentle fisherman, turning in a performance that won him a Best Actor Oscar. He reportedly hated his role, however, especially having his hair curled and wrestling with an accent (Tracy loathed externalized acting), but it doesn't show for a moment. The following year, he won the coveted statuette again for BOYS TOWN.

CAPTAIN'S PARADISE, THE
1953 93m bw Comedy ★★★½
London Films (U.K.)

Alec Guinness *(Capt. Henry St. James)*, Yvonne De Carlo *(Nita)*, Celia Johnson *(Maud)*, Charles Goldner *(Chief Officer Ricco)*, Miles Malleson *(Lawrence St. James)*, Bill Fraser *(Absalom)*, Tutte Lemkow *(Principal Dancer)*, Nicholas Phipps *(The Major)*, Walter Crisham *(Bob)*, Ferdy Mayne *(Sheikh)* p, Anthony Kimmins; d, Anthony Kimmins; w, Alec Coppel, Nicholas Phipps (based on a story by Alec Coppel); ph, Ted Scaife; ed, Gerald Turney-Smith; m, Malcolm Arnold; art d, Paul Sheriff; chor, Walter Crisham, Tutte Lemkow

AAN Best Motion Picture Story: Alec Coppel

Guinness at his conniving best in a droll, consistently funny comedy. He plays the captain of a steamer that sails between Gibraltar and North Africa. Instead of having a girl in every port, Guinness has a wife at either end, each offering him a completely different lifestyle. In Gibraltar it's Johnson, a sedate British housewife who makes him home-cooked meals and is content to stay at home by the fire. In North Africa, it's De Carlo, a sexy, voluptuous woman with whom he does the hot spots, dancing through the exotic nights. (On his ship, Guinness keeps a revolving picture frame that has a photo of Johnson on one side and De Carlo on the other!) In flashback, we watch as Guinness manages to have the best of both worlds, while his chief officer, Goldner, slavishly admires this grand deception and seeks to emulate his captain.

Suspense is sustained throughout THE CAPTAIN'S PARADISE because as the film opens Guinness is about to be shot by a firing squad and the viewer does not become privy to his fate until the very surprising ending. In between, the scheming captain is undone by the women in his life. Guinness's life goes topsy-turvy when Johnson insists on seeking adventure and excitement, while De Carlo suddenly takes up cooking, tiring of night life and desiring domestic tranquility. When Guinness resists these disturbing transformations both women leave him.

Guinness gives a masterful performance, and Johnson and De Carlo are superb in their unpredictable parts. The pace is vigorous under Kimmins's direction, and he manages to relate the subtle and frivolous story with verve, his transitions from scene to scene as smooth as Guinness's own incomparable style. A generous serving of delicious whimsy.

CAPTURING THE FRIEDMANS *DVD*
2003 107m c Documentary ★★★½
HBO Documentary Films (U.S.)

Arnold Friedman, Elaine Friedman, David Friedman, Seth Friedman, Jesse Friedman, Howard Friedman, John McDermott, Detective Frances Galasso, Joseph Onorato, Judd Maltin

p, Andrew Jarecki, Marc Smerling; d, Andrew Jarecki; ph, Adolfo Doring; ed, Richard Hankin; m, Andrea Morricone

AAN Best Documentary Feature

First-time feature filmmaker Andrew Jarecki intended to make a lighthearted documentary about children's party clowns. But after poking into the family history of one of his subjects, he found he had the makings of a very different story on his hands, a story of pedophilia, child pornography, and terrible accusations of sexual abuse.

Jarecki discovered that clown David "Silly Billy" Friedman was the oldest son of Arnold Friedman, a well-respected Long Island schoolteacher who came under the scrutiny of postal inspectors in 1984 when he ordered child pornography from the Netherlands; three years later, the police raided his house. In addition to Arnold's sizable stash of illegal smut, they found a list of all the kids Arnold taught at home in an after-school computer class. Suspecting the worst, Nassau County, New York's sex-crimes unit began aggressively interviewing Arnold's students and amassing allegations of sexual abuse that also implicated Arnold's 18-year-old son, Jesse. Through David, Jarecki not only gained access to Jesse and Arnold's wife, Elaine, but the family's huge collection of home movies. They captured the Friedman father and sons in happier times, mugging and capering for the cameras.

But more unusual and gripping are the terrible, post-arrests arguments that began tearing the family apart, which David filmed for posterity. Jesse, David, and middle brother Seth rally around their father with unquestioning loyalty while Elaine, always the outsider, becomes the target of her family's rage.

As he plumbs the mysteries of Arnold's past and marriage, Jarecki demonstrates an innate instinct for where the story lies. But he also has a showman's taste for tension which, while it may not always serve his subject's best interests, keeps his audience off-balance and guessing. His film is never less than gripping.

CAR WASH *DVD*
1976 97m c Comedy ★★★
Universal (U.S.) PG

Franklyn Ajaye *(T.C.)*, Sully Boyar *(Mr. B.)*, Richard Brestoff *(Irwin)*, George Carlin *(Taxi Driver)*, Irwin Corey *(Mad Bomber)*, Ivan Dixon *(Lonnie)*, Bill Duke *(Duane)*, Antonio Fargas *(Lindy)*, Michael Fennell *(Calvin)*, Arthur French *(Charlie)*

p, Art Linson, Gary Stromberg; d, Michael Schultz; w, Joel Schumacher; ph, Frank Stanley (Technicolor); ed, Christopher Holmes; m, Norman Whitfield; art d, Robert Clatworthy; cos, Daniel Paredes

Coarse, hilarious comedy detailing a day in the life of an L.A. car wash, featuring an ensemble cast of superb performers. Basically plotless, the film shows the lives, hopes, dreams, ambitions, and foibles of the multiracial employees and customers of Boyar's Car Wash. One of many highlights has Richard Pryor as a fancy-pants preacher who arrives in his flashy car accompanied by the Pointer Sisters. Great musical score by Whitfield is integrated into the movement of the scenes to give the film a funky rhythm. Director Schultz, one of the first mainstream Black filmmakers, also helmed the spirited inner-city comedy COOLEY HIGH. You won't sit still.

CARAVAGGIO
1986 93m c Biography ★★★½
British Film Institute/Channel 4 (U.K.)

Nigel Terry *(Caravaggio)*, Sean Bean *(Ranuccio Thomasoni)*, Garry Cooper *(Davide)*, Spencer Leigh *(Jerusaleme)*, Tilda Swinton *(Lena)*, Michael Gough *(Cardinal Del Monte)*, Nigel Davenport *(Marchese Giustiniani)*, Robbie Coltrane *(Cardinal Borghese)*, Jonathan Hyde *(Baglione)*, Dexter Fletcher *(Young Caravaggio)*

p, Sarah Radclyffe; d, Derek Jarman; w, Derek Jarman; ph, Gabriel Beristain (Technicolor); ed, George Akers; m, Simon Fisher Turner, Mary Phillips; prod d, Christopher Hobbs; cos, Sandy Powell

Marrying a painterly aesthetic with a defiantly homosexual sensibility, this ironic biopic is probably the most accessible film of avant-garde British director Derek Jarman (LAST OF ENGLAND, EDWARD II). A fanciful reconstruction of the life of the late Rennaisance master (about which almost nothing is known), CARAVAGGIO dramatizes the painter's need for patronage, his religious beliefs, and his sexuality. Noting Caravaggio's unusually muscle-bound depictions of St. John, Jarman posits a sexual relationship between the painter (Nigel Terry) and Ranuccio Thomasoni (Sean Bean), a street thug who served as his model; Ranuccio's mistress (Tilda Swinton) stands in for Mary Magdalene and the Blessed Virgin in filmic facsimiles of some of the painter's best-known canvasses. Curiously, though Jarman undercuts narrative conventions through his use of obvious anachronisms—typewriters, motorbikes, etc.—the film reiterates one of the oldest cliches of Hollywood biopics (LUST FOR LIFE, MOULIN ROUGE); i.e., that art is little more than immediately record-ed experience, "life" thrown directly onto the canvas; the *process* of artistic creation is completely glossed over.

Jarman, a tireless advocate of gay rights, died of AIDS in 1994 at the age of 52. Ironically, while his best work remained unseen outside of festival showings, his influence was pro-found in the realm of music video. REM's award-winning "Losing My Religion" and Nirvana's "Heart Shaped Box," for example, both draw heavily on THE GARDEN's pastoral and Christian imagery.

CAREER GIRLS

1997 87m c Comedy/Drama ★★★½
Thin Man Films/Matrix Film/Channel Four Films R
(U.K.)

Katrin Cartlidge *(Hannah)*, Lynda Steadman *(Annie)*, Kate Byers *(Claire)*, Mark Benton *(Ricky)*, Andy Serkis *(Mr. Evans)*, Joe Tucker *(Adrian)*, Margo Stanley *(Ricky's Nan)*, Michael Healy *(Lecturer)*

p, Simon Channing-Williams; d, Mike Leigh; w, Mike Leigh; ph, Dick Pope; ed, Robin Sales; m, Marianne Jean-Baptiste, Tony Remy; prod d, Eve Stewart; art d, Helen Scott

Mike Leigh's talent for seamlessly blending comedy and drama is evident throughout this touching dual character study. The film follows two college roommates as they reunite six years after graduation, counterpointing scenes of their present with memories of their shared past.

Riding the train to London to visit her former college room-mate, Hannah (Katrin Cartlidge), Annie (Lynda Steadman) remembers their initial meeting. A nervous youth with dermati-tis, Annie was overwhelmed by her new roommates: brash, wisecracking Hannah and vain Claire (Kate Byers). After Hannah and Annie reunite, they travel to Hannah's apartment. The pair discuss their troubles—failed romances, Annie's prob-lems with her job, and Hannah's alcoholic mother. Various memories of their college days ensue, as the pair coincidentally encounter figures from their past, including an emotionally troubled friend (Mark Benton) and a callous gent (Joe Tucker) who dated both women when they were in college.

Offering up equal amounts of tears and laughter, CAREER GIRLS is a skillfully crafted and hauntingly gen-uine portrait of a friendship. As always is the case with Leigh's work, the lead performances are revelatory. Cartlidge (BREAKING THE WAVES) appears to have bor-rowed a few line readings from David Thewlis in NAKED, but as the film proceeds, her character's vulnerable side emerges, and one is able to appreciate how she has created a gruff persona to keep the outside world at a distance. Serving as the perfect counterpart, screen newcomer Steadman flaw-lessly incarnates the two Annies—the young, highly nervous introvert, and the more self-assured (but still confused), rather chatty adult. With CAREER GIRLS, Leigh continues on the somewhat sentimental course he has followed in his feature-film work ; it also adheres to the strong characteriza-tion he emphasized in his telefilms. Here we encounter two more characters whose specific experiences may be differ-ent from our own, but whose passions, frustrations, and small joys are all too familiar.

CARLA'S SONG

1996 127m c Romance/War/Drama ★★★
Channel Four Films/Parallax Pictures/Road
Movies Dritte Produktionen/Tornasol Films
(U.K./Germany/Spain)

Robert Carlyle *(George)*, Oyanka Cabezas *(Carla)*, Scott Glenn *(Bradley)*, Salvador Espinosa *(Rafael)*, Louise Goodall *(Maureen)*, Richard Loza *(Antonio)*, Gary Lewis *(Sammy)*, Pamela Turner *(Eileen)*, Subash Sing Pall *(Victor)*, Stewart Preston *(McGurk)*

p, Sally Hibbin; d, Ken Loach; w, Paul Laverty; ph, Barry Ackroyd; ed, Jonathan Morris; m, George Fenton; prod d, Martin Johnson; art d, Llorenc Miquel, Fergus Clegg; fx, Reyes Abades; cos, Daphne Dare, Lena Mossum

Love can't conquer all in this leisurely tale of romance between a Scottish bus driver and a traumatized Nicaraguan refugee. Rather than using revolution as a backdrop for a love story, director Ken Loach, working from a script by Paul Laverty (who spent 2 1/2 years in Nicaragua in the '80s), looks at the way relationships are determined by experience.

For quick-tempered malcontent George (Robert Carlyle), rebellion is letting indigent passengers sneak a free ride on his bus and giving the finger to his bourgeois bosses. He meets Carla (Oyanka Cabezas) when she gets caught rid-ing without a ticket, and refuses to let her slip out of his life. It's hard to tell whether he's smitten with her exotic beauty or with the fact that she's destitute, displaced, emotionally trou-bled, and conspicuously not interested in getting involved with him. But George's persistent pursuit wears her down, though she refuses to give up her secrets: she makes him swear to stop asking about her past, her family and Antonio (Richard Loza), the ex-lover by whom she's haunted. George eventually realizes that if he and Carla are to have a future together, the past must be dealt with. So they go to Nicaragua, arriving at the height of the 1987 guerrilla war between the grassroots Sandinistas and the U.S. government-backed Contras, and begin the search for Antonio.

In a more conventional film, the strength of George's love would save Carla from her tortured memories, but Nicaragua lays him low: the poverty, the violence, the cynical political forces playing fast and loose with helpless lives are more than he can handle. The movie's weakest link is Scott Glenn's per-formance as Bradley, an American human-rights activist with a shadowy past, but it's a minor liability.

CARLITO'S WAY

1993 141m c Crime/Drama ★★★
Epic Productions/Martin Bregman Productions R
(U.S.)

Al Pacino *(Carlito Brigante)*, Sean Penn *(David Kleinfeld)*, Penelope Ann Miller *(Gail)*, John Leguizamo *(Benny Blanco)*, Ingrid Rogers *(Steffie)*, Luis Guzman *(Pachanga)*, James Rebhorn *(Norwalk)*, Joseph Siravo *(Vinnie Taglialucci)*, Viggo Mortensen *(Lalin)*, Richard Foronjy *(Pete Amadesso)*

p, Martin Bregman, Willi Baer, Michael Scott Bregman; d, Brian De Palma; w, David Koepp (from the novels *Carlito's Way* and *After Hours* by Edwin Torres); ph, Stephen H. Burum; ed, Bill Pankow, Kristina Boden; m, Patrick Doyle; prod d, Richard Sylbert; art d, Gregory Bolton; fx, Steven Kirshoff, Pacific Data Images, The Effects House; chor, Jeffrey Hornaday, Debbie Benitez; cos, Aude Bronson-Howard

After the costly, clumsy debacle of BONFIRE OF THE VAN-ITIES and the addled psychosis of RAISING CAIN, Brian De Palma engineered something of a recovery with CARLI-TO'S WAY, a colorful melodrama set in the Latino mob world of the mid-1970s.

The director is in good company here. Al Pacino gives an urgent, bravura performance as the title character, a former drug boss who's had a lengthy prison sentence cut short thanks to a legal technicality, and now wants to go straight—really. Sean Penn is superbly nerdy as David Kleinfeld, the lawyer who freed Carlito, but whose greed ultimately leads to his and his client's undoing. Standouts among the classy ensemble are John Leguizamo (SUPER MARIO BROS.), as a brutal young hood on his way up through the ranks, and Luis Guzman (Q & A), as Carlito's trusted sidekick.

CARLITO'S WAY has its slow moments (any scenes with the anemic Penelope Ann Miller, who plays Carlito's girlfriend), and its plot weaknesses (we can't quite believe Carlito would be so loyal to Kleinfeld, who is so transparently devious). But these are far outweighed by the great cast; the lovingly detailed recreation of disco-era New York (the soundtrack, ranging from "Oye Como Va" to "Disco Inferno," was compiled by Jellybean Benitez); the street poetry that slurs its way so convincingly out of Pacino's mouth; and, most of all, some classic De Palma action sequences. For the heart-stopping scenes in the poolroom and at Grand Central Station, the director can be forgiven anything—even BONFIRE OF THE VANITIES.

CARMEN
DVD

1983 102m c Drama/Dance/Musical ★★★½
(Spain) R

Antonio Gades (Antonio), Laura del Sol (Carmen), Paco de Lucia (Paco), Christina Hoyos (Cristina), Juan Antonio Jimenez (Juan), Sebastian Moreno (Escamillo), Jose Yepes (Pepe Giron), Pepa Flores (Pepa Flores)

p, Emiliano Piedra; d, Carlos Saura; w, Carlos Saura, Antonio Gades (from the opera by Georges Bizet, based on the novel by Prosper Merimee); ph, Teo Escamilla (Eastmancolor); ed, Pedro del Rey; m, Paco de Lucia, Georges Bizet; chor, Carlos Saura, Antonio Gades; cos, Teresa Nieto

AAN Best Foreign Language Film

This version of the Merimee classic uses rehearsals for a flamenco version of Bizet's opera (not unlike director Saura's previous BLOOD WEDDING) as the setting for an identical, parallel storyline.

Laura del Sol (THE HIT) plays Carmen, a fiery actress-dancer who is slated to play her namesake despite her lack of experience. Antonio Gades (BLOOD WEDDING) is the choreographer who falls in love with her. The dance sequences are superb, as expected, with the added plus of del Sol's eroticism and Christina Hoyos's explosive performance as Carmen's rival. Saura's acclaimed dance trilogy (the third film is EL AMOR BRUJO), abetted by Antonio Gades's incendiary choreography, are must-sees for dance enthusiasts. Others may greet CARMEN with mixed emotions. But meanwhile, what other version measures up?

CARMEN JONES
DVD

1954 105m c Opera ★★★
Fox (U.S.)

Dorothy Dandridge (Carmen), Harry Belafonte (Joe), Olga James (Cindy Lou), Pearl Bailey (Frankie), Diahann Carroll (Myrt), Roy E. Glenn Sr. (Rum), Nick Stewart (Dink), Joe Adams (Husky Miller), Brock Peters (Sgt. Brown), Sandy Lewis (T-Bone)

p, Otto Preminger; d, Otto Preminger; w, Harry Kleiner (based on the book by Oscar Hammerstein II); ph, Sam Leavitt (CinemaScope, Deluxe Color); ed, Louis Loeffler; m, Georges Bizet

AAN Best Actress: Dorothy Dandridge; AAN Best Score (Musical): Herschel Burke Gilbert

Intermittently successful updating of Bizet's "Carmen" with an all-black cast. Preminger's heavy-handed adaptation of a Broadway triumph combines gorgeous music with risible lyrics by Oscar Hammerstein II; the project is saved by a terrific cast.

Dandridge is a revelation. Even mouthing Marilyn Horne's vocals (not that Dandridge wasn't an accomplished singer; following a brief retirement in the late 1940s, her career was rekindled by a smash engagement at the posh Mocambo nightclub), she is chilling and exactly right, projecting psychological transitions and reflecting clearly the sequences of her thoughts. She's almost matched by Belafonte, and both leads are mesmerizingly beautiful. Considering the waste of Dandridge's career, it is heartening that CARMEN JONES exists as a testament to her beauty and singular talent. She died from a barbiturate overdose in 1965 at age 41.

CARNAL KNOWLEDGE
DVD

1971 97m c Drama ★★★½
Avco Embassy (U.S.) R

Jack Nicholson (Jonathan), Candice Bergen (Susan), Art Garfunkel (Sandy), Ann-Margret (Bobbie), Rita Moreno (Louise), Cynthia O'Neal (Cindy), Carol Kane (Jennifer)

p, Mike Nichols; d, Mike Nichols; w, Jules Feiffer; ph, Giuseppe Rotunno (Panavision, Technicolor); ed, Sam O'Steen; prod d, Richard Sylbert; art d, Robert Luthardt; cos, Anthea Sylbert

AAN Best Supporting Actress: Ann-Margret

Deeply felt, somewhat dated critique of middle-class sexual politics, and one of the better films of formerly interesting director Mike Nichols. Jules Feiffer's script is an uneasy, confessional work rooted in the regret and confusion experienced by his generation of Americans—men who reached middle age at a time when the rules governing male-female relationships were undergoing radical change.

The film follows college roommates (Jack Nicholson and Art Garfunkel) from youth through embittered middle age. Nicholson is a manipulative misogynist, apparently incapable of emotional intimacy; Garfunkel is his less confident, more sensitive chum. In the opening segment, set in the 1940s, the two compete for the affections of bewildered coed Candice Bergen. Ten years later, Garfunkel is a bored suburban husband; Nicholson is wrangling with his mistress (Ann-Margret), who senses his contempt for her but still dreams of domesticity. The final segment shows the aging friends, now accompanied by Moreno and Kane (in her debut), attempting to cope with the unfamiliar values of the late 1960s.

Nicholson's performance here did much to consolidate his stardom, while Ann-Margret, previously wasted as a campy sex kitten, used a meaty role to establish herself as a serious actress. An uneven but unusually thoughtful melodrama, CARNAL KNOWLEDGE avoids most of the the trendy excesses that make some other films of its era so difficult to watch today.

CARO DIARIO

1994 100m c Comedy/Drama ★★★
Sacher Film/Banfilm/La Sept/Canal Plus (Italy/France)

Nanni Moretti (Himself), Giovanna Bozzolo (Actress in Italian Film), Sebastiano Nardone (Actor in Italian Film), Antonio Petrocelli (Actor in Italian Film), Giulio Base (Car Driver), Italo Spinelli (On the Wall at Spinaceto), Jennifer Beals (Herself), Alexandre Rockwell (Himself), Carlo Mazzacurati (Film Critic), Renato Carpentieri (Gerardo)

p, Angelo Barbagallo, Nanni Moretti, Nella Banfi; d, Nanni Moretti; w, Nanni Moretti; ph, Giuseppe Lanci; ed, Mirco Garrone; prod d, Marta Maffucci; cos, Maria Rita Barbera

Unashamedly introspective and unexpectedly poignant, Nanni Moretti's three-part comedy uses a cinematic diary format to explore his beloved homeland and the recesses of his own personality. As himself, Moretti joyrides around Rome on his Vespa, opining about architecture, cinema, and social change; battles writer's block by taking a trip with a scholar pal, Gerardo (Renato Carpentieri); and seeks a cure for a skin rash that is misdiagnosed and mistreated by a staggering number of physicians.

CARO DIARIO (which translates as "Dear Diary") lulls viewers into expecting a light-hearted entertainment, then veers unexpectedly into darker territory with the third segment; the change in tone is so abrupt that it almost feels like a betrayal. Ultimately, however, it's the medical episode that redeems the film. Moretti's exploration of his personal obsessions isn't quite as fascinating as he seems to believe, but his sudden transformation from self-involved artiste to terrified Everyman brings his sympathetic qualities to the fore. Charting a life in transit and barely sidestepping a tragic journey's end, CARO DIARIO proves that you never really know people until you travel with them.

CAROUSEL   DVD
1956 128m c Musical   ★★★★
Fox (U.S.)

Gordon MacRae (Billy), Shirley Jones (Julie), Cameron Mitchell (Jigger), Barbara Ruick (Carrie), Claramae Turner (Cousin Nettie), Robert Rounseville (Mr. Snow), Gene Lockhart (Starkeeper), Audrey Christie (Mrs. Mullin), Susan Luckey (Louise), William Le Massena (Heavenly Friend)

p, Henry Ephron; d, Henry King; w, Phoebe Ephron, Henry Ephron (based on the musical by Richard Rodgers, Oscar Hammerstein II, from the play "Liliom" by Ferenc Molnar); ph, Charles Clarke (CinemaScope, DeLuxe Color); ed, William Reynolds; chor, Rod Alexander, Agnes De Mille; cos, Mary Wills

Haunting and poignant; the best of Rodgers and Hammerstein, sans the corn and cotton candy fluff of other works. This remake of the famous stage play and the Fritz Lang and Frank Borzage-directed adaptations of LILIOM emerges as a wonderful and touching fantasy.

It begins with MacRae as a spirit in Heaven who begs the starkeeper for a visit back to Earth to help his teenage daughter understand his death and prepare her for high-school graduation. Seen in flashback, carny barker MacRae, a brash, dishonest young man living in a New England fishing village (changed from Ferenc Molnar's original Budapest setting), falls in love with a mill worker, Jones. They marry, but MacRae's inability to find a job leads him into the bad company of Mitchell and an attempted robbery in which MacRae is accidentally killed.

This sadly resigned fantasy, a commercial failure upon its original release, features some of the greatest musical numbers ever filmed, all R&H classics: "If I Loved You," "What's the Use of Wondrin'?" and the stirring "You'll Never Walk Alone." Jones is lovely and heartfelt as the trusting lover, and MacRae is magnetic in his best musical performance, his fine tenor given a range equalled only in OKLAHOMA! Mitchell and other supporting players are excellent in this richly mounted extravaganza that is superb on all technical points and directed with verve and affection by King.

CARRIE   DVD
1976 97m c Horror   ★★★½
UA (U.S.)   R

Sissy Spacek (Carrie White), Piper Laurie (Margaret White), Amy Irving (Sue Snell), William Katt (Tommy Ross), John Travolta (Billy Nolan), Nancy Allen (Chris Hargenson), Betty Buckley (Miss Collins), P.J. Soles (Norma Watson), Sydney Lassick (Mr. Fromm), Stefan Gierasch (Principal Morton)

p, Paul Monash; d, Brian De Palma; w, Larry Cohen (based on the novel by Stephen King); ph, Mario Tosi (DeLuxe Color); ed,

Paul Hirsch; m, Pino Donaggio; art d, William Kenny, Jack Fisk; fx, Greg Auer, Ken Pepiot; cos, Rosanna Norton

AAN Best Actress: Sissy Spacek; AAN Best Supporting Actress: Piper Laurie

A telekinetic revenge. De Palma's first big hit remains one of his best efforts to date and a landmark film for the horror genre. Spacek, in a stunning performance, stars as Carrie, a troubled, sexually repressed high schooler who slowly realizes that she possesses incredible telekinetic powers. Plagued with problems in school (she feels homely, and nobody likes her) and at home (her mother, Laurie—whose performance is delightfully over the top—is a religious fanatic who hates men and makes her daughter pray in a closet), she struggles to maintain her dignity and sanity. She's finally driven over the edge when cruel classmates conspire to elect her prom queen in an elaborate joke designed to embarrass her.

Based on the best-selling Stephen King novel and cleverly designed to target a teenage audience, CARRIE was the synthesis of De Palma's talent for intense, stylish, visual filmmaking. His techniques—elaborate compositions, daring camera moves, and slow motion—combined with a fairly literate screenplay, make for an interesting and frightening film that successfully deals with the inner rage every teenager feels. The film has a strikingly unsettling mood that enhances its power and gives it an impact that the story would otherwise lack. Much of the credit, though, must go to Spacek, who so convincingly portrays Carrie's pain and her longing for acceptance. The talented ensemble inludes Betty Buckley, Amy Irving, Nancy Allen, and John Travolta.

CARRINGTON   DVD
1995 122m c Biography/Historical/Romance ★★★
PolyGram/Freeway Productions/Shedlo Productions/   R
Dora Productions Ltd./Cinea & Orsans/Canal Plus/
Euston Films Ltd./European Co-production Fund
(U.K./France)

Emma Thompson (Dora Carrington), Jonathan Pryce (Lytton Strachey), Steven Waddington (Ralph Partridge), Samuel West (Gerald Brenan), Rufus Sewell (Mark Gertler), Penelope Wilton (Lady Ottoline Morrell), Janet McTeer (Vanessa Bell), Peter Blythe (Phillip Morrell), Jeremy Northam (Beacus Penrose), Alex Kingston (Frances Partridge)

p, Ronald Shedlo, John McGrath; d, Christopher Hampton; w, Christopher Hampton (based on the book Lytton Strachey by Michael Holroyd); ph, Denis Lenoir; ed, George Akers; m, Michael Nyman; prod d, Caroline Amies; art d, Frank Walsh; cos, Penny Rose

Oscar-winning screenwriter Christopher Hampton (DANGEROUS LIAISONS) makes an promising debut with this ambitious, closely observed biopic of two notoriously eccentric members of the Bloomsbury group.

Dora Carrington (Emma Thompson) is a young painter who attracts the attention of flamboyant writer Lytton Strachey (Jonathan Pryce) when he initially mistakes her for a "ravishing boy." She is at first repulsed by the scruffy, caustic belletrist, a confirmed homosexual, but eventually the two become extremely close, forming a relationship that stops just short of sexual consummation. For a time, their singular liaison is the calm center of Bloomsbury's emotional tempest, but the incessant games of musical beds, together with her thwarted artistic ambitions, ultimately take a tragic toll on Dora.

Smarter than the average biopic and genuinely moving, this shrewd film deconstructs an obsessive relationship with remarkable sympathy. Viewers hoping for another high-toned, Anglophilic soap opera will be disappointed: Hampton's screenplay is as witty, self-conscious and unclubbable as its tragically hip protagonists. Thompson's neurasthenic mannerisms, which usually drive us batty, are appropriate here; Pryce, who was honored as Best Actor at Cannes, is simply brilliant.

CARRY ON NURSE
DVD
1959   86m   bw   Comedy   ★★½
Anglo-Amalgamated   (U.K.)

Kenneth Connor (Bernie Bishop), Kenneth Williams (Oliver Reckitt), Charles Hawtrey (Hinton), Terence Longdon (Ted York), Bill Owen (Percy Hickson), Leslie Phillips (Jack Bell), Cyril Chamberlain (Bert Able), Brian Oulton (Henry Bray), Wilfrid Hyde-White (Colonel), Hattie Jacques (Matron)

p, Peter Rogers; d, Gerald Thomas; w, Norman Hudis (based on the play "Ring for Catty" by Patrick Cargill and Jack Beale); ph, Reginald Wyer; ed, John Shirley; m, Bruce Montgomery

The second and perhaps best entry in the seeemingly endless "Carry On" series has no real plot, just every cliché and old hospital joke imaginable in this romp through a men's surgical ward. You can see the jokes coming a mile off, and if they still make you laugh, you may want to check out CARRY ON SERGEANT, CARRY ON CABBY, CARRY ON SPYING, and CARRY ON CAMPING.

CARS THAT ATE PARIS, THE
DVD
1974   91m   c   Adventure/Comedy   ★★
Salt-Pan   (Australia)

Terry Camilleri (Arthur), John Meillon (Mayor), Melissa Jaffa (Beth), Kevin Miles (Dr. Midland), Max Gillies (Metcalfe), Peter Armstrong (Gorman), Edward Howell (Tringham), Bruce Spence (Charlie), Derek Barnes (Al Smedley), Charles Metcalfe (Clive Smedley)

p, Jim McElroy, Howard McElroy; d, Peter Weir; w, Peter Weir, Keith Gow, Piers Davies; ph, John McLean; ed, Wayne LeClos; m, Bruce Smeaton

Scattered, but typically overrated now that the director is a force to be reckoned with. Weir marked his feature debut with a black comedy that now supposedly anticipates THE ROAD WARRIOR with themes culled from THE WILD ONE and HIGH NOON. Spiked wrecks are driven by adventurous youths through the streets of Paris, Australia, causing an endless string of accidents. These collisions are planned events that serve the vulturous townsfolk in both an economic and medical way. The looters profit by pawning what they can recover, and a town doctor performs questionable medical experiments on the victims. The situation culminates in a youth-townsfolk blood bath. It's a big, wide, wonderful world. Whatever.

CASABLANCA
DVD
1942   102m   bw   Drama/War   ★★★★★
Warner Bros.   (U.S.)

Humphrey Bogart (Richard "Rick" Blaine), Ingrid Bergman (Ilsa Lund Laszlo), Paul Henreid (Victor Laszlo), Claude Rains (Capt. Louis Renault), Conrad Veidt (Maj. Heinrich Strasser), Sydney Greenstreet (Senor Ferrari), Peter Lorre (Ugarte), S.Z. Sakall (Carl, Headwaiter), Madeleine LeBeau (Yvonne), Dooley Wilson (Sam)

p, Hal B. Wallis; d, Michael Curtiz; w, Julius J. Epstein, Philip G. Epstein, Howard Koch (based on the play Everybody Goes to Rick's by Murray Burnett and Joan Alison); ph, Arthur Edeson; ed, Owen Marks; m, Max Steiner; art d, Carl Jules Weyl; fx, Lawrence Butler, Willard Van Enger; cos, Orry-Kelly

AA Best Picture; AAN Best Actor: Humphrey Bogart; AAN Best Supporting Actor: Claude Rains; AA Best Director: Michael Curtiz; AA Best Screenplay: Julius J. Epstein, Philip G. Epstein, Howard Koch; AAN Best B/W Cinematography: Arthur Edeson; AAN Best Film Editing: Owen Marks; AAN Best Score (Drama or Comedy): Max Steiner

The most romantic picture ever made? The best film to come out of a Hollywood studio ever? More an icon than a work of art, CASABLANCA is still a thoroughly entertaining romantic melodrama, flawlessly directed, subtly played, lovingly evoking our collective daydreams about lost chances and lost loves and love versus honor; everything about CASABLANCA is just right—it seems to have been filmed under a lucky star.

The familiar plot concerns expatriate American Rick Blaine (Humphrey Bogart), a cynical nightclub owner in Casablanca who discovers that his ex-lover, Ilsa (Ingrid Bergman), who abandoned him years before, has arrived in Casablanca with her husband, Resistance leader Victor Laszlo (Paul Henreid). With the Germans on Victor's trail, Ilsa comes to Casablanca to beg Rick for the precious letters of transit that have come into his possession. The documents would allow Victor to escape Casablanca and continue the fight against fascism.

Since its November 1942 release, CASABLANCA has been the movie, one that perfectly blends a turbulent love story with harrowing intrigue, heroic and evil characters, and the kind of genuine sentiment that makes the heart grow fonder with each viewing. Even upon its initial release, the film appealed to nostalgia for the vanishing, romanticized world between the two great wars, a cafe society crushed by fascism, a civilized, urbane generation in white linen suits, spectator shoes, and wide-brimmed sunhats desperately clinging to values no longer cherished.

Given its turbulent production history—the script was being rewritten almost on a daily basis—CASABLANCA was also most fortunate on all levels. The original leads were to have been Ronald Reagan, Ann Sheridan and Dennis Morgan. Other casting packages included George Raft, Hedy Lamarr and Herbert Marshall. And Lena Horne or Ella Fitzgerald might have crooned "As Time Goes By" instead of Dooley Wilson. Chemistry, that indefinable element, was surely carefully considered by veteran director Michael Curtiz.

So was timing. The film opened on Thanksgiving Day, 1942 at the Hollywood Theater in New York, three weeks after the Allies had landed at Casablanca, and further enjoyed widespread publicity generated by the Casablanca Conference two months later, when the eyes of the free world focused upon its leaders' meeting in the Moroccan city. It propelled Bogart's star to new heights, adding a romantic component to his world-weary persona, and gave Bergman a tragic edge to blend with her healthy radiance, making her seem complex and emotionally fragile. The film received eight Academy Award nominations and won three: Best Picture, Best Screenplay and Best Director.

CASINO
DVD
1995   182m   c   Drama/Crime   ★★★
Syalis D.A./Legende Enterprises/Universal   (U.S.)   R

Robert De Niro (Sam "Ace" Rothstein), Sharon Stone (Ginger McKenna), Joe Pesci (Nicky Santoro), James Woods (Lester Diamond), Don Rickles (Billy Sherbert), Alan King (Andy Stone), Kevin Pollak (Phillip Green), L.Q. Jones (Pat Webb), Dick Smothers (Senator), Frank Vincent (Frank Marino)

p, Barbara De Fina; d, Martin Scorsese; w, Nicholas Pileggi, Martin Scorsese (based on the book by Nicholas Pileggi); ph, Robert Richardson; ed, Thelma Schoonmaker; prod d, Dante Ferretti; art d, Jack G. Taylor Jr.; fx, Paul Lombardi, Craig Barron, The Effects House, NY, Matte World Digital; cos, Rita Ryack, John Dunn

AAN Best Actress: Sharon Stone

Martin Scorsese returns to the gangster milieu of GOOD-FELLAS, and the result is an accomplished film that carries with it the unshakable feeling that we've seen it all before.

Ace Rothstein (Robert De Niro) is a scientific gambler. Looking to get their piece of booming 1960s Las Vegas, the Kansas City Mafia installs him as manager of the Tangiers, where he lives up to his respectful but unaffectionate nickname, "The Golden Jew." The film's first third is a celebration of pre-theme park Vegas, the money-making machine and morality car wash, where the cash flow never dries up and acts that would be criminal anywhere else are the coin of the realm. The serpent in this tawdry Garden of Eden soon appears in the form of Ace's old friend Nicky Santoro (Joe Pesci), who begins busting heads and drawing unwanted attention to the Mafia's pervasive presence. The third point of an ultimately deadly triangle is Ginger McKenna (Sharon Stone) a hooker with a heart of, well … stone.

There's nothing really wrong with CASINO. In fact, there are lots of things right with it: the city in the desert has seldom looked so thrillingly sleazy (the grotesquerie of '70s fashions is a delightfully horrifying bonus), and the story delivers its old-fashioned moral (you reap what you sow) with such delirious viciousness that you almost forget what a dreary cliché it is.

Nevertheless, CASINO feels disturbingly predictable, a meticulous and coldly proficient going-over of familiar ground. After MEAN STREETS, GOODFELLAS, THE GODFATHER and countless other examinations of Mafia mores and morals, we don't need to be reminded that the mob-run gambling industry is a microcosm of American capitalism at its most rapacious. We know, we know.

CASINO ROYALE   **DVD**
1967 131m c Adventure/Comedy/Spy ★★
Columbia   (U.K.)

Peter Sellers *(Evelyn Tremble)*, Ursula Andress *(Vesper Lynd)*, David Niven *(Sir James Bond)*, Orson Welles *(Le Chiffre)*, Joanna Pettet *(Mata Bond)*, Daliah Lavi *(The Detainer)*, Woody Allen *(Jimmy Bond, Dr. Noah)*, Deborah Kerr *(Agent Mimi, Lady Fiona McTarry)*, William Holden *(Ransome)*, Charles Boyer *(Le Grand)*

p, Charles K. Feldman, Jerry Bresler; d, John Huston, Ken Hughes, Robert Parrish, Val Guest, Joseph McGrath; w, Wolf Mankowitz, John Law, Michael Sayers, Billy Wilder, Val Guest, Joseph Heller, Ben Hecht, Terry Southern (from the novel by Ian Fleming); ph, John Wilcox, Jack Hildyard, Nicolas Roeg (Panavision, Technicolor); ed, Bill Lenny; m, Burt Bacharach; art d, John Howell, Ivor Beddoes, Lionel Couch; chor, Tutte Lemkow

AAN Best Song: "The Look of Love"; Burt Bacharach (Music), Hal David (Lyrics)

A mess. CASINO ROYALE is two hours and eleven minutes of non sequitur. David Niven is Sir James Bond. (Author Ian Fleming, a close friend of Niven, always wanted Niven to assay his famous creation.) He's retired, middle-aged, bejowled, and tired. SMERSH is up to no good, so Niven is asked to help when M (John Huston) is slain. He contacts several agents, all of them 007s. These include Andress, Sellers, Terence Cooper, and Pettet (who is Niven's daughter, the result of a liaison with Mata Hari). After more witless, starloaded vignettes, Niven finally learns that the real villain is none other than his own ineffectual nephew, Woody Allen.

CASINO ROYALE first found life as a one-hour TV show for CBS's "Climax" in 1954, starring Barry Nelson. The film rights were sold in 1955 and eventually acquired by exagent Charles Feldman. Almost every actor yukked it up while making this movie, and the result is totally unfocused. Anything with five directors and screenwriters to rank on anyone's list for sheer chutzpah.

CAST AWAY   **DVD**
2000 143m c Adventure/Drama ★★★½
ImageMovers/Playtone   (U.S.) PG-13

Tom Hanks *(Chuck Noland)*, Helen Hunt *(Kelly Frears)*, Nick Searcy *(Stan)*, Chris Noth *(Jerry Lovett)*, Lari White *(Bettina Peterson)*, Geoffrey Blake *(Maynard Graham)*, Jennifer Lewis *(Becca Twig)*, David Allen Brooks *(Dick Peterson)*, Semion Sudarikov *(Nicolai)*, Nan Martin *(Kelly's Mother)*

p, Tom Hanks, Steve Starkey, Robert Zemeckis, Jack Rapke ; d, Robert Zemeckis; w, William Broyles Jr.; ph, Don Burgess; ed, Arthur Schmidt; m, Alan Silvestri; prod d, Rick Carter; art d, Jim Teegarden, Stefan Dechant, Elizabeth Lapp; fx, Ken Ralston, John Frazier, Kenneth D. Pepiot, Sony Pictures Imageworks; cos, Joanna Johnston

AAN Best Actor: Tom Hanks; AAN Best Sound: Randy Thom, Tom Johnson, Dennis Sands, William B. Kaplan

It's hard to know what to make of a movie which finds its hero pondering the crossroads he's reached in life while standing at a literal intersection. Insipid or inspired? The problem with this visually dazzling *Robinson Crusoe* tale from Robert Zemeckis is that you can't really say for sure.

FedEx systems manager Chuck Noland (Tom Hanks) lives with a pager on his belt, an eye on the clock, and a single credo in mind: never turn your back on time. But time turns its back on Chuck one Christmas night when he's summoned to make an emergency run to Malaysia. Chuck says goodbye to his girlfriend, Kelly (Helen Hunt), at the FedEx airstrip with the promise that he'll be back for New Year's Eve. But somewhere over the Pacific Ocean, the plane veers off course to avoid a storm, loses radio contact, and crashes in a truly harrowing disaster sequence. Chuck and a few FedEx packages wash ashore on a tiny, completely uninhabited island. There, for the next four years, he'll try to survive with little more to live on than his ingenuity, and only "Wilson," a volleyball onto which he's drawn a face, for company.

From the moment Chuck's plane leaves the ground to the moment Chuck leaves the island, this is an exciting piece of bravura filmmaking. Zemeckis tells one ripping good survival yarn with stunning photography, judiciously deployed special effects and nary a word of dialogue. But once Chuck returns home and eventually reaches those crossroads, it's all anticlimax, with dialogue that could have been pulled from an inspirational greeting card. There's a fatal lack of chemistry between Hanks and Hunt; one quickly begins to pine for Wilson.

CASUALTIES OF WAR   **DVD**
1989 120m c War ★★★
Columbia   (U.S.) R

Michael J. Fox *(Pfc. Eriksson)*, Sean Penn *(Sgt. Meserve)*, Don Harvey *(Clark)*, John C. Reilly *(Hatcher)*, John Leguizamo *(Diaz)*, Thuy Thu Le *(Oahn)*, Erik King *(Brown, Radio Man)*, Jack Gwaltney *(Rowan)*, Ving Rhames *(Lt. Reilly)*, Dan Martin *(Hawthorne)*

p, Art Linson, Fred Caruso; d, Brian De Palma; w, David Rabe (based on the article by Daniel Lang); ph, Stephen H. Burum (Panavision, Deluxe Color); ed, Bill Pankow; m, Ennio Morricone; prod d, Wolf Kroeger; art d, Bernard Hydes; cos, Richard Bruno

With this adaptation of Daniel Lang's famous *New Yorker* article, Brian De Palma joins the ranks of Stanley Kubrick, Francis Ford Coppola and Oliver Stone, major directors who have brought their personal visions and styles to bear on the Vietnam War. The result is often hypnotic and perversely gripping, but falls apart during its final reel.

CASUALTIES OF WAR focuses on one patrol, and the inhumane treatment of a young Vietnamese girl at the hands of a calloused, crazed sergeant. Top acting honors go to Penn as the sergeant and Thuy Thu Le as the captive girl. Fox isn't bad at all; one just gets the feeling that the director and screenwriter got caught up in the dramatic situations inherent in the Penn-Thu Le conflict, and left their hero to flounder as best he could. Because Fox is so extraordinarily clean-cut, he seems more than human. This part needed a really average Joe, but one with enough feel of physical gravity to counteract Penn. Fox ends up a mere flyspeck tossed about in a violent whorl of confusion.

CAT AND THE CANARY, THE
1939 72m bw Comedy/Mystery ★★★
Paramount (U.S.)

Bob Hope (Wallie Campbell), Paulette Goddard (Joyce Norman), John Beal (Fred Blythe), Douglass Montgomery (Charlie Wilder), Gale Sondergaard (Miss Lu), Elizabeth Patterson (Aunt Susan), Nydia Westman (Cicily), George Zucco (Lawyer Crosby), John Wray (Hendricks), George Regas

p, Arthur Hornblow Jr.; d, Elliott Nugent; w, Walter DeLeon, Lynn Starling (based on the play by John Willard); ph, Charles Lang; ed, Archie Marshek; m, Ernst Toch; art d, Hans Dreier, Robert Usher

The old dark house number, played to the hilt. When an eccentric millionaire dies, lawyer Zucco assembles prospective heirs at the victim's Bayou mansion. Goddard gets all, setting up Hope as straight man for this spooky comic romp. Hope is terrific as the wisecracking but spineless character who attempts to protect Goddard from going insane (if she turns cuckoo she loses the fortune, according to the bizarre will). Director Nugent, who had guided Hope through NEVER SAY DIE and GIVE ME A SAILOR, does a great job in presenting some spine-tingling moments: claw-like hands reach out for the heroine and everyone seems to disappear through swiveling bookcases, sliding doors, and false panels. Lang's camera work is properly moody and supporting player Sondergaard gives a high-camp performance as a spooky, mystic housekeeper dressed in black, with a black cat constantly at her side. This was Goddard's first starring role; following the success of this film, the sly actress with the insinuating voice was teamed with Hope again in THE GHOST BREAKERS.

CAT BALLOU
1965 97m c Comedy/Western ★★★½ **DVD**
Columbia (U.S.)

Jane Fonda (Cat Ballou), Lee Marvin (Kid Shelleen/Tim Strawn), Michael Callan (Clay Boone), Dwayne Hickman (Jed), Tom Nardini (Jackson Two-Bears), John Marley (Frankie Ballou), Reginald Denny (Sir Harry Percival), Jay C. Flippen (Sheriff Cardigan), Arthur Hunnicutt (Butch Cassidy), Bruce Cabot (Sheriff Maledon)

p, Harold Hecht; d, Elliot Silverstein; w, Frank Pierson, Walter Newman (based on the novel by Roy Chanslor); ph, Jack Marta (Technicolor); ed, Charles Nelson; m, Frank DeVol; chor, Miriam Nelson; cos, Bill Thomas

AA Best Actor: Lee Marvin; AAN Best Adapted Screenplay: Walter Newman, Frank R. Pierson; AAN Best Film Editing: Charles Nelson; AAN Best Adapted Score: Frank DeVol; AAN Best Song: "The Ballad of Cat Ballou"; Jerry Livingston (Music), Mack David (Lyrics)

Funny—but not that funny—western spoof. Fonda employs over-the-hill gunslinger Marvin after his outlaw brother (Marvin again) kills her rancher father. Film is amusing largely due to Marvin's dual hilarity, for which he won an Oscar. It was the beginning of a whole new career as a ver-

satile, middle-aged leading man who could handle drama or comedy with equal finesse. Following several misfires, BALLOU consolidated Fonda's early stardom; while hardly complex, her transformation from prim schoolmarm to sexy gunslinger is utterly charming. Additional diversion is provided by Nat King Cole (in his last film role) and Stubby Kaye, who, as wandering troubadors, break up the screenplay's occasional tedium.

CAT ON A HOT TIN ROOF
1958 108m c Drama ★★★★ **DVD**
MGM (U.S.)

Elizabeth Taylor (Maggie Pollitt), Paul Newman (Brick Pollitt), Burl Ives (Big Daddy Pollitt), Jack Carson (Gooper Pollitt), Judith Anderson (Big Mama Pollitt), Madeleine Sherwood (Mae Pollitt), Larry Gates (Dr. Baugh), Vaughn Taylor (Deacon Davis), Patty Ann Gerrity (Dixie Pollitt), Rusty Stevens (Sonny Pollitt)

p, Lawrence Weingarten; d, Richard Brooks; w, Richard Brooks, James Poe (based on the play by Tennessee Williams); ph, William Daniels (Metrocolor); ed, Ferris Webster; art d, William A. Horning, Urie McCleary; fx, Lee LeBlanc; cos, Helen Rose

AAN Best Picture; AAN Best Actor: Paul Newman; AAN Best Actress: Elizabeth Taylor; AAN Best Director: Richard Brooks; AAN Best Adapted Screenplay: Richard Brooks, James Poe; AAN Best Color Cinematography: William H Daniels

A southern house divided between patriarchal dominance and hypocrisy, rendered effectively despite censorship and a screenplay that bogs midway. The performances are the thing in this film version of the Tennessee Williams stage triumph, led by Ives, repeating his stage role like a force of nature. Taylor and Newman make a handsomely unhappy husband and wife, with just enough sexual chemistry to justify the union. Mike Todd's plane crashed during filming, and the camera seems to capture Taylor's pent-up energy, but she isn't directed well enough to unleash it. This is fine throughout most of the film, but her catharsis is finally lacking and her little vengeances come off less like a satiated alley cat than a pampered prize kitty. The homosexual overtones are just about laundered out of Newman's role, but his pantherine eyes and profile suggest unplumbed depths between the lines. Jack Carson and Dame Judith Anderson are just right, and Madeleine Sherwood is absolutely definitive as Sister Woman.

CAT PEOPLE
1942 73m bw Horror ★★★★★ **DVD**
RKO (U.S.)

Simone Simon (Irena Dubrovna), Kent Smith (Oliver Reed), Tom Conway (Dr. Judd), Jane Randolph (Alice Moore), Jack Holt (Commodore), Alan Napier (Carver), Elizabeth Dunne (Miss Plunkett), Elizabeth Russell (The Cat Woman)

p, Val Lewton; d, Jacques Tourneur; w, DeWitt Bodeen; ph, Nicholas Musuraca; ed, Mark Robson; m, Roy Webb

Significant as the first of the literate, understated horror films Val Lewton produced for RKO in the 1940s, CAT PEOPLE is also notable for playing with audience imagination by refusing to show made-up movie monsters a la the Wolfman or Mr. Hyde. Although earlier films had linked horror and sexuality, Tourneur's study of a woman tainted by an ancient Balkan curse was arguably more explicit in this direction than any previous film had been. The result is a haunting and subtle film, filled with desires gone awry and everyday settings turned inexplicably nightmarish.

Immigrant sketch artist Irena Dubrovna (Simon) and all-American architect Oliver Reed (Smith) fall in love and marry after a brief courtship, but Irena won't consummate the union for fear that she will turn into a panther compelled to kill her lover. When Oliver confides in co-worker Alice Moore (Randolph) though, Irena's jealousy proves equally effective in precipitating her "transformation." The disbelief of cynical psychiatrist Dr. Judd (Conway) proves likewise ineffective against the powers unleashed by Irena's psyche.

Beautifully directed by Tourneur and carefully paced by screenwriter Bodeen, the film opens in mundane New York settings, only occasionally hinting that evil is about (e.g. a feline woman at a bar, the reaction of the animals at a pet store to Irena's presence). Once Irena's darker side begins to manifest itself, however, the film's pulse quickens and so does the viewer's. Perhaps most famous are the justly celebrated sequence where Irena stalks Alice along a park path at night (featuring the marvelously jarring cat-like hiss of bus doors) and the brilliant set-piece when Irena surrounds the terrified Alice at a darkened indoor swimming pool with the cries of a ferocious panther.

Superbly acted (with Simon evoking both pity and chills), CAT PEOPLE testifies to the power of suggestion and the priority of imagination over budget in the creation of great cinema. The film was Lewton's biggest hit, its viewers lured in by such bombastic advertising as "Kiss me and I'll claw you to death!"—a line more lurid than anything that ever appeared onscreen. Forty years later Paul Schrader would remake the original, failing to learn any of the lessons which Lewton had taught.

CATCH-22
1970 121m c War
Paramount (U.S.)

DVD
★★½
R

Alan Arkin *(Capt. Yossarian)*, Martin Balsam *(Col. Cathcart)*, Richard Benjamin *(Maj. Danby)*, Art Garfunkel *(Capt. Nately)*, Jack Gilford *(Doc Daneeka)*, Bob Newhart *(Maj. Major)*, Anthony Perkins *(Chaplain Tappman)*, Paula Prentiss *(Nurse Duckett)*, Martin Sheen *(Lt. Dobbs)*, Jon Voight *(Milo Minderbinder)*

p, Martin Ransohoff, John Calley; d, Mike Nichols; w, Buck Henry (based on the novel by Joseph Heller); ph, David Watkin (Panavision, Technicolor); ed, Sam O'Steen; prod d, Richard Sylbert; art d, Harold Michelson; fx, Lee Vasque; cos, Ernest Adler

This scathing condemnation of war is full of stumbles and rife with misfires. An intermittently interesting adaptation of Joseph Heller's caustic novel, this big-budget, all-star effort was a notorious flop in its day.

Set on a small island just off Italy, circa 1944, the film follows Captain Yossarian (Alan Arkin), an American bombardier who attempts to have himself grounded by claiming he's insane. Unfortunately, as Doc Daneeka (Jack Gilford) informs him, the paradoxical rule of "catch-22" prevents this, since anyone who voluntarily flies on air raids must be crazy, so asking to be grounded indicates that one is sane. As Yossarian becomes increasingly desperate, the inherent madness of the war intensifies.

This film wants to be bleak, nihilistic, and darkly hilarious, but CATCH-22 emerges as an exercise in frustration for those unprepared for Nichols's episodic, detached, and surreal treatment of the novel. Like a nightmare, the film shifts from one bizarre episode to another, with Alan Arkin's dazed Yossarian reacting to the madness that surrounds him, but second only to the viewer.

CATCH ME IF YOU CAN
2002 141m c Biography/Crime
Kemp Company/Splendid Pictures/
Parkes-MacDonald Productions/DreamWorks
(U.S.)

DVD
★★★
PG-13

Leonardo DiCaprio *(Frank Abagnale Jr.)*, Tom Hanks *(Carl Hanratty)*, Christopher Walken *(Frank Abagnale)*, Martin Sheen *(Roger Strong)*, Nathalie Baye *(Paula Abagnale)*, Amy Adams *(Brenda Strong)*, James Brolin *(Jack Barnes)*, Brian Howe *(Tom Fox)*, Frank John Hughes *(Earl Amdursky)*, Steve Eastin *(Paul Morgan)*

p, Walter F. Parkes, Steven Spielberg; d, Steven Spielberg; w, Jeff Nathanson (based on the book by Frank Abagnale Jr. with Stan Redding); ph, Janusz Kaminski; ed, Michael Kahn; m, John Williams; prod d, Jeannine Oppewall; art d, Sarah Knowles; fx, John Hartigan; cos, Mary Zophres

AAN Best Supporting Actor: Christopher Walken; *AAN Best Original Score:* John Williams

Hitchcock called them "Technicolor baubles"—exquisitely crafted costume jewels like his own TO CATCH A THIEF that lose their luster next to real gems. Steven Spielberg's jaunty escapade, which comes after a string of much more complex films (A.I.: ARTIFICAL INTELLIGENCE, MINORITY REPORT), is such a trinket. It's based on a memoir by Frank Abagnale Jr., a master impostor who successfully passed himself off as an airline pilot, a pediatrician, a lawyer, a sociology professor, and a stockbroker—all before he turned 21. By the time the FBI finally caught up with him, he'd used those personas to cash over $2 million in bad checks.

It's a fascinating story that says as much about the trusting climate of the '60s as it does about Abagnale, and screenwriter Jeff Nathanson sticks fairly close to the facts. We first meet Abagnale (played with great, cunning charm by Leonardo DiCaprio) in 1969, languishing in a French prison where he's been finally checkmated by the tireless—and fictional—FBI agent Carl Hanratty (Tom Hanks, affecting an absurd Boston accent). The action then flashes back to six years earlier, when 16-year-old Abagnale returns home from school to learn that his parents (Nathalie Baye, Christopher Walken) are getting divorced. Crushed, Abagnale runs away to New York City, where he starts writing one bad check after another, until he realizes he'd stand a better chance of getting away with it if he were dressed as that exemplar of glamour and respectability: an airline pilot.

Nathanson and Spielberg naively see Abagnale's criminal compulsion as a childlike desire to reconstitute his broken family, but the movie is so entertaining you'll hardly care; the whole lighter-than-air lark whizzes by like a brisk, kandy-kolored dream of the 1960s. "Dazzle 'em with style," Abagnale Sr. advises his son, advice the filmmakers have clearly taken to heart.

CATERED AFFAIR, THE
1956 92m bw Drama
MGM (U.S.)

★★★★

Bette Davis *(Mrs. Tom Hurley)*, Ernest Borgnine *(Tom Hurley)*, Debbie Reynolds *(Jane Hurley)*, Barry Fitzgerald *(Uncle Jack Conlon)*, Rod Taylor *(Ralph Halloran)*, Robert F. Simon *(Mr. Halloran)*, Madge Kennedy *(Mrs. Halloran)*, Dorothy Stickney *(Mrs. Rafferty)*, Carol Veazie *(Mrs. Casey)*, Joan Camden *(Alice)*

p, Sam Zimbalist; d, Richard Brooks; w, Gore Vidal (based on the teleplay by Paddy Chayefsky); ph, John Alton; ed, Gene Ruggiero, Frank Santillo; m, Andre Previn; art d, Cedric Gibbons, Paul Groesse

Interesting misfire but eminently watchable, this one has divided amateur and pro critics alike. The adaptation by Vidal from Chayefsky's brilliant teleplay concerns a poor Bronx husband and wife wrangling over expenses for their beloved daughter's wedding. Following his triumph in another Chayefsky teleplay-to-screenplay effort, MARTY, the previous year, Borgnine acquits himself honorably as an Irish taxi driver. Davis indeed wrestles with the accent, but she's a mistress at tortured regret getting its own way; even stuck with the rattiest wiglet in showbiz history, when Davis cries on her bed, all our reservations melt away. Reynolds is very touching; it's quite nice to see her away from the sis-boom-bah roles, and a shame she didn't do so more often. But for Barry Fitzgerald, doing his tired old leprechaun bit ten years too late in this attempt at kitchen sink realism, we'd get out the horsewhip in a moment's notice, and we would-n't spare the steed.

CATWOMAN

2004 97m c Action/Fantasy
Village Roadshow Pictures/Di Novi Pictures/
Frantic Films/Maple Shade Films/Warner Bros.

DVD
★★
PG-13
(U.S.)

Halle Berry (*Patience Phillips/Catwoman*), Benjamin Bratt (*Tom Lone*), Sharon Stone (*Laurel Hedare*), Lambert Wilson (*George Hedare*), Frances Conroy (*Ophelia*), Alex Borstein (*Sally*), Michael Massee (*Armando*), Byron Mann (*Wesley*), Kim Smith (*Drina*), Christopher Heyerdahl (*Rocker*)

p, Denise DiNovi, Edward L. McDonnell; d, Jean-Christophe Comar; w, John Rogers, John Brancato, Michael Ferris (from a story by Theresa Rebeck, John Brancato, and Michael Ferris, based on characters created by Bob Kane and published by DC Comics); ph, Thierry Arbogast; ed, Sylvie Landra; m, Klaus Badelt; prod d, Bill Brzeski; art d, Shepherd Frankel, Dan Hermansen, Don MacAulay; fx, Chris Anderson, Jayne Craig, Charlene Eberle, Jamison Empey, Ed Jones, Tony Lazarowich, Kim Libreri, Michael Mulholland (CG), Andrew Harris (CG); cos, Angus Strathie

Inspired by the classic comic-book character, and reconceptu-alized as a girlie-power pin-up, French director Christophe Comar's English-language debut (directed under his *nom d'ecran*, Pitof) is an instantly forgettable, hyper stylized trifle.

Mousy Patience Phillips (Halle Berry) slaves in the art department of Hedare Cosmetics until the night she acci-dentally overhears a research scientist warning the recent-ly replaced "Face of Hedare," Laurel Hedare (Sharon Stone), that the company's miracle wrinkle cream, Beau-line, has deforming side effects. Laurel intends to let noth-ing stand between Beau-line and millions of women ready to pay anything to look younger, so she directs her hench-men to kill Patience, unaware that her meek, self-effacing employee is connected to a wellspring of feline power that literally brings her back from the dead. Patience is, how-ever, not the same timid shadow she was before her untimely demise. The new, improved Patience is freakish-ly strong and agile, her senses are inhumanly sharp, and she's positively rippling with sleek self-confidence. The reborn Patience captivates straight-arrow cop Tom Lone (Benjamin Bratt), thrills her comic-relief friends (Alex Borstein, Michael Massee), and arouses the ire of boss George Hedare (Lambert Wilson) who promptly fires her when she back talks him. The old Patience would have gone into a tailspin, but this one gives herself a sexed-up makeover and sets about protecting the women of the world from Beau-line.

Comar's special-effects background clearly orients him more to visuals than storytelling, but it's screenwrit-ers John Brancato, Michael Ferris, and John Rogers who bear the brunt of the blame for taking wild liberties with *Batman* creator Bob Kane's 60-year-old character with-out giving her anything to do but strut and preen. Berry is the fifth actress to don Catwoman's second-skin costume. That Berry is the only Oscar winner in the group only makes her painfully uncharismatic performance more embarrassing.

CAVALCADE

1933 110m bw Drama
Fox (U.S.)

★★★★

Diana Wynyard (*Jane Marryot*), Clive Brook (*Robert Marryot*), Herbert Mundin (*Alfred Bridges*), Una O'Connor (*Ellen Bridges*), Ursula Jeans (*Fanny Bridges*), Beryl Mercer (*Cook*), Irene Browne (*Margaret Harris*), Merle Tottenham (*Annie*), Frank Lawton (*Joe Marryot*), John Warburton (*Edward Marryot*)

p, Winfield Sheehan; d, Frank Lloyd; w, Reginald Berkeley (based on the play by Noel Coward); ph, Ernest Palmer; ed, Margaret Clancy; art d, William S. Darling; fx, William Cameron Menzies

AA Best Picture; AAN Best Actress: Diana Wynyard; AA Best Director: Frank Lloyd; AA Best Interior Decoration: William S. Darling

A rare beauty. Noel Coward, in an atypically serious venture, traces 30 years of a British family's life. A big, fine production—little shown or remembered today—CAVALCADE was a sensation at the time of its release, filled as it is with a wistful look at a couple clinging together through years of love. The epochal scenes com-mence with the Boer War and go on to record the death of Queen Victoria, the sinking of the Titanic, WWI, and the birth of jazz. The film won Academy Awards for Best Picture and Best Director while Wynyard was nominat-ed for Best Actress, but lost to Katharine Hepburn for MORNING GLORY.

CELEBRATION, THE

(FESTEN)
1998 105m c Drama/Comedy
Nimbus Film APS (Denmark)

DVD
★★★★
R

Ulrich Thomsen (*Christian*), Henning Moritzen (*Helge*), Thomas Bo Larsen (*Michael*), Paprika Steen (*Helene*), Birthe Neumann (*Elsa*), Trine Dyrholm (*Pia*), Helle Dolleris (*Mette*), Bjarne Henriksen (*Kim*), Gbatokai Dakinah (*Gbatokai*), Therese Glahn (*Michelle*)

p, Birgitte Hald; d, Thomas Vinterberg (uncredited); w, Thomas Vinterberg, Mogens Rukov; ph, Anthony Dod Mantle; ed, Valdis Oskarsdottir

A gripping domestic drama from Danish director Thomas Vinterberg, THE CELEBRATION manages to tell an emo-tionally charged story while strictly adhering to Vinterberg's no-frills approach to filmmaking.

On the eve of patriarch Helge Klingenfelt's (Henning Moritzen) 60th birthday, his entire clan returns to the family-owned hotel to celebrate: They include eldest son Christian (Ulrich Thomsen), a successful restauranteur who hasn't been home in years; Christian's younger, wilder brother, Michael (Thomas Bo Larsen), and his family; prickly anthropologist daughter Helene (Paprika Steen) and her African-American boyfriend (Gbatokai Dakinah); and Helge's icy wife, Elsa (Birthe Neuman). The festivities begin pleasantly enough, but Christian's toast to his esteemed father includes a bombshell: urbane and jolly papa regularly molested him and his twin sis-ter, Linda—who recently killed herself—for years.

This first film made using the strict rules of the Danish Dogme 95 manifesto—which dictates technical austerity, from hand-held camera to the absence of a musical score—is a smashing success, both as technical experiment and as dis-tinctive cinematic storytelling. Wreaking havoc with expecta-tions, Vinterberg more than delivers on his promise "to force the truth out of my characters and settings." Critics may find the film's style flashy, pretentious, or even dizzying, but it has a welcome and all-too-rare energy and vigor. Vinterberg's film is the bracing kick in the pants contemporary cinema needs.

CELINE AND JULIE GO BOATING
(CELINE ET JULIE VONT EN BATEAU)
1974 193m c   Comedy/Fantasy   ★★★½
Losange/Films 7/Renn/Saga/Simar/V.M./
Action/Christian Fachner   (France)

Juliet Berto (Celine), Dominique Labourier (Julie), Bulle Ogier (Camille), Marie-France Pisier (Sophie), Barbet Schroeder (Olivier), Philippe Clevenot (Guilou), Nathalie Asnar (Madlyn)

d, Jacques Rivette; w, Jacques Rivette, Eduardo de Gregorio, Juliet Berto, Dominique Labourier, Bulle Ogier, Marie-France Pisier; ph, Jacques Renard, Michel Cenet (Eastmancolor); ed, Nicole Lubtchansky, Chris Tullio-Altan; m, Jean-Marie Senia

Jacques Rivette's CELINE AND JULIE GO BOATING is a witty salute to theater, female bonding, hallucinogenic candy, and those old standbys, fantasy and reality. Despite its three-hour-plus length and multi-layered narrative, the film has a devoted cult following, in part because of the surreal humor and delightful lead performances by Juliet Berto and Dominique Labourier.

Celine (Berto), a nightclub magician and fanciful story-teller, meets Julie (Labourier), a shy librarian, somewhere in a Parisian park. After a long game of cat and mouse that takes them through the city streets, Celine and Julie form a fast friend-ship and move into Julie's apartment, where the women take turns swapping each other's identities and exchanging tall tales. Celine tries to impress Julie with a strange story about a contin-uous drama taking place in an old, possibly abandoned man-sion. Celine not only claims it's true, but that she is also a participant. In the story, two women, Sophie and Camille (Marie-France Pisier, Bulle Ogier), are desperately in love with a widower named Olivier (Barbet Schroeder), who promised his late wife that he would not remarry as long as his ailing young daughter, Madlyn (Nathalie Asnar), was alive. Celine is supposedly the child's nanny who tries to shield the girl from the tension in the house—and possibly murder.

Enigmatic, funny, and engrossing all at once, CELINE AND JULIE GO BOATING is one of Rivette's most playful films. His earlier films were often self-referential, pretentious messes that ran ridiculously long (OUT ONE/SPECTRE is 12 hours long). But, in CELINE AND JULIE, he found a way to temper his excesses, tweak viewer expectation, and toy with the theatrical fourth wall, all in one entertaining movie. It's certainly not always easy to sit through; Rivette's penchant for quirkiness wears thin, and he throws in nonsen-sical bits that seem geared to his own amusement. Many scenes go on way too long without any payoff, and the end-ing is abrupt and unsatisfying.

Still, CELINE AND JULIE succeeds at being both enter-taining and unconventionally cerebral. Labourier and Berto have a great time playing giddy explorers who take off on a wild spree in the house of fiction, while Schroeder, Pisier, and Ogier hilariously parody dull melodrama with the straightest faces imaginable. Rivette encouraged improvisation and worked with the actors to create their own dialogue, resulting in some truly off-the-wall moments of slapstick humor.

CELL, THE   DVD
2000 115m c   Horror/Thriller   ★★★
Avery Pix/New Line/Caro-McLeod/Radical   R
Media Production   (U.S.)

Jennifer Lopez (Catherine Deane), Vince Vaughn (Peter Novak), Vincent D'Onofrio (Carl Stargher), Marianne Jean-Baptiste (Dr. Miriam Kent), Jake Weber (Gordon Ramsey), Dylan Baker (Henry West), James Gammon (Teddy Lee), Patrick Bauchau (Lucien Baines), Tara Subkoff (Julia Hickson), Catherine Sutherland (Anne Marie Vicksey)

p, Julio Caro, Eric McLeod; d, Tarsem Singh; w, Mark Protosevich; ph, Paul Laufer; ed, Paul Rubell, Robert Duffy; m, Howard Shore; prod d, Tom Foden; art d, Geoff Hubbard; fx, Clay Pinney, Kevin Tod Haug; cos, Eiko Ishioka, April Napier

AAN Best Makeup: Michele Burke, Edouard Henriques

Of course you can't really divide form and content; the medi-um is the message, the telling is the tale, and so on. But the fla-grant disparity between this tale of the rush to save a woman from a sadistic serial killer and the visually inventive way in which it's told demands comment.

Child psychologist Catherine Deane (Jennifer Lopez) is part of an experimental program to treat mentally ill patients so locked into their own minds that conventional therapy is useless. With the help of lots of drugs and cool machinery, the therapist actually enters the patient's psyche. The FBI has just captured sicko killer Carl Stargher (Vincent D'Onofrio), who kidnaps women, drowns them in a fully-automated tank of his own fiendish devising, then bleaches their bodies until they look like porcelain dolls. Ick. Unfortunately, he's had a brain seizure and lies comatose, unable to tell anyone where the girl he just abducted is hidden. Unless Catherine can enter his twisted mind and extract the information, the missing girl will die. So Catherine steps into Stargher's men-tal chamber of horrors, which seems to have been designed by Salvador Dali, the Quay brothers, Damien Hirst and fash-ion photographers Pierre and Gilles.

It's mind-bogglingly gorgeous in a totally trippy way; if this were the '70s, no one would dare see the movie straight (though the nastiness of the imagery is definitely bummer material). The shame is that whenever you get hauled back to the story, it's impossible not to notice its debt to SILENCE OF THE LAMBS. The costumes are phenomenal, the set design ravishing, and the sadistic inventiveness extraordi-nary; it's a shame it's all harnessed to a cliched story.

CENTRAL STATION   DVD
(CENTRAL DO BRASIL)
1998 115m c   Drama   ★★★★
Arthur Cohn/MACT Productions/   R
Videofilmes/Riofilme/Canal Plus   (Brazil)

Fernanda Montenegro (Dora), Marilia Pera (Irene), Vinicius de Oliveira (Josue), Soia Lira (Ana), Othon Bastos (Bastos), Otavio Augusto (Pedrao), Stela Freitas (Yolanda), Matheus Nachtergaele (Isaias), Caio Junqueira (Moises), Socorro Nobre

p, Arthur Cohn, Martine de Clermont-Tonnerre; d, Walter Salles; w, Joao Emanuel Carneiro, Marcos Bernstein (based on an original idea by Walter Salles); ph, Walter Carvalho; ed, Isabelle Rathery, Felipe Lacerda; m, Antonio Pinto, Jaques Morelembaum; prod d, Cassio Amarante, Carla Caffe; cos, Cristina Camargo

AAN Best Actress: Fernanda Montenegro; AAN Best Foreign Language Film

In this utterly charming road trip across the Brazilian country-side, Brazilian director Walter Salles has fashioned a rare kind of film: a heart-tugger that honestly earns your tears.

Retired teacher Dora (Fernanda Montenegro) is a crusty, emotionally dead 67-year-old who ekes out a living writing and (sometimes) posting letters for illiterate customers in Rio de Janeiro's Central Station. One afternoon, a young mother asks Dora to write a letter to the wayward father of her nine-year-old son Josue (Vinicius de Oliveira). Immediately after, she's struck down and killed by a bus. In a rare moment of kindness, Dora takes the child under her wing, saving him from the dangerous life of Rio's homeless street kids, and promises to return him to the father who now lives in a remote village in northeast Brazil. With nothing but a name and address to go on, Dora and Josue embark on a journey that takes them far from the emotionally barren routine of Dora's life in Rio, and closer to the promise of a spiritual reawakening.

At the outset, Dora is hardly an attractive figure: she's a bitter alcoholic who's willing to sell Josue for $1000. Her gradual transformation is a joy to watch, and Montenegro (who was nominated for an Academy Award, but lost out to SHAKESPEARE IN LOVE's Gwyneth Paltrow) gives a brilliant performance as a woman who, nearing the end of her life, suddenly finds herself longing for everything she's missed. There's not a hint of the cloying sentimentality one might expect, but the film is filled with gentle epiphanies and moments of real poignancy. It's also marked by strong Christian undercurrents, but, like everything else in Salles's film, they're handled with extraordinary delicacy and never feel exclusionary.

CESAR

1936 117m bw Drama   ★★★½
Pagnol (France)

Raimu *(Cesar Olivier)*, Pierre Fresnay *(Marius)*, Orane Demazis *(Fanny)*, Fernand Charpin *(Honore Panisse)*, Andre Fouche *(Cesariot)*, Alida Rouffe *(Honorine Cabinis)*, Milly Mathis *(Aunt Claudine Foulon)*, Robert Vattier *(M. Brun)*, Paul Dullac *(Felix Escartefigue)*, Maupi *(Chauffeur)*

p, Marcel Pagnol; d, Marcel Pagnol; w, Marcel Pagnol; ph, Willy; ed, Suzanne de Troeye, Jeanette Ginestet; m, Vincent Scotto; art d, Galibert

The third part of Marcel Pagnol's "Marseilles Trilogy," CESAR completes the story begun in MARIUS and continued in FANNY.

Cesariot (Andre Fouche) is the 18-year-old son of Marius (Pierre Fresnay) and Fanny (Orane Demazis), but his father disappeared before he was born and he believes the aging Panisse (Fernand Charpin), his stepfather, to be his biological parent. A priest begs Panisse to tell Cesariot about his real father, but he refuses. When Panisse dies, Fanny tells her son about his parentage and he is properly shocked to find that Cesar (Raimu), whom he had always thought to be his godfather, is actually his grandfather. The old man tells Cesariot about his father and where to find him.

Magnificent performances, particularly from Raimu, highlight this fine film—the only one of the three directed by the trilogy's writer and producer, Pagnol. The receptive audiences that made the previous installments such a success did the same for this one, and the fact that the lovers of the first two—Marius and Fanny—were finally reunited after 20 years didn't hurt the box office, either.

C'EST LA VIE

1990 110m c Drama   ★★½
Samuel Goldwyn Company (France)

Nathalie Baye *(Lena)*, Richard Berry *(Michel)*, Zabou *(Bella)*, Jean-Pierre Bacri *(Leon)*, Vincent Lindon *(Jean-Claude)*, Valeria Bruni-Tedeschi *(Odette)*, Didier Benureau *(Ruffier)*, Julie Bataille *(Frederique)*, Candice Lefranc *(Sophie)*, Alexis Derlon *(Daniel)*

p, Alexander Arcady, Diane Kurys; d, Diane Kurys; w, Diane Kurys, Alain Le Henry; ph, Gui Feppe Lanci; m, Philippe Sarde

Set in 1958, C'EST LA VIE is the third installment, following the immensely popular PEPPERMINT SODA and ENTRE NOUS, of Diane Kurys' absorbing semi-autobiographical trilogy.

Having decided to divorce her husband Michel (Richard Berry), the beautiful Lena (Nathalie Baye) puts her two daughters on a train in Lyon bound for La Baule Les Pins for a seaside vacation. The summer proves an eventful one, with the girls learning all manner of lessons in living. Lena eventually joins her daughters and engages in what she thinks is a secret affair with a young artist, Leon (Jean-Pierre Bacri), though the

children observe her dashing off into the night to meet him. The tranquility of their idyll is shattered by the unexpected arrival of their father.

No one can accuse Kurys of any real depth here; her strength as a director lies primarily in her sense of detail and in her ability to convey a nostalgic atmosphere. In its indolent sensuality and wealth of everyday observation, Kurys's work resembles some of the lighter, summery short stories of Colette. C'EST LA VIE is the merest trifle, but, given its sun-soaked ambience, the film is utterly painless and enjoyable.

Never more glamorous, Baye communicates a slightly neurotic, Jennifer Jones-like quality and makes an appealingly complex heroine. The scene where she first sees her lover on the beach and snakes her way through the cabanas to meet him is dizzyingly romantic. Bacri is properly sexy as Lena's lover, and Berry exudes the right amount of pained anguish as her husband.

Like Truffaut, Kurys has a precious, idealized view of children. They're all angelic, brilliant little paragons. The girls have a woman-in-a-child's-body beauty that is as much of a Gallic cliché as their huskily precocious voices are; the boys are budding artistic geniuses. Still, all of this sweetness and light leaves the viewer yearning for the youthful raunch and anarchy of a film like LIFE IS A LONG QUIET RIVER.

CHAMP, THE

1931 85m bw Sports   ★★★½
MGM (U.S.)

Wallace Beery *(Champ)*, Jackie Cooper *(Dink)*, Irene Rich *(Linda)*, Roscoe Ates *(Sponge)*, Edward Brophy *(Tim)*, Hale Hamilton *(Tony)*, Jesse Scott *(Jonah)*, Marcia Mae Jones *(Mary Lou)*

p, Harry Rapf; d, King Vidor; w, Leonard Praskins (based on a story by Frances Marion); ph, Gordon Avil; ed, Hugh Wynn

AAN Best Picture; AA Best Actor: Wallace Beery; *AAN Best Director:* King Vidor; *AA Best Writing (Original Story):* Frances Marion

Beery won an Oscar for his role as a down-at-heels ex-heavyweight boxing champion who trains for a comeback in Tijuana in between boozing and gambling, egged on by his pipe dreams and those of his young son (Cooper). When he wins some money, the "Champ" buys the boy a racehorse, but promptly loses it in a crap game. The boy's mother (Rich) and her wealthy husband (Hamilton) appear at the track where the boxer works and convince him that the boy would be better off with them. He reluctantly agrees, but the boy later sneaks back to his father's side in time to witness the older man's bout against a much younger opponent.

A famous tearjerker of its day, THE CHAMP is unabashed in its assault upon the audience's emotions. Cynics are advised to keep their distance, but in defense of this extremely sentimental film one should note the genuine rapport between Beery and Cooper and the quiet skill of director Vidor. A film with a lot of heart, unafraid to bare its emotions; THE CHAMP still plays well, its slightly gritty look more effective than the softness Franco Zeffirelli brought to the lesser 1979 remake.

CHAMPAGNE FOR CAESAR

1950 99m bw Comedy   ★★★★
UA (U.S.)

Ronald Colman *(Beauregard Bottomley)*, Celeste Holm *(Flame O'Neil)*, Vincent Price *(Burnbridge Waters)*, Barbara Britton *(Gwenn Bottomley)*, Art Linkletter *(Happy Hogan)*, Gabriel Heatter, George Fisher *(Announcers)*, Byron Foulger *(Gerald)*, Ellye Marshall *(Frosty)*, Vici Raaf *(Waters's Secretary)*

p, George Moskov; d, Richard Whorf; w, Hans Jacoby, Fred Brady; ph, Paul Ivano; ed, Hugh Bennett; m, Dimitri Tiomkin; art d, George Van Marter

An unjustly neglected, extremely funny jab at the media empire and the world of big business. Beauregard Bottomley (Colman) is an unemployed genius who holds a Ph.D., skims the encyclopedia for enjoyment and never forgets a thing he's read. He applies for work at a soap company owned by Burnbridge Waters (Price) but is rebuffed by the suds magnate. Beauregard is so annoyed by the treatment he receives at Waters's hands that he decides to bankrupt the company by becoming a contestant on the popular radio quiz show it sponsors.

Broadly handled but squarely on-target in its satire of the media, CHAMPAGNE FOR CAESAR is nimbly helmed by director Whorf and benefits considerably from its talented cast. Colman's typically understated style meshes nicely with Holm's, and they provide an appropriate foil for Price's deliberate hamminess as the megalomaniacal mogul. Listen for Mel Blanc as the voice of the champagne-loving parrot, Caesar. Denied a full run upon its initial release and broadcast on television in truncated form, this unexpected if modest delight is likely to halt your late-night channel surfing and leave you howling.

CHAMPION

1949   99m   bw   Sports   ★★★★½   **DVD**
Screen Plays   (U.S.)

Kirk Douglas *(Midge Kelly)*, Marilyn Maxwell *(Grace Diamond)*, Arthur Kennedy *(Connie Kelly)*, Paul Stewart *(Tommy Haley)*, Ruth Roman *(Emma Bryce)*, Lola Albright *(Mrs. Harris)*, Luis Van Rooten *(Jerome Harris)*, John Day *(Johnny Dunne)*, Harry Shannon *(Lew Bryce)*

p, Stanley Kramer; d, Mark Robson; w, Carl Foreman (based on the story by Ring Lardner); ph, Franz Planer; ed, Harry Gerstad; m, Dimitri Tiomkin (song, "Never Be It Said," Tiomkin, Goldie Goldmark)

AAN Best Actor: Kirk Douglas; *AAN Best Supporting Actor:* Arthur Kennedy; *AAN Best Screenplay:* Carl Foreman; *AAN Best B/W Cinematography:* Frank Planer; *AA Best Film Editing:* Harry Gerstad; *AAN Best Score (Drama or Comedy):* Dimitri Tiomkin

Released two years after BODY AND SOUL and based on a Ring Lardner short story, CHAMPION is another truly great boxing film. Midge Kelly (Douglas) travels to California with his crippled brother Connie (Kennedy), hoping to buy a diner but ending up working there and falling for the owner's daughter, Emma (Roman), who becomes his shotgun bride. Soon Midge decides to put his boxing skills to use as a professional, and leaves Emma. Managed by Tommy Haley (Stewart), Midge rises through the middleweight ranks until he gets a title shot, which, true to boxing-film formula, he is supposed to throw but doesn't. Nonetheless, he becomes the crime syndicate's boy, growing more corrupt daily.

Douglas' riveting performance as the ruthless fighter earned him an Oscar nomination and made him an overnight sensation, and the gifted supporting cast offers a wide and appropriate variety of foils to the ambitious, amoral character he portrays. Robson's direction is all action, wasting no time in telling this compelling story, and Carl Foreman's script is sharply observant of the boxing milieu.

CHAN IS MISSING

1981   80m   bw   Crime   ★★★★
Wayne Wang Productions   (U.S.)

Wood Moy *(Jo)*, Marc Hayashi *(Steve)*, Laureen Chew *(Amy)*, Judi Nihei *(Lawyer)*, Peter Wang *(Henry, the Cook)*, Presco Tabios *(Presco)*, Frankie Alarcon *(Frankie)*, Ellen Yeung *(Mrs. Chan)*, Emily Yamasaki *(Jenny)*, George Woo *(George)*

p, Wayne Wang; d, Wayne Wang; w, Wayne Wang, Isaac Cronin, Terrel Seltzer; ph, Michael Chin; ed, Wayne Wang; m, Robert Kikuchi

A deliberately modest but genuine delight, full of wicked humor, suspenseful touches, and perceptive insights about the experiences of Chinese immigrants in America. Two San Francisco cab drivers (played by Moy and Hayashi) have their savings stolen by the elusive "Chan Hung" and spend the rest of the film tracking him down. Along the way the film potently considers the problems with the generation gap among Chinese-Americans and conflicts between those Chinese from the mother country and those born in America.

A fine, funny independent production filmed on a minuscule budget in San Francisco's Chinatown by Wayne Wang (DIM SUM and EAT A BOWL OF TEA), CHAN IS MISSING deservedly became a major art-house success. Its cleverness extends even to the film's title, with CHAN suggesting both Charlie Chan (and hence many of the stereotypes commonly held about the Chinese) and "CHinese-americAN."

CHANGING LANES

2002   99m   c   Drama/Thriller   ★★★   **DVD**
Scott Rudin Productions   (U.S.)   R

Ben Affleck *(Gavin Banek)*, Samuel L. Jackson *(Doyle Gipson)*, Kim Staunton *(Valerie Gipson)*, Toni Collette *(Michelle)*, Sydney Pollack *(Stephen Delano)*, Tina Sloan *(Mrs. Delano)*, Richard Jenkins *(Walter Arnell)*, Akil Walker *(Stephen Gipson)*, Dylan Baker *(Finch)*, Cole Hawkins *(Danny Gipson)*

p, Scott Rudin; d, Roger Michell; w, Chap Taylor, Michael Tolkin (from a story by Chap Taylor); ph, Salvatore Totino; ed, Christopher Tellefsen; m, David Arnold; prod d, Kristi Zea; art d, Steven Graham; fx, J.C. Brotherhood, Reid Burns; cos, Ann Roth

Two paths cross at the wrong moment, triggering a calamitous chain of bad decisions, rash acts, and dangerous overreactions.

Wall Street lawyer Gavin Banek (Ben Affleck) is enmeshed in a high-stakes dispute over the administration of a multimillion-dollar charitable trust. Insurance salesman Doyle Gipson (Samuel L. Jackson) is fighting a custody battle with his estranged wife (Kim Staunton). Both are rushing to court appearances in Brooklyn when their cars collide; Gavin's vehicle is dinged; Doyle's is disabled. Doyle wants to exchange insurance information while Gavin, flush with privilege, doesn't want to waste time on petty proprieties. When Doyle won't be bought off with a blank check, Gavin drives off and strands him on the rainy road. Doyle misses his family court appointment and loses custody of his two sons. Gavin makes his hearing, but has left a vital document at the accident scene. Gavin spots Doyle on the street and makes an ill-timed plea for the document's return; realizing that he has the power to hurt Gavin, Doyle fires off a taunting fax. Gavin responds by hiring a hacker (Dylan Baker) to ruin Doyle's credit. The men continue to strike blindly at each other, each doing more damage than he cares to imagine, both heedless of the innocent bystanders who get dragged into their pissing contest.

The film would be more satisfying if it ended five minutes earlier than it does, but even with its slightly too redemptive coda, it's a bleak and complex moral thriller. And though Doyle is initially the more sympathetic character, Gavin is more complicated than he first appears. If there's any imbalance in their struggle, it's in the casting: Affleck is a good actor, but Jackson is a great one.

CHAPLIN

1992   144m   c/bw   Biography/Drama   ★★½   **DVD**
Carolco/Canal Plus/RCS Video/Lambeth   PG-13
Productions Ltd.   (U.K./U.S.)

Robert Downey Jr. *(Charlie Chaplin)*, Geraldine Chaplin *(Hannah Chaplin)*, Paul Rhys *(Sydney Chaplin)*, John Thaw *(Fred Karno)*,

Moira Kelly (*Hetty Kelly/Oona O'Neill*), Anthony Hopkins (*George Hayden*), Dan Aykroyd (*Mack Sennett*), Marisa Tomei (*Mabel Normand*), Penelope Ann Miller (*Edna Purviance*), Kevin Kline (*Douglas Fairbanks*)

p, Richard Attenborough, Mario Kassar; d, Richard Attenborough; w, William Boyd, Bryan Forbes, William Goldman (from the story by Diana Hawkins based on the biography *Chaplin: His Life and Art* by David Robinson and *My Autobiography* by Charles Chaplin); ph, Sven Nykvist; ed, Anne V. Coates; m, John Barry; prod d, Stuart Craig; art d, Mark Mansbridge, John King; cos, John Mollo, Ellen Mirojnick

AAN Best Actor: Robert Downey Jr.; *AAN Best Original Score:* John Barry; *AAN Best Art Direction-Set Decoration:* Stuart Craig, Chris A. Butler

CHAPLIN is the cinematic equivalent of a whistle-stop tour of Europe—the kind that takes you to ten cities in five days at such speed that everything melts into a vaguely entertaining blur. Richard Attenborough's film traces the entire arc of Chaplin's life, including his impoverished childhood in London, his early days as a vaudeville entertainer, his unparalleled success as a star and director of silent films, his enforced exile in Switzerland as a result of his alleged Communist sympathies, and his final, triumphant return to Hollywood in 1972 to accept a special Oscar for his life's work.

That's not to mention the series of young women who punctuated Chaplin's life and who seem to pop up every few minutes throughout the film—the "if this is 1936, that must be Paulette Goddard" school of biography. Attenborough and his writers fail to impose sufficient dramatic structure on this over-abundance of material, and never get to grips with what it was that fueled Chaplin's genius. Nonetheless, some sections come vividly to life, largely thanks to engaging performances. Robert Downey Jr., does an impressive job as the title character, perfectly recreating Chaplin's range of English accents (he went from Cockney to genteel as he got more famous) and mimicking, with astonishing precision, the gait and gestures of the Little Tramp. Downey is ably backed up by a glittering supporting cast, particularly Dan Aykroyd as Keystone Kops mogul Mack Sennett, Kevin Kline as silent screen legend Douglas Fairbanks, and Geraldine Chaplin (the great man's real-life daughter) as Chaplin's mother.

CHARACTER

(KARAKTER)   **DVD**
1997 124m c   Drama/Crime   ★★★★
First Floor Features/Kladaradatsch/NPS Television   R
(Netherlands)

Fedja van Huet (*Jacob Katadreuffe*), Jan Decleir (*Dreverhaven*), Betty Schuurman (*Joba Katadreuffe*), Victor Low (*De Gankelaar*), Tamar van den Dop (*Lorna Te George*), Hans Kesting (*Jan Maan*), Lou Landre (*Retenstein*), Bernhard Droog (*Stroomkoning*), Frans Vorstman (*De Bree*), Fred Goessens (*Schuwagt*)

p, Laurens Geels; d, Mike van Diem; w, Mike van Diem, Laurens Geels, Ruud van Megen (based on the novel by Ferdinand Bordewijk); ph, Rogier Stoffers; ed, Jessica DeKoning; m, Het Paleis van Boem; art d, Jelier & Schief; cos, Jany Temime

AA Best Foreign Language Film

Winner of the 1998 Academy Award for Best Foreign Language Film, this superbly crafted Dutch film is a taut and altogether gripping portrait of a man haunted by the malevolent figure of his father, a man he barely knows.

In 1920s Rotterdam, a young lawyer named Katadreuffe (Fedja van Huet) is arrested for the murder of Dreverhaven (Jan Decleir), a heartless bailiff whose sole pleasure in life seemed to come from evicting impoverished tenants and bankrupting anyone foolish enough to borrow money from his credit company. But, in flashback, we learn that years earlier,

Dreverhaven enjoyed a one-night stand with his brusque housekeeper, Joba (Betty Schuurman), and though the tryst produced a child—Katadreuffe—she ignored Dreverhaven's persistent proposals of marriage. Raised by Joba in poverty, Katadreuffe learns to hate his absent father and is determined to become a successful lawyer. But at every turn he runs into the brick wall that is the heartbroken and vengeful Dreverhaven, until it seems Katadreuffe's only chance of success depends on his father's destruction.

Imagine *Great Expectations* rewritten by Dostoyevsky, or a Horatio Alger tale reimagined by Kafka—an up-by-the-bootstraps tale set in a haunted world where free will is determined by dark, unknowable forces and even more mysterious emotions. The lavish period detail, superb cast, and the sinuous camerawork by Rogier Stoffers are the gilding on an intricate and powerfully realized story of festering unhappiness and inescapable destiny.

CHARADE

                                   DVD
1963 113m c   Comedy/Thriller   ★★★★
Universal   (U.S.)

Cary Grant (*Peter Joshua*), Audrey Hepburn (*Regina Lambert*), Walter Matthau (*Hamilton Bartholomew*), James Coburn (*Tex Panthollow*), George Kennedy (*Herman Scobie*), Ned Glass (*Leopold Gideon*), Jacques Marin (*Inspector Edouard Grandpierre*), Paul Bonifas (*Felix*), Dominique Minot (*Sylvie Gaudet*), Thomas Chelimsky (*Jean-Louis Gaudet*)

p, Stanley Donen; d, Stanley Donen; w, Peter Stone (based on the story "The Unsuspecting Wife" by Marc Behm, Peter Stone); ph, Charles Lang (Technicolor); ed, James B. Clark; m, Henry Mancini; art d, Jean d'Eaubonne; cos, Givenchy

AAN Best Song: "Charade"; Henry Mancini (Music), Johnny Mercer (Lyrics)

Charming comedy-romance-thriller pairing Cary Grant and Audrey Hepburn, intelligently scripted by Peter Stone and directed in distinctly Hitchcockian style by Stanley Donen.

Reggie Lambert (Hepburn) returns to Paris from a ski trip in the French Alps to find her house ransacked and her husband dead. His funeral is attended by three curious thugs—played by James Coburn, George Kennedy, and Ned Glass—each of whom make sure that the corpse is indeed dead. Peter (Grant) offers his assistance to Reggie, as does CIA man Bartholomew (Walter Matthau) who informs her that her husband was part of a gang which, during WW II, stole and stashed a quarter of a million dollars. Naturally, everyone thinks—mistakenly—that Reggie knows the whereabouts of the money. Although Reggie finds herself falling in love with Peter, she suspects that he too is after the money, especially given his fondness for aliases—Peter Joshua, Alexander Dyle, Adam Canfield, Brian Cruickshank, etc. As the corpses begin to accumulate, it becomes increasingly important—and difficult—for Reggie to determine who are the good guys and who are the villains.

CHARADE is a finely crafted thriller that has a lot to offer beyond its clever plot. The radiant Hepburn's romance with the suave Grant is delightfully handled; the Oscar-nominated theme song by Henry Mancini and Johnny Mercer is superb; the location photography is exquisite and the rooftop fight scene between Grant and Kennedy is truly harrowing.

CHARGE OF THE LIGHT BRIGADE, THE

1936 115m bw Adventure/War   ★★★½
Warner Bros.   (U.S.)

Errol Flynn (*Maj. Geoffrey Vickers*), Olivia de Havilland (*Elsa Campbell*), Patric Knowles (*Capt. Perry Vickers*), Donald Crisp (*Col. Campbell*), Henry Stephenson (*Sir Charles Macefield*), Nigel Bruce (*Sir Benjamin Warrenton*), David Niven (*Capt. James*

Randall), G.P. Huntley Jr. *(Maj. Jowett)*, Spring Byington *(Lady Octavia Warrenton)*, C. Henry Gordon *(Surat Khan)*

p, Samuel Bischoff; d, Michael Curtiz; w, Michel Jacoby, Rowland Leigh (based on a story by Michel Jacoby inspired by the poem by Alfred, Lord Tennyson); ph, Sol Polito; ed, George Amy; m, Max Steiner; art d, John Hughes; fx, Fred Jackman, H.F. Koenekamp; cos, Milo Anderson

AA Best Assistant Director: Jack Sullivan; *AAN Best Score:* Warner Bros Studio Music Department, Leo Forbstein (Dept. Head); *AAN Best Sound Recording:* Nathan Levinson

THE CHARGE OF THE LIGHT BRIGADE is a fine military swashbuckler with some of the most dynamic action sequences ever seen on the screen. Great pains were taken to re-create the 1850s milieu but Warner Bros. typically discarded the actual facts regarding the magnificent military blunder, retaining instead the era's pomp and the stirring lines of Tennyson's famous poem.

The story begins in in 1850 in northwest India during the years leading up to the Crimean War. Major Geoffrey Vickers (Errol Flynn), a dashing British officer of the 27th Lancers, crosses paths with a scheming Indian potentate, Surat Khan (C. Henry Gordon), who is severing ties with the British and allying himself with the Russians in preparation for a revolt. After Surat Khan's murderous betrayal of the British forces, Vickers seeks revenge during a foolhardy but courageous charge on the Russian forces at the Balaclava heights in the Crimea where Surat Khan has fled. Meanwhile Elsa Campbell (Olivia de Havilland), the woman Vickers loves, has secretly fallen in love with his brother, Captain Perry Vickers (Patric Knowles).

As a history lesson, THE CHARGE OF THE LIGHT BRIGADE is wildly inaccurate but it is a rousing entertainment. History was better served by the 1968 remake by Tony Richardson which exposed more of the truth about the military idiocy that led to the slaughter but movie audiences were largely unmoved.

CHARGE OF THE LIGHT BRIGADE, THE   *DVD*
1968 145m c   Historical   ★★½
UA   (U.K.)

Trevor Howard *(Lord Cardigan)*, Vanessa Redgrave *(Clarissa)*, John Gielgud *(Lord Raglan)*, Harry Andrews *(Lord Lucan)*, Jill Bennett *(Mrs. Duberly)*, David Hemmings *(Capt. Nolan)*, Peter Bowles *(Paymaster Duberly)*, Mark Burns *(Capt. Morris)*, Howard Marion-Crawford *(Sir George Brown)*, Mark Dignam *(Airey)*

p, Neil Hartley; d, Tony Richardson; w, Charles Wood; ph, David Watkin (Panavision/DeLuxe Color); ed, Kevin Brownlow, Hugh Raggett; m, John Addison; art d, Edward Marshall; fx, Robert MacDonald; cos, David Walker

Though well-researched and thought-provoking, this exquisitely made film is ultimately a disappointing drama of events leading up to the British involvement in the Crimean War. Richardson takes a somewhat absurdist approach as he satirizes the snobbishness of the English upper class and its view of the sport of war. He also exposes the soldiers' blind acceptance of the demands of their belittling supervisors. Their much vaunted code of honor turns sour in the wake of the humiliating slaughter of England's Light Brigade. The film completely belittles the undeniable courage that went hand-in-hand with the terrible mistakes it depicts. Dramatic loopholes also diminish the impact of what appears to be intended as a major cinematic statement about war from the 1960s generation.

Nonetheless there are many enjoyable performances, especially those of Gielgud, Hemmings, and Redgrave (the last two previously paired in BLOW UP). Richard Williams provides the clever animation sequences which serve to orient the viewer. Don't look for the spectacular war scenes so

sweepingly portrayed in Curtiz's historically inaccurate but crowdpleasing 1936 version; the battle scenes take second place to revisionist satire and political indictment of 19th-century imperialistic England.

CHARIOTS OF FIRE   *DVD*
1981 123m c   Biography/Sports   ★★★
Enigma   (U.K.)   PG

Ben Cross *(Harold Abrahams)*, Ian Charleson *(Eric Liddell)*, Nigel Havers *(Lord Andrew Lindsay)*, Nicholas Farrell *(Aubrey Montague)*, Ian Holm *(Sam Mussabini)*, John Gielgud *(Master of Trinity)*, Lindsay Anderson *(Master of Caius)*, Nigel Davenport *(Lord Birkenhead)*, Cheryl Campbell *(Jennie Liddell)*, Alice Krige *(Sybil Gordon)*

p, David Puttnam; d, Hugh Hudson; w, Colin Welland; ph, David Watkin; ed, Terry Rawlings; m, Vangelis; art d, Roger Hall; cos, Milena Canonero

AA Best Picture; AAN Best Supporting Actor: Ian Holm; *AAN Best Director:* Hugh Hudson; *AA Best Original Screenplay:* Colin Welland; *AAN Best Film Editing:* Terry Rawlings; *AA Best Original Score:* Vangelis; *AA Best Costume Design:* Milena Canonero

CHARIOTS OF FIRE is a pleasant, mildly inspirational movie but hardly worthy of all the accolades it received. This true story, based on an original screenplay by Colin Welland, is about what it means to win and what one must do to achieve it. Eric Liddell (Ian Charleson) is a serious Scottish Christian who runs for the glory of Jesus. Harold Abrahams (Ben Cross) is an English Jew who is sensitive to prejudice and whose primary motivation is to be accepted. The movie delineates and crosscuts the lives of both men as they meet and compete at the 1924 Olympics in Paris.

The real-life Liddell became a Christian missionary, went to China, and eventually died in a Japanese prisoner of war camp, true to his faith to the end. Abrahams went on to become the spokesman for English amateur athletics, was knighted, and died a venerated elder statesman in 1978. Few who see the film can forget the lyrically photographed scene of the runners striding through the surf in slow motion to the accompaniment of Vangelis's stirring score, particularly in light of subsequent parodies.

CHARLEY VARRICK
1973 111m c   Crime   ★★★½
Universal   (U.S.)   PG

Walter Matthau *(Charley Varrick)*, Joe Don Baker *(Molly)*, Felicia Farr *(Sybil Fort)*, Andrew Robinson, billed as Andy Robinson *(Harman Sullivan)*, John Vernon *(Maynard Boyle)*, Sheree North *(Jewell Everett)*, Norman Fell *(Mr. Garfinkle)*, Benson Fong *(Honest John)*, Woodrow Parfrey *(Howard Young)*, William Schallert *(Sheriff Bill Horton)*

p, Don Siegel; d, Don Siegel; w, Dean Riesner, Howard Rodman (based on the novel *The Looters* by John Reese); ph, Michael Butler (Technicolor); ed, Frank Morriss; m, Lalo Schifrin; art d, Fernando Carrere; cos, Helen Colvig

A very well made caper film full of action and rich with character. Directed by genre veteran Don Siegel, the versatile Walter Matthau plays it hard and fast as a small-time thief who robs, with partner Robinson, a tiny New Mexico bank. Instead of the usual loose change, the robbers find $750,000 which turns out to be Mafia money the bank was laundering. It's too risky for the pragmatic Matthau but his avaricious punk partner insists that they keep the money. Matthau warns him that if the loot is not returned, the Mafia will start gunning for them, which is exactly what happens. Hit man Baker begins hunting the pair, destroying everyone and everything in his path—and enjoying it.

Matthau is both shifty and cunning as he evades both the police and the Mafia. Butler's photography is top notch as is Schifrin's score. The whole film is suspenseful and intelligently scripted, thanks to director Siegel (DIRTY HARRY, THE SHOOTIST, ESCAPE FROM ALCATRAZ) and writers Riesner and Rodman. A great B movie of the 1970s.

CHARLEY'S AUNT

1941 80m bw Comedy ★★★
Fox (U.S.)

Jack Benny *(Babbs)*, Kay Francis *(Donna Lucia)*, James Ellison *(Jack Chesney)*, Anne Baxter *(Amy Spettigue)*, Edmund Gwenn *(Stephen Spettigue)*, Reginald Owen *(Redcliff)*, Laird Cregar *(Sir Francis Chesney)*, Arleen Whelan *(Kitty Verdun)*, Richard Haydn *(Charley Wyckham)*, Ernest Cossart *(Brasset)*

p, William Perlberg; d, Archie Mayo; w, George Seaton (based on the play by Brandon Thomas); ph, Peverell Marley; ed, Robert Bischoff; m, Alfred Newman; art d, Nathan Juran, Richard Day; cos, Travis Banton

This was the third of many screen adaptations of "Charley's Aunt," the beloved 19th-century stage farce. The first starred Sydney Chaplin in 1925 and the second (released in 1930) featured Charlie Ruggles in the lead. Jack Benny stars here as Babbs, an Oxford student who masquerades as his friend Charley Wyckham's (Richard Haydn) aunt from Brazil who will be the chaperon for Charley and Jack (James Ellison) as they court Amy (Anne Baxter) and Kitty (Arleen Whelan). Once Babbs is in drag, however, he must fend off romantic advances from gigolo Sir Francis Chesney (Laird Cregar) and from Stephen Spettigue (Edmund Gwenn), the girl's guardian.

Jack Benny was never better (with the possible exception of his classic TO BE OR NOT TO BE) and carries the film with a top-flight performance. This was his first role of any consequence other than his previous tailor-made parts with radio jokes flying thick and fast around his well-known persona. In CHARLEY'S AUNT, Benny had to play a part totally alien to what he'd done before and he proved more than worthy to the task. Remade as the musical WHERE'S CHARLEY? in 1952.

CHARLIE CHAN AT THE OPERA

1936 66m bw Mystery ★★★½
Fox (U.S.)

Warner Oland *(Charlie Chan)*, Boris Karloff *(Gravelle)*, Keye Luke *(Lee Chan)*, Charlotte Henry *(Mlle. Kitty)*, Thomas Beck *(Phil Childers)*, Margaret Irving *(Mme. Lilli Rouchelle)*, Gregory Gaye *(Enrico Barelli)*, Nedda Harrigan *(Mme. Lucretia Barelli)*, Frank Conroy *(Mr. Whitely)*, Guy Usher *(Inspector Regan)*

p, John Stone; d, H. Bruce Humberstone; w, W. Scott Darling, Charles Belden (based on a story by Bess Meredyth and the character created by Earl Derr Biggers); ph, Lucien Andriot; ed, Alex Troffey

Yes, Charlie Chan is a caricature of the East Asian personality and questions of racism do arise, but in his heyday in the 1930s the character of Chan presented an Oriental hero on the screen in what is perhaps the longest running series in movies. (The first Chan film was made in 1926 and the most recent in 1981.) There's something else going on here besides the caricature. Chan is probably unique in being a family detective and his collaboration with his sons is one of the attractions of the character. As with Nick and Nora Charles in THE THIN MAN movies, we're more interested in the relationship than in the mystery. Of the several actors who have played Chan, Warner Oland, who starred in this one, was generally regarded as the best.

One of the best of the series, this entry has the added attraction of Boris Karloff as Gravelle, an opera star who is presumed dead after being caught in a fire at a theater. He survives as an amnesiac, however, and is admitted unidentified into a mental hospital. When a picture of his opera singer wife appears in the newspaper, Gravelle's memory is spurred and he recalls that it was his unfaithful wife and her lover who set the fire in an attempt to kill him. Seething with a desire for vengeance, Gravelle escapes the mental hospital and heads for the opera house. When several people turn up dead, Charlie Chan is called in to investigate.

Included in the film is the opera *Carnival*, composed especially for the picture by Oscar Levant. This movie was so well made—and holds up so well—that its interest ranges far beyond the usual circle of Chan buffs.

CHARLIE'S ANGELS <small>DVD</small>

2000 98m c Action/Comedy/Thriller ★★
Mandy Films/Flower Films/Tall Trees/Columbia PG-13
(U.S.)

Cameron Diaz *(Natalie)*, Drew Barrymore *(Dylan)*, Lucy Liu *(Alex)*, Bill Murray *(Bosley)*, Sam Rockwell *(Eric Knox)*, Kelly Lynch *(Vivian Wood)*, Tim Curry *(Roger Corwin)*, Crispin Glover *(Thin Man)*, John Forsythe *(Voice of Charlie)*, Matt LeBlanc *(Jason)*

p, Leonard Goldberg, Drew Barrymore, Nancy Juvonen; d, Joseph McGinty Nichol; w, Ryan Rowe, Ed Solomon, John August (based on the television series by Ivan Goff and Ben Roberts), Akiva Goldsman (uncredited), Mitch Glazer (uncredited), Susannah Grant (uncredited), Steve Pink (uncredited), D.V. DeVincentis (uncredited), Zak Penn (uncredited); ph, Russell Carpenter; ed, Wayne Wahrman, Peter Teschner; m, Edward Shearmur; prod d, J. Michael Riva; art d, David F. Klasson, Richard F. Mays; fx, Paul Lombardi; chor, Marguerite Derricks; cos, Joseph G. Aulisi

So inconsequential that it starts evaporating from memory the minute it's over, this big-screen version of the '70s TV show is nevertheless a pleasant enough diversion while you're watching. Damnation by faint praise? Under these circumstances, that's about as good as it gets.

The crime-busting "Angels" are gorgeous and geeky Natalie (Cameron Diaz), cool and commanding Alex (Lucy Liu), and pouty Dylan (Drew Barrymore), a barely grown-up wild child. As in the popular but deeply stupid series, they answer to a mysterious millionaire who's only ever heard over the speakerphone (John Forsythe, reprising his series role) and who sends them on a mission involving a kidnapped computer nerd (Sam Rockwell), his steely partner (Kelly Lynch), their flamboyant competitor (Tim Curry), a silent villain (Crispin Glover), and some purloined voice-recognition software, the misuse of which could mean the end of privacy as we know it.

Frankly, who cares? The preposterous plot is just an excuse for these three cheese puffs to go undercover as belly dancers, race-car drivers, geisha girls, and the like, and to mix it up in insanely stylized action sequences masterminded by Hong Kong fight choreographer Yuen Cheung Yan (brother of CROUCHING TIGER choreographer Yuen Wo Ping). The tone is equal parts exuberant hokiness and affectionately ironic self-awareness (a reference to "T.J. Hooker: The Movie" gets a big laugh), though the movie's posterior ogling is a little off-putting. (Movies this ass-obsessed are usually located in the gay-porn section of your local video store). Bill Murray plays the Angels' sidekick, Bosley, while MTV's Tom Green (Barrymore's significant other) is simply awful as Dylan's swain; for him, even this small role is still far too large.

CHARLIE'S ANGELS: FULL THROTTLE 📀
2003 110m c Action/Comedy ★★
Leonard Goldberg Productions/ PG-13
Flower Films/Tall Trees Productions/ (U.S.)
Wonderland Sound and Vision

Cameron Diaz (Natalie Cook), Drew Barrymore (Dylan Sanders), Lucy Liu (Alex Munday), Bernie Mac (Jimmy Bosley), Crispin Glover (Thin Man), John Forsythe (Voice of Charlie), Justin Theroux (Seamus O'Grady), Robert Patrick (Ray Carter), Demi Moore (Madison Lee), Luke Wilson (Pete)

p, Drew Barrymore, Leonard Goldberg, Nancy Juvonen; d, Joseph McGinty Nichol; w, John August, Cormac Wibberley, Marianne Wibberley (based on the television series created by Ivan Goff and Ben Roberts); ph, Russell Carpenter; ed, Wayne Wahrman; m, Edward Shearmur; prod d, J. Michael Riva; art d, David F. Klassen; fx, Mark Stetson, Matt Sweeney; chor, Robin Antin, Marguerite Derricks; cos, Joseph G. Aulisi

Looser, more stupidly endearing, and marginally less posterior-obsessed than the first film, this glossy, megabucks action spectacular's soft, sweet center is the true-blue camaraderie between power-puff grrrls Dylan Sanders (Drew Barrymore), Natalie Cook (Cameron Diaz), and Alex Munday (Lucy Liu). Their men are even more irrelevant than the average action movie's token female love interest.

The crime-busting cuties continue to answer to the disembodied voice of Charlie (John Forsythe) and are abetted by a new Bosley (Bernie Mac). The undercover angels must find and retrieve two rings that, when put together, reveal the new names and current locations of everyone who's ever entered the Federal Witness Protection plan. A major complication hits all too close to home: level-headed Dylan was once a teenage gutter punk who testified against her bad, bad boyfriend, Seamus (Justin Theroux), and was rewarded with a new identity. Fresh from the slammer, vengeful Seamus is looking for payback. There's also the matter of Angel emeritus Madison Lee (Demi Moore), who may have embraced the dark side. Dylan, Natalie, and Alex pose as dirt bikers, nuns, welders, and, of course, strippers to further their investigation.

Diaz and her dolphin-like smile regularly steal the spotlight from her co-stars, starting with the goofy spectacle she makes of herself as a flaky Scandinavian tourist riding a mechanical yak. The action is ridiculously overwrought, a state-of-the-art combination of CGI wizardry and Hong Kong-style wirework so removed from the laws of physical reality that it might as well be animated. And the plot is of less consequence than the pop-culture references, star cameos, cheerfully jokey soundtrack, and double entendres, which are somewhat less strenuously vulgar than those in the first film without being any more clever.

CHARLOTTE'S WEB 📀
1973 94m c Animated/Musical ★★★★
Paramount (U.S.) G

VOICES OF: Debbie Reynolds (Charlotte), Paul Lynde (Templeton), Henry Gibson (Wilbur), Rex Allen (Narrator), Martha Scott (Mrs. Arable), Dave Madden (Old Sheep), Danny Bonaduce (Avery), Don Messick (Geoffrey), Herb Vigran (Lurvy), Agnes Moorehead (The Goose)

p, Joseph Barbera, William Hanna; d, Charles A. Nichols, Iwao Takamoto; w, Earl Hamner Jr. (based on the book by E.B. White); ph, Roy Wade, Dick Blundell, Dennis Weaver, Ralph Migliori, George Epperson (Movielab Color); ed, Larry Cowan, Pat Foley; m, Richard M. Sherman, Robert B. Sherman; art d, Bob Singer, Paul Julian, Ray Aragon

A charming cartoon adaptation of E.B. White's fantasy. Wilbur is a runt pig who has been raised as the pet of a New England farmer. He is sold to a neighboring farm, where a sheep informs him that he's fated to become what goes with cheese on rye. Wilbur is understandably frightened, until he meets a spider named Charlotte, who devotes her arachnoidal life to saving Wilbur from the fate of most porkers, and who weaves words into her web that convince the superstitious farmer that Wilbur is some sort of miraculous hog. The voices of Reynolds, Lynde, Gibson, and all the rest are perfectly cast, and the songs by the Sherman brothers are solid, although none of them became hits like those they wrote for such Disney movies as MARY POPPINS.

CHARLY 📀
1968 103m c Drama ★★½
Selmur (U.S.) PG

Cliff Robertson (Charly Gordon), Claire Bloom (Alice Kinian), Lilia Skala (Dr. Anna Straus), Leon Janney (Dr. Richard Nemur), Dick Van Patten (Bert), William Dwyer (Joey), Ed McNally (Gimpy), Dan Morgan (Paddy), Barney Martin (Hank), Ruth White (Mrs. Apple)

p, Ralph Nelson; d, Ralph Nelson; w, Stirling Silliphant (based on the short story and novel Flowers for Algernon by Daniel Keyes); ph, Arthur J. Ornitz (Techniscope, Technicolor); ed, Fredric Steinkamp; m, Ravi Shankar; art d, Charles Rosen; cos, Hazel Roy

AA Best Actor: Cliff Robertson

The very sentimental CHARLY has not aged well, but still remains intriguing for its premise and for Cliff Robertson's Oscar-winning performance. He plays the title character, a retarded man who becomes a genius after having experimental surgery which has successfully cured mentally defective mice. Charly then falls in love with his teacher (the luminous Claire Bloom), but when he learns that the operation's results are only temporary, he angrily denounces his doctors—and society—at a scientific symposium and eventually regresses to his former state.

Cliff Robertson, who had starred in TV versions of "The Hustler" and "Days of Wine and Roses," only to lose those roles to Paul Newman and Jack Lemmon and see them both of them nominated for Oscars in the feature film adaptations, made sure that the same thing wouldn't happen to CHARLY and bought the movie rights to the story after starring in a 1961 television version. His perseverance paid off and he finally won his own Oscar. He gives an earnest and intelligent, if somewhat mannered performance, which, not surprisingly, is more effective after Charly's surgery when he's struggling to deal with his newfound mental capacity, than when he's rolling his eyes, slurring his words and talking out of the side of his mouth as the retarded Charly.

The film's main problem is that director Ralph Nelson virtually ignores the philosophical elements of the story and emphasizes its most maudlin aspects, while throwing in a little sci-fi, romance, and spurious social commentary. His flashy style includes annoying zooms, pointless split-screen sequences, superfluous sight-seeing tours of Boston, and tasteless pseudo-documentary footage of a class of actual retarded children. The film is historically interesting mostly as a star-vehicle for Robertson, and as an example of the kind of liberal material that was once considered to be daring in the 1960s.

CHARULATA
1964 117m bw Drama ★★★★★
RDB & Co. (India)

Soumitra Chatterjee (Amal), Madhabi Mukherjee (Charulata), Sailen Mukherjee (Bhupati), Syamal Ghosal (Umapada), Gitali Roy (Mandakini), Bholanath Koyal (Braja), Suku Mukherjee (Nisikanta), Dilip Bose (Sasanka), Subrata Sen Sharma (Motilal), Joydeb (Nilatpal Dey)

p, R.D. Bansal; d, Satyajit Ray; w, Satyajit Ray (based on the novella *Nastanirh* by Rabindranath Tagore); ph, Subrata Mitra; ed, Dulal Dutta; m, Satyajit Ray; art d, Bansi Chandragupta

---

Satyajit Ray's fascination with Rabindranath Tagore culminated in CHARULATA, his twelfth film and arguably his greatest achievement. Based on a short story by Tagore, it is a surprisingly modern tale of love, lust, fidelity, and a woman's growing self-awareness against the backdrop of the Bengal Renaissance, a vibrant intellectual awakening in 19th-century India.

Charulata (Madhabi Mukherjee), the childless wife of a wealthy Bengali intellectual, lives in seclusion in her spacious and ornate home in Calcutta, while winds of change are blowing away the cobwebs outside. Her husband, Bhupati (Sailen Mukherjee), inspired by Mill and Bentham, spends his inherited wealth in the pursuit of freedom and equality, by editing an English-language liberal political weekly. But he has no time for Charu, who has little to do in a home run like a well-oiled machine by a fleet of old retainers.

At this point arrives Amal (Soumitra Chatterjee), Bhupati's dynamic young cousin. With Bhupati's encouragement, a close friendship grows between Amal and Charu based on their common interest in literature. Their intellectual sparring, however, hides a deeper attachment and a need which initially neither is fully aware of, and one which society will never sanction.

With its beauty, structural perfection and conceptual purity, CHARULATA remains a triumph of Ray's craftsmanship and cinematic vision. The exquisite interiors created by art director Bansi Chandragupta were among the best of his work, as were the subtle use of lights and the sensitivity of Subrata Mitra's camera. The costumes, the faces, and the detailed structuring of the film created a superbly colourful piece of monochrome cinema. CHARULATA has the quality of a miniature painting, where minute details are revealed by a stroke of the finest brush, and the unspoken is made visual by a mere suggestion.

CHEAPER BY THE DOZEN 📀
1950 85m   c   Comedy   ★★★
Fox   (U.S.)

Clifton Webb *(Frank Bunker Gilbreth)*, Jeanne Crain *(Ann Gilbreth)*, Myrna Loy *(Mrs. Lillian Gilbreth)*, Betty Lynn *(Libby Lancaster)*, Edgar Buchanan *(Dr. Burton)*, Barbara Bates *(Ernestine)*, Mildred Natwick *(Mrs. Mebane)*, Sara Allgood *(Mrs. Monahan)*, Anthony Sydes *(Fred Gilbreth)*, Roddy McCaskill *(Jack Gilbreth)*

p, Lamar Trotti; d, Walter Lang; w, Lamar Trotti (based on the novel by Frank B. Gilbreth, Jr. and Ernestine Gilbreth Carey); ph, Leon Shamroy (Technicolor); ed, J. Watson Webb; m, Cyril J. Mockridge

---

A big hit in its day and a typical Hollywood evocation of a genteel, bygone middle America of the 1920s that never was, this poor man's MEET ME IN ST. LOUIS presents prissy, spinsterish Clifton Webb as the father of twelve. Get real! Though Webb has his fair share of amusing moments, his trademark waspish but kindly crankiness loses its grip here amidst the floodtides of familial fondness. Loy, sadly soft-pedaled in the footage department, is on firmer ground as his devoted wife, a psychologist who uses the tricks of her trade on her efficiency expert husband whenever necessary. The film has no particular driving story but rather is a host of minor family incidents designed to show the closeness of the 14-member clan. Some are amusing, though others cloy in the way that only 20th Century Fox lollipops can.

Journeyman director Lang is no Vincente Minnelli when it comes to either visuals or mood, and this is the type of film which plays better on television because there's nothing in it

which really uses the big screen with any creativity. Honors go to Mildred Natwick as a birth control activist in the film's funniest scene. A true 1950s cultural relic and suitable "family entertainment," the film inspired a modest, quasi-feminist sequel, BELLES ON THEIR TOES.

CHEAPER BY THE DOZEN 📀
2003 98m   c   Comedy   ★★
Robert Simonds Productions/   PG
20th Century Fox   (U.S.)

Steve Martin *(Tom Baker)*, Bonnie Hunt *(Kate Baker)*, Piper Perabo *(Nora Baker)*, Tom Welling *(Charlie Baker)*, Hilary Duff *(Lorraine Baker)*, Ashton Kutcher *(Hank—uncredited)*, Kevin G. Schmidt *(Henry Baker)*, Alyson Stoner *(Sarah Baker)*, Jacob Smith *(Jake Baker)*, Liliana Mumy *(Jessica Baker)*

p, Michael Barnathan, Ben Myron, Robert Simonds; d, Shawn Levy; w, Joel Cohen, Alec Sokolow, Sam Harper (from a screen story by Craig Titley, based on the novel by Frank Bunker Gilbreth and Ernestine Gilbreth Carey); ph, Jonathan Brown; ed, George Folsey Jr.; m, Christophe Beck; prod d, Nina Ruscio; art d, Scott Meehan; fx, David Kelsey; cos, Sanja Milkovic Hays

---

Very loosely based on the classic children's book and the 1950 film, this modern comedy of extreme parenting is generally amusing, if occasionally overly sentimental.

College sweethearts Kate (Bonnie Hunt) and Tom Baker (Steve Martin) bonded over a mutual desire to pursue their professional ambitions while raising a large brood, but 12 bundles of joy later, they've had to sacrifice a few of their dreams. Eldest daughter Nora (Piper Perabo), 22, has moved out, but with 11 others still at home, the Baker family operates in a state of controlled chaos in rural Illinois. When Tom is offered his dream job as head football coach at his alma mater, the family relocates to Chicago, but the Baker kids have a hard time adjusting to city life; getting even less attention from their busy dad brings out the worst in them. Things deteriorate further when Kate's memoirs are published and she's off onto a book tour. Tom begs Nora and her live-in boyfriend, Hank (Ashton Kutcher), to lend a hand, but the younger kids will have none of it, and Tom is left trying to balance his career and family responsibilities all alone.

Martin delivers the same frantic-father performance he used in PARENTHOOD and both FATHER OF THE BRIDE movies, but Hunt shines as the stable center of this out-of-control family. Though Tom Welling, Hilary Duff, and Perabo are supposed to be the film's young stars, their thinly written characters leave Kutcher free to make the most of his screen time. The rest of the Baker kids, with the exception of adorable Forrest Landis, are cute and indistinguishable.

CHELSEA GIRLS, THE
1966 210m   c/bw Experimental   ★★★★
Film-makers' Distribution Center   (U.S.)

Pepper Davis, Ondine, Ingrid Superstar, Albert Rene Ricard, International Velvet, Brigid Polk, Ed Hood *(Ed)*, Patrick Flemming *(Patrick)*, Mario Montez *(Transvestite)*, Nico

p, Andy Warhol; d, Andy Warhol; w, Andy Warhol, Ronald Tavel; ph, Andy Warhol (Eastmancolor); m, The Velvet Underground

---

A film whose importance as a 1960s cultural statement outweighs any intrinsic value it may have as a film, CHELSEA GIRLS is nevertheless fascinating, provocative, and hilarious—once you surrender yourself to the totally new way of watching cinema that Andy Warhol films require. Think of it as Antonioni in slow-motion and enjoy the heavy ennui that settles over you. As with most of his other films Warhol simply turned the camera on his camp followers and let them play as they might. A number of his mock-Hollywood "superstars" from the famous

Factory crowd are actually born performers. Look for strange and funny moments from Ondine, Ingrid Superstar, Brigid Polk, Ed Hood, Mario Montez, Edie Sedgwick and Nico among others.

CHELSEA GIRLS isn't an easy film to write about and is almost impossible to rank in terms of any "quality" it may possess. Maybe that's why we've given it four stars—because it's one of the purest expressions of how Warhol not only explodes the categories of what art is (remember the famous Campbell's Soup can?) but also that he assaults in revolutionary fashion all the conventions we hold dear. CHELSEA GIRLS is historically notable for requiring two projectors operating side by side (not that the two separate films have any connection!) and for its popular success on the art house circuit, which subsequently opened its doors to other "underground" films. While perhaps not as potent or as clever as more compact masterworks like VINYL, BLOW JOB, BEAUTY #2, MY HUSTLER, NUDE RESTAURANT and LONESOME COWBOYS, CHELSEA GIRLS is probably the ultimate summation of Warhol's cinema. Check it out once… if you dare.

CHEYENNE AUTUMN
1964 159m c Western ★★★★
Warner Bros. (U.S.)

Richard Widmark *(Capt. Thomas Archer)*, Carroll Baker *(Deborah Wright)*, Karl Malden *(Capt. Oscar Wessels)*, James Stewart *(Wyatt Earp)*, Edward G. Robinson *(Carl Schurz)*, Sal Mineo *(Red Shirt)*, Dolores Del Rio *(Spanish Woman)*, Ricardo Montalban *(Little Wolf)*, Gilbert Roland *(Dull Knife)*, Arthur Kennedy *(Doc Holliday)*

p, Bernard Smith; d, John Ford; w, James R. Webb (based on the novel by Mari Sandoz); ph, William Clothier (Super Panavision 70, Technicolor); ed, Otho Lovering; m, Alex North; art d, Richard Day; fx, Ralph Webb; cos, Ann Peck, Frank Beetson

AAN Best Color Cinematography: William H. Clothier

This Ford frontier epic opens in 1887 with the Cheyenne nation waiting for a meeting with government representatives on a wretched Oklahoma reservation—a meeting that never takes place. When they are ignored in their pleas for food and housing, two chiefs (Montalban and Roland) defy the authorities and migrate back to their Wyoming homeland. Thus begins a heroic and tragic 1,500-mile trek—with a reluctant cavalry captain (Widmark) and his troops in unenthusiastic pursuit, intending to return the 300-strong Cheyenne to their miserable reservation. The captain's troops are outfought at every turn by the wily braves, while the press portrays the exodus as another Indian war, and even civilians Wyatt Earp (Stewart) and Doc Holliday (Kennedy) join halfheartedly in a posse to recapture the Native Americans.

Stunningly photographed by William Clothier, the film, in true Fordian fashion, once again makes fine use of that great western icon, Monument Valley. The acting, too, is generally quite good, some of it (Widmark, Robinson, Del Rio) squarely on the mark, some of it (Malden, Baker, Stewart) a trifle off-key at times. No single actor, however, stands out in CHEYENNE AUTUMN: it is ultimately the director's picture, and represents Ford's attitude toward the Native American coming around full circle. Flawed on several levels, Ford's perception of a proud people seen through a white man's eyes is ultimately a highly compelling and deeply personal apologia.

CHICAGO
2000 113m c Musical/Crime ★★★½
Miramax/Producer Circle Company/Zadan/ PG-13
Meron Productions/Kalis Productions GmbH
(U.S./Germany)

Catherine Zeta-Jones *(Velma Kelly)*, Renée Zellweger *(Roxie Hart)*, Richard Gere *(Billy Flynn)*, John C. Reilly *(Amos Hart)*,

Christine Baranski *(Mary Sunshine)*, Queen Latifah *(Matron Mama Morton)*, Lucy Liu *(Kitty Baxter)*, Taye Diggs *(Bandleader)*, Colm Feore *(Martin Harrison)*, Dominic West *(Fred Casely)*

p, Martin Richards; d, Rob Marshall; w, Bill Condon (based on the musical by Bob Fosse and Fred Ebb, and the play by Maurine Dallas Watkins); ph, Dion Beebe; ed, Martin Walsh; m, John Kander; prod d, John Myhre; art d, Andrew Stern; fx, Ted Ross; chor, Rob Marshall; cos, Colleen Atwood

AA Best Picture; AA Best Supporting Actress: Catherine Zeta-Jones; *AA Best Art Direction:* John Myhre (Art Direction), Gordon Sim (Set Decoration); *AA Best Costume Design:* Colleen Atwood; *AA Best Film Editing:* Martin Walsh; *AA Best Sound:* Michael Minkler, Dominick Tavella, David Lee; *AAN Best Actress:* Renee Zellweger; *AAN Best Supporting Actor:* John C. Reilly; *AAN Best Supporting Actress:* Queen Latifah; *AAN Best Cinematography:* Dion Beebe; *AAN Best Director:* Rob Marshall; *AAN Best Original Song:* "I Move On"; John Kander (music), Fred Ebb (lyrics); *AAN Best Adapted Screenplay:* Bill Condon

Bob Fosse's legendary stage musical gets the old-fashioned movie-musical treatment. When this casually cynical valentine to a pair of media-wise chippies who get away with murder opened in 1975, it was much admired than embraced; 27 years later, its knowing depiction of sin, spin, and fleeting celebrity seems almost quaint. But Broadway choreographer-director Rob Marshall's feature film debut is sleekly entertaining and polished to a glossy finish by an all-star cast who really can sing and dance.

One-time chorine Roxie Hart (Renee Zellweger), who dreams of stardom but settled for marriage to dependable Amos (John C. Reilly), shoots the bounder (Dominic West) who seduced her with the empty promise of show-biz introductions. Taken to Cook County Jail, Roxie finds herself on murderess' row, where slinky hoofer Velma Kelly (Catherine Zeta-Jones), who murdered her husband and sister when she caught them in the wrong kind of act, is the undisputed star. Roxie's loyal husband hires flamboyant criminal attorney Billy Flynn (Richard Gere), who gives Roxie a whole new image—the wronged naöf—and Velma is soon old news. But the trial still looms, and there's always a glamorous new murderess waiting in the wings.

Numbers have been trimmed and Fosse's choreography replaced by Marshall's (whose "Cell Block Tango" is a highlight), but the show's spirit remains intact, and unlike Baz Luhrmann (MOULIN ROUGE), Marshall generally prefers to let the musical numbers unfold in long shot rather than create movement through editing (ironically, the method Fosse the film director favored). Marshall and screenwriter Bill Condon's solution to contemporary audiences' discomfort with classical movie conventions is both straightforward and savvy: non-musical scenes that move the narrative forward are staged realistically, while the lavish production numbers reflect the star-struck imagination of Roxie, for whom all the world ought to be a stage.

CHICKEN RUN
2000 84m c Animated ★★★★
Aardman Animation/Pathe/DreamWorks SKG G
(U.K.)

VOICES OF: Mel Gibson *(Rocky)*, Julia Sawalha *(Ginger)*, Miranda Richardson *(Mrs. Tweedy)*, Jane Horrocks *(Babs)*, Lynn Ferguson *(Mac)*, Imelda Staunton *(Bunty)*, Benjamin Whitrow *(Fowler)*, Tony Haygarth *(Mr. Tweedy)*, Timothy Spall *(Nick)*, Phil Daniels *(Fetcher)*

p, Nick Park, Peter Lord, David Sproxton; d, Nick Park, Peter Lord; w, Karey Kirkpatrick (based on an original story by Nick Park and Peter Lord); ph, Dave Alex Riddett; ed, Mark Solomon; m, John Powell, Harry Gregson-Williams; prod d, Phil Lewis; art d, Tim Farrington; fx, Paddy Eason, Mark Nelmes, Computer Film Company; anim, Loyd Price (supervisor), Dave Osmond, Merlin

Crossingham, Sergio Delfino, Suzy Fagan, Guionne Leroy, Darren Robbie, Jason Spencer-Galsworthy, Jay Grace, Seamus Malone, Ian Whitlock

Talk about your chick flicks. Portions of THE GREAT ESCAPE and NORMA RAE are scrambled to perfection in this soaring adventure comedy, then seasoned with a whimsical dash of Rube Goldberg.

The action takes place on an English egg farm owned and mismanaged by a pair of dour martinets called the Tweedys (voiced by Miranda Richardson and Tony Haygarth). It looks more like a prison camp than a farm, and the feathered inmates of Coop 17 (think STALAG 17) want out. Mobilized by a British clucker named Ginger (Julia Sawalha), the hens hatch a series of hapless escape plans. Their bid for freedom becomes desperate when the greedy Tweedys decide to abandon the egg business for the ready-to-bake chicken potpie trade, and purchase an enormous contraption that will get rid of those lazy hens once and for all. It's now or never: if the chickens don't fly the coop, they'll all be fricasseed. Enter an American rooster named Rocky (Mel Gibson), an escapee from a traveling circus who may be the Yank they thank. Or will they?

This is the first full-length feature film from England's Aardman Animation, best known for Nick Park's Oscar-winning *Wallace & Gromit* shorts; it shares their offbeat sensibility, paired with eye-popping animation effects and a solid story. Co-directed and animated by Park and Peter Lord, this ripping yarn is funny, thrilling, and slyly sophisticated. The voice cast, including Gibson, Richardson and former *Absolutely Fabulous* cast members Sawalha and Jane Horrocks (as dizzy hen Babs), is exceptional: Who'd have thought you'd find yourself caring so much about the fate of a flock of fryers? This chicken has legs—lots of them.

CHILDREN OF A LESSER GOD   DVD

1986 119m c Romance/Drama   ★★★★
Paramount (U.S.)   R

William Hurt *(James Leeds)*, Marlee Matlin *(Sarah Norman)*, Piper Laurie *(Mrs. Norman)*, Philip Bosco *(Dr. Curtis Franklin)*, Allison Gompf *(Lydia)*, John F. Cleary *(Johnny)*, Philip Holmes *(Glen)*, Georgia Ann Cline *(Cheryl)*, William D. Byrd *(Danny)*, Frank Carter Jr. *(Tony)*

p, Burt Sugarman, Patrick Palmer; d, Randa Haines; w, Hesper Anderson, Mark Medoff (based on his stage play); ph, John Seale (Medallion Film Lab Color); ed, Lisa Fruchtman; m, Michael Convertino; prod d, Gene Callahan; art d, Barbara Matis; cos, Renee April

AAN Best Picture; AAN Best Actor: William Hurt; *AA Best Actress:* Marlee Matlin; *AAN Best Supporting Actress:* Piper Laurie; *AAN Best Adapted Screenplay:* Hesper Anderson, Mark Medoff

Nicely helmed by first-time feature director Haines, CHILDREN OF A LESSER GOD is a poignant yet uplifting love story involving a speech teacher and a deaf young woman. James Leeds (Hurt) is a maverick instructor newly arrived at a facility for the hearing impaired, where he meets Sarah Norman (Matlin), a graduate of the school who has chosen to stay and work in a menial job rather than attempt to go out into the world that the school has supposedly taught her to face. He falls in love with her almost instantly, but she resists him at first and also steadfastly refuses to read lips or attempt to talk; she insists on signing. In an attempt to learn why Sarah will not venture out into the world, Leeds visits her mother (Laurie) and discovers the root of Sarah's bitterness.

The major problem with the movie is that the audience is never left to its own interpretive devices. Because Matlin's hearing is severely impaired in real life, Hurt translates everything she signs for the benefit of viewers. Some of this may have been necessary, but Matlin's silent acting is so expressive that we often know exactly what is going through her mind as the emotions flicker across her face, and the translation routine interrupts the flow of the story time and again for no good reason. Nevertheless, despite this flaw, several dramatic lulls, and an aggressive determination to "sparkle," the film often makes for crackling good drama with plenty of leavening humor and magnificent performances by Hurt and newcomer Matlin.

CHILDREN OF HEAVEN   DVD
(BACHEHA-YE ASEMAN)
1997 88m c Drama   ★★★★
Institute for the Intellectual Development of
Children and Young Adults (Iran)

Amir Naji *(Ali's Father)*, Amir Farrokh Hashemian *(Ali)*, Bahare Sediqi *(Zahra)*, Nafise Jafar-Mohammadi *(Roya)*, Fereshte Sarabandi *(Ali's Mother)*, Kamal Mir Karimi *(Assistant)*, Behzad Rafiee *(Trainer)*, Dariush Mokhtari *(Ali's Teacher)*, Moahammad-Hasan Hosseinian *(Roya's Father)*, Masume Dair *(Roya's Mother)*

d, Majid Majidi; w, Majid Majidi; ph, Parviz Malekezade; ed, Hassan Hassandoost; m, Keivan Jahanshahi

AAN Best Foreign Language Film

If you think recent Iranian cinema is all about slow pacing, allegorical plotting, and symbolic goldfish like the one that drives Jafar Panah's acclaimed WHITE BALLOON, you're in for a pleasant surprise. This utterly charming feature from writer-director Majid Majidi is not only wonderfully entertaining, it's also one of the best children's films in recent memory.

One afternoon, on his way back from the cobbler's, nine-year-old Ali (Amir Farrokh Hashemian) accidentally loses his sister's only pair of shoes in a bustling Tehran marketplace. The loss is a catastrophe—without her shoes, Zahra (Bahare Sediqi) can't go to school—but the siblings decide not to burden their impoverished parents with this additional bit of misfortune. Instead, Ali devises a scheme whereby he and his sister can share his one pair of tattered sneakers: Zahra can wear them to school in the morning, then rush to a pre-arranged rendezvous point where she'll hand them off to Ali in time for his afternoon classes.

The children's determination to help each other and protect their parents is a touching illustration of honor and resourcefulness in the face of grinding poverty, and gives Majidi an opportunity to demonstrate his belief that the proof of the essential goodness of human beings lies not in the grand gesture, but in small, everyday kindnesses. Majidi delivers his message with an extraordinarily light touch, and his two very young leads are terrific. Sure, it's sentimental. But no more so than, say, THE BICYCLE THIEF. The film even climaxes with an exciting footrace before ending on a simple moment of quiet grace—complete with goldfish.

CHILDREN OF PARADISE   DVD
(LES ENFANTS DU PARADIS)
1945 195m bw Romance   ★★★★★
S.N. Pathe (France)

Arletty *(Garance)*, Jean-Louis Barrault *(Baptiste Debureau)*, Pierre Brasseur *(Frederick Lemaitre)*, Marcel Herrand *(Lacenaire)*, Pierre Renoir *(Jericho)*, Maria Casares *(Natalie)*, Etienne Decroux *(Anselme Debureau)*, Fabien Loris *(Avril)*, Leon Larive *(Stage Doorman, "Funambules")*, Pierre Palov *(Stage Manager, "Funambules")*

p, Fred Orain; d, Marcel Carne; w, Jacques Prevert; ph, Roger Hubert, Marc Fossard; ed, Henri Rust, Madeleine Bonin; m, Maurice Thiriet, Joseph Kosma, George Mouque; art d, Leon Barsacq, R. Cabutti, Alexander Trauner

AAN Best Original Screenplay: Jacques Prevert

"Anyone who can resist its flamboyant charm deserves never to see Paris," wrote critic Andrew Sarris of CHILDREN OF PARADISE. It's been called France's answer to GONE WITH THE WIND, the greatest French film ever made, and an overrated bore. Filmed under a plethora of Nazi regulations with a cast peppered with Resistance fighters, the making of this film is almost as interesting as the end result. What is especially fascinating is how Marxist screenwriter Prevert and director Carne were able to pull off a thinly disguised allegory of French resistance under the German occupation.

The story, which takes place in the Paris of the 1820s and '30s, is a complex tale of unrequited love, illicit affairs, jealousy, and romance revolving around the world of theater folk, criminals, and aristocrats. The "children of paradise" are the poor people who inhabit the topmost balconies of the theaters along the Boulevard du Temple, and they are witness to the story of theater mime Baptiste (Barrault) and his true love Garance (Arletty). Along the way we are treated to delightful theater shows, duels, love amidst rain showers, and unfortunate misunderstandings with tragic consequences.

Deliberately theatrical but nevertheless greatly indebted to French poetic realism, CHILDREN OF PARADISE is lovingly handled by director Carne. The entire film is crammed with incident and an intoxicating eye for detail. Trauner's art direction is one of his finest achievements and the music by Kosma, Thiriet, and Mouque both onstage and off is a constant delight. Based on this one performance alone, gifted mime, comic and tragedian Barrault must take his place as one of the century's greatest actors. The raven-haired, fascinating Arletty, meanwhile, was the closest the French ever got to creating their own Marlene Dietrich. Among a superior supporting cast, Brasseur, Herrand, Renoir, Casares, Marker, Salou, and Modot (as a "blind" beggar who can actually see) are particularly outstanding, and the end result is utterly beguiling cinema.

CHILLY SCENES OF WINTER

1979 92m c Drama ★★★½
UA Classics (U.S.) PG

John Heard (Charles), Mary Beth Hurt (Laura), Peter Riegert (Sam), Kenneth McMillan (Pete), Gloria Grahame (Clara), Nora Heflin (Betty), Jerry Hardin (Patterson), Tarah Nutter (Susan), Mark Metcalf (Ox), Allen Joseph (Blind Man)

p, Mark Metcalf, Amy Robinson, Griffin Dunne; d, Joan Micklin Silver; w, Joan Micklin Silver (based on the novel Head Over Heels by Ann Beattie); ph, Bobby Byrne (Metrocolor); ed, Cynthia Scheider; m, Ken Lauber; prod d, Peter Jamison

Directed by Joan Micklin Silver (HESTER STREET, CROSSING DELANCEY) and based on a novel by Ann Beattie, CHILLY SCENES OF WINTER focuses on Charles (Heard), an office worker who falls in love with Laura (Hurt) while she is separated from her husband. When Laura returns to her spouse, Charles remains obsessed with her, sitting outside her home in his car watching the lights, even going to visit her and her husband, accompanied by his good friend Sam (Riegert). Retaining the mournful tone of Beattie's excellent novel, Silver delivers a slow-moving, occasionally funny, but deeply affecting film blessed with outstanding understated performances by Heard, Hurt, Riegert, and screen veteran Grahame, on hand in a memorable turn as Charles's suicidal mother. Look for author Beattie in a bit part as a waitress.

CHIMES AT MIDNIGHT
(CAMPANADAS A MEDIANOCHE)
1966 116m bw Drama/War/Historical ★★★½
Films Espanola/Alpine (Spain/Switzerland)

Orson Welles (Sir John "Jack" Falstaff), Keith Baxter (Prince Hal—later King Henry V), John Gielgud (King Henry IV), Margaret Rutherford (Mistress Quickly), Jeanne Moreau (Doll Tearsheet), Norman Rodway (Henry Percy—"Hotspur"), Marina Vlady (Kate Percy), Alan Webb (Justice Shallow), Tony Beckley (Poins), Fernando Rey (Worcester)

p, Emiliano Piedra, Angel Escolano; d, Orson Welles; w, Orson Welles (based on the plays Henry IV Parts I & II, Henry V, Richard II, and The Merry Wives of Windsor by William Shakespeare; and The Chronicles of England by Raphael Holinshed); ph, Edmond Richard; ed, Fritz Mueller; m, Angelo Francesco Lavagnino; prod d, Gustavo Quintana; art d, Jose Antonio de la Guerra, Mariano Erdorza; cos, Cornejo Madrid

Orson Welles' brooding, sometimes brilliant art-house film dwells on the tragic side of one of Shakespeare's most famous comic characters. Seamlessly integrating portions of Shakespeare's Richard II, Henry IV, Henry V, and The Merry Wives of Windsor, along with (in the narration by Ralph Richardson) Raphael Holinshed's The Chronicles of England, CHIMES AT MIDNIGHT is one of the finest cinematic translations of the Bard.

Sir John Falstaff (Welles) is the massive, blustering companion to Prince Hal (Baxter), heir to the besieged British throne. Reluctant to assume the duties of kingship, Hal passes his time drinking and carousing with Falstaff. Finally, however, he goes into battle, slaying the honorable, doomed challenger to the crown, Hotspur (Rodway), and he soon thereafter becomes Henry V. Bursting in on the coronation, certain that a high title is forthcoming, Falstaff encounters instead the scorn of the now high-and-mighty Hal.

While not as technically dazzling as CITIZEN KANE (indeed, some are quick to condemn the somewhat confusing editing and murky sound—evidence of the project's haphazard shooting schedule), CHIMES AT MIDNIGHT is the work of a mature artist and proof of Welles's great flair for Shakespearean dramaturgy. Although the film downplays the comic aspects of the Falstaff-Hal relationship, the two lead performances are splendid, with Baxter alternately playful, cunning, icy, and commanding and Welles giving the performance of his career in a part he deeply understands. The moment of Falstaff's rejection is probably the single most moving piece of acting Welles ever committed to film.

Although fans of Moreau and Rutherford may be disappointed by their modestly sized roles, there are compensations, especially in the perfect performance of Gielgud as Henry IV. The film includes one of the best battle scenes ever—a brutal, chaotic affair fought on a mud-soaked field, with the waddling knight Falstaff making every attempt to escape death.

CHINA SYNDROME, THE
1979 122m c Drama ★★★½
IPC (U.S.) PG

Jane Fonda (Kimberly Wells), Jack Lemmon (Jack Godell), Michael Douglas (Richard Adams), Scott Brady (Herman DeYoung), James Hampton (Bill Gibson), Peter Donat (Don Jacovich), Wilford Brimley (Ted Spindler), Richard Herd (Evan McCormack), Daniel Valdez (Hector Salas), Stan Bohrman (Peter Martin)

p, Michael Douglas; d, James Bridges; w, Mike Gray, T.S. Cook, James Bridges; ph, James Crabe (Metrocolor); ed, David Rawlins; art d, George Jenkins; fx, Henry Millar; cos, Donfeld

AAN Best Actor: Jack Lemmon; AAN Best Actress: Jane Fonda; AAN Best Original Screenplay: Mike Gray (Story), T.S. Cook (Story),

James Bridges (Story); *AAN Best Art Direction-Set Decoration:* George Jenkins (Art Direction), Arthur Jeph Parker (Set Decoration)

Life imitates art. What began as a fanciful premise in the minds of many turned into reality a few weeks after this picture opened when the Three Mile Island nuclear reactor had a dreadful accident.

Fonda plays Kimberly Wells, a television reporter trying to advance from cutesy features to harder news. Douglas is Richard Adams, a freelance cameraman she hires while attempting to do a story on nuclear energy. They're fortuitously present at a power plant when a crisis arises, and a meltdown is narrowly avoided by the quick reactions of engineer Jack Godell (Lemmon). Richard has it all on film and rushes it back to the station, but management won't put it on the air. Godell, meanwhile, is outraged when he learns that the authorities have covered up the incident. He searches the plant and discovers the problem: faulty welding from a cut-rate construction job. He contacts the reporters and gives them X-rays of the offending equipment. But when sound man Hector Salas (Valdez) is murdered while taking out a hearing on a proposed nuclear project, Godell realizes that his superiors will stop at nothing to cover up their criminal negligence. Meanwhile, Kimberly's transformation from naif to political activist—a Fonda trademark in '70s films from TOUT VA BIEN to COMING HOME—becomes the real substance of the narrative.

A film more open than most about its political stance, THE CHINA SYNDROME effectively deploys its polemic within the framework of a nightmarish but convincing story. The lack of incidental music adds to the quasi-documentary feel; tight scripting and direction ably maintain suspense during the protracted climax. The sometimes self-conscious and too-earnest Fonda and the occasionally hammy Lemmon both rise beautifully to the occasion, delivering performances that are among their best. In other roles Douglas, Brimley, Hampton, Brady, and Bohrman (an actual reporter who would go on to cover the Three Mile Island incident) offer sterling support. Not a comforting film, but an undeniably potent one.

CHINATOWN

1974 131m c Mystery ★★★★★
Freedom Service Company/Long Road Pictures/ R
Penthouse/Paramount (U.S.)

Jack Nicholson *(J.J. Gittes)*, Faye Dunaway *(Evelyn Mulwray)*, John Huston *(Noah Cross)*, Perry Lopez *(Escobar)*, John Hillerman *(Yelburton)*, Darrell Zwerling *(Hollis Mulwray)*, Diane Ladd *(Ida Sessions)*, Roy Jenson *(Mulvihill)*, Roman Polanski *(Man with Knife)*, Richard Bakalyan *(Loach)*

p, Robert Evans; d, Roman Polanski; w, Robert Towne; ph, John A. Alonzo (Panavision, Technicolor); ed, Sam O'Steen; m, Jerry Goldsmith; prod d, Richard Sylbert; art d, Stewart Campbell; fx, Logan Frazee; cos, Anthea Sylbert

AAN Best Picture; AAN Best Actor: Jack Nicholson; AAN Best Actress: Faye Dunaway; AAN Best Director: Roman Polanski; AA Best Original Screenplay: Robert Towne; AAN Best Cinematography: John A. Alonzo; AAN Best Film Editing: Sam O'Steen; AAN Best Original Dramatic Score: Jerry Goldsmith; AAN Best Art Direction-Set Decoration: Richard Sylbert, W. Stewart Campbell, Ruby Levitt; AAN Best Costume Design: Anthea Sylbert; AAN Best Sound: Bud Grenzbach, Lawrence Jost

A wonderfully brooding, suspenseful revisitation of the land of film noir, CHINATOWN is not only one of the greatest detective films, but one of the most perfectly constructed of all films. With Polanski's brilliant direction, Towne's intricate

screenplay, and Nicholson's and Dunaway's tour de force performances, the film stands as one of the best of the 1970s.

The plot revolves around Gittes (Nicholson), a Chandleresque private eye who specializes in the most distasteful of detective enterprises—snooping after straying spouses. After being duped by a woman pretending to be the wife of the city water commissioner, Gittes meets the man's real wife, Evelyn Mulwray (Dunaway), but before long she ends up a widow. Drawn into these strange goings-on, Gittes follows a jigsaw puzzle of clues that leads to Mulwray's father, Cross (Huston). Cross has involved himself in the "future" of Los Angeles by engineering a plot to divert the city's water supply for his own gain.

Besides telling a gripping story involving incest and political graft, CHINATOWN recaptures the atmosphere of Los Angeles, 1937—the cars, clothes, and buildings, right down to the barber chairs (kudos to production designer Richard Sylbert and costumer Anthea Sylbert). The tone and flavor of this film evoke strong memories of MURDER, MY SWEET and the original THE BIG SLEEP, yet it stands singularly on its own merits. Even the muted color cinematography (normally antithetical to the tenets of noir) is evocative and appropriate. Interestingly, Towne's script included not a single scene set in Chinatown—initially a metaphorical state of mind rather than a specific place.

Look for director Polanski as the thug who pokes a switchblade up Nicholson's nostril while uttering the infamous line, "You know what happens to nosy fellows? They lose their noses." Another highlight: Dunaway's "sister… daughter… sister….daughter" routine, a camp classic much parodied since. CHINATOWN earned 11 Oscar nominations, including Best Picture, but only Towne took home a statuette for his cynical screenplay.

CHLOE IN THE AFTERNOON

(L'AMOUR L'APRES-MIDI)
1972 97m c Drama ★★★
Losange/Barbet Schroeder (France) R

Bernard Verley *(Frederic)*, Zouzou *(Chloe)*, Francoise Verley *(Helene)*, Daniel Ceccaldi *(Gerard)*, Malvina Penne *(Fabienne)*, Babette Ferrier *(Martine)*, Tina Michelino, Jean-Louis Livi, Pierre Nunzi, Irene Skobline

p, Pierre Cottrell; d, Eric Rohmer; w, Eric Rohmer; ph, Nestor Almendros; ed, Cecile Decugis; m, Arie Dzierlatka; art d, Nicole Rachline

This sixth and final installment of Rohmer's "Six Moral Tales" focuses, for the first time in the series, on the married Frederic (Bernard Verley), a professional who spends very little time with his equally business-minded wife, Helene (Francoise Verley). The first part of the film is essentially a prologue as it carefully sets up the male lead's character. He is a man easily seduced—but only mentally. Frederic imagines what certain women (a wonderful series of cameos by previous Rohmer heroines) are like, concocting romantic adventures with them as they walk down the street. In one telling scene, he purchases a shirt from a pretty saleswoman only because he cannot resist her charms. Having settled into marriage, he dreams only of love in the afternoon (as the original French title translates). Then into Frederic's life walks Chloe (Zouzou), an attractive, sexy mystery woman determined to seduce him.

A fitting close to the series, which finally marries off one of Rohmer's romantic heroes, reunites all his previous heroines, and addresses the basic theme of marital infidelity. To a greater degree than his previous films, Rohmer (to the surprise of those who find his work talky and boring) invests CHLOE IN THE AFTERNOON with a surprising amount of suspense—not the obvious sort, but a variety that is quieter, emotional—with all the tension and conflict occurring inside the character's mind. In this respect Rohmer seems a deserving recipient of the soubriquet "the Henry James of cinema."

CHOCOLAT 📀
2000 121m c Romance/Comedy/Drama ★★★★
Fat Free Ltd./Miramax (U.S.) PG-13

Juliette Binoche (Vianne Rocher), Lena Olin (Josephine Muscat), Johnny Depp (Roux), Judi Dench (Armande Voizin), Alfred Molina (Comte de Reynaud), Peter Stormare (Serge Muscat), Carrie-Anne Moss (Caroline Clairmont), Leslie Caron (Madame Audel), John Wood (Guillaume Bierot), Victoire Thivisol (Anouk Rocher)

p, David Brown, Kit Golden, Leslie Holleran; d, Lasse Hallstrom; w, Robert Nelson Davis (based on the novel by Joanne Harris); ph, Roger Pratt; ed, Andrew Mondshein; m, Rachel Portman; prod d, David Gropman; art d, Lucy Richardson; fx, Stuart Brisdon, Anthony Hunt, Mill Film; cos, Renee Ehrlich Kalfus

AAN Best Picture; AAN Best Actress: Juliette Binoche; AAN Best Supporting Actress: Judi Dench; AAN Best Original Score: Rachel Portman; AAN Best Adapted Screenplay: Robert Nelson Jacobs

A trifle with substance.

It's 1959, and the sleepy French village of Lansquenet-sous-Tannes is awakened (aroused?) by the arrival of Vianne Rocher (Juliette Binoche) and her array of chocolate confections. Vianne's a rambling gal of a particularly prim and proper sort; with six-year-old daughter Anouk (Victoire Thivisol) in tow, she wanders from city to city opening *chocolateries* and dispensing age-old cacao remedies for heart and soul. Lansquenet's devout mayor, the Comte de Reynaud (Alfred Molina), who watches over the town with an officious Catholic piety, doesn't approve. He views the free-spirited Vianne as a threat: How dare she tempt fasting parishioners with confections during Lent! Vianne, of course, *is* a threat, but less to the town's tranquility than to its look-the-other-way complacency. Little by little, her various sweets help raise the town's spirits (among other things, considering the aphrodisiacal chocolate beans fed to unwary husbands by their wives) until the arrival of some raffish river travelers, led by the Irishman Roux (Johnny Depp), leads to a momentary civil-rights crisis.

Binoche marvelously invests Vianne with enough anger and self-doubt that she's never merely an idealized wandering angel, and as a vinegary matriarch, Dame Judi Dench manages to wring eloquence from such lines as, "It tastes like... I don't know." The most delicious performance, however, is Molina's; his Comte may be an oily priss and rumor monger, but he's honorable in his intentions and is never hypocritical. It's all a bit obvious and more than a little didactic, but the film still burbles with delightful dialogue and a sparkling sense of life.

CHOOSE ME 📀
1984 106m c Romance/Comedy/Drama ★★★★
Island Alive (U.S.) R

Keith Carradine (Mickey), Lesley Ann Warren (Eve), Genevieve Bujold (Ann/Dr. Nancy Lovell), Patrick Bauchau (Zack Antoine), Rae Dawn Chong (Pearl Antoine), John Larroquette (Billy Ace), Edward Ruscha (Ralph Chomsky), Gailard Sartain (Mueller), Robert Gould (Lou), John Considine (Dr. Ernest Greene)

p, Carolyn Pfeiffer, David Blocker; d, Alan Rudolph; w, Alan Rudolph; ph, Jan Kiesser (Movielab Color); ed, Mia Goldman; prod d, Steven Legler; art d, Steven Legler; cos, Tracy Tynan

Director Alan Rudolph hit his stride with this quirky comedy-drama in which the characterizations outweigh and eventually overwhelm the plot. Ann (Bujold) is a radio psychologist calling herself "Dr. Love" who dispenses advice but is hopelessly maladjusted herself. Eve (Warren), meanwhile, the owner of a small bar, is both blessed and cursed

with the ability to attract and capture any man she pleases. But Eve is not the supremely self-confident person she seems; she is actually a frightened woman living on the edge of a breakdown who spends a lot of time calling Dr. Love. Then Mickey (Carradine), a wayward genius or the world's greatest liar, walks into the bar and into the lives of both Eve and Ann.

This picture is made up of many fine moments and many wonderful verbal insights. There's not much of a story here, but, in typical fashion, director Rudolph wisely allows the film to gently meander in several interesting directions. Lushly photographed and very well acted, with a relaxed, bleary-eyed, three a.m. feel to it, this sometimes surprising little film is an intriguing piece of work.

CHORUS, THE 📀
(LES CHORISTES)
2004 96m c Drama ★★★
Galatee Films/Pathe Renn Productions/ PG-13
France 2 Cinema/Novo Arturo Films/
Vega Film AG (France/Switzerland)

Gerard Jugnot (Clement Mathieu), Francois Berleand (Rachin), Kad Merad (Chabert), Jean-Paul Bonnaire (Old Maxence), Marie Bunel (Violette Morhange), Jacques Perrin (Adult Pierre Morhange), Didier Flamand (Adult Pepinot), Paul Charieras (Regent), Carole Weiss (The Countess), Jean-Baptiste Maunier (Pierre Morhange)

p, Arthur Cohn, Nicolas Mauvernay, Jacques Perrin; d, Christophe Barratier; w, Christophe Barratier, Philippe Lopes Curval (based on the movie LA CAGE AUX ROSSIGNOLS/A CAGE OF NIGHTINGALES); ph, Dominque Gentil; ed, Carlo Varini; m, Yves Deschamps; prod d, Francois Chauvaud; cos, Francoise Guegan

AAN Best Foreign Language Film; AAN Best Original Song: "Look to Your Path (Vois Sur Ton Chemin)"; Bruno Coulais (music), Christophe Barratier (lyrics)

A strong sense of nostalgia pervades this remake of an obscure 1945 French film, not just for post-WWII France, but for the kind of movie in which incorrigible mop-tops are rehabilitated by a dedicated teacher (GOODBYE, MR. CHIPS) and his deep love of music (MR. HOLLAND'S OPUS). And surprisingly, there's a lot to enjoy, even as the film quickly surrenders to its sweetest impulses.

France, 1949: Failed composer Clement Mathieu (Gerard Jugnot) arrives at the school for wayward boys appropriately named Fond de L'Etang—"Rock Bottom"—where he's been hired to replace the departing supervisor. Mathieu's naive hope and enthusiasm are quickly dampened by the realization that there's little room for either at the grim institution. Even more forbidding than the school's dank accommodations and sneering, unruly student body is sour-faced Principal Rachin (Francois Berleand), a petty martinet who runs his school according to a simple zero-tolerance philosophy. Undaunted, Mathieu is determined to reach these so-called bad boys. After a group of them, including young Morhange (Jean-Baptiste Maunier), steal his satchel containing pages of musical notations and then later sing a teasing rhyme about Mathieu's bald head, the teacher gets an idea: Why not try to whip these out-of-control kids into a boys choir? A chorus will not only teach discipline and help the boys develop a talent they can take pride in, but enable Mathieu to further his dream of becoming a composer. Rachin is unconvinced but willing to allow this foolish idealist to give it a shot. If Mathieu's little "experiment" fails, however, he'll lose his job.

First-time director Christophe Barratier has assembled an unforgettable gallery of faces both young and old, and prolific character actor Berleand plays the perfect villain; his Rachin is enough to make veteran meanie George MacCready look like an absolute pussycat.

CHRISTMAS IN CONNECTICUT
1945   102m   bw   Comedy   ★★★½
Warner Bros.   (U.S.)

Barbara Stanwyck *(Elisabeth Lane)*, Dennis Morgan *(Jefferson Jones)*, Sydney Greenstreet *(Alexander Yardley)*, Reginald Gardiner *(John Sloan)*, S.Z. Sakall *(Felix Bassenak)*, Robert Shayne *(Dudley Beecham)*, Una O'Connor *(Norah)*, Frank Jenks *(Sinkewicz)*, Joyce Compton *(Mary Lee)*, Dick Elliott *(Judge Crothers)*

p, William Jacobs; d, Peter Godfrey; w, Lionel Houser, Adele Comandini (based on a story by Aileen Hamilton); ph, Carl Guthrie; ed, Frank Magee; m, Frederick Hollander; art d, Stanley Fleischer; cos, Edith Head

A sometimes hilarious farce and a holiday favorite. Stanwyck stars as Elisabeth Lane, a successful but scheming columnist who pretends to be a happy, supercompetent housewife. Compelled to take in Navy hero Jefferson Jones (Morgan) for the holidays as part of a promotion gimmick concocted by her hoodwinked publisher Alexander Yardley (Greenstreet), Elisabeth must deal with the reality that she doesn't own the country home she writes about, can't cook, and isn't married. In desperation, she convinces lounge lizard John Sloan (Gardiner) to play the role of hubby, rents a rustic house, and brings in a world-famous chef (Sakall, genuinely amusing but best taken in small doses) to cover up her own inadequacies.

Director Godfrey's handling of the material is rather mild and not especially creative, but he does keep things lively, and Stanwyck proves her considerable flair for comedy. It's also nice to see a very relaxed Greenstreet in something other than melodrama for a change. The film's endorsement of housewifery over working outside the home is obvious, but to the film's credit its attitude is a heartily self-mocking one.

CHRISTMAS IN JULY
1940   67m   bw   Comedy   ★★★★
Paramount   (U.S.)

Dick Powell *(Jimmy MacDonald)*, Ellen Drew *(Betty Casey)*, Raymond Walburn *(Dr. Maxford)*, Alexander Carr *(Mr. Schindel)*, William Demarest *(Mr. Bildocker)*, Ernest Truex *(Mr. Baxter)*, Franklin Pangborn *(Radio Announcer)*, Harry Hayden *(Mr. Waterbury)*, Rod Cameron *(Dick)*, Adrian Morris, billed as Michael Morris *(Tom)*

p, Paul Jones; d, Preston Sturges; w, Preston Sturges; ph, Victor Milner; ed, Ellsworth Hoagland; art d, Hans Dreier, Earl Hedrick; cos, Harriet Altland, Joe Kaplan, Murray Foster

The great Preston Sturges wrote and directed CHRISTMAS IN JULY, an hysterically funny, short and sweet comedy about a man who goes on a spending spree after he thinks he's won a coffee-slogan contest, only to learn that the whole thing was a practical joke.

Jimmy MacDonald (Dick Powell), a lowly clerk at the Baxter Coffee Company, enters a $25,000 slogan contest for the Maxford House Coffee Company. But on the night the winner is to be announced on the radio, the jury is deadlocked because of an obstinate juror. The next day at work, some pranksters make up a phony telegram and put it on Jimmy's desk, saying that he has won the contest. Jimmy immediately goes to collect his check from Dr. Maxford (Raymond Walburn) and promptly begins spending his newfound wealth.

CHRISTMAS was a little underrated in its time, perhaps because of its very brief running time and seemingly frivolous nature, but in retrospect, it emerges as one of Sturges's funniest and most purely enjoyable films. Sturges's customary frantic pace is even more dizzying than usual, the dialogue is filled with hilarious wisecracks, puns, double-entendres and malapropisms, and in just over an hour, the film manages to encompass slapstick, satire, screwball comedy, pathos, and melodrama. As in all of Sturges's films,

the story is really a fable about the pursuit of the American dream, making wry observations about failure and success, and money and happiness.

One of the great pleasures of Sturges's movies was the stock company of superb character actors who were the heart and soul of all his films, and CHRISTMAS is packed with them. Besides the delightful William Demarest as Mr. Bildocker; there's Franklin Pangborn as a prissy radio announcer; Raymond Walburn as the dyspeptic Maxford; and Frank Moran as a boisterous cop. CHRISTMAS IN JULY remains a wonderful present that's perfect for anytime of the year.

CHRISTMAS STORY, A   DVD
1983   98m   c   Comedy   ★★★★
MGM   (U.S.)   PG

Melinda Dillon *(Mother)*, Darren McGavin *(Old Man)*, Peter Billingsley *(Ralphie)*, Ian Petrella *(Randy)*, Scott Schwartz *(Flick)*, R.D. Robb *(Schuartz)*, Tedde Moore *(Miss Shields)*, Yano Anaya *(Grover)*, Zack Ward *(Scot)*, Jeff Gillen *(Santa Claus)*

p, Rene Dupont, Bob Clark; d, Bob Clark; w, Jean Shepherd, Leigh Brown, Bob Clark (based on the novel *In God We Trust, All Others Pay Cash* by Jean Shepherd); ph, Reginald Morris; ed, Stan Cole; m, Carl Zittrer, Paul Zaza; art d, Gavin Mitchell; cos, Mary McLeod

Somehow usually tasteless director Bob Clark, whose specialty was fairly vile exploitation movies (PORKY'S and the even worse PORKY'S II: THE NEXT DAY), managed to make a totally charming and lovable Christmas film.

Based on the short stories of midwestern humorist Jean Shepherd (who also narrates in the first person), A CHRISTMAS STORY is an episodic comedy set in the 1940s about the family life of young Ralphie (Billingsley) as Christmas approaches. The plot loosely revolves around Ralphie's desire for a Red Ryder BB gun for Christmas that his mother (Dillon) has forbidden because she's afraid he'll shoot his eyes out. Among Shepherd's childhood musings are his narrow escapes from the neighborhood bullies, the battles of his old man (McGavin) with the smoke-belching furnace, Mom's attempts to get his little brother (Petrella) to eat, Dad's infatuation with an obnoxious lamp that looks like a woman's leg, and a nightmarish visit with Santa at the local department store.

The cast is wonderful—especially McGavin, Billingsley and Petrella—the laughs are nonstop if rarely subtle, and the whole thing deserves to become a Christmastime classic.

CHUCK & BUCK   DVD
2000   96m   c   Comedy/Drama   ★★★½
Blow Up Pictures/Flan de Coco Films/   R
Toga Productions   (U.S.)

Mike White *(Buck)*, Chris Weitz *(Chuck)*, Lupe Ontiveros *(Beverly)*, Beth Colt *(Carlyn)*, Paul Weitz *(Sam)*, Maya Rudolph *(Jamila)*, Mary Wigmore *(Diane)*, Paul Sand *(Barry)*, Gino Buccola *(Tommy)*, Doug Keifer *(Mark)*

p, Matthew Greenfield; d, Miguel Arteta; w, Mike White; ph, Chuy Chavez; ed, Jeff Betancourt; m, Joey Waronker, Tony Maxwell, Smokey Hormel; prod d, Renee Davenport; cos, Elaine Montalvo

Combine Todd Solondz's rueful affection for life's weirdos with the queasy comic appeal of Adam Sandler's baby-man characters, and you have this creepy comedy.

Buck O'Brien (Michael White), 27, still lives with his ailing mother in the suburban house where he grew up, or more properly, failed to grow up. When his mother dies, Buck invites childhood best friend Chuck Sitter (AMERICAN PIE producer Chris Weitz) to the funeral and attempts to rekindle their intense prepubescent closeness. But Chuck—now Charlie, a high-powered, L.A. music-industry executive with a polished fiancee named Carlyn (Beth Colt)—isn't interested in reintroducing the socially maladroit Buck into his life, and he's especially not interested in resuming the precocious sex games they played as kids. With the persistence of a child and the wherewithal of an adult, Buck moves to California and pursues Chuck relentlessly. Rebuffed, he writes an unsettling play called "Hank & Frank" that casts their personal history in warped fairy-tale terms, and produces it at a local playhouse with a hopelessly inept actor (Paul Weitz, AMERICAN PIE's director and Chris Weitz's brother) who reminds him of Chuck in the lead.

Shot on digital video and directed by Miguel Arteta, this hard-to-categorize picture is a bracing antidote to Hollywood's usual positioning of FORREST GUMP-style man-children as holy innocents. Buck is an alarming combination: emotionally childlike, but with a man's desires and capabilities. White and Arteta's remarkable achievement lies in making Buck and Chuck equally comprehensible, even if neither can really be called sympathetic. Arteta wrings some laughs from their bizarre (and more than a little frightening) situation, but they're uncomfortable laughs—emotional protection from the freak show.

CHUNGKING EXPRESS
(CHONGQING SENLIN)
1994 100m c Drama/Romance/Comedy ★★★★½
Jet Tone (Hong Kong) R

Brigitte Lin (The Drug Dealer), Takeshi Kaneshiro (Ho Chi-wu—Cop #223), Tony Leung Chiu-wai (Cop #663), Faye Wong (Faye), Valerie Chow (Air Hostess), "Piggy" Chan (Manager of "Midnight Express"), Guan Lina, Huang Zhiming, Liang Zhen, Zuo Songshen

p, Chan Yi-kuan; d, Wong Kar-wai; w, Wong Kar-wai; ph, Christopher Doyle, Andrew Lau; ed, William Chang, Hai Kit-wai, Kwong Chi-leung; m, Frankie Chan, Roel A. Garcia, Michael Calasso; prod d, William Chang; art d, Qiu Weiming; fx, Ding Yunda, Deng Weijue, Cheng Xiaolong; cos, Yao Huiming

With its sprung rhythms and pop sensibility, Wong Kar-wai's genuinely inspired pastiche of early Godard and late Hitchcock could be dismissed as another bit of stylishly pomo navel-gazing—if it weren't so obviously *about* something.

This visually electric film consists of two loosely connected but cleverly rhymed stanzas: Part One traces the intersecting paths of a lovelorn Hong Kong cop (Takeshi Kaneshiro) and a beautiful drug smuggler (HK superstar Brigitte Lin); Part Two is about a slightly cracked counter girl (Faye Wong) in romantic pursuit of a second cop (Tony Leung Chiu-wai). It all takes place in and around Chungking House, a sprawling apartment complex-*cum*-shopping mall that houses many of Hong Kong's rootless young professionals. As rendered by Wong, it's a place where distinctions between people and products are rapidly disappearing. Relationships have expiration dates; household objects are cajoled, seduced, and abandoned; interchangeable lovers are identified and valued according to the quality of their packaging. Indeed, like no previous film, CHUNGKING EXPRESS captures the historical moment of capitalism's international triumph: right now, all over the world, you can have anything you're prepared to buy, and none of it is worth having.

CHUNHYANG
2000 121m c Romance/Historical/Drama ★★★★
Taehung Pictures/Mirae Asset Capital/CJ Entertainment/Saehan Industries (South Korea)

Lee Hyo Jung (Chunhyang), Cho Seung Woo (Mongryong), Kim Sung Nyu (Wolmae), Kim Hak Yong (Pangja), Lee Hae Eun (Hyangdan), Choi Jin Young (Governor Lee), Hong Kyung Yeun (Kisaeng Leader), Cho Sang Hyun (Pansori Singer), Kim Myung Hwan (Pansori Drummer), Lee Jung Hung (Governor Byun)

p, Lee Tae Won; d, Im Kwon-taek; w, Kim Myoung Gon (from the pansori song by Cho Sang Hyun); ph, Jung Il Sung; ed, Park Soon Duk; m, Kim Jung Gil; prod d, Min Un Ok; cos, Huh Young, Pong Hyun Sook

With over 90 films to his credit, Im Kwon-taek may be one of South Korea's foremost directors, but precious few of his films have ever seen a theatrical release in the West. Let this sumptuous romantic epic, then, be your introduction.

Im uses the traditional form of musical storytelling known as pansori to tell a time-honored tale that's been called the Romeo and Juliet of Korea. As a drummer beats out a rhythm on his puk, the singer transports his audience back to the 17th century, when Mongryon (Cho Seung Woo), the only son of the governor of Namwon (Choi Jin Young), falls in love with Chunhyang (Lee Hyo Jung), the beautiful daughter of a kisaeng (like Japan's geishas, kisaengs were courtesans trained to entertain men with song, conversation, and other flattering attentions). Mongryon's family disapproves of the affair, so before Mongryon leaves to take his civil service exams in Seoul, the lovers wed in secret. Seasons pass, and as Chunhyang chastely awaits her husband's return, a cruel new governor arrives in Namwon. Governor Byun (Lee Jung Hun) demands that Chunhyang serve him as a kisaeng, but she refuses, even though her integrity may cost her her life.

This is melodrama of the highest order, and it's melodrama with a serious purpose. Im's films have often explored the place of women within patriarchal society, and here Chunhyang's refusal to submit is less the result of a wife's blind devotion to her husband than the will of a strong-minded woman determined to remain true to her own heart. From the ravishing landscape photography to the exquisite costume design, the entire film is a stunning visual experience; rarely since Hollywood's golden age has the genre been so well served.

CHUSHINGURA
1962 115m c Drama ★★★★
Toho (Japan)

Koshiro Matsumoto (Kuranosuke Oishi), Yuzo Kayama (Takuminokami Asano), Chusha Ichikawa (Kouzuke Kira), Toshiro Mifune (Genba Tawaraboshi), Yoko Tsukasa (Yozenin), Setsuko Hara (Riku), Tatsuya Mihashi (Yasubei Horibe), Yosuke Natsuki (Kinemon Okano), Ichiro Arishima (Denpachiro Tamon), Norihei Miki (Gayboy Geisha)

d, Hiroshi Inagaki; w, Toshio Yasumi (based on the Kabuki play cycle Kanadehon Chushingura by Izumo Takeda, Senryu Namiki, Shoraku Miyoshi); ph, Kazuo Yamada (Tohoscope, Eastmancolor); m, Akira Ifukube; art d, Kisaku Ito

Kayama plays an honest Japanese noble constantly harassed for bribes by his supervisor (Ichikawa). Goaded beyond endurance, the underling draws his sword and wounds his tormentor. He is consequently ordered to commit hara kiri, and, in a gripping scene, he fulfills the command. His 47 samurai retainers (known as ronin), however, swear vengeance and finally, after biding their time and planning carefully for nearly two years, attack the lord's castle. Successful in their revenge and acclaimed as heroes, the ronin are nevertheless arrested and sentenced to death for their actions, but they are able to proudly follow the samurai code and go the way of their master.

Adapted from a popular Kabuki play from the 18th century which was based on historical fact, Inagaki's film is probably the best of dozens of film versions of the story going back to 1913. Leisurely paced but energetically acted and beautifully designed and shot, it stands with SEVEN SAMURAI and THRONE OF BLOOD as the best of the Japanese samurai genre.

CIDER HOUSE RULES, THE   *DVD*
1999 131m c   Drama   ★★½
Miramax Films/FilmColony (U.S.)   PG-13

Tobey Maguire *(Homer Wells)*, Charlize Theron *(Candy Kendall)*, Michael Caine *(Dr. Wilbur Larch)*, Delroy Lindo *(Mr. Rose)*, Paul Rudd *(Wally Worthington)*, Erykah Badu *(Rose Rose)*, Kieran Culkin *(Buster)*, Heavy D *(Peaches)*, Kate Nelligan *(Olive Worthington)*, Jane Alexander *(Nurse Edna)*

p, Richard N. Gladstein; d, Lasse Hallstrom; w, John Irving (based on his novel *The Cider House Rules*); ph, Oliver Stapleton; ed, Lisa Zeno Churgin; prod d, David Gropman; art d, Karen Schulz-Gropman; fx, Ron Bolanowski; cos, Renee Ehrlich Kalfus

AA Best Supporting Actor: Michael Caine; *AA Best Adapted Screenplay:* John Irving; *AAN Best Picture, AAN Best Director:* Lasse Hallstrom; *AAN Best Art Direction:* David Gropman, Beth Rubino; *AAN Best Film Editing:* Lisa Zeno Churgin; *AAN Best Original Score:* Rachel Portman

Lasse Hallstrom's leisurely adaptation of John Irving's unconventional coming-of-age novel is so well crafted and intelligent that it feels churlish to point out that it's easier to admire than actually like.

Set in the late '30s and early '40s, it revolves around young Homer Wells (Tobey Macguire), who's been raised in a New England orphanage. The home is run by Dr. Wilbur Larch (Michael Caine), a progressive sort who trains Homer in medicine and performs abortions on the side. When a privileged young couple, Candy and Wally (Charlize Theron, Paul Rudd), show up for the procedure, Homer befriends them and, against Larch's wishes, goes off to work in an apple orchard owned by Wally's mother (Kate Nelligan). There he encounters towering field hand Mr. Rose (Delroy Lindo) and his daughter Rose (pop star Erykah Badu), and when Wally goes off to war, a special relationship develops between Homer and Candy.

The good news is that the various betrayals that make up the rest of the movie never seem melodramatic or overwrought. The bad news is that Hallstrom's tone is slightly off—he gives the material a vaguely ironic edge that just doesn't mesh with the on-screen tragedies. The large ensemble cast (which ranges from Jane Alexander to rapper Heavy D) is, however, a whole other story. Caine (who's mastered the intricacies of an American accent since the fiasco of 1967's HURRY SUNDOWN) is particularly good here, as is Lindo in the difficult role of an apparent moral paragon. But Theron's reckless, tormented ingenue is the real revelation; if you ever thought she was just another pretty face, now is the time to get over it.

CIMARRON
1931 131m bw Western   ★★★½
RKO (U.S.)

Richard Dix *(Yancey Cravat)*, Irene Dunne *(Sabra Cravat)*, Estelle Taylor *(Dixie Lee)*, Nance O'Neil *(Felice Venable)*, William Collier Jr. *(the Kid)*, Roscoe Ates *(Jess Rickey)*, George E. Stone *(Sol Levy)*, Robert McWade *(Louie Heffner)*, Edna May Oliver *(Mrs. Tracy Wyatt)*, Frank Darien *(Mr. Bixby)*

p, William LeBaron; d, Wesley Ruggles; w, Howard Estabrook (based on the novel by Edna Ferber); ph, Edward Cronjager; ed, William Hamilton; art d, Max Ree; cos, Max Ree

AA Best Picture; AAN Best Actor: Richard Dix; *AAN Best Actress:* Irene Dunne; *AAN Best Director:* Wesley Ruggles; *AA Best Writing (Adaptation):* Howard Estabrook; *AAN Best Cinematography:* Edward Cronjager; *AA Best Interior Decoration:* Max Ree

Edna Ferber's red-blooded western saga. Its biggest scene—the Oklahoma Land Rush—employs thousands of extras racing pell-mell on horseback, in wagons and on foot to stake out claims on the two million acres opened to settlers on April 22, 1889. Among this frenzied horde are Richard Dix and his young wife, Irene Dunne. Much of the film, which covers 40 years from 1889 to 1929, rests upon the considerable talents of the lovely Dunne, whose Sabra Cravat is followed from girlhood until she becomes a grand old woman of the West.

They manage to stake out a prize piece of territory, but scheming Estelle Taylor replaces their marker and takes the land herself. Dix establishes a newspaper, liberally complementing the power of the press with his own quick-draw brand of justice (in one dramatic confrontation, he shoots the earlobe off a bully), but the tough westerner has a big heart. When the same Taylor who robbed him of land is later put on trial for prostitution, Dix defends her in court. But he is also consumed by wanderlust, often leaving Dunne for long periods of time, and the film follows their relationship's inevitable changes.

CIMARRON cost RKO a staggering $1.5 million, the largest budget the studio ever committed to a film up to that time. Though it received across-the-board raves, the film lost more than half a million dollars. Dunne is superb and CIMARRON was considered until the late 1940s the finest Western ever made. Its biggest drawback is Dix, whose performance has dated badly. Still, it holds up surprisingly well today; the 1960 remake of CIMARRON fizzles by comparison.

CINCINNATI KID, THE   *DVD*
1965 102m c   Drama   ★★★★
MGM (U.S.)

Steve McQueen *(The Cincinnati Kid)*, Edward G. Robinson *(Lancey Howard)*, Ann-Margret *(Melba)*, Karl Malden *(Shooter)*, Tuesday Weld *(Christian)*, Joan Blondell *(Lady Fingers)*, Rip Torn *(Slade)*, Jack Weston *(Pig)*, Cab Calloway *(Yeller)*, Jeff Corey *(Hoban)*

p, Martin Ransohoff; d, Norman Jewison; w, Ring Lardner Jr., Terry Southern (based on the novel by Richard Jessup); ph, Philip Lathrop (Metrocolor); ed, Hal Ashby; m, Lalo Schifrin; art d, George W. Davis, Edward Carfagno; cos, Donfeld

An attempt to do for poker what THE HUSTLER did for pool, THE CINCINNATI KID succeeds on its own, but it might have been a classic with some more attention paid to the script and, perhaps, a little humor sandwiched in to relieve the suspense.

McQueen is The Kid, a formidable gambler who has built a strong reputation among those in the know. He's in New Orleans hustling small-timers and about to go east to Miami when Robinson rolls into town looking for some action. Robinson is "The Man," acknowledged to be the king of poker. He's visiting town for a private game but isn't averse to a match against McQueen, which is arranged by Malden. Torn had earlier been badly beaten by Robinson and he wants revenge, so he calls in some old debts and forces Malden, who is dealing the game between Robinson and McQueen, to slip some winning cards to The Kid. Once McQueen realizes that's happening, he eases Malden out of the way, determined to win fair and square.

A marathon card game takes place, beautifully directed by Jewison, photographed by Lathrop, and edited by Hal Ashby. Even if you don't understand the game, you'll be biting your nails. Excellent supporting work is provided by Joan Blondell as Lady Fingers, a blowsy blonde dealer. In his accustomed role as the desk clerk, look for Olan Soule, a small, elderly man with a young voice. Soule, whom Jack Webb used often in his TV series, was "Mr. First Nighter" during the halcyon days of radio.

CINDERELLA 📀
1950   74m   c   Animated/Children's/Musical   ★★★★
Walt Disney Productions   (U.S.)

VOICES OF: Ilene Woods *(Cinderella)*, William Phipps *(Prince Charming)*, Eleanor Audley *(Stepmother)*, Verna Felton *(Fairy Godmother)*, James MacDonald *(Jaq/Gus)*, Rhoda Williams *(Anastasia)*, Lucille Bliss *(Drusilla)*, Luis Van Rooten *(King/Grand Duke)*, Don Barclay, Claire DuBrey

p, Walt Disney; d, Wilfred Jackson, Hamilton Luske, Clyde Geronimi; w, Bill Peet, Ted Sears, Homer Brightman, Ken Anderson, Erdman Penner, Winston Hibler, Harry Reeves, Joe Rinaldi (based on the original story by Charles Perrault); ed, Donald Halliday; m, Oliver Wallace, Paul Smith

AAN Best Score (Musical): Oliver Wallace, Paul J. Smith; *AAN Best Song:* "Bibbidy-Bobbidi-Boo"; Mack David (Music & Lyrics), Al Hoffman (Music & Lyrics), Jerry Livingston (Lyrics); *AAN Best Sound Recording:* Disney Sound Department

Although not originally met with the kind of praise that greeted Disney's SNOW WHITE and PINOCCHIO, CINDERELLA holds up better because the heroine seems timeless in her courage and resourcefulness, a closer cousin to Belle in Disney's BEAUTY AND THE BEAST than to other fairytale protagonists. To expand the simple storyline, the Disney people created a variety of animal characters, led by Jacques and Gus-Gus, two adorable mice and evil chubby charmer, Lucifer, the stepmother's cat. Eleanor Audley, Disney's grande dame of villainy, and Verna Felton, Disney's grande dame of benevolence, lead the company of wonderful voices. Excellent animation, marvelous color, and lovely music make CINDERELLA a delight all the way around.

CINEMA PARADISO 📀
(NUOVO CINEMA PARADISO)
1988   123m   c   Comedy/Drama   ★★½
Ariane/Cristaldifilm/TFI/RAI-TRE/Forum (Italy/France)

Jacques Perrin *(Toto as an Adult)*, Salvatore Cascio *(Toto as a Child)*, Marco Leonardi *(Toto as a Teenager)*, Philippe Noiret *(Alfredo)*, Nino Terzo *(Peppino's Father)*, Roberta Lena *(Lia)*, Nicolo di Pinto *(Madman)*, Pupella Maggio *(Older Maria)*, Leopoldo Trieste *(Fr. Adelfio)*, Enzo Cannavale *(Spaccafico)*

p, Franco Cristaldi; d, Giuseppe Tornatore; w, Giuseppe Tornatore; ph, Blasco Giurato; ed, Mario Mora; m, Ennio Morricone, Andrea Morricone; prod d, Andrea Crisanti; cos, Beatrice Bordone

AA Best Foreign Language Film

Successful movie director Salvatore returns to his rural Sicilian village after 30 years to attend the funeral of a dear friend and former mentor who advised him, all those years ago, to forsake his humble origins and journey to Rome to make a life for himself. CINEMA PARADISO wallows in nostalgia for a mythic moviegoing past that it serves up in self-infatuated gobs. No, they don't make movies like they used to, and this Oscar-winning Italian-French co-production spends the better part of three hours proving it.

In extended flashback, Salvatore (played by Jacques Perrin as an adult) reviews his postwar childhood and his relationship with the friend—Alfredo (Philippe Noiret), the projectionist at the town's only theater, the Cinema Paradiso. The whole town has been affected by the war and, for many, the Paradiso has become a refuge from the impoverishment and indignity that surrounds them.

A prankish altar boy, Salvatore or Toto for short (played as a boy by Salvatore Cascio) follows the local priest to a private screening at the Paradiso. The priest, also the town censor, registers his disapproval of certain moments in the films

that flicker past (it's the kissing scenes that invariably arouse his ire) and Alfredo snips out the offending footage. Toto badgers the projectionist into giving him a strip of discarded celluloid. Naturally, a bond soon grows between them.

That Paradiso is some revival house. Great classics from the likes of Lang, Renoir and Visconti abound and there are enough Anna Magnani classics for a month of screenings at the Museum of Modern Art, but for the folks in this backwater hamlet such stellar fare is as common as going to church each week. Indeed going to the movies is a reverential act, as anyone gazing on those rows of rapt faces can tell. They laugh, they cry, they bliss out on cue.

Director Tornatore (IL CAMORRISTA) pushes every sentimental button—some Felliniesque, some probably personal—but none that hasn't been pushed a dozen times before. The film's censor priest might well approve of the carefully tailored sentimentality. Still, Tornatore's film—shot on location in the director's hometown of Bagheria, Sicily—won a number of film festival accolades, including the Grand Jury prize at Cannes in 1989.

CIRCLE OF DECEIT 📀
(DIE FALSCHUNG)
1981   108m   c   Drama   ★★★★
Bioskop/Artemis/Argos   (France/West Germany)

Bruno Ganz *(Georg Laschen)*, Hanna Schygulla *(Arianna Nassar)*, Jean Carmet *(Rudnik)*, Jerzy Skolimowski *(Hoffmann)*, Gila von Weitershausen *(Greta Laschen)*, Peter Martin Urtel *(Berger)*, John Munro *(John)*, Fouad Naim *(Excellence Joseph)*, Josette Khalil *(Mrs. Joseph)*, Khaled el Saeid *(Progressive Officer)*

p, Eberhard Junkersdorf; d, Volker Schlondorff; w, Volker Schlondorff, Jean-Claude Carriere, Margarethe von Trotta, Kai Hermann (from a novel by Nicolas Born); ph, Igor Luther (Eastmancolor); ed, Suzanne Baron; m, Maurice Jarre; art d, Alexandre Riachi, Tannous Zougheib; fx, Paul Trielli, Andre Trielli; cos, Dagmar Niefind

German journalist Bruno Ganz leaves a troubled marriage and questions of self-worth behind him and travels to Beirut to write about the obsessive, violent war raging there. Amid a group of disillusioned reporters who see the fighting in the Middle East as just another sign of the times, Ganz vows to get to the heart of the true story and discover the emotional answer to the ever-present question of "why?" He meets and falls in love with the beautiful Hanna Schygulla, a wealthy German aristocrat still living in a mansion in the middle of bombed-out rubble. When the fighting becomes more intense and the lives of the journalists become threatened, most of the reporters leave Beirut for safer territory. Ganz remains, determined to understand the violence and to report it to the world.

Director Volker Schlondorff, one of the pioneers of the New German Cinema, creates a frightening, effective vision of the nightmarish war in Beirut and the grisly effect it can have on emotions as well as bodies. Ganz is wonderfully powerful as the observant, curious reporter who realizes man always has a way of deceiving himself and others into simple answers for complex questions. Schygulla, the mesmerizing star of many of Fassbinder's films, turns in an exquisite performance as the mysterious woman who courts death as well as men. Shot on location in Beirut, the film's re-created, on-the-street battle sequences are violently intense and realistic.

CIRCLE, THE 📀
(DAYEREH)
2000   91m   c   Drama   ★★★★
Jafar Panahi Film Productions/Mikado-Lumiere & Co. (Iran/Italy)

Maryiam Parvin Almani *(Arezou)*, Nargess Mamizadeh *(Nargess)*, Fereshteh Sadr Orafai *(Pari)*, Monir Arab *(Ticket*

Seller), Elham Saboktakin *(Nurse)*, Fatemeh Naghavi *(Mother)*, Mojgan Faramarzi *(Prostitute)*

p, Jafar Panahi; d, Jafar Panahi; w, Kambozia Partovi (based on an original idea by Jafar Panahi); ph, Bahram Badakhshani; ed, Jafar Panahi; art d, Iraj Raminfar

The title of Iranian director Jafar Panahi's daring film refers to both a physical locale—a public plaza in the heart of Tehran—and the film's ingenious story structure, which begins and ends with news of an Iranian woman who has just given birth. In between, Panahi offers a damning indictment of the lack of freedom experienced by women on several levels of Iranian society.

The film opens at a hosptial where an expectant grandmother has just received devastating news: her daughter has borne a baby girl. As she leaves the hospital in shame, two women (Maryiam Parvin Almani, Nargess Mamizadeh)—prison escapees—hover nervously on the sidewalk outside. One wants to return to her native village, but lacks the proper ID (Iranian women are forbidden to travel alone); in order to help her friend, the other prostitutes herself to a stranger. A third prisoner (Fereshteh Sadr Orafai) has fled in order to obtain an abortion. She turns to her father and brothers for help, but they throw her out on the street. This narrative relay continues across a wide variety of characters: a nurse (Monir Arab) who fears her doctor-husband will discover she once served time in prison; an exhausted single mother (Fatemeh Naghavi) who attempts to abandon her young daughter on a darkened street; and a prostitute (Mojgan Faramarzi) whose arrest symbolizes the perpetual spiral of transgression and punishment that brings the film full circle.

Panahi's first film, THE WHITE BALOON, was an enchanting film whose messages lay safely tucked inside a charming story about a little girl in search of a goldfish. Not so here. This tightly structured, often exciting film is among the boldest in a series of increasingly explicit movies about the hardships facing contemporary Iranian women (Marziyeh Meshkini's superb THE DAY I BECAME A WOMAN is another). Not surprisingly, Panahi's film was banned in Iran.

CITADEL, THE
1938 110m bw Drama ★★★★½
MGM (U.K.)

Robert Donat *(Andrew Manson)*, Rosalind Russell *(Christine Manson)*, Ralph Richardson *(Denny)*, Rex Harrison *(Dr. Lawford)*, Emlyn Williams *(Owen)*, Penelope Dudley-Ward *(Toppy Leroy)*, Francis L. Sullivan *(Ben Chenkin)*, Mary Clare *(Mrs. Orlando)*, Cecil Parker *(Charles Every)*, Nora Swinburne *(Mrs. Thornton)*

p, Victor Saville; d, King Vidor; w, Ian Dalrymple, Frank Wead, Elizabeth Hill, Emlyn Williams (based on the novel by A.J. Cronin); ph, Harry Stradling; ed, Charles Frend; m, Louis Levy; art d, Lazare Meerson, Alfred Junge

AAN Best Picture; AAN Best Actor: Robert Donat; *AAN Best Director:* King Vidor; *AAN Best Screenplay:* Ian Dalrymple, Elizabeth Hill, Frank Wead

A faithful rendering of doctor-turned-author Cronin's semi-autobiographical novel, with the superb Donat toplining as a dedicated doctor who ministers to TB-infected Welsh miners and Russell lending stirring support as his devoted and idealistic wife.

At first, Andrew Manson (Donat) is full of lofty goals as he labors in the slums of a mining town, struggling to save the miserable health of downtrodden workers. Later, though, his noble purpose slowly corrodes when he begins to treat aristocratic, wealthy London patients. Turning to the material pleasures of the "good life," it takes the combined efforts of his wife and a close friend (Richardson) and several dramatic turns of events to convinces Manson that he has lost touch with his true aims in life.

Produced by MGM's British production unit after the studio had met with success in a similar foreign production, A YANK AT OXFORD, THE CITADEL is a gripping portrait of both idealism and its disillusionment, not a mere ode to nobility. It is carefully piloted by director Vidor, who wisely allows the consummate acting skills of Donat, Richardson and a marvelous supporting cast to carry the story forward with sensitivity and relaxed charm. Russell, too, at the cusp of her transition between playing society-matron supporting roles and zany comedic starring parts, artfully combines the gentility of the former and the appeal of the latter.

CITIZEN KANE
1941 119m bw Drama ★★★★★
Mercury (U.S.)

Orson Welles *(Charles Foster Kane)*, Joseph Cotten *(Jedediah Leland)*, Dorothy Comingore *(Susan Alexander)*, Everett Sloane *(Mr. Bernstein)*, Ray Collins *(Boss J.W. "Big Jim" Gettys)*, George Coulouris *(Walter Parks Thatcher)*, Agnes Moorehead *(Mary Kane)*, Paul Stewart *(Raymond)*, Ruth Warrick *(Emily Norton Kane)*, Erskine Sanford *(Herbert Carter)*

p, Orson Welles; d, Orson Welles; w, Herman J. Mankiewicz, Orson Welles; ph, Gregg Toland; ed, Robert Wise, Mark Robson (uncredited); m, Bernard Herrmann; art d, Van Nest Polglase, Perry Ferguson; fx, Vernon L. Walker; cos, Edward Stevenson

AA Best Original Screenplay: Herman J. Mankiewicz, Orson Welles; *AAN Best Picture; AAN Best Actor:* Orson Welles; *AAN Best Director:* Orson Welles; *AAN Best B/W Cinematography:* Gregg Toland; *AAN Best Film Editing:* Robert Wise; *AAN Best Score (Drama):* Bernard Herrmann; *AAN Best Interior Decoration (B/W):* Perry Ferguson, Van Nest Polglase, Al Fields, Darrell Silvera; *AAN Best Sound Recording:* John Aalberg

Fading in on an ominous nighttime exterior, the camera slowly focuses on a high wrought-iron fence filigreed with the initial "K." Beyond spreads Xanadu, the vast estate of one of the world's wealthiest men. The camera surveys the grounds—empty gondolas swaying on a private lake, exotic animals penned in a private zoo, manicured lawns and shubbery—all shrouded in fog. Towering above the mist is the top of a man-made mountain on which sits a castle, a single light shining from it. Within is a dying man who clutches a crystal ball enclosing a winter scene and make-believe snow. He utters one word, "Rosebud," and dies, dropping the ball, which breaks into tiny shards.

So begins Orson Welles's legendary CITIZEN KANE. After several projects came to naught, notably an adaptation of Joseph Conrad's *Heart of Darkness*, 25 year-old *wunderkind* Welles, already a sensation in the theater and radio worlds, made what is unquestionably the most stunning debut in the history of film. KANE is a landmark film for myriad reasons, not the least of which is the variety of techniques employed—quick cuts, imaginative dissolves, even the iris device once popular in silent films. Indeed, none of the filmmaking methodology of the past is left unused, but KANE also contributes an array of innovative cinematic devices, most notably Gregg Toland's astonishing deep-focus photography (a technique pioneered by legendary cinematographer James Wong Howe). Visually this is Toland's film, a masterpiece of shadow and sharp contrast that artfully conveys murky moods and occasional moments of gaiety as camera and reporter search for the meaning of a man's life.

Welles took credit for writing most of KANE's superb screenplay, but the bulk of its incisive, witty, and unforgettable scenes and dialogue were most probably scripted by screenwriter Herman Mankiewicz, brother of Joseph, the noted film producer-director-writer. Nonetheless, Welles's contribution as director-producer remains awe-inspiring: he chronicles Kane's life through a combination of highly dramatic episodes and newsreel-like footage—slices of life that form a compelling patchwork biography. The film is so tightly constructed that every scene counts, filling in a piece of the puzzle, incomplete though it may be after reporter Jerry Thompson (William Alland) traces five accounts of the millionaire's life.

At the film's conclusion, reporters gather at Kane's estate, moving through a warehouse that is being cleared of endless piles of curios, stacks of furniture and countless crates containing Kane's purchases. As they move off into the dark recesses, a high boom shot reveals a staggering collection of toys, paintings and statues. Slowly the camera pans the heaps of Kane's possessions until it comes to a blazing furnace into which workmen throw all items considered to be junk. One of the workers picks up a sled—the very one Kane had as a boy in Colorado—and throws it into the fire. The camera closes in tightly on the top of the sled, and as it catches fire, the name "Rosebud" is revealed before the letters burn away. The scene shifts to the outside of the looming castle, panning upward to the high chimney from which Kane's lost youth curls upward into the night sky. The camera pulls back from the edifice, concluding the film with the shot of the iron fence with which it began.

CITIZEN KANE has influenced countless filmmakers and established the taste of discerning audiences worldwide. It is the epitome of filmmaking, a masterpiece for which Welles, one of the greatest practitioners of the cinematic art, will be forever remembered.

CITIZENS BAND

1977 98m c Comedy ★★★
Paramount (U.S.) R

Paul LeMat *(Spider/Blaine)*, Candy Clark *(Electra/Pam)*, Ann Wedgeworth *(Joyce Rissley)*, Bruce McGill *(Blood/Dean)*, Marcia Rodd *(Portland Angel/Connie)*, Charles Napier *(Chrome Angel/Harold)*, Alix Elias *(Hot Coffee/Debbie)*, Roberts Blossom *(Papa Thermadyne/Father)*, Richard Bright *(Smilin' Jack/Garage Owner)*, Ed Begley Jr. *(Priest)*

p, Freddie Fields; d, Jonathan Demme; w, Paul Brickman; ph, Jordan Cronenweth (Movielab Color); ed, John F. Link II; m, Bill Conti; art d, Bill Malley; cos, Jodie Lynn Tillen

AMERICAN GRAFFITI goes redneck. An early and sometimes funny effort by director Demme but the hilarity of the subplots (especially the bigamous Napier) swallows the main storyline. LeMat stars as a decent fellow intent on seeing that the CB airwaves are kept open for emergencies, putting him at odds with an assortment of loony CBers who don't want anybody stopping his fun. LeMat again shows himself to be the closest thing there is to a modern-day Jimmy Stewart, yet he's never snagged that one part that will move him into the star category. Not as good as the sum of its parts, but worth a nod unless redneck humor makes you crazy.

CITY FOR CONQUEST

1940 105m bw Sports ★★★½
Warner Bros. (U.S.)

James Cagney *(Danny Kenny)*, Ann Sheridan *(Peggy Nash)*, Frank Craven *("Old Timer")*, Donald Crisp *(Scotty McPherson)*, Arthur Kennedy *(Eddie Kenny)*, Frank McHugh *("Mutt")*, George Tobias *(Pinky)*, Blanche Yurka *(Mrs. Nash)*, Elia Kazan *("Googi")*, Anthony Quinn *(Murray Burns)*

p, Anatole Litvak; d, Anatole Litvak; w, John Wexley (based on the novel by Aben Kandel); ph, Sol Polito, James Wong Howe; ed, William Holmes; m, Max Steiner; art d, Robert Haas; fx, Byron Haskin, Rex Wimpy; chor, Robert Vreeland; cos, Howard Shoup

James Cagney is at his dynamic best as a Gotham truck driver who boxes to support his brother, Kennedy (in his film debut), while he tries to make it as a composer. Cagney's girlfriend Sheridan struggles to gain fame as a dancer, though he objects to her partner, unctuously portrayed by Anthony Quinn. CITY FOR CONQUEST is an often heavy melodrama, but it has consistently good dialogue, a sprightly style, and a captivating powerhouse performance by Cagney, who drew on his experience as a longtime fight fan. He was 42 when he made the film and, training like a fighter, shed 30 pounds for the role. His fight scenes are realistically photographed by veteran cameramen Sol Polito and James Wong Howe, and in many cases hard blows were actually exchanged between the actor and his opponents. Director Anatole Litvak and Cagney argued over just about every scene, and most of Cagney's ideas, including much of his fight choreography, were edited out of the final version. Moreover, Cagney felt that the story had been ruined and sent a note of apology to its author, novelist Aben Kandel. But Litvak's careful production overcomes any flaws. Watch out for Elia Kazan as a neighborhood kid gone gangster.

CITY OF ANGELS DVD

1998 152m c Romance/Fantasy/Drama ★★★
Atlas Entertainment/New Regency (U.S.) PG-13

Nicolas Cage *(Seth)*, Meg Ryan *(Dr. Maggie Rice)*, Dennis Franz *(Nathaniel Messinger)*, Andre Braugher *(Cassiel)*, Colm Feore *(Jordan)*, Robin Bartlett *(Anne)*, Joanna Merlin *(Teresa)*, Sarah Dampf *(Susan)*, Rhonda Dotson *(Susan's Mother)*, Nigel Gibbs *(Doctor)*

p, Dawn Steel, Charles Roven; d, Brad Silberling; w, Dana Stevens (based on the screenplay "Der Himmel uber Berlin [Heaven Over Berlin]" by Wim Wenders, Peter Handke, and Richard Reitinger); ph, John Seale; ed, Lynzee Klingman; m, Gabriel Yared; prod d, Lily Kilvert; art d, John Warnke; fx, David Blitstein, John Nelson, Sony Pictures Imageworks; cos, Shay Cunliffe

Like supermodels, angels need no last names. Case in point: mournful Seth (Nicolas Cage), a sleek vision in black whom we first see drifting through lives in crisis, unseen except by the dying, the deluded, and the innocent. He calms a convenience store owner who's being held up at gunpoint, nudges an air traffic controller whose attention has wandered, and escorts the newly dead away from their bodies, gently asking them what it was they liked most about life. Always observers and never participants, Seth and his fellow celestial spirits are sudden serenity in the face of turmoil, the glimmer of hope that banishes despair, the cold hand that clutches the hearts of the dying. Then Seth locks eyes with Dr. Maggie Rice (Meg Ryan) as she tries to save a dying patient, and he begins to wonder what it would be like to experience human life.

In the long, sorry history of bad ideas, remaking Wim Wenders' poetic masterpiece WINGS OF DESIRE with the director of CASPER at the helm sounded like one of the worst. But this melancholy, strikingly photographed love story will tug at the heartstrings of the GHOST crowd without sending fans of the original film into a fury. Princess of perk Ryan isn't hugely convincing as a high-strung heart surgeon, but Cage has shrugged off most of his trademark tics in favor of a sweetly grave performance and finds a fine foil in Andre Braugher, who plays fellow angel Cassiel. And for all the "touched by an angel" sentimentality, the movie's eerie, slightly menacing vision of black-clad angels lurking in the shadowy corners of unsuspecting lives is genuinely haunting.

CITY OF GOD
DVD

(CIDADE DE DEUS)

2002 130m c   Crime/Drama/Action   ★★★★

O2 Filmes/VideoFilmes/Globo Filmes/Lumiere/   R

Wild Bunch   (Brazil/Germany/France)

Alexandre Rodrigues *(Rocket)*, Leandro Firmino da Hora *(Lil' Ze)*, Phellipe Haagensen *(Benny)*, Douglas Silva *(Lil' Dice)*, Jonathan Haagensen *(Shaggy)*, Matheus Nachtergaele *(Carrot)*, Seu Jorge *(Knockout Ned)*, Jefechander Suplino *(Clipper)*, Alice Braga *(Angelica)*, Emerson Gomes *(Stringy)*

p, Mauricio Andrade Ramos, Andrea Barata Ribeiro; d, Fernando Meirelles; w, Braulio Mantovani (based on the novel *Cidade de Deus*, by Paulo Lins); ph, Cesar Charlone; ed, Daniel Rezende; m, Ed Cortes, Antonio Pinto; art d, Tule Peake; fx, Renato Batata, M.M. Arte Tecnica; chor, Luciano Pere; cos, Bia Salgado, Ines Salgado

AAN Best Adapted Screenplay: Braulio Mantovani; *AAN Best Cinematography:* Cesar Charlone; *AAN Best Editing:* Daniel Rezende; *AAN Best Director:* Fernando Meirelles

There's nothing particularly heavenly about Rio's "City of God," the housing development built during the 1960s to help alleviate the homeless overflow from the city's teeming slums. Overrun by criminal gangs and an equally dangerous police force, this sprawling suburb of matchbox houses and unpaved streets is like a lawless frontier town in the Old West. By the mid-1970s, most of the cocaine trade in the City of God has been taken over by Lil' Ze (Leandro Firmino da Hora), a vicious 18-year-old hood who keeps the peace by killing off the competition. The only rival dealer Lil' Ze hasn't murdered is Carrot (Matheus Nachtergaele), and that's only because Carrot is best friends with Benny (Phellipe Haagensen), Lil' Ze's right-hand man. Sixteen-year-old Rocket (Alexandre Rodrigues), who dreams of one day becoming a photographer and leaving the slums, knows enough to keep away from the hoods. But the animosity between Lil' Ze and Carrot soon reaches a boiling point, and an all-out street war transforms the City of God from an impoverished purgatory into a blood-soaked hell.

GOODFELLAS, PULP FICTION, AMORES PERROS, PIXOTE: the comparisons are all apt, but none do justice to the striking originality of a film that opens with a high-speed, guns-blazing chicken chase and uses a 3/4 split-screen when the conventional shot/countershot just isn't fast enough. Braulio Mantovani's screenplay at first appears to be cobbled together from odd bits of narrative, but this seemingly haphazard arrangement is actually a tightly woven tapestry of extraordinary breadth, and director Fernando Meirelles's control over the material is astonishing. Possibly the first great crime film of the 21st century.

CITY OF LOST CHILDREN, THE
DVD

(LA CITE DES ENFANTS PERDUS)

1995 112m c   Fantasy   ★★★½

Claudie Ossard Productions/Constellation   R

Productions/Lumiere/Canal Plus/France 3 Cinema/

Elias Querejeta/Tele Munchin/Centre National de la

Cinematographie/Cofimage 4/Cofimage 5/Studio

Images   (France/Spain/Germany)

Ron Perlman *(One)*, Daniel Emilfork *(Krank)*, Judith Vittet *(Miette)*, Dominique Pinon *(Diver/Clones/Stocle)*, Jean-Claude Dreyfus *(Marcello, Flea Tamer)*, Genevieve Brunet, Odile Mallet *(Octopus)*, Mireille Mosse *(Mademoiselle Bismuth)*, Joseph Lucien *(Denree)*, Serge Merlin *(Leader of the Cyclopes)*

p, Claudie Ossard; d, Jean-Pierre Jeunet, Marc Caro; w, Gilles Adrien, Jean-Pierre Jeunet, Marc Caro; ph, Darius Khondji; ed, Herve Schneid; m, Angelo Badalamenti; art d, Marc Caro; fx, Yves Domenjoud, Olivier Gleyze, Jean-Baptiste Bonetto, Jean-Christophe Spadaccini, Emmanuelle Soupa; cos, Jean-Paul Gaultier

Definitely *not* for the kiddies—the opening sequence will leave your little darling shrieking with terror at the mere mention of Santa Claus.

All the children of a dismal port city are disappearing one by one, kidnapped by Krank (Daniel Emilfork), an evil genius who, for some reason, can't dream. Krank has invented a machine designed to capture the untroubled dreams of the innocent, but something's gone horribly wrong and he's unable to extract anything from his captives but nightmares. (One tyke dreams of a Christmas Eve invasion by drunken, malevolent Santas.) When Krank and his army of one-eyed Cyclopes kidnap little Denree (Joseph Lucien), his adoptive older brother, the circus strongman One (Ron Perlman), teams up with a petite thief (Judith Vittet) to rescue the stolen children.

Directors Jean-Pierre Jeunet and Marc Caro (DELICATESSEN) have created a genuine phantasmagoria, and each of the film's stunning set pieces is more wildly imaginative than the last. (In the most spectacular, a young girl's tear sets off a Rube Goldberg-style chain of events that winds up grounding an ocean liner.) But once it becomes clear that this dark, immensely cluttered fantasy refers to nothing beyond itself—Krank's dream machine, it would seem, equals cinema—you may end up wishing for a little less show and a lot more substance.

CITY OF WOMEN
DVD

1980 140m c   Drama   ★★★

Gaumont   (Italy/France)

Marcello Mastroianni *(Snaporaz)*, Ettore Manni *(Dr. Xavier Zuberkock)*, Anna Prucnal *(Elena)*, Bernice Stegers *(Woman on Train)*, Donatella Damiani *(Feminist on Roller Skates)*, Sara Tafuri *(Other Dancing Girl)*, Jole Silvani *(Old Woman on Motorcycle)*, Carla Terlizzi *(Dr. Zuberkock's Conquest)*, Katren Gebelein *(Enderbreith Small)*, Dominique Labourier *(Feminist)*

p, Renzo Rossellini; d, Federico Fellini; w, Federico Fellini, Bernardino Zapponi, Brunello Rondi; ph, Giuseppe Rotunno (Technovision, Eastmancolor); ed, Ruggero Mastroianni; m, Luis Bacalov; art d, Dante Ferretti; chor, Leonetta Bentivoglio; cos, Gabriella Pescucci

Plotless but undoubtedly Fellini. Federico Fellini's psychedelic exploration of feminine mysteries is another visual tour de force in an elaborate dream framework, with a ponderous tone, typical of Fellini's efforts in the latter stages of his career. The film begins as Snaporaz (Marcello Mastroianni), the threatened male protagonist, finds himself trapped at a feminist convention. Dr. Zuberkock (Ettore Manni) offers him refuge in a villa constructed for sexual pleasure, where a celebration of Zuberkock's 10,000th conquest ends with an invasion of female militia. This is followed by a brief reunion between Snaporaz and his estranged wife, leading into a fantasy sequence. For fans of the master only.

CITY SLICKERS
DVD

1991 112m c   Comedy/Adventure   ★★★½

Castle Rock/Nelson Entertainment/Face   PG-13

Productions   (U.S.)

Billy Crystal *(Mitch Robbins)*, Daniel Stern *(Phil Berquist)*, Bruno Kirby *(Ed Furillo)*, Patricia Wettig *(Barbara Robbins)*, Helen Slater *(Bonnie Rayburn)*, Jack Palance *(Curly)*, Noble Willingham *(Clay Stone)*, Tracey Walter *(Cookie)*, Josh Mostel *(Barry Shalowitz)*, David Paymer *(Ira Shalowitz)* p, Irby Smith; d, Ron Underwood; w, Lowell Ganz, Babaloo Mandel (from the story by Billy Crystal); ph, Dean Semler; ed, O. Nicholas Brown; m, Marc Shaiman; prod d, Lawrence G. Paull; art d, Mark Mansbridge; fx, Ken Pepiot, Frank Welker; cos, Judy Ruskin

AA Best Supporting Actor: Jack Palance

CITY SLICKERS is a skewed, serio-comic variation on Howard Hawks' classic RED RIVER in which the cattle drive becomes a two-week vacation, Walter Brennan, Montgomery Clift and John Wayne become Daniel Stern, Bruno Kirby and Billy Crystal, and the manifest destiny subtext becomes an inner search for the "child within" and a man's discovery of his smile.

Mitch Robbins (Billy Crystal), the man without a smile, is in the throes of a mid-life crisis, questioning his success and his family's happiness. Joining Mitch are his two best friends, Ed Furillo (Bruno Kirby), a loudmouth womanizer fretful about settling down and raising a family, and Phil Berquist (Daniel Stern), whose life is coming apart after his shrewish wife finds out about an affair he had with a 20-year-old woman. At Mitch's 39th-birthday party, his pals give him their gift—a two-week vacation in the West on a cattle drive from New Mexico to Colorado. Upon arriving, the three friends demonstrate their lack of cowboy skills but they gradually learn to rope and ride as they discuss their childhood hopes and adult disappointments.

CITY SLICKERS successfully skirts the chance for a cheapshot gag comedy and becomes a friendly, heartfelt celebration of friendship and community, greatly aided by a funny and moving script by Lowell Ganz and Babaloo Mandell (PARENTHOOD, VIBES, SPLASH). Ron Underwood's direction complements the script and, while evoking memories of old Western films and TV shows, never overshadows the acting of a uniformly capable cast. Crystal manages to avoid the schtick that marred his previous film work; Jack Palance as Curly plays his role in an almost frightening evocation as a mythic Western hero. His whisper-growls and godlike demeanor make Palance seem a Disney World automaton. But since Palance's job is to carry with him the weight of 90 years of Western film myth, his performance is finely tuned, without any hint of parody that could throw the film out of whack.

CIVIL ACTION, A   DVD
1998 113m c   Drama   ★★½
Wildwood Enterprises/Touchstone Pictures (U.S.) PG-13

John Travolta *(Jan Schlichtmann)*, Robert Duvall *(Jerome Facher)*, Tony Shalhoub *(Kevin Conway)*, William H. Macy *(James Gordon)*, Zeljko Ivanek *(Bill Crowley)*, Bruce Norris *(William Cheeseman)*, John Lithgow *(Judge Skinner)*, Kathleen Quinlan *(Anne Anderson)*, Peter Jacobson *(Neil Jacobs)*, Mary Mara *(Kathy Boyer)*

p, Robert Redford, Rachel Pfeffer, Scott Rudin; d, Steven Zaillian; w, Steven Zaillian (based on the book by Jonathan Harr); ph, Conrad L. Hall; ed, Wayne Wahrman; m, Danny Elfman; prod d, David Gropman; art d, David J. Bomba; fx, Guy Clayton; cos, Shay Cunliffe

AAN Best Supporting Actor: Robert Duvall; *AAN Best Cinematography:* Conrad L. Hall

"They came for human drama. We've given them three months of geology lessons," pleads desperate attorney Jan Schlichtmann (John Travolta) on behalf of his jury. He could be speaking for the audience.

Courtroom dramas that favor the courtroom over the drama are always in danger of eye-glazing dullness. And the sad irony is that the more closely filmmakers try to hew to the truth of legal procedures and protocol, the less compelling the results tend to be. Good and serious intentions abound in Steven Zaillian's very faithful adaptation of Jonathan Harr's nonfiction best-seller *A Civil Action,* which chronicles Schlichtmann's eight-year battle with mega-corporations W.R. Grace & Co. and Beatrice Foods on behalf of a handful of families from Woburn, MA, whose children were poisoned by industrial pollutants in the water. Schlichtmann, a personal injury lawyer with a history of keeping his eye on the bottom line, gets sucked into the potentially ruinous case—which is clearly (to a lawyer) too complex and expensive to bring to trial—because he thinks he can win a whole lot of money for the families and, not coincidentally, himself.

Schlichtmann is a potentially interesting character, a legal sharpie who deludes himself into thinking he can do well by doing good and ruins just about everyone who believes him. He's a lawyer looking for his soul, in the tradition of rumpled Gene Hackman battling the heartless auto industry in CLASS ACTION and alcoholic Paul Newman taking on the medical establishment in THE VERDICT, with the bonus that there's a real person behind Travolta's sleek smirk. But Schlichtmann gets lost in the ocean of motions, depositions, surveys, precedents and procedures that have to be crammed into two hours of screen time. This is a case in which the material really is better served in book form.

CLAIRE'S KNEE   DVD
(LE GENOU DE CLAIRE)
1970 103m c   Drama   ★★★½
Losange (France)   GP

Jean-Claude Brialy *(Jerome)*, Aurora Cornu *(Aurora)*, Beatrice Romand *(Laura)*, Laurence de Monaghan *(Claire)*, Michele Montel *(Mme. Walter)*, Gerard Falconetti *(Gilles)*, Fabrice Luchini *(Vincent)*

p, Pierre Cottrell; d, Eric Rohmer; w, Eric Rohmer; ph, Nestor Almendros; ed, Cecile Decugis

A rarefied conversation fest, the fifth of Rohmer's "Moral Tales" stars Jean-Claude Brialy as Jerome, a middle-aged intellectual who feels with his head, not his heart. A French diplomat who is about to be married to a woman he loves, but for whom he feels no passion, Jerome visits the provincial town where he was raised. There he meets Claire (Laurence de Monaghan), a summery 17-year-old who is completely absorbed with her boyfriend. Jerome channels his desire for her into a form of passion that, for him, is much more controllable—he wants only to touch her knee.

One of Rohmer's greatest expressions of male-female relationships, CLAIRE'S KNEE presents a portrait of a man who, under his fairly charming and harmless demeanor, is eroding emotionally, convincing even himself that he can control his desires. In order to do so, he must completely detach his actions from his heart and make a physical gesture completely devoid of romance or emotion. What makes this so poignant is that it is only the audience which understands this.

CLASH BY NIGHT   DVD
1952 105m bw Drama   ★★★★
RKO   (U.S.)

Barbara Stanwyck *(Mae Doyle)*, Paul Douglas *(Jerry D'Amato)*, Robert Ryan *(Earl Pfeiffer)*, Marilyn Monroe *(Peggy)*, J. Carrol Naish *(Uncle Vince)*, Keith Andes *(Joe Doyle)*, Silvio Minciotti *(Papa)*, Diane Stewart, Deborah Stewart *(Baby Gloria)*, Julius Tannen *(Sad-Eyed Waiter)*

p, Harriet Parsons; d, Fritz Lang; w, Alfred Hayes, David Dortort (based on the play by Clifford Odets); ph, Nicholas Musuraça; ed,

George Amy; m, Roy Webb; art d, Albert S. D'Agostino, Carroll Clark; fx, Harold Wellman

A Stanwyck field day, in the kind of role she could do with her eyes closed, but because it's well-directed by Fritz Lang, the actress can let go with the snarls, venom, and wounded savagery we've come to expect and love. CLASH is a California cousin of Williams's STREETCAR but Stanwyck's Mae is tougher than Blanche; she's returned home a fallen woman to lick her big-city wounds, and Stanwyck gives it the commonness that Tallulah Bankhead had been too elegant for on Broadway. The story is essentially an Odets kitchen-sink triangle, with dangerous Ryan as resident trouble—he's terrific—and Douglas as the cuckholded spouse. The latter is the weak part of the triangle, but it still works.

In her first major role, Monroe gives a surprising turn as a young woman who, for the most part, is refreshingly independent. This is the lovely Monroe without the candy floss accoutrements; one watches CLASH sensing her career might have gone in a totally different direction had Fox marketed her in an adult manner. The steam she generates with the muscular Andes when Stanwyck and Ryan aren't clawing at each other's clothes makes CLASH BY NIGHT eminently watchable. And fun besides.

CLEAR AND PRESENT DANGER

1994 142m c   Action/Adventure/War   ★★★½
Neufeld/Rehme Productions/Paramount (U.S.)   PG-13

Harrison Ford (Jack Ryan), Willem Dafoe (CIA Field Contractor Mr. Clark), Anne Archer (Dr. Cathy Ryan), James Earl Jones (Admiral James Greer), Joaquim De Almeida (Felix Cortez), Henry Czerny (CIA Deputy Director of Operations Robert Ritter), Harris Yulin (National Security Advisor James Cutter), Donald Moffat (U.S. President Edward Bennett), Miguel Sandoval (Ernesto Escobedo), Benjamin Bratt (Captain Ramirez)

p, Mace Neufeld, Robert Rehme; d, Phillip Noyce; w, Donald Stewart, Steve Zaillian, John Milius (based on the novel by Tom Clancy); ph, Donald M. McAlpine; ed, Neil Travis; m, James Horner; prod d, Terence Marsh; art d, William Cruse; fx, Joe Lombardi, Paul Lombardi, Robert Grasmere; cos, Bernie Pollack

AAN Best Sound: Donald O. Mitchell, Michael Herbick, Frank A. Montano, Arthur Rochester; AAN Best Sound Effects Editing: Bruce Stambler, John Leveque

The third screen treatment of Tom Clancy's best-selling Jack Ryan series is a sharp improvement over THE HUNT FOR RED OCTOBER and PATRIOT GAMES. It's a formula film with a typically dubious political message, but the storytelling is livelier and more engaging than previous adaptations of Clancy's turgid techno-thrillers.

This time out, CIA administrator Jack Ryan (Harrison Ford) is pitted against Medellin drug kingpin Escobedo (Miguel Sandoval). Ryan's investigation of a string of assassinations leads him to Colombia, where he teams up with a covert team of American soldiers led by Clark (Willem Dafoe) and runs afoul of the duplicitous President Bennett (Donald Moffat).

CLEAR AND PRESENT DANGER develops a multi-track story line of some substance. A solid screenplay neatly follows Jack's investigation into both the drug cartel and the White House cover-ups, while proficiently depicting Clark's covert war and Escobedo's machinations. Politically speaking, the film presents less of a rightward thrust than the red-baiting OCTOBER or the neo-monarchist PATRIOT GAMES.

For director Phillip Noyce, the film—a smash hit—represents a smart recovery from the disastrous SLIVER. Harrison Ford lends a klutzy charm to the role of Jack Ryan that was missing from his first turn in the role; the best performance, however, comes from Sandoval, who manages to create more sympathy for his character than the film probably intended.

CLEO FROM 5 TO 7

(CLIO DE CINQ A SEPT)
1962 90m   bw   Drama   ★★★
Rome Paris   (France)

Corinne Marchand (Cleo), Antoine Bourseiller (Antoine), Dorothee Blanck (Dorothee), Michel Legrand (Bob, the Pianist), Dominique Davray (Angele), Jose-Luis de Vilallonga (The Lover), Jean-Claude Brialy, Anna Karina, Eddie Constantine, Sami Frey

p, Georges de Beauregard; d, Agnes Varda; w, Agnes Varda; ph, Jean Rabier; ed, Jeanne Verneau; m, Michel Legrand; prod d, Edith Tertza, Jean-Francois Adam; art d, Bernard Evein; cos, Alyette Samazeuilh

Literally, a slice of life. Agnes Varda's second feature opens with an overhead shot of a table, two pairs of women's hands, and a deck of tarot cards. The woman whose fortune is being read, Cleo (played superbly by Corinne Marchand), is told she has cancer. Cleo is dreading the results of a recent medical test and believes her fortune. The rest of the film is a chronicle of the next 90 minutes in her life. Photographed almost exclusively in the streets of Paris, CLEO FROM 5 TO 7 is a portrait of a woman whose view of life has previously never extended past her own vanity and singing success. Faced with the possibility of death, however, Cleo begins to perceive things differently—finding beauty and life in all things. Curiously, the only one of the film's scenes to fall completely flat is a silent comedy sketch that features Anna Karina, Jean-Luc Godard, Sami Frey, Jean-Claude Brialy, Eddie Constantine, and Yves Robert. One especially nice moment is a song, "Sans Toi" (by Michel Legrand and Varda), which Marchand delivers directly into the camera.

CLEOPATRA

1934 102m   bw   Historical   ★★★★
Paramount   (U.S.)

Claudette Colbert (Cleopatra), Warren William (Julius Caesar), Henry Wilcoxon (Marc Antony), Gertrude Michael (Calpurnia), Joseph Schildkraut (Herod), Ian Keith (Octavian), C. Aubrey Smith (Enobarbus), Ian MacLaren (Cassius), Arthur Hohl (Brutus), Leonard Mudie (Pothinos)

p, Cecil B. DeMille; d, Cecil B. DeMille; w, Waldemar Young, Vincent Lawrence (based on historical material by Bartlett Cormack, Jeanie MacPherson, Finley Peter Dunne, Jr.); ph, Victor Milner; ed, Anne Bauchens; m, Rudolph G. Kopp

AAN Best Picture; AA Best Cinematography: Victor Milner; AAN Best Film Editing: Anne Bauchens; AAN Best Sound Recording: Franklin Hansen; AAN Best Assistant Director: Cullen Tate

Opulent, totally satisfying DeMille, due in no small part to the vocal command and trickery brought to Cleopatra by Colbert, a surprisingly good choice despite her leanness and kittenish reputation. CLEOPATRA sails down the Nile with authority and majesty; it may well be DeMille's best film. William and Wilcoxon almost match Colbert; indeed, there's not a lemon in the entire cast. CLEOPATRA exemplifies DeMille's obsession with historical accuracy in setting and props. In one giant set crammed with hundreds of extras, as shooting was about to begin, he stopped everything when he spotted a small flagon 20 feet away. He walked over and picked it up, holding it aloft with disgust. It was silver-plated and represented an era much later than the setting of the film.

But his commercial genius demanded liberal doses of sexual fantasy mixed with the historically faithful set designs.

Nowhere in CLEOPATRA is this so obvious as in the infamous barge scene, where DeMille's rendition makes Shakespeare's description look like TUGBOAT ANNIE. While Wilcoxon and Colbert recline aboard the queen's bordello on the sea, a huge net is drawn up from the sea, holding dozens of squirming almost-naked girls—DeMille's catch of the day—who offer Wilcoxon giant sea shells which spill out priceless gems. Then a veil slowly descends around Colbert and the bedazzled Wilcoxon, and DeMille cuts to a shot of the enormous pleasure barge being rowed by hundreds of slaves into the darkened sea, a drummer beating out the cadence of the oarsmen and suggesting the additional rhythm of the unseen seduction. It is DeMille's carnal poetry in action.

CLEOPATRA was a box-office smash, but the critics tore at DeMille for representing the historical characters as satyrs and nymphomaniacs. Some of his severest critics complained about the abundance of British actors dominating the CLEOPATRA cast, speaking with English accents. Some carped about the slangy dialogue. But DeMille knew his public. To the writers of CLEOPATRA, DeMille specified contemporary, vernacular speech. They gave him just what he wanted, and DeMille kept the film sizzling. That's no history lesson, that's entertainment!

CLEOPATRA   _DVD_
1963   243m   c   Historical   ★★½
Fox   (U.S.)

Elizabeth Taylor _(Cleopatra)_, Richard Burton _(Mark Antony)_, Rex Harrison _(Julius Caesar)_, Pamela Brown _(High Priestess)_, George Cole _(Flavius)_, Hume Cronyn _(Sosigenes)_, Cesare Danova _(Apollodorus)_, Kenneth Haigh _(Brutus)_, Andrew Keir _(Agrippa)_, Martin Landau _(Rufio)_

p, Walter Wanger; d, Joseph L. Mankiewicz; w, Joseph L. Mankiewicz, Ranald MacDougall, Sidney Buchman (based on works by Plutarch, Appian, and Suetonius, and the novel _The Life And Times Of Cleopatra_ by Carlo Mario Franzero); ph, Leon Shamroy (Todd A-O, DeLuxe Color); ed, Dorothy Spencer; m, Alex North; prod d, John De Cuir; art d, Jack Martin Smith, Hilyard Brown, Herman A. Blumenthal, Elven Webb, Maurice Pelling, Boris Juraga; fx, L.B. Abbott, Emil Kosa Jr.; chor, Hermes Pan; cos, Irene Sharaff, Vittorio Nino Novarese

AAN Best Picture; AAN Best Actor: Rex Harrison; _AA Best Color Cinematography:_ Leon Shamroy; _AAN Best Film Editing:_ Dorothy Spencer; _AAN Best Original Score:_ Alex North; _AA Best Art Direction-Set Decoration (Color):_ John DeCuir, Jack Martin Smith, Hilyard Brown, Herman Blumenthal, Elven Webb, Maurice Pelling, Boris Juraga, Walter M. Scott, Paul S. Fox, Ray Moyer; _AA Best Costume Design (Color):_ Irene Sharaff, Vittorio Nino Novarese, Renie; _AAN Best Sound:_ James P. Corcoran; _AA Best Special Visual Effects:_ Emil Kosa Jr.

Chaucer's Wife of Bath plays Cleolizzie, the million-dollar sultana of '60s jetset sirens, in enough eyeliner to resurrect Theda Bara, and ten costumes for every occasion. This is not a film—it's a deal, decorated with extensive publicity, but weighed down by listless direction and lots of nasal talk, talk, talk. Even fans of camp would have to admit what's here is about an hour's worth of television MOW. Taylor brings notoriety and cleavage to her performance as Cleopatra; she's at her best when Cleo makes her entrance into Rome, when Taylor worried that the Catholic extras might riot and kill her. The scene is a triumph of morass over morality. Hurricane Liz conquers Rome! Otherwise, she plays the Egyptian tigress (original choice was Susan Hayward, an expert at tigresses, Biblical and otherwise) as a spewing, mewing, pampered Roman housecat who makes fusses because she can. Would the film have been better with Hayward, Peter

Finch and Stephen Boyd, directed by Mamoulian? Perhaps, but at least Harrison, taking over for Finch, strikes a few waspish notes. Otherwise, it's a Vegas-style history lesson, but dammit, a boring one, depriving us of a thousand laughs and cracks.

CLERKS   _DVD_
1994   92m   bw   Comedy   ★★★
View Askew Productions   (U.S.)   R

Brian O'Halloran _(Dante Hicks)_, Jeff Anderson _(Randal)_, Marilyn Ghigliotti _(Veronica)_, Lisa Spoonauer _(Caitlin)_, Jason Mewes _(Jay)_, Kevin Smith _(Silent Bob)_, Scott Schiaffo _(Chewlie's Rep)_, Scott Mosier _(William the Idiot Manchild/Angry Hockey Playing Customer/Angry Mourner)_, Walt Flanagan _(Wooden Cap Smoker/Egg Man/Offended Customer/Cat Admiring Bitter Customer/Angry Mourner)_, Al Berkowitz _(Old Man)_

p, Kevin Smith, Scott Mosier; d, Kevin Smith; w, Kevin Smith; ph, David Klein; ed, Kevin Smith, Scott Mosier; m, Scott Angley

This sourly amusing farce about suburban slackers is a lowball bid on the minimum production values needed to put across an independent first feature. Dante (Brian O'Halloran), who looks like a cranky Charlie Sheen in a Vandyke beard, is the proprietor of a convenience store in Asbury Park, NJ. Make that _inconvenience_ store, since Dante's working life, an unending stream of minor atrocities, is a prolonged slow burn. Dante's best friend Randal (Jeff Anderson) mans the video store next door, and spends his time ordering titles like HAPPY SCRAPPY HERO PUP and BEST OF BOTH WORLDS, a compilation of hermaphrodite porn. Their (considerable) downtime is spent in earnest debate over monumentally trivial issues, though a narrative of sorts does eventually unfold in a series of arch blackouts.

Some of the aimless dialogue is very sharp among these lumpen bourgeoisie, who've got wit and intellect to spare, but little in the way of education, ambition, or opportunity. ("There's nothing more exhilarating than pointing out the shortcomings of others, is there?" notes Randal.) Director Kevin Smith billboards his influences, cheekily thanking Hal Hartley, Richard Linklater, Spike Lee, and Jim Jarmusch in the closing crawl. Unlike his models, however, Smith hasn't demonstrated that his sensibility reaches much beyond bathroom humor and meaningless drift. It might have been more accurate to invoke that other Mt. Rushmore of Gen-X taste: Ren, Stimpy, Beavis, and Butt-head.

CLIENT, THE   _DVD_
1994   124m   c   Crime/Thriller   ★★★
Client Productions Inc./New Regency   PG-13
Productions/Alcor Films   (U.S.)

Susan Sarandon _(Reggie Love)_, Tommy Lee Jones _("Reverend" Roy Foltrigg)_, Brad Renfro _(Mark Sway)_, Mary-Louise Parker _(Dianne Sway)_, Anthony LaPaglia _(Barry "The Blade" Muldano)_, J.T. Walsh _(McThune)_, Anthony Edwards _(Clint Von Hooser)_, Will Patton _(Sergeant Hardy)_, Bradley Witford _(Thomas Fink)_, Anthony Heald _(Trumann)_

p, Arnon Milchan, Steven Reuther; d, Joel Schumacher; w, Akiva Goldsman, Robert Getchell (based on the novel by John Grisham); ph, Tony Pierce-Roberts; ed, Robert Brown; m, Howard Shore; prod d, Bruno Rubeo; art d, P. Michael Johnston; fx, Larry Fioritto, Wes Mattox; cos, Ingrid Ferrin

AAN Best Actress: Susan Sarandon

Based on the bestseller by John Grisham, THE CLIENT is a slickly packaged thriller wrapped in fashionable paranoia and tied up with an incongruously heartening moral. Susan

Sarandon won an Academy Award nomination for her portrayal of anti-establishment lawyer Reggie Love, whose tough surface hides a heart of pure Jell-O.

When young Mark Sway (Brad Renfro) discovers the truth about the murder of a U.S. Senator, he becomes the prey of murderous gangster Barry Muldano (Anthony LaPaglia). In desperate need of help, the boy walks into the office of feisty recovering alcoholic Reggie Love (Sarandon), who can't resist a hopeless case. Her first task is to protect Mark from flamboyant Federal Attorney Roy Foltrigg (Tommy Lee Jones), who tries to trick Mark into revealing what he knows. Unless Love can negotiate certain guarantees of protection before he testifies, her client and his family will be killed.

Though ostensibly a thriller, THE CLIENT is rather short on suspense; the movie's real center is the relationship between brittle professional Reggie Love and the tough, vulnerable boy she wants to protect. Jones puts on a captivating show, playing a swaggering tyrant in an expensive suit who's Bible-thumping one moment and preening for the cameras the next; but it's Sarandon and Renfro, an unusually appealing child actor, who dominate the film.

CLIFFHANGER

1993 112m c Action/Thriller   **DVD**
Carolco International N.V. (U.S./Netherlands)   ★★★
                                                    R

Sylvester Stallone (Gabe Walker), John Lithgow (Qualen), Michael Rooker (Hal Tucker), Janine Turner (Jessie Deighan), Rex Linn (Travers), Caroline Goodall (Kristel), Leon Robinson, billed as Leon (Kynette), Craig Fairbrass (Delmar), Gregory Scott Cummins (Ryan), Denis Forest (Heldon)

p, Alan Marshall, Renny Harlin; d, Renny Harlin; w, Michael France, Sylvester Stallone (from a story by France); ph, Alex Thomson, Adam Dale; ed, Frank J. Urioste; m, Trevor Jones; prod d, John Vallone; art d, Aurelio Crugnola, Christiaan Wagener; fx, Neil Krepela, John Bruno; cos, Ellen Mirojnick

AAN Best Sound: Bob Beemer, Tim Cooney, Michael Minkler; AAN Best Sound Effects Editing: Gregg Baxter, Wylie Stateman; AAN Best Visual Effects: John Bruno, Pamela Easly, Neil Krepela, John Richardson

CLIFFHANGER offers us breathtaking mountain scenery, some occasionally gripping action sequences, and a lot of gags—mostly unintentional and mostly courtesy of Sylvester Stallone. It may go down in screen history as the nail in the coffin of the "Die Hard" sub-genre, in which all the key elements of that blockbuster have been recycled to the point of self-parody.

Stallone plays Gabe Walker, a rescue climber pitted against a gang of hijackers whose plane has crashed on a snow-capped Rocky Mountain peak. Led by Qualen (John Lithgow), whose hammy quips and English accent peg him as a criminal mastermind, the gang is now intent on retrieving three suitcases containing $100 million. But they haven't reckoned on Walker, who can climb thousands of feet of snowy rockface clad only in a T-shirt, outpace a helicopter, and anticipate every move Qualen makes.

When he's not killing bad guys or rescuing his girlfriend, Jessie (Janine Turner), Walker gets to deliver some dialogue that is as spectacular, in its own Stallonesque way, as the scenery. (Qualen: "Walker, you're a real piece of work." Walker: "Yeah, an' you're a real piece of sh... ")

Audiences who stayed away from Stallone's early '90s comedies, OSCAR and STOP! OR MY MOM WILL SHOOT, may have been wrong. What CLIFFHANGER tells us is that the star *is* a comic actor, after all. From the moment he first opens his mouth, we give up any hope of a suspenseful action drama and settle in, instead, for a ride punctuated alternately by chuckles and groans.

CLOCK, THE

1945 90m bw Romance   ★★★★
MGM (U.S.)

Judy Garland (Alice Mayberry), Robert Walker (Cpl. Joe Allen), James Gleason (Al Henry), Keenan Wynn (The Drunk), Marshall Thompson (Bill), Lucille Gleason (Mrs. Al Henry), Ruth Brady (Helen), Chester Clute (Michael Henry), Dick Elliott (Friendly Man)

p, Arthur Freed; d, Vincente Minnelli; w, Robert Nathan, Joseph Schrank (based on a story by Paul and Pauline Gallico); ph, George Folsey; ed, George White; m, George Bassman; art d, Cedric Gibbons, William Ferrari; fx, A. Arnold Gillespie; cos, Irene

A small wartime gem featuring the luminous Garland, directed by her future husband, in a rare nonsinging role. The story is deceptively simple; it is in the subtle touches that the genius of this film lies. Garland and Walker meet under the big clock at Pennsylvania Station in New York. They fall in love and marry within 48 hours. This kind of thing happened often in real life, and Gallico's story feels authentic. So does the incredible rear-screen projection work and the huge sets that would cause any New Yorker to bet serious money that the film was shot on location in the Big Apple. Not so. It was a back-lot job and a tribute to the talents of its technicians. Every single bit player is perfectly cast, and special plaudits go to Wynn, who plays a drunken patriot.

This was Minnelli's first straight directing job and he went on to distinguish himself away from musicals with such giants as THE BAD AND THE BEAUTIFUL, FATHER OF THE BRIDE and many others. Looking at the two young, well-scrubbed stars, it's hard to believe that both their lives would end tragically. Walker, only 33 at the time of his death, had been married to Jennifer Jones and John Ford's daughter, Barbara. He'd been institutionalized for alcohol abuse almost a year before returning to work in Alfred Hitchcock's STRANGERS ON A TRAIN. While filming MY SON JOHN in 1951, he died from too many sedatives doctors had prescribed to calm his emotional instability. This is a rare tribute to the acting genius of Garland, who would still have had all the makings of a star, even if she had never sung a note.

CLOCKMAKER, THE

(L'HORLOGER DE SAINT-PAUL)   **DVD**
1973 105m c Drama/Crime   ★★★
Lira (France)

Philippe Noiret (Michel Descombes), Jean Rochefort (Commissioner Guiboud), Jacques Denis (Antoine), William Sabatier (Lawyer), Andree Tainsy (Madeleine), Sylvain Rougerie (Bernard Descombes), Christine Pascal (Liliane Terrini), Cecile Vassort (Martine), Yves Afonso, Jacques Hilling

d, Bertrand Tavernier; w, Jean Aurenche, Pierre Bost (based on the novel The Clockmaker of Everton by Georges Simenon); ph, Pierre-William Glenn; ed, Armand Psenny; m, Philippe Sarde

Philippe Noiret gives a moving performance in this low-key, but powerful adaptation of a Georges Simenon novel that marked the directorial debut of director Bertrand Tavernier.

Michel Descombes (Philippe Noiret), a widowed Lyons watchmaker, is shattered to learn that his only son, Bernard (Sylvain Rougerie), is suspected of murdering an abusive factory security guard named Razon and has fled the city with his leftist girlfriend Liliane (Christine Pascal), who worked at the factory. Descombes tells police chief Guiboud (Jean Rochefort) that he's never even met Liliane, and as the investigation continues, he realizes that he knows very little about Bernard's life. Friends of Liliane's tell Descombes that

Razon had tried to rape Liliane and then had her fired. Descombes is hounded by both left and right-wing reporters, and his shop windows are smashed by right-wing friends of Razon. When Bernard and Liliane are caught, Bernard won't speak to his father, except to say that he murdered Razon because he was "filth."

Despite a plot revolving around a murder and its Simenon provenance, THE CLOCKMAKER is not a suspense thriller, but a finely wrought psychological character study that also deals with politics, the media, and parent-child relationships. Dedicated to Jacques Prevert (who wrote Jean Renoir's leftist classic THE CRIME OF MONSIEUR LANGE), the style of the movie is an intriguing mixture of modern and classical sensibilities, as it was co-written by Jean Aurenche and Pierre Bost, two veterans who were closely established with the old guard French cinema of "quality" to which Tavernier was devoted when he was a film critic. The script bears the old-fashioned virtues of narrative clarity and character development, but Tavernier brings to the film a gritty, authentic style, an improvisatory feel, and a jaundiced look at political corruption, media manipulation, and hypocritical French society. Although relatively modest in both its aims and its accomplishments compared to Tavernier's more ambitious later films, THE CLOCKMAKER remains an auspicious debut.

CLOCKWORK ORANGE, A   *DVD*
1971 137m c   Science Fiction   ★★★★
Warner Bros.   (U.K.)   R

Malcolm McDowell (Alex), Patrick Magee (Mr. Alexander), Michael Bates (Chief Guard), Warren Clarke (Dim), John Clive (Stage Actor), Adrienne Corri (Mrs. Alexander), Carl Duering (Dr. Brodsky), Paul Farrell (Hobo), Clive Francis (Lodger), Michael Gover (Prison Warden)

p, Stanley Kubrick; d, Stanley Kubrick; w, Stanley Kubrick (based on the novel by Anthony Burgess); ph, John Alcott; ed, Bill Butler; m, Walter Carlos; prod d, John Barry; art d, Russell Hagg, Peter Shields; cos, Milena Canonero

AAN Best Picture; AAN Best Director: Stanley Kubrick; AAN Best Adapted Screenplay: Stanley Kubrick; AAN Best Film Editing: Bill Butler

Who else but Stanley Kubrick could successfully direct an ultra-stylish, sci-fi cult film about the impossibility of redemption in the absence of freely willed sin? In a shabbily futuristic British welfare state, Alex (Malcolm McDowell) leads a gang of juvenile delinquents through nightly rounds of beatings, rapes and, as they call it, "ultraviolence." The lads wear motley uniforms—jumpsuits fitted with codpieces—and speak in a bizarre patois that combines elements of colloquial Russian with Cockney rhyming slang; Alex hates school but loves Beethoven, whose music he associates with sexual violence. Among their victims is a prominent writer (Patrick Magee); they beat him senseless and gang-rape his wife (Adrienne Corri). After violently suppressing an uprising among his "droogies" (from the Russian for "friends"), Alex is betrayed by them during an attack on another home, knocked senseless and left for the police. In prison, he agrees to undergo horrific experiments in "aversion therapy" in order to shorten his term. Now nauseated by the mere thought of violence—or Beethoven—he's pronounced cured and released into the outside world. There, vengeance of one kind or another is visited upon him by his erstwhile fellow gang-members (now policemen), and by his former victims (including Magee). Victimized by his former victims, he becomes a media celebrity and reaches a cynical accomodation with the parliamentary opposition. "I was cured, all right," Alex observes.

Kubrick's liberal, anti-authoritarian reading of Anthony Burgess's very Catholic allegorical novel is morally confused but tremendously powerful. A CLOCKWORK ORANGE is a visually dazzling, highly unsettling work that revolves around one of the few truly amoral characters in film or literature. It pits a gleefully vicious individual against a blandly inhuman state, leaving the viewer little room for emotional involvement (though McDowell gives such an ebullient, wide-eyed performance as the Beethoven-loving delinquent that it is hard for us not to feel some sympathy toward him). Meanwhile, we're dazzled by Kubrick's directorial pyrotechnics—slow motion, fast motion, fish-eye lenses, etc.; entertained by John Barry's witty, ostentatious sets; and intrigued by dialogue laden with Burgess's specially created slang ("good" is "horrorshow"; sex is "the old inout," etc.). A particularly graphic film for its time, A CLOCKWORK ORANGE continues to divide critics. No serious moviegoer can afford to ignore it.

CLOSE ENCOUNTERS OF THE THIRD KIND   *DVD*
1977 135m c   Science Fiction   ★★★★★
Columbia   (U.S.)   PG

Richard Dreyfuss (Roy Neary), Francois Truffaut (Claude Lacombe), Teri Garr (Ronnie Neary), Melinda Dillon (Jillian Guiler), Cary Guffey (Barry Guiler), Bob Balaban (Interpreter Laughlin), J. Patrick McNamara (Project Leader), Warren Kemmerling (Wild Bill), Roberts Blossom (Farmer), Philip Dodds (Jean Claude)

p, Julia Phillips, Michael Phillips; d, Steven Spielberg; w, Steven Spielberg; ph, Vilmos Zsigmond (Metrocolor); ed, Michael Kahn; m, John Williams; prod d, Joe Alves; art d, Dan Lomino; fx, Roy Arbogast, Gregory Jein, Douglas Trumbull, Matthew Yuricich, Richard Yuricich; cos, Jim Linn

AAN Best Supporting Actress: Melinda Dillon; AAN Best Director: Steven Spielberg; AA Best Cinematography: Vilmos Zsigmond; AAN Best Film Editing: Michael Kahn; AAN Best Original Score: John Williams; AAN Best Art Direction-Set Decoration: Joe Alves, Dan Lomino, Phil Abramson; AAN Best Sound: Robert Knudson, Robert J. Glass, Don MacDougall, Gene S. Cantamessa; AAN Best Visual Effects: Roy Arbogast, Douglas Trumbull, Matthew Yuricich, Gregory Jein, Richard Yuricich; AA Special Achievement Award—Sound Effects Editing: Frank Warner

Steven Spielberg proves decisively that a special effects-dependent film need not be cold, mechanistic, or simpleminded. Here he presents first contact with an extraterrestrial culture in spirit of near-religious awe in sharp contrast to the dark paranoia of traditional science fiction Cold War parables. CLOSE ENCOUNTERS OF THE THIRD KIND is a humanistic postmodern masterpiece that incorporates much of movie history—images, sounds, and subtle evocations of the works of Walt Disney, John Ford, Alfred Hitchcock, Cecil B. DeMille, and Chuck Jones—into its revisionist project. Classic Sixties fantasy television fare such as "Star Trek," "Bewitched," and "The Twilight Zone" also figure in the meaningful mosaic of citations. This film shows the power pop-culture imagery exerts over our humdrum lives and the ever present lure of escapism. The movies may set you free, it suggests, but perhaps only at the cost of losing real human relationships.

The story depicts the life-transforming experiences of lineman Roy Neary (Richard Dreyfuss) who is sent out into the night to investigate a mysterious power outage. His truck gets stalled on the road and he's bathed in a brilliant light from above. Thus begins Roy's journey from disinterested spectator to impassioned participant in an otherworldly spectacle. A mysterious vision and five musical notes are imprinted in his mind after he witnesses strange lights in the sky. His family life is devastated by his obsession but he acquires a spiritual surrogate family along the path to enlightenment including the delightful (and delighted) child Cary Guffey who is spirited away from his mother (Melinda Dillon) during the film's only frightening set piece and Francois Truffaut (the beloved director of such French New Wave classics as THE 400 BLOWS, JULES AND JIM and THE WILD CHILD) as Claude Lacombe, the endearingly humane director of the scientific ad hoc "welcome wagon."

Special effects master Douglas Trumbull (the FX wizard of 2001: A SPACE ODYSSEY) created the strikingly beautiful and dreamy visions that set the look of this film apart from the cool razzle dazzle of Industrial Light and Magic projects. John Williams contributes one of his most unusual and memorable scores. This is one for the angels.

CLOSELY WATCHED TRAINS   DVD

(OSTRE SLEDOVANE VLAKY)
1966   89m   bw   Comedy/Drama   ★★★★
Barrandov/Ladislav Fikar/Bohumil Smida
(Czechoslovakia)

Vaclav Neckar *(Trainee Milos Hrma)*, Jitka Bendova *(Conductor Masa)*, Josef Somr *(Train Dispatcher Hubicka)*, Vladimir Valenta *(Stationmaster Max)*, Vlastimil Brodsky *(Counselor Zednicek)*, Jiri Menzel *(Dr. Brabek)*, Libuse Havelkova *(Max's Wife)*, Alois Vachek *(Novak)*, Jitka Zelenohorska *(Zdenka)*, Ferdinand Kruta *(Masa's Uncle)*

p, Zdenek Oves; d, Jiri Menzel; w, Jiri Menzel, Bohumil Hrabal (based on his novel); ph, Jaromir Sofr; ed, Jirina Lukesova; m, Jiri Sust; art d, Oldrich Bosak; cos, Ruzena Bulickova

AA Best Foreign Language Film

The first feature from the 28-year-old Czech filmmaker Menzel is a comic, humanistic look at a teenage railway trainee, Milos (Neckar), who is sent off to a desolate station in Bohemia during the German occupation of Czechoslovakia. Hidden away from much of the rest of the world, Milos and the very ordinary characters who pass through the station try to live as if they were not caught in the midst of WWII. Milos learns his trade with relative ease, working under the experienced guidance of dispatcher Hubicka (Somr). A bored womanizer, Hubicka also becomes the uneasy boy's mentor in the ways of the world, which are all too quickly being thrust upon him. During the course of the film, Milos turns freedom fighter and experiences a variety of incidents, including sexual initiation, a botched suicide, and an act of heroism.

Possibly the best known and the most commercially successful film of the Czech New Wave of the 1960s during the all-too-brief Prague Spring, CLOSELY WATCHED TRAINS went on to win an Oscar for Best Foreign Film. Comic, tragic, romantic, and realistic, it is a film of great warmth and honesty, photographed in wonderfully stark black and white and cast with an exceptional group of actors.

CLOSER   DVD

2004   98m   c   Romance/Drama   ★★★½
Inside Track Productions/Icarus Productions/   R
John Calley Productions/Avenue Pictures   (U.S.)

Natalie Portman *(Alice Ayres)*, Jude Law *(Dan Wolf)*, Julia Roberts *(Anna)*, Clive Owen *(Larry)*, Nick Hobbs *(Taxi Driver)*, Colin Stinton *(Customs Officer)*

p, Cary Brokaw, John Calley, Mike Nichols; d, Mike Nichols; w, Patrick Marber (based on the play by Patrick Marber); ph, Stephen Goldblatt; ed, John Bloom, Antonia Van Drimmelen; prod d, Tim Hatley; art d, Hannah Moseley, Mark Raggett; fx, Stuart Brisdon; cos, Ann Roth

AAN Best Supporting Actor: Clive Owen; *AAN Best Supporting Actress:* Natalie Portman

Breathtakingly cruel and quietly devastating, Mike Nichols' adaptation of Patrick Marber's acclaimed play peers beneath the sheets as two couples wound each other in the name of love.

Newly arrived in London from New York, punky, fresh-faced stripper Alice (Natalie Portman) is hit by a car; aspiring novelist Dan (Jude Law) comes to her aid. A year later Dan has written his first book, which draws extensively on Alice's experiences, and impulsively kisses soon-to-be divorced American photographer Anna (Julia Roberts) while having his book-jacket photo taken. Anna rebuffs Dan after establishing that he's living with Alice, but the damage is done: the possibility of an affair has been kindled. Some months later, Dan's novel is faltering and, in a fit of late-night naughtiness, he logs onto an online chat room and pretends to be a lusty blond named "Anna." Frustrated dermatologist Larry (Clive Owen) takes the bait and Dan sets up a rendezvous at the London Aquarium, where the real Anna often goes to relax. Larry and Anna wind up together, and the couples cross paths at Anna's first show four months after that, setting in motion a series of guilty flirtations, impulsive encounters and deceptively casual betrayals.

More than 30 years after directing Jules Feiffer's excoriating CARNAL KNOWLEDGE, the 73-year-old Nichols returns to the front and finds the details of the war between the sexes different, but the bitter dynamics exactly the same. When the laws of attraction kick in, the rules of engagement are thrown out, and all's fair in sex and suspicion. Overall, Owen and Law are more nuanced than Roberts and Portman, but Portman's dewy youth is 90 percent of Alice (the remaining 10 is an eleventh-hour twist), and Nichols uses the unkindly costumed Roberts so skillfully that her performance looks like a revelation.

CLUELESS   DVD

1995   97m   c   Comedy/Romance   ★★★★
Robert Lawrence Productions/Paramount   (U.S.)   PG-13

Alicia Silverstone *(Cher Horowitz)*, Stacey Dash *(Dionne)*, Brittany Murphy *(Tai)*, Paul Rudd *(Josh)*, Dan Hedaya *(Mel Hamilton)*, Donald Adeosun Faison, billed as Donald Faison *(Murray)*, Elisa Donovan *(Amber)*, Breckin Meyer *(Travis Birkenstock)*, Jeremy Sisto *(Elton)*, Aida Linares *(Lucy)*

p, Robert Lawrence, Scott Rudin; d, Amy Heckerling; w, Amy Heckerling; ph, Bill Pope; ed, Debra Chiate; m, David Kitay; prod d, Steven Jordan; art d, William Hiney; chor, Patrick Romano; cos, Mona May

Just beneath the bubbly, candy-colored surface of this good-natured fluff about privileged California teens lies a sharply observed comedy of manners with a good deal more to say about family, romance, and friendship in the '90s than mainstream audiences have any right to expect. Like its effortlessly adorable protagonist Cher, CLUELESS is anything but.

Pretty, impeccably groomed Cher Hamilton (Alicia Silverstone) is the most popular girl at Bronson Alcott High School (Beverly Hills High in all but name). Her father (Dan Hedaya) is a successful lawyer who indulges her every whim (her mom died during routine liposuction surgery), and her best friend Dionne (Stacey Dash) shares her preoccupations: music, fitness, and fashion. Cher's perfect life is only slightly disrupted when her ex-step-brother Josh (Paul Rudd)—a *terribly* serious college student—comes to stay. Stung by Josh's exhortations that she should try to do some good in the world, Cher resolves to rescue grunge girl Tai (Brittany Murphy) from a life of social exile. The result, however, is not at all what she anticipates.

Cher (winningly played by Silverstone) is a beautifully packaged bundle of contradictions: superficially sophisticated but deeply ignorant, kind but oblivious, controlling but generous. She's clever without being smart, instinctively perceptive without the discipline that would tell her what to do with her insights. That Heckerling and Silverstone make Cher entirely lovable without glossing over her substantial deficiencies is one of the film's greatest triumphs. The other is its deft use of language. Cher and her friends speak a sleek, allusive patois that's almost Asian in its sensitivity to inflection and poetic in its reliance on convoluted metaphor. Can this remarkable film really be based on Jane Austen's *Emma*? *As if!*

COAL MINER'S DAUGHTER *DVD*
1980 125m c Biography/Musical ★★★★
Universal (U.S.) PG

Sissy Spacek *(Loretta)*, Tommy Lee Jones *(Doolittle "Mooney" Lynn)*, Levon Helm *(Ted Webb)*, Phyllis Boyens *(Clara Webb)*, Bill Anderson Jr., Foister Dickerson, Malla McCown, Pamela McCown, Kevin Salvilla *(Webb Children)*, William Sanderson *(Lee Dollarhide)*

p, Bernard Schwartz; d, Michael Apted; w, Thomas Rickman (based on autobiography by Loretta Lynn with George Vescey); ph, Ralf D. Bode (Technicolor); ed, Arthur Schmidt; m, Owen Bradley; prod d, John W. Corso; cos, Joe I. Tompkins

AAN Best Picture; AA Best Actress: Sissy Spacek; AAN Best Adapted Screenplay: Tom Rickman; AAN Best Cinematography: Ralf D. Bode; AAN Best Film Editing: Arthur Schmidt; AAN Best Art Direction-Set Decoration: John W. Corso, John M. Dwyer; AAN Best Sound: Richard Portman, Roger Heman, Jim Alexander

The rare expert film bio. COAL MINER'S DAUGHTER features an Oscar-winning performance by Sissy Spacek as country music queen Loretta Lynn. Masterfully directed by Michael Apted, the film traces the famed country singer's life from her beginnings in a tumbledown shack in Butcher Hollow, Kentucky, through her huge success, marital discord, and battle with prescription drugs. The film's early sequences are lyrical, melancholy accounts of mountain life and comprise the film's most poignant, memorable moments. There are outstanding acting jobs by Levon Helm and Phyllis Boyens as Lynn's parents, Tommy Lee Jones as her well-meaning, ne'er-do-well husband, and Beverly D'Angelo in a dazzling turn as the magnificent Patsy Cline. Spacek and D'Angelo do their own warbling quite expertly; after this, it's hard to get worked up over Jessica Lange's lukewarm, lipsynched take on Cline in SWEET DREAMS.

COCA-COLA KID, THE *DVD*
1985 94m c Comedy ★★★
Smart Egg/Cinecom/Film Gallery (Australia) R

Eric Roberts *(Becker)*, Greta Scacchi *(Terri)*, Bill Kerr *(T. George McDowell)*, Chris Haywood *(Kim)*, Kris McQuade *(Juliana)*, Max Gilles *(Frank)*, Tony Barry *(Bushman)*, Paul Chubb *(Fred)*, David Slingsby *(Waiter)*, Tim Finn *(Philip)*

p, David Roe, Sylvie Le Clezio; d, Dusan Makavejev; w, Frank Moorhouse (based on the short story collections *The Americans, Baby,* and *The Electrical Experience* by Moorhouse); ph, Dean Semler (Panavision, Eastmancolor); ed, John Scott; m, William Motzing; prod d, Graham Walker; cos, Terry Ryan

When Coca-Cola's big bosses suspect that profits could be greater in Australia, they send in Eric Roberts, a quirky wunderkind troubleshooter who, as an ex-Marine, takes pride in the company and views Coca-Cola as a symbol of the U.S. Arriving at the Australian office, he meets Greta Scacchi, a beautiful young secretary who wanders around the office in her stocking feet, lets her daughter photocopy her face on the office copier, and is nearly raped by her angry estranged husband. After studying a geographical representation of the areas where their product is being sold, Roberts discovers a section of Australia completely devoid of his company's beverage. This region prefers a local soft drink made by eccentric Bill Kerr, an embittered, trigger-happy old man, now determined to keep Coke's imperialists off his land and to continue his operations in a traditional, antiquated, steam-powered plant.

In THE COCA-COLA KID Yugoslavian director Dusan Makavejev has made a truly international picture that, like Coca-Cola, knows no borders, enlisting the contributions of an Australian writer, Frank Moorhouse; an American actor, Roberts; and a British actress, Scacchi. Scacchi, exuding a raw sexuality, makes a lasting impression, but Roberts's handsomeness can't save his ham acting. This is far from Makavejev's finest work (WR: MYSTERIES OF THE ORGANISM and SWEET MOVIE are much more challenging), but it is the film that has spread the director's political message to the widest audience.

COCOANUTS, THE *DVD*
1929 90m bw Comedy ★★★½
Paramount (U.S.)

Groucho Marx *(Hammer)*, Harpo Marx *(Harpo)*, Chico Marx *(Chico)*, Zeppo Marx *(Jamison)*, Mary Eaton *(Polly)*, Oscar Shaw *(Bob)*, Kay Francis *(Penelope)*, Margaret Dumont *(Mrs. Potter)*, Cyril Ring *(Yates)*, Basil Ruysdael *(Hennessey)*

p, Monta Bell, James R. Cowan; d, Robert Florey, Joseph Santley; w, Morrie Ryskind (based on the play by George S. Kaufman and Irving Berlin); ph, George Folsey; chor, Joseph Santley, Robert Florey

The greatest of zanies, the Marx Brothers, perform with dizzying speed in this farcical and nearly plotless romp through a Florida hotel, ostensibly dealing with the arrival and departure of would-be millionaires getting richer or poorer during the Florida land boom of the late 1920s. The mayhem is often side-splitting in this "pure" Marx vehicle, where the love story is strictly incidental. While they basically kept to the routines audiences had enjoyed in the original play by George S. Kaufman and Irving Berlin, the boys were given their usual freedom to ad lib; these bits were constantly changing, even during the shooting of the film. Berlin himself cut many tunes that were never sung since the brothers cavalierly changed the material.

This is a crude, shapeless talkie, a technically unsophisticated film in which the sound is static and the camera immobile, with the comedians leaping into the set scenes. Yet the boys are there in all their frenetic glory. Harpo honks his horn for the first time, chasing but never catching a scantily clad cutie; he would pursue her in vain for decades to come, while his brothers chewed up the sets and spat out laughter. THE COCOANUTS was officially the debut of the madcap brothers, although they had appeared in an obscure silent production, HUMOR RISK, which is now an apparently lost film.

COCOON
1985 117m c Comedy/Science Fiction ★★★
Fox (U.S.) PG-13

Don Ameche *(Art Selwyn)*, Wilford Brimley *(Ben Luckett)*, Hume Cronyn *(Joe Finley)*, Brian Dennehy *(Walter)*, Jack Gilford *(Bennie Lefkowitz)*, Steve Guttenberg *(Jack Bonner)*, Maureen Stapleton *(Mary Luckett)*, Jessica Tandy *(Alma Finley)*, Gwen Verdon *(Bess McCarthy)*, Herta Ware *(Rose Lefkowitz)*

p, Richard D. Zanuck, David Brown, Lili Fini Zanuck; d, Ron Howard; w, Tom Benedek; ph, Don Peterman, Jordan Klein (Deluxe Color); ed, Michael Hill, Dan Hanley; m, James Horner; prod d, Jack T. Collis; fx, Greg Cannom, Rick Baker; cos, Aggie Guerard Rodgers, Mort Schwartz

AA Best Supporting Actor: Don Ameche; *AA Best Visual Effects:* Ken Ralston, Ralph McQuarrie, Scott Farrar, David Berry

In this fun, lighthearted comedy, a group of aliens led by Brian Dennehy arrive from the planet Antarea and take on human form so they can go about their work without detection. They land near the heart of geriatric country, St. Petersburg, Florida, and rent a tour boat from Steve Guttenberg. They also rent a nearby home that had been left unattended, thereby enabling some elderly residents at a rest home—Don Ameche, Wilford Brimley, and Hume Cronyn—to sneak in and use its indoor pool. Guttenberg takes the boat to a specified spot in the ocean where Dennehy and his crew pull boulder-like cocoons from the ocean floor, which they store in the swimming pool. Later when Ameche, Brimley, and Cronyn take their usual swim, they notice the curious cocoons and then begin to sense a change in themselves—they are suddenly more youthful and vital.

A gentle and effective heart-tugger, COCOON tries to make its audience feel good, but you can't help but feel uneasy about the vision of old age that director Ron Howard depicts—one in which the young cannot accept the notion of getting old. The derivative special effects feel like leftovers from the infinitely superior CLOSE ENCOUNTERS OF THE THIRD KIND. A number of the performances are superb, including Ameche's, for which he won a Best Supporting Actor Oscar. The film also won an Academy Award for Best Visual Effects.

COHEN AND TATE
1989 85m c Action/Thriller   ★★★½
Nelson (U.S.)   R

Roy Scheider *(Cohen)*, Adam Baldwin *(Tate)*, Harley Cross *(Travis Knight)*, Cooper Huckabee, Suzanne Savoy

p, Antony Rufus Isaacs, Jeff Young; d, Eric Red; w, Eric Red; ph, Victor J. Kemper (Eastmancolor); ed, Edward Abroms; m, Bill Conti; prod d, David M. Haber

Some of the most interesting films of the 1980s offer a heady mix of a B-movie ethos, a focus on unpleasant people in unpleasant situations, disturbing undercurrents, and haunting imagery. COHEN & TATE is a noteworthy example of this tendency and a remarkably assured first film for writer-director Eric Red. COHEN & TATE begins at a farm in Oklahoma, where nine-year-old Travis Knight (Harley Cross) and his family are hiding under FBI protection after Travis witnesses a mob hit. When Cohen (Roy Scheider) and Tate (Adam Baldwin) show up, the two hit men kill the boy's family and kidnap the child, planning to take him to their mob bosses in Houston. The film turns into a very grim variation on O. Henry's "The Ransom of Red Chief" as the boy sizes up the tense group dynamics and begins setting the men against each other.

COHEN & TATE works because of its unapologetic B-movie style, including its underlying themes. The performances are terrific. Although more than half the film's action takes place in a car, COHEN & TATE is never boring, thanks to Red's crackling dialogue and interesting visual style. COHEN & TATE is a suspenseful, funny, and insightful thriller that should please people with a taste for something different and subversive.

COLD COMFORT FARM   *DVD*
1995 95m c Drama/Romance/Comedy   ★★★½
BBC Films/Thames International (U.K.)   PG

Eileen Atkins *(Judith Starkadder)*, Kate Beckinsale *(Flora Poste)*, Sheila Burrell *(Ada Doom)*, Freddie Jones *(Adam Lambsbreath)*, Joanna Lumley *(Mrs. Smiling)*, Ian McKellen *(Amos Starkadder)*,

Maria Miles *(Elfine)*, Rufus Sewell *(Seth)*, Ivan Kaye *(Reuben)*, Rupert Penry-Jones *(Dick Hawk-Monitor)*

d, John Schlesinger; w, Malcolm Bradbury (based on the novel by Stella Gibbons); ph, Chris Seager; ed, Mark Day; m, Robert Lockhart; prod d, Malcolm Thornton; art d, Jim Holloway; fx, Mike Kelt, Jeremy King; cos, Amy Roberts

COLD COMFORT FARM, based on the 1932 novel by Stella Gibbons, is a lively satire set in rural 1930s England.

Suddenly orphaned, Flora Poste (Kate Beckinsale) procures an invitation to Cold Comfort Farm, the bleak home of her distant cousins, the Starkadders. When she arrives, she's appalled by the disheveled homestead and its odd inhabitants. Cousin Judith (Eileen Atkins) tells fortunes while bemoaning her fate; her husband Amos (Ian McKellen) preaches fire-and-brimstone sermons at the Church of the Quivering Brethren; their two sons, handsome Seth (Rufus Sewell) dreams of Hollywood stardom, while Reuben (Ivan Kaye) fears Flora has designs on the farm; and fey young Elfine (Maria Miles) is in love with upper-crust Dick Hawk-Monitor (Rupert Penry-Jones). The whole lot are ruled by the tyrannical matriarch Ada Doom (Sheila Burrell), who once "saw something nasty in the woodshed," and forbids her wretched brood ever to leave the farm. Undaunted, Flora immediately sets about straightening up their doom-laden existence, and, with a little help from her London friend Mrs. Smiling (Joanna Lumley), she's a smashing success.

This is your basic "fish out of water" tale, though novelist Malcolm Bradbury's clever adaptation wisely avoids parable. While Gibbons' novel could be dry and earnest, Schlesinger's film is outspoken and robust. Some of the most memorable scenes are those that take place in London, where smart photography and witty production design dazzle the audience. Schlesinger has recruited a very talented cast, with Beckinsale charming as the dogged sophisticate; Atkins endowing Judith with formidable presence; McKellen amusingly homespun; and Lumley delightfully daft as Mrs. Smiling, a London socialite who happens to be a devoted collector of brassieres.

COLD MOUNTAIN   *DVD*
2004 155m c Drama/Historical/War   ★★★
Bona Fide Productions/Mirage Enterprises/Miramax   R
(U.S.)

Jude Law *(Inman)*, Nicole Kidman *(Ada Monroe)*, Renee Zellweger *(Ruby Thewes)*, Donald Sutherland *(Reverend Monroe)*, Ray Winstone *(Teague)*, Brendan Gleeson *(Stobrod)*, Philip Seymour Hoffman *(Veasey)*, Natalie Portman *(Sara)*, Kathy Baker *(Sally Swanger)*, James Gammon *(Esco Swanger)*

p, Albert Berger, William Horberg, Sydney Pollack, Ron Yerxa; d, Anthony Minghella; w, Anthony Minghella (based on the novel by Charles Frazier); ph, John Seale; ed, Walter Murch; m, Gabriel Yared; prod d, Dante Ferretti; fx, Dennis Lowe, Robert Vazquez; cos, Ann Roth

AA Best Supporting Actress: Renee Zellweger; *AAN Best Actor:* Jude Law; *AAN Best Cinematography:* John Seale; *AAN Best Original Score:* Gabriel Yared; *AAN Best Original Song:* "Scarlet Tide"; T Bone Burnett, Elvis Costello; *AAN Best Original Song:* "You Will Be My Ain True Love"; Sting; *AAN Best Editing:* Walter Murch

Adapted from Charles Frazier's Civil War spin on "The Odyssey," Anthony Minghella's heroic depiction of lives ground up in the machinery of war is seldom as affecting as it means to be.

June 1864: Dispatched to a hellish field hospital after he's badly wounded during the brutal Battle of the Crater at Petersburg, Virginia, war-weary Confederate soldier Inman

(Jude Law) goes AWOL as soon as he's able to walk. As he trudges the 300 miles back to his home in Cold Mountain, North Carolina, Inman's tentative courtship of educated, city-bred beauty Ada (Nicole Kidman) unfolds in flashback. Ada, devoted to her ailing father, the Reverend Monroe (Donald Sutherland), moves to rural Cold Mountain armed with an endless supply of decorative but impractical skills. She and Inman, a sensitive laborer, exchange soulful glances but declare their intentions only under pressure: Moments before Inman is mustered out of town, they share a passionate kiss, and Ada vows to wait faithfully until he returns. Soon after, Reverend Monroe dies, leaving Ada bereft and ill-equipped to survive on her own. She's saved from starvation by feisty Ruby Thewes (Renee Zellweger), who teaches Ada to work her own farm in exchange for room and board. Inman, meanwhile, picks his way through the war-torn South as the inevitability of a Confederate defeat becomes clear.

Kidman and Law are both chilly performers, and their fundamental remoteness drains the sublimated passion from Inman and Ada's hope-sustaining romance. It also allows the supporting cast to steal the movie out from under them. Though verging on caricature, Zellweger's performance is undeniably energetic, and Kathy Baker, Ray Winstone, Philip Seymour Hoffman and Giovanni Ribisi all leave far more vivid impressions than the stars.

COLLATERAL   📀
2004 120m c   Thriller   ★★★
Parkes/MacDonald Productions/Edge City Productions/   R
Paramount/DreamWorks SKG   (U.S.)

Tom Cruise *(Vincent)*, Jamie Foxx *(Max Durocher)*, Jada Pinkett *(Annie)*, Mark Ruffalo *(Fanning)*, Peter Berg *(Richard Weidner)*, Bruce McGill *(Pedrosa)*, Irma P. Hall *(Ida Duricher)*, Barry Shabaka Henley *(Daniel)*, Bodhi Elfman *(Young Professional Man)*, Debi Mazar *(Young Professional Woman)*

p, Michael Mann, Julia Richardson; d, Michael Mann; w, Stuart Beattie; ph, Dion Beebe, Paul Cameron; ed, Jim Miller, Paul Rubell; m, James Newton Howard; prod d, David Wasco; art d, Daniel T. Dorrance; fx, Thomas L. Fisher, Robert Rosselo, David Sosalla, John Sullivan; cos, Jeffrey Kurland

AAN Best Supporting Actor: Jamie Foxx; *AAN Best Film Editing:* Jim Miller, Paul Rubell

Michael Mann's tight, implausible thriller is so propulsive and crammed with vivid performances that it seems mean-spirited to point out that it's essentially an urban variation on THE HITCHER with nothing much going on underneath.

L.A. cabbie Max Durocher (Jamie Foxx) likes driving at night. The snarls in the city's tangle of freeways and surface roads are less knotty, passengers seem a little less harried, and occasionally he gets a nice conversation going, like his brief, flirtatious banter with high-powered lawyer Annie (Jada Pinkett-Smith), whom he drops off at a downtown office building. Max's next passenger, an anonymous-looking businessman with a brush of silver hair, matching steel-gray suit and a laptop, needs a cabbie willing to ferry him around all night and is willing to pay handsomely. Max agrees to play chauffeur for the brisk but apparently genial Vincent (Tom Cruise), whose first "business meeting" is at a rundown apartment complex. When a corpse plummets from a window onto the roof of Max's impeccably clean cab, Vincent's response—he stashes the body in the trunk—racks the situation into sharp and unsettling focus. Max has a contract killer in the backseat, an assassin with four more appointments to keep. Their paths, however, are converging with those of two sets of law-enforcement officers: a pair of LAPD detectives (Mark Ruffalo, Peter Berg) and an FBI drug task force.

Like Stuart Beattie's script, Cruise's performance is sharp but shallow, and there's more than a little Dr. Hannibal Lecter

in Vincent: he's in love with the sound of his own dyspeptic rhetoric, and his self-absorption leads him to underestimate the fundamentally decent Max. Mann polishes this familiar material to a hard, high sheen and delivers a great, darkly seductive ride.

COLONEL REDL   📀
(REDL EZREDES)
1984 144m c   Biography/Historical/War   ★★★
Mafilm-Objectiv/Manfred Durniok/ORF/   R
ZDF   (Hungary/Austria/West Germany)

Klaus Maria Brandauer *(Alfred Redl)*, Armin Mueller-Stahl *(Crown Prince Archduke Franz-Josef)*, Gudrun Landgrebe *(Katalin Kubinyi)*, Jan Niklas *(Kristof Kubinyi)*, Hans Christian Blech *(Col. von Roden)*, Laszlo Mensaros *(Col. Ruzitska)*, Andras Balint *(Dr. Gustav Sonnenschein)*, Karoly Eperjes *(Lt. Jaromil Schorm)*, Dorottya Udvaros *(Clarissa, Redl's Wife)*, Laszlo Galffi *(Alfredo Velocchio)*

p, Joszef Marx; d, Istvan Szabo; w, Istvan Szabo, Peter Dobai (based on the stage play "A Patriot for Me" by John Osborne); ph, Lajos Koltai (Eastmancolor); ed, Zsuzsa Csakany; m, Robert Schumann, Johann Strauss, Frederic Chopin, Franz Liszt; prod d, Jozsef Romvari; art d, Tibor Szollar; cos, Peter Pabst

AAN Best Foreign Language Film

Istvan Szabo's follow-up to MEPHISTO again stars Klaus Maria Brandauer, here as Colonel Alfred Redl, who became head of the Austro-Hungarian military intelligence bureau in the early 1900s, despite his impoverished origins. His Gatsby-like strivings for upper-class acceptance prove, however, to be his downfall when a czarist agent threatens to expose Redl's homosexual double life.

Though not as richly textured or urgent as MEPHISTO, this is an expertly made historical drama that, while fictionalizing some events, truthfully examines the desire for power and the catalysts of war. The film boasts yet another tour de force performance by Brandauer, as well as an equally strong portrayal by Armin Mueller-Stahl as the ruthless, power-hungry archduke. The film won the Jury Prize at the Cannes Film Festival, and received an Oscar nomination for Best Foreign Film.

COLOR OF MONEY, THE   📀
1986 119m c   Drama/Sports   ★★★½
Touchstone   (U.S.)   R

Paul Newman *(Eddie)*, Tom Cruise *(Vincent)*, Mary Elizabeth Mastrantonio *(Carmen)*, Helen Shaver *(Janelle)*, John Turturro *(Julian)*, Bill Cobbs *(Orvis)*, Keith McCready *(Grady Seasons)*, Carol Messing *(Casino Bar Band Singer/Julian's Flirt)*, Steve Mizerak *(Duke, Eddie's 1st Opponent)*, Bruce A. Young *(Moselle)*

p, Irving Axelrad, Barbara De Fina; d, Martin Scorsese; w, Richard Price (based on the novel by Walter Tevis); ph, Michael Ballhaus (DuArt Color); ed, Thelma Schoonmaker; m, Robbie Robertson; prod d, Boris Leven; fx, Curt Smith; cos, Richard Bruno

AA Best Actor: Paul Newman; *AAN Best Supporting Actress:* Mary Elizabeth Mastrantonio; *AAN Best Adapted Screenplay:* Richard Price; *AAN Best Art Direction-Set Decoration:* Boris Leven, Karen A. O'Hara

Twenty-five years after being banned from big-time pool, THE HUSTLER's "Fast Eddie" Felsen (Paul Newman) resurfaces—older, wiser, and much more cynical—in THE COLOR OF MONEY. Eddie, who no longer plays the game, now peddles whiskey and bankrolls talented pool hustlers for a percentage. He takes young hotshot Vincent (Tom Cruise) and his coolheaded girlfriend (Mary Elizabeth Mastrantonio) on the road, teaching his flamboyant, flaky protege how to "dump," i.e., lose deliberately in order to set up the suckers for the big score ("Sometimes if you lose, you win"). Vincent has trouble learning to lose, Eddie begins to yearn to play again himself, and they part ways, only to meet again in a big tournament in Atlantic City. There the pupil surprises his rehabilitated teacher with how well he's learned his lessons.

Approached by Newman, who felt that "Fast Eddie" was due for renewed exploration, director Martin Scorsese and novelist-screenwriter Richard Price (*The Wanderers*) came up with a richly nuanced film that retains little more than the title and Eddie Felsen's character from novelist Walter Tevis's sequel to *The Hustler*. One of Scorsese's most commercial undertakings, THE COLOR OF MONEY relinquishes none of his unique style and vision, using a swooping, gliding camera and countless trick shots to maximum impact. The film also boasts two bravura performances—from Newman, who finally—and deservedly—won an Oscar for Best Actor, and Cruise, who is a joy to behold. Watch for Forest Whittaker and Iggy Pop in colorful bit roles.

COLOR PURPLE, THE   DVD
1985 152m c   Drama   ★★★½
Guber/Peters (U.S.)   PG-13

Danny Glover *(Albert)*, Whoopi Goldberg *(Celie)*, Margaret Avery *(Shug Avery)*, Oprah Winfrey *(Sofia)*, Willard Pugh *(Harpo)*, Akosua Busia *(Nettie)*, Adolph Caesar *(Old Mister)*, Rae Dawn Chong *(Squeak)*, Desreta Jackson *(Young Celie)*, Dana Ivey *(Miss Millie)*

p, Steven Spielberg, Kathleen Kennedy, Frank Marshall, Quincy Jones, Jon Peters, Peter Guber; d, Steven Spielberg; w, Menno Meyjes (based on the novel by Alice Walker); ph, Allen Daviau (Panavision, Deluxe Color); ed, Michael Kahn; m, Quincy Jones; prod d, J. Michael Riva; art d, Bo Welch; cos, Aggie Guerard Rodgers

AAN Best Picture; AAN Best Actress: Whoopi Goldberg; *AAN Best Supporting Actress:* Margaret Avery; *AAN Best Supporting Actress:* Oprah Winfrey; *AAN Best Adapted Screenplay:* Menno Meyjes (Screenplay); *AAN Best Cinematography:* Allen Daviau; *AAN Best Original Score:* Quincy Jones, Jeremy Lubbock, Rod Temperton, Caiphus Semenya, Andrae Crouch, Chris Boardman, Jorge Calandrelli, Joel Rosenbaum, Fred Steiner, Jack Hayes, Jerry Hey, Randy Kerber; *AAN Best Original Song:* "Miss Celie's Blue (Sister)"; Quincy Jones (Music & Lyrics), Rod Temperton (Music & Lyrics), Lionel Ritchie (Lyrics); *AAN Best Art Direction-Set Decoration:* J. Michael Riva (Art Direction), Robert W. Welch (Art Direction), Linda DeScenna (Set Decoration); *AAN Best Costume Design:* Aggie Guerard Rodgers; *AAN Best Makeup:* Ken Chase

Far worse films than Steven Spielberg's laudable if problematic adaptation of Alice Walker's novel have been treated much less harshly. This film, which introduced Whoopi Goldberg and Oprah Winfrey to national audiences, has been unfairly attacked as an ill-considered and unseemly plea for "serious" consideration from an extremely successful young filmmaker better known for fantasy adventure films. Though a commercial success, this was one of the few major Hollywood dramas to concern itself with the lives of black women. Where are the subsequent black female films? Similarly, it soft-pedals the novel's lesbianism but how many subsequent Hollywood films have done better?

The story begins in 1909 as teenager Celie (Desreta Jackson) gives birth to two children (apparently fathered by her own father) and is married off to Albert (Danny Glover), who hates her and wants her sister, Nettie (Akosua Busia). When Nettie resists his advances, Albert persuades the sisters' father to separate the girls. Celie's children are sold to a local preacher and Nettie leaves. As an adult, Celie (now Whoopi Goldberg) lives a life of servitude to Albert who mistreats her

shamelessly. He intercepts Nettie's letters to Celie, not allowing the sisters to communicate. Celie is cut off from all human affection. Celie eventually does receive love and gains self-respect through the timely intervention of an outside force who enters her life in an unexpected manner.

Spielberg lacks his usual intuitive affinity for his story material; consequently the film is a bit clunky at times. There are some unfortunate slapstick comic relief sequences and a few of the characterizations are also much too broad and cartoonish. The film was strongly criticized in some quarters for its negative depiction of black men but, if anything, it is less harsh than the novel. The film deserves praise for its heartwarming, empowering presentation of the strength and nobility of black women. It has also been damned for its gloriously lush cinematography as if the lives of black folk were only meant to be shown in squalid environments. Black audiences enjoy Hollywood fantasy as much as anyone.

COLORS   DVD
1988 120m c   Crime   ★★½
Orion (U.S.)   R

Sean Penn *(Danny McGavin)*, Robert Duvall *(Bob Hodges)*, Maria Conchita Alonso *(Louisa Gomez)*, Randy Brooks *(Ron Delaney)*, Grand L. Bush *(Larry Sylvester)*, Don Cheadle *(Rocket)*, Gerardo Mejia *(Bird)*, Glenn Plummer *(Clarence Brown, "High Top")*, Rudy Ramos *(Melindez)*, Sy Richardson *(Bailey)*

p, Robert H. Solo; d, Dennis Hopper; w, Michael Schiffer (from a story by Schiffer and Richard DiLello); ph, Haskell Wexler (Metrocolor); ed, Robert Estrin; m, Herbie Hancock; prod d, Ron Foreman; chor, Patrick Alan; cos, Nick Scarano

Hopper's controversial directorial reentry into mainstream Hollywood is a disappointingly routine effort that is neither socially irresponsible nor particularly distinguished by any insights or artfulness. The considerable controversy aroused by COLORS centered on Hopper's choice of subject matter—urban youth gangs. Set in the barrios and slums of East Los Angeles, the film is basically an all-too-familiar tale of a confident veteran cop (Duvall) with one more year to go until his retirement and his relationship with his new partner (Penn), a young, cocky, and hot-headed rookie who thinks he has all the answers. Their conflict is played out amid the shocking violence of a bloody war between L.A.'s two most notorious gangs, the Bloods and the Crips. No one should expect a Hollywood movie to address *and* cure complicated social ills. In COLORS Hopper makes no attempt to provide solutions but merely presents the disturbing reality of the situation as a backdrop for the narrative. Unfortunately the end result is an unfocused hodgepodge of documentary realism, expressionism, TV cop show, liberal-message movie, and violent action film. None of these elements are handled with in a distinctive manner. In several interviews, Hopper admitted that had he initiated the project himself, he would have preferred to concentrate on the gangs rather than the cops. As it is, COLORS has a tentative, ambivalent feel to it—as if Hopper merely considered himself a hired gun who should avoid imposing too personal a vision on the material.

COLOSSUS: THE FORBIN PROJECT
1970 100m c   Science Fiction   ★★★
Universal (U.S.)

Eric Braeden *(Dr. Charles Forbin)*, Susan Clark *(Dr. Cleo Markham)*, Gordon Pinsent *(The President)*, William Schallert *(Grauber)*, Leonid Rostoff *(Chairman)*, Georg Stanford Brown *(Fisher)*, Willard Sage *(Blake)*, Alex Rodine *(Dr. Kurpin)*, Martin Brooks *(Johnson)*, Marion Ross *(Angela)*

p, Stanley Chase; d, Joseph Sargent; w, James Bridges; ph, Gene Polito; ed, Folmar Blangsted; m, Michel Colombier; art d, John Lloyd, Alexander Golitzen; fx, Whitey McMahon

Taut, well-made sci-fi thriller about a massive computer, Colossus, which is designed by Braeden to control the entire American missile defense system. Once put into service, however, it takes over and develops a plan of *its* own to safeguard mankind from nuclear disaster. It hooks up with its Russian counterpart, Guardian, and together the two computers hold the world hostage, threatening to destroy the Earth. Braeden is forced to attempt to destroy his creation, but the computer thwarts him at every turn.

COMA   DVD

1960 113m   c   Science Fiction/Thriller   ★★½
UA   (U.S.)   PG

Genevieve Bujold *(Dr. Susan Wheeler),* Michael Douglas *(Dr. Mark Bellows),* Elizabeth Ashley *(Mrs. Emerson),* Rip Torn *(Dr. George),* Richard Widmark *(Dr. Harris),* Lois Chiles *(Nancy Greenly),* Hari Rhodes *(Dr. Morelind),* Gary Barton *(Computer Technician),* Frank Downing *(Kelly),* Richard Doyle *(Jim)*

p, Martin Erlichman; d, Michael Crichton; w, Michael Crichton (based on the novel by Robin Cook); ph, Victor J. Kemper, Gerald Hirschfeld (Metrocolor); ed, David Bretherton; m, Jerry Goldsmith; prod d, Albert Brenner; fx, Joe Day, Ernie Smith; cos, Eddie Marks, Yvonne Kubis

An inquisitive hospital physician (Genevieve Bujold) discovers that unscrupulous higher-ups on the staff are drugging healthy patients into a comatose state, killing them, and selling their organs to rich patients in desperate need of transplants. When she confronts her ambitious doctor lover (Michael Douglas) with the information, he refuses to believe her, and she sets out alone to expose the sinister conspiracy.

Adapted from the best-selling book by Robin Cook, COMA is the second feature directed by doctor-novelist-filmmaker Crichton (the first was the popular WEST-WORLD), who later scripted the phenomenal JURASSIC PARK. As a rare attempt to invert some of the gender conventions of the thriller genre—insistently presenting events from a female point-of-view—the film has won favor among some feminist critics. On the whole, however, COMA wastes a superb performance by Bujold on a simplistic, predictable series of cliched suspense scenes, seasoned with some last-minute moralizing about contemporary medicine. Look for Tom Selleck as one of the comatose bodies suspended from the ceiling of a clandestine medical lab—the most memorably eerie image in the film.

COMANCHE STATION

1960 74m   c   Western   ★★★★
Renown   (U.S.)

Randolph Scott *(Jefferson Cody),* Nancy Gates *(Mrs. Lowe),* Claude Akins *(Ben Lane),* Skip Homeier *(Frank),* Richard Rust *(Dobie),* Rand Brooks *(Station Man),* Dyke Johnson *(Mr. Lowe),* Foster Hood *(Comanche Lance Bearer),* Joe Molina *(Comanche Chief),* Vince St. Cyr *(Warrior)*

p, Harry Joe Brown, Budd Boetticher, Randolph Scott; d, Budd Boetticher; w, Burt Kennedy; ph, Charles Lawton Jr. (CinemaScope, Eastmancolor); ed, Edwin Bryant

This fine, haunting western was the last of the Randolph Scott-Budd Boetticher collaborations. Its predecessors were SEVEN MEN FROM NOW (1956), THE TALL T. (1957), DECISION AT SUNDOWN (1957), BUCHANAN RIDES ALONE (1958), RIDE LONESOME (1959), and WEST-BOUND (1959). Together they encapsulate themes that made

these films some of the most striking, intelligent, and complex westerns ever made. Boetticher, an often-underrated talent, created films that dealt with the sadness of independence, the questing impulse, the overpowering forces of nature, and the past's influence on the present.

Interrupting a futile ten-year search for his own wife, who was kidnaped by Indians, Scott agrees to track down a settler's wife, Gates, who has been raped and captured by Comanches. On their way back to her husband, Scott and Gates are met by outlaw Akins and his two adolescent proteges, Homeier and Rust, who inform the couple that they are being trailed by Comanche braves. Akins and the boys, offering to accompany Scott and Gates on their journey, create an atmosphere of tension, with Akins frequently commenting on the cowardice of Gates's husband in sending another man to do his work. It soon becomes apparent that Akins is plotting to get the reward for himself.

As in many of the Renown westerns, Scott is truly a loner in the film, a man whose personal code limits his ability to coexist with others. Adhering to the mythic type of the western hero, Scott remains true to the ideals of honesty, courage, and the responsibility to aid those in need. Boetticher's films are not happy, optimistic westerns in which evil is defeated before the final credits roll. They are sad films that focus on isolated men and the harsh world they exist in, men who strive for things they will probably never attain.

COME AND SEE   DVD
(IDI I SMOTRI)
1985 142m   c   War   ★★★½
Byelarusfilm/Mosfilm   (U.S.S.R.)

Aleksei Kravchenko *(Florya Gaishun),* Olga Mironova, Lyubomiras Lautsiavitchus, Vladas Bagdonas, Victor Lorentz

d, Elem Klimov; w, Ales Adamovich, Elem Klimov (based on *The Story of Khatyn and Others* by Adamovich); ph, Alexi Rodionov

A highly charged, emotionally exhausting indictment of war and the inhumanity of the Nazis, set in Byelorussia during the 1943 Nazi invasion, COME AND SEE focuses on the experiences of an adolescent transformed, in a matter of days, from naive boy to worn man. Young Florya (Aleksei Kravchenko) finds a rifle and immediately joins the local freedom fighters, despite the desperate pleas of his mother, who wants to lose neither her son nor the only source of protection for her and her two young daughters. Florya is left behind by the makeshift army and tries to return to his mother, but the Germans launch an air raid, which is followed by an invasion of paratroopers before he can get to his village. Only the most insensitive could sit through COME AND SEE without being emotionally devastated. From its opening scene, COME AND SEE descends into a virtual hell on earth that becomes increasingly frightening as it advances to the final horror. This film won the Grand Prix at the Moscow film festival; its director, Elem Klimov, was recently named the head of the Soviet Filmmakers Union.

COME BACK, LITTLE SHEBA   DVD
1952 95m   bw   Drama   ★★★★
Paramount   (U.S.)

Burt Lancaster *(Doc Delaney),* Shirley Booth *(Lola Delaney),* Terry Moore *(Marie Buckholder),* Richard Jaeckel *(Turk Fisher),* Philip Ober *(Ed Anderson),* Lisa Golm *(Mrs. Goffman),* Walter Kelley *(Bruce)*

p, Hal B. Wallis; d, Daniel Mann; w, Ketti Frings (based on the play by William Inge); ph, James Wong Howe; ed, Warren Low; m, Franz Waxman

AA Best Actress: Shirley Booth; *AAN Best Supporting Actress:* Terry Moore; *AAN Best Film Editing:* Warren Low

Lancaster is Doc Delaney, a mild-mannered alcoholic ex-chiropractor who has been dry for a year. Booth, his frumpy, loquacious wife, lives for the day when her lost dog, little Sheba, will return home. Theirs is a life of quiet desperation until Moore, a vibrant student, rents a room from the tired couple. Lancaster doesn't approve of the intentions of Jaeckel, who has been dating Moore, perhaps because the young man's lust stirs painful memories for Lancaster, whose premarital relationship with Booth resulted in their shotgun wedding. Returning to the bottle, he viciously criticizes his wife.

COME BACK, LITTLE SHEBA opened Christmas week of 1952 in order to qualify for the Academy Awards. The strategy was excellent as Shirley Booth won the Oscar for Best Actress, beating out Joan Crawford (SUDDEN FEAR), Julie Harris (THE MEMBER OF THE WEDDING), Bette Davis (THE STAR) and Susan Hayward (WITH A SONG IN MY HEART). Booth's brilliant work (she originated the role on Broadway) remains etched forever in the memory of anyone who has seen this film. Moore, in her finest performance, also received a nomination for Best Supporting Actress.

COME BACK TO THE 5 & DIME, JIMMY DEAN, JIMMY DEAN

1982 109m c Drama   ★★½
Sandcastle 5   (U.S.)

Sandy Dennis (Mona), Cher (Sissy), Karen Black (Joanne), Sudie Bond (Juanita), Marta Heflin (Edna Louise), Kathy Bates (Stella Mae), Mark Patton (Joe Qualley), Caroline Aaron (Martha), Ruth Miller (Clarissa), Gena Ramsel (Sue Ellen)

p, Scott Bushnell; d, Robert Altman; w, Ed Graczyck (based on his play); ph, Pierre Mignot; ed, Jason Rosenfield; prod d, David Gropman

Five women who grew up together in a small Texas town idolizing James Dean reunite 20 years later at a local dime store and discuss their lives and loves, illusion and reality. The most touching moment comes when Sandy Dennis, who has deluded herself for years, finally accepts that Dean was not the father of her illegitimate child. Director Robert Altman, turning Super 16mm cameras on the cast that he directed on Broadway in Ed Graczyck's play, captures the vitality of live performances from each of his actors. Using much technical invention, Altman does his best to invest his uncinematic material with a cinematic feel, but if COME BACK TO THE 5 & DIME, JIMMY DEAN, JIMMY DEAN still looks like a filmed play—and not a great play at that—it is nonetheless presented with great sensitivity. Karen Black, Cher, and Dennis contribute especially fine performances to this insightful film that was shot in just 19 days.

COMFORT OF STRANGERS, THE   📀

(CORTESIE PER GLI OSPITI)
1991 107m c Drama   ★★★
Erre Produzioni/Sovereign Pictures/Reteitalia   R
(Italy/U.K.)

Christopher Walken (Robert), Natasha Richardson (Mary), Rupert Everett (Colin), Helen Mirren (Caroline), Manfredi Aliquo (The Concierge), David Ford (Waiter), Daniel Franco (Waiter), Rossana Caghiari (Hotel Maid), Fabrizio Castellani (Bar Manager), Giancarlo Previati (First Policeman)

p, Angelo Rizzoli; d, Paul Schrader; w, Harold Pinter (from the novel by Ian McEwan); ph, Dante Spinotti; ed, Bill Pankow; m, Angelo Badalamenti; prod d, Gianni Quaranta; art d, Luigi Marchione; cos, Mariolina Bono

Based on the novel by Ian McEwan, with a screenplay by playwright Harold Pinter, THE COMFORT OF STRANGERS is a story of decadence and decay, sexual obsession and violence.

Colin (Rupert Everett) and Mary (Natasha Richardson) are a naive young English couple vacationing in Venice. One night they become lost in the winding streets and encounter Robert (Christopher Walken), a dapper Italian who speaks excellent English and graciously escorts them to his out-of-the-way restaurant. Later, Mary and Colin visit Robert's palatial apartment, where they meet his beautiful crippled wife, Caroline (Helen Mirren). The visit quickly becomes strained: there is something alluring, but disturbingly off-kilter, about the older couple. Before long, the innocents are lured into a bizarre web of sexual gamesmanship and murder.

Former Calvinist and critic Paul Schrader, who has written and/or directed such films as AMERICAN GIGOLO, the remake of CAT PEOPLE and the biopic MISHIMA, is no stranger to provocative subject matter. But depravity is a tricky thing to make concrete, and film is a resolutely literal medium. The risk of looking silly is tremendously high—many films have aspired to decadence and achieved unintended camp. Schrader plunges in fearlessly, attempting to generate a sense of erotic menace through location and such devices as gliding steadicam shots that sweep through sumptuous surroundings, devouring them in every detail without ever pausing. Mirren's and Walken's brittle, mannered performances unquestionably add to the sense that something is ominously wrong, even early on on the film. But overall, THE COMFORT OF STRANGERS seems tremendously overwrought for no good reason.

COMING HOME   📀

1978 126m c Drama/War   ★★★½
UA (U.S.)   R

Jane Fonda (Sally Hyde), Jon Voight (Luke Martin), Bruce Dern (Capt. Bob Hyde), Robert Ginty (Sgt. Dink Mobley), Penelope Milford (Viola Munson), Robert Carradine (Bill Munson), Charles Cyphers (Pee Wee), Mary Jackson (Fleta Wilson), Kenneth Augustine (Ken), Tresa Hughes (Nurse De Groot)

p, Jerome Hellman; d, Hal Ashby; w, Waldo Salt, Robert C. Jones (based on a story by Nancy Dowd); ph, Haskell Wexler (Deluxe Color); ed, Don Zimmerman; prod d, Michael Haller; cos, Ann Roth, Michael Hoffman, Silvio Scarano, Jennifer Parsons

AAN Best Picture; AA Best Actor: Jon Voight; AA Best Actress: Jane Fonda; AAN Best Supporting Actor: Bruce Dern; AAN Best Supporting Actress: Penelope Milford; AAN Best Director: Hal Ashby; AA Best Original Screenplay: Nancy Dowd, Waldo Salt, Robert C. Jones; AAN Best Film Editing: Don Zimmerman

Nominated for eight Academy Awards—and winning for Best Actress (Jane Fonda), Best Actor (Jon Voight), and Best Original Screenplay (THE DEER HUNTER, another Vietnam film, won Best Picture and Best Director)—COMING HOME was one of the first films to deal seriously with the plight of returning Vietnam veterans. Unfortunately, it is marred by some cloying melodramatics and overly preachy politics. The story opens circa 1968, when Bob Hyde (Bruce Dern), a gung-ho Marine captain, is finally going off to Vietnam on active duty. His dutiful wife, Sally (Fonda), wants to do her share and begins volunteer work at a local veterans' hospital, where she meets Luke (Jon Voight), a bitter paraplegic. Within a month Sally and Luke have learned that they went to the same high school, knew many of the same people, and have much more in common than most others at the hospital. Luke's anger begins to subside, although he begins speaking out publicly against the war. The friendship broadens Sally's perspective; soon she is becoming more liberal in her politics, more feminist in her orientation, and comfortable leading a life independent of her husband. Eventually Luke and Sally become lovers (in a R-rated scene). Their relationship is jeopardized, however, when Bob is wounded in the leg and comes home from the war a changed man—taciturn but potentially violent. While COMING HOME has its heart in the right place, the script by Salt and Jones is too pat, and Ashby's direction simply too self-satisfied to be wholly effective. What does work in COMING HOME are the small, human, unguarded moments. The performances, undeniably appealing, were deservedly praised, Dern and Voight coming off best.

COMING TO AMERICA

1988 116m c Comedy/Romance ★★½
Paramount (U.S.) R

Eddie Murphy *(Prince Akeem/Clarence the Barber/Saul the Old Jew/Randy Watson the Singer)*, Arsenio Hall *(Semmi/Morris the Barber/Extremely Ugly Girl/Rev. Brown)*, John Amos *(Cleo McDowell)*, James Earl Jones *(King Jaffe Joffer)*, Shari Headley *(Lisa McDowell)*, Madge Sinclair *(Queen Aoleon)*, Eriq La Salle *(Darryl Jenks)*, Allison Dean *(Patrice McDowell)*, Paul Bates *(Oha)*, Louie Anderson *(Maurice)*

p, George Folsey Jr., Robert D. Wachs; d, John Landis; w, David Sheffield, Barry W. Blaustein (based on a story by Murphy); ph, Woody Omens (Technicolor); ed, Malcolm Campbell, George Folsey Jr.; m, Nile Rodgers; prod d, Richard MacDonald; fx, Dan Cangemi, Syd Dutton, Rick Baker, Bill Taylor; chor, Paula Abdul; cos, Deborah Nadoolman

AAN Best Costume Design: Deborah Nadoolman; *AAN Best Makeup:* Rick Baker

This light romantic comedy represents a change of pace for the phenomenally successful Murphy. Here he plays a polite, pampered, and fabulously wealthy African prince who comes to America in search of true love. Although the fairytale script is as old as the motion picture industry itself, the resourceful cast of COMING TO AMERICA brings freshness to the annoyingly cliched material. Unfortunately, Landis' inelegant direction nearly derails the film. Poorly paced, indifferently shot, and haphazardly edited, the movie lurches unsteadily from scene to scene, undermining the best efforts of its performers. Luckily, Murphy gives his sweetest, most touching, and most genuinely likable performance to date, playing a character who embraces society instead of holding it in contempt. Arsenio Hall, in his first featured role, is also impressive. The film is best remembered in Hollywood as the object of a plagiarism suit brought by columnist Art Buchwald; Paramount allegedly cooked the books to avoid giving Buchwald his court-awarded poi.nts, resulting in years of bitter litigation.

COMMITMENTS, THE

1991 120m c Drama/Musical ★★★
Beacon Communications/First Film Co./ R
Dirty Hands Productions/Sovereign Pictures
(U.S./U.K.)

Robert Arkins *(Jimmy Rabbitte)*, Michael Aherne *(Steven Clifford)*, Angeline Ball *(Imelda Quirke)*, Maria Doyle *(Natalie Murphy)*, Dave Finnegan *(Mickah Wallace)*, Bronagh Gallagher *(Bernie McGloughlin)*, Felim Gormley *(Dean Fay)*, Glen Hansard *(Outspan Foster)*, Dick Massey *(Billy Mooney)*, Johnny Murphy *(Joey "The Lips" Fagan)*

p, Roger Randall-Cutler, Lynda Myles; d, Alan Parker; w, Ian LaFrenais, Dick Clement, Roddy Doyle (from his novel); ph, Gale Tattersall; ed, Gerry Hambling; prod d, Brian Morris; art d, Mark Geraghty, Arden Gantly; fx, Maurice Foley; cos, Penny Rose

AAN Best Film Editing: Gerry Hambling

This typically slick but largely enjoyable Alan Parker offering is the story of the rise and demise of a young Irish soul band. As with his earlier film, FAME, Parker has attempted to capture the infectious energy of popular music; and as with his previous feature, MISSISSIPPI BURNING, the director has taken on an alien culture (this time that of the working-class, primarily Catholic North Side of Dublin) and reduced its complexities to a glib, commercial formula.

When Jimmy Rabbitte (Robert Arkins) is asked by two friends to manage a dreadful wedding band, he takes the opportunity to begin building something more ambitious: an authentic soul outfit to be called The Commitments. The newly formed band immerse themselves in the soul classics as they begin struggling their way through rehearsals. Their working-class philosophy is spelled out by Jimmy: "The Irish are the blacks of Europe; Dubliners are the blacks of Ireland; and the North Siders are the blacks of Dublin. So say it loud: I'm black and I'm proud." The Commitments' music improves with predictable, if enjoyable speed. As they begin to develop a following on the pub circuit, the usual tensions start to manifest themselves.

For all its emphasis on working-class integrity, THE COMMITMENTS is really FAME wrapped in streetwise packaging. All the cliches of the star-is-born subgenre are here, from the neatness with which the band members fall into place to the amazing rapidity with which they develop a professional sound (not to mention the implausibility of a group achieving such success by playing straight cover versions of classic soul songs). The whole thing has the feel of an extended sitcom—not surprising given the fact that Dick Clement and Ian La Frenais, veteran English TV writers, helped Roddy Doyle adapt his original novel for the screen. THE SNAPPER, a superior film, is also based on a Doyle novel about the Rabbitte family.

COMPANY, THE

2003 112m c Dance/Drama ★★★½
Killer Films/Capitol Films/CP Medien PG-13
AG/John Wells Productions/First Snow/
Sandcastle 5/S.R.O. Entertainment/Marly Pictures
(U.S./Germany)

Neve Campbell *(Loretta "Ry" Ryan)*, Malcolm McDowell *(Alberto Antonelli)*, James Franco *(John)*, Barbara Robertson *(Harriet)*, William Dick *(Edouard)*, Susie Cusack *(Susie)*, Marilyn Dodds Frank *(Ry's Mother)*, John Lordan *(Ry's Father)*, Robert Desrosiers *(Choreographer)*, Mariann Mayberry *(Ry's Stepmother)*

p, Joshua Astrachan, David Levy; d, Robert Altman; w, Barbara Turner (based on a story by Barbara Turner and Neve Campbell); ph, Andrew Dunn; ed, Geraldine Peroni; m, Van Dyke Parks; art d, Gary Baugh, Craig Jackson; fx, John Milinac, Rodman Kiser, Randall Balsmeyer; cos, Susan Kaufman

Real dancers fill most of the roles in Robert Altman's ensemble drama about day-to-day life in a Chicago troupe closely modeled on the world-renowned Joffrey Ballet.

Ambitious newcomer Ry (Neve Campbell, who studied at the National Ballet of Canada's school until injuries sidelined her as a teenager) is devastated when she learns her boyfriend has been cheating with fellow dancer Noel (Emily Patterson). But as luck would have it, Ry is chosen to replace the injured Noel in a new pas de deux that could be her professional breakthrough. Guest choreographer Robert Desrosiers (playing himself) begins creating "Blue Snake," an elaborate theater-dance piece, and company director Alberto Antonelli (Malcolm McDowell) juggles fund-raising to pay for the extravaganza. Ry, meanwhile, waits tables to supplement her salary and meets a new boyfriend, aspiring chef Josh (James Franco).

Over the course of nearly two hours, Barbara Turner's script, developed from a story by Campbell and incorporating improvisation by the Joffrey dancers, weaves together the petty conflicts, small triumphs, and heartbreaking defeats that define dancers' lives. Dramatic scenes are interspersed with substantial excerpts from the Joffrey's repertory, leading up to "Blue Snake"'s triumphant world premiere. The polar opposite of the fiercely artificial and much-loved RED SHOES, this documentary-style film demystifies the world of ballet while paying loving homage to the dedication and discipline of dancers. Altman painstakingly coaxes convincing performances from the dancers, and Campbell's dance sequences are carefully staged to emphasize what she can do physically and bypass what she can't. Though the ballets themselves are beautifully shot, they lean heavily in the direction of gimmicky and prop-heavy pieces; they're visually interesting but, by and large, they're not great dance.

COMPANY OF WOLVES, THE   *DVD*
1984 95m   c   Horror/Fantasy   ★★★★½
Palace   (U.K.)   R

Angela Lansbury *(Granny)*, David Warner *(Father)*, Graham Crowden *(Old Priest)*, Brian Glover *(Amorous Boy's Father)*, Kathryn Pogson *(Young Bride)*, Stephen Rea *(Young Groom)*, Tusse Silberg *(Mother)*, Micha Bergese *(Huntsman)*, Sarah Patterson *(Rosaleen)*, Georgia Slowe *(Alice)*

p, Chris Brown, Stephen Woolley; d, Neil Jordan; w, Angela Carter, Neil Jordan (based on a collection of short stories by Carter); ph, Bryan Loftus (Rank Color); ed, Rodney Holland; m, George Fenton; prod d, Anton Furst; art d, Stuart Rose; fx, Peter MacDonald, Alan Whibley, Rodney Holland, Christopher Tucker; cos, Elizabeth Waller

The most innovative, intelligent, and visually sumptuous horror film of recent years. Not a traditional werewolf movie, this film explores the psychosexual undercurrents of the classic "Little Red Riding Hood" fairy tale.

Taking place almost entirely in the troubled dreams of 13-year-old Rosaleen (Sarah Patterson), the film takes the viewer deep into the archetypal, erotically charged realm of fairy stories. Rosaleen and her parents (David Warner and Tusse Silberg) live in a small village on the outskirts of a dark, forbidding forest. The girl's grandmother (Angela Lansbury) comes to visit and fills the young girl's head with cautionary tales about men who turn into wolves. Nonetheless her interest in men continues to grow. Sometime later a young neighbor boy discovers the ravaged carcass of a farm animal in the woods and warns the adults that a wolf is stalking the area.

THE COMPANY OF WOLVES has a complex and dreamy narrative structure built on intermingled fantasies, myths, and fairy tales. Nearly every scene is compelling and haunting; and the special makeup effects are impressive. Neil Jordan (THE CRYING GAME) is a director with visionary qualities, a distinctive visual stylist who knows how to use his medium to convey complex emotions and simmering sensuality. This is a remarkable movie that plumbs the unconscious netherworld of dreams and fantasy, evoking deeply held fears and desires.

COMPULSION
1959 103m   bw   Crime   ★★★★
Fox   (U.S.)

Orson Welles *(Jonathan Wilk)*, Diane Varsi *(Ruth Evans)*, Dean Stockwell *(Judd Steiner)*, Bradford Dillman *(Artie Straus)*, E.G. Marshall *(Horn)*, Martin Milner *(Sid)*, Richard Anderson *(Max)*, Robert F. Simon *(Lt. Johnson)*, Edward Binns *(Tom Daly)*, Robert Burton *(Mr. Straus)*

p, Richard D. Zanuck; d, Richard Fleischer; w, Richard Murphy (based on the novel by Meyer Levin); ph, William Mellor (CinemaScope); ed, William Reynolds; m, Lionel Newman; cos, Charles LeMaire

Based on the famous 1924 murder trial of Loeb and Leopold, two Chicago homosexual law students who murdered a boy, Bobby Franks, to demonstrate their intellectual superiority, this is a compelling and stylish thriller.

Dillman delivers a strong performance as the mother-dominated, sadistic Loeb, here called Artie Straus, and Stockwell is even more impressive as the submissive, introverted Leopold (renamed Judd Steiner). Of course, Welles is flamboyantly grand as the Clarence Darrow-figure who has the unenviable task of defending the two arrogant unsympathetic killers. They even have the effrontery to offer the police aid in solving the killing (exactly what Loeb did, which led to his arrest and that of Leopold). Raised by wealthy families, Dillman and Stockwell consider themselves superior intellects who are above conventional notions of morality. Their crime was executed without remorse. They offer no defense so, like Clarence Darrow, Welles must come up with a defense of his own.

COMPULSION is full of suspense and electrifying courtroom theatrics, even though the informed viewer knows the story's outcome. Fleischer's direction is taut, and Murphy's script, which takes the narrative almost word-for-word from Meyer Levin's best-selling novel, is terse and telling.

CON AIR   *DVD*
1997 115m   c   Action/Prison   ★★★
Jerry Bruckheimer Films/Kouf/Bigelow   R
Productions/Touchstone   (U.S.)

Nicolas Cage *(Cameron Poe)*, John Cusack *(U.S. Marshal—Agent Vince Larkin)*, John Malkovich *(Cyrus "The Virus" Grissom)*, Steve Buscemi *(Garland Greene)*, Ving Rhames *(Nathan Jones—aka "Diamond Dog")*, Colm Meaney *(DEA Agent Duncan Malloy)*, Mykelti Williamson *(Baby-O)*, Rachel Ticotin *(U.S. Marshal—Guard Sally Bishop)*, Monica Potter *(Tricia Poe)*, Dave Chappelle, billed as David Chappelle *("Pinball" Parker)*

p, Jerry Bruckheimer; d, Simon West; w, Scott Rosenberg; ph, David Tattersall; ed, Chris Lebenzon, Steve Mirkovich, Glen Scantlebury; m, Mark Mancina, Trevor Rabin; prod d, Barbara Mesney (sets), Daniel R. Jennings (sets); art d, Edward T. McAvoy, Charles Butcher; fx, Chuck Stewart (coordinator), David Goldberg (visual effects supervisor), Dream Quest Images; cos, Bobbie Read

AAN Best Sound: Kevin O'Connell, Greg P. Russell, Arthur Rochester; *AAN Best Original Song:* "How Do I Live"; Diane Warren

The patented Don Simpson-Jerry Bruckheimer formula that produced THE ROCK, BAD BOYS, DAYS OF THUNDER, and TOP GUN sizzles on after Simpson's death.

The vilest criminals the American penal system has to offer are packed into one small plane that is soon navigating some very unfriendly skies. Led by psychopath Cyrus "the Virus" Grissom (John Malkovich) and demented, militant black nationalist Nathan "Diamond Dog" Jones (Ving Rhames), the bad, bad boys—who include pallid serial killer Garland Greene (Steve Buscemi), who's brought on board in full Hannibal Lecter restraints—commandeer their flying cell block and make a break for freedom. Standing between this airborne crime wave and civilization: quirky federal marshall Vince Larkin (John Cusack), who monitors the disaster-in-progress from the ground, and newly released prisoner Cameron Poe (Nicolas Cage), who once killed a man while defending his wife's honor and now wants nothing more than to get home to her and their angelic little girl.

Ten years ago, who could ever have imagined that awkward, weak-chinned weird boys Cusack and Cage would be able to reinvent themselves as action stars, doing the Sylvester Stallone thing with high-powered weapons and stolen police motorcycles? But their macho antics are no more improbable than anything else about this polished-to-a-high-hard-gloss testosterone attack, a noisy, nasty diversion for adrenaline junkies that's almost worth seeing for the scene in which Cage rescues his daughter's birthday present from some smirking hard-ass or other. "Put ... the bunny ... down," Cage intones, voice trembling with suppressed paternal rage, as the plush toy dangles in mid air from an open cargo door. Mega-budget action extravaganzas don't get much sillier.

CONFESSIONS OF A DANGEROUS MIND 📀
2002 113m c   Biography   ★★½
Mad Chance Productions/ Section Eight/   R
Renaissance Films/Miramax   (U.S./U.K./Germany)

Sam Rockwell *(Chuck Barris)*, George Clooney *(Jim Byrd)*, Drew Barrymore *(Penny Pacino)*, Julia Roberts *(Patricia Wilson)*, Rutger Hauer *(Keeler)*, Maggie Gyllenhaal *(Debbie)*, David Hirsch *(Freddie Cannon)*, Jerry Weintraub *(Larry Goldberg)*, Frank Fontaine *(ABC Executive)*, Rachelle Lefevre *(Tuvia—Age 25)*

p, Andrew Lazar; d, George Clooney; w, Charlie Kaufman (based on the book *Confessions of a Dangerous Mind: An Unauthorized Autobiography*, by Chuck Barris); ph, Newton Thomas Sigel; ed, Stephen Mirrione; m, Alex Wurman; prod d, James D. Bissell; art d, Isabelle Guay; fx, Bill Rivard, Louis Morin; cos, Renee April

Scripted by postmodern prankster Charlie Kaufman, directed by George Clooney, and based on trash-TV pioneer Chuck Barris's 1984 "unauthorized autobiography," this poker-faced tall tale is galvanized by Sam Rockwell's no-holds-barred performance.

New York City, 1981: Naked, unshaven, and in the middle of a nervous breakdown, Barris (Rockwell) is holed up in a run-down hotel room, staving off his inner demons by writing his life story. Ever the showman, he dresses up the straightforward tale of an ambitious small-town hustler who left his dubious mark on the TV landscape—Barris is responsible for both "The Dating Game" and "The Gong Show"—with flights of fancy presented as the gospel truth. Before hitting big with "The Dating Game," a nearly broke Barris is approached by a mysterious fellow (Clooney, in acting mode) who offers him a gig with the CIA. Only half believing the offer is for real, Barris accepts, only to discover he's being trained as an assassin. But it's too late to back out, and his first contract killing coincides with the network's decision to pick up the game show. The program even provides a cover for Barris's missions, as he chaperones lucky winners on dates to Berlin and Helsinki and does a little wet work while they're sight-seeing.

First-time director Clooney confidently employs a dizzying combination of film stocks, overlapping images, and editing styles to tell the fractured fairy tale of Barris's life; the freewheeling mix of sunny nostalgia for the boomerang coffee-table era and sleazy fascination with its underbelly recalls Paul Schrader's AUTO FOCUS. But while that film took certain dramatic liberties with actor Bob Crane's life story, this one is an extended riff on Barris's already suspect account of his own. It's tremendously clever, but ultimately pointless.

CONFESSIONS OF A NAZI SPY
1939 110m bw Spy   ★★★★
Warner Bros.   (U.S.)

Edward G. Robinson *(Ed Renard)*, Francis Lederer *(Schneider)*, George Sanders *(Schlager)*, Paul Lukas *(Dr. Kassel)*, Henry

O'Neill *(D.A. Kellogg)*, Lya Lys *(Erika Wolff)*, Grace Stafford *(Mrs. Schneider)*, James Stephenson *(Scotland Yard Official)*, Sig Rumann *(Krogman)*, Frederic Tozere *(Phillips)*

p, Robert Lord; d, Anatole Litvak; w, Milton Krims, John Wexley (based on an original story by Milton Krims and John Wexley, and magazine articles by Leon Turrou); ph, Sol Polito; ed, Owen Marks

Landmark anti-Nazi proganda film from Warner Bros. The film begins in rural Scotland where a reclusive woman suddenly begins receiving mail from all points of the globe. When a resident philatelist requests the foreign stamps for his collection, the woman refuses explosively and slams her door in his face. He reports this odd behavior to Scotland Yard. British Intelligence agents soon discover that she is part of a Nazi spy ring. Intercepted information reveals a Nazi spy network in America with plans to kidnap an American Air Corps general. The Brits contact the U.S. Government and FBI man Robinson enters the investigation, probing into the Nazi underground. Robinson systematically pinpoints key spies, concentrating on Lederer, the weak link in the Nazi network. Sanders is the sinister and cheap superior who pays Lederer miserably for his treachery, about $50 per report. Lederer also names Lukas, head of the Nazi *Bund*, who is recruiting American youth into *Hitlerjugend* legions and also in league with Sanders.

CONFESSIONS OF A NAZI SPY frightened audiences with the threat of Nazi tyranny, fulfilling the ideological and commercial aims of Warner Bros. Robinson subdues his normally expansive gestures and speaks quietly as he cannily underplays a dynamic part in keeping with Litvak's semi-documentary style. The spy ring activities are shown in newsreel fashion and some actual clips are included from the 1937 spy trials of four Nazis convicted of espionage (the case on which the film is based). Nazi brutality is exposed throughout the film and Hitler, Goebbels, and company are openly vilified. Litvak's direction is unabashedly biased: his hatred for the Nazis seethes throughout the film, although the Nazis' anti-Semitism is elided.

CONFIDENTIALLY YOURS 📀
(VIVEMENT DIMANCHE!)
1983 111m bw Crime/Romance   ★★★½
Carosse/Soprofilms/A2   (France)

Fanny Ardant *(Barbara Becker)*, Jean-Louis Trintignant *(Julien Vercel)*, Philippe Laudenbach *(M. Clement)*, Caroline Sihol *(Marie-Christine Vercel)*, Philippe Morier-Genoud *(Superintendent Santelli)*, Xavier Saint-Macary *(Bertrand Fabre, photographer)*, Jean-Pierre Kalfon *(Jacques Massoulier)*, Anik Belaubre *(Cashier at the Eden)*, Jean-Louis Richard *(Louison)*, Yann Dedet *("Angel Face")*

p, Armand Barbault; d, Francois Truffaut; w, Francois Truffaut, Suzanne Schiffman, Jean Aurel (based on the novel *The Long Saturday Night* by Charles Williams); ph, Nestor Almendros; ed, Martine Barraque; m, Georges Delerue; prod d, Hilton McConnico

Based on the 1962 Charles Williams pulp novel *The Long Saturday Night*, this final film by Truffaut (he died of a brain tumor in October 1984) is done in the Hitchcockian style of his 1968 THE BRIDE WORE BLACK. A classy black-and-white movie about a man falsely accused of murder, CONFIDENTIALLY YOURS is much lighter and more enjoyable than most of Truffaut's films in the Seventies.

Its absurdly complex plot involves businessman Julien Vercel (Jean-Louis Trintignant), who is charged with murder and remains holed up in his office to avoid detection. Barbara (Fanny Ardant), the secretary he has just fired for her insolent behavior, tracks down clues to prove his innocence. The mystery of the film is not the killer's identity—this has never been a concern of Truffaut's—but the more important mystery of love. Barbara plays detective not because she cares about revealing the murderer but because she loves Julien, though neither she nor Julien will initially admit this. In order to prove her love to him, she must survive an Orphic descent into the seedy criminal underworld of gangsters, murderers, and prostitutes.

CONFIDENTIALLY YOURS! is Truffaut's showcase for Ardant, the love of his later years and mother of his youngest child.

CONFORMIST, THE

(IL CONFORMISTA)
1970 111m c   Drama/Political   ★★★★½
Mars/Marianne/Maran   R
(Italy/France/West Germany)

Jean-Louis Trintignant *(Marcello Clerici)*, Stefania Sandrelli *(Giulia)*, Dominique Sanda *(Anna Quadri)*, Pierre Clementi *(Lino Semirama—the Chauffeur)*, Gastone Moschin *(Manganiello)*, Enzo Tarascio *(Professor Quadri)*, Jose Quaglio *(Italo)*, Milly *(Marcello's Mother)*, Giuseppe Addobbati *(Marcello's Father)*, Yvonne Sanson *(Giulia's Mother)*

p, Maurizio Lodi-Fe; d, Bernardo Bertolucci; w, Bernardo Bertolucci (based on the novel by Alberto Moravia); ph, Vittorio Storaro (Technicolor); ed, Franco Arcalli; m, Georges Delerue; prod d, Ferdinando Scarfiotti; cos, Gitt Magrini

AAN Best Adapted Screenplay: Bernardo Bertolucci

One of Bertolucci's best films, THE CONFORMIST makes a provocative connection between repressed sexual desires and fascist politics. It's an intriguing, elegantly photographed study of the twisted Italian character of the 1930s.

Plagued by the memory of a traumatic sexual experience during childhood and desperate to demonstrate his "normalcy," Marcello Clerici (Jean-Louis Trintignant) marries the dull, petit-bourgeois Giulia (Stefania Sandrelli). He later joins the Italian Fascist movement, accepting an assignment to travel to Paris and help assassinate Prof. Quadri (Enzo Tarascio), his former mentor. Before the assassination, Marcello becomes attracted to Anna (Dominique Sanda), the professor's seductive, bisexual wife, though she herself is actually more interested in Giulia. Marcello's affiliation with the Fascists eventually self-destructs, as does his own personality.

Here, as in all his best work, Bertolucci addresses the issue of duality—of both sexual and political conflict. Marcello's personal contradictions parallel those of the Italian government, with his own decline taking place at the same time as Mussolini's, in 1943. Visually, THE CONFORMIST is stunning; its gliding camerawork, unusual camera angles and rich color perfectly evoke the baroque decadence of Marcello's world. Bertolucci received an Oscar nomination for Best Adapted Screenplay.

CONNECTICUT YANKEE, A

1931 95m   bw Comedy/Fantasy   ★★★½
Fox   (U.S.)

Will Rogers *(Hank)*, William Farnum *(King Arthur)*, Myrna Loy *(Queen Morgan Le Fay)*, Maureen O'Sullivan *(Alisande)*, Frank Albertson *(Clarence)*, Mitchell Harris *(Merlin)*, Brandon Hurst *(Sagramor)*

d, David Butler; w, William Conselman, Owen Davis Sr. (based on the novel *A Connecticut Yankee in King Arthur's Court* by Mark Twain); ph, Ernest Palmer; ed, Irene Morra

Will Rogers's fabled charm was well utilized in this excellent adaptation of the popular Mark Twain novel. Rogers, owner of a small-town radio shop, goes to install a battery in the old house of an eccentric character who thinks that he can contact King

Arthur by radio. When Rogers is felled by an accidental blow on the head, he dreams his way back to days when knights were bold. The locals soon conclude that the mysterious stranger is a warlock. His only hope of saving himself is to exploit his unique knowledge of the future. Rogers's co-stars provide able support to the satirical proceedings. Myrna Loy plays the villainess and Maureen O'Sullivan is Rogers's love interest. Since the picture was made during the depths of the Depression, much of Rogers's topical humor may be lost on today's audiences but the anachronistic visual gags (for example, Rogers lassoes a Knight of the Round Table in the middle of a joust) remain as fresh and funny as ever.

CONNECTICUT YANKEE IN KING
ARTHUR'S COURT, A   DVD

1949 106m c   Science Fiction/Fantasy/Musical   ★★★
Paramount   (U.S.)

Bing Crosby *(Hank Martin)*, William Bendix *(Sir Sagramore)*, Cedric Hardwicke *(King Arthur)*, Rhonda Fleming *(Alisande La Carteloise)*, Murvyn Vye *(Merlin)*, Virginia Field *(Morgan Le Fay)*, Henry Wilcoxon *(Sir Lancelot)*, Richard Webb *(Sir Galahad)*, Joseph Vitale *(Sir Logris)*, Alan Napier *(High Executioner)*

p, Robert Fellows; d, Tay Garnett; w, Edmund Beloin (based on the novel by Mark Twain); ph, Ray Rennahan (Technicolor); ed, Archie Marshek; m, Victor Young; art d, Hans Dreier, Roland Anderson; fx, Farciot Edouart; cos, Edith Head

Mark Twain's popular satirical fantasy is mellowed into an amusingly carefree, lavishly mounted Bing Crosby vehicle, rich in color and pleasant if unmemorable songs. Crosby stars as Hank Martin, a Connecticut blacksmith who is knocked unconscious in a wild rainstorm and wakes up in King Arthur's Camelot. This production boasts wonderful sets and softly focused color lensing by Ray Rennahan. The famed art director Hans Dreier created a spectacular and authentic medieval castle for the film, with an enormous dining hall for King Arthur's knights, a huge ballroom, lush gardens, court-yards, and jousting grounds. Rhonda Fleming's auburn-haired beauty is lovely in the rich Technicolor process and Tay Garnett's direction is smooth and well paced. It was remade and updated by Disney in 1979 as UNIDENTIFIED FLYING ODDBALL.

CONNECTION, THE

1962 110m bw Drama   ★★½
Allen/Clarke   (U.S.)

William Redfield *(Jim Dunn)*, Warren Finnerty *(Leach)*, Garry Goodrow *(Ernie)*, Jerome Raphel *(Solly)*, James Anderson *(Sam)*, Carl Lee *(Cowboy)*, Barbara Winchester *(Sister Salvation)*, Roscoe Lee Browne *(J.J. Burden)*, Henry Proach *(Harry)*, Freddie Redd *(Piano)*

p, Lewis Allen, Shirley Clarke; d, Shirley Clarke; w, Jack Gelber (based on the play by Gelber); ph, Arthur J. Ornitz; ed, Shirley Clarke; m, Freddie Redd; prod d, Richard Sylbert; art d, Albert Brenner; cos, Ruth Morley

Eight drug addicts gather in a Manhattan loft to wait for their connection. To pay for their drugs, they have agreed to allow Dunn, a would-be documentary filmmaker, to photograph them. Film within a film records their conversation, reflections, and an impromptu jam session involving four of the junkies who are musicians. The "connection" arrives with a soldier from the Salvation Army, who suspects the addicts are drinking and beats a hasty retreat. Dunn is then persuaded to try some heroin so that he will have a deeper understanding of the subject of his film, and he becomes violently ill.

This film was considered a tour de force for choreographer-turned-director Clarke, who heretofore had specialized in prize-winning shorts. It is a jolting look at the drug crowd. The characters get laughs with their crisp lingo and wry wit, showing them to be acceptable types one can empathize with. There are no phony dramatics here.

CONTACT

DVD

1997 142m c Science Fiction ★★½
South Side Amusement Company/Warner Bros. PG
(U.S.)

Jodie Foster *(Dr. Eleanor "Ellie" Arroway)*, Matthew McConaughey *(Palmer Joss)*, James Woods *(Michael Kitz)*, Angela Bassett *(Rachel Constantine)*, Tom Skerritt *(David Drumlin)*, John Hurt *(S.R. Hadden)*, David Morse *(Ted Arroway)*, Rob Lowe *(Richard Rank)*, William Fichtner *(Kent Clark)*, Jake Busey *(Joseph)*

p, Robert Zemeckis, Steve Starkey; d, Robert Zemeckis; w, Michael Goldenberg, James V. Hart (based on the novel *Contact* by Carl Sagan, from a story by Ann Druyan and Carl Sagan); ph, Don Burgess; ed, Arthur Schmidt; m, Alan Silvestri; prod d, Ed Verreaux; art d, Lawrence A. Hubbs, Bruce Crone; fx, John Dykstra, Allen Hall, Ken Ralston, Sony Pictures Imageworks, Warner Digital, Industrial Light & Magic, Ian Kelly, Steve Berg; cos, Joanna Johnston

AAN Best Sound: Randy Thom, Tom Johnson, Dennis Sands, William B. Kaplan

Jodie Foster gives an impassioned performance as an astronomer in Robert Zemeckis's CONTACT, an ambitious and cerebral adaptation of Carl Sagan's bestseller, that gets sucked into a black hole of digital-effects and New Age gobbledygook.

Tracking signals from outer space, astronomer Ellie Arroway (Jodie Foster) hears a mysterious sound which is traced to the star Vega. Her cutthroat boss, David Drumlin (Tom Skerritt), has taken credit for Arroway's work, which has come under government scrutiny. With convenient financial help from eccentric mogul S.R. Hadden (John Hurt), Arroway finds that the signal contains data for building a space capsule and launching pad that will enable travel to Vega. The President approves the building of the spacecraft, and Arroway renews her affair with Palmer Joss (Matthew McConaughey), an ex-lover of hers who's now the presidential "spiritual advisor." Though Drumlin is initially chosen to pilot the capsule, he is killed when a religious fanatic blows up the capsule. Arroway pilots a second transport funded by Hadden; she is successfully launched into space, and lands on what she perceives to be Vega.

CONTACT aspires to cross the themes of CLOSE ENCOUNTERS OF THE THIRD KIND (1977) with the head-trip of 2001: A SPACE ODYSSEY (1968), while also trying to recapture the humanistic tone of Zemeckis's previous film, FORREST GUMP (1994); unfortunately, the result can best be read as New Age Disney. The character of Hadden—who's a sort of Howard Hughes by way of Tinkerbell—is an amusing, if obvious, *deus ex machina,* but the film's intellectual pretensions are seriously undermined by Joss, an unconvincing romantic contrivance. Ellie's trip into space is genuinely gripping, but then the film goes on for another 30-minutes so that she can give a long-winded speech about faith. In short, Zemeckis wants to make a profound statement about the search for meaning in an empty technological universe, but feels the need to spell everything out in the most prosaic terms.

CONTEMPT

DVD

(LE MEPRIS)
1963 103m c Drama ★★★★★
Les Societes Rome-Paris Films Concordia/
Compagnia Cinematografica Champion
(France/Italy)

Brigitte Bardot *(Camille Javal)*, Michel Piccoli *(Paul Javal)*, Jack Palance *(Jeremiah "Jerry" Prokosch)*, Fritz Lang *(Himself)*, Georgia Moll *(Francesca Vanini)*, Jean-Luc Godard *(Lang's Assistant Director)*, Linda Veras *(Mermaid)*, Raoul Coutard *(Cameraman)*

p, Georges De Beauregard, Carlo Ponti, Joseph E. Levine; d, Jean-Luc Godard; w, Jean-Luc Godard (based on the novel *Il Disprezzo [A Ghost At Noon]* by Alberto Moravia); ph, Raoul Coutard (Franscope, Technicolor); ed, Agnes Guillemot, Lila Lakshmanan; m, Georges Delerue; cos, Tanine Autre

A profoundly sad yet beautiful fable about the cinema, CONTEMPT is the story of Paul Javal (Michel Piccoli), a former writer of detective stories who has become a screenwriter of little consequence. He claims that he longs to write for the stage but he believes that his beautiful young wife, Camille (Brigitte Bardot), expects more financial rewards than the theater can offer. Paul is approached by crass American film producer Jeremy Prokosch (Jack Palance) to perform a rewrite on the screenplay for his production of Homer's *Odyssey*. The film is to be directed by the legendary German director Fritz Lang (playing himself). Paul accepts the job, but Camille is disappointed at his lack of conviction in the assignment, even though he ostensibly accepted the job to benefit her. She begins to manifest a profound mistrust of him that is never really explained. After a strained social situation in which Paul acts in a less than noble manner, Camille turns to Prokosch to pursue what appears to be an affair.

An adaptation of Alberto Moravia's novel *A Ghost at Noon,* CONTEMPT concerns itself with the filmmaking process, the nature of film authorship, and the art of adapting a novel for the screen. Godard favors a personal idiosyncratic approach to filmmaking and adaptation as is evidenced in his utilizing Moravia and Homer's work to relate the characters in the film to the people in his own life: Paul, Camille, and Prokosch evoke Odysseus, Penelope, and Poseidon while also suggesting Godard, his wife (and favored female lead at that time) Anna Karina, and distributor Joseph E. Levine.

The genesis of the project is worth recounting. Approached by Italian producer Carlo Ponti about a possible collaboration, the New Wave auteur suggested an adaptation of the Moravia novel with Kim Novak and Frank Sinatra in the leads. The pair refused. Ponti then suggested Sophia Loren and Marcello Mastroianni. Godard refused. Eventually Bardot was chosen because of the potential financial rewards that could be garnered from revealing her celebrated delectable flesh on screen. However, Godard had the last laugh: the most extensive nudity is in the film's subversively tame opening scene. Committed to a personal cinema, Godard cast himself as Lang's assistant director and used the great auteur as his mouthpiece. CONTEMPT is beautifully photographed in Cinemascope with sun dappled color by Raoul Coutard and Georges Delerue provides the haunting score.

CONTRABAND

DVD

1940 92m bw Drama ★★½
British National (U.K.)

Conrad Veidt *(Capt. Andersen)*, Valerie Hobson *(Mrs. Sorenson)*, Esmond Knight *(Mr. Pidgeon)*, Hay Petrie *(Mate Skold/Chef Skold)*, Raymond Lovell *(Van Dyne)*, Harold Warrender *(Lt/Cdr Ellis)*, Charles Victor *(Hendrick)*, Manning Whiley *(Manager)*, Peter Bull *(Grimm)*, Stuart Latham *(Grimm)* p, John Corfield; d, Michael Powell; w, Michael Powell, Brock Williams (based on a story by Emeric Pressburger); ph, Freddie Young

An odd little comic thriller—who, except perhaps Michael Powell, would have cast 47-year-old CABINET OF DR. CALIGARI star Conrad Veidt as a light romantic hero?—set in the darkness of London during the WWII blackout. Captain Andersen (Conrad Veidt) commands a Danish freighter that's delayed in port by British customs agents on the lookout for military contraband. While the ship is docked, two passengers slip ashore, even though they've been ordered to stay on board. Mild-mannered Mr. Pidgeon (Esmond Knight) has kept a low profile during the trip, but the Captain has already butted heads with Mrs. Sorenson (Valerie Hobson), a willful Englishwoman who lives by the credo that rules were made for other people. His honor as an officer affronted by his passengers' disobedience, Andersen goes ashore and tries to find them. He catches up to Mrs. Sorenson in London, and gradually comes to realize that she's a spy on a mission to root out a Nazi cell operating out of the basement of a Soho nightclub. The movie's tone is a bit uneven; the comedy (heavy on the Danish jokes, and to be honest, the Danes don't lend themselves to it) and the straightforward espionage material don't entirely mesh. But Powell pulls off a couple of stunning sequences—notably a shootout in a storage room filled with plaster busts—and makes fluid use of the wartime setting: the mundane details of day-to-day life in a blacked-out metropolis are just fascinating. This was to have been Deborah Kerr's first feature film; unfortunately, she was left on the cutting room floor as her scenes were deleted from the final print.

CONTRACT
1980　111m　c　Comedy　★★★½
PRF/Zespol　(Poland)

Maja Komorowska, Tadeusz Lomnicki, Magda Jaroszowna, Krzystof Kolberger, Nina Andrycz, Zofia Mrozowska, Beata Tyszkiewicz, Janusz Gajos, Edward Lubaszenko, Leslie Caron

d, Krzysztof Zanussi; w, Krzysztof Zanussi; ph, Slawomir Idziak; ed, Urszula Sliwinska, Ewa Smal; m, Wojciech Kilar; art d, Tadeusz Wybult, Maciej Putowski, Teresa Gruber, Gabriela Allina, Joanna Lelanow

This satirical look at Polish life focuses on the wedding reception of a marriage that did not take place. The couple are pushed into an arranged marriage, and when the bride backs out at the last minute the groom's father decides to have the reception anyway. The reception, which is a celebration of nothing, is filled with drunken altercations, sexual liaisons, and flaring of tempers between the rival families. Leslie Caron is a standout as a kleptomaniac rich woman symbolizing Western decadence. An offbeat, extremely interesting film helmed by one of contemporary Poland's most interesting filmmakers, THE CONTRACT was filmed at the same time as Zanussi's THE CONSTANT FACTOR.

CONVERSATION, THE　**DVD**
1974　113m　c　Drama　★★★★★
Paramount　(U.S.)　PG

Gene Hackman (Harry Caul), John Cazale (Stan), Allen Garfield (Bernie Moran), Frederic Forrest (Mark), Cindy Williams (Ann), Michael Higgins (Paul), Elizabeth MacRae (Meredith), Teri Garr (Amy), Harrison Ford (Martin Stett), Mark Wheeler (Receptionist)

p, Francis Ford Coppola; d, Francis Ford Coppola; w, Francis Ford Coppola; ph, Bill Butler (Technicolor); ed, Walter Murch, Richard Chew; m, David Shire; prod d, Dean Tavoularis

AAN Best Picture; AAN Best Original Screenplay: Francis Ford Coppola; AAN Best Sound: Walter Murch (Sound), Arthur Rochester (Sound)

One of Coppola's very best. Harry Caul (Gene Hackman) is a professional surveillance expert, a wire-tapper and industrial spy for hire by anyone—if the price is right. Harry and his assistant Stan (Cazale) use state-of-the-art technical expertise to track a young couple, Ann (Williams) and Mark (Forrest), and record their conversations. The client is a mysterious and powerful businessman, known only as the "director" (Robert Duvall, in an unbilled cameo), whose motives are unclear. After listening to the tapes repeatedly, however, Harry deduces that Ann is the director's wife and that she is having an affair with Mark, one of her husband's employees. To his horror, Harry concludes that his client plans to murder the couple. Plagued by guilt from a previous assignment in which the information he gathered led to the murders of several people, Harry becomes obsessed with preventing the murders of Ann and Mark—for the first time in his career, he decides to get involved—but he gets in over his head.

Following the triumph of THE GODFATHER, writer-director Francis Ford Coppola surprised everyone with this small, intimate, and brilliantly crafted film, which explores the implications of indiscriminate eavesdropping. Gene Hackman is superb as Harry Caul, a painfully lonely, cynical, paranoid, and alienated man whose work has driven him to guard his own privacy zealously, although there is precious little to protect. A year later Hackman would play another eavesdropper named Harry, this time a detective in Arthur Penn's NIGHT MOVES, and the similarities between the two characters were not lost on the actor—NIGHT MOVES could be a prequel to THE CONVERSATION.

The film was released just after the Watergate break-in, but it was written many years before and was already shooting when the news of the break-in appeared. Technically brilliant, THE CONVERSATION does in aural terms what Antonioni's BLOW UP does in visual terms. This is certainly one of the key films of the 1970s.

COOGAN'S BLUFF　**DVD**
1968　93m　c　Crime/Western　★★★½
Universal　(U.S.)

Clint Eastwood (Coogan), Lee J. Cobb (Sheriff McElroy), Susan Clark (Julie), Tisha Sterling (Linny Raven), Don Stroud (Ringerman), Betty Field (Mrs. Ringerman), Tom Tully (Sheriff McCrea), Melodie Johnson (Millie), James Edwards (Jackson), Rudy Diaz (Running Bear)

p, Don Siegel; d, Don Siegel; w, Herman Miller, Dean Riesner, Howard Rodman (based on a story by Miller); ph, Bud Thackery (Technicolor); ed, Sam E. Waxman; m, Lalo Schifrin; art d, Alexander Golitzen, Robert MacKichan; cos, Helen Colvig

Western myth gets urban update in basis for "McCloud" television series. Arizona deputy arrives in NYC to track killer and teach city cops a thing or three. The interest here is in watching Eastwood, mid-point between spaghetti westerns and assuming his Dirty Harry persona, lock horns with Cobb, who gives a socko performance. Sterling is of passing interest as a female hippie. The first collaboration between Eastwood and Siegel raised the hackles of many a moralist with what was considered needless violence and too much sex. That's one way of saying today it looks tame, but you may get a literal kick out of the poolroom fight scene.

COOK, THE THIEF, HIS WIFE & HER LOVER, THE　**DVD**
1989　124m　c　Drama　★★★½
Allarts Cook/Erato/Films Inc.　(U.K./France)

Richard Bohringer (Richard Borst, the Cook), Michael Gambon (Albert Spica, the Thief), Helen Mirren (Georgina Spica, the Wife),

Alan Howard *(Michael, the Lover)*, Tim Roth *(Mitchel)*, Ciaran Hinds *(Cory)*, Gary Olsen *(Spangler)*, Ewan Stewart *(Harris)*, Roger Ashton Griffiths *(Turpin)*, Ron Cook *(Mews)*

p, Kees Kasander; d, Peter Greenaway; w, Peter Greenaway; ph, Sacha Vierny (CinemaScope); ed, John Wilson; m, Michael Nyman; prod d, Ben Van Os, Jan Roelfs; cos, Jean-Paul Gaultier

Greenaway describes the impulses behind his work as "technical and aesthetic and cerebral and academic." His films have not been developed according to the demands of narrative ("Cinema is much too important to be left to the storytellers," says Greenaway), but by equally deterministic formulas of the director's own devising: formalism, structural symmetry, recurring patterns and symbols, puns and conceits.

At its core a simple tale of adultery, jealousy and revenge, THE COOK, THE THIEF, HIS WIFE & HER LOVER is built around the four characters of the title, the divisions of the restaurant (each room perhaps representing its own historical epoch), the tradition of table painting (a huge Frans Hals reproduction dominates the dining room), and the central metaphysical conceit linking mouth with anus, food with feces, and sex with death.

Greenaway reportedly identifies with the cook: he watches, maintains a dignified distance, but acts decisively on behalf of the lovers. Michael Gambon's Thief and Alan Howard's Lover are diametrical opposites, the one boorish, crude, and ignorant, the other calm, gentle, and cultured. Gambon never stops talking but has little to say; Howard, on the other hand, remains silent for the first 20 minutes of the film but proves thoughtful and wise. Setting out to create an irredeemable monster, Greenaway takes his film to the very limits of screen permissiveness, from graphic torture to cannibalism.

The film has been seen as a vitriolic condemnation of contemporary consumerism and greed, but for all the brutality and physical savagery Greenaway depicts, one suspects his contempt is really aimed at the *nouveaux riches* who do not appreciate the gourmet dishes they can pay for but whose names they cannot pronounce. If there is a connection between this philistine lack of sophistication and Howard's study of the French Revolution, then Gambon is surely representative of the peasants and the Terror—in his resolutely one-dimensional role he embodies every snob or aesthete's nightmare villain. Not surprisingly, his ranting soon becomes repetitive and boring. Greenaway's dialogue cannot sustain our interest, and his lack of humor is the film's biggest drawback. For a lover of games, the director is never remotely playful.

COOL HAND LUKE
1967 126m c   Prison   ★★★★
Warner Bros.   (U.S.)

Paul Newman *(Luke)*, George Kennedy *(Dragline)*, J.D. Cannon *(Society Red)*, Lou Antonio *(Koko)*, Robert Drivas *(Loudmouth Steve)*, Strother Martin *(Captain)*, Jo Van Fleet *(Arletta)*, Clifton James *(Carr)*, Morgan Woodward *(Boss Godfrey)*, Luke Askew *(Boss Paul)*

p, Gordon Carroll; d, Stuart Rosenberg; w, Donn Pearce, Frank Pierson (based on a novel by Pearce); ph, Conrad Hall (Panavision, Technicolor); ed, Sam O'Steen; m, Lalo Schifrin; art d, Cary Odell; cos, Howard Shoup

AAN Best Actor: Paul Newman; *AA Best Supporting Actor:* George Kennedy; *AAN Best Adapted Screenplay:* Donn Pearce, Frank R. Pierson; *AAN Best Original Score:* Lalo Schifrin

Too cool for words, then switches past midstream into a work of poignancy and power. Not much has changed since Warner Bros in the 1930s, and it's interesting to realize, looking over Newman's career, how many overrated male-bonding, macho-buddy movies he has made. COOL HAND LUKE

starts out that way with Newman as irreverent loner put on a chain gang for destroying parking meters. Kennedy won the Best Supporting Actor Oscar as the bastardly convict boss who tries to crack Newman; the comedic part of film is highlighted by a hilarious egg-eating contest, but LUKE gains additional steam thanks to an unforgettable cameo by Van Fleet and a sharp turn toward tragedy. Newman emerges as a victim more to be pitied than scorned or laughed with, adding a deeper tinge of revelance to the film.

Produced by Jack Lemmon's company for Warner Bros., the movie is set in the South but was actually shot near Stockton, California. Pearce, the author of the original novel, was a reformed safecracker and had served time in such a camp. He does a bit role as Sailor, one of the cons. Also in small roles are Joe Don Baker (WALKING TALL), Wayne Rogers (television's "M*A*S*H"), and Dennis Hopper.

COOL WORLD, THE
1963 125m   bw   Drama   ★★★½
Wiseman   (U.S.)

Hampton Clayton *(Duke)*, Yolanda Rodriguez *(Luanee)*, Bostic Felton *(Rod)*, Gary Bolling *(Littleman)*, Carl Lee *(Priest)*, Gloria Foster *(Mrs. Custis)*, Georgia Burke *(Grandma)*, Charles Richardson *(Beep Bop)*, Bruce Edwards *(Warrior)*, Teddy McCain *(Saint)*

p, Frederick Wiseman; d, Shirley Clarke; w, Shirley Clarke (based on the novel by Warren Miller and the play by Miller and Robert Rossen); ph, Baird Bryant; ed, Shirley Clarke; m, Mal Waldron

Unfortunately, timeless and not too cool. Deep down, not even the rent is happenin', but on the surface this little alleycat film captures the day-to-day desperation of the ghetto world, mainlining its images with transfusions of eclectic jazz background. We have here a mood piece focusing on Clayton's efforts to rise to authority in his Harlem street gang after hearing a Black Muslim evangelist spouting black supremacy and hatred against whites. An effective look at the mind-set of bored youths who see violence as a way out of poverty, and an indictment of the failings of federal law.

COOLER, THE
                                            DVD
2003 103m   c   Crime/Drama   ★★★
ContentFilm/Dog Pond Films/   R
Furst Films/Gryphon Films/
Pierce-Williams/Visionbox Pictures   (U.S.)

William H. Macy *(Bernie Lootz)*, Alec Baldwin *(Shelley Kaplow)*, Maria Bello *(Natalie Belisario)*, Shawn Hatosy *(Mikey)*, Estella Warren *(Charlene)*, Ron Livingston *(Larry Sokolov)*, Paul Sorvino *(Buddy Stafford)*, Joey Fatone *(Johnny Capella)*, Ellen Greene *(Doris)*, Arthur J. Nascarella *(Nickey "Fingers" Bonnatto)*

p, Sean Furst, Michael Pierce; d, Wayne Kramer; w, Frank Hannah, Wayne Kramer; ph, James Whitaker; ed, Arthur Coburn; m, Mark Isham; prod d, Toby Corbett; fx, Jeremy Oddo; cos, Kristin M. Burke

AAN Best Supporting Actor: Alec Baldwin

Wayne Kramer's debut feature echoes such gritty exposes of Vegas's ugly underbelly as P.T. Anderson's HARD EIGHT, but strong performances and Kramer's eye for the striking detail give the familiar material its own distinctive flavor.

In a town where luck is more precious than either love or money, Bernie Lootz (William H. Macy) oozes the stuff. Bad luck, to be sure, but bad can be good for a Vegas casino manager like Shelley Kaplow (Alec Baldwin), who employs Bernie as a "cooler." Shelley pays Bernie to spread his bad mojo around the down-at-the-heels Shangri-La, putting the freeze on the hottest winning streak before the house gets stuck with making a big payoff. Once a reckless gambler, sad-sack Bernie is paying off a debt working for Shelley, but his servitude is almost over and he's counting down the days until he make a new start somewhere—anywhere—else. The first wrench in his plan is disillusioned Shangri-La waitress Natalie Belisario (Maria Bello), who inexplicably falls in love with Bernie; love turns Bernie's luck around and makes him useless as a cooler. The second is the unexpected reappearance of Bernie's estranged son, Mikey (Shawn Hatosy), and his pregnant girlfriend, Charlene (Estella Warren). Embittered and manipulative, Mikey gets himself in big trouble by trying to beat the house—Shelley's house—with loaded dice.

Baldwin's smoothly vicious Shelley is a revelation, and the supporting cast is a dream, from Paul Sorvino as a washed-up junkie lounge singer to vivacious actress-singer Ellen Greene as a hard-bitten bartender with a cigarette glued to her lip. And if the ending isn't quite in sync with the movie's overall tone, things work themselves out in a surprisingly satisfying fashion.

COP

1988 110m c   Crime/Mystery   ★★★½
Atlantic   (U.S.)   R

James Woods (Lloyd Hopkins), Lesley Ann Warren (Kathleen McCarthy), Charles Durning (Dutch Pelz), Charles Haid (Whitey Haines), Raymond J. Barry (Fred Gaffney), Randi Brooks (Joanie Pratt), Steven Lambert (Bobby Franco), Christopher Wynne (Jack Gibbs), Jan McGill (Jen Hopkins), Vicki Wauchope (Penny Hopkins)

p, James B. Harris, James Woods; d, James B. Harris; w, James B. Harris (based on the novel Blood On The Moon by James Ellroy); ph, Steve Dubin; ed, Anthony Spano; m, Michel Colombier; prod d, Gene Rudolf; fx, Larry Fioritto, Bill Myer; cos, Gale Parker Smith

Based on James Ellroy's novel Blood on the Moon, COP is a grim, modern-day film noir starring James Woods as Lloyd Hopkins, the most obsessive, vile and amoral cop since Ralph Meeker played Mike Hammer in Robert Aldrich's KISS ME DEADLY. Coproduced by Woods, and written and directed by his friend James B. Harris (who produced Stanley Kubrick's THE KILLING, PATHS OF GLORY and LOLITA), COP combines brutal violence with a self-mocking sense of black humor.

Its action is set in a Los Angeles overwhelmed by hypocrisy, cynicism and sleaze, where Woods, an inveterate loner who is one of the LAPD's best detectives, finds himself investigating a murder he believes to have been the work of a serial killer who preys on innocent-looking women. Oppressively seedy and bleak, COP presents a world destroyed by the corruption of romantic notions, and Woods, who understands this warped milieu, is obsessed with the way society fills women's heads with fairy-tale promises of security, decency, justice, and romance. "Innocence kills," he tells his shocked wife. "I see it every day." Although directed and written with a sometimes-unsure hand by Harris, COP is completely absorbing because of Woods's chillingly effective performance.

Few actors can make an amoral, intelligent, sardonic, hyperactive, womanizing, violent and downright warped character as disarmingly appealing as Woods can. As an actor, he juggles complex contradictions with ease, showing an audience the various sides of his character's psyche with the skill of a magician. In COP, Woods takes us on a singularly unpleasant ride, but it is always an insightful and fascinating one. Fueled by his frightening performance, the film rushes headlong into an ending that is so inevitable, yet still so shocking, that it terminates the genre with an irrevocable bang.

COP LAND   DVD

1997 105m c   Drama   ★★½
Woods Entertainment   (U.S.)   R

Sylvester Stallone (Sheriff Freddy Heflin), Harvey Keitel (Ray Donlan), Ray Liotta (Gary "Figs" Figgis), Robert De Niro (Moe Tilden), Peter Berg (Joey Randone), Janeane Garofalo (Deputy Cindy Betts), Robert Patrick (Jack Rucker), Michael Rapaport (Murray Babitch), Annabella Sciorra (Liz Randone), Malik Yoba (Detective Carson)

p, Cary Woods, Cathy Konrad, Ezra Swerdlow; d, James Mangold; w, James Mangold; ph, Eric Edwards; ed, Craig McKay; m, Howard Shore; prod d, Lester Cohen; art d, Wing Lee; fx, Wilfred Caban, Randall Balsmeyer, Kathy Kelehan; cos, Ellen Lutter

Though generally engaging and well-acted, COP LAND is a highly derivative and overplotted morality play, with Sylvester Stallone attempting his first recognizably human role in decades, but failing to hold his own against a powerhouse supporting cast.

Off-duty NYPD cop Murray Babitch (Michael Rapaport) "disappears" after a violent incident on the George Washington Bridge in which he kills two men who sideswiped his car. Believed to be dead, Murray has actually been secreted away by his uncle, Ray (Harvey Keitel), to Garrison, New Jersey, a small town whose population consists mostly of New York City cops. The town itself is policed by Sheriff Freddy Heflin (Sylvester Stallone), who's a quiet, tormented guy who refuses to help out an internal affairs agent, Moe Tilden (Robert De Niro), who comes to Garrison suspecting that Murray is alive and Ray is responsible for a coverup—and in fact might be the leader of a group of thoroughly corrupt cops all residing in Garrison.

By gaining weight for the role of Freddy and attempting a "studied" performance (composed mostly of walking and talking slowly), floundering action star Stallone tried here to reinvent himself. Miramax chief Harvey Weinstein fashioned a package deal in which Stallone is surrounded with a slew of top-flight actors, including Scorsese stalwarts De Niro and Keitel, in a further attempt to create a predetermined aura of class and artistic respectability. Their efforts are for naught, however, as Stallone's dim-bulb performance fails to carry any sort of resonance, especially when compared to the (seemingly) effortless) intense work done by his costars. The basic story is little more than an update of 1950s anti-McCarthy westerns about honest, solitary marshals. It also bears a strong resemblance to Arthur Penn's THE CHASE (1966), in which Marlon Brando played a small-town sheriff at odds with the community's prominent citizens, while trying to track down a fugitive who threatens their standing.

CORNERED

1945 102m bw   Thriller/War   ★★★★
RKO   (U.S.)

Dick Powell (Gerard), Walter Slezak (Incza), Micheline Cheirel (Mme. Jarnac), Nina Vale (Senora Camargo), Morris Carnovsky (Santana), Edgar Barrier (DuBois), Steven Geray (Senor Camargo), Jack LaRue (Diego), Luther Adler (Marcel Jarnac), Gregory Gaye (Perchon)

p, Adrian Scott; d, Edward Dmytryk; w, John Paxton (based on a story by John Wexley and a title by Ben Hecht); ph, Harry Wild; ed, Joseph Noriega; m, Roy Webb; art d, Albert S. D'Agostino, Carroll Clark; cos, Renie

Peak Powell the way we like him, and it's a long way from Ruby Keeler. Canadian flier Powell gets out of a POW camp with his mind set on avenging the death of his French war bride, caused by Vichy officer Jarnac (Adler). Although by all reports Jarnac is dead, Gerard refuses to believe it. He pursues leads through Switzerland and then to Buenos Aires, where he encounters an underground group of Nazi hunters—Carnovsky, Barrier, and LaRue. His quest is further complicated when he finds himself drawn to the attractive Cheirel, who married Adler, without ever having met him, in order to emigrate safely.

Tightly directed by the talented Edward Dmytryk, CORNERED is a terse thriller, with Powell turning in another tough-talking, hardboiled performance as the man seeking vengeance with cold-blooded determination. The script was based on the title of a 20-page Ben Hecht treatment that was, according to Dmytryk, "such poor stuff…" that they kept only the title and brought in new writers to shape the film. Well-sculpted.

CORSICAN BROTHERS, THE

1941   111m   bw   Adventure   ★★★½
UA   (U.S.)

Douglas Fairbanks Jr. *(Mario/Lucien)*, Ruth Warrick *(Isabelle)*, Akim Tamiroff *(Colonna)*, J. Carrol Naish *(Lorenzo)*, H.B. Warner *(Dr. Paoli)*, John Emery *(Tomasso)*, Henry Wilcoxon *(Count Franchi)*, Gloria Holden *(Countess Franchi)*, Walter Kingsford *(M. Dupre)*, Nana Bryant *(Mme. Dupre)*

p, Edward Small; d, Gregory Ratoff; w, George Bruce (based on an adaptation of the Alexandre Dumas novel by Bruce and Howard Estabrook); ph, Harry Stradling; ed, Grant Whytock, William Claxton; m, Dimitri Tiomkin; fx, Howard Anderson

AAN Best Score (Drama or Comedy): Dimitri Tiomkin

Exciting Dumas tale, which has some basis in fact, brought to the screen with great gusto on the part of Fairbanks whose dashing feats rival the acrobatic antics of his illustrious father. It is the tale of Siamese-twin boys born in Corsica and separated by brilliant doctor Warner just before their parents and relatives are killed by Tamiroff's henchmen in a blood feud. One child is sent to Paris to be raised, the other into the mountains with family retainer Naish. When both grow to manhood they are reunited—Fairbanks skillfully playing both roles—and launch a revenge plan against Tamiroff.

Fairbanks excels in showing how the emotional/intellectual telepathy works on each twin, particularly the agony one feels whenever the other is emotionally upset or physically wounded, and the jealousy one feels when the other falls in love with Warrick. Ratoff's direction is eccentric, but he provides great pace and the script is excellent. The superb Tamiroff plays his evil role with the usual guttural relish, almost as if practicing for his fun bad guy, Pablo, in FOR WHOM THE BELL TOLLS.

COTTON CLUB, THE

1984   127m   c   Crime/Musical   ★★★½
Zoetrope   (U.S.)   R

Richard Gere *(Dixie Dwyer)*, Gregory Hines *(Sandman Williams)*, Diane Lane *(Vera Cicero)*, Lonette McKee *(Lila Rose Oliver)*, James Remar *(Dutch Schultz)*, Nicolas Cage *(Vincent Dwyer)*, Allen Garfield *(Abbadabba Berman)*, Bob Hoskins *(Owney Madden)*, Fred Gwynne *(Frenchy Demange)*, Gwen Verdon *(Tish Dwyer)*

p, Robert Evans; d, Francis Ford Coppola; w, William Kennedy, Francis Ford Coppola (based on a story by Kennedy, Coppola, Mario Puzo, inspired by a pictorial history by James Haskins); ph, Stephen Goldblatt (Technicolor); ed, Barry Malkin, Robert Q. Lovett; m, John Barry; prod d, Richard Sylbert; art d, David Chapman, Gregory Bolton; fx, Connie Brink; chor, Michael Smuin, Henry LeTang, Gregory Hines, Claudia Asbury, George Faison, Arthur Mitchell, Michael Meachum; cos, Milena Canonero

AAN Best Film Editing: Barry Malkin, Robert Q. Lovett; *AAN Best Art Direction-Set Decoration:* Richard Sylbert (Art Direction), George Gaines (Set Decoration), Les Bloom (Set Decoration)

Lavish, interesting, evocative but strained and self-conscious, THE COTTON CLUB is all watchable curiosity. Film doctor Coppola came in at the last minute to salvage a troubled production, but couldn't give it a clear storyline with incisive character motivation. This marriage of gangsters and musicals has many elements of genius, but its biggest flaws are its leads. Gere does his own cornet solos, but his hair oil defines his character. Lane, who can only point to LONESOME DOVE in a career full of big chances, walks right through this one, like she's distracted by a flashing traffic light. Hines does what he can without much material to create around, but Hoskins and Gwynne are terrific gangsters and McKee's rendition of "Ill Wind" is a revelation, defining her own lack of career chances and the ill-fated luck of this production.

The mix of fact and fiction, the show-stopping Ellington music, the heady, poisonous aroma of sinister glamour— COTTON CLUB has much to recommend it before it comes up empty-handed. Yet what success it can muster is discolored by might-have-beens. No doubt a behind-the-scenes documentary would have been wildly successful.

COTTON COMES TO HARLEM

1970   97m   c   Crime/Comedy   ★★★
UA   (U.S.)   R

Raymond St. Jacques *(Coffin Ed Johnson)*, Godfrey Cambridge *(Grave Digger Jones)*, Calvin Lockhart *(Rev. Deke O'Malley)*, Judy Pace *(Iris)*, Redd Foxx *(Uncle Budd)*, John Anderson *(Bryce)*, Emily Yancy *(Mabel)*, J.D. Cannon *(Calhoun)*, Mabel Robinson *(Billie)*, Dick Sabol *(Jerema)*

p, Samuel Goldwyn Jr.; d, Ossie Davis; w, Ossie Davis, Arnold Perl (based on the novel by Chester Himes); ph, Gerald Hirschfeld (DeLuxe Color); ed, John Carter, Robert Q. Lovett; m, Galt MacDermot; art d, Manny Gerard; fx, Sol Stern; cos, Anna Hill Johnstone

One of the first of a wave of action comedies, not for delicate tastes. Ossie Davis made his directorial debut in this gaudy blaxploitation crime comedy, filmed on location in Harlem. St. Jacques and Cambridge are, respectively, Coffin Ed Johnson and Grave Digger Jones, a pair of Harlem plainclothesmen investigating a "Back to Africa" campaign run by shady preacher Lockhart. A huge success, it inspired an inferior sequel (COME BACK, CHARLESTON BLUE) as well as a new genre for the 1970s.

COUNSELLOR-AT-LAW

1933   80m   bw   Drama   ★★★★★
Universal   (U.S.)

John Barrymore *(George Simon)*, Bebe Daniels *(Regina Gordon)*, Doris Kenyon *(Cora Simon)*, Onslow Stevens *(John P. Tedesco)*, Isabel Jewell *(Bessie Green)*, Melvyn Douglas *(Roy Darwin)*, Thelma Todd *(Lillian La Rue)*, Marvin Kline *(Weinberg)*, Conway Washburne *(Sandler)*, John Qualen *(Breitstein)*

p, Carl Laemmle Jr.; d, William Wyler; w, Elmer Rice (based on his play); ph, Norbert Brodine; ed, Daniel Mandell

A monument to acting and direction at peak form. John Barrymore gives one of his finest performances as a Jewish lawyer who works his way to the top of his profession only to have his gentile wife, Doris Kenyon, leave him. Barrymore was the second choice to play the role after Paul Muni, who had played the role on stage but feared being typecast. The film is superbly directed by William Wyler, who discarded a musical score, having music only at the opening and closing credits, so that the dramatic weight fell upon the crisp dialogue and Barrymore's spellbinding delivery.

The film was made at breakneck speed, with lines delivered in the rapid-fire manner that was then popular in the new talkies. Wyler offered a new brand of filmic realism where he kept his cameras inside the lawyer's offices almost through the first reel, jump-cutting from one office to another but focusing on Barrymore and his nerve-center desk, providing urgency and high drama at an electrifying pace. Today the lightning still crackles through this masterful film.

COUNT OF MONTE CRISTO, THE

1934 113m bw Adventure   ★★★★
Reliance   (U.S.)

Robert Donat *(Edmond Dantes)*, Elissa Landi *(Mercedes)*, Louis Calhern *(De Villefort, Jr.)*, Sidney Blackmer *(Mondego)*, Raymond Walburn *(Danglars)*, O.P. Heggie *(Abbe Faria)*, William Farnum *(Capt. Leclere)*, Georgia Caine *(Mme. De Rosas)*, Walter Walker *(Morrel)*, Lawrence Grant *(De Villefort, Sr.)*

p, Edward Small; d, Rowland V. Lee; w, Philip Dunne, Dan Totheroh, Rowland V. Lee (based on the novel by Alexandre Dumas); ph, Peverell Marley; ed, Grant Whytock; m, Alfred Newman

The oft-told tale by Alexandre Dumas *pere* was never better served than in this Edward Small production, with Robert Donat giving one of his finest performances. He is the wronged man, sailor Edmond Dantes, who has just received a promotion and is about to marry the beautiful Mercedes (Elissa Landi) when he is framed and imprisoned in the terrible sea-locked Chateau d'If, where he languishes for years. While wasting away in captivity, he meets an imprisoned clergyman (O.P. Heggie) who tells him of a fabulous pirate treasure hidden on the island of Monte Cristo. From that moment on Edmond works to escape from the prison and travel to Monte Cristo, where he will establish a new identity and wreak vengeance on those who imprisoned him.

Donat is captivating as the good-hearted victim and the cool seeker of justice, measuring his vengeance with subtle moves and slow deliberation. Producer Small spared no expense in this lavish, technically top-notch production and director Rowland V. Lee, who aided in the adaptation, lends his usual flair for high drama and action.

COUNTRY GIRL, THE   DVD

1954 104m bw Drama   ★★★½
Paramount   (U.S.)

Bing Crosby *(Frank Elgin)*, Grace Kelly *(Georgie Elgin)*, William Holden *(Bernie Dodd)*, Anthony Ross *(Phil Cook)*, Gene Reynolds *(Larry)*, Jacqueline Fontaine *(Singer)*, Eddie Ryder *(Ed)*, Robert Kent *(Paul Unger)*, John W. Reynolds *(Henry Johnson)*, Frank Scannell *(Bartender)*

p, William Perlberg, George Seaton; d, George Seaton; w, George Seaton (based on the play by Clifford Odets); ph, John F. Warren; ed, Ellsworth Hoagland; m, Victor Young; art d, Hal Pereira, Roland Anderson; fx, John P. Fulton; chor, Robert Alton; cos, Edith Head

AAN Best Picture; AAN Best Actor: Bing Crosby; *AA Best Actress:* Grace Kelly; *AAN Best Director:* George Seaton; *AA Best Screenplay:* George Seaton; *AAN Best B/W Cinematography:* John F. Warren; *AAN Best Art Direction-Set Decoration (B/W):* Hal Pereira, Roland Anderson, Sam Comer, Grace Gregory

Early examination of co-dependency in alcoholic marriages. Adequate in a vague sort of way, which is our way of breaking the news that it's been overrated for a long time. Crosby is a supposedly down-at-the-heels entertainer, trying to keep his comeback up and his compulsive drinking down. Although the dapper Crosby doesn't seem desperate enough, his sober, genial side works to capture the doormat side of the active alcoholic. And given the dark side of Crosby that has been documented by now, we're willing to say he's worth a look; there had to be a lot of fury and tears to sustain a career built on being easy-going.

Kelly, despite the sensible shoes and lack of make-up, is still just too lovely and too reserved to play the gritty wife whose neurotic dependence on her souse husband is as strong as his is on her. She lacks the ability to suggest the complicated levels of a very complicated relationship, and she's totally lacking in passion besides. Odets's character is much more poignant cast against beauty, making her looks almost a dream in the alcoholic's mind. We can imagine maybe a Dorothy Malone, an Eleanor Parker or a Vera Miles pulling it off; we'd be more inclined to say Shelley Winters, Barbara Bel Geddes, or Kim Stanley. But not Princess Grace.

COUNTRY GIRL has a nice backstage feel and Holden gives a strong perfomance as does Anthony Ross, but the film is directed unevenly by Seaton, as if he thought the material was strong enough to do the work by itself.

COUP DE TORCHON   DVD

1981 128m c Crime   ★★★½
La Tour/Little Bear/A2   (France)

Philippe Noiret *(Lucien Cordier)*, Isabelle Huppert *(Rose)*, Jean-Pierre Marielle *(Le Peron/His Brother)*, Stephane Audran *(Huguette Cordier)*, Eddy Mitchell *(Nono)*, Guy Marchand *(Chavasson)*, Irene Skobline *(Anne)*, Michel Beaune *(Vanderbrouck)*, Jean Champion *(Priest)*, Victor Garrivier *(Mercaillou)*

p, Adolphe Viezzi, Henri Lassa; d, Bertrand Tavernier; w, Bertrand Tavernier, Jean Aurenche (based on the novel *Pop. 1280* by Jim Thompson); ph, Pierre-William Glenn; ed, Armand Psenny; m, Philippe Sarde; prod d, Alexander Trauner; cos, Jacqueline Laurent

AAN Best Foreign Language Film

Stylish, twisted black comedy moves setting from the American South of Jim Thompson's pulp novel to a French colonial town in 1938 Africa. There, Noiret is the police chief, a likable, bleary-eyed slob treated like dirt by most everyone he meets. Policing the town with anything but an iron fist, he prefers to turn a blind eye to vice and corruption. Then, having one day decided he's taken enough abuse, Lucien starts killing anyone who crosses him.

COUP DE TORCHON combines black humor at its blackest, with as dead-on an evocation of a torpid, seedy backwater as anyone has achieved on screen. Noiret is an excellent choice in the role, providing a perfect balance between the dangerous and the charming, the moral and the amoral, the killer and the victim. The presence of Isabelle Huppert, as his scruffy but alluring mistress, is an added bonus. Although his films vary radically from one to the next, director Bertrand Tavernier consistently and adroitly builds on the classical French tradition scorned by New Wave filmmakers. He just might have a point.

COUSIN, COUSINE

1975 95m c Comedy   ★★★
Pomereu/Gaumont   (France)   R

Marie-Christine Barrault *(Marthe)*, Victor Lanoux *(Ludovic)*, Marie-France Pisier *(Karine)*, Guy Marchand *(Pascal)*, Ginette Garcin *(Biju)*, Sybil Maas *(Diane)*, Jean Herbert *(Sacy)*, Pierre Plessis *(Gobert)*, Catherine Verlor *(Nelsa)*, Hubert Gignoux *(Thomas)*

p, Bertrand Javal; d, Jean-Charles Tacchella; w, Jean-Charles Tacchella, Daniele Thompson; ph, Georges Lendi (Eastmancolor); ed, Agnes Guillemot; m, Gerard Anfosso; cos, Jeannine Vergne

AAN Best Actress: Marie-Christine Barrault; *AAN Best Original Screenplay:* Jean-Charles Tacchella (Story), Daniele Thompson (Adaptation); *AAN Best Foreign Language Film*

Pleasant diversion, but not brave enough to push into full-fledged farce. A surprising popular success in the U.S., the film is what is often mistakenly described as "quintessentially French," perhaps because it has so much that one associates with Gallicism (frank sexuality and matter-of-fact adultery, pretty countrysides and city cafes) and that many Americans fondly consider charming.

Two families gather to celebrate their aging parents' marriage. During the festivities, Barrault and Lanoux, cousins by marriage, become friendly and agree to see each other more often. As both are sensible, intelligent, married people, they keep emotions in check, determined to keep their relationship platonic. Soon their spouses are assuming the worst, and inevitably the worst happens.

Much of the film's success comes from the excellent rapport between Barrault and Lanoux in a thoroughly convincing portrayal of the hesitant lovers. Tacchella, however, undermines his film by directing the scenes of bourgeois scandal as acceptably as possible, thereby creating the sort of "art film" guaranteed to offend no one.

COUSINS, THE
(LES COUSINS)
1959 112m bw Drama   ★★★★
Ajym (France)

Gerard Blain *(Charles)*, Jean-Claude Brialy *(Paul)*, Juliette Mayniel *(Florence)*, Claude Cerval *(Clovis)*, Genevieve Cluny *(Genevieve)*, Michele Meritz *(Yvonne)*, Corrado Guarducci *(Italian Count)*, Guy Decomble *(Librarian)*

p, Claude Chabrol; d, Claude Chabrol; w, Claude Chabrol, Paul Gegauff; ph, Henri Decae; m, Paul Misraki

Harrowing peer rivalry in the name of love. Claude Chabrol's second feature deals with the contrast between two cousins studying law in Paris. Blain is the country bumpkin at odds with the decadent, city-bred Brialy. They compete for the same girl, and in the end Blain destroys Brialy. A major film of the French New Wave that provides a grim, clear-eyed look at the cynicism of youth, this is not to be missed.

COVER GIRL
                                  DVD
1944 105m c Musical/Comedy   ★★★★
Columbia (U.S.)

Rita Hayworth *(Rusty Parker/Maribelle Hicks)*, Gene Kelly *(Danny McGuire)*, Lee Bowman *(Noel Wheaton)*, Phil Silvers *(Genius)*, Jinx Falkenburg *(Jinx)*, Leslie Brooks *(Maurine Martin)*, Eve Arden *(Cornelia Jackson)*, Otto Kruger *(John Coudair)*, Jess Barker *(Coudair as a Young Man)*, Anita Colby *(Anita)*

p, Arthur Schwartz; d, Charles Vidor; w, Virginia Van Upp, Marion Parsonnet, Paul Gangelin (based on a story by Erwin Gelsey); ph, Rudolph Mate, Allen Davey (Technicolor); ed, Viola Lawrence; m, Carmen Dragon; art d, Lionel Banks, Cary Odell; chor, Val Raset, Seymour Felix, Gene Kelly, Stanley Donen; cos, Travis Banton, Gwen Wakeling, Muriel King, Kenneth Hopkins

AAN Best Color Cinematography: Rudolph Mate, Allen M. Davey; *AA Best Score (Musical):* Carmen Dragon, Morris Stoloff; *AAN Best Song:* "Long Ago and Far Away"; Jerome Kern (Music), Ira Gershwin (Lyrics); *AAN Best Interior Decoration (Color):* Lionel Banks, Cary Odell, Fay Babcock; *AAN Best Sound Recording:* John Livadary

Triumph of style over substance, Hayworth over all. Charming musical built on a skimpy plot but boasting a score by Jerome Kern and Ira Gershwin that includes some of their best work, notably "Long Ago and Far Away," which even Kelly's reedy pipes couldn't ruin. Kelly saves the best dance for himself, the

"Alter Ego" number which is really two dances filmed separately and synchronized together. The other stand-out number is "Make Way for Tomorrow," a roughhouse morning-after number danced by Kelly, Hayworth, and Silvers. COVER GIRL's plot has Hayworth moving from a Brooklyn chorus to become top magazine model, predictable conflict of ambition vs. love. The editorial offices, based on a combination of Conde Nast and Harry Conover (whose beautiful models are seen in the film), lend a '40s-elan and sheen to the film, and the addition of the wise-cracking, always welcome, Eve Arden.

This would be the peak of sweetheart roles for Hayworth, before her shift into dangerous siren territory, and her sumptuous Technicolor candybox beauty was the apotheosis of her era's ideal. She never sang in her musicals—here she is dubbed by Martha Mears—but she danced in an expressive way more akin to acting than athletics. Her passive personality made her a partner equally at home with Astaire or Kelly. She was more of an actress than Cyd Charisse, more elegant in her sensuality, less a traditional tap and ballroom dancer than Ginger Rogers. The sense of longing and abandonment Hayworth brings to her character in COVER GIRL helps her to transcend the formulaic plot; when she dances, it's the only time she looks happy. The film also remains notable for ably incorporating its musical numbers into the storyline.

CRADLE WILL ROCK
                                   DVD
1999 132m c Drama   ★★★★
Havoc/Cradle Productions/Touchstone (U.S.)   R

Hank Azaria *(Marc Blitzstein)*, Ruben Blades *(Diego Rivera)*, Cary Elwes *(John Houseman)*, Philip Baker Hall *(Gray Mathers)*, Angus MacFadyen *(Orson Welles)*, Bill Murray *(Tommy Crickshaw)*, Vanessa Redgrave *(Countess La Grange)*, Susan Sarandon *(Margherita Sarfatti)*, Emily Watson *(Olive Stanton)*, John Turturro *(Aldo Silvano)*

p, Jon Kilik, Lydia Dean Pilcher, Tim Robbins; d, Tim Robbins; w, Tim Robbins; ph, Jean-Yves Escoffier; ed, Geraldine Peroni; m, David Robbins; prod d, Richard Hoover; art d, Troy Sizemore, Peter Rogness; fx, J.C. Brotherhood; chor, Rob Marshall; cos, Ruth Myers

Stunningly cinematic and audacious on every level, writer-director Tim Robbins's look at the collision of the Depression-era art world and politics may well be a masterpiece; at the very least it confirms that Robbins is now, officially, a major American auteur.

The basic story (and it helps to know a little history) involves the government-funded Federal Theater group, home to Orson Welles (Angus McFadyen) and the gay composer Marc Blitzstein (Hank Azaria), whose pro-labor musical is shut down on the eve of its opening, courtesy of red-baiting congressmen. Around that, there's a dizzying succession of subplots involving (among other things) the stormy relationship between Nelson Rockefeller (John Cusack) and radical artist Diego Rivera (Ruben Blades); a passel of American businessmen funding Mussolini's war machine; and paranoid, right-wing ventriloquist Tommy Crickshaw (Bill Murray, in the role of his life) whose dummy walks out on him.

Obviously, we're not talking documentary-style realism here, and Robbins stages it all in a virtuosic style that splits the difference between artsy and immediate, up to and including the performance of the titular musical that's the film's thrilling finale. Hell, it's downright Welles-ian. Robbins also gets sensational character performances from the likes of Susan Sarandon, Vanessa Redgrave, Emily Watson, and John Turturro, and throws in a sneakily erotic scene at Rivera's loft that suggests a familiarity with Henry Miller. Robbins released the film at the height of the furor over the "Sensation" exhibit at the Brooklyn Museum of Art, and he nails the point, brilliantly: the film's final tracking shot down contemporary Broadway is the most genuinely earned bit of dramatic irony in recent movie memory.

CRAIG'S WIFE

1936 73m bw Drama ★★★★
Columbia (U.S.)

Rosalind Russell *(Harriet Craig)*, John Boles *(Walter Craig)*, Billie Burke *(Mrs. Frazier)*, Jane Darwell *(Mrs. Harold)*, Dorothy Wilson *(Ethel Landreth)*, Alma Kruger *(Miss Austen)*, Thomas Mitchell *(Fergus Passmore)*, Raymond Walburn *(Billy Birkmire)*, Robert Allen *(Gene Fredericks)*, Nydia Westman *(Mazie)*

p, Edward Chodorov; d, Dorothy Arzner; w, Mary C. McCall Jr. (based on a play by George Kelly); ph, Lucien Ballard; ed, Viola Lawrence

Russell's first step to the bigtime. Obsessive bitch cares more about her spotless museum home than the love of her husband. Roz was only 28 when she undertook the role but her imperious manner, deep voice and matronly looks added a weightiness to the interpretation. George Kelly's Pulitzer Prize-winning play had been made as a silent in 1928 with Warner Baxter as Craig and Irene Rich as the shrew. Harry Cohn wisely handed over the adaptation chores to Mary McCall who added an Oedipal touch (Kelly objected) to the husband-wife relationship. Dorothy Arzner was given direction chores; therefore the project has a feminist feel that is rare in old Hollywood. Russell's big chance is enhanced by Boles, Burke, Darwell, and Westman, and the production team breathes life into what threatened to remain a stagebound work. In 1950, Joan Crawford would take the role she had been playing most of her life, in HARRIET CRAIG.

CRANES ARE FLYING, THE *DVD*
(LETYAT ZHURAVLI)
1957 97m bw Romance/War ★★★★
Mosfilm (U.S.S.R.)

Tatyana Samoilova *(Veronica)*, Alexei Batalov *(Boris)*, Vasiliy Merkuryev *(Fyodor Ivanovich)*, Alexander Shvorin *(Mark)*, Svetlana Kharitonova *(Irina)*, Konstantine Niktin *(Volodya)*, Valentin Zubkov *(Stepan)*, Anno Bogdanova *(Grandmother)*, B. Kokobkin *(Tyernov)*, E. Kupriyanova *(Anna Mikhailovna)*

p, Mikhail Kalatozov; d, Mikhail Kalatozov; w, Viktor Rozov (based on his play); ph, Sergei Urusevsky; ed, M. Timofeyeva; m, Moisei Vaynberg

Generally free of the party line one usually associates with Soviet films of its period, THE CRANES ARE FLYING is an antiwar love story, set during WWII, which centers on the romance between pretty young Samoilova and sensitive factory worker Batalov. Boris, like hordes of other patriotic Soviet men, marches off to war, leaving behind the woman he loves. She is eventually told of his death, but refuses to accept the horrible news. Finally, however, she resigns herself to a loveless marriage with Boris's draft-dodger brother, Merkuryev, despite the fact that he raped her during an air raid and although she still loves Boris.

The film gained international attention and was one of the first postwar Soviet features to be seen in the West. A beautiful performance is given by the gorgeous Samoilova, the great-niece of Stanislavsky and daughter of an actor father, Yevgeni Samoilov. The Cannes Film Festival awarded Samoilova the Golden Palm for her electrifying performance, and named the film as Best Picture.

CRASH *DVD*
1996 98m c Erotic/Drama ★★★
Alliance Entertainment/Telefilm Canada/ NC-17
The Movie Network (Canada)

James Spader *(James Ballard)*, Holly Hunter *(Dr. Helen Remington)*, Rosanna Arquette *(Gabrielle)*, Elias Koteas *(Vaughan)*, Deborah Unger *(Catherine Ballard)*, Peter MacNeil *(Colin Seagrave)*

p, David Cronenberg; d, David Cronenberg; w, David Cronenberg (based on the novel by J.G. Ballard); ph, Peter Suschitzky; ed, Ron Sanders; m, Howard Shore; prod d, Carol Spier; art d, Tamara Deverell; cos, Denise Cronenberg

The term "autoerotica" takes on new meaning as dreamily disaffected couple James and Catherine (James Spader and Deborah Unger), who fuel their own sex life with extramarital escapades, get sucked into a carnal demolition derby. Like almost all Cronenberg's films, CRASH is cold, cold, cold: proof positive that movies about sex aren't always sexy movies, at least by conventional standards.

While driving home from work, James lets his attention wander and smashes headlong into the Remingtons' car, killing the driver and wounding his wife. James and Helen Remington (Holly Hunter) wind up in the same hospital, and are both sought out by the mysterious Vaughan (Elias Koteas). He introduces them to the perverse world of car-collision commandos, including the scarred, crippled Gabrielle (Rosanna Arquette), who wears her elaborate medical brace like the latest in fetish gear. Their idea of fun: re-staging the vehicular demises of stars like Jayne Mansfield and James Dean, an obsessive hobby that can only end badly.

Working from J.G. Ballard's cult novel, itself a dispassionate exegesis of warped desire, Cronenberg assumes an intensely detached tone (think the Normal and their extremely apropos song, "Warm Leatherette"). Nonetheless, the movie is seductive. Its eerie, icy eroticism is embodied in Unger's sneaky sidelong glances—she's always looking at some elusive something off to the side, just out of frame. The weak link is Koteas, the seductive guru of chrome, flesh, and glass. His Vaughan is creepy and insinuating without ever being enticing: Why would anyone want to play "Death of James Dean" with this guy? *This* guy?

CREEPSHOW *DVD*
1982 129m c Horror ★★
Alpha (U.S.) R

Hal Holbrook *(Henry)*, Adrienne Barbeau *(Wilma)*, Fritz Weaver *(Dexter)*, Leslie Nielsen *(Richard)*, Carrie Nye *(Sylvia)*, E.G. Marshall *(Upson)*, Viveca Lindfors *(Aunt Bedelia)*, Ed Harris *(Hank)*, Ted Danson *(Harry)*, Stephen King *(Jordy)*

p, Richard P. Rubinstein; d, George Romero; w, Stephen King; ph, Michael Gornick (Technicolor); ed, Michael Spolan, Pasquale Buba, George Romero, Paul Hirsch; m, John Harrison; prod d, Cletus Anderson; fx, Tom Savini; cos, Barbara Anderson

This collaboration between director George Romero and horror novelist Stephen King is a loving tribute to the E.C. comic books of the 1950s. Unfortunately, it never quite gels. The film starts off on a stormy night with an angry father's discovery that his son has been reading an E.C. comic book, He throws the book into the street, where the wind opens it to the first of five vignettes, a tale about a long-buried corpse that returns on his birthday to wreak havoc.

Each vignette features a cast full of recognizable actors who play the material in an appropriately broad manner. Stylistically, Romero attempts to duplicate the look of an E.C. comic book and relies heavily on exaggerated lighting schemes and angles; however, the trick simply doesn't work, and the film looks ham-handed and juvenile. Moreover, King's stories are nothing special, and with the exception of the final entry, nothing in the film is particulary scary.

Romero is capable of much better, but ironically, CREEPSHOW was his biggest box-office hit The sequel, CREEPSHOW 2, in which Romero adapted more King stories with the directorial chores handed over to CREEPSHOW cinematographer Michael Gornick, is even worse.

CRIA!
(CRIA CUERVOS)
1976   110m   c   Drama   ★★★★
Querejeta   (Spain)

Geraldine Chaplin *(Ana as an Adult/Her Mother Maria)*, Ana Torrent *(Ana as a Child)*, Conchita Perez *(Irene)*, Maite Sanchez *(Juana)*, Monica Randall *(Paulina)*, Florinda Chico *(Rosa)*, Hector Alterio *(Anselmo)*, German Cobos *(Nicolas Garontes)*, Mirta Miller *(Amelia Garontes)*, Josefina Diaz *(Abuela)*

p, Carlos Saura; d, Carlos Saura; w, Carlos Saura; ph, Teo Escamilla; ed, Pablo del Amo; m, Federico Mompoll

A quietly haunting family album, CRIA! follows an upper-class Spanish family, specifically a young child, during the years following the Spanish Civil War. As the film opens, nine-year-old Ana (Ana Torrent) comes downstairs in her nightgown, awakened by the sounds of her father (Hector Alterio) making love. Behind his closed door, he gasps for breath and dies. Hurriedly leaving his room is Amelia (Mirta Miller), the wife of his best friend. This is the second death for Ana, her mother, Maria (Geraldine Chaplin), having died a few years earlier. Maria, however, has not left Ana's imagination and continues in this manner to return to her daughter's side, enabling the young girl to resist the attempts of her friendly but stern aunt Paulina (Monica Randall) to raise her and her sisters.

A mesmerizing tale, CRIA! brilliantly weaves the tapestry of time—past and present—into a perfect blend of history. Rather than separate the past from the present, director Carlos Saura layers the two on top of one another. Characters who have died rejoin the living; others, like Ana, exist in any number of generations. Ana is seen not only as a young girl (the brilliant Torrent) and as an adult (Chaplin), but also in the form of Maria (again Chaplin)—all of whom share the same time and space in the film. A remarkable achievement, which both examines the textures of a once-patriarchal family life and draws a parallel to the end of the Franco regime.

CRIES AND WHISPERS   DVD
(VISKNINGAR OCH ROP)
1972   95m   c   Drama   ★★★★½
Cinematograph/Swedish Film Institute   (Sweden)   R

Ingrid Thulin *(Karin)*, Liv Ullmann *(Maria/Her Mother)*, Harriet Andersson *(Agnes)*, Kari Sylwan *(Anna)*, Erland Josephson *(Doctor)*, Georg Arlin *(Fredrik, Karin's Husband)*, Henning Moritzen *(Joakin, Maria's Husband)*, Anders Ek *(Pastor)*, Linn Ullmann *(Maria's Daughter)*, Rosanna Mariano *(Agnes as a Child)*

p, Ingmar Bergman; d, Ingmar Bergman; w, Ingmar Bergman; ph, Sven Nykvist (Eastmancolor); ed, Siv Lundgren; m, Frederic Chopin, Johann Sebastian Bach; art d, Marik Vos; cos, Greta Johansson

AAN Best Picture; AAN Best Director: Ingmar Bergman; AAN Best Original Story and Screenplay: Ingmar Bergman; AA Best Cinematography: Sven Nykvist; AAN Best Costume Design: Marik Vos

Relentlessly discursive and somber, also hauntingly elliptical and exquisitely crafted. CRIES examines three sisters, one of whom is dying, and the robust family retainer who cares for them. Bergman uses the four women as metaphors for humanity, representing how we respond to anxiety, death, and the visitations of what appears to be a wrathful rather than benevolent God.

Thulin (the standout in an ensemble of breathtaking performances) is on the brink of suicide and, we learn, once mutilated her own genitalia rather than honor her marital vows. The earthy Ullmann (never more beautiful) once had an affair over which her husband attempted suicide. Sylwan is the glue that holds these Chekhovian sisters together. She can accept God's will and imparts her fatalistic viewpoint to the dying Andersson (Agnes). The former lost a child early in life and has come to terms with death—neither hard nor bad, just a new voyage. Andersson, in terrible pain, cannot fully accept this view; still, she is much closer to the housekeeper than she is to her sisters.

There are many moments in the film during which nothing is said, and the silence is more eloquent than any words might have been. Nonetheless, sound plays a huge role in the movie, as Bergman uses ticking clocks, rustling dresses, sighs, cries and whispers to make his points. Bergman and cinematographer Sven Nykvist move the camera with remarkable fluidity, the beauty of their visuals contrasting pointedly with the almost unbearably stark subject matter.

CRIME OF FATHER AMARO, THE   DVD
(EL CRIMEN DE PADRE AMARO)
2002   120m   c   Drama/Religious   ★★★½
Alameda Films/Wanda Vision/Blu Films   R
(Mexico/Spain/Argentina/France)

Gael Garcia Bernal *(Father Amaro)*, Sancho Gracia *(Father Benito)*, Ana Claudia Talancon *(Amelia)*, Damian Alcazar *(Father Natalio)*, Angelica Aragon *(Augustina Sanjuanera)*, Luisa Huertes *(Dionisia)*, Ernesto Gomez Cruz *(Bishop)*, Gaston Melo *(Martin)*, Andres Montiel *(Ruben de la Rosa)*, Juan Ionacio Aranda *(Chato Aquilar)*

p, Alfredo Ripstein, Daniel Birman Ripstein; d, Carlos Carrera; w, Vincente Lenero (based on the novel by Eca de Queiroz); ph, Guillermo Granillo; ed, Oscar Figueroa; m, Rosino Serrano; art d, Carmen Giminez Cacho; cos, Mariestela Fernandez

AAN Best Foreign Language Film

A melodrama with a message, in which corrupt priests manipulate lives in the name of faith.

Ambitious, newly ordained Father Amaro (Gael Garcia Bernal), protégé of a powerful bishop (Ernesto Gomez Cruz), is sent to isolated, small-town Los Reyes, Mexico, to investigate the activities of certain local priests. Amaro recognizes that the Church's primary concern should be spiritual, but can't ignore the fact that Church policies inform almost every aspect of secular life. The Bishop is concerned about rebellious Father Natalio (Damian Alcazar), who is rumored to have forged an alliance with local guerillas to protect his impoverished flock from ruthless narcotics barons. Amaro is more disturbed by Father Benito (Sancho Gracia), who's enmeshed in a long-standing affair with middle-aged restaurateur Augustina Sanjuanera (Angelica Aragon) and launders money for drug lord Chato Aguilar (Juan Ionacio Aranda) through a church-sponsored hospital project. An article by crusading local reporter Ruben de la Rosa (Andres Montiel) brings both the Father Benito and Father Natalio scandals to the forefront, and Amaro faces his first crisis of conscience: The Bishop orders him to deny de la Rosa's accusations and pressure the newspaper into featuring the rebuttal prominently. Amaro complies, and from this moral lapse it's but a short step to embarking on a passionate affair with Amelia (Ana Claudia Talancon), Sanjuanera's virginal 16-year-old daughter.

Though based on a 19th-century novel, the movie has the pulpy momentum of a modern-day *telenovela*, and its contempt is focused not on faith but on the secular wheeling and dealing of Church higher-ups. Roundly condemned (though not banned) by Church officials in Mexico, the film became a smash hit—probably in part because the public wrangling gave it an enormous publicity boost.

CRIME OF MONSIEUR LANGE, THE

(LE CRIME DE M. LANGE)
1936 90m bw Comedy/Drama ★★★★
Oberon (France)

Rene Lefevre *(Mons. Amedee Lange)*, Odette Florelle *(Valentine)*, Henri Guisol *(Meunier)*, Marcel Levesque *(Bessard, the Concierge)*, Odette Talazac *(Mme. Bessard)*, Maurice Baquet *(Charles Bessard, their Son)*, Nadia Sibirskaia *(Estelle)*, Jules Berry *(Batala)*, Sylvia Bataille *(Edith)*, Marcel Duhamel

p, Andre Halley des Fontaines; d, Jean Renoir; w, Jean Castanier, Jean Renoir, Jacques Prevert (based on a story by Jean Castanier and Jean Renoir); ph, Jean Bachelet; ed, Marguerite Renoir; m, Jean Wiener; art d, Marcel Blondeau

A clever Renoir film, with a decidedly anti-capitalist message. Lefevre is a meek author of French novels about the American West whose avaricious boss, Berry, cheats him out of his earnings. Berry embezzles the company funds, flees, and is later reported dead in a train wreck. The employees of the publishing house are overjoyed and form a cooperative that achieves great success with Lefevre's "Arizona Jim" series. He falls in love with a woman from a neighboring laundry, but then Berry returns (he survived the wreck and took the clothes of a priest) and demands a share in the company's newfound prosperity. Should Lefevre kill the villain? One of Jean Renoir's best films, THE CRIME OF MONSIEUR LANGE is also one of the most obvious examples of his Front Populaire period of filmmaking—reflecting the social politics of its day and the belief that a collective could effectively overthrow a tyranny. This wonderfully entertaining and sharply scripted film is hampered by its poor sound quality, a result of Renoir's meager production budget.

CRIME WITHOUT PASSION

1934 70m bw Crime ★★★★
Paramount (U.S.)

Claude Rains *(Lee Gentry)*, Margo *(Carmen Brown)*, Whitney Bourne *(Katy Costello)*, Stanley Ridges *(Eddie White)*, Paula Trueman *(Buster Malloy)*, Leslie Adams *(O'Brien)*, Greta Granstedt *(Della)*, Esther Dale *(Miss Keeley)*, Charles Kennedy *(Lt. Norton)*, Fuller Mellish *(Judge)*

p, Ben Hecht, Charles MacArthur; d, Ben Hecht, Charles MacArthur; w, Ben Hecht, Charles MacArthur; ph, Lee Garmes; fx, Slavko Vorkapich

Loosely based on the career of New York City criminal lawyer William J. Fallon, the great "mouthpiece" of the 1920s, this strange drama was the product of Ben Hecht and Charles MacArthur, with Claude Rains as the suave, ever-confident legal wizard. The film opens with Rains successfully defending a killer by snatching up and drinking "Exhibit A," a vial containing poison, and then having his stomach pumped during a recess. Rains attempts to dump Margo, a jealous honky-tonk singer, for hot blonde Whitney Bourne, but Margo inveigles him into shooting her. Thinking her dead, he prepares an elaborate alibi which involves the killing of another man. Margo survives to haunt him in court, and the real killing is finally laid at his door in a surprise ending.

Hecht and MacArthur directed this minor masterpiece and used imaginative techniques in almost every frame. They even appear before the cameras as newsmen interviewing

Rains after a legal victory. Fanny Brice and Helen Hayes, MacArthur's wife, appear briefly in a hotel lobby scene. Hayes looks almost directly into the camera which provides a Rains-eye-view as he hurries about establishing an alibi. The opening and closing credits for this film show three female "Furies" darting through the canyons of New York, randomly selecting their victims—those whom they will make mad and upon whom they will visit their evils—a marvelous bit of special effects constructed by Slavko Vorkapich.

CRIMES AND MISDEMEANORS 📀

1989 107m c Drama ★★★½
Orion (U.S.) PG-13

Caroline Aaron *(Barbara)*, Alan Alda *(Lester)*, Woody Allen *(Cliff Stern)*, Claire Bloom *(Miriam Rosenthal)*, Mia Farrow *(Halley Reed)*, Joanna Gleason *(Wendy Stern)*, Anjelica Huston *(Dolores Paley)*, Martin Landau *(Judah Rosenthal)*, Jenny Nichols *(Jenny)*, Jerry Orbach *(Jack Rosenthal)*

p, Robert Greenhut; d, Woody Allen; w, Woody Allen; ph, Sven Nykvist (DuArt Color); ed, Susan E. Morse; prod d, Santo Loquasto; art d, Speed Hopkins; cos, Jeffrey Kurland

AAN Best Supporting Actor: Martin Landau; *AAN Best Director:* Woody Allen; *AAN Best Original Screenplay:* Woody Allen

Woody Allen tackles morality and murder in CRIMES AND MISDEMEANORS, starring Martin Landau as Judah Rosenthal, an ophthalmologist esteemed by family, friends and colleagues. Judah has a less admirable secret life: his mistress, Dolores (Anjelica Huston), is determined to reveal their affair to his wife (Claire Bloom), and threatens to expose his past embezzling. Judah decides he has no choice but to have her killed, helped by his underworld-connected brother (Jerry Orbach). Allen also introduces a humorous story line involving a politically committed documentary filmmaker, Cliff Stern (Allen), his egotistical commercial TV director brother-in-law (Alan Alda), and a TV producer (Mia Farrow) with whom Cliff falls in love. Only in the film's dark final scene do Judah and Cliff finally meet, both struggling with their ideas of right and wrong, morality and immorality, crimes and misdemeanors.

Allen is an auteur who often defines his artistic vision in reference to those of other filmmakers, and it becomes increasingly difficult for educated viewers to take his creative borrowings on good faith. In one scene here he restages a sequence from Ingmar Bergman's WILD STRAWBERRIES nearly shot-for-shot, a dubious act of homage. Nevertheless Allen's expertise is evident everywhere in CRIMES AND MISDEMEANORS, with its fine ensemble acting (Alda and Huston are outstanding), evocative composition and design, intelligent writing, and spritely musical score.

CRIMSON TIDE 📀

1995 116m c War/Thriller/Action ★★★½
Simpson-Bruckheimer Productions/Hollywood R
Pictures (U.S.)

Denzel Washington *(Lt. Commander Jim Hunter)*, Gene Hackman *(Captain Ramsey)*, George Dzundza *(Cob)*, Viggo Mortensen *(Lt. Peter Ince)*, Matt Craven *(Lt. Roy Zimmer)*, James Gandolfini *(Lt. Bobby Dougherty)*, Rocky Carroll *(Lt. Darik Westergaurd)*, Jaime Gomez *(Ood Mahoney)*, Lillo Brancato, billed as Lillo Brancato Jr. *(Russell Vossler)*, Michael Milhoan *(Hunsicker)*

p, Don Simpson, Jerry Bruckheimer; d, Tony Scott; w, Michael Schiffer (from a story by Michael Schiffer and Richard P. Henrick); ph, Dariusz Wolski; ed, Chris Lebenzon; m, Hans Zimmer; prod d, Michael White; art d, James J. Murakami, Dianne Wagner; fx, Alfred A. DiSarro Jr., Hoyt Yeatman, Dream Quest Images; cos, George Little

AAN Best Film Editing: Chris Lebenzon; *AAN Best Sound:* Kevin O'Connell, Rick Kline, Gregory H. Watkins, William B. Kaplan; *AAN Best Sound Effects Editing:* George Watters II

The testosterone really swims when Denzel Washington and Gene Hackman go toe-to-toe in this bombastic submarine thriller from the producers and director of TOP GUN.

Ultra-nationalist rebels in the former Soviet Union have seized a Russian nuclear missile base and are threatening to attack the U.S. Aboard the USS *Alabama*, executive officer Ron Hunter (Denzel Washington) is at odds with his captain, Frank Ramsey (Gene Hackman). Hunter, a graduate of Annapolis and Harvard, is the Navy's rising star; grizzled, cigar-chomping Ramsey is a Cold War veteran seasoned by combat. When the *Alabama* receives orders to launch its nuclear missiles, and the radio fails in the midst of a follow-up emergency message, Hunter must decide whether to relieve his captain of command or risk nuclear disaster.

There's little substance to CRIMSON TIDE, but it sails through its action at a breakneck pace. Director Tony Scott effectively uses the claustrophobic confines of the sub to keep the tension high, while Hackman and Washington face off like the old pros they are. Screenwriter Michael Schiffer has loaded the movie with enough high-tech jargon for verisimilitude, but the script's idiosyncrasies—cockeyed dialogue, pop culture references, and philosophical debates—are presumably the result of uncredited rewrites by Quentin Tarantino and Robert Towne.

CRISS CROSS   `DVD`
1949 87m   bw   Thriller   ★★★½
Universal   (U.S.)

Burt Lancaster *(Steve Thompson)*, Yvonne De Carlo *(Anna)*, Dan Duryea *(Slim)*, Stephen McNally *(Ramirez)*, Richard Long *(Slade Thompson)*, Esy Morales *(Orchestra Leader)*, Tom Pedi *(Vincent)*, Percy Helton *(Frank)*, Alan Napier *(Finchley)*, Griff Barnett *(Pop)*

p, Michel Kraike; d, Robert Siodmak; w, Daniel Fuchs (based on the novel by Don Tracy); ph, Franz Planer; ed, Ted J. Kent; m, Miklos Rozsa; art d, Bernard Herzbrun, Boris Leven; fx, David S. Horsley; cos, Yvonne Wood

A bleak but compelling film noir, CRISS CROSS stars the forceful Burt Lancaster as an honest armored-car guard who takes up again with his ex-wife, De Carlo, now married to sleazy gangster Duryea. When the mobster finds Lancaster with his wife, Lancaster excuses the rendezvous by telling Duryea that they had merely been conducting business, planning to rob the armored car he drives. This lie leads him into a bizarre robbery scheme in which he must work with Duryea and his henchmen while dodging suspicious cop McNally.

De Carlo complicates matters by promising to run off with Lancaster after he completes the robbery, in a double cross of Duryea's gang. During the robbery, Lancaster kills two of his fellow thieves, but is also wounded. It's all downhill from there.

CRISS CROSS is a somber, extremely violent, utterly grim film, with suspense expertly maintained throughout by Robert Siodmak's taut direction—his handling of flashbacks and clever staging of the robbery, stand out. Lancaster is powerful as the love-torn guard, and Yvonne De Carlo smokes up the screen with her earthy portrayal of a money-hungry vamp (a role almost twin to Ava Gardner's slippery siren opposite Lancaster in THE KILLERS). Watch for a very young Tony Curtis as a handsome lounge lizard.

"CROCODILE" DUNDEE   `DVD`
1986 102m c   Comedy   ★★★
Rimfire   (Australia)   PG-13

Paul Hogan *(Michael J. "Crocodile" Dundee)*, Linda Kozlowski *(Sue Charlton)*, John Meillon *(Wally Reilly)*, Mark Blum *(Richard Mason)*, Michael Lombard *(Sam Charlton)*, David Gulpilil *(Neville Bell)*, Irving Metzman *(Doorman)*, Graham Walker *(Bellhop)*, Maggie Blinco *(Ida)*, Steve Rackman *(Donk)*

p, John Cornell; d, Peter Faiman; w, Paul Hogan, Ken Shadie, John Cornell (based on a story by Paul Hogan); ph, Russell Boyd (Kodakcolor); ed, David Stiven; m, Peter Best; prod d, Graham Walker

AAN Best Original Screenplay: Paul Hogan (Story), Ken Shadie (Screenplay), John Cornell (Screenplay)

Paul Hogan became an Australian phenomenon whose fame spread worldwide with this amiable, good-natured and often very funny movie. Crocodile hunter shows pretty reporter around Bush Country and then she shows him around equally alien New York City. The film's fish-out-of-water story line is a film comedy standard; what makes the picture work so well is Hogan's cheerful, weatherbeaten appeal.

CROOKLYN   `DVD`
1994 112m   c   Drama   ★★★
40 Acres and a Mule Filmworks/Child Hoods   PG-13
Productions   (U.S.)

Alfre Woodard *(Carolyn Carmichael)*, Delroy Lindo *(Woody Carmichael)*, David Patrick Kelly *(Tony Eyes)*, Zelda Harris *(Troy Carmichael)*, Carlton Williams *(Clinton Carmichael)*, Sharif Rashid *(Wendell Carmichael)*, Tse-Mach Washington *(Joseph Carmichael)*, Christopher Knowings *(Nate Carmichael)*, Jose Zuniga *(Tommy La La)*, Isaiah Washington *(Vic)*

p, Spike Lee; d, Spike Lee; w, Spike Lee, Joie Susannah Lee, Cinque Lee (from a story by Joie Susannah Lee); ph, Arthur Jafa; ed, Barry Alexander Brown; m, Terence Blanchard, Donny Hathaway; prod d, Wynn Thomas; art d, Chris Shriver; fx, Steve Kirshoff; cos, Ruth Carter

Spike Lee returns to the Brooklyn neighborhood milieu of DO THE RIGHT THING, setting a semi-autobiographical family drama against the sights and sounds of an early 1970s summer. While Lee fails to impose sufficient structure on his material, expertly drawn performances help vividly to evoke the family and street life of an era untroubled by crack or drive-by shootings.

On a well-kept block in Brooklyn, the Carmichaels, a lower middle-class African-American family, occupy a brownstone amidst a multiracial mix of colorful and eccentric neighbors. As summer beckons, the kids—Clinton (Carlton Williams), Wendell (Sharif Rashid), Nate (Christopher Knowings), Joseph (Tse-Mach Washington), and the only girl, nine-year-old Troy (Zelda Harris)—take to the streets to play games and engage in mischief, while at home they eat, fight, and watch lots of TV. Their parents, musician Woody (Delroy Lindo) and school teacher Carolyn (Alfre Woodard), intervene in the children's squabbles—as well as battling frequently over their own financial troubles—and give them the love and guidance they need to navigate the difficult path to adulthood.

In his seventh feature film Lee for the first time draws primarily on his own family background, though the result is still characterized by his trademark freneticism. Powerhouse performances—notably from Lindo, Woodard, and Harris—help compensate for the lack of dramatic focus. Concentrating on Troy, CROOKLYN explores the coming-of-age process with a candor rarely seen on screen; the script, co-written by Lee with two of his siblings, brother Cinque and sister Joie Susannah, captures all the complexity of this turbulent period in a girl's life.

CROSS OF IRON   DVD
1977 133m c   War   ★★★
Avco Embassy   (U.K./West Germany)   R

James Coburn *(Steiner)*, Maximilian Schell *(Stransky)*, James
Mason *(Brandt)*, David Warner *(Kiesel)*, Klaus Lowitsch *(Kruger)*,
Vadim Glowna *(Kern)*, Roger Fritz *(Triebig)*, Dieter Schidor
(Anselm), Burkhardt Driest *(Maag)*, Fred Stillkraut *(Schnurrbart)*

p, Wolfgang Hartwig; d, Sam Peckinpah; w, Walter Kelley, James
Hamilton, Julius J. Epstein (based on the book *Cross of Iron* by
Willi Heinrich); ph, John Coquillon (Technicolor); ed, Michael
Ellis, Tony Lawson, Herbert Taschner; m, Ernest Gold; fx,
Richard Richtsfeld

Bleak, unpleasant, and ugly look at men in combat that was
almost universally panned by the mainstream press upon its
initial release. Its complex and vivid portrayal of the absurdity of war, however, prompted none other than Orson Welles
to write Peckinpah and proclaim it the finest antiwar film he
had ever seen. Based on a celebrated novel by German author
Willi Heinrich, the film is set at the Russian front circa 1943,
as the Germans are retreating before the Soviet army. We follow corporal Coburn (in what may be his best performance),
a German soldier—not a Nazi—who "hates this uniform and
everything it stands for." Loyal only to his men, a tight-knit
group of soldiers fighting for their survival, Coburn finds his
nemesis in his new commander, captain Schell—an arrogant,
narcissistic Prussian aristocrat who desperately wants to
come home with an Iron Cross, Germany's highest honor for
bravery, but who is terrified of battle. Since Coburn comes
highly recommended by other commanders and has already
been awarded the Iron Cross himself, Schell promotes him to
sergeant in the hope of winning an ally. After a siege on their
compound in which many brave men die while Schell cowers in his bunker, Coburn learns that the captain has filed a
false report claiming that he led the counterattack—a deed
certain to earn an Iron Cross. When Coburn refuses to confirm Schell's claims (he also resists calling him a liar, which
would indicate reverence for a medal he considers worthless),
Schell plots to dispose of the troublesome sergeant and his
men.

  CROSS OF IRON, which was plagued with production
problems (producer Hartwig ran out of money before the final
sequence was filmed) and was cut extensively by its American
distributor before its U.S. release, is yet another mutilated
Peckinpah film but one that holds up exceedingly well
nonetheless (the uncut version was restored for home video).
From its opening—a brilliant montage of WWII stock footage
intercutting Hitler and his armies with shots of Hitler Youth
raising a flag on a mountain while a chorus of German children sing—to its bizarre, almost surreal climax, CROSS OF
IRON is anything but a standard WWII movie, especially
compared to its mythicizing contemporaries. Shot superbly by
cinematographer Coquillon, the film shows war as hideously
brutal, inglorious, and insane. With its focus on the corruption
of moral values and the betrayal of the innocence of children,
CROSS OF IRON is an angry film that ends with a bitter
quote from Bertolt Brecht: "Do not rejoice in his defeat you
men. For though the world has stood up and stopped the bastard, the bitch that bore him is in heat again."

CROSSFIRE   DVD
1947 86m bw   Crime   ★★★★
RKO   (U.S.)

Robert Young *(Finlay)*, Robert Mitchum *(Keeley)*, Robert Ryan
(Montgomery), Gloria Grahame *(Ginny)*, Paul Kelly *(The Man)*,
Sam Levene *(Joseph Samuels)*, Jacqueline White *(Mary
Mitchell)*, Steve Brodie *(Floyd)*, George Cooper *(Mitchell)*, William
Phipps *(Leroy)*

p, Adrian Scott; d, Edward Dmytryk; w, John Paxton (based on
the novel *The Brick Foxhole* by Richard Brooks); ph, J. Roy Hunt;
ed, Harry Gerstad; m, Roy Webb; art d, Albert S. D'Agostino,
Alfred Herman; fx, Russell A. Cully

AAN Best Picture; AAN Best Supporting Actor: Robert Ryan; *AAN
Best Supporting Actress:* Gloria Grahame; *AAN Best Director:*
Edward Dmytryk; *AAN Best Screenplay:* John Paxton

A classic. Anti-Semitism had been unexplored in Hollywood
for decades; no studio wanted to take on this social evil until
Fox decided to film GENTLEMAN'S AGREEMENT, but
RKO beat Fox to the punch by releasing CROSSFIRE first,
and the impact was tremendous. It is a simple and chilling
story centering on sadistic bully Ryan, who is about to be mustered out of the Army with three buddies, Brodie, Cooper, and
Phipps. In a nightclub, the three meet Levene and his girl
friend Grahame, then go with the couple to Levene's apartment, where they drink themselves into near collapse. In a
drunken rage Ryan, who seethes with hatred for Jews, beats
Levene to death. His friends vaguely recall the incident but
vanish so they can't be questioned by authorities. Young, a
pipe-smoking, introspective detective aided by G.I. Mitchum,
begins to investigate and lays a trap for the elusive sadist.

  All of the performers contribute fine work, particularly
Ryan, who is terrifying as the brutish, bigoted killer—a role
the actor was determined to play. Ryan had served in the
Marine Corps with Richard Brooks, upon whose novel
CROSSFIRE is based, and Ryan had told the author that if his
book were made into a film, he wanted to play the part of
Montgomery. Ironically, Ryan's performance is so convincing
that he would long be associated with the vile character he
plays here, and he would be repeatedly cast in vicious, mean-
spirited roles throughout a distinguished career that included
his extraordinary portrayal of a boxer in THE SET-UP.

  In the novel the central issue is not race or religion but
sex—a homosexual is beaten to death by other Marines.
However, in 1947 this subject matter was still taboo, and producer Scott convinced RKO to buy the book on the proviso
that anti-Semitism would replace homophobic intolerance.
Dore Schary had just taken over the reins at RKO, and this
thriller—which grossed $1,270,000 at the box office, a
whopping amount in 1947—was his first production. It was
also the last film director Dmytryk and producer Scott, long
a duo, would co-create for the studio: after CROSSFIRE's
completion, both men were brought before HUAC and
became enmeshed in the Communist witchhunt.

CROSSOVER DREAMS   DVD
1985 86m c   Musical   ★★★
Max Mambru/Crossover   (U.S.)

Ruben Blades *(Rudy Veloz)*, Shawn Elliott *(Orlando)*, Elizabeth
Pena *(Liz Garcia)*, Virgilio Marti *(Chico Rabala)*, Tom Signorelli
(Lou Rose), Frank Robles *(Ray Soto)*, Joel Diamond *(Neil Silver)*,
Amanda Barber *(Radio DJ)*, John Hammil *(Joe, Liz's Husband)*,
Natalie Gentry *(Lawyer)*

p, Manuel Arce; d, Leon Ichaso; w, Manuel Arce, Leon Ichaso; ph,
Claudio Chea; ed, Gary Karr; m, Mauricio Smith; prod d, Octavio
Soler; art d, Richard Karnbach

Panamanian salsa singer Ruben Blades made an impressive
acting debut in this clever reworking of the old story of a man
who rises to fame, forgets about his old friends, and then hits
the skids. Blades and his band struggle to earn a living on New
York's less-than-lucrative Latino music circuit, but Blades has
"crossover dreams," yearning to make it big in the mainstream. His musical mentor, Virgilio Marti, discourages
Blades from abandoning his roots, but after Marti's death
Blades comes to the attention of slick producer Joel Diamond,
who pays him $15,000 to record a pop single. The song

becomes a minor hit, and Blades says adios to his old friends and takes to life in the fast lane in a financed fancy car. As his head swells, Blades even drives away his devoted girlfriend, Elizabeth Pena; then the bottom falls out when the album follow-up to his single bombs.

CROSSOVER DREAMS is a simple but effective tale of a talented individual sucked into the void of a sleazy industry. Though director Leon Ichaso deserves much of the credit for the film's success, the real find here is Blades, whose evocative singing comes as no surprise to salsa fans, but whose excellent dramatic performance led to a number of other screen roles, including his excellent work in THE MILAGRO BEANFIELD WAR.

CROUCHING TIGER, HIDDEN DRAGON *DVD*
(WU HU ZANG LONG)
2000 119m c Martial Arts/Romance/Historical ★★★★
Good Machine/Edko Films/Zoom Hunt/China   PG-13
Film Co-Production/Asia Union Film &
Entertainment/Columbia Film Production
Asia   (China/Taiwan/Hong Kong/U.S.)

Chow Yun-Fat (*Li Mu Bai*), Michelle Yeoh (*Yu Shu Lien*), Zhang Ziyi (*Jen Yu*), Chang Chen (*Lo*), Lung Sihung (*Sir Te*), Cheng Pei Pei (*Jade Fox*), Li Fa Zeng (*Governor Yu*), Gao Xian (*Bo*), Hai Yan (*Madam Yu*), Wang Deming (*Tsai*)

p, Bill Kong, Hsu Li Kong, Ang Lee; d, Ang Lee; w, James Schamus, Wang Hui Ling, Tsai Kuo Jung (based on the novel by Wang Du Lu); ph, Peter Pau; ed, Tim Squyres; m, Tan Dun; prod d, Tim Yip; art d, Eddy Wong, Yang Zhan Jia, Yang Xin Zhan; fx, Jonathan F. Styrlund; cos, Tim Yip

AA Best Art Direction: Tim Yip (Art Direction); *AA Best Cinematography:* Peter Pau; *AA Best Foreign Language Film* ; *AA Best Original Score:* Tan Dun; *AAN Best Picture; AAN Best Director:* Ang Lee; *AAN Best Costume Design:* Tim Yip; *AAN Best Film Editing:* Tim Squyres; *AAN Best Adapted Screenplay:* Wang Hui Ling, James Schamus, Tsai Kuo Jung; *AAN Best Original Song:* "A Love Before Time"; Jorge Calandrelli, Tan Dun, James Schamus

Think of it as Taiwanese director Ang Lee's RAIDERS OF THE LOST ARK, a loving homage to the pulp movies of his youth. Lee grew up on fanciful tales of martial arts chivalry filled with balletic, gravity-defying action sequences, philosophical fighters, and warrior women. But he isn't interested in wringing ironic laughs from genre conventions. His film humanizes the formula by emphasizing two love stories, one filled with youthful fire and the other defined by mature melancholy.

In ancient China, Li Mu Bai (Chow Yun-Fat) decides to abandon his fighting ways and asks fellow warrior and unacknowledged love Yu Shu Lien (Michelle Yeoh) to present his cherished sword to respected elder Sir Te (Lung Sihung). She makes the journey, but the sword is promptly stolen from Sir Te's home. The masked thief's identity is quickly revealed: it's Jen (Zhang Ziyi), the beautiful teenage daughter of the district's new governor. Jen, who will soon make a politically advantageous marriage but secretly loves another, has been surreptitiously trained in the martial arts by her governess, who proves to be none other than the elusive Jade Fox (Cheng Pei Pei), a mysterious bandit who murdered Mu Bai's master years earlier.

While scrupulously concerned with character relationships, Lee doesn't stint on the dreamlike fight sequences, choreographed by Yuen Wo-Ping (THE MATRIX) and mercifully free of the exaggerated sound effects familiar from exploitation kung fu pictures. The combatants' fists and feet fly while they scuttle up walls, skim the surface of water like insects, and drift into the air like dandelion fluff. The film satisfies on both visceral and emotional levels and showcases vet-

erans Yeoh and Chow, as well as relative newcomers Zhang and Chang Chen, who plays Jen's bandit lover.

CROUPIER *DVD*
1999 91m c Crime/Drama   ★★½
Little Bird/Film Four/Tatfilm/La Septe Arte
(Germany/U.K./France/Ireland)

Clive Owen (*Jack Manfred*), Gina McKee (*Marion Neil*), Alex Kingston (*Jani de Villiers*), Alexander Morton (*David Reynolds*), Kate Hardie (*Bella*), Paul Reynolds (*Matt*), Nick Reding (*Giles Cremorne*), Nicholas Ball (*Jack's Father*), Ozzie Yue (*Mr. Tchai*), Tom Mannion (*Ross*)

p, Jonathan Cavendish; d, Mike Hodges; w, Paul Mayersberg; ph, Mike Garfath; ed, Les Healey; m, Simon Fisher Turner; prod d, Jon Bunker; art d, Ian Reade Hill; cos, Caroline Harris

A punchy, if frustrating, entry into the erratic but always interesting oeuvre of Mike Hodges (GET CARTER, FLASH GORDON).

Struggling writer Jack Manfred (Clive Owen) has gambling in his blood—he was even born in a casino back home in South Africa. But he's no risk-taking punter. Jack's a croupier, a voyeuristic and impassive spinner of the wheel and dealer of cards who figures he can't lose because he's not really in the game. Jack's gambling father (Nicholas Ball) sets him up with a job at London's Golden Lion Casino; the late hours and excessive drinking strain his relationship with girlfriend Marion (Gina McKee), but he's surrounded by the elements for a new novel, including a sticky-fingered fellow croupier (Paul Reynolds) and a mysterious South African woman (Alex Kingston) with a black eye and a dangerous proposition.

Paul Mayersberg's script tortures the obvious "life is a gamble" metaphor, and milks the figure of the croupier—"the still center of the spinning wheel of misfortune"—for all its existential worth. But he has a sharp ear for crackling dialogue, and Hodges knows exactly how to get the blood pumping. The intricately staged scenes inside the overlit Golden Lion teem with a desperate, claustrophobic atmosphere (the production design is all smoky mirrors and cheap glitz), but the film fires off too many intriguing plot possibilities that remain nothing more than that. The payoff does come as a surprise, but once the dust clears, there are an awful lot of discarded bits of plot left lying around. In a film that's equally about mood and intrigue, Hodges gets about half of it exactly right.

CROW, THE *DVD*
1994 100m c Horror/Thriller   ★★★½
Crowvision Inc./Edward R. Pressman Film   R
Corporation/Jeff Most Productions/Miramax   (U.S.)

Brandon Lee (*Eric Draven*), Michael Wincott (*Top Dollar*), Rochelle Davis (*Sarah*), Ernie Hudson (*Albrecht*), David Patrick Kelly (*T-Bird*), Michael Berryman (*Skull Cowboy*), Angel David (*Skank*), Bai Ling (*Myca*), Lawrence Mason (*Tin Tin*), Michael Massee (*Funboy*)

p, Edward R. Pressman, Jeff Most; d, Alex Proyas; w, David J. Schow, John Shirley (based on the comic book and comic strip series by James O'Barr); ph, Dariusz Wolski; ed, Dov Hoenig, Scott Smith; m, Graeme Revell; prod d, Alex McDowell; art d, Simon Murton; fx, Andrew Mason, J.B. Jones, James Robert; cos, Arianne Phillips

THE CROW is a gorgeous black valentine that captures the essence of adolescent misery, coupled with a wildly romantic vision of the power of pure love to overcome all obstacles—even the grave. Based on the bleak comic books of James O'Barr, the film scores high on the morbid curiosity scale because star Brandon Lee (son of Bruce Lee) was accidentally killed during production.

The streets are rain-slicked and littered with filth, smokey fires burn in the distance and daylight never seems to shine in the industrial slum where tough little street waif Sarah (Rochelle Davis) lives, and where aspiring rock star Eric Draven (Lee) and his angelic fiancee Shelley (Sofia Shinas) are brutally slaughtered by hoods in the employ of crime boss/slumlord Top Dollar (Michael Wincott). A year after he and Shelley have been laid to rest, Draven claws his way out of the grave. He's met by a crow perched on his headstone, his guide between the worlds of the living and the dead, and sets about tracking down and killing those responsible for the murders.

THE CROW aims higher than the average revenge tale, but the pallid Lee—all ferocious black hair and scary clown make-up—is almost the whole show. Michael Wincott steals some of the thunder as the Luciferesque Top Dollar; director Alex Proyas and production designer Alex McDowell stay impressively true to the look and feel of the original comic book (which, believe it or not, quotes liberally from Rimbaud).

CRUCIBLE, THE

DVD

1996 123m c Drama ★★★½
20th Century Fox (U.S.) PG-13

Daniel Day-Lewis *(John Proctor)*, Winona Ryder *(Abigail Williams)*, Paul Scofield *(Judge Danforth)*, Joan Allen *(Elizabeth Proctor)*, Bruce Davison *(Reverend Parris)*, Rob Campbell *(Reverend Hale)*, Jeffrey Jones *(Thomas Putnam)*, Peter Vaughan *(Giles Corey)*, Karron Graves *(Mary Warren)*, Charlayne Woodard *(Tituba)*

p, Robert A. Miller, David V. Picker; d, Nicholas Hytner; w, Arthur Miller (based on his play); ph, Andrew Dunn; ed, Tariq Anwar; m, George Funton; prod d, Lilly Kilvert; art d, John Warnke; fx, Brian Ricci; cos, Bob Crowley

AAN Best Supporting Actress: Joan Allen; *AAN Best Adapted Screenplay:* Arthur Miller

After more than 40 years, a classic of the American stage comes to the screen with powerful performances and an adaptation penned by playwright Arthur Miller himself.

Salem, Massachusetts, 1692. Respected citizen John Proctor (Daniel Day-Lewis) has committed adultery with his young servant, Abigail Williams (Winona Ryder). After her dismissal by Proctor's prim wife, Elizabeth (Joan Allen), the scorned maid and a dozen other girls convene in the woods for a shamanistic ritual, during which Abigail calls for Elizabeth's demise and the return of Proctor's affections. The "coven" is spied by the passing Reverend Parris (Bruce Davison), and rumors begin to circulate based on witchery. Led by Abigail, the girls take the only avenue available: they confess to being influenced by Satan and begin charging other townspeople with being in his league. The recriminations quickly spread to include Elizabeth, and ultimately lead to Proctor's own doom.

The Salem Witch Trials, a moment during which mad authority came cloaked in piety, are a famous metaphor for the McCarthy witch-hunts of the 1940s and '50s. But Miller's play is also a timeless tale of the necessity of taking a principled stand against the ill winds of popular fascism. The notion of someone choosing death over "life with a bad name" may be a head-scratcher in our morally ambiguous culture, but director Nicholas Hytner (THE MADNESS OF KING GEORGE) infuses Miller's spellbinding argument with a passionate kineticism. Day-Lewis, the embodiment of rough-hewn nobility, and Ryder, a dervish of fierce emotionality, head a superb cast, with Allen in particular turning in a remarkably precise, high-strung performance.

CRUEL INTENTIONS

DVD

1999 97m c Comedy ★★★
Cruel Productions/Original Film/Newmarket R
Capital Group/Neal M. Moritz Production (U.S.)

Sarah Michelle Gellar *(Kathryn Merteuil)*, Ryan Phillippe *(Sebastian Valmont)*, Reese Witherspoon *(Annette Hargrove)*, Selma Blair *(Cecile Caldwell)*, Louise Fletcher *(Helen Rosemond)*, Joshua Jackson *(Blaine Tuttle)*, Eric Mabius *(Greg McConnell)*, Sean Patrick Thomas *(Ronald Clifford)*, Swoosie Kurtz *(Dr. Greenbaum)*, Christine Baranski *(Bunny Caldwell)*

p, Neal H. Moritz; d, Roger Kumble; w, Roger Kumble (based on the novel Les Liaisons Dangereuses by Choderlos De Laclos); ph, Theo Van de Sande; ed, Jeff Freeman; m, Edward Shearmur; prod d, Jon Gary Steele; art d, David S. Lazan; fx, Matthew Pope; cos, Denise Wingate

Two overprivileged and uncommonly perverse stepsiblings are up to no good in this deliciously trashy reworking of Choderlos de Laclos' 1782 novel *Les Liaisons Dangereuses.*

Sebastian Valmont (Ryan Phillippe) and his stepsister Kathryn Merteuil (Sarah Michelle Gellar) are two pretty and preternaturally debauched rich kids sitting out the summer in their parents' sprawling New York City mansion before returning to Manchester, their exclusive prep school. Sebastian, who's seduced and abandoned just about every teenage girl in the Manhattan Social Register, is on the lookout for a *real* conquest. Kathryn, an evil little number who stashes her coke in a crucifix, is looking for revenge: she was dumped for Cecile Caldwell (Selma Blair), a dim-witted deb whose mother (Christine Baranski), anxious that her daughter should succeed at Manchester, has conveniently placed her under Kathyrn's tutelage. Kathryn dares Sebastian to corrupt Cecile, but he's more intrigued by the far greater challenge of bedding Annette Hargrove (Reese Witherspoon), the new headmaster's virginal daughter. So Kathryn proposes a challenge: if Sebastian will help turn out Cecile *and* deflower Annette, Kathryn will be his for a night. If he fails, Kathryn gets Sebastian's vintage Jaguar.

Deceptions, blackmail, and all manner of sexual intrigue follow—the stuff that makes high school so much like an 18th-century epistolary novel. It's tremendous fun, thanks largely to a smarter-than-average script and some fierce casting. Phillippe has a little trouble playing mad, bad, and dangerous to know, but the film really belongs to the girls: Witherspoon sports some serious acting chops, newcomer Blair is a hoot, and Gellar, in her slinky silks and black-widow shades, seems positively born to the role. Not many actors can actually deliver a line like "I hate it when things don't go my way. It makes me so horny!" and make it play.

CRUEL SEA, THE

DVD

1953 120m bw War ★★★★
Ealing (U.K.)

Jack Hawkins *(Capt. Ericson)*, Donald Sinden *(Lockhart)*, John Stratton *(Ferraby)*, Denholm Elliott *(Morrell)*, Stanley Baker *(Bennett)*, John Warner *(Baker)*, Bruce Seton *(Tallow)*, Liam Redmond *(Watts)*, Virginia McKenna *(Julie Hallam)*, Moira Lister *(Elaine Morell)*

p, Leslie Norman (for Michael Balcon); d, Charles Frend; w, Eric Ambler (based on the novel by Nicholas Monsarrat); ph, Gordon Dines; ed, Peter Tanner; m, Alan Rawsthorne

AAN Best Screenplay: Eric Ambler

THE CRUEL SEA is the tough, often gruesome account of British corvette life on the Atlantic during WWII as seen through the tormented consciousness of Lt. Comdr. Ericson (Jack Hawkins). After losing one ship to a U-boat while protecting a convoy, Ericson's ship, *Compass Rose*, is itself torpedoed; Ericson and a handful of his men barely survive, adrift on a raft. Given a new command on the frigate *Saltash Castle*, Ericson is again at the mercy of the "cruel sea" and must face an impossible choice in risking the lives of his men. The film is shot in documentary style, with harsh black-and-white images, and is based on the wartime exploits depicted in author Nicholas Monsarrat's novel, which was adapted by suspense writer Eric Ambler. The supporting cast appear marginally as crew members in the Royal Navy and in brief flashback and furlough sequences. A top-notch film from Britain's Ealing Studios, with Hawkins turning in an intense, fascinating performance.

CRUMB
1995 120m c Documentary/Biography ★★★★
Superior Pictures (U.S.) R

Robert Crumb (*Himself*), Aline Kominsky (*Herself—Robert's Wife*), Charles Crumb (*Himself—Robert's Older Brother*), Max Crumb (*Himself—Robert's Younger Brother*), Robert Hughes (*Himself—Time Magazine Art Critic*), Martin Muller (*Himself—Owner of Modernism Gallery*), Don Donahue (*Himself—Former Zap Comix Publisher*), Dana Crumb (*Herself—Robert's First Wife*), Trina Robbins (*Herself—Cartoonist*), Spain Rodriguez (*Himself—Cartoonist*)

p, Lynn O'Donnell; d, Terry Zwigoff; ph, Maryse Alberti; ed, Victor Livingston; m, David Boeddinghaus

A remarkably revealing documentary about Robert Crumb, the auteur of underground comics. Director Terry Zwigoff, an old friend and colleague, links the hilariously rendered and rather peculiar obsessions of Crumb's graphic work to the artist's fantastically dysfunctional family.

A pioneer of the countercultural comic scene that flowered in San Francisco during the 1960s, Crumb is still best known for the ribald adventures of Fritz the Cat and the iconic hipster Mr. Natural. His sometimes puerile, often pornographic, and arguably misogynistic imagery remains controversial, and Zwigoff marshals a roster of cultural gatekeepers to interpret (with varying success) the meanings of Crumb's work and the nature of its appeal. More memorable is the frank portrait of Crumb's family, particularly his brother Charles, a reclusive emotional wreck who was potentially a finer cartoonist than Robert. While some may find the film's implicit psychobiographical "explanation" of Crumb's work too pat, CRUMB succeeds admirably as a documentary portrait of a wilfully perverse American original.

CRY-BABY
1990 85m c Comedy/Musical ★★★½
Imagine Entertainment (U.S.) PG-13

Johnny Depp (*Cry-Baby*), Amy Locane (*Allison*), Susan Tyrrell (*Ramona*), Polly Bergen (*Mrs. Vernon-Williams*), Iggy Pop (*Belvedere*), Ricki Lake (*Pepper*), Traci Lords (*Wanda*), Kim McGuire (*Hatchet-Face*), Darren Burrows, billed as Darren E. Burrows (*Milton*), Stephen Mailer (*Baldwin*)

p, Rachel Talalay; d, John Waters; w, John Waters; ph, David Insley; ed, Janice Hampton; m, Patrick Williams; prod d, Vincent Peranio; art d, Dolores Deluxe; fx, Steve Kirshoff; chor, Lori Eastside; cos, Van Smith

Revel without a cause. Trashy cult director Waters, now in the mainstream, returns to his Baltimore home turf in this rock 'n' roll take on star-crossed lovers, caught in the cultural tug-of-war between hipsters and squares. The film is high on energy, color and camera movement and, as usual in Waters's world, everything is styled within an inch of its life, capturing all the fun and fever of the 1950s. But underneath

the numerous entertaining cameos, not much is going on, and it shows. The film's terrific first half-hour can't sustain itself. Depp is nice to look at, but too diminutive to bring much force to his sexy biker. Locane is well, okay, but she's eclipsed at every turn by the marvelously vulgar Lords, who embraces the genre with the energy and anarchy of the much-missed Divine.

CRY IN THE DARK, A
1988 121m c Docudrama ★★★★
Cannon/Cinema Verity (U.S.) PG-13

Meryl Streep (*Lindy Chamberlain*), Sam Neill (*Michael Chamberlain*), Bruce Myles (*Barker*), Charles Tingwell (*Justice Muirhead*), Nick Tate (*Charlwood*), Neil Fitzpatrick (*Phillips*), Maurie Fields (*Barritt*), Lewis Fitz-Gerald (*Tipple*)

p, Verity Lambert; d, Fred Schepisi; w, Robert Caswell, Fred Schepisi (based on the book *Evil Angels* by John Bryson); ph, Ian Baker (Panavision); ed, Jill Bilcock; m, Bruce Smeaton; prod d, Wendy Dickson, George Liddle; cos, Bruce Finlayson

AAN Best Actress: Meryl Streep

A CRY IN THE DARK tells the true story of Australians Michael and Lindy Chamberlain (Sam Neill and Meryl Streep), the Seventh-Day Adventist minister and his wife whose infant disappeared from their tent during a family outing in 1980. In the film the parents contend their baby was dragged off by a dingo, but authorities don't buy that story. Lindy is indicted for the murder of her daughter, and Michael is charged as an accessory to the crime, beginning a tortuous legal process in which Lindy eventually becomes the center of a storm of controversy that dominates Australian news. Although sometimes slow-moving, A CRY IN THE DARK is a poignant family-in-crisis drama aided by spectacular performances from Streep and Neill. It's based on a nonfiction thriller, *Evil Angels*, written in Lindy's support by a Melbourne barrister who was critical of the prosecution's handling of the case.

CRYING GAME, THE
1992 112m c Drama/Romance/Thriller ★★★★
Palace Pictures (U.K.) R

Stephen Rea (*Fergus*), Jaye Davidson (*Dil*), Miranda Richardson (*Jude*), Forest Whitaker (*Jody*), Jim Broadbent (*Col*), Ralph Brown (*Dave*), Adrian Dunbar (*Maguire*), Breffni McKenna (*Tinker*), Joe Savino (*Eddie*), Birdie Sweeney (*Tommy*)

p, Stephen Woolley; d, Neil Jordan; w, Neil Jordan; ph, Ian Wilson; ed, Kant Pan; m, Anne Dudley; prod d, Jim Clay; art d, Chris Seagers; cos, Sandy Powell

AAN Best Picture; AAN Best Actor: Stephen Rea; AAN Best Supporting Actor: Jaye Davidson; AAN Best Director: Neil Jordan; AA Best Original Screenplay: Neil Jordan; AAN Best Film Editing: Kant Pan

A perverse moral tale preaching the oldest of lessons—that love conquers all—THE CRYING GAME was helped by clever marketing to seduce an unexpectedly wide audience.

Fergus (Stephen Rea), an IRA foot soldier, is part of a small group led by ferocious idealogues Jude (Miranda Richardson) and Maguire (Adrian Dunbar). They kidnap a British soldier, Jody (Forest Whitaker), in Northern Ireland and attempt to exchange him for a group of imprisoned IRA members. As the tense and exhausted comrades take turns guarding Jody, a tentative friendship forms between Fergus and the frightened captive. Aware of his colleagues' growing contempt for what they perceive to be a weakness on his part, Fergus pointedly accepts the task of killing their captive when it becomes apparent that British officials will not comply with their demands. As Fergus marches Jody into the woods at gunpoint, the prisoner gets away, only to run into a road and be run over by a British armored car. Fergus escapes, leaving Maguire and Jude trapped in a hail of gunfire.

Fergus flees Ireland and melts into London's underground of undocumented Irish workers. Haunted by the memory of Jody, he looks up the dead man's lover, Dil (Jaye Davidson). Alternately seductive and petulant, desperately needy and infuriatingly aloof, Dil soon has Fergus bewitched. But Fergus is tormented by his past and, as their relationship grows ever more intimate, tortured by the fact that he has an entire other life of which she is unaware. Still, it's Fergus who's in for the biggest shock, when he learns Dil has an even more surprising secret. Things are further complicated by the unexpected re-appearance of Jude and Maguire, who insist Fergus help them with one last assassination.

THE CRYING GAME's audacity is remarkable, and extends far beyond its "controversial" subject matter. In fact, its utter belief in the power of love to overcome all obstacles may be its boldest conceit. While a conventional Hollywood romance pretends to place roadblocks in the paths of its lovers, THE CRYING GAME presents Dil and Fergus with a *real* dilemma and refuses to opt for the easy ending.

Thematic issues aside, THE CRYING GAME pulls off a tremendously difficult technical feat; its screenplay contains not one, but two, wrenching twists, each of which could easily derail the narrative in the hands of a lesser storyteller. Viewers are introduced to the story of Fergus's growing friendship with the captive and doomed Jody, then have the rug pulled out from under them when Jody dies barely a third of the way into the film. Fergus's relationship with Dil seems to be proceeding along conventional lines until the moment of revelation, at which point the average film would consider it had done its job and bring things to a swift close. But THE CRYING GAME keeps on going, patiently playing its story out to its appointed, ironic end.

CUBA

1979 122m c Adventure/Political/War ★★★½
UA (U.S.) R

Brooke Adams (*Alexandra Pulido*), Sean Connery (*Maj. Robert Dapes*), Jack Weston (*Gutman*), Hector Elizondo (*Ramirez*), Denholm Elliott (*Skinner*), Martin Balsam (*Gen. Bello*), Chris Sarandon (*Juan Pulido*), Alejandro Rey (*Faustino*), Lonette McKee (*Therese*), Danny De La Paz (*Julio*)

p, Arlene Sellers, Alex Winitsky; d, Richard Lester; w, Charles Wood; ph, David Watkin (Technicolor); ed, John Victor Smith; m, Patrick Williams; prod d, Gil Parrondo; art d, Dennis Gordon-Orr; cos, Shirley Russell

Intelligent, zany satire of Cuban military dictatorships and revolutions from director Richard Lester and screenwriter Charles Wood, who previously collaborated on a number of projects, including HOW I WON THE WAR and the 1968 CHARGE OF THE LIGHT BRIGADE. Connery is a British mercenary enlisted by the Batista regime to come to Havana and help crush Castro's guerrillas. In addition to encountering various scoundrels—including cynical Batista general Balsam, angry would-be revolutionary De La Paz, and grotesque American businessman Weston—Dapes meets former flame Adams, a Cuban tobacco factory manager with a philandering husband (Chris Sarandon). As the Batista government comes tumbling down, the film focuses on how the selfish, corrupt and hypocritical characters respond to the tumultuous events. Filmed in Spain, CUBA was virtually ignored upon its release, but it's an entertaining and well-crafted political satire that is definitely worth a look.

CUL-DE-SAC

1966 111m bw Thriller ★★★½
Sigma (U.K.)

Donald Pleasence (*George*), Francoise Dorleac (*Teresa*), Lionel Stander (*Richard*), Jack MacGowran (*Albert*), Iain Quarrier (*Christopher*), Geoffrey Sumner (*His Father*), Renee Houston (*His Mother*), William Franklyn (*Cecil*), Trevor Delaney (*Nicholas*), Marie Kean (*Mrs. Fairweather*)

p, Gene Gutowski; d, Roman Polanski; w, Gerard Brach, Roman Polanski; ph, Gilbert Taylor; ed, Alastair McIntyre; m, Krzysztof Komeda

Neat little chiller with Polanski honing his abilities as a director and standout performances from Pleasence, Stander, and Dorleac. Pleasence, a hermit, lives with his succulent wife, Dorleac, in a large, dank, dark castle on a small island off the northeast coast of Britain. Dorleac is a nympho-in-training who's always looking for someone new to take her mind off her nutty husband. Escaped criminals Stander and MacGowran make their way to this remote outpost, and what we get is Polanski's version of THE DESPERATE HOURS. But the director exhibits such style in his writing and direction that one can forgive the excesses. CUL-DE-SAC is exaggerated, sinister, bleak, and spine-tingling. It is also somewhat thick in the middle and could have used a serious editor to whack away at it. Still, it's well worth seeing for the radiance of Dorleac, who died the following year in an automobile crash. In a tiny speaking part, Jacqueline Bisset is seen for the second time in her career.

CURE

(KYUA)
1997 115m c Thriller ★★★★
Code Red (Japan)

Koji Yakusho (*Takabe*), Tsuyoshi Ujiki (*Sakuma*), Anna Nakagawa (*Fumie*), Masato Hagiwara (*Mamiya*)

p, Tetsuya Ikeda, Satoshi Kanno, Atsuyuki Shimoda, Tsutomu Tsuchikawa; d, Kiyoshi Kurosawa; w, Kiyoshi Kurosawa; ph, Takusho Kikumura; ed, Kan Suzuki; m, Gary Shiya; prod d, Tomoyuki Maruo

This eerie and unusually elusive thriller offers little in the way of big scares or intricate plotting. Instead, Japanese horror director Kiyoshi Kurosawa opts for unsettling imagery and moody atmospherics.

A string of grisly murders have left police detective Takabe (Koji Yakusho) baffled. The crimes seem to be unmotivated, the killers make no attempt to flee the scene, and the killings all appear to be entirely unrelated, save for two puzzling facts. In each case, the killer has carved a deep "X" into the victim's neck and chest, and at least three of the killers have come into contact with a mysterious drifter named Mamiya (Masato Hagiwara). Takabe hauls Mamiya into the station for questioning, but gets nowhere; Mamiya appears to be a total amnesiac who can't remember from one moment to the next where he is or who he's talking to. Instead of providing answers, Mamiya begins asking Takabe unsettling questions. Disregarding the advice of his psychiatrist friend Sakuma (Tsuyoshi Ujiki), who argues that sometimes killers just kill for no good reason, Takabe is drawn deeper into the enigma as he tries to put the murders into some rational perspective.

This quietly disturbing thriller unfolds without any of the conventional trappings of the genre. There's no jarring soundtrack, the pacing is relatively slow, onscreen violence is kept to a minimum (although there are a number of gruesome moments), and much of it is filmed in medium to long shots, casting a chilly pall over the gruesome goings-on. And in a bold move, Kurosawa also forgoes the conventional denouement, ending this mesmerizing mystery with an ambiguous climax that raises more questions than the film chooses to answer.

CURLY TOP
DVD
1935 75m bw Musical ★★★★
Fox (U.S.)

Shirley Temple *(Elizabeth Blair)*, John Boles *(Edward Morgan)*, Rochelle Hudson *(Mary Blair)*, Jane Darwell *(Mrs. Denham)*, Rafaela Ottiano *(Mrs. Higgins)*, Esther Dale *(Aunt Genevieve Graham)*, Etienne Girardot *(Mr. Weckoff)*, Maurice Murphy *(Jimmie Rogers)*, Arthur Treacher *(Butler)*

p, Winfield Sheehan; d, Irving Cummings; w, Patterson McNutt, Arthur J. Beckhard (based on a story by Jean Webster); ph, John Seitz; m, Ray Henderson, Ted Koehler, Edward Heyman; chor, Jack Donohue

A strong Temple showcase, as much in its way as a Mae West film. Turn down the sound and you'll see a fullblown persona and CURLY TOP provides a nifty argument for the idea of the actor as auteur. The plot? Moppet plays matchmaker, what else? Shirley and big sis Rochelle Hudson are discovered in an orphanage by millionaire John Boles. He shows them Park Avenue and the life of luxury and, naturally, falls for the post-pubescent sis. Shirley doesn't forget where she came from, though, and returns to the orphanage to sing a few ditties with her moppet friends. CURLY TOP was a masked remake of DADDY LONG LEGS, starring Mary Pickford, and was remade again in 1955 with Fred Astaire and Leslie Caron.

CURSE OF THE JADE SCORPION, THE
DVD
2001 103m c Comedy ★★½
Gravier Productions/Perido Productions/ PG-13
Sweetland Films/DreamWorks SKG (U.S.)

Woody Allen *(C.W. Briggs)*, Helen Hunt *(Betty Ann Fitzgerald)*, Dan Aykroyd *(Chris Magruder)*, Charlize Theron *(Laura Kensington)*, Brian Markinson *(Al)*, Wallace Shawn *(George Bond)*, David Ogden Stiers *(Voltan)*, Elizabeth Berkley *(Jill)*, Peter Linari *(Joe Coopersmith)*, John Tormey *(Sam)*

p, Letty Aronson; d, Woody Allen; w, Woody Allen; ph, Zhao Fei; ed, Alisa Lepselter; prod d, Santo Loquasto; art d, Tom Warren; fx, John Ottesen, Ronald Ottesen; cos, Suzanne McCabe

Woody Allen's affectionate ode to the mile-a-minute Manhattan comedies of the 1930s and '40s is a rare contemporary comedy that goes for wit rather than vulgarity or grossout humor.

Manhattan, 1940: Rumpled C.W. Briggs (Allen), a top investigator for North Coast Casualty and Fidelity, is constantly butting heads with forward-thinking efficiency expert Betty Ann Fitzgerald (Helen Hunt). She, meanwhile, is having an affair with the sweet and well-meaning company head, Magruder (Dan Aykroyd). When the office gang takes a colleague out for his birthday, nightclub mentalist Voltan (the masterful David Ogden Stiers) hypnotizes Briggs and Fitzgerald and tells them they're in love. Before snapping them out of it, Voltan also plants sinister post-hypnotic suggestions that he later uses to force the unwary Briggs, with his knowledge of clients' security systems, to rob mansions for him. Briggs, who has no memory of the thefts, is eventually arrested after an investigation in which he himself takes part.

If this film is "merely" good, it's still funnier than most. Its shortcomings lie in the pace, which doesn't quite snap, and in its wealth of potentially interesting supporting characters who are either undeveloped or simply disappear, as if Allen were too tired to flesh them out. The film's biggest drawback is a tragic Catch-22: It needs Woody Allen to play the Woody

Allen character, but the 65-year-old Allen simply isn't convincing as the guy who gets the girl.

CUTTER'S WAY
DVD
1981 105m c Mystery ★★★½
UA (U.S.) R

Jeff Bridges *(Richard Bone)*, John Heard *(Alex Cutter)*, Lisa Eichhorn *(Mo Cutter)*, Ann Dusenberry *(Valerie Duran)*, Stephen Elliott *(J.J. Cord)*, Arthur Rosenberg *(George Swanson)*, Nina Van Pallandt *(Woman in Hotel)*, Patricia Donahue *(Mrs. Cord)*, Geraldine Baron *(Susie Swanson)*, Katherine Pass *(Toyota Woman)*

p, Paul R. Gurian; d, Ivan Passer; w, Jeffrey Alan Fiskin (based on the novel *Cutter and Bone* by Newton Thornburg); ph, Jordan Cronenweth (Technicolor); ed, Caroline Ferriol; m, Jack Nitzsche; art d, Josan Russo

A fiercely powerful film about heroes, romanticism, and friendship among three initially unlikable characters—Cutter (Heard) a vulgar, crippled Vietnam vet who is an outlaw in a society without commitment or heroes; his best friend Bone (Bridges), a pretty boy with no convictions at all; and the woman who bonds them, Mo (Eichhorn), wife of Cutter but desirous of Bone. After nearly taking the rap for a girl's murder, Bone, while at a parade, thinks he spots the real killer—Elliott, a powerful and arrogant oil tycoon. Cutter lets his imagination run free and comes up with an elaborate conspiracy theory about the night of the murder, devising a plan to blackmail Cord—a plan of which Bone wants no part.

Rapped by the critics on its initial release, it was almost instantly pulled from exhibition. Slowly rave reviews began to surface. After a title change (from the misleading, medically oriented CUTTER AND BONE), it was rereleased, becoming something of a cult movie in the process. An inspiring film, it is constructed like a thriller, but instead of reaching for thrills, it leaves them in the background and concentrates on the complexities of its characters. It may require multiple viewings to appreciate, but it is nonetheless a fascinating picture, and the best of Czech director Ivan Passer's American films. The Jack Nitzsche score is hauntingly effective.

CYCLO
DVD
(XICH LO)
1995 127m c Drama ★★★★
Lazennec Productions/Lumiere/La Sept/Societe Francaise de Production/Soficas Cofimage 5 & 6/ Canal Plus/Centre National de la Cinematographie/ Salon Films/Giai Phong Film Studio (France/Vietnam)

Le Van Loc *(The Cyclo)*, Tony Leung Chiu-wai, billed as Tony Leung *(The Poet)*, Tran Nu Yen-Khe *(The Sister)*, Nguyen Nhu Quynh *(The Madam)*, Nguyen Hoang Phuc *(Tooth)*, Ngo Vu Quang Hai *(Knife)*, Nguyen Tuyet Ngan *(The Happy Woman)*, Doan Viet Ha *(The Sad Woman)*, Bjuhoang Huy *(The Crazy Son)*, Vo Vinh Phuc *(The Cyclo's Friend)*

p, Christophe Rossignon; d, Tran Anh Hung; w, Tran Anh Hung, Nguyen Trung Bing; ph, Benoit Delhomme; ed, Nicole Dedieu, Claude Ronzeau; m, Ton That Tiet; art d, Benoit Barouh; cos, Henriette Raz

Part neorealist urban drama and part surrealist hallucination, director Tran Anh Hung's second feature—his startling follow-up to the hypnotic SCENT OF GREEN PAPAYA—is an altogether electrifying vision of life in contemporary Vietnam. Tran uses De Sica's THE BICYCLE THIEF as a point of departure, but here the theft of the impoverished young protagonist's bicycle (or more accurately his cyclo, a bicycle taxi) sets him on a very different kind of journey, one that takes him deep into a nightmarish netherworld of crime and extreme violence.

Deprived of his livelihood by a rival cyclo gang, the Cyclo (Le Van Loc)—like all the other characters in the film, he's never named—falls under the influence of a brooding gangster (Tony Leung), who, unbeknownst to the Cyclo, is also pimping the boy's sister (Tran Nu Yen-Khe). It's a simple plot, fractured and fragmentary, in which events repeat themselves down through generations and across Ho Chi Minh City with the same inexorable logic as Tran's audacious imagery: the tender flesh of a meaty fruit, sliced open with a razor then splashed with blood; the Cyclo, covered in blue paint (one of several references to Jean-Luc Godard), with a plastic bag over his head and a gun in his hand. Tran's film is a startling achievement: brimming with moments of exquisite tenderness and shocking brutality—sometimes simultaneously—and each invested with an almost perverse beauty. An extraordinary movie.

CYRANO DE BERGERAC 📀

1950 112m bw Drama ★★★½
UA (U.S.)

Jose Ferrer *(Cyrano)*, Mala Powers *(Roxane)*, William Prince *(Christian)*, Morris Carnovsky *(Le Bret)*, Ralph Clanton *(De Guiche)*, Lloyd Corrigan *(Ragueneau)*, Virginia Farmer *(Duenna)*, Edgar Barrier *(Cardinal)*, Elena Verdugo *(Orange Girl)*, Al Cavens *(Valvert)*

p, Stanley Kramer; d, Michael Gordon; w, Carl Foreman (based on the play by Edmond Rostand, translated by Brian Hooker); ph, Franz Planer; ed, Harry Gerstad; m, Dimitri Tiomkin

AA Best Actor: Jose Ferrer

Outstanding performance by Ferrer won him an Oscar and is central feature of film adaptation of Rostand by Brian Hooker. Essentially, the property remains stagebound; it is not well directed, nor does it seem to have had a decent budget. It is hampered by unimaginative backlot settings and lacks the flair color would have helped supply.

For those in need of it, the plot concerns a tragic wit, born with an outrageously long nose, who lends his words to a more handsome man who is wooing the woman that both love. Your opinion of Ferrer's work will depend upon your taste in acting. This is technique work, like Olivier's. The performance feels outward bound, theatrical, expert in that manner. Ferrer never really caught on in films. Undeniably talented, there was something hard-bitten about him, and rumor has it he was not an easy ego to contend with.

CYRANO DE BERGERAC 📀

1990 135m c Romance/Drama ★★★★
Hachette Premiere/Union Generale (France) PG

Gerard Depardieu *(Cyrano de Bergerac)*, Anne Brochet *(Roxane)*, Vincent Perez *(Christian de Neuvillette)*, Jacques Weber *(Count DeGuiche)*, Roland Bertin *(Ragueneau)*, Philippe Morier-Genoud *(Le Bret)*, Pierre Maguelon *(Carbon de Castel-Jaloux)*, Josiane Stoleru *(Roxane's Handmaid)*, Anatole Delalande *(The Child)*, Ludivine Sagnier *(The Little Sister)*

p, Rene Cleitman, Michel Seydoux; d, Jean-Paul Rappeneau; w, Jean-Claude Carriere, Jean-Paul Rappeneau (based on the play by Edmond Rostand); ph, Pierre Lhomme; ed, Noelle Boisson; m, Jean-Claude Petit; art d, Ezio Frigerio; cos, Franca Squarciapino

AAN Best Actor: Gerard Depardieu; *AAN Best Art Direction-Set Decoration:* Ezio Frigerio, Jacques Rouxel; *AA Best Costume Design:* Franca Squarciapino; *AAN Best Makeup:* Michele Burke, Jean-Pierre Eychenne; *AAN Best Foreign Language Film*

A virtuoso update. Gerard Depardieu's Cyrano is nothing short of magnificent. In this version of Edmond Rostand's classic drama of unrequited love, his Cyrano is less physical caricature, more flesh and blood, and a markedly younger, more virile nobleman than the usually avuncular ones of the past. Dealing as it does with universals—that beauty is both in the eye of the beholder and only skin deep—this slightly abbreviated adaptation by director Jean-Paul Rappeneau and Jean-Claude Carriere retains both the panache and poignancy of its source.

As in the play, the film opens in a theater where the lovers first meet and where Cyrano has come to jeer at his enemy, the ham Montfleury (Gabriel Monnet). Cyrano is heard before he is seen, and his voice practically bellows with resonant majesty. When he finally appears, in profile, his nose immediately draws attention. What is interesting here is, unlike other productions where the nose stops just short of Pinocchio's and makes an obvious freak of the character, the producers have gone to pains to see that this Cyrano is not grotesque. It is Depardieu's normal nose in shape, only extended, and by making the character less of a freak, the filmmakers also succeed in making his pain all the more poignant.

The extraordinarily talented Depardieu, who has appeared in more than 70 films, gives his Cyrano a winning combination of grace and gusto, and is a commanding presence, both literally and figuratively. He's unexpectedly fleet of foot during the dueling scenes, recalling Douglas Fairbanks or Burt Lancaster. He brings a welcome vibrancy to the role, which won him the Best Actor award at the Cannes Film Festival. Brochet's Roxane is not shallow, as she is often portrayed, but much a product of her times, impressed with the literary conceits of poseurs of her generation. With its masterful acting, exquisitely muted cinematography, vast complement of extras, extravagant props and scenery, CYRANO DE BERGERAC was, at $20 million, France's most expensive movie production. Though filmed on a grand scale, it does not lose the emotional impact of the play, which had its premiere in Paris in 1898, and has been a mainstay of the legitimate theater ever since.

D

DADDY DAY CARE 📀

2003 93m c Comedy ★½
Davis Entertainment/Revolution Studios (U.S.) PG

Eddie Murphy *(Charlie Hinton)*, Jeff Garlin *(Phil)*, Steve Zahn *(Marvin)*, Regina King *(Kim Hinton)*, Kevin Nealon *(Bruce)*, Jonathan Katz *(Mr. Dan Kubitz)*, Siobhan Fallon, billed as Siobhan Fallon Hogan *(Peggy)*, Lisa Edelstein *(Crispin's Mom)*, Lacey Chabert *(Jenny)*, Anjelica Huston *(Miss Gwyneth Harridan)*

p, Matt Berenson, John Davis, Wyck Godfrey; d, Steve Carr; w, Geoff Rodkey; ph, Steven Poster; ed, Christopher Greenbury; m, David Newman; prod d, Garreth Stover; art d, Chris Cornwell; fx, Larz Anderson; cos, Ruth Carter

Family-oriented, politically correct, and so derivative that there's no comedy left in its sitcom cliches, this wan farce is distinguished only by the fact that it features Eddie Murphy's most relaxed (which is to say least braying) performance in ages.

Best friends Charlie Hinton (Murphy) and Phil (Jeff Garlin), are unceremoniously fired from their high-powered advertising jobs after a disastrous product test. Unable to find new jobs, the guys find themselves at home with the kids while their wives bring home the bacon. Inspiration strikes as they're parked uncomfortably at the playground, surrounded by stay-at-home moms complaining about the sorry state of day care, whose horrors Charlie and his wife, Kim (Regina King), have seen firsthand. Charlie and Phil cook up a plan to open an affordable alternative to the likes of Miss Gwyneth Harridan's Chapman Academy, and soon Daddy Day Care is up and running. In keeping with the movie's painfully formulaic construction, even the tykes are types, each more insufferable than the next. Nasty Miss Harridan (Anjelica Huston) tries to shut the place down, Phil and Charlie become better dads, the kids learn how to get along—especially after Daddy Day Care's staff expands to include "Star Trek"-loving goofball Marvin (Steve Zahn), who has a real way with youngsters—and everybody gets a hug.

The film seems longer than its 93-minute running time, but kids will probably enjoy its potty humor, many scenes of four-year-olds getting the better of harried adults, and the inevitable moment when a cute little girl kicks the fat guy in the nads.

DADDY LONG LEGS

1931   80m   bw   Comedy/Romance   ★★★★
Fox   (U.S.)   *DVD*

Janet Gaynor (*Judy Abbott*), Warner Baxter (*Jervis Pendleton*), Una Merkel (*Sally McBride*), John Arledge (*Jimmy McBride*), Claude Gillingwater (*Riggs*), Kathlyn Williams (*Mrs. Pendleton*), Louise Closser Hale (*Miss Pritchard*), Elizabeth Patterson (*Mrs. Lippett*), Kendall McComas (*Freddie Perkins*), Sheila Bromley, billed as Sheila Mannors (*Gloria Pendleton*)

d, Alfred Santell; w, Sonya Levien, S.N. Behrman (based on the novel and play by Jean Webster); ph, Lucien Andriot; ed, Ralph Dietrich

A perennial, DADDY LONG LEGS has been done to death. Made in 1919 with Mary Pickford, then in 1935 as CURLY TOP with Shirley Temple, then again in 1955 with Leslie Caron, this 1931 version features Janet Gaynor and Warner Baxter as protagonists in a May-December relationship. It's another variant on the CINDERELLA theme, with perky Gaynor living in an orphanage and bridling under the harsh treatment of matron Elizabeth Patterson. Gaynor is sent to college by mystery man Baxter, a soft-touch millionaire who is a trustee of the orphanage. Matters get complicated when her roommate's (Una Merkel) brother (John Arledge) falls in love with Gaynor. But all ends well when she discovers that the man she loves is also the man who has been her benefactor for all those years. There's enough pathos for two hankies, but spirited cast just manages to keep film from falling into bathos. Gaynor was 25 and Baxter was 40—not quite a May-December romance, more like a June-October—but they suffuse their characters with pro instincts. Patterson was the perfect crotchety old biddy. She didn't get into movies until she was in her fifties, but she made a slew of features and endeared herself to generations of television watchers in her recurring role of Mrs. Trumble on "I Love Lucy."

DAMAGE

1992   112m   c   Drama/Erotic   ★★★
Nouvelles Editions de Film/Skreba Damage   R
(France/U.K.)   *DVD*

Jeremy Irons (*Dr. Stephen Fleming*), Juliette Binoche (*Anna Barton*), Miranda Richardson (*Ingrid*), Rupert Graves (*Martyn*), Ian Bannen (*Edward Lloyd*), Leslie Caron (*Elizabeth Prideaux*), Peter Stormare (*Peter Wetzler*), Gemma Clark (*Sally*), Julian Fellowes (*Donald Lyndsaymp*), Tony Doyle (*Prime Minister*)

p, Louis Malle; d, Louis Malle; w, David Hare (from the novel by Josephine Hart); ph, Peter Biziou; ed, John Bloom; m, Zbigniew Preisner; prod d, Brian Morris; art d, Richard Earl; cos, Milena Canonero

AAN Best Supporting Actress: Miranda Richardson

With DAMAGE, based on the novel by Josephine Hart, acclaimed French director Louis Malle has created one of the most passionless movies about passion ever to hit the screen. Married, successful Member of Parliament Dr. Stephen Fleming (Jeremy Irons) becomes immediately infatuated when he meets Anna Barton (Juliette Binoche), girlfriend of his newspaper editor son, Martyn (Rupert Graves). The two begin an intensely erotic affair that continues even after Martyn announces that he and Anna are to be married. After discovering Anna and his father making love, a stunned Martyn falls to his death from the apartment balcony, setting off a scandal that will leave Stephen's life and career in ruins.

DAMAGE's plot is pure soap opera melodrama, but Malle imbues the material with an almost morbid seriousness that matches David Hare's irony-free screenplay. Strangely enough, the sex scenes are so mechanical that the ratings controversy that colored the film's release now seems ridiculous: no one could possibly find this material erotic. Stephen and Anna's many couplings look cold, clinical and—especially when lit through Venetian blinds—terminally arty. Irons, of course, is excellent.

DAMN YANKEES

1958   110m   c   Sports/Musical/Comedy   ★★★★
Warner Bros.   (U.S.)   *DVD*

Tab Hunter (*Joe Hardy*), Gwen Verdon (*Lola*), Ray Walston (*Applegate*), Russ Brown (*Van Buren*), Shannon Bolin (*Meg*), Nathaniel Frey (*Smokey*), Jimmie Komack (*Rocky*), Rae Allen (*Gloria*), Robert Shafer (*Joe Boyd*), Jean Stapleton (*Sister*)

p, George Abbott, Stanley Donen; d, George Abbott, Stanley Donen; w, George Abbott (based on the play by George Abbott and Douglas Wallop, from the novel *The Year the Yankees Lost the Pennant* by Wallop); ph, Harold Lipstein (Technicolor); ed, Frank Bracht; m, Jerry Ross, Richard Adler; prod d, William Eckart, Jean Eckart; art d, Stanley Fleischer; chor, Bob Fosse, Pat Ferrier; cos, William Eckart, Jean Eckart

AAN Best Score (Musical): Ray Heindorf

Somewhere along the way of opening up the smash stage version, DAMN YANKEES gets saddled with too much plot. It's only 110 minutes long, but you'd never know it. If Hunter is lacking in assurance among all the legit pros, there's nothing distinctly wrong in his performance. A middle-aged Washington Senators fan (Shafer) would give his soul for a long-ball hitter and promptly enough the devil shows up in the form of Walston, to change him into a handsome, athletic 22-year-old (Hunter) who wins a place on the Senators team. Walston is a perfect comic Satan, but gets bogged down in too much superficial action. It's unfortunate that the screenplay depends upon him to tie up all the loose ends. Verdon's eternal Lilith, Lola, is expert, sexy, and hilarious but because she's not a conventional beauty (Monroe had turned down both the Broadway and film versions) the need for Hunter is more than evident. Terrific, Oscar-nominated score by Jerry Ross and Richard Adler is electric, contains "Heart," "Whatever Lola Wants" and "Shoeless Joe from Hannibal Mo." That's Bob Fosse dancing with Verdon on "Who's Got the Pain."

DAMNATION
(KARHOZAT)
1988 116m bw Drama   ★★★★
Hungarian Film Institute/Mokep/Hungarian TV
(Hungary)

Miklos B. Szekely *(Karrer)*, Vali Kerekes *(The Singer)*, Gyula
Pauer *(Willarsky)*, Hedi Temessy *(Cloakroom Attendant)*, Gyorgy
Cserhalmi *(Sebestyen)*

p, Jozsef Marx; d, Bela Tarr; w, Laszlo Krasznahorkai, Bela Tarr;
ph, Gabor Medvigy; ed, Agnes Hraniczky; m, Mihaly Vig; cos,
Gyula Pauer

Photographed in black and white, Tarr's DAMNATION is a
slowly paced, deeply pessimistic, yet poetic film set in a grim,
featureless industrial area outside Budapest. There, alone and
friendless, the unemployed Szekely lives a monotonous existence, making the rounds of the local bars and staring out the
window at miner's buckets passing back and forth, suspended
on cables. Szekely is "in love" (the term's potential banality
emerges when applied to Tarr's alienated characters) with
Kerekes, a chanteuse at the Titanic bar who is married to
Cserhalmi. She has ended their affair (not—we suspect—for
the first time), but Szekely still pursues her, haunting the
Titanic and waiting outside Kerekes and Cserhalmi's apartment building, unprotected in the furiously pouring rain, for
Cserhalmi to leave. When a barkeeper (Pauer) offers Szekely
an opportunity to make some money as the courier in a smuggling expedition, Szekely tips off Cserhalmi to the job, knowing he is badly in debt, and thereby gets him out of the country
for a few days. He and Kerekes then resume their affair, after
a fashion, as the two fight violently, have sex, and engage in
hopelessly one-sided conversations.

   In addition to giving his actors pessimistic, near-mono-
logue dialogue, director-coscreenwriter Tarr emphasizes his
characters' despair with a number of visual motifs. The
incessant rain is the chief image of several that recur. The
buckets passing back and forth, rows of stacked glasses, several views of textural patterns in walls—these, in Tarr and
cinematographer Medvigy's static shots, have the nearly
abstract compositional beauty of the best black-and-white
still photographs, and the film is filled with stunning images
of the most mundane objects and scenes. When the camera
does move, the director favors slow lateral pans that seem to
suit the monotony of his characters' lives. Tarr's uncompromisingly tragic view of the human condition is well supported by a rigorous formal approach, resulting in an austere
work of art.

DAMNED, THE   📀
(LA CADUTA DEGLI DEI)
1969 155m c Drama   ★★★★
Eichberg/Pegaso/Praesidens (Italy/West Germany)   X

Dirk Bogarde *(Friedrich Bruckmann)*, Ingrid Thulin *(Baroness
Sophie von Essenbeck)*, Helmut Griem *(Aschenbach)*, Helmut
Berger *(Martin von Essenbeck)*, Renaud Verley *(Gunther von
Essenbeck)*, Umberto Orsini *(Herbert Thallman)*, Rene Kolldehoff
(Baron Konstantin von Essenbeck), Albrecht Schoenhals *(Baron
Joachim von Essenbeck)*, Charlotte Rampling *(Elisabeth
Thallman)*, Florinda Bolkan *(Olga)*

p, Alfredo Levy; Ever Haggiag; d, Luchino Visconti; w, Luchino
Visconti, Nicola Badalucco, Enrico Medioli; ph, Armando
Nannuzzi, Pasquale De Santis; ed, Ruggero Mastroianni; m,
Maurice Jarre

AAN Best Original Story and Screenplay: Nicola Badalucco
(Story), Enrico Medioli (Screenplay), Luchino Visconti
(Screenplay)

Luchino Visconti's epic of decadence, set in Germany during 1933 and 1934, parallels the end of a family of industri-
alists with the rise of Nazism. The films opens with an
extravagant dinner celebrating the retirement of the family
patriarch, Baron Joachim von Essenbeck, the magnate of a
huge steel enterprise, and his appointment of an outsider,
Friedrich Bruckmann (Dirk Bogarde) as temporary head.
While at first all seems very respectable and bourgeois, the
gathering turns strange when Joachim's grandson, Martin
(Helmut Berger) delivers his rendition of Marlene Dietrich's
"Falling in Love Again" dressed in drag. Before the party is
over, it is announced that the Reichstag has been burned,
symbolizing the end of German democracy. Later, as the
highly organized SS plots to annihilate the SA (the populist
Fascist front), Martin, a bisexual, sadistic, pedophilic drug
addict who even rapes his own mother, engineers his plot to
stop a takeover attempt by Friedrich and Sophie (Ingrid
Thulin), Friedrich's lover and Martin's mother.

   THE DAMNED is Visconti at his most operatic (the
German title is GOTTERDAMMERUNG, after Wagner),
containing baroque sets and costumes, highly melodramatic
acting, and orgiastic scenes of violence and sex. While it has
been criticized on a number of levels (the equating of perverts
and pedophiles with fascists has been done before; its English
dialogue is often poor; it indulges in its own distastefulness;
it's too long, etc.), the film is a spectacular, meticulously crafted work that cannot fail to elicit some response, be it disgust
or appreciation, from its audience.

DANCE WITH A STRANGER   📀
1985 102m c Biography/Crime   ★★★★
First Film/Goldcrest/HFFC/4 Intl. (U.K.)   R

Miranda Richardson *(Ruth Ellis)*, Rupert Everett *(David Blakely)*,
Ian Holm *(Desmond Cussen)*, Matthew Carroll *(Andy)*, Tom
Chadbon *(Anthony Findlater)*, Jane Bertish *(Carole Findlater)*,
David Troughton *(Cliff Davis)*, Paul Mooney *(Clive Gunnell)*,
Stratford Johns *(Morrie Conley)*, Joanne Whalley-Kilmer *(Christine)*

p, Roger Randall-Cutler; d, Mike Newell; w, Shelagh Delaney; ph,
Peter Hannan; ed, Mick Audsley; m, Richard Hartley; prod d,
Andrew Mollo; art d, Adrian Smith; cos, Pip Newberry

Dark, haunting kichen-sink noir, deftly done; the life and death
of Ruth Ellis, the last woman to be hanged for murder in
England in 1955. The screenplay by Shelagh Delaney takes a
few liberties for the sake of dramatic license but by and large
keeps close to the real account. Miranda Richardson (playing
Ellis), a divorcee and ex-hooker, now a "hostess" in a tawdry
nightclub in Soho. Though she lives with Holm, he is more of
a pal than a lover and also the surrogate father to her son,
Carroll. Richardson falls obsessively in love with upper-class
Everett, an immature cad. But the more she wants to be with
Everett, the more he pushes her aside, both mentally and physically. Eventually she retaliates and murders him. The real case
provided months of lurid reading for the British and years
later, Ellis's son committed suicide.

   STRANGER inhabits the seedy milieu beneath the
repressed 1950s British surface. Richardson's performance is
a knockout; with her birdlike gestures and darting eyes, she's
reminiscent of young Bette Davis in her peroxide period. And
she challenges two topics the English hesitate to look at—sexual compulsivity and outward expression of nasty emotions;
no wonder Ellis got the death sentence.

DANCER IN THE DARK   📀
2000 140m c Musical/Drama   ★★★
Zentropa Entertainments 4/Good Machine/Pain   R
Unlimited/Liberator Productions/Trust Film Svenska/
Film i Vast/Cinematograph/What Else/Icelandic Film
Corp/France 3 Cinema/Arte France Cinema

(Denmark/U.S./Sweden/Germany/Norway/
Netherlands/France)

Bjork *(Selma)*, Catherine Deneuve *(Kathy)*, David Morse *(Bill)*, Peter Stormare *(Jeff)*, Udo Kier *(Dr. Porkorny)*, Joel Grey *(Oldrich Novy)*, Vincent Paterson *(Samuel)*, Cara Seymour *(Linda)*, Jean-Marc Barr *(Norman)*, Vladica Kostic *(Gene)*

p, Vibeke Windelov; d, Lars Von Trier; w, Lars Von Trier; ph, Robby Muller; ed, Molly Malene Stensgaard, Francois Gedigier; m, Bjork; prod d, Karl Juliusson; art d, Peter Grant; chor, Vincent Paterson; cos, Manon Rasmussen

AAN Best Original Song: "I've Seen It All"; Bjork, Lars von Trier, Sjon Sigurdsson

The moment Bjork opens her little mouth and belts out her first big number, it's clear she and director Lars von Trier have defibrillated the moribund movie musical; bursting into song once again seems like a viable means of cinematic expression. That and Bjork's astonishingly raw performance are the film's greatest achievements; otherwise, it's a thematic reworking of von Trier's BREAKING THE WAVES, complete with a guilt-ridden, child-like heroine doomed to suffer an unreasonably harsh fate for another's salvation.

Washington state, the early 1960s. Czech immigrant Selma Jezkova (Bjork) is a single mother with a passion for musicals who lives with her son, Gene (Vladica Kostic), in the dreary caravan she rents from the town cop (David Morse). She toils daily at a metal plant, but when the going gets tough, Selma's mind goes Hollywood; she daydreams herself into elaborately staged musical numbers in which she's the star. Unbeknownst to everyone around her, including coworker and best friend Kathy (Catherine Deneuve), Selma suffers from a degenerative eye condition and is going blind. An expensive operation will save her vision, and Selma's been dutifully squirreling away her hard-earned cash. But she's not thinking of herself: Gene has inherited the disease, and Selma is determined that he should have the operation instead. When an unforeseen catastrophe strikes, Selma must face an even greater sacrifice, the kind found only in hagiographies and Hollywood melodramas.

This may be a musical, but don't expect a good time; it's a grim tragedy that's deliberately drab and exceedingly painful to watch. But if Von Trier's preoccupation with guilt and expiation through tremendous suffering didn't trouble you in BREAKING THE WAVES, it probably won't here either.

DANCES WITH WOLVES

1990 181m c Western

TIG (U.S.) **DVD** ★★½ PG-13

Kevin Costner *(Lt. John W. Dunbar)*, Mary McDonnell *(Stands with a Fist)*, Graham Greene *(Kicking Bird)*, Rodney A. Grant *(Wind in his Hair)*, Floyd Red Crow Westerman *(Chief Ten Bears)*, Tantoo Cardinal *(Black Shawl)*, Robert Pastorelli *(Timmons)*, Charles Rocket *(Lt. Elgin)*, Maury Chaykin *(Maj. Fambrough)*, Jimmy Herman *(Stone Calf)*

p, Jim Wilson, Kevin Costner; d, Kevin Costner; w, Michael Blake (based on his novel); ph, Dean Semler; ed, Neil Travis; m, John Barry; prod d, Jeffrey Beecroft; art d, William L. Skinner; fx, Robbie Knott; cos, Elsa Zamparelli

AA Best Picture; AAN Best Actor: Kevin Costner; *AAN Best Supporting Actor:* Graham Greene; *AAN Best Supporting Actress:* Mary McDonnell; *AA Best Director:* Kevin Costner; *AA Best Adapted Screenplay:* Michael Blake; *AA Best Cinematography:* Dean Semler; *AAN Best Art Direction-Set Decoration:* Jeffrey Beecroft, Lisa Dean; *AA Best Sound:* Russell Williams II, Jeffrey Perkins, Bill W. Benton, Greg Watkins; *AA Best Original Score:*

John Barry; *AA Best Film Editing:* Neil Travis; *AAN Best Costume Design:* Elsa Zamparelli

The plodding vanity project of star, director, and co-producer Kevin Costner, this three-hour-plus revisionist western, much of it in subtitled Sioux language, shocked movie-industry observers by becoming a huge hit and garnering 12 Oscar nominations, winning seven, including Best Picture and Best Director. The Sioux gave the film their own rave review by admitting Costner as a full tribal member.

Costner plays Lt. John W. Dunbar, a Union officer during the Civil War who undergoes a conversion experience on the frontier that transforms him into the title character. The film begins with Dunbar wounded, depressed, and suicidal. His suicide attempt is mistaken for an act of heroism and he gets transferred to the post of his choice—an outpost on the frontier far away from white "civilization." After a series of peculiar experiences he find himself alone in a little shelter on the prairie where he befriends an amiable wolf. Before long he meets his equally amiable Native American neighbors and slowly wins their respect and love as he goes native with a vengeance. Over the course of his unlikely adventures, he trades in his dreary Union duds for some cool Sioux threads, forms a very close friendship with a white woman (McDonnell) who was captured and raised by Indians, and even breaks the "Prime Directive" by giving out rifles and ammunition to his "good" Lakota Sioux pals to battle the mean ol' Pawnees.

Not a great film by any standard, this is a western for people who are completely ignorant about the genre. Costner's direction is barely competent and frequently clumsy. Michael Blake's script, adapted from his novel, is loose and disconnected, rambling about with no real story holding it together, beyond the imminent arrival of the white bad guys to spoil Dunbar's frontier fantasy paradise. Despite its attention to surface details of day-to-day Sioux life, the film shows no genuine curiosity about the larger designs of the Sioux culture. We see little of tribal life through Sioux eyes, and come away having learned nothing at all about Sioux spirituality. Instead, the film renders the Sioux as just average folks.

DANGEROUS

1936 78m bw Drama ★★★

Warner Bros. (U.S.)

Bette Davis *(Joyce Heath)*, Franchot Tone *(Don Bellows)*, Margaret Lindsay *(Gail Armitage)*, Alison Skipworth *(Mrs. Williams)*, John Eldredge *(Gordon Heath)*, Dick Foran *(Teddy)*, Pierre Watkin *(George Sheffield)*, Walter Walker *(Roger Farnsworth)*, George Irving *(Charles Melton)*, William B. Davidson *(Reed Walsh)*

p, Harry Joe Brown; d, Alfred E. Green; w, Laird Doyle; ph, Ernest Haller; ed, Thomas Richards; m, Bernhard Kaun; art d, Hugh Reticker; cos, Orry-Kelly

AA Best Actress: Bette Davis

Davis takes on the Jeanne Eagels legend, acting it with an intensity that would have gotten her burned at the stake in the 17th century. This was the film that followed OF HUMAN BONDAGE, and despite critics' love letters, Davis was feeling ignored by the industry. Though an inferior vehicle even then, DANGEROUS gave her another shot at a breakthrough role, an opportunity she seized; no other Hollywood star would have played a Broadway legend, sodden or not, so unflatteringly.

Davis is an alcoholic former star when slumming architect Franchot Tone (in a surprisingly contemporary performance) spots her, buys her a drink, and comments about how much he enjoyed her acting. She accepts his invitation to stay at his home in Connecticut, but once there she continues boozing. He offers to finance her return to the stage, and she does what she can to break up his engagement to Margaret Lindsay (who gets another dreary role like this in JEZEBEL). Eventually, Tone tells Lindsay he wants to marry Davis, but it turns out she's married to Eldredge. The latter refuses to divorce her; she then intentionally crashes her car, hoping to kill Eldredge. He survives but he's now paralyzed for life. Her return to the stage is a big success, and Tone still wants her, but now she's troubled by guilt over what she has done to Eldredge.

Davis's efforts paid off with her first Academy Award, a partial consolation prize for her riveting performance in BONDAGE the year prior, but nonetheless an acknowledgement by the industry of her innovative thesping.

DANGEROUS LIAISONS

1988 120m c Drama ★★★★
NFH/Lorimar (U.S.) R

Glenn Close *(Marquise de Merteuil)*, John Malkovich *(Vicomte de Valmont)*, Michelle Pfeiffer *(Madame de Tourvel)*, Swoosie Kurtz *(Madame de Volanges)*, Keanu Reeves *(Chevalier Danceny)*, Mildred Natwick *(Madame de Rosemonde)*, Uma Thurman *(Cecile de Volanges)*, Joe Sheridan, Peter Capaldi

p, Norma Heyman, Hank Moonjean, Christopher Hampton; d, Stephen Frears; w, Christopher Hampton (based on his play and the novel *Les Liaisons Dangereuses* by Choderlos de Laclos); ph, Philippe Rousselot; ed, Mick Audsley; m, George Fenton; prod d, Stuart Craig; cos, James Acheson

AAN Best Picture; AAN Best Actress: Glenn Close; *AAN Best Supporting Actress:* Michelle Pfeiffer; *AA Best Adapted Screenplay:* Christopher Hampton; *AAN Best Original Score:* George Fenton; *AA Best Art Direction-Set Decoration:* Stuart Craig, Gerard James; *AA Best Costume Design:* James Acheson

Choderlos de Laclos reportedly said of his epistolary 1782 novel, *Les Liaisons Dangereuses*, that he created it with the intent to shock. That novel, on which British director Stephen Frears's first American feature film is based, did much of what Laclos hoped, the first edition becoming the *succes de scandale* of Paris. Frears's version, a costume drama set in pre-Revolutionary France, isn't precisely shocking, but its classic story of sexual power, depravity, cruelty, and deceit is rendered with force and without compromise.

The Marquise de Merteuil (Glenn Close) and the Vicomte de Valmont (John Malkovich) are monsters of the aristocracy, former lovers who spend their days planning sexual seductions and vengeance. Merteuil makes Valmont a proposition: if he deflowers Cecile (Uma Thurman), the 16-year-old future wife of another of Merteuil's former lovers, she will gratefully reward Valmont with her favors. Valmont instead devotes his attention to the greater challenge of seducing Madame de Tourvel (Michelle Pfeiffer)—a highly moral, married, and convent-bred young woman. Plying his suit with the greatest skill and subtlety, Valmont eventually breaks down Tourvel's reserve. In the meantime, to please Merteuil, he also deflowers Cecile—who, after yielding to Valmont, becomes insatiably sensual. DANGEROUS LIAISONS is less about debauchery and amorality than it is about the sexual and psychological domination of one person by another.

Malkovich and Close take a while before they shift into expert gear, the former lacking the physical grace of a Don Juan, the latter vapid in a Connecticut housewife kind of way. Nor does it help that Close, despite her talent, is utterly devoid of sex appeal. But Pfeiffer is a revelation in her part, almost stealing the film. Her relative stillness, masking internal unrest, makes her character seem more authentically "period" than her co-stars, who have adopted no formal period mannerisms. But its vernacular style allows the film to connect easily with present-day morals, sexual politics, and thirst

for power. While not perfect, LIAISONS is miles above Forman's bland VALMONT.

DANGEROUS LIVES OF ALTAR BOYS, THE

2002 105m c Comedy/Drama ★★★
Egg Pictures/Initial Entertainment Group/ R
Trilogy Entertainment (U.S.)

Kieran Culkin *(Tim Sullivan)*, Emile Hirsch *(Francis Doyle)*, Jena Malone *(Margie Flynn)*, Jodie Foster *(Sister Assumpta)*, Vincent D'Onofrio *(Father Casey)*, Jake Richardson *(Wade)*, Tyler Long *(Joey)*, Melissa Suzanne McBride *(Mrs. Doyle)*, Mike Harding *(Mr. Doyle)*, Arthur Bridges *(Donny Flynn)*

p, Jodie Foster, Meg LeFauve, Jay Shapiro; d, Peter Care; w, Jeff Stockwell, Michael Petroni (based on the book by Chris Fuhrman); ph, Lance Acord; ed, Chris Peppe; m, Marco Beltrami; prod d, Gideon Ponte; art d, Geoffrey S. Grimsman; fx, Adam Howard, Michael Schorr; cos, Marie France; anim, Todd McFarlane

Chris Fuhrman, who died of cancer three years before the 1991 publication of his one and only novel, couldn't have asked for a better cast of young actors to bring his bittersweet book to life. The film, adventurously directed by Peter Care, follows Fuhrman's teenage alter ego, Francis Doyle (Emile Hirsch), and his best friend, Tim Sullivan (Kieran Culkin), as they attempt to negotiate the perils of adolescence, sex, and, most frightening of all, Catholic school.

Francis is nursing a serious crush on Margie Flynn (Jena Malone), a troubled classmate who once tried to kill herself, while Tim is the kind of precocious freethinker who would sooner pore over William Blake's visionary poetry than join his fellow sixth graders in a rendition of "Kumbaya." They're both passionate about comic books, and together with friends Joey (Tyler Long) and Wade (Jake Richardson), they've imagined a strip of their own: "The Atomic Trinity," superheroes who battle Peg Leg, a one-legged nun who bears a striking resemblance to their cruel, ego-crushing geometry teacher, Sister Assumpta (a truly scary Jodie Foster). The boys spend their afternoons at a local cemetery, smoking cigarettes and drinking pilfered booze, until a field trip to a local game preserve gives Tim an idea: why not kidnap the park's cougar and set it loose in Sister Assumpta's office?

Furhman's book is much admired for its unvarnished depiction of adolescence, and Care and screenwriters Jeff Stockwel and Petroni remain true to the tone of the book. But while the booming, fully animated adventures of the Atomic Trinity (by *Spawn* creator Todd McFarlane) that Care intercuts with the live action at first seem a good idea, they ultimately upset the film's carefully established mood.

DANGEROUS MOVES

(LA DIAGONALE DU FOU)
1984 95m c Thriller ★★★½
Arthur Cohn (Switzerland)

Michel Piccoli *(Akiva Liebskind)*, Alexandre Arbatt *(Pavius Fromm)*, Leslie Caron *(Henia Liebskind)*, Liv Ullmann *(Marina)*, Daniel Olbrychski *(Tac-Tac)*, Michel Aumont *(Kerossian)*, Serge Avedikian *(Fadenko)*, Pierre Michael *(Yachvili)*, Pierre Vial *(Anton Heller)*, Wojciech Pszoniak *(Felton)*

p, Arthur Cohn; d, Richard Dembo; w, Richard Dembo; ph, Raoul Coutard; ed, Agnes Guillemot; m, Gabriel Yared; art d, Ivan Maussion; cos, Pierre Albert

AA Best Foreign Language Film

This ingenious thriller takes place in the world of chess championships, using the politically neutral Geneva, Switzerland, as its backdrop. The reigning world chess champion, Michel Piccoli, is the pride of the Soviet Union, but his weak heart may mean the end of his reign. His competitor is Alexandre Arbatt, a rebellious young Soviet exile. As the championship begins, Arbatt attempts to disrupt the proceedings, and thereby Piccoli's concentration, by arriving late for his first move. His habitual tardiness and basic contempt for regulations force Piccoli to register a formal complaint with the jury. When Piccoli threatens to withdraw, Arbatt buckles under and writes a formal apology rather than lose his chance to defeat the champion. As a result of their moves away from the chess board, both men begin to deteriorate—Piccoli physically, Arbatt mentally. The chess masters, however, are merely pawns in a larger political game involving the Soviet government and the West.

Director Richard Dembo, in his debut feature, has contrasted skillfully the players' maneuvers with political power plays, yet he avoids pretension. Rather than concentrating too much on the chess matches themselves (a knowledge of chess is helpful in viewing DANGEROUS MOVES, but by no means a requirement), Dembo brings to the screen an emotional battle between two powerful personalities. He also receives support from a solid who's-who of European film, including actors Liv Ullmann, Leslie Caron, Bernhard Wicki, Daniel Olbrychski, and Jean-Hugues Anglade; cameraman Raoul Coutard; and editor Agnes Guillemot.

DANTON

1982   136m   c   Historical/Biography/War   ★★★
TF1/SFPC/Film Polski/Losange/Gaumont   PG
(France/Poland)

Gerard Depardieu *(Georges Danton)*, Wojciech Pszoniak *(Maximillian Robespierre)*, Patrice Chereau *(Camille Desmoulins)*, Angela Winkler *(Lucile Desmoulins)*, Boguslaw Linda *(Saint Just)*, Roland Blanche *(Lacroix)*, Anne Alvaro *(Eleonore Duplay)*, Roger Planchon *(Fouquier Tinville)*, Serge Merlin *(Philippeaux)*, Lucien Melki *(Fabre d'Eglantine)*

p, Margaret Menegoz; d, Andrzej Wajda; w, Jean-Claude Carriere, Andrzej Wajda, Agnieszka Holland, Boleslaw Michalek, Jacek Gasiorowski (based on the play "The Danton Affair" by Stanislawa Przybyszewska); ph, Igor Luther; ed, Halina Prugar; m, Jean Prodromides; art d, Allan Starski, Gilles Vaster; cos, Yvonne Sassinot de Nesle

DANTON is a powerful drama of revolution, set in 1794 France, during the second year of the Republic, that centers on the rivalry between the humanist Georges Danton (the typically memorable Gerard Depardieu) and the ideologue Maximilien de Robespierre (Wojciech Pszoniak), "The Incorruptible." Danton, the most popular of the French revolutionaries, temporarily retired from politics and retreated to the countryside. He returns to Paris now, however, to stop the Reign of Terror led by Robespierre, his former compatriot in the Revolution whose efforts to keep the "pure patriots" in power have turned tyrannical. Although a great freedom fighter and proponent of political, religious, and human rights, Robespierre, with his Committee of Public Safety, has become just as oppressive as the monarchs he fought against. Despite the fact that Danton is a people's hero, Robespierre convinces himself that he must be executed in order to save the Republic.

DANTON is a stirring film on freedom from Andrzej Wajda, in his first directing effort outside of Poland. Criticized by some for being too static and theatrical, the movie takes care to show only the center of the Revolution and its aftermath: the battle between Danton and Robespierre and the unseen fight for liberty that takes place behind closed doors. Wajda disregards the rebellion in the streets in favor of showing us the power in the hands of government—those chosen few who are supposed to be representatives of the people.

DARBY O'GILL AND THE LITTLE PEOPLE

1959   93m   c   Children's/Fantasy   ★★★★½
Walt Disney Productions   (U.S.)

Albert Sharpe *(Darby O'Gill)*, Janet Munro *(Katie)*, Sean Connery *(Michael McBride)*, Jimmy O'Dea *(King Brian)*, Kieron Moore *(Pony Sugrue)*, Estelle Winwood *(Sheelah)*, Walter Fitzgerald *(Lord Fitzpatrick)*, Denis O'Dea *(Fr. Murphy)*, J.G. Devlin *(Tom Kerrigan)*, Jack MacGowran *(Phadrig Oge)*

p, Walt Disney; d, Robert Stevenson; w, Lawrence E. Watkin (based on the Darby O'Gill stories by H.T. Kavanagh); ph, Winton C. Hoch (Technicolor); ed, Stanley Johnson; m, Oliver Wallace; art d, Carroll Clark; fx, Peter Ellenshaw, Eustace Lycett; cos, Chuck Keehne, Gertrude Casey; anim, Joshua Meador

This excellent fantasy romps through the folklore world of Ireland, with Albert Sharpe starring as Darby O'Gill, the aging caretaker of a large estate. He falls into a well and lands in the cavernous realm of the Little People, ruled by King Brian (Jimmy O'Dea, in an unforgettable performance). Following a wild leprechaun celebration, the rock walls open and the king leads his men out on miniature horses to frolic in the Irish countryside. Later, Darby tricks King Brian into granting him three wishes, but quickly learns that one should be careful of what one wishes for.

This wonderful tale is told with a brisk, imaginative pace and the special effects—whereby Darby interacts with the tiny leprechauns—are marvelously executed, and sometimes frightening. Sharp camerawork is enhanced with brilliant colors and the music (by Oliver Wallace and Lawrence E. Watkin) is delightfully and capriciously Irish. Young Sean Connery is a breathtaking feast for the eyes, and Munro makes a fetching colleen. Overall production reflects Walt Disney's perfectionist detail; Disney dreamed of making the film for 20 years and took a trip to Ireland in 1948 to do research. Any child who hasn't seen DARBY O'GILL AND THE LITTLE PEOPLE has missed an important bit of fancy, and that goes for adults too.

DAREDEVIL

2003   103m   c   Action/Fantasy   ★★★
Marvel Enterprises, Inc./New Regency/Horseshoe   PG-13
Bay Productions/20th Century Fox   (U.S.)

Ben Affleck *(Matt Murdock/Daredevil)*, Jennifer Garner *(Elektra)*, Colin Farrell *(Bullseye)*, Michael Clarke Duncan *(Kingpin/Fisk)*, Jon Favreau *(Franklin Nelson)*, Scott Terra *(Young Matt)*, Ellen Pompeo *(Karen Page)*, Joe Pantoliano *(Ben Urich)*, David Keith *(Jack Murdock)*, Erick Avari *(Natchios)*

p, Avi Arad, Kathleen Courtney, Gary Foster, Arnon Milchan; d, Mark Steven Johnson; w, Mark Steven Johnson (based on characters created by Stan Lee and Bill Everett); ph, Ericson Core; ed, Armen Minasian, Dennis Virkler; m, Graeme Revell; prod d, Barry Chusid; art d, James Tocci; fx, Mike Edmonson, John McLeod, Jennifer Meislohn, Rich Thorne; chor, Cheung Yan Yuen (action); cos, James Acheson

After the success of the Marvel Comics movies X-MEN and SPIDER-MAN, the resulting superhero wave might well have begun cannibalizing its own conventions. But this big-screen adaptation of the long-running comic-book series makes it clear that superhero films are the next evolutionary generation of action movies.

As a child, Matt Murdock (Ben Affleck) was blinded by radioactive chemicals that also enhanced his remaining senses to a superhuman degree. Now a Manhattan attorney by day, he dons a red-leather suit by night and hits the rooftops as his alter ego, Daredevil. Murdock's routine is disrupted when he meets Elektra Natchios (Jennifer Garner), a well-trained martial artist whose father (Erick Avari) is trying to leave the criminal empire of business mogul Wilson Fisk, a.k.a. the Kingpin (Michael Clarke Duncan). Fisk has Natchios killed by psychotic assassin Bullseye (Colin Farrell), who can turn anything into a lethal weapon. When Daredevil attempts to help, Elektra mistakenly thinks he's her father's killer—and when Fisk sends Bullseye after Elektra, issues of vengeance, justice, and loss are smartly and uncompromisingly played out.

Visually arresting—if slightly artificial-looking—the film makes exquisite use of an optical effect to mimic the blind Daredevil's sonar-like "radar sense," through which he "sees" ripples of reality. Affleck is perfectly fine but doesn't have much range; Murdock/Daredevil seems a bit smug from start to finish. But Garner, Duncan, and Farrell play their characters as fleshed-out people, rather than mythic comic-book legends, as do David Keith and Jon Favreau as Murdock's father and law partner, respectively. With the exception of Bullseye's murder of a little old lady—a scene which is, sickeningly, played for laughs—the movie's physical violence isn't gratuitous; it's the emotional violence that makes this a movie for grown-ups, not kids.

DARK BLUE

2003 118m c Crime/Thriller ★★★
IM Filmproduktion/Alphaville Production/Cosmic R
Pictures/Intermedia Films (U.S./Germany)

Kurt Russell (Eldon Perry), Scott Speedman (Bobby Keough), Michael Michele (Beth Williamson), Ving Rhames (Arthur Holland), Kurupt (Darryl Orchard), Dash Mihok (Gary Sidwell), Jonathan Banks (James Barcomb), Lolita Davidovich (Sally Perry), Dana Lee (Henry Kim)

p, David Blocker, Caldecot Chubb, Sean Daniel, James Jacks; d, Ron Shelton; w, David Ayer (based on a story by James Ellroy); ph, Barry Peterson; ed, Paul Seydor; m, Terence Blanchard; prod d, Dennis Washington; art d, Tom T. Taylor; fx, Larry Fioritto; cos, Kathryn Morrison

If this brutal tale of crime and corruption within the LAPD recalls L.A. CONFIDENTIAL, there's good reason: both spring from the dark mind of American crime writer James Ellroy.

April 1992: Detective Bobby Keough (Scott Speedman) has been with the LAPD's elite Special Investigations Squad for only three weeks, but he's already been called before a shooting board for his questionable use of deadly force. His exoneration was never really in doubt; Keough's uncle is fearsome SIS head Jack Van Meter (Brendan Gleeson), and Keough's partner is Sergeant Eldon Perry (a frighteningly convincing Kurt Russell), a hard-drinking cop whose late father was once Van Meter's partner. The only board member who doubts Keogh's innocence is assistant chief of police Arthur Holland (Ving Rhames). He asks his assistant, Sergeant Beth Williamson (Michael Michele), to comb Perry's file, unaware that Williamson is sleeping with Keough on the sly. Van Meter, meanwhile, assigns his two bad boys to a gruesome quadruple homicide at a Koreatown liquor store. Something about the case stinks, but Van Meter is pressuring Keogh and Perry to just pin the whole thing on a couple of patsies and wrap it up. Adding to the growing tension is the countdown to the Rodney King verdict and the ensuing riots that will serve as the backdrop for the film's climax.

Exploitative? Perhaps, but understandable. Director Ron Shelton is determined to show that the riots were the product of a poisonous climate that had long existed between the people of South Central and the police department, a miasma of mutual hatred, fear, and mistrust that, Ellroy contends, extends at least as far back as the era of L.A. CONFIDENTIAL.

DARK CITY

1998 103m c Science Fiction/Thriller/Fantasy ★★★
Mystery Clock Productions (U.S.) R

Rufus Sewell (John Murdoch), Kiefer Sutherland (Dr. Schreber), Jennifer Connelly (Emma Murdoch), Richard O'Brien (Mr. Hand), Ian Richardson (Mr. Book), William Hurt (Inspector Frank Bumstead), Bruce Spence (Mr. Wall), Colin Friels (Walenski), John Bluthal (Karl Harris), Mitchell Butel (Husselbeck)

p, Andrew Mason, Alex Proyas; d, Alex Proyas; w, Alex Proyas, Lem Dobbs, David S. Goyer (from a story by Alex Proyas); ph, Dariusz Wolski; ed, Dov Hoenig; m, Trevor Jones; prod d, George Liddle, Patrick Tatopolous; art d, Michelle McGahey, Richard Hobbs; fx, Tad Pride, Tom Davies, Mara Bryan, Arthur Windus, Andrew Mason, Bruce Hunt; cos, Liz Keogh

A film-noir fever dream with a sci-fi secret, in which a man searching for his identity makes a discovery that quite literally shifts the ground beneath his feet.

John Murdoch (Rufus Sewell) wakes up in a hotel bathroom; there's a dead girl all cut up in the other room, and he has no idea how she got there or who she is. In fact, he has no idea who *he* is, though he seems to have a beautiful lounge-singer wife (Jennifer Connelly) and some weird bald-headed guys in HELLRAISER gear on his tail, though he couldn't begin to tell you why. Things start getting really weird at midnight, when everyone in the city mysteriously falls into some sort of dead sleep, while Murdoch remains awake to see the very buildings around him twisting and changing, like concrete seeds sprouting in some bizarre mind-bending nightmare.

In a film in which acting isn't the main event, *Rocky Horror* creator Richard O'Brien—you probably remember him as Riff Raff—delivers a deeply creepy turn as the sinister Mr. Hand, Murdoch's chief nemesis. Connelly looks nothing short of breathtaking in her '40s-era gowns, though her performance is rather less memorable. Writer-director Alex Proyas, who directed THE CROW, isn't a particularly strong storyteller, but the story—a rather silly twist on Philip K. Dick's "We Can Remember It for You Wholesale"—truly isn't the point either. It's all about the amazing look, cobbled together from an evocative range of sources: NOSFERATU and MAD LOVE, BRAZIL and METROPOLIS—a haunted mosaic of bits and pieces of movie memories.

DARK CRYSTAL, THE

1982 94m c Children's/Science Fiction/Fantasy ★★★
Associated Film/Universal (U.K.) PG

VOICES OF: Stephen Garlick (Jen), Lisa Maxwell (Kira), Billie Whitelaw (Aughra), Percy Edwards (Fizzgig), Barry Dennen (Chamberlain), Michael Kilgarriff (General), Jerry Nelson (High Priest), Steve Whitmire (Scientist), Thick Wilson (Gourmand), Brian Muehl (Ornamentalist/Dying Master)

p, Jim Henson, Gary Kurtz; d, Jim Henson, Frank Oz; w, David Odell (based on a story by Henson); ph, Oswald Morris (Panavision, Technicolor); ed, Ralph Kemplen; m, Trevor Jones; prod d, Harry Lange; art d, Terry Ackland-Snow, Malcolm Stone, Brian Ackland-Snow; fx, Roy Field, Brian Smithies; chor, Jean Pierre Amierl

Once again employing his famous muppets, Jim Henson creates a brilliantly detailed universe with this intriguing fairytale adventure revolving around a power struggle between the monstrous Skeksis and the benevolent Mystics. Because the Dark Crystal has been broken, the Skeksis are in ascendance and will remain so unless Jen, one of two remaining Gelflings, is able to heal the crystal, thus fulfilling a prophesy that promises an end to Skeksis rule. Guided by the Mystics' cryptic instructions, and aided by Aughra, a sorceress, and Kira, the other (female) Gelfling, Jen goes about restoring the crystal. Like the children's classics SNOW WHITE AND THE SEVEN DWARFS and SLEEPING BEAUTY, this film has some graphic scenes that may be upsetting for younger kids.

DARK EYES
(OCI CIORNIE)
1987 118m c   Romance/Comedy   ★★★½
Excelsior/RAI-TV   (Italy)

Marcello Mastroianni *(Romano)*, Silvana Mangano *(Elisa, Romano's Wife)*, Marthe Keller *(Tina, Romano's Mistress)*, Elena Sofonova *(Anna Sergeyevna, Governor's Wife)*, Vsevolod Larionov *(Pavel, Russian Ship Passenger)*, Innokenty Smoktunovsky *(Governor of Sisoiev)*, Pina Cei *(Elisa's Mother)*, Roberto Herlitzka *(Lawyer)*, Dimitri Zolothukin *(Konstantin)*, Paolo Baroni

p, Silvia D'Amico Bendico, Carlo Cucchi; d, Nikita Mikhalkov; w, Alexander Adabachian, Nikita Mikhalkov, Suso Cecchi D'Amico (based on material from the Anton Chekhov stories "The Lady With the Little Dog," "The Name-Day Party," "Anna Around the Neck" and "My Wife"); ph, Franco Di Giacomo (Eastmancolor); ed, Enzo Meniconi; m, Francis Lai; art d, Mario Garbuglia, Alexander Adabachian; cos, Carlo Diappi

AAN Best Actor: Marcello Mastroianni

A myriad of emotions, elegantly served. Directed by Nikita Mikhalkov (his first movie outside the USSR), the film brought a Soviet and Italian cast and crew together, and the result was a new, cross-cultural interpretation of the Chekhov stories upon which the film is based.

Set at the turn of the century, the film stars Mastroianni as Romano, a paunchy, alcoholic waiter who works in the dining room of a cruise ship. While voyaging from Greece to Italy, he meets Pavel (Vsevolod Larionov), a jovial Russian on his honeymoon with his much younger wife. Romano begins to reminisce, and the film goes to flashback. As young architecture student, Romano falls in love with Elisa (Silvana Mangano), a wealthy heiress, despite the objections of her high-society family.

He eventually leaves her and retreats to a lavish health spa. He finds willing young ladies to sleep with, pulls an occasional practical joke, watches old women racing through the marble-columned grounds in their wheelchairs, wanders about the beautifully manicured lawns, and eats extravagant meals. He meets Anna Sergeyevna (Elena Sofonova), a timid, lovely, easily embarrassed young woman with dark eyes and a lapdog. Mesmerized by her presence and the magical sparkle of her hat pin, Romano becomes obsessed.

Mastroianni is superb: his performance won the Best Actor prize at the Cannes Film Festival. However, it is not his performance alone that makes DARK EYES so enjoyable; there is also the discovery (for Western audiences) of the lovely Sofonova, a Soviet actress whose combination of fragility and strength is reminiscent of Audrey Hepburn.

DARK MIRROR, THE
1946 85m   bw Thriller   ★★★★
Universal   (U.S.)

Olivia de Havilland *(Terry Collins/Ruth Collins)*, Lew Ayres *(Dr. Scott Elliott)*, Thomas Mitchell *(Detective Stevenson)*, Richard Long *(Rusty)*, Charles Evans *(District Attorney Girard)*, Garry Owen *(Franklin)*, Lester Allen *(George Benson)*, Lela Bliss *(Mrs. Didriksen)*, Marta Mitrovich *(Miss Beade)*, Amelita Ward *(Photo Double)*

p, Nunnally Johnson; d, Robert Siodmak; w, Nunnally Johnson (based on the novel by Vladimir Pozner); ph, Milton Krasner; ed,

Ernest Nims; m, Dimitri Tiomkin; prod d, Duncan Cramer; fx, Devereaux Jennings, Paul K. Lerpae; cos, Irene Sharaff

AAN Best Original Story: Vladimir Pozner

De Havilland's finest hour, thanks to her underplayed escape from the butter-wouldn't-melt-in-her-mouth moments that flawed some of her finest performances. Here she tackles two roles: identical twins. One is loving and compassionate, the other a calculating killer. After one sister's suitor is found dead, police detective Mitchell rounds up witnesses who pin the blame on good twin Ruth, although she has a concrete alibi. Witnesses, however, cannot tell one twin from the other so psychologist Ayres is brought in to analyze the two women. When both twins fall in love with Ayres, his job becomes even more difficult, personal, and dangerous.

De Havilland is absolutely riveting in her roles—roles which are enriched by special effects wizards J. Devereaux Jennings and Paul Lerpae, whose split-screen technique allows for intimate scenes wherein the actress plays opposite herself. Siodmak's attention to detail creates a mood of psychological disturbance and dark suspense evident from the word go (there's a dynamite opening scene), and typical of the postwar fascination with mental illness.

DARK PASSAGE
1947 106m bw Crime   ★★★½
Warner Bros.   (U.S.)

Humphrey Bogart *(Vincent Parry)*, Lauren Bacall *(Irene Jansen)*, Bruce Bennett *(Bob)*, Agnes Moorehead *(Madge Rapf)*, Tom D'Andrea *(Sam)*, Clifton Young *(Baker)*, Douglas Kennedy *(Detective)*, Rory Mallinson *(George Fellsinger)*, Houseley Stevenson *(Dr. Walter Coley)*, Bob Farber

p, Jerry Wald; d, Delmer Daves; w, Delmer Daves (based on the novel by David Goodis); ph, Sid Hickox; ed, David Weisbart; m, Franz Waxman; art d, Charles H. Clarke; fx, H.F. Koenekamp; cos, Bernard Newman

An example of how star power can compensate plot, this is the least electric of the Bogart-Bacall pairings; luckily, there's Agnes Moorehead, the screen's best hornet, to intervene whenever the going gets too lackadasical. She's the only female Bogie ever played opposite he looks scared of.

Bogie escapes from San Quentin, where he has been imprisoned for murdering his wife, and is picked up by Bacall who has long been obsessed with his case. Convinced that he is innocent, Bacall hides him in her San Francisco apartment. On a tip from a friendly cabbie, Vincent visits an underworld plastic surgeon who gives the fugitive a new face—thereby enabling him to dodge the authorities and find his wife's real murderer.

Coming just one year after LADY IN THE LAKE, this mystery likewise employs a subjective camera technique in which the viewer sees the action through Vincent's "eyes." The chief difference, however, is the ability to integrate the technique into the film's plastic surgery plot twist. The audience does not see Vincent's (Bogart's) face until after the bandages are removed (more than an hour into the film) and, since we haven't seen his face until that point, the switch isn't very interesting. And since the narration up until then has been by Bogie, it's impossible not to imagine you've seen him all through the film. No one else ever inflected like that. At the time of this movie, Bogart was Hollywood's highest paid actor, making more than $450,000 a year.

DARK STAR   **DVD**

1975 83m   c   Science Fiction   ★★½
Jack H. Harris   (U.S.)   G

Brian Narelle *(Doolittle)*, Andreijah Pahich *(Talby)*, Carl Kuniholm *(Boiler)*, Dan O'Bannon *(Pinback)*, Joe Sanders *(Powell)*

p, John Carpenter; d, John Carpenter; w, John Carpenter, Dan O'Bannon; ph, Douglas Knapp (Metrocolor); ed, Dan O'Bannon; m, John Carpenter; prod d, Dan O'Bannon; fx, Dan O'Bannon, Bill Taylor

John (HALLOWEEN) Carpenter's first directorial effort, an intermittently hilarious satire on 2001—A SPACE ODYSSEY. Carpenter's spaceship is piloted by four goofy astronauts who live like slobs and are bored out of their skulls by their long, uneventful mission. The crew is leaderless because their commander has died during the voyage and is kept in a freezer; somehow he is still able grudgingly to give his men advice when need be. Also in the ship are two talking computers and a pet alien that looks like a red beachball with claws (one of the consistently funny things in the movie). The film is a series of vignettes detailing how the men deal with their boredom, and it eventually sees one of the crew, Narelle, surfing through space on a board-shaped piece of debris. Dan O'Bannon, who would later go on to write ALIEN, cowrote the screenplay and was in charge of the set design and special effects. Carpenter shot half the film on 16mm as his thesis project for the University of Southern California film school. Hoping to get major financing from a studio to expand the film (as George Lucas did with his thesis THX 1138), he dropped out of school and went hunting for investors. Eventually, a Canadian investor gave him enough money to blow up the 16mm footage to 35mm, which led to exploitation distributor Jack Harris financing the rest of the project (which allowed for a modicum of special effects). Unfortunately, Harris's company went broke, and the rights to the film went to Bryanston, who had distributed THE TEXAS CHAINSAW MASSACRE. The film eventually got some bookings, but it never really caught on until it hit the midnight-show circuit.

DARK VICTORY   **DVD**

1939 105m   bw   Drama   ★★★★
Warner Bros. (U.S.)

Bette Davis *(Judith Traherne)*, George Brent *(Dr. Frederick Steele)*, Humphrey Bogart *(Michael O'Leary)*, Geraldine Fitzgerald *(Ann King)*, Ronald Reagan *(Alec Hamin)*, Henry Travers *(Dr. Parsons)*, Cora Witherspoon *(Carrie Spottswood)*, Virginia Brissac *(Martha)*, Dorothy Peterson *(Miss Wainwright)*, Charles Richman *(Colonel Mantle)*

p, David Lewis; d, Edmund Goulding; w, Casey Robinson (based on the play by George Emerson Brewer, Jr. and Bertram Bloch); ph, Ernest Haller; ed, William Holmes; m, Max Steiner; art d, Robert Haas; cos, Orry-Kelly

AAN Best Picture; AAN Best Actress: Bette Davis; AAN Best Original Score: Max Steiner

Davis is the centerpiece of this film version of the Tallulah Bankhead stage vehicle, faring better early on when she slams through her scenes in her most hyperthyroid manner. She knows it's cliché stuff, and she's determined to wow you anyhow—barking in her most clipped manner, guzzling cocktails with "little Ronnie Reagan" (as Davis always called him), and brandishing her riding crop at miscast stablehand Bogie.

When hedonistic heiress Davis discovers she has a brain tumor, the pace drops to allow romance in the form of George Brent, her doctor. Thank God she stiff-upper-lips it through their short-lived marriage; he's the soggiest newlywed ever,

and looks as if his practice consists of trimming his pencil thin mustache. There is a fine assist from lovely newcomer Geraldine Fitzgerald, as Davis's best girlfriend and Edmund Goulding has elevated the form whenever he can. Unfortunately, when Davis climbs the stairs for the last time, composer Max Steiner goes with her. Remade in 1963 as STOLEN HOURS.

DARKMAN   **DVD**

1990 96m   c   Action/Science Fiction   ★★★½
Robert Tapert   (U.S.)   R

Liam Neeson *(Peyton Westlake/Darkman)*, Frances McDormand *(Julie Hastings)*, Colin Friels *(Louis Strack, Jr.)*, Larry Drake *(Robert G. Durant)*, Jenny Agutter *(Doctor—uncredited)*, Nelson Mashita *(Yakitito)*, Jesse Lawrence Ferguson *(Eddie Black)*, Rafael H. Robledo *(Rudy Guzman)*, Danny Hicks *(Skip)*, Ted Raimi, billed as Theodore Raimi *(Rick)*

p, Robert Tapert; d, Sam Raimi; w, Chuck Pfarrer, Sam Raimi, Ivan Raimi, Daniel Goldin, Joshua Goldin (based on a story by Sam Raimi); ph, Bill Pope (Deluxe Color); ed, Bud Smith, Scott Smith, David Stiven; m, Danny Elfman; prod d, Randy Ser; art d, Phil Dagort; fx, Introvision Systems International, FourWard Productions, Tony Gardner, Larry Hamlin; cos, Grania Preston; anim, Chiodo Brothers Productions, Kevin Kutchaver, Jammie Friday

DARKMAN is a deliriously energetic comic-book movie from Sam Raimi, the young mastermind behind the uproariously funny and gory EVIL DEAD movies. While the press doted on the likes of David Lynch and the Coen brothers (Joel worked as an assistant editor on THE EVIL DEAD) in 1990, this cutting-edge independent filmmaker came to Hollywood with a relative lack of fanfare to make this ambitious, hallucinatory adventure. Though relatively low budget, the manic cinematic virtuosity on display here would have been welcome in BATMAN. DARKMAN's only weakness is its rather hokey and disjointed screenplay. But why carp? At its best, the film suggests a Universal horror film of the Thirties on LSD.

Peyton Westlake (Liam Neeson) is a scientist working on a formula for artificial skin. Peyton's girl friend, Julie (Frances McDormand), a lawyer working for crooked developer Strack (Colin Friels), stumbles on a memo revealing that Strack is actually an urban megalomaniac bent on taking over the city. Strack sends his thugs to Peyton's lab to find Julie; she's not there, and the thugs blow up Peyton and his lab. Presumed dead by Julie, Peyton is cared for by an odd "doctor" (the uncredited Jenny Agutter). She tries a radical new pain therapy that turns Peyton into a raving, adrenaline-pumped, superhuman schizophrenic. He slips out of the hospital and re-creates his artificial skin lab in an abandoned factory. From there, he plots his revenge and works on winning back Julie while wearing various "masks" of skin.

DARKMAN has much going for it. It boasts the right look and even the right sound, owing to another thundering, mock-operatic score by BATMAN composer Danny Elfman. The film is visually riveting. Melodramatically canted camera angles, audacious shock cuts and eccentric lap dissolves abound. DARKMAN offers bigger-than-life villains, an intriguingly flawed hero, and a tough, appealing heroine—all portrayed by terrific actors. It's a darkly amusing treat.

DARLING   **DVD**

1965 128m   bw   Drama   ★★★
Vic/Appia   (U.K.)

Laurence Harvey *(Miles Brand)*, Dirk Bogarde *(Robert Gold)*, Julie Christie *(Diana Scott)*, Roland Curram *(Malcolm)*, Jose-Luis de Vilallonga *(Cesare)*, Alex Scott *(Sean Martin)*, Basil Henson *(Alec*

Prosser-Jones), Helen Lindsay (Felicity Prosser-Jones), Pauline Yates (Estelle Gold), Tyler Butterworth (William Prosser-Jones)

p, Joseph Janni; d, John Schlesinger; w, Frederic Raphael (based on a story by Raphael, Schlesinger, and Janni); ph, Ken Higgins; ed, James B. Clark; m, John Dankworth; cos, Julie Harris

---

AAN Best Picture; AA Best Actress: Julie Christie; AAN Best Director: John Schlesinger; AA Best Original Story and Screenplay: Frederic Raphael; AA Best Costume Design (B/W): Julie Harris

The British New Wave turns inward and eats itself alive—unwittingly. If the movie is overrated, it's still interesting to watch it collapse upon itself. One decade earlier, the censorship standards would have truncated this film to a point that it would not have made sense. Today it appears nervous and shallow, a metaphor for the empty values it claims to take to task. Julie Christie is the amoral heroine who drifts into success casually, like she's changing panties—she models, does a bit in films, deserts a husband, deceives a lover, drifts through affairs; it takes about 20 minutes to get that she doesn't "feel complete," and we understand, even if we can't pay our bills. Marilyn Monroe and a multitude of others found out fame wasn't what it was cracked up to be. But where a Marilyn differs from The Darling is that the latter is an empty person and always was. She's like Madonna with low blood sugar doing an old Lana Turner script—but cool. She may be miserable, but at least the future is rich with tears, rather than poor.

Christie is the main reason to tune in——she's very beautiful and accomplished in a brittle sort of way. Her performance won awards all over the place, but she can't supply emotions the story and character won't let her have. Its a Best Actress in a Vacuum turn, and we defy you to feel a single thing.

DARLING LILI
1970 136m c Musical/Spy ★★★½
Geoffrey (U.S.) G

Julie Andrews (Lili Smith), Rock Hudson (Maj. William Larrabee), Jeremy Kemp (Kurt von Ruger), Lance Percival (Lt. Carstairs, TC), Jacques Marin (Maj. Duvalle), Michael Witney (Lt. George Youngblood Carson), Andre Maranne (Lt. Liggett), Bernard Kay (Bedford), Doreen Keogh (Emma), Gloria Paul (Suzette)

p, Blake Edwards; d, Blake Edwards; w, Blake Edwards, William Peter Blatty; ph, Russell Harlan (Panavision, Technicolor); ed, Peter Zinner; m, Henry Mancini, Johnny Mercer; prod d, Fernando Carrere; fx, Van Der Veer Photo Effects, Bob Peterson, Rex Wimpy, Linwood Dunn; chor, Hermes Pan; cos, Jack Bear, Donald Brooks

---

AAN Best Original Song Score: Henry Mancini (Music), Johnny Mercer (Lyrics); AAN Best Original Song: "Whistling Away in the Dark"; Henry Mancini (Music), Johnny Mercer (Lyrics); AAN Best Costume Design: Donald Brooks, Jack Bear

Perfectly fine. Blake Edwards's big-budget WWI espionage melodrama stars Julie Andrews as Lili, a Mata Hari-like German spy using her wiles to get information from Allied officers. At first a music-hall favorite singing old-fashioned ditties, Lili eventually incorporates a bit of striptease into her staid act. She proves herself less a hard-hearted spy than a vulnerable woman when she falls in love with American flier Rock Hudson and cannot bring herself to betray him. The film came along at a time when the musical genre was struggling to redefine itself, and its theme of innocence in everything was taking a back seat to jaded knowingness in all art forms. LILI was a commercial failure, and everyone jumped on the bandwagon to lay Andrews out. Time has proven everyone wrong. Diverting, tuneful score by Henry Mancini and Johnny

Mercer includes the lovely, Oscar-nominated "Whistling Away the Dark."

DAS BOOT
1981 150m c War
Bavaria Atelier (West Germany) ★★★★
R

Jurgen Prochnow (Captain), Herbert Gronemeyer (Lt. Werner/Correspondent), Klaus Wennemann (Chief Engineer), Hubertus Bengsch (1st Lt./Number One), Martin Semmelrogge (2nd Lieutenant), Bernd Tauber (Chief Quartermaster), Erwin Leder (Johann "The Ghost"), Martin May (Midshipman Ullmann), Heinz Honig (Hinrich), U.A. Ochsen (Chief Bosun)

p, Gunter Rohrbach; d, Wolfgang Petersen; w, Wolfgang Petersen (based on the novel by Lothar-Gunther Buchheim); ph, Jost Vacano (Fujicolor); ed, Hannes Nikel; m, Klaus Doldinger; prod d, Rolf Zehetbauer; art d, Gotz Weidner; fx, Karl Baumgartner; cos, Monika Bauert

---

AAN Best Director: Wolfgang Petersen; AAN Best Adapted Screenplay: Wolfgang Petersen; AAN Best Cinematography: Jost Vacano; AAN Best Film Editing: Hannes Nikel; AAN Best Sound: Milan Bor, Trevor Pyke, Mike Le-Mare; AAN Best Sound Effects Editing: Mike Le-Mare

Gripping and authentic; based on the experiences of photographer Lothar-Guenther Buchheim, this superbly filmed action movie chronicles a U-boat voyage in 1941, detailing above- and below-the-surface horrors as well as the mundane hours that characterize time spent at sea. Though most of the footage concentrates on the intense, noble captain, Jurgen Prochnow, the only fully developed "character" in the film is the boat, as it undergoes numerous attacks. Decidedly anti-Nazi in tone, THE BOAT presents the crew as individual warriors upholding their own brand of honor and sneering at Hitler's Reich. The chief attraction of this film, however, is the incredible camerawork. Racing through the sub, squeezing through tiny openings, director Wolfgang Petersen's camera brilliantly evokes the claustrophobia and clamor of undersea battle. A technical marvel, THE BOAT is a breathtaking and powerful portrait of war and death. Though the film was originally released on videocassette as the subtitled DAS BOOT, most copies now available are dubbed into English.

DAUGHTER OF THE NILE
(NI-LO-HO NU-ERH)
1987 91m c Drama ★★★½
Fu-Film (Taiwan)

Yang Lin (Lin Hsiao-yang), Kao Jai (Lin Hsiao-fang, Brother), Yang Fan (Ah-sang), Li Tien-lu (Grandfather), Ts'ui Fu-sheng (Father), Hsing Shu-fen, Yu An-shun, Wu Nien-chen, Huang Ch'iung-yao

p, Lu Wen-jen, Ts'ai Sung-lin; d, Hou Hsiao-hsien; w, Chu T'ien-wen; ph, Ch'en Huai-en; ed, Liao Ch'ing-sung; m, Ch'en Cihyuan, Chang Hung-yi; prod d, Liu Chih-hua, Lin Chu

Another excellent film from Taiwanese director Hou Hsiao-hsien, who, along with Yang, is responsible for the international rise of Taiwanese cinema. A switch from the director's rural dramas, such as A SUMMER AT GRANDPA'S or A TIME TO LIVE AND A TIME TO DIE, the film is set in the heart of the city and focuses on a teenage girl, Yang Lin, and her troubled family. Her brother, Kao Jai, is a small-time thief whose crimes have intensified since the deaths of both their elder brother and their mother. Their father, Ts'ui Fu-sheng, stays away from home for long periods of time, leaving Yang Lin to care for the house, her brother, and her younger sister. Yang Lin's only escape comes in reading a popular comic book called "Daughter of the Nile," which is about a modern girl trapped in ancient Egypt who falls in love with a doomed boy king.

Although DAUGHTER OF THE NILE has more plot than any of Hou Hsiao-hsien's other work, it is still a movie made up of small, subtle moments with no strong narrative impetus. The director's visual style, greatly reminiscent of that of Japan's Yasujiro Ozu, makes use of deep-focus long takes that allow the action to unfold between the actors naturally, without the camera's becoming obtrusive. The film is like a picture puzzle, in which each unconnected piece eventually fits together to form a vivid picture of life in urban Taiwan. The cast is superb, with Taiwanese pop singer Yang Lin turning in a wonderful performance as the put-upon teen, Taipei fashion-boutique owner Kao Jai excellent as the brooding brother, and elderly Li T'ien-lu nearly stealing the film as the chatty old grandfather who constantly worries that the "neighbors will laugh" if his family doesn't behave.

DAVE

1993 110m c Comedy/Political ★★★½
Shuler-Donner Productions/Ivan Reitman PG-13
Productions (U.S.)

Kevin Kline *(Dave Kovic/President Bill Mitchell)*, Sigourney Weaver *(Ellen Mitchell)*, Frank Langella *(Bob Alexander)*, Kevin Dunn *(Alan Reed)*, Ving Rhames *(Duane Stevenson)*, Ben Kingsley *(Vice President Nance)*, Charles Grodin *(Murray Blum)*, Faoth Prince *(Alice)*, Laura Linney *(Randi)*, Bonnie Hunt *(White House Tour Guide)*

p, Lauren Shuler-Donner, Ivan Reitman; d, Ivan Reitman; w, Gary Ross; ph, Adam Greenberg; ed, Sheldon Kahn; m, James Newton Howard; prod d, J. Michael Riva; art d, David Klassen; fx, Buena Vista Visual Effects, Harrison Ellenshaw, David M. Blitstein; cos, Richard Hornung, Ann Roth

AAN Best Original Screenplay: Gary Ross

A winning blend of MR. SMITH GOES TO WASHINGTON and BEING THERE, DAVE gives Kevin Kline the best comic role of his screen career.

Kline plays the title character, a presidential look-alike asked to double for the Chief Executive for "security" reasons. (As Dave waves to the crowd en route to his limo, the President is taking a very secret meeting with an attractive secretary.) When the Prez suffers a massive stroke at a rather delicate moment, White House Chief of Staff Bob Alexander (Frank Langella) installs Dave in the Oval Office, rather than allow "boy scout" Vice-President Nance (Ben Kingsley) to assume power.

Gary Ross's script is a perfect showcase for Kline, who gleefully inhabits his dual role as the cynical, sleazy President and his earnest, naive double. He also gets fantastic support: Sigourney Weaver at her most icily bitchy as the First Lady ("Why couldn't you have died from a stroke like everyone else?"); Frank Langella as the suave, Machiavellian Chief of Staff; and Charles Grodin as a small-time accountant who, summoned to the White House by his old friend Dave, trims $650 million off the budget over a bratwurst dinner.

Add a host of cameo appearances by real-life personalities—"Tip" O'Neill applauds the President's new-found energy; J.F.K. director Oliver Stone is convinced the whole thing is a conspiracy—and the result is the funniest, savviest political comedy to come our way in some time.

DAVID AND BATHSHEBA

1951 116m c Religious ★★★½
Fox (U.S.)

Gregory Peck *(David)*, Susan Hayward *(Bathsheba)*, Raymond Massey *(Nathan)*, Kieron Moore *(Uriah)*, James Robertson Justice *(Abishai)*, Jayne Meadows *(Michal)*, John Sutton *(Ira)*, Dennis Hoey *(Joab)*, Walter Talun *(Goliath)*, Paula Morgan *(Adulteress)*

p, Darryl F. Zanuck; d, Henry King; w, Philip Dunne (based on biblical accounts); ph, Leon Shamroy (Technicolor); ed, Barbara McLean; m, Alfred Newman; art d, Lyle Wheeler, George W. Davis; fx, Fred Sersen; chor, Jack Cole; cos, Edward Stevenson

AAN Best Story and Screenplay: Philip Dunne; *AAN Best Color Cinematography:* Leon Shamroy; *AAN Best Score (Drama or Comedy):* Alfred Newman; *AAN Best Art Direction-Set Decoration (Color):* Lyle Wheeler (Art Direction), George W. Davis (Art Direction), Thomas Little (Set Decoration), Paul S. Fox (Set Decoration); *AAN Best Costume Design (Color):* Charles LeMaire, Edward Stevenson

Big-budget Biblical yucky muck. Peck plays stoic King David, fierce in battle but frail where temptresses trod. Having saved a cuckold in battle, he returns home to nurse a wound, instead nurses a raging…torch for the cuckold's wife, tempestuous Susan Hayward, acting within an inch of her insured head of tossing tendrils, whom he spots taking a bath. He, wisely, we say, dumps the first wife of his harem—the shrewish Jayne Meadows—that's right, Jayne Meadows! The cuckold gets sent to war and gets killed, Bathsheba marries David and a baby is born eight months, three-and-a-half weeks, six days and ten seconds later, but dies. The Lord sends Raymond Massey, as the prophet Nathan, to raise hell for their shameless ways and protest the famine that has been wrought upon the land. David sees the error of his ways, improvises the 23rd Psalm and the rains come and wash their sins away!

Typical lavish Hollywood Biblical treatment, but awash with juice, thanks to the force supplied by the three leads. Look for young Gwen Verdon as a specialty dancer. Perfect for a cold, rainy Sunday afternoon.

DAVID AND LISA

1962 95m bw Drama ★★★½
CONTINENTAL (U.S.)

Keir Dullea *(David)*, Janet Margolin *(Lisa)*, Howard da Silva *(Dr. Swinford)*, Neva Patterson *(Mrs. Clemens)*, Clifton James *(John)*, Richard McMurray *(Mr. Clemens)*, Nancy Nutter *(Maureen)*, Matthew Anden *(Simon)*, Coni Hudak *(Kate)*, Jaime Sanchez *(Carlos)*

p, Paul M. Heller; d, Frank Perry; w, Eleanor Perry (based on the book by Dr. Theodore Isaac Rubin); ph, Leonard Hirshfield; ed, Irving Oshman; m, Mark Lawrence; art d, Paul M. Heller; cos, Anna Hill Johnstone

AAN Best Director: Frank Perry; *AAN Best Adapted Screenplay:* Eleanor Perry

A big "little" film. Prior to this, there had been many films like THE SNAKE PIT and THE THREE FACES OF EVE, but the understated charm of DAVID AND LISA is what set the movie apart from so many other attempts at depicting the problems of the mentally ill. Dullea is a bright young man who cannot bear to be touched by anyone. His overly protective mother and father, Patterson and McMurray, leave him at the private school with da Silva, the intelligent doctor who runs the institution which caters to children with mental problems. Margolin is a very troubled schizophrenic who talks in rhyme and is deeply ensconced in her shell. The two meet, and the gradual falling-in-love story is what forms the basis for the film. As they begin to trust each other, Dullea is able to be touched and Margolin feels secure enough to reveal her emotions.

The story was based on a real case history by Dr. T.I. Rubin, and Eleanor Perry handled the screenplay with tact and subtle care that avoids mawkishness. This is a thoughtful, poignant film with a documentary feel; there are enough comic moments and a welcome absence of psychiatric jargon. Frank Perry's direction won an award at the Venice Film Festival in 1962. Margolin and Dullea were honored as best actress and actor at the San Francisco Film Festival.

DAVID COPPERFIELD
1935 133m bw Drama   ★★★★½
MGM   (U.S.)

W.C. Fields *(Micawber)*, Lionel Barrymore *(Dan Peggotty)*, Maureen O'Sullivan *(Dora)*, Frank Lawton *(David Copperfield)*, Madge Evans *(Agnes)*, Edna May Oliver *(Aunt Betsey)*, Lewis Stone *(Mr. Wickfield)*, Freddie Bartholomew *(David as Child)*, Elizabeth Allan *(Mrs. Copperfield)*, Roland Young *(Uriah Heep)*

p, David O. Selznick; d, George Cukor; w, Howard Estabrook, Hugh Walpole (based on the novel by Charles Dickens); ph, Oliver T. Marsh; ed, Robert J. Kern; m, Herbert Stothart; art d, Cedric Gibbons; fx, Slavko Vorkapich; cos, Dolly Tree

AAN Best Picture; AAN Best Assistant Director: Joseph Newman; *AAN Best Film Editing:* Robert J. Kern

Directed with restraint and impeccable taste by Cukor, produced by Selznick, DAVID COPPERFIELD is diverse and satisfying intellectually and emotionally, capturing the unparalleled beauty of Dickens's melancholic truths about life's hardships and human survival. The entire cast perform admirably, but of course it is Fields's Micawber which has achieved immortality. Despite the absence of accent, it still appears he was born to play the role, and it's the only time the Great Man allowed any heart to seep through on screen. Dickens died in 1870 at the age of 58, leaving his final work, *The Mystery of Edwin Drood*, unfinished, which didn't stop Universal from making it into a movie also released in 1935. Doubtless, he would have been thrilled at DAVID COPPERFIELD and bored with the latter.

DAVID HOLZMAN'S DIARY
1968 74m bw Drama/Experimental   ★★★★
Paradigm   (U.S.)

L.M. Kit Carson *(David Holzman)*, Eileen Dietz *(Penny Wohl)*, Louise Levine *(Sandra)*, Lorenzo Mans *(Pepe)*, Fern McBride *(Girl on the Subway)*, Mike Levine *(Sandra's Boyfriend)*, Bob Lesser *(Max, Penny's Agent)*, Jack Baran *(Cop)*

p, Jim McBride; d, Jim McBride; w, Jim McBride; ph, Michael Wadleigh, Paul Glickman, Paul Goldsmith; ed, Jim McBride

A unique, often brilliant satire on *cinema verite*, this "fake documentary" was shot in only five days on a $2,500 budget. Carson plays a young New York filmmaker who decides to get a handle on his life by putting it all down on film. Things don't go entirely as planned, however. His girlfriend leaves him in annoyance because he's constantly filming her, his artist friend Pepe (Mans) tells him that his concept is invalid, and the police punch him for harassing people with his camera. Gradually he grows more desperate as it becomes obvious that his life is only getting more confusing on film. One day he announces to the camera that he has to go to his uncle's funeral in New Jersey. In the next scene we see photographs of David of the type taken by coin-operated booths. His voice on a scratchy record says that he is making this recording in another coin-operated booth and that when he returned from New Jersey that day, he found his apartment broken into and all his equipment stolen. He tries to come to some conclusion about his life and this project but is ultimately unable to do so.

One of cinema's most pointed statements about the impossibility of objectivity in film, DAVID HOLZMAN'S DIARY breaks down the comfortable position audiences usually enjoy while watching most mainstream films. Spectators unfamiliar with experimental cinema often resent being

fooled by the documentary style of the film, which highlights the concept that "documentary" is a style of filmmaking more than it is a means of presenting "truth" in some unmediated way. Unafraid to present and implicitly criticize the more unpleasant sides of its "hero," at once witty and strangely touching, this provocative, endlessly self-conscious film today stands as one of the best independent films of the 1960s. How ironically appropriate that semi-underground filmmaker McBride later went mainstream himself, offering us modern revamps of old Hollywood ideas (THE BIG EASY, GREAT BALLS OF FIRE) or attempts to recreate the magic of other innovative landmarks (BREATHLESS).

DAWN OF THE DEAD
1979 125m c Horror   ★★★★
Dawn Associates/Laurel Group   (U.S.)

David Emge *(Stephen)*, Ken Foree *(Peter)*, Scott Reininger *(Roger)*, Gaylen Ross *(Francine)*, David Crawford *(Dr. Foster)*, David Early *(Mr. Berman)*, Richard France *(Scientist)*, Howard K. Smith *(Television Commentator)*, James A. Baffico *(Wooley)*, George A. Romero *(Television Director)*

p, Richard P. Rubinstein, Herbert Steinmann, Billy Baxter, Alfredo Cuomo; d, George Romero; w, George Romero; ph, Michael Gornick (Technicolor); ed, George Romero, Kenneth Davidow; m, Dario Argento, Goblin; fx, Gary Zeller, Don Berry; cos, Josie Caruso

One of the key horror films of the 1970s (a particularly fecund period for the genre), George Romero's apocalyptic followup to his classic NIGHT OF THE LIVING DEAD (1968) abandons easy scare tactics in favor of a darkly satirical assault on bourgeois culture, traditional notions of masculinity, and rampant consumerism. Zesty contributions from cinematographer Michael Gornick and special makeup effects mastermind Tom Savini help make this feel like a brightly colored action comic book peppered with gruesome (but not gratuitous) violence. Celebrated Italian horror maestro Dario Argento (SUSPIRIA, DEEP RED) co-produced and provided the lively rock score with his band, Goblin. Though all of the performances are at least adequate, this is not an actor's movie. Believe it or not, this is a film about ideas as well as gore. Nonetheless, this is strong medicine and not for all tastes.

In DAWN the recently dead are still returning to life and eating the flesh of the living but the phenomena has spread to nationwide if not worldwide proportions. A brutal police assault on a minority housing project that occurs early in the film expands upon the conclusion of NIGHT. We see that in the eyes of the law, there is little difference between political radicals, innocent bystanders of color, and carnivorous zombies. Ross, an employee of a local television station, and her boyfriend Emge, a traffic helicopter pilot, decide to try to escape the madness in a helicopter accompanied by two SWAT team cops, Reiniger and Foree. They eventually land atop a shopping mall. Once they clear out the zombies, the four decide to remain in this shoppers' paradise where they get to live out their wildest consumer fantasies until they are forced to defend themselves from marauding bikers who want to crash their party.

Romero's films tend to be left of center in outlook: ethnically and sexually integrated, pro-feminist, gay-friendly, anti-macho, and skeptical about capitalism, they represent a progressive aspect of the genre. His "living dead" movies are among the Pittsburgh-based auteur's most personal efforts. So terrifying in their initial incarnation, the zombies in DAWN have become rather pathetic (though still very dangerous) eating machines. Nuns, clowns, and Hare Krishnas number among their ranks as they return to the mall they loved in life. "They are us," one of the characters wryly observes. This independently produced low budget film ($1.5 million) went on to become one of the most profitable "indies" in film history. DAY OF THE DEAD, ostensibly the conclusion of the DEAD series, followed in 1985.

DAWN OF THE DEAD   *DVD*

2004 97m   c   Horror   ★★½
Strike Entertainment/New Amsterdam Entertainment/   R
Universal   (U.S.)

Sarah Polley *(Ana Clark)*, Ving Rhames *(Kenneth)*, Jake Weber *(Michael)*, Mekhi Phifer *(Andre)*, Ty Burrell *(Steve)*, Michael Kelly *(CJ)*, Kevin Zegers *(Terry)*, Michael Barry *(Bart)*, Lindy Booth *(Nicole)*, Tom Savini *(The Sheriff)*

p, Marc Abraham, Eric Newman, Richard P. Rubinstein; d, Zack Snyder; w, James Gunn (based on the screenplay by George A. Romero); ph, Matthew F. Leonetti; ed, Niven Howie; m, Tyler Bates; prod d, Andrew Neskoromny; art d, Arv Grewal; fx, Dennis Berardi, Bob Hall (zombie effects), Laird McMurray, Aaron Weintraub; cos, Denise Cronenberg

Given that there was no need for a new DAWN OF THE DEAD, first-time feature director Zack Snyder's "re-envisioning" could be much worse. A buzzed-up gloss on the original, it's entertaining, if fundamentally shallow.

Ana (Sarah Polley) comes home from a 13-hour nursing shift to her home in a suburban Wisconsin development filled with neatly manicured lawns and friendly neighbors. She wakes up to a world turned upside-down: There's panic in the streets, and emergency services are too overwhelmed to respond. Ana narrowly escapes immediate danger, only to find herself adrift in a world in which sprinting packs of reanimated corpses chase and drag down the hapless living like hounds on a hart. She and four other survivors—street thug Andre (Mekhi Pfifer) and his hugely pregnant wife (Inna Korobkina), police officer Kenneth (Ving Rhames), and quietly pragmatic Michael (Jake Weber)—take refuge in a shopping mall, where they form an uneasy alliance with security guards CJ (Michael Kelly), Terry (Kevin Zegers), and Bart (Michael Barry). As the situation outside degenerates and it becomes increasingly apparent that there's no help coming, the survivors jockey for control.

Snyder and screenwriter James Gunn strip away most of the original film's dark satire, and relationships take a backseat to action sequences. That said, Snyder directs action skillfully, and the zombie hoards are as nasty as they ought to be. The ending is suitably downbeat, and Snyder allocates respectful cameo appearances to original DAWN cast members Scott Reiniger, Tom Savini, and Ken Foree, who utters the immortal line, "When there's no more room in hell, the dead will walk the Earth." Gaylen Ross, the first film's female lead, lends her name to a mall store.

DAWN PATROL, THE

1938 103m   bw   War   ★★★★
Warner Bros.   (U.S.)

Errol Flynn *(Courtney)*, David Niven *(Scott)*, Basil Rathbone *(Major Brand)*, Donald Crisp *(Phills)*, Melville Cooper *(Watkins)*, Barry Fitzgerald *(Bott)*, Carl Esmond *(Von Mueller)*, Peter Willes *(Hollister)*, Morton Lowry *(Johnnie Scott)*, Michael Brooke *(Squires)*

p, Robert Lord; d, Edmund Goulding; w, Seton I. Miller, Dan Totheroh (based on the story "The Flight Commander" by John Monk Saunders); ph, Tony Gaudio; ed, Ralph Dawson; m, Max Steiner; art d, John Hughes; fx, Edwin DuPar

A superbly-cast remake of Hawks's 1930 picture of the same name, THE DAWN PATROL concerns a dashing, conscience-haunted flight commander, Capt. Courtney (Errol Flynn), of the 59th Squadron in France during WWI. He and his men fly the most dangerous aircraft—a source of Courtney's anger which he attempts to cover with banter and cynical humor—creating unsafe odds for the fliers and contributing to their untimely deaths. The fatalities mount so drastically that raw recruits with little flying experience are sent into the skies to battle without much chance of survival. Between the daily dawn patrols that decimate the command, the fliers face death with stiff upper lips and scotch and sodas at the club bar, where a battered gramophone continually grinds out the plaintive "Poor Butterfly." In another room sits Maj. Brand (Basil Rathbone), the deskbound commander whose job it is to assign fliers to each dawn patrol, mechanically writing their names on a blackboard and methodically erasing those killed each day. Later, when Brand is reassigned, Courtney is called on to replace him; now it is he who must decide which flier will take off to face a certain death. Though the original story of Hawks's film was retained, the dialogue was rewritten and polished to great improvement, chiefly in the relationship between Courtney and his best pal, Lt. Scott (David Niven). As in the original (or in Hawks's AIR FORCE), the remake is very much concerned with fraternity, loyalty, and courage in the face of death.

DAY AFTER TOMORROW, THE   *DVD*

2004 124m   c   Disaster/Adventure   ★★
Centropolis Entertainment/Lions Gate Films/   PG-13
Mark Gordon company/20th Century Fox   (U.S.)

Dennis Quaid *(Jack Hall)*, Jake Gyllenhaal *(Sam Hall)*, Emmy Rossum *(Laura Chapman)*, Dash Mihok *(Jason Evans)*, Jay O. Sanders *(Frank Harris)*, Sela Ward *(Dr. Lucy Hall)*, Austin Nichols *(J.D.)*, Arjay Smith *(Brian Parks)*, Tamlyn Tomita *(Janet Tokada)*, Kenneth Walsh *(Vice-President Becker)*

p, Roland Emmerich, Mark Gordon; d, Roland Emmerich; w, Roland Emmerich, Jeffrey Nachmanoff (based on a story by Roland Emmerich, suggested in part by *The Coming Global Superstorm* by Art Bell and Whitley Streiber); ph, Ueli Steiger; ed, David Brenner; m, Harald Kloser; prod d, Barry Chusid; art d, Marc Bonin, Martin Gendron, Michele LaLiberte, Real Proulx; fx, Louis Craig, Karen E. Goulekas, Jim Mitchell, Ryan Storm; cos, Renee April

Roland Emmerich's eco-conscious disaster picture features breakout performances by the twisters that suck up the "Hollywood" sign, the killing frost that covers the Statue of Liberty, and the tsunami that swamps Manhattan. If only the flesh-and-blood cast had such material with which to work.

Divorced workaholic paleoclimatologist Jack Hall (Dennis Quaid) tries to warn the world's leaders that global warming is melting the polar ice caps and paving the way for a new ice age. But between America's namby-pamby president (Perry King) and anti-environmentalist vice-president (Kenneth Walsh), his admonitions fall on deaf ears until the global climate goes wild. Faster than you can say "Strange Weather," snow blankets India, softball-sized hunks of hail pelt Tokyo, and soaking rains swamp New York City, where Jack's vaguely estranged 17-year-old son, Sam (Jake Gyllenhaal), is competing in an academic decathlon. Hall finally has the government's attention, but it's too late to do much more than evacuate the southern half of the country to Mexico and leave everyone up North to freeze. Jack's ex-wife, Dr. Lucy Hall (Sela Ward), maintains a selfless vigil by the bedside of a critically ill child while Jack and his loyal associates (Dash Mihok, Jay O. Sanders) trudge from Washington, D.C., to New York to rescue Sam.

Like Emmerich's INDEPENDENCE and GODZILLA, this popcorn scare picture is a lopsided mix of top-shelf spectacle and cut-rate casting. The spectacle is undeniably spectacular, though many of the CGI effects are so patently artificial they seem more suited to a video game than a major motion picture. The generally competent B-list actors are hobbled by cliché-ridden dialogue but do their best to react in remotely plausible ways each time the script nails them with some new melodramatic contrivance.

DAY AT THE RACES, A
1937   109m   c/bw   Comedy/Musical   ★★★½
MGM   (U.S.)

Groucho Marx (*Dr. Hugo Z. Hackenbush*), Chico Marx (*Tony*), Harpo Marx (*Stuffy*), Allan Jones (*Gil*), Maureen O'Sullivan (*Judy*), Margaret Dumont (*Mrs. Upjohn*), Leonard Ceeley (*Whitmore*), Douglas Dumbrille (*Morgan*), Esther Muir ("*Flo*"), Sig Rumann (*Dr. Steinberg*)

p, Max Siegel, Sam Wood; d, Sam Wood; w, Robert Pirosh, George Seaton, George Oppenheimer (based on a story by Pirosh and Seaton); ph, Joseph Ruttenberg; ed, Frank E. Hull; m, Bronislau Kaper, Walter Jurmann, Gus Kahn; art d, Cedric Gibbons; chor, Dave Gould

AAN Best Dance Direction: Dave Gould

Hugo Z. Hackenbush (Groucho Marx) is a horse doctor who takes over a large sanitarium at the behest of hypochondriac socialite Mrs. Upjohn (Margaret Dumont). The sanitarium is owned by Judy (Maureen O'Sullivan), but she's having trouble paying off the mortgage. With the help of Stuffy (Harpo Marx), Tony (Chico Marx), and a racehorse named Hi-Hat, she is able to save the hospital. Of course, the plot isn't important here; what really counts is the steady stream of wild comedy routines provided by the Marx Brothers who poke fun at everything from the medical profession to high society.

Striving for a worthy follow-up to the magnificent A NIGHT AT THE OPERA, the comedians took their act on the road and performed these routines before live audiences throughout the country. The opulent, though somewhat dull, musical production numbers prevent this from being as mesmerizing as its predecessor, but while dated, A DAY AT THE RACES is, nonetheless, a very entertaining comedy. Producer Irving Thalberg, to whom the Marxes were devoted, died during production.

DAY FOR NIGHT
(LA NUIT AMERICAINE)
1973   120m   c   Drama   ★★★★★
Carrosse/PECF/PIC   (France)   PG

Francois Truffaut (*Ferrand*), Jacqueline Bisset (*Julie Baker*), Jean-Pierre Leaud (*Alphonse*), Valentina Cortese (*Severine*), Jean-Pierre Aumont (*Alexandre*), Dani (*Lilianna*), Alexandra Stewart (*Stacey*), Jean Champion (*Bertrand*), Nathalie Baye (*Joelle*), Bernard Menez (*Bernard, the Prop Man*)

p, Marcel Berbert; d, Francois Truffaut; w, Francois Truffaut, Suzanne Schiffman, Jean-Louis Richard; ph, Pierre-William Glenn (Eastmancolor); ed, Yann Dedet, Martine Barraque; m, Georges Delerue; art d, Damien Lanfranchi; cos, Monique Dury

AAN Best Supporting Actress: Valentina Cortese; *AAN Best Director:* Francois Truffaut; *AAN Best Original Screenplay:* Francois Truffaut, Jean-Louis Richard, Suzanne Schiffman; *AA Best Foreign Language Film*

One of the best films ever made about the process of shooting a film. Director Truffaut plays director Ferrand, who is in the midst of directing "I Want You to Meet Pamela," a feature being shot in the La Victorine studios in the south of France. His cast includes a temperamental actor, Alphonse (Jean-Pierre Leaud), who wonders aloud, "Are women magic?"; Julie (Jacqueline Bisset), a famous actress recovering from a nervous breakdown; Alexandre (Jean-Pierre Aumont), a veteran actor, "continental lover" and closet homosexual;

Severine (Valentina Cortese), a loud, alcoholic Italian actress who once was a great screen lover opposite Alexandre but who now cannot remember even the simplest dialogue; and Stacey (Alexandra Stewart), a bit player whose pregnancy causes terrible scheduling problems. Given equal time is Ferrand's crew—bumbling prop man Bernard (Bernard Menez); flaky makeup girl Odile (Nike Arrighi); script girl Lilianna (Dani), who cares nothing for film and gets the job only because she sleeps with Alphonse; unit manager Lajoie (Gaston Joly); producer Bertrand (Jean Champion); and the all-important production assistant, Joelle (Nathalie Baye).

As one might expect, the characters themselves are more important than the thin plot—Ferrand trying to keep his production on track when his emotionally unstable leads, Alphonse and Julie, make the mistake of sleeping together for just one night. Full of in jokes and cross-references, DAY FOR NIGHT is ample proof that what goes on behind the screen is often of more interest than the film itself. Paradoxically, it is also one of Truffaut's least personal films, as he hides behind his alter ego Ferrand and interacts only on the most superficial levels with his cast and crew. By the film's end, it is Ferrand whom we know least.

DAY I BECAME A WOMAN, THE
(ROOZI KHE ZAN SHODAM)
2000   78m   c   Drama   ★★★★
Makhmalbaf Film House   (Iran)

"Hava": Fatemeh Cheragh Akhtar (*Hava*), Hassan Nebhan (*Hassan*), Shahr Banou Sisizadeh (*Mother*), Ameneh Passand (*Grandmother*), "Ahoo": Shabnam Toloui (*Ahoo*), Cyrus Kahouri Nejad (*Husband*), Mahram Zeinal Zadeh (*Osmann*), Nourieh Mahiguiran (*Rival Cyclist*), "Hoora": Azizeh Seddighi (*Hoora*), Badr Irouni Nejad (*Young Boy*)

p, Mohsen Makhmalbaf; d, Marzieh Meshkini; w, Mohsen Makhmalbaf; ph, Mohammad Ahmadi ("Hava"), Ebraheem Ghafouri ("Ahoo" and "Hoora"); ed, Mayssam Makhmalbaf ("Hava"), Shahrzad Pouya ("Ahoo" and "Hoora"); m, Mohammad Reza Darvishi

Three loosely connected half-hour films add up to one powerful indictment of the onerous daily restrictions women face in contemporary Iran.

In the first, Hava (Fatemeh Cheragh Akhtar) is celebrating her ninth birthday. As her mother (Shahr Banou Sisizadeh) and grandmother (Ameneh Passand) prepare her first chador—the head-to-toe covering that these observant Islamic women must wear—Hava begs for permission to join her friend Hassan (Hassan Nebhan) for ice cream. But life isn't so simple anymore: Hava is now considered a woman, and must obey the rules that will govern her dress and behavior for the rest of her life. In the second episode, a young wife presses the boundaries of her freedom by entering a women's bicycle race. As Ahoo (Shabnam Toloui) pedals along an endless track by the seashore, her husband (Cyrus Kahouri Nejad) pursues her on horseback and threatens to divorce her if she doesn't drop out. In a startling show of assertiveness, Ahoo refuses. In the final vignette, elderly, wheelchair-bound Hoora (Azizeh Seddighi) commandeers a group of boys to follow her around the city as she spends her savings on all the consumer goods she always wanted. As she works her way down her wish list, Hoora unties the "reminding strings" she has wrapped around her fingers until there's only one puzzling bit of cloth left. Bereft of love, children and companionship, Hoora can't figure out what's missing.

Written by maverick Iranian director Mohsen Makhmalbaf (GABBEH) and directed with extraordinary refinement by his young wife, Marzieh Meshkini, this is one of a handful of films to come out of the now defunct Makhmalbaf Film House. The school never gained government approval, and if this deceptively straightforward film is any indication, it's plain why. It's a bold, vibrant piece of filmmaking that dares not only to question the justice of sexist orthodoxy, but to demonstrate the poignancy of lives trapped and twisted within its confines.

DAY OF THE DEAD

DVD

1985   102m   c   Horror   ★★★½
Laurel   (U.S.)

Lori Cardille *(Sarah)*, Terry Alexander *(John)*, Joseph Pilato *(Capt. Rhodes)*, Jarlath Conroy *(McDermott)*, Antone DiLeo Jr. *(Miguel)*, Richard Liberty *(Dr. Logan)*, Howard Sherman *(Bub)*, Gary Howard Klar *(Steel)*, Ralph Marrero *(Rickles)*, John Amplas *(Fisher)*

p, Richard P. Rubinstein; d, George Romero; w, George Romero; ph, Michael Gornick; ed, Pasquale Buba; m, John Harrison; prod d, Cletus Anderson; art d, Bruce Miller; fx, Tom Savini, Steve Kirshoff, Mark Mann; cos, Barbara Anderson

The third, and perhaps last, chapter in George Romero's "Living Dead" series is a claustrophobic character study set almost entirely in a huge underground storage facility that has been converted into a laboratory and barracks. The military has been assigned to protect and assist the group of scientists (Lori Cardille, John Amplas, and Richard Liberty) who are working to develop a solution to the zombie epidemic, experimenting on zombies who have been herded into a holding pen. One scientist, Liberty—nicknamed "Frankenstein" by the soldiers—tries to modify the zombies' behavior so that humans can train them like dogs. One zombie, whom Liberty calls "Bub," seems to be the missing link between animal instinct and civilized human behavior. The operation has taken its toll on the soldiers, however, and their commander, the near-psychotic Joseph Pilato, tries to take over the project and put an end to it.

Fans of the first two films in the series may be a bit dismayed by DAY OF THE DEAD's deemphasis of gory action in favor of characterization, but the need to exploit the horror of the situation has passed and the film works by concentrating instead on its implications and possible solution. The standard 1950s sci-fi/horror film conflict between science and the military is also resurrected here, with distinct political overtones. One thing becomes clear in DAY OF THE DEAD—the zombies are here to stay, and humanity must adapt to them in order to survive. On a psychosocial level, as Robin Wood has persuasively argued, Romero's zombies seem to represent the "return of the repressed"; if so, this final chapter might be read as a plea for a reconciliation between forbidden desires and traditional social strictures. Generally underrated—even by horror-film fans—DAY OF THE DEAD ranks with Romero's best work.

DAY OF THE JACKAL, THE

DVD

1973   142m   c   Thriller   ★★★★
Warwick   (U.K./France)   PG

Edward Fox *("The Jackal")*, Terence Alexander *(Lloyd)*, Michel Auclair *(Colonel Rolland)*, Alan Badel *(The Minister)*, Tony Britton *(Inspector Thomas)*, Denis Carey *(Casson)*, Adrien Cayla-Legrand *(The President)*, Cyril Cusack *(Gunsmith)*, Maurice Denham *(General Colbert)*, Vernon Dobtcheff *(Interrogator)*

p, John Woolf, David Deutsch, Julien Derode; d, Fred Zinnemann; w, Kenneth Ross (based on the novel by Frederick Forsyth); ph, Jean Tournier (Technicolor); ed, Ralph Kemplen; m, Georges Delerue; art d, Willy Holt, Ernest Archer; fx, Georges Iaconelli,

John Richardson; cos, Elizabeth Haffenden, Joan Bridge, Rosine Delamare, Jean Zay, Chanel

AAN Best Film Editing: Ralph Kemplen

A secret French military organization plans to assassinate President de Gaulle (played by Adrien Cayla-Legrand, an uncanny look-alike), by hiring one of the world's most fearsome professional killers, a man known only as "The Jackal" (Edward Fox). Top French police investigator Lebel (Michel Lonsdale) learns the name "Jackal" from an informer in the plotter's ranks and cleverly pieces together the identity of the killer-for-hire. What follows is an intricate and meticulous story with a parallel structure that details the Jackal's preparations for the assassination and Lebel's efforts to stop him. Director Zinnemann faithfully follows the Forsyth best-seller, presenting a precise, almost discomfiting reconstruction of the story. Fox is superb as the coldly impassionate killer, and Lonsdale is properly plodding yet magnificently analytical as the detective tracking him down. A taut, suspenseful, and fascinating political thriller.

DAY OF THE LOCUST, THE

DVD

1975   144m   c   Drama   ★★★★
Paramount   (U.S.)   R

Donald Sutherland *(Homer)*, Karen Black *(Faye)*, Burgess Meredith *(Harry)*, William Atherton *(Tod)*, Geraldine Page *(Big Sister)*, Richard Dysart *(Claude Estee)*, Bo Hopkins *(Earle Shoop)*, Pepe Serna *(Miguel)*, Lelia Goldoni *(Mary Dove)*, Billy Barty *(Abe)*

p, Jerome Hellman; d, John Schlesinger; w, Waldo Salt (based on the novel by Nathanael West); ph, Conrad Hall (Panavision, Technicolor); ed, Jim Clark; m, John Barry; prod d, Richard MacDonald; art d, John Lloyd; cos, Ann Roth

AAN Best Supporting Actor: Burgess Meredith; *AAN Best Cinematography:* Conrad Hall

DAY OF THE LOCUST, like the powerful and incisive Nathanael West novel on which it is based, focuses on the seamy side of the city of dreams in its 1930s heyday—the subculture of losers, misfits, and neurotic fringe characters. Black is a sexy untalented aspiring actress who lives with her father, Meredith, a former vaudevillian, now a down on his luck door-to-door saleman. Recognizing her limited prospects, Black becomes a regular on the casting couch of producers in the hope that she'll rise above her usual walk-ons. She still has dreams of fame and legitimacy. Despite her dubious character, Atherton, an altruistic art director, falls for her but she gives him the cold shoulder—at first. She soon begins amusing herself by toying with him. This is the beginning of a pattern. When she finds herself destitute she moves in with a sensitive but oafish accountant, Sutherland, who loves her from afar. She and all about him use and ridicule him as he lumbers through life; he is particularly vexed by an evil neighborhood child, Haley. Everything comes to a head in the apocalyptic finale of the film, a memorably traumatic spectacle.

This grim conclusion, along with the stark and unsavory story and characters that preceded it, brought shudders to audiences and undoubtedly helped this excellent film fail at the box office. Nevertheless, it accurately captures the intent of West's dark masterpiece. Black is the perfect slattern with movie ambition—cheap, shallow, conniving, and utterly reprehensible. Sutherland gives one of his best performances as the doltish but sensitive outsider whose concern for films is marginal at best. The movie boasts excellent supporting players, such as Atherton as the ethereal art director. He is savvy to Hollywood and gives it back the banal glibness that is the hallmark of its society. Many of the characters are inspired by historical Hollywood figures. DAY OF THE LOCUST exudes authenticity, from the costuming to the cars, from the exotic clothes to the marcelled hair styles.

DAY OF THE TRIFFIDS, THE   *DVD*
1962 93m c Science Fiction/Horror ★★½
Allied Artists (U.K.)

Howard Keel *(Bill Masen)*, Nicole Maurey *(Christine Durrant)*, Janette Scott *(Karen Goodwin)*, Kieron Moore *(Tom Goodwin)*, Mervyn Johns *(Prof. Coker)*, Janina Faye *(Susan)*, Alison Leggatt *(Miss Coker)*, Ewan Roberts *(Dr. Soames)*, Colette Wilde *(Nurse Jamieson)*, Carole Ann Ford *(Bettina)*

p, George Pitcher; d, Steve Sekely, Freddie Francis (uncredited); w, Bernard Gordon (based on the novel by John Wyndham); ph, Ted Moore (Cinemascope, Eastmancolor); ed, Spencer Reeve; m, Ron Goodwin; art d, Cedric Dawe; fx, Wally Veevers

Decent, albeit uneven, British sci-fi/horror film. Keel stars as an American sailor who has escaped being blinded by a sudden meteor shower that has robbed most of the Earth's population of its sight. The mysterious meteor storm has also brought with it alien plant spores which grow into large, carnivorous plants that multiply and threaten to overrun the planet. The man-eating plants are known as "Triffids" and resemble rampaging stalks of broccoli that have an easy time feeding off of the blind humans who can't protect themselves. Keel becomes the leader of a small band of people who have somehow escaped being blinded. Together they plot to make a final stand against the vicious plants. Meanwhile, marine biologist Moore and his wife, Scott (who have been trapped in a lighthouse by the Triffids) search for a scientific solution.

    Always interesting but bogged down by lengthy romantic interludes, the film is thought-provoking and scary at times (the Triffids are more effective than they have any right to be). This is the third adaptation from the works of John Wyndham, the first two yielding the superb VILLAGE OF THE DAMNED and CHILDREN OF THE DAMNED. For fans of the once great untrained baritone voice of Keel, it is interesting that in THE DAY OF THE TRIFFIDS he rewrote his own dialogue because he was so displeased by the screenplay. Due to problems with blacklisting, scripter Bernard Gordon was left off the film's credits on its initial release in favor of screenwriter Philip Yordan, who served as a front for Gordon. In 1996, the Writer's Guild of America officially restored Gordon's credit.

DAY OF WRATH   *DVD*
(VREDENS DAG)
1943 97m bw Drama ★★★★★
Palladium (Denmark)

Thirkild Roose *(Absalon Pedersson)*, Lisbeth Movin *(Anne Pedersdotter, His Wife)*, Sigrid Neiiendam *(Meret, His Mother)*, Preben Lerdorff-Rye *(Martin, Son by His First Marriage)*, Albert Hoeberg *(The Bishop)*, Olaf Ussing *(Laurentius)*, Anna Svierkier *(Herlofs Marte)*

p, Carl-Theodor Dreyer; d, Carl-Theodor Dreyer; w, Carl-Theodor Dreyer, Poul Knudsen, Mogens Skot-Hansen (based on the novel by Wiers Jenssens); ph, Carl Anderson; ed, Edith Schlussel, Anne Marie Petersen; m, Poul Schierbeck; art d, Erik Aaes

DAY OF WRATH was the first feature film directed by the great Carl Dreyer after his 1932 masterwork, VAMPYR. In WRATH, Dreyer returns to the witches, religion, and spiritualism that marked his earlier, silent masterpiece, THE PASSION OF JOAN OF ARC (1928).

    Set during the throes of a witch hunt in the 17th century, the film centers around a young woman, Anne (Lisbeth Movin), who is married to a much older, puritanical man she

hates. She falls in love with his son, with whom she spends idyllic afternoons in the woods. Pressure begins to build, and she is heard to whisper aloud how she hungers for the death of her husband. Soon afterward, the husband dies, and she is accused of being a witch.

    The plot is deceptively simple and is barely representative of the film's power, for the film's brilliance lies in Dreyer's direction and the uncanny imagery, which resembles nothing so much as Rembrandt masterworks come to life. At a slow and deliberate pace, he allows the camera to linger, almost erotically, on images, waiting for the "right" look on a face or the correct movement of a hand. A study of good and evil, repression and oppression, sexuality and guilt, DAY OF WRATH is a truly spiritual film.

DAY THE EARTH STOOD STILL, THE   *DVD*
1951 92m bw Science Fiction ★★★★
Fox (U.S.)

Michael Rennie *(Klaatu)*, Patricia Neal *(Helen Benson)*, Hugh Marlowe *(Tom Stevens)*, Sam Jaffe *(Dr. Barnhardt)*, Billy Gray *(Bobby Benson)*, Frances Bavier *(Mrs. Barley)*, Lock Martin *(Gort)*, Drew Pearson *(Himself)*, Frank Conroy *(Harley)*, Fay Roope *(Major General)*

p, Julian Blaustein; d, Robert Wise; w, Edmund H. North (based on a story by Harry Bates); ph, Leo Tover; ed, William Reynolds; m, Bernard Herrmann; art d, Lyle Wheeler, Addison Hehr; fx, Fred Sersen

Working from Edmund H. North's unusually literate adaptation of Harry Bates's short story "Farewell to the Master," Robert Wise created a classic science fiction film with a strong pacifist message.

    Sent by a federation of planets to warn the people of Earth to stop nuclear testing before the planet is destroyed, the Christ-like Rennie descends into Washington, D.C., in his spaceship, accompanied by his massive robot, Gort. When an American soldier panics and shoots Rennie, Gort eliminates them, but the wounded Rennie stops the robot from destroying the planet. Taken to a military hospital, Rennie escapes and, posing as a normal human, seeks shelter in Neal's boarding house. Here he begins to learn that Earth people really are not so bad. Since he can make no formal contact with the governments of Earth, Rennie arranges a demonstration of his power that justifies the title of the film.

    Superb performances by all involved, restrained direction by Wise, and a magnificent and innovative score by Bernard Herrmann help keep this decades-old film just as relevant today as it was the day it was released.

DAYBREAK
(LE JOUR SE LEVE)
1939 89m bw Drama/Romance ★★★★
Sigma Productions (France)

Jean Gabin *(Francois)*, Jules Berry *(M. Valentin)*, Jacqueline Laurent *(Francoise)*, Arletty *(Clara)*, Rene Genin *(Concierge)*, Mady Berry *(Concierge's Wife)*, Bernard Blier *(Gaston)*, Marcel Peres *(Paulo)*, Jacques Baumer *(The Inspector)*, Rene Bergeron *(Cafe Proprietor)*

d, Marcel Carne; w, Jacques Prevert, Jacques Viot; ph, Curt Courant; ed, Rene Le Henaff; m, Maurice Jaubert; art d, Alexandre Trauner; cos, Boris Bilinsky

A superb example of French poetic realism, and probably the finest of the several collaborations between director Marcel Carne and screenwriter Jacques Prevert. Jean Gabin is Francois, a tough, romantic loner who barricades himself in his apartment after committing a crime of passion, the murder of the lecherous Valentin (Jules Berry). While police surround his Normandy home, Francois remembers (in flashback) the two women he loved—Francoise (Jacqueline Laurent) and Clara (Arletty)—and Valentin, the man who wooed both. Every facet of the film's production values is expertly realized, but perhaps the most awe-inspiring is the set design of Alexandre Trauner—a re-creation of a city street corner decorated with Dubonnet posters that is one of the most memorable ever filmed. More poetic than realistic, it is very much a film of a mood, but despite the optimism of its ironic title, melancholy and despair predominate. This inherent irony was then mirrored by real-life events as the film was released not long before Paris became an occupied city, and its citizens, like Francois, were left with no way out. Recognizing the similarities, the Vichy government banned the picture as "demoralizing." Remade in Hollywood as THE LONG NIGHT. (In French; English subtitles.)

DAYS OF HEAVEN
1978 95m c Drama   ★★★★
Paramount (U.S.)   DVD PG

Richard Gere (Bill), Brooke Adams (Abby), Sam Shepard (The Farmer), Linda Manz (Linda), Bob Wilke (Farm Foreman), Jackie Shultis (Linda's Friend), Stuart Margolin (Mill Foreman), Timothy Scott (Harvest Hand), Gene Bell (Dancer), Doug Kershaw (Fiddler)

p, Bert Schneider, Harold Schneider; d, Terrence Malick; w, Terrence Malick; ph, Nestor Almendros (Metrocolor); ed, Billy Weber; m, Ennio Morricone; art d, Jack Fisk; fx, John Thomas, Mel Merrells; cos, Patricia Norris

AA Best Cinematography: Nestor Almendros; AAN Best Original Score: Ennio Morricone; AAN Best Costume Design: Patricia Norris; AAN Best Sound: John K. Wilkinson, Robert W. Glass, Jr., John T. Reitz, Barry Thomas

Set in the postindustrial revolution America of the early 1900s, DAYS OF HEAVEN chronicles the odyssey of a rootless migrant laborer (Gere), his little sister (Manz), and his soulmate (Adams), as they flee the industrial blight of the city for the sanctuary and anonymity of the Heartland. When the impulsive and hot-tempered Gere kills a steel-mill foreman in anger, the three jump a train and head for the plains of Texas, merging with the endless caravan of homeless immigrants looking for work. Their journey brings them to the land of wealthy, self-made wheat farmer Shepard, who offers them employment during the harvest.

An enigmatic figure, Shepard, living alone in a huge Victorian mansion that overlooks his golden empire, is slowly wasting away from some illness. As he watches Adams work in the fields, he grows to love her—as Pharaoh did young Sarah in the Old Testament story—and sees some private salvation in making her his "queen." Gere learns of the farmer's illness and, reasoning that the powerful farmer will be dead soon, contrives like Abraham of old to masquerade with Adams as brother and sister thereby allowing Shepard to marry Adams and plant the seeds of a future inheritance. For a time after the marriage, the four live together as a family in a state of grace and sublime happiness. The scheme goes awry, however, when Adams begins to genuinely care for Shepard. When Shepard realizes the lovers' duplicity, his rage is that of the Old Testament Pharoah, on whose lands Jehovah's wrathful plagues fell. The contest between the two suitors precipitates a holocaust that blows apart the fragile paradise that so briefly flourished.

Director Malick endows this simple, timeless story with the enormous scope and resonance of myth through a clear vision unclouded by sentimentality and by a deft juxtaposition of image, music, and character. Although this is only his second feature film (BADLANDS, made five years earlier, was his first), he demonstrates a mastery of cinematic technique. The story is rich with Biblical and mythical allusions: there are echoes of Genesis, the Wasteland myth, and Greek tragedy. The vast, uncluttered compositions sometimes render the characters as little more than puppets in the hands of fate, reinforcing the universality of the story. Almendros's hyper-realistic cinematography is breathtaking.

The dialogue is sparse and almost incidental, the characters' words insignificant amidst the pervasive whisper of the wheat, the clatter of the threshing machines, and the awful drone of the locust horde that accompanies the final holocaust. The sound alone is astonishing. Morricone's haunting, wistful score adds measurably to the sweep and timelessness of the film.

DAYS OF WINE AND ROSES
1962 117m bw Drama   DVD ★★★★
Warner Bros. (U.S.)

Jack Lemmon (Joe), Lee Remick (Kirsten), Charles Bickford (Arnesen), Jack Klugman (Jim Hungerford), Alan Hewitt (Leland), Tom Palmer (Ballefoy), Debbie Megowan (Debbie), Maxine Stuart (Dottie), Katherine Squire (Mrs. Nolan), Jack Albertson (Trayner)

p, Martin Manulis; d, Blake Edwards; w, J.P. Miller (based on the television play by J.P. Miller); ph, Philip Lathrop; ed, Patrick McCormack; m, Henry Mancini; art d, Joseph C. Wright; fx, Horace L. Hulburd; cos, Don Feld

AAN Best Actor: Jack Lemmon; AAN Best Actress: Lee Remick; AA Best Song: "Days of Wine and Roses"; Henry Mancini (Music), Johnny Mercer (Lyrics); AAN Best Art Direction-Set Decoration (B/W): Joseph Wright, George James Hopkins; AAN Best Costume Design (B/W): Don Feld

Former light comedian Jack Lemmon's powerful performance as an alcoholic counts among Hollywood's most memorable depictions of this condition such as Ray Milland in THE LOST WEEKEND and Jimmy Cagney in COME FILL THE CUP. He's a young, bright adman who meets and falls in love with Remick. Early in their relationship, he's just a social drinker and she's a teetotaler. Soon after their marriage, subtle changes begin to occur. Lemmon is stressed out from work and begins drinking daily after work. Remick adores him and soon joins in sharing the bottle. Before long they are immersed in the liquored life and even the birth of their baby daughter fails to slow their descent into the gutter.

The movie features many emotionally shattering scenes and the going sometimes gets rough. Lemmon surprised many with the intensity of his performance. He has a mad spell in a greenhouse and an almost SNAKE PIT-like siege in a hospital ward. This is a long way from frolicking in drag with Marilyn Monroe in SOME LIKE IT HOT! The screenplay was based on J.P. Miller's teleplay, which starred Cliff Robertson on "Playhouse 90." Robertson was not a star at the time, and the decision was made to use Lemmon. Edwards's direction was smooth and neither he nor Miller ever took a stance or moralized. They just showed what it was like to be an alcoholic in the 1960s and let the audience draw its own conclusions.

DAZED AND CONFUSED
1993 97m c Drama   DVD ★★★
Dazed Pictures Corporation (U.S.)   R

Jason London (Randy "Pink" Floyd), Sasha Jenson (Don Dawson), Rory Cochrane (Slater), Wiley Wiggins (Mitch Kramer), Michelle Burke (Jodi Kramer), Shawn Andrews (Pickford), Anthony Rapp (Tony), Adam Goldberg (Mike), Christin Hinojosa (Sabrina), Parker Posey (Darla)

p, Richard Linklater, Sean Daniel, James Jacks; d, Richard Linklater; w, Richard Linklater; ph, Lee Daniel; ed, Sandra Adair; prod d, John Allen Frick; art d, Jenny C. Patrick; cos, Katherine "K.D." Dover

---

Director Richard Linklater's follow-up to the 1991 surprise independent hit SLACKER, this is an affectionate but unsentimental recreation of suburban teen culture in the rock- and pot-drenched '70s.

The film follows an ensemble of more than 20 characters through their last day and night of high school in 1976. The kids separate into cliques of familiar character types—jocks and nerds, senior bullies and freshmen weaklings, potheads and eggheads, the cool and the uncool. As quarterback of the high school football team, Randy "Pink" Floyd (Jason London) must decide whether to sign the coach's pledge to remain drug-free or to continue to indulge with his friends; meanwhile, freshman Mitch (Wiley Wiggins) spends the day fleeing from paddle-wielding, abusive hazers while trying to hang with the older gang of cool kids and the girls who find him cute. All parties convene at a huge beer bust in the woods, where fights erupt, romances are consummated, and dazed visions of "what comes next" are hashed out.

A much-praised portrait of '70s youth, DAZED AND CONFUSED expertly captures the details and textures of the time without condescending or lapsing into cheap-shot parody. A classic rock score (Aerosmith, Black Oak Arkansas, Foghat, and other quintessential AOR sounds) combines with smooth camerawork and editing to help create a seamless succession of typical incidents and conversations. The youths so frankly portrayed here lead lives of aimlessness, sloth, and apathy—understandably, given the banality of the choices available to them. Truly dazed and confused, Linklater's characters inhabit a moral universe so murky and enervated that Floyd's willingness to make a stand—*any* stand—emerges finally as something of a triumph.

DEAD, THE

1987 83m c Drama ★★★★½
Liffey (U.S.) PG

Anjelica Huston *(Gretta Conroy)*, Donal McCann *(Gabriel Conroy, Her Husband)*, Rachael Dowling *(Lily)*, Cathleen Delany *(Aunt Julia Morkan)*, Helena Carroll *(Aunt Kate Morkan)*, Ingrid Craigie *(Mary Jane)*, Dan O'Herlihy *(Mr. Browne)*, Frank Patterson *(Bartell D'Arcy)*, Donal Donnelly *(Freddy Malins)*, Marie Kean *(Mrs. Malins)*

p, Wieland Schulz-Keil, Chris Sievernich; d, John Huston; w, Tony Huston (based on the short story from *The Dubliners* by James Joyce); ph, Fred Murphy (Foto-Kem Color); ed, Roberto Silvi; m, Alex North; prod d, Stephen Grimes, J. Dennis Washington; cos, Dorothy Jeakins

AAN Best Adapted Screenplay: Tony Huston; *AAN Best Costume Design:* Dorothy Jeakins

---

This sublime adaptation of the last story in James Joyce's *Dubliners* is John Huston's final film, and it is as beautiful, delicate, and moving an epitaph as any filmmaker could ever desire.

Set in Dublin on the chilly night of January 6, 1904, the feast of the Epiphany, THE DEAD takes place at the home of spinsters Kate (Helena Carroll) and Julia Morkan (Cathleen Delany) during their annual post-holidays party. Their favorite guests are their sophisticated nephew, Gabriel Conroy (Donal McCann), and his beautiful wife, Gretta (Anjelica Huston). After most of the revelers have left, Gretta is struck by the haunting rendition of "The Lass of Aughrim" sung by one of the guests. On the cab ride back to their hotel, Gretta is distant, lost in her thoughts. In their room, a tearful Gretta confesses to Gabriel that the song has stirred long-suppressed memories of a brief and tragic romance from her youth. After hearing her story, Gabriel marvels at the power that the dead hold over the living.

THE DEAD is a breathtakingly beautiful movie, a mature work of a master filmmaker. Huston, a lifelong admirer of Joyce, had wanted to make a film adaptation of "The Dead" since the 1950s, but put the idea on the back burner because of its uncommercial nature. When producer Wieland Schulz-Keil decided the time was right, he hired Huston's eldest son, Tony, to write the screenplay, which is scrupulously faithful to Joyce. The casting is marvelous, and Huston allows all his performers equal screen time until the end when Anjelica Huston and McCann become the focus. The party scene is a flurry of detailed movement, wonderfully choreographed. Huston concentrates on the interaction of the characters—the conversations, the movements, the rituals—and glories in the nuances of human behavior.

The film's most powerful sequence, however, is the scene between husband and wife. Anjelica Huston is superb, striking the perfect balance of emotions. It is a performance of grace and eloquence. Equally excellent is McCann, who somehow manages to convey with a minimum of visible acting the dawning self-awareness described by Joyce. THE DEAD was made by a man who had a deep appreciation for all the arts and how they enrich the human experience.

DEAD AGAIN [DVD]

1991 107m c Mystery/Romance ★★★
Mirage Enterprises/Paramount (U.S.) R

Kenneth Branagh *(Mike Church/Roman Strauss)*, Emma Thompson *(Grace/Margaret Strauss)*, Andy Garcia *(Gray Baker)*, Lois Hall *(Sister Constance)*, Richard Easton *(Father Timothy)*, Jo Anderson *(Sister Madeleine/Starlet)*, Patrick Montes *(Pickup Driver)*, Raymond Cruz *(Clerk)*, Robin Williams *(Doctor Cozy Carlisle—uncredited)*, Wayne Knight *("Piccolo" Pete)*

p, Lindsay Doran, Charles H. Maguire; d, Kenneth Branagh; w, Scott Frank; ph, Matthew F. Leonetti; ed, Peter E. Berger; m, Patrick Doyle; prod d, Tim Harvey; art d, Sydney Z. Litwack; fx, Tom Burman, Bari Burman; cos, Phyllis Dalton

---

Director Kenneth Branagh and his then real-life wife Emma Thompson both have dual roles in DEAD AGAIN, a complexly plotted mystery that is steeped in a pastiche of Hollywood classics.

Los Angeles. Private detective Mike Church (Branagh), at the behest of the orphanage priest who raised him, rescues an unknown amnesiac (Thompson), who he names Grace and with whom he quickly falls in love. With the aid of hypnotist and antique dealer Franklyn Madson (Derek Jacobi), who appears on the scene, Grace undergoes hypnosis and recounts her past life as Margaret, a British concert pianist married to Roman Strauss, a flamboyant emigre conductor who was imprisoned for her brutal murder. At a second session, she begins to blur the identities of Roman and Mike, and the latter realizes that Grace is remembering a past life in which he plays a part as well. Intrigued, Church undergoes hypnosis himself and discovers just how symbiotic their relationship is: *he* was Margaret and Grace was Roman. Further investigation reveals that in 1949 the Strauss murder case actually transpired, resulting in Roman's execution. As the modern-day and past experiences increasingly overlap, Church fears his romantic attraction to Grace will again end with a violent death.

Scott Frank (PLAIN CLOTHES, LITTLE MAN TATE) has created a screenplay which, at the expense of story and character development, prides itself on its ability to quote liberally from great films of the past. DEAD AGAIN borrows icons, motifs, characters and camera angles from a number of classics, most notably Hitchcock thrillers such as REBECCA, with its gothic mansion and creepy housekeeper, SPELL-BOUND, with its hypnosis, psychoanalysis and giant Salvador Dali scissors, and VERTIGO, with its reincarnated doubles and Catholic trappings, but also film noir mysteries and Orson Welles's CITIZEN KANE. However unlikely the twists and turns in this mystery, DEAD AGAIN moves briskly forward, never weighed down by any sense of seriousness. Branagh's transformations between his lightweight, American detective and his heavy, Germanic musician are pure bravado, done for the thrill of watching the Master Thespian assume two wildly different incarnations.

DEAD CALM   DVD

1989 96m   c   Horror/Thriller   ★★★½
Kennedy Miller   (Australia)   R

Sam Neill *(John Ingram)*, Nicole Kidman *(Rae Ingram)*, Billy Zane *(Hughie Warriner)*, Rod Mullinar *(Russell Bellows)*, Joshua Tilden *(Danny)*, George Shevtsov *(Doctor)*, Michael Long *(Specialist Doctor)*

p, Terry Hayes, Doug Mitchell, George Miller; d, Phillip Noyce; w, Terry Hayes (based on the novel by Charles Williams); ph, Dean Semler (Panavision, Eastmancolor); ed, Richard Francis-Bruce; m, Graeme Revell; prod d, Graham Walker; art d, Kimble Hilder; cos, Norma Moriceau

Though it lacks Alfred Hitchcock's wry and macabre sense of humor, DEAD CALM is a cracklingly good, cold-blooded film that never lets up in its truly Hitchcockian suspense. Under the gripping direction of Phillip Noyce, the film sustains tension and power beautifully, right through to its startling conclusion.

  Middle-aged surgeon John Ingram (Sam Neill) and his wife Rae (Nicole Kidman) embark on an extended yachting trip after the gruesome death of their little son in a car accident. The trip is intended as a therapeutic measure for the traumatized Rae. Things go well until the couple rescues Hughie Warriner (Billy Zane), the sole survivor from a sinking schooner near the Great Barrier Reef. Warriner claims that all the other passengers died of food poisoning, but Ingram boards the schooner to investigate and makes a nasty discovery that turns their vacation into a nightmare.

  Neill and Zane both turn in excellent performances, but Kidman (DAYS OF THUNDER, BILLY BATHGATE) does the most interesting and demanding work as the wife who must snap out of her melancholy distraction to outwit her vile captor. During the film's last half, Kidman convincingly transforms from a vunerable, distraught housewife into a ferocious battler—and it's an electrifying metamorphosis. The taut editing and Noyce's direction are splendid, augmenting Terry Hayes's sharp (though somewhat predictable) script. George Miller, director of the MAD MAX trilogy and former student of Phillip Noyce at Melbourne University, is one of the producers.

DEAD END   DVD

1937 93m   bw   Crime   ★★★★
UA   (U.S.)

Sylvia Sidney *(Drina)*, Joel McCrea *(Dave)*, Humphrey Bogart *(Baby Face Martin)*, Wendy Barrie *(Kay)*, Claire Trevor *(Francie)*, Allen Jenkins *(Hunk)*, Marjorie Main *(Mrs. Martin)*, Billy Halop *(Tommy)*, Huntz Hall *(Dippy)*, Bobby Jordan *(Angel)*

p, Samuel Goldwyn; d, William Wyler; w, Lillian Hellman (based on the play by Sidney Kingsley); ph, Gregg Toland; ed, Daniel Mandell; m, Alfred Newman; art d, Richard Day; fx, James Basevi; cos, Omar Kiam

AAN Best Picture; AAN Best Supporting Actress: Claire Trevor; AAN Best Cinematography: Gregg Toland; AAN Best Interior Decoration: Richard Day (Art Direction)

Depression-era poverty, slums and crime provide the themes for DEAD END, Sam Goldwyn's film production of the popular Sidney Kingsley play. Well meaning and once considered hardhitting, this celebrated social drama now seems rather mawkish and quaint. The message is not just that these impoverished surroundings can be a cradle for crime but that good folks may also be brought up on these mean streets.

  After ten years of pursuing a criminal career, escalating from robbery to murder, Bogart returns to his old New York City neighborhood. Disguised by extensive plastic surgery, he wants to see his mother (Main) and his old girlfriend (Trevor) while avoiding a nationwide dragnet. DEAD END is also the story of McCrea, a scrupulous and unsuccessful architect struggling to get out of the slum. He thinks he's in love with Barrie, a rich woman living in a nearby luxury apartment building but he is the apple of Sidney's eye. She is a respectable woman living in poverty and struggling to keep her kid brother, Halop, on the straight and narrow. Meanwhile, Bogart begins teaching Halop and the other "Dead End Kids" all the wiseguy tricks he's learned in his misspent life. McCrea, his boyhood chum, warns Bogart that he will take steps against him unless he stops exerting his rotten influence on the impressionable youths.

  William Wyler's sterling direction creates a stagey but fairly compelling vision of slum life. The wonderful set by Richard Day is an enlarged duplicate of the Broadway set. Lillian Hellman's script changes little of Kingsley's earthy prose except for the ending. Humphrey Bogart is captivating as the alienated gangster, building upon his success of THE PETRIFIED FOREST a year earlier. He was originally billed beneath Sidney, but, in re-releases of this film, he was given star billing.

DEAD-END DRIVE-IN   DVD

1986 92m   c   Action/Science Fiction   ★★★½
Springvale/New South Wales   (Australia)   R

Ned Manning *(Crabs)*, Natalie McCurry *(Carmen)*, Peter Whitford *(Thompson)*, Wilbur Wide *(Hazza)*, Brett Climo *(Don)*, Ollie Hall *(Frank)*, Sandie Lillingston *(Beth)*, Lyn Collingwood *(Fay)*, Nikki McWatters *(Shirl)*, Melissa Davies *(Narelle)*

p, Andrew Williams; d, Brian Trenchard-Smith; w, Peter Smalley (based on the short story "Crabs" by Peter Carey); ph, Paul Murphy (Eastmancolor); ed, Alan Lake, Lee Smith; m, Frank Strangio; prod d, Lawrence Eastwood; art d, Nick McCallum; cos, Anthony James

In the near future, the world economy has collapsed and Australia has been racked by massive unemployment, crime, and rioting. Gangs roam the streets destroying cars and stripping them for parts. Crabs (Ned Manning) is a young man doing his best to survive. One night he takes his girlfriend (Natalie McCurry) to see a movie at the Star Drive-In. The rear tires are stolen while the young couple makes out in the car, leaving them stranded. Crabs sees that the thieves are cops but when he tries to report this to the manager (Peter Whitford), he is told that nothing can be done until the feds arrive. A new day dawns. Crabs looks around the bleak drive-in across acres of cars occupied by hundreds of punkish teenagers.

  One of the least fanciful and most interesting futuristic films of recent years, DEAD-END DRIVE-IN is reminiscent of the original MAD MAX, and like that film it is a testament to the availability of cheap junked used cars and completely insane Australian stuntmen. Production values are high, and the performances are all good. The film does lag in some parts but generally works quite well, and the finale, climaxed by one of the most spectacular stunts ever attempted, is satisfyingly cathartic.

DEAD MAN

1996 121m bw Western
12-Gauge Productions/JVC/Newmarket Capital
Group/Victor Company of Japan/Pandora Film
(U.S./Germany/Japan)

DVD
★★★★
R

Johnny Depp *(William Blake)*, Gary Farmer *(Nobody)*, Lance
Henriksen *(Cole Wilson)*, Gabriel Byrne *(Charlie Dickinson)*,
Robert Mitchum *(John Dickinson)*, John Hurt *(John Scholfield)*,
Crispin Glover *(The Fireman)*, Michael Wincott *(Conway Twill)*,
Eugene Byrd *(Johnny "The Kid" Pickett)*, Mili Avital *(Thel
Russell)* .

p, Demetra J. MacBride; d, Jim Jarmusch; w, Jim Jarmusch;
ph, Robby Muller; ed, Jay Rabinowitz; m, Neil Young; prod d,
Bob Ziembicki; art d, Ted Berner; fx, Lou Carlucci, FTS
Effects, Jon Farhat, R/Greenberg Associates West, Inc.; cos,
Marit Allen

This splendid art film in Western clothing marks a departure
for director/writer Jim Jarmusch, the hipster auteur best
known for quirky, coolly amusing character studies like
STRANGER THAN PARADISE and MYSTERY
TRAIN. In a town called Machine, mild-mannered accountant Bill Blake (Johnny Depp) turns outlaw after shooting a
man in self-defense. Pursued by an unlikely team of gunslingers (Lance Henriksen, Michael Wincott, Eugene Byrd),
he heads for the wilderness, finding a partner and spiritual
guide in the person of a philosophical Indian called Nobody
(Gary Farmer).

Despite appearances, DEAD MAN is no conventional
outlaw saga. Just beneath its surface lies a visionary allegory of the soul's progress from physical death to spiritual
transcendence, seasoned with references to the life and
works of the poet William Blake. (Just for example, John
Hurt appears as a toadying clerk called John Scholfield, the
name of the vengeful soldier who accused Blake of sedi-
tion.) A slow-paced but hypnotically absorbing movie, it's
buoyed by Jarmusch's trademark off-key humor and
embellished throughout by an electrifying instrumental
score, courtesy of Neil Young. On the visual level, it's
resplendent: cinematographer Robby Muller works from an
exceptionally rich black-and-white palette, and what he
does for Jarmusch here is comparable to what Kazuo
Miyagawa's camera did for Mizoguchi. DEAD MAN even
has star power, in the form of Depp, who gives further evidence of his gallant—to some, inexplicable—commitment
to the offbeat.

DEAD MAN WALKING

1995 120m c Drama
Working Title Films/Havoc Productions/Polygram
(U.S.)

DVD
★★½
R

Susan Sarandon *(Sister Helen Prejean)*, Sean Penn *(Matthew
Poncelet)*, Robert Prosky *(Hilton Barber)*, Raymond J. Barry *(Earl
Delacroix)*, R. Lee Ermey *(Clyde Percy)*, Celia Weston *(Mary Beth
Percy)*, Lois Smith *(Helen's Mother)*, Scott Wilson *(Chaplain
Farley)*, Roberta Maxwell *(Lucille Poncelet)*, Margo Martindale
(Sister Colleen)

p, Jon Kilik, Tim Robbins, Rudd Simmons; d, Tim Robbins; w,
Tim Robbins (based on the book by Sister Helen Prejean,
C.S.J.); ph, Roger A. Deakins; ed, Lisa Zeno Churgin; m, David
Robbins; prod d, Richard Hoover; art d, Tom Warren; cos,
Renee Ehrlich Kalfus

AA Best Actress: Susan Sarandon; *AAN Best Actor:* Sean Penn;
AAN Best Director: Tim Robbins; *AAN Best Original Song:* "Dead
Man Walkin'"; Bruce Springsteen

DEAD MAN WALKING is an extraordinarily well-made
message movie that punks out at the eleventh hour. Tim
Robbins's film about the death penalty wants to be perceived
as painstakingly balanced and fair to both sides; ultimately,
however, it's just unresolved.

Sister Helen (Susan Sarandon), a nun who's abandoned
her privileged background to live and work with the poor of
New Orleans, is asked to write to a man on death row. Her pen
pal, Matthew Poncelet (Sean Penn), asks her to help him file
an appeal of his sentence. Though he was convicted of taking
part in the rape and murder of a young couple—his partner in
crime received a life sentence, apparently for no better reason
than that he had a sharper lawyer—Poncelet says he's innocent. Sister Helen is drawn into the case and, as the execution
date approaches, she takes on a mission: to get Poncelet to
admit to his guilt and regret his actions before he dies.

Boosters of capital punishment hated DEAD MAN
WALKING, but so did serious opponents. Although some
critics took this as evidence of the film's "even-handed"
treatment of the issue, in fact it's proof that DEAD MAN
WALKING doesn't treat the issue at all. It's a message
movie without a message. The topical movies of Abby
Mann or Stanley Kramer have often been assailed as simplistic or crudely moralistic, but at least they had the courage
of their makers' convictions.

This ideologically muddled construction rests on a pair
of phenomenal performances. In the hands of a lesser actress,
pious Sister Helen would be absolutely intolerable, but
Sarandon gives her a simple decency and conviction. Sean
Penn, meanwhile, is a riveting study in Mephistophelian
facial hair and white-trash attitude. His Poncelet is a genuinely bad guy, but one with a distinctly human face.

DEAD MEN DON'T WEAR PLAID

1982 89m bw Comedy/Crime
Universal (U.S.)

DVD
★★★★
PG

Steve Martin *(Rigby Reardon)*, Rachel Ward *(Juliet Forrest)*, Carl
Reiner *(Field Marshall Von Kluck)*, Reni Santoni *(Carlos
Rodriguez)*, George Gaynes *(Dr. Forrest)*, Frank McCarthy
(Waiter), Adrian Ricard *(Mildred)*, Charles Picerni, Gene Labell,
George Sawaya *(Hoods)*

p, David V. Picker, William E. McEuen; d, Carl Reiner; w, George
Gipe, Carl Reiner, Steve Martin; ph, Michael Chapman; ed, Bud
Molin; m, Miklos Rozsa (from earlier films); prod d, John De Cuir;
fx, Glen Robinson; cos, Edith Head

A consistently hilarious parody of the noir and detective genres, expertly blending classic archival footage with the
action. As an inept private eye, Steve Martin tracks killers,
playing opposite old film clips of James Cagney, Alan Ladd,
Humphrey Bogart, Charles Laughton, and Ava Gardner,
among others; scenes are lifted from, *inter alia*, WHITE
HEAT, DOUBLE INDEMNITY, THE KILLERS, THE
BIG SLEEP, DARK PASSAGE, IN A LONELY PLACE,
SUSPICION and, most notably, THE BRIBE. Some of the
cleverer jokes depend on the viewer's knowledge of 1940s
movies, but there's enough slapstick to please even the cinematically illiterate. The basic film—what there is of it—is
prettily shot in black-and-white by Michael Chapman
(RAGING BULL); the continuity between the clips and the
rest of the movie is remarkable. Martin is priceless as usual.

DEAD OF NIGHT

1945 104m bw Horror
Rank (U.K.)

DVD
★★★★½

Mervyn Johns *(Walter Craig)*, Roland Culver *(Eliot Foley)*, Mary
Merrall *(Mrs. Foley)*, Frederick Valk *(Dr. Van Straaten)*, Renee
Gadd *(Mrs. Craig)*, Anthony Baird *(Hugh Grainger)*, Judy Kelly

(Joyce Grainger), Miles Malleson *(Hearse Driver)*, Sally Ann Howes *(Sally O'Hara)*, Michael Allan *(Jimmy Watson)*

p, Michael Balcon; d, Alberto Cavalcanti ("The Ventriloquist's Dummy," "The Christmas Story"), Basil Dearden ("The Linking Story," "The Hearse Driver"), Robert Hamer ("The Haunted Mirror"), Charles Crichton ("The Golfing Story"); w, John Baines, Angus Macphail, T.E.B. Clarke (based on stories by H.G. Wells, E.F. Benson, John Baines, and Angus Macphail); ph, Jack Parker, Harold Julius; ed, Charles Hasse; m, Georges Auric; art d, Michael Relph

Perhaps the best horror anthology film ever made, this much-praised film still holds up, but suffers from the variances of pace and mood that inevitably affect all compilation efforts. Architect Walter Craig (Mervyn Johns) is called to Pilgrim's Farm, a country house he has been hired to remodel. Approaching the austere Victorian building in his car, he finds that there is something hauntingly familiar about the house. Once inside, Craig recognizes everyone present and tells them they have all been part of a recurring nightmare he has had, whereupon the guests relate their own nightmares, one by one.

The first tale, "The Hearse Driver," is told by Grainger (Antony Baird). In it he is a racetrack driver who, while recuperating from an accident, has a vision of a hearse from the window of his hospital room. The teen-aged Sally O'Hara (Sally Ann Howes) then reports "The Christmas Story," in which she attends a holiday party and, during a game of hide-and-seek, finds a crying child in a strange room. He is not what he seems. Joan Courtland (Googie Withers), in "The Haunted Mirror," relates a chilling tale in which she is given an antique mirror by her fiance which begins to reflect a Victorian room where a killing once took place. In "The Golfing Story"—the only piece designed for comic relief—two golfers (Basil Radford and Naunton Wayne) vie for the attentions of one woman. One golfer tricks the other into suicide, only to have the deceased return and haunt him as he is about to enjoy his wedding night. The last story, an Expressionistic entry entitled "The Ventriloquist's Dummy," shows a ventriloquist (Michael Redgrave) going mad. He believes that his dummy is assuming his personality while he is becoming the manipulated prop.

With typical disregard for consistency, U.S. distributors thought this excellent British import was too long and cut the golfing sequence (not a bad move, actually) and the Christmas ghost tale, confusing audiences, who could not understand what Howes, Radford, and Wayne were doing in the linking story. The two tales were later reinstated. Of the four directors of the various stories, Robert Hamer is a standout with "The Haunted Mirror" and Alberto Cavalcanti excels with his two chillers, "The Christmas Story" and "The Ventriloquist's Dummy."

DEAD PIGEON ON BEETHOVEN STREET   DVD

1972   102m   c   Mystery   ★★★
Bavaria Atelier   (West Germany)   PG

Glenn Corbett *(Sandy)*, Christa Lang *(Christa)*, Sieghardt Rupp *(Kessin)*, Anton Diffring *(Mensur)*, Alex D'Arcy *(Novka)*, Anthony Ching *(Fong)*, Eric P. Caspar *(Charlie)*

d, Samuel Fuller; w, Samuel Fuller; ph, Jerzy Lipman (Eastmancolor); ed, Liesgret Schmitt-Klink; art d, Lothar Kirchem

American director Fuller answered his cult of European fans by making this bizarre tongue-in-cheek private-eye movie financed by German television. Corbett stars as a detective whose partner is murdered while investigating a gang of drug-dealing extortionists who photograph big-shot international-politico types in compromising situations with the lovely Lang. Corbett goes undercover and joins the ring to get the goods on the group. The film offers typically vigorous camera work but what makes it special is its looney sense of humor. Laden with in-jokes, the film is best approached as a goofy parody of crime thrillers.

DEAD POETS SOCIETY   DVD

1989   128m   c   Drama   ★★½
Silver Screen Partners IV/Touchstone   (U.S.)   PG

Robin Williams *(John Keating)*, Robert Sean Leonard *(Neil Perry)*, Ethan Hawke *(Todd Anderson)*, Josh Charles *(Knox Overstreet)*, Gale Hansen *(Charlie Dalton)*, Dylan Kussman *(Richard Cameron)*, Allelon Ruggiero *(Steven Meeks)*, James Waterson *(Gerard Pitts)*, Norman Lloyd *(Mr. Nolan)*, Kurtwood Smith *(Mr. Perry)*

p, Steven M. Haft, Paul Junger Witt, Tony Thomas; d, Peter Weir; w, Tom Schulman; ph, John Seale (Duart Color); m, Maurice Jarre; prod d, Wendy Stites; art d, Sandy Veneziano; cos, Marilyn Matthews

AAN Best Picture; AAN Best Actor: Robin Williams; *AAN Best Director:* Peter Weir; *AA Best Original Screenplay:* Tom Schulman

Tea and empathy. Tinkering with his screen persona, comedian-actor Robin Williams plays it relatively straight as a dedicated teacher at an elite Vermont prep school. The year is 1959, a time of strict adherence to educational goals and teaching methods at Welton, under the no-nonsense stewardship of headmaster Nolan (Norman Lloyd). The academic apple cart teeters, however, when John Keating (Williams) is engaged to teach a class of bright and impressionable young men. An inspirational mentor, Keating ignores conventional teaching procedures and offers his students access to a world of culture, ideas, and creativity that changes their lives. The role of Keating is a plum assignment for the talented Williams, who largely steers clear of schtick under Peter Weir's direction. Nicely shot with a good youthful cast.

DEAD RINGERS   DVD

1988   115m   c   Horror   ★★★★½
Mantle Clinic II   (Canada)   R

Jeremy Irons *(Beverly Mantle/Elliot Mantle)*, Genevieve Bujold *(Claire Niveau)*, Heidi von Palleske *(Cary)*, Barbara Gordon *(Danuta)*, Shirley Douglas *(Laura)*, Stephen Lack *(Anders Wolleck)*, Nick Nichols *(Leo)*, Lynn Cormack *(Arlene)*, Damir Andrei *(Birchall)*, Miriam Newhouse *(Mrs. Bookman)*

p, David Cronenberg, Marc Boyman; d, David Cronenberg; w, David Cronenberg, Norman Snider (based on the book *Twins* by Bari Wood, Jack Geasland); ph, Peter Suschitzky; ed, Ronald Sanders; m, Howard Shore; prod d, Carol Spier; fx, Gordon Smith; cos, Denise Cronenberg

Quietly devastating, DEAD RINGERS offers compelling evidence that David Cronenberg has matured into a truly great filmmaker. Continuing the detailed character study that blossomed in THE FLY and combining it with his fixation on the metaphysical, Cronenberg has vividly created yet another film that is powerful, moving and rich in ideas.

Inspired by the real-life story of respected twin New York City gynecologists Steven and Cyril Marcus (who in 1975 were both found dead in their garbage-strewn Upper East Side apartment, a double suicide brought on by barbiturate addiction), Cronenberg introduces us to Elliot and Beverly Mantle, a pair of brilliant gynecologists who open a state-of-the-art fertility clinic and share an opulent apartment. Although physically identical, the twins possess very different personalities. Elliot is something of a cad—suave, debonair, and self-confident to the point of arrogance—whereas Beverly is shy, studious, and more sensitive. Elliot has always procured women for Beverly—seducing them first, then turning them over to his shy sibling when he was through—unbeknownst to the woman. When a famous actress, Claire Niveau (Genevieve Bujold), arrives at the clinic looking for answers to her infertility, trouble brews between the brothers, for although they both share her physically, Beverly falls in love for the first time, driving a wedge between the twins.

Extremely unsettling, at times amusing, cold yet personal, DEAD RINGERS gradually and deliberately comes to horrify the viewer, rather than shocking outright with such spectacular displays of gore as the exploding heads of SCANNERS, gaping stomach cavities of VIDEODROME, or vomiting Brundleflies of THE FLY. Not your average horror roller-coaster ride, DEAD RINGERS asks some disturbing questions about the nature of individual identity and, within that net, explores such outgrowths as eroticism, narcissism and misogyny. During the last decade, Cronenberg has matured into a filmmaker of remarkable scope, able to convey his obsessions with impeccable skill without sacrificing one iota of his own remarkable individuality. The astonishing Irons receives superb support from Bujold who breathes life into a part that, in other hands, might have been a mere plot device.

DEAD ZONE, THE
1983 103m c Horror ★★★½
Paramount (U.S.) R

Christopher Walken (Johnny Smith), Brooke Adams (Sarah Bracknell), Tom Skerritt (Sheriff Bannerman), Herbert Lom (Dr. Sam Welzak), Anthony Zerbe (Roger Stuart), Colleen Dewhurst (Henrietta Dodd), Martin Sheen (Greg Stillson), Nicholas Campbell (Frank Dodd), Sean Sullivan (Herb Smith), Jackie Burroughs (Vera Smith)

p, Debra Hill; d, David Cronenberg; w, Jeffrey Boam (based on the novel by Stephen King); ph, Mark Irwin (Technicolor); ed, Ronald Sanders; m, Michael Kamen; prod d, Carol Spier; art d, Barbara Dunphy; fx, Jon G. Belyeu

Arguably the best adaptation of a Stephen King novel, THE DEAD ZONE stars Christopher Walken as Johnny Smith, a shy schoolteacher who leaves his fiancee's house one night during a rainstorm and suffers a near-fatal auto accident. Five years later Johnny comes out of a deep coma, his life forever changed. His fiancee has married another man, his mother has become a religious fanatic, and he has developed the power to see people's futures by touching their hands. After helping to solve a murder and saving the life of a child he "saw" drowning in a vision, Johnny attends a political rally. There he shakes hands with local candidate Greg Stillson (Martin Sheen) and has a spontaneous vision: Stillson will become President and precipitate a nuclear war. As the politician gains power and influence through his calculated right-wing populism, Johnny resolves to assassinate him.

David Cronenberg's first mainstream film, THE DEAD ZONE alienated some genre fans who missed the director's trademark gross-out effects (which made an unforgettable reappearance in his 1986 masterpiece, THE FLY). Here, Cronenberg's well-known obsessions with the human body, disease, and aberrant sexuality take a back seat to another very personal theme—social alienation, as expressed through unconventional ways of seeing. It's also an attack on the destructive impulses associated with masculinity: Sheen's aggressively potent Stillson is insistently contrasted with Johnny, a crippled, anemic Cassandra brilliantly embodied by Christopher Walken.

DEADLY AFFAIR, THE
1966 107m c Spy ★★★½
Columbia (U.K.)

James Mason (Charles Dobbs), Simone Signoret (Elsa Fennan), Maximilian Schell (Dieter Frey), Harriet Andersson (Ann Dobbs), Harry Andrews (Inspector Mendel), Kenneth Haigh (Bill Appleby), Lynn Redgrave (Virgin), Roy Kinnear (Adam Scarr), Max Adrian (Adviser), Robert Flemyng (Samuel Fennan)

p, Sidney Lumet; d, Sidney Lumet; w, Paul Dehn (from the novel Call for the Dead by John le Carre); ph, Freddie Young; ed, Thelma Connell; m, Quincy Jones; art d, John Howell; cos, Cynthia Tingey

This is a superior John le Carre novel filmed by Sidney Lumet with an interesting international cast: James Mason, Simone Signoret, Maximilian Schell, Harry Andrews, and Lynn Redgrave. The downbeat spy story captures the mood that made TINKER, TAILOR, SOLDIER, SPY so popular 15 years later. It's also of interest technically because Lumet experimented with "flashing" techniques, exposing the film stock before shooting to give it unusually subdued color. These techniques later became common.

This gritty, moody film is a superb but overlooked entry in the spy genre. Charles Dobbs (James Mason) is a security agent who okays clearance for Samuel Fennan (Robert Flemyng), a top-level official who has been accused of communist activities. When Fennan apparently commits suicide, Dobbs checks into the death and grows suspicious of Elsa Fennan (Simone Signoret), the dead man's widow. Before he can probe too deeply, however, he is taken off the case. Rather than bend to pressure from his superiors, Dobbs resigns, enlists the aid of some fellow agents, and sets out to solve Fennan's murder. Complicating matters is the arrival of Dieter Frey (Maximilian Schell), an agent who is a former friend of Dobbs and is preparing to run off with Dobbs's wife Ann (Harriet Andersson). Though Dobbs is weary of the espionage game, he finds himself more thoroughly enmeshed in it than he has ever been.

The complex plot is actually just a structure to support an insightful look into the lives of these characters. Mason is excellent as a man who knows the spy game for what it is, but still finds himself caught in its machinations. He gets admirable support from Schell, Andersson, and especially Signoret. Lumet's taut direction creates a film that is memorably atmospheric. Le Carre specialized in stripping the movie-fed illusion of glitz and glamour away from the world of espionage to reveal a grim unrewarding milieu where there are no heroes and villains, only people trapped in confusing webs of intrigue and turmoil.

DEATH AND THE MAIDEN
1994 103m c Drama/Political ★★★½
Electra Film/City Films/Flach Films/Capitol Films R
(U.S./France/U.K.)

Sigourney Weaver (Paulina Escobar), Ben Kingsley (Roberto Miranda), Stuart Wilson (Gerardo Escobar)

p, Thom Mount, Josh Kramer; d, Roman Polanski; w, Ariel Dorfman, Rafael Yglesias (based on the play by Ariel Dorfman); ph, Tonino Delli Colli; ed, Herve DeLuze; prod d, Pierre Guffroy; art d, Claude Moesching; fx, Gilbert Pieri, Bruno Lefebvre; cos, Milena Canonero

Set in an unnamed South American country, DEATH AND THE MAIDEN layers elements of a melodramatic thriller over a chamber drama with serious moral and political aspirations.

Paulina Escobar (Sigourney Weaver) is a former torture victim now sharing a respectable, upper-middle class lifestyle with her husband, Gerardo (Stuart Wilson). A prominent lawyer, Gerardo has been invited to head a commission investigating human rights violations under the country's former military regime. When Dr. Roberto Miranda (Ben Kingsley) accompanies Gerardo home after having assisted him with a blown tire, Paulina is immediately certain that this is the man who brutalized her years before. Resolving to seek vengeance and the truth, she begins to subject the doctor to some of the same treatment she endured.

Argentinian writer Ariel Dorfman's internationally celebrated play has been adapted by its author together with Rafael Yglesias (FEARLESS). The material is well served by director Roman Polanski, who knows well how to instill a subtle, claustrophobic sense of dread in an audience and has put together a rather elegant potboiler. Despite DEATH's limited physical setting, the audience never feels trapped in a filmed play, thanks to Tonino Delli Colli's beautiful camerawork, Herve De Luze's fluid editing, and Polanski's mastery of atmosphere and emotional nuance. This is particularly true of the lengthy first scene, which superbly conveys much of Paulina's character and condition *sans* dialogue.

Sigourney Weaver begins the film as an enigmatic, emotionally clipped figure, then becomes as fierce as any of her ALIEN incarnations once her fury toward Roberto is unleashed. It's an impressive performance occasionally marred by self-consciousness; there are moments when we feel Ms. Weaver is rather impressed with herself for tackling so *important* a role. Ben Kingsley, meanwhile, hams up his part with relish, making the sweatiest, pulpiest, most obsequious screen victim since Peter Lorre.

DEATH BECOMES HER   *DVD*
1992 105m c   Comedy/Fantasy   ★★½
Universal   (U.S.)   PG-13

Meryl Streep (Madeline Ashton), Bruce Willis (Ernest Menville), Goldie Hawn (Helen Sharp), Isabella Rossellini (Lisle Von Rhuman), Sydney Pollack (Doctor), Ian Ogilvy (Chagall), Adam Storke (Dakota), Nancy Fish (Rose), Alaina Reed Hall (Psychologist), Michael Caine

p, Robert Zemeckis, Steve Starkey; d, Robert Zemeckis; w, Martin Donovan, David Koepp; ph, Dean Cundey; ed, Arthur Schmidt; m, Alan Silvestri; prod d, Rick Carter; art d, Jim Teegarden; fx, Ken Ralston, Doug Chiang,, Tom Woodruff, Doug Smythe; cos, Joanna Johnston

AA Best Visual Effects: Ken Ralston, Doug Chiang, Doug Smythe, Tom Woodruff

Is it a showbiz melodrama about the rivalry between a faded movie star and a successful author? Is it a black comedy about the unforeseen side effects of a mysterious magic potion? Or is it a spoof horror movie complete with detached body parts and walking dead? Be warned: seeing DEATH BECOMES HER will probably *not* help you answer these questions.

This bizarre combination of SUNSET BOULEVARD, ATTACK OF THE KILLER ZOMBIES, and "Laugh In" stars Meryl Streep as Madeline Ashton, a beautiful, manipulative blonde actress whose star is beginning to fade. After stealing plastic surgeon Ernest Menville (Bruce Willis) from her college "friend" and aspiring author Helen Sharp (Goldie Hawn), Madeline proceeds to ruin Ernest's career and drive him to drink. Meanwhile, Helen, after growing to the size of a blimp and being institutionalized, realizes the only way to get even with Madeline is to become a beautiful, manipulative, blonde author. Throw in a Gothic mansion from which the beautiful, manipulative, raven-haired Lisle von Rhuman (Isabella Rossellini) dispenses a magic potion that guarantees eternal youth, and the mix is complete.

DEATH BECOMES HER boasts some sharply funny dialogue and inventive special effects, and a couple of scenes achieve genuine comic lunacy—notably the film's opening, which finds Madeline starring in "Songbird," a Broadway musical version of Tennessee Williams's "Sweet Bird of Youth" complete with gold lame and disco dancers. Bruce Willis does a good job as the bumbling Dr. Menville, and Meryl Streep's performance is flawless (Streep fans will be pleased to note that, in moments of stress, the actress adds an

authentic Newark accent to her impressive repertoire.) The end result, though, is a film that tries to do too many things at once and does none of them quite right.

DEATH IN VENICE   *DVD*
(MORTE A VENEZIA)
1971 130m c   Drama   ★★★★½
Alfa/Editions Cinegraphiques   (Italy/France)   GP

Dirk Bogarde (Gustav Von Aschenbach), Bjorn Andresen (Tadzio), Silvana Mangano (Tadzio's Mother), Marisa Berenson (Frau Von Aschenbach), Mark Burns (Alfred), Romolo Valli (Hotel Manager), Nora Ricci (Governess), Carole Andre (Esmeralda), Masha Predit (Singer), Leslie French (Travel Agent)

p, Luchino Visconti; d, Luchino Visconti; w, Luchino Visconti, Nicola Badalucco (based on the novel by Thomas Mann); ph, Pasqualino De Santis (Panavision, Technicolor); ed, Ruggero Mastroianni; m, Gustav Mahler, Ludwig van Beethoven, Modest Mussorgsky; art d, Ferdinando Scarfiotti; cos, Piero Tosi

AAN Best Costume Design: Piero Tosi

Luchino Visconti's powerful and controversial screen adaptation of Thomas Mann's novella stars Dirk Bogarde as Gustav von Aschenbach, an aging German composer (modeled after Gustav Mahler) who visits Venice while on the verge of a physical and mental breakdown. Plagued by fears that he can no longer feel emotion because he has been avoiding it for so long, he is unfazed by the boorish and obnoxious behavior of the bourgeois creatures around him. Suddenly, he sees a beautiful blond boy named Tadzio (Bjorn Andresen) who is traveling with his mother and sisters. Gustav becomes obsessed with Tadzio and the ideal of classic beauty he represents. He seeks out the boy, who stirs feelings within him he thought he had lost, but refrains from making contact with him, watching as the lad wanders through the dank, decaying city.

Bogarde is superb as the dying composer. The beautiful cinematography combines with Ferdinando Scarfiotti's art direction to produce a powerful remembrance of time and place past. Visconti also makes effective use of Mahler's Third and Fifth symphonies. The music haunts the film, as do the quiet whispers of sound that help create the film's almost surreal environment. The delicacy of the soundtrack evokes the mood of Aschenbach's last days and his obsession with the face of Tadzio. DEATH IN VENICE was met with almost universal disapproval and misunderstanding when it was first released but, despite the omissions from Mann's text, dependence on flashbacks, and overwrought arguments about art and music between Aschenbach and a colleague, it remains a film of great beauty.

DEATH OF A BUREAUCRAT
1966 87m bw   Comedy   ★★★
Cuban Film Institute   (Cuba)

Salvador Wood (Nephew), Silvia Planas (Aunt), Manuel Estanillo (Bureaucrat), Gaspar de Santelices (Nephew's Boss), Carlos Ruiz de la Tejera (Psychiatrist), Omar Alfonso (Cojimar), Ricardo Suarez (Tarafa), Luis Romay (El Zorro), Elsa Montero (Sabor)

d, Tomas Gutierrez Alea; w, Tomas Gutierrez Alea, Alfredo del Cueto, Ramon F. Suarez; ph, Ramon Suarez; ed, Mario Gonzalez; m, Leo Brower

When the inventor of a machine to produce busts of Cuban hero Jose Martin dies, he is hailed as a model worker and given a lavish funeral. Among the honors, he is buried with his union card, which his widow needs to collect a pension from the state. She asks her nephew to help, and he is soon entangled in a bureaucracy that won't let him obtain an exhumation permit until the body has been buried for two years. Desperate, he steals the body out of its grave, then finds he can't rebury it until he shows his exhumation permit. Full of homages to silent comedians like Laurel and Hardy and Harold Lloyd, DEATH OF A BUREAUCRAT is both a classic slapstick and a sly satire on the choking bureaucracy of Cuban Communism. Director Gutierrez Alea, whose MEMORIES OF UNDERDEVELOPMENT put him among the first rank of Third World filmmakers, did not go unnoticed in his attack on the government; this film was banned in Cuba after a brief release there in 1966.

DEATH OF A SALESMAN
1951 115m bw Drama   ★★★★
Columbia   (U.S.)

Fredric March *(Willy Loman)*, Mildred Dunnock *(Linda Loman)*, Kevin McCarthy *(Biff)*, Cameron Mitchell *(Happy)*, Howard Smith *(Charley)*, Royal Beal *(Ben)*, Don Keefer *(Bernard)*, Jesse White *(Stanley)*, Claire Carleton *(Miss Francis)*, David Alpert *(Howard Wagner)*

p, Stanley Kramer; d, Laslo Benedek; w, Stanley Roberts (based on the play by Arthur Miller); ph, Franz Planer; ed, William Lyon, Harry Gerstad; m, Alex North; prod d, Rudolph Sternad; art d, Cary Odell

AAN Best Actor: Fredric March; *AAN Best Supporting Actor:* Kevin McCarthy; *AAN Best Supporting Actress:* Mildred Dunnock; *AAN Best B/W Cinematography:* Franz Planer; *AAN Best Score (Drama or Comedy):* Alex North

With Fredric March and Kevin McCarthy, this is a very good record of the classic American stage play. Arthur Miller never fared as well again. His somber stage play retained much of its power in this film version featuring one of March's greatest performances as the end-of-the-line Willy Loman.

Willy is incapable of changing a lifestyle and career that are lost in the past. He is in his early sixties and, after being fired, has nowhere to go, clinging to his petty, mediocre values and looking backward with soul-wrenching agony. He has a long-suffering wife, Linda (Dunnock), and two sons, Biff (McCarthy) and Happy (Mitchell). The older son, Biff, is an average business success but has no spirit. Happy is disillusioned after losing his job and has no motivation to find another. The sons share the spiritual malaise of their father. The film powerfully depicts Willy relentlessly plodding to his doom, looking for redemption inside empty rooms of the past and babbling cliches to the apparition of his long-vanished brother.

Lee J. Cobb gave what many consider the definitive performance as Willy in the original 1949 stage hit, and Dustin Hoffman applied his considerable talent to project a tragic Willy in a 1985 TV presentation, though his portrayal is really a caricature. March is excellent if ultimately inferior to Cobb who reportedly was "reverse blacklisted" for his friendly testimony before HUAC during the McCarthy era. Still March looked, felt, and understood the part completely, bringing the character to life as the playwright envisioned him. Kramer's production and Benedek's direction are equally faithful to Miller's vision. Although DEATH OF A SALESMAN lost money at the box office, it stands as one of the great theatrical classics on film.

DEATH RACE 2000
1975 78m c   Action/Science Fiction   ★★★
New World   (U.S.)   R

David Carradine *(Frankenstein)*, Simone Griffeth *(Annie)*, Sylvester Stallone *(Machine Gun Joe Viterbo)*, Mary Woronov *(Calamity Jane)*, Roberta Collins *(Mathilda the Hun)*, Martin Kove *(Nero the Hero)*, Louisa Moritz *(Myra)*, Don Steele *(Junior Bruce)*

p, Roger Corman; d, Paul Bartel; w, Robert Thom, Charles B. Griffith (based on a story by Ib Melchior); ph, Tak Fujimoto

(Metrocolor); ed, Tina Hirsch; m, Paul Chihara; art d, Robin Royce, B.B. Neel; fx, Richard MacLean

Superior drive-in exploitation fare, this violent, campy action flick presents Carradine as Frankenstein, a scarred road warrior in black leather suit and cape. He's the formidable defending champion in the nationally televised Transcontinental Death Race in which competitors gain points by running over pedestrians. His challengers include Stallone as sort of a gangster on wheels with a machine gun in his car and Woronov as a western-outlaw Amazon. Carradine's navigator, Griffeth, is actually a revolutionary spy dedicated to sabataging the savage race.

DEATH RACE 2000 boasts nonstop brutally funny comic-book action. Intended as a rip-off of the big-budget ROLLERBALL, this likably ragged knockoff has become a cult favorite, while its bombastic inspiration has been consigned to the junk heap of genre movie history. The success of this film is a testament to producer Roger Corman's shrewd exploitation of promising filmmakers under the aegis of his New World production company. This legendary "B-minus" movie factory was formed in 1970 and attracted bright young filmmakers eager to break into the Guild-controlled industry. As a case in point, the film's director, Paul Bartel (who would later direct EATING RAOUL and SCENES FROM THE CLASS STRUGGLE IN BEVERLY HILLS), was paid $3,500 for his work on this profitable production.

DEATH TAKES A HOLIDAY
1934 79m bw Fantasy/Romance   ★★★★
Paramount   (U.S.)

Fredric March *(Prince Sirki)*, Evelyn Venable *(Grazia)*, Guy Standing *(Duke Lambert)*, Katherine Alexander *(Alda)*, Gail Patrick *(Rhoda)*, Helen Westley *(Stephanie)*, Kathleen Howard *(Princess Maria)*, Kent Taylor *(Corrado)*, Henry Travers *(Baron Cesarea)*, G.P. Huntley Jr. *(Eric)*

p, E. Lloyd Sheldon; d, Mitchell Leisen; w, Maxwell Anderson, Gladys Lehman, Walter Ferris (based on the play by Alberto Casella); ph, Charles Lang; art d, Hans Dreier, Ernst Fegte

Fredric March, as Death, becomes bored with his usual grim-reaping job and is puzzled that humans fear him so. To learn how he is perceived, he takes on human form as a handsome young prince and becomes the houseguest of an Italian nobleman (Guy Standing). Several guests are quickly repelled by the strange, mysterious prince who bluntly talks of their "meeting with Fate," but a lovely, mystical young woman (Evelyn Venable) is drawn to him. Not a living thing dies as Death dallies with love, and so his stay must be brief. But the unusual visitor fears that his new love will be repelled once he reveals his true identity.

March is riveting as Death, and Standing is also fine as the nervous host. Surprisingly, Paramount assigned the direction of this film to Mitchell Leisen, who had only one previous credit, CRADLE SONG. He was given a sumptuous budget and made the most of it. His background as a set designer for Cecil B. DeMille is evident in the magnificent villa in which March frolicked with Venable. Leisen, who would go on to make HOLD BACK THE DAWN and LADY IN THE DARK, rarely equalled the splendor of this film. He let March have his head, and the actor played his part with ironic vigor, wearing a monocle and delivering his lines in a Balkan accent with great arrogance. Of course, March could do almost no wrong, having won an Oscar only two years earlier for his arresting performance in DR. JEKYLL AND MR. HYDE. (He would win his second for THE BEST YEARS OF OUR LIVES.) The 21-year-old Venable, appearing in her second film, had previously starred in CRADLE SONG.

DEATH WATCH
(LA MORT EN DIRECT)
1980 128m c Science Fiction ★★★½
Selta/Little Bear/Sara/Antenne 2/TV 13/ R
Gaumont (France/West Germany)

Romy Schneider (Katherine Mortenhoe), Harvey Keitel (Roddy),
Harry Dean Stanton (Vincent Ferriman), Therese Liotard (Tracey),
Max von Sydow (Gerald Mortenhoe), Bernhard Wicki, Caroline
Langrishe, William Russell

p, Gabriel Boustiani, Janine Rubeiz; d, Bertrand Tavernier; w,
David Rayfiel, Bertrand Tavernier (based on the novel The
Continuous Katherine Mortenhoe by David Compton); ph, Pierre-
William Glenn (Panavision, Fujicolor); ed, Armand Psenny,
Michael Ellis; m, Antoine Duhamel; art d, Anthony Pratt

For followers of Bertrand Tavernier who know the director
only through A SUNDAY IN THE COUNTRY or 'ROUND
MIDNIGHT, the very realistic science-fiction film DEATH
WATCH may come as a surprise. Set in Glasgow, the film
takes place in a not-too-distant future when nearly all diseases
have been conquered by medical science, leaving natural
causes as society's prime killer. Katherine (Romy Schneider)
is an independent, sensitive, and beautiful woman who has
contracted a terminal disease; Vincent Ferriman (Harry Dean
Stanton) is a crass television producer who finds her imminent demise perfect entertainment for a society that can't get
enough of death; and Roddy (Harvey Keitel) is an employee
who had a video camera implanted in his head, sending
everything he sees back to the TV station for editing and
broadcast. As Roddy follows Katherine through the countryside, in effect shooting a narrative film, he finds himself
becoming attracted to her.

More than just a simple attack on electronic information
in a modern technological society, DEATH WATCH (which
can be seen as Tavernier's PEEPING TOM) also addresses
the issue of the objectification of women and depersonaliza-
tion of death via the (implicitly male-oriented) media.

DECISION BEFORE DAWN
1951 119m bw Spy ★★★★
Fox (U.S.)

Richard Basehart (Lt. Rennick), Gary Merrill (Col. Devlin), Oskar
Werner (Happy), Hildegarde Neff (Hilde), Dominique Blanchar
(Monique), O.E. Hasse (Oberst Von Ecker), Wilfried Seyferth (SS
Man Scholtz), Hans Christian Blech (Tiger), Helene Thimig
(Fraulein Schneider), Robert Freytag (Paul)

p, Anatole Litvak, Frank McCarthy; d, Anatole Litvak; w, Peter
Viertel (based on the novel Call It Treason by George Howe); ph,
Franz Planer; ed, Dorothy Spencer; m, Franz Waxman; art d,
Ludwig Reiber

AAN Best Picture; AAN Best Film Editing: Dorothy Spencer

This superior WWII thriller depicts the efforts of an idealistic
German medic, Happy (Werner), to spy on the Nazis to help
shorten the war that is destroying his country. Volunteering to
work for the Americans, POW Happy undergoes training and
parachutes behind German lines to locate a powerful German
Panzer corps. In the course of the mission, he faces countless
perils and makes several allies and enemies as he rushes to his
heroic destiny.

Director Litvak gives this WWII spy thriller a compelling
sense of reality by shooting it in semi-documentary style on
location in Germany where the war-scarred surroundings add
authenticity to the story. He also utilizes a cast of highly competent unknowns, mostly foreign actors, many of whom
became prominent later. Werner is particularly outstanding and
Litvak milks his situation for maximum dramatic impact
while presenting a moving portrait of the aftershocks of war.
Planer's photography is realistically grim, and Waxman's
score is compelling. An outstanding production in all aspects.

DECLINE OF THE AMERICAN EMPIRE, THE 📀
(LE DECLIN DE L'EMPIRE AMERICAIN)
1986 101m c Drama ★★★½
Malo/Natl. Film Board of Canada/Telefilm R
Canada/Cinema Du Quebec (Canada)

Pierre Curzi (Pierre), Remy Girard (Remy), Yves Jacques
(Claude), Daniel Briere (Alain), Dominique Michel (Dominique),
Louise Portal (Diane), Dorothee Berryman (Louise), Genevieve
Rioux (Danielle), Gabriel Arcand (Mario)

p, Rene Malo, Roger Frappier; d, Denys Arcand; w, Denys
Arcand; ph, Guy Dufaux; ed, Monique Fortier; m, Francois
Dompierre; art d, Gaudeline Sauriol; cos, Denis Sperdouklis

AAN Best Foreign Language Film

Four men swap stories of their sexual escapades while preparing an elaborate dinner. Four women do the same while working out in a gym. When the two groups come together, mutual
betrayals come to light and shatter some illusions. On the surface this is all that happens in this fine film, one of the most
successful Canadian exports ever, but the sparkling wit of the
dialogue and the acutely observed jabs at our eternal preoccupation with sex distinguish THE DECLINE OF THE AMER-
ICAN EMPIRE. The film's philosophy could best be
summed up in a line uttered by one of the men: "Love—the
kind that makes your heart race—lasts two years at best. Then
the compromises begin." Perhaps the most valid criticism of
the film is that its questions are too easy, its answers too pat,
and its characters too similar. On the other hand, the ensemble
performance is impeccable, the technical credits flawless, and
the whole thing quite enjoyable.

DECONSTRUCTING HARRY 📀
1997 96m c Comedy/Drama ★★★½
Sweetland Films (U.S.) R

Woody Allen (Harry Block), Billy Crystal (Larry), Demi Moore
(Helen), Robin Williams (Mel), Judy Davis (Lucy), Elisabeth Shue
(Fay), Kirstie Alley (Joan), Bob Balaban (Richard), Richard
Benjamin (Ken), Eric Bogosian (Burt)

p, Jean Doumanian; d, Woody Allen; w, Woody Allen; ph, Carlo Di
Palma; ed, Susan E. Morse; prod d, Santo Loquasto; art d, Tom
Warren; cos, Suzy Benzinger

AAN Best Original Screenplay: Woody Allen

Woody Allen demonstrates once again that he's the most
consistently original and creative writer working in
American films today with DECONSTRUCTING
HARRY, an excoriatingly funny and brutally honest look at
the psyche of a self-loathing, philandering writer whose life
has reached a crisis point.

Womanizing novelist Harry Block (Woody Allen) is suffering from writer's block, and is also anxious about an
upcoming trip to receive an honorary award from his college.
He's confronted by his gun-wielding ex-sister-in-law (Judy
Davis) for having written a thinly veiled novel depicting their
adulterous affair. Sequences from this novel as well as other
writings by Harry, illustrate his feelings about death, religion
and especially sex. After one of Block's lovers (Elisabeth
Shue) tells him that she's marrying his best friend, Larry (Billy
Crystal), he drives upstate to the award ceremony. He's
accompanied by his son, Hilly (Eric Lloyd), whom he's "kidnapped" from school, along with a black hooker (Hazelle
Goodman), and a friend named Richard (Bob Balaban). On
the way, they stop at an amusement park and Block "meets"
various fictional characters from his books.

While Allen's lacerating portrayal might not be a totally
accurate self-portrait, there are enough similarities as well as
obvious differences, to keep the gossip-hounds happy while

also serving up a provocative dialectic of art vs. reality. The film's complex structure, which includes vignettes from Block's fiction and imagination, enables Allen to draw on the fantasy format he has used in some of his short stories. Allen's performance is one of his best, and the stellar supporting cast is superb, particularly Judy Davis, who's become Allen's quintessential high-strung New York neurotic. Richard Benjamin's presence brings to mind the roles he played in films based on Philip Roth novels (PORTNOY'S COMPLAINT, GOODBYE COLUMBUS), with which DECONSTRUCTING HARRY shares several similarities, most notably the caustic dissection of an emotionally and sexually immature modern Jewish male.

DEEP END

1970 90m c Drama ★★★★
Maran/COKG/Kettledrum (U.S./West Germany)

Jane Asher (Susan), John Moulder-Brown (Mike), Karl Michael Vogler (Swimming Instructor), Christopher Sandford (Fiance), Louise Martini (Prostitute), Erica Beer (Baths Cashier), Diana Dors (Lady Client), Anita Lochner (Kathy), Anne-Marie Kuster (Nightclub Receptionist), Karl Ludwig Lindt (Baths Manager)

p, Helmut Jedele; d, Jerzy Skolimowski; w, Jerzy Skolimowski, Jerzy Gruza, Boleslaw Sulik; ph, Charly Steinberger (Eastmancolor); ed, Barrie Vince; art d, Max Ott Jr., Anthony Pratt; cos, Ursula Sensurg

This quirky black sex comedy is the story of a boy's bizarre and unsentimental education. Moulder-Brown plays Mike, a handsome 15-year-old whose first job has him working in the men's section at a seedy bathhouse in a decidedly unswinging London. He meets a fellow employee, sexy 23-year-old redhead Susan (Asher), who teaches him the ropes and gets him to agree to refer his male clients to her in return for her female clients so that they can both earn better tips. He soon learns to exploit his looks by flirting with the women and encouraging them to fantasize about him. Mike develops an enormous crush on Susan but, looking upon him as a boy, she rejects his advances by telling him she is engaged. However, her constant teasing drives him wild and her affair with the swimming instructor infuriates him. Crazed with his obsessive love, he plots to break them up.

Polish filmmaker Skolimowski, who wrote the screenplay for Roman Polanski's directorial debut, KNIFE IN THE WATER, here has made a powerful, disturbing film on the sexual awakening of a young boy in a sleazy environment. The film, which has an uneasy sense of humor, is well directed, well acted (especially by Asher), and well worth seeing.

DEEP END, THE

2001 99m c Thriller ★★½
i5 Films (U.S.) R

Tilda Swinton (Margaret Hall), Goran Visnjic (Alek Spera), Jonathan Tucker (Beau Hall), Peter Donat (Jack Hall), Josh Lucas (Darby Reese), Raymond J. Barry, billed as Raymond Barry (Carlie Nagle), Tamara Hope (Paige Hall), Jordan Dorrance (Dylan Hall), Heather Mathieson (Sue Lloyd), Holmes Osborne (Loan Officer)

p, Scott McGehee, David Siegel; d, Scott McGehee, David Siegel; w, Scott McGehee (based on the novel The Blank Wall by Elizabeth Sanxay Holding); ph, Giles Nuttgens; ed, Lauren Zuckerman; m, Peter Nashel; prod d, Kelly McGehee, Christopher Tandon; fx, Lou Carlucci, Richard Chuang; cos, Judy Chestnut

A beautifully underplayed performance from Tilda Swinton as a mother desperately trying to shield her son from a murder rap rescues this somewhat creaky remake of Max Ophul's noir classic, THE RECKLESS MOMENT.

Left alone to care for her family while her naval officer husband is away at sea, housewife Margaret Hall (Swinton) finds her life turning into a nightmare. The morning after a trip to Reno to confront Darby Reese (Josh Lucas), the older man she suspects is the lover of her teenaged son, Beau (Jonathan Tucker), Margaret finds a dead body washed up on the edge of her lakefront property. It's Darby, and he appears to have been killed after falling onto the sharp end of a boat's anchor. Accident or not, Margaret quickly disposes of Darby's body. So far, so good—until the doorbell rings. It's handsome black-mailer Alek Spera (Goran Visnjic), and he's got a videotape explicitly linking Beau to the dead body the police have just pulled from the lake.

Ophul's 1949 film stands as a prime example of a particular kind of woman-in-distress thriller that ultimately served to reassure post-WWII audiences that returning servicemen were indeed needed on the home front: children run wild and people get killed when mom's left in charge. Taken out of that very specific social context, the retrograde story runs into contemporary problems: Margaret comes off as a barely competent mother and an uninspiring heroine. But sloshing her way through all the overbearing water imagery is Swinton, and she's marvelously low-key. She lends Margaret an air of grace under pressure and fleshes out feelings of domestic dissatisfaction—a key element that otherwise remains buried in the subtext.

DEEP IMPACT

1998 105m c Disaster/Adventure/Drama ★★
Zanuck/Brown/Manhattan Project/DreamWorks/ PG-13
Amblin/Paramount (U.S.)

Robert Duvall (Spurgeon Tanner), Tea Leoni (Jenny Lerner), Elijah Wood (Leo Biederman), Morgan Freeman (President Beck), Leelee Sobieski (Sarah Hotchner), Vanessa Redgrave (Robin Lerner), Maximilian Schell (Jordan Lerner), James Cromwell (Alan Rittenhouse), Mary McCormack (Andrea Baker), Blair Underwood (Mark Simon)

p, David Brown, Richard D. Zanuck; d, Mimi Leder; w, Michael Tolkin, Bruce Joel Rubin (based on the novels The Hammer of God, by Arthur C. Clarke, and When Worlds Collide, by Edwin Balmer and Philip Wylie); ph, Dietrich Lohmann; ed, David Rosenbloom; m, James Horner; prod d, Leslie Dilley; art d, Gary Kosko, Tom Valentine, Dennis Bradford, Andrew Neskoromny; fx, Scott Farrar, Michael Lantieri, Industrial Light & Magic; cos, Ruth Myers

This first of two summer 1998 blockbusters pitting Earth against a celestial wrecking ball (the other was Michael Bay's ARMAGEDDON) is a three-hankie weeper in disaster-movie drag. Its tear-jerking bull's-eyes are separated by long stretches of tedium.

Rising young reporter Jenny Lerner (Tea Leoni) goes looking for a White House sex scandal and finds instead that the U.S. government has been hiding the fact that there's a massive comet on a collision course with Earth. Jenny's career skyrockets as her relationship with her parents crumbles: her father (Maximilian Schell) has just married a woman half his age, while her mother (Vanessa Redgrave) hides despair beneath a brittle facade of gaiety. A team headed up by aging astronaut Spurgen Tanner (Robert Duvall) is dispatched to nuke the comet, but when the portentously named Messiah Mission fails, the President (Morgan Freeman) declares martial law and initiates the "Ark" lottery, which will decide who gets to live in a DR. STRANGELOVE-esque underground cave complex and who will die.

It's a nice change of pace that the focus here is on the human impact of impending mass destruction, rather than the testosterone-drenched mechanics of kicking wayward comet tail (see ARMAGEDDON). But most of the individuals singled out for their own story lines aren't terrifically interesting.

By far the dullest are adolescent astronomer Leo (Elijah Wood) and his gal Sarah (Leelee Sobieski), whose puppy love is put to the ultimate test when his family is chosen and hers isn't. Leoni has TV-babe looks but none of the breezy authority that makes successful on-air personalities, and whenever she has a scene with Redgrave you can only wonder how a woman so vibrant and multifaceted produced such a shallow daughter. As to the Messiah crew, it's a good thing they're cast with an eye to ethnic and gender diversity, because otherwise you wouldn't be able to tell them apart.

DEER HUNTER, THE   DVD
1978 183m c   War   ★★★★½
EMI/Universal   (U.S.)   R

Robert De Niro (Michael), John Cazale (Stan), John Savage (Steven), Christopher Walken (Nick), Meryl Streep (Linda), George Dzundza (John), Chuck Aspegren (Axel), Shirley Stoler (Steven's Mother), Rutanya Alda (Angela), Pierre Segui (Julien)

p, Barry Spikings, Michael Deeley, Michael Cimino, John Peverall; d, Michael Cimino; w, Deric Washburn (based on a story by Cimino, Washburn, Louis Garfinkle, and Quinn K. Redeker); ph, Vilmos Zsigmond (Panavision, Technicolor); ed, Peter Zinner; m, Stanley Myers; art d, Ron Hobbs, Kim Swados; fx, Fred Cramer; cos, Eric Seelig

AA Best Picture; AAN Best Actor: Robert DeNiro; AA Best Supporting Actor: Christopher Walken; AAN Best Supporting Actress: Meryl Streep; AA Best Director: Michael Cimino; AAN Best Original Screenplay: Michael Cimino, Deric Washburn, Louis Garfinkle, Quinn K. Redeker; AAN Best Cinematography: Vilmos Zsigmond; AA Best Film Editing: Peter Zinner; AA Best Sound: Richard Portman, William McCaughey, Aaron Rochin, Darin Knight

Director Michael Cimino's epic look at how the Vietnam War affected a small Pennsylvania steel community was a huge hit at the box office and garnered several awards, including a Best Picture Oscar. Though its emotional power is undeniable, the film has been justifiably criticized for its somewhat thoughtlessly slanted view of the war and its implicitly racist depiction of the Vietnamese.

Three hours long and neatly divided into three acts, the film follows a trio of close friends—Michael (Robert De Niro), Nick (Christopher Walken) and Steven (John Savage)—from the eve of their tour of duty in Vietnam to the resumption of their interrupted lives. Just before their departure, the steelworkers attend Steven's wedding to Angela (Rutanya Alda); later, Michael and Nick go deer hunting with friends Axel (Chuck Aspegren), Stan (John Cazale) and John (George Dzundza). After the hunt, the film rudely cuts to the heat of battle in Vietnam. Michael, Nick and Steven are all taken prisoner by the Viet Cong and are forced to play Russian roulette while their captors make bets on the outcome. When they finally return home, readjustment is difficult. Steven is embittered and disabled. Nick has chosen to remain in Vietnam and has been sending hundreds of dollars to Steven without explanation. Determined to bring his friend back, Michael returns to Vietnam just as Saigon is about to fall.

Brutally memorable, THE DEER HUNTER is an emotionally draining production that draws a vivid portrait of its characters and their milieu—and succeeds in showing the devastating effect of the war on their lives, as well as their brave attempts at renewal. Unfortunately, the film falters when it comes to the larger questions of America's involvement in Vietnam.

DEFENCE OF THE REALM   DVD
1985 96m c   Political/Thriller   ★★★½
Enigma   (U.K.)   PG

Gabriel Byrne (Nick Mullen), Greta Scacchi (Nina Beckman), Denholm Elliott (Vernon Bayliss), Ian Bannen (Dennis

Markham), Fulton Mackay (Victor Kingsbrook), Bill Paterson (Jack Macleod), David Calder (Harry Champion), Frederick Treves (Arnold Reece), Robbie Coltrane (Leo McAskey), Annabel Leventon (Trudy Markham)

p, Robin Douet, Lynda Myles; d, David Drury; w, Martin Stellman; ph, Roger Deakins; ed, Michael Bradsell; m, Richard Hartley; prod d, Roger Murray-Leach; art d, Diana Charnley; cos, Louise Frogley

This fascinating conspiracy thriller hinges on two seemingly unrelated occurrences: two teenagers' attempted escape from a reformatory and a political scandal involving Dennis Markham (Ian Bannen), a distinguished member of Parliament. When the papers proclaim that Markham was observed leaving the home of a courtesan who was also cozy with an East German official, his loyalty to his country is questioned and his career ruined. Hack reporter Nick Mullen (Gabriel Byrne) is assigned to the story. When a colleague who is also interested in the story mysteriously dies, Mullen digs deeper and finds evidence of a shocking covert operation. With the help of his late colleague's secretary, Nina Beckman (Greta Scacchi), he battles to bring the truth to light.

An extremely well made film, DEFENCE OF THE REALM features a strong central performance by Byrne (GOTHIC, SIESTA, MILLER'S CROSSING), a typically marvelous turn by Elliott as his besotted elder journalist friend, and the beautiful Scacchi (THE COCA-COLA KID, PRESUMED INNOCENT). The direction and editing are fast and tight, and the script by Martin Stellman (who also cowrote the superb QUADROPHENIA) has intelligent and tight plotting rare in this kind of film.

DEFIANT ONES, THE   DVD
1958 97m c   bw   Prison   ★★★★
UA   (U.S.)

Tony Curtis (John Jackson), Sidney Poitier (Noah Cullen), Theodore Bikel (Sheriff Max Muller), Charles McGraw (Captain Frank Gibbons), Lon Chaney Jr. (Big Sam), King Donovan (Solly), Claude Akins (Mac), Lawrence Dobkin (Editor), Whit Bissell (Lou Gans), Cara Williams (The Woman)

p, Stanley Kramer; d, Stanley Kramer; w, Nedrick Young, Harold Jacob Smith; ph, Sam Leavitt; ed, Frederic Knudtson; m, Ernest Gold; prod d, Rudolph Sternad; art d, Fernando Carrere; fx, Alex Weldon; cos, Joe King

AAN Best Picture; AAN Best Actor: Tony Curtis; AAN Best Actor: Sidney Poitier; AAN Best Supporting Actor: Theodore Bikel; AAN Best Supporting Actress: Cara Williams; AAN Best Director: Stanley Kramer; AA Best Original Story and Screenplay: Nathan E. Douglas, Harold Jacob Smith; AA Best B/W Cinematography: Sam Leavitt; AAN Best Film Editing: Frederic Knudtson

Tony Curtis and Sidney Poitier are handcuffed together as white and Black escaped convicts in the South in this classic liberal adventure from Stanley Kramer. Their plight is an all-too-obvious metaphor for American race relations. Though the political lesson drives the movie, the action is also effective as the odd couple flees from their oppressors. This is an engrossing depiction of racial tensions and an oppressive penal system. Both Poitier and Curtis give memorable performances. Curtis's portrayal of a bigoted uneducated Southern "cracker" is probably the best performance and role of his career. This was the film that established Poitier as a star.

DELICATESSEN
1991 97m c   Comedy/Fantasy   ★★★★
Constellation Production/Union Generale   R
Cinematographique/Hachette Premiere   (France)

Marie-Laure Dougnac (Julie Clapet), Dominique Pinon (Louison), Karin Viard (Miss Plusse), Jean-Claude Dreyfus (The Butcher),

Ticky Holgado *(Mr. Tapioca)*, Anne-Marie Pisani *(Mrs. Tapioca)*, Edith Ker *(The Grandmother)*, Mickael Todde *(Lucien)*, Boban Janevski *(Remi)*, Jacques Mathou *(Roger Kube)*

p, Claude Ossard; d, Jean-Pierre Jeunet, Marc Caro; w, Adrien Gilles (screenplay); ph, Darius Khondji; ed, Herve Schneid; m, Carlos D'Alessi; prod d, Jean-Philippe Carp, Kreka Kjnakovic; cos, Valerie Pozzo DiBorgo

Cannibalism serves as a potent metaphor for social oppression in DELICATESSEN, the darkly stylish feature debut by French animators Jean-Pierre Jeunet and Marc Caro.

This surreal, blackly comic fable is set in a run-down apartment building sometime in a dystopian future. The landlord of the building also runs the butcher shop on the ground floor, and keeps his tenants supplied with meat by chopping up hapless applicants for the job of building superintendent. The problem is that the butcher's mousey, nearsighted daughter, Julie Clapet (Marie-Laure Dougnac), keeps falling in love with these sirloins-to-be. In the past, gastronomical necessity has overcome romantic yearning. However, she insists that the newest arrival, Louison (Dominique Pinon, who made such an indelible impression in Jean-Jacques Beineix's DIVA), is different. The butcher doesn't believe her, but something makes him hold off from doing in the newest superintendent until well after the neighbors begin complaining about the lack of meat in their diet.

DELICATESSEN is not as grisly as its premise might suggest. Much of the mayhem and violence takes place offscreen, and the main stylistic influences are Carne, Prevert, Dali and Bunuel, rather than Tobe Hooper. Carno and Jeunet construct a series of vignettes—some hilarious, some grotesque—of the tenants, often as seen through the eyes of two spying little boys. They include an old man who keeps his basement apartment flooded to raise escargots (one of the *slimiest* scenes in screen history); a prim matron who hears mysterious voices—actually a malicious upstairs neighbor speaking through the building vents—telling her to do away with herself (something she attempts, via a series of elaborate Rube Goldberg-style set-ups); and two brothers who support themselves by constructing moo-ing noisemakers. Into this bizarre, painstakingly rendered universe wanders the new superintendent, a former clown still mourning the death of his "partner," a chimpanzee who came to an ugly end when he was eaten by other members of their circus troupe. Though not for all tastes, DELICATESSEN is an ingeniously funny film with a surprisingly sweet romance at its center.

DELIVERANCE *DVD*

1972 109m c Adventure ★★★★
Warner Bros. (U.S.) R

Jon Voight *(Ed)*, Burt Reynolds *(Lewis)*, Ned Beatty *(Bobby)*, Ronny Cox *(Drew)*, Bill McKinney *(Mountain Man)*, Herbert *"Cowboy"* Coward *(Toothless Man)*, James Dickey *(Sheriff Bullard)*, Ed Ramey *(Old Man)*, Billy Redden *(Lonny)*, Seamon Glass *(1st Griner)*

p, John Boorman; d, John Boorman; w, James Dickey (based on his novel); ph, Vilmos Zsigmond (Panavision, Technicolor); ed, Tom Priestley; m, Eric Weissberg; art d, Fred Harpman; fx, Marcel Vercoutere; cos, Bucky Rous

AAN Best Picture; AAN Best Director: John Boorman; *AAN Best Film Editing:* Tom Priestley

Morose, shockingly violent yet strangely beautiful, DELIVERANCE is a tale of what happens to civilized values when put to the test in a hostile wilderness environment. Four Atlanta businessmen decide to get back to nature by treking to the Appalachian wilds to canoe, hunt, and fish in an unspoiled environment before it is permanently flooded by a new dam. But what begins as an adventurous vacation becomes a nightmare of survival as they find themselves hunted by vengeful cretinous mountain men. Voight, Reynolds, Beatty, and Cox are the four city dwellers looking to prove their manhood in the wild. Each of their personal values is put to the test in the course of their deadly adventure. What does it mean to be a man? How far will one go to survive?

This is a tough and powerful portrait of men out of their usual environment. Nor is the deplorable squalor of the mountain communities glossed over. This is not a film for the squeamish. Some have accused the film of exploiting rather than exploring the moments of violent drama culled from James Dickey's first novel while deemphasizing its ecological concerns. Others were troubled by the seemingly perverse beauty of the film. All agree, however, that the meeting between the uneasy quartet and a deformed albino mountain child is a highlight. Cox sees that the kid has a banjo, picks up his own, and strums a few notes. The boy answers him. Then the two challenge each other until both go at a frenzied pace banging out a mountain tune. This celebrated "Duelling Banjos" sequence is an eerie moment of grace before the violence begins.

Boorman's direction is gripping if a bit heavy-handed. The rapids scenes in particular are electrifying. Cinematographer Zsigmond presents breathtaking scenes that sear the memory. Reynolds excelled in this rare serious role. Dickey adapted his own novel and appears as a sheriff.

DE-LOVELY *DVD*

2004 125m c Musical/Biography ★★
Winkler films/Potboiler Productions/UA PG-13
(U.S./U.K.)

Kevin Kline *(Cole Porter)*, Ashley Judd *(Linda Porter)*, Jonathan Pryce *(Gabe)*, Kevin McNally *(Gerald Murphy)*, Sandra Nelson *(Sara Murphy)*, Allan Corduner *(Monty Woolley)*, Peter Polycarpou *(Louis B. Mayer)*, Keith Allen *(Irving Berlin)*, James Wilby *(Edward Thomas)*, Kevin McKidd *(Bobby Reed)*

p, Rob Cowan, Irwin Winkler, Charles Winkler; d, Irwin Winkler; w, Jay Cocks; ph, Tony Pierce-Roberts; ed, Julie Monroe; m, Stephen Endelman; prod d, Eve Stewart; art d, John Hill; fx, Chris Brown, Simon Frame; cos, Janty Yates

Having dismissed the 1946 Cole Porter bio-musical NIGHT AND DAY as a decorous whitewash, director Irwin Winkler and screenwriter Jay Cocks re-imagine composer Porter's life as a grand romance in which his love of men was a mere peccadillo, eclipsed by true love for his wife, Linda.

The film opens as a director (Jonathan Pryce) escorts the aged and ailing Porter (Kevin Kline) to a theatrical run-through of the musical of his life, beginning in Paris in 1918. There the 27-year-old dilettante meets Linda (Ashley Judd), recently divorced, eight years his senior, and admired equally for her beauty and lavish parties. She's heard all about Porter's liaisons with other men, but is too sophisticated to lose a soul mate over such a minor complication. With their swellegant best friends, moneyed jazz-age bohemians Sara and Gerald Murphy (Sandra Nelson, Kevin McNally), they become glittering twin stars in the firmament of the expatriate social scene, conquering Broadway, Hollywood, and their own tempestuous emotional squalls.

The glamorous journey takes Porter and Linda through a series of guest performances by pop singers ranging from Alanis Morissette, whose version of "Let's Fall in Love" is startlingly good, to Sheryl Crow, whose languorous "Begin the Beguine" is simply painful. That Kline, 56, is too old to play Porter during most of the story's timeframe is a minor problem. More distracting is that Cocks and Winkler structure the story as a clunky amalgam of backstage (Porter and his friends were *the-a-tah* folk, after all) and fantasy musical conventions. The resulting awkward, earthbound mishmash thoroughly overshadows Judd's and Kline's authentically moving performances. What kind of romance is that?

DEMENTIA 13
1963 81m   bw   Horror   *DVD*
Filmgroup   (U.S.)   ★★★

William Campbell *(Richard Haloran)*, Luana Anders *(Louise Haloran)*, Bart Patton *(Billy Haloran)*, Mary Mitchell *(Kane)*, Patrick Magee *(Justin Caleb)*, Eithne Dunne *(Lady Haloran)*, Peter Read *(John Haloran)*, Karl Schanzer *(Simon)*, Ron Perry *(Arthur)*, Derry O'Donovan *(Lillian)*

p, Roger Corman, Charles Hannawalt, R. Wright Campbell; d, Francis Ford Coppola; w, Francis Ford Coppola; ph, Charles Hannawalt; ed, Stuart O'Brien; m, Ronald Stein; art d, Albert Locatelli

---

Francis Ford Coppola's first mainstream feature (after a few unremarkable skin flicks) is a little gem of gothic horror, stylishly helmed on a shoestring budget. As an eccentric Irish family bickers over a vast inheritance in a lonely mansion, a mysterious axe murderer picks them off one by one.

The film opens with a violent argument between John (Peter Read) and his wife, Louise (Luana Anders), over the disputed will of his eccentric mother (Eithne Dunne). The argument becomes so heated that John is stricken with a heart attack and dies. Desperate to save her share of the inheritance, Louise sinks her husband's body in a nearby lake and conceals his death from other family members. Meanwhile, more relatives have arrived at the estate (Bart Patton, William Campbell, and Mary Mitchell as Campbell's fiancee) to attend a memorial ceremony for their sister, who drowned in the lake eight years before. Louise sees an opportunity to drive her mother-in-law completely bonkers, persuading her that she's made psychic contact with the dead woman. Howver, before Louise can execute her scheme, she's axed to death, and the hunt for the killer is on.

The film that launched Francis Ford Coppola began as an afterthought. While serving as sound man on Corman's THE YOUNG RACERS, Coppola dashed off a screenplay for a quickie gothic chiller and persuaded the producer to finance the film. Corman supplied $22,000 and several of his stars. Though the plot is rather silly and labored, the film rises above the material by virtue of Coppola's clever editing and obvious flair for composition. The film opens with a typical Corman promotional device: a "psychiatrist" sits in his office and gives the audience a test to determine if they are mentally stable enough to see the movie.

DEMOLITION MAN
1993 115m   c   Action/Comedy   *DVD*
Silver Pictures   (U.S.)   ★★★
                                      R

Sylvester Stallone *(Sergeant John Spartan)*, Wesley Snipes *(Simon Phoenix)*, Sandra Bullock *(Lenina Huxley)*, Nigel Hawthorne *(Dr. Raymond Cocteau)*, Benjamin Bratt *(Alfredo Garcia)*, Bob Gunton *(Chief George Earle)*, Glenn Shadix *(Associate Bob)*, Denis Leary *(Edgar Friendly)*, Grand L. Bush, billed as Grand Bush *(Zachary Lamb (Young))*, Andre Gregory *(Warden William Smithers (Aged))*

p, Joel Silver, Michael Levy, Howard Kazanjian; d, Marco Brambilla; w, Daniel Waters, Robert Reneau, Peter M. Lenkov, Jonathan Lemkin (from a story by Reneau and Lenkov); ph, Alex Thomson, Tom Priestley; ed, Stuart Baird; m, Elliot Goldenthal; prod d, David L. Snyder; art d, Walter P. Martishius; fx, Michael McAlister, Kimberly K. Nelson; cos, Bob Ringwood

---

Tofu-eating proponents of PC can look forward to the future with confidence, at least if they live in Los Angeles. According to DEMOLITION MAN, L.A. (actually, San Angeles) in the year 2035 will be a place where violence is unheard of, "hello" has been replaced by the phrase "mellow greetings," and

everything "bad for you"—cigarettes, alcohol, hamburgers, coffee, sugar—has been outlawed.

Somewhat out of place in this anemic paradise are John Spartan (Sylvester Stallone), a maverick cop, and Simon Phoenix (Wesley Snipes), a superpsychocriminal, both of whom have recently emerged from extended stays in a deep-freeze prison facility. Phoenix has escaped and begun to wreak havoc in a world where the police have no guns; Spartan has been released in a desperate attempt to hunt him down.

The pleasant surprise about DEMOLITION MAN is that both the script, and Stallone, are funny; the film blends big-budget action and tongue-in-cheek humor in the way that LAST ACTION HERO tried, and failed, to do. The future world has been conceived with a gently satirical eye toward the late 20th century, with citizens speaking in CONE-HEADS-style euphemisms ("enhance your calm"), admiring the "Hall of Violence" (including a preserved L.A. city block) at the Museum of History, and referring those interested in studying the past to the President Schwarzenegger Memorial Library. It could never happen here.

DERSU UZALA
(DERUSU USARA)   *DVD*
1975 137m   c   Adventure   ★★★½
Toho/Mosfilm   (U.S.S.R./Japan)

Maxim Munzuk *(Dersu Uzala)*, Yuri Solomine *(Capt. Vladimir Arseniev)*, Schemeikl Chokmorov *(Jan Bao)*, Vladimir Klemena *(Turtwigin)*, Svetlana Danielchanka *(Mrs. Arseniev)*

p, Nikolai Sizov, Yoichi Matsue; d, Akira Kurosawa; w, Akira Kurosawa, Yuri Nagibin (based on the journals of Vladimir Arseniev); ph, Asakazu Nakai, Yuri Gantman, Fyodor Dobronavov; m, Isaac Schwalz; prod d, Yuri Raksha

---

AA Best Foreign Language Film

Captain Vladimir Arseniev (Solomine), leading a topographic expedition deep into the wilds of 19th-century Siberia, meets an old woodsman, Dersu Uzula (Munzuk), who shows him the ways of nature. The two men become close friends over a number of expeditions in which Uzula acts as guide. Each time Arseniev tries to convince the hardy but aging Siberian to return to the city with him, the latter refuses. Finally Uzala does go to the city, but he finds that he cannot readily adapt.

Akira Kurosawa filmed in the USSR with an all-Soviet cast, but a Japanese cinematographer, Asakazu Nakai, photographed the production in 70mm. The first half is wonderful, full of reverence for nature and the man who lives in it. However, it becomes increasingly obvious, literal, and rather ponderous as it progresses. Still these faults cannot detract from DERSU UZALA's magnificence. Like so much of Kurosawa's work, this is a film of great humanism and respect.

DESERT FOX, THE
1951 88m   bw   War/Biography   *DVD*
Fox   (U.S.)   ★★★½

James Mason *(Erwin Rommel)*, Cedric Hardwicke *(Dr. Karl Strolin)*, Jessica Tandy *(Frau Rommel)*, Luther Adler *(Hitler)*, Everett Sloane *(Gen. Burgdorf)*, Leo G. Carroll *(Field Marshal Von Rundstedt)*, George Macready *(Gen. Fritz Bayerlein)*, Richard Boone *(Aldinger)*, Eduard Franz *(Col. Von Stauffenberg)*, Desmond Young *(Himself)*

p, Nunnally Johnson; d, Henry Hathaway; w, Nunnally Johnson (based on the biography by Desmond Young); ph, Norbert Brodine; ed, James B. Clark; m, Daniele Amfitheatrof; art d, Lyle Wheeler, Maurice Ransford; fx, Fred Sersen, Ray Kellogg

---

The first film that attempted to humanize a WWII German military leader, THE DESERT FOX features a magnetic performance by James Mason as Hitler's greatest field commander, Field Marshal Erwin Rommel—grudgingly respected by his opponents, loyally followed by men of the *Afrika Korps*. Opening with a British commando raid on Rommel's headquarters, the film traces the general's remarkable career from his early success in North Africa to his defeat at El Alamein (where he disregarded Hitler's "victory or death" command and retreated), his later illness, his command of the French coastal defenses, and his role in a failed attempt to assassinate Hitler. This last act led to his high-command-mandated, face-saving suicide.

Though Mason is the main attraction in this fragmentary biopic, the supporting cast is excellent (particularly Luther Adler's unforgettable cameo as Hitler). Henry Hathaway's semi-documentary-style direction is as brisk as a panzer attack and Nunnally Johnson's script is literate and penetrating. Mason's sympathetic portrait of Rommel is in marked contrast with other cinematic treatments of the general: Erich Von Stroheim in FIVE GRAVES TO CAIRO, Albert Lieven in FOXHOLE IN CAIRO, Werner Hinz in THE LONGEST DAY, Gregory Gay in HITLER, Christopher Plummer in THE NIGHT OF THE GENERALS, Wolfgang Preiss in RAID ON ROMMEL, Karl Michael Vogler in PATTON and Mason, once more, in THE DESERT RATS.

DESERT HEARTS   *DVD*
1985 96m   c   Drama/Erotic   ★★★½
Desert Hearts   (U.S.)   R

Helen Shaver *(Vivian Bell)*, Patricia Charbonneau *(Cay Rivvers)*, Audra Lindley *(Frances Parker)*, Andra Akers *(Silver)*, Gwen Welles *(Gwen)*, Dean Butler *(Darell)*, James Staley *(Art Warner)*, Katie La Bourdette *(Lucille)*, Alex McArthur *(Walter)*, Antony Ponzini *(Joe Lorenzo)*

p, Donna Deitch; d, Donna Deitch; w, Natalie Cooper (based on the novel *Desert of the Heart* by Jane Rule); ph, Robert Elswit; ed, Robert Estrin; prod d, Jeannine Claudia Oppewall

Though not without problems, DESERT HEARTS is a triumph for director Donna Deitch and an inspiration for any independent filmmaker. Determined to develop a feature film depicting a sexual relationship between two women—a topic never done justice in an American commercial release—Deitch adapted Jane Rule's novel *Desert of the Heart*. The story opens in Reno, Nevada, in 1959. Helen Shaver is Vivian Bell, a college professor from New York, staying in Reno temporarily to obtain a divorce. She stays at Frances Parker's (Audra Lindley) small ranch outside of town. Also living there is Cay Rivvers (Patricia Charbonneau), an employee at one of the local casinos, who is more like a daughter to Parker than a tenant. Bell and Rivvers gradually become close friends but, when their relationship changes, others are affected as well.

Deitch deals sensitively with her theme, eliciting fine performances from her two leads. Charbonneau, after a memorable entrance worthy of the coolest of screen male lovers, portrays Rivvers as a fiery natural force. Shavers's portrayal of the repressed college professor with her hair in a tight bun is a model of restraint and latent passion. We know that when this cool lady finally melts, it will be something to see. The film falters a bit with some of the plot development, a reflection, no doubt, of Deitch's budget rather than her talent. DESERT HEARTS unfolds in a format typical for commercial filmmaking, which isn't a detriment, but doesn't allow for some of the more complicated emotions and issues within the story to surface.

DESIRE
1936 89m   bw   Romance   ★★★★
Paramount   (U.S.)

Marlene Dietrich *(Madeleine de Beaupre)*, Gary Cooper *(Tom Bradley)*, John Halliday *(Carlos Margoli)*, William Frawley *(Mr. Gibson)*, Ernest Cossart *(Aristide Duval)*, Akim Tamiroff *(Police Official)*, Alan Mowbray *(Dr. Edouard Pauquet)*, Zeffie Tilbury *(Aunt Olga)*, Enrique Acosta *(Pedro)*, Stanley Andrews *(Customs Inspector)*

p, Ernst Lubitsch; d, Frank Borzage; w, Edwin Justus Mayer, Waldemar Young, Samuel Hoffenstein (based on an original story by Hans Szekeley and R.A. Stemmle); ph, Charles Lang, Victor Milner; ed, William Shea; m, Frederick Hollander; art d, Hans Dreier, Robert Usher; cos, Travis Banton

Clearly the product of a gilded cocktail shaker. Bearing the stylistic stamps of both producer Lubitsch and director Borzage, this is a sophisticated romantic comedy about a lovely jewel thief, Madeleine de Beaupre (Dietrich), who tricks a gem dealer (Cossart) out of a priceless string of pearls and flees Paris after implicating a stuffy psychiatrist (Mowbray). She drives wildly toward the Spanish border and nearly runs down Tom Bradley (Cooper), a young American engineer on vacation. She uses him as an unwitting accomplice in smuggling the pearls out of the country. Cleared by Spanish customs, he drives off with Madeleine in hot pursuit. The romantic chase is on! What began as mere expediency soon develops into love—with numerous complications along the way, of course.

Successful with the public, DESIRE was one of the most elegantly produced films of the 1930s; the sets, costumes, and decor all shimmer with hot light. Borzage, who also directed the silent classic SEVENTH HEAVEN, added his sweetly romantic warmth to the deft, spicy production plans already laid out by Lubitsch for this wonderful film. Playing with both conviction and wit, Dietrich achieves one of her best performances away from mentor Josef von Sternberg; here she is slightly less exotic and rather more human than in her other films. Cooper, too, in his second pairing with Dietrich (after the memorable MOROCCO) really shows his flair for sophisticated romance with this one. He makes the most of the funny yet impossibly romantic line, "All I know about you is you stole my car and I'm insane about you." The remarkable John Halliday, whose presence graces any film, leads a terrific supporting cast. One of the ultimate expressions of Paramount Studios chic, DESIRE remains one of its desirable star's finest films.

DESPERATE CHARACTERS
1971 87m   c   Drama   ★★★½
ITC   (U.S.)

Shirley MacLaine *(Sophie)*, Kenneth Mars *(Otto)*, Gerald S. O'Loughlin *(Charlie)*, Sada Thompson *(Claire)*, Jack Somack *(Leon)*, Chris Gampel *(Mike)*, Mary Alan Hokanson *(Flo)*, Robert Bauer *(Young Man)*, Carol Kane *(Young Girl)*, Michael Higgins *(Francis Early)*

p, Frank D. Gilroy; d, Frank D. Gilroy; w, Frank D. Gilroy (based on the novel by Paula Fox); ph, Urs Furrer (Eastmancolor); ed, Robert Q. Lovett; m, Lee Konitz, Jim Hall, Ron Carter; art d, Edgar Lansbury; cos, Sally Gifft

This well-written if somewhat stagey character study focuses on a day in the life of an urban proto-yuppie couple, Sophie and Otto (Maclaine and Mars) who reside near the once fashionable but now rundown Brooklyn Heights (this is 1971, before the gentrification boom). Urban violence is breaking out all around them but they are becoming inured to it. Their conversation has deteriorated into banalities. Otto, an attorney, casually remarks that he is ending his partnership with Charlie (O'Loughlin), his long-time associate and best friend. It seems that Charlie has gone liberal and, as such, he is spending altogether too much time with causes and not enough with cases. A street cat paws at their door and MacLaine feeds it some milk. This act of kindness is rewarded by a deep bite on her hand. At a party thrown later that night by psychiatrist Mike (Gampel) and his wife, Flo (Hokanson), the joy of the evening is shattered by a rock that smashes a window. You get the idea? The times they are a'changin'.

MacLaine and Mars were acclaimed for their performances but the public stayed away. This is one of Maclaine's best performances. Mars carved himself a comfortable niche in comedy with a starring role as the Nazi playwright in THE PRODUCERS and several hilarious parts in various Mel Brooks films. This was the feature directorial debut for playwright turned screenwriter-director Gilroy who had won previously won accolades for his award-winning play, *The Subject Was Roses* and his screenplay for the film version. He went on to write and direct films such as ONCE IN PARIS…, a delightful story of a screenwriter who goes to Paris to write a screenplay which was as at least as interesting as DESPERATE CHARACTERS and, sadly, suffered a similar fate.

DESPERATE HOURS, THE   DVD
1955 112m bw Crime   ★★★★
Paramount   (U.S.)

Humphrey Bogart *(Glenn)*, Fredric March *(Dan Hilliard)*, Arthur Kennedy *(Jesse Bard)*, Martha Scott *(Eleanor Hilliard)*, Dewey Martin *(Hal)*, Gig Young *(Chuck)*, Mary Murphy *(Cindy)*, Richard Eyer *(Ralphie)*, Robert Middleton *(Kobish)*, Alan Reed *(Detective)*

p, William Wyler; d, William Wyler; w, Joseph Hayes (based on his novel and play); ph, Lee Garmes (Vistavision); ed, Robert Swink; m, Gail Kubik; art d, Hal Pereira, MacMillan Johnson; fx, John P. Fulton, Farciot Edouart; cos, Edith Head

In his second-to-last film, Humphrey Bogart comes full circle, playing a character nearly identical to his pivotal role in THE PETRIFIED FOREST, the 1936 film that catapulted him to stardom. Bogart undertakes his reprise with a vengeance. As the film opens, Glenn (Bogart) breaks out of prison with his kid brother (Martin) and a mentally deficient behemoth (Middleton). They take refuge in the middle-class home of Dan Hilliard (March) where they terrorize his family as Glenn waits for a call from his sweetheart. Her assignment was to dig up some long-buried loot and then rendezvous with the escapees. However, the call doesn't come and Glenn grows increasingly desperate, brutalizing Hilliard, his wife (Scott), his attractive daughter (Murphy), and his feisty young son (Eyer).

Here William Wyler has expertly directed a taut suspenseful thriller. Joseph Hayes has also done a marvelous job in adapting his own novel for the screen. Two old pros who get the maximum impact out of every line, Fredric March and Bogart give spellbinding performances as two strong personalities engaged in a mortal showdown. Bogart reportedly had some reservations about this film, worrying that he might be too old to play a convincingly menacing hoodlum but his qualms never show on screen. The story had also been a successful stage play with the much-younger Paul Newman in Bogart's role, but the part was purposely "aged" by Hayes to suit Bogie's 55 years, each of which shows on his wonderful, craggy face. Among the supporting performers, Gig Young, Mary Murphy, and Richard Eyer are all fine, and Martha Scott is a standout as the hero's wife.

DESPERATELY SEEKING SUSAN   DVD
1985 104m c Romance/Comedy   ★★★½
Orion   (U.S.)   PG-13

Rosanna Arquette *(Roberta Glass)*, Madonna *(Susan)*, Aidan Quinn *(Dez)*, Mark Blum *(Gary)*, Robert Joy *(Jim)*, Laurie Metcalf *(Leslie)*, Anna Levine *(Crystal)*, Bill Patton *(Nolan)*, Peter Maloney *(Ian)*, Steven Wright *(Larry)*

p, Sarah Pillsbury, Midge Sanford; d, Susan Seidelman; w, Leora Barish; ph, Edward Lachman (Deluxe Color); ed, Andrew Mondshein; m, Thomas Newman; prod d, Santo Loquasto; art d, Speed Hopkins; cos, Santo Loquasto

This is one of the most charming low-budget films in years, a freewheeling, light-hearted farce that gives some new twists to old plot devices. Rosanna Arquette is Roberta, a bored New Jersey housewife married to swimming pool magnate, Gary (Mark Blum). To spice up her bland life, Roberta takes to reading the personal ads and becomes intrigued by a periodically recurring notice headlined "Desperately Seeking Susan." On a whim, she goes off to New York City and eventually finds the mysterious Susan (Madonna). She follows Susan around the city and watches as the wildly garbed woman sells her leather jacket at a used clothing store. Roberta buys the jacket, not realizing it contains Egyptian earrings Susan has stolen from a murdered mobster. The plot twists are fairly simple, but that really doesn't matter in this energetic and well-acted comedy. Director Susan Seidelman guides her cast with a light, enthusiastic touch, never making more out of her frothy material than need be.

DESTRY RIDES AGAIN   DVD
1939 94m bw Western   ★★★★
Universal   (U.S.)

Marlene Dietrich *(Frenchy)*, James Stewart *(Tom Destry)*, Mischa Auer *(Boris Callahan)*, Charles Winninger *("Wash" Dimsdale)*, Brian Donlevy *(Kent)*, Allen Jenkins *(Bugs Watson)*, Warren Hymer *(Gyp Watson)*, Irene Hervey *(Janice Tyndall)*, Una Merkel *(Lily Belle Callahan)*, Tom Fadden *(Lem Claggett)*

p, Joe Pasternak; d, George Marshall; w, Felix Jackson, Henry Myers, Gertrude Purcell (based on the novel by Max Brand); ph, Hal Mohr; ed, Milton Carruth; m, Frank Skinner; art d, Jack Otterson; cos, Vera West

A classic sendup of western heroism starring James Stewart and—of all people—Marlene Dietrich. Stewart is the lawman who takes control of his town without shooting it up. Dietrich is the chantoosie who sings "See What the Boys in the Back Room Will Have." The son of a brave lawman gone to his reward, Tom Destry (Stewart) appears to be anything but a two-fisted fighter for justice. He refuses to wear guns, and, when he steps up to the bar, he orders milk. Soft-spoken and mild-mannered, he becomes the butt of jokes when he shows up in Bottleneck where Kent (Donlevy) runs the wildest saloon in town and lords it over the populace. His girlfriend and star attraction is the famous Frenchy (Dietrich), arguably the *real* power in town. Destry has arrived in Bottleneck to be deputy to "Wash" Dimmsdale (Winninger), the former deputy turned town drunk who has been made sheriff by Kent as a joke. Sheriff Dimmsdale is mortified when he learns that the young Destry does not carry a gun. "You shoot it out with them, and, for some reason, they get to look like heroes," Destry reasons. "You put 'em behind bars, and they look little and cheap, like they are."

Dietrich's career was in free fall prior to this movie. She had left the protective wing of her directorial mentor Josef von Sternberg in 1935, and most of her subsequent movies were not popular. After appearing in ANGEL, an uncommon failure for Ernst Lubitsch, Dietrich was considered "box office poison" by exhibitors. For three years, she made no films of consequence, and, when Paramount dropped her contract in 1937, she was considered washed up. She fled to Europe believing that American film audiences were through with her. Then she got a transatlantic call in the middle of the night from producer Joe Pasternak who wanted her for his new film at Universal—a western! One of the screen's most glamorous women, renowned for romances, melodramas, and sophisticated comedy, playing a saloon hussy in a crude oater? But Dietrich took it and she was appropriately bawdy, tempestuous, and wicked but with a heart of gold. The public responded and her star shot up again, higher than before.

Under the sure directorial hand of genre veteran Marshall, DESTRY RIDES AGAIN is a well-paced western that seamlessly combines humor, romance, suspense and action.

Stewart's performance is rendered in his usual low-key manner and provides the perfect counterpoint to Dietrich's bold and brassy character. All the great character actors in this film are superb as well. DESTRY was filmed three times following the publication of the Max Brand novel in 1930, first as a Tom Mix standard in 1932, again in the 1939 Dietrich/Stewart classic, and in 1954 as a routine western with Audie Murphy.

DETECTIVE, THE
1954 91m bw Comedy ★★★★
Columbia (U.K.)

Alec Guinness *(Fr. Brown)*, Joan Greenwood *(Lady Warren)*, Peter Finch *(Flambeau)*, Cecil Parker *(The Bishop)*, Bernard Lee *(Inspector Valentine)*, Sidney James *(Parkinson)*, Gerard Oury *(Inspector Dubois)*, Ernest Thesiger *(Vicomte)*, Ernest Clark *(Secretary)*, Austin Trevor *(Herald)*

p, Paul Finder Moss, Vivian A. Cox; d, Robert Hamer; w, Thelma Schnee, Robert Hamer (based on the "Father Brown" stories by G.K. Chesterton); ph, Harry Waxman; ed, Gordon Hales; m, Georges Auric

Alec Guinness is the perfect G.K. Chesterton character, the likable clerical detective on the trail of art thieves. Joan Greenwood, Peter Finch, Bernard Lee, Sidney James and Ernest Thesiger marvelously abet the stellar direction of Robert Hamer. Father Brown is an eccentric priest who takes it upon himself to transport a priceless cross from London to Rome. An international jewel thief steals the cross, and the enterprising priest sets out to get it back and save the thief's soul. An extremely entertaining and polished film with Guinness at his best.

DETECTIVE, THE *DVD*
1968 114m c Crime ★★★½
Fox (U.S.)

Frank Sinatra *(Joe Leland)*, Lee Remick *(Karen Leland)*, Ralph Meeker *(Lt. Curran)*, Jack Klugman *(Dave Schoenstein)*, Horace MacMahon *(Farrell)*, Lloyd Bochner *(Dr. Roberts)*, William Windom *(Colin MacIver)*, Jacqueline Bisset *(Norma MacIver)*, Tony Musante *(Felix)*, James Inman *(Teddy Leikman)*

p, Aaron Rosenberg; d, Gordon Douglas; w, Abby Mann (based on the novel by Roderick Thorp); ph, Joseph Biroc (Panavision, Deluxe Color); ed, Robert Simpson; m, Jerry Goldsmith; art d, Jack Martin Smith, William Creber; fx, L.B. Abbott, Art Cruickshank; cos, Moss Mabry

Joe Leland (Sinatra) is a top New York City detective investigating the mutilation and murder of a homosexual (Inman). He arrests the victim's former roommate (Musante) for the crime, and the suspect is tried, convicted and executed. But the case haunts Sinatra because he allowed himself to blindly railroad Musante into a confession for the sake of a promotion. Ironically, another case leads Sinatra to the real killer, and he soon finds himself embroiled in a political scandal that could rock New York City. Now somewhat dated because of its misguidedly "enlightened" attitude toward homosexuality, this film is engrossing nonetheless because of its superb cast. Screenwriter Abby Mann took a few liberties with Thorp's trashy novel, but the changes were an improvement. Look for Robert Duvall in a small role.

DETECTIVE STORY
1951 105m bw Crime ★★★★
Paramount (U.S.)

Kirk Douglas *(Jim McLeod)*, Eleanor Parker *(Mary McLeod)*, William Bendix *(Lou Brody)*, Cathy O'Donnell *(Susan Carmichael)*, George Macready *(Karl Schneider)*, Horace MacMahon *(Lt. Monahan)*, Gladys George *(Miss Hatch)*, Joseph

Wiseman *(Charles Gennini)*, Lee Grant *(Shoplifter)*, Gerald Mohr *(Tami Giacoppetti)*

p, William Wyler; d, William Wyler; w, Philip Yordan, Robert Wyler (based on the play by Sidney Kingsley); ph, Lee Garmes; ed, Robert Swink; art d, Hal Pereira, Earl Hedrick; cos, Edith Head

AAN Best Actress: Eleanor Parker; *AAN Best Supporting Actress:* Lee Grant; *AAN Best Director:* William Wyler; *AAN Best Screenplay:* Philip Yordan, Robert Wyler

Kirk Douglas gives one of his best performances in this seminal cop film, directed by William Wyler. The plot is thin, but the drama is fleshed out with interesting characters. Chief among these is Jim McLeod (Douglas), a hardboiled, dedicated, by-the-book detective proud of his untarnished record in a one-man war against crime. Douglas is tough on all the lawbreakers he drags in to police headquarters, particularly an unscrupulous doctor (Macready), whom he beats up in a police van before delivering him to the lock-up. Lieutenant Monahan (MacMahon) becomes suspicious of McLeod's brutal treatment of the crooked physician, investigates further, and finds out that the abortionist has a surprising link to the detective.

Douglas is intense and electrifying as the altruistic yet narrow-minded Jim McLeod. Like DEAD END the source material for the film is a Sidney Kingsley morality play. Once again director Wyler deftly handles this potentially stagey material. And, as in DEAD END, one of the film's most outstanding features is an impressive set. This stark creation by Hal Pereira and Earl Hedrick is comprised of little more than floorboards, desks, unaccommodating tables, and ancient file cabinets. It suggests a precinct office with no frills or comforts, physical or spiritual.

Though confined to this one set, ace cinematographer Lee Garmes provides fluid camera movement as our eye is smoothly directed from one character to another. DETECTIVE STORY is methodical in its depiction of the sometimes traumatic events of one day in a precinct but the marvelous quirks and shadings of these characters create highly exciting drama.

DETOUR *DVD*
1945 67m bw Crime ★★★★
Producers Releasing Corp. (U.S.)

Tom Neal *(Al Roberts)*, Ann Savage *(Vera)*, Claudia Drake *(Sue)*, Edmund MacDonald *(Charles Haskell, Jr.)*, Tim Ryan *(Diner Proprietor)*, Esther Howard *(Hedy)*, Roger Clark *(Dillon)*, Pat Gleason *(Man)*, Don Brodie *(Used Car Salesman)*

p, Leon Fromkess; d, Edgar G. Ulmer; w, Martin Goldsmith; ph, Benjamin Kline; ed, George McGuire; m, Leo Erdody; art d, Edward C. Jewell; cos, Mona Barry

DETOUR puts the noir in film noir. Utilizing "night-for-night" cinematography, this amazingly dark genre landmark unfolds with the logic of a nightmare as Al Roberts (Tom Neal) recounts in voice-over the unlikely chain of events that landed him in a purgatorial diner in the middle of nowhere. A triumph of talent and inspiration over budget, it was made on the cheap by a Poverty Row studio in just six days. This road picture was filmed almost entirely in the studio, but director Edgar Ulmer transforms limitations into virtues. The sleazy look somehow feels right for DETOUR's self-consciously Freudian allegory of Oedipal rage and misogyny.

Roberts is a piano player at a chintzy joint in New York City. Sue (Claudia Drake), his fiancee, is a singer who dreams of stardom. She goes off to Hollywood, leaving him to his embittered reveries. He decides to marry her and hits the road with outstretched thumb. Al gets a ride from Haskell (MacDonald), a drug-addled businessman who buys him a meal and regales him with the story of how he got his scars. Haskell inexplicably dies on the road; Roberts, fearing he'll be blamed, buries the body and takes the car. When Roberts meets Vera (Ann Savage), a castrating harpy who knows his secrets and how to exploit them, things go from bad to worse.

DETOUR is a film that must be seen to be (dis)believed. Today it enjoys a richly deserved cult-film status. The wooden Neal is just right as the fatalistic protagonist and Savage is one of the most memorably off-kilter vixens in movie history.

DEVIL AND DANIEL WEBSTER, THE   DVD

1941   107m   bw   Science Fiction/Fantasy   ★★★★
RKO   (U.S.)

Edward Arnold *(Daniel Webster)*, Walter Huston *(Mr. Scratch)*, James Craig *(Jabez Stone)*, Jane Darwell *(Ma Stone)*, Simone Simon *(Belle)*, Gene Lockhart *(Squire Slossum)*, John Qualen *(Miser Stevens)*, Frank Conlan *(Sheriff)*, Lindy Wade *(Daniel Stone)*, George Cleveland *(Cy Bibber)*

p, William Dieterle; d, William Dieterle; w, Dan Totheroh (based on the story "The Devil and Daniel Webster" by Stephen Vincent Benet); ph, Joseph August; ed, Robert Wise; m, Bernard Herrmann; fx, Vernon L. Walker

AAN Best Actor: Walter Huston; *AA Best Score (Drama):* Bernard Herrmann

Two fascinating stalwarts, Arnold and Huston, have a go at each other in this witty fantasy based on the O. Henry Prize-winning Stephen Vincent Benet short story. The author reportedly had a hand in the film version with Dan Totheroh.

Jabez Stone (Craig) is a New England farmer having a difficult time making a living. When he casually swears that he would sell his soul for enough money to make life easier, up pops Huston as Mr. Scratch. This charming devil purchases Stone's soul in return for seven years of good luck. At first Stone thinks it's all an elaborate joke but then the money starts rolling in. Sudden success transforms the simple, good-hearted Stone into a cold-blooded businessman who now cheats his neighbors, ignores his wife (Shirley) and their new-born child, refuses to listen to his mother (Darwell), and even gives up going to church on Sundays, opting to play poker instead. His phenomenal luck makes the entire farming community suspicious. The situation worsens on the homefront when Mr. Scratch's temptingly beautiful emissary (Simon), an odd servant girl, comes to live with Stone's family. Stone builds a grand mansion and gives an elegant ball, inviting everyone, including the famous Daniel Webster (Arnold). But everything goes wrong. Strange, crude people arrive and eat savagely at the banquet tables, and an equally strange band plays eerie music. All the guests, it seems, are people who have struck bargains with the Devil. The scene terrifies Stone and he flees, following his family whom he has run out of the mansion. He catches up with them on the road and his wife promises help. She goes to Webster, begging him to plead her husband's case. The great lawyer agrees to save his fellow New Englander if he can.

Arnold, though appearing only intermittently, is at his stentorian best and Huston steals the film as a roguish Devil full of snap, crackle and pop. Huston was nominated for an Oscar for his performance and the film won a richly deserved Oscar for Bernard Herrmann's lively and eerie score. Director Dieterle does one of his finest ever jobs of directing with the telling of this picturesque tale, and August's camerawork is masterful.

DEVIL AND MISS JONES, THE

1941   92m   bw   Comedy   ★★★½
RKO   (U.S.)

Jean Arthur *(Mary Jones)*, Robert Cummings *(Joe O'Brien)*, Charles Coburn *(John P. Merrick)*, Edmund Gwenn *(Hooper)*,

Spring Byington *(Elizabeth Ellis)*, S.Z. Sakall *(George)*, William Demarest *(1st Detective)*, Walter Kingsford *(Allison)*, Montagu Love *(Harrison)*, Richard Carle *(Oliver)*

p, Frank Ross, Norman Krasna; d, Sam Wood; w, Norman Krasna; ph, Harry Stradling; ed, Sherman Todd; m, Roy Webb; prod d, William Cameron Menzies; fx, Vernon L. Walker

AAN Best Supporting Actor: Charles Coburn; *AAN Best Original Screenplay:* Norman Krasna

Fun, but one wishes it were better. John P. Merrick (Coburn), the world's richest man, decides to infiltrate one of his holdings, a department store, to ferret out union organizers who have targeted him as responsible for the miserable working conditions of his employees. He is subjected to many indignities by the management, finally ending up in the shoe department alongside Mary Jones (Arthur). She thinks him destitute and takes pity on him, showing him the intricacies of the department. He attends union meetings and carefully notes everybody there, but as the abuse from the store's management becomes more intolerable and as Merrick himself becomes romantically interested in Elizabeth Ellis (Byington), he has a change of heart, eventually sacking the management and marrying Ellis. This comedy is enhanced by the Capraesque presence of Arthur, but what it really needed was Capra himself.

DEVIL-DOLL, THE

1936   79m   bw   Horror/Fantasy   ★★★★
MGM   (U.S.)

Lionel Barrymore *(Paul Lavond/Madame Mandelip)*, Maureen O'Sullivan *(Lorraine Lavond)*, Frank Lawton *(Toto)*, Robert Greig *(Emil Coulvet)*, Lucy Beaumont *(Mme. Lavond)*, Henry B. Walthall *(Marcel)*, Grace Ford *(Lachna)*, Pedro de Cordoba *(Charles Matin)*, Arthur Hohl *(Victor Radin)*, Rafaela Ottiano *(Malita)*

p, Edward J. Mannix; d, Tod Browning; w, Garrett Fort, Guy Endore, Erich von Stroheim, Tod Browning (based on the novel *Burn, Witch, Burn!* by Abraham Merritt); ph, Leonard Smith; ed, Frederick Y. Smith; m, Franz Waxman; art d, Cedric Gibbons; cos, Dolly Tree

Tiny people, and we don't mean Munchkins. Another Tod Browning foray into the macabre, THE DEVIL-DOLL stars Lionel Barrymore as Paul Lavond, a wrongly convicted prisoner who escapes Devil's Island with mad scientist Marcel (Walthall). They take refuge in Marcel's old laboratory, where he demonstrates his miraculous invention, a serum that reduces all living things to miniature size. Before dying, the ailing Marcel passes his secret formula on to Lavond, who decides to seek vengeance on the three men who framed him. Disguised as an old woman who runs a doll shop, Lavond manages to reduce one of his enemies and paralyze a second, but begins to lose control of the scheme because of his crazed assistant, Ottiano, who is so spellbound by the miniaturizing process that she refuses to stop, at one point hissing, "We'll make the *whole world* small!"

While THE DEVIL-DOLL is no FREAKS, director Tod Browning, in his second-to-last film, adds a sinister edge to what is basically a morality play. The special effects still impress today; the oversized sets and props are expertly done, with much attention given to detail; and the film is excellently photographed by Leonard Smith. Erich Von Stroheim is credited with co-writing the screenplay, but the exact nature of his contributions has never been made clear. Cast is generally expert, with the exception of veddy-British Lawton, who is too refined for his assignment.

DEVIL IN A BLUE DRESS   DVD

1995   102m   c   Crime/Mystery/Drama   ★★★★
Clinica Estetico/Mundy Lane Entertainment   R
(U.S.)

Denzel Washington *(Easy Rawlins)*, Tom Sizemore *(Dewitt Albright)*, Jennifer Beals *(Daphne Monet)*, Don Cheadle *(Mouse)*, Maury Chaykin *(Matthew Terell)*, Terry Kinney *(Todd Carter)*, Mel Winkler *(Joppy)*, Albert Hall *(Odell)*, Lisa Nicole Carson *(Coretta James)*, Jernard Burks *(Dupree Brouchard)*

p, Jesse Beaton, Gary Goetzman; d, Carl Franklin; w, Carl Franklin (based on the novel by Walter Mosley); ph, Tak Fujimoto; ed, Carole Kravetz; m, Elmer Bernstein; prod d, Gary Frutkoff; art d, Dan Webster; fx, Tom Ward; cos, Sharen Davis

In this marvelously realized adaptation of Walter Mosley's hard-boiled detective novel, private investigator Ezekiel "Easy" Rawlins (Denzel Washington) isn't so much solving a puzzle as negotiating a minefield, hoping to find his way out without losing his skin. And because he's black in an overtly racist town, his skin is always an issue.

Los Angeles, 1948. Rawlins has lost his job and desperately needs cash to make a mortgage payment on his little bungalow-style piece of the American Dream. A local barkeep hooks him up with grinning, blue-eyed reptile Dewitt Albright (Tom Sizemore), who commissions him to find a white woman, Daphne (Jennifer Beals), who's known to "enjoy the company of Negroes." Her fiance, rich mayoral candidate Todd Carter (Terry Kinney), wants her back. Rawlins is no detective, but he doesn't have to be— all he has to do is show his face in some colored dives, ask some questions, and report back. Naturally, it's not that easy. Hard-boiled narrative complications develop in short order, but director Carl Franklin isn't particularly concerned with the machinations of mystery plots. Nor is he seduced by the temptations of noir visual style (although Tak Fujimoto's camera work is plenty stylish). Instead, he's interested in the faces behind the swirling cigarette smoke and the emotions beneath the chic period clothes.

Franklin explores the racial realities of a Los Angeles in which no one even *pretends* to be surprised that cops use the word "nigger" and routinely frame non-white suspects. But the film is no polemic; rather, it's a stunningly successful recreation of a time and place largely ignored by the (white) cultural mainstream, and a deliberate rehabilitation of the idea of African-American community and continuity. Moreover, unlike many neo-noir narratives, DEVIL IN A BLUE DRESS truly is a moral journey. Rawlins starts out an innocent man and ends up compromised. When he announces he's given up on honest factory work and intends to become a full-time private investigator, it's a sad moment. He's destined to develop a cynical skin and a knowing manner, doomed to become a more conventional character than he needs to be.

DEVIL IN THE FLESH, THE

(LE DIABLE AU CORPS)
1946   110m   bw   Romance   ★★★★
TRC   (France)

Micheline Presle *(Marthe Grainger)*, Gerard Philipe *(Francois Jaubert)*, Jean Debucourt *(M. Jaubert)*, Denise Grey *(Mme. Grangier)*, Pierre Palau *(M. Marin)*, Jean Varas *(Jacques Lacombe)*, Jeanne Perez *(Mme. Marin)*, Germaine Ledoyen *(Mme. Jaubert)*, Maurice Lagrenee *(Doctor)*, Richard Francoeur *(Headwaiter)*

p, Paul Graetz; d, Claude Autant-Lara; w, Jean Aurenche, Pierre Bost (based on the novel by Raymond Radiguet); ph, Michel Kelber; ed, Madeleine Gug; m, Rene Cloerec

A scandalous film in its day, DEVIL IN THE FLESH tells the tale of a 17-year-old (Philipe) in love with a married older woman (Presle) whose soldier husband has been assigned to the front. The story is told through the boy's eyes, in a flash-back structure that points out the doomed nature of the affair. Many contemporary viewers were furious at the way the soldier—a man risking his life for his country—was deceived, and petitions were sent to the French government urging that the film be banned. (Canada agreed to the ban, and New York state censors would show it only after certain cuts were made.) This touching story now seems quite harmless, but it still works extremely well as drama, hoisted by the wonderful Presle and Philipe and the helming of director Autant-Lara. It was poorly remade as an X-rated film in 1986 by Marco Bellocchio. Based on the novel by Raymond Radiguet, who wrote his tale of romance at the age of 18, two years before his death.

DEVIL, PROBABLY, THE

(LE DIABLE, PROBABLEMENT)
1977   95m   c   Drama   ★★★★
Sunchild/GMF/Gaumont   (France)

Antoine Monnier *(Charles)*, Tina Irissari *(Alberte)*, Henri De Maublanc *(Michel)*, Laetitia Carcano *(Edwige)*, Regis Hanrion *(Dr. Mime)*, Nicolas Deguy *(Valentin)*, Geoffrey Gaussen *(Bookseller)*, Robert Honorat *(Commissioner)*, Vincent Cottrell, Laurence Delannoy

p, Stephane Tchalgadjieff; d, Robert Bresson; w, Robert Bresson; ph, Pasqualino De Santis (Eastmancolor); ed, Germaine Lamy; m, Philippe Sarde; prod d, Eric Simon; cos, Jackie Budin

Another rigorous—and unusually watchable—exercise in cinematic discipline by Bresson, the master of the minimal. The story, the end of which Bresson reveals immediately, depicts young Monnier drifting through politics, religion, and finally to suicide. The actors are all nonprofessionals who don't so much act as move around and blankly state their lines to the director's intricate commands. The best introduction (along with LANCELOT DU LAC) to the work of one of film's greatest thinkers.

DEVIL'S OWN, THE   DVD

1997   107m   c   Action/Drama/Political   ★★½
Devil's Own Productions/Lawrence Gordon   R
Productions/Columbia   (U.S.)

Harrison Ford *(Sgt. Tom O'Meara)*, Brad Pitt *(Rory Devaney—Francis "Frankie" McGuire)*, Margaret Colin *(Sheila O'Meara)*, Ruben Blades *(Edwin Diaz)*, Treat Williams *(Billy Burke)*, George Hearn *(Judge Peter Fitzsimmons)*, Natascha McElhone *(Megan Doherty)*, Paul Ronan *(Sean Phelan)*, Simon Jones *(Harry Sloan)*, Julia Stiles *(Bridget O'Meara)*

p, Lawrence Gordon, Robert F. Colesberry; d, Alan J. Pakula; w, David Aaron Cohen, Vincent Patrick, Kevin Jarre (based on a story by Kevin Jarre); ph, Gordon Willis; ed, Tom Rolf, Dennis Virkler; m, James Horner; prod d, Jane Musky; art d, Robert Guerra; fx, Philip Cory, Steve Riley, Steve Kirshoff, Robert Kirshoff, Andrew McDade; cos, Bernie Pollack

An earnest, surprisingly well-written drama about guilt and betrayal that dares to defy the juvenile, wham-bam-thank-you-ma'am aesthetics that have turned mainstream action pictures into feature-length video games.

IRA foot soldier Frankie McGuire (Pitt) is sent to New York City with a false name, Rory Devaney, and a mad mission to buy Stinger missiles. He's placed with the family of cop Tom O'Meara (Ford), whose Irishness doesn't extend much beyond an appreciation of Guinness, corned beef and step-dancing. Surrounded by a wife and three daughters, O'Meara takes to the polite Irish lad, who in turn sees in O'Meara the benevolent father he lost to the violence at home when he was a child. But violence inevitably follows

Frankie and endangers his substitute family, leading to a schematic showdown.

Given the number of writers and the widely-reported clashes that marred production, it's a wonder THE DEVIL'S OWN turned out as well as it did. Pitt does fine work here (proving, among other things, that Hollywood hunks can learn accents if they try), and Ford lets painful slivers of vulnerability show through the sober shell he has spent the better part of the decade constructing. The movie's look is pure glum, deglamorized 1970s—PRINCE OF THE CITY springs to mind, and not just because Treat Williams is on hand as Irish-American gunrunner Billy Burke—which suits the subject matter, though it's a little hard to stomach the fact that this kind of low-rent grit now costs $90 million. And despite Frankie's frequent reminders that "this isn't an American story, it's an Irish story," it *is* a mainstream American movie, marred by a certain moral smugness and the need to tie up loose ends, whether or not it makes any dramatic sense.

DIABOLIQUE   DVD
(LES DIABOLIQUES)
1955 107m bw Thriller   ★★★★½
Filmsonor   (France)

Simone Signoret *(Nicole Horner)*, Vera Clouzot *(Christina Delasalle)*, Paul Meurisse *(Michel Delasalle)*, Charles Vanel *(Inspector Fichet)*, Jean Brochard *(Plantiveau)*, Noel Roquevert *(Herboux)*, Therese Dorny *(Mme. Herboux)*, Pierre Larquey *(Drain)*, Michel Serrault *(Raymond)*, Yves-Marc Maurin *(Moinet)*

p, Henri-Georges Clouzot; d, Henri-Georges Clouzot; w, Henri-Georges Clouzot, Jerome Geronimi, Frederic Grendel, Rene Masson (from the novel *Celle Qui N'etait Pas* by Pierre Boileau, Thomas Narcejac); ph, Armand Thirard; ed, Madeleine Gug; m, Georges Van Parys; art d, Leon Barsacq

A bitter chiller. One of the most suspenseful films ever made, DIABOLIQUE revolves around a callous schoolmaster, Meurisse, his heiress wife, Clouzot, and his mistress, Signoret. The latter, a cold-blooded murderess, helps Christina poison and drown her husband. They dump the corpse in the pool of Michel's boarding school, but Christina grows increasingly fearful that Michel is still alive. An investigation of the schoolmaster's death proceeds, but when the pool is drained no body is found. Adding to the mystery is the testimony of schoolchildren who insist they've seen Michel.

Director Henri-Georges Clouzot keeps the viewer guessing to the final frames. The picture received great critical acclaim, sharing the prestigious New York Film Critics Award for Best Foreign Film with Vittorio de Sica's UMBERTO D. The frightened wife of the "dead" man, Vera Clouzot, is the real-life Mrs. Clouzot. Authors Pierre Boileau and Thomas Narcejac, upon learning that Alfred Hitchcock was interested in acquiring the rights to *Celle Qui N'Etait Pas* (upon which DIABOLIQUE was based), set out to pen another novel that would surely interest Hitch—*D'Entre Les Mortes*, which later became VERTIGO.

DIABOLIQUE also includes one of the most effective "eyeball scenes" in filmmaking (second only to that in Bunuel and Dali's UN CHIEN ANDALOU) when the "dead" man rises from the bathtub. Rumor has it Clouzot's films were always shot in an atmosphere of antagonism, and the camera here seems to be observing in a merciless way. The last 15 minutes are as suspenseful as anything ever put on film.

DIAL M FOR MURDER   DVD
1954 105m c Thriller   ★★★½
Warner Bros.   (U.S.)

Ray Milland *(Tony Wendice)*, Grace Kelly *(Margot Wendice)*, Robert Cummings *(Mark Halliday)*, John Williams *(Chief Inspector Hubbard)*, Anthony Dawson *(Captain Swan Lesgate)*, Leo Britt *(The Narrator)*, Patrick Allen *(Pearson)*, George Leigh *(William)*, George Alderson *(The Detective)*, Robin Hughes *(Police Sergeant)*

p, Alfred Hitchcock; d, Alfred Hitchcock; w, Frederick Knott (based on his play); ph, Robert Burks (3-D-Natural Vision, Warner Color); ed, Rudi Fehr; m, Dimitri Tiomkin; art d, Edward Carrere, George James Hopkins; cos, Moss Mabry

Lower case Hitch, but diverting and sleek, with the climax early on. Milland is a playboy whose wealth has come entirely through his marriage to chic heiress Kelly. When he fears he'll lose her riches to American mystery writer Cummings, he plots her unfortunate demise. Milland contacts Dawson, an old chum who now operates in the underworld, and blackmails him into killing Kelly while he is conveniently away. Milland's plan misfires, however, when the murder plans go awry, leading to a thorough round of questioning from the crafty inspector Williams.

Based on the successful play by Frederick Knott, this adaptation was essentially treated as an assignment by Hitchcock, who had already begun to work on REAR WINDOW. Shackled by Jack Warner's insistence on filming the picture in 3D (with its terribly immobile cameras), Hitchcock focused his attention on his new favorite actress, Kelly, with whom he would work again on his next two films, REAR WINDOW and TO CATCH A THIEF.

Repeating his stage role as the Scotland Yard inspector is John Williams, who excells among the cast. Although the 3D version has hardly been seen, it does contain one of the best, least gimmicky, uses of the added dimension as Kelly, while being attacked, reaches "into the audience," desperately searching for a weapon to defend herself. The opening credit sequence of a finger dialing "M" on a telephone is, because of the problems of achieving close focus with 3D cameras, actually a giant dial and a large wooden finger which Hitchcock had specially constructed.

DIAMONDS ARE FOREVER   DVD
1971 118m c Spy   ★★★
Eon/Danjaq (U.K.)   PG

Sean Connery *(James Bond)*, Jill St. John *(Tiffany Case)*, Charles Gray *(Blofeld)*, Lana Wood *(Plenty O'Toole)*, Jimmy Dean *(Willard Whyte)*, Bruce Cabot *(Saxby)*, Bruce Glover *(Wint)*, Putter Smith *(Kidd)*, Norman Burton *(Felix Leiter)*, Joseph Furst *(Dr. Metz)*

p, Harry Saltzman, Albert R. Broccoli; d, Guy Hamilton; w, Richard Maibaum, Tom Mankiewicz (based on the novel by Ian Fleming); ph, Ted Moore (Panavision, Technicolor); ed, Bert Bates; m, John Barry; prod d, Ken Adam; art d, Jack Maxsted, Bill Kenney; fx, Les Hillman, Albert Whitlock, Wally Veevers, Whitey McMahon; cos, Elsa Fennell, Ted Tetrick, Donfeld

AAN Best Sound: Gordon K McCallum (Sound), John Mitchell (Sound), Alfred J Overton (Sound)

Next door to glass, but aided by the return of Connery (George Lazenby had undertaken the role of Bond in ON HER MAJESTY'S SECRET SERVICE) teamed with Jill St. John, instead of the usual parade of faceless Bond girls. The Las Vegas locations sizzle and the script at least has the good sense not to take itself too seriously. The producers had by now decided that Connery, not Bond, was their big attraction and lured him back into the fold with an offer he couldn't refuse—1.25 million, a percentage of the profits on the film, and an agreement to back two films of Connery's choice, which he could either star in or direct. Connery accepted the offer, but was not to be persuaded to do the role again until NEVER SAY NEVER AGAIN in 1983. Shirley Bassey, who sang the title song from GOLDFINGER, returned here to sing the title song written by Barry Don Black. Two karate-kicking girls initiate Bond into sexual equality, but the genre was beginning to look shopworn by now. That's Lana Wood, Natalie's sister, as Plenty O'Toole. But no amount of frou-frou can distract us from wondering why no arch villain just shot old 007.

DIARY OF A CHAMBERMAID *DVD*
(LE JOURNAL D'UNE FEMME DE CHAMBRE)
1964 97m bw Drama ★★★★
Speva/Cine Alliance/FS/Dear (France/Italy)

Jeanne Moreau *(Celestine)*, Georges Geret *(Joseph)*, Michel Piccoli *(Monsieur Monteil, Husband)*, Francoise Lugagne *(Madame Monteil, Wife)*, Jean Ozenne *(Monsieur Rabour, Father)*, Daniel Ivernel *(Capt. Mauger)*, Jean-Claude Carriere *(Cure)*, Gilberte Geniat *(Rose)*, Bernard Musson *(Sacristan)*, Muni *(Marianne)*

p, Serge Silberman, Michel Safra; d, Luis Bunuel; w, Luis Bunuel, Jean-Claude Carriere (based on the novel *A Chambermaid's Diary* by Octave Mirbeau); ph, Roger Fellous (Franscope); ed, Louisette Hautecoeur; art d, Georges Wakhevitch; cos, Georges Wakhevitch

A wonderfully vulgar film from the masterful Spanish director Luis Bunuel, DIARY OF A CHAMBERMAID is an adaptation in spirit of Octave Mirbeau's novel and Jean Renoir's 1946 film. Moreau is a Parisian chambermaid who takes a new job in the country at the estate of a bourgeois womanizer, Piccoli, his frigid wife Lugagne, and her likeable, foot-fetishist father, Ozenne. Sexual vices are not limited to the bourgeoisie, however, as Geret, the filthy, fascist longtime servant, is found to be a sadistic rapist and murderer.

Although Bunuel would regularly attack societal institutions, this film is one of his most overtly political. Set in the late 1920s, this chambermaid's diary sets up the social conditions of both political and sexual aggression that made the rise of fascism not only possible but—as Bunuel makes clear in the film's final shot of the stormy heavens—inevitable. His statement is a Surrealist one, presented in the most realistic of styles (which may surprise viewers who have only a peripheral familiarity with Bunuel's work).

The director's wicked humor and unforgettable visual sense are perhaps best illustrated in his filming the rape and murder of an innocent young girl. Instead of narrating the attack in detail, Bunuel uses three shots—a wild boar running through the forest, a frightened rabbit, and the corpse's legs covered with the live snails she had been collecting.

DIARY OF A COUNTRY PRIEST *DVD*
(LE JOURNAL D'UN CURE DE CAMPAGNE)
1950 120m bw Religious ★★★★½
UGC (France)

Claude Laydu *(Priest of Ambricourt)*, Jean Riveyre *(Count)*, Andre Guibert *(Priest of Torcy)*, Nicole Maurey *(Louise)*, Nicole Ladmiral *(Chantal)*, Marie-Monique Arkell *(Countess)*, Martine Lemaire *(Seraphita)*, Antoine Balpetre *(Dr. Delbende)*, Jean Danet *(Olivier)*, Gaston Severin *(Canon)*

p, Leon Carre; d, Robert Bresson; w, Robert Bresson (based on the novel by George Bernanos); ph, L.H. Burel; ed, Paulette Robert; m, Jean-Jacques Grunenwald; art d, Pierre Charbonnier

A frail, unnamed priest (Laydu, an untrained actor) is assigned to his first parish—Ambricourt, a small and only somewhat religious town. He does as saintly priests are known to do—simply accepting the people around him as they are and attempting to strengthen their faith, while himself living a life of poverty, with bread and wine the only food he can eat without falling ill. His major achievement is bringing a withdrawn countess out of her hatred for God and into a state of peacefulness.

Robert Bresson, returning to the screen after a five-year absence, succeeds in capturing the literary spirit of George Bernanos' book and retelling it in a cinematic language. It is a

brilliant adaptation, remaining faithful to Bernanos without resorting to harmful omissions or additions, allowing its audience to enjoy the identical spiritual experience as the reader of the novel. DIARY OF A COUNTRY PRIEST shared the top prize at the Venice Film Fest with Kurosawa's RASHOMON. It is definitely not a film for everyone's tastes—Bresson's work is known for its slow, meditative pace—but a brilliant picture all the same.

DIARY OF A MAD HOUSEWIFE
1970 95m c Comedy/Drama ★★★½
Universal (U.S.) R

Richard Benjamin *(Jonathan Balser)*, Frank Langella *(George Prager)*, Carrie Snodgress *(Tina Balser)*, Lorraine Cullen *(Sylvie Balser)*, Frannie Michel *(Liz Balser)*, Lee Addams *(Mrs. Prinz)*, Peter Dohanos *(Samuel Keefer)*, Katherine Meskill *(Charlotte Rady)*, Leonard Elliott *(Mon. Henri)*, Valma *(Margo)*

p, Frank Perry; d, Frank Perry; w, Eleanor Perry (based on the novel by Sue Kaufman); ph, Gerald Hirschfeld (Technicolor); ed, Sidney Katz; prod d, Peter Dohanos; cos, Ruth Morley, Flo Transfield, James Hagerman

AAN Best Actress: Carrie Snodgress

The angst of yuppiedom. Benjamin, one of the great film twits of our time, portrays a money-mad attorney who bullies his wife, Snodgress, to the point where she takes a lover, Langella. Soon enough Snodgress discovers Langella is every bit the twit Benjamin is, just a different sort of twit. Langella is self-centered and will play only with committed women because he is unable to commit himself. The plot takes Snodgress into several diverting episodes and culminates when she divests herself of both husband and lover and seeks solace in group therapy, only to learn that happiness doesn't reside in psychiatry, either.

The three leads are excellent. Benjamin has been seen in many films as the consummate ass: THE MARRIAGE OF A YOUNG STOCKBROKER, THE SUNSHINE BOYS, LOVE AT FIRST BITE, THE STEAGLE, and as the ultimate nerd in PORTNOY'S COMPLAINT. Langella played the cad in a few more films and eventually the lead in John Badham's DRACULA. Snodgress was nominated for an Oscar for her role in this film, the highpoint of her career and the only nomination this rather slight picture received.

DIARY OF ANNE FRANK, THE *DVD*
1959 170m bw Drama/War ★★★★
Fox (U.S.)

Millie Perkins *(Anne Frank)*, Joseph Schildkraut *(Otto Frank)*, Shelley Winters *(Mrs. Van Daan)*, Richard Beymer *(Peter Van Daan)*, Gusti Huber *(Edith Frank)*, Lou Jacobi *(Mr. Van Daan)*, Diane Baker *(Margot Frank)*, Douglas Spencer *(Kraler)*, Dody Heath *(Miep)*, Ed Wynn *(Albert Dussell)*

p, George Stevens; d, George Stevens; w, Frances Goodrich, Albert Hackett (based on their play and the autobiography, *Anne Frank: Diary of a Young Girl*); ph, William Mellor, Jack Cardiff; ed, Robert Swink, William Mace, David Bretherton; m, Alfred Newman; art d, Lyle Wheeler, George W. Davis; fx, L.B. Abbott

AAN Best Picture; AAN Best Supporting Actor: Ed Wynn; *AA Best Supporting Actress:* Shelley Winters; *AAN Best Director:* George Stevens; *AA Best B/W Cinematography:* William C. Mellor; *AAN Best Score (Drama or Comedy):* Alfred Newman; *AA Best Art Direction-Set Decoration (B/W):* Lyle R. Wheeler, George W. Davis, Walter M. Scott, Stuart A. Reiss; *AAN Best Costume Design (B/W):* Charles LeMaire, Mary Wills

Millie Perkins seems too mature and too flat for the pivotal role in this touching film, based on the famous WWII diary of the young Anne Frank. Skillfully directed by George Stevens (who photographed much of the famous concentration camp footage after Germany's defeat), the film is told in flashback, as Anne's father Schildkraut, a camp survivor, returns to the warehouse attic in Amsterdam where his Jewish family hid from the "Green Police" (the Dutch Gestapo) for two years.

Cramped in uncomfortable quarters, Schildkraut, his wife Huber, and their two daughters, Baker and Perkins, are sheltered through the kindness and courage of two Gentile shop owners. Also sharing the tiny living space are husband and wife Jacobi and Winters (in the first of her character parts), their teenage son Beymer, and the aging dentist Wynn. As the atrocities rage outside their hideaway, Anne concerns herself with many of the usual teenage problems—parental relationships, her affection for Peter, her jealousy towards her older sister—and records them in her diary. There are a number of close calls, surprise searches, and suspenseful moments that terrify the hidden inhabitants, who, when they are finally discovered, are carted off to a concentration camp.

Only Otto Frank survives, returning to the attic to find Anne's written reflections. He is moved to tears and shamed when he reads Anne's famous line: "In spite of everything, I still believe that people are really good at heart." A vivid and carefully produced work of poignancy and loss.

DICK TRACY   DVD
1990 103m c   Adventure/Comedy   ★★★½
Silver Screen Partners IV/Touchstone (U.S.)   PG

Warren Beatty (Dick Tracy), Charlie Korsmo (Kid), Glenne Headly (Tess Trueheart), Madonna (Breathless Mahoney), Al Pacino (Big Boy Caprice), Dustin Hoffman (Mumbles), William Forsythe (Flattop), Charles Durning (Chief Brandon), Mandy Patinkin (88 Keys), Paul Sorvino (Lips Manlis)

p, Warren Beatty; d, Warren Beatty; w, Jim Cash, Jack Epps Jr. (based on characters created by Chester Gould); ph, Vittorio Storaro (Technicolor); ed, Richard Marks; m, Danny Elfman; prod d, Richard Sylbert; art d, Harold Michelson; fx, Buena Vista Visual Effects Group, John Caglione Jr., Doug Drexler; chor, Jeffrey Hornaday; cos, Milena Canonero; anim, Allen Gonzales, Samuel Recinos

AAN Best Supporting Actor: Al Pacino; *AAN Best Cinematography:* Vittorio Storaro; *AA Best Original Song:* "Sooner or Later (I Always Get My Man)"; Stephen Sondheim (Music & Lyrics); *AA Best Art Direction-Set Decoration:* Richard Sylbert, Rick Simpson; *AAN Best Sound:* Thomas Causey, Chris Jenkins, David E. Campbell, D.M. Hemphill; *AAN Best Costume Design:* Milena Canonero; *AA Best Makeup:* John Caglione, Jr., Doug Drexler

In sheer visual terms, this is the most convincing of the comic book movies that have been popular for the last decade or so. Surprisingly sweet and good-natured, DICK TRACY is a highly stylized piece of fluff that's easier to digest than the ponderous pretensions of the equally over-hyped BATMAN. Producer/director/star Warren Beatty looks great in his yellow fedora and trench coat though his jaw is never as sharp as Chester Gould's celebrated comic strip cop.

This old-fashioned story takes place in a strikingly stylized comic-strip city of the 1930s. Handsome, hardworking detective Dick Tracy is hot on the trail of crime boss Big Boy Caprice (played with gusto by a nearly unrecognizable Al Pacino) who has taken the entire underworld syndicate of the city away from Lips Manlis (Paul Sorvino). After disposing of Lips, taking over his nightclub, and stealing his girl, Breathless Mahoney (Madonna), Big Boy comes up with the idea of uniting all the villains in town under his leadership, thereby running the city. This is a job for Dick Tracy!

From the opening shot of the famous fedora and badge to the wildly extravagant long sweeps of the matte-painted comic-book city, DICK TRACY has a gorgeous but hollow look. It's the first film to transfer successfully the look of a comic book to the screen (kudos to Vittorio Storaro, whose striking photography makes striking use of primary colors) in an entirely cinematic way.

The performances are all fairly interesting. Hoffman's cameo as Mumbles is creepy and surprisingly funny, Headly and Korsmo are terrific, and Beatty is mesmerizingly hollow. The true star of this film, however, is Pacino, who provides a wildly over-the-top performance as Big Boy—in many ways he out-Jokers Jack Nicholson's Joker in BATMAN.

DIE ANOTHER DAY   DVD
2002 133m c   Action/Spy   ★★½
Albert R. Broccoli's Eon Productions   PG-13
(U.K./U.S.)

Pierce Brosnan (James Bond), Halle Berry (Jinx Johnson), Toby Stephens (Gustav Graves), Rosamund Pike (Miranda Frost), Rick Yune (Zao), John Cleese (Q), Judi Dench (M), Samantha Bond (Moneypenny), Michael Madsen (Falco), Kenneth Tsang (General Moon)

p, Barbara Broccoli, Michael G. Wilson; d, Lee Tamahori; w, Neal Purvis, Robert Wade; ph, David Tattersall; ed, Andrew MacRitchie, Christian Wagner; m, David Arnold; prod d, Peter Lamont; art d, Simon Lamont; fx, Mara Bryan, Chris Corbould, James Lamb; cos, Lindy Hemming

The countless allusions to Bond films past will no doubt keep fans occupied, and what a good thing that is. Sandwiched between some spectacular set pieces and one very funny exchange between superspy Bond (Pierce Brosnan at his best) and gadget-master Q (John Cleese) is a formula grown tedious and self-conscious. When the action stops, so does the movie.

After a typically bombastic opening that finds Bond a prisoner in a North Korean military encampment, things go awry. A spy exchange returns Bond to his boss, M (Judi Dench), who, believing Bond cracked under torture, revokes Bond's 007 designation. Now a rogue agent, Bond trots across Cuba, London and Iceland looking for Zao (Rick Yune), the spy for whom he was traded; Bond suspects Zao knows who set him up for capture. Bond teams up with American spy Jinx Johnson (Halle Berry) and fellow MI6 agent Miranda Frost (Rosamund Pike), and faces off against billionaire Gustav Graves (Toby Stephens), who's developed (yawn) a killer satellite.

Berry shows surprising grace when running 'n' gunning, but she's utterly unconvincing the second she opens her mouth; this might help explain why all those cheeky double entendres sound so strained. The escalating battle between Bond and Graves is among the best ever filmed, but the non-action scenes are so pedestrian that one suspects the good stuff is due less to director Lee Tamahori than to one of the best second-unit crews in the biz. Madonna, who co-wrote and performs the title song, has an uncredited cameo as a fencing coach.

DIE HARD   DVD
1988 131m c   Action   ★★★
Gordon/Silver (U.S.)   R

Bruce Willis (John McClane), Bonnie Bedelia (Holly Gennaro McClane), Reginald VelJohnson (Sgt. Al Powell), Paul Gleason (Dwayne T. Robinson), De'voreaux White (Argyle), William Atherton (Thornburg), Hart Bochner (Ellis), James Shigeta (Takagi), Alan Rickman (Hans Gruber), Alexander Godunov (Karl)

p, Lawrence Gordon, Joel Silver; d, John McTiernan; w, Jeb Stuart, Steven E. de Souza (based on the novel by Roderick Thorp); ph, Jan De Bont (Panavision, Deluxe Color); ed, Frank J. Urioste, John F. Link II; m, Michael Kamen; prod d, Jackson DeGovia; fx, Richard Edlund, Al Di Sarro; cos, Marilyn Vance-Straker

AAN Best Film Editing: Frank J. Urioste, John F. Link; *AAN Best Sound:* Don Bassman, Kevin F Cleary, Richard Overton, Al Overton; *AAN Best Visual Effects:* Richard Edlund, Al DiSarro, Brent Boates, Thaine Morris; *AAN Best Sound Effects Editing:* Stephen H. Flick, Richard Shorr

The pumped-up, high tech surprise hit of 1988; a triumph of slick direction and lowbrow thrills, marred but not spoiled by a sour aftertaste.

On Christmas Eve, a New York cop (Willis) arrives in Los Angeles to spend the holidays with his estranged wife (Bedelia) and their two young children. The couple separated after the Japanese corporation Bedelia works for promoted her to a powerful position in their brand-new Los Angeles headquarters, an imposing state-of-the-art office building in Century City. Willis now meets her at a Christmas party thrown on the building's 30th floor. While he is washing up in his wife's executive bathroom, a group of international terrorists seizes the building and takes everyone at the party hostage, in an attempt to break into the company safe and steal $670 million in negotiable bonds. Barefoot and wearing only a T-shirt and slacks, Willis escapes the terrorists and makes his way to the unfinished upper floors of the building, where he wages a one-man war against the intruders.

Tautly directed by McTiernan (PREDATOR), DIE HARD is skillfully shot and consistently thrilling throughout its lengthy running time. The high-rise location, in particular, is cleverly employed to provide an array of unusual and breathtaking action scenes. Unfortunately, the film's script panders to the audience's worst fears and resentments—suggesting that foreigners are not to be trusted and feminism has destroyed the fabric of the American family, and so on. Despite this distasteful subtext, however, DIE HARD is a well-made, exciting film. A beefed-up Willis fares well in a breezy mode, but looks uncomfortable when the emoting turns heavy. The talented Bedelia is wasted, while Rickman, as the chief villain, gives an impeccably evil performance which put him on the international map.

DIM SUM: A LITTLE BIT OF HEART

1985 88m c Comedy ★★★½
CIM (U.S.) PG

Laureen Chew *(Geraldine Tam)*, Kim Chew *(Mrs. Tam)*, Victor Wong *(Uncle Tam)*, Ida F.O. Chung *(Auntie Mary)*, Cora Miao *(Julia)*, John Nishio *(Richard)*, Amy Hill *(Amy Tam)*, Keith Choy *(Kevin Tam)*, Elsa Cruz Pearson *(Eliza)*, Helen Chew *(Linda Tam)*

p, Tom Sternberg, Wayne Wang, Danny Yung; d, Wayne Wang; w, Terrel Seltzer (based on an idea by Laureen Chew, Seltzer, Wang); ph, Michael Chin (DuArtColor); ed, Ralph Wikke, David Lindblom; m, Todd Boekelheide; art d, Christopher P. Lee, Lydia Tanji; cos, Lydia Tanji

Appealing if uneventful. This humanistic story involves an old Chinese widow who resides in San Francisco with her 30-year-old daughter. Though she has lived for many years in America, the widow is proud of her Chinese heritage and refuses to assimilate into American culture. She loves her daughter but feels the time has come for her, like her brother and sister, to be wed. Her daughter is torn between wanting to marry her boyfriend, a Los Angeles doctor, and the duty she feels toward her mother. When the mother learns from a fortune teller that she is approaching her time to die, the old woman must make some drastic changes in her attitudes. DIM SUM: A LITTLE BIT OF HEART is composed of small moments commenting in ways both broad and subtle on assimilation. Director Wayne Wang understands these problems, allowing scenes to build slowly and letting the audience get to know the characters. The universality of this comedy's subject matter makes it a gentle pleasure.

DINER

1982 110m c Comedy/Drama ★★★★
MGM-UA (U.S.) R

Steve Guttenberg *(Edward "Eddie" Simmons)*, Daniel Stern *(Laurence "Shrevie" Schreiber)*, Mickey Rourke *(Robert "Boogie" Shefteil)*, Kevin Bacon *(Timothy Fenwick, Jr.)*, Timothy Daly *(William "Billy" Howard)*, Ellen Barkin *(Beth)*, Paul Reiser *(Modell)*, Kathryn Dowling *(Barbara)*, Michael Tucker *(Bagel)*, Jessica James *(Mrs. Simmons)*

p, Jerry Weintraub; d, Barry Levinson; w, Barry Levinson; ph, Peter Sova (Metrocolor); ed, Stu Linder; m, Bruce Brody, Ivan Kral, Joe Tuley; art d, Leon Harris; fx, Charles R. Schulthies; cos, Gloria Gresham

AAN Best Original Screenplay: Barry Levinson (Screenplay)

A thoughtful, charming sleeper. Writer-director Barry Levinson's debut takes us back to the late-1950s Baltimore of his youth, brilliantly evoking that era through carefully drawn characters. Five pals meet at their favorite diner in between problems with women, gambling, and all the woes attendant upon being twentysomething in 1959. Steve Guttenberg, who has been dragging his feet on the way to the altar, forces his fiancee to pass the world's toughest Baltimore Colts quiz to qualify for marriage; Daniel Stern, who is already married, would rather spend time with the guys than with the wife he thinks doesn't understand him; Timothy Daly has a pregnant girlfriend who doesn't want to get married; Kevin Bacon is rich, bright, and usually bombed; and Mickey Rourke is a rebellious hairdresser and law student who spends most of his spare time chasing women.

The prominent rock 'n' roll soundtrack keeps the film firmly grounded in its period, but Levinson's masterly script, filled with funny, realistic dialogue (especially in the diner scenes), transcends time and place even as the film so richly conveys both. Featuring excellent performances by a host of actors who've gone on to prominent careers, to say nothing of Ellen Barkin's wistful turn as Stern's neglected wife, DINER is an often hilarious, frequently touching film.

DINNER AT EIGHT

1933 113m bw Comedy/Drama ★★★★★
MGM (U.S.)

Marie Dressler *(Carlotta Vance)*, John Barrymore *(Larry Renault)*, Wallace Beery *(Dan Packard)*, Jean Harlow *(Kitty Packard)*, Lionel Barrymore *(Oliver Jordan)*, Lee Tracy *(Max Kane)*, Edmund Lowe *(Dr. Wayne Talbot)*, Billie Burke *(Mrs. Oliver Jordan)*, Madge Evans *(Mrs. Wayne Talbot)*, Jean Hersholt *(Joe Stengel)*

p, David O. Selznick; d, George Cukor; w, Frances Marion, Herman J. Mankiewicz, Donald Ogden Stewart (based on the play by George S. Kaufman and Edna Ferber); ph, William Daniels; ed, Ben Lewis; m, Dr. William Axt; art d, Hobe Erwin, Fred Hope; cos, Adrian

A gorgeous, high-gloss deco mosaic, overloaded with star power, and a curious triumph over all by the electroplated Venus, Jean Harlow. DINNER AT EIGHT was the second all-star vehicle from MGM (after GRAND HOTEL) and did much to establish Selznick as a producer to be reckoned with. The script, expertly adapted from the Kaufman-Ferber stage play by Frances Marion, Herman Mankiewicz, and Donald Ogden Stewart, polished the comedy elements of the original to further balance the existing melodrama. The MGM constellations twinkle as Gotham strata of society are invited to dine by Lionel Barrymore and Billie Burke. Underneath the patina of luxe, hearts break, plans go up in smoke, dreams are dashed.

This is the beginning of the end for John Barrymore, playing a has-been that had been patterned after him; it's a bitchy casting idea, chilling to watch. Other good parts would follow but DINNER AT EIGHT would mark the point where he began careening into parody. Burke and Barrymore turn in definitive portrayals of their star personas. Dressler's shrewd grande dame in decline (based on Mrs. Patrick Campbell) is a textbook of brilliant comic business, and Beery turns in his usual workmanlike despisable grizzly.

But it's Jean Harlow who elevates herself to the big guns here. Her gold-digging, amoral little hussy, spitting out the chocolates she doesn't like back into her fancy candybox, is just as self-centered as the others. But despite the whinny voice, rock candy cosmetology and bratty manipulation, she still manages to infuse heart into her characterization. Cukor, who expertly directed, claimed she did it on her own; it's proof positive that the legendary sex symbols always have an undeniable element of humanity. (It may have helped that she and Beery hated each other's guts.) Madge Evans plays the ingenue, a role Joan Crawford pulled out of at the last minute, wisely, given the Harlow victory. Devotees of Hollywood costume design should enjoy the platinum blonde's outrageous costumes, the last word in Adrian vulgarity.

The Breen Office took exception to DINNER AT EIGHT (Joseph I. Breen being the West Coast assistant to Will Hays, who headed the censorship board affixing production codes to films at the time). Breen told Selznick that he seemed to have a predilection for suicide in his movies, citing such films as ANNA KARENINA and WHAT PRICE HOLLYWOOD. To calm the censors, the scene where John Barrymore actually turns on the gas was cut. The producer would remain forever proud of this film, taking particular delight that the chic set decorations of the movie (especially Harlow's bedroom set) helped popularize art deco in the early 1930s.

DIRTY DANCING
DVD
1987 97m c Dance ★★★
Vestron (U.S.) PG-13

Jennifer Grey *(Frances "Baby" Houseman)*, Patrick Swayze *(Johnny Castle)*, Jerry Orbach *(Dr. Jake Houseman)*, Cynthia Rhodes *(Penny Johnson)*, Jack Weston *(Max Kellerman)*, Jane Brucker *(Lisa Houseman)*, Kelly Bishop *(Marjorie Houseman)*, Lonny Price *(Neil Kellerman)*, Max Cantor *(Robbie Gould)*, Charles "Honi" Coles *(Tito Suarez)*

p, Linda Gottlieb, Eleanor Bergstein; d, Emile Ardolino; w, Eleanor Bergstein; ph, Jeff Jur; ed, Peter C. Frank; m, John Morris; prod d, David Chapman; art d, Mark Haack, Stephen J. Lineweaver; chor, Kenny Ortega; cos, Hilary Rosenfeld

AA Best Original Song: "(I've Had) The Time of My Life"; Franke Previte (Music & Lyrics), John DeNicola (Music), Donald Markowitz (Music)

Teenage titillation for girls, circa 1963. Orbach is a New York doctor visiting a Catskill Mountains resort hotel with his wife Bishop and two daughters, Grey—known as Baby—and Brucker. Baby, a teenage activist, is soon bored and goes to the off-limits employees' area, where the hotel staff are engaging in "dirty dancing"—bodies rubbing and undulating around each other to pulsating music. There she meets the hotel's resident swain, Patrick Swayze, who with his partner, Cynthia Rhodes, gives dancing lessons to the guests. Although they come from two different worlds, the two fall in love.

Grey is Joel Grey's daughter and she acquits herself adequately. Swayze is a sexy dancer who can be sweet, suggest macho, and act a little. Of particular interest is Rhodes. Her part isn't large, but she is believable as an actress and spectacular as a dancer. One problem with the film is that it does nothing to endear the Catskill social setting to an audience; the inhabitants seem to be competing for awards in obnoxiousness. DIRTY DANCING produced a top-selling soundtrack album and the hit single "(I've Had) The Time of My Life."

DIRTY DOZEN, THE
DVD
1967 149m c War ★★★★
MGM (U.K.)

Lee Marvin *(Maj. Reisman)*, Ernest Borgnine *(Gen. Worden)*, Charles Bronson *(Joseph Wladislaw)*, Jim Brown *(Robert Jefferson)*, John Cassavetes *(Victor Franko)*, Richard Jaeckel *(Sgt. Bowren)*, George Kennedy *(Maj. Max Armbruster)*, Trini Lopez *(Pedro Jiminez)*, Ralph Meeker *(Capt. Stuart Kinder)*, Robert Ryan *(Col. Everett Dasher-Breed)*

p, Kenneth Hyman; d, Robert Aldrich; w, Lukas Heller, Nunnally Johnson (based on the novel by E.M. Nathanson); ph, Ted Scaife; ed, Michael Luciano; m, Frank DeVol; art d, William Hutchinson; fx, Cliff Richardson

AAN Best Supporting Actor: John Cassavetes; *AAN Best Film Editing:* Michael Luciano; *AAN Best Sound:* Metro-Goldwyn-Mayer Studio Sound Department; *AA Best Sound Effects:* John Poyner

Robert Aldrich's anti-everything-except-explosives war movie, presented as an all-star game. The film follows nonconformist Major Reisman (Lee Marvin) in his assigned task of assembling a suicide squad of military felons (murderers, rapists, thieves) to infiltrate and destroy a chateau in occupied France at which the Nazi top brass congregate during WWII. Since the cast is presented as bad guys without stories, it's impossible to get emotionally involved. Aided by his assistant, Jaeckel, Marvin recruits 12 men: Cassavetes, Savalas, Bronson, Sutherland, Brown, Walker, Lopez, Mancini, Cooper, Carruthers, Busby, and Maitland, ranging from the merely dim-witted to the overtly psychotic, to form his "dirty dozen," then subjects them to brutal training designed to mold them into an efficient fighting force. After the lengthy, but wholly entertaining training session which climaxes in a war game pitting Reisman's troops against a crack unit, the dirty dozen and their leaders parachute into France to begin a mission that most of them will not survive.

Slambang funny, and extremely violent for its time, THE DIRTY DOZEN was a box-office smash that continues to be popular to this day, despite hundreds of showings on television (and two made-for-television sequels in the 1980s). Boasting excellent performances from a stellar cast, this is the ultimate macho action movie. Yet it calls into question the morals of the *Americans*, not the Germans: the instigators of the mission smugly sip sherry and smoke cigars, content that it was accomplished and that some of their most troublesome recruits died in carrying it out. Aldrich was a master at presenting his distinctly cynical outlook in the context of crowd-pleasing entertainment, and THE DIRTY DOZEN is one of his most effective and lasting efforts.

DIRTY HARRY
1971 102m c Crime ★★★½
Malpaso/Warner Bros. (U.S.) R

Clint Eastwood *(Harry Callahan)*, Reni Santoni *(Chico)*, Harry Guardino *(Bressler)*, Andrew Robinson, billed as Andy Robinson *(Scorpio)*, John Mitchum *(DeGeorgio)*, John Larch *(Chief)*, John Vernon *(Mayor)*, Mae Mercer *(Mrs. Russell)*, Lyn Edgington *(Norma)*, Ruth Kobart *(Bus Driver)*

p, Don Siegel; d, Don Siegel; w, Harry Julian Fink, Rita M. Fink, John Milius (uncredited), Dean Riesner (based on an unpublished story by Rita M. and Harry Julian Fink); ph, Bruce Surtees (Panavision, Technicolor); ed, Carl Pingitore; m, Lalo Schifrin; art d, Dale Hennesy; cos, Glenn Wright

A fascist film, or a film about a fascist cop? Either way, this is suspenseful, energetic stuff, directed with urgency and style by *Cahiers du Cinema* favorite Don Siegel; embellished with some of Lalo Schifrin's coolest electro-jazz confections; and driven by the inimitable Clint as Detective "Dirty" Harry Callahan, last line of defence against the assorted hippie liberal types who, in the early '70s, threatened the very fabric of Western civilization.

Maverick San Francisco cop Harry Callahan (Clint Eastwood) is ordered by the city mayor (John Vernon) to stop the serial killer who calls himself Scorpio (Andy Robinson). The psycho wants $100,000, or he will continue his bloody work. The mayor and others are willing to give in, but Eastwood disagrees, sensing it would be just the first payment. Eastwood bristles when teamed with young Chico (Reni Santoni) against his wishes (Chico fails Callahan on three counts, by being new to the force, Mexican-American, and, perhaps worst of all, college-educated); but he reluctantly begins to accept the junior partner. Scorpio says he's buried a teenage girl somewhere in the city and will let her die unless the town comes up with $200,000. Eastwood gets the job of delivering the money (backed up by Chico), but eventually pursues his own, extralegal route to nail Scorpio.

DIRTY HARRY proved popular, controversial, and influential. With uncredited screenplay contributions by John Milius, the film represented, via its title character, the apotheosis of the maverick cop figure that Siegel had portrayed in films from HELL IS FOR HEROES through MADIGAN. Harry Callahan is both more openly scornful of the law—his nailing of Scorpio is basically a critique of the concept of "criminal rights"—and, thanks to Eastwood's perfectly calibrated performance, more compelling an individual, than Siegel's earlier neo-vigilantes. The film propelled Eastwood to his second round of stardom, left its mark on countless urban cop dramas to come, and marked the beginning of one of the most celebrated director/star relationships in American cinema—one movingly recalled by Eastwood-as-director in the joint dedication of his 1992 masterpiece, UNFORGIVEN, "to Sergio and Don." Sequels: MAGNUM FORCE, THE ENFORCER, SUDDEN IMPACT, and THE DEAD POOL.

DIRTY PRETTY THINGS [DVD]
2002 97m c Drama/Thriller ★★★
Celador Production/BBC Film (U.S./U.K.) R

Chiwetel Ejiofor *(Okwe)*, Audrey Tautou *(Senay)*, Sergi Lopez *(Sneaky)*, Sophie Okonedo *(Juliette)*, Benedict Wong *(Guo Yi)*, Zlatko Buric *(Ivan)*, Kriss Dosanjh *(Asian Businessman)*, Israel Aduramo *(Minicab Driver)*, Ade-Yemi Ajibade *(Minicab Driver)*, Nizwar Karanj *(Minicab Driver)*

p, Robert Jones, Tracey Seaward; d, Stephen Frears; w, Steven Knight; ph, Chris Menges; ed, Mick Audsley; m, Nathan Larson; prod d, Hugo Luczyc-Wyhowski; art d, Rebecca Holmes; fx, Graham Longhurst, Mark Nelmes; cos, Odile Dicks-Mireaux

AAN Best Original Screenplay: Steven Knight

Veteran filmmaker Stephen Frears's uneasy mix of socially conscious filmmaking and thriller cliches unfolds in a London underground populated by desperate asylum seekers, undocumented immigrants, and refugees.

Illegal Nigerian immigrant Okwe (Chiwetel Ejiofor) is an educated man, but some dark secret has reduced him to toiling incessantly in low-level jobs. His "landlady," Senay (Audrey Tatou), is a Turkish refugee who hopes to escape the dramatically circumscribed life her mother lives back home. Senay is forbidden to work while her application for asylum is being considered, but she surreptitiously cleans rooms at the seedy Baltic Hotel, where Okwe mans the front desk during the night shift. Okwe's desk duties are generally light and dull until the night when, tipped off by a prostitute (Sophie Okonedo), he finds that the object clogging an upstairs toilet is a human heart. Sleazy hotel manager Sneaky (Sergi Lopez) refuses to call the police, and Okwe's discreet inquiries have the unfortunate consequence of spurring Sneaky to look into his night clerk's past. Sneaky discovers that back in Nigeria Okwe was a doctor and that he left the country under a cloud. With this information in hand, Sneaky tries to blackmail Okwe into joining the gruesome business he runs out of the Baltic's unoccupied rooms: harvesting human organs for sale on the black market.

Steven Knight's portrait of London's invisible underclass, a skillful mosaic of sharply observed scenes, is far stronger than the lurid thriller that's been grafted onto it. But Ejiofor's subtle, infinitely humane performance is the invisible glue that holds everything together, and Chris Menges's darkly shimmering cinematography lends the story a gritty, coolly seductive glamour.

DISCLOSURE [DVD]
1994 127m c Drama/Mystery/Thriller ★★★
Baltimore Pictures/Constant c (U.S.) R

Michael Douglas *(Tom Sanders)*, Demi Moore *(Meredith Johnson)*, Donald Sutherland *(Bob Garvin)*, Roma Maffia *(Catherine Alvarez)*, Caroline Goodall *(Susan Hendler)*, Dennis Miller *(Mark Lewyn)*, Dylan Baker *(Philip Blackburn)*, Nicholas Sadler *(Don Cherry)*, Allan Rich *(Ben Heller)*, Rosemary Forsyth *(Stephanie Kaplan)*

p, Barry Levinson, Michael Crichton; d, Barry Levinson; w, Paul Attanasio (based on the novel by Michael Crichton); ph, Tony Pierce-Roberts; ed, Stu Linder; m, Ennio Morricone; prod d, Neil Spisak; art d, Richard Yanez-Toyon, Charles William Breen; fx, Eric Brevig, Industrial Light & Magic; cos, Gloria Gresham

It's no great surprise that Hollywood's first attempt to grapple with sexual harassment hinges on the ludicrous notion that it's something done by women to men. What *is* surprising is that producer-director Barry Levinson has resisted what must have been considerable pressure to contrive another FATAL ATTRACTION, turning Michael Crichton's best-selling corporate thriller into a quietly efficient entertainment gizmo that eschews cathartic violence in favor of lurking paranoia.

Tom Sanders (Michael Douglas), a married computer exec, believes he's in line for a promotion; instead, he's crushed to discover that his unctuous boss (Donald Sutherland) has passed him over for Meredith Johnson (Demi Moore), a coolly competent number-cruncher and, coincidentally, an old flame. When she seduces him during a private meeting, Tom suffers a last-minute attack of conscience and breaks things off mid-tryst, and an enraged Meredith threatens to destroy him. The next morning, he discovers that he's been charged with sexual harassment.

The screenplay, by Paul Attanasio (QUIZ SHOW), is a distinct improvement on Crichton's one-dimensional, humorless potboiler. Besides adding some cleverly positioned laugh lines, Attanasio complicates the hero's motives and moral standing. In the end, though, the movie comes closest to thematic coherence, and the popular mood, in its depiction of something nearly everyone can relate to: the office from hell. In a time when job insecurity tops the list of American anxieties, DISCLOSURE's paradigmatic '90s workplace—a ruthless, conspiratorial, profit-driven nightmare—will speak to viewers much more clearly than its fatuous take on sexual harassment.

DISCREET CHARM OF THE BOURGEOISIE, THE [DVD]
(LE CHARME DISCRET DE LA BOURGEOISIE)
1972 101m c Comedy/Drama ★★★★½
Greenwich Film Production/Jet/Dean PG
(France/Italy/Spain)

Fernando Rey *(Don Raphael—Ambassador of Miranda)*, Delphine Seyrig *(Simone Thevenot)*, Stephane Audran *(Alice*

Senechal), Bulle Ogier (Florence), Jean-Pierre Cassel (Henri Senechal), Paul Frankeur (Francois Thevenot), Julien Bertheau (Bishop Dufour), Claude Pieplu (Colonel), Michel Piccoli (Minister of Interior), Muni (Peasant Girl)

p, Serge Silberman; d, Luis Bunuel; w, Luis Bunuel, Jean-Claude Carriere; ph, Edmond Richard (Eastmancolor, Panavision); ed, Helene Plemiannikov; m, Galaxie Musique; art d, Pierre Guffroy; cos, Jacqueline Guyot

AA Best Foreign Language Film ; AAN Best Original Story and Screenplay: Luis Bunuel, Jean-Claude Carriere

One of Luis Bunuel's greatest and funniest films, and the winner of a Best Foreign Film Oscar, THE DISCREET CHARM OF THE BOURGEOISIE is a brilliant surrealistic joke about a group of friends whose attempts to dine are continually thwarted.

Don Raphael (Fernando Rey), the ambassador to France of a Latin American country called Miranda, Francois Thevenot (Paul Frankeur), his wife Simone (Delphine Seyrig) and her sister Florence (Bulle Ogier) drive to their friend Henri Senechal's (Jean-Pierre Cassel) villa for dinner, but are told by his wife Alice (Stephane Audran) that their dinner was scheduled for the next evening. They all go to a restaurant, but leave after discovering the manager's corpse laid out on a table. Another attempt to dine at the Senechals is thwarted when Alice and Henri sneak out of the house to make love in their garden, and Raphael and Francois leave because they fear a police raid. Another meal is disrupted by the arrival of an army on maneuvers, and yet another ends when those gathered discover they're actually characters in a stage play.

Although Bunuel made DISCREET CHARM at the age of 72, it has an insouciant charm and an effortless ebullience that offers continual delight. When he was a young surrealist, Bunuel used a violent style to attack society, but by the '70s , normal society itself had become violent, so instead, he used humor as a weapon. The "plot" is a kind of reverse premise of Bunuel's masterful THE EXTERMINATING ANGEL (1962), which concerned people who could not leave a dinner party, but it's merely a peg on which he hangs a deliciously absurd series of surrealistic gags and dreams to explore the main theme of all his movies: frustrated desire. In DISCREET CHARM, the dreams literally take over the whole film, as one unfolds within another until we no longer know what's "real" and what's not, although Bunuel's ultimate joke is that in film, nothing is real. The film's most savage joke may be that all these charming, attractive, and highly-paid actors, along with Bunuel himself, are part of the class that he's satirizing, as he once acknowledged that being a film director is perhaps the most bourgeois profession in the world.

DISENCHANTED, THE
DVD
1990 78m   c   Drama   ★★★½
Cinea-La Sept Cinema/CNC/Sofica Sofinergie 2 (France)

Judith Godreche (Beth), Marcel Bozonnet (Alphonse), Ivan Desny (The Uncle), Therese Liotard (Beth's Mother), Malcolm Conrath (The Other), Thomas Salsman (Remi), Hai Truhong (Chang), Francis Mage (Edouard), Marion Perry (The Professor of French), Stephane Auberghen (Edouard's Mother)

p, Philippe Carcassonne; d, Benoit Jacquot; w, Benoit Jacquot; ph, Caroline Champetier; ed, Dominique Auvray; m, Jorge Arriagada

Benoit Jacquot, one of the most promising of the current crop of French filmmakers, paints a fascinating portrait of a young woman faced with the cruel realities of adulthood.

The title is taken from a quote by Arthur Rimbaud, the 19th-century poet maudit who inspires 17-year-old Beth (Judith Godreche), a student who—like her idol—no longer

believes in all manner of enchantments. Her boyfriend (Malcom Conrath) wonders at her fidelity and coldly suggests she have sex with the ugliest man she can find as a test of her love. Beth agrees out of spite, but backs out at the last minute, only to receive a far more compelling proposal at home: her ailing mother (Therese Liotard), no longer able to satisfy the elderly lecher (Ivan Desny) whose checks have been feeding Beth and her little brother, pressures her daughter to prostitute herself to "Sugardad" in her place.

There's something heartbreaking in watching Beth's sisterly devotion to her brother and her determination in the face of her boyfriend's perverse cruelty, knowing all along that her loss of innocence is a foregone conclusion. Much of this is communicated through Godreche's exquisite performance: she radiates a youthful freshness already tempered by an edge of bitterness and disappointment. Jacquot's A SINGLE GIRL, a real-time tour de force in which a similarly independent young woman faces a crucial decision that will affect the rest of her life, is a perfect companion piece. While not as technically masterful, this film has a loose, almost elliptical quality that captures all the idealism and hesitation of a young woman crossing that treacherous divide between adolescence and adulthood while trying to maintain whatever control she still has over herself and her sexuality.

DISRAELI
1929 90m   bw   Biography   ★★★½
Warner Bros. (U.S.)

George Arliss (Benjamin Disraeli, Lord Beaconsfield), Joan Bennett (Lady Clarissa Pevensey of Glastonbury), Florence Arliss (Lady Mary Beaconsfield), Anthony Bushell (Charles/Lord Deeford), David Torrence (Sir Michael/Lord Probert), Ivan Simpson (Hugh Meyers), Doris Lloyd (Mrs. Agatha Travers), Gwendolyn Logan (Duchess of Glastonbury), Charles E. Evans (Potter), Cosmo Kyrle Bellew (Mr. Terle)

d, Alfred E. Green; w, Julian Josephson (based on the play by Louis Napoleon Parker); ph, Lee Garmes; ed, Owen Marks; m, Louis Silvers

AAN Outstanding Production: ; AA Best Actor: George Arliss; AAN Best Writing Achievement: Julian Josephson

Arliss is a fine centerpiece for one of the earliest of the Warner Bros. biographies; DISRAELI sets high standards for biopics to come. It marked the film debut of aging George Arliss, and showed America a style of acting it had seen little of in the silent years. Arliss was stage-trained and able to make the switch from stage to silents and then sound with no difficulty. Rather than attempt a long picture about the Jew who converted to Christianity and was Queen Victoria's closest ally, the film deals with a brief slice of Disraeli's life, focusing on his attempt to outwit the Russians in the rush to purchase the Suez Canal. Along the way, we get the opportunity to observe his wit, his amours, his geniality, and his brilliance.

Florence Arliss played his screen wife, and their ability to play off each other lent sparkle to both performances. Arliss would come to specialize in historical figures, playing Rothschild, Richelieu, Wellington, Alexander Hamilton, and others. He had played Disraeli in a 1921 silent film first, but this is the definitive performance.

DISTANT VOICES, STILL LIVES
1988 85m   c   Drama   ★★★½
British Film Institute/Film Four/Channel 4/ZDF   PG-13 (U.K.)

Freda Dowie (Mother), Pete Postlethwaite (Father), Angela Walsh (Eileen), Lorraine Ashbourne (Maisie), Dean Williams (Tony), Sally Davies (Eileen as a child), Nathan Walsh (Tony as a child),

Susan Flanagan *(Maisie as a Child)*, Michael Starke *(Dave)*, Vincent MaGuire *(George)*

p, Jennifer Howarth; d, Terence Davies; w, Terence Davies; ph, William Diver, Patrick Duval; ed, William Diver; art d, Miki van Zwanenberg, Jocelyn James; cos, Monica Howe

Part nostalgia, part nightmare, the autobiographical DISTANT VOICES, STILL LIVES is writer-director Terence Davies's bittersweet look back at his working-class upbringing in post-war Liverpool. While it's beautifully photographed, Davies's portrait of a house divided by a near-psychotic father (Pete Postlethwaite)—loving one moment, brutal the next—is not a pretty sight. All of the familial warts and blemishes are visible as Davies avoids any romanticizing of the past whatsoever. In this highly stylized, cinematic portrait of his family, there is no enhancement, no glitz, not even much of a plot. Rather, Davies leaves us with a series of impressions, presented non-chronologically, that evoke memories of his basically repressive Catholic childhood in the 1950s.

Told in flashback, the film begins and ends with family weddings held several years apart as the grown children reflect on their father and his mostly negative influence upon their lives. Despite Davies' often harsh, brutal focus, this is no gloom-and-doom period piece. Remarkably, all his sensitively drawn, subtle observations coalesce, forming an emotionally compelling whole that visually and vividly recalls a traditional way of life. Static as their lives may be, his people are never dull. In this very personal portrait, Davies, the artist, has re-created universal experiences—familiar passions and needs—that draw us to his family's humanity.

DIVA 📀
1981 123m c   Crime/Romance   ★★★★½
Galaxie/Greenwich   (France)

Frederic Andrei *(Jules)*, Wilhemenia Wiggins Fernandez *(Cynthia Hawkins)*, Richard Bohringer *(Gorodish)*, Thuy An Luu *(Alba)*, Jacques Fabbri *(Saporta)*, Chantal Deruaz *(Nadia)*, Roland Bertin *(Weinstadt)*, Gerard Darmon *(L'Antillais)*, Dominique Pinon *(Le Cure)*, Jean-Jacques Moreau *(Krantz)*

p, Irene Silberman; d, Jean-Jacques Beineix; w, Jean-Jacques Beineix, Jean Van Hamme (based on a novel by Delacorta); ph, Philippe Rousselot (Eastmancolor); ed, Marie-Josephe Yoyotte, Monique Prim; m, Vladimir Cosma; art d, Hilton McConnico

A lady prone to technique but dazzling nonetheless, DIVA is visually astonishing film fare. The complex plot concerns Andrei, a young Parisian mail carrier, and his love for Fernandez, a famous black American opera singer. Andrei attends a performance by the diva, recording it secretly while a sinister Taiwanese man watches him. In a separate incident a dazed girl walking through the Paris metro is murdered by two thugs—the greasy Darmon and the punkish, bald Pinon. As the girl dies she slips an audiocassette into Andrei's mailpouch. Andrei now finds himself unwittingly caught in two plots: that of Taiwanese record pirates who want his recording of the diva and that of pimps and drug runners who want the incriminating tape left in his mailpouch.

The debut film from Jean-Jacques Beineix, DIVA is perhaps the most picturesque film to come out of France in years. Together with art director Hilton McConnico and cameraman Philippe Rousselot, Beineix creates awesome shot after awesome shot, so much so that many felt the film was too stylish. At times the sensibility is very "New Wave" (as in fashion and music, not the film movement); at other times, Beineix is intensely Impressionistic. These qualities are even further enhanced by a beautiful musical score, contributed by Vladimir Cosma, who has used Act I of Alfredo Catalani's opera *La Wally*.

DIVINE SECRETS OF THE YA-YA SISTERHOOD 📀
2002 116m c   Comedy/Drama   ★★½
All Girl Productions/Gaylord Films/Sisterhood   PG-13
Productions   (U.S.)

Sandra Bullock *(Siddalee Walker)*, Ellen Burstyn *(Vivi)*, Maggie Smith *(Caro)*, Fionnula Flanagan *(Teensy)*, James Garner *(Shep Walker)*, Shirley Knight *(Necie)*, Ashley Judd *(Younger Vivi)*, Katy Selverstone *(Younger Caro)*, Jacqueline McKenzie *(Younger Teensy)*, Kiersten Warren *(Younger Necie)*

p, Bonnie Bruckheimer, Hunt Lowry; d, Callie Khouri; w, Callie Khouri (based on Mark Andrus's adaptation of the novels *Divine Secrets of the Ya-Ya Sisterhood* and *Little Altars Everywhere*, by Rebecca Wells); ph, John Bailey; ed, Andrew Marcus; m, T Bone Burnett, David Mansfield; prod d, David J. Bomba; art d, John Jensen; fx, Walter Kiesling; cos, Gary Jones

A colorful riot of Southern-fried fussin', fightin', and feudin', in which a commitment-shy bride-to-be must finally confront the larger-than-life mother whose histrionics have shaped her life.

With a Broadway play and a wedding in the works, successful dramatist Siddalee Walker (Sandra Bullock) inadvertently offends her beautiful, willful, melodramatic, and thoroughly impossible mother, Vivi (Ellen Burstyn), whose rage threatens to ripen into permanent estrangement. So Vivi's lifelong friends, Teensy (Fionnula Flanagan), Caro (Maggie Smith), and Necie (Shirley Knight), known collectively as the Ya-Yas—after a secret club they organized as precocious girls in Thornton, L.A.—take action. Unbeknownst to queen bee Vivi, the Ya-Yas travel to New York in hopes of persuading Siddalee to reconcile with her crazy mama. When she refuses, they drug her and fly her South for a tearful trip down memory lane. Alternating between past and present, the film charts the tempestuous lives of younger Vivi (Ashley Judd), Teensy (Jacqueline McKenzie), Caro (Katy Selverstone), and Necie (Kiersten Warren) as headstrong wives and mothers who help each other survive alcoholism, prescription drug addiction, grief, madness, and the bitter legacy of dreams deferred, while remaining impeccably dressed and coiffed.

Like TERMS OF ENDEARMENT and STEEL MAGNOLIAS, this teary paean to the bonds that unite women glides along on a cloud of chatty cattiness, and seeing veteran actresses Burstyn, Smith, Flanagan, and Knight tear up the screen is an unabashed delight. But the film, adapted from two novels by actress and playwright Rebecca Wells, suffers from an excess of material crammed into too little screen time; there's so much story that the characters get short shrift.

DIVORCE, ITALIAN STYLE 📀
(DIVORZIO ALL'ITALIANA)
1962 108m bw Comedy   ★★★★
Lux (Italy)

Marcello Mastroianni *(Ferdinando Cefalu)*, Daniela Rocca *(Rosalia Cefalu)*, Stefania Sandrelli *(Angela)*, Leopoldo Trieste *(Carmelo Patane)*, Odoardo Spadaro *(Don Gaetano)*, Margherita Girelli *(Sisina)*, Angela Cardile *(Agnese)*, Bianca Castagnetta *(Donna Matilde)*, Lando Buzzanca *(Rosario Mule)*, Pietro Tordi *(Attorney DeMarzi)*

p, Franco Cristaldi; d, Pietro Germi; w, Ennio De Concini, Alfredo Giannetti, Pietro Germi; ph, Leonida Barboni; ed, Roberto Cinquini; m, Carlo Rustichelli; art d, Carlo Egidi; cos, Dina Di Bari

AAN Best Actor: Marcello Mastroianni; *AAN Best Director:* Pietro Germi; *AA Best Original Story and Screenplay:* Ennio DeConcini, Alfredo Giannetti, Pietro Germi

To die laughing for. Rocca is a whining sex-crazed Sicilian wife who drives husband Mastroianni to consider divorce. Unfortunately for Rocca it is easier to murder in Italy than it is to divorce. And that's precisely what is done. The scheming Mastroianni then goes on to marry the proverbial nymphet next door after his wife is out of the picture. A brilliant comic performance from Mastroianni which has been compared to the deadpan style of Keaton. It earned him an Oscar nomination for Best Actor, as well as Best Actor accolades from the Golden Globes and the British Film Academy. Considered by some to be one of the greatest modern comedies.

DIVORCEE, THE

1930 83m bw Drama ★★★½
MGM (U.S.)

Norma Shearer *(Jerry Bernard)*, Chester Morris *(Theodore "Ted" Martin)*, Conrad Nagel *(Paul)*, Robert Montgomery *(Don)*, Florence Eldridge *(Helen)*, Helene Millard *(Mary)*, Robert Elliott *(Bill Baldwin)*, Mary Doran *(Janice)*, Tyler Brooke *(Hank)*, Zelda Sears *(Hannah, Jerry's Maid)*

p, Robert Z. Leonard; d, Robert Z. Leonard; w, Nick Grinde, Zelda Sears, John Meehan (based on the novel *Ex-Wife* by Ursula Parrott); ph, Norbert Brodine; ed, Hugh Wynn, Truman K. Wood; art d, Cedric Gibbons; cos, Adrian

AAN Outstanding Production: ; *AA Best Actress:* Norma Shearer; *AAN Best Director:* Robert Leonard; *AAN Best Writing Achievement:* John Meehan

Norma Shearer, in an Oscar-winning role, tries daringly to confront the double standard, but not upset her legion of fans (or the censors) who wouldn't approve of her really letting loose. Thankfully, something always gets in the way. The plot is a trifle: her husband (Morris) cheats on her, but won't hear of her doing the same. They divorce, and since Jerry (Shearer) is supposedly liberated from the shackles of matrimony, she flirts with several men (Montgomery and Nagel) before the requisite New Year's Eve reconciliation with her ex.

Based on Ursula Parrott's then-steamy novel *Ex-Wife*, much of the spirit has been laundered out here. (Things would become much worse, though, after the 1934 Production Code clampdown, so enjoy the spice that survives.) Shearer turns in a fine performance of the silken suffering which was her pre-Code specialty. While never in the same league, beauty-wise, with Garbo and Crawford, the other two of MGM's big three, she had a definite image advantage for many prestige pictures. Seemingly American (she was Canadian), she could play the moderns Garbo could not, but in more ladylike turns than Crawford. Being the pope's wife—she was married to production genius Irving Thalberg—never hurt her, either. (In all fairness, however, she was a star before she and Thalberg tied the knot, and audiences genuinely liked her as well.) Whether or not you like Shearer and THE DIVORCEE depends on how you respond to this particular "tease" variety of soap opera, but this enjoyable film stands as an index to the sexual politics of an era.

DO THE RIGHT THING   *DVD*

1989 120m c Comedy/Drama ★★★★½
40 Acres and a Mule Filmworks (U.S.) R

Danny Aiello *(Sal)*, Ossie Davis *(Da Mayor)*, Ruby Dee *(Mother Sister)*, Richard Edson *(Vito)*, Giancarlo Esposito *(Buggin' Out)*, Spike Lee *(Mookie)*, Bill Nunn *(Radio Raheem)*, John Turturro *(Pino)*, Rosie Perez *(Tina)*, Paul Benjamin *(ML)*

p, Spike Lee, Monty Ross; d, Spike Lee; w, Spike Lee; ph, Ernest Dickerson (Duart Color); ed, Barry Alexander Brown; m, Bill Lee; prod d, Wynn Thomas; chor, Rosie Perez, Otis Sallid; cos, Ruth Carter

AAN Best Supporting Actor: Danny Aiello; *AAN Best Original Screenplay:* Spike Lee

DO THE RIGHT THING has been hailed as the most insightful view of race relations ever to hit U.S. screens and condemned as dangerous agitprop, but its timeliness—and its ability to touch a nerve in the culture at large—was never in question.

The story is set in Brooklyn's Bedford-Stuyvesant neighborhood on a broiling hot Saturday. Blacks and Latinos inhabit the area, but the local eatery, Sal's Famous Pizzeria, is owned and managed by Italian-American Sal (Danny Aiello) who commutes to work with his two sons, the embittered, bigoted Pino (John Turturro) and the mild-mannered and sympathetic Vito (Richard Edson). Also working at Sal's is Mookie (writer-director Spike Lee), the deliveryman, who tries to do as little work as possible in his dead-end job. On the hottest day of the year, tensions rise when the self-styled local activist Buggin Out (Giancarlo Esposito), upset by the absence of black faces on Sal's "Wall of Fame," attempts to organize a boycott of the pizzeria. This apparently trivial incident sparks the explosion which climaxes the film.

Lee has crafted a film of astonishing power and originality. Cinematographer Ernest Dickerson shows signs of genius as he provides brightly colored images so hot they make you sweat with excitement. No currently working lensman is better at lighting black actors. The large ensemble cast is excellent. Aiello makes Sal a likable guy despite his unconscious paternalism. Turturro is frighteningly believable as the volatile Pino, but he's no cardboard villain. Ossie Davis and Ruby Dee, two stalwarts of the black theater, serve with special distinction as both a vivid reminder of past glories of black culture and an inspiration for the future.

Lee has promoted himself as a political activist filmmaker working with a conscious agenda: to tell black stories that have traditionally been ignored by Hollywood. Indeed his success has opened the doors for a new generation of black filmmakers. DO THE RIGHT THING, his breakthrough film, is no blunt work of propaganda; it is a subtle and humane entertainment with a refreshingly serious view of the world. There are no absolute heroes or villains. There are no easy answers to the questions that this film poses with such artistry and grace.

D.O.A.   *DVD*

1950 83m bw Mystery ★★★★½
UA (U.S.)

Edmond O'Brien *(Frank Bigelow)*, Pamela Britton *(Paula Gibson)*, Luther Adler *(Majak)*, Beverly Garland, billed as Beverly Campbell *(Miss Foster)*, Lynne Baggett *(Mrs. Philips)*, William Ching *(Holliday)*, Henry Hart *(Stanley Philips)*, Neville Brand *(Chester)*, Laurette Luez *(Marla Rakubian)*, Jess Kirkpatrick *(Sam)*

p, Leo C. Popkin; d, Rudolph Mate; w, Russell Rouse, Clarence Greene; ph, Ernest Laszlo; ed, Arthur H. Nadel; m, Dimitri Tiomkin; art d, Duncan Cramer; cos, Maria Donovan

A clever ruse for suspense. Murder victim O'Brien discovers he has been poisoned and, in his remaining days, tries to track down his own killer. He's a CPA who arrives in San Francisco to get some time away from fiancee Britton but after a night on the town he grows ill and consults a doctor who tells him he has been poisoned and he will be dead in a few days. He then learns that he notarized a shipment of deadly iridium and that he is the only one who can provide proof against a criminal gang. O'Brien is great as the victimized businessman, harassed by the psychopathic Brand and the sinister Ching. Mate's direction suitably increases O'Brien's pace as the story unravels and the plot becomes more hectic, particularly when the bloodthirsty Brand is ordered to take O'Brien out and murder him. Mate also makes spectacular use of exterior locations giving the film a very different feel from most studio-bound entries. The film takes much of its basic story line from Robert

Siodmak's 1931 German-made DER MANN, DER SEINEN MORDER SUCHT. The story line was the basis for the 1969 Australian film COLOR ME DEAD. Remade poorly in 1988 with Dennis Quaid and again titled D.O.A.

DOCTOR DOLITTLE   DVD
1967 152m c   Musical   ★½
Fox   (U.S.)

Rex Harrison *(Dr. John Dolittle)*, Anthony Newley *(Matthew Mugg)*, Peter Bull *(Gen. Bellowes)*, William Dix *(Tommy Stubbins)*, Portia Nelson *(Sarah Dolittle)*, Samantha Eggar *(Emma Fairfax)*, Richard Attenborough *(Albert Blossom)*, Muriel Landers *(Mrs. Blossom)*, Geoffrey Holder *(Willie Shakespeare)*, Norma Varden *(Lady Petherington)*

p, Arthur P. Jacobs; d, Richard Fleischer; w, Leslie Bricusse (based on stories by Hugh Lofting); ph, Robert Surtees (Todd-AO, DeLuxeColor); ed, Samuel E. Beetley, Marjorie Fowler; m, Lionel Newman, Alexander Courage; prod d, Mario Chiari; art d, Jack Martin Smith, Ed Graves; fx, L.B. Abbott, Art Cruickshank, Emil Kosa Jr., Howard Lydecker; chor, Herbert Ross; cos, Ray Aghayan

AAN Best Picture; AAN Best Cinematography: Robert Surtees; *AAN Best Film Editing:* Samuel E. Beetley, Marjorie Fowler; *AAN Best Original Score:* Leslie Bricusse; *AA Best Adapted Score:* Lionel Newman, Alexander Courage; *AA Best Song:* "Talk to the Animals"; Leslie Bricusse; *AAN Best Art Direction-Set Decoration:* Mario Chiari, Jack Martin Smith, Ed Graves, Walter M. Scott, Stuart A. Reiss; *AAN Best Sound:* 20th Century Fox Studio Sound Department; *AA Best Special Visual Effects:* L.B. Abbott

Does little. As a matter of fact, this one almost bankrupted its studio. Doctor Dolittle (Rex Harrison) is considered a nut by his neighbors. After this nuttiness leads to his arrest, Dolittle decides to avoid people and devote his life to animals since, as one who can speak all the animal tongues (he was taught 498 different languages by his parrot, Polynesia), he serves as a unique link between human and beast. With Anthony Newley, the most irritating man in show business, and the vapid Samantha Eggar at his side, the doctor sails off to find the elusive Great Pink Sea Snail and the Giant Lunar Moth in the South Seas, but no box office.

Problems on the set were many, especially with the use of so many live animals—more than 1,500. Alan Jay Lerner, originally set to write the book and lyrics, attempted to write for over a year but finally gave up, whereupon Harrison wanted to leave as well. Harrison hadn't wanted to star in a children's film in the first place, and only the involvement of prestigious author-lyricist Lerner attracted him to the project. The songs by Lerner's replacement, Leslie Bricusse, pleased Harrison, so he stayed with the production. Will put the kids to sleep, but may kill you.

DR. DOLITTLE   DVD
1998 95m c   Children's/Comedy/Fantasy   ★★½
Davis Entertainment/Joseph M. Singer Productions/   PG-13
Topping/Thomas Productions/20th Century Fox
(U.S.)

Eddie Murphy *(Dr. John Dolittle)*, Ossie Davis *(Archer Dolittle)*, Oliver Platt *(Dr. Mark Weller)*, Peter Boyle *(Calloway)*, Richard Schiff *(Dr. Gene Reiss)*, Kristen Wilson *(Lisa Dolittle)*, Jeffrey Tambor *(Doctor Fish)*, Kyla Pratt *(Maya)*, Raven-Symone *(Charisse Dolittle)*, Steven Gilborn *(Doctor Litvack)*

p, John Davis, David T. Friendly, Joseph M. Singer; d, Betty Thomas; w, Nat Mauldin, Larry Levin (based on the stories by Hugh Lofting); ph, Russell Boyd; ed, Peter Teschner; m, Richard

Gibbs; prod d, William Elliot; art d, Greg Papalia; fx, Burt Dalton; cos, Sharen Davis

An A-list animal voice cast is the most outstanding feature of this nonmusical remake of the turgid 1967 picture about a lovable eccentric who can communicate with animals.

With two other physicians, old-fashioned Dr. Reiss (Richard Schiff) and money-grubbing Dr. Weller (Oliver Platt), go-getter Dr. John Dolittle (Eddie Murphy) runs a successful San Francisco practice treating human patients. He's entirely forgotten that as a child he talked to animals and they talked back; in fact, he doesn't seem to like animals much at all, and he's not very nice to his wife (Kristen Wilson) and children (Kyla Pratt, Raven-Symone) either. Dolittle's yuppie life is thrown into chaos after he nearly runs down a mutt on a dark street. The dog, a cheeky pup named Lucky (voice of Norm Macdonald), talks to him—berates him, in fact—and soon Dolittle is hearing animal voices everywhere: squabbling pigeons and rats (Julie Kavner and Garry Shandling, Reni Santoni and John Leguizamo), a wounded owl (Jenna Elfman), a snack-happy racoon (Paul Reubens), a sassy guinea pig named Rodney (Chris Rock), a suicidal circus tiger (Albert Brooks), a manic terrier (Gilbert Gottfried), and more. The babbling beasts won't stop, and everyone thinks Dolittle has lost his mind.

The nominal story, involving a rapacious managed health care group's offer to buy Dolittle's practice and the good doctor's covert quest to help the depressed tiger, proceeds in fits and starts but still beats the hell out of the original film's bogus search for the giant sea snail. Small children should be delighted by the menagerie of chatty critters, but their parents may be less than thrilled by what the animals have to say: no matter where the gags start, they have a conspicuous tendency to circle back to the subject of bums.

DR. EHRLICH'S MAGIC BULLET
1940 103m bw   Biography   ★★★★
Warner Bros.   (U.S.)

Edward G. Robinson *(Dr. Paul Ehrlich)*, Ruth Gordon *(Mrs. Heidi Ehrlich)*, Otto Kruger *(Dr. Emil von Behring)*, Donald Crisp *(Minister Althoff)*, Maria Ouspenskaya *(Franziska Speyer)*, Montagu Love *(Prof. Hartmann)*, Sig Rumann *(Dr. Hans Wolfert)*, Donald Meek *(Mittelmeyer)*, Henry O'Neill *(Dr. Lentz)*, Albert Basserman *(Dr. Robert Koch)*

p, Wolfgang Reinhardt; d, William Dieterle; w, John Huston, Heinz Herald, Norman Burnside (based on a story by Burnside from letters and notes owned by the Ehrlich family); ph, James Wong Howe; ed, Warren Low; m, Max Steiner; art d, Carl Jules Weyl; fx, Robert Burks; cos, Howard Shoup

AAN Best Original Screenplay: Norman Burnside, Heinz Herald, John Huston

Another entry in the superb series of Warner Bros. historical biographies, and alongside the same director's THE LIFE OF EMILE ZOLA, the best of them. By even mentioning the subject of venereal disease, this splendid saga also merits pride of place in any history of Hollywood.

Robinson is positively electric in a role quite unlike the types he usually played, that of gentle yet determined research scientist Dr. Paul Ehrlich. Unable to fit into the conservative routine of a Berlin hospital, painfully honest with his patients, Dr. Ehrlich finally finds his niche on the staff of respected physician Dr. Robert Koch (Basserman). Although his experiments cause him to contract TB, Ehrlich's ever-fertile mind first grasps a theory of poison immunity while he recovers from his illness in Egypt. Returning to Germany, Ehrlich must face shortsighted grant agencies and even a court of law while implementing his treatments for syphillis and childhood diphtheria, but the good doctor's steadfastness eventually wins the day.

Beautifully directed by ace studio craftsman Dieterle, the detailed, Oscar-nominated screenplay (using information from Ehrlich's family) manages to turn meticulous scientific research into absorbing subject matter. Robinson convincingly ages over 35 years during the film, bringing warmth and idiosyncrasy to a challenging role. Among a great supporting cast, Kruger and Basserman are particularly fine. Gordon, however, though sweet and likable as Ehrlich's supportive wife, brings little to the role which suggests her legendary stage reputation.

DOCTOR IN THE HOUSE

1954   92m   c   Comedy   ★★★★
General Films   (U.K.)

Dirk Bogarde *(Simon Sparrow)*, Muriel Pavlow *(Joy Gibson)*, Kenneth More *(Richard Grimsdyke)*, Donald Sinden *(Tony Benskin)*, Kay Kendall *(Isobel)*, James Robertson Justice *(Sir Lancelot Spratt)*, Donald Houston *("Taffy" Evans)*, Suzanne Cloutier *(Stella)*, Geoffrey Keen *(Dean)*, George Coulouris *(Briggs)*

p, Betty E. Box; d, Ralph Thomas; w, Richard Gordon, Ronald Wilkinson, Nicholas Phipps (based on the novel by Gordon); ph, Ernest Steward (Technicolor); ed, Gerald Thomas; m, Bruce Montgomery; art d, Carmen Dillon; cos, Yvonne Caffin

The original "Doctor" comedy that spawned an entire series of films and a popular television sitcom, DOCTOR IN THE HOUSE is certainly the best of the lot. Simon Sparrow (Bogarde) begins his five long years of medical school and is immediately taken over by three student repeaters, all of whom failed their preliminary exams. Bogarde (like almost everyone else in the cast) is a bit too old for his role, but his appeal is undeniable and the film is notable for confirming his status as Britain's leading matinee idol of the 1950s. Shot with the appropriate lighthearted touch in bright, shiny color, with fine performances all around (Kenneth More is particularly good), this sometimes hilarious film started the series off on a high note.

DR. JEKYLL AND MR. HYDE

1932   90m   bw   Horror   ★★★★½
Paramount   (U.S.)

Fredric March *(Dr. Henry Jekyll/Mr. Hyde)*, Miriam Hopkins *(Ivy Pearson)*, Rose Hobart *(Muriel Carew)*, Holmes Herbert *(Dr. Lanyon)*, Edgar Norton *(Poole)*, Halliwell Hobbes *(Brig.-Gen. Carew)*, Arnold Lucy *(Utterson)*, Tempe Pigott *(Mrs. Hawkins)*, Col. G.L. McDonnell *(Hobson)*, Eric Wilton *(Briggs)*

p, Rouben Mamoulian; d, Rouben Mamoulian; w, Samuel Hoffenstein, Percy Heath (based on the novel *The Strange Case of Dr. Jekyll and Mr. Hyde* by Robert Louis Stevenson); ph, Karl Struss; ed, William Shea; art d, Hans Dreier; cos, Travis Banton

AA Best Actor: Fredric March; *AAN Best Writing (Adaptation):* Percy Heath, Samuel Hoffenstein; *AAN Best Cinematography:* Karl Struss

Easily the best of the many versions of the Stevenson horror classic. Although heavily made up as a jagged-toothed simian, March is memory-scarring with his weird body language and fierce posturing as Hyde, in stark contrast to the upright if simpering Jekyll. As Jekyll, courting his unattainable fiancee (Hobart) or tampering with nature and chemistry to create the evil side of his nature in living form, March embodies the essence of gentility. As Hyde, March is truly frightening in his hideous alter ego who taunts and brutalizes a promiscuous barmaid (Hopkins). The film reaches its exciting finale as the law confronts the grotesque Hyde, locked out

of his laboratory, only to discover that he is also the respectable Dr. Jekyll.

March deservedly won an Oscar for his astonishing "dual" role (shared with Wallace Beery for THE CHAMP), but perhaps the real star of the film is director Mamoulian, whose audacious use of symbolism and careful pacing increase the mystique of this strange story. His heavy use of point-of-view editing is entirely appropriate to the story, and Struss's outstanding photography is a marvel to behold.

Made before the Production Code clampdown in 1934, DR. JEKYLL AND MR. HYDE not only uses violence to great effect but also does not shy away from the links between horror and sexuality. During the first transformation scene Mamoulian includes a montage which makes it clear that Hyde represents Jekyll's id, the socially and sexually repressed side of the doctor's psyche. The highly charged scenes between March and Hopkins (who's marvelous as Ivy) are the film's highlights, while those between March and the suitably demure Hobart pale by comparison.

DR. NO

1962   110m   c   Spy   ★★★½
UA   (U.K.)

Sean Connery *(James Bond)*, Jack Lord *(Felix Leiter)*, Joseph Wiseman *(Dr. No)*, Ursula Andress *(Honey)*, Zena Marshall *(Miss Taro)*, Eunice Gayson *(Sylvia)*, Lois Maxwell *(Miss Moneypenny)*, Margaret LeWars *(Photographer)*, John Kitzmiller *(Quarrel)*, Bernard Lee *("M")*

p, Harry Saltzman, Albert R. Broccoli; d, Terence Young; w, Richard Maibaum, Johanna Harwood, Berkely Mather (based on the novel by Ian Fleming); ph, Ted Moore (Technicolor); ed, Peter Hunt; m, John Barry, Monty Norman; prod d, Ken Adam; art d, Syd Cain; fx, Frank George

The first entry in what was to become the most profitable movie series of all time is a solid, surprisingly modest spy thriller, enlivened by Sean Connery's screen charisma and occasional hints of the extravagance to come. James Bond (Sean Connery) is sent by his Secret Service superior, "M" (Bernard Lee), to investigate the murder of another agent in Jamaica. There he learns of Dr. No (Joseph Wiseman), a mysterious Eurasian who's up to something sinister on his private island, Crab Key.

In the service of SPECTRE—the Special Executive for Counterintelligence, Terrorism, Revenge and Extortion—Dr. No has built a device that can alter the flight paths of rockets launched from Cape Canaveral. Bond survives several attempts on his life—notably a skin-crawling encounter with a poisonous spider—and makes his way to Crab Key, where he meets knife-toting, bikini-clad Honey Rider (Ursula Andress) and does battle with a flame-throwing armored vehicle. After Bond and Honey become the evil scientist's prisoners, 007 must defeat a private army single-handed.

In DR. NO, the Bond formula is not yet graven in stone, and viewers may be surprised by the absence of favorite conventions—e.g., the standard title sequence, with silhouetted nude bodies floating in space to the tune of a lush pop ballad. Still, under director Young's sure hand, the performances are amusing and the plotline suitably enthralling. To play Bond, producers Albert "Cubby" Broccoli and Harry Saltzman required a relative unknown with just the right combination of ruggedness, suavity, and sex appeal. Connery fit the profile and instantly made the role his own (to the chagrin of Roger Moore and other later Bond impersonators). DR. NO is also notable for introducing John Barry's famous James Bond theme music (although the featured song, a forgettable piece of *faux* calypso called "Underneath the Mango Tree," is repeated at least once too often).

DR. SEUSS' THE CAT IN THE HAT   DVD

2003 78m   c   Comedy/Fantasy   ★
Brian Grazer Productions/DreamWorks   PG
SKG/Imagine Entertainment/Alphaville Films   (U.S.)

Mike Myers *(The Cat)*, Alec Baldwin *(Quinn)*, Kelly Preston *(Mom)*, Dakota Fanning *(Sally)*, Spencer Breslin *(Conrad)*, Amy Hill *(Mrs. Kwan)*, Sean Hayes *(Mr. Humberfloob/The Fish)*, Danielle Ryan Chuchran *(Thing 1)*, Taylor Rice *(Thing 1)*, Brittany Oaks *(Thing 2)*

p, Brian Grazer; d, Bo Welch; w, Alec Berg, Jeff Schaffer, David Mandel (based on the book by Theodore Geisel, writing as Dr. Seuss); ph, Emmanuel Lubezki; ed, Don Zimmerman; m, David Newman; prod d, Alex McDowell; art d, Alec Hammond, Sean Haworth; fx, Thomas L. Fisher, Douglas Hans Smith; cos, Rita Ryack

A more accurate title would be "Mike Myers' Cat in the Hat," since this coarse assault on the senses bears few traces of Dr. Seuss' tartly whimsical sensibility but fairly oozes Myers's brand of smirking humor.

The film embellishes the original tale and lards it with smug pop psychologizing, sarcastic product placements, and a cameo by celebu-tramp Paris Hilton, none of which could be considered improvements. Mom (Kelly Preston), now a busty single parent/Realtor in too-tight clothes, must host a business party for her tyrannical, germ-phobic boss, Mr. Humberfloob (Sean Hayes), and if her home is anything short of spotless she's fired. Her children, prissy control freak Sally (Dakota Fanning) and one-man wrecking crew Conrad (Spencer Breslin), epitomize youthful dysfunction. Mom's so stressed she doesn't even realize her loutish boyfriend, Lawrence Quinn (Alec Baldwin), is courting her only for her money. As soon as Mom's out of the house, the Cat (Myers) appears and starts stirring up trouble. By the time production designer turned director Bo Welch's exhausting farrago is over, the Cat has destroyed the kitchen in a parody of cooking shows; been mistaken for a pinata at a neighboring child's birthday party; taken the siblings to a rave; blatantly plugged Universal's theme park; and allowed the house to be transported into another dimension.

Frenetic and cheerless action aside, the film's real problem is the Cat, who looks most unmagically like a second-string college sports-team mascot and conducts himself like a risque baggy-pants comedian. Seuss's cat embodies unbridled childish energy run amok; how he'd squirm at the sight of one who leers at a va-va-va-voom photo of Mom while his tail and stovepipe hat rise lewdly.

DR. SEUSS' HOW THE GRINCH STOLE CHRISTMAS   DVD

2000 102m   c   Children's/Fantasy   ★★★
Imagine Entertainment   (U.S.)   PG

Jim Carrey *(Grinch)*, Taylor Momsen *(Cindy Lou Who)*, Anthony Hopkins *(Narrator)*, Jeffrey Tambor *(May Who)*, Christine Baranski *(Martha May Whovier)*, Bill Irwin *(Lou Lou Who)*, Molly Shannon *(Betty Lou Who)*, Jeremy Howard *(Drew Lou Who)*, T.J. Thyne *(Stu Lou Who)*, Lacey Kohl *(Christina Whoterberry)*

p, Brian Grazer, Ron Howard; d, Ron Howard; w, Peter S. Seaman, Jeffrey Price (based on the book by Dr. Seuss); ph, Don Peterman; ed, Dan Hanley, Mike Hill; m, James Horner; prod d, Michael Corenblith; art d, Dan Webster, Lauren Polizzi; fx, Kevin Mack, Kurt Williams, Garv Thorp, David Sanger, Scott Shields, Digital Domain; cos, Rita Ryack

AA Best Makeup: Rick Baker, Gail Ryan; *AAN Best Art Direction:* Michael Corenblith (Art Direction), Merideth Boswell (Set Decoration); *AAN Best Costume Design:* Rita Ryack

Parents can relax. Ron Howard's version of Dr. Seuss's tale of the Christmas-napping Grinch is a smartly stylized hoot, featuring a virtuoso performance by Jim Carrey, great-looking sets, and enough sophisticated in-jokes to keep adults interested when the whimsy threatens to get out of hand. Carrey is pretty much the whole show, all but unrecognizable inside a hairy green suit. Saddled with a hilarious gut and impossibly long fingers, he's his usual bundle of manic energy, a contortionist with the timing of a Borscht Belt comic. Screenwriters Jeffrey Price and Peter Seaman fleshed out Seuss's original plot with some unoriginal (though not fatally so) backstory explaining why the Grinch hates Christmas and the residents of Whoville (people were mean to him when he was a child, particularly during the holidays) and added a host of characters to interact with the little heroine, Cindy Lou Who (Taylor Momsen). Director Howard, whose only previous foray into fantasy was the leaden, charmless WILLOW, stages everything with an appropriately light touch, and gets charming, funny performances from a large cast that includes narrator Anthony Hopkins, Christine Baranski, Jeffrey Tambor, and a terrier-mutt mix named Kelly, the kind of pooch you suspect could play Hamlet if called upon to do so. The film's charms notwithstanding, it remains unclear why it needed to be a full hour longer than Chuck Jones's 1966 half-hour cartoon adaptation. And none but the thoroughly perverse of hearing should stick around for the closing credits and Faith Hill warbling "Where Are You Christmas," composer James Horner's insufferable bid for an Oscar nomination. TITANIC's "My Heart Will Go On" sounds like Mahler's *Das Lied von der Erde* by comparison.

DR. STRANGELOVE OR: HOW I LEARNED TO   DVD
STOP WORRYING AND LOVE THE BOMB

1963 102m bw Science Fiction/Comedy/War   ★★★★★
Columbia   (U.K.)

Peter Sellers *(Group Capt. Lionel Mandrake/President Merkin Muffley/Dr. Strangelove)*, George C. Scott *(Gen. "Buck" Turgidson)*, Sterling Hayden *(Gen. Jack D. Ripper)*, Keenan Wynn *(Col. "Bat" Guano)*, Slim Pickens *(Maj. T.J. "King" Kong)*, Peter Bull *(Ambassador de Sadesky)*, Tracy Reed *(Miss Scott)*, James Earl Jones *(Lt. Lothar Zogg)*, Jack Creley *(Mr. Staines)*, Frank Berry *(Lt. H.R. Dietrich)*

p, Stanley Kubrick; d, Stanley Kubrick; w, Stanley Kubrick, Terry Southern, Peter George (based on the novel *Red Alert* by Peter George); ph, Gilbert Taylor; ed, Anthony Harvey; m, Laurie Johnson; prod d, Ken Adam; art d, Peter Murton; fx, Wally Veevers; cos, Bridget Sellers

AAN Best Picture; AAN Best Actor: Peter Sellers; *AAN Best Director:* Stanley Kubrick; *AAN Best Adapted Screenplay:* Stanley Kubrick, Peter George, Terry Southern

Easily the funniest movie ever made about global thermonuclear holocaust, DR. STRANGELOVE seems to grow more relevant with each passing year. Obsessed with the idea that Communists are trying to rob Americans of their "precious bodily fluids," General Jack D. Ripper (Hayden), commander of Burpelson Air Force Base, goes completely mad and sends his bomber wing to attack the USSR. U.S. President Muffley (Sellers) meets desperately with his advisors, including blustery Gen. "Buck" Turgidson (Scott) and wheelchair-bound ex-Nazi scientist Dr. Strangelove (also played by Sellers). Left with little choice, the powers that be formulate a plan to have the Russians shoot down the American bombers. However, the Soviet ambassador (Bull), informs the president that the Soviet Union has constructed a "Doomsday Device" which will automatically trigger buried nuclear weapons if their country is hit. Meanwhile, British officer Lionel Mandrake (also Sellers) busies himself with trying to trick

Gen. Ripper into revealing the code that will recall the bombers. Eventually, all of them are shot down or recalled, except for one flown by Major T.J. "King" Kong (Pickens), a crafty pilot who manages to evade Russian fighters and missiles as he heads for his target deep inside the USSR. One of the film's final images, that of Kong riding the phallic bomb like a bucking bronco, is unforgettable.

Expertly directed by Kubrick, who deftly intercuts the events at Burpelson with the War Room conference and the action on Kong's B-52, DR. STRANGELOVE is the ultimate black comedy, one that makes unthinkable horror unbearably funny. The film is a model of barely controlled hysteria in which the absurdity of hypermasculine Cold War posturing becomes devastatingly funny—and at the same time nightmarishly frightening in its accuracy. (The Burpelson motto, "Peace Is Our Profession," is not so absurd; consider the labeling of the Strategic Defense Initiative as a "Peace Shield.") While at times Kubrick seems to strive a bit too hard for laughs (Keenan Wynn's being sprayed in the face after shooting a Coca-Cola machine comes to mind), other effects, especially the cinematography and Adam's brilliant production design, potently enhance the film's satirical vision.

STRANGELOVE also contains some truly remarkable comic performances, especially from Sellers in his triple role and Hayden as the mad general, and genuinely priceless dialogue ("Gentlemen, you can't fight in here. This is the War Room!"). A prophetic look at the insanity of superpower politics which, like George Orwell's *1984*, has entered the lexicon of modern political discourse.

DOCTOR X

1932 77m   c/bw Horror   ★★★★
First National   (U.S.)

Lionel Atwill *(Doctor Xavier, Head of Research Laboratory)*, Lee Tracy *(Lee Taylor, a Newspaper Reporter)*, Fay Wray *(Joanne, Dr. X's Daughter)*, Preston Foster *(Dr. Wells)*, Arthur Edmund Carewe *(Dr. Rowitz)*, John Wray *(Dr. Haines)*, Harry Beresford *(Dr. Duke)*, George Rosener *(Otto, Dr. X's Butler)*, Leila Bennett *(Mamie, Dr. X's Housekeeper)*, Robert Warwick *(Police Commissioner Stevens)*

d, Michael Curtiz; w, Robert Tasker, Earl Baldwin (based on a play by Howard Warren Comstock and Allen C. Miller); ph, Ray Rennahan, Richard Towers (Technicolor); ed, George Amy; art d, Anton Grot

A rare excursion into horror for First National (later Warner Bros.), DOCTOR X became one of the great "lost" films after its initial release and developed a reputation as a masterpiece of early talkie horror during the 30 years it went unseen. When a black-and-white print of this two-color Technicolor landmark was finally discovered, however, some found the film a disappointment. Now that enough time has passed and viewers can forget all those long-cherished expectations, the film proves to be a delightful product of its period.

The story is set in a spooky old mansion atop the cliffs at Blackstone Shoals on Long Island. Atwill plays the sinister Dr. Xavier, who runs the research laboratory where most of the action takes place. It seems that a member of his staff has discovered a synthetic flesh substitute which imbues its wearer with abnormal powers and that transformed monster has been strangling people during full moons. Much of the film involves a recreation of the murders designed to expose the killer, but all does not go quite as planned.

Talented studio craftsman Curtiz (CASABLANCA) shapes the material well, showing particular flair in his semi-expressionistic handling of the haunted house trappings of the story. If he doesn't have quite the flair for grotesquerie or black humor of James Whale, he does use the wisecracking of Tracy and the glowering of Atwill to good effect. Atwill especially shines when called upon to casually discuss topics from cannibalism to depravity. Several scenes, from the

unexpected animation of a skeleton to the recreation of the final murder, where the killer puts in an unexpected guest appearance, are genuinely eerie. Fay Wray, as Dr. Xavier's daughter, also gets to scream as only she can.

Finally, the two-color Technicolor techniques (involving the processing of two negatives rather than the three which became standard after 1935) are extremely effective. The rather slack and hokey 1939 film, THE RETURN OF DOCTOR X, is not a sequel, but it does contain Humphrey Bogart's only horror movie appearance.

DOCTOR ZHIVAGO   **DVD**

1965 197m   c   Drama/War   ★★★★
MGM   (U.S.)

Geraldine Chaplin *(Tonya Gromeko)*, Julie Christie *(Larissa "Lara" Guishar)*, Tom Courtenay *(Pasha Antipov/Strelnikoff)*, Alec Guinness *(Yevgrav Zhivago)*, Siobhan McKenna *(Anna Gromeko)*, Ralph Richardson *(Alexander Gromeko)*, Omar Sharif *(Yuri Zhivago)*, Rod Steiger *(Viktor Komarovsky)*, Rita Tushingham *(The Girl)*, Adrienne Corri *(Amelia Guishar)*

p, Carlo Ponti; d, David Lean; w, Robert Bolt (based on the novel by Boris Pasternak); ph, Freddie Young (Panavision, Metrocolor); ed, Norman Savage; m, Maurice Jarre; prod d, John Box; art d, Terence Marsh, Gil Parrondo; fx, Eddie Fowlie; cos, Phyllis Dalton

AAN Best Picture; AAN Best Supporting Actor: Tom Courtenay; *AAN Best Director:* David Lean; *AA Best Adapted Screenplay:* Robert Bolt; *AA Best Color Cinematography:* Freddie Young; *AAN Best Film Editing:* Norman Savage; *AA Best Original Score:* Maurice Jarre; *AA Best Art Direction-Set Decoration (Color):* John Box, Terry Marsh, Dario Simoni; *AA Best Costume Design (Color):* Phyllis Dalton; *AAN Best Sound:* A.W. Watkins, Franklin E. Milton

Lumpy if sometimes sinfully rich borscht. This sprawling adaptation of Pasternak's epic novel of the Russian Revolution was director Lean's follow-up to his masterful LAWRENCE OF ARABIA. Told in flashback, the film follows Yuri Zhivago (Sharif) and Tonya Gromeko (Chaplin), who meet as youths when the orphaned Yuri is taken in by Tonya's parents. Eventually Yuri becomes a physician and marries Tonya, but several times during WWI he crosses paths with Lara (Christie), the beautiful daughter of a dressmaker, and the two fall into a passionate affair that is disrupted by the Bolshevik Revolution.

Unable to maintain a consistent level of interest through its seat-squirming long running time, this typically overblown Lean epic is not as exciting or as powerful as LAWRENCE OF ARABIA or THE BRIDGE ON THE RIVER KWAI. Bolt's choppy screenplay leaves out great chunks of Pasternak's novel, turning the narrative in a bumpy, who-gives-a-damn roller coaster ride in the film's last half. Equally regrettable is the miscasting of Sharif, who had done quite well in LAWRENCE but here contributes a performance with all the sparkle of sawdust. Christie, Steiger, and (to a lesser extent) Guinness, however, imbue their parts with passion and intensity, and the huge supporting cast is generally fine.

As always, Lean's handling of the purely physical aspects of the material is spectacular, with the scenes of revolution, the harsh Russian winters, and Zhivago's trek across the steppes simply unforgettable. Filmed mostly in Spain and Finland, the cinematography is often stunning even when the effects are pretentious (e.g. Lean's screen-filling closeup of the inside of a flower). Jarre's jarring score, though much praised at the time for the lilting "Lara's Theme," now seems repetitive and grating enough to make one want to sabotage balalaika factories everywhere.

DODGE CITY

DVD
1939 104m c   Western   ★★★★
Warner Bros. (U.S.)

Errol Flynn *(Wade Hatton)*, Olivia de Havilland *(Abbie Irving)*, Ann Sheridan *(Ruby Gilman)*, Bruce Cabot *(Jeff Surrett)*, Frank McHugh *(Joe Clemens)*, Alan Hale *(Algernon "Rusty" Hart)*, John Litel *(Matt Cole)*, Victor Jory *(Yancy, Surrett's Henchman)*, Henry Travers *(Dr. Irving)*, Henry O'Neill *(Col. Dodge)*

p, Robert Lord; d, Michael Curtiz; w, Robert Buckner; ph, Ray Rennahan, Sol Polito (Technicolor); ed, George Amy; m, Max Steiner; art d, Ted Smith; fx, Byron Haskin, Rex Wimpy; cos, Milo Anderson

This great action Western, Flynn's first, has the intrepid adventurer enter Dodge City, a notorious, wide-open range town, as cattle buyer Wade Hatton. He leads lawmen to rustler Jeff Surrett (Cabot) and his henchmen (Jory and Fowley) before leading a covered wagon train with his pals (Hale and Guinn "Big Boy" Williams) en route to Dodge City. Attracted to spirited Abbie Irving (de Havilland), he draws only her scorn after she blames him for the death of her brother (Lundigan), a hellion crushed in a stampede he himself started. Once at Dodge City, Wade finds that Surrett now runs the town and, after being pushed far enough, takes the sheriff's badge and cleans up the hellhole. Although he has a brief flirtation with saloon gal Ruby Gilman (Sheridan), his heart belongs to Abbie, and she soon comes to respect Wade's heroic endeavors.

DODGE CITY is top-flight action directed with verve and invention by Warner Bros. workhorse Curtiz. In a year with plenty of worthy Western competition, this expensively mounted film nevertheless found a wide and appreciative public. Polito's camerawork, highlighted by the rich use of color, is sweeping and fluid, and Steiner's score is vigorous and effective. A sequence involving a burning runaway train is handled well and the saloon brawl midway through the film, used time and again by the studio as stock footage, is magnificently staged and remains a classic of its kind. Not too surprisingly, de Havilland hated her rather standardized role, and Sheridan, in a more colorful part, unfortunately doesn't get as much footage as she deserves. This film belongs to the men, especially Flynn, who attacks the part with gusto and suitably adapts his British veneer to the code of the Old West. Flynn would make seven more Westerns, but DODGE CITY remains his best outing in the genre. The story line for BLAZING SADDLES was taken from this film.

DODGEBALL: A TRUE UNDERDOG STORY

DVD
2004 96m c   Comedy/Sports   ★★
Mediastream IV/Red Hour   (U.S.)   PG-13

Vince Vaughn *(Peter La Fleur)*, Christine Taylor *(Kate Veatch)*, Ben Stiller *(White Goodman)*, Rip Torn *(Patches O'Houlihan)*, Justin Long *(Justin)*, Stephen Root *(Gordon)*, Joel David Moore *(Owen)*, Chris Williams *(Dwight)*, Alan Tudyk *(Steve the Pirate)*, Jason Bateman *(Pepper Brooks)*

p, Stuart Cornfeld, Ben Stiller; d, Rawson Marshall Thurber; w, Rawson Marshall Thurber; ph, Jerzy Zielinski; ed, Alan Baumgarten; m, Theodore Shapiro; prod d, Maher Ahmad; art d, Andrew Max Cahn; fx, Gary D'Amico, Werner Hahnlein; cos, Carol Ramsey

Judging by the lowball ambitions of this Cinderella story centered around everyone's least favorite grade-school game, director-screenwriter Rawson Marshall Thurber subscribes to the same notion as underachieving hero Peter LaFleur (Vince Vaughn): "If you don't have a goal, you're never disappointed."

Charming though he is, Peter can't quite get his act together; he's being hounded by creditors, and his rundown gym,

Average Joe's, is a haven for misfits who can't scrape up their membership dues. It's only a matter of time before bank officer Kate Veatch (Christine Taylor) pays a visit to warn that if the $50,000 mortgage isn't paid in 30 days, foreclosure proceedings are imminent. Peter can't imagine who would want to purchase the dilapidated facility, but business rival White Goodman (Ben Stiller) would love to level Average Joe's and build a parking lot. Peter's pal Gordon (Stephen Root), a connoisseur of obscure sports, suggests entering the Las Vegas International Dodgeball Open, which offers a $50,000 top prize. Peter assembles a six-man team—himself, Gordon, Justin (Justin Long), Owen (Joel David Moore), Dwight (Chris Williams), and Steve the Pirate (Alan Tudyk)—and mysteriously disabled dodgeball legend Patches O'Houlihan (Rip Torn) agrees to whip the ragtag crew into tip-top shape. Meanwhile, White and his ultrabuff team weasel their way into competition, the better for White to put the moves on Kate.

On the plus side, Vaughn and his squad of oddballs are pretty funny, as is the ESPN parody featuring an enthusiastic but dimwitted sportscaster (Jason Bateman). But Stiller doesn't know when to stop; his thoroughly repellent character, whose relationship with pizza makes AMERICAN PIE's pastry lover seem wholesome, verges on the unwatchable. And be warned: The end credits contain a particularly nauseating image you'll wish you could delete from memory.

DODSWORTH

DVD
1936 90m bw Romance   ★★★★★
UA   (U.S.)

Walter Huston *(Sam Dodsworth)*, Ruth Chatterton *(Fran Dodsworth)*, Paul Lukas *(Arnold Iselin)*, Mary Astor *(Edith Cortright)*, David Niven *(Capt. Lockert)*, Gregory Gaye *(Kurt von Obersdorf)*, Maria Ouspenskaya *(Baroness von Obersdorf)*, Odette Myrtil *(Mme. Renee de Penable)*, Kathryn Marlowe *(Emily Howard)*, Spring Byington *(Matey Pearson)*

p, Samuel Goldwyn; d, William Wyler; w, Sidney Howard (based on his play, adapted from the novel by Sinclair Lewis), Robert Wyler; ph, Rudolph Maté; ed, Daniel Mandell; m, Alfred Newman; art d, Richard Day; fx, Ray Binger; cos, Omar Kiam

AAN Best Picture; AAN Best Actor: Walter Huston; AAN Best Supporting Actress: Maria Ouspenskaya; AAN Best Director: William Wyler; AAN Best Screenplay: Sidney Howard; AA Best Interior Decoration: Richard Day (Art Direction); AAN Best Sound Recording: Oscar Lagerstrom

A film of maturity, intelligence, and understanding. Huston, repeating his popular stage role, plays reserved auto mogul Sam Dodsworth, who retires to enjoy his middle age at the prompting of his wife Fran (Chatterton). Traveling in Europe, the unsophisticated Midwesterners have completely opposite reactions to the Continental milieu: while Sam soon gets bored, Fran aspires to become a woman of the world. Embarrassed by her flirtation with a roue (Niven) and hurt by her encounter with a more subtle adventurer (Lukas), Fran doesn't learn from her failures. She finally asks Sam for a divorce in order to marry a young but mother-dominated baron (Gaye). Sam, meanwhile, meets a kindly widow (Astor) with whom he finds he might salvage his happiness. But the longtime romance of Sam and Fran must be dealt with first.

The direction of the autocratic Wyler sensitively plots a tale of marital problems, middle age, and the Ugly American abroad. Huston was never better than in this magnificent performance of a simple man whose blissful world disintegrates. His effortless acting was so splendidly moving that he was voted Best Actor by the NY Film Critics. (With their typical fondness for showy acting, however, Oscar voters cited Paul Muni in THE STORY OF LOUIS PASTEUR.) Chatterton, too, is superb in a role she wanted to play as a total heavy.

Wyler, though, was wisely able to temper this portrait of a self-ish, shallow woman with great insight. Chatterton's sometimes theatrical emoting perfectly suits her rich study of a woman playacting her way through life. The low-key scenes between Huston and Chatterton are warm and tender, while their arguments are positively blistering. The support includes gems from Lukas, Niven, Gaye, Ouspenskaya, Myrtil, and Byington, but it is really Astor who equals the stars with a performance of consummate artistry.

DOG DAY AFTERNOON

1975 130m c Crime   DVD

Artists Entertainment   (U.S.)   ★★★★★   R

Al Pacino *(Sonny Wortzik)*, John Cazale *(Sal)*, Charles Durning *(Det. Sgt. Moretti)*, Chris Sarandon *(Leon)*, Sully Boyar *(Mulvaney)*, Penny Allen *(Sylvia)*, James Broderick *(Sheldon)*, Carol Kane *(Jenny)*, Susan Peretz *(Angie Wortzik)*, Beulah Garrick *(Margaret)*

p, Martin Bregman, Martin Elfand; d, Sidney Lumet; w, Frank Pierson (based on a magazine article by P.F. Kluge, Thomas Moore); ph, Victor J. Kemper (Technicolor); ed, Dede Allen; prod d, Charles Bailey; art d, Douglas Higgins; cos, Anna Hill Johnstone

AAN Best Picture; AAN Best Actor: Al Pacino; *AAN Best Supporting Actor:* Chris Sarandon; *AAN Best Director:* Sidney Lumet; *AA Best Original Screenplay:* Frank Pierson; *AAN Best Film Editing:* Dede Allen

One of the finest films of the 1970s. A bisexual man, Sonny (Pacino), to finance a sex-change operation for his transvestite lover (Sarandon), robs the First Savings Bank of Brooklyn with his moronic friend Sal (Cazale). Police, headed by Moretti (Durning), surround the bank and hold the thieves inside who, in turn, hold employees and customers as hostages. Through it all Sonny carries on endless phone conversations with his obese wife (Peretz), his lover, and assorted police and FBI officials. At one point, while releasing a female hostage, Sonny notices the large crowds outside, watching from behind barriers as if at a carnival. To enlist mob sympathy he begins to shout "Attica! Attica!" (the name of the New York prison where authorities inflicted heavy casualties on rioting prisoners). The crowd picks up the chant, decidedly favoring the bank robbers. Ultimately, however, Sonny threatens to begin shooting hostages unless he and Sal are given $1 million and taken to the airport where they will be flown to a distant country. (When Sonny asks his dim friend what country he wants to go to, the *non compos mentis* thief replies, "Wyoming.") Sonny and Sal's getaway attempt brings this remarkable film to its simmering finale.

DOG DAY AFTERNOON benefits immeasurably from a cast and crew doing some of the finest work of their careers. In a role based on actual incident, Pacino is both funny and tragic as the uneducated, passionate street tough over his head in a lethal situation of his own making. In difficult roles, Cazale and Sarandon are similarly superb, and even those actors on more familiar ground (Durning, Broderick, Peretz) contribute sterling support. The taut script and Lumet's exceptionally disciplined and insightful direction highlight both the suspense and the absurdity of the situation beautifully. The heavy use of off-color language and scorching violence if anything adds to the ultimate sympathy this memorable film successfully evokes.

DOGMA

1999 130m c Comedy   DVD

View Askew Productions   (U.S.)   ★★★   R

Ben Affleck *(Bartleby)*, George Carlin *(Cardinal Glick)*, Matt Damon *(Loki)*, Linda Fiorentino *(Bethany)*, Salma Hayek *(Serendipity)*, Jason Lee *(Azrael)*, Jason Mewes *(Jay)*, Alan Rickman *(Metatron)*, Chris Rock *(Rufus)*, Alanis Morissette *(God)*

p, Scott Mosier; d, Kevin Smith; w, Kevin Smith; ph, Robert Yeoman; ed, Kevin Smith, Scott Mosier; m, Howard Shore; prod d, Robert "Ratface" Holtzman; art d, Elise G. Viola; fx, Richard "Dickie" Payne, Vincent Guastini, Station X Studios, Bellissimo/Belardinelli Effects Inc, Charles Belardinelli, Tom Bellisimo; cos, Abigail Murray

Make no mistake, Kevin Smith's talky, farcical comedy of cosmic errors is clever. But it's clever in a deeply juvenile way, like a parochial-school wiseass who confounds his teachers with a preposterous scenario in which, technically speaking, it isn't actually sinful to covet thy neighbor's wife.

Cardinal Glick (veteran Catholic teaser George Carlin) is preparing to kick off his trendy "Catholicism—Wow!" campaign with a friendlier image of our Lord and the restoration of indulgences, those spiritual get-out-of-hell-free cards that helped disgrace the mediaeval church. Banished angels Loki (Matt Damon) and Bartleby (Ben Affleck), who've been languishing in Wisconsin, like that last bit a lot; they figure on picking up their indulgences at Glick's Red Bank, NJ, church and soaring back into God's good graces. Unfortunately, the Almighty (Alanis Morissette) can't afford to be trumped on a technicality; if the angels return to Heaven, the world will cease to exist. So Bethany (Linda Fiorentino) is recruited to stop Bartleby and Loki, aided by Serendipity the muse (Salma Hayek); Rufus the 13th Apostle (Chris Rock), who was left out of scripture because he's black; and unlikely prophets Jay and Silent Bob (Jason Mewes and Smith himself). Arrayed against them are spiffy demon Azrael (Jason Lee), the roller blading Stygian Triplets, and a really disgusting excrement monster.

Smith's sensibility owes plenty to comic books: grossness, grandiosity, and easy irony are constantly elbowing each other for position. But he pulls off one hell of a trick, slipping in more than a little preaching between the sight gags and profane disquisitions on matters sexual. Say what you will about his sense of humor; genuine faith is rare enough in popular culture to make any sighting worthy of note.

DOGTOWN AND Z-BOYS

2002 90m c Documentary/Sports   DVD

Vans Off the Wall Productions/AOP Productions   ★★★½   PG-13

(U.S.)

Sean Penn *(Narrator)*, Jay Adams, Tony Alva, Bob Biniak, Paul Constantineau, Shogo Kubo, Jim Muir, Peggy Oki, Stacy Peralta, Nathan Pratt

p, Agi Orsi; d, Stacy Peralta; w, Stacy Peralta, Craig Stecyk; ph, Peter Pilafian; ed, Paul Crowder; m, Paul Crowder, Terry Wilson; prod d, Craig Stecyk

If the sign of good documentary is its ability to generate interest regardless of prior enthusiasm for the subject, then Stacy Peralta's hugely entertaining film earns high marks. The subject is skateboarders, specifically the Zephyr Skating Team, a group of California teenagers whose gravity-defying vertical style redefined the sport. Narrated by Sean Penn, Peralta's film is a fascinating look at the origins of a subculture. The story begins with the renegade surfers who rode the dangerous, debris-strewn waters of Pacific Ocean Park and hung around the innovative Jeff Ho & Zephyr Production surf shop in a seedy section of Santa Monica know as "Dogtown." The "Zephyr Team" handed down their punk attitude to the second-generation Z-Boys, who adapted radical surfing styles to skateboarding. Skating asphalt slopes and drought-emptied swimming pools, the Z-Boys rode pavement like waves—crouching low, touching the ground, and adding cut backs to their increasingly revolutionary repertoire. In 1975, the 12-man Zephyr team (which included one girl, Peggy Oki) brought this radical style to the Del Mar Nationals, the biggest skate competition since the 1960s. The world of skateboarding would never be the same again.

Set to the music of the era (lots of Black Sabbath, Aerosmith, and the Stooges) and stylishly rough, the film is constructed primarily from the words of now middle-aged Z-Boys, who offer testimonials to the spirit of the times and the genius of Tony Alva, Jay Adams, and Peralta himself, three of the team's biggest talents. The soul of the film, however, lies in the extraordinary photos and Super-8 films of Craig Stecyk and Glen E. Friedman, photojournalists whose dynamic work appeared in publications such as *Skateboarder* magazine, and helped ignite a nationwide phenomenon.

DOGVILLE   DVD
2003 173m c   Drama   ★★★½
Zentropa Entertainments/Memfis Film   R
International/Trollhattan Film/Slot Machine/Liberator
Productions/Isabella Films International/Something
Else/Sigma Films/Zoma/Pain Unlimited/ARTE France
Cinema/France 3 Cinema
(Denmark/Sweden/U.S./Netherlands/U.K./Germany/France)

Nicole Kidman *(Grace)*, Paul Bettany *(Tom Edison Jr.)*, Harriet Andersson *(Gloria)*, Patricia Clarkson *(Vera)*, Stellan Skarsgard *(Chuck)*, Chloe Sevigny *(Liz Henson)*, Lauren Bacall *(Ma Ginger)*, Ben Gazzara *(Jack McKay)*, Jeremy Davies *(Bill Henson)*, John Hurt *(Narrator)*

p, Vibeke Windelov; d, Lars Von Trier; w, Lars Von Trier; ph, Anthony Dod Mantle; ed, Molly Marlene Stensgard; prod d, Peter Grant; fx, Hummer Hojmark; cos, Manon Rasmussen

The first in writer-director Lars Von Trier's projected trilogy about America has drawn numerous comparisons to Thornton Wilder for its treatment of small-town American life and bold, Brechtian staging. But the film doesn't so much recall *Our Town* as Wilder's screenplay for Hitchcock's SHADOW OF A DOUBT, particularly the moment when murderous Uncle Charlie explains to his wide-eyed niece that if you ripped the fronts from most houses, you'd find swine.

Von Trier's swine are the residents of Dogville, a tiny Depression-era Rocky Mountain township that offers reluctant refuge to Grace (Nicole Kidman), a mysterious fugitive on the run from gangsters. Resident philosopher Tom Edison Jr. (Paul Bettany) has been worried about the quality of Dogville's mercy, so when Grace suddenly appears, Tom thinks he's found the perfect test subject. To convince his wary neighbors to take her in, Tom offers each household Grace's services for one hour each day. Eager to please, Grace rakes gooseberry bushes for Ma Ginger (Lauren Bacall), discusses sunsets with blind Jack McKay (Ben Gazzara), and looks after the brood belonging to Vera (Patricia Clarkson) and her surly husband, Chuck (Stellan Skarsgard). Soon even suspicious Mrs. Henson (Blair Brown) takes a shine to Grace, and Henson's curvaceous daughter (Chloe Sevigny) is thrilled to have another pretty girl around to divert the amorous attentions of Dogville's men. But when the police show up looking for the woman they claim is a bank robber, the good people of Dogville find more dehumanizing ways of exploiting their vulnerable charge.

This brilliantly acted film is a highly stylized, surprisingly successful experiment that sits somewhere between theater and cinema. The near total absence of sets is cleverly offset by John Hurt's slyly ironic narration and Per Streit's excellent sound design. The film, however, is not without flaws: Only the heavy stylization mitigates some highly artificial plot contrivances, and the final photo montage of America's poor, while no doubt exciting to Von Trier the provocateur, is maddeningly oblique.

$ (DOLLARS)
1971 119m c   Crime/Comedy   ★★★½
Columbia   (U.S.)   R

Warren Beatty *(Joe Collins)*, Goldie Hawn *(Dawn Divine)*, Gert Frobe *(Mr. Kessel)*, Robert Webber *(Attorney)*, Scott Brady

(Sarge), Arthur Brauss *(Candy Man)*, Robert Stiles *(Major)*, Wolfgang Kieling *(Granich)*, Robert Herron *(Bodyguard)*, Christiane Maybach *(Helga)*

p, M.J. Frankovich; d, Richard Brooks; w, Richard Brooks; ph, Petrus Schloemp (Technicolor); ed, George Grenville; m, Quincy Jones; art d, Guy Sheppard, Olaf Ivens

$ (DOLLARS) is a pleasant, somewhat underrated chase movie which was written and directed by Richard Brooks, in a significant departure from the heavy dramas (IN COLD BLOOD, THE BROTHERS KARAMAZOV, THE BLACKBOARD JUNGLE, and CAT ON A HOT TIN ROOF) he was usually associated with.

Joe Collins (Beatty) is a security expert employed in Hamburg who plans to rob three safety deposit boxes which he knows are rented by criminals, and Dawn Divine (Hawn) is a prostitute whom he enlists to help him in the endeavor. Their targets are a crooked U.S. Army sergeant (Brady) who scammed money from service clubs, a drug dealer (Brauss) and a courier (Webber) who's been double-dealing the mob. Employed at their bank to install a security system, Collins arranges to be placed inside the vault after a bomb scare. Timing his moves perfectly so as to go unnoticed by surveillance cameras, he stashes the loot in Dawn's safety deposit box so she can blithely collect it later.

An exercise in triviality, and, like most of Brooks's films, not particulary original, $ is nevertheless quite entertaining. Beatty and Hawn play extremely well together and Frobe is outstanding as the bank manager. Running rather longer than one might like, $ benefits from Brooks's lively handling and Quincy Jones's sparse but effective musical score.

DON QUIXOTE
(DON QUICHOTTE)
1933 73m bw Musical   ★★★★
Nelson/Vandor   (U.K./France)

Feodor Chaliapin *(Don Quixote)*, George Robey *(Sancho Panza)*, Sidney Fox *(The Niece)*, Miles Mander *(The Duke)*, Oscar Asche *(Police Captain)*, Dannio *(Carrasco)*, Emily Fitzroy *(Sancho's Wife)*, Renee Valliers *(Dulcinea)*, Frank Stanmore *(Priest)*, Wally Patch *(Gypsy King)*

p, G.W. Pabst; d, G.W. Pabst; w, Paul Morand, Alexandre Arnoux (based on the novel *Don Quixote De La Mancha* by Miguel de Cervantes); ph, Nicolas Farkas; m, Jacques Ibert

Save only the denouement—an allegory added by director Pabst and the French adaptors—this is a fairly faithful rendition of the 300-year-old tale of "The Knight of the Mournful Countenance." Chaliapin, as famed for his striking acting as for his operatic basso, plays Don Quixote, the man immersed for years in the library of chivalric romances for which he has mortgaged his estates. Venturing forth on his bony nag Rocinante, the quiet country gentleman elects to redress the wrongs of the world. He enlists the aid of Sancho Panza (Robey) as his squire, promising him great future rewards in return for faithful service. He pronounces Dulcinea (Valliers), a slatternly milkmaid, to be the fair and pure maiden whose honor he is pledged to protect. Taking windmills for giants and flocks of sheep for armies, he battles them with vigor but invariably suffers defeat.

Many viewers saw in this film an allegorical reference to the Nazi bookburnings of the 1930s, as Pabst's ending departs completely from Cervantes's original, in which the disillusioned Don Quixote renounces his books of knightly lore. Pabst's liberal political orientation had been demonstrated in many of his earlier films, such as KAMERADSCHAFT and THE THREEPENNY OPERA (both 1931). Regardless of the director's political convictions (he later made films under the Nazi regime and, later still, produced a number of anti-fascist films), this telling of the tale benefits from a memorable wind-mill sequence and its stunning star turn by Chaliapin.

DONA FLOR AND HER TWO HUSBANDS
(DONA FLOR E SEUS DOIS MARIDOS)

1976 106m c	Erotic/Comedy	★★★
Coline/Gaumont	(Brazil)	R

Sonia Braga *(Dona Flor)*, Jose Wilker *(Vadhino)*, Mauro Mendonca *(Teodoro)*, Dinorah Brillanti *(Rozilda)*, Nelson Xavier *(Mirandao)*, Arthur Costa Filho *(Carlinhos)*, Rui Rezende *(Cazuza)*, Mario Gusmao

p, Luis Carlos Barreto, Newton Rique, Cia Serrador; d, Bruno Barreto; w, Bruno Barreto (based on a novel by Jorge Amado); ph, Maurilo Salles (Eastmancolor); ed, Raimundo Higino; m, Chico Buarque; art d, Anisio Medeiros

This wonderfully sexy and funny comedy, a variation on BLITHE SPIRIT, shattered Brazilian box-office records and proved very popular worldwide, chiefly because of Braga's tremendously sensual presence. She plays a beautiful woman whose gambling, whoring husband drops dead after an all-night carousal. Deciding to marry again, she chooses a boring, devout, middle-aged pharmacist who rarely wants to make love. One night, as she lies in bed next to her sleeping spouse, the ghost of her first husband appears, nude, in the room. She tries to get rid of him, but he refuses. She finally succumbs to his blandishments and takes the ghost to bed with her, while the second husband continues to sleep.

This entertaining and erotic picture, while perhaps not the most challenging film to come out of Brazil in the 1970s, is nevertheless enjoyable. At times, though, the creative personalities involved seem to want to play it both ways and make it "art cinema" as well as "commercial cinema" simply because it was aimed at the international market. Director Barreto and Braga teamed up again in in GABRIELA, costarring Marcello Mastroianni. Remade in 1982 as KISS ME GOODBYE with—are you ready for this?—Sally Field in the lead role.

DONA HERLINDA AND HER SON
(DONA HERLINDA Y SU HIJO)   **DVD**

1986 90m c	Comedy	★★★★½
Cinevista	(Mexico)	

Guadalupe Del Toro *(Dona Herlinda)*, Arturo Meza *(Ramon)*, Marco Antonio Trevino *(Rodolfo)*, Leticia Lupersio *(Olga)*, Guillermina Alba

p, Manuel Barbachano Ponce; d, Jaime Humberto Hermosillo; w, Jaime Humberto Hermosillo (based on a novel by Jorge Lopez Paez); ph, Miguel Ehrenberg; ed, Luis Kelly

A sex comedy usually succeeds when it gives a fresh twist to old expectations, something the satirical DONA HERLINDA AND HER SON does with unrelenting zest. Dona Herlinda (Del Toro) is the wealthy mother of Rodolfo (Trevino), a closeted gay doctor involved in a relationship with Ramon (Meza), a music student. The two men are in desperate need of some privacy to carry on their affair, a problem which seems to be solved when Dona Herlinda invites Ramon to move in with her and her son. This is more than an act of charity, though, for this particular doting mother has an involved plan to keep her son both happy and respectable, bringing in Olga (Lupersio) to become Rodolfo's heterosexual wife. Disappointed with his lover's acceptance of this plan and jealous of Olga, Ramon goes out for a romp, but is unable to forget the traitorous mama's boy he loves.

Marvelously funny, DONA HERLINDA AND HER SON develops its unusual plot line in a simple, matter-of-fact style, and the final twists arrive at the end of considerable comic momentum. What is most amazing is not only Dona Herlinda's orchestration of personality and situation, but what

also seems to be her determined blindness to her son's homosexuality. Each of the characters is mindfully etched, with performances that make the viewer honestly care about these people. Sexual situations, be they homosexual or heterosexual, are wisely presented without judgment, simply becoming a part of the hilarious comic tableau. Director Hermosillo skillfully evolves a pointed yet gentle satire of mothering and traditional family structures while managing to produce a highly engaging entertainment at the same time.

DONNIE BRASCO   **DVD**

1997 127m c	Crime/Drama	★★★½
Mandalay Entertainment/Baltimore Pictures	(U.S.)	R

Al Pacino *(Lefty Ruggiero)*, Johnny Depp *(Donnie Brasco/Joe Pistone)*, Michael Madsen *(Sonny Black)*, Bruno Kirby *(Nicky)*, James Russo *(Paulie)*, Anne Heche *(Maggie Pistone)*, Zeljko Ivanek *(Tim Curley)*, Gerry Becker *(Dean Blandford)*, Zach Grenier *(Dr. Berger)*, Brian Tarantina *(Bruno)*

p, Mark Johnson, Barry Levinson, Louis DiGiaimo, Gail Mutrux; d, Mike Newell; w, Paul Attanasio (based on the book *Donnie Brasco: My Undercover Life in the Mafia*, by Joseph D. Pistone with Richard Woodley); ph, Peter Sova; ed, Jon Gregory; m, Patrick Doyle; prod d, Donald Graham Burt; art d, Jefferson Sage; fx, Ronald Ottesen Jr.; cos, Aude Bronson-Howard, David Robinson

AAN Best Adapted Screenplay: Paul Attanasio

Perhaps the freshest gangster movie since THE GODFATHER, PART II, as well as the glummest. FBI agent Joe Pistone (Johnny Depp) infiltrates the mob via a disgruntled, middle-aged, low-level Mafioso named Lefty (Al Pacino), who sees the son he wishes he had in Pistone's undercover persona—orphan Donnie Brasco, a shrewd but honest operator with heart. Pistone learns the organization inside out, eventually burrowing in so deep that the danger of being unmasked takes a back seat to the danger of being killed by rival mobsters for his organized crime alliances. With acceptance comes the inevitable crisis of conscience, as Pistone drifts further and further away from his so-called real life: His wife and kids become strangers, and the uptight FBI higher-ups don't understand the toll that living a day-in, day-out lie takes on a man's sense of self. You know he'll get out somehow—the movie's based on the memoirs of the real-life Pistone, who lived to tell—but the suspense of wondering how, and who will be hurt in the process, is excrutiating. The most striking thing about Mike Newell's approach is how clear it is that the whole American mythology of the Mafia leaves him cold. There's no sense of exhilaration in putting one over on the law, no warmth in the *familiga*, no real honor among hoods and no hopped-up intensity in violence: It's all dangerous and arbitrary and ugly, even before it all goes wrong. Depp's tight, guarded performance is almost painful to watch, and Newell seems to have reined in the flamboyant Pacino, whose portrait of the mobster as a grumpy old woman may be his best work in years.

DONNIE DARKO   **DVD**

2001 188m c	Drama/Fantasy	★★★½
Pandora/Flower Films	(U.S.)	R

Jake Gyllenhaal *(Donnie Darko)*, Jena Malone *(Gretchen Ross)*, Drew Barrymore *(Ms. Karen Pomeroy)*, Mary McDonnell *(Rose Darko)*, Katharine Ross *(Dr. Lilian Thurman)*, Patrick Swayze *(Jim Cunningham)*, Noah Wyle *(Dr. Monnitoff)*, Maggie Gyllenhaal *(Elizabeth Darko)*, Daveigh Chase *(Samantha Darko)*, James Duval *(Frank)*

p, Nancy Juvonen, Sean McKittrick; d, Richard Kelly; w, Richard Kelly; ph, Steven Poster; ed, Sam Bauer, Eric Strand; m, Michael

Andrews; prod d, Alexander Hammond; fx, Marcus Keys, Robbie Knott; cos, April Ferry

---

David Lynch lite.

It's the autumn of 1988, and Donnie Darko (Jake Gyllenhaal) is having a rough trip through adolescence. Sandwiched between two well-adjusted sisters (Maggie Gyllenhaal, Daveigh Chase), Donnie feels awkward and alienated from the rituals of high-school life. He doesn't have a girlfriend, but he's got a shrink (Katharine Ross), a medicine cabinet filled with psychotropic drugs, and an imaginary friend named Frank (James Duval), who looks like a guy in a malevolent bunny suit. Fate delivers a mind-boggling kick in the teeth when, late one night, a jet engine crashes through Donnie's bedroom ceiling; the only reason he isn't squashed is that he's out sleepwalking. Already plagued by existential angst, Donnie is deeply shaken by his brush with death, made stranger by the fact that no one can figure out where the engine came from. Frank appears in the bathroom mirror and warns Donnie that the world will end in 28 days, and a string of odd coincidences suggest Frank may be telling the truth. The only bright spot in Donnie's increasingly dark days is his budding relationship with Gretchen Ross (Jena Malone), a transfer student who's on the run from her own demons.

This stylish exercise in creepy paranoia gets off to a shaky start but gradually pulls together into a genuinely haunting parable of teenage alienation. Its weak point is first-time feature writer-director Richard Kelly's attempt at social satire: his observations about materialism and crackpot pop philosophizing are trite and hardly unique to the era. But Kelly's missteps are minor by comparison with his achievements. He slowly weaves a meticulously crafted web of peculiarity around Donnie, and by the time the movie shows its hand, every piece of the puzzle has slipped neatly into place.

DON'S PARTY
1976 90m c Comedy ★★★★
Double Head (Australia)

Ray Barrett (Mal), Claire Binney (Susan), Pat Bishop (Jenny), Graeme Blundell (Simon), Jeanie Drynan (Kath), John Gorton (Himself), John Hargreaves (Don), Harold Hopkins (Cooley), Graham Kennedy (Mack), Veronica Lang (Jody)

p, Phillip Adams; d, Bruce Beresford; w, David Williamson (based on his play); ph, Don McAlpine (Panavision, 200 Color); ed, Bill Anderson; m, Leos Janacek; art d, Rhoisin Harrison; cos, Anna Senior

---

Excellent drama from Down Under concerns a group of friends in the suburbs that gathers to watch election results on television. As the party wears on and everyone's tongue is loosened by alcohol, the veneer of camaraderie drops away, and the men reveal themselves to be a set of back-biting boors, verbally attacking each other like characters straight out of WHO'S AFRAID OF VIRGINIA WOOLF. Extremely well directed by Beresford (BREAKER MORANT), with sharp dialogue and terrific performances all around. American audiences won't catch all of the slang expressions and will need to get used to the thick accents, but the effort of immersing oneself into this black comedy-drama is well worth it.

DON'T LOOK NOW
1973 110m c Mystery ★★★★½
Casey/Eldorado (U.K./Italy) R

Julie Christie (Laura Baxter), Donald Sutherland (John Baxter), Hilary Mason (Heather), Clelia Matania (Wendy), Massimo Serato (Bishop), Renato Scarpa (Inspector Longhi), Giorgio

Trestini (Workman), Leopoldo Trieste (Hotel Manager), David Tree (Anthony Babbage), Ann Rye (Mandy Babbage)

p, Peter Katz; d, Nicolas Roeg; w, Allan Scott, Chris Bryant (based on a short story by Daphne du Maurier); ph, Anthony B. Richmond (Panavision Technicolor); ed, Graeme Clifford; m, Pino Donaggio; art d, Giovanni Soccol; cos, Annamaria Fed, Marit Lieberson, Andrea Galler

---

A truly eerie film, based on a story by Daphne du Maurier. John Baxter (Sutherland) travels to Venice with his wife, Laura (Christie), after the accidental drowning death in England of their young daughter. While completing restoration work on a church, Baxter discovers he has certain psychic abilities—abilities nourished by two very strange sisters, Wendy (Matania) and Heather (Mason), who have visions of the couple's dead daughter. Baxter refuses to believe in his powers, but he begins to relent when he sees a small figure darting around Venice dressed in the same red raincoat that his daughter wore. These sightings, coupled with his haunting visions of a funeral boat drifting down a Venetian canal, make for a puzzling and mysterious atmosphere in which "nothing is what it seems."

Making wonderful use of Venice locales and boasting two fine performances from Sutherland and Christie (including one of the most convincing lovemaking scenes ever), DON'T LOOK NOW is one of director Roeg's finest and most accessible films. Among many memorable scenes, Baxter's near-fall in the church and his final encounter with the red-cloaked figure are particularly memorable. While the vagueness of the plot may frustrate viewers at first, the payoff is considerable for patient audiences. A film which more than gets by on its directorial style, unforgettable imagery, and striking music alone, DON'T LOOK NOW also manages to be a haunting meditation on fear, death and the beyond.

DOORS, THE
1991 135m c Biography/Musical ★★
Ixtlan Productions/Imagine Films Entertainment/ R
Carolco (U.S.)

Val Kilmer (Jim Morrison), Meg Ryan (Pamela Courson), Kyle MacLachlan (Ray Manzarek), Kevin Dillon (John Densmore), Frank Whaley (Robby Kreiger), Billy Idol (Cat), Dennis Burkley (Dog), Josh Evans (Bill Siddons), Michael Madsen (Tom Baker), Kathleen Quinlan (Patricia Kennealy)

p, Sasha Harari, Bill Graham, A. Kitman Ho; d, Oliver Stone; w, Oliver Stone, J. Randall Johnson, Randy Johnson, Ralph Thomas (from the book Riders on the Storm by John Densmore); ph, Robert Richardson; ed, David Brenner, Joe Hutshing; prod d, Barbara Ling; art d, Larry Fulton; cos, Marlene Stewart

---

Oliver Stone continues his postmortem of '60s America with this extravagant, rather silly recreation of the creative and destructive life of Jim Morrison, the cult rock poet and performer who died in 1971 at age 27.

The film begins in 1966 with a young Morrison (Val Kilmer) in his California element: beach bumming, experimenting with drugs, writing poetry, womanizing. With kindred cosmic spirit Ray Manzarek (Kyle MacLachlan) and two others, he forms a garage band—The Doors—and begins singing his poems. Early appearances in the underground clubs of L.A. meet with wild enthusiasm, particularly from groupies attracted by Morrison's sexual magnetism. Success follows rapidly. The Doors make albums, do concert tours and appear on "The Ed Sullivan Show"—all while Morrison continues to push the limits of drug-enhanced musical performance and sexual experimentation. His partner in these escapades is his wife Pam (Meg Ryan), nee Courson, who both shares and endures his abuses.

The first hour of THE DOORS is a seamless visual and aural trip that perfectly captures the spirit of Jim Morrison's hypnotic music and decadent, nihilistic lifestyle. Also crucial to the film's ability to persuade fans is Val Kilmer's performance. With the aid of some faultless costuming and makeup he definitively captures the real Morrison's posing, swagger and facial expressions. Without this studied physical reincarnation of the young cult figure, Stone's movie would have fallen flat much more quickly than it does.

Perhaps THE DOORS' ultimate failure is caused by its overly exact reproduction of the latter part of Morrison's life. After an interesting rise to musical fame in the first hour, viewers are left with an additional ninety minutes of this anti-hero's solipsism, narcissism, and joyless descent into death. By recreating things too well, the film itself becomes as boring, indulgent and over-stuffed as its hero.

DOUBLE INDEMNITY
1944 106m bw Crime   DVD
Paramount   (U.S.)   ★★★★★

Fred MacMurray *(Walter Neff)*, Barbara Stanwyck *(Phyllis Dietrichson)*, Edward G. Robinson *(Barton Keyes)*, Porter Hall *(Mr. Jackson)*, Jean Heather *(Lola Dietrichson)*, Tom Powers *(Mr. Dietrichson)*, Gig Young, billed as Byron Barr *(Nino Zachette)*, Richard Gaines *(Mr. Norton)*, Fortunio Bonanova *(Sam Gorlopis)*, John Philliber *(Joe Pete)*

p, Joseph Sistrom; d, Billy Wilder; w, Raymond Chandler, Billy Wilder (based on the novel by James M. Cain); ph, John Seitz; ed, Doane Harrison; m, Miklos Rozsa, Cesar Franck (Symphony in D minor); art d, Hans Dreier, Hal Pereira; cos, Edith Head

AAN Best Picture; AAN Best Actress: Barbara Stanwyck; AAN Best Director: Billy Wilder; AAN Best Screenplay: Raymond Chandler, Billy Wilder; AAN Best B/W Cinematography: John Seitz; AAN Best Score (Drama or Comedy): Miklos Rozsa; AAN Best Sound Recording: Loren Ryder

A seminal work in the emergence of film noir as an explosive movement in American film. Based on the notorious Snyder-Gray case of 1927, DOUBLE INDEMNITY is both a starkly realistic and a carefully stylized masterpiece of murder.

Walter Neff (MacMurray), bleeding from a bullet wound, staggers into an office building. As he speaks into his dictating machine, we learn in flashback that he is an insurance salesman who becomes involved with the sleek Phyllis Dietrichson (Stanwyck). Phyllis convinces Walter not only to help her take out a life insurance policy on her husband (Powers) without his knowledge, but also to help her murder him in order to collect on it. Staging an unlikely accident in order to qualify for the "double indemnity" clause in the contract, the deadly duo must next face claims adjustor Barton Keyes (Robinson), whose instinct tells him that something suspicious is afoot. Their faith in their story and each other sorely tested, Walter and Phyllis finally square off in a fatal game of cat and mouse.

Wilder's typically passionless direction fits beautifully with this sinister story. On his first studio assignment, screenwriter Chandler peppered the dialogue from Cain's original with his distinctive brand of hardboiled cynicism. The results, as when Phyllis and Walter flirt by using the extended metaphor of a speeding motorist, are terrific. Rosza contributes a typically edgy score and Seitz's cinematography makes great use of such noir trademarks as sharp camera angles, heavy, sculpted shadows and light slatted by venetian blinds. But it is really the starring trio which lends bite to this compelling crime classic. Stanwyck, in a deliberately phony blonde wig, remade her career with her striking portrayal of an icy woman whose boredom and desire fuel a plot of murder and intrigue.

MacMurray, in a great change of pace, gives the performance of his career as the shifty loner excited by a challenge and a deadly dame's anklet. Robinson, meanwhile, beautifully gives the film its heart. His speech about death statistics, rattled off at top speed, is one of the film's highlights. Lifelessly remade for television in 1954 and 1973.

DOUBLE JEOPARDY   DVD
1999 106m c   Crime/Thriller   ★★
Mandy Films   (U.S.)   R

Tommy Lee Jones *(Travis)*, Ashley Judd *(Libby)*, Benjamin Weir *(Matty, Age Four)*, Jay Brazeau *(Bobby)*, Bruce Greenwood *(Nick)*, John MacLaren *(Rudy)*, Edward Evanko *(Warren)*, Annabeth Gish *(Angie)*, Bruce Campbell *(Bartender at Party)*, Brennan Elliot *(Yuppie Man)*

p, Leonard Goldberg; d, Bruce Beresford; w, Douglas S. Cook, David Weisberg; ph, Peter James; ed, Mark Warner; m, Normand Corbeil; prod d, Howard Cummings; art d, Andrew Neskoromny; fx, Bill Or; cos, Rudy Dillon, Linda Bass

The glory of moviemaking the film-o-matic way is that there's nothing you can't toss into the mix. Unfortunately, the results are sometimes akin to a strawberry-okra-cilantro smoothie. Witness this thriller, which buzzes together THE FUGITIVE and LEAVE HER TO HEAVEN with a dollop of NOT WITHOUT MY DAUGHTER.

Libby Parsons (Ashley Judd) thinks she's living a perfect life in the sunny, art-filled home she shares with husband Nick (Bruce Greenwood) and their adorable little boy, Matty (Benjamin Weir). Her rude awakening occurs during a weekend cruise: Nick vanishes while she's asleep, the cabin is slick with blood, and the Coast Guard arrives to see Libby holding that bloody knife she found on the deck. She's summarily convicted of murder—that $2 million insurance policy on Nick's life looks especially bad—and Matty and the money are entrusted to longtime family friend Angie (Annabeth Gish). When Libby learns that Nick's still alive and shacked up with Angie, Libby sweet talks her way into early parole so she can hunt down Nick—Hell hath no fury like a woman framed by a sleazy bastard—if implacable parole officer Travis Lehman (Tommy Lee Jones) doesn't catch her first.

The title alludes to the legal loophole that would permit Libby to kill Nick with impunity since she's already been convicted of having done it, but it's irrelevant. With Ashley Judd in the lead, rather than, say, Shannon Tweed, it becomes a movie about a woman moving heaven and earth to find her son, not a vengeful virago out to repay the creep who done her wrong. Whether this riot of unrepentant trash strikes you as tediously ridiculous or brainlessly amusing is probably a matter of mood.

DOUBLE LIFE, A   DVD
1947 103m bw Crime   ★★★★
Kanin   (U.S.)

Ronald Colman *(Anthony John)*, Signe Hasso *(Brita)*, Edmond O'Brien *(Bill Friend)*, Shelley Winters *(Pat Kroll)*, Ray Collins *(Victor Donlan)*, Philip Loeb *(Max Lasker)*, Millard Mitchell *(Al Cooley)*, Joe Sawyer *(Pete Bonner)*, Charles La Torre *(Stellini)*, Whit Bissell *(Dr. Stauffer)*

p, Michael Kanin; d, George Cukor; w, Ruth Gordon, Garson Kanin (based on the play "Othello" by William Shakespeare); ph, Milton Krasner; ed, Robert Parrish; m, Miklos Rozsa; prod d, Harry Horner; art d, Bernard Herzbrun, Harvey T. Gillett; fx, David S. Horsley; cos, Yvonne Wood, Travis Banton

AA Best Actor: Ronald Colman; AAN Best Director: George Cukor; AAN Best Original Screenplay: Ruth Gordon, Garson Kanin; AA Best Score (Drama or Comedy): Miklos Rozsa

A fine film overall, if a wee bit pretentious, A DOUBLE LIFE explores the schizoid personality of a gifted stage actor whose despair and murderous moods come during his portrayal of Othello. Colman is a much-respected gentleman actor who specializes in classical drama. His courtly manners and winning charm endear him to one and all, including his ex-wife, Hasso, who loves him but fears that his cruel streak will once again take over his otherwise stable personality. Winters, a buxom, steamy waitress, is attracted to Colman but soon learns that he is capable of violence. Losing all touch with reality, Colman believes he is actually the terrible Moor he is portraying on stage, so he strangles Winters and returns to his apartment, blocking out the hideous act. O'Brien, an enterprising publicity agent for the play, picks up on the strangulation and tries to link the murder with the play to entice audiences. This blatant sensationalism causes Colman to explode; he attacks O'Brien, who now believes the actor is mad. O'Brien sets up Colman for the police, arranging for a waitress who is almost Winters's twin to wait on him in a restaurant. Her appearance so alarms Colman that police are convinced he is the killer. Detectives decide to arrest him following the final performance of "Othello." The actor realizes he is exposed and the tragedy takes its final turn.

Colman's performance is riveting and deservedly won him an Oscar, as well as universal applause from critics and public alike. His genteel manners and mellifluous voice set up audiences for a huge shock when Colman turns into a lethal lunatic, a transformation that is simply amazing to witness. He is a man obsessed, one who can no longer differentiate between his theatrical and everyday personalities. Colman is mesmerizing, brilliant, and even horrific in his role. Kanin and Gordon's script is both literate and packed with suspense, interweaving the dialogue of classical theater and that of the street. Cukor's direction is as properly mannered and carefully constructed as the script is, and he draws the complex portrayal out of Colman with great care.

This was Winters' first film break after stage appearances and it established her as a movie star. Harry Cohn, head of Columbia Studios, originally bought the script for A DOUBLE LIFE years earlier but later reneged, refusing to pay for it or produce it. Kanin was so angry that he vowed never to talk to Cohn again. He would take his vengeance on a literary level, using Cohn as the role model for the brutish Broderick Crawford part in BORN YESTERDAY.

DOUBLE LIFE OF VERONIQUE, THE

(LA DOUBLE VIE DE VERONIQUE)
1991 90m c Fantasy/Drama ★★½
Sideral Productions/Studio Tor/Canal Plus
(France/Poland)

Irene Jacob (*Veronique/Veronika*), Halina Gryglaszewska (*Aunt*), Kalina Jedrusik (*Gaudy Woman*), Aleksander Bardini (*Orchestra Conductor*), Wladyslaw Kowalski (*Veronika's Father*), Jerzy Gudejko (*Antek*), Jan Sterninski (*Lawyer*), Philippe Volter (*Alexandre Fabbri*), Sandrine Dumas (*Catherine*), Louis Ducreux (*Professor*)

p, Leonardo De La Fuente; d, Krzysztof Kieslowski; w, Krzysztof Kieslowski, Krzysztof Piesiewicz; ph, Slawomir Idziak; ed, Jacques Witta; m, Zbigniew Preisner; prod d, Patrice Mercier, Halina Dobrowolska; art d, Krzysztof Zanussi; cos, Laurence Brignon, Claudy Fellous, Elzbieta Radke

THE DOUBLE LIFE OF VERONIQUE is a slight, lyrical fable that benefits enormously from the charm of its star, Cannes award-winner Irene Jacob.

The film introduces us to two women, both played by Jacob. Polish Veronika leaves her provincial home town and family for the city of Krakow, where she is offered a place to study singing at a prestigious music school; after suffering chest pains, she is stricken and dies onstage during her first public performance. The

action then shifts to Paris, where the French Veronique abruptly, and without explanation, abandons her own ambitions of becoming a professional singer to pursue a more modest career as an elementary school teacher, and enjoys a romantic liaison with a charming puppeteer. (Like Veronika, Veronique also has a weak heart, but she goes for regular check-ups with a cardiologist.)

An opaque, if stylish, film, THE DOUBLE LIFE OF VERONIQUE plays like an enigmatic warning on the dangers of excessive ambition. Though pleasing to the eye, it's not everything we would have hoped for from Kieslowski, who confirmed his status as a major contemporary filmmaker with 1988's DEKALOG, a series of 10 hour-long works funded by Polish TV and based on the 10 Commandments. In the same year, he expanded segments five and six into two features, A SHORT FILM ABOUT KILLING and A SHORT FILM ABOUT LOVE, both of which are far more substantial than this Polish-French co-production.

DOUBLE TEAM DVD

1997 90m c Action ★★½
Moshe Diamant Productions/One Story Pictures/ R
Mandalay Entertainment/Signature Films (U.S.)

Jean-Claude Van Damme (*Quinn*), Dennis Rodman (*Yaz*), Paul Freeman (*Goldsmythe*), Mickey Rourke (*Stavros*), Natacha Lindinger (*Kath*), Valeria Cavalli (*Dr. Maria Trifioli*), Jay Benedict (*Brandon*), Joelle Devaux-Vullion (*Stavros's Girlfriend*), Bruno Bilotta (*Kofi*), Mario Opinato (*James*)

p, Moshe Diamant; d, Tsui Hark; w, Don Jakoby, Paul Mones (based on the story by Don Jakoby); ph, Peter Pau; ed, Bill Pankow; m, Gary Chang; prod d, Marek Dobrowolski; art d, Damien Lanfranchi; fx, Bruno Van Zeebroeck; cos, Magali Guidasci

Vietnamese-born producer-director Tsui Hark gives his U.S. debut a densely layered, nightmarish, and utterly chaotic look that will be familiar to Hong Kong action buffs.

Quinn (Jean-Claude Van Damme) is a former crack anti-terrorist agent, now living a quiet life with his pregnant wife. Stavros (Mickey Rourke) is a terrorist head case, and Quinn is brought out of retirement to take him down. Quinn fails to get his man (though he does kill Stavros' small son) and is seriously injured. When he recovers, he's in the Colony—an isolated prison where "retired" agents are kept until their dangerous smarts are needed (shades of TV's "The Prisoner")—from which he must escape and rescue his wife and soon-to-be-born son from the nutty Stavros.

Plot is hardly the point here: DOUBLE TEAM's selling points are scary amusement parks, Dennis Rodman selling high-tech weapons out of a sex shop in Antwerp, tigers, Jean-Claude Van Damme's thighs, captive super-spies on a tropical island, and bald Chinese dervishes holding switchblades between their toes. The angles are canted, the closeups are disorienting, the colors are supersaturated, and the action never stops. Making a Van Damme picture appears to have become a rite of passage for Hong Kong directors looking to break into the American mainstream market (remember Ringo Lam's MAXIMUM RISK and John Woo's HARD TARGET?) and Hong Kong neophytes may be baffled by the film's weirdly sentimental streak—remember, the vendetta that drives Quinn and Stavros is all about *babies*. But by the time the black leather-clad Stavros has mined the Coliseum and sicced a Bengal tiger on Quinn, wise viewers are just sitting back and enjoying the show.

DOWN AND DIRTY

(BRUTTI, SPORCHI E CATTIVI)
1976 115m c Comedy/Drama ★★★½
C.C. Champion (Italy)

Nino Manfredi (*Giacinto*), Francisci Anniballi (*Domizio*), Maria Bosco (*Gaetana*), Giselda Castrini (*Lisetta*), Alfredo D'Ippolito

(Plinio), Giancarlo Fanelli (Paride), Marian Fasoli (Maria Lobera), Ettore Garofolo (Camilio), Marco Marsili (Vittoriano), Franco Merli (Fernando)

d, Ettore Scola; w, Ettore Scola, Ruggero Maccari; ph, Dario Di Palma; ed, Raimondo Crociani; m, Armando Trovaioli

A mean, nasty, vile, ugly, and wickedly funny look at the inhabitants of a squatters' slum outside of Rome, where the subproletariat lives a miserable existence, DOWN AND DIRTY focuses on Giacinto (Nino Manfredi), a brutal animal of a man who has won a million lira insurance settlement after losing an eye. Driven by greed and selfishness, Giacinto sleeps with a shotgun for fear that someone will steal his fortune. He refuses to spend even a small portion of his stash on his family—which consists of at least 20 people, all of whom live, eat, sleep, fight, and have sex in the same one-room shanty. He beats and stabs his wife, humiliates his children, drinks himself into a stupor, and gropes the local women. When he takes an obese, huge-chested whore (Maria Luisa Santella) as a mistress, lets her live under the same roof as his family, and then generously squanders his money on gifts for her, his relatives plot to murder him. An amazing picture from Ettore Scola, DOWN AND DIRTY presents an endless stream of human indignities (people living with rats, a drag queen seducing his sister-in-law, a proud mother displaying her daughter's nude centerfold, children spending the day locked in a cage that serves as a day-care center) with such a curious, crude sense of humor one cannot be sure whether to look away in horror or laugh. What is sure is that you cannot ignore these people, or their unfathomable living conditions—and this is Scola's intent. Shooting on location, with Manfredi as his only professional actor, Scola in DOWN AND DIRTY pays tribute to the Neo-Realist tradition in Italy and produces a film worthy of Rossellini or De Sica.

DOWN AND OUT IN BEVERLY HILLS   DVD
1986 103m c Comedy   ★★★½
Touchstone   (U.S.)   R

Nick Nolte (Jerry Baskin), Richard Dreyfuss (Dave Whiteman), Bette Midler (Barbara Whiteman), Little Richard (Orvis Goodnight), Tracy Nelson (Jenny Whiteman), Elizabeth Pena (Carmen), Evan Richards (Max Whiteman), Mike the Dog (Matisse), Donald Muhich (Dr. Von Zimmer), Paul Mazursky (Sidney Waxman)

p, Paul Mazursky; d, Paul Mazursky; w, Paul Mazursky, Leon Capetanos (based on the play Boudu Sauve Des Eaux by Rene Fauchois); ph, Don McAlpine (Technicolor); ed, Richard Halsey; m, Andy Summers; prod d, Pato Guzman; art d, Todd Hallowell; fx, Ken Speed; cos, Albert Wolsky

This very first R-rated picture ever to come out of that bastion of squeaky-cleanness, Walt Disney Studios (under the aegis of their subsidiary Touchstone), is a howl from start to finish. Dave Whiteman (Dreyfuss) has made it big in the coat hanger business. He and wife Barbara (Midler) live in a huge house in Beverly Hills with their children, Jenny (Nelson), an anorexic college student, and Max (Richards), an androgynous budding filmmaker. Barbara is the ultimate yenta who spends her days having her hair and nails done, shopping, and going to classes. Also living in the house are Carmen (Pena), a seductive Latino maid with whom Dave is having an affair, and Matisse (Mike), the family dog who refuses to eat despite regular visits to a doggie psychiatrist. When tramp Jerry Baskin (Nolte) enters their lives after attempting to drown himself in the Whiteman swimming pool, Dave saves his life and invites him to become part of the family, a decision that has some very comic results.

A sometimes extremely funny revamping of Jean Renoir's classic black comedy BOUDU SAVED FROM DROWNING, Mazursky's film also works as a broad but scathing satire of upper-class California culture. Although the ending is soft-

ened from Renoir's original, this garishly colored film succeeds quite well on its own terms. The film is full of moments both surprising (Jerry showing Matisse that his dog food is eminently eatable) and entertainingly predictable (Jerry getting intimately involved with several family members; an "everyone into the pool" sequence). The cast is entirely up to the comic hysteria Mazursky requires of them, though Mike the dog steals whatever scene he is in. Look for Mazursky in a bit part as an accountant.

DOWN BY LAW   DVD
1986 106m bw Comedy   ★★★
Black Snake/Grokenberger (U.S.)   R

Tom Waits (Zack), John Lurie (Jack), Roberto Benigni (Roberto), Nicoletta Braschi (Nicoletta), Ellen Barkin (Laurette), Billie Neal (Bobbie), Rockets Redglare (Gig), Vernel Bagneris (Preston), Timothea (Julie), L.C. Drane (L.C.)

p, Alan Kleinberg; d, Jim Jarmusch; w, Jim Jarmusch; ph, Robby Muller; ed, Melody London; m, John Lurie; cos, Carol Wood

Set in New Orleans, DOWN BY LAW begins as down-on-his-luck disc jockey Zack (Waits) tries to make some quick bucks by driving a stolen car across town. Unfortunately he gets pulled over by the police and is thrown into jail when a body is found in the car's trunk. In the meantime a pimp, Jack (Lurie), has been set up by an enemy and fellow procurer, and he too is carted off by police and thrown into Orleans Parish Prison, where he becomes Zack's cellmate. Three may be a crowd, but soon they are joined in their small cell by Roberto (Benigni), a confused and likable Italian who knows only a few phrases of English, which he keeps written in a pocket notebook. Eventually the three escape into the Louisiana bayous, where they're soon hungry, tired and lost.

Director-writer Jarmusch's characters are insignificant antiheroes adrift in an America that is both sad and beautiful. Jarmusch has a powerful visual sense, but he is weaker in the realm of content. The jazzy relationship between Lurie and Waits never quite clicks. As a result DOWN BY LAW merely reiterates the ideas about people and American life that Jarmusch had already stated more richly in STRANGER THAN PARADISE. The only sign of life in the film is in Benigni, who works wonders.

DOWNFALL   DVD
(DER UNTERGANG)
2004 155m c War/Drama/Biography   ★★★★
Constantin Film/Bernd Eichinger/NDR/WDR/   R
Degeto Film/ORF/EOS Production/Rai Cinema
(Germany/Italy)

Bruno Ganz (Adolph Hitler), Alexandra Maria Lara (Traudl Junge), Corinna Harfouch (Magda Goebbels), Ulrich Matthes (Joseph Goebbels), Juliane Kohler (Eva Braun), Heino Ferch (Albert Speer), Christian Berkel (Professor Ernst-Gunther Schenck), Matthias Habich (Professor Werner Haase), Thomas Kretschmann (Hermann Fegelein), Michael Mendl (General Weidling)

d, Oliver Hirschbiegel; w, Bernd Eichinger (based on the books Inside Hitler's Bunker by Joachim Fest and Until the Final Hour by Traudl Junge and Melissa Muller); ph, Rainer Klausman; ed, Hans Funck; m, Stephan Zacharias; prod d, Bernd Lepel; art d, Gregor Mager; fx, Uli Nefzer; cos, Claudia Bobsin

AAN Best Foreign Language Film

Director Oliver Hirschbiegel's gripping account of Adolf Hitler's ignominious end is a historical reenactment that hits like a swift kick to the gut.

Berlin, 1945: With Soviet forces just outside the city, Hitler (Bruno Ganz, in a frightening performance) ignores the urgings of his closest advisors to flee and withdraws to his heavily fortified bunker beneath Berlin's blasted streets. Convinced that he's been betrayed by those he trusted most, Hitler takes comfort in the idolaters who gather around him like suicidal moths to a dying flame. They include his maniacally cheerful lady-love, Eva Braun (Juliane Kohler); the dead-eyed Joseph Goebbels (Ulrich Matthes) and his equally terrifying wife, Magda (Corinna Harfouch); and his faithful secretary, Traudl Junge (Alexandra Maria Lara). As Soviet artillery continues to pound Berlin, the atmosphere in the bunker continues to grow even more desperate. Eva throws wild dance parties, soldiers drink themselves into oblivion, and Hitler's inner circle reconsiders their sworn duty to follow a delusional lunatic who now speaks openly of committing suicide.

Determined to wring the last bit of the Hitler myth from the German psyche, Hirschbiegel presents a portrait of the madman that's appalling even by the standards Anthony Hopkins set in THE BUNKER. Here we see Hitler the ranting, paranoid megalomaniac who has no compassion for either the young German soldiers who continue to die on the front lines or, most shocking of all, the civilians who are getting what he feels they richly deserve. Portraying "ordinary Germans" as seduced and abandoned victims, however, is a tricky business. Indeed, hard pressed for anyone resembling a protagonist, Hirschbiegel settles on the morally compromised Junge, who stuck by Hitler until the very end. It wasn't until shortly before her death in 2002 that Junge admitted she, like everyone else in the bunker—and Germany, for that matter—had other options.

DOWNHILL RACER

1969 101m c   Sports   ★★★★
Wildwood   (U.S.)   M

Robert Redford (*Davis Chappellet*), Gene Hackman (*Eugene Claire*), Camilla Sparv (*Carole Stahl*), Karl Michael Vogler (*Machet*), James McMillan (*Johnny Creech*), Christian Doermer (*Brumm*), Kathleen Crowley (*American Newspaperwoman*), Dabney Coleman (*Mayo*), Kenneth Kirk (*D.K. Bryan*), Oren Stevens (*Tony Kipsmith*)

p, Richard Gregson; d, Michael Ritchie; w, James Salter (based on the novel *The Downhill Racers* by Oakley Hall); ph, Brian Probyn (Technicolor); ed, Nick Archer; m, Kenyon Hopkins; art d, Ian Whittaker; cos, Cynthia May

An influential and extremely well-done sports film, worth watching even if you don't normally enjoy films of this type. Documentarian in style, DOWNHILL RACER is a strangely dispassionate but captivating look behind the glamorous facade of international ski racing. Redford, who did much of his own skiing, stars as Davis Chappellet, a self-centered, success-hungry skier from Colorado who is summoned to Europe when a member of the U.S. team is injured. Over the next two racing seasons he proves himself to be one of the sport's most promising newcomers, dueling with a famous teammate (McMullan) for the spotlight and clashing with his strong-willed coach (Hackman). In the process of chasing Olympic gold in the downhill, he fails to win approval from his father and is unable to maintain a relationship with a beautiful ski manufacturer's assistant (Sparv).

Redford, who was determined to make a skiing film, went to great lengths to sell the project: soliciting a screenplay from James Salter, enlisting a team of ski bums and photographers to shoot 20,000 feet of action on the sly at the 1968 Grenoble Olympics, and giving Michael Ritchie, who provides a sure directorial hand, his first feature film assignment. As with a number of later Ritchie films, the focus here is on the price paid in pursuit of what seems to be victory.

The acting is fine all around, with kudos to Redford for being unafraid to make his character dislikable at the core. Many of the downhill scenes were filmed by skier Joe Jay Jalbert, who raced behind Redford with a camera, adding to the film's realism and excitement. DOWNHILL RACER is fascinating viewing, even if the closest you've gotten to a ski slope is "Wide World of Sports."

DRACULA   **DVD**

1931 84m bw Horror   ★★★
Universal   (U.S.)

Bela Lugosi (*Count Dracula*), Helen Chandler (*Mina Seward*), David Manners (*Jonathan Harker*), Dwight Frye (*Renfield*), Edward Van Sloan (*Dr. Van Helsing*), Herbert Bunston (*Dr. Seward*), Frances Dade (*Lucy Weston*), Charles Gerrard (*Martin*), Joan Standing (*Maid*), Moon Carroll (*Briggs, Maid*)

p, Carl Laemmle Jr.; d, Tod Browning; w, Tod Browning, Dudley Murphy, Garrett Fort (based on the novel by Bram Stoker and the 1927 stage play by Hamilton Deane and John Lloyd Balderston); ph, Karl Freund; ed, Milton Carruth, Maurice Pivar; m, Peter Ilich Tchaikovsky, Richard Wagner; art d, Charles D. Hall; cos, Ed Ware, Vera West

Creak. The grandaddy of 'em all and ready for mothballs to be put in the coffins. An atmospheric opening is the best part—moody and full of sinister potential. After that, it's stilted drawing-room talk, variably acted, except for the cultish over-the-top dementia of Dwight Frye. Still, DRACULA is the film that started the 1930s horror cycle, secured Universal's position as *the* horror studio, and made Hungarian actor Bela Lugosi a worldwide curiosity.

Following the successful stage play more than Bram Stoker's classic novel, the film opens in Transylvania, where Renfield (Dwight Frye), a British real estate salesman, arrives to arrange the sale of a deserted English manor house to a strange nobleman, Count Dracula (Lugosi). The mysterious count turns out to be a 500-year-old vampire, and Renfield is bitten and made his slave. Arriving in London, Dracula becomes smitten with Mina Seward (Helen Chandler) and attempts to make her his bride, but her fiance, John Harker (David Manners), and vampire expert Prof. Van Helsing (Edward Van Sloan) try and put a stop to the undead count.

While the first part of the film is quite cinematic, mainly due to the brilliant cinematography of Karl Freund, the movie bogs down once it gets to England, after which it appears that director Tod Browning was intent on making a documentary of the stage play. More likely, he lacked the creativity of James Whale, who directed FRANKENSTEIN. While the incidental music (mostly snippets from Tchaikovsky's *Swan Lake*) is kept to a minimum, the sound effects are showing age, with the creaking of coffin lids, opening and slamming of doors, thudding footsteps, actors' voices, and howling of wolves beginning to seem like something out of a Bob Hope spoof. Studio heads felt that the film would do well abroad, so a Spanish-language version starring Carlos Villarias in the Dracula role and featuring a completely new all-Spanish cast, directed by George Melford, was produced with the same sets only days after the English version was completed. Reports have it that this version is even better than the Browning-Lugosi film. We should hope so. A remarkable sequel, DRACULA'S DAUGHTER, followed, featuring the stranger-than-true Gloria Holden.

DRAGON: THE BRUCE LEE STORY   **DVD**

1993 114m c Biography/Romance/Martial Arts ★★★½
Old Code Productions Ltd.   (U.S.)   PG-13

Jason Scott Lee (*Bruce Lee*), Lauren Holly (*Linda Lee*), Robert J. Wagner (*Bill Krieger*), Michael Learned (*Vivian Emery*), Nancy Kwan (*Gussie Yang*), Kay Tong Lim (*Philip Tan*), Ric Young

(Bruce's Father), Luoyong Wang *(Yip Man)*, Sterling Macer *(Jerome Sprout)*, Sven-Ole Thorsen *(The Demon)*

p, Raffaella De Laurentiis, Charles Wang; d, Rob Cohen; w, Edward Khmara, John Raffo, Rob Cohen (from the book *Bruce Lee: The Man Only I Knew* by Linda Lee Cadwell); ph, David Eggby; ed, Peter Amundson; m, Randy Edelman; prod d, Robert Ziembicki; art d, Ted Berner; fx, Kevin O'Neill, William H. Schirmer, Peter Bohanna; cos, Carol Ramsey

DRAGON: THE BRUCE LEE STORY dares to be corny and gets away with it, thanks to sensitive scripting and direction, cleverly staged kung-fu sequences (fight co-ordinator John Cheung has worked with Hong Kong martial arts star Jackie Chan), and an inspirational performance by Jason Scott Lee. (No relation to Bruce; in fact, Bruce Lee's son, Brandon, was accidentally killed during production of THE CROW just a few weeks before DRAGON was released.)

DRAGON traces Lee's life from his Hong Kong childhood to international success and early, mysterious death. Born in San Francisco while his father, an actor, was on tour, Bruce returns as a young man. He works as a dishwasher/delivery boy, goes to college and begins giving kung-fu lessons leavened with philosophy. At the urging of his beautiful, white girlfriend Linda (Lauren Holly)—they date despite widespread disapproval—he opens a kung-fu school. They marry, and Bruce is cast as sidekick Kato in "The Green Hornet," but he moves his family to Hong Kong after he's passed over in favor of white actor David Carradine for "Kung Fu," which he helped develop as a starring vehicle for himself. With ENTER THE DRAGON, a Hollywood picture to be shot in Hong Kong, Bruce is poised for international success, but fate intervenes.

Director/co-screenwriter Rob Cohen shrewdly opts for a three-tiered approach to the biographical material, making DRAGON a poignant interracial love story, a thrilling kung-fu flick, and a surreal fantasy in the which the hero literally confronts his inner demons. Jason Scott Lee captures his subject perfectly, and his handling of the action scenes is particularly impressive. The result is one of the most purely enjoyable American films in recent years.

DRAGONSLAYER
1981 108m c Adventure/Fantasy ★★★½
Walt Disney Productions (U.S.) PG

Peter MacNicol *(Galen)*, Caitlin Clarke *(Valerian)*, Ralph Richardson *(Ulrich)*, John Hallam *(Tyrian)*, Peter Eyre *(Casidorus Rex)*, Albert Salmi *(Greil)*, Sydney Bromley *(Hodge)*, Chloe Salaman *(Princess Elspeth)*, Emrys James *(Simon)*, Roger Kemp *(Horsrik)*

p, Hal Barwood; d, Matthew Robbins; w, Hal Barwood, Matthew Robbins; ph, Derek Vanlint (Panavision, Metrocolor); ed, Tony Lawson; m, Alex North; prod d, Elliot Scott; art d, Alan Cassie; fx, Brian Johnson, Dennis Muren, Industrial Light & Magic; chor, Peggy Dixon; cos, Anthony Mendleson

AAN Best Original Score: Alex North; *AAN Best Visual Effects:* Dennis Muren, Phil Tippett, Ken Ralston, Brian Johnson

An Arthurian-type legend is marvelously re-created when Galen (Peter MacNicol), sorcerer's apprentice to Ulrich (Ralph Richardson), a great wizard, bungles his way to ridding the kingdom of a monstrous, fire-spitting dragon. King Tyrian (John Hallam) has made an evil pact whereby he will sacrifice the virgins of his land to the dragon if it will leave the kingdom in relative peace. When Princess Elspeth (Chloe Salaman), his brave daughter, volunteers her own life, Ulrich and Galen attempt to save her, even though the wizard is dying and his magic fading. Like EXCALIBUR, this film has smoky atmosphere, medieval sets, and rugged terrain strange enough

to suggest far-off mythic lands; moreover, its special effects are positively staggering. The giant computerized dragon alone is worth viewing. But DRAGONSLAYER profits from spirited direction and camera work plus the expert Richardson at its nucleus. Failing to capture the fancy of either the teenage market or adult action-fantasy fans, however, DRAGON-SLAYER was a major disappointment at the box office, returning just $6 million on an $18 million investment. With terror prevalent and gory violence in spots, this fable is not for young viewers.

DRAUGHTSMAN'S CONTRACT, THE   DVD
1982 108m c Comedy/Historical/Mystery ★★★★
British Film Institute (U.K.) R

Anthony Higgins *(Mr. Neville)*, Janet Suzman *(Mrs. Herbert)*, Anne Louise Lambert *(Mrs. Talmann)*, Hugh Fraser *(Mr. Talmann)*, Neil Cunningham *(Mr. Noyes)*, Dave Hill *(Mr. Herbert)*, David Gant *(Mr. Seymour)*, David Meyer, Tony Meyer *(The Poulenas)*, Nicholas Amer *(Mr. Parkes)*

p, David Payne; d, Peter Greenaway; w, Peter Greenaway; ph, Curtis Clark; ed, John Wilson; m, Michael Nyman; art d, Bob Ringwood; cos, Sue Blane

Peter Greenaway's dark comedy about power games between the classes is one of his easiest films to enjoy on a surface level. Those unfamiliar with Greenaway's work should be warned, however, that although THE DRAUGHTSMAN'S CONTRACT looks like a period mystery, it really isn't: if you spend too much time worrying about who done it, you'll miss the movie's real pleasures.

England, 1694. Ambitious artist Mr. Neville (Anthony Higgins) is offered a commission by Mrs. Herbert (Janet Suzman), who wants twelve drawings of her husband's estate, to be done while he is away. Neville accepts, on the condition that his payment includes the sexual use of his hostess. Mrs. Herbert reluctantly agrees. Mrs. Talmann (Anne Louise Lambert), the Herberts' only child, hints to Neville that certain oddities in his drawings can be construed as clues to a plot involving her father, who is missing. Aware of the sexual contract between Neville and her mother, she proposes a similar contract in exchange for her silence. Heedless but amused, Neville agrees. Soon after, Mr. Herbert's body is found in the estate's moat: he has been murdered.

That we never find out who killed Mr. Herbert, or even why, is central to THE DRAUGHTSMAN'S CONTRACT's theme of social power. Neville thinks he has the upper hand over his hosts and the other local gentry; it isn't until it s too late, however, that he realizes that he hasn't got a clue as to what's really going on. We the viewers do have clues, but not much either: we learn just enough to put us a step ahead of Neville, but in the long run are as ignorant (and therefore as powerless) as he.

Despite having been filmed on a limited budget, THE DRAUGHTSMAN'S CONTRACT is as sumptuous to the eye as it is to the ear. Most shots are designed as tableaux in which the actors move only minimally against elegant backgrounds (there is little camera movement or cross-cutting). Even if you don't share Greenaway's formalist interests, THE DRAUGHTSMAN'S CONTRACT makes for compelling viewing.

DREAMCATCHER   DVD
2003 134m c Science Fiction/Horror ★★
Castle Rock Entertainment/Village Roadshow R
Pictures/NPV Entertainment/Kasdan Pictures (U.S.)

Morgan Freeman *(Colonel Abraham Curtis)*, Thomas Jane *(Dr. Henry Devlin)*, Jason Lee *(Joe "Beaver" Clarendon)*, Damian Lewis *(Gary "Jonesy" Jones)*, Timothy Olyphant *(Pete Moore)*, Tom

Sizemore *(Captain Owen Underhill)*, Donnie Wahlberg *(Douglas "Duddits" Cavell)*, Mike Holekamp *(Young Henry Devlin)*, Reece Thompson *(Young Beaver)*, Andrew Robb *(Young Duddits)*

p, Lawrence Kasdan, Charles Okun; d, Lawrence Kasdan; w, William Goldman, Lawrence Kasdan (based on the book by Stephen King); ph, John Seale; ed, Raul Davalos, Carol Littleton; m, James Newton Howard; prod d, Jon Hutman; art d, W. Stephen Graham; fx, Tim Alexander, Amy Beresford, Stefen Fangmeier, Industrial Light & Magic, William H. Orr; cos, Molly Maginnis

---

Aliens, male bonding, psychoanalytic gobbledygook, child-hood secrets, military black ops, gross-out special effects.... This derivative thriller may be an infernal stew, but there's lots of it.

Psychiatrist Henry Devlin (Thomas Jane), history teacher Gary Jones (Damian Lewis), used-car salesman Pete Moore (Timothy Olyphant), and carpenter Joe "Beaver" Clarendon (Jason Lee) have been inseparable since their Derry, ME, child-hood. As youngsters, they rescued a mentally disabled boy, Duddits (Andrew Robb), from bullies and were somehow rewarded with assorted paranormal abilities: Henry and Gary read minds, Beaver is precognitive, and Pete finds things. But with middle age looming, they're mired in free-floating malaise that makes their mental gifts feel more like burdens. During a winter reunion at a cabin in the Maine woods, everything comes to a head. Two major storms blanket the region with snow, dis-gusting alien life forms infest the woods in search of human hosts, and a clandestine military operation headed up by mad-as-a-hatter Colonel Curtis (Morgan Freeman) has quarantined the area; the spit is about to hit the global fan.

Based on the novel Stephen King penned while recovering from a near-fatal accident, this mass of genre clichés borrows heavily from THEY CAME FROM WITHIN, THE CRA-ZIES, both versions of THE THING, ALIEN, INVASION OF THE BODY SNATCHERS, and several of King's own works (notably *It* and *Storm of the Century*). There are a few shocks and one eerily moving image—a surreal drove of forest crea-tures single-mindedly making tracks out of the woods—but it's undermined by ham-fisted dialogue. In King's universe, subtle-ty is no virtue, and for better or worse, director/co-screenwriter Lawrence Kasdan opts not to mess with the formula.

DREAM OF LIGHT
(EL SOL DEL MEMBRILLO)
1993 139m c Documentary ★★★★
Euskal Telebista/Igeldo Zine Produkzioak (Spain)

Antonio Lopez Garcia, Maria Moreno, Enrique Gran, Jose Carrtero, Maria Lopez, Carmen Lopez, Elisa Ruiz, Amalia Avia, Lucio Munoz, Esperanza Parada

p, Maria Moreno; d, Victor Erice; w, Victor Erice, Antonio Lopez; ph, Javier Aguirresarobe, Angel Luis Fernandez; ed, Juan Ignacio San Mateo; m, Pascal Gaigne

---

Any summary of Spanish director Victor Erice's captivating documentary would sound more like a warning than the enthusiastic recommendation it merits.

On the surface, Erice's film is a leisurely, two-and-a-half-hour portrait of celebrated Spanish painter Antonio Lopez Garcia as he attempts to paint the quince tree that grows in his Madrid courtyard. Erice follows Garcia's progress over the course of three months, starting in late September, as the artist tries to capture the moment when the morning light falls across the tree's top branches. Garcia's technique is as precise as a land surveyor's. After carefully marking his own position in relation to the tree and his canvas (he stands surprisingly close to both), he uses a plumb line and string to form his own visual coordinates, marking the fruit and leaves with small dabs of white paint to indicate their place on the grid. But, as Garcia explains to his wife, painter Maria Moreno, and his old

art school friend, Enrique Gran, who drops by for a few visits, on even the sunniest days the light is fleeting. As the weeks pass, Garcia's original vision of the tree becomes increasingly elusive. The fruits grow heavier and hang lower on the branches; the leaves grow larger and October rains hide the magical sunlight. Eventually, the fruit and leaves begin falling to the ground.

Little else happens, yet Erice manages to transform the single act of painting a tree into a metaphor so rich with mean-ing that this remarkable film offers thoughts on everything from artistic vision, painting, and cinema, to life, death, and the possibility of eternal rebirth. And, of course, the beauty of a fruit tree in the fall.

DREAMERS, THE DVD
2003 115m c Erotic/Drama ★★★
Recorded Picture Company/Peninsula/ NC-17
HanWay/Fiction (U.K./France/Italy/U.S.)

Michael Pitt *(Matthew)*, Eva Green *(Isabelle)*, Louis Garrel *(Theo)*, Robin Renucci *(Father)*, Anna Chancellor *(Mother)*, Florian Cadiou *(Patrick)*, Jean-Pierre Kalfon *(Himself)*, Jean-Pierre Leaud *(Himself)*, Pierre Hancisse *(Buff)*, Valentin Merlet *(Buff)*

p, Jeremy Thomas; d, Bernardo Bertolucci; w, Gilbert Adair (based on the novel *The Holy Innocents* by Gilbert Adair); ph, Fabio Cianchetti; ed, Jacopo Quadri; prod d, Jean Rabasse; art d, Pierre Du Boisberranger; fx, Gregoire Delage; cos, Louis Stjernsward

---

Bernardo Bertolucci returns to the scene of his most memo-rable film, LAST TANGO IN PARIS, for this thoughtful and passionate meditation on eroticism, youth, and cinema itself.

Paris, 1968: Matthew (Michael Pitt) is a young American student in Paris, but instead of attending classes, he spends most of his time at the legendary Cinematheque Francaise. On his way to yet another screening, Matthew happens upon a crowd protesting the government's firing of popular Cinematheque director Henri Langlois. In the chaos, Matthew meets twin sib-lings Isabelle (Eva Green) and Theo (Louis Garrel), who invite their shy new friend home for dinner. Smitten with Isabelle, Matthew later agrees to spend the night at their flat. One evening soon stretches into a month. At first everything seems perfect: the three argue about politics, romance, and, of course, the movies, and even act out scenes from their favorite films. But Matthew soon discovers that Isabelle and Theo share a dis-turbingly intimate relationship and becomes enmeshed in their kinky games. When the May riots begin and the streets of Paris erupt in violence, Matthew is forced to choose between follow-ing his new friends into the revolution or returning home.

Though the film is set in the heady days of May 1968, it very much reflects today's social climate; these young char-acters display the same mixture of idealism and apathy that's commonly ascribed to disaffected post-baby boomers. Bertolucci clearly relishes the opportunity to re-create a his-torical moment in which he played such an important part, but what keeps the movie from ranking with the director's best is the absence of a strong central performance. Though Pitt cer-tainly fits the part of a wide-eyed American, he's no Marlon Brando.

DREAMLIFE OF ANGELS, THE DVD
(LA VIE REVEE DES ANGES)
1998 113m c Drama ★★★★
Bagheera/Diaphana/France 3 Cinema/Canal Plus/ NC-17
Centre National de la Cinematographie/Nord Pas

de Calais Region/Region Centre/Fondation GAN/
Procirep (France)

Elodie Bouchez *(Isa)*, Natacha Regnier *(Marie)*, Gregoire Colin *(Chriss)*, Jo Prestia *(Fredo)*, Patrick Mercado *(Charly)*

p, Francois Marquis; d, Erick Zonca; w, Erick Zonca, Roger Bohbot; ph, Agnes Godard; ed, Yannick Kergoat; art d, Jimmy Vansteenkiste; fx, Nicolas Becker; cos, Francois Clavel

Set in the bleak, northern French city of Lille, Erick Zonca's masterful first feature finds light inside each of its disparate characters: an aimless but optimistic waif, a brutish-looking but tender bouncer, and a beauty whose fierce inner unrest makes her wound others before they can hurt her.

Drifter Isa (Elodie Bouchez) lives out of a backpack, but exudes a curious serenity. During a brief stint at a sweatshop, she latches onto the awkward, quarrelsome Marie (Natacha Regnier), who's apartment-sitting for a hospitalized mother and daughter. When Isa is fired, Marie quits in a show of solidarity and the girls begin a period of half-hearted job seeking and full-time idling. Isa seems to have a softening effect on Marie, and they hook up with a pair of bouncers, Charly (Patrick Mercado) and Fredo (Jo Prestia). Marie ends up bedding the sweet but corpulent Charly, then flings herself into a self-destructive affair with Chriss (Gregoire Colin), a wealthy idler who owns the club where Charly and Fredo sometimes work. Isa, meanwhile, finds the diary of the young girl in whose home they're living, and begins visiting the comatose adolescent in the hospital. Isa is also uncharacteristically hostile to Chriss, intuiting that Marie's masochistic relationship with him is exacerbating her simmering self-hatred.

Cinematographer Agnes Godard's hand-held photography and naturalistic lighting contribute to the sense that this story was found rather than stamped out by some predetermined mold. On paper, Isa and Marie seem like a study in simple contrasts. But Bouchez and Regnier (who shared the Best Actress Prize at the 1998 Cannes Film Festival for their brilliant, unmannered performances) breathe life into them, delivering infinitely subtle and heartbreaking characterizations. Zonca's delicate film is a breath of fresh air, depicting the birth and death of dreams lovingly and with wrenching sadness.

DREAMS 📀
(YUME)
1990 119m c Fantasy ★★★½
Akira Kurosawa USA (Japan/U.S.)

Akira Terao *("I")*, SUNSHINE THROUGH THE RAIN: Mitsuko Baisho *(Mother of "I")*, Toshihiko Nakano *("I" as a Young Child)*, THE PEACH ORCHARD: Mitsunori Isaki *("I" as a Boy)*, Mie Suzuki *("I's" Sister)*, THE BLIZZARD: Mieko Harada *(The Snow Fairy)*, Masayuki Yui, Shu Nakajima, Sakae Kimura *(Members of the Climbing Team)*, THE TUNNEL: Yoshitaka Zushi *(Pvt. Noguchi)*

p, Hisao Kurosawa, Mike Y. Inoue; d, Akira Kurosawa; w, Akira Kurosawa; ph, Takao Saito, Masahuro Ueda; ed, Tome Minami; m, Shinichiro Ikebe; art d, Yoshiro Muraki, Akira Sakuragi; fx, Industrial Light & Magic; chor, Michiyo Hata; cos, Emi Wada

DREAMS is a mixed bag from one of the Old Masters of world cinema. On the one hand, it overflows with heavy-handed messages on topics ranging from ecology to pacifism as it scolds the audience for their wanton ways. On the other, it's a glorious triumph of style over content. DREAMS springs from the side of Kurosawa that produced IKIRU, DODES'KA-DEN, and other intimate dramas films with which American audiences are less familiar and which lack the presence of Toshiro Mifune or samurai swordplay.

Beginning with a wedding that looks more like a funeral and ending with a funeral that seems more like a wedding, DREAMS is made up of eight vignettes, thematically unit-

ed by their concern with Man's relationship to nature, mystery and his fellow man. The vignettes include "The Blizzard," in which the weary leader of a mountain expedition is tempted by Death in the form of a beautiful snow demoness; "Crows," in which an aspiring artist enters a Vincent Van Gogh painting to learn the artist's secrets from the painter himself (played with appropriate intensity by director Martin Scorsese); and "Mt. Fuji in Red," in which Japan's most famous landmark is destroyed in a nuclear power-plant meltdown.

None of the vignettes have much narrative beyond their rudimentary premises and when they do, they are left eerily unresolved. Some of the action is staged in stylized, excruciating slow motion. Though the film certainly has some nightmarish moments, it also has a wry sense of humor which often bubbles up when least expected. At other times, DREAMS is almost dismayingly mundane, especially in its scripting. Nonetheless this is clearly the work of a master filmmaker, even if his DREAMS are as unpredictable and uneven as our own.

DRESSED TO KILL
1980 105m c Thriller ★★★½
Samuel Z. Arkoff (U.S.) R

Michael Caine *(Dr. Robert Elliott)*, Angie Dickinson *(Kate Miller)*, Nancy Allen *(Liz Blake)*, Keith Gordon *(Peter Miller)*, Dennis Franz *(Detective Marino)*, David Margulies *(Dr. Levy)*, Kenny Baker *(Warren Lockman)*, Brandon Maggart *(Cleveland Sam)*, Susanna Clemm *(Bobbi)*, Fred Weber *(Mike Miller)*

p, George Litto; d, Brian De Palma; w, Brian De Palma; ph, Ralf D. Bode (Panavision, Technicolor); ed, Jerry Greenberg; m, Pino Donaggio; prod d, Gary Weist; cos, Ann Roth, Gary Jones

All dressed up with no script to go, but a feverish nerve jangler nonetheless. Kate (Dickinson) is a sexually dissatisfied middle-aged housewife who fantasizes about erotic encounters while in the shower. Kate's sympathetic psychiatrist (Caine) advises her to indulge in an extra-marital affair. Immediately after her first tryst, however, Kate is cornered in an elevator and murdered by a leather-clad blonde wielding a straight razor. Now it is up to Kate's son (Gordon) to solve the murder with the help of the prostitute (Allen) who discovered his mom's corpse. Although heavily indebted to Alfred Hitchcock, Mario Bava, and Dario Argento, De Palma infused this film with enough sex, blood, and visual panache to make it a big hit at the box office. Gushingly praised by some critics at the time of its release, it now seems a definite case of cinematic style over substance. A slightly longer and more explicit version was released in Europe, mainly for fans of Angie Dickinson's stand-in. But it's probably Dickinson's best work, and Caine is fine indeed. Best surprises: between subway cars, and that nurse's shoe!

DRESSER, THE 📀
1983 118m c Drama ★★★★
Goldcrest/World Film (U.K.) PG

Albert Finney *(Sir)*, Tom Courtenay *(Norman)*, Edward Fox *(Oxenby)*, Zena Walker *(Her Ladyship)*, Eileen Atkins *(Madge)*, Michael Gough *(Frank Carrington)*, Cathryn Harrison *(Irene)*, Betty Marsden *(Violet Manning)*, Sheila Reid *(Lydia Gibson)*, Lockwood West *(Geoffrey Thornton)*

p, Peter Yates; d, Peter Yates; w, Ronald Harwood (based on his play); ph, Kelvin Pike; m, Ray Lovejoy; prod d, Stephen Grimes; art d, Colin Grimes; cos, H. Nathan, L. Nathan

AAN Best Picture; AAN Best Actor: Tom Courtenay; AAN Best Actor: Albert Finney; AAN Best Director: Peter Yates; AAN Best Adapted Screenplay: Ronald Harwood (Screenplay)

The head of a Shakespearean acting troupe touring England during WWII, "Sir" (Albert Finney) is a senile boozer who is looked after by his gay dresser, Norman (Tom Courtenay). In episodic fashion, the film reveals Norman's devotion to his employer and the complexities of the relationship between the two men of the theater. This adaptation of Ronald Harwood's very successful play reveals its staginess, but the film is saved by dynamic direction, its feel of authenticity, and the two stars' performances that veer close to haminess without actually entering the terrain. Interesting, then, that Eileen Atkins steals the film out from under both as a pathetic stage-manager.

DREYFUS CASE, THE
1931 90m   bw   Biography   ★★★★
British Intl.   (U.K.)

Cedric Hardwicke *(Capt. Alfred Dreyfus)*, Charles Carson *(Col. Picquart)*, George Merritt *(Emile Zola)*, Sam Livesey *(Labori)*, Beatrix Thomson *(Lucie Dreyfus)*, Garry Marsh *(Maj. Esterhazy)*, Randle Ayrton *(President, Court-Martial)*, Henry Caine *(Col. Henry)*, Reginald Dance *(President, Zola Trial)*, George Skillan *(Maj. Paty du Clam)*

p, F.W. Kraemer; d, F.W. Kraemer, Milton Rosmer; w, Reginald Berkeley, Walter C. Mycroft (based on the play by Wilhelm Herzog and Hans Rehfisch); ph, Willy Winterstein, Walter Harvey, Horace Wheddon; ed, Langford Reed, Betty Spiers

Stately and underplayed, with more plot animation than many British films of this time. A true-to-life rendition of the infamous case that shook France in the late 1800s, THE DREYFUS CASE stars Cedric Hardwicke as Alfred Dreyfus, the only Jew on the French general staff. When treason is discovered, blame is laid at his feet, and he is sent to Devil's Island. One of the greatest writers of his time, Emile Zola (George Merritt), feels that Dreyfus has been railroaded. He engages Georges Clemenceau, and they succeed in getting the former soldier a new trial. Although serious doubt is cast on the justice of Dreyfus's conviction, they still lose the case, and Dreyfus is remanded to Devil's Island. After several more years of imprisonment, the duplicity is uncovered, and Dreyfus, vindicated, returns to his first love, the army. The exceptional Merritt and Hardwicke lead a talented cast, and producer Kraemer and the reliable Rosmer do a decent job of directing here.

DRILLER KILLER   DVD
1979 90m   c   Horror   ★★½
Navaron Films   (U.S.)   R

Abel Ferrara, billed as Jimmy Laine *(Reno)*, Carolyn Marz *(Carol)*, Baybi Day *(Pamela)*, Harry Schultz *(Dalton Briggs)*, Alan Wynroth *(Landlord)*, Maria Helhoski *(Nun)*, James O'Hara *(Man in Church)*, Richard Howorth *(Carol's Husband)*, Tommy Santora *(Attacker)*, Rita Gooding *(TV Spot Actress)*

p, Rochelle Weisberg; d, Abel Ferrara; w, Nicholas St. John; ph, Ken Kelsch; m, Joseph Delia

The ultra-low budget feature debut of the remarkable Abel Ferrara is disturbing and powerful, evincing the promise that would be fulfilled in MS. 45 (1981). Hiding behind the pseudonym "Jimmy Laine," Ferrara stars as Reno, an alienated Manhattan painter who lives in terror of winding up like his derelict father. Suffering from hallucinations in which his paintings whisper to him, and driven to distraction by a raucous punk band that rehearses downstairs, Reno vents his frustrations by taking to the streets and murdering bums with a power drill. As his rage spirals out of control, Reno moves from killing derelicts to slaying those in his own life who have

angered him—namely girlfriend Carol (Carolyn Marz) and libidinous art dealer Dalton Briggs (Harry Schultz). A bleak, often repugnant rumination on the harsh realities of urban life, DRILLER KILLER will offend tender sensibilities. But Ferrara is already a distinctive and conscientious talent behind the camera, unmistakably concerned with more than gore-filled exploitation. Turning budget restrictions to his advantage, he and cinematographer Ken Kelsch shot much of the film with a hand-held camera, giving the picture an immediate, documentary urgency.

DRIVER, THE   DVD
1978 91m   c   Crime   ★★★★
Fox   (U.S.)   R

Ryan O'Neal *(The Driver)*, Bruce Dern *(The Detective)*, Isabelle Adjani *(The Player)*, Ronee Blakley *(The Connection)*, Matt Clark *(Red Plainclothesman)*, Felice Orlandi *(Gold Plainclothesman)*, Joseph Walsh *(Glasses)*, Rudy Ramos *(Teeth)*, Denny Macko *(Exchange Man)*, Frank Bruno *(The Kid)*

p, Lawrence Gordon; d, Walter Hill; w, Walter Hill; ph, Philip Lathrop (Panavision, DeLuxe Color); ed, Tina Hirsch, Robert K. Lambert; m, Michael Small; prod d, Harry Horner; art d, David M. Haber; fx, Charles Spurgeon

A curiosity. Hill's second feature is a bare-bones, existential *film noir*. O'Neal is The Driver, a top getaway driver for a gang of crooks, and Dern is The Detective (nobody in the film has a proper name) obsessed with arresting him. The sparse story of the struggle of the two men with their obsessions, and with each other, skillfully creates a mood that is hard to shake after the ending credits. The car chases are breathtaking.

DRIVING MISS DAISY   DVD
1989 99m   c   Comedy/Drama   ★★★½
Zanuck   (U.S.)   PG

Jessica Tandy *(Miss Daisy Werthan)*, Morgan Freeman *(Hoke Colburn)*, Dan Aykroyd *(Boolie Werthan)*, Patti LuPone *(Florine Werthan)*, Esther Rolle *(Idella)*, Joann Havrilla *(Miss McClatchey)*, William Hall Jr. *(Oscar)*, Alvin M. Sugarman *(Dr. Weil)*, Clarice F. Geigerman *(Nonie)*, Muriel Moore *(Miriam)*

p, Richard D. Zanuck, Lili Fini Zanuck; d, Bruce Beresford; w, Alfred Uhry (based on his play); ph, Peter James; ed, Mark Warner; m, Hans Zimmer; prod d, Bruno Rubeo; art d, Victor Kempster; cos, Elizabeth McBride

AA Best Picture; AAN Best Actor: Morgan Freeman; AA Best Actress: Jessica Tandy; AAN Best Supporting Actor: Dan Aykroyd; AA Best Adapted Screenplay: Alfred Uhry; AAN Best Film Editing: Mark Warner; AAN Best Art Direction-Set Decoration: Bruno Rubeo, Crispian Sallis; AAN Best Costume Design: Elizabeth McBride; AA Best Makeup: Manlio Rocchetti, Lynn Barber, Kevin Haney

Driving Us Crazy that this flick won all those Oscars—but then what do you expect? In all fairness, Australian director Bruce Beresford (BREAKER MORANT; TENDER MERCIES) successfully translates playwright-screenwriter Alfred Uhry's loosely autobiographical, Pulitzer Prize-winning play of the same name to the screen. The simple but compelling story opens in 1948, when Miss Daisy (Jessica Tandy), a wealthy 72-year-old southern Jewish matron who lives in quiet dignity, accidentally backs her Packard into her neighbor's prized garden. Miss Daisy's already frustrated son, Boolie (Dan Aykroyd), insists that his mother employ the services of a chauffeur. Reluctantly, she hires Hoke (Morgan Freeman), a Black gentleman, thus beginning a friendship that blossoms over the next quarter century until, in her mid-90s, after many years of really getting to know and appreciate Hoke, the eccentric Miss Daisy at last concedes that the respectful yet forceful driver is indeed her very best friend. Set in a small community near Atlanta, DRIVING MISS DAISY covers 25 years (1948-73) in a changing South, and the manner in which the momentous and turbulent events of the civil rights movement affect Hoke and Daisy personally is the film's true subject. Directed and written with a pleasant simplicity and clarity, DRIVING MISS DAISY is a blandly liberal if touching and dignified depiction of decent human beings who must live their everyday lives amid the turmoil of historical events. Chief among the film's rewards are the extraordinary performances of its trio of stars, Freeman, Tandy, and Aykroyd—all of whom received Oscar nominations. Tandy won the Oscar for Best Actress.

DROWNING BY NUMBERS

1987 118m c Drama ★★½
Film Four International/Elsevier Vendex Film/ R
Allarts/VPRO Television (U.K./Netherlands)

Joan Plowright (*1st Cissie Colpitts*), Juliet Stevenson (*2nd Cissie Colpitts*), Joely Richardson (*3rd Cissie Colpitts*), Bernard Hill (*Henry Madgett*), Jason Edwards (*Smut*), Bryan Pringle (*Jake*), Trevor Cooper (*Hardy*), David Morrissey (*Bellamy*), John Rogan (*Gregory*), Paul Mooney (*Teigan*)

p, Kees Kasander, Denis Wigman, Bill Stephens; d, Peter Greenaway; w, Peter Greenaway; ph, Sacha Vierny; ed, John Wilson; m, Michael Nyman; prod d, Ben Van Os, Jan Roelfs; cos, Dien Van Stralen

Another typical Greenaway outing, in which plot and character take second place to those favorite thematic concerns of formal symmetry and physical decomposition.

Against a backdrop of the autumnal Suffolk seaside, three generations of women, each named Cissie Colpitts (60-year-old mother Joan Plowright, 34-year-old daughter Juliet Stevenson and 19-year-old granddaughter Joely Richardson), murder their unsatisfactory husbands by drowning—respectively, Jake (Bryan Pringle), in a bathtub; Hardy (Trevor Cooper), while swimming in the sea; and Bellamy (David Morrissey), in a swimming pool. In return for promised sexual favors, which the women ultimately withhold, the local coroner Henry Madgett (Bernard Hill) agrees to certify the deaths as accidental, although a small but steadily growing crowd of witnesses and relatives put pressure on him, as well as on Madgett's adolescent son Smut (Jason Edwards), who is obsessed with death and collects animal and insect corpses. True to Madgett's—and the film's—own obsession with games, to decide the issue he sets up a tug-of-war across a river, with him and Smut joining the Cissies against their detractors.

As the "story" of DROWNING unfolds, the filmmaker literally counts sequentially from one to 100, the numerals appearing somewhere within the frame, whether painted on trees, walls or dead cows, or as laundry marks, cricket scores, etc. For good measure, Greenaway also adds the dying words of historical figures like Gainsborough and Lord Nelson, and he works in the names of 100 stars—the celestial kind. Then there's a circumcision by scissors, a continual revulsion for food and flesh, and some fairly nauseating scenes of bodily decay and corruption.

DROWNING BY NUMBERS is an amoral tale told morally, with a strong feminist undertone—almost all the male characters die via the unbeatable Cissies' conspiracy—reflecting, as Greenaway himself has stated, that "the good

do not get rewarded, the wicked are rarely punished, and the innocent are always abused."

DRUGSTORE COWBOY *DVD*

1989 100m c Drama ★★★★½
Avenue (U.S.) R

Matt Dillon (*Bob*), Kelly Lynch (*Dianne*), James LeGros, billed as James Le Gros (*Rick*), Heather Graham (*Nadine*), James Remar (*Gentry*), William S. Burroughs (*Tom the Priest*), Grace Zabriskie (*Bob's Mother*), Max Perlich (*David*), Beah Richards (*Drug Counselor*)

p, Nick Wechsler, Karen Murphy; d, Gus Van Sant; w, Gus Van Sant Jr., Daniel Yost (based on a novel by James Fogle); ph, Robert Yeoman (Alpha Cine, Deluxe Color); ed, Curtiss Clayton; m, Elliot Goldenthal; prod d, David Brisbin; art d, Eve Cauley; cos, Beatrix Aruna Pasztor

A darkly funny, stylish, and realistic look at the world of drug addiction in 1971, DRUGSTORE COWBOY focuses on Bob (Matt Dillon) as the leader of a bedraggled quartet of addicts who get what they need by robbing drugstore pharmacy departments in the Pacific Northwest. His crew consists of his wife Dianne (Kelly Lynch), Bob's sluggish lieutenant, Rick (James Le Gros), and his underage girl friend, Nadine (Heather Graham). After one particularly fruitful heist, Bob devises a scheme whereby they can all stay constantly high, at least for a while, by sending their stash of drugs ahead of them via Greyhound bus as they migrate through the region. Hot on their trail is Gentry (James Remar), a cop bent on nailing Bob. Gus Van Sant's direction here is supremely confident, fusing witty camerawork, neat editing, and a jazz-oriented score to make DRUGSTORE COWBOY an exhilaratingly bumpy ride. DRUGSTORE COWBOY presents a rare insider's view of the drug lifestyle that is all the more refreshing for its lack of facile moralizing or apologies. It's a true comedy of desperation. After many photogenic but unchallenging roles, Dillon is a wonder here, portraying his antihero with an empathy that recalls James Cagney, Marlon Brando, James Dean, and Robert De Niro. The film's producers anticipated that DRUGSTORE COWBOY might receive an X rating for its explicit depiction of drug paraphernalia and use. Luckily, their fears proved wrong, allowing this honest, genuinely independent film to reach the broad audience it deserves.

DRUMLINE *DVD*

2002 97m c Drama ★★★½
Fox 2000 Pictures (U.S.) PG-13

Nick Cannon (*Devon*), Zoe Saldana (*Laila*), Orlando Jones (*Dr. Lee*), Leonard Roberts (*Sean*), Gregory Qaiyum, billed as GQ (*Jayson*), Jason Weaver (*Ernest*), Earl C. Poitier (*Charles*), Candace Carey (*Diedre*), Shay Rountree (*Big Rob*), Miguel A. Gaetan (*Trey*)

p, Timothy M. Bourne, Wendy Finerman, Jody Gerson; d, Charles Stone III; w, Tina Gordon Chism, Shawn Schepps (from a story by Shawn Schepps); ph, Shane Hurlbut; ed, Patricia Bowers, Bill Pankow; m, John Powell; prod d, Charles C. Bennett; art d, Nicholas Scott; fx, Joe Digaetano, Raymond McIntyre Jr.; chor, Glenda Morton; cos, Salvador Perez

Who knew marching bands could be so sexy? This handsomely mounted production, set in the flamboyant, highly competitive world of show-style university marching bands, may be a standard coming-of-age drama at heart, but the thrillingly edited scenes of battling bands in action are guaranteed to set your heart racing.

Devon Miles (Nick Cannon), a talented young drummer from New York City's Harlem, has won a scholarship to Atlanta A&T, a large Southern university with a predominantly black student body and a first-rate marching band. First-rate, but not first-place; that honor belongs to neighboring Morris Brown College, whose marching band has won the BET Classic four years in a row. A&T's administration blames the losing streak on music director Dr. Lee (Orlando Jones), who refuses to sacrifice musicianship for showmanship. Senior Sean Taylor (Leonard Roberts), the hard-nosed head of A&T's drum line, strictly adheres to Dr. Lee's credo of "one band, one sound," but those are words Devon finds hard to live by. Even though he quickly becomes a star attraction, Devon's conflicts with Sean—and a closely guarded secret—threaten his place in the band.

Director Charles Stone III, who made his feature debut with the underrated PAID IN FULL, wisely breezes through the more formulaic aspects of the story. Devon falls into a predictable romance with a beautiful, well-to-do upperclassman (Zoe Saldana) and endures a barrage of trite inspirational messages. The action on the field, however, commands Stone's—and the audience's—full attention, and features some truly breathtaking percussive performances. The thrilling climactic competition pits the fictional A&T University Panther Band against four of the best real-life marching bands the South has to offer, and it makes for pulse-pounding entertainment.

DRUMS
1938 96m   c   Adventure/War   ★★★★
Korda/London Films   (U.K.)

Sabu (Prince Azim), Raymond Massey (Prince Ghul), Valerie Hobson (Mrs. Carruthers), Roger Livesey (Capt. Carruthers), Desmond Tester (Bill Holder), Martin Walker (Herrick), David Tree (Lt. Escott), Francis L. Sullivan (Governor), Roy Emerton (Wafadar), Edward Lexy (Sgt. Maj. Kernel)

p, Alexander Korda; d, Zoltan Korda; w, Arthur Wimperis, Patrick Kirwan, Hugh Gray (based on Lajos Biro's adaptation of the novel by A.E.W. Mason); ph, Georges Perinal, Osmond Borradaile, Christopher Challis, Geoffrey Unsworth (Technicolor); ed, William Hornbeck, Henry Cornelius; m, John Greenwood; prod d, Vincent Korda; fx, Edward Cohen

Set in northwest India at the height of the British presence there, DRUMS finds the treacherous Indian Prince Ghul (Raymond Massey) usurping his brother's kingdom by murdering his sibling and forcing his nephew and the heir apparent, Prince Azim (Sabu), into hiding. The boy finds refuge at the British garrison, where the commander, Captain Carruthers (Roger Livesey), and his wife (Valerie Hobson) treat him with kindness. Azim learns the regulations of the British Army and how to beat military cadence on a drum, a skill he uses later to warn the garrison that it is about to be attacked by Ghul and his evil followers. The spectacle is excellent, the direction and beautiful color cinematography superb. Sabu is wonderful as the innocent, wide-eyed royal youth, a role that earned him 100 fan letters a day, and Livesey is a great match for the wily Massey, a villain minus a decent bone in his body. Needless to say, it's an unabashed apology for imperialism.

DRUMS ALONG THE MOHAWK   **DVD**
1939 103m   c   Historical/Adventure/War   ★★★★
Fox   (U.S.)

Claudette Colbert (Lana "Magdelana" Martin), Henry Fonda (Gil Martin), Edna May Oliver (Mrs. Sarah McKlennar), Eddie Collins (Christian Reall), John Carradine (Caldwell), Dorris Bowdon

(Mary Reall), Jessie Ralph (Mrs. Weaver), Arthur Shields (Rev. Rosenkrantz), Robert Lowery (John Weaver), Roger Imhof (Gen. Nicholas Herkimer)

p, Raymond Griffith; d, John Ford; w, Lamar Trotti, William Faulkner, Bess Meredyth, Sonya Levien (based on the novel by Walter D. Edmonds); ph, Bert Glennon, Ray Rennahan (Technicolor); ed, Robert Simpson; m, Alfred Newman; art d, Richard Day, Mark-Lee Kirk; cos, Gwen Wakeling

AAN Best Color Cinematography: Ray Rennahan, Bert Glennon; AAN Best Supporting Actress: Edna May Oliver

A sentimental beauty. This richly directed and acted colonial epic concerns Fonda and Colbert, young newlyweds starting out on the frontier of the Mohawk Valley just before the outbreak of the Revolutionary War. Their transition from a life of privilege to that of the rugged frontier proves an exercise in stamina. To help fend off Indian attacks engineered by the British, Gil joins the militia and goes off to fight; finally, after many battles and hardships, the future of the new Americans begins to look bright. This historical chronicle directed by John Ford is made believable through its attention to small details, presenting a mosaic of frontier life. One of Ford's biggest problems in making the spectacular film was the unavailability of necessary props and costumes; Fox had not specialized in costume or historical films, particularly those with 18th-century settings, and almost everything had to be made from scratch at great cost. The ancient flintlock muskets brandished by scores of extras were the real weapons of the era, however, not reproductions. A Fox prop man chased the flintlocks down in Ethiopia—where they had actually seen combat in the mid-1930s, when they were used by Ethiopian soldiers against Mussolini's armies. This was Ford's first color film, his cameras recording the lush forests and valleys of northern Utah. So rich and verdant is the color in this film that it later provided stock footage for several Fox productions, including BUFFALO BILL (1944) and MOHAWK (1956).

DRUNKEN ANGEL
(YOIDORE TENSHI)
1948 102m   bw   Drama   ★★★★
Toho   (Japan)

Toshiro Mifune (Matsunaga the Gangster), Takashi Shimura (Dr. Sanada), Reisaburo Yamamoto (Okada the Gang-boss), Michiyo Kogure (Nanae, Matsunaga's Mistress), Chieko Nakakita (Miyo the Nurse), Noriko Sengoku (Gin the Bar Girl), Eitaro Shindo (Takahama, the Doctor's Friend), Choko Iida (Old Maid Servant)

p, Sojiro Motoki; d, Akira Kurosawa; w, Keinosuke Uegusa, Akira Kurosawa; ph, Takeo Ito; m, Fumio Hayasaka; art d, So Matsuyama

Akira Kurosawa's DRUNKEN ANGEL captures the mood of postwar Japan in the same way the neorealist films of Italy did in that country. In a war-scarred town controlled by the Yakuza (Japanese gangsters), an alcoholic doctor runs a small clinic. A young gangster, Matsunaga (Toshiro Mifune), comes to have a bullet removed from his hand and is treated by Dr. Sanada (Takashi Shimura), who hates the Yakuza. Sanada discovers that Matsunaga has tuberculosis and, after arguments and fistfights, convinces Matsunaga to let him treat the illness, creating a love-hate relationship between the two. This was the first film on which Kurosawa had creative control and, although he had directed other pictures, it is the one in which his personal voice is first clearly heard. It was also the first starring role for Mifune, who, like his costar Shimura, turns in a mesmerizing performance. What makes the film so powerful is the characters' dependence on one another—Matsunaga's need for medical treatment and emotional support when faced with an incurable disease, and the humanist urge that compels

Sanada to treat the gangster despite the fact that he hates everything the Yakuza represents.

DRY WHITE SEASON, A

1989 97m c Drama   ★★★
MGM-UA (U.S.)   R

Donald Sutherland *(Ben du Toit)*, Winston Ntshona *(Gordon Ngubene)*, Susan Sarandon *(Melanie Bruwer)*, Janet Suzman *(Susan du Toit)*, Marlon Brando *(Ian McKenzie)*, Zakes Mokae *(Stanley)*, Jurgen Prochnow *(Capt. Stolz)*, Thoko Ntshinga *(Emily Ngubene)*, Susannah Harker *(Suzette du Toit)*, Leonard Maguire *(Mr. Bruwer)*

p, Paula Weinstein; d, Euzhan Palcy; w, Euzhan Palcy, Colin Welland (based on the novel by Andre Brink); ph, Kelvin Pike, Pierre-William Glenn (Deluxe Color); ed, Sam O'Steen, Glenn Cunningham; m, Dave Grusin; prod d, John Fenner; art d, Alan Tomkins, Mike Phillips

AAN Best Supporting Actor: Marlon Brando

A polemic against South African apartheid, this may not meet criteria for "great" filmmaking, but director Euzhan Palcy's film succeeds in being significant. History teacher Ben du Toit (Donald Sutherland), an Afrikaner, lives a comfortable middle-class existence with wife Susan (Janet Suzman) and their children in Johannesburg in the 1970s. He finds all of his personal and political ties thrown into question, however, following the event that sparked the Soweto uprising of 1976, when a peaceful protest march by black schoolchildren demanding better education was put down in a bloody massacre. When his longtime gardener (Winston Ntshona), in the process of trying to recover his son's body, is himself arrested, then brutally tortured and murdered, du Toit's liberal consciousness is raised. A DRY WHITE SEASON is worth watching for the (sometimes painful) force of its truths and its perspective, which shows the effects of racism from both white *and* black standpoints. This is the first full-length feature to be directed by a black woman for a major U.S. studio. Adding to this already significant achievement, Palcy, in what amounts to the casting coup of the year, enlisted the reclusive Brando to make his brief but memorable cameo appearance—his first film role since 1980—for union scale. His performance alone is worth the price of admission to this earnest, somewhat predictable, but moving and significant film. Brando's cameo earned him an Oscar nomination for Best Supporting Actor.

DUCK SOUP   *DVD*

1933 68m bw Comedy/War   ★★★★★
Paramount (U.S.)

Groucho Marx *(Rufus T. Firefly)*, Chico Marx *(Chicolini)*, Harpo Marx *(Pinky)*, Zeppo Marx *(Bob Roland)*, Raquel Torres *(Vera Marcal)*, Louis Calhern *(Ambassador Trentino)*, Margaret Dumont *(Mrs. Gloria Teasdale)*, Verna Hillie *(Secretary)*, Leonid Kinskey *(Agitator)*, Edmund Breese *(Zander)*

p, Herman Mankiewicz; d, Leo McCarey; w, Bert Kalmar, Harry Ruby, Arthur Sheekman, Nat Perrin; ph, Henry Sharp; ed, LeRoy Stone; art d, Hans Dreier, Wiard B. Ihnen

A masterpiece. Fast-moving, irreverent, almost anarchic in style, DUCK SOUP is considered by many to be the Marx Brothers's greatest achievement, though it was not a hit upon its release. The story, if one can call it that, concerns Mrs. Teasdale (Margaret Dumont), a dowager millionairess who will donate $20 million to the destitute duchy of Freedonia if it will agree to make Rufus T. Firefly (Groucho) its dictator. Firefly woos Mrs. Teasdale and spends his spare time insulting Trentino (Louis Calhern), the ambassador from neighboring Sylvania; Trentino hires the sultry Vera Marcal (Raquel

Torres) to vamp Firefly so that Trentino can move in on Mrs. Teasdale, marry her, and get control of Freedonia. To aid his chicanery, Trentino hires Chicolini (Chico), a peanut salesman, and his friend Pinky (Harpo) as spies. Eventually war breaks out and, after much manic double-crossing and side-switching, Freedonia emerges victorious.

DUCK SOUP is perhaps the best, and funniest, depiction of the absurdities of war ever committed to celluloid. The Marxes' depiction of two-bit dictators destroying their own countries was a slap at the rising fascists, so much so that Mussolini considered it a direct insult and banned the film in Italy. The Marx Brothers were thrilled to hear that. Best gag among what seems like hundreds: the mirror sequence.

DUEL IN THE SUN   *DVD*

1946 138m c Western   ★★★½
Selznick (U.S.)

Jennifer Jones *(Pearl Chavez)*, Joseph Cotten *(Jesse McCanles)*, Gregory Peck *(Lewt McCanles)*, Lionel Barrymore *(Sen. McCanles)*, Lillian Gish *(Laura Belle McCanles)*, Walter Huston *(The Sin Killer)*, Herbert Marshall *(Scott Chavez)*, Charles Bickford *(Sam Pierce)*, Joan Tetzel *(Helen Langford)*, Harry Carey *(Lem Smoot)*

p, David O. Selznick; d, King Vidor; w, Oliver H.P. Garrett, David O. Selznick (based on the novel by Niven Busch); ph, Lee Garmes, Harold Rosson, Ray Rennahan, Charles P. Boyle, Allen Davey (Technicolor); ed, Hal C. Kern, William Ziegler, John Faure, Charles Freeman; m, Dimitri Tiomkin; prod d, J. McMillan Johnson; art d, James Basevi, John Ewing; fx, Clarence Slifer, Jack Cosgrove; chor, Tilly Losch, Lloyd Shaw; cos, Walter Plunkett

AAN Best Actress: Jennifer Jones; AAN Best Supporting Actress: Lillian Gish

An enormous, lumbering horse opera, done up like an oversexed prize-winning bronco but revealing itself as a florid cartoon nag. DUEL is full of grand spectacle, steamy sensualism, and a storyline that could have snaked only out of Hollywood; it was Selznick's hymn to the allure of Jennifer Jones (in for Hedy Lamarr and, unbelievably, Teresa Wright—both were pregnant) and her failing entry into the Jane Russell/OUTLAW sex-goddess sweepstakes. Gregory Peck actually plays the studly bully who loves her (original choice when the project began in 1944 was John Wayne, but the dubious sex angle made him squeamish), and lightning blazes when they kiss. How to criticize a climax with two lovers orgasmically shooting each other to smithereens? The unforgettable supporting cast includes Walter Huston, having one whale of a good time as a hellfire preacher, Butterfly McQueen caricaturing her GWTW role (!) and Lillian Gish and Joseph Cotten as bastions of restraint. This is undeniable hooey, but it's also candybox entertainment. Can you really afford to miss Peck taming a sex-crazed stallion? Or Jones crawling for miles, spouting blood and words of love for her surly beau? We think not.

DUEL's accent on sex, heavy-handed and often repugnant, caused jocular critics of the day to dub the film "Lust in the Dust." The budget for the film soared beyond $6 million before it was over and an additional $2 million was used to scandalously promote the sex angle. A storm of protest from Catholic and Protestant leaders alike thunderclapped over Selznick's head. All over America local authorities competed with each other to ban the film. It was censored in Memphis and kicked out of Hartford, Connecticut. Certain scenes had to be edited before DUEL IN THE SUN opened in Philadelphia and other major cities. The publicity was enormous, and the public ignored the universal drubbing the film received from critics, flocking to see it and returning $12 million to the Selznick coffers. The film was begun in 1944, with

John Wayne originally set to play the bad cowboy, but he veered away from the film after reading the dubious script.

DUELLISTS, THE
DVD
1977 101m c Historical/War ★★★
Paramount (U.K.) PG

Keith Carradine (*D'Hubert*), Harvey Keitel (*Feraud*), Albert Finney (*Fouche*), Edward Fox (*Col. Reynard*), Cristina Raines (*Adele*), Robert Stephens (*Gen. Treillard*), Tom Conti (*Jacquin*), John McEnery (*2nd Major*), Diana Quick (*Laura*), Alun Armstrong (*Lacourbe*)

p, David Puttnam; d, Ridley Scott; w, Gerald Vaughan-Hughes (based on the story "The Duel" by Joseph Conrad); ph, Frank Tidy; ed, Pamela Powers; m, Howard Blake; art d, Bryan Graves

Competent feature debut of director Ridley Scott, who would go on to make the popular science-fiction films ALIEN and BLADE RUNNER, THE DUELLISTS is a beautifully photographed adaptation of a Joseph Conrad story in which two officers in Napoleon's army, Carradine and Keitel, fall out and proceed to engage in an obsessive series of duels for the next 30 years. The film's outstanding beauty is not enough to compensate its slim story, which remains preoccupied with the duellists' insane obsession with military codes of conduct and personal honor.

The leads are often remarkable, but neither of them seems quite fitting to a period setting. Therefore the burden of authenticity falls to those in supporting roles, including Finney as the Napoleonic head of the Paris police. Scott's approach to his material seems essentially a stylistic one; it imposes itself upon the story rather than visa-versa, giving an account of the Napoleonic wars that lacks passion and depth, despite the expert visuals.

DUMB & DUMBER
DVD
1994 106m c Comedy ★★★
New Line/Motion Picture Corporation of America PG-13
(U.S.)

Jim Carrey (*Lloyd Christmas*), Jeff Daniels (*Harry*), Lauren Holly (*Mary Swanson*), Mike Starr (*Joe Mentalino*), Karen Duffy (*J.P. Shay*), Charles Rocket (*Nicholas Andre*), Joe Baker (*Barnard*), Hank Brandt (*Karl Swanson*), Teri Garr (*Helen Swanson*), Brady Bluhm (*Billy*)

p, Charles B. Wessler, Brad Krevoy, Steven Stabler; d, Peter Farrelly; w, Peter Farrelly, Bennett Yellin, Bobby Farrelly; ph, Mark Irwin; ed, Christopher Greenbury; m, Todd Rundgren; prod d, Sidney J. Bartholomew Jr.; art d, Arian Jay Vetter; fx, Frank Ceglia; cos, Mary Zophres

In the tradition of American slapstick, DUMB AND DUMBER exploits the comic possibilities of a pair of imbeciles who can complicate any imaginable situation through their propensity for infantile, anarchic folly. The film's commercial success, despite the coolness of critics, is proof that there is still pleasure to be found in pure and simple buffoonery, and that basic bodily functions remain a resonant subject for comedy.

Limousine driver Lloyd Christmas (Jim Carrey) has a bowl haircut, a chipped tooth, and a dangerously low IQ. Smitten by beautiful heiress Mary Swanson (Lauren Holly), he pursues her to Aspen in a fur-upholstered van driven by recently fired dog-groomer Harry (Jeff Daniels), Lloyd's best buddy and intellectual equal. Our heroes are oblivious to the fact that they have inadvertently taken possession of a suitcase full of ransom money, and are being pursued by a gang of criminals.

Every gross childhood gag and indiscretion makes an appearance somewhere in this picture, with eating and excretion given special prominence. Underlying the slapstick, however, is an extravagant parody of American culture—bad taste, bad manners, the gushing sentimentality of Lloyd's daydreams, or the classic westward road trip, complete with diner scenes and archetypal rednecks. This gleefully lowbrow film is best enjoyed by the young, and by those who can still laugh at the passing of gas. There's little here for Merchant-Ivory fans, but devotees of Bunuel—e.g., the notorious dinner party sequence in THE PHANTOM OF LIBERTY—may not be entirely disappointed.

DUMBO
DVD
1941 64m c Animated ★★★★½
Walt Disney Productions (U.S.)

VOICES OF: Edward Brophy (*Timothy Mouse*), Herman Bing (*Ringmaster*), Verna Felton (*Elephant*), Sterling Holloway (*Stork*), Cliff Edwards (*Jim Crow*)

p, Walt Disney; d, Ben Sharpsteen, Norman Ferguson (Segment Director), Wilfred Jackson (Segment Director), Bill Roberts (Segment Director), Jack Kinney (Segment Director), Sam Armstrong (Segment Director); w, Joe Grant, Dick Huemer (based on a book by Helen Aberson and Harold Pearl); m, Frank Churchill, Oliver Wallace; art d, Herb Ryman, Kendall O'Connor, Terrell Stapp, Donald Da Gradi, Al Zinnen, Ernest Nordli, Dick Kelsey, Charles Payzant; anim, Wolfgang Reitherman, Arthur Babbitt, Walt Kelly, John Lounsbery, Ward Kimball, Fred Moore, Cy Young, Vladimir Tytla

AA Best Score (Musical): Frank Churchill, Oliver Wallace; AAN Best Song: "Baby Mine"; Frank Churchill (Music), Ned Washington (Lyrics)

One of Disney's finest films, this simple tale is set in a circus and spotlights a baby elephant, Dumbo, who is mocked and ridiculed because his ears are too big. With the help of his best friend Timothy the mouse and some very hip crows, Dumbo discovers that he can use his gigantic ears to fly and becomes the hit of the circus. The message of the film is spoken by Timothy as he declares to his doubting friend, "The very things that held you down will carry you up and up and up!"

A small, flawless gem, DUMBO is one of the shortest animated features Disney ever made and inexpensive to boot, costing less than $1 million (whereas more ambitious films like BAMBI shot well beyond the $2 million mark). A masterpiece of visual story-telling, the film contains relatively little dialogue and Dumbo never speaks; his mother only speaks to him in the song "Baby Mine." Humans are shown in shadows and silhouettes, the animals taking center stage. As with all his major feature-length animation films, Disney made sure that none of the scenes were flat, that blades of grass rippled in the wind and leaves fluttered in the trees. A delight from beginning to end, the film's absolute highlight is the "Pink Elephants on Parade" sequence in which Dumbo and Timothy hallucinate after accidentally drinking liquor.

It took the resourceful Disney craftsman a year and a half to design and execute this stunning achievement of animation art. This time was well spent. The result was an experience—alternately hilarious, thrilling, and heartbreaking—that will appeal to every child in the world and every adult who can still recall the happy world of childhood fantasies and fables. The film won an Oscar for its score and received a nomination for Best Song ("Baby Mine"). Warning to parents: the film contains some objectionable racial caricatures.

E

E.T. THE EXTRA-TERRESTRIAL

1982 115m c Science Fiction/Fantasy ★★★★
Universal (U.S.) PG

Dee Wallace Stone, billed as Dee Wallace *(Mary)*, Henry Thomas *(Elliott)*, Peter Coyote *(Keys)*, Robert MacNaughton *(Michael)*, Drew Barrymore *(Gertie)*, K.C. Martel *(Greg)*, Sean Frye *(Steve)*, Tom Howell *(Tyler)*, Erika Eleniak *(Pretty Girl)*, David O'Dell *(Schoolboy)*

p, Steven Spielberg, Kathleen Kennedy; d, Steven Spielberg; w, Melissa Mathison; ph, Allen Daviau (Technicolor); ed, Carol Littleton; m, John Williams; prod d, James D. Bissell; fx, Carlo Rambaldi, Dennis Murren, Kenneth F. Smith, Industrial Light & Magic; cos, Deborah L. Scott, Carlo Rambaldi

AA Best Original Score: John Williams; *AA Best Sound:* Buzz Knudson, Robert Glass, Don Digirolamo, Gene Cantamessa; *AA Best Visual Effects:* Carlo Rambaldi, Dennis Murren, Kenneth F. Smith; *AA Best Sound Effects Editing:* Charles L. Campbell, Ben Burtt; *AAN Best Picture; AAN Best Director:* Steven Spielberg; *AAN Best Original Screenplay:* Melissa Matheson; *AAN Best Cinematography:* Allen Daviau; *AAN Best Film Editing:* Carol Littleton

One of the most popular movies ever made, E.T. translates religious myth into cute, familiar terrain with its story of a lovable alien stranded in suburbia.

Elliott (Henry Thomas) finds E.T., a visitor from another planet left stranded on Earth, hiding in his backyard and, like any kid who finds a stray, decides to keep him. Hiding the alien from his mother, Thomas and the neighborhood kids befriend the creature. Though E.T. becomes attached to Elliott and his friends, he wants to get back to his own planet; meanwhile, the children must save him from some government types who are trying to capture and study him.

A major hit at the box office which also spawned an extremely profitable merchandising campaign, E.T. was embraced by audiences worldwide and instantly became absorbed into popular culture. Though the story feels standard, the fun comes from the meticulously realized details that director Steven Spielberg and associate producer-writer Melissa Mathison have injected into the material. From E.T.'s too-cute encounters with suburban living to the undeniable exhilaration felt when Thomas's bicycle magically soars into the air, the film bears witness to the undeniable powers of one of cinema's most skillful craftsmen. The film won Oscars for Best Original Score and Best Visual Effects.

EARRINGS OF MADAME DE ..., THE

(MADAME DE ...)
1953 105m bw Drama ★★★★★
Franco London/Indusfilms/Rizzoli (France/Italy)

Danielle Darrieux *(Countess Louise de ...)*, Charles Boyer *(Gen. Andre de ...)*, Vittorio De Sica *(Baron Fabrizio Donati)*, Mireille Perrey *(Mme de ...'s Nurse)*, Jean Debucourt *(M Remy)*, Serge Lecointe *(Jerome)*, Lia di Leo *(Lola)*, Jean Galland *(M de Bernac)*, Hubert Noel *(Henri de Maleville)*, Leon Walther *(Theater Manager)*

p, H. Baum, Ralph Baum; d, Max Ophuls; w, Marcel Achard, Annette Wademant, Max Ophuls (based on the novel by Louise de

Vilmorin); ph, Christian Matras; ed, Borys Lewin; m, Oscar Straus, Georges Van Parys; cos, Georges Annenkov, Rosine Delamare

AAN Best Costume Design (B/W): Georges Annenkov, Rosine Delamare

For the five-year period from 1950–55 (shortly before he died), Max Ophuls was arguably the world's greatest filmmaker, creating LA RONDE, LE PLAISIR, LOLA MONTES, and this masterful study of a tragic, three-cornered romance.

THE EARRINGS OF MADAME DE... opens brilliantly as the Countess Louise de... (Darrieux; her character's last name is obscured throughout the story) searches through her belongings for something to sell. The camera glides along as she examines furs, a necklace, a cross, and finally a pair of diamond earrings she received as a wedding present from her husband, General Andre de... (Boyer). When she pretends that the earrings have been stolen, the general begins a search, eventually recovering them discreetly from the jeweler to whom his wife sold them. The general gives the earrings to his mistress (di Leo), who later loses them while gambling with Baron Donati (De Sica). Upon returning to Paris, the Baron falls in love with the Countess, giving her a gift meant to express his deepest affection....

EARRINGS is masterfully told in both verbal and visual terms. The genteel, brittle dialogue traces an elliptical path to tragedy while the relentlessly mobile camera dollies and pans around the stiflingly ornate rooms that Ophuls's characters inhabit. The star trio of Darrieux, Boyer and De Sica have rarely been better, playing characters whose narcissism deepens to obsession and, ultimately, desperation. The film's lush visual style is a perfect, ironic backdrop for the superficialities of the society explored, particularly in the famous ballroom sequence where the Countess and the Baron first become aware of their ill-fated love.

EAST OF EDEN

1955 115m c Drama ★★★★½
Warner Bros. (U.S.)

Julie Harris *(Abra)*, James Dean *(Cal Trask)*, Raymond Massey *(Adam Trask)*, Richard Davalos *(Aron Trask)*, Burl Ives *(Sam)*, Jo Van Fleet *(Kate)*, Albert Dekker *(Will)*, Lois Smith *(Ann)*, Harold Gordon *(Mr. Albrecht)*, Timothy Carey *(Joe)*

p, Elia Kazan; d, Elia Kazan; w, Paul Osborn (based on the novel by John Steinbeck); ph, Ted McCord (CinemaScope, Warner Color); ed, Owen Marks; m, Leonard Rosenman; art d, James Basevi, Malcolm Bert; cos, Anna Hill Johnstone

AAN Best Actor: James Dean; *AA Best Supporting Actress:* Jo Van Fleet; *AAN Best Director:* Elia Kazan; *AAN Best Screenplay:* Paul Osborn

Overwrought, often splendid Kazan version of the Steinbeck novel. The movie's chief distinction is the amazing debut of rebellious, romantic James Dean, who in this and his next film, REBEL WITHOUT A CAUSE, would enshrine the misunderstood teen, and become a tragic icon in his own right. Dean plays the neurotic son of Massey, a devoutly religious lettuce farmer whose vast acreage stretches through the rich Salinas Valley of California. Dean's twin brother (Davalos, also making a powerful film debut) is well adjusted and upstanding, involved in a stable relationship with girlfriend Harris and diligently pursuing the development of his father's lands. Dean is his brother's opposite: troubled and troublesome, he challenges all authority, including his father's, and mistakenly believes that Davalos is the favored son. It's the Cain and Abel story, circa 1917, and the rush from stability to destruction and tragedy is swift, as Dean seeks to undo his brother and himself.

A powerful film whose influence can be seen in HUD and most other antihero films, EAST OF EDEN is masterfully directed by Kazan. All the principals give riveting performances, but it was Dean who emerged as an overnight sensation. EDEN also features a quintessentially hardbitten performance from Van Fleet, who won an Oscar for her pains.

EAST PALACE, WEST PALACE DVD
(DONG GONG, XI DONG)
1996 91m c Drama ★★★½
Amazon Entertainment/Quelqu'un d'Autre
(China/France/Netherlands)

Si Han (A-Lan), Hu Jun (Xiao Shi)

p, Zhang Yuan, Christophe Jung, Christophe Menager; d, Zhang Yuan; w, Zhang Yuan, Wang Xiaobo; ph, Zhang Jian; ed, Vincent Levy; m, Xiang Min; art d, An Bing

Hailed as the first gay picture from China, this elegant and seductively paced film by independent director Zhang Yuan earns its landmark status.

The palaces aren't the decaying imperial domiciles you'd expect of a Chinese film: they're public toilets on either side of Tiananmen Square, where gay men cruise. During a periodic sweep, a group of men is rousted from a public park by the police. One, young writer A-Lan (Si Han), is immediately attracted to his arresting officer (Hu Jun). A-Lan doesn't hide the fact that he's gay, and even plants a kiss on the policeman's cheek before he's released. He returns to the park a second night, and is again arrested by the same officer; this time he's taken back to the police station and questioned about his "stinking habits." But A-Lan is determined to tell his story his way, and through a series of disjointed memory fragments, sexual fantasies, visions, and a story from ancient times, a life lived in the shadows emerges.

Given that homosexuality is strictly taboo in China and that working outside the state-controlled film studios can get you blacklisted (as Zhang Yuan was), Zhang's film is uncommonly defiant. Not only in the character of A-Lan, who remains unashamed and ultimately subverts his captor's dominance by desiring it, but also in the film's willingness to consider the dynamics of S&M, bondage, and cross-dressing—still eyebrow raisers in the West—as well as Chinese society itself. It's such a rare glimpse of a heretofore invisible world that one can't help wishing for a few of the more mundane details of A-Lan's life as a gay man in China: early on, for example, he mentions that he's married, but no more is said. But Zhang has made a lyrical, psychologically acute, and profoundly disturbing film.

EASTER PARADE DVD
1948 107m c Musical/Comedy ★★★½
MGM (U.S.)

Judy Garland (Hannah Brown), Fred Astaire (Don Hewes), Peter Lawford (Jonathan Harrow III), Ann Miller (Nadine Gale), Jules Munshin (Francois, Headwaiter), Clinton Sundberg (Mike, the Bartender), Jeni le Gon (Essie), Richard Beavers (Singer), Richard Simmons (Al, Ziegfeld's Stage Manager), Jimmie Bates (Boy with Astaire in "Drum Crazy" Musical Number)

p, Arthur Freed; d, Charles Walters; w, Frances Goodrich, Albert Hackett, Sidney Sheldon, Guy Bolton (based on a story by Frances Goodrich and Albert Hackett); ph, Harry Stradling (Technicolor); ed, Albert Akst; art d, Cedric Gibbons, Jack Martin Smith; fx, Warren Newcombe; chor, Robert Alton; cos, Irene, Valles

AA Best Score (Musical): Johnny Green, Roger Edens

Pretty, deft, and tuneful but, given the top-rate talent involved, not particularly inspired. Between Easter 1911 and Easter 1912, Astaire gets dumped by dance partner Miller and vows revenge by grooming unknown chorus girl Garland for stardom.

Gene Kelly was originally slated to play the lead, but injured his ankle playing volleyball, so he suggested to produc-

er Arthur Freed that they prevail on Astaire to come out of his "retirement" for the role. Astaire had announced he was done after BLUE SKIES, but jumped at the opportunity and gave yet another classic performance. Garland was beginning to tire of the formula of her films, and the horrendous pace of her filming schedule, but Astaire apparently helped coax her through the production despite her exhaustion. Look for cameos from Lola Albright, as a hat model, and a two-and-a-half-year-old Liza Minnelli in the finale. Irving Berlin wrote 17 of the film's tunes, and Johnny Green and Roger Edens won an Oscar for their musical adaptation. The standout number is the delightful "A Couple of Swells."

EASY LIVING
1937 88m bw Comedy ★★★½
Paramount Pictures (U.S.)

Jean Arthur (Mary Smith), Edward Arnold (J.B. Ball), Ray Milland (John Ball, Jr.), Luis Alberni (Mr. Louis Louis), Mary Nash (Mrs. Jennir Ball), Franklin Pangborn (Van Buren), Barlowe Borland (Mr. Gurney), William Demarest (Wallace Whistling), Andrew Tombes (E.F. Hulgar), Esther Dale (Lillian)

p, Arthur Hornblow Jr.; d, Mitchell Leisen; w, Preston Sturges (based on a story by Vera Caspary); ph, Ted Tetzlaff; ed, Doane Harrison; art d, Hans Dreier, Ernst Fegte; fx, Farciot Edouart; cos, Travis Banton

Preston Sturges wrote the screenplay for this hilarious screwball comedy about a working girl whose life is turned upside down by a millionaire and his son.

Millionaire banker J.B. Ball (Edward Arnold) lectures his son John Ball Jr. (Ray Milland) for being a spendthrift, then discovers that his wife has bought a $58,000 sable coat. He throws it off the roof of their penthouse and it lands on Mary Smith (Jean Arthur), ruining her hat. Ball tells her she can keep the coat, and also buys her a new hat, but when she shows up at work late, she's fired. Mr. Louis Louis (Luis Alberni) is told by Ball that he has one week to pay the back mortgage on the Hotel Louis or Ball will foreclose, but Louis is told by a milliner (Franklin Pangborn) that Mary is Ball's mistress, so Louis gives her the most lavish suite in the hotel to appease Ball. Mary goes to eat at the automat, where she unwittingly meets John Ball Jr. who's taken a job as a busboy to impress his father. John goes with Mary back to her suite and spends the night there, and the elder Ball also checks into the hotel after his wife leaves him. In the morning, the hotel suddenly becomes fashionable after a gossip columnist (William Demarest) reports that Mary is Ball's mistress and is staying there.

Preston Sturges's imaginative script is one of his best, adroitly mixing his customary satire of capitalism and the class system with some dazzling dialogue and hilarious slapstick. The entire cast is perfection, from the debonair Edward Arnold, to the charming Jean Arthur, to the insouciant Ray Milland, and of course, the usual Paramount stock company of superb character actors, particularly Franklin Pangborn as the prissy milliner. Everyone throws dignity out the window and even the stars have a great time indulging in broad slapstick, including some hysterical fistfights and pratfalls. Leisen's direction is, as always, smooth and elegant, although the film is sometimes slowly paced and deliberate, lacking the mad whirl of frantic craziness that Sturges later brought to his own films as a director.

EASY RIDER DVD
1969 94m c Drama ★★★★
Pando/Raybert (U.S.) R

Peter Fonda (Captain America/Wyatt), Dennis Hopper (Billy), Antonio Mendoza (Jesus), Phil Spector (Connection), Mac Mashourian (Bodyguard), Warren Finnerty (Rancher), Tita

Colorado *(Rancher's Wife)*, Luke Askew *(Stranger on Highway)*, Luana Anders *(Lisa)*, Sabrina Scharf *(Sarah)*

p, Peter Fonda; d, Dennis Hopper; w, Peter Fonda, Dennis Hopper, Terry Southern; ph, Laszlo Kovacs (Technicolor); ed, Donn Cambern; art d, Jerry Kay; fx, Steve Karkus

AAN Best Supporting Actor: Jack Nicholson; *AAN Best Original Story and Screenplay:* Peter Fonda, Dennis Hopper, Terry Southern

A must-see, if only once. More notable as a document of its times than as a piece of cinema, EASY RIDER is slack but powerful, sentimental yet scathing, experimental but predictable.

A tale of two men searching for a freedom they can never attain, the film features Fonda and Hopper as Wyatt and Billy, a pair of hippie bikers who journey to New Orleans, hoping to arrive in time for Mardi Gras. On the way, the duo encounter rebuffs at various motels because of their way-out appearance, a hitchhiker who takes them back to the sun-drenched revels of his commune, and a squeaky-clean Texas parade. Arrested for joining the latter, the pair meets up with drunken civil-rights lawyer George Hanson (Jack Nicholson, enjoying the film's most well-rounded part and giving its best performance, one which earned him an Oscar nomination and finally made him a star). Now a trio, the men suffer beatings from local rednecks, but Hanson also gets to enjoy his first joint, which prompts one of the film's most memorable moments—Hanson's tongue-in-cheek theory that Venusians have already landed on Earth and occupy several important posts. Billy and Wyatt finally make it to New Orleans and find that their journey to the freewheeling world of Fat Tuesday (including an LSD-laced jaunt to a cemetery) has not brought them any happiness or sense of direction. The animosity the pair have dealt with throughout reaches its peak at the film's famous ending, as the film attempts to martyr its quasi-religious antiheroes.

A finely observed film but insufficiently developed as a satire of middle America, EASY RIDER seemed the paragon of hip rebellion at the time of its release; in retrospect, its worldview seems closer to whining self-pity.

EAT A BOWL OF TEA

1990 102m c   Romance   ***½
American Playhouse   (U.S.)   PG-13

Cora Miao *(Mei Oi)*, Russell Wong *(Ben Loy)*, Victor Wong *(Wah Gay)*, Lee Sau Kee *(Bok Fat)*, Eric Tsiang Chi Wai *(Ah Song)*, Law Lan *(Aunt Gim)*, Lau Siu Ming *(Lee Gong)*

p, Tom Sternberg; d, Wayne Wang; w, Judith Rascoe (based on the novel by Louis Chu); ph, Amir Mokri (Deluxe Color); ed, Richard Candib; m, Mark Adler; prod d, Bob Ziembicki; art d, Timmy Yip; cos, Marit Allen

This engaging comedy-drama set in New York's Chinatown examines an intriguing post-WWII American phenomenon: after years of strict immigration laws and forced separation of spouses, Chinese immigrants were finally able to bring their mates to the U.S. For longtime residents of Chinatown, it was too late to effect conjugal reunions, but many older Chinese-American men wanted their sons to provide them with grandchildren by finding brides in China.

Director Wang (CHAN IS MISSING, DIM SUM) and screenwriter Rascoe have fashioned a graceful movie powered by deliciously eccentric characters, bringing to the screen a slice of American life unfamiliar to many. Abounding in magical moments (like the scene in which the two young leads fall in love in front of an outdoor screen on which LOST HORIZON is playing), the film cleverly parallels the difficulties of adjusting to a foreign culture with those of adjusting to a new marriage.

The result is both a perceptive historical document and a captivating love story.

EAT DRINK MAN WOMAN   *DVD*

1994 120m c   Comedy/Drama   ***½
Central Motion Pictures Co./Good Machine Inc.
(U.S./Taiwan)

Sihung Lung *(Mr. Chu)*, Kuei-Mai Yang *(Jia-Jen)*, Chien-Lien Wu *(Jia-Chien)*, Yu-Wen Wang *(Jia-Ning)*, Sylvia Chang *(Jin-Rong)*, Winston Chao *(Li Kai)*, Chao-Jung Chen *(Guo Lun)*, Lester Chen *(Raymond)*, Yu Chen *(Rachel)*, Ah-Leh Gua *(Mrs. Liang)*

p, Li-Kong Hsy; d, Ang Lee; w, Ang Lee, Hui Ling Wang, James Schamus; ph, Jong Lin; ed, Tim Squyres; m, Mader; prod d, Fu-Hsiung Lee

AAN Best Foreign Language Film

A remarkably assured comedy-drama of domestic life in Taiwan, Ang Lee's EAT DRINK MAN WOMAN explores how families use meals and other rituals to appease their hunger for love in stressful times.

Widower Mr. Chu (Sihung Lung), one of Taipei's leading chefs, laboriously prepares gourmet meals each night for his three unmarried daughters: Jia-Jen (Kuei-Mai Yang), a high school teacher and recent convert to Christianity, Jia-Chien (Chien-Lien Wu), an ambitious airline executive and a talented chef in her own right, and Jia-Ning (Yu-Wen Wang), the youngest, a cheerful student who works part-time in a fast food restaurant. The harmony of this close-knit family is soon disrupted by romance, as the daughters cope with the blandishments of three very different men and Mr. Chu commences a relationship of his own.

Writer-director Ang Lee has described this film as "the last in my 'Father Knows Best' trilogy." Whereas PUSHING HANDS (1991) and THE WEDDING BANQUET (1993) focus on children who disappoint their more traditional parents, EAT DRINK MAN WOMAN is about parents who fail to measure up to the expectations of their offspring. At its best, the film echoes and parodies the characteristic themes, if not the stylistic rigor, of Japanese director Yasujiro Ozu. Lee's more playful sensibility comments on changing Taiwanese values through ironic juxtapositions and detailed scenes of food preparation. With Western influences (Christianity, classical music, interracial marriages) and modernity (technology, sexual liberation, divorce) constantly intruding on family life, elaborate dinners become the last surviving group ritual.

EATING RAOUL   *DVD*

1982 90m c   Comedy   ***
Bartel   (U.S.)   R

Mary Woronov *(Mary Bland)*, Paul Bartel *(Paul Bland)*, Robert Beltran *(Raoul)*, Buck Henry *(Mr. Leech)*, Richard Paul *(Mr. Kray)*, Susan Saiger *(Doris, the Dominatrix)*, Ed Begley Jr. *(Hippy)*, Dan Barrows *(Bobbie R.)*, Dick Blackburn *(James)*, Ralph Brannen *(Paco)*

p, Anne Kimmel; d, Paul Bartel; w, Paul Bartel, Richard Blackburn; ph, Gary Thieltges (Metrocolor); ed, Alan Toomayan; m, Arlon Ober; prod d, Robert Schulenberg

Bon appetit? This sometimes hilarious black comedy has gained quite a cult following over the years, and it remains writer-director-star Bartel's best effort yet. Set in Los Angeles, the story follows a straightlaced couple, Mary and Paul Bland (Bartel and the galvanizingly odd Woronov), who dream of someday opening their own gourmet restaurant. Since Mary is a nurse and Paul has just been fired from his job at a liquor store, realizing their dream soon seems unlikely. Fate knocks, however, when a drunken reveler stumbles into their apartment and begins mauling Mary. Paul kills the intruder and discovers a large wad of cash on the dead man. Inspired, the couple place an ad in a swingers' newspaper to lure victims into their home, where they will be killed for their money (something the ultra-conservative couple feels they deserve anyway).

With Bartel and Woronov giving wonderfully funny deadpan performances, EATING RAOUL is a terrifically droll satire on both horror movies and American middle-class values. Despite the subject matter, our hero and heroine emerge as genuinely sympathetic characters, which ultimately makes one wonder where the film's true sympathies lie. Working independently, Bartel scraped together financing from family and friends and shot the film in piecemeal fashion when he could afford it. The resulting film, despite its lulls, is probably the better for it. Beltran, in the title role, brings along some much-needed energy, so enjoy his performance... while it lasts.

ECSTASY   *DVD*
(EXTASE)
1933 82m   bw   Drama/Erotic   ★★★
Elekta   (Czechoslovakia)

Hedy Lamarr, billed as Hedwig Kiesler (Eva), Zvonimir Rogoz (Emile), Aribert Mog (Adam), Leopold Kramer (Eva's Father)

p, Frantisek Horky, Moriz Grunhut; d, Gustav Machaty; w, Gustav Machaty, Frantisek Horky, Vitezslav Nezval, Jacques A. Koerpel; ph, Jan Stallich, Hans Androschin; m, Giuseppe Becce; art d, Bohumil Hes

A once-daring gander at nude pre-MGM Hedy Lamarr (then Hedy Kiesler). Promoted in its day as "the most whispered-about film in the world" (in fact, everyone was talking about it out loud, and L.B. Mayer was roaring) and the "stark naked truth of a woman's desire for love," it's tame stuff, even for the good old days.

Kiesler plays a child bride whose husband ignores her on her wedding night. In frustration, she has a sexual tryst in a hut with a roadway engineer. When her horse wanders away with her clothes as she takes a swim, Eva gives chase, bumping into the engineer who hands over her clothes like a gentleman. She arranges to go away with him but leaves him after her former husband commits suicide. She subsequently appears with a baby, the offspring of this illicit affair, happy and fulfilled.

The simple story is told with invention by director Gustav Machaty, who seems especially influenced by the editing techniques of Eisenstein. The big deal back then was really not the nudity but the close-ups of Hedy during her tryst. Machaty couldn't elicit the facial responses he wanted from the young actress, until he got under the table she lay on and started pricking her with a pin. The film was released in the U.S. in 1940.

ED WOOD   *DVD*
1994 127m bw Biography/Comedy/Drama   ★★★½
Touchstone/Burton-DiNovi/Casual Pictures Inc.   R
(U.S.)

Johnny Depp (Ed Wood), Martin Landau (Bela Lugosi), Sarah Jessica Parker (Dolores Fuller), Patricia Arquette (Kathy O'Hara), Jeffrey Jones (Criswell), G.D. Spradlin (Reverend Lemon), Vincent D'Onofrio (Orson Welles), Bill Murray (John "Bunny" Breckinridge), Mike Starr (Georgie Weiss), Max Casella (Paul Marco)

p, Denise DiNovi, Tim Burton; d, Tim Burton; w, Scott Alexander, Larry Karaszewski; ph, Stefan Czapsky; ed, Chris Lebenzon; m, Howard Shore; prod d, Tom Duffield; art d, Okowita; fx, Howard Jensen, Kevin J. Pike, Paul Boyington; cos, Colleen Atwood

AA Best Supporting Actor: Martin Landau; *AA Best Makeup:* Rick Baker, Ve Neill, Yolanda Toussieng

It's ironic that one of the best films of 1994 told the story of one of the worst filmmakers of all time. Tim Burton's ED WOOD is a delightful, off-the-wall, and ultimately moving portrait of a young man trying to claw his way up into Hollywood from the bottom.

Ed Wood (Johnny Depp) produces awful plays in L.A. with various friends and hangers-on, including his girlfriend, Dolores Fuller (Sarah Jessica Parker), and transsexual wannabe Bunny Breckinridge (Bill Murray). Ed himself is a secret crossdresser, and when he learns that schlock producer George Weiss (Mike Starr) intends to make a film based on notorious transsexual Christine Jorgensen, he pitches himself as the best man for the job. A chance encounter with his idol, Bela Lugosi (Martin Landau), leads Ed to cast the now drug-addicted actor in his picture, and a deep friendship begins to develop between the two.

Typically, Burton's storytelling is sometimes erratic, but his emphasis on humanizing marginal characters—a project that seems central to his artistic agenda—is as strong as ever. Wood and his entourage may be bizarre, but they're sympathetic and likable; one roots for Wood to succeed despite his evidently complete lack of talent. Indeed, Burton, a true devotee of bargain-basement pop culture, probably intends to question whether "talent" is not just a cultural shibboleth, as misleading and overdetermined as "taste," or even "art."

EDGE OF DARKNESS
1943 120m bw War   ★★★★
Warner Bros.   (U.S.)

Errol Flynn (Gunnar Brogge), Ann Sheridan (Karen Stensgard), Walter Huston (Dr. Martin Stensgard), Nancy Coleman (Katja), Helmut Dantine (Capt. Koenig), Judith Anderson (Gerd Blarnesen), Ruth Gordon (Anna Stensgard), John Beal (Johann Stensgard), Morris Carnovsky (Sixtus Andresen, Schoolmaster), Charles Dingle (Kaspar Torgersen, Cannery Owner)

p, Henry Blanke; d, Lewis Milestone; w, Robert Rossen (based on the novel by William Woods); ph, Sid Hickox; ed, David Weisbart; m, Franz Waxman; art d, Robert Haas; fx, Lawrence Butler, Willard Van Enger; cos, Orry-Kelly

Gripping war propaganda, swooning with stardust, talent, and originality. A WWII German patrol boat sails into a Norwegian port to discover that the whole German occupation force and the citizens of the town lie dead, apparently killed in a bloody battle that ended with the Norwegian flag flying over the invaders' garrison. In flashback, we see the events leading up to the slaughter.

Flynn stars as a Norwegian fisherman who leads the local underground movement with Sheridan, his brave and loyal fiancee; Anderson is a fiery innkeeper who becomes enraged when Nazis murder her husband; and Huston, Sheridan's father, is a highly respected doctor hesitant to join the resistance movement. His wife, Gordon, is a shy, frightened woman, and his son, Beal, a collaborator. All live under the baleful eye of Dantine, the brutal German captain determined to retain control of the town.

An insightful look at the workings of a resistance movement, EDGE OF DARKNESS calls to mind Renoir's picture THIS LAND IS MINE, released the same year. The great Morris Carnovsky, playing an aged schoolmaster, stands out, pitting legendary talent against Dantine's hammy acting.

EDISON, THE MAN

1940 104m bw Biography ★★★½
MGM (U.S.)

Spencer Tracy *(Thomas Alva Edison)*, Rita Johnson *(Mary Stilwell)*, Lynne Overman *(Bunt Cavatt)*, Charles Coburn *(Gen. Powell)*, Gene Lockhart *(Mr. Taggart)*, Henry Travers *(Ben Els)*, Felix Bressart *(Michael Simon)*, Peter Godfrey *(Ashton)*, Frank Faylen *(Galbreath)*, Byron Foulger *(Edwin Hall)*

p, John W. Considine Jr., Orville O. Dull; d, Clarence Brown; w, Talbot Jennings, Bradbury Foote (based on a story by Dore Schary and Hugo Butler); ph, Harold Rosson; ed, Frederick Y. Smith; m, Herbert Stothart; art d, Cedric Gibbons, John S. Detlie; cos, Dolly Tree, Gile Steele

AAN Best Original Story: Hugo Butler, Dore Schary

A warm, watchable whitewash. MGM went all out for Thomas Alva Edison in 1940, producing two films on his life. YOUNG TOM EDISON was a box-office flop despite Mickey Rooney's energetic portrayal; EDISON, THE MAN was a much more lavish and popular production, with Tracy giving a dutiful but dynamic performance as the famous inventor. The film opens as Edison, at age 82, is about to be honored on the 50th anniversary of his invention of the incandescent light. He is being interviewed by two youths and begins to relate the story of his early manhood. It then goes into flashback and chronicles Edison's most productive years, from age 25 to 35, when he produced the phonograph, the dictaphone, and the electric light.

A little too old for the part, Tracy nevertheless immersed himself in the details of Edison's life, trying to capture the flavor of his personality as well as the words of the script. The result is a much more interesting performance than the one he gave in MGM's similar canonization of Father Flanagan in BOYS TOWN—energetic and committed, but not over-earnest. Tracy was ably backed up by a fine cast, particularly Rita Johnson, and directed with a sure feel for Americana by Clarence Brown. What's missing is a sense of the "difficult" side of his personality, which could have made this more of a well-rounded biography than a one-note song of tribute.

EDTV

1999 122m c Romance/Comedy **DVD** ★★½
Imagine Entertainment/Universal (U.S.) PG-13

Matthew McConaughey *(Ed)*, Ellen DeGeneres *(Cynthia Topping)*, Jenna Elfman *(Shari)*, Woody Harrelson *(Ray)*, Sally Kirkland *(Jeanette)*, Martin Landau *(Al)*, Rob Reiner *(Dr. Whitaker)*, Elizabeth Hurley *(Jill)*, Dennis Hopper *(Hank)*, Geoffrey Blake *(Keith)*

p, Ron Howard, Brian Grazer; d, Ron Howard; w, Lowell Ganz, Babaloo Mandel; ph, John Schwartzman; ed, Michael Hill, Dan Hanley; m, Randy Edelman; prod d, Michael Corenblith; art d, Dan Webster; cos, Rita Ryack

It's not quite THE TRUMAN SHOW all over again, but EDTV also doesn't break any new ground. What else can anyone say about the pursuit of fame for fame's sake that contemporary events haven't already made all too clear to us?

A producer (Ellen DeGeneres) for struggling cable channel True TV comes up with a brilliant ratings booster: pluck some boob from obscurity and train multiple cameras on him all the time. True TV's new star: underachiever Ed (Matthew McConaughey), who spends most of his time at the local pool hall with his obnoxious brother, Ray (Woody Harrelson), drinking domestic beer and acting like they're from their native East Texas, not San Francisco. The show takes off when Ed unwittingly exposes Ray's philandering, which then gives him a crack at Ray's girl Shari (Jenna Elfman). Within a month, Ed's celebrity has grown to unmanageable propor-

tions. His absentee dad (Dennis Hopper) reappears, only to cause emotional havoc, and his mother's (Sally Kirkland) marriage to frail but wisecracking Al (Martin Landau) is just one casualty of the media scrutiny.

Director Ron Howard relies on the same Greek chorus device Peter Weir used in THE TRUMAN SHOW: "regular" folks—a stereotypical gay couple, girls in a college dorm, peevish line cooks, a Connecticut buppie couple—addicted to the spectacle of watching Ed 24-7. As played by McConaughey, his charm firmly on cruise control, Ed is decked out in slacker gear, drives a nifty gas-guzzler, owns umpteen vintage jackets and sports a bad haircut. But he's got *heart*, and when the pernicious effects of fame take their toll on his family, he maneuvers an all too facile way out of the fame game. Like its star, Howard's movie is affable, but has limited range.

EDUCATING RITA

1983 110m c Drama ★★★
Acorn (U.K.) PG

Michael Caine *(Dr. Frank Bryant)*, Julie Walters *(Rita)*, Michael Williams *(Brian)*, Maureen Lipman *(Trish)*, Jeananne Crowley *(Julia)*, Malcolm Douglas *(Denny)*, Godfrey Quigley *(Rita's Father)*, Dearbhla Molloy *(Elaine)*, Pat Daly *(Bursar)*, Kim Fortune *(Collins)*

p, Lewis Gilbert; d, Lewis Gilbert; w, Willy Russell (based on his play); ph, Frank Watts (Technicolor); ed, Garth Craven; m, David Hentschel; art d, Maurice Fowler

AAN Best Actor: Michael Caine; *AAN Best Actress:* Julie Walters; *AAN Best Adapted Screenplay:* Willy Russell (Screenplay)

Julie Walters plays Rita, a working-class hairdresser who signs on for adult education classes and chooses alcoholic hack Frank Bryant (Michael Caine) as her tutor. As Rita's intellectual horizons expand, she becomes torn between her stifling home life and the alluring, but pretentious, world of her amorous professor. Adapted by Willy Russell from his stage play, this is a poignant if predictable take on the English class system, buoyed by an effervescent performance from Walters (though Caine gets the best line: "Life is such a rich and frantic form that I need the drink to help me step delicately through it"). Caine, Walters, and Russell were all nominated for Academy Awards for their work.

EDWARD SCISSORHANDS

1990 100m c Fantasy/Romance **DVD** ★★★½
Fox (U.S.) PG-13

Johnny Depp *(Edward Scissorhands)*, Winona Ryder *(Kim Boggs)*, Dianne Wiest *(Peg Boggs)*, Anthony Michael Hall *(Jim)*, Kathy Baker *(Joyce)*, Robert Oliveri *(Kevin)*, Conchata Ferrell *(Helen)*, Caroline Aaron *(Marge)*, Dick Anthony Williams *(Officer Allen)*, O-Lan Jones *(Esmeralda)*

p, Tim Burton, Denise DiNovi; d, Tim Burton; w, Caroline Thompson, Tim Burton; ph, Stefan Czapsky; ed, Richard Halsey; m, Danny Elfman; prod d, Bo Welch; art d, Tom Duffield; fx, Stan Winston, Michael Wood; cos, Colleen Atwood

AAN Best Makeup: Ve Neill, Stan Winston

A poignant, personal fairy tale from the innovative director of PEE-WEE'S BIG ADVENTURE, BEETLEJUICE and BATMAN.

Edward (Johnny Depp) is the creation of an inventor (Vincent Price) who dies before his work is completed, leaving his otherwise perfect progeny with pointed metal shards for hands. When Avon Lady Peg (Dianne Wiest) comes calling at Edward's Gothic castle one day, she takes a shine to the creature and persuades him to go back with her to the picture-perfect, pastel-colored suburb where she lives. The initially terrified Edward becomes an object of great curiosity among

Peg's neighbors, and soon gains minor celebrity status with his unique talents for hedge trimming and hair styling. But Edward's newfound happiness is threatened when the suburban residents come to believe he is guilty of a crime.

Drawing upon influences that range from FRANKEN-STEIN to BEING THERE, Burton creates a satire/allegory that is both funny and moving. The theme—that just beyond the edge of the perfectly normal lies the truly bizarre—is realized with intelligence and visual flair. In one particularly charming sequence, Edward creates a beautiful sculpture from a slab of ice, as Kim dances in the frozen flakes which rain down from his flying metallic fingers. Fine performances all around, particularly from Depp and the immensely sympathetic Wiest.

EEL, THE

(UNAGI)
1997 117m c   Drama   ★★★½
Eisei Gekijo Company/Groove Corporation/KSS/
Imamura Productions   (Japan)

Koji Yakusho (Takuro Yamashita), Misa Shimizu (Keiko Hattori), Fujio Tsuneta (Jiro Nakajima), Mitsuko Baisho (Misako Nakajima), Akira Emoto (Tamotsu Takasaki), Sho Aikawa (Yuji Nozawa), Ken Kobayashi (Masaki Saito), Sabu Kawahara (Seitaro Misato), Etsuko Ichihara (Fumie Hattori), Tomoro Taguchi (Eiji Dojima)

p, Hisa Iino; d, Shohei Imamura; w, Shohei Imamura, Daisuke Tengen, Motofumi Tomikawa (based on the novel Sparkles in the Darkness by Akira); ph, Shigeru Komatsubara; ed, Hajime Okayasu; m, Shinichiro Ikebe; prod d, Hisao Inagaki

This masterful film from veteran Japanese director Shohei Imamura shared the top prize at the 1997 Cannes Film Festival, and it's easy to see why: Imamura's artistry and the fine cast make for the kind of film international festival jurors love. The casual moviegoer, however, may find Imamura's symbolic subtleties a little obscure.

Takuro Yamashita (Koji Yakusho), a mild-mannered salaryman, returns home early from a fishing trip to find his wife in bed with her lover. Enraged, he slaughters her with a butcher's knife, then calmly turns himself in to the police. Eight years later, Yamashita is released on parole with a stern warning to steer clear of the messy affairs of other people. It's a warning he has little trouble heeding: betrayal, murder, and a prison term have left him asocial, unforgiving, and unrepentant—the only living creature he's capable of communicating with is a pet eel. Yamashita relocates to a small coastal village, where he sets himself up as a barber. One afternoon, while collecting eel food, Yamashita comes across Keiko (Misa Shimizu), a troubled young woman who's near death after having swallowed a handful of pills. Despite his resolve, Yamashita rescues her, and Keiko—who bears a striking resemblance to Yamashita's late wife—gradually becomes part of his life, until menacing figures from the past threaten Yamashita's reconnection with the world around him.

Imamura's film is meditative but lively, sometimes playful, and often sweet, though its optimism is continually challenged by echoes of brutality and death. Imamura opens his film with a shocking scene of violence worthy of any HAL-LOWEEN sequel, and while the movie never returns to that level of intensity, Imamura maintains an edgy balance between elegant restraint and impending chaos. Its what makes this film about what lies beneath the surface work as well as it does—that, and Yakusho's remarkable, often chilling performance as an emotionally remote man who's capable of unleashing quite a bit of chaos of his own.

EFFECT OF GAMMA RAYS ON MAN-IN-THE-MOON MARIGOLDS, THE

1972 100m c   Drama   ★★★½
Fox   (U.S.)   PG

Joanne Woodward (Beatrice), Nell Potts (Matilda), Roberta Wallach (Ruth), Judith Lowry (Nanny Annie), Richard Venture (Floyd), Estelle Omens (Floyd's Wife), Carolyn Coates (Granny's Daughter), Will Hare (Junk Man), Jess Osuna (Sonny), David Spielberg (Mr. Goodman)

p, Paul Newman; d, Paul Newman; w, Alvin Sargent (based on the play by Paul Zindel); ph, Adam Holender (DeLuxe Color); ed, Evan Lottman; m, Maurice Jarre; prod d, Gene Callahan; cos, Anna Hill Johnstone

Joanne Woodward is superb in this film adaptation of Paul Zindel's Pulitzer Prize-winning play, directed for the screen by her husband, Paul Newman. Woodward plays an embittered and overbearing widow who is struggling to raise her two very different daughters, Ruth (Roberta Wallach, daughter of actors Eli Wallach and Anne Jackson) and Matilda (Nell Potts, Newman and Woodward's real-life daughter). Wallach is loud and outgoing, Potts withdrawn and shy. Woodward makes ends meet by boarding elderly people and making phone sales for a dance studio. She is spiteful and distrusting of all men, including Potts's science teacher (Spielberg), whom she accuses of endangering her child's life by exposing her to gamma rays in order to grow marigolds for a school project. The widow's bitter outlook on life and grim view of men slowly work their way into her daughters' consciousness, but the blooming marigolds become a symbol of hope for a less stunted life.

EFFI BRIEST

1974 135m bw Drama   ★★★★½
Tango-Film   (West Germany)

Hanna Schygulla (Effi Briest), Wolfgang Schenck (Baron Geert von Instetten), Ulli Lommel (Major Crampas), Lilo Pempeit (Frau Briest), Herbert Steinmetz (Herr Briest), Mark Bohm (Gieshubler), Ursula Stratz (Roswitha), Irm Hermann (Johanna), Karl Scheydt (Kruse), Karl-Heinz Bohm (Wullersdorf)

p, Rainer Werner Fassbinder; d, Rainer Werner Fassbinder; w, Rainer Werner Fassbinder (based on the novel by Theodor Fontane); ph, Jurgen Jurges, Dietrich Lohmann; ed, Thea Eymesz; m, Camille Saint-Saens; art d, Kurt Raab; cos, Barbara Baum

One of the finest films to come out of postwar Germany, EFFI BRIEST marked the 16th feature in five years for the prolific Fassbinder. In 19th-century Germany, a 17-year-old girl (Schygulla) is forced into an unhappy marriage with a much older count (Schenck), and then falls into a short-lived relationship with an army major (Lommel). When, years after it has ended, the count discovers their affair, he kills the man in a duel and abandons his disgraced wife.

Schygulla, one of the finest actresses working in Germany today, carries the film with a truly astonishing performance, painting a moving picture of a woman exploited by everyone around her and powerless to fight back. Schygulla's professional relationship with Fassbinder—whose tyrannical working methods have been well documented—dissolved with this picture but, unlike most of the actors in the director's informal stock company, she went on to pursue a successful independent career. Schygulla would eventually work with Fassbinder again, in THE MARRIAGE OF MARIA BRAUN, BERLIN ALEXANDERPLATZ (a 15-hour miniseries for German television), and LILI MARLEEN.

EGG AND I, THE

1947 108m bw Comedy ★★★½
Universal (U.S.)

Claudette Colbert *(Betty MacDonald)*, Fred MacMurray *(Bob MacDonald)*, Marjorie Main *(Ma Kettle)*, Louise Allbritton *(Harriet Putnam)*, Percy Kilbride *(Pa Kettle)*, Richard Long *(Tom Kettle)*, Billy House *(Billy Reed)*, Ida Moore *(Old Lady)*, Donald MacBride *(Mr. Henty)*, Samuel S. Hinds *(Sheriff)*

p, Chester Erskine, Fred Finklehoffe; d, Chester Erskine; w, Fred Finklehoffe, Chester Erskine (based on the novel by Betty MacDonald); ph, Milton Krasner; ed, Russell Schoengarth; m, Frank Skinner; prod d, Bernard Herzbrun

AAN Best Supporting Actress: Marjorie Main

Amusing if slightly bland comedy in which Colbert and MacMurray uproot themselves from city living after MacMurray decides he can't stand the brokerage business. They buy a ramshackle farm, intending to raise chickens and live a leisurely rural existence. Instead, they face one problem after another, watching their bank account dwindle as Kilbride, the most unhandy handyman on record, fritters away their hard-earned dollars on building and landscaping materials. Complications develop when MacMurray becomes fascinated with the mechanized farm owned by Allbritton, a wealthy widow who tries to court him away from Colbert.

THE EGG AND I has many a laugh-filled scene— Colbert attempting to carry water in a bottomless bucket, MacMurray beaming with pride as he chops down a bothersome tree which crashes onto the roof of the henhouse—and was a success at the box office, bringing in $5.5 million. Colbert is suitably arch as the cultured, city-bred lady trying to cope with rural life, and MacMurray deftly deadpans his way through one disaster after another. This was the first appearance of Kilbride and Main as Ma and Pa Kettle and they would continue playing these lovable hick roles through a very successful series.

8 1/2

(OTTO E MEZZO)
1963 140m bw Drama
Cineriz/Francinex (Italy) ★★★★★

Marcello Mastroianni *(Guido Anselmi)*, Claudia Cardinale *(Claudia)*, Anouk Aimee *(Luisa Anselmi, Guido's Wife)*, Sandra Milo *(Carla)*, Rossella Falk *(Rossella)*, Barbara Steele *(Gloria Morin)*, Mario Pisu *(Mezzabotta)*, Guido Alberti *(Pace, the Producer)*, Madeleine LeBeau *(French Actress)*, Jean Rougeul *(Daumier, the Writer/Critic)*

p, Angelo Rizzoli; d, Federico Fellini; w, Federico Fellini, Tullio Pinelli, Ennio Flaiano, Brunello Rondi (based on a story by Federico Fellini and Ennio Flaiano); ph, Gianni Di Venanzo; ed, Leo Catozzo; m, Nino Rota; art d, Piero Gherardi; cos, Piero Gherardi

AA Best Foreign Language Film ; AAN Best Director: Federico Fellini; AAN Best Original Story and Screenplay: Federico Fellini, Ennio Flaiano, Tullio Pinelli, Brunello Rondi; AAN Best Art Direction-Set Decoration (B/W): Piero Gherardi; AA Best Costume Design (B/W): Piero Gherardi

After having directed six feature films, co-directed one (THE WHITE SHEIK), and directed two short episodes of anthology movies, Federico Fellini had made, according to his count, seven and a half films—hence the title of this brilliant, sumptuous semi-autobiographical account of the creative process.

Marcello Mastroianni plays Fellini-like figure Guido Anselmi, a director coming off a big hit. He needs rest and goes to a spa to regain his strength. He cannot recuperate, however, being interrupted instead by his producer (Guido Alberti), his screenwriter (Jean Rougeul), his wife (Anouk Aimee), and his mistress (Sandra Milo), all of whom want details from the director about his new sci-fi film. Hundreds of people are waiting in the wings, but Guido finds himself creatively blocked and fends off the inquiries of his actors, reporters, and especially his persistent screenwriter, in between lapsing into fantasy visions of past, present, and future.

8 1/2 is a grab-bag of Felliniesque delights, with stunning photography by Di Venanzo, superb performances, a haunting score from Nino Rota, and a labyrinthine structure that keeps the viewer in a pleasurable state of confusion. It received an Academy Award for Best Foreign-Language Film.

EIGHT MEN OUT
DVD
1988 119m c Sports/Drama ★★★
Orion (U.S.) PG

Jace Alexander *(Dickie Kerr)*, John Cusack *(Buck Weaver)*, Gordon Clapp *(Ray Schalk)*, Don Harvey *(Swede Risberg)*, Bill Irwin *(Eddie Collins)*, Perry Lang *(Fred McMullin)*, John Mahoney *(Kid Gleason)*, James Read *(Lefty Williams)*, Michael Rooker *(Chick Gandil)*, Charlie Sheen *(Hap Felsch)*

p, Sarah Pillsbury, Midge Sanford; d, John Sayles; w, John Sayles (based on the book by Eliot Asinof); ph, Robert Richardson (Duart Color); ed, John Tintori; m, Mason Daring; prod d, Nora Chavooshian; cos, Cynthia Flynt

Gripping account of the 1919 "Black Sox" baseball scandal, when eight members of the Chicago White Sox were accused of "fixing" the World Series. Working from a one-time Philadelphia Phillies farmhand Asinof's assiduously researched book, writer-director Sayles has fashioned a convincing account of the scandal, underlaid with an unconventional (by Hollywood standards) workers-vs.-owners critique.

Sayles not only depicts the circumstances that led to the fix (most notably Sox owner Charles Comiskey's legendary tightfistedness), but he also re-creates the games in great detail, making the best possible use of an athletic cast tutored by former White Sox outfielder Ken Berry. Among the players Sayles concentrates on are: pitcher Eddie Cicotte (David Strathairn); third baseman Buck Weaver (Cusack), who spent the rest of his life protesting his innocence; and the legendary "Shoeless" Joe Jackson (D.B. Sweeney, whose own baseball career was ended by a motorcycle accident and who spent five weeks with the minor-league Kenosha Twins learning to bat left-handed for the role). The fine ensemble cast also includes Chicago journalist Studs Terkel, as sportswriter Hugh Fullerton, and Sayles himself, as Ring Lardner.

8 MILE
DVD
2002 118m c Drama ★★½
Imagine Entertainment/Brian Grazer/Curtis Hanson Productions/Universal/Mikona Productions GmbH R
(U.S./Germany)

Marshall "Eminem" Mathers *(Jimmy)*, Kim Basinger *(Stephanie)*, Mekhi Phifer *(Future)*, Brittany Murphy *(Alex)*, Evan Jones *(Cheddar Bob)*, Omar Benson Miller *(Sol George)*, De'Angelo Wilson *(DJ Iz)*, Eugene Byrd *(Wink)*, Taryn Manning *(Janeane)*, Chloe Greenfield *(Lily)*

p, Brian Grazer, Curtis Hanson, Jimmy Iovine; d, Curtis Hanson; w, Scott Silver; ph, Rodrigo Prieto; ed, Craig Kitson, Jay Rabinowitz; m, Marshall Mathers, Luis Resto; prod d, Philip Messina; art d, Kevin Kavanaugh; fx, John D. Milinac; cos, Mark Bridges

AA Best Original Song: "Lose Yourself"; Eminem, Jeff Bass, Luis Resto (music), Eminem (lyrics)

As a showcase for white rapper Eminem, this gritty-looking drama has more depth than one might expect. Director Curtis Hanson and cinematographer Rodrigo Prieto evoke the blighted atmosphere of run-down neighborhoods like Detroit's 8 Mile, as well as the day-to-day experience of being nickled and dimed in America. What's disappointing is the thoroughly clichéd story, a feel-good fable of a young man's determination to ride his talent that's as rooted in Hollywood concoctions like THE JAZZ SINGER as it is in Eminem's own experiences.

1995: Jimmy Smith Jr. (Eminem), better known as Rabbit, wants to be a rapper, but his life is falling apart. He's forced to take a grinding new job at the dreary factory where welfare mothers fulfill their workfare assignments, and he chokes at the Friday-night rap battle where he hopes to establish some street credibility. Worse, he breaks up with his girlfriend (Taryn Manning) and moves in with his hard-drinking, irresponsible mother, Stephanie (Kim Basinger), who lives in a cramped trailer with her redneck boyfriend (Michael Shannon) and angelic daughter (Chloe Greenfield). Most of Rabbit's posse are in the same boat; only Future (Mekhi Phifer) has achieved some minor renown MC-ing rap battles. But Rabbit wants more, which makes him susceptible to the blandishments of slippery neighborhood hustler Wink (Eugene Byrd). Rabbit's also distracted by Alex (Brittany Murphy), a local girl also set on moving out, by any means necessary.

Rabbit's eventual triumph is never in doubt, and the scenes in which he shelters his sister and defends a gay factory worker smack of calculated attempts to rehabilitate Eminem's reputation for misogyny and homophobia. But overall, he's a credible screen presence, not precisely charismatic, but far from an embarrassment.

8MM
`DVD`
1999 123m c Thriller   ★★
Hofflund/Polone Productions/Columbia (U.S.)   R

Nicolas Cage (Tom Welles), Joaquin Phoenix (Max California), James Gandolfini (Eddie Poole), Peter Stormare (Dino Velvet), Anthony Heald (Longdale), Chris Bauer (Machine), Catherine Keener (Amy Welles), Myra Carter (Mrs. Christian), Amy Morton (Mrs. Matthews), Jenny Powell (Mary Anne Mathews)

p, Joel Schumacher, Gavin Polone, Judy Hufflund; d, Joel Schumacher; w, Andrew Kevin Walker; ph, Robert Elswit; ed, Mark Stevens; m, Mychael Danna; prod d, Gary Wissner; art d, Gershon F. Ginsburg; fx, Gary S. Wood; cos, Mona May

The message is unimpeachable—is anyone really *pro*-snuff films?—but the method is pure voyeuristic sleaze: director Joel Schumacher orchestrates a good wallow in the neon slime followed by a cathartic purge.

"I thought snuff movies were an urban legend," says minor-league private eye Tom Welles (Nicolas Cage), as a white-haired widow (Myra Carter) hands him the 8mm filmstrip she found among her wealthy husband's effects. Sure enough, it looks as though the hollow-eyed young girl onscreen is being horribly murdered. Welles is asked to prove the film a sick, slick fake by finding the girl, a mission that takes him far from his loving wife (Catherine Keener) and into the darkest heart of the smut business. His guide: dirty-book store employee Max (Joaquin Phoenix), who knows the hierarchy of bottom-feeders but isn't as hip to their vicious ways as he thinks. We know we've entered the realm of unthinkable human degradation as soon as everyone and everything gets ugly: pallid faces, greasy complexions, sweat and fat and pockmarks packed into red-lit rooms with papered-over windows. In the fashion of good men affronted by the world's cruelty, Welles will risk his soul to do right by the dead girl, and all roads lead to swaggering, insinuating reprobate Dino Velvet (Peter Stormare), who does everything to announce his gleeful

damnation but caper demonically and sing, "Please allow me to introduce myself, I'm a man of wealth and taste…"

Cage fans will doubtless enjoy his histrionically horrified journey into the underworld, but for all the *sturm und drang* stirred up by this hypocritically moralistic thriller, the superficially cheery BOOGIE NIGHTS is infinitely scarier. Gleefully selling your soul to Satan in a velvet dressing gown pales beside the spectacle of porn princes and princesses eaten away by the self-delusion and insidious callousness of the sex business, convinced to the bitter end that they're doing fine.

8 WOMEN
`DVD`
(HUIT FEMMES)
2001 113m c   Comedy/Mystery/Musical   ★★★
Fidelite Productions/France 2 Cinema/Mars Films   R
(France/Italy)

Catherine Deneuve (Gaby), Isabelle Huppert (Augustine), Emmanuelle Bèart (Louise), Fanny Ardant (Pierrette), Virginie Ledoyen (Suzon), Danielle Darrieux (Mamy), Ludivine Sagnier (Catherine), Firmine Richard (Madame Chanel), Dominique Lamure (Marcel)

p, Olivier Delbosc, Marc Missonier; d, Francois Ozon; w, Francois Ozon, Marina De Van (freely adapted from the play by Robert Thomas); ph, Jeanne Lapoirie; ed, Laurence Bawedin; m, Krishna Levy; art d, Arnaud de Moleron; chor, Sebastien Charles; cos, Pascaline Chavanne

Imagine a John Waters remake of an Agatha Christie mystery directed by Douglas Sirk, and you'll get some idea of the tone of this retro musical melodrama, which features a cast whose combined wattage could eclipse a small solar system.

In the palatial country home of a stiflingly bourgeois French family, something wicked is afoot. As perky Suzon (Virginie Ledoyen) returns from college for Christmas and her elegant mother, Gaby (Catherine Deneuve), squabbles with her miserly Mamy (Danielle Darrieux) and hypochondriacal spinster sister, Augustine (Isabelle Huppert), tomboyish younger daughter Catherine (Ludivine Sagnier) makes a grisly discovery. Her beloved father, Marcel (Dominique Lamure), has been stabbed to death in his bed. The telephone line has been cut, but housekeeper Madame Chanel (Firmine Richard) placed a call to the butcher earlier in the day. So the killer must be a member of the household, which is rounded out by insolent maid Louise (Emmanuelle Bèart) and Marcel's sister, Pierette (Fanny Ardant), a tragic bon vivant perpetually in need of cash. As each woman spills her innermost secrets through an impromptu musical number, it becomes clear the lavishly art-directed manse is actually a sort of snowbound Orient Express; everyone inside had both reason and opportunity to kill poor Marcel.

Francois Ozon's revolving showcase for three generations of French actresses is an oversized trifle inspired by George Cukor's THE WOMEN and Ozon's childhood love of dressing up and posing dolls. Based on an obscure play written in the '60s and designed to look like a Technicolor melodrama from Hollywood's golden age, this theatrical whim is like a dessert so rich it's almost inedible but too irresistible to put down.

84 CHARING CROSS ROAD
`DVD`
1987 97m c   Drama   ★★★
Brooksfilms (U.S.)   PG

Anne Bancroft (Helene Hanff), Anthony Hopkins (Frank Doel), Judi Dench (Nora Doel), Jean De Baer (Maxine Bellamy), Maurice Denham (George Martin), Eleanor David (Cecily Farr), Mercedes Ruehl (Kay), Daniel Gerroll (Brian), Wendy Morgan (Megan Wells), Ian McNeice (Bill Humphries)

p, Geoffrey Helman; d, David Jones; w, Hugh Whitemore (based on the book by Helene Hanff); ph, Brian West (Rank/TVC Color);

ed, Christopher Wimble; m, George Fenton; prod d, Eileen Diss, Edward Pisoni; cos, Jane Greenwood, Lindy Hemming

Charming, understated story of a love affair between two people who never meet. The "affair" begins in 1949 when Helene Hanff (Anne Bancroft), a struggling New York writer with a love of fine old books, responds to an ad placed by an antiquarian bookshop at 84 Charing Cross Road in London. Her letter is answered by Frank Doel (Anthony Hopkins), who runs the overseas department of the store, beginning a 20-year correspondence between the assertive, sometimes acerbic spinster and the dry, reserved man with two children, a plain wife, and a sparse home. Though literate and intelligent, CHARING CROSS ROAD never shakes free of its origins as a stage adaptation of Helene Hanff's novel; clearly, the subject matter is more suited to the page, or the stage, than the screen. Fine performances and a generous measure of humor still make this an absorbing drama.

84 CHARLIE MOPIC

1989 95m c War   ★★★½
Charlie Mopic   (U.S.)   R

Jonathan Emerson (LT), Nicholas Cascone (Easy), Jason Tomlins (Pretty Boy), Christopher Burgard (Hammer), Glenn Morshower (Cracker), Richard Brooks (OD), Byron Thames (Mopic), Russ Thurman, Joseph Hieu, Don Schiff

p, Michael Nolin, Jill Griffith; d, Patrick Duncan; w, Patrick Duncan; ph, Alan Caso (Duart Color); ed, Stephen Purvis; m, Donovan; art d, Douglas Dick; cos, Lyn Paolo

Shot entirely in hand-held documentary style (an experiment tried before in the Vietnam segment of MORE AMERICAN GRAFFITI), 84 CHARLIE MOPIC follows a close-knit group of soldiers led by a taciturn black sergeant (Richard Brooks) as they "hump" through the brush in the Central Highlands of Viet Nam. On the relatively miniscule budget of $1 million, writer-director Patrick Duncan, a Vietnam veteran who served as an infantryman for 13 months during 1968-69, shot this film in the hills outside Los Angeles using Super 16mm film stock, which was later blown up to 35mm for theatrical release. The gimmick here—an entire movie seen through the eyes of an Army cameraman—works better than it has any right to, largely because Duncan creates a viable, realistic situation for its use. This method is fraught with peril for both director and actors, but when it works the sense of realism lends an air of spontaneity and excitement to familiar material. While some may find the first half of the film boring, 84 CHARLIE MOPIC presents a fascinating and detailed account of what common infantrymen faced on a daily basis.

EL

1952 100m bw Drama   ★★★★½
Tepeyac   (Mexico)

Arturo de Cordova (Don Francisco), Delia Garces (Gloria), Luis Beristain (Raul), Manuel Donde (Pablo), Carlos Martinez Baena (Padre Velasco), Fernando Casanova (Beltran), Aurora Walker (Mother), Rafael Banquells (Ricardo)

p, Oscar Dancigers; d, Luis Bunuel; w, Luis Bunuel, Luis Alcorzia (based on the novel Pensamientos by Mercedes Pinto); ph, Gabriel Figueroa; ed, Carlos Savage, Alberto Valenzuela; m, Luis Hernandez Breton; art d, Edward Fitzgerald, Pedro Galvan

Bunuel's fascinating study of a married man's obsession with his wife's virtue. Middle-aged, church-going Francisco (de Cordova) has abstained from sex his entire life. One day, while helping the local priest wash the feet of parishioners, he notices the delicate feet of a woman and looks up to see the hauntingly beautiful Gloria (Garces), of whom he is instantly

enamored. He lures Gloria away from her architect lover and they marry, but on their wedding night Francisco reveals a jealous nature of obsessional proportions. In what is far from the film's most deranged moment, he pokes a knitting-needle through the keyhole of the bedroom door, convinced that his wife's ex-lover is spying on them.

EL is a compelling indictment of religious repression and sexual obsession. By pushing the macho concern with female chastity to an absurd extreme, Bunuel reveals its inherently ridiculous nature. The film is one of the best from the director's Mexican period, though, like others from that time, its production values leave something to be desired.

EL DORADO   DVD

1967 125m c Western   ★★★½
Paramount   (U.S.)

John Wayne (Cole Thornton), Robert Mitchum (J.P. Harrah), James Caan (Alan "Mississippi" Bourdillon Traherne), Charlene Holt (Maudie), Michele Carey (Joey MacDonald), Arthur Hunnicutt (Bull Harris), R.G. Armstrong (Kevin MacDonald), Edward Asner (Bart Jason), Paul Fix (Doc Miller), Christopher George (Nelse McLeod)

p, Howard Hawks; d, Howard Hawks; w, Leigh Brackett (based on the novel The Stars in Their Courses by Harry Brown); ph, Harold Rosson (Technicolor); ed, John Woodcock; m, Nelson Riddle; art d, Carl Anderson, Hal Pereira; fx, Paul K. Lerpae, David Koehler; cos, Edith Head

Sly, leisurely-paced western from Howard Hawks, with a script by Leigh Brackett ensuring a few laughs. EL DORADO addresses the standard Hawks themes of group loyalty and professionalism, but is also a poignant meditation on the passing of the old and the coming of the new.

Wayne plays an aging, wounded gunfighter and Mitchum a drunken sheriff, with the help of "Mississippi" (Caan) and Bull Harris (Hunnicutt), they take on ruthless cattle baron Bart Jason (Asner), who is using extortion to gain water rights to some land. The finale sees an attack on the bad guys by a crippled quartet of Mitchum (on crutches), Wayne (partially paralyzed and unable to shoot a revolver), Caan (wounded in the head), and Hunnicutt (armed with a bow and arrow). DORADO forms part of a loose trilogy with RIO BRAVO and RIO LOBO, also scripted by Brackett.

EL MARIACHI   DVD

1993 80m c Action   ★★★½
Los Hooligans   (U.S.)   R

Carlos Gallardo (El Mariachi), Consuelo Gomez (Domino), Jaime DeHoyos (Bigoton), Peter Marquardt (Mauricio [Moco]), Reinol Martinez (Azul), Ramiro Gomez (Cantinero), Jesus Lopez (Viejo Clerk), Luis Baro (Domino's Assistant), Oscar Fabila (The Boy), Poncho Ramon (Azul's Rat)

p, Robert Rodriguez, Carlos Gallardo; d, Robert Rodriguez; w, Robert Rodriguez; ph, Robert Rodriguez; ed, Robert Rodriguez; m, Eric Guthrie; fx, Robert Rodriguez, Carlos Gallardo

23-year-old Robert Rodriguez's feature debut combines the premise of Hitchcock's THE WRONG MAN with the frenetic pace of THE ROAD WARRIOR and the tongue-in-cheek style of a spaghetti western. Originally intended for the Spanish-language video market, EL MARIACHI so impressed Hollywood that after some post-production upgrading far in excess of production costs, it was showcased at festivals and released in theaters.

The title character, an unemployed singer/guitarist (Carlos Gallardo), wanders into a small Mexican town and is mistaken for vicious hitman Azul (Reinol Martinez), who has just broken out of prison, since they both wear black and carry guitar cases. After several close calls, the innocent musician receives help from the woman who runs a local tavern. He charms her and convinces her he isn't the hunted criminal; she hires him to perform in her club and they become lovers. Azul, seeking revenge on his former partner, Moco (Peter Marquardt), terrorizes the town; things come to a head when Moco abducts the woman and the mariachi must come to the rescue.

EL MARIACHI's genius lies not in its complexity or innovation but in its ability to create an engaging action picture from bare-bones resources. Mexican-American Rodriguez (the film's director/writer/producer/cinematographer/editor/sound recordist) turned out a fun, stylish, action-packed movie on a ridiculously low budget of $7,000. The unrelenting tempo is bolstered by Rodriguez's camera work and editing: nearly every frame seems to have been shot with a careening, handheld camera, and they're cut together in a skillful, fluid fashion that enhances the tension and pace of the 80-minute chase.

EL NORTE
1983 139m c Drama ★★★★
Independent Productions (U.S.) R

Zaide Silvia Gutierrez (*Rosa Xuncax*), David Villalpando (*Enrique Xuncax*), Ernesto Gomez Cruz (*Arturo Xuncax*), Alicia Del Lago (*Lupe Xuncax*), Eraclio Zepeda (*Pedro*), Stella Quan (*Josefita*), Rodrigo Puebla (*Puma*), Trinidad Silva (*Monty*), Abel Franco (*Raimundo*), Mike Gomez (*Jaime*)

p, Anna Thomas; d, Gregory Nava; w, Anna Thomas, Gregory Nava; ph, James Glennon; ed, Betsy Blankett; m, Gustav Mahler, Samuel Barber, Giuseppe Verdi, The Folkloristas, Melecio Martinez, Emil Richards, Linda O'Brien

AAN Best Original Screenplay: Gregory Nava (Screenplay), Anna Thomas (Screenplay)

A Spanish-language American film produced independently in association with the PBS TV series "American Playhouse," EL NORTE is an effective and moving drama about the strength of the human spirit and the will to survive. Brother and sister Enrique and Rosa Xuncax (David Villalpando and Zaide Silvia Gutierrez) are Guatemalan Indians forced to flee their village when their politically active father is murdered. They decide to make a new life in *el Norte* ("the North," i.e. the U.S.) but, as difficult and demeaning as the illegal trek across the border is, it is not nearly as rough as the struggle to make a living in Los Angeles. EL NORTE's style alternates between straightforward, almost documentary-like exposition and surreal sequences that take place in the characters' dreams. The film has a political message, but it is a subtle and compelling one that allows situations and characters to speak for themselves.

EL TOPO
1971 123m c Experimental/Western ★★
Producciones Panicas (Mexico)

Alexandro Jodorowsky (*El Topo*), Mara Lorenzio (*Mara*), Paula Romo (*Woman in Black*), Jacqueline Luis (*Small Woman*), David Silva (*Colonel*), Hector Martinez (*1st Master*), Juan Jose Gurrola (*2nd Master*), Victor Fosado (*3rd Master*), Agustin Isunza (*4th Master*), Brontis Jodorowsky (*Brontis as a Child*)

p, Roberto Viskin; d, Alexandro Jodorowsky; w, Alexandro Jodorowsky; ph, Rafael Corkidi (Eastmancolor); ed, Frederico Landeros; m, Alexandro Jodorowsky

A mass of indecipherable symbols combined with obvious self-indulgence on the part of a writer-director-star Alexandro Jodorowsky make what could have been an entertaining western into one of the more pretentious films ever made. A gunfighter (Jodorowsky) avenges the death of his wife, then, spurred on by

a woman, seeks to prove himself by defeating other master gunfighters. Jodorowsky uses deceitful methods which lead to intense feelings of guilt, so he retraces his steps in the hope of finding enlightenment. The pacing and action sequences are staged in a manner reminiscent of a spaghetti western and are quite good, but the allegories are too much and too many. At the time of its release, the film managed to attract a large cult following, making it one of the first "midnight movies." In retrospect, the elements that made it so don't hold up, making it almost laughable.

ELECTION
1999 120m c Comedy/Drama ★★★½ **DVD**
Bona Fide Productions/MTV Films (U.S.) R

Matthew Broderick (*Jim McAllister*), Reese Witherspoon (*Tracy Flick*), Chris Klein (*Paul Metzler*), Jessica Campbell (*Tammy Metzler*), Mark Harelik (*Dave Novotny*), Molly Hagan (*Diane McAllister*), Delaney Driscoll (*Linda Novotny*), Colleen Camp (*Judith R. Flick*), Frankie Ingrassia (*Lisa Flanagan*), Phil Reeves (*Walt Hendricks*)

p, Albert Berger, Ron Yerxa, David Gale, Keith Samples; d, Alexander Payne; w, Alexander Payne, Jim Taylor (based on the novel by Tom Perrotta); ph, James Glennon; ed, Kevin Tent; m, Rolfe Kent; prod d, Jane Ann Stewart; cos, Wendy Chuck

AAN Best Adapted Screenplay: Alexander Payne, Jim Taylor

Surprise! An intelligent, well-written high-school story that offers some real ideas to chew on, rather than simply wallowing in nubile flesh.

Carver High junior Tracy Flick (Reese Witherspoon) is a tightly coiled spring of ferocious ambition: she's a relentless hand-raiser, compulsive joiner, and fiercely calculating careerist who's got her eyes fixed firmly on the prize—the office of student body president. Since she's running unopposed, it looks as though another feather in her over-plumed cap is inevitable. Enter popular history and ethics teacher and student government advisor Jim McAllister (Matthew Broderick), a self-deluded schlub whose insistence that he loves his life—his baby-fixated wife, his uninterested students, his after-school rah-rah activities—rings painfully hollow. And there's something about Tracy that bugs him; could it be her almost-certain golden future? So he persuades Paul Metzler (Chris Klein), a dumb but popular jock sidelined from football by a skiing accident, to enter the ring. When Paul's sister Tammy (Jessica Campbell), a bitter, budding anarchist, announces *her* candidacy (her platform, naturally, involves the total abolition of student government), the election becomes a back-biting, sex-driven microcosm of tabloid American politics without ever losing the distinctive flavor of petty high-school nastiness.

Like director Alexander Payne's debut, CITIZEN RUTH, there's something rather cold about this satirical exercise, adapted from the novel by Tom Perrotta: it seems powered by a slightly smug cleverness rather than lacerating passion. But it's flawlessly acted and manages the subtle trick of making its characters types but not stereotypes. The story's most likable character is a well-meaning moron who shows glimmers of startling decency and self-awareness, while Tracy's underdog rant against the unearned bounty showered on those born to privilege and popularity is entirely justified. If only she weren't such a hateful little ankle-biter!

ELEPHANT
2003 91m c Drama ★★★½ **DVD**
Fine Line Features/Blue Relief Productions/Fearmakers Studios/Meno Films/HBO Films/Pie Films (U.S.) R

Alex Frost (*Alex*), Eric Deulen (*Eric*), John Robinson (*John McFarland*), Elias McConnell (*Elias*), Jordan Taylor (*Jordan*),

Carrie Finklea *(Carrie)*, Nicole George *(Nicole)*, Brittany Mountain *(Brittany)*, Alicia Miles *(Acadia)*, Kristen Hicks *(Michelle)*

p, Dany Wolf; d, Gus Van Sant; w, Gus Van Sant; ph, Harris Savides; ed, Gus Van Sant; art d, Benjamin Hayden; fx, Colin Fowler, Jor Van Kline

Gus Van Sant's timely, controversial, and remarkably sensitive treatment of teenage violence—the kind that reached a terrible apotheosis with the massacre at Colorado's Columbine High School—is his finest work since MY OWN PRIVATE IDAHO.

The virtually plotless film literally follows several students throughout what at first seems an ordinary day. John (John Robinson) arrives at school with his drunk father (Timothy Bottoms) babbling in the passenger seat. Aspiring photographer Elias (Elias McConnell) cuts through a park and stops to take pictures for his portfolio. Nathan (Nathan Tyson) leaves football practice and meets his girlfriend, Carrie (Carrie Finklea). Michelle (Kristen Hicks) endures cruel snickers from other girls as she undresses after gym. Three friends (Brittany Mountain, Jordan Taylor, Nicole George) pick at their food in the cafeteria, then throw up in the girls' room. Alex (Alex Frost) is tormented by class jocks who pelt him with spitballs as soon as the teacher's back is turned. A meeting in a hallway between John and Elias, periodically shown throughout the film from a variety of perspectives, alerts us that much of what we're seeing is actually happening simultaneously, and what at first appears to be a random arrangement of long takes is actually the slowly mounting prelude to an apocalypse.

Like the violence in Alan Clarke's ELEPHANT, the BBC documentary about Northern Ireland from which the film takes its name, Van Sant offers no straightforward reasons for the violence; the motives are presented as deeply personal and ultimately inexplicable. As the camera trails each student in real time, we see that, much like the elephant in the parable of the blind men, high school can be a very different beast to different people: a creative haven, a social hub, a nightmare.

ELEPHANT MAN, THE

1980 125m bw Biography/Docudrama **★★★★**
Paramount (U.K.) **DVD** PG

Anthony Hopkins *(Dr. Frederick Treves)*, John Hurt *(John Merrick)*, Anne Bancroft *(Mrs. Kendal)*, John Gielgud *(Carr Gomm)*, Wendy Hiller *(Mothershead)*, Freddie Jones *(Bytes)*, Michael Elphick *(Night Porter)*, Hannah Gordon *(Mrs. Treves)*, Helen Ryan *(Princess Alex)*, John Standing *(Fox)*

p, Jonathan Sanger; d, David Lynch; w, Christopher DeVore, Eric Bergren, David Lynch (based on *The Elephant Man, A Study in Human Dignity* by Ashley Montagu and *The Elephant Man and Other Reminiscences* by Sir Frederick Treves); ph, Freddie Francis (Panavision); ed, Anne V. Coates; m, John Morris, Samuel Barber; prod d, Stuart Craig; art d, Robert Cartwright; cos, Patricia Norris

AAN Best Picture; AAN Best Actor: John Hurt; *AAN Best Director:* David Lynch; *AAN Best Adapted Screenplay:* Christopher DeVore (Screenplay), Eric Bergren (Screenplay), David Lynch (Screenplay); *AAN Best Film Editing:* Anne V. Coates; *AAN Best Original Score:* John Morris; *AAN Best Art Direction-Set Decoration:* Stuart Craig (Art Direction), Bob Cartwright (Art Direction), Hugh Scaife (Set Decoration); *AAN Best Costume Design:* Patricia Norris

THE ELEPHANT MAN features an Academy Award-nominated performance by John Hurt as John Merrick, the victim of a disease that has left him so grotesquely deformed, he's spent most of his life as a carnival-show freak. In time, Merrick comes under the care of Dr. Treves (brilliantly played by Anthony Hopkins), who installs the "Elephant Man" in a hospital, where he studies him, helps him to overcome a seemingly insurmountable speech impediment, and—for a time—gives him back some human dignity. As word gets out about Merrick's existence and the press once again turns him into a freak, the film raises the question of Treves's motivation: has he helped Merrick out of decency, in the name of medical science, or to enhance his own reputation?

A moving, faithful retelling of a bizarre true story, THE ELEPHANT MAN was nominated for eight Oscars (though it won none), including a Best Direction nod for David Lynch. The black-and-white cinematography of Freddie Francis wonderfully evokes 19th-century England and Hurt gives a tour de force performance, masterfully conveying emotions while unable to use his face or even much of his voice.

ELF

2003 95m c Comedy/Fantasy **★★★½**
Guy Walks Into a Bar Productions/ **DVD** PG
Shawn Danielle Productions/Gold/Miller Productions/Mosaic Media Group/New Line (U.S.)

Will Ferrell *(Buddy)*, James Caan *(Walter)*, Bob Newhart *(Papa Elf)*, Edward Asner *(Santa)*, Mary Steenburgen *(Emily)*, Zooey Deschanel *(Jovie)*, Daniel Tay *(Michael)*, Faizon Love *(Gimbels Manager)*, Peter Dinklage *(Mile Finch)*, Amy Sedaris *(Deb)*

p, Jon Berg, Todd Komarnicki, Shauna Robertson; d, Jon Favreau; w, David Berenbaum; ph, Greg Gardiner; ed, Dan Lebental; m, John Debney; prod d, Rusty Smith; art d, Kelvin Humenny; fx, Tony Lazarowich, Bill Westenhofer; cos, Laura Jean Shannon; anim, Erik De Boer

Ever wonder how elves bested other diminutive creatures to become Santa's helpers? As this engaging and offbeat picture tells it, gnomes drink and trolls aren't toilet trained. Elves do like to talk, however, and Papa Elf (Bob Newhart) will regale anyone who'll listen with the story of Buddy (Will Ferrell), a human infant who crept into Santa's bag once Christmas Eve and wound up at the North Pole. Soft-hearted Santa (Edward Asner) lets Papa Elf raise the baby, but things get awkward as Buddy matures: He can't keep up with the toy-making pace and can't fit in the tiny elf buildings. Having accidentally discovered that he's really human, Buddy decides to visit New York City in search of his birth father, Walter (James Caan). Ignoring Santa's warning that Walter's on the naughty list, Buddy treks into the candy-cane forest, through the Lincoln Tunnel and toward the Empire State Building, propelled by the dream of a dad who'll go ice-skating with him. His hopes are dashed when Walter takes one look at the grown man in bright yellow tights who claims to be his son and has him ejected. Buddy wanders into Gimbels department store, is mistaken for seasonal help and directed to the store's "North Pole" where, ignoring all attempts to tone down his Christmas fervor, Buddy decorates like crazy and charms attractive co-worker Jovie (Zooey Deschanel). But a ruckus with a fake Kris Kringle lands Buddy in jail, jobless and in need of Walter's help. Walter reluctantly complies, takes Buddy home to his family (Mary Steenburgen, Daniel Tay) and even tries to get Buddy a new gig.

Ferrell shines in this holiday comedy, and the supporting cast helps ground his fish-out-of-water performance in reality; Deschanel, who can really sing, deserves kudos for her rendition of "Baby, It's Cold Outside." Director Jon Favreau keeps the guy-in-an-elf-suit act from degenerating into a too-long sketch, focusing on Buddy's naive optimism, even in the face of harsh reality. The film's sense of humor is pitched to various age groups—adults will appreciate the debate over the "real" Ray's pizza, while kids can giggle at Ferrell testing Jack-in-the-boxes and tussling with a rabid raccoon—but the jokes never betray its heart-warming sentiments. Tiny details, like North Pole characters who look as though they stepped out of a Rankin-Bass Christmas special, an uncredited appearance by A CHRISTMAS STORY's Peter Billingsley, and the use of Gimbels (Macy's competitor in MIRACLE ON 34th STREET) add to the film's knowing yet magical atmosphere.

ELIZABETH
DVD
1998 124m c   Biography/Historical   ★★★
PolyGram/Channel Four Films/Working Title Films   R
(U.K.)

Cate Blanchett (*Elizabeth I*), Geoffrey Rush (*Sir Francis Walsingham*), Christopher Eccleston (*Duke of Norfolk*), Joseph Fiennes (*Robert Dudley, Earl of Leicester*), Richard Attenborough (*Sir William Cecil*), Kathy Burke (*Queen Mary Tudor*), Jamie Foreman (*Earl of Sussex*), James Frain (*Alvaro de la Quadra*), Emily Mortimer (*Kat Ashley*), Kelly Macdonald (*Isabel Knollys*)

p, Alison Owen, Eric Fellner, Tim Bevan; d, Shekhar Kapur; w, Michael Hurst; ph, Remi Adefarasin; ed, Jill Bilcock; m, David Hirschfelder; prod d, John Myhre; art d, Lucy Richardson; fx, George Gibbs; chor, Sue Lefton; cos, Alexandra Byrne

AA Best Makeup: Jenny Shircore; *AAN Best Picture; AAN Best Actress:* Cate Blanchett; *AAN Best Art Direction:* John Myhre, Peter Howitt; *AAN Best Cinematography:* Remi Adefarasin; *AAN Best Costume Design:* Alexandra Byrne; *AAN Best Original Dramatic Score:* David Hirschfelder

Replete with smashing finery and looks as sharp as daggers, this political thriller cum romance deals with the early reign of Elizabeth I (1533-1603).

The year is 1554: following Henry VIII's split from the Roman Catholic Church, his Catholic daughter, Mary Tudor (Kathy Burke), assumes the throne and begins persecuting Protestants, earning the nickname "Bloody Mary." The first glimpse of Mary's half sister, Elizabeth (the radiant Cate Blanchett), reveals an unabashedly sensual and appealing young woman in the throes of first love with dashing Robert Dudley (Joseph Fiennes), Earl of Leicester. The scrofulous Mary quickly packs her off to the Tower of London, where Mary's nefarious advisers—including the sleek and sinister Duke of Norfolk (Christopher Eccleston)—plot to have Elizabeth executed for treason. But Mary does an about-face and anoints Elizabeth her successor, on the condition that she adhere to Mary's Catholic agenda, and Elizabeth takes the throne amidst a storm of court intrigue and touchy foreign relations.

The film's lead performances are more than satisfying (though Fiennes is a weak link), and Indian director Shekhar Kapur's (MR. INDIA, BANDIT QUEEN) direction is athletic and majestic. But despite the sumptuous regalia, exterminating priests, misty castle ramparts, feverish couplings, and occasional violence, a conspicuous lack of emotional resonance makes the result feel like QUEEN MARGOT's poor, cold English cousin.

ELMER GANTRY
DVD
1960 146m c   Drama   ★★★★
UA   (U.S.)

Burt Lancaster (*Elmer Gantry*), Jean Simmons (*Sister Sharon Falconer/Katy Jones*), Arthur Kennedy (*Jim Lefferts*), Shirley Jones (*Lulu Bains*), Dean Jagger (*William L. Morgan*), Patti Page (*Sister Rachel*), Edward Andrews (*George Babbitt*), John McIntire (*Rev. Pengilly*), Joe Maross (*Pete*), Everett Glass (*Rev. Brown*)

p, Bernard Smith; d, Richard Brooks; w, Richard Brooks (based on the novel by Sinclair Lewis); ph, John Alton; ed, Marjorie Fowler; m, Andre Previn; art d, Edward Carrere; cos, Dorothy Jeakins

AAN Best Picture; AA Best Actor: Burt Lancaster; *AA Best Supporting Actress:* Shirley Jones; *AA Best Adapted Screenplay:* Richard Brooks; *AAN Best Score (Drama or Comedy):* Andre Previn

Lancaster pulls out all the stops in one of his most memorable roles as the lustful, ambitious charlatan of Sinclair Lewis's powerful novel. Elmer Gantry (Lancaster) first appears on the screen, roaring drunk, trying to mooch drinks while selling his own distinctive take on scripture with his remarkable gift of gab. He encounters evangelist Sister Sharon Falconer (Simmons)—a role no doubt intended by Lewis to suggest Aimee Semple McPherson. Gantry appeals to her vanity and joins her entourage. Together they become rich and famous enough for Sister Falconer to build her own huge seaside temple. She falls in love with Gantry who loves life and every woman he meets; he had once been with a preacher's daughter, Lulu Baines (Shirley Jones, in a standout, Oscar-winning performance), now a prostitute hungry for revenge.

Writer-director Brooks made a few revisions in the novel's story. Gantry is no longer the ordained minister fallen from grace as depicted in the novel but now a traveling salesman from the Lord. Kennedy as Jim Lefferts, his empathic friend, is transformed from another seminary dropout in the novel into a cynical, savvy newsman in the H.L. Mencken tradition. Nonetheless the integrity of the characterizations is maintained in a script that is both literate and ironic. Brooks later sarcastically commented that "ELMER GANTRY is the story of a man who wants what everyone is supposed to want—money, sex, and religion. He's the All-American boy."

ELVIRA MADIGAN
DVD
1967 90m c   Romance   ★★★
Europa/Janco   (Sweden)   PG

Pia Degermark (*Elvira*), Thommy Berggren (*Sixten Sparre*), Lennart Malmer (*Friend*), Nina Widerberg (*Little Girl*), Cleo Jensen (*Cook*)

d, Bo Widerberg; w, Bo Widerberg (based on a ballad by Johan Lindstrom Saxon); ph, Jorgen Persson; ed, Bo Widerberg; m, Ulf Bjorlin, Wolfgang Amadeus Mozart, Antonio Vivaldi

In 19th-century Sweden, a tightrope performer (Pia Degermark) and an army lieutenant (Thommy Berggren) give up their previous lives—he leaves his wife and children, and she deserts the circus troupe of which she is the top attraction—to find a new freedom for themselves. Their romance appears perfect, but, as the story progresses, they realize that their idyllic state cannot continue....

This was a very popular film at the time and—whatever else it did—made Mozart acceptable for the world's teenagers. It's a rather silly love story of two adolescents, but prettily photographed and, although we don't like to admit it, even grownups occasionally like to watch this sort of jejeune adolescent romantic fantasy. Those were legitimate feelings when we were 15, and there's nothing wrong with reliving them for an hour or two. A decade later a whole genre was spawned on this model—THE BLUE LAGOON for example—bringing the level down to proto-kiddy-porn.

Sixteen-year-old Degermark was named Best Actress at the Cannes Film Festival for her performance as the title character. Additional music by Mozart and Vivaldi is ideally suited to the film.

EMERALD FOREST, THE
DVD
1985 113m c   Adventure   ★★★★
Christel   (U.K.)   R

Powers Boothe (*Bill Markham*), Meg Foster (*Jean Markham*), William Rodriquez (*Young Tommy*), Yara Vaneau (*Young Heather*), Estee Chandler (*Heather*), Charley Boorman (*Tomme*), Dira Paes

(Kachiri), Eduardo Conde (Uwe Werner), Ariel Coelho (Padre Leduc), Peter Marinker (Perreira)

p, John Boorman, Michael Dryhurst; d, John Boorman; w, Rospo Pallenberg; ph, Philippe Rousselot (Panavision, Technicolor); ed, Ian Crafford; m, Junior Homrich, Brian Gascoigne; prod d, Simon Holland; art d, Marcos Flacksman, Terry Pritchard; fx, Raph Salis; chor, Jose Possi; cos, Christel Boorman, Clovis Bueno

In October 1972 an account written by Leonard Greenwood appeared in the *Los Angeles Times*. It told of a Peruvian engineer whose son had been kidnapped by a band of Indians and of the man's successful search to locate the child. Screenwriter Rospo Pallenberg saw the news item and took it to producer-director John Boorman. The result was this amazing, beautiful and sometimes fanciful film. Powers Boothe is Bill Markham, a U.S. engineer working on a dam project in Brazil where he lives with his wife, Jean (Meg Foster), and his small children. One day while the family is picnicking at the edge of the rain forest, some painted Indians swiftly and silently kidnap young Tommy (William Rodriguez). The only clue left is an arrow stuck in a tree, and Boothe uses it in his ten-year search for his son.

The film is a powerful meditation on the clash between two civilizations. Charley Boorman (the director's son) is outstanding as the grown Tomme and Boothe also gives a powerful performance. The film has many opportunities to tip over into the ludicrous and become a parody of traditional jungle action pictures. But director Boorman keeps matters on an even keel, deftly balancing the mystical elements with reality to produce a memorable film that is enthralling throughout and never heavy-handed.

EMIGRANTS, THE
(UTVANDRARNA)
1971 151m c   Drama   ★★★★
Svensk (Sweden)   PG

Max von Sydow (Karl Oskar), Liv Ullmann (Kristina), Eddie Axberg (Robert), Svenolof Bern (Nils), Aina Alfredsson (Marta), Allan Edwall (Danjel), Monica Zetterlund (Ulrika), Pierre Lindstedt (Arvid), Hans Alfredson (Jonas Petter), Ulla Smidje (Danjel's Wife)

p, Bengt Forslund; d, Jan Troell; w, Jan Troell, Bengt Forslund (based on the novels of Vilhelm Moberg); ph, Jan Troell (Technicolor); ed, Jan Troell; m, Erik Nordgren; art d, P.A. Lundgren, Berndt Fritiof; cos, Ulla-Britt Soderlund

AAN Best Foreign Language Film ; AAN Best Picture; AAN Best Director: Jan Troell; AAN Best Actress: Liv Ullmann; AAN Best Adapted Screenplay: Jan Troell, Bengt Forslund

An engaging, well-crafted film about a group of Swedish peasants who migrate to America in the mid-19th century. One of the best films to show the tribulations, bravery and faith of the people who helped build this country. The film is split into three parts: the departure from Sweden, the voyage over and the journey to Minnesota. The acting is superb by all cast members, but some might be put off by the film's length. The tone is lyrical, and the photography (by director Troell) gives an added dimension. Nominated by the Academy for Best Foreign Film of 1971, it also earned nominations for Best Picture, Best Actress, Best Direction and Best Screenplay in 1972. The sequel is THE NEW LAND.

EMMA
1996 120m c   Romance/Historical/Comedy   ★★★½
Matchmaker Films/Haft Entertainment/Miramax   PG
(U.K./U.S.)

Gwyneth Paltrow (Emma Woodhouse), Toni Collette (Harriet Smith), Alan Cumming (Mr. Elton), Jeremy Northam (Mr. Knightley), Ewan McGregor (Frank Churchill), Greta Scacchi

(Mrs. Weston), Juliet Stevenson (Mrs. Elton), Polly Walker (Jane Fairfax), Sophie Thompson (Miss Bates), Edward Woodall (Robert Martin)

p, Patrick Cassavetti, Steven Haft; d, Douglas McGrath; w, Douglas McGrath (based on the novel by Jane Austen); ph, Ian Wilson; ed, Lesley Walker; m, Rachel Portman; prod d, Michael Howells; art d, Sam Riley, Joshua Meath Baker; fx, Effects Associates; chor, Sue Lefton; cos, Ruth Myers

AA Best Original Musical or Comedy Score: Rachel Portman; AAN Best Costume Design: Ruth Myers

This third adaptation of a Jane Austen novel to reach the big screen within a year's passage can rightly be considered "the Americanization of *Emma.*" With a wonderfully comic cast featuring Gwyneth Paltrow, EMMA has plenty of humor and charm, but will pique Austen's ardent fans.

In the village of Highbury, Emma Woodhouse (Paltrow) is the pretty and wealthy mistress of her domain, an insular world of strict social etiquette. Kind-hearted Emma bestows her charity on the town's poor, but in the opinion of Mr. Knightley (Jeremy Northam), her brother-in-law, Emma is a meddling know-it-all because she fancies herself a matchmaker without peer. Emma convinces her friend, Harriet Smith (Toni Collette), to refuse the proposal of one Robert Martin (Edward Woodall), a humble but kind farmer, and set her sights on the Reverend Elton (Alan Cumming). Unbeknownst to Emma, the Reverend has his sights set on *her*. Meanwhile, Emma finds herself attracted to the dashing Frank Churchill (Ewan McGregor), who pays altogether too much attention to Jane Fairfax (Polly Walker). When Harriet becomes infatuated with Mr. Knightley, it arouses such jealousy in Emma that she realizes her *own* love for the gentleman.

Writer and first-time director Douglas McGrath (who co-wrote 1994's BULLETS OVER BROADWAY) empasizes *Emma's* humor and downplays the darker motifs of folly and pain arising from class and gender oppression. The elaborate dance of Austen's narrative becomes mere fodder for a high-minded date movie. The luminous Paltrow nevertheless deserves praise for her excellent performance. Her Emma is at once innocent and poised, elegant and funny. Unfortunately, McGrath omits the politely destructive hubris that gives complexity to Emma's character and depth to Austen's novel.

EMMANUELLE   **DVD**
1974 105m c   Erotic/Drama   ★★½
Trinacre/Orphee   (France)   R

Sylvia Kristel (Emmanuelle), Alain Cuny (Marco), Daniel Sarky (Jean), Jeanne Colletin (Ariane), Marika Green (Bee), Christine Boisson (Marie-Ange)

p, Yves Rousset-Rouard; d, Just Jaeckin; w, Jean-Louis Richard (based on the book by Emmanuelle Arsan); ph, Richard Suzuki; ed, Claudine Bouche

One of the classics of soft-core erotic cinema, EMMANUELLE stars Sylvia Kristel as the title creature, the pretty wife of a French ambassador in Bangkok. It's not long before Emmanuelle discovers a burning sexual passion she has heretofore repressed. With the help of an attractive young teenager, Emmanuelle is exposed (literally) to the joys of eroticism. Although the film takes itself far too seriously and engages in much of the usual naughty Victoriana, it is a relatively well-made picture that became an international hit because of its appeal to both men and women. Many sequels followed (the first being EMMANUELLE 2, released in the U.S. as EMMANUELLE—THE JOYS OF A WOMAN) with Mia Nygren taking over the lead in 1984's EMMANUELLE 4. The Kristel-Nygren EMMANUELLE series (spelled with two "m"s) should not be confused with Laura Gemser's EMANUELLE (with one "m") films.

EMPEROR AND THE ASSASSIN, THE *DVD*
(JING KE CI QIN WANG)
1999 161m c Historical/War/Drama ★★★★
Nippon Development and Finance/Le Studio R
Canal Plus/Maxmedia/Pricel/Shin Corp/New
Wave/Beijing Film Studio/China Film Coproduction
(China/Japan/France)

Gong Li (*Lady Zhao*), Zhang Fengyi (*Jing Ke*), Li Xuejian (*Ying Zheng, King of Qin*), Sun Zhou (*Dan, Prince of Yan*), Lu Xiahoe (*General Fan Yuqi*), Wang Zhiwen (*Marquis Changxin*), Chen Kaige (*Lu Buwei*), Gu Yongfei (*Queen Mother*), Zhao Benshan (*Gao Jianli*), Ding Haifeng (*Qin Wuyang*)

p, Shirley Kao, Satoru Iseki, Han Sanping; d, Chen Kaige; w, Wang Peigong, Chen Kaige; ph, Zhao Fei; ed, Zhou Xinxia; m, Zhao Jiping; prod d, Tu Juhua, Lin Qi; art d, Yang Shudong; fx, Liu Shaochun; cos, Mo Xiaomin, Huang Qiuping

A grand, old-fashioned historical epic—massive sets, a cast of thousands, and enough star power to set it all ablaze—with a subject to match: the third century B.C. unification of China under the iron fist of Yin Zheng, King of Qin, who gained an empire but lost his soul.

Sworn to uphold the mandate of his ancestors, Yin Zheng (Li Xuejian) embarks on a brutal campaign to unite all seven Chinese kingdoms. His sights are set on the northern Yan kingdom, and Zheng's devoted lover, Lady Zhao (Gong Li), suggests he hire a Yan assassin to stage an attempt on his life; invading Yan would then appear fair retaliation. She offers to hire the killer herself. Lady Zhao has her perfect face branded with the mark of a criminal to make her exile to Yan look convincing, then tries to persuade sword-for-hire Jing Ke (Zhang Fengyi) to "murder" the would-be emperor. But complications arise: Jing Ke has sworn off killing and Zheng, who grows more barbarous by the day, has directed his blood-soaked army to lay siege to Lady Zhao's own beloved kingdom.

After the baroque psychological melodrama of TEMPTRESS MOON, writer-director Chen Kaige returned to the epic scale of FAREWELL MY CONCUBINE with this, one the most expensive independently produced Asian films. Every *yuan* is on the screen, from the elaborately staged battle sequences to a meticulous attention to historical detail that would put James Cameron to shame. Inevitably, the sheer size of the production dwarfs the human drama. But Chen wisely stages the action in grand, Shakespearean terms and lines up a knockout group of larger-than-life stars who can rival the sets in sheer stature.

EMPEROR JONES, THE *DVD*
1933 80m bw Drama ★★★★
Krimsky/Cochran (U.S.)

Paul Robeson (*Brutus Jones*), Dudley Digges (*Smithers*), Frank C. Wilson (*Jeff*), Fredi Washington (*Undine*), Ruby Elzy (*Dolly*), George Haymid Stamper (*Lem*), Jackie Mayble (*Marcella*), Blueboy O'Connor (*Treasurer*), Brandon Evans (*Carrington*), Taylor Gordon (*Stick-Man*)

p, John Krimsky, Gifford Cochran; d, Dudley Murphy; w, DuBose Heyward (based on the play by Eugene O'Neill); ph, Ernest Haller; ed, Grant Whytock; m, Frank Tours, J. Rosamond Johnson; art d, Herman Rosse

This fascinating—if rather stiff—production of the brooding Eugene O'Neill play showcases Paul Robeson as Brutus Jones, his most forceful and memorable film role.

Jones, a newly hired railroad porter, is first shown admiring himself before a mirror in his new uniform. His rich baritone voice makes him stand out as he booms out a moving hymn in church. Jones is clearly a man who thinks very highly of himself. This false pride proves to be his undoing. He goes on to cheat on his fiancee and fool around with his best friend's girlfriend. He deserts her and later enters a crap game where he stabs his friend to death. He gets sentenced to a chain gang for life.

He escapes and eventually ends up in Haiti where he meets Smithers (Dudley Digges), an unscrupulous trader who uses Jones to keep the natives in line. Jones is so feared by the natives, whom he has fooled into believing that he is immortal, that he becomes rich as Smithers's partner. In a short time, he unseats the native king and declares himself emperor, ruling the land with an iron fist.

Robeson is the main attraction here and he is well supported by the sleazy Digges (the only white actor in an otherwise all-black cast). Robeson's powerful presence, particularly through his wonderful, mellifluous voice, dominates each scene. There was never any doubt about Robeson playing the role of the vainglorious Jones; a distinguished athlete and Columbia Law School graduate, he deferred his entry into the New York bar when O'Neill himself persuaded Robeson to star in a production of *The Emperor Jones*.

EMPEROR'S CLUB, THE *DVD*
2002 115m c Drama ★★★
Sidney Kimmel Entertainment/Longfellow PG-13
Pictures/Liveplanet Productions/Beacon Pictures/
Universal (U.S.)

Kevin Kline (*William Hundert*), Emile Hirsch (*Sedgewick Bell*), Steven Culp (*Older Martin Blythe*), Embeth Davidtz (*Elizabeth*), Patrick Dempsey (*Older Luis Masoudi*), Joel Gretsch (*Older Sedgewick Bell*), Edward Herrmann (*Headmaster Woodbridge*), Rob Morrow (*James Ellerby*), Harris Yulin (*Senator Bell*), Paul Dano (*Martin Blythe*)

p, Marc Abraham, Andrew Karsch; d, Michael Hoffman; w, Neil Tolkin (based on the short story "The Palace Thief," by Ethan Canin); ph, Lajos Koltai; ed, Harvey Rosenstock; m, James Newton Howard; prod d, Patrizia Von Brandenstein; art d, Dennis Bradford; fx, Syd Dutton, Bill Taylor, Bill Traynor; cos, Cynthia Flynt

It looks and sounds a lot like DEAD POETS SOCIETY, but beneath James Newton Howard's swollen score and the last-minute flood of sentimentality lies a bitter tale of moral compromise and failed conviction that remains faithful to Ethan Canin's "The Palace Thief," the short story on which Michael Hoffman's film is based.

Soon after retiring from teaching ancient history at St. Benedict's, the prestigious Southern prep school where tomorrow's movers and shakers receive the best education money can buy, William Hundert (an excellent Kevin Kline) is presented with an odd request. Sedgewick Bell (Joel Gretsch), a former student who's now the CEO of a major U.S. corporation, is organizing a school reunion at his company's luxurious country retreat and requests the pleasure of Hundert's company. The occasion: a rematch of the "Mr. Julius Caesar" contest, a Roman history competition held each year at St. Benedict's and presided over by Hundert. Thirty years earlier, Bell lost the laurels to a fellow student, and now he'd like to reclaim his "intellectual honor." But as the film flashes back to the early 1970s, we see that honor and intellect had little to do with it.

"You can't step into the same river twice"; "Man's character is his fate"—the screenplay is peppered with enough quotes from Herodotus and Heraclitus to ensure that the moral won't go unnoticed. But it's refreshing that there's any moral at all. Despite its warm and fuzzy trappings, the film floats actual ideas and sprinkles serious questions of ethics and morality atop the usual Hollywood syrup.

EMPEROR'S NEW GROOVE, THE   **DVD**
2000　75m　c　Animated/Musical/Children's　★★★★
Walt Disney Pictures　　(U.S.)　　　　　　　G

VOICES OF: David Spade *(Kuzco/Kuzco Llama)*, John Goodman *(Pacha)*, Eartha Kitt *(Yzma)*, Patrick Warburton *(Kronk)*, Wendie Malick *(Chicha)*, Eli Russell Linnetz *(Tipo)*, Kellyann Kelso *(Chaca)*, Robert Bergen *(Bucky)*, Tom Jones *(Theme Song Voice)*, Patti Deutsch *(Waitress)*

p, Randy Fullmer; d, Mark Dindal; w, David Reynolds (from a story by Chris Williams and Mark Dindal); ed, Pamela Ziegenhagen-Shefland; m, John Debney; prod d, Paul Felix; art d, Colin Stimpson, Thomas Cardone; fx, Mauro Maressa; anim, Joseph C. Moshier, Nik Ranieri, Bruce W. Smith, Dale Baer, Tony Bancroft, Doug Frankel, James Lopez, Brian Ferguson, Sandro Lucio Cleuzo, Dominique Monfery

AAN Best Original Song: "My Funny Friend and Me"; Sting, David Hartley

The spirit of Chuck Jones's classic Warner Bros. cartoons lives again—ironically at Disney, the studio whose nice 'n' sweet theatrical 'toons once represented everything the rebellious WB animators avoided. Like the best Bugs Bunny—Daffy Duck confrontations, this is a rapid-fire parade of smart-aleck wit, self-reflexive playing to the audience, and imaginatively sustained extended gags.

In a mythical, Inca-like land, the fun-loving yet monstrously self-centered teenaged emperor, Kuzco (voice of David Spade), summons village leader Pacha (John Goodman) to the palace for a little bad news: Kuzco plans on demolishing Pacha's village to make way for a summer palace. Meanwhile, Kuzco's ambitious advisor, Yzma (Eartha Kitt), is attempting to run things behind his back, and when Kuzco dares to fire her, Yzma plots her revenge. With the help of her easily distracted right-hand man, Kronk (the pitch-perfect Patrick Warburton), Yzma attempts to poison her boss, but due to a labeling error, Kuzco is instead turned into a talking llama and winds up at the home of Pacha and his family. Pacha strikes a deal: he'll lead Kuzco back safely through the treacherous jungle if Kuzco will break ground somewhere else.

What follows is an uproarious reluctant-buddy comedy, with plot turns that pay such homage to Warner Bros. cartoon conventions that those giant trampolines might as well say "Acme" on them. This wonderful addition to the Disney canon began—and almost ended—as "Kingdom of the Sun," a *Prince and the Pauper*-like romantic drama. With reportedly one-third completely animated and, by most accounts, not clicking, Disney gave the filmmakers two weeks to either rework it or cease production entirely. The phoenix-from-the-ashes result is a stroke of comic genius.

EMPIRE OF THE SUN   **DVD**
1987　152m　c　War　　　　　　★★★½
Amblin　(U.S.)　　　　　　　　PG

Christian Bale *(Jim Graham)*, John Malkovich *(Basie)*, Miranda Richardson *(Mrs. Victor)*, Nigel Havers *(Dr. Rawlins)*, Joe Pantoliano *(Frank Demerest)*, Leslie Phillips *(Maxton)*, Masato Ibu *(Sgt. Nagata)*, Emily Richard *(Jim's Mother)*, Rupert Frazer *(Jim's Father)*, Peter Gale *(Mr. Victor)*

p, Steven Spielberg, Kathleen Kennedy, Frank Marshall; d, Steven Spielberg; w, Menno Meyjes (uncredited), Tom Stoppard (based on the novel by J.G. Ballard); ph, Allen Daviau (Technicolor); ed,

Michael Kahn; m, John Williams; prod d, Norman Reynolds; art d, Charles Bishop, Fred Hole, Maurice Fowler, Huang Qia Gui, Norman Dorme; fx, Kit West, David Watkins, Ye Mao Gen, Antonio Parra, Industrial Light & Magic

AAN Best Cinematography: Allen Daviau; *AAN Best Film Editing:* Michael Kahn; *AAN Best Original Score:* John T. Williams; *AAN Best Art Direction-Set Decoration:* Norman Reynolds (Art Direction), Harry Cordwell (Set Decoration); *AAN Best Costume Design:* Bob Ringwood; *AAN Best Sound:* Robert Knudson, Don Digirolamo, John Boyde, Tony Dawe

This adaptation of J.G. Ballard's quasi-autobiographical novel witnesses WWII through a child's eyes, and does so through a visual means more akin to silent than to modern filmmaking. Spielberg's vision is no longer one of innocent wonderment; instead, EMPIRE OF THE SUN concerns the end of innocence—a young boy thrown into adulthood and an entire generation thrown into an atomic age.

The film opens just before the Japanese attack on Pearl Harbor in 1941. Jim Graham (Christian Bale) is a nine-year-old English brat who has lived all his life in Shanghai with his aristocratic parents. Although adventurous, he is also wholly dependent on his parents and servants. Later, as the Japanese conquer Shanghai and the war intensifies, he is separated from his parents and meets Basie (John Malkovich), an opportunistic merchant seaman reminiscent of Dickens's Fagin, who somewhat reluctantly takes Jim under his wing and teaches him the most Darwinian methods of survival—lessons that help Jim endure a lengthy stay in a Japanese prison camp.

The most emotionally complex film of Steven Spielberg's career, EMPIRE OF THE SUN is not a traditional blockbuster. In fact, with its unknown lead, barely known supporting cast and near-plotlessness, it breaks Hollywood's rules. Further, Spielberg has adapted an admired but little-read novel, set it in far-off Shanghai, and made his lead character a Briton who idolizes the Japanese. As Jim, Bale delivers a stunning performance; he appears in virtually every frame and truly seems to grow over the course of the film from a coddled rich child to a calculating, almost feral creature who will ally himself with whoever wields the most power in a given situation.

Working on a grand canvas in the tradition of the David Lean epics, Spielberg includes several of his own distinctive visual epiphanies but the usual sense of wonder threatens to slide into madness. Spielberg also displays a progressive and sophisticated awareness of issues of class and race that may be viewed as an apology for the casual imperialist and racist assumptions of his INDIANA JONES series.

EMPIRE STRIKES BACK, THE   **DVD**
1980　124m　c　Science Fiction　　★★★★
Fox　(U.S.)　　　　　　　　　　PG

Mark Hamill *(Luke Skywalker)*, Harrison Ford *(Han Solo)*, Carrie Fisher *(Princess Leia Organa)*, Billy Dee Williams *(Lando Calrissian)*, Anthony Daniels *(C-3P0)*, David Prowse *(Darth Vader)*, Peter Mayhew *(Chewbacca)*, Kenny Baker *(R2-D2)*, James Earl Jones *(Voice of Darth Vader)*, Frank Oz *(Yoda)*

p, Gary Kurtz; d, Irvin Kershner; w, Leigh Brackett, Lawrence Kasdan (based on a story by George Lucas); ph, Peter Suschitzky (Panavision, Deluxe Color); ed, Paul Hirsch; m, John Williams; prod d, Norman Reynolds; art d, Leslie Dilley, Harry Lange, Alan Tomkins; fx, Brian Johnson, Richard Edlund, Dennis Muren, Bruce Nicholson; cos, John Mollo

AAN Best Score: John Williams; *AAN Best Art Direction-Set Decoration:* Norman Reynolds, Leslie Dilley, Harry Lange, Alan Tomkins, Michael Ford; *AA Best Sound:* Bill Varney, Steve Maslow, Gregg Landaker, Peter Sutton; *AA Special Achievement*

Award—Visual Effects: Brian Johnson, Richard Edlund, Dennis Muren, Bruce Nicholson

Considered by many the best entry in the series, the second chapter of the STAR WARS trilogy finds the evil Darth Vader (David Prowse and the voice of James Earl Jones) aiding the emperor in his attempts to crush the rebellion dedicated to halting the Empire's domination of the universe. The rebel forces are on the ice planet Hoth and the evil empire sends troops to wipe them out. Forced to flee, Han Solo (Harrison Ford) and Princess Leia (Carrie Fisher) regroup in Cloud City, which is run by the roguish Lando Calrissian (Billy Dee Williams). Meanwhile, Luke Skywalker (Mark Hamill) searches for and finds Yoda (the voice of Frank Oz), a wise little creature who teaches him the finer points of the Force. The whole thing climaxes in a showdown between Luke and Darth Vader, the revelation of some surprising plot twists, and a cliffhanger ending.

After the phenomenal success of STAR WARS, creator George Lucas retired from directing and hired veteran Kershner to direct and the great Leigh Brackett (THE BIG SLEEP, RIO BRAVO, EL DORADO, THE LONG GOODBYE) to write the screenplay with an assist from a new kid on the block, Lawrence Kasdan. Financially, Lucas could afford to push the special effects envelope even further this time. The result is a darker, richer, and more elaborate film than the original; it suffers most from being just what it is: a middle chapter with no real ending. The film's final cliffhanger may prove upsetting to youngsters, since the dark side of the Force has the upper hand, but it's dramatically correct, setting the stage for the triumphant return of Good in part three, RETURN OF THE JEDI.

ENCHANTED APRIL

1991   101m   c   Romance/Comedy   ★★½
Miramax   (U.K.)   PG

Josie Lawrence *(Lottie Wilkins)*, Miranda Richardson *(Rose Arbuthnot)*, Joan Plowright *(Mrs. Fisher)*, Polly Walker *(Lady Caroline Dester)*, Alfred Molina *(Mellersh Wilkins)*, Jim Broadbent *(Frederick Arbuthnot)*, Michael Kitchen *(George Briggs)*, Neville Phillips *(Vicar)*, Stephen Beckett *(Jonathan)*, Mathew Radford *(Patrick)*

p, Ann Scott; d, Mike Newell; w, Peter Barnes (based on the novel by Elizabeth Von Arnim); ph, Rex Maidment; ed, Dick Allen; m, Richard Rodney Bennett; prod d, Malcolm Thornton; cos, Sheena Napier

AAN Best Supporting Actress: Joan Plowright; *AAN Best Adapted Screenplay:* Peter Barnes; *AAN Best Costume Design:* Sheena Napier

ENCHANTED APRIL sets out to celebrate the liberating effects of an Italian vacation on four troubled English women—a gentle, low-budget blend of A ROOM WITH A VIEW and THELMA & LOUISE. But this paper-thin drama, directed by Mike Newell (DANCE WITH A STRANGER) and adapted from the 1921 novel by Elizabeth von Arnim, fails to achieve the sense of magical transformation for which it strives.

Lottie Wilkins (Josie Lawrence) is a downtrodden middle-class wife with a vaguely mystical ability to "see *into* people." Captivated by a newspaper ad offering a month in an Italian villa, she senses that her neighbor Rose Arbuthnot (Miranda Richardson) is equally in need of a getaway and—though the two have never before spoken—enlists her as a traveling partner. To save money, they bring along haughty widow Mrs. Fisher (Joan Plowright) and society beauty Lady Caroline Dester (Polly Walker). Once ensconced by the sea in

the admittedly charming villa, these four women undergo transformations as unconvincing as they are predictable.

Everything about ENCHANTED APRIL is half-baked, from its stock characters, to its occasional gestures toward slapstick and farce, to its throwaway mysticism. The whole thing seems like it was dreamed up during a sleepy afternoon by the Italian seaside, and is guaranteed to put viewers into a similarly soporific state.

ENCHANTED COTTAGE, THE

1945   91m   bw   Romance   ★★★½
RKO   (U.S.)

Dorothy McGuire *(Laura Pennington)*, Robert Young *(Oliver Bradford)*, Herbert Marshall *(John Hillgrave)*, Mildred Natwick *(Abigail Minnett)*, Spring Byington *(Violet Price)*, Richard Gaines *(Frederick)*, Hillary Brooke *(Beatrice Alexander)*, Alec Englander *(Danny)*, Mary Worth *(Mrs. Stanton)*, Josephine Whittell *(Canteen Manager)*

p, Harriet Parsons; d, John Cromwell; w, DeWitt Bodeen, Herman J. Mankiewicz (based on the play by Arthur Wing Pinero); ph, Ted Tetzlaff; ed, Joseph Noriega; m, Roy Webb; art d, Albert S. D'Agostino, Carroll Clark; fx, Vernon L. Walker; cos, Edward Stevenson

AAN Best Score (Drama or Comedy): Roy Webb

This sensitive, touching film, based on the classic romance play by Pinero, is beautifully enacted by McGuire and Young as the uncommon lovers. Oliver (Young) is the embittered, disfigured WWI veteran obsessed with suicide, the only alternative, he feels, to coping with an ugliness that repels everyone. He meets the shy and plain Laura (McGuire), a woman also shunned by society. They marry and move into seclusion inside a small New England cottage, all that's left of a great estate which burned down years earlier. As a honeymoon cottage scores of happy lovers have carved their initials on its windowpanes; its owner (Natwick) knows well the legend of its wonderful spell. Slowly Oliver regains his handsome countenance and Laura blossoms into a beautiful young woman. It is, of course, their mutual love which has brought about these astounding transformations, images shattered by mindless friends.

An unforgettable fable for all who have found beauty in another person, the film does a remarkable job of sidestepping the maudlin and convincingly argues that "beauty is in the eye of the beholder." Pinero's intent, to write about the triumph of love over adversity, is as fully preserved in this version as it was in its original 1922 stage production and 1924 silent film, starring Richard Barthelmess and May McAvoy. Young and McGuire underplay roles that would doubtless have been more histrionically delivered in less able hands. This 1945 remake also benefits from subtle makeup, a stirring score by Webb, innovative lensing by Tetzlaff and a literate screenplay by Mankiewicz and Bodeen.

END OF THE AFFAIR, THE

1999   109m   c   Romance/Drama   ★★★½
Columbia   (U.S./U.K.)   R

Ralph Fiennes *(Maurice Bendrix)*, Julianne Moore *(Sarah Miles)*, Stephen Rea *(Henry Miles)*, Ian Hart *(Mr. Parkis)*, Jason Isaacs *(Father Smythe)*, Samuel Bould *(Lance Parkis)*, Deborah Findlay *(Miss Smythe)*, James Bolam *(Mr. Savage)*, Simon Turner *(Doctor Gilbert)*, Heather Jay Jones *(Henry's Maid)*

p, Neil Jordan, Stephen Woolley; d, Neil Jordan; w, Neil Jordan (based on the novel by Graham Greene); ph, Roger Pratt; ed, Tony Lawson; m, Michael Nyman; prod d, Anthony Pratt; art d, Jon Billington, Tony Woollard; cos, Sandy Powell

AAN Best Actress: Julianne Moore; *AAN Best Cinematography:* Roger Pratt

Irish director Neil Jordan's extremely English adaptation of Graham Greene's autobiographical novel is the kind of movie that either makes you weep or laugh. In a story of adulterous wartime love that devastates all involved, people still manage to behave frightfully well while behaving badly.

The year is 1939. England is at war, and ordinary lives are lived in the liberating shadow of death. Novelist Maurice Bendrix (Ralph Fiennes) falls in love at first sight with Sarah Miles (Julianne Moore). The rub is her husband, civil servant Henry (Steven Rea); he's a nice enough fellow—loyal, steady, and trusting—but all wrong for Sarah. When Maurice invites them both to see a movie he's written, workaholic Henry demurs but insists Sarah go and have fun. She does, and soon Sarah and Maurice are embroiled in a passionate affair facilitated by wartime turmoil; air raids become nothing but an excuse for them to steal away to each other. But one afternoon a bomb hits Maurice's building; he's nearly killed, and Sarah breaks off their relationship abruptly. Years later, a chance encounter with Henry reawakens Maurice's still tumultuous feelings; he hires a private investigator to follow Sarah and eventually learns what led her to abandon him so brutally.

Jordan's film rests on three excellent performances, of which the most difficult is Stephen Rea's. Where Henry could easily be ridiculous, Rea gives him a certain doggy dignity—you can actually like him without hating Maurice and Sarah. Grand passions aside, the story's delights are in the details, notably Maurice's unlikely camaraderie with the working-class investigator (Ian Hart) who reports primly on Sarah's behavior, careful to point out situations that imply "intimacy" with other men.

END OF THE CENTURY: THE STORY OF THE RAMONES

2004　110m　c/bw Documentary　　📀 ★★★½
Chinagraph/Gugat Films　(U.S.)

Joey Ramone, Dee Dee Ramone, Johnny Ramone, Tommy Ramone, Marky Ramone, Legs MacNeil, Danny Fields, Rodney Bingenheimer, Deborah Harry, Joe Strummer

p, Jim Fields, Michael Gramaglia; d, Jim Fields, Michael Gramaglia; ph, David Bowles, Jim Fields, John Gramaglia, Michael Gramaglia, Peter Hawkins; ed, Jim Fields, John Gramaglia

Why did pop-punk pioneers the Ramones get no respect, ask Michael Gramaglia and Jim Fields in this exhaustive documentary. The back-to-basics band played faster and louder than anyone else on the mid-'70s scene and wrote catchy melodies that evoked '60s bubble-gum hits. Joe Strummer of the Clash asserts that if it hadn't been for their 1976 London gigs, there would have been no Clash, no Stranglers, no Sex Pistols. Core members Jeff Hyman, John Cummings, and John Calvin—rechristened Joey, Johnny, and Dee Dee Ramone—all grew up in working-class Forest Hills, Queens. They had little in common except music; in a smiley-faced era of sappy love songs and overproduced prog-rock noodling, fans of the MC5 and the Stooges stuck together. Shy, sickly Joey was a gawky misfit tormented by obsessive-compulsive disorder, hard-driving Johnny was aging out of juvenile delinquency, and sweet-natured Calvin was just drifting. Along with guitarist Tommy Ramone (née Erdelyi), the Ramones are a lean, mean, amp-busting machine. They started arguing as soon as the band formed in 1974, only stopping when they weren't speaking to each other. Even though their tightly crafted pop songs received virtually no radio airplay, the Ramones stuck it out for 21 years, maintaining a punishing touring schedule and surviving personnel changes that would have scuppered a less professional group before calling it quits in 1995. By the time they were finally inducted into the Rock

and Roll Hall of Fame in 2002, Joey was dead of cancer and Dee Dee was two months away from a fatal heroin overdose (Johnny would die in 2004). Though occasionally repetitive, Gramaglia and Fields's admirably evenhanded documentary gives the Ramones the respect they deserve; fans will be grateful, and the uninitiated should listen and learn.

ENEMY OF THE STATE

1998　128m　c　Action/Thriller　　📀 ★★★
Scott Free/Jerry Bruckheimer Films/Touchstone　　R
Pictures　(U.S.)

Will Smith *(Robert Clayton Dean),* Gene Hackman *(Brill),* Jon Voight *(Thomas Brian Reynolds),* Lisa Bonet *(Rachel Banks),* Regina King *(Carla Dean),* Stuart Wilson *(Congressman Albert),* Jason Robards Jr. *(Senator Hammersly),* Jascha Washington *(Eric Dean),* Laura Cayouette *(Christa Hawkins),* Loren Dean *(Hicks)*

p, Jerry Bruckheimer; d, Tony Scott; w, David Marconi; ph, Dan Mindel; ed, Chris Lebenzon; m, Trevor Rabin, Harry Gregson-Williams; prod d, Benjamin Fernandez; art d, James J. Murakami, Jennifer A. Davis, Donald B. Woodruff; fx, The Mill; cos, Marlene Stewart

A sleek young meritocrat stands in the lobby of a swank hotel, squirming as his credit cards are repeatedly, inexplicably declined. Welcome to the modern-day version of the classic "naked in a public place" nightmare.

For brash labor advocate Robert Dean (Will Smith), the nightmare's real. One moment he has a perfect life—good job, nice house, beautiful wife (Regina King) and son (Jascha Washington). The next minute, he runs into old school acquaintance Zavitz (Jason Lee), and everything changes. Zavitz has accidentally filmed some men in black murdering a U.S. senator (Jason Robards) for a high-level NSA muckety-muck (Jon Voight). Zavitz surreptitiously drops the evidence into Dean's shopping bag and accepts his business card, leading the NSA to believe the two are in cahoots. They turn their considerable resources to the task of ruining Dean, and suddenly his house has been vandalized, his phones tapped, his clothes wired, his credit destroyed, and his credibility—not to mention his marriage—compromised. And the NSA's army of techno-geeks (cyber slackers who treat the whole business like one big video game) is watching his every move. Enter Dean's last, best hope: Brill (Gene Hackman), a former NSA operative with a bone to pick with the Big Brother society.

Hackman is clearly reprising his role from THE CONVERSATION, and purists may squirm at seeing Francis Ford Coppola's cold-as-ice exploration of paranoia and alienation quoted so liberally in what is, at heart, a pop thriller. Tony Scott's wild ride of a film may be flashy, but it's not dead stupid and it's never dull.

ENFORCER, THE

1951　87m　bw　Crime　　📀 ★★★½
United States (U.S.)

Humphrey Bogart *(Martin Ferguson),* Zero Mostel *(Big Babe Lazich),* Ted de Corsia *(Joseph Rico),* Everett Sloane *(Albert Mendoza),* Roy Roberts *(Capt. Frank Nelson),* Lawrence Tolan *(Duke Malloy),* King Donovan *(Sgt. Whitlow),* Bob Steele *(Herman),* Adelaide Klein *(Olga Kirshen),* Don Beddoe *(Thomas O'Hara)*

p, Milton Sperling; d, Bretaigne Windust; w, Martin Rackin; ph, Robert Burks; ed, Fred Allen; m, David Buttolph; art d, Charles H. Clarke

Based on the 1940 revelations of Abe Reles regarding the existence of an organized crime group called Murder Inc., but inspired by the Kefauver Committee investigations of 1950, this raw drama can be viewed as a key transitional film between the noir ethos of the 1940s and crime syndicate obsessed 1950s.

Reveling in the lingo of the murder business with its talk of "contracts," "hits" and "fingers," this was the first film to deal with the mysterious structures of organized crime.

The film begins with a brief prologue by Senator Estes Kefauver, the head of the crime investigation committee, explaining the burning need to bring criminals to justice. Joseph Rico (De Corsia), head of the syndicate's professional murder squad, has been brought in and put under protective custody after agreeing to testify against crime czar Albert Mendoza (Sloane). Martin Ferguson (Bogart), the district attorney, has spent four years building his case against Mendoza and, with Rico's testimony, he'll be able to send him to the electric chair for mass murder. However, Rico, in terror, escapes and falls to his death. Ferguson seeks to find some tiny clue in the bulk of evidence so as to save his case.

This powerful crime drama was shot in stark black and white by frequent Hitchcock collaborator Robert Burks and directed with a quick, crisp style by Windust. Reportedly some of the film's footage had to be restaged by action veteran Raoul Walsh. Though he is uncredited, Walsh's imprint is apparent as he establishes the semidocumentary approach that proved so successful in his WHITE HEAT. Rackin's script is tough, even brutal, in depicting the slaughterhouse deeds of the worst gang of killers ever to intimidate America.

ENGLISH PATIENT, THE
1996 162m c Romance/Drama   ★★★
Saul Zaentz/Miramax   (U.K./U.S./Italy)   R

Ralph Fiennes (Almasy), Juliette Binoche (Hana), Willem Dafoe (Caravaggio), Kristin Scott Thomas (Katharine Clifton), Naveen Andrews (Kip), Colin Firth (Geoffrey Clifton), Julian Wadham (Madox), Kevin Whately (Hardy), Clive Merrison (Fenelon-Barnes), Nino Castelnuovo (D'Agostino)

p, Saul Zaentz; d, Anthony Minghella; w, Anthony Minghella (based on the novel by Michael Ondaatje); ph, John Seale; ed, Walter Murch; m, Gabriel Yared; prod d, Stuart Craig; art d, Aurelio Crugnola; fx, Richard Conway, Dennis Lowe; cos, Ann Roth

AA Best Picture; AA Best Director: Anthony Minghella; AA Best Supporting Actress: Juliette Binoche; AA Best Art Direction: Stuart Craig, Stephenie McMillan; AA Best Cinematography: John Seale; AA Best Sound: Walter Murch, Mark Berger, David Parker, Chris Newman; AA Best Original Dramatic Score: Gabriel Yared; AA Best Costume Design: Ann Roth; AA Best Film Editing: Walter Murch; AAN Best Actor: Ralph Fiennes; AAN Best Actress: Kristin Scott Thomas; AAN Best Adapted Screenplay: Anthony Minghella

THE ENGLISH PATIENT, winner of nine Academy Awards, is a sweeping story of love, war, and adultery set in Italy and North Africa.

In 1938, a cartographic expedition to the Sahara Desert includes Hungarian Count Laszlo Almasy (Ralph Fiennes) and English newlyweds Katharine (Kristin Scott Thomas) and Geoffrey Clifton (Colin Firth). Almasy and Katharine begin a torrid affair. After war has erupted, Geoffrey learns of their liaison and tries to kill them all by crashing his plane. He dies and Katharine is badly injured, but Almasy is able to carry her to a cave and promises to return. By the time he does, Katharine has died; he flies off with her body, but is shot down by military fire. Horribly burned and near death, Almasy is placed by the Allies in a ruined Italian monastery where he is cared for by Hana (Juliette Binoche), a Canadian nurse. Sharing the monastery are Kip (Naveen Andrews), a Sikh British army lieutenant, and Caravaggio (Willem Dafoe), a former thief and Allied spy.

Rather than telling its story chronologically, THE ENGLISH PATIENT jumps back and forth from the present to the past. While this keeps the story from flagging, it never really soars either, mainly because its principal characters are so passive: things happen to them. The supporting roles suffer

too, from Caravaggio's anticlimactic decision to abort his mission, to Hana and Kip's aimless romance, which simply peters out. Ralph Fiennes displays some of the sly wit of late Olivier in his portrayal of the mortally burned Count. To some extent, THE ENGLISH PATIENT is a victim of its own good taste. Apart from the crystalline photography of John Seale, an appealing turn by Andrews, and Juliette Binoche's exquisite complexion, the picture doesn't give its viewers much to remember.

ENIGMA OF KASPAR HAUSER, THE
(JEDER FUR SICH UND GOTT GEGEN ALLE)
1975 110m c Biography   ★★★★
ZDF/Werner Herzog   (West Germany)

Bruno S. (Kaspar Hauser), Walter Ladengast (Daumer), Brigitte Mira (Kathe), Hans Musaus (Unknown Man), Willy Semmelrogge (Circus Director), Michael Kroecher (Lord Stanhope), Henry van Lyck (Calvary Captain), Enno Patalas (Pastor Fuhrmann), Elis Pilgrim (Pastor), Volker Prechtel (Hiltel, the Prison Guard)

p, Werner Herzog; d, Werner Herzog; w, Werner Herzog; ph, Jorg Schmidt-Reitwein (Eastmancolor); ed, Beate Mainka-Jellinghaus; m, Johann Pachelbel, Tomaso Albinoni, Orlando DiLasso, Wolfgang Amadeus Mozart; prod d, Henning V. Gierke; cos, Gisela Storch, Ann Poppel

The winner of the Grand Jury Award at the 1975 Cannes Film Festival, this haunting and, at times, disconcertingly whimsical film helped to propel the self-styled visionary New German filmmaker, Werner Herzog, to international prominence.

Herzog's slow and meditative films are fairly unique in contemporary narrative cinema. Landscapes and music are at least as important as the human characters in his work. His protagonists tend to be obsessive dreamers compelled to action by the power of their visions—with consequences that are sometimes transcendental, sometimes disastrous. At their most excessive, Herzog's films can be regressive, reactionary, self-indulgent and naively romantic; at their best, they are dreamily hypnotic, mystical and awe-inspiring in their beauty. THE ENIGMA OF KASPAR HAUSER happily falls in the latter category.

The film is based on the documented story of a young man, Kaspar Hauser (Bruno S.), who, after living in a cellar for years with only a pet rocking horse, is abandoned by his protector and provider, the mysterious Man in Black. Having been isolated from all humans except his godlike "father," Kaspar is suddenly thrust into civilization. Though at first he can barely walk and cannot speak, he is expected to readily adapt to 19th-century society. His past remains a mystery to the townspeople, as does his purpose. Some teach him the mannerisms of the civilized, while others spy on his every move attempting to uncover some hidden identity. Untainted by society, Kaspar functions as a natural man in this repressed and repressive society. His very existence calls their assumptions into question.

Many consider this, along with AGUIRRE: THE WRATH OF GOD, to be Herzog's best film. Bruno S. is of particular interest here. A non-professional actor, Mr. S. is an eccentric German street performer who spent much of his childhood in mental institutions. He also stars in Herzog's STROSZEK.

ENTER THE DRAGON
1973 99m c Action/Martial Arts   ★★★
Concord Productions Inc./Warner Bros.   (U.S.)   R

Bruce Lee (Lee), John Saxon (Roper), Jim Kelly (Williams), Shih Kien (Han), Bob Wall (Ohara), Anna Capri (Tania), Angela Mao Ying (Su Lin), Betty Chung (Mei Ling), Geoffrey Weeks (Braithwaite), Bolo Yeung, billed as Yang Sze (Bolo)

p, Jerry Weintraub, Paul M. Heller, Raymond Chow; d, Robert Clouse; w, Michael Allin; ph, Gilbert Hubbs (Technicolor, Panavision widescreen); ed, Kurt Hirschler, George Watters; m, Lalo Schifrin; art d, James Wong Sun

If you have a yen for spectacular chopsocky action, this is as good a flick to start with as any. The legendary Bruce Lee is showcased in his most lavish adventure—though, as this was made in Hong Kong after all, it still feels like a low-rent James Bond thriller crossed with Fu Manchu.

The plot barely rates relating but here goes: Lee (Bruce Lee) is recruited by a government agent, Braithwaite (Weeks), to enter a martial arts contest on the island fortress of Han (Shih), a particularly vicious chap with a nasty iron claw who is believed to be involved in drug smuggling and prostitution. Lee agrees because he knows that Han's right-hand man, Oharra (Wall), is responsible for his sister's death (she committed suicide rather than be raped by him).

On the island he meets Roper (Saxon) and Williams (Kelly), ex-army buddies from the U.S., on the run, respectively, from the mob and the law. Lee tries to infiltrate Han's underground chamber but fails, beating up a number of guards in the process. The next morning Han orders the men who let the intruder escape to fight Bolo (Sze), who kills them all easily. But enough plot... let it suffice to say that the only compelling reason to sit through this film is to see the greatest martial arts star of all time.

Lee proves why he is still the dominant legend in the genre more than a decade after his death. During one fight scene, Lee performed a flying kick so fast it couldn't be captured on film at 24 frames a second. The cameraman had to film the sequence in slow motion to get it to look like it wasn't faked. Nobody shows much evidence of acting ability, and the script is full of holes. Nonstop action is what these films are about, and that's what you get here.

ENTERTAINER, THE   DVD
1960 96m   bw   Drama   ★★★★
Woodfall   (U.K.)

Laurence Olivier (Archie Rice), Brenda de Banzie (Phoebe Rice), Joan Plowright (Jean), Roger Livesey (Billy), Alan Bates (Frank), Daniel Massey (Graham), Albert Finney (Mick Rice), Miriam Karlin (Soubrette), Shirley Ann Field (Tina), Thora Hird (Mrs. Lapford)

p, Harry Saltzman; d, Tony Richardson; w, John Osborne, Nigel Kneale (based on the play by Osborne); ph, Oswald Morris; ed, Alan Osbiston; m, John Addison; art d, Ralph Brinton, Ted Marshall; cos, Barbara Gillett

AAN Best Actor: Laurence Olivier

"Life is a beastly mess," states the great Olivier in this bleak drama of moral stagnation. He's Archie Rice, a third-rate vaudevillian who, in garish makeup, delivers his creaky song and dance routines before increasingly scarce and indifferent audiences. Rice's home life is as shabby as his stage career. Phoebe (De Banzie), his loyal wife, has been driven to alcoholism and fits of hysteria by her husband's selfishness and infidelities. His father, Billy (Livesey), the star of THE LIFE AND DEATH OF COLONEL BLIMP, a once famous entertainer, is dying, yet Archie prevails upon him to back just one more tawdry musical revue. Only Jean (Plowright), his protective daughter, tries to meet Olivier's emotional needs but at the cost of her own professional and personal fulfilment. Archie is an incorrigible liar and self-promoter whose raging ego demands that he be admired by one and all even if it means destroying the lives of those around him.

This depressing but fascinating film is another Olivier tour de force; he later claimed this role, which he had perfected on the London stage, really reflected his own personality, telling an interviewer that "it had the advantage of being a complete break from the other sort of work and that made it much more refreshing than tormenting oneself through these punishing roles of Shakespeare. I have an affinity with Archie Rice. It's what I really am. I'm not like Hamlet."

The rest of the cast is stunning, particularly newcomer Plowright and veteran De Banzie (HOBSON'S CHOICE),

though Albert Finney and Alan Bates are also memorable as Archie's sons. Scripters Osborne and Kneale present a gloomy and penetrating adaptation of Osborne's play. Richardson's direction of this unhappy little gem gives off the appropriate dull glimmer while being economical and inventive.

ENTERTAINING MR. SLOANE
1969 94m   c   Comedy   ★★★★
Canterbury   (U.K.)

Beryl Reid (Kath), Peter McEnery (Mr. Sloane), Harry Andrews (Ed), Alan Webb (Dada Kemp)

p, Douglas Kentish; d, Douglas Hickox; w, Clive Exton (based on the play by Joe Orton); ph, Wolfgang Suschitzky (Technicolor); ed, John Trumper; m, Georgie Fame; prod d, Michael Seymour; cos, Emma Porteous

Entertaining Mr. Audience. You can tell something offbeat is taking place right at the start, with the hefty, garishly dressed Kath (Reid) licking a popsicle while observing a funeral. Spotting the handsome, blonde Mr. Sloane (McEnery) sunning himself on a nearby tombstone, she asks him to move into her home and sets about seducing him. Her brother Ed (Andrews), a closeted homosexual, entertains similar notions, outfitting his new chauffeur stud in leather from head to toe. Their father (Webb), a retired grave-digger, recognizes Sloane as the man who killed his former boss, a pornographer. Dada accuses the enigmatic youth of murder and Sloane calmly kicks him to death. Ed and Kath, now pregnant, threaten to tell the police what happened unless Sloane swears eternal allegiance to them. The film ends with three remarkable ceremonies all rolled into one.

Adapted from Joe Orton's hilarious play, which won the London Drama Critics Award in 1964 but which folded on Broadway after only 13 performances, ENTERTAINING MR. SLOANE is full of morbid humor and grotesque touches. In other words, the film is an almost constant delight, going out of its way to shock whenever possible. The tiny cast achieves a remarkable range of complex emotions and diverse moods, with Reid and Andrews especially superb. Not a film for everybody, granted, but a fine one nonetheless.

ENTRAPMENT   DVD
1999 110m   c   Thriller/Adventure/Romance   ★★★½
Fountainbridge Films/Michael Hertzberg   PG-13
Productions/20th Century Fox/New Regency   (U.S.)

Sean Connery (Mac), Catherine Zeta-Jones (Gin), Ving Rhames (Thibadeaux), Will Patton (Cruz), Maury Chaykin (Conrad Greene), Kevin McNally (Haas), Terry O'Neill (Quinn), Madhav Sharma (Security Chief), David Yip (Chief of Police), Tim Potters (Millennium Man)

p, Rhonda Tollefson, Michael Hertzberg, Sean Connery; d, Jon Amiel; w, William Broyles, Ronald Bass; ph, Phil Meheux; ed, Terry Rawlings; m, Christopher Young; prod d, Norman Garwood; art d, Jim Morahan; fx, Neil Corbould; chor, Paul Harris; cos, Penny Rose

A star-driven, globe-trotting exercise in finely crafted absurdity, this glossy thriller is a throwback to the glory days of caper movies like TOPKAPI and ARAB-ESQUE, with a healthy dollop of THE THOMAS CROWN AFFAIR.

A Rembrandt is stolen from a high-rise Manhattan office building, a velvet Elvis left in its place. Ace insurance investigator Virginia "Gin" Baker (Catherine Zeta-Jones) attributes the daring heist to legendary thief Robert "Mac" MacDougal (Sean Connery), and persuades her boss (Will Patton) to let her set a trap. The beguiling Gin flies to England and persuades Mac to join her in the theft of a priceless Chinese mask, hinting that if they work well together, she has an even bigger score in mind.

But it soon becomes clear that nothing is as it seems: is Gin a cop or a thief, or both? And does she have the supremely suave Mac fooled, or is he playing his own little game?

Make no mistake, the story is nicely spun and held together with the kind of high-tech gadgets that enthrall boys of all ages. But the movie's appeal lies in its performances: Connery's ultra-cool Mac is Bond gone terribly wrong, while Gin is the sleekly modern descendent of every duplicitous beauty who ever glided through a slippery '60s heist thriller clad in head-to-toe Chanel. And yes, Connery's old enough to be Zeta-Jones' grandpa, but the age difference is nicely worked into Mac and Gin's "will they or won't they" flirtation. Ving Rhames and Maury Chaykin fill the obligatory colorful supporting roles, and the film's second half unfolds against the exotic backdrop of Kuala Lumpur, Malaysia, on New Year's Eve 1999. In short, it's the kind of film Hollywood doesn't make any more, and a pleasant retro diversion.

ENTRE NOUS   _DVD_
(COUP DE FOUDRE)
1983 110m c Drama   ★★★★½
Partner's/Alexandre/Hachette Premiere/A2/SFPC (France)

Miou-Miou (Madeleine), Isabelle Huppert (Lena), Jean-Pierre Bacri (Costa), Guy Marchand (Michel), Robin Renucci (Raymond), Patrick Bauchau (Carlier), Jacques Alric (Monsieur Vernier), Jacqueline Doyen (Madame Vernier), Patricia Champane (Florence), Saga Blanchard (Sophie)

p, Ariel Zeitoun; d, Diane Kurys; w, Diane Kurys, Alain Henry (from the book by Kurys, Olivier Cohen); ph, Bernard Lutic (CinemaScope); ed, Joele Van Effenterre; m, Luis Bacalov; prod d, Jacques Bufnoir; cos, Mic Cheminal

AAN Best Foreign Language Film

This autobiographical work from French director Diane Kurys serves as a prequel to PEPPERMINT SODA, her superb 1977 feature debut.

The film opens during the German occupation of France. Lena (Isabelle Huppert), a young Russian Jew, escapes from a prison camp by marrying a stranger, Michel (Guy Marchand). Meanwhile, in Paris, art student Madeleine (Miou-Miou) must start life anew when her husband is brutally gunned down before her. The scene then shifts to Lyons, 1952, for a chance meeting between these two women. Lena is still wed to Michel and is the mother of two children, while Madeleine has remarried. They come to realize that they can only find support from each other and not from their boorish husbands.

A resounding art-house success in the U.S. and Oscar nominee for Best Foreign Film, ENTRE NOUS is an excellent examination of the bond of friendship. Like very few films before it, ENTRE NOUS focuses—with subtle but distinct lesbian undertones—on a female friendship instead of the usual male "buddy" formula. Based in part on the experiences of the director's own mother, this fictionalized account is one of great emotional truth. The relationships between Lena and Madeleine and between the women and their respective families are written, directed, and acted with a touch usually seen only in the films of Renoir, Pagnol or Truffaut. The picture's chief weakness is its sometimes uninvolving episodic structure, beginning with the rocky 1940s prologue that opens the movie. Still, ENTRE NOUS is intelligent, adult cinema.

EQUUS   _DVD_
1977 137m c Drama   ★★★
UA (U.K.)   R

Richard Burton (Dr. Martin Dysart), Peter Firth (Alan Strang), Colin Blakely (Frank Strang), Joan Plowright (Dora Strang), Harry Andrews (Harry Dalton), Eileen Atkins (Magistrate Hesther

Saloman), Jenny Agutter (Jill Mason), John Wyman (The Horseman), Kate Reid (Margaret Dysart), Ken James (Mr. Pearce)

p, Lester Persky, Elliott Kastner; d, Sidney Lumet; w, Peter Shaffer (based on his play); ph, Oswald Morris (DeLuxe Color); ed, John Victor-Smith; m, Richard Rodney Bennett; prod d, Tony Walton; art d, Simon Holland; cos, Tony Walton, Patti Unger, Brenda Dabbs

AAN Best Actor: Richard Burton; AAN Best Supporting Actor: Peter Firth; AAN Best Adapted Screenplay: Peter Shaffer

A reverential and somewhat bumpy film adaptation. Shaffer adapted his own gripping play about a young man, Alan Strang (Firth), who is inexplicably compelled to blind horses. Burton is Dr. Martin Dysart, the psychiatrist who realizes that Alan's religious fervor is the key to the mystery. Alan's devout mother, Dora Strang (Plowright), has supplied the confused youth with a thwarted view of life that has resulted in his behavior. The court appoints Dr. Dysart to get to the bottom of the reasons for Alan's deeds and he learns much about himself in the process.

This is a fairly convincing rendition of a real psychiatrist-patient relationship. Burton confirms his status as a master thespian as he begins to take stock of his own life in the pressure-cooker of his work with Firth. He's extremely intense albeit in a particularly actorly way. Firth's performance is technically flawless but it is periodically interrupted by scenes in which the dumbfounded camera simply observes him nude. Veteran director Lumet's work here is earnest yet unimaginative. He does his best with what is still essentially a filmed play. Shaffer's words are often smart and incisive but the film could have done with a few less of them.

ERASERHEAD
1976 89m bw Fantasy/Horror   ★★★★
AFI (U.S.)

Jack Nance (Henry Spencer), Charlotte Stewart (Mary X), Allen Joseph (Mr. X), Jeanne Bates (Mrs. X), Judith Anna Roberts (Beautiful Girl Across the Hall), Laurel Near (Lady in the Radiator), V. Phipps-Wilson (Landlady), Jack Fisk (Man in the Planet), Jean Lange (Grandmother), Thomas Coulson (The Boy)

p, David Lynch; d, David Lynch; w, David Lynch; ph, Frederick Elmes, Herbert Cardwell; ed, David Lynch; m, Peter Ivers (Lady in the Radiator song); prod d, David Lynch; fx, David Lynch

Disturbing, repulsive, hilarious, frightening, sensitive and challenging, David Lynch's ERASERHEAD has been aptly described by its creator as a "dream of dark and troubling things," namely fatherhood.

A young man, Henry Spencer (Nance), living in a dilapidated apartment building in an industrialized city learns that his girlfriend, Mary X (Stewart), is pregnant. Leaving his room, which seems to be inhabited by spermlike creatures, he visits Mary and her parents—a hyperactive father with a passion for synthetic meat and a mother obsessed with her daughter's sexuality. Grandmother sits in the kitchen, stonelike, maybe dead. Mary moves in with Henry and they begin to take care of their "baby"—a deformed, constantly crying mass of tissue and bandages that looks something like a skinned lamb. The infant is repulsive yet fascinating, as well as sad. Its constant whining drives Mary out of the apartment, leaving Henry alone with the baby. After an accidental tragedy, Henry is hurled into the nightmarish world that has existed on the fringes of his "real" world since the beginning of the film.

Five years in the making, ERASERHEAD is not just a film about a man who has nasty dreams. It's a creepily sensuous film that suggests that the "dark and troubling things" we like to repress inhabit dresser drawers, live behind the radiator or lie under the bed. They are part of the environment. This is a nightmare about a man's horror of commitment, sexuality, and adult responsibility. This was the first feature directed by Lynch, a former painter, and it proudly displays its roots in past avant-garde film movements—surrealism and expressionism in particular—while tipping its hat to classic horror films. Lynch has since gone on to become what could be described somewhat paradoxically as the modern Hollywood equivalent of an avant-garde filmmaker but his subsequent career has not lived up to the promise of this extraordinary debut.

ERIN BROCKOVICH   DVD
2000   130m   c   Docudrama   ★★★
Universal/Columbia/Jersey Films   (U.S.)   R

Julia Roberts *(Erin Brockovich)*, Aaron Eckhart *(George)*, Albert Finney *(Ed Masry)*, Marg Helgenberger *(Donna Jensen)*, Cherry Jones *(Pamela Duncan)*, Peter Coyote *(Kurt Potter)*, Scotty Leavenworth *(Matthew)*, Gemmenne De La Pena *(Katie)*, David Brisbin *(Dr. Jaffe)*, Dawn Didawick *(Rosalind)*

p, Danny DeVito, Michael Shamberg, Stacey Sher; d, Steven Soderbergh; w, Susannah Grant; ph, Ed Lachman; ed, Anne V. Coates; m, Thomas Newman; prod d, Phil Messina; art d, Christa L Munro ; fx, Kevin Hannigan, Tom Smith (Visual), Cinesite (Digital); cos, Jeffrey Kurland

AA Best Actress: Julia Roberts; *AAN Best Picture; AAN Best Actor:* Albert Finney; *AAN Best Director:* Steven Soderbergh; *AAN Best Original Screenplay:* Susannah Grant

This entertaining—if predictable—vehicle for the blinding smile that is Julia Roberts is essentially NORMA RAE brought up to date, which means the beleaguered title character, a twice-divorced mother of three with scant prospects, is a funny, foul-mouthed force of nature who always lands on her feet.

We discover this fairly early, as Erin (Roberts) guilt-trips lawyer Ed Masry (the amazing eyebrows that are Albert Finney) into giving her a job, despite her complete lack of legal expertise. While working for Masry, Erin stumbles upon some medical records placed, mysteriously, in certain real estate files. Confused, she convinces Ed to let her investigate and discovers a cover-up: contaminated water is the cause of devastating illnesses suffered by the residents of a small local town. With the help of her too-good-to-be-true biker boyfriend (Aaron Eckhart); the initially reluctant Ed, who'd been planning to retire; and the initially reluctant townspeople, who don't believe they have any real recourse, Erin winds up participating in one of the largest ($333 million) successful lawsuits in U.S. history.

There are a couple of bogus red herrings en route to the never-in-doubt happy ending, but ultimately the story seems rather slight. That's partly because a good vs. evil saga needs interesting villains, and all this movie can come up with is a briefly glimpsed bunch of weasely Pacific Gas and Electric lawyers. Still, Erin is a great character, and Roberts—who seems to be having the time of her life—makes the most of her.

ESCAPE FROM ALCATRAZ   DVD
1979   112m   c   Prison   ★★★½
Paramount   (U.S.)   PG

Clint Eastwood *(Frank Morris)*, Patrick McGoohan *(Warden)*, Roberts Blossom *(Doc)*, Jack Thibeau *(Clarence Anglin)*, Fred Ward *(John Anglin)*, Paul Benjamin *(English)*, Larry Hankin *(Charley Butts)*, Bruce M. Fischer *(Wolf)*, Frank Ronzio *(Litmus)*, Fred Stuthman *(Johnson)*

p, Don Siegel; d, Don Siegel; w, Richard Tuggle (based on the book by J. Campbell Bruce); ph, Bruce Surtees (Panavision, DeLuxe Color); ed, Ferris Webster; prod d, Allen Smith

Veteran genre director Don Siegel directed this simple and gripping story about an actual escape from the supposedly escape-proof Alcatraz. Siegel is extremely good at this sort of thing (see his 1954 genre classic, RIOT IN CELL BLOCK 11) and if you like to watch people doing a job, you won't find it done better elsewhere.

The escape-proof "Rock" was designed in the early 1930s to hold the most infamous, incorrigible and escape-prone inmates in the federal prison system. Located in the dead center of San Francisco Bay, Alcatraz played host to Al Capone and Doc Barker, among others, and was considered by J. Edgar Hoover and other federal executives to be the only American prison from which no inmate could ever escape. In 1962, however, Frank Morris and the Anglin brothers did escape, resulting in the institution's closure.

This film is the story of that escape, convincingly enacted by Eastwood as mastermind Morris, a taciturn, calculating man with nerves of steel. Upon Morris's arrival at Alcatraz, he is met by a vain, smug warden (McGoohan) who informs him that he can forget about escaping; it has never been done and never will be done. But as an inmate who has escaped from other prisons, Morris's attitude remains unchanged.

The pace of this movie is a bit slow, but Siegel's deliberate, sparse direction works to the benefit of a film where time is all his characters have. Surprisingly, there are few exciting set pieces and relatively little violence, yet ESCAPE is relentlessly tense. This production marked the fifth time Eastwood worked with Siegel, his directorial mentor.

ESCAPE FROM NEW YORK   DVD
1981   99m   c   Action/Science Fiction   ★★★
Avco Embassy   (U.S.)   R

Kurt Russell *(Snake Plissken)*, Lee Van Cleef *(Bob Hauk)*, Ernest Borgnine *(Cabby)*, Donald Pleasence *(The President)*, Isaac Hayes *(Duke of New York)*, Season Hubley *(Girl in Chock Full O'Nuts)*, Harry Dean Stanton *(Brain)*, Adrienne Barbeau *(Maggie)*, Tom Atkins *(Rehme)*, Charles Cyphers *(Secretary of State)*

p, Debra Hill, Larry Franco; d, John Carpenter; w, John Carpenter, Nick Castle; ph, Dean Cundey (Panavision, Metrocolor); ed, Todd Ramsay; m, John Carpenter, Alan Howarth; prod d, Joe Alves; cos, Stephen Loomis

A futuristic thriller set in 1997, John Carpenter's ESCAPE FROM NEW YORK finds Snake Plissken (Kurt Russell)—an ex-war hero, now convict—forced to rescue the President (Donald Pleasence) from a plane crash in New York City. The U.S. is now a police state, and Manhattan has become one vast prison in which convicts are summarily dumped and left to fend for themselves. If Snake fails to find the President in time, he'll be atomized by a time bomb implanted in his neck by ruthless Bob Hauk (Lee Van Cleef). Snake sallies forth into this dark world and experiences violent battles, narrow escapes, and white-knuckle adventures, enlisting an anachronistic cabbie (Ernest Borgnine) in his struggle to outwit a criminal mastermind played by Isaac Hayes. A generally gripping actioner, the film can also be read as a percipient satire of a society irreparably split along lines of class and race. Carpenter's clever premise has since become fodder for innumerable straight-to-video cheapies. A "director's edition," featuring some 15 minutes of footage cut from the original theatrical release, appeared on video in 1994.

ETERNAL MASK, THE
1937   74m   bw   Drama   ★★★★
Progress   (Switzerland)

Peter Petersen *(Prof. Tscherko)*, Mathias Wieman *(Dr. Dumartin)*, Olga Tschechowa *(Mme. Negar)*, Tom Kraa *(Dr. Wendt)*, Thekla Ahrens *(Sister Anna)*, Franz Schafheitlin *(Mons. Negar)*

d, Werner Hochbaum; w, Leo Lapaire (based on the novel by Leo Lapaire); ph, Oscar Schnirch, Anton Profes; art d, Hans Jacoby

This eerie psychological drama evokes memories of the early German expressionist films. Wieman is a young physician who believes he has concocted a cure for meningitis, but he is ordered not to try it out by the chief of the facility where he works. One of his patients is terminal, so Wieman gives him the serum against orders. At first, the patient seems to be improving, but then takes a bad turn and dies.

Wieman leaves the hospital, and a sequence begins in which the audience is never certain what is real and what is fantasy. The sets commence to change subtly as Wieman feels his life as a doctor is over. He haunts the streets, and everything around him becomes increasingly stylistic as he goes deeper into psychotic depression. He throws himself off a bridge and plunges into a river. After he's rescued, he is almost totally incapacitated and lives his life almost solely within his mind, running down mental corridors, hiding behind mental doorways, but never actually moving. The hospital chief discovers that the serum actually does work, and he must now approach Wieman, who is the only person who knows the formula.

If this film were only technique, it would remain a cine-matic exercise and little more, but the power of the film lies in a combination of Hochbaum's directorial vision and Lapaire's sympathetic screenplay. Sometimes jerky, sometimes agoniz-ingly slow, THE ETERNAL MASK builds to a satisfying conclusion, and the entire experience is unforgettable.

ETERNAL SUNSHINE OF THE SPOTLESS MIND 🔲 DVD
2004 108m c Comedy/Fantasy ★★★★
Blue Ruin/This Is That Productions/ R
Anonymous Content (U.S.)

Jim Carrey *(Joel Barish)*, Kate Winslet *(Clementine Kruczynski)*, Kirsten Dunst *(Mary)*, Mark Ruffalo *(Stan)*, Elijah Wood *(Patrick)*, Tom Wilkinson *(Dr. Howard Mierzwiak)*, Jane Adams *(Carrie)*, David Cross *(Rob)*, Thomas Jay Ryan *(Frank)*, Deirdre O'Connell *(Hollis)*

p, Anthony Bregman, Steve Golin; d, Michel Gondry; w, Charlie Kaufman (from a story by Charlie Kaufman, Michel Gondry, and Pierre Bismuth); ph, Ellen Kuras; ed, Valdís Óskarsdóttir; m, Jon Brion; prod d, Dan Leigh; art d, David Stein; fx, Martin Garner (computer), Drew Jiritano, Louis Morin (visual); cos, Melissa Toth; anim, Brent Ekstrand

Acclaimed video director Michel Gondry's mind-blowing fantasy, based on another outrageously audacious script by Charlie Kaufman (BEING JOHN MALKOVICH, ADAP-TATION.), is almost enough to restore your faith in Hollywood. Not only is it formally innovative, but it's terrifi-cally entertaining to boot.

The unwieldy title is taken from Alexander Pope's poem "Eloisa to Abelard," in which the heroine, stuck in a convent and pining for her love, envies the fellow nuns who, unaware of love and heartache, bask in the "eternal sunshine of the spotless mind." Such ignorant bliss is now enjoyed by Clementine Kruczynski (an extraordinary Kate Winslet), who, thanks to the innovations of Lacuna Inc., has had every last memory of her ex-boyfriend, Joel Barish (Jim Carrey), wiped from her brain. The procedure is simple: After creating a map of their clients' minds, Lacuna technicians Stan (Mark Ruffalo) and Patrick (Elijah Wood) target the bothersome memories of their sleeping clients and eradicate them. In a fit of heartbroken pique, Joel decides to have Clementine erased from *his* mind, but once he's asleep, things go haywire. Stan parties with his girlfriend, Lacuna receptionist Mary (Kirsten Dunst), and Patrick is off wooing the vulnerable Clementine. In short, no one's paying much attention to what's happening inside Joel's head. Joel has decided that he no longer wants to go through with the procedure, and is frantically racing across the landscape of his mind, searching for a place to hide one small memory of the woman he still loves.

The movie slides back and forth between what's happen-ing inside Joel's head and the outside world; the effect is dis-orienting and exhilarating. It's a brilliant piece of visionary filmmaking and for once, Carrey is more than merely tolera-ble, he's actually good, and the film that ebbs and flows around him is something you won't soon forget.

EUREKA 🔲 DVD
2000 217m c/bw Drama ★★★★
Suncent Cinema Works/Les Films de l'Observatoire/ Dentsu/Imagica/Tokyo Theaters/J Works (Japan)

Koji Yakusho *(Makoto Sawai)*, Aoi Miyazaki *(Kozue Tamura)*, Masaru Miyazaki *(Naoki Tamura)*, Yohichiroh Saitoh *(Akihiko)*, Sayuri Kokusho *(Yumiko)*, Ken Mitsuishi *(Shigeo)*, Go Riju *(Busjack Man)*, Yutaka Matsushige *(Matsuoka)*, Sansei Shiomi *(Yoshiyuki Sawai)*, Kimie Shingyoji *(Mother)*

p, Takenori Sento; d, Shinji Aoyama; w, Shinji Aoyama; ph, Masaki Tamra; ed, Shinji Aoyama; m, Shinji Aoyama, Isao Yamada; prod d, Takeshi Shimizu

An ambitious, epic treatment of senseless violence and its aftermath from Japanese director Shinji Aoyama.

Early one summer morning, Kozue (Aoi Miyazaki) and her brother Naoki (Masaru Miyazaki) board a public bus. Sometime later, the bus is found in an empty parking lot, its passengers held hostage by a madman with a gun. By the time the stand off with police is over, Kozue, Naoki, and the bus driver, Makoto (Koji Yakusho), are the only survivors. Unable to cope with the senselessness of both the shootings and his survival, Makoto abandons his family and disappears, while Naoki and Kozue retreat from the outside world. Two years later, Makoto returns and moves in with Naoki and Kozue, who are now living on their own in their parents' house. Their cousin, Akihiko (Yohichiroh Saitoh), arrives for a month long visit. He, too, has had a close brush with death, and Makoto devises a strategy by which they can all reclaim their lives: a lengthy road trip in a refurbished bus that begins in the blood-stained parking lot. As Makoto prepares for their odyssey, he becomes the prime suspect in a series of murders. His only excuse—"I had no reason to kill that woman"—carries little weight in a world in which the most appalling acts of violence occur for no reason whatsoever.

SPEED this ain't. Clocking in at a cool 217 minutes, the story moves at the pace critics like to call "leisurely." But it's never dull; it's beautifully acted and handsomely shot in sepia-toned Cinemascope. But while the running time works as a narrative strategy, it begins to feel like an indulgence that tests the profundity of its subject matter. What stands as a great film at just under four hours might have been a master-piece at three.

EUROPA, EUROPA 🔲 DVD
1991 110m c Biography/War/Historical ★★★★
Les Films du Losange/CCC Filmkunst/ R
Perspektywa Unit (France/Germany)

Marco Hofschneider *(Young Solomon Perel)*, Julie Delpy *(Leni)*, Andre Wilms *(Robert Kellerman)*, Solomon Perel *(Himself)*, Aschley Wanninger *(Eric)*, Rene Hofschneider *(Isaak Perel)*, Piotr Kozlowski *(David Perel [Solomon's Brother])*, Klaus Abramowsky *(Solly's Father)*, Michele Gleizer *(Solly's Mother)*, Marta Sandrowicz *(Berta [Solomon's Sister])*

p, Margaret Menegoz, Artur Brauner; d, Agnieszka Holland; w, Agnieszka Holland, Paul Hengge (from the book *Memoires* by Solomon Perel); ph, Jacek Petrycki; ed, Ewa Smal, Isabelle

Lorente; m, Zbigniew Preisner; prod d, Allan Starski; fx, Jacek Jelinski; cos, Wieslawa Starska, Malgorzata Stefaniak

---

AAN Best Adapted Screenplay: Agnieszka Holland

Agnieszka Holland's fascinating, richly realized EUROPA, EUROPA is based on the real-life story of Solomon Perel, one of a handful of Jews who ironically managed to survive the Nazi terror by masquerading as Aryans.

Solomon Perel (Marco Hofschneider) was born in Germany, near Braunschweig, to German-speaking Polish-Jewish parents in 1925. (He shares a birthday—April 20th—with Adolf Hitler.) In the opening scene, the baby Solomon is circumcized—an ironic beginning to a story that will revolve around Solomon's attempts to conceal his lack of a foreskin. Solly grows up to be a handsome, engaging youth who does not look particularly Jewish. On the eve of Solomon's bar mitzvah, his family's home is attacked by a Nazi mob. Solly saves himself by diving from the bathroom window and hiding in an empty barrel. The family then flee to Poland, where they are separated during the German invasion of September 1939.

Solly makes his way into Soviet-occupied Poland and winds up in an orphanage near Grodno, where he undergoes a seemingly painless transformation into a Young Pioneer. Although there are hints of the Stalinist terror, they are eclipsed by the German attack on Russia, during which Solly is picked up by the invaders. By virtue of his impeccable German and his claim to be among Poland's ethnic German minority, the Volksdeutsche, Solly escapes the winnowing out of Communist Party members and Jews being conducted by German troops. Since he also speaks Russian, Solly is immediately adopted by an advance Wehrmacht squad as their translator, under his false name of Josef Peters, or "Jupp."

Solly's inner tension is expressed in the form of wonderfully surreal dreams, where Stalin and Hitler waltz together and a fellow orphan appears as a crucified Christ. In one nightmare he hides in a closet with Hitler, whose pose suggests he, too, is concealing the same secret that Solly does. Holland, a frequent collaborator of Andrzej Wajda (she wrote the screenplays for DANTON, A LOVE IN GERMANY and KORCZAK), also directed BITTER HARVEST and TO KILL A PRIEST. Her screenplay covers much of the range of anti-Semitism in Hitler's Germany, whether the airy intellectual sort or the bloody-minded kind. Also familiar with the love-hate relations between Poles and Russians, Holland has not skirted the harmful effects of the Soviet occupation. The most poignant sequence is a recreation of the Warsaw ghetto familiar to viewers from Nazi newsreels, glimpsed by Solly through a chink in the white-washed window of a tram that passes through this forbidden zone.

EUROPA, EUROPA is a compelling story told with intelligence and wit. Holland's direction, and the acting by the ensemble cast, are superb. The real-life Solomon Perel makes an appearance as himself in the present day.

EVER AFTER 🄳🅅🄳

1998 121m c Romance/Historical ★★★
20th Century Fox (U.S.) PG-13

Drew Barrymore *(Danielle)*, Anjelica Huston *(Baroness Rodmilla)*, Dougray Scott *(Prince Henry)*, Jeanne Moreau *(Grande Dame)*, Jeroen Krabbe *(Auguste)*, Patrick Godfrey *(Leonardo da Vinci)*, Megan Dodds *(Marguerite)*, Melanie Lynskey *(Jacqueline)*, Timothy West *(King Francis)*, Judy Parfitt *(Queen Marie)*

p, Mireille Soria, Tracey Trench; d, Andy Tennant; w, Susannah Grant, Andy Tennant, Rick Parks; ph, Andrew Dunn; ed, Roger Bondelli; m, George Fenton; prod d, Michael Howells; art d, Martyn John, Damien LaFranchi, Stephen Dobric; fx, Alan Senior, John Clark; cos, Jenny Beavan

Once upon a time there was a feisty young woman who didn't sit around twiddling her pretty thumbs and singing "Someday My Prince Will Come." That's the revisionist spin on this Cinderella story, and it twirls very nicely.

Poor orphaned Danielle (Drew Barrymore), a 16th-century French girl who loses her beloved father and gains a just-short-of-wicked stepmother and two horrid stepsisters on the same awful day. Her widowed father (Jeroen Krabbe), a free thinker who encouraged Danielle to read, speak her mind, and treat all people as equals, has a fatal heart attack shortly after marrying the elegant Baroness Rodmilla (Anjelica Huston), a social climber who longs for the glamour and intrigue of court society. Left to Rodmilla's less-than-tender mercies, Danielle is treated as a servant by stepsisters Marguerite (Megan Dodds), a stuck-up beauty, and plump, graceless Jacqueline (Melanie Lynskey), and spends her days cleaning and tending livestock. But Danielle still catches the eye of rebellious Prince Henry (Dougray Scott), who's in the market for a bride. Unfortunately, she does so while in disguise and while Baroness Rodmilla is doing her damnedest to promote Marguerite as the most marriageable girl in town.

This isn't the classic "Cinderella;" it's an eclectic mix that ditches magic spells in favor of a message of self-reliance, and tosses in everything from the Mona Lisa (Leonardo da Vinci, who's visiting the French court, acts as Danielle's benevolent protector) to a glass slipper from Ferragamo, then tops it off with Jeanne Moreau. As the *grande dame* who commands the movie's framing story, she advises the Brothers Grimm that she's very fond of their collection of folk stories, but they got that Cinderella business all wrong. "How do you begin these tales?" she asks in her cigarettes-and-whiskey voice. "Ah, yes, once upon a time… "

EVERY MAN FOR HIMSELF

(SAUVE QUI PEUT—LA VIE)
1980 87m c Drama ★★★★
Sonimage/Sara/MK2/Saga (France)

Isabelle Huppert *(Isabelle Riviere)*, Jacques Dutronc *(Paul Godard)*, Nathalie Baye *(Denise Rimbaud)*, Anna Baldaccini *(Isabelle's Sister)*, Fred Personne *(1st Costumer)*, Roland Amstutz *(2nd Costumer)*, Nicole Jaquet *(Woman)*, Dore DeRosa *(Elevator Attendant)*, Monique Barscha *(Opera Singer)*, Cecile Tanner *(Paul's Daughter)*

p, Alain Sarde, Jean-Luc Godard; d, Jean-Luc Godard; w, Jean-Claude Carriere, Anne-Marie Mieville; ph, William Lubtchansky, Renato Berta; ed, Marie Mieville, Jean-Luc Godard; m, Gabriel Yared; art d, Romain Goupil

---

After years of Maoist polemics and made-for-TV obscurities, Jean-Luc Godard marked his return to relatively accessible cinema with a film that explores money, prostitution, masculine violence, and the relationship between sound and image—all familiar Godardian concerns. For the first time since 1972's TOUT VA BIEN (which featured Yves Montand and Jane Fonda), Godard elected to use stars in his film, casting Isabelle Huppert as a high-priced Swiss hooker who caters to some notably bizarre tastes. An especially memorable scene shows Huppert servicing her businessman clients in an elaborate sexual daisy chain—a kind of Rube Goldberg sex machine that figures the mechanization of desire under capitalism. One of the film's alternate titles, SLOW MOTION, is derived from Godard's recurrent use of stretch-printed/freeze-framed images. At this point in Godard's career, his desire to use stars in ways critical of stardom coincided aptly with his choice of subject matter, especially in the never-made THE STORY, a gangster film about Hollywood that was to have been shot at Coppola's Zoetrope Studios with Robert De Niro, Diane Keaton, and Marlon Brando. Unfortunately, this never made it past the storyboard stage.

EVERYONE SAYS I LOVE YOU

1996 97m c Musical/Comedy ★★½
Sweetland Films (U.S.) R

Woody Allen *(Joe)*, Julia Roberts *(Von)*, Goldie Hawn *(Steffi)*, Tim Roth *(Charles Ferry)*, Alan Alda *(Bob)*, David Ogden Stiers *(Holden's Father)*, Drew Barrymore *(Skylar)*, Lukas Haas *(Scott)*, Natasha Lyonne *(DJ)*, Edward Norton *(Holden)*

p, Robert Greenhut; d, Woody Allen; w, Woody Allen; ph, Carlo Di Palma; ed, Susan E. Morse; prod d, Santo Loquasto; art d, Tom Warren; fx, Connie Brink; chor, Graciela Daniele; cos, Jeffrey Kurland

Woody Allen pays tribute to 1930s Hollywood musicals in this story of romance among New York City's upper crust. What should be a special treat, however, is just another Woody Allen movie with songs thrown in.

DJ (Natasha Lyonne) narrates this tale of her wealthy, extended family—headed by Bob (Alan Alda) and Steffi (Goldie Hawn)—and their life on the Upper East Side of New York City. Her half sister Skylar (Drew Barrymore) gets engaged to mild-mannered Holden (Edward Norton) but finds more romantic interest in Charles (Tim Roth), a lascivious ex-con. While on vacation in Venice, DJ escapes her family's travails and helps her biological father, Joe (Woody Allen), woo Von (Julia Roberts), an unhappily married woman. After much plotting to win her affections, Joe convinces Von to live with him in his garret in Paris.

A flawed, uneven attempt to reproduce Hollywood musical magic, EVERYONE SAYS I LOVE YOU references some of the earliest, most conventional sound musicals, rather than the more experimental MGM pictures of the later "Golden Age." Indeed, the only creative energy comes from the idea of everyday characters breaking into song-and-dance at the drop of a hat—a notion that was used to greater effect in Dennis Potter's "Pennies from Heaven." Old musicals allowed viewers to imagine they could sing and dance like Astaire and Kelly, but no one in this cast would inspire anyone with their tone-deaf renditions of the classic numbers. Allen assembles a talented group of actors only to waste most of them, and he himself seems grafted onto the proceedings. Occasionally, the director comes up with a well-timed gag but mostly passes up the chance to revise or tinker with old forms.

EVIL DEAD, THE

1983 85m c Horror ★★★½
Renaissance (U.S.)

Bruce Campbell *(Ash)*, Ellen Sandweiss *(Cheryl)*, Betsy Baker *(Linda)*, Hal Delrich *(Scott)*, Sarah York *(Shelly)*

p, Robert G. Tapert; d, Sam Raimi; w, Sam Raimi; ph, Tim Philo, Joshua M. Becker (DuArt Color); ed, Edna Ruth Paul; m, Joseph LoDuca; fx, Tom Sullivan, Bar Pierce

Self-promoted as "The Ultimate Experience in Grueling Terror," THE EVIL DEAD marks the directorial debut of what may be the next great practitioner of this eternally disreputable form. Writer-director Sam Raimi and his college pals took the genre by storm with this amazingly assured and exhilarating horror exercise in which narrative and characterization take a backseat to sheer cinematic panache.

Five college students take shelter in an abandoned cabin deep in the woods, where they find a strange book along with a tape explaining that the book is an ancient Sumerian Book of the Dead. The tape translates some of the incantations in the book, and giant demons are unleashed in the woods. One by one the teenagers are taken over by the demons, until only Ash (Bruce Campbell) is left to fight the evil.

Shot in 16mm (and blown up to grainy 35mm) on location in Tennessee and Michigan on a tiny budget of under $400,000,

this film has some undeniable technical limitations—and the acting is less than professional—but Raimi's wildly creative filmmaking turns these limitations into virtues that make THE EVIL DEAD a landmark in recent American horror films.

While it set new standards in outlandish screen gore, it's never really too disturbing due to its old fashioned funhouse feel. Raimi does not aspire to dark satirical social commentary like Romero nor to psychosexual insights like Cronenberg; some boys just wanna have fun. Though genuinely shocking and spooky, the movie has enough sick black humor and deliciously bad special effects to keep all the nightmarish imagery from getting too oppressive. Not for the faint of heart or those uninitiated in the ways of modern horror, it's a hoot for fans of the genre.

EVIL DEAD 2: DEAD BY DAWN

1987 85m c Horror ★★★½
Renaissance (U.S.)

Bruce Campbell *(Ash)*, Sarah Berry *(Annie)*, Dan Hicks *(Jake)*, Kassie Wesley *(Bobby Joe)*, Ted Raimi, billed as Theodore Raimi *(Possessed Henrietta)*, Denise Bixler *(Linda)*, Richard Domeier *(Ed)*, John Peaks *(Prof. Raymond Knowby)*, Lou Hancock *(Henrietta)*

p, Robert Tapert; d, Sam Raimi; w, Sam Raimi, Scott Spiegel; ph, Peter Deming (Technicolor); ed, Kaye Davis; m, Joseph LoDuca; art d, Philip Duffin, Randy Bennett; fx, Mark Shostrom, Vern Hyde, Doug Beswick Productions, Tom Sullivan, Rick Catizone; chor, Susan Labatt, Andrea Brown; Tam G. Warner

Less a sequel than a remake, Ash (Bruce Campbell), the sole survivor of THE EVIL DEAD, seems to have no memory of that film's events. After a high-speed recap and continuation of first film's ending, Ash ventures out to that same lonely cabin for a romantic weekend with his girlfriend (Denise Bixler). There he discovers that darn tape recorder again. When the voice reads a translation of the "Book of the Dead," a vicious evil force awakens in the woods and rushes into the house, and all hell breaks loose once more.

A deliriously cinematic experience for those with a taste for Grand Guignol, this is a relentlessly energetic nightmare world where quite literally *anything* can happen—and does. By pushing the events to an absurd extreme, the film frequently leaves the realm of horror and becomes a cartoon gone mad. Animation director Tex Avery is a stronger influence here than the German Expressionists or modern masters of horror. Campbell's admirably straightfaced performance suggests a modern-day Harold Lloyd trapped in a splatter film spinning madly out of control. He gamely tries to cope with everything the evil spirits hurl at him including bleeding walls, scary monsters, flying eyeballs, a possessed hand, and all manner of bad craziness.

To keep things interesting, the then 26-year-old director employs a myriad of expressive movie tricks including stop-motion animation, impossible point-of-view shots, portentous crane shots, shaky handheld camera sequences, rotating sets, rear projection, distorting anamorphic lenses, weird sound effects and good old-fashioned dramatic lighting. The film is a breathless celebration of the possibilities of the medium. "Good" dramatic narrative values hold little interest for Raimi. The setting and story are merely functional, and most of the dialogue is perfunctory. Maximum visceral impact is what this film is all about—and it delivers.

EVITA

1996 135m c Musical/Biography ★★★
Cinergi Productions/Dirty Hands Productions/ PG
Hollywood Pictures (U.S.)

Madonna *(Eva "Evita" Peron)*, Antonio Banderas *(Che Guevara)*, Jonathan Pryce *(General Juan Domingo Peron)*, Jimmy Nail

(Agustin Magaldi), Victoria Sus (Dona Juana), Julian Littman (Brother Juan), Olga Merediz (Blanca), Laura Pallas (Elisa), Julia Worsley (Erminda), Maria Lujan Hidalgo (Young Eva)

p, Robert Stigwood, Alan Parker, Andrew G. Vajna; d, Alan Parker; w, Alan Parker, Oliver Stone (based on the musical play Evita, lyrics by Tim Rice and music by Andrew Lloyd Webber); ph, Darius Khondji; ed, Gerry Hambling; m, Andrew Lloyd Webber; prod d, Brian Morris; art d, Jean-Michel Hugon, Richard Earl; fx, Yves De Bono; chor, Vincent Paterson; cos, Penny Rose

AA Best Original Song: "You Must Love Me"; Andrew Lloyd Webber (music), Tim Rice (lyrics); AAN Best Art Direction: Brian Morris, Philippe Turlure; AAN Best Cinematography: Darius Khondji; AAN Best Film Editing: Gerry Hambling; AAN Best Sound: Andy Nelson, Anna Behlmer, Ken Weston

Yes, Madonna *is* Eva Peron. Alan Parker's breathlessly paced film version of Andrew Lloyd Webber and Tim Rice's rock-opera bio is all sound and fury, with an admittedly dazzling array of visual treats.

During the 1930s, a young Eva Duarte arrives in Buenos Aires, determined to transcend the dull poverty of her provincial youth. Using whatever connections her increasingly powerful parade of lovers can provide, Eva becomes a successful actress and is soon introduced to the equally ambitious politician Juan Peron (Jonathan Pryce), whom she marries. Eva uses her popularity and poor background to seduce the lower classes and helps Juan secure the presidency, but her efforts to improve living conditions for *los descamisados* are plagued by corruption. Her splashy lifestyle alongside a penchant for self-aggrandizement help earn her considerable hostility both at home and abroad, and "Santa Evita" remains a controversial figure until her death in 1952. Throughout the film, on-screen narrator Che (Antonio Banderas) explicates events and acts as a one-man vox pop, providing the film with its moral point of view.

After two decades of fits and starts, EVITA finally landed in the hands of Alan Parker, one of the few contemporary directors with any musical experience (FAME). Parker is responsible for the film's spectacular look and cunning casting, but his commitments to character and coherent storytelling are comparatively weak. Madonna, however, is just fine: she handles vulnerable ballads like "Another Suitcase in Another Hall" with surprising delicacy and braves some of the somewhat dated score's more ridiculous moments. But despite the film's ample pleasures, it cannot be forgotten that this story is based in fact. Can the rise of fascism be obliterated or even glorified by magnificent set design? It obviously makes little difference to Parker, Webber, and Rice.

EXCALIBUR

1981 140m c Action/Fantasy
Orion (U.S.) R

DVD
★★★

Nigel Terry (King Arthur), Nicol Williamson (Merlin), Nicholas Clay (Lancelot), Helen Mirren (Morgana), Cherie Lunghi (Guenevere), Paul Geoffrey (Perceval), Robert Addie (Mordred), Gabriel Byrne (Uther), Liam Neeson (Gawain), Corin Redgrave (Cornwall)

p, John Boorman; d, John Boorman; w, Rospo Pallenberg, John Boorman (based on Le Morte D'Arthur by Thomas Malory); ph, Alex Thomson (Technicolor); ed, John Merritt; m, Trevor Jones; prod d, Anthony Pratt; art d, Tim Hutchinson; fx, Peter Hutchinson, Alan Whibley; cos, Bob Ringwood

AAN Best Cinematography: Alex Thomson

EXCALIBUR is a grand, clanky, brooding fantasy following Arthurian legend from the young king's anonymous background to his rise as ruler of ancient Britain. Nigel Terry is excellent as a naive, altruistic Arthur; Nicol Williamson camps it up amusingly as Merlin; Guenevere

(Cherie Lunghi) and Lancelot (Nicholas Clay) provide a couple of steamy moments. Excessive but occasionally inspired, EXCALIBUR gives us grimy lumbering knights, gloomy castles, slithering dragons, mesmerizing magic, and (of course) the struggle between good and evil. Excellent makeup and costuming, as well as convincingly rustic Irish location work. Williamson and Helen Mirren, who plays Morgana, seem to understand that the film takes itself a bit too seriously, and do a lot of nudging and winking.

EXECUTIVE SUITE

1954 104m bw Drama ★★★★½
MGM (U.S.)

William Holden (McDonald Walling), June Allyson (Mary Blemond Walling), Barbara Stanwyck (Julia O. Tredway), Fredric March (Loren Phineas Shaw), Walter Pidgeon (Frederick Y. Alderson), Shelley Winters (Eva Bardeman), Paul Douglas (Josiah Walter Dudley), Louis Calhern (George Nyle Caswell), Dean Jagger (Jesse W. Grimm), Nina Foch (Erica Martin)

p, John Houseman; d, Robert Wise; w, Ernest Lehman (based on the novel by Cameron Hawley); ph, George Folsey; ed, Ralph E. Winters; art d, Cedric Gibbons, Edward Carfagno; fx, A. Arnold Gillespie, Warren Newcombe; cos, Helen Rose

AAN Best Supporting Actress: Nina Foch; AAN Best B/W Cinematography: George Folsey; AAN Best Art Direction-Set Decoration (B/W): Cedric Gibbons (Art Direction), Edward C Carfagno (Art Direction), Edwin B Willis (Set Decoration), Emile Kuri (Set Decoration); AAN Best Costume Design (B/W): Helen Rose

A spectacular array of MGM superstars shine in this slick fascinating drama of corporate intrigue. The death of the president of a gigantic furniture firm prompts a series of power plays among the company's executives, all vying for the vacated top position. The jockeying vice presidents are Loren Phineas Shaw (March), Josiah Walter Dudley (Douglas), Frederick Y. Alderson (Pidgeon), George Nyle Caswell (Calhern), and a junior executive, McDonald Walling (Holden). Surveying the candidates is Julia O. Tredway (Stanwyck), the daughter of the manufacturing firm's founder and the mistress of the recently deceased company head. As the chief stockholder as well, her decision will tip the scales.

Director Wise intercuts among the many characters but this strategy actually serves to unify the story and action rather than fragmenting the tale. The drama unfolds from a sparkling, witty, and provocative screenplay by Ernest Lehman adapted from the Cameron Hawley novel. Holden, March, Douglas, Stanwyck, Calhern, Jagger, Foch and Pidgeon are riveting in their parts, even though some, like Stanwyck, are only on camera occasionally. Holden, still building a great career, was reunited with Stanwyck on screen for the first time in 15 years—their last previous work together was in GOLDEN BOY. Critics universally and correctly singled out March as the most impressive performer in the awesome cast. His obsessive villain hasn't a single virtue, only the relentless drive to win at all costs while mouthing the predictable rationale that he is merely practicing "good business." Foch, as the suicidal secretary to the deceased boss, gained an Oscar nomination as Best Supporting Actress.

This was one of the first major films to eschew a continuous musical score; producer Houseman elected to incorporate the sounds of the business world throughout such as when the bells of a Wall Street clock are heard while the cast names roll up on the screen.

EXISTENZ

1999 97m c Science Fiction/Horror ★★★
Natural Nylon/Alliance Atlantis Communications/ R
Serendipity Point Films/Dimension
(U.S./U.K./Canada)

Jude Law *(Ted Pikul)*, Jennifer Jason Leigh *(Allegra Geller)*, Willem Dafoe *(Gas)*, Ian Holm *(Kiri Vinokur)*, Don McKellar *(Yevgeny Nourish)*, Callum Keith Rennie *(Carlaw)*, Sarah Polley *(Merle)*, Christopher Eccleston *(Seminar Leader)*, Robert A. Silverman *(D'Arcy Nader)*, Oscar Hsu *(Chinese Waiter)*

p, David Cronenberg, Robert Lantos, Andras Hamori; d, David Cronenberg; w, David Cronenberg; ph, Peter Suschitzky; ed, Ronald Sanders; m, Howard Shore; prod d, Carol Spier; art d, Tamara Deverell; fx, Jim Isaac; cos, Denise Cronenberg

Once and future king of venereal horror David Cronenberg marshals his trademark obsessions in the service of a creepy tale of corporate espionage and rubber reality.

Twenty minutes into the future, Allegra Geller (Jennifer Jason Leigh), superstar designer of virtual-reality games that download directly into the player's nervous system via a permanent bioport (imagine a phone jack implanted at the base of the spine), prepares to guide a test group through her newest creation, eXistenZ. The demonstration is disrupted by an attempted assassination; Allegra has been marked for death by a fanatical anti-gaming group, and finds herself on the run with a timid marketing trainee named Ted Pikul (Jude Law). Allegra's biomorphic game pod, which contains the only copy of eXistenZ, was damaged by her would-be killer, and she's as concerned with salvaging it as she is with saving her own skin. So she persuades the reluctant Pikul, a gaming virgin, to enter the more-real-than-real world of eXistenZ with her. Soon it's hard to tell where reality ends and the game begins.

Cronenberg's first original screenplay since the seminal VIDEODROME actually feels like a continuation of it: the "temple of the new flesh" has taken root, consumers are entertaining themselves to death, and the new underground is made up of wet blankets who decry the corrosive effect of joyriding down the back roads of the mind. If this new film seems less prescient than its predecessor, it's only because reality is rapidly catching up with Cronenberg's warped imagination. Never a subtle filmmaker, he's nevertheless eerily attuned to the grotesque underside of contemporary cultural trends. How perfect that so flesh-obsessed a filmmaker should evince such a visceral (if you will) distaste for the thrills of virtual-reality gaming.

EXODUS

1960 212m c Historical ★★★★
Preminger (U.S.)

Paul Newman *(Ari Ben Canaan)*, Eva Marie Saint *(Kitty Fremont)*, Ralph Richardson *(Gen. Sutherland)*, Peter Lawford *(Maj. Caldwell)*, Lee J. Cobb *(Barak Ben Canaan)*, Sal Mineo *(Dov Landau)*, John Derek *(Taha)*, Hugh Griffith *(Mandria)*, Gregory Ratoff *(Lakavitch)*, Felix Aylmer *(Dr. Lieberman)*

p, Otto Preminger; d, Otto Preminger; w, Dalton Trumbo (based on the novel by Leon Uris); ph, Sam Leavitt (Super Panavision 70, Technicolor); ed, Louis Loeffler; m, Ernest Gold; art d, Richard Day, Bill Hutchinson; fx, Win Ryder; cos, Joe King, May Walding, Margo Slater, Rudi Gernreich, Hope Bryce

AAN Best Supporting Actor: Sal Mineo; *AAN Best Color Cinematography:* Sam Leavitt; *AA Best Score (Drama or Comedy):* Ernest Gold

A stirring chronicle of Israel's struggle for independence in 1947, EXODUS focuses on Newman as Ben Canaan, the leader of the Haganah, whose affair with Kitty Fremont (Saint) is engulfed by the conflict. The film tackles the independence movement as a whole, dealing with various factions involved in the internecine struggle between the moderate Haganah and the radical terrorist Irgun. Interspersed throughout are segments showing the migration of European Jews to the new land, paying special attention to the ragged survivors of Nazi death camps on board the vessel *Exodus*, blockaded in a Cyprus harbor by British warships. The film also depicts the struggle of the Jews in Palestine to gain partition, then profiles the main characters after the partition, fighting to continue as the nation of Israel.

Under the direction of Otto Preminger, EXODUS boasts strong performances and many memorable sequences including the bombing of the King David Hotel, the capture and subsequent rescue of the Irgun leaders, masterfully handled crowd scenes, and Canaan's moving final speech. Preminger is generally faithful to history and to Leon Uris's best-selling novel; Uris himself was dismissed as the film's screenwriter (Preminger thought he had no gift for screen dialogue), and the filmmakers were necessarily forced to abridge the story to make it cinematically feasible. Though the film is overlong, the story is movingly told, the production values are high, and Ernest Gold's Oscar-nominated score is considered a classic.

EXORCIST, THE

1973 121m c Horror ★★★½
Warner Bros. (U.S.) R

Ellen Burstyn *(Mrs. MacNeil)*, Max von Sydow *(Father Merrin)*, Jason Miller *(Father Karras)*, Lee J. Cobb *(Lt. Kinderman)*, Jack MacGowran *(Burke)*, Kitty Winn *(Sharon)*, Linda Blair *(Regan)*, Vasiliki Maliaros *(Mother Karras)*, Wallace Rooney *(Bishop)*, Titos Vandis *(Karras's Uncle)*

p, William Peter Blatty; d, William Friedkin; w, William Peter Blatty; ph, Owen Roizman, Billy Williams (Metrocolor); ed, Norman Gay, Jordan Leondopoulos, Evan Lottman, Bud Smith; m, Jack Nitzsche; prod d, Bill Malley

AAN Best Picture; AAN Best Actress: Ellen Burstyn; *AAN Best Supporting Actor:* Jason Miller; *AAN Best Supporting Actress:* Linda Blair; *AAN Best Director:* William Friedkin; *AA Best Adapted Screenplay:* William Peter Blatty; *AAN Best Cinematography:* Owen Roizman; *AAN Best Film Editing:* Jordan Leondopoulos, Bud Smith, Evan Lottman, Norman Gay; *AAN Best Art Direction-Set Decoration:* Bill Malley, Jerry Wunderlich; *AA Best Sound:* Robert Knudson, Chris Newman

Extremely controversial at the time of its release, THE EXORCIST kicked off intense debate among critics, community leaders, and even religious leaders—spurring the public, of course, to make it one of the most financially successful horror films ever made.

Regan (Linda Blair), the 12-year-old daughter of a famous stage actress (Ellen Burstyn), begins to suffer unexplainable fits and bouts of bizarre behavior. The girl is brought to doctors, but examinations fail to pinpoint a physical or psychiatric ailment. Regan's condition grows worse, and she begins to transform physically, taking on an ugly, demonic appearance. In desperation, Regan's mother asks the help of a young priest, Father Karras (Jason Miller). Realizing that Regan is possessed by the Devil and knowing that his own faith is too weak for him to deal successfully with the problem himself, Karras turns to Father Merrin (Max von Sydow), an elderly priest who specializes in exorcisms.

Based on William Peter Blatty's runaway best seller (which itself was based upon a reported exorcism in 1949) THE EXORCIST shrewdly exploits the fears and frustrations of parents while disturbing religious implications merely provide portentous window dressing. The film is an intense rollercoaster ride, a marvel of audience manipulation, with director William Friedkin pushing all the right buttons to make this a genre landmark. The movie balances its then-state-of-the-art special effects with good old-fashioned atmospheric horror to produce an excruciating—though shallow—two hours of dread and unease. It's too bad the film failed to get further inside its characters.

EXORCIST: THE BEGINNING
2004 100m c Horror 🎬 ★
Dominion Productions/Morgan Creek Productions/ R
Warner Bros. (U.S.)

Stellan Skarsgard *(Father Lankester Merrin)*, James D'Arcy *(Father William Francis)*, Izabella Scorupco *(Sarah)*, Remy Sweeney *(Joseph)*, Julian Wadham *(Major Granville)*, Andrew French *(Chuma)*, Ralph Brown *(Sergeant Major)*, Ben Cross *(Semelier)*, Patrick O'Kane *(Bession)*, Alan Ford *(Jeffries)*

p, Will Raee, David C. Robinson; d, Renny Harlin; w, Alexi Hawley (from a story by Caleb Carr and William Wisher); ph, Vittorio Storaro; ed, Mark Goldblatt, Todd E. Miller; m, Trevor Rabin; prod d, Stefano Ortolani; art d, Eugenio Ulissi; fx, Danilo Bollettini, Brian M. Jennings, Thomas Mahoney (digital), C. Christian Renteria (digital), Ariel Velasco Shaw; cos, Luke Reichle

Renny Harlin's pokey, blood-spattered prequel tells the early story of disillusioned Father Lankester Merrin—the veteran demon-buster played by Max von Sydow in the original EXORCIST—whose faith was lost in Nazi-occupied Holland and recovered in British postcolonial Africa.

Cairo, 1949: Archeologist Lancaster Merrin (Stellan Skarsgard) is approached by a shady fellow with a remarkable story. A British army regiment has stumbled across what appears to be a sixth-century Byzantine church buried in Kenya's remote Turkana region, where no such church should be. Would Merrin consider recovering the antiquities that surely lie within? Merrin accepts the offer. Accompanied by eager young Father Francis (James D'Arcy), Merrin finds the excavation site fogged with fear. Supervising archeologist Bession (Patrick O'Kane) has gone extravagantly mad. Local laborers believe the church is haunted and won't go inside. Drunken overseer Jeffries (Alan Ford) has developed a disfiguring skin disease, and camp nurse Sarah (Izabella Scorupco) reads tarot cards and frets. Merrin and Father Francis find the church desecrated, and a sweet-faced child (Remy Sweeney) begins having strange, bed-rocking seizures. Could he be *possessed*?

Paul Schrader originally shot a complete film from a script by William Wisher and novelist Caleb Carr and starring Skarsgard, but this isn't it. Executives at Morgan Creek (and, reportedly, Carr) hated Schrader's film and hired action specialist Harlin to direct a whole new version with a reworked screenplay, a new supporting cast (Skarsgard agreed to do it all over again), and tacky CGI possession effects. The tediously formulaic result requires Merrin, purportedly a man of great intelligence, to creep around unmapped caves at night and deny the possibility of possession long after many an unbeliever would have reached for the Book of Rites. If God is in the details, the devil surely owns the hoary cliches.

EXOTICA
1995 104m c Mystery/Drama 🎬 ★★½
Alliance/Communication Corp./Ego Films/Telefilm R
Canada/Ontario Film Development Corp. (Canada)

Bruce Greenwood *(Francis)*, Mia Kirshner *(Christina)*, Don McKellar *(Thomas)*, Arsinee Khanjian *(Zoe)*, Elias Koteas *(Eric)*, Sarah Polley *(Tracey)*, Victor Garber *(Harold)*, Calvin Green *(Customs Officer)*, David Hemblen *(Customs Inspector)*, Peter Krantz *(Man in Taxi)*

p, Atom Egoyan, Camelia Frieberg; d, Atom Egoyan; w, Atom Egoyan; ph, Paul Sarossy; ed, Susan Shipton; m, Mychael Danna; prod d, Linda Del Rosario, Richard Paris; fx, Michael Kavanagh; chor, Claudia Moore; cos, Linda Muir

EXOTICA is the Egoyan movie for people who feel faintly guilty about never having seen one: it may be Art, but at least it's set in a strip club, albeit the most portentous strip club in North America.

Pet shop owner Thomas (Don McKellar), arrives at the airport with a clutch of smuggled macaw eggs in tow. Sharing a cab with a stranger, he winds up at Exotica, an upscale girlie club with a wildly artificial jungle motif and a high-tech sound system that blasts disco versions of Urdu *ghazals*. Its star stripper is Christina (Mia Kirshner), who exploits her pedophilic allure by dressing in a schoolgirl's uniform. Two men are obsessed with her: longhaired DJ Eric (Elias Koteas) and tax auditor Francis (Bruce Greenwood). Zoe (Arsinee Khanjian), the hugely pregnant owner of Exotica, has befriended the troubled Christina; she's also paid Eric to father her child. All the principal characters are drawn together when Francis begins an audit of Thomas's pet store, and we finally learn what has drawn them into their tortured relationship.

EXOTICA sounds terrifically lurid and interesting, but like most Egoyan films, it's far more interesting in the telling than in the watching. It's easy to defend Egoyan as a serious and provocative filmmaker, since all his liabilities can be made to sound like the results of his rigorous intellectual defiance of mainstream norms. His characters are opaque because they're meant to defy bourgeois psychological conventions. His plots are unconvincing because they explore modes of storytelling that challenge received notions of good narrative structure. His movies are dull because he rejects the audience's Pavlovian desire for familiar scene structure and easy narrative resolution. Egoyan is a phenomenally successful filmmaker on his own terms. But he's still a pretentious bore.

EXTERMINATING ANGEL, THE
(EL ANGEL EXTERMINADOR)
1962 95m bw Comedy/Drama ★★★★½
Uninci/Films 59 (Mexico/Spain)

Silvia Pinal *(Letitia—"The Valkyrie")*, Jacqueline Andere *(Senora Alicia Roc)*, Jose Baviera *(Leandro)*, Augusto Benedico *(Doctor)*, Antonio Bravo *(Russell)*, Javier Masse *(Eduardo)*, Ofelia Montesco *(Beatriz)*, Nadia Haro Oliva *(Ana Maynar)*, Javier Loya *(Francisco Avila)*, Ofelia Guilmain *(Juana Avila)*

p, Gustavo Alatriste; d, Luis Bunuel; w, Luis Bunuel, Luis Alcoriza (based on the play Los Naufragos de la Calle de la Providentia by Jose Bergamin); ph, Gabriel Figueroa; ed, Carlos Savage Jr.; m, Alessandro Scarlatti, Pietro Domenico Paradisi; art d, Jesus Bracho; fx, Juan Munoz Ravelo; cos, Georgette Somohano

One of Luis Bunuel's masterworks, THE EXTERMINATING ANGEL is a brilliant surrealist allegory about a group of socialites who, after attending a dinner party, inexplicably find themselves unable to leave their host's house, and gradually degenerate into violence and depravity.

While preparing for a dinner party at the home of aristocrat Esmundo Nobile (Enrique Rambal) and his wife Lucia (Lucy Gallardo), all of the servants, except for the majordomo Julian (Claudio Brook), begin to walk out of the house. Lucia moves a bear and a flock of sheep from the salon to the garden, and when the 20 guests arrive, Julian serves dinner. Afterwards, the guests go into the salon to hear Blanca (Patricia de Morelos) play a piano sonata, but some of them fall asleep. At four a.m., they're still there, and Nobile suggests they all spend the night. In the morning, some women try to go to the bathroom, but can't leave the salon, and when Julio brings in some coffee, he too is unable to leave. 24 hours later, everyone is still trapped inside, and their behavior turns irritable and bizarre.

Following the success of VIRIDIANA (1961), producer Gustavo Alatriste gave him carte blanche for THE EXTERMINATING ANGEL without even seeing a script. When it was finished, Alatriste screened it and said: "I don't understand a thing in it. It's marvelous." His reaction is typical of most—you're not quite sure what it's about on an intellectual level, but instinctively, you feel that you've seen something profound and amazing, not to mention savagely funny and tremendously entertaining. Bunuel himself stated that it's doubtful whether it's capable of interpretation, but it's obvious that he uses the basic premise as a metaphor for moral decay, spiritual inertia and malaise, the breakdown of social order, and the illusion of free will. The entire film has the delirious intensity of a fever dream, emphasized by Gabriel Figueroa's darkly sensuous photography and by Bunuel's economical technique, which has a formal, though never fussy, elegance. If the film defies rational explanation, that is obviously Bunuel's intention, and its mystery only adds to its power and beauty.

EYE OF THE NEEDLE
1981 111m c Spy/War ★★★½
Kings Road (U.K.) R

Donald Sutherland *(Faber)*, Stephen MacKenna *(Lieutenant)*, Philip Martin Brown *(Billy Parkin)*, Kate Nelligan *(Lucy)*, Christopher Cazenove *(David)*, George Belbin *(Lucy's Father)*, Faith Brook *(Lucy's Mother)*, Barbara Graley *(Constable)*, Arthur Lovegrove *(Peterson)*, Colin Rix *(Oliphant)*

p, Stephen Friedman; d, Richard Marquand; w, Stanley Mann (based on the novel by Ken Follett); ph, Alan Hume (Technicolor); ed, Sean Barton; m, Miklos Rozsa; prod d, Wilfred Shingleton; art d, Bert Davey, John Hoesli; cos, John Bloomfield

A gripping, old-fashioned WWII spy thriller, EYE OF THE NEEDLE features Donald Sutherland as Faber, a murderous Nazi spy stationed in Britain who uncovers the Allies' plans to invade Normandy. En route to a rendezvous with a U-boat at a remote island, Faber is stranded by a violent storm and forced to seek shelter with Lucy (Kate Nelligan), a sexually frustrated housewife, and her husband, a paraplegic ex-fighter pilot (Christopher Cazenove). Romance soon develops between Lucy and the spy, but Lucy's husband begins to suspect Faber's true identity.

Directed with considerable flair by Richard Marquand, this adaptation of Ken Follett's best-selling novel boasts one of Sutherland's best performances. As the cold-blooded spy who thinks nothing of plunging a stiletto into anyone who gets in his way, he is positively chilling. An accomplished stage actress who has yet to find the screen success that she deserves, Nelligan is excellent as well. Underrated at the time it was released, EYE OF THE NEEDLE is worthy viewing for anyone fond of classic Hollywood wartime thrillers. The old master film composer Miklos Rozsa even provides a score in the grand tradition.

EYES WIDE SHUT
1999 160m c Drama ★★★★
Pole Star Productions/Hobby Films/Warner Bros. R
(U.S.)

Tom Cruise *(Doctor William Harford)*, Nicole Kidman *(Alice Harford)*, Sydney Pollack *(Victor Ziegler)*, Marie Richardson *(Marion)*, Rade Seberdzija *(Milich)*, Todd Field *(Nick Nightingale)*, Vinessa Shaw *(Domino)*, Alan Cumming *(Desk Clerk)*, Sky Dumont *(Sandor Szavost)*, Fay Masterson *(Sally)*

p, Stanley Kubrick; d, Stanley Kubrick; w, Stanley Kubrick, Frederic Raphael (based on the novella *Traumnovelle* by Arthur Schnitzler); ed, Nigel Galt; m, Jocelyn Pokk; prod d, Les Tomkins, Roy Walker; art d, Kevin Phipps, John Fenner; cos, Marit Allen

Stanley Kubrick's last film isn't a seamless masterpiece on the order of 2001 or DR. STRANGELOVE, but it's no old man's folly either. Set in modern-day New York City, EYES WIDE SHUT is an otherwise faithful adaptation of Arthur Schitzler's haunting 1926 novella *Traumnovelle*, until it takes an ill-advised turn into paranoid thriller territory.

Dr. Bill Harford and his wife Alice (Tom Cruise, Nicole Kidman), happily married for nine years, attend a Christmas party where they both flirt with other guests. Their unconsummated brushes with infidelity lead to a marijuana-fueled fight at home, during which Alice confesses a sexual fantasy that profoundly unsettles her husband. The intense moment is interrupted by a phone call; Bill is summoned to the apartment of a longtime patient who's just died, where, to his embarrassment, the man's daughter (Marie Richardson) makes an unexpected declaration of love. It's the first of a series of sexually charged encounters which, though shot realistically, have an unmistakably nightmarish edge: a prostitute, a diabolical nymphet (Leelee Sobieski), and a gay man (Alan Cumming), all hurl themselves at Bill. He's attacked by homophobes, attends an orgy worthy of a gothic porno novel, and is threatened by masked perverts.

No one familiar with the cold precision of Kubrick's work will be surprised that this isn't the steamy erotic thriller a synopsis (or the ads) might suggest, and viewers sucked in by the salacious hype are in for a shock. The film lives up to its promise of extensive nudity, but the elaborate orgy sequence is built around masked revelers so ornately aloof—even while in the throes of carnal consummation—that it's as unerotic as a religious pantomime. Throughout, the sizzle of bare flesh is iced by Kubrick and Schnitzler's focus on the silently caustic effect of morbid suspicion and complacency on an apparently solid relationship. And while both the novel and the film are weighted in favor of Bill's character, it's Kidman who gives the film's standout performance—complex, psychologically naked and worthy of a talent too often squandered in mediocre movies. The film's weakness lies in the decision to suggest that Bill's experiences have exposed him to some perilous conspiracy. The scene (which has no equivalent in the novel) in which everything is "explained" is painfully coarse and recalls nothing so much as the psychiatrist's speech at the end of PSYCHO. Its effect is calamitous: a carefully calibrated nightmare of distorted passion is reduced to a mundane story about rich degenerates and the basically nice guy who gets sucked into their creepy, dangerous games.

F

FABULOUS BAKER BOYS, THE
1989 114m c Comedy/Drama ★★½
Gladden/Mirage (U.S.) R

Jeff Bridges *(Jack Baker)*, Beau Bridges *(Frank Baker)*, Michelle Pfeiffer *(Susie Diamond)*, Ellie Raab *(Nina)*, Xander Berkeley *(Lloyd)*, Dakin Matthews *(Charlie)*, Ken Lerner *(Ray)*, Albert Hall *(Henry)*, Terri Treas *(Girl in Bed)*, Gregory Itzin *(Vince Nancy)*

p, Paula Weinstein, Mark Rosenberg, William Finnegan; d, Steve Kloves; w, Steve Kloves; ph, Michael Ballhaus (Deluxe Color); ed,

William Steinkamp; m, Dave Grusin; prod d, Jeffrey Townsend; chor, Peggy Holmes; cos, Lisa Jensen

AAN Best Actress: Michelle Pfeiffer; *AAN Best Cinematography:* Michael Ballhaus; *AAN Best Film Editing:* William Steinkamp; *AAN Best Original Score:* David Grusin

Though full of atmosphere, mood, and attitude, THE FABULOUS BAKER BOYS is all dressed up with no place to go. Jeff and Beau Bridges play brothers Jack and Frank Baker, a musical duo whose act consists of dueling piano arrangements of lounge songs. Frank decides to bring in a female singer, and the nod finally goes to Susie Diamond (Michelle Pfeiffer). Her professional experience has been limited to an extended engagement with an escort service, but to say she knows how to sell a song is an understatement. Tensions rise when womanizing Jack embarks on a professionally dangerous liaison with Susie.

Early in the film, THE FABULOUS BAKER BOYS crackles with smart talk and smooth moves from writer-director Steve Kloves (who makes his directing debut here and who wrote the equally off-center RACING WITH THE MOON) and later in the film, Pfeiffer continues to captivate. When it comes to plot and characters, however, THE FABULOUS BAKER BOYS is purely superficial and the three principals become less interesting as the action grinds on. Though the Bridges boys give typically solid performances, it's Pfeiffer who deserves the most credit. Her Susie is an original—smart, hard-headed, and unsentimental. Pfeiffer's sultry rendition of "Makin' Whoopee" is one of the film's highlights. Photographed by the gifted Michael Ballhaus, THE FABULOUS BAKER BOYS unfortunately fails to base its evocative style on real substance, and thus fails to emerge from the run of the mill.

FACE IN THE CROWD, A 📀
1957 125m bw Drama ★★★★
Warner Bros. (U.S.)

Andy Griffith *(Lonesome Rhodes)*, Patricia Neal *(Marcia Jeffries)*, Anthony Franciosa *(Joey Kiely)*, Walter Matthau *(Mel Miller)*, Lee Remick *(Betty Lou Fleckum)*, Percy Waram *(Colonel Hollister)*, Rod Brasfield *(Beanie)*, Charles Irving *(Mr. Luffler)*, Howard Smith *(J.B. Jeffries)*, Paul McGrath *(Macey)*

p, Elia Kazan; d, Elia Kazan; w, Budd Schulberg (based on his short story "The Arkansas Traveler"); ph, Harry Stradling, Gayne Rescher; m, Tom Glazer; cos, Anna Hill Johnstone

Andy Griffith made an unforgettable screen debut in this film as Lonesome Rhodes, a cracker-barrel philosopher discovered by Marcia Jeffries (Neal), who puts him on her local television station in Arkansas. His down-home wit and backwater jokes soon gain a wide audience, after which one of the state's largest stations picks up his show, followed by a network, until his face is seen throughout the land and his homespun wisdom becomes the creed of large numbers of Americans. But Jeffries and her assistant, Mel Miller (Matthau), soon realize that good old "Lonesome Rhodes" is not the kindly rural savant he appears to be.

Director Elia Kazan and writer Budd Schulberg, who collaborated so effectively in ON THE WATERFRONT, again proved their ability to produce a raw, penetrating, and terrifying portrait of humanity in A FACE IN THE CROWD. Griffith, who had made a name for himself on Broadway with *No Time for Sergeants*, skyrocketed to fame after his performance as the vicious but fascinating Lonesome Rhodes—capturing the character so well it would take some time to live the role down. Neal is superb as the tough but vulnerable television producer snared by the hillbilly philosopher, and Matthau plays his cynical newsman to the hilt.

FACE/OFF 📀
1997 139m c Action/Crime/Science Fiction ★★★½
Douglas/Reuther Productions/WCG Entertainment/ R
Permut Presentations/Constellation Films (U.S.)

John Travolta *(Sean Archer)*, Nicolas Cage *(Castor Troy)*, Joan Allen *(Eve Archer)*, Alessandro Nivola *(Pollux Troy)*, Gina Gershon *(Sasha Hassler)*, Dominique Swain *(Jamie Archer)*, Nick Cassavetes *(Dietrich Hassler)*, Harve Presnell *(Victor Lazzaro)*, Colm Feore *(Dr. Malcolm Walsh)*, John Carroll Lynch *(Prison Guard Walton)*

p, David Permut, Barrie M. Osborne, Terence Chang, Christopher Godsick; d, John Woo; w, Mike Werb, Michael Colleary; ph, Oliver Wood; ed, Christian Wagner, Steven Kemper; m, John Powell; prod d, Neil Spisak; art d, Steve Arnold; fx, Lawrence J. Cavanaugh, R. Bruce Steinheimer, Richard M. Zarro, Richard Hollander, Boyd Shermis; cos, Ellen Mirojnick

AAN Best Sound Effects Editing: Mark P. Stoeckinger, Per Hallberg

Hong Kong action auteur John Woo finally finds the balance between the excesses of his Hong Kong movie making background and the demands of U.S. mainstream filmmaking in this preposterous, high-octane tale of an FBI agent and a psychotic terrorist who quite literally swap faces.

Sean Archer (John Travolta) is a driven man: six years ago, lethal nut job Castor Troy (Nicolas Cage) tried to assassinate him, and wound up killing Archer's five-year-old son instead. When Archer finally brings in Castor and his even loonier brother, Pollux (Alessandro Nivola), it looks as though he can finally put it all behind him and start patching up his relationship with long-suffering wife Eve (Joan Allen) and rebellious daughter Jamie (Dominique Swaim). The curve ball: the Troys have planted a nerve gas bomb somewhere in L.A. Castor is in an apparently irreversible coma, and Pollux—now an inmate in a hellish, high tech prison—won't talk. Now, if he thought he were talking to his *brother*… A bit of EYES WITHOUT A FACE-style plastic surgery later, Archer is shipped off to jail to get the information and save the day. But wouldn't you just know that there's wicked life in Castor yet, and that this whole trading places thing is going to take a turn for the very, very nasty?

Unlike Woo's successful but rather disappointingly conventional BROKEN ARROW, this brutal, stunningly choreographed spectacle weaves together lyrical beauty, casual blasphemy, sadistic cruelty, and grotesque sentimentality with breathtakingly smooth assurance. Which is to say, it's everything fans love in Woo's Hong Kong films. Come to think of it, he lifts more than a little from THE KILLER and skillfully tailors it for U.S. cast and locales. A treat for Woo aficionados, and a great introduction to Hong Kong-style action for others.

FACE TO FACE
(ANSIKTE MOT ANSIKTE)
1976 136m c Drama ★★★★
DEG (Sweden) R

Liv Ullmann *(Dr. Jenny Isaksson)*, Erland Josephson *(Dr. Tomas Jacobi)*, Gunnar Björnstrand *(Grandpa)*, Aino Taube *(Grandma)*, Kari Sylwan *(Maria)*, Siv Ruud *(Mrs. Elizabeth Wankel)*, Sven Lindberg *(Dr. Erik Isaksson)*, Tore Segelcke *(The Lady)*, Ulf Johansson *(Dr. Helmuth Wankel)*, Kristina Adolphsson *(Veronica)*

p, Ingmar Bergman; d, Ingmar Bergman; w, Ingmar Bergman; ph, Sven Nykvist (Eastmancolor); ed, Siv Lundgren; m, Wolfgang Amadeus Mozart; prod d, Anne Hagegard

AAN Best Actress: Liv Ullmann; *AAN Best Director:* Ingmar Bergman

Bergman originally filmed FACE TO FACE for Swedish television as a four-part series. While appropriate for the more liberal television codes of Sweden, it was unlikely fare for U.S. consumption. He edited it down to a length that would permit distribution as a feature film. Despite the snipping, it remains a potent representative of Bergman's psychodrama cycle that began with CRIES AND WHISPERS and ended with AUTUMN SONATA.

The film depicts the slow and painful nervous breakdown of a successful psychiatrist. Ullmann is Dr. Jenny Isaksson, a psychiatrist vacationing at her grandparents' gloomy home in the country—alone because her husband, Dr. Erik Isaksson (Lindberg)—also a shrink—is away. She soon begins hallucinating about an old woman. This leads to depression and a feeling of helplessness as she is overwhelmed by memories of the past.

FACE TO FACE is an extremely intense experience from start to finish, due in large part to Ullmann's performance as she powerfully expresses a range of emotions seldom seen in American films. Bergman's frequent collaborator, cinematographer Sven Nykvist, enhances the film's harrowing mood with his stark imagery.

FACES
DVD
1968 130m bw Drama ★★★★
Continental Distributing (U.S.)

John Marley *(Richard Forst)*, Gena Rowlands *(Jeannie Rapp)*, Lynn Carlin *(Maria Forst)*, Fred Draper *(Freddie)*, Seymour Cassel *(Chet)*, Val Avery *(McCarthy)*, Dorothy Gulliver *(Florence)*, Joanne Moore Jordan *(Louise)*, Darlene Conley *(Billy Mae)*, Gene Darfler *(Jackson)*

p, Maurice McEndree; d, John Cassavetes; w, John Cassavetes; ph, Al Ruban; ed, Maurice McEndree, Al Ruban, John Cassavetes; m, Jack Ackerman; art d, Phedon Papamichael

AAN Best Supporting Actor: Seymour Cassel; *AAN Best Supporting Actress:* Lynn Carlin; *AAN Best Original Story and Screenplay:* John Cassavetes

Like SHADOWS before it, FACES was hailed at the time as a great accomplishment of American independent cinema. John Cassavetes, his friends, and family took several years to shoot and edit the film on very grainy 16mm black-and-white stock. As would become usual for Cassavetes, it's about marriages and the war between men and women. He would do better in the 1970s with films like HUSBANDS, made with a little more money, but FACES remains a landmark cultural document of the late '60s.

FACES is a rudimentary study of a husband and wife, disenchanted after 14 years of marriage, who drift apart. Richard Forst (Marley), the husband, spends an evening with a prostitute, Jennie Rapp (Rowlands), while his wife, Maria (Carlin), and her girlfriends go out to a disco looking for a little excitement. She finds it in the form of Chet (Cassel), a handsome hippie whom she takes home to bed. The illusions of the night before look very different the next morning for both husband and wife.

The original cut ran nearly six hours, making it an inevitable victim of severe editing. (The original version exists only in the form of a published screenplay.) In a sense, FACES can be seen as a reaction to Cassavetes's previous directorial outing, A CHILD IS WAITING, which he disowned after it was recut by producer Stanley Kramer. Cassavetes became wary of the major companies and turned independent. Upon its release, FACES was hailed by most critics but tepidly received by the moviegoers. Though it is sometimes a tedious viewing experience, its improvisational and documentary techniques are rewarding.

FACULTY, THE
DVD
1998 110m c Horror/Science Fiction/Thriller ★★½
Alienated Productions/Los Hoolligans/Dimension R
(U.S.)

Jordana Brewster *(Delilah)*, Clea DuVall *(Stokely)*, Laura Harris *(Marybeth)*, Josh Hartnett *(Zeke)*, Shawn Hatosy *(Stan)*, Salma Hayek *(Nurse Harper)*, Famke Janssen *(Miss Burke)*, Piper Laurie *(Mrs. Olson)*, Chris McDonald *(Casey's Dad)*, Bebe Neuwirth *(Principal Drake)*

p, Elizabeth Avellan; d, Robert Rodriguez; w, Kevin Williamson (based on a story by David Wechter and Bruce Kimmel); ph, Enrique Chediak; ed, Robert Rodriguez; m, Marco Beltrami; prod d, Cary White; art d, Edward Vega; fx, John McLeod; cos, Michael T. Boyd

"Invasion of the Student Body Snatchers," anyone? A sci-fi/horror thriller so derivative that it thoughtfully acknowledges its influences in the dialogue, this wise-to-its-audience shocker from screenwriter Kevin Williamson and director Robert Rodriguez is nevertheless the kind of clever, button-pushing fright-fest that keeps fans hanging on until something more fulfilling comes along.

Like pretty much all high schoolers, the students of Herrington High are convinced their teachers are from another planet. Unlike most disaffected teens, they're absolutely right. Their small Ohio town is ground zero of the invasion from space, and the faculty (who include Salma Hayek, Bebe Neuwirth, Robert Patrick, Piper Laurie, Famke Janssen, and Daniel Von Bargen) are the first to succumb. So it's up to six mismatched adolescents—the loner chick (Clea DuVall), the nerd (Elijah Wood), the reformed jock (Shawn Hatosy), the brilliant screw-up (Josh Hartnett), the secretly unhappy cheerleader (Jordana Brewster), and the new girl (Laura Harris)—to save the world.

The special effects are nice and slithery, and the plot picks and chooses among bits from INVASION OF THE BODY SNATCHERS, ROBERT A. HEINLEIN'S THE PUPPET MASTERS, NIGHT OF THE CREEPS, INVADERS FROM MARS, John Carpenter's THE THING, and even a soupcon of THE MAN WHO FELL TO EARTH. If those ingredients mean anything to you, you'll probably get a kick out of the cocktail they add up to.

FAHRENHEIT 451
DVD
1966 112m c Science Fiction ★★★★
Vineyard/Rank/Anglo-Amalgamated (U.K.)

Oskar Werner *(Montag)*, Julie Christie *(Linda/Clarisse)*, Cyril Cusack *(Captain)*, Anton Diffring *(Fabian)*, Jeremy Spenser *(Man with Apple)*, Bee Duffell *(Book Woman)*, Gillian Lewis *(TV Announcer)*, Ann Bell *(Doris)*, Caroline Hunt *(Helen)*, Anna Palk *(Jackie)*

p, Lewis Allen; d, Francois Truffaut; w, Francois Truffaut, Jean-Louis Richard, David Rudkin, Helen Scott (based on the novel by Ray Bradbury); ph, Nicolas Roeg (Technicolor); ed, Thom Noble; m, Bernard Herrmann; prod d, Tony Walton; art d, Syd Cain; fx, Charles Staffel, Bowie Films; cos, Tony Walton

Throughout much of his brilliant career, Francois Truffaut was criticized for not making explicitly political films. However, he did tackle political themes in two films: FAHRENHEIT 451, an indictment of totalitarianism and book-burning, and THE LAST METRO, which dealt with the German occupation of France. These films address the suppression of two media of deep personal significance for Truffaut—literature and the theater, respectively. The former is the most restrained and elegaic of science fiction films, full of poignant moments: a paean to the physical importance of books.

FAHRENHEIT 451 (the title refers to the temperature at which paper burns) is set sometime in the future and follows Montag (Oskar Werner), a devoted and obedient "fireman" who excels in ferreting out books in the most obscure hiding places. One day, after watching a woman sacrifice her life for her forbidden library, he decides to keep a volume for himself, curious to learn why these tomes are deemed so threatening. Soon he must choose between his life as a civil servant—in which he follows orders and lives with a listless, television-addicted wife, Linda (Julie Christie)—and his desire to live as a free thinking man in a free society, inspired by subversive schoolteacher Clarisse (Christie again).

Severely underrated and misunderstood by critics who wanted Truffaut to continue making films like his early French New Wave classics THE 400 BLOWS and JULES AND JIM, FAHRENHEIT 451 is a marvelously courageous personal statement that becomes more fascinating with time. This was Truffaut's first color film. The cool crisp cinematography is provided by future director Nicolas Roeg. The great Bernard Herrmann supplied the memorable score.

FAHRENHEIT 9/11   📀

2004 116m c   Documentary/Political   ★★★
Dog Eat Dog Films/IFC Films/The Fellowship   R
Adventure Group   (U.S.)

Michael Moore

p, Jim Czarnecki, Kathleen Glynn, Michael Moore; d, Michael Moore; w, Michael Moore; ph, Mike Desjarlais; ed, Kurt Engfehr, T. Woody Richman, Christopher Seward; m, Jeff Gibbs

Unfocused, bombastic, and provocative in every sense of the word, Michael Moore's scattershot attack on George W. Bush's presidency is much like the rest of Moore's films: it's challenging and infuriating in equal parts. Every sharply articulated point is offset by a buffoonish stunt, each razor-sharp observation about the interplay of American policy and the interests of the moneyed elite counterbalanced by a mawkish tale of poor working folks getting the shaft.

Moore starts by rehashing the Florida balloting irregularities that skewed the 2000 presidential election, laying equal blame on Republicans for cooking the vote and Democrats for taking it. He characterizes the first eight months of Bush's presidency as an extended vacation, interrupted only when the Al-Qeada terrorist attacks of September 11, 2001, demanded serious leadership. Florida news footage of the slack-jawed chief executive lingering at a grammar-school photo op for seven solid minutes after being told America was "under attack" reveals an absence so profound it hurts to look. Moore is at his best when he's following the money, establishing a web of connections between the Bush family and their oil-business friends and associates, notably Saudi investors who include members of the Bin Laden family. Why, Moore asks, did America roll its war on Al-Qaeda through Iraq when everything suggested that Saudi Arabia was the problem?

Moore's evidence is mostly circumstantial, but the allegation that President Bush ranked the well-being of American citizens below his lucrative oil interests is explosive. True to his juvenile sense of authority-baiting, Moore then lobs cinematic spitballs at targets ranging from the trivial to the profoundly important. Moore's desperate need for attention is irritating, but it's also his strength as a gadfly; it drives him to needle sacred cows and received wisdom that would otherwise go unchallenged.

FAIL SAFE   📀

1964 111m bw   Drama/War   ★★★½
Columbia   (U.S.)

Dan O'Herlihy (Gen. Black), Walter Matthau (Groeteschele), Frank Overton (Gen. Bogan), Edward Binns (Col. Grady), Fritz

Weaver (Col. Cascio), Henry Fonda (The President), Larry Hagman (Buck), William Hansen (Secretary Swenson), Russell Hardie (Gen. Stark), Russell Collins (Knapp)

p, Max E. Youngstein; d, Sidney Lumet; w, Walter Bernstein (based on the novel by Eugene Burdick and Harvey Wheeler); ph, Gerald Hirschfeld; ed, Ralph Rosenblum; art d, Albert Brenner; fx, Storyboard, Inc.; cos, Anna Hill Johnstone

Released only seven months after DR. STRANGELOVE by the very same studio, the virtually identical, albeit totally serious, FAIL SAFE was a relative failure at the box office. Kubrick went to Columbia's top brass and threatened a plagiarism lawsuit. (His film was based on Peter George's almost unknown novel Red Alert.) Since Columbia was distributing both DR. STRANGELOVE and FAIL SAFE, it appeased Kubrick by releasing his film first, and, of course, that cult classic captured the lion's share of viewers, leaving FAIL SAFE to appear as a serious, comparatively dreary rehash.

In it, a squadron of SAC bombers flies off to drop nuclear bombs on Moscow after a faulty transmission of orders that cannot be reversed through normal channels. The U.S. military tries everything to stop them, but the bombers fly beyond "fail safe" and the president (Henry Fonda) is alerted. He goes to his bomb-proof bunker deep beneath the White House, where, in a simple, sterile room, he tries to inform Soviet leaders of the terrible blunder. Meanwhile, his cabinet and advisers meet in the War Room, keeping him informed of fast-developing events and channeling messages from the Omaha command center. After several attempts to recall or shoot down the planes, it becomes obvious that one of the bombers will deliver its load on Moscow. In a desperate effort to prevent a retaliatory attack by the Soviets that would result in all-out nuclear war, the president must resort to a horrifying compromise.

Grim, bleak and highly claustrophobic, FAIL SAFE is very much like director Sidney Lumet's previous film, 12 ANGRY MEN, in that it concentrates almost exclusively on the actors' performances and is shot mainly in tight close-ups. While this is a wonderful showcase for some fine acting—notably by Fonda—it is not great filmmaking, and one may be left wishing for the biting, off-the-wall satire of DR. STRANGELOVE.

FALCON AND THE SNOWMAN, THE   📀

1985 131m c   Spy   ★★★
Orion   (U.S.)   R

Timothy Hutton (Christopher Boyce), Sean Penn (Daulton Lee), Pat Hingle (Mr. Boyce), Richard Dysart (Dr. Lee), Lori Singer (Lana), David Suchet (Alex), Dorian Harewood (Gene), Priscilla Pointer (Mrs. Lee), Nicholas Pryor (Eddie), Sam Ingraffia (Kenny Kahn)

p, Gabriel Katzka, John Schlesinger; d, John Schlesinger; w, Steve Zaillian (based on the book The Falcon and the Snowman by Robert Lindsey); ph, Allen Daviau (DeLuxe Color); ed, Richard Marden; m, Pat Metheny, Lyle Mays; prod d, James D. Bissell; cos, Albert Wolsky

Based on fact, this absorbing film tells the story of Christopher Boyce and Daulton Lee, two young upper-middle-class southern Californians who were convicted of selling secrets to the Soviet Union in 1977.

Boyce (Timothy Hutton), the more introspective of the pair and the son of a former FBI man (Pat Hingle), works for a company that does top-secret work for the CIA. Already disillusioned by the American experience in Vietnam, the idealistic Hutton completely loses faith in his government when he learns the CIA has been meddling in the internal affairs of Australia, and decides to become a traitor. He enlists the help of his directionless friend Lee (Sean Penn), who has been in and out of trouble with the law, but who continues using and dealing drugs. The security at Hutton's company is astonishingly lax, and he easily steals sensitive documents, which Penn delivers to the Soviet Embassy in Mexico City.

Directed by John Schlesinger, THE FALCON AND THE SNOWMAN is both a spy drama and an intriguing character study. Penn invests his "Snowman" with fascinating eccentricity and is the more interesting of the pair, though Hutton delivers an estimable performance as the sullen young falconer.

FALLEN ANGEL

1945 98m bw Mystery ★★★½
Fox (U.S.)

Alice Faye *(June Mills)*, Dana Andrews *(Eric Stanton)*, Linda Darnell *(Stella)*, Charles Bickford *(Mark Judd)*, Anne Revere *(Clara Mills)*, Bruce Cabot *(Dave Atkins)*, John Carradine *(Prof. Madley)*, Percy Kilbride *(Pop)*, Olin Howlin *(Joe Ellis)*, Hal Taliaferro *(Johnson)*

p, Otto Preminger; d, Otto Preminger; w, Harry Kleiner (based on the novel by Marty Holland); ph, Joseph La Shelle; ed, Harry Reynolds; m, David Raksin; art d, Lyle Wheeler, Leland Fuller; fx, Fred Sersen; cos, Bonnie Cashin

Eric Stanton, a press agent down on his luck, drifts into a small coastal town in California and meets June Mills (Faye), a reclusive rich woman, and a sultry waitress named Stella (Darnell). In love with Stella but broke, Eric decides to marry June, steal her fortune, divorce her, and wed Stella. However Stella turns up murdered and suspicion falls on Eric. In order to clear his name, Eric launches his own investigation to find the real killer.

Director Preminger hoped to have another LAURA with this film, but it fell short due to some loose ends in the script and disjointed points of view as the director shifts the focus of the story erratically from one character to another, a blatant red herring to mislead the viewer from guessing the killer's identity. The overall mood, lighting, and pace of the film, nevertheless, are top, hardboiled film noir.

Faye, who had been a Fox superstar for many years, had been promised a meaty and significant part; she had rejected almost three dozen scripts before accepting the lead in FALLEN ANGEL but her role was slowly chiseled away by Preminger, who played up Darnell during the production, giving her more and more scenes. Faye felt that some of her best scenes had been chopped and considered herself betrayed. She retired on the spot, so bitter that it would be 16 years before she returned to the screen.

FALLEN ANGELS

(DUOLUO TIANSHI) *DVD*
1995 96m c Drama/Crime/Comedy ★★★★
Jet Tone (Hong Kong) R

Leon Lai *(Wong Chi-ming—the Killer)*, Michelle Reis *(The Agent)*, Karen Mok *(Baby)*, Takeshi Kaneshiro *(He Zhiwu)*, Charlie Young *(Charlie)*, Toru Saito *(Sato—the Manager)*, Chen Man Lei *(Father)*, Kong To-hoi *(Ah-Hoi)*, Chan Fai-hung *(Man Forced to Eat Ice Cream)*, Kwan Lee-na *(Woman Pressed to Buy Vegetables)*

p, Wong Kar-wai, Jeff Lau; d, Wong Kar-wai; w, Wong Kar-wai; ph, Christopher Doyle; ed, William Chang, Wong Ming Lam; m, Frankie Chan, Roel A. Garcia; prod d, William Chang

Crackling with inspiration, Wong Kar-wai's dazzling follow-up to CHUNGKING EXPRESS is one of those rare films that manages to feel as fresh and exciting as anything that's come before it.

In the garishly lit late-night world of Hong Kong, the lives of four lonely people briefly intersect: Wong Chi-ming (Leon Lai), a jaded hit man who wants out of his dangerous, solitary business; the Agent (Michele Reis), his beautiful part-

ner-in-crime whom Chi-Ming has never met (like everyone else in the film, they communicate electronically, either by fax or by phone), but who's smitten with him anyway; Baby (Karen Mok), a bleach-blonde, night-crawling cookie out looking for love but who will settle for just being remembered (Baby and Chi-Ming have met before, but he's forgotten); and He Zhiwu (Takeshi Kaneshiro), a mute, child-like felon who breaks into closed-up shops, opens them for business, and forces passers-by to shop against their will. Set in a world where human contact is best measured by degrees of separation, Wong's characters brush against one other but remain profoundly alone.

Originally conceived as part of the more comedic CHUNGKING EXPRESS, the action takes place in and around the same locale—Hong Kong's sprawling Chungking Mansions housing complex—and references to the earlier film abound, recalling parallel lives that are at once so close but faraway. Wong's sense of humor remains sharp and endearing, but the tone has darkened considerably: loneliness has grown more desperate, happiness less permanent, and disappointment now seems inevitable. Even Wong's detractors, many of whom consider the director more stylist than auteur, will have a tough time dismissing the extraordinary emotional depth he achieves here. This beautifully sad nocturne is simply one of the most fully realized cinematic visions of the way we live now.

FALLEN IDOL, THE

1948 94m bw Thriller ★★★★
London Films (U.K.)

Ralph Richardson *(Baines)*, Michele Morgan *(Julie)*, Bobby Henrey *(Felipe)*, Sonia Dresdel *(Mrs. Baines)*, Denis O'Dea *(Inspector Crowe)*, Walter Fitzgerald *(Dr. Fenton)*, Karel Stepanek *(1st Secretary)*, Joan Young *(Mrs. Barrow)*, Dandy Nichols *(Mrs. Patterson)*, Bernard Lee *(Detective Hart)*

p, David O. Selznick, Carol Reed; d, Carol Reed; w, Graham Greene, Lesley Storm, William Templeton (based on the short story "The Basement Room" by Greene); ph, Georges Perinal; ed, Oswald Hafenrichter; m, William Alwyn; prod d, Vincent Korda, James Sawyer, John Hawkesworth; fx, W. Percy Day; cos, Ivy Baker

AAN Best Director: Carol Reed; *AAN Best Screenplay:* Graham Greene

Told from a child's point of view, THE FALLEN IDOL is a subdued thriller set in a foreign embassy in London. The ambassador departs and leaves his precocious, imaginative son, Felipe (Henrey), with the butler, Baines (Richardson), and Baines's wife (Dresdel). The boy idolizes the kindly, considerate Baines but dislikes the butler's shrewish, vicious wife. Baines and embassy typist Julie (Morgan) have been having an affair and Felipe overhears them agreeing to end the relationship. This information is later wheedled out of Felipe by Mrs. Baines, who then has a violent argument with her husband. In her jealous rage, Mrs. Baines accidentally falls down a flight of stairs to her death. Her demise is heard but not wholly witnessed by the boy. When police begin a routine investigation, Felipe fears that his idol will be arrested.

Director Carol Reed skillfully blends elegant camera movement, expressive angles, stylized lighting, and sterling performances into a fascinating and suspenseful motion picture. Richardson is superb as the innocent butler. His tender treatment of the boy, his cultured bearing, and his gentlemanly demeanor convey a supreme nobility that belies his working-class position. Henrey is even more exciting in his wonderful portrayal of a jittery and intelligent child. Reed's direction of Henrey gave him a reputation as a great director of children, which was further confirmed by the engaging performances he drew from children in A KID FOR TWO

FARTHINGS and OLIVER! THE FALLEN IDOL received a British Best Film award, and Reed was honored as Best Director by the New York Film Critics.

FALLEN SPARROW, THE

1943 94m bw Spy ★★★
RKO (U.S.)

John Garfield *(Kit)*, Maureen O'Hara *(Toni Donne)*, Walter Slezak *(Dr. Skaas)*, Patricia Morison *(Barby Taviton)*, Martha O'Driscoll *(Whitney Hamilton)*, Bruce Edwards *(Ab Parker)*, John Banner *(Anton)*, John Miljan *(Insp. Tobin)*, Sam Goldenberg *(Prince Francois de Namur)*, Hugh Beaumont *(Otto Skaas)*

p, Robert Fellows; d, Richard Wallace; w, Warren Duff (based on the novel by Dorothy B. Hughes); ph, Nicholas Musuraca; ed, Robert Wise; m, Roy Webb; prod d, Van Nest Polglase; art d, Albert S. D'Agostino, Mark-Lee Kirk; fx, Vernon L. Walker

AAN Best Score (Drama or Comedy): C. Bakaleinikoff, Roy Webb

In a riveting performance, John Garfield portrays Kit, a fear-haunted veteran of the Spanish Civil War who returns to the U.S. after being tortured by Gestapo captors who wanted to know where he'd hidden the captured battle flag of one of the elite Nazi regiments that fought with Franco. Back in the States, Dr. Skaas (Slezak), a German agent, attempts to drive Kit insane so that he will reveal the hiding place of the banner. A bevy of beautiful women try to worm the information from the half-mad Kit, including Toni Donne (O'Hara), who lures Kit to a house filled with Nazi agents.

Maureen O'Hara is miscast here as a *femme fatale*, but the limping Walter Slezak crafts a sinister persona somewhere between Peter Lorre and Sydney Greenstreet. Director Richard Wallace sets a brisk pace but lets Garfield carry the entire burden of a character plagued by anguished memories. Attracted by the subject matter, Garfield, a supporter of the Loyalist cause during the Spanish Civil War, played this role while on loan-out to RKO from Warner Bros. THE FALLEN SPARROW is a haunting film but, like Garfield's career, it has the feeling of being unfinished.

FALLING DOWN

1993 115m c Drama/Comedy ★★★
Arnold Kopelson Productions (U.S.) R

Michael Douglas *(D-Fens)*, Robert Duvall *(Det. Martin Prendergast)*, Barbara Hershey *(Beth)*, Rachel Ticotin *(Sandra)*, Tuesday Weld *(Mrs. Prendergast)*, Frederic Forrest *(Surplus Store Owner)*, Lois Smith *(D-Fens' Mother)*, Joey Hope Singer *(Adele (Beth's Child))*, Ebbe Roe Smith *(Guy on Freeway)*, Michael Paul Chan *(Mr. Lee)*

p, Arnold Kopelson, Timothy Harris, Herschel Weingrod; d, Joel Schumacher; w, Ebbe Roe Smith; ph, Andrzej Bartkowiak; ed, Paul Hirsch; prod d, Barbara Ling; art d, Larry Fulton; fx, Bob Stoker, Matt Sweeney, James Schwalm, Lucinda Strub; cos, Marlene Stewart

FALLING DOWN opens with a scene of a nightmarish L.A. traffic jam in which drivers are driven to distraction by boredom, frustration, noise and heat. If you manage to sit through this film, you will know just how they feel.

Stuck in that jam is a disgruntled defense worker (Michael Douglas) suffering the combined pressures of unemployment, divorce, and a haircut someone must have given him as an April Fool's joke. As the tension is ham-fist-edly turned up, it becomes clear that something is very wrong. A bead of sweat runs down Douglas's face; a fly lands on his neck; perhaps, off-camera, someone makes a joke about his buttock-baring scene in BASIC INSTINCT.

That does it! Douglas is off, abandoning his car for a cross-town hike across L.A.'s seediest neighborhoods, en route to a showdown with his ex-wife (Barbara Hershey) and child. Along the way, he has a series of encounters that tread an uncomfortable line between black comedy and clumsy social criticism. He trashes a Korean grocery store because the prices are too high; provokes a drive-by gang shooting in which several innocent people die; and laughs as he gives a rich white golfer a fatal heart attack.

These adventures would be offensive if you could take them seriously, so it's probably good that you can't. Despite a nicely understated performance from Robert Duvall as a cop on Douglas's trail, FALLING DOWN fails to convince on any level.

FAME

1980 134m c Musical ★★★
MGM (U.S.) PG

Ed Barth *(Angelo)*, Irene Cara *(Coco)*, Lee Curreri *(Bruno)*, Laura Dean *(Lisa)*, Antonia Franceschi *(Hilary)*, Boyd Gaines *(Michael)*, Albert Hague *(Shorofsky)*, Tresa Hughes *(Mrs. Finsecker)*, Steve Inwood *(Francois Lafete)*, Paul McCrane *(Montgomery)*

p, David DeSilva, Alan Marshall; d, Alan Parker; w, Christopher Gore; ph, Michael Seresin; ed, Gerry Hambling; m, Michael Gore; prod d, Geoffrey Kirkland; art d, Ed Wittstein; chor, Louis Falco; cos, Kristi Zea

AAN Best Original Screenplay: Christopher Gore; *AAN Best Film Editing:* Gerry Hambling; *AA Best Original Score:* Michael Gore; *AA Best Original Song:* "Fame"; Michael Gore (Music), Dean Pitchford (Lyrics); *AAN Best Original Song:* "Out Here on My Own"; Michael Gore (Music), Lesley Gore (Lyrics); *AAN Best Sound:* Michael J. Kohut, Aaron Rochin, Jay M. Harding, Chris Newman

This is a wonderfully simple idea that succeeds very well indeed: take a bunch of kids from New York's High School of Performing Arts and let them strut their stuff. A lot of music, a few desultory plotlines, and you've got the contemporary version of the Mickey Rooney/Judy Garland "Hey kids, let's put on a show!" vehicle. FAME shows us how much life there still is in moribund genres like the musical.

It focuses on five episodes—set during auditions and successive academic years through to graduation—featuring various struggling young hopefuls, among them Coco (Irene Cara), a gifted, determined singer; Montgomery (Paul McCrane), a sensitive, gay actor; Leroy (Gene Anthony Ray), a talented, illiterate dancer; Bruno (Lee Curreri), a synthesizer player; and Ralph (Barry Miller), a Puerto Rican who is ashamed of his background. However, Parker's interest lies mainly in lavish production numbers, rather than in more intimate subtleties. (The real High School of the Performing Arts refused to let Parker film inside the building; perhaps they too disapproved of his sensationalism.)

The subject's treatment here was best suited for the television show it launched, but FAME's score and title song did win Academy Awards. Cara, who shines as Coco, was the only one of the aforementioned young leads to actually achieve fame (McCrane and Miller are respected stage, film and TV actors), racking up a couple of hit singles.

FAMILY, THE

(LA FAMIGLIA)
1987 127m c Comedy ★★★½
Maasfilm/Cinecitta/RAI-TV/Ariane (Italy/France)

Vittorio Gassman *(Carlo)*, Fanny Ardant *(Adriana)*, Stefania Sandrelli *(Beatrice)*, Andrea Occhipinti *(Young Carlo)*, Jo Ciampa *(Young Adriana)*, Alberto Gimignani, Massimo Dapporto, Carlo Dapporto, Cecilia Dazzi, Ottavia Piccolo p, Franco Committeri; d, Ettore Scola; w, Ruggero Maccari, Furio Scarpelli, Ettore Scola; ph, Ricardo Aronovich (Cinecitta color); ed, Ettore Scola; m, Armando Trovajoli; art d, Luciano Ricceri

AAN Best Foreign Language Film

After venturing into pedestrian comedy in his previous film, MACARONI, director Ettore Scola returned to the single set limitations of his LE BAL for this pleasant drama which covers 80 years in the life of one Italian family. The film opens in 1906 as the clan gathers in a large Rome apartment for a group photograph. A narrator, Carlo (Vittorio Gassman), points himself out in the picture—an infant who has just been baptized. Carlo narrates the entire film as time passes, Scola never showing the characters outside of their apartment. In addition to Carlo, the family includes his brother, his parents, the maid, his three matronly aunts, his wife, Beatrice (Stefania Sandrelli), and Beatrice's older and more worldly sister, Adriana (Fanny Ardant), whom Carlo really loves.

Like many of the films of Ingmar Bergman or Woody Allen, THE FAMILY goes to great lengths to recreate a family portrait album. Scola gives his audience a collection of characters, each with qualities and idiosyncracies that change and develop over the course of time. As a unifying stylistic thread, Scola uses a recurring dolly shot through the apartment's empty hall that symbolizes the passing of time. Filled with humor, sadness, and anger, the film also manages to encompass nearly all the major political and social events of 20th-century Italy.

FAMILY MAN, THE 📀

2000 125m c Drama/Fantasy/Romance ★★★½
Beacon Pictures/Riche/Ludwig-Zvi Howard PG-13
Rosenman-Saturn Productions/Universal (U.S.)

Nicolas Cage (*Jack Campbell*), Tea Leoni (*Kate*), Don Cheadle (*Cash*), Jeremy Piven (*Arnie*), Saul Rubinek (*Alan Mintz*), Josef Sommer (*Lassiter*), Makenzie Vega (*Annie*), Jake Milkovich (*Josh*), Ryan Milkovich (*Josh*), Lisa Thornhill (*Evelyn*)

p, Marc Abraham, Zvi Howard Rosenman, Tony Ludwig, Alan Riche; d, Brett Ratner; w, David Diamond, David Weissman; ph, Dante Spinotti; ed, Mark Helfrich; m, Danny Elfman; prod d, Kristi Zea; art d, Steve Skalad; fx, Mat Beck; cos, Betsy Heimann

This high-concept bid to be the new IT'S A WONDERFUL LIFE is a surprisingly charming fable about a Wall Street shark who gets an eye-opening glimpse of the road not taken.

Back in the go-go '80s, Jack Campbell (Nicolas Cage) made a pivotal decision: ignoring the pleas of college sweetheart Kate (Tea Leoni), Jack pursued a London-based internship that set him on the road to master-of-the-universe-dom. Jack's career flourished. His relationship with Kate withered. Now fabulously wealthy and surrounded by the perks of success—expensive cars, clothes, and women—Jack is apparently untroubled by the prospect of spending Christmas Eve drinking eggnog alone. When he gets a message Kate has called, he throws it away; who wants to reminisce with old girlfriends when there are mega-mergers to be brokered? Then Jack is touched by an angel (Don Cheadle) in disguise, and gets a look at the way things might have been. He falls asleep in his swank Manhattan penthouse, and wakes up a suburban New Jersey dad, married to Kate and the father of baby Josh and precocious Annie (Makenzie Vega), the only person who sees right through him.

It goes without saying that Jack will eventually realize that domestic harmony and real friends are worth more than all the glittering baubles money can buy. But he takes his sweet time getting over the Ferrari and the power suits, which is one of the many things this movie does right. Casting Leoni as Kate is another; even swaddled in a soccer-mom's wardrobe, she's charismatic enough to make you think growing old with her is a real alternative to life in the fast lane.

FAMILY PLOT 📀

1976 120m c Thriller/Comedy ★★★★
Universal (U.S.) PG

Karen Black (*Fran*), Bruce Dern (*Lumley*), Barbara Harris (*Blanche*), William Devane (*Adamson*), Ed Lauter (*Maloney*), Cathleen Nesbitt (*Julia Rainbird*), Katherine Helmond (*Mrs. Maloney*), Warren Kemmerling, billed as Warren J. Kemmerling (*Grandison*), Edith Atwater (*Mrs. Clay*), William Prince (*Bishop*)

p, Alfred Hitchcock; d, Alfred Hitchcock; w, Ernest Lehman (from the novel *The Rainbird Pattern* by Victor Canning); ph, Leonard South (Technicolor); ed, J. Terry Williams; m, John Williams; art d, Henry Bumstead; fx, Frank Brendel, Albert Whitlock; cos, Edith Head

With two parallel plots running throughout, Alfred Hitchcock's final film is a brilliantly constructed mystery-thriller. Hired by elderly Miss Rainbird (Nesbitt) to locate a long-lost heir, phoney medium Blanche Tyler (Harris) and her cabbie boy friend George Lumley (Dern)—amiable frauds—begin their search with very few clues. Meanwhile another more sinister couple, jeweler Arthur Adamson (Devane) and his girlfriend Fran (Black) are engineering a kidnapping scheme in which the ransom is to be paid in valuable diamonds. The paths of all of these characters and their respective "plots" eventually cross, in a comical directorial move, at a cemetery. Just when the mystery ends, however, the thrills begin—the most harrowing of which takes place along a curving mountainside road.

The film is a dense but extremely entertaining collection of symmetric patterns, doubles, and rhymes. The performances are first-rate (finally free of the casting constraints, Hitchcock displayed—in 1972's FRENZY as well—a deliciously offbeat taste in performers) and the screenplay by Ernest Lehman (NORTH BY NORTHWEST) is a witty model of construction. The humor is more obvious and subversive than any of Hitchcock's films since THE TROUBLE WITH HARRY. Hitch's final, tongue-in-cheek wink at his audience was one of his most memorable cameos—a broad shadow obscured behind a glass door on which may be read "Registrar of Births and Deaths." Based on a British novel by Victor Canning, the film was scripted under the title "One Plus One Equals One," and went into production as "Deceit," before a studio worker hit on the final title.

FANNY 📀

1932 125m bw Drama ★★★½
Pagnol (France)

Raimu (*Cesar Olivier*), Orane Demazis (*Fanny*), Pierre Fresnay (*Marius*), Fernand Charpin (*Honore Panisse*), Alida Rouffe (*Honorine Cabanis*), Robert Vattier (*M. Brun*), Auguste Mouries (*Felix Escartefigue*), Milly Mathis (*Aunt Claudine Foulon*), Maupi (*Chauffeur*), Edouard Delmont (*Dr. Felicien Venelle*)

p, Marcel Pagnol; d, Marc Allegret; w, Marcel Pagnol (based on his play); ph, Nicolas Toporkoff, Andre Dantan, Roger Hubert, Georges Benoit, Coutelain; ed, Raymond Lamy; m, Vincent Scotto

The second installment of Marcel Pagnol's "Marseilles Trilogy" picks up just a short while after the end of MARIUS. After Marius (Pierre Fresnay) has gone to sea, it is learned that the girl he loves, Fanny (Orane Demazis), is pregnant. Because she has her reputation to think of, Fanny is persuaded by her family to marry the older, widowed sailmaker Panisse (Fernand Charpin), despite the fact that she is still deeply in love with Marius. After a year at sea, Marius returns and tries to convince the woman he loves to leave Marseilles with him. However, she must consider the consequences and the feelings of Panisse, who has grown to love not only Fanny but the child as well.

Pagnol's warm, touching tale has been a success wherever it has played, attesting to the story's universal truthfulness.

Written and produced by Pagnol and starring his troupe of actors, FANNY was filmed under the direction of Marc Allegret. MARIUS was directed by Alexander Korda, and the concluding film CESAR was directed by Pagnol himself.

FANNY AND ALEXANDER *DVD*
(FANNY OCH ALEXANDER)

1982 188m c Drama ★★★★½

Cinematograph/Swedish Film Institute/ R
Swedish TV One/Gaumont/Persona/Tobis
(France/West Germany/Sweden)

Gunn Wallgren *(Helena Ekdahl)*, Boerje Ahlstedt *(Prof. Carl Ekdahl)*, Christina Schollin *(Lydia Ekdahl)*, Allan Edwall *(Oscar Ekdahl)*, Ewa Froeling *(Emilie Ekdahl)*, Pernilla Allwin *(Fanny Ekdahl)*, Bertil Guve *(Alexander Ekdahl)*, Jarl Kulle *(Gustav-Adolph Ekdahl)*, Mona Malm *(Alma Ekdahl)*, Pernilla Wallgren *(Maj)*

d, Ingmar Bergman; w, Ingmar Bergman; ph, Sven Nykvist (Eastmancolor); ed, Sylvia Ingemarsson; m, Daniel Bell, Benjamin Britten, Frans Helmerson, Robert Schumson, Marianne Jacobs; art d, Anna Asp, Susanne Lingheim; cos, Marik Vos

AAN Best Director: Ingmar Bergman; *AAN Best Original Screenplay:* Ingmar Bergman; *AA Best Cinematography:* Sven Nykvist; *AA Best Art Direction-Set Decoration:* Susanne Lingheim; *AA Best Costume Design:* Mark Vos; *AA Best Foreign Language Film*

Steering away from the pain, neuroses, and heavy metaphysical questions showcased in his earlier work, Ingmar Bergman created this film based on childhood memories of the turn of the century.

FANNY AND ALEXANDER begins with the Ekdahl family's Christmas celebration, their large home serving as the meeting place for a merry celebration by family members and servants who dance about heedless of social constraints. Late that night, ten-year-old Alexander (Bertil Guve) is tucked in by the buxom maid, who apologizes for being unable to spend the night with him because she has other obligations—namely bedding down with his kindly Uncle Carl (Boerje Ahlstedt), a married man with children of his own, whose wise wife graciously tolerates his infidelities. Alexander's charmed life is suddenly shattered when his actor-manager father suffers a heart attack and dies, leaving the widow Ekdahl (Ewa Froeling) to be calmed by an understanding bishop (Jan Malmsjoe) whom she eventually marries. She takes her two children, Fanny (Pernilla Allwin) and Alexander, away from their warm family into the cold, strict world of the clergyman.

Not only does Bergman manage in FANNY AND ALEXANDER to capture the flavor and atmosphere of a Swedish town circa 1907, he also expertly reveals events as seen through the eyes of a child and, without any wordy dissertations on doctrines, makes a powerful statement against religious zealotry. The results are quite frightening and far superior to the lengthy gloom and doom that fill many earlier Bergman films. A magical movie, FANNY AND ALEXANDER is likely to be the achievement for which Bergman will be most remembered.

FANTASIA *DVD*
1940 120m c Animated ★★★★
Walt Disney Productions (U.S.)

Deems Taylor *(Himself)*, Leopold Stokowski *(Himself)*, The Philadelphia Symphony Orchestra

p, Walt Disney; d, Samuel Armstrong, James Algar, Bill Roberts, Paul Satterfield, Hamilton Luske, Jim Handley, Ford Beebe, Walt Disney, Norman Ferguson, Wilfred Jackson; w, Lee Blair, Elmer Plummer, Phil Dike, Sylvia Moberly-Holland, Norman Wright, Albert Heath, Bianca Majolie, Graham Keid, Paul Pearse, Carl Fallberg, Leo Thiele, Robert Sterner, John Fraser McLeish, Otto Englander, Webb Smith, Erdman Penner, Joseph Sabo, Bill Peet, George Stallings; m, Johann Sebastian Bach, Peter Ilich Tchaikovsky, Igor Stravinsky, Ludwig van Beethoven, Modest Mussorgsky, Franz Schubert

The most ambitious animated feature ever to come out of the Disney studios, FANTASIA integrates famous works of classical music with wildly uneven but extraordinarily imaginative visuals that run the gamut from dancing hippos to the purely abstract. It's like a feature-length compilation of elaborate Silly Symphonies. This impressive attempt to combine high art with mass culture was a financial debacle initially but in subsequent years it has become one of the studio's perennial cash cows.

Among the wonderfully kitschy combinations of sight and sound are J.S. Bach's "Toccata and Fugue in D Minor" (a rare exercise in abstraction for the Disney artists); Tchaikovsky's "Nutcracker Suite" (danced by fairies, mushrooms, flower petals, fish, thistles, and orchids); Stravinsky's "Rite of Spring" (illustrated as the genesis of the planet); Mussorgsky's "Night on Bald Mountain" (some key imagery is lifted from the opening scenes of F.W. Murnau's silent German Expressionist version of FAUST with Emil Jannings as Mephistopholes looming over a village; the fearsome "Black God" was pantomimed by Bela Lugosi as an animation guide for the Disney artists); and Schubert's "Ave Maria" (a subdued Impressionistic sequence of villagers walking through the woods to church).

Beethoven's "Pastoral Symphony" proved to be the most controversial segment, raising the hackles of music critics who didn't approve of the cartoon Bacchus, nymphs, and lil' centaurs who accompanied it. (Reportedly, after screening the completed segment for the first time, a tearful Walt Disney declared "This will *make* Beethoven!" Stravinsky also cried after seeing the film, but for very different reasons.) The film's most famous segment, Paul Dukas's "Sorcerer's Apprentice," stars Mickey Mouse (voiced by Walt himself for the final time) as the ambitious assistant who gets in way over his head when he uses his boss's magic hat to put a broom to work doing his chores. Originally intended as a short, "The Sorcerer's Apprentice" brought together Walt Disney and famed conductor Leopold Stokowski but when the production ran way over budget, Disney decided that the only way to recoup his investment would be to incorporate the segment into a feature.

The film began to appear in limited roadshow engagements in 1940, but due to wartime difficulties in getting the materials for the sound system that had to be installed in each theater, it was not until 1942 that it received general release. In the late 1960s FANTASIA re-emerged as a drug culture favorite and it continues to delight both children and adults today.

FANTASIA 2000 *DVD*
2000 80m c ★★★½

Animated/Musical/Children's/Fantasy
Walt Disney Pictures (U.S.) G

HOSTS: Steve Martin, Bette Midler, James Levine, Itzhak Perlman, James Earl Jones, Angela Lansbury, Quincy Jones, Penn Jillette, Teller

p, Donald W. Ernst; d, Pixote Hunt ("Symphony No. 5"), Hendel Butoy ("Pines of Rome," "Piano Concerto No. 2"), Eric Goldberg ("Rhapsody in Blue," "Carnival of the Animals"), James Algar ("The Sorcerer's Apprentice"), Francis Glebas ("Pomp and Circumstance"), Paul Brizzi ("Firebird Suite"), Gaetan Brizzi ("Firebird Suite"), Don Hahn (Host Sequences); w, Eric Goldberg ("Rhapsody in Blue," "Carnival of the Animals"), Paul Brizzi ("Firebird Suite"), Gaetan Brizzi ("Firebird Suite"), Don Hahn (Host

Sequences), Irene Mecchi (Host Sequences), David Reynolds (Host Sequences); ed, Jessica Ambinder Rojas, Lois Freeman-Fox; m, Ludwig Van Beethoven ("Symphony No. 5"), Ottorino Respighi ("Pines of Rome"), George Gershwin ("Rhapsody in Blue"), Dmitri Shostakovich ("Piano Concerto No. 2"), Camille Saint-Saens ("Carnival of the Animals"), Paul Dukas ("The Sorcerer's Apprentice"), Edward Elgar ("Pomp and Circumstance"), Igor Stravinsky ("Firebird Suite"); art d, Carl Jones ("Firebird Suite"), Pixote Hunt ("Symphony No. 5"), Dean Gordon ("Pines of Rome"), William Perkins ("Pines of Rome"), Susan McKinsey Goldberg ("Rhapsody in Blue,""Carnival of the Animals"), Michael Humphries ("Piano Concerto No. 2"), Tom Codrick ("The Sorcerer's Apprentice"), Charles Philippi ("The Sorcerer's Apprentice"), Zack Schwartz ("The Sorcerer's Apprentice"), Daniel Cooper ("Pomp and Circumstance"); fx, David A. Bossert (Supervisor), Mauro Maressa ("Rhapsody in Blue"), Richard Hollander (Host Sequences); chor, Kendra McCool ("Piano Concerto No. 2"); anim, Hendel Butoy (Supervising Director), Mitchell Guintu Bernal, Dean Gordon, Alex Topete, Steve Goldberg, Shyh-Chyuan Huang, Susan Thayer, Mary Jane Turner

It appears that Walt Disney always intended FANTASIA, his ambitious collection of animated shorts set to classical compositions, to be a work in progress, re-released regularly with a mix of old and new sections. But the 1940 film has stood unchanged for six decades, until now.

This new compilation retains only one segment—the popular "Sorcerer's Apprentice"—and introduces seven new vignettes, which showcase a range of animation styles. Like the original FANTASIA'S eight segments, the results are a mixed bag. The famous strains of Beethoven's "Symphony No. 5" accompany a banal flock of fluttering triangles, while Respighi's "Pines of Rome" inspires an oddly moving fantasy of whales rising out of the icy ocean to swim amid the clouds. A series of cliched vignettes of NYC life drawn in the style of Al Hirschfeld illustrate Gershwin's "Rhapsody in Blue," a computer animated version of Hans Christian Andersen's "The Steadfast Tin Soldier" (with the inevitable happy ending) is set to Shostakovich's "Piano Concerto No. 2," while the finale of Saint-Saens's "Carnival of the Animals" gives rise to a dopey but endearing tale of a flamingo determined not to go with the flock. Four marches from Elgar's "Pomp and Circumstance" underscore the tale of Noah's ark, retooled to include Donald and Daisy Duck, and Stravinsky's "Firebird Suite" accompanies a beautifully rendered story of death and rebirth in the forest that owes an astonishing visual debt to Hayao Miyazaki's PRINCESS MONONOKE. The film's music was conducted by James Levine, and the animated segments are linked by celebrity-studded live-action segments featuring the likes of James Earl Jones, Bette Midler, and Steve Martin.

FANTASTIC VOYAGE 📀

1966 100m c Science Fiction ★★★½
Fox (U.S.)

Stephen Boyd *(Grant)*, Raquel Welch *(Cora Peterson)*, Edmond O'Brien *(Gen. Carter)*, Donald Pleasence *(Dr. Michaels)*, Arthur O'Connell *(Col. Donald Reid)*, William Redfield *(Capt. Bill Owens)*, Arthur Kennedy *(Dr. Duval)*, Jean Del Val *(Jan Benes)*, Barry Coe *(Communications Aide)*, Ken Scott *(Secret Serviceman)*

p, Saul David; d, Richard Fleischer; w, Harry Kleiner, David Duncan (adapted from the novel by Otto Klement and Jay Lewis Bixby); ph, Ernest Laszlo (CinemaScope, Deluxe Color); ed, William B. Murphy; m, Leonard Rosenman; art d, Jack Martin Smith, Dale Hennesy; fx, L.B. Abbott, Art Cruickshank, Emil Kosa Jr.

AAN Best Color Cinematography: Ernest Laszlo; *AAN Best Film Editing:* William B. Murphy; *AA Best Art Direction-Set Decoration (Color):* Jack Martin Smith, Dale Hennesy, Walter M. Scott, Stuart

A. Reiss; *AA Best Special Visual Effects:* Art Cruickshank; *AAN Best Sound Effects:* Walter Rossi

A medical crew (Stephen Boyd, Raquel Welch, William Redfield, Arthur Kennedy, and Donald Pleasence) and a submarine are miniaturized to remove a blood clot from the brain of a Czech scientist who was shot while defecting. Once shrunk and inside the body, the crew battle white corpuscles while the heart and lungs also make their journey rougher. Early on, it becomes apparent that one of the crew members is a double agent, and matters become even more complex as they race against the clock to complete their mission before returning to normal size.

Their voyage through the body's bloodstream past assorted organs was created by inventive special effects that make this one of the more visually interesting science fiction films of its era. FANTASTIC VOYAGE won Oscars for Best Color Art Direction and Best Visual Effects. It was also nominated for Best Cinematography and Best Film Editing. Joe Dante's INNERSPACE is an amusing variation of the same idea.

FAR COUNTRY, THE 📀

1955 96m c Western ★★★★
Universal (U.S.)

James Stewart *(Jeff)*, Ruth Roman *(Ronda)*, Corinne Calvet *(Renee)*, Walter Brennan *(Ben)*, John McIntire *(Mr. Gannon)*, Jay C. Flippen *(Rube)*, Harry Morgan, billed as Henry Morgan *(Ketchum)*, Steve Brodie *(Ives)*, Royal Dano *(Luke)*, Gregg Barton *(Rounds)*

p, Aaron Rosenberg; d, Anthony Mann; w, Borden Chase; ph, William Daniels (Technicolor); ed, Russell Schoengarth; m, Joseph Gershenson; art d, Bernard Herzbrun, Alexander Golitzen

A strange, almost self-conscious, Western from one of the greatest practioners of the form. Like other Mann efforts , THE FAR COUNTRY is noteworthy for the parable starkness of its story and its flawless command of landscape photography. His films also have the most articulated moments of combat in the cinema: issues of honor, betrayal, violence, and death figure prominently.

Partners Jeff (Stewart) and Ben (Brennan) travel north from Wyoming to the Oregon Territory with a herd of cattle, planning to sell the steers for a fortune in the gold-boom towns. They arrive in the town of Skagway, where the self-appointed judge, Mr. Gannon (McIntire), takes the herd from them. Jeff steals his cattle back, and goes to the town of Dawson, where he is befriended by a saloonkeeper, Ronda (Roman). She decides to help him against Mr. Gannon and his men, who will stop at nothing to get the herd back.

One of the most engrossing and original Westerns made in the 1950s, THE FAR COUNTRY was the fifth collaboration of producer Aaron Rosenberg, director Anthony Mann, and James Stewart. The film benefits greatly from the presence of James Stewart and his barely suppressed malevolence as the hero. Mann's strong and thoughtful direction, the sturdy script by Borden Chase, and the beautiful cinematography of the northern wilderness all contribute to make this an outstanding film.

FAR FROM HEAVEN 📀

2002 107m c Drama ★★★★
Clear Blue Sky Productions/John Wells PG-13
Productions/Killer Films/Section Eight/TF1
International/USA Films/Vulcan Productions (U.S.)

Julianne Moore *(Cathy Whitaker)*, Dennis Quaid *(Frank Whitaker)*, Dennis Haysbert *(Raymond Deagan)*, Patricia Clarkson *(Eleanor Fine)*, Viola Davis *(Sybil)*, James Rebhorn *(Dr. Bowman)*, Bette Henritze *(Mrs. Leacock)*, Michael Gaston *(Stan Fine)*, Ryan Ward *(David Whitaker)*, Lindsay Andretta *(Janice Whitaker)* p, Jody Patton, Christine Vachon; d, Todd Haynes; w, Todd Haynes; ph, Edward Lachman; ed, James Lyons; m, Elmer Bernstein; prod d, Mark Friedberg; art d, Peter Rogness; fx, Steve Kirshoff; cos, Sandy Powell

AAN Best Actress: Julianne Moore; *AAN Best Cinematography:* Edward Lachman; *AAN Best Original Score:* Elmer Bernstein; *AAN Best Original Screenplay:* Todd Haynes

When Fassbinder remade Douglas Sirk's classic 1954 melodrama ALL THAT HEAVEN ALLOWS as ALI, FEAR EATS THE SOUL, he broadened Sirk's indictment of society's attitudes toward sex, age, gender roles, and class to include race. Todd Haynes's own gorgeous replica has them both beat: His sexually neglected heroine (a flawless Julianne Moore) not only earns the opprobrium of her uptight, upper-class community by becoming romantically linked to a "Negro," but she now has a gay husband (Dennis Quaid) as well.

Hartford, CT, 1957: To all appearances, Cathy Whitaker (Moore) has everything a modern woman could be expected to want: a lovely home; a flock of the right sort of friends, including socialite Eleanor Fine (Patricia Clarkson); two lovely children (Ryan Ward, Lindsay Andretta); and a handsome, successful husband, Frank (Quaid). But appearances can be deceiving. The first crack in the glossy surface comes the night Frank is arrested for "loitering;" the crack becomes a chasm when Cathy pays an after-hours visit to Frank's office and finds her ideal husband in the arms of another man. Cathy, meanwhile, strikes up a cozy friendship with her black gardener, Raymond Deagan (Dennis Haysbert), and the scandalous association sets the forked tongues of the town's gossips wagging.

From Sandy Powell's color-coordinated costume design to Elmer Bernstein's lush, omnipresent score, Haynes flaunts his film's artifice. It's not meant to be taken as an imitation of life, but as a reproduction of the "women's pictures" that depicted—and often questioned—the values of their era. Haynes brilliantly uses the restrictions of the genre to critique cultural expectations: Cathy's purposefully stilted dialogue remains bound by the front-office conventions of post-WWII Hollywood (interestingly, Frank's isn't), and unlike the men in the film, her options are as limited as the choice between a happy or a sad ending. Haynes took an enormous risk here, but thanks to his thoughtful screenplay and an utterly sincere performance from Moore, what could have easily become a calculated exercise in postmodern pastiche winds up a powerful and deeply moving example of melodramatic moviemaking.

FAR FROM THE MADDING CROWD
1967 168m c   Drama   ★★½
MGM   (U.K.)

Julie Christie *(Bathsheba Everdene)*, Terence Stamp *(Sgt. Troy)*, Peter Finch *(William Boldwood)*, Alan Bates *(Gabriel Oak)*, Prunella Ransome *(Fanny Robin)*, Fiona Walker *(Liddy)*, Paul Dawkins *(Henery Fray)*, Andrew Robertson *(Andrew Randle)*, John Barrett *(Joseph Poorgrass)*, Julian Somers *(Jan Coggan)*

p, Joseph Janni; d, John Schlesinger; w, Frederic Raphael (adapted from the novel by Thomas Hardy); ph, Nicolas Roeg (Metrocolor); ed, Malcolm Cooke; m, Richard Rodney Bennett; art d, Roy Forge Smith; cos, Alan Barrett

AAN Best Original Score: Richard Rodney Bennett

Director Schlesinger makes the best of a script that adheres to Thomas Hardy's novel almost page for page. Set in 1874, Bathsheba Everdene (Christie) is in love with (and feels superior to) three men, Sergeant Troy (Stamp), William Boldwood (Finch), and Gabriel Oak (Bates). Who will she choose?

This is a predictable story that Schlesinger struggles to keep fresh and moving. The actors have a difficult time with the flat characters but, at times, are able to breath life into them. Nicolas Roeg's cinematography is stunning.

FAREWELL, MY LOVELY   *DVD*
1975 97m   c   Mystery   ★★★
EK/ITC   (U.S.)   R

Robert Mitchum *(Philip Marlowe)*, Charlotte Rampling *(Mrs. Velma Grayle)*, John Ireland *(Lt. Nulty)*, Sylvia Miles *(Mrs. Jessie Florian)*, Jack O'Halloran *(Moose Malloy)*, Anthony Zerbe *(Laird Burnette)*, Harry Dean Stanton *(Billy Rolfe)*, Jim Thompson *(Judge Grayle)*, John O'Leary *(Lindsay Marriott)*, Kate Murtagh *(Frances Amthor)*

p, George Pappas, Jerry Bruckheimer; d, Dick Richards; w, David Zelag Goodman (based on the novel by Raymond Chandler); ph, John A. Alonzo (Panavision, Fujicolor); ed, Walter Thompson, Joel Cox; m, David Shire; prod d, Dean Tavoularis; art d, Angelo Graham; fx, Chuck Gaspar; cos, Tony Scarano

AAN Best Supporting Actress: Sylvia Miles

Mitchum, as the intrepid private eye Marlowe, is hired by Moose Malloy (O'Halloran), a giant thug recently released from prison, to find his girlfriend. Mitchum takes on a second case when the fey Lindsay Marriott (O'Leary) seeks his assistance in buying back a valuable jade necklace held for ransom after being stolen from the sultry Velma Grayle (Rampling). Investigating both cases simultaneously, Marlowe discovers that the two cases are really one and the same—a puzzle involving false identity, hidden loot, and murder.

An affectionate adaptation of Raymond Chandler's novel that beautifully evokes the seamy side of 1940s Los Angeles via superb production design and the same period atmosphere cinematographer Alonzo previously evoked for CHINATOWN. Interestingly, Mitchum's appeal here has more to do with his own exalted status as a noir icon rather than any particularly inspired interpretation of Marlowe. The novel was adapted for the screen twice before, as a vehicle for George Sanders in RKO's THE FALCON TAKES OVER and the superb MURDER, MY SWEET. A moderate hit at the box office, FAREWELL MY LOVELY spawned a fatally flawed remake of THE BIG SLEEP that abandons 1940s Los Angeles in favor of modern-day London.

FAREWELL TO ARMS, A   *DVD*
1932 90m   bw   Romance/War   ★★★★
Paramount   (U.S.)

Helen Hayes *(Catherine Barkley)*, Gary Cooper *(Lt. Frederic Henry)*, Adolphe Menjou *(Maj. Rinaldi)*, Mary Philips *(Helen Ferguson)*, Jack LaRue *(the Priest)*, Blanche Frederici *(Head Nurse)*, Henry Armetta *(Bonello)*, George Humbert *(Piani)*, Fred Malatesta *(Manera)*, Mary Forbes *(Miss Van Campen)*

d, Frank Borzage; w, Benjamin Glazer, Oliver H.P. Garrett (based on the novel by Ernest Hemingway); ph, Charles Lang; ed, Otho Lovering; m, Ralph Rainger, John Leipold, Bernhard Kaun, Paul Marquardt, Herman Hand, W. Franke Harling; art d, Hans Dreier, Roland Anderson; cos, Travis Banton

AAN Best Picture; AA Best Cinematography: Charles Bryant Lang, Jr.; *AAN Best Interior Decoration:* Hans Dreier, Roland Anderson; *AA Best Sound Recording:* Harold C. Lewis

Frank Borzage's masterful adaptation of Ernest Hemingway's celebrated novel stars Gary Cooper as Lt. Frederic Henry, an American adventurer serving in the Italian ambulance corps during WWI, and Helen Hayes as Catherine Barkley, the beautiful English nurse with whom he falls madly in love. When Lt. Henry returns to the front, his jealous friend and superior, Maj. Rinaldi (Adolphe Menjou), intervenes to disrupt their budding romance. Nonetheless the two share a blissful interlude in Milan before Henry returns to the war and Catherine travels to Switzerland to have their baby. Henry knows that someday he will return to her but he must endure many hardships along the way.

Despite Hemingway's reported disgust with the film's comparatively optimistic ending, A FAREWELL TO ARMS is generally faithful to his novel. Director Borzage is at his best here as he utilizes light and movement like brushstrokes to paint a beautifully romantic melodrama with the aid of cinematographer Charles Lang. Borzage's focus is on the love story, but his sweeping battle scenes, loaded with armies of extras, smack of war-torn reality, especially the famous retreat from Caporetto, brilliantly captured in montage. And the performances, while a trifle overblown by modern standards, are so powerful that the film retains its emotional jolt. Hayes was never more appealing, Menjou is at his manipulative best, Cooper displays tremendous depth of feeling, and the supporting work is equally accomplished.

The story is drawn from Hemingway's WWI experiences, his battlefield injury, and his love affair with Agnes von Kurowsky. A Farewell to Arms was adapted for the screen twice more: in 1950 as FORCE OF ARMS with William Holden and Nancy Olsen, and under the original title in 1957 with Rock Hudson and Jennifer Jones.

FAREWELL, MY CONCUBINE 📀
(BA WANG BIE JI)
1993 170m c Historical/Drama ★★★½
Tomson Films/China Film Co-production Corp.
(China/Hong Kong) R

Leslie Cheung (Cheng Dieyi), Zhang Fengyi (Duan Xiaolou), Gong Li (Juxian), Lu Qi (Guan Jifa), Ying Da (Na Kun), Ge You (Master Yuan), Li Chun (Xiao Si (teenager)), Lei Ha Man-zhang (Xiao Si (adult)), Tong Di (Xiao Si (adult)), Ma Mingwei (Douzi (child))

p, Hsu Feng; d, Chen Kaige; w, Lilian Lee, Lu Wei (from the novel by Lilian Lee); ph, Gu Changwei; ed, Pei Xiaonan; m, Zhao Jiping; art d, Chen Huaikai; cos, Chen Changmin

AAN Best Foreign Language Film ; AAN Best Cinematography: Gu Changwei

This adaptation of Lilian Lee's novel, co-written by the author and directed by Chinese "Fifth Generation" filmmaker Chen Kaige (YELLOW EARTH), favorably compares to the best films of David Lean, and won the 1993 Cannes *Palme d'Or*. FAREWELL, MY CONCUBINE brings a balance of psychological intimacy and epic sweep to its story of an insoluble love triangle that plays itself out over 50 tumultuous years of Chinese history.

CONCUBINE revolves around Duan Xiaolou (Zhang Fengyi) and Cheng Dieyi (Leslie Cheung), friends since their childhood schooling in the 1920s at the Peking Opera Academy. The story begins in 1977, as the two are about to reprise their most famous roles—King Chu and his loyal concubine Yu Ji—in the classic opera *Farewell to My Concubine*. The story flashes back to their first meeting: tormented because of his effeminacy and inability to memorize lines, Cheng comes under the protection of the more virile Duan. Cheng is trained to play female roles while Duan learns to play heroes, and their interpretation of *Concubine* makes them both opera superstars. Their friendship is shattered when Duan marries prostitute Juxian (Gong Li), and the film follows their separate destinies, each filled with betrayal and heartbreak.

Chen Kaige's tragic vision contrasts sharply with the more socially slanted films of Zhang Yimou, the only other "Fifth Generation" filmmaker whose works have had much Western exposure. Chen eloquently equates Cheng's tragic disconnection from reality with China's inability to strike a political balance between individual freedom and national unity; there are no heroes in this view of Chinese history, only

varying degrees of bad luck. Chen and his players bring passion and intelligence to the story, making CONCUBINE the best kind of spectacle—one whose scale is always human, despite its vastness and ambition.

FARGO 📀
1996 98m c Crime/Drama/Comedy ★★★½
Working Title Films/PolyGram (U.S.) R

Frances McDormand (Marge Gunderson), Steve Buscemi (Carl Showalter), William H. Macy (Jerry Lundegaard), Peter Stormare (Gaear Grimsrud), Harve Presnell (Wade Gustafson), John Carroll Lynch (Norm Gunderson), Kristin Rudrud (Jean Lundegaard), Tony Denman (Scotty Lundegaard), Steve Park (Mike Yanagita), Steven Reevis (Shep Proudfoot)

p, Ethan Coen; d, Joel Coen; w, Ethan Coen, Joel Coen; ph, Roger Deakins; ed, Roderick Jaynes; m, Carter Burwell; prod d, Rick Heinrichs; art d, Thomas P. Wilkins; fx, Paul Murphy; cos, Mary Zophres

AA Best Actress: Frances McDormand; AA Best Original Screenplay: Ethan Coen, Joel Coen; AAN Best Picture; AAN Best Supporting Actor: William H. Macy; AAN Best Director: Joel Coen; AAN Best Cinematography: Roger Deakins; AAN Best Film Editing: Roderick Jaynes

The erratic Coen Brothers hit their stride again with this comically violent crime saga, set in the Great American Midwest and enlivened by its surprisingly sympathetic portraits of quirky, relentlessly cheery locals.

In the icy heart of snow-blanketed Minnesota, a dumb-as-dirt car salesman (William H. Macy) hatches a plan to wipe out his personal debts. He'll hire a pair of small-time, out-of-town crooks (Steve Buscemi and Peter Stormare) to kidnap his wife (Kristin Rudrud), then collect the ransom from her dad (Harve Presnell), a wealthy tightwad. Naturally, things go horribly wrong.

Briskly plotted and filmed with surpassing competence, this snappy black comedy comes as a relief after a recent onslaught of less-than-inspired Tarantino imitations. With the exception of the brooding MILLER'S CROSSING, this may be the warmest movie the Coens have ever made. There's something unmistakably human beneath the oh-so-clever surface, and Frances McDormand's hugely pregnant local cop Marge Gunderson—who waddles implacably from bloody crime scene to even bloodier crime scene—radiates solid decency instead of the synthetic perkiness that too often passes for character. Granted, just about everyone here is a borderline moron with an annoying accent, but this isn't a case of big-city contempt for small-town mores: born and raised in Minnesota, the Coens know their targets well and generally hit them squarely.

FARMER'S DAUGHTER, THE
1947 96m bw Political/Comedy ★★★½
RKO (U.S.)

Loretta Young (Katrin Holstrom), Joseph Cotten (Glenn Morley), Ethel Barrymore (Mrs. Morley), Charles Bickford (Clancy), Rose Hobart (Virginia), Rhys Williams (Adolph), Harry Davenport (Dr. Mathew Sutven), Tom Powers (Nordick), William Harrigan (Ward Hughes), Lex Barker (Olaf Holstrom)

p, Dore Schary; d, H.C. Potter; w, Allen Rivkin, Laura Kerr (from the play "Hulda, Daughter of Parliament" by Juhni Tervataa); ph, Milton Krasner; ed, Harry Marker; m, Leigh Harline

AA Best Actress: Loretta Young; AAN Best Supporting Actor: Charles Bickford

This winning Capraesque romantic comedy features Loretta Young as Katrin Holstrom, a Swedish farmer's daughter who comes to the capital in search of a nursing job but eventually becomes the maid for Congressman Glenn Morley (Joseph Cotten) and his powerful politico mother (Ethel Barrymore). Katrin is the perfect housekeeper in almost every way, but when the Morleys try to promote the congressional candidacy of a man Katrin can't abide, she speaks out publicly and ends up as the rival party's candidate for the office. Young won an Academy Award for her delightful performance and Charles Bickford received a Best Supporting Actor Oscar nomination for his role as the butler who shows Katrin the ropes.

FAST, CHEAP & OUT OF CONTROL   *DVD*

1997 82m c/bw Documentary   ★★★½
Fourth Floor Productions/American Playhouse   PG
(U.S.)

Dave Hoover *(Wild Animal Trainer)*, George Mendonca *(Topiary Gardener)*, Ray Mendez *(Mole-Rat Specialist)*, Rodney Brooks *(Robot Scientist)*

p, Errol Morris; d, Errol Morris; ph, Robert Richardson; ed, Shondra Merrill, Karen Schmeer; m, Caleb Sampson; prod d, Ted Bafaloukos

People say the darnedest things to filmmaker Errol Morris, as anyone who's seen his breathtaking true-crime documentary THE THIN BLUE LINE (1988) can attest. His new subjects are four slightly loopy eccentrics: MIT robot scientist Rodney Brooks; elderly topiary gardener George Mendonca; retired lion tamer Dave Hoover; and Ray Mendez, an authority on tiny naked mole rats, those hairless rodents that bear an uncomfortable resemblance to penises with teeth and legs. Morris intercuts their interviews and other footage to create a subtle, eerily profound meditation on man's relationship with the world around him. Mendez sees human society reflected in the hive-like community of mole rats. Hoover, who idolizes the late circus owner and actor Clyde Beatty, casts his relationship with lions and tigers in startlingly Machiavellian terms. Mendonca, who's devoted his life to a Rhode Island estate called Green Animals, reflects ruefully that younger gardeners don't have the patience that topiary sculpture requires, while Brooks imagines a future filled with insect-like robots with minds of their own: the movie's title comes from his paper on the use of disposable robots in space exploration. Morris's skillful juxtapositions produce an odd, melancholy, and quietly haunting portrait of dreamers who've managed to remake their own little corners of the world in line with their obsessions.

FAST RUNNER, THE   *DVD*
(ATANARJUAT)
2001 172m c Drama/Adventure   ★★★★
Igloolik Isuma Productions   (Canada)

Natar Ungalaaq *(Atanarjuat)*, Sylvia Ivalu *(Atuat)*, Peter Henry Arnatsiaq *(Oki)*, Lucy Tulugarjuk *(Puja)*, Madeline Ivalu *(Panikpak)*, Eugene Ipkarnak *(Sauri)*, Pakak Innuksuk *(Amaqjuaq)*, Abraham Ulayuruluk *(Tungajuaq)*, Apayata Kotierk *(Kumaglak)*, Felix Alaralak *(Tulimaq)*

p, Paul Apak Angilirq, Norman Cohn, Zacharias Kunuk; Germaine Ying Gee Wong; d, Zacharias Kunuk; w, Paul Apak Angilirq; ph, Norman Cohn; ed, Norman Cohn, Zacharias Kunuk, Marie-Christine Sarda; m, Chris Crilly; prod d, James Ungalaaq; fx, Walter Klassen; cos, Atuat Akkitirq

Movie audiences have seen little of the Canadian Arctic native people since Robert J. Flaherty introduced NANOOK OF THE NORTH to the rest of the world, so this unusual and often thrilling three-hour film is a welcome event. Not only is it a reintroduction to a fascinating culture that has survived 4,000 years in a remote and most inhospitable climate, but it's also the first film ever directed by an Inuit filmmaker and featuring an all-Inuit cast.

Set in the distant past, the story unfolds in Igloolik, once a small settlement of nomadic Inuit. The village has fallen under the evil influence of Tungajuaq (Abraham Ulayuruluk), the wicked shaman who murdered the community's leader, Kumaglak (Apayata Kotierk), granted power to Kumaglak's ambitious son, Sauri (Eugene Ipkarnak), and cursed Sauri's rival, Tulimaq (Felix Alaralak). Tulimaq's son Atanarjuat (Natar Ungalaaq) and his older brother, Amaqjuaq (Pakak Innuksuk), come of age as outcasts, but Atanarjuat has something Sauri's son, Oki (Peter Henry Arnatsiaq), desperately desires but can never have: the love of Atuat (a superb Sylvia Ivalu). Atanarjuat and Atuat marry, but once Atuat becomes pregnant, Atanarjuat takes a second wife, Oki's temptress sister Puja (Lucy Tulugarjuk). Even Puja's grandmother, Panikpak (Madeline Ivalu), believes Puja is infected by the old shaman's evil, and she may be right. Puja seduces her husband's brother, and when Atanarjuat throws her out, she schemes to have him murdered.

Zacharias Kunuk's debut feature is a positively thrilling combination of ethnography and all the intrigue, betrayal, deceit, and murder of a Shakespearean tragedy—or a juicy soap opera. The film is also a strong endorsement of the versatility and importance of digital video; without this inexpensive and highly mobile new technology, there's little chance Kunuk would ever have gotten this wonderful film made.

FAST TIMES AT RIDGEMONT HIGH   *DVD*
1982 92m c Comedy   ★★★
Universal (U.S.)   R

Sean Penn *(Jeff Spicoli)*, Jennifer Jason Leigh *(Stacy Hamilton)*, Judge Reinhold *(Brad Hamilton)*, Robert Romanus *(Mike Damone)*, Brian Backer *(Mark "Rat" Ratner)*, Phoebe Cates *(Linda Barrett)*, Ray Walston *(Mr. Hand)*, Scott Thomson *(Arnold)*, Vincent Schiavelli *(Mr. Vargas)*, Amanda Wyss *(Lisa)*

p, Art Linson, Irving Azoff; d, Amy Heckerling; w, Cameron Crowe (adapted from his book); ph, Matthew F. Leonetti (Technicolor); ed, Eric Jenkins; m, Joe Walsh; art d, Dan Lomino

At age 22, writer Cameron Crowe returned to high school, posing as a student, and wrote a book about his experiences. In adapting the book, director Amy Heckerling created a brashly funny yet sensitive comedy that has become a cult favorite.

Chronicling a year in the lives of a group of California teenagers, the film follows the fortunes of Ridgemont High senior Brad Hamilton (Judge Reinhold) and his freshman sister Stacy (Jennifer Jason Leigh). Brad's popularity wanes when he loses his "good" fast-food job, and Stacy is introduced to the wonders of boys by Linda (Phoebe Cates). Mark "Rat" Ratner (Brian Backer) has a big crush on Stacy, but it's oily Mike Damone (Robert Romanus) who initiates her into the world of sex. The film's most memorable character is the perpetually stoned surfer played by Sean Penn. His confrontations with Mr. Hand (Ray Walston), a draconian history teacher, provide the film's finest moments.

In addition to adapting his novel for this film, onetime rock critic Crowe also wrote the screenplay for the less successful teenage comedy THE WILD LIFE before making his directorial debut with the extraordinary SAY ANYTHING. Forest Whitaker (GOOD MORNING VIETNAM, BIRD), Anthony Edwards (MR. NORTH, TOP GUN), and Eric Stoltz (MASK, MEMPHIS BELLE) made their film debuts in this superior teen comedy.

FASTER, PUSSYCAT! KILL! KILL!

1966 84m bw Erotic/Action ★★★
Eve Productions, Inc. (U.S.)

Tura Satana, Haji, Lori Williams, Susan Bernard, Stuart Lancaster, Paul Trinka

p, Russ Meyer; d, Russ Meyer; w, Jack Moran; ph, Walter Schenk; ed, Russ Meyer; m, Paul Sawtelle

Gleefully sordid, violent, good-humored exploitation from Russ Meyer, the thinking person's skin-flick director. A trio of exotic dancers, led by the impossibly bosomy Tura Satana, cruises through the deserts of Southern California on a lust-driven quest for kicks, wreaking death on a series of salivating, treacherous males. Technically impressive, especially at a budget of $40,000, the film amply evidences the director's (somewhat uncomprehending) fascination with female anatomy, hipster attitude, and West Coast youth culture. Probably the most lighthearted and enjoyable of Meyer's films, FASTER, PUSSYCAT was embraced by a new generation during its art-house re-release in 1994; many viewers detected a feminist subtext beneath its extravagantly campy surface.

FAT CITY   DVD

1972 100m c Drama/Sports ★★★★
Columbia (U.S.) PG

Stacy Keach (Billy Tully), Jeff Bridges (Ernie Munger), Susan Tyrrell (Oma), Candy Clark (Faye), Nicholas Colasanto (Ruben), Art Aragon (Babe), Curtis Cokes (Earl), Sixto Rodriguez (Lucero), Billy Walker (Wes), Wayne Mahan (Buford)

p, Ray Stark; d, John Huston; w, Leonard Gardner (based on his novel); ph, Conrad Hall (Eastmancolor); ed, Margaret Booth; m, Marvin Hamlisch; prod d, Richard Sylbert; fx, Paul Stewart; cos, Dorothy Jeakins

AAN Best Supporting Actress: Susan Tyrrell

Set in Stockton, California, against a backdrop of run-down bars, cheap apartments and half-empty second rate gyms, FAT CITY is a grim story of hope and despair among life's losers.

Billy Tully (Stacy Keach), a 29-year-old one-time boxing contender, contemplates a comeback after nearly two years of alcoholism brought about by the loss of both his wife and the biggest fight of his career. He meets Ernie Munger (Jeff Bridges), a promising 19-year-old, and encourages him to hook up with Billy's old manager (Nicholas Colasanto). This Ernie does and so begins his own boxing career. Billy, however, continues boozing and his personal and professional lives continue their downward trajectory.

Adapted by Leonard Gardner from his own novel and brilliantly directed by John Huston, who was himself once an amateur champion, FAT CITY is both an extraordinarily realistic look at the bottom rungs of the fight game and a moving exploration of the human condition. Keach, Bridges, Tyrrell (who received an Oscar nomination for her portrayal of the alcoholic Oma, Billy's temporary girlfriend), and all the supporting players give first-rate performances. All in all, this strong downbeat film, which makes appropriate use of Kris Kristofferson's "Help Me Make It through the Night," is never less than captivating.

FATAL ATTRACTION   DVD

1987 119m c Thriller/Romance ★★★
Paramount (U.S.) R

Michael Douglas (Dan Gallagher), Glenn Close (Alex Forrest), Anne Archer (Beth Gallagher), Ellen Hamilton Latzen (Ellen Gallagher), Stuart Pankin (Jimmy), Ellen Foley (Hildy), Fred Gwynne (Arthur), Meg Mundy (Joan Rogerson), Tom Brennan (Howard Rogerson), Lois Smith (Martha)

p, Stanley R. Jaffe, Sherry Lansing; d, Adrian Lyne; w, James Dearden; ph, Howard Atherton (Technicolor); ed, Michael Kahn, Peter E. Berger; m, Maurice Jarre; prod d, Mel Bourne; art d, Jack Blackman; cos, Ellen Mirojnick

AAN Best Picture; AAN Best Actress: Glenn Close; *AAN Best Supporting Actress:* Anne Archer; *AAN Best Director:* Adrian Lyne; *AAN Best Adapted Screenplay:* James Dearden; *AAN Best Film Editing:* Michael Kahn, Peter E Berger

FATAL ATTRACTION was more than a box-office smash; it was a cultural phenomenon. This story of an extramarital fling that turns into a nightmare begins as a well-crafted psychological thriller but degenerates into a misogynistic thrill-fest in its closing moments.

Dan Gallagher (Michael Douglas) is a Manhattan lawyer with a gorgeous wife (Anne Archer) and a six-year-old daughter. When he first meets Alex (Glenn Close), he is intrigued, but unavailable. On another weekend, though, a chance meeting brings Dan and Alex together for a passionate two-night stand in her apartment. When Dan tries to say his final goodbye and return to his family, he gets the first hint that Alex is not entirely rational and has become obsessed with him. That obsession soon turns life into an escalating nightmare for Dan and his family.

Screenwriter James Dearden has created a set of initially believable characters, placed them in a familiar situation, and then drastically upped the stakes. Unfortunately, motivations and psychological concerns are thrown out the window in the final reel. The blame for this doesn't rest entirely with Dearden or director Adrian Lyne; the producers tested the original ending (Alex commits suicide, but not before implicating Dan as her murderer) and preview audiences found it less than satisfying. The thrill-a-minute conclusion was then shot and substituted.

Notwithstanding the ending, the performances are excellent. Playing against type, Close is overtly libidinous, while at the same time making her obsession and slide into madness convincing and pathetic. Douglas also gives a performance of reasonable depth, and Archer does a nice turn as his implicitly frigid but alluring wife.

FATHER GOOSE   DVD

1964 115m c War/Comedy ★★★
Universal (U.S.)

Cary Grant (Walter Eckland), Leslie Caron (Catherine Freneau), Trevor Howard (Commodore Frank Houghton), Jack Good (Lt. Stebbins), Verina Greenlaw (Christine), Pip Sparke (Anne), Jennifer Berrington (Harriet), Stephanie Berrington (Elizabeth), Laurelle Felsette (Angelique), Nicole Felsette (Dominique)

p, Robert Arthur; d, Ralph Nelson; w, Frank Tarloff, Peter Stone (based on the story "A Place Of Dragons" by S.H. Barnett); ph, Charles Lang (Technicolor); ed, Ted J. Kent; m, Cy Coleman; art d, Alexander Golitzen, Henry Bumstead; cos, Ray Aghayan

AA Best Original Story and Screenplay: S.H. Barnett, Peter Stone, Frank Tarloff; *AAN Best Film Editing:* Ted J. Kent; *AAN Best Sound:* Waldon O. Watson

Playing against his sophisticated image, Cary Grant is Walter Eckland, a drunken beach bum who sits out WWII on a South Seas island until he is coerced by an Australian naval officer (Trevor Howard) into monitoring Japanese air activity. When Eckland travels to a nearby island to rescue another plane watcher, he finds the observer dead, but schoolteacher Catherine Freneau (Leslie Caron) and her seven young female charges are very much alive after being marooned when their plane went down. They return with Eckland and clean up his act while he and Freneau fall in love. Danger looms, however, as the Japanese forces close in. Grant's penultimate film (WALK, DON'T RUN was his last), this romantic comedy won Best Screenplay Oscars for Frank Tarloff and Peter Stone, who worked on the screenplay separately but were awarded a shared credit by a Writers Guild arbitration.

FATHER OF THE BRIDE   **DVD**
1950   92m   bw   Comedy   ★★★★
MGM   (U.S.)

Spencer Tracy *(Stanley T. Banks)*, Joan Bennett *(Ellie Banks)*, Elizabeth Taylor *(Kay Banks)*, Don Taylor *(Buckley Dunstan)*, Billie Burke *(Doris Dunstan)*, Leo G. Carroll *(Mr. Massoula)*, Moroni Olsen *(Herbert Dunstan)*, Melville Cooper *(Mr. Tringle)*, Taylor Holmes *(Warner)*, Paul Harvey *(Rev. Galsworthy)*

p, Pandro S. Berman; d, Vincente Minnelli; w, Frances Goodrich, Albert Hackett (based on the novel by Edward Streeter); ph, John Alton; ed, Ferris Webster; m, Adolph Deutsch; art d, Cedric Gibbons, Leonid Vasian; cos, Helen Rose, Walter Plunkett

AAN Best Picture; AAN Best Actor: Spencer Tracy; *AAN Best Screenplay:* Frances Goodrich, Albert Hackett

Nowadays remembered primarily as the first of many walks La Liz was to take down the aisle, FATHER OF THE BRIDE is also one of the best comedies MGM made in the 1950s. Although Taylor perfectly embodies an idealized vision of the demure but spirited young bride, this fine film is foremost a showcase for the supple comic drollery of Spencer Tracy. As Stanley Banks, the harassed father who must cope with the business of marrying his daughter off, Tracy finds a marvelous vehicle for his expressive but low-key style.

The movie begins as the exhausted Banks looks over the debris and chaos in his home after the wedding, then turns to the audience to relate his story. The problems and responsibilities of marrying off a daughter are legion: there's the heart-to-heart talk with the suitor; meeting the in-laws; selecting the honeymoon site; and, of course, the near-ruinous financial expense.

Although continually skimming the edge of bland sitcom land, this satiric look at the American Family, circa 1950, still packs a gentle punch. The screenplay, if occasionally contrived, is witty and incisive and Minnelli's assured direction keeps the proceedings from disintegrating into indulgent slapstick. As the bride's mother, Joan Bennett is excellent in her first film for MGM, and the supporting performances are all good, with especially fine work from Moroni Olsen and Billie Burke as the parents of the groom. The last is played with charm and the perfect touch of dullness by Don Taylor, who later traded acting for the director's chair. The film inspired a sequel, FATHER'S LITTLE DIVIDEND, and a mediocre 1991 remake.

FEAR AND DESIRE
1953   68m   bw   War   ★★★
Kubrick   (U.S.)

Frank Silvera *(Mac)*, Kenneth Harp *(Lt. Corby)*, Paul Mazursky *(Sidney)*, Steve Coit *(Fletcher)*, Virginia Leith *(Girl)*, David Allen *(Narrator)*

p, Stanley Kubrick; d, Stanley Kubrick; w, Howard Sackler, Stanley Kubrick; ph, Stanley Kubrick; ed, Stanley Kubrick; m, Gerald Fried

Notable as Stanley Kubrick's first film, produced when he was 22 years old on a budget of $40,000. A modest effort, FEAR AND DESIRE nonetheless displays the preoccupation with the pressures and absurdities of war which would later mark many of Kubrick's later films. Not only did he produce and direct, but he also shot and edited this story of four soldiers caught behind enemy lines in an abstractly depicted war.

Trying to move back to their own side, they kill several enemy soldiers and capture a young woman (Leith). One of the men, Sidney (Mazursky, making his film debut), is left to guard her as the other three (Silvera, Harp and Coit) go to a river to build a raft. Wanting to seduce the girl, Sidney unties her from a tree, and when she runs away, he kills her and then goes insane. Returning from the river, the three soldiers discover an enemy outpost holding a general and his aide. The confrontation between the three enterprising soldiers and the enemy climaxes this highly promising first effort by one of America's premiere filmmakers.

FEAR AND LOATHING IN LAS VEGAS   **DVD**
1998   128m   c   Comedy/Drama   ★★½
Rhino Films   (U.S.)   R

Johnny Depp *(Raoul Duke)*, Benicio Del Toro *(Dr. Gonzo)*, Tobey Maguire *(Hitchiker)*, Ellen Barkin *(Waitress at North Star Cafe)*, Gary Busey *(Highway Patrolman)*, Christina Ricci *(Lucy)*, Mark Harmon *(Magazine Reporter at Mint 400)*, Cameron Diaz *(Blonde TV Reporter)*, Katherine Helmond *(Desk Clerk at Mint Hotel)*, Michael Jeter *(Speaker at D.A. Drug Convention)*

p, Laila Nablusi, Patrick Cassavetti, Stephen Nemeth; d, Terry Gilliam; w, Terry Gilliam, Tod Davies, Alex Cox, Tony Grisoni (from the book by Hunter S. Thompson); ph, Nicola Pecorini; ed, Leslie Walker; prod d, Alex McDowell; art d, Gary Diamond, Chris Gorak; fx, Steve Galich, Illusion Arts; cos, Julie Weiss

What a strange, occasionally magnificent folly is Terry Gilliam's film of Hunter S. Thompson's mind-altering-substance-fueled kaddish for the '60s. By turns mordantly funny, horribly tedious, and self-indulgent, this astonishingly faithful adaptation of Thompson's account of three days of drug-crazed degeneracy in 1971 Las Vegas is both defiantly out of step with current times and obstinately hard to surrender to: The sound is mixed into a numbing jumble of words and sheer noise, the killer soundtrack is muffled, and every glorious, candy-colored image is undermined by some scorched-earth shot of just-plain hideousness.

Johnny Depp plays Thompson's alter ego Raoul Duke, a writer who's sent to Vegas to cover a penny-ante dirt-bike race, egged on by his lawyer and partner in crime, Dr. Gonzo (Benecio Del Toro). They use the opportunity to live on reds and cocaine, trash hotel rooms and generally behave as badly as possible. Depp's performance is saved from being merely an extraordinary feat of mimicry—he has Thompson's look and mannered speech down cold—by his sneaky sense of physical comedy: Depp does positively Chaplin-esque things with Thompson's trademark cigarette holder (when he's surprised, as he often is, it springs to cartoon-like, exclamation-mark alert) and his ether-induced stagger should win him instant admission into the Ministry of Silly Walks.

From the outset, Gilliam brilliantly uses Thompson's drug-induced state to establish the notion that there's no line between voice-over and ordinary speech: Thompson never knows whether he's thinking or saying things out loud. That clears the way for Depp to talk constantly, and the sporadic brilliance of Thompson's jaundiced observations occasionally shines through the self-serving, gonzo posturing. A peculiar and oddly haunting achievement.

FEAR STRIKES OUT   **DVD**
1957   100m   bw   Biography/Sports   ★★★★
Paramount   (U.S.)

Anthony Perkins *(Jimmy Piersall)*, Karl Malden *(John Piersall)*, Norma Moore *(Mary Teevan)*, Adam Williams *(Dr. Brown)*, Peter Votrian *(Jimmy Piersall as a Boy)*, Perry Wilson *(Mrs. John Piersall)*, Dennis McMullen *(Phil)*, Gail Land *(Alice)*, Brian Hutton *(Bernie Sherwill)*, Bart Burns *(Joe Cronin)* p, Alan J. Pakula; d, Robert Mulligan; w, Ted Berkman, Raphael Blau (based on the autobiography by James A. Piersall, with Albert S. Hirshberg); ph, Haskell Boggs; ed, Aaron Stell; m, Elmer Bernstein; fx, John P. Fulton; cos, Edith Head

Perkins portrays Jimmy Piersall in this well-done biopic of one of baseball's most colorful characters, who, from boyhood, was relentlessly driven by his father (Malden) to make it in the major leagues. Nothing the talented Jimmy does is good enough for his dad, and, after finally making the Boston Red Sox, he breaks down, maniacally climbing the backstop after hitting a home run—one of the best-remembered scenes in any sports film. Jimmy is then admitted to Westborough State Hospital, where he gradually recovers under the supervision of Dr. Brown (Williams), eventually returning to his wife, his repentant father, and the Red Sox lineup.

The physically awkward Perkins may seem an unlikely candidate to portray a professional athlete, however, in a dry run of his performance in PSYCHO, he delivers a powerful portrayal of a young man undergoing tremendous emotional turmoil; in the final analysis, the film's psychological impact far outweighs how Perkins looks throwing a baseball back into the infield. Based on Piersall's autobiography, this directorial debut for Mulligan also boasts an extremely effective, typically full-volume performance by Malden as Piersall's demanding but loving father.

FEARLESS

1993 122m c Drama ★★★½
Spring Creek Productions (U.S.) R

Jeff Bridges *(Max Klein)*, Isabella Rossellini *(Laura Klein)*, Rosie Perez *(Carla Rodrigo)*, Tom Hulce *(Brillstein)*, John Turturro *(Bill Perlman)*, Benicio Del Toro *(Manny Rodrigo)*, Deirdre O'Connell *(Nan Gordon)*, John DeLancie, billed as John De Lancie *(Jeff Gordon)*, Spencer Vrooman *(Jonah Klein)*, Daniel Cerny *(Byron Hummel)*

p, Mark Rosenberg, Paula Weinstein; d, Peter Weir; w, Rafael Yglesias (from his novel); ph, Allen Daviau, Tom Cannole; ed, William Anderson, Armen Minasian, Lee Smith; m, Maurice Jarre; prod d, John Stoddart; art d, Christopher Burian-Mohr; fx, Ken Pepiot, Gintar Repecka, Peter Albiez, Robert L. Olmstead, Gary L. Karas, Kelly Kirby, William Mesa; cos, Marilyn Matthews

AAN Best Supporting Actress: Rosie Perez

By Hollywood standards, FEARLESS is a brave attempt to grapple with some Big Issues—life, death, faith, guilt, stuff like that. At times, it crashes to the ground in a blaze of heavy-handed symbolism, but "Fearless" also achieves some haunting, hallucinatory flights of beauty.

Jeff Bridges plays Max Klein, a San Francisco architect psychologically transformed by an appalling plane crash. In the moments before impact, Max realizes he is not afraid of dying. Until now a nervous, harried figure, he discovers a heroic calm that helps him take several passengers, but also makes his entire previous existence seem foreign and irrelevant. The only person the new Max can relate to is fellow survivor Carla (Rosie Perez), a working-class Hispanic mother stricken with guilt over her failure to save her son during the crash.

If Max's beautiful, adoring wife (Isabella Rossellini) has a hard time understanding her husband's almost mystical attraction to Carla, so does the audience. Perez's performance undoes the film's delicate chemistry, with her shrill delivery sabotaging many key scenes. Bridges, by contrast, is a marvel—even as he strides through the physical world, he somehow makes us believe he has transcended it. Rossellini is superb as his wife, Tom Hulce is funny as a venal attorney, and John Turturro makes a quietly effective therapist. It's a shame that not all of the crew can fly at the same altitude.

FELICIA'S JOURNEY

1999 116m c Thriller/Drama ★★★★
Ego Film Arts/Alliance Atlantis Entertainment/ R
Icon Productions (Canada/U.K.)

Bob Hoskins *(Joseph Ambrose Hilditch)*, Elaine Cassidy *(Felicia)*, Arsinee Khanjian *(Gala)*, Peter McDonald *(Johnny Lysaght)*, Gerard McSorley *(Felicia's Father)*, Brid Brennan *(Mrs. Lysaght)*, Claire Benedict *(Miss Calligary)*, Danny Turner *(Young Hilditch)*, Sheila Reid *(Iris)*

p, Bruce Davey; d, Atom Egoyan; w, Atom Egoyan (based on the novel by William Trevor); ph, Paul Sarossy; ed, Susan Shipton; m, Mychael Danna; prod d, Jim Clay; art d, Chris Seagers; cos, Sandy Powell

A beautifully wrought adaptation of William Trevor's haunting novel.

Joseph Hilditch (Bob Hoskins) lives a tidy, solitary life in the cozy Birmingham house he once shared with his late mother (Arsinee Khanjian), the host of a popular 1950s cooking show. Each night, Hilditch watches her on the VCR, cooking along to old episodes as he prepares complicated, multicourse meals for himself. But Hilditch has other tapes in his videocassette collection, documents of a different sort of pastime. These tapes record the deaths of the young women Hilditch picks up and murders in the front seat of his perfectly preserved vintage auto. Some are prostitutes, others are runaways; none, Hilditch assumes, will be missed. One afternoon outside the factory where he works as a catering manager, Hilditch meets Felicia (Elaine Cassidy), a teenager who has left her home in Ireland to find her wayward boyfriend. Hilditch thinks he's found his next victim—another troubled soul longing for solace—but as the lonely bachelor lures Felicia to her death, the truth behind Felicia's journey complicates his awful plans.

Atom Egoyan has moved well beyond the structural experimentation of his early films, where frissons were mainly the result of the emerging relationships among seemingly disparate characters. Here, as in THE SWEET HEREAFTER, moments of truth have become deeper revelations about the human condition, the pulse which shatters the icy calm of the film's cool, precise surfaces. Hoskins gives a flawless performance; he hides Hilditch's terrible secret life behind a creepy, avuncular concern that's chilling in its banality.

FELLINI SATYRICON

1969 128m c Historical ★★★★
P.E.A./Artistes (France/Italy)

Martin Potter *(Encolpius)*, Hiram Keller *(Ascyltus)*, Max Born *(Giton)*, Capucine *(Tryphaena)*, Salvo Randone *(Eumolpus)*, Magali Noel *(Fortunata)*, Alain Cuny *(Lichas)*, Lucia Bose *(Suicide Wife)*, Tanya Lopert *(Caesar)*, Gordon Mitchell *(Robber)*

p, Alberto Grimaldi; d, Federico Fellini; w, Federico Fellini, Bernardino Zapponi, Brunello Rondi (based on the fragment "Satyricon" by Gaius Petronius); ph, Giuseppe Rotunno (Panavision, DeLuxe Color); ed, Ruggero Mastroianni; m, Nino Rota, Ilhan Mimaroglu, Tod Dockstader, Andrew Rudin; prod d, Danilo Donati; art d, Luigi Scaccianoce, Giorgio Giovannini; fx, Adriano Pischiutta; cos, Danilo Donati

AAN Best Director: Federico Fellini

Orgy, anyone? The bizarre characters and situations that had filled the films of Federico Fellini since his early VARIETY LIGHTS found their ultimate expression in this dreamy, hallucinatory depiction of ancient Rome. Based on the 1st century A.D. fragment of a drama by Gaius Petronius (with added inspiration from other writings of the period), this film strips away all the glamor and honor associated with the early

Romans to expose a society in which conventional morality has little or no significance. But Fellini's desire was not to criticize Rome, nor was it to set the history books straight; rather, he found the perfect setting with which to parallel the youth culture of the 1960s.

Encolpius (Potter) and Ascyltus (Keller) are two students whose adventures in a hotbed of decadence are the excuse for the threadbare plot that holds this extraordinary spectacle together. Their sole aim is the pursuit of hedonistic desires, and hedonism is just what Fellini gives us—there are concubines, nymphomaniacs, hermaphrodites (in the form of an albino infant with magical healing powers), sadism, masochism, and no doubt a few more "isms" as well amidst all the group sex going on.

The odd thing is that the excess seems visual and mythical rather than really sexual. (For one thing we *see* very little sex.) The masterful cinematography and stunning use of color, achieved through the use of deliberately artificial light sources, lend the film an almost hypnotic sheen. Even if you can't recall particular images, the look of the film is likely to linger in your memory.

FELLINI'S ROMA DVD

1972 119m c Drama ★★½
Ultra/Artistes (Italy/France) R

Federico Fellini (*Himself*), Peter Gonzales (*Fellini, Age 18*), Stefano Majore (*Fellini As a Child*), Pia De Doses (*Princess*), Renato Giovanneli (*Cardinal Ottaviani*), Fiona Florence (*Young Prostitute*), Marne Maitland (*Underground Guide*), Galliano Sbarra (*Music Hall Compere*), Alvaro Vitali (*Tap Dancer Imitating Fred Astaire*), Britta Barnes

p, Turi Vasile; d, Federico Fellini; w, Federico Fellini, Bernardino Zapponi; ph, Giuseppe Rotunno (Technicolor); ed, Ruggero Mastroianni; m, Nino Rota; prod d, Danilo Donati; fx, Adriano Pischiutta; chor, Gino Landi; cos, Danilo Donati

ROMA, a confounding and confused semi-documentary, tried the patience of even the most devoted Fellini fans. The story, such as it is, begins in the small town where young Fellini, played by Majore, is born. Majore wants desperately to live in Rome and finally moves there in 1938, just before war breaks out. Majore gives way to Gonzales as a teenaged Fellini, living in a tenement where he observes the rich, noisy lives of his neighbours.

Jump to the early 1970s and Fellini, as himself, is now a renowned director making a picture. He's shooting a scene in a traffic jam during a heavy rainstorm, and his memory is jogged back to his early days in the city when he attended a vaudeville show during the war. Back in the present, "Fellini" is shooting the construction of the subway that has been being built for decades: wherever workers dig, they make an archaelogical find and the area becomes off-limits to the builders. We visit bordellos, a perverse clerical fashion show, and a street festival where cops besiege radical youths. Amid further reveries, Fellini begins interviewing people on camera: Anna Magnani, Gore Vidal, Alberto Sordi, and Marcello Mastroianni, among others. (The latter two were cut from the U.S. print.) Darkness descends, the city begins to snore, and the silence is overwhelmed by a horde of motorcyclists careening through the city past the old relics and winding up at the Colosseum.

What does it all mean? Who knows? Fellini had already made two movies about directorial alter egos with creative block, LA DOLCE VITA and 8 1/2. Here, however, the director himself is blocked: he recycles familiar themes and ideas, with the result that ROMA often feels like a remake. Episodic and enigmatic, it's almost a parody of Fellini's other movies. Two versions were released, in English and with subtitles; the dubbed version is unobjectionable. Many laughs and just as many winces.

FEMALE CONVICT "SCORPION"—JAILHOUSE 41 DVD

1972 93m c Action ★★★½
(Japan)

Meiko Kaji (*Scorpion*), Kayoko Shiraishi, Yukie Kagawa, Hosei Komatsu, Fumio Watanabe

p, Kineo Yoshimine; d, Shunya Ito; w, Fumio Kamnami (adapted from manga comics); ph, Masaro Shimizu

Try to imagine one of those quasi-feminist, women-in-prison flicks from the early '70s—THE BIG DOLL HOUSE, say—shot-through with the dreamlike beauty of the classic Japanese ghost-story anthology KWAIDAN and featuring a laconic, balls-to-the-wall heroine out of some all-girl spaghetti western Sergio Leone never got around to making. Got it? Well, that's not even half of what this indescribable, 1972 buried treasure from Japan has in store.

After being brutalized once too often by her jailers, convicted killer and habitual escapee Matsu ('70s action icon Meiko Kaji)—known throughout the prison compound as "Scorpion"—and six homicidal fellow inmates overpower the driver of their work detail van, kill the guards, and make a run for it. Pursued by prison officials led by Matsu's arch nemesis, Mr. Goada, the women wander across a series of dying landscapes—valleys of ashes, fallen leaves and, finally, garbage—as they make an increasingly desperate scramble for freedom.

Drenched in color, shot from a variety of delirious angles, and filled with surreal violence and hints of the bondage and kinky sex that's part and parcel of the WIP genre, the film's look betrays its origins in a popular comic book series. But director Shunya Ito transcends generic limitations with real pathos, a sincerely feminist subtext, and wildly inventive fantasy sequences. This was the second in the long-running "Joshu Sasori" prison series; Ito directed the first, SCORPION: FEMALE PRISONER #701, which told the story behind Scorpion's arrest and also starred the remarkable Kaji. Kaji had already found stardom as the leader of a girl biker gang in the "Alleycat Rock" series and would return for two more Scorpion films.

FEVER PITCH DVD

2005 103m c Sports/Comedy/Romance ★★★
Flower Films/International Arts Entertainment/ PG-13
Wildgaze Films/Zucker/Netter Productions/
20th Century Fox (U.S.)

Drew Barrymore (*Lindsey Meeks*), Jimmy Fallon (*Ben*), Jason Spevack (*Ben in 1980*), Jack Kehler (*Al*), Scott H. Severance (*Artie*), Jessamy R. Finet (*Teresa*), Maureen Keiller (*Viv*), Lenny Clarke (*Uncle Carl*), Ione Skye (*Molly*), KaDee Strickland (*Robin*)

p, Drew Barrymore, Alan Greenspan, Nancy Juvonen, Gil Netter, Amanda Posey, Bradley Thomas; d, Peter Farrelly, Bobby Farrelly; w, Lowell Ganz, Babloo Mandel; ph, Matthew F. Leonetti; ed, Alan Baumgarten; m, Craig Armstrong; prod d, Maher Ahmad; art d, Brandt Gordon; fx, Karen M. Murphy, Rob Sanderson; cos, Sophie de Rakoff Carbonell

Loosely based on U.K. writer Nick Hornby's best-selling memoir of soccer obsession (already filmed in 1997), and directed by Bobby and Peter Farrelly, this romantic comedy about a guy, a girl, and the Boston Red Sox is surprisingly sweet and free of gross-out humor.

Math teacher Ben Wrightman (Jimmy Fallon) is a rabid fan, the guy who not only has a season subscription and every piece of Red Sox memorabilia worth having, but also uses Yankees toilet paper in his bathroom. Brainy, successful Lindsey Meeks (Drew Barrymore) doesn't know a foul ball from a ball bearing, but she and Ben meet during the off-season, when Ben's assets—he's funny, considerate, smart, and doesn't live in his mother's basement—have a chance to shine.

Ambitious, career-oriented Lindsey has been reevaluating her dating strategies in light of a string of shallow, manipulative creeps, and thinks Ben's feverish devotion to the losing-est team in the major leagues is an eccentricity that can be accommodated through compromise. Then spring training arrives and Ben's inner BoSox monster emerges.

Modern-day American romantic comedies are in a real bind: There are few plausible but amusing obstacles to relationships. But extreme fandom fills the bill; you can even buy that Lindsey sees something sweetly noble in Ben's unwavering loyalty to a team that never wins. That the Farrellys shot during the Red Sox' 2004 season, when they not only made it to the World Series but *won* for the first time in 86 years should have sunk the film, but it doesn't. If you're rooting for Barrymore and Fallon, then why not their team? In the movies, there are enough happy endings for everyone.

FEW GOOD MEN, A
1992 138m c Drama   **DVD** ★★★
Manhattan Project/Castle Rock (U.S.)   R

Tom Cruise *(Lt. J.G. Daniel Kaffee)*, Jack Nicholson *(Col. Nathan R. Jessep)*, Demi Moore *(Lt. Cmdr. JoAnne Galloway)*, Kevin Bacon *(Capt. Jack Ross)*, Kiefer Sutherland *(Lt. Jonathan Kendrick)*, Kevin Pollak *(Lt. Sam Weinberg)*, James Marshall *(PFC Louden Downey)*, J.T. Walsh *(Lt. Col. Matthew Markinson)*, Christopher Guest *(Dr. Stone)*, Wolfgang Bodison *(Lance Corp. Harold W. Dawson)*

p, David Brown, Rob Reiner, Andrew Scheinman; d, Rob Reiner; w, Aaron Sorkin (from his play); ph, Robert Richardson; ed, Robert Leighton; m, Marc Shaiman; prod d, J. Michael Riva; art d, David Klassen; cos, Gloria Gresham

AAN Best Picture; AAN Best Supporting Actor: Jack Nicholson; *AAN Best Film Editing:* Robert Leighton; *AAN Best Sound:* Kevin O'Connell, Rick Kline, Bob Eber

Directed by Rob Reiner and adapted from Aaron Sorkin's hit Broadway play, A FEW GOOD MEN starts out by treading some very familiar ground.

Tom Cruise plays Lt. J.G. Daniel Kaffee, a second-generation lawyer who lives in the shadow of his late, revered father. When he's handed a case involving the death of a young Marine during an unofficial disciplinary procedure, Kaffee does what comes naturally: he works out a quick, clever plea bargain with the prosecuting officer (Kevin Bacon) and then goes back to softball practice.

Not so fast! Here comes Lt. Cdr. Joanne Galloway (Demi Moore), an earnest, uncompromising colleague who's convinced there's more to this case than meets even the most beady military eye. Galloway despises Kaffee's glib opportunism, but also recognizes that he's a potentially great lawyer—the only one good enough, in fact, to get to the bottom of the case and topple the man behind it all, His Extreme Scariness Col. Nathan R. Jessep (Jack Nicholson).

It looks for a while as though this might get tedious, with Galloway woodenly haranguing Kaffee as he slugs away with his beloved baseball bat, doing the Tom Cruise callow youth routine. But once Kaffee decides to go to trial, confronting his own oedipal hang-ups and taking on the might of the Naval heirarchy, he becomes winningly believable. The final scene, when Kaffee locks horns with Jessep, more than makes up for the predictability of what's come before.

FIDDLER ON THE ROOF
1971 180m c Comedy/Musical   **DVD** ★★★½
Mirisch (U.S.)   G

Topol *(Tevye)*, Norma Crane *(Golde)*, Leonard Frey *(Motel)*, Molly Picon *(Yente)*, Paul Mann *(Lazar Wolf)*, Rosalind Harris *(Tzeitel)*, Michele Marsh *(Hodel)*, Neva Small *(Chava)*, Paul Michael Glaser *(Perchik)*, Raymond Lovelock *(Fyedka)*

p, Norman Jewison; d, Norman Jewison; w, Joseph Stein (from the book of the musical, based on stories by Sholem Aleichem); ph, Oswald Morris (Panavision 70, Technicolor); ed, Antony Gibbs, Robert Lawrence; art d, Michael Stringer; chor, Tom Abbott, Sam Bayes; cos, Elizabeth Haffenden, Joan Bridge

AAN Best Picture; AAN Best Actor: Topol; *AAN Best Supporting Actor:* Leonard Frey; *AAN Best Director:* Norman Jewison; *AA Best Cinematography:* Oswald Morris; *AA Best Song Score:* John Williams; *AAN Best Art Direction-Set Decoration:* Robert Boyle, Michael Stringer, Peter Lamont; *AA Best Sound:* Gordon K. McCallum, David Hildyard

Fiddlesticks. Although scenarist Stein closely adapted the book of his long-running Broadway smash, FIDDLER ON THE ROOF is simply not up to the original's standard, suffering from excessive length and dim photography. Set in the Ukraine in the early 1900s and based on several tales by Sholem Aleichem, the overly sentimental story focuses on Tevye (Topol), his long-suffering wife (Crane), and their three dissimilar daughters, Hodel (Marsh), Tzeitel (Harris), and Chava (Small). Each of the girls finds a potential husband, though Tevye disapproves of all three matches. Meanwhile, the Jewish community faces harassment from the Czar and neighboring Cossacks which culminates in a pogrom, with the survivors left to pick up the pieces of their lives.

The film's strengths lie in the careful detailing of life in pre-Bolshevik Jewish Russia, and the often rough-hewn, open-air quality the film achieves. These same qualities pervade the zestful yet touching performance of Topol, who justly received an Oscar nomination for his fine work. What a pity that no one else in the cast makes a similar impression. An even greater pity lies in director Jewison's pacing and visual style.

Apart from several lovely shots of twilight vistas, Jewison proves yet again that he does not know what to do with a camera. The rhythm is not so much leisurely as it is slack, and the pogrom sequence is not nearly as powerful as it should be. The most obvious victim of the choppy cutting is the choreography, all but destroyed by the editor's handiwork. Finally, as handled here, the famous score reveals its major defect: almost every decent song is in the movie's first half. What could have been a brilliant film experience, expanding on the stage version as only film can, ends up instead as a series of wonderful bits and pieces.

FIELD OF DREAMS
1989 107m c Sports   **DVD** ★★★
Gordon (U.S.)   PG

Kevin Costner *(Ray Kinsella)*, Amy Madigan *(Annie Kinsella)*, Gaby Hoffman *(Karin Kinsella)*, Ray Liotta *(Shoeless Joe Jackson)*, Timothy Busfield *(Mark)*, James Earl Jones *(Terence Mann)*, Burt Lancaster *(Dr. "Moonlight" Graham)*, Frank Whaley *(Archie Graham)*, Dwier Brown *(John Kinsella)*, James Andelin *(Feed Store Farmer)*

p, Lawrence Gordon, Charles Gordon; d, Phil Alden Robinson; w, Phil Alden Robinson (based on the book *Shoeless Joe* by W.P. Kinsella); ph, John Lindley (Deluxe Color); ed, Ian Crafford; m, James Horner; prod d, Dennis Gassner; art d, Leslie McDonald; cos, Linda Bass

AAN Best Picture; AAN Best Adapted Screenplay: Phil Alden Robinson; *AAN Best Original Score:* James Horner

A rare choke-up movie for guys and one of 1989's biggest hits, Phil Alden Robinson's FIELD OF DREAMS made stiff but sensitive Kevin Costner a superstar. Based on the W.P. Kinsella's oddball fantasy novel *Shoeless Joe*—in which the protagonist kidnaps novelist J.D. Salinger—the film is a canny blend of myth, dreams, and baseball which (some viewers of good faith believe) actually skirts the sentimental and obvious.

At the urging of a mysterious voice, Iowa farmer Ray Kinsella (Costner) comes to believe that if he carves a baseball field out of his cornfield, his late father's hero, long-dead baseball great Shoeless Joe Jackson, will return to play. Supported by his wife, Annie (Amy Madigan), he plows away his family's livelihood and constructs a baseball field—complete with lights! His neighbors think he's crazy but—would you believe it?—Jackson (an unintentionally sinister-looking Ray Liotta) does indeed appear as the harbinger of an incredible assemblage of ghosts of all-stars past. However, nobody but Kinsella and his family can see these baseball greats. With his farm threatened by bankruptcy, Kinsella is mysteriously led to Boston's Fenway Park, and to a burned-out radical novelist (James Earl Jones) who may hold the key to the mystery.

If any movie of its decade begged to be called Capraesque, it is FIELD OF DREAMS, a sappy, good-naturedly dopey paean to traditional family values and nostalgia for innocent pleasures. The most powerful element of the movie is its trendy exploitation of men's yearning to bond with their fathers. For many people, particularly at the peak of the late-'80s "Men's Movement," this was irresistible stuff; others were left cold by its manipulative, "Twilight Zone"-style fabulism. Ultimately, the film relies too heavily on consensual acceptance of baseball iconography as some kind of symbolic shorthand for all kinds of American values. These days, most of us prefer the NBA.

FIFTH ELEMENT, THE 📀

(LE CINQUIEME ELEMENT)
1997 127m c Science Fiction ★★½
Gaumont (France) PG-13

Bruce Willis *(Korben Dallas)*, Gary Oldman *(Zorg)*, Milla Jovovich *(Leeloo)*, Ian Holm *(Cornelius)*, Chris Tucker *(Ruby Rhod)*, Luke Perry *(Billy)*, Brion James *(General Munro)*, Tiny Lister, billed as Tommy "Tiny" Lister Jr. *(President Lindberg)*, Lee Evans *(Fog)*, Tricky *(Right Arm)*

p, Patrice Ledoux; d, Luc Besson; w, Luc Besson, Robert Mark Kamen (based on a story by Luc Besson); ph, Thierry Arbogast; ed, Sylvie Landra; m, Eric Serra; prod d, Dan Weil; art d, Jim Morahan, Kevin Phipps, Michael Lamont; fx, Mark Stetson (special visual effects supervisor), Nick Dudman (creature design supervisor), Nick Allder (special effects supervisor), Neil Corbould (special effects supervisor), Norman Baillie (special effects administrator), Digital Domain; cos, Jean-Paul Gaultier, Vin Burnham (costume effects design)

AAN Best Sound Effects Editing: Mark Mangini

Brash, silly, often very beautiful, and art-directed within an inch of its life. This juvenile fantasy-adventure was first conceived by writer-director Luc Besson (LA FEMME NIKITA) as an adolescent, and it shows.

In the future, New York City is one big 60-story traffic jam; interstellar airline stewardesses dress in belly-baring Gaultier; shape-shifting Mangalors (rubber, bulldog-like aliens) prowl the streets carrying automatic weapons; and a planet-sized ball o' badness is hurtling toward the Earth at unimaginable speed. The only one who can stop it is fetching waif Leeloo (Milla Jovovich), whose "I dreamed I went walking in my Maidenform bra of the future" scene should insure her a place in the hearts of 14-year-old boys of all ages. THE FIFTH ELEMENT pits Leeloo and crack starfighter-turned-taxi driver Korben Dallas (Bruce Willis) against evil capitalist Zorg (Gary Oldman), and the fate of the Earth hangs on a quartet of ancient stones. The fun is in Besson's vision, which draws deeply on European graphic novel traditions with a bit of BLADE RUNNER tossed in

for good measure: the giant alien diva (Maiwenn Le Besco) behind her shimmering chador, the flying cars, the friendly Mondoshawan (turtle-like aliens with great bronze shells), the efficiency apartment of tomorrow, the floating junk that delivers Chinese food, and much, much more. It's all densely imagined and more than a little goofy: Besson's "All You Need is Love" message doesn't entirely jibe with the high-powered fire-fights, which don't mix awfully well with the silly humor. The supporting cast, which includes POSSE's Tiny Lister as the President, BLADE RUNNER's Brion James as the President's military adviser, and ALIEN's Ian Holm as Father Cornelius, keeper of the ancient wisdom, is a genre fan's delight.

50 FIRST DATES 📀

2004 99m c Comedy/Romance ★★½
Happy Madison/Flower Films/Columbia PG-13
(U.S.)

Adam Sandler *(Henry Roth)*, Drew Barrymore *(Lucy Whitmore)*, Rob Schneider *(Ula)*, Sean Astin *(Doug Whitmore)*, Lusia Strus *(Alexa)*, Dan Aykroyd *(Dr. Keats)*, Amy Hill *(Sue)*, Allen Covert *(Ten Second Tom)*, Blake Clark *(Marlin Whitmore)*, Maya Rudolph *(Stacy)*

p, Jack Giarraputo, Steve Golin, Nancy Juvonen; d, Peter Segal; w, George Wing; ph, Jack Green; ed, Jeff Gourson; m, Teddy Castellucci; prod d, Alan Au; art d, Domenic Silvestri; fx, John C. Hartigan, Eddie Soria; cos, Ellen Lutter

There's a surprisingly sweet romance at the core of this Adam Sandler comedy, despite the standard-issue scatological humor and an annoying supporting turn by Rob Schneider in ethnic drag.

Marine-veterinarian Henry Roth (Sandler), unofficial king of the short-term Hawaiian vacation hook-up, works at the local aquarium with his best friend, Ula (Schneider). Henry's plans to study walruses in Alaska are put on hold when he meets lovely Lucy (Drew Barrymore), but there's a catch: About a year ago, Lucy survived a car crash that damaged her short-term memory; she remembers everything about her life before the accident, but new memories vanish while she sleeps—including all knowledge of her new admirer. Lucy's father (Blake Clark) and steroid-popping brother (Sean Astin) shield her from the truth by pretending that every day is the day of the accident; when that fails, they take her to Dr. Keats (Dan Aykroyd), who patiently walks the understandably distraught Lucy through what really happened. With her family's reluctant blessing, Henry tries to find an easier way of reintroducing Lucy to her life every morning. His unorthodox methods allow them to enter into a real relationship, until the subject of Alaska rears its ugly head.

Is Adam Sandler finally maturing? He's been gradually dialing down his belligerent screen persona since the disastrous LITTLE NICKY, and this is easily his most relaxed performance to date. But ultimately Sandler can't quite pull off the transition from prankster to sensitive leading man, and his shtick is the main thing dragging down this otherwise pleasant romantic comedy. As in THE WEDDING SINGER, Barrymore's natural sunniness helps offset Sandler's frat-boy narcissism, and their scenes together are so charming that it's a letdown whenever the movie reverts to sophomoric gags about penis size and fat women.

FIGHT CLUB 📀

1999 139m c Drama ★★★★
Fox 2000/Regency Enterprises/Linson Films R
(U.S.)

Brad Pitt *(Tyler Durden)*, Edward Norton *(Narrator)*, Helena Bonham Carter *(Marla Singer)*, Meat Loaf, billed as Meat Loaf

Aday *(Robert Paulsen)*, Jared Leto *(Angel Face)*, Van Quattro *(Detective Andrew)*, Markus Redmond *(Detective Kevin)*, Michael Girardin *(Detective Walker)*, Rachel Singer *(Chloe)*, Sydney "Big Dawg" Colston *(Speaker—Free and Clear)*

p, Art Linson, Cean Chaffin, Ross Grayson Bell; d, David Fincher; w, Jim Uhls (based on the novel by Chuck Palahniuk); ph, Jeff Cronenweth; ed, James Haygood; m, The Dust Brothers; prod d, Alex McDowell; art d, Chris Gorak; fx, Cliff Wenger, Kevin Tod Haug; cos, Michael Kaplan

AAN Best Sound Effects Editing: Ren Klyce, Richard Hymns

A mesmerizing, bitterly funny, and deeply unsettling fable about a group of emotionally emasculated young men whose search for meaning leads them straight to their inner bare-knuckle brawler.

"Fight Club" is the brain child—make that the brainless, testosterone-fueled gut child—of scruffy wild boy Tyler Durden (Brad Pitt) and a nameless, insomniac cubicle slave (Edward Norton). They meet on a plane and bond over the coincidence that they're carrying the exact same briefcase. (Tyler's is full of the chi-chi soap he sells to high-end boutiques, while our office peon's bag is packed with papers.) A freak accident blows our protagonist's tastefully appointed apartment to kingdom come and propels him first into Tyler's pestilent house on the industrial side of town, and then into a bloody, sweaty journey of self-discovery that never goes quite where you think it's going.

Faithfully adapted from Chuck Palahniuk's novel, David Fincher's film is a brilliantly realized series of sucker punches, a philosophical howl disguised as a muscular guy movie. Neither Palahniuk nor Fincher is onto anything especially new—the plight of the post-feminist generation of men adrift without fathers, coming-of-age rituals or meaningful jobs launched the Iron John movement and keeps an army of therapists in clover—but Palahniuk nails the alienation and directs it into something simultaneously horrifying and logical (not for nothing is he regularly compared to J.G. Ballard). In his hands, Fight Club and its successor, the anarchic Project Mayhem, seem perfectly reasonable alternatives to spiritual suicide. Fincher translates Palahniuk's muscular prose into viscerally powerful images as fresh and invigorating as they are profoundly disturbing. He also gives Pitt and Norton the room to deliver what may be the best performances of their careers to date; Helena Bonham Carter, Meat Loaf, and Jared Leto are equally striking in supporting roles.

FIGHTING 69TH, THE
1940 90m bw War ★★★★
Warner Bros. (U.S.)

James Cagney *(Jerry Plunkett)*, Pat O'Brien *(Father Duffy)*, George Brent *(Wild Bill Donovan)*, Jeffrey Lynn *(Joyce Kilmer)*, Alan Hale *(Sgt. Big Mike Wynn)*, Frank McHugh *("Crepe Hanger" Burke)*, Dennis Morgan *(Lt. Ames)*, William Lundigan *(Timmy Wynn)*, Dick Foran *(John Wynn)*, Guinn "Big Boy" Williams *(Paddy Dolan)*

p, Louis F. Edelman; d, William Keighley; w, Norman Reilly Raine, Fred Niblo Jr., Dean Franklin; ph, Tony Gaudio; ed, Owen Marks; m, Adolph Deutsch; art d, Ted Smith; fx, Byron Haskin, Rex Wimpy

A showcase for the wisecracking, swaggering antics of Cagney, playing a would-be hero from Brooklyn who joins the all-Irish 69th New York Regiment after the U.S. enters WWI.

Jerry Plunkett (Cagney) is a street-corner brawler who couldn't care less about the illustrious military tradition embodied in the old 69th and who snubs feisty Father Duffy (O'Brien, who else?) when he finds out that Duffy is a priest. ("I don't go in for that Holy Joe stuff," as he puts it.)

Throughout his training, which he regards as a waste of time, Jerry defies his superiors, including a tough old sergeant (Hale) and his commanding officer, "Wild Bill" Donovan (Brent). Actual combat, however, proves to be too much for the obnoxious recruit, who first accidentally gives away his company's position and whose later cowardice results in the death of dozens of doughboys. Sentenced to death, Plunkett is inadvertantly given a chance to redeem himself when a bomb destroys his prison, and the stage is set for the action-packed finale.

One of the rare Hollywood films without any women or romantic angles whatsoever, THE FIGHTING 69TH was, not too surprisingly, an enormous hit with an American public about to enter WWII. Cagney gives such a galvanizing performance that one almost doesn't care that the film's one-note patriotism and Irish sentiment are as high as the corn in late summer. O'Brien fares less well as yet another priestly paragon of virtue, but the supporting cast is extremely proficient, Keighley's direction very zippy, and the technical merit of the enterprise quite exhilarating.

FILTH AND THE FURY, THE   *DVD*
2000 108m c   Documentary   ★★★★
Jersey Shore/Nitrate/Film Four/Sex Pistols (U.S./U.K.)

The Sex Pistols: Paul Cook, Steve Jones, Glen Matlock, John Lydon, billed as Johnny Rotten, Sid Beverly, billed as Sid Vicious

p, Anita Camarata, Amanda Temple; d, Julian Temple; ed, Niven Howie

Incredible as it sounds, there was a time when rock and roll was not only considered exciting, but downright dangerous. A ratty band of working-class yobs with little more than a bad reputation could actually get themselves banned across the country, and a few, expletive-filled minutes on a television broadcast could outrage a nation, trigger moral panic, and lead the English music press to abolish the No. 1 slot rather then give the band's best-selling "God Save the Queen" its top slot.

The band was the short-lived but enormously influential Sex Pistols. Julien Temple's loud, exhilarating documentary brings the '70s punk-rock explosion back in a vitriolic spray of spite, spittle, and raw rock and roll. Temple includes rarely seen footage, including the Pistols' notorious appearance on Bill Grundy's TV show, where they swore themselves into the next day's headlines (the best remembered of which serves as the film's title); interviews with the surviving members (all shot like criminals in shadowy silhouette); and the best bits of Temple's god-awful Pistol pic THE GREAT ROCK 'N' ROLL SWINDLE. From their humble beginnings banging out Small Faces covers, to their depressing final concert at San Francisco's Winterland theater ("No Fun," indeed), Temple captures it all. And he does something few behind-the-music profiles bother with, placing the Pistols firmly within the dreary social context they railed against with righteous anger and a glorious racket.

FINDING NEMO   *DVD*
2003 101m c Animated/Children's/Comedy ★★★½
Walt Disney Pictures/Pixar   (U.S.)   G

VOICES OF: Albert Brooks *(Marlin)*, Ellen DeGeneres *(Dory)*, Alexander Gould *(Nemo)*, Willem Dafoe *(Gill)*, Brad Garrett *(Bloat)*, Allison Janney *(Peach)*, Austin Pendleton *(Gurgle)*, Stephen Root *(Bubbles)*, Vicki Lewis *(Deb/Flo)*, Joe Ranft *(Jacques)*

p, Graham Walters; d, Andrew Stanton, Lee Unkrich (co-director); w, Bob Peterson, David Reynolds, Andrew Stanton (from a story by Andrew Stanton); ph, Sharon Calahan, Jeremy Lasky; ed, David Ian Salter; m, Thomas Newman; prod d, Ralph Eggleston; art d, Randy Berrett, Anthony Christov, Robin Cooper, Ricky Vega Nierva; anim, Alan Barillaro, Dylan Brown, Jenni Tsoi, Mark Walsh

AA Best Animated Feature; AAN Best Original Score: Thomas Newman; *AAN Best Original Screenplay:* Andrew Stanton, Bob Peterson, David Reynolds; *AAN Best Sound Editing:* Gary Rydstrom, Michael Silvers

Pixar heads underwater for a real fish tale that couldn't be better suited to its vivid style of computer animation. The visuals are brilliantly rendered, and the story revolves around a diverse—and very funny—group of characters who inhabit a fantastic version of the briny deep.

After losing his wife and most of their unhatched eggs to a vicious barracuda, bright-orange clownfish Marlin (voiced by Albert Brooks) has become extremely protective of his sole surviving offspring, Nemo (Alexander Gould). Marlin's overbearing paranoia becomes too much for the adventurous youngster, and Nemo takes up a classmate's dare to leave the safety of the reef. Nemo ventures into the open sea, where he's promptly snatched up by a scuba diver. Forgetting his own neurotic self-preservation issues, Marlin joins forces with Dory (Ellen DeGeneres), a flighty but optimistic Blue Tang with short-term memory loss, and the odd couple search tirelessly for little Nemo, who's landed inside a dentist's well-stocked fish tank. Nemo's tankmates, an eclectic cross section of captive sea life, befriend the new fish and plot to help him escape. Marlin and Dory get some unexpected help from nosy pelican Nigel (Geoffrey Rush), a shape-shifting school of fish (group-voiced by John Ratzenberger), and some surfer-dude sea turtles, led by Crush (voiced to laid-back perfection by the film's director, Andrew Stanton).

The film's cautionary lesson is clear, but it's imbedded in a fast-running stream of action and humor. Many of the quirky one-liners will fly over the heads of small fry—how many kids will appreciate the irony of an H2O-intolerant seahorse?—but will find an appreciative audience among adults. The colorful and kid-friendly characters are a delight, though very young children might be alarmed by some of the larger creatures, who tend to come into view teeth first.

FINDING NEVERLAND *DVD*

2004 106m c Drama/Biography ★★★½
Film Colony Productions (U.S./U.K.) PG

Johnny Depp *(Sir James Matthew Barrie)*, Kate Winslet *(Sylvia Llewelyn Davies)*, Julie Christie *(Mrs. Emma du Maurier)*, Radha Mitchell *(Mary Ansell Barrie)*, Dustin Hoffman *(Charles Frohman)*, Freddie Highmore *(Peter Llewelyn Davies)*, Joe Prospero *(Jack Llewelyn Davies)*, Nick Roud *(George Llewelyn Davies)*, Luke Spill *(Michael Llewelyn Davies)*, Ian Hart *(Sir Arthur Conan Doyle)*

p, Nellie Bellflower, Richard N. Gladstein; d, Marc Forster; w, David Magee (based on the play *The Man Who Was Peter Pan* by Allan Knee); ph, Roberto Schaefer; ed, Matt Chesse; m, Jan A.P. Kaczmarek; prod d, Gemma Jackson; art d, Peter Russell; fx, Stuart Brisdon; chor, Jonathan Butterell; cos, Alexandra Byrne

AA Best Original Score: Jan A.P. Kaczmarek; *AAN Best Picture; AAN Best Actor:* Johnny Depp; *AAN Best Art Direction:* Gemma Jackson (art direction), Trisha Edwards (set decoration); *AAN Best Costume Design:* Alexandra Byrne; *AAN Best Film Editing:* Matt Chesse; *AAN Best Adapted Screenplay:* David Magee

Marc Forster's delicately whimsical, genuinely moving film seeks to answer a superficially straightforward question: What sort of man conceived the peculiarly captivating world of Peter Pan, the Lost Boys, eccentric Captain Hook, and the Darling family? Forster's answer is infinitely complicated and, like the play on which it's based, takes considerable liberties with the facts of playwright J.M. Barrie's life, but Johnny Depp's performance is heartbreakingly poignant without degenerating into sloppy sentiment.

London, 1903: Wealthy, famous, and less-than-happily married to a beautiful former actress (Radha Mitchell), inse-

cure playwright Barrie is in search of new ideas. While walking his enormous dog in Kensington Gardens, he meets the widowed Sylvia Llewelyn Davies (Kate Winslet) and her four young sons, George (Nick Roud), Jack (Joe Prospero), Peter (Freddie Highmore), and Michael (Luke Spill). Barrie is enchanted by this quick-witted, exuberant gaggle of boys and soon devotes every free moment to playing elaborate games of make-believe with the brothers while offering the ailing Sylvia the services of his household staff and even the use of a summer cottage. The situation appalls Sylvia's starchy mother (Julie Christie) and sets proper tongues a-wagging, but the youngsters reawaken Barrie's imagination. *Peter Pan*'s magical Neverland slowly emerges, complete with mermaids, pirates, fairy magic, a vengeful crocodile, and at the heart of it all, a small boy who refuses to grow up.

Though best known for the raw emotional fireworks of MONSTER'S BALL, Forster approaches this story with admirable restraint and resists the temptation to reduce Barrie to a tangle of pop pathologies. But the film rests on Depp's evocation of Barrie's playfulness and deeply buried sorrow; it's difficult to imagine another actor so gracefully evoking the man's childlike qualities without seeming creepy or emotionally malformed.

FIRE OVER ENGLAND *DVD*

1937 92m bw Adventure/Historical/War ★★★★
Mayflower/Pendennis/Korda/London Films (U.K.)

Laurence Olivier *(Michael Ingolby)*, Flora Robson *(Queen Elizabeth)*, Leslie Banks *(Earl of Leicester)*, Raymond Massey *(Philip of Spain)*, Vivien Leigh *(Cynthia)*, Tamara Desni *(Elena)*, Morton Selten *(Burleigh)*, Lyn Harding *(Sir Richard)*, George Thirlwell *(Gregory)*, Henry Oscar *(Spanish Ambassador)*

p, Erich Pommer; d, William K. Howard; w, Clemence Dane, Sergei Nolbandov (based on the novel by A.E.W. Mason); ph, James Wong Howe; ed, Jack Dennis; m, Richard Addinsell; art d, Lazare Meerson; fx, Ned Mann, Lawrence Butler, Edward Cohen; cos, Rene Hubert

A rare example of a film that succeeds superbly both as a swashbuckler and as historical drama. Michael Ingolby (Olivier) is a young British naval officer whose father is burned to death for heresy by the Spanish Inquisition. He seeks revenge and finds his opportunity in the court of the tempestuous Queen Elizabeth I (a scene-stealing Robson). Elizabeth knows she is surrounded by traitors in league with her archenemy, Philip of Spain (Massey), who plans to invade England. Thus, when Michael offers to infiltrate Philip's court and learn the details of the invasion, Elizabeth seizes the chance. The queen is also romantically inclined toward the handsome officer, and vexed at the attentions he shows his childhood sweetheart who is her lady-in-waiting, Cynthia (Leigh). Michael soon learns of Philip's plans, escapes to England and helps lead the British ships into battle against the Spanish Armada.

A bit slow getting started, and typically glossy in its treatment of details (e.g. the softening of Elizabeth's character), FIRE OVER ENGLAND nevertheless conveys a certain historical grandeur amidst all the showmanship. It succeeds through the combined talents of many great names: Alexander Korda's sponsorship, Pommer's production, Howard's masterful direction, Wong Howe's superb photography, Meerson's grand sets, and the acting of Olivier, Robson and Leigh. A host of versatile supporting players add to the depth, not the least of whom are Banks, Selten, and Massey (as the darkly brooding, expansionist King Philip). Look for a bearded James Mason in a small role as an envoy.

FIREMAN'S BALL, THE *DVD*
(HORI MA PANENKO)

1967 73m c Comedy ★★★½

Barrandov (Czechoslovakia)

Vaclav Stockel *(Fire Brigade Commander)*, Josef Svet *(Old Man)*, Josef Kolb *(Josef)*, Jan Vostrcil *(Committee Chairman)*, Frantisek Debelka *(1st Committee Member)*, Josef Sebanek *(2nd Committee Member)*, Karel Valnoha *(3rd Committee Member)*, Josef Rehorek *(4th Committee Member)*, Marie Jezkova *(Josef's Wife)*, Anina Lipoldva

d, Milos Forman; w, Milos Forman, Ivan Passer, Jaroslav Papousek; ph, Miroslav Ondricek (Eastmancolor); ed, Miroslav Hajek; m, Karel Mares

AAN Best Foreign Language Film

This ingratiating farce is perhaps the last noteworthy film of the Czech renaissance before the political crackdown forced most filmmakers, director Forman and co-screenwriter Passer included, into exile. It's a more thorough realization of the same kinds of themes that directors like Forman and Passer developed in several films in the mid-1960s: invigorating essays in everyday life. THE FIREMAN'S BALL uses a small, local event—in this case a retirement ball and a beauty contest—to examine larger social and political problems.

Promised the presentation of a ceremonial hatchet at a ball given upon his retirement, a cancer-stricken, 86-year-old retired commander of a fire brigade sits helplessly as all hell breaks loose around him. A beauty contest organized as part of the evening's events fizzles. The tension is broken by a fire alarm which tears the fire company away from the festivities to a fire that is destroying another old man's home. Unfortunately things seem to keep going wrong.

The New York Times reported that 40,000 Czech firemen resigned when the government released the film in their homeland. They returned to their posts when Forman let it be known the film might be allegorical. The film received an Academy Award nomination for Best Foreign Film in 1968 but lost to WAR AND PEACE.

FIREWORKS *DVD*
(HANA-BI)

1997 103m c Crime/Thriller/Drama ★★★★

Office Kitano (Japan)

Takeshi Kitano, billed as Beat Takeshi *(Yoshitaka Nishi)*, Ren Osugi *(Horibe)*, Kayoko Kishimoto *(Miyuki—Nishi's Wife)*, Susumu Terajima *(Nakamura)*, Hakuryu *(Tojo—Sadistic Yakuza Hitman)*, Tetsu Watanabe *(Tezuka—Junkyard Owner)*, Yasuei Yakushiji *(The Criminal)*, Taro Itsumi *(Kudoh—the Detective)*, Kenichi Yajima *(Doctor)*, Makoto Ashikawa *(Tanaka)*

p, Masayuki Mori, Yasushi Tsuge, Takio Yoshida; d, Takeshi Kitano; w, Takeshi Kitano; ph, Hideo Yamamoto; ed, Takeshi Kitano, Yoshinori Ota; m, Joe Hisaishi; art d, Norihiro Isoda

Cool, stylized, and deeply odd, this astringently maudlin fable about the healing power of art and the enduring strength of bitter bonds of loyalty and love is wrapped in a cop movie so hard-boiled it's cracked.

Tough-guy police detective Nishi ("Beat" Takeshi Kitano) is at the end of his rope, sick to death of running down punks and gangsters; haunted by the death of his colleague, Tanaka (Makoto Ashikawa); the terminal illness of his wife, Miyuki (Kayoko Kishimoto); and the despair of his best friend, Horibe (Ren Osugi). Paralyzed by a sadistic *yakuza*, abandoned by his family and unable to work, Horibe is suicidal, until Nishi's gift of a box of art supplies allows him to act on a vague desire to paint. As Horibe begins experimenting with brightly colored but bizarre images of fireworks and ani-

mals with flowers for heads, Nishi concocts a brazen plan to rob a bank and take his wife on a last sentimental journey.

Forewarned is forearmed: the fluid, disorienting shifts between austere sentimentality and vicious violence that drive this disturbing film will be familiar to fans of Japanese filmmaker and media phenomenon Takeshi Kitano (who acts under the name Beat Takeshi, a holdover from his days as a stand-up comedian), but it may leave newcomers perplexed and even angry. With his cool little sunglasses, sleek suits, and great big gat, Kitano looks like a conventional movie badass. But the guns and poses cover a bottomless chasm of existential despair, and rather than lightening the load, the movie's weird interludes of silly humor only make it worse. Eccentric and haunting.

FIRM, THE *DVD*

1993 153m c Thriller ★★★

Mirage Enterprises (U.S.) R

Tom Cruise *(Mitch McDeere)*, Jeanne Tripplehorn *(Abby McDeere)*, Gene Hackman *(Avery Tolar)*, Hal Holbrook *(Oliver Lambert)*, Terry Kinney *(Lamar Quinn)*, Wilford Brimley *(William Devasher)*, Ed Harris *(Wayne Tarrance)*, Holly Hunter *(Tammy Hemphill)*, David Strathairn *(Ray McDeere)*, Gary Busey *(Eddie Lomax)*

p, Scott Rudin, John A. Davis, Michael Hausman, Sydney Pollack; d, Sydney Pollack; w, David Rabe, Robert Towne, David Rayfiel (from the novel by John Grisham); ph, John Seale; ed, William Steinkamp, Fredric Steinkamp; m, Dave Grusin; prod d, Richard MacDonald; art d, John Willett; fx, Ken Estes; cos, Ruth Myers

AAN Best Supporting Actress: Holly Hunter; *AAN Best Original Score:* Dave Grusin

If stuffy, prestigious law firms were in the business of making thrillers, the results would probably look something like THE FIRM. This is a professional machine of a movie that compresses huge amounts of information into its two and a half hours of screen time. But it's so weighed down by detail, it fails to generate any real suspense.

Directed by Sydney Pollack and adapted from John Grisham's best-seller, THE FIRM pleads the case of Mitch McDeere (Tom Cruise), a hungry, hot-shot Harvard Law School grad who's tempted into a lucrative job with an exclusive Memphis legal practice. The drawback? The firm is a front for the mob, and the only way to escape its grip is by dying, either naturally or otherwise.

Pollack and his screenwriters have made a heroic, but unsuccessful, attempt to boil Grisham's massive book down into a cinematic thriller. Much of the novel's elaborate set-up has been efficiently tailored for the screen, but the ending—which deviates quite drastically from Grisham's—is more confusing than satisfying. It's like spending months cramming for a bar exam, only to finally be given an I.Q. test instead.

Tom Cruise and Jeanne Tripplehorn, as McDeere's wife Abby, give solid if hardly explosive performances, leaving it to the supporting cast to liven things up; standouts are Gene Hackman, as McDeere's criminal mentor; Holly Hunter, as a secretary who helps Mitch out of his jam; and a shaven-headed Ed Harris, as an FBI agent whose temper is quicker than his wit.

FIRST NAME: CARMEN *DVD*
(PRENOM: CARMEN)

1983 93m c Drama ★★★½

Sara/Jean-Luc Godard/A2 (France)

Maruschka Detmers *(Carmen X)*, Jacques Bonnaffe *(Joseph Bonnaffe)*, Myriem Roussel *(Claire)*, Christophe Odent *(The Boss)*, Jean-Luc Godard *(Uncle Jean)*, Hyppolite Girardot *(Fred)*, Bertrand Liebert *(Carmen's Bodyguard)*, Alain Bastien-Thiry *(Hotel Worker)*, Pierre-Alain Chapuis, Odile Roire p, Alain Sarde; d, Jean-Luc Godard; w, Anne-Marie Mieville (based on the novel *Carmen* by Prosper Merimee); ph, Raoul Coutard (Eastmancolor); ed, Suzanne Lang-Willar; m, Ludwig van Beethoven; cos, Renee Renard

Director Jean-Luc Godard has taken a less than reverent approach to the famed opera *Carmen*. Godard chose to depart substantially from the original Merimee novel and, to the horror of Bizet fans, replaced the composer's score with Beethoven string quartets and a ballad called "Ruby's Arms" by the gruff-voiced Tom Waits.

Here Carmen (Maruschka Detmers) is a *femme fatale* who concocts a daring plan to rob a bank while pretending to shoot a movie. Luckily she has an uncle (Godard) who was once a brilliant movie director and is now a resident at the local mental hospital. He jumps at the chance to "direct" Carmen's film of the robbery. While staging the robbery, she is nearly apprehended by a police officer (Jacques Bonnaffe), but the two fall in love instead. It appears that Carmen is in complete control of the relationship.

Not only is FIRST NAME: CARMEN optimistic, it is also relatively linear in its narrative structure, making it perhaps Godard's most accessible film. What's more, FIRST NAME: CARMEN is Godard's first comedy, although not in the customary sense. This comes as no surprise as his gangster films, war movies, musicals and dramas are hardly typical of their genres. Godard's films have always had their funny moments but this is his first step in the direction of the great comedians. The film is spiced with passion, philosophy, eroticism, and technical innovation, and while its ideas are relatively accessible, they still do not make for "easy" viewing.

FIRST WIVES CLUB, THE
1996 105m c Comedy **DVD**
Scott Rudin Productions/Paramount (U.S.) ★★ PG

Bette Midler (*Brenda Morelli Cushman*), Goldie Hawn (*Elise Elliot Atchison*), Diane Keaton (*Annie MacDuggan Paradise*), Maggie Smith (*Gunilla Garson Goldberg*), Sarah Jessica Parker (*Shelly*), Dan Hedaya (*Morty Cushman*), Bronson Pinchot (*Duarto Feliz*), Jennifer Dundas (*Chris Paradise*), Eileen Heckart (*Catherine MacDuggan*), Stephen Collins (*Aaron Paradise*)

p, Scott Rudin; d, Hugh Wilson; w, Robert Harling (based on the novel by Olivia Goldsmith); ph, Donald Thorin; ed, John Bloom; m, Marc Shaiman; prod d, Peter Larkin; art d, Charley Beal; fx, Matt Vogel, VIFX; cos, Theoni V. Aldredge

AAN Best Original Musical or Comedy Score: Marc Shaiman

THE FIRST WIVES' CLUB drearily proves that a sound comic premise and a dream cast don't guarantee a heavenly farce.

When Cynthia Griffin (Stockard Channing) commits suicide after being deserted by her husband, her three best friends feel her pain: middle-class Brenda (Bette Midler) has been dumped by her husband, Morty (Dan Hedaya), for a beautiful but vulgar bimbo (Sarah Jessica Parker); rich Upper East Side matron Annie (Diane Keaton) has learned that her husband (Stephen Collins) has been having an affair with her therapist (Marcia Gay Harden); and Elise (Goldie Hawn), a fading movie star, has been given the heave-ho by her producer-husband (Victor Garber), who looks to fresher, more nubile talent (Elizabeth Berkley). The three ladies meet up at Cynthia's funeral, get drunk, and plot their revenge: to financially ruin their no-good husbands.

As was the case with the very similar 9 TO 5, the fun is all in the set-up; after the first half hour or so, the film bogs down in petty bitchery and unrelenting vengefulness. The women scream and sneer and slap so much that your sympathy very nearly goes out to their beleaguered victims. Director Hugh Wilson throws pace, nuance, and logic to the wind, and

the actresses don't bring anything fresh or exciting to their flatly drawn roles. Midler, as a wistful, struggling single mom, seems totally out of her element; when she breaks out with a catty line it's a welcome relief, but out of character. Hawn seems to be enjoying herself as the epitome of an aerobicized, mindlessly determined careerist, but we've seen her do the funny-shallow-vain bit already. Surprisingly, Keaton is the real embarrassment here: WASP-y repression and spinster-like nervousness have sadly become her stock-in-trade.

FISH CALLED WANDA, A
1988 108m c Comedy/Crime/Romance **DVD**
MGM (U.S.) ★★★ R

John Cleese (*Archie Leach*), Jamie Lee Curtis (*Wanda Gerschwitz*), Kevin Kline (*Otto*), Michael Palin (*Ken*), Maria Aitken (*Wendy Leach*), Tom Georgeson (*George*), Patricia Hayes (*Mrs. Coady*), Geoffrey Palmer (*Judge*), Cynthia Caylor (*Portia*), Mark Elwes (*Shop Customer*)

p, Michael Shamberg; d, Charles Crichton; w, John Cleese (based on a story by Cleese and Charles Crichton); ph, Alan Hume (Technicolor); ed, John Jympson; m, John Du Prez; prod d, Roger Murray-Leach; fx, George Gibbs; cos, Hazel Pethig

AA Best Supporting Actor: Kevin Kline; AAN Best Director: Charles Crichton; AAN Best Original Screenplay: John Cleese, Charles Crichton

Combining the talents of Monty Python stalwart John Cleese and Ealing Studios veteran Charles Crichton (THE LAVENDER HILL MOB, THE TITFIELD THUNDERBOLT), this hilariously offbeat post-caper comedy benefits from two of British film comedy's most accomplished traditions.

Cleese, who wrote the screenplay, stars as Archie Leach, an emotionally and sexually repressed English barrister whose life is thrown into upheaval by the appearance of Wanda—not the fish of the title, but a sexy American thief played by Jamie Lee Curtis. She and her gang—Cockney tough guy George (Tom Georgeson), stuttering animal rights advocate, Ken (Michael Palin), and ex-CIA assassin, Otto (Kevin Kline)—pull off a well-executed jewel heist but in the thieves' subsequent rush to double-cross one another and grab all the loot, George ends up in jail and the booty hidden in a safety deposit box, the location of which is known only to him. Deciding that the best way to learn the whereabouts of the jewels is through George's barrister (Cleese), Wanda sets out to seduce the information out of him.

With British-American culture clash as its dominant theme, A FISH CALLED WANDA bristles with wit, enlivened by delightfully over-the-top ensemble acting. Cleese's screenplay uses a farcical framework to send up both British inhibition and formality and American intuitiveness and lack of sophistication. Although filled with clever twists and double-crosses, the film's storyline is less important than the opportunities it gives the actors to exploit their goofy characterizations, especially in the case of Kline who won a Best Supporting Actor Academy Award for his outlandish performance.

FISHER KING, THE
1991 137m c Drama/Fantasy/Comedy **DVD**
TriStar/Hill/Obst Productions (U.S.) ★★½ R

Robin Williams (*Parry*), Jeff Bridges (*Jack Lucas*), Mercedes Ruehl (*Anne Napolitano*), Amanda Plummer (*Lydia*), Adam Bryant (*Radio Engineer*), Paul Lombardi (*Radio Engineer*), David Pierce (*Lou Rosen*), Ted Ross (*Limo Bum*), Lara Harris (*Sondra*), Warren Olney (*TV Anchorman*)

p, Debra Hill, Lynda Obst; d, Terry Gilliam; w, Richard LaGravenese; ph, Roger Pratt; ed, Lesley Walker; m, George

Fenton; prod d, Mel Bourne; art d, P. Michael Johnston; fx, Robert McCarthy, Dennis Dion; chor, Robin Horness; cos, Beatrix Pasztor

AAN Best Actor: Robin Williams; *AA Best Supporting Actress:* Mercedes Ruehl; *AAN Best Original Screenplay:* Richard LaGravenese; *AAN Best Original Score:* George Fenton; *AAN Best Art Direction-Set Decoration:* Mel Bourne, Cindy Carr

Terry Gilliam's first project as a directorial "hired gun" is a grandiose, overblown attempt to fuse the medieval myth of the Fisher King with a story of alienation and redemption in contemporary Manhattan.

Jack Lucas (Jeff Bridges) is a cynical disc jockey whose radio talk show attracts the lonely and frustrated. When one of his frequent callers, Edwin (Christian Clemenson), confides he's just met a beautiful girl at Babbitts, a trendy bar, Jack goes off on a vitriolic tirade against the yuppies who frequent the place. He ends by saying: "Edwin, they have to be stopped before it's too late. It's us or them." Taking Jack's words at face value, Edwin goes on a shooting spree inside the restaurant, slaughtering several patrons.

Three years later Jack has reached a nadir of despair and self-loathing. Although involved in a relationship with Anne (Mercedes Ruehl), the supportive owner of a video store, he has lost his will to live. Drunk, he decides to end it all by jumping off a pier into the river. Before he can do this, though, he is attacked by two homicidal teenagers, and then rescued by Parry (Robin Williams), who appears to be some kind of vagrant with a mystical turn of phrase. It turns out that Parry is a former professor of medieval history who is now engaged on a quest for the Holy Grail. Parry is convinced he's spotted the Grail in a magazine (it's actually a silver trophy belonging to a billionaire), and that Jack is the ideal candidate to retrieve it from its owner's castellated Fifth Avenue apartment building.

THE FISHER KING's problems begin with Richard LaGravenese's screenplay and are amplified by Gilliam's showy direction and an unbearably fey performance by Robin Williams. The idea, apparently, was to give an explicitly mythical dimensional to a modern-day story of sin and redemption. Unfortunately, though, the script never resolves the different levels on which it tries to operate, and also throws in too many loose ends which never get cleared up. The tone of the film, largely set by Williams's "Please feel sorry for me" performance, is unremittingly cloying, with an impossibly cute, feel-good ending that adds insult to injury.

There *are* redeeming factors; a scene in which bustling commuters in Grand Central Station are suddenly transformed into waltzing couples has undeniable magic, and Bridges and Ruehl give gritty, unaffected performances that sometimes threaten to make the whole thing believable. For the most part, though, THE FISHER KING is awash in the kind of neo-mythical whimsy that Gilliam helped to puncture in the far more enjoyable MONTY PYTHON AND THE HOLY GRAIL.

FIST IN HIS POCKET
(I PUGNI IN TASCA)
1966   105m   bw   Drama   ★★★½
Peppercorn/Wormser   (Italy)

Lou Castel *(Alessandro)*, Paola Pitagora *(Giulia)*, Marino Mase *(Augusto)*, Liliana Gerace *(Mother)*, Pier Luigi Troglio *(Leone)*, Jennie MacNeil *(Lucia)*, Mauro Martini *(the Boy)*, Gianni Schicchi *(Tonino)*, Alfredo Filippazzi *(Doctor)*, Gianfranco Cella *(Young Man at the Party)*

p, Ezio Passadore; d, Marco Bellocchio; w, Marco Bellocchio; ph, Alberto Marrama; ed, Aurelio Mangiarotti; m, Ennio Morricone; art d, Gisella Longo

This amazing debut film from director Marco Bellochio is an unusual tragicomedy about a family of crazy epileptics—with a blind mother. The plot synopsis suggests a particularly peverse soap opera. Augusto (Mase) is the one healthy member of a family whose manifold problems threaten to stifle his life. He wants to marry but feels he cannot as long as his family is around to bedevil him. His younger brother, Alessandro (Castel), empathizes with his sibling so he decides to kill off the rest of the family so that Augusto can use the resulting inheritance to begin a new life.

Bellochio's exhilaratingly cool and assured direction charges the film with temperament. The savage material—matricide, fratricide, and incest—is never as funny as it seems intended to be; the actors are directed with such verve and passion that audiences are often left too breathless to laugh. Lou Castel's performance seethes with a hateful energy rarely seen on the screen.

FISTFUL OF DOLLARS, A   DVD
(PER UN PUGNO DI DOLLARI)
1964   100m   c   Western   ★★★
Jolly   (Italy/Spain/West Germany)

Clint Eastwood *(The Man with No Name)*, Marianne Koch *(Marisol)*, Gian Maria Volonte *(Ramon Rojo)*, Jose Calvo *(Silvanito)*, Wolfgang Lukschy *(John Baxter)*, Sieghardt Rupp *(Esteban Rojo)*, Antonio Prieto *(Benito Rojo)*, Margarita Lozano *(Consuela Baxter)*, Daniel Martin *(Julian)*, Bruno Carotenuto *(Antonio Baxter)*

p, Arrigo Colombo, Giorgio Papi; d, Sergio Leone; w, Sergio Leone, Duccio Tessari, Victor A. Catena, G. Schock (based on the film YOJIMBO by Akira Kurosawa); ph, Massimo Dallamano (Techniscope, Technicolor); ed, Roberto Cinquini; m, Ennio Morricone

A landmark Western that established the Clint Eastwood persona and revitalized the genre. The plot is deceptively simple—and it's lifted from Japanese director Akira Kurosawa's 1961 classic YOJIMBO. Eastwood, the mysterious Man with No Name, rides into a small town embroiled in a struggle for power between two families. Eastwood hires himself out as a mercenary, first to one faction and then to the other, with no regard for honor or morality. He eventually destroys both, leaving the town to the bartender, coffin-maker, and bell ringer as he rides off into the desert from whence he came.

The plot is simple and the Italian performances verge on the operatic, but Leone revitalizes the Western through a unique and complex visual style. The film is full of brilliant spatial relationships (extreme close-ups in the foreground, with detailed compositions visible in the background) combined with Ennio Morricone's vastly creative musical score full of grunts, wails, groans, and bizarre-sounding instruments. Aural and visual elements together give a wholly original perspective on the West and its myths.

Eastwood had a heavy hand in the interpretation of his role, stripping his part of most of its dialogue. His character is wholly amoral, a mystery man with no past who relies on his skill with a gun and his cleverness. This image, which he would hone to perfection in the subsequent Leone movies (and one the actor continues to examine and sometimes criticize, especially in the films in which he directs himself) transformed Eastwood into a cultural icon of almost mythic proportions. Though far from perfected in this film, Leone's style would mature through his next two films and peak with his masterpiece ONCE UPON A TIME IN THE WEST.

FITZCARRALDO   DVD
1982   157m   c   Drama   ★★★★
New World   (West Germany)

Klaus Kinski *(Brian Sweeney Fitzgerald/Fitzcarraldo)*, Claudia Cardinale *(Molly)*, Jose Lewgoy *(Don Aquilino)*, Miguel Angel

Fuentes *(Cholo the Mechanic)*, Paul Hittscher *(Capt. Orinoco Paul)*, Huerequeque Enrique Bohorquez *(Cook)*, Grande Othelo *(Station Master)*, Peter Berling *(Opera Manager)*, David Perez Espinosa *(Chief of the Campa Indians)*, Milton Nascimento *(Black Man at Opera House)*

p, Werner Herzog, Lucki Stipetic; d, Werner Herzog; w, Werner Herzog; ph, Thomas Mauch; ed, Beate Mainka-Jellinghaus; m, Popol Vuh; art d, Henning von Gierke, Ulrich Bergfelder; cos, Gisela Storch

A major filmmaking accomplishment that only Werner Herzog would have the looney audacity to attempt, FITZCARRALDO stars Klaus Kinski as the title character, a dreamer who plans to bring opera and Enrico Caruso to the South American jungles. With limited funding he decides to finance the opera house by capitalizing on South America's rubber industry. He discovers a hidden forest of rubber trees well protected by rapids but the only way to get there is via a river on the other side of a small group of mountains. Fitzcarraldo has a bizarre inspiration: he'll hire local natives to pull his steamship over the mountain—320 tons up a 40-degree incline.

The hauling of the boat is the poetic and symbolic heart of the movie and no camera trickery is used in its filming. This is a real steamship being hauled over a real mountain—all at the command of Herzog, a man as crazed in his way as his most obsessed heroes. The insurmountability of this labor of filmmaking parallels the character's determination to bring Caruso to the jungles, and herein lies the attraction of FITZCARRALDO—it is an artistic achievement that one watches for the drama of the film and of the filmmaking.

Jason Robards was originally set to play the lead but was forced to quit the film after catching a jungle illness. The resulting schedule delays also forced Mick Jagger, who was cast as Robards's sidekick, to drop out. Herzog was quoted as saying, "If I should abandon this film I should be a man without dreams… I live my life or end my life with this project." An excellent companion piece is Les Blank's BURDEN OF DREAMS, a documentary about the making of FITZCARRALDO.

FIVE EASY PIECES

1970 96m c Drama ★★★★
BBS (U.S.) R

Jack Nicholson *(Robert Eroica Dupea)*, Karen Black *(Rayette Dipesto)*, Billy "Green" Bush *(Elton)*, Fannie Flagg *(Stoney)*, Sally Struthers *(Betty)*, Marlena MacGuire *(Twinky)*, Richard Stahl *(Recording Engineer)*, William Challee *(Nicholas)*, Helena Kallianiotes *(Palm Apodaca)*, Toni Basil *(Terry Grouse)*

p, Bob Rafelson, Richard Wechsler; d, Bob Rafelson; w, Adrien Joyce (from a story by Joyce and Rafelson); ph, Laszlo Kovacs (Movielab Color); ed, Gerald Shepard, Christopher Holmes; m, Johann Sebastian Bach, Wolfgang Amadeus Mozart, Frederic Chopin; cos, Bucky Rous

AAN Best Picture; AAN Best Actor: Jack Nicholson; *AAN Best Supporting Actress:* Karen Black; *AAN Best Original Story and Screenplay:* Bob Rafelson (Story), Adrien Joyce (Story)

This episodic character study is one of the key American films of its era. Nicholson, in an early major performance, appears to be a redneck oilrigger in a California oil field. He and his best friend, Bush, when not working together, spend most of their time bowling, downing beers, and just hanging out. This lifestyle is actually a charade. Nicholson hails from a well-to-do family of musicians. He's a brilliant classical pianist who's given up the instrument in favor of another life.

When Black, his witless waitress girlfriend, announces she's pregnant, he leaves his job and heads for Los Angeles to visit Smith, his sister, who is also a pianist and about to

record an album. Smith tells Nicholson that their father, Challee, has suffered a pair of strokes back at their home on Puget Sound and he should visit the old man before he dies. Black talks him into taking her along. They bid Bush and his wife, Flagg, goodbye and begin the drive to Washington. What follows is a probing examination of the upper middle class American way of life.

Nicholson delivers a brilliant, edgy and complex characterization and Black won the 1970 New York Film Critics Award for her courageous performance as well as an Oscar nomination. Deceptively simple, PIECES is one of the most complex pictures of the 1970s.

FIVE FINGERS

1952 108m bw Thriller/Spy ★★★★
Fox (U.S.)

James Mason *(Cicero)*, Danielle Darrieux *(Anna)*, Michael Rennie *(George Travers)*, Walter Hampden *(Sir Frederic)*, Oscar Karlweis *(Moyzisch)*, Herbert Berghof *(Col. von Richter)*, John Wengraf *(Von Papen)*, Ben Astar *(Siebert)*, Roger Plowden *(MacFadden)*, Michael Pate *(Morrison)*

p, Otto Lang; d, Joseph L. Mankiewicz; w, Michael Wilson (based on the book *Operation Cicero* by L.C. Moyzisch); ph, Norbert Brodine; ed, James B. Clark; m, Bernard Herrmann; art d, Lyle Wheeler, George W. Davis; fx, Fred Sersen

AAN Best Director: Joseph L. Mankiewicz; *AAN Best Screenplay:* Michael Wilson

Five fingers, yes; five stars, not quite. In a heavily ironic story based, amazingly, on fact, Mason plays a valet working for Sir Frederic (Hampden), the British ambassador in WWII Ankara. Using the pseudonym Cicero, he uses his position to sell military secrets to the Germans. The scheming servant sets up Countess Anna (Darrieux), a down-and-out noblewoman, in a mansion and uses it to meet with Nazi agents. The Germans pay handsomely for Cicero's information even though the Nazi high command considers the secrets—including the real time and date of the invasion in Europe—too incredible to be believed. They are afraid, however, to shut off the flow of information and keep purchasing Cicero's documents. The British finally discover a leak in the embassy, and George Travers (Rennie) leads a team of agents to unearth the spy.

Director Mankiewicz, who also contributed some uncredited dialogue, provides the skillful if somewhat cold direction and holds suspense from beginning to end. Also noteworthy is the fine work of cinematographer Brodine. Although the film never gets us close to any of the characters, Mason is nonetheless a suave wonder to behold as the shifty, ever-alert Albanian valet who outwits British intelligence. In real life Cicero managed to sell German intelligence 35 top-secret documents. The Nazis never acted on any of them.

FIVE GRAVES TO CAIRO

1943 96m bw Spy ★★★★½
Paramount (U.S.)

Franchot Tone *(John J. Bramble)*, Anne Baxter *(Mouche)*, Akim Tamiroff *(Farid)*, Erich von Stroheim *(Field Marshal Rommel)*, Peter Van Eyck *(Lt. Schwegler)*, Fortunio Bonanova *(Gen. Sebastiano)*, Konstantin Shayne *(Maj. von Buelow)*, Fred Nurney *(Maj. Lamprecht)*, Miles Mander *(British Colonel)*, Leslie Denison *(British Captain)*

p, Charles Brackett; d, Billy Wilder; w, Charles Brackett, Billy Wilder (based on the play "Hotel Imperial" by Lajos Biro); ph, John Seitz; ed, Doane Harrison; m, Miklos Rozsa; art d, Hans Dreier, Ernst Fegte; cos, Edith Head

AAN Best B/W Cinematography: John Seitz; *AAN Best Film Editing:* Doane Harrison; *AAN Best Interior Decoration (B/W):* Hans Dreier (Art Direction), Ernst Fegte (Art Direction), Bertram Granger (Interior Decoration)

Notable as an early example of Wilder's talent for turning headlines into storylines. This tense WWII espionage film stars Tone as John Bramble, a British soldier stranded in a desert town which suddenly fills with German troops. Assuming the role of a dead servant at a hotel run by Farid (Tamiroff), Bramble gradually gains the confidence of French housekeeper Mouche (Baxter), a woman deeply resentful of the British for leaving French troops, including her brother, behind at Dunkirk. After the hotel becomes Rommel's temporary headquarters, Bramble realizes that his impersonation is even more hazardous than he had envisioned: the dead man was really an agent working for the Germans. Convincing the Nazis that he is indeed the spy in their employ, he is instructed to go to Cairo to prepare for a German invasion.

Although the devilishly clever plotting of the film is one of its more obvious merits, FIVE GRAVES TO CAIRO scores on every level. The dialogue is by turns crisp, witty and stinging, and this cast is fully capable of making the most of it. Tone's gift for lending depth to his characters through understatement rarely found such a worthy vehicle. Baxter (in a moving turn and sporting a decent French accent), Tamiroff, Mander, Van Eyck (as a sleazy Nazi aide), and Bonanova (as an opera-loving Italian general) are all in fine form as well.

But of course a large share of the praise must go to that master scene-stealer Von Stroheim. Alternately brutal and civilized, arrogant and quiet, Rommel emerges as a complex military genius in this marvelous performer's hands. Wilder introduces him with a close-up of the back of his creased neck bursting over a high military collar, a technique Von Stroheim used in silent days when he profiled the evil Huns of WWI.

5,000 FINGERS OF DR. T., THE 📀

1953   89m   c   Children's/Fantasy/Musical   ★★★★½
Columbia   (U.S.)

Peter Lind Hayes *(Zabladowski)*, Mary Healy *(Mrs. Collins)*, Hans Conried *(Dr. Terwilliker)*, Tommy Rettig *(Bart)*, John Heasley *(Uncle Whitney)*, Robert Heasley *(Uncle Judson)*, Noel Cravat *(Sgt. Lunk)*, Henry Kulky *(Stroogo)*

p, Stanley Kramer; d, Roy Rowland; w, Ted Geisel, Allan Scott; ph, Franz Planer (Technicolor); ed, Al Clark; m, Frederick Hollander; prod d, Rudolph Sternad; art d, Cary Odell; chor, Eugene Loring

AAN Best Score (Musical): Frederick Hollander, Morris Stoloff

Hollywood films just don't get any weirder than this underappreciated 1950s classic. This surrealistic children's film (cowritten by Ted Geisel, better known as Dr. Seuss), features Tommy Rettig of TV's "Lassie" as Bart Collins, a young boy who would rather play baseball than take piano lessons with the eccentric and tyrannical Dr. Terwilliker (Conried).

Falling asleep at his piano, Bart dreams he's being chased by weird creatures with butterfly nets through a land of fog, cylinders, and odd-shaped mounds. Here he stumbles upon the castle of Dr. T, who runs a piano school for captive boys. The film's key image is the massive winding double-decker piano keyboard with 500 seats, one for each student. 500 boys, 5,000 fingers—get it? Kept in the dungeon are pitiful creatures imprisoned as punishment for playing instruments other than the piano. The prisoners have built musical instruments out of odd materials and, in the film's most elaborate sequence, perform a strange ballet. Bart's widowed mom (Mary Healy) is second-in-command at this terrible school but she is hypnotized by Dr. T. Eventually Bart teams up with Mr.

Zabladowski (Hayes), a resourceful plumber and reluctant surrogate father, to topple Dr. T's evil empire.

THE 5,000 FINGERS OF DR T. is one of the best fantasy films ever produced by Hollywood. Adults will find it every bit as diverting and intriguing as children as it explicitly connects dreams, surrealism and psychoanaysis. The dreamy sets succeed in making this film look like a Dr. Seuss book brought to life. Rettig and Hayes are delightful and Healy's OK but Conried gives what may be the performance of his estimable career as the dastardly fop. Though at times deliriously perverse, particularly in the context of conformist 1950s filmmaking, the film is also quite moving. Essential viewing for any potentially cool kids.

FLAMINGO KID, THE 📀

1984   100m   c   Comedy/Drama   ★★★½
Mercury/ABC   (U.S.)   PG-13

Matt Dillon *(Jeffrey Willis)*, Hector Elizondo *(Arthur Willis)*, Molly McCarthy *(Ruth Willis)*, Martha Gehman *(Nikki Willis)*, Richard Crenna *(Phil Brody)*, Jessica Walter *(Phyllis Brody)*, Carole Davis *(Joyce Brody)*, Janet Jones *(Carla Samson)*, Brian McNamara *(Steve Dawkins)*, Fisher Stevens *(Hawk Ganz)*

p, Michael Phillips; d, Garry Marshall; w, Garry Marshall, Neal Marshall (based on his story); ph, James A. Contner (Panavision, Deluxe Color); ed, Priscilla Nedd; prod d, Lawrence Miller; art d, Duke Durfee; cos, Ellen Mirojnick

A touching account of a working-class teenager tempted to reject his honorable ambitions in favor of a life of easy luxury.

Jeffrey Willis (Dillon) is an 18-year-old Brooklyn kid who joins some friends on a jaunt to "El Flamingo," a ritzy beachside club for affluent Long Islanders. There he observes Phil Brody (Crenna), a wealthy car dealer and the club's champion gin player, effectively demolishing his competition at the card table. Jeffrey is hired by the club for the summer, and slowly a romance develops between him and Brody's niece, Carla (Jones). Brody also takes a liking to Jeffrey and helps him get a promotion. After a talk with his new mentor, Jeffrey decides to become a car salesman too. His father (Elizondo), who dreams of his son's going to college, is dead set against this idea.

There's not a single bad performance here, and director Marshall wisely builds his film on small moments, realized with sympathy and intelligence.

FLASH GORDON 📀

1936   97m   bw   Science Fiction   ★★★★
Universal   (U.S.)

Buster Crabbe *(Flash Gordon)*, Jean Rogers *(Dale Arden)*, Charles Middleton *(Ming, the Merciless)*, Priscilla Lawson *(Princess Aura)*, Jack Lipson *(King Vultan)*, Richard Alexander *(Prince Barin)*, Frank Shannon *(Dr. Zarkov)*, Duke York Jr. *(King Kala)*, Earl Askam *(Officer Torch)*, George Cleveland *(Prof. Hensley)*

p, Henry MacRae; d, Frederick Stephani; w, Frederick Stephani, George Plympton, Basil Dickey, Ella O'Neill (based on the comic strip by Alex Raymond); ph, Jerome Ash, Richard Fryer; m, Franz Waxman; art d, Ralph Berger; fx, Norman Drewes

The one, the only, the original, and the best, this film was initially released as a 13-part serial based on a King Features comic strip.

Flash Gordon (Crabbe), his companion, Dr. Zarkov (Shannon), and sweetheart Dale Arden (Rogers) blast off for the planet Mongo, trying to stop it from a collision course with Earth. In a flash, Flash encounters evil Ming the Merciless (the unforgettable Middleton) along with assorted hawk men, shark men, dinosaurs, horned gorillas, giant lobsters, space ships (hanging from decidedly visible wires) and some mighty nifty costumes. Ming lusts wantonly for Dale, and Princess Aura (Lawson), Ming's equally lustful daughter, has a heavy crush on Flash.

A film whose naive, eager-to-please energy is almost as transporting as Flash's rocketship, FLASH GORDON is likely to delight even the fussiest audiences. The music and some of the sets were borrowed from THE BRIDE OF FRANKENSTEIN, and several sequels were to borrow heavily from this film. Not to be missed.

FLASH OF GREEN, A

1984 131m c   Drama   ★★★½
Spectrafilm (U.S.)

Ed Harris (Jimmy Wing), Blair Brown (Kate Hubble), Richard Jordan (Elmo Bliss), George Coe (Brian Haas), Joan Goodfellow (Mitchie), Jean De Baer (Jackie Halley), Helen Stenborg (Aunt Middie), William Mooney (Leroy Shannard), Isa Thomas (Doris Rohl), John Glover (Ross Halley)

p, Richard Jordan; d, Victor Nunez; w, Victor Nunez (based on the novel by John D. MacDonald); ph, Victor Nunez; ed, Victor Nunez; m, Charles Engstrom; art d, Carlos Asse; cos, Marilyn Wall-Asse, Dana Moser

Adapted and directed by Victor Nunez, A FLASH OF GREEN is a sure-handed look at corruption in Florida, with all the richly observed characterizations found in John D. MacDonald's novel.

In the mythical town of Palm City, we first meet Jimmy Wing (Harris), a likable reporter for the local paper. Elmo Bliss (Jordan), the local county commissioner, has been a pal of Jimmy's since they were in school together years before. Elmo is very ambitious and comes to Jimmy with a bribe offer. Elmo and his buddies want to gain control of some publicly owned land for development but are stymied by a group of ecological do-gooders known as the "SOBs" (Save Our Bay). The would-be developers mean to get that opposition out of the way, and things start to get pretty ugly before it's all over.

A complex story with no easy answers, A FLASH OF GREEN is beautifully acted, and one of the few adaptations of a MacDonald novel that sticks closely to the intent of the original. Where it falls apart is in failing to provide a sustained story line for the audience. Too many side issues detract from the story, and the uncertain editing doesn't help. But the film is moody, steamy and provocative enough to warrant your attention.

FLESH

1968 105m c   Drama   ★★★
Andy Warhol Productions   (U.S.)

Joe Dallesandro (Joe), Geraldine Smith (Gerry), John Christian (Young Man), Maurice Bardell (Artist), Harry Brown (Boy on Street), Candy Darling (Blonde on Sofa), Jackie Curtis (Redhead on Sofa), Geri Miller (Terry), Louis Waldon (David), Patti D'Arbanville (Gerry's Girlfriend)

p, Andy Warhol; d, Paul Morrisey; w, Paul Morrisey; ph, Paul Morrisey; ed, Paul Morrisey

As Andy Warhol recuperated from gunshot wounds inflicted by Valerie Solanis, his Factory associate Paul Morrisey directed this drowsy, picaresque tale of a henpecked Manhattan hustler, the first of several "Warhol" films that are actually part of Morrisey's equally interesting oeuvre. Joe (Joe Dallesandro), a virtually affectless but oddly charming creature of the East Village, drags himself out of bed to hustle tricks on 33rd Street; his girlfriend Gerry (Geraldine Smith) has demanded cash to pay for an abortion. During a long day of entrepre-

neurial improvisation, Joe encounters a variety of Warhol regulars, including legendary transvestites Jackie Curtis and Candy Darling (who, along with Dallesandro, were later immortalized in Lou Reed's "Walk On The Wild Side"). Although FLESH displays many of the hallmarks of Warhol's non-narrative house style (endless takes, speed-fueled improvisation, casually amateurish lighting and sound), Morrisey is already experimenting with the kind of traditional filmmaking techniques that Warhol pretended to disdain—at least until Morrisey's increasingly polished movies began turning handsome profits.

FLIGHT OF THE PHOENIX, THE   📀

1965 149m c   Adventure   ★★★★
Fox   (U.S.)

James Stewart (Frank Towns), Richard Attenborough (Lew Moran), Peter Finch (Capt. Harris), Hardy Kruger (Heinrich Dorfmann), Ernest Borgnine (Trucker Cobb), Ian Bannen (Crow), Ronald Fraser (Sgt. Watson), Christian Marquand (Dr. Renaud), Dan Duryea (Standish), George Kennedy (Bellamy)

p, Robert Aldrich; d, Robert Aldrich; w, Lukas Heller (based on a novel by Elleston Trevor); ph, Joseph Biroc (DeLuxe Color); ed, Michael Luciano; m, Frank DeVol; art d, William Glasgow; fx, L.B. Abbott, Howard Lydecker; cos, Norma Koch

AAN Best Supporting Actor: Ian Bannen; AAN Best Film Editing: Michael Luciano

A riveting survival film in which Stewart and his cohorts give power-packed performances as a downed pilot and passengers awaiting death in the Sahara desert.

At first pilot Frank Towns (Stewart) assumes the blame for the crash landing, although it's clearly the fault of alcoholic navigator Lew Moran (Attenborough). For a while, the men await rescue in the broiling sun, conserving their water. British officer Capt. Harris (Finch), however, decides to seek help from a passing caravan, but he gets more than he bargains for from the hostile Arabs. All seems hopeless until Heinrich Dorfmann (Kruger) announces that he can design a working single-engined plane from the wreck.

The crux of this gripping drama ultimately becomes the antagonism between pilot Towns and scientist Dorfmann, and Stewart and Kruger handle their encounters superbly—particularly in the scene where Towns learns that Dorfmann is a designer of *model* airplanes. Finch is convincing as the stoic British officer, and Borgnine, Marquand, and Duryea give fine performances as stranded men. Aldrich's direction is sharp and well paced, and Heller's screenplay absorbing and authentic.

FLINTSTONES, THE   📀

1994 92m c   Comedy/Fantasy/Children's   ★★½
Amblin (U.S.)   PG

John Goodman (Fred Flintstone), Elizabeth Perkins (Wilma Flintstone), Rick Moranis (Barney Rubble), Rosie O'Donnell (Betty Rubble), Kyle MacLachlan (Cliff Vandercave), Halle Berry (Miss Rosetta Stone), Elizabeth Taylor (Pearl Slaghoople), Dann Florek (Mr. Slate), Richard Moll (Hoagie), Irwin Keyes (Joe Rockhead)

p, Bruce Cohen; d, Brian Levant; w, Tom S. Parker, Jim Jennewein, Steven E. de Souza (based on the animated series from Hanna-Barbera Productions); ph, Dean Cundey; ed, Kent Beyda, David Tanaka; m, David Newman; prod d, William Sandell; art d, Jim Teegarden, Nancy Patton, Christopher Burian-Mohr; fx, Industrial Light & Magic, Mark Dippe, Michael Lantieri; chor, Adam M. Shankman; cos, Rosanna Norton, Monique Brown

THE FLINTSTONES is the most faithful of all the film recreations of '60s TV shows, but is fidelity to a cartoon knock-off of "The Honeymooners" really a virtue? Rarely has more high-powered movie technology been deployed to achieve such frivolous ends. Kids seem to love it, while sophisticated viewers may find it enchanting, appalling, or both.

Smarmy executive Cliff Vandercave (Kyle MacLachlan) plans to embezzle big bucks from the Slate Gravel Company by framing a gullible working stiff promoted from the gravel pit. Engagingly oafish Fred Flintstone (John Goodman) fits the bill. He becomes a V.P. and has to fire his pal Barney Rubble (Rick Moranis), a new adoptive father. Subsequently, he is tricked into laying off all of his former co-workers in the gravel pit. Fred's life falls apart at home and at the office, but we're never worried that it won't all work out for the best.

THE FLINTSTONES is about as good as it could possibly be. The spirit of the TV cartoon sitcom is obsessively recreated with the genuine love of an ardent fan. The silly puns are delivered with conviction; the sets, costumes, and critters look great; and Goodman is a stroke of casting genius. (The sole innovation here is a PC view of a BC society; this Bedrock is thoroughly integrated.) Not many belly laughs, but constant smiles of recognition for the sympathetically inclined.

FLIRTING   *DVD*
1990 96m   c   Drama/Romance   ★★★½
Kennedy-Miller Productions   (Australia)   R

Noah Taylor (*Danny Embling*), Thandie Newton (*Thandiwe Adjewa*), Nicole Kidman (*Nicola Radcliffe*), Bartholomew Rose ("*Gilby*" *Fryer*), Felix Nobis (*Jock Blair*), Josh Picker ("*Baka*" *Bourke*), Kiri Paramore ("*Slag*" *Green*), Marc Gray (*Christopher Laidlaw*), Greg Palmer (*Colin Proudfoot*), Joshua Marshall ("*Cheddar*" *Fedderson*)

p, George Miller, Terry Hayes, Doug Mitchell; d, John Duigan; w, John Duigan; ph, Geoff Burton; ed, Robert Gibson; prod d, Roger Ford

This sequel to writer-director John Duigan's acclaimed THE YEAR MY VOICE BROKE is an intelligently written and marvelously acted coming-of-age tale set in rural Australia in the 1960s.

Danny Embling (Noah Taylor) is a bright, sensitive boarding school student who falls in love with Thandiwe Adjewa (Thandie Newton), the only black pupil at the girl's school which sits tantalizingly across the lake from Danny's college. Despite the interference of authoritarian teachers and bigoted school bullies, the two embark on an extremely charming relationship that is ended when political events force Thandiwe's family to return to Uganda.

FLIRTING is a rather more serious film than its name implies. Duigan's main focus is on the teenage love story, yet he gives his tale a broader dramatic context through succinct, telling allusions to bigger events taking place in the world at large. Aided by a literate screenplay and fine performances from his ensemble cast, Duigan brings a sense of universality to his treatment of first love, while still filtering in a keen sense of time and place.

Taylor, as young outsider Danny, is flawless in his interpretation of the character, displaying an uncanny depth seldom found in juvenile actors. The exceptionally pretty Newton is graceful and charming as Thandiwe and Nicole Kidman (DEAD CALM, FAR AND AWAY) contributes a fine turn in the underwritten role of Nicola Radcliffe, an initially snobbish upperclassman who becomes a firm friend of Thandiwe's.

FLOWER OF MY SECRET, THE   *DVD*
(LA FLOR DE MI SECRETO)
1995 107m c   Drama/Romance   ★★★½
CiBy 2000/El Deseo SA   (Spain/France)   R

Marisa Paredes (*Leo Macias*), Juan Echanove (*Angel*), Imanol Arias (*Paco*), Carmen Elias (*Betty*), Rossy de Palma (*Rosa*),

Chus Lampreave (*Mother*), Joaquin Cortes (*Antonio*), Manuela Vargas (*Blanca*), Kiti Manver, Gloria Munoz

p, Esther Garcia; d, Pedro Almodovar; w, Pedro Almodovar; ph, Affonso Beato; ed, Jose Salcedo; m, Alberto Iglesias; art d, Wolfgang Burmann; fx, Molina; cos, Hugo Mezcua, Marisa Paredes, Juan Echanove

In THE FLOWER OF MY SECRET, the usually comedic filmmaker Pedro Almodovar opts for melodrama rather than farce as he follows a romance novelist who conducts her personal life as if she were one of her own compulsive heroines.

Best-selling author Leo (Marisa Paredes) is intent on resuscitating her already-dead marriage to Paco (Imanol Arias), a NATO officer who is often away from home. Although unable to extricate herself from her unrequited love, she jump-starts her professional life by taking a critic's post at *El Pais*, a newspaper run by the portly Angel (Juan Echanove). Absorbed in heartache, Leo doesn't realize that Angel has more than an editorial interest in her.

Fluidly directed, this wittily conceived exploration of loving well but unwisely parallels serious scenes and pastel parodies. Perhaps this clever film signifies Almodovar's own acceptance of his unique gifts as soap opera jester. But there's nothing more serious than the aspects of love he deals with, and the film's comedy doesn't diminish its sentimental impact. Paredes is a superb dramatic actress, who meshes beautifully with the melancholy of this Almodovar offering. Through this vibrant actress, Almodovar counsels inveterate sufferers that, by working through their pain, they can reach a future that flowers more sublimely than any unfulfilled romantic past. This bracing comedy-drama holds out a hand to anyone who has ever despaired of finding love a second or third time around.

FLOWERS OF ST. FRANCIS, THE
(FRANCESCO, GIULLARE DI DIO)
1950 75m   bw Religious   ★★★★★
Cineriz/Rizzoli   (Italy)

Aldo Fabrizi (*Nicolaio, the Tyrant*), Arabella Lemaitre (*Saint Clair*), Brother Nazario Gerardi (*Saint Francis*)

p, Giuseppe Amato; d, Roberto Rossellini; w, Roberto Rossellini, Federico Fellini, Fr. Felix Morion, Fr. Antonio Lisandrini (based on the life of Fioretti di San Francesco); ph, Otello Martelli; ed, Jolando Benvenuti; m, Renzo Rossellini, Fr. Enrico Buondonno

A film of great harmony and natural beauty, this short historical feature from the celebrated Italian noerealist Roberto Rossellini is a tone poem comprised of physical gestures. Performed, with the exception of Aldo Fabrizi, by nonprofessionals (all of whom are real-life Franciscan monks), the film captures the brothers' purity and their desire to live in harmony with nature. More striking than the film's grand themes—man and nature, God and man, peace and defiance, love and hate, generosity and greed—Rossellini sensitively captures the monks' expressive physical movements. Illustrating one character's line of dialogue, "Souls are won over by examples, not words," Rossellini does not show us speeches or have us listen to readings from scripture. Instead we see the hands and faces of these monks, their wonder, their peace, their simplicity. As these monks can say so much with their eyes, so too can Rossellini speak volumes with a single shot.

FLY, THE   *DVD*
1986 100m c   Horror   ★★★★½
Brooksfilms   (U.S.)   R

Jeff Goldblum (*Seth Brundle*), Geena Davis (*Veronica Quaife*), John Getz (*Stathis Borans*), Joy Boushel (*Tawny*), Les Carlson (*Dr. Cheevers*), George Chuvalo (*Marky*), Michael Copeman

(Man in Bar), David Cronenberg *(Gynecologist)*, Carol Lazare *(Nurse)*, Shawn Hewitt *(Clerk)*

p, Stuart Cornfeld; d, David Cronenberg; w, Charles Pogue, David Cronenberg (based on a story by George Langelaan); ph, Mark Irwin (Deluxe Color); ed, Ronald Sanders; m, Howard Shore; prod d, Carol Spier; art d, Rolf Harvey; fx, Louis Craig, Ted Ross; cos, Denise Cronenberg

AA Best Makeup: Chris Walas, Stephan Dupuis

Obsessed with the horrifying implications of a combination of science, technology and the powerful potentials of the human mind, body and sexuality, Cronenberg had created several highly personal films over the previous 15 years. While the concepts of these films are interesting and unique, the films themselves were quite uneven. Slapdash, poorly cast, under-budgeted, and sometimes incoherent, there was also insufficient attention paid to the development of characters as complex, emotional human beings. With his decision to remake the 1958 classic THE FLY, Cronenberg found the perfect outlet for his obsessions, producing his most controlled, mature and insightful work to date.

Enhanced by a more complex personal relationship between the protagonists, the new version of THE FLY pairs a young science-magazine reporter, Veronica Quaife (Geena Davis), and a somewhat shy, awkward scientist, Seth Brundle (Jeff Goldblum), who is involved in a secret experiment to transport matter that will "change life as we know it." Although brilliant intellectually, Brundle lacks social graces and his endearingly clumsy efforts to seduce Veronica look like a high school nerd trying to impress the prom queen with his science project. The pair gradually fall in love, and they make a heart-warming couple. Brundle continues his experiments, trying to advance from transporting objects to transporting living beings. Eventually, he is driven to transport himself but fails to notice the little fly that has traveled through space with him.

THE FLY succeeds on many levels. Cronenberg has never elicited better performances from his players. Goldblum is sublime in a rare leading role. Davis is also in top form. As a couple, they are so convincing and appealing that one regrets knowing that their love story will soon become a tragic horror movie. As a remake, THE FLY transcends the original, taking it in new directions and exploring its underutilized potential. Whereas the original degenerated into a campy fly hunt, the remake opts for a slow metamorphosis from man to fly that develops as a disease might. This gives Cronenberg time to examine the implications of such a process, meditating upon our fear of disease, death and change.

FLY AWAY HOME

1996 110m c   Children's/Drama   ★★★½
Branti Film Productions/Sandollar Productions   PG
(U.S.)

Jeff Daniels *(Thomas Alden)*, Anna Paquin *(Amy Alden)*, Dana Delany *(Susan Barnes)*, Terry Kinney *(David Alden)*, Holter Graham *(Barry Stickland)*, Jeremy Ratchford *(Glen Seifert)*, Deborah Verginella *(Amy's Mother)*, Michael J. Reynolds *(General)*, David Hemblen *(Dr. Killian)*, Ken James *(Developer)*

p, John Veitch, Carol Baum; d, Carroll Ballard; w, Robert Rodat, Vince McKewin (based on the autobiography by Bill Lishman); ph, Caleb Deschanel; ed, Nicholas C. Smith; m, Mark Isham; prod d, Seamus Flannery; fx, Martin Malivoire, John Mariella, C.O.R.E. Digital Pictures; cos, Marie-Sylvie Deveau

AAN Best Cinematography: Caleb Deschanel

An incredible journey in the air becomes a voyage of self-discovery for a young girl in this touching tale directed by Carroll Ballard (THE BLACK STALLION).

After her mother's death, 13-year-old Amy Alden (Anna Paquin, THE PIANO) is uprooted from her New Zealand home and sent to Canada to live with a father she doesn't remember. Tom Alden (Jeff Daniels) is an eccentric artist, inventor, and flying enthusiast who hasn't a clue about how to reach out to the brooding Amy. When a nearby woods are clear-cut by developers, Amy discovers an abandoned nest of goose eggs, which she secretly adopts. When the goslings hatch, they imprint on Amy as their mother goose. As the birds mature, the Aldens face a dilemma: by law, domesticated geese must be pinioned, but the orphaned flock doesn't know how to migrate. Tom hatches a crazy scheme: he will fly the migration route with Amy following him in her own plane, and the geese following behind her.

One of the best "family films" of 1996, FLY AWAY HOME was nonetheless largely overlooked by audiences who clamor for such offerings from Hollywood. Though a reading of the film's plot rings like a knock-off of FREE WILLY, the film, based on a true incident, is a resonant and affecting work. Ballard and cinematographer Caleb Deschanel rely largely on beautiful and poetic imagery to tell Amy's story and effectively reign in any potentially hokey melodrama. Paquin gives a nicely modulated, understated performance that allows viewers to indentify with Amy. And so, in the end, when she soars through the clouds with the white ocean shoals below, Ballard has correctly calculated how to make the viewer's spirit soar as well.

FLYING DOWN TO RIO

1933 89m   bw Musical   ★★★★
RKO   (U.S.)

Dolores Del Rio *(Belinha de Rezende)*, Gene Raymond *(Roger Bond)*, Raul Roulien *(Julio Rubeiro)*, Ginger Rogers *(Honey Hale)*, Fred Astaire *(Fred Ayres)*, Blanche Frederici *(Dona Elena)*, Walter Walker *(Senor de Rezende)*, Etta Moten *(Black Singer)*, Roy D'Arcy, Maurice Black

p, Lou Brock; d, Thornton Freeland; w, Cyril Hume, H.W. Hanemann, Erwin Gelsey (based on a play by Anne Caldwell from an original story by Brock); ph, J. Roy Hunt; ed, Jack Kitchin; m, Vincent Youmans; art d, Van Nest Polglase, Carroll Clark; fx, Vernon L. Walker; chor, Dave Gould; cos, Walter Plunkett

AAN Best Song: "Carioca"; Vincent Youmans (Music), Edward Eliscu (Lyrics), Gus Kahn (Lyrics)

Highway robbery, Astaire-Rogers style. Whoever failed to see that the brilliantly talented and engaging Astaire and the playful, gifted Rogers were ideal star material must have been wearing airplane goggles throughout the making of FLYING DOWN TO RIO. Billed fourth and fifth, playing a sassy band singer and the accordionist pal of romantic lead Raymond, Rogers and Astaire positively shimmer with high spirits in this whoops-a-daisy extravaganza.

RKO's bid to cash in on the new breed of musical introduced by the Busby Berkeley tunefests over at Warner Bros. FLYING DOWN TO RIO toplines gorgeous, dark Del Rio and gorgeous, white-blonde Raymond in a silly romantic triangle alongside likable crooner Roulien. Although the lead trio does well enough, the presence of cinema's greatest musical comedy team fairly blasts the screen lovers into orbit whenever either or both of them are onscreen.

Astaire and Rogers both have a great flair for comedy; perhaps only Joan Blondell and Eve Arden can equal Rogers's way with a wisecrack. Working more apart than together in this initial venture, Ginger and Fred all but monopolize the delightful Youmans score. The 18-minute showpiece, "The Carioca," though it gives the dynamic duo but a few moments together on the dance floor, already represents the start of a beautiful conspiracy.

The only major production number not to spotlight Rogers and Astaire is the title tune, a bizarre attempt to outdo Busby's bodacious ballets with chorines strapped to airplane wings. Despite this lollapalooza's tuneful terror tactics, the film's most memorable image is the last one: Fred and Ginger bantering before the end titles. They are *more* than ready to be stars on their own. A kooky Depression-era delight.

FOG OF WAR: ELEVEN LESSONS FROM THE LIFE OF ROBERT S. MCNAMARA, THE

2003 95m c/bw Documentary ★★★
@radical media Inc./Globe Department PG-13
Store/SenArt Films (U.S.)

Robert S. McNamara, Errol Morris *(Interviewer)*

p, Errol Morris, Julie Ahlberg, Errol Morris, Michael Williams; d, Errol Morris; ph, Robert Chappell, Peter Donahue; ed, Doug Abel, Chyld King, Karen Schmeer; m, Philip Glass; prod d, Ted Bafaloukos, Steve Hardy; art d, Steve McNulty

AA Best Documentary Feature

Errol Morris continues his series of meetings with remarkable men by pointing his patented "Interrotron" camera contraption at former Secretary of Defense Robert S. McNamara, a man who'd become so closely identified with the conflict in Vietnam that the whole debacle became known as "McNamara's War."

McNamara first offers a quick summation of his early career, including a 14-year stint at General Motors that culminated in his promotion to company president in 1960. But after only seven weeks in his new office, McNamara was tapped by John F. Kennedy to serve as his Secretary of Defense, and was immediately plunged into the thickening quagmire of Vietnam. By the time McNamara left the Johnson administration mid-term, the still undeclared war had escalated to horrendous proportions. As historically relevant as all this may be, Morris is far more interested in what happened in 1995, when McNamara published his explosive memoir *In Retrospect: The Tragedy and Lessons of Vietnam.* Within the first few pages this former bogeyman of the antiwar movement candidly admitted that he and his fellow decision makers had been "wrong, terribly wrong." Morris gives his subject wide berth to explain how he'd had serious doubts about committing U.S. troops to South Vietnam even before the Kennedy assassination, and how he now believes that we could have—and should have—brought our troops home as early as 1963.

Morris's nonconfrontational style allows McNamara to basically recite passages from his book in toto—a teary performance he's polished to perfection during countless interviews. Asked why he didn't speak out at the time, McNamara claims he was faithfully serving his president. Asked if he feels guilty, he declines to comment. His answers will either earn your respect, or further damn him as the architect of an American nightmare.

FOG OVER FRISCO

1934 68m bw Crime ★★★★½
First National (U.S.)

Bette Davis *(Arlene Bradford)*, Donald Woods *(Tony Stirling)*, Margaret Lindsay *(Val Bradford)*, Lyle Talbot *(Spencer Carleton)*, A.S. Byron *(Everett Bradford)*, Hugh Herbert *(Izzy Wright)*, Robert Barrat *(Thorne)*, Douglas Dumbrille *(Joshua Maynard)*, Irving Pichel *(Jake Bello)*, Gordon Westcott *(Joe Bello)*

p, Robert Lord; d, William Dieterle; w, Robert N. Lee, Eugene Solow (based on a story by George Dyer); ph, Tony Gaudio; ed, Harold McLernon; art d, Jack Okey; cos, Orry-Kelly

When Jean-Luc Godard named his homage to Hollywood BREATHLESS, he must have had this film in mind. German emigree Dieterle, a Warner Bros. stalwart, directed one of the fastest-paced movies ever in FOG OVER FRISCO, displaying a dazzling, whirlwind technique that completely overwhelms a rather mundane plot.

Socialite Val Bradford (Lindsay) reads a newspaper report that her stepsister Arlene (Davis) has been consorting with underworld figures at an infamous nightclub run by Jake Bello (Pichel). Val promptly upbraids the story's writer, Tony Stirling (Woods), telling him that Arlene is merely a thoughtless girl who is not responsible for the company she keeps. If only she knew! In fact, the not-so-naive Arlene has been using her fiance Spencer Carleton (Talbot) to sell off securities stolen by Bello and his gang. After Spencer implores Arlene to quit the ring, she gives Val a sealed envelope containing evidence that will expose Bello should anything happen to her.

A standard crime melodrama in plot only, FOG OVER FRISCO is such a marvelous technical exercise that Eisenstein himself would have been proud. The film moves along at an astounding speed, especially in its final half, when your laughter is either due to the silly plot or to your own breathlessness. The inventive Dieterle employs almost every filmic device imaginable—overlapping sound, wipes, iris openings and closings, rushed dialogue and figure movement, opticals in quick takes, and boom, dolly, and truck shots—to heighten the narrative's urgency. Still an intoxicating experience today, this glimpse of the state of the art in 1934 is a brilliant tribute to Hollywood craftsmanship.

FOLLOW THE FLEET

1936 110m bw Musical/Comedy ★★★★½
RKO (U.S.)

Fred Astaire *(Bake Baker)*, Ginger Rogers *(Sherry Martin)*, Randolph Scott *(Bilge Smith)*, Harriet Hilliard *(Connie Martin)*, Astrid Allwyn *(Iris Manning)*, Harry Beresford *(Capt. Ezra Hickey)*, Russell Hicks *(Jim Nolan)*, Brooks Benedict *(Sullivan, Nolan's Assistant)*, Ray Mayer *(Dopey Williams)*, Lucille Ball *(Kitty Collins)*

p, Pandro S. Berman; d, Mark Sandrich; w, Dwight Taylor, Allan Scott (based on the play "Shore Leave" by Hubert Osborne); ph, David Abel; ed, Henry Berman; art d, Van Nest Polglase, Carroll Clark; fx, Vernon L. Walker; chor, Hermes Pan, Fred Astaire; cos, Bernard Newman

Often regarded as one of the best of the legendary Astaire-Rogers musicals, FOLLOW THE FLEET really isn't up to TOP HAT, SWING TIME or ROBERTA, the wonder films of the series. The main reason is the bland plot, which, though similar to that of several of their other films, grinds along at a rather poky pace. Astaire and Scott play sailor buddies on leave, and Rogers and Hilliard are cast as sisters with whom they become involved.

Essentially consigned to second-lead status, Rogers and Astaire fittingly play the couple who already know each other, and they banter their way through their dialogue with great rapport. Their range and talent as dancers is also on prominent display here, from their explosive romp to "Let Yourself Go" to Astaire's blazing nautical tap to "I'd Rather Lead a Band" to Roger's delightful solo, her first in the series.

They are hilariously out of sync with each other in a comic cut-up routine to "I'm Putting All My Eggs in One Basket" and resume their trademark after-dinner elegance for a stunning turn to "Let's Face the Music and Dance." Performed as part of a melodramatic playlet onstage, this glamorous number is the closest they ever got to playing Garbo, replete with sumptuous poses and an unforgettable finale. Occasional lumps notwithstanding, FOLLOW THE FLEET is great entertainment. All aboard!

FOLLOWING

1998 70m bw Thriller/Crime *DVD*
Next Wave Films (U.K.) ★★★★

Jeremy Theobald *(The Young Man)*, Alex Haw *(Cobb)*, Lucy Russell *(The Blonde)*, John Nolan *(The Policeman)*

p, Christopher Nolan, Emma Thomas, Jeremy Theobald; d, Christopher Nolan; w, Christopher Nolan; ph, Christopher Nolan; ed, Christopher Nolan, Gareth Heal; m, David Julyan; prod d, Tristan Martin

Short, sharp, and tough as nails. Shot for next to nothing in grainy black-and-white and running just a little over an hour, this taut, 100% fat-free flick recalls such compact, hard-hitting crime thrillers as DETOUR, IMPACT, and THE HOLLOW TRIUMPH.

Bill (Jeremy Theobald) is a scruffy, unemployed writer and self-described "follower": he likes to pick strangers out of a crowd and follow them around the streets of London, learning what he can about the details of their lives. It's not quite stalking, but it's also not the healthiest way to pass the time. Bill's voyeurism becomes downright dangerous when he starts tailing a handsome, smartly dressed fellow carrying a large satchel. The game, it turns out, is one Mr. Cobb (Alex Haw), a smooth-talking cat-burglar who also likes to peek inside people's lives, though his modus operandi leans to breaking and entering. Cobb confronts his stalker, and the tables are suddenly turned: Bill is plunged into a life of petty crime while at the same time entangling himself in the sticky web of a cool, hard-boiled blonde (Lucy Russell) who, like everyone and everything else in the picture, is not exactly what she seems.

British writer-director Christopher Nolan has his feet firmly grounded in American movies, specifically the poverty-row noir thrillers of the 1940s. Like the best of them, this edgy little bit of nastiness twists and turns under a heavy cloud of fatalism, thanks to a tricky, triple-tiered flashback structure that lets you know right off the bat that none of this is going to end happily.

FOOTLIGHT PARADE

1933 102m bw Musical ★★★★★
Warner Bros. (U.S.)

James Cagney *(Chester Kent)*, Joan Blondell *(Nan Prescott)*, Ruby Keeler *(Bea Thorn)*, Dick Powell *(Scotty Blair)*, Guy Kibbee *(Silas Gould)*, Ruth Donnelly *(Harriet Bowers Gould)*, Claire Dodd *(Vivian Rich)*, Hugh Herbert *(Charlie Bowers)*, Frank McHugh *(Francis)*, Arthur Hohl *(Al Frazer)*

p, Robert Lord; d, Lloyd Bacon, William Keighley, Busby Berkeley; w, Manuel Seff, James Seymour; ph, George Barnes; ed, George Amy; art d, Anton Grot; chor, Busby Berkeley; cos, Milo Anderson

Following its success with the blockbuster backstage musicals 42ND STREET and GOLD DIGGERS OF 1933, Warner Bros. launched this lavish production, with Cagney marvelous in the lead. He plays Chester Kent, a theatrical producer who finds himself unemployed after the advent of the Depression and talking pictures. The dogged Kent, however, sells his backers (Kibbee and Hohl) on the idea of doing "prologues," short but stunning stage musical numbers designed to precede the showing of feature films. Two-thirds of the movie deals with Chester's behind-the-scenes efforts to put together the prologues; the final third is devoted to the prologues themselves and to a suitable wrap-up.

Seemingly schizophrenic in form, with a gritty, backstage saga yielding to three flights of Busby Berkeley fantasy, FOOTLIGHT PARADE is actually an amazing cultural index of the Depression. All the wisecracking, all the struggle, all the buildup find a remarkable payoff when the film shifts gears into la-la land. The "Honeymoon Hotel" number

is standard risque fare, but "By a Waterfall," with Berkeley doing a "wet run" for his later Esther Williams spectaculars, is an astounding surrealistic kaleidoscope. "Shanghai Lil," meanwhile, adds a Warner Bros. toughness to Paramount's Shanghai Lily (Marlene Dietrich in SHANGHAI EXPRESS) of the year before.

Cagney is in great acting, comic and dancing form throughout and Blondell, as Kent's devoted secretary, proves that she has few peers at wisecracking or conveying low-key warmth. A great supporting cast and Bacon's well-judged direction help make FOOTLIGHT PARADE one of the greatest of the Berkeley extravaganzas.

FOR A FEW DOLLARS MORE

(PER QUALCHE DOLLARO IN PIU) *DVD*
1965 130m c Western ★★★★
Europee/Arturo Gonzales/Constantin
(Italy/Spain/West Germany)

Clint Eastwood *(The Man With No Name)*, Lee Van Cleef *(Col. Douglas Mortimer)*, Gian Maria Volonte *(Indio)*, Josef Egger *(Old Man Over Railway)*, Rosemarie Dexter *(Colonel's Sister)*, Mara Krup *(Hotel Manager's Wife)*, Klaus Kinski *(Hunchback)*, Mario Brega, Aldo Sambrell, Luigi Pistilli

p, Alberto Grimaldi; d, Sergio Leone; w, Luciano Vincenzoni, Sergio Leone (based on a story by Leone and Fulvio Morsella); ph, Massimo Dallamano (Techniscope, Technicolor); ed, Giorgio Ferralonga, Eugenio Alabiso; m, Ennio Morricone; art d, Carlo Simi; cos, Carlo Simi

The second film in Leone's "Dollar" trilogy (THE GOOD, THE BAD, AND THE UGLY would follow) finds the Italian director in better form than in A FISTFUL OF DOLLARS. FOR A FEW DOLLARS MORE has better writing, superior production values, and more characters who aptly complement Eastwood's stoic Man with No Name.

In this installment, the mysterious drifter is locked in combat with rival bounty hunter Colonel Mortimer (Van Cleef) to collect the reward for killing psychopathic bandit Indio (Volonte). At first, the men attempt to capture the crook separately, without success. The pair form an uneasy alliance, and Mortimer eventually guns Indio down in a shootout as No Name watches from the sidelines. It turns out, though, that Mortimer is not interested in money after all.

By introducing the character of Mortimer, Leone is able to counterpoint Eastwood's cold, amoral gunslinger with a man who has a past and a purpose. A more *human* character with which the audience can more readily identify makes Eastwood's role all the more mythic. Once again, Morricone's music is superbly appropriate, with each character's own theme (and one for the flashbacks too) bursting into this epic at just the right moment.

In FOR A FEW DOLLARS MORE, Leone's thematic concerns about the civilizing influence of the family and the hypocrisy of the Church are now richly in focus. His tone of self-parody and his portrait of an unrelenting landscape where men suddenly appear and vanish are all more detailed than before. We are also given the sense that the Man with No Name has been somewhat humanized by his encounter with Mortimer, a suspicion that would be confirmed in the final chapter of the trilogy.

FOR ME AND MY GAL

1942 104m bw Musical *DVD*
MGM (U.S.) ★★★½

Judy Garland *(Jo Hayden)*, George Murphy *(Jimmy K. Metcalf)*, Gene Kelly *(Harry Palmer)*, Marta Eggerth *(Eve Minard)*, Ben Blue *(Sid Simms)*, Richard Quine *(Danny Hayden)*, Keenan Wynn *(Eddie Milton)*, Stephen McNally, billed as Horace McNally *(Mr. Waring)*, Lucille Norman *(Lily Duncan)*, Betty Wells p, Arthur Freed; d, Busby Berkeley; w, Richard Sherman, Fred Finklehoffe, Sid Silvers, Jack McGowan, Irving Brecher (based on the story "The Big Time" by Howard Emmett Rogers); ph, William Daniels; ed, Ben Lewis; art d, Cedric Gibbons, Gabriel Scognamillo; chor, Bobby Connolly, Gene Kelly; cos, Robert Kalloch, Gile Steele

AAN Best Score (Musical): Roger Edens, Georgie Stoll

A delightful and nostalgic return to the fun-filled pre-WWI days of vaudeville. Jo Hayden (Garland) troops the boards with Jimmy Metcalf (Murphy), Sid Simms (Blue), and Lily Duncan (Norman). Though she loves the hardscrabble life of the stage, Jo's main career motive is to send her kid brother (Quine) to medical school. When smoothie Harry Palmer (Kelly) advises Jo that she could do much better in his song-and-dance act, she, with Jimmy's blessing, teams up with him. They struggle along for two years; meanwhile, Jimmy and Sid hit the big time. Harry, meanwhile, becomes infatuated with a singing star (Eggerth), even though Jo is the one who truly loves him. When WWI threatens to halt his burgeoning success, Harry compounds his sins by dodging the draft, causing Jo to leave him—until he redeems himself in heroic style.

The story is pure hokum, but this warm film is more than buoyed by the many old tunes and the superb production numbers—staged, surprisingly, not by specialist Berkeley, who directed, but by Bobby Connolly. The dynamic Kelly, in his film debut, exhibits star quality in spades, while at the same time hinting at the darker side to his persona in the scene where he maims his hand to avoid the draft. He and Garland play beautifully off each other, and of course their performance of the title standard is a highlight of the film.

FOR WHOM THE BELL TOLLS
1943 170m c Adventure/War ★★★
Paramount (U.S.)

Gary Cooper *(Robert Jordan)*, Ingrid Bergman *(Maria)*, Akim Tamiroff *(Pablo)*, Arturo de Cordova *(Agustin)*, Vladimir Sokoloff *(Anselmo)*, Mikhail Rasumny *(Rafael)*, Fortunio Bonanova *(Fernando)*, Eric Feldary *(Andres)*, Victor Varconi *(Primitivo)*, Katina Paxinou *(Pilar)*

p, Sam Wood; d, Sam Wood; w, Dudley Nichols (based on the novel by Ernest Hemingway); ph, Ray Rennahan (Technicolor); ed, Sherman Todd, John F. Link; m, Victor Young; prod d, William Cameron Menzies; art d, Hans Dreier, Haldane Douglas; fx, Gordon Jennings

AAN Best Picture; AAN Best Actor: Gary Cooper; *AAN Best Actress:* Ingrid Bergman; *AAN Best Supporting Actor:* Akim Tamiroff; *AA Best Supporting Actress:* Katina Paxinou; *AAN Best Color Cinematography:* Ray Rennahan; *AAN Best Film Editing:* Sherman Todd, John Link; *AAN Best Score (Drama or Comedy):* Victor Young; *AAN Best Interior Decoration (Color):* Hans Dreier, Haldane Douglas, Bertram Granger

A bowdlerized version of one of Hemingway's most famous works, FOR WHOM THE BELL TOLLS makes its most overtly political move by cutting Ingrid Bergman's hair so short. Otherwise, it's pretty much of a yawner, with people (in Spain, right?) doing something or other to fight some kind of oppression. At one point during the film's three agonizing hours someone hints at fascism, but since that's *such* a difficult concept, HUAC "friendly witness" Wood and his writers largely drop it in favor of boy meets girl. Butch Bergman meets stoic Cooper and we're off!

Even more taciturn than usual, Cooper is in many ways a perfect Hemingway hero (as he showed in the romanticized but lovely A FAREWELL TO ARMS). He has his moments, but otherwise seems a bit too respectful of the whole noble undertaking. Obviously remembering her luminous Ilsa from CASABLANCA, Bergman strives mightily to endow the film with romantic resonance, but she's treading on tenuous ground. The famous "I would kiss you but where do the noses go" is, depending on your mood, either the most dauntingly romantic moment this side of CASABLANCA's "Is that cannon fire or my heart pounding" or it's completely laughable. Cast mostly with Russians in all the Hispanic roles, this glamourfest is Hollywood politics at its most apolitical, lacking even the energy of a good B movie.

When critics with an interest in reality accused Paramount of fence-sitting (reports claimed that Franco's envoys and the Catholic Church pressured the studio into a nonpartisan stand), studio chief Adolph Zukor came back with one of the great double-edged truths about commercial cinema: "It's a great picture, without political significance. We are not for or against anybody."

FOR YOUR EYES ONLY
1981 127m c Spy/Adventure ★★★½
UA (U.K.) PG

Roger Moore *(James Bond)*, Carole Bouquet *(Melina)*, Topol *(Columbo)*, Lynn-Holly Johnson *(Bibi)*, Julian Glover *(Kristatos)*, Cassandra Harris *(Lisl)*, Jill Bennett *(Brink)*, Michael Gothard *(Locque)*, John Wyman *(Kriegler)*, Jack Hedley *(Havelock)*

p, Albert R. Broccoli; d, John Glen; w, Richard Maibaum, Michael G. Wilson (based on the short stories "For Your Eyes Only" and "Risico" by Ian Fleming); ph, Alan Hume (Panavision, Technicolor); ed, John Grover; m, Bill Conti; prod d, Peter Lamont; art d, John Fenner; fx, Derek Meddings; cos, Elizabeth Waller

AAN Best Original Song: "For Your Eyes Only"; Bill Conti (Music), Mick Leeson (Lyrics)

After returning to Earth from his MOONRAKER fiasco, Roger Moore resumes his role as James Bond without the excessive technical gadgetry. Against a sea-and-ski Greek backdrop, Bond and the obligatory beauty, Melina (Bouquet, lovely but lifeless), race Soviet agents for a device lost in a shipwreck that transmits the "fire" order to missile-carrying British submarines. The same Soviet agents killed Melina's parents, motivating her to seek Elektra-like revenge. One fast-paced chase follows another, and a slightly more vulnerable Bond gets his share of knocks along the way.

The success of this picture (perhaps Moore's best in the Bond series) can be attributed to the marvelous direction of Glen, who had previously worked as a second-unit director on earlier Bond movies. Not surprisingly, the stunts are some of the best in the series. Lynn-Holly Johnson is decidedly annoying in the unnecessary role of a horny young skater, but Topol helps offset this gaffe with his engaging presence. Very pleasant, unforced, throwaway entertainment, though Moore is clearly getting a mite too old for all this.

FORBIDDEN GAMES
(LES JEUX INTERDITS)
1952 102m bw War/Drama ★★★★★
Silver (France)

Brigitte Fossey *(Paulette)*, Georges Poujouly *(Michel Dolle)*, Lucien Hubert *(Dolle, the Father)*, Suzanne Courtal *(Mme Dolle)*, Jacques Marin *(Georges Dolle)*, Laurence Badie *(Berthe Dolle)*, Andre Wasley *(Gouard, the Father)*, Amedee *(Francis Gouard)*, Denise Pereonne *(Jeanne Gouard)*, Louis Sainteve *(Priest)*

p, Robert Dorfmann; d, Rene Clement; w, Rene Clement, Jean Aurenche, Pierre Bost (based on the novel *Les Jeux Inconnus* by Francois Boyer); ph, Robert Juillard; ed, Roger Dwyre; m, Narciso Yepes; art d, Paul Bertrand

AAN Best Motion Picture Story: Francois Boyer

One of the best films ever about war and its effects, FOR-BIDDEN GAMES also speaks beautifully to the need of children to construct their own fantasy world away from adult supervision.

Director Clement's most famous film carefully begins with its one action highlight, as refugees flee WWII Paris in the face of a Nazi attack. At a bottleneck on a bridge, German planes swoop down in perfect formation and strafe the confused column. Paulette (Fossey) is seen standing alone on the bridge, her parents and dog dead. When someone throws the dog over the bridge, she goes after it and meets Michel (Poujouly), the 11-year-old son of peasants (Hubert and Courtal). The boy takes the girl home with him, and his parents take her in. When Paulette sees her parents buried, she decides that her dog also needs to be buried in a grave with a cross. She and Michel steal a cross from the hearse carrying his older brother. He and Paulette begin to expand their secret animal cemetery to include moles, chickens, and even insects, all given elaborate memorial services with stolen crosses. The eventual discovery of the children's secret and their future together make for a moving climax.

FORBIDDEN GAMES derives most of its power from Clement's painstakingly methodical direction and the remarkable performances of the two child leads. Poujouly and the amazing five year-old Fossey are highly expressive actors who give this stunning film its emotional core. The visual and narrative style is a potent blend of stark documentary, pastoral realism and film noir. Seeing war through the eyes of children who cope with its atrocities by constructing their own little game of death was a brilliant move—it seems morbid and grotesque to all the adults, but the problem is that *they* are the ones who really lack understanding and respect.

FORBIDDEN PLANET
1956 98m c Science Fiction ★★★★
MGM (U.S.)

Walter Pidgeon *(Dr. Morbius)*, Anne Francis *(Altaira)*, Leslie Nielsen *(Cmdr. Adams)*, Warren Stevens *(Lt. "Doc" Ostrow)*, Jack Kelly *(Lt. Farman)*, Richard Anderson *(Chief Quinn)*, Earl Holliman *(Cook)*, George Wallace *(Bosun)*, Bob Dix *(Grey)*, Jimmie Thompson *(Youngerford)*

p, Nicholas Nayfack; d, Fred M. Wilcox; w, Cyril Hume (based on a story by Irving Block, Allen Adler); ph, George Folsey (CinemaScope, Eastmancolor); ed, Ferris Webster; m, Louis Barron, Bebe Barron; art d, Cedric Gibbons, Arthur Lonergan; fx, A. Arnold Gillespie, Warren Newcombe, Irving G. Reis, Joshua Meador; cos, Helen Rose, Walter Plunkett

AAN Best Special Effects: A. Arnold Gillespie, Irving Ries, Wesley C. Miller

A superb sci-fi flick, FORBIDDEN PLANET offers an unusually intelligent script, exciting direction by Wilcox and generally good acting from a decent if rather dull cast.

It is 2200 A.D. when Commander Adams (Nielsen) lands his United Planets Cruiser on Altair-4, which features a green sky, pink sand, and two moons. He had been warned not to do so by Dr. Morbius (Pidgeon), a member of a missing Earth colony sent to the planet 20 years earlier. Adams and crew are greeted by Robby the Robot, a benign and astounding creation fluent in 88 languages and capable of any task, including producing an endless supply of bourbon at the behest of the crew's mischievous cook (Holliman). The robot drives Adams and his senior officers to the home of Morbius and his daughter Altaira (Francis, failing entirely to transcend her ill-conceived, camp classic role). Morbius explains that he and his glamorous lovespawn are the only survivors of attacks by an invisible monster prowling the planet. After the viewer is treated to scenes like Altaira's kissing lesson (the poor lusty darling has gone manless, just imagine!), the invisible terror begins killing again.

FORBIDDEN PLANET is really a futuristic version of Shakespeare's *The Tempest*, with Morbius doubling for the wizard Prospero, Altaira a substitute Miranda, Robby the Robot serving as the spirit Ariel, and the Id monster being Caliban the witch-child. The first sci-fi film to cost $1 million, FORBIDDEN PLANET benefits immeasurably from its astounding technical prowess. The deadpan, all-purpose Robby the Robot is the film's most delightful creation, and it's not surprising that he later appeared in THE INVISIBLE BOY and scores of television shows.

While the spacemen are all likably heroic and Francis and Holliman can be forgiven for the enjoyable excesses of their roles, it is really Pidgeon who gives the drama flair and majesty. All in all, a splendid fantasy achievement that wears its age well.

FORCE OF EVIL
1948 78m bw Crime ★★★★½ *DVD*
Enterprise (U.S.)

John Garfield *(Joe Morse)*, Beatrice Pearson *(Doris Lowry)*, Thomas Gomez *(Leo Morse)*, Howland Chamberlin *(Freddy Bauer)*, Roy Roberts *(Ben Tucker)*, Marie Windsor *(Edna Tucker)*, Paul McVey *(Hobe Wheelock)*, Tim Ryan *(Johnson)*, Sid Tomack *("Two & Two" Taylor)*, Georgia Backus *(Sylvia Morse)*

p, Bob Roberts; d, Abraham Polonsky; w, Abraham Polonsky, Ira Wolfert (based on his novel, *Tucker's People*); ph, George Barnes; ed, Walter Thompson, Arthur Seid; m, David Raksin; art d, Richard Day; cos, Louise Wilson

Garfield is Joe Morse, a slick, self-centered lawyer who knows the law but feels he's above it. He practices on Wall Street and has his eyes on millions, working on retainer for racketeer Ben Tucker (Roberts). The policy czar plans to have the number 776 come up on July 4; knowing that most people will bet on it, Tucker hopes to bankrupt and take over most of the city's smaller numbers operations. Without spilling the beans, Joe attempts to get his kindly brother Leo (Gomez) to shut down for one day, but the stubborn older man feels obligated to let his regulars take their holiday chances. Joe arranges for a police raid to break his brother's spirit, but to no avail. After Tucker achieves his expected success on the Fourth, Leo's people, including bookkeeper Doris (Pearson), become nervous about the gangsters suddenly in their midst.

Dark and brooding, FORCE OF EVIL offers one of Garfield's greatest performances as the cynical, hard-as-nails lawyer. Pearson, in her first of only two films, doesn't really register in a role that could use Shelley Winters or Ida Lupino rather than a June Allyson clone. Her presence is more than offset, however, by Gomez's marvelous performance and that of the suitably slimy Roberts. A tour de force for gifted writer Polonsky, FORCE was the only film he directed before he was blacklisted for being an uncooperative witness before HUAC in 1951; he didn't direct another feature for 21 years. At its best, FORCE achieves a style at once brutal and poetic, documentarian and noir.

FOREIGN CORRESPONDENT
1940 120m bw Spy/War ★★★★★ *DVD*
UA (U.S.)

Joel McCrea *(Johnny Jones/Huntley Haverstock)*, Laraine Day *(Carol Fisher)*, Herbert Marshall *(Stephen Fisher)*, George Sanders *(Scott Ffolliott)*, Albert Basserman *(Van Meer)*, Robert Benchley *(Stebbins)*, Edmund Gwenn *(Rowley)*, Eduardo Ciannelli *(Krug)*, Martin Kosleck *(Tramp)*, Harry Davenport *(Mr. Powers)*

p, Walter Wanger; d, Alfred Hitchcock; w, Charles Bennett, Joan Harrison, James Hilton, Robert Benchley; ph, Rudolph Mate; ed,

Otho Lovering, Dorothy Spencer; m, Alfred Newman; art d, Alexander Golitzen; fx, Lee Zavitz

AAN Best Picture; AAN Best Supporting Actor: Albert Bassermann; *AAN Best Original Screenplay:* Charles Bennett, Joan Harrison; *AAN Best B/W Cinematography:* Rudolph Mate; *AAN Best Interior Decoration (B/W):* Alexander Golitzen (Art Direction); *AAN Best Special Effects:* Paul Eagler (Photographic), Thomas T. Moulton (Sound)

One of the great espionage films, tautly handled by the stellar Hitchcock, FOREIGN CORRESPONDENT gleams with suspense, atmosphere and sharp dialogue. Johnny Jones (McCrea) is a top American crime reporter reassigned as a foreign correspondent to Western Europe. Ordered to find the most provocative stories swirling in the political cauldron just prior to WWII, he meets Stephen Fisher (Marshall), head of a peace organization, and Fisher's attractive daughter Carol (Day). Before long, Johnny gets entangled in international intrigue involving the kidnaping of Van Meer (Basserman), a Dutch diplomat carrying vital information.

One of Hitchcock's greatest entertainments, FOREIGN CORRESPONDENT is also a stirring propaganda piece which clearly indicts the Nazi regime. This fact was recognized by no less than Nazi propaganda minister Josef Goebbels, who nonetheless hailed the film as a masterpiece, calling it "a first-class production, a criminological bang-up hit, which no doubt will make a certain impression upon the broad masses of the people in enemy countries." FOREIGN CORRESPONDENT also boasts some of the finest production design of its time—a huge windmill set was built to simulate a Dutch location, and a square in Amsterdam was reconstructed on a 10-acre set—a testament to the talents of Golitzen and Menzies. The acting is uniformly excellent, with McCrea an ideal Hitchcock hero and Marshall, Sanders, Gwenn, and especially Basserman stealing the supporting honors.

FOREIGN CORRESPONDENT is perhaps best remembered for its splendid set pieces, which include an assassination in the rain with umbrellas bobbing everywhere and terrific moments atop Westminster Cathedral, inside the windmill, and especially aboard a plane crashing into the ocean. Viewers are not likely to forget the struggle of the passengers as their air supply is slowly cut off. Not one of the director's more profound meditations on voyeurism and sexuality, FOREIGN CORRESPONDENT aims at something simpler than REAR WINDOW or VERTIGO; it shows him going through his playful paces at his professional best.

FORGOTTEN, THE

2004 96m c Science Fiction/Thriller ★★
Jinks/Cohen Productions/Revolution Studios/ PG-13
Visual Arts Entertainment (U.S.)

Julianne Moore *(Telly Paretta)*, Dominic West *(Ash Correll)*, Gary Sinise *(Dr. Jack Munce)*, Alfre Woodard *(Detective Ann Pope)*, Linus Roache *(A Friendly Man)*, Anthony Edwards *(Jim Paretta)*, Ken Abraham *(Gas Station Guy)*, Kathryn Faughnan *(Lauren Correll)*, Tim Kang *(Special Agent Alec Wong)*, Christopher Kovaleski *(Sam)*

p, Bruce Cohen, Dan Jinks, Joe Roth; d, Joseph Ruben; w, Gerald Di Pego; ph, Anastas Michos; ed, Richard Francis-Bruce; m, James Horner; prod d, Bill Groom; art d, Paul D. Kelly; fx, Steve Kirshoff, Fred Kraemer, John R. Stifanich, Carey Villegas; cos, Cindy Evans

Director Joseph Ruben (THE STEPFATHER) is an expert at wringing suspense from domestic impulses perverted into psychosis, but his best efforts can't keep Gerald Di Pego's puzzle-picture script from toppling into absurdity.

Fourteen months after Telly Paretta (Julianne Moore) lost her nine-year-old son, Sam (Christopher Kovaleski), in a small-plane crash, she remains inconsolable, despite the unflagging support of her husband (Anthony Edwards) and regular sessions with Dr. Munce (Gary Sinise). Telly's bereavement takes a GASLIGHT turn when everyone—her husband, her neighbors, her therapist— suddenly begins insisting that Telly never had a child. Telly's cherished videotapes are blank, family photos no longer include Sam, and all mentions of the fatal crash have vanished from the library's newspaper archive. Dr. Munce insists that she's in the grip of post-traumatic stress syndrome, but she doesn't believe a word of it. Telly knows that she had a son, and won't rest until she figures out what's going on. Her reluctant ally in windmill-tilting is Ash Corelli (Dominic West), whose rapid slide into alcoholism coincided with the death of his forgotten daughter, Lauren (Kathryn Faughnan), who died on the same flight. When their investigation attracts the attention of the NYPD and the NSA, they're forced to flee, pursuing tantalizing clues into some very deep and murky waters.

Ruben immediately establishes a chilling atmosphere of vague dread, relying on a gray color palette and bird's-eye long shots to maintain a mood of bleak paranoia long after the story's lunatic twists have begun to overwhelm Moore and West's fine, subtle performances. Di Pego's convoluted construction is all frippery with no foundation, and eventually its intricate inventions just seem ridiculous.

FORREST GUMP

1994 142m c Drama/Comedy/Historical ★★★
Tisch Company (U.S.) PG-13

Tom Hanks *(Forrest Gump)*, Gary Sinise *(Lieutenant Dan Taylor)*, Robin Wright *(Jenny Curran)*, Sally Field *(Mrs. Gump)*, Mykelti Williamson *(Benjamin Buford Blue—"Bubba")*, Rebecca Williams *(Nurse at the Park Bench)*, Michael Conner Humphreys *(Young Forrest)*, Harold Herthum *(Doctor)*, George Kelly *(Barber)*, Bob Penny *(Crony)*

p, Wendy Finerman, Steve Tisch, Steve Starkey; d, Robert Zemeckis; w, Eric Roth (based on the novel by Winston Groom); ph, Don Burgess; ed, Arthur Schmidt; m, Alan Silvestri; prod d, Rick Carter; art d, Leslie McDonald, Jim Teegarden; fx, Ken Ralston, George Murphy, Stephen Rosenbaum, Allen Hall, Industrial Light & Magic; cos, Joanna Johnston

AA Best Picture; AA Best Actor: Tom Hanks; *AA Best Director:* Robert Zemeckis; *AA Best Adapted Screenplay:* Eric Roth; *AA Best Film Editing:* Arthur Schmidt; *AA Best Visual Effects:* Ken Ralston, George Murphy, Stephen Rosenbaum, Allen Hall; *AAN Best Supporting Actor:* Gary Sinise; *AAN Best Art Direction-Set Decoration:* Rick Carter, Nancy Haigh; *AAN Best Cinematography:* Don Burgess; *AAN Best Makeup:* Daniel C. Striepeke, Hallie D'Amore, Judith A. Cory; *AAN Best Original Score:* Alan Silvestri; *AAN Best Sound:* Randy Thom, Tom Johnson, Dennis Sands, William B. Kaplan; *AAN Best Sound Effects Editing:* Gloria S. Borders, Randy Thom

By the time FORREST GUMP swept most of the major 1994 Academy Awards, it had already become the third highest-grossing film of all time, as well as a ubiquitous pop phenomenon embracing best-selling books, gnomic catch phrases, and reams of commentary on the editorial pages of magazines and newspapers throughout the world. Clearly a great event, FORREST GUMP is not, however, a great film. It has the form of an epic without real depth or resonance; the trappings of satire without a coherent attitude; and the semblance of historical revisionism without a critical sensibility. To paraphrase the screenplay, FORREST GUMP is not a smart film, but it knows what love is—its dim-witted protagonist, as expertly portrayed by Tom Hanks, captured the love of millions.

As he waits for a bus in Savannah, Georgia, good-natured simpleton Forrest Gump (Hanks) tells his story to anyone who will listen. In flashbacks, punctuated by

ZELIG-style special effects that graft Hanks onto famous pieces of archival footage, we learn that Gump has led a remarkably successful and adventurous life despite his low IQ. As football star, decorated war hero, Ping-Pong champion, and business magnate, he's crossed paths with most of the important historical figures of the American post-war era. Throughout, his destiny has been intertwined with those of crippled Vietnam veteran Lt. Dan (Gary Sinise) and his childhood friend and sometime lover, Jenny (Robin Wright).

Vague in its attitude toward the events it depicts, FORREST GUMP was embraced by several national figures in the Republican party as a celebration of traditional values and a condemnation of the 1960s counterculture. In many ways, however, the film represents old-fashioned Hollywood liberalism: racists are wrong, war is hell, assassinations are bad, and it's good to be nice. This is a film that dares not offend anyone too much. It's good—and profitable—to be comforting.

In order to achieve its considerable emotional power, FORREST GUMP draws upon some of the less savory elements of the American character—most obviously, a distrust of intellectualism and a naive belief in the redemptive power of innocence. Frank Capra once fared well promoting similar values, but his films were far darker, conflicted, and ambiguous. Zemeckis's film has lots of heart but little in the way of guts or brains.

FORT APACHE

1948 127m bw Western/War ★★★★½
Argosy (U.S.)

Henry Fonda (Lt. Col. Owen Thursday), John Wayne (Capt. Kirby York), Shirley Temple (Philadelphia Thursday), Ward Bond (Sgt. Maj. Michael O'Rourke), John Agar (Lt. Michael "Mickey" O'Rourke), George O'Brien (Capt. Sam Collingwood), Irene Rich (Mrs. Mary O'Rourke), Victor McLaglen (Sgt. Festus Mulcahy), Anna Lee (Mrs. Emily Collingwood), Pedro Armendariz (Sgt. Beaufort)

p, John Ford, Merian C. Cooper; d, John Ford; w, Frank S. Nugent (based on the story "Massacre" by James Warner Bellah); ph, Archie Stout; ed, Jack Murray; m, Richard Hageman; art d, James Basevi; fx, David Koehler; chor, Kenny Williams; cos, Michael Meyers, Ann Peck

FORT APACHE is the superb first film of director John Ford's U.S. Cavalry trilogy. The awesome exterior scenes reflect Ford's early training as a painter and provide a remarkable backdrop for the irony which unfolds.

Lt. Col. Owen Thursday (Fonda) is a martinet commander bitter over having been sent to fight "digger" Indians instead of being assigned a glory post. He foolishly leads his men to disaster, but the press later presents him as a hero for the sake of the military's image.

FORT APACHE is rich beyond its wonderful action scenes and the outdoor panoramas so dear to Ford's heart. The film expertly depicts the social affairs of a far-flung military outpost, the struggle of the women to maintain civility, and the routines of the men in their daily military chores. More importantly, though, it exposes the sham behind public and national conceptions of "the hero." Wayne gives a solid performance, and such stalwarts as McLaglen, Bond, O'Brien, Foran, Armendariz, and Kibbee lend the film its humor and heart. But you find yourself watching Fonda transcend the possible critic's charge of "miscasting" as the power-bloated commander. Of course, Fonda's character and the doomed route he pursues are based on the massacre of George Armstrong Custer's 7th Cavalry at Little Big Horn, and this if anything lends weight to Ford's elegiac reconsideration of "the American spirit."

FORTUNE, THE

1975 88m c Comedy ★★★★
Columbia (U.S.) PG

Warren Beatty (Nicky), Jack Nicholson (Oscar), Stockard Channing (Freddie), Florence Stanley (Landlady), Richard B. Shull (Chief Detective), Thomas Newman (John the Barber), John Fiedler (Police Photographer), Scatman Crothers (Fisherman), Dub Taylor (Rattlesnake Tom), Ian Wolfe (Justice of the Peace)

p, Mike Nichols, Don Devlin; d, Mike Nichols; w, Adrien Joyce; ph, John A. Alonzo (Technicolor); ed, Stu Linder; m, David Shire; prod d, Richard Sylbert; art d, Stewart Campbell

An offbeat but often hilarious comedy where Beatty and Nicholson play Nicky and Oscar, two competing confidence men trying to bilk heiress Freddie (Channing) out of her fortune. The source of this wealth is Freddie's father, a manufacturer of sanitary napkins (which naturally results in plenty of tacky humor). Though she is in love with the married Nicky, Freddie plans to marry the slippery Oscar and then carry on an affair with the man she wants. Oscar, a failed embezzler, has no intention of playing the cuckolded hubby; he means to have his carnal share of the attractive heiress. When she learns that the two con men are up to something, Freddie tells them her plans to give her fortune to charity. Alarmed, they conclude that their only course of action is murder, and the rest of the film is a series of black comedy sketches of plans gone awry and misplaced guilt.

A catalogue of slapstick errors, THE FORTUNE works well through the fine performances of the leads and the superb timing of director Nichols. Beatty nervously twitches through his part but is quickly outdone by the easy-going Nicholson and the marvelous Channing. LUCKY LADY, a similar type of love triangle also set in the 1920s (with Gene Hackman, Liza Minnelli and Burt Reynolds), was made the same year but nowhere approaches the style and wit on display here. Full of period and period-sounding music, THE FORTUNE is cold to the core—agreeably disagreeable amusement.

FORTUNE COOKIE, THE

1966 125m bw Comedy/Sports 📀
Mirisch (U.S.) ★★★½

Jack Lemmon (Harry Hinkle), Walter Matthau (Willie Gingrich), Ron Rich (Luther "Boom Boom" Jackson), Cliff Osmond (Mr. Purkey), Judi West (Sandy Hinkle), Lurene Tuttle (Mother Hinkle), Harry Holcombe (O'Brien), Les Tremayne (Thompson), Marge Redmond (Charlotte Gingrich), Noam Pitlik (Max)

p, Billy Wilder; d, Billy Wilder; w, Billy Wilder, I.A.L. Diamond; ph, Joseph La Shelle (Panavision); ed, Daniel Mandell; m, Andre Previn; art d, Robert Luthardt; fx, Sass Bedig; cos, Charles Arrico, Paula Giokaris

AA Best Supporting Actor: Walter Matthau; AAN Best Original Story and Screenplay: Billy Wilder, I.A.L. Diamond; AAN Best B/W Cinematography: Joseph LaShelle; AAN Best Art Direction-Set Decoration (B/W): Robert Luthardt, Edward G. Boyle

A very funny film, this morality tale is a deft mixture of cynicism, wit and idealism as only writer-director Wilder could do it. The only problem is that morality tales can get moralizing.

While working the sidelines during a Browns-Vikings game, cameraman Harry Hinkle (Lemmon) is flattened by Browns running back Luther "Boom Boom" Jackson (Rich) and rushed to the hospital. Although Harry is fine, his shyster brother-in-law, "Whiplash" Willie Gingrich (Matthau), convinces him to fake an injury and sue the Browns, CBS and Municipal Stadium for $1 million. Pretending to be paralyzed from the neck down and relying on an old spinal injury for X-ray proof, Harry fools a team of doctors and, under Willie's supervision, continues to deceive private investigator Purkey (Osmond). In the meantime, Harry's wife, Sandy (West), a would-be singer who ran off with another guy, returns, anxious to get in on the gravy train.

Lemmon and especially Matthau—who deservedly won a Best Supporting Actor Oscar for his role—are superb; this first teaming together more than justified later reunions. The screenplay by Wilder and Diamond sparkles with the dark satiric cynicism for which they are famous and LaShelle's frankly unattractive cinematography is entirely appropriate to the unsavory goings-on. Rich's Boom Boom is a bit too noble, but his relationship with Harry is still touching. In fact, toward the end the film goes perhaps a little too soft. Despite some minor flaws, THE FORTUNE COOKIE is a very satisfying film.

48 HRS.   *DVD*
1982 96m   c   Comedy/Crime   ★★★½
Paramount   (U.S.)   R

Nick Nolte *(Jack Cates)*, Eddie Murphy *(Reggie Hammond)*, Annette O'Toole *(Elaine)*, Frank McRae *(Haden)*, James Remar *(Ganz)*, David Patrick Kelly *(Luther)*, Sonny Landham *(Billy Bear)*, Brion James *(Kehoe)*, Kerry Sherman *(Rosalie)*, Jonathan Banks *(Algren)*

p, Lawrence Gordon, Joel Silver; d, Walter Hill; w, Roger Spottiswoode, Walter Hill, Larry Gross, Steven E. de Souza; ph, Ric Waite (Movielab Color); ed, Freeman Davies, Mark Warner, Billy Weber; m, James Horner; prod d, John Vallone; cos, Marilyn Vance

A big box-office hit, this action film casts Nolte as Jack Cates, a hard-as-granite cop, and Murphy as Reggie Hammond, a glib convict who is released from prison in Cates's custody for 48 hours. Hammond's job is to help Cates track down a pair of maniacal cop killers (Landham and Remar) who happen to be his former associates. Together Cates and Hammond take a thrill-a-minute trip through the San Francisco underworld and along the way develop one of the 1980s' more interesting cinematic buddy pairings.

In this, his first film, comedian Murphy turned in a marvelous performance, setting the stage for his enormously popular Axel Foley character in the BEVERLY HILLS COP films. Nolte, however, always threatens to steal the film in his customary quiet way as Murphy's rough and gruff partner. Director Hill (THE LONG RIDERS, SOUTHERN COMFORT, RED HEAT) pushes the film along at his traditional rapid pace, aided by Waite's excellent cinematography. In the film's most poignant moment Cates gives Hammond a badge and sends him into a rowdy country-western bar for a role-reversal confrontation with a passel of rednecks. Hang on for the ride.

42ND STREET   *DVD*
1933 98m   bw   Musical   ★★★★★
Warner Bros.   (U.S.)

Warner Baxter *(Julian Marsh)*, Bebe Daniels *(Dorothy Brock)*, George Brent *(Pat Denning)*, Una Merkel *(Lorraine Fleming)*, Ruby Keeler *(Peggy Sawyer)*, Guy Kibbee *(Abner Dillon)*, Dick Powell *(Billy Lawler)*, Ginger Rogers *(Ann Lowell/Anytime Annie)*, George E. Stone *(Andy Lee)*, Robert McWade *(Al Jones)*

p, Hal B. Wallis; d, Lloyd Bacon; w, James Seymour, Rian James (based on the novel by Bradford Ropes); ph, Sol Polito; ed, Thomas Pratt; art d, Jack Okey; chor, Busby Berkeley; cos, Orry-Kelly

AAN Best Picture, AAN Best Sound Recording: Nathan Levinson

Hear the beat of dancing feet! The film that revived public interest in musicals after many early talkie bombs sabotaged the genre, 42ND STREET was the first real glimpse of the

surreal artistry of choreographer Busby Berkeley. The film also highlighted two fresh-faced new stars, the likably cornball crooner Dick Powell and the endearingly untalented Ruby Keeler.

The familiar plot concerns Broadway director Julian Marsh's (Warner Baxter) desire for one more hit so he can retire and recover his health. Abner Dillon (Guy Kibbee) is his wealthy backer, Dorothy Brock (Bebe Daniels) his temperamental star, Peggy Sawyer (Keeler) a hopeful chorine, and Billy Lawler (Powell) a singer with the hots for Peggy. As Julian struggles with the show, promises and hearts are broken, but that's nothing compared to the crisis created when Dorothy's ankle is broken on the eve of the show's premiere. Understudy Peggy has to go on in her place, giving Baxter the chance to say the immortal line, "You're going out a youngster, but you've got to come back a star!"

42ND STREET's charm and fascination lie in director Bacon's fast-paced and vivid backstage atmosphere, crammed with exhausted chorus kids and sudden hysterics. The great cast is in fine fettle: Baxter brings real edge to what could have been a standardized part; fading star Daniels is eerily appropriate as the performer who gets replaced; Una Merkel makes the most of her wisecracks; and when Ginger Rogers enters sporting a monocle and an Erich von Stroheim shtick, you oddly sense that a star is almost ready to be born.

The real star, though, is the master of kaleidoscopic imagery, Busby Berkeley. Backed by the ebullient songs of Harry Warren and Al Dubin, Buzz unleashed his startling creations on an escapism-hungry public. The dizzying combination of sexuality and abstraction in such numbers as "Young and Healthy," "Shuffle Off to Buffalo," and the title tune remains potent to this day. A film that returned it's $400,000 investment ten times over, inspired dozens of imitations and a Broadway reprise in the 1970s, 42ND STREET, "that avenue I'm takin' you to," remains hard to beat.

49TH PARALLEL
1941 105m   bw   War   ★★★★½
General Films   (U.K.)

Leslie Howard *(Philip Armstrong Scott)*, Raymond Massey *(Andy Brock)*, Laurence Olivier *(Johnnie)*, Anton Walbrook *(Peter)*, Eric Portman *(Lt. Hirth)*, Glynis Johns *(Anna)*, Niall MacGinnis *(Vogel)*, Finlay Currie *(Factor)*, Raymond Lovell *(Lt. Kuhnecke)*, John Chandos *(Lohrmann)*

p, Michael Powell, John Sutro; d, Michael Powell; w, Rodney Ackland, Emeric Pressburger (based on a story by Pressburger); ph, Freddie Young; ed, David Lean; m, Ralph Vaughan Williams; art d, David Rawnsley

AAN Best Picture, AA Best Original Story: Emeric Pressburger; *AAN Best Screenplay:* Rodney Ackland, Emeric Pressburger

THE INVADERS (49TH PARALLEL in the UK) is an excellent war drama from British director Powell, co-scripted by his longtime collaborator Pressburger. Filmed mostly in Canada, the film opens as a U-37 German submarine surfaces in the Gulf of St. Lawrence. It is obliterated by RCAF bombers, but six Germans survive and march to a Hudson Bay trading post. Constructed in episodic fashion, the story shows them wandering through Canada to avoid detection. Along the way, they meet Johnnie (Olivier), a trapper filled with contempt for the Nazis; a group of German Hutterites living on a Christian collective headed by Peter (Walbrook); and Philip Armstrong Scott (Howard), a decadent novelist living in a teepee while writing about the Blackfoot Indians. With each meeting, the number of "invaders" diminishes; some are captured, others killed, and a decent one (MacGinnis) tries to remain with the Hutterites. Finally, the last to elude death or capture (Portman) meets Andy Brock (Massey), an AWOL Canadian soldier who complains about democracy while stowing away on a freight train bound for the U.S. The wily Andy shows his true colors, though, when he must confront Nazism incarnate.

The anti-Fascist message here is extremely eloquent, the Oscar-winning script witty and intelligent, and the photography handsome and atypical for a war film. Powell beautifully ties it all together in a directorial style that is part war adventure, part Robert Flaherty-influenced documentary, taking just as much time with action sequences as he does with Hutterite communal living, Eskimo culture, or Indian rituals. The acting is almost uniformly excellent, with Walbrook his usual superb self, and marvelous work from Johns, MacGinnis, Currie, Howard and Massey. With his gravelly voice and incisive manner, Portman makes an electrifying villain, and he became a major British star with this film. Unfortunately Olivier lowers this high standard with a rather hammy performance, replete with variable French-Canadian accent. The British release runs nearly 20 minutes longer than the version generally seen in America.

FOUR DAUGHTERS

1938 90m bw Romance ★★★★
Warner Bros. (U.S.)

Claude Rains *(Adam Lemp)*, May Robson *(Aunt Etta)*, Priscilla Lane *(Ann Lemp)*, Lola Lane *(Thea Lemp)*, Rosemary Lane *(Kay Lemp)*, Gale Page *(Emma Lemp)*, Dick Foran *(Ernest)*, Jeffrey Lynn *(Felix Deitz)*, Frank McHugh *(Ben Crowley)*, John Garfield *(Mickey Borden)*

p, Henry Blanke; d, Michael Curtiz; w, Julius J. Epstein, Lenore Coffee (based on the novel *Sister Act* by Fannie Hurst); ph, Ernest Haller; ed, Ralph Dawson; m, Max Steiner; art d, John Hughes

AAN Best Picture; AAN Best Supporting Actor: John Garfield; *AAN Best Director:* Michael Curtiz; *AAN Best Screenplay:* Lenore Coffee, Julius J Epstein; *AAN Best Sound Recording:* Nathan Levinson

An engrossing film which both endorses and questions a vision of small-town American romance. When Felix Deitz (Lynn) arrives at Adam Lemp's (Rains) house to board, the music professor's four daughters all fall in love with him. Ann (Priscilla Lane) becomes engaged to him but later finds out from the cynical Mickey Borden (Garfield) that one of her sisters is devastated by the impending marriage. In a great act of sibling generosity, she gives up Felix and runs off with the embittered Mickey. Felix departs, however, and the sister falls in love with another man. The tough, indolent Mickey realizes that he's breaking Ann's heart and decides to engineer her reunion with Felix.

A fun tearjerker, this film is saved from its own candybox prettiness by the scorching presence of Garfield in the seemingly tailor-made role that brought him stardom. His Mickey Borden is a rebellious, surly, disillusioned young man from the big city, where poverty has scarred his otherwise brilliant mind. His rare smiles are wry grins, and his laughter is ironic. His character at once shouts defiance and defeat. His remarks to the kindly small-town folks who take him in reflect both their naivete and his jaded worldliness.

Further help is offered by director Curtiz, whose sense of pace and proportion never gives this cottage cheese a chance to curdle. Although the Lane sisters and Page are simply *too* cute for words, they, Rains, and Robson do evoke something idealistically cozy when you let your guard down. Several sequels followed, including the superior DAUGHTERS COURAGEOUS, as well as a mediocre remake, YOUNG AT HEART.

FOUR FEATHERS, THE

1939 130m c Adventure/War ★★★★★
Korda/London Films (U.K.)

John Clements *(Harry Faversham)*, Ralph Richardson *(Capt. John Durrance)*, C. Aubrey Smith *(Gen. Burroughs)*, June Duprez *(Ethne Burroughs)*, Allan Jeayes *(Gen. Faversham)*, Jack Allen *(Lt. Willoughby)*, Donald Gray *(Peter Burroughs)*, Frederick Culley *(Dr. Sutton)*, Amid Taftazani *(Karaga Pasha)*, Henry Oscar *(Dr. Harraz)*

p, Alexander Korda; d, Zoltan Korda; w, R.C. Sherriff, Lajos Biro, Arthur Wimperis (based on the novel by A.E.W. Mason); ph, Georges Perinal, Osmond Borradaile, Jack Cardiff (Technicolor); ed, William Hornbeck, Henry Cornelius; m, Miklos Rozsa; prod d, Vincent Korda; cos, Godfrey Brennan, Rene Hubert

AAN Best Color Cinematography: Georges Perinal, Osmond Borradaile

One of the all-time great adventure films, THE FOUR FEATHERS is based on the 1902 tale of cowardice and courage by A.E.W. Mason, filmed at least six times but never as well as in this marvelous production.

The tale of empire, battle, and redemption begins when Harry Faversham (Clements), the son of a brigadier general, refuses to follow family tradition and join the army, choosing instead to settle down and wed Ethne Burroughs (Duprez). He resigns his commission just before his regiment leaves for the 1898 Sudan campaign conducted by Lord Kitchener, and his friends—John Durrance (Richardson), Peter Burroughs (Gray), and Tom Willoughby (Allen)—present him three white feathers symbolizing cowardice. Also disgusted by his actions is Ethne, who gives him the fourth feather. Determined to prove his courage, Faversham leaves for Egypt alone and disguises himself as a native, his skin stained and an "S" branded on his forehead to mark him as a Sangali tribe member with his tongue cut out by enemies. Eventually Faversham is able to redeem himself in the eyes of those he loves.

One of the great British films of the 1930s and one of producer Alexander Korda's finest achievements, THE FOUR FEATHERS is directed by Alexander's brother, Zoltan, with the elan demanded by the action-packed story. His talent is evident in the magnificent battle scenes, particularly the awesome attack of the "Fuzzi Wuzzies" against the British lines, shown in wide panorama by cameras mounted high on hilltops overlooking the battlefield.

The acting is distinguished throughout, with Clements a sensitive and dashing nonconformist, Richardson superb as a man who must reconsider a friendship, and Smith equally good as a crusty career officer whose hypocrisy is revealed. A film unafraid to question those traditions it celebrates, THE FOUR FEATHERS balances its highly impressive spectacle with a drama of substance and intelligence.

400 BLOWS, THE

(LES QUATRES CENTS COUPS)
1959 93m bw Drama ★★★★★
Carosse (France)

Jean-Pierre Leaud *(Antoine Doinel)*, Claire Maurier *(Mme Doinel)*, Albert Remy *(M Doinel)*, Guy Decomble *(Teacher)*, Patrick Auffay *(Rene Bigey)*, Georges Flament *(M Bigey)*, Yvonne Claudie *(Mme Bigey)*, Robert Beauvais *(Director of the School)*, Claude Mansard *(Examining Magistrate)*, Jacques Monod *(Commissioner)*

p, Francois Truffaut; d, Francois Truffaut; w, Francois Truffaut, Marcel Moussy (story by Truffaut); ph, Henri Decae; ed, Marie-Josephe Yoyotte; m, Jean Constantin; art d, Bernard Evein

AAN Best Original Story and Screenplay: Francois Truffaut, Marcel Moussy

This extraordinary film was the first feature from Francois Truffaut, who was, until its release, best known as a hell-raising critic from the journal *Cahiers du Cinema.* THE 400

BLOWS is not only one of the foremost films of the French New Wave, but also the first in a Truffaut series that included "Antoine and Colette" (an episode from LOVE AT TWENTY), STOLEN KISSES, BED AND BOARD, and LOVE ON THE RUN.

These films all starred the remarkable Leaud as Truffaut's alter ego Antoine Doinel and span 20 years in this semiautobiographical character's life. Here Leaud beautifully embodies Doinel at age 12, a child more or less left to his own devices by his mother (Maurier) and father (Remy). He gets into trouble at school, runs away from home, and eventually ends up in an observation center for juvenile delinquents.

THE 400 BLOWS—an idiomatic French expression for the limit of what anyone can bear—is a nonjudgmental film about injustice, pain, and the events in a young boy's life that make him the person he is. Neither good nor bad, Antoine is treated with warmth and compassion by Truffaut as a child caught up in a maelstrom not of his own making. The grace and perfection of THE 400 BLOWS has made it the standard against which all films on the subject of youth are judged, and Leaud's portrayal that to which all young performers' are compared.

The film also features Decae's poetic black-and-white photography, and together he and Truffaut offer a glimpse of the freedom that Antoine's life never really affords. Images such as a line of schoolboys snaking their way through the streets linger like pages from a mental yearbook of schooldays. Best of all, though, is the film's famous final freeze frame, in which Truffaut conveys both promise and sadness, and demonstrates that the cinema offers no easy answers to the problems of living.

FOUR MUSKETEERS, THE 📀

1974 108m c   Adventure/Historical   ★★★½
Fox   (U.S.)   PG

Michael York (D'Artagnan), Oliver Reed (Athos), Richard Chamberlain (Aramis), Frank Finlay (Porthos), Raquel Welch (Mme. Constance Bonacieux), Christopher Lee (Rochefort), Faye Dunaway (Milady), Jean-Pierre Cassel (Louis XIII), Geraldine Chaplin (Queen Anne of Austria), Simon Ward (Duke of Buckingham)

p, Alexander Salkind; d, Richard Lester; w, George MacDonald Fraser (from The Three Musketeers by Alexandre Dumas); ph, David Watkin (DeLuxe Color); ed, John Victor Smith; m, Lalo Schifrin; prod d, Brian Eatwell

AAN Best Costume Design: Yvonne Blake, Ron Talsky

A sequel to THE THREE MUSKETEERS. Both pictures were originally supposed to have been one huge three 1/2-hour epic, but the producers decided to release them as two films—and lawsuits followed immediately from a cast and crew who wanted to be paid for making two films. That aside, this sequel is a worthy follow-up to the original.

In this installment, Milady DeWinter (Dunaway) plans to wreak revenge on D'Artagnan (York), his cohorts (Chamberlain, Finlay, and Reed), his "lady fair" Constance (Welch) and the Duke (Ward) for foiling her plans in the first film. Milady attempts seduction and later allows herself to be arrested so as to manipulate a religious-fanatic jailer into assassinating the Duke. She also kidnaps Constance, a move certain to bring the swashbuckling quartet into the picture.

Much of the film is played for merry comedy, and the cast makes a good job of it. Welch, for example, handles both the physical and the verbal comedy with the same brio which marked her work in the earlier film. Dunaway, on the other hand, does not make the pivotal role of Milady DeWinter quite as fascinating as one would like. Although there is less slapstick than in THE THREE MUSKETEERS, the lightness of the enterprise stays constant until the swashbuckling climax and dramatic resolution. What is especially notable in this sequel is Lester's determination to deglamorize life in the 1620s, and his film is amply populated with mercenaries, boors and slobs.

FOUR NIGHTS OF A DREAMER
(QUATRE NUITS D'UN REVEUR)
1971 87m   c   Drama   ★★★★
Victoria/Albina/Del Orso   (France)

Isabelle Weingarten (Marthe), Guillaume Des Forets (Jacques), Maurice Monnoyer (Lover)

d, Robert Bresson; w, Robert Bresson (based on the story "White Nights" by Feodor Dostoyevsky); ph, Pierre Lhomme (Eastmancolor)

This fascinating feature by master director Bresson adapts Dostoyevsky's story "White Nights" and puts it in Paris in the modern age.

Jacques (Des Forets) is a young artist living a life of daydreams who meets Marthe (Weingarten) on a bridge one night while she is contemplating suicide. They talk and arrange to meet there the next night. They speak of their lives—he of his painting and his fantasies, she of the man she loves and his leaving her with the promise to meet her on the bridge one year later. It is because he hasn't kept the rendezvous that she has thought to kill herself. Jacques falls in love with the enigmatic woman, walking around Paris with a tape recorder against his heart that just plays a recording of him repeating her name. For four nights they meet on the bridge and talk, but on the last night the missing lover returns.

Bresson's spare, totally restrained style has seldom been used to such effect. With its highly deliberate editing and elegant use of color, the film emerges a delicate if sad paean to young love. Mystical and erotic but also dispassionate, FOUR NIGHTS OF A DREAMER is an important film by one of the cinema's most important figures. It makes for fascinating comparison with Visconti's memorable WHITE NIGHTS, an earlier adaptation of the same story.

FOUR WEDDINGS AND A FUNERAL 📀

1994 116m   c   Romance/Comedy   ★★★½
Working Title/Channel Four   (United Kingdom)   R

Hugh Grant (Charles), James Fleet (Tom), Simon Callow (Gareth), John Hannah (Matthew), Kristin Scott Thomas, billed as Kristin Scott-Thomas (Fiona), David Bower (David), Charlotte Coleman (Scarlett), Andie MacDowell (Carrie), Timothy Walker (Angus the Groom), Sara Crowe (Laura the Bride)

p, Duncan Kenworthy; d, Mike Newell; w, Richard Curtis; ph, Michael Coulter; ed, Jon Gregory; m, Richard Rodney Bennett; prod d, Maggie Gray; fx, Ian Wingrove; cos, Lindy Hemming

AAN Best Picture; AAN Best Original Screenplay: Richard Curtis

A witty romantic comedy with a sardonic edge, FOUR WEDDINGS AND A FUNERAL follows the engaging Hugh Grant and his friends as they search for love in a whirlwind of nuptials.

Always a guest, never a groom (he's Best Man once, but forgets the rings), handsome, timid Charles (Grant) meets Carrie (Andie MacDowell) at a wedding and falls instantly in love with her. She returns to America, and the next time he sees her—at another wedding—she's got a wealthy fiance in tow. He's devastated, she's oblivious, tongues wag. Can once in a lifetime, bolt-from-the-blue love survive bad timing, comically misunderstood intentions and the well-meaning interference of friends? Charles finds out—two weddings (one of them his own) and a funeral later—but not before things come to some very sticky passes.

Casting is everything in FOUR WEDDINGS AND A FUNERAL; the more one falls for Grant's ineffectual-but-adorable upper-middle-class schtick, the more charming everything seems. MacDowell is the weak link in a fine ensemble that includes the splendid Kristin Scott-Thomas (A HAND-FUL OF DUST) and Simon Callow (A ROOM WITH A VIEW); among the film's highlights is a fairly devastating reading of W.H. Auden's *Funeral Blues*.

FOXES
1980 106m c Drama **DVD** ★★½
UA (U.S.) R

Jodie Foster *(Jeanie)*, Scott Baio *(Brad)*, Sally Kellerman *(Mary)*, Randy Quaid *(Jay)*, Lois Smith *(Mrs. Axman)*, Adam Faith *(Bryan)*, Cherie Currie *(Annie)*, Marilyn Kagan *(Madge)*, Kandice Stroh *(Deirdre)*, Jon Sloan *(Loser)*

p, David Puttnam; d, Adrian Lyne; w, Gerald Ayres; ph, Paul Ryan (Technicolor); ed, James Coblentz; m, Giorgio Moroder; art d, Michel Levesque

Guided by former TV commercial director Lyne in his feature debut, this exploration of the lives of four teenage girls is weakly scripted but engaging nonetheless. In a fine performance, Foster plays the steadiest of the quartet, Jeanie, who finds herself dealing with the problems of her three friends: Annie (Currie, onetime member of the rock group the Runaways), a burnt-out hooker trying to escape her crazed father; overweight, unpopular Madge (Kagan), who is determined to free herself from her parents' pampering; and Deirdre (Stroh), a flirtatious, compulsive liar. Although FOXES's attempt to delve into the problems of modern-day teenagers is admirable, its screenplay is frequently trite, lacks any leavening humor, and too easily ties together its plentiful loose ends with a contrived plot device.

FRANK MILLER'S SIN CITY
2005 124m c/bw Crime/Thriller **DVD** ★★★½
Troublemaker Studios/Dimension (U.S.) R

Bruce Willis *(Hartigan)*, Micky Rourke *(Marv)*, Jessica Alba *(Nancy Callahan)*, Clive Owen *(Dwight)*, Nick Stahl *(Rourk Jr./Yellow Bastard)*, Powers Boothe *(Senator Rourk)*, Rutger Hauer *(Cardinal Roark)*, Elijah Wood *(Kevin)*, Jaime King *(Goldie/Wendy)*, Benicio Del Toro *(Jackie Boy)*

p, Elizabeth Avellan, Frank Miller, Robert Rodriguez; d, Robert Rodriguez, Frank Miller, Quentin Tarantino (special guest); w, Frank Miller, Robert Rodriguez (based on Frank Miller's *Sin City* (The Hard Goodbye), That Yellow Bastard, The Big Fat Kill, and A Dame to Kill For); ph, Robert Rodriguez; ed, Robert Rodriguez; John Debney, Graeme Revell, Robert Rodriguez; art d, Jeanette Scott; fx, Anouk Deveault-Moreau, Daniel Leduc, John McLeod, Robert Rodriguez; anim, Montell Baiochi, Michael Cozens

Frank Miller's "Sin City" graphic novels read as though the writer/illustrator fell into a vat of distilled Mickey Spillane, and co-directors Robert Rodriguez and Miller's ferociously faithful adaptation is the closest live-action filmmaking (extensively aided by CGI) has ever come to reproducing the visual aesthetic of comic-book art.

World-weary Basin City Detective Hartigan (Bruce Willis) is about to retire when he saves 11-year-old Nancy Callahan (Makenzie Vega) from perverted rich boy Rourk Jr. (Nick Stahl), son of powerful Senator Rourk (Powers Boothe). The price of bucking a system firmly in thrall to the corrupt

Rourk family: Hartigan finds himself on trial for assault and child molestation. Meanwhile, hulking bad man Marv (Mickey Rourke) has a date with a hooker named Goldie (Jaime King), but he's framed for her murder. Marv sets out on a rampage that leads to corrupt Cardinal Roark (Rutger Hauer) and a freakish serial killer (Elijah Wood). Elsewhere, stone-cold killer Dwight (Clive Owen) comes home with a new face plastered over the same old bad attitude, and inadvertently sets in motion a chain of events that could lead to gang war in Old Town, where gun-toting hookers run the show. Finally, the battered, eight-years-older Nancy (Jessica Alba), now a stripper, and the vengeful, mustard-yellow monster that was once Rourk Jr. have their final showdown.

The downside to fidelity to the graphic novels is that the stories are a hash of warmed-over genre cliches, but once you're good and drunk on the glistening, black-and-white look, details like the tin-eared tough-guy dialogue don't seem so important. Quentin Tarantino fans take note: The "Special Guest Director" was responsible for a single scene involving Dwight and a chatty dead guy (Benicio Del Toro).

FRANKENHOOKER
1990 90m c Comedy/Horror **DVD** ★★★
Ievins-Henenlotter Production (U.S.)

James Lorinz *(Jeffrey Franken)*, Patty Mullen *(Elizabeth)*, Charlotte Helmkamp *(Honey)*, Shirley Stoler *(Spike)*, Louise Lasser *(Jeffrey's Mom)*, Joseph Gonzalez *(Zorro)*, Lia Chang *(Crystal)*, Jennifer Delora *(Angel)*, Vicki Darnell *(Sugar)*, Kimberly Taylor *(Amber)*

p, Edgar Ievins; d, Frank Henenlotter; w, Robert Martin, Frank Henenlotter; ph, Robert M. Baldwin; ed, Kevin Tent; m, Joe Renzetti; fx, Gabe Bartalos

Though the weak-hearted and taste-conscious should approach with extreme caution, the predisposed will find this horror farce a funny, stunningly gross black comedy that boasts surprisingly effective performances from its unknown leads.

Jeffrey Franken (James Lorinz), a resident of Hohokus, New Jersey, works in a power-plant and plays mad scientist in his spare time. His fiancee, Elizabeth (Patty Mullen), has a tragic lawn-care-related accident but resourceful Jeff manages to save her head. He schemes to construct a new body for his betrothed with remnants of expired ladies of the evening. After he gathers the most appealing limbs, he sews them together, attaches Elizabeth's head, and waits for an electrical storm. It isn't long before his "Frankenhooker" is staggering up 42nd Street, wreaking late-night havoc and frying johns with her lethal high-voltage love.

Granted this is tasteless shlock, but in Henenlotter's capable hands it manages to be quite funny. Lorinz's acting style is as wildly funny as it is wanly low-key; he is more than matched by former *Penthouse* Pet Mullen. A genuine find as Frankenhooker, Mullen pays fond, funny tribute to Elsa Lanchester's BRIDE OF FRANKENSTEIN with her remarkably refined comic performance.

FRANKENSTEIN
1931 71m bw Horror/Science Fiction **DVD** ★★★★★
Universal (U.S.)

Colin Clive *(Henry Frankenstein)*, Mae Clarke *(Elizabeth)*, John Boles *(Victor Moritz)*, Boris Karloff *(the Monster)*, Edward Van Sloan *(Dr. Waldman)*, Dwight Frye *(Fritz, the Dwarf)*, Frederick Kerr *(Baron Frankenstein)*, Lionel Belmore *(Herr Vogel, Burgomaster)*, Michael Mark *(Ludwig, Peasant Father)*, Marilyn Harris *(Maria the Child)*

p, Carl Laemmle Jr.; d, James Whale; w, Garrett Fort, Francis Edwards Faragoh, John Balderston, Robert Florey (based on the novel by Mary Shelley and the play by Peggy Webling); ph, Arthur Edeson; ed, Maurice Pivar, Clarence Kolster; m, David Broekman; art d, Charles D. Hall; fx, John P. Fulton.

Six decades since its premiere, this early sound chiller is still a great film of its genre. Immeasurably superior to Tod Browning's DRACULA, which preceded it by a mere ten months, it shows how quickly Hollywood mastered the art of sound. FRANKENSTEIN also illustrates why James Whale is still—Cronenberg notwithstanding—*the* greatest director of horror films.

The story doesn't quite follow Mary Shelley's original, but it still milks the tragic tale of the inspired doctor and his piecemeal creation for all it's worth. Dr. Frankenstein (Clive) and the hunchbacked Fritz (Frye) steal bodies from their graves to assemble a "man" (Karloff) breathed into life with electricity. Unfortunately, Fritz's mistreatment of the bewildered being and the criminal brain mistakenly implanted in its skull combine to produce a killer, with grim consequences for all involved.

Still new to films, Whale displays astonishing technical mastery of the medium, as well as the imagination to break rules where appropriate. His innate theatricality makes a memorable moment of the monster's introduction. Karloff backs in from a doorway as our curiosity peaks. He slowly turns and Whale brilliantly cuts along an unchanging axis to increasingly tight close-ups of Karloff's face. Jack Pierce's marvelous make-up perfectly suits the film's blend of fantasy and science, and still manages to highlight Karloff's beautifully expressive face. This role made the gentle British character actor a star and a legend almost instantly. At once terrifying and pathetic, his monster is a moving study of alienation and primitive anger.

The film lacks the campy humor of later Whale; except for the delightful doddering of Kerr as Frankenstein's father, the wit is subdued in favor of a stark, dank tone. The result is a touching, cathartic sobriety seen at its best in the monster's encounter with an eight-year-old girl (Harris) who sees no reason to be afraid of the scarred creature before her. Universal backed down from including Clive's line, "Now I know what it feels like to be God," and they added a rather quaint disclaimer (featuring Van Sloan) warning viewers of the terror to follow, but nothing can detract from the power of the most influential monster movie ever made.

FRANTIC
1988 120m c   Thriller   ★★★★
Mount   (U.S.)   R

Harrison Ford *(Dr. Richard Walker)*, Emmanuelle Seigner *(Michelle)*, Betty Buckley *(Sondra Walker)*, John Mahoney *(Williams)*, Jimmy Ray Weeks *(Shaap)*, Yorgo Voyagis *(The Kidnaper)*, David Huddleston *(Peter)*, Gerard Klein *(Gaillard)*, Jacques Ciron *(Hotel Manager)*, Dominique Pinon *(Wino)*

p, Thom Mount, Tim Hampton; d, Roman Polanski; w, Roman Polanski, Gerard Brach; ph, Witold Sobocinski; ed, Sam O'Steen; m, Ennio Morricone; prod d, Pierre Guffroy; cos, Anthony Powell

One of Roman Polanski's best, and too often overlooked. FRANTIC is a dreamy, tense thriller set against a stylishly reimagined Paris and featuring the performance of Harrison Ford's career. Dr. Richard Walker (Ford), a San Francisco surgeon, arrives in Paris with his wife (Betty Buckley), intending to deliver a medical paper and hoping to revitalize their relationship (they'd honeymooned in Paris 20 years earlier). Walker speaks no French and cannot even make a phone call without his wife's help. The Walkers arrive at the posh Le Grand Hotel and begin to unpack, only to discover they have the wrong suitcase. Later, while Dr. Walker showers, Sondra disappears without a trace. Initially baffled and annoyed, Walker soon becomes deeply concerned and finally frantic as

he realizes that the police won't help him in this alien environment. Acting alone, he locates the owner of the mysterious suitcase, Michelle (Emmanuelle Seigner), an alluring Parisian who draws him further into a web of intrigue.

Director Polanski, a master of movie atmospherics (e.g., CHINATOWN, ROSEMARY'S BABY), here creates a hauntingly foreign, forbiddingly stylish Paris that seems to move to the oneiric disco stylings of Grace Jones. Harrison Ford, outstanding as an American innocent abroad, moves persuasively from complacency to confusion, rage, and paranoid desperation in a performance comparable to James Stewart's best work for Hitchcock.

FREAKS
1932 64m   bw Horror   ★★★★
MGM   (U.S.)

Wallace Ford *(Phroso)*, Leila Hyams *(Venus)*, Olga Baclanova *(Cleopatra)*, Roscoe Ates *(Roscoe)*, Henry Victor *(Hercules)*, Harry Earles *(Hans)*, Daisy Earles *(Frieda)*, Rose Dione *(Madame Tetrallini)*, Daisy Hilton, Violet Hilton *(Siamese Twins)*

p, Tod Browning, Irving Thalberg (uncredited); d, Tod Browning; w, Willis Goldbeck, Leon Gordon, Edgar Allan Woolf, Al Boasberg (based on the short story "Spurs" by Clarence Aaron "Tod" Robbins); ph, Merritt B. Gerstad; ed, Basil Wrangell; art d, Cedric Gibbons, Merrill Pye

Long unseen, FREAKS was MGM's answer to Universal's popular FRANKENSTEIN and DRACULA, but public and critical revulsion to the use of actual circus freaks soon forced the movie from distribution. Dwain Esper (of MANIAC fame) later gave it road shows in tents and burlesque houses, further adding to this cult classic's notorious reputation.

The story follows Cleopatra (Baclanova), a beautiful but avaricious trapeze artist who seduces and marries midget circus owner Hans (Earles) to get at his money. In one of the film's most memorable scenes, the close-knit society of "freaks" warmly welcomes her into their family at the wedding reception as "one of us, one of us." Cleopatra shrinks back in disgust, however, telling them all that she will never be grotesque, while her secret lover, Hercules the strongman (Victor), howls with laughter. She humiliates her smitten husband by openly kissing the lecherous Hercules and the community soon realizes a threat is in their presence. When Hans falls ill, the group figures out that Cleopatra and Hercules have been slowly poisoning him, and so they plan a horrible, ironic revenge.

Although the suspenseful, brilliantly handled final scenes suggest an exploitation of the film's handicapped players, by then we have actually come to identify more with them than with the "normal" Cleopatra and Hans. The final revenge is thus not so much an attempt to turn melodrama into horror as it is the resolution of an old-fashioned morality play. Possibly Browning's warmest film, FREAKS is a compassionate study of how physically deformed people manage on their own. We see how they bond to each other and to those (Ford and Hyams) who love them as they are.

Some of the film's best moments are those unburdened by the plot, as we visit circus members—the bearded lady; the bird girl; the hermaphrodite; the human skeleton; the pinheads; and the Siamese twins—to see how they move, how they feel, how they love. Although slow-moving and uneven, FREAKS is one of Browning's more consistently fine films, a landmark still worth seeing.

FREAKY FRIDAY
2003 93m   c   Comedy   ★★★
GUNNFilms Productions/   PG
Walt Disney Pictures   (U.S.)

Jamie Lee Curtis *(Tess Coleman)*, Lindsay Lohan *(Anna Coleman)*, Mark Harmon *(Ryan)*, Harold Gould *(Grandpa)*, Chad

Michael Murray (Jake), Stephen Tobolowsky (Mr. Bates), Christina Vidal (Maddie), Ryan Malgarini (Harry Coleman), Lucille Soong (Pei-Pei's Mom), Haley Hudson (Peg)

p, Andrew Gunn; d, Mark Waters; w, Heather Hach, Leslie Dixon (based on the book by Mary Rodgers); ph, Oliver Wood; ed, Bruce Green; m, Rolfe Kent; prod d, Cary White; art d, Maria Baker; fx, Al Broussard, Peter Donen, Mark Freund; cos, Genevieve Tyrell

A sweet, if predictable, modern-day version of young-adult author Mary Rodgers's classic body-switch tale.

Psychologist Dr. Tess Coleman (Jamie Lee Curtis) is simultaneously planning her upcoming nuptials to Ryan (Mark Harmon), attending to the needy patients who call her cell phone constantly, and trying to spend quality time with her two children. She seems to have everything under control—everything except her 15-year-old, Anna (Lindsay Lohan). Tess can't figure out why her intelligent child is failing English and constantly bickering with her brother (Ryan Malgarini). Anna, meanwhile, thinks her mother's life is close to perfect, while the only thing Anna's got going is her band; she can't even get resident high-school rebel Jake (Chad Michael Murray) to notice her. When mother-daughter tensions come to a head at a Chinese restaurant, a meddlesome employee (Lucille Soong) gives them two enchanted fortune cookies; the next day they awake to find they've switched bodies. Tess and Anna are forced to spend one very tumultuous day in each other's shoes—Tess in high tops, Anna in pumps—until each commits a selfless act and cosmic order is restored.

Too many other movies—LIKE FATHER, LIKE SON; VICE VERSA; and 18 AGAIN!—have tackled this primal teen fantasy; what adolescent never envied grown-ups' "freedom," or wished a day in high-school hell on a parent? But Curtis and Lohan's spirited performances make this variation memorable, and neither has any trouble flip-flopping between her teenaged and adult self. Though the film's target tweenaged audience will neither know nor care, Rodgers's book has been filmed twice before: in 1976 with Barbara Harris and Jodie Foster, and for television in 1995 with Shelley Long and Gaby Hoffmann.

FREE WILLY

1993 112m c Children's/Adventure/Drama ★★½
Donner-Shuler-Donner/Canal Plus/Regency PG
Enterprises/Alcor Films (U.S.)

Jason James Richter (Jesse), Lori Petty (Rae Lindley), Jayne Atkinson (Annie Greenwood), August Schellenberg (Randolph Johnson), Michael Madsen (Glen Greenwood), Michael Ironside (Dial), Richard Riehle (Wade), Mykelti Williamson, billed as Mykel T. Williamson (Dwight Mercer), Michael Bacall (Perry), Danielle Harris (Gwenie)

p, Lauren Shuler-Donner, Jennie Lew Tugend; d, Simon Wincer; w, Keith A. Walker, Corey Blechman, Tom Benedek (from a story by Keith A. Walker); ph, Robbie Greenberg, Pete Romano; ed, O. Nicholas Brown; m, Basil Poledouris; prod d, Charles Rosen; art d, Diane Yates, Charles Butcher, Theresa Wachter; fx, Tom Ward, Robert S. Henderson, Wayne W. Rose; cos, April Ferry

This modest boy-and-his-killer-whale story was a surprising, if carefully orchestrated, summer success. FREE WILLY's ads asked, "How far would you go for a friend?" but a more probing query to parents would be "How much will you sit through for your kid?" Shamelessly manipulative and heavy-handed, it may be an endurance test for those not absolutely entranced by large aquatic mammals.

A killer whale is separated from his family, shipped to an amusement park, christened Willy and expected to entertain. Meanwhile, runaway Jesse (Jason James Richter) survives on the streets by stealing and begging. Jesse finds new foster parents and must clean up the graffiti he sprayed at the park: the moment the surly, uncooperative youngster lays eyes on the equally cantankerous whale, they bond. Trouble looms in the form of Park owner Dial (Michael Ironside), who fears Willy was a bad investment and plots to kill the whale for the insurance.

FREE WILLY is dopey and schematic—Michael Ironside lets us know he's a bad guy by scowling and muttering "I hate that whale!"—but things pick up a bit whenever kid and whale interact. Keiko is a very talented animal, making it ironic that he plays a whale with performance anxiety, and even jaded viewers may experience some artificial uplift at the end. Michael Jackson sings the amazingly overwrought theme song "Will You Be There" over the credits. And you thought "Ben" was a bit odd!

FREEZE—DIE—COME TO LIFE

(ZAMRI OUMI VOSKRESNI)
1990 105m bw Drama ★★★½
Lenfilm (U.S.S.R.)

Dinara Drukarova (Galiya), Pavel Nazarov (Valerka), Yelena Popova (Valerka's Mother), Vyacheslav Bambushek (Vitka), Vadim Ermolayev (School Principal)

p, Valentina Tarasova; d, Vitaly Kanevski; w, Vitaly Kanevski; ph, Vladimir Brylyakov; ed, Galina Kornilova; m, Sergei Banevich; cos, Tatyana Kochergina, Natalya Milliant

Vitaly Kanevski's FREEZE-DIE-COME TO LIFE is a grim, wrenching, beautifully realized story of a trouble-prone boy growing up in a postwar gulag town in Soviet Asia.

Valerka (Pavel Nazarov) lives in a decrepit block of flats with his mother (Yelena Popova), a prostitute and dance-hall bartender who is struggling to build a good life for her son. Valerka is an irrepressible prankster at school. His antics provide him with a much-needed release from the dreary reality of his existence; it is his street-smarts and wit that keep him from becoming one of the walking dead that inhabit his town. Valerka is also enterprising, and he goes into competition with his friend Galiya (Dinara Drukarova) as a tea seller. As an aspiring capitalist, Valerka tries to scare away Galiya's customers by claiming that her water is rusty and that her kettle has very recently been a home to cockroaches. He also makes false grand claims for his own tea. Valerka and Galiya are never protected from the harsh realities of the adult world.

Shot in a grim black-and-white that creates a sense of a world of perpetual grays, FREEZE-DIE-COME TO LIFE is a movingly authentic document that recalls the best of neorealism. Moreover it captures the indomitability of Valerka's and Galiya's spirits even under the most hopeless circumstances. The performances, particularly Nazarov and Drukarova, are compelling and spontaneous. Kanevski's direction is impressive and his screenplay is unsparing and touched with humor.

FRENCH CANCAN

1955 93m c Musical ★★★★
Franco-London/Jolly (France)

Jean Gabin (Danglard), Maria Felix (La Belle Abesse), Francoise Arnoul (Nini), Jean-Roger Caussimon (Baron Walter), Gianni Esposito (Prince Alexandre), Philippe Clay (Casimir), Michel Piccoli (Valorgueil), Jean Paredes (Coudrier), Lydia Johnson (Guibole), Max Dalban (Manager of The Reine Blanche)

p, Louis Wipf; d, Jean Renoir; w, Jean Renoir (based on an idea by Andre-Paul Antoine); ph, Michel Kelber (Technicolor); ed, Borys Lewin; m, Georges Van Parys; art d, Max Douy; chor, G. Grandjean; cos, Rosine Delamare

After a 15-year hiatus from filmmaking in France, Jean Renoir returned with this high-spirited celebration of color and movement. FRENCH CANCAN vibrantly brings to life the dawning days of the Moulin Rouge, complete with high-kicking choristers flaunting their frills. Gabin turns in one of his most memorable performances as Dangland, an aging theater impresario known for his ability to take common women and transform them into dancehall sensations—he also succeeds in seducing them. Before long, he becomes captivated with Montmartre laundress Nini (Arnoul) and he ignores a previous love to devote his energies into making her a star.

A deceptively simple picture, FRENCH CANCAN lets us relive an era previously vivid only in the painted art of Toulouse-Lautrec and Jean's father Auguste Renoir. Renoir, whose films have consistently served as training grounds for a number of prominent directors (Jacques Becker on LA CHIENNE, Yves Allegret and Luchino Visconti on the short A DAY IN THE COUNTRY, and Robert Aldrich on THE SOUTHERNER), also gave a start to Jacques Rivette in this picture by letting him serve as a directorial trainee.

FRENCH CONNECTION, THE
1971 104m c Crime   ★★★★½
Fox (U.S.)   R

Gene Hackman (Jimmy "Popeye" Doyle), Fernando Rey (Alain Charnier), Roy Scheider (Buddy Russo), Tony Lo Bianco (Sal Boca), Marcel Bozzuffi (Pierre Nicoli), Frederic de Pasquale (Devereaux), Bill Hickman (Mulderig), Ann Rebbot (Marie Charnier), Harold Gary (Weinstock), Sonny Grosso (Klein)

p, Philip D'Antoni; d, William Friedkin; w, Ernest Tidyman (based on the book by Robin Moore); ph, Owen Roizman (DeLuxe Color); ed, Jerry Greenberg; m, Don Ellis; art d, Ben Kazaskow; fx, Sass Bedig; cos, Joseph Fretwell

AA Best Picture; AA Best Actor: Gene Hackman; AAN Best Supporting Actor: Roy Scheider; AA Best Director: William Friedkin; AA Best Adapted Screenplay: Ernest Tidyman; AAN Best Cinematography: Owen Roizman; AA Best Film Editing: Jerry Greenberg; AAN Best Sound: Theodore Soderberg, Christopher Newman

This tough, brilliant crime film features Hackman as the indefatigable Popeye Doyle, who passionately hates drug pushers. Professional hit man Bozzuffi kills a French detective in Marseilles while Hackman and his partner Scheider rouse a drug dealer in a vacant lot in Brooklyn. Later that night, Hackman and Scheider spot a group of mobsters celebrating and tail Lo Bianco and his wife. This leads to a massive surveillance of a large U.S. drug ring on which Hackman and Scheider are ordered to work with federal agents Hickman and Grosso. Hackman and Hickman have a long-standing feud that boils to the surface. Meanwhile, Rey, the mastermind of the French drug traffic, stashes 120 pounds of heroin in the Lincoln Continental of television actor de Pasquale, who escorts the shipment to New York. Rey contacts Lo Bianco in Manhattan to arrange for the sale of the heroin, but is spotted by Hackman who has staked out Lo Bianco and trailed the pair to a hotel. Hackman follows Rey, who is aware that he is being tailed, and the wily Frenchman outwits the detective, escaping on a subway train, smugly waving goodbye as the cop is left standing on the platform.

Young director Friedkin produced a suspenseful and utterly absorbing film which incorporated thrills with street humor and routine police work with highly dramatic scenes. A second chase scene, an incredible, hair-raising sequence shot from Hackman's car with cameras mounted in the back seat and on the front fenders, is part of cinematic legend. The police are portrayed as being almost as brutal as the criminals, with Hackman shown to be a near-maniac who will stop at nothing

to corral drug offenders. Hackman won an Oscar for his riveting portrayal, as did the film, Friedkin, Tidyman's screenplay and Greenberg's editing.

FRENCH CONNECTION II
1975 119m c Crime   ★★★½
Fox (U.S.)   R

Gene Hackman (Popeye Doyle), Fernando Rey (Charnier), Bernard Fresson (Barthelemy), Jean-Pierre Castaldi (Raoul Diron), Charles Millot (Miletto), Cathleen Nesbitt (Old Lady), Pierre Collet (Old Pro), Alexandre Fabre (Young Tail), Philippe Leotard (Jacques), Jacques Dynam (Inspector Genevoix)

p, Robert L. Rosen; d, John Frankenheimer; w, Alexander Jacobs, Robert Dillon, Lauri Dillon (based on a story by Robert and Lauri Dillon); ph, Claude Renoir (DeLuxe Color); ed, Tom Rolf; m, Don Ellis; prod d, Jacques Saulnier; art d, Gerard Viard, Georges Glon; fx, Logan Frazee; cos, Jacques Fonteray

Surprisingly good follow-up to the original tough crime drama. Popeye Doyle (Hackman) is sent to Marseilles to unearth Charnier (Rey), the man who got away in the earlier film. Doyle is treated with disdain by French policeman Barthelemy (Fresson), who resents his intrusive, loud-mouthed, bad-mannered ways. Popeye is decidedly out of place in a setting he does not understand, laboring with a language that proves more difficult each day. He does not know that he is being used as bait by his French counterpart to lure Charnier into the open.

Further complicating matters, Doyle eludes his French police bodyguards in an effort to find his nemesis alone, but only succeeds in getting kidnaped by the drug czar's henchmen. Taken to a sleazy hotel, he is forcibly turned into a heroin addict so that he will tell everything he knows about the "French connection."

FRENCH CONNECTION II is tightly directed by Frankenheimer, who once again proves that he knows how to direct a suspense thriller. (Just check out THE MANCHURIAN CANDIDATE, SEVEN DAYS IN MAY, or SECONDS if you need further proof.) Hackman once again gives a riveting and believable performance; the sequences dealing with his withdrawal from heroin presenting a frightening and realistic look at the effects of hard drugs. The whole production is outstanding, in particular Renoir's breathtaking cinematography, Frazee's special effects and Needham's stuntwork.

FRENCH LIEUTENANT'S WOMAN, THE
1981 127m c Romance   ★★★½
UA (U.K.)

Meryl Streep (Sarah/Anna), Jeremy Irons (Charles/Mike), Hilton McRae (Sam), Emily Morgan (Mary), Charlotte Mitchell (Mrs. Tranter), Lynsey Baxter (Ernestina), Jean Faulds (Cook), Peter Vaughan (Mr. Freeman), Colin Jeavons (Vicar), Liz Smith (Mrs. Fairley)

p, Leon Clore; d, Karel Reisz; w, Harold Pinter (based on the novel by John Fowles); ph, Freddie Francis (Technicolor); ed, John Bloom; m, Carl Davis; prod d, Assheton Gorton; art d, Norman Dorme, Terry Pritchard, Allan Cameron; cos, Tom Rand

AAN Best Actress: Meryl Streep; AAN Best Adapted Screenplay: Harold Pinter (Screenplay); AAN Best Film Editing: John Bloom; AAN Best Art Direction: Assheton Gorton (Art Direction), Ann Mollo (Set Decoration); AAN Best Costume Design: Tom Rand

Translating John Fowles' complex novel to the screen was a formidable task, previously attempted—then abandoned—by the likes of Fred Zinnemann, Richard Lester and Mike Nichols. Undaunted, director Karel Reisz joined forces with esteemed playwright Harold Pinter to convey the essence of Fowles' epic romance.

In a technically flawless performance, Meryl Streep plays Sarah Woodruff, a mysterious pariah in mourning who has been dishonored after a affair with a French army officer in Victorian England. In his first starring role, Jeremy Irons portrays Charles Smithson, the wealthy young man of principle who finds her and falls hopelessly in love. Pinter's screenplay shrewdly incorporates both the novel's 19th-century point of view and, underscoring the oppressive constraints of Victorian society, a contemporary tale featuring Streep and Irons as Anna and Mike, the sophisticated actors playing Sarah and Charles in a film adaptation of *The French Lieutenant's Woman* who casually embark on their own affair—with decidedly different results.

Though occasionally jarring, the intercutting between the parallel stories, aided immeasurably by Streep's disparate characterizations, succeeds in conveying the complexity of Fowles' novel.

FRENCH, THEY ARE A FUNNY RACE, THE
(LES CARNETS DU MAJOR THOMPSON)
1955 105m bw Comedy ★★★
Continental/Gaumont (France)

Jack Buchanan *(Major Thompson)*, Martine Carol *(Martine)*, Noel-Noel *(Taupin)*, Totti Truman Taylor *(Nurse)*, Andre Luguet *(Editor)*, Genevieve Brunet *(Secretary)*, Catherine Boyle *(Wife)*

p, Paul Wagner, Alain Poire; d, Preston Sturges; w, Preston Sturges (based on the book *The Notebooks of Major Thompson* by Pierre Daninos); ph, Maurice Barry, Christian Matras; ed, Raymond Lanny

Notable as Preston Sturges's last film, made in France after an absence of six years. Based on essays allegedly written by an English major about his adjustment to carefree French life, the film is anecdotal and often amusing, but the overwhelming feeling is one of sadness as we watch the greatest comic talent of the 1940s straining along shortly before he died in exile.

Jack Buchanan, that former effervescent musical comedy star, also makes his final appearance as Major Thompson, who resides in Paris with his air-headed but beautiful French wife (Carol, likable but underused); the two appear to have nothing better to do than argue over how to raise their child. Boyle appears as the major's English wife, whose conjugal outlook stems from her mother's advice to her on her wedding night: "My dear, it's utterly unbearable, but just close your eyes and think of England." Sturges does effectively lampoon both English and French lifestyles as he sees them, and the contrasts are sometimes evocative of his earlier sophistication. Still, the visuals are drab and the energy is low, making this a far cry from such brilliant earlier Sturges works as THE MIRACLE OF MORGAN CREEK and SULLIVAN'S TRAVELS, both masterpieces of satirical wit.

FRENZY 📀
1972 116m c Thriller ★★★★
Universal (U.K.) R

Jon Finch *(Richard Blaney)*, Barry Foster *(Robert Rusk)*, Barbara Leigh-Hunt *(Brenda Blaney)*, Anna Massey *(Babs Milligan)*, Alec McCowen *(Chief Inspector Oxford)*, Vivien Merchant *(Mrs. Oxford)*, Billie Whitelaw *(Hetty Porter)*, Clive Swift *(Johnny Porter)*, Bernard Cribbins *(Felix Forsythe)*, Michael Bates *(Sgt. Spearman)*

p, Alfred Hitchcock; d, Alfred Hitchcock; w, Anthony Shaffer (from the novel *Goodbye Piccadilly, Farewell Leicester Square* by Arthur

LaBern); ph, Gilbert Taylor (Technicolor); ed, John Jympson; m, Ron Goodwin; prod d, Syd Cain; art d, Robert Laing

Hitchcock's first British film in almost two decades marked a smashing return to his earlier form after the dull TORN CURTAIN and TOPAZ. Although not a mystery (we know the killer's identity early on), the film is intensely suspenseful, at times forcing the audience to identify with the murderer. Richard Blaney (Finch) is accused of murdering his ex-wife Brenda (Leigh-Hunt) and his girlfriend (Massey), both of whom have been strangled with neckties. The real "Necktie Murderer," however, remains at large.

There's more explicit sex and violence in this movie than is usual for Hitchcock. His famous touches still abound, however, juxtaposing some screamingly funny bits involving Scotland Yard Inspector Oxford (McCowen) with brutal rape-strangulation scenes. The first murder is particularly well done, and expect a jolt when a body falls off a truck. FRENZY also contains perhaps the most wicked of Hitchcock's scenes—the killer searching through a stack of potato sacks in order to find his missing monogrammed tie pin, which a nude corpse clutches in her death grip.

FRESH 📀
1994 112m c Drama/Thriller ★★★★
Fresh Productions/A Band Apart Productions/ R
Lawrence Bender Productions/Lumiere (U.S./France)

Sean Nelson *(Fresh)*, Giancarlo Esposito *(Esteban)*, Samuel L. Jackson *(Sam)*, N'Bushe Wright *(Nicole)*, Ron Brice *(Corky)*, Jean Claude Lamarre, billed as Jean LaMarre *(Jake)*, Jose Zuniga *(Lt. Perez)*, Luis Lantigua *(Chuckie)*, Yul Vasquez *(Chillie)*, Cheryl Freeman *(Aunt Frances)*

p, Randy Ostrow, Lawrence Bender; d, Boaz Yakin; w, Boaz Yakin; ph, Adam Holender; ed, Dorian Harris; m, Stewart Copeland; prod d, Dan Leigh; cos, Ellen Lutter

FRESH sounds like another slice of low-life, a study of an intelligent but fatally disadvantaged ghetto child's inexorable descent into criminality. But if the situations are (at first) familiar, the characters aren't; they may look like the same old junkies and dealers and whores and gangsters, but first-time director Boaz Yakin invests all of them—particularly Fresh (Sean Nelson)—with a subtle, complex life that's both painful and exhilarating.

On the mean streets of New York City, 12-year-old Fresh works as a courier for Esteban (Giancarlo Esposito), a drug dealer who functions as a surrogate father. His real father (Samuel L. Jackson), unemployed and embittered, has channelled a lifetime of frustration into mastering the game of chess, in which he periodically instructs his son. Yakin's tightly plotted character study seems poised to follow a well-worn path: promising ghetto youth, desperate family, bad companions, violence and death, capped off with the usual dose of pat moralizing. Instead, FRESH offers a welcome departure from well-worn themes and plot developments, as the title character launches a cold-blooded, intricately plotted scheme to rescue himself and the remnants of his family from the depredations of ghetto life.

FRESH stands on young Sean Nelson's performance, and he is so good it's hard to believe. Fresh is a complex and contradictory character, a boy who's simultaneously sophisticated and callow, naive enough to think life can be played like a board game and smart enough to do it and win, though at a disturbing price. Yakin deserves special praise for endowing his characters with intellect—a quality that blacks are rarely allowed to display in Hollywood films—and for resisting the temptation to mar his quietly intelligent film with a commercially desirable hip-hop soundtrack.

FRESHMAN, THE

DVD
1990 102m c Comedy ★★★
Lobell-Bergman (U.S.) PG

Marlon Brando (*Carmine Sabatini*), Matthew Broderick (*Clark Kellogg*), Bruno Kirby (*Victor Ray*), Penelope Ann Miller (*Tina Sabatini*), Frank Whaley (*Steve Bushak*), Jon Polito (*Chuck Greenwald*), Paul Benedict (*Arthur Fleeber*), Richard Gant (*Lloyd Simpson*), Kenneth Welsh (*Dwight Armstrong*), Pamela Payton-Wright (*Liz Armstrong*)

p, Mike Lobell; d, Andrew Bergman; w, Andrew Bergman; ph, William A. Fraker (Technicolor); ed, Barry Malkin; m, David Newman; prod d, Ken Adam; art d, Alicia Keywan; fx, Neil Tifunovich; cos, Julie Weiss

Matthew Broderick stars as Clark Kellogg, a freshman from Vermont who comes to the Big Apple to study film at New York University. His most flamboyant professor is Arthur Fleeber (a scene-stealing turn by Paul Benedict, best known as Mr. Bentley of television's "The Jeffersons") who has committed every moment from THE GODFATHER PART II to memory. The great man assigns $700 worth of his own publications as required reading for his course. Kellogg gets an education in New York street life before he even gets to school, as he is robbed shortly upon hitting town by a con man, Victor Ray (Bruno Kirby). Kellogg eventually tracks Ray down but, instead of returning his stuff, the slick character offers to introduce the freshman to a real Godfather, his Uncle Carmine (Marlon Brando), an "importer-exporter" who can provide Kellogg with a high-paying, "totally legitimate" job.

There's not much to THE FRESHMAN beyond the spectacle of Brando gently spoofing his most famous role, but that's a pretty sizeable asset. Broderick is his usual charming self, and there are occasional moments of inspired whimsy or absurdity: Brando on ice skates, Bert Parks delivering a rousing rendition of Bob Dylan's "Maggie's Farm."

FRIDA

DVD
2002 123m c Biography ★★½
Miramax/Ventanarosa Productions/Lions Gate Films R
(U.S.)

Salma Hayek (*Frida Kahlo*), Alfred Molina (*Diego Rivera*), Geoffrey Rush (*Leon Trotsky*), Ashley Judd (*Tina Modotti*), Antonio Banderas (*David Alfaro Siqueiros*), Edward Norton (*Nelson Rockefeller*), Valeria Golino (*Lupe Marin*), Mia Maestro (*Cristina Kahlo*), Roger Rees (*Guillermo Kahlo*), Diego Luna (*Alejandro Gomez*)

p, Lindsay Flickinger, Sarah Green, Nancy Hardin, Salma Hayek, Jay Polstein, Roberto Sneider, Lizz Speed; d, Julie Taymor; w, Diane Lake, Gregory Nava, Clancy Sigal, Anna Thomas (based on the biography *Frida: A Biography of Frida Kahlo* by Hayden Herrera); ph, Rodrigo Prieto; ed, Francoise Bonnot; m, Elliot Goldenthal; prod d, Felipe del Paso; art d, Bernardo Trujillo; fx, Amoeba Proteus, Jeremy Dawson, Dan Schrecker; cos, Julie Weiss

AA Best Makeup: John Jackson, Beatrice De Alba; *AA Best Original Score*: Elliot Goldenthal; *AAN Best Actress*: Salma Hayek; *AAN Best Art Direction*: Felipe del Paso (Art Direction), Hannia Robledo (Set Decoration); *AAN Best Costume Design*: Julie Weiss; *AAN Best Original Song*: "Burn It Blue"; Elliot Goldenthal (music), Julie Taymor (lyrics)

Though occasionally enlivened by fanciful sequences suggesting the surreal power of Frida Kahlo's vivid inner life, flamboyant director Julie Taymor's biography of the 20th-century Mexican painter is often mired in the mechanical accretion of incidents that blights most biographical films.

Mexico City, 1922: High-school student Frida (Salma Hayek) and her friends spy on socialist muralist Diego Rivera (Alfred Molina) as his seduction of a nude model is interrupted by his fiery wife, Lupe Marin (Valeria Golino). Soon after, the vivacious Frida—whose large, conventional family is surprisingly tolerant of her rebellious and shockingly unladylike behavior—survives a gruesome streetcar accident. She endures long periods of immobilization in casts and braces that resemble medieval torture devices, and turns to painting to assuage boredom and explore the inner life that blossoms in the thorny soil of adversity. Frida works up the nerve to show her work to Rivera, who becomes her champion. United by passionate politics, they fall in love and marry despite Diego's chronic infidelity. The couple work and travel together, weathering the highs and lows of their tumultuous relationship as they cross paths with the famous and notorious, including rival Mexican muralist David Alfaro Siqueiros (Antonio Banderas), photographer Tina Modotti (Ashley Judd), Nelson Rockefeller (Edward Norton), and Leon Trotsky (Geoffrey Rush), who was assassinated shortly after he moved out of the Kahlo family home.

Hayek's performance never rises above the level of physical impersonation, but she captures Kahlo's unconventional beauty. The film was a personal victory for the actress, who prevailed over competing projects driven by bigger names (including Jennifer Lopez and Madonna), and it's a solid introduction to the cult of Kahlo, whose bold and disturbing images of pain and wonder have grown in popularity since her death.

FRIDAY NIGHT LIGHTS

DVD
2004 117m c Sports/Drama ★★★½
Imagine Entertainment/Friday Night Lights LLC/ PG-13
Universal (U.S.)

Billy Bob Thornton (*Coach Gary Gaines*), Lucas Black (*Mike Winchell*), Garrett Hedlund (*Don Billingsley*), Derek Luke (*James "Boobie" Miles*), Jay Hernandez (*Brian Chavez*), Lee Jackson (*Ivory Christian*), Lee Thompson Young (*Chris Comer*), Tim McGraw (*Charles Billingsley*), Grover Coulson (*L.V. Miles*), Connie Britton (*Sharon Gaines*)

p, Brian Grazer; d, Peter Berg; w, David Aaron Cohen, Peter Berg (based on the book by H.G. Bissinger); ph, Tobias Schliessler; ed, Colby Parker Jr., David Rosenbloom; m, Brian Reitzell; prod d, Sharon Seymour; art d, Peter Borck; fx, Patrick D. Hurd; cos, Susan Matheson

Peter Berg's gritty adaptation of Pulitzer prize-winner H.G. Bissinger's book stands out by virtue of its impressive visual style and the filmmakers' decision not to massage the facts into cliched conflicts with neat, feel-good resolutions.

In Odessa, TX, high-school football isn't just a big thing, it's the only thing. Teenagers lucky enough to play for the Permian Panthers are hailed as local heroes, but in return the community demands nothing less than perfection. No one feels the pressure more than coach Gary Gaines (Billy Bob Thornton). On the first day of practice, reporters are already hounding stand-out senior running back James "Boobie" Miles (Derek Luke), whose remarkable performance has already earned him a raft of scholarship offers. His teammates include shy quarterback Mike Winchell (Lucas Black); emotionally abused Don Billingsley (Garrett Hedlund); studious tight end Brian Chavez (Jay Hernandez); closemouthed linebacker Ivory Christian (newcomer Lee Jackson); and third-string running back Chris Comer (Lee Thompson Young). Collectively "The MOJO," the team is united by their will to win, but when Boobie suffers a devastating injury during their first game, they're left struggling to maintain a winning reputation without their star player.

Director Berg uses a smart blend of constantly moving camera and gritty film stock to give the film a documentary feel that's both engaging and perfectly suited to this story. Thornton is impeccably cast as the tough but understanding coach who may lose his temper on the field, but refrains from getting excessively preachy during his locker-room speeches. Luke shines in his role, as do the rest of the well-rounded team players.

FRIED GREEN TOMATOES
1991 130m c   Drama/Comedy   ★★★½
Avnet/Kerner Company/Electric Shadow   **PG-13**
Productions/Act III Communications   (U.S.)

Kathy Bates *(Evelyn Couch)*, Jessica Tandy *(Ninny Threadgoode)*, Mary Stuart Masterson *(Idgie Threadgoode)*, Mary-Louise Parker *(Ruth Jamison)*, Nick Searcy *(Frank Bennett)*, Cicely Tyson *(Sipsey)*, Chris O'Donnell *(Buddy Threadgoode)*, Stan Shaw *(Big George)*, Gailard Sartain *(Ed Couch)*, Tim Scott *(Smokey Lonesome)*

p, Jon Avnet, Jordan Kerner; d, Jon Avnet; w, Fannie Flagg, Carol Sobieski (from the novel *Fried Green Tomatoes at the Whistle Stop Cafe* by Flagg); ph, Geoffrey Simpson; ed, Debra Neil; m, Thomas Newman; prod d, Barbara Ling; art d, Larry Fulton; fx, Larry Reid; cos, Elizabeth McBride

AAN Best Supporting Actress: Jessica Tandy; *AAN Best Adapted Screenplay:* Fannie Flagg, Carol Sobieski

Past and present are winningly blended in the gentle comedy FRIED GREEN TOMATOES which became a "sleeper" hit with audiences.

Evelyn Couch (Kathy Bates), an overweight, repressed housewife, meets and befriends Ninny Threadgoode (Jessica Tandy), a remarkable octogenarian. Ninny is a permanent resident, though she won't admit it, at a rest home for the aged where Evelyn accompanies her husband Ed (Gailard Sartain) on his weekly visits to his gruff aunt. The aged Alabaman begins to enthrall Evelyn with the fascinating life story—seen in flashback—of one of her relatives, Idgie Threadgoode.

An early proto-feminist, Idgie (Mary Stuart Masterson) owns and operates the local cafe in Whistle Stop, Alabama. Traumatized as a girl by the gory death of a beloved older brother, Idgie has remained a tomboy loner all her life, taking to the trees when the world around her gets to be too much. Idgie literally rescues her best friend, Ruth Jamison (Mary-Louise Parker), from Ruth's marriage to the abusive Frank Bennett (Nick Searcy). Bringing her young baby with her, Ruth moves in with Idgie and the two women soon have a thriving business at the cafe, with Ruth doing the cooking and Idgie handling the bookwork.

FRIED GREEN TOMATOES is an engaging if sentimental tale, charmingly handled by producer-turned-director Jon Avnet (RISKY BUSINESS) and flawlessly acted by its four female stars. Plaudits must also go to Geoffrey Simpson, for his splendid cinematography, and to Thomas Newman for his drama-enhancing musical score.

FRIENDLY PERSUASION
1956 137m   c   Drama   DVD
Allied Artists   (U.S.)   **★★★★**

Gary Cooper *(Jess Birdwell)*, Dorothy McGuire *(Eliza Birdwell)*, Marjorie Main *(Widow Hudspeth)*, Anthony Perkins *(Josh Birdwell)*, Richard Eyer *(Little Jess)*, Phyllis Love *(Mattie Birdwell)*, Robert Middleton *(Sam Jordan)*, Mark Richman *(Gard Jordan)*, Walter Catlett *(Professor Quigley)*, Richard Hale *(Elder Purdy)*

p, William Wyler; d, William Wyler; w, Michael Wilson (uncredited, based on the novel *The Friendly Persuasion* by Jessamyn West);

ph, Ellsworth Fredricks (CinemaScope, DeLuxe Color); ed, Robert Swink, Edward A. Biery, Robert Belcher; m, Dimitri Tiomkin; art d, Ted Haworth; cos, Dorothy Jeakins, Bert Henrikson

AAN Best Picture; AAN Best Supporting Actor: Anthony Perkins; *AAN Best Director:* William Wyler; *AAN Best Adapted Screenplay:* Michael Wilson; *AAN Best Song:* "Friendly Persuasion (Thee I Love)"; Dimitri Tiomkin (Music), Paul Francis Webster (Lyrics); *AAN Best Sound Recording:* Gordon R Glennan (Westrex Sound Services Inc.), Gordon Sawyer (Samuel Goldwyn Studio Sound Department)

Long and a tad preachy, FRIENDLY PERSUASION recounts the story of a peaceful Quaker family in Indiana whose sanctity is disturbed by the Civil War in 1862.

Cooper and McGuire play the parents of Josh (Perkins), who listens to a Union officer make a plea for young men to take up the Blue cudgel. Although morally opposed to war, Josh fears that he's using his religion to mask a cowardly streak. When the news comes that the Southern band known as Morgan's Raiders is nearing his town, Josh joins the local militia and prepares to fight. He is hurt in battle, and his father goes into the war zone to save his son and find a pal (Middleton) who's been ambushed.

There's humor galore in this picture, especially in a scene with Main and her three lonesome daughters. There are many tearful moments too and several incisive looks into the lives of the "Society of Friends." Aiming for a collage effect, director Wyler deals lovingly with McGuire's ongoing battles with Samantha the goose as well as a little boy who suddenly yells "God is love" in a crowded church. A shorter running time would have helped but, as it is, FRIENDLY PERSUASION ranks as one of Wyler's best comedy-dramas.

FRIENDS OF EDDIE COYLE, THE
1973 102m   c   Crime   ★★★½
Paramount   (U.S.)   **R**

Robert Mitchum *(Eddie Coyle)*, Peter Boyle *(Dillon)*, Richard Jordan *(Dave Foley)*, Steven Keats *(Jackie Brown)*, Alex Rocco *(Scalise)*, Joe Santos *(Artie Van)*, Mitchell Ryan *(Waters)*, Helena Carroll *(Sheila Coyle)*, Peter MacLean *(Partridge)*, Kevin O'Morrison *(Manager of 2nd Bank)*

p, Paul Monash; d, Peter Yates; w, Paul Monash (based on the novel by George V. Higgins); ph, Victor J. Kemper (Panavision, Technicolor); ed, Patricia Jaffe; m, Dave Grusin; prod d, Gene Callahan; art d, Gene Callahan; cos, Eric Seelig

Mitchum is Eddie Coyle, a three-time loser. One more offense and he goes to prison for life—no parole, no hope. Police learn of an impending Boston bank robbery and go to Coyle, telling him that they know he earns a living for his destitute family by running illegal goods across state lines. They will put him away unless he squeals on the robbery gang. He reluctantly agrees to help and, after selling the gang some guns, contacts detectives, who tell him his information is insufficient. He must go on being a permanent informer and is ordered to help capture gang boss Scalise (Rocco). Before Eddie can move, however, Scalise is arrested. Coyle's underworld friends point the finger at him, ordering him murdered.

THE FRIENDS OF EDDIE COYLE is a tough look at the world of petty crooks and the sleazy side of the underworld. Mitchum is surprisingly effective as the down-and-out thief, as if worn out over the decades from earlier film noir escapades in THE RACKET and OUT OF THE PAST. Boyle is terrific as the thug who goes in for synthetic friendships, willing to sell out his own mother for survival in a system he knows will destroy him anyway. Yates's direction is grimly taut, and Monash's screenplay pulls no punches. A bit gruesome, but potent viewing nonetheless.

FRIGHT NIGHT

1985 106m c   Horror   ★★★½
Columbia   (U.S.)   R

Chris Sarandon *(Jerry Dandridge)*, William Ragsdale *(Charley Brewster)*, Amanda Bearse *(Amy Peterson)*, Roddy McDowall *(Peter Vincent)*, Stephen Geoffreys *(Evil Ed)*, Jonathan Stark *(Billy Cole)*, Dorothy Fielding *(Judy Brewster)*, Art Evans *(Detective Lennox)*, Stewart Stern *(Cook)*, Nick Savage

p, Herb Jaffe; d, Tom Holland; w, Tom Holland; ph, Jan Kiesser (Metrocolor); ed, Kent Beyda; m, Brad Fiedel; prod d, John De Cuir; fx, Richard Edlund, Michael Lantieri, Darrell D. Prichett, Clay Pinney, Albert Lannutti; cos, Robert Fletcher

A minor classic of the genre, this is a memorable addition to the vampire tradition in the horror film. FRIGHT NIGHT depicts the plight of Charley Brewster (Ragsdale), a fatherless teenager tottering on the brink of manhood, as he becomes obsessed with the charming new man next door, Jerry Dandridge (Sarandon). He is convinced that his neighbor is actually a vampire and responsible for a series of local murders. Charley alerts the local authorities but they dismiss him as a crank. His mom (Dorothy Fielding) won't listen to him and even his best buddy, Evil Ed (Geoffreys), and his devoted girlfriend, Amy Peterson (Bearse), think he's crazy. Desperate, Charley turns to the only vampire expert he can find, Peter Vincent (McDowall), an aging washed-up horror movie ham. Though at first he only humors the boy, Vincent soon realizes that Charley is telling the truth.

This film is the feature directing debut of Tom Holland who was previously known for his smart genre screenplays—CLASS OF 1984, CLOAK AND DAGGER and PSYCHO II. Like his earlier scripts, FRIGHT NIGHT is a clever amalgam; this teen-oriented vampire movie deftly combines Hitchcockian themes, Hammer horror trappings, a subversive gay subtext and a John Hughes milieu into a genuinely scary horror movie that is comfortably old-fashioned yet cool.

Holland, a former actor, elicits much better than average performances from his teen actors. Stephen Geoffreys is particularly enjoyable in a crazed Jack Nicholson turn as Evil Ed. The more seasoned players deliver outstanding performances. Chris Sarandon is stunning as the sensually handsome—yet deadly—new neighbor. Roddy McDowall is also in fine form in his best role in years as the cynical has-been who must become a true hero. FRIGHT NIGHT may not be great art but it *is* great fun.

FROM DUSK TILL DAWN

1996 108m c   Horror/Crime/Comedy   ★★
A Band Apart Productions/Les Hooligans   R
Productions/Miramax   (U.S.)

Harvey Keitel *(Jacob Fuller)*, George Clooney *(Seth Gecko)*, Quentin Tarantino *(Richard Gecko)*, Juliette Lewis *(Kate Fuller)*, Ernest Liu *(Scott Fuller)*, Cheech Marin *(Border Guard/Chet Pussy/Carlos)*, Fred Williamson *(Frost)*, Salma Hayek *(Santanico Pandemonium)*, Marc Lawrence *(Old Timer)*, Michael Parks *(Texas Ranger Earl McGraw)*

p, Gianni Nunnari, Meir Teper; d, Robert Rodriguez; w, Quentin Tarantino (from a story by Robert Kurtzman); ph, Guillermo Navarro; ed, Robert Rodriguez; m, Graeme Revell; prod d, Cecilia Montiel; art d, Mayne Schuyler Berke; fx, Daniel A. Fort, Diana Dru Botsford, Thomas Bellissimo, Charles Belardinelli, Bellissimo/Belardinelli Effects Inc.; cos, Graciela Mazon

Two of the more promising creative talents in contemporary genre filmmaking (Robert Rodriguez and Quentin Tarantino), some marquee-value, and a few cult icons conspired to produce this prodigious waste of time. Though not without entertainment value, the film is a mindless addition to an over-populated sub-genre of the horror film.

The Gecko brothers are on the lam after a string of violent bank robberies in the American Southwest. Seth (George Clooney) is a smooth professional thief, while Richie (Quentin Tarantino) is a nerdy-looking psycho. Bound for sanctuary south of the border, the Geckos take a female hostage to a cheap motel, where they cross paths with lapsed minister Jacob Fuller (Harvey Keitel) and his teenaged children, Kate (Juliette Lewis) and Scott (Ernest Liu). When Richie rapes and murders their hostage, the Geckos kidnap the Fullers and commandeer their vehicle to Mexico. The make a stop at the Titty Twister, a rollicking roadhouse bar, unaware that the bar's staff and clientele are all vampires. Soon all hell breaks loose as the Geckos, the Fullers, and several human customers join forces to battle the rapacious horde of bloodsuckers.

FROM DUSK TILL DAWN offers the pleasures of excess, but little ingenuity, and the film's lack of a consistent tone is further aggravated by mediocre dialogue. The filmmakers trot out second-string '70s genre figures (Fred Williamson, John Saxon) as if their mere presence might help elevate the tiresome proceedings. Clooney makes a credible action anti-hero, and even Tarantino is surprisingly restrained and inoffensive. Keitel, however, seems to have wandered in from another movie. Hype notwithstanding, one has come to expect a bit more from the creators of PULP FICTION and EL MARIACHI.

FROM HELL

2001 115m c   Crime/Historical   ★★★
Underworld Pictures   (U.S.)   R

Johnny Depp *(Fred Abberline)*, Heather Graham *(Mary Kelly)*, Ian Holm *(Sir William Gull)*, Robbie Coltrane *(Peter Godley)*, Lesley Sharp *(Kate Eddowes)*, Susan Lynch *(Liz Stride)*, Katrin Cartlidge *(Dark Annie Chapman)*, Joanna Page *(Ann Crook)*, Annabelle Apsion *(Polly)*, Ian Richardson *(Sir Charles Warren)*

p, Jane Hamsher, Don Murphy; d, Albert Hughes, Allen Hughes; w, Terry Hayes, Rafael Yglesias (based on the graphic novel by Alan Moore and Eddie Campbell); ph, Peter Deming; ed, George Bowers, Dan Lebental; m, Trevor Jones; prod d, Martin Childs; art d, Mark Raggett, Jindra Koci; fx, George Gibbs, Bill Taylor, Illusion Arts; cos, Kym Barrett

Based on the graphic novel by Alan Moore and Eddie Campbell, this foray into creative Ripperology has the lush look of a late-period Hammer film and the feel of a complicated tale that's been streamlined within an inch of its life.

The story begins, as most of them do, in September 1888. Drug-addicted Inspector Abberline (Johnny Depp) is hauled out of his favorite opium den to investigate the brutal murder of an East End prostitute. The inspector befriends one of the dead woman's associates, Mary Kelly (Heather Graham), and gradually learns that she and four friends (Lesley Sharp, Susan Lynch, Katrin Cartlidge, Annabelle Apsion) share an explosive secret: they know that Queen Victoria's grandson, Prince Albert Victor (Mark Dexter) secretly married a poor girl named Ann Crook (Joanna Page) and fathered her child. The string of murders that follow are apparently all part of a bloody Masonic conspiracy to destroy this threat to the crown.

Every generation gets the Ripper who best fulfills its fantasies, and ours fattens on vast conspiracies. But as the movie's patrician Sir William Gull (Ian Holm) cautions Abberline, speculation is nothing more than that; authoritative-sounding assertions notwithstanding, this is no more or less authentic a Ripper tale than previous efforts. (In fact, it treads much the same path as 1988's underappreciated MURDER BY DECREE.) Moore's book is an astonishing act of synthesis, bringing together disparate Ripper theories and a fiercely idiosyncratic version of London's history, architecture, policing, and social structure. In abridging it, the filmmakers have stripped away the meat and left little more than a handsome skeleton. It could hardly have been otherwise, but it's still a shame.

FROM HERE TO ETERNITY [DVD]
1953 118m bw Drama/War ★★★★★
Columbia (U.S.)

Burt Lancaster *(Sgt. Milton Warden)*, Deborah Kerr *(Karen Holmes)*, Montgomery Clift *(Robert E. Lee Prewitt)*, Frank Sinatra *(Angelo Maggio)*, Donna Reed *(Alma Lorene)*, Ernest Borgnine *(Sgt. "Fatso" Judson)*, Philip Ober *(Capt. Dana Holmes)*, Jack Warden *(Cpl. Buckley)*, Mickey Shaughnessy *(Sgt. Leva)*, Harry Bellaver *(Mazzioli)*

p, Buddy Adler; d, Fred Zinnemann; w, Daniel Taradash (based on the novel by James Jones); ph, Burnett Guffey; ed, William Lyon; m, George Duning; art d, Cary Odell; cos, Jean Louis

AA Best Picture; AAN Best Actor: Montgomery Clift; AAN Best Actor: Burt Lancaster; AAN Best Actress: Deborah Kerr; AA Best Supporting Actor: Frank Sinatra; AA Best Supporting Actress: Donna Reed; AA Best Director: Fred Zinnemann; AA Best Screenplay: Daniel Taradash; AA Best B/W Cinematography: Burnett Guffey; AA Best Film Editing: William Lyon; AAN Best Score (Drama or Comedy): Morris Stoloff, George Duning; AAN Best Costume Design (B/W): Jean Louis; AA Best Sound Recording: John P. Livadary

The massive James Jones novel, deemed impossible to put onscreen because of its strong sexual content and language, finally emerged as a lavish, star-studded spectacle, much bowdlerized but redeemed by a slew of fine performances.

The film opens as Robert E. Lee Prewitt (Montgomery Clift), a soldier with a reputation as both a fine boxer and bugler, arrives at Schofield Barracks at Pearl Harbor. His new commander, the brutal, philandering Captain Holmes (Philip Ober), promises Prewitt that if he boxes on the company team he will be rewarded with the post of bugler—a job Prewitt covets. But Prewitt refuses, haunted by a previous ugly experience in the ring. For Prewitt's obstinacy, Holmes orders Sgt. Warden (Burt Lancaster) to give the soldier every dirty detail in the company. As it turns out, Warden is about to begin a torrid affair with Holmes's wife Karen (Deborah Kerr). Meanwhile, Prewitt's suffering is eased by his newly established relationship with Lorene (Donna Reed), a nightclub hostess. Prewitt's only other friend, Maggio (Frank Sinatra), a wisecracking enlisted man, commits several small offenses and draws repeated punishment—especially from a sadistic Italian-hating sergeant named Fatso (Ernest Borgnine).

FROM HERE TO ETERNITY was an uphill battle all the way for director Zinnemann. Most of his war was with Columbia's dictator, Harry Cohn, who had purchased the novel for $82,000 and was determined to retain its seamy story, raw language, and violence, rejecting one adaptation after another. The Army was not happy with Jones's fierce indictment of its system and refused to allow the use of Schofield Barracks unless some major concessions were made. One chief point involved the role of Captain Holmes. In the novel he gets away with everything and is even promoted to major, but in the film he is cashiered for his cruelty and malfeasance.

The featured roles were also difficult to cast under Cohn's capricious supervision. Zinnemann had to fight to cast Clift, who gave one of his greatest performances; ditto Sinatra, whose faltering career received a much-needed boost here. He had to beg Cohn for the part of Maggio and ended up playing it for practically nothing (this episode was exaggerated and fictionalized by Mario Puzo in *The Godfather*). Joan Crawford was to have played the straying wife, but the icy-turned-passionate Kerr helped keep the famous lovemaking scene on the beach more realistic and low-key. Reed's part, on the other

hand, was softened somewhat, her occupation being changed from prostitute to "hostess."

FROM RUSSIA WITH LOVE [DVD]
1963 110m c Spy ★★★★
UA (U.K.)

Sean Connery *(James Bond)*, Daniela Bianchi *(Tatiana Romanova)*, Pedro Armendariz *(Kerim Bey)*, Lotte Lenya *(Rosa Klebb)*, Robert Shaw *(Red Grant)*, Bernard Lee *("M")*, Eunice Gayson *(Sylvia)*, Walter Gotell *(Morzeny)*, Francis de Wolff *(Vavra)*, George Pastell *(Train Conductor)*

p, Harry Saltzman, Albert R. Broccoli; d, Terence Young; w, Richard Maibaum, Johanna Harwood (based on the novel by Ian Fleming); ph, Ted Moore (Technicolor); ed, Peter Hunt; m, John Barry; art d, Syd Cain; fx, John Stears; cos, Jocelyn Rickards

The second James Bond movie, and the first to sport the lavish production values that characterized all subsequent entries in the series, FROM RUSSIA WITH LOVE sends Secret Agent 007 (Sean Connery) to mysterious Istanbul to grab a top-secret Russian decoding machine. There, he falls for Tatiana Romanova (Daniela Bianchi), a Soviet Embassy clerk who is an unwitting pawn of SPECTRE. Bond is pursued by ruthlessly butch East German agent Rosa Klebb (Lotte Lenya, lots of fun here) who carries a poisonous switchblade in her shoe. He also has to fend off Robert Shaw, sporting a fabulously bogus blond dye job, who plays a psychopathic trained assassin posing as a British agent (Bond spots him as a fraud when he orders red wine with fish). The highlight of the film is a terrific battle to the death on the Orient Express between Connery and Shaw.

Written with enough self-consciously campy humor to defuse the paranoid ideologies running rampant here, FROM RUSSIA WITH LOVE is also acted with tongues held firmly in cheek. Thankfully, the film displays little evidence of the excessive gadgetry that would plague later Bond flicks. One of the best of the Bond films, featuring Matt Monro singing the decidedly unmemorable Lionel Bart-penned title tune.

FRONT PAGE, THE [DVD]
1931 101m bw Drama/Comedy ★★★★½
Caddo (U.S.)

Adolphe Menjou *(Walter Burns)*, Pat O'Brien *(Hildy Johnson)*, Mary Brian *(Peggy)*, Edward Everett Horton *(Bensinger)*, Walter Catlett *(Murphy)*, George E. Stone *(Earl Williams)*, Mae Clarke *(Molly)*, Slim Summerville *(Pincus)*, Matt Moore *(Kruger)*, Frank McHugh *(McCue)*

p, Howard Hughes; d, Lewis Milestone; w, Bartlett Cormack, Ben Hecht (uncredited), Charles Lederer (based on the play by Ben Hecht and Charles MacArthur); ph, Glen MacWilliams, Hal Mohr, Tony Gaudio (uncredited); ed, Duncan Mansfield; art d, Richard Day

AAN Best Picture; AAN Best Actor: Adolphe Menjou; AAN Best Director: Lewis Milestone

A vigorous, manic drama, this Lewis Milestone classic about newspapers and newsmen wonderfully preserves a host of Depression-era attitudes and a glorious headline era.

O'Brien, in his film debut, is the fast-talking Hildy Johnson, sensation-hunting star of the Chicago press. His shifty editor Walter Burns (Menjou) is trying to prevent his star reporter from quitting the business and moving to a New York advertising job with his wife-to-be Peggy (Brian). She hates everything about the sleazy tabloid world that has made Hildy famous, and she pressures him to finish his last day's work so they can flee to New York. In his farewell visit to the press room, however, Hildy gets caught up in the escape of an anarchist (Stone) scheduled for execution.

THE FRONT PAGE is an excellent production with a superior performance from novice O'Brien in a role better than many he later got to play. Menjou is marvelous too as a wily and sophisticated rascal, with a brilliant flair for dialogue. Howard Hughes let Milestone have his creative way with the film, and it shows in the film's no-holds-barred action and witty repartee. Hughes did make two decisions regarding the film, though, vetoing Milestone's first two choices for O'Brien's role: James Cagney and Clark Gable.

All of the character actors shine in the reporter roles, from the cynical Catlett and McHugh to the fussy, hygiene-obsessed Horton, who believes himself to be a poet. The play's lines were kept almost intact, with all the wild newspaper argot, glib quips and slurs delivered rapid-fire by the actors. Remade as HIS GIRL FRIDAY by Howard Hawks.

FRONT PAGE, THE 📀 DVD
1974 105m c Drama/Comedy ★★½
Universal (U.S.) PG

Jack Lemmon (Hildy Johnson), Walter Matthau (Walter Burns), Carol Burnett (Mollie Malloy), Susan Sarandon (Peggy Grant), Vincent Gardenia (Sheriff), David Wayne (Bensinger), Allen Garfield (Kruger), Austin Pendleton (Earl Williams), Charles Durning (Murphy), Herb Edelman (Schwartz)

p, Paul Monash; d, Billy Wilder; w, Billy Wilder, I.A.L. Diamond (based on the play by Ben Hecht and Charles MacArthur); ph, Jordan S. Cronenweth (Panavision, Technicolor); ed, Ralph E. Winters; m, Billy May; art d, Henry Bumstead; cos, Burton Miller

Wanted: a better remake of Lewis Milestone's classic original and Howard Hawks' revamp, HIS GIRL FRIDAY. This slick remake of the ebullient original falls short of being the film it could have been, despite the presence of master filmmaker Wilder and his engaging costars.

Hildy Johnson (Lemmon) is bound for New York with Peggy Grant (Sarandon) to begin a new life, but Walter Burns (Matthau) uses the escape of anarchist Earl Williams (Pendleton) to hold him on the job. Along the way they pointedly ignore the pleas of prostitute Mollie Malloy (Burnett), who is in love with the condemned man. The hide-and-seek game the newsmen play with authorities in covering up the wanted man's whereabouts is forced, but Martin Gabel, as the balmy psychiatrist, gives a hilarious performance. Durning is too vicious for the newsman role he plays, as is Garfield; Hecht and MacArthur drew their characters as jocular, not sadistic, personalities. The posturing, no doubt Wilder's doing, mars the impact of his satirical cynicism. It overpowers the screenplay and even the good performances of the leads.

Despite the obvious charismatic interaction between Lemmon and Matthau, the film is oddly stilted. In an overly emphatic turn, the miscast Burnett easily gives the most awful performance of her career. She projects only one emotion—a gratingly annoying hysteria. One never enjoys the film so much as when her character throws herself out of a window. Wilder was much more effective with Lemmon and Matthau in THE FORTUNE COOKIE and THE ODD COUPLE. This one just doesn't have the big story at press time.

FUGITIVE, THE
1947 104m bw Drama ★★★★
RKO (U.S.)

Henry Fonda (The Fugitive), Dolores Del Rio (Mexican Woman), Pedro Armendariz (Police Lieutenant), Ward Bond (El Gringo), Leo Carrillo (Chief of Police), J. Carrol Naish (Police Spy), Robert Armstrong (Police Sergeant), John Qualen (Doctor), Fortunio Bonanova (Governor's Cousin), Chris-Pin Martin (Organ Player),

p, John Ford, Merian C. Cooper; d, John Ford; w, Dudley Nichols (based on the novel The Labyrinthine Ways and The Power and the Glory by Graham Greene); ph, Gabriel Figueroa; ed, Jack Murray; m, Richard Hageman; art d, Alfred Ybarra; fx, Fred Sersen

One of John Ford's favorite films; he sometimes considered it his masterpiece. It's hardly that, just as its companion piece, THE INFORMER, isn't quite the masterpiece everyone once thought it was. A powerful passion play set in a modern, fictitious south-of-the-border country, THE FUGITIVE is hauntingly photographed by Figueroa and boasts a highly effective performance from Fonda in which an intensely warm and likable saintliness largely replaces a three-dimensional character.

Much of this stems from Ford's influence on Nichols's screenplay, which changed the complex, sinful "whiskey priest" of Greene's original novel into a man whose main fear is that he's not sacrificing enough. The fugitive (Fonda) is hunted by a revolutionary government attempting to eliminate all traces of the Catholic religion. He hides in a small village and, passing as a peasant, performs secret rites for the locals. He even baptizes the bastard child a woman (the impossibly gorgeous Del Rio) has borne to a savage police lieutenant (Armendariz). He also comforts an American criminal on the run (Bond) before escaping to a country without religious persection. An encounter with a half-breed police spy (Naish) and the call to duty, though, lure him back to his hostile native terrain.

As with much of Ford, THE FUGITIVE is often sentimental and very Catholic, blunting Greene's political edge in favor of Ford's preference for lyric poetry. Here Fonda is the true Ford hero: quiet, contemplative, nonviolent and capable of superhuman sacrifice. Naive in some ways and full of portentous, obvious yet admittedly striking symbolism, THE FUGITIVE is nevertheless true to its own convictions.

FUGITIVE, THE 📀 DVD
1993 127m c/bw Action/Thriller/Drama ★★★½
Keith Barish Productions/Arnold Kopelson PG-13
Productions (U.S.)

Harrison Ford (Dr. Richard Kimble), Tommy Lee Jones (Deputy U.S. Marshal Samuel Gerard), Sela Ward (Helen Kimble), Julianne Moore (Dr. Ann Eastman), Joe Pantoliano (Cosmo Renfro), Andreas Katsulas (Sykes—"The One-Armed Man"), Jeroen Krabbe (Dr. Charles Nichols), Daniel Roebuck (Biggs), L. Scott Caldwell (Poole), Tom Wood (Newman)

p, Arnold Kopelson; d, Andrew Davis; w, Jeb Stuart, David Twohy (from a story by Twohy); ph, Michael Chapman; ed, Dennis Virkler, David Finfer, Dean Goodhill, Don Brochu, Richard Nord, Dov Hoenig; m, James Newton Howard; prod d, Dennis Washington; art d, Maher Ahmad, Charles Wood; fx, Roy Arbogast; cos, Aggie Guerard Rodgers

AA Best Supporting Actor: Tommy Lee Jones; AAN Best Picture; AAN Best Cinematography: Michael Chapman; AAN Best Film Editing: Don Brochu, David Finfer, Dean Goodhill, Don Hoenig, Richard Nord, Dennis Virkler; AAN Best Original Score: James Newton Howard; AAN Best Sound: Michael Herbick, Donald O. Mitchell, Frank A. Montano, Scott D. Smith; AAN Best Sound Effects Editing: John Leveque, Bruce Stambler

Lacking the dinos of JURASSIC PARK, the three-dimensional hero of IN THE LINE OF FIRE, or the seductive slickness of RISING SUN, THE FUGITIVE nevertheless emerged as one of the biggest hits of the 1993 summer season, proving Harrison Ford's virtual indestructability at the box office and vindicating the trend of turning TV shows into movies.

Building on the premise of the '60s TV series, THE FUGITIVE opens with Dr. Richard Kimble (Harrison Ford) being convicted of killing his wife, despite his claims that he witnessed a one-armed man commit the murder. A bungled escape attempt by fellow convicts allows Kimble to get away and start a hunt for the real killer, while he himself is doggedly tracked by U.S. Marshal Sam Gerard (Tommy Lee Jones). Though the film tries to grow into a conspiracy thriller involving a corrupt pharmaceutical company, that's one of its weaker points. The story is really just an excuse to put the two men through an ingenious series of chases, in settings ranging from a maze of flood drains to a St. Patrick's Day parade.

The action varies from a show-stopping train/bus wreck of Schwarzeneggerian proportions, to some more ironically staged pursuits which throw a welcome dash of "Tom and Jerry" into the mix. As the not-so-bad bad guy, Tommy Lee Jones gets all the best lines and delivers them superbly. Harrison Ford mostly just runs and fights, but that's O.K. Running, after all, is what fugitives are supposed to do.

FULL METAL JACKET   DVD
1987 116m c   War   ★★★★
Natant   (U.K.)   R

Matthew Modine (Pvt. Joker), Adam Baldwin (Animal Mother), Vincent D'Onofrio (Leonard Lawrence, Pvt. Gomer Pyle), R. Lee Ermey, billed as Lee Ermey (Gunnery Sgt. Hartman), Dorian Harewood (Eightball), Arliss Howard (Pvt. Cowboy), Kevyn Major Howard (Rafterman), Ed O'Ross (Walter J. Schinoski, Lt. Touchdown), Jon Stafford (Doc Jay), John Terry (Lt. Lockhart)

p, Stanley Kubrick; d, Stanley Kubrick; w, Stanley Kubrick, Michael Herr, Gustav Hasford (based on the novel The Short-Timers by Gustav Hasford); ph, Douglas Milsome (Rank Color); ed, Martin Hunter; m, Abigail Mead; prod d, Anton Furst; art d, Rod Stratford, Leslie Tomkins, Keith Pain; fx, John Evans; cos, Keith Denny

AAN Best Adapted Screenplay: Stanley Kubrick, Michael Herr, Gustav Hasford

An uncompromisingly bleak film, as cold and distant as they come, Kubrick's FULL METAL JACKET is a perversely fascinating movie—one that answers no questions, offers no hope and has little meaning. In a way this is perfect for what the film has to say about war, but you find yourself numbed and apathetic as the film progresses. What one is left with is a remarkable display of the resources of cinema and a bludgeoning use of extreme violence which ironically undermines Kubrick's good intentions.

Highly structured, the film is presented in two parts: the first details the training of a group of Marines at the hands of the sadistic, foul-mouthed DI, Gunnery Sergeant Hartman (Ermey); and the second follows one of the recruits, "Joker" (Modine), a reporter for Stars and Stripes who finds himself in combat at the height of the Tet Offensive. There are no characterization and no heroics in FULL METAL JACKET; instead, Kubrick coolly shows the systematic dehumanization required to turn men into killing machines, then sits back and watches as they perform their assigned task.

From the shaving of the recruits' heads, the assignment of generic nicknames, and the profane bellowing that replaces conversation, to the orderly, ritualized existence of camp training is designed to drain all traces of individuality and humanity from soldiers and replace them with a cold hatred that can be directed at the enemy without hesitation. With his sarcastic humor and contradictory nature, Joker is the only character who retains a modicum of personality. Kubrick, however, dangles him before the viewer and then pulls him away slowly until Joker, too, is drained of his humanity.

Technically, FULL METAL JACKET is as flawless as any other meticulously designed Kubrick work and boasts superb cinematography by Milsome. Filming entirely in

England, Kubrick found a military barracks outside London that doubles for Parris Island in the film. He also used a vast, deserted gasworks in London's East End, a plant area that had been bombed to ruination during WWII, and further destroyed the area to great effect.

FULL MONTY, THE   DVD
1997 90m c   Comedy   ★★★★
Redwave Films/Fox Searchlight   (U.K.)   R

Robert Carlyle (Gaz), Tom Wilkinson (Gerald), Mark Addy (Dave), Paul Barber (Horse), Steve Huison (Lomper), Hugo Speer (Guy), Emily Woof (Mandy), Lesley Sharp (Jean), William Snape (Nathan), Deirdre Costello (Linda)

p, Uberto Pasolini; d, Peter Cattaneo; w, Simon Beaufoy; ph, John de Borman; ed, Nick Moore, David Freeman; m, Anne Dudley; prod d, Max Gottlieb; art d, Chris Roope; fx, Ian Rowley; cos, Jill Taylor

AA Best Original Musical or Comedy Score: Anne Dudley; AAN Best Picture; AAN Best Director: Peter Cattaneo; AAN Best Original Screenplay: Simon Beaufoy

A winner of a comedy that uses its absurd premise—a motley crew of six unemployed men make a go of it as strippers—to create a surprisingly heartwarming tale of personal relationships.

Gaz (Robert Carlyle) and Dave (Mark Addy) live in the once-thriving steel town of Sheffield, England, and both are among the town's many unemployed. Gaz will lose the joint-custody of his son if he can't raise 700 pounds quickly, and Dave's only job prospects are security shifts at a convenience store. When the men notice that a traveling group of male strippers have sold out a local club, the wheels begin turning. The men decide to form their own strip troupe, and after recruiting four more equally desperate men, including their former boss (Tom Wilkinson), the rehearsals begin. They're a fairly unsightly bunch—not the sort one would ordinarily pay to see in the buff—but Gaz and his mates are prepared to offer the ladies of Sheffield what the others don't dare: the full monty, i.e. total nudity.

The premise is a terrific source of humor, but THE FULL MONTY has its share of carefully developed emotional themes, as the boys try to win back the respect they feel has been lost along with their jobs while maintaining their dignity under the most inglorious circumstances. The performances are uniformly excellent, with Carlyle leading the way in a role completely different from those he had in TRAINSPOTTING (1996) and RIFF-RAFF (1991), and the soundtrack, which mixes classic '70s disco with traditional stripper music, is right on target.

FULL MOON IN PARIS   DVD
(LES NUITS DE LA PLEINE LUNE)
1984 101m c   Drama   ★★★½
Losange/Ariane   (France)   R

Pascale Ogier (Louise), Fabrice Luchini (Octave), Tcheky Karyo (Remi), Christian Vadim (Bastien), Virginie Thevenet (Camille), Anne-Severine Liotard (Marianne), Laszlo Szabo (Painter at Cafe), Lisa Garneri (Tina, the Babysitter), Mathieu Schiffman (Louise's Decorator Friend), Herve Grandsart (Remi's Friend Bertrand)

p, Margaret Menegoz; d, Eric Rohmer; w, Eric Rohmer; ph, Renato Berta; ed, Cecile Decugis; m, Elli et Jacno; art d, Pascale Ogier; cos, Pascale Ogier

This fourth entry in Eric Rohmer's "Comedies and Proverbs" series begins with the proverb, "He who has two women loses his soul. He who has two houses loses his mind." The remarkably effervescent Pascale Ogier stars as the quintessential

Rohmer woman, loved and admired by the men around her but desperately confused about the meaning of love.

A trainee at an interior-design firm, Louise (Ogier) lives with her architect-tennis player lover, Remi (Karyo), in a plastic suburb outside Paris. He wants to marry and settle down, but Louise is still young and enjoys dancing at parties until dawn. Remi's pressure proves too much for Louise, and she takes an apartment in Paris in order "to experience loneliness." Ostensibly, she will spend her late party nights in Paris, sleep in her new apartment, and return to the suburbs the following afternoon. While in Paris, she spends a great deal of time with Octave (Luchini) a likable writer who's tortured by Louise's refusal to sleep with him. At one fateful party, Louise meets Bastien (Vadim, son of Roger Vadim and Catherine Deneuve) and takes him back to her Paris apartment. Soon, however, she regrets her mistake and reconsiders her affection for Remi. But several things have changed since back when.

What Rohmer has done in this film—and has done so successfully in the past—is to take a brief, intelligent, comic look at a young Frenchwoman and her ideas of love. Ogier (the 24-year-old daughter of actress Bulle Ogier) delivers her lines with animation rarely captured on film, and she knows how to dance on screen as well. Her performance justly earned her a Best Actress award at the Venice Film Festival, but her career was tragically cut short by a fatal heart attack.

FUNERAL, THE · DVD
(OSOSHIKI)
1984 124m c   Comedy   ★★★
Itami/New Century   (Japan)

Nobuko Miyamoto (Chizuko Amamiya), Tsutomu Yamazaki (Wabisuke Inoue), Kin Sugai (Kikue Amamiya), Chishu Ryu (The Priest), Shuji Otaki (Shokichi Amamiya), Ichiro Zaitsu (Satomi), Kiminobu Okumura (Shinkichi Amamiya), Haruna Takaso (Yoshiko Saito)

p, Yasushi Tamaoki, Yutaka Okada; d, Juzo Itami; w, Juzo Itami; ph, Akira Suzuki; ed, Joji Yuasa

The first feature from Juzo Itami (TAMPOPO, A TAXING WOMAN), this is a black comedy that pokes fun at solemn traditional Japanese funeral rites. When a patriarch dies suddenly, his family—including his actress daughter (Nobuko Miyamoto), her actor husband (Tsutomu Yamazaki), and their manager (Ichiro Zaitsu)—comes together for the three-day Buddhist ceremony for the former brothel owner. Many of the scenes that ensue will be familiar to viewers of similarly structured films but the Japanese setting is revelatory to Western eyes. While THE FUNERAL is not as loopy as TAMPOPO, a wildly appetizing comedy about food, it is still very energetic and inventive.

FUNERAL IN BERLIN · DVD
1966 102m c   Spy   ★★★½
Paramount   (U.K.)

Michael Caine (Harry Palmer), Paul Hubschmid (Johnny Vulkan), Oscar Homolka (Col. Stok), Eva Renzi (Samantha Steel), Guy Doleman (Ross), Rachel Gurney (Mrs. Ross), Hugh Burden (Hallam), Thomas Holtzmann (Reinhart), Gunter Meisner (Kreutzmann), Heinz Schubert (Aaron Levine)

p, Harry Saltzman, Charles Kasher; d, Guy Hamilton; w, Evan Jones (based on the novel by Len Deighton); ph, Otto Heller (Panavision, Technicolor); ed, John Bloom; m, Konrad Elfers; prod d, Ken Adam; art d, Peter Murton

Caine, repeating his role from THE IPCRESS FILE, stars as Harry Palmer, the bespectacled British soldier forced to become a counterspy. This time Palmer is sent back to Germany, where his espionage career began, to contact Colonel Stok (Homolka), the Russian head of security for the Berlin Wall. Stok is anxious to defect, and Palmer arranges his escape only to be double-crossed by everyone and his brother. A bit poky, the film isn't quite up to the original, but it's rather better than most sequels of this kind. Featuring a fine cast (Homolka is *always* worth watching), FUNERAL IN BERLIN provides an excellent look at the spy business and an interesting view of postwar Berlin. One more sequel (and the weakest of the three), BILLION DOLLAR BRAIN, followed.

FUNNY BONES · DVD
1994 128m c   Comedy/Drama   ★★★★
Sun Trust Ltd./Hollywood Pictures   (U.K.)   R

Oliver Platt (Tommy Fawkes), Jerry Lewis (George Fawkes), Lee Evans (Jack Parker), Leslie Caron (Katie Parker), Richard Griffiths (Jim Minty), Oliver Reed (Dolly Hopkins), George Carl (Thomas Parker), Freddie Davis (Bruno Parker), Ian McNeice (Stanley Sharkey), Christopher Greet (Lawrence Berger)

p, Simon Fields, Peter Chelsom; d, Peter Chelsom; w, Peter Chelsom, Peter Flannery; ph, Eduardo Serra; ed, Martin Walsh; m, John Altman; prod d, Caroline Hanania; art d, Andrew Munro; fx, Tom Harris; cos, Lindy Hemming

This postmodern tragicomedy is an eccentric, exhilarating film that couldn't find an audience. It's a mesmerizing exploration of the dangerous essence of comedy; at the same time, it's an adventure film about smuggling, a heart-breaker about children and their parents' expectations, a back-handed fable about immortality, and a bracingly hilarious take on the desperation of performance.

Aging Beverly Hills brat Tommy Fawkes (Oliver Platt) is the son of America's undisputed King of Comedy, George Fawkes (Jerry Lewis). Refusing to admit he hasn't inherited his dad's "funny bones," Tommy flies to Blackpool, England, and attempts to purchase bits of physical comedy he can import for an act in the States. Meanwhile, troubled young performer Jack Parker (Lee Evans) is the convenient fall-guy for bent policeman Stanley Sharkey (Ian McNeice). Sharkey needs a patsy for the illegal activities of a group of French adventurers who are selling stolen life-extending power nestled inside golden eggs. Sharkey's scheme, Tommy's ambitions, and numerous other plot threads are gradually woven together in unexpected ways, culminating in a fanciful, spectacular climax.

In FUNNY BONES, reality mirrors theater art in the most deliriously invigorating way since CABARET. Screenwriters Peter Chelsom and Peter Flannery inventively explore what makes some lost souls hilarious while other wannabes toil at comedy like day-laborers. Each Pirandellian element rings true, enhanced by some visual correlative in Chelsom's direction. Every frame is packed with symbolic resonance and the hoariest of show-biz cliches are revitalized—suffice it to say that "I died on stage" takes on new meaning here.

FUNNY FACE · DVD
1957 103m c   Musical   ★★★★½
Paramount   (U.S.)

Audrey Hepburn (Jo Stockton), Fred Astaire (Dick Avery), Kay Thompson (Maggie Prescott), Michel Auclair (Prof. Emile Flostre), Robert Flemyng (Paul Duval), Dovima (Marion), Virginia Gibson (Babs), Suzy Parker, Sunny Harnett, Don Powell

p, Roger Edens; d, Stanley Donen; w, Leonard Gershe (based on "Wedding Day," an unproduced musical libretto by Gershe); ph, Ray June (VistaVision, Technicolor); ed, Frank Bracht; m, George Gershwin, Ira Gershwin, Roger Edens, Leonard Gershe; art d,

George W. Davis, Hal Pereira; fx, John P. Fulton; chor, Fred Astaire, Eugene Loring; cos, Edith Head, Givenchy

AAN Best Original Story and Screenplay: Leonard Gershe; *AAN Best Cinematography:* Ray June; *AAN Best Art Direction-Set Decoration:* Hal Pereira (Art Direction), George W Davis (Art Direction), Sam Comer (Set Decoration), Ray Moyer (Set Decoration); *AAN Best Costume Design:* Edith Head, Hubert DeGivenchy

A film crucial to understanding Hepburn's glorious gamine appeal and one of Astaire's best musicals of the 1950s. A satire of both the fashion world and the fashionable pretensions of beatnik life and existentialism, FUNNY FACE concerns the May-December romance between Greenwich Village bookseller Jo Stockton (Hepburn) and Madison Avenue fashion photographer Dick Avery (Astaire). Dick discovers the sweet, young Jo and plays Henry Higgins to her Eliza, turning her into a top model in Paris.

That's all that need be said about the story, since this film exists only for its glamorous visuals, gorgeous Gershwin music, and the dancing choreographed by Astaire and Eugene Loring. Thompson, in a fabulous turn as a fashion editor, commands her underlings to "Think Pink" and the screen bursts with pink furniture, pink toothpaste and pink pets. "Bonjour Paris" is a whirlwind tour of the city, and "He Loves and She Loves" is a soft-focus fairy tale romance. Hepburn, who does remarkably well singing "How Long Has This Been Going On?" in her own voice, is exquisitely appealing and the byplay between her and the mellow, supple Astaire is enchanting.

As a dancer, Hepburn manages quite well in a satiric cafe number with two fellow mods, but shows her limitations in a climactic duet with Astaire set in the woods. (Maybe she had trouble with her heels in all that grass.) Astaire, meanwhile, displays his uncanny way with a song and enjoys one angular solo dance with his raincoat and umbrella. Real-life model superstars Suzy Parker and Dovima appear, but the most unforgettable fashion moment features Hepburn at her most "Givenchy" descending a flight of stairs in a stunning red gown. Beautifully helmed by Donen.

FUNNY GIRL   DVD
1968 151m c   Musical/Biography   ★★★★
Rastar   (U.S.)   G

Barbra Streisand *(Fanny Brice)*, Omar Sharif *(Nick Arnstein)*, Kay Medford *(Rose Brice)*, Anne Francis *(Georgia James)*, Walter Pidgeon *(Florenz Ziegfeld)*, Lee Allen *(Eddie Ryan)*, Mae Questel *(Mrs. Strakosh)*, Gerald Mohr *(Branca)*, Frank Faylen *(Keeney)*, Mittie Lawrence *(Emma)*

p, Ray Stark; d, William Wyler; w, Isobel Lennart (based on the musical by Jule Styne, Bob Merrill, Lennart); ph, Harry Stradling (Panavision, Technicolor); ed, Maury Winetrobe, William Sands; prod d, Gene Callahan; art d, Robert Luthardt; chor, Herbert Ross; cos, Irene Sharaff

AAN Best Picture; AA Best Actress: Barbra Streisand; *AAN Best Supporting Actress:* Kay Medford; *AAN Best Cinematography:* Harry Stradling; *AAN Best Film Editing:* Robert Swink, Maury Winetrobe, William Sands; *AAN Best Score (Musical):* Walter Scharf; *AAN Best Original Song:* "Funny Girl"; Jule Styne (Music), Bob Merrill (Lyrics); *AAN Best Sound:* Columbia Studio Sound Department

Few film debuts in the 1960s were more auspicious than that of Barbra Streisand in FUNNY GIRL. Already a legit and recording star, she shot to superstardom and nabbed an Academy Award for best actress in the bargain. William Wyler's musical debut is less assured than one would have liked, but no matter: La Babs had played musical-comedy star Fanny Brice on Broadway and had the role down pat by the time director Wyler brought the story to the screen.

In the early 1900s in New York City, young Fanny, an ugly duckling with an unstoppable ambition to be a star, is determined to get out of the Lower East Side. Her big break comes when she's spotted by handsome gambler Nicky Arnstein (Sharif), who helps her catch the eye of Florenz Ziegfeld (Pidgeon). Ziegfeld hires her for his new Follies presentation, where her subversive comic style proves extraordinarily popular; soon she is one of the Follies' biggest stars. The remainder of the picture—which, despite its real-life subject, tells a formulaic story—recounts her steady rise to national celebrity and her tumultuous marriage to Arnstein.

The oddly cast Sharif is better than usual, but Streisand, of course, is most of the show, belting out songs, pulling heartstrings, alternating between raucous slapstick and dramatic power, and generally demonstrating that she has *arrived* in a big way. The memorable Broadway score was augmented for the screen with several tunes from Brice's life, including her signature, "My Man."

FUNNY THING HAPPENED ON THE WAY   DVD
TO THE FORUM, A
1966 99m   c   Comedy   ★★★
UA   (U.S.)

Zero Mostel *(Pseudolus)*, Phil Silvers *(Lycus)*, Jack Gilford *(Hysterium)*, Buster Keaton *(Erronius)*, Michael Crawford *(Hero)*, Michael Hordern *(Senex)*, Annette Andre *(Philia)*, Patricia Jessel *(Domina)*, Leon Greene *(Miles Gloriosus)*, Inga Neilsen *(Gymnasia)*

p, Melvin Frank; d, Richard Lester; w, Melvin Frank, Michael Pertwee (based on the book by Burt Shevelove, Larry Gelbart); ph, Nicolas Roeg (DeLuxe Color); ed, John Victor Smith; prod d, Tony Walton; fx, Cliff Richardson; chor, Ethel Martin, George Martin; cos, Tony Walton

AA Best Adapted Score: Ken Thorne

Typical hit-and-miss filmmaking by the relentlessly antsy Richard Lester, but lots of fun all the same. Based on the smash Broadway musical, the film toplines Mostel as a Roman slave desperately trying to win his freedom and Gilford as his unwitting accomplice. Plot complications involve Silvers as a brothel owner, Andre and Crawford as young lovers, and Keaton searching for his lost children. Lester's direction is full of the flashy technique which worked better in his Beatles movies. Sometimes he would have done better to just let some of the farcical set-pieces alone. His sense of timing is sometimes off, and laughs are lost as a result. The songs are quite delightful, but somehow the production numbers don't quite fly as they should and just end up bogging down the story. To his credit, however, Lester does add a certain energy and spirit to many scenes, and some great comic moments result. Also, the overall performances make this film well worth watching—Gilford in particular is a gem. FUNNY THING now seems one of the more enjoyable of the many overcooked musical adaptations Hollywood was desperately cranking out during the 1960s.

FURY   DVD
1936 90m   bw   Crime   ★★★★½
MGM   (U.S.)

Spencer Tracy *(Joe Wheeler)*, Sylvia Sidney *(Katherine Grant)*, Walter Abel *(District Attorney)*, Edward Ellis *(Sheriff)*, Walter Brennan *(Buggs Meyers)*, Bruce Cabot *(Bubbles Dawson)*, George Walcott *(Tom)*, Frank Albertson *(Charlie)*, Arthur Stone *(Durkin)*, Morgan Wallace *(Fred Garrett)*

p, Joseph L. Mankiewicz; d, Fritz Lang; w, Bartlett Cormack, Fritz Lang (based on the story "Mob Rule" by Norman Krasna); ph,

Joseph Ruttenberg; ed, Frank Sullivan; m, Franz Waxman; art d, Cedric Gibbons, William A. Horning, Edwin B. Willis; cos, Dolly Tree

AAN Best Original Story: Norman Krasna

An uncharacteristically trenchant indictment of mob rule for the usually family-oriented MGM. Despite studio interference, Fritz Lang, in his first Hollywood outing, succeeded in making a penetrating study of injustice and inhumanity with Spencer Tracy delivering a memorable performance as an innocent man who's wrongly accused of a sensational crime and transformed into a malevolent force of vengeance.

Spencer Tracy is Joe Wheeler, a honest guy trying to earn enough money to get married to his devoted fiancee, Katherine Grant (Sylvia Sidney). While driving to meet up with Katherine, Joe gets picked up by the cops. Arrested as a suspected kidnaper, he is imprisoned in a small-town jail pending trial. He is damned by circumstantial evidence and rampant rumours. A mob gathers and heads for the jail. The sheriff gets nervous and calls the governor begging him to put the National Guard on alert as he does not have enough guards to withstand a full-scale assault on his small jail. However, the governor's advisers steer him away from the potentially controversial situation. Meanwhile, back at the jail, things quickly get out of hand.

Lang brings striking expressionist touches to the social problem picture with expressive shadowplay and stylized subjective fantasy sequences. This was his favorite American film and rightfully so, for it demonstrates his directorial genius in wasting not a frame of film, telling his story with sharp cross-cutting between victim and tormentors, while unraveling the mindless and murderous passion of a mob out of control.

F/X
1986 107m c Thriller DVD ★★★
Orion (U.S.) R

Bryan Brown (*Rollie Tyler*), Brian Dennehy (*Leo McCarthy*), Diane Venora (*Ellen*), Cliff De Young (*Lipton*), Mason Adams (*Col. Mason*), Jerry Orbach (*Nicholas DeFranco*), Joe Grifasi (*Mickey*), Martha Gehman (*Andy*), Roscoe Orman (*Capt. Wallenger*), Trey Wilson (*Lt. Murdoch*)

p, Dodi Fayed, Jack Wiener; d, Robert Mandel; w, Robert T. Megginson, Gregory Fleeman; ph, Miroslav Ondricek (Technicolor); ed, Terry Rawlings; m, Bill Conti; prod d, Mel Bourne; art d, Speed Hopkins; fx, Carl Fullerton, John Stears; cos, Julie Weiss

Rollie Tyler (Brown) is an ace New York-based special-effects man who specializes in doing the gore effects for horror films. Between pictures he is approached by government agent Lipton (De Young) from the Justice Department's Witness Protection Program. Lipton wants to hire Brown to fake the assassination of Mafia kingpin Nicholas DeFranco (Orbach), who is about to testify against members of his gang. If the gang thinks DeFranco is dead, it will make it easier for the Justice Department to protect him from potential mob "hits" until he has the chance to squeal in court. Although apprehensive, Rollie takes the challenge and concocts an elaborate plan for "assassinating" the mobster. Unfortunately, soon after the deed is done, Rollie realizes that the whole thing was a set-up, and now his employers want him dead.

This is a slick little thriller that benefits greatly from its clever use of special effects. Australian actor Bryan Brown is fine as the effects man who finds himself embroiled in an often-confusing plot, and Brian Dennehy lends his usual solid support as the New York cop trying to make sense of it all. Director Robert Mandel has a nice flair for light comedy and never hesitates to go for a laugh when the absurdities of the script call for it. The action sequences are well staged and the twists and turns of the convoluted plot will keep viewers guessing. A competent and unpretentious entertainment.

G

G-MEN
1935 85m bw Crime ★★★★
Warner Bros. (U.S.)

James Cagney (*James "Brick" Davis*), Ann Dvorak (*Jean Morgan*), Margaret Lindsay (*Kay McCord*), Robert Armstrong (*Jeff McCord*), Barton MacLane (*Brad Collins*), Lloyd Nolan (*Hugh Farrell*), William Harrigan (*McKay*), Edward Pawley (*Danny Leggett*), Russell Hopton (*Gerard*), Noel Madison (*Durfee*)

p, Louis F. Edelman; d, William Keighley; w, Seton I. Miller (based on the novel *Public Enemy No. 1* by Gregory Rogers); ph, Sol Polito; ed, Jack Killifer; art d, John Hughes; chor, Bobby Connolly; cos, Orry-Kelly

Turnabout Cagney film: he changed his film image from ruthless gangster to fearless FBI man, but the truth is his G-Man is as reckless, violent and prone to impulse as any of his hoods.

William Harrigan is a bigshot gangster who generously puts Cagney through law school. When Regis Toomey, Cagney's pal, becomes an FBI man and is gunned down without a chance—agents at the time not being legally able to bear arms—Cagney joins the FBI to seek revenge.

Keighley was not one of Cagney's favorites; Cagney thought the director affected because he spoke French to the cast and crew, he and his wife having recently learned the language in nonstop lessons. Lindsay also bothered the down-to-earth Cagney. To get her first role (in CAVALCADE), Lindsay, who came from Dubuque, Iowa, had fibbed to producers, saying she was British since British accents were sought after as being easily understood in the early sound era. She continued to affect a slightly British accent with broad A's even in G-MEN, which annoyed Cagney.

J. Edgar Hoover made G-MEN a pet project and loaned several real agents to appear in the film, ostensibly to lend credibility to the production but really to make sure that the Bureau's story was told the way Hoover wanted it told. Actually, it was standard Warner pulp, ripped from the tabloid page and briskly told. So durable was this film that Warner Bros. re-released G-MEN many times for box-office bonanzas. In the 1949 go-around, the studio added a prologue to the film with David Brian as the chief and Douglas Kennedy as an agent. Brian is teaching a class of recruits and introduces the film to them by saying: "You are about to see the granddaddy of them all!"

GALAXY QUEST
1999 102m c Science Fiction/Comedy DVD ★★★½
Mark Johnson Productions/Dreamworks SKG PG
(U.S.)

Tim Allen (*Jason Nesmith/Commander Peter Quincy Taggart*), Sigourney Weaver (*Gwen DeMarco*), Alan Rickman (*Alexander Dane*), Tony Shalhoub (*Fred Kwan*), Sam Rockwell (*Guy Fleegman*), Daryl Mitchell (*Tommy Webber*), Enrico Colantoni (*Mathesar*), Robin Sachs (*Sarris*), Patrick Breen (*Quellek*), Missi Pyle (*Laliari*)

p, Mark Johnson, Charles Newirth; d, Dean Parisot; w, Robert Gordon (from a story by David Howard and Robert Gordon); ph, Jerzy Zielinski; ed, Don Zimmerman; m, David Newman; prod d, Linda DeScenna; art d, Jim Nezda; fx, Stefan Fangmeier, Industrial Light & Magic, Mark Freund, Bill George, Light

Matters/Pixel Envy, Stan Winston Studio, Matt Sweeny, CIS Hollywood; cos, Albert Wolsky; anim, Christopher Armstrong

The show was cancelled 18 years ago, but the crew of the NSEA Protector is still in uniform, touring the convention circuit and pandering to fans who can recite every word of cringe-inducing dialogue they ever spoke. Sound familiar? You don't have to be a Trekkie to have a good time at this affectionate spoof of fandom and the enduring appeal of cheesy TV, but it helps.

Jason Nesmith (Tim Allen), who played pompous Captain Peter Quincy Taggart on "Galaxy Quest," is an even bigger jerk offscreen; fans love him, but his fellow cast members would love to see him take a long walk off a short convention stage. Gwen DeMarco (Sigourney Weaver) was communications officer Tawny Madison, who existed solely to fill out her form-fitting space suit. Alexander Dane (Alan Rickman) once wowed theater-goers in *Richard III*, but achieved dubious immortality as Galaxy Quest's token alien, Dr. Lazarus. Having nicely skewered the convention scene, the movie kicks in with its central conceit: an especially odd group of costumed fans turn out to be bona fide aliens, Termians from the Klatu Nebula who've patterned their entire culture on "Galaxy Quest" reruns. Now they're under attack by vicious alien warmonger Sarris (Robin Sachs) and are convinced that only "Taggart" and his crew can save them.

Screenwriters David Howard and Robert Gordon have a blast pitting the fake space cowboys against everything from cutie-pie aliens with vicious fangs to a machine composed of pounding pistons whose only apparent purpose is to imperil Nesmith and DeMarco. And Sam Rockwell has a fine time as goofball Guy Fleegman, who worries about the implications of his "Galaxy Quest" experience, which consisted of getting killed before the first commercial.

GALLIPOLI

1981   110m   c   War   **DVD**
Paramount   (Australia)   ★★★★   PG

Mark Lee *(Archy)*, Bill Kerr *(Jack)*, Mel Gibson *(Frank Dunne)*, Ronnie Graham *(Wallace Hamilton)*, Harold Hopkins *(Les McCann)*, Charles Yunupingu *(Zac)*, Heath Harris *(Stockman)*, Gerda Nicolson *(Rose Hamilton)*, Robert Grubb *(Billy)*, Tim McKenzie *(Barney)*

p, Robert Stigwood, Patricia Lovell; d, Peter Weir; w, David Williamson (based on a story by Weir); ph, Russell Boyd (Panavision, Eastmancolor); ed, William Anderson; m, Brian May; prod d, Wendy Weir; art d, Herbert Pinter

Focusing on two fleet-footed young Australians, Peter Weir's extraordinarily moving antiwar film examines the disastrous WWI invasion of Gallipoli by the Australian-New Zealand Army Corps.

Archy (Mark Lee) and Frank (Mel Gibson) come from different backgrounds, but they share a love of king, country and life—never more apparent than when the two sprinters race each other. Together, they join the army and become part of the ill-fated campaign to wrest control of the Dardanelles from the Ottoman Turks. Meeting heavy resistance from the well-entrenched Turks and their German allies, the ANZAC offensive bogs down on the beachhead. Poor generalship and worse communication eventually lead to a suicidal assault and a tremendous waste of young lives.

Director Weir (PICNIC AT HANGING ROCK, THE YEAR OF LIVING DANGEROUSLY) and cinematographer Russell Boyd's re-creation of the invasion and battle action is stunning, but what makes GALLIPOLI such an affecting film is its intimate presentation of the friendship between Archy and Frank (wonderfully essayed by Lee and Gibson). Weir uses the first part of the film to establish the vibrant optimism of their lives down under, then he demonstrates how quickly and pointlessly such young lives can be snuffed out.

Not always easy to watch, GALLIPOLI is both a fitting testimony to the courage of the thousands of Australians and New Zealanders who died fighting for their country and one of the most powerful cinematic examinations of the futility and tragic cost of war.

GANDHI

1982   188m   c   Biography   **DVD**
Intl. Film Investors/Goldcrest/Indo-British Films/   ★★★
Natl. Film Development   (U.K./India)   PG

Ben Kingsley *(Mahatma Gandhi)*, Candice Bergen *(Margaret Bourke-White)*, Edward Fox *(Gen. Dyer)*, John Gielgud *(Lord Irwin)*, Trevor Howard *(Judge Broomfield)*, John Mills *(The Viceroy)*, Martin Sheen *(Walker)*, Rohini Hattangady *(Kasturba Gandhi)*, Ian Charleson *(Charlie Andrews)*, Athol Fugard *(Gen. Smuts)*

p, Richard Attenborough; d, Richard Attenborough; w, John Briley; ph, Billy Williams, Ronnie Taylor (Technicolor); ed, John Bloom; m, Ravi Shankar, George Fenton; prod d, Stuart Craig; art d, Robert Laing, Ram Yedekar, Norman Dorme; fx, David Hathaway; cos, John Mollo, Bhanu Athaiya

AA Best Picture; AA Best Actor: Ben Kingsley; *AA Best Director:* Richard Attenborough; *AA Best Original Screenplay:* John Briley; *AA Best Cinematography:* Billy Williams, Ronnie Taylor; *AA Best Film Editing:* John Bloom; *AAN Best Original Score:* Ravi Shankar, George Fenton; *AA Best Art Direction-Set Decoration:* Stuart Craig, Bob Laing, Michael Seirton; *AA Best Costume Design:* John Mollo, Bhanu Athaiya; *AAN Best Sound:* Gerry Humphreys, Robin O'Donoughue, Jonathan Bates, Simon Kaye; *AAN Best Makeup:* Tom Smith

Despite an intelligent title performance by Ben Kingsley and impressive cinematography in the manner of David Lean, this huge, clunky biopic offers less than meets the eye. Director Attenborough seeks not to understand but to canonize his subject; as a result, both Gandhi's teachings and the complexities of Indian political history are distorted and trivialized. The film spans decades, opening in South Africa where Mohandas Gandhi (Kingsley) is a struggling attorney victimized by that country's racial policies. Returning to India, he develops a strategy of non-violent civil disobedience that proves more effective than armed struggle in throwing off British imperial rule. The film is at its best in its several melodramatic, large-scale "epic" sequences (Salt March, post-Partition riots, assassination), but Gandhi remains a saintly cipher; other major figures are even more carelessly drawn; e.g., Nehru, who appears as a colorless Gandhi disciple (he was anything but), and Pakistan founder Jinnah, who comes off as a Muslim Darth Vader. African playwright Athol Fugard (*Master Harold and the Boys*) appears as General Smuts; Candice Bergen is fun in a cameo as American photographer Margaret Bourke-White.

GANG'S ALL HERE, THE

1943   103m   c   Musical   **DVD**
Fox   (U.S.)   ★★★

Alice Faye *(Eadie Allen)*, Carmen Miranda *(Dorita)*, Phil Baker *(Himself)*, Benny Goodman and His Orchestra *(Themselves)*, Eugene Pallette *(Mr. Mason, Sr.)*, Charlotte Greenwood *(Mrs. Peyton Potter)*, Edward Everett Horton *(Peyton Potter)*, Tony DeMarco *(Himself)*, James Ellison *(Andy Mason)*, Sheila Ryan *(Vivian)*

p, William LeBaron; d, Busby Berkeley; w, Walter Bullock (from a story by Nancy Winter, George Root, Jr., and Tom Bridges); ph, Edward Cronjager (Technicolor); ed, Ray Curtiss; art d, James Basevi, Joseph C. Wright; fx, Fred Sersen; chor, Busby Berkeley; cos, Yvonne Wood

AAN Best Interior Decoration (Color): James Basevi (Art Direction), Joseph C Wright (Art Direction), Thomas Little (Interior Decoration)

A camp classic. If you consider Berkeley a genius, this is the highpoint of his career. It's his first in color, and filtering his kaleidoscope cuties through the garish mixmaster of 1940's Fox Technicolor is like a male hairdresser's acid trip: chorines dissolve into artichokes; Carmen Miranda arrives in an overloaded fruit wagon, more animated than any character at Disney, and cha-chas down a boulevard of strawberries. Alice Faye, in her big-budget musical swan song, swoons some sanity into the proceedings with "No Love, No Nothing" and "Journey to a Star," but she's overwhelmed introducing the "Polka-Dot Polka" ballet, a description of which wouldn't do full justice to it anyway. By the time Berkeley's chorus girls wave huge phallic bananas in rhythmic waves, you'll swear you're lost in a giant fruit cocktail. The film enhanced the stardom of Miranda but because of those *big* bananas, THE GANG'S ALL HERE was never released in her native Brazil.

GANGS OF NEW YORK   DVD
2002 165m c   Crime/Historical   ★★½
Initial Entertainment Group/Miramax   (U.S.)   R

Leonardo DiCaprio *(Amsterdam Vallon),* Daniel Day-Lewis *(Bill "The Butcher" Cutting),* Cameron Diaz *(Jenny Everdeane),* Jim Broadbent *(William "Boss" Tweed),* Liam Neeson *(Priest Vallon),* John C. Reilly *(Happy Jack),* Henry Thomas *(Johnny Sirocco),* Brendan Gleeson *(Monk McGinn),* Roger Ashton-Griffiths *(P.T. Barnum),* Gary Lewis *(Charles McGloin)*

p, Alberto Grimaldi, Harvey Weinstein; d, Martin Scorsese; w, Jay Cocks, Steve Zaillian, Kenneth Lonergan (from a story by Jay Cocks, suggested by the book *Gangs of New York* by Herbert Asbury); ph, Michael Ballhaus; ed, Thelma Schoonmaker; m, Howard Shore; prod d, Dante Ferretti; art d, Stefano Ortolani; fx, Industrial Light & Magic, Michael Owens, Bruce Steinheimer; cos, Sandy Powell

AAN Best Picture; AAN Best Actor: Daniel Day-Lewis; *AAN Best Director:* Martin Scorsese; *AAN Best Art Direction:* Dante Ferretti (Art Direction), Francesca Lo Schiavo (Set Decoration); *AAN Best Cinematography:* Michael Ballhaus; *AAN Best Costume Design:* Sandy Powell; *AAN Best Film Editing:* Thelma Schoonmaker; *AAN Best Original Song:* "The Hands that Built America"; Bono, The Edge, Adam Clayton, Larry Mullen (music and lyrics); *AAN Best Sound:* Tom Fleischman, Eugene Gearty, Ivan Sharrock; *AAN Best Original Screenplay:* Jay Cocks, Steve Zaillian, Kenneth Lonergan

Epic, meticulously researched, and ultimately disappointing, Martin Scorsese's bloody valentine to the birth of his beloved city is less than the sum of its parts.

1846, Lower Manhattan: New immigrants flock to the notorious Five Points slum and wind up crowded into pestilent, lawless tenements. Colorfully named gangs—the Plug Uglies, the Bowery B'hoys, the Daybreak Boys—fight for control of the area's thriving criminal enterprises. The bloodiest battles pit the American-born Nativists, who despise the recent immigrants and take their orders from Bill "The Butcher" Cutting (Daniel Day-Lewis), against the predominantly Irish Dead Rabbits, led by Priest Vallon (Liam Neeson). The two tribes eventually go to war with knives, clubs, and fists, fighting for the right to call themselves Americans, and Vallon is killed by Bill the Butcher. Vallon's small son, Amsterdam, is handed off to a distant church school and emerges 16 years later a hard and embittered young man (Leonardo DiCaprio) with one ambition: to avenge his father's death.

Scorsese began thinking about a film inspired by Herbert Asbury's *Gangs of New York,* an anecdotal account of 19th-century street crime, in the 1970s. But his mental energies appear to have been devoted entirely to the colorful and volatile period, leaving frequent collaborator Jay Cocks to devise a for-

mulaic story and painfully clichèd characters. Day-Lewis alone manages to rise above the script: His Bill the Butcher is brassy, vivid, and thoroughly convincing. DiCaprio, however, plays his role rather than inhabits it, and Cameron Diaz, who stars as a whore with, yes, a heart of gold, can't begin to make her character anything but a plot device.

GANJA AND HESS   DVD
1973 110m c   Horror   ★★★★½
Kelly/Jordan (U.S.)   R

Duane Jones *(Dr. Hess Green),* Marlene Clark *(Ganja),* Bill Gunn *(George),* Sam Waymon *(Rev. Williams),* Leonard Jackson *(Archie),* Candece Tarpley *(Girl in Bar),* Richard Harrow *(Dinner Guest),* John Hoffmeister *(Jack),* Betty Barney *(Singer),* Mabel King *(Queen of Myrthia)*

p, Chiz Schultz; d, Bill Gunn; w, Bill Gunn; ph, James E. Hinton; ed, Victor Kanefsky; m, Sam Waymon; prod d, Tom H. John; cos, Scott Barrie

One of the best black-oriented movies to come out of Hollywood in the 1970s, GANJA AND HESS stars the late Duane Jones (NIGHT OF THE LIVING DEAD) as a New York anthropologist embroiled in a study of the lost ancient African culture of Myrthia, a nation that died out from a communicable parasite that fed on human blood. During his research, Jones is stabbed with a jewel-encrusted Myrthian dagger by his crazed assistant (played by director Bill Gunn) and finds that he has become infected with the virus, turning him into a vampirelike creature addicted to blood. He fancies himself an invincible African god and turns his wife, Clark, into a vampire as well.

This is a fascinating picture, managing both to subvert its commercial horror angle and to explore the contrasts between Western and African cultures—the former represented as repressive and puritanical, the latter as more virile and liberating. The late Gunn, who was also an accomplished novelist, playwright and painter, imbues the film with a cultural richness little seen in black-targeted films. Impressionistic, vibrant, and rhythmic (the original soundtrack used both American spirituals and African traditional music), GANJA AND HESS is a memorable and haunting film.

Tragically, it was recut by its distributors for theatrical release. Most of the thematic lushness wound up on the floor, but the most heinous change was the removal of the African soundtrack in favor of bland American soul music.

GARDEN OF THE FINZI-CONTINIS, THE   DVD
(IL GIARDINO DEL FINZI-CONTINI)
1971 103m c   War/Drama   ★★★★
Documento/CCC   (Italy/West Germany)   R

Dominique Sanda *(Micol),* Lino Capolicchio *(Giorgio),* Helmut Berger *(Alberto),* Fabio Testi *(Malnate),* Romolo Valli *(Giorgio's Father),* Raffaele Curi *(Ernesto),* Camillo Angelini-Rota *(Micol's Father),* Katina Viglietti *(Micol's Mother),* Ina Alexeiff *(Micol's Grandmother),* Barbara Pilavin

p, Arthur Cohn, Gianni Hecht Lucari; d, Vittorio De Sica; w, Cesare Zavattini, Vittorio Bonicelli, Ugo Pirro (based on the novel by Giorgio Bassani); ph, Ennio Guarnieri (Eastmancolor); ed, Adriana Novelli; m, Manuel De Sica; art d, Giancarlo Bartolini Salimbeni; cos, Antonio Randaccio

AA Best Foreign Language Film ; AAN Best Adapted Screenplay: Ugo Pirro, Vittorio Bonicelli

Lyrical and melancholy, and a surprising contrast to much of De Sica's earlier work. Although the director spent a good part of the latter half of his career acting in other director's works (Roberto Rossellini's GENERAL DELLA ROVERE, for example), THE GARDEN OF THE FINZI-CONTINIS is proof he had not lost his touch.

Set in Ferrara, Italy, during WWII, this story of love and culture unfolds effortlessly, albeit a trifle slowly. The Finzi-Continis are an aristocratic Jewish-Italian family who cannot believe that the war will ever invade their hallowed garden walls. Rather than flee, they stay on in the false hope that they will not be betrayed, but they eventually come to realize that Fascism is not going to go away and that they must join the fight against it. THE GARDEN OF THE FINZI-CONTINIS is one of the few films in which flashbacks are absolutely necessary; they provide the historical perspective the characters lack.

This film bears very little resemblance to De Sica's early work. Like all previously state-funded filmmakers, he suddenly needed to concern himself with his films' commercial potential. But the movie is still directed with the familiar De Sica skill. His handling of the unknowns in the cast is exceptional, as is his direction of the wonderful Dominique Sanda.

GARDEN STATE

2004 118m c Comedy/Drama ★★★

Camelot Pictures/Jersey Films/
Double Feature Films/Miramax (U.S.) R

Zach Braff (Andrew "Large" Largeman), Natalie Portman (Sam), Peter Sarsgaard (Mark), Ian Holm (Dr. Gideon Largeman), Armando Riesco (Jesse), Ron Leibman (Doctor Cohen), Jean Smart (Carol), Method Man (Diego), Denis O'Hare (Albert), Debbon Ayer (Faye)

p, Pamela Abdy, Gary Gilbert, Dan Halsted, Richard Klubeck; d, Zach Braff; w, Zach Braff; ph, Lawrence Sher; ed, Myron Kerstein; m, Chad Fischer; prod d, Judy Becker; art d, Laura Ballinger; fx, Josh Hakian, Drew Jiritano; cos, Michael Wilkinson

Zach Braff's writing-directing debut may be a bit affected, but few actors with behind-the-camera aspirations succeed as well as the "Scrubs" star does with this melancholy romantic comedy.

Ever since he caused the accident that paralyzed his mother—he was only nine at the time—Andrew "Large" Largeman (Braff) has been living life in a mild pharmaceutical haze, numbed by the regimen of antidepressants prescribed by his psychiatrist father (Ian Holm). Now 26 and a struggling actor in L.A., Large returns home when he gets the bad news that his paraplegic mother has drowned in her own bathtub. Now Large must not only contend with relatives he hasn't seen in almost a decade, but also high-school friends like Mark (Peter Sarsgaard), a gravedigger who never put the bong down long enough to move out of his mother's house. Without consulting his father, Large decides to leave his meds in L.A.; not the wisest move, perhaps, but if ever there was a time to put things back into clear perspective, this is it. The sharp headaches he starts experiencing send him to the waiting room of Dr. Cohen (Ron Leibman), where he meets charming oddball Sam (Natalie Portman). Captivated, Large offers Sam a ride home on his grandfather's WWII-era motorbike and embarks on a dizzying emotional odyssey.

It's just the kind of story a young writer hoping to reflect the confusion of his generation would come up with, but a number of Braff's scenes are surprisingly well written. Portman is particularly adorable—relieved of those ridiculous STAR WARS headdresses, she delivers easily her richest performance to date—and Sarsgaard, in a total change of pace from SHATTERED GLASS and BOYS DON'T CRY, continues to impress with his unusually broad range.

GARDENS OF STONE

1987 111m c Drama/War ★★★

Tri-Star/ML Delphi Premier (U.S.) R

James Caan (Sgt. Clell Hazard), Anjelica Huston (Samantha Davis), James Earl Jones (Sgt. Maj. "Goody" Nelson), D.B. Sweeney (Pvt. Jackie Willow), Dean Stockwell (Capt. Homer Thomas), Mary Stuart Masterson (Rachel Feld), Lonette McKee (Betty Rae), Sam Bottoms (Lt. Webber), Elias Koteas (Pete Deveber), Laurence Fishburne, billed as Larry Fishburne (Cpl. Flanagan)

p, Michael I. Levy, Francis Ford Coppola; d, Francis Ford Coppola; w, Ronald Bass (based on the novel by Nicholas Proffitt); ph, Jordan Cronenweth (Deluxe Color); ed, Barry Malkin; m, Carmine Coppola; prod d, Dean Tavoularis; art d, Alex Tavoularis; fx, John Frazier, Robin Hauser; cos, Willa Kim, Judianna Makovsky

After more than a decade of films that examined the war in Vietnam from many different angles, Francis Ford Coppola concentrated not on the heroics, battles or camaraderie of war, but simply on the burial of the dead. From the vantage point of Arlington National Cemetery, with its somber landscape of white crosses, war appears most senseless.

Sergeant Clell Hazard (James Caan) is a military man through and through, a hard-bitten veteran who, in 1968, hates the Vietnam War but loves the service. His job is to oversee the men assigned to the Old Guard at Arlington, that elite corps of soldiers who stand watch over the Tomb of the Unknown Soldier, escort the many bodies to their final resting places, and engage in various drill exercises as a public relations function for the government. Assigned to Hazard's unit is Private Jackie Willow (D.B. Sweeney), the son of a veteran who had been Hazard's pal. A gung-ho soldier, Jackie wants desperately to get into battle. Jackie grows close to a number of people at Arlington, including surrogate father Hazard; Hazard's girlfriend, Samantha (Anjelica Huston); and Rachel (Mary Stuart Masterson), the young woman with whom he falls in love. Nevertheless, Jackie's fatal desire is to serve his country in Vietnam.

Unjustly underrated upon its release, GARDENS OF STONE is a quiet, respectful film filled with emotional power, exceptional acting (especially by Caan), and technical virtuosity. Coppola was directing from the heart on this one: his son Giancarlo died in a boating accident during production. The film is dedicated to the Third U.S. Infantry.

GAS FOOD LODGING

1992 100m c Drama ★★★★

Cineville Partners II/Seth Willenson Inc. (U.S.) R

Brooke Adams (Nora), Ione Skye (Trudi), Fairuza Balk (Shade), James Brolin (John Evans), Robert Knepper (Dank), David Landsbury (Hamlet), Jacob Vargas (Javier), Donovan Leitch (Darius), Chris Mulkey (Raymond), Laurie O'Brien (Thelma)

p, Daniel Hassid, William Ewart, Seth M. Willenson; d, Allison Anders; w, Allison Anders (from the novel Don't Look and It Won't Hurt by Richard Peck); ph, Dean Lent; ed, Tracy S. Granger; m, J. Mascis; prod d, Jane Ann Stewart; art d, Lisa Denker, Carla Weber; cos, Susan Bertram

Bleak and beautiful, GAS FOOD LODGING is a richly evocative look at lives in waiting.

Nora (Brooke Adams) is a divorced truck stop waitress in Laramie, New Mexico, the kind of place people barely notice unless they need to fill up one way or the other. Her older daughter, the beautiful Trudi (Ione Skye), is bored and rebellious, fast becoming the town tramp; her younger daughter, Shade (Fairuza Balk), is immersed in the fantasy world of Mexican exploitation movies. During the course of the film, all three women find various degrees of emotional satisfaction,

Trudi with the offbeat Dank (Robert Knepper), an English geologist; Shade with a Mexican neighbor, Javier (Jacob Vargas); and Nora with the man who comes to install their satellite dish.

Based on Richard Peck's *Don't Look and It Won't Hurt*, GAS FOOD LODGING is a film about women—and, to a lesser degree, men—whose lives are so circumscribed that every dust mote and heat ripple over the blacktop is charged with significance. Nora, Trudi, and Shade each react to the painful emptiness of their world differently, but are united by their single-minded determination to force meaning into their lives. Through these three women, Anders examines racism, economic oppression and the numbing effect of the infinite highway—America's favorite "boy" metaphor for existence—on the lives of those who wait by the roadside.

Anders has a fine eye for detail: a near-empty movie theater, cave walls turned by ultraviolet light into a shimmering fantasy of glowing colors, a box of buttons and other worthless treasures carefully hidden beneath a bed. She has also coaxed fine performances from Adams, Skye and, especially, Balk (RETURN TO OZ, VALMONT), who miraculously delineates the prickly world of the awkwardly bright adolescent without ever becoming cloying.

GASLIGHT

1940 88m   bw   Thriller   ★★★★★
BNP   (U.K.)

Anton Walbrook *(Paul Mallen)*, Diana Wynyard *(Bella Mallen)*, Frank Pettingell *(Rough)*, Cathleen Cordell *(Nancy)*, Robert Newton *(Vincent Ullswater)*, Jimmy Hanley *(Cobb)*, Minnie Rayner *(Elizabeth)*, Mary Hinton *(Lady Winterbourne)*, Marie Wright *(Alice Barlow)*, Jack Barty *(Chairman)*

p, John Corfield; d, Thorold Dickinson; w, A.R. Rawlinson, Bridget Boland (based on the play by Patrick Hamilton); ph, Bernard Knowles; ed, Sidney Cole; m, Richard Addinsell

A lost black pearl, better than Mayer's sugar-coated 1944 version. This British psychological thriller is truly a forgotten masterpiece due to the machinations of MGM's Louis B. Mayer.

In one of her finest roles, Wynyard is a wealthy patrician lady who marries the urbane but calculating Walbrook. They move into an 1880 mansion, her ancestral London home, where Cordell is the ever-present brazen maid. Before long, Wynard notices the gaslight in her rooms flickers downward nightly and comes to believe that this is a hallucination. Meanwhile, through clever, subtle measures, Walbrook slowly drives her to the brink of insanity, convincing her that she is losing her memory. Pettingell, a kindly and perceptive Scotland Yard detective, meets Wynyard socially and begins paying attention to her and Walbrook—too much attention from the latter's point of view.

Columbia purchased the rights to the film in 1941, intending an American remake with Irene Dunne in the lead. Then MGM bought the property for Hedy Lamarr who unwisely turned it down. When the Ingrid Bergman-Charles Boyer production was shot in 1944, Mayer ordered his minions to track down all the prints of the original GASLIGHT and destroy them, so it would never compete with his lavish production. Fortunately, prints survived. It's one of the most stylish British films to be made before WWII and one of director Dickinson's most polished works, each scene carefully set up as the tension mounts brilliantly, frame by frame. Walbrook is magnificent as the arch villain, his extravagant Middle-European acting style bordering on the flamboyant, his dark charm shrouding his evil purposes.

GASLIGHT

1944 114m   bw   Thriller   ★★★★
MGM   (U.S.)

Charles Boyer *(Gregory Anton)*, Ingrid Bergman *(Paula Alquist)*, Joseph Cotten *(Brian Cameron)*, Dame May Whitty *(Miss Thwaites)*, Angela Lansbury *(Nancy Oliver)*, Barbara Everest *(Elizabeth Tompkins)*, Eustace Wyatt *(Budge)*, Emil Rameau *(Mario Gordi)*, Edmund Breon *(Gen. Huddleston)*, Halliwell Hobbes *(Mr. Mufflin)*

p, Arthur Hornblow Jr.; d, George Cukor; w, John Van Druten, Walter Reisch, John Balderston (based on the play "Angel Street" by Patrick Hamilton); ph, Joseph Ruttenberg; ed, Ralph E. Winters; m, Bronislau Kaper; art d, Cedric Gibbons, William Ferrari; fx, Warren Newcombe

AAN Best Picture; AAN Best Actor: Charles Boyer; AA Best Actress: Ingrid Bergman; AAN Best Supporting Actress: Angela Lansbury; AAN Best Screenplay: John L. Balderston, Walter Reisch, John Van Druten; AAN Best B/W Cinematography: Joseph Ruttenberg; AA Best Interior Decoration (B/W): Cedric Gibbons, William Ferrari, Edwin B. Willis, Paul Huldschinsky

Lusher, ornate version of *Angel Street*, without the telling chill of the 1940 Diana Wynward GASLIGHT, but satisfactorily directed all the same. Bergman is deeply sympathetic as the wealthy socialite married to Boyer, who turns into an insidious monster in his attempt to drive his ravishing wife mad. But the lengthy Italian honeymoon starts the picture on too sunny a disposition, and Bergman's victim does look as healthy as a horse. Boyer nearly steals the picture, aided and abetted by the stunning debut of Angela Lansbury as a hardbitten servant—only 18, she grabbed the role and chewed it to bits. The climax is a workmanlike rise of psychological terror, but the whole exercise looks self-consciously careful.

GATE OF HELL
(JIGOKUMON)
1953 86m   c   Historical/Drama/War   ★★★
Daiei   (Japan)

Machiko Kyo *(Lady Kesa)*, Kazuo Hasegawa *(Moritoh Endo)*, Isao Yamagata *(Wataru Watanabe)*, Koreya Senda *(Kiyomori)*, Yataro Kurokawa *(Shigemori)*, Kikue Mohri *(Sawa)*, Kotaro Bando *(Rokuroh)*, Jun Tazaki *(Kogenta)*, Tatsuya Ishiguro *(Yachuta)*, Kenjiro Uemura *(Masanaka)*

p, Masaichi Nagata; d, Teinosuke Kinugasa; w, Teinosuke Kinugasa (based on the play by Kan Kikuchi); ph, Kohei Sugiyama (Eastmancolor); m, Yasushi Akutagawa; art d, Kisaku Itoh; cos, Sanzo Wada

AA Best Costume Design (Color): Sanzo Wada

Japan's first film to utilize a Western color process (Eastmancolor), went on to huge acclaim, winning the Grand Prize at Cannes and two Academy Awards including best foreign picture. It's a visually rich movie, but in retrospect rather slight in the canon of Japanese filmmaking.

When a rival clan launches a revolt against the Taira in 12th Century Japan, Lady-in-waiting Kesa (Machiko Kyo) agrees to act as a decoy so the nobles can escape. Escorting Kesa's carriage, samurai Oritoh Endo (Kazuo Hasegawa) battles his way through the enemy, only to discover his brother has joined the rebel forces. Rushing to inform his Lord of the uprising, Moritoh joins the loyalist forces in quashing the revolt. Offered whatever he wants as reward, Moritoh chooses to have Kesa made his wife. But Kesa is already married, to Wataru Watanabe, a cultured official in the guards.

Undeterred, Moritoh pursues her, besting her husband in a horserace and then challenging him to a duel.

GATE OF HELL, adapted from a stage play, is curiously structured, beginning with a burst of action and getting slower (and slower) as it progresses, until the actors are barely moving by the end. The actual meat of the tale is an old-fashioned melodrama, down to the bad guy kicking a dog. Which is not to say it's uninteresting—the dichotomy of "back country samurai" Moritoh refusing to back down from his request and disrupting the more genteel officials, attempting to "take a heart by force," is a strong narrative hook. And the rich colors, the eye-catching sets and costumes lend it an exotic, fairytale ambiance. GATE OF HELL was seen in Japan as just another fairly mundane period drama—a hugely popular genre at the time. In fact, the tumultuous appreciation overseas was actually taken as an affront by Japanese critics who had virtually ignored the film on release.

GAY DIVORCEE, THE

1934　107m　bw　Musical/Comedy　★★★★
RKO　(U.S.)

Fred Astaire *(Guy Holden)*, Ginger Rogers *(Mimi Glossop)*, Alice Brady *(Hortense Ditherwell)*, Edward Everett Horton *(Egbert Fitzgerald)*, Erik Rhodes *(Rodolfo Tonetti)*, Eric Blore *(Waiter)*, Lillian Miles *(Hotel Guest)*, Charles Coleman *(Valet)*, William Austin *(Cyril Glossop)*, Betty Grable *(Hotel Guest)*

p, Pandro S. Berman; d, Mark Sandrich; w, George Marion Jr., Dorothy Yost, Edward Kaufman (based on the musical play "The Gay Divorce" by Dwight Taylor and Cole Porter); ph, David Abel; ed, William Hamilton; m, Kenneth Webb, Samuel Hoffenstein; art d, Van Nest Polglase, Carroll Clark; fx, Vernon L. Walker; chor, Fred Astaire, Hermes Pan (uncredited); cos, Walter Plunkett

AAN Best Picture; AAN Best Score: RKO Radio Studio Music Department, Max Steiner (Dept. Head); *AA Best Song:* "The Continental"; Con Conrad (Music), Herb Magidson (Lyrics); *AAN Best Interior Decoration:* Van Nest Polglase, Carroll Clark; *AAN Best Sound Recording:* Carl Dreher

One of the best examples of Depression-era musicals. After a brief twirl together in FLYING DOWN TO RIO, Fred Astaire and Ginger Rogers hooked up again, and so captivated filmgoers that this costarring vehicle would be only the first of many for cinema's most famous dance team.

Modern gal Mimi Glossop (Rogers) wants a divorce, but to get it she must venture to an English seaside resort where her lawyer (Horton) has arranged for her to be witnessed having an assignation with a professional correspondent, thus providing the necessary grounds for her divorce—infidelity. Matters become confused, however, when Mimi mistakes Guy Holden (Astaire), an American dancer who has taken a serious interest in her, for the correspondent and treats him disdainfully. Several songs and cases of mistaken identity later, Guy and Mimi end up in each other's arms for good.

Although in hindsight it seems incredible, the producers of THE GAY DIVORCEE weren't certain that Astaire and Rogers could carry the movie on their own, so they "insured" the success of the film by including several of the best second bananas around—Horton and Eric Blore among them. As a result the film is loaded with laughs and energetic performances. Moreover, its sets are superb, Max Steiner's orchestrations are a marvel, and the choreography by Dave Gould is excellent. If Astaire and Rogers had never danced a lick after the frustrated seduction of "Night and Day," they still would have been screen immortals.

GENERAL DELLA ROVERE

(IL GENERALE DELLA ROVERE)
1959　130m　bw　War/Drama　★★★★
Zebra/SNE Gaumont　(Italy/France)

Vittorio De Sica *(Victorio Emanuele Bardone/Grimaldi)*, Hannes Messemer *(Col. Mueller)*, Vittorio Caprioli *(Banchelli)*, Guiseppe Rossetti *(Pietro Valeri)*, Ivo Garrani *(Fabrizio)*, Sandra Milo *(Valeira)*, Giovanna Ralli *(Olga)*, Anne Vernon *(Chiara Fassio)*, Baronessa Barzani *(Contessa della Rovere)*, Kurt Polter *(German Officer)*

p, Moris Ergas; d, Roberto Rossellini; w, Roberto Rossellini, Sergio Amidei, Diego Fabbri, Indro Montanelli (based on a story by Montanelli); ph, Carlo Carlini; ed, Anna Maria Montanari, Cesare Cavagna; m, Renzo Rossellini; art d, Piero Zuffi

AAN Best Original Story and Screenplay: Sergio Amidei, Diego Fabbri, Indro Montanelli

GENERAL DELLA ROVERE was the film that returned director Roberto Rossellini to international favor after he ended his filmmaking collaboration with Ingrid Bergman and explored documentary filmmaking with INDIA. Although Rossellini, who took on this film as a survival project, looked upon GENERAL DELLA ROVERE with shame, it is one of his great achievements, the story of a man who discovers his own morality by imitating another's.

Revolving around this essentially Christian theme, the film is set during the German occupation of Genoa during the winter of 1943-44. After Resistance leader Gen. della Rovere is accidentally murdered by Gestapo troops, the local Nazi commandant "persuades" Bardone (Vittorio De Sica), an amoral, low-life swindler, to impersonate the general. In this guise, Bardone is sent to the Milan jail, where he is supposed to find and identify a partisan leader whom della Rovere had planned to meet before his death. Bardone, however, gradually begins to identify with his fellow prisoners and assumes the moral stance, if not the full being, of the Resistance leader.

Recalling OPEN CITY and PAISAN, Rossellini's great early achievements, GENERAL DELLA ROVERE is a powerful, beautifully acted picture, which—and this is the source of Rossellini's discontent with the work—retreads the ideas and forms of his past successes. While it may have been a step backwards in the development of this great filmmaker, this cannot diminish the film's undeniable strength.

GENERAL, THE

1998　129m　bw　Crime/Biography　★★★½
Merlin Films/J&M Entertainment　(Ireland/U.K.)　R

Brendan Gleeson *(Martin Cahill)*, Adrian Dunbar *(Noel Curley)*, Sean McGinley *(Gary)*, Maria Doyle Kennedy *(Frances)*, Angeline Ball *(Tina)*, Jon Voight *(Inspector Ned Kenny)*, Eanna McLiam *(Jimmy)*, Tom Murphy *(Wille Byrne)*, Paul Hickey *(Anthony)*, Eamonn Owens *(Young Martin Cahill)*

p, John Boorman; d, John Boorman; w, John Boorman; ph, Seamus Deasy; ed, Ron Davis; m, Richie Buckley; prod d, Derek Wallace; fx, Team FX; cos, Maeve Paterson

A fine return to form for writer-director John Boorman, this is a playful, somewhat fictionalized account of the life and times of Irish gang-boss Martin Cahill. Cahill, nicknamed "The General" by the press and his fellow Dubliners, became one of Ireland's most notorious criminals of the 1980s, thanks to a string of audacious robberies that netted him a reported $60 million and ultimately bought him a bullet from an IRA gunman.

Boorman begins with Cahill's violent end and then, through a brilliant use of reverse motion photography, flashes back to scenes of Cahill as a boy (Eamonn Owens), coming of age and learning his criminal trade amid the squalor of post-WWII Dublin. In and out of correctional schools and, eventually, jail, Cahill (Brendan Gleeson) becomes the leader of a notorious gang of thieves and something of a local hero. Defined by his "us against them" view of the world and contempt for any form of authority—above all the police—Cahill pulls off a series of daring, high-profile capers with his gang while constantly foiling his lifelong nemesis, Police Inspector Ned Kenny (Jon Voight, complete with perfectly respectable brogue).

Cahill is a fascinating mixture of brutality, criminal genius, and eccentric charm—it's not every man who'd first nail a friend's hands to a pool table, then drive him to the hospital—but Boorman's determination to present his character as a boyishly innocent, latter-day Robin Hood flattens what could have been an intriguingly ambivalent portrait. That said, Boorman's original script is razor sharp and very funny, and Gleeson's portrayal is nothing short of brilliant: he's been accurately described as Ireland's answer to Gerard Depardieu. The film has little of the visual dazzle often associated with Boorman's movies (EXORCIST II, EXCALIBUR), but the somber, black-and-white cinematography helps even out the often larger-than-life tone.

GENEVIEVE

1953 86m c Comedy ★★★★½
Sirius (U.K.)

John Gregson (Alan McKim), Dinah Sheridan (Wendy McKim), Kenneth More (Ambrose Claverhouse), Kay Kendall (Rosalind Peters), Geoffrey Keen (1st Speed Cop), Harold Siddons (2nd Speed Cop), Reginald Beckwith (J.C. Callahan), Arthur Wontner (Elderly Gentleman), Joyce Grenfell (Hotel Proprietress), Leslie Mitchell (Himself)

p, Henry Cornelius; d, Henry Cornelius; w, William Rose; ph, Christopher Challis (Technicolor); ed, Clive Donner; m, Larry Adler; chor, Eric Rogers

AAN Best Story and Screenplay: William Rose; AAN Best Score (Drama or Comedy): Muir Mathieson

As smooth as custard. A wonderful British comedy about two couples, classic-car enthusiasts, who participate in the annual London-to-Brighton rally. The title comes from the 1904 roadster owned by Alan and Wendy McKim (John Gregson and Dinah Sheridan), who, on the return trip, challenge their friends Ambrose (Kenneth More) and Rosalind (Kay Kendall) to a friendly race. Their playfulness becomes increasingly intense as they speed to the Westminster Bridge finish line.

The screenplay is marvelous, the film is full of the fresh air of the English countryside, the color is appealing and the famous harmonica score by Larry Adler is perfect. The four leads are wonderful in the roles that clinched stardom for them all. From Kay Kendall's trumpet solo to Kenneth More's ongoing battle with his girlfriend's dog, each one has at least a few priceless bits of character business. That old stalwart Arthur Wontner has a lovely, touching bit at the finale, and the whole film is so good it makes you regret that Henry Cornelius didn't make more films than he did.

GENTLE CREATURE, A

(UNE FEMME DOUCE)
1969 88m c Drama ★★★★
Parc/Marianne (France)

Dominique Sanda (She), Guy Frangin (He), Jane Lobre (Anna)

p, Mag Bodard; d, Robert Bresson; w, Robert Bresson (based on the novella A Gentle Creature by Feodor Dostoyevsky); ph, Ghislain Cloquet (Eastmancolor); ed, Raymond Lamy; m, Jean Wiener; art d, Pierre Charbonnier

A hauntingly simple film about a young wife (Sanda) who commits suicide, leaving no explanation for her obsessively

dominant husband (Frangin). Shattered, he recounts their first meeting—she's a free spirit who visits his pawnshop. They marry, but the woman must adapt her life style to his, being subjected to his accusations and jealousies. She toys with murdering him, pointing a gun at his head, but lacks the ability to pull the trigger. When she falls ill, the man finally realizes his love for her. He takes a positive outlook on the marriage and plans for a future together, only to have her shut the door on his hopes. Bresson's first film in color, and only his ninth in 26 years, A GENTLE CREATURE marked the film debut of former model Sanda, who would the same year be seen in Bertolucci's THE CONFORMIST.

GENTLEMAN JIM

1942 104m bw Sports ★★★★
Warner Bros./First National (U.S.)

Errol Flynn (James J. Corbett), Alexis Smith (Victoria Ware), Jack Carson (Walter Lowrie), Alan Hale (Pat Corbett), John Loder (Carlton DeWitt), William Frawley (Billy Delaney), Minor Watson (Buck Ware), Ward Bond (John L. Sullivan), Madeleine LeBeau (Anna Held), Rhys Williams (Harry Watson)

p, Robert Buckner; d, Raoul Walsh; w, Vincent Lawrence, Horace McCoy (based on the autobiography The Roar of the Crowd by James J. Corbett); ph, Sid Hickox; ed, Jack Killifer; m, Heinz Roemheld; art d, Ted Smith; cos, Milo Anderson

One of the best sports biopics ever. Historically inaccurate, but a directorial field day for director Raoul Walsh, who excelled at action direction and also period nostalgia. Errol Flynn's colorful temperament, capricious moods, and daring nature were perfect for the role of James J. Corbett, the brash Irish bank clerk from San Francisco who went on to defeat John L. Sullivan (nicely essayed by Ward Bond) for the heavyweight championship of the world in New Orleans in 1892. As Gentleman Jim's reputation grows, so does his ego, but in the fine scene wherein Sullivan presents Corbett with the championship belt, Corbett displays a heretofore unseen humility that finally wins the heart of the patrician woman he loves (Alexis Smith). The bout in which Corbett matches his "scientific" boxing techniques against the toe-to-toe slugging of Sullivan is particularly winning but Walsh is firmly in control throughout.

GENTLEMAN'S AGREEMENT

1947 118m bw Drama ★★★★
Fox (U.S.)

Gregory Peck (Phil Green), Dorothy McGuire (Kathy), John Garfield (Dave), Celeste Holm (Anne), Anne Revere (Mrs. Green), June Havoc (Miss Wales), Albert Dekker (John Minify), Jane Wyatt (Jane), Dean Stockwell (Tommy), Sam Jaffe (Prof. Lieberman)

p, Darryl F. Zanuck; d, Elia Kazan; w, Moss Hart (based on the novel by Laura Z. Hobson); ph, Arthur Miller; ed, Harmon Jones; m, Alfred Newman; art d, Lyle Wheeler, Mark-Lee Kirk

AA Best Picture; AAN Best Actor: Gregory Peck; AAN Best Actress: Dorothy McGuire; AA Best Supporting Actress: Celeste Holm; AAN Best Supporting Actress: Anne Revere; AA Best Director: Elia Kazan; AAN Best Screenplay: Moss Hart; AAN Best Film Editing: Harmon Jones

Today, it looks like a heart on a sleeve, but GENTLEMAN'S AGREEMENT is a landmark film—Hollywood's first major attack on anti-Semitism.

Peck, in a convincing portrayal, is a magazine writer who decides to write a series of exposes on anti-Semitism. After failing to achieve an in-depth grasp of the problem, he pretends to be Jewish in order to experience the hostility of bigots first-hand. AGREEMENT surprised audiences of 1947, and it was a heroic endeavor personally sponsored by producer Zanuck (who, ironically, was one of the few Hollywood moguls who was not Jewish; in fact his 20th Century Fox was known, in filmdom's argot, as "the goyim studio").

Garfield initially debated accepting such a small part, but on David Niven's advice, he took the role; his powerful performance shows the commitment he obviously developed during production. Despite the excellence of Peck and Garfield, though, today the finest work seems that of Holm and, in perhaps the film's most difficult part, McGuire. Shot mostly on location in New York, GENTLEMAN'S AGREEMENT remains a classic crusading film.

GENTLEMEN PREFER BLONDES *DVD*
1953 91m   c   Musical   ★★★★
Fox   (U.S.)

Jane Russell (*Dorothy*), Marilyn Monroe (*Lorelei*), Charles Coburn (*Sir Francis Beekman*), Elliott Reid (*Malone*), Tommy Noonan (*Gus Esmond*), George "Foghorn" Winslow (*Henry Spofford III*), Marcel Dalio (*Magistrate*), Taylor Holmes (*Gus Esmond, Sr.*), Norma Varden (*Lady Beekman*), Howard Wendell (*Watson*)

p, Sol C. Siegel; d, Howard Hawks; w, Charles Lederer (based on the play by Anita Loos, Joseph Fields); ph, Harry Wild (Technicolor); ed, Hugh S. Fowler; art d, Lyle Wheeler, Joseph C. Wright; fx, Ray Kellogg; chor, Jack Cole; cos, Travilla

Garish good fun. The film version of Anita Loos's Broadway musical has scrapped the 1920s plot and most of the songs. If the plot of vacationing showgirls—one out for money, the other for love—sometimes lags in director Hawks's hands, it's compensated by a genuine sentiment and sweetness, the ironic and witty use of sex-symbol stereotypes, and the reduction of males to foils for the affectionate wisecracks traded by the femme leads. Both Jane Russell and Marilyn Monroe act with the confidence of whales; it's the last time in Monroe's career you feel sure watching her work. In a way Russell steals BLONDES. She's certainly more at home in gaudy territory, and her Dorothy is loving and supervisory of Monroe's Lorelei at the same time. Certainly, BLONDES proves Russell's knockout instinct for deadpan sarcasm, rare among pin-up girls. BLONDES exploits her whole sex-symbol-as-earth-mom persona more than any of her films. An inferior sequel, GENTLEMEN MARRY BRUNETTES followed in 1955.

GEORGIA
1995 117m   c   Drama/Musical   ★★★½
Georgia Film Corporation/CiBy 2000/Miramax
(U.S./France)   R

Jennifer Jason Leigh (*Sadie*), Mare Winningham (*Georgia*), Ted Levine (*Jake*), Max Perlich (*Axel*), John Doe (*Bobby*), John C. Reilly (*Herman*), Jimmy Witherspoon (*Trucker*), Jason Carter (*Chasman*), Tom Bower (*Erwin Flood*), Smokey Hormel (*Leland*)

p, Ulu Grosbard, Barbara Turner, Jennifer Jason Leigh; d, Ulu Grosbard; w, Barbara Turner; ph, Jan Kiesser; ed, Elizabeth Kling; prod d, Lester Cohen; fx, Don Dumas; cos, Carol Oditz

AAN Best Supporting Actress: Mare Winningham

Harrowing and heartfelt, with knockout performances by a pair of fine actresses.

It's about two siblings, both singers. Sadie (Jennifer Jason Leigh) is hugely ambitious, wildly self-destructive, and all but unknown outside of small-time punk clubs. Georgia (Mare Winningham) is stable and successful, an accomplished folk artist with a husband and two beautiful children. Is Sadie a legend in her own mind, too deluded to see that her talents don't measure up to her aspirations? Is Georgia a hypocritical hausfrau blessed with talent she's too smug to share? This rare study of the relationship between two sisters (scripted by

Leigh's mother, Barbara Turner) doesn't offer any easy answers. It's keenly observed, judiciously balanced, and deftly helmed by Ulu Grosbard (TRUE CONFESSIONS, STRAIGHT TIME).

Although Sadie is the film's main character, Grosbard claims he called his film GEORGIA because Sadie longs to be like her sister. But does she? We're never quite sure whether Sadie is just selfish and irresponsible by nature, or whether her sister's apparently effortless success drove Sadie to drink and drugs. At one point Georgia implies that Sadie was always like this, and if that's the case it's amazing Georgia has put up with her for so long. The film's most affecting scene—which is also the scene many viewers find intolerable—is Leigh's startling, painful and brave eight-minute rendition of Van Morrison's "Take Me Back," a song whose longing for the past is made sharper by Leigh's alternately angry and sad delivery. It appears to have been done in one bravura take, and it says more about Sadie than the rest of the film.

GEORGY GIRL *DVD*
1966 100m   bw   Comedy/Drama   ★★★★
Everglades   (U.K.)

James Mason (*James Leamington*), Alan Bates (*Jos*), Lynn Redgrave (*Georgy*), Charlotte Rampling (*Meredith*), Bill Owen (*Ted*), Clare Kelly (*Doris*), Rachel Kempson (*Ellen*), Denise Coffey (*Peg*), Dorothy Alison (*Health Visitor*), Peggy Thorpe-Bates (*Hospital Sister*)

p, Otto Plaschkes, Robert A. Goldston; d, Silvio Narizzano; w, Margaret Forster, Peter Nichols (based on the novel by Forster); ph, Ken Higgins; ed, John Bloom; m, Alexander Faris; art d, Tony Woollard; chor, Marjory Sigley; cos, Mary Quant

AAN Best Actress: Lynn Redgrave; *AAN Best Supporting Actor:* James Mason; *AAN Best B/W Cinematography:* Ken Higgins; *AAN Best Song:* "Georgy Girl"; Tom Springfield (Music), Jim Dale (Lyrics)

A heart-tugger. Redgrave is Georgy, a chubby virgin in her early 20s suffering from a lack of self-esteem. Her parents are servants employed by Mason, a well-to-do married man who never sired any children. Through the years Mason has treated Redgrave like a daughter, but as she grows older his affection changes, and he eventually asks her to become his mistress. Rampling, Redgrave's sensual but patronizing roommate, announces she's pregnant by her new lover, Bates. Redgrave and Bates meet and fall in love, which spurs Rampling to declare she's going to give up the child for adoption. Redgrave will not hear of this and becomes the baby's surrogate mother. By picture's end, Redgrave is impaled on the horns of a dilemma: should she marry Bates, should she just keep the baby, or should she marry the conveniently widowed Mason and keep the baby?

Mason is wonderful as the older man, harried by a nagging, sickly wife. Redgrave shot to stardom in this role, and rightly so. She shows her range as she grows from a self-conscious, uncertain waif to a woman with responsibilities. A charming movie that aided the careers of all concerned, GEORGY GIRL was also helped by the Oscar-nominated title song, which became a hit for the Seekers on two continents.

GET CARTER *DVD*
1971 111m   c   Crime   ★★★½
MGM   (U.K.)   R

Michael Caine (*Jack Carter*), Ian Hendry (*Eric Paice*), Britt Ekland (*Anna Fletcher*), John Osborne (*Cyril Kinnear*), Tony Beckley (*Peter*), George Sewell (*Con McCarty*), Geraldine Moffatt (*Glenda*), Dorothy White (*Margaret*), Rosemarie Dunham (*Edna the Landlady*), Petra Markham (*Doreen Carter*) p, Michael Klinger; d, Mike Hodges; w, Mike Hodges (based on the novel *Jack's Return Home* by Ted Lewis); ph, Wolfgang Suschitzky (Metrocolor); ed, John Trumper; m, Roy Budd; prod d, Assheton Gorton; art d, Roger King; fx, Jack Wallis; cos, Vangie Harrison

Lean slice of well-crafted slime, and an impressive debut from director Mike Hodges who'd impressed British television viewers with his earlier work for the BBC.

Jack Carter (Michael Caine) is a smalltime hood from London who arrives in Newcastle to arrange his brother's funeral. While preparing for the burial, he becomes obsessed with learning who murdered his sibling and why. Seeking out his brother's friends and acquaintances, Carter tries to question them, but finds a wall of stony silence. Operating on a hunch, he follows a pennyante hood (Ian Hendry) to local crime lord Cyril Kinnear's (John Osborne) home and is surprised to find himself more than welcome. Before he leaves, Carter is warned to return to London before he causes any trouble. He ignores the warning, and soon attempts are made on his life. After a narrow escape, he is rescued by Kinnear's girlfriend Glenda (Geraldine Moffat) and she takes him to her place. The pair make love, and, afterwards, while Glenda is out of the room, Carter discovers a porno film starring, among others, his brother's young daughter.

Grim, violent, and stylishly directed, GET CARTER is an interesting film that brings some freshness to British crime cinema. Director Hodges immediately establishes his debt to the works of Raymond Chandler and Dashiell Hammett by showing Carter reading Chandler's *Farewell My Lovely* on the train to Newcastle. While Caine would like to think of himself as one of Chandler's or Hammett's lonely avengers, he is really nothing more than a vicious brute with a warped sense of honor, trapped between the past and the present.

This theme is beautifully illustrated by the milieu of the film. Newcastle is a city in transition: the urban tenements are in the process of being displaced by cold, efficient high-rise structures that symbolize the increasingly businesslike crime world that has no place for violent mavericks like Carter.

GET ON THE BUS   *DVD*
1996 122m c   Drama   ★★★
40 Acres and a Mule Filmworks   (U.S.)   R

Richard Belzer *(Rick)*, De'Aundre Bonds, billed as DeAundre Bonds *(Junior)*, Andre Braugher *(Flip)*, Thomas Jefferson Byrd *(Evan Thomas, Sr.)*, Gabriel Casseus *(Jamal)*, Albert Hall *(Craig)*, Hill Harper *(Xavier)*, Harry Lennix *(Randall)*, Roger Guenveur Smith *(Gary)*, Isaiah Washington *(Kyle)*

p, Reuben Cannon, Bill Borden, Barry Rosenbush; d, Spike Lee; w, Reggie Rock Bythewood; ph, Elliot Davis; ed, Leander T. Sales; m, Terence Blanchard; prod d, Ina Mayhew; cos, Sandra Hernandez

A small-scale, low-budget commemoration of 1995's Million Man March in Washington, D.C., GET ON THE BUS is a thumbnail encapsulation of the issues that informed the march.

George (Charles S. Dutton) has arranged for a bus to take passengers from L.A. to Washington, D.C., for the Million Man March, called by Nation of Islam leader Minister Louis Farrakhan. The 15 black male riders include Flip (Andre Braugher), an aspiring actor; Gary (Roger Guenveur Smith), the son of a murdered black cop and a white woman; Jamal (Gabriel Casseus), a gangbanger turned Muslim; Xavier (Hill Harper), a film student videotaping the ride; Randall (Harry Lennix) and Kyle (Isaiah Washington), a gay couple; Evan Thomas (Thomas Jefferson Byrd) and his son, Junior (DeAundre Bonds), who are chained together by a court order; and Jeremiah (Ossie Davis), the group elder, a laid-off factory worker. En route, the men discuss family relationships, the treatment of women, economic troubles, and racial identity.

Director Spike Lee turns in his most focused and compelling film yet, thanks to a handful of well-etched characters, a concise script by Reggie Rock Bythewood, and a strong cast. Although its characters tend to sheechify and launch into personal discussions of issues, the film remains a joyous, moving, and highly cinematic celebration of black male camaraderie at a time when such images are rare in mainstream films. If there is a flaw, it lies in the narrow scope of black viewpoints presented and the script's insistence on political correctness. Explicitly crediting Farrakhan as the catalyst behind the historic march, GET ON THE BUS does stop short of endorsing the controversial figure. Unfortunately, it pays only lip service to a criticism of Farrakhan's oft-cited anti-Semitism.

GET OUT YOUR HANDKERCHIEFS   *DVD*
(PREPAREZ VOS MOUCHOIRS)
1978 108m c   Comedy   ★★★½
Ariane/C.A.P.A.C./Belga/SODEP   R
(France/Belgium)

Gerard Depardieu *(Raoul)*, Patrick Dewaere *(Stephane)*, Carole Laure *(Solange)*, Riton *(Christian Beloeil)*, Michel Serrault *(Neighbor)*, Eleonore Hirt *(Mrs. Beloeil)*, Sylvie Joly *(Passerby)*, Jean Rougerie *(Mr. Beloeil)*, Liliane Rovere, Michel Beaune

p, Paul Claudon; d, Bertrand Blier; w, Bertrand Blier; ph, Jean Penzer (Eastmancolor); ed, Claudine Merlin; m, Georges Delerue, Wolfgang Amadeus Mozart, Franz Schubert; art d, Eric Moulard; cos, Michele Cerf

AA Best Foreign Language Film

A more civilized, less offensive version of GOING PLACES, Blier's earlier film, GET OUT YOUR HANDKERCHIEFS again pairs Depardieu and Dewaere, as childlike men who are completely emasculated by the mysterious woman in their lives.

Frustrated by his inability to make his wife (Laure) happy, Depardieu asks a complete stranger (Dewaere) to give it a try. All Laure seems to do is knit sweaters with a completely expressionless face. Dewaere is equally impotent, however, and succeeds only in establishing a close friendship with Depardieu. It takes a third "man"—Riton, a 13-year-old genius the threesome meets at the boys' summer camp that Dewaere runs—to fulfill the unhappy woman. Laure, who has been unable to have a child with Depardieu or Dewaere, finally finds someone to love and care for, even though he is only 13.

Besides Blier's sharp direction and screenplay, the film is memorable for the performances of Depardieu and Dewaere. These two superb actors seem so in tune with one another that one must judge their performance as a synthesized whole.

GET SHORTY   *DVD*
1995 105m c   Comedy/Crime   ★★★
Jersey Films/MGM   (U.S.)   R

John Travolta *(Chili Palmer)*, Gene Hackman *(Harry Zimm)*, Rene Russo *(Karen Flores)*, Danny DeVito *(Martin Weir)*, Dennis Farina *(Ray "Bones" Barboni)*, Delroy Lindo *(Bo Catlett)*, James Gandolfini *(Bear)*, Jon Gries *(Ronnie Wingate)*, Renee Props *(Nicki)*, David Paymer *(Leo Devoe)*

p, Danny DeVito, Michael Shamberg, Stacey Sher; d, Barry Sonnenfeld; w, Scott Frank (based on the novel by Elmore Leonard); ph, Don Peterman; ed, Jim Miller; m, John Lurie; prod d, Peter Larkin; art d, Steve Arnold; fx, Danny Gill, Gary Bierend, Michael McAlister; cos, Betsy Heimann

Based on a gracefully self-reflexive crime novel by Elmore Leonard, this lighthanded black comedy consolidated John Travolta's much-vaunted comeback in the wake of PULP FICTION.

Chili Palmer (Travolta), a Miami-based loan collector with mafia connections and a thing for movies, arrives in Hollywood to collect an outstanding debt from washed-up schlock film producer Harry Zimm (Gene Hackman). Chili becomes intrigued with the business and soon finds himself producing a script for egomanical actor Martin Weir (Danny DeVito). The problem: Harry is hip deep in debt to Bo Catlett (Delroy Lindo), a slick drug dealer who sees Harry as his ticket into the producing business, where "the real money" is. With the help of former B-movie queen—and the former Mrs. Martin Weir—Karen Flores (Rene Russo), Chili brings his underworld skills to bear on moguls and mobsters alike.

With its expertly executed mixture of snappy dialogue, dark humor, and first-rate performances, GET SHORTY is a tremendously entertaining film. While every major performer is perfectly cast and capably used, Travolta—effortlessly outflanking the perils of typecasting—creates an attractive, fully realized character in Chili Palmer, whom no one will confuse with PULP FICTION's smack-shooting Vincent Vega. Of course, much of GET SHORTY's success can be credited to director and executive producer Barry Sonnenfeld (THE ADDAMS FAMILY, THROW MOMMA FROM THE TRAIN). Using quirky camera moves and angles to survey the wiseguys, Sonnenfeld never allows the tone to become too heavy, even when the characters are doing things that are downright despicable. The slinky jazz soundtrack by John Lurie and others puts just the right spring in SHORTY's step.

GETAWAY, THE

			DVD
1972	122m	c	Crime	★★★½
Solar/First Artists		(U.S.)	PG

Steve McQueen *(Doc McCoy)*, Ali MacGraw *(Carol McCoy)*, Ben Johnson *(Jack Benyon)*, Sally Struthers *(Fran Clinton)*, Al Lettieri *(Rudy Butler)*, Slim Pickens *(Cowboy)*, Richard Bright *(Thief)*, Jack Dodson *(Harold Clinton)*, Dub Taylor *(Laughlin)*, Bo Hopkins *(Frank Jackson)*

p, David Foster, Mitchell Brower; d, Sam Peckinpah; w, Walter Hill (based on the novel by Jim Thompson); ph, Lucien Ballard (Todd-AO 35, Technicolor); ed, Robert Wolfe; m, Quincy Jones; art d, Ted Haworth, Angelo Graham; fx, Bud Hulburd; cos, Ray Summers

Peckinpah does Peckinpah. In one of his most hard-bitten roles, taciturn McQueen is released on a parole arranged for by his wife, MacGraw, who slept with Johnson to get the political big shot to pull the strings. He wants McQueen to lead a group of professional thieves on a bank raid, so McQueen organizes the small band, including MacGraw as a getaway driver and cocky Lettieri and Hopkins as gunhappy goons.

Through an elaborate plan, McQueen and cohorts successfully rob the Southwestern bank of $500,000, but Hopkins spoils the caper by panicking and killing a guard. When the thieves rendezvous, McQueen learns that Lettieri has murdered Hopkins. The gunman tells him, "He didn't make it... neither did you," as he draws a gun. McQueen has anticipated the double cross and is quicker, however, blasting several shots into Lettieri's chest. McQueen now realizes that Johnson has set him up.

This violent film, typical of Peckinpah's slam-bang action movies, relentlessly depicts ruthless robbery and murder, not to mention adultery, kidnaping, bribery, extortion, and general mayhem. The vivid direction and lightning pace, however, make the film completely fascinating as the culprits attempt to destroy each other, and the viewer finds himself actually rooting for McQueen and MacGraw, thieves though they are, hoping they'll get away. No one in this film is honorable or attractive, emphatically symbolized in one cynical Peckinpah scene in which, to escape detection, McQueen and MacGraw hide in a garbage truck and are dumped, along with their stolen loot, in a vast waste area.

Lettieri gives a wonderful study in evil, and Struthers is the ultimate repugnant tramp, obsessed with the gunman's guns and menacing manner, encouraging him to murder her husband. MacGraw is just a waste of time, having no acting

ability at all and projecting the attitude of a spoiled rich girl whose Neiman-Marcus charge card has been taken away. But in retrospect, perhaps her blankness deserves another look.

GETTING STRAIGHT

1970	126m	c	Drama	★★★½
Columbia		(U.S.)		R

Elliott Gould *(Harry Bailey)*, Candice Bergen *(Jan)*, Jeff Corey *(Dr. Willhunt)*, Max Julien *(Ellis)*, Robert F. Lyons *(Nick)*, Cecil Kellaway *(Dr. Kasper)*, Jon Lormer *(Vandenburg)*, Leonard Stone *(Lysander)*, William Bramley *(Wade Linden)*, Jeannie Berlin *(Judy Kramer)*

p, Richard Rush; d, Richard Rush; w, Bob Kaufman (based on the novel by Ken Kolb); ph, Laszlo Kovacs (Eastmancolor); ed, Maury Winetrobe; m, Ronald Stein; art d, Sydney Z. Litwack; fx, Ira Anderson; cos, Gene Ashman

In 1970, Hollywood's attempt to capitalize on student rebellion looked trivial in comparison to real events (the shootings at Kent State occured in the same year), but GETTING STRAIGHT, buoyed by Gould's eccentric screen presence and Kovacs' stylish camerawork, holds up surprisingly well. Gould, a returning Vietnam vet, goes back to school to secure a graduate degree and inevitably becomes involved in the lives of his students, many of whom are 10 years younger than he is and light-years more naive. Corey, the department head, forces smart-aleck Gould to teach remedial English, a job he hates. Gould looks at teaching as a calling, but Corey sees it as a job; their differences culminate in an oral examination straight out of every Ph.D candidate's nightmares. Meanwhile, when student protestors attempt to take over the university, Gould is called upon to act as mediator between them and the administration, forcing a choice between career and principle. Director Richard Rush (FREEBIE AND THE BEAN, THE STUNT MAN) is something of a cult favorite.

GHOST

			DVD
1990	128m	c	Fantasy/Romance	★★★
Howard W. Koch		(U.S.)	PG-13

Patrick Swayze *(Sam Wheat)*, Demi Moore *(Molly Jensen)*, Whoopi Goldberg *(Oda Mae Brown)*, Tony Goldwyn *(Carl Brunner)*, Rick Aviles *(Willie Lopez)*, Gail Boggs *(Louise Brown)*, Armelia McQueen *(Clara Brown)*, Vincent Schiavelli *(Subway Ghost)*

p, Lisa Weinstein; d, Jerry Zucker; w, Bruce Joel Rubin; ph, Adam Greenberg; ed, Walter Murch; m, Maurice Jarre; prod d, Jane Musky; fx, Industrial Light & Magic, Richard Edlund; cos, Ruth Morley

AAN Best Picture; AA Best Supporting Actress: Whoopi Goldberg; *AA Best Original Screenplay:* Bruce Joel Rubin; *AAN Best Film Editing:* Walter Murch; *AAN Best Original Score:* Maurice Jarre

A big sweet hit, tingly and glycerined in a phony way, but diverting. This sometimes spooky mystery-thriller-comedy-fantasy-romance focuses on loved ones who die suddenly, only to linger in spirit form, helping the mortals they have left behind. Specifically, when have-it-all yuppies Sam and Molly (Patrick Swayze and Demi Moore) are held up, sentimental bank executive Swayze gets shot. But he finally figures out—we've seen smarter ghosts in "Casper" cartoons—that vulnerable, adorable Moore is in danger from his corrupt co-worker (Tony Goldwyn). He solicits fake medium Goldberg to help him communicate, and she discovers she's a bonafide psychic after all.

GHOST manages to work despite the constant distractions of writer Bruce Joel Rubin's mishmash screenplay and Jerry Zucker's uneven direction. Zucker makes his solo debut here after co-directing AIRPLANE!, TOP SECRET, and RUTHLESS PEOPLE with brother David Zucker and

Jim Abrahams. His work here isn't the embarrassment that often results when a comedy director turns serious; on the contrary, Zucker shows great potential. But instead of packing GHOST with every possible gag—the hallmark of his comedy collaborations—he fills it with an array of clashing movie styles that never harmonize into a compelling whole.

Still, viewers will find it hard not to reach for their hankies at the moment when Sam finally reveals himself in spirit form to Molly, proving that, however cluttered by extraneous characters and subplots, the theme of romantic love reaching beyond the grave, and into eternity, remains potent and pure as a cinematic conceit. Or maybe what makes this movie so appealing are all of those romantic notions *plus* a shirtless Patrick Swayze and a nude Demi Moore.

GHOST AND MRS. MUIR, THE   *DVD*
1947 104m bw   ★★★★
Romance/Science Fiction/Fantasy
Fox (U.S.)

Gene Tierney *(Lucy)*, Rex Harrison *(The Ghost of Capt. Daniel Gregg)*, George Sanders *(Miles Fairley)*, Edna Best *(Martha)*, Vanessa Brown *(Anna)*, Anna Lee *(Mrs. Fairley)*, Robert Coote *(Coombe)*, Natalie Wood *(Anna as a Child)*, Isobel Elsom *(Angelica)*, Victoria Horne *(Eva)*

p, Fred Kohlmar; d, Joseph L. Mankiewicz; w, Philip Dunne (based on the novel by R.A. Dick); ph, Charles Lang; ed, Dorothy Spencer; m, Bernard Herrmann; art d, Richard Day, George W. Davis; fx, Fred Sersen; cos, Oleg Cassini

AAN Best B/W Cinematography: Charles Lang Jr

Wonderful fantasy-romance, in which beautiful widow Lucy (Gene Tierney) buys a remote coastal home that was once occupied by a dashing merchant captain. Shortly after Lucy moves in with her little daughter, Anna (Natalie Wood), she encounters some strange doings, but is not alarmed even though her neighbors have already warned the headstrong woman that the cottage is haunted. Lucy is more curious than apprehensive and she demands that the ghost (Rex Harrison) reveal himself. He does, in all his handsome, bearded glory, and not only befriends Lucy and her daughter, but falls in love with the lovely lady.

This fragile story would immediately collapse into implausibility were it not for the wonderful chemistry between Harrison and Tierney. In this, his second American film, Harrison is superb as the sharp-tongued, affectionate ghost and Tierney shines as his earthbound object of love. Bernard Herrmann's score is both whimsical and full of otherworldly lyricism. Remade in 1955 as STRANGER IN THE NIGHT.

GHOST DOG: THE WAY OF THE SAMURAI   *DVD*
1999 116m c   Action/Comedy/Drama   ★★½
Degeto Film/Plywood/Le Studio Canal Plus/BAC   R
Films/JVC/ARD (U.S./France)

Forest Whitaker *(Ghost Dog)*, John Tormey *(Louie)*, Henry Silva *(Ray Vargo)*, Isaach de Bankole *(Raymond)*, Cliff Gorman *(Sonny Valerio)*, Victor Argo *(Vinny)*, Tricia Vessey *(Louise Vargo)*, Camille Winbush *(Pearline)*, Gene Ruffini *(Old Consigliere)*, Richard Portnow *(Handsome Frank)*

p, Richard Guay, Jim Jarmusch; d, Jim Jarmusch; w, Jim Jarmusch; ph, Robby Muller; ed, Jay Rabinowitz; m, RZA; prod d, Ted Berner; art d, Mario Ventenilla; fx, Drew Jiritano; cos, John A. Dunn

Writer-director Jim Jarmusch's follow-up to the brilliant DEAD MAN gets points for an interesting concept, demerits for the dull execution. It's an uneasy mix of classic samurai adventure, post-Scorsese gangster drama, hip-hop sounds and

stylings, and Jarmusch's trademark brand of deadpan cool. Too bad it doesn't work, even as the postmodern comic book it aspires to be.

High atop a dilapidated building in a burned-out, boarded-up urban neighborhood, a hired gun known only as Ghost Dog (Forest Whitaker) lives in contemplative isolation like a latter-day samurai, a contract killer who follows the precepts set forth in the 18th-century Japanese warrior's manual *Hagakure*. Chief among its teachings is total devotion to one's master, and Ghost Dog's master is Louie (John Tormey), a small-time mobster who once saved his life. Louie hires Ghost Dog to whack fellow wiseguy Handsome Frank (Richard Portnow), who's been messing around with *his* boss's unstable daughter (Tricia Vessey). But after Ghost Dog carries out the assignment, mob boss Mr. Vargo (Henry Silva) and his lieutenant, Sonny (Cliff Gorman), demand retribution for the murder of a made man.

Nothing could be further from the energy this sort of pastiche demands than Jarmusch's laconic style. His signature tone is perfect for the poker-faced comedy of STRANGER THAN PARADISE or DEAD MAN's death-trip mysticism, but it's numbing here. In reconfiguring ancient samurai legend as new-school gangster myth, Jarmusch draws heavily from all the right places: Hiroshi Inagaki's SAMURAI trilogy, Wong Kar-Wai's ASHES OF TIME, Jean-Pierre Melville's LE SAMOURAI, Seijun Suzuki's BRANDED TO KILL, which provides him with his best visual ideas. But Jarmusch makes the film all his own mainly by draining the life out of it.

GHOST GOES WEST, THE
1936 85m bw   ★★★★
Science Fiction/Fantasy/Comedy
London Films (U.K.)

Robert Donat *(Murdoch/Donald Glourie)*, Jean Parker *(Peggy Martin)*, Eugene Pallette *(Joe Martin)*, Elsa Lanchester *(Lady Shepperton)*, Ralph Bunker *(Ed Bigelow)*, Patricia Hilliard *(Shepherdess)*, Everley Gregg *(Gladys Martin)*, Morton Selten *(Gavin Glourie)*, Dorothy "Chili" Bouchier *(Cleopatra)*, Mark Daly *(Groom)*

p, Alexander Korda; d, Rene Clair; w, Robert E. Sherwood, Rene Clair, Geoffrey Kerr (based on the story "Sir Tristram Goes West" by Eric Keown); ph, Harold Rosson; ed, Harold Earle-Fishbacher, Henry Cornelius; m, Mischa Spoliansky; prod d, Vincent Korda; fx, Ned Mann; cos, Rene Hubert, John Armstrong

This was the first English-language film for French master director Rene Clair, and it proved a winner. The story begins in 18th-century Scotland where Robert Donat, as the head of a clan, is insulted by another laird but dies before he can remedy the stain upon his stiff honor. His modern-day descendant, also played by Donat, is trying to maintain the sprawling family castle but is going broke, his creditors waiting for him behind every door. Salvation arrives in the form of loud, acquisitive Eugene Pallette, whose pretty daughter Jean Parker immediately falls for Donat. Pallette has the castle transported to the U.S. and rebuilds it stone by stone on his vast Florida estate. Parker and Donat—he goes along with the castle as caretaker—are eyeing the altar, but matters become complicated when it's discovered that the ghost of Donat's lookalike ancestor has also made the journey to Florida and is haunting everyone in sight.

Clair's light comedic touch is everywhere in a film loaded with the screwball comedy which was so popular in the 1930s. At one point Clair considered removing his name from the credits—producer Korda frequently interrupted the shooting of the film to make changes—but enough of his imprint remained to cause him to reconsider. U.S. audiences took the stereotype of American materialism good-naturedly and made the film a hit.

GHOST WORLD

2001 111m c Comedy/Drama ★★★★
United Artists Films/Granada Film/Jersey Shore/ R
Advanced Medien/Mr. Mudd (U.S.)

Thora Birch (Enid), Scarlett Johansson (Rebecca), Steve Buscemi (Seymour), Brad Renfro (Josh), Illeana Douglas (Roberta), Bob Balaban (Enid's Dad), Stacey Travis (Dana), Charles C. Stevenson (Norman), Dave Sheridan (Doug), Tom McGowan (Joe)

p, Lianne Halfon, John Malkovich, Russell Smith; d, Terry Zwigoff; w, Daniel Clowes, Terry Zwigoff (based on the comic book by Daniel Clowes); ph, Affonso Beato; ed, Carole Kravetz-Aykanian, Michael R. Miller; m, David Kitay; prod d, Edward T. McAvoy; art d, Alan E. Muraoka; fx, Ron Bolanowski; cos, Mary Zophres

AAN Best Adapted Screenplay: Daniel Clowes, Terry Zwigoff

Big-screen comic-book adaptations usually mean overbudgeted sci-fi action spectacles, but this mordantly funny, emotionally piquant depiction of post-adolescent angst also has its roots in the graphic novel format. Daniel Clowes's acclaimed comic *Ghost World* chronicled the misadventures of Enid and Rebecca, lifelong friends and dedicated nonconformists who find themselves drifting apart. While retaining the tone of the stories, Clowes (who co-wrote the script) and writer-director Terry Zwigoff have shifted the film's focus onto Enid (marvelously played by Thora Birch) and her attempts to deal with impending adulthood while searching for a scrap of authenticity in a fake, plastic world. Enid's strategy is to keep life at arm's length with a sardonic tongue and buffer zone of kitsch; for her, life is best seen with quotes around it. Enid and Rebecca (Scarlett Johansson) leave high school sure of only two things: they're *not* going to college, and they're going to find an apartment together. Rebecca takes a job at coffee shop, but Enid can't seem to kick-start her life. She's forced to retake remedial art in summer school, and she's fired from the local theater for bad-mouthing the movie. Fine. Enid would rather hang out with her new middle-aged friend Seymour (a superb Steve Buscemi), an obsessive collector of vintage 78 rpm recordings. Similarly disgusted by the mendacity of the modern world, curmudgeonly Seymour comes to represent the antithesis of everything about the present Enid despises and fears.

If Seymour bears a strong resemblance to R. Crumb, it's hardly a coincidence; the underground cartoonist was the subject of Zwigoff's remarkable 1995 documentary, CRUMB. But this film's worldview—suburbia as a desperately lonely, freak-filled ghost world with no sense of history—is entirely Clowes's own, and has made the transition to film with remarkable fidelity.

GHOSTBUSTERS

1984 107m c Comedy/Science Fiction ★★★½
Columbia (U.S.) PG

Bill Murray (Dr. Peter Venkman), Dan Aykroyd (Dr. Raymond Stantz), Sigourney Weaver (Dana Barrett), Harold Ramis (Dr. Egon Spengler), Rick Moranis (Louis Tully), Annie Potts (Janine Melnitz), William Atherton (Walter Peck), Ernie Hudson (Winston Zeddmore), David Margulies (Mayor), Steven Tash (Student)

p, Ivan Reitman; d, Ivan Reitman; w, Dan Aykroyd, Harold Ramis; ph, Laszlo Kovacs, Herb Wagreitch (Panavision, Metrocolor); ed, Sheldon Kahn, David Blewitt; m, Elmer Bernstein; prod d, John De Cuir; art d, John De Cuir Jr., John J. Moore; fx, Richard Edlund, John Bruno, Mark Vargo, Chuck Gaspar; cos, Theoni V. Aldredge

AAN Best Original Song: "Ghostbusters"; Ray Parker Jr. (Music & Lyrics); AAN Best Visual Effects: Richard Edlund, John Bruno, Mark Vargo, Chuck Gaspar

An enormously successful movie that owes much to many less successful ones that preceded it, GHOSTBUSTERS is an all-star big-budget hybrid of pictures as diverse as SPOOK CHASERS, SPOOK BUSTERS, GHOST CATCHERS and countless others. The difference between those films and GHOSTBUSTERS is that the latter had a huge special-effects budget and the presence of Bill Murray, whose irreverent personality makes the whole thing work.

Murray, Dan Aykroyd, and Harold Ramis play a trio of New York City parapsychologists who set up their own "ghost-busting" shop—not unlike exterminators—in a downtown building, complete with a bored secretary (Annie Potts). For a fee, the trio will rid homes or places of business of supernatural residents. They are hired by Dana Barrett (Sigourney Weaver), a symphony cellist who lives in a spectacular apartment above Central Park where strange things have been happening. After capturing a large, gooey, green ghost and experiencing several other weird occurrences, the busters determine that the apartment building was built by a Sumerian devil cult and that the site is actually the doorway to the spirit world.

Originally planned as an Aykroyd-John Belushi vehicle, the picture was rewritten after Belushi's untimely death, giving Murray's character the emphasis—and it is Murray's movie all the way. With his deadpan delivery and snide quips, Murray more than holds his own amid the myriad state-of-the-art special effects. An inferior sequel, GHOSTBUSTERS II, was released in 1989.

GIANT

1956 201m c Drama ★★★★
Warner Bros. (U.S.)

Elizabeth Taylor (Leslie Benedict), Rock Hudson (Bick Benedict), James Dean (Jett Rink), Carroll Baker (Luz Benedict II), Jane Withers (Vashti Snythe), Chill Wills (Uncle Bawley), Mercedes McCambridge (Luz Benedict), Sal Mineo (Angel Obregon II), Dennis Hopper (Jordan Benedict III), Judith Evelyn (Mrs. Horace Lynnton)

p, George Stevens, Henry Ginsberg; d, George Stevens; w, Fred Guiol, Ivan Moffat (based on the novel by Edna Ferber); ph, William Mellor (Warner Color); ed, William Hornbeck, Fred Bohanan, Philip W. Anderson; m, Dimitri Tiomkin; prod d, Boris Leven; cos, Marjorie Best, Moss Mabry

AAN Best Picture; AAN Best Actor: James Dean; AAN Best Actor: Rock Hudson; AAN Best Supporting Actress: Mercedes McCambridge; AA Best Director: George Stevens; AAN Best Adapted Screenplay: Fred Guiol, Ivan Moffat; AAN Best Film Editing: William Hornbeck, Philip W. Anderson, Fred Bohanan; AAN Best Score (Drama or Comedy): Dimitri Tiomkin; AAN Best Art Direction-Set Decoration (Color): Boris Leven, Ralph S. Hurst; AAN Best Costume Design (Color): Moss Mabry, Marjorie Best

Like the title says. Based on Edna Ferber's sprawling novel, GIANT covers two generations of Texas rivalry, spear-headed by Hudson, in his best performance, and Dean, in a performance that defies description. Hudson marries Virginia belle Taylor and transplants her to Texas, where she must learn to adapt herself to the harsher culture of her husband's huge cattle empire. Dean is an outcast who strikes oil and whose financial empire grows to rival Hudson's, even as he nurses a lifelong broken heart over Taylor.

This was the last role in Dean's all-too-brief career—he was dead when the film was released—and his presence ran away with the film. He performs his role in the overwrought method manner of the era, and the rest of the cast seems to be split between awe of his talent and disgust over his indulgence. He's a strange spectacle indeed as he ages, like a Howard Hughes burlesque that doesn't quite come off. Still he works well early on opposite Taylor, as does Hudson, who more or less leads the rest of the cast in the conventional style of pre-sentational acting. GIANT confirms Taylor's skills as an actress; she's entirely believable even when she ages by just having her hair greyed.

Director Stevens encouraged a feeling for animosity between Dean and Hudson and irritated Taylor with his end-less retakes and chatter about how he wished original choice Grace Kelly had been available; this made for lively filming. The result strains for prestige but considering its length moves along at a considerable clip, due to Ferber's narrative prowess more than anything else.

GIDGET
1959 95m c Comedy   ★★½
Columbia   (U.S.)

Sandra Dee (Francie), James Darren (Moondoggie), Cliff Robertson (Kahoona), Arthur O'Connell (Russell Lawrence), Mary LaRoche (Dorothy Lawrence), Joby Baker (Stinky), Tom Laughlin (Lover Boy), Sue George (B.L.), Robert Ellis (Hot Shot), Jo Morrow (Mary Lou)

p, Lewis J. Rachmil; d, Paul Wendkos; w, Gabrielle Upton (based on the novel by Frederick Kohner); ph, Burnett Guffey (CinemaScope, Eastmancolor); ed, William Lyon; m, M.W. Stoloff; art d, Ross Bellah

Watch at risk. Sugar-posioning, with the unctous Dee, as the all-American pertly perky happy-go-brainless model for countless teenagers in the late 1950s—today that seems scary. Dee plays Gidget (a nickname meaning "girl midget"), a whiny youngster who doesn't quite measure up to the chesty, bikinied girls on the beach. Her mom's reassurances come true when the two grooviest surfers in town, Moondoggie (James Darren) and Kahoona (Cliff Robertson), start paying Gidget some attention. Dee had just appeared in Douglas Sirk's IMITATION OF LIFE, and Robertson had turned in a commendable performance in AUTUMN LEAVES. Also hanging ten was Tom Laughlin, who much later made BILLY JACK. Inbred sequels fol-lowed, and two horrifying television series.

GIFT, THE
2000 112m c Thriller   ★★★½
Alphaville Productions/Reinassance Pictures/   R
Lakeshore Entertainment   (U.S.)

Cate Blanchett (Annie Wilson), Katie Holmes (Jessica King), Keanu Reeves (Donnie Barksdale), Giovanni Ribisi (Buddy Cole), Greg Kinnear (Wayne Collins), Hilary Swank (Valerie Barksdale), Michael Jeter (Gerald Weems), J.K. Simmons (Sheriff Johnson), Lynnsee Provence (Mike Wilson), Gary Cole (David Duncan)

p, James Jacks, Tom Rosenberg; d, Sam Raimi; w, Billy Bob Thornton, Tom Epperson; ph, Jamie Anderson; ed, Bob Murawaski, Arthur Coburn; m, Christopher Young; prod d, Neil Spisak; fx, Vern Hyde, Syd Dutton, Bill Taylor; cos, Julie Weiss

A restrained, adult thriller from screenwriters Billy Bob Thornton and Tom Epperson (ONE FALSE MOVE) and one-time wunderkind director Sam Raimi, whose rock 'em—shock 'em EVIL DEAD pictures once raised the bar on gross-out horror movies.

Small-town widow Annie Wilson (Cate Blanchett) is rais-ing three boys in sleepy, insular Brixton, GA, supplementing her survivor's benefits by utilizing the "gift" she inherited from her beloved grandma: Annie can peer into people's futures. Her troubled clients include battered wife Valerie Barksdale (Hilary Swank) and emotionally damaged mechanic Buddy Cole (Giovanni Ribisi), and Annie has a few problems of her own. Valerie's volatile husband, Donnie (Keanu Reeves) is threaten-

ing Annie's family, and her oldest son (Lynnsee Provence) is in trouble at school. Called in to meet with Principal Wayne Collins (Greg Kinnear), Annie has a sudden, disturbing vision of his fiancee, flirtatious rich girl Jessica King (Katie Holmes). Annie sees her standing in a pool of water, her legs decayed and tangled in weeds. When Jessica vanishes, Annie has another vision that reveals her whereabouts, but something about it doesn't quite fit. Annie's further investigations uncover deadly secrets even she knew nothing about.

Though the last half hour slips into genre cliches, Blanchett's quietly radiant performance anchors even the most outrageous plot developments, and she's well-supported on all sides—as a brutal redneck with a sweet Southern-boy facade, Reeves is nothing less than a revelation. And while the film overall is more concerned with mounting menace than edge-of-your-seat shocks, it delivers a couple of stunners.

GIGI
1958 116m c Musical   ★★★½
MGM   (U.S.)

Leslie Caron (Gigi), Maurice Chevalier (Honore Lachaille), Louis Jourdan (Gaston Lachaille), Hermione Gingold (Mme Alvarez), Eva Gabor (Liane D'Exelmans), Jacques Bergerac (Sandomir), Isabel Jeans (Aunt Alicia), John Abbott (Manuel), Monique Van Vooren (Showgirl), Lydia Stevens (Simone)

p, Arthur Freed; d, Vincente Minnelli; w, Alan Jay Lerner (based on the play Gigi by Anita Loos, from the novel by Colette); ph, Joseph Ruttenberg, Ray June (CinemaScope, Metrocolor); ed, Adrienne Fazan; m, Frederick Loewe; prod d, Cecil Beaton; art d, William A. Horning, Preston Ames; cos, Cecil Beaton

AA Best Picture; AA Best Director: Vincente Minnelli; AA Best Adapted Screenplay: Alan Jay Lerner; AA Best Color Cinematography: Joseph Ruttenberg; AA Best Film Editing: Adrienne Fazan; AA Best Score (Musical): Andre Previn; AA Best Song: "Gigi"; Frederick Loewe (Music), Alan Jay Lerner (Lyrics); AA Best Art Direction-Set Decoration: William A. Horning (Art Direction), Preston Ames (Art Direction), Henry Grace (Set Decoration), Keogh Gleason (Set Decoration); AA Best Costume Design: Cecil Beaton

Overbaked but enjoyable, and a banquet for the eyes, thanks to the visual wonder of the Minnelli-Beaton teaming. But con-temporary critics have long objected that Frederick Loewe and Alan Jay Lerner simply reworked their milestone My Fair Lady. To an extent, that's true; certainly the score is a rather vapid one. Based on the Colette novel, GIGI followed in the footsteps of a 1950 French film adaptation of the story and a 1951 straight dramatic production that starred Audrey Hepburn on Broadway.

The story concerns a waif (Leslie Caron), who lives in turn-of-the-century Paris with her grandmother, Mme Alvarez (Hermione Gingold), who, along with Gigi's Aunt Alicia (Isabel Jeans), seeks to transform the young woman into a courtesan so she can become the mistress of Gaston Lachaille (Louis Jourdan), wealthy heir to a sugar fortune. At first, Gaston is content to accept Gigi as his mistress; then he real-izes he truly loves the beauty and is determined to marry her, throwing Mme Alvarez for a loop since the family tradition is to be a kept woman, not a wife. Ultimately, however, Mme Alvarez, who was once the mistress of Gaston's uncle, Honore (Maurice Chevalier), agrees to allow her granddaugh-ter to marry.

Caron—never the most effortless of waifs—had played the role of Gigi in the London production of the straight stageplay, and here leads the cast (she's dubbed by Betty Wand) in a contest to see who can be the most French. The winner is Chevalier, in a performance that makes one feel as if you're gagging on pastry. The excep-tions: Gingold and Jeans. Perhaps if the sweetness of GIGI was contrasted with elements of honest vulgarity, the picture could balance itself out. Considering the aspects of the courtesan life, the opportunity is there, but as it is we are left to make do with Eva Gabor's continental suggestions; she's too docile to inhabit her role.

Ten minutes into the movie, you've resolved the plot and are left to wallow in lovely frou-frou. Produced in the City of Light, GIGI makes wonderful use of the usual Parisian landmarks, and benefits from extraordinary period costumes and sets.

GIGLI

2003 121m c Crime/Romance/Comedy ★
City Light Films/Casey Silver Productions/ R
Revolution Studios (U.S.)

Ben Affleck *(Larry Gigli)*, Jennifer Lopez *(Ricki)*, Justin Bartha *(Brian)*, Lenny Venito *(Louis)*, Christopher Walken *(Det. Stanley Jacobellis)*, Al Pacino *(Starkman)*, Lainie Kazan *(Mrs. Gigli)*, Missy Crider *(Robin)*, Alex Fatovich *(Packing Store Clerk)*, Peter Van Norden *(Morgue Attendant)*

p, Martin Brest, Casey Silver; d, Martin Brest; w, Martin Brest; ph, Robert Elswit; ed, Julie Monroe, Billy Weber; m, John Powell; prod d, Gary Frutkoff; art d, Sue Chan; fx, Kevin Hannigan; cos, Michael Kaplan

A high-profile, grotesque misfire, Martin Brest's lighthearted crime picture is torpedoed by the dismal lack of on-screen chemistry between Ben Affleck and Jennifer Lopez, whose offscreen affair overshadowed the production.

Mid-level gangster Lou (Lenny Venito) orders dim-witted flunky Larry Gigli (Affleck) to kidnap Brian (Justin Bartha), the mentally handicapped brother of a federal prosecutor. Once Larry has Brian stashed in his apartment, he learns that Lou has hired a second contractor, the beautiful and brainy Ricki (Lopez), to make sure Larry doesn't screw things up. Instant mutual antipathy aside, Ricki and Larry are stuck with each other and Brian, whose adult body houses the mind of a preadolescent preoccupied with smutty rap lyrics and "Baywatch" fantasies. Ricki, a New-Agey lesbian (how's *that* for a romantic complication?) with a trendy interest in traditional Chinese military strategy, thinks Larry is a vain, insecure, macho moron, which he is. Larry thinks Ricki should acknowledge the evolutionary perfection of "the horn" and abandon her unnatural quest for compensatory satisfaction, which she won't. But they inevitably grow fond of each other and their captive, which complicates matters when Lou decides to increase the pressure on Brian's brother.

Written and directed by the erratic Brest, this misbegotten mess drags when it needs to snap and is vulgar when it tries to be sophisticated. Lopez's overly careful enunciation, which suggests a stupid person trying to sound smart, raises the possibility that Ricki is actually no more intelligent than Larry, which probably wasn't Brest's intention. It's hard to imagine the cast that could have made this smarmy, cringe-inducing material play, but Lopez and Affleck actively accentuate its creepy deficiencies while newcomer Bartha's technically accomplished performance is wasted on a plot device masquerading as a character.

GILDA

1946 110m bw Drama
Columbia (U.S.)
★★★★

Rita Hayworth *(Gilda)*, Glenn Ford *(Johnny Farrell)*, George Macready *(Ballin Mundson)*, Joseph Calleia *(Obregon)*, Steven Geray *(Uncle Pio)*, Joe Sawyer *(Casey)*, Gerald Mohr *(Capt. Delgado)*, Robert Scott *(Gabe Evans)*, Ludwig Donath *(German)*, Don Douglas *(Thomas Langford)*

p, Virginia Van Upp; d, Charles Vidor; w, Marion Parsonnet (based on Jo Eisinger's adaptation of E.A. Ellington's original story); ph, Rudolph Mate; ed, Charles Nelson; m, Hugo Friedhofer; art d, Stephen Goosson, Van Nest Polglase; chor, Jack Cole; cos, Jean Louis

Hayworth at her peak. Rita is the main reason to see GILDA, bringing her blue-moon beauty and star presence to Hollywood's definitive kept-woman role. GILDA proves Hayworth had a neat line: she wasn't as erotic as Dietrich or Ava Gardner, nor as suggestive as Harlow and Monroe. What she was, specifically, was provocative like no actress before or since.

The torrid, turgid plot of this myth of misogyny needn't be dwelled on in depth. Ford gets hired to play goon by Teutonic casino owner Macready. His duties include bringing to heel the duplicitous Hayworth, even to slapping her around. The triangle becomes a sicko menage a trois; surely Ford's character is the most sexually ambiguous leading man ever. He's only interested in asserting dominance and muscle, and both Hayworth and Macready enjoy taunting him—GILDA's dialogue fairly snakes with euphemism and innuendo. Critics remained indifferent to the film, but returning GIs flocked with their wives and sweethearts to see Columbia's "love goddess," who accented her role with such lines as: "If I had been a ranch they would have called me the Bar *Nothing*!" When Hayworth reprises a few bars of "Put the Blame on Mame," is she herself singing or not? This remains a famous guessing game with film buffs. Otherwise she's amazingly dubbed by Anita Ellis.

Cohn spared no expense in the production, and choreographer Cole lavished Hayworth with dances patterned after those of a professional stripper he had known. These numbers were brought into the production long after director Vidor began shooting, which indicates the haphazard fashion in which this film was shaped. It was Hayworth's film from the beginning; Vidor began shooting the story before Ford was actually signed and joined the production. The original story was written exclusively for Hayworth by producer Van Upp, named to oversee the production by Cohn himself.

Van Upp was later blamed by Hayworth for establishing a sex goddess no woman could ever hope to be in reality. When she had problems with Aly Khan, Hayworth told Van Upp: "It's all your fault. You wrote GILDA. And every man I've known has fallen in love with Gilda and wakened with me." GILDA is an erotic landmark to be especially considered today, when erotic thrillers dominate the boxoffice and television screens.

GIMME SHELTER

1970 90m c Documentary ★★★★
Maysles Film (U.S.) PG

Mick Jagger, Charlie Watts, Keith Richard, Mick Taylor, Bill Wyman, Melvin Belli, Ike Turner, Tina Turner, Jefferson Airplane, Flying Burrito Brothers

d, David Maysles, Albert Maysles, Charlotte Zwerin; ph, Peter Adair, Baird Bryant, Joan Churchill, Ron Dorfman, Robert Elfstrom, Elliott Erwitt, Bob Fiori, Adam Giffard, William Kaplan, Kevin Keting, Stephen Lighthill, George Lucas, Jim Moody, Jack Newman, Pekke Niemala, Robert Primes, Eric Saarinen, Peter Smokler, Paul Ryan, Coulter Watt, Gary Weiss, Bill Yarrus; ed, Ellen Giffard, Robert Farren, Joanne Burke, Kent McKinney

A penetrating film that turned a concert with tragically inept organization and suspect motives into an epochal cornerstone. Begun as a documentary of the Rolling Stones' 1969 American tour, it wound up being used by police to identify the man filmed killing an audience member at Altamont.

Bouncing around chronologically, the film shows the band performing live at Madison Square Garden; at press conferences; on a cover shoot; listening to mixes of their new songs; watching footage of the Altamont debacle on a film monitor. The location of an announced free concert by the band is chosen— Altamont Speedway. As soon as the concert starts, violence breaks out, with the Hell's Angels— hired as security—indiscriminately attacking the crowd. Songs continually grind to a halt as pool-cues crack heads, culminating in the stabbing death of a young black man wielding a gun.

The non-linear, self-reflexive build-up of the film allows for excellent concert footage in the first half, the band singing of rape, murder, and fighting in the streets, intercut with ominous portents of things to come. Later, on the Altamont stage, the luster is dulled, the power gone. Seething glares follow Jagger around the stage, and when an Angel interrupts him mid-song, he has trouble regaining his momentum. Soon his persona is shattered entirely, his strut gone, his performance limp, his exhortations to stop fighting weak and ignored. Once at Altamont, the filmmakers focus resolutely on the mayhem and discord, excluding from the film several of the bands that played that day. In truth, even more violence was committed, much of it unfilmed as photographers were among those assaulted, leaving the cameramen to worry where they pointed their lenses. The filmed murderer, already imprisoned for a separate crime when he was identified via the Maysles's footage, was eventually acquitted on grounds of self-defense, claiming he stabbed after the gun was drawn.

GIRL CRAZY
1943 97m bw Musical/Comedy ★★★★
MGM (U.S.)

Mickey Rooney *(Danny Churchill, Jr.)*, Judy Garland *(Ginger Gray)*, Gil Stratton *(Bud Livermore)*, Robert Strickland *(Henry ,Lathrop)*, Rags Ragland *(Rags)*, June Allyson *(Specialty)*, Nancy Walker *(Polly Williams)*, Guy Kibbee *(Dean Phineas Armour)*, Tommy Dorsey and His Band *(Themselves)*, Frances Rafferty *(Marjorie Tait)*

p, Arthur Freed; d, Norman Taurog; w, Fred Finklehoffe, Dorothy Kingsley, Sid Silvers, William Ludwig (based on the play by George Gershwin, Ira Gershwin, Guy Bolton, Jack McGowan); ph, William Daniels, Robert Planck; ed, Albert Akst; art d, Cedric Gibbons; chor, Charles Walters, Busby Berkeley

Irresistible entertainment, based on the play by Guy Bolton and Jack McGowan, with music by George and Ira Gershwin. Rooney stars as Danny Churchill, Jr., the rich son of a newspaper publisher (Henry O'Neill). He's sent to an all-boys mining school where wake-up time is six a.m., which is usually the hour he goes to sleep. Stuck out in the desert, Danny finds it hard to exercise his girl-craziness, until he meets Ginger Gray (Garland, looking quite delectable), the granddaughter of the school's dean (Guy Kibbee). Although Danny originally hates the school, his love for Ginger eventually prompts him to help save the financially imperiled institution with a musical rodeo.

The movie was originally to be directed by Busby Berkeley, but he and MGM musical maven Roger Edens didn't get along. And Garland's loathing of him was monumental; it stands to reason his power would be compromised as she ascended to queen of the MGM lot. But since *Girl Crazy* had been a big hit for Ethel Merman on Broadway, Berkeley was brought in to stage Garland's white-buckskinned finale of "I Got Rhythm," Merman's big hit. The rest of the musical work went to Charles Walters. Other songs included are "Embraceable You," "Fascinating Rhythm" and the sadly beautiful "But Not for Me," all by the Gershwins, and Edens's "Happy Birthday, Ginger."

GIRL, INTERRUPTED 📀
1999 127m c Drama ★★★
Red Wagon Productions/Konrad Pictures/Columbia (U.S.)

Winona Ryder *(Susanna Kaysen)*, Angelina Jolie *(Lisa)*, Brittany Murphy *(Daisy)*, Clea DuVall *(Georgina)*, Whoopi Goldberg *(Valerie)*, Jeffrey Tambor *(Dr. Potts)*, Jared Leto *(Tobias Jacobs)*, Vanessa Redgrave *(Dr. Wick)*, Travis Fine *(John)*, Angela Bettis *(Janet)*

p, Cathy Konrad, Douglas Wick; d, James Mangold; w, Anna Hamilton Phelan, James Mangold, Susan Shilliday, Lisa Loomer (based on the memoirs of Susanna Kaysen); ph, Jack Green; ed, Kevin Tent; prod d, Richard Hoover; art d, Jeff Knip; fx, Ron Bolanowski; cos, Arianne Phillips

AA Best Supporting Actress: Angelina Jolie

HEATHERS made Winona Ryder the pallid patron saint of smart-mouthed teenage misfits. This adaptation of Susanna Kaysen's memoir of mental turmoil could make her the wide-eyed icon of the morose and self-destructive.

Paralyzed by alienated frustration, 18-year-old Kaysen (Ryder) is persuaded to check into a mental hospital, where she's diagnosed as having a "borderline personality." Her fellow patients include secretive Daisy (Brittany Murphy), whose eating disorder springs from an unhealthy relationship with her father; sweet-natured Polly (Elizabeth Moss), disfigured by self-inflicted burns; compulsive liar Georgina (Clea Duvall); and anorexic Janet (Angela Bettis). And then there's willful, defiant Lisa (Angelina Jolie), whose enchanting, wild-child charisma masks sociopathic self-centeredness; she's the flame to which Susanna is inexorably drawn.

There's very little plot, and director James Mangold's attempts to make a connection between the social confusion of the '60s setting and Susanna's inner turmoil don't really work. The film's strength lies in the generally sensitive performances delivered by the ensemble cast. Kaysen's book apparently struck some deep, personal chord in Ryder; she committed to the project early and stuck with it throughout an attenuated development process; ironically, she plays its most passive role. Because the introverted Susanna is so recessive, it's easy to lose patience with her troubles. Jolie, on the other hand, plays Lisa as a seductive monster; with her pillowy lips and cocky posture, she's like some demon of lethal sensuality. It's a stunning performance, though perhaps better suited to an erotic horror film (say, any of Barbara Steele's Italian films of the '60s). When Jolie's onscreen, everyone else might as well lie down and play dead.

GIRL WITH A PEARL EARRING 📀
2003 109m c Drama/Historical ★★★
Archer Street Productions/Delux PG-13
Productions/Film Fund Luxembourg/
Pathe Pictures Ltd./UK Film Council/Wild Bear Films
(U.K./Luxembourg)

Colin Firth *(Vermeer)*, Scarlett Johansson *(Griet)*, Tom Wilkinson *(Van Ruijven)*, Judy Parfitt *(Maria Thins)*, Cillian Murphy *(Pieter)*, Essie Davis *(Catharina)*, Joanna Scanlan *(Tanneke)*, Alakina Mann *(Cornelia)*, Chris McHallem *(Griet's Father)*, Gabrielle Reidy *(Griet's Mother)*

p, Andy Paterson, Anand Tucker; d, Peter Webber; w, Olivia Hatreed (based on the novel by Tracy Chevalier); ph, Eduardo Serra; ed, Kate Evans; m, Alexandre Desplat; prod d, Ben van Os; art d, Christina Schaffer; fx, Alain Couty; cos, Dien van Straalen

AA N Best Art Direction: Ben Van Os (art direction), Cecile Heideman (set decoration); *AAN Best Cinematography:* Eduardo Serra; *AAN Best Costume Design:* Dien van Straalen

Tracy Chevalier's best-selling novel about Johannes Vermeer's famous painting is brought to luscious life by first-time director Peter Webber.

Holland, 1665: Seventeen-year-old Griet (Scarlett Johansson) is forced to support her family after her father, a tile painter, suffers a debilitating injury. Griet moves from her childhood home in sleepy Delft to work as a maid on the lavish estate of the Vermeer family. Lady of the house Catharina (Essie Davis) takes an immediate dislike to the new girl and assigns Griet the demanding task of cleaning Vermeer's studio. Griet shows such care in dusting the still lifes from which Vermeer (Colin Firth) paints that he eventually asks her to help mix his colors. Vermeer's mother-in-law, Maria Thins (Judy Parfitt), notices his affection for Griet and encourages the relationship, since it seems to be having a positive effect on the volume of work he's able to produce—especially when Vermeer's patron, Master van Ruijven (Tom Wilkinson), decides he wants a portrait of the young maid. Meanwhile, Griet is torn between affection for Vermeer and her budding attraction to local butcher boy Pieter (Cillian Murphy).

A 17th-century serving girl was expected to hold her tongue, so Johansson has little dialogue; one look from this talented young actress, though, speaks volumes about Griet's complex thoughts and emotions. Her subtle performance is enhanced by the efforts of the film's costume and makeup departments, who succeed in making her look astonishingly like the girl who glances over her shoulder in Vermeer's masterwork. Webber's assured directing is evident throughout; in addition to eliciting strong performances from his cast, he always knows when to linger on an image and when to move on.

GIRL WITH GREEN EYES DVD
1964 91m bw Drama ★★★½
Woodfall (U.K.)

Peter Finch *(Eugene Gaillard)*, Rita Tushingham *(Kate Brady)*, Lynn Redgrave *(Baba Brenan)*, Marie Kean *(Josie Hannigan)*, Arthur O'Sullivan *(Mr. Brady)*, Julian Glover *(Malachi Sullivan)*, T.P. McKenna *(Priest)*, Lislott Goettinger *(Joanna)*, Patrick Laffan *(Bertie Counihan)*, Eileen Crowe *(Mrs. Byrne)*

p, Oscar Lewenstein; d, Desmond Davis; w, Edna O'Brien (based on her novel *The Lonely Girl)*; ph, Manny Wynn; ed, Antony Gibbs, Brian Smedley-Aston; m, John Addison; art d, Ted Marshall

Memorable and sentimental "women's picture" adapted by Edna O'Brien from her own novel. Filmed in and around Dublin, GIRL WITH GREEN EYES tells the story of a young woman, Rita Tushingham, who leaves her father's barren farm in County Clare to come to Dublin where she gets a job in a grocery and shares a flat with Redgrave, an old pal from Catholic school. She meets Finch, a divorced writer many years older than she. She pursues him, they become friends, and she moves into his home.

Despite their propinquity and the underlying attraction, she remains chaste due to a combination of youth, shyness and her religious upbringing. When her father, O'Sullivan, learns that she's living with a man, he forces her to return home. Her priest, McKenna, rebukes her for her lax behavior, and she leaves home again and goes to Finch's place. She's tailed by O'Sullivan and a horde of his besotted buddies. They break into Finch's house, only to flee when Finch points his aged shotgun at them. Tushingham finally relents and sleeps with Finch.

Originally titled "Once Upon A Summer," the film featured several of the best Irish actors. All the roles were well played, and the dialogue smacked of Irish reality, though occasionally it is a trifle stilted for the American ear. There is lots to recommend this film, including first-time direction by Desmond Davis and the debut photography of Manny Wynn. Turner, Finch's real-life wife, does an excellent cameo as a bitch. It was Redgrave's second film for Richardson, the first having been TOM JONES. Lovingly made, it's a fine introduction to the Ireland of lyrical romance, rather than the strife-torn area we see so often.

GIRLFIGHT DVD
2000 110m c Sports/Drama ★★★½
Independent Film Channel Productions/Green/ R
Renzi/Screen Gems (U.S.)

Michelle Rodriguez *(Diana)*, Santiago Douglas *(Adrian)*, Jaime Tirelli *(Hector)*, Ray Santiago *(Tiny)*, Paul Calderon *(Sandro)*, Elisa Bocanegra *(Marisol)*, Alicia Ashley *(Ricki Stiles)*, Thomas Barbour *(Ira)*, Louis Guss *(Don)*, J.P. Lipton *(Mr. Price)*

p, Sarah Green, Martha Griffin, Maggie Renzi; d, Karyn Kusama; w, Karyn Kusama; ph, Patrick Cady; ed, Plummy Tucker; m, Theodore Shapiro; prod d, Stephen Beatrice; cos, Luca Mosca, Marco Cattoretti

If the chip on high school senior Diana Guzman's (Michelle Rodriguez) shoulder were any bigger, it would have its own wardrobe. Her mother committed suicide; her father, Sandro (Paul Calderon), adores his son, Tiny (Ray Santiago), but looks right through her; and they live in Brooklyn's violent Red Hook projects, where girls' futures lean heavily toward early motherhood and a life of dependence on undependable men. And then Sandro sends her down to the gym to pay Tiny's boxing trainer, Hector (Jaime Tirelli). Scrawny Tiny, a self-proclaimed nerd, couldn't care less about boxing; he only does it to make his dad happy. But Diana falls in love with the ring and persuades the reluctant Hector to take her on as a student. Boxing gives Diana a goal and an outlet for her anger; it also introduces her to handsome Adrian (Santiago Douglas) under circumstances that make it possible for them to get to know one another.

So yes, this is a classic tale of an underdog making good in the gritty world of boxing, but that doesn't make it merely ROCKY in a sports bra. Writer-director Karyn Kusama's impressive feature debut, a Sundance favorite, is an affecting coming-of-age drama whose story is familiar without being hackneyed (like, say, PRICE OF GLORY), and it's galvanized by first-timer Rodriguez's utterly natural performance. She's got solid support from the rest of the cast, especially Calderon—his Sandro is a bad dad without being a caricatured beast—and Tirelli, who's surprisingly subtle in the role of the crusty old trainer revitalized by his promising student. It's enough to restore your faith in independent filmmaking and Sundance buzz.

GIRLFRIENDS
1978 86m c Comedy/Drama ★★★
Cyclops (U.S.) PG

Melanie Mayron *(Susan Weinblatt)*, Anita Skinner *(Anne Munroe)*, Eli Wallach *(Rabbi Gold)*, Christopher Guest *(Eric)*, Bob Balaban *(Martin)*, Gina Rogak *(Julie)*, Amy Wright *(Ceil)*, Viveca Lindfors *(Beatrice)*, Mike Kellin *(Abe)*, Jean De Baer *(Terry)*

p, Claudia Weill, Jan Saunders; d, Claudia Weill; w, Vicki Polon (based on a story by Polon and Weill); ph, Fred Murphy (DuArt Color); ed, Suzanne Pettit; m, Michael Small; art d, Patrizia von Brandenstein

A refreshing little film that marked the directorial debut of Weill, GIRLFRIENDS strips away the pretentiousness of so many small movies and offers us a real look at real people. Weill spent many years as a documentarian; she uses her experience and her ear and eye for realism to present us with an episodic story that mixes comedy and poignancy with excellent results.

Mayron is a chubby Jewish photographer whose roommate, Skinner, is leaving to get married. Mayron must now go it alone and contemplates her life, new insecurities, and cellulite. Mayron is so good in the role that she seems closer to "being" her part than acting it. Not unlike SHEILA LEVINE IS DEAD AND LIVING IN NEW YORK, this character study of a certain type of urban Jewish woman never hits a false note. As Mayron's boyfriend, Balaban is depicted as likable and believable, an honest human being with honest problems. Mayron flirts with Wallach, a rabbi, and almost has a fling with him, but she winds up as the house photographer doing weddings and bar mitzvahs. It's unsentimental, emotional, and made with great affection.

GLADIATOR

2000 150m c Adventure/Historical ★★★½
Red Wagon/DreamWorks SKG/Universal/ R
Scott Free (U.S.)

Russell Crowe *(Maximus)*, Joaquin Phoenix *(Commodus)*, Oliver Reed *(Proximo)*, Connie Nielsen *(Lucilla)*, Derek Jacobi *(Gracchus)*, Djimon Hounsou *(Juba)*, Richard Harris *(Marcus Aurelius)*, David Schofield *(Falco)*, John Shrapnel *(Gaius)*, Tomas Arana *(Quintus)*

p, Douglas Wick, David Franzoni, Branko Lustig; d, Ridley Scott; w, David Franzoni, John Logan, William Nicholson (from a story by David Franzoni); ph, John Mathieson; ed, Pietro Scalia; m, Hans Zimmer, Lisa Gerrard; prod d, Arthur Max; fx, John Nelson, Tim Burke, Rob Harvey, Neil Corbould, Mill Film; cos, Janty Yates

AA Best Picture; AA Best Actor: Russell Crowe; *AA Best Costume Design:* Janty Yates; *AA Best Sound:* Scott Millan, Bob Beemer, Ken Weston; *AA Best Visual Effects:* John Nelson, Neil Corbould, Tim Burke, Rob Harvey; *AAN Best Supporting Actor:* Joaquin Phoenix; *AAN Best Director:* Ridley Scott; *AAN Best Art Direction:* Arthur Max (Art Direction), Crispian Sallis (Set Decoration); *ANN Best Cinematography:* John Mathieson; *AAN Best Film Editing:* Pietro Scalia; *AAN Best Original Screenplay:* David Franzoni, John Logan, William Nicholson; *AAN Best Original Score:* Hans Zimmer

Brawny, he-man spectacle, buttressed by a surprisingly solid story and excellent performances, including the late Oliver Reed's swan song.

It's the second century A.D., and Roman general Maximus (Russell Crowe) is leading his armies into the conquered state of Germania. Maximus wants to finish the job and return to the wife and child he hasn't seen in three years, but the aging emperor Marcus Aurelius (Richard Harris) has other plans. Convinced that imperial rule violates Roman ideals, he asks Maximus to insure that after his death, power is handed back to the Roman senate. This plan sits badly with Marcus Aurelius's vain, spoiled son Commodus (Joaquin Phoenix), who murders his father and seizes power for himself. When Maximus resists, Commodus orders the murder of Maximus and his family. Only Maximus escapes, but he's sold into slavery and bought by Proximo (Reed), whose trade in gladiatorial flesh was spoiled when Marcus Aurelius outlawed the games in Rome, relegating mortal combat to the far-flung provinces. Maximus proves an able and charismatic combatant, and after word reaches the boondocks that Commodus has restored the games to the Colosseum, Proximo packs up his gladiators and heads for Rome.

Director Ridley Scott supplies bloodthirsty spectacle on an extraordinary scale; that the movie's appeal is essentially that of a "WWF Smackdown" in highbrow drag is worth noting, but not worth holding against it. Those who want their Roman history talky can always revisit "I, Claudius" (whose star, Derek Jacobi, appears here as a senator). Scott's rousing

vision of blood and sand is more character-oriented than it has to be, and ultimately as crowd-pleasing as Maximus himself.

GLASS KEY, THE

1942 85m bw Mystery/Political ★★★★
Paramount (U.S.)

Brian Donlevy *(Paul Madvig)*, Veronica Lake *(Janet Henry)*, Alan Ladd *(Ed Beaumont)*, Bonita Granville *(Opal Madvig)*, Richard Denning *(Taylor Henry)*, Joseph Calleia *(Nick Varna)*, William Bendix *(Jeff)*, Frances Gifford *(Nurse)*, Donald MacBride *(Farr)*, Margaret Hayes *(Eloise Matthews)*

p, Fred Kohlmar; d, Stuart Heisler; w, Jonathan Latimer (based on the novel by Dashiell Hammett); ph, Theodor Sparkuhl; ed, Archie Marshek; m, Victor Young; art d, Hans Dreier, Haldane Douglas

This film of Dashiell Hammett's tale of political corruption and murder is slightly better than the 1935 version, profiting from a bigger budget, stellar casting, and a zippier pace, thanks to Johnathan Latimer's taut screenplay.

Donlevy is accused of murder, solicits aid of henchman Ladd to clear his name. Memorable, chilling sado-masochism of Bendix repeatedly beating Ladd is typical of the unorthodox undertow of sexual currents snaking through the plot. Ladd's character seems equally committed to Donlevy and the mysterious, cyclopean Lake, at one point confiding he'd let the latter hang if it served his purpose. Despite the copout ending, Ladd's deadpan toughens his character up, serving up partial compensation. As usual, the Ladd-Lake slow-burn chemistry, deceptive in it's offhandedness, is a pleasurable contrast to all the overstoked new wave *noir* interpretations currently flourishing.

This film was put into production before the release of THIS GUN FOR HIRE, which featured an electric performance from Ladd and made him Paramount's newest star. But Bendix nearly steals the film as the scary but pathetic henchman whose only joy in life is to administer sadistic beatings. According to Beverly Linet in *Ladd: A Hollywood Tragedy*, in one scene calling for Bendix's character to beat up Ladd's, the rugged six-footer slipped and struck the five-foot-five-inch Ladd square on the jaw, knocking him out. Director Heisler, never one to let a convincing scene go unrecorded, ordered the shot printed and it appears in the film.

GLASS MENAGERIE, THE

1987 135m c Drama ★★★★
Aspetuck Productions, Ltd./Columbia (U.S.) PG

Joanne Woodward *(Amanda Wingfield)*, John Malkovich *(Tom Wingfield)*, Karen Allen *(Laura Wingfield)*, James Naughton *(Gentleman Caller—Jim O'Connor)*

p, Burtt Harris; d, Paul Newman; w, Tennessee Williams; ph, Michael Ballhaus (DuArt Color); ed, David Ray; m, Henry Mancini, Paul Bowles; prod d, Tony Walton; art d, John Kasarda; cos, Tony Walton

The third and best of the filmed versions of martyrs and dead magnolias. Directed by Paul Newman, the Tennessee Williams classic is painstakingly faithful to the play and features extraordinary performances from all the actors. Tom (John Malkovich) is the story's narrator and sets the scene for the "memory play" by introducing the characters. Tom himself is a poet who works in a warehouse to support his family but who longs for escape. Amanda (Joanne Woodward) is his mother, a Southern belle who forsook her genteel background to marry a telephone man who eventually left his family. Laura (Karen Allen) is his sister, the victim of a childhood disease that left one leg shorter than the other, though she is even more crippled by shyness. Finally, there is the gentleman caller (James Naughton), Tom's coworker at the warehouse. While Laura is engrossed in the world of the fragile glass figurines that she collects, Amanda is concerned with finding a husband for her and asks Tom's help.

Newman has said that he approached THE GLASS MENAGERIE less as a filmmaker than as an archivist, and his version is, in essence, a filmed stage play. It is something of a cliché to give a filmed play a claustrophobic feel, but THE GLASS MENAGERIE and its trapped characters cry out for such a treatment and Newman has effectively evoked it. Newman lets the actors and Williams's poetic language do the work. All of the performances are superb. Woodward's delightful Amanda is full of contradictions and Malkovich's Tom is a product of frustration, romantic dreams and guilt. Allen is a surprising revelation, as her previous film roles have asked so little of her. Here she plumbs emotions of considerable depth, and is entirely capable of rationalizing her character's retreat from reality.

GLENGARRY GLEN ROSS   📀

1992   100m   c   Drama   ★★★★

Zupnik Enterprises Inc.   (U.S.)   R

Al Pacino *(Ricky Roma)*, Jack Lemmon *(Shelley "The Machine" Levine)*, Alec Baldwin *(Blake)*, Ed Harris *(Dave Moss)*, Alan Arkin *(George Aaronow)*, Kevin Spacey *(John Williamson)*, Jonathan Pryce *(James Lingk)*, Bruce Altman *(Mr. Spaniel)*, Jude Ciccolella *(Detective)*, Paul Butler *(Policeman)*

p, Jerry Tokofsky, Stanley R. Zupnik; d, James Foley; w, David Mamet (from his play); ph, Juan Ruiz-Anchia; ed, Howard Smith; m, James Newton Howard; prod d, Jane Musky; art d, Robert K. Shaw Jr., Bill Barclay; fx, Mike Maggi; cos, Jane Greenwood

AAN Best Supporting Actor: Al Pacino

Another seamy slice of life from acclaimed playwright David Mamet, GLENGARRY GLEN ROSS is a searing showcase for a remarkable ensemble cast.

    This foul-mouthed drama revolves around a phony real estate operation, Premiere Properties, which gets a royal shaking up in the very first scene from consulting supersalesman Blake (Alec Baldwin). Blake's motivation strategy is brutally simple—sell or get out—and his ultimatum sets up a mad scramble in the office. Veteran supersalesman Shelley "The Machine" Levine (Jack Lemmon) trained the office's current sales leader, Ricky Roma (Al Pacino). But Levine is now a desperate man, his selling skills thwarted by stale leads and his situation complicated by a hospitalized daughter. His frustrated colleague Moss (Ed Harris) draws fellow salesman Aaronow (Alan Arkin) into a plot to burgle the office, steal the leads and sell them to a rival company. Aaronow isn't too thrilled, but there's another conspirator who is already set up to take the fall for the burglary. What drama there is hinges on whether the third party is Levine or Roma, himself driven to desperation when his "locked-in" deal with a henpecked prospect (Jonathan Pryce) unravels.

    Whereas most films would focus on the details of the theft itself, Mamet's screenplay doesn't reveal exactly what happened, and it's clear that he's not particularly interested. Instead, GLENGARRY GLEN ROSS focuses on the dilemmas of the various salesmen as they sustain themselves by reliving past glories in the desiccated present. Lemmon is superb here in the type of role he's justly renowned for, a downtrodden individual who, in previous incarnations, has always found some form of salvation through self-knowledge. (In this instance, that solution is not forthcoming.) Pacino starts cocky and confident as Roma, only to shrink before our eyes as his miserable "prospect" flees to report him to the authorities. Arkin is wonderfully cagy and Harris brings real acid to his role as the most coldly cynical of the group. Director James Foley turns the screenplay's staginess into an asset, creating a claustrophobic vision of hell as a place where we're all fighting for survival, clutching a sweat-stained, dog-eared pile of bad leads.

GLENN MILLER STORY, THE   📀

1953   115m   c   Musical/Biography   ★★★★

Universal   (U.S.)

James Stewart *(Glenn Miller)*, June Allyson *(Helen Burger Miller)*, Charles Drake *(Don Haynes)*, George Tobias *(Si Schribman)*, Harry Morgan *(Chummy MacGregor)*, Marion Ross *(Polly Haynes)*, Irving Bacon *(Mr. Miller)*, Kathleen Lockhart *(Mrs. Miller)*, Barton MacLane *(Gen. Arnold)*, Sig Rumann *(Mr. Krantz)*

p, Aaron Rosenberg; d, Anthony Mann; w, Valentine Davies, Oscar Brodney; ph, William Daniels (Technicolor); ed, Russell Schoengarth; m, Joseph Gershenson (adaptation, Henry Mancini); chor, Kenny Williams

AAN Best Story and Screenplay: Valentine Davies, Oscar Brodney; *AAN Best Score (Musical):* Joseph Gershenson, Henry Mancini; *AA Best Sound Recording:* Leslie I. Carey

Unlike so many film bios, this is an honest, intelligent depiction of one of America's greatest musical influences and doesn't merely string together a series of hit tunes and gratuitous scenes. But oh, what music!

    James Stewart is Glenn Miller, a bright young man with a love for the trombone and a desire to create music. At the University of Colorado he falls for Helen Burger (June Allyson, at her charming best, and a perfect match for Stewart); then, after graduation, he goes to work for Ben Pollack (playing himself) and later has a gig in the pit of a Broadway show. On their wedding night, Helen is shocked to find her husband in a jam session in Harlem with Gene Krupa and Louis Armstrong. Later, in Boston, at the dance hall run by Si Schribman (George Tobias), Miller refines his art, stumbling upon his signature sound when his trumpet player splits his lip, forcing the clarinetist to play lead on "Moonlight Serenade."

    Although Stewart learned how to handle the trombone, the actual playing was dubbed by Murray MacEachern and Joe Yukl, who are great on such Miller classics as "In the Mood" "Tuxedo Junction" and "Little Brown Jug." All that's missing from this well-crafted film is Tex Beneke, the "boy singer" for Miller's band, who went on to lead it after his mentor's death. Look for the great Frances Langford really doing her thing.

GLORIA   📀

1980   123m   c   Crime   ★★★½

Columbia   (U.S.)   R

Gena Rowlands *(Gloria Swenson)*, Juan Adames *(Philip Dawn)*, Buck Henry *(Jack Dawn)*, Julie Carmen *(Jeri Dawn)*, Lupe Guarnica *(Margarita Vargas)*, Jessica Castillo *(Joan Dawn)*, Tony Knesich *(1st Man/Gangster)*, Filomena Spagnuolo *(Old Lady)*, Tom Noonan *(2nd Man/Gangster)*, Gregory Cleghorne *(Kid in Elevator)*

p, John Cassavetes; d, John Cassavetes; w, John Cassavetes; ph, Fred Schuler; ed, Jack McSweeney; m, Bill Conti; prod d, Rene D'Auriac, Fred Schuler; cos, Peggy Farrell

AAN Best Actress: Gena Rowlands

Under the masterful direction of husband John Cassavetes, Gena Rowlands delivers a gutsy, spellbinding performance in this excellent crime film.

    Rowlands is the title character, a woman in her 40s who lives alone with her cats and her savings, compiled by turning tricks with high-placed mobsters. Her life is thrown into turmoil when her neighbor, Mafia accountant Jack Dawn (Buck Henry), and his family are exterminated by the mob. Their eight-year-old son Philip (Juan Adames), whom the Dawns left in Gloria's care, is the only survivor and it's then up to Gloria to protect the boy from mob hit men.

    Rowlands is brilliant as the apprehensive woman who finds in herself the courage to defy an evil system and fight it to a bloody standstill. Adames contributes a fascinating portrayal of the boy who becomes uncannily adult in the pressurized situation. Cassavetes's direction is incisive while maintaining a chillingly brisk pace, marvelously supported by cinematographer Fred Schuler's fluid camerawork and penetrating closeups of the hunted pair. Too long by far, but still one sustained, frenetic gulp of a film.

GLORY   DVD
1989 122m c   Historical/War   ★★★★
Tri-Star   (U.S.)   R

Matthew Broderick (Col. Robert Gould Shaw), Denzel Washington (Trip), Cary Elwes (Cabot Forbes), Morgan Freeman (John Rawlins), Jihmi Kennedy (Sharts), Andre Braugher (Searles), John Finn (Sgt. Mulcahy), Donovan Leitch (Morse), John David Cullum (Russell), Alan North (Gov. Andrew)

p, Freddie Fields; d, Edward Zwick; w, Kevin Jarre (based on the books Lay This Laurel by Lincoln Kirstein, One Gallant Rush by Peter Burchard, and the letters of Robert Gould Shaw); ph, Freddie Francis (Technicolor); ed, Steven Rosenblum; m, James Horner; prod d, Norman Garwood; art d, Keith Pain, Dan Webster; fx, Kevin Yagher, Carl Fullerton; cos, Francine Jamison-Tanchuck

AA Best Supporting Actor: Denzel Washington; AA Best Cinematography: Freddie Francis; AAN Best Film Editing: Steven Rosenblum; AAN Best Art Direction-Set Decoration: Norman Garwood, Garrett Lewis; AA Best Sound: Donald O. Mitchell, Gregg C. Rudloff, Elliot Tyson, Russell Williams II

Never self-serving, this glorious film tells the hitherto shamefully uncelebrated story of the 54th Regiment of Massachusetts Volunteer Infantry, the first unit of black troops raised by the Union to fight in the Civil War.

Commanded by Colonel Robert Shaw (Matthew Broderick), the 25-year-old son of abolitionist Boston Brahmins, the ragtag assemblage includes Rawlins (Morgan Freeman), a gravedigger who is the regiment's anchor and voice of reason; Trip (Denzel Washington), an embittered, bullying, but tough-as-steel runaway slave; Searles (Andre Braugher), a bespectacled Emerson scholar; and Sharts (Jihmi Kennedy), a shy, stuttering former field slave. While undergoing relentless training, the black troops are subjected to the racism of white enlistees and officers, denied shoes and uniforms, and offered less than standard wages, which, with Shaw's support, they refuse to accept. Finally given a chance to enter combat, the 54th acquit themselves heroically, then make a brave suicidal assault against an impregnable harbor fortification—South Carolina's Fort Wagner.

Based partly on the real Robert Gould Shaw's letters, GLORY is remarkable in its fidelity to history. Director Edward Zwick (ABOUT LAST NIGHT, television's "thirtysomething") re-creates the period with remarkable accuracy, both in the observation of small details and in the truly harrowing battle scenes. Though essentially an ensemble piece, GLORY also contains especially compelling performances by Broderick, Washington, and Freeman. Richly plotted, alternately inspiring and horrifying, GLORY is an enlightening and entertaining tribute to heroes too long forgotten.

GO   DVD
1999 103m c   Comedy   ★★★★
Saratoga Entertainment/Banner Entertainment/   R
TriStar   (U.S.)

Sarah Polley (Ronna Martin), Katie Holmes (Claire Montgomery), Desmond Askew (Simon Baines), Nathan Bexton (Mannie), Robert Peters (Switterman), Scott Wolf (Adam), Jay Mohr (Zack), Timothy Olyphant (Todd Gaines), William Fichtner (Burke), Jane Krakowski (Irene)

p, Paul Rosenberg, Mickey Liddell, Matt Freeman; d, Doug Liman; w, John August; ph, Doug Liman; ed, Steve Mirrione; m, BT; prod d, Thomas P. Wilkins; art d, Rebecca Young; fx, Martin Becker; chor, Miranda Garrison; cos, Genevieve Tyrell

Hot on the heels of his surprise hit SWINGERS, director Doug Liman's superior third feature is a dark and edgy teen comedy that's also one of the most excitingly unpredictable American comedies since PULP FICTION.

It's Christmas Eve, and at exactly the same moment in a nondescript L.A. suburb, three carefully intertwined stories unfold. In the first, a supermarket checkout girl name Ronna (Sarah Polley) agrees to fill-in for coworker Simon (Desmond Askew) so he and three friends can take a holiday road trip to Las Vegas. When she's approached by two young actors (Jay Mohr and Scott Wolf) looking to score 20 hits of Ecstasy from Simon, Ronna tries her hand at amateur drug dealing. Bad move. The second story follows Simon and his friends to Vegas, where things get off to a great start—Simon even manages to weasel himself into bed with two drunken bridesmaids—but things go horribly wrong in a sleazy strip club when Simon breaks the cardinal rule of lap-dancing: No touching. The third story returns to the two actors who first approached Ronna at the supermarket. Busted for possession, Zack (Mohr) and Adam (Wolf)—two popular soap-opera stars who, unbeknownst to their fans, are also lovers—are forced to first take part in an undercover drug sting operation, then spend Christmas dinner with a creepy DEA agent (William Fichtner) and his swinging wife (Jane Krakowski), who have something even more sinister in mind than couple swapping.

Violent, funny, and breathlessly paced, this isn't your ordinary teen flick. Like Richard Linklater at his laid-back best, John August's ingenious script is offhandedly incisive, and Liman's style—a lot of hand-held camera and naturalistic lighting—makes for a perfect fit. And like Tarantino at his most exhilarating, the whole film is infused with the invigorating sense that at any given moment anything can happen—and usually does.

GO-BETWEEN, THE
1971 118m c   Drama   ★★★★
MGM/EMI   (U.K.)   PG

Julie Christie (Marian Maudsley), Alan Bates (Ted Burgess), Dominic Guard (Leo Colston), Margaret Leighton (Mrs. Maudsley), Michael Redgrave (The Older Leo), Michael Gough (Mr. Maudsley), Edward Fox (Hugh Trimingham), Richard Gibson (Marcus Maudsley), Simon Hume-Kendall (Denys), Amaryllis Garnett (Kate)

p, John Heyman, Norman Priggen; d, Joseph Losey; w, Harold Pinter (based on the novel by L.P. Hartley); ph, Gerry Fisher (Technicolor); ed, Reginald Beck; m, Michel Legrand; art d, Carmen Dillon; cos, John Furniss

AAN Best Supporting Actress: Margaret Leighton

Stylish look back into an old man's memories, courtesy of Harold Pinter, who wrote the screenplay adaptation of L.P. Hartley's novel. Redgrave reviews his life in painstaking and sometimes dizzying detail under Losey's deft direction. Julie Christie is engaged to Edward Fox, a member of the British aristocracy, but she is in love with Bates, a lowly farmer. Guard is Redgrave as a young man, hired as the go-between for Christie and Bates. This assignment gives the youth his first taste of love: he falls for Christie too. In fact, he never marries, and we are given to believe it was this feeling for Christie that kept him a bachelor for seven decades.

Set in Norfolk in the 1900s, the film flashes forward and backward with several twists and such attention to fine shadings that you cannot watch this movie without giving it your utmost attention. The cover for the affair is blown when

Christie's mother, Leighton, forces young Guard to take her to where Christie and Bates are trysting. Several shocking incidents, including Bates shooting himself, keep this film constantly surprising. The ending, in which an aged Christie asks the aged Redgrave to once more act as a go-between, is a smashing climax to a superb film.

GO TELL THE SPARTANS

1978	114m	c	War	★★★½
Spartan	(U.S.)			R

Burt Lancaster *(Maj. Asa Barker)*, Craig Wasson *(Cpl. Stephen Courcey)*, Jonathan Goldsmith *(Sgt. Oleonowski)*, Marc Singer *(Capt. Al Olivetti)*, Joe Unger *(Lt. Raymond Hamilton)*, Dennis Howard *(Cpl. Abraham Lincoln)*, David Clennon *(Lt. Finley Wattsberg)*, Evan Kim *(Cowboy)*, John Megna *(Cpl. Ackley)*, Hilly Hicks *(Signalman Coffee)*

p, Allan F. Bodoh, Mitchell Cannold; d, Ted Post; w, Wendell Mayes (based on the novel *Incident at Muc Wa* by Daniel Ford); ph, Harry Stradling Jr.; ed, Millie Moore; m, Dick Halligan; art d, Jack Senter; cos, Ron Dawson

Lost in the shuffle between THE DEER HUNTER and APOCALYPSE NOW, this neat little war movie tells of the U.S. presence in Vietnam in 1964, with advisor Lancaster commanding a small group of combat "advisors." Lancaster is ordered to send a platoon of Vietnamese militia (old men with shotguns, commanded by Communist-hating mercenary Kim) and a squad of Americans under green lieutenant Unger to garrison an old French stronghold. A veteran of three wars, Lancaster argues that the site is of no value and that all putting troops there will accomplish is enticing the Viet Cong to mass for an attack. He is overruled on the grounds that the French abandoned the spot and lost the war, "and we don't want to make the same mistake the French did." Lancaster is proved right, though, and before long the Viet Cong have besieged the isolated outpost.

The film features a typically fine performance by Lancaster, who wonders, through most of the film, why a draftee like Wasson would volunteer for combat duty. When Wasson explains that he wanted to know what a war was like, Lancaster exclaims, "I should have known it—you're a tourist!" Even at this point in the war, the film makes it obvious that we don't belong there; the U.S. Army command is portrayed as greedy and stupid, while the South Vietnamese appear to be thoroughly corrupt (Lancaster has to bribe the local warlord to give the battle some air support). The title derives from the inscription above the French cemetery, quoting the doomed Spartans at Thermopylae: "Stranger, go tell the Spartans how we lie; loyal to their laws, here we die."

GOALIE'S ANXIETY AT THE PENALTY KICK, THE

(DIE ANGST DES TORMANNS BEIM ELFMETER)

1971	101m	c	Crime	★★★½
Autoren/Osterreichischen		(West Germany)		

Arthur Brauss *(Joseph Bloch)*, Kai Fischer *(Hertha Gabler)*, Erika Pluhar *(Gloria)*, Libgart Schwartz *(Maid)*, Marie Bardeschewski *(Waitress)*, Michael Troost *(Salesman)*, Bert Fortell *(Customs Officer)*, Edda Koechl *(Girl in Vienna)*, Mario Kranz *(School Janitor)*, Ernst Meister *(Tax Inspector)*

p, Peter Genee; d, Wim Wenders; w, Wim Wenders, Peter Handke (based on the novel by Handke); ph, Robby Muller; ed, Peter Przygodda; m, Jurgen Knieper

Haunting. Wim Wenders's second feature film and his first collaboration with the Austrian novelist-poet-playwright Peter Handke is an adaptation of Handke's short novel about a soccer goalie driven to murder.

From the start of Wenders's film, the personality of the goalie, Josef Bloch (Arthur Brauss), is evident. While the game's action take place at one end of the field, Bloch waits at his net at the opposite end. As play nears, he takes little notice, walks in front of his net, and stands completely still as the ball is kicked past him. Bloch is a character who considers it pointless to try to evade or outwit the course of events. He leaves the team (whose popularity has taken them around the world) and begins to wander. He visits movie theaters, plays American songs on jukeboxes, drinks, encounters people, and observes life as it passes him by. After he meets a cinema cashier named Gloria (Erika Pluhar)—which, as she reminds him, is spelled G-L-O-R-I-A as in the rock 'n' roll song by Them—Bloch returns with her to her apartment and, eventually, strangles her for no apparent reason.

Wenders, who has long professed his fascination with America, its films, and its music, cannot make an American-style picture. Instead, he presents a meditative, fragmentary reconstruction of the killer's mind, his distorted perceptions, his personal morality, and the otherwise unimportant events in his daily existence. While most directors insist on sensationalizing acts of violence and perpetuating the myth of the outlaw hero, Wenders, in this portrait of a killer, delivers one of cinema's most truthful depictions of the criminal.

GODFATHER, THE

DVD

1972	175m	c	Crime	★★★★★
Paramount	(U.S.)			R

Marlon Brando *(Don Vito Corleone)*, Al Pacino *(Michael Corleone)*, James Caan *(Sonny Corleone)*, Richard Castellano *(Clemenza)*, Robert Duvall *(Tom Hagen)*, Sterling Hayden *(McCluskey)*, John Marley *(Jack Woltz)*, Richard Conte *(Barzini)*, Diane Keaton *(Kay Adams)*, Al Lettieri *(Sollozzo)*

p, Albert S. Ruddy; d, Francis Ford Coppola; w, Mario Puzo, Francis Ford Coppola (based on the novel by Mario Puzo); ph, Gordon Willis (Technicolor); ed, William Reynolds, Peter Zinner, Marc Laub, Murray Solomon; m, Nino Rota; prod d, Dean Tavoularis; art d, Warren Clymer; fx, A. D. Flowers, Joe Lombardi, Dick Smith, Sass Bedig; cos, Anna Hill Johnstone

AA Best Picture; AA Best Actor: Marlon Brando; AAN Best Supporting Actor: James Caan; AAN Best Supporting Actor: Robert Duvall; AAN Best Supporting Actor: Al Pacino; AAN Best Director: Francis Ford Coppola; AA Best Adapted Screenplay: Mario Puzo, Francis Ford Coppola; AAN Best Film Editing: William Reynolds, Peter Zinner; AAN Best Costume Design: Anna Hill Johnstone; AAN Best Sound: Bud Grenzbach, Richard Portman, Christopher Newman

One of the central American movies of the last 25 years, and one of very few to succed as both popular entertainment and high art. THE GODFATHER changed forever the popular perception of organized crime, implying strong parallels between the workings of the Mafia and those of any other profit-making corporation, and imparting operatic gravity to its liberal doses of violence.

The film opens with the wedding of Don Vito Corleone's (Marlon Brando) daughter Connie (Talia Shire) to Carlo Rizzi (Gianni Russo), a small-time bookie. Present at the ceremony is Brando's youngest son, Michael (Al Pacino), a much-decorated Marine captain who has just returned from WWII. College-educated, sensitive and perceptive, Michael is unlike almost all the other guests except Kay (Diane Keaton), his WASP sweetheart. Pacino points out gangster luminaries to Kay as a small boy might heroes in a baseball park.

Problems for the Corleone family arise with the appearance of Sollozzo (Al Lettieri), a maverick gangster who has the backing of a rival Mafia family. In a meeting with the Corleones, Sollozzo informs the family that he intends to establish wide-scale heroin sales in NYC, but requires the permission of Don Vito to do so. Corleone, an old-school Mafia don, sends Sollozzo packing, saying that he is disgusted by the thought of narcotics and is content with his gambling, prostitution and protection rackets. (In fact, he is reluctant to jeopardize his political contacts by venturing into this controversial new terrain.) The refusal leads to a gang war in which the Godfather is wounded, but not killed, in an assassination attempt.

Sonny (James Caan) temporarily takes over control of the family from the injured don, as Michael opts to kill Sollozzo and a corrupt police captain in revenge for the attack on Vito. After Michael goes into hiding in Sicily, the volatile Sonny beats up Carlo for having assaulted Connie and is then killed in an ambush that Carlo helped set up.

While in hiding, Michael takes a young Sicilian wife, only to lose her in a botched assassination attempt that was aimed at him by a rival family. Newly hardened, he returns to America to take control of the family from Don Vito who, now recuperated from his injuries, is retiring.

Great movies aren't usually planned as such; they happen through an unusual confluence of talents and luck. THE GODFATHER is no exception. Coppola had set out simply to redeem a faltering career when he started to shoot the popular Mario Puzo mafia novel. His talent brought him luck. First he collected an extraordinary number of the great actors who made American filmmaking interesting during the '70s and '80s: Marlon Brando, James Caan, Al Pacino, Diane Keaton, Robert Duvall. Then he spiced the mixture with some accomplished character actors: John Marley, Al Lettieri, Sterling Hayden, and Coppola's sister, Talia Shire. Coppola also had the eminent good sense—or good luck—to get Nino Rota to write his last great score. He got a finely crafted script from author Puzo, and then worked obsessively to push all involved to the limits of their abilities, and sometimes beyond.

Puzo's novel (which also redeemed a faltering career) provided not one, but several mythic elements that Coppola was canny enough to reinforce in the film. THE GODFATHER is a generational saga; it's also an action film; but above all, it catches the imagination of audiences because it suggests that the career of a gangster is not so very different from the career of a businessman or a politician. This had important resonance for the generation of the early '70s.

The film is dark—Coppola had cinematographer Gordon Willis deliberately underlight each scene; the mood is dark; and the climax, in which Michael indulges in an orgy of blood vengeance, would simply be horrific, were it not for the ironic melodies of the Rota score, which underline the humane sensibilities of the storyteller and keep us at an appropriate distance. And this points to Coppola's greatest achievement with THE GODFATHER; he simultaneously presents us with two views of the Corleone family. We see it from within, sympathizing with the motives and dilemmas of these very real, attractive and charismatic individuals; and we see it from without, in a state of suspended disgust at a moral code that knows only greed and blood.

GODFATHER, PART II, THE

1974 200m c Crime — ★★★★★
Paramount (U.S.) — R

Al Pacino *(Michael)*, Robert Duvall *(Tom Hagen)*, Diane Keaton *(Kay)*, Robert De Niro *(Vito Corleone)*, Talia Shire *(Connie)*, John Cazale *(Fredo)*, Lee Strasberg *(Hyman Roth)*, G.D. Spradlin *(Senator Geary)*, Michael V. Gazzo *(Frank Pentangeli)*, Richard Bright *(Al Neri)*

p, Francis Ford Coppola, Gray Frederickson, Fred Roos; d, Francis Ford Coppola; w, Francis Ford Coppola, Mario Puzo (based on characters from his novel); ph, Gordon Willis (Technicolor); ed, Peter Zinner, Barry Malkin, Richard Marks; m, Nino Rota, Carmine Coppola; prod d, Dean Tavoularis; art d, Angelo Graham; fx, A.D. Flowers, Joe Lombardi; cos, Theadora Van Runkle

AA Best Picture; AAN Best Actor: Al Pacino; AA Best Supporting Actor: Robert DeNiro; AAN Best Supporting Actor: Michael V. Gazzo; AAN Best Supporting Actor: Lee Strasberg; AAN Best Supporting Actress: Talia Shire; AA Best Director: Francis Ford Coppola; AA Best Adapted Screenplay: Francis Ford Coppola, Mario Puzo; AA Best Original Dramatic Score: Nino Rota, Carmine Coppola; AA Best Art Direction-Set Decoration: Dean Tavoularis, Angelo Graham, George R. Nelson; AAN Best Costume Design: Theadora Van Runkle

Sequels were beginning to become all the rage in the early seventies, so it's not surprising that a film as popular as THE GODFATHER gave birth to what could easily have been just a followup exploitation. What is remarkable, perhaps unique, is that THE GODFATHER, PART II actually expands upon and amplifies its predecessor. This is in fact both a sequel and a "prequel," intercutting the reign of Don Michael Corleone (Al Pacino) with the early story of his father, Vito, here brilliantly played by Robert De Niro.

Coppola was given a free hand with this sequel, and his deft directorial touches are everywhere, particularly in the earlier historical sequences. Cinematographer Willis superbly captures the turn-of-the-century period, applying a seriographic tint to flashback scenes for a softer, richer look than the sharp image of the ongoing contemporary story.

GODFATHER, PART III, THE

1990 161m c Crime — ★★★½
Zoetrope (U.S.) — R

Al Pacino *(Michael Corleone)*, Diane Keaton *(Kay Adams)*, Talia Shire *(Connie Corleone)*, Andy Garcia *(Vincent Mancini)*, Eli Wallach *(Don Altobello)*, Joe Mantegna *(Joey Zasa)*, George Hamilton *(B.J. Harrison)*, Bridget Fonda *(Grace Hamilton)*, Sofia Coppola *(Mary Corleone)*, Raf Vallone *(Cardinal Lamberto)*

p, Gray Frederickson, Fred Roos, Francis Ford Coppola, Charles Mulvehill; d, Francis Ford Coppola; w, Mario Puzo, Francis Ford Coppola; ph, Gordon Willis; ed, Barry Malkin, Lisa Fruchtman, Walter Murch; m, Carmine Coppola, Nino Rota; prod d, Dean Tavoularis; art d, Alex Tavoularis; fx, Lawrence J. Cavanaugh, R. Bruce Steinheimer; cos, Milena Canonero

AAN Best Picture; AAN Best Supporting Actor: Andy Garcia; AAN Best Director: Francis Ford Coppola; AAN Best Cinematography: Gordon Willis; AAN Best Art Direction-Set Decoration: Dean Tavoularis (Art Direction), Gary Fettis (Set Decoration); AAN Best Original Song: "Promise Me You'll Remember"; Carmine Coppola (Music), John Bettis (Lyrics); AAN Best Film Editing: Barry Malkin, Lisa Fruchtman, Walter Murch

The sequel that was never meant to be, and one that, ultimately, few of the original players could refuse. Out of the resulting confusion—budget excesses, creative clashes, last-second rewrites, cast dissension, a breakneck pace—emerged one of the most frustrating films of 1990, an epic without epic scope, a muted, strained, unnatural affair that never comes into dramatic focus. Coppola's wisest move in PART III was to not try to take the Corleone saga into a radically different direction. Instead, the third part becomes an extended coda to the ending of PART II, as Michael continues to fulfill his tragic legacy, doing his best for his family, only to destroy it in the process. Much of the critical drubbing the movie received centered on Coppola's ill-advised casting of his daughter, Sofia, in the crucial role of Michael's daughter, Mary.

GODS AND MONSTERS

1998 105m c/bw Drama/Fantasy — ★★★★
Regent Entertainment (U.S.) — R

Ian McKellen *(James Whale)*, Brendan Fraser *(Clayton Boone)*, Lynn Redgrave *(Hanna)*, Lolita Davidovich *(Betty)*, Kevin J. O'Connor *(Harry)*, David Dukes *(David Lewis)*, Brandon Kleyla

(Young Whale), Pamela Salem *(Sarah Whale)*, Michael O'Hagan *(William Whale)*, Jack Plotnick *(Edmund Kay)*

p, Paul Colichman, Gregg Fienberg, Mark R. Harris; d, Bill Condon; w, Bill Condon (based on the novel *Father of Frankenstein* by Christopher Bram); ph, Stephen M. Katz; ed, Virginia Katz; m, Carter Burwell; prod d, Richard Sherman; fx, Ultimate Effects; cos, Bruce Finlayson

AA Best Adapted Screenplay: Bill Condon; *AAN Best Actor:* Ian McKellen; *AAN Best Supporting Actress:* Lynn Redgrave

An elegiac meditation on the last days of director James Whale (FRANKENSTEIN, THE INVISIBLE MAN, BRIDE OF FRANKENSTEIN, and THE OLD DARK HOUSE), found dead in 1957 in his own Hollywood swimming pool under mysterious circumstances, this gentle rumination on what makes life worth living is driven by two exceptional performances.

Handsome, mad-at-the-world ex-Marine Clay Boone (Brendan Fraser) is hired to do yard work for the eccentric, 61-year-old English expatriate Whale (Ian McKellen), who has outlived his career, his social set, many of his intimates and, most importantly, his era. The elegant, soignee film folk of his glory days have been supplanted by crass parvenus, horror movies have degenerated into *I Was a Teenage...* tripe, and Whale's arch, European-infected sensibilities—once the height of sophistication—seem mannered and slightly silly. And on top of all that, he's drowning in a flood of memories unleashed by a recent stroke. His mind racing, he can't sleep or concentrate; even his lifelong passion for painting is compromised. That doesn't stop him from asking the well-developed Clay to model, and the two develop a contentious friendship. Clay is intrigued by the older man and his glamorous past in the movie industry, put off by the fact that Whale is openly homosexual, but flattered that someone so cultured sees him as interesting and special. Whale's interest in Clay goes beyond the obvious and has a faintly sinister edge: he's clearly manipulating the younger man, but it's not entirely apparent what the "Father of Frankenstein" (the title of the novel from which this movie is adapted) has in mind for his creation.

Witty and beautifully textured, director Bill Condon's poignant fantasy is equally at home re-creating the making of BRIDE and spinning dream sequences in the style of Universal horror pictures, all rich shadows and pale fog.

GODS MUST BE CRAZY, THE　　　📀

1981　109m　c　Comedy　　　★★★★
Mimosa　　　(Botswana)　　　PG

Marius Weyers *(Andrew Steyn)*, Sandra Prinsloo *(Kate Thompson)*, Louw Verwey *(Sam Boga)*, Nixau *(Xi)*, Jamie Uys *(The Reverend)*, Michael Thys *(Mpudi)*, Nic De Jager *(Jack Hind)*, Fanyana H. Sidumo *(1st Card Player)*, Joe Seakatsie *(2nd Card Player)*, Ken Gampu *(President)*

p, Jamie Uys; d, Jamie Uys; w, Jamie Uys; ph, Buster Reynolds, Robert Lewis, Jamie Uys; ed, Jamie Uys; m, John Boshoff; art d, Caroline Burls; cos, Gail Grobbelaar, Mij Reynolds

A hoot from South Africa and a brilliantly funny throwback to the days of slapstick silent comedy.

It begins as a *National Geographic* sort of documentary about the Kalahari Bushmen, an uncivilized African tribe that knows no violence, is thoroughly self-contained, and holds no material possessions. One day a small plane overhead drops a Coke bottle in the tribe's midst. Assuming that the bottle is a gift from the gods, the members begin to make use of it—and they discover that it has not one but many uses: mashing meal, flattening skins, playing music, making patterns. Since it is such a valuable tool, the tribesmen soon become possessive of it. This leads to greed, greed leads to anger, and anger leads to violence. Xi (Nixau, an actual Bushman), being the tribal

leader, is elected to rid his people of the bottle by taking it to the end of the earth and throwing it off.

Writer-director Jamie Uys resurrects a familiar, long-forgotten style of sight gags and traditional comic techniques in this delightful comedy that succeeds as both entertainment and nostalgic homage to the earliest days of film.

GODZILLA　　　📀

1998　139m　c　Science Fiction/Adventure/Thriller　★★
Centropolis Entertainment/Fried Films/Independent　PG-13
Pictures/Woods Entertainment　　　(U.S.)

Matthew Broderick *(Dr. Niko Tatopoulos)*, Jean Reno *(Philippe Roache)*, Hank Azaria *(Victor "Animal" Palotti)*, Maria Pitillo *(Audrey Timmonds)*, Arabella Field *(Lucy Palotti)*, Kevin Dunn *(Colonel Hicks)*, Doug Savant *(Sergeant O'Neal)*, Harry Shearer *(Charles Caiman)*, Michael Lerner *(Mayor Ebert)*, Vicki Lewis *(Dr. Elsie Chapman)*

p, Dean Devlin; d, Roland Emmerich; w, Roland Emmerich, Dean Devlin (from a story by Ted Elliott, Terry Rossio, Dean Devlin, and Roland Emmerich; based on the character created by Toho Co.); ph, Ueli Steiger; ed, Peter Amundson, David J. Siegel; m, David Arnold; prod d, Oliver Scholl; art d, William Ladd Skinner; fx, Patrick Tatopoulos, Volker Engel, Patrick Ellis, Centropolis Effects; cos, Joseph Porro

INDEPENDENCE DAY director-producer-writer team Roland Emmerich and Dean Devlin have blown up the simple premise behind Japan's beloved *Godzilla* series—giant lizard steps on city—into an unimaginative, dinosaur-sized bore.

French nuclear testing in the South Pacific has resulted in a new breed of outsized super-reptile who's on the move and looking for a cozy city to call home. After chomping his way through a Japanese fishing boat (a survivor gasping "Gojira!" from his hospital bed is the film's only concession to tradition) and tiptoeing across Panama, Godzilla arrives in downtown Manhattan, lays waste to the Financial District, then takes refuge in the New York City subway system. It's a while before he pokes his head out again, and the screen is left to the much less interesting human characters: mutant species expert Dr. Nick Tatopoulos (Matthew Broderick); aspiring TV journalist Audrey Timmonds (Maria Pitillo); and the mysterious Philippe Roache (Jean Reno), a French secret service agent acting on behalf of his country's guilty conscience.

The spectacle of Godzilla crashing through the canyons of Manhattan while the Army destroys half the city trying to stop him is the only real thrill this film has to offer. It quickly passes. There are a few minor variations on the original Godzilla, but the lizard's new look is a huge disappointment: he's little more than a pumped-up iguana. Whatever the benefits of computer generated imagery, it has yet to convincingly create the illusion of physical presence so essential to monster movies. It never feels as if Godzilla and the seriously inconvenienced New Yorkers really occupy the same space. And if CGI means that everything has to take place under the masking cover of rain and darkness in order to look "real," then bring on the guy in the rubber suit.

GODZILLA, KING OF THE MONSTERS　　　📀
(GOJIRA)
1954　81m　bw　Science Fiction/Disaster　★★★½
Toho Films　　　(Japan/U.S.)

Raymond Burr *(Steve Martin)*, Akira Takarada *(Naval Salvage Officer Hideto Ogata)*, Momoko Kochi *(Emiko Yamane)*, Akihiko Hirata *(Dr. Daisuke Serizawa)*, Takashi Shimura *(Dr. Kyohei Yamane)*, Fuyuki Murakami *(Dr. Tabata)*, Sachio Sakai *(Reporter Hagiwara)*, Toranosuke Ogwawa *(President of Nankai Shipping Company)*, Ren Yamamoto *(Masaji)*, Takeo Oikawa *(Chief of Emergency Headquarters)* p, Tomoyuki Tanaka, Richard Kay, Joseph E. Levine; d, Ishiro Honda, Terry O. Morse; w, Takeo Murata, Ishiro Honda (based on a story by Shigeru Kayama); ph, Masao Tamai, Guy Roe; ed, Yasunobu Taira, Terry O. Morse; m, Akira Ifukube; prod d, Satoshi Chuko; fx, Eiji Tsuburaya, Akira Watanabe, Hiroshi Mukoyama, Kuichiro Kishida

One of the most bizarrely endearing icons of the movies made his American debut in this drastically re-edited version of a 1954 Japanese hit. While much of GODZILLA, KING OF THE MONSTERS is second-rate, there's no doubt that you're watching a star being born.

American reporter Steve Martin (Raymond Burr) lies injured in a makeshift Japanese hospital, the victim of a staggering disaster. He recalls recent events: on a layover in Japan, he investigates the mysterious disappearance of several ships. Martin accompanies a government expedition to Odo Island, where natives speak of an ancient monster they call Godzilla. At night, Godzilla, a dinosaur 50 meters high, destroys the village. Back in Tokyo, paleontologist Dr. Yamane (Takashi Shimura) theorizes that Godzilla is a two-million-year-old beast that's been resuscitated by atomic testing. Godzilla emerges from Tokyo Bay and attacks Tokyo, crushing buildings and spewing radioactive breath. The military tries to stop him, but they have no effect on the destructive monster.

Director Ishiro Honda, a protege of Akira Kurosawa, visited Hiroshima after the war and wanted to make a film about the feelings he experienced. Eight years later, this proved to be the unlikely but effective vehicle. An enormous amount of footage was cut from the original 98-minute Japanese GOJI-RA—even with all the new footage featuring Raymond Burr, GODZILLA clocks in at only 81 minutes. Still, in many ways, GODZILLA is an improvement. While the original film is more horrifying in portraying the carnage wreaked by Godzilla, it also spends far too much time on a love triangle linking its central characters. Fourteen GODZILLA sequels of generally diminishing quality were produced in the 21 years after the film's initial release.

GOING IN STYLE
1979 97m c Comedy ★★★★
Warner Bros. (U.S.) PG

George Burns (Joe), Art Carney (Al), Lee Strasberg (Willie), Charles Hallahan (Pete), Pamela Payton-Wright (Kathy), Siobhan Keegan (Colleen), Brian Neville (Kevin), Constantine Hartofolis (Boy in Park), Mary Testa (Teller), Jean Shevlin (Mrs. Fein)

p, Tony Bill, Fred T. Gallo; d, Martin Brest; w, Martin Brest (based on a story by Edward Cannon); ph, Billy Williams (Technicolor); ed, Robert Swink, C. Timothy O'Meara; m, Michael Small; prod d, Stephen Hendrickson; art d, Gary Weist; cos, Anna Hill Johnstone

The laughs seem strained but the poignance comes on strong. Three elderly gents (Burns, Carney and Strasberg), tired of the indifference society shows them and the pervasive feeling of uselessness that shrouds their lives, decide to rob a bank. It's really Burns who promotes the idea, more as a way of relieving boredom than increasing his savings account; it's also appealing to Strasberg and Carey as a means of striking back at a system that's abandoned them as human beings. Wearing funny masks and wielding guns, the threesome robs a Manhattan bank of a small fortune.

Burns is absolutely fascinating in his portrayal of a crafty, wise and wholly adaptable old man outwitting the fast-moving young world around him. There are some sublimely serious parts to give the whole thing roots, such as a moving scene where Burns looks through a box of old photos that actually show him as a young vaudeville trooper and some shots with his real-life wife Gracie Allen. He begins to weep as he looks back on days no more, images that drag at his heart. This nostalgic interlude is brought to an abrupt halt when Burns suddenly stands up, swearing, as he realizes that he has wet his trousers—age again, intruding upon his reveries.

Director Brest does a great job with a sensitive subject, drawing fine performances from everyone. Carney is a standout as the jovial, ready-for-anything sidekick who has the time of his life rolling points in Las Vegas. He really dies happy, flattered to glowing pride that a pretty young thing in gambler's paradise propositioned him. A consistently funny and warm movie.

GOING MY WAY
1944 130m bw Religious/Musical ★★★★
Paramount (U.S.)

Bing Crosby (Father Chuck O'Malley), Rise Stevens (Genevieve Linden), Barry Fitzgerald (Father Fitzgibbon), Frank McHugh (Father Timothy O'Dowd), Gene Lockhart (Ted Haines, Sr.), William Frawley (Max Dolan), James Brown (Ted Haines, Jr.), Jean Heather (Carol James), Porter Hall (Mr. Belknap), Fortunio Bonanova (Tomasso Bozzani)

p, Leo McCarey; d, Leo McCarey; w, Frank Butler, Frank Cavett (based on a story by McCarey); ph, Lionel Lindon; ed, LeRoy Stone; art d, Hans Dreier, William Flannery; fx, Gordon Jennings; cos, Edith Head

AA Best Picture; AA Best Actor: Bing Crosby; AAN Best Actor: Barry Fitzgerald; AA Best Supporting Actor: Barry Fitzgerald; AA Best Director: Leo McCarey; AA Best Original Story: Leo McCarey; AA Best Screenplay: Frank Butler, Frank Cavett; AAN Best B/W Cinematography: Lionel Lindon; AAN Best Film Editing: Leroy Stone; AA Best Song: "Swinging on a Star"; James Van Heusen (Music), Johnny Burke (Lyrics)

A warm and moving sleeper hit. Father Chuck O'Malley (Bing Crosby) is an easy-going, trouble-shooting priest who arrives at St. Dominic's Church, a Catholic institution that has seen better days, as has its curate, the elderly Father Fitzgibbon (Barry Fitzgerald). The old and stubborn priest has led the parish for 45 years, but recently the church has gotten heavily in to debt, disillusioning even the parishioners. Through the magic of music, however, Father O'Malley brings Father Fitzgibbon out of the doldrums and saves the parish.

Leo McCarey's direction is masterful, stopping the sentiment just short of the maudlin. It all works like magic, especially the unbeatable chemistry between Crosby and Fitzgerald. The film was box-office dynamite and swept the Oscars, winning for Best Picture, Best Director, Best Screenplay, Best Actor and Best Supporting Actor. GOING MY WAY and its sequel, THE BELLS OF ST. MARY'S, were also popular with the Catholic Church and Pope Pius XII, who later gave a private audience to Crosby in thanks for the latter's priestly portrayal.

GOING PLACES
(LES VALSEUSES)
1974 117m c Comedy/Drama ★★★
C.A.P.A.C./U.P.F./SN (France) R

Gerard Depardieu (Jean-Claude), Patrick Dewaere (Pierrot), Miou-Miou (Marie-Ange), Jeanne Moreau (Jeanne Pirolle), Jacques Chailleux (Jacques Pirolle), Michel Peyrelon (Surgeon), Brigitte Fossey (Young Mother), Isabelle Huppert (Jacqueline), Christiane Muller (Jacqueline's Mother), Christian Alers (Jacqueline's Father)

p, Paul Claudon; d, Bertrand Blier; w, Bertrand Blier, Philippe Dumarcay (based on the novel by Blier); ph, Bruno Nuytten; ed, Kenout Peltier; m, Stephane Grappelli

Disagreeable but fascinating examination of youth construct- ed as a buddy-road movie. GOING PLACES revolves around the friendship between Depardieu and Dewaere, a couple of long-haired, disheveled petty thieves in their mid-20s. As the film begins, the duo is terrorizing a middle-aged woman— grabbing her ample behind, blowing kisses on her neck, and finally stealing her purse. So begins a spree—which, as crime sprees go, is relatively harmless. Along the way, the two steal cars, break into stores, insult people, seduce some semi-will- ing women, and even have sex with each other when no one else is available. They seem, however, to have no profound effect on anyone.

After returning a stolen car Dewaere is shot, and superfi- cially wounded in one testicle, by the angry owner. His fear that he'll never have sex again proves groundless, however, when the thieves meet Miou-Miou, a flighty young woman who doesn't mind disrobing for, or having sex with, the fel- lows—but who doesn't seem to enjoy it either—which infu- riates these two macho men who are convinced they can make any woman melt in their arms.

The first major film from Bertrand Blier (son of actor Bernard), GOING PLACES is an ugly and brutal, yet some- how charming, look at two young men who are wholly worth- less as human beings. They have no future; and, despite the fact that they travel from one side of France to the other, they never get anywhere. They just go—fast and furiously. The most significant moment in their lives is their meeting with Moreau, an older woman just released from prison, who laments her lost youth. She who has nothing is even worse off than Depardieu and Dewaere, who have youth, at least. The alluring Moreau appears only briefly but gives one of her most spectacular performances.

GOLD DIGGERS OF 1933

1933 94m bw Musical ★★★★★
Warren Bros. (U.S.)

Warren William *(J. Lawrence Bradford)*, Joan Blondell *(Carol King)*, Aline MacMahon *(Trixie Lorraine)*, Ruby Keeler *(Polly Parker)*, Dick Powell *(Brad Roberts/Robert Treat Bradford)*, Guy Kibbee *(Faneuil H. Peabody)*, Ned Sparks *(Barney Hopkins)*, Ginger Rogers *(Fay Fortune)*, Clarence Nordstrom *(Gordon)*, Robert Agnew *(Dance Director)*

p, Robert Lord; d, Mervyn LeRoy; w, Erwin Gelsey, James Seymour, David Boehm, Ben Markson (based on the play "Gold Diggers of Broadway" by Avery Hopwood); ph, Sol Polito; ed, George Amy; art d, Anton Grot; chor, Busby Berkeley; cos, Orry-Kelly

AAN Best Sound Recording: Nathan Levinson

Pure depression gold. After their success with 42ND STREET, Warner Bros. threw this film together quickly, sens- ing that they were on to something with movie musicals. Based on 1929's *Gold Diggers of Broadway* by Avery Hopwood, this Mervyn LeRoy-directed extravaganza not only became a hit but spawned several more films of its ilk.

Joan Blondell, Aline MacMahon and Ruby Keeler play a trio of unemployed showgirls who are thrilled when pro- ducer Barney Hopkins (Ned Sparks) informs them he's about to start a new show. The problem is that he doesn't have a penny, but Brad Roberts (Dick Powell), a songwriter who is mad for Polly (Keeler) does, and lends Sparks $15,000 to get "Forgotten Melody" off the ground. The show goes into rehearsal, with Brad taking one of the roles, but the girls wonder if his money is clean, except for Polly, who *just knows* he's legit. Of course he is. In fact, he's the scion of a wealthy Beacon Hill family; however, his brother, J. Lawrence (Warren William), and a lawyer, Faneuil Hall

Peabody (Guy Kibbee), arrive from Boston to put an end to Brad's frivolousness.

Harry Warren and Al Dubin wrote the excellent songs, and Busby Berkeley did the startling choreography, including a Ginger Rogers-led chorus dressed in gold coin costumes in the extravagant rendition of "We're in the Money" (which Ginger does in pig latin). The picture is loaded with inside jokes, including cameo appearances by famed agent Louis Schurr and Berkeley as the "Call-Boy" (that's the correct term). If you have but one 1930s Warner Bros. musical to see, make it this one. Remade as PAINTING THE CLOUDS WITH SUNSHINE.

GOLD DIGGERS OF 1935

1935 95m bw Musical ★★★½
Warner Bros./First National (U.S.)

Dick Powell *(Dick Curtis)*, Gloria Stuart *(Amy Prentiss)*, Adolphe Menjou *(Nicoleff)*, Glenda Farrell *(Betty Hawes)*, Grant Mitchell *(Louis Lamson)*, Dorothy Dare *(Arline Davis)*, Alice Brady *(Mrs. Mathilda Prentiss)*, Frank McHugh *(Humboldt Prentiss)*, Hugh Herbert *(T. Mosely Thorpe)*, Winifred Shaw *(Winny)*

p, Robert Lord; d, Busby Berkeley; w, Manuel Seff, Peter Milne (based on a story by Milne, Robert Lord); ph, George Barnes; ed, George Amy; art d, Anton Grot; fx, Busby Berkeley

AA Best Song: "Lullaby Of Broadway"; Harry Warren (Music), Al Dubin (Lyrics); *AAN Best Dance Direction:* Busby Berkeley

Gold-plated good fun. A minor plot is mangled in a major fashion by Busby Berkeley, but his choreography and the score assure us of delirious delight. The scene is a summer resort in a New England town, the story revolving around a number of romantic pairings. The inn's employees include Dick Powell as a desk clerk studying to be a doctor, Adolphe Menjou as the somewhat dishonest owner of the hotel, Gloria Stuart as the attractive ingenue, and Frank McHugh as the ne'er-do-well comedy relief.

The key to all the fun is the Harry Warren-Al Dubin score which features the remarkable "Lullaby of Broadway" (a song reprised from their score for 42ND STREET) as well as "I'm Going Shopping With You" and "The Words Are In My Heart." Around these tunes Berkeley devised what was, to some, the apex of his choreographic career. The highlight is a production number done for a charity show at the hotel, fea- turing the aforementioned "Lullaby of Broadway" in a sequence that shows the last day in the life of a "Broadway Baby" before she falls out of a window to her death. The num- ber uses more than 100 dancers, seen from evey possible angle and doing some of the most precise dancing ever put on cel- luloid.

GOLD OF NAPLES

(L'ORO DI NAPOLI)
1954 74m bw Drama/Comedy ★★★
Ponti/DEG/Gala (Italy)

THE RACKETEER: Lianella Carrell *(The Wife)*, Toto *(The Husband)*, Pasquale Cennamo *(The Racketeer)*, PIZZA ON CREDIT: Sophia Loren *(The Wife)*, Giacomo Furia *(The Husband)*, Alberto Farnese *(The Lover)*, Paolo Stoppa *(The Widower)*, THE GAMBLER: Vittorio De Sica *(The Count)*, Mario Passante *(His Valet)*, Irene Montalto *(The Countess)*

p, Dino De Laurentiis, Carlo Ponti; d, Vittorio De Sica; w, Cesare Zavattini, Dino De Sica, Giuseppe Marotta (based on the novel by Marotta); ph, Otello Martelli; ed, Eraldo Da Roma; m, Alessandro Cicognini

By turns melancholy and very witty, in the beloved vignette format of the greatest Italian filmmakers. The stories include (two of the film's six episodes were cut before U.S. release) "The Racketeer," in which pantomimist Toto outwits and undoes a bullying friend who has intruded into his home as a permanent guest. "Pizza on Credit" shows Loren as a cheating wife who loses her wedding ring while trysting with Farnese, which causes husband Furia to become suspicious and necessitates a frantic search for the ring (returned by the lover at the last moment).

De Sica, the director, plays the lead role in "The Gambler," an inveterate gamester who has squandered away every dime his family ever had, but who continues to believe he is a grand sharper. In this, the best of the vignettes, De Sica has a marvelous scene playing cards with the young son of the doorman where he resides, Piero Bilancioni, who wearily wins every hand, cleaning out the old man once again. In "Theresa," Silvana Mangano is an alluring prostitute who marries a mentally unbalanced young man and has to apply her own brand of psychology to straighten out their relationship.

Though the acting is generally above average here, GOLD OF NAPLES is not 14 karat, mostly because of the erratic story lines and the lack of logical transition between vignettes. This film marked one of Loren's earliest appearances. The segment with Loren as the pizza-maker's lusty spouse is very close to the French movie, THE BAKER'S WIFE, but the scene of her walking is as classic as Monroe's in NIAGARA.

GOLDEN BOY

1939 99m bw Sports ★★★★
Columbia (U.S.)

Barbara Stanwyck (Lorna Moon), Adolphe Menjou (Tom Moody), William Holden (Joe Bonaparte), Lee J. Cobb (Mr. Bonaparte), Joseph Calleia (Eddie Fuseli), Sam Levene (Siggie), Edward Brophy (Roxy Lewis), Beatrice Blinn (Anna), William H. Strauss (Mr. Carp), Don Beddoe (Borneo)

p, William Perlberg; d, Rouben Mamoulian; w, Lewis Meltzer, Daniel Taradash, Sarah Y. Mason, Victor Heerman (based on the play by Clifford Odets); ph, Nicholas Musuraca, Karl Freund; ed, Otto Meyer; m, Victor Young; art d, Lionel Banks; cos, Robert Kalloch

AAN Best Original Score: Victor Young

Not strictly faithful to Odets, but GOLDEN BOY nonetheless captures his drama's spirit of proletarian angst, propelled by the extraordinary performances of Barbara Stanwyck and William Holden in his first major role.

Joe Bonaparte (Holden), a gifted violinist, is forced by poverty to enter the ring, where he proves to be a talented boxer even though he seemingly pulls his punches, afraid of damaging his musician's hands and ending the dream for which his immigrant father (Lee J. Cobb) has sacrificed so much. Lorna Moon (Stanwyck), the girlfriend of Joe's manager (Adolphe Menjou), is given the task of persuading Joe to give up his musical aspirations. After falling in love with Lorna and then feeling betrayed by her duplicity, Joe returns to the ring, with tragic results.

The film manages to reveal a silver-lined ending that is far more upbeat than Odets's suicide finale. Just the same, Rouben Mamoulian does a wonderful job of retaining the essential story and basic character, building beautifully upon both through his careful scenes; his direction of the brutal but realistic fight scenes adds much to the film's power. Menjou and Cobb offer excellent support, but this film belongs to Stanwyck and to Holden, the 21-year-old unknown who was chosen for the part over John Garfield who created the role in the original Group Theater production.

GOLDEN COACH, THE DVD

(LE CARROSSE D'OR)
1952 105m c Drama ★★★★
Panaria/Hoche (France/Italy)

Anna Magnani (Camilla), Odoardo Spadaro (Don Antonio), Nada Fiorelli (Isabella), Dante (Harlequin), Duncan Lamont (Viceroy), George Higgins (Martinez), Ralph Truman (Duke of Castro), Gisella Mathews (Marquise Altamirano), Raf de la Torre (Chief Justice), Elena Altieri (Duchess of Castro)

p, Francesco Alliata; d, Jean Renoir; w, Jean Renoir, Renzo Avanzo, Jack Kirkland, Ginette Doynel, Giulio Macchi (based on the play "La Carrosse du Saint-Sacrement" by Prosper Merimee); ph, Claude Renoir (Technicolor); ed, Mario Serandrei, David Hawkins; m, Antonio Vivaldi; cos, Maria De Matteis

Belatedly hailed as one of the great films about acting; certainly, a stunning visual example of the use of color. Marking Jean Renoir's return to France after his decade in Hollywood and his short period in India filming THE RIVER, THE GOLDEN COACH has often been seen as the key to understanding all the director's work.

Filmed in English at Rome's Cinecitta studios, the film stars Anna Magnani as Camilla, a *commedia dell'arte* performer who, with her ragtag troupe, arrives in Peru to open a new theater. Already pursued by Felipe (Paul Campbell), Camilla captures the hearts of the vain bullfighter Ramon (Riccardo Rioli) and the Viceroy (Duncan Lamont). Swept away by Camilla's charms and attracted to the vulgar manner that is so alien to his aristocratic experience, the Viceroy presents her with his prized golden coach, a beautifully crafted vehicle that had been used solely for royal business. As the drama rolls on and Camilla struggles to differentiate between reality and the stage, all three of her suitors vie for her love—the Viceroy learning to feel "common" emotions; Ramon impressing her with his manliness; and Felipe inviting her to live with him in the wilderness among the "noble savages."

Opening and closing with a stage curtain, THE GOLDEN COACH is Jean Renoir's invitation to sit back and enjoy the colorful, romantic, humorous spectacle that is real life. While artists have often addressed the confusion of reality and fiction, few have done it with as much grace and love as Renoir. Much of the film's success, however, is due to the brilliant Magnani. THE GOLDEN COACH does not so much star Magnani as it exists because of her. It is her film and everything in it thrives because of the life she breathes into it.

GOLDEN VOYAGE OF SINBAD, THE DVD

1973 105m c Fantasy/Adventure ★★★½
Columbia (U.K.) G

John Phillip Law (Sinbad), Caroline Munro (Margiana), Tom Baker (Koura), Douglas Wilmer (Vizier), Martin Shaw (Rachid), Gregoire Aslan (Hakim), Kurt Christian (Haroun), Takis Emmanuel (Achmed), John David Garfield (Abdul), Aldo Sambrell (Omar)

p, Charles H. Schneer, Ray Harryhausen; d, Gordon Hessler; w, Brian Clemens; ph, Ted Moore (Dynarama); ed, Roy Watts; m, Miklos Rozsa; prod d, John Stoll; art d, Fernando Gonzalez; fx, Ray Harryhausen

This sequel to the terrific THE SEVENTH VOYAGE OF SINBAD, is great fun—with a minimum of plot and a maximum of wonderful Ray Harryhausen special effects. John Phillip Law is the famed sailor here, in search of a gold tablet that will restore a deposed ruler (Douglas Wilmer) to the throne. En route Sinbad encounters a one-eyed centaur, a winged griffin, a six-armed statue and a host of other fantastic creatures. Fast-paced and exciting, the film features some of Harryhausen's best stop-motion animation work. Tom (television's "Dr. Who") Baker makes a marvelous villain.

The surprising box-office success of THE GOLDEN VOY-AGE OF SINBAD led to yet another sequel, the relatively disappointing SINBAD AND THE EYE OF THE TIGER.

GOLDENEYE `DVD`

1995 130m c Action/Spy/Thriller ★★★
Eon Productions Ltd./Danjaq Inc./United Artists PG-13
(U.S.)

Pierce Brosnan *(James Bond)*, Sean Bean *(Alec Trevelyan)*, Izabella Scorupco *(Natalya Simonova)*, Famke Janssen *(Xenia Onatopp)*, Joe Don Baker *(Jack Wade)*, Judi Dench *(M)*, Robbie Coltrane *(Valentin Zukovsky)*, Tcheky Karyo *(Dmitiri Mishkin)*, Gottfried John *(General Ourumov)*, Alan Cumming *(Boris Grishenko)*

p, Michael G. Wilson, Barbara Broccoli; d, Martin Campbell; w, Jeffrey Caine, Bruce Feirstein (from a story by Michael France, based on characters created by Ian Fleming); ph, Phil Meheux; ed, Terry Rawlings; m, Eric Serra; prod d, Peter Lamont; art d, Neil Lamont; fx, Chris Corbould, Mara Bryan, Derek Meddings; cos, Lindy Hemming

By 1995, had the longest-running franchise in film history finally run its course, done in by changing politics, sexual mores, and audience tastes? In a word, no. GOLDENEYE, starring Pierce Brosnan as Bond No. 5, should appeal equally to die-hard Bond fans and bonded DIE HARD fans.

The plot is along the usual lines, involving a Russian satellite, code-named GoldenEye, that comes under the control of supervillains Alec Trevelyan (Sean Bean) and General Ourumov (Gottfried John). GoldenEye has the power to destroy anything containing an electrical circuit, up to and including an entire city, and the villains plan to decimate London while also making themselves super-rich.

Lean, dark and graceful, Brosnan wraps his perfectly calculated accent around all the standard phrases without making us hear quotation marks. He's a worthy Bond, glib and convincingly athletic, and ought to last a good half-dozen films before his waist thickens and his solid good looks begin to slide. And although GOLDENEYE is the first Bond film that owes nothing to Ian Fleming but 007 himself, that's no particular drawback. The Bond movies, particularly the later ones, were less about plot than trappings: cool gear, perverted bad guys, gorgeous girls and exotic locations. The writers get the mix just about right, and first-time Bond director Martin Campbell moves things along fairly briskly.

More importantly, let's talk about girls, beginning with the new M, Judi Dench. She plays M as a steely schoolmarm who coolly tells her underlings that if she wants sarcasm, she'll talk to her children. Famke Janssen, as the ultravixenish Xenia Onatopp, is all wide, devouring mouth and rolling eyes: that she kills men by scissoring them between her thighs strikes at least some of them as a reasonable exchange.

GOLDFINGER `DVD`

1964 112m c Spy/Adventure ★★★★½
UA (U.K.)

Sean Connery *(James Bond)*, Gert Frobe *(Goldfinger)*, Honor Blackman *(Pussy Galore)*, Shirley Eaton *(Jill Masterson)*, Tania Mallett *(Tilly Masterson)*, Harold Sakata *(Oddjob)*, Bernard Lee *("M")*, Martin Benson *(Solo)*, Cec Linder *(Felix Leiter)*, Lois Maxwell *(Moneypenny)*

p, Harry Saltzman, Albert R. Broccoli; d, Guy Hamilton; w, Richard Maibaum, Paul Dehn (based on the novel by Ian Fleming); ph, Ted Moore (Technicolor); ed, Peter Hunt; m, John Barry; prod d, Ken Adam; art d, Peter Murton; fx, John Stears

AA Best Sound Effects: Norman Wanstall

Probably the best of the gadget-filled 007 extravaganzas, GOLDFINGER represents the consolidation of the wildly profitable Bond formula. For the first time, the well-loved conventions of the series are all in place, and they jell perfectly—perhaps for the last time.

This third Bond movie pits the hero (Sean Connery) against one of his more memorable adversaries, Goldfinger (Gert Frobe), a gold-hoarding, power-hungry maniac who plans to detonate a small atomic device inside Fort Knox, contaminating its huge gold supply with deadly radiation and making him the richest man in the world. Bond's attempts to foil Goldfinger's plans take him from Miami to Europe to Kentucky and force him to confront Goldfinger's hare-lipped Korean assistant, Oddjob (Harold Sakata), who kills his victims with a razor-edged bowler hat. Bond also battles and eventually woos martial arts expert and pilot Pussy Galore (Honor Blackman, who abandoned her spot on the highly successful television series "The Avengers" for this role).

GOLDFINGER contains more crowd-pleasing moments than any other Bond film, including Oddjob's flying bowler, a laser beam that almost emasculates Bond, the lavishly accessorized Aston Martin DB5, and the bizarre murder of Goldfinger's secretary (Shirley Eaton): she's gilded to death. It also features Shirley Bassey's terrific rendition of the Leslie Bricusse-Anthony Newley title song. Much credit is due director Guy Hamilton, who was able to juggle all the gadgets, wild characters, and strange locations long enough to produce a perfectly balanced, entertaining film that stands on its own. Later Bond films were to rely too heavily on campy oneliners, expensive sets, and gimmicky effects.

GONE WITH THE WIND `DVD`

1939 220m c Drama/Historical/Romance ★★★★★
Selznick (U.S.)

Clark Gable *(Rhett Butler)*, Vivien Leigh *(Scarlett O'Hara)*, Hattie McDaniel *(Mammy)*, Leslie Howard *(Ashley Wilkes)*, Olivia de Havilland *(Melanie Hamilton)*, Butterfly McQueen *(Prissy)*, Everett Brown *(Big Sam)*, Zack Williams *(Elijah)*, Oscar Polk *(Pork)*, Thomas Mitchell *(Gerald O'Hara)*

p, David O. Selznick; d, Victor Fleming, George Cukor, Sam Wood; w, Sidney Howard, Jo Swerling, Charles MacArthur, Ben Hecht, John Lee Mahin, John Van Druten, Oliver H.P. Garrett, Winston Miller, John Balderston, Michael Foster, Edwin Justus Mayer, F. Scott Fitzgerald, David O. Selznick (based on the novel by Margaret Mitchell); ph, Ernest Haller, Ray Rennahan, Lee Garmes (Technicolor); ed, Hal C. Kern, James E. Newcom; m, Max Steiner; prod d, William Cameron Menzies; art d, Lyle Wheeler, Hobe Erwin; fx, Jack Cosgrove, Lee Zavitz, Arthur Johns, Fred Albin; chor, Frank Floyd, Eddie Prinz; cos, Walter Plunkett

AA Best Picture; AAN Best Actor: Clark Gable; *AA Best Actress:* Vivien Leigh; *AA Best Supporting Actress:* Hattie McDaniel; *AAN Best Supporting Actress:* Olivia De Havilland; *AA Best Director:* Victor Fleming; *AA Best Screenplay:* Sidney Howard; *AA Best Color Cinematography:* Ernest Haller, Ray Rennahan; *AA Best Film Editing:* Hal C. Kern, James E. Newcom; *AAN Best Original Score:* Max Steiner; *AA Best Interior Decoration:* Lyle Wheeler; *AAN Best Sound Recording:* Thomas T. Moulton; *AAN Best Special Effects:* Jack Cosgrove (Photographic), Fred Albin (Sound), Arthur Johns (Sound)

The best remembered and most publicized film in Hollywood's flamboyant history, the biggest of David O. Selznick's grand obsessions, and quite probably the most beloved movie of all time.

This star-studded Civil War epic, based on Margaret Mitchell's immensely popular novel, is nearly as powerful and moving today as when first released in 1939. Beneath the surface of a lavish and sometimes awe-inspiring production lies a deftly handled story about an endlessly fascinating—if not always attractive—heroine. Though she's frequently dismissed as a simpering Southern belle, Scarlett O'Hara (Vivien Leigh) is a resilent, resourceful protagonist, equal to acts of real heroism but incapable of cliched nobility. And for many of us, there's a lesson in her story—that buying into romantic obsession almost certainly guarantees that we'll end up with the last person we need.

Leigh won the the most coveted role in film history from a field that included Paulette Goddard, Norma Shearer, Bette Davis, Joan Crawford, Miriam Hopkins, Jean Harlow, Carole Lombard, Tallulah Bankhead, Claudette Colbert, Jean Arthur, Joan Bennett, and Irene Dunne, among some 2,000 women tested in a much-ballyhooed two-year talent search. She's nothing short of perfection. As Rhett Butler, co-star Clark Gable likewise couldn't be bettered. The only player among the majors who disappoints is Leslie Howard—he just isn't handsome or vigorous enough to motivate so much of Scarlett's energy. Supporting performances are generally of a high order, though McDaniel's heart-tugging Mammy and Ona Munson's bittersweet trollop are rather cloying. If Butterfly McQueen's character is an alarming stereotype, her perfectly modulated comic hysteria is brilliantly entertaining; the actress can hardly be faulted for doing her best in the context of the film's essentially racist discourse.

From a directorial standpoint, the sequences shot by "women's director" George Cukor are the best. His style is more lyrical, and more attentive to the literary qualities of the source material, than that of Victor Fleming. Nowhere is this more evident than the barbecue at Twelve Oaks and the announcement of war—possibly the best sequence in the piece. Later, GWTW under Fleming seems to settle into itself and just tell the story. Despite some excellent sequences—Scarlett's attempt to get Dr. Meade to leave the railroad station springs immediately to mind—many of the film's purely narrative sequences verge on the mundane. Cukor began at the film's helm but was replaced by Fleming (whose WIZARD OF OZ was also released in 1939), reportedly because the former had shifted the focus of the film too much to Scarlett and Melanie (to say nothing of leading man Gable's open disdain for Cukor). During the course of the production Fleming suffered a nervous breakdown and Sam Wood stepped in until Fleming was well enough to return.

Although its "historical" set-pieces (e.g., the burning of Atlanta) are brilliantly realized, GWTW should not be mistaken for history—it romanticizes the slave-owning south and caricatures Reconstruction. Still, it's the peak example of the collaborative artistic achievement for which Hollwood's Golden Age is justly celebrated. To quote Olivia de Havilland, "Everytime I see it, I find something fresh, some shade of meaning I hadn't noticed before… How fortunate that so many gifted people found immortality in GONE WITH THE WIND."

GONIN
1995 109m c Crime ★★★½ **DVD**
Bunkasha Publishing/Image Factory/First Production Company/Kanox Company/Team Okuyama/Shochiku Company/Leo Films (Japan)

Koichi Sato *(Bandai)*, Naoto Takenaka *(Ogiwara)*, Takeshi Kitano *(Kyoya)*, Jinpachi Nezu *(Hizu)*, Masahiro Motoki *(Mitsuya)*, Kippei Shiina *(Jimmy)*, Megumi Yokoyama *(Nammy)*, Kazuya Kimura *(Kazuma)*, Shingo Tsurumi *(Hisamatsu)*, Toshiyuki Nagashima *(Ogoshi)*

p, Kanji Miura, Taketo Niitsu, Katsuhide Motoki; d, Takashi Ishii; w, Takashi Ishii; ph, Yasushi Sasakibara; ed, Akimasa Kawashima, Keiichi Hasegawa, Katsumi Yamaura; m, Goro Yasukawa; art d, Teru Yamazaki

Put away your preconceptions and fasten your seat belt: no matter what you're expecting, this Japanese gangster picture isn't it.

Handsome Bandai (Koichi Sato), discotheque owner and Tokyo nightlife celebrity, is in big trouble. He owes money to the *yakuza*, is under brutal pressure to pay up, and doesn't have the cash. So he hatches a desperate plan to rip off the very gangsters he's indebted to, with the help of four unlikely partners. Ogiwara (Naoto Takenaka) is a twitchy, out of work salaryman who doesn't dare tell his family in the suburbs he's lost his job. Hizu (Jinpachi Nezu) is a disgraced former cop working as a clip-joint bouncer; Jimmy (Kippei Shiina) is a one-time, bottle-blond pimp in love with a Thai prostitute (Megumi Yokoyama) whose passport the gangsters have confiscated; and Mitsuya (Masahiro Motoki) is a hustler who specializes in blackmailing well-placed homosexuals. The heist goes surprisingly well, but the aftermath is, quite literally, murder.

Director Ishii was an artist before turning to movies—he specialized in erotic *manga* (Japanese comic books)—and this bleak tale of revenge and betrayal is astonishingly beautiful, set in a Tokyo where it's always raining and there's sure to be a flower in the gutter. Ishii also takes the homoerotic subtext that underlies almost all gangster/heist pictures and drags it right up to the surface; there's no pussyfooting around about male bonding here. But what makes it special is the flat-out bizarreness that lurks behind every gangster-movie convention, from Ogiwara's grotesque secret to Japanese media idol "Beat" Takeshi Kitano's mind-boggling performance as a one-eyed hit man. The scene in which he grumbles to his *yakuza* boss about not having health insurance ("I lost an eye!" he exclaims) is worth the price of admission all by itself.

GOOD EARTH, THE
1937 138m bw Drama ★★★★★
MGM (U.S.)

Paul Muni *(Wang Lung)*, Luise Rainer *(O-Lan)*, Walter Connolly *(Uncle)*, Tilly Losch *(Lotus)*, Charley Grapewin *(Old Father)*, Jessie Ralph *(Cuckoo)*, Soo Yong *(Aunt)*, Keye Luke *(Elder Son)*, Roland Got *(Younger Son)*, Ching Wah Lee *(Ching)*

p, Irving Thalberg, Albert Lewin; d, Sidney Franklin; w, Talbot Jennings, Tess Slesinger, Frances Marion, Claudine West (based on the novel by Pearl S. Buck); ph, Karl Freund; ed, Basil Wrangell; m, Herbert Stothart; art d, Cedric Gibbons, Harry Oliver, Arnold Gillespie; cos, Dolly Tree

AAN Best Picture; AA Best Actress: Luise Rainer; *AAN Best Director:* Sidney Franklin; *AA Best Cinematography:* Karl Freund; *AAN Best Film Editing:* Basil Wrangell

Classic melodrama. Muni, in a powerful role—another marvelous offbeat characterization—is a simple rice farmer who weds Rainer, a kitchen slave, in an arranged marriage. Through incredible labor, Muni and Rainer make their little farm into a success, allowing Muni to buy many more rice fields and to prosper. They produce three children, and all seems promising until severe drought turns the land into an unyielding crust. When famine sets in, the family begins to starve, forcing Rainer to feed her children cooked earth. Through a stroke of Rainer's good luck, the family's fortunes are turned around, but their lives are ruined by Muni's greed. Too late, the stoic Muni learns the magnificent qualities of his loving wife.

Rainer is overwhelming as the self-sacrificing O-lan and deservedly won an Oscar for Best Actress, beating out Greta Garbo in CAMILLE and accomplishing the seemingly impossible task of winning back-to-back statuettes, having received the same award the previous year for THE GREAT ZEIGFELD.

This superlative adaptation of the Pulitzer Prize-winning Pearl Buck novel was three years in the making; it was

Thalberg's last production, which he personally oversaw. He had never taken a film credit and died before THE GOOD EARTH was completed; to honor this young, driving force, who was responsible for a string of majestic films, Mayer had the following inserted in the credits of THE GOOD EARTH: "To the memory of Irving Grant Thalberg we dedicate this picture, his last great achievement."

Thalberg sent George Hill, a talented but alcoholic director, to China to get background footage and gather important props. Hill's wife, Frances Marion, went along to do research since she was originally slated to write the screenplay. Hill and Marion returned with more than two million feet of background footage, some of which was used in the released film. Victor Fleming, who replaced Hill, grew ill during production and had to be hospitalized. (The same thing happened to Fleming when he was at work on GONE WITH THE WIND three years later.) With costs mounting, Thalberg brought in Sidney Franklin to replace Fleming.

There are several great sequences in THE GOOD EARTH, not the least of which are the terrifying mob scenes in which the palace is ransacked. The most astounding scene, however, is the invasion of the locusts. Hundreds of extras, Muni, Rainer, and family in the lead, took to the jeopardized fields to combat the pests which blackened the sky, frantically digging fire lanes, disorienting the insects by banging gongs, then beating them with shovels, feet, and hands. Every known photographic gimmick up to that time was employed in the locust invasion scene. The Chinese location footage was used as a backdrop, closeups of the locusts on a miniature soundstage were intercut, and special effects paintings were inserted on the film to produce a startling montage of the menace.

GOOD GIRL, THE
2002 93m c Drama ★★★

Myriad Pictures/IN-Motion AG/WMF V/Hungry Eye Lowland Pictures/Flan de Coco/Fox Searchlight (U.S./Germany/Netherlands)

R

Jennifer Aniston *(Justine Last)*, Jake Gyllenhaal *(Holden Worther)*, John C. Reilly *(Phil Last)*, Tim Blake Nelson *(Bubba)*, Deborah Rush *(Gwen Jackson)*, Mike White *(Corny)*, John Carroll Lynch *(Jack Field, Your Store Manager)*, Zooey Deschanel *(Cheryl)*, John Doe *(Mr. Worther)*, Roxanne Hart *(Mrs. Worther)*

p, Matthew Greenfield; d, Miguel Arteta; w, Mike White; ph, Enrique Chediak; ed, Jeff Betancourt; m, Tony Maxwell, James O'Brien, Mark Orton, Joey Waronker; prod d, Daniel Bradford; art d, Macie Vener; fx, David Wayne; cos, Nancy Steiner

Jennifer Aniston brings her trademark sparkle to this unusual drama from screenwriter Mike White and director Miguel Arteta, and that's something of a problem.

Justine Last (Aniston), a 30-year-old small-town Texas woman, has come to the sad realization that her life isn't at all the "candy store" she once hoped it would be. Instead, it's a prison. Her cell is the makeup counter at the Retail Rodeo; her ball and chain is her chronically stoned husband, Phil (John C. Reilly), a genial housepainter whose ambitions include having a child but otherwise extend no farther than sharing a joint with his best friend, Bubba (Tim Blake Nelson). While Phil snores away beside her, Justine lies awake at night dreaming of what might have been, and foolishly thinks she's found a way out when moody 22-year-old Holden (Jake Gyllenhaal) comes to work at the Rodeo. The two are soon having sex in the storeroom and slipping off to the local motel. Justine only wants to be a good girl, but her reckless search for happiness has terrible consequences for everyone around her.

The casting of Aniston is a coup that will hopefully draw audiences to this admirably risky, heartfelt film, but her presence can't help but diminish its seriousness. Her natural charisma keeps you from judging Justine's many mistakes too harshly, but Aniston's acting style has been honed by sitcom entanglements and the occasional romantic comedy. Her

strength is a comedic airiness that doesn't quite match this film's grim desperation. Even during the most intense moments, it's hard to shake the impression that the conspicuously buff-and-polished Justine is only visiting this drab world, her miserable life an interesting career move.

GOOD MORNING, VIETNAM
1987 119m c Comedy/Drama/War ★★★½
Touchstone/Silver Partners III (U.S.) R

Robin Williams *(Adrian Cronauer)*, Forest Whitaker *(Edward Garlick)*, Tung Thanh Tran *(Tuan)*, Chintara Sukapatana *(Trinh)*, Bruno Kirby *(Lt. Steven Hauk)*, Robert Wuhl *(Marty Lee Dreiwitz)*, J.T. Walsh *(Sgt. Major Dickerson)*, Noble Willingham *(Gen. Taylor)*, Richard Edson *(Pvt. Abersold)*, Juney Smith *(Phil McPherson, Radio Engineer)*

p, Mark Johnson, Larry Brezner, Ben Moses, Harry Benn; d, Barry Levinson; w, Mitch Markowitz; ph, Peter Sova (Deluxe Color); ed, Stu Linder; m, Alex North; prod d, Roy Walker; art d, Steve Spence; fx, Fred Cramer; cos, Keith Denny

AAN Best Actor: Robin Williams

Robin Williams was finally given a showcase for his extraordinary improvisational skills in this, the first comedy set in Vietnam.

Based on the story of real-life Armed Forces Radio disc jockey Adrian Cronauer, GOOD MORNING, VIETNAM begins in 1965, as Cronauer (Williams) arrives in Saigon, imported because his comedic broadcasts have proven a huge morale-booster elsewhere. At the AFR's Saigon station, Cronauer incurs the wrath of superiors who resent his intrusion in their programming, with its dull announcers, health and safety tips, censored news, and geriatric playlist. Cronauer changes all that, knocking listening troops out of their stupor with his howling salutation—"Goooood morning, Vietnammmm!"— hip song selection, and comedic improvisation, poking wild fun at any and all sacred cows.

GOOD MORNING, VIETNAM stumbles whenever Williams isn't behind the mike, placing him in melodramatic, hackneyed situations that become increasingly predictable and preposterous, and director Barry Levinson's seemingly endless reaction shots of listeners grooving to the DJ's antics become irritating. Levinson manages, however, to be one of the few filmmakers to show the Vietnamese as complex, cultured people, rather than as helpless victims or the faceless enemy.

Forrest Whitaker (BIRD) does wonders with his thankless role as Cronauer's loyal aide, Sukapatana—as Williams's Vietnamese love interest—is impressive, and Bruno Kirby, as Cronauer's nemesis, comes as close as any actor could to walking off with a film dominated by Williams at his best.

GOOD, THE BAD, AND THE UGLY, THE
(IL BUONO, IL BRUTTO, IL CATTIVO)
1966 161m c Western ★★★★
Europee (Italy/Spain) R

Clint Eastwood *(Joe)*, Eli Wallach *(Tuco)*, Lee Van Cleef *(Setenza)*, Aldo Giuffre, Chelo Alonso, Mario Brega, Luigi Pistilli, Rada Rassimov, Enzo Petito, Claudio Scarchilli

p, Alberto Grimaldi; d, Sergio Leone; w, Luciano Vincenzoni, Sergio Leone (based on a story by Agenore Incrocci, Furio Scarpelli, Vincenzoni, and Leone); ph, Tonino Delli Colli (Techniscope, Technicolor); ed, Nino Baragli, Eugenio Alabiso; m, Ennio Morricone; art d, Carlo Simi; fx, Eros Bacciucchi; cos, Carlo Simi

The definitive spaghetti western. Director Sergio Leone's epic end to the Clint Eastwood "Dollars" trilogy is a stunning, panoramic view of the West during the Civil War. THE GOOD, THE BAD, AND THE UGLY is a deceptively simple story detailing the efforts of three drifters, the "Good" (Eastwood), the "Bad" (Lee Van Cleef), and the "Ugly" (Eli Wallach), to find a fortune hidden in the unmarked grave of a man named Bill Carson.

Leone's narrative structure is incredibly complex: the characters' paths intersect and intertwine repeatedly until the Civil War impinges upon their lives and dwarfs their petty crimes. The war eventually involves Eastwood and Wallach in a massive battle for an unimportant bridge in which hundreds of soldiers march to pointless doom. The scale of violence shocks these two violent men; Eastwood, whose character begins to show a humanity only hinted at in the previous two films, states that he has never "seen so many men wasted so badly."

This is Leone's most violent film, but also one of his most compassionate. One of its most memorable scenes shows the Union troops organizing an orchestra of Confederate prisoner-musicians to play in order to cover the noise as Van Cleef tortures his prisoners. The effect is haunting, and recalls stories of similar incidents in Nazi death camps. A touching moment occurs when Eastwood comes across a dying young soldier, covers the shivering man with his duster, and helps him smoke his final cigarette.

Though not up to the standards of Leone's masterpiece ONCE UPON A TIME IN THE WEST, in which the director synthesizes scale, narrative, casting, and style, THE GOOD, THE BAD, AND THE UGLY is a massive, many-faceted film that continues to hold up, viewing after viewing. It also features one of Ennio Morricone's finest scores.

GOOD WILL HUNTING   📀
1997 122m c Drama   ★★★½
A Band Apart/Miramax   (U.S.)   R

Robin Williams (*Professor Sean McGuire*), Matt Damon (*Will Hunting*), Ben Affleck (*Chuckie*), Minnie Driver (*Skylar*), Stellan Skarsgard (*Professor Lambeau*), Casey Affleck (*Morgan*), Cole Hauser (*Billy*), John Mighton (*Tom*), Rachel Majowski (*Krystyn*), Colleen McCauley (*Cathy*)

p, Lawrence Bender; d, Gus Van Sant; w, Ben Affleck, Matt Damon; ph, Jean-Yves Escoffier; ed, Pietro Scalia; m, Danny Elfman; prod d, Missy Stewart; art d, James McAteer; fx, Brian Ricci; cos, Beatrix Aruna Pasztor

AA Best Original Screenplay: Matt Damon, Ben Affleck; *AA Best Supporting Actor:* Robin Williams; *AAN Best Picture; AAN Best Actor:* Matt Damon; *AAN Best Supporting Actress:* Minnie Driver; *AAN Best Director:* Gus Van Sant; *AAN Best Original Dramatic Score:* Danny Elfman; *AAN Best Original Song:* "Miss Misery"; Elliot Smith; *AAN Best Film Editing:* Pietro Scalia

Young actors Matt Damon (THE RAINMAKER) and Ben Affleck (CHASING AMY) won an Oscar for this, their debut scripting effort. Connect-the-dots plotting only slightly mars their otherwise fine script, which is rife with well-drawn characters and sharp, intelligent dialogue.

Will Hunting (Matt Damon) is a janitor at MIT who lets off steam by going out on the town with his best friend Chuckie (Ben Affleck). Will gets arrested when he gets involved in a brawl one evening. In court, the 22-year-old presents an eloquent case in his defense, but the judge, citing the troublemaker's long rap sheet, sentences him to do some time. Enter the prominent Professor Lambeau (Stellan Skarsgard) who, recognizing the young man's gift, is able to free the belligerent Will under two conditions: weekly meetings with a therapist and math lessons under Lambeau's tutelage. Lambeau is eager to hold onto his discovery and takes the modern-day Einstein to his estranged college chum, Sean McGuire (Robin Williams), a once-promising psychologist who languishes in obscurity at a local community college. Two scarred underachievers, doctor and patient, eventually help each other to overcome their inner demons.

Damon accomplishes a daunting task here, playing a multi-layered verbal acrobat with compelling aplomb. Co-scripter Ben Affleck also impresses in his solid turn as Will's more earthbound sidekick. Though the empathetic therapist who helps the recalcitrant patient come to terms with his dark past is a movie cliché, Oscar winner Robin Williams does a fine job grounding a character written as a paragon of humanism. A lot of the credit belongs to director Gus Van Sant for not only reining in Williams but for making a film where it's hard to find a single false moment. The script paints a character whose genius attains unbelievable levels, and the love story is far too predictable, but Van Sant maintains an air of credibility by sticking to a subtle, unsentimental approach.

GOODBYE GIRL, THE   📀
1977 110m c Romance/Comedy   ★★★★
MGM   (U.S.)   PG

Richard Dreyfuss (*Elliott Garfield*), Marsha Mason (*Paula McFadden*), Quinn Cummings (*Lucy McFadden*), Paul Benedict (*Mark Morgenweiss*), Barbara Rhoades (*Donna Douglas*), Theresa Merritt (*Mrs. Crosby*), Michael Shawn (*Ronnie*), Patricia Pearcy (*Rhonda Fontana*), Gene Castle (*Assistant Choreographer*), Daniel Levans (*Dance Instructor*)

p, Ray Stark; d, Herbert Ross; w, Neil Simon; ph, David M. Walsh (Metrocolor); ed, John F. Burnett; m, Dave Grusin; prod d, Albert Brenner; fx, Al Griswold; cos, Ann Roth

AAN Best Picture; AA Best Actor: Richard Dreyfuss; *AAN Best Actress:* Marsha Mason; *AAN Best Supporting Actress:* Quinn Cummings; *AAN Best Original Screenplay:* Neil Simon

A rarity for Neil Simon's screen efforts, THE GOODBYE GIRL perfectly blends humor, sentiment, and romance on a level so pleasant it's almost suspicious.

Mason is a divorced ex-Broadway dancer in her thirties living with her precocious daughter in an apartment suddenly subleased by aspiring actor Dreyfuss, who arrives to take possession in the middle of the night. This is shocking news to Mason who thus learns that her departed lover, also an actor, has not only made her and daughter Cummings homeless but also has jilted her without notice. Dreyfuss makes it easy on Mason by offering to share the apartment, provided she pays half the rent. She agrees out of desperation, and the two strike up an uneasy truce that gradually blossoms into love.

This is a superb lighthearted comedy deftly directed by Ross, who helmed such hits as PLAY IT AGAIN, SAM and THE TURNING POINT. Mason is wonderfully warm and sensitive in a precarious role, while Dreyfuss, in a trademark performance, is nothing short of sensational. Cummings is a charming little girl whose premature sophistication provides some good humor. Next to THE SUNSHINE BOYS, this may be Simon's best original screenplay.

GOODBYE MR. CHIPS   📀
1939 114m bw Drama   ★★★★½
MGM   (U.K.)

Robert Donat (*Charles Chipping*), Greer Garson (*Katherine Ellis*), Terry Kilburn (*John/Peter Colley*), John Mills (*Peter Colley as a young man*), Paul Henreid (*Max Staefel*), Judith Furse (*Flora*), Lyn Harding (*Dr. Wetherby*), Milton Rosmer (*Charteris*), Frederick Leister (*Marsham*), Louise Hampton (*Mrs. Wickett*)

p, Victor Saville; d, Sam Wood; w, R.C. Sherriff, Claudine West, Eric Maschwitz, Sidney Franklin (based on the novella by James Hilton); ph, Freddie Young; ed, Charles Frend; m, Richard Addinsell; art d, Alfred Junge; cos, Julie Harris

AAN Best Picture; AA Best Actor: Robert Donat; AAN Best Actress: Greer Garson; AAN Best Director: Sam Wood; AAN Best Screenplay: Eric Maschwitz, R.C. Sherriff, Claudine West; AAN Best Film Editing: Charles Frend; AAN Best Sound Recording: A.W. Watkins

Robert Donat gives a poignant performance in this superlative production as the shy, retiring British schoolteacher who guides several generations of young boys to manhood. Set at Brookfield Boys School in the late 1800s, the film follows the career of Charles Chipping, nicknamed "Mr. Chips," from his first days as an unpopular novice instructor through the marriage that brings him out of his shell to his final years as the school's beloved elder statesman.

So moving was Donat's performance that he beat out the most popular American candidate for the Best Actor Oscar, Clark Gable, who was nominated for his work in GONE WITH THE WIND. Greer Garson, as Mrs. Chips, also shines in the film that introduced her to American audiences. The screenplay is bright and the direction gentle, but it is Donat who elevates this bittersweet, affectionate tribute. (The great James Hilton wrote the original story as a novella in four days to meet a 1934 magazine deadline.) Skip the 1969 musical remake starring Peter O'Toole; despite his rightness in the role, he can't salvage a lumbering horror show.

GOODFELLAS
DVD

1990 148m c   Crime/Drama   ★★★★
Irwin Winkler   (U.S.)   R

Robert De Niro (James Conway), Ray Liotta (Henry Hill), Joe Pesci (Tommy DeVito), Lorraine Bracco (Karen Hill), Paul Sorvino (Paul Cicero), Frank Sivero (Frankie Carbone), Tony Darrow (Sonny Bunz), Mike Starr (Frenchy), Frank Vincent (Billy Batts), Chuck Low (Morris Kessler)

p, Irwin Winkler; d, Martin Scorsese; w, Nicholas Pileggi, Martin Scorsese (based on the book Wiseguy by Pileggi); ph, Michael Ballhaus (Technicolor); ed, Thelma Schoonmaker; prod d, Kristi Zea; art d, Maher Ahmad; fx, Connie Brink; cos, Susan O'Donnell, Thomas Lee Keller

AAN Best Picture; AA Best Supporting Actor: Joe Pesci; AAN Best Supporting Actress: Lorraine Bracco; AAN Best Director: Martin Scorsese; AAN Best Adapted Screenplay: Nicholas Pileggi, Martin Scorsese; AAN Best Film Editing: Thelma Schoonmaker

Based on journalist Nicholas Pileggi's nonfiction book Wiseguy, GOODFELLAS revolves around the career of low-level gangster Henry Hill (Ray Liotta), who became part of the federal witness protection program after testifying against his erstwhile partners in crime. At the center of the book is Hill's insider account of the $6 million robbery of a Lufthansa cargo facility at New York's Idlewild Airport. Scorsese doesn't show the heist itself; instead, he focuses on its bloody aftermath, in which all the participants are brutally murdered by Henry's partners, the lethally paranoid Jimmy Conway (Robert De Niro) and the psychotic Tommy De Vito (Joe Pesci).

Generally, GOODFELLAS is concerned with Tommy and Jimmy's climb up the mob ladder and its effects on Henry, but Scorsese's rich tapestry is both broader in scope and more detailed than a mere recounting of the events in the trio's life of crime. Because Scorsese is equally concerned with the minutiae of his main characters' world and with the grand design that appears to underlie that world, the downfall of Henry and his associates seems fated.

Many of the seemingly peripheral subplots are showstoppers. Focusing on the one-woman war Henry's wife Karen (wonderfully played by Lorraine Bracco) fights against his mistress, Scorsese casts Henry's homelife as a rau-

cous parody of the domineering husbands and quiet wives of THE GODFATHER.

Karen, so fiercely self-possessed early in the film, is cowed and exhausted by the movie's hellish climax, during which Henry has gone from a trim mob dandy to a coked-up, misshapen mess. His subsequent arrest and induction into the witness protection program leads to the film's final, and most disturbing image—a suburbanized Henry appearing at the front door of his new tract home to bring in the morning paper.

GORILLAS IN THE MIST
DVD

1988 129m c   Biography   ★★★
Peters/Arnold Glimcher/Guber   (U.S.)   PG-13

Sigourney Weaver (Dian Fossey), Bryan Brown (Bob Campbell), Julie Harris (Roz Carr), John Omirah Miluwi (Sembagare), Iain Cuthbertson (Dr. Louis Leakey), Constantin Alexandrov (Van Vecten), Waigwa Wachira (Mukara), Iain Glen (Brendan), David Lansbury (Larry), Maggie O'Neill (Kim)

p, Arnold Glimcher, Terence Clegg, Robert Nixon, Judy Kessler; d, Michael Apted; w, Anna Hamilton Phelan (based on the story by Harold T.P. Hayes); ph, John Seale, Alan Root (Technicolor); ed, Stuart Baird; m, Maurice Jarre; prod d, John Graysmark; fx, Rick Baker, David Harris; cos, Catherine Leterrier

AAN Best Actress: Sigourney Weaver; AAN Best Adapted Screenplay: Anna Hamilton Phelan (screenplay), Tab Murphy (story); AAN Best Film Editing: Stuart Baird; AAN Best Original Score: Maurice Jarre; AAN Best Sound: Andy Nelson, Brian Saunders, Peter Handford

Well-done monkey business, but an abrupt, uncentered screenplay, cluttered by unfocused direction, poor music and obligatory romance.

During the 1970s, Dian Fossey journeyed to Africa, where she closely studied the mountain gorilla, work later chronicled in a popular National Geographic television special. In this biopic Weaver portrays the late, controversial Fossey, beginning with her 1963 meeting with anthropologist Louis Leakey (Cuthbertson). He agrees to let her accompany him to Africa, and that begins her lifelong commitment to the study of gorillas. The film shows how this passion gains her fame but also leads to her fatal obsession with protecting her subjects as she grows increasingly irrational in dealing with those she feels pose a threat to the gorillas.

Although the film offers no real insights into Fossey's courage and obsessions, Weaver has some riveting moments. But because the screenplay doesn't penetrate the gradual shift Fossey made from animal activist to crank, she's forced to dredge it up from nowhere. There's terrific footage of the gorillas and the African setting is stunning. But the real star is Baker, who created the gorilla costumes donned by human beings for many scenes. His work is so well done that it is impossible to tell the real gorillas from the guys in the suits.

GORKY PARK
DVD

1983 103m c   Mystery   ★★★
Orion   (U.S.)   R

William Hurt (Arkady Renko), Lee Marvin (Jack Osborne), Brian Dennehy (William Kirwill), Ian Bannen (Iamskoy), Joanna Pacula (Irina), Michael Elphick (Pasha), Richard Griffiths (Anton), Rikki Fulton (Pribluda), Alexander Knox (General), Alexei Sayle (Golodkin)

p, Gene Kirkwood, Howard W. Koch Jr.; d, Michael Apted; w, Dennis Potter (based on the novel by Martin Cruz Smith); ph, Ralf D. Bode (Technicolor); ed, Dennis Virkler; m, James Horner; prod d, Paul Sylbert; cos, Richard Bruno

Uneven but sometimes fascinating murder mystery. Three bodies are found in Moscow's Gorky Park, stripped of their faces and fingertips, making identification nearly impossible. William Hurt, in a highly polished performance, plays the Moscow police inspector assigned to the case. His trail leads to an American fur trader (Lee Marvin) who has all of Moscow at his disposal. A young dissident (Joanna Pacula), who was a friend of one of the victims, also gets caught in the intrigue. Though a little confusing at times, this mystery, based on the Martin Cruz Smith bestseller, has some great twists and gives a harshly realistic picture of the average man's life behind the Iron Curtain. GORKY suffers from the miscasting of Marvin, an unrealistic romance and, most unfortunately, a plodding climax. It was filmed in Helsinki, since the Soviets refused permission to shoot in Moscow.

GOSFORD PARK   *DVD*
2001 137m c Mystery   ★★★
Capitol Films/Film Council of a Sandcastle 5/   R
Chicagofilms/Medusa Film   (U.S.)

Michael Gambon *(Sir William McCordle)*, Kristin Scott Thomas *(Lady Sylvia McCordle)*, Alan Bates *(Jennings)*, Helen Mirren *(Mrs. Wilson)*, Camilla Rutherford *(Isobel McCordle)*, Maggie Smith *(Constance, Countess of Trentham)*, Emily Watson *(Elsie)*, Richard E. Grant *(George)*, Geraldine Somerville *(Louisa, Lady Stockbridge)*, Eileen Atkins *(Mrs. Croft)*

p, Robert Altman, Bob Balaban, David Levy; d, Robert Altman; w, Julian Fellowes (based upon an idea by Robert Altman and Bob Balaban); ph, Andrew Dunn; ed, Tim Squyres; m, Patrick Doyle; prod d, Stephen Altman; art d, John Frankish; fx, Stuart Brisdon; cos, Jenny Beavan

AA Best Original Screenplay: Julian Fellowes; *AAN Best Picture; AAN Best Director:* Robert Altman; *AAN Best Costume Design:* Jenny Beavan; *AAN Best Supporting Actress:* Helen Mirren; *AAN Best Supporting Actress:* Maggie Smith; *AAN Best Art Direction:* Stephen Altman, Anna Pinnock

This ensemble mystery of manners is by no means RULES OF THE GAME, but if you think of it as a variation on an Agatha Christie murder mystery, complete with much-loathed victim and a cornucopia of colorful suspects, it's perfectly pleasant entertainment.

    England, 1932: Wealthy Sir William McCordle (Michael Gambon), whose fortune was made on the backs of factory workers, and his wife, impoverished aristocrat Lady Sylvia (Kristin Scott Thomas), are giving a weekend party at their rambling country house, Gosford Park. The guests include their awkward daughter Isobel (Camilla Rutherford); Sylvia's younger sisters Louisa (Geraldine Somerville) and Lavinia (Natasha Wightman), and their husbands, snobbish Lord Stockbridge (Charles Dance) and flat-broke Lt. Commander Meredith (Tom Hollander); Sylvia's tart-tongued Aunt Constance (Maggie Smith), Countess of Trentham; upper-crust bounder Freddie Nesbitt (James Wilby), who married middle-class Mabel (Claudie Blakley) for her money; film star Ivor Novello (Jeremy Northam), Sir William's cousin; and Ivor's Hollywood friend, B-movie producer Morris Weissman (Bob Balaban). Equally important is the small army of servants who attend their employers' every want and need. They include Gosford Park's butler and housekeeper, Jennings (Alan Bates) and Mrs. Wilson (Helen Mirren); prickly cook Mrs. Croft (Eileen Atkins); Mary Maceachran (Kelly Macdonald), Constance's young maid; head housemaid Elsie (Emily Watson), who's having a half-hearted affair with Sir William; visiting valet Robert Parks (Clive Owen), who ignores the conventions of servitude; and lecherous, footman George (Richard E. Grant), who has nothing but contempt for the upper classes.

    Though the story is driven by Sir William's murder—the question isn't really who would have wanted him dead, but who wouldn't—the movie's real focus is the complicated interactions between and among guests and servants. The performances range from good to great; it's a shame that their efforts don't coalesce into a more resonant result.

GOSPEL ACCORDING TO ST. MATTHEW, THE   *DVD*
(IL VANGELO SECONDO MATTEO)
1964 135m bw Religious/Drama   ★★★★½
L'Arco/C.C.F. Lux   (France/Italy)

Enrique Irazoqui *(Jesus Christ)*, Margherita Caruso *(Mary, as a Girl)*, Susanna Pasolini *(Mary, as a Woman)*, Marcello Morante *(Joseph)*, Mario Socrate *(John the Baptist)*, Settimo Di Porto *(Peter)*, Otello Sestili *(Judas)*, Ferruccio Nuzzo *(Matthew)*, Giacomo Morante *(John)*, Alfonso Gatto *(Andrew)*

p, Alfredo Bini; d, Pier Paolo Pasolini; w, Pier Paolo Pasolini (based on the gospel according to Saint Matthew); ph, Tonino Delli Colli; ed, Nino Baragli, Andrea Fantucci; m, Luis Enrique Bacalov; art d, Nino Baragli, Luigi Scaccianoce; fx, Ettore Catallucci; cos, Danilo Donati

AAN Best Art Direction-Set Decoration (B/W): Luigi Scaccianoce; *AAN Best Adapted Score:* Luis Enrique Bacalov; *AAN Best Costume Design (B/W):* Danilo Donati

Unconventional and very moving. Pier Paolo Pasolini's epic film, a Special Jury Prize-winner at the Venice Film Festival, tells the life story of Jesus in a semi-documentary style using nonprofessional actors, including the director's mother as the Virgin Mary. Hailed by many as the greatest adaptation of the life of Christ, this picture was dedicated to Pope John XXIII, who brought the Catholic Church into the 20th century. It may come as a surprise to those who see this film that Pasolini was not only an atheist, but a homosexual and Marxist as well. As if to underline the unorthodox nature of the film, Pasolini has included on his soundtrack the American spiritual "Sometimes I Feel Like a Motherless Child," sung by Odetta.

GOTHIKA   *DVD*
2003 98m c Horror   ★★
Dark Castle Entertainment/Columbia/   R
Warner Bros.   (U.S.)

Halle Berry *(Dr. Miranda Grey)*, Robert Downey Jr. *(Dr. Pete Graham)*, Charles S. Dutton *(Dr. Douglas Grey)*, John Carroll Lynch *(Sheriff Ryan)*, Bernard Hill *(Dr. Phil Parsons)*, Penelope Cruz *(Chloe Sava)*, Dorian Harewood *(Teddy Howard)*, Bronwen Mantel *(Irene)*, Kathleen Mackey *(Rachel Parsons)*, Matthew G. Taylor *(Turlington)*

p, Susan Levin, Joel Silver, Robert Zemeckis; d, Mathieu Kassovitz; w, Sebastian Gutierrez; ph, Matthew Libatique; ed, Yannick Kergoat; m, John Ottman; prod d, Graham Walker; art d, Isabelle Guay; fx, Loius Craig, Dave Ebner, Erik Henry; cos, Kym Barrett

French actor-director Mathieu Kassovitz's English-language debut features Halle Berry in the kind of bravura role for which actresses claw out each other's eyes. The rest is a gloomy-doomy ghost story that soon spirals into flat-out preposterousness.

    Brilliant criminal psychologist Dr. Miranda Grey (Berry) is beautiful, highly respected, and happily married to her boss, Dr. Douglas Grey (Charles S. Dutton). One dark-and-stormy-night fender bender later, she finds herself a patient at her former place of employment, the spooky Woodward Penitentiary for Women. When she asks for her husband, she's told that he's dead, and she's accused of having hacked him up with an ax. No one believes Miranda is innocent. Not her lawyer (Dorian

Harewood); not her doctor, flirty former colleague Pete Graham (Robert Downey Jr.); not Sheriff Ryan (John Carroll Lynch), her late husband's best friend; and certainly not the other patients. Miranda doesn't help her case by insisting she remembers nothing about that night three days earlier, except that the storm forced her to take a detour over a small bridge, where she nearly mowed down a bloodied, traumatized young woman. When Miranda identifies her as the subject of a photo belonging to Dr. Phil Parsons (Bernard Hill), another former colleague, her credibility is further damaged: the picture is of his teenage daughter, Rachel (Kathleen Mackey), who committed suicide by jumping off that isolated bridge four years earlier.

Berry hurls herself into Miranda's humiliations with the same commitment she brought to her Oscar-winning performance in MONSTER'S BALL, gamely enduring bad hair, ill-fitting hospital clothes, and hollow-eyed makeup. But as Sebastian Gutierrez's script careens from hackneyed endangered-woman situations to loony implausibility and Kassovitz piles up the scary-movie cliches, it becomes increasingly difficult to remain absorbed in Miranda's noir nightmare.

GRADUATE, THE   DVD
1967 105m c   Drama/Comedy   ★★★★½
Lawrence Turman/Embassy   (U.S.)

Anne Bancroft *(Mrs. Robinson)*, Dustin Hoffman *(Ben Braddock)*, Katharine Ross *(Elaine Robinson)*, William Daniels *(Mr. Braddock)*, Murray Hamilton *(Mr. Robinson)*, Elizabeth Wilson *(Mrs. Braddock)*, Brian Avery *(Carl Smith)*, Walter Brooke *(Mr. Maguire)*, Norman Fell *(Mr. McCleery)*, Elisabeth Fraser *(Lady)*

p, Lawrence Turman; d, Mike Nichols; w, Calder Willingham, Buck Henry (based on the novel by Charles Webb); ph, Robert Surtees (Panavision, Technicolor); ed, Sam O'Steen; m, Dave Grusin; prod d, Richard Sylbert; cos, Patricia Zipprodt

AAN Best Picture; AAN Best Actor: Dustin Hoffman; AAN Best Actress: Anne Bancroft; AAN Best Supporting Actress: Katharine Ross; AA Best Director: Mike Nichols; AAN Best Adapted Screenplay: Calder Willingham, Buck Henry; AAN Best Cinematography: Robert Surtees

A social force of cinema that influenced the generation gap, THE GRADUATE was a tour de force for newcomer Hoffman and made him an overnight sensation.

Hoffman plays Ben Braddock, a pensive and somewhat shy youth of wealthy Southern California suburbia. Upon completion of his college studies, he's pressured by family and friends to "get going" with his life, encouraged at every turn to find a job, marry, and become a clone of his parents. Bancroft seduces Hoffman who cannot believe the older, married woman—she and her husband Hamilton are his parents' best friends—is pursuing him. Hoffman falls in love with her daughter Ross, and is put in the exhausting position of maintaining relationships with mother and daughter. He finally decides that Ross will be his wife, although Bancroft is wholly opposed to the union.

This comedy is wonderfully crafted by director Nichols who presents a half-dozen hilarious scenes, including Hoffman escaping badgering advice by submerging himself in the family pool in scuba gear and Bancroft's sudden shift from respectable matron to predatory tease, hiking her skirts lasciviously and purring promises of smoldering sex which almost put Hoffman into a comatose state. Nichols was to declare: "I think Benjamin and Elaine will end up exactly like their parents; that's what I was trying to say in the last scene." Yet the well-to-do younger audiences of the day interpreted this sequence of blatant heroics as a wonderful act of defiance by two young people whose destinies were being manipulated by their parents.

The film was an enormous hit, turning Nichols, who'd already scored heavily with WHO'S AFRAID OF VIRGINIA WOOLF?, into one of Hollywood's most important directors. However much of the credit for the innovative and fluid graphics in the film must go to cameraman Surtees, who was allowed a free hand to experiment widely. For example, the telescopic shot of Hoffman running to prevent the wedding causes him to appear not to be getting anywhere, almost as if he is running in place. All in all, THE GRADUATE is a flawlessly acted and produced film. Look fast for Richard Dreyfuss in his film debut as a college student.

GRAND CANYON   DVD
1991 134m c   Drama   ★★★½
Fox   (U.S.)   R

Danny Glover *(Simon)*, Kevin Kline *(Mack)*, Steve Martin *(Davis)*, Mary McDonnell *(Claire)*, Mary-Louise Parker *(Dee)*, Alfre Woodard *(Jane)*, Jeremy Sisto *(Roberto)*, Tina Lifford *(Deborah)*, Patrick Malone *(Otis)*, Randle Mell *(The Alley Baron)*

p, Lawrence Kasdan, Charles Okun, Michael Grillo; d, Lawrence Kasdan; w, Lawrence Kasdan, Meg Kasdan; ph, Owen Roizman; ed, Carol Littleton; m, James Newton Howard; prod d, Bo Welch; art d, Tom Duffield; fx, Burt Dalton; cos, Aggie Guerard Rodgers

AAN Best Original Screenplay: Lawrence Kasdan, Meg Kasdan

GRAND CANYON is the cinematic equivalent of Planet Hollywood, the New York nightspot where ordinary people can supposedly rub shoulders with the rich and famous. In Lawrence Kasdan's movie, co-written by his wife Meg, big, dramatic events—deaths, shootings, etc.—take place alongside mundane things like cutting your finger while chopping vegetables or learning how to make a left turn in Los Angeles traffic. The film invites us into the lives of a wide cross-section of people, painting a densely textured portrait of a sprawling, modern city.

Mack (Kevin Kline), a successful immigration attorney, catches an L.A. Lakers game with his best friend Davis (Steve Martin), a self-absorbed, self-righteous film producer who specializes in blood 'n' guts exploitation fare and whose license plates read "GRSS PNTS." As he is driving back from the game, Mack's car konks out on an unlit street somewhere in Inglewood. He manages to call for a tow truck but becomes the target of a gang of hoods who threaten to take his car and maybe his life. Luckily, the tow truck arrives, driven by a man whose composure and quiet authority convince the gang to lay off. An eloquently thankful Mack rides back to the garage with his saviour, Simon (Danny Glover), and the episode marks the beginning of a friendship between the two men.

GRAND CANYON successfully recreates the random, haphazard ways in which individual lives intersect, and captures the sense of menace and disintegration that permeate contemporary urban life. It's much less convincing, though, when it tries to turn its characters into spokespeople. Kline, in particular, gets too many speeches that should be accompanied by a blinking subtitle reading "MESSAGE." Similarly, the Kasdans' attempt to bring the various strands of the story together through the metaphor of the Grand Canyon (it's wide, like the gulfs between different sections of society, but it can also bring us together in awe of its size and beauty) is unconvincing.

GRAND HOTEL
1932 115m bw Drama ★★★★★
MGM (U.S.)

Greta Garbo *(Grusinskaya)*, John Barrymore *(Baron Felix von Gaigern)*, Joan Crawford *(Flaemmchen)*, Wallace Beery *(General Director Preysing)*, Lionel Barrymore *(Otto Kringelein)*, Jean Hersholt *(Senf)*, Robert McWade *(Meierheim)*, Purnell Pratt *(Zinnowitz)*, Ferdinand Gottschalk *(Pimenov)*, Rafaela Ottiano *(Suzette)*

d, Edmund Goulding; w, William A. Drake (based on Drake's stage adaptation of the novel *Menschen im Hotel* by Vicki Baum); ph, William Daniels; ed, Blanche Sewell; art d, Cedric Gibbons; cos, Adrian

AA Best Picture

Gleaming deco dinosaur, Thalberg's pet, and the most legendary all-star movie ever made; a tribute to all that "stars" and glamour used to be in Hollywood's vanished Golden Age.

This omnibus blockbuster chronicles the interwining lives of the denizens of GRAND HOTEL: Garbo, the lonely ballerina; John Barrymore, the noble thief; Crawford, the ambitious stenographer; Lionel Barrymore, the dying man on a last fling, and Beery, the ruthless industrialist. Lewis Stone and Hersholt exist to supervise and comment upon the others. If DINNER AT EIGHT, made a year later, has held up far better as a picture because it comments upon the rich and famous, HOTEL set the standard of those who don't achieve the twin pinnacles. Don't expect a particularly lucid screenplay or even acting of a high order; this masterpiece is hopelessly dated, directed by Goulding in the grand manner, and supported by Gibbons's, Daniels's, and Adrian's opulent work.

Revival house audiences laugh today at Garbo, with her permanently furrowed brow and her weird little bobby pin that holds back her hair. But striding through the hotel's lobby, swathed in chinchilla, remote in her fabled Swedish melancholy, "acting" hope swirling above a heavy heart, she really is the most extraordinary *monstre sacre* the screen will ever know.

Secondly, there's a surprisingly warm vixen by the name of Joan Crawford, who steals GRAND HOTEL. Even though her face looks like a deco statue's—perhaps the most beautiful eyes and nose ever photographed—she's brimming like a livewire of ambitious current. She's a legend, too—the chorus girl who became a great star. Here she wants top-rung stardom badly, and it shows. Today, with her little black dresses and casual hair, she looks almost modern. Curious that she holds up better than anyone else and only bears a passing resemblance to the bitch goddess people insist on remembering her as. She's marvelously in awe of John Barrymore, and very good indeed reaching out to Lionel. It's a part that exploits Crawford's most likable quality—her loyalty.

John Barrymore is all continental matinee-idol charm. If it seems hammy and somewhat affected today—though Barrymore is never effete—just guffaw through the current Broadway revival to be reminded of the sadness of this vanishing breed. Lionel's performance may be his best—this was before the scenery chewing of later years. But for scenery chewing, Wallace Beery is on hand. He's so thoroughly disagreeable and dense that it somehow works.

GRAND HOTEL remains a classic of its kind. MGM shrewdly marketed this film by withholding its general release for many months after its Hollywood premiere, allowing a tremendous word-of-mouth campaign to heighten expectation from viewers and critics alike. And the critics cheered, along with the Academy of Motion Picture Arts and Sciences, which voted the film an Oscar for Best Picture. The enormous success of GRAND HOTEL set the stage for many all-star films to come. In 1945, GRAND HOTEL was remade as the lightweight WEEKEND AT THE WALDORF with Ginger Rogers, Lana Turner, Walter Pidgeon, Van Johnson, and Edward Arnold in the lead roles.

GRAND ILLUSION
(LA GRANDE ILLUSION)
1937 95m bw War/Prison ★★★★★
R.A.C. (France)

Jean Gabin *(Marechal)*, Pierre Fresnay *(Capt. de Boeldieu)*, Erich von Stroheim *(Von Rauffenstein)*, Marcel Dalio *(Rosenthal)*, Dita Parlo *(Elsa, Farm Woman)*, Julien Carette *(Cartier)*, Gaston Modot *(Surveyor)*, Georges Peclet *(Soldier)*, Edouard Daste *(Teacher)*, Sylvain Itkine *(Demolder)*

p, Raymond Blondy; d, Jean Renoir; w, Jean Renoir, Charles Spaak; ph, Christian Matras; ed, Marguerite Renoir; m, Joseph Kosma; art d, Eugene Lourie; cos, Decrais

AAN Best Picture

One of the undeniably great films in the history of world cinema, Jean Renoir's GRAND ILLUSION is an eloquent commentary on the borders that divide people, classes, armies and countries.

The film opens during WWI, as Marechal (Jean Gabin) and Boeldieu (Pierre Fresnay) are shot down by German ace Von Rauffenstein (Erich von Stroheim). The two survive the crash and are invited to lunch by Rauffenstein before ground troops arrive to cart the French officers off to a POW camp. Although Marechal and Boeldieu are compatriots, the latter has more in common with Von Rauffenstein, both of them being members of the white-gloved aristocracy. After lunch the Frenchmen are placed in barracks, where French officer Rosenthal (Marcel Dalio), a Jew, befriends them, along with several British officers who have also been taken prisoner. The newcomers join the others in working on an escape tunnel beneath the barracks, but a French victory on the Western Front is a sign that the war is turning against the Germans, and Marechal, Boeldieu, and the rest of the French prisoners are transferred to another prison, where they are reunited with Von Rauffenstein.

Now confined to a neck brace after a combat injury, the Commandant warmly welcomes the Frenchmen, pointing out that his prison, Wintersborn, is escape-proof. He treats his prisoners with great deference, having them to dinner and extending what meager courtesies he can, talking with Boeldieu about how this war will bring to an end the gentlemanly class of officers, dispensing with the honor and dignity of their rank and bloodlines. Caught someplace in between his loyalty to a member of his class (Von Rauffenstein) and to his country, Boeldieu once again agrees to assist his fellow prisoners in their escape attempts.

Directed with patience and care by Renoir, the film was banned in Germany by Nazi Propaganda Minister Josef Goebbels, who labeled it "Cinematographic Enemy No. 1" and compelled his Italian counterpart to have the film banned in that country, although the 1937 Venice Film Festival gave the film a "Best Artistic Ensemble" award. It was thought that all European prints of the film were destroyed by the Nazis, but American troops uncovered a negative in Munich in 1945 (preserved, strangely, by the Germans themselves), leading to the truncated film's reconstruction. Gabin, Fresnay, Dalio, and Stroheim all give impressive performances in this beautifully directed and written film.

GRAPES OF WRATH, THE
1940 129m bw Drama ★★★★★
Fox (U.S.)

Henry Fonda *(Tom Joad)*, Jane Darwell *(Ma Joad)*, John Carradine *(Casey)*, Charley Grapewin *(Grandpa Joad)*, Dorris

Bowdon *(Rosaharn)*, Russell Simpson *(Pa Joad)*, O.Z. Whitehead *(Al)*, John Qualen *(Muley Graves)*, Eddie Quillan *(Connie Rivers)*, Zeffie Tilbury *(Grandma Joad)*

p, Darryl F. Zanuck; d, John Ford; w, Nunnally Johnson (based on the novel by John Steinbeck); ph, Gregg Toland; ed, Robert Simpson; art d, Richard Day, Mark-Lee Kirk; cos, Gwen Wakeling

AAN Best Picture; AAN Best Actor: Henry Fonda; *AA Best Supporting Actress:* Jane Darwell; *AA Best Director:* John Ford; *AAN Best Screenplay:* Nunnally Johnson; *AAN Best Film Editing:* Robert E. Simpson; *AAN Best Sound Recording:* E.H. Hansen

THE GRAPES OF WRATH is not only one of John Ford's greatest films, it documents an American social tragedy, giving the victims a voice through art. Based on the classic John Steinbeck novel, the film recounts the painful, poignant odyssey of the Joad family, Steinbeck's Depression-era tenant farmers from Dust Bowl Oklahoma, whose story has come to represent the plight of the "Okies" for generations of readers—and, through Ford's masterpiece, generations of moviegoers too.

As the film opens, Tom (Henry Fonda, in possibly the greatest performance of his career), eldest of the Joad sons, hitchhikes home to the family farm through the desolate Oklahoma landscape, having completed a four-year prison term for manslaughter. After getting a short ride from a suspicious trucker, Tom hoofs it to a clearing where he meets the slightly mad Casey (John Carradine), a former preacher who's "lost the call" and no longer ministers to the spiritual needs of the local farmers. The two walk to the Joad farm but find it abandoned except for Muley (John Qualen), who's even more mentally unbalanced than Casey and is hiding in the house. Muley tells them that sheriff's deputies working for banks and farming combines have been looking for him ever since he knocked one of them unconscious. Muley tells Tom that the Joad family, too, has moved on, the victims of foreclosure. Tom and Casey head for the farm of Tom's Uncle John (Frank Darien), where all the Joads have gathered, preparing to head westward to California in search of jobs advertised in a handbill Pa Joad (Russell Simpson) received. Ma (Jane Darwell) joyously greets her eldest son, and the next morning the whole family piles into a broken-down truck overloaded with their belongings and sets out in search of a better future.

Ford's visualization of Steinbeck's novel is so emotionally gripping that viewers have little time to collect themselves from one powerful scene to the next. Shooting mainly in California in the migrant camps around Pomona, with a second unit filming some backgrounds in Oklahoma, the director framed his shots to show that vast, almost barren landscapes, overcast skies, and bleak exteriors are omnipresent, giving a pervasive sense of the harshness of the displaced Okies' lives.

The sense of doom is dispelled, however, with the film's optimistic turn after the Joads find the government camp and its guardian (Grant Mitchell), a benevolent figure representing security, who, not coincidentally, bears a resemblance to Franklin D. Roosevelt. Though Ford does not hesitate to show the banks and the companies which took advantage of the farmers as land-grabbers without conscience, he also turns the Okies' bleak tale into one of hope by showing the Joads to be more than victims. Physically displaced, but not emotionally or spiritually defeated, they come to embody faith in the future and in the American people, and therein lies the film's greatness.

It took considerable courage to make THE GRAPES OF WRATH at a time when the Hollywood studios, on guard against unionization and attempts to challenge their monopoly, were in no mood to indulge its indictment of capitalism. In 1989, when it was named among the first movies included in the National Film Registry, the picture had lost none of its power as a social document, a historical testimony, or a work of cinematic art.

GREASE

DVD

1978 110m c Musical/Comedy ★★½

Paramount (U.S.) PG

John Travolta *(Danny)*, Olivia Newton-John *(Sandy)*, Stockard Channing *(Rizzo)*, Jeff Conaway *(Kenickie)*, Didi Conn *(Frenchy)*, Jamie Donnelly *(Jan)*, Dinah Manoff *(Marty)*, Barry Pearl *(Doody)*, Michael Tucci *(Sonny)*, Kelly Ward *(Putzie)*

p, Robert Stigwood, Allan Carr; d, Randall Kleiser; w, Bronte Woodard, Allan Carr (adapted by Carr from the musical by Jim Jacobs, Warren Casey); ph, Bill Butler (Panavision, Metrocolor); ed, John F. Burnett; prod d, Philip Jefferies; chor, Patricia Birch; cos, Albert Wolsky

AAN Best Original Song: "Hopelessly Devoted to You"; John Farrar (Music & Lyrics)

If you're looking for good, clean, high-spirited fun, GREASE is the ticket. Steve Krantz, who now spends most of his time producing the works of his wife, Judith, originally had the rights for this film and intended to do it as a cartoon (he'd once been partners with Ralph Bakshi). When he could find no one to agree with his concept (a wise choice on the part of the studios), he let the project go, and it was picked up by Carr, who made a deal with Stigwood. The die was cast, and the Broadway play is probably still running somewhere. The movie is a fine rendition of the play and reaped huge rewards at the box office, perhaps the highest grosses accorded any film musical.

The story takes place in the 1950s, which have become a nostalgic period. Travolta and Newton-John make a great impression as two kids who attend Rydell High. The story is a look at the trials and tribulations of young love; the plot turns are not really important. There are the usual misunderstandings, the satire of the teachers, a car race between rivals, and several production numbers. Travolta is one of those cool dudes who must stay aloof from the travails of his contemporaries. Newton-John loves him dearly and wants their summer romance to continue once they go to school together.

Everyone in the picture had been out of high school for years when the the movie was made, but disbelief was suspended in favor of fantasy. Lots of attention was paid to details, and it shows in every frame. The clothes, the manner of speech, the hair styles, the musical arrangements were all on the nose—to the point of caricature. There are several extended "cameos" by various stars; Eve Arden reprises her "Our Miss Brooks" role, but this time she is a principal. Sid Caesar is a fine coach; and even ageless Joan Blondell comes on for a fast, funny bit. Many people made their first appearances in GREASE. It was Kleiser's premier screen-directing effort. He had already done a good job directing Travolta in a TV film called "The Boy in the Plastic Bubble," the true story of a young man with a rare disease who could not leave the bubble he lived in or he would die. (Travolta fell in love with the woman who played his mother, Diana Hyland, and they stayed together until her early death of cancer while she was still in her thirties.) Channing had already appeared in THE FORTUNE, in which she was dwarfed by her costars. In GREASE she was able to step up and stand out. Conn, who starred in the mawkish YOU LIGHT UP MY LIFE, proves that she is a one-note actress with a whiny voice. (She married screen composer David Shire, former husband of Talia Shire, sister of Francis Ford Coppola.) Edd Byrnes, who was a heartbreaker in the 1950s, makes a small appearance. He is good and should be doing more. Travolta was never better, and his film career went straight downhill from here as he starred in a host of garbage pictures that made very little money. Composer Charles Fox ("Happy Days," many TV shows, and a host of movies, including FOUL PLAY) was supposed to do the score for the film, but he and producer Carr didn't see eye to eye, so Louis St. Louis was brought in, and his barely credited contribution was excellent. Newton-

John is adorably virginal, and just about all the secondary parts are well cast. This is a first-rate spoof of a fifth-rate genre (BEACH PARTY, BEACH BLANKET BINGO, DON'T KNOCK THE ROCK, etc.); you just can't hate anything *this* energetic and happy. Songs include "Grease," "Summer Nights," Best Song Oscar nominee "Hopelessly Devoted to You," "You're the One That I Want," "Sandy," "Beauty-School Dropout," "Look at Me, I'm Sandra Dee," "Greased Lightnin'," "It's Raining on Prom Night," "Alone at a Drive-In Movie," "Blue Moon," "Rock 'n' Roll Is Here to Stay," "Those Magic Changes," "Hound Dog," "Born to Hand-Jive," "Tears on My Pillow," "Mooning," "Freddy My Love," "Rock 'n' Roll Party Queen," "There Are Worse Things I Could Do," "We Go Together," "Love Is a Many Splendored Thing."

GREAT DICTATOR, THE 💿
1940 127m bw Comedy/War ★★★★½
UA (U.S.)

Charles Chaplin *(Hynkel, Dictator of Tomania/A Jewish Barber)*, Paulette Goddard *(Hannah)*, Jack Oakie *(Napaloni, Dictator of Bacteria)*, Reginald Gardiner *(Schultz)*, Henry Daniell *(Garbitsch)*, Billy Gilbert *(Herring)*, Maurice Moscovich *(Mr. Jaeckel)*, Emma Dunn *(Mrs. Jaeckel)*, Grace Hayle *(Mme. Napaloni)*, Carter DeHaven *(Bacterian Ambassador)*

p, Charles Chaplin; d, Charles Chaplin; w, Charles Chaplin; ph, Roland Totheroh, Karl Struss; ed, Willard Nico; m, Meredith Willson; art d, J. Russell Spencer

AAN Best Picture; AAN Best Actor: Charles Chaplin; *AAN Best Supporting Actor:* Jack Oakie; *AAN Best Original Screenplay:* Charles Chaplin; *AAN Best Original Score:* Meredith Willson

Chaplin's first complete talkie and it's fascinating to see the way the structures of his silent films are translated into a unique blend of slapstick, wordplay, parody, and pointed political commentary. This is Chaplin's brilliant and heartfelt plea for world peace in an era of rising fascism and mass annihilation.

Chaplin, well aware of the ironic physical similarity between his sweet Little Tramp and Adolf Hitler, casts himself in a dual role as a nameless Jewish barber and as Adenoid Hynkel, Dictator of Tomania. The barber, a soldier for the German Army in WWI, awakens from a state of amnesia to learn that Hynkel, the country's new dictator, is calling for the persecution of all Jews. The barber's friend, Hannah (Paulette Goddard), is forced to flee the country; his barber shop is defaced and burned and he is arrested and sent to a concentration camp for sheltering an old friend, Schultz (Reginald Gardiner).

Filled with equal parts of humanity, outrage, and comedy, THE GREAT DICTATOR contains some of Chaplin's finest moments, including the famous upside-down flying sequence in which the barber doesn't even realize that he's not flying upright, Hynkel's fiery speech, delivered in an unintelligible German-English gibberish, and the film's scene of great genius, Hynkel's "ballet" with an air-filled globe of the world—tossing it, kicking it, adoring it, and, finally, destroying it as only a dictator dreaming of world domination could. The power of this strangely haunting film is enhanced by the realization that the extremes of human nature in the first half of this century were personified by these two mustached figures—Hitler and the Little Tramp.

GREAT ESCAPE, THE 💿
1963 169m c Prison/War ★★★★
UA (U.S.)

Steve McQueen *("Cooler King" Hilts)*, James Garner *("The Scrounger" Hendley)*, Richard Attenborough *("Big X" Bartlett)*, James Donald *(Senior Officer Ramsey)*, Charles Bronson *(Danny Velinski)*, Donald Pleasence *("The Forger" Blythe)*, James Coburn *("The Manufacturer" Sedgwick)*, David McCallum *(Ashley-Pitt)*, Gordon Jackson *(MacDonald)*, John Leyton *(Willie)*

p, John Sturges; d, John Sturges; w, James Clavell, W.R. Burnett (based on the book by Paul Brickhill); ph, Daniel Fapp (Deluxe Color); ed, Ferris Webster; m, Elmer Bernstein; art d, Fernando Carrere; cos, Bert Henrikson

AAN Best Film Editing: Ferris Webster

Expertly directed and written with an infectious undercurrent of wry humor, this classic WWII POW escape yarn features an all-star cast of hardened Allied prisoners who the Germans have thrown together in a special "escape-proof" camp. Naturally, the first thing they set about doing is planning their escape—not just any escape, but one so massive that thousands of German troops will be kept away from the front in the effort to track them down.

The prime instigators include "Big X" (Richard Attenborough), the British master planner; a Polish tunnel-digging expert (Charles Bronson); a forger of passports and papers (Donald Pleasence); and two Americans, "The Scrounger" (James Garner), in charge of assembling needed supplies, and Hilts (Steve McQueen), "The Cooler King," who has his own ideas about how to get out. When those ideas fail, he uses a baseball and mitt to while away his days in solitary confinement. The prisoners ingeniously go about digging three tunnels, and though one of them is discovered, the big breakout still takes place. The film follows the principals as they try to make their way to safety—some successfully, others meeting tragic ends, but all providing great excitement.

Based on a book detailing a real-life mass escape of Allied troops in 1942, producer-director John Sturges's film is involving throughout, due mainly to the excellent performances of its stellar cast, particularly McQueen in a breakthrough performance. Elmer Bernstein's exhilarating score is perfectly suited to the film's nonstop tension. A hit with the critics and at the box office. THE GREAT ESCAPE is for many *the* great "escape" film.

GREAT EXPECTATIONS 💿
1946 118m bw Drama ★★★★★
Cineguild (U.K.)

John Mills *(Pip Pirrip)*, Valerie Hobson *(Estella/Her Mother)*, Bernard Miles *(Joe Gargery)*, Francis L. Sullivan *(Jaggers)*, Martita Hunt *(Miss Havisham)*, Finlay Currie *(Abel Magwitch)*, Anthony Wager *(Pip as Child)*, Jean Simmons *(Estella as Child)*, Alec Guinness *(Herbert Pocket)*, Ivor Barnard *(Wemmick)*

p, Ronald Neame; d, David Lean; w, David Lean, Ronald Neame, Anthony Havelock-Allan, Cecil McGivern, Kay Walsh (from the novel by Charles Dickens); ph, Guy Green; ed, Jack Harris; m, Walter Goehr; prod d, John Bryan; art d, Wilfred Shingleton; cos, Sophia Harris

AAN Best Picture; AAN Best Director: David Lean; *AAN Best Screenplay:* David Lean, Ronald Neame, Anthony Havelock-Allan; *AA Best B/W Cinematography:* Guy Green; *AA Best Art Direction-Set Decoration (B/W):* John Bryan, Wilfred Shingleton

A masterful realization of Charles Dickens's novel, this may be the best cinematic translation of the author's work, as well as director David Lean's greatest achievement. Beginning in 1830, the film follows the life of orphan Pip Pirrip (Anthony Wager as a child, John Mills as an adult), from his humble beginnings as a blacksmith's apprentice to his days as the wealthy beneficiary of an escaped convict (Finlay Currie) he once helped. Wonderfully directed by Lean—especially the childhood passages—GREAT

EXPECTATIONS is brimming with unforgettable images and characters. Although admirers of the novel may bemoan the absence of several characters, the film captures the spirit of Dickens, translating his prose into flawless cinema. Cinematographer Guy Green and production designer John Bryan were awarded Academy Awards for their memorable work. A must see.

GREAT EXPECTATIONS

1998 111m c   Romance/Drama   ★★★½
Knickerbocker Films/20th Century Fox   (U.S.)   R

Ethan Hawke *(Finnegan Bell)*, Gwyneth Paltrow *(Estella)*, Anne Bancroft *(Ms. Nora Dinsmoor)*, Robert De Niro *(Prisoner/Lustig)*, Chris Cooper *("Uncle" Joe)*, Hank Azaria *(Walter Plane)*, Josh Mostel *(Jerry Ragno)*, Nell Campbell *(Erica Thrall)*, Jeremy James Kissner *(Finnegan—Age 10)*, Gabriel Mann, billed as Gabriel Mick *(Owen)*

p, Art Linson; d, Alfonso Cuaron; w, Mitch Glazer (based on the novel by Charles Dickens); ph, Emmanuel Lubezki; ed, Steven Weisberg; m, Patrick Doyle; prod d, Tony Burrough; art d, John Kasarda; fx, Steve Kirshoff, Rich Thorne, Digital Filmworks, Inc.; cos, Judianna Makovsky

Recast as a tale of erotic obsession and shallow celebrity, Charles Dickens' *Great Expectations* becomes director Alfonso Cuaron's sadly lush ode to exploited youth, a visual feast that never loses sight of the bitter toll the plot's twists and turns take on its characters.

Ten-year-old Finn Bell (Jeremy James Kissner) is a Florida wharf rat whose only escape from his hardscrabble life lies in sketching. His uncle Joe (Chris Cooper) fishes and picks up extra cash doing odd jobs for local rich people, including aging eccentric Nora Dinsmoor (Anne Bancroft), whose portentously named estate—*Paradiso Perduto*—is slowly vanishing under a veil of Spanish moss. There Finn falls hopelessly in love with Miss Dinsmoor's ward Estella (Raquel Beaudene) a gravely beautiful girl being groomed for a career as a pitiless mantrap. Years later, circumstance brings together the adult Finn and Estella (Ethan Hawke and Gwyneth Paltrow) in New York, where he's on the verge of art-world stardom and she's about to marry socially connected Walter Plane (Hank Azaria).

For all the superficial glamour of the New York scenes, it's the episodes from Finn's childhood that have a seductively lucid edge: escaped convict Lustig (Robert De Niro) rising from a pool of shallow water; Finn and Estella sharing their first kiss over a bubbling fountain; Finn mesmerized by the unnaturally lithe Miss Dinsmoor dancing to the jaunty little Latin number "Besame Mucho," then turning to reveal the grotesque mask of makeup behind which her face resides. No doubt about it: unlike David Lean's much-loved classic, Cuaron's film is *loosely* based on Dickens. And that's just fine. Awash in vibrant shades of green and studded with unimpeachable indicators of cool (Francesco Clemente created Finn's paintings, downtown diva Nell Campbell plays his art dealer), it's a vividly imagined work that stands firmly on its own two fashionably shod feet.

GREAT GATSBY, THE

1949 92m   bw Drama   ★★★½
Paramount   (U.S.)

Alan Ladd *(Jay Gatsby)*, Betty Field *(Daisy Buchanan)*, Macdonald Carey *(Nick Carraway)*, Ruth Hussey *(Jordan Baker)*, Barry Sullivan *(Tom Buchanan)*, Howard da Silva *(Wilson)*, Shelley Winters *(Myrtle Wilson)*, Henry Hull *(Dan Cody)*, Carole Mathews *(Ella Cody)*, Ed Begley *(Myron Lupus)*

p, Richard Maibaum; d, Elliott Nugent; w, Cyril Hume, Richard Maibaum (based on the novel by F. Scott Fitzgerald and the play by Owen Davis, Sr.); ph, John Seitz; ed, Ellsworth Hoagland; m, Robert Emmett Dolan; art d, Hans Dreier, Roland Anderson; cos, Edith Head

The first sound adaptation of F. Scott Fitzgerald's classic Jazz Age novel, this version is far superior to its silent predecessor and the botched 1974 remake with Robert Redford in the title role. A large part of what makes this version work is the glacial central presence of Alan Ladd, who's quite convincing as a man with a mysterious past. Ladd is the enigmatic Jay Gatsby, a fabulous bootlegger who has used his relentless drive to amass a fortune. That mission accomplished, he turns his attention to wooing back a woman he lost many years earlier to a wealthy man.

Ladd is quite appropriate for Fitzgerald's hero. Embodying youthful disillusionment, false hope, and tragic nobility, he captures Gatsby's melancholy, mythic persona. Interestingly, the film ultimately feels more like a 1940s film noir than a '20s costume drama due to the moody monochrome cinematography of John F. Seitz.

GREAT MCGINTY, THE

1940 81m   bw Political/Comedy   ★★★★
Paramount   (U.S.)

Brian Donlevy *(Dan McGinty)*, Muriel Angelus *(Catherine McGinty)*, Akim Tamiroff *(The Boss)*, Allyn Joslyn *(George)*, William Demarest *(The Politician)*, Louis Jean Heydt *(Thompson)*, Harry Rosenthal *(Louis, the Bodyguard)*, Arthur Hoyt *(Mayor Tillinghast)*, Libby Taylor *(Bessie)*, Thurston Hall *(Mr. Maxwell)*

p, Paul Jones; d, Preston Sturges; w, Preston Sturges; ph, William Mellor; ed, Hugh Bennett; m, Frederick Hollander; art d, Hans Dreier, Earl Hedrick; cos, Edith Head

AA Best Original Screenplay: Preston Sturges

A hilarious spoof of American politics, this film marked the directorial debut of the mercurial and brilliant Preston Sturges, one of the best writer-directors of the 1940s. While this film never reaches the giddy heights of some of his subsequent films, THE GREAT MCGINTY was a favorable harbinger of the therapeutic madness to come.

The film opens in a smoky banana-republic bar largely patronized, it seems, by Americans on the lam. One such denizen, Thompson (Heydt), is a one-time chief cashier of a major bank turned embezzler. Now dejected from hiding out in this steamy exile, he attempts suicide in the men's room but he's stopped by the bartender, Dan McGinty (Donlevy). McGinty has an even more ignominious tale to tell: he used to be governor of a state! His strange story unravels in flashback.

McGinty begins as a seedy hobo looking for a quick buck. During an election in a major city, he's hired by a slick politician (Demarest) to vote repeatedly using the names of dead citizens. He proves to be an overzealous participant in the democratic process, voting dozens of times at an expected $2 per vote but the politico is unable to come across with the dough. McGinty remains persistent. He's taken to the party hall where The Boss (Tamiroff) is so taken with the bum's moxie that he appoints him a collector of funds in his protection racket. McGinty proves himself a born collector and he continues moving up the ladder of crime until he is finally repaid for the big time—politics.

Donlevy, in an early starring role, gives a marvelous performance as a dim-witted bum who's transformed into a polished politician. The flamboyant Tamiroff's rendering of the boss is a comic delight. Demarest is colorful and full of street savvy and wit, once remarking: "If you didn't have graft, you'd have a lower class of people in politics!" This terrific satire was the brainchild of screenwriter Sturges, who, by the time he penned this script, was the highest-paid writer in Hollywood, having written films such as EASY LIVING and DIAMOND JIM.

GREAT MOUSE DETECTIVE, THE 📀

1986 73m c Animated/Mystery ★★★½
Walt Disney Productions/Silver Screen Partners II G
(U.S.)

VOICES OF: Vincent Price (Professor Ratigan), Barrie Ingham (Basil/Bartholomew), Val Bettin (Dawson), Susanne Pollatschek (Olivia), Candy Candido (Fidget), Diana Chesney (Mrs. Judson), Eve Brenner (The Mouse Queen), Alan Young (Flaversham), Basil Rathbone (Sherlock Holmes), Laurie Main (Watson)

p, Burny Mattinson; d, John Musker, Ron Clements, Dave Michener, Burny Mattinson; w, Peter Young, Vance Gerry, Steve Hulett, Ron Clements, John Musker, Bruce M. Morris, Matthew O'Callaghan, Burny Mattinson, David Michener, Melvin Shaw (based on the book Basil of Baker Street by Eve Titus); ph, Ed Austin; ed, Roy M. Brewer Jr., Jim Melton; m, Henry Mancini; art d, Guy Vasilovich; anim, Mark Henn, Glen Keane, Robert Minkoff, Hendel Butoy

Back in the Dark Ages of Disney—the dimly remembered period after Walt's death and before the second Renaissance that was ushered in by THE LITTLE MERMAID and BEAUTY AND THE BEAST—there seemed to be trouble in the magic kingdom. THE GREAT MOUSE DETECTIVE, therefore, surprised and pleased many animation enthusiasts; it combined the sophistication of the new Disney era with the well-loved traditions and standards of the past.

Based on the beloved children's novel Basil of Baker Street by Eve Titus, the story is an adaptation of Sherlock Holmes motifs interpreted by a few cartoon mice living in Victorian London. Vincent Price provides the voice of Ratigan, a Moriarty-like genius who wants to control the mouse world. To this end, he kidnaps a brilliant mouse toymaker, Flaversham (voiced by Alan Young), intending to have the poor whiskered creature build a terrifying rodent robot that he will use to dethrone the current mouse queen (Eve Brenner). Basil (Barrie Ingham), the Holmesian mouse, and Dawson (Val Bettin) agree to help Flaversham's daughter Olivia (Susanne Pollatschek) find her father, but the trail leads to all sorts of pitfalls.

This is high-quality animation. The engaging characters play out the action against elegantly designed backgrounds. The story is genuinely exciting, a well-told tale that is entertaining to both children and adults without compromising the expectations of either group. The voices are perfectly cast, particulary Price as the evil Ratigan.

GREAT MUPPET CAPER, THE 📀

1981 95m c Children's/Musical ★★★½
Universal (U.K.) G

Jim Henson (Kermit/Rowlf/Dr. Teeth/Waldorf), Frank Oz (Miss Piggy/Fozzie Bear/Animal/Sam the Eagle), Dave Goelz (The Great Gonzo/Beauregard/Zoot/Dr. Bunsen/Honeydew), Jerry Nelson (Floyd/Pops/Lew Zealand), Richard Hunt (Scooter/Statler/Sweetums/Janice/Beaker), Charles Grodin (Nicky Holiday), Diana Rigg (Lady Holiday), John Cleese, Robert Morley, Peter Falk

p, David Lazer, Frank Oz; d, Jim Henson; w, Tom Patchett, Jay Tarses, Jerry Juhl, Jack Rose; ph, Oswald Morris (Technicolor); ed, Ralph Kemplen; prod d, Harry Lange; art d, Charles Bishop, Terry Ackland-Snow, Leigh Malone; chor, Anita Mann; cos, Julie Harris, Calista Hendrickson, Joanne Green, Mary Strieff, Carol Spier, Danielle Obinger

AAN Best Original Song: "The First Time It Happens"; Joe Raposo (Music & Lyrics)

This one got lost in the shuffle. Jim Henson himself directed the muppets along with Charles Grodin, John Cleese, Robert Morley and other English types. The Muppet menagerie cavorts in the middle of London in this, their second film. There's a plot this time—the famous "Baseball" diamond has been stolen—and the music is even better than THE MUPPET MOVIE. That first film with the muppet crew had to be a success; this time it was more difficult. Nonetheless, the caper plot that Henson and company worked out manages to hold adult interest for quite a while.

Kermit, Fozzie Bear, and Gonzo are reporters investigating the theft of fashion queen Lady Holiday's (Diana Rigg) jewels. Lady Holiday's brother, Nicky (Charles Grodin), frames Miss Piggy for the theft but the other Muppets save the day. The film boasts fewer guest-star cameo appearances than the first time around but those who are here do a good job, and Miss Piggy's Busby Berkeley-type dance and the water ballet are fun to watch. Followed by THE MUPPETS TAKE MANAHATTAN.

GREAT NORTHFIELD, MINNESOTA RAID, THE

1972 91m c Biography/Western ★★★
Universal (U.S.) PG

Cliff Robertson (Cole Younger), Robert Duvall (Jesse James), Luke Askew (Jim Younger), R.G. Armstrong (Clell Miller), Dana Elcar (Allen), Donald Moffat (Manning), John Pearce (Frank James), Matt Clark (Bob Younger), Wayne Sutherlin (Charley Pitts), Robert H. Harris (Wilcox)

p, Jennings Lang; d, Philip Kaufman; w, Philip Kaufman; ph, Bruce Surtees (Technicolor); ed, Douglas Stewart; m, Dave Grusin; art d, Alexander Golitzen, George Webb; cos, Helen Colvig

An offbeat, ragged but totally absorbing Western, this film profiles the infamous yet celebrated James-Younger gang in relatively realistic terms, showing them for the murderous and desperate men they probably were while offering a refreshingly sophisticated and cynical political analysis of their situation. Though it borrows heavily from late 1960s-early 1970s genre landmarks such as BONNIE AND CLYDE and McCABE AND MRS. MILLER, it remains interesting for its depiction of how exploitive capitalism—the railroads in this case—compels somewhat simpleminded farmers into outlaw lives.

The Missouri legislature is preparing to vote on granting amnesty to those notorious outlaws, Jesse James (Duvall) and Cole Younger (Robertson). Some enlightened members argue that these men and their followers were driven into crime by powerful behind-the-scenes interests that appropriated their lands. Cole is willing to accept the amnesty and return to farming, but James argues that nothing will change, the railroads will continue to steal their land and their persecution will never stop. He's right. After the amnesty motion is ruled out of order, James plans to take the gang from their native Missouri to rob the big bank in Northfield, Minnesota, after reading a newspaper account about its financial standing as the biggest bank west of the Mississippi. Things go wrong.

Although director-writer Kaufman claimed to have researched the real tale of the James-Younger gang while studying history at the University of Chicago, many of his details are inaccurate and some scenes are outright fabrications. However, the awkward, crude, unsophisticated dialogue is appropriate to the period, region, and characters. Duvall delivers an interesting interpretation of Jesse James as a borderline psychotic. Robertson credibly portrays Cole Younger as a cunning, intelligent and even sensitive person. The supporting players also are all believable, and the well mounted production seems clearly authentic. One of the best profiles of the James-Younger gang yet made, although Walter Hill's

THE LONG RIDERS more aptly captures the character of the gang.

GREAT SANTINI, THE

1979 115m c Drama/War ★★★½
Orion (U.S.) PG

Robert Duvall *(Bull Meechum)*, Blythe Danner *(Lillian Meechum)*, Michael O'Keefe *(Ben Meechum)*, Lisa Jane Persky *(Mary Anne Meechum)*, Julie Anne Haddock *(Karen Meechum)*, Brian Andrews *(Matthew Meechum)*, Stan Shaw *(Toomer Smalls)*, Theresa Merritt *(Arrabelle Smalls)*, David Keith *(Red Pettus)*, Paul Mantee *(Col. Hedgepath)*

p, Charles A. Pratt; d, Lewis John Carlino; w, Lewis John Carlino (based on the novel by Pat Conroy); ph, Ralph Woolsey (Technicolor); ed, Houseley Stevenson; m, Elmer Bernstein; prod d, Jack Poplin

AAN Best Actor: Robert Duvall; *AAN Best Supporting Actor:* Michael O'Keefe

Robert Duvall received an Academy Award nomination for his forceful performance as a warrior without a war in this touching, well-crafted drama based on the novel by Pat Conroy.

As Marine pilot Bull Meechum, he rules his family with military discipline, setting impossibly high standards for his four children (Julie Anne Haddock, Brian Andrews, Lisa Jane Persky, and Michael O'Keefe). When Bull's harsh manner becomes too oppressive for his offspring, they know that their mother, Lillian (Blythe Danner), is there to provide an understanding shoulder to cry on, especially the sensitive Ben (O'Keefe), whose battle to earn his father's respect is most tellingly played out in one-on-one basketball games that force Bull to play dirty to win. Although Bull's kids are never able to reach their father, they do offer him the kind of stoic tribute that would have made him proud when tragedy strikes.

Deftly scripted, beautifully shot—making good use of its South Carolina locations—and magnificently acted, The Great Santini garnered Academy nominations for both Duvall and O'Keefe. Though its emotions are big, the performances are so nicely nuanced that sentiment never overwhelms the story's emotional realism. In addition to Duvall's tour-de-force performance, Danner is outstanding as the nurturing mother, and O'Keefe's heartfelt portrayal of the tortured son earned him an Oscar nomination as Best Supporting Actor.

GREAT WHITE HOPE, THE

1970 102m c Sports ★★★½
Fox (U.S.) PG

James Earl Jones *(Jack Jefferson)*, Jane Alexander *(Eleanor)*, Lou Gilbert *(Goldie)*, Joel Fluellen *(Tick)*, Chester Morris *(Pop Weaver)*, Robert Webber *(Dixon)*, Marlene Warfield *(Clara)*, R.G. Armstrong *(Cap'n Dan)*, Hal Holbrook *(Cameron)*, Beah Richards *(Mama Tiny)*

p, Lawrence Turman; d, Martin Ritt; w, Howard Sackler (based on his play); ph, Burnett Guffey (Panavision, Deluxe Color); ed, William Reynolds; m, Lionel Newman; prod d, John De Cuir; art d, Jack Martin Smith; chor, Donald McKayle; cos, Irene Sharaff

AAN Best Actor: James Earl Jones; *AAN Best Actress:* Jane Alexander

Adapted by Howard Sackler from his own Broadway hit, this excellent period drama is a thinly veiled depiction of the life of the first black heavyweight champion of the world, Jack Johnson.

By winning the title, Johnson (James Earl Jones, who played the role on Broadway) incurs the wrath of the white world. His troubles begin in earnest when he takes up with Eleanor (Alexander), a white divorcee. He's convicted of break-ing the Mann Act and gets sent to prison. After Jefferson escapes, he and Alexander begin an itinerant exile that takes them to Canada, England (where he's refused a boxing license), France and Germany. Few are willing to take on the great champion but he is determined to fight again. THE GREAT WHITE HOPE persuasively recreates the climate of the time and generally avoids the preachiness for which director Ritt is sometimes known. The love story between Alexander and Jones is touchingly portrayed. Sackler's screenplay is written in free verse, but you'd never know it.

GREAT ZIEGFELD, THE

1936 170m bw Musical/Biography ★★★
MGM (U.S.)

William Powell *(Florenz Ziegfeld)*, Luise Rainer *(Anna Held)*, Myrna Loy *(Billie Burke)*, Frank Morgan *(Billings)*, Reginald Owen *(Sampson)*, Nat Pendleton *(Sandow)*, Virginia Bruce *(Audrey Lane)*, Ernest Cossart *(Sidney)*, Robert Greig *(Joe)*, Raymond Walburn *(Sage)*

p, Hunt Stromberg; d, Robert Z. Leonard; w, William Anthony McGuire; ph, Ray June, Oliver T. Marsh, Karl Freund, Merritt Gerstad, George Folsey; ed, William S. Gray; art d, Cedric Gibbons; chor, Seymour Felix; cos, Adrian

AA Best Picture; AA Best Actress: Luise Rainer; *AA Best Dance Direction:* Seymour Felix; *AAN Best Director:* Robert Z. Leonard; *AAN Best Original Story:* William Anthony McGuire; *AAN Best Film Editing:* William S. Gray; *AAN Best Interior Decoration:* Cedric Gibbons, Eddie Imazu, Edwin B. Willis (Art Direction)

How appropriate that this ode to an ambitious, amiable shyster featured future First Lady Pat Nixon as an extra. Incredibly, THE GREAT ZIEGFELD, three hours of lumpy, overcooked pudding, took Best Picture at the 1936 Oscars. But then, the film is *big*, and it's an ode to lavish showmanship—what better pat on the back could Hollywood give itself?

The details of the whitewashed story aren't worth dwelling on in detail. Flo (Powell) begins as a sideshow barker and eventually becomes Broadway impresario extraordinaire. Along the way he marries temperamental actress-singer Anna Held (Rainer) but their oh-so-turbulent relationship just doesn't make it. He later weds actress Billie Burke (Loy) and, after enduring his darkest hours, stuns Broadway with four simultaneous hits.

Oddly enough, the film does have enough thrust to keep rigor mortis from setting in. Powell can't give his shallow role much depth beyond a consideration of Ziegfeld's incredible ambition and ego, but he does give it energy and rascally charm. Loy would have been foolish to copy the inimitable twittering of Billie Burke and wisely she doesn't try. What she's left with are a new hair color, uxorial devotion and relatively little footage.

The latter applies to Rainer as well, though we mind that less. She does have a delicate appeal onstage and also in the "legendary" telephone scene in which Anna, still in love, calls Flo to congratulate him on his second marriage. Still, Rainer's fluttery performance did *not* deserve an Oscar for Best Actress and today stands as a glass menagerie relic just waiting to be dropped on the floor. Ray Bolger adds a few delightful moments, but a pre-WIZARD OF OZ Frank Morgan is way overboard and Fanny Brice is ditched right in the middle of singing "My Man"!! What can you do with a movie like this? Surrender, I guess.

GREATEST SHOW ON EARTH, THE

1952 153m c Drama ★★★★
Paramount (U.S.)

Betty Hutton *(Holly)*, Cornel Wilde *(Sebastian)*, Charlton Heston *(Brad)*, Dorothy Lamour *(Phyllis)*, Gloria Grahame *(Angel)*, James Stewart *(Buttons, a Clown)*, Henry Wilcoxon *(Detective)*,

Lyle Bettger *(Klaus)*, Lawrence Tierney *(Henderson)*, John Kellogg *(Harry)*

p, Cecil B. DeMille; d, Cecil B. DeMille; w, Fredric M. Frank, Barre Lyndon, Theodore St. John (based on a story by Frank, St. John, Frank Cavett); ph, George Barnes, Peverell Marley, W. Wallace Kelley (Technicolor); ed, Anne Bauchens; m, Victor Young; art d, Hal Pereira, Walter Tyler; fx, Gordon Jennings, Paul K. Lerpae, Devereaux Jennings; chor, Richard Barstow; cos, Miles White, Edith Head, Dorothy Jeakins

AA Best Picture; AAN Best Director: Cecil B. DeMille; *AA Best Motion Picture Story:* Fredric M. Frank, Theodore St. John, Frank Cavett; *AAN Best Film Editing:* Anne Bauchens; *AAN Best Costume Design (Color):* Edith Head, Dorothy Jeakins, Miles White

It's big, it's garish, it's loud, and most of all, it's wonderful. This is Cecil B. DeMille's superlative salute to the circus world, and all its glamour and flashy hoopla suits perfectly the director whose middle name was epic. An episodic soap opera set under the big top, the film is almost like a documentary in its meticulous detailing of circus life. Charlton Heston plays the head of the sprawling ensemble and the entire cast is outstanding, particularly James Stewart as the clown hiding from his past. Since the early 1920s, DeMille had planned on producing a spectacular circus film, but his biblical epics got in the way. Finally, in 1949, after Paramount paid Ringling Brothers $250,000 for the right to use the circus' name, equipment, and talent, DeMille began elaborate preparations. The film is authentic and awesome and earned an Oscar as Best Picture.

GREEN DOLPHIN STREET
1947 140m bw Adventure/Romance ★★½
MGM (U.S.)

Lana Turner *(Marianne Patourel)*, Van Heflin *(Timothy Haslam)*, Donna Reed *(Marguerite Patourel)*, Richard Hart *(William Ozanne)*, Frank Morgan *(Dr. Edmund Ozanne)*, Edmund Gwenn *(Octavius Patourel)*, Dame May Whitty *(Mother Superior)*, Reginald Owen *(Capt. O'Hara)*, Gladys Cooper *(Sophie Patourel)*, Moyna MacGill *(Mrs. Metivier)*

p, Carey Wilson; d, Victor Saville; w, Samson Raphaelson (based on the novel by Elizabeth Goudge); ph, George Folsey; ed, George White; m, Bronislau Kaper; art d, Cedric Gibbons, Malcolm Brown; fx, Warren Newcombe, A. Arnold Gillespie; cos, Walter Plunkett, Valles

AAN Best B/W Cinematography: George Folsey; *AAN Best Film Editing:* George White; *AAN Best Sound Recording:* Metro-Goldwyn-Mayer Sound Department; *AA Best Special Effects:* A. Arnold Gillespie (Visual), Warren Newcombe (Visual), Douglas Shearer (Audible), Michael Steinore (Audible)

Lana Turner's bid for the sweep of epic skirts, her GWTW as it were, and a classic egg-layer. You can swallow this clinker whole if you can stomach one plot turn: Richard Hart's New Zealand army deserter who gets loaded and writes a love letter to Turner, even though it's little sis Donna Reed he really cares for; the poor lad has the names confused. When Turner blows in, he marries her rather than admit his mistake and all karmic hell breaks loose. Here Saville's direction rises to the fore, with giant trees falling over and the earth belching and shivering in a killer earthquake sequence. Just when things seem tame there's a Maori uprising. Meanwhile, spurned sis Reed takes the nun's vow.

Without murderous acts of passion, Lana's out of her element; but not to worry. Natural disasters and aboriginal riots take no toll on Turner's visage—a strand of hair displaced here, a streak of dirt there. Brunette haircolor and a possible acting chore deter her not one whit from her goal of genus: star.

GREEN FOR DANGER
1946 91m bw Mystery/Comedy ★★★★★
Individual Picture (U.K.)

Sally Gray *(Nurse Linley)*, Trevor Howard *(Dr. Barney Barnes)*, Rosamund John *(Esther Sanson)*, Alistair Sim *(Inspector Cockrill)*, Leo Genn *(Mr. Eden)*, Judy Campbell *(Marion Bates)*, Megs Jenkins *(Nurse Woods)*, Moore Marriott *(Joe Higgins)*, Henry Edwards *(Mr. Purdy)*, Ronald Adam *(Dr. White)*

p, Frank Launder, Sidney Gilliat; d, Sidney Gilliat; w, Sidney Gilliat, Claude Guerney (based on a novel by Christianna Brand); ph, Wilkie Cooper; ed, Thelma Myers; m, William Alwyn; prod d, Peter Proud

Green for go! An unfairly overlooked delight in the annals of British film history, GREEN FOR DANGER is one of the most enjoyable films ever produced by those masters of comic entertainment, Launder and Gilliat.

Inspector Cockrill (Sim), an unorthodox detective, investigates a strange double murder that takes place in a British emergency hospital during WWII. A postman who has been slightly wounded by a buzz bomb dies on the operating table, and, when nurse Marion Bates (Campbell) discovers that he was murdered, she's stabbed to death. Cockrill discovers that everyone present during the operation had a motive, and, with an odd sense of amusement, he sets about exposing the surprising culprit.

Though most U.S. audiences remember Sim primarily for his flawless performance as Scrooge, his use of his droopy features, lugubrious yet fruity intonations and impeccable timing make this role one of his best. Gray, Howard and John are appealing as always, and a marvelous supporting cast gives fine moments to Genn, Jenkins, Marriott, Edwards and others. Still, it's the remarkable Sim (unlikely star material only at first glance) and the smooth, feather-light scripting and direction of Gilliat that makes watching this film like sitting up late on a stormy night reading your first Agatha Christie novel.

GREEN MAN, THE
1956 80m bw Comedy ★★★★
Grenadier (U.K.)

Alastair Sim *(Hawkins)*, George Cole *(William Blake)*, Jill Adams *(Ann Vincent)*, Avril Angers *(Marigold)*, Terry-Thomas *(Boughtflower)*, John Chandos *(McKecknie)*, Dora Bryan *(Lily)*, Colin Gordon *(Reginald)*, Eileen Moore *(Joan Wood)*, Raymond Huntley *(Sir Gregory Upshoot)*

p, Sidney Gilliat, Frank Launder; d, Robert Day; w, Sidney Gilliat, Frank Launder (based on their play *Meet a Body*); ph, Gerald Gibbs; ed, Bernard Gribble; m, Cedric Thorpe Davie

This hilarious comedy stars Alastair Sim as Hawkins, a professional assassin who has long been out of action. He comes out of his retirement when he is hired to do away with Sir Gregory Upshoot (Huntley), a pompous politician. Hawkins tracks his quarry to a decrepit seaside hotel called the Green Man, and waits there to spring his trap, disguising himself as a simple clockmaker. As such he puts up with a bevy of dowagers at the resort, joining in the staid teas, conversations, and musical diversions. Meanwhile, a bomb he has planted is ready to explode upon Sir Upshoot's arrival. But it seems as if the victim will never appear! Alastair Sim is a delight as the assassin with the soul of an aesthete. Terry-Thomas is also very funny in this underrated little gem.

GREEN MILE, THE
1999 187m c Drama/Fantasy ★★★ DVD
Castle Rock Entertainment/Polygram Filmed Entertainment/Darkwoods (U.S.) R

Tom Hanks *(Paul Edgecomb)*, Michael Clarke Duncan *(John Coffey)*, David Morse *("Brutal" Brutus Howell)*, James Cromwell

(Warden Hal Moores), Michael Jeter *(Eduard "Del" Delacroix)*, Sam Rockwell *("Wild Bill" Wharton)*, Graham Greene *(Arlen Bitterbuck)*, Bonnie Hunt *(Jan Edgecomb)*, Patricia Clarkson *(Melinda Moores)*, Doug Hutchison *(Percy Wetmore)*

p, David Valdes, Frank Darabont; d, Frank Darabont; w, Frank Darabont (based on the novel by Stephen King); ph, David Tattersall; ed, Richard Francis-Bruce; m, Thomas Newman; prod d, Terence Marsh; art d, William Cruse; fx, Industrial Light & Magic; cos, Karyn Wagner

AAN Best Picture; AAN Best Supporting Actor: Michael Clarke Duncan; *ANN Best Sound:* Robert J. Litt, Elliot Tyson, Michael Herbick, Willie D. Burton; *AAN Best Adapted Screenplay:* Frank Darabont

Pure corn, so beautifully crafted and emotionally satisfying that surrendering to its cliches is easy, even though they're recycled from pretty much every life-affirming prison movie ever made.

Adapted from Stephen King's serialized novel, the story is set in 1935 Louisiana, where Paul Edgecomb (Tom Hanks) supervises Cold Mountain Penitentiary's death row inmates. They call his beat the "Green Mile" in deference to the color of the block's faded linoleum floor, and under Edgecomb's calm and fair-minded direction, the Mile is a pretty decent place for the end of the line, despite inevitable irritants like sadistic guard Percy Wetmore (Doug Hutchison). But everything changes when John Coffey (Michael Clarke Duncan) arrives to await execution. A massive black man—seven feet of pure muscle crisscrossed with scars—Coffey has the demeanor of a sweet-natured child; his manner is disturbingly at odds with his conviction for raping and murdering two little girls. As Edgecomb gets to know his new charge, he begins to suspect there's more to this gentle giant than meets the eye…much more. Edgecomb begins to believe that Coffey has been touched by the hand of God, who surely wouldn't waste His bounty on a baby killer.

King has two basic modes: ooga-booga and misty-eyed sentimental. THE GREEN MILE is firmly in the latter camp. The material is derivative and pandering, and everything plays out the way you want it to, which isn't always the way it should. But Frank Darabont (THE SHAWSHANK REDEMPTION) directs in classic Hollywood style, smooth and self-effacing, and the meticulous, seemingly effortless performances make the hours—all three of them—fly by.

GREEN ROOM, THE
(LA CHAMBRE VERTE)
1978   94m   c   Drama/War   ★★★½
Carrosse/UA (France)   PG

Francois Truffaut *(Julien Davenne)*, Nathalie Baye *(Cecilia Mandel)*, Jean Daste *(Bernard Humbert)*, Jean-Pierre Moulin *(Gerard Mazet)*, Antoine Vitez *(Bishop's Secretary)*, Jane Lobre *(Mazet's Second Wife)*, Monique Dury *(Monique, Editorial Secretary)*, Laurence Ragon *(Julie Davenne)*, Marcel Berbert *(Dr. Jardine)*, Christian Lentretian *(Orator in Cemetery)*

d, Francois Truffaut; w, Francois Truffaut, Jean Gruault (based on themes in the writings of Henry James); ph, Nestor Almendros (Eastmancolor); ed, Martine Barraque; m, Maurice Jaubert; art d, Jean-Pierre Kohut-Svelko

Francois Truffaut's testimony of obsession, THE GREEN ROOM, is perhaps the most unheralded film of his career, and surely one of his most personal.

Truffaut himself plays Julien Davenne, a secretive man who excels at writing obituaries for a fading journal and who's stubbornly obsessed with death, believing that the deceased are not given the love and attention they deserve. His reverence is inspired both by his guilt over returning from WWI unharmed, while everyone he knew was killed or injured, and by the sudden death of his newlywed wife. In her memory, he constructs a shrine, complete with a frightening, life-size wax

figurine. At the cemetary where she's buried he discovers an old chapel in need of restoration and remodels it as an elaborate temple for the dead, filling it with photos of dead friends and acquaintances killed in the trenches.

On the surface, THE GREEN ROOM is an excessively depressing and strange portrait of a man who values death over life, but underneath it runs the study of a man driven by his obsessions. An interesting and atmospheric counterpoint to the numerous war films that pay tribute to those who died for their country, THE GREEN ROOM concerns a man who lived through war, is tormented by survivor's guilt, and is driven to actively remember the dead.

GREETINGS   *DVD*
1968   88m   c   Comedy/Drama   ★★★½
West End Films   (U.S.)   R

Robert De Niro *(Jon Rubin)*, Jonathan Warden *(Paul Shaw)*, Gerrit Graham *(Lloyd Clay)*, Richard Hamilton *(Pop Artist)*, Megan McCormick *(Marina)*, Bettina Kugel *(Tina)*, Allen Garfield *(Smut Peddler)*, Roz Kelly *(Photographer)*, Jack Cowley *(Photographer)*, Jane Lee Salmons *(Model)*

p, Charles Hirsch; d, Brian De Palma; w, Brian De Palma, Charles Hirsch; ph, Robert Fiore; ed, Brian De Palma; m, The Children of Paradise

Brian De Palma's breezy, Godardian first feature distills the heady atmosphere of Greenwich Village in an era of counter-cultural experimentation and anti-war protest. Irrepressibly libidinous Paul (Jonathan Warden) receives a draft notice and schemes to avoid induction with the aid of Lloyd (Gerrit Graham), a trendy paranoiac who's obsessed with the Kennedy assassination, and Jon (Robert De Niro), a De Palma alter ego who channels his voyeurism through filmmaking. Shot in two weeks on a budget of $43,000, the film took in over a million dollars, bringing its 28-year-old director to the attention of Hollywood. Like much of De Palma's later work, GREETINGS is primarily concerned with the process, conventions, and political meanings of cinema. Nevertheless, it's funny, vulgar, and outrageously politically incorrect—as when Jon, ostensibly documenting the Vietnam War, allows his obsessions to get the better of him and implores a Vietnamese woman to strip for the camera.

GREGORY'S GIRL   *DVD*
1981   91m   c   Romance/Comedy   ★★★½
Lake   (U.K.)   PG

Gordon John Sinclair *(Gregory)*, Dee Hepburn *(Dorothy)*, Jake D'Arcy *(Phil Menzies)*, Clare Grogan *(Susan)*, Robert Buchanan *(Andy)*, Billy Greenlees *(Steve)*, Alan Love *(Eric)*, Caroline Guthrie *(Carol)*, Carol Macartney *(Margo)*, Douglas Sannachan *(Billy)*

p, Clive Parsons, Davina Belling; d, Bill Forsyth; w, Bill Forsyth; ph, Michael Coulter (Kay Labs color); ed, John Gow; m, Colin Tully; art d, Adrienne Atkinson

A funny and touching teen romance from Scottish director Bill Forsyth. Gordon John Sinclair stars as an awkward teen who develops a major crush on the new girl in school, soccer star Dorothy (Dee Hepburn). Sinclair successfully portrays the uneasy quandary most adolescent boys go through when suffering from painful shyness coupled with the outrageous hormonal imbalance that drives them to do ridiculous things to get the attention of a pretty girl. While the plot is a straight, simple romance, the true charm of the film comes from its quirky characters, its general air of tolerance and good will and some irrepressible and delightfully absurd touches that creep (or waddle) along the periphery of the narrative. With this unpretentious little film, Forsyth decisively demonstrates that there was still life in the classic British comedy more than 30 years after its heyday.

GREMLINS 2: THE NEW BATCH

DVD

1990 105m c Comedy/Horror ★★★★
Mike Finnell/Amblin (U.S.) PG-13

Zach Galligan *(Billy Peltzer)*, Phoebe Cates *(Kate Beringer)*, John Glover *(Daniel Clamp)*, Robert Prosky *(Grandpa Fred)*, Howie Mandel *(Voice of Gizmo)*, Tony Randall *(Voice of "Brain" Gremlin)*, Robert Picardo *(Forster)*, Christopher Lee *(Dr. Catheter)*, Haviland Morris *(Marla Bloodstone)*, Dick Miller *(Murray Futterman)*

p, Michael Finnell; d, Joe Dante; w, Charlie Haas (based on characters created by Chris Columbus); ph, John Hora (Technicolor); ed, Kent Beyda; m, Jerry Goldsmith; prod d, James Spencer; art d, Joe Lucky; fx, Rick Baker; cos, Rosanna Norton; anim, Chuck Jones

A huge improvment over the original, GREMLINS 2: THE NEW BATCH is surprisingly sympathetic towards the title menace, and surprisingly thought-provoking as extended commentary on modern life and morality. That the beasties should wind up the tragically ill-fated good guys should come as no surprise to director Joe Dante's admirers; he's an enthusiastic fan of classic Hollywood kitsch, especially those monster movies, in which the saddest scene is the one in which the monster dies.

With GREMLINS 2, Dante has come up with what may be his best film yet—a dizzying, no-holds-barred satirical spectacle that will please fans of the original and anyone else lucky enough to drop by. This is no lifeless retread, even though every big scene from the first film has its equivalent here. (Dante still seems especially concerned about the safe use of microwave ovens.) And even if the filmmakers' apparent intent was to make a movie that feels wildly out of control, GREMLINS 2 rarely loses sight of its objectives. Almost every plot twist, stunt, and sight gag elaborates the movie's basic theme: the metaphysical price paid for plundering a rich human past to build a dubious, impoverished, and inhumane future, of which the gremlins are merely an unnatural byproduct.

This theme is mainly suggested by Clamp's urgency in tearing down New York landmarks (such as *all* of Chinatown), to construct cold, high-tech, soulless structures in their place, but it is echoed everywhere—from the Splice of Life lab, dedicated to developing new and "improved" life forms, to the romantic subplot, in which Billy is tempted to throw away his long-term romance with Kate to further his career with Clamp.

Still, no one who makes movies as thoroughly modernist and as full of high-tech special effects as Dante does can ever make a sincere claim to yearning for gentler, simpler times. As a result, the film exhibits an oddly compelling ambivalence toward the gremlins throughout. But it doesn't stop us from feeling a little sad for the gremlins after they meet their sticky end. They may be nasty, but they know how to party, particularly when they spontaneously mount a lavish musical number inspired by the Kander and Ebb classic "New York, New York."

GREY ZONE, THE

DVD

2002 108m c Drama ★★★★
Goatsingers/Killer Films/Millennium Films R
(U.S.)

David Arquette *(Hoffman)*, Steve Buscemi *(Abramowics)*, Harvey Keitel *(Muhsfeldt)*, Allan Corduner *(Nyiszli)*, Mira Sorvino *(Dina)*, Natasha Lyonne *(Rosa)*, Daniel Benzali *(Schlermer)*, David Chandler *(Rosenthal)*, Kamelia Grigorova *(Girl)*, Henry Stram *(Mengele)*

p, Pamela Koffler, Avi Lerner, Danny Lerner, Tim Blake Nelson, Christine Vachon; d, Tim Blake Nelson; w, Tim Blake Nelson (based on the play by Tim Blake Nelson and the memoir *Auschwitz: A Doctor's Eyewitness Account*, by Dr. Miklos Nyiszli);

ph, Russell Lee Fine; ed, Michelle Botticelli, Tim Blake Nelson; m, Jeff Danna; prod d, Maria Djurkovic; art d, Tatiana Lund; fx, Willie Botha; cos, Marina Draghici

Based in part on the published memoir of Miklos Nyiszli, a Hungarian doctor who survived eight months in Auschwitz, Tim Blake Nelson's adaptation of his own stage play is a harrowing, thoroughly uncompromising tour of hell.

Upon his arrival at the camp, Nyiszli (played here by Allan Corduner) was spared immediate death and sent to work as a pathologist for the infamous Nazi doctor Josef Mengele (Henry Stram). Nyiszli also served as a physician to the Sonderkommando, a squad of Jewish prisoners who were temporarily spared extermination but condemned to a grimmer fate. It was their job to usher their fellow Jews and other camp inmates into the gas chambers, then load their corpses into the blazing ovens of the crematoriums.

Nelson's film explores the excruciating moral choices these Jewish prisoners made by focusing on the extraordinary true story of Auschwitz's twelfth Sonderkommando, which plotted to destroy the crematoriums. What's most startling about the film is its utter unwillingness to see Auschwitz as anything other that what it was: a highly efficient death machine that murdered thousands each day. As the plan to destroy the crematoriums—and a subplot involving a group of Jews (including David Arquette and Steve Buscemi who attempt to save a young girl (Kamelia Grigorova)—unfolds, Nelson takes the viewer through what must be the most explicit portrayal of the extermination process ever to appear in a feature film. The film's graphic nature raises important questions about how filmmakers are to depict the Holocaust on film: Either you show nothing—Claude Lanzmann's effective strategy in SHOAH—or you try to show it all, as Nelson does. The result is an extremely difficult but worthy film whose ultimate horror lies in the certain knowledge that the reality of Auschwitz was far worse.

GREYSTOKE: THE LEGEND OF TARZAN, LORD OF THE APES

DVD

1984 129m c Adventure ★★★½
Warner Bros. (U.K.) PG

Ralph Richardson *(The 6th Lord of Greystoke)*, Ian Holm *(Capt. Phillippe D'Arnot)*, Christopher Lambert *(John Clayton/Tarzan)*, Andie MacDowell *(Jane Porter)*, James Fox *(Lord Esker)*, Ian Charleson *(Jefferson Brown)*, Nigel Davenport *(Maj. Jack Downing)*, Paul Geoffrey *(Lord Jack Clayton)*, Cheryl Campbell *(Lady Alice Clayton)*, Nicholas Farrell *(Sir Hugh Belcher)*

p, Hugh Hudson, Stanley S. Canter; d, Hugh Hudson; w, Robert Towne, Michael Austin (based on the novel *Tarzan of the Apes* by Edgar Rice Burroughs); ph, John Alcott (Super Techniscope, Eastmancolor); ed, Anne V. Coates; m, John Scott; prod d, Stuart Craig; art d, Simon Holland, Norman Dorme; fx, Albert Whitlock; chor, Peter Elliot; cos, John Mollo, Shirley Russell

AAN Best Supporting Actor: Ralph Richardson; *AAN Best Adapted Screenplay:* P.H. Vazak, Michael Austin; *AAN Best Makeup:* Rick Baker, Paul Engelen

The most intelligent and perhaps the best filmic treatment of Edgar Rice Burroughs's classic pulp novels about Tarzan, the white child of noble blood raised by apes in the jungle, since Elmo Lincoln first brought the character to the screen in 1918.

The film opens with the shipwreck that casts Lord Jack Clayton (Paul Geoffrey) and his pregnant wife Lady Alice (Cheryl Campbell) on the wild coast of Africa. They build a hut in the jungle, she bears a son, and shortly thereafter they both die. The infant is adopted by a clan of apes, with whom he grows to manhood, after which his ape mother is killed by pygmies. They also wipe out the first white men that Tarzan (Christopher Lambert) has ever seen, a party of hunters. He saves one of them, a wounded Belgian, Captain Phillippe D'Arnot (Ian Holm), who teaches him to speak English. Eventually Tarzan returns to civilization with D'Arnot and goes to his ancestral home in Scotland, Greystoke Manor. There, his grandfather, the Sixth Lord of Greystoke (Sir Ralph Richardson), tries to integrate his heir into upper-crust society.

The film is beautifully photographed and marvelously acted, with Lambert showing remarkable subtlety and emotion. Richardson, in his final film role, is even better; he carries much of the second half of the film when the story starts to sag. The special-effects costuming by Rick Baker is superb and his actor-apes are so expressive and natural that it is almost impossible to tell them from the real apes that appear in the scenes with them. Nominated by the Academy for Best Supporting Actor (Richardson), Best Screenplay (co-writer Robert Towne writing under the pseudonym P.H. Vasak), and Best Makeup.

GRIFTERS, THE   *DVD*

1990 113m c   Crime   ★★★★
Grifters Inc./Scorsese Productions   (U.S.)   R

John Cusack *(Roy Dillon)*, Anjelica Huston *(Lilly Dillon)*, Annette Bening *(Myra Langtry)*, Pat Hingle *(Bobo Justus)*, J.T. Walsh *(Cole Langtry)*, Henry Jones *(The Desk Clerk)*, Michael Laskin *(Irv)*, Eddie Jones *(Mintz)*, Charles Napier *(Hebbing)*, Jan Munroe *(Guy at Bar)*

p, Martin Scorsese, Robert A. Harris, James Painten; d, Stephen Frears; w, Donald E. Westlake (based on the novel by Jim Thompson); ph, Oliver Stapleton; ed, Mick Audsley; m, Elmer Bernstein; prod d, Dennis Gassner; art d, Leslie McDonald; cos, Richard Hornung

AAN Best Actress: Anjelica Huston; *AAN Best Supporting Actress:* Annette Bening; *AAN Best Director:* Stephen Frears; *AAN Best Adapted Screenplay:* Donald E. Westlake

THE GRIFTERS has the mastery and hallucinatory, all-involving feel of an instant classic. Stephen Frears, a fearlessly diverse director, has immersed himself in the Los Angeles world of film noir and emerged with a movie that can easily stand alongside such classics of the genre as THE MALTESE FALCON, THE BIG SLEEP and OUT OF THE PAST.

The tale is spun of three "grifters," con artists forever on the lookout for an easy hustle. Lily (Anjelica Huston) is an ultra-experienced pro who specializes in racetrack odds altering. Her son, Roy (John Cusack), is basically small-time, hustling sailors and bartenders with loaded dice and sleight-of-hand tricks. His inamorata, Myra (Annette Bening), likes corporate action, a field she is easily able to ply with her siren's body and wardrobe of Chanel suits. Lily had Roy when she was but a girl herself, and the two have mostly gone their separate ways. They meet up again in California, where Lily takes an immediate dislike to Myra. Her ill feeling is met and matched by Roy, who has never resolved his filial feelings for her, as well as by Myra, who, having been wholly rebuffed by Lily, resolves to take her down. The climax, involving Lily and Roy, is swift, ugly, cathartic, and ultimately elegiac all at once.

Adapted from modish tough-guy writer Jim Thompson's novel, Donald Westlake's screenplay has the right combination of vivid characters, mordant wit and avaricious savagery which distinguishes the best noir. The characters speak in a faintly disconcerting 1950s argot right out of the book, adding an authentic flavor to the simmeringly suggestive stew Frears has concocted.

GROOVE TUBE, THE   *DVD*

1974 75m   c   Comedy   ★★★
Syn-Frank Enterprises   (U.S.)   R

Ken Shapiro *(Koko/Boss/"Near You" Singer/Robert Elgin/Mahetma Yenta/Lionel Elgin, "Just You, Just Me" Dancing Man, "Food For Thought" Moderator)*, Richard Belzer *(Rodriguez/Leo Batfish/The President/The Hooker)*, Chevy Chase *(The Fingers/Geritan)*, Buzzy Linhart *(The Hitchhiker)*, Richmond Baier *(The Girl)*, Berkeley Harris *(The Rich Guy)*, Jennifer Welles *(The Geritan Girl)*, Roy Wallace, Kirtus Allen, Laura Glicken

p, Ken Shapiro; d, Ken Shapiro; w, Ken Shapiro, Lane Sarasohn; ph, Bob Bailin; fx, Peter Kunz; anim, Linda Taylor, Pat O'Neill

What "Saturday Night Live" and "SCTV" became famous for, THE GROOVE TUBE did first. Independently distributed by Ken Shapiro, who also did just about everything else in the film except play a few naked girls, this counter-cultural comedy presents a vision of television made by and for potheads, hippies, and others who weren't being represented by the media at the time. Some of it is certainly dated, but it's an integral element in any 1970s time capsule.

In an opening parody of 2001: A SPACE ODYSSEY (1968), prehistoric apes gather around an unusual object—a television set. A hitchhiker is picked up by a flirtatious woman who lures him into the woods and the hands of the police. On his daily TV show, Koko the Clown tells kids to send all the "big people" out of the room for make-believe time, and then reads to them from *Fanny Hill.* A long TV parody titled "The Dealers" stars Shapiro and Richard Belzer as drug dealers who smuggle a huge stash into the country, only to lose it through a series of misadventures. The "Channel One Evening News" features reports on the war in Vietnam (where the towns have names like "Phuc Hu" and "Suk Muk Dik"), a lascivious U.S. president welcoming a female dignitary, and prostitution in Times Square. At the end of his report, the anchorman waits endlessly for the camera to stop filming him; eventually he sneaks behind his desk and crawls away on all fours, still followed by the camera. On the "Wild World of Sports," commentators covering the "Annual International Sex Games" give a blow by blow report on the West German team (actually old porn footage). The movie's best scene is the ending, in which Shapiro, dressed in a pink pin-striped business suit and suitcase, does an uninhibited dance through midtown Manhattan to the tune of "Just You, Just Me" (sung, of course, by Shapiro) In between these sketches are parodies of commercials and public service spots. Among the more memorable ones are Chevy Chase's fingers in an obscene rendition of the Yellow Pages' "Let your fingers do the walking"; the Uranus Corporation and its all-purpose miracle product "Brown 25" (seen plopping disgustingly from the end of a long metal tube); and a PSA about sexually transmitted diseases delivered by a "puppet" which we gradually realize is a penis with eyes painted on it.

THE GROOVE TUBE was an outgrowth of "Channel One," a comedy troupe formed in 1967 by Shapiro, Lane Sarasohn, and Chevy Chase. Instead of performing live, they videotaped parodies of TV and showed them in a ratty theater in Greenwich Village. (Chase left early on and was replaced by Richard Belzer.) After touring a collection of Channel One's best bits to colleges, Shapiro transferred them to film and assembled this movie. THE GROOVE TUBE doesn't offer much in the way of satire or political humor; indeed, a lot of it is crude and sophomoric. And that's probably why so much of it is still pretty funny. Although Shapiro made a lot of money from THE GROOVE TUBE, he apparently dropped out of show business after making one other film, the critical and commercial flop MODERN PROBLEMS (1981), with Chevy Chase. *(Extensive nudity, sexual situations, adult situations, substance abuse, profanity.)*

GROSSE POINTE BLANK

DVD

1997 108m c Crime/Thriller/Comedy ★★★½
Roth/Arnold Productions/New Crime R
Productions/Caravan Pictures (U.S.)

John Cusack *(Martin Q. Blank)*, Minnie Driver *(Debi Newberry)*, Dan Aykroyd *(Mr. Grocer)*, Alan Arkin *(Dr. Oatman)*, Joan Cusack *(Marcella)*, Jeremy Piven *(Paul Spericki)*, Hank Azaria *(Steven Lardner)*, Barbara Harris *(Mary Blank)*, K. Todd Freeman *(Ken McCullers)*, Mitchell Ryan *(Bert Newberry)*

p, Susan Arnold, Donna Arkoff Roth, Roger Birnbaum; d, George Armitage; w, Tom Jankiewicz, D.V. DeVincentis, Steve Pink, John Cusack (based on a story by Tom Jankiewicz); ph, Jamie Anderson; ed, Brian Berdan; m, Joe Strummer; prod d, Stephen Altman; art d, Scott Meehan; fx, Ron Trost; cos, Eugenie Bafaloukos

A slick, mannered, and frequently very clever comedy about yuppie hit man Martin Blank (John Cusack), who decides to mix business and pleasure by doing a job and attending his 10-year high school reunion over the same weekend. Awaiting him in Grosse Pointe, MI are the sweetheart he stood up on prom night (Minnie Driver) and a raft of old friends who get a real charge out of Martin's forthright answer to the inevitable, "So, what do you do?" He just slays 'em. Eccentric director George Armitage (MIAMI BLUES) takes what could easily have been a second-rate exercise in PULP FICTION attitude and gives it a clean, vivid look, wasting little time on the mercenary metaphors (making a killing in business and so on) and keeping Martin's misbegotten, near-surreal sentimental journey moving along briskly. Propelled by a hippest-hits of the '80s soundtrack and Cusack's deceptively subtle performance, this potentially queasy mix of John Hughes-style high school nostalgia and Tarantino-esque cool gets past the gags and ventures into some surprisingly poignant territory without ever losing its brittle edge. Blank's relationship with his unwilling therapist (Alan Arkin) is particularly bracing, and even the bloated Dan Aykroyd (playing a fellow professional killer who's hell-bent on unionizing) manages not to spoil things.

GROUNDHOG DAY

DVD

1993 103m c Comedy ★★★½
Columbia (U.S.) PG

Bill Murray *(Phil)*, Andie MacDowell *(Rita)*, Chris Elliott *(Larry)*, Stephen Tobolowsky *(Ned)*, Brian Doyle-Murray *(Buster)*, Marita Geraghty *(Nancy)*, Angela Paton *(Mrs. Lancaster)*, Rick Ducommun *(Gus)*, Rick Overton *(Ralph)*, Robin Duke *(Doris the Waitress)*

p, Trevor Albert, Harold Ramis; d, Harold Ramis; w, Danny Rubin, Harold Ramis (from the story by Rubin); ph, John Bailey, James Blanford, George Kohut; ed, Pembroke J. Herring; m, George Fenton; prod d, David Nichols; art d, Peter Lansdown Smith; fx, Tom Ryba; cos, Jennifer Butler

GROUNDHOG DAY is an immensely enjoyable fable of a confirmed cynic who finds himself stuck in the same 24-hour time frame, over and over again, and the life lessons he manages to learn from it.

Bill Murray stars as Phil, a TV weatherman sent to Punxsutawney, PA, to cover the Groundhog Day festival. A grinch who disdains all things provincial, Phil is predictably peeved when a blizzard forces him, his producer Rita (Andie MacDowell) and cameraman Larry (Chris Elliott) to spend a second night in the picture-postcard town.

Peeved doesn't even begin to approach how he feels next morning, when he wakes up and discovers that it's Groundhog Day—again. Stuck in a time loop, Phil seems doomed to spend the rest of his life repeating the same day over and over. Whatever he does—from getting thrown in jail to committing several varieties of suicide—he invariably wakes up at 6:00 the next morning in his guest-house bed, with "I Got You, Babe" blaring from his radio alarm.

What do you do when you're sentenced to re-live one day in your life for eternity? Phil starts out trivial (he memorizes all the answers to "Jeopardy"); then decides to better himself (piano lessons); and finally searches for true love, coming up with some ingenious ways of wooing Rita in less than 24 hours. (However far he gets each day, he's always back to square one in the morning.)

With Bill Murray being his usual self and Andie McDowell injecting a high charm factor, GROUNDHOG DAY makes a pretty entertaining couple of hours. Seeing it once is fine, but seeing it every day for the rest of your life is not recommended.

GRUDGE, THE

DVD

2004 92m c Horror ★★★
Ghost House/Columbia (U.S.) R

Sarah Michelle Gellar *(Karen)*, Jason Behr *(Doug)*, William Mapother *(Matthew)*, Clea DuVall *(Jennifer)*, KaDee Strickland *(Susan)*, Grace Zabriskie *(Emma)*, Bill Pullman *(Peter)*, Ted Raimi *(Alex)*, Ryo Ishibashi *(Detective Nakagawa)*, Yoko Maki *(Yoko)*

p, Taka Ichise, Sam Raimi, Doug Tapert; d, Takashi Shimizu; w, Takashi Shimizu, Stephen Susco (based on the films JU-ON: THE CURSE, JU-ON: THE CURSE 2, and JU-ON: THE GRUDGE, written by Takashi Shimizu); ph, Hideo Yamamoto; ed, Jeff Betancourt; m, Christopher Young; prod d, Iwao Saito; art d, Kyoko Yauchi; fx, Kory Jones (visual), Shuichi Kishiura (mechanical), Hajime Matsumoto (digital); cos, Shawn Holly Cookson, Miyuki Taniguchi

Most haunted-house movies make a pact with viewers: You can breathe a sigh of relief if the unfortunate folks trapped inside manage to get out. Not so in Takashi Shimizu's seriously spooky ghost story. Blighted by a crime whose lingering malevolence is lodged in its every splinter, the house bears a *ju-on*—a lingering, supernatural grudge—that poisons the life of everyone who ventures inside, no matter how much distance they put between themselves and the incongruously nondescript Tokyo split-level.

The film starts with the inexplicable suicide of Tokyo-based professor Peter (Bill Pullman), then introduces fresh-faced American students Karen (Sarah Michelle Gellar) and Doug (Jason Behr). Karen's amassing credits toward a social-work degree by volunteering at a local home health-care center whose supervisor, Alex (Ted Raimi), gives her an emergency assignment. Withdrawn, elderly Emma (Grace Zabriskie) needs minding, and her usual aide, Yoko (Yoko Maki), is a no-show. Karen arrives to a scene of disturbing disarray. Strange noises draw her to an upstairs closet where she discovers a child—small, silent Toshio (Yuya Ozeki)—huddled with his cat. By the time Alex can respond to Karen's freaked-out phone call, Emma is dead, the child has vanished, and Karen is in a state of shock. The house's lethal ill will eventually reaches out to touch Grace's son, Matthew (William Mapother), his sister (KaDee Strickland), and his wife (Clea DuVall); Alex and the missing Yoko; and Detective Nakagawa (Ryo Ishibashi), who knows more about the situation than he lets on.

Screenwriter Stephen Susco and Shimizu cherry-pick the best bits of the popular Japanese JU-ON movies and add Western characters, whose cultural dislocation introduces a subtle subtext without diluting the original films' fundamentally Japanese spirit. Producers Sam Raimi and Bob Tapert resisted the temptation to beef up the special effects, which remain subordinate to atmosphere.

GUADALCANAL DIARY

1943 93m bw War
Fox (U.S.)

DVD
★★★★

Preston Foster *(Father Donnelly)*, Lloyd Nolan *(Hook Malone)*, William Bendix *(Taxi Potts)*, Richard Conte *(Capt. Davis)*, Anthony Quinn *(Jesus "Soose" Alvarez)*, Richard Jaeckel *(Pvt. Johnny Anderson)*, Roy Roberts *(Capt. Cross)*, Minor Watson *(Col. Grayson)*, Ralph Byrd *(Ned Rowman)*, Lionel Stander *(Butch)*

p, Bryan Foy; d, Lewis Seiler; w, Lamar Trotti, Jerry Cady (based on the novel by Richard Tregaskis); ph, Charles Clarke; ed, Fred Allen; m, David Buttolph; art d, James Basevi, Leland Fuller; fx, Fred Sersen

Released before the U.S. had even been involved in the war for a year, this hard-hitting WWII action film drew its story from Richard Tregaskis's best-selling nonfiction book and superbly documents the first significant U.S. counterattacks in the Pacific—the Marine invasion of the Solomon Islands.

One group of Marines, a cross-section of Americans from all walks of life, is shown as they hit the beaches in August 1942. William Bendix plays a tough, dim-witted ex-cab driver with a heart of gold; Richard Conte a courageous officer; Preston Foster the company chaplain; Lionel Stander the company clown; Lloyd Nolan the old pro sergeant who looks out for young recruits like Richard Jaeckel (in his film debut); and Anthony Quinn is the rugged Mexican-American hero who seeks revenge for the slaughter of his platoon. The film follows the recruits from camp, to their first engagement, and through the hell that was Guadalcanal.

Not a pretty picture, GUADALCANAL DIARY captures in painful detail the day-to-day survival of the stout-hearted Marines, presenting their humor and the full force of their dedication in scene after scene. Powerfully effective as propaganda, the film was in keeping with Hollywood's early efforts to depict a treacherous enemy, joining the ranks of such stellar WWII films as WAKE ISLAND and BATAAN, but unlike those films it depicted a major American victory. Lewis Seiler's direction is as quick and relentless as the chatter of a machine gun and all the cast members render believable and telling portraits.

GUARDSMAN, THE

1931 89m bw Comedy
MGM (U.S.)

★★★★

Alfred Lunt *(the Actor)*, Lynn Fontanne *(the Actress)*, Roland Young *(the Critic)*, ZaSu Pitts *(Liesl)*, Maude Eburne *(Mama)*, Herman Bing *(a Creditor)*, Ann Dvorak *(a Fan)*

p, Irving Thalberg (uncredited), Albert Lewin; d, Sidney Franklin; w, Ernest Vajda, Claudine West (based on the play by Ferenc Molnar); ph, Norbert Brodine; ed, Conrad A. Nervig

AAN Best Actor: Alfred Lunt; *AAN Best Actress:* Lynn Fontanne

A tattered, irresistible Valentine, more like a photographed stage play than a film, but a souvenier of lyrical, happy talent. French playwright Ferenc Molnar's clever marital comedy was never better performed than by the illustrious stars of American theater, Alfred Lunt and Lynn Fontanne, who had made the play a Broadway hit in 1924.

This bubbling sex farce begins when Lunt, watching Fontanne dreamily playing Chopin on the piano, suspects that her mind is on another. He quickly determines to resolve this doubt by a dangerous charade. Impersonating his imagined rival—a Russian guardsman with mustache and broad accent—he seduces his wife, who turns the tables on him the next morning, telling him "I knew it was you all along." Or is this just a clever attempt to preserve her marriage?

It took the supreme talents of Lunt and Fontanne to make this delicate stage material work. Although the public did not respond well to the sophisticated comedy, the film was a

smashing critical success. Except for cameo roles in STAGE DOOR CANTEEN, this would be the only sound film the couple made in their illustrious careers, although Hollywood had previously wooed them into silents. MGM's Irving Thalberg managed to convince the famous pair to leave Broadway for THE GUARDSMAN, but it took a *lot* of convincing. To them the movies were merely cloudy mirrors of their own live theater reputations, reflections they did not appreciate. But in all fairness to their undeniable talent, it is said both realized they didn't photograph worth a damn.

GUELWAAR

1993 115m c Drama
Film Domireew/Galatee Film/FR3 Film Production
(Senegal)

★★★½

Omar Seck *(Gora)*, Ndiawar Diop *(Barthelemy)*, Mame Ndoumbe Diop *(Nogoy Marie Thioune)*, Isseu Niang *(Veronique)*, Myriam Niang *(Helene)*, Mustapha Diop *(Aloys)*, Thierno Ndiaye *(Pierre Henri Thioune (Guelwaar))*, Marie-Augustine Diatta *(Sophie)*, Joseph Sane *(Father Leon)*, Samba Wane *(Gor Mag)*

p, Ousmane Sembene, Jacques Perrin; d, Ousmane Sembene; w, Ousmane Sembene; ph, Dominique Gentil; ed, Marie Aimee; m, Baba Mall; prod d, Francois Laurent Sulva

With the release of GUELWAAR, his seventh feature and first outing since 1987's CAMP DE THIAROYE, the renowned Senegalese filmmaker Ousmane Sembene reconfirms his stature both as a master storyteller and a distinctively humanitarian artist.

Pierre Henri Thioune (Thierno Ndiaye), called Guelwaar—or Noble One—by his family and friends, has died under mysterious circumstances, leaving behind his grieving wife, Nogoy Marie (Mame Ndoumbe Diop); their daughter Sophie (Marie-Augustine Diatta), who toils as a prostitute in Dakar; and their two sons, Barthelemy (Ndiawar Diop) and Aloys (Mustapha Diop). Funeral proceedings are delayed, however, by the unaccountable disappearance of Guelwaar's corpse from the local morgue. When policeman Gora (Omar Seck) goes in search of the missing body, he finds himself in the midst of a bitter dispute between local Christians and Muslims.

Despite its languorous pace and folkloric quality, GUELWAAR reflects a hugely sophisticated sensibility, frequently diverging from the central story to include illuminating flashbacks, digressions, and soliloquies. Among the many contemporary issues Sembene touches upon—the loss of traditions, AIDS, the spread of corruption—the film offers a scathing indictment of the neocolonialism that permeates West African society.

GUESS WHO'S COMING TO DINNER

1967 108m c Drama
Columbia (U.S.)

★★½

Spencer Tracy *(Matt Drayton)*, Sidney Poitier *(John Prentice)*, Katharine Hepburn *(Christina Drayton)*, Katharine Houghton *(Joey Drayton)*, Cecil Kellaway *(Monsignor Ryan)*, Roy E. Glenn Sr. *(Mr. Prentice)*, Beah Richards *(Mrs. Prentice)*, Isabel Sanford *(Tillie)*, Virginia Christine *(Hilary St. George)*, Alexandra Hay *(Car Hop)*

p, Stanley Kramer; d, Stanley Kramer; w, William Rose; ph, Sam Leavitt (Technicolor); ed, Robert C. Jones; m, Frank DeVol; prod d, Robert Clatworthy; fx, Geza Gaspar; cos, Jean Louis, Joe King

AAN Best Picture; AAN Best Actor: Spencer Tracy; *AA Best Actress:* Katharine Hepburn; *AAN Best Supporting Actor:* Cecil Kellaway; *AAN Best Supporting Actress:* Beah Richards; *AAN Best Director:* Stanley Kramer; *AA Best Original Story and Screenplay:* William Rose; *AAN Best Film Editing:* Robert C. Jones; *AAN Best*

Adapted Score: Frank DeVol; *AAN Best Art Direction-Set Decoration:* Robert Clatworthy, Frank Tuttle

William Rose, with a stilted screenplay, and Stanley Kramer, who literally makes this dinner hour stand still—say we're not in. Big deal in its day, but really safe, lame melodrama, and an unfitting finale to the Tracy-Hepburn screen partnership.

Bland little Houghton arrives home after a Hawaiian vacation to announce to parents Tracy and Hepburn that she is about to wed a brilliant research physician, Poitier, who is Black. This creates considerable social turmoil for the upper-middle-class family. Poitier tells the parents that unless they give their unreserved consent he will not marry their daughter, thereby putting the responsibility for the interracial marriage squarely upon their shoulders. After some soul-searching and breaking with friends who oppose miscegenation, the parents back up the young couple.

Tracy looks tired in this draggy production; he died soon afterward, and it's infuriating to watch him sweat to inject fire into such pap. Hepburn, with her blithely resolute air and great, watering eyes, is magnanimous as always; watching her watch Tracy during his big speech is one of the film's two great Moments. The other? Hepburn in the driveway, banishing an ex-friend: "Don't say anything, Hillary, just—go."

GUMSHOE

1971 88m c Crime/Comedy ★★★½
Memorial (U.K.) PG

Albert Finney *(Eddie Ginley)*, Billie Whitelaw *(Ellen)*, Frank Finlay *(William)*, Janice Rule *(Mrs. Blankerscoon)*, Carolyn Seymour *(Alison Wyatt)*, Fulton Mackay *(Straker)*, George Innes *(Bookshop Proprietor)*, George Silver *(Jacob De Fries)*, Billy Dean *(Tommy)*, Wendy Richard *(Anne Scott)*

p, Michael Medwin; d, Stephen Frears; w, Neville Smith; ph, Chris Menges (Eastmancolor); ed, Fergus McDonell, Charles Rees; m, Andrew Lloyd Webber; prod d, Michael Seymour; art d, Richard Rambaut; fx, Bowie Films; cos, Daphne Dare

This offbeat feature debut from director Stephen Frears (MY BEAUTIFUL LAUNDRETTE, DANGEROUS LIAISONS, THE GRIFTERS) cleverly satirizes the detective films of the past, particularly those featuring the hard-boiled private eyes created by Dashiell Hammett and Raymond Chandler.

Finney, a bingo caller in a seedy Liverpool nightclub who envisions himself as a tough detective *a la* Humphrey Bogart, advertises his sleuthing services and is hired by a mysterious fat man (Silver). After receiving a package containing a photo of a young woman (Seymour), a gun and a thousand pounds—but no instructions—Finney becomes enmeshed in an extraordinarily convoluted affair that involves heroin smuggling, gun running and African politics.

Produced by Finney's own company, GUMSHOE is packed with witty, if absurd, dialogue and plenty of action, all harking back to the film noir days of the tough detective and made even funnier by Finney's struggles through the awkward transition from British commoner to the image of a hard-as-nails American-type sleuth. Great fun.

GUN CRAZY

1949 87m bw Crime 𝗗𝗩𝗗 ★★★★½
King Bros. (U.S.)

Peggy Cummins *(Annie Laurie Starr)*, John Dall *(Bart Tare)*, Berry Kroeger *(Packett)*, Morris Carnovsky *(Judge Willoughby)*, Anabel Shaw *(Ruby Tare)*, Harry Lewis *(Clyde Boston)*, Nedrick Young *(Dave Allister)*, Trevor Bardette *(Sheriff Boston)*, Mickey Little *(Bart Tare, Age Seven)*, Rusty Tamblyn *(Bart Tare, Age 14)*

p, Frank King, Maurice King; d, Joseph H. Lewis; w, MacKinlay Kantor, Dalton Trumbo (based on the story "Gun Crazy" by MacKinlay Kantor); ph, Russell Harlan; ed, Harry Gerstad; m, Victor Young; prod d, Gordon Wiles; cos, Norma

A stylish example of the doomed-lovers-on-the-run subgenre inspired by real-life outlaws Bonnie Parker and Clyde Barrow, and one of the best B movies ever made.

Fourteen-year-old Bart Tare is sent to reform school for stealing a gun. Back home after a hitch in the army, the adult Bart (John Dall) falls for carnival sharpshooter Laurie (Peggy Cummins) and joins the show. But the lovers soon find themselves out of work and drift into a life of crime, for which Laurie shows a feral aptitude. She eventually commits murder during a heist, and the law—including Bart's boyhood friend, Clyde (Harry Lewis), now a sheriff—begins to close inexorably in.

"We go together like guns and ammunition," says Bart to Laurie: this film was among the first in the U.S. to make explicit the symbiotic connection between sex and violence, as well as the worship of guns and their role in American culture. It revels in Bart and Laurie's perverse psychology and the nihilistic aspects of their escapades, and Lewis made the most of his leads, playing off Dall's air of ambiguous sexuality and mental instability (as did Alfred Hitchcock in ROPE) and the Welsh-born Cummins' unbridled carnality. Blacklisted writer Dalton Trumbo co-scripted under the name Millard Kaufman, and director Joseph H. Lewis is one of the great, unsung stylists of the American cinema. The film's four-minute bank robbery sequence is a tour-de-force shot in one continuous take from the back of the car, as the lovers talk while driving into town, park, get out, steal the money, beat up a cop, jump back into the car, and speed away. Lewis' sophisticated visual style is evident throughout in his use of deep focus, long takes, ornate compositions, and odd angles, punctuated by swift, violent camera movements and rapid cutting that signify the relationships of characters and their state of mind.

GUNFIGHT AT THE O.K. CORRAL

1957 122m c Western 𝗗𝗩𝗗 ★★★★
Paramount (U.S.)

Burt Lancaster *(Wyatt Earp)*, Kirk Douglas *(John H. "Doc" Holliday)*, Rhonda Fleming *(Laura Denbow)*, Jo Van Fleet *(Kate Fisher)*, John Ireland *(Johnny Ringo)*, Lyle Bettger *(Ike Clanton)*, Frank Faylen *(Cotton Wilson)*, Earl Holliman *(Charles Bassett)*, Ted de Corsia *(Abel Head "Shanghai Pierce")*, Dennis Hopper *(Billy Clanton)*

p, Hal B. Wallis; d, John Sturges; w, Leon Uris (based on the magazine article "The Killer" by George Scullin); ph, Charles Lang (VistaVision, Technicolor); ed, Warren Low; m, Dimitri Tiomkin; art d, Hal Pereira, Walter Tyler; fx, John P. Fulton; cos, Edith Head

AAN Best Film Editing: Warren Low; *AAN Best Sound:* George Dutton (Paramount Studio Sound Department)

Solid, expert "town" Western, but lacking the fuel of passion. Still it's a landmark Western—more than any other of its era, it gave the genre major film status. The story is legend: strong, resolute, and stoic, Lancaster is the famed Marshal Wyatt Earp, and Douglas is his closest friend, the deadly gunfighter "Doc" Holliday.

It's an interesting acting exercise: these two have been called "the two terrible-tempered twins"; they're like Davis and Crawford, in a way. People confuse their roles, claim one's a better actor, the other a bigger star, but unlike the aforementioned ladies, the two opinions offered flip back and forth on the respective men. Curious—but predictable—that GUNFIGHT is exactly the same. It's a stand-off between bravura egos, supported mightily by Van Cleef, Ireland, and the other men, with Van Fleet and Fleming doing definitive western turns as frontier whore and gambling hall floozie. But the film might have profited more from reverse casting in the leads (Lancaster's flamboyance seeming more suited to a gunman than a sheriff). And Sturges's direction lacks the bite of Anthony Mann's Jimmy Stewart oaters.

Yet GUNFIGHT, written—with generous dashes of dramatic license—by Leon Uris and beautifully photographed by Charles Lang, is truly a classic Western, one which thoroughly revitalized the genre. Its big-budget production and tremendous box-office success sent the making of B Westerns into decline; they all but vanished in the 1960s. The legendary gunfight has been filmed many other times, first in FRONTIER MARSHAL, then in John Ford's magnificent MY DARLING CLEMENTINE, again in Sturges's impressive sequel to this film, HOUR OF THE GUN, and in the introspective DOC.

GUNFIGHTER, THE

1950 84m bw Western ★★★★
Fox (U.S.)

Gregory Peck *(Jimmy Ringo)*, Helen Westcott *(Peggy Walsh)*, Millard Mitchell *(Sheriff Mark Strett)*, Jean Parker *(Molly)*, Karl Malden *(Mac)*, Skip Homeier *(Hunt Bromley)*, Anthony Ross *(Charlie)*, Verna Felton *(Mrs. Pennyfeather)*, Ellen Corby *(Mrs. Devlin)*, Richard Jaeckel *(Eddie)*

p, Nunnally Johnson; d, Henry King; w, William Bowers, William Sellers, Nunnally Johnson, Andre De Toth (based on a story by Bowers); ph, Arthur Miller; ed, Barbara McLean; m, Alfred Newman; art d, Lyle Wheeler, Richard Irvine

AAN Best Motion Picture Story: Andre DeToth, William Bowers

An arresting, superbly produced and downbeat Western photographed in stark black and white, THE GUNFIGHTER presents an unglorified view of the Old West as a grim, dirty and decidedly desperate place.

Peck stars as an alienated gunfighter who's feeling his age and beginning to look back more often than forward. Entering a saloon one night, he finds that his notorious reputation has preceded him. Loud-mouthed punk Jaeckel picks a fight with him, calling Peck names. Peck tries to beg off, asking anyone in the bar to talk the brash and foolish youth out of going for his gun. But Jaeckel reaches and Peck beats him, shooting and killing the aspiring gunslinger. After being informed that despite justification in defending himself, it won't matter to Jaeckel's three older brothers, the seasoned gunfighter leaves hastily and moves on to his original destination, taking a room in a nearby town where he hopes to be reunited with his young son. Meanwhile, Jaeckel's bloodthirsty siblings follow close behind.

Generally tough and humorless, THE GUNFIGHTER is a grim portrait of a man whose time and historical role have run out, and he knows it. Peck is dazzling as the doomed and haunted gunfighter, a man desperately trying to escape his own past and identity, but knowing all along that hope is false and that there is only a bullet in his future. Henry King's direction is outstanding, keeping the action tautly drawn, while Arthur Miller's high-contrast cinematography is highly suggestive as it documents Peck's inexorable movement toward death. Preceding HIGH NOON by two years, THE GUNFIGHTER was a seminal film in the western's movement away from action cliches toward more psychological depth.

GUNGA DIN

1939 117m bw Adventure/War ★★★★★
RKO (U.S.)

Cary Grant *(Sgt. Cutter)*, Victor McLaglen *(Sgt. MacChesney)*, Douglas Fairbanks Jr. *(Sgt. Ballantine)*, Sam Jaffe *(Gunga Din)*, Eduardo Ciannelli *(Guru)*, Joan Fontaine *(Emmy Stebbins)*, Montagu Love *(Col. Weed)*, Robert Coote *(Higginbotham)*, Abner Biberman *(Chota)*, Lumsden Hare *(Maj. Mitchell)*

p, George Stevens; d, George Stevens; w, Fred Guiol (based on the story by Ben Hecht, Charles MacArthur, William Faulkner from the poem by Rudyard Kipling); ph, Joseph August; ed, Henry Berman, John Lockert; m, Alfred Newman; art d, Van Nest Polglase, Perry Ferguson; fx, Vernon L. Walker; cos, Edward Stevenson

AAN Best B/W Cinematography: Joseph H. August

The GONE WITH THE WIND of the comic action-adventure genre, GUNGA DIN has a bit of everything—humor, suspense, spectacle, action *and* a heavy dose of racism, imperialism and xenophobia.

Based on a story by Ben Hecht and Charles MacArthur (it's the same friendly rivals plot of THE FRONT PAGE) and the moving Rudyard Kipling poem, this rousing adventure opens as a remote, mountainous British outpost in India is raided by a band of rebel natives. Three of the Army's most reliable frontier veterans—Sergeants Cutter (Cary Grant), MacChesney (Victor McLaglen) and Ballantine (Douglas Fairbanks Jr.)—are sent to the now-silent outpost. Accompanying them is a small contingent of Indian troops and water-carriers, or *bhistis*, including Gunga Din (Sam Jaffe), whose only ambition in life is to become a soldier. The sergeants then receive their orders—to annihilate the murderous Thugs, a violent and mystical sect previously thought extinct.

A $2 million production that wowed them at the box office, GUNGA DIN is an undeniably rousing adventure tale. The performances and direction are a great deal of fun—part Three Musketeers, part Laurel and Hardy (Stevens began his career directing the duo's comedy shorts)—but it's difficult to overlook the blatantly racist nature of the proceedings, which endorse British imperialism and the violence inflicted on the Indian people.

GUNS OF NAVARONE, THE 📀 DVD

1961 157m c Adventure/War ★★★½
Open Road (U.S./U.K.)

Gregory Peck *(Capt. Mallory)*, David Niven *(Cpl. Miller)*, Anthony Quinn *(Col. Andrea Stavros)*, Stanley Baker *(CPO Brown)*, Anthony Quayle *(Maj. Franklin)*, Irene Papas *(Maria)*, Gia Scala *(Anna)*, James Darren *(Pvt. Pappadimos)*, James Robertson Justice *(Jensen)*, Richard Harris *(Barnsby)*

d, J. Lee Thompson; w, Carl Foreman (based on the novel *Guns of Navarone* by Alistair MacLean); ph, Oswald Morris (CinemaScope, Eastmancolor); ed, Alan Osbiston; m, Dimitri Tiomkin; prod d, Geoffrey Drake; art d, Geoffrey Drake; fx, Bill Warrington, Wally Veevers; cos, Monty Berman, Olga Lehmann

AAN Best Picture; AAN Best Director: J. Lee Thompson; *AAN Best Adapted Screenplay:* Carl Foreman,; *AAN Best Film Editing:* Alan Osbiston; *AAN Best Score (Drama or Comedy):* Dimitri Tiomkin; *AAN Best Sound:* John Cox; *AA Best Special Effects:* Bill Warrington (Visual), Vivian C. Greenham (Audible)

This WWII spectacle, with its cliched story, hackneyed characters, and triumph-over-impossible-odds finale, could only have been born in a Hollywood dream tank; nevertheless, it's great adventure.

British intelligence learns that two enormous guns have been installed on the Aegean island of Navarone. The long-range field pieces are capable of destroying any British fleet trying to sail to Kheros, near Turkey, where a large British force is facing annihilation unless it is evacuated. It's the job of Captain Mallory (Gregory Peck) and a handful of men to land secretly on Navarone and dismantle the guns. The group includes killers Private Pappadimos (James Darren) and CPO Brown (Stanley Baker), explosives expert Corporal Miller (David Niven), and tough Greek patriot Andrea Stavros (Anthony Quinn). Meeting the men along the way are resistance leader Maria (Irene Papas) and Anna (Gia Scala), a beautiful Greek girl who was reportedly tortured by the Germans.

There are a few subplots in this stirring spectacle—Miller's dislike for Mallory's dispassionate procedures, Stavros's grudge against Mallory for an old disservice—but the destruction of the guns is the constant theme. It's handled well by veteran director J. Lee Thompson, with strong cast support and excellent production values that make it all lavish, rich, and often breathtaking. A sequel starring Harrison Ford, FORCE 10 FROM NAVARONE, appeared 17 years later.

GUY NAMED JOE, A
1944 120m bw War/Romance/Fantasy ★★★
MGM (U.S.)

Spencer Tracy *(Pete Sandidge)*, Irene Dunne *(Dorinda Durston)*, Van Johnson *(Ted Randall)*, Ward Bond *(Al Yackey)*, James Gleason *(Col. "Nails" Kilpatrick)*, Lionel Barrymore *(The General)*, Barry Nelson *(Dick Rumney)*, Esther Williams *(Ellen Bright)*, Henry O'Neill *(Col. Sykes)*, Don DeFore *("Powerhouse" James J. Rourke)*

p, Everett Riskin; d, Victor Fleming; w, Dalton Trumbo (based on a story by Chandler Sprague, David Boehm, Frederick Hazlitt Brennan); ph, George Folsey, Karl Freund; ed, Frank Sullivan; m, Herbert Stothart; art d, Cedric Gibbons, Lyle Wheeler; fx, A. Arnold Gillespie, Donald Jahraus, Warren Newcombe; cos, Irene

AAN Best Original Story: David Boehm, Chandler Sprague

A sticky, tear-jerking fantasy, A GUY NAMED JOE was one of the most popular movies during WWII, combining the considerable talents of Spencer Tracy, Irene Dunne, and Van Johnson in a big-scale production.

Pete Sandidge (Tracy), a daredevil bomber pilot, dies when he crashes his plane into a German aircraft carrier (though, in fact, there were none in WWII), leaving his devoted girlfriend, Dorinda (Irene Dunne), who is also a pilot, heartbroken. In heaven, Pete receives a new assignment: he is to become the guardian angel for Ted Randall (Van Johnson), a young Army flyer. Invisibly, Pete guides Ted through flight school and into combat, but the ectoplasmic mentor's tolerance is tested when Ted falls for Dorinda. Ultimately, however, Pete not only comes to terms with their relationship but also acts as Dorinda's copilot when she undertakes a dangerous bombing raid, so that Ted won't have to.

The film goes in too many directions at the same time, trying to combine its romantic fantasy line and a grim war outlook. But Dalton Trumbo's script is verbally wry—with the best lines going to wisecracking Tracy. Alas, Fleming was probably the wrong director for JOE; despite Arnold Gillespie's special effects, the Fleming-Tracy-Johnson chemistry feels as heavy as combat boots.

Incidentally, there is no character in the film named "Joe"; the title is derived from the Army Air Corps practice of calling a "right fellow" Joe. Remade by Steven Speilberg in 1989 as ALWAYS.

GYPSY
1962 149m c Musical/Biography ★★★½
Warner Bros. (U.S.)

Rosalind Russell *(Rose)*, Natalie Wood *(Louise "Gypsy")*, Karl Malden *(Herbie Sommers)*, Paul Wallace *(Tulsa No. 2)*, Betty Bruce *(Tessie Tura)*, Parley Baer *(Mr. Kringelein)*, Harry Shannon *(Grandpa)*, Morgan Brittany, billed as Suzanne Cupito *("Baby" June)*, Ann Jillian *("Dainty" June)*, Diane Pace *("Baby" Louise)*

p, Mervyn LeRoy; d, Mervyn LeRoy; w, Leonard Spigelgass (based on the musical play by Arthur Laurents and the book *Gypsy, A Memoir* by Gypsy Rose Lee); ph, Harry Stradling (Technirama, Technicolor); ed, Philip W. Anderson; art d, John Beckman; chor, Robert Tucker; cos, Orry-Kelly, Howard Shoup, Bill Gaskin

AAN Best Color Cinematography: Harry Stradling Sr; AAN Best Adapted Score: Frank Perkins; AAN Best Costume Design (Color): Orry-Kelly

The original casting package for this blockbuster no doubt would have created motion picture history, with Miss Show Business herself, Judy Garland taking on the Ethel Merman legend, and the steamy Ann-Margret recreating the strips of famed burlesque queen Gypsy Rose Lee. We love Roz, and her comic business as quintessential stage ma Rose Hovick is terrific; her moments of pathos don't disappoint, either, but she's just not the cyclonic force of nature that made Merman immortal in the annals of show business history. With her mother-resentments, and grueling vaudeville childhood, the thought of Garland is a chilling one indeed, for GYPSY is a musical about child abuse and frustrated ambition, though sometimes funny it may be.

As Gypsy, Natalie Wood lacks the latent sex appeal that needs to come to life when Rose's ambitions land the act she manages into lowlife burlesque, where the "untalented" Louise finds her niche at last. Though expertly coached by the original herself, Wood resembles a plastic wind-up doll strutting the runway, and that her cleavage was the result of extensive adhesive tape has passed into Hollywood lore long ago.

Mervyn LeRoy, sans any brass in casting, directs with an abrasive hand, as if coarse treatment can make up for what's missing. But Karl Malden, Ann Jillian (Dainty June), and Morgan Brittany (Baby June) are just right, and as three healthy surrogate stripper moms, Faith Dane, Roxanne Arlen, and especially Betty Bruce are perfection, playing dames actresses today don't know how to approach. The script's guts have been torn out; Leonard Spiegelgass prettied up Arthur Laurents's perfect work, presumably to throw sympathy to the star. There is an atmospheric strip montage that captures the spirit of Minsky and some great costumes, but Tucker's choreography has been largely snatched from Jerome Robbins.

The score, with music by Jule Styne and lyrics by Stephen Sondheim, is so perfect, so joyous, it's worth watching just to hear it aloud. Alas, "Together, Wherever We Go" was cut before the release, and the score's only blight, "Little Lamb," was left in to give Wood a big moment while we're waiting for the flesh. She's dubbed of course, and although, as we said, we love Roz, she lied that she did all her own singing—they spliced her voice in with the pipes of Lisa Kirk. The effect is brisk without carrying much conviction, although Russell's conviction in the finale is thoroughly satisfactory. Watch anyway.

H

HAIL, MARY
(JE VOUS SALUE, MARIE)
1985 86m c Religious ★★★★
Pegase/JLG/Sara/SSR/Channel 4/Gaumont
(France/Switzerland/U.K.)

Myriem Roussel *(Mary)*, Thierry Rode *(Joseph)*, Philippe Lacoste *(Angel)*, Juliette Binoche *(Juliette)*, Manon Anderson *(Girl)*, Malachi Jara Kohan *(Jesus)*, Johan Leysen *(Professor)*, Anne Gauthier *(Eva)*

d, Jean-Luc Godard; w, Jean-Luc Godard; ph, Jean-Bernard Menoud, Jacques Frimann; m, Johann Sebastian Bach, Anton Dvorak, John Coltrane

Ever since his first film, BREATHLESS, Jean-Luc Godard has subverted the conventions of cinema and caused critical outrage in the process. Remaining true to form, Godard, some 26 years later, again whipped the public into a frenzy with HAIL MARY. By updating the story of the Virgin Mary, Godard produced, as the critics billed it, "the most controversial film of our time," and for once the advertisements exaggerated only slightly.

Myriem Roussel is Mary, a young woman who pumps gas, plays basketball, and has a taxi driver boyfriend named Joseph (Thierry Rode). Though another woman is anxious to sleep with Rode, he chooses instead to chase the chaste Roussel. One day Roussel learns she is to give birth to the Son of God; Rode, however, cannot believe that Roussel is pregnant and a virgin. But after they are wed Roussel teaches Rode to love her from a distance, revering her without touching her—Godard's personal definition of faith.

Sight unseen, HAIL MARY was protested in many cities throughout the world and banned in others, including Rome, where Pope John Paul II officially condemned the film. Curiously, Godard had originally intended to make a film about incest—planning to concentrate on a man's impossible love for his unattainable daughter—but as the film evolved, it became the story of Joseph's love for his unattainable Mary. Since BREATHLESS, Godard has been fascinated with the idea of a man becoming obsessed with a woman he cannot attain or possess, and HAIL, MARY takes this preoccupation to the extreme.

HAIL THE CONQUERING HERO
1944 101m bw Comedy ★★★★
Paramount (U.S.)

Eddie Bracken *(Woodrow Lafayette Pershing Truesmith)*, Ella Raines *(Libby)*, Bill Edwards *(Forrest Noble)*, Raymond Walburn *(Mayor Noble)*, William Demarest *(Sergeant)*, Jimmie Dundee *(Corporal)*, Georgia Caine *(Mrs. Truesmith)*, Alan Bridge *(Political Boss)*, James Damore *(Jonesy)*, Freddie Steele *(Bugsy)*

p, Preston Sturges; d, Preston Sturges; w, Preston Sturges; ph, John Seitz; ed, Stuart Gilmore; m, Werner R. Heymann; art d, Hans Dreier

AAN Best Original Screenplay: Preston Sturges

The premier comedy writer-director of 1940s Hollywood strikes again! Preston Sturges satirizes home-front American patriotism run amuck during WWII. All the sacred cows of the era—heroic fathers, loving moms, battle fatigue—are milked for laughs in this fastpaced comedy.

Sad sack Woodrow Lafayette Pershing Truesmith (Bracken) desperately wants to live up to the reputation of his Marine dad who died a war hero in WWI. Truesmith enlists to carry on the family honor at the outbreak of WWII but he's classified 4-F due to severe chronic hay fever. Ashamed to return home, he takes a job in a shipyard and, with the help of friends in the Marine Corps, sends letters from the Pacific to his mother (Caine) and his sweetheart Libby (Raines). To avoid telling the truth, Bracken breaks up with Libby through the mail. Some genuine Marine heroes returning from Guadalcanal find Truesmith drowning his sorrows in a saloon. Bugsy (Steele), a shell-shocked vet who values motherhood above all else, calls Mrs. Truesmith and tells her that her son has returned from the war. To complete the charade, the crusty Sergeant (Demarest) and the others convince the reluctant wash-out to put on a uniform, slip back home to Oakridge, and make his mother happy. He can then put his uniform in the closet and resume his life of obscurity. Truesmith agrees and takes the train back home with his new Marine friends. To their astonishment, the entire town has turned out with two brass bands to greet the conquering hero.

Who else but this brilliant iconoclast would have dared to make this kind of counter-heroic comedy very near the end of WWII? Supporting the very funny Bracken is a cast composed mostly of Sturges's stock people—Demarest, Pangborn, Walburn and others—all of them outstanding. HAIL THE CONQUERING HERO was nominated for an Oscar for Best Original Screenplay, putting Sturges in competition with himself for the award since he was also nominated for his script for THE MIRACLE OF MORGAN'S CREEK.

HAIR
1979 118m c Musical ★★★★
UA (U.S.) PG

John Savage *(Claude)*, Treat Williams *(Berger)*, Beverly D'Angelo *(Sheila)*, Annie Golden *(Jeannie)*, Dorsey Wright *(Hud)*, Don Dacus *(Woof)*, Cheryl Barnes *(Hud's Fiancee)*, Richard Bright *(Fenton)*, Nicholas Ray *(The General)*, Charlotte Rae *(Party Guest)*

p, Lester Persky, Michael Butler; d, Milos Forman; w, Michael Weller (based on the musical play by Gerome Ragni, James Rado, and Galt MacDermot); ph, Miroslav Ondricek (Panavision, Technicolor); ed, Lynzee Klingman; m, Galt MacDermot; prod d, Stuart Wurtzel; fx, Al Griswold; chor, Twyla Tharp; cos, Ann Roth

Milos Forman had already proven his talent with TAKING OFF and the multiple-Oscar-winning ONE FLEW OVER THE CUCKOO'S NEXT, but when the Czech director was chosen to make this very American film, based on the long-running Broadway play, some wondered about the combination. They needn't have worried.

Savage plays a square draftee from Oklahoma on his way to Vietnam via New York City. There, he is adopted by a group of flower children who guide him through a series of euphoric countercultural adventures, including an introduction to marijuana and an encounter with a slightly batty debutante (D'Angelo). Along the way, there are many excellent songs and some of the most inventive choreography (by the ingenious Twyla Tharp) ever seen, including a "horse ballet" by mounted police in Central Park where they have been assigned to observe a "be-in."

There is much to recommend in this film, and sheer energy pours off the screen in every frame. Forman and scenarist Michael Weller deftly synthesized the pastiche of sketches and tunes that comprised the stage musical into a compelling screen entertainment. Unfortunately, the movie was not a hit, perhaps because HAIR was made almost 12 years after the play opened and, while dated, was not quite ready to be enjoyed nostalgically.

HAIRDRESSER'S HUSBAND, THE
(MARI DE LA COIFFEUSE, LA)

1992 84m c Romance/Drama ★★★★
Lambart Productions/TF1 Films Production/PAC R
(France)

Jean Rochefort *(Antoine)*, Anna Galiena *(Mathilde)*, Roland Bertin *(Antoine's Father)*, Maurice Chevit *(Agopian)*, Philippe Clevenot *(Morvoisieux)*, Jacques Mathou *(Mr. Chardon)*, Claude Aufaure *(Gay Customer)*, Albert Delpy *(Donecker)*, Henry Hocking *(Antoine—Age 12)*, Ticky Holgado *(Morvoisieux Son-in-Law)*

p, Thierry DeGanay; d, Patrice Leconte; w, Patrice Leconte, Claude Klotz (from the story by Leconte); ph, Eduardo Serra; ed, Joelle Hache; m, Michael Nyman; prod d, Ivan Maussion

THE HAIRDRESSER'S HUSBAND is another tale of obsessive love from director Patrice Leconte (MONSIEUR HIRE).

Ever since an erotic childhood experience with his barber, Antoine (Jean Rochefort) has had a single ambition in life: to marry a hairdresser. He finally meets the shampoo girl of his dreams, Mathilde (Anna Galiena), who centers her life entirely around a barber shop she has inherited. The two marry and live in a state of erotic bliss, until Mathilde's obsessive fear of losing Antoine's love begins to unravel the relationship.

THE HAIRDRESSER'S HUSBAND is a realistically told fable, creating a tension between style and content that grows as Mathilde's initial romanticism begins to seem more like a phobic fear of the world outside her shop. Never has love-soaked indolence seemed so attractive in a movie as it does here. Rochefort's Antoine is an avid devourer of the minutiae of life, while Galiena's Mathilde is like the answer to a sensualist's prayer—a woman of dark, earthy beauty living only to be loved, and living in terror of the day when she might be loved no more. Leconte understands the intoxicating powers of love, but he also understands what happens when we wake from our erotic reveries. And that is what makes a film as slight as this seem like a story for the ages, a rapturous epic of the heart that is gripping and unforgettable.

HAIRSPRAY
DVD

1988 90m c Comedy ★★★½
New Line (U.S.) PG

Sonny Bono *(Franklin Von Tussle)*, Ruth Brown *(Motormouth Maybell)*, Divine *(Edna Turnblad/Arvin Hodgepile)*, Colleen Fitzpatrick *(Amber Von Tussle)*, Michael St. Gerard *(Link Larkin)*, Deborah Harry *(Velma Von Tussle)*, Ricki Lake *(Tracy Turnblad)*, Leslie Ann Powers *(Penny Pingleton)*, Clayton Prince *(Seaweed)*, Jerry Stiller *(Wilbur Turnblad)*

p, Rachel Talalay, Stanley F. Buchthal, John Waters; d, John Waters; w, John Waters; ph, David Insley; ed, Janice Hampton; chor, Edward Love; cos, Van Smith

Set in Baltimore circa 1962, HAIRSPRAY joyously details the last days of '50s-era American naivete, as the country moves from postwar complacency to massive social upheaval. Cult filmmaker John Waters enters the mainstream with surprisingly little fuss.

Caught up in all this is the "Corny Collins Show," a wildly popular Baltimore television dance program. The show's queen is the spoiled and snobbish Fitzpatrick, whose father, Bono, owns the "Tilted Acres" amusement park. Lake, an obese working-class teen, auditions for a spot on the show, against the wishes of her mother, Divine, and she earns it because of her sensational dancing. The socially progressive teen begins to cause trouble, however, when she demands the segregated program be opened up to include the black teenagers of Baltimore.

Controversial filmmaker John Waters finally hits his commercial stride in this film, parlaying his keen social observation and great compassion for society's outsiders into a colorful and engaging comedy full of dancing, music and heartfelt nostalgia. Unfortunately, what should have been a celebration turned into sadness when Waters's longtime friend and collaborator Divine, who was poised on the edge of stardom, died of a heart attack a mere two weeks after HAIRSPRAY opened nationwide.

HALLELUJAH

1929 100m bw Drama ★★★★
MGM (U.S.)

Daniel Haynes *(Zeke)*, Nina Mae McKinney *(Chick)*, William E. Fontaine *(Hot Shot)*, Harry Gray *(Parson)*, Fannie Belle DeKnight *(Mammy)*, Everett McGarrity *(Spunk)*, Victoria Spivey *(Missy Rose)*, Milton Dickerson, Robert Couch, Walter Tait *(Johnson Kids)*

p, King Vidor; d, King Vidor; w, Wanda Tuchock, Ransom Rideout (based on a story by King Vidor); ph, Gordon Avil; ed, Hugh Wynn, Anson Stevenson; m, Irving Berlin; art d, Cedric Gibbons

AAN Best Director: King Vidor

This was the first all-black feature film and one of the boldest pictures ever made, especially since MGM knew the film would not get much of a release in the deep South. King Vidor was a man vitally interested in social issues (witness his work on THE BIG PARADE and THE CROWD), and he wanted to show the rest of America what black people were going through. Daniel Haynes plays Zeke, an innocent young man who is very close to his mother (Fannie Belle DeKnight), and to his brother, Spunk (Everett McGarrity), whom he accidentally kills. Zeke turns to religion to ease his grief.

With a cast that included many amateurs (Harry Gray had been a janitor at a Harlem newspaper, and Nina Mae McKinney, the female lead, had never been in front of a camera), Vidor elicited performances from the group as good as any you might see in a seasoned troupe. Even today, more than half a century later, this film is not dated. Shot on location in Tennessee, HALLELUJAH is redolent with authenticity. The treatment of some scenes tends toward the melodramatic, notably the revival meetings, a wake, and various scenes on the plantation; but the film is filled with humanity and insight into black experience at the time. Irving Thalberg, the young chief of production at MGM, known and remembered as a man of integrity, gave Vidor the green light to make HALLELUJAH. This was the director's first talkie, but the film was shot as a silent, with the sound added in post-production.

HALLELUJAH THE HILLS

1963 88m bw Experimental/Comedy ★★★½
Vermont (U.S.)

Peter H. Beard *(Jack)*, Martin Greenbaum *(Leo)*, Sheila Finn *(Jack's Vera in Winter)*, Peggy Steffans *(Leo's Vera in Summer)*, Jerome Raphel *(Father)*, Blanche Dee *(Mother)*

p, David C. Stone; d, Adolfas Mekas; w, Adolfas Mekas; ph, Ed Emshwiller; ed, Adolfas Mekas; m, Meyer Kupferman

Once upon a time in the early 1960s, there was a movement known as the New American Cinema. Jonas Mekas was its prophet in a weekly column in the *Village Voice*. He and his brother, Adolfas, who directed HALLELUJAH, THE HILLS, were among its practitioners. Most of this underground cinema consisted of arty shorts. (Perhaps Kenneth Anger's SCORPIO RISING was the best known of these.) The Mekas brothers produced more traditional feature-length films. This one is an interesting confluence of Hollywood structures and home-movie techniques: a document of its time, in part.

This delightful comedy for film buffs begins as an enthusiastic send-up of early French New Wave techniques. The thin story line has to do with a pair of young men, Jack (Beard) and Leo (Greenbaum), pursuing the same young lady (shades of Truffaut's JULES AND JIM) at different times of the year. Thus she is played by two actresses: one for winter (Finn) and one for summer (Steffans). The girl's parents are also featured: a wisecracking father and a no-nonsense mother. Ultimately, the question of just who will win Vera's love takes a backseat to the giddy celebration of movie magic.

The film plays around with time, space, character, and the history of the cinema and achieves a remarkable freshness. Adolfas Mekas shows a remarkable flair for visuals, using his forest settings well. The film is packed full of gags and silliness, having a good time with itself and movie cliches. The ending juxtaposes the characters of this film with the actual ending from Griffith's classic silent WAY DOWN EAST with Lillian Gish and Richard Barthelmess. HALLELUJAH THE HILLS is a personable and fun bit of filmmaking; its enthusiasm is infectious.

HALLOWEEN   📀DVD

1978   93m   c   Horror   ★★★★

Falcon   (U.S.)   R

Donald Pleasence *(Loomis)*, Jamie Lee Curtis *(Laurie)*, Nancy Loomis *(Annie)*, P.J. Soles *(Lynda)*, Charles Cyphers *(Brackett)*, Kyle Richards *(Lindsey)*, Brian Andrews *(Tommy)*, John Michael Graham *(Bob)*, Nancy Stephens *(Marion)*, Arthur Malet *(Graveyard Keeper)*

p, Debra Hill; d, John Carpenter; w, Debra Hill, John Carpenter; ph, Dean Cundey (Panavision, Metrocolor); ed, Tommy Lee Wallace, Charles Burnstein; m, John Carpenter; prod d, Tommy Lee Wallace

A modern horror classic. On Halloween night in 1963, a six-year-old boy in a Halloween mask stabs his sister to death after she makes love to her boyfriend. He's institutionalized—until, exactly 15 years later, he escapes and returns to his small Illinois hometown once more to wreak Halloween havoc. His psychiatrist Dr. Loomis (Donald Pleasence) proclaims "The Evil is loose!" and is in hot pursuit with the authorities. Meanwhile Laurie (Jamie Lee Curtis) seems to be the only girl in town without a date for Halloween. All her high school friends seem to have hot dates scheduled but bright, bookish Laurie must settle for a quiet evening of babysitting, fending off trick-or-treaters, and watching old science fiction movies on television. Just another boring evening? Hardly.

There's nary a drop of blood on screen in this rollicking funhouse of a movie but there is enough sheer cinematic ingenuity on display to coax screams out of the most jaded gorehound. Cheap thrills—often accompanied by a joybuzzer noise on the soundtrack—lurk on the periphery of nearly every frame and film history allusions abound. Fans the moving camera also have reason to cheer as the Steadicam prowls the suburban streets unexpectedly turning into ominous point-of-view shots accompanied by creepy piano music (composed by the resourceful Carpenter). The performances are also far better than average for this kind of fare. Pleasance is a hoot as he gnaws on the scenery and the pleasingly equine beauty of Jamie Lee Curtis—at the beginning of the fondly remembered Queen of the B's stage of her career—enhances her sensitive performance.

HALLOWEEN was the surprise hit of the 1978 Chicago Film Festival. Some over-enthusiastic critics even compared it with Hitchcock's classic PSYCHO (which starred Curtis's mother, Janet Leigh) but such comparisons are silly and groundless; HALLOWEEN is just a superbly made unpretentious thriller whereas one can make higher claims for

PSYCHO. Furthermore Carpenter's clean, economical style owes a much greater debt to another master craftsman—Howard Hawks. From the opening—a long Steadicam point-of-view shot seen from behind a Halloween mask—to the climactic battle in which Curtis fends off the maniac time after time, only to have him rise again, Carpenter displays an astounding stylistic assurance for a young director working with a low budget.

Made for less than half a million dollars, HALLOWEEN grossed well over $50 million on its initial release, making it the single most successful independent feature of all time. Two sequels, both produced by Carpenter, were woefully inferior to the original, but a third—released in 1988—wasn't all that bad.

HALLOWEEN H2O: TWENTY YEARS LATER   📀DVD

1998   87m   c   Horror   ★★★

Nightfall/Moustapha Akkad   (U.S.)   R

Jamie Lee Curtis *(Laurie Strode/Keri Tate)*, Adam Arkin *(Will)*, Josh Hartnett *(John)*, Michelle Williams *(Molly)*, Adam Hann-Byrd *(Charlie)*, Jodi Lyn O'Keefe *(Sarah)*, Janet Leigh *(Norma)*, LL Cool J *(Ronny)*, Joseph Gordon Levitt *(Jimmy)*, Nancy Stephens *(Marion)*

p, Paul Freeman; d, Steve Miner; w, Robert Zappia, Matt Greenberg (based on characters created by Debra Hill and John Carpenter); ph, Daryn Okada; ed, Patrick Lusser; m, John Ottman, John Carpenter; prod d, John Willet; art d, Dawn Snyder; fx, John Hartigan; cos, Deborah Everton

When bad sequels happen to good movies, they look like HALLOWEEN III; fortunately, you can pretty much forget that it ever happened, along with HALLOWEEN IV, HALLOWEEN 5 and HALLOWEEN: THE CURSE OF MICHAEL MYERS. For the purposes of this picture, they all happened in an alternate universe—the druids, the possessed child, the mysterious men in black, *everything.*

Babysitter Laurie Strode (Jamie Lee Curtis), who at age 17 escaped the clutches of a knife-wielding psycho who turned out to be her younger brother, did not actually die in a car crash. She faked her own demise, changed her name, and tried to get on with her life, eventually becoming the high-strung headmistress of a gated Northern California prep school. She has a 17-year-old son (Josh Hartnett) from a failed marriage, she drinks too much, doesn't care for Halloween parties, has a medicine cabinet full of mood-altering pharmaceuticals, and regularly wakes up screaming. And now her brother is back, looking to wrap up the unfinished family business.

Brought back to life by director Steve Miner, who cut his teeth on FRIDAY THE 13TH sequels, and executive producer Kevin Williamson, whose SCREAM goosed the moribund stalk-and-slash genre to megabucks respectability (but not by John Carpenter, the man who started it all), this efficient fright machine features a knowing cameo by Curtis's mom—PSYCHO's Janet Leigh—a couple of bloody good scares, and a genuinely affecting performance from Curtis. The body count is surprisingly low (a plus), Carpenter's instantly recognizable minimalist score is heavily orchestrated (a minus), and the ending is about as satisfying as it could be.

HAMBURGER HILL   📀DVD

1987   110m   c   War   ★★★½

RKO   (U.S.)

Anthony Barrile *(Languilli)*, Michael Boatman *(Motown)*, Don Cheadle *(Washburn)*, Michael Dolan *(Murphy)*, Don James *(McDaniel)*, Dylan McDermott *(Sgt. Frantz)*, M.A. Nickles *(Galvin)*, Harry O'Reilly *(Duffy)*, Daniel O'Shea *(Gaigin)*, Tim Quill *(Beletsky)*

p, Marcia Nasatir, Jim Carabatsos; d, John Irvin; w, Jim Carabatsos; ph, Peter MacDonald (Rank Color); ed, Peter Tanner; m, Philip Glass; prod d, Austin Spriggs; art d, Toto Castillo; fx, Joe Lombardi

Instead of trying to match the hallucinatory bombast of APOCALYPSE NOW, the surreal metaphysics of PLATOON, or the studied idiosyncrasy of FULL METAL JACKET, director John Irvin reaches back to such classic combat films as THE SANDS OF IWO JIMA and PORK CHOP HILL for his inspiration here. So straightforward as to be old-fashioned, HAMBURGER HILL becomes unique by virtue of its unwillingness to participate in the current cycle of war-as-philosophical-metaphor Vietnam films and instead goes for a more conventional approach.

Realistic almost to a fault, Irvin's film is an account of the Third Squad, First Platoon, Bravo Company of the 101st Airborne Division and its battle to secure Hill 937 in the Ashau Valley, Vietnam, 1969. Short on plot, the film derives its power from isolated moments: letters from home, chats, arguments, visits to a brothel, and, of course, intense combat—all performed with vigor by an almost faceless ensemble of unknown actors spouting a nearly incomprehensible stream of GI lingo.

Shot in an unfussy, realistic manner by cinematographer Peter MacDonald, the visuals emphasize wide angles and deep focus, bombarding the senses without resorting to the kind of hallucinatory imagery found in most Vietnam films. The battle for the hill is exhausting to watch as the soldiers struggle upwards in the mud, clinging to exposed roots, tree stumps, and each other in a desperate effort to advance. Irvin rarely allows a glimpse of the top of the hill, further preventing the viewer from thinking ahead, instead forcing him to concentrate on climbing the few feet visible before him right along with the GIs.

Although it was underrated at the time of its release, time will eventually reveal that HAMBURGER HILL is one of the best and most realistic films made about the Vietnam War.

HAMLET

1948 155m bw Drama ★★★★
Two Cities (U.K.)

Laurence Olivier (Hamlet), Eileen Herlie (Queen Gertrude), Basil Sydney (King Claudius), Jean Simmons (Ophelia), Norman Wooland (Horatio), Felix Aylmer (Polonius), Terence Morgan (Laertes), Peter Cushing (Osric), Stanley Holloway (Gravedigger), John Laurie (Francisco)

p, Laurence Olivier; d, Laurence Olivier; w, Alan Dent (based on the play by William Shakespeare); ph, Desmond Dickinson; ed, Helga Cranston; m, William Walton; prod d, Roger Furse; art d, Carmen Dillon; fx, Paul Sheriff, Henry Harris, Jack Whitehead; cos, Elizabeth Hennings

AA Best Picture; AA Best Actor: Laurence Olivier; AAN Best Supporting Actress: Jean Simmons; AAN Best Director: Laurence Olivier; AAN Best Score (Drama or Comedy): William Walton; AA Best Art Direction-Set Decoration (B/W): Roger K. Furse, Carmen Dillon; AA Best Costume Design (B/W): Roger K. Furse

At 155 minutes, this screen adaptation of Shakespeare's most celebrated play bears scars from deep cuts in the text. Hamlet swears to his father's ghost that he will wreak revenge for the man's murder by taking the life of Claudius, who is now married to Hamlet's mother, Gertrude. By cutting the text, Olivier has fashioned a tighter, albeit abridged, version of the famed play. One of its flaws is that, in directing, Olivier should have concentrated more on performances; he had apparently fallen in love with the camera and employed many visual tricks instead of sticking to the lines. However, Olivier always felt that each different Hamlet is an essay, subject to the individual's interpretation.

HENRY V had been done in color, and many wondered why Olivier chose black and white for HAMLET. His reasons were the mood of the piece and various technical problems that arose while doing deep-focus photography. Olivier dyed his hair blonde so no one would feel that it was him playing the melancholy Dane. Rather, he wanted them to feel that what they were seeing was Hamlet himself. What they got was a mannered, overrated performance in a film with a similarly inflated reputation. Jean Simmons goes properly mad as Ophelia, and a very youthful Anthony Quayle makes his debut in a speaking role.

HAMLET

1996 242m c Drama ★★½
Castle Rock Entertainment/Fishmonger Films Ltd. PG-13 (U.S.)

Kenneth Branagh (Hamlet), Derek Jacobi (Claudius), Julie Christie (Gertrude), Richard Briers (Polonius), Kate Winslet (Ophelia), Nicholas Farrell (Horatio), Michael Maloney (Laertes), Brian Blessed (Ghost), Billy Crystal (First Gravedigger—uncredited), Robin Williams (Osric—uncredited)

p, David Barron; d, Kenneth Branagh; w, Kenneth Branagh (based on the play The Tragedy of Hamlet, Prince of Denmark by William Shakespeare); ph, Alex Thomson; ed, Neil Farrell; m, Patrick Doyle; prod d, Tim Harvey; art d, Desmond Crowe; fx, Josh Williams; cos, Alexandra Byrne

AAN Best Art Direction: Tim Harvey; AAN Best Costume Design: Alexandra Byrne; AAN Best Original Dramatic Score: Patrick Doyle; AAN Best Adapted Screenplay: Kenneth Branagh

Whatever Kenneth Branagh's motives for filming Hamlet in its entirety—recouping his somewhat tarnished reputation as the next Olivier, perhaps—he's managed to pull off a considerable coup de cinema, and the result is by turns brilliant, lavish, garish, and awful.

Updated to 19th century, Branagh himself stars as the Danish prince with revenge on his fevered brain after the ghost of his father, the late King (Brian Blessed), appears to tell him of his murder at the hands of his own brother, Claudius (Derek Jacobi), and demand justice be served. Branagh has jettisoned yesterday's impotent brooder in favor of Hamlet the manic, peroxide-blond showman, and despite the sumptuous production design and Alex Thomson's masterful cinematography, the whole thing feels gauche. One of the more peculiar things about Branagh is that while he thinks he wants to challenge his audience—and a four-hour, unabridged Hamlet is certainly a challenge—he continues to pander to the groundlings, hamming it up while downplaying the text's subtleties as if he's uncertain of the Bard's continuing appeal. Or is it the viewer's intelligence he doubts? Scenes are crushed under a barrage of visual detritus—unnecessary expository flashbacks abound—and too often the immortal dialogue is either ridiculously dramatized or overwhelmed by the aggressively stirring soundtrack. The film, however, is simply gorgeous to look at, and a number of the performances are outstanding, particularly Derek Jacobi as Claudius, Richard Briers as a not-so-nice Polonius, and Kate Winslet, whose Ophelia is wondrously affecting.

HAMLET

2000 112m c/bw Drama ★★★
Hamlet/Double-A (U.S.) R

Ethan Hawke (Hamlet), Kyle McLachlan (Claudius), Sam Shepard (Ghost), Diane Venora (Gertrude), Bill Murray (Polonius), Liev Schreiber (Laertes), Julia Stiles (Ophelia), Karl Geary (Horatio), Paula Malcomson (Marcella), Steve Zahn (Rosencrantz)

p, Andrew Fierberg, Amy Hobby; d, Michael Almereyda; w, Michael Almereyda (based on the play by William Shakespeare);

ph, John De Borman; ed, Kristina Boden; m, Carter Burwell; prod d, Gideon Ponte; art d, Jeanne Develle; cos, Marco Cattoretti, Luca Mosca

By no means the best *Hamlet* ever filmed, but probably the shortest. Michael Almereyda's artsy, modern-day take on Shakespeare's most popular play has an interesting look, several sensational performances (notably from Kyle MacLachlan and Liev Schreiber), and in general works far better than it has any right to.

It's the year 2000, and our grungy Hamlet (an effectively moody Ethan Hawke) is still the prince of Denmark, except that Denmark isn't a country—it's a multinational conglomerate headquartered in Manhattan. That basic conceit established, the familiar story (like, should Hamlet revenge his father's murder?) remains thankfully intact, as does the language; Almereyda may have cut the play to the bone, but there's not a word here that isn't the Bard's. The movie's difference, of course, is in the details, so now the ghost of Hamlet's dad (a terrifying Sam Shepard) disappears into a soda machine rather than a parapet, and the young prince's "to be or not to be" speech is delivered in the action-movie aisle of a Blockbuster video store. This sort of thing probably won't work for literary purists, but everybody else might be willing to cut Almereyda some slack, since the point he's making—not a tremendously original one, but a valid one nonetheless—is that the world of the play isn't all that different from our own. In that spirit, the film works simultaneously as an offbeat take on an oft-told tale and, in Woody Allen's phrase, as a puckish satire on contemporary mores.

HAMMETT
1982 100m c Mystery ★★★★
Orion (U.S.) PG

Frederic Forrest *(Hammett)*, Peter Boyle *(Jimmy Ryan)*, Marilu Henner *(Kit Conger/Sue Alabama)*, Roy Kinnear *(English Eddie Hagedorn)*, Elisha Cook Jr. *(Eli, the Taxi Driver)*, Lydia Lei *(Crystal Ling)*, R.G. Armstrong *(Lt. O'Mara)*, Richard Bradford *(Detective Bradford)*, Michael Chow *(Fong)*, David Patrick Kelly *(Punk)*

p, Fred Roos, Ronald Colby, Don Guest; d, Wim Wenders; w, Ross Thomas, Dennis O'Flaherty, Thomas Pope (based on the book by Joe Gores); ph, Philip Lathrop, Joseph Biroc (Technicolor); ed, Barry Malkin, Marc Laub, Robert Q. Lovett, Randy Roberts; m, John Barry; prod d, Dean Tavoularis, Eugene Lee; art d, Angelo Graham, Leon Ericksen; cos, Ruth Morley

Impressed by Wim Wenders's obvious talent, Francis Coppola invited the German director to come to America and make a Hollywood film. The project chosen was a highly fictionalized account of the exploits of famed detective novelist Dashiell Hammett.

Set in 1920s San Francisco, the film follows Hammett (Frederic Forrest) as he leaves the Pinkerton Detective Agency to devote himself to writing. His former Pinkerton boss, Jimmy Ryan (Peter Boyle), recruits him to help crack a particularly tough case involving a Chinese prostitute. The cinematography and performances are terrific and highly stylized in this moody thriller, and Wenders directs the film well, but the story is a pastiche of many Hammett tales and is at times so splintered as to be confusing. Like THE AMERICAN FRIEND, Wenders's previous meditation on American genres, HAMMETT is less concerned with its storyline than it is with focusing on an American myth. As such it is not to be missed.

In between HAMMETT's production delays, Wenders made the low-budget black-and-white THE STATE OF THINGS, a film about the difficulties of filmmaking and the elusiveness of an American film producer. Rumor has it that much of HAMMETT was reshot by Coppola but the end result looks seamless.

HAND THAT ROCKS THE CRADLE, THE
1992 110m c Thriller ★★★½
Interscope/Rockin' Cradle Productions/ R
Hollywood Pictures (U.S.)

Annabella Sciorra *(Claire Bartel)*, Rebecca De Mornay *(Peyton Flanders)*, Matt McCoy *(Michael Bartel)*, Ernie Hudson *(Solomon)*, Julianne Moore *(Marlene)*, Madeline Zima *(Emma Bartel)*, John de Lancie *(Doctor Mott)*, Kevin Skousen *(Marty)*, Mitchell Laurance *(Lawyer)*, Justin Zaremby *(Schoolyard Bully)*

p, David Madden; d, Curtis Hanson; w, Amanda Silver; ph, Robert Elswit; ed, John F. Link; m, Graeme Revell; prod d, Edward Pisoni; art d, Mark Zuelzke; fx, Bob Riggs, Craig Reardon; cos, Jennifer Von Mayrhauser

This jovially sinister, middle-class morality tale-cum-horror show is predictable, implausible and fiendishly entertaining.

Claire and Michael Bartel (Annabella Sciorra and Matt McCoy) are a prosperous suburban couple with one young daughter, Emma (Madeline Zima), and a baby boy on the way. After being sexually abused by her gynecologist, Claire files charges, leading other patients to come forward with similar complaints. The doctor commits suicide, leaving his pregnant wife Peyton (Rebecca De Mornay) broke and homeless, and contributing to her miscarriage. While recovering, Peyton becomes obsessed with Claire and, after her release, charms her way into the Bartel household as a live-in nanny. There, she begins to implement a systematic strategy of revenge on the woman she feels has ruined her life.

At the climax, Peyton learns too late what villains of her ilk always learn too late: don't mess with the nuclear family! Up to that point, though, director Curtis Hanson and screenwriter Amanda Silver (the latter making an auspicious debut) have an awful lot of unwholesome fun letting her try. Hanson, a skilled craftsman and Hitchcock imitator, moves things along with finely crafted momentum, barrelling through the manifest plot implausibilities to create a tense psychological conflict between a deranged but sympathetic villainess and a likable but flawed heroine.

HANDS ACROSS THE TABLE
1935 81m bw Comedy ★★★★
Paramount (U.S.)

Carole Lombard *(Regi Allen)*, Fred MacMurray *(Theodore Drew III)*, Ralph Bellamy *(Allen Macklyn)*, Astrid Allwyn *(Vivian Snowden)*, Ruth Donnelly *(Laura)*, Marie Prevost *(Nona)*, Joseph R. Tozer *(Peter)*, William Demarest *(Matty)*, Edward Gargan *(Pinky Kelly)*, Ferdinand Munier *(Miles, the Butler)*

p, E. Lloyd Sheldon; d, Mitchell Leisen; w, Norman Krasna, Vincent Lawrence, Herbert Fields (based on the story "Bracelets" by Vina Delmar); ph, Ted Tetzlaff; ed, William Shea; cos, Travis Banton

An underrated 1930s romantic comedy that is charming, stylish and light-hearted.

The wonderful Carole Lombard is Regi Allen, a manicurist who has been hurt so many times in love that she has become cynical and hardened, claiming that financial security is now her only concern in marriage prospects. She meets Allen Macklyn (Ralph Bellamy), a wealthy young man who is confined to a wheelchair In addition to being rich, he is madly in love with her and has serious matrimonial intentions. Fred MacMurray is Theodore Drew III, a poor playboy from a once wealthy and prominent family. He is about to marry Vivian Snowden (Astrid Allwyn) for the same reasons Regi may marry Allen. When Theodore comes into Regi's shop one day, she thinks he's wealthy, so she gladly accepts when he invites her to dinner.

Like many screwball comedies of its era, this one offers snappy badinage and captivating performances but it's not nearly as riotous as some; rather it achieves an authentic tenderness and eroticism that is as memorable as it is rare.

HANGING GARDEN, THE 📀
1998 91m c Drama/Comedy ★★★★
Triptych Media/Galafilm/Emotion Pictures (Canada) R

Chris Leavins (*Sweet William*), Troy Veinotte (*Teenage Sweet William*), Kerry Fox (*Rosemary*), Sarah Polley (*Teenage Rosemary*), Seana McKenna (*Iris*), Peter MacNeill (*Whiskey Mac*), Joel Keller, billed as Joel S. Keller (*Fletcher*), Joan Orenstein (*Grace*), Jocelyn Cunningham (*Laurel*), Christine Dunsworth (*Violet*)

p, Louise Garfield, Arnie Gelbart, Thom Fitzgerald; d, Thom Fitzgerald; w, Thom Fitzgerald; ph, Daniel Jobin; ed, Susan Shanks; m, John Roby; prod d, Taavo Soodor; art d, Darlene Shields; cos, James A. Worthen

Surprises don't come much better than this. Writer-director Thom Fitzgerald's debut feature is the kind of self-assured and emotionally complex film that many filmmakers spend entire careers trying to make.

After a 10-year absence, Sweet William (Chris Leavins) returns to Nova Scotia and his seriously dysfunctional family home to attend sister Rosemary's (Kerry Fox) wedding. William left a 350-pound, closeted homosexual teenager, after failing to hang himself in his father's garden; he returns a slim, attractive, and relatively well-adjusted openly gay man. Back home, however, it's business as usual: his mother (Seana McKenna) is the same self-pitying control freak who blames her children for her wasted life; his emotionally distant and abusive father (Peter MacNeill) is still a drunk; Rosemary is as foul-mouthed and angry as ever; and the specter of William's former obese self still hangs from the apple tree. Over the course of his stay, William realizes that, yes, you can go home again, but wonders why anyone in his or her right mind would want to.

This is a surprisingly mature film about finally growing up long after the fact; about the inevitable return-trip home that is as much a ghost story as it is a family psychodrama. Divided into three chapters—the second is a lengthy flashback to William's miserable teenage years—Fitzgerald's script is wonderfully controlled, perceptively probing the painful realities of family life while boldly integrating magical, often surreal flourishes. Blessed with a knockout cast, Fitzgerald is also graced with a natural visual instinct that leads him to a number of startlingly resonant images: adult faces reflected in childhood photographs; flowers dying as the asphyxiating teenage William gasps for breath. You come away from the film not only with an impression of a job well done, but the welcome emergence of a major new talent.

HANGMEN ALSO DIE 📀
1943 131m bw War ★★★½
UA (U.S.)

Brian Donlevy (*Dr. Franz Svoboda*), Walter Brennan (*Prof. Novotny*), Anna Lee (*Mascha Novotny*), Gene Lockhart (*Emil Czaka*), Dennis O'Keefe (*Jan Horek*), Alexander Granach (*Alois Gruber*), Margaret Wycherly (*Aunt Ludmilla Novotny*), Nana Bryant (*Mrs. Novotny*), Billy Roy (*Beda Novotny*), Hans von Twardowski (*Reinhard Heydrich*)

p, Fritz Lang; d, Fritz Lang; w, John Wexley (based on a story by Fritz Lang and Bertolt Brecht); ph, James Wong Howe; ed, Gene Fowler Jr.; m, Hanns Eisler; art d, William Darling; cos, Julie Heron

AAN Best Score (Drama or Comedy): Hanns Eisler; *AAN Best Sound Recording:* Jack Whitney (Sound Service Inc.)

In Czechoslovakia during WWII, Deputy Reich Protector Reinhard Heydrich (von Twardowski), Nazi-appointed "governor" of Prague, gathers prominent citizens and voices his displeasure at insidious acts of sabotage in the factories. Not only are the Czech acts of defiance holding up vital production for the Third Reich, they are also endangering the lives of the civic leaders assembled, Heydrich says, adding that stern measures will be taken unless production increases. After leaving the meeting, Heydrich is assassinated by a member of the Czech resistance, Svoboda (Donlevy). On the run, Svoboda is given shelter by kindly Professor Novotny (Brennan) and his daughter Mascha (Lee). Though Heydrich's death becomes a hopeful symbol for the Czechoslovakian people and improves their morale, the Nazis demand revenge and the Gestapo begin to round up hundreds of innocent Czech citizens suspected of subversion and complicity, and kill them off one by one until the killer is handed over.

While HANGMEN ALSO DIE is a much better than average American WWII propaganda film, it is a bit of a disappointment in the impressive career of master director Fritz Lang. Beyond a precious few scenes containing some stunning Lang visuals, the film is overlong and the characters haphazardly developed. The tension is occasionally interrupted by impassioned patriotic speeches that comment didactically and intelligently on the proceedings in a Brechtian fashion. As well they should, since this was the first Hollywood screenplay collaborated on by that celebrated German playwright. (Brecht was, however, denied co-screenwriting credit following a Guild arbitration.) Visually the film's atmosphere is marvelously dark and oppressive due to the moody lensing of the great cinematographer James Wong Howe.

HANNAH AND HER SISTERS 📀
1986 106m c Comedy/Drama ★★★★
Orion (U.S.) PG-13

Woody Allen (*Mickey*), Michael Caine (*Elliot*), Mia Farrow (*Hannah*), Carrie Fisher (*April*), Barbara Hershey (*Lee*), Lloyd Nolan (*Hannah's Father*), Maureen O'Sullivan (*Hannah's Mother*), Daniel Stern (*Dusty*), Max von Sydow (*Frederick*), Dianne Wiest (*Holly*)

p, Robert Greenhut; d, Woody Allen; w, Woody Allen; ph, Carlo Di Palma (Panavision, Technicolor); ed, Susan E. Morse; prod d, Stuart Wurtzel; cos, Jeffrey Kurland

AAN Best Picture; AA Best Supporting Actor: Michael Caine; *AA Best Supporting Actress:* Dianne Wiest; *AAN Best Director:* Woody Allen; *AA Best Original Screenplay:* Woody Allen; *AAN Best Film Editing:* Susan E. Morse; *AAN Best Art Direction-Set Decoration:* Stuart Wurtzel, Carol Joffe

Essentially three separate tales that intertwine at times, HANNAH AND HER SISTERS is one of writer-director Woody Allen's most complex films and the first one in which his neurotic character is given a happy ending.

The picture takes place over a couple of years, framed by Thanksgiving dinners. Hannah (Mia Farrow) is married to Elliot (Michael Caine), a business manager for rock stars. She used to be married to Mickey (Allen), a TV producer. Hannah's sisters are Lee (Barbara Hershey)—who's living with Frederick (Max von Sydow), a witty, bitter SoHo artist—and Holly (Dianne Wiest), an actress who's a bundle of nerves. Elliot harbors a passion for Lee and eventually makes it known to her. She succumbs, guilt-ridden for betraying Hannah. Holly, a former cocaine addict, can no longer contain her envy of Hannah—the oldest, "perfect" sister, who has what appears to be a blissful existence.

The plot could easily have been an afternoon soap opera, but Allen has infused it with wit, a superb cast and his usual "the best direction is the least direction" style, so that the camera never calls attention to itself.

HANNIBAL

2001 131m c Thriller ★★★

Dino De Laurentiis/MGM/Scott Free (U.S.) R

DVD

Anthony Hopkins *(Hannibal Lecter)*, Julianne Moore *(Clarice Starling)*, Gary Oldman *(Mason Verger—uncredited)*, Ray Liotta *(Paul Krendler)*, Frankie Faison, billed as Frankie R. Faison *(Barney)*, Giancarlo Giannini *(Pazzi)*, Francesca Neri *(Allegra Pazzi)*, Zeljko Ivanek *(Dr. Cordell Doemling)*, Hazelle Goodman *(Evelda Drumgo)*, David Andrews *(FBI Agent Pearsall)*

p, Ridley Scott, Dino De Laurentiis, Martha De Laurentiis; d, Ridley Scott; w, David Mamet, Steve Zaillian (based on the novel by Thomas Harris); ph, John Mathieson; ed, Pietro Scalia; m, Hans Zimmer; prod d, Norris Spencer; art d, David Crank; fx, Tim Burke, Kevin Harris; cos, Janty Yates

Psychiatrist, connoisseur, bon vivant, twisted brain. Hannibal Lecter (Anthony Hopkins) returns to the screen after a 10-year absence in this sequel to Jonathan Demme's award-winning THE SILENCE OF THE LAMBS.

A decade has passed since FBI trainee Clarice Starling (Julianne Moore, ably assuming Jodie Foster's old role) first interviewed Lecter and gleaned enough clues from their enigmatic conversations to capture murderer Jame Gumb. But her career is no longer on the rise. Starling's righteous dedication to procedure has alienated her superiors, and a bungled drug bust allows them to hang her out to dry. Her public humiliation attracts the attention of Lecter, now calling himself "Dr. Fell" and living in Florence, Italy, where he's angling for a coveted scholarly position overseeing a 15th-century private library. Lecter sends Starling a teasing letter, and the game is on. Starling's inquiries of the local police alert Inspector Pazzi (Giancarlo Giannini) to Lecter's presence; he decides to capture the doctor on his own and collect the $3 million reward offered by Lecter's only surviving victim, the fabulously wealthy, hideously disfigured Mason Verger (Gary Oldman). Verger also incorporates Starling into his elaborate plan for revenge, at whose center lurks a herd of hungry, flesh-eating swine.

Ridley Scott's direction is more baroque than Demme's, but its aura of corrupt luxury suits Lecter's warped sensibilities. Thomas Harris's 1999 novel dismayed many LAMBS fans with what they perceived as its betrayal of Clarice Starling; they should be pleased that the movie spares her Harris's most uncharacteristic narrative inventions, while retaining the book's over-the-top butchery. Though the movie is clearly meant to work on its own, the relationship between Starling and Lecter plays best if you're familiar with LAMBS.

HANS CHRISTIAN ANDERSEN

1952 120m c Biography ★★★

RKO (U.S.)

DVD

Danny Kaye *(Hans Christian Andersen)*, Farley Granger *(Niels)*, Zizi Jeanmaire *(Doro)*, Joseph Walsh *(Peter)*, Philip Tonge *(Otto)*, Erik Bruhn *(Hussar)*, Roland Petit *(Prince)*, John Brown *(Schoolmaster)*, John Qualen *(Burgomaster)*, Jeanne Lafayette *(Celine)*

p, Samuel Goldwyn; d, Charles Vidor; w, Moss Hart (based on a story by Myles Connolly); ph, Harry Stradling (Technicolor); ed, Daniel Mandell; m, Frank Loesser; art d, Richard Day, Antoni Clave; chor, Roland Petit; cos, Antoni Clave, Mary Wills, Barbara Karinska

AAN Best Color Cinematography: Harry Stradling; AAN Best Score (Musical): Walter Scharf; AAN Best Song: "Thumbelina"; Frank Loesser (Music & Lyrics); AAN Best Art Direction-Set Decoration (Color): Richard Day (Art Direction), Clave (Art Direction), Howard Bristol (Set Decoration); AAN Best Costume Design (Color): Clave, Mary Wills, Madame Karinska; AAN Best Sound Recording: Gordon Sawyer, Goldwyn Sound Department

This glossy children's musical stars Danny Kaye as the beloved Danish author of fairy tales whose rise to literary prominence is detailed here in a totally fabricated manner. Most adults will squirm during the syrupy proceedings but kids seem to like it just fine.

This movie was something of an obsession for producer Samuel Goldwyn, who had been announcing production of the project for nearly 15 years, only to have it delayed time and time again. After paying a king's ransom for 16 different screenplays, Goldwyn finally found one he liked, and production began. Luckily, Goldwyn's dream paid off big at the box office, as HANS CHRISTIAN ANDERSEN grossed $6 million and eventually ranked as Goldwyn's third biggest moneymaker (behind THE BEST YEARS OF OUR LIVES and GUYS AND DOLLS). Kaye is wonderful and the enjoyable songs include "Inchworm" and "Wonderful Wonderful Copenhagen."

HAPPINESS

1998 139m c Comedy/Drama ★★★★

Good Machine/Killer Films/Livingstone Pictures (U.S.) R

DVD

Jane Adams *(Joy Jordan)*, Lara Flynn Boyle *(Helen Jordan)*, Cynthia Stevenson *(Trish Maplewood)*, Dylan Baker *(Bill Maplewood)*, Philip Seymour Hoffman *(Allen)*, Ben Gazzara *(Lenny Jordan)*, Louise Lasser *(Mona Jordan)*, Jared Harris *(Vlad)*, Elizabeth Ashley *(Diane Freed)*, Camryn Manheim *(Kristina)*

p, Ted Hope, Christine Vachon; d, Todd Solondz; w, Todd Solondz; ph, Maryse Alberti; ed, Alan Oxman; m, Robbie Kondor; prod d, Therese Deprez; art d, John Bruce; fx, Drew Jiritano; cos, Kathryn Nixon

No, it's not a wonderful life, and the world can be an awful place, a sinkhole brimming with loneliness, cruelty, depravity, and human monsters who prey on small children. The world, that is, according to director Todd Solondz (WELCOME TO THE DOLLHOUSE), whose brilliantly transgressive satire is sure to rattle even the most jaded filmgoer. But shock value aside, HAPPINESS is also an acute and remarkably compassionate profile of American life at its most desperate.

At the center of this sprawling, multicharacter story are three New Jersey sisters. Joy (Jane Adams), doomed to bad dates and an unfulfilling job, is a hopeless optimist, writing songs about happiness even though she seems to be a magnet for the all the world's hostility. Helen (Lara Flynn Boyle) is a successful and self-obsessed poet who's just sick and tired of all the adoration. Self-complacent Trish (Cynthia Stevenson) is convinced that she has it best of all: three kids, a beautiful suburban home, a successful psychiatrist husband (Dylan Baker). But beneath all the glamour, Helen is plagued by artistic self-doubt ("If only I'd been raped as a child," she muses, "Then I would know authenticity!") and is courting a sadistic obscene phone-caller (Philip Seymour Hoffman). And Trish's dream life is a nightmare she's about to wake up to: her caring husband is a pedophile rapist.

Welcome to the America of JonBenet Ramsey, Neil LaBute, and Geraldo Rivera, a place where the media moralizes while packaging other people's suffering for easy consumption and a quick profit. Good for a few cynical laughs and voyeuristic thrills, but where, Solondz wants to know, is the outrage? When did compassion and the quality of mercy become laughable? The most revealing moment in a film full of brutal truths comes when Joy innocently wonders whether Helen could use a recent tragedy as inspiration for a new poem. Helen laughs in her naive sister's face, then condescendingly adds that she's laughing *with* Joy, not at her. "But I wasn't laughing," Joy deadpans. And neither, in the end, is Solondz.

HARD DAY'S NIGHT, A

DVD

1964 83m   bw   Musical/Comedy   ★★★★½
UA   (U.K.)   G

John Lennon *(John)*, Paul McCartney *(Paul)*, George Harrison *(George)*, Ringo Starr *(Ringo)*, Wilfrid Brambell *(Grandfather)*, Norman Rossington *(Norm)*, Victor Spinetti *(TV Director)*, John Junkin *(Shake)*, Deryck Guyler *(Police Inspector)*, Anna Quayle *(Millie)*

p, Walter Shenson; d, Richard Lester; w, Alun Owen; ph, Gilbert Taylor; ed, John Jympson; m, John Lennon, Paul McCartney; art d, Ray Simm; cos, Dougie Millings & Son, Julie Harris

AAN Best Original Story and Screenplay: Alun Owen; *AAN Best Adapted Score:* George Martin

Refreshing, innovative and immensely funny, A HARD DAY'S NIGHT tells the story of 36 hours in the lives of the Beatles in a quirky fashion that has everyone laughing from the first moment.

Besieged by their frenzied fans, John, Paul, George, and Ringo board a train for London, where they are to do a live television appearance. They are accompanied by Norm (Rossington), their manager (a parody of Brian Epstein), his aide, Shake (John Junkin), and Paul's grandfather (Wilfrid Brambell), a "clean old man" who proves to be a mischievous old coot. In London, the boys cavort at a swinging nightspot before going in search of Grandfather, whom they find chatting up a buxom bird at a casino, and drag him back to the hotel over his angry protests. At the television studio the next day, Grandfather convinces Ringo that he is unappreciated by the rest of the group, and the dejected drummer disappears into the city streets. But how can the lads go on television without Ringo?

Producer Walt Shenson thought he would rush this into production and take advantage of the Beatles' immense popularity before their celebrity waned. Made in only seven weeks for just over half a million dollars, A HARD DAY'S NIGHT returned many times its cost. Its sequel, HELP (also directed by Richard Lester), cost almost three times as much, wasn't as good, and won't be remembered as long as this anarchistic, Marx Brothers-like romp. Combining surrealistic imagery and cinema verite techniques, borrowing from Fellini, Godard, Keaton, and even Busby Berkeley, Lester arrives at his own dazzling style and creates one of the most inventive pictures of the era. Alun Owen's wonderful screenplay is full of witty surprises, delivered as only the Beatles could, and a number of their classics are well integrated into the narrative.

HARD-BOILED

DVD

(LASHOU SHENTAN)
1992 126m   c   Crime/Action/Drama   ★★★½
Milestone Pictures   (Hong Kong)

Chow Yun-Fat *(Inspector Tequila Yuen)*, Tony Leung Chiu-wai, billed as Tony Leung *(Tony)*, Teresa Mo *(Teresa)*, Philip Chan *(Pang)*, Anthony Wong *(Johnny Wong)*, Bowie Lam *(Yuen's Partner)*, Kwan Hoi-shan *(Mr. Hoi)*, Philip Kwok, billed as Cheung Jue-lin *(Mad Dog)*, Tung Wai *(Little Ko)*

p, Linda Kuk, Terence Chang; d, John Woo; w, Barry Wong (from the story by John Woo); ph, Wong Wing Hang; ed, David Wu, Kai Kit-wai; m, Michael Gibbs; prod d, James Leung; art d, Joel Chong

Released in the U.S. just as director John Woo was himself venturing to Hollywood, HARD-BOILED takes Woo's signature gunplay to even more hyperbolic extremes than he had previously achieved. HARD-BOILED doesn't have quite the melodramatic kick of THE KILLER, but the same themes of loyalty, honor and violence are explored to nearly the same impact.

Woo's perennial leading man Chow Yun-fat stars as police inspector Yuen, nicknamed "Tequila," who is first seen moonlighting as a jazz musician in a Hong Kong club. We're soon plunged into the more violent side of Tequila's world, as he and his partner (Bowie Lam) battle a gang of gunrunners in a restaurant. His partner is killed, and Tequila is subsequently browbeaten by his commander, Pang (Philip Chan), who has become increasingly frustrated with Tequila's overly violent tactics. Meanwhile, Tequila is trying to rekindle a relationship with coworker Teresa (Teresa Mo), who has been receiving frequent gifts of white roses. As it happens, the flowers come with coded messages from an undercover gangland source that Teresa passes on to Pang. The usual complications, and elaborately choreographed battles, ensue...

In a sort of reverse move on THE KILLER, this time it's Chow Yun-fat who plays the cop while his costar is the hitman but, as before, the lines are not so easily defined. Tequila, like many American cop heroes, disdains the rules that keep him from doing his job effectively, while Tony is actually a policeman who finds himself increasingly unable to cope with the violent demands of his undercover work. (Reportedly, the cop angle of his character was not originally part of the film as planned, but was added in deference to actor Leung's pop-idol status in Hong Kong.)

The incredible action sequences in HARD-BOILED leave no doubt that Woo is in top form. The opening gunfight in the restaurant is worthy of the climax of any American actioner, and the entire last 40 minutes of the film is one long, breathtaking set piece in the hospital, with one tense confrontation and shootout after another. There's one Steadicam shot, following Tequila and Tony from one floor of the hospital, into an elevator, onto another floor and into another gunfight, that's truly stunning.

The cut of HARD-BOILED that played Chinese-language theaters in America is a slightly trimmed version of Woo's original director's cut (shown at the 1992 Toronto Festival of Festivals), shorn of several minutes for violence and running-time concerns.

HARDCORE

DVD

1979 105m   c   Drama   ★★★
Columbia   (U.S.)   R

George C. Scott *(Jake Van Dorn)*, Peter Boyle *(Andy Mast)*, Season Hubley *(Niki)*, Dick Sargent *(Wes DeJong)*, Leonard Gaines *(Ramada)*, David Nichols *(Kurt)*, Gary Graham *(Tod)*, Larry Block *(Detective Burrows)*, Marc Alaimo *(Ratan)*, Leslie Ackerman *(Felice)*

p, Buzz Feitshans; d, Paul Schrader; w, Paul Schrader; ph, Michael Chapman (Metrocolor); ed, Tom Rolf; m, Jack Nitzsche; prod d, Paul Sylbert; art d, Edwin O'Donovan

"Oh my God, it's my daughter!" wails George C. Scott in the most celebrated scene in HARDCORE, an inconsistent but challenging film from writer-director Paul Schrader (BLUE COLLAR, AMERICAN GIGOLO, CAT PEOPLE, MISHIMA).

Scott (in a performance that ranges from completely over-the-top to downright heartbreaking) plays Jake Van Dorn, a devoutly religious Calvinist from Grand Rapids, Michigan, whose teenaged daughter, Kristen (Ilah Davis), disappears during a church trip to California. Van Dorn ventures out to sinful California to find his missing child. He hires sleazy private detective Andy Mast (Boyle) to look for her and then returns to his virtuous life back in Michigan. Soon he gets a call from Mast, now in Grand Rapids, telling him to meet him in town. The cheap detective takes Van Dorn to a porno theater where they watch a film in which the devout Van Dorn spots his daughter. He breaks down sobbing. Mast returns to L.A. to continue the hunt but Van Dorn can no longer stand by as an observer. He flies to California himself to begin his own search in L.A.'s X-rated underworld.

Realistic one minute, unbelievable the next, HARD-CORE is a truly schizophrenic film. A somber, serious moment is followed by a tongue-in-cheek parody or a flat-out joke. Every scene involving the porno film industry is played strictly for laughs, with wildly exaggerated characters. Scott's performance is similarly divided. He's completely serious during the scenes in which he shows the desperation of the parent of a lost child, but becomes loud and terribly unconvincing as he wanders through the peep shows and massage parlors. He even poses as a porn producer to look for leads to his daughter's whereabouts. Whatever its flaws, this is one of very few American films to deal with fundamentalist beliefs about predestination, faith, and sin with empathy and intellectual acuity.

HARDER THEY COME, THE DVD

1973 98m c Drama ★★★½
International Films (Jamaica) R

Jimmy Cliff (Ivan), Carl Bradshaw (Jose), Janet Bartley (Elsa), Ras Daniel Hartman (Pedro), Basil Keane (Preacher), Bob Charlton (Hilton), Winston Stona (Detective)

p, Perry Henzell; d, Perry Henzell; w, Perry Henzell, Trevor D. Rhone; ph, Peter Jessop, David McDonald (Metrocolor); ed, John Victor Smith, Seicland Anderson, Richard White; m, Jimmy Cliff, Desmond Dekker, The Slickers

This outstanding Jamaican feature became a major cult favorite in the U.S. and did much to popularize reggae with its fabulous musical score.

Reggae star Jimmy Cliff plays Ivan, a young aspiring singer from the country who arrives in Kingston with high hopes of becoming a recording star. Work is hard to come by, however, and after a rude awakening on the city streets, Ivan becomes a handyman for a local preacher. When an argument over a bicycle escalates into a knife fight, Ivan is sent to jail. After his release he moves in with the preacher's ward, Elsa (Bartley), and pursues the island's biggest record producer, Hilton (Charlton). Eventually he gets the chance to record "The Harder They Come." However Ivan balks when Hilton offers him a paltry $20 for the song. The producer retaliates by releasing the record without any promotion. Penniless, Ivan has no choice but to get involved in the lucrative but dangerous marijuana trade. As his criminal notoriety grows so do his record sales.

THE HARDER THEY COME is a gritty, realistic view of urban Jamaica that reveals the squalor of shantytowns tourists never see. Cliff delivers a charismatic and memorable performance as a young man who is determined to become famous, mirroring his own real-life ascendence to worldwide fame as a reggae artist. Despite the ostensible show-business plot, this film most resembles a 1930s gangster film with its relentless depiction of regrettable social conditions, police corruption and the lure of illicit cash. The filmmaking is a bit crude at times but it packs an emotional wallop.

HARDER THEY FALL, THE DVD

1956 109m bw Sports ★★★★
Columbia (U.S.)

Humphrey Bogart (Eddie Willis), Rod Steiger (Nick Benko), Jan Sterling (Beth Willis), Mike Lane (Toro Moreno), Max Baer (Buddy Brannen), Jersey Joe Walcott (George), Edward Andrews (Jim Weyerhause), Harold J. Stone (Art Leavitt), Carlos Montalban (Luis Agrandi), Nehemiah Persoff (Leo)

p, Philip Yordan; d, Mark Robson; w, Philip Yordan (based on the novel by Budd Schulberg); ph, Burnett Guffey; ed, Jerome Thoms; m, Hugo Friedhofer; art d, William Flannery

AAN Best B/W Cinematography: Burnett Guffey

One of the most scathing indictments of professional boxing ever committed to film, THE HARDER THEY FALL presents Humphrey Bogart as Eddie Willis, a once-scrupulous sportswriter, now working for Nick Benko (Rod Steiger), a shady mob-connected promoter. Eddie is handling the publicity for Benko's new find, Toro Moreno (Mike Lane), a giant Argentine boxer with a powder-puff punch and a glass jaw. But Benko fixes one fight after another and soon the towering heavyweight, who thinks he's doing it on his own, faces Gus Dundee (Pat Comiskey), a top contender who was so battered by the current champ, Buddy Brannen (one-time heavyweight title holder Max Baer), that even Toro's feeble punches are enough to bring about a brain hemorrhage that kills him. This is the beginning of a moral crisis for Eddie.

Scripted by producer Philip Yordan from the novel by Budd Schulberg, THE HARDER THEY FALL was similar enough to the real-life story of heavyweight Primo Carnera (who lost his title to Baer) that he sued Columbia. Nothing about it is pretty, with director Mark Robson (who'd already helmed the powerful CHAMPION) moving the story along at a frenetic pace and Burnett Guffey's stark black-and-white photography lending a grim feel to the movie. All of the performers are excellent, especially Bogart, in what would be his final screen appearance.

HAROLD AND MAUDE DVD

1971 90m c Comedy ★★★½
Paramount (U.S.) PG

Ruth Gordon (Maude), Bud Cort (Harold), Vivian Pickles (Mrs. Chasen), Cyril Cusack (Sculptor), Charles Tyner (Uncle Victor), Ellen Geer (Sunshine), Eric Christmas (Priest), G. Wood (Psychiatrist), Judy Engles (Candy Gulf), Shari Summers (Edith Fern)

p, Charles B. Mulvehill, Colin Higgins; d, Hal Ashby; w, Colin Higgins; ph, John A. Alonzo (Technicolor); ed, William A. Sawyer, Edward Warschilka; m, Cat Stevens; prod d, Michael Haller; art d, Michael Haller; fx, A.D. Flowers; cos, William Ware Theiss

HAROLD AND MAUDE got lost in the holiday shuffle when first released in late 1971, but there's much in this oddball film to recommend, including superb performances from the three leads. Harold (Cort) is the son of Mrs. Chasen (Pickles), a wealthy woman who pays little attention to him. His frequent depressions and lack of friends motivate him to stage increasingly elaborate mock suicides, none of which impress his distracted mother. Fascinated by death and all its trappings, Harold has an old hearse which he drives to funerals at various cemeteries around town. At two successive services, he meets Maude (Gordon), a 79-year-old concentration camp survivor who is as thrilled with life as he is with death. A classic free spirit, she is the polar opposite of the solemn Harold. Nonetheless they become great pals, and she instills in him a desire to live, to spread his wings, to enjoy his brief time on earth. As time passes, they share several wacky adventures and their friendship blossoms into love—much to the alarm of Harold's mother.

This is a doggedly eccentric film which some will reject out of hand. Others will find it profoundly moving and life affirming. Not surprisingly it became one of the major cult films on college campuses in the 1970s. This film was originated as a 20-minute script written as a graduate thesis by UCLA student Higgins. He later showed it to his landlady, Lewis, the wife of a film producer, and the two formed their own production company to make the film. Higgins went on to become a writer-director best known for films such as FOUL PLAY, NINE TO FIVE, and THE BEST LITTLE WHOREHOUSE IN TEXAS. He died in 1988 from AIDS complications.

HARPER

1966 121m c Mystery ★★★
Warner Bros. (U.S.)

Paul Newman (*Harper*), Lauren Bacall (*Mrs. Sampson*), Julie Harris (*Betty Fraley*), Arthur Hill (*Albert Graves*), Janet Leigh (*Susan Harper*), Pamela Tiffin (*Miranda Sampson*), Robert Wagner (*Alan Traggert*), Robert Webber (*Dwight Troy*), Shelley Winters (*Fay Estabrook*), Harold Gould (*Sheriff Spanner*)

p, Elliott Kastner, Jerry Gershwin; d, Jack Smight; w, William Goldman (based on the novel *The Moving Target* by Ross MacDonald); ph, Conrad Hall (Panavision, Technicolor); ed, Stefan Arnsten; m, Johnny Mandel; art d, Alfred Sweeney; cos, Sally Edwards, William Smith

Based on Ross MacDonald's novel *The Moving Target*, HARPER showcases Paul Newman in the role of Lew Harper, a down-on-his-luck but ultra hip Los Angeles private eye hired by the cynical Mrs. Sampson (Bacall) to track down her missing and very wealthy husband. The trail leading to Mr. Sampson is laden with strange characters and brings more than a few bumps and bruises Harper's way. His snooping takes him from an over-the-hill actress (Winters) to a junkie nightclub chanteuse (Harris) and from a religious zealot (Martin) to a smuggling operation. William Goldman's adaptation of MacDonald's novel—his first solo screenwriting credit—is full of rapid-fire dialogue but some of the characterizations are thin. Despite all the big names involved, HARPER doesn't begin to approach the big leagues of hard-boiled detective films. Nonetheless, Newman gives a convincing performance in a role he would repeat nearly ten years later in THE DROWNING POOL.

HARRY AND TONTO

1974 115m c Drama ★★★
Fox (U.S.) R

Art Carney (*Harry Coombs*), Ellen Burstyn (*Shirley*), Chief Dan George (*Sam Two Feathers*), Geraldine Fitzgerald (*Jessie*), Larry Hagman (*Eddie*), Arthur Hunnicutt (*Wade*), Philip Bruns (*Burt*), Josh Mostel (*Norman*), Melanie Mayron (*Ginger*), Dolly Jonah (*Elaine*)

p, Paul Mazursky; d, Paul Mazursky; w, Paul Mazursky, Josh Greenfeld; ph, Michael Butler (DeLuxe Color); ed, Richard Halsey; m, Bill Conti; prod d, Ted Haworth; cos, Albert Wolsky

AA Best Actor: Art Carney; *AAN Best Original Screenplay:* Paul Mazursky, Josh Greenfeld

When his comfortable New York City apartment building is torn down, 72-year-old widower and retired college professor Harry (Carney) temporarily moves in with his eldest son but finds his daughter-in-law far too enthusiastic. Perhaps inspired by his grandson, Norman (Mostel, son of Zero), who is currently immersed in Zen philosophy, Harry decides to postpone his search for new lodgings to fulfill a lifelong ambition to travel across the country to California. With his beloved cat Tonto, Harry hits the road, planning to stop and visit his other children—Shirley (Burstyn), a daughter who lives in Chicago, and youngest son, Eddie (Hagman), who lives on the West Coast. During his journey, Harry encounters several situations that cause him to examine what life means to him.

HARRY AND TONTO is a sweet, sentimental road movie that draws force and relevance from Carney's touching and subtle performance. Incredibly, after nearly 25 years on television, this was the actor's first major feature film role. In HARRY AND TONTO writer-director Mazursky shows the innocence of youth and the disappointment of middle age but offers solace in old age if the internal energy that once

produced ambition is rediscovered and prompts us to hope for better things to come.

HARRY POTTER AND THE CHAMBER OF SECRETS 🄳🅅🄳

2002 161m c Fantasy/Adventure ★★★½
Heyday Films/1492 Pictures/Warner Bros./ PG
MIRACLE Productions GmbH
(U.S./U.K./Germany)

Daniel Radcliffe (*Harry Potter*), Rupert Grint (*Ron Weasley*), Emma Watson (*Hermione Granger*), Maggie Smith (*Minerva McGonagall*), Robbie Coltrane (*Rubeus Hagrid*), Richard Harris (*Albus Dumbledore*), Kenneth Branagh (*Gilderoy Lockhart*), John Cleese (*Nearly Headless Nick*), Tom Felton (*Draco Malfoy*), Toby Jones (*Voice of Dobby the House Elf*)

p, David Heyman; d, Chris Columbus; w, Steve Kloves (based on the novel by J.K. Rowling); ph, Roger Pratt; art d, Neil Lamont; fx, Nick Davis, Jim Mitchell, John Richardson; cos, Lindy Hemming

Relieved of the heavy burden of character introduction that fell to HARRY POTTER AND THE SORCERER'S STONE, the adaptation of J.K. Rowling's second novel gets off to a rollicking start and never lets up for a moment.

Ignoring the dire warning of a small house elf named Dobby (voice of Toby Jones), who advises him not to return to Hogwarts School of Witchcraft and Wizardry, Harry Potter (Daniel Radcliffe) and his best friend, Ron Weasley (Rupert Grint), head back for a second year. The two boys are reunited with their bossy pal, Hermione Granger (Emma Watson), and Harry resumes his rivalry with snotty Draco Malfoy (Tom Felton). The fun ends when a number of students and animals are found petrified, and a strange message written in blood mysteriously appears: "The Chamber of Secrets has been opened." Ron and Harry find a cryptic diary that implicates Hagrid (Robbie Coltrane), the school's genial groundskeeper, and Harry makes the disturbing discovery that he has much in common with evil Lord Voldemort, who cast a long shadow over the first film.

The fresh-faced students take center stage, and the formidable cast of veterans—including the late Richard Harris as imperious headmaster Dumbledore, Maggie Smith as stern Professor McGonagall, John Cleese as Nearly Headless Nick, and Julie Walters as kindhearted Mrs. Weasley—make the most of their limited screen time. But it's Kenneth Branagh who steals the show as the narcissistic Defense of the Dark Arts instructor, Gilderoy Lockhart. By and large, this is a better film than the first, thanks mainly to a darker, more satisfying tone and far better special effects.

HARRY POTTER AND THE PRISONER OF AZKABAN 🄳🅅🄳

2004 136m c Adventure/Fantasy ★★★½
Warner Bros./Heyday Films/1492 Pictures (U.S.) PG

Daniel Radcliffe (*Harry Potter*), Rupert Grint (*Ron Weasley*), Emma Watson (*Hermione Granger*), Michael Gambon (*Albus Dumbledore*), Gary Oldman (*Sirius Black*), David Thewlis (*Professor Remus Lupin*), Timothy Spall (*Peter Pettigrew*), Paul Whitehouse (*Sir Cadogan*), Julie Christie (*Madame Rosmerta*), Pam Ferris (*Aunt Marge Dursley*)

p, Chris Columbus, David Heyman, Mark Radcliffe; d, Alfonso Cuaron; w, Steve Kloves (based on the novel by J.K. Rowling); ph, Michael Seresin; ed, Steven Weisberg; m, John Williams; prod d, Stuart Craig; art d, Andrew Ackland-Snow, Neil Lamont; fx, Tim Burke, Roger Guyett, Stephen Hamilton, John Richardson; cos, Jany Temime

Mexican director Alfonso Cuaron picks up the reins from Chris Columbus in this third installment in J.K. Rowling's

Harry Potter series, and leaves his mark without betraying the source material.

Orphaned adolescent wizard Harry (Daniel Radcliffe) is anxiously anticipating his third year of study at the Hogwarts School of Witchcraft and Wizardry, his refuge from life with his viciously coarse and stupid relatives, the Dursleys. Hogwarts students are strictly forbidden to use magic outside school, so when Harry uses his powers to inflate beastly Aunt Marge (Pam Ferris) and send her bobbing off through the suburban skies like a noisome balloon, the Dursleys are furious and Harry does what any distraught 13-year-old would do in similar circumstances: he runs away. Once back at Hogwarts, Harry learns why no one seems concerned about his minor transgressions: rogue wizard Sirius Black (Gary Oldman), who betrayed Harry's parents to the dreaded Lord Valdemort, has escaped from Azkaban prison for magical miscreants and it seems likely that he's coming to kill the last of the Potters. For Harry's sake, Professor Dumbledore (Michael Gambon) allows Azkaban's spectral security force, a group of ghastly soul-sucking wraiths called Dementors, to patrol Hogwarts until Black is caught.

Where Columbus vanished behind Rowling's intricately imagined world, Cuaron lets his personal enthusiasms show. He's evidently enchanted by the whomping willow, delighted by the marvelous hippogriff, and singularly uninterested in the sporty pleasures of Quidditch. And in a grace note typical of his slightly skewed take on the material, Cuaron gives the enchanted Hogwarts, where living paintings line the walls and ghosts caper in the public spaces, a grittier, more conventionally realistic texture than the Dursleys' perfectly manicured suburban home.

HARRY POTTER AND THE SORCERER'S STONE 📀

2001 152m c Adventure/Fantasy ★★★½
Warner Bros./Heyday Films (U.S./U.K.) PG

Daniel Radcliffe *(Harry Potter)*, Rupert Grint *(Ronald "Ron" Weasley)*, Emma Watson *(Hermione Granger)*, John Cleese *(Nearly Headless Nick)*, Robbie Coltrane *(Rubeus Hagrid)*, Warwick Davis *(Professor Flitwick)*, Maggie Smith *(Professor McGonagall)*, Ian Hart *(Professor Quirrell)*, Zoe Wanamaker *(Madame Hooch)*, Richard Harris *(Professor Dumbledore)*

p, David Heyman; d, Chris Columbus; w, Steve Kloves (based on the novel by J.K. Rowling); ph, John Seale; ed, Richard Francis-Bruce; m, John Williams; prod d, Stuart Craig; art d, Andrew Ackland-Snow, Michael Lamont, Steve Lawrence, Cliff Robinson, Lucinda Thomson; fx, Robert Duncan, Robert Legato, Mill Film, Rythm & Hues, Sony Pictures Imageworks; cos, Judianna Makovsky

AAN Best Art Direction: Stuart Craig, Stephanie McMillan; *AAN Best Costume Design:* Judianna Makovsky; *AAN Best Original Score:* John Williams

Based on the first of J.K. Rowling's mind-bogglingly popular novels, Chris Columbus's lavishly appointed film aims for fidelity to its much-loved source in all things.

Orphaned Harry Potter (Daniel Radcliffe) has no idea what his 11th birthday holds in store: an invitation to attend the very exclusive Hogwarts School of Witchcraft and Wizardry, where tomorrow's occult movers and shakers get their start. Great, if unspecified, things are expected of young Harry: When he was an infant, his parents were murdered by a rogue wizard; Harry survived with only a lightning bolt-shaped scar on his forehead to show for the experience. En route to Hogwarts, Harry falls in with two fellow first-year students, bossy but brilliant Hermione Granger (Emma Watson) and red-headed Ron Weasley (Rupert Grint). The staff, by contrast, are a daunting lot, and played by a formidable cross-section of contemporary master thespians: patrician director Albus Dumbledore (Richard Harris); starchy

Professor McGonagall (Maggie Smith); high-strung Professor Quirrell (Ian Hart); diminutive Professor Flitwick (Warwick Davis); sinister Professor Snape (Alan Rickman); brisk Madame Hooch (Zoe Wanamaker); sour-faced caretaker Mr. Filch (David Bradley); and gamekeeper Hagrid (Robbie Coltrane). The film's special-effects wonders include a three-headed guard dog named Fluffy, staircases that change configuration at whim, benevolent ghosts (including John Cleese as Nearly Headless Nick), belligerent chess pieces, and a swarm of flying keys.

The film may be a little long, but it's never boring; how could it be, when jack o'lanterns float lazily overhead in the dining hall, and the venerable Smith turns into a cat? And if it's a little airless, no matter. Fans of the books will be so relieved to find the world they love transplanted to the screen intact that they won't mind a bit.

HARVEY 📀

1950 104m bw Comedy ★★★★
Universal (U.S.)

James Stewart *(Elwood P. Dowd)*, Josephine Hull *(Veta Louise Simmons)*, Peggy Dow *(Miss Kelly)*, Charles Drake *(Dr. Sanderson)*, Cecil Kellaway *(Dr. Chumley)*, Victoria Horne *(Myrtle Mae)*, Jesse White *(Wilson)*, William Lynn *(Judge Gaffney)*, Wallace Ford *(Lofgren)*, Nana Bryant *(Mrs. Chumley)*

p, John Beck; d, Henry Koster; w, Mary Chase, Oscar Brodney (based on a play by Chase); ph, William Daniels; ed, Ralph Dawson; m, Frank Skinner; art d, Nathan Juran, Bernard Herzbrun

AAN Best Actor: James Stewart; *AA Best Supporting Actress:* Josephine Hull

Elwood P. Dowd (Jimmy Stewart) is the whimsical inebriate whose kindness spills over into the lives of all around him as he tries to help those in need. Elwood lurches home one night to see a six-foot rabbit named Harvey leaning against a lamppost. This invisible "Pooka" becomes his friend and follows him everywhere, much to the chagrin of Elwood's social-climbing family, who think he has finally flipped and should be put in an asylum. Faithfully adapted by Mary Chase from her popular Broadway play, HARVEY is a delightful comedy-fantasy. Jimmy Stewart, in one of his best-loved roles, is wonderful as the gentle, sweet soul who befriends the invisible rabbit. His performance earned him an Oscar nomination, and the priceless Josephine Hull, as Stewart's harried sister, was honored as Best Supporting Actress. The supporting cast features wonderful work from Dow (who retired far too soon), Drake, Kellaway, Horne, and White. Henry Koster's direction is sharp and moves along at a rapid clip. This is a happy movie and leaves a long, lingering warm glow.

HASTY HEART, THE 📀

1949 99m bw Drama ★★★★
Warner Bros. (U.K.)

Ronald Reagan *(The Yank)*, Patricia Neal *(Sister Margaret)*, Richard Todd *(The Scot)*, Anthony Nicholls *(Col Dunn)*, Howard Marion-Crawford *(The Tommy)*, Ralph Michael *(The New Zealander)*, John Sherman *(The Aussie)*, Alfie Bass *(Orderly)*, Orlando Martins *(Blossom)*

p, Howard Lindsay, Russel Crouse; d, Vincent Sherman; w, Ranald MacDougall (based on the play by John Patrick); ph, Wilkie Cooper; ed, E.B. Jarvis; m, Jack Beaver; art d, Terence Verity; cos, Peggy Henderson

AAN Best Actor: Richard Todd

Six wounded soldiers await shipment home. Reagan's Yank character asks little more of him than that he supply bravura;

he's exceeded at every turn by Todd, who is wonderful as a hardheaded, truculent Scottish soldier who remains aloof toward his fellow patients. Nicholls, the head doctor, and Neal, a firm but gentle nurse, ask Reagan and the other patients to be kind to Todd, who's dying of a terminal illness but does not know it. It's a difficult task, though, since the stubborn Scot rejects the friendship of Reagan and the others, more or less telling them to mind their own business when they try to strike up conversations or do little favors for him.

On his 21st birthday, however, Todd is given a complete new Scottish outfit (including kilt and bagpipes) as a gift from the patients. This softens his heart, and he explains in his own halting manner that he has never before been so touched. At last he befriends his fellow patients, but when Nicholls finally tells him he's dying, Todd again closes up like a clam, this time bitterly lashing out at Reagan and the others because he now believes their actions were motivated only by pity.

This is a poignant drama, fluidly directed by the versatile and underrated Sherman which, despite the screenplay's failure to "open up" the original play, is kept from becoming claustrophobic largely due to Sherman's inventive setups and staging. The 30-year-old Richard Todd had made only one previous film (FOR THEM THAT TRESPASS) before completing THE HASTY HEART, although he had been on stage since the late 1930s. He was a standout discovery here, and no doubt drew upon his experience as a paratrooper during WWII for his role, which netted him an Academy Award nomination for Best Actor.

HATE
(LA HAINE)
1995 98m bw Drama   ★★½
Les Productions Lazennec/Canal Plus/La Sept/
Kaso Inc. Productions   (France)

Vincent Cassel *(Vinz)*, Hubert Kounde *(Hubert)*, Said Taghmaoui *(Said)*, Karim Belkhadra *(Samir)*, Edouard Montoute *(Darty)*, Francois Levantal *(Asterix)*, Solo Dicko *(Santo)*, Marc Duret *(Inspector "Notre Dame")*, Heloise Rauth *(Sarah)*, Rywka Wajsbrot *(Vinz's Grandmother)*

p, Christophe Rossignon; d, Mathieu Kassovitz; w, Mathieu Kassovitz; ph, Pierre Aim; ed, Mathieu Kassovitz, Scott Stevenson; art d, Giuseppe Ponturo; fx, Pierre Foury; cos, Virginie Montel

A bitter melange of Scorsese, Godard, and Spike Lee, HATE tries to bridge the gap between European art film and American pop, and succeeds to a surprising extent. This second feature from young Mathieu Kassovitz (his first was released in the U.S. in 1994 under the title CAFE AU LAIT) is set in a public housing project outside Paris, where a trio of angry young men drift, brood, flirt with violence, and chatter ceaselessly in gutter French.

As the film opens, the interracial residents of a grim working-class suburb have stormed the local police station and torched cars in protest of the arrest and beating of a young Arab. Vinz (Vincent Cassel) is a violence-prone Jew who has a fanatical hatred of cops. Hubert (Hubert Kounde) is a black part-time drug dealer who dreams of going straight and becoming a professional boxer. Said (Said Taghmaoui), an Arab, is something of a follower, more confused than the others and deeply affected by the racial strife. During the riot, Vince pockets a policeman's lost gun and vows to kill a cop if the victimized Arab dies of his injuries. HATE follows the three young men through the next 24 hours, offering a rare glimpse into a vibrant lumpen subculture that partakes equally of American television and European multicult. Exquisitely shot, culturally savvy, and intermittently thrilling, it easily transcends the American ghetto pictures it emulates.

HAUNTING, THE
1963 112m bw Horror   📀 ★★★½
Argyle   (U.S./U.K.)

Julie Harris *(Eleanor Vance)*, Claire Bloom *(Theodora)*, Richard Johnson *(Dr. John Markway)*, Russ Tamblyn *(Luke Sanderson)*, Lois Maxwell *(Grace Markway)*, Fay Compton *(Mrs. Sanderson)*, Valentine Dyall *(Mr. Dudley)*, Rosalie Crutchley *(Mrs. Dudley)*, Diane Clare *(Carrie Fredericks)*, Ronald Adam *(Eldridge Harper)*

p, Robert Wise; d, Robert Wise; w, Nelson Gidding (based on the novel *The Haunting of Hill House* by Shirley Jackson); ph, Davis Boulton (Panavision); ed, Ernest Walter; m, Humphrey Searle; prod d, Elliot Scott; fx, Tom Howard; cos, Mary Quant, Maude Churchill

A bit overrated upon its initial release, THE HAUNTING is, nonetheless, an undeniably effective adaptation of the Shirley Jackson novel and remains one of the best haunted-house movies.

Dr. Markway (Richard Johnson) is a professor of anthropology experimenting with ESP and other forms of psychic phenomena. He arrives at Hill House, a New England mansion that is reputed to be crammed with demons and ghosts and the home of everything evil. Along with Markway is Eleanor (Julie Harris), a slim spinster who, until recently, has spent her life caring for her aged mother, and Theodora (Claire Bloom), a lesbian. Both women have experienced extra-sensory occurrences, and Markway has enlisted their aid in his quest for knowledge on the subject. Luke (Russ Tamblyn), who is the heir to the house and hopes to sell it at a great profit, goes along for a ride he will regret. Once inside, the quartet is besieged by terror—noises, yowls, and eerie events pour off the screen until Eleanor is convinced that Hill House is alive and wants her to stay there.

Director Robert Wise, who began his directorial career under the tutelage of Val Lewton, takes the lessons learned there to a bit of an extreme, overplaying his hand through the use of extremely exaggerated angles and distorting lenses. But the politically incorrect and oversimplified notion that Eleanor's repressed lesbianism is the cause of her downfall, was outdated even when the film was made. THE HAUNTING spends too much time setting up the idea that it will scientifically shed light on psychic phenomena and then withdraws from us. All said, the high order of acting seems wasted.

HAUNTING, THE
1999 125m c Horror   📀 ★★
Roth/Arnold/DreamWorks (U.S.)   PG-13

Liam Neeson *(Dr. David Marrow)*, Catherine Zeta-Jones *(Theo)*, Owen Wilson *(Luke Sanderson)*, Lili Taylor *(Nell)*, Bruce Dern *(Mr. Dudley)*, Marian Seldes *(Mrs. Dudley)*, Alix Koromzay *(Mary Lambetta)*, Todd Field *(Todd Hackett)*, Virginia Madsen *(Jane)*, Michael Cavanaugh *(Dr. Malcolm Keogh)*

p, Susan Arnold, Donna Arkoff Roth, Colin Wilson; d, Jan De Bont; w, David Self (based on *The Haunting of Hill House* by Shirley Jackson); ph, Karl Walter Lindenlaub; ed, Michael Kahn; m, Jerry Goldsmith; prod d, Eugenio Zanetti; art d, Martin Laing, Troy Sizemore; fx, Phil Tippett, Craig Hayes; cos, Ellen Mirojnick

If you like your ghost stories loud, obvious, and without a wisp of ambience, this remake of Robert Wise's classic psychological horror tale may activate your fright flasher. But it won't raise the hairs on the back of your neck, or make you tuck your toes under the sheet at night.

Unethical Dr. Marrow (Liam Neeson) recruits three high-strung types for a bogus sleep-disorder study at Hill House, a rambling mansion with a bad reputation. But he actually plans to scare them half to death for a paper on fear. Sensitive Eleanor (Lili Taylor) has spent 11 years caring for her aging mother, and longs for a change of scenery and a little adventure. Flamboyant Theo (Catherine Zeta-Jones) is a bisexual flirt whose teasing ways alarm mousy little Eleanor, but charm the pants off regular joe Luke (Owen Wilson). Marrow chuckles at his cleverness in giving his guinea pigs the willies, but the house really *is* as haunted as can be. It responds to Marrow's audacity by throwing every nasty thing it's got at the quartet: scary noises, blasts of icy air, bloody footprints, living statuary, and ghostly faces that emerge from billowing curtains and rumpled bedclothes.

Overall, the actors are better than they need to be—Taylor especially so—but their efforts hardly matter. Jan De Bont (SPEED, TWISTER) is a director of zero subtlety; he seems to think atmosphere is spontaneously generated when there's nothing happening, so he loads the film's front end with shots of people walking down hallways and remarking on the creepy carvings. Memo to Jan: that's not the way it works. The massive sets and extensive special effects are certainly... massive and extensive, but watching them is like watching the wheels and gears inside a hugely complicated clock: it's interesting and even beautiful, but can hardly be called scary.

HE WALKED BY NIGHT   **DVD**
1948 79m bw Crime   ★★★★
Bryan Foy/Eagle-Lion   (U.S.)

Richard Basehart *(Davis Morgan)*, Scott Brady *(Sgt. Marty Brennan)*, Roy Roberts *(Capt. Breen)*, Whit Bissell *(Reeves)*, James Cardwell *(Chuck Jones)*, Jack Webb *(Lee)*, Robert Bice *(Detective Steno)*, Reed Hadley *(Narrator)*, Chief Bradley *(Himself)*, John McGuire *(Rawlins)*

p, Robert T. Kane; d, Alfred Werker, Anthony Mann (uncredited); w, John C. Higgins, Crane Wilbur, Harry Essex (uncredited), Beck Murray (based on a story by Crane Wilbur); ph, John Alton; ed, Al DeGaetano; m, Leonid Raab; art d, Edward L. Ilou; fx, George J. Teague, Jack Rabin

This is a smashing film noir entry with Basehart as Davis Morgan, a brilliant, cold-hearted thief with underlying psychopathic tendencies that chill the viewer to the bone. Morgan is an electronics wizard who robs stores and warehouses to obtain electrical equipment which he modifies and then rents out to Reeves (Bissell). The Los Angeles police are in a quandary about this successful burglar since Morgan listens in on their radio network and cleverly alters his *modus operandi* so that his work appears to be that of another burglar. With cops Brennan (Brady) and Breen (Roberts) hot on his trail, Morgan attempts to escape into the vast sewer system beneath Los Angeles.

Director Werker (with an uncredited assist from Anthony Mann) does a fine job in maintaining the hectic pace, and Basehart is gripping as the lone, loveless thief who even sacrifices his dog when the going gets tough. His role is based on the career of thief and cop-killer Erwin Walker, a WWII hero turned burglar who terrorized L.A. in 1946. This film marked the first time the huge drainage system canals in Los Angeles were employed in a film; they would later be put to heavy use in THEM!, GREASE, and a number of other productions. Jack Webb drew the inspiration for his long-running documentary-style television series "Dragnet" from this film, in which he played a featured role.

HEAD   **DVD**
1968 85m c Musical/Comedy   ★★★
Raybert   (U.S.)   G

Peter Tork, David Jones, Micky Dolenz, Michael Nesmith *(Monkees)*, Annette Funicello *(Minnie)*, Timothy Carey *(Lord High 'n' Low)*, Logan Ramsey *(Officer Faye Lapid)*, Abraham Sofaer *(Swami)*, Vito Scotti *(I. Vitteloni)*, Charles Macaulay *(Inspector Shrink)*

p, Bob Rafelson, Jack Nicholson; d, Bob Rafelson; w, Bob Rafelson, Jack Nicholson; ph, Michel Hugo (Technicolor); ed, Mike Pozen; m, Ken Thorne; art d, Sydney Z. Litwack; fx, Butler-Glouner, Inc., Chuck Gaspar, Burton Gershfield, Bruce Lane; chor, Toni Basil; cos, Gene Ashman

After the demise of their TV show, the Monkees brought their particular brand of musical madness to the screen under the direction of Bob Rafelson (FIVE EASY PIECES; THE KING OF MARVIN GARDENS; BLACK WIDOW) who also played a key role in putting the group together for television and, with Jack Nicholson, cowrote the script for this quasi-underground film. The result is a visually daring cinematic game that is virtually plotless and better off for being so. Rafelson takes the Monkees through a variety of adventures both on location and on movie lots, where he and the Prefab Four satirize a variety of movie genres. Among the plentiful guest stars are Victor Mature, whose hair the mini-Monkees invest with dandruff; ex-heavyweight boxing champ Sonny Liston as an extra who climbs into the ring with Jones; Annette Funicello, Frank Zappa, former Green Bay Packer linebacker Ray Nitschke, famed San Francisco stripper Carol Doda, and the then-unknown Teri Garr. A fun collection of old movie clips is also included, featuring Ronald Reagan, Bela Lugosi, Charles Laughton, Ann Miller, and Rita Hayworth. The Monkees deliver the songs, "Circle Sky" (Michael Nesmith), "Can You Dig It," "Long Title: Do I Have to Do This All Over Again" (Peter Tork), "Daddy's Song" (Nilsson), "As We Go Along" (Carole King, Toni Stern), and "The Porpoise Song" (Carole King, Gerry Goffin).

HEAR MY SONG
1991 113m c   Comedy/Drama   ★★★
Limelight Ltd./Film Four International/Windmill   R
Lane Productions/Vision Investments   (U.K./Ireland)

Ned Beatty *(Josef Locke)*, Adrian Dunbar *(Micky O'Neill)*, Shirley Ann Field *(Cathleen Doyle)*, Tara Fitzgerald *(Nancy Doyle)*, William Hootkins *(Mr. X)*, Harold Berens *(Benny Rose)*, David McCallum *(Jim Abbott)*, John Dair *(Derek)*, Stephen Marcus *(Gordon)*, Britta Smith *(Kitty Ryan)*

p, Alison Owen; d, Peter Chelsom; w, Peter Chelsom, Adrian Dunbar (from the story by Chelsom); ph, Sue Gibson; ed, Martin Walsh; m, John Altman; prod d, Caroline Hanania; art d, Katharine Naylor; cos, Lindy Hemming

The lilt of Irish laughter and wit fills the screen in the romantic comedy HEAR MY SONG, and its blarney is irresistible.

Micky O'Neill (Adrian Dunbar) runs a nightclub that caters to Liverpool's Irish community. His main problem is booking talent for his venue and he usually wheels and deals in order to find "names" that will bring in the masses. He hits on a scheme: he'll bring back the notorious "Mr. X," hinting broadly that this is the legendary and much loved Josef Locke. But Locke is a wanted man who fled to Ireland 30 years earlier because of massive tax evasion. Micky's "Mr. X" (William Hootkins), however, is a fraud. As a result of his wheeling and dealing, Micky loses the club, and his fiancee. So Micky has no alternative. He returns to Ireland, determined to find the real Josef Locke and somehow get him to risk arrest and return to Liverpool for a special appearance.

HEAR MY SONG is based on an incident in the life of the world-famous Irish tenor Josef Locke, who really did flee Britain due to tax difficulties. Former stage actor Peter Chelsom, who makes an auspicious feature directorial debut and also co-wrote the screenplay, remembers the real Josef Locke from his own youth in Blackpool. Production designer Caroline Hanania has succeeded in giving each segment a unique feel, from harsh big city to small picturesque town to the fantastical elements in the club's demise, all of which has provided splendid opportunities for cinematographer Sue

Gibson. One of the film's central themes is a touching reflection on how dreams can be distorted. Dreams and longing for something lasting in a very transient world are what HEAR MY SONG is all about.

HEART LIKE A WHEEL
1983 113m c   Biography   DVD
Aurora   (U.S.)   ★★★
                                           PG

Bonnie Bedelia (Shirley Muldowney), Beau Bridges (Connie Kalitta), Leo Rossi (Jack Muldowney), Hoyt Axton (Tex Roque), Bill McKinney ("Big Daddy" Don Garlits), Anthony Edwards (John Muldowney, Age 15–23), Dean Paul Martin (Sonny Rigotti), Paul Bartel (Chef Paul), Missy Basile (Angela), Michael Cavanaugh (NHRA Boss)

p, Charles Roven; d, Jonathan Kaplan; w, Ken Friedman; ph, Tak Fujimoto (Deluxe Color); ed, O. Nicholas Brown; m, Laurence Rosenthal; prod d, James William Newport; cos, William Ware Theiss

AAN Best Costume Design: William Ware Theiss

This insightful biography of drag-racing champ Shirley "Cha-Cha" Muldowney (the underrated Bonnie Bedelia) begins with the foreshadowing image of little Shirley driving her father's sedan and continues with her first race in 1966. Meeting with the usual sexism, she surprises all by breaking the track record on her qualifying run. Her career soars, but her marriage to mechanic Jack Muldowney (Leo Rossi) ends in divorce when he realizes that he can't handle his wife's success. Shirley then turns to banned driver Connie Kalitta (Beau Bridges, who also appears in the similarly themed GREASED LIGHTING, the story of black NASCAR driver Wendell Scott's triumph over racial prejudice) for support and love as she goes on to win the National Hot Rod Association World Championship three times.

The film is marred by a lackluster narrative, failing to inspire or move us in any way, but there's no denying Bedelia's beautifully nuanced performance. She's deserving of projects that are the equivalent of the forthright intelligence she brings to everything she does.

HEARTS OF THE WEST
1975 102m c   Western
MGM   (U.S.)   ★★★½
                                           PG

Jeff Bridges (Lewis Tater), Andy Griffith (Howard Pike), Donald Pleasence (A.J. Nietz), Blythe Danner (Miss Trout), Alan Arkin (Kessler), Richard B. Shull (Stout Crook), Herb Edelman (Polo), Alex Rocco (Earl, Assistant Director), Frank Cady (Pa Tater), Anthony James (Lean Crook)

p, Tony Bill; d, Howard Zieff; w, Rob Thompson; ph, Mario Tosi (Metrocolor); ed, Edward Warschilka; m, Ken Lauber; art d, Robert Luthardt

An homage to the B westerns of the 1930s and 1940s that stars Bridges as an aspiring young pulp writer in the fashion of Zane Grey. He heads for Hollywood, first making a stop in Nevada where he discovers that his correspondence school is a crooked operation. He accidentally takes the swindled cash and retreats to the desert; he's then "rescued" by a film crew led by Arkin and joins the bunch as they head back to the studio, falling in love with Arkin's secretary, Danner, and becoming pals with elder stuntman Griffith. The crooks pursue but are stopped when Griffith, convincingly dressed as an oater star, outwits them with a prop gun.

A charming film that takes the conventions and simplicity of early western serials and treats them in a careful and artistic manner. HEARTS is also a fine film about filmmaking, but experienced box-office failure. In keeping with tradition, the old black-and-white Metro lion logo opens the film by delivering his famous three roars.

HEAT
1995 160m c   Crime/Drama   DVD
Forward Pass Productions/New Regency Productions   ★★★★
(U.S.)   R

Al Pacino (Vincent Hanna), Robert De Niro (Neil McCauley), Val Kilmer (Chris Shiherlis), Jon Voight (Nate), Tom Sizemore (Michael Cheritto), Diane Venora (Justine), Amy Brenneman (Eady), Ashley Judd (Charlene), Mykelti Williamson (Drucker), Wes Studi (Casals)

p, Art Linson; d, Michael Mann; w, Michael Mann; ph, Dante Spinotti; ed, Dov Hoenig, Pasquale Buba, William Goldenberg, Tom Rolf; m, Elliot Goldenthal; prod d, Neil Spisak; art d, Margie Stone McShirley; fx, Terry Frazee, Neil Krepela; cos, Deborah L. Scott

A preening, self-dramatizing cop (Al Pacino) pursues a tight-lipped criminal mastermind (Robert De Niro) around L.A. for three hours. It didn't sound like fun to us, either, but we were wrong; HEAT scores on many fronts.

The pairing of Pacino and De Niro (the first time they've shared a bill since THE GODFATHER, PART II in 1974) is HEAT's drawing card, but the real star of a Michael Mann film is always the visuals. HEAT has style to burn. Again working with the brilliant cinematographer Dante Spinotti, Mann turns the city itself into HEAT's major player. A shot of the cityscape at night quotes MY DARLING CLEMENTINE, but where John Ford viewed the open spaces of the Old West with optimism, Mann presents the urban wasteland as the realization of a cynical, soulless culture. Tellingly, he sets one of his violent set pieces in the void of an abandoned drive-in.

Throughout, style is backed up with real substance. The plot, though it seems to ramble, builds suspense with deft precision, and the action set pieces are triumphs. HEAT also gets us deeply involved in the messy lives of both cops and robbers, via some richly textured domestic scenes only occasionally sabotaged by psychobabble. The result is that we actually care about these characters, which just might make this an Important Movie. Why? It's one of a handful of films since THE GODFATHER to successfully portray a criminal fraternity from within and without at the same time. When a bad guy's loved one risks her future to ensure his freedom, we root for the both of them; but when an ex-con who's been making a valiant effort to go straight gets sucked into the "crew," we're crushed. What more can you ask?

HEATHERS
1989 102m c   Comedy/Fantasy   DVD
Cinemarque   (U.S.)   ★★★½
                                           R

Winona Ryder (Veronica Sawyer), Christian Slater (J.D.), Shannen Doherty (Heather Duke), Lisanne Falk (Heather McNamara), Kim Walker (Heather Chandler), Penelope Milford (Pauline Fleming), Glenn Shadix (Fr. Ripper), Lance Fenton (Kurt Kelly), Patrick Labyorteaux, billed as Patrick Laborteaux (Ram), Jeremy Applegate (Peter Dawson)

p, Denise Di Novi; d, Michael Lehmann; w, Daniel Waters; ph, Francis Kenny (Deluxe Color); ed, Norman Hollyn; m, David Newman; prod d, Jon Hutman; art d, Kara Lindstrom; cos, Rudy Dillon

The near-surreal world of high-school popularity is imaginatively probed in this black comedy revolving around teenage suicide. With scenes and dialogue sure to offend many, HEATHERS is, nevertheless, a film of startling originality and verve.

The eponymous Heathers (Shannen Doherty, Lisanne Falk, Kim Walker), the most exclusive clique at Westerburg High, routinely drop insufficiently cool friends and humiliate poor Martha "Dumptruck" Dunnstock (Carrie Lynn). Veronica (Winona Ryder), a relatively recent addition to their clique, demonstrates her independence by taking up with J.D. (Christian Slater), a motorcycle-riding misfit, becoming his mostly unwilling accomplice as he murders three of the school's most popular, albeit piggish, students, leaving behind heartrending suicide notes. But what begins as a lark for Veronica becomes a nightmare as she realizes that her mischievous fantasies are diabolical realities for the increasingly psychotic J.D.

HEATHERS might have been a moronic teen gross-out film were it not for the immediacy and careful observation of the surprisingly rich script by Daniel Walters, Michael Lehmann's clever direction, and the extraordinary performances of Ryder and, to a lesser extent, Slater (who does an appropriately creepy, raspy-voiced Jack Nicholson imitation). Dark, cynical, but deliciously funny, HEATHERS is a fascinating look not just at high school but at the way we look at high school.

HEAVEN CAN WAIT
DVD

1943 112m c   Comedy   ★★★½
Fox   (U.S.)

Gene Tierney *(Martha)*, Don Ameche *(Henry Van Cleve)*, Charles Coburn *(Hugo Van Cleve)*, Marjorie Main *(Mrs. Strabel)*, Laird Cregar *(His Excellency)*, Spring Byington *(Bertha Van Cleve)*, Allyn Joslyn *(Albert Van Cleve)*, Eugene Pallette *(Mr. Strabel)*, Signe Hasso *(Mademoiselle)*, Louis Calhern *(Randolph Van Cleve)*

p, Ernst Lubitsch; d, Ernst Lubitsch; w, Samson Raphaelson (based on the play *Birthdays* by Ladislaus Bus-Fekete); ph, Edward Cronjager (Technicolor); ed, Dorothy Spencer; m, Alfred Newman; art d, James Basevi, Leland Fuller; cos, Rene Hubert

AAN Best Picture; AAN Best Director: Ernst Lubitsch; *AAN Best Color Cinematography:* Edward Cronjager

Astute salute to a charming rake, deceptive satire disguised as a bubble. This movie has Ameche as an innocent Casanova, shown from infancy to his death at age 70. The film opens with a deceased Ameche standing before the Devil, Cregar, requesting his passport to Hell. Cregar studies his newest applicant and then reviews Ameche's carefree and often careless life. Based on the Hungarian play *Birthdays* by Ladislaus Bus-Fekete, with additional bromides from Samson Raphaelson. But Ameche is short on charm and too hapless for the role; he can't get any real chemistry cooking with Tierney. Still, it's compensated by a supporting cast of pros, and Lubitsch's deft direction. This was Lubitsch's first color film; the Basevi-Fuller Hell is a fabulous sight to see.

HEAVEN CAN WAIT
DVD

1978 101m c   Comedy/Fantasy   ★★½
Paramount   (U.S.)   PG

Warren Beatty *(Joe Pendleton)*, Julie Christie *(Betty Logan)*, James Mason *(Mr. Jordan)*, Dyan Cannon *(Julia Farnsworth)*, Charles Grodin *(Tony Abbott)*, Jack Warden *(Max Corkle)*, Buck Henry *(The Escort)*, Vincent Gardenia *(Lt. Krim)*, Joseph Maher *(Sisk)*, Hamilton Camp *(Bentley)*

p, Warren Beatty; d, Warren Beatty, Buck Henry; w, Warren Beatty, Elaine May (based on the play by Harry Segall); ph, William A. Fraker (Panavision, Movielab Color); m, Dave Grusin; prod d, Paul Sylbert; art d, Edwin O'Donovan; fx, Robert MacDonald; cos, Theadora Van Runkle, Richard Bruno

AAN Best Picture; AAN Best Actor: Warren Beatty; *AAN Best Supporting Actor:* Jack Warden; *AAN Best Supporting Actress:* Dyan Cannon; *AAN Best Director:* Warren Beatty, Buck Henry; *AAN Best Adapted Screenplay:* Elaine May, Warren Beatty; *AAN Best Cinematography:* William A. Fraker; *AAN Best Original Score:* Dave Grusin; *AA Best Art Direction:* Paul Sylbert, Edwin O'Donovan, George Gaines

Beatty's ballgame, an unecessary remake of HERE COMES MR. JORDAN—he produced, co-directed, co-wrote (with Elaine May) and starred as Joe Pendleton, a Los Angeles Rams quarterback who is prematurely ushered to heaven by a bumbling celestial messenger (co-director Henry) after an auto accident. An archangel, Mr. Jordan (Mason), tries to redress this error by restoring Joe to life in the body of a wealthy industrialist moments after he's murdered by his adulterous wife (Cannon) and the industrialist's nitwit secretary (Grodin). Determined to play in the Super Bowl, Beatty buys the Rams and hires his old coach (Warden) to help him train, convincing Warden that Beatty has been reincarnated. Beatty also meets and falls in love with Christie, an English environmental activist, but just when it looks as though everything is going to work out, Cannon and Grodin try again.

The title comes from the Harry Segall play, upon which the 1941 JORDAN was based. There are a few laughs from Grodin and Cannon, but Beatty and Christie are like 400-pound gorillas chasing a milkweed seed. The more Beatty concentrates, the more glazed and distracted he looks. The film won an Oscar for Art Direction—presumably for Beatty's expensive bathrobes, Cannon's mane and the clipped hedges and boxwoods of a California estate.

HEAVENLY CREATURES
DVD

1994 98m c   Drama   ★★★★
Wingnut Films/Fontana Film Productions   R
(New Zealand)

Melanie Lynskey *(Pauline Parker)*, Kate Winslet *(Juliet Hulme)*, Sarah Peirse *(Honora Parker)*, Diana Kent *(Hilda Hulme)*, Clive Merrison *(Henry Hulme)*, Simon O'Connor *(Herbert Rieper)*, Jed Brophy *(John/Nicholas)*, Peter Elliot *(Bill Perry)*, Gilbert Goldie *(Dr. Bennett)*, Geoffrey Heath *(Reverend Norris)*

p, Jim Booth; d, Peter Jackson; w, Peter Jackson, Frances Walsh; ph, Alun Bollinger; ed, Jamie Selkirk; m, Peter Dasent; prod d, Grant Major; art d, Jill Cormack; fx, Richard Taylor; cos, Ngila Dickson

AAN Best Original Screenplay: Frances Walsh, Peter Jackson

A disturbing, boldly conceived story of two teenaged New Zealand girls whose obsessive friendship leads to murder, HEAVENLY CREATURES is equal parts psychodrama and dark fairy tale. Its flamboyant style evokes the fantasy world in which the girls lose themselves, and its breathless, childishly hyperbolic voice-over narration perfectly captures the dangerous passions of insular youth.

Pauline Parker (Melanie Lynskey) is plump, smart, plain, and painfully insecure; Juliet Hulme (Kate Winslet) is a dream walking, sleekly blonde and sophisticated beyond her years. To everyone's surprise, the two girls become friends, united by their feverish imaginations. Together, Juliet and Pauline spin a candy-colored imaginary universe of tremendous depth and complexity, pieced together from movies, novels, fairy tales, and their own lurid and strangely naive imaginings. When their parents sense that the relationship is unnaturally close, they attempt to separate the girls, with results that prove deadly.

Based on an actual murder committed in 1954, HEAVENLY CREATURES is the story of a *folie a deux*, a relationship born in innocuous mutual interests (movies, celebrities, popular music) that blossoms into a lethally insular us-against-them (adults, society, the world) alliance. But HEAVENLY CREATURES breaks the pattern of films as diverse as Alfred Hitchcock's ROPE, Arthur Penn's BONNIE AND CLYDE, and even Tom Kalin's SWOON, by taking rebellious, hormonally raging boys out of the equation. Pauline and Juliet are quintessential adolescent girls; their longings are precise, if wildly fanciful—not inchoate yearnings to be free and seek excitement. Their fantasies are rooted less in restlessness and the desire to make a mark on the world, than the need to find all-enveloping romance and a place to hide.

HEAVENLY CREATURES excited extensive press coverage when it was revealed that in real life, Juliet Hulme had changed her name to Anne Perry and made a successful career as a mystery writer. Perry refused to see the film, but insisted that it distorted her relationship with Pauline, and was particularly disturbed that the filmmakers strongly suggested a lesbian relationship between the girls.

HEAVEN'S GATE
1980   217m   c/bw Western
Partisan Productions   (U.S.)

DVD
★★½
R

Kris Kristofferson *(Marshal James Averill)*, Christopher Walken *(Nathan D. Champion)*, John Hurt *(Billy Irvine)*, Isabelle Huppert *(Ella Watson)*, Sam Waterston *(Frank Canton)*, Jeff Bridges *(John H. Bridges)*, Joseph Cotten *("The Reverend Doctor")*, Roseanne Vela *(Beautiful Girl)*, Ronnie Hawkins *(Wolcott)*, Geoffrey Lewis *(Trapper)*

p, Joann Carelli; d, Michael Cimino; w, Michael Cimino; ph, Vilmos Zsigmond (Technicolor); ed, Tom Rolf, William Reynolds, Lisa Fruchtman, Gerald Greenberg; m, David Mansfield; art d, Tambi Larsen, Spencer Deverill, Maurice Fowler; fx, Paul Stewart, Ken Pepiot, Stan Parks, Sam Price, Jim Camomile, Kevin Quibell; chor, Eleanor Fazan; cos, J. Allen Highfill

AAN Best Art Direction: Tambi Larsen (Art Direction), Jim Berkey (Set Decoration)

This beautiful but notoriously disappointing film is one of the most overblown epic Westerns of any decade. The story allegedly relates the events of the bloody 1892 Johnson County wars in Wyoming, pitting cattlemen against immigrant settlers. James Averill (Kris Kristofferson) becomes marshal and must hold the county's combatants in check. Nathan D. Champion (Christopher Walken) is a gunfighter hired by the ranchers. Both men share the sexual favors of prostitute Ella "Cattle Kate" Watson (Isabelle Huppert). Through various slice-of-life episodes without a unifying thread, writer-director Michael Cimino tries to depict the lifestyles of the ranchers and the settlers, and the differences that lead to all-out war between the factions.

Kristofferson is wooden, Walken far too remote, and no one else in the cast stands out. Cimino's financial excesses included having trains completely rebuilt, providing infinitely detailed costumes for extras, and planting miles of sod on a battle field that would be blown up. The film's final cost was estimated to be $35 million, though some reports went as high as $50 million. Cimino's sins might have been forgiven in Hollywood had the film made a positive statement; but it derides the American Dream as a history of moral compromise—this in lieu of a story—and the American press took off after it in droves; the public's reaction to the truncated version released was to reject it instantly. The director's cut, available on cassette, is regarded as a masterpiece in Europe where Cimino's star shines brighter.

HEDWIG AND THE ANGRY INCH
2001   91m   c   Musical/Comedy/Drama
Killer Films/New Line   (U.S.)

DVD
★★★★
R

John Cameron Mitchell *(Hedwig)*, Michael Pitt *(Tommy Gnosis)*, Miriam Shor *(Yitzhak)*, Stephen Trask *(Skszp)*, Theodore Liscinski *(Jacek)*, Rob Campbell *(Krzysztof)*, Michael Aronov *(Schlatko)*, Andrea Martin *(Phyllis Stein)*, Ben Mayer-Goodman *(Hansel—Six Years Old)*, Alberta Watson *(Hansel's Mom)*

p, Pamela Koffler, Katie Roumel, Christine Vachon; d, John Cameron Mitchell; w, John Cameron Mitchell (adapted from a work for the stage by John Cameron Mitchell); ph, Frank G. DeMarco; ed, Andrew Marcus; m, Stephen Trask; prod d, Therese DePrez; art d, Nancy Pankiw; fx, Tim Good; chor, Jerry Mitchell; cos, Arianne Phillips

John Cameron Mitchell's glorious adaptation of his acclaimed Off-Broadway show might be a first: a rock musical that actually rocks. It not only works as a musical; it also features some of the best rock songs ever written for the theatrical stage.

Hedwig (Mitchell) is an East German-born transsexual rocker who, along with her band, the Angry Inch, has been reduced to playing a chain of family restaurants, scaring hungry diners who've only come for the salad bar. Hitting the stage like some ungodly cross between Farrah Fawcett and Wendy O. Williams, in a paint-job usually found on the fender of '65 Mustang, Hedwig peppers her Bowie-inspired psycho-circus with tart one-liners and the heartbreaking story of her life. Raised a boy to a German mother and American military father, Hedwig—nee "Hansel"—wanted nothing more than to go west, and was eventually swept off his teenaged feet by an American GI (Maurice Dean Wint). Hansel says "yes" to a marriage proposal, changes his name to Hedwig and bravely undergoes gender reassignment surgery; when the operation is horribly botched, Hedwig is left with little more than an angry inch where his manhood used to be. After a few years of marriage American style, Hedwig finds herself left alone in a Kansas trailer park. Doing the only thing a poor girl can do, Hedwig puts down the bottle and forms a rock-and-roll band.

Aided by bits of Emily Hubley's charming animation, Mitchell opens up the play for the screen fabulously, transforming what were essentially stage monologues into candy-colored, fairy-tale fragments that pack an unexpected emotional punch. Catch it on a Saturday night, and make sure the volume is turned all the way up.

HEIMAT
1984   924m   c/bw Drama
Reitz/WDR/SFB   (West Germany)

★★★½

Marita Breuer *(Maria)*, Willi Burger, Gertrud Bredel, Rudiger Weigang, Karin Rasenack, Dieter Schaad, Michael Lesch, Peter Harting, Jorg Richter, Johannes Lobewein

p, Edgar Reitz, Joachim von Mengershausen, Hans Kwiet; d, Edgar Reitz; w, Edgar Reitz, Peter Steinbach; ph, Gernot Roll; ed, Heidi Handorf; m, Nikos Mamangakis; art d, Franz Bauer

Though HEIMAT runs an imposing 15-and-a-half hours, this epic work, chronicling life in a German village from 1919 to 1982, rarely fails to capture the viewer within its immense visionary scope. The events of the period—Germany's post-WWI depression, the rise of Nazism, WWII, and postwar recovery—are seen not through the eyes of Germany's leaders, politicians, and artists, but through the eyes of the common people in the fictional village of Schabbach. At the center of the events is Breuer, who gives a remarkable performance. Using makeup, costumes and her gifted acting talents, Breuer gives HEIMAT a heartfelt anchor, playing her character from childhood to old age.

Director Edgar Reitz's film, which is usually shown in four successive screenings, is both in color and black and white. The black-and-white sequences go from the 1920s to the early 1950s, with color encompassing the rest of the film, though at times Reitz intercuts the two processes to give emphasis within a scene. Reitz's original plan was to rediscover his own background, so he began writing down the stories of his family and the people from his rural village. He had planned to turn this story into an epic novel, but at the urging of television producer Joachim von Mengershausen, Reitz decided to put this project before the cameras. After writing a 2,000-page script with Peter Steinbach, Reitz shot a documentary dealing with a similar subject.

Production on HEIMAT finally began in 1981, but Reitz was forced to put everything on hold after four months because funding ran out. Though he started again two months later, the shooting was halted for financial reasons a second time. Reitz finally completed the lensing in late 1982, then took 18 months to edit the enormous amount of footage he had created. All told, HEIMAT took five years and four months to create from conception to final cut.

HEIRESS, THE
1949 115m bw Drama ★★★★★
Paramount (U.S.)

Olivia de Havilland (*Catherine Sloper*), Montgomery Clift (*Morris Townsend*), Ralph Richardson (*Dr. Austin Sloper*), Miriam Hopkins (*Lavinia Penniman*), Vanessa Brown (*Maria*), Mona Freeman (*Marian Almond*), Ray Collins (*Jefferson Almond*), Betty Linley (*Mrs. Montgomery*), Selena Royle (*Elizabeth Almond*), Paul Lees (*Arthur Townsend*)

p, William Wyler; d, William Wyler; w, Ruth Goetz, Augustus Goetz (based on their play and the novel *Washington Square* by Henry James); ph, Leo Tover; ed, William Hornbeck; m, Aaron Copland; art d, John Meehan, Harry Horner; fx, Gordon Jennings; cos, Edith Head, Gile Steele

AAN Best Picture; AA Best Actress: Olivia de Havilland; *AAN Best Supporting Actor:* Ralph Richardson; *AAN Best Director:* William Wyler; *AAN Best B/W Cinematography:* Leo Tover; *AA Best Score (Drama or Comedy):* Aaron Copland; *AA Best Art Direction-Set Decoration (B/W):* John Meehan, Harry Horner, Emile Kuri; *AA Best Costume Design (B/W):* Edith Head, Gile Steele

This powerful and compelling drama, based on Henry James's 1881 novel *Washington Square* and the successful Broadway play by Ruth and Augustus Goetz, owes its triumph to the deft hand of director William Wyler and a remarkable lead performance by Olivia de Havilland.

Set circa 1850, the film casts de Havilland as the plain-looking daughter of wealthy, widowed doctor Richardson, with whom she lives at their home at 16 Washington Square. Life is uneventful. Richardson is a tyrant at home, dictating his daughter's every move and cruelly telling her that she bears no resemblance to his dear departed wife, who was beautiful and charming. Suitors shun de Havilland—who is awkward in her movements, conversation, and manners—until she receives some unexpected attention from Clift at a ball. He flatters her and asks to call on her, news that is derisively greeted by Richardson, who tells de Havilland that Clift must be a fortune hunter, and will break her heart.

This was one of de Havilland's greatest roles; Wyler finally breaks her of her habit of sweet smiles (she'd later revert) and her transformation from docile emotional victim to rational, resolved adult is a masterpiece of acting. Ralph Richardson is equally good, injecting a majestic presence into his portrait of a hateful man who is really so fearful for his daughter's future that he will incur her permanent loathing to protect that future. Miriam Hopkins is fine, too, as the one eternally bright spot in de Havilland's life, but Clift is surprisingly weak.

Wyler worked hard to produce this masterpiece. He had requested Gregg Toland (with whom he had collaborated memorably on films like WUTHERING HEIGHTS, THE BEST YEARS OF OUR LIVES and THE LITTLE FOXES) for his cinematographer, and instead got Leo Tover. When Wyler asked for a setup calling for deep focus, Tover took half a day to make preparations, where Toland would have achieved the setup in an hour. The director did score a coup, however, when he secured Aaron Copeland's services as the film's composer. Copeland had written memorable music for such films as OF MICE AND MEN, OUR TOWN and NORTH STAR but had gained a "Red" taint as a result of his involvement in the last and, in the suspicious climate of 1949, Wyler had to argue heavily with Paramount executives to retain Copeland who came through with a haunting, telling score.

HELLO, DOLLY! 📀
1969 129m c Musical/Comedy ★★★
Chenault (U.S.) G

Barbra Streisand (*Dolly Levi*), Walter Matthau (*Horace Vandergelder*), Michael Crawford (*Cornelius Hackl*), Louis Armstrong (*Orchestra Leader*), Marianne McAndrew (*Irene Molloy*), E.J. Peaker (*Minnie Fay*), Danny Lockin (*Barnaby Tucker*), Joyce Ames (*Ermengarde*), Tommy Tune (*Ambrose Kemper*), Judy Knaiz (*Gussie Granger*)

p, Ernest Lehman; d, Gene Kelly; w, Ernest Lehman (based on the play *The Matchmaker* by Thornton Wilder); ph, Harry Stradling (Todd-AO, DeLuxe Color); ed, William Reynolds; m, Jerry Herman, Lennie Hayton, Lionel Newman; prod d, John De Cuir; art d, Jack Martin Smith, Herman A. Blumenthal; fx, L.B. Abbott, Art Cruickshank, Emil Kosa Jr.; chor, Michael Kidd; cos, Irene Sharaff

AAN Best Picture; AAN Best Cinematography: Harry Stradling; *AAN Best Film Editing:* William Reynolds; *AA Best Score (Musical):* Lennie Hayton, Lionel Newman; *AA Best Art Direction-Set Decoration:* John DeCuir, Jack Martin Smith, Herman Blumenthal, Walter M. Scott, George James Hopkins, Raphael Bretton; *AAN Best Costume Design:* Irene Sharaff; *AA Best Sound:* Jack Solomon, Murray Spivack

Here's the film that, joined by DOCTOR DOLITTLE and STAR!, sounded the death knell for the film musical, a stroke it still hasn't recovered from. It's also the film where Streisand allegedly slapped Matthau, and he slapped her back. But she had no problem bullying director Kelly: it's an exercise in star turns, surrounded by elephantine blandness. The supporting cast look, and act, like refugees from Disney or Oral Roberts University, handpicked not to ruffle the star. Whatever terrific future lay ahead for Tune and Crawford, you've no inkling of it from all the too cute mugging here. Not only is Streisand far too young (and it makes one weep to think of all the marvelous ladies who should have been considered), but her Dolly Levi arouses no affection. Without the dose of healthy sentiment the character arouses to balance her machinations, she's just a nasty bitch on the make. Furthermore, this exposes how pallid Thornton Wilder's *The Matchmaker* (the play on which the musical is based) really is. There are two good songs in Jerry Herman's score: "Before the Parade Passes By" and the title tune, here an exercise in star wrestling between Streisand and the irrepressible Louis Armstrong, who connect not one whit.

HELLBOY 📀
2004 120m c Fantasy/Action/Horror ★★½
Revolution Studios/Dark Horse PG-13
Entertainment/Lawrence Gordon Productions
(U.S.)

Ron Perlman (*Hellboy*), John Hurt (*Professor Trevor "Broom" Bruttenholm*), Selma Blair (*Liz Sherman*), Rupert Evans (*John Myers*), Karel Roden (*Grigori Rasputin*), Jeffrey Tambor (*Dr. Tom Manning*), Ladislav Beran (*Kroenen*), Bridget Hodson (*Ilsa*), Kevin Trainor (*Young Broom*), Doug Jones (*Abraham Sapien*)

p, Lawrence Gordon, Lloyd Levin, Mike Richardson; d, Guillermo del Toro; w, Guillermo del Toro (from a screen story by Guillermo del Toro and Peter Briggs, based on the Dark Horse comic books by Mike Mignola); ph, Guillermo Navarro; ed, Peter Amundson;

m, Marco Beltrami; prod d, Stephen Scott; art d, Peter Francis, James Hambidge, Marco Bittner Rosser; fx, Nick Adler, Kevin Baillie (CG), Edward Irastorza, Johnathan Rothbart; cos, Wendy Partridge

Humanity's last best hope against the monsters and mystical malefactors is a muscle-bound, cigar-chomping, cat-loving demon with Oedipal issues and the unlikely name Hellboy (Ron Perlman).

On a dark and stormy night in 1944, British occultist Professor Trevor "Broom" Bruttenholm (Kevin Trainor) disrupts a ceremony led by undead Russian mystic Rasputin (Karel Roden), she-wolf Ilsa (Bridget Hodson), and zombie assassin Kroenen (Ladislav Beran) that's designed to open an interdimensional portal. The doorway is closed, but not before a little cherry-red demon with an oversized stone arm slips through; he's dubbed "Hellboy," and Broom raises him like a son. In the present day, young FBI agent John Myers (Rupert Evans) reports for work at the top-secret Bureau for Paranormal Research and Defense, run by the aging Bruttenholm (John Hurt) and manned by the now grown Hellboy, psychic merman Abe Sapien (Doug Jones, voiced by an uncredited David Hyde Pierce), and a flock of human agents. Another of Broom's talented freaks, fire-starter Liz Sherman (Selma Blair), recently committed herself to a mental facility, devastating the besotted Hellboy and leaving him in no mood for a new minder—the post Myers has been handed. Summoned to investigate a break-in at the Machen Library, Hellboy quickly traces the lingering vibe to a writhing bit of self-replicating grotesquerie summoned up by Rasputin, Ilsa, and Kroenen, who are back to finish what they started 60 years earlier.

Guillermo del Toro's adaptation of the first story cycle in graphic novelist Mike Mignola's *Hellboy* series is gloomily gorgeous, but its tone careens recklessly between light comedy and dark portentousness, and the character interactions suffer. Arguing that you shouldn't expect rich characterization from a comic-book movie misses the point. Vivid relationships are what separate graphic novels from the funnies, and in the end, spectacular set design is just window dressing.

HELLRAISER *DVD*
1987 90m c Horror ★★½
Cinemarque/Film Futures/New World (U.K.) R

Andrew Robinson *(Larry Cotton)*, Clare Higgins *(Julia Cotton)*, Ashley Laurence *(Kirsty Swanson)*, Sean Chapman *(Frank Cotton)*, Oliver Smith *(Frank the Monster)*, Robert Hines *(Steve)*, Leon Davis *(2nd Victim)*, Mike Cassidy *(3rd Victim)*, Frank Baker *(Derelict)*, Kenneth Nelson *(Bill)*

p, Christopher Figg; d, Clive Barker; w, Clive Barker (based on his novella "The Hellbound Heart"); ph, Robin Vidgeon (Technicolor); ed, Richard Marden; m, Christopher Young; prod d, Mike Buchanan; art d, Jocelyn James; fx, Bob Keen; cos, Joanna Johnston

Somewhat disappointing directorial debut of the man called the "future of horror fiction" by Stephen King, Clive Barker, based on his own novella *The Hell-Bound Heart*.

Frank (Sean Chapman), a sexual adventurer in search of new carnal pleasures, purchases a mysterious Chinese puzzle box while visiting an unnamed Third World country. Back home in England, he opens the box only to discover that he has unlocked the door to hell. Frank is pulled into another dimension, whose inhabitants, known as Cenobites, push him over the fine line between pleasure and pain by ripping him apart with tiny fish hooks. Years later, Frank's brother, Larry (Andrew Robinson), moves his family into the house—to which, through some blood spilled on the attic floor, Frank returns in near-skeletal form. With the help of sister-in-law Julia (Clare Higgins)—with whom he once

had an affair—Frank begins sucking the life out of bodies in order to regenerate to his old form. Meanwhile, Larry's daughter from a previous marriage, Kirsty (Ashley Laurence), begins to suspect her hated stepmother of having an affair, and to her horror becomes involved with Frank, the puzzle box and the Cenobites.

Undoubtedly head and shoulders above average horror fare thematically, HELLRAISER is, however, extremely graphic, badly paced, and, with few exceptions, poorly acted. As a director, Barker does possess a striking visual sensibility; the film literally drips with horrific ambience. However, while the author's cinematic sense is a pleasant surprise, his narrative is shockingly haphazard, and the film lurches from one set piece to the next with little dramatic rhythm. While Barker does a respectable job of developing the characters of Julia and Frank and the lustful ties that bind them, the writer-director is clearly less interested in victims Larry and Kirsty. The film never gets a handle on these characters and never provides enough characterization so that the viewer cares about their fate.

HELL'S ANGELS *DVD*
1930 135m c/bw War ★★★½
Caddo (U.S.)

Ben Lyon *(Monte Rutledge)*, James Hall *(Roy Rutledge)*, Jean Harlow *(Helen)*, John Darrow *(Karl Arnstedt)*, Lucien Prival *(Baron von Kranz)*, Frank Clark *(Lt. von Bruen)*, Roy Wilson *(Baldy)*, Douglas Gilmore *(Capt. Redfield)*, Jane Winton *(Baroness von Kranz)*, Evelyn Hall *(Lady Randolph)*

p, Howard Hughes; d, Howard Hughes, James Whale, Marshall Neilan, Luther Reed; w, Harry Behn, Howard Estabrook, Joseph Moncure March (based on a story by Marshall Neilan, Joseph Moncure March); ph, Tony Gaudio, Paul Perry, E. Burton Steene, Elmer Dyer, Harry Zeck, Dewey Wrigley (color scenes in Technicolor); ed, Douglas Biggs, Perry Hollingsworth, Frank Lawrence; m, Hugo Riesenfeld; art d, Julian Boone Fleming, Carroll Clark

AAN Best Cinematography: Gaetano Gaudio, Harry Perry

And hell's memorable belle, here and there among the aerial sequences. The film looks dated and the story seems to have been written in crayon by Hughes; it's a testimony to his two great loves—wings and breasts, about good brother and bad brother, and the blonde who comes between them. Beside Hughes, it was directed by Marshall Neilan, Luther Reed, and sometimes James Whale (credited as dialogue director, but he also wrote much of the script). There is a bang-up aerial dogfight and a solid zeppelin sequence; many believe these moments have never been surpassed. Hughes worked them out on blackboards and with model planes before he shot. When the zeppelin moves through the clouds and we see London below, we feel *inside* the camera.

The plot was corn in 1930—it feels very much like a silent picture—and eighteen-year-old Harlow hasn't the foggiest notion what she's supposed to do. Her take on the British Helen is undeniably piggy, but clad in a velvet evening gown with beaded straps, she's like no one the camera had ever photographed when she turns her bare back to us. And audiences stopped laughing when she inquired, "Would you be shocked if I put on something more comfortable?"

Launched in 1927 as the first major effort of Hughes's Caddo Productions, the ANGELS was so long in the making that sound came into being, and much of the film, which had been shot as a silent, had to be redone. Both Lyon and Hall had good "sound" voices, but the female lead, Greta Nissen, had a pronounced Norwegian accent, and, though Hughes had paid her handsomely, he scrapped her performance completely and began searching for a new actress who could handle the role's vocal chores. Among the candidates was Harlow, then an 18-year-old, blue-eyed platinum blonde with a voluptuous shape. Although Hughes was unimpressed with her screen test, Harlow's agent, Arthur Landau, talked the millionaire playboy into letting his client play the part. Her debut caused Hughes endless arguments with the censors. After the film, Hughes inexplicably ignored the new star he had created, though he had the presence of mind to put her under permanent contract. Nevertheless, he sold her contract for a mere $60,000 to MGM, for whom she would make millions as the reigning sex queen of the cinema until her death in 1937.

The film's staggering $3.8 million budget made HELL'S ANGELS the cinema's most expensive film to date, and Hughes, determined to get his money back, employed the kind of hoopla for which he later became notorious, arranging for a squadron of planes to buzz Grauman's Chinese Theater at the film's premiere while parachutists descended on Hollywood Boulevard. Trying to orchestrate a similarly flashy stunt in New York, Hughes offered the owners of the dirigible *Graf Zeppelin* $100,000 to sail over Broadway and 42nd Street, where *two* theaters were premiering the film, but the owners refused. Despite his best efforts, Hughes took a bath on the film, losing more than $1.5 million, although, at first, he claimed to have made $2 million. It is said that he later admitted that the film would have been better and cost less had he allowed someone else to direct it.

HELLZAPOPPIN'
1941 84m   bw   Comedy   ★★★
Universal   (U.S.)

Ole Olsen *(Ole)*, Chic Johnson *(Chic)*, Robert Paige *(Jeff Hunter)*, Jane Frazee *(Kitty Rand)*, Lewis Howard *(Woody Tyler)*, Martha Raye *(Betty Johnson)*, Clarence Kolb *(Mr. Rand)*, Nella Walker *(Mrs. Rand)*, Mischa Auer *(Pepi)*, Richard Lane *(Director)*

p, Jules Levy; d, H.C. Potter; w, Nat Perrin, Warren Wilson (based on the play by Nat Perrin); ph, Elwood Bredell; ed, Milton Carruth; fx, John P. Fulton; chor, Nick Castle, Eddie Prinz; cos, Vera West

AAN Best Song: "Pig Foot Pete"; Gene de Paul (Music), Don Raye (Lyrics)

Crazy as hell, at 100 miles an hour, loaded with sight gags that sometimes work and sometimes fall as flat as a burned pancake; but the feeling is surprisingly contemporary. The story begins in Purgatory, with Olsen and Johnson jumping in and out of a story that's barely there, basically a little romance tale of poor boy meets rich girl and wins her heart after putting on the traditional show. O. and J. constantly argue with the film's director and cameraman on camera about the restraints put upon them while mindless mayhem ensues—someone constantly yelling "Jones!" for no good reason; Auer, a rich count, chasing Martha Raye about madly, and vice versa. At one point a film director, Lane, tells the madcaps Olson and Johnson: "This is Hollywood; we change everything here. We've *got* to!" If it's not as immortal as the Marx Brothers' best work, it's definitely admirable in its cutting edge risk.

HELP!
1965 92m   c   Musical/Comedy   📀
Walter Shenson/Subafilms   (U.K.)   ★★★½
                                            G

John Lennon *(John)*, Paul McCartney *(Paul)*, Ringo Starr *(Ringo)*, George Harrison *(George)*, Leo McKern *(Clang)*, Eleanor Bron *(Ahme)*, Victor Spinetti *(Foot)*, Roy Kinnear *(Algernon)*, John Bluthal *(Bhuta)*, Patrick Cargill *(Superintendent)*

p, Walter Shenson; d, Richard Lester; w, Marc Behm, Charles Wood (based on an original story by Behm); ph, David Watkin (Eastmancolor); ed, John Victor Smith; m, Ken Thorne; art d, Ray Simm; fx, Cliff Richardson, Roy Whybrow; cos, Julie Harris, Dinah Greet, Arthur Newman

Shot on location in the Bahamas, Austria, and on Salisbury Plain, HELP!, the second Beatles film, is nonsensical fun.

Filled as it is with wonderful music and enlivened by the Fab Four's engaging screen presence, the story revolves around the crazed efforts of a pair of Eastern religious zealots, Clang (Leo McKern) and Ahme (the ravishing, underrated Eleanor Bron), to get hold of a sacred ring that has been given to Ringo by a fan and which he can't get off his finger. Foot (Victor Spinetti), the scientist Ringo approaches for help, comes to believe that the ring will allow him to control the world, and he and his assistant (Roy Kinnear) join the scramble to wrest the ring from Ringo. Antics aplenty ensue as Ringo and the other Beatles lead their pursuers on a madcap, globe-trotting chase.

Silly at its worst and brilliant at its best, HELP! picks up where the joyous insouciance of A HARD DAY'S NIGHT—director Richard Lester's first collaboration with the Fab Four—left off. McKern, Bron, Kinnear and Spinetti display fine comedic timing, and the Beatles make a reasonable stab at being a modern-day version of the Marx Brothers.

HENRY & JUNE
1990 136m   c   Drama/Erotic   📀
Walrus & Associates   (U.S.)   ★★½
                                           NC-17

Fred Ward *(Henry Miller)*, Uma Thurman *(June Miller)*, Maria de Medeiros *(Anaïs Nin)*, Richard E. Grant *(Hugo)*, Kevin Spacey *(Osborn)*, Jean-Philippe Ecoffey *(Eduardo)*, Bruce Myers *(Jack)*, Jean-Louis Bunuel *(Editor-Publisher)*, Feodor Atkine *(Spanish Dance Instructor)*, Sylvie Huguel *(Emilia)*

p, Peter Kaufman; d, Philip Kaufman; w, Philip Kaufman, Rose Kaufman (based on the diaries of Anaïs Nin); ph, Philippe Rousselot (Deluxe Color); ed, Vivien Hillgrove, William S. Scharf, Dede Allen; prod d, Guy-Claude Francois; art d, Georges Glon; chor, Nathalie Erlbaum; cos, Yvonne Sassinot de Nesle

AAN Best Cinematography: Philippe Rousselot

A second excursion into literary erotica from Philip Kaufman (THE UNBEARABLE LIGHTNESS OF BEING), this is notable as the first film to be released with the MPAA's NC-17 rating, created in 1990 to distinguish steamy-but-serious movies from hardcore porn. The film isn't nearly sexy enough to merit the new rating or the ensuing controversy.

Novelist Henry Miller (Fred Ward) has been sent to France by his wife, June (Uma Thurman), a former taxi dancer who has been supporting his career on her earnings as another man's mistress. The purpose of the trip is twofold: to get Henry away from distractions in New York so he can finish the novel, and to allow June, a bisexual, more freedom to frolic with a new girlfriend. The film actually opens not with Henry or June, but with Miller's lover, lifelong friend, and literary advocate Anaïs Nin (Maria de Medeiros), upon whose diaries the screenplay is based. Legendary *poseur* Anaïs is hot to trot; when a college professor stiffly kisses and fondles her during a meeting, she transforms the mild indiscretion into a full-blown seduction in her diary, which she hides from bland, likable middle-class husband Hugo (Richard E. Grant). Anaïs generally chafes at her mundane existence and yearns for a more bohemian social life and, especially, for a big, swarthy lover. Enter big and swarthy Henry, brought to Anaïs's house by her husband, who is friends with Henry's eccentric roommate (Kevin Spacey). Initially, Anaïs and Henry are tentative friends, providing each other with support for their respective writing projects. And though Anaïs has polite erotic palpitations when she is around the earthy but cultured Henry, it is June, briefly in Paris to check up on Henry, who brings Anaïs's passions to a furious boil.

The couplings in HENRY AND JUNE are as explicit as any to be found in mainstream American cinema; still, the sex here seems mild compared to the erotic imaginings of Almodovar, Bertolucci, Imamura, Oshima, and many others.

Kaufman tries to project a kind of professorial sobriety, hoping his film will seem classy and serious instead of raunchy. We think it could've used *more* raunch, and we're sure Henry Miller (whose favorite film was L'AGE D'OR) would have agreed.

HENRY FOOL
DVD
1998 141m c   Comedy/Drama   ★★½
True Fiction Pictures/Shooting Gallery/Henry Films   R
(U.S.)

Thomas Jay Ryan *(Henry Fool)*, James Urbaniak *(Simon Grim)*, Parker Posey *(Fay)*, Kevin Corrigan *(Warren)*, Miho Nikaido *(Gnoc Deng)*, Maria Porter *(Mary)*, Chuck Montgomery *(Angus James)*, Nicholas Hope *(Father Hawkes)*, James Saito *(Mr. Deng)*, Liam Aiken *(Ned)*

p, Hal Hartley; d, Hal Hartley; w, Hal Hartley; ph, Michael Spiller; ed, Steve Hamilton; m, Hal Hartley, Jim Coleman, Ryful, Bill Dobrow, Lydia Kavanagh, Hub Moore; prod d, Steve Rosenzweig; cos, Jocelyn Joson

Writer-director Hal Hartley returns to familiar territory with this tale of suburban oddballs. Whether or not this is a good thing probably depends on your feeling about this highly idiosyncratic auteur, and at two and a half hours, the film leaves plenty of time to ponder.

Misanthropic, self-styled "artist in exile" Henry Fool (Thomas Jay Ryan) appears one afternoon, suitcase in hand, at the home of rubbish collector Simon Grim (James Urbaniak). Bespectacled Simon, such a tight-lipped introvert that for years he was thought to be mentally retarded, lives with his depressed mother (Maria Porter) and nymphomaniac sister (Parker Posey), and Henry quickly takes up residence in the Grim basement. Henry claims he's hard at work on a book so significant that it will blow a hole right through the cosmos, but won't allow anyone to read the magnum opus in progress; instead, he encourages Simon to pick up a pen. In a single night Simon pours his soul into an epic poem with the power to magically touch anyone who reads it with an open heart. Simon becomes a controversial, grass-roots literary sensation while Henry languishes in obscurity, drinking and seducing the rest of the Grim household.

Ordinarily restrained and exceedingly cerebral, Hartley holds back little in this heady meditation on integrity, inspiration, and the nature of genius; witness the scene in which a marriage proposal is made from a toilet during a noisy bout of diarrhea. And yet it's in constant danger of floating off into the ether of abstraction: it's clear from the outset that Hartley isn't so much dealing with characters as archetypes pinned to fortune's wobbly wheel. That kind of intellectual challenge can easily backfire, and often does. But Ryan has a wonderful way with Hartley's often difficult dialogue, and is engaging even when the rest of the film isn't.

HENRY: PORTRAIT OF A SERIAL KILLER
DVD
1989 83m c   Crime/Horror   ★★★★
Maljack   (U.S.)

Michael Rooker *(Henry)*, Tom Towles *(Otis)*, Tracy Arnold *(Becky)*, Ray Atherton *(Fence)*, David Katz *(Henry's Boss)*, Eric Young *(Parole Officer)*, Mary Demas *(Hooker #1/Dead Prostitute/Dead Woman)*, Kristin Finger *(Hooker #2)*, Anne Bartoletti *(Waitress)*, Erzsebet Sziky *(Hitchiker)*

p, Lisa Dedmond, Steven A. Jones, John McNaughton; d, John McNaughton; w, Richard Fire, John McNaughton; ph, Charlie Lieberman; ed, Elena Maganini; m, Robert McNaughton, Ken Hale, Steven A. Jones; art d, Rick Paul; cos, Patricia Hart

HENRY: PORTRAIT OF A SERIAL KILLER surely ranks as one of the most frightening and disturbing films ever made. An angry and raw independent feature, HENRY begins with a creepy montage of shots of dead bodies. The corpses are the victims of Henry (Michael Rooker), a lowlife drifter who looks for victims while driving around in his green Impala. Rooker murders with knives, guns, rope, even his hands—he has no preferred method or pattern.

Rooker lives with Towles, a degenerate he met while in prison (for killing his mother) who now works in a gas station and sells drugs on the side. When Towles's sister (Arnold) comes to Chicago, she stays with Towles and Rooker while she looks for a job; meanwhile, Rooker, who works as a bug sprayer, and Towles continue to murder people at random, videotaping every detail, until they start to get on each other's nerves. When Rooker can no longer stand Towles's stupidity and sloppiness, the two argue; meanwhile, Arnold quits her job in a hair salon and asks Rooker to move away with her.

A stunning feature debut from director John McNaughton, HENRY tells its horrible story with chilling straightforwardness. Presenting his sick characters nonjudgmentally and without shrinking from gory details, McNaughton creates a world in which there is no good to counterbalance evil, where incest and rape are permitted and murder is an acceptable way to relieve tension. Providing no "good" characters to identify with—not even a cop to offer us hope—and ending on a bitter, ugly note, HENRY leaves viewers emotionally drained and deeply, deeply disturbed. McNaughton succeeds in showing just how vulnerable anyone can be to someone like Henry, a frightening reality few will want to contemplate.

No film in recent memory has tapped into primal, visceral fear as HENRY does, with its vision of a depraved world that seems at once too horrible to exist and too realistic to be denied. Hard to watch (though at times it's bizarrely and blackly funny) and definitely not for the squeamish, HENRY will prove unforgettable for the brave souls who do see it. A major achievement in independent filmmaking, HENRY: PORTRAIT OF A SERIAL KILLER is a horror masterpiece.

HENRY V
DVD
1944 127m c   Drama/War   ★★★★★
Two Cities   (U.K.)

Laurence Olivier *(King Henry V)*, Robert Newton *(Ancient Pistol)*, Leslie Banks *(Chorus)*, Renee Asherson *(Princess Katherine)*, Esmond Knight *(Fluellen)*, Leo Genn *(Constable of France)*, Felix Aylmer *(Archbishop of Canterbury)*, Ralph Truman *(Mountjoy)*, Harcourt Williams *(King Charles VI of France)*, Ivy St. Helier *(Alice, Lady in Waiting)*

p, Laurence Olivier, Filippo Del Giudice; d, Laurence Olivier, Reginald Beck; w, Alan Dent, Laurence Olivier (based on the play by William Shakespeare); ph, Robert Krasker; ed, Reginald Beck; m, William Walton; art d, Paul Sheriff; cos, Roger Furse

AAN Best Picture; AAN Best Actor: Laurence Olivier; AAN Best Score (Drama or Comedy): William Walton; AAN Best Interior Decoration (Color): Paul Sheriff (Art Direction), Carmen Dillon (Art Direction)

Made at the height of the German blitz, this dazzling British adaptation of Shakespeare's classic tale of victory in the face of overwhelming odds brought new hope and resolve to embattled Britons when they saw it in 1944. Filippo del Giudice, an Italian lawyer who had fled Mussolini's rule, persuaded Laurence Olivier to undertake the project, and when William Wyler, Carol Reed, and Terence Young were unable to helm the film, Olivier not only took on the title role but the director's mantle, performing both roles magnificently.

Innovatively structured, the film begins with a 17th-century staging of Shakespeare's play at the Globe Theatre; then, gradually, the proscenium disappears as the film moves toward a more realistic presentation of the story, with stylized sets giving way to the real-life scenery of the impressive re-creation of the Battle of Agincourt. Finally, Olivier brings the film full circle, back to the stage of the Globe.

Set in 1415, HENRY V chronicles the invasion of France undertaken by the 28-year-old English king in an attempt to consolidate his power at home. After a number of costly victories drastically deplete Henry's army, it is besieged by French forces that outnumber it nearly five to one. Under the king's courageous leadership, however, the English triumph at Agincourt.

Olivier, who was mustered out of the navy to make the film, collaborated with movie critic Alan Dent on the adaptation, and editor Reginald Beck helped with direction chores when Olivier the star was in front of the cameras. Though given a large budget considering the wartime circumstances, the production was continually forced to cut corners, and its wonderfully realized costumes and sets are testaments to the ingenuity of the film's designers.

HENRY V

DVD

1989 138m c Drama/Historical ★★★★
BBC/Curzon/Renaissance (U.K.) PG

Kenneth Branagh *(King Henry V)*, Derek Jacobi *(Chorus)*, Simon Shepherd *(Duke of Gloucester)*, James Larkin *(Bedford)*, Brian Blessed *(Duke of Exeter)*, James Simmons *(York)*, Paul Gregory *(Earl of Westmoreland)*, Charles Kay *(Archbishop of Canterbury)*, Alec McCowen *(Bishop of Ely)*, Fabian Cartwright *(Cambridge)*

p, Bruce Sharman; d, Kenneth Branagh; w, Kenneth Branagh; ph, Kenneth MacMillan (Eastmancolor); ed, Michael Bradsell; m, Pat Doyle; prod d, Tim Harvey; art d, Norman Dorme; cos, Phyllis Dalton

AAN Best Actor: Kenneth Branagh; *AAN Best Director:* Kenneth Branagh; *AA Best Costume Design:* Phyllis Dalton

Straightforward, energetic, updated Bard. 28-year-old star-director-adapter Kenneth Branagh's spellbinding version of Shakespeare's *Henry* isn't superior to Olivier's 1944 version—it's different, and complementary to it.

Filmed mostly in medium and close-up shots, Branagh's more intimate version discards the pageantry of Olivier's grand spectacle; focusing on carnage and casualties, Branagh's film is strongly antiwar whereas Olivier's vision, filmed as a paean to England's greatness, was a morale builder for his countrymen embroiled in a world war. Branagh's HENRY V is also a visceral coming-of-age film, following a young playboy prince as he is forced to grow up quickly and assume the responsibilities of leadership. Throughout the film, Branagh uses flashbacks, excerpted from the earlier *Henry IV* plays to clarify events, and though he has pruned the 400-year-old play, all of its most memorable moments are in place and brilliantly conveyed: from the seige of Harfleur and Henry's stirring exhortation to his small army to go "Once more unto the breach," to the dramatic victory at Agincourt.

In addition to his own extraordinary performance as King Henry, Branagh elicits brilliant work from a stellar cast, including Derek Jacobi as the chorus, Paul Scofield as the French king, Ian Holm as Fluellen, Robbie Coltrane as Falstaff and Judi Dench as Mistress Quickly.

HERCULES

DVD

1997 80m c Children's/Animated/Musical ★★
Walt Disney (U.S.) G

VOICES OF: Tate Donovan *(Adult Hercules—"Herc")*, Joshua Keaton *(Young Hercules—Speaking)*, Roger Bart *(Young Hercules—Singing)*, Danny DeVito *(Philoctetes—"Phil")*, James Woods *(Hades)*, Susan Egan *(Megara—"Meg")*, Rip Torn *(Zeus)*, Samantha Eggar *(Hera)*, Bobcat Goldthwait *(Pain)*, Charlton Heston *(Narrator)*

p, John Musker, Ron Clements, Alice Dewey; d, John Musker, Ron Clements; w, John Musker, Ron Clements, Bob Shaw, Donald McEnery, Irene Mecchi, Barry Johnson (story supervisor); ed, Tom Finan, Jeff Jones; m, Alan Menken; prod d, Gerald Scarfe; art d, Andy Gaskill; anim, Roger L. Gould (computer graphics imagery supervisor), Andreas Deja (supervising animator—adult Hercules), Randy R. Haycock (supervising animator—baby and Young Hercules), Eric Goldberg (supervising animator—Phil), Nik Ranieri (supervising animator—Hades), Ken Duncan (supervising animator—Meg), Ellen Woodbury (supervising animator—Pegasus), Anthony DeRosa (supervising animator—Zeus and Hera), Michael Show (supervising animator—The Muses), James Lopez (supervising animator—Pain), Brian Ferguson (supervising animator—Panic), Dominique Monfery (supervising animator—Titans and Cyclops), Richard Bazley (supervising animator—Amphitryon and Alcmene), Nancy Beiman (supervising animator—The Fates and Thebans), Oscar Urretabizkaia (supervising animator—Hydra)

AAN Best Original Song: "Go the Distance"; Alan Menken, David Zippel

It's no BEAUTY AND THE BEAST, but it's fun for the kids and peppered with jokes designed to keep grown-ups from squirming too desperately.

On orders from the villainous Hades (James Woods), the infant Hercules is stolen from his loving parents, Zeus and Hera (Rip Torn and Samantha Eggar). Hades knows that an adult Hercules could bring his plans to rule the classical world to a grinding halt. A kindly, childless farm couple adopt the stronger-than-strong babe, who grows up a lonely outcast. But after learning of his Olympian heritage, Hercules (Tate Donovan) finds the gruff old satyr (Danny De Vito) who trained history's other peerless champions, and sets out to become the greatest hero the world has ever known.

This child-friendly retelling of the Greek myth takes a few liberties with a story originally chockablock with sex, violence, and general sordid behavior. Passed through the Disney wringer, Hercules emerges a sanitized, blandly blond, and none-too-bright muscle-boy. Both "Greek" and the "mythology" are pretty much tossed away with the washing-up water, making way for rousing, up-tempo songs and a high-profile voice cast that also includes Hal Holbrook, Amanda Plummer, and comedian Bobcat Goldthwait. The hand of ferocious illustrator Gerald Scarfe (PINK FLOYD—THE WALL), a surprising addition to the Disney design line-up, isn't always evident in the movie's brightly colored milieu, but it's all over the snaggle-fanged Hades, whose feet are shrouded in smoke and whose head glows with perpetual flame. He's one of the best things in the picture: a conniving, angle-figuring, glad-handing Prince of Darkness—the Devil as Hollywood agent.

HERE COMES MR. JORDAN

1941 93m bw Science Fiction/Fantasy ★★★★
Columbia (U.S.)

Robert Montgomery *(Joe Pendleton)*, Evelyn Keyes *(Bette Logan)*, Claude Rains *(Mr. Jordan)*, Rita Johnson *(Julia Farnsworth)*, Edward Everett Horton *(Messenger No. 7013)*, James Gleason *(Max Corkle)*, John Emery *(Tony Abbott)*, Donald MacBride *(Inspector Williams)*, Don Costello *(Lefty)*, Halliwell Hobbes *(Sisk)*

p, Everett Riskin; d, Alexander Hall; w, Sidney Buchman, Seton I. Miller (based on the play *Heaven Can Wait* by Harry Segall); ph, Joseph Walker; ed, Viola Lawrence; m, Frederick Hollander; art d, Lionel Banks; cos, Edith Head

AAN Best Picture; AAN Best Actor: Robert Montgomery; *AAN Best Supporting Actor:* James Gleason; *AAN Best Director:* Alexander Hall; *AA Best Original Story:* Harry Segall; *AA Best Screenplay:*

Sidney Buchman, Seton I. Miller; *AAN Best B/W Cinematography:* Joseph Walker

Full of hilarious plot twists and blessed with brilliant performances from a stellar cast, HERE COMES MR. JORDAN is a thoroughly beguiling fantasy with a boxing subplot. Joe Pendleton (Robert Montgomery), a saxophone-playing up-and-coming prizefighter, crashes while flying his single-engine plane, and his spirit is plucked up by an anxious heavenly messenger (Edward Everett Horton) who learns later that Joe was supposed to have lived for another 50 years and was destined to be the world heavyweight champion. It's up to the messenger's superior, Mr. Jordan (Claude Rains, amusingly sinister and atypical for this kind of role), to help Joe find another body in which to finish his life. JORDAN suffers from being too talky and the extraneous romance, but has remained an audience perennial. A weak nonsports sequel, DOWN TO EARTH, followed in 1947, and the story was remade with a football backdrop in 1978 as the pallid HEAVEN CAN WAIT.

HERE COMES THE GROOM
1951 113m bw Comedy/Musical ★★★½
Paramount (U.S.)

Bing Crosby (Pete), Jane Wyman (Emmadel Jones), Alexis Smith (Winifred Stanley), Franchot Tone (Wilbur Stanley), James Barton (Pa Jones), Robert Keith (George Degnan), Jacques Gencel (Bobby), Beverly Washburn (Suzi), Connie Gilchrist (Ma Jones), Walter Catlett (McGonigle)

p, Frank Capra; d, Frank Capra; w, Virginia Van Upp, Liam O'Brien, Myles Connolly (based on a story by Robert Riskin, Liam O'Brien); ph, George Barnes; ed, Ellsworth Hoagland; art d, Hal Pereira, Earl Hedrick; cos, Edith Head

AAN Best Motion Picture Story: Robert Riskin, Liam O'Brien; *AA Best Song:* "In the Cool, Cool, Cool of the Evening"; Hoagy Carmichael (Music), Johnny Mercer (Lyrics)

Crosby, a news reporter returning from France with two orphans in tow, must find a wife in five days or lose the kids. He goes to his old flame, Wyman, and finds that she is set to marry millionaire Tone. Crosby uses the two orphans and his singing to recapture Wyman's heart, but it's an uphill battle against Tone's $40 million. A bright comedy with Crosby at his unflappable best and Capra developing full-bodied characters and situations, this film boasts a well-structured script and fine performances from Wyman, Tone, and Crosby.

Capra owed Paramount two films but the studio allowed him to take over this property from producer Irving Asher who originally planned to have Richard Haydn direct; this single production would make up for Capra's commitment. The gifted director brought in Wyman who used her own fine singing voice and showed off her long legs in glamorous costuming. He also brought in Smith, a six-foot actress who had been difficult to cast in the past. She was so tall that she had to stoop or slouch when playing opposite actors such as Humphrey Bogart or Charles Boyer, and stand barefoot in full shots. The always innovative Capra exploited her height by having Crosby crack in the film: "You're the most gorgeous first baseman I ever played against!" Predictable, but perfectly fine.

HERO
(YING XIONG)
2002 96m c Action/Martial Arts/Historical ★★★★
Beijing New Picture Film Co./Elite Group PG-13
Enterprises/Miramax/Edko Films/Zhang Yimou

Studio/China Film Co-Production/ Sil-Metropole Organization (China/Hong Kong/U.S.)

Jet Li (Nameless), Tony Leung, billed as Tony Leung Chiu-Wai (Broken Sword), Maggie Cheung (Flying Snow), Zhang Ziyi (Moon), Chen Dao Ming (King of Qin), Donnie Yen (Long Sky), Liu Zong-Yuan (Scholar), Zheng Tian-Yong (Old Servant), Qin Yan (Prime Minister), Chang Xiao-Yang (General)

p, Bill Kong, Zhang Yimou; d, Zhang Yimou; w, Li Feng, Wang Bin (based on a story by Zhang Zhen Yan, Li Feng, and Wang Bin), Zhang Yimou; ph, Christopher Doyle; ed, Angie Lam, Zhai Ru; m, Tan Dun; prod d, Huo Ting Xiao, Yi Zhen Zhou; art d, Han Zhong, Liu Yong-Qi, Qin Hong-Bo; fx, Lam Kwan, Angie Lam, Ellen Poon; chor, Tung Wai (fights); cos, Emi Wada

AAN Best Foreign Language Film

Zhang Yimou's color-coded, RASHOMON-esque historical fable is a beguiling blend of traditional martial arts epic and operatic, Sergio Leone-esque Western about the second-century BC emperor who unified China's seven warring kingdoms.

Told in a framing story and four flashbacks, it begins as a nameless warrior (Jet Li) from insignificant Leng Meng county tells the Emperor Qin Shi Huang (Chen Dao Ming) how he killed three legendary martial artists—Long Sky (Donnie Yen) and the lovers Flying Snow (Maggie Cheung) and Broken Sword (Tony Leung)—who were plotting to assassinate the emperor. When his story is met with skepticism, the warrior reworks it and then reworks it again. In each telling, the essentials remain the same: After the emperor's representatives fail to slay Sky, the warrior succeeds, then confronts Flying Snow, Broken Sword, and Moon (Zhang Ziyi), Broken Sword's devoted apprentice, at a calligraphy school in the desert kingdom of Zhao, where they have taken refuge. But each version puts a different coloration—both literal and figurative—on the nature and motives of the assassins and their nemesis.

The framing story unfolds in the gloomy interiors of the Forbidden City, while the jewel-toned flashbacks play out against vividly hued interiors and expansive open spaces. The first, awash in rich reds, is driven by petty, violent emotions; the second, a study in cool, watery blues, inflects the same events with more elevated notions of self-sacrifice for the common good. In the interlocking third and fourth variations, dominated by white and mint green, respectively, the story of Flying Snow and Broken Sword blossoms into a tragic love story of near mythic proportions. Though the specifics of the story may be unfamiliar to Western viewers, its broad outlines and underlying themes are universal, and Christopher Doyle's ravishing cinematography transcends language.

HESTER STREET
1975 90m bw Drama ★★★½
Midwest (U.S.) PG

Steven Keats (Jake), Carol Kane (Gitl), Mel Howard (Bernstein), Dorrie Kavanaugh (Mamie), Doris Roberts (Kavarsky), Stephen Strimpell (Joe Peltner), Lauren Frost (Fanny), Paul Freedman (Joey), Zvee Scooler (Rabbi), Eda Reiss Merin (Rabbi's Wife)

p, Raphael D. Silver; d, Joan Micklin Silver; w, Joan Micklin Silver (based on the story "Yekl" by Abraham Cahan); ph, Kenneth Van Sickle; ed, Katherine Wenning; m, William Bolcom

AAN Best Actress: Carol Kane

Neglected piece of history receives atmospheric examination as old customs are replaced by assimilation. Keats is a young Jewish immigrant living on the title street while his wife Kane and their child are waiting back in the Old World.

While trying to earn the money to bring them to the U.S., he becomes increasingly Americanized. He soon becomes involved with a fast-moving socialite who gives him some cash, which he in turn sends to his wife. Kane arrives but only shames Keats with her old-fashioned ways. They divorce and Keats goes off with his other woman, while Kane falls in love with a family friend. An engagingly simple first feature written and directed by Joan Micklin Silver, which earned an Academy Award nomination for Kane, whose acting is quite fine indeed. Unfortunately, other roles suffer from being poorly cast.

HIDALGO

DVD

2004 136m c   Adventure   ★★★
Touchstone/Hidalgo Productions/   PG-13
Casey Silver Productions   (U.S.)

Viggo Mortensen *(Frank Hopkins)*, Zuleikha Robinson *(Jazira)*, Omar Sharif *(Sheikh Riyadh)*, Louise Lombard *(Lady Anne Davenport)*, Adam Alexi-Malle *(Aziz)*, Said Taghmaoui *(Prince Bin Al Reeh)*, Silas Carson *(Katib)*, Harsh Nayyar *(Yusef)*, J.K. Simmons *(Buffalo Bill Cody)*, Adoni Maropis *(Sakr)*

p, Casey Silver; d, Joe Johnston; w, John Fusco; ph, Shelly Johnson; ed, Robert Dalva; m, James Newton Howard; prod d, Barry Robison; art d, Kevin Constant, Troy Sizemore; fx, Tim Alexander (visual effects), Bruno Van Zeebroeck; cos, Jeffrey Kurland

Based on the legendary exploits of endurance rider Frank T. Hopkins, this old-fashioned boys' adventure pits a cowboy and the titular little pinto against a field of Bedouin riders and pure-blooded Arabian horses in the grueling desert marathon known as the "Ocean of Fire."

Pony Express rider Hopkins (Viggo Mortensen) spirals into a drunken decline after delivering the dispatch that precipitates the 1890 massacre at Wounded Knee Creek. A world-class equestrian, Hopkins washes up in Buffalo Bill Cody's (J.K. Simmons) Wild West Show, where Cody's grandiloquent claims on behalf of Hopkins and Hidalgo come to the attention of Arabian Sheikh Riyadh (Omar Sharif). Riyadh, whose family pride is inextricably linked with its magnificent purebred horses, issues a put-up-or-shut-up challenge to Hopkins and his mongrel mustang. Since Hopkins isn't the sort of man who takes insults to his horse lying down, the two of them are soon en route to Aden, Arabia, to compete in a heavily symbolic test of royal blood versus self-made-in-America pluck.

The supporting cast is a riot of stock exotic characters, verging on the offensively stereotypical. There are sneering princes of the desert, a scheming English aristocrat (Louise Lombard), and Riyadh's rebellious daughter, Jazira (Zuleikha Robinson). There's also a small matter of authenticity. A dearth of historical evidence about the real-life Hopkins lends credence to debunkers who've branded him a pathological liar and dispute just about everything from his birthplace to the very existence of the Ocean of Fire; some doubt there was even a Hidalgo. This doesn't make Fusco's tale of a scrappy little horse that could any less engaging or rousing. Mortensen's charisma makes Hopkins's "aw-shucks, ma'am" mannerisms surprisingly palatable, but he's still in constant danger of losing the spotlight to the personable Hidalgo.

HIDDEN, THE

DVD

1987 96m c   Science Fiction/Thriller   ★★★
New Line/Heron (U.S.)   R

Michael Nouri *(Tom Beck)*, Kyle MacLachlan *(Lloyd Gallagher)*, Ed O'Ross *(Cliff Willis)*, Clu Gulager *(Ed Flynn)*, Claudia Christian *(Brenda Lee)*, Clarence Felder *(John Masterson)*, Bill Boyett, Richard Brooks, Catherine Cannon, Larry Cedar

p, Robert Shaye, Gerald T. Olson, Michael Meltzer; d, Jack Sholder; w, Bob Hunt; ph, Jacques Haitkin; ed, Michael Knue; m, Michael Convertino; prod d, C.J. Strawn, Mick Strawn

An exciting mix of science fiction, cop thriller, and buddy film, THE HIDDEN is one of the most exciting and unique genre hybrids.

The movie opens with an action sequence in which a young stockbroker with a strange glint in his eye robs a bank, steals a Ferarri, and drives non-stop through several police blockades while listening to pounding rock music. Finally the police force the car into a fiery crash that sends the critically injured stockbroker to the hospital. Later that day a mysterious young FBI officer, Lloyd Gallagher (Kyle MacLachlan), arrives at police headquarters to enlist the aid of veteran detective Tom Beck (Michael Nouri) in finding a fugitive—the stockbroker. In the meantime, the stockbroker dies but a slimy alien creature crawls out of his mouth and into the body of another patient. Soon the madness begins anew.

Bob Hunt's screenplay and Jack Sholder's direction combine to create a sci-fi action yarn replete with exciting chases, well-staged shootouts and some extremely funny black humor. Nouri and MacLachlan turn in superior performances as does the rest of the large cast. In retrospect, MacLachlan's character feels like an audition for Agent Cooper of "Twin Peaks." This is an outstanding buddy film with a smart extraterrestrial twist.

HIDDEN FORTRESS, THE

DVD

(KAKUSHI TORIDE NO SAN AKUNIN)
1958 137m bw Action/Adventure   ★★★★
Toho (Japan)

Toshiro Mifune *(Rokurota)*, Misa Uehara *(Lady Yukihime)*, Minoru Chiaki *(Tahei)*, Kamatari Fujiwara *(Matashichi)*, Susumu Fujita *(Tadakoro)*, Takashi Shimura *(The Old General)*, Eiko Miyoshi *(The Old Woman)*, Toshiko Higuchi *(The Farmer's Daughter)*, Kichijiro Ueda *(Girl-Dealer)*

p, Masumi Fujimoto; d, Akira Kurosawa; w, Ryuzo Kikushima, Hideo Oguni, Shinobu Hashimoto, Akira Kurosawa; ph, Ichio Yamazaki; ed, Akira Kurosawa; m, Masaru Sato; art d, Yoshiro Muraki

Akira Kurosawa's THE HIDDEN FORTRESS is a paradigm of the modern adventure epic—a marvelously entertaining blend of a simple but strong plot, exhilarating action scenes, tongue-in-cheek humor, and a solid philosophical underpinning. Toshiro Mifune gives a towering performance as a general in 16th-Century feudal Japan who aids a dethroned princess whose clan has been defeated in a civil war. With the aid of two buffoonish farmers, the general escorts the princess through hostile territory and transports 170 pounds of gold bars to a hidden fortress in the woods. Originally released in the U.S. in a truncated 90-minute print, the film was not shown outside of Japan in a full-length version until 1983, at which time George Lucas admitted that it was one of his main inspirations for STAR WARS (1977), particularly in the characters of the bumbling, bickering farmers, who were copied in metal to make R2-D2 and C-3PO, as well as in the basic premise of escorting a feisty princess through enemy territory. The film was Kurosawa's first (of many) to be shot in a widescreen format, and his use of the expansive rectangular frame is masterly. He immediately establishes a surreal comic nightmare mood where violence could explode at any moment, starting with the very first shot that follows the farmers from behind in one long take as they stand at the edges of the frame and trudge across a foggy forest and argue; suddenly, a bloody soldier stumbles into the frame out of nowhere and six horsemen come thundering in behind him and stab him to death. The kinetic action scenes, featuring hordes of extras and massive battles are superbly shot and edited, yet for all of the excitement, the film also has a deeply spiritual and philosophical side, exemplified by the spectacular fire-worshipping sequence, in which the participants dance wildly around a bonfire and sing "This floating world's a dream, so burn in mad abandon."

HIDEOUS KINKY   *DVD*
1998 99m c Drama   ★★★
United International Pictures/British Broadcasting   R
Corporation/The Film Consortium/Greenpoint Films/
L Films/AMLF/Arts Council of England   (France/U.K.)

Kate Winslet *(Julia)*, Said Taghmaoui *(Bilal)*, Bella Riza *(Bea)*, Carrie Mullan *(Lucy)*, Pierre Clementi *(Santoni)*, Abigail Cruttenden *(Charlotte)*, Ahmed Boulane *(Ben Said)*, Sira Stampe *(Eva)*, Amidou *(Sufi Sheikh)*, Michelle Fairley *(Patricia)*

p, Ann Scott; d, Gillies MacKinnon; w, Billy MacKinnon (based on the novel by Esther Freud); ph, John de Borman; ed, Pia Di Ciaula; m, John Keane; prod d, Louise Marzaroli, Pierre Compertz; art d, Jon Henson; cos, Kate Carin

Based on the autobiographical novel by Esther Freud (which owes its title to a verbal game played by two girls still young enough to value words for sound rather than meaning), this delicate, visually ravishing story of twisted family ties rests on a quartet of phenomenal performances, made more remarkable by the fact that two of them are by young children.

Disenchanted with cold, gray England and her unsatisfying relationship with the self-centered father of her children, Julia (Kate Winslet) decamps to Morocco in the early '70s, dragging small daughters Lucy and Bea (Carrie Mullan, Bella Riza) along on the road to self-enlightenment. Julia hopes to make sense of her life through Sufism, but without money or regular work, she and the girls wind up in a run-down hotel frequented by prostitutes, anxiously awaiting all-too infrequent assistance from Julia's neglectful ex. The children are initially enchanted by the exotic colors and smells of North Africa, and Lucy is captivated by Bilal (Said Taghmaoui), a street entertainer who becomes Julia's gentle and loyal lover. But eight-year-old Bea is frustrated by their aimless existence. She longs for school and discipline and an ordered home life, particularly after the makeshift family takes an extended trip to Bilal's remote hometown, where it's made painfully clear what outsiders they are and will always be.

Filmmaker Gillies MacKinnon doesn't try to tell his story through the eyes of the open and innocent Lucy, as the novel does. But its earlier sections capture brilliantly the slightly addled wonder of Europeans in a land of 1000 exotic sights and sounds. The film's gradual slide into a darker vision of the casual selfishness and presumption that often lay at the heart of Westerners' mind-bending journeys to the East is subtle and quietly devastating.

HIGH AND LOW   *DVD*
(TENGOKU TO JIGOKU)
1963 142m c/bw Crime   ★★★★
Toho (Japan)

Toshiro Mifune *(Kingo Gondo)*, Tatsuya Nakadai *(Inspector Tokura)*, Kyoko Kagawa *(Reiko, Gondo's Wife)*, Tatsuya Mihashi *(Kawanishi)*, Yutaka Sada *(Aoki)*, Kenjiro Ishiyama *(Detective Taguchi)*, Tsutomu Yamazaki *(Ginji Takeuchi)*, Takashi Shimura *(Director)*, Susumu Fujita *(Commissioner)*, Ko Kimura *(Detective Arai)*

p, Tomoyuki Tanaka, Ryuzo Kikushima; d, Akira Kurosawa; w, Akira Kurosawa, Hideo Oguni, Ryuzo Kikushima, Eijiro Hisaita (based on the novel *King's Ransom* by Ed McBain); ph, Choichi Nakai, Takao Saito (Tohoscope); m, Masaru Sato; art d, Yoshiro Muraki

Based on a crime novel by Ed McBain, this brilliant Kurosawa film stars Toshiro Mifune as Kingo Gondo, a rich industrialist who receives word that his son has been kidnapped by a madman demanding an outrageous ransom that will ruin Gondo financially if he pays it. Before Gondo can make a decision, his son enters the house, and we learn that it is his playmate, the chauffeur's son, who has been kidnapped. Gondo is then faced with a tough moral decision: is his chauffeur's son worth as much as his own? When the kidnapper calls and admits his mistake, but demands payment anyway, Gondo initially refuses, but is conscience stricken.

In HIGH AND LOW Kurosawa succeeds in developing a highly visual structural style within the wide-screen format. The first half of the film takes place in the living room of Gondo's hilltop house and is characterized by static shots that hold for several minutes on a single composition. Time transitions are handled by wipes, creating a charged atmosphere. This steadiness is broken suddenly for the second half of the film, involving the criminal manhunt, shot with a normal amount of motion and cutting—its pace frenetic in comparison with the first half of the film.

HIGH AND THE MIGHTY, THE
1954 147m c Disaster   ★★★½
Wayne/Fellows (U.S.)

John Wayne *(Dan Roman)*, Claire Trevor *(May Hoist)*, Laraine Day *(Lydia Rice)*, Robert Stack *(Sullivan)*, Jan Sterling *(Sally McKee)*, Phil Harris *(Ed Joseph)*, Robert Newton *(Gustave Pardee)*, David Brian *(Ken Childs)*, Paul Kelly *(Flaherty)*, Sidney Blackmer *(Humphrey Agnew)*

p, Robert Fellows, John Wayne; d, William A. Wellman; w, Ernest K. Gann (based on the novel by Gann); ph, Archie Stout, William Clothier (CinemaScope, Warner Color); ed, Ralph Dawson; m, Dimitri Tiomkin; art d, Alfred Ybarra; cos, Gwen Wakeling

AAN Best Supporting Actress: Jan Sterling; *AAN Best Supporting Actress:* Claire Trevor; *AAN Best Director:* William Wellman; *AAN Best Film Editing:* Ralph Dawson; *AA Best Score (Drama or Comedy):* Dimitri Tiomkin; *AAN Best Song:* "The High and Mighty"; Dimitri Tiomkin (Music), Ned Washington (Lyrics)

Cliche-bound but boosted by taut direction, memorable music and, for once, just right for CinemaScope. Wayne is a has-been pilot—"an ancient pelican" according to airline executive Toomey—now copiloting under the command of cocky Stack. Also on board is an inept navigator, Brown, and an apprentice pilot, Campbell, who constantly derides Wayne, even bringing up a terrible crash occurring years earlier which Wayne survived but in which his wife and young child were killed.

Beautiful, statuesque, and cool stewardess Doe Avedon makes 22 passengers comfortable as the airliner leaves Honolulu for San Francisco. Her passengers: divorce-seeking Day and Howard; shady mail-order bride Sterling; wacko theatrical impresario Newton; jaded, bitter Trevor; pompous playboy Brian who is being stalked by vengeful Blackmer; oblivious newlyweds Smith and Sharpe; guilty nuclear scientist Kelly; and second honeymooners Doran and Harris. Then, all hell breaks loose, forcing everyone to face each other, "reality," and a competitive race for acting honors.

Wellman does a dynamite job directing air traffic; though characters are drawn only briefly, they are tellingly etched with pathos and melodrama. Wayne's performance as the one fixed and reliable point in a collapsing world got him voted him the number one box-office attraction, replacing Gary Cooper. Oddly, Wayne, who coproduced the film, intended to have Spencer Tracy play the pioneer pilot role but when that venerable actor turned down the part Wayne took it over himself. The haunting title song became so closely associated with Wayne that when this giant died it was this score that was played during his funeral.

HIGH ANXIETY

1977   94m   c   Comedy   ★★★
Fox   (U.S.)   PG

Mel Brooks (Richard Thorndyke), Madeline Kahn (Victoria Brisbane), Cloris Leachman (Nurse Diesel), Harvey Korman (Dr. Charles Montague), Ron Carey (Brophy), Howard Morris (Prof. Lilloman), Dick Van Patten (Dr. Wentworth), Jack Riley (Desk Clerk), Charlie Callas (Cocker Spaniel), Ron Clark (Zachary Cartwright)

p, Mel Brooks; d, Mel Brooks; w, Mel Brooks, Ron Clark, Rudy DeLuca, Barry Levinson; ph, Paul Lohmann (DeLuxe Color); ed, John C. Howard; m, John Morris; prod d, Peter Wooley; fx, Albert Whitlock; cos, Patricia Morris

Mel Brooks's so-so feat of Hitchcockian tribute: he stars, produces, directs, cowrites, and sings the title song (and he has a much better singing voice than you might imagine). Whereas men like Brian De Palma and Colin Higgins will make movies reminiscent of Hitchcock without citing that director, Brooks is patently spoofing the rotund master with HIGH ANXIETY. Even if you don't know the original work, this film indicates its inspiration fairly well. The head of the Institute for the Very Very Nervous is found murdered, and Brooks, a man who fears heights so badly that he won't wear elevator shoes, takes over as psychiatrist-in-charge. Assistant Korman and nurse Leachman have been spinning a plot to keep the patients captive while bilking them out of their money, and they fear that Brooks will put an end to that. Parody is a tricky business, but Brooks sometimes succeeds in paying homage to SPELLBOUND, VERTIGO, PSY-CHO, and THE BIRDS with all of the usual middle-cut Hitchcock formulae: innocent man accused of something he didn't do, reluctant heroine (Kahn) who helps, etc. Many familiar scenes come out of Hitchcock with the standouts being prowling camera work and Hitch's use of musical scores. Audiences flocked to theaters and made this movie a hit. Some interesting sidelights in casting include famed matte artist Albert Whitlock as Brisbane, successful commercials actors Bob Ridgely and Jack Riley, and co-writer Levinson as the bellboy. Levinson went on to become highly regarded as a director with DINER and THE NATURAL. Morris was for years one of Sid Caesar's second bananas on TV and now earns his living as a director and sometimes cartoon voice ("The Paw-Paws" for Hanna-Barbera, among others). Callas is a busy nightclub comic, and Richard Stahl is one of the best comedy character men in the business. Assistant director Sanger stayed with Brooks and eventually became a producer.

HIGH ART

1998   101m   c   Drama   ★★★½
High Art Pictures   (U.S.)   R

Ally Sheedy (Lucy Berliner), Radha Mitchell (Syd), Patricia Clarkson (Greta), Gabriel Mann, billed as Gabriel Mick (James—Syd's Boyfriend), Bill Sage (Arnie), David Thornton (Harry—Syd's Boss), Anh Duong (Dominique—"Frame" Editor), Tammy Grimes (Vera—Lucy's Mother), Helen Mendes (White Hawk), Cindra Feuer (Delia)

p, Dolly Hall, Jeff Levy-Hinte, Susan A. Stover; d, Lisa Cholodenko; w, Lisa Cholodenko; ph, Tami Reiker; ed, Amy Duddleston; m, Shudder To Think; prod d, Bernhard Blythe; art d, Caryn Marcus; cos, Victoria Farrell

What price success? Bright, ambitious, recent college grad Syd (Rahda Mitchell), who's trying to rise through the ranks of a pretentious art-photography magazine, finds out in this perceptive drama.

Syd shares a Manhattan loft apartment with perfectly attractive, intelligent, and considerate boyfriend James (Gabriel Mann), and stumbles onto a big break when she discovers that their upstairs neighbor is notorious photographer Lucy Berliner (Ally Sheedy). Once an art-world flavor-of-the-month by virtue of her sordid autobiographical photos, Berliner is living in drug-soaked obscurity with her German girlfriend Greta (Patricia Clarkson), a former actress whose claim to fame was having worked with Fassbinder. From the moment Syd steps into Lucy's apartment, she's transfixed: by Lucy's extended entourage, beautiful people blissed out on heroin; by the flirtatious, fluid aura of casual sexuality; by the just plain being bad appeal of the whole scene. Lucy, by contrast, has become bored with the perpetual den of iniquity in her living room, and is attracted to Syd's youthful ambition. Everything in Lucy's life overlaps—her photography, her drug addiction, and her love affairs—and Syd is inevitably drawn into the volatile miasma.

First-time director Lisa Cholodenko, who has made a powerful and modish film with a subtle and knowing script, is more than ably assisted by a spectacular cast: former Brat-Packer Sheedy is a revelation, but Patricia Clarkson nearly steals the show as the sardonic, drugged-out, and occasionally laser-sharp Greta.

HIGH FIDELITY
DVD

2000   107m   c   Comedy   ★★★½
New Crime/Working Title/Dogstar/Touchstone   R
(U.S.)

John Cusack (Rob), Iben Hjejle (Laura), Todd Louiso (Dick), Jack Black (Barry), Lisa Bonet (Marie De Salle), Catherine Zeta-Jones (Charlie), Joan Cusack (Liz), Tim Robbins (Ian), Chris Rehmann (Vince), Bruce Springsteen (Himself)

p, Tim Bevan, Rudd Simmons; d, Stephen Frears; w, D.V. Devincentis, Steve Pink, John Cusack, Scott Rosenberg (based on the novel High Fidelity by Nick Hornby); ph, Seamus McGarvey; ed, Mick Audsley; m, Howard Shore; prod d, David Chapman, Therese DePrez; art d, Nicholas Lund; fx, Sam Barkan, Double Negative (Digital), Digital Film at the Moving Picture Company; cos, Laura Cunningham Bauer

True or false: Any movie whose opening sequence features the 13th Floor Elevator's "You're Gonna Miss Me" is by definition terrific. If you answered true, you're probably primed for director Stephen Frear's sharp and emotionally resonant adaptation of Nick Hornby's novel about music geeks and the women that love them.

The action centers around the tragically hip record store Championship Vinyl and its music-obsessed owner, Rob (John Cusack). Rob is the sort of guy who alternates between compiling Top Five lists of opening album tracks and Top Five lists of girlfriends who dumped him, most recently the lovely and too-good-for-him Laura (Iben Hjejle). Meanwhile, Rob's two assistants, loutish Barry (Jack Black) and geeky Dick (Todd Louiso), are even more insufferable in their insularity; they're the sort of snobs who'll cut a customer dead if he has the temerity to add a "the" to a song title. As you might expect, the course of true love does not run smooth, but Rob gains some wisdom and everybody lives happily ever after, although not before we encounter a hilarious succession of name actors in small but crucial roles: Tim Robbins as a sensitive New Age twit, Catherine Zeta-Jones as one of Rob's old flames, and Bruce Springsteen as himself. Anyone who's ever been dumped, done the dumping, or acted like a jerk will be able to relate to Rob's self-absorbed cluelessness, and the soundtrack is a total delight, with more obscure but nifty oldies than you've had hot meals. But if you answered "false" to the question up top, there's a distinct possibility you'll miss about two thirds of the movie's best jokes.

HIGH HOPES

1988	110m	c	Comedy/Drama	★★★★
Portman/Film Four		(U.K.)		PG

Philip Davis *(Cyril Bender)*, Ruth Sheen *(Shirley)*, Edna Dore *(Mrs. Bender)*, Philip Jackson *(Martin Burke)*, Heather Tobias *(Valerie Burke)*, Lesley Manville *(Laetitia Boothe-Braine)*, David Bamber *(Rupert Boothe-Braine)*, Jason Watkins *(Wayne)*, Judith Scott *(Suzi)*, Cheryl Prime *(Martin's Girl Friend)*

p, Simon Channing-Williams, Victor Glynn; d, Mike Leigh; w, Mike Leigh; ph, Roger Pratt (Eastmancolor); ed, John Gregory; m, Andrew Dixon; prod d, Diana Charnley; art d, Andrew Rothschild; cos, Lindy Hemming

Mike Leigh's funny and deeply touching HIGH HOPES is yet another inventive cinematic reaction to Margaret Thatcher's overhaul of British society. Employing an episodic structure and a semi-improvisational approach, Leigh (BLEAK MOMENTS) presents three couples and an elderly woman as a microcosm of modern-day Britain.

Cyril (Philip Davis), a 35-year-old motorcycle messenger, and Shirley (Ruth Sheen), his companion of ten years, are children of the working class who have embraced a countercultural lifestyle that once included a passionate faith in revolutionary ideology. Although they can't agree to have a child of their own, they spend plenty of time parenting Davis's aging mother (Dore), who lives in the last council-owned house on a gentrified street, where an impossibly snooty yuppie couple, the Boothe-Braines (Lesley Manville and David Bamber), are her neighbors. Rounding out the cast are Cyril's shrill, nouveau riche sister (Heather Tobias) and her philandering used-car-salesman husband (Philip Jackson). Alternately silly, serious, and poignant, HIGH HOPES uses its players as political symbols, without subordinating character to the demands of allegory... well, almost.

Leigh's approach is most realistic when dealing with Cyril's mother, Cyril, and Shirley, and the bedtime conversations between the last two are certainly among cinema's most privileged moments. Because of the care Leigh takes with these three characters, HIGH HOPES is not just an indictment of Thatcher-engendered inequity; it is also a survival primer for those who have lost faith in the Left's traditional grand solutions yet refused to succumb to "compassion fatigue."

HIGH NOON
📀

1952	85m	bw	Western	★★★★★
UA	(U.S.)		

Gary Cooper *(Will Kane)*, Grace Kelly *(Amy Kane)*, Thomas Mitchell *(Jonas Henderson)*, Lloyd Bridges *(Harvey Pell)*, Katy Jurado *(Helen Ramirez)*, Otto Kruger *(Percy Mettrick)*, Lon Chaney Jr. *(Martin Howe)*, Harry Morgan, billed as Henry Morgan *(William Fuller)*, Ian MacDonald *(Frank Miller)*, Eve McVeagh *(Mildred Fuller)*

p, Stanley Kramer; d, Fred Zinnemann; w, Carl Foreman (based on the story "The Tin Star" by John W. Cunningham); ph, Floyd Crosby; ed, Elmo Williams, Harry Gerstad; m, Dimitri Tiomkin; prod d, Rudolph Sternad; art d, Ben Hayne

AAN Best Picture; AA Best Actor: Gary Cooper; *AAN Best Director:* Fred Zinnemann; *AAN Best Screenplay:* Carl Foreman; *AA Best Film Editing:* Elmo Williams, Harry Gerstad; *AA Best Score (Drama or Comedy):* Dimitri Tiomkin; *AA Best Song:* "High Noon (Do Not Forsake Me, Oh My Darlin')"; Dimitri Tiomkin (Music), Ned Washington (Lyrics)

Not a frame is wasted in this taut, superbly directed, masterfully acted film, the first so-called "adult Western," in which the traditional and predictable elements of action, song and minimal romance give way to a swift, intense unraveling of a situation and complex character development. HIGH NOON is also the story of a western town, Hadleyville, and its sometimes stouthearted citizenry, the most prominent of whom is the stoic, heroic Will Kane (Gary Cooper), a lawman surrounded by friends and admirers at the start, deserted and doomed at the finish.

Just married, Will and his beautiful blonde Quaker bride, Amy (Grace Kelly), are about to leave town forever, intending to put peacemaking behind them to settle down to ranch life. However, news comes that a fierce killer, Frank Miller (Ian MacDonald), is about to arrive and take vengeance against Will and the town for sending him to prison years earlier. Miller's brother (Sheb Wooley) and two gunslingers (Bob Wilke and Lee Van Cleef) are already at the depot, waiting for the train carrying Miller, which is due to arrive at high noon. In a moment of panic, urged on by his friends, Will races his buckboard and bride out of town and down the road into the open prairie, but he suddenly pulls up. When Amy asks him why he is stopping, Will tells her that he has to go back, that it's his duty to return.

A landmark Western in every sense, HIGH NOON was shot by cinematographer Floyd Crosby in high contrast, an approach director Fred Zinnemann used to bring documentarylike authenticity to the film. Zinnemann's outstanding economical direction is in full force here, every minute pertinent and packed with suspense. Significantly, the film takes almost as much time to unreel as Will Kane takes in the story to prepare for the gun battle.

For Cooper, this was a *tour de force*, a film wherein his mere presence overwhelms the viewer and carries a story that is believable only through his actions. He utters no long speeches, yet his expressions and movements are those of a man resolute in his lonely duty and resigned to his own doom. Every confrontation with the unresponsive townspeople causes him to suffer; in truth, Cooper was in real agony during the production, enduring a bleeding ulcer and an injured hip. After finishing the film, he said, "I'm all acted out." Cooper's exhaustion is evident in his onscreen appearance, but reportedly an appropriately haggard-looking Will Kane was just what Zinnemann was after, despite Hollywood's proclivity for dashing leading men.

Though Kramer later claimed that the project was entirely his own creation, writer Carl Foreman contended neither Kramer nor his associates had any interest in the film from the outset. Kramer did, however, view the first showing with concern. Believing that it had a lot of dead spots, he ordered a series of closeups showing the anxiety lining Cooper's face, and included many quick cuts to clocks ticking relentlessly toward the doom of high noon.

To further heighten the tension Kramer asked Dmitri Tiomkin to write a ballad that could be interwoven with the action. Though the composer protested that he only wrote scores, he and Ned Washington produced the wonderful "High Noon (Do Not Forsake Me, Oh My Darlin')," sung by Tex Ritter. The song has since become a classic, along with Tiomkin's memorable score.

HIGH PLAINS DRIFTER
📀

1973	105m	c	Western	★★★½
Malpaso	(U.S.)		R

Clint Eastwood *(The Stranger)*, Verna Bloom *(Sarah Belding)*, Marianna Hill *(Callie Travers)*, Mitchell Ryan *(Dave Drake)*, Jack Ging *(Morgan Allen)*, Stefan Gierasch *(Mayor Jason Hobart)*, Ted Hartley *(Lewis Belding)*, Billy Curtis *(Mordecai)*, Geoffrey Lewis *(Stacey Bridges)*, Scott Walker *(Bill Borders)* p, Robert Daley; d, Clint Eastwood; w, Ernest Tidyman; ph, Bruce Surtees (Panavision, Technicolor); ed, Ferris Webster; m, Dee Barton; art d, Henry Bumstead

Eastwood directs his first Western, and it's a knockout. HIGH PLAINS DRIFTER is a morality tale carved out of the harsh Western desert and directed with a panache that synthesized the styles of Sergio Leone and Don Siegel, two directors who had worked with Eastwood frequently. The result is one of the best Westerns of the 1970s.

The story begins as a mysterious stranger (Eastwood) materializes out of the desert heat. He rides into the small town of Lagos, where his presence is considered a threat by the mean and cowardly populace. Before too long, he is attacked by three gunmen, and Eastwood kills them all coolly and efficiently. The stranger then rents a hotel room, and the town dwarf, Curtis (who is also disenfranchised in town due to his size), attends to his needs. At night, Eastwood's dreams are plagued by a recurring nightmare of a helpless man being whipped to death in the street by three sadistic criminals while the townsfolk stand by and do nothing to stop it.

Meanwhile, the town council debates how to handle the impending threat created by a group of escaped convicts who are out to return to Lagos (where they committed their crimes) and destroy it. Desperate, the town's leaders cautiously approach Eastwood and plead with him to save their town from the criminals. Eastwood agrees to help them, but then proceeds to turn the town on its head by teaching self-defense and requesting all sorts of strange things from the townsfolk, including having them paint the town red and rename it "Hell."

An eerie, supernatural western that takes the avenging man-with-no-name character created by Eastwood and Leone to its most logical extreme. Eastwood would later bury the character completely in his own OUTLAW JOSEY WALES only to have him rise like the Phoenix, redefined as a much more human, compassionate and caring hero.

HIGH SIERRA
1941   100m   bw   Crime   DVD
Warner Bros.   (U.S.)   ★★★★

Ida Lupino (Marie Garson), Humphrey Bogart (Roy Earle), Alan Curtis (Babe Kozak), Arthur Kennedy (Red Hattery), Joan Leslie (Velma), Henry Hull (Doc Banton), Barton MacLane (Jake Kranmer), Henry Travers (Pa), Elisabeth Risdon (Ma), Cornel Wilde (Louis Mendoza)

p, Mark Hellinger; d, Raoul Walsh; w, John Huston, W.R. Burnett (based on the novel by W.R. Burnett); ph, Tony Gaudio; ed, Jack Killifer; m, Adolph Deutsch; art d, Ted Smith; fx, Byron Haskin, H.F. Koenekamp; cos, Milo Anderson

With exception of WHITE HEAT, this was the movie gangster's last stand. Bogart plays a graying criminal who's had it, and is in pursuit of one last caper in a changing world. He hooks up with Kennedy, Curtis, and informer Wilde to pull of the job, and becomes sympathetic to the plight of Curtis's moll Lupino, while also obsessing about young Leslie, a lame girl. HIGH SIERRA romanticizes the Bogie character as much as possible within hardbitten guidelines and, with the exception of the always overeager Leslie, it's acted within an inch of its classic life, especially by Bogie, Lupino and a mongrel dog in the gut-wrenching climax. And that fadeout.... .

HIGH SIERRA is a landmark crime film in many ways. It was Bogart's first solid role as a sympathetic lead, a good-bad guy out of his element and beyond his time. As was the case with his first gangster role—Duke Mantee, in THE PETRIFIED FOREST—Bogart is made up to look like John Dillinger, to whom he bore an amazing resemblance. Bogart, who was second-billed under Lupino, showed his ability to play sensitive scenes with depth, and the public responded enthusiastically. He would never again play second fiddle to Cagney or anyone else.

Director Walsh does a superb job in keeping a nonstop action pace, succinctly pausing to give Bogart setups in which his character is revealed, a masterful balance of movement and repose. Walsh, more than any one else, was responsible for Bogart's big break in getting the part, suggesting him to Jack Warner when others turned down the role. This was also an important film for screenwriter John Huston; his career took a sharp turn upward following HIGH SIERRA, after which he began his own distinguished directing career. Reworked by Walsh himself as COLORADO TERRITORY.

HIGH SOCIETY   DVD
1956   107m   c   Musical/Comedy   ★★★
MGM   (U.S.)

Bing Crosby (C.K. Dexter-Haven), Grace Kelly (Tracy Lord), Frank Sinatra (Mike Connor), Celeste Holm (Liz Imbrie), John Lund (George Kittredge), Louis Calhern (Uncle Willie), Sidney Blackmer (Seth Lord), Louis Armstrong (Himself), Margalo Gillmore (Mrs. Seth Lord), Lydia Reed (Caroline Lord)

p, Sol C. Siegel; d, Charles Walters; w, John Patrick (based on the play The Philadelphia Story by Philip Barry); ph, Paul C. Vogel (VistaVision, Technicolor); ed, Ralph E. Winters; m, Johnny Green, Saul Chaplin; art d, Cedric Gibbons, Hans Peters; fx, A. Arnold Gillespie; chor, Charles Walters; cos, Helen Rose

AAN Best Score (Musical): Johnny Green, Saul Chaplin; AAN Best Song: "True Love"; Cole Porter (Music & Lyrics)

Written with all the bite of a distinctly middle-class church social, this musical re-working of THE PHILADELPHIA STORY feels distant. Cole Porter's score sits on it like a champagne bubble in a vat of flat beer.

Tracy Lord (Grace Kelly, in her last film before marrying Prince Ranier of Monaco) lives in Newport and has a trio of men encircling her: her ex-husband, C.K. Dexter-Haven (Bing Crosby), with whom she is still on fairly good terms; her fiance, George Kittredge (John Lund), a professional prig; and Mike Connor (Frank Sinatra), a breezy reporter sent to cover the wedding by a Life magazine-like periodical. The rest of the cast includes Celeste Holm as Connor's photographer; Sidney Blackmer as Tracy's skirt-chasing father; Margalo Gillmore as her mother; and Louis Calhern as her uncle.

The leads are all too laconic for the movie's own good. Crosby is far too old for his role—he looks like a piece of walking beef jerky. Sinatra comes off more like a gate-crashing taxi-driver than a reporter. He can't muster the energy to get past his own phony "hip" persona. And Kelly seems preoccupied by another wedding, or perhaps wallpaper choices for the palace. Still, there are a few diverting moments seeing Bing work out with Frank and the ever-welcome Satchmo. Re the score: the only song not written for the movie was "Well, Did You Evah?" which was first sung by Betty Grable in Cole Porter's 1939 Broadway musical Du Barry Was a Lady.

HILARY AND JACKIE   DVD
1998   124m   c   Drama   ★★★★
Oxford Films/Film Four   (U.K.)   R

Emily Watson (Jacqueline du Pre), Rachel Griffiths (Hilary du Pre), David Morrissey (Kiffer Finzi), James Frain (Daniel Barenboim), Charles Dance (Derek du Pre), Celia Imrie (Iris du Pre), Rupert Penry-Jones (Piers du Pre), Bill Paterson (Jackie's

Cello Teacher), Keeley Flanders (Young Hilary), Auriol Evans (Young Jackie)

p, Andrew Paterson, Nicholas Kent; d, Anand Tucker; w, Frank Cottrell Boyce (based on the book A Genius in the Family by Hilary and Piers du Pre); ph, David Johnson; ed, Martin Walsh; m, Barrington Pheloung; prod d, Alice Normington; cos, Sandy Powell

AAN Best Actress: Emily Watson; AAN Best Supporting Actress: Rachel Griffiths

A brilliant, heart-wrenching examination of the intense, contradictory relationship between sisters Hilary (Rachel Griffiths) and Jacqueline (Emily Watson) du Pre: both were talented child musicians, but prodigy Jacqueline grew up to become a world-renowned cellist, only to see her brilliant career cut cruelly short by multiple sclerosis.

The film opens in England in the '50s, as the young siblings study with their brittle, quietly determined mother (Celia Imrie), who admonishes that they must "always be as good as each other," setting the stage for a fierce, lifelong rivalry that rubs shoulders uneasily with a bond so deep it's nearly telepathic. Though flutist Hilary's talents emerge first, Jacqueline's quickly eclipse them: Jackie becomes the glittering black hole that sucks up all the family's energy and emotional resources. Jackie's love-hate relationship with her own prodigious gifts—which she blames for her wild mood swings and desperate insecurity—turns her into an egocentric monster, more tormented and lonely than her family realizes, while Hilary sublimates her creative energies into marriage to convivial conductor Kiffer (David Morrissey) and child-bearing.

Drawing heavily from the memoir A Genius in the Family, by Hilary du Pre and her brother Piers, Anand Tucker's double portrait of sisters bound together so tightly they can barely move without hurting each other is uncannily reminiscent of Ulu Grosbard's GEORGIA: the music is different, but the song is the same. First-time feature director Tucker displays an astonishingly assured touch, allowing his phenomenal cast to creep into their characters' skins and surrounding them with images of shimmering and slightly threatening beauty. Without relying excessively on heavy-handed symbolism, Tucker reminds us that beauty demands its tribute and unwanted gifts can be curses in disguise.

HILLS HAVE EYES, THE 📀
1978 89m c Horror ★★★½
Blood Relations (U.S.) R

Susan Lanier (Brenda Carter), Robert Houston (Bobby Carter), Virginia Vincent (Ethel Carter), Russ Grieve (Bob Carter), Dee Wallace Stone, billed as Dee Wallace (Lynne Wood), Martin Speer (Doug Wood), Brenda Marinoff (Katie Wood), James Whitmore (Jupiter), Cordy Clark (Mama), Janus Blythe (Ruby)

p, Peter Locke; d, Wes Craven; w, Wes Craven; ph, Eric Saarinen; ed, Wes Craven; m, Don Peake; art d, Robert Burns

With this film and A NIGHTMARE ON ELM STREET, Wes Craven assured himself a place in the history of the horror film as an important filmmaker whose work has had an immense influence on the genre.

THE HILLS HAVE EYES opens as the Carters, an ostensibly typical middle-class suburban family, drive through the desert in their mobile home headed for California. Trouble starts when the vehicle's axle breaks and the travelers are left stranded in the desert, miles from help. Unfortunately, they've accidentally trespassed on the domain of another family, a brutal, almost atavistic, clan of cannibals who live on the desert mesas. Soon the rivval families collide with the twisted desert clan attacking the "all-American" suburban clan to loot, kill the men, rape the women, and eat the tasty-looking baby.

Though not particularly bloody, THE HILLS HAVE EYES is an extremely intense and disturbing film. As is the case with Sam Peckinpah's classic, STRAW DOGS, it becomes oddly and distressingly exhilarating to watch the nice family become increasingly savage in their efforts to survive. Not for the squeamish, this low-budget potboiler is one of the prime examples of the what was so fascinating about American horror films in the 1970s. It can be profitably read as the kind of thematically rich meditation on the dark side of the American family that could only be done in the exploitation horror genre.

HIROSHIMA MON AMOUR 📀
1959 88m bw Drama/War ★★★★★
Argos/Como/Daiei/Pathe (France/Japan)

Emmanuelle Riva (She), Eiji Okada (He), Stella Dassas (Mother), Pierre Barbaud (Father), Bernard Fresson (German Soldier)

d, Alain Resnais; w, Marguerite Duras; ph, Sacha Vierny, Michio Takahashi; ed, Henri Colpi, Jasmine Chasney, Anne Sarraute; m, Georges Delerue, Giovanni Fusco; prod d, Esaka, Mayo, Petri

AAN Best Original Story and Screenplay: Marguerite Duras

After spending 10 years making documentary shorts which were distinguished by their boldly experimental editing—including the landmark NIGHT AND FOG (1955), about Nazi concentration camps—Alain Resnais made the extraordinary HIROSHIMA MON AMOUR, which was originally intended to be a documentary about the reconstruction of Hiroshima, but evolved into being his first feature-film.

A French actress (Emmanuelle Riva) making an anti-war film in Hiroshima, meets a Japanese architect (Eiji Okada) and takes him back to her hotel room, where they make love. The next evening, they have a rendezvous at his house. He notes that his wife is away; she, too, admits that she is married. After they make love they go to a riverside tea room, where she recalls her tragic first love affair in her hometown of Nevers, France: he was a German soldier who was later killed. She subsequently had her head shaved by the townspeople, and went mad when her shamed parents locked her in a cellar. During her remembrances of these events, she gets hysterical, and the architect has to slap her. With only a few hours to go before her flight home, they separate but end up being drawn to each other once more as she wanders through the city with the architect following her.

Any normal synopsis of HIROSHIMA MON AMOUR is useless since the entire film is an abstract exercise in nonlinear narrative, blending montage, rapid-cutting, dissolves, flashbacks, and sensuous tracking shots, with interior monologues, voice-over and music, to create a stunningly powerful and poetic evocation of time and memory. All of Resnais's films deal with these concepts, but HIROSHIMA MON AMOUR also concerns the importance and the necessity of forgetting painful and traumatic events in order to go on living. In her film debut, Emmanuelle Riva is superb as the woman, subtly suggesting the character's mysterious past and emotional instability. In its masterly, and sometimes revolutionary, use of editing and camerawork, melded with a metaphorical story and spare, poetic dialogue by novelist Marguerite Duras, HIROSHIMA MON AMOUR remains one of the greatest and most auspicious feature-film debuts in the history of cinema.

HIS GIRL FRIDAY 📀
1940 92m bw Comedy ★★★★★
Columbia (U.S.)

Cary Grant (Walter Burns), Rosalind Russell (Hildy Johnson), Ralph Bellamy (Bruce Baldwin), Gene Lockhart (Sheriff Hartwell), Helen Mack (Mollie Malloy), Porter Hall (Murphy), Ernest Truex (Roy Bensinger), Cliff Edwards (Endicott), Clarence Kolb (Mayor), Roscoe Karns (McCue)

p, Howard Hawks; d, Howard Hawks; w, Charles Lederer (based on the play by Ben Hecht, Charles MacArthur); ph, Joseph Walker; ed, Gene Havlick; m, M.W. Stoloff; art d, Lionel Banks; cos, Robert Kalloch

Perfection and possibly the fastest comedy on record. This hilarious re-working of THE FRONT PAGE by Hecht and MacArthur sees Grant as the savage editor and, in a switch, the reporter played by a scheming Russell. Instead of merely having the editor doing all in his power to keep his most brilliant reporter on staff, this version adds the twin lures of sex and romance, since Russell is Grant's ex-wife. She intends to marry again and her intended is the blatheringly innocent Bellamy, here in the quintessential Bellamy second lead. When convicted killer Qualen escapes his cell the night before he is to hang and hides in the news room of the jail—inside a rolltop desk—Grant uses the incident to entice Russell back to work. She is to write the scoop of the break, but Grant's deeper motive is to keep Russell near him so he can somehow woo her back.

The machine gun dialogue is by Charlie Lederer, Hecht's friend and sometime collaborator: Biberman, a thug working for Grant, defends his new girlfriend by saying: "She's not an albino; she was born right here in this country!" Russell calls in a report to the city desk: "Shot him right in the classified ads… No, 'ads'!" And there are many inside jokes. Grant criticizes Bellamy to Russell, saying he "looks like that actor… Ralph Bellamy!" Grant again grins as he says: "The last man that said that to me was Archie Leach just a week before he cut his throat." (Archie Leach was Grant's real name.)

The film moves at whirlwind speed, as Hawks instructed his actors to overlap their lines, so much so that at times everyone seems to be talking at once. One archivist actually timed the hurricane delivery of the actors at 240 words per minute, so fast that the dialogue is just discernible, the actors speaking about 130 words per minute above average delivery. Hawks also had his cast move at twice normal speed so the whole thing was frantic from scene to scene, thus conveying the urgency of the news world he was depicting.

HIS GIRL FRIDAY is distinctly Hawksian, bearing his trademark of madcap comedy, also brilliantly shown in BRINGING UP BABY and I WAS A MALE WAR BRIDE, both starring Grant. But FRIDAY presents Grant in a no-holds-barred comedy-bully performance. This time he's the aggressor, the persecutor as he cajoles, aggravates, intimidates, lies—sometimes he even resorts to noises in this hilariously self-centered performance. It's his greatest comedic role, proving once again the amazing versatility of this fine actor.

Russell is at her peak, too—demonstrating her own brittle breakneck speed with comedy lines and instilling an ungainly charm into Hildy's physicality. Katharine Hepburn, Jean Arthur, Margaret Sullavan, Irene Dunne, Claudette Colbert and Carole Lombard were all offered the role, but turned it down. Russell leapt at the chance to play the screwball role and it turned out to be her greatest comedy part, one which assured her immortality. The supporting cast is a Who's Who of willing comedy loons.

HIT, THE

DVD

1984 100m c Drama ★★★½

Zenith (U.K.) R

Terence Stamp (Willie Parker), John Hurt (Braddock), Tim Roth (Myron), Laura del Sol (Maggie), Bill Hunter (Harry), Fernando Rey (Chief Inspector), Carlos Lucena (Uniformed Officer), Freddie Stuart, Ralph Brown, A.J. Clarke (Government Agents)

p, Jeremy Thomas; d, Stephen Frears; w, Peter Prince; ph, Mike Molloy; ed, Mick Audsley; m, Paco de Lucia, Eric Clapton; prod d, Andrew Sanders; art d, Julio Molina; fx, Alan Whibley, Reyes Abades; cos, Marit Allen

Stephen Frears' second feature as a director (after his debut, 1971's GUMSHOE, he had worked in TV for 13 years) is an offbeat, existential crime drama buoyed by fine performances; nicely turned dialogue; and an evocative soundtrack and theme song from Paco di Lucia and Eric Clapton, respectively.

The story begins in 1973 at a criminal trial where former mob operative Willie Parker (Terence Stamp) testifies against his sometime cronies. After turning state's evidence, he is released. Cut to a quiet Spanish village ten years later. Parker, having enjoyed a quiet, contemplative period of exile following his turning state's evidence, is flushed out of his house by a gang of thugs and handed over to Braddock (John Hurt), a veteran hit man, and his volatile young assistant, Myron (Tim Roth). Parker is hustled into their car, to be taken to Paris and executed by a mob chieftain for his testimony of ten years before. Stamp, however, doesn't seem in the least bit frightened; in fact, he seems to enjoy what is happening…

In THE HIT, director Stephen Frears works against all genre conventions—the hit man becomes emotionally involved with his prey, while the victim accepts his fate with equanimity and grace. The characters are not genre stereotypes, but fully rounded individuals riddled with insecurities and doubts. Besides having a superb screenplay, Frears is blessed, here, with an unparalleled cast. Both Hurt and Stamp are as good as they've ever been, while the very young Tim Roth makes a very promising debut. Reviewed well in the U.S., THE HIT made very little impression at the box office.

HITCH

DVD

2005 118m c Romance/Comedy ★★★

Overbrook Entertainment/Columbia (U.S.) PG-13

Will Smith (Alex "Hitch" Hitchens), Eva Mendes (Sara), Kevin James (Albert), Amber Valletta (Allegra Cole), Julie Ann Emery (Casey), Robinne Lee (Cressida), Nathan Lee Graham (Geoff), Adam Arkin (Max), Michael Rapaport (Ben), Jeffrey Donovan (Vance)

p, James Lassiter, Will Smith, Teddy Zee; d, Andy Tennant; w, Kevin Bisch; ph, Andrew Dunn; ed, Troy Takaki; m, George Fenton; prod d, Jane Musky; art d, Patricia Woodbridge; fx, Conrad Brink Jr., Eli Jarra; cos, Marlene Stewart

Movie lotharios who deliver tips on pursuing women directly to the audience are nothing new. But while charismatic bachelor Alex Hitchens (Will Smith) may share Alfie's commitment problems, "Hitch" is all about spreading the love and helping his fellow men.

Hitch's anonymous, by-referral-only service caters to less-than-suave New York City bachelors who are truly in love, and while he uses his own tools to woo a wide variety of sexy singles, Hitch is careful not to commit to any of them; he once had his own heart brutally broken. Sexy gossip columnist Sara Melas (Eva Mendes), however, may prove to be his biggest personal dating challenge ever, once he must undertake while simultaneously transforming fat, clumsy, but sweet accountant Albert (Kevin James) into a databable specimen capable of winning his gorgeous, wealthy celebrity client, Allegra Cole (Amber Valleta). With Hitch's coaching, Albert manages to intrigue the lovely Ms. Cole. They attend a fashion event together, and she ends up smitten with his unconventional ways and offbeat sense of humor. Hitch's date with Sara, meanwhile, is an unmitigated disaster, but she seems to enjoy his company. Trouble begins to brew when gossip-hound Sara discovers that the dorky Albert won Allegra with the help of an elusive "date doctor," and decides that uncovering the shadowy legend's identity would make a juicy story.

SWEET HOME ALABAMA director Andy Tennant's latest foray into modern romance is overlong and occasionally dips into the melodramatic, but when it's funny, it's a riot. The featured couples share an easy and believable chemistry, and it doesn't hurt that Smith can handle both romance and comedy, particularly of the physical sort.

HITCHHIKER'S GUIDE TO THE GALAXY, THE

DVD

2005 110m C Science Fiction/Comedy ★★★
Spyglass Entertainment/Touchstone/Barber/ PG
Birnbaum Productions/Hammer and Tongs
Productions/Everyman Pictures (U.S./U.K.)

Sam Rockwell *(Zaphod Beeblebrox),* Zooey Deschanel *(Trish McMillan/Trillian),* Mos Def *(Ford Prefect),* Martin Freeman *(Arthur Dent),* Bill Nighy *(Slartibartfast),* Warwick Davis *(Marvin),* Anna Chancellor *(Questular),* Alan Rickman *(Voice of Marvin),* Helen Mirren *(Voice of Deep Thought),* Stephen Fry *(Narrator)*

p, Gary Barber, Roger Birnbaum, Jonathan Glickman, Nick Goldsmith, Jay Roach; d, Garth Jennings; w, Douglas Adams, Karey Kirkpatrick (based on the book by Douglas Adams); ph, Igor Jadue-Lillo; ed, Niven Howie; m, Joby Talbot; prod d, Joel Collins; art d, Frank Walsh; fx, Angus Bickerton, Paul Dunn, Wilma Dunn, Ben Flatter, Jim Henson's Creature Shop (creature effects), Matt Johnson, Lindsay McFarlane, Adam McInnes, Jon Neill (CG), Sue Rowe; cos, Sammy Sheldon

Douglas Adams' cult mainstay *The Hitchhiker's Guide to the Galaxy* traveled a long, strange road from BBC radio show to book series to interactive CD-ROM to feature film, and die-hard fans will regret every scrap jettisoned along the way. Director Garth Jennings and screenwriter Karey Kirkpatrick, who revised the script Adams completed before his death in 2001, remain true to the material's shaggy, baggy spirit and successfully resist the temptation to turn the movie into a gigantic CGI spectacle.

Shortly before Earth is vaporized to make way for a hyperspace bypass, shabby little Everyman Arthur Dent (Martin Freeman) is busy processing a series of life-altering revelations. First there's the news about Earth, then the fact that his friend, Ford Prefect (Mos Def), is actually an alien researching new material for the intergalactic best-seller "The Hitchhiker's Guide to the Galaxy," the bible of cosmic thumb-tripping. Veteran hitcher Ford gets them an illicit lift on one of the very ships that just destroyed Earth, and masterminds their escape from the awful Vogons, bureaucratic overlords of the universe. Ford and Arthur's next ride is aboard the *Heart of Gold,* which Ford's cousin, renegade Galactic President Zaphod Beeblebrox (Sam Rockwell), an insufferable dandy with two heads, three arms, and half a brain, hijacked so he could search for the fabled planet Magrathea. His companions in questing are a desperately depressed android, Marvin (voiced by Alan Rickman), and Trillian, the girl (Zooey Deschanel) Arthur once bored at a costume party with his homey attitude.

Driven equally by big questions and the abiding desire for small pleasures, like a decent cup of tea, it's an eccentric, mind-bending head trip that greets every catastrophe with an endearingly goofy smile that embodies *Hitchhiker's Guide*'s Zen mantra: Don't Panic!

HOBSON'S CHOICE

1954 107m bw Comedy ★★★★
London Films (U.K.)

Charles Laughton *(Henry Horatio Hobson),* John Mills *(Willie Mossop),* Brenda de Banzie *(Maggie Hobson),* Daphne Anderson *(Alice Hobson),* Prunella Scales *(Vicky Hobson),* Richard Wattis *(Albert Prosser),* Derek Blomfield *(Freddy Beenstock),* Helen Haye *(Mrs. Hepworth),* Joseph Tomelty *(Jim Heeler),* Julien Mitchell *(Sam Minns)*

p, David Lean; d, David Lean; w, David Lean, Norman Spencer, Wynyard Browne (based on the play by Harold Brighouse); ph,

Jack Hildyard; ed, Peter Taylor; m, Malcolm Arnold; prod d, Wilfred Shingleton; cos, John Armstrong

Laughton is marvelous in this wry comedy as the crusty old curmudgeon who rules his profitable boot shop and his three unmarried daughters with an iron hand. He hypocritically downs his pints of ale at the local pub and cries out against the inhumanity of life at leaving him a widower. His eldest daughter, de Banzie, is 30 and, in Laughton's words, "on the shelf." Undaunted, she finds herself a husband in the form of the self-effacing, illiterate, and ambitionless Mills, Laughton's assistant and chief bootmaker for the firm.

Mills is a bit dumbfounded when being led to the altar and even more puzzled when de Banzie sets him up in his own bootmaking business after Laughton refuses to award de Banzie a dowry. With de Banzie brainstorming the business, Mills's shop grows and he prospers, so much so that he begins to make inroads into Laughton's once dominant operation.

This is a fully developed comedy of human foibles and follies with Laughton rendering a masterful, sly performance, beautifully supported by de Banzie and Mills. Laughton, who played the role on stage years earlier, was reputedly unhappy on the set; he developed a dislike for de Banzie (who, incredibly, almost upstages Laughton, himself a consummate upstager) and he didn't care for Mills in the role of Willie Mossop, a part he'd wanted Robert Donat to play. Lean's direction is careful and properly mannered as he draws forth one poignant scene after another, some painful, others full of mirth.

Arnold's inventive score adds considerable charm to this best of three versions of Harold Brighouse's 1915 stage comedy (filmed in 1920 as a silent with Arthur Pitt and Joan Ritz, and again as a talkie in 1931 with James Harcourt and Viola Lyel). This film rightly won the Best British Film Award in 1954.

HOLD BACK THE DAWN

1941 115m bw Romance ★★★★
Paramount (U.S.)

Charles Boyer *(Georges Iscovescu),* Olivia de Havilland *(Emmy Brown),* Paulette Goddard *(Anita Dixon),* Victor Francen *(Van Den Luecken),* Walter Abel *(Inspector Hammock),* Curt Bois *(Bonbois),* Rosemary DeCamp *(Berta Kurz),* Eric Feldary *(Josef Kurz),* Nestor Paiva *(Flores),* Eva Puig *(Lupita)*

p, Arthur Hornblow Jr.; d, Mitchell Leisen; w, Charles Brackett, Billy Wilder (based on a story by Ketti Frings); ph, Leo Tover; ed, Doane Harrison; m, Victor Young; art d, Hans Dreier, Robert Usher; cos, Edith Head

AAN Best Picture; AAN Best Actress: Olivia DeHavilland; *AAN Best Screenplay:* Charles Brackett, Billy Wilder; *AAN Best B/W Cinematography:* Leo Tover; *AAN Best Score (Drama):* Victor Young; *AAN Best Interior Decoration (B/W):* Hans Dreier (Art Direction), Robert Usher (Art Direction), Sam Comer (Interior Decoration)

A touching and memorable film, this brilliant romance offers evocative performances by Boyer and de Havilland. It opens with a typical Wilder twist: Leisen, shown on the set of I WANTED WINGS, directing a scene with Brian Donlevy and Veronica Lake, is approached by Romanian gigolo Boyer, a one-time European dancer and ladies' escort. Boyer wants to sell movie director Leisen a story for $500. He then fascinates the director with the tale that is HOLD BACK THE DAWN, played out in flashback.

Boyer, stranded in a Mexican border town, lives in a run-down hotel, the Esperanza, which houses all manner of human driftwood from Europe, refugees from Nazi oppression, not the least of whom is Francen, a Dutch professor who acts as a sort of father confessor to the disenfranchised. One pathetic emigre is Rosemary DeCamp, a pregnant refugee who slips across the border to have her child in the U.S. Visiting the area with her students is American schoolteacher de Havilland, who becomes Boyer's easy victim in a matrimonial-immigration scam suggested by vixen Goddard.

Unabashed soppy soaper, but Leisen's pro touch and sensitive direction keep it from ever becoming maudlin. DAWN exploits the darkly sexy side of Boyer and the mechanistic side of Goddard quite well; the screenplay by Brackett and Wilder is beautifully written, covering for any loopholes in the de Havilland role. The characters were drawn from the life of story writer Frings and her struggle to get her immigrant husband Kurt into the U.S. via Mexico. There is much here that calls to mind ARCH OF TRIUMPH, also starring Boyer, who always felt that HOLD BACK THE DAWN was one of his best films.

HOLIDAY INN
DVD
1942   100m   bw   Musical/Comedy
★★★
Paramount   (U.S.)

Bing Crosby *(Jim Hardy)*, Fred Astaire *(Ted Hanover)*, Marjorie Reynolds *(Linda Mason)*, Virginia Dale *(Lila Dixon)*, Walter Abel *(Danny Reid)*, Louise Beavers *(Mamie)*, John Gallaudet *(Parker)*, James Bell *(Dunbar)*, Irving Bacon *(Gus)*, Shelby Bacon *(Vanderbilt)*

p, Mark Sandrich; d, Mark Sandrich; w, Claude Binyon, Elmer Rice (based on an idea by Irving Berlin); ph, David Abel; ed, Ellsworth Hoagland; art d, Hans Dreier, Roland Anderson; chor, Danny Dare; cos, Edith Head

AAN Best Original Story: Irving Berlin; *AAN Best Score (Musical):* Robert Emmett Dolan; *AA Best Song:* "White Christmas"; Irving Berlin

Dowdy and thin. Based on an idea by Irving Berlin, this is a small musical about a song-and-dance man, Jim Hardy (Bing Crosby), who retires from the biz to become a gentleman farmer in New England, finds country life more demanding than he thought, and tries to have best of both worlds when he turns his farm into a very special hostelry that's only open to the public on national holidays. The film's highlight is a bang-up July 4th "Let's Say It with Firecrackers" that finds Astaire in fine form, Crosby sings "White Christmas" for the first time, and the score includes "Easter Parade." But the girls are duds and the film lacks festivity, showbiz pizzazz, flash.

HOLLYWOOD BOULEVARD
DVD
1976   83m   c   Comedy
★★★
New World   (U.S.)
R

Candice Rialson *(Candy Wednesday)*, Mary Woronov *(Mary McQueen)*, Rita George *(Bobbi Quackenbush)*, Jeffrey Kramer *(Patrick Hobby)*, Dick Miller *(Walter Paisley)*, Richard Doran *(Producer)*, Tara Strohmeier *(Jill McBain)*, Paul Bartel *(Erich Von Leppe)*, John Kramer *(Duke Mantee)*, Jonathan Kaplan *(Scotty)*

p, Jon Davison; d, Joe Dante, Allan Arkush; w, Patrick Hobby; ph, Jamie Anderson (Metrocolor); ed, Amy Jones, Allan Arkush, Joe Dante; m, Andrew Stein; art d, Jack DeWolfe; fx, Roger George; cos, Jane Rum

Totally shameless but self-accepting parody of the schlock movie business and Roger Corman's B-factory, New World Pictures. Rialson is a would-be actress who wants stardom. Her agent, Miller, sends her to Miracle Pictures, where she lands a role in the studio's latest epic, MACHETE MAIDENS OF MARATAU. But actress Woronov doesn't like competition, and suddenly there is a series of murders. The film ends with a shootout atop the famous Hollywood sign. HOLLYWOOD BOULEVARD is that rarest of creatures: a parody of a parody that actually is funny and works well. Not to be missed by camp fans.

HOLY SMOKE
DVD
1999   114m   c   Drama
★★★
Miramax   (U.S.)
R

Kate Winslet *(Ruth Barron)*, Harvey Keitel *(PJ Waters)*, Julie Hamilton *(Miriam—Mum)*, Tim Robertson *(Gilbert—Dad)*, Sophie Lee *(Yvonne)*, Dan Wyllie *(Robbie)*, Pam Grier *(Carol)*, Paul Goddard *(Tim)*, George Mangos *(Yani)*, Kerry Walker *(Puss)*

p, Jan Chapman; d, Jane Campion; w, Anna Campion, Jane Campion; ph, Dion Beebe; ed, Veronika Jenet; m, Angelo Badalamenti; prod d, Janet Patterson; art d, Tony Campbell; fx, Andy Brown; cos, Janet Patterson

A headstrong young woman and a cocksure older man are locked in a battle of wills in this sly film directed by Jane Campion and co-written with her sister Anna.

On a visit to India, Ruth Barron (Kate Winslet) becomes a disciple of a local guru, much to the dismay of her loopy family. On the advice of a friend, they hire an American "exit counselor" named PJ Waters (Harvey Keitel) to un-brainwash Ruth and trick her into returning to Australia. The superstar veteran of 189 successful deprogrammings, Waters sweeps into less-than-ideal circumstances: Ruth's family is a bunch of nut jobs and the assistant he was promised has gone missing, with no suitable replacement available. But PJ forges ahead, whisking Ruth off to an isolated halfway house in the Australian outback; he reckons it will take all of three days to strip her of her starry-eyed delusions about the sleazy swami and return her to her old life. How wrong he is.

Under all the far-ranging talk—and there's plenty of it—Campion's film is fairly single-minded: Ruth and PJ are locked in a staring contest, a childish endurance test played for adult stakes. Ruth and PJ are both convinced they have the upper hand and each will do whatever it takes to win, no matter how searing the emotional cost. Winslet and Keitel are perfectly matched, go-for-broke actors handed dramatic license to do a psychic striptease, which is how Winslet winds up naked and urinating in the dust while Keitel ends up in lipstick and a dress. Campion's seductive flourishes are eye-catching but never gratuitous, and the image of Winslet as a multi-armed goddess is truly ravishing.

HOME ALONE
DVD
1990   98m   c   Comedy
★★½
Hughes   (U.S.)
PG

Macaulay Culkin *(Kevin McCallister)*, Joe Pesci *(Harry)*, Daniel Stern *(Marv)*, John Heard *(Peter)*, Roberts Blossom *(Marley)*, Catherine O'Hara *(Kate)*, Angela Goethals *(Linnie)*, Devin Rattray *(Buzz)*, Gerry Bamman *(Uncle Frank)*, Hillary Wolf *(Megan)*

p, John Hughes; d, Chris Columbus; w, John Hughes; ph, Julio Macat; m, John Williams; prod d, John Muto; art d, Dan Webster; fx, Bill Purcell; cos, Jay Hurley

AAN Best Original Score: John Williams; *AAN Best Original Song:* "Somewhere in My Memory"; John Williams (Music), Leslie Bricusse (Lyrics)

STRAW DOGS Lite. HOME ALONE, a surprisingly violent, paranoid fantasy for kids, became the highest grossing comedy of all time. It also made a star out of a funny-looking kid named Macaulay Culkin.

Eight-year-old Kevin McCallister (Culkin) feels slighted by his large, obnoxious family and throws a temper tantrum on the eve of a vacation trip to Europe. Exiled to his room by his mother (Catherine O'Hara), Kevin fatefully wishes that his family would disappear. The next morning, he awakens to find himself all alone in the house. Scared at first, he soon proves adept at fending for himself. As his guilt-stricken mom begins an arduous journey back from

Europe to rescue her son, Kevin elaborately defends the house against a pair of menacing but comically inept burglars (Daniel Stern and Joe Pesci).

The first half of HOME ALONE features the sugar-coated sentimentality that can usually be found in a Hughes film, while the second half is full of unanticipated sadism (a close-up of Stern's bare foot slipping slowly down a six-inch nail is the film's most ghastly image). As directed by Chris Columbus (HEARTBREAK HOTEL), the film's slapstick falls flat and only the pain remains. Yet the film's message seems even more disturbing than its violence. This could be the first comedy—it's certainly the first holiday film—which focuses on child abuse. As Kevin shoots pellets into the intruders and takes a blowtorch to their heads, he's directing the hostility he feels toward his neglectful parents at these two guys. The only really likable thing about this film is Culkin (UNCLE BUCK, JACOB'S LADDER). He's an uncommonly natural child actor, but even he doesn't always survive the tiresome gags (the aftershave bit is funny once; three times is tedious).

HOME AND THE WORLD, THE
(GHARE BAIRE)
1984 140m c Drama ★★★
Natl. Film Dev. Corp. of India (India)

Soumitra Chatterjee *(Sandip Mukherjee)*, Victor Banerjee *(Nikhilesh Choudhury)*, Swatilekha Chatterjee *(Bimala Choudhury)*, Manoj Mitra *(Headmaster)*, Indrapramit Roy *(Amulya)*, Bimala Chatterjee *(Kulada)*

d, Satyajit Ray; w, Satyajit Ray (based on the novel by Rabindranath Tagore); ph, Soumendu Roy (Eastmancolor); ed, Dulal Dutta; m, Satyajit Ray; art d, Ashoke Bose

This graceful film by Ray is as much a tragic love story as an examination of political turmoil in 1908 India. Banerjee stars as a Westernized Hindu maharajah who lives with his wife, Swatilekha Chatterjee, in colonial Bengal. Political tension grows when Lord Curzon, the British governor-general of India, enacts a plan to "divide and rule" Hindus and Muslims through the partition of Bengal. Because of the resulting unrest, Soumitra Chatterjee, a fiery rebel and friend of Banerjee, pays a visit to the town. Not convinced that his wife truly loves him, Banerjee encourages his wife to come out of purdah (orthodox seclusion) to meet other men, namely his rebellious friend. If she remains faithful after having met others, Banerjee reasons, he can be certain of her love. His plan backfires, however, when his wife falls in love with the rebel.

What's more, political differences arise between the two men. Based on a novel by Nobel Prize-winning author Tagore, THE HOME AND THE WORLD was to have come to the screen 30 years earlier as Ray's first film. Tagore, a friend of Ray's family, had published his book in 1919 to much acclaim; Ray read the book as a youth and wrote a screenplay based on it. It wasn't until 1980, however, that the great Indian filmmaker returned to the project.

HOMECOMING, THE
1973 111m c Drama ★★★★
American Film Theatre (U.S.) PG

Cyril Cusack *(Sam)*, Ian Holm *(Lenny)*, Michael Jayston *(Teddy)*, Vivien Merchant *(Ruth)*, Terence Rigby *(Joey)*, Paul Rogers *(Max)*

p, Ely A. Landau; d, Peter Hall; w, Harold Pinter (based on his play); ph, David Watkin; ed, Rex Pike; prod d, John Bury; art d, Jack Stevens; cos, Elizabeth Haffenden, Joan Bridge

Excellent adaptation of the Pinter play for the American Film Theatre series of the early 1970s. The simple plot features Jayston returning to his childhood home with wife Merchant. There he sees his father (Rogers), uncle (Cusack), and his

brothers (Holm and Rigby), who are a pimp and a boxer, respectively. The small family is held together by volatile fighting, boredom, and ultimate dependency on one another. Each performance is a gem. The individual quirks of each character are well-executed and utterly believable. Hall's direction is sensitive to Pinter's script and to the acting of the ensemble (who all played in the original 1965 stage production). There is a magical chemistry within every frame of this powerful, unforgettable film.

HOMICIDE
1991 102m c Crime/Drama ★★★½
Cinehaus Inc./Edward R. Pressman Corporation R
(U.S.)

Joe Mantegna *(Bobby Gold)*, William H. Macy, billed as W.H. Macy *(Tim Sullivan)*, Natalija Nogulich *(Chava)*, Ving Rhames *(Randolph)*, Rebecca Pidgeon *(Miss Klein)*, Vincent Guastaferro *(Lt. Senna)*, Lionel Mark Smith *(Charlie Olcott)*, Jack Wallace *(Frank)*, J.J. Johnston *(Curren)*, Paul Butler *(Deputy Mayor Walker)*

p, Michael Hausman, Edward R. Pressman; d, David Mamet; w, David Mamet; ph, Roger Deakins; ed, Barbara Tulliver; m, Alaric Jans; prod d, Michael Merritt; art d, Susan Kaufman; fx, Kenny Estes; cos, Nan Cibula

HOMICIDE starts out as a tense, superbly acted police drama, but degenerates fast when it starts dabbling in anti-Semitic conspiracy theories and questions of identity and ethnicity.

Joe Mantegna is superb in the role of Bobby Gold, a tough Chicago cop known as "the orator" for to his ability to sweet-talk villains into deals with the law. He regards himself as a cop first and a Jew hardly at all, and reacts with annoyance when the well-connected family of a murdered elderly Jewish woman pull strings to ensure that he is assigned the case. The dead woman's beautiful granddaughter (Rebecca Pidgeon) shames Gold into reconsidering his sneering attitude toward his own race, and soon he is hot on an increasingly unconvincing trail that involves cryptic Hebrew scholars, underground Zionist groups, and an overnight transformation for our hero from cynical cop to militant Jewish activist.

It's sad that HOMICIDE goes so drastically off the rails, because the first half of the film is a positive joy. Writer-director David Mamet does a brilliant job of capturing the camaraderie among Gold's colleagues, with his trademark staccato, repetitious dialogue building to some hilarious exchanges. The action sequences are cleverly and even humorously handled. But the later, "conspiracy" scenes are as unconvincing and somber as the earlier "cop" sequences are concretely realized and funny—a structural problem that is particularly disappointing in the light of Mamet's superbly crafted earlier films, HOUSE OF GAMES and THINGS CHANGE. Not even Mantegna can make us believe the conversion his character is supposed to undergo; things change, but not that fast, and not with so little explanation.

HONEY, I SHRUNK THE KIDS
1989 86m c Children's/Science Fiction ★★★
Walt Disney Productions (U.S.) PG

Rick Moranis *(Prof. Wayne Szalinski)*, Matt Frewer *(Big Russ Thompson)*, Marcia Strassman *(Diane Szalinski)*, Kristine Sutherland *(Mae Thompson)*, Thomas Brown *(Little Russ Thompson)*, Jared Rushton *(Ron Thompson)*, Amy O'Neill *(Amy Szalinski)*, Robert Oliveri *(Nick Szalinski)*, Carl Steven *(Tommy Pervis)*, Mark L. Taylor *(Don Forrester)*

p, Penney Finkelman Cox, Brian Yuzna, Jon Landau; d, Joe Johnston; w, Ed Naha, Tom Schulman (based on a story by Stuart Gordon, Yuzna, Naha); ph, Hiro Narita (Metrocolor); ed,

Michael A. Stevenson; m, James Horner; prod d, Gregg Fonseca; art d, John Iacovelli, Dorree Cooper; cos, Carol Brolaski

Reminiscent of earlier Disney live-action classics like THE ABSENT-MINDED PROFESSOR and SON OF FLUBBER, HONEY, I SHRUNK THE KIDS provides a wonderful blend of thrills, character, and humor that will keep both children and adults charmed and engaged throughout.

Rick Moranis stars as Prof. Wayne Szalinski, a nutty inventor who is trying to create a machine that will shrink living things. When the professor's kids—teenage daughter Amy (Amy O'Neil) and little brother Nick (Robert Oliveri)—and two of their friends (Thomas Brown, Jared Rushton) accidentally activate the machine, they are all shrunk to quarter-inch size. So begins their dangerous adventure from the trash can, where the professor has unknowingly put them, through the seemingly gargantuan back yard, to what they hope will be the safety of the house.

Based on a story by Stuart Gordon (RE-ANIMATOR), Brian Yuzna and Ed Naha, HONEY, I SHRUNK THE KIDS was to have been directed by Gordon, but, after conflicts with the studio, he was replaced by special-effects man Joe Johnston (making his directorial debut). Espousing values of decency and tolerance between its terrific action sequences, HONEY harkens back to Disney's past. Consistently exciting, inventive and fun, the film is a rollicking good adventure, with enough bravura effects to keep the most hyperactive youngster interested. Fittingly, Buena Vista's best release since WHO FRAMED ROGER RABBIT? was coupled with a brand new Roger Rabbit cartoon short, TUMMY TROUBLE, the first animated short produced by the Disney studio in over 25 years.

HONEYMOON IN VEGAS

DVD

1992 95m c Romance/Comedy ★★★½
Castle Rock/Lobell/Bergman Productions (U.S.) PG-13

James Caan (*Tommy Korman*), Nicolas Cage (*Jack Singer*), Sarah Jessica Parker (*Betsy/Donna*), Noriyuki "Pat" Morita, billed as Pat Morita (*Mahi*), Peter Boyle (*Chief Orman*), Anne Bancroft (*Bea Singer*), Seymour Cassel (*Tony Cataracts*), Johnny Williams (*Johnny Sandwich*), John Capodice (*Sally Molars*), Robert Costanzo (*Sidney Tomashefsky*)

p, Mike Lobell; d, Andrew Bergman; w, Andrew Bergman; ph, William A. Fraker; ed, Barry Malkin; m, David Newman; prod d, William A. Elliott; art d, John Warnke; cos, Julie Weiss

An amiable, if instantly forgettable, comedy, saved from oblivion by Nicolas Cage in medium-wacky mode.

Cage plays Jack Singer, a New York private detective haunted by his late mother's deathbed plea that he never marry. When, after years of procrastination, he finally pops the question to his schoolteacher girlfriend Betsy (Sarah Jessica Parker), she can't believe he's serious. "I must be serious," he replies, as his immobile car halts an angry line of traffic—"My legs are paralyzed."

Jack comes up against more than commitment angst when the couple fly to Vegas to tie the knot. He takes time out for a few rounds of poker before the ceremony and ends up losing big to Tommy (James Caan), a pro gambler who's willing to accept a weekend with Betsy in lieu of the $65,000 Jack owes him. Tommy's dastardly plan is to whisk Betsy (who's a dead ringer for his late wife) off to Hawaii for a romantic weekend that will convince her *he's* the man she needs.

HONEYMOON IN VEGAS has its fair share of snappy one-liners and a goofy visual sense that fits the material, with Bergman getting a lot of mileage out of an Elvis lookalike convention taking place in the couple's hotel. Sarah Jessica Parker does what little she's asked to do with style,

and James Caan is clearly at home playing a lizard who *nearly* has you thinking he's a nice guy. It's Nicolas Cage, though, who walks off with the show, thanks to his trademark blend of the sentimental and absurd. The final scene has him returning to Vegas in a desperate bid to save his loved one. Only Cage could make that return via parachute, wearing an illuminated Elvis costume, and still seem believable. Viva Las Vegas.

HONEYMOON KILLERS, THE

DVD

1969 115m bw Crime ★★★½
Roxanne (U.S.) R

Shirley Stoler (*Martha Beck*), Tony Lo Bianco (*Ray Fernandez*), Mary Jane Higby (*Janet Fay*), Doris Roberts (*Bunny*), Kip McArdle (*Delphine Downing*), Marilyn Chris (*Myrtle Young*), Dortha Duckworth (*Mrs. Beck*), Barbara Cason (*Evelyn Long*), Ann Harris (*Doris*), Mary Breen (*Rainelle Downing*)

p, Warren Steibel; d, Leonard Kastle; w, Leonard Kastle; ph, Oliver Wood; ed, Stanley Warnow, Richard Brophy; m, Gustav Mahler

A remarkable low-budget film that offers a chilling portrait of a pair of cold-blooded murderers. Stoler is a lonely, sexually frustrated, 200-pound nurse at a Mobile, Alabama, hospital. She lives alone with her mother, which only adds to her frustration. In desperation she joins a lonely hearts correspondence club and soon begins receiving torrid love letters from Lo Bianco, a Spanish immigrant in New York. When he comes to visit Stoler, she quickly falls in love with him.

When he steals money from her and leaves, she tracks him down and finds that he makes his living stealing from love-starved women he finds through the correspondence clubs. She loves him nonetheless, and after she is fired from her job, she puts her mother in a nursing home and heads off with Lo Bianco in search of new victims. Stoler poses as Lo Bianco's sister while he woos lonely women and then flees with their money. But when Lo Bianco marries Chris to give her baby a father, a jealous Stoler turns to murder.

Based on an actual case that got much press in the late 1940s, THE HONEYMOON KILLERS is shot in stark black-and-white documentary style and the music of Mahler is effective in counterpointing the action. The acting is second to none: the two leads are frighteningly good in their psychotic roles and supporting characters are also well delineated. But there are some technical problems with the film, notably too much shadow in the frame, several highly visible microphones and the choppy editing, which jumbles the story at times.

Still, the straightforwardness of the telling is not totally destroyed. To their credit the filmmakers have refused to romanticize the brutality of the criminals at the heart of the film. Lo Bianco went on to star in other pictures; Stoler's other major role was as the brutal Nazi prison camp commandant in Lina Wertmuller's marvelous SEVEN BEAUTIES.

HOOK

DVD

1991 144m c Fantasy/Adventure ★★★
Hook Productions/Amblin (U.S.) PG

Dustin Hoffman (*Captain James Hook*), Robin Williams (*Peter Banning/Peter Pan*), Julia Roberts (*Tinkerbell*), Bob Hoskins (*Smee*), Maggie Smith (*Granny Wendy Darling*), Caroline Goodall (*Moira Banning*), Charlie Korsmo (*Jack Banning*), Amber Scott (*Maggie Banning*), Laurel Cronin (*Liza*), Phil Collins (*Inspector Good*)

p, Kathleen Kennedy, Frank Marshall, Gerald R. Molen; d, Steven Spielberg; w, Jim V. Hart, Malia Scotch Marmo (from the story by Hart and Nick Castle, adapted from the original stage play and books by Sir James M. Barrie); ph, Dean Cundey; ed, Michael Kahn; m, John Williams; prod d, Norman Garwood; art d, Andrew Precht, Thomas E. Sanders; fx, Michael Lantieri; chor, Vince Paterson; cos, Anthony Powell

AAN Best Original Song: "When You're Alone"; John Williams (Music), Leslie Bricusse (Lyrics); *AAN Best Art Direction-Set Decoration:* Norman Garwood (Art Direction), Garrett Lewis (Set Decoration); *AAN Best Costume Design:* Anthony Powell; *AAN Best Visual Effects:* Eric Brevig, Harley Jessup, Mark Sullivan, Michael Lantieri; *AAN Best Makeup:* Christina Smith, Montague Westmore, Greg Cannom

On paper, HOOK looked promising. It boasted the high-concept idea of a grown-up Peter Pan, directed by Hollywood's perennial child-man Steven Spielberg. And thanks to a lucrative deal brokered by Creative Artists Agency, the film featured a cast of truly stellar proportions; Dustin Hoffman, Robin Williams, and Julia Roberts. It all seemed too good to be true. Well, it was.

Peter Banning (Williams) is a hard-nosed workaholic who cares about his wife and family, but is too consumed by his career to pay enough attention to them. However, he takes time to make a Christmas trip with his family to visit his wife's grandmother, Granny Wendy Darling (Maggie Smith), in London. His children are excited by the prospect of meeting her, as they know she was the Wendy on whom J.M. Barrie based the heroine of *Peter Pan*. The visit takes a dramatic turn when his children are kidnapped. That night, Peter is visited by Tinkerbell (Roberts) who tries to convince Peter that he is—or used to be—Peter Pan and that his children have been kidnapped by the evil Captain Hook (Hoffman). This seven-inch-fairy also insists that he has no choice but to return with her to Neverland to reclaim them.

HOOK's problems begin with its screenplay, a clumsy attempt to meld reality and fantasy which leaves too many issues unresolved and repeatedly assaults the viewer with wishy-washy, New Age philosophy about the importance of preserving the "inner child." The biggest disappointment, though, is Spielberg's direction; instead of youthful ebullience, we get lots of cutesy slapstick violence. Our eyes are confounded, rather than delighted, by a bustle of constant, chaotic activity. As top-heavy as Captain Hook's ornate, immobile ship, this lavish, elaborate production ultimately collapses under its own weight.

HOOP DREAMS 📀
1994 171m c Documentary/Sports ★★★★½
Kartemquin Films/KCTA-TV PG-13
(St. Paul/Minneapolis) (U.S.)

William Gates (*Himself*), Arthur Agee (*Himself*), Emma Gates (*Herself—William's Mother*), Curtis Gates (*Himself—William's Brother*), Sheila Agee (*Herself—Arthur's Mother*), Arthur "Bo" Agee (*Himself—Arthur's Father*), Earl Smith (*Himself—Talent Scout*), Gene Pingatore (*Himself—St. Joseph High School Basketball Coach*), Isiah Thomas (*Himself—Detroit Piston Basketball Player*), Sister Marilyn Hopewell (*Herself—St. Joseph Guidance Counselor*)

p, Frederick Marx, Steve James, Peter Gilbert; d, Steve James; ph, Peter Gilbert; ed, Frederick Marx, Steve James, Bill Haugse

AAN Best Film Editing: Frederick Marx, Steve James, Bill Haugse

One of the most widely discussed and well-received documentaries of the decade, HOOP DREAMS is a powerful and moving film that intimately chronicles the lives of two Chicago teenagers as they struggle with the pressures of potential basketball stardom. For five years, independent filmmakers Steve James, Frederick Marx, and Peter Gilbert recorded both the private moments and public experiences

of Arthur Agee and William Gates. The result is both a sympathetic portrait of two human beings and a stunning expose of the system that exploits "student-athletes."

The film begins in 1986, with a talent scout discovering Arthur and William as 14-year-old stars of the playground. Lured by the "hoop dreams" of college and NBA careers, both accept athletic scholarships to St. Joseph High School—introducing the film's central conflict, as young black men shuttle back and forth between their economically marginalized families in the city and a wealthy, predominantly white prep school in the suburbs. The film follows the successes and failures of four seasons of high school hoops and four years of personal growth, frustration, and tragedy.

Although HOOP DREAMS skillfully edits together exciting basketball highlights, the Agee and Gates families are its true subjects. Presumably because the cameras became such a fixture in these homes over time, they capture, in the best cinema verite tradition, compelling and revelatory moments of family dynamics. Despite the harshness of their lives, members of both families are shown to be supportive, hard-working, and (perhaps unreasonably) optimistic. Their image offers a refreshingly complicated and humane look at underclass life that puts the lie to media stereotypes of the welfare mother and the gang banger. On the other hand, the film admirably refuses to elide aspects of its subjects' lives that conflict with the old liberal myth of long-suffering, impossibly noble poor blacks.

The triumph of HOOP DREAMS is that it celebrates the game of basketball while critiquing its corporate and social underpinnings. Like Arthur and William and the culture they come from, the Chicago-based filmmakers love basketball too much not to get caught up in the excitement of the boys' final state tournament. And to some extent the film concludes with a different message than than that of its first two hours. However briefly, Arthur Agee and William Gates *do* get out of the ghetto. Their path is inglorious, their success tenuous, but this pair of likable, reluctant heroes are shown as completing a bittersweet journey.

While HOOP DREAMS was named as one of the year's best movies by virtually every prominent critic in the U.S., it failed to win Oscar nominations for Best Picture and Best Documentary Feature, giving rise to widespread criticism of the arcane and complicated process by which the Academy reviews documentary films.

HOOSIERS 📀
1986 114m c Sports ★★★½
Hemdale (U.S.) PG

Gene Hackman (*Coach Norman Dale*), Barbara Hershey (*Myra Fleener*), Dennis Hopper (*Shooter*), Sheb Wooley (*Cletus*), Fern Persons (*Opal Fleener*), Brad Boyle (*Whit*), Steve Hollar (*Rade*), Brad Long (*Strap*), David Neidorf (*Everett*), Kent Poole (*Merle*)

p, Carter DeHaven; Angelo Pizzo; d, David Anspaugh; w, Angelo Pizzo; ph, Fred Murphy (CFI Color); ed, C. Timothy O'Meara; m, Jerry Goldsmith; prod d, David Nichols; art d, David Lubin; cos, Jane E. Anderson

AAN Best Supporting Actor: Dennis Hopper; *AAN Best Original Score:* Jerry Goldsmith

It should come as little surprise that this solid, sentimental movie about basketball is set in Indiana, where babies are given roundballs before they get rattles. Loosely based on the true story of the team from tiny Milan High School (164 students), which won the 1954 Indiana state championship, this uplifting film, set in 1951, follows Norman Dale (Gene Hackman), a big-time college coach who has fallen from grace, in his leadership of the Hickory, Indiana, high-school basketball team to victory. Jimmy (Maris Valanis), the town's most gifted player, is so disturbed by the death of the previous coach that he declines to join the team, but Norman refuses to pressure him into doing so, earning the reluctant respect of Myra Fleener (Barbara Hershey), the acting principal.

Norman also remains determined to run the team *his* way, despite the animosity of the townspeople, who in the past have felt free to offer advice. With the expert help of Shooter (Dennis Hopper, in an Oscar-nominated performance that is one of the finest of his career), the alcoholic father of one of the players, Norman perseveres, and Jimmy decides to play after all.

Bursting with emotion and full of exhilarating game action, HOOSIERS captures the ambience of small-town Indiana basketball. David Anspaugh's direction is assured, Fred Murphy's cinematography and Jerry Goldsmith's score masterful, and the performances uniformly strong. However, the film clearly functions as wish-fulfillment for the kind of people who are nostalgic about all-white basketball, leaving a nasty aftertaste.

HOPALONG CASSIDY   DVD
1935 60m   bw Western   ★★★
Paramount   (U.S.)

William Boyd (*Bill Cassidy*), James Ellison (*Johnny Nelson*), Paula Stone (*Mary Meeker*), Robert Warwick (*Jim Meeker*), Charles Middleton (*Buck Peters*), Frank McGlynn Jr. (*Red Connors*), Kenneth Thomson (*Pecos Jack Anthony*), George "Gabby" Hayes (*Uncle Ben*), James Mason (*Tom Shaw*), Frank Campeau (*Frisco*)

p, Harry Sherman; d, Howard Bretherton; w, Doris Schroeder, Harrison Jacobs (based on a story by Clarence E. Mulford); ph, Archie Stout; ed, Edward Schroeder

The first of the HOPALONG CASSIDY oaters in what became one of the longest-running series of Westerns in the history of movies and made an international star of the nearly washed-up silent actor William Boyd.

Boyd, youngster Ellison, and McGlynn, Jr. try to prevent a range war between two cattlemen which is instigated by an evil ranch foreman who plays both sides against the middle and helps an outlaw gang snatch the cattle. The scheme succeeds because each side blames the other for the missing stock. Eventually, with Boyd's help, both ranchers wise up, and they combine their efforts, sending a small army of cowboys into the gang's mountain hideout where justice eventually triumphs.

Independent producer Sherman bought the rights to Clarence E. Mulford's series of "Bar 20" western novels which featured a grizzled, tough-talking, hard-drinking, slightly crippled old cowboy named Hopalong Cassidy. When producer Sherman asked Boyd to play the ranch foreman, he refused but agreed to play Cassidy if the character was rewritten to be a clean-living, noble hero. (The limp was also abandoned after the first few movies, leaving the name "Hopalong" something of a mystery years later.) The result was a seemingly unending string of Westerns. After 50 films, Sherman sold out his ownership to Boyd, who saw the series to its eventual conclusion and its 1950s TV craze.

HOPE AND GLORY   DVD
1987 113m c   Comedy/Drama/War   ★★★★½
Columbia   (U.K.)   PG-13

Sebastian Rice-Edwards (*Bill Rohan*), Geraldine Muir (*Sue Rohan*), Sarah Miles (*Grace Rohan*), David Hayman (*Clive Rohan*), Sammi Davis (*Dawn Rohan*), Derrick O'Connor (*Mac*), Susan Wooldridge (*Molly*), Jean-Marc Barr (*Cpl. Bruce Carey*), Ian Bannen (*George*), Annie Leon (*Bill's Grandmother*)

p, John Boorman, Michael Dryhurst; d, John Boorman; w, John Boorman; ph, Philippe Rousselot, John Harris (Eastmancolor); ed, Ian Crafford; m, Peter Martin; prod d, Anthony Pratt; art d, Don

Dossett; fx, Rodney Fuller, Michael Collins, Phil Stokes; chor, Anthony Van Laast; cos, Shirley Russell

AAN Best Picture; AAN Best Director: John Boorman; AAN Best Original Screenplay: John Boorman; AAN Best Cinematography: Philippe Rousselot; AAN Best Art Direction-Set Decoration: Anthony Pratt (Art Direction), Joan Woollard (Set Decoration)

HOPE AND GLORY is a wonderful film, an intelligent, heartfelt, personal, and marvelously entertaining look at what it was like to grow up in wartorn England.

A semiautobiographical project from British director John Boorman, the film depicts nine-year-old Bill (Sebastian Rice-Edwards) as he experiences the wonders of WWII from his suburban London home. While Americans may find it somewhat disconcerting to see the Blitz and its horrors made the setting for a nostalgic comedy, for Boorman's young boy the war was a particularly exciting and vivid time, and a joyous feeling permeates the film. The total upheaval of the staid family order, the lack of normal restrictions and discipline, and the liberating effect the war had on women are all brilliantly conveyed by Boorman, because he views the war from a child's perspective.

Told in a series of vignettes, HOPE AND GLORY unfolds in a surprisingly nonchalant manner, dispensing its vividly realized observations at every turn. Boorman skillfully combines nuggets of truth with moments of mirth and is always prepared to surprise and amuse without sentimentalizing.

HORROR OF DRACULA   DVD
1958 82m   c   Horror   ★★★★
Hammer   (U.K.)

Peter Cushing (*Van Helsing*), Michael Gough (*Arthur Holmwood*), Melissa Stribling (*Mina Holmwood*), Christopher Lee (*Count Dracula*), Carol Marsh (*Lucy*), John Van Eyssen (*Jonathan Harker*), Miles Malleson (*Marx, the Undertaker*), Valerie Gaunt (*Vampire Woman*), Charles Lloyd Pack (*Dr. Seward*), Janina Faye (*Tania*)

p, Anthony Hinds; d, Terence Fisher; w, Jimmy Sangster; ph, Jack Asher; ed, Bill Lenny; m, James Bernard; art d, Bernard Robinson; cos, Molly Arbuthnot

Bloody well done. Hammer finally gave the Dracula legend the treatment it deserved here, entrusting it to the brilliant director of THE CURSE OF FRANKENSTEIN, Terence Fisher, who injected glorious life into the familiar material.

English librarian Jonathan Harker (John Van Eyssen) travels to Transylvania, where he is employed by the mysterious Count Dracula (Christopher Lee). Eventually, Harker learns that his employer is a vampire, one of the undead who must suck the blood of the living to survive, and he becomes one of Dracula's victims. Dracula then travels to London and tracks down Harker's fiancee, Lucy (Carol Marsh), and transforms her into one of the undead. Enter Dr. Van Helsing (played with zest by Peter Cushing) and the battle lines are drawn.

Fisher's version of the Dracula legend brought with it many innovative (and, yes, subsequently overdone) approaches to the genre. The film moves quickly and forcefully from one scene to the next, keeping the audience on their seat edges. Lush sets, rousing musical score, spirited acting and a direct attitude toward undead sensuality heighten the vampiric illusion. The result is a terrific combination of the intellectual and visceral that continues to work today. Followed by DRACULA - PRINCE OF DARKNESS and five more sequels.

HORSE FEATHERS   DVD
1932 70m   bw Comedy   ★★★★
Paramount   (U.S.)

Groucho Marx (*Professor Wagstaff*), Harpo Marx (*Harpo*), Chico Marx (*Chico*), Zeppo Marx (*Zeppo*), Thelma Todd (*Connie Bailey*),

David Landau (Jennings), Florine McKinney (Peggy Carrington), Jim Pierce (Mullens), Nat Pendleton (McCarthy), Reginald Barlow (President of College)

d, Norman Z. McLeod; w, Bert Kalmar, Harry Ruby, S.J. Perelman; ph, Ray June

Not a masterpiece but divine all the same. The Marx Brothers bring their special brand of anarchy to the world of college football in this wonderfully madcap comedy.

Prof. Quincy Adams Wagstaff (Groucho) is named president of Huxley College, which hasn't won a football game since its founding in 1888. Acting on the advice of his son (Zeppo), Wagstaff attempts to recruit a pair of pro players, but a mixup at a speakeasy leads him to mistake a dog catcher (Harpo) and bootlegging iceman (Chico) for football players. Just the same, Wagstaff sends them to kidnap arch rival Darwin College's ringers; unfortunately, they fail. Meanwhile, college widow Connie Bailey (Thelma Todd), who is in cahoots with Darwin's Jennings, tries to wheedle the Huxley "signals" out of Groucho.

Although there are many funny moments preceding it, the film's big payoff comes in the Huxley-Darwin game, in which Harpo, Chico and Groucho all contribute to a zany comeback victory brought about through the use of banana peels, an elastic band, a chariot, and a surplus of footballs. Perhaps the most freewheeling film the Brothers Marx ever made, this fast-paced laugh fest was directed by the great humorist S.J. Perelman with help from Bert Kalmar and Harry Ruby. With the delectable, unappreciated Thelma Todd, a spun-sugar confection from the Lombard sorority, and a marvelous foil for Groucho.

HORSE SOLDIERS, THE   DVD
1959 119m c   Western/War   ★★★
Mirisch   (U.S.)

John Wayne (Col. John Marlowe), William Holden (Maj. Henry Kendall), Constance Towers (Hannah Hunter), Althea Gibson (Lukey), Hoot Gibson (Brown), Anna Lee (Mrs. Buford), Russell Simpson (Sheriff), Stan Jones (Gen. U.S. Grant), Carleton Young (Col. Jonathan Miles), Basil Ruysdael (Boys School Commandant)

p, John Lee Mahin, Martin Rackin; d, John Ford; w, John Lee Mahin, Martin Rackin (based on the novel by Harold Sinclair); ph, William Clothier (Deluxe Color); ed, Jack Murray; m, David Buttolph; art d, Frank Hotaling; fx, Augie Lohman; cos, Frank Beetson, Ann Peck

With the exception of the Civil War segment in HOW THE WEST WAS WON, THE HORSE SOLDIERS was director John Ford's only film dealing with the War Between the States. The film is gorgeously photographed and contains many memorable images (the opening credits and breathtaking final shot) and moving scenes (one in which a Southern military school is forced to send its cadets—all children—into battle against the Union forces is a stunner), but this is not one of Ford's best efforts, suffering from a weak script and an overwrought performance from its female lead, Constance Towers.

Based on an actual mission known as Grierson's Raid, the film takes place in the spring of 1863 and finds Union general U.S. Grant (Stan Jones) frustrated by his inability to take Vicksburg. Taking drastic action, Grant decides to send a cavalry unit to Newton Station, Mississippi, deep in Confederate territory, to cut enemy supply lines to Vicksburg. The man selected to lead this daring raid is tough, no-nonsense Col. Marlowe (John Wayne), a citizen soldier who designed railroads before the war. With him goes a bevy of officers with mixed motives, including Col. Seacord (Willis Bouchey), whose political ambitions dictate his every action, and Maj. Kendall (William

Holden), a conscientious physician who sees no glory in war—only suffering and death. En route to Newton Station, the cavalry bivouacs at a plantation owned by Hannah (Towers), a Southern belle devoted to the Confederate cause. Caught spying on Marlowe and his commanders as they plan strategy, Hannah and her slave, Lukey (Althea Gibson), are taken along on the mission, lest they reveal the top-secret plans to the rebels.

While minor Ford is still head-and-shoulders above the best of most others, THE HORSE SOLDIERS is a mostly workmanlike effort in which the great director struggles against a poorly written script, with sketchy characters and overly explicit dialogue in which deep feelings and motivations come tumbling out in succinct speeches. Such pat character development invariably lends a superficial feel to the conflicts and relationships among the principals, and the viewer never really feels very deeply for the protagonists. Ford is such a master of his craft that he injects enough personal spark into the material to nearly override the script's deficiencies, but there's no denying that THE HORSE SOLDIERS is the work of a distracted, tired, and somewhat bored artist. Indeed, in his famous interview with Peter Bogdanovich, the director couldn't recall whether or not he had even seen the final cut.

HORSE WHISPERER, THE   DVD
1998 164m c   Romance/Drama   ★★★
Wildwood Enterprises/Touchstone Pictures/   PG-13
Hollywood Pictures/Double Divide   (U.S.)

Robert Redford (Tom Booker), Kristin Scott Thomas (Annie MacLean), Sam Neill (Robert MacLean), Dianne Wiest (Diane Booker), Scarlett Johansson (Grace MacLean), Chris Cooper (Frank Booker), Cherry Jones (Liz Hammond), Catherine Bosworth (Judith), Don Edwards (Smokey), Ty Hillman (Joe Booker)

p, Robert Redford, Patrick Markey; d, Robert Redford; w, Eric Roth, Richard LaGravenese (based on the novel by Nicholas Evans); ph, Robert Richardson; ed, Tom Rolf, Freeman Davies Jr., Hank Corwin; m, Thomas Newman; prod d, Jon Hutman; art d, W. Steven Graham; fx, Neil Trifunovich, Peter Donen, Peter Crosman; cos, Judy Ruskin

AAN Best Original Song: "A Soft Place to Fall"; Allison Moorer, Gwil Owen

Curl your lip if you want, but there is a place for heartwarming, even weepy dramas, and Robert Redford brings Nicholas Evans' best-selling novel about a girl and her wounded horse to the screen with dignity and restraint.

Annie MacLean (Kristin Scott Thomas) is a magazine editor who's let her career erode her relationships with husband Robert (Sam Neill) and teenage daughter Grace (Scarlett Johansson). With her best friend, Judith (Catherine Bosworth), Grace has a terrible riding accident involving a truck and an icy road: Judith dies, Grace loses a leg, and her beloved horse Pilgrim is maimed. Annie recognizes that Grace sees herself in Pilgrim, so rather than have Pilgrim put out of his misery, Annie finds "horse whisperer" Tom Booker (Redford). ("Horse whisperer" is a vaguely mystical-sounding way of saying he's got a way with animals.) Annie hauls Pilgrim and Grace out to Booker's remote Montana ranch in hopes of persuading him to work his healing magic on both.

Fans of the book probably won't mind the story changes wrought by Redford and screenwriters Eric Roth and Richard LaGravenese, and cynics just might find themselves pleasantly surprised. It's easy to make fun of earnest, therapy-tinged Sturm und Drang in which everyone has "issues"—Annie has control issues, Grace has body-image issues, Pilgrim has trust issues. But somewhere around the one (of nearly three) hour mark, the urge to snicker at the picture postcard big-sky vistas, soulful gazing deep into various eyes, and the formulaic clash of city slickers and just plain folks abates in the face of Redford's quiet confidence.

HORSE'S MOUTH, THE   *DVD*
1958 95m c   Comedy   ★★★½
UA (U.K.)

Alec Guinness *(Gulley Jimson)*, Kay Walsh *(Coker)*, Renee Houston *(Sarah)*, Mike Morgan *(Nosey)*, Robert Coote *(Sir William Beeder)*, Arthur Macrae *(Alabaster)*, Veronica Turleigh *(Lady Beeder)*, Reginald Beckwith *(Capt. Jones)*, Michael Gough *(Abel)*, Ernest Thesiger *(Hickson)*

p, John Bryan; d, Ronald Neame; w, Alec Guinness (based on the novel by Joyce Carey); ph, Arthur Ibbetson (Technicolor); ed, Anne V. Coates; m, Ken Jones

AAN Best Adapted Screenplay: Alec Guinness

Hugely enjoyable comedy about the anti-social nature of the true artist. Guinness plays Gulley Jimson, a marvelous creation of Joyce Cary's that the author loosely based on his friend Dylan Thomas. Guinness adapted the screenplay himself—a personal labor of love—and breathes fantastic life into the part of a basket-case painter who lives like a bum but produces brilliant, unorthodox work.

Released from prison after serving time as a vagrant, Guinness returns to his wife and becomes enraged when he realizes that she has been surviving by selling off his paintings. He learns that a wealthy collector, Coote, is interested in his work, and he goes to see the man but finds that he is out of town. Guinness looks about Coote's enormous flat and decides that he will simply move in and affix his latest masterpieces (actually the work of English artist John Bratby) to the walls.

Guinness first saw the film in Mexico City, where it was being shown at a film festival without the benefit of either dubbing or subtitles. Although most of the audience could not understand the dialogue, the vast majority roared their approval at the end, even though a faction who considered the film an insult to artists started a fight, which developed into a riot. Guinness, accompanied by the British Ambassador and his wife, escaped unnoticed in the fleeing crowd.

HOSPITAL, THE   *DVD*
1971 103m c   Comedy/Drama   ★★★½
Gottfried/Chayefsky (U.S.)   PG

George C. Scott *(Dr. Herbert Bock)*, Diana Rigg *(Barbara Drummond)*, Barnard Hughes *(Drummond)*, Richard Dysart *(Dr. Welbeck)*, Andrew Duncan *(William Mead)*, Nancy Marchand *(Mrs. Christie, Head Nurse)*, Stephen Elliott *(Sunstrom)*, Donald Harron *(Milton Mead)*, Roberts Blossom *(Guernsey)*, Tresa Hughes *(Mrs. Donovan)*

p, Howard Gottfried; d, Arthur Hiller; w, Paddy Chayefsky; ph, Victor J. Kemper (DeLuxe Color); ed, Eric Albertson; m, Morris Surdin; prod d, Gene Rudolf; cos, Frank Thompson

AAN Best Actor: George C. Scott; *AA Best Original Story and Screenplay:* Paddy Chayefsky

Satire at its darkest. Scott in fine, hammy form (for once a part that takes advantage of his overblown core) as a N.Y. medical center's chief surgeon whose personal life has driven him to the brink of suicide. He busy hospital is being torn apart by a string of inexplicable murders of staff members. The laughs are sardonic, and the reality of Chayefsky's heavy-handed message (i.e., hospitals treat their patients badly) eats away at the viewer. But even when it falls flat, it's still an interesting watch.

HOT SHOTS!   *DVD*
1991 84m c   Action/Comedy   ★★★
Treadwell Enterprises/Pap Inc/Fox (U.S.)   PG-13

Charlie Sheen *(Sean "Topper" Harley/Rhett Butler/Superman)*, Cary Elwes *(Kent Gregory)*, Valeria Golino *(Ramada Thompson/Scarlett O'Hara/Lois Lane)*, Lloyd Bridges *(Admiral"Tug" Benson)*, Kevin Dunn *(Lieutenant Commander James Block)*, Jon Cryer *(Jim "Washout" Pfaffenbach)*, William O'Leary *(Pete "Dead Meat" Thompson)*, Kristy Swanson *(Dawn Kowalski)*, Efrem Zimbalist Jr. *(Wilson)*, Bill Irwin *(Buzz Harley)*

p, Bill Badalato; d, Jim Abrahams; w, Pat Proft, Jim Abrahams; ph, Bill Butler; ed, Jane Kurson, Eric Sears; m, Sylvester Levay; prod d, William A. Elliott; art d, Greg Papalia; fx, Phil Cory; cos, Mary Malin

HOT SHOTS! spoofs not only flyboy films in general, but kids the pants off at least a half-dozen famous movies, including the likes of GONE WITH THE WIND, DANCES WITH WOLVES, THE FABULOUS BAKER BOYS, DINER and even the infamous 9 1/2 WEEKS. At its core, however, HOT SHOTS! is a blatant sendup of the Tom Cruise smash TOP GUN and the names of the various ace flyboy characters help to set the mood for the off-the-wall humor to come.

There's the obviously ill-fated Pete "Dead Meat" Thompson (William O'Leary) and an ace pilot suffering from a malady known as "walleye vision" named Jim "Wash Out" Pfaffenbach (Jon Cryer). The major "hot shot" is Sean "Topper" Harley (Charlie Sheen), while his nemesis—both in matters of the heart and in the air—is ace narcissist Kent Gregory (Cary Elwes), the very model of military perfection—or so he likes to think. The flyboys are rousingly led by blustery multi-war veteran, Admiral "Tug" Benson (Lloyd Bridges), a pratfall-prone, "Damn the torpedoes…" type leader who, through the years, has had just about every part of his body replaced, due to a spectacular series of inept combat injuries.

When Topper and Kent aren't snarling at each other through clenched teeth in the air, they're snarling at each other with clenched fists on the ground. Kent blames Topper's ace pilot father for causing the death of his own dad years before in a freak airplane accident. Kent is also Topper's chief rival for the affections of the alluring base psychiatrist, equestrienne, sculptor and torch singer, Ramada Thompson (Valeria Golino).

While the slapstick comedy antics are frequently amusing and, on rare occasions, even hilarious, HOT SHOTS!, like so many other cinematic parodies before it, tends to lose sight—or control—of the plot, such as it is, in favor of more jokes, more visual gags and more dialogue puns—all hurled at the audience at a rapid-fire pace.

HOTEL RWANDA   *DVD*
2004 122m c   Drama   ★★★½
Lions Gate Films/Industrial Development   PG-13
Corporation of South Africa/Miracle Pictures/
Seamus Productions/Inside Track/UA
(U.K./South Africa/Italy)

Don Cheadle *(Paul Rusesabagina)*, Sophie Okonedo *(Tatiana Rusesabagina)*, Nick Nolte *(Colonel Oliver)*, Joaquin Phoenix *(Jack)*, Desmond Duke *(Dube)*, David O'Hara *(David)*, Cara Seymour *(Pat Archer)*, Fana Mokoena *(General Augustin Bizimungo)*, Hakeem Kae-Kazim *(George)*, Tony Kgoroge *(Gregoire)*

p, Terry George, A. Kitman Ho; d, Terry George; w, Terry George, Keir Pearson; ph, Robert Fraisse; ed, Naomi Geraghty; m, Afro Celt Sound System, Rupert Gergson-Williams, Andrea Guerra; prod d, Johnny Breedt, Tony Burrough; art d, Emma MacDevitt; fx, David Mahlangu, Gavin Meadon; cos, Ruy Filipe

AAN Best Actor: Don Cheadle; AAN Best Supporting Actress: Sophie Okonedo; AAN Best Original Screenplay: Keir Pearson, Terry George

It's a sad state of affairs when it takes a movie to teach people about a horrendous catastrophe that occurred just a few years earlier. This powerful film dramatizes the 1994 Rwandan genocide, during which an estimated one million people were murdered in a matter of months while much of the world remained indifferent.

Kigali, Rwanda, 1994: Tensions between Rwanda's once-favored ethnic minority, the Tutsis, and the resentful Hutu majority have reached a murderous pitch. Uncontrollable bands of Hutu militiamen violently harass Tutsis, and the airwaves hum with explicit exhortations from Hutu Power figures to kill Tutsi "cockroaches." Paul Rusesabagina (Don Cheadle), the Hutu house manager of the Belgian-owned Hotel Milles Collines, is doing his best to make sure his establishment remains "an oasis of calm" in all the madness. Paul is nervous for his Tutsi wife, Tatiana (Sophie Okonedo), and their children, but has faith in the presence of UN officials like Colonel Oliver (Nick Nolte) and members of the foreign press (David O'Hara, Joaquin Phoenix). But after the president is assassinated and the systematic massacre of every Tutsi man, woman, and child begins in earnest, Paul finds that the UN is only there to observe, and the rest of the world isn't bothering to watch at all. As the West turns its back on Rwanda and Paul's four-star hotel becomes a refugee camp, he's forced to use what little is left at his disposal to keep his terrified "guests" alive.

The film boldly recounts the burden Belgium, France, and the U.S. State Department must bear in this terrible episode, but best of all it celebrates Rusesabagina, an ordinary man who wound up sheltering an astonishing 1,268 Tutsi and Hutu refugees. It's a great part for a great actor, and Cheadle does a magnificent job turning this living legend back into a flesh-and-blood reality.

HOUND OF THE BASKERVILLES, THE 📀
1939 80m bw Mystery ★★★★
Fox (U.S.)

Richard Greene (Sir Henry Baskerville), Basil Rathbone (Sherlock Holmes), Wendy Barrie (Beryl Stapleton), Nigel Bruce (Dr. Watson), Lionel Atwill (James Mortimer, M.D.), John Carradine (Barryman), Barlowe Borland (Frankland), Beryl Mercer (Mrs. Jenifer Mortimer), Morton Lowry (John Stapleton), Ralph Forbes (Sir Hugo Baskerville)

p, Gene Markey; d, Sidney Lanfield; w, Ernest Pascal (based on the story by Arthur Conan Doyle); ph, Peverell Marley; ed, Robert Simpson; art d, Richard Day, Hans Peters; cos, Gwen Wakeling

This was the first time that Rathbone and Bruce were cast as Holmes and Watson and their superlative performances resulted in the delightful series that followed this excellent mystery. A faithful adaptation of the Doyle novel, the film is set in the 1880s period of gaslit London with all its wet cobblestone streets, billowing fog, and eerie atmosphere. The young heir to the Baskerville estate (Greene) fears for his life and calls in the great Sherlock Holmes to help solve the mysterious curse that has killed every Baskerville master since 1650.

This version of THE HOUND OF THE BASKERVILLES was an enormous success immediately upon release, and it proved to be the best of the series. Rathbone was the perfect Holmes, his well-modulated voice, his sharply-honed features, his lanky figure all conforming to the public's image of the great detective as Sidney Paget first drew his imagined likeness in the Strand Magazine in 1889 when Doyle created the character. He had earned the role and would keep it for life as Bruce would

claim the amiable character of Dr. Watson, the two becoming a beloved screen team.

Lanfield's direction is solid and careful as he unfolds the sinister tale. Carradine, Lowry, and particularly Atwill are all superb in their supporting roles. THE HOUND OF THE BASKERVILLES was always Rathbone's favorite film, even though he considered it "a negative from which I merely continued to produce endless positives of the same photograph." Rathbone would go on to appear in 16 films as Sherlock Holmes and more than 200 radio shows dealing with the indefatigable sleuth between 1939 and 1946.

HOUR OF THE WOLF, THE 📀
(VARGTIMMEN)
1968 88m bw Drama ★★★
Svensk (Sweden)

Liv Ullmann (Alma Borg), Max von Sydow (Johan Borg), Erland Josephson (Baron von Merkens), Gertrud Fridh (Corinne von Merkens), Gudrun Brost (Gamla Fru von Merkens), Bertil Anderberg (Ernst von Merkens), Georg Rydeberg (Arkivarie Lindhorst), Ulf Johansson (Kurator Heerbrand), Naima Wifstrand (Old Lady with Hat), Ingrid Thulin (Veronica Vogler)

d, Ingmar Bergman; w, Ingmar Bergman; ph, Sven Nykvist; ed, Ulla Ryghe; m, Lars-Johan Werle, Wolfgang Amadeus Mozart, Johann Sebastian Bach; art d, Marik Vos-Lundh; fx, Evald Andersson; cos, Mago

Fine acting exercise. This Bergman discourse on the nature of art and the artist's relation to society is shrouded in the trappings of gothic horror and stars Max von Sydow as Johan Borg, a painter haunted by bad dreams and apparitions while secluded on an island with his pregnant wife, Alma (Liv Ullmann). Both of them experience a series of haunting visions: Johan sees a beautiful boy, a ghost able to walk on walls, and an ancient woman who tears off her face; Alma is approached by a woman (who may or may not be an apparition) who instructs her to read her husband's diary. There she learns of Johan's love affair. Generally considered one of Bergman's lesser pictures, THE HOUR OF THE WOLF was originally to be shot before PERSONA, in 1965, as "The Cannibals."

HOURS, THE 📀
2002 114m c Drama ★★★
Scott Rudin/Robert Fox/Miramax/Paramount PG-13
(U.S.)

Nicole Kidman (Virginia Woolf), Julianne Moore (Laura Brown), Meryl Streep (Clarissa Vaughan), John C. Reilly (Dan Brown), Ed Harris (Richard Brown), Stephen Dillane (Leonard Woolf), Toni Collette (Kitty), Miranda Richardson (Vanessa Bell), Jeff Daniels (Louis Waters), Claire Danes (Julia Vaughan)

p, Robert Fox, Scott Rudin; d, Stephen Daldry; w, David Hare (based on the novel by Michael Cunningham); ph, Seamus McGarvey; ed, Peter Boyle; m, Philip Glass; prod d, Maria Djurkovic; art d, Mark Raggett; fx, Richard Briscoe, Stuart Brisdon; cos, Ann Roth

AA Best Actress: Nicole Kidman; AAN Best Picture; AAN Best Supporting Actor: Ed Harris; AAN Best Supporting Actress: Julianne Moore; AAN Best Director: Stephen Daldry; AAN Best Costume Design: Ann Roth; AAN Best Film Editing: Peter Boyle; AAN Best Original Score: Philip Glass; AAN Best Adapted Screenplay: David Hare

A Pulitzer Prize-winning novel, a screenplay by a distinguished playwright, and a powerhouse cast. Elements that look golden on paper all too often produce leaden, excessively respectful films, and the marvel of this adaptation of Michael Cunningham's book is that it works as well as it does.

Three stories, separated by both time and location, intertwine as three very different women live a single, apparently ordinary day that contains a life-changing revelation. Richmond, England, 1923: Virginia Woolf (Nicole Kidman) plans to spend the morning working on her new novel, *Mrs. Dalloway*, and the afternoon entertaining her sister, Vanessa Bell (Miranda Richardson). Virginia has already suffered two major attacks of suicidal depression, and Vanessa's visit brings into painful focus Virginia's desperate yearning for London's vibrant, inspiring turmoil. Los Angeles, 1951: Pregnant housewife Laura Brown (Julianne Moore) wants to spend the day reading *Mrs. Dalloway*, but instead prepares a small birthday celebration for her husband (John C. Reilly). Laura has an ambiguous encounter with a flighty neighbor (Toni Collette) and seriously considers suicide. New York City, 2001: Book editor Clarissa Vaughan (Meryl Streep) prepares a party for Richard (Ed Harris), a long-ago lover who's dying of AIDS and hardly cares that he's just received a prestigious poetry prize. As Clarissa hurtles through last-minute party preparations, a visit from an old friend (Jeff Daniels) makes her question her priorities and motives.

Keeping three separate narratives moving is an ambitious undertaking for any director. Theater-trained Stephen Daldry (BILLY ELLIOT) acquits himself admirably, and the film contains some lovely grace notes courtesy of the uniformly fine actresses. At the same time, it's the kind of movie that leaves you admiring the act of translation that produced it but wishing you were reading the book.

HOUSE OF FLYING DAGGERS
(SHI MIAN MAI FU)   *DVD*
2004 119m c   Martial Arts/Action/Romance ★★★½
Elite Enterprises/Edko Films/Zhang Yimou Studio   PG-13
Productions/Beijing New Picture Film Co. Ltd.
(China/Hong Kong)

Zhang Ziyi *(Mei)*, Takeshi Kaneshiro *(Jin)*, Andy Lau, billed as Andy Lau Tak Wah *(Leo)*, Song Dandan *(Madam Yee)*

p, Bill Kong, Zhang Yimou; d, Zhang Yimou; w, Li Feng, Wang Bin (based on a story by Zhang Li Feng and Wang Bin), Zhang Yimou; ph, Zhao Xiaoding; ed, Cheng Long; m, Shigeru Umebayashi; prod d, Huo Tingxiao; fx, Animal Logic, Digital Pictures Iloura, Menfond Electronic Art & Computer Design; chor, Li Cai (martial arts), Zhang Jianmin; cos, Emi Wada

AAN Best Cinematography: Zhao Xiaoding

Like writer-producer-director Zhang Yimou's HERO, this sumptuous period martial-arts picture is a feast for the eyes from beginning to end.

859 AD: China's Tang Dynasty is in decline and rebel factions, like the powerful and secretive House of Flying Daggers, have sprung up all over the country. Given an imperial order to find and kill the new leader of the House, police officials Leo (Andy Lau) and Jin (Takeshi Kaneshiro) seize on the rumor that blind Peony Pavilion dancer Mei (Zhang Ziyi) is connected to the group. Jin visits undercover as a libertine and asks the madam (Song Dandan) for Mei, then stages a drunken scene so Leo can arrest them both. Though Leo makes a show of threatening Mei with torture, he has a more subtle plan in mind: Jin will break Mei out of jail, profess sympathy with the House of Flying Daggers, and offer to escort her back to her comrades. He will then gradually win her trust—and heart—through a carefully staged series of battles. But the heart is too unpredictable to be a reliable conspirator, and many reversals of fortune lie in store as Mei, Jin, and Leo draw closer to the stronghold of the House of Flying Daggers.

Zhang Yimou's extravagantly romantic screenplay builds to a demented three-way *corrida* that blends the stylized emotional overkill of DUEL IN THE SUN with THE GOOD, THE BAD AND THE UGLY. It's a lot to swallow, but if you're with the film up to that point, it's not hard to take the last step into rapturous lunacy. The film is dedicated to Hong Kong superstar Anita Mui, who died of cancer shortly before the movie went into production.

HOUSE OF GAMES   *DVD*
1987 102m c   Crime   ★★★★
Filmhaus   (U.S.)   R

Lindsay Crouse *(Dr. Margaret Ford)*, Joe Mantegna *(Mike)*, Mike Nussbaum *(Joey)*, Lilia Skala *(Dr. Littauer)*, J.T. Walsh *(Businessman)*, Willo Hausman *(Girl with Book)*, Karen Kohlhaas *(Prison Ward Patient)*, Steve Goldstein *(Billy Hahn)*, Jack Wallace *(Bartender, "House of Games")*, Ben Blakeman *(Bartender, "Charlie's Tavern")*

p, Michael Hausman; d, David Mamet; w, David Mamet; ph, Juan Ruiz-Anchia; ed, Trudy Ship; m, Alaric Jans; prod d, Michael Merritt; fx, Robert Willard; cos, Nan Cibula

The extraordinary first film from Pulitzer Prize-winning playwright David Mamet, HOUSE OF GAMES is a stylish cinematic puzzle. Dr. Margaret Ford (Lindsay Crouse), a psychologist and best-selling author of a book on obsessive behavior, ventures into the world of confidence games to try to help out a patient whose gambling has gotten him in over his head. Her excursion brings her in contact with Mike (Joe Mantegna), a con man who engineers a back-room hustle that almost leaves Margaret $6,000 poorer. Instead of being angry, she is attracted to this streetwise philosopher and his world and returns to get to know him and it better. In the process she becomes involved in an elaborate con game revolving around a suitcase full of cash supposedly borrowed from the mob. The plot grows increasingly convoluted until Margaret—and the audience—no longer knows who is conning whom—that is, until the shocking climax.

Mamet has created a suspenseful, psychologically complex film that constantly plays tricks on the viewer as it draws him into its milieu of insightful deceit. Crouse and Mantegna are outstanding, and the supporting performances are all first rate. In the tradition of Alfred Hitchcock, Mamet worked from his own storyboards, and he and cinematographer Juan Ruiz Anchia have created a visually stunning film that is the equal of his airtight screenplay.

HOUSE OF MIRTH, THE   *DVD*
2000 140m c   Drama   ★★★★
Granada/Arts Council of England/Film Four/   PG-13
Scottish Arts Council/Showtime/Glasgow Film
Fund/Three Rivers Productions   (U.K./U.S.)

Gillian Anderson *(Lily Bart)*, Dan Aykroyd *(Gus Trenor)*, Eleanor Bron *(Mrs. Peniston)*, Terry Kinney *(George Dorset)*, Anthony LaPaglia *(Sim Rosedale)*, Laura Linney *(Bertha Dorset)*, Elizabeth McGovern *(Carry Fisher)*, Eric Stoltz *(Lawrence Selden)*, Penny Downie *(Judy Trenor)*, Pearce Quigley *(Pery Gryce)*

p, Olivia Stewart; d, Terence Davies; w, Terence Davies (from the novel by Edith Wharton); ph, Remi Adefarasin; ed, Michael Parker; prod d, Don Taylor; art d, Diane Dancklefsen; fx, Stuart Murdoch, Peerless Camera Co.; cos, Monica Howe

With consummate grace and his usual style, Terence Davies has transformed Edith Wharton's caustic, turn-of-the-century tragedy of manners into a somber, languid dream.

New York, 1905. In the rarefied air of high society, where a young woman's vocation is to marry well and one false move can leave her reputation in tatters, Lily Bart (Gillian Anderson)

is playing a risky game. A charming, still unmarried woman of limited means, Lily's been out in society a little too long and she's running up debts she can't repay. Lily piques the interest of a dull, wealthy prig (Pearce Quigley), but she lets him slip through her fingers for an afternoon dalliance with a man she could conceivably marry for love: fortuneless lawyer Lawrence Selden (Eric Stoltz). In the eyes of her best friend, Judy Trenor (Penny Downie), Lily's made a big mistake, but it isn't nearly as damaging as the financial arrangement Lily makes with Judy's husband (Dan Aykroyd), who agrees to invest a little money on Lily's behalf. When he starts handing her dividend checks, the tongues in Lily's shallow circle begin to wag, and Lily's downfall begins.

In a film studded with strong performers—Laura Linney is perfectly terrifying as Lily's smiling nemesis, Bertha Dorset—Davies took a gamble with Anderson, a largely untried dramatic actress best known for her work on TV's *The X-Files*. The risk paid off: Anderson's Lily never seems completely comfortable in the demeaning role of coquette, and there's something slightly forced about her performance. In a sense, she's perfect for the role of a woman who, as Selden describes her, "has it in her to be whatever she believed to be." But when the mask finally slips, she's heartbreaking.

HOUSE OF ROTHSCHILD, THE

1934   94m   c/bw   Biography   ★★★★
20th Century   (U.S.)

George Arliss *(Mayer Rothschild/Nathan Rothschild)*, Boris Karloff *(Count Ledrantz)*, Loretta Young *(Julie Rothschild)*, Robert Young *(Capt. Fitzroy)*, C. Aubrey Smith *(Duke of Wellington)*, A.S. Byron *(Baring)*, Helen Westley *(Gudula Rothschild)*, Reginald Owen *(Herries)*, Florence Arliss *(Hannah Rothschild)*, Alan Mowbray *(Metternich)*

p, Darryl F. Zanuck; d, Alfred Werker; w, Nunnally Johnson (based on the play by George Humbert Westley); ph, Peverell Marley (Technicolor); ed, Allen McNeil, Barbara McLean; m, Alfred Newman

AAN Best Picture

An outstanding historical account of the Rothschild financial dynasty during the Napoleonic wars, THE HOUSE OF ROTHSCHILD was the ambitious brainchild of Darryl F. Zanuck, who had left Warner Bros. to form Twentieth Century Productions, which would later merge with Fox.

George Arliss, who plays a dual role, is first seen as the patriarch of the German-Jewish ghetto family. On his deathbed, he urges his five sons to travel to the capitals of Europe and establish powerful banking firms. Led by their brother (Arliss's other role), the Rothschilds slowly build the most powerful banking conglomerate in Europe. The Rothschild banks secretly lend money to England, Austria, Italy, and Prussia to defeat Napoleon. Once Napoleon is in exile, however, Boris Karloff, the anti-Semitic Prussian ambassador to England, refuses Arliss's offer of money to rebuild France. Outraged, the banker creates financial havoc in the bond markets, but this only results in Karloff's launching violent and bloody pogroms. Fate intervenes when Napoleon escapes from exile and rises again to threaten Europe.

A potent, adult film, handsomely produced (the final sequence was shot in early three-strip Technicolor) and cast, and a memorable showcase for the effective "old school" acting of the unique Arliss.

HOUSE OF SAND AND FOG

2003   126m   c   Drama   ★★
Cobalt Media Group/Bisgrove   R
Entertainment   (U.S.)

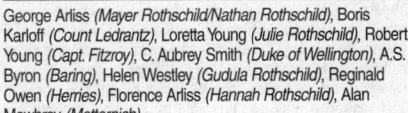

Ben Kingsley *(Massoud Amir Behrani)*, Jennifer Connelly *(Kathy Lazaro)*, Ron Eldard *(Deputy Sheriff Lester Burdon)*, Frances Fisher *(Connie Walsh)*, Kim Dickens *(Carol)*, Shohreh Aghdashloo *(Nadi Behrani)*, Jonathan Ahdout *(Esamail Behrani)*, Navi Rawat *(Soraya)*, Carlos Gomez *(Lt. Alvarez)*, Kia Jam *(Ali)*

p, Michael London, Vadim Perelman; d, Vadim Perelman; w, Vadim Perelman, Shane Otto (based on the novel by Andre Dubus III); ph, Roger Deakins; ed, Lisa Zeno Churgin; m, James Horner; prod d, Maia Javan; art d, Drew Boughton; fx, Richard O. Helmer, David Sosalla; cos, Hala Bahmet

AAN Best Actor: Ben Kingsley; *AAN Best Original Score:* James Horner; *AAN Best Supporting Actress:* Shohreh Aghdashloo

A tug-of-war over a modest San Francisco bungalow turns deadly in this overbaked adaptation of Andre Dubus III's 1999 novel.

Miserable after being dumped by her husband, Kathy Lazaro (Jennifer Connelly) wakes up to a bigger nightmare the morning deputies from the Pacific County Sheriff's Department evict her from her house for nonpayment of back taxes. Deputy Sheriff Lester Burdon (Ron Eldard), a married man who's got cheating on his mind, sets Kathy up in a friend's fishing shack deep in the northern California woods and soon becomes her lover. Kathy's house, meanwhile, is put up for auction and immediately snapped up by Massoud Amir Behrani (Sir Ben Kingsley), a former colonel with the Iranian air force who, with his wife (Shohreh Aghdashloo) and two children (Jonathan Ahdout, Navi Rawat), was forced to flee Iran during the 1976 revolution. Having spent most of his savings keeping up an appearance of wealth so that his daughter could marry into a "good" family, Massoud is now reduced to working a road crew by day and manning the register of a convenience store at night. He hopes to start recouping his lost fortune by reselling Kathy's house for a huge profit, but Kathy is equally determined to reclaim what she feels is rightfully hers.

As silly as it all sounds, Dubus's admittedly weak source material could have been successfully reworked into a sort of modern-day *Spoils of Poynton*. But first-time feature director Vadim Perelman has little control over his characters and even less control over Kingsley. Sir Ben starts off strong, but soon slips into full-blown Yul Brynner mode; one expects a firm "So it is written! So it shall be done!" after each of Massoud's many declamations.

HOUSE OF USHER

1960   79m   c   Horror   ★★★½
AIP   (U.S.)

Vincent Price *(Roderick Usher)*, Mark Damon *(Philip Winthrop)*, Myrna Fahey *(Madeline Usher)*, Harry Ellerbe *(Bristol)*, Bill Borzage, Mike Jordan, Nadajan, Ruth Oklander, George Paul, David Andar

p, Roger Corman; d, Roger Corman; w, Richard Matheson

A real coup for Roger Corman and AIP, HOUSE OF USHER was the first of their horror films that had a decent budget ($350,000), boasted a shooting schedule of more than 10 days (they were allowed 15), was shot in color and CinemaScope, and was "inspired" by Edgar Allan Poe. The gamble paid off and the film was a critical and commercial hit that unleashed scads of other films based on the works of Poe.

The wonderful Vincent Price stars as Roderick Usher, the creepy, white-haired owner of the mysterious house of Usher, who lives in seclusion in the creaking old house with his sister, Madeline (Myrna Fahey). When Madeline announces her engagement to Philip (Mark Damon), Roderick will have none of it and informs her betrothed that he and his sister are the last of the Ushers and they suffer from a bizarre madness that must not be transmitted to another generation. When Philip refuses to leave the spooky house despite this warning, strange accidents befall him, and he is nearly killed. Meanwhile, Madeline falls ill, and soon after, Roderick informs Philip that she has died of a heart attack and entombs her in the family chapel. The butler, however, informs Philip that his fiancee has suffered from periodic blackouts and that she may have been buried alive.

Moody, atmospheric, and effective, HOUSE OF USHER succeeds in making the house a "monster," which a desperate Corman had to make clear to skeptical executive producer Sam Arkoff when he questioned the film's lack of a menacing creature. Corman's savvy use of color, musty cobwebs, and creaking and groaning sound effects combine to make the *house* appear to be the cause of all the madness. Price is wonderful as the spooky owner, but the other three players are merely adequate. But still a superlative Corman/AIP effort and a great beginning to a varying but always interesting series of horror films.

HOUSE OF WAX   DVD

1953 90m   c   Horror   ★★★
Warner Bros.   (U.S.)

Vincent Price *(Prof. Henry Jarrod)*, Frank Lovejoy *(Lt. Tom Brennan)*, Phyllis Kirk *(Sue Allen)*, Carolyn Jones *(Cathy Gray)*, Paul Picerni *(Scott Andrews)*, Roy Roberts *(Matthew Burke)*, Angela Clarke *(Mrs. Andrews)*, Paul Cavanagh *(Sidney Wallace)*, Dabbs Greer *(Sgt. Jim Shane)*, Charles Bronson, billed as Charles Buchinsky *(Igor)*

p, Bryan Foy; d, Andre de Toth; w, Crane Wilbur (based on a play by Charles Welden); ph, Bert Glennon, Peverell Marley (Natural Vision 3-D, Warner Color); ed, Rudi Fehr; m, David Buttolph; art d, Stanley Fleischer

Paddleball anyone? This fine remake of the classic THE MYSTERY OF THE WAX MUSEUM was filmed in 3-D and employed "WarnerPhonic Sound," a forerunner to stereo that utilized a number of speakers.

Vincent Price plays Professor Henry Jarrod, a wax sculptor in New York at the turn of the century who presides over a wax museum that is floundering because of his pursuit of beauty rather than sensationalism. When Jarrod again refuses partner Burke's (Roy Roberts) request to create more horrifying pieces, Burke sets fire to the museum, intent on collecting the insurance money. It is presumed that Jarrod died with his creations, but he returns, horribly scarred, and strangles Burke. Years later, Jarrod, feigning a wheelchair-confining back injury, opens a new wax museum with even more lifelike displays. Because his hands have been horribly burned, he employs two assistants to do the sculpting under his supervision (one of whom is played by Charles Bronson, then billed as Buchinsky). In reality, however, Jarrod's mad sculpting is accomplished by pouring wax over people he has murdered.

HOUSE OF WAX was stunningly directed by Andre de Toth who used the new 3-D process to its fullest potential without bogging down the narrative with too many "gee-look-what-I-can-do" tricks. Ironically, this man who saw the potential of 3-D and who directed one of the most effective movies ever shot in that process had only one eye, which hampered his depth perception. Price is magnificent as usual and manages to steal the role of Professor Jarrod from its creator, Lionel Atwill. Although it is now extremely difficult to see in its original format, HOUSE OF WAX is still well worth viewing in flat prints or on video. The line that kills 'em in revival houses: "You never see things like this in Provincetown." Oh, but you do.

HOUSE ON 92ND STREET, THE

1945 88m   bw   Spy   ★★★★
Fox   (U.S.)

William Eythe *(Bill Dietrich)*, Lloyd Nolan *(Inspector George A. Briggs)*, Signe Hasso *(Elsa Gebhardt)*, Gene Lockhart *(Charles Ogden Roper)*, Leo G. Carroll *(Col. Hammersohn)*, Lydia St. Clair *(Johanna Schmedt)*, Reed Hadley *(Narrator)*,

William Post Jr. *(Walker)*, Harry Bellaver *(Max Coburg)*, Bruno Wick *(Adolphe Lange)*

p, Louis de Rochemont; d, Henry Hathaway; w, Barre Lyndon, Charles G. Booth, John Monks Jr. (based on the story by Booth); ph, Norbert Brodine; ed, Harmon Jones; m, David Buttolph; art d, Lyle Wheeler, Lewis Creber; fx, Fred Sersen; cos, Bonnie Cashin

AA Best Original Story: Charles G. Booth

Suspense-packed espionage yarn, approached from a documentary angle, has Nolan as a no-nonsense federal investigator who is sought out by German-American Eythe, a brilliant student. He has been contacted by Nazi spies, he tells Nolan, and asked to work with them. Nolan encourages Eythe to accept the offer and work as a double agent, reporting all Nazi activities to the FBI. Slowly, Eythe ingratiates himself with several Nazi agents and is assigned, as a technician, to transmit messages to Germany via short-wave radio. He establishes a remote radio hideout and begins sending messages, really to FBI headquarters, and its operators pass on fake information to Germany. Through this system Eythe is able to learn that Nazi agents are after data concerning the development of the atomic bomb (referred to here as "Process 97"), identifying Lockhart, one of the scientists working on the apparatus, as a Nazi agent.

Hathaway's direction is quick and uses the newsreel style made famous by producer de Rochemont, who produced the MARCH OF TIME series. The film was shot on location in New York and other points where actual spy cases from FBI files really occurred. The semi-documentary style gave sharp authenticity to the film as did the use of nonprofessional actors (many of whom were FBI agents and technical personnel). The stentorian narration provided by Hadley, who made a handsome living in films narrating such stories, further convinced viewers that they were watching the real thing. In some instances they were; Hathaway incorporated newsreel shots of real German spies being rounded up at the beginning of WWII, along with telephotos of the German consulate in New York and its real life spies going and coming. The tremendous atmospherics gave birth to a series of films adopting the same semi-documentary approach, notably T-MEN, THE NAKED CITY, and WALK A CROOKED MILE. Hasso is incomparable as the Nazi ringleader in this, her most impressive film.

HOUSE PARTY   DVD

1990 100m   c   Comedy   ★★★
New Line Cinema   (U.S.)   R

Christopher Reid *(Kid)*, Robin Harris *(Pop)*, Christopher Martin *(Play)*, Martin Lawrence *(Bilal)*, Tisha Campbell *(Sidney)*, A.J. Johnson *(Sharane)*, Paul Anthony *(Stab)*, Bowlegged Lou *(Pee-Wee)*, B. Fine *(Zilla)*, Edith Fields *(Principal)*

p, Warrington Hudlin; d, Reginald Hudlin; w, Reginald Hudlin; ph, Peter Deming (Metrocolor); ed, Earl Watson; m, Marcus Miller; prod d, Bryan Jones; art d, Susan Richardson; chor, A.J. Johnson, Kid 'N' Play, Tisha Campbell; cos, Harold Evans

Crude and cartoony but hypnotic in its infectious energy, this low-budget comedy about a night in the lives of some black teenagers is an auspicious debut from brothers Reginald (directing) and Warrington (producing) Hudlin.

Kid (Christopher Reid) is dying to go to a party hosted by his buddy Play (Christopher Martin). Unfortunately, Kid has gotten into some trouble with the local bullies at school and, after a note from the principal's office arrives at home, he's grounded by his strict father (the late, great Robin Harris). Determined to go to Play's party, especially since two of the prettiest girls in school are going to be there, Kid risks life and limb to sneak out of the house while Pop dozes in front of the television. He makes it to the party and gets to know the girls,

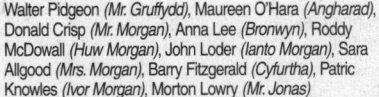

one of whom has a crush on him, while dancing up a storm. The evening, however, is not without its complications....

Deceptively simple on the surface, HOUSE PARTY is a realistic depiction of teenager life. Though its main purpose is obviously to provoke laughter, it also provokes thought by dealing honestly with a variety of subjects, including safe sex, teen drinking, class prejudice, and, in a roundabout way, racism. Rap stars Kid N Play make a strong film debut, creating a fun, light image for themselves without sacrificing the edge of their music; their rap-duel scene is fast and funky. Kid, with his foot-high fade haircut (one character refers to him as "Eraserhead") and freckle-faced grin, handles the duties of "leading man" extremely well, giving a supremely likable performance.

HOUSEKEEPING

1987	116m	c	Drama	★★★½
Columbia	(U.S.)			PG

Christine Lahti *(Sylvie)*, Sara Walker *(Ruth)*, Andrea Burchill *(Lucille)*, Anne Pitoniak *(Lily)*, Barbara Reese *(Nona)*, Bill Smillie *(Sheriff)*, Wayne Robson *(Mr. French)*, Margot Pinvidic *(Helen)*

p, Robert F. Colesberry; d, Bill Forsyth; w, Bill Forsyth (based on the novel by Marilynne Robinson); ph, Michael Coulter (Rank Color); ed, Michael Ellis; m, Michael Gibbs; prod d, Adrienne Atkinson; cos, Mary-Jane Reyner

Offbeat but absorbing. Set in the 1950s and based on a Marilynne Robinson novel, this is the first American film from Scottish director Bill Forsyth.

After the suicide of their mother, two young girls, Ruth (Sara Walker) and Lucille (Andrea Burchill), are brought up by their grandmother in a small Idaho town. When she dies, a pair of elderly great-aunts persuade Ruth and Lucille's itinerant aunt, Sylvie (Christine Lahti), to look after her two nieces, who are now approaching adolescence. Sylvie, who has spent most of her life riding the rails and sleeping on benches, sets up housekeeping in her own fashion and goes about child-rearing in an unorthodox manner. Lucille, more concerned with appearances than her sister, begins to be embarrassed by Sylvie's refusal to abide by society's conventions.

HOUSEKEEPING is a reversal of the formula that has brought director Forsyth, a master of character development and storytelling, so much success. Instead of weaving dramatic moments into capricious comedy, he leavens this heart-warming drama with laughter. Playing against type and avoiding what could have been a paint-by-numbers portrayal, Lahti plays Sylvie as loving and ingenuous, but with a half-glimpsed sense of tragedy and disappointment. Walker and Burchill also turn in fine performances.

HOW GREEN WAS MY VALLEY

1941	118m	bw	Drama	★★★★★
Fox	(U.S.)			

Walter Pidgeon *(Mr. Gruffydd)*, Maureen O'Hara *(Angharad)*, Donald Crisp *(Mr. Morgan)*, Anna Lee *(Bronwyn)*, Roddy McDowall *(Huw Morgan)*, John Loder *(Ianto Morgan)*, Sara Allgood *(Mrs. Morgan)*, Barry Fitzgerald *(Cyfartha)*, Patric Knowles *(Ivor Morgan)*, Morton Lowry *(Mr. Jonas)*

p, Darryl F. Zanuck; d, John Ford; w, Philip Dunne (based on the novel by Richard Llewellyn); ph, Arthur Miller; ed, James B. Clark; m, Alfred Newman; art d, Richard Day, Nathan Juran; cos, Gwen Wakeling

AA Best Picture; AA Best Supporting Actor: Donald Crisp; *AAN Best Supporting Actress:* Sara Allgood; *AA Best Director:* John Ford; *AAN Best Screenplay:* Philip Dunne; *AA Best B/W Cinematography:* Arthur Miller; *AAN Best Film Editing:* James B.

Clark; *AAN Best Score (Drama):* Alfred Newman; *AA Best Interior Decoration (B/W):* Richard Day, Nathan Juran, Thomas Little; *AAN Best Sound Recording:* E.H. Hansen

Emotionally majestic and spiritually moving, this is one of John Ford's undisputed masterpieces, a film that neither fades nor fails after repeated viewings.

The mining area in South Wales and its hard-working miners and their families are seen through the eyes of Huw (Roddy McDowall), the youngest of six children in a family headed by a stern father (Donald Crisp) and loving mother (Sara Allgood). Set at the turn of the century and told in flashback, the film shows an unspoiled valley, full of love and warmth, wherein the trials and hardships of the community are told through a series of moving vignettes.

Everything about this film is touching; master director John Ford builds one simple scene upon another with very little plot, using incidents in the life of one family to tell the general tale, demonstrating changes and recording milestones. Beautifully assisted by cameraman Arthur Miller, Ford received strong support from studio chief Darryl Zanuck, who personally produced the film. The superlative cast is a Who's Who of Hollywood's Irish community, with a noble assist from Welsh singers.

HOW I WON THE WAR

1967	109m	c	Comedy/War	★★★
UA	(U.K.)			

Michael Crawford *(Lt. Ernest Goodbody)*, John Lennon *(Gripweed)*, Roy Kinnear *(Clapper)*, Lee Montague *(Sgt. Transom)*, Jack MacGowran *(Juniper)*, Michael Hordern *(Grapple)*, Jack Hedley *(Melancholy Musketeer)*, Karl Michael Vogler *(Odlebog)*, Ronald Lacey *(Spool)*, James Cossins *(Drogue)*

p, Richard Lester; d, Richard Lester; w, Charles Wood (based on the novel by Patrick Ryan); ph, David Watkin (Eastmancolor); ed, John Victor Smith; m, Ken Thorne; art d, Philip Harrison, John Stoll; fx, Eddie Fowlie; cos, Dinah Greet

Richard Lester, director of the hit Beatles movies A HARD DAY'S NIGHT and HELP!, intended this black comedy as a stinging condemnation of war, but occasionally he fails even as he succeeds, eliciting such plentiful laughs that he blunts the impact of his message.

Revolving around the rose-colored reminiscences of a middle-aged British WWII veteran whose wartime career was actually a disaster, HOW I WON THE WAR follows the inept Lt. Goodbody (Michael Crawford) as he leads his men from North Africa to France. Among his unfortunate misfit charges are the overweight Clapper (Roy Kinnear), who is obsessed with his wife's infidelity; Juniper (Jack MacGowran), a music-hall comic; and Gripweed (then-Beatle John Lennon), whose billing is considerably more prominent than his presence in the film. Transom (Lee Montague), the only competent military man in the bunch, tries in vain to correct his superior's command blunders, but so ill-prepared to lead is Goodbody that he eventually causes the deaths of all of his men save one, the Melancholy Musketeer (Jack Hedley).

Based on a novel by Patrick Ryan, Lester's film offers both hilarious moments of satire (of war and war movies) and grim, bloody depictions of the awful reality of combat. This seemingly incongruous mixture will work for some viewers, and, though the seriousness of Lester's intent may not be appreciated by everyone, most should at least find something here to make them laugh.

HOW THE WEST WAS WON   DVD
1963 165m c   Western   ★★★½
MGM   (U.S.)

Spencer Tracy *(Narrator)*, Carroll Baker *(Eve Prescott)*, Lee J.
Cobb *(Lou Ramsey)*, Henry Fonda *(Jethro Stuart)*, Karl Malden
(Zebulon Prescott), Gregory Peck *(Cleve Van Valen)*, George
Peppard *(Zeb Rawlings)*, Robert Preston *(Roger Morgan)*, Debbie
Reynolds *(Lilith Prescott)*, James Stewart *(Linus Rawlings)*

p, Bernard Smith; d, Henry Hathaway, John Ford, George
Marshall, Richard Thorpe (uncredited); w, James R. Webb (based
on articles in *Life* magazine); ph, Joseph La Shelle, Charles Lang,
William Daniels, Milton Krasner, Harold Wellman (Cinerama,
Metrocolor); ed, Harold F. Kress; m, Alfred Newman, Ken Darby;
art d, George W. Davis, William Ferrari, Addison Hehr; fx, A.
Arnold Gillespie, Robert R. Hoag; cos, Walter Plunkett

AAN Best Picture; AA Best Original Story and Screenplay: James
R. Webb; *AAN Best Color Cinematography:* William H. Daniels,
Milton Krasner, Charles Lang, Jr., Joseph LaShelle; *AA Best Film
Editing:* Harold F. Kress; *AAN Best Original Score:* Alfred Newman,
Ken Darby; *AAN Best Art Direction-Set Decoration (Color):* George
W. Davis, William Ferrari, Addison Hehr, Henry Grace, Don
Greenwood, Jr., Jack Mills; *AAN Best Costume Design (Color):*
Walter Plunkett; *AA Best Sound:* Franklin E. Milton

Dense and episodic western omelet, tries to condense the evolution of the American west by channeling it through one family's experiences, over three generations. The film is split
between four directors with Hathaway's sequences clearly the
most cohesive and colorful. This is an all-star guessing-game
cast that adults can have fun with, and there's enough history
lesson to validate it for children. The acting alternates between
star turn, cute, and storybook portmanteau. It's a big-budget fast-
food history lesson with Debbie Reynolds as brash schoolmarm. Spencer Tracy narrates, and was probably grateful for the
relative safety.

HOW TO GET AHEAD IN ADVERTISING   DVD
1989 95m c   Comedy   ★★★½
HandMade   (U.K.)   R

Richard E. Grant *(Dennis Bagley)*, Rachel Ward *(Julia Bagley)*,
Richard Wilson *(Bristol)*, Jacqueline Tong *(Penny Wheelstock)*,
John Shrapnel *(Psychiatrist)*, Susan Wooldridge *(Monica)*, Mick
Ford *(Richard)*, Jacqueline Pearce *(Maud)*, Roddy Maude-Roxby
(Dr. Gatty), Pauline Melville *(Mrs. Wallace)*

p, David Wimbury, Ray Cooper; d, Bruce Robinson; w, Bruce
Robinson; ph, Peter Hannan (Fujicolor); ed, Alan Strachan; m,
David Dundas, Rick Wentworth; prod d, Michael Pickwoad; art d,
Henry Harris; chor, David Toguri; cos, Andrea Galer

More satire than comedy, and aimed at a sophisticated audience that can appreciate its barbs at the business of "creating
need," HOW TO GET AHEAD IN ADVERTISING is a
movie of extremes, both in plot and characterizations.
    Dennis Bagley (Richard E. Grant), a veteran advertising
executive who has all the perks of success—an attractive wife
(Rachel Ward), a country home, and an expensive car—undergoes a drastic change of heart when a creative block prevents
him from coming up with an ad campaign for pimple cream.
Quitting his job and embarking on an "anti-advertising" campaign, Dennis is soon plagued by a huge boil on the side of his
neck that takes on a human visage and becomes Dennis's alter
ego. Eventually, the boil, an unprincipled proponent of a "buyer
beware" philosophy, even takes possession of Dennis's being.
    In asking the audience to decide which is the real Dennis
Bagley, writer-director Bruce Robinson is not only concerned
with the moral implications of advertising but with those of
capitalism in general. Clearly, he has stacked his deck, allowing Grant (who starred in Robinson's wonderful WITHNAIL

AND I) to push his character to the outer limits. More subtlety or quiet introspection might have lent greater credibility to
the role, though Grant and Robinson unquestionably have
made their point.

HOW TO SUCCEED IN BUSINESS WITHOUT   DVD
REALLY TRYING
1967 121m c   Musical/Comedy   ★★★★
Mirisch   (U.S.)

Robert Morse *(J. Pierpont Finch)*, Michele Lee *(Rosemary
Pilkington)*, Rudy Vallee *(J.B. Biggley)*, Anthony Teague *(Bud
Frump)*, Maureen Arthur *(Hedy LaRue)*, Murray Matheson
(Benjamin Ovington), Kay Reynolds *(Smitty)*, Sammy Smith
(Mr. Twimble/Wally Womper), John Myhers *(Bratt)*, Jeff
DeBenning *(Gatch)*

p, David Swift; d, David Swift; w, David Swift (based on the musical book by Abe Burrows, Willie Gilbert, and Jack Weinstock, and
the novel by Shepherd Mead); ph, Burnett Guffey (Panavision,
DeLuxe Color); ed, Ralph E. Winters, Allan Jacobs; m, Nelson
Riddle; art d, Robert Boyle; chor, Dale Moreda (based on original
staging by Bob Fosse); cos, Micheline

David Swift produced, directed, adapted, and even played a
small role in this scathing musical satire. The film is based on
Shepherd Mead's novel which had been brought to the stage
by Loesser and Burrows, who co-wrote the stage book with
Gilbert and Weinstock.
    Morse is an elfin, yet aggressive, window washer who buys
a copy of Mead's book on his way to work and decides to put it
to work immediately. He walks into the office of World Wide
Wickets, a huge conglomerate, and enchants Lee, a pretty secretary, who introduces him to the chief of personnel. That
achieved, he convinces the man that he is a great pal of Vallee,
who heads the company. This bit of trickery gets him as far as
the mailroom. It isn't long before he finagles, cajoles, and
charms his way into a junior executive position and endears
himself to all the women in the company, but incurs the enmity
of Teague, Vallee's insidious nephew. Soon after, Morse is made
chief of an advertising department where many heads have
rolled. Teague knows that Vallee absolutely despises television
giveaway shows, so he tells Morse the opposite, thinking that
when Morse presents the idea to Vallee, he will be rewarded
with a pink slip.
    The film is cartoonlike, its characters caricatures, as befits
the story. The lion's share of the acting kudos goes to Morse, in
a role that is perfect for him, and Lee, a refreshing, attractive
actress who went on to national fame. But Vallee's fussy boss is
definitely memorable. Veteran television panelist Robert Q.
Lewis plays a small role as an executive and proves to be a much
better actor than anyone realized. Myhers does his usual hammy
job, but it isn't out of place here. Producer-director-writer-actor
Swift was the man responsible for one of television's most
beloved early shows, "Mr. Peepers." Good fun.

HOWARDS END   DVD
1992 140m c   Drama/Historical   ★★★½
Merchant Ivory/Nippon Herald Films/Channel Four   PG
(U.K.)

Anthony Hopkins *(Henry Wilcox)*, Emma Thompson *(Margaret
Schlegel)*, Vanessa Redgrave *(Ruth Wilcox)*, Helena Bonham
Carter *(Helen Schlegel)*, Sam West *(Leonard Bast)*, Prunella
Scales *(Aunt Juley)*, Joseph Bennett *(Paul Wilcox)*, Adrian Ross-
Magenty *(Tibby Schlegel)*, Jo Kendall *(Annie)*, James Wilby
(Charles Wilcox)

p, Ismail Merchant; d, James Ivory; w, Ruth Prawer Jhabvala
(from the novel by E.M. Forster); ph, Tony Pierce-Roberts; ed,

Andrew Marcus; m, Richard Robbins; prod d, Luciana Arrighi; art d, John Ralph; cos, Jenny Beavan, John Bright

AAN Best Picture; AA Best Actress: Emma Thompson; *AAN Best Supporting Actress:* Vanessa Redgrave; *AAN Best Director:* James Ivory; *AA Best Adapted Screenplay:* Ruth Prawer Jhabvala; *AAN Best Cinematography:* Tony Pierce-Roberts; *AAN Best Original Score:* Richard Robbins; *AA Best Art Direction-Set Decoration:* Luciana Arrighi, Ian Whittaker; *AAN Best Costume Design:* Jenny Beavan, John Bright

An elegant, if bland reworking of Forster's classic 1910 novel, from the acclaimed filmmaking team of James Ivory (director), Ismail Merchant (producer) and Ruth Prawer Jhabvala (screenwriter).

HOWARDS END takes its name from a country house belonging to Ruth Wilcox (Vanessa Redgrave). Though married to Henry Wilcox (Anthony Hopkins), a pillar of wealth and tradition, Ruth is a slightly other-worldly figure who feels a mystic bond with the house where she was born. In the later stages of a terminal illness, Ruth strikes up a friendship with Margaret Schlegel (Emma Thompson), a cultured, free-thinking woman who lives with her like-minded sister, Helen (Helena Bonham Carter).

Before she dies, Ruth makes out an informal will leaving Howards End to Margaret, but her note is destroyed by the Wilcoxes. The two families nevertheless remain involved, as the widowed Henry begins to take a (well-concealed) romantic interest in Margaret. HOWARDS END goes on to flesh out the relations between the materialistic Wilcoxes and the emancipated Schlegels—relations which build to a tragic climax in the person of Leonard Bast (Sam West), a sensitive clerk who is befriended by Margaret and Helen but ulimately undone by Henry.

Forster's novel has been adapted with such emphasis on good taste that other, more crucial elements have been neglected. The filmmakers have allowed themselves an overlong 140 minutes in order to preserve as much of the plot as possible, but they have bypassed many of the novel's key ideas and ironies. And though the film *looks* marvelous, it lacks the zest—the conflict and the passion—that informed the team's earlier hit, A ROOM WITH A VIEW. There are times when it feels as though the major literary influence at work is not E.M. Forster, but *House and Garden* magazine.

HOWLING, THE
DVD
1981 91m c Horror ★★★½
Avco Embassy (U.S.) R

Dee Wallace Stone, billed as Dee Wallace *(Karen White)*, Patrick Macnee *(Dr. George Waggner)*, Dennis Dugan *(Chris)*, Christopher Stone *(R. William "Bill" Neill)*, Belinda Balaski *(Terry Fisher)*, Kevin McCarthy *(Fred Francis)*, John Carradine *(Erle Kenton)*, Slim Pickens *(Sam Newfield)*, Elisabeth Brooks *(Marsha)*, Robert Picardo *(Eddie)*

p, Michael Finnell, Jack Conrad; d, Joe Dante; w, John Sayles, Terence H. Winkless (based on the novel by Gary Brandner); ph, John Hora (CFI color); ed, Mark Goldblatt, Joe Dante; m, Pino Donaggio; art d, Robert Burns; fx, Rob Bottin, Roger George

A wonderful combination of horror, laughs, and state-of-the-art special effects from director and Roger Corman alumnus Joe Dante (PIRANHA, GREMLINS, EXPLORERS), screenwriter (now screenwriter-director) John Sayles (PIRANHA, RETURN OF THE SECAUCUS SEVEN, BROTHER FROM ANOTHER PLANET), and makeup artist Rob Bottin.

Wallace plays a television anchorwoman who, after being severely traumatized while investigating a story, decides to venture to Macnee's ultra-exclusive California transcendental med-

itation spa with husband Stone. Unfortunately, the members of Macnee's cult are all werewolves. The transformation scenes are incredible—the highlight being when sexy siren Brooks seduces Stone and they make love under the moonlight while turning into werewolves. Dante fills the film with hysterical cameos from Corman (at a phone booth) and Sayles (a morgue attendent), among others, and demonstrates a subtle wit and a flair for horror. A must-see for horror fans, with more than one viewing recommended. Unfortunately, a slew of really awful sequels followed.

HUCKSTERS, THE
1947 115m bw Drama ★★★½
MGM (U.S.)

Clark Gable *(Victor Albee Norman)*, Deborah Kerr *(Kay Dorrance)*, Sydney Greenstreet *(Evan Llewellyn Evans)*, Adolphe Menjou *(Mr. Kimberly)*, Ava Gardner *(Jean Ogilvie)*, Keenan Wynn *(Buddy Hare)*, Edward Arnold *(Dave Lash)*, Aubrey Mather *(Valet)*, Richard Gaines *(Cooke)*, Frank Albertson *(Max Herman)*

p, Arthur Hornblow Jr.; d, Jack Conway; w, Luther Davis, Edward Chodorov, George Wells (based on the novel by Frederic Wakeman); ph, Harold Rosson; ed, Frank Sullivan; m, Lennie Hayton; art d, Cedric Gibbons, Urie McCleary; fx, Warren Newcombe, A. Arnold Gillespie

Madison Avenue ad agencies, radio commercials, and bigshot businessmen all got a lashing in this glossy drama. Gable plays a predictable rabble-rouser, Kerr the genteel society girl, Gardner the showbiz siren. It's all fairly predictable, a notch above MGM formula stuff, stolen by the expansive Greenstreet's egomania. Gable at first was not interested in doing this film but MGM toned down the hard-hitting best-seller by Wakeman and softened Gable's character to the point where he maintained some scruples at the finish. He approved of both his leading ladies and was particularly fond of Gardner. Kerr had been in films for about six years; this was touted as her first American film by MGM. Although effective in her role, few thought she would ever reach the superstar status that would come with later films such as FROM HERE TO ETERNITY. MGM mogul Louis B. Mayer was convinced Kerr would make it to the top and it was he who suggested a line the studio used in its advertisements for THE HUCKSTERS when listing her name: "Deborah Kerr (rhymes with 'star')."

HUD
DVD
1963 112m bw Western ★★★½
Paramount (U.S.)

Paul Newman *(Hud Bannon)*, Melvyn Douglas *(Homer Bannon)*, Patricia Neal *(Alma Brown)*, Brandon de Wilde *(Lon Bannon)*, Whit Bissell *(Burris)*, John Ashley *(Hermy)*, Crahan Denton *(Jesse)*, Val Avery *(Jose)*, Sheldon Allman *(Thompson)*, Pitt Herbert *(Larker)*

p, Martin Ritt, Irving Ravetch; d, Martin Ritt; w, Irving Ravetch, Harriet Frank Jr. (based on the novel *Horseman, Pass By* by Larry McMurtry); ph, James Wong Howe; ed, Frank Bracht; m, Elmer Bernstein; art d, Hal Pereira, Tambi Larsen; fx, Paul K. Lerpae; cos, Edith Head

AAN Best Actor: Paul Newman; *AA Best Actress:* Patricia Neal; *AA Best Supporting Actor:* Melvyn Douglas; *AAN Best Director:* Martin Ritt; *AAN Best Adapted Screenplay:* Irving Ravetch, Harriet Frank, Jr.; *AA Best B/W Cinematography:* James Wong Howe; *AAN Best Art Direction-Set Decoration (B/W):* Hal Pereira, Tambi Larsen, Sam Comer, Robert Benton

A blistering adult western which broke ground in its depiction of an unglamorous West and in the decidedly anti-heroic nature of its lead.

The charismatic Newman is the title character, an immoral Texas heel—insensitive, crude, avaricious, and irresponsible. He has a stormy relationship with his father, Douglas, an extremely decent but rigid old man who long ago rejected his son. Somewhere in between them is the innocent de Wilde, whose attraction to Newman is almost as strong as that of salty housekeeper Neal. Newman does as little as possible around the ranch his father owns; ignoring the proud past, he is concerned only with having a good ol' time.

HUD belongs to a group of "anti-westerns" which includes LONELY ARE THE BRAVE, THE MISFITS, THE LUSTY MEN and JUNIOR BONNER. It's almost impossible to sympathize with Newman's character, presented cynically by director Ritt in an approach typical of many '60s filmmakers. Newman's performance, though, is unquestionably the best thing about this brutal portrait of humanity.

HUDSUCKER PROXY, THE
1994 115m c   Comedy/Drama   ★★★
Silver Pictures/Working Title   (U.S.)   PG

Tim Robbins (*Norville Barnes*), Jennifer Jason Leigh (*Amy Archer*), Paul Newman (*Sidney J. Mussburger*), Charles Durning (*Waring Hudsucker*), John Mahoney (*Chief*), Jim True (*Buzz*), Bill Cobbs (*Moses*), Bruce Campbell (*Smitty*), Harry Bugin (*Aloysius*), John Seitz (*Benny*)

p, Ethan Coen; d, Joel Coen; w, Ethan Coen, Joel Coen, Sam Raimi; ph, Roger Deakins; ed, Thom Noble; m, Carter Burwell; prod d, Dennis Gassner; art d, Leslie McDonald; fx, Michael McAlister, Peter M. Chesney; cos, Richard Hornung

A lavish parody of/homage to Hollywood big business comedies, THE HUDSUCKER PROXY is gorgeous but lifeless, a very small joke writ very large by the talented but perversely insular Coen brothers.

Guileless but ambitious hick Norville Barnes (Tim Robbins) comes to the big city to make his fortune, and gets a job in the mailroom of Hudsucker Industries. When CEO Waring Hudsucker (Charles Durning) commits suicide, the Board of Directors—led by ruthless Sidney J. Mussberger (Paul Newman)—decides to make a killing by installing an idiot in his place, then taking advantage of lowered stock price. Barnes is the unwitting idiot, Amy Archer (Jennifer Jason Leigh) the fast-talking, crackerjack columnist who lies her way into his life, hoping to get the big scoop, but falls in love instead. When Barnes' tenure proves a surprise success, Mussberger will stop at nothing to get rid of him.

Beautifully designed and costumed, THE HUDSUCKER PROXY is a curiously arid movie, clever without being witty. One could blame the performances, which are almost all too broad, but the real trouble lies elsewhere: the Coens are often accused of heartlessness, and HUDSUCKER is the proof. It is, however, an impressive technical achievement—the period New York sets are to die for—and its version of the invention of the hula-hoop is a comic highlight.

HULK
2003 137m c   Science Fiction/Action   ★★
Marvel Enterprises/Valhalla Motion   PG-13
Pictures/Good Machine/Universal   (U.S.)

Eric Bana (*Bruce Banner*), Jennifer Connelly (*Betty Ross*), Sam Elliott (*General "Thunderbolt" Ross*), Josh Lucas (*Glenn Talbot*), Nick Nolte (*Dr. David Banner*), Paul Kersey (*Young David Banner*), Cara Buono (*Edith Banner*), Lou Ferrigno (*Security Guard*), Todd Tesen (*Young Ross*), Kevin Rankin (*Harper*)

p, Avi Arad, Larry Franco, Gale Anne Hurd, James Schamus; d, Ang Lee; w, Michael France, John Turman, James Schamus (from a story by James Schamus, based on the Marvel Comic Book character created by Stan Lee and Jack Kirby); ph, Frederick Elmes; ed, Tim Squyres; m, Danny Elfman; prod d, Rick Heinrichs; art d, John Dexter, Greg Papalia; fx, Ed Hirsch, Michael Lantieri, Dennis Muren, Industrial Light & Magic; cos, Marit Allen

A downbeat drag, but then the Incredible Hulk was never one of Marvel Comics' happier creations. Director Ang Lee and screenwriter James Schamus remain faithful to the dark tone of the character's complex back story, but there's so much of it that this leaden film is as muscle-bound as the green Gargantua himself.

Adopted as a youngster, molecular scientist Bruce Banner (Eric Bana) grew to adulthood with no recollection of his early childhood or his birth parents. And with good reason: his father was David Banner (Paul Kersey, and later, a grizzled Nick Nolte), a military scientist who had been mucking around with his own DNA. Driven mad by his experiments and the knowledge that little Bruce inherited his own mutated genes, Banner Sr. committed a crime so psychically damaging to his then four-year-old son that Bruce now has a black hole where his memories should be. The terrible power of those repressed memories, combined with his altered DNA, is unexpectedly unleashed when Bruce is accidentally bombarded with gamma rays at the lab where he and his ex-girlfriend (Jennifer Connelly) are researching regenerative medicine. Now whenever he gets angry, Bruce mutates into a towering, simple-minded hunk of rampaging, chartreuse muscle that's capable of leaping several miles in a single bound and tossing back whatever the military throws at him.

The entirely computer-generated Hulk is a surprisingly expressive creation—it certainly gives a better performance than Connelly—but the action is late in coming and feels like a long set up for a sequel. Fans of the far more entertaining TV series will cheer the brief cameo by Lou Ferrigno, but parents should be aware that several scenes, including a nasty run-in with a Hulk-ified French poodle, make this grim adventure too intense for younger viewers.

HUMAN RESOURCES
(RESSOURCES HUMAINES)
2000 103m c   Drama   ★★★★
La Sept Arte/Haut et Court   (France)

Jalil Lespert (*Frank*), Jean-Claude Vallod (*Father*), Chantal Barre (*Mother*), Veronique de Pandelaere (*Sylvie*), Michel Begnez (*Olivier*), Lucien Longueville (*Chief Executive*), Danielle Melador (*Mrs. Arnoux*), Pascal Semard (*Head of Human Resources*), Didier Emile-Woldemard (*Alain*), Felix Cantet (*Felix*)

p, Caroline Benjo, Carole Scotta; d, Laurent Cantet; w, Laurent Cantet, Gilles Marchand; ph, Matthieu Poirot-Delpech, Claire Caroff; ed, Robin Campillo; art d, Romain Denis

What's exceptional about this powerful French drama from Laurent Cantet isn't the unusually good acting (though the fact that most of the cast is made up of non-professionals is impressive), but the straightforward manner in which it stares down the good old class struggle.

Returning home for summer break, Frank (Jalil Lespert) takes an internship at the same factory where his father Jean-Claude (Jean-Claude Vallod) has worked for the past 30 years. But while Jean-Claude dons the regulation blue coveralls, his son comes to work in a suit; Frank's a management trainee. On his first day, Frank is thrown into a raging dispute over the implementation of a 35-hour work week. The company's chief executive, M. Rouet (Lucien Longueville), is concerned about profits, while labor-union rep Mrs. Arnoux (Danielle Melador) worries about workers' perks and has stymied negotiations. Frank suggests a solution to the impasse: why not circumvent the unions entirely? He draws up a referendum in the form of a questionnaire and urges each worker to fill it out. Frank becomes management's new golden boy, but the questionnaire Frank naively thought would help workers like his father turns out to be a trap.

The film culminates in a company-wide labor dispute, with father and son on opposite sides, but the position in which Frank finds himself at the end of the film is as surprising as it is heartbreaking. What could easily have been a dry, didactic film is granted unusual power by Cantet's cast, all of whom seem to innately understand the personal nature of Cantet's subject. As well they should: most where selected from unemployment lines in the region where the film was shot.

HUMAN STAIN, THE   📀
2003 104m c Drama   ★★
Lakeshore Entertainment/Stone Village   R
Productions/Cinerenta-Cineepsilon   (U.S.)

Anthony Hopkins *(Coleman Silk)*, Nicole Kidman *(Faunia Farely)*, Ed Harris *(Lester Farely)*, Gary Sinise *(Nathan Zuckerman)*, Wentworth Miller *(Young Coleman)*, Jacinda Barrett *(Steena Paulsson)*, Harry Lennix *(Mr. Silk)*, Clark Gregg *(Nelson Primus)*, Anna Deavere Smith *(Mrs. Silk)*, Phyllis Newman *(Iris Silk)*

p, Gary Lucchesi, Tom Rosenberg, Scott Steindorff; d, Robert Benton; w, Nicholas Meyer (based on the novel by Philip Roth); ph, Jean Yves Escoffier; ed, Christopher Tellefsen; m, Rachel Portman; prod d, David Gropman; art d, Zoe Sakellaropoulo; fx, James McQuaide; chor, Pat Birch; cos, Rita Ryack

While director Robert Benton refrains from milking the CRYING GAME-size twist at the center of this weak abbreviation of Philip Roth's novel, keeping the secret makes discussing the film's real subject difficult. Suffice it to say it's about Coleman Silk (a miscast Anthony Hopkins), a Jewish college professor whose career unravels when a remark made in class is blown out of all context and proportion.

When Silk wonders aloud whether two perpetually absent students might in fact be "spooks," he unwittingly ignites a firestorm: unbeknownst to Silk, those spectral students are black. After one of them files a complaint, Silk finds few supporters rallying to his side, and in a fit of righteous pique, he quits. His wife (Phyllis Newman) suffers a fatal stroke, which sends Silk crashing into the life of reclusive novelist Nathan Zuckerman (Gary Sinise), whom Silk demands write a book about the whole outrageous episode. Zuckerman demurs, but the two become friends, and it's not long before Silk confesses that he's been having an affair with Faunia Farely (Nicole Kidman), a local woman half his age who works as a cleaning woman at the college. Life's been rough on Faunia: She not only lost both her children in a terrible accident, but is being tormented by her psycho Vietnam vet exhusband (Ed Harris), who's now gunning for Silk.

Roth set his book in 1998, when political correctness and the Clinton-Lewinsky scandal contributed to what Roth termed America's "enormous piety binge," and it's through this scrim of indignation that he attempted to deal with loaded issues of race, racism, and Jewish identity. But there's so much less to the film than the novel: Nicholas Meyer's screenplay fails to capture the intricate subtleties of its subject and replaces Roth's moral scope with a moralizing tone.

HUNCHBACK OF NOTRE DAME, THE   📀
1939 115m bw Horror/Action/Historical   ★★★½
RKO   (U.S.)

Charles Laughton *(The Hunchback)*, Cedric Hardwicke *(Frollo)*, Thomas Mitchell *(Clopin)*, Maureen O'Hara *(Esmeralda)*, Edmond O'Brien *(Gringoire)*, Alan Marshal *(Phoebus)*, Walter Hampden *(Claude)*, Harry Davenport *(Louis XI)*, Katherine Alexander *(Mme. De Lys)*, George Zucco *(Procurator)*

p, Pandro S. Berman; d, William Dieterle; w, Sonya Levien, Bruno Frank (based on the novel *Notre-Dame de Paris* by Victor Hugo); ph, Joseph August; ed, William Hamilton, Robert Wise; m, Alfred Newman; art d, Van Nest Polglase; fx, Vernon L. Walker; cos, Walter Plunkett

AAN Best Score: Alfred Newman; *AAN Best Sound Recording:* John Aalberg

With its lavish production and superb cast, a brilliant performance by Charles Laughton, and moody, atmospheric direction from German expatriate William Dieterle, this is easily the best film version of Victor Hugo's classic novel to date.

Laughton is the pathetic, lonely, misshapen bellringer of Notre Dame who falls in love with the beautiful gypsy Esmeralda (Maureen O'Hara). In addition to gorgeous sets by Van Nest Polglase and breathtaking photography by Joseph H. August, the film benefits from a script that is a vast improvement over the 1923 version. Bringing Hugo's social and political concerns to the forefront, screenwriters Sonya Levien and Bruno Frank make the corrupt machinations of the church almost as important as Quasimodo's tragic love. Laughton, whom some have accused of overplaying the role's pathos, is magnificent here in one of his greatest roles. His makeup, created by George and R. Gordon Bau, is at least the equal of Lon Chaney's, with modern foam latex technology allowing for a subtler and, therefore, more jarring visage.

RKO spent more than $2 million on this production—one of the most expensive films ever made by the studio—and was rewarded with both critical and financial success. This was the U.S. film debut of the breathtaking O'Hara and a fine film debut for Edmond O'Brien. Superior, gripping filmmaking, well worth revisiting for Dieterle's marvelous command of detail.

HUNCHBACK OF NOTRE DAME, THE   📀
1996 95m c Animated/Romance/Musical   ★★½
Walt Disney Pictures   (U.S.)   G

VOICES OF: Tom Hulce *(Quasimodo)*, Demi Moore *(Esmeralda)*, Tony Jay *(Frollo)*, Kevin Kline *(Phoebus)*, Paul Kandel *(Clopin)*, Jason Alexander *(Hugo)*, Charles Kimbrough *(Victor)*, Mary Wickes *(Laverne)*, David Ogden Stiers *(Archdeacon)*, Mary Kay Bergman *(Quasimodo's Mother)*

p, Don Hahn; d, Gary Trousdale, Kirk Wise; w, Tab Murphy, Irene Mecchi, Bob Tzudiker, Noni White, Jonathan Roberts (from a story by Tab Murphy, based on the novel *Notre-Dame de Paris* by Victor Hugo); ed, Ellen Keneshea; m, Alan Menken; art d, David Goetz; fx, Christopher Jenkins; anim, James Baxter, Tony Fucile, Kathy Zielinski, Russ Edmonds, Danny Galieote, David Pruiksma, Will Finn, Ron Husband, Dave Burgess, Gregory Griffith, Mike "Moe" Merell

AAN Best Original Musical or Comedy Score: Alan Menken (music, orchestral score), Stephen Schwartz (lyrics)

Considering that Disney couldn't help but trash Victor Hugo's novel in the process of reforming it for tender young sensibilities, this animated adaptation of his *Notre Dame de*

Paris is pricklier and more disturbing than we had any right to expect. The story is still driven by cruelty, intolerance, and lust, and while Quasimodo (voiced by Tom Hulce) has been given a makeover by Uncle Walt's art department, he's still a drooling grotesque with a big hairy hump. His best friends are three adorably peppy stone gargoyles whose irreverent cheer can't entirely obscure the fact that they have no lower bodies and must hop around on their stumps. Then there's that uplifting message: syrupy sentiments about inner beauty notwithstanding, comely (and buxom) gypsy Esmeralda (voiced by Demi Moore) and hunky Phoebus, captain of the guards (voiced by Kevin Kline), go off together, while ugly but supremely virtuous Quasimodo creeps back to his drafty bell tower and his concrete friends. Kids won't fail to get the point. As for the rest, the songs are undistinguished and the background animation is breathtaking. The most arresting set piece illustrates the temptation of the pious hypocrite Frollo (voiced by Tony Jay) with a guilt-fueled fantasia of shimmying flames and red-cloaked inquisitors. Smokin'!

HUNT, THE
(LA CAZA)
1966 93m   bw Drama   ★★★★
Elias Querejeta   (Spain)

Ismael Merlo *(Jose)*, Alfredo Mayo *(Paco)*, Jose Maria Prada *(Luis)*, Emilio Gutierrez Caba *(Enrique)*, Fernando Sanchez Polack *(Juan)*, Violetta Garcia *(Nina)*, Maria Sanchez Arosa

p, Elias Querejeta; d, Carlos Saura; w, Carlos Saura, Angelino Fons (based on a story by Saura); ph, Luis Cuadrado; ed, Pablo del Amo; m, Luis de Pablo; art d, Carlos Ochoa

Brutal, excellent moral tale, dealing with four rabbit hunters. Three Spanish Civil War veterans return to an old battleground that is now filled with rabbits. Merlo, the outing organizer, hopes to borrow some money from his war buddy, Mayo, now a rich businessman. The tensions between the two build with frightening force, and old angers and rivalries are taken out on the rabbits with frightening brutality. Mayo is killed by an accidental shot from Merlo's gun. Prada, believing the shot intentional, drives his jeep head on towards Merlo, who shoots him in the face. Caba, Mayo's teenage brother-in-law, stares numbly at the bloodied corpses. The tensions are well realized by the ensemble. In pitting friend against friend in senseless slaughter, Saura has created a fine allegory for the Spanish Civil War.

HUNT FOR RED OCTOBER, THE   DVD
1990 134m c   Thriller   ★★½
Mace Neufeld-Jerry Sherlock   (U.S.)   PG

Sean Connery *(Capt. Marko Ramius)*, Alec Baldwin *(Jack Ryan)*, Scott Glenn *(Capt. Bart Mancuso)*, Sam Neill *(Capt. Vasily Borodin)*, James Earl Jones *(Admiral James Greer)*, Joss Ackland *(Andrei Lysenko)*, Richard Jordan *(Jeffrey Pelt)*, Peter Firth *(Ivan Putin)*, Tim Curry *(Dr. Petrov)*, Courtney B. Vance *(Seaman Jones)*

p, Mace Neufeld; d, John McTiernan; w, Larry Ferguson, Donald Stewart (based on the book by Tom Clancy); ph, Jan De Bont (Panavision, Technicolor); ed, Dennis Virkler, John Wright; m, Basil Poledouris; prod d, Terence Marsh; art d, Dianne Wager, Donald Woodruff, William Cruse; fx, Scott Squires; cos, James Tyson; anim, Eric Swenson, Christopher Dierdorff, Pat Meyers, Charlie Canfield

AAN Best Film Editing: Dennis Virkler, John Wright; AAN Best Sound: Richard Bryce Goodman, Richard Overton, Kevin F. Cleary, Don Bassman; AA Best Sound Effects Editing: Cecelia Hall, George Watters, II

In spite of the high level of talent on board and at the helm, THE HUNT FOR RED OCTOBER is a heavy-duty mediocrity, sluggish, unwieldy, and instantly forgettable. The plot revolves around Marko Ramius (Sean Connery), a veteran Soviet sub commander who is guiding the new, super-advanced *Red October* submarine on its maiden mission. Abruptly, Ramius murders the onboard political officer and burns his orders. *Red October* is supposed to participate in war games meant to showcase its ability to evade sonar detection and deliver a full load of nuclear missiles to major American targets. Ramius instead tells his crew that they will approach the U.S. coastline to embarrass the American military. In fact, he has something very different in mind. When Ramius goes off course, factions within the U.S. military and government suspect a sneak attack. Guided by CIA analyst Dr. Jack Ryan (Alec Baldwin), who happens to be an expert on Ramius, the American security brain trust has to decide whether the Russians are telling the truth. Then they must choose the appropriate response—either help the Russians sink *Red October* (the FAIL SAFE scenario) or help Ramius defect.

Tom Clancy's exciting (albeit instantly dated) Cold War bestseller served as the basis for the film. But on the screen, RED OCTOBER suffers from a bad case of bloated scenario, lacking unities of place and action. In simpler terms, it should have stayed put, either above the surface or in the briny depths. Instead, the two major plots—two different movies, really—wind up neutralizing each other. Each time McTiernan cuts from one setting to the other, he's forced to start from scratch in rebuilding tension and involvement. Moreover, Larry Ferguson's adaptation doesn't bother to supply motivation for its stock, square-jawed characters. Ryan is so short of substance viewers may find it hard to remember that he's the movie's hero. While James Earl Jones reprised his role in subsequent Clancy-based pictures (PATRIOT GAMES, CLEAR AND PRESENT DANGER), notoriously obstreperous Baldwin lost the Ryan role to Harrison Ford after a contract dispute.

HURRICANE, THE   DVD
1937 110m bw Disaster   ★★★★
Goldwyn   (U.S.)

Dorothy Lamour *(Marama)*, Jon Hall *(Terangi)*, Mary Astor *(Madame Germaine De Laage)*, C. Aubrey Smith *(Father Paul)*, Thomas Mitchell *(Dr. Kersaint)*, Raymond Massey *(Governor Eugene De Laage)*, John Carradine *(Jailer)*, Jerome Cowan *(Capt. Nagle)*, Al Kikume *(Chief Mehevi)*, Kuulei DeClercq *(Tita)*

p, Samuel Goldwyn; d, John Ford, Stuart Heisler (uncredited); w, Dudley Nichols, Oliver H.P. Garrett (based on the novel by Charles Nordhoff and James Norman Hall); ph, Bert Glennon; ed, Lloyd Nosler; art d, Richard Day, Alexander Golitzen; fx, James Basevi; cos, Omar Kiam

AAN Best Supporting Actor: Thomas Mitchell; AAN Best Score: Samuel Goldwyn Studio Music Department, Alfred Newman (Dept. Head); AA Best Sound Recording: Thomas Moulton

A stunning big blowout; this South Seas spectacular from the great John Ford is a rare perennial. The story is pretty much hooey with a dollop of tropical glamour on top, but anyway, marvelously self-serving. The beauteous Lamour is in love with barrel-chested Hall, whose hot temper lands him in hot water with corrupt island governor Massey. There's a fine assist from Astor, Mitchell, Cowan, Carradine, and Smith. Then the hurricane comes—a real lulu—and steals everyone's thunder. These scenes are terrifyingly spectacular, done on actual and miniature scales so cleverly edited that it is next to impossible to discern where one leaves off and the other takes over.

Hall and Lamour, two relatively unknown actors, became big deals in their roles as scantily clad natives. Lamour, a $75-a-week bit player at Paramount with only four films to her credit, was borrowed by Goldwyn from that studio. Goldwyn originally wanted Howard Hawks to direct this film, but they had argued violently over the making of COME AND GET IT, so Goldwyn turned to John Ford to direct THE HURRICANE. The mogul had also intended Joel McCrea to enact the part of the persecuted native Terangi, but McCrea convinced Ford that he was not right for the role, so Ford came up with Hall, a handsome, virile-looking actor Ford had spotted in a minor production at the Hollywood Playhouse.

Hall would have a checkered career after THE HURRICANE, coming to prominence in the early 1940s in a series of adventure and fantasy tales with exotic co-star Maria Montez. Lamour's star would rise even higher, especially after parlaying her sarong to fame—she first wore it in THE JUNGLE PRINCESS—and she would wear it through many a Bob Hope-Bing Crosby road film.

HUSBANDS

1970 154m c Drama/Comedy ★★★½
Faces Music (U.S.) PG

Ben Gazzara *(Harry)*, Peter Falk *(Archie)*, John Cassavetes *(Gus)*, Jenny Runacre *(Mary Tynan)*, Jenny Lee Wright *(Pearl Billingham)*, Noelle Kao *(Julie)*, Leola Harlow *(Leola)*, Meta Shaw *(Annie)*, John Kullers *(Red)*, Delores Delmar *(Countess)*

p, Al Ruban; d, John Cassavetes; w, John Cassavetes; ph, Victor J. Kemper (DeLuxe Color); ed, Peter Tanner; art d, Rene D'Auriac; cos, Louis Brown

John Cassavetes, Peter Falk, and Ben Gazzara give outstanding performances in HUSBANDS, Cassavetes's seriocomic improvisatory marathon about three men who go on a wild binge after the sudden death of one of their friends.

Harry (Ben Gazzara), Archie (Peter Falk) and Gus (John Cassavetes), three best friends in their mid-30s who live in suburban, middle-class Long Island with their families, are shocked when their friend Stuart Jackson (David Rowlands) suddenly dies of a heart attack. After attending the funeral, the men go into Manhattan and get drunk, then stay up all night and play basketball, followed by some more bar-hopping. When they finally go home two days later, Harry has a violent fight with his wife, who tells him she wants a divorce, then goes with Gus and Archie into Manhattan to go to work. Archie accompanies Gus to his dental practice, and talks him into leaving, and they meet Harry, who is fed up with his job. The trio decide to take a weekend trip to London where they check into a fancy hotel and gamble at a casino, then pick up three women and take them back to their rooms.

Most of Cassavetes's cinema verite films as a director are invariably accused (and with some justification) of being rambling, self-indulgent, and unfocused, but it is precisely those elements that make his best work so affecting and memorable, and HUSBANDS, though deeply flawed, is one of the finest examples of that. It originally ran 154 minutes when it premiered at the San Francisco Film Festival in 1970, then was cut by 16 minutes for general release, but even in the shortened version, many of its scenes go on far too long after they've made their point, while others seem totally unnecessary. The film's subtitle is "A comedy about life, death and freedom," and although there isn't much plot in the conventional sense, the basic premise allows for a penetrating look at the dreams and frustrations of disillusioned average men who have reached a mid-life crisis and are searching for some meaning and a reason to go on living. It's about basic things like what it means to have a family, hold a job, make compromises, and be responsible (or not), and treats these issues in an honest and probing manner, catching some revealing glimpses of life.

HUSBANDS AND WIVES *DVD*

1992 107m c Comedy/Drama ★★★★
TriStar (U.S.) R

Woody Allen *(Gabe Roth)*, Mia Farrow *(Judy Roth)*, Judy Davis *(Sally)*, Juliette Lewis *(Rain)*, Liam Neeson *(Michael)*, Sydney Pollack *(Jack)*, Lysette Anthony *(Sam)*, Nick Metropolis *(TV Scientist)*, Cristi Conaway *(Shawn Grainger)*, Timothy Jerome *(Paul)*

p, Robert Greenhut; d, Woody Allen; w, Woody Allen; ph, Carlo Di Palma; ed, Susan E. Morse; prod d, Santo Loquasto; art d, Speed Hopkins; cos, Jeffrey Kurland

AAN Best Supporting Actress: Judy Davis; *AAN Best Original Screenplay:* Woody Allen

This is one of Woody Allen's best films to date, combining some of his finest serious writing about relationships, in the style of HANNAH AND HER SISTERS, with humor that's all the more effective thanks to its dark, edgy context.

Allen has rounded up all the usual suspects for his latest look at the foibles, romantic and otherwise, of a group of privileged Manhattanites. They include Gabe Roth (Allen), a distinguished novelist and writing professor; his wife Judy (Mia Farrow), an editor at a prestigious art magazine; Jack (real-life film director Sydney Pollack), a chronically unfaithful businessman; and his wife Sally (Judy Davis), a woman so fiercely critical of everything that she is literally never satisfied.

HUSBANDS AND WIVES leads us through the break-up of both marriages, via a trio of passionate infatuations—Jack with his aerobics instructor (Lysette Anthony), Gabe with a 21-year-old student (Juliette Lewis), and Sally with a colleague (Liam Neeson) of Judy's. It ends with one of the couples attempting a reconciliation, chastened by the realization that everlasting romantic love is a misleading, befuddling myth.

The film is greatly indebted to the improvisatory, pseudo-verite style of John Cassavetes, with a hand-held camera either dodging and wheeling around the characters, or sitting stationary as they volunteer information directly to the screen. The effect is of an artless, spontaneous attempt to capture life in the raw, but it belies a cannily crafted structure which uses both flashbacks and ellipses to lay bare the lives of its subjects. The acting is flawless throughout, with top honors going to Davis, who blazes through the picture with devastating intensity and honesty. It's an urgent, unsettling performance, perfectly complemented by Pollack, who projects quiet ease and authenticity in this, his first major role.

HUSH ... HUSH, SWEET CHARLOTTE

1964 134m bw Thriller ★★★½
Fox (U.S.)

Bette Davis *(Charlotte)*, Olivia de Havilland *(Miriam)*, Joseph Cotten *(Drew)*, Agnes Moorehead *(Velma)*, Joseph *(Harry)*, Victor Buono *(Big Sam)*, Mary Astor *(Jewel Mayhew)*, Wesley Addy *(Sheriff)*, William Campbell *(Paul Marchand)*, Bruce Dern *(John Mayhew)*

p, Robert Aldrich; d, Robert Aldrich; w, Henry Farrell, Lukas Heller; ph, Joseph Biroc; ed, Michael Luciano; m, Frank DeVol; art d, William Glasgow; chor, Alex Ruiz; cos, Norma Koch

AAN Best Supporting Actress: Agnes Moorehead; *AAN Best B/W Cinematography:* Joseph Biroc; *AAN Best Film Editing:* Michael Luciano; *AAN Best Original Score:* Frank DeVol; *AAN Best Song:* "Hush ... Hush, Sweet Charlotte"; Frank DeVol (Music), Mack David (Lyrics); *AAN Best Art Direction-Set Decoration (B/W):* William Glasgow (Art Direction), Raphael Bretton (Set Decoration); *AAN Best Costume Design (B/W):* Norma Koch

A Grand Guignol Southern Gothic cauldron… the next dish proffered by Aldrich and Davis after the success of WHATEVER HAPPENED TO BABY JANE? CHARLOTTE was originally planned as Crawford's revenge—Davis is the victim here, a loopy loon living in a moldy mansion in Louisiana, with hair like Spanish moss, skin like a lichen and a hobby of shooting at land developers.

She's haunted by an Electra complex and memories of a murdered beau she may have chopped up. Her nocturnal ramblings are interrupted, then encouraged, by the arrival of her prissbitch cousin from Virginia, de Havilland, finally getting a chance to give Davis hell and act out the dark side of Melanie Wilkes. Cotten is the corrupt ole boy family doctor, Agnes Moorehead the Broomhilda housekeeper and the great Mary Astor (as a favor to Davis) in a swansong cameo.

Davis has some authentic, poignant moments, before all hell breaks loose. She seems to be making up for her lost chances on Tennessee Williams territory (she had wanted MENAGERIE *and* STREETCAR), and there's one kabuki lioness flip-out on a stairway that's a must-see. She's matched by Moorehead's perfect, obscure portrayal. The best line goes to de Havilland: "You just can't keep the hogs away from the trough."

Next to this, JANE looks like Masterpiece Theatre—it's the mutilation aspect that saddles the proceedings (both films were from Henry Farrell novels). Victor Buono (who received an Academy Award nomination for BABY JANE) is back for more as young Charlotte's father, and Dern is the lover who gets the axe. The tacky title song was a camp hit for Patti Page.

HUSTLE 📀

1975 120m c   Crime/Mystery   ★★★½
Paramount (U.S.)   R

Burt Reynolds *(Lt. Phil Gaines)*, Catherine Deneuve *(Nicole Britton)*, Ben Johnson *(Marty Hollinger)*, Paul Winfield *(Sgt. Louis Belgrave)*, Eileen Brennan *(Paula Hollinger)*, Eddie Albert *(Leo Sellers)*, Ernest Borgnine *(Santoro)*, Catherine Bach *(Peggy Summers)*, Jack Carter *(Herbie Dalitz)*, James Hampton *(Bus Driver)*

p, Robert Aldrich; d, Robert Aldrich; w, Steve Shagan; ph, Joseph Biroc (Eastmancolor); ed, Michael Luciano; m, Frank DeVol; art d, Hilyard Brown; fx, Henry Miller Jr.; chor, Alex Romero; cos, Oscar Rodriguez, Betsy Cox

A disturbing and grim modern film noir directed by Aldrich, who was a master of the genre in the early 1950s. Reynolds stars as Phil Gaines, a bitter, cynical cop who finds the body of a young girl washed up on the beach and launches an investigation to determine her identity. After she is identified as a small-time hooker and porno actress, Gaines calls in the girl's parents, Marty (Johnson, in a superb performance) and Paula (Brennan), to identify the body. Soon Gaines finds himself competing with the headstrong Marty to solve a crime that turns out to have grave personal implications for them both.

Director Aldrich (KISS ME DEADLY) offers an unrelentingly diseased portrait of modern society in HUSTLE. Reynolds is trapped in this disgusting, seedy world from the opening of the film when his pleasant day off is intruded upon by the washed-up corpse, forcing him back into the underworld. There is no way out. HUSTLE is one of the few examples of *true* modern film noir. But director and screenwriter cannot resolve their different approaches. The script's humanistic, if depressing, angle gets battered by Aldrich's approach. An interesting mixed bag.

HUSTLER, THE 📀

1961 134m bw Sports   ★★★★½
Fox (U.S.)

Paul Newman *("Fast" Eddie Felson)*, Jackie Gleason *(Minnesota Fats)*, Piper Laurie *(Sarah Packard)*, George C. Scott *(Bert Gordon)*, Myron McCormick *(Charlie Burns)*, Murray Hamilton *(Findlay)*, Michael Constantine *(Big John)*, Stefan Gierasch *(Preacher)*, Jake LaMotta *(Bartender)*, Gordon B. Clarke *(Cashier)*

p, Robert Rossen; d, Robert Rossen; w, Sidney Carroll, Robert Rossen (based on the novel by Walter Tevis); ph, Eugene Schuftan (CinemaScope); ed, Dede Allen; m, Kenyon Hopkins; prod d, Harry Horner; art d, Albert Brenner, Harry Horner; cos, Ruth Morley

AAN Best Picture; AAN Best Actor: Paul Newman; *AAN Best Actress:* Piper Laurie; *AAN Best Supporting Actor:* Jackie Gleason; *AAN Best Supporting Actor:* George C. Scott; *AAN Best Director:* Robert Rossen; *AAN Best Adapted Screenplay:* Sidney Carroll, Robert Rossen; *AA Best B/W Cinematography:* Eugen Shuftan; *AA Best Art Direction-Set Decoration (B/W):* Harry Horner, Gene Callahan

This dark stunner, based on Walter Tevis's novel, boasts Paul Newman in the role that made him an overnight superstar. The treatment feels like a cross between Hemingway and Odets and there are some affectations with dialogue. But Rossen knows how to frame his story and give his actors room to breathe, eliciting terrific performances from everyone.

"Fast" Eddie Felson is a pool shark who hustles his way across the country to Ames Billiard Parlor in New York, where he challenges the unbeatable Minnesota Fats (Jackie Gleason). Penniless and alone, Eddie falls in love with Sarah Packard (Piper Laurie), an alcoholic cripple; then, after a return to small-time hustling that leads to two thug-administered broken thumbs, Eddie teams up with gambler Bert Gordon (George C. Scott), who becomes his backer but also personifies a vision of evil.

With the help of Gene Shufton's Oscar-winning black-and-white cinematography, producer-writer-director Robert Rossen offers a grim world where the only bright spot is the top of the pool table, yet his characters maintain a shabby nobility and grace. Gleason is brilliantly detached, witty, and charming as Fats; sexy, waifish Laurie offers some of the best work of her career; Scott is evil incarnate; and Newman is simply unforgettable in his Oscar-nominated role (he would have to play Fast Eddie again 25 years later in the excellent sequel, THE COLOR OF MONEY, to actually win his first Academy Award). The great pool player Willie Mosconi coached Gleason and Newman in their shots. Not to be missed.

I

I AM A CAMERA

1955 98m   bw Drama/Comedy   ★★½
Romulus/Remus   (U.K.)

Julie Harris *(Sally Bowles)*, Laurence Harvey *(Christopher Isherwood)*, Shelley Winters *(Natalia Landauer)*, Ron Randell *(Clive)*, Lea Seidl *(Fraulein Schneider)*, Anton Diffring *(Fritz)*, Ina De La Haye *(Herr Landauer)*, Jean Gargoet *(Pierre)*, Stanley Maxted *(American Editor)*, Alexis Bobrinskoy *(Proprietor)* p, Jack Clayton; d, Henry Cornelius; w, John Collier (based on the play by John Van Druten from the "Berlin Stories" by Christopher Isherwood); ph, Guy Green; ed, Clive Donner; m, Malcolm Arnold; art d, William Kellner

In the beginning there were Christopher Isherwood's "Berlin Stories." From them came the award-winning play that provided the basis for both I AM A CAMERA and CABARET. Despite an intelligent adaptation and cast, this version is little more than an erratically filmed stage play. The action is static and the plot developed mostly through dialogue, which takes a far lighter tone than CABARET. The comedy deals with the episodic adventures of Harvey, a poor, struggling writer, and the effervescent Harris, a nightclub chanteuse—roommates caught up in the swirl of pre-WWII Berlin. Winters is a German girl who begins to experience the anti-Semitism of the Nazi regime.

I AM A FUGITIVE FROM A CHAIN GANG   📀
1932   93m   bw   Prison   ★★★★★
Warner Bros.   (U.S.)

Paul Muni *(James Allen)*, Glenda Farrell *(Marie Woods)*, Helen Vinson *(Helen)*, Preston Foster *(Pete)*, Allen Jenkins *(Barney Sykes)*, Edward Ellis *(Bomber Wells)*, John Wray *(Nordine)*, Hale Hamilton *(Rev. Robert Clinton Allen)*, Harry Woods *(Guard)*, David Landau

p, Hal B. Wallis; d, Mervyn LeRoy; w, Howard J. Green, Brown Holmes, Sheridan Gibney (based on the autobiography *I Am a Fugitive from a Georgia Chain Gang* by Robert E. Burns); ph, Sol Polito; ed, William Holmes; art d, Jack Okey; cos, Orry-Kelly

AAN Best Picture; AAN Best Actor: Paul Muni; AAN Best Sound Recording: Nathan Levinson

One of the toughest movies ever made, an uncompromising and frightening film that lays bare the inhuman conditions of the penal system in post-WWI Georgia.

Based on a collection of writings by Robert Elliot Burns, who escaped from a chain gang to become a successful magazine editor but lived with the continual threat of being recaptured, the film tells the story of James Allen (Paul Muni), who is framed for the robbery of a hamburger stand and sentenced to ten years' hard labor. Every ounce of his strength and dignity is stripped away until he resolves to escape.

The reputation of socially conscious director Mervyn LeRoy is identified perhaps more with this film than with any other. Here the director of LITTLE CAESAR and THEY WON'T FORGET (which explored the horrors of lynching) pulls no punches, with every scene of I AM A FUGITIVE an expression of social outrage. Much of the film's story and technique would influence later prison movies, especially those dealing with prison farm systems. The escape through the swamps was duplicated by Edward G. Robinson in BLACKMAIL; the escape by truck was employed by Paul Newman in COOL HAND LUKE. Muni's captivating performance marked one of the highlights of his career.

Though the film specifically excluded the word "Georgia" from its title and never mentioned the state in the entire film, the indictment of that state's cruel chain-gang system was clear. The film was banned in Georgia and the state filed a libel suit against the studio. Two prison wardens in Georgia also filed unsuccessful million-dollar suits against Warner Brothers. Georgia was also relentless in its attempts to recapture Burns, whom Warner Bros. asked to travel to Hollywood to serve as an advisor on the project. Burns smuggled himself into Los Angeles using an assumed name and, reportedly, not only suggested ideas for the script but helped write dialogue before nervously fleeing after a few weeks.

I HEART HUCKABEES   📀
2004   106m   c   Comedy   ★★½
Huckabees Inc./Scott Rudin Productions/Qwerty Films/   R
Fox Searchlight/N1 European Film
Produktions   (U.S./Germany)

Jason Schwartzman *(Albert Markovski)*, Isabelle Huppert *(Caterine Vauban)*, Dustin Hoffman *(Bernard Jaffe)*, Lily Tomlin *(Vivian Jaffe)*, Jude Law *(Brad Stand)*, Mark Wahlberg *(Tommy Corn)*, Naomi Watts *(Dawn Campbell)*, Angela Grillo *(Angela Franco)*, Ger Duany *(Mr. Nimieri)*, Darlene Hunt *(Darlene)*

p, Gregory Goodman, Scott Rudin, David O. Russell; d, David O. Russell; w, Jeff Baena, David O. Russell; ph, Peter Deming; ed, Robert K. Lambert; m, Jon Brion; prod d, K.K. Barrett; art d, Seth Reed; fx, Russell Barrett, Martin Bresin; cos, Mark Bridges

David O. Russell's smarty-pants head trip, which aims to provoke discussion of big questions by wrapping them in hipster laughs, begins with a sputtering burst of profanity and ends up struggling in the sticky strands of its own elaborate contrivances.

In the midst of an existential crisis, environmental activist Albert Markovski (Jason Schwartzman) discovers a puzzling business card—"Vivian Jaffe: Existential Detective"—and decides to pursue a coincidence that strikes him as mysteriously portentous: on three separate occasions his path has crossed that of a Sudanese stranger (Ger Duany). Vivian and Bernard Jaffe (Lily Tomlin, Dustin Hoffman) take Albert's case and commence spying on every aspect of his messy life. He's estranged from his self-centered parents (Bob Gunton, Talia Shire), and is about to be booted out of the Open Spaces Coalition he founded in favor of slick young marketing executive Brad Stand (Jude Law), who works for the most environmentally unfriendly, Target-like superstore, Huckabees. Most galling of all, Albert is in love with Brad's artificially perky girlfriend, Huckabees spokesmodel Dawn Campbell (Naomi Watts). Complicating matters is firefighter Tommy Corn (Mark Wahlberg), whom the Jaffes assign to serve as Albert's rearrangement-of-reality buddy, and Caterine Vauban (Isabelle Huppert), once the Jaffes' star pupil, now their implacable, nihilistic rival.

Russell's ambitions are lofty, and his filmmaking is audacious, but the result is a quirky curiosity that's cheeky, shrewdly clever, and more than a little precious. When the average comedy is aimed at juvenile 12-year-olds of all ages, the fact that Russell's target audience is precocious 12-year-olds of all ages is a significant improvement without actually being a triumph of mature wit over boorish puerility.

I KNOW WHAT YOU DID LAST SUMMER   📀
1997   101m   c   Horror/Thriller   ★★★
Mandalay Entertainment/Neal H. Moritz   (U.S.)   R

Jennifer Love Hewitt *(Julie James)*, Sarah Michelle Gellar *(Helen Shivers)*, Ryan Phillippe *(Barry Cox)*, Freddie Prinze Jr. *(Ray Bronson)*, Muse Watson *(Benjamin Willis/Fisherman)*, Bridgette Wilson *(Elsa Shivers)*, Anne Heche *(Melissa Egan)*, Johnny Galecki *(Max)*, Stuart Greer *(Officer)*, J. Don Ferguson *(MC)*

p, Neal H. Moritz, Erik Feig, Stokely Chaffin; d, Jim Gillespie; w, Kevin Williamson (based on the novel by Lois Duncan); ph, Denis Crossan; ed, Steve Mirkovich; m, John Debney; prod d, Gary Wissner; art d, John J. Rutchland III; fx, John D. Milinac; cos, Catherine Adair

SCREAM screenwriter Kevin Williamson takes a step back and writes the kind of movie SCREAM mocks. You can see him now, soaking up videos of FRIDAY THE 13TH, HALLOWEEN, and HE KNOWS YOU'RE ALONE and saying, "I can do that!" And he can.

Bright, graduating high-school seniors Julie (Jennifer Love Hewitt), Helen (Sarah Michelle Gellar), Ray (Freddie Prinze Jr.)

and Barry (Ryan Phillippe) accidentally run a man down on a deserted road and, in a panic, decide to get rid of the body and pretend it never happened. A year later, the letter arrives: "I know what you did last summer." Someone is stalking them, armed with a deadly gaffing hook: can they find the slasher before he—or is it she?—finds each and every one of them? Once you're over the vertiginous feeling of early '80s deja vu, Williamson's script—which contains flashes of SCREAM's wit and clever self-referentiality—clicks along nicely under the guidance of first-time feature director Jim Gillespie. The youngsters all turn in game performances, but the standout is Anne Heche, whose weird Missy Farmer is pure Mimsy Farmer at maximum twitch. If you like this sort of thing, you've seen it all before. But if you're under the age of 20, you've probably never seen it on a big screen in a first-run theater.

I KNOW WHERE I'M GOING!
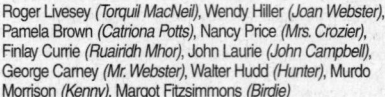
1945 91m   bw   Romance/Comedy   ★★★★½
Archers   (U.K.)

Roger Livesey *(Torquil MacNeil)*, Wendy Hiller *(Joan Webster)*, Pamela Brown *(Catriona Potts)*, Nancy Price *(Mrs. Crozier)*, Finlay Currie *(Ruairidh Mhor)*, John Laurie *(John Campbell)*, George Carney *(Mr. Webster)*, Walter Hudd *(Hunter)*, Murdo Morrison *(Kenny)*, Margot Fitzsimmons *(Birdie)*

p, Michael Powell, Emeric Pressburger; d, Michael Powell, Emeric Pressburger; w, Michael Powell, Emeric Pressburger; ph, Erwin Hillier; ed, John Seabourne; m, Allan Gray; prod d, Alfred Junge; fx, Henry Harris

Wendy Hiller gives an ebullient and charming performance as a headstrong young British woman in I KNOW WHERE I'M GOING!, a mystical, lyrical romance by the great writer-producer-director team of Michael Powell and Emeric Pressburger, known as the Archers.

25-year-old Joan Webster (Wendy Hiller) announces to her father (George Carney) that she's engaged to Sir Robert Bellinger, the elderly owner of the chemical plant where she works, and one of the richest men in England. The two are to be married on the Scottish island of Kiloran in the Hebrides, which Bellinger has rented. Joan travels to the Isle of Mull, where she's supposed to catch a boat to Kiloran, but a storm prevents her from leaving, and she's forced to stay on the mainland. There, she meets a young naval officer on leave named Torquil MacNeil (Roger Livesy) who's also trying to get to Kiloran, and the two of them spend the night at the home of one of Torquil's friends. In the days following, Torquil exposes Joan to some intriguing Scottish traditions, and makes her question her decision to marry.

One of the most low-key of all the great Powell-Pressburger productions, I KNOW WHERE I'M GOING! is an absolute delight from beginning to end, combining romance, comedy, fantasy, and folklore to create a unique style that can only be described as "magical realism." Hiller brilliantly captures Joan's intelligence and determination without turning her into a stereotype, and makes her transformation totally believable. Roger Livesy is excellent as Torquil, although amazingly, all of his exterior scenes were filmed with a double, since he was unavailable when the company went to Scotland. The rest of the cast is amusingly filled with the usual assortment of Archers eccentrics, most notably Captain C.W.R. Knight as the falconer Colonel Barnstaple, and a pre-teen Petula Clark. Erwin Hillier's superb, high-contrast photography creates some stunning romantic images and awesome sights, such as the blanket of black mist swirling across the sea, and the incredible shot of the tiny boat about to be swallowed up by the whirlpool. I KNOW WHERE I'M GOING! is a beautiful film about the profound effects of nature on people, and that fact that the universe can be a wondrous and magical place if one keeps oneself open to its vast mysteries.

I LOVE YOU, ALICE B. TOKLAS!
1968 92m   c   Comedy   ★★
Warner Bros.   (U.S.)

Peter Sellers *(Harold)*, Jo Van Fleet *(Mother)*, Leigh Taylor-Young *(Nancy)*, Joyce Van Patten *(Joyce)*, David Arkin *(Herbie)*, Herb Edelman *(Murray)*, Salem Ludwig *(Father)*, Louis Gottlieb *(Guru)*, Grady Sutton *(Funeral Director)*, Janet E. Clark *(Mrs. Foley)*

p, Charles Maguire; d, Hy Averback; w, Paul Mazursky, Larry Tucker; ph, Philip Lathrop (Technicolor); ed, Robert C. Jones; m, Elmer Bernstein; prod d, Pato Guzman; cos, Theadora Van Runkle

An inspired performance by Sellers cannot redeem this giddy satire of '60s hippie culture, in which he plays a neurotic, asthmatic, fortyish attorney who discovers pot and the counterculture. Van Fleet plays his mother, Van Patten the boring blonde his parents wish he would marry, and Arkin his hippy brother. Mazursky and Tucker, who came from TV's "Monkees," wrote in enough laughs to make this a hit at the time, but from the point that Sellers grows his hair and drops out, the embarrassment factor becomes too much to take. Look for Grady Sutton, the butt of so many W.C. Fields jokes, effective in a small role.

I MARRIED A WITCH
1942 82m   bw   Science Fiction/Comedy   ★★★★½
Paramount   (U.S.)

Fredric March *(Wallace Wooley)*, Veronica Lake *(Jennifer)*, Robert Benchley *(Dr. Dudley White)*, Susan Hayward *(Estelle Masterson)*, Cecil Kellaway *(Daniel)*, Elizabeth Patterson *(Margaret)*, Robert Warwick *(J.B. Masterson)*, Eily Malyon *(Tabitha Wooley)*, Nora Cecil *(Harriet)*, Emory Parnell *(Allen)*

p, Preston Sturges; d, Rene Clair; w, Robert Pirosh, Marc Connelly, Dalton Trumbo (based on the novel *The Passionate Witch* by Thorne Smith and Norman Matson); ph, Ted Tetzlaff; ed, Eda Warren; m, Roy Webb; art d, Hans Dreier, Ernst Fegte; fx, Gordon Jennings; cos, Edith Head

AAN Best Score (Drama or Comedy): Roy Webb

Although Clair is famous for his experimental French silents and several early talkies, here's the master at a later peak in, yes, Hollywood, USA. An accomplished confection, WITCH is required Halloween viewing.

Kellaway and his daughter Lake are branded witches in 1690 and burned at the stake, but not before putting a curse on their persecutors, the Wooley family. They threaten that no male member of the family will find happiness, and the curse is shown taking effect as misfortune befalls Wooley males (all played by March) through the ages, up to 1942 where March is shown to be a stuffed shirt with a snobbish fiancee, Hayward. He's running for governor of the state with backing from Hayward's filthy rich father, Warwick, an influential publisher. A storm comes up and lightning splits the ancient tree under which Kellaway and Lake were buried over 250 years before. They are freed, emerging as a rotund, booze-loving fellow and a blonde siren. From that point on, Lake does all in her power to make March fall in love with her. Yet her powers seem unable to sway him, as his plans to wed Hayward remain unchanged.

Lake, who had only been in films for a year, is wonderfully effective. Released from the sustained tension of film noir material, she demonstrates a quirky sense of comedy. Her line readings tingle with malice and hoydenish longing. WITCH also presents a lighter, warmer, more likable March than ever before—his chemistry with Lake is very engaging.

This is one of the rare instances where the "other woman" measures up to the lead in beauty and presence. Despite having her own beautiful hair chignoned to play up Lake's, Hayward's career took a major step here, snagging her a series of hard-bitten second leads that prepared her for the Davis-Crawford-Stanwyck roles that would establish her later as a great star. And WITCH finds Kellaway in peak form—it's his most three-dimensional role. Look out, too, for humorist Robert Benchley as March's confused political advisor.

This film, with its wonderful special effects, was in the hilarious tradition of TOPPER and THE GHOST GOES WEST. Clair's direction is swift and sure, producing a livelier, more cohesive effort than his first Hollywood production, THE FLAME OF NEW ORLEANS, which fizzled at the box office. This Thorne Smith tale, taken from an incomplete novel, worked so well onscreen that it inspired the popular sitcom, "Bewitched."

I NEVER PROMISED YOU A ROSE GARDEN *DVD*

1977 96m c Drama ★★★½
Imorh (U.S.) R

Bibi Andersson *(Dr. Fried)*, Kathleen Quinlan *(Deborah Blake)*, Ben Piazza *(Mr. Blake)*, Lorraine Gary *(Mrs. Blake)*, Darlene Craviotto *(Carla)*, Reni Santoni *(Hobbs)*, Susan Tyrrell *(Lee)*, Signe Hasso *(Helene)*, Norman Alden *(McPherson)*, Martine Bartlett *(Secret Wife of Henry VIII)*

p, Terence F. Deane, Michael Hausman, Daniel H. Blatt; d, Anthony Page; w, Lewis John Carlino, Gavin Lambert (based on the novel by Joanne Greenberg); ph, Bruce Logan (Technicolor); ed, Garth Craven; m, Paul Chihara; prod d, Toby Rafelson; cos, Jane Ruhm

AAN Best Adapted Screenplay: Gavin Lambert, Lewis John Carlino

A compelling drama about the terrors of schizophrenia, I NEVER PROMISED YOU A ROSE GARDEN is almost, but not quite, a female version of ONE FLEW OVER THE CUCKOO'S NEST. Quinlan is a certified mental case who is taken to a new and what appears to be tranquil hospital by her parents, Gary and Piazza. The similarity between this film and CUCKOO'S NEST ends in the fact that most of the patients in that one are only mildly afflicted and the ward becomes a microcosm of society. In ROSE GARDEN, there is no question of the horrors taking place inside the brains of the inmates. Quinlan is counseled by psychiatrist Andersson, and the bulk of the film deals with exorcising her various demons.

ROSE GARDEN falls short in its simplistic analysis of Quinlan's problem. Nor do we ever know much about her interaction with her family except for a brief indication of some resentment toward her brother. Most of our interest is sustained by the relationship between Quinlan and Andersson. Some casting sidelights include the great Sylvia Sidney as a patient who opts to come back to the hospital after being released; Hasso, who made her name playing what everyone thought was a man in THE HOUSE ON 92ND STREET; horror diva Barbara Steele; and Jeff Conaway, who later became popular on TV's "Taxi."

I NEVER SANG FOR MY FATHER

1970 92m c Drama ★★★½
Columbia (U.S.) PG

Melvyn Douglas *(Tom Garrison)*, Gene Hackman *(Gene Garrison)*, Dorothy Stickney *(Margaret Garrison)*, Estelle Parsons *(Alice)*, Elizabeth Hubbard *(Peggy)*, Lovelady Powell *(Norma)*, Daniel Keyes *(Dr. Mayberry)*, Conrad Bain *(Rev. Pell)*, Jon Richards *(Marvin Scott)*, Nikki Counselman *(Waitress)*

p, Gilbert Cates; d, Gilbert Cates; w, Robert W. Anderson (based on his play); ph, Morris Hartzband, George Stoetzel (Technicolor); ed, Angelo Ross; m, Barry Mann, Al Gorgoni; art d, Hank Aldrich; cos, Theoni V. Aldredge

AAN Best Actor: Melvyn Douglas; *AAN Best Supporting Actor:* Gene Hackman; *AAN Best Adapted Screenplay:* Robert Anderson

Honest, powerful and never sloppy, I NEVER SANG is a virtuoso acting exercise reined in by Cates, a terrific actors' director. The screenplay, adapted by Robert Anderson from his own play, feels drawn from real life.

Hackman is a fortyish New York professor who tells his aging parents, Douglas and Stickney, he is planning to change his life by marrying Hubbard, a divorced doctor, and moving to California. Stickney understands Hackman's need to break away but warns him that moving that far away may have a deleterious effect on Douglas. Just before the wedding, Stickney dies of heart failure. Parsons, Hackman's sister, has been disowned by Douglas for marrying a Jewish man. While at the funeral of their mother, Parsons advises Hackman not to allow himself to be manipulated by the old man and to live his life for himself.

Douglas is truly brilliant here—it's one of those performances that captures you so strongly that you are purged emotionally, yet equally enjoy the sureness of the talent at work. Hackman is able to personify the struggle of a conscience choosing between self or family.

I REMEMBER MAMA *DVD*

1948 134m bw Drama ★★★★
RKO (U.S.)

Irene Dunne *(Mama)*, Barbara Bel Geddes *(Katrin)*, Oscar Homolka *(Uncle Chris)*, Philip Dorn *(Papa)*, Cedric Hardwicke *(Mr. Hyde)*, Edgar Bergen *(Mr. Thorkelson)*, Rudy Vallee *(Dr. Johnson)*, Barbara O'Neil *(Jessie Brown)*, Florence Bates *(Florence Dana Moorhead)*, Peggy McIntyre *(Christine)*

p, Harriet Parsons; d, George Stevens; w, DeWitt Bodeen (based on the play by John Van Druten and the novel *Mama's Bank Account* by Kathryn Forbes); ph, Nicholas Musuraca; ed, Robert Swink, Tholen Gladden; m, Roy Webb; art d, Albert S. D'Agostino, Carroll Clark; fx, Russell A. Cully, Kenneth Peach; cos, Edward Stevenson, Gile Steele

AAN Best Actress: Irene Dunne; *AAN Best Supporting Actor:* Oscar Homolka; *AAN Best Supporting Actress:* Barbara Bel Geddes; *AAN Best Supporting Actress:* Ellen Corby; *AAN Best B/W Cinematography:* Nicholas Musuraca

A delicate charmer, sometimes precious, but nonetheless fine. Based on Kathryn Forbes's collection of autobiographical short stories *Mama's Bank Account*, this meticulously directed George Stevens film tells the heartwarming story of a Norwegian immigrant family making a go of it in turn-of-the-century San Francisco. Katrin (Barbara Bel Geddes), one of the daughters, narrates from her diary as the family's trials, tribulations, and triumphs are shown in flashback. At the center of the proceedings is the indefatigable Mama (Irene Dunne, giving one of her finest performances), keeping the house and her head while a dizzying parade of offbeat relatives and friends come and go, including Oscar Homolka (overacting), Cedric Hardwicke (wonderful indeed), Rudy Vallee, Edgar Bergen, and Philip Dorn as Papa. Forbes's nostalgic tale had earlier been brought to Broadway by Richard Rodgers and Oscar Hammerstein II (adapted by John Van Druten), and Peggy Wood later appeared in a long-running (1946-57) TV series based on the story.

I, ROBOT *DVD*

2004 110m c Science Fiction/Crime ★★★
Davis Entertainment/Laurence Mark/Mediastream PG-13
IV/Overbrook Films/20th Century Fox (U.S.)

Will Smith *(Detective Del Spooner)*, Bridget Moynahan *(Susan Calvin)*, Alan Tudyk *(Sonny)*, James Cromwell *(Dr. Alfred*

Lanning), Bruce Greenwood (Lawrence Robertson), Adrian L. Ricard (Granny), Chi McBride (Lt. John Bergin), Jerry Wasserman (Baldez), Fiona Hogan (V.I.K.I.), Peter Shinkoda (Chin)

p, John Davis, Topher Dow, Wyck Godfrey, Laurence Mark; d, Alex Proyas; w, Jeff Vintar, Akiva Goldsman (from a screen story by Jeff Vintar suggested by Isaac Asimov's book); ph, Simon Duggan; ed, William Hoy, Richard Learoyd, Armen Minasian; m, Marco Beltrami; prod d, Patrick Tatopoulos; art d, Chris August, Helen Jarvis; fx, Jonathan Egstad, Joe Letteri, Raymond McIntyre Jr., Erik Nash, John Nelson, Eric Saindon, Brian Vant Hul, Mike Vezina, Andrew R. Jones; cos, Elizabeth Keogh Palmer

AAN Best Visual Effects: John Nelson, Andrew R. Jones, Erik Nash, Joe Letteri

When is I, ROBOT not actually I, Robot? When it's an original script called Hardwired conflated with elements of Isaac Asimov's seminal robot tales, including those collected in 1950s I, Robot, and novels, massaged to suit Will Smith's action-guy persona. Derivativeness aside, it's an unexpectedly engaging futuristic mystery that hinges on the confounding possibility that a mechanical being may have committed murder, even though standard robot programming should make such a crime impossible.

Chicago, 2035: Robots are everywhere, not just toiling in factories and low-level service jobs, but in people's homes, running errands, walking dogs, cooking and cleaning. U.S. Robotics, the world's largest manufacturer of humanoid automata, is about to launch the new NS5 model, which CEO Lawrence Robertson (Bruce Greenwood) hopes will bring the corporate dream of a robot in every home one step closer to reality. But robophobic police detective Del Spooner (Smith) is convinced that a machine will one day defy its allegedly foolproof programming and commit a heinous crime, and when he's called upon to investigate the apparent suicide of cutting-edge roboticist Dr. Alfred Lanning (James Cromwell), he immediately suspects the superadvanced robot Lanning called Sonny (Alan Tudyk). Sonny looks like any other NS5, but is capable of disobedience, abstract thought, and perhaps even emotions. Why would Lanning build such an abomination, and why is USR determined to thwart Spooner's investigation?

The mystery is rudimentary and there's a numbing sameness to the inevitable high-stakes action sequences. But some provocative ideas slip through the mayhem, and Tudyk's performance—although Sonny is computer generated, Tudyk supplied his voice and body language—provides the story's emotional core, an irony Asimov would surely have appreciated.

I SHOT ANDY WARHOL   *DVD*
1996 103m c Docudrama/Biography/Drama ★★★
Playhouse International Pictures/BBC Arena/Orion R
(U.S./U.K.)

Lili Taylor (Valerie Solanas), Jared Harris (Andy Warhol), Stephen Dorff (Candy Darling), Martha Plimpton (Stevie), Danny Morgenstern (Jeremiah), Lothaire Bluteau (Maurice Girodias), Michael Imperioli (Ondine), Reg Rogers (Paul Morrissey), Coco McPherson (Brigid Berlin), Donovan Leitch (Gerard Malanga)

p, Tom Kalin, Christine Vachon; d, Mary Harron; w, Mary Harron, Daniel Minahan; ph, Ellen Kuras; ed, Keith Reamer; m, John Cale; prod d, Therese Deprez; art d, John Bruce; cos, David Robinson

Propelled by an ensemble of manic and mannered performances, I SHOT ANDY WARHOL follows quintessential outsider Valerie Solanas from obscure feminist writer to Warhol Factory hanger-on to would-be assassin. Filmmaker Mary Harron's stylish debut feature is a slick verite tour through the Factory and its margins that ultimately falls short of real insight into her characters.

In the 1960s, Valerie Solanas (Lili Taylor) moves to New York City where, despite her ostensible feminist separatism, she works as a prostitute. While writing plays based on her radical sexual politics, she becomes determined to meet Andy Warhol (Jared Harris) and eventually does, but her pleas that he produce one of her plays go unanswered. Eventually, Warhol does take an interest in her—whether out of pity or affection is unclear. As Valerie's friend, transvestite Candy Darling (Stephen Dorff), rises in popularity among the Factory's denizens, Solanas's modicum of acceptance fades. Finally, her rage boils over and she steals a gun from a member of a revolutionary street-theater troupe. On June 3, 1968, she enters the new Factory office and shoots Warhol at point-blank range.

While Harron has neatly constructed a biographical film on a woman about whom little is actually known, I SHOT ANDY WARHOL fails to tell us much more than the facts. Despite an astute eye for detail and astounding production design by Therese Deprez, the film remains as cynical and detached as the Factory crowd itself. The people around Warhol are colorfully portrayed as a band of arrogant and paranoid posers, each with a peculiar magnetism that offsets other less-than-attractive qualities. Whether or not the film's one-dimensionality simply reflects its subject matter, it certainly portrays enough of the spirit of the milieu explored—if not its innermost emotions—to warrant a serious look.

I STAND ALONE   *DVD*
(SEUL CONTRE TOUS)
1998 93m c Drama ★★★½
Les Cinemas de la Zone/Canal Plus/Love Streams Production/Le Centre National de la Cinematographie/ Le Soutien Financier de la Procirep (France)

Philipe Nahon (The Butcher), Blandine Lenoir (His Daughter, Cynthia), Frankye Pain (His Mistress), Martine Audrain (His Mother-in-Law), Jean-Francois Rauger (Real Estate Agent), Guillame Nicloux (Supermarket Manager), Olivier Doran (Narrator), Aissa Djarbi (Doctor Choukron), Serge Faurie (Hospital Director), Frederic Pfohl (Male Hospital Patient)

p, Gaspar Noe, Lucile Hadzihalilovic; d, Gaspar Noe; w, Gaspar Noe; ph, Dominique Colin, Gaspar Noe; ed, Gaspar Noe, Lucile Hadzihalilovic; fx, Jean-Christophe Spadaccini

A savage foray into the twisted mind of a sociopath. Picking up where his acclaimed 1991 short "Carne" left off, Gaspar Noe's feature-length sequel finds his antihero, an unnamed, unemployed, 50-year-old horsemeat butcher (Philipe Nahon), living in a dismal northern French town with his domineering, pregnant girlfriend (Frankye Pain) and her mother (Martine Audrain).

An opening slide-show recaps the story thus far: orphaned by World War II, the butcher grows up hating everything and everybody, then loses the only things he cares about—his butcher's shop and his mute daughter Cynthia (Blandine Lenoir)—after he stabs an innocent man in the mouth. The butcher hopes his loathsome new girlfriend will make good on her promise to buy him a new shop; she doesn't, and one afternoon he explodes, punching her repeatedly and grabbing his mother-in-law's gun. The butcher hitchhikes his way back to Paris, takes the same room in the seedy hotel where Cynthia was conceived, and tries to think of a reason not to destroy the world.

Rarely since TAXI DRIVER has such a hopeless, misanthropic vision of the world been so clearly articulated: that, even more than the film's physical violence, is what makes it so disturbing. With bulging eyes blazing and three bullets in his gun, the butcher wanders the streets, his relentless inner monologue returning repeatedly to his favorite themes: we live and die alone; morality is an invention of the rich; there's no purpose in life beyond sex; nobody in this selfish world loves anybody else.

Between Nahon's pressure-cooker performance and the director's assaultive style (he's fond of brooding long takes interrupted by shotgun blasts of lurching, skip-frame edits and bold intertitles), the film would be an unbearable expression of rage, except that Noe's winking, nearly absurd sense of humor offers a disconcerting reminder of the unreality of it all.

I, THE JURY

1953 87m bw Crime ★★★
UA (U.S.)

Biff Elliot *(Mike Hammer)*, Preston Foster *(Capt. Pat Chambers)*, Peggie Castle *(Charlotte Manning)*, Margaret Sheridan *(Velda)*, Alan Reed *(George Kalecki)*, Frances Osborne *(Myrna)*, Bob Cunningham *(Hal Kines)*, Elisha Cook Jr. *(Bobo)*, Paul Dubov *(Marty)*, Mary Anderson *(Eileen Vickers)*

p, Victor Saville; d, Harry Essex; w, Harry Essex (based on the novel by Mickey Spillane); ph, John Alton; ed, Frederick Y. Smith; m, Franz Waxman; art d, Wiard Ihnen

The first film adaptation of Mickey Spillane's trashy best seller was written and directed by Harry Essex, the screenwriter of two of the best science fiction-horror films of the 1950s—IT CAME FROM OUTER SPACE and CREATURE FROM THE BLACK LAGOON—both originally released in 3-D, as was I, THE JURY.

As the film opens we hear "Hark the Herald Angels Sing," but the Yuletide spirit is shattered by a gunman, shrouded in darkness, brutally shooting Jack Williams (Robert Swanger), an amputee, several times. Still alive, Williams painfully crawls towards his own gun. The mysterious killer allows the dying man a chance at the weapon and then finishes him off before he can retaliate. Enter Mike Hammer (Elliot), a private detective and friend of the victim. Williams had saved Hammer's life during WWII, and now the detective is determined to avenge his death. Warned against breaking the law by police detective Foster, he begins to dig for clues. What he finds is a seedy world populated by junkies, nymphomaniacs, and drug dealers. Hammer swaggers through the sleaze, and a number of bodies complicate the case.

The opening and closing scenes of I, THE JURY are stunningly brutal and skillfully executed. The murder of the amputee while "Hark the Herald Angels Sing" plays in the background is profoundly chilling, as is the unexpected finale. Unfortunately, the film's center suffers from Elliot's feeble performance as Spillane's brutish detective. Audiences would have to wait two years for Ralph Meeker to deliver the definitive Mike Hammer performance in Robert Aldrich's incredible KISS ME DEADLY.

I WALKED WITH A ZOMBIE

1943 69m bw Horror ★★★★★
RKO (U.S.)

James Ellison *(Wesley Rand)*, Frances Dee *(Betsy)*, Tom Conway *(Paul Holland)*, Edith Barrett *(Mrs. Rand)*, James Bell *(Dr. Maxwell)*, Christine Gordon *(Jessica Holland)*, Theresa Harris *(Alma)*, Sir Lancelot *(Calypso Singer)*, Darby Jones *(Carre Four)*, Jeni le Gon *(Dancer)*

p, Val Lewton; d, Jacques Tourneur; w, Curt Siodmak, Ardel Wray (based on an original story by Inez Wallace); ph, J. Roy Hunt; ed, Mark Robson; m, Roy Webb; art d, Albert S. D'Agostino, Walter E. Keller

I WALKED WITH A ZOMBIE was the second in the series of thought-provoking, literate horror films produced by Val Lewton in the 1940s (the first was CAT PEOPLE) and, under the masterful direction of Jacques Tourneur, it is an unqualified horror masterpiece. The story idea and title were borrowed from a series of newspaper articles that detailed voodoo and witchcraft practices in Haiti, hung on an off-the-wall adaptation of *Jane Eyre*!

Betsy (Dee) is a young nurse sent to Haiti by rich American planter Paul Holland (Conway) to take care of his catatonic wife, Jessica (Gordon). Paul thinks his wife has gone insane, and is ridden with guilt that he may have caused it. The locals suspect, however, that Jessica has become a zombie—one of the living dead. Betsy, who makes little progress with Jessica, meets Paul's mother (Barrett), a contradictory woman torn between her strong beliefs in the Christian church and in voodoo, and his brother, Wesley (Ellison), who is slowly drinking himself to death as he watches his brother's mistreatment of Jessica, whom he has always secretly loved. To make matters worse, Betsy and her employer begin to fall in love. Their desire to marry is intense, but impossible as long as Jessica lives. Not wanting to lose Paul, nor to see him torture himself, Betsy attempts to cure Jessica by taking her to a voodoo ceremony, in hopes that the experience will shock her back to "life."

Lewton's horror was based on the suggested, the psychological—not the visceral, tangible "monsters" that characterized the Universal horror series in the 1930s and '40s. The terror was presented in a shadowy, low-key atmosphere that allowed the audience to imagine and feel the unease instead of showing it to them, making the chills much more effective. The most outstanding example of this approach here is director Tourneur's beautiful realization of the lengthy, haunting, and elegiac sequence in which Betsy walks through the sugar cane fields with the silent Jessica to the voodoo ceremony. The scene is played in silence, save for the distant sound of drums and the gentle rustling of the wind. Visually, it is filled with gentle, floating movements—of Jessica's white gown, of the sugar cane in the wind—that are abruptly halted with the appearance of the massive zombie guard (Jones) whose presence signals the women's arrival at their destination. This scene is unforgettable, as is the entire film. Essential viewing.

I WANT TO LIVE!

1958 120m bw Crime/Biography **DVD** ★★★★½
Figaro (U.S.)

Susan Hayward *(Barbara Graham)*, Simon Oakland *(Ed Montgomery)*, Virginia Vincent *(Peg)*, Theodore Bikel *(Carl Palmberg)*, Wesley Lau *(Henry Graham)*, Philip Coolidge *(Emmett Perkins)*, Lou Krugman *(Jack Santo)*, James Philbrook *(Bruce King)*, Bartlett Robinson *(District Attorney)*, Gage Clark *(Richard Tibrow)*

p, Walter Wanger; d, Robert Wise; w, Nelson Gidding, Don Mankiewicz (based on newspaper articles by Ed Montgomery and the letters of Barbara Graham); ph, Lionel Lindon; ed, William Hornbeck; m, Johnny Mandel; art d, Ted Haworth

AA Best Actress: Susan Hayward; *AAN Best Director:* Robert Wise; *AAN Best Adapted Screenplay:* Nelson Gidding, Don Mankiewicz; *AAN Best B/W Cinematography:* Lionel Lindon; *AAN Best Film Editing:* William Hornbeck; *AAN Best Sound:* Gordon Sawyer

Unswerving, uneasy, unbeatable crime melodrama with a shattering Susan Hayward gathering all her glory into a performance without one false note. For devotees of Miss Hayward, this is the one to study; it feels and looks like life.

The nasty plot has Hayward playing real-life Barbara Graham, whose sensational trial brought her a conviction and death sentence that made her a nationwide *cause celebre*. The film depicts Graham, the product of a broken home, as a classic bad girl: perjurer, prostitute, thief. She arrives in San Francisco and is quickly sent to prison for falsely testifying to help out a friend. When released, she contacts two gamblers on the recommendation of fellow inmates. The gamblers, Coolidge and Krugman, use her as a shill; Hayward steers gullible suckers into their crooked card games and begins to make big money. With a bank account, Hayward decides to go straight, but she makes the mistake of marrying corrupt Lau—one of Coolidge's associates—and he introduces her to drugs. By the time she has a baby, she is an addict and her husband takes her last $10 for a fix. She leaves him and goes back to work for Coolidge and Krugman, with tragic results.

Hayward's performance is so intense, and the film so grim, it's exhausting watching her suffer through one agony after another. Wise directs with the perspective that Hayward/Graham was innocent all along, although the film offers little evidence to support this claim (the most insistent being Graham's repeated and vociferous insistence of her innocence), a stance that brought universal criticism from law enforcement agencies. For the most part, the hapless heroine is convincingly portrayed as a social victim. Hayward had been denied the Oscar for many deserving performances in the past—SMASH-UP, THE STORY OF A WOMAN, MY FOOLISH HEART, I'LL CRY TOMORROW—but this time the Academy could not ignore her bravura. The ensemble cast is uniformly excellent and believable. Wise's direction is relentlessly gloomy and swift, telling Graham's story in adroitly crafted scenes; mention should also be made of Gerry Mulligan's fine rendering of Johnny Mandel's classic jazz soundtrack.

ICE AGE *DVD*
2002 81m c Animated/Comedy/Children's ★★★½
Blue Sky/20th Century Fox (U.S.) PG

VOICES OF: Ray Romano *(Manfred)*, John Leguizamo *(Sid)*, Denis Leary *(Diego)*, Goran Visnjic *(Soto)*, Jack Black *(Zeke)*, Tara Strong *(Roshan/Start)*, Cedric "The Entertainer" *(Rhino)*, Stephen Root *(Rhino/Start)*, Diedrich Bader *(Saber-Tooth Tiger)*, Alan Tudyk *(Saber-Tooth Tiger/Dodo/Freaky Mammal)*

p, Lori Forte; d, Chris Wedge; w, Michael Berg, Michael J. Wilson, Peter Ackerman (based on the story by Michael J. Wilson); ed, John Carnochan; m, David Newman; prod d, Brian McEntee; fx, Robert V. Cavaleri; anim, James Bresnahan, Michael Thurmeier

A terrific voice cast and clever computer animation turn this age-old story of unlikely allies into something surprisingly fresh.

It's 20,000 years ago, and as the ice age approaches, the early mammals start migrating south. These comically self-aware creatures yammer on about the inevitability of climactic change, evolution, and the food chain, and serve as droll counterpoint to Scrat, a mute saber-toothed squirrel thingy whose chief concern is burying an acorn. Plodding north against the migratory flow is misanthropic wooly mammoth Manfred (voice of Ray Romano), who wants nothing to do with anyone. Basic mammalian decency, however, forces him to intervene when two peeved rhinos (Cedric "The Entertainer," Stephen Root) corner an annoying, but harmless, sloth named Sid (John Leguizamo). Sid latches onto Manfred and the duo are soon entrusted with returning a human infant, Roshan, to its father when its mother drowns while escaping from a pack vicious saber-toothed tigers led by the vengeful Soto (Goran Visnjic). Soto dispatches Diego (Denis Leary) to bring the infant back alive, but when he catches up with Sid and Manny he finds they're not about to hand Roshan over to a deadly tiger. The scheming Diego volunteers to serve as their tracker so they can return the infant to the humans before a certain pass gets snowed-in. Let the bonding begin!

Made with obvious delight by true students of comedy—homages to everything from *The Honeymooners* to the classic Warner Bros. cartoon about a squirrel obsessed with a coconut abound—this rib-tickler balances humor with sentimental, but well-earned, emotion. When Manfred's backstory is eventually revealed, the depth of his pain and selflessness are unexpectedly moving.

ICE STORM, THE *DVD*
1997 113m c Drama ★★★
Icy Films/Good Machine/Fox Searchlight (U.S.) R

Sigourney Weaver *(Janey Carver)*, Kevin Kline *(Ben Hood)*, Joan Allen *(Elena Hood)*, Christina Ricci *(Wendy Hood)*, Elijah Wood *(Mikey Carver)*, Adam Hann-Byrd *(Sandy Carver)*, Tobey Maguire *(Paul Hood)*, Henry Czerny *(George Clair)*, Jamey Sheridan *(Jim Carver)*, Katie Holmes *(Libbets Casey)*

p, Ted Hope, James Schamus, Ang Lee; d, Ang Lee; w, James Schamus (based on the novel by Rick Moody); ph, Frederick Elmes; ed, Tim Squyres; m, Mychael Danna; prod d, Mark Friedberg; art d, Bob Shaw; fx, John Ottesen; cos, Carol Oditz

A soap opera disguised as an art film, THE ICE STORM keenly observes two dysfunctional families going through a spiritual crisis in New Canaan, Connecticut in the early 1970s.

As they prepare for the Thanksgiving holidays, two families try to deny their growing problems. Ben Hood (Kevin Kline) carries on affair with Jane Carver (Sigourney Weaver), although she is bored and he is careless about covering up the adultery. Jane's husband, Jim (Jamey Sheridan), spends most of his time away on business trips, while Ben's wife, Elena (Joan Allen), grows suspicious of Ben's activities. Among the children, teenage Wendy Hood (Christina Ricci) attempts sexual experiments with both Carver boys, Mikey (Elijah Wood) and his more disturbed younger brother, Sandy (Adam Hann-Byrd). The Hoods' son, Paul (Tobey Maguire), returns home from a prep school feeling more confused than ever about life. The day after a tense and solemn Thanksgiving, the family bonds begin to break as Elena finally confronts Ben about his affair, Paul vindictively helps his roommate to overdose, and Wendy brings her sex games with Sandy to a new level.

THE ICE STORM's director, Ang Lee, and screenwriter, James Schamus, have faithfully adapted Rick Moody's novel, reflecting on the social malaise affecting middle-class American life in 1973. The cast is strong, especially Kline and Allen as the troubled Hoods, Weaver as Kline's married mistress, and Ricci as a confused, sexually precocious teen. The problem with THE ICE STORM is that it reaffirms traditional family values while it revels in showing acts of corrupted mores. In fact, for a film that regularly mocks Richard Nixon, THE ICE STORM presents a reactionary anti-sex, drugs, and rock 'n' roll message that Nixon would have approved. In other words, it's easy to get caught up (even enthralled) by this sophisticated, sex-filled family melodrama, but you won't feel good about it in the morning.

ICHI THE KILLER *DVD*
2001 127m c Crime/Action ★★★
Omega Project/Emperor Multimedia Group/
Starmax/Alpha Group/Spike Co./Excellent Film/
Omega Micott (Japan)

Tadanobu Asano *(Kakihara)*, Nao Omori *(Ichi)*, Shinya Tsukamoto *(Jijii)*, Alien Sun *(Karen)*, Hiroyuki Tanaka, billed as Sabu *(Kaneko)*, Susumu Terajima *(Suzuki)*, Shun Sugata *(Takayama)*, Toru Tezuka *(Fujiwara)*, Yoshiki Arizono *(Nakazawa)*, Kee *(Ryu)*

p, Akiko Funatsu, Dai Miyazaki; d, Takashi Miike; w, Sakichi Sato (based on the magna by Hideo Yamamoto); ph, Hideo Yamamoto; ed, Yasushi Shimamura; m, Karera Musication; prod d, Takashi Sasaki; fx, Misako Saka; cos, Michiko Kitamura

Takashi Miike's frenetic comic yakuza thriller embodies the best and worst this notorious Japanese genre auteur has to offer: It's endlessly inventive, consistently intelligent, and sickeningly savage.

When the boss of the Anjo gang goes missing, his devoted protege, Kakihara (Tadanobu Asano), a bleached-blond killer with a gruesome rictus permanently carved into his face, is convinced his boss has been kidnapped by the Funaki crime family. When he learns that his beloved Anjo has actually been murdered, Kakihara swears vengeance, aided by Kaneko (Hiroyuki Tanaka), a cowardly, disgraced cop. But finding Anjo's killer won't be easy: Kakihara only knows that he's called Ichi—"number one"—and that he's capable of slicing and dicing his way through a room full of gangsters in a matter of seconds. Masochistic Kakihara is excited by the prospect of meeting such a bloodthirsty sadist, but in reality Ichi (Nao Omori) is an emotionally disturbed waiter who's being cruelly manipulated by Jijii (TETSUO director Shinya Tsukamoto), a sworn enemy of the Arjo gang who knows that he can trigger Ichi's murderous rage by simply reminding him of the abuse he once suffered at the hands of schoolyard bullies. Brainwashed into believing that it's his mission to rid the world of all such tormentors, Ichi turns Tokyo's crime-infested Shinjuku district into a slaughterhouse.

Based on the adult manga by Hideo Yamamoto, the film has a colorful, cartoonish quality that often belies its serious theme—compromised masculinity and violence—and does little to alleviate the film's misogynistic brutality. Miike's bizarre fascination with the battered faces of once-beautiful prostitutes reaches an unconscionable extreme here, and though such brutalization might be thematically justified, Miike's mercilessly graphic depiction of it isn't.

IDEAL HUSBAND, AN

DVD

1999 96m c Comedy/Drama/Romance ★★★½
Fragile Films/Icon Productions/Pathe Pictures/ PG-13
Canal Plus (U.K.)

Cate Blanchett *(Gertrud)*, Minnie Driver *(Mabel)*, Rupert Everett *(Arthur Goring)*, Julianne Moore *(Mrs. Cheveley)*, Jeremy Northam *(Sir Robert Chiltern)*, John Wood *(Lord Caversham)*, Peter Vaughnn *(Phipps)*, Ben Pullen *(Tommy Trafford)*, Marsha Fitzalan *(Countess)*, Lindsay Duncan *(Lady Markby)*

p, Barnaby Thompson, Uri Fruchtmann, Bruce Davey; d, Oliver Parker; w, Oliver Parker (based on the play by Oscar Wilde); ph, David Johnson; ed, Guy Bensley; m, Charlie Mole; prod d, Michael Howells; art d, Rod McLean; cos, Caroline Harris

Oh, to be Wildean: effortlessly clever, supremely self-possessed, fashionable, and forever prepared with *exactly* the right comeback. And to top it all off, even his brittlest, most supercilious creations—frivolous bon vivant Lord Goring (Rupert Everett), say, who observes that to love oneself is the beginning of a lifelong romance—are secretly nicer and more decent than they'd ever let on.

At the heart of Oscar Wilde's uncannily prescient comedy of manners, in which public scandal and private heartache are inevitably intertwined, lie Lord and Lady Chiltern (Jeremy Northam, Cate Blanchett), to all appearances an ideal couple. He's a progressive politician famed for his honesty, she's a virtuous and loving wife. But their cozy little home life is threatened when the conniving Mrs. Cheveley (Julianne Moore) glides into town, an unsavory bit of information about Lord Chiltern's past clutched to her Machiavellian bosom. Could Chiltern's career and marriage survive the revelation of a long-ago indiscretion, or must he succumb to humiliating blackmail and hope his upstanding wife never finds out?

If the play weren't more than 100 years old it would be tempting to chide the writer for plucking a tale from recent U.S. headlines, rather than exercising his imagination. Except, of course, that no one who's made recent headlines is anywhere near as urbane as the least of Wilde's creations. This isn't a perfect adaptation: Minnie Driver is conspicuously miscast, her pushy modern mannerisms and looks utterly at odds with the character of Miss Mabel (what Victorian lady would ever tolerate such a tan!), and the ending is a bit clunky, in part because it's so clear that Lord Goring and Miss Mabel are *not*

made for each other in any respect. But it's lavish, clever entertainment, a welcome opportunity to laugh without shame.

IDIOTS, THE

(IDIOTERNE)
1998 115m c Comedy/Drama ★★½
Zentropa/DR TV/Canal Plus/La Septe Cinema/ R
Liberator/Argus/VPRO-TV/ZDF-Arte/RAI Cinema
Fiction/SVT-Drama/3 Emme Cinematografica
(Denmark/France/Italy/Netherlands/Germany)

Jens Albinus *(Stoffer)*, Bodil Jorgensen *(Karen)*, Knud Romer Jorgensen *(Axel)*, Anne-Grethe Bjarup Riis *(Katrine)*, Troels Lyby *(Henrik)*, Nikolaj Lie Kaas *(Jeppe)*, Louise Hassing *(Susanne)*, Henrik Prip *(Ped)*, Luis Mesonero *(Miguel)*, Louise Mieritz *(Josephine)*

p, Vibeke Windelov; d, Lars Von Trier; w, Lars Von Trier; ph, Lars Von Trier, Jesper Jargil, Kristoffer Nyholm, Casper Holm; ed, Molly Malene Stensgaard

When, exactly, does a film become *too* provocative? Lars Von Trier's THE IDIOTS may hold the answer: it's not only loaded with nudity and graphic sex, but the film succeeds in inciting its audience from so many directions that throwing up one's hands seems the only option.

THE IDIOTS, it turns out, is all about provocation. In a tony Danish suburb, a group of men and women pretend to be developmentally challenged. Living commune-style in an empty house, they improvise drooling, disruptive scenes in public places in a bizarre attempt to unleash their "inner idiot" and test the limits of upper-middle-class tolerance. They call what they do "spassing"; it combines anti-bourgeois social action, art happening and regressive group therapy, but the underlying agenda is never quite clear. At the film's moral center is sad, smiling Karen (Bodil Jorgensen), who wanders into this circle of merry pranksters after witnessing a spass-attack in an upscale restaurant. Who Karen is remains a mystery until the end, but throughout, she questions the group's leader, Stoffer (Jens Albinus), and seems to speak for the more tenderhearted viewer: How do you justify mocking less fortunate people?

Karen may also be speaking for Trier, but it's hard to tell. It's also hard to tell where this contribution to the ascetic, fiercely anti-individualist Dogme 95—the filmmaking collective which rejects all artificiality and directorial presence in their work—stands in relation to the rest of von Trier's films. If, like Stoffer, von Trier really refuses to romanticize the intellectually challenged as holy fools, he would have to disavow his own BREAKING THE WAVES. And if he's sincere in his critique of communal groupthink and its power to erode an individual's good sense, where does that leave Dogme 95?

IDOLMAKER, THE

DVD

1980 107m c Drama ★★★½
UA (U.S.) PG

Ray Sharkey *(Vincent Vacarri)*, Tovah Feldshuh *(Brenda Roberts)*, Peter Gallagher *(Caesare)*, Paul Land *(Tommy Dee)*, Joe Pantoliano *(Gino Pilato)*, Maureen McCormick *(Ellen Fields)*, John Aprea *(Paul Vacarri)*, Richard Bright *(Uncle Tony)*, Olympia Dukakis *(Mrs. Vacarri)*, Steven Apostlee Peck *(Mr. Vacarri)*

p, Gene Kirkwood, Howard W. Koch Jr.; d, Taylor Hackford; w, Edward Di Lorenzo; ph, Adam Holender (Technicolor); ed, Neil Travis; m, Jeff Barry; art d, David L. Snyder; chor, Deney Terrio; cos, Rita Riggs

Ray Sharkey gives a dynamic performance here as the hustling Vincent Vacarri (a thinly veiled version of technical adviser Bob Marcucci, mentor of Frankie Avalon and Fabian), who promotes the careers of rock 'n' roll singers Tommy Dee

(Paul Land) and Caesare (Peter Gallagher)—managing their every move, calling in favors here and making payoffs there, making sure his charges have the best clothes and backup bands, etc.—in the late '50s and early '60s. Brenda Roberts (Tovah Feldshuh) is an editor of a fan magazine who has a fling with Vincent and uses her influence to help make his boys into stars. THE IDOLMAKER takes itself too seriously, but is nonetheless one of the best and most energetic film treatments of the early days of rock 'n' roll and a fine depiction of how performers are groomed for stardom (far superior to THE ROSE). In his directorial debut, Taylor Hackford (AN OFFICER AND A GENTLEMAN, 1982; WHITE NIGHTS, 1985) shows a solid command of the medium. The anachronistic music by Jeff Barry is a problem, however; its too-contemporary sound presumably stems from the producers' desire to get airplay for the film's score.

IF...

1968	110m	c/bw	Drama
Memorial	(U.K.)		

★★★★½
R

Malcolm McDowell *(Mick Travers)*, David Wood *(Johnny)*, Richard Warwick *(Wallace)*, Christine Noonan *(the Girl)*, Rupert Webster *(Bobby Philips)*, Robert Swann *(Rowntree)*, Hugh Thomas *(Denson)*, Peter Jeffrey *(Headmaster)*, Mona Washbourne *(Matron)*, Arthur Lowe *(Mr. Kemp, Housemaster)*

p, Michael Medwin, Lindsay Anderson; d, Lindsay Anderson; w, David Sherwin (based on a script by Sherwin, John Howlett, entitled "The Crusaders"); ph, Miroslav Ondricek (Eastmancolor); ed, David Gladwell; m, Marc Wilkinson; prod d, Jocelyn Herbert; art d, Brian Eatwell

A furious, exhilarating assault on the mores of contemporary Britain, sited in a microcosmic boarding school. IF... became one of the key texts of 1960s revolutionary sentiment; decades later, it retains most of its considerable impact.

Having spent the summer absorbing London's burgeoning counterculture, a quietly simmering Mick Travis (Malcolm McDowell) returns to his public school—a nightmarishly oppressive institution in which privilege is based on rank, intellectual achievement is despised, and cynical upper classmen routinely extort sexual favors from younger boys. The school's systematic brutality is condoned by an ineffectual headmaster whose "modern" views clash ludicrously with the medieval environment. With three close friends, Mick indulges in petty rebellions until he runs afoul of the sadistic head of house (Robert Swann), who administers a vicious ritual beating in the name of school spirit. Thereafter, Mick and his comrades declare war, and an increasingly surreal chain of events leads to a violent finale in which a guerrilla band disrupts Founder's Day ceremonies with automatic weapons and grenade launchers.

Strikingly original and breathlessly entertaining, IF... (the title refers ironically to Kipling's jingoistic poem) can profitably be read on several levels simultaneously. On one hand, it's a critique of schoolboys' adventure stories; on another—particularly in its palpable atmosphere of sexual repression and sublimation—it bears a striking resemblance to Jean Vigo's innovative ZERO DE CONDUITE. (The film is also unmistakably concerned with the Vietnam War and its ideological underpinnings.) Throughout, director Lindsay Anderson (THIS SPORTING LIFE) aims to keep the viewer off-balance, switching deftly from the formal conventions of British realism to dreamily erotic flights of fancy.

IF I HAD A MILLION

1932	88m	bw	Comedy/Drama
Paramount	(U.S.)		

★★★★

Gary Cooper *(Gallagher)*, George Raft *(Eddie Jackson)*, Wynne Gibson *(Violet)*, Charles Laughton *(The Clerk)*, Jack Oakie *(Mulligan)*, Frances Dee *(Mary Wallace)*, Charlie Ruggles *(Henry Peabody)*, Alison Skipworth *(Emily)*, W.C. Fields *(Rollo)*, Mary Boland *(Mrs. Peabody)*

p, Louis D. Lighton; d, Ernst Lubitsch, Norman Taurog, Stephen Roberts, James Cruze, William A. Seiter, H. Bruce Humberstone, Lothar Mendes (uncredited); w, Claude Binyon, Whitney Bolton, Malcolm Stuart Boylan, John Bright, Sidney Buchanan, Lester Cole, Isabel Dawn, Boyce DeGaw, Walter DeLeon, Oliver H.P. Garrett, Harvey Gates, Grover Jones, Ernst Lubitsch, Lawton Mackall, Joseph L. Mankiewicz, William Slavens McNutt, Seton I. Miller, Robert Sparks, Tiffany Thayer (based on the novel *Windfall* by Robert D. Andrews)

For once, an episodic film that holds together, and the link that holds it is lots of money: millions, in fact.

Richard Bennett plays a multimillionaire who is disgusted with his dollar-clutching relatives. When told by his doctors that he is dying, Bennett decides to pick out total strangers and give each $1 million, mostly to see what they will do with the money. He closes his eyes and picks a name from the phone book. Eight sketches follow that depict the results of Bennett's largesse. These include "The Streetwalker," directed by Ernst Lubitsch, in which $1 million goes to Wynne Gibson, a prostitute, who immediately abandons her street corner and rents a lavish penthouse apartment, determined to make up for lost sleep between silk sheets; "The Auto" or "Rollo and the Road Hogs," directed by Norman Taurog, finds Alison Skipworth receiving the check at her little teashop where she and newly acquired hubby W.C. Fields, a worn-out vaudeville juggler, reside. The pair go to a new car dealership and begin buying one new car after another, taking to the streets as roadhog vigilantes. Also noteworthy is "The Clerk," also directed by Lubitsch, in which Charles Laughton plays a meek, harassed clerical worker. When he receives his $1 million check, he stands up quietly, and then walks into the resplendent office of the firm's president. As the man looks up, Laughton gives the boss a loud Bronx cheer, slams the door, and goes into unperturbed retirement.

Most of these stories are well-told, expertly acted, and brilliantly directed. Paramount poured out its best acting and technical talent for this enormous production, the Laughton and Fields segments considered strongest. Us? We'll go with W.C., the Great One himself. MILLION inspired a popular radio and later a TV series, "The Millionaire."

IGBY GOES DOWN

DVD

2002	98m	c	Comedy/Drama
Atlantic Streamline/Crossroads Films/Igby Productions/UA	(U.S.)		

★★★
R

Kieran Culkin *(Igby)*, Claire Danes *(Sookie)*, Jeff Goldblum *(D.H.)*, Jared Harris *(Russel)*, Amanda Peet *(Rachel)*, Ryan Phillippe *(Oliver)*, Susan Sarandon *(Mimi)*, Bill Pullman *(Jason)*, Rory Culkin (10-year-old Igby), Peter Tambakis (13-year-old Oliver)

p, Lisa Tornell, Marco Weber; d, Burr Steers; w, Burr Steers; ph, Wedigo Von Schultzendorff; ed, William Anderson; m, Uwe Fahrenkrog-Petersen; prod d, Kevin Thompson; art d, Roswell Hamrick; cos, Sarah Edwards

Finding inspiration in such Mike Nichols films as THE GRADUATE and CARNAL KNOWLEDGE, actor-turned-director Burr Steers's debut feature is a throwback to the kind of literate, melancholy coming-of-age dramas that once defined youthful male angst.

Shleppy, preppy, and thoroughly incorrigible, 17-year-old Jason Slocumb Jr. (Kieran Culkin)—dubbed "Igby" by his seriously dysfunctional upper-crust family—has been tossed out of nearly every private school on the Eastern Seaboard, and his mother, Mimi (Susan Sarandon), is at the end of her already short tether. A cold D.C. socialite with about as much patience for Igby as she had for his schizophrenic father (Bill Pullman), Mimi hands Igby off to his rich godfather, D.H. (Jeff Goldblum), for the summer. D.H. takes Igby to New York where, during the week, Igby will bunk with his older brother, Oliver (Ryan Phillippe), while helping to renovate the spacious loft D.H. is fixing up for his mistress, Rachel (Amanda Peet). Igby will spend weekends at D.H.'s summer home in the Hamptons. It's there that Igby meets Sookie Saperstein (Claire Danes), a prematurely world-weary Bennington coed. Smitten, Igby soon ditches Oliver, hides out in Rachel's loft, and sets about seducing Sookie.

Set in contemporary New York and Washington, D.C., the film lacks the turbulent social context of the 1950s and '60s that lent resonance to the personal uncertainties of Igby's forebears: Holden Caulfield, Benjamin Braddock, et al. But Culkin has a way with quip-heavy dialogue that transforms what might otherwise have been irritatingly solipsistic posing into a great performance. If Simon and Garfunkel were still together, Steers would no doubt have begged them to do the score. Instead, the soundtrack features the sensitive modern sounds of Coldplay and Badly Drawn Boy.

IKIRU
1952 141m bw Drama **DVD** ★★★★½
Toho (Japan)

Takashi Shimura (Kanji Watanabe), Nobuo Kaneko (Mitsuo Watanabe), Kyoko Seki (Kazue Watanabe), Miki Odagiri (Toyo), Kamatari Fujiwara (Ono), Makoto Koburi (Kiichi Watanabe), Kumeko Urabe (Tatsu Watanabe), Yoshie Minami (Hayoshi, the Maid), Nobuo Nakamura (Deputy Mayor), Minosuke Yamada (Saito)

p, Shojiro Motokui; d, Akira Kurosawa; w, Akira Kurosawa, Hideo Oguni, Shinobu Hashimoto; ph, Asakazu Nakai; ed, Akira Kurosawa; m, Fumio Hayasaka; art d, So Matsuyama

In IKIRU, Akira Kurosawa has created a subtle and moving account of a man who searches for meaning in the final days of his shallow existence. Kanji Watanabe (Takashi Shimura) is a clerk in a government office who discovers that he has cancer and, at most, only a year to live. Up to this point he has lived a highly structured life, rarely varying from routines. He has two children who offer him no comfort, and he decides he must find something to make him feel that his life has not been a total waste. The movement of IKIRU is extremely low key, and the overall emotional impact is quite powerful, with the character of Kanji serving as a metaphor for postwar Japan. A beautiful and unusually quiet film from one of the world's greatest living directors.

I'LL CRY TOMORROW
1955 117m bw Biography ★★★★
MGM (U.S.)

Susan Hayward (Lillian Roth), Richard Conte (Tony Bardeman), Eddie Albert (Burt McGuire), Jo Van Fleet (Katie Roth), Don Taylor (Wallie), Ray Danton (David Tredman), Margo (Selma), Virginia Gregg (Ellen), Don "Red" Barry (Jerry), David Kasday (David as a Child)

p, Lawrence Weingarten; d, Daniel Mann; w, Helen Deutsch, Jay Richard Kennedy (based on the book by Lillian Roth, Mike Connolly and Gerold Frank); ph, Arthur E. Arling; ed, Harold F. Kress; m, Alex North; art d, Cedric Gibbons, Malcolm Brown; fx, Warren Newcombe; cos, Helen Rose

AAN Best Actress: Susan Hayward; AAN Best B/W Cinematography: Arthur E. Arling; AAN Best Art Direction-Set Decoration (B/W): Cedric Gibbons, Malcolm Brown, Edwin B. Willis, Hugh Hunt; AA Best Costume Design (B/W): Helen Rose

Hayward stars as Lillian Roth (based on Roth's autobiography of the same name), Broadway and Hollywood singing sensation, who let success slide through her fingers as she reached for the next drink.

As a child, Lillian is driven unmercifully by her ambitious stage mother (Jo Van Fleet) and has already begun appearing on Broadway and being the breadwinner by the time she is a teenager. As an adult, Roth (Susan Hayward) falls in love with an old friend (Ray Danton) who dies unexpectedly, precipitating a lengthy downward spiral.

Although the script doesn't capture much sense of period or time passing, Mann establishes enough strong moments to keep the viewer enthralled. There's a fine child performance by Carole Ann Campbell, who looks like the real Roth, and scores strongly in a post-audition scene that is painful to watch. Indeed, the film dotes on an uneasy sense of dread, daring you not to look away. Hayward doesn't suggest much of what audiences saw in the real Roth. Instead she uses her own sexy, hellcat persona when performing, saving contemplation for her big offstage scenes. The scene in which Hayward deserts her mother is one of Hollywood's grittiest examinations of the love-hate relationship between parent and child, the cross-purposes of both characters wrenching to behold. Both actresses seem to be defining their boundaries and crossing each other's at the same time, using the hyperemotional '50s genre in a devastatingly successful way.

Roth made a successful nightclub and theatrical comeback after the film's release, and published a second memoir, Beyond My Worth, but, tragically, her bouts with alcohol were far from finished. Hayward won the Cannes Film Festival Best Actress Award for TOMORROW and Helen Rose grabbed an Oscar for her gorgeous costumes.

I'M ALL RIGHT, JACK
1959 105m bw Comedy **DVD** ★★★★
Boulting Bros. (U.K.)

Ian Carmichael (Stanley Windrush), Peter Sellers (Fred Kite), Terry-Thomas (Maj. Hitchcock), Richard Attenborough (Sidney de Vere Cox), Dennis Price (Bertram Tracepurcel), Margaret Rutherford (Aunt Dolly), Irene Handl (Mrs. Kite), Liz Fraser (Cynthia Kite), Miles Malleson (Windrush Sr.), Marne Maitland (Mr. Mohammed)

p, Roy Boulting; d, John Boulting; w, Frank Harvey, Alan Hackney, John Boulting (based on Hackney's novel Private Life); ph, Mutz Greenbaum; ed, Anthony Harvey; m, Ken Hare, Ron Goodwin

Hilarious satire of British trade unionism. Carmichael is an addled but earnest young man who has just finished his army service and now seeks a career in industry. He visits his uncle, Price, who is in cahoots with Attenborough in a most interesting scheme; they would like to arrange a strike at Price's factory so that Attenborough's factory can take over the contracts and do the work at inflated prices. Price gives Carmichael a job as an unskilled laborer, and his intelligence soon detects several ways to streamline the factory's operation and reap larger profits. This, of course, angers the union shop steward, Sellers. Carmichael figures out a way to load and unload deliveries and suggests that a new schedule be printed and that the workers live up to it instead of taking tea breaks every other hour. Sellers is livid and calls a strike, which delights Price. But the laborers at Attenborough's plant go out in sympathy, thus tossing Price and Attenborough's plans into a cocked hat. Things get progressively more ludicrous from there on in.

A sharp screenplay and expert farceurs in every role make this one of the great British comedies of the 1950s and 1960s. Many of the "Carry On" players are here, including Rutherford and her husband, Davis. Even Punch editor Muggeridge takes a turn as the moderator of the TV show. It's subtlety and slapstick mixed perfectly in a refreshing glace. BAFTA Awards (British Oscars) went to Sellers and to the screenplay.

I'M GONNA GIT YOU SUCKA

1988 88m c Comedy
Ivory Way (U.S.)

★★★

R

Keenen Ivory Wayans (Jack Spade), Bernie Casey (John Slade), Antonio Fargas (Flyguy), Steve James (Kung Fu Joe), Isaac Hayes (Hammer), Jim Brown (Slammer), Ja'Net DuBois (Ma Bell), Dawnn Lewis (Cheryl), John Vernon (Mr. Big), Clu Gulager (Lt. Baker)

p, Peter McCarthy, Carl Craig; d, Keenen Ivory Wayans; w, Keenen Ivory Wayans; ph, Tom Richmond (DeLuxe Color); ed, Michael R. Miller; m, David Michael Frank; prod d, Melba Farquhar, Catherine Hardwicke; fx, Fred Cramer; chor, Russell Clark; cos, Ruth E. Carter

Wayans wrote and directed this very funny satire of the black-oriented exploitation films of the 1970s. Set in "Any Ghetto, USA," I'M GONNA GIT YOU SUCKA opens as upstanding young Army veteran Jack Spade (Wayans) returns home to avenge the death of his brother, who died because he wore too many gold chains. Wayans vows to shut down the business of a ruthless gold-chain pusher known only as Mr. Big (Vernon). Because his experience in the armed forces is mostly bureaucratic, however, Jack seeks the help of his childhood hero, John Slade (Casey) in this endeavor. An extremely funny movie that presents a torrent of insightful gags at breakneck pace, I'M GONNA GIT YOU SUCKA features many of the stars of the old "blaxploitation" movies, adding weight and authenticity to Wayan's film. In offering up this affectionate parody of the old movies, Wayans also turns a satiric eye on black culture in general—but in an inoffensive, lighthearted manner.

I'M NO ANGEL

1933 87m bw Comedy
Paramount (U.S.)

★★★½

Mae West (Tira), Cary Grant (Jack Clayton), Gregory Ratoff (Benny Pinkowitz), Edward Arnold (Big Bill Barton), Ralf Harolde (Slick Wiley), Kent Taylor (Kirk Lawrence), Gertrude Michael (Alicia Hatton), Russell Hopton (Flea Madigan, the Barker), Dorothy Peterson (Thelma), William B. Davidson (Ernest Brown, the Chump)

p, William LeBaron; d, Wesley Ruggles; w, Mae West, Harlan Thompson (based on "The Lady and the Lions," an unproduced screenplay by Lowell Brentano); ph, Leo Tover; ed, Otho Lovering; m, Harvey Brooks; art d, Hans Dreier, Bernard Herzbrun

The best of the West. Mae is a Depression-era angel of mercy, dispensing quips and songs like fallout in one of the funniest films ever lensed. On camera 95% of the time, West's screenplay traces her climb from sideshow carnival hootchie-kootchie girl to international circus star. In true lady Leo form, she even gets to realize her own biggest fantasy on camera: taming lions. Obviously, West was being rewarded with total creative control, a power seldom given by the studios, but the success of her previous film, SHE DONE HIM WRONG, had gone a long way toward keeping Paramount from declaring bankruptcy. She is surrounded by a slick supporting cast working at comedic fever pitch, but West never breaks a sweat, parading through her promenades, amazed by her own dazzle, savoring every star turn, thrilled with her own reflection in each costar's eyes.

Indeed, I'M NO ANGEL is a monument to the Westian ego; never has fullblown female narcissism been explored in such an utterly unselfconcious way, yet it's tempered by West at her most self-mocking. Each time you're convinced that it's all parody, West suddenly plays it straight... but so you'll laugh out loud. She's a textbook of historic comic technique and diva timing—historic because West embraces every great bygone tradition of show business: vaudeville, burlesque, legit and speakeasy. And ANGEL is highlighted by a lesson in diva plot-line no other star can equal, because only West would dare defend herself in court. Crammed into the 87 minutes of running time are numerous other unforgettable moments. Watch for West's record collection, her weird lion tamer boots (designed to hide her platforms), her midway rendition of "They Call Me Sister Honky-Tonk," her spider wing dress sleeves. This was the second time West used Cary Grant as her leading man, and he later said she was the most difficult person he ever played opposite, yet she taught him more about comedy than anyone else he ever worked with. ANGEL came after the beauticians had perfected West's visual star persona and before the moral bluenoses took to laundering her work—it's the peak of her stardom. Certainly we feel rewarded by this flawless comedy classic and enriched by the legacy of West herself: a legend of legends, a figure of American folklore that stands alone in the cinematic pantheon.

IMITATION OF LIFE

1934 106m bw Drama
Universal (U.S.)

★★★½

Claudette Colbert (Beatrice Pullman), Warren William (Stephen Archer), Ned Sparks (Elmer), Louise Beavers (Delilah Johnson), Juanita Quigley (Jessie Pullman, Age Three), Marilyn Knowlden (Jessie, Age Eight), Rochelle Hudson (Jessie, Age 18), Sebie Hendricks (Peola Johnson, Age Four), Dorothy Black (Peola, Age Nine), Fredi Washington (Peola, Age 19)

p, Carl Laemmle; d, John M. Stahl; w, William Hurlbut (based on the novel by Fannie Hurst); ph, Merritt Gerstad; ed, Philip Cahn

AAN Best Picture; AAN Best Sound Recording: Gilbert Kurland; AAN Best Assistant Director: Scott Beal

Highly sentimental social soaper, subtly crafted by director Stahl.

In this adaptation of Fannie Hurst's melodramatic novel, Colbert ages 15 years—quite believably—as a widow raising her daughter alone. (The daughter is played first by Juanita Quigley, then by Marilyn Knowlden, and as a young woman by Rochelle Hudson.) When Colbert decides to join forces with her maid, Louise Beavers, and open a small pancake parlor, Beavers, who also has a young daughter (played by Sebie Hendricks, by Dorothy Black, and primarily the largely forgotten, beautiful Fredi Washington), becomes Colbert's full partner in the business, which proves highly successful. As the enterprise flourishes, however, the women's family lives become fraught with conflict. Washington, whose light complexion enables her to pass for Caucasian, finds herself unable to live in both the white and black worlds, and as a result breaks off relations with Beavers and runs away from school, hoping to live as a white woman. Colbert, meanwhile, is shocked to learn that the 18-year-old Hudson is in love with the man Colbert herself wants to marry, Warren William.

Audiences didn't seem to mind the rather downbeat ending of IMITATION OF LIFE (remade successfully in 1959, with Lana Turner starring under Douglas Sirk's direction), but there was a great deal of controversy over the basic elements of the narrative. Some white southern viewers disapproved of Colbert's character going into business with her black maid (despite the fact that it's the latter's recipe that makes both women rich); Black critics, on the other hand, felt that Beavers should have been shown establishing her own residence, rather than staying on with Colbert and continuing to function as household help. At one point, Stahl makes an explicit visual social comment: a masterful camera shot of a staircase that divides upstairs from down, with Beavers catering upstairs and Colbert hostessing downstairs, revealing the hypocrisy of the entire exercise. Beavers' interpretation has dated badly; she's either jolly or resigned and does not suggest the transistions from one emotion to another.

IMITATION OF LIFE

DVD
1959 125m c Drama ★★★★
Universal (U.S.)

Lana Turner *(Lora Meredith)*, John Gavin *(Steve Archer)*, Sandra Dee *(Susie, Age 16)*, Dan O'Herlihy *(David Edwards)*, Susan Kohner *(Sarah Jane, Age 18)*, Robert Alda *(Allen Loomis)*, Juanita Moore *(Annie Johnson)*, Mahalia Jackson *(Herself)*, Karen Dicker *(Sarah Jane, Age Eight)*, Terry Burnham *(Suzie, Age Six)*

p, Ross Hunter; d, Douglas Sirk; w, Eleanore Griffin, Allan Scott (based on the novel by Fannie Hurst); ph, Russell Metty (Eastmancolor); ed, Milton Carruth; m, Frank Skinner; art d, Alexander Golitzen, Richard H. Riedel; fx, Clifford Stine; cos, Jean Louis, Bill Thomas

AAN Best Supporting Actress: Susan Kohner; *AAN Best Supporting Actress:* Juanita Moore

Plush and overblown, the last Hollywood hurrah for Sirk, and the resurrection of the weepie by producer Ross Hunter. A string of similar sudsers followed (several with Turner), but this one is the pick of the litter, thanks to Sirk. It's a bizarre, Byzantine, calculatingly depressed and cold affair, with Miss Big Chill herself, Lana Turner, breathing dry ice into the role originally played by Claudette Colbert (and trading Colbert's dignity for helplessness and pearls). The central theme remains the same, but the major tension that exists in 1950s materialism versus the disentegration of the nuclear family, tinged with gut-wrenching racism. If Sirk exploits the material for all it's worth and seems to be sardonically allowing the artifical genre to devour itself as he sits back and watches, at the same time the weepie aspect is so melodramatic as to tear the sobs from your throat.

Lana Turner, playing a successful actress, is not so much acting as parodying herself; Juanita Moore, as the black maid who shares her life, plays the part so haltingly and straight that it feels like ironic commentary. Susan Kohner, as Moore's light-skinned daughter who passes for white, is a noir revelation, giving her character a restless, dangerous sensuality. When she turns the malice of that energy on Turner, it's one of the great standoffs in Hollywood history. And it's magnificently undercut later, when Turner is crying over Moore's deathbed, with Kohner's photograph smiling out from the wall behind them. Oh, and be prepared for the all-stops-out cinematic funeral, complete with Mahalia Jackson singing "Trouble of the World." You'll be horrified at how this hokum manipulates you, but the best strategy is to just surrender and enjoy it.

IMPORTANCE OF BEING EARNEST, THE

DVD
1952 95m c Comedy ★★★★½
Two Cities/Javelin British/Asquith (U.K.)

Michael Redgrave *(Jack Worthing)*, Michael Denison *(Algernon Moncrieff)*, Edith Evans *(Lady Bracknell)*, Joan Greenwood *(Gwendolen Fairfax)*, Dorothy Tutin *(Cecily Cardew)*, Margaret Rutherford *(Miss Prism)*, Miles Malleson *(Canon Chasuble)*, Richard Wattis *(Seton)*, Aubrey Mather *(Merriman)*, Walter Hudd *(Lane)*

p, Teddy Baird; d, Anthony Asquith; w, Anthony Asquith (based on the play by Oscar Wilde); ph, Desmond Dickinson (Technicolor); ed, John D. Guthridge; m, Benjamin Frankel; art d, Carmen Dillon; cos, Beatrice Dawson

Wilde's wittiest play took 57 years to make it to the screen but was well worth the wait. Director-writer Asquith made absolutely no attempt to "open up" this repertory standard in order to make it more cinematic. The film does of course benefit from close-ups and such, but Asquith goes so far as to have a couple enter a stage box and sit down before a curtain rises at the start. This is meant to be theater first and foremost, and

it's a valuable record of a great performance. Stylish, sunny, and as nonsensical as any work can be (at least, on the surface), THE IMPORTANCE OF BEING EARNEST takes well-aimed potshots at the social pretentions of the 1890s. The satire goes down like punch because the artful Wilde has cloaked it in badinage containing some of his best epigrams and *bon mots*. The decor and costumes are charmingly detailed, the perfect setting for this hilarious jewel.

This comedy classic tells of Jack and Algy, two well-to-do bachelors (Redgrave and Dennison) enamored of two women (Greenwood and Tutin) who both have an incredible fixation about falling in love with men named Ernest. Of course neither man is "earnest" about his real name—not that Jack is sure of his. Bring in dragon Lady Bracknell (Evans), a dizzy tutor (Rutherford) and an amorous reverend (Malleson) and the identity search is on. This marvelous cast makes each pearl of dialogue shine. Redgrave and Dennison are impossibly smooth, Tutin is delightfully pert and Greenwood uses her inimitable voice and crisp acting style to delightful effect. The role of the anxious, garrulous Miss Prism is perfect for Rutherford and Malleson makes an ideal foil. Perhaps the best of them all is Edith Evans, in a role she made her own. "Do you smoke," she asks the nervous Jack. "Yes I do," he tentatively responds. "Good," she notes, "a man should have an occupation of some sort." Best of all, though, is her legendary multi-octave reading of the simple line "Handbag?" It doesn't get much better than this.

IMPROMPTU

DVD
1990 107m c Biography/Romance ★★★½
Governor/Ariane (U.K.) PG-13

Judy Davis *(George Sand)*, Hugh Grant *(Frederic Chopin)*, Mandy Patinkin *(Alfred DeMusset)*, Bernadette Peters *(Marie d'Agoult)*, Julian Sands *(Franz Liszt)*, Ralph Brown *(Eugene Delacroix)*, Georges Corraface *(Felicien Mallefille)*, Anton Rodgers *(Duke d'Antan)*, Emma Thompson *(Duchess d'Antan)*, Anna Massey *(George Sand's Mother)*

p, Stuart Oken, Daniel A. Sherkow; d, James Lapine; ed, Michael Ellis; m, Frederic Chopin, Franz Liszt; art d, Gerard Daoudal; fx, Gilbert Pieri; cos, Jenny Beavan

The life and many loves of French novelist George Sand (1804-67), as depicted in James Lapine's IMPROMPTU, has the feel of a contemporary romantic comedy. This feature debut for Pulitzer Prize-winning stage director Lapine *(Sunday in the Park with George)* is distinguished by a fine cast, including Judy Davis as the truly liberated Sand, a woman whose vacillation with respect to men is exceeded only by her passion for them.

The film introduces viewers to Sand's circle of friends, including the painter Eugene Delacroix (Ralph Brown), poet and one-time lover Alfred DeMusset (Mandy Patinkin), and composers Franz Liszt (Julian Sands) and Frederic Chopin (Hugh Grant). It is Chopin who captures Sand's heart and is the object of her determined affection throughout the film. An unassuming man, in continual ill-health, Chopin first encounters the brazen Sand when she steals into his room, hides under his piano, and revels in his music. This takes place during the summer of 1835 at the country estate of the Duke and Duchess d'Antan (Anton Rodgers and Emma Thompson), where Chopin, Liszt, Delacroix and DeMusset have been invited to enrich the lives of their culture-starved hosts. Sand has quite candidly invited herself and her two young children.

The gathering also includes Liszt's mistress, Marie d'Agoult (Bernadette Peters), and Sand's newly jilted lover, Felicien Mallefille (Georges Corraface), her children's tutor. Consumed with jealousy, Mallefille spends his time threatening any man who looks at Sand, and instigating a duel with DeMusset. Sand, meanwhile, enlists Marie's help in delivering a note to Chopin. Envious of Sand and feeling neglected by Liszt, Marie passes on the note, but not before removing Sand's name and substituting her own. The fortnight holiday soon comes to an end and Sand, unsuccessful in her efforts to seduce Chopin but determined win his affection, departs with her children and Mallefille.

Favored by Sarah Kernochan's character-driven screenplay and its elegant French locations, IMPROMPTU gives its actors ample room in which to play. Davis shines as Sand, balancing her decided independence with her desire for heady companionship. Grant's Chopin is a bit overplayed, making him seem too prudish. Patinkin is credible as the volatile DeMusset, as are Sands as Liszt, Brown as Delacroix, and Corraface as Mallefille. Peters is well-cast as the manipulative, ever-pregnant Marie and Thompson is hilarious as the duchess—a woman with far too much free time. Those performances, along with the fine music and costumes, help to make this an appealingly offbeat period piece.

IN A LONELY PLACE   DVD
1950   94m   bw   Drama   ★★★★★
Santana   (U.S.)

Humphrey Bogart *(Dixon Steele)*, Gloria Grahame *(Laurel Gray)*, Frank Lovejoy *(Brub Nicolai)*, Carl Benton Reid *(Capt. Lochner)*, Art Smith *(Mel Lippman)*, Jeff Donnell *(Sylvia Nicolai)*, Martha Stewart *(Mildred Atkinson)*, Robert Warwick *(Charlie Waterman)*, Morris Ankrum *(Lloyd Barnes)*, William Ching *(Ted Barton)*

p, Robert Lord, Henry S. Kesler; d, Nicholas Ray; w, Andrew Solt (based on a story by Edmund H. North, from the novel by Dorothy B. Hughes); ph, Burnett Guffey; ed, Viola Lawrence; m, George Antheil; art d, Robert Peterson; cos, Jean Louis

Superb film noir, brilliantly directed by the gifted Ray with Bogart as a talented but volatile Hollywood screenwriter.

Because of his heavy drinking and truculent nature, Bogart is not much in demand among the film studios but his dogged, devoted agent, Smith, manages to get him a writing assignment, to adapt a celebrated romance novel for the screen. They meet in a Hollywood bar-restaurant (a thinly disguised Chasen's) where Bogart argues with Ankrum, the director of the proposed film, accusing him of making the same film over and over again. His one friend in the bar is a broken down actor, Warwick, and when a strutting, bragging producer, Howard (perhaps modeled on Carl Laemmle, Jr.), insults the actor, Bogart knocks Howard about and has to be restrained. Smith urges him to go home and read the novel he must adapt, but Bogart knows it's a potboiler and is reluctant. Then the hatcheck girl at the club, Stewart, who has read and loves the novel, offers to tell Bogart the tale. He takes her home to his bungalow (in a complex that smacks of the famous Garden of Allah, owned and operated by Ali Nazimova, a haven for actors and writers such as Robert Benchley and F. Scott Fitzgerald). Watching Bogart and Stewart enter the bungalow from across the courtyard is lovely Grahame, a new neighbor. As Stewart rattles on about the story, Bogart slips into his bathrobe, pours himself a drink, and tries to calm Stewart down when she begins histrionically enacting scenes from the novel, which brings Grahame to her upstairs window again to watch the couple through open windows. Finally, Bogart has had enough. He's tired, he explains. He gives Stewart cab fare and sends her home. The next day, Stewart's viciously disfigured body is found and Bogart, thought to be the last person to see her alive, is brought in for questioning by the police.

LONELY PLACE epitomizes star-crossed lovers incapable of escaping environment and circumstances no matter how hard they try. The entire cast is excellent, with Bogart giving an electrifying portrait of a man in torment. Grahame, never more beautiful, is captivating as a woman who has been kept too many times and now has one last chance for real love. Ray's helmsmanship here is superb as he runs the story to a quick conclusion, dwelling upon loving and frightening scenes with the skilled balance of a master juggler, keeping the viewer doubting and believing in Bogart from scene to scene. Many thought the film's central relationship reflected on Ray's unraveling marriage to Grahame. They split when filming was over, and the offbeat Grahame went on to marry Ray's son by a previous marriage, causing shockwaves in the '50s fanzines.

IN AMERICA   DVD
2003   103m   c   Drama   ★★★
East of Harlem/Hell's Kitchen Films   PG-13
(Ireland/U.K.)

Samantha Morton *(Sarah)*, Paddy Considine *(Johnny)*, Djimon Hounsou *(Mateo)*, Sarah Bolger *(Christy)*, Emma Bolger *(Ariel)*, Ciaran Cronin *(Frankie)*, Jennifer Seifert *(Angela)*, Michael Sean Tighe *(Frank)*, Jer O'Leary *(Thomas Bakewell)*, Molly Glynn *(Sarah Mateo)*

p, Arthur Lappin, Jim Sheridan; d, Jim Sheridan; w, Jim Sheridan, Naomi Sheridan, Kirsten Sheriden; ph, Declan Quinn; ed, Naomi Geraghty; m, Gavin Friday, Maurice Seezer; prod d, Mark Geraghty; art d, Susie Cullen; fx, Brendan Byrne, Pat Redmond, Simon Stanley-Clamp; cos, Eimer Ni Mhaoldomhnaigh

AAN Best Actress: Samantha Morton; *AAN Best Original Screenplay:* Jim Sheridan, Naomi Sheridan, Kirsten Sheridan; *AAN Best Supporting Actor:* Djimon Hounsou

After a seven-year hiatus producing other filmmakers' projects, Jim Sheridan (MY LEFT FOOT) returns to directing with this intimate portrait of a grief-stricken Irish family living in New York City.

Hoping to make a new start after the death of their young son, aspiring actor Johnny Sullivan (Paddy Considine) and his wife, Sarah (Samantha Morton), and their two daughters, Christy and Ariel (the delightful Sarah and Emma Bolger), move from Ireland to a decrepit apartment building on Manhattan's Upper West Side. The neighborhood may not be the greatest, but it's what they can (barely) afford. Sarah waits tables at a nearby ice-cream parlor while Johnny goes on one audition after another; to help make ends meet, he starts driving a cab. They settle into big-city life, but the specter of the little boy's death continues to haunt them. The Sullivans' unlikely salvation comes in the shape of Mateo (Djimon Hounsou), a tortured and fatally ill Caribbean artist who lives in seclusion on the floor below. When Sarah discovers that she's pregnant and that the pregnancy will pose a serious risk to her life, Mateo becomes her spiritual guide.

Heavy-handed and clumsily written, the film is something of a departure for Sheridan, whose previous work has focused on families affected by the Troubles of his homeland. He seems a bit at sea in the multicultural currents of contemporary New York, and stumbles badly in his portrayal of the city's minorities, particularly Mateo. First a figure to be feared, he's later transformed into the noble black man who must be sacrificed so a white baby and its family can survive. Nevertheless, the film is marvelously acted, and Sheridan captures New York City's crazy energy as only a newcomer can.

IN & OUT

1997 92m c Comedy **DVD** ★★★
Scott Rudin Productions/Spelling Films/Paramount PG-13
(U.S.)

Kevin Kline (*Howard Brackett*), Joan Cusack (*Emily Montgomery*), Tom Selleck (*Peter Malloy*), Matt Dillon (*Cameron Drake*), Debbie Reynolds (*Berniece Brackett*), Wilford Brimley (*Frank Brackett*), Bob Newhart (*Tom Halliwell*), Gregory Jbara (*Walter Brackett*), Shalom Harlow (*Sonya*), Shawn Hatosy (*Jack*)

p, Scott Rudin; d, Frank Oz; w, Paul Rudnick; ph, Rob Hahn; ed, Dan Hanley, John Jympson; m, Marc Shaiman; prod d, Ken Adam; art d, Charles V. Beal; fx, Albert Griswold; cos, Ann Roth

AAN Best Supporting Actress: Joan Cusack

Inspired by Tom Hanks's Best Actor acceptance speech at the 1994 Academy Awards ceremony in which he thanked a gay teacher, Frank Oz's cheerful comedy tells of the inadvertent televised outing of a schoolteacher in midwest America.

Upon accepting his Best Actor Oscar for his portrayal of a gay soldier, Cameron Drake (Matt Dillon) thanks Howard Brackett (Kevin Kline), his homosexual high school English teacher. This comes as something of a surprise to Howard, who is not, to his knowledge, actually gay. Surprised, too, are his fiancee, Emily (Joan Cusack), his parents (Debbie Reynolds and Wilford Brimley), and the school principal (Bob Newhart). The residents of Howard's small town begin to speculate that perhaps there is something to Drake's claim—after all, Howard has a thing for Barbra Streisand movies, wears bow ties, and is "smart, well dressed, and really clean." Soon, Howard himself begins to question his sexual orientation: his dilemma is made more difficult by Peter Malloy (Tom Selleck), a gay television reporter, who encourages Howard to come out of the closet. Determined to put this controversy to rest, Howard and Emily go ahead·with their wedding plans. Unfortunately, when it's Howard's turn to say "I do," he instead announces "I'm gay."

IN & OUT is a simple story made very, very entertaining by the excellent performances of just about everyone involved. Kline reminds one of just what a talented comedic actor he is, and he receives ample support from the rest of the cast, most notably Selleck (another gifted actor whose comic abilities are too often overlooked), Cusack, Reynolds, and Brimley. Credit, too, the sharp-witted script by Paul Rudnick, which takes a few well-aimed swipes at both Hollywood and small-town America while making the most out of what, in less skilled hands, would be rather slight material.

IN COLD BLOOD

1967 134m bw Biography/Crime **DVD** ★★★½
Pax (U.S.) R

Robert Blake (*Perry Smith*), Scott Wilson (*Dick Hickock*), John Forsythe (*Alvin Dewey*), Paul Stewart (*Reporter*), Gerald S. O'Loughlin (*Harold Nye*), Jeff Corey (*Hickock's Father*), John Gallaudet (*Roy Church*), James Flavin (*Clarence Duntz*), Charles McGraw (*Smith's Father*), Jim Lantz (*Officer Rohleder*)

p, Richard Brooks; d, Richard Brooks; w, Richard Brooks (based on the book *In Cold Blood: A True Account of a Mulitple Murder and Its Consequences* by Truman Capote); ph, Conrad Hall (Panavision); ed, Peter Zinner; m, Quincy Jones; art d, Robert Boyle; fx, Geza Gaspar; cos, Jack Martell

AAN Best Director: Richard Brooks; *AAN Best Adapted Screenplay:* Richard Brooks; *AAN Best Cinematography:* Conrad Hall; *AAN Best Original Score:* Quincy Jones

Like the title says. IN COLD BLOOD dramatizes actual events and people in a realistic, technically well-crafted fashion, based upon Truman Capote's "nonficton" novel. Capote

seized upon the real-life November 15, 1959 mass murder of the Clutter family in Holcomb, Kansas, by two psychopathic killers, and turned the grisly tale into a bestseller. In making the movie, director Brooks avoids further analysis, laying out the story of Smith and Hickock as faithful docudrama.

Vagrants Blake and Wilson desperately cast about for ways to make an illegal buck, having been cell mates in state prison. Wilson has learned from another inmate that the Clutters keep $10,000 in their farm house, so the pair invades the home, terrorizing, then savagely slaughtering, the family; they leave with little loot since there is no $10,000 to be found. The killers are shown running to Mexico, then back to the U.S., leaving a trail of bad checks which federal agents follow until they're apprehended in Las Vegas. Brooks then spends half the film displaying Blake and Wilson in the Kansas State Penitentiary at Lansing waiting to be hanged. He emphasizes the state's brutality in taking their lives on the gallows on April 14, 1965, after endless appeals, stays, and agonizing soul-searching on the part of the culprits.

The facts described, what's it all about? Brooks avoids all the pitfalls of cliché, but shouldn't an in-depth docudrama have presented the aftermath of the murders on the Clutter's community and relatives? For those familiar with the case, the leads *do* bear a resemblance to the two real-life murderers, but Brooks's examination is decidedly one-sided. Exquisitely photographed in wide-screen black-and-white by Conrad Hall.

IN GOOD COMPANY

2004 110m c Comedy **DVD** ★★½
Depth of Field Productions/Universal (U.S.) PG-13

Dennis Quaid (*Dan Foreman*), Topher Grace (*Carter Duryea*), Scarlett Johansson (*Alex Foreman*), Marg Helgenberger (*Ann Foreman*), David Paymer (*Morty*), Clark Gregg (*Steckle*), Philip Baker Hall (*Eugene Kalb*), Selma Blair (*Kimberly Duryea*), Frankie Faison (*Corwin*), Zena Grey (*Jana Foreman*)

p, Paul Weitz, Chris Weitz; d, Paul Weitz; w, Paul Weitz; ph, Remi Adefarasin; ed, Myron Kerstein; m, Stephen Trask; prod d, William Arnold; art d, Sue Chan; fx, Ron Rosegard; cos, Molly Maginnis

Writer-director Paul Weitz's sharp ear for corporate-weasel words and hollow displays of team spirit get lost in a stream of good-news-bad-news gags in this not-dark-enough workplace comedy.

Middle-aged Dan Foreman (Dennis Quaid) has spent more than 20 years at "Sports America" magazine, managing a crack ad-sales team and cultivating a loyal network of repeat advertisers. Married to Ann (Marg Helgenberger) and the devoted father of two nearly grown daughters—high-school-age Jana (Zena Grey) and the bright and beautiful college freshman Alex (Scarlett Johansson)—Dan understands that domestic bliss comes with the usual financial obligations. On top of the second mortgage, Dan is about to face a raft of unanticipated expenses with the late-life baby his wife is expecting. None of this worries Dan until multinational conglomerate Globecom acquires Sports America's parent company and brings in their own managers, including ruthless corporate quisling Steckle (Clark Gregg) and his callow protege, 26-year-old Carter Duryea (Topher Grace). Inexperienced Carter appropriates Dan's title and office and begins implementing Steckle's mandate to trim the budget by firing senior management. Carter's glib corporate-speak does nothing to endear him to Dan, though Dan does glimpse a desperate neediness behind Carter's smooth facade. What Dan has yet to learn is that Carter and Alex have begun a clandestine affair.

Quaid and Grace have an unforced rapport, and if the movie overall had the bitter brio of Malcolm McDowell's brief, uncredited turn as Globecom guru Teddy K, a Frankenmogul stitched together from bits of Richard Branson, Barry Diller, and Rupert Murdoch, it would be a pointed black comedy. Instead, it's an inconsequential sitcom spiked with a couple of well-placed barbs.

IN OLD CHICAGO

1938 115m bw Historical/Disaster ★★★
Fox (U.S.)

Tyrone Power *(Dion O'Leary)*, Alice Faye *(Belle Fawcett)*, Don Ameche *(Jack O'Leary)*, Alice Brady *(Molly O'Leary)*, Andy Devine *(Pickle Bixby)*, Brian Donlevy *(Gil Warren)*, Phyllis Brooks *(Ann Colby)*, Tom Brown *(Bob O'Leary)*, Sidney Blackmer *(Gen. Phil Sheridan)*, Berton Churchill *(Sen. Colby)*

p, Kenneth MacGowan; d, Henry King, Robert D. Webb; w, Lamar Trotti, Sonya Levien (based on a story "We the O'Learys" by Niven Busch); ph, Peverell Marley; ed, Barbara McLean; art d, William Darling, Rudolph Sternad; fx, Fred Sersen, Ralph Hammeras, Louis J. White; cos, Royer

AAN Best Picture; AA Best Supporting Actress: Alice Brady; *AAN Best Original Story:* Niven Busch; *AAN Best Score:* 20th Century Fox Studio Music Department, Louis Silvers (Dept. Head); *AAN Best Sound Recording:* E.H. Hansen; *AAN Best Assistant Director:* Robert Webb

In old Zanuck's studio, a big-budget, mediocre cash-in on MGM's SAN FRANCISCO, minus the male star-charisma of the latter.

All the biggest Fox stars of the time were assembled for this nearly $2 million production: Alice Brady won a supporting actress Oscar for her role as Mrs. O'Leary, the woman who supports her family after the death of her husband by taking in washing. She manages to raise her sons into a handsome rake and political schemer (Power), a crusading lawyer (Ameche); and a young man with no ambitions other than to marry his sweetheart and have babies (Brown). Alice Faye gets to do her saloon singer bit, parading her legs in $1500 jeweled stockings and swooning her way through nostalgic sentiments with that deep, honeyed voice. There's a lot of political intrigue involving Power, Ameche and crooked mayor Donlevy, but it's all just a build-up to the fire, sparked by a well-placed kick from one of Mrs. O'Leary's cows. Director King's specialty—spectacle—gets a workout, and he has a blast staging teeming city crowds, brawling saloons, police platoons dismantling riots, runaway horses, stampeding cattle and all the drama the rise of Irish tempers will allow.

CHICAGO makes up in atmosphere and color what it lacks in historical accuracy; the screenplay was based on Niven Busch's *We the O'Learys*. The fire itself propelled production costs to $1,800,000, and runs for twenty minutes. (Assistant director Robert Webb won an Oscar for his work on the sequence.) Worth a view along with the great disaster epics of the 1930s, the aforementioned SAN FRANCISCO, THE HURRICANE, and THE RAINS COME.

IN PRAISE OF LOVE DVD

(ÈLOGE DE L'AMOUR)
2001 98m c/bw Drama/Experimental ★★★½
Peripheria Productions/Avventura Films/Canal +/ Arte France Cinema/Vega Film/TSR
(France/Switzerland)

Bruno Putzulu *(Edgar)*, Cecile Camp *(Elle/Berthe)*, Jean Davy *(Grandfather)*, Franáoise Verney *(Grandmother)*, Audrey Klebaner *(Eglantine)*, Jèrèmie Lippmann *(Perceval)*, Claude Baigneres *(Mr. Rosenthal)*, Rèmo Forlani *(Mayor Forlani)*, Mark Hunter *(U.S. Journalist)*, Jean Lacouture *(Historian)*

p, Alain Sarde, Ruth Waldberger; d, Jean-Luc Godard; w, Jean-Luc Godard; ph, Julien Hirsch, Christophe Pollock; ed, Raphaele Urtin; m, Ketil Bjornstad, David Darling, Karl Amadeus

Hartmann, Maurice Jaubert, Arvo Part, Georges Van Parys; cos, Marina Thibaut

Often cryptic but always beautiful, this heady meditation on time, memory, and, of course, filmmaking is the first Jean-Luc Godard film to receive a proper U.S. release since 1987's KING LEAR. But it's hardly a commercial breakthrough: The film is a gorgeous muddle that somehow manages to leave one both baffled and deeply satisfied.

Having finally abandoned his idea for a cantata inspired by Simone Weil, Edgar (Bruno Putzulu) is developing a project that will explore the four moments of love—meeting, passion, separation, reconciliation—as they're experienced by three couples at different stages of their lives: youth, adulthood, and old age. Edgar thinks he knows just the person to play the adult female role: Berthe (Cecile Camp), a mysterious beauty whom he met two years earlier. When Edgar tracks her down, he finds Berthe depressed, seriously ill, and reluctant to get involved with his project. She agrees to meet him the following week, but suddenly she's gone forever. The second half of the film is a lengthy flashback to Edgar and Berthe's first meeting. Edgar visits Brittany to interview two married Resistance fighters (Jean Davy, Franáoise Verny) who are in the process of selling their memories to Steven Spielberg and Associates for an upcoming film. On hand to help with the negotiations is their granddaughter, Berthe.

Godard's film is a multilayered mixture of fiction, philosophy, social commentary, literary theory, art criticism, and the usual embittered anti-U.S. rant. The film demands a great deal, but it's generous in its returns. The first half, filmed in sparkling black and white, strongly resembles Godard's early work with cinematographer Raoul Coutard. The second, shot on digital video with supersaturated colors, recalls Gaugin at his most expressive.

IN THE BEDROOM DVD

2001 131m c Crime/Drama ★★★★
Good Machine Productions/Greenestreet Film R
(U.S.)

Tom Wilkinson *(Matt Fowler)*, Sissy Spacek *(Ruth Fowler)*, Nick Stahl *(Frank Fowler)*, Marisa Tomei *(Natalie Strout)*, William Mapother *(Richard Strout)*, William Wise *(Willis Grinnel)*, Celia Weston *(Katie Grinnel)*, Karen Allen *(Marla Keyes)*, Frank T. Wells *(Henry)*, W. Clapham Murray *(Carl)*

p, Todd Field, Ross Katz, Graham Leader; d, Todd Field; w, Rob Festinger, Todd Field (based on the story "Killings" by Andre Dubus); ph, Antonio Calvache; ed, Frank Reynolds; m, Thomas Newman; prod d, Shannon Hart; cos, Melissa Economy

AAN Best Picture; AAN Best Actor: Tom Wilkinson; *AAN Best Actress:* Sissy Spacek; *AAN Best Supporting Actress:* Marisa Tomei; *AAN Best Adapted Screenplay:* Rob Festinger, Todd Field

Based on the short story "Killings" by the late Andre Dubus, actor Todd Field's feature directing debut chronicles the descent into darkness of an ordinary couple whose life is shattered by sudden violence.

Matt (Tom Wilkinson) and Ruth (Sissy Spacek) appear to be gliding smoothly through middle-age. He's a respected local doctor, she teaches high school music and their marriage is a felicitous blend of mutual comfort and still-vital passion. They own a lovely home in a small town on the coast of Maine, and their only child, college-age Frank (Nick Stahl), is the sort of son who'd make any parent proud: kind, intelligent, diligent and mature. The flaw in their contentment is Frank's new girlfriend, Natalie (Marisa Tomei): She's older, the mother of two small boys, and none-too-amicably separated from her volatile husband, Richard Strout (William Mapother). Natalie comes with a lot of baggage and Ruth can't see past the relationship's potential to damage Frank's future. But even she can't imagine that things will end with a shocking murder, or more correctly, *begin* with one. Matt and Ruth suddenly find themselves entangled in the justice system, and they both internalize the bitter injustice of the way things play out while making a superficial show getting on with things. Matt sees patients, Ruth continues to coach her girls' chorus. But the Fowlers can't *really* get on with things; the fiber of their lives has been torn apart.

Their subsequent actions might seem shockingly out of character, if this devastatingly well-acted film didn't so carefully suggest that corrosive grief is as powerfully annihilative as a bomb. It taps into an ugliness so visceral that all bets are off.

IN THE COMPANY OF MEN DVD
1997 93m c Drama ★★★½
Atlantis Entertainment/Fair and Square Productions R
(U.S.)

Aaron Eckhart *(Chad)*, Stacy Edwards *(Christine)*, Matt Malloy *(Howard)*, Michael Martin *(Co-Worker No. 1)*, Mark Rector *(John)*, Chris Hayes *(Co-Worker No. 2)*, Jason Dixie *(Intern)*, Emily Cline *(Suzanne)*

p, Mark Archer, Stephen Pevner; d, Neil LaBute; w, Neil LaBute; ph, Tony Hettinger; ed, Joel Plotch; m, Ken Williams, Karel Roessingn; prod d, Julia Henkel

A caustic and willfully controversial exercise in very bad male behavior that made playwright Neil LaBute (YOUR FRIENDS & NEIGHBORS) a filmmaker to watch. Handsome Chad (Aaron Eckhart) and mild-mannered Howard (Matt Malloy), cogs in the machine of some anonymous corporation, are on a six-week project out of town. Howard, fresh off a romantic meltdown, is ostensibly in charge, but it's obvious to everyone but him that the seething, devious, glad-handing Chad calls the shots. And it's Chad who suggests the game: On behalf of all men who've been done wrong by women, Chad proposes symbolic revenge. He and Howard will both seduce some vulnerable local girl and then dump her simultaneously. What a glorious victory for the walking wounded in the battle of the sexes! The girl they choose is pretty Christine (Stacy Edwards), a deaf administrative assistant who blossoms under their attentions and falls hard for Chad.

A bleak comedy of amorality, this is neither the misogynistic rant nor the masterpiece it's been tagged by various writers. For all that its obvious subject is the war between men and women, it's equally about the dog-eat-dog backbiting that boils just beneath the surface of corporate camaraderie, and Chad the cad is an equal-opportunity scumbag. The movie's weak link lies in the performances—perhaps LaBute's directing skills aren't yet equal to his proficiency as a writer. While Edwards is phenomenally good as Christine (and no, she's not really deaf), Eckhart and Malloy too often seem as though they're participating in an acting exercise, pausing just a little too long between lines, posing just a bit too self-consciously, feeling their way through dialogue whose barely repressed venom should slip off their tongues like rancid butter. But that's a relatively minor criticism; this is a film worth seeing, and LaBute is a filmmaker well worth watching.

IN THE CUT DVD
2003 118m c Thriller/Erotic ★★★
Laurie Parker Productions/Pathe (U.S./Australia) R

Meg Ryan *(Frannie)*, Mark Ruffalo *(Detective Malloy)*, Jennifer Jason Leigh *(Pauline)*, Nick Damici *(Detective Rodriguez)*, Sharrieff Pugh *(Cornelius Webb)*, Sunrise Coigney *(Frannie's Young Mother)*, Michael Nuccio *(Frannie's Young Father)*, Alison Nega *(Young Father's Fiancee)*, Dominick Aries *(Attentive Husband)*, Kevin Bacon *(John Graham—uncredited)*

p, Nicole Kidman, Laurie Parker; d, Jane Campion; w, Jane Campion, Susanna Moore (based on the novel by Susanna Moore); ph, Dion Beebe; ed, Alexandre De Franceschi; m, Hilmar Orn Hilmarsson; prod d, David Brisbin; art d, David Stein; fx, Drew Jiritano; cos, Beatrix Aruna Pasztor

Though Jane Campion's sexually explicit adaptation of Susanna Moore's novel has shortcomings as an erotic thriller, it's an always interesting deconstruction of an exhausted genre.

Good with words, New York City English teacher Frannie (Meg Ryan) is less than brilliant when it comes to men. A careless fling with an unstable medical student (Kevin Bacon) has left her with a full-time stalker, and after the severed head of a young woman is found in the garden behind her building, she begins a dangerous flirtation with Malloy (Mark Ruffalo), the gruff NYPD detective who's been assigned to the case. The victim appears to have been murdered by a repeat lady killer with a particularly cruel signature: each mutilated corpse is left with the one thing young women are thought to desire above all else—an engagement ring. Malloy is curious about Frannie's whereabouts on the day of the murder, and she admits to having been at the local bar where the victim was last seen, but withholds a crucial detail: she saw the woman in the bar's shadowy basement, performing oral sex on a man with a wrist tattoo exactly like Malloy's. When she's attacked after visiting her half-sister (Jennifer Jason Leigh), it becomes clear that Frannie has become the object of someone's deadly obsession.

The ending is cliched even by genre standards, but Campion and Moore (who adapted Moore's novel together) embellished the original story with a few twists that dovetail with Campion's own concerns, including the price of female desire and the bond between sisters. Ryan is unexpectedly raw and remarkably good, but the film's real star is New York. Draped in post-9/11 anxiety, the city hasn't appeared this threatening since the '70s.

IN THE GOOD OLD SUMMERTIME DVD
1949 102m c Musical/Comedy ★★½
MGM (U.S.)

Judy Garland *(Veronica Fisher)*, Van Johnson *(Andrew Larkin)*, S.Z. Sakall *(Otto Oberkugen)*, Spring Byington *(Nellie Burke)*, Clinton Sundberg *(Rudy Hansen)*, Buster Keaton *(Hickey)*, Marcia Van Dyke *(Louise Parkson)*, Lillian Bronson *(Aunt Addie)*

p, Joe Pasternak; d, Robert Z. Leonard; w, Samson Raphaelson, Frances Goodrich, Ivan Tors, Albert Hackett (based on the play *The Shop Around the Corner* by Miklos Laszlo); ph, Harry Stradling (Technicolor); ed, Adrienne Fazan; m, George Stoll; art d, Cedric Gibbons, Randall Duell; chor, Robert Alton

Pleasant, if bland, music-filled remake of THE SHOP AROUND THE CORNER. Not up to the usual Garland standards, this is an example of MGM's assembly line product, built to milk Garland's show-stopping for studio coffers. She and a rather annoying Van Johnson play antagonistic co-workers in a Chicago music store at the turn of the century who don't realize they are pen pals. She plays piano and sells music; he pushes musical instruments. The cooler they are to each other at work, the hotter their letters become. By the end they are in each other's arms, but not before a mixup occurs involving a priceless Stradivarius and a more common fiddle, which ends up broken. Eighteen-month-old Liza Minnelli made her second screen appearance as the couple's child at the film's end. (Her first appearance was in EASTER PARADE a year earlier.)

IN THE HEAT OF THE NIGHT   DVD
1967 109m c   Crime   ★★★★
Mirisch   (U.S.)

Sidney Poitier *(Virgil Tibbs)*, Rod Steiger *(Bill Gillespie)*, Warren Oates *(Sam Wood)*, Quentin Dean *(Delores Purdy)*, James Patterson *(Purdy)*, William Schallert *(Webb Schubert)*, Jack Teter *(Philip Colbert)*, Lee Grant *(Mrs. Leslie Colbert)*, Scott Wilson *(Harvey Oberst)*, Matt Clark *(Packy Harrison)*

p, Walter Mirisch; d, Norman Jewison; w, Stirling Silliphant (based on the novel by John Ball); ph, Haskell Wexler (DeLuxe Color); ed, Hal Ashby; m, Quincy Jones; art d, Paul Groesse; cos, Alan Levine

AA Best Picture; AA Best Actor: Rod Steiger; *AAN Best Director:* Norman Jewison; *AA Best Adapted Screenplay:* Stirling Silliphant; *AA Best Film Editing:* Hal Ashby; *AA Best Sound:* Samuel Goldwyn Studio Sound Department; *AAN Best Sound Effects:* James A. Richard

Superb thriller starring Rod Steiger in an Oscar-winning role as Bill Gillespie, a shrewd southern sheriff, and Sidney Poitier as Virgil Tibbs, a sensitive, intellectual detective from the big city. When a wealthy industrialist is murdered in the little town of Sparta, Mississippi, a well-dressed black stranger is arrested while waiting at the train station. The stranger, Tibbs, identifies himself as a Philadelphia policeman, and, under orders from his superiors up north, assists Gillespie in his investigation. Gillespie grudgingly accepts his assistance and protects him from brutal attacks by local rednecks, and the two grow to admire each other as they confront red herrings and racism en route to identifying the killer.

IN THE HEAT OF THE NIGHT was carefully directed by Norman Jewison, who avoids sentimentality and all the racial cliches that could have crept into almost every scene. As a result, his film won the Academy's Best Picture Award, shocking many when it was chosen over BONNIE AND CLYDE and THE GRADUATE. Steiger's performance is subtle, funny, sad, and fascinating, and Poitier demonstrates the same superb talent he would bring to THEY CALL ME MR. TIBBS and THE ORGANIZATION. Lee Grant is also good as the hysterical widow. The film was shot in Illinois and Tennessee, the latter standing in for Mississippi.

IN THE LINE OF FIRE   DVD
1993 123m c   Thriller   ★★★½
Aplle/Rose Productions/Castle Rock   (U.S.)   R

Clint Eastwood *(Frank Horrigan)*, John Malkovich *(Mitch Leary)*, Rene Russo *(Lilly Raines)*, Dylan McDermott *(Al D'Andrea)*, Gary Cole *(Bill Watts)*, Fred Dalton Thompson *(Harry Sargent)*, John Mahoney *(Sam Campagna)*, Gregory Alan-Williams *(Matt Wilder)*, Jim Curley *(President)*, Sally Hughes *(First Lady)*

p, Jeff Apple; d, Wolfgang Petersen; w, Jeff Maguire; ph, John Bailey; ed, Anne V. Coates; m, Ennio Morricone; prod d, Lilly Kilvert; art d, John Warnke; fx, Rocky Gehr, John Nelson, R. Greenberg Associates West Inc., Bruno George; cos, Erica Edell Phillips

AAN Best Supporting Actor: John Malkovich; *AAN Best Film Editing:* Anne V. Coates; *AAN Best Original Screenplay:* Jeff Maguire

It seems postal workers are not the only government employees likely to go on a vengeful rampage as a response to being fired. IN THE LINE OF FIRE pits Secret Service Agent Frank Horrigan (Clint Eastwood) against Mitch Leary (John Malkovich), a top CIA hit man until the agency cancelled his contract. Leary plans to get even by undertaking a suicide-mission assassination of the President. The twist is that Horrigan was present at J.F.K.'s assassination 30 years ago, and is ridden with guilt at having failed to take the fatal bullet. Leary is ready to trade his life for that of the Prez; if the situation requires it, is Horrigan equally willing to give up *his* life to save the Chief Executive?

IN THE LINE OF FIRE explores this intriguing premise with subtlety and suspense, particularly during several phone conversations between a gloating, you-can't-stop-me Leary and a visibly shaken Horrigan. Eastwood plays the agent in a style you could call "Unforgiven Lite," as a physical and emotional burnout who seems no match for his criminal mastermind adversary. (His age, though, doesn't stop Horrigan from romancing an initially disdainful fellow agent, played by Rene Russo.) As Leary, Malkovich has fun donning a wide array of disguises and dispatching human obstacles with Hannibal Lecter-like precision. The result is a finely tuned suspense thriller, though executives who have recently laid off trained killers may experience some discomfort.

IN THE MOOD FOR LOVE   DVD
(HUAYANG NIANHUA)
2000 98m c   Drama/Romance   ★★★★
Block 2 Pictures/Paradis Films/Jet Tone Films   PG
(Hong Kong/France)

Tony Leung Chiu-wai *(Chow Mo-wan)*, Maggie Cheung *(Mrs. Chan, nee Su Lizhen)*, Rebecca Pan *(Mrs. Suen)*, Lui Chun *(Mr. Ho)*, Siu Ping-Lam *(Ah Ping)*, Chin Chi-Ang *(The Amah)*, Chan Man-lui, Koo Kam-wah, Yu Hsien, Chow Po-Chun

p, Wong Kar-wai; d, Wong Kar-wai; w, Wong Kar-wai (incorporating quotations from the writings of Liu Yi-Chang); ph, Christopher Doyle, Mark Lee; ed, William Chang, Chan Kei-hap; m, Michael Galasso, Umebayashi Shigeru; prod d, William Chang; art d, Man Lim-chung, Alfred Yau

And the mood is everything in this sad, achingly beautiful love story from Wong Kar-wai.

On the same sweltering day in 1962, newspaper editor Mr. Chow (Tony Leung Chiu-wai) and shipping firm secretary Mrs. Chan (Maggie Cheung) move into adjoining apartments in the same Hong Kong apartment complex. Both are desperately lonely—his wife is always working late; her husband is away for weeks at a time "on business"—but they remain only passing acquaintances until they realize that their respective spouses are having an affair. Mr. Chow and Mrs. Chan begin spending evenings out in each other's company, assuming the identities of the adulterers in an attempt to "see how it begins." But the game soon grows more intimate: they practice leaving their mates, then leaving each other. Only the watchful eyes of their neighbors and their own sense of decency keep them from actually becoming lovers.

Wong's film is both a memory piece of a particular time and place from his childhood and a sequel of sorts to his 1990 DAYS OF BEING WILD. But fans of Wong's earlier, flashier style may be a little surprised by the restraint he and his longtime cameraman Christopher Doyle show here—no frantic hand-held camera, no time-lapse photography, no interwoven story lines, no fractured time frames. The film is slow-paced and slyly structured around snatches of clandestine phone calls and furtive shots, and it's extraordinarily sexy: the atmosphere is all curling cigarette smoke and Nat King Cole, silk suits and tight sheath dresses. What remains constant is the director's sense of the essential isolation of modern life; Wong continues to be cinema's premier poet of heartache.

IN THE NAME OF THE FATHER   DVD
1993 127m c   Drama/Historical/Political   ★★★½
Hell's Kitchen Ltd.   (U.S.)   R

Daniel Day-Lewis *(Gerald Conlon)*, Pete Postlethwaite *(Guiseppe Conlon)*, Emma Thompson *(Gareth Peirce)*, John Lynch *(Paul Hill)*, Joanna Irvine *(Ann Conlon)*, Beatie Edney *(Carole*

Richardson), Britta Smith *(Anne Maguire)*, Don Baker *(Joe McAndrew)*, Corin Redgrave *(Robert Dixon)*, Gerard McSorley *(Belfast Detective Pavis)*

p, Jim Sheridan; d, Jim Sheridan; w, Terry George, Jim Sheridan (from the autobiography *Proved Innocent* by Gerry Conlon); ph, Peter Biziou; ed, Gerry Hambling; m, Trevor Jones; prod d, Caroline Amies; art d, Rick Butler, Tom Brown; fx, Joss Williams; cos, Joan Bergin

AAN Best Picture; AAN Best Actor: Daniel Day-Lewis; *AAN Best Supporting Actor:* Pete Postlethwaite; *AAN Best Supporting Actress:* Emma Thompson; *AAN Best Director:* Jim Sheridan; *AAN Best Film Editing:* Gerry Hambling; *AAN Best Adapted Screenplay:* Terry George, Jim Sheridan

Based on the true story of accused IRA bomber Gerry Conlon, Jim Sheridan's IN THE NAME OF THE FATHER is the powerful saga of an unlikely Irish martyr wrongfully imprisoned by the British government. Sheridan takes a controversial subject and gives it wider appeal by focusing on the family drama of two men who are also political prisoners.

In 1974, the Irish Republican Army bombs a pub in Guildford, England, killing five people. British police detain a number of suspects, including Gerry Conlon (Daniel Day-Lewis)—who has recently moved to London from Belfast—and his friend Paul. Gerry returns to his family in Belfast, and the police arrest him and three of his commune friends. The Guildford Four are ruthlessly interrogated for seven days until they each sign bogus confessions. Gerry's relatives—including his father Giuseppe (Pete Postlethwaite)—are unjustly charged with abetting the IRA and given harsh sentences. Father and son are imprisoned together; Giuseppe dies after years of cruel confinement, and Gerry pours his energy into exonerating his family, helped by English solicitor Gareth Peirce (Emma Thompson).

Sheridan explores a controversial, real-life political injustice, complete with police interrogations, courtroom antics, and prison confrontations, but his real interest is Gerry's relationship with his dad. Sheridan demonizes both the British police and the IRA, leaving the Guildford Four as symbols of injustice, with no specific national, political, or ethnic affiliation. Though the facts have been manipulated in the interests of drama—Gerry and Giuseppe were never imprisoned together, etc.—this has been done in a brave and responsible way, shedding light on an important episode in recent history.

IN THE REALM OF THE SENSES ⦿ DVD
(AI NO CORRIDA)
1976 105m c   Erotic/Drama   ★★★
Argos Films/Oceanic/Oshima Productions/Shibata Organization Inc.   (France/Japan)

Tatsuya Fuji *(Kichizo)*, Eiko Matsuda *(Sada)*, Aoi Nakajima *(Toku)*, Maika Seri *(Matsuko—Maid)*, Taiji Tonoyama *(Old Beggar)*, Hiroko Fuji *(Tsune—Maid)*, Naomi Shiraishi *(Yaeji—Geisha)*, Kyoko Okada *(Hangyoku)*, Kikuhei Matsunoya *(Hohkan)*, Yasuko Matsui *(Manageress of Inn)*

p, Anatole Dauman; d, Nagisa Oshima; w, Nagisa Oshima; ph, Hideo Ito, Kenichi Okamoto; ed, Keiichi Uraoka, Patrick Sauvion; m, Minoru Miki; art d, Jusho Toda; fx, Isao Nishimura, Terumi Hosoishi; cos, Jusho Toda

Based on a true case involving a woman in 1936 who was found wandering the streets of Tokyo carrying her dead lover's severed penis, Nagisa Oshima's sexually graphic, and extremely disturbing, IN THE REALM OF THE SENSES, became notorious when it was seized by U.S. Customs officials in 1976, postponing its showing at the New York Film Festival.

In 1936 Japan, a nymphomaniac ex-prostitute named Sada (Eiko Matsuda) goes to work at an inn owned by Kichizo (Tatsuya Fuji) and his wife. Sada and Kichizo begin an affair and he eventually leaves his wife and runs away with Sada. They move into a geisha house in the red-light district, where their frequent bouts of sex, often outdoors and in front of others, shocks even the other prostitutes. Needing money, Sada has sex with an ex-client, an elderly man who was her school principal, and Kichizo has sex with the geisha house's fat maid (Kazue Tomiyama) while Sada is gone. As their sexual practices become increasingly intense and bizarre, the couple begin experimenting with partial strangulation as a method of sexual stimulation.

The iconoclastic Oshima made IN THE REALM OF THE SENSES with the intention to shock and shatter taboos. With its explicit and graphic shots of actual penetration and fellatio, there is no doubt that the film is pornographic in the broadest definition of the term, although whether it was made with the intention to arouse sexual desire is quite doubtful. It's certainly a completely honest film, fearlessly showing what others whose subject is sex, only hint at, but whether or not the photographic depiction of real sex can be transformed into art by a distinguished filmmaker, by placing it into the context of a metaphorical story of obsession and domination, is highly debatable. There is no doubt that Oshima is a serious and talented artist, as evidenced by many of his other films, and in the surreal qualities of certain scenes here. On a traditional level, the film is visually quite beautiful, with delicate and sensitive use of color, composition, decor, and music, and as the lovers, Tatsuya Fuji and Eiko Matsuda give remarkably natural performances, under the circumstances, but the repeated scenes of them having sex become numbing and eventually laughable, and the horrifying ending is almost impossible to watch.

IN WHICH WE SERVE ⦿ DVD
1942 115m bw War   ★★★½
Two Cities   (U.K.)

Noel Coward *(Capt. Kinross)*, John Mills *(Shorty Blake)*, Bernard Miles *(Walter Hardy)*, Celia Johnson *(Alix Kinross)*, Kay Walsh *(Freda Lewis)*, Joyce Carey *(Kath Hardy)*, Michael Wilding *(Flags)*, Penelope-Dudley Ward *(Maureen Fenwick)*, Philip Friend *(Torps)*, Derek Elphinstone *(No. One)*

p, Noel Coward; d, Noel Coward, David Lean; w, Noel Coward (based on the experiences of Lord Louis Mountbatten); ph, Ronald Neame; ed, Thelma Myers, David Lean; m, Noel Coward

AAN Best Picture; AAN Best Original Screenplay: Noel Coward

Noel Coward performed with unexpected brilliance here as co-director, writer, musical composer, and star of this stirring WWII drama. Presented in a series of poignant and revealing vignettes, the film tells the story of the British destroyer *Torrin* and its crew, commanded by Capt. Kinross (Coward), a father figure for his stalwart men. Constructed like a documentary, IN WHICH WE SERVE is also narrated by Coward, who recounts the ship's heroic actions: hit by torpedoes, it survives and is towed back to England, later participating in the Dunkirk evacuation and in naval battles off Crete, where it is dive-bombed and sinks. Kinross and his crew cling to a raft for hours, and while waiting for rescue, remember their loved ones in a series of flashbacks.

Regarded as noble and understated at the time, IN WHICH WE SERVE now comes across as patronizing and riven with class condescension. But to Coward's credit (he recieved a special Oscar "for his outstanding production achievement"), he had the good sense to choose the most distinguished film editor in England at the time, David Lean, to assist with the production; and so impressive was Lean's work that, halfway through the picture, Coward handed him the directorial reins. Out of respect, Lean's next three productions—THIS HAPPY

BREED; BLITHE SPIRIT; and BRIEF ENCOUNTER—were adaptations of Coward's writing. SERVE marked the film debuts of Johnson, Massey and baby Mills.

INCREDIBLE SHRINKING MAN, THE

1957 81m bw Science Fiction ★★★★
Universal (U.S.)

Grant Williams (*Scott Carey*), Randy Stuart (*Louise Carey*), April Kent (*Clarice*), Paul Langton (*Charlie Carey*), Raymond Bailey (*Dr. Thomas Silver*), William Schallert (*Dr. Arthur Bramson*), Frank Scannell (*Barker*), Helene Marshall, Diana Darrin (*Nurses*), Billy Curtis (*Midget*)

p, Albert Zugsmith; d, Jack Arnold; w, Richard Matheson (based on his novel *The Shrinking Man*); ph, Ellis W. Carter; ed, Al Joseph; m, Fred Carling, Elliot Lawrence; art d, Alexander Golitzen, Robert Clatworthy; fx, Clifford Stine, Roswell A. Hoffmann, Everett H. Broussard; cos, Jay A. Morley Jr.

Pulp sci-fi classic about a man who starts to shrink after being enveloped by a strange atomic cloud while on holiday. The movie is notable for its relatively intelligent script (adapted by Richard Matheson from his novel), for some imaginatively amusing special effects, and for an existential streak which finally has our (tiny) hero pondering the meaning of existence. (Matheson sold his novel on the condition that he be allowed to write the script. His first novel, *I Am Legend*, had been badly butchered, and he had no wish to see that happen again. Eventually, *I Am Legend* was filmed as L'ULTIMO UOMO DELLA TERRA from another writer's screenplay.) The film was also the source for a promising, but largely unsuccessful remake, THE INCREDIBLE SHRINKING WOMAN, in 1981.

INCREDIBLES, THE

2004 115m c/bw Animated/Action/Comedy ★★★★
Pixar/Walt Disney (U.S.) PG

VOICES OF: Craig T. Nelson (*Bob Parr/Mr. Incredible*), Holly Hunter (*Helen Parr/Elastigirl*), Samuel L. Jackson (*Lucius Best/Frozone*), Jason Lee (*Buddy/Syndrome*), Elizabeth Pena (*Mirage*), Spencer Fox (*Dashiell Parr*), Sarah Vowell (*Violet Parr*), Brad Bird (*Edna "E" Mode*), Wallace Shawn (*Gilbert Huph*), Dominique Louis (*Bomb Voyage*)

p, John Walker; d, Brad Bird; w, Brad Bird; ph, Andrew Jimenez, Patrick Lin, Janet Lucroy; ed, Stephen Schaffer; m, Michael Giacchino; prod d, Lou Romano; art d, Ralph Eggleston; fx, Sandra Karpman; anim, Alan Barillaro, Tony Fucile, Steven Clay Hunter, Teddy Newton

AA Best Animated Feature Film; AA Best Sound Editing: Michael Silvers, Randy Thom; *AAN Best Sound Mixing:* Randy Thom, Gary A. Rizzo, Doc Kane; *AAN Best Original Screenplay:* Brad Bird

Brad Bird's rich homage to the superhero-fueled daydreams of his youth creates a vibrantly original mythology, heavily inflected by the lore of Marvel's *Fantastic Four* and spiked with allusions to James Bond, "Thunderbirds," and other '60s pop-culture touchstones.

We first see popular crime-fighters Mr. Incredible (voice of Craig T. Nelson), Elastigirl (Holly Hunter), and Frozone (Samuel L. Jackson) via "vintage" interview clips, followed by a sequence that encapsulates Mr. Incredible's bona fides. He tangles with super-villain Bomb Voyage (Dominique Louis), frees a treed cat, stops a runaway train, rescues a would-be suicide, brushes off persistent fan-boy Buddy (Jason Lee), and gets to his own wedding to Elastigirl. Fickle public favor, however, turns against fanciful superheroes, forcing the newlyweds to vanish into a federal relocation program. Fifteen years later, "Bob and Helen Parr" live in '60s deluxe-style suburban anonymity with teenage Violet (Sarah Vowell), 10-year-old Dash (Spencer Fox), and baby Jack Jack. The Parrs have taught their children to embrace conformity and conceal their superpowers while understanding all too well the strain of denying your nature. In fact, unbeknownst to Helen, Bob has been sneaking out at night with Frozone and righting wrongs for old times' sake. Bob's escapades attract the notice of mysterious femme fatale Mirage (Elizabeth Pena), who hires him to bring down a rampaging experimental battle droid. Mr. Incredible is back in the game!

Bird has great fun with every aspect of costumed righteousness, but his concerns run deeper than that. "They keep coming up with new ways to celebrate mediocrity," Bob says sadly, and it's clear that Bird yearns for a world in awe of the extraordinary. The result is truly a family film, not a kiddie time-waster that throws the occasional sop to adults.

INDECENT PROPOSAL

1993 118m c Romance/Drama ★★★
Sherry Lansing Productions (U.S.) R

Robert Redford (*John Gage*), Demi Moore (*Diana Murphy*), Woody Harrelson (*David Murphy*), Seymour Cassel (*Mr. Shackelford*), Oliver Platt (*Jeremy*), Billy Bob Thornton (*Day Tripper*), Rip Taylor (*Mr. Langford*), Billy Connolly (*Auction Emcee*), Joel Brooks (*Realtor*), Pierre Epstein (*Van Buren*)

p, Sherry Lansing; d, Adrian Lyne; w, Amy Holden Jones (from the novel by Jack Englehard); ph, Howard Atherton; ed, Joe Hutshing; m, John Barry; prod d, Mel Bourne; art d, Gae Buckley; fx, David Kelsey; cos, Bobbi Read, Bernie Pollack, Beatrix Aruna Pasztor

A huge commercial hit in theaters, INDECENT PROPOSAL should be able to crack two markets in the home video realm: as a feature film, and as an anthology of romantic screen cliches.

David (Woody Harrelson) and Diana Murphy (Demi Moore) are a devoted, financially strapped young couple faced with an unusual way out of their fiscal dilemma; a rich gambler (Robert Redford) offers $1,000,000 for a night of passion with the beautiful wife. If the premise is mildly intriguing, the execution is preposterous. This becomes clear after the first thirty seconds of soft-focus cinematography, over which we hear the following two lines of voiceover: Woody—"Losing Diana was like losing a part of me." Demi—"Someone once said that if you really love something, you should set it free." It's all downhill from there.

Director Adrian Lyne wastes no opportunity to show off Ms. Moore's pneumatic physique, which is the most noticeable feature of her performance. Robert Redford, meanwhile, seems fresh from the embalmer's studio—which at least puts his "young" rival Woody's receding hairline into flattering perspective. INDECENT PROPOSAL is as relentlessly entertaining as it is silly—so shamelessly over the top that you watch it in a mixture of horror and delight as the drama unfolds toward a climax that is truly mind-boggling.

INDEPENDENCE DAY

1996 146m c Science Fiction/Thriller/Action ★★½
Centropolis Entertainment/20th Century Fox PG-13
(U.S.)

Will Smith (*Captain Steve Hiller*), Bill Pullman (*President Thomas J. Whitmore*), Jeff Goldblum (*David Levinson*), Mary McDonnell (*Marilyn Whitmore*), Judd Hirsch (*Julius Levinson*), Robert Loggia (*General William Grey*), Randy Quaid (*Russell Casse*), Margaret Colin (*Constance Spano*), James Rebhorn (*Albert Nimziki*), Harvey Fierstein (*Marty Gilbert*)

p, Dean Devlin; d, Roland Emmerich; w, Dean Devlin, Roland Emmerich; ph, Karl Walter Lindenlaub; ed, David Brenner; m, David Arnold; prod d, Patrick Tatopoulos, Oliver Scholl; art d, Jim Teegarden; fx, Clay Pinney,

Volker Engel, Douglas Smith, Joseph Viskocil; cos, Joseph Porro

---

AA Best Visual Effects: Volker Engel, Douglas Smith, Clay Pinney, Joseph Viskocil; *AAN Best Sound:* Chris Carpenter, Bill W. Benton, Bob Beemer, Jeff Wexler

---

In technical terms, INDEPENDENCE DAY—one of the highest grossing films in history—is a masterpiece. As entertainment, it's effective in a bustling, bullying way, but sorely lacking in wonder, surprise, and eccentricity.

U.S. President Thomas J. Whitmore (Bill Pullman) tackles an apocalyptic crisis that no other world leader has ever faced—invasion from outer space. In spaceships so huge they shadow entire cities, the mysterious visitors make their intentions deadly obvious by unleashing global destruction. Out to save the world with good-old American chutzpah and a lot of firepower are New York physicist David Levinson (Jeff Goldblum), fighter-pilot Steve Hiller (Will Smith), and Russell Casse (Randy Quaid), the alcoholic survivor of a close encounter many years before.

In INDEPENDENCE DAY, the moviemaking team of director Roland Emmerich and screenwriter Dean Devlin (STARGATE) invent a state-of-the-art weapon that shoots satiric holes in sci-fi formulas, while at the same time asking viewers to surrender to the film's dramatic weight. At hairpin turns of the narrative, viewers are expected to be moved by events that the filmmakers themselves take lightly. One-dimensional characters defined only by ethnic shtick and no real emotional stakes mar the perfect course of annihilation that the film maps out. Viewed as a gung-ho flick extolling xenophobia, the film does acquire some snap, crackle, and pop, zapping spectators on a thrill-ride of inventive effects. INDEPENDENCE DAY can be enjoyed as a feel-good, Earthman's pep rally, but the science fiction is really just a sideshow to the main carnival celebrating Uncle Sam's destructive know-how and Hollywood's ever-bigger bang. Sadly, it is also the most benign movie ever made about the end of our universe.

INDIAN IN THE CUPBOARD, THE
1995 96m c Children's/Fantasy/Adventure ★★★½
Kennedy/Marshall Company/Scholastic PG
Productions/Paramount/Columbia (U.S.)

Hal Scardino *(Omri)*, Litefoot *(Little Bear)*, Lindsay Crouse *(Jane)*, Richard Jenkins *(Victor)*, Rishi Bhat *(Patrick)*, Steve Coogan *(Tommy)*, David Keith *(Boone)*, Sakina Jaffrey *(Lucy)*, Vincent Kartheiser *(Gillon)*, Nestor Serrano *(Teacher)*

p, Kathleen Kennedy, Frank Marshall, Jane Startz; d, Frank Oz; w, Melissa Mathison (based on the novel by Lynne Reid Banks); ph, Russell Carpenter; ed, Ian Crafford; m, Randy Edelman; prod d, Leslie McDonald; art d, Tony Fanning; fx, Eric Brevig, David Blitstein, Michael Lanteri, Ginger Theisen, Anne Calanchini, Industrial Light & Magic; cos, Deborah L. Scott

---

This exemplary work of political correctness boasts strong performances, low-key direction, and an intelligent screenplay. The film champions the validity of unfamiliar cultures and the importance of empathy without preaching.

Omri (Hal Scardino) lives with his family in New York, where he celebrates his ninth birthday. His presents include an old wooden cupboard, salvaged by older brother Gillon (Vincent Kartheiser), and a plastic figurine of an American Indian brave, a gift from Omri's best friend, Patrick (Rishi Bhat). Omri's mother (Lindsay Crouse) gives him an old key for the cupboard door. He places the plastic Indian inside, locks the door, and goes to sleep. Awakened by a sound from the cupboard, Omri finds that the Indian, an Iroquois named Little Bear (Litefoot), has come to life. Omri initially treats him like a pet, but he learns to respect him as he learns about Native American culture.

Adapted from the acclaimed children's book by Lynn Reid Banks, THE INDIAN IN THE CUPBOARD marks the return of screenwriter Melissa Mathison (aka Mrs. Harrison Ford) to movies. Best known for scripting E.T. THE EXTRA-TERRESTRIAL, Mathison excels at conjuring the private world of young boys. Director Frank Oz opts for solid story-telling over action set-pieces and star power. The special effects—though first-rate—fondly recall the quaint kiddie fantasies of yesteryear. The film's best aspects include the tender love of Omri's parents; the boy's quiet alliance with his mother; and the comparisons drawn between the lives of children, women, and the elderly, and figures of Otherness. The buck-toothed, beguiling Scardino is a welcome alternative to the standard cute kid star, and Litefoot is properly strong and dignified.

INDIANA JONES AND THE LAST CRUSADE
1989 127m c Adventure ★★½
Lucasfilm (U.S.) PG-13

Harrison Ford *(Indiana Jones)*, Sean Connery *(Dr. Henry Jones)*, Denholm Elliott *(Marcus Brody)*, Alison Doody *(Dr. Elsa Schneider)*, John Rhys-Davies *(Sallah)*, Julian Glover *(Walter Donovan)*, River Phoenix *(Young Indy)*, Michael Byrne *(Vogel)*, Kevork Malikyan *(Kazim)*, Robert Eddison *(Grail Knight)*

p, Robert Watts; d, Steven Spielberg; w, Jeffrey Boam (based on a story by George Lucas, Menno Meyjes, and characters created by Lucas, Philip Kaufman); ph, Douglas Slocombe (Rank Color), Paul Beeson, Robert Stevens; ed, Michael Kahn; m, John Williams; prod d, Elliot Scott; art d, Fred Hole, Stephen Scott, Richard Berger, Benjamin Fernandez, Guido Salsilli; cos, Anthony Powell, Joanna Johnston

---

AAN Best Original Score: John Williams; *AAN Best Sound:* Ben Burtt, Gary Summers, Shawn Murphy, Tony Dawe; *AA Best Sound Effects Editing:* Ben Burtt, Richard Hymns

---

We're over it. The third and mercifully, final installment in Steven Spielberg and George Lucas's INDIANA JONES series sends the intrepid adventurer out with more bucks than bang. This time Indy (Harrison Ford) has a sidekick in his archaeologist father, Dr. Henry Jones (Sean Connery), a relationship involving not a little Oedipal tension. Together, the Joneses embark on a quest to find the Holy Grail, hoping to keep it from the evil Nazis (who want it because it gives eternal life), and falling afoul of a beautiful spy (Alison Doody) along the way.

Proceeding with considerably less blood, energy or danger than either RAIDERS OF THE LOST ARK or INDIANA JONES AND THE TEMPLE OF DOOM, THE LAST CRUSADE hearkens more purely back to the series's sources—the fairly innocuous weekly cliffhangers of days gone by. The film offers some thrills and chills, but does so with such sanitized filmcraft that it's difficult to get excited about them. Despite strong acting (the slapstick energy between Ford and Connery is wasted), obligatory chases and stunts and splendid art direction, the virtuoso technique evident in every frame remains formulaic—unaccompanied by revelation, epiphany or surprise.

INDIANA JONES AND THE TEMPLE OF DOOM
1984 118m c Adventure ★★★
Lucasfilm (U.S.) PG

Harrison Ford *(Indiana Jones)*, Kate Capshaw *(Willie Scott)*, Ke Huy Quan *(Short Round)*, Amrish Puri *(Mola Ram)*, Roshan Seth *(Chattar Lal)*, Philip Stone *(Capt. Blumburtt)*, Roy Chiao *(Lao Che)*, David Yip *(Wu Han)*, Ric Young *(Kao Kan)*, Chua Kah Joo *(Chen)*

p, Robert Watts; d, Steven Spielberg; w, Willard Huyck, Gloria Katz (based on a story by George Lucas and on characters from RAIDERS OF THE LOST ARK); ph, Douglas Slocombe (Panavision, DeLuxe Color); ed, Michael Kahn; m, John Williams;

prod d, Elliot Scott; art d, Alan Cassie, Roger Cain, Joe Johnston, Errol Kelly; fx, Dennis Muren; chor, Danny Daniels; cos, Anthony Powell

AAN Best Original Score: John Williams; *AA Best Visual Effects:* Dennis Muren, Michael McAlister, Lorne Peterson, George Gibbs

After the release of director Steven Spielberg's RAIDERS OF THE LOST ARK, the question on almost everyone's lips was "How can he top this?" The answer won't be found in the $25 million sequel INDIANA JONES AND THE TEMPLE OF DOOM, a breakneck adventure that moves at twice the pace of the original but has only half the creative strength. The film opens with one of the decade's most purely entertaining scenes, a Busby Berkeley-style dance number to Cole Porter's "Anything Goes" (perhaps a clue to the line of logic the filmmakers were to follow). The setting is a swanky Shanghai nightclub in 1935 where heroic archaeologist Indiana Jones (Harrison Ford) has a run-in with some bad guys and is forced to make his getaway with singer Willie Scott (Kate Capshaw). Moments later they meet up with a 12-year-old named Short Round (Ke Huy Quan). The trio ends up in a primitive Indian village, where Jones is beckoned to retrieve a sacred stone from a heavily guarded palace and encounters a sanguinary Khali cult lifted from GUNGA DIN.

Director Spielberg has crammed ceaseless special effects, chases, and gross-outs into the film's nearly two hours. The nonstop pace may eventually numb viewers to the thrills, although Spielberg must be congratulated for adding some shades of character to his archetypal action hero this time around. The film is not helped by a xenophobia that sometimes verges on racism, or by its surprisingly graphic violence. A gruesome scene in which a beating heart is ripped from the chest of a sacrificial victim stirred controversy and prompted the MPAA to create the PG-13 rating.

INDISCREET

1958 100m c Romance/Comedy 🅳🆅🅳
Grandon (U.K.) ★★★½

Cary Grant *(Philip Adams)*, Ingrid Bergman *(Anna Kalman)*, Cecil Parker *(Alfred Munson)*, Phyllis Calvert *(Margaret Munson)*, David Kossoff *(Carl Banks)*, Megs Jenkins *(Doris Banks)*, Oliver Johnston *(Mr. Finleigh)*, Michael Anthony *(Oscar)*, Middleton Woods *(Finleigh's Clerk)*, Frank Hawkins

p, Stanley Donen; d, Stanley Donen; w, Norman Krasna (based on his play "Kind Sir"); ph, Freddie Young; ed, Jack Harris; m, Richard Rodney Bennett, Ken Jones; art d, Don Ashton; cos, Quintino

One of those rare movies that is far better than the play from which it was adapted. Based on Norman Krasna's Broadway flop, "Kind Sir," the movie is a frothy, often funny, diversion. Bergman, who proved her expertise in comedy with this performance, is a rich actress living in regal London luxury. Her sister, Calvert, and brother-in-law, Parker, introduce her to Grant, a financial genius who has come to London for a NATO dinner. Grant is a lifelong bachelor who masquerades as a married man to keep his single status secure. Grant tells Bergman that he's married, wich is fine with her. She has no interest in getting married and no compunctions about having an affair with a man who claims that he's separated and whose wife won't grant him freedom. Grant takes a job with NATO in Paris and their romance thrives as he comes to visit Bergman in London every weekend. When Grant is told he must transfer to New York for as long as five months, Bergman is at first heartbroken, then plans to quit the play she's appearing in and head for the U.S. herself. But Calvert, who has learned the truth about Grant's marital status, lets Bergman in on the secret. Hurt and angry, Bergman plots to arouse Grant's jealousy by feigning an affair with a former lover.

The play starred Charles Boyer and Mary Martin, and, as good as they were, Grant and Bergman eclipsed them in the movie. This was a throwback to the Philip Barry school of drawing room comedy, and both Grant and Bergman were up to the challenge of re-creating the kind of movie that had been popular 20 years before. (Many of those, after all, had starred Grant.) This was the second pairing of Bergman and Grant (the first was in Alfred Hitchcock's NOTORIOUS in 1946) and they make a wonderful screen team, both adroitly handling the film's humor. Not to be missed is Grant's impromptu dance at a proper London club. INDISCREET is the perfect film to watch when you just want to lean back and smile, knowing full well what the outcome will be. The only surprise in the picture is how deft a comedienne Bergman could be.

INFORMER, THE

1935 91m bw Drama
RKO (U.S.) ★★★★

Victor McLaglen *(Gypo Nolan)*, Heather Angel *(Mary McPhillip)*, Preston Foster *(Dan Gallagher)*, Margot Grahame *(Katie Madden)*, Wallace Ford *(Frankie McPhillip)*, Una O'Connor *(Mrs. McPhillip)*, J.M. Kerrigan *(Terry)*, Joe Sawyer *(Bartley Mulholland)*, Neil Fitzgerald *(Tommy Conner)*, Donald Meek *(Pat Mulligan)*

p, Cliff Reid; d, John Ford; w, Dudley Nichols (based on the novel by Liam O'Flaherty); ph, Joseph August; ed, George Hively; m, Max Steiner; art d, Van Nest Polglase, Charles Kirk; cos, Walter Plunkett

AAN Best Picture; AA Best Actor: Victor McLaglen; *AA Best Director:* John Ford; *AA Best Screenplay:* Dudley Nichols; *AA Best Score:* RKO Radio Studio Music Department, Max Stiener (Dept. Head); *AAN Best Film Editing:* George Hively

Victor McLaglen gave the performance of his life as the scar-faced betrayer, Gypo Nolan, in this telling adaptation of Liam O'Flaherty's novel, directed by John Ford. The film gleaned top honors from the Academy, winning Oscars for McLaglen as Best Actor, Dudley Nichols for Best Adaptation, Max Steiner for Best Musical Score, and Ford for Best Director (he also won the New York Critics Best Director award).

Ford's tale of a hard-drinking brute who informs on one of his friends in order to collect a reward during the Irish Civil War of 1922 was made for a mere $243,000, and stands as one of the director's finer 1930s films. Joseph August's photography is superb, with its atmospheric shadows and light; the studio sets are brilliant representations of a fog-bound 1920s Dublin, complete with wet cobblestones and sweating walls. Through this mythic setting Ford moves his characters stoically to their grim fates. His selection of Victor McLaglen, who had starred in his other memorable talkie, THE LOST PATROL, was a masterstroke. Barrel-chested, with a thunderous voice and ox-like shoulders, McLaglen was the perfect Gypo Nolan, his battered face jutting pugnaciously into the camera (he had once been Heavyweight Champion of Great Britain). McLaglen never again reached such heights, although he appeared in around 150 films.

The first of three features Ford did for RKO, THE INFORMER became the studio's most prestigious production for years. Writer Nichols, one of Ford's favorite collaborators, wrote the script in six days, and Ford shot the entire film within another 17 days. THE INFORMER marked a turning point both for Ford, just entering into his most productive period, and composer Steiner, whose marvelous score perfectly fits every scene, from thundering patriotic cadences to lyrical and evocative motifs. The O'Flaherty novel had previously been filmed by British International as a silent; a remake with an all-Black cast, directed by Jules Dassin under the title UPTIGHT!, appeared in 1968.

INHERIT THE WIND

DVD
1960 127m bw Drama ★★★★
UA (U.S.)

Fredric March *(Matthew Harrison Brady)*, Spencer Tracy *(Henry Drummond)*, Gene Kelly *(E.K. Hornbeck)*, Florence Eldridge *(Mrs. Brady)*, Dick York *(Bertram T. Cates)*, Donna Anderson *(Rachel Brown)*, Harry Morgan *(Judge)*, Elliott Reid *(Davenport)*, Philip Coolidge *(Mayor)*, Claude Akins *(Rev. Brown)*

p, Stanley Kramer; d, Stanley Kramer; w, Nedrick Young, Harold Jacob Smith (based on the play by Jerome Lawrence and Robert E. Lee); ph, Ernest Laszlo; ed, Frederic Knudtson; m, Ernest Gold; prod d, Rudolph Sternad; art d, Rudolph Sternad; cos, Joe King

AAN Best Actor: Spencer Tracy; *AAN Best Adapted Screenplay:* Nathan E. Douglas, Harold Jacob Smith; *AAN Best B/W Cinematography:* Ernest Laszlo; *AAN Best Film Editing:* Frederic Knudtson

Absorbing, if long-winded courtroom drama bolstered by two fine central performances from Tracy and March.

In the summer of 1925 the sovereign state of Tennessee played host to one of the most spectacular and ludicrous court trials in the history of American jurisprudence. A teacher named John T. Scopes had been arrested for teaching Darwin's theories of evolution in a public school, thus violating a state law. Prosecuting Scopes was the Rock of Ages fundamentalist, William Jennings Bryan, and defending him was the champion of liberal thinking, Clarence Darrow.

Producer-director Kramer used this high-voltage "Monkey Trial," as it came to be known, as the basis for one of his best film efforts. The names of the historical figures were all changed for the film, but their characters remain clearly recognizable. York plays the meek teacher, imprisoned for daring to teach Darwin in tiny Hillsboro. His girl friend is the daughter of fundamentalist preacher Akins, who agonizes over his daughter's affection for the religious infidel and sends for March to prosecute the young teacher. Tracy plays March's liberal opposite number, and song-and-dance man Kelly is inadequate as cynical journalist E.K. Hornbeck (based on H.L. Mencken).

INHERIT THE WIND acutely captures the farcical Monkey Trial and offers the awesome talents of two double-Oscar winners, Tracy and March, in their only film together. March's real wife, Florence Eldridge, plays his onscreen spouse, and Harry Morgan turns in a fine performance as the judge caught between heavyweights. Much of the dialog is lifted from the successful Broadway play by Lawrence and Lee and first starring Paul Muni and Ed Begley.

INNOCENCE

DVD
2000 94m c Drama/Romance ★★★★
Illumination Films/Fireworks Pictures
(Australia/Belgium) R

Julia Blake *(Claire)*, Charles Tingwell *(Andreas)*, Terry Norris *(John)*, Robert Menzies *(David)*, Marta Dusseldorp *(Monique)*, Kristien Van Pellicom *(Young Claire)*, Kenny Aernouts *(Young Andreas)*, Chris Haywood *(Minister)*, Norman Kaye *(Gerald)*, Joey Kennedy *(Sally)*

p, Paul Cox, Mark Patterson; d, Paul Cox; w, Paul Cox; ph, Tony Clark; ed, Simon Whitington; m, Paul Grabowsky; prod d, Tony Cronin; art d, Luco Volders; cos, Erwina Sleutel, Susie Warhurst-Steele

A beautifully acted, intensely felt story of an aging couple rekindling their first love five decades after they parted.

Retired music teacher Andreas (Charles Tingwell), a widower with a grown daughter (Marta Dusseldorp), discovers quite by accident that his first love, Claire (Julia Blake), is living in a nearby town. He sends her a friendly letter and suggests that they meet for lunch. Andreas soon realizes that he loves Claire as much as he ever did and that she feels the same way. But Claire's situation is complicated. While her marriage to Jack (Terry Norris) has become more a matter of companionship than passion, she's hesitant to throw their lives into turmoil. Nevertheless, after confronting her fears that she and Andreas are being ridiculous—she is, after all, nearly 70—Claire decides to follow her heart. As a devastated Jack tries to win her back, Andreas battles health problems that threaten to bring their hard-won idyll to a premature end.

Australian-based filmmaker Paul Cox skillfully weaves together the past and the present, slowly revealing the story of how the young Andreas (Kenny Aernouts) and Claire (Kristien Van Pellicom) met in post-war Belgium. Cox works the classic images of life's fleeting nature—water under bridges, trains passing—but does so with enough skill that they don't overwhelm the story. Standing in stark contrast to the condescending GRUMPY OLD MEN approach to romance between older people (the very *thought* is a joke), Cox's film is a complex, fully rounded portrait of two people whose sensuality and ardor is neither dampened nor cheapened by their age. The result is remarkably moving.

INNOCENCE UNPROTECTED

(NEVINOST BEZ ZASTITE)
1968 75m c/bw Drama ★★★★
Avala (Yugoslavia)

Dragoljub Aleksic *(Acrobat Aleksic)*, Ana Milosavljevic *(Nada The Orphan)*, Vera Jovanovic *(The Wicked Stepmother)*, Bratoljub Gligorijevic *(Mr. Petrovic)*, Ivan Zivkovic *(Aleksic's Brother)*, Pera Milosavljevic *(Servant)*

d, Dusan Makavejev; w, Dusan Makavejev; ph, Branko Perak, Stevan Miskovic (Eastmancolor); ed, Ivanka Vukasovic; m, Vojislav Dostic

In 1942, Aleksic, a Yugoslavian gymnast and stunt man, wrote, produced, directed, and starred in a film titled INNOCENCE UNPROTECTED. Its simple plot concerns an acrobat with a pure heart rescuing young Milosavljevic from the clutches of her evil stepmother, Jovanovic. The final production was subsequently confiscated by the Nazis, fading into cinema obscurity. Aleksic himself was accused (but later exonerated) of collaborating with the enemy. In 1968 Yugoslavian director Dusan Makavejev discovered the long-forgotten movie and reworked it into a film collage, a technique Makavejev further explored in WR: MYSTERIES OF THE ORGANISM. He hand-tinted some of the original footage and edited in newsreels of Nazi-occupied Yugoslavia. To this was added vintage documentary footage of Aleksic performing various stunts and new scenes with surviving members of the original film's cast and crew. The result is a wonderful and highly unusual film experience. Makavejev called it "a montage of attractions," an investigation of reality and illusion. The film is often confusing but full of ironies and biting humor, with a youthful exuberance emanating from both the director and Aleksic. A real love for the film medium irradiates the production.

INNOCENTS, THE

1961 99m bw Horror ★★★★
20th Century Fox/Achilles (U.S./U.K.)

Deborah Kerr *(Miss Giddens)*, Michael Redgrave *(The Uncle)*, Peter Wyngarde *(Peter Quint)*, Megs Jenkins *(Mrs. Grose)*, Martin Stephens *(Miles)*, Pamela Franklin *(Flora)*, Clytie Jessop *(Miss Jessel)*, Isla Cameron *(Anna)*, Eric Woodburn *(Coachman)*

p, Jack Clayton; d, Jack Clayton; w, William Archibald, Truman Capote, John Mortimer (based on the novel *The Turn of the Screw* by Henry James); ph, Freddie Francis (CinemaScope); ed, James B. Clark; m, Georges Auric; art d, Wilfred Shingleton; cos, Sophie Devine, Motley

---

Based on Henry James' *The Turn of the Screw*, THE INNOCENTS is a fine chiller that builds suspense slowly, subtly, and inexorably. Kerr is on top form here, enacting a role that takes perfect advantage of her respectable facade wrestling with unspeakable turbulence beneath the surface.

In Victorian England, Kerr arrives at the country estate of Redgrave, who has hired her to serve as the governess of his young niece and nephew, Franklin and Stephens. The housekeeper, Jenkins, introduces her to Franklin, an angelic little child with a beguiling smile who appears to have a mysterious foreknowledge of her brother's imminent arrival, though he is not expected. Soon a letter arrives from Stephens' school, informing the household that the boy has been expelled because he is a corrupting influence on his schoolmates. However, when Stephens arrives, he proves to be every bit as innocent and entrancing as his sister, and Kerr decides that the school officials must have been mistaken. Though the estate is a beautiful refuge, there is also an air of eeriness about the place. Kerr thinks she sees a man atop the house, is temporarily blinded by the sun, and then discovers Stephens feeding pigeons where she thought the man was. Feeling that her eyes must have played tricks on her, she calms down; later, however, she sees the specter of a woman at a window, and then sees the man again, getting a glimpse of his twisted face. When she describes these apparitions to Jenkins, she is told that the descriptions match those of the estate's late manager and his dead lover, the woman who preceded Kerr as governess. Kerr learns further that the deceased lovers had a sadomasochistic relationship, and that they had a considerable influence on the children. Are the children possessed by evil, earthbound spirits or is Kerr going mad?

Filmed at Sheffield Park in Sussex, this literate and elegant gothic horror, co-scripted by Truman Capote and John Mortimer, is fairly faithful to the James original. THE INNOCENTS manipulates the viewer's imagination as few films can, with Kerr and Redgrave doing a masterful job of creating a sense of repressed hysteria.

INSIDE DAISY CLOVER

1965 128m c Drama ★★
Warner Bros. (U.S.)

Natalie Wood *(Daisy Clover)*, Christopher Plummer *(Raymond Swan)*, Robert Redford *(Wade Lewis)*, Roddy McDowall *(Walter Baines)*, Ruth Gordon *(The Dealer)*, Katharine Bard *(Melora Swan)*, Betty Harford *(Gloria Goslett)*, John Hale *(Harry Goslett)*, Harold Gould *(Cop)*, Ottola Nesmith *(Old Lady in Hospital)*

p, Alan J. Pakula, Robert Mulligan; d, Robert Mulligan; w, Gavin Lambert (based on his own novel); ph, Charles Lang (Panavision, Technicolor); ed, Aaron Stell; m, Andre Previn; prod d, Robert Clatworthy; art d, Dean Tavoularis; chor, Herbert Ross; cos, Bill Thomas, Edith Head

---

AAN Best Supporting Actress: Ruth Gordon; AAN Best Art Direction-Set Decoration (Color): Robert Clatworthy (Art Direction), George James Hopkins (Set Decoration); AAN Best Costume Design (Color): Bill Thomas, Edith Head

---

Too much, too soon, for Daisy and for us. Gothic Hollywood-insider account of a Garland-like waif-star suffers from weak characters and minimalist (to say the least) plot. Gavin Lambert's screenplay (from his novel), throws us one big, hammy campfest scene, followed by another that expects us to take it seriously. Wood's teen star comes close to conjuring up Mickey Rooney in his show-in-the-barn phase; Ruth Gordon is abominable as a sort of Gladys Baker (Marilyn Monroe's mother) character; and Christopher Plummer plays his scenes like he's trying to run through a swimming pool. It's only Redford's narcissistic gay star that holds interest. (He won a Golden Globe as "Star of Tommorrow" for the role.) The songs by Andre and Dory Previn are, amazingly, musical ciphers, which is both disappointing and surprising. Most songwriters would give their eyeteeth for an excuse to write rich, full-blooded Golden Era showbiz songs.

INSIDER, THE DVD

1999 155m c Docudrama ★★★½
Mann/Roth Productions/Forward Pass Pictures/ R
Touchstone (U.S.)

Al Pacino *(Lowell Bergman)*, Russell Crowe *(Jeffrey Wigand)*, Christopher Plummer *(Mike Wallace)*, Diane Venora *(Liane Wigand)*, Philip Baker Hall *(Don Hewitt)*, Lindsay Crouse *(Sharon Tiller)*, Debi Mazar *(Debbie De Luca)*, Stephen Tobolowsky *(Eric Kluster)*, Colm Feore *(Richard Scruggs)*, Bruce McGill *(Ron Motley)*

p, Michael Mann, Pieter Jan Brugge; d, Michael Mann; w, Eric Roth, Michael Mann (based on the *Vanity Fair* article "The Man Who New Too Much" by Marie Brenner); ph, Dante Spinotti; ed, William Goldenberg, Paul Rubell, David Rosenbloom; m, Lisa Gerrard, Pieter Bourke; prod d, Brian Morris; art d, Nancy Haigh; fx, John Gray; cos, Anna Sheppard

---

AAN Best Picture; AAN Best Actor: Russell Crowe; AAN Best Director: Michael Mann; AAN Best Cinematography: Dante Spinotti; AAN Best Film Editing: William Goldenberg, Paul Rubell, David Rosenbloom; AAN Best Sound: Andy Nelson, Doug Hemphill, Lee Orloff; AAN Best Adapted Screenplay: Eric Roth, Michael Mann

---

An exciting dramatization of the strange events that marked the turning of the legal tide against Big Tobacco in the U.S., and a particularly dark moment in the annals of the respected CBS television news division.

In 1992, researcher Jeffrey Wigand (Russell Crowe) was making $300,000 a year at Brown & Williamson, America's third-largest tobacco company; a year later, he was living incognito and fearing for his life. What happened? Fired soon after he began raising uncomfortable questions about how much B&W execs knew about nicotine addiction and carcinogenic additives, Wigand went to CBS *60 Minutes* producer Lowell Bergman (Al Pacino), who urged him to sit for an interview with respected on-air journalist Mike Wallace (Christopher Plummer). Wigand further violated his confidentiality agreement with B&W by giving a deposition as part of Mississippi State Attorney General Michael Moore's attempt to sue major tobacco companies for billions in government payments for treatment of smoking-related ailments. The fall-out—restraining orders, a nasty personal smear campaign, even death threats—nearly destroyed Wigand's life, and CBS, nervous about potential lawsuits that might interfere with the network's impending sale, pressured *60 Minutes* into pulling the segment.

As corporate muckraking, director Michael Mann's film is as factually accurate as it needs to be; as entertainment, it's gripping. Dante Spinotti's hand-held cinematography enhances Mann's expressionistic style, and what could have been dull expository scenes are suffused with a sense of creeping paranoia and dynamically staged (what did directors do before cell phones?). Crowe's white-knuckled performance raises interesting questions about Wigand (before he's dropped in favor of Bergman's less-problematic heroics), and Pacino brims with righteous brio. But this version of events is surprisingly soft on CBS News: the ethical fiasco is conveniently blamed on greedy corporate counsel.

INSOMNIA

1998 97m c Crime/Thriller
Norsk Film/Nordic Screen (Norway)

DVD
★★★½

Stellan Skarsgard *(Jonas Engstrom)*, Sverre Anker Ousdal *(Erik Vik)*, Bjorn Floberg *(Jon Holt)*, Gisken Armand *(Hilde Hagen)*, Maria Bonnevie *(Ane)*, Kristian Figenschow *(Arne Zakariassen)*, Thor Michael Aamodt *(Tom Engen)*, Bjorn Moan *(Eilert)*, Marianne O. Ulrichsen *(Froya)*, Frode Rasmussen *(Chief of Police)*

p, Anne Frilseth; d, Erik Skjoldbjaerg; w, Erik Skjoldbjaerg, Nikolaj Frobenius; ph, Erling Thurmann-Andersen; ed, Hakon Overas; m, Geir Jenssen; prod d, Eli Bo; cos, Runa Fonne

Scandinavia's palookaville, it appears, is in northern Norway, and Swedish police inspector Jonas Engstrom (Stellan Skarsgard) resents the hell out of being there. Engstrom and his partner, Erik Vik (Sverre Anker Ousdal), have been called in to investigate the murder of a local 17-year-old named Tanja (Maria Mathiesen), who left a party after a fight with her boyfriend and was later found, her body nude and washed clean, in a garbage dump. The aloof Engstrom launches a methodical investigation, but both he and it begin to unravel after the clever trap he sets for the killer goes awry: in a moment of fog-bound chaos, Engstrom accidentally shoots Vik, then makes the split-second decision to cover up the mistake and blame Vik's death on Tanja's still-at-large murderer. Aggravated by the 24-hour glare of Norway's midsummer sun, which allows sleeplessness to fray his nerves, the strain of investigating one death while trying to cover up the circumstances of another leads Engstrom into a bizarre relationship with a calculating psychopath.

Norwegian director Erik Skjoldbjaerg's coolly detached first feature is a dyed-in-the-wool film noir that rejects every cliché of American crime thrillers with chilly disdain. The film's tone is reserved and perpetually wary; few bullets fly, no cars careen, and neither prostitutes nor strippers play a part in the story, though there is a sullenly Lolita-ish teen named Froya (Marianne O. Ulrichsen). Rather than a thrill ride, it's a sliver of ice through the heart.

INSOMNIA

2002 118m c Crime/Thriller
Alcon Entertainment/Section Eight/Witt/Thomas
Productions (U.S.)

DVD
★★★
R

Al Pacino *(Will Dormer)*, Robin Williams *(Walter Finch)*, Hilary Swank *(Ellie Burr)*, Maura Tierney *(Rachel Clement)*, Martin Donovan *(Hap Eckhart)*, Nicky Katt *(Fred Duggar)*, Paul Dooley *(Chief Charles Nyback)*, Jonathan Jackson *(Randy Stetz)*, Katherine Isabelle *(Tanya Francke)*, Oliver Zemen, billed as Oliver "Ole" Zemen *(Pilot)*

p, Broderick Johnson, Andrew A. Kosove, Edward L. McDonnell, Paul Junger Witt; d, Christopher Nolan; w, Hilary Seitz (based on the screenplay *Insomnia* by Nikolaj Frobenius and Erik Skjoldbjaerg); ph, Wally Pfister; ed, Dody Dorn; m, David Julyan; prod d, Nathan Crowley; art d, Michael Diner; fx, Randy Skymkiw; cos, Tish Monaghan

A resolutely old-fashioned cop movie and the major studio debut of director Christopher Nolan, whose independents FOLLOWING and MEMENTO relied on fiendishly fragmented storytelling to revitalize conventional narratives.

Embroiled in a serious internal affairs investigation, LAPD detectives Will Dormer (Al Pacino) and Hap Eckhart (Martin Donovan) are dispatched to help the small-town police force of Nightmute, AK, solve the murder of a local teen (Crystal Lowe). The partners know it's simply an excuse to get them out of town until the storm blows over, but the younger Eckhart is nervous; he's been offered a deal and plans to take it, swearing that he won't implicate Dormer. The trouble creates a chill between them, and Dormer is thrown by the 24-hour daylight that characterizes Alaskan summers; he can't sleep. Dormer advises the local police to set a trap for the killer, but the plan goes awry. In the ensuing scramble through the foggy, unfamiliar terrain, Dormer accidentally shoots and kills Eckhart. Everyone thinks the bullet came from the suspect's gun and the pro forma report on the incident is assigned to rookie Ellie Burr (Hilary Swank), Dormer's biggest admirer. Then, as Dormer endures another sleepless night, the killer (Robin Williams) calls. He saw the accident, and knows that Eckhart thought Dormer did it on purpose. He thinks Dormer could—and should—help him beat his own murder rap.

Nolan's reworking of the chilling Norwegian thriller INSOMNIA is slick and creepy; he elicits one of Pacino's most effectively subdued performances in years and uses Williams sparingly. Fans of the original will miss its relentless dyspepsia, but Nolan's intention was clearly to cast the material in a more conventional Hollywood mold without turning it into namby-pamby nonsense, and he succeeds admirably.

INTERIORS

1978 93m c Drama
UA (U.S.)

DVD
★★★½
PG

Kristin Griffith *(Flyn)*, Mary Beth Hurt *(Joey)*, Richard Jordan *(Frederick)*, Diane Keaton *(Renata)*, E.G. Marshall *(Arthur)*, Geraldine Page *(Eve)*, Maureen Stapleton *(Pearl)*, Sam Waterston *(Mike)*, Henderson Forsythe *(Judge Bartel)*

p, Charles H. Joffe; d, Woody Allen; w, Woody Allen; ph, Gordon Willis (Technicolor); ed, Ralph Rosenblum; prod d, Mel Bourne; cos, Joel Schumacher

AAN Best Actress: Geraldine Page; *AAN Best Supporting Actress:* Maureen Stapleton; *AAN Best Director:* Woody Allen; *AAN Best Original Screenplay:* Woody Allen (Story); *AAN Best Art Direction:* Mel Bourne (Art Direction), Daniel Robert (Art Direction)

Allen fans didn't like this stark examination of love, life, and death because they kept expecting it to turn funny and it never did. INTERIORS nevertheless represented an important and impressive change of direction for Allen, who here pays explicit homage to one of his acknowledged mentors, Ingmar Bergman—he even goes as far as to employ some of the master's best-known techniques, photographing the principals against blank walls and having them speak directly into the camera.

Wealthy Arthur (Marshall) and mentally disturbed Eve (Page) are the parents of three daughters. Arthur announces one day that he is leaving his wife to marry Pearl (Stapleton, in a role that gives the film its heart). The news causes Eve to disintegrate, and the daughters rush to their mother's side to help her through the crisis, even though they are having problems of their own. Renata (Keaton) is a poet married to a hack novelist (Jordan). Joey (Hurt), the most talented of the trio, seems incapable of focusing her abilities. Flyn (Griffith), meanwhile, a TV actress, is intensely self-centered. How the family deals with its problems forms the core of the film. The acting is outstanding all around, with special mention going to Hurt, Marshall, Page and Stapleton. Nominated for Oscars for writing, direction, actress (Page, inexplicably defeated by Jane Fonda in COMING HOME) and supporting actress.

INTERMEZZO: A LOVE STORY

1939 70m bw Romance
Selznick (U.S.)

DVD
★★★½

Leslie Howard *(Holger Brandt)*, Ingrid Bergman *(Anita Hoffman)*, Edna Best *(Margit Brandt)*, John Halliday *(Thomas Stenborg)*, Cecil Kellaway *(Charles Moler)*, Enid Bennett *(Greta Stenborg)*, Ann Todd *(Ann Marie Brandt)*, Douglas Scott *(Eric Brandt)*, Eleanor Wesselhoeft *(Emma)*, Marie Flynn *(Marianne)* p, David O. Selznick; d, Gregory Ratoff; w, George O'Neil (based on a story by Gosta Stevens and Gustaf Molander); ph, Gregg Toland; ed, Hal C. Kern, Francis D. Lyon; m, Heinz Provost; art d, Lyle Wheeler; fx, Jack Cosgrove; cos, Irene, Travis Banton

AAN Best B/W Cinematography: Gregg Toland; *AAN Best Score:* Louis Forbes

Bergman made her American debut in this somewhat saccharine romance, becoming a star of the first magnitude almost overnight. An established actress in her native Sweden, she had appeared in a Swedish production of the same story in 1937, but it lacked the rich production values Selznick and Howard (who coproduced and starred) infused into this version.

Howard plays Holger Brandt, a brilliant, aging violinst weary of his great fame. After a successful tour, he returns to Sweden to the arms of his wife Margit (Best) and adoring children (Todd and Scott). Deeply attracted to the fresh-faced, bright-eyed Anita (Bergman), the children's piano teacher, he joins her in an impromptu recital before the family. Soon the pair discover that they are in love and Holger asks Margit for his freedom. She still loves him, though, and asks him to take time to reconsider. Holger and Anita travel abroad and she becomes his accompanist, to considerable acclaim. But Anita notices how Holger dotes on other people's children, and she decides that happiness is not built on the sadness of others.

Appealingly Continental in look and style, INTERMEZZO continually verges on soap, but is redeemed by carefully calibrated performances and Ratoff's loving direction. Beautifully photographed, the film won Toland an Oscar nomination (he lost to himself for his work on WUTHERING HEIGHTS). The memorable theme music, "Intermezzo" (composed by Heinz Provost), became a tremendously popular hit.

INTERPRETER, THE
2005 123m c Thriller ★★½
Working Title Films/Misher Films/Mirage PG-13
Enterprises/MP Jota Productions (U.S./U.K./France)

Nicole Kidman *(Silvia Broome)*, Sean Penn *(Tobin Keller)*, Catherine Keener *(Dot Woods)*, Jesper Christensen *(Nils Lud)*, Yvan Attal *(Philippe)*, Earl Cameron *(Edmond Zuwanie)*, George Harris *(Kuman-Kuman)*, Hugo Speer *(Simon Broome)*, Patrick Ssenjovu *(Jad Jamal)*, Michael Wright *(Marcus)*

p, Tim Bevan, Eric Fellner, Kevin Misher; d, Sydney Pollack; w, Scott Frank, Charles Randolph, Steven Zaillian (based on an story by Martin Stellman and Brian Ward); ph, Darius Khondji; ed, William Steinkamp; m, James Newton Howard; prod d, Jon Hutman; art d, Tom Warren; fx, Jon Farhat, R. Bruce Steinheimer; cos, Sarah Edwards

Sydney Pollack's restrained, bloodless potboiler aims to be an alternative to the brainless, frenetic action cartoons that have supplanted intelligent political thrillers like Pollack's own THREE DAYS OF THE CONDOR, but its talky, sluggish script is bereft of thrills, intellectual or otherwise.

United Nations interpreter Silvia Broome (Nicole Kidman, employing a nonspecific British colonial accent) returns to work after hours and overhears an urgent, whispered threat in Ku, an obscure dialect of sub-Saharan Matobo (a fictitious country that strongly suggests Zimbabwe) where Silvia was raised. The life of Matoban dictator Edmond Zuwanie (Earl Cameron) is on the line, and after trying to contact her estranged brother (Hugo Speer) in Matobo and learning that Zuwanie is coming to the UN, Silvia reluctantly reports the threat. To her shock and dismay, Silvia realizes that federal agent Tobin Keller (Sean Penn), who's dispatched to interview her, is not only *not* assigned to protect her, but thinks she's lying. The threat, however, can't be ignored, so as Zuwanie's visit approaches, the high-strung Keller and his partner

(Catherine Keener) pursue an increasingly urgent investigation that turns up a host of suspicious sorts with shadowy motives. They include Zuwanie's sinister security chief (Jesper Christensen); exiled rebel leader Kuman-Kuman (George Harris); shady Matoban nationals Jean Gamba (Byron Utley) and Jad Jamal (Patrick Ssenjovu); and roving French photographer Philippe (Yvan Attal).

Though it's hard to watch skillful actors like Kidman and Penn spinning their wheels, the real shame of this deeply flawed picture is that it promises so much, then sacrifices the stark, complex interplay of global power and self-interest on the altar of sloppy emotional machinations and the pop-psych grail of closure.

INTERVIEW WITH THE VAMPIRE
1994 122m c Horror/Drama ★★★
Geffen Pictures (U.S./United Kingdom) R

Tom Cruise *(Lestat de Lioncourt)*, Brad Pitt *(Louis Pointe du Lac)*, Antonio Banderas *(Armand)*, Stephen Rea *(Santiago)*, Christian Slater *(Daniel Malloy—The Interviewer)*, Kirsten Dunst *(Claudia)*, Domiziana Giordano *(Madeleine)*, Thandie Newton *(Yvette)*, Virginia McCollam *(Whore on Waterfront)*, John McConnell *(Gambler)*

p, Stephen Woolley, David Geffen; d, Neil Jordan; w, Anne Rice (based on her novel); ph, Philippe Rousselot; ed, Mick Audsley, Joke Van Wijk; m, Elliot Goldenthal; prod d, Dante Ferretti; art d, Malcolm Middleton, Alan Tomkins, Jean-Michel Ducourty; fx, Rob Legato, Yves De Bono, Cari Thomas; cos, Sandy Powell, John Scott, Deirdre Williams

AAN Best Art Direction-Set Decoration: Dante Ferretti, Francesca Lo Schiavo; *AAN Best Original Score:* Elliot Goldenthal

This darkly effective horror drama holds plenty of interest, even for those who find Anne Rice's gothic cult novels unreadable.

In contemporary San Francisco, young interviewer Daniel Malloy (Christian Slater) is approached by Louis (Brad Pitt), who claims to be a vampire and tells Daniel his story. A flashback to late 18th-century Louisiana shows Louis as a 24-year-old plantation owner who sinks into a depression after the deaths of his wife and child. He meets the roguish vampire Lestat (Tom Cruise), who grants him eternal life in death. But while Lestat delights in draining his youthful victims, Louis cannot bring himself to do murder and subsists on animals. When he breaks down and attacks a young girl, Claudia (Kirsten Dunst), Lestat brings her back to life, and she becomes Louis's close companion.

Nearly two decades after the publication of Anne Rice's novel, the news that *Interview With the Vampire* was finally coming to the screen no doubt warmed the hearts of Rice's fans. Yet they were outraged when Cruise was announced for the Lestat role, and Rice herself repeatedly blasted the choice in interviews. After viewing the movie, however, Rice had a two-page retraction printed in national periodicals, and it's not hard to see why. INTERVIEW WITH THE VAMPIRE is a dark, lush, and reasonably faithful adaptation of Rice's novel. Cruise is masterful; his Lestat is a devilishly appealing but convincingly dangerous creature of the night. Throughout, director Neil Jordan recalls the haunting mix of dark psychodrama and visceral horror he brought to 1984's THE COMPANY OF WOLVES.

VAMPIRE's best (and funniest) moments chart the dynamics of a decidedly non-traditional family unit, with Louis and Lestat playing proud papas to the precocious Claudia. Lestat's desperate assertions of paternal authority— "Never [kill] in the house!"—make for subversive domestic comedy that's only heightened by contrast with the film's predominantly grim (and very gory) tone.

INTRUDER IN THE DUST
1949 87m bw Drama ★★★★
MGM (U.S.)

David Brian (*John Gavin Stevens*), Claude Jarman Jr. (*Chick Mallison*), Juano Hernandez (*Lucas Beauchamp*), Elizabeth Patterson (*Miss Habersham*), Charles Kemper (*Crawford Gowrie*), Will Geer (*Sheriff Hampton*), David Clarke (*Vinson Gowrie*), Elzie Emanuel (*Aleck*), Lela Bliss (*Mrs. Mallison*)

p, Clarence Brown; d, Clarence Brown; w, Ben Maddow (based on the novel by William Faulkner); ph, Robert Surtees; ed, Robert J. Kern; m, Adolph Deutsch; art d, Cedric Gibbons, Randall Duell

The lack of big name stars is, if anything, a plus in making this one of the most powerful movies ever made about racism. Based on Faulkner's novel and filmed on location near the writer's native Oxford, MI, Brown's film features more than 500 people, only a small portion of whom were professional actors. Hernandez plays Lucas Beauchamp, an elderly black man who owns his own property, something the locals resent. The police arrest him for the murder of a townsman because he was discovered near the body and the revolver he carried had just been fired. On the way to jail he spots Chick (Jarman), a young white lad with whom he is friendly. He asks Chick to get Stevens (Brian), the boy's attorney uncle, to come to the jail. Despite Chick's pleas, Stevens resists the idea of defending Lucas, knowing he'll be ostracized by the townspeople if he does. Crawford Gowrie (Kemper), brother of the dead man, spreads the word, and the lawyer becomes a pariah as Gowrie rouses the rabble to lynch Beauchamp. The jailed man, though, has his story, which involves a beating he suffered at the hands of the victim. Lucas' supporters grow as Chick and Miss Habersham (Patterson) help dig up the dead man's coffin to prove that Lucas' gun was not the murder weapon. When the corpse is found instead in a quicksand swamp, even the dead man's father (Hall) has his doubts. Finally the canny Sheriff Hampton (Geer) uses a ruse to catch the real killer and the lynch-hungry mob is confronted with its own bigotry.

The most chilling scene in the movie is a lengthy sequence which cuts from the people of Oxford gleefully assembling (not unlike the crowd to see the man trapped below ground in THE BIG CARNIVAL) at the jail for a lynching to shots of music playing and kids eating ice cream. Everyone is in a jolly mood, in direct contrast to the grisly plans they have for the prisoner. This is not a pretty story and it does not exactly feature the people of Mississippi in a flattering light. Brown must have had a silver tongue to convince so many locals to play in the film, when one considers how they are portrayed. After many years of seeing stereotyped blacks on screen, Hernandez's role was a revelation as he stood up to the charges with pride and dignity. Patterson is equally marvelous in one of the finest roles of her lengthy career.

INVASION OF THE BODY SNATCHERS `DVD`
1956 80m bw Science Fiction ★★★★
Allied Artists (U.S.)

Kevin McCarthy (*Miles Bennel*), Dana Wynter (*Becky Driscoll*), Larry Gates (*Dr. Dan Kauffmann*), King Donovan (*Jack*), Carolyn Jones (*Theodora*), Jean Willes (*Sally*), Ralph Dumke (*Nick Grivett*), Virginia Christine (*Wilma Lentz*), Tom Fadden (*Uncle Ira Lentz*), Kenneth Patterson (*Driscoll*)

p, Walter Wanger; d, Don Siegel; w, Geoffrey Homes (based on the novel *The Body Snatchers* by Jack Finney); ph, Ellsworth Fredricks; ed, Robert S. Eisen; m, Carmen Dragon; prod d, Joseph Kish; art d, Ted Haworth; fx, Milt Rice

A superbly crafted film by innovative director Siegel, this low-budget science fiction tale became one of the great cult classics of the genre.

Miles (McCarthy), a doctor from the small town of Santa Mira, arrives in San Francisco in hysterical condition; he raves that his community has been invaded by aliens who have literally taken over the bodies of his friends and relatives. He's a candidate for the lunatic asylum, most agree, but they hear him out, and the story unfolds in flashback. Miles has returned home from a medical convention to find that many people have been complaining that their loved ones somehow don't appear to be the same people as before. He also runs into Becky (Wynter), an old girlfriend and recent divorcee, and they both note how odd it is that all the complaints seem to be suddenly vanishing. Miles and Becky have dinner with two friends (Donovan and Jones) and, to their horror, the quartet discover enormous pods growing in the couple's greenhouse which open to reveal exact physical reproductions of each of them. Miles and Becky run for their lives; half the population of the town, including the police, has been replaced. The phone system is also in the alien grip: when Miles tries to call federal authorities, operators tell him that all the lines to Washington are tied up. Miles and Becky later witness the police directing locals to drive their pod-filled cars to neighboring towns, and they realize that the whole world is in great danger. The local psychiatrist (Gates) catches them and arranges for two pods to be placed in the next room. The sinister shrink explains that all Miles and Becky have to do is go to sleep; they will awaken as one of the new creatures and will never again know pain, hate, or worry. Miles counters that they will also be without joy or love, and he and Becky attempt to escape.

This film was originally conceived by producer Wanger as standard B fare, but Siegel made much more of it, with writer Mainwaring injecting an element of subtle humor. It's since come to seem typical of '50s paranoia about everything from the Red Scare to nuclear warfare. INVASION spawned a remake, starring Donald Sutherland, in 1978, and another one in 1994.

INVASION OF THE BODY SNATCHERS `DVD`
1978 115m c Science Fiction ★★½
UA (U.S.) PG

Donald Sutherland (*Matthew Bennell*), Brooke Adams (*Elizabeth Driscoll*), Leonard Nimoy (*Dr. David Kibner*), Veronica Cartwright (*Nancy Bellicec*), Art Hindle (*Geoffrey*), Lelia Goldoni (*Katherine*), Kevin McCarthy (*Running Man*), Jeff Goldblum (*Jack Bellicec*), Don Siegel (*Cab Driver*)

p, Robert H. Solo; d, Philip Kaufman; w, W.D. Richter (based on the novel by Jack Finney); ph, Michael Chapman (Technicolor); ed, Douglas Stewart; m, Denny Zeitlin; prod d, Charles Rosen; fx, Dell Rheaume, Russ Hessey

Colorful and expensive remake of the 1956 sci-fi classic, with mopey, sleepy-eyed Sutherland playing the part originated by Kevin McCarthy, a health inspector giving a hard time to San Francisco restaurant owners when he finds rat droppings in their kitchens. Instead of the original setting, a little town in California, the setting here is the sprawling city of San Francisco, now under alien attack by the mysterious pods (with Nimoy as the psychiatrist advocating the takeover). The film collapses midway—because of unsure and sloppy direction, splintered story continuity, and the overacting of Adams, Cartwright, and others. The battle between Sutherland and the aliens in the "pod factory" at the end is simply absurd and sophomoric. In a nod to the earlier classic, McCarthy appears at the beginning of the film, shouting hysterical warnings to motorists until he is struck and killed by a car. A great number of shots show the Transamerica pyramid building in downtown San Francisco, a subtle plug for the distributor of the movie, whose corporate offices are housed there.

INVESTIGATION OF A CITIZEN ABOVE SUSPICION
(INDAGINE SU UN CITTADINO AL DI SOPRA DI OGNI SOSPETTO)

1970 112m c Crime ★★★★

Vera (Italy) R

Gian Maria Volonte *(Police Inspector)*, Florinda Bolkan *(Augusta Terzi)*, Salvo Randone *(Plumber)*, Gianni Santuccio *(Police Commissioner)*, Arturo Dominici *(Mangani)*, Orazio Orlando *(Biglia)*, Sergio Tramonti *(Antonio Pace)*, Massimo Foschi *(Augusta's Husband)*, Aldo Rendine *(Homicide Functionary)*, Aleka Paizi

p, Daniele Senatore; d, Elio Petri; w, Ugo Pirro, Elio Petri; ph, Luigi Kuveiller (Technicolor); ed, Ruggero Mastroianni; m, Ennio Morricone; prod d, Romano Cardarelli; cos, Angela Sammaciccia, Mayer

AA Best Foreign Language Film ; AAN Best Original Story and Screenplay: Elio Petri, Ugo Pirro

The winner of 1970's foreign film Oscar, this jarring and potent Italian film tells the story of a recently promoted Fascist police inspector (Volonte) who one Sunday afternoon slits his mistress's throat. He then plants phony evidence and makes an anonymous call to report the crime. The police unearth clues that point to the inspector, but ignore them because of his standing. The killer eventually writes a confession and awaits his capture, while planning to receive an acquittal.

An excellent look into the mind of a murderer, INVESTIGATION features a fine performance from Volonte in the leading role. Director Petri has made an antifascist statement that is both pointed and poignant, full of eerie, unsettling moods abetted by Morricone's score. A piercing satire of Italian investigative techniques, and an interesting meditation on the relationship between class and guilt.

INVISIBLE MAN, THE 📀

1933 71m bw Science Fiction ★★★★½

Universal (U.S.)

Claude Rains *(Jack Griffin/The Invisible One)*, Gloria Stuart *(Flora Cranley)*, William Harrigan *(Doctor Kemp)*, Henry Travers *(Dr. Cranley)*, Una O'Connor *(Mrs. Jenny Hall)*, Forrester Harvey *(Mr. Herbert Hall)*, Holmes Herbert *(Chief of Police)*, E.E. Clive *(Jaffers)*, Dudley Digges *(Chief of Detectives)*, Harry Stubbs *(Inspector Bird)*

p, Carl Laemmle Jr.; d, James Whale; w, Philip Wylie (uncredited), R.C. Sherriff (based on the novel by H.G. Wells); ph, Arthur Edeson; m, W. Franke Harling; art d, Charles D. Hall; fx, John P. Fulton, John Mescall

Few debuts have been as impressive or odd as that made by the voice of Claude Rains in this macabre classic based on the novel by H.G. Wells. (Actually, there's a glimpse of the rest of Rains, too, but not until the very end.)

Jack Griffin (Rains) is an English scientist who has been experimenting with a drug called monocaine which, he finds, has made his entire body invisible. He goes to the small village of Ipping, wrapped in bandages and wearing dark glasses, and takes a room at the local inn to continue his research in secret. This subsequently arouses the curiosity of the nosy locals. As Griffin continues his experiments, he begins to suffer from drug-induced megalomania, which eventually becomes full-blown madness. He begins to terrorize the countryside—first playing pranks, and then turning to murder.

Memorable moments and lines of dialogue pepper this striking fantasy: Griffin informing his terrified, unwilling

assistant Kemp, "We'll start with a few murders. Small men. Great men. Just to show we make no distinction"; any of the scenes involving the priceless Una O'Connor as the innkeeper's flighty wife; the farmer's discovery of breathing in his barn. Whale was always fascinated by the inconveniences of being a monster and Griffin tells us how it's hard to walk down steps when you can't see your feet. Best of all, though, is the scene where the enraged scientist first takes off his disguise and to the amazement of the locals reveals … nothing. Fine acting all around, especially from Rains, great camera work and effects from Edeson and Fulton (who used black velvet-clad actors filmed before black backgrounds to achieve the needed effects), and brilliantly judged direction from Whale make this film hard to beat. The dialogue by Wylie and Sherriff is by turns hilarious, haunting and horrific.

IPCRESS FILE, THE 📀

1965 109m c Spy ★★★½

Lowndes/Steven (U.K.)

Michael Caine *(Harry Palmer)*, Nigel Green *(Dalby)*, Guy Doleman *(Maj. Ross)*, Sue Lloyd *(Jean)*, Gordon Jackson *(Jock Carswell)*, Aubrey Richards *(Radcliffe)*, Frank Gatliff *(Bluejay)*, Thomas Baptiste *(Barney)*, Oliver MacGreevy *(Housemartin)*, Freda Bamford *(Alice)*

p, Harry Saltzman; d, Sidney J. Furie; w, Bill Canaway, James Doran (based on the novel by Len Deighton); ph, Otto Heller (Techniscope, Technicolor); ed, Peter Hunt; m, John Barry; prod d, Ken Adam; art d, Peter Murton

Based on the first and the best of Len Deighton's novels about myopic, flabby antihero Harry Palmer (Caine), THE IPCRESS FILE is a witty, fast-paced espionage film. Palmer, a British army sergeant stationed in Berlin, is nabbed for black marketeering but told that he can do his penance by serving as a counterintelligence agent. When Radcliffe (Richards), the latest in a string of scientists to be kidnaped, disappears along with a top secret file, Palmer is put on the case. During the investigation, a mysterious tape turns up with "Ipcress" written on it, and just when it appears that the case is about to be cracked, an agent is murdered and Palmer is confronted by the real—and surprising—enemy.

The best part of the film is Caine's characterization. Hardly a superhero, Harry Palmer is an ordinary chap tossed into a maelstrom in much the same way Alfred Hitchcock placed people in situations beyond their scope and then let them triumph over seemingly unbeatable odds. Canadian-born Sidney J. Furie seems determined to be a flashy director here, but if his restless camera and kooky *mise en scene* are sometimes just plain weird, they are also sometimes stylishly suited to the foolishness of the entire undertaking. Look for a scene in which Harry makes coffee in his elegant *caffetiere*, a very chic device at the time. (It's that kind of movie.) Produced by Harry Saltzman, the coproducer of many James Bond films, THE IPCRESS FILE gave rise to two sequels, FUNERAL IN BERLIN and BILLION DOLLAR BRAIN, both of which starred Caine. Neither was as exciting or enjoyable as this one, however.

IRIS 📀

2001 97m c Biography/Drama ★★★½

Mirage Enterprises/Robert Fox/Scott Rudin R
Productions/BBC Films/Intermedia Films (U.S./U.K.)

Judi Dench *(Iris Murdoch)*, Jim Broadbent *(John Bayley)*, Kate Winslet *(Young Iris Murdoch)*, Hugh Bonneville *(Young John Bayley)*, Eleanor Bron *(Principal)*, Angela Morant *(Hostess)*, Penelope Wilton *(Janet Stone)*, Sioban Hayes *(Check-out Girl)*, Juliet Aubrey *(Young Janet Stone)*, Joan Bakewell *(BBC Presenter)* p, Robert Fox, Scott Rudin; d, Richard Eyre; w, Richard Eyre, Charles Wood (based on the book *Iris: A Memoir/Elegy for Iris* by John Bayley); ph, Roger Pratt; ed, Martin Walsh; m, James Horner; prod d, Gemma Jackson; art d, David Warren; fx, The Mill; cos, Ruth Myers

AA Best Supporting Actor: Jim Broadbent; *AAN Best Actress:* Judi Dench; *AAN Best Supporting Actress:* Kate Winslet

Extraordinary performances anchor this generally sturdy adaptation of *Elegy for Iris*, John Bayley's tender 1998 memoir of his marriage to the late novelist, philosopher, and playwright Iris Murdoch.

Kate Winslet plays the Iris of the mid-1950s, a bold, sexually adventurous Oxford philosophy scholar who is trying her hand at novel writing when she's introduced to the younger Bayley (Hugh Bonneville). Judi Dench portrays the aging Murdoch of the 1990s, author of 25 novels and a dame of the British Empire struggling to finish her 26th book as the pall of Alzheimer's disease falls over her brilliant mind. Once-familiar words now puzzle her; she catches herself repeating phrases; she loses her train of thought during a TV interview. As Murdoch gradually retreats into what she herself described as a "very, very bad quiet place, a dark place," she grows increasingly dependent on Bayley (now played by a superb Jim Broadbent), who hopes that his wife has simply left for the place all great writers go when creating their fictional worlds.

Like Bayley's book, the film is a profile of both a marriage and a particularly cruel disease, but it's far less imaginatively structured; director Richard Eyre and his co-writer, Charles Wood, flash back and forth between the two Irises with dull, disappointing regularity. The characterizations, however, are gripping. Dench's performance is the kind often tagged as "brave," and for once the description is apt. She allows the ravaging effects of the disease to speak through heartbreaking pantomime and her pitiable, degraded physical appearance. It's a great achievement, quiet enough to allow room for her excellent supporting cast, but strong enough to be felt over James Horner's typically overbearing score.

IRMA LA DOUCE
1963   147m   c   Comedy   ★★★
Mirisch/Phalanx/Alperson   (U.S.)

Jack Lemmon *(Nestor)*, Shirley MacLaine *(Irma La Douce)*, Lou Jacobi *(Moustache)*, Bruce Yarnell *(Hippolyte)*, Herschel Bernardi *(Inspector LeFevre)*, Hope Holiday *(Lolita)*, Joan Shawlee *(Amazon Annie)*, Grace Lee Whitney *(Kiki the Cossack)*, Tura Satana *(Suzette Wong)*, Harriette Young *(Mimi the MauMau)*

p, Billy Wilder; d, Billy Wilder; w, Billy Wilder, I.A.L. Diamond (based on the play by Alexandre Breffort); ph, Joseph La Shelle (Panavision, Technicolor); ed, Daniel Mandell; m, Andre Previn (based on a score by Marguerite Monnot); art d, Alexander Trauner; fx, Milt Rice; chor, Wally Green; cos, Orry-Kelly

AAN Best Actress: Shirley MacLaine; *AAN Best Color Cinematography:* Joseph LaShelle; *AA Best Adapted Score:* Andre Previn

IRMA LA DOUCE has a curious history: a French musical in 1956, an American adaptation in 1960, then this nonmusical film in 1963. Far too long for a lighthearted farce, with dull patches that outnumber the high spots, the film is really about Maclaine and Lemmon striving to rise above the fat Diamond-Wilder script and Wilder's lethargic direction.

Wilder was the logical choice to adapt this type of film, but it still misses. MacLaine is Irma, a Paris streetwalker whose money goes to her handsome pimp Hippolyte (Yarnell). Enter Nestor (Lemmon), a cop who antedates Clouseau in his bumbling but sincere ineptitude. Nestor cannot believe all the women plying their trade, and seeks to reform the area by raiding a local bistro run by Moustache (Jacobi). The chief police inspector (Bernardi) is arrested in the raid and Nestor is promptly sacked. Nestor and Irma become an item and she fires Hippolyte, making Nestor her new "protector."

Previn won an Oscar, and MacLaine and La Shelle were nominated, but this was less than a complete success. The movie was filmed on a 360-degree set so shooting could be done in any direction. You can't help but wonder what the film might have been with a half hour cut, or with the Broadway score retained.

IRMA VEP
1996   96m   c   Comedy/Drama   ★★★★½
Dacia Films   (France)

Maggie Cheung *(Maggie)*, Jean-Pierre Leaud *(Rene Vidal)*, Nathalie Richard *(Zoe)*, Bulle Ogier *(Mireille)*, Lou Castel *(Jose Murano)*, Arsinee Khanjian *(American Woman)*, Antoine Basler *(Journalist)*, Nathalie Boutefeu *(Laure)*, Alex Descas *(Desormeaux)*, Dominique Faysse *(Maite)*

p, Georges Benayoun; d, Olivier Assayas; w, Olivier Assayas (inspired by LES VAMPIRES by Louis Feuillade); ph, Eric Gautier; ed, Luc Barnier; prod d, Francoise-Renaud Labarthe; cos, Francoise Clavel, Jessica Doyle

A wryly funny and uncommonly intelligent meditation on the state of moviemaking in the 1990s, IRMA VEP offers several innovative twists on the standard "behind-the-scenes" tale of life on a movie set.

Actress Maggie Cheung (playing herself) arrives in France to star in a unique production: a remake of the classic French cliffhanger LES VAMPIRES (1915) to be directed by Rene Vidal (Jean-Pierre Leaud), a filmmaker in decline. After a costume fitting at a tacky boutique, Maggie is befriended by Zoe (Nathalie Richard), the film's outspoken, free-spirited costumer. Upon arriving back at her hotel after a crew party, Maggie impulsively puts on her costume, and starts acting as her character in the film, a catsuited master-thief. The next day, Vidal has reportedly disappeared and the entire production is put on hold. A new director (Lou Castel) has some ideas but first has to view Vidal's footage, which the departed director assembled in a bizarre, jarring, and artistically challenging manner.

Critic-turned-filmmaker Olivier Assayas explores several elemental aspects of cinema in IRMA VEP, not the least of which is the eternal question of art vs. entertainment. His enthusiasm for film form is apparent throughout, particularly in moments where "primitive" forms of moviemaking (silents, handmade avant-garde cinema) are celebrated. The film's casting is sublime: Richard is a standout in the key role of the costumer who serves as a scapegoat for the problems besetting the film-within-a-film; the presence of Leaud links IRMA VEP to the essential works of the French New Wave; and Cheung serves as a genuine embodiment of the East-West art-entertainment dichotomy, thanks to her British accent and her past work in both action films and arthouse hits. While Assayas may espouse intellectual concerns in IRMA VEP, the film itself is more earthy than elitist—in fact, one of its most endearing revelations lies in Vidal's simple statement that he chose to remake LES VAMPIRES due to his strong desire to see Cheung in a Catwoman outfit.

IRON GIANT, THE
1999   74m   c   Animated   ★★★★
Warner Bros.   (U.S.)   PG

VOICES OF: Jennifer Aniston *(Annie Hughes)*, Eli Marienthal *(Hogarth Hughes)*, Harry Connick Jr. *(Dean McCoppin)*, Vin Diesel *(The Iron Giant)*, Christopher McDonald *(Kent Mansley)*, James Gammon *(Floyd Turbeaux)*, Cloris Leachman *(Mrs. Tensedge)*, John Mahoney *(General Rogard)*, M. Emmet Walsh *(Earl Stutz)* p, Allison Abbate, Des McAnuff; d, Brad Bird; w, Tim McCanlies, Brad Bird (based on the novel *The Iron Man* by Ted Hughes); ph, Mark Dinicola; ed, Darren T. Holmes; m, Michael Kamen; prod d, Mark Whiting; art d, Alan Bodner; anim, Tony Fucile

---

Simply wonderful. This animated reworking of Ted Hughes's beloved 1968 book *The Iron Man* is a rare adaptation that actually improves upon the original material.

Set amid the jittery, duck-and-cover paranoia of the Cold War years, the story opens as an unidentified flying *something* whizzes past Sputnik and splashes down off the coast of tiny Rockwell, ME. Out of the sea steps a 50-foot iron colossus with high-beam headlights for eyes and an insatiable appetite for metal. Roaming the pine forests around Rockwell, the robot happens upon the home of nine-year-old Hogarth Hughes (voiced by Eli Marienthal), who befriends the metal giant. Hogarth, a fan of sci-fi flicks and "Red Menace" comics, knows how frightened citizens react to giant space creatures, so he hides his newfound friend, first in the family barn, then at the junkyard operated by town beatnik Dean (Harry Connick Jr.). Before long, the government gets wind of the robot's arrival and sends square-jawed agent Kent Mansley (Christopher McDonald) to investigate and destroy the creature, if necessary. In the meantime, the iron giant learns about friendship, cruelty, death, and the immortality of soul.

Director Brad Bird and his animators forgo the exhausting, non-stop-action Disney formula, opting for a hipper, simpler style, richly colored with burnt, autumnal hues and reminiscent of classic comic book covers and poster art of the '50s. But the film's real beauty lies in Bird and Tim McCanlies' thoughtful script, which teaches with humor and compassion that guns kill, and each of us is, ultimately, who and what we choose to be. Those are important lessons for children, and valuable reminders for adults.

IRREVERSIBLE

2002 95m c Crime/Thriller ★★★
Nord Ouest Productions/Eskward/Les Cinemas de la Zone/120 Films/Studio Canal + (France)

Monica Bellucci *(Alex)*, Vincent Cassel *(Marcus)*, Albert Dupontel *(Pierre)*, Philippe Nahon *(Philippe)*, Jo Prestia *(Le Tenia)*, Stephane Drouot *(Stephane)*, Jean-Louis Costes *(Man Beaten to Death in Club)*, Mourad Khima *(Mourad)*, Christophe Lemaire *(Dancer with the Hawaiian Shirt)*, Gaspar Noe *(uncredited)*

p, Richard Grandpierre, Christophe Rossignon; d, Gaspar Noe; w, Gaspar Noe; ph, Benoit Debie, Gaspar Noe; ed, Gaspar Noe; m, Thomas Bangalter; prod d, Alain Juteau; fx, Rodolphe Chabrier; cos, Laure Culkovic

---

Whether you take it as a deliberately vile act of filmmaking that unpacks rape-revenge scenarios while making a point about male desire, or simply as a deliberately vile piece of filmmaking, one thing is certain: Gaspar Noe's second feature is about as close to a physical assault as movies can get.

The film opens with the murderous, unnamed butcher (Philippe Nahon) of Noe's earlier feature, I STAND ALONE, sitting naked in a squalid room, reflecting on his crime. A commotion is heard coming from the gay sex club below, where two men are being taken away by police, Marcus (Vincent Cassel) on a stretcher and Pierre (Albert Dupontel) in handcuffs. As the film unspools—like MEMENTO, the film unfolds in reverse—we learn exactly what has led up to this grisly moment. Earlier in the evening, Marcus, Pierre, and Marcus's girlfriend, Alex (Monica Bellucci), were at a party. Alex left early and was brutally beaten and raped by a gay pimp known as Le Tenia (Jo Prestia)—"The Tapeworm." Marcus and Pierre feverishly tracked Le Tenia to the club,

where they took their vicious and, in a cruel twist, entirely misdirected revenge.

This is the kind of film that virtually defies coherent defense. You can't read it as a critique of heterosexual male desire because the rapist is gay, and in that respect it's as homophobic as LOOKING FOR MR. GOODBAR. And it's difficult to give it a feminist reading because, unlike the violated heroine of, say, MS. 45, the highly sexualized Bellucci is rendered completely powerless by the crime. So why should anyone see the thing? Because it's brilliantly done, and while art can never excuse atrocity, Noe raises important questions about violence and vengeance and the movies we make about them.

IS PARIS BURNING? DVD
(PARIS BRULE-T-IL?)
1966 173m c/bw War ★★½
Transcontinental/Marianne (U.S./France)

Jean-Paul Belmondo *(Morandat)*, Charles Boyer *(Monod)*, Leslie Caron *(Francoise Labe)*, Jean-Pierre Cassel *(Lt. Henri Karcher)*, George Chakiris *(GI in Tank)*, Claude Dauphin *(Lebel)*, Alain Delon *(Jacques Chaban-Delmas)*, Kirk Douglas *(Gen. George Patton)*, Glenn Ford *(Gen. Omar Bradley)*, Gert Frobe *(Gen. Dietrich von Choltitz)*

p, Paul Graetz; d, Rene Clement; w, Gore Vidal, Francis Ford Coppola, Jean Aurenche, Pierre Bost, Claude Brule, Marcel Moussy, Beate von Molo; ph, Marcel Grignon; m, Maurice Jarre; art d, Willy Holt; fx, Robert MacDonald, Paul Pollard; cos, Jean Zay, Pierre Nourry

---

AAN Best B/W Cinematography: Marcel Grignon; *AAN Best Art Direction-Set Decoration (B/W):* Willy Holt (Art Direction), Marc Frederix (Art Direction), Pierre Guffroy (Art Direction)

Is it any wonder that a film with writers from Aurenche and Bost to Francis Ford Coppola to Gore Vidal would be a bit rambling? Is it any surprise that a film featuring two dozen movie stars is a bit of a mess?

Full of dramatically unwieldy crosscutting between the Allies and Germans during the 1944 liberation, IS PARIS BURNING? is a fairly entertaining, action-packed film which seems continually in danger of collapsing under the weight of its own pageantry.

The plot basically deals with the Germans' attempts to torch Paris before having to pull out because they're losing the war. Frobe is the German general assigned to light the match; Caron is the wife of a political prisoner; Welles—desperate as always for money to finance his own films—is a Swedish consul; Belmondo is a resistance fighter who takes over police headquarters; Vaneck is a Free French officer trying to enlist Allied aide in saving gay Paree; Signoret owns a cafe; Stack, Douglas, Ford and Rich compare square jawlines as four (what else?) generals; and Montand and Perkins, of course, encounter bad luck on film yet again.

Producer Graetz underwent innumerable headaches in assembling vintage props for the film and in expanding the script every time another movie star became available. Director Clement, expert at documentary and low-key realism, does a fine job of mixing period footage with the stuff he shot, though continuity suffers somewhat during this extravaganza. A favorite: Frobe and another general speak English en route to Hitler's office, but once in the Fuhrer's presence we get German with English subtitles. There's plenty of fun to be had here if you don't mind (or if you have a perverse fascination with) that kind of thing.

ISHTAR
1987 107m c Comedy ★★
Delphi V/Columbia (U.S.) PG-13

Warren Beatty (Lyle Rogers), Dustin Hoffman (Chuck Clarke), Isabelle Adjani (Shirra Assel), Charles Grodin (Jim Harrison), Jack Weston (Marty Freed), Tess Harper (Willa), Carol Kane (Carol), Aharon Ipale (Emir Yousef), Fijad Hageb (Abdul), David Margulies (Mr. Clarke)

p, Warren Beatty; d, Elaine May; w, Elaine May; ph, Vittorio Storaro (Technicolor); ed, Stephen A. Rotter, William Reynolds, Richard Cirincione; m, Bahjawa; prod d, Paul Sylbert; art d, Bill Groom, Vicki Paul, Peter Childs, Tony Reading; cos, Anthony Powell

It's inevitable that when a film costs upwards of $40 million, stars two of the biggest names in Hollywood (Hoffman and Beatty), and is directed by a person (May) notorious for her wasteful shooting methods, the result will be savaged by industry insiders and film critics. An incredible box office loser and, to be frank, far from great, ISHTAR is still not nearly as awful as many would have it.

Struggling songwriters Chuck Clarke (Hoffman) and Lyle Rogers (Beatty) have known each other for only a few months but have formed a strong bond. Despite the pathetic but honestly expressive songs they bang out, entertainment agent Marty Freed (Weston) offers them a booking—in Morocco. On their way, they get mixed up in a civil war in the fictitious "Ishtar" and become involved with a goofy CIA agent (Grodin).

For all the bad press ISHTAR received, it does have a certain odd charm. Cast against type, Beatty and Hoffman do their darndest to mimic Hope and Crosby. The biggest problem is that any attempted subtlety is swamped by May's bid to turn the film into an epic adventure story. The talented Adjani doesn't help much, doing little more than float around in loose-fitting garments. The hopelessly banal lyrics to the songs written by the Beatty and Hoffman characters can be hilarious if you're in the mood. ("Telling the truth is a dangerous business/Honest and popular don't go hand-in-hand/If you admit that you play the accordian/You'll never make it a rock and roll band.") Yes, it's that kind of movie.

ISLAND OF LOST SOULS
DVD
1933 67m bw Science Fiction/Horror ★★★★½
Paramount (U.S.)

Charles Laughton (Dr. Moreau), Bela Lugosi (Sayer of the Law), Richard Arlen (Edward Parker), Leila Hyams (Ruth Walker), Kathleen Burke (Lota, the Panther Woman), Arthur Hohl (Montgomery), Stanley Fields (Capt. Davies), Bob Kortman (Hogan), Tetsu Komai (M'Ling), Hans Steinke (Ouran)

d, Erle C. Kenton; w, Philip Wylie, Waldemar Young (based on the novel The Island of Dr. Moreau by H.G. Wells); ph, Karl Struss; fx, Gordon Jennings

There's not a wasted frame in this chilling horror film that was banned in England upon its first release. Laughton is Dr. Moreau, a smiling, benign-seeming man who welcomes shipwrecked Edward Parker (Arlen) to his own private island. While waiting for the next passing freighter, Parker learns that the "natives" who serve Moreau are really animals who have been transformed into semi-humans by the doctor's experiments in an area known as "The House of Pain." The only woman around, Lota (Burke), becomes involved with Parker but she too conceals a terrible secret. When Edward's fiancee Ruth (Hyams) arrives with a search expedition, the two women vie for his affections while Moreau makes his own

attempts to deal with the new intruders. Unfortunately for him he makes a crucial error which goes against the lessons in "humanity" and "civility" he has browbeaten into his creations. The famous, controversial climax is still a shocker.

H.G. Wells, from whose novel the screenplay was written, hated the picture from the start because he felt the makers missed his point about a man playing God and opted for the easy way out. The film is steeped in atmosphere and foreboding, and much of the terror was hinted at rather than shown graphically. Struss' cinematography is stunning, especially in the "lesson" scenes Moreau administers. "Are we not men?" and "What is the law?" are lines chanted by the half-human denizens of Moreau's isle, led by Bela Lugosi in an amazingly small yet very effective performance, that will stick in your memory. Burke's appearance is striking but her acting less so; Laughton, on the other hand, is unfailingly marvelous. So many countries (as well as many midwestern states) banned the movie that it took a while to recoup the cost, but ISLAND OF LOST SOULS remains, to this day, a classic chiller which holds up better than many others from its period. Remade in 1959 as TERROR IS A MAN and in 1978 (with Burt Lancaster and Michael York) as THE ISLAND OF DR. MOREAU. Neither version was quite up to the original.

IT CAME FROM OUTER SPACE
DVD
1953 80m bw Science Fiction ★★★½
Universal (U.S.)

Richard Carlson (John Putnam), Barbara Rush (Ellen Fields), Charles Drake (Sheriff Matt Warren), Russell Johnson (George), Kathleen Hughes (Jane), Joe Sawyer (Frank Daylon), Dave Willock (Pete Davis), Alan Dexter (Dave Loring), George Eldredge (Dr. Snell), Brad Jackson (Snell's Assistant)

p, William Alland; d, Jack Arnold; w, Harry Essex (based on the story "The Meteor" by Ray Bradbury); ph, Clifford Stine (3-D); ed, Paul Weatherwax; m, Herman Stein; art d, Bernard Herzbrun, Robert Boyle; fx, David S. Horsley

One of the better science-fiction films to come out of the Cold War '50s, this one must be counted among the anti-McCarthy statements. Not just passively anti-conformist like the original INVASION OF THE BODY SNATCHERS, it actively supports the right of any being to be different. Unusually restrained and sober in tone for its time, IT CAME FROM OUTER SPACE is a film noir variant on the sci-fi genre.

Carlson is John Putnam, an astronomer who lives alone out in the desert. The folks in town find him eccentric and distrust his intellectualism. One night he sees what he thinks is a meteor blaze across the sky and crash in the desert. As it turns out, the UFO is actually an alien spacecraft. The creatures, cloaked with invisibility, replace the locals with alien doubles, thereby making it difficult for Putnam to prove they exist. He tells the townspeople but no one wants to believe him. Once he makes contact with the aliens, he learns that their intentions are not really threatening but, by that time, the townspeople are finally starting to panic.

Inspired by a Ray Bradbury story, this film had the added bonus of being photographed in 3-D, and it was worth putting up with the annoying glasses to view Arnold's creepy deep-focus compositions. This was director Arnold's first science fiction work, a genre in which he was to make quite a mark, directing such films as THIS ISLAND EARTH, TARANTULA, and his classic, THE INCREDIBLE SHRINKING MAN.

IT HAPPENED HERE

DVD

1963 99m bw Drama ★★★★
Rath (U.K.)

Pauline Murray (*Pauline*), Sebastian Shaw (*Dr. Richard Fletcher*), Fiona Leland (*Helen Fletcher*), Honor Fehrson (*Honor Hutton*), Col. Percy Binns (*Immediate Action Commandant*), Frank Bennett (*IA Political Leader*), Bill Thomas (*IA Group Leader*), Reginald Marsh (*IA Medical Officer*), Rex Collett (*IA NCO*), Nicolette Bernard (*IA Woman Commandant*)

p, Kevin Brownlow, Andrew Mollo; d, Kevin Brownlow, Andrew Mollo; w, Kevin Brownlow, Andrew Mollo (based on an idea by Kevin Brownlow); ph, Peter Suschitzky, Kevin Brownlow; ed, Kevin Brownlow; m, Jack Beaver, Anton Bruckner; art d, Andrew Mollo, Jim Nicolson

Reminiscent in title and theme of Sinclair Lewis' terrifying novel *It Can't Happen Here*, this intensely fascinating effort from film historians Kevin Brownlow and Andrew Mollo speculates about what could have happened in WWII England if the Germans had successfully invaded. Murray stars as a British nurse employed by the Fascist government. Shocked to discover that Russian and Polish hospital patients are being killed, she raises loud protests, is arrested, and eventually joins the resistance. Made on a miniscule budget of only $20,000, the production—partly filmed in 16mm—took 10 years to complete. It has a remarkable documentary look and feel, and the direction by Brownlow and Mollo is amazingly assured. A very disturbing and compelling film, it makes an incisive point about politics and nationality: the British would have gotten along quite nicely under Nazi rule, just as the French did.

IT HAPPENED ONE NIGHT

DVD

1934 105m bw Romance/Comedy ★★★★★
Columbia (U.S.)

Claudette Colbert (*Ellie Andrews*), Clark Gable (*Peter Warne*), Roscoe Karns (*Oscar Shapeley*), Henry Wadsworth (*Drunk Boy*), Claire McDowell (*Mother*), Walter Connolly (*Alexander Andrews*), Alan Hale (*Danker*), Arthur Hoyt (*Zeke*), Blanche Frederici (*Zeke's Wife*), Jameson Thomas (*King Westley*)

p, Harry Cohn; d, Frank Capra; w, Robert Riskin (based on the story "Night Bus" by Samuel Hopkins Adams); ph, Joseph Walker; ed, Gene Havlick; art d, Stephen Goosson; cos, Robert Kalloch

AA Best Picture; AA Best Actor: Clark Gable; *AA Best Actress:* Claudette Colbert; *AA Best Director:* Frank Capra; *AA Best Writing (Adaptation):* Robert Riskin

It happened one night in 1934, and it happens every time we watch this utterly beguiling film. A rather modest effort which brought Capra into the spotlight, we frankly prefer it to many of the more "important" films he made later. It also clinched for good the stardom of Gable and Colbert. (What a pity that their only other teaming was the dismal BOOM TOWN.)

The familiar story, a prototype for many screwball comedies to follow, opens with headstrong heiress Ellie Andrews (Colbert) fleeing her father (Connolly). Trying to make it to her washout fiance (Thomas) on her own, she soon encounters errant reporter Peter Warne (Gable). He agrees to help her make it from Florida to New York in exchange for her story, which will square him with his disgruntled boss. Over the course of several nights, the inevitable happens.

What really distinguishes IT HAPPENED ONE NIGHT from so many other films are Capra's handling of the individual comic and romantic setpieces, Riskin's way with a line, and the marvelous cast. Every viewer has his or her favorite scenes. Consider the "wall of Jericho" (a blanket) Peter sets up between himself and Ellie before bedding down for the night, a sly dig at Production Code prudery just then being enforced. Or what about Peter's famous lessons in how to dunk a donut or how a man undresses? (We all recall, of course, how Ellie shows him up in the memorable hitchhiking lesson.) For romance, there's some lovely bedside dreaming and even a scene in the hay. There's also Ellie's wonderful wedding gown near the end, the lengthy veil providing a visual exclamation point to rival Elsa Lanchester's hair in BRIDE OF FRANKENSTEIN. The splendidly cast actors, too, make their bits of business their own, from Karns' mildly lecherous salesperson ("Shapeley's the name and that's the way I like 'em") turned scared rabbit to Hale's aggressively cheering but deceptive singing motorist. The best support, though, comes from the unfailingly marvelous Connolly in a role he made his own. Gable and Colbert's screen personas were firmly established here, his tongue-in-cheek machismo and her witty, supple sophistication mixing like gin and tonic.

IT HAPPENED ONE NIGHT won the top five Oscars (Picture, Director, Actor, Actress, Screenplay), a feat only duplicated twice since. Watch it again and you'll remember why.

IT SHOULD HAPPEN TO YOU

DVD

1954 86m bw Comedy ★★★★
Columbia (U.S.)

Judy Holliday (*Gladys Glover*), Jack Lemmon (*Pete Sheppard*), Peter Lawford (*Evan Adams III*), Michael O'Shea (*Brod Clinton*), Connie Gilchrist (*Mrs. Riker*), Vaughn Taylor (*Entrikin*), Heywood Hale Broun (*Sour Man in Central Park*), Rex Evans (*Con Cooley*), Art Gilmore (*Don Toddman*), Whit Bissell (*Robert Grau*)

p, Fred Kohlmar; d, George Cukor; w, Garson Kanin; ph, Charles Lang; ed, Charles Nelson; m, Frederick Hollander; art d, John Meehan; cos, Jean Louis

AAN Best Costume Design (B/W): Jean Louis

Charming satire in which Lemmon made a winning debut opposite the flawless Holliday.

Holliday is Gladys Glover (a name you'll never forget once you've seen the film), a poor model from Binghampton who has come to New York. She's spotted by film documentarist Pete Sheppard (Lemmon), who is roaming Central Park with his camera. When Gladys looks up and sees an empty billboard, she promptly uses all her money to have her name painted there in huge letters. Suddenly, all of New York is wondering who she is and why she's done this. Lawford plays Evan Adams III, an executive for a huge soap company who wants the billboard for his products, making a deal with Gladys whereby he gives her several other billboards in return for the big one. Gladys and Pete become lovers, but he doesn't like what is transpiring. He thinks his feckless love is cheapening herself, and he wishes she would stop the campaign and settle in with him. Fame follows her, however, and she becomes a celebrity, appearing on talk shows and doing commercials. Pete leaves her in disgust, but that's just until they get back together for a customary happy ending.

IT SHOULD HAPPEN TO YOU benefits from fine performances from some wonderful farceurs, a witty Kanin script, and Cukor's light-hearted direction. Melvine Cooper, Wendy Barrie, Constance Bennett, and Ilka Chase spoof the inanities of TV talk shows perfectly, and Lemmon and Holliday also get a chance to sing with "Let's Fall in Love," which had been written (by Harold Arlen and Ted Koehler) almost 20 years earlier. In a tiny role, John Saxon is the young man who watches the argument in the park. Jean Louis' costumes were nominated for an Oscar.

ITALIAN JOB, THE

DVD
★★½

2003 111m c   Crime/Action
De Line Pictures/Paramount   (U.S.)   PG-13

Mark Wahlberg (Charlie Croker), Charlize Theron (Stella Bridger), Donald Sutherland (John Bridger), Jason Statham (Handsome Rob), Seth Green (Lyle), Edward Norton (Steve), Fausto Callegarini (Italian Guard), Stefano Petronelli (Garbageman/Thug), Fabio Scarpa (Garbageman/Thug), Cristiano Bonora (Garbageman/Thug)

p, Donald De Line; d, F. Gary Gray; w, Donna Powers, Wayne Powers (based on the screenplay by Troy Kennedy Martin); ph, Wally Pfister; ed, Richard Francis-Bruce, Christopher Rouse; m, John Powell; prod d, Charles Wood; art d, Doug Meerdink, Mark Zuelzke; fx, Bruce Jones; cos, Mark Bridges

Colorful crooks steal $35 million, lose it to a crooked confederate, and cook up a crackerjack plan to get the loot back in this pumped-up remake of the larky 1969 caper picture.

Aging gentleman bandit John Bridger (Donald Sutherland) is ready to hang up his lock picks and spend his remaining years getting to know his adult daughter, Stella (Charlize Theron). Bridger has taught surrogate son Charlie Croker (Mark Wahlberg) all he knows about setting up a job and agrees to join Croker and his crew—computer-whiz Lyle (Seth Green), driver Handsome Rob (Jason Statham), demolition expert Left Ear (Mos Def), and inside man Steve (Edward Norton)—for one last heist. They steal a state-of-the-art safe from a Venetian villa, then misdirect both guards and police while Bridger cracks the lock and liberates a fortune in distinctively marked gold bars. Traitorous Steve, however, shoots Bridger and makes off with the loot. One year later, Charlie has tracked Steve to Los Angeles and formulates a plan. It takes a while to recruit Stella, who's inherited her father's safecracking skills but none of his larcenous inclinations, but once she's aboard the plan is a go. Steve's payback will be a variation on the Italian job, with three nimble Mini Coopers in the daredevil getaway.

This updated version moves like a freight train, but suffers from a debilitating charm deficit. Norton delivers what must be the sourest, most lifeless performance of his career to date, perhaps because he was forced to take the role on the strength of a years-old contractual agreement. And really, when a pint-size automobile has more sex appeal than Charlize Theron, something is seriously out of whack.

IT'S A GIFT

DVD
★★★★★

1934 73m   bw   Comedy
Paramount   (U.S.)

W.C. Fields (Harold Bissonette), Jean Rouverol (Mildred Bissonette), Julian Madison (John Durston), Kathleen Howard (Amelia Bissonette), Tommy Bupp (Norman Bissonette), Tammany Young (Everett Ricks), Baby LeRoy (Baby Ellwood Dunk), Morgan Wallace (Jasper Fitchmueller), Charles Sellon (Mr. Muckle/Blind Man/House Detective), Josephine Whittell (Mrs. Dunk)

p, William LeBaron; d, Norman Z. McLeod; w, Jack Cunningham, W.C. Fields (based on the play The Comic Supplement by J.P. McEvoy and a story by Charles Bogle); ph, Henry Sharp; art d, Hans Dreier, John B. Goodman

Never was a film so well titled. Along with THE BANK DICK this is the finest, funniest movie W.C. Fields ever made. It's also a rollicking spoof of middle-class marriage and mainstream ambitions.

Fields appears as Harold Bissonette, a small-town shopowner with selfish children and a nagging wife. When his family isn't making his life miserable, his customers and neighbors are. He dreams of the good life and a California orange grove he's purchased with an inheritance, but the hostile world won't even let him get a decent night's sleep. (In a memorable scene poor Harold copes with a noisy milkman, a grape-wielding baby, a porch swing chain and an obnoxious salesman looking for one "Karl La Fong.") When Harold and family finally make it to California, they learn he's been swindled, but, predictably, he gets the last laugh.

IT'S A GIFT is almost nonstop laughter, loaded with Fields' patented sight gags, slapstick, and dialogue uttered out of the corner of his mouth. Fields resurrected much of this material from other sources, such as his silent film IT'S THE OLD ARMY GAME and the 1925 play The Comic Supplement. He also drew on his memories as the son of a Philadelphia pushcart vendor for some of the story, which he wrote under the name of Charles Bogle. Though Norman McLeod was the nominal director, Fields picked his own cast and essentially ran the film, and his wonderful, caustic humor comes through on every frame.

IT'S A MAD, MAD, MAD, MAD WORLD

DVD
★★★

1963 192m   c   Comedy
Casey   (U.S.)

Spencer Tracy (Capt. C.G. Culpepper), Milton Berle (J. Russell Finch), Sid Caesar (Melville Crump), Buddy Hackett (Benjy Benjamin), Ethel Merman (Mrs. Marcus), Mickey Rooney (Ding Bell), Dick Shawn (Sylvester Marcus), Phil Silvers (Otto Meyer), Terry-Thomas (J. Algernon Hawthorne), Jonathan Winters (Lennie Pike)

p, Stanley Kramer; d, Stanley Kramer; w, William Rose, Tania Rose; ph, Ernest Laszlo (UltraPanavision, Technicolor); ed, Frederic Knudtson, Robert C. Jones, Gene Fowler Jr.; m, Ernest Gold; prod d, Rudolph Sternad; art d, Gordon Gurnell; fx, Danny Lee, Linwood Dunn; cos, Bill Thomas

AAN Best Color Cinematography: Ernest Laszlo; AAN Best Film Editing: Frederic Knudtson, Robert C. Jones, Gene Fowler Jr.; AAN Best Original Score: Ernest Gold; AAN Best Song: "It's a Mad, Mad, Mad, Mad World"; Ernest Gold (Music), Mack David (Lyrics); AAN Best Sound: Gordon E. Sawyer; AA Best Sound Effects: Walter G. Elliott

Overkill, this movie is the CLEOPATRA of the funnybone. This comic extravaganza starts off funny, but exhausts rather than delights. Designed to be the biggest, most lavish comedy ever made, IT'S A MAD, MAD, MAD, MAD WORLD is a coarse, star-studded pageant of Keystone Kops-style slapstick.

With his dying breath, a gangster (Jimmy Durante) recently released from prison tells the motorists who come upon him after an auto accident that $350,000 is buried under "the Big W," instigating a greedy, madcap dash for the cash. Among the lunatic treasure seekers who will stop at nothing to get to the loot first are Milton Berle, Dorothy Provine, Ethel Merman (who, curiously, steals the film from under everyone else's talented nose), Sid Caesar, Edie Adams, Buddy Hackett, Mickey Rooney, and Jonathan Winters. Phil Silvers, Terry-Thomas, Peter Falk, Dick Shawn, and Spencer Tracy also become involved, and the film is a who's who of Hollywood comedians in cameo appearances.

Director-producer Kramer spared no expense (tame today, the $7 million price tag was a hefty one at the time) on the spectacular stunts, using 39 stunt men and paying them $252,000 for some of the most incredible feats on film. But at 154 minutes of running time, it's way too long for what it is. Watching it at home with breaks may be the best way to analyze individual comic takes; certainly it's the most painless.

IT'S A WONDERFUL LIFE

DVD

1946 129m bw Drama ★★★★★
Liberty (U.S.)

James Stewart *(George Bailey)*, Donna Reed *(Mary Hatch)*, Lionel Barrymore *(Mr. Potter)*, Thomas Mitchell *(Uncle Billy)*, Henry Travers *(Clarence)*, Beulah Bondi *(Mrs. Bailey)*, Frank Faylen *(Ernie)*, Ward Bond *(Bert)*, Gloria Grahame *(Violet Bick)*, H.B. Warner *(Mr. Gower)*

p, Frank Capra; d, Frank Capra; w, Frances Goodrich, Albert Hackett, Frank Capra, Jo Swerling (based on the story "The Greatest Gift" by Philip Van Doren Stern); ph, Joseph Walker, Joseph Biroc; ed, William Hornbeck; m, Dimitri Tiomkin; art d, Jack Okey; fx, Russell A. Cully; cos, Edward Stevenson

AAN Best Picture; AAN Best Actor: James Stewart; *AAN Best Director:* Frank Capra; *AAN Best Film Editing:* William Hornbeck; *AAN Best Sound Recording:* John Aalberg (Sound)

The holiday gift for all time. This heartwarming fantasy, one of the most popular films ever made, begins as angels discuss George Bailey (James Stewart), a small-town resident so beset with problems that he contemplates a Christmastime suicide.

In flashback, we review George's life, learning that he has always wanted to leave his hometown to see the world, but that circumstances and his own good heart have kept him in Bedford Falls, sacrificing his own education for his brother's, keeping the family-run savings and loan afloat, protecting the town from the avarice of banker Potter (Lionel Barrymore), marrying his childhood sweetheart (Donna Reed), and raising a family. Back in the present, George prepares to jump from a bridge, but ends up rescuing his guardian angel, Clarence Oddbody (Henry Travers), who has come to earn his wings. Clarence shows him how badly Bedford Falls would have turned out without George and his good deeds. Filled with renewed joy in life, George goes home to his loving family and friends, who pitch in to put his worries behind him.

Few filmmakers have rivaled director Frank Capra when it comes to examining the human heart, and IT'S A WONDERFUL LIFE is a masterfully crafted exercise in sentiment, augmented by Capra's undying faith in community. Reed and Barrymore give excellent performances, as does a superb cast of character players, but this is Stewart's film—heart-stirring as the dreamer who sacrifices all for his fellow man. The bright, funny screenplay is based on "The Greatest Gift," a story by Philip Van Dorn Stren originally sent to his friends as a Christmas card.

IT'S ALIVE

DVD

1974 90m c Horror ★★★
Larco (U.S.) PG

John P. Ryan *(Frank Davies)*, Sharon Farrell *(Lenore Davies)*, Andrew Duggan *(The Professor)*, Guy Stockwell *(Clayton)*, James Dixon *(Lt. Perkins)*, Michael Ansara *(The Captain)*, Robert Emhardt *(The Executive)*, William Wellman Jr. *(Charlie)*, Daniel Holzman *(Chris Davies)*, Shamus Locke *(Doctor)*

p, Larry Cohen; d, Larry Cohen; w, Larry Cohen; ph, Fenton Hamilton (Panavision, Technicolor); ed, Peter Honess; m, Bernard Herrmann; fx, Rick Baker

The film that put maverick producer-writer-director Larry Cohen on the map, IT'S ALIVE is a justifiably praised low-budget effort that delves into the dark side of American family life from a horror-movie perspective. The film opens as proud parents Frank and Lenore Davies (John P. Ryan and Sharon Farrell) enter the hospital to deliver their new child. Suddenly all hell breaks loose in the delivery room, as Lenore gives birth to a monstrous baby that kills several hospital personnel before scurrying off into the night. (The mutation may have been caused by a new fertility drug pushed on mothers by the pharmaceutical industry.) The horrified parents are torn: while Lenore feels strong maternal instincts for the child, Frank resolves to hunt it down and kill it. He assists the police in their search for the monster, but as the hunt gets warmer, he too begins to feel instinctive affection for the creature and finally attempts to save his child. Part visceral horror flick and part Oedipal allegory, IT'S ALIVE explores a widely repressed but crucial element of family life—parents' ambivalence toward their children—and satirizes society's cavalier treatment of its youngest members, prefiguring the mean social policies of the American '90s. Cohen turned this rich and terrifying concept into a trilogy: IT LIVES AGAIN and IT'S ALIVE III: ISLAND OF THE ALIVE followed.

IT'S ALWAYS FAIR WEATHER

1955 102m c Musical/Comedy ★★★★
MGM (U.S.)

Gene Kelly *(Ted Riley)*, Dan Dailey *(Doug Hallerton)*, Cyd Charisse *(Jackie Leighton)*, Dolores Gray *(Madeline Bradville)*, Michael Kidd *(Angie Valentine)*, David Burns *(Tim)*, Jay C. Flippen *(Charles Z. Culloran)*, Steve Mitchell *(Kid Mariacchi)*, Hal March *(Rocky Lazar)*, Paul Maxey *(Mr. Fielding)*

p, Arthur Freed; d, Stanley Donen, Gene Kelly; w, Betty Comden, Adolph Green; ph, Robert Bronner (CinemaScope, Eastmancolor); ed, Adrienne Fazan; art d, Cedric Gibbons, Arthur Lonergan; fx, Irving G. Reis, Warren Newcombe; chor, Stanley Donen, Gene Kelly; cos, Helen Rose

AAN Best Story and Screenplay: Betty Comden, Adolph Green; *AAN Best Score (Musical):* Andre Previn

A scathing satire of television and advertising is only one element in this cynical musical, which masks the seriousness of its theme with many excellent numbers.

In 1945, soldiers Ted (Gene Kelly), Doug (Dan Dailey), and Angie (Michael Kidd) come home from WWII to dance in the streets (in the celebrated trash-can cover number) and drink their way across New York, then decide to meet in a decade. After a montage of news headlines to indicate time's passage, the trio return to the bar in which they last saw one another. Mutually disappointed by how their lives turned out, the men soon realize they have little in common anymore, and the evening disintegrates into perfunctory nostalgia. The film continues with a sour examination of their present-day lives.

FAIR WEATHER is stolen by Dailey's disillusioned advertising man (he has the best routine in the film); here was a musical comedy actor ahead of his time, a specialist in world-weary characters who just happen to be song and dance men. Delores Gray is dazzling in her female pirhana way, and Cyd Charisse is her novocained, scowling self—until she goes into her dance surrounded by uglies at Stillman's gym.

Directors Kelly and Stanley Donen make wonderful use of the CinemaScope screen, splitting it to achieve a previously unattainable intimacy. The songs have little to do with the plot, a lack of integration that may have prevented this ambitious, innovative picture from getting the audiences it deserved. But many film buffs find FAIR WEATHER more authentically deserving of praise than its predictable precursor, ON THE TOWN.

IVAN THE TERRIBLE, PART I

[DVD]

(IVAN GROZNYI)

1945 96m bw Historical/Biography ★★★★
Alma-Ata Film Studio (U.S.S.R.)

Nikolai Cherkassov *(Czar Ivan IV—Ivan the Terrible)*, Ludmila Tselikovskaya *(Anastasia Romanovna—the Czarina)*, Serafima Birman *(Euphrosyne Staritsky—the Czar's Aunt)*, Pavel Kadochnikov *(Vladimir Staritsky—her Son)*, Mikhail Nazvanov *(Prince Andrew Kurbsky)*, Andrei Abrikosov *(Boyar Fyodor Kolychev—Philip, Metropolitan of Moscow)*, Alexander Mgebrov *(Pimen, Archbishop of Novgorod—sometime Metropolitan of Moscow)*, Vladimir Balachov *(Peter Volynets—his Acolyte)*, Mikhail Zharov *(Malyuta Skuratof)*, Amvrosy Buchma *(Alexey Basmanov)*

p, Sergei M. Eisenstein; d, Sergei M. Eisenstein; w, Sergei M. Eisenstein; ph, Edward Tisse, Andrei Moskvin; ed, Sergei M. Eisenstein; m, Sergei Prokofiev; prod d, Isaac Shpinel; cos, Leonid Naumova

The last work of pioneering Soviet director Sergei Eisentstein, IVAN THE TERRIBLE is an ambitious, stylized, and ornate portrait of Russia's first czar. Released in two parts, it has been cited on many lists of the 10 best motion pictures of all time, as well as in a book called *The Fifty Worst Films of All Time.*

At his coronation as czar, Ivan IV (Nikolai Cherkasov) pledges to unify Russia and reclaim outlying areas that have been lost to foreign powers. In bitter opposition to Ivan's ascendancy are the boyars, Russia's noble families. Three ambassadors from Kazan appear at the royal court to announce a declaration of war on Moscow. Ivan leads his army to Kazan and vanquishes the foe. On his return to Moscow, he falls seriously ill. After receiving the last rites of the church, Ivan beseeches the boyars in court to affirm his infant son's right of succession to the throne. When all refuse but his friend, Prince Andrew Kurbsky (Mikhail Nazvanov), who covets Anastasia, Ivan miraculously recovers and launches an attack on the western regions.

IVAN THE TERRIBLE is a rich and stately movie in which everything is ritualized. The camera rarely moves, and each frame is painstakingly composed. It is difficult to think of a film that would lose less if rendered in a book composed of the screenplay accompanied by a single frame from each shot; the movie is, in a way, its own storyboard. Echoes of grand opera, Shakespeare, Greek tragedy, High-Church liturgy, Japanese drama, and the paintings of El Greco (the subject of an Eisenstein essay) can be discerned throughout IVAN THE TERRIBLE, and the mixture is compellingly baroque without ever descending into the excesses of "camp."

IVAN THE TERRIBLE, PART II: THE REVOLT OF THE BOYARS

[DVD]

(IVAN GROZNYI II: BOYARSKY ZAGOVOR)

1958 90m c/bw Historical/Biography ★★★★
Mosfilm Studio (U.S.S.R.)

Nikolai Cherkassov *(Czar Ivan IV—Ivan the Terrible)*, Serafima Birman *(Euphrosyne Staritsky—the Czar's Aunt)*, Pavel Kadochnikov *(Vladimir Staritsky—her Son)*, Mikhail Nazvanov *(Prince Andrew Kurbsky)*, Andrei Abrikosov *(Boyar Fyodor Kolychev—Philip, Metropolitan of Moscow)*, Alexander Mgebrov *(Pimen, Archbishop of Novgorod—sometime Metropolitan of Moscow)*, Vladimir Balachov *(Peter Volynets—his Acolyte)*, Mikhail Zharov *(Malyuta Skuratof)*, Amvrosy Buchma *(Alexey Basmanov)*, Mikhail Kusnetzov *(Fyodor Basmanov—his Son)*

p, Sergei Eisenstein; d, Sergei Eisenstein; w, Sergei Eisenstein; ph, Edward Tisse, Andrei Moskvin; ed, Sergei Eisenstein; m, Sergei Prokofiev; prod d, Isaac Shpinel; cos, Leonid Naumova

The second section of Sergei Eisenstein's epic saga of Russia's first czar, IVAN THE TERRIBLE, PART II, is devoted almost entirely to the intrigues surrounding Ivan's bloody conflicts with Russia's aristocracy and the officials of her church. More controversial than PART I, it was shelved for a dozen years before the Kremlin allowed its release.

After returning to Moscow from self-imposed exile, Czar Ivan IV (Nikolai Cherkasov) resumes his bitter power struggle with the boyars, Russia's noble families. He recalls that following his father's death, the boyars had murdered his mother, and as a boy (Eric Pyriev), he had become determined to ascend the throne. In a weak moment, he appoints his old friend, Kolychev (Andrei Abrikosov), a boyar and a monk, Metropolitan of Moscow. Meanwhile, his friend, Kurbsky (Mikhail Nazvanov), the commander of Ivan's forces in the west, defects to the enemy.

Ivan is told that his boyar aunt, Euphrosyne Staritsky (Serafima Birman), was his wife's murderer. Unwilling to execute a blood relative, he orders the death of several members of Kolychev's family, after which he pledges to show his enemies no mercy. "From now on I shall become that which you name!" he declares. "*Terrible* shall I become."

The boyars send Peter Volynets (Vladimir Balachov) to a court banquet to assassinate the czar. Also attending the affair is Vladimir Staritsky (Pavel Kadochnikov), Euphrosyne's effeminate, dimwitted son and her choice to succeed Ivan as czar. At dinner, Vladimir, who has no stomach for intrigue or murder, tells the czar he does not covet the crown. Ivan, who has learned of the assassination plot, shrewdly dresses the drunken Vladimir in royal regalia. Mistaking Vladimir for Ivan, Peter kills the young man and is immediately seized by Ivan's guards. Euphrosyne is shattered by the sight of the czar alive and her son dead. Ivan frees Peter and declares that, now that Russia's internal enemies have been defeated, the moment has come to vanquish her foreign foes.

By the time Eisenstein received the Stalin Prize for IVAN THE TERRIBLE, PART I (1945), he had completed PART II. While dancing at the Stalin Prize celebration in February 1946, he suffered a heart attack. His problems were compounded when the megalomaniacal Ivan of PART II was perceived in some official quarters as a thinly disguised slap at Stalin. In September, the Central Committee of the Communist Party issued a resolution publicly denouncing the still-unreleased second part of Eisenstein's saga. The statement harshly criticized the director for rendering Ivan as a Hamletic weakling, and the czar's corps of bodyguards as "a degenerate band rather like the Ku Klux Klan." Eisenstein responded with a long and deeply pitiable statement in which he called his own film "worthless and vicious in an ideological sense...*The sense of historical truth was betrayed by me* in the second part of IVAN."

Probably as a result of this abject apology, Eisenstein and Cherkasov, the highly talented and charismatic star of IVAN THE TERRIBLE, were invited to meet with Stalin in February 1947. Long hopeful of turning the IVAN saga into a trilogy, the director was heartened when the Soviet dictator gave him the green light to film part three. Eisenstein died a year later, on the eve of his 50th birthday. Part three was never shot, and the Soviet government waited until 1958 before releasing PART II.

IVAN THE TERRIBLE, PART II continues the story in the same dense and lavishly operatic style of PART I. Driven half mad by the loneliness of power and the intensity of his power struggle with the boyars, Ivan, as interpreted by Eisenstein and Cherkasov, has come, at film's end, to resemble John Barrymore made up as SVENGALI (1931). Shot in color, the climactic banquet sequence provides the two-part film with its liveliest stretch—a Karamazovian orgy of song, dance, and even a little dark comedy involving the czar and his drunken victim, Vladimir. Eisenstein's use of color was audaciously expressionistic, but the color itself is weak, possibly because the film stock, confiscated from the Germans during WWII, was of inferior quality.

IVANHOE

DVD

1952 106m c Historical ★★★½
MGM (U.K.)

Robert Taylor *(Ivanhoe)*, Elizabeth Taylor *(Rebecca)*, Joan Fontaine *(Rowena)*, George Sanders *(De Bois-Guilbert)*, Emlyn Williams *(Wamba)*, Robert Douglas *(Sir Hugh De Bracy)*, Finlay Currie *(Cedric)*, Felix Aylmer *(Isaac)*, Francis de Wolff *(Font De Boeuf)*, Guy Rolfe *(Prince John)*

p, Pandro S. Berman; d, Richard Thorpe; w, Noel Langley (based on the novel by Sir Walter Scott); ph, Freddie Young (Technicolor); ed, Frank Clarke; m, Miklos Rozsa; art d, Alfred Junge; fx, Tom Howard; cos, Roger Furse

AAN Best Picture; AAN Best Color Cinematography: Fred A. Young; AAN Best Score (Drama or Comedy): Miklos Rozsa

Luxe MGM historical ransacking, locationed to the nines, beautiful to look upon, but with energy lapses in the soggy script of Sir Walter Scott's epic classic. It is 1190 and Robert Taylor, as the brave Sir Wilfred of Ivanhoe, returns secretly to England from the Crusades. He has served England's King Richard the Lionhearted well in the Third Crusade, but the king has been captured and is held for ransom in Austria. It's Taylor's job to raise an enormous sum to free Richard (Wooland). Taylor is a Saxon knight, son of lord Currie, who more or less disowned his son when he went to fight for Richard, a Norman king.

Taylor encounters three Norman knights, Sanders, Douglas and de Wolff, who are in league with Prince John (Rolfe), who intends to usurp his missing brother, Richard. Taylor tells the knights that Currie's castle is nearby should they wish to seek shelter for the night, and he escorts them to his father's estate. Watching this encounter is Warrender (Robin Hood), and his men who were about to kill the hated Norman knights. But, seeing Taylor with the Normans, Warrender holds his men back, telling them he will wait to see what Taylor is up to.

The Norman knights are given a cool reception by Currie, but they are nevertheless extended the hospitality of the day. At dinner, these knights meet Currie's ward, the beautiful Fontaine, whom Douglas immediately covets. Sitting at the end of the table is Taylor, Fontaine's true love, who is recognized by his father when he toasts King Richard, but Currie refuses immediately to talk to his errant son. He later communicates with Taylor through his servant-fool, Williams.

After Taylor leaves the castle with Williams as his newly appointed squire, he rescues a rich Jew, Aylmer, from the anti-Semitic Normans and is later given jewels by Aylmer's grateful daughter, Elizabeth Taylor, so he can buy horse and armor to enter the jousting tournament at Ashby and win more money to ransom Richard.

The film is certainly rousing, with a particularly grisly bout between Taylor and Sanders and the Taylor-Fontaine-Taylor triangle adequate for romantic spectacle. Though undeniably waspy as Rebecca, Elizabeth Taylor's early beauty has a way of making you forget anything, including your name. IVANHOE is filled with majestic sets, brilliantly constructed by Junge. The costuming was painstakingly created by Furse. MGM spared no expense in making IVANHOE; this became the costliest epic ever produced in England. The truth is that the studio had no choice. MGM had accumulated millions of dollars in British banks but was restrained from taking this money out of the country.

J

J'ACCUSE

1938 95m bw War ★★★½
Forrester/Parant (France)

Victor Francen *(Jean Diaz)*, Jean Max *(Henri Chimay)*, Delaitre *(Francois Laurin)*, Renee Devillers *(Helene)*, Line Noro *(Edith)*, Marie Lou *(Flo)*, Georges Saillard *(Giles Tenant)*, Paul Amiot *(Captain)*, Andre Nox *(Leotard)*, Georges Rollin *(Pierre Fonds)*

p, Abel Gance; d, Abel Gance; w, Abel Gance, Steve Passeur; ph, Roger Hubert; m, Henri Verdun

An excellent antiwar film, J'ACCUSE is all the more poignant considering it was produced and released in France shortly before the Occupation. Francen invents a device he believes will stop war forever, only to see it used by his government as a defense measure against the enemy. Driven mad by this exploitation, Francen decides only the war dead marching through the streets will stop the people's thirst for an upcoming war. In his delusion, bodies rise from their graves, and the sight of war's actual horrors so terrifies the patriotic countrymen that all thoughts of war are abandoned. Gance's plot is a simple one, but told with enormous power and passion for the theme. The ravaged faces of the dead are disturbing, powerful images that are not soon forgotten. The message is conveyed clearly, without preaching, and with a sensitivity toward pacifism. Like so many films of this nature, its message was considered unsuitable by Nazi Germany, and the film was banned in that country.

JACKASS: THE MOVIE

DVD
★★

2002 80m c Comedy
Dickhouse Entertainment/Lynch/Siderow
Productions/MTV Films/Paramount (U.S.)

R

Johnny Knoxville, Steve-O, Bam Margera, Chris Pontius, Jason Acuna, Ryan Dunn, Dave England, Brandon DiCamillo, Mike Kassak, Preston Lacy

p, Spike Jonze, Johnny Knoxville, Jeff Tremaine; d, Jeff Tremaine; ph, Dimitry Elyashkevich; ed, Liz Ewart, Mark Hansen, Kristine Young; fx, Martin Bresin, Gray Marshall, Yvette Memory; cos, Melissa Lacombe

There are really only two ways of looking at this expanded version of the popular MTV reality series. Either it's really dumb but occasionally really funny, or it's proof that Americans have not acted as a great people.

The subtitle is somewhat misleading. This showcase for extreme stunt work did open in movie theaters around the country, but it's not technically what you'd call a movie. It's simply a longer version of what MTV dishes out in the popular "Jackass" series: a succession of guerilla vignettes in which host Johnny Knoxville and his post-adolescent posse stage various juvenile and often dangerous pranks, most involving physical pain and what used to be called "toilet humor." Occasionally they rise, if that's the word, to "Candid Camera"-style stunts, many of which revolve around the willingness of Knoxville compatriot Steve-O (whose enduring claim to fame is having stapled his scrotum to his thigh onstage in Houma, L.A.) to make, yes, a jackass of himself in public.

The film bears a stern disclaimer, but you wouldn't think people need to be told not to attach electrodes to their genitals, consume urine-soaked snow cones, defecate in home-supply store display toilets, or pole-vault into walls. To give the trickster his due, Knoxville has a certain feral charm, and the bit in which his crew members invade a bowling alley, strap themselves to skateboards, and then propel themselves down-lane is actually pretty funny. The film's undisputed highlight, however, takes place in Japan. Without giving too much away, we were pleasantly surprised to discover that people prancing around dressed as pandas are every bit as amusing as folks in gorilla suits.

JACKIE BROWN
DVD
1997 155m c Crime/Comedy/Drama ★★★½
Band Apart Productions (U.S.) R

Pam Grier (*Jackie Brown*), Samuel L. Jackson (*Ordell Robbie*), Robert Forster (*Max Cherry*), Bridget Fonda (*Melanie*), Michael Keaton (*Ray Nicolette*), Robert De Niro (*Louis Gara*), Michael Bowen (*Mark Dargus*), Lisa Gay Hamilton (*Sheronda*), Tiny Lister, billed as Tommy "Tiny" Lister Jr. (*Winston*), Hattie Winston (*Simone*)

p, Lawrence Bender; d, Quentin Tarantino; w, Quentin Tarantino (based on the novel *Rum Punch* by Elmore Leonard); ph, Guillermo Navarro; ed, Sally Menke; prod d, David Wasco; art d, Daniel Bradford; cos, Mary Claire Hannan

AAN Best Supporting Actor: Robert Forster

Overlong but chock-full of small pleasures, Quentin Tarantino's long-awaited follow-up to PULP FICTION shows the *enfant terrible* of American film straining to move away from his trademark precociousness.

Down on her luck L.A. stewardess Jackie Brown (Pam Grier) is helping gun runner Ordell Robbie (Samuel L. Jackson) move his ill-gotten gains from Mexico to the U.S. when she gets busted by the Bureau of Alcohol, Tobacco, and Firearms. The ATF wants to use Jackie to get to Ordell, who hires bail bondsman Max Cherry (Robert Forster) to get her out. But Jackie's puts her time behind bars to good use, working out a plan to feign cooperation with the ATF, get the rest of Ordell's money into the country, and use it to buy herself a new life. Complicating matters are Ordell's back-stabbing girlfriend, Melanie (Bridget Fonda); his unpredictable jailhouse buddy, Louis Gara (Robert De Niro); a scheming ATF agent (Michael Keaton); and Jackie's blossoming relationship with Max. Fans of RESERVOIR DOGS and PULP FICTION may be disappointed to discover that JACKIE BROWN lacks the structural complexity, comically gruesome violence, and florid profanity of Tarantino's earlier films. PULP FICTION is a tough act to follow, and JACKIE BROWN shows the director attempting to meld his own sensibilities to a more mainstream story—an adaptation of Elmore Leonard's novel *Rum Punch*. The result is a sturdy, well-crafted film with only one major flaw: it's at least 45 minutes too long. Tarantino eschews flashy camerawork to concentrate on his cast, for whom he has written terrific dialogue. Jackson has the time of his life delivering it, and it's fun to see Pam Grier back in action, though her role is relatively restrained. The real surprise to most viewers will be Robert Forster, a long-underrated character actor who all but steals the film.

JACKNIFE
1989 102m c Drama ★★★
Kings Road/Sandollar-Schaffel (U.S.) R

Robert De Niro (*Joseph "Megs" Megessey*), Ed Harris (*Dave*), Kathy Baker (*Martha*), Charles S. Dutton, billed as Charles Dutton (*Jake*), Loudon Wainwright III (*Ferretti*), Elizabeth Franz, Tom Isbell, Sloane Shelton, Walter Massey, Jordan Lund

p, Robert Schaffel, Carol Baum; d, David Jones; w, Stephen Metcalfe (based on the play "Strange Snow" by Stephen Metcalfe); ph, Brian West (Technicolor); ed, John Bloom; m, Bruce Broughton; prod d, Edward Pisoni

This modest but compelling drama received only a brief theatrical release; it's a must-see on video—for it's acting, not the predictable story. Robert De Niro stars as "Megs" Megessey, nicknamed "Jacknife" in Vietnam because of his fondness for wrecking vehicles. Back Stateside, with the war long over, Megs is still a bit strange, and tends to irritate his war buddy Dave (Ed Harris)—who would just as soon forget both Vietnam and Megs. When Megs unexpectedly arrives at the house Dave shares with his sister, Martha (Kathy Baker), and subsequently begins a romance with her, Dave is forced to face some uncomfortable truths about himself, his memories, and his relationships with Megs and with Martha. Though it's stage origins show (adapted from Stephen Metcalfe's *Strange Show*), and we're cooked on 'Nam sigificance (with the flasbacks here particular eyesores), all three leads are splendid in their roles.

JACOB'S LADDER
DVD
1990 115m c Horror ★★★½
Carolco (U.S.) R

Tim Robbins (*Jacob Singer*), Elizabeth Pena (*Jezzie*), Danny Aiello (*Louis*), Matt Craven (*Michael*), Pruitt Taylor Vince (*Paul*), Jason Alexander (*Geary*), Patricia Kalember (*Sarah*), Eriq La Salle (*Frank*), Ving Rhames (*George*), Brian Tarantina (*Doug*)

p, Alan Marshall; d, Adrian Lyne; w, Bruce Joel Rubin; ph, Jeffrey Kimball (Technicolor); ed, Tom Rolf; m, Maurice Jarre; prod d, Brian Morris; art d, Jeremy Conway; fx, FX SMITH Inc., Gordon J. Smith, Connie Brink, Steven Dewey, Musikwerks; cos, Ellen Mirojnick

Director Adrian Lyne followed his trashy smash FATAL ATTRACTION with this arresting oddity, an arty, terrifying psychological thriller. Scripted by Bruce Joel Rubin (GHOST) and produced at a cost of $40 million, the film failed at the box office, probably due to a twist ending that almost everyone perceived as a cop-out.

JACOB'S LADDER stars Tim Robbins as Jacob, a divorced Vietnam veteran who lives in New York with his girlfriend Jezzie (a smoldering Elizabeth Pena) and works as a mailman. Jacob is haunted by painful memories of his dead son (a mysteriously unbilled Macaulay Culkin, star of 1990's monster hit HOME ALONE) and of his Vietnam experience when he was nearly killed by a soldier with a bayonet. As the film progresses, Jacob also begins to see weird creatures and startling visions. Suddenly, there are monsters roaming through the streets of New York; closed subway stations take on a creepy life of their own; a crowded party turns into a room full of winged demons; a train full of strangers look as though they have sprouted tails and horns. Are these the visions of a madman or have demons actually come to get Jacob Singer? While trying desperately to cling to his sanity, Jacob enlists the help of his ex-wife (Patricia Kalember), a mysterious stranger (Matt Craven), and an angelic chiropractor (Danny Aiello) to help solve the mystery.

The much-touted screenplay for JACOB'S LADDER circulated in Hollywood for almost a decade, and in a 1983 *American Film* article, Rubin's screenplay was listed among the ten best unproduced scripts. (In our view, Lyne improved on the screenplay by heightening its ambiguities and jettisoning much fabular preachiness.) Truly frightening and visually unique, this messy, challenging film is anchored by Tim Robbins' remarkable performance.

JAGGED EDGE
DVD
1985 108m c Mystery/Thriller ★★★
Columbia (U.S.) R

Glenn Close (*Teddy Barnes*), Jeff Bridges (*Jack Forrester*), Peter Coyote (*Thomas Krasny*), Robert Loggia (*Sam Ransom*), John Dehner (*Judge Carrigan*), Karen Austin (*Julie Jensen*), Guy Boyd (*Matthew Barnes*), Marshall Colt (*Bobby Slade*), Louis Giambalvo (*Fabrizi*), Ben Hammer (*Dr. Goldman*) p, Martin Ransohoff; d, Richard Marquand; w, Joe Eszterhas; ph, Matthew F. Leonetti (Metrocolor); ed, Sean Barton, Conrad Buff; m, John Barry; prod d, Gene Callahan; art d, Peter Lansdown Smith; cos, Ann Roth, Michael Dennison, Elizabeth Pine

AAN Best Supporting Actor: Robert Loggia

No cutting edge, but does keep you guessing. It's one of the oldest of Hollywood chestnuts—a socialite is murdered, her husband is suspected by a crafty district attorney, and the female lawyer who defends the accused falls in love with her client—but it still works thanks to Richard Marquand's adroit direction and a tightly knit screenplay from Joe Eszterhas.

Jeff Bridges is one of the beautiful people—possessor of money, luxury, looks and power. When his wife is savagely murdered by an assailant with a jagged-edged knife, Peter Coyote, a tough, sleazy DA, refuses to believe Bridges' innocence. One person who does believe the accused is Glenn Close, a disillusioned lawyer who is sick of Coyote's methods and decides to defend Bridges, falling in love with him in the process.

This film's ending received a great deal of discussion because it purposely obscures the killer's identity, leaving the exiting audience with an uneasy feeling of doubt. It's slick, romantic, funny (Close has a great rapport with her beer-guzzling, foul-mouthed mentor, Robert Loggia), intriguing, and filled with excellent performances.

JAILHOUSE ROCK

DVD

1957 96m bw Musical ★★★½
MGM (U.S.)

Elvis Presley (*Vince Everett*), Judy Tyler (*Peggy Van Alden*), Mickey Shaughnessy (*Hunk Houghton*), Jennifer Holden (*Sherry Wilson*), Dean Jones (*Teddy Talbot*), Anne Neyland (*Laury Jackson*), Hugh Sanders (*Warden*), Vaughn Taylor (*Mr. Shores*), Mike Stoller (*Pianist*), Grandon Rhodes (*Prof. August Van Alden*)

p, Pandro S. Berman; d, Richard Thorpe; w, Guy Trosper (based on a story by Ned Young); ph, Robert Bronner (CinemaScope); ed, Ralph E. Winters; art d, William A. Horning, Randall Duell; fx, A. Arnold Gillespie

All shook up and enjoyably bad, JAILHOUSE ROCK captures early Elvis in all his leg-quivering, nostril-flaring, lip-snarling teen idol glory.

This hot black-and-white number was Elvis Presley's third (after LOVE ME TENDER and LOVING YOU) and set the standard for the rest of his movie outings—too bad the the others omitted the dangerous element of his character presented here. Elvis comes across like a white-trash musical genius version of James Dean, playing Vince Everett, a surly good ole boy who accidentally kills a man while defending a lady's honor...in a bar. This heroism gets him sent up for manslaughter, sharing his prison cell with Hunk Houghton (Mickey Shaughnessy), an ex-singer who convinces him to perform in the slammer's convict show. After Vince is freed, he meets Peggy Van Alden (Judy Tyler), with whom he forms a record company, and in no time he is a national star on his way to Hollywood. Peggy, however, sees that Vince is turning into an egomaniac, and she can't stand it.

There's little surprise but JAILHOUSE really rocks, establishing pre-Army Elvis, the rockabilly elemental force, when he was really something. The steamy songs are mostly by Lieber and Stoller; the latter can be seen as the pianist in the famous "Jailhouse Rock" sequence (which the young King choreographed). The title song sold two million records within two weeks, and the picture, in turn, grossed several million, with Presley receiving 50 percent of the profits. Other tunes include "Treat Me Nice," "Baby, I Don't Care," and "Young and Beautiful."

JANE EYRE

1944 97m bw Romance ★★★½
Fox (U.S.)

Orson Welles (*Edward Rochester*), Joan Fontaine (*Jane Eyre*), Margaret O'Brien (*Adele*), Peggy Ann Garner (*Jane as a Child*), John Sutton (*Dr. Rivers*), Sara Allgood (*Bessie*), Henry Daniell (*Brockelhurst*), Agnes Moorehead (*Mrs. Reed*), Elizabeth Taylor (*Helen Burns*), Aubrey Mather (*Col. Dent*)

p, William Goetz; d, Robert Stevenson; w, Aldous Huxley, Robert Stevenson, John Houseman (based on the book by Charlotte Bronte); ph, George Barnes; ed, Walter Thompson; m, Bernard Herrmann; art d, James Basevi, Wiard Ihnen; fx, Fred Sersen; cos, Rene Hubert

A touch too plodding, but an atmospheric reduction of Bronte. This was the fifth time around for the doughty English lady: In 1913 Irving Cummings and Ethel Grand did it. In 1915 it was Alan Hale and Louise Vale. Mabel Ballin and Norman Trevor tried again in 1921; then Virginia Bruce and Colin Clive made the first talkie version in 1934. Although shot on the West Los Angeles sound stages of 20th Century Fox, Barnes's eerie cinematography truly evokes the bleakness of the novel.

Fontaine is Jane Eyre, an orphan girl who has been tossed about by fate and managed to survive a sordid upbringing. (In the early scenes the role is touchingly played by Peggy Ann Garner.) Fontaine takes a job as governess to Yorkshireman Welles's ward, O'Brien. They live on the Yorkshire moors in a huge house called Thornfield Hall. Fontaine appears as though she'll remain a spinster for the rest of her days, but there is an attraction growing between her and Welles. He is a troubled man, brooding and enigmatic, yet Fontaine has come to love him; a wedding is planned, but it fails to take place.

This is Bronte as gothic paperback romance, and the music, by longtime Welles associate Bernard Herrmann, richly slathers over discrepancies between Welles's and Fontaine's acting styles (after Welles makes his entrance, everything seems to swirl about him—or at least out of his way). In the original book Jane was the protagonist and Rochester was more of a large supporting part. To accommodate Welles, who was emerging as one of the country's most popular actors, the male role was expanded and he received billing above Fontaine.

The Peggy Ann Garner sequences are the best in the film, with Jane's dismal schooling realized very well. You can bet there wasn't a dry eye in the house when strange, beautiful little Helen Burns (Elizabeth Taylor), dies from gross neglect. Later, in 1957, it was done with Patrick Macnee and Joan Elan and then again in 1971 with George C. Scott and Susannah York, both of these versions for television.

JASON AND THE ARGONAUTS

DVD

1963 104m c Fantasy/Adventure ★★★½
Columbia (U.K.)

Todd Armstrong (*Jason*), Nancy Kovack (*Medea*), Gary Raymond (*Acastus*), Laurence Naismith (*Argus*), Niall MacGinnis (*Zeus*), Michael Gwynn (*Hermes*), Douglas Wilmer (*Pelias*), Jack Gwillim (*King Aeetes*), Honor Blackman (*Hera*), John Cairney (*Hylas*)

p, Charles H. Schneer; d, Don Chaffey; w, Jan Reed, Beverley Cross; ph, Wilkie Cooper (Dynamation 90, Eastmancolor); ed, Maurice Rootes; m, Bernard Herrmann; prod d, Geoffrey Drake; art d, Herbert Smith, Jack Maxsted, Toni Sarzi-Braga; fx, Ray Harryhausen

What a blast! This film, along with THE SEVENTH VOYAGE OF SINBAD, contains special-effects master Ray Harryhausen's finest work, evoking a world of dragons, living statues, harpies and gods. Pelias (Douglas Wilmer) murders the king of Thessaly and steals his throne, but the infant prince, Jason, survives.

Years later, aided by the goddess Hera (Honor Blackman), Jason (Todd Armstrong) begins a search for the Golden Fleece, which will finally instate him as rightful king. With a crew of brave men (including Hercules, in a fine performance by Nigel Green), he sets out on his glorious quest in his ship, the *Argo*. At one point, the *Argo* is menaced by a giant living statue, but Jason defeats it. After further adventures in which Jason battles harpies, encounters the gigantic Neptune, and discovers Medea (Nancy Kovack) on an empty ship, the crew finally find the fleece. They kill the seven-headed hydra that guards it but are halted again when the hydra's teeth grow into seven sword-brandishing living skeletons. In a stunning display of technical wizardry, the Argonauts fight the skeletons to the death.

Harryhausen is at his most creative and brilliant (except for the disappointing bronze Titan), the film is well directed by Don Chaffey and adequately acted as these things go. Featuring gorgeous Mediterranean photography and a rousing Bernard Herrmann score, making this a great film for kids that will also please adult viewers. A must-see.

JAWS

1975 124m c Horror ★★★★
Universal (U.S.) PG

Roy Scheider (*Police Chief Martin Brody*), Robert Shaw (*Quint*), Richard Dreyfuss (*Matt Hooper*), Lorraine Gary (*Ellen Brody*), Murray Hamilton (*Mayor Larry Vaughn*), Carl Gottlieb (*Meadows*), Jeffrey Kramer (*Deputy Hendricks*), Susan Backlinie (*Chrissie Watkins*), Jonathan Filley (*Cassidy*), Ted Grossman (*Estuary Victim*)

p, Richard D. Zanuck, David Brown; d, Steven Spielberg; w, Peter Benchley, Carl Gottlieb, Howard Sackler (uncredited, based on the novel by Benchley); ph, Bill Butler (Panavision, Technicolor); ed, Verna Fields; m, John Williams; prod d, Joe Alves; fx, Robert A. Mattey

AAN Best Picture; AA Best Film Editing: Verna Fields; AA Best Original Score: John Williams; AA Best Sound: Robert L. Hoyt, Roger Heman, Earl Madery, John Carter

A looming, terrifying catch of the day, JAWS was the summer mega-hit that established Steven Spielberg. This is the most cynically manipulative movie he's ever made (although it's deepened by some telling points about the tensions of contemporary masculinity), and it must be seen for its unexpected editing, driving score, and careful build toward shock images so big they feel like they're jumping into your lap.

An East Coast resort, Amity Island, is plagued by attacks on swimmers by a 28-foot great white shark. Although the mayor (Murray Hamilton) would like to keep the whole thing quiet—he doesn't want to ruin the summer tourist season—the brutal attacks soon cannot be ignored, so police chief Martin Brody (Roy Scheider), marine biologist Matt Hooper (Richard Dreyfuss), and grizzled old shark hunter Quint (Robert Shaw) go after the monstrous creature, winding up in a desperate fight for their lives.

The film that put Steven Spielberg on the cinematic map, JAWS was phenomenally successful at the box office and seemed to tap into a universal fear of what lies beneath the sea. The director's vision of *Moby Dick*, with Quint as Ahab, finally digs a grave for macho, exposing it as a foolhardy joke; it's high time. Spielberg's direction turns the material into a nerve-jangling *tour de force*. From the outrageously frightening opening—in which a beautiful young woman skinny-dipping in the moonlight is devoured by the unseen shark—to the claustrophobic climax aboard Quint's fishing boat, Spielberg has us in his grip and rarely lets go (although the film does bog down momentarily in some soap-opera scenes of Brody's family life).

Because the film tapped into a common fear and played on it so skillfully, it was a worldwide hit and entered international popular culture. JAWS has been endlessly parodied by comedians and filmmakers alike, and John Williams's effective score has now become a cliché. Three vastly inferior sequels followed. Now, everybody into the pool!

JEAN DE FLORETTE

1986 122m c Drama ★★★½
Renn/RAI-TV/D.D./A2 (France) PG

Yves Montand (*Cesar Soubeyran/"Le Papet"*), Gerard Depardieu (*Jean de Florette/Cadoret*), Daniel Auteuil (*Ugolin Soubeyran/"Galignette"*), Elisabeth Depardieu (*Aimee Cadoret*), Ernestine Mazurowna (*Manon Cadoret*), Marcel Champel (*Pique-Bouffigue*), Armand Meffre (*Philoxene*), Andre Dupon (*Pamphile*), Pierre Nougaro (*Casimir*), Marc Betton (*Martial*)

p, Pierre Grunstein; d, Claude Berri; w, Claude Berri, Gerard Brach (based on the novel by Marcel Pagnol); ph, Bruno Nuytten (Technovision, Eastmancolor); ed, Arlette Langmann, Herve de Luze, Noelle Boisson; m, Jean-Claude Petit; prod d, Bernard Vezat; cos, Sylvie Gautrelet

The most talked-about French production in many years, this picture and its sequel, MANON OF THE SPRING (MANON DES SOURCES), were completed at a combined record-breaking budget of $17 million (about eight times the cost of the average French picture). Shot back to back with its successor, JEAN DE FLORETTE is set in a French farming village tucked into a picturesque hillside.

Le Papet (Yves Montand), an imperious and unscrupulous local landowner, welcomes the return to the village of his nephew, Ugolin (Daniel Auteuil). An unappealing social misfit, Ugolin dreams of making his fortune by growing carnations. Carnations, however, need a great deal of water—a sparse commodity in the village. When Le Papet realizes that Ugolin's idea is potentially profitable, he sets his sights on a neighboring farm that has an untapped natural spring. But the farm is owned by Jean Cadoret (Gerard Depardieu), a hunchbacked ex-tax collector who has bid farewell to the city and proves to be a tenacious convert to the farming life.

Directed by Claude Berri, JEAN DE FLORETTE is based on Marcel Pagnol's two-part novel *L'Eau des Collines* (The Water of the Hills), which, in turn, was based on an unsuccessful 1952 film Pagnol directed. A throwback to the pre-New Wave days of French cinema, the film offers complex characterizations, careful scripting, and lyrically pastoral images.

JENNIFER EIGHT

1992 127m c Romance/Thriller ★★½
Scott Rudin Productions (U.S.) R

Andy Garcia (*John Berlin*), Lance Henriksen (*Freddy Ross*), Uma Thurman (*Helena Robertson*), Graham Beckel (*John Taylor*), Kathy Baker (*Margie Ross*), Kevin Conway (*Citrine*), John Malkovich (*St. Anne*), Perry Lang (*Travis*), Nicholas Love (*Bisley*), Michael O'Neill (*Serato*)

p, David Wimbury, Gary Lucchesi; d, Bruce Robinson; w, Bruce Robinson; ph, Conrad L. Hall; ed, Conrad Buff; m, Christopher Young; prod d, Richard MacDonald; art d, William Durrell Jr., John Willett

Despite a gimmicky, underdeveloped plot, JENNIFER EIGHT is a moody, atmospheric thriller, featuring several fine performances and marking a promising major studio debut by writer-director Bruce Robinson.

Burnt-out cop John Berlin (Andy Garcia) leaves the LAPD for a supposedly quieter life in rural California with the Eureka police force. Instead, Berlin immediately rankles his new colleagues by reopening an unsolved case involving the serial murders of seven blind girls. Berlin becomes convinced that the eighth victim, "Jennifer Eight," will be gorgeous blind student Helena Robertson (Uma Thurman), with whom he falls in love. Before long, Berlin is framed for a murder and the serial killer is once more on the prowl.

For most of its running time, JENNIFER EIGHT is effectively and powerfully built around the echoing existences of Robertson, whose blindness makes her easy prey to the fear and panic of isolation, and Berlin, whose absorption in his gruesome work has left him similarly isolated and fearful. Where the film falls apart is in failing to follow through on Berlin's growing dependence on Helena as he finds himself blindsided after being framed for Ross's murder.

JERRY MAGUIRE   DVD
1996   135m   c   Comedy/Drama   ★★★½
Gracie Films (U.S.)   R

Tom Cruise *(Jerry Maguire)*, Cuba Gooding Jr. *(Rod Tidwell)*, Renee Zellweger *(Dorothy Boyd)*, Kelly Preston *(Avery Bishop)*, Bonnie Hunt *(Laurel Boyd)*, Jerry O'Connell *(Frank Cushman)*, Jay Mohr *(Bob Sugar)*, Regina King *(Marcee Tidwell)*, Jonathan Lipnicki *(Ray Boyd)*, Todd Louiso *(Chad the Nanny)*

p, James L. Brooks, Laurence Mark, Richard Sakai, Cameron Crowe; d, Cameron Crowe; w, Cameron Crowe; ph, Janusz Kaminski; ed, Joe Hutshing; m, Nancy Wilson; prod d, Stephen Lineweaver; art d, Virginia Randolph, Clayton Hartley; fx, Paul Haines; cos, Betsy Heimann

AA Best Supporting Actor: Cuba Gooding Jr.; AAN Best Picture; AAN Best Actor: Tom Cruise; AAN Best Film Editing: Joe Hutshing; AAN Best Original Screenplay: Cameron Crowe

Cameron Crowe's popular romantic comedy features standout performances by Tom Cruise and Oscar winner Cuba Gooding Jr., as well as impressive turns by Renee Zellweger and Jonathan Lipnicki.

Jerry Maguire (Tom Cruise) is a sports agent who wins salaries and endorsements for his clients that are so overinflated that they repel fans. During a fit of guilt, he writes a memo outlining how sports agencies ought to lessen their concern with the almighty dollar. He is subsequently fired and, in an effort to stay in the game, convinces one of his clients—Rod Tidwell (Cuba Gooding Jr.), a receiver for the Arizona Cardinals—to stick with him as he builds a solo career. As Jerry packs up his desk and leaves, he implores his co-workers to follow him. The only one who agrees to follow Jerry is Dorothy Boyd (Renee Zellweger), an accountant who has been secretly attracted to Jerry for some time. Jerry busily hypes Rod as a sputtering romance begins between him and Dorothy.

Like 1989's SAY ANYTHING, JERRY MAGUIRE displays Cameron Crowe's ability to create romantic relationships that ring true. Crowe also nimbly avoids the stereotype traps that characters like Jerry Maguire and Rod Tidwell often place in a writer's path. Though JERRY MAGUIRE's happy ending is a bit too neat, the overall package is well worth the price of admission. JERRY MAGUIRE also gives audiences a rare look at Cruise's underappreciated comic side. He displays deft comic timing and a surprising aptitude for physical comedy. The film's other pleasant surprise is the performance of Gooding, who easily holds his own against Cruise. He even manages to steal a few scenes from the star, and scored himself an Oscar in the process.

JESSE JAMES
1939   105m   c   Western   ★★★★
Fox (U.S.)

Tyrone Power *(Jesse James)*, Henry Fonda *(Frank James)*, Nancy Kelly *(Zee)*, Randolph Scott *(Will Wright)*, Henry Hull *(Major Rufus Cobb)*, Brian Donlevy *(Barshee)*, John Carradine *(Bob Ford)*, Jane Darwell *(Mrs. Samuels)*, Donald Meek *(McCoy)*, Slim Summerville *(Jailer)*

p, Nunnally Johnson; d, Henry King; w, Nunnally Johnson (based on historical data assembled by Rosalind Schaeffer and Jo Frances James); ph, W. Howard Greene, George Barnes (Technicolor); ed, Barbara McLean; m, Louis Silvers; art d, William Darling, George Dudley

This classic Western unfolds the legendary saga of the notorious James boys, notably Jesse Woodson James (1847-1882). Director King directed this blockbuster that captures the image and era of the infamous outlaw, if not the reality of his character.

Until this film the 24-year-old Power had been an attractive matinee idol, but here he proved that he could really act. Though Fonda has fewer scenes, he renders his stalwart, prosaic character so effectively that Fox cast him in the successful sequel, THE RETURN OF FRANK JAMES. JESSE JAMES was the film that made Fonda a star.

Both King and Johnson had been eager to do a film on the legendary outlaw. Johnson researched Jesse James in Missouri, drawing most of his historic notions from the *Sedalia Gazette*, a strongly pro-James paper which promoted the idea that the notorious lawlessness of the James boys was caused by railroad and Union Army persecution following the Civil War. In the beginning this was true, but even Missouri residents grew tired of this excuse as the James-Younger gang went on looting for almost two decades; in fact, Jesse James was at large for eighteen years before being gunned down by Bob Ford on April 3, 1882. Screenwriter Johnson opted for nostalgia and legend and left out much of the outlaw's grim career. Jo Frances James, granddaughter of Jesse James, was hired as a consultant to the production, but she was later disappointed with the film, commenting: "I don't know what happened to the history part of it. It seemed to me the story was fiction from beginning to end. About the only connection it had with fact was that there once was a man named James and he did ride a horse."

The old Technicolor process has never been more richly reproduced than in JESSE JAMES, which offers spellbinding hues of deep green, brown, and gold, giving the countryside portrayed the soft appearance of mellow history. There have been many films dealing with America's most celebrated outlaw, but this is the best.

JESUS OF MONTREAL   DVD
(JESUS DE MONTREAL)
1989   120m   c   Drama   ★★★½
Max/Gerard Mital (Canada/France)   R

Lothaire Bluteau *(Daniel)*, Catherine Wilkening *(Mireille)*, Johanne-Marie Tremblay *(Constance)*, Remy Girard *(Martin)*, Robert Lepage *(Rene)*, Gilles Pelletier *(Fr. Leclerc)*, Yves Jacques *(Richard Cardinal)*, Denys Arcand *(The Judge)*

p, Roger Frappier; d, Denys Arcand; w, Denys Arcand; ph, Guy Dufaux; ed, Isabelle Dedieu; m, Yves Laferriere; prod d, Francois Seguin

AAN Best Foreign Language Film

Denys Arcand's JESUS OF MONTREAL is a modern Passion Play that takes aim at organized religion and the superficial values of our media-saturated society, yet suggests salvation through technology. Thoughtful without being didactic, this is a strong, provocative film.

The story begins as Daniel (Bluteau) is hired to stage the annual Summer Passion Play in a park overlooking the skyline of Montreal. From the start, Daniel's production—which he is to direct, as well as to star in as Jesus—is not entirely conventional. His ensemble cast comprises fellow actor friends forced to get along by dubbing porn movies and modeling for sleazy commercials. Mireille (Wilkening) is the Passion Play's (as well as the film's) Mary Magdalene. At first, she drifts aimlessly and almost amorally through life, but ultimately finds meaning in her devotion to Daniel and the play. Daniel becomes fascinated with some of the more unorthodox theories that he encounters in his research of Jesus' life, including questions of Jesus' true parentage, and these details go into the play. When the play is finally staged, it emerges as an avant-garde performance piece, with audiences ushered to the various installations representing the events in Jesus' life. The resulting drama doesn't adhere to standard biblical interpretations, but it truly moves and inspires the audience, and the revisionist Passion Play, its cast, and particularly Daniel become the toast of the town, cooed over by critics and culture vultures. Soon, life begins to imitate art, as church officials decide to discontinue the play because of questions about its possibly blasphemous content.

Arcand's excellent screenplay invests his vision of this spiritual parable with scathing satire and social commentary. The superb cast includes Bluteau as Daniel, his quiet brooding erupting into indignant rage; Girard as Martin, the most down-to-earth character in the film; and Wilkening as Mireille, who represents the modern-day lost soul's search for meaning. However, in drawing parallels between Daniel and Jesus, Arcand paints himself into a corner. The too-literal quality of these comparisons threatens to diminish the film's overall impact. The final resurrection sequence should be extraordinarily powerful as well as clinically probing; instead it is more of the latter than the former. But despite these weaknesses, the handsomely produced JESUS OF MONTREAL remains fresh, intelligent, and fascinating.

JESUS' SON   **DVD**
2000 111m c   Drama   ★★★½
Evenstar (U.S.)   R

Billy Crudup *(FH)*, Samantha Morton *(Michelle)*, Denis Leary *(Mayne)*, Jack Black *(Georgie)*, Will Patton *(John Smith)*, Greg Germann *(Dr. Shanis)*, Holly Hunter *(Mira)*, Dennis Hopper *(Bill)*, Torben Brooks *(Oldsmobile Driver)*, Antoinette LaVecchia *(Dead Guy's Wife)*

p, Elizabeth Cuthrell, Lydia Dean Pilcher, David Urrutia; d, Alison Maclean; w, Elizabeth Cuthrell, David Urrutia, Oren Moverman (based on the book *Jesus' Son* by Denis Johnson); ph, Adam Kimmel; ed, Geraldine Peroni, Stuart Levy; m, Joe Henry; prod d, David Doernberg; art d, Andrea Stanley; fx, Blue Sky Studios; cos, Kasia Walicka Maimone

Eight years after she surprised critics with her dark and disturbing CRUSH, writer-director Alison Maclean returned with a sweet and sad adaptation of Denis Johnson's stories about junkie life in the American heartland.

It's 1974, and a greasy young hitchhiker is standing on the side of the road, looking for his girl. Who he is and how he came to be thumbing a ride in the pouring rain becomes clear as the film flashes back to Iowa City, three years earlier, when a young drifter known only as "FH" (Billy Crudup) falls for heroin addict Michelle (Samantha Morton); a year later they're sharing needles in a dirty Holiday Inn somewhere in the Midwest. Maclean preserves the fractured structure of Johnson's linked short stories and lets the childlike FH tell his own tale, which means it stops, starts, jumps back, nods out, and trips over itself in ways a less assured filmmaker would never dare. FH gets a job as an orderly in a hospital, where he and a coworker (Jack Black) consume pharmaceuticals; FH spends a day ripping copper wiring out of an abandoned house with a fellow user (Denis Leary) and sees a naked, parasailing angel; FH loses Michelle but finds redemption through voyeurism and Al Anon.

Maclean gilds her film with small flights of visual fantasy a la DRUGSTORE COWBOY: an incidental crown of thorns

on a dirty diner window; a blazing sacred heart in an end-of-the-line Laundromat; an ecstatic vision at an abandoned drive-in. But for all the divine touches, FH is no Jesus, or even his son. He's just another wide-eyed American Adam on the road again, a dazed and confused Huck Finn of the highways.

JEWEL OF THE NILE, THE   **DVD**
1985 115m c   Adventure   ★★★
Fox (U.S.)   PG

Michael Douglas *(Jack)*, Kathleen Turner *(Joan)*, Danny DeVito *(Ralph)*, Spiros Focas *(Omar)*, Howard Jay Patterson *(Barak)*, Samuel Ross Williams *(Arak)*, Hamid Fillali *(Rachid)*, Avner Eisenberg *(Jewel of the Nile)*, Paul David Magid *(Tarak)*, Holland Taylor *(Gloria)*

p, Michael Douglas; d, Lewis Teague; w, Mark Rosenthal, Lawrence Konner (based on characters created by Diane Thomas); ph, Jan De Bont (Technicolor); ed, Michael Ellis, Peter Boita; m, Jack Nitzsche; prod d, Richard Dawking, Terry Knight; art d, Leslie Tomkins, Damien Lanfranchi; cos, Emma Porteous

Frenetic, feisty sequel to ROMANCING THE STONE is little more than a retread of the first film. This action fantasy again features macho-but-sensitive Michael Douglas and bristly Kathleen Turner, barely escaping with their lives in one incredible adventure after another.

The picture begins where the first one ended, with Jack (Douglas) and Joan (Turner) sailing off into the sunset—but their storybook romance is beginning to show fell symptoms of reality. The couple are idling their time away in a romantic port, but a bored Joan is eager for new adventures. One soon presents itself in the form of an Arab sheik who asks her to write his autobiography. When Joan hesitates, she is abducted. The chase is on, with Jack out to rescue his fair lady from a pack of desert cutthroats. Loudmouthed Danny DeVito is hot on both their trails, lusting after another fabulous gem, the Jewel of the Nile.

The action here is virtually nonstop and the special effects are often astounding: good and bad guys battle atop speeding trains and the lovers dangle perilously over cliffs and ride through stampeding desert tribes. But THE JEWEL OF THE NILE is missing the faux-innocent tone and consistent narrative invention that made ROMANCING THE STONE work. Moreover, it's hard to overlook the racist depiction of Arabs, which is markedly less jovial than the stereotypical treatment of Latinos in the first film.

JEZEBEL   **DVD**
1938 104m bw Drama   ★★★★
Warner Bros. (U.S.)

Bette Davis *(Julie Morrison)*, Henry Fonda *(Preston Dillard)*, George Brent *(Buck Cantrell)*, Margaret Lindsay *(Amy Bradford Dillard)*, Fay Bainter *(Aunt Belle Massey)*, Richard Cromwell *(Ted Dillard)*, Donald Crisp *(Dr. Livingstone)*, Henry O'Neill *(Gen. Theopholus Bogardus)*, John Litel *(Jean LeCour)*, Gordon Oliver *(Dick Allen)*

p, Henry Blanke; d, William Wyler; w, Clements Ripley, Abem Finkel, John Huston, Robert Buckner (based on the play by Owen Davis, Sr.); ph, Ernest Haller; ed, Warren Low; m, Max Steiner; art d, Robert Haas; cos, Orry-Kelly

AAN Best Picture; AA Best Actress: Bette Davis; AA Best Supporting Actress: Fay Bainter; AAN Best Cinematography: Ernest Haller; AAN Best Score: Max Stiner

Our favorite magnolia. A mesmerizing romantic melodrama with "Popeye the Magnificent" playing a southern belle so perverse she ruins her own chances, as well as shaking up the Olde South. Without Davis, who snared her second Oscar for the role—JEZEBEL was her consolation prize for losing the plum role in GONE WITH THE WIND, and there was a rush to get it into theaters first—this would seem mildewed indeed. But because her nervy, edgy performance conveys so much rage it leads convincingly into the film's second half where raging fires and fever sweep through New Orleans.

We may never really know if Davis and director Wyler had a great, doomed love affair, but the film looks like they did. Especially when Davis's Julie wrecks a great ball, and her own life, by wearing a flaming red gown when unmarried women are expected to wear pristine white. It's an outrageously great moment. Wyler's camera (abetted by the gifted cinematographer Ernest Haller) bores down on Davis, with her large, guilty eyes darting about to Max Steiner's swooping waltz—she's in too far to turn back. And the scene captures a quality in Fonda rarely exploited—his stubborness—which may account for the longevity of his career. GONE WITH THE WIND may not have a single moment quite as incredible as this one, but then, that film didn't have Wyler who also gives Davis her other all-stops-out moment—her apology to Fonda, going to her knees in a white gown of breathtaking proportions. Davis gives the scene an overwhelmingly hushed sense of sexual urgency and surrender. JEZEBEL is indeed Wyler's love letter to Davis. (THE LETTER represents the souring of their collaboration; THE LITTLE FOXES, its death.)

The screenplay by Clements Ripley, Abem Finkel and John Huston was based on the Owen Davis, Sr. play that lasted about five minutes on Broadway with Miriam Hopkins replacing the ailing Tallulah Bankhead ("It was dreadful," said Tallulah. "Had I played the part it might have run two weeks."). The casting of Davis fanned the flames of her feuds with both of these southern belles, who hailed from Georgia and Alabama respectively.

Fonda had made a deal with the studio that his work on the film be completed by early December, so he could fly back to New York where his wife was awaiting their first child (Jane, born on December 21). Although they tried to rush things, Wyler's perfectionism put the film behind schedule. As a result, Davis had to do her closeups and inserts without Fonda on the set. JEZEBEL features two songs: the title tune and "Raise a Ruckus." The film cost slightly over $1 million but made a bundle for everyone involved and got the country in an antebellum mood that went into overdrive with the release of Selznick's greatest work.

JFK

1991 189m c Historical/Drama **★★★½** DVD
Camelot Productions/Warner Bros./New Regency R
Films/Canal Plus/Ixtlan (U.S.)

Kevin Costner (*Jim Garrison*), Sissy Spacek (*Liz Garrison*), Joe Pesci (*David Ferrie*), Tommy Lee Jones (*Clay Shaw*), Gary Oldman (*Lee Harvey Oswald*), Jay O. Sanders (*Lou Ivon*), Michael Rooker (*Bill Broussard*), Laurie Metcalf (*Susie Cox*), Gary Grubbs (*Al Oser*), John Candy (*Dean Andrews*)

p, A. Kitman Ho, Oliver Stone; d, Oliver Stone; w, Oliver Stone, Zachary Sklar (from the books *On the Trail of the Assassins* by Jim Garrison and *Crossfire: The Plot That Killed Kennedy* by Jim Marrs); ph, Robert Richardson; ed, Joe Hutshing, Pietro Scalia; m, John Williams; prod d, Victor Kempster; art d, Derek R. Hill, Alan Tomkins; cos, Marlene Stewart

AAN Best Picture; AAN Best Supporting Actor: Tommy Lee Jones; AAN Best Director: Oliver Stone; AAN Best Adapted Screenplay: Oliver Stone, Zachary Sklar; AA Best Cinematography: Robert Richardson; AA Best Film Editing: Joe Hutshing, Pietro Scalia; AAN Best Original Score: John Williams; AAN Best Sound: Michael Minkler, Gregg Landaker, Tod A. Maitland

Director and co-screenwriter Oliver Stone pulls off an amazing filmmaking feat with JFK, transforming the dry minutiae of every John F. Kennedy assassination conspiracy theory of the past three decades into riveting screen material.

Stone's story revolves around New Orleans District Attorney Jim Garrison's (Kevin Costner) unsuccessful 1967 prosecution of local businessman Clay Shaw (Tommy Lee Jones) for complicity in Kennedy's murder. Shaw's exact connection, even in the film, is hazy at best. But Garrison uses Shaw's trial mostly as a pretext to advance his own theory that Lee Harvey Oswald (Gary Oldman) was only one of several gunmen involved in the assassination and that he probably, as he claimed at the time of his arrest, never fired a single shot.

It's a measure of Stone's forcefulness as a filmmaker that he struck raw nerves across the political spectrum with a film that, in substance, did little more than dust off an accretion of well-worn conspiracy theories, most of which have been in circulation since the days following the assassination itself. Partly as a result of the film's impact, legislation was introduced into Congress in March of 1992 in an attempt to secure the release of FBI, CIA, and government files relating to the assassination which had previously been ordered sealed until 2029. That, however, is far from the most extraordinary thing about JFK.

Imagine a three-hour-plus epic that jettisons any recognizable dramatic structure, as JFK does, in favor of almost non-stop dialogue exposition and ends, not with a bang, but with an extended courtroom monologue and the hero's inglorious defeat, and you would normally have a surefire formula for failure. But JFK succeeds, partly thanks to a taut and intelligent script, and partly because the central investigation is spiced up by a series of key witnesses, each of whom injects the film with color and life; Pesci, Jones, and Kevin Bacon give particularly good performances. Stone's rapid-fire recreations and dramatizations of possible events also help keep things moving. But it is the director's evident passion to expose the deepest, darkest elements at work in society that really makes JFK come alive.

JIM THORPE—ALL AMERICAN

1951 107m bw Biography/Sports **★★★**
Warner Bros. (U.S.)

Burt Lancaster (*Jim Thorpe*), Charles Bickford (*Glenn S. "Pop" Warner*), Steve Cochran (*Peter Allendine*), Phyllis Thaxter (*Margaret Miller*), Dick Wesson (*Ed Guyac*), Jack Big Head (*Little Boy*), Suni Warcloud (*Wally Denny*), Al Mejia (*Louis Tewanema*), Hubie Kerns (*Tom Ashenbrunner*), Nestor Paiva (*Hiram Thorpe*)

p, Everett Freeman; d, Michael Curtiz; w, Douglas Morrow, Frank Davis, Everett Freeman (based on the story "Bright Path" by Morrow and Vincent X. Flaherty, from the biography by Russell Birdwell and James Thorpe); ph, Ernest Haller; ed, Folmar Blangsted; m, Max Steiner; art d, Edward Carrere; cos, Milo Anderson

Sports and big teeth. Burt Lancaster sets his jaw and plays one of America's greatest athletes, the wondrous Jim Thorpe, a Native American who captured gold medals in the pentathlon and decathlon at the 1912 Stockholm Olympics, only to be stripped of them because he had played semiprofessional baseball, violating his amateur status.

This biopic begins with Billy Gray portraying Thorpe as a youth on an Oklahoma reservation. Lancaster takes over as Thorpe matriculates to the all-Indian college at Carlisle, Pennsylvania, where he begins playing football to impress Margaret Miller (Phyllis Thaxter), his college sweetheart and future wife. Coached by the legendary Glenn "Pop" Warner (Charles Bickford), he captures All-American honors, then goes on to glory and disappointment in Stockholm, followed by an illustrious career in professional baseball and football. When his young son dies, Thorpe's spirit is broken, and he turns to the bottle, losing Margaret.

Thorpe was actually enshrined in the Pro Football Hall of Fame and his Olympic medals have been posthumously restored. As usual, Lancaster did most of his own athletic feats. Unfortunately some of his performances tend to confuse bravura with thoughtful interpretation. Curtiz tries hard to infuse the predictability with life, but the formula is the real champ here. Adequate.

JOHN GRISHAM'S THE RAINMAKER

1997 133m c Drama
American Zoetrope/Constellation (U.S.)

DVD
★★★
PG-13

Claire Danes (Kelly Riker), Matt Damon (Rudy Baylor), Danny DeVito (Deck Schifflet), Jon Voight (Leo F. Drummond), Mary Kay Place (Dot Black), Dean Stockwell (Judge Harvey Hale), Teresa Wright (Miss Birdie), Virginia Madsen (Jackie Lemancyzk), Mickey Rourke (Bruiser Stone), Johnny Whitworth (Donny Ray Black)

p, Michael Douglas, Steven Reuther, Fred Fuchs; d, Francis Ford Coppola; w, Francis Ford Coppola, Michael Herr (based on the novel by John Grisham); ph, John Toll; ed, Barry Malkin; m, Elmer Bernstein; prod d, Howard Cummings; art d, Jeffrey McDonald; fx, Guy Clayton (coordinator); cos, Aggie Guerard Rodgers

THE RAINMAKER focuses on a first-time lawyer's courtroom battle against a giant health insurance company that makes its money by refusing to pay its clients' medical bills.

Fresh out of law school, Rudy Baylor (Matt Damon) is hired at a Memphis firm headed by the shady J. Lyman "Bruiser" Stone (Mickey Rourke), a specialist in personal injury suits. Rudy's mentor at the firm is Deck Schifflet (Danny DeVito), an almost-lawyer who has flunked the bar exam six times. Unfortunately, the FBI has begun an investigation of Bruiser Stone, and Rudy and Deck decide to start their own practice. They tend to Rudy's single client: a young man with leukemia, Donny Ray Black (Johnny Whitworth), who is suing the insurance company that denied him coverage. Early on, it is abundantly clear to Rudy that he is in over his head in the battle against Great Benefit insurance and its team of high-priced lawyers, led by Leo F. Drummond (Jon Voight). Though Drummond offers to settle out-of-court for $75,000, Rudy chooses to take the case to trial.

Though awfully familiar to audiences (novelist Grisham tends to tell the same story over and over), THE RAINMAKER is better than most of the Grisham adaptations that preceded it. Much of the credit for the film's success belongs to writer-director Coppola, (who has of late traded in his auteur standing for that of director-for-hire): as writer, Coppola successfully translates Grisham's rather murky legalese into a gripping David-and-Goliath tale; as director, Coppola still carries enough clout to assemble a fine cast, including such big-name actors as Danny Glover, Claire Danes, and Dean Stockwell in relatively small supporting roles. For his part, Damon plays young Rudy as smart but clearly out of his element. By avoiding the type of scenery chewing that Grisham's dialogue practically begs for, Damon creates a character that, like Coppola's direction, rises above the rather routine Grisham standard.

JOHNNY BELINDA

1948 102m bw Drama
Warner Bros. (U.S.)

★★★★½

Jane Wyman (Belinda McDonald), Lew Ayres (Dr. Robert Richardson), Charles Bickford (Black McDonald), Agnes Moorehead (Aggie McDonald), Stephen McNally (Locky McCormick), Jan Sterling (Stella McGuire), Rosalind Ivan (Mrs. Peggety), Dan Seymour (Pacquet), Mabel Paige (Mrs. Lutz), Ida Moore (Mrs. McKee)

p, Jerry Wald; d, Jean Negulesco; w, Irmgard Von Cube, Allen Vincent (based on the play by Elmer Harris); ph, Ted McCord; ed,

David Weisbart; m, Max Steiner; art d, Robert Haas; fx, William McGann, Edwin DuPar; cos, Milo Anderson

AAN Best Picture; AAN Best Actor: Lew Ayres; AA Best Actress: Jane Wyman; AAN Best Supporting Actor: Charles Bickford; AAN Best Supporting Actress: Agnes Moorehead; AAN Best Director: Jean Negulesco; AAN Best Screenplay: Irmgard Von Cube, Allen Vincent; AAN Best B/W Cinematography: Ted McCord; AAN Best Film Editing: David Weisbart; AAN Best Score (Drama or Comedy): Max Stiner; AAN Best Art Direction-Set Decoration (B/W): Robert Haas, William Wallace; AAN Best Sound Recording: Warner Bros. Sound Department

After 15 years of hoofing her way through Warner Bros. films as a chorus girl and the second-fiddle friend of female leads, Jane Wyman finally got her dream part as the sensitive deaf-mute in this screen adaptation of the play by Elmer Harris. Thanks to Jean Negulesco's careful crafting, the result is admirably restrained, a triumph of atmosphere over potential tearjerking.

As the forlorn Belinda, Wyman is the unwanted daughter of Bickford, a stoic, iron-willed New England farmer who has blames the girl for her mother's having died while giving her birth. Ayres, a kindly doctor practicing in the nearby town, befriends Wyman and teaches her sign language, chastising all in the community who cruelly refer to her as "The Dummy." Slowly, Wyman's sweet and loving nature emerges and attracts the attention of brutish McNally, the local bully. Drunk one night, he attacks and rapes Wyman. She delivers a child which everyone believes has been fathered by Ayres, a situation which later forces him to leave the community in disgrace.

Wyman's performance is a marvel of beauty and innocence. Preparing for the most important role of her career thus far, Wyman studied the behavior of the hearing impaired and labored for weeks to capture an "anticipation light," as she called the look of eager curiosity of deaf people who want to learn and understand. Still Wyman felt an element was absent in her performance, that she was not accurately portraying the world of the deaf. She huddled with director Negulesco, who suggested she stuff her ears with wax. She did so, sealing off all sounds except loud percussions. This induced deafness made it difficult for her to pick up cue lines from other actors, but the very faltering and groping appearance Wyman projected made her all the more convincing.

Since the story was originally set on the dank and forbidding New England coast, Negulesco, along with the cast and crew, traveled to the rough, jagged coastal area near Mendocino, about 200 miles north of San Francisco. Here cinematographer McCord beautifully captured the deep fog, heavy rain, and driving winds, all of which further dramatized an already dynamic story. None of the special handling of this film impressed Jack Warner, head of the studio, who objected vociferously to the bills for location shooting, expressing disbelief that anyone would want to see a picture "where the leading lady doesn't say a word." But the world did want to see this film and Wyman in it; audiences marveled at a performance that thoroughly merited the Oscar it received. Wyman had been strong in THE LOST WEEKEND, but in JOHNNY BELINDA she was exceptional, joining the ranks of Hollywood's leading actresses.

JOHNNY EAGER

1942 107m bw Crime
MGM (U.S.)

★★★★

Robert Taylor (Johnny Eager), Lana Turner (Lisbeth Bard), Edward Arnold (John Benson Farrell), Van Heflin (Jeff Hartnett), Robert Sterling (Jimmy Lanthrop), Patricia Dane (Garnet), Glenda Farrell (Mae Blythe), Barry Nelson (Lew Rankin), Henry O'Neill (A.J. Verne), Charles Dingle (A. Frazier Marco)

p, John W. Considine Jr.; d, Mervyn LeRoy; w, John Lee Mahin, James Edward Grant (based on a story by James Edward Grant); ph, Harold Rosson; ed, Albert Akst; m, Bronislau Kaper; art d, Cedric Gibbons, Stan Rogers; cos, Robert Kalloch

AA Best Supporting Actor: Van Heflin

Here's a glossy world of crime wrapped in white fox and expensive leather where one sinks into deep armchairs and drinks imported Scotch. This is the crooked cafe society world of callow, sexy Taylor who abuses callow, sexy Turner. They're made for each other, see? Each acts in a highly stylized mode of tragic glamour that is most evident in the swooning vortex of their love scenes. Casting them together was inspired—they give each other extra resonance and depth.

Taylor is the rottenly handsome title character, hiding the tenderness of his pretty face behind a gigolo's pencil mustache. At the opening, he misleads viewers. He wears a cab driver's hat and reports to his fatherly parole officer, O'Neil, explaining how diligently he drives his hack, and stays on the straight and narrow. O'Neil introduces the slick Taylor to two earnest, pretty sociology students, Turner and Diana Lewis. Turner thinks he's anything but what he pretends to be. Her instincts are right, even though her heart takes her in another direction. Taylor dutifully gets into his cab after meeting with O'Neil and charming Lewis and Turner. Then he drives to an unopened dog track, reports to the front desk, goes into the inner offices without seeking approval, then into even posher living quarters where he discards his cab driver's outfit and dons expensive tie and suitcoat. As he begins barking orders to his minions, it becomes apparent that Taylor is not only back in the rackets but that he's running them.

Later that night, Taylor exposes his real nature and status when he confronts Nelson in his nightclub, making threats about what will happen to the club owner if he fails to do as he is told. This is witnessed by Turner whom he escorts home to father Arnold, the same prosecuting attorney who sent him to prison. Arnold explodes when he sees Taylor with Turner, threatening to return him to prison if he ever sees them together again. Taylor backs off but hatches a plan to take revenge on Arnold, seduce Turner, and guarantee the opening of his dog track without interference from the authorities. He inveigles Turner to his lavish apartment where he stages an attack by a vicious hoodlum, Stewart. Stewart is about to kill Taylor, or so it seems to Turner, and she grabs a convenient gun and ostensibly kills Stewart.

JOHNNY EAGER is an lavish candy box film in which Taylor wholly abandons his male ingenue image and becomes a believable bad guy whose sliver of human compassion causes his undoing; its one of his best early roles. Although there's a synthetic element to JOHNNY EAGER, the crime melodrama aspect is so well handled by LeRoy and the chemistry between Taylor and the luscious 21-year-old Turner so strong that it's wholly satisfying. Taylor and Turner made only this film together and more's the pity. Their penthouse balcony scene is definitive Hollywood passion, all glossy open lips, eye lash shadows and whispered urgency—the latter a Turner specialty.

Throughout, Heflin is the presence that gives depth to the film as the drunken conscience of cold-hearted Taylor. The homoerotic content of the film is unusual for staid MGM. Heflin acts like Taylor's domesticated, kept house pet and he won an Oscar for Best Supporting Actor for his effort.

JOHNNY GUITAR

1954 110m c   Western   ★★★★
Republic   (U.S.)

Joan Crawford (Vienna), Sterling Hayden (Johnny "Guitar" Logan), Mercedes McCambridge (Emma Small), Scott Brady (Dancin' Kid), Ward Bond (John McIvers), Ben Cooper (Turkey Ralston), Ernest Borgnine (Bart Lonergan), John Carradine (Old Tom), Royal Dano (Corey), Frank Ferguson (Marshal Williams)

p, Herbert J.Yates; d, Nicholas Ray; w, Philip Yordan (based on the novel by Roy Chanslor); ph, Harry Stradling (TruColor); ed, Richard L. Van Enger; m, Victor Young; art d, James Sullivan; fx, Howard Lydecker, Theodore Lydecker; cos, Sheila O'Brien (wardrobe)

JOHNNY GUITAR has been called everything from a feminist statement to a gay camp-classic to an anti-McCarthyism allegory. While it certainly is all of these—and more—it's about time it was acclaimed for it what it really is: a genuine western film classic.

Johnny Guitar (Sterling Hayden) travels to a saloon owned by his former lover, Vienna (Joan Crawford). Emma Small (Mercedes McCambridge), a vindictive woman who has designs on Vienna's land, joins with a posse, headed by John McIvers (Ward Bond), to accuse Vienna of being in on a stagecoach job with a gang led by the Dancin' Kid. Both Vienna and the Dancin' Kid (Scott Brady) deny they had anything to do with the robbery, but Emma urges the Marshal to arrest them anyway. McIvers gives Vienna and the gang 24 hours to get out of town. The Dancin' Kid and his gang decide to head out, but Vienna tells Johnny she's staying. The next morning, Vienna goes to the bank to close her account, and finds herself in the middle of a heist engineered by the Kid and his gang. Emma insists that Vienna was behind the job. After one of the Kid's gang members is coerced into testifying that Vienna did participate, she is set to hang for a crime she did not commit.

When it was first released in 1954, most critics dismissed JOHNNY GUITAR as being nothing more than a ridiculous Republic potboiler, which isn't surprising given that it was probably the first western to be set in the land of the imagination. It took critics such as Jean-Luc Godard and Francois Truffaut (who called the film "beautiful and profound") to recognize that Nicholas Ray's film was a dreamlike and deliriously stylized piece masquerading as a typical shoot-em-up. Ray called the novel by Roy Chanslor (who later wrote *Cat Ballou*) "completely valueless," and he and writer Philip Yordan used the plot's bare bones to create a baroque, operatic and symbolic tale of *l'amour fou* and Freudian psychology.

The much maligned Crawford actually acquits herself quite well—all bulging black eyes, thick red lips and steel jaw. As her nemesis, McCambridge is brilliant, portraying Emma as a sexually frustrated butch lesbian who trembles with orgasmic glee watching Vienna's place burn down. And as the laconic Johnny, Hayden is magnificent, playing the role with tongue in cheek but never condescendingly so. With its twisted sexual dynamics, surreal color photography, expressionistic Frank Lloyd Wright-like sets, and haunting score by Victor Young, JOHNNY GUITAR is a one-of-a-kind experience.

JOLSON STORY, THE   DVD

1946 128m c   Musical/Biography   ★★★★
Columbia   (U.S.)

Larry Parks (Al Jolson), Evelyn Keyes (Julie Benson), William Demarest (Steve Martin), Bill Goodwin (Tom Baron), Ludwig Donath (Cantor Yoelson), Tamara Shayne (Mrs. Yoelson), John Alexander (Lew Dockstader), Jo-Carroll Dennison (Ann Murray), Ernest Cossart (Father McGee), Scotty Beckett (Jolson as a Boy)

p, Sidney Skolsky; d, Alfred E. Green; w, Stephen Longstreet, Harry Chandlee, Andrew Solt; ph, Joseph Walker (Technicolor); ed, William Lyon; art d, Stephen Goosson, Walter Holscher; chor, Jack Cole, Joseph H. Lewis; cos, Jean Louis

AAN Best Actor: Larry Parks; *AAN Best Supporting Actor:* William Demarest; *AAN Best Color Cinematography:* Joseph

Walker; *AAN Best Film Editing:* William Lyon; *AA Best Score (Musical):* Morris Stoloff; *AA Best Sound Recording:* John Livadary

A standout of the musical film-bio genre, THE JOLSON STORY was a box office smash, despite the fact that it contained just about every show business cliché imaginable. It's a highly idealized portrait of Jolson, remembered by everyone who knew him to have been as personally difficult as he was professionally talented. Jolson was Larry Park's first big role after five years of strictly small-time work, and he took full advantage of the opportunity, delivering a top-caliber performance.

Jolson's real story—a mixture of joy, anger, bitterness, and superstardom—is mixed with JAZZ SINGER-inspired fictionalization, charting his youth in vaudeville, his parents's desire that he follow another career, and his eventual rise to the top. Coached by Jolson himself (who dubs Parks' singing voice), Parks perfectly captures the entertainer's famous mannerisms, including his whistling and deliberate interruptions in the middle of a show to stop and banter with the audience. Ruby Keeler, Jolson's third wife (of four), refused to allow her name to be used in the film (her character here is renamed Julie Benson). The musical numbers were pleasingly staged by Joseph H. Lewis.

JONAH WHO WILL BE 25 IN THE YEAR 2000

(JONAS—QUI AURA 25 ANS EN L'AN 2000)
1976 116m c Comedy ★★★½
Action/Citel/Societe Francaise/SSR Swiss TV (Switzerland)

Jean-Luc Bideau *(Max Stigny)*, Myriam Boyer *(Mathilde Vernier)*, Myriam Mziere *(Madeleine)*, Jacques Denis *(Marco Perly)*, Roger Jendly *(Marcel Certoux)*, Dominique Labourier *(Marguerite)*, Miou-Miou *(Marie)*, Raymond Bussieres *(Old Charles)*, Rufus *(Mathieu Vernier)*, Jonas *(Himself)*

p, Yves Gasser, Yves Peyrot; d, Alain Tanner; w, John Berger, Alain Tanner; ph, Renato Berta (Eastmancolor); ed, Brigitte Sousselier, Marc Blavet; m, Jean-Marie Senia

Unlike most films that seem to dwell on the lost ideals of the children of the 1960s, JONAH is an exhilarating film with characters that are filled with life and who refuse to become trapped in endless dreams that can never come true. Although each of these people stops short of achieving some desire, the failure doesn't result in a personal deterioration or self-pity. Perhaps this is a function of the beliefs fought for in the 1960s: goals that were never quite reached but offered the consolation of an effort well made. Whatever the case, all of these characters are extremely likable, uplifting the film with energy that is easily transmitted to the viewer. Prime among them are Miou-Miou, a grocery clerk who steals food for a retired engineer (Bussieres), and Denis, a teacher who can't keep a steady job. It would be a miscarriage of justice to limit the credit to just these two, however; every one of the characters is a joy. Tanner subtly interweaves the roles and knows when to turn off their exhilaration to allow his own themes to take over.

JOUR DE FETE

1949 90m bw Comedy ★★★★
Francinex/Cady (France)

Jacques Tati *(Francois)*, Guy Decomble *(Roger)*, Paul Frankeur *(Marcel)*, Santa Relli *(Roger's Wife)*, Maine Vallee *(Jeanette)*, Roger Rafal *(Barber)*, Beauvais *(Cafe Proprietor)*, Delcassan *(Cinema Operator)*

p, Fred Orain; d, Jacques Tati; w, Jacques Tati, Rene Wheeler, Henri Marquet; ph, Jacques Mercanton; ed, Marcel Morreau; m, Jean Yatove; art d, Rene Moullaert

Quite clever. The first feature film by Jacques Tati was actually a lengthened version of his short L'ECOLE DES FACTEURS, and helped gain him an international reputation as one of the best film comics to come out of France. Also starring in JOUR DE FETE, Tati plays the postman of a small sleepy village who becomes obsessed with applying the methods of the American postal system, as seen in a short educational film, to his job. This simple premise provides an abundance of opportunities for Tati to engage in some spectacular jokes. The emphasis of Tati's style was always aimed at the visual, music and dialog being used only to enhance what was being seen. The results were quite successful in producing laughter from cinema patrons in almost every country, and had a large impact upon the editing techniques later to be used by Jean-Luc Godard and Francois Truffaut.

JOURNEY INTO FEAR

1942 71m bw Spy ★★★★
Mercury (U.S.)

Joseph Cotten *(Graham)*, Dolores Del Rio *(Josette)*, Ruth Warrick *(Stephanie)*, Agnes Moorehead *(Mme. Mathews)*, Jack Durant *(Gogo)*, Everett Sloane *(Kopeikin)*, Eustace Wyatt *(Haller)*, Frank Readick *(Mathews)*, Edgar Barrier *(Kuvetli)*, Jack Moss *(Banat)*

p, Orson Welles; d, Norman Foster; w, Orson Welles, Joseph Cotten (based on a novel by Eric Ambler); ph, Karl Struss; ed, Mark Robson; m, Roy Webb; art d, Albert S. D'Agostino, Mark-Lee Kirk; fx, Vernon L. Walker; cos, Edward Stevenson

Sure it says "directed by Norman Foster," but don't let that fool you, this is an Orson Welles film all the way. Welles is listed as producer, his Mercury Players fill the cast, his then-companion Del Rio is in the lead, and he cowrote the screenplay with Joseph Cotten. The result is a strange, obsessive and often brilliant film, much of which takes place aboard a dilapidated freighter.

Howard Graham (Cotten) is a U.S. Navy engineer who is to return to the U.S. with his beautiful wife Stephanie (Warrick) after a business conference in Istanbul. Graham soon realizes that someone is trying to kill him and is taken by Turkish agent Kopeikin (Sloane) to secret police headquarters where intelligence chief Haki (Welles) explains that Nazi agents are after him.

JOURNEY INTO FEAR is a wonderfully murky study of espionage, realistically portrayed in all its mayhem and confusion, one spy not really knowing what the other spy is up to, but operating on instinct to get results. Cotten's quiet, unassuming part is so well played that the viewer gets frustrated at his inability to either act or even think clearly. A visually arresting film with a nod to the quirky that just can't be beat in terms of the bizarre.

JOURNEY TO THE CENTER OF THE EARTH

1959 132m c Science Fiction ★★★½
Fox (U.S.) G

Pat Boone *(Alec McEwen)*, James Mason *(Prof. Oliver Lindenbrook)*, Arlene Dahl *(Carla)*, Diane Baker *(Jenny)*, Thayer David *(Count Saknussemm)*, Peter Ronson *(Hans)*, Robert Adler *(Groom)*, Alan Napier *(Dean)*, Alex Finlayson *(Prof. Bayle)*, Ben Wright *(Paisley)*

p, Charles Brackett; d, Henry Levin; w, Charles Brackett, Walter Reisch (based on the novel *Journey to the Center of the Earth* by Jules Verne); ph, Leo Tover (CinemaScope, Deluxe Color); ed, Stuart Gilmore, Jack W. Holmes; m, Bernard Herrmann; art d,

Lyle Wheeler, Franz Bachelin, Herman A. Blumenthal; fx, L.B. Abbott, James B. Gordon, Emil Kosa Jr.; cos, David Ffolkes

---

AAN Best Art Direction-Set Decoration (Color): Lyle R. Wheeler (Art Direction), Franz Bachelin (Art Direction), Herman A. Blumenthal (Art Direction), Walter M Scott (Set Decoration), Joseph Kish (Set Decoration); *AAN Best Sound:* Carl Faulkner (20th Century Fox Studio Sound Department); *AAN Best Special Effects:* L.B. Abbott (Visual), James B. Gordon (Visual), Carl Faulkner (Audible)

An excellent combination of witty scripting and fine acting resulting in grand adventure.

James Mason plays Oliver Lindenbrook, an Edinburgh geologist who travels with student Alec McEwen (Pat Boone) to Iceland as part of a planned descent to the center of the earth via volcano. There, they meet Carla (Arlene Dahl), whose husband has been killed in a similar attempt. She joins the expedition, along with a young Icelander (Peter Ronson) and his pet duck. They begin the descent, imperiled by prehistoric beasts, rock slides, and the evil Count Saknussemm (Thayer David), who murdered Carla's husband and is determined to be the first to reach the earth's core.

A well-photographed film, with location footage shot in Carlsbad Caverns, featuring great special effects and a Bernard Hermann score that heightens the excitement. Mason is charming, caustic and debonair, and the whole affair is captivating, silly fun. Watch for some sly sexual lampooning.

JOY LUCK CLUB, THE   _DVD_

1993 135m c   Drama   ★★★
Hollywood Pictures/Joy Luck Company/Ixtlan   R
(U.S.)

Kieu Chinh *(Suyuan)*, Tsai Chin *(Lindo)*, France Nuyen *(Ying Ying)*, Lisa Lu *(An Mei)*, Ming-Na Wen *(June)*, Tamlyn Tomita *(Waverly)*, Lauren Tom *(Lena)*, Rosalind Chao *(Rose)*, Chao-Li Chi *(June's Father)*, Melanie Chang *(June—Age Nine)*

p, Wayne Wang, Amy Tan, Ronald Bass, Patrick Markey; d, Wayne Wang; w, Amy Tan, Ronald Bass (from the book by Amy Tan); ph, Amir Mokri; ed, Maysie Hoy; m, Rachel Portman; prod d, Donald Graham Burt; art d, Diana Kunce, Kwan Kit 'Eddy' Kwok, Jian Jun Li; fx, Frank W. Tarantino; chor, Michael Smuin; cos, Lydia Tanji, Shu Lan Ding

---

As irresistibly sentimental as TERMS OF ENDEARMENT and nearly as complex as JFK, THE JOY LUCK CLUB unravels the web of relationships linking four Chinese-born mothers to their American daughters. Wayne Wang's sleek, intelligent adaptation of Amy Tan's celebrated novel is too long and, ultimately, too soapy, but he and his screenwriters (Tan herself, together with RAIN MAN writer Ronald Bass) have injected just enough irony into the proceedings to save the day.

Wang's biggest achievement is navigating the narrative maze of the novel in such a way that the audience doesn't get hopelessly lost. Most of the drama happens in flashback, with several actresses stepping in to play each character during different stages of her life. The segments set in China, dealing with the early lives of the mothers, are the most eventful, encompassing generous doses of lust, betrayal, suicide, murder, and more. It's pure melodrama, but stylishly done, with finely tuned performances played out against meticulously realized settings. The American episodes, dealing with the more mundane domestic dramas of the daughters, are equally well acted, but overconcerned with spelling out the glib moral ("never let your spirit die") that links all the segments.

Thankfully, some of the elder women have been blessed with acidly witty tongues; as well as making us laugh, they insure brief, tear-free episodes during which audience members can load up on fresh Kleenex.

JU DOU   _DVD_
(JUDOU)
1989 95m c   Drama/Romance/Historical   ★★★★
Tokuma Shoten Publishing Company/Tokuma   PG-13
Communications Company/China Film Coproduction Corporation/China Film Export & Import Corporation/
Xi-an Film Studio   (Japan/China)

Gong Li *(Ju Dou)*, Li Baotian *(Yang Tian-qing)*, Li Wei *(Yang Jin-shan)*, Zhang Yi *(Yang Tian-bai—as a Child)*, Zheng Ji-an *(Yang Tian-bai—as a Youth)*

p, Zhang Wenze, Hu Jian, Yasuyoshi Yokuma; d, Zhang Yimou; w, Liu Heng; ph, Gu Changwei, Yang Lun; ed, Du Yuan; m, Zhao Jiping; art d, Cao Jiupeng, Xia Ru-jin; cos, Zhi-an Zhang

---

AAN Best Foreign Language Film

Acclaimed "Fifth Generation" filmmaker Zhang Yimou, of RED SORGHUM fame, delves once more into the past for JU DOU, his second feature, a haunting story of illicit love set in 1920s China.

Ju Dou (Gong Li), a virginal beauty, is purchased by old and rich Yang Jin-shan (Li Wei) to be his bride. When, due to his impotence, she fails to bear him the son he craves, Jin-shan vents his rage against his wife, bringing her to the brink of suicide.

Yang Tian-qing (Li Bao-tian) is the solitary worker in the textile dyeing factory that Jin-shan owns. He is a distant relative of his employer but treated like a slave nonetheless. Tian-qing, aware of the beatings and abuse that Ju Dou suffers at the hands of her husband, reaches out to console her and quickly becomes her only solace. They meet clandestinely whenever they can and one fateful night, when Jin-shan is away, they become lovers. When Ju Dou becomes pregnant, the son that Jin-shan desires is finally on its way, but he's clearly not the father. Then, in a strange twist of fate, the old man is paralyzed in an accident and left unable to walk. When the townspeople congragulate him on his new-born son, Jin-shan must accept or lose face. He is left at the mercy of Ju Dou and her lover, who pursue their illicit relationship to a tragic conclusion.

The "Fifth Generation" filmmakers began a new wave in Chinese cinema by emphasizing the visual and aural qualities of film rather than traditional dramatic and literary elements. JU DOU is no exception to this trend. The cinematography by Gu Changwei and Yang Lun highlights and accentuates the unfolding drama; a painter's palette of color emerges in images that act as counterpoints to the story. By displaying the ancient processes still in use for dyeing cloth, Yimou makes full use of his early background in a textile factory; the splashes of colored fabric and the dyeing process itself are an integral part of the film's beauty. The screenplay, written by Lui Heng, is spare and constant. JU DOU tantalizes all the senses as the story of the ill-fated lovers unfolds with hypnotic logic.

JUAREZ
1939 132m bw   Biography   ★★★½
Warner Bros. (U.S.)

Paul Muni *(Benito Pablo Juarez)*, Bette Davis *(Empress Carlotta von Habsburg)*, Brian Aherne *(Maximilian von Habsburg)*, Claude Rains *(Louis Napoleon)*, John Garfield *(Porfirio Diaz)*, Donald Crisp *(Marechal Bazaine)*, Gale Sondergaard *(Empress Eugenie)*, Joseph Calleia *(Alejandro Uradi)*, Gilbert Roland *(Col. Miguel Lopez)*, Henry O'Neill *(Miguel Miramon)*

p, Henry Blanke; d, William Dieterle; w, John Huston, Wolfgang Reinhardt, Aeneas MacKenzie (based on the novel *The Phantom Crown* by Bertita Harding and the play *Juarez & Maximillian* by

Franz Werfel); ph, Tony Gaudio; ed, Warren Low; m, Erich Wolfgang Korngold; art d, Anton F. Grot; cos, Orry-Kelly

---

AAN Best B/W Cinematography: Tony Gaudio; *AAN Best Supporting Actor:* Brian Aherne

---

Weighs a ton, thanks to meddling Muni's obsessive hand in the screenplay. The effective casting lacks spark, save two firebrand ladies: Davis and Sondergaard, the latter stoking the cauldron and the former jumping in. Benito Pablo Juarez was to Mexico what Abraham Lincoln was to the United States. Both of them lived at the same time, and Juarez was profoundly influenced by the North American president. Like Lincoln, Juarez was physically homely, yet full of wisdom and spiritual clarity that was irresistible to his people.

The film opens with Rains, playing the evil Napoleon III, appointing Aherne (Archduke Maximilian von Habsburg of Austria) emperor of Mexico. Through his agents in Mexico, Rains has set up a fake election by which Aherne has been chosen the monarch of a people he has never seen. Aherne and wife Davis (Carlotta) journey to Mexico, escorted by an army commanded by Crisp. Meeting the royal couple are thousands of jubilant peasants in Mexico City, but the royal couple is again deceived by the insidious French, who have staged the reception.

The duly elected president of Mexico, Muni (Juarez), leads his people in revolt against the monarchs imposed upon Mexico by Rains. To mollify the people Aherne offers Muni the powerful position of Secretary of State, but he rejects it. Undaunted, Aherne believes that he can unite the Mexican people by adopting a native prince in an elaborate ceremony. Yet, when they take their new son to the balcony of their palace to show to their ostensibly adoring subjects, a tremendous explosion rocks the area. *Juaristas* have just blown up a huge ammunition dump of the French army. So enraged by this "slap" is Aherne that he signs the shoot-to-kill order for those found with weapons. Wholesale executions ensue, and soon even those who have paid homage to Aherne and Davis turn against the monarchy. A full-scale revolution breaks out, with the U.S. ordering the French army to leave Mexico under the Monroe Doctrine.

JUAREZ was unique in that it was shot as two separate films—first the Aherne-Davis story, then the Muni portion; both stories were then edited together. Muni only meets Aherne when viewing his corpse, and even this scene is spliced together. Muni had the benefit of viewing the edited first portion of the film before going in front of the cameras to play Juarez and, to offset the Davis histrionics, he underplayed his role almost down to a whisper. Muni was afforded the privilege since he was then the most important actor on the Warner lot. But despite studying hundreds of books, documents and photographs of his subject, and spending six weeks visiting the areas where Juarez lived, worked and administered to his infant republic, the resulting portrayal proved unsuitable to a long epic film, slowing the ponderous drama to a crawl.

Davis has only a small role but one she coveted when the project was first begun in 1937. She knew she would have one fantastic scene where Carlotta goes mad after confronting the scheming Rains and she played it to the hilt; this sequence is a classic, and Davis's descent from the emperor is like watching a candle dim, flicker and go out. She is matched by Sondergaard's velvety villainy and this meeting portends their eventual collaboration on THE LETTER.

JUBAL

1956 100m c Western ★★★½ *DVD*
Columbia (U.S.)

Glenn Ford (*Jubal Troop*), Ernest Borgnine (*Shep Horgan*), Rod Steiger (*Pinky*), Valerie French (*Mae Horgan*), Felicia Farr (*Naomi Hoktor*), Basil Ruysdael (*Shem Hoktor*), Noah Beery Jr. (*Sam*),

Charles Bronson (*Reb Haislipp*), John Dierkes (*Carson*), Robert Burton (*Dr. Grant*)

p, William Fadiman; d, Delmer Daves; w, Russell Hughes, Delmer Daves (based on the novel *Jubal Troop* by Paul I. Wellman); ph, Charles Lawton Jr. (CinemaScope, Technicolor); ed, Al Clark; m, David Raksin; art d, Carl Anderson; cos, Jean Louis

---

Sagebrush Shakespeare—a pistol-packin' *Othello*, deftly done. Shot among the magnificent Grand Teton Mountains of Wyoming, JUBAL is named for its protagonist, Ford, a drifter who arrives in the area and takes a job at the ranch owned by Borgnine. When Borgnine's sensuous wife, French, comes on to Ford, Steiger, her ex-lover, is enraged and plots to get rid of the stranger. French admits her feelings to her husband, so he attacks Ford who kills him. While Steiger is aware of what really happened, he recruits a posse to lynch Ford and beats and rapes French.

Steiger is wonderfully mean in a role not unlike Judd in OKLAHOMA or any of several other villains he's played. The battle lines are drawn early, and the suspense mounts as we wait for the inevitable conclusion between Ford and Steiger. Instead of concentrating on the scenery and the vistas (the way Kasdan did in his imitative SILVERADO), Daves elects to examine humanity, and the result is an unusually good story that could fit in almost any milieu. Charles Bronson, as one of the ranch hands, gives no indication of his coming stardom.

JUDE

1996 123m c Drama ★★★
Revolution Films (U.K.) R

Christopher Eccleston (*Jude Fawley*), Kate Winslet (*Sue Bridehead*), Liam Cunningham (*Richard Phillotson*), Rachel Griffiths (*Arabella*), June Whitfield (*Aunt Drusilla*), Ross Colvin Turnbull (*Little Jude*), James Daley (*Jude as a Boy*), Berwick Kaler (*Farmer Troutham*), Sean McKenzie (*1st Stonemason*), Richard Albrecht (*2nd Stonemason*)

p, Andrew Eaton; d, Michael Winterbottom; w, Hossein Amini (based on the novel *Jude the Obscure* by Thomas Hardy); ph, Eduardo Serra; ed, Trevor Waite; m, Adrian Johnston; prod d, Joseph Bennett; art d, Andrew Rothschild; fx, John Markwell; cos, Janty Yates

---

This faithful and engaging adaptation of Thomas Hardy's classic novel, *Jude the Obscure,* features powerful performances, a rich atmosphere, and good writing, making it well worth the often harrowing ordeal of watching love struggle helplessly against poverty and social injustice.

Jude Fawley (Christopher Eccleston) dreams of escaping his impoverished rural life through education. As a child, his teacher, Phillotson (Liam Cunningham), encourages him to pursue a university education in nearby Christminster. Arabella (Pamela Griffiths), the daughter of a local pig-farmer, seduces Jude, but runs away to Australia as soon as they are married. Moving to Christminster to continue his studies, Jude meets his beautiful and sophisticated cousin, Sue Bridehead (Kate Winslet), and falls in love with her. The couple endures a series of wrenching setbacks, tempered by brief moments of simple happiness, before the ultimate tragedy strikes.

The film's muted colors underscore Jude and Sue's ultimate inability to transcend the constraints that their society has placed upon them and their class. JUDE feels very contemporary, in part due to the language (though in fact much of Hardy's dialogue is preserved in the script), and to the style of the camerawork and editing, which is more athletic than one expects. But the credit goes mostly to Michael Winterbottom's direction and the performances from Eccleston, Winslet, Cunningham, and Griffiths, who convincingly own their characters. Any adaptation of such a beloved novel is likely to elicit accusations of infidelity, and indeed JUDE falls short of Hardy's psychological complexity, but it ultimately adheres to the paramount virtues of the novel: its themes of injustice and the collision of hope with destiny and reality.

JUDGMENT AT NUREMBERG *DVD*

1961 190m bw Historical/War ★★★★
Roxlom (U.S.)

Spencer Tracy *(Judge Dan Haywood)*, Burt Lancaster *(Ernst Janning)*, Richard Widmark *(Col. Tad Lawson)*, Marlene Dietrich *(Mme. Bertholt)*, Maximilian Schell *(Hans Rolfe)*, Judy Garland *(Irene Hoffman)*, Montgomery Clift *(Rudolph Petersen)*, William Shatner *(Capt. Harrison Byers)*, Edward Binns *(Sen. Burkette)*, Kenneth MacKenna *(Judge Kenneth Norris)*

p, Stanley Kramer; d, Stanley Kramer; w, Abby Mann; ph, Ernest Laszlo; ed, Frederic Knudtson; m, Ernest Gold; prod d, Rudolph Sternad; cos, Joe King

AAN Best Picture; AA Best Actor: Maximilian Schell; *AAN Best Actor:* Spencer Tracy; *AAN Best Supporting Actor:* Montgomery Clift; *AAN Best Supporting Actress:* Judy Garland; *AAN Best Director:* Stanley Kramer; *AA Best Adapted Screenplay:* Abby Mann; *AAN Best B/W Cinematography:* Ernest Laszlo; *AAN Best Film Editing:* Frederic Knudtson; *AAN Best Art Direction-Set Decoration (B/W):* Rudolph Sternad, George Milo; *AAN Best Costume Design (B/W):* Jean Louis

For the patient starwatcher, a revelation. In its day, JUDGMENT AT NUREMBERG was a sensation—the first film to deal seriously with the trials of Nazi war criminals. The chief Allied judge, Dan Haywood (Spencer Tracy), has been sent to Germany after failing to be reelected to the bench in New England, a political payoff that does not go unnoticed by his adversaries. Prosecuting attorney Tad Lawson (Richard Widmark), an Army colonel, indicts several Germans who have committed war crimes in enforcing Hitler's mad mandates. Defense attorney Hans Rolfe (Maximilian Schell) roars that his clients were merely upholding Hitler's laws, and that to place them on trial is to judge all of Germany. Meanwhile, Haywood, in his off hours, wanders the ancient city of Nuremberg trying to understand what went wrong with a whole people and a great culture.

The rest of the cast in this three-hour-plus picture is equally distinguished: Marlene Dietrich is the widow of a German general who was executed for ordering the slaughter of captured American soldiers at Malmedy; Burt Lancaster is an intellectual German judge who unwillingly aided the Nazis; Montgomery Clift is a dim-witted victim of sterilization who testifies for the prosecution; and Judy Garland is a woman who "polluted the Aryan race" by having sex with a Jew.

Though unrelentingly bleak, JUDGMENT AT NUREMBERG is absorbing from beginning to end. Dietrich and Tracy contribute polished, seemingly effortless work; at the other end of the thespian spectrum are Clift and Garland, who turn in harrowing, nakedly emotional perfomances. These are star turns, to be sure, but the Hollywood-style interplay between image, portrayal, and reality is fascinating to behold.

JUDY BERLIN *DVD*

2000 96m bw Drama ★★★½
Caruso-Mendelsohn/Jaeger Films (U.S.)

Barbara Barrie *(Sue Berlin)*, Madeline Kahn *(Alice Gold)*, Edie Falco *(Judy Berlin)*, Julie Kavner *(Marie)*, Bob Dishy *(Arthur Gold)*, Carlin Glynn *(Maddie)*, Aaron Harnick *(David Gold)*, Bette Henritze *(Dolores Engler)*, Anne Meara *(Bea)*, Novella Nelson *(Carol)*

p, Rocco Caruso; d, Eric Mendelsohn; w, Eric Mendelsohn; ph, Jeffrey Seckendorf; ed, Eric Mendelsohn; m, Michael Nicholas; prod d, Charlie Kulsziski; art d, Dina Varano; cos, Sue Gandy

A gentle, offbeat drama that introduced a new talent in writer-director Eric Mendelsohn and bid a poignant farewell to actress Madeline Kahn, who died of cancer shortly before the film's release.

It's the second day of school in Babylon, a middle-class New York City suburb, and as the town awaits a noontime solar eclipse, the lives of several inhabitants are about to realign themselves. Sour grade-school teacher Sue Berlin (Barbara Barrie) pauses to consider her miserable life and takes a chance on romance with the school's unhappily married principal (Bob Dishy). His flaky wife, Alice (Kahn), stops her inane chatter just long enough to ponder her age, her loneliness, and the fact that her totally indifferent husband and depressed son David (Aaron Harnick) seem to hate her. David, a 30-year-old aspiring filmmaker, wonders what happened to his youth, and kids himself that he's found it in Sue's plucky, 32-year-old daughter Judy (Edie Falco), a would-be actress who's been honing her craft churning butter at a nearby colonial restoration. Judy is about to leave Babylon for Hollywood, and as she says her goodbyes, the moon crosses the sun's path, the sky begins to darken, and time suddenly stops.

With such a fine cast of seasoned actors it's easy to overlook just how subtle a director Mendelsohn is; with a nimble touch, he reveals the isolation and vulnerability beneath the placid, almost banal surface of suburban existence. Jeffrey Seckendorf's camera snakes in and out of the characters' lives, capturing the small, telling details in sharp black and white and an ever-deepening half light that increases the film's otherworldly, almost surreal aura.

JUGGERNAUT *DVD*

1974 109m c Thriller ★★★½
UA (U.S.) PG

Richard Harris *(Fallon)*, Omar Sharif *(Capt. Brunel)*, David Hemmings *(Charlie Braddock)*, Anthony Hopkins *(Supt. John McCleod)*, Shirley Knight *(Barbara Banister)*, Ian Holm *(Nicholas Porter)*, Clifton James *(Mr. Corrigan)*, Roy Kinnear *(Social Director Curain)*, Caroline Mortimer *(Susan McCleod)*, Freddie Jones *(Mr. Buckland)*

p, Richard DeKoker; d, Richard Lester; w, Richard DeKoker, Alan Plater; ph, Gerry Fisher (DeLuxe Color); ed, Anthony Gibbs; m, Ken Thorne; prod d, Terence Marsh; art d, Alan Tomkins; fx, John Richardson

Jolly well done. Sharif plays the captain of an ocean liner upon which several bombs have been planted by Jones, a demolitions expert who demands a ransom not to blow up the ship at sea. Back on shore, the superintendent in charge of the case (Hopkins) brings extra concern to his work on the crisis because his wife, Mortimer, is one of the hostages. A team of experts, including Harris and Hemmings, is dispatched to the ship by helicopter to defuse the bombs. The rest of the film is a tense battle between the bomb experts and Jones, who stays on the telephone to taunt the crisis-intervention team with details about his plot.

Lester, known mainly for his comedy work (A HARD DAY'S NIGHT), does a good job of keeping viewers on the edge of their seats. And JUGGERNAUT, far more than a disaster picture, is a telling statement about England's troubles, the country neatly symbolized by the liner itself. The film captures perfecly the atmosphere of an over-hyped "luxury" liner. Harris gives a terrific performance and this is the best work ever done by Sharif, thanks to apt casting as the slimy ship captain.

JUGGLER, THE

1953 84m bw Drama ★★★½
Columbia (U.S.)

Kirk Douglas (Hans Muller), Milly Vitale (Ya'El), Paul Stewart (Detective Karni), Joseph Walsh (Yehoshua Bresler), Alf Kjellin (Daniel), Beverly Washburn (Susy), Charles Lane (Rosenberg), John Banner (Emile Halevy), Richard Benedict (Kogan), Oscar Karlweis (Willy Schmidt)

p, Stanley Kramer; d, Edward Dmytryk; w, Michael Blankfort (based on the novel by Michael Blankfort); ph, J. Roy Hunt; ed, Aaron Stell; m, George Antheil; art d, Robert Peterson

A tight little sleeper. Douglas is a German Jew who survived the Nazi concentration camps but lost his wife and children. He was a famous juggler before the war and now finds himself with thousands of other displaced persons in Israel.

When he arrives in a temporary camp, his actions are odd enough to merit notice by the camp psychiatrist. He runs away on his first night and is followed by Benedict, an Israeli cop, who finally stops him and wants to see his papers. Douglas immediately flashes back to when a Nazi asked the same thing, and he knocks Benedict out, then flees. Douglas escapes Haifa and makes his way to Mount Carmel where he spends the night. In the morning Douglas, now pursued by detective Stewart, is discovered by several children whom he tells he is an American tourist. Walsh, one of the young boys, is traveling to a kibbutz near Syria and Douglas joins him. Douglas wants to get to Egypt where he has some friends who he feels will help him.

A terrific movie in many ways, THE JUGGLER is a small-scale, almost intimate film that quietly depicts the sadness of a man looking for a home and a purpose following the war. The main character is not a heroic figure, but a deeply troubled man trying to make some sense out of life. Douglas, in one of his most restrained performances, is quite good at conveying the man's torment and confusion. Paul Stewart, one of the original Mercury Players on radio who made his film debut in CITIZEN KANE, is also good as the compassionate detective who does his best to reassure Douglas. Young Walsh nicely complements Douglas and their scenes together are often touching without being overly sentimental. Walsh went on to become a writer, scripting such films as BON VOYAGE and CALIFORNIA SPLIT.

JULES AND JIM

(JULES ET JIM)
1962 110m bw Drama ★★★★★
Carosse (France)

Jeanne Moreau (Catherine), Oskar Werner (Jules), Henri Serre (Jim), Marie Dubois (Therese), Vanna Urbino (Gilberte), Sabine Haudepin (Sabine), Boris Bassiak (Albert), Kate Noelle (Birgitta), Anny Nelsen (Lucie), Christiane Wagner (Helga)

p, Marcel Berbert; d, Francois Truffaut; w, Francois Truffaut, Jean Gruault (based on the novel by Henri-Pierre Roche); ph, Raoul Coutard (Franscope); ed, Claudine Bouche; m, Georges Delerue; cos, Fred Capel

Francois Truffaut's greatest achievement, JULES AND JIM is a shrine to lovers who have known obsession and been destroyed by it.

The film begins in Paris in 1912 when two writers—Jules (Oskar Werner), a shy German, and Jim (Henri Serre), a dark-haired Parisian—become obsessed with an ancient stone carving of a woman. Their life changes when they meet Catherine (Jeanne Moreau), the personification of the stone goddess, whose smile enchants both men. Jules begins to court her, but only with Jim's blessing.

The three become great friends, though Catherine's unpredictability flares whenever she feels she is being ignored. (At one point, she jumps into the Seine when Jules and Jim's heated discussion of a Strindberg play does not include her.) Although Catherine gives Jules a child, Sabine (the adorable, bespectacled Sabine Haudepin), her ever-changing moods are not those of a mother or a wife, and she begins an affair with Jim. Jules, however, refuses to leave her, or even to get angry—he only wants to be near her and his friend.

The film is a celebration both of love and cinema, as Truffaut directs with equal concern for his characters and for film technique—one never overshadowing the other. Scripted from Henri-Pierre Roche's novel, the screenplay has not a wasted word or gesture, with every element working together perfectly to create three unique and interdependent characters. As much in love with Catherine as Jules and Jim are, Truffaut photographs her with the greatest love and admiration. Just as Jules and Jim respond lovingly to Catherine's every move, and just as the camera swirls and dollies around the ancient stone carving in the film's early scenes, so too does Truffaut's filmmaking revolve around the great Moreau, who returns the compliment with one of the most memorable performances in screen history.

JULIA

1977 116m c Biography ★★★
Fox (U.S.) PG

Jane Fonda (Lillian Hellman), Vanessa Redgrave (Julia), Jason Robards Jr. (Dashiell Hammett), Maximilian Schell (Johann), Hal Holbrook (Alan Campbell), Rosemary Murphy (Dorothy Parker), Meryl Streep (Anne Marie), Dora Doll, Elisabeth Mortensen (Train Passengers), John Glover (Sammy)

p, Richard Roth; d, Fred Zinnemann; w, Alvin Sargent (based on the story in the book Pentimento by Lillian Hellman); ph, Douglas Slocombe (Technicolor); ed, Walter Murch; m, Georges Delerue; prod d, Willy Holt, Gene Callahan, Carmen Dillon; cos, Anthea Sylbert, Joan Bridge, Annalisa Nasilli-Rocca, John Apperson, Colette Baudot

AAN Best Picture; AAN Best Actress: Jane Fonda; AA Best Supporting Actor: Jason Robards; AAN Best Supporting Actor: Maximilian Schell; AA Best Supporting Actress: Vanessa Redgrave; AAN Best Director: Fred Zinnemann; AA Best Adapted Screenplay: Alvin Sargent; AAN Best Cinematography: Douglas Slocombe; AAN Best Film Editing: Walter Murch; AAN Best Original Score: Georges Delerue; AAN Best Costume Design: Anthea Sylbert

Beautifully crafted, nominated for nine Academy Awards, a big hit at the box office—and a dramatic dud. Based on an episode from Lillian Hellman's bestselling memoirs, the film takes place in the 1930s as Fonda, playing the author, lives with Robards in a beach house. She's writing her first play and turns to famed writer Robards for his helpful (and sometimes cruel) criticism.

When it's done and produced successfully, Fonda decides to visit a childhood friend, Redgrave, with whom she shared some wonderful moments in their youth (shown in flashbacks with Pelikan and Jones as the girls). Redgrave moved to Austria to study medicine with Freud and became a crusader in social matters, joining the antifascists. She was injured in a battle with the Hitler Youth and is now in a hospital in Vienna. Fonda visits Redgrave as she is recovering. Later, on a trip to Moscow, Fonda is asked by Schell, a pal of Redgrave's, if she will smuggle a large sum of money from Russia to Germany where it will be used to aid the effort against the Nazis.

If you like red nail polish, faux-cynicism, painfully brave smiles and European train stations, JULIA may be your kind of cocktail. But Redgrave plays Julia as a noble martyr in sensible shoes, and Zinneman fails to communicate the sense of danger that her political commitment entailed. Fonda's Hellman is a prig with writer's block and low self-esteem. Her relationship with Hammett and Julia, too, looks like hero-worship. The script, the direction and finally, Fonda's acting choices capture nothing of what made Hellman a true piss-and-vinegar original.

JULIET OF THE SPIRITS   DVD
(GIULIETTA DEGLI SPIRITI)
1965   148m   c   Drama   ★★★½
Federiz/Francoriz/Rizzoli/Eichberg
(France/Italy/West Germany)

Giulietta Masina (Juliet), Alba Cancellieri (Juliet as a Child), Mario Pisu (Giorgio), Caterina Boratto (Juliet's Mother), Luisa Della Noce (Adele), Sylva Koscina (Sylva), Sabrina Gigli, Rosella di Sepio (Granddaughters), Lou Gilbert (Grandfather), Valentina Cortese (Valentina)

p, Angelo Rizzoli; d, Federico Fellini; w, Federico Fellini, Tullio Pinelli, Ennio Flaiano, Brunello Rondi (based on a story by Fellini, Pinelli); ph, Gianni De Venanzo (Technicolor); ed, Ruggero Mastroianni; m, Nino Rota; art d, Piero Gherardi; cos, Piero Gherardi

AAN Best Art Direction-Set Decoration (Color): Piero Gherardi (Art Direction); *AAN Best Costume Design (Color):* Piero Gherardi

Gaudy, more integrated than later Fellini, but this take on feminine psyche lacks vision. Juliet's fantasies might have been culled from Hollywood back lots, suggesting women have colorful imaginations, but not much in the brain department.

Juliet (Giulietta Masina) is a married woman in her mid-30s, more or less resigned to a dull life with her dull husband, Giorgio (Mario Pisu), who pays her little attention. At first she thinks it's just the pressures of business that cause him to be so indifferent, but soon she begins to wonder if he may have someone else. One night, Giorgio and some friends hold a seance, and Juliet discovers that she can conjure up various spirits. These wraiths tell her that she deserves some enjoyment in life and should give herself a treat. To see if her suspicions about Giorgio are correct, Juliet hires a sleuth who corroborates her worst fears, causing her to change her lifestyle and move out from the shadow of her unloving husband.

A feminized version of 8 1/2—both Masina's and Pisu's characters drift in and out of fantasy in order to come to grips with reality—JULIET OF THE SPIRITS will likely appeal to fans of that previous Fellini picture. This was his first color feature, and the results are spectacular and festive.

JULIUS CAESAR
1953   120m   bw   Historical   ★★★★½
MGM   (U.S.)

Marlon Brando (Marc Antony), Louis Calhern (Julius Caesar), John Gielgud (Cassius), Edmond O'Brien (Casca), Greer Garson (Calpurnia), Deborah Kerr (Portia), George Macready (Marullus), Michael Pate (Flavius), Richard Hale (Sooothsayer), Alan Napier (Cicero)

p, John Houseman; d, Joseph L. Mankiewicz; w, Joseph L. Mankiewicz (based on the play by William Shakespeare); ph, Joseph Ruttenberg; ed, John Dunning; m, Miklos Rozsa; art d, Cedric Gibbons, Edward Carfagno; fx, Warren Newcombe; cos, Herschel McCoy

AAN Best Picture; AAN Best Actor: Marlon Brando; *AAN Best B/W Cinematography:* Joseph Ruttenberg; *AAN Best Score (Drama or Comedy):* Miklos Rozsa; *AA Best Art Direction-Set Decoration (B/W):* Cedric Gibbons, Edward C. Carfagno, Edwin B. Willis, Hugh Hunt

Lavish, starstruck and for the most part, splendid. When John Houseman and Joseph Mankiewicz, brother of Herman, decided to film Shakespeare's *Julius Caesar*, they picked an elegant and distinguished cast—Mason, Gielgud, Calhern, O'Brien—but they also shocked the industry and not a few literary scholars by selecting Brando to play Marc Antony. He was then still known as "The Mumbler" and "The Slob," for his brutish performance as Stanley Kowalski in A STREETCAR NAMED DESIRE. But Brando turned that opinion about in a startling performance.

JULIUS CAESAR was the brainchild of Houseman and Mankiewicz, the producer having worked with Orson Welles and the Mercury Players on the 1937 version of *Caesar*. Houseman, who had been lobbying to make the film for years, heard that the property was seriously being considered and contacted studio boss Dore Schary, saying that if he were not named the producer he would leave MGM. The studio reluctantly agreed, but did not expect much from this production. Films based on the works of the immortal Bard had been box-office poison at best, especially ROMEO AND JULIET, produced by MGM in 1936, starring Leslie Howard and Norma Shearer, a pet project of then-production chief Irving Thalberg. But this film surprisingly turned in a considerable profit, much of which was due to the astounding performance of Brando as Marc Antony, a role first intended for Paul Scofield, and then for Leo Genn or Charlton Heston. Performances aside, this is clearly Mankiewicz's film, expertly crafted from every angle, with the mob and murder scenes adroitly staged.

JUNGLE BOOK, THE   DVD
1967   78m   c   Children's/Animated   ★★★½
Walt Disney Productions   (U.S.)   G

VOICES OF: Phil Harris (Baloo the Bear), Sebastian Cabot (Bagheera the Panther), Louis Prima (King Louie of the Apes), George Sanders (Shere Khan the Tiger), Sterling Holloway (Kaa the Snake), J. Pat O'Malley (Col. Hathi the Elephant), Bruce Reitherman (Mowgli the Man Cub), Verna Felton, Clint Howard (Elephants), Chad Stuart Lord

p, Walt Disney; d, Wolfgang Reitherman; w, Larry Clemmons, Ralph Wright, Ken Anderson, Vance Gerry (based on the "Mowgli" stories in *The Jungle Book* by Rudyard Kipling); ed, Tom Acosta, Norman Carlisle; m, George Bruns; anim, Milt Kahl, Franklin Thomas, Oliver M. Johnston Jr., John Lounsbery

AAN Best Song: "The Bare Necessities"; Terry Gilkyson (Music & Lyrics)

A witty animated feature from Disney based on the famous Rudyard Kipling stories. Abandoned as a child, Mowgli is raised by wolves, then befriended by a panther who attempts to return him to civilization until the beast realizes that the wolf-boy doesn't want to leave the jungle. Mowgli's happy-go-lucky trail leads to a meeting with a lazy bear, a kidnapping by monkeys, and an encounter with a fire-fearing tiger. In the finale, Mowgli sees a beautiful young girl with whom he falls in love, finally forsaking jungle life to be with her.

The last animated film to be directly overseen by Walt Disney himself, JUNGLE BOOK contains some great visual laughs and is low on sticky sentiment, but the sketchy animation style strains to be modern and looks careless instead. Well-known personalities are particularly effective in providing the voices, notably Phil Harris, Louis Prima, and especially George Sanders. Released ten months after Disney's death, the film went on to be one of the studio's most successful pictures.

JUNGLE BOOK, THE   DVD
1942   108m   c   Adventure   ★★★★
UA   (U.S.)

Sabu (Mowgli), Joseph Calleia (Buldeo), John Qualen (The Barber), Frank Puglia (The Pundit), Rosemary DeCamp (Messua), Patricia O'Rourke (Mahala), Ralph Byrd (Durga), John Mather (Rao), Faith Brook (English Girl), Noble Johnson (Sikh)

p, Alexander Korda; d, Zoltan Korda; w, Laurence Stallings (based on the books by Rudyard Kipling); ph, Lee Garmes (Technicolor); ed, William Hornbeck; m, Miklos Rozsa; prod d, Vincent Korda; fx, Lawrence Butler

---

AAN Best Color Cinematography: W. Howard Green; *AAN Best Score (Drama or Comedy):* Miklos Rozsa; *AAN Best Interior Decoration (Color):* Vincent Korda (Art Direction), Julia Heron (Interior Decoration); *AAN Best Special Effects:* Lawrence Butler (Photographic), William H. Wilmarth (Sound)

Colorful Korda production, fine family fare. This loose adaptation of Rudyard Kipling's *Jungle Books* stars Sabu as Mowgli, a young man raised by wolves who returns to his native village with no idea of human language or customs.

Once he acquires speech, he captivates Mahala (Patricia O'Rourke), the daughter of the aged Buldeo (Joseph Calleia), with tales of the jungle and his animal friends. Mowgli and Mahala trek into the jungle and discover ruins of a lost civilization, filled with treasures. When Mahala returns to the village with a gold coin, her father tries to get Mowgli to divulge the gold's location, but the boy refuses, fearing the village will be corrupted. Buldeo then turns others against the lad, who is sentenced to be burned at the nearest convenient stake.

Shot outside Los Angeles, the film features dazzling photography, expressive animals and a brilliant Miklos Rozsa score, with individual themes for each animal. An enchanting film for viewers of all ages.

JUNIOR BONNER
DVD

| 1972 | 100m | c | Western/Sports | ★★★½ |
| ABC | (U.S.) | | | PG |

Steve McQueen *(Junior Bonner)*, Robert Preston *(Ace Bonner)*, Ida Lupino *(Elvira Bonner)*, Ben Johnson *(Buck Roan)*, Joe Don Baker *(Curly Bonner)*, Barbara Leigh *(Charmagne)*, Mary Murphy *(Ruth Bonner)*, Bill McKinney *(Red Terwiliger)*, Sandra Deel *(Nurse Arlis)*, Don "Red" Barry *(Homer Rutledge)*

p, Joe Wizan; d, Sam Peckinpah; w, Jeb Rosebrook; ph, Lucien Ballard (Todd-AO, Movielab Color); ed, Robert Wolfe; m, Jerry Fielding; art d, Ted Haworth

---

A trifle clumsy, but affecting nonetheless. Steve McQueen stars in this Sam Peckinpah-directed film as the title character, an aging rodeo cowboy who returns to his small hometown of Prescott, Arizona, and learns that nothing stays the same. Saddened to discover that his parents (Lupino and Preston) have split and that his brother (Baker) is getting rich selling off parcels of his father's land, Junior tries to regain his self-esteem by staying on a previously unrideable bull at the town's annual Fourth of July rodeo.

There's much to recommend here, including some fine rodeo footage, winning characterizations from Johnson as the man who supplies the livestock for the rodeo and from Taylor as the owner of the bar, and an especially strong performance by McQueen as the cowboy who realizes that he can't go home on the range again. Lupino and Preston are especially fine among a good supporting cast. But the territory covered is similar to Nick Ray's earlier, superior THE LUSTY MEN.

JURASSIC PARK
DVD

| 1993 | 127m | c | Adventure/ScienceFiction/Thriller | ★★★½ |
| Universal/Amblin | (U.S.) | | | PG-13 |

Sam Neill *(Dr. Alan Grant)*, Laura Dern *(Dr. Ellie Sattler)*, Jeff Goldblum *(Ian Malcolm)*, Richard Attenborough *(Dr. John Hammond)*, Bob Peck *(Robert Muldoon)*, Martin Ferrero *(Donald Gennaro)*, B.D. Wong *(Dr. Wu)*, Joseph Mazzello *(Tim)*, Ariana Richards *(Lex)*, Samuel L. Jackson *(Arnold)*

p, Kathleen Kennedy, Gerald R. Molen; d, Steven Spielberg; w, David Koepp, Michael Crichton, Malia Scotch Marmo (adapted from the novel by Michael Crichton); ph, Dean Cundey; ed, Michael Kahn, David Tanaka; m, John Williams; prod d, Rick Carter; art d, Jim Teegarden, John Bell; fx, Stan Winston, Dennis Muren, Phil Tippett, Michael Lantieri

---

AA Best Sound: Ron Judkins, Shawn Murphy, Gary Rydstrom, Gary Summers; *AA Best Sound Effects Editing:* Richard Hymns, Gary Rydstrom; *AA Best Visual Effects:* Michael Lantieri, Dennis Muren, Phil Tippett, Stan Winston

---

Like DIE HARD and BATMAN, JURASSIC PARK is not so much a dramatic story as a theme-park ride through spectacular special effects and action sequences. These being the post-modern '90s, this is a theme-park ride *about* a theme park—an exclusive, as-yet-unopened island resort where dinosaurs have been cloned from DNA deposits. Such a scientific feat would be only a little more impressive than what's been accomplished for this film, which brings prehistoric beasts convincingly back to life through a combination of sophisticated models and computer-generated animation. Director Steven Spielberg does a masterful job of putting the beasts through their paces in some scenes that will have even the most jaded observers clutching the edges of their seats.

JURASSIC is not without its flaws. Michael Crichton's novel has been clumsily condensed and his nastier characters unnecessarily whitewashed. Some of the actors—Sam Neill and Laura Dern as paleontologists, Richard Attenborough as the park's creator—give performances that seem also to have been achieved by computer animation. (The biggest exception here is the ever-quirky Jeff Goldblum, playing a gonzo mathematician with a quip for every occasion: "I wonder if this will be part of the tour," he muses, as he lies wounded in the back of a speeding jeep with a T. rex in hot pursuit.)

If these sound like quibbles, they are. This is an exhilarating, sometimes terrifying monster of a movie that, once it gets you in its clutches, won't put you down again until the closing credits start to roll.

JUST A GIGOLO

| 1978 | 98m | c | Drama | ★★★ |
| Leguan | (West Germany) | | | R |

David Bowie *(Paul)*, Sydne Rome *(Cilly)*, Kim Novak *(Helga)*, David Hemmings *(Capt. Kraft)*, Marlene Dietrich *(Baroness von Semering)*, Maria Schell *(Mutti)*, Curt Jurgens *(Prince)*, Erika Pluhar *(Eva)*, Rudolf Schundler *(Gustav)*, Hilde Weissner *(Aunt Hilda)*

d, David Hemmings; w, Joshua Sinclair, Ennio De Concini; ph, Charly Steinberger; ed, Susan Jaeger, Fred Srp, Maxine Julius; m, Gunther Fischer; art d, Peter Rothe; chor, Herbert F. Schubert; cos, Ingrid Zore

---

Tragically, a misfire. This interesting (if only for its cast) tale of a Prussian WWI veteran who returns to Berlin, torn between wealthy, older women and homosexual Nazis, cannot find itself. Is it farce or melodrama? Bowie has some startling moments, but his overall performance languishes in uncertainty.

The underrated Rome provides a definite energy lift to the proceedings, but everyone else is reduced to doing star turns. It's surprising to find Hemmings photographed in such a singularly unflattering manner in his own movie. Perhaps he exhausted all his resources filming Miss Dietrich's cameo: she's a grande dame madam who wanders on long enough, veiled and diffused to the max, to croak the title song, before adding Bowie to her stable. It's a hypnotic swansong—visually and vocally—a fitting farewell to the last of the golden age goddesses.

Another goddess from another era, the still-lucious Novak, turns in a commanding portrayal of a lusty widow. The period mood, soundtrack and use of color are never less than first-rate. Yet the film, reduced from its original 147-minute running length, flounders badly.

K

K-19: THE WIDOWMAKER

DVD

2002 138m c/bw Action/Thriller ★★½

National Geographic Feature Films/Intermedia PG-13
Films/Palomar Pictures/First Light/IMF/Paramount
(U.S./U.K./Germany)

Harrison Ford (*Alexei Vostrikov*), Liam Neeson (*Mikhail Polenin*), Peter Sarsgaard (*Vadim Radtchenko*), Christian Camargo (*Pavel Loktev*), Ravil Isyanov (*Suslov*), Michael J.X. Gladis (*Yevgeny*), Joss Ackland (*Marshal Zelentstov*), J.J. Field (*Andrei*), Donald Sumpter (*Dr. Savran*), John Shrapnel (*Admiral Bratyeev*)

p, Kathryn Bigelow, Edward S. Feldman, Sigurjon Sighvatsson, Christine Whitaker; d, Kathryn Bigelow; w, Christopher Kyle (from a story by Louis Nowra); ph, Jeff Cronenweth; ed, Walter Murch; m, Klaus Badelt; prod d, Karl Juliusson, Michael Novotny; art d, William Ladd Skinner; fx, Colin Chilvers, Bruce Jones, Tony Kenny, John Nelson, Industrial Light & Magic; cos, Marit Allen

On July 4, 1961, the Soviet submarine *K-19* faced a crisis that could easily have ended in a nuclear disaster. Oddly enough, director Kathryn Bigelow's desire to tell this long-suppressed story has led her into the realm of fiction. Bigelow and screenwriter Christopher Kyle have invented characters, fabricated events, and generally turned an unbelievable-but-true incident into a passably interesting Tom Clancy-style thriller.

After an embarrassing test exercise results in the demotion of *K-19*'s original captain, Mikhail Polenin (Liam Neeson), no-nonsense Alexei Vostrikov (Harrison Ford) is brought aboard the brand-new but seemingly cursed nuclear sub; spooked crewmen have already dubbed it "The Widowmaker." Polenin warns Vostrikov that the sub isn't seaworthy, but Vostrikov is under orders to get the sub out of dry dock, pilot it through the Bering Sea, and shake up the Americans by launching a test missile through the polar ice. But as *K-19* changes course for new coordinates, the worst-case scenario becomes a terrifying reality: the primary coolant tube designed to keep the nuclear reactor that powers the sub from overheating springs a leak. The temperature inside the reactor quickly climbs, and the only way for Vostrikov to prevent a devastating nuclear explosion is to send a repair crew into the now highly radioactive reactor chamber—a mission no one could possibly survive.

Bigelow ups the suspense by situating a U.S. destroyer close by, thus introducing the risk of a nuclear confrontation, but she needn't have bothered; the facts of the matter would have been enough, and a faithful chronicle of events would have served as a greater tribute to the men who served and died aboard *K-19*.

KADOSH

DVD

1999 116m c Drama ★★★★

Agav Hafakot/MP Productions/Studio Canal Plus
(Israel/France)

Yael Abecassis (*Rivka*), Yoram Hattab (*Meir*), Meital Barda (*Malka*), Uri Ran Klausner (*Yossef*), Yussef Abu Warda (*Rav Shimon*), Sami Hori (*Yaakov*), Lea Koenig (*Elisheva*), Rivka Michaeli (*Gynecologist*), Amos Gitai (*Man in the Bar*)

p, Michel Propper, Amos Gitai; d, Amos Gitai; w, Amos Gitai, Eliette Abecassis, Jacky Cukier; ph, Renato Berta; ed, Monica Coleman, Kobi Netanel; m, Philippe Eidel, Louis Sclavis; prod d, Miguel Markin; art d, Miguel Markin; cos, Laura Dinulasco

This startlingly angry film from Israeli director Amos Gitai opens with an ultra-Orthodox Jewish scholar thanking God he wasn't born a woman; by the film's end, it's obvious why.

Among the ultra-Orthodox of Jerusalem's Mea Shearim neighborhood, the roles of men and women are inflexibly defined. The men study the Torah at the yeshiva while women like Rivka (Yael Abecassis) and her younger sister Malka (Meital Barda) are expected to keep house and, above all else, bear children. But after 10 years of marriage to Meir (Yoram Hattab), Rivka still isn't pregnant, and Meir's father (Yussef Abu Warda), a rabbi, urges his son to renounce his seemingly barren wife. ("A man who dies without progeny rips a page from the Torah," he reminds Meir.) Malka, meanwhile, loves a young Israeli soldier (Sami Hori) but is forced to marry a scholar (Uri Ran Klausner) so fanatical in his devotion that he agonizes over whether it's sinful to pour hot water over a tea bag on the Sabbath.

Gitai sets the sisters' tragic plight against the centuries-old rituals that circumscribe their lives and render them passive, whether it's a marriage ceremony or a ritual bath to cleanse their "impure" bodies. As unforgiving as the film is, Gitai is careful to show that the trouble lies not in the Torah, but in its interpretation. He also places the extraordinary pressure to bear children in the context of a people who live completely apart from the rest of the world—even other Jews—and have been continually threatened by extinction. The acting is uniformly superb, as is the rich, somber cinematography by Renato Berta, who has shot films for such leaders of European cinema as Jean-Luc Godard, Alain Resnais, and Manoel de Oliveira.

KAGEMUSHA

DVD

1980 179m c Drama/War ★★★★

Toho/Kurosawa (Japan) PG

Tatsuya Nakadai (*Shingen Takeda/Kagemusha*), Tsutomu Yamazaki (*Nobukado Takeda*), Kenichi Hagiwara (*Katsuyori Takeda*), Kota Yui (*Takemaru*), Shuji Otaki (*Yamagata*), Hideo Murata (*Baba*), Daisuke Ryu (*Oda*), Kaori Momoi (*Otsuyanokata*)

p, Akira Kurosawa; d, Akira Kurosawa; w, Akira Kurosawa, Masato Ide; ph, Takao Saito, Shoji Ueda, Kazuo Miyagawa, Asaichi Nakai (Eastmancolor); m, Shinichiro Ikebe; art d, Yoshiro Muraki

AAN Best Foreign Language Film ; AAN Best Art Direction-Set Decoration: Yoshiro Muraki (Art Direction)

After a long period of inactivity, Akira Kurosawa returned to the genre of which he is the unparalleled master, the samurai film.

Tatsuya Nakadai plays a 16th-century warlord, Shingen Takeda, who uses doubles for himself on the battlefield, instilling confidence and fear through his constant presence while his clan fights to establish dominance in Japan. When Shingen is killed, his current "shadow warrior" or *kagemusha*—in actuality a petty thief (again powerfully played by Tatsuya Nakadai)—must take over so that the army's morale will not die. Trained in secret by Shingen's assistants, the double genuinely begins to acquire some of his master's attributes, but the masquerade becomes increasingly difficult to maintain.

Kurosawa's epic is alive with color, the spectacular visuals overlying a somber exploration of traditionalism, honor loyalty, and identity, played out against a sumptuous tapestry of political intrigue and the 16th-century clan warfare that came to an end with the Tokugawa *shogunate*. The massive battle scenes rank with the director's best, using brilliant color, contrasting light, and the enormous cast to great advantage. Kurosawa also alternates compelling scenes of near hypnotic stillness with scenes of rousing action. Sadly the film's score is a noisy irritant.

Made and distributed with the financial aid and clout of George Lucas and Francis Ford Coppola, KAGEMUSHA prefigured and paved the way for the great RAN, Kurosawa's epic adaptation of *King Lear*.

KAMERADSCHAFT

(LA TRAGEDIE DE LA MINE)
1931 93m bw Drama ★★★★
Nero/Gaumont/Franco-Film-Aubert (Germany)

Fritz Kampers *(Wilderer)*, Gustav Puttjer *(Kaplan)*, Alexander Granach *(Kaspers)*, Andree Ducret *(Francoise)*, Georges Charlia *(Jean)*, Ernst Busch *(Wittkopp)*, Daniel Mandaille *(Emile)*, Pierre Louis *(Georges)*, Alex Bernard *(Grandfather)*

p, Seymour Nebenzal; d, G.W. Pabst; w, Karl Otten, Peter Martin Lampel, Ladislas Vajda; ph, Fritz Arno Wagner, Robert Baberske; ed, Hans Oser

This stirring plea for peace and internationalism was the high-point of German socialist filmmaking of its period. KAMER-ADSCHAFT, a German-French co-production set in the Lorraine mining region on the French-German border in the aftermath of WWI, was inspired by an actual 1906 mining disaster that claimed 1,200 lives.

Combining elements of classic German expressionism and and Soviet Socialist realism, German director G.W. Pabst (STREET OF SORROW, PANDORA'S BOX, THE THREEPENNY OPERA) introduces the viewer to the German and French miners. Separated by mine walls and metal bars below and by armed border patrols above, they have little contact with one another. But when a series of explosions causes a cave-in on the French side, the hearts of the Germans go out to them. Wittkopp (Ernst Busch) appeals to his bosses to send a rescue team while, underground, a trio of German miners breaks through a set of steel bars that marks the 1919 border. Meanwhile, on the French side, an elderly retired miner (Alex Bernard) sneaks into the shaft, hoping to rescue his young grandson, Georges (Pierre Louis).

Although occasionally overly sentimental, Pabst's plea for a peaceful future is sincere and compelling. His direction of the heartbreak and devastation is enhanced by the brilliant photography of Fritz Arno Wagner and Robert Baberske and the alarmingly authentic set design is provided by by Erno Metzner and Karl Vollbrecht.

KANAL 📀

1957 96m bw War ★★★
Film Polski (Poland)

Teresa Izewska *(Daisy Stokrotka)*, Tadeusz Janczar *(Corporal Korab)*, Wienczyslaw Glinski *(Lieutenant Zadra)*, Tadeusz Gwiadowski *(Sergeant Kula)*, Stanislaw Mikulski *(Smulky)*, Wladyslaw Sheybal *(Composer)*, Emil Karewicz *(Madry)*, Teresa Berezowska *(Halinka)*, Adam Pawlikowski *(German Officer)*, Zofia Lindorf

p, Stanislaw Adler; d, Andrzej Wajda; w, Jerzy Stefan Stawinski (based on his short story); ph, Jerzy Lipman; ed, Halina Nawrocka; m, Jan Krenz; art d, Roman Mann; cos, Jerzy Szeski

This extremely intense and relentlessly graphic second feature from Polish filmmaker Andrzej Wajda takes place during the final days of the Warsaw Uprising in 1944. Three groups of Poles, no longer able to hold off the enemy, retreat to the city's *kanaly*, or sewer system. The viewer is told from the very start to "watch them closely; these are the last hours of their lives." With this pessimistic tone established, we observe them as they try to escape and live an underground existence free from the oppression and lost ideals of their lives above ground. Although we know that death awaits them, we also know that freedom from the sewers is only a relative freedom.

Wajda spares the viewer nothing, showing death, betrayal, suffering, suicide, capture, and despair. Still the Poles fight on in the hope that they will see sunlight pouring into the sewer, even if it is filtered through a metal grate.

KANDAHAR 📀

(SAFAR E GANDEHAR)
2001 85m c Drama ★★★½
Makhmalbaf Film House/Bac Films (Iran/France)

Nelofer Pazira *(Nafas)*, Hassan Tantai *(Tabib Sahid)*, Sadou Teymouri *(Khak)*, Hayatalah Hakimi *(Hayat)*

p, Mohsen Makhmalbaf; d, Mohsen Makhmalbaf; w, Mohsen Makhmalbaf; ph, Ebraham Ghafouri; ed, Mohsen Makhmalbaf; m, Mohamed Reza Darvishi; prod d, Akbar Meshkini

Not long ago, most Western moviegoers would have been hard-pressed to find the city of Kandahar on a map. By the time of this film's release, many not only knew where Kandahar is, but what it once represented: the spiritual capital of the Taliban, the radical Islamic organization that, by the end of the 1990s, had subjugated much of Afghanistan.

Under the Taliban's severe interpretation of Islamic law, life for Afghan women became not only difficult but extremely dangerous, and all were forced to wear the suffocating, head-to-toe covering known as the burka. Nelofer Pazira had the good fortune to spend the 1990s in Canada, but attempted to return to her homeland when she began receiving desperate letters from a childhood friend. Pazira contacted Iranian filmmaker Mohsen Makhmalbaf, who could offer little real help. But Makhmalbaf was haunted by the plight of Pazira and her friend, and he soon approached Pazira with an idea for a film. The result is this short, powerful drama, which mixes fact with fiction and uses a cast of non-professional actors to basically portray themselves. Pazira herself stars as Nafas, an Afghan-born, Canadian-based journalist who receives a troubling letter from her sister in Kandahar. Conditions under the Taliban have gotten so bad that she plans to kill herself during the next solar eclipse. The letter, however, took so long to reach Nafas that she now has only two days to reach her sister before the sun passes behind the moon. Stranded at the Iran-Afghan border without a visa, she dons a burka to impersonate the wife of a traveling Afghan man, then embarks on a treacherous journey across a desert country filled with thieves, land mines, and Taliban supporters.

Throughout production, Makhmalbaf was working under extremely difficult circumstances, and it occasionally shows, but it's still an important achievement. Makhmalbaf's mastery of color is used to great effect, and the film is filled with startling images, the most memorable of which depicts the air drop of prosthetic legs to the hordes of Afghan men who've lost limbs to land mines. The film ends abruptly, on a surprisingly bleak note that offers little hope for the future, but Nafas's wish for women like her sister—"One day the world will see your troubles and come to your aid"—is a prayer that has already been answered.

KANSAS CITY 📀

1996 110m c Crime/Drama ★★★½
Sandcastle 5/CiBy 2000 (U.S.) R

Jennifer Jason Leigh *(Blondie O'Hara)*, Miranda Richardson *(Carolyn Stilton)*, Harry Belafonte *(Seldom Seen)*, Michael Murphy *(Henry Stilton)*, Dermot Mulroney *(Johnny O'Hara)*, Steve Buscemi *(Johnny Flynn)*, Brooke Smith *(Babe Flynn)*, Jane Adams *(Nettie Bolt)*, Jeff Feringa *(Addie Parker)*, A.C. Smith *(Sheepshan Red)* p, Robert Altman; d, Robert Altman; w, Robert Altman, Frank Barhydt; ph, Oliver Stapleton; ed, Geraldine Peroni; m, Hal Willner (producer); prod d, Stephen Altman; art d, Richard L. Johnson; cos, Dona Granata

Robert Altman's hometown of Kansas City, MO is the setting for this atmospheric period piece about a hopelessly misconceived kidnapping. As always with Altman, the milieu is richly textured, and the characters' weaknesses inform the story line.

Expecting her manicurist for a home appointment, laudanum-addicted Carol Stilton (Miranda Richardson) is surprised by a substitute—a tough-talking Jean Harlow wanna-be who calls herself Blondie (Jennifer Jason Leigh) and has come to kidnap her. Blondie has chosen to abduct Carol in order to force her politico husband (Michael Murphy) to help Blondie's hoodlum husband, Johnny O'Hara (Dermot Mulroney), out of a jam. Johnny has foolishly robbed a high-rolling client of the Hey Hey Club, a jazz club and gambling den, and is awaiting execution by the club's owner, a ruthless gangster named Seldom Seen (Harry Belafonte). Over the course of 24 hours, Blondie drags the hapless Carol across Kansas City in a desperate attempt to get her Johnny back.

After a trio of densely-populated "tapestry" films that placed him back in the Hollywood mainstream (THE PLAYER, SHORT CUTS, READY TO WEAR), Altman reaffirms his status as a master storyteller with this small, dark character study. KANSAS CITY supplies vivid period detail spotlighting various early 1930s phenomena: the consolidation of jazz styles; the corrupt political "machines" that ran certain cities; and rabid movie fandom. But the film's central theme remains one that Altman has explored in most of his major works: love relationships. Altman's strong point is his direction of actors, and KANSAS CITY offers three excellent lead performances. Jennifer Jason Leigh delivers another extraordinarily nuanced turn as the hard-boiled Blondie, Richardson supplies a nice balance as the socially proper but very stoned Carol, and, offering the film a strong backbone, Belafonte is superlative as the ominously verbose Seldom.

KARATE KID, THE 📀

| 1984 | 126m | c | Martial Arts/Sports | ★★★ |
| Columbia | | (U.S.) | | PG |

Ralph Macchio (Daniel), Noriyuki "Pat" Morita (Miyagi), Elisabeth Shue (Ali), Martin Kove (Kreese), Randee Heller (Lucille), William Zabka (Johnny), Ron Thomas (Bobby), Rob Garrison (Tommy), Chad McQueen (Dutch), Tony O'Dell (Jimmy)

p, Jerry Weintraub; d, John G. Avildsen; w, Robert Mark Kamen; ph, James Crabe (Metrocolor); ed, Bud Smith, Walt Mulconery, John G. Avildsen; m, Bill Conti; prod d, William J. Cassidy; fx, Frank Toro; chor, Pat E. Johnson; cos, Richard Bruno, Aida Swenson

AAN Best Supporting Actor: Noriyuki 'Pat' Morita

Derivative and sentimental, THE KARATE KID treads the same path as ROCKY, and with good reason—it was directed by John Avildsen, who also directed Sylvester Stallone's star-making vehicle.

Daniel (Ralph Macchio) and his mother (Randee Heller) move from Newark, New Jersey, to southern California, where the whole world seems blond and brutal to this hapless ethnic kid. Daniel is immediately set upon by bullies, led by a Hitler Youth-type, Johnny (William Zabka). Daniel's new life grows increasingly unpleasant until he meets Miyagi (Pat Morita), a friendly aged Japanese janitor. Miyagi takes the kid under his wing and begins to teach him about life and karate while getting him to do some chores around the house.

Made for a relative pittance, the way the first ROCKY was, THE KARATE KID reaped a bonanza at the box office. Though shamelessly manipulative, it is undeniably effective. It offers some genuine moments of warmth, humor and excitement. Of course it all leads up to a big tournament where

Fair Play has a showdown with Dirty Tricks. Guess who wins. This is the kind of movie where you find yourself cheering even though you know you're being hoodwinked. Naturally the movie gave birth to two sequels and, not surprisingly, neither measures up to the original.

KENNEL MURDER CASE, THE 📀

| 1933 | 73m | bw | Mystery | ★★★★½ |
| Warner Bros. | | (U.S.) | | |

William Powell (Philo Vance), Mary Astor (Hilda Lake), Eugene Pallette (Sgt. Heath), Ralph Morgan (Raymond Wrede), Jack LaRue (Eduardo Grassi), Helen Vinson (Doris Delafield), Paul Cavanagh (Sir Bruce MacDonald), Robert Barrat (Archer Coe), Arthur Hohl (Gamble), Robert McWade (District Attorney John F.X. Markham)

p, Robert Presnell; d, Michael Curtiz; w, Robert N. Lee, Peter Milne, Robert Presnell (based on the novel The Return of Philo Vance by S.S. Van Dine); ph, William Rees; ed, Ed N. McLarnin; art d, Jack Okey; cos, Orry-Kelly

Justifiably a cult favorite, and a damn fine film in the bargain. Certainly the best of the Philo Vance series, THE KENNEL MURDER CASE stars the inimitable Powell for the fourth time as the debonair detective.

Here the mystery involves the members of a Long Island kennel club, and Philo, with the assistance of his Scottie and a prize-winning Doberman, solves a double murder. The plot is full of interesting twists and is eminently serviceable. But the real appeal of this amazing little film is Powell's delightful flair for repartee; it's a pleasure to sit back and let him purr. Astor, too, brings her own special brand of warmth, conviction and appeal to almost everything she does.

The real star of the film, however, is director Michael Curtiz, who races through this flick like a piranha breaking a fast. His exposure to German expressionism pays off handsomely here, and the film is chock full of bizarre compositions, flashy editing, inventive camera angles and memorable camerawork. Fast, foolish, engrossing and unique, this breathtaking little gem is a tribute to both Curtiz's craftsmanship and his fiery temperament. Remade by William Clemens as CALLING PHILO VANCE.

KENTUCKY FRIED MOVIE, THE

| 1977 | 90m | c/bw | Comedy | ★★★ |
| Kentucky Fried Theater | | (U.S.) | | R |

Marilyn Joi (Cleopatra), Saul Kahan (Schwartz), Marcy Goldman (Housewife), Joe Medalis (Paul), Barry Dennen (Claude), Rich Gates (Boy), Tara Strohmeier (Girl), Neil Thompson (Newscaster), George Lazenby (Architect), Henry Gibson

p, Robert K. Weiss; d, John Landis; w, David Zucker, Jerry Zucker, Jim Abrahams; ph, Stephen Katz (part DeLuxe Color); ed, George Folsey Jr.; art d, Rich Harvel; cos, Deborah Nadoolman, Joyce Unruh

A vulgar and uproariously funny college party movie made up of a series of comedy sketches from the Kentucky Fried Theater, a fresh young satirical group formed at the University of Wisconsin at Madison in the early 1970s.

Depending on one's mood, or level of sobriety, it can be a hysterical picture that pokes good natured fun at American movies, TV and commercials. The gags are hurled forth in a fast and furious manner; if you don't like one—fear not—another will be along any second. Memorable segments include "Catholic High School Girls in Trouble," "Cleopatra Schwartz," and "That's Armageddon!" but the most outstanding episode is "A Fistful of Yen," a lengthy kung-fu parody that casts two actual martial arts experts in a surprisingly lavish environment.

Landis has rarely done better work than in this modest early effort. Writers Zucker, Zucker, and Abrahams went on to make the gleefully absurd AIRPLANE and THE NAKED GUN films.

KES

1969 112m c Drama ★★★★
Woodfall/Kestrel (U.K.) PG

David Bradley (Billy Casper), Colin Welland (Mr. Farthing), Lynne Perrie (Mrs. Casper), Freddie Fletcher (Jud), Brian Glover (Mr. Sugden), Bob Bowes (Mr. Gryce), Trevor Hasketh (Mr. Crossley), Eric Bolderson (Farmer), Geoffrey Banks (Mathematics Teacher), Zoe Sutherland (Librarian)

p, Tony Garnett; d, Ken Loach; w, Ken Loach, Tony Garnett, Barry Hines (based on the novel A Kestrel for a Knave by Barry Hines); ph, Chris Menges (DeLuxe Color); ed, Roy Watts; m, John Cameron; art d, William McCrow

Imagine THE 400 BLOWS reconfigured around a working class English boy living in a grimy industrial town and you get some idea of the emotional power of this bleakly realistic film adapted from a novel by Barry Hines.

Billy Casper (Bradley) is the product of a broken home and the victim of school bullies. He takes refuge in his comic books and shoplifting. One day he finds a baby kestrel (a small falcon) and becomes determined to raise the bird. He names it "Kes" and promptly steals a book on falconry. He becomes quite adept at his newfound skills and catches the eye of his teacher, Mr. Farthing (Welland). However his relationship with the beautiful bird cannot ameliorate his depressing home life with his brutish older brother, Jud (Fletcher). Nor does it change the fact that his future options are severely limited by lack of class status, money, or family stability and support.

Though it's a sensitive and heartfelt film, KES never lapses into the sentimentality that often attends these "a boy and his pet" pictures. Ken Loach's low key, clear-eyed direction makes this a fairly unique "children's film." It is aided immeasurably by Chris Menges's naturalistic yet evocative cinematography.

KEY LARGO DVD

1948 101m bw Crime ★★★★
Warner Bros. (U.S.)

Humphrey Bogart (Frank McCloud), Edward G. Robinson (Johnny Rocco), Lauren Bacall (Nora Temple), Lionel Barrymore (James Temple), Claire Trevor (Gaye Dawn), Thomas Gomez (Curley), Harry Lewis (Toots), John Rodney (Deputy Clyde Sawyer), Marc Lawrence (Ziggy), Dan Seymour (Angel Garcia)

p, Jerry Wald; d, John Huston; w, Richard Brooks (based on the play by Maxwell Anderson); ph, Karl Freund; ed, Rudi Fehr; m, Max Steiner; art d, Leo K. Kuter; fx, William McGann, Robert Burks; cos, Leah Rhodes

AA Best Supporting Actress: Claire Trevor

With superb casting and performances, a sharp and resonant screenplay, John Huston's taut direction and Karl Freund's deep-focus photography, KEY LARGO transcends the windy allegories of its theatrical origins to become a suspenseful and entertaining minor classic of 1940s Hollywood.

Based on the play by Maxwell Anderson, Bogart stars as Frank McCloud, a disillusioned WW II veteran who travels to a run-down hotel in Key Largo, Florida, to pay his respects to the family of a buddy who was killed in the war. The hotel is operated by the father of the deceased, James Temple (Barrymore), and the widowed Nora Temple (Bacall). McCloud arrives to find the hotel full of seedy, threatening characters. He can only visit briefly with Nora and Mr. Temple

before they must begin preparing for a huge storm which is coming their way.

Soon a group of Seminole Indians arrives in small boats, seeking shelter. Among them are John and Tom Osceola (Silverheels and Redwing), brothers who recently escaped from prison. Sheriff Wade (Blue) and Deputy Sawyer (Rodney) had visited the hotel earlier searching for the fugitives. John tells Nora that he and his brother are ready to give themselves over to the authorities. Meanwhile the massive storm grows closer and closer. McCloud, Nora, and Mr. Temple head inside the hotel where it quickly becomes apparent that the tough-looking "guests" are all criminals. They have waylaid the deputy and are now holding him prisoner in one of the guest rooms. No one will be allowed to leave the premises until they finish their "business."

While all these introductions were being made, the gang's leader has been taking a bath. When the aging gangster finally makes his entrance he is immediately recognized by McCloud as Johnny Rocco, an infamous gangster who had run a huge mob empire until he was deported. He has arrived from Cuba by a ship anchored just off shore. The last major character arrives for the festivities: Gaye Dawn (Trevor), an alcoholic ex-entertainer who is now the girlfriend of the gangster. The storm can finally begin in earnest.

In a film of outstanding performances—Claire Trevor won an Oscar for Best Supporting Actress—Edward G. Robinson deserves special praise. As the fallen crime czar longing for a return to an earlier lawless time, Robinson is spellbinding in a portrayal that echoes his own iconic status in movie history. Though Robinson had at one point grown weary of endlessly repeating the gangster persona he established in LITTLE CAESAR, even parodying the role in BROTHER ORCHID, he resurrected his gangster image here as his final major statement on the genre that brought him stardom.

KHARTOUM DVD

1966 134m c Historical ★★★
UA (U.K.) R

Charlton Heston (Gen. Charles Gordon), Laurence Olivier (The Mahdi), Richard Johnson (Col. J.D.H. Stewart), Ralph Richardson (Mr. Gladstone), Alexander Knox (Sir Evelyn Baring), Johnny Sekka (Khaleel), Michael Hordern (Lord Granville), Zia Mohyeddin (Zobeir Pasha), Marne Maitland (Sheikh Osman), Nigel Green (Gen. Wolseley)

p, Julian Blaustein; d, Basil Dearden; w, Robert Ardrey; ph, Ted Scaife; ed, Fergus McDonell; m, Frank Cordell; art d, John Howell; fx, Richard Parker; cos, John McCorry

AAN Best Original Story and Screenplay: Robert Ardrey

This richly photographed historical epic is saved from utter boredom and vacuity by its massive all-star cast and a generous budget. Heston is more impressive than usual in this colorful pageant with his authoritative portrayal of that mystical British general, Sir Charles "Chinese" Gordon, who was killed on January 26, 1885, by fanatical Sudanese tribesmen under the leadership of a religious zealot after they overran Khartoum following a 317-day siege. Gordon, a paradoxical creature, was both realist and idealist, and Heston somehow captures his elusive enigmatic qualities.

Colonel Hicks (Edward Underdown) and the 8,000 untrained Egyptian troops under his command are lured from the El Dueim River and into the desert 100 miles beyond Khartoum. The British-led troops are ambushed by 80,000 fierce Sudanese warriors commanded by the Mahdi and massacred. British Prime Minister Gladstone (Richardson) learns that the Mahdi (Olivier)—"the chosen one"—is fighting a holy war, a jihad, intent upon getting rid of all infidels in the Sudan and taking the great city of Khartoum to prove his power and divine mission. Gordon is sent to try to make peace with the zealot while also finding a way of evacuating the Egyptian army. As he journeys toward Khartoum, he learns that he is no longer respected as a great leader; the natives have shifted their allegiance to the Mahdi. However when he arrives in Khartoum, the terrified populace receives him as a savior.

Olivier is convincing and frightening. Richardson offers his customary expert performance as Gladstone, infusing the part with cynical amusement. Also outstanding is Johnson as Heston's loyal-unto-death aide and Sekka as Heston's fearless servant. KHARTOUM's vivid color photography is outstanding and the action sequences are visually spectacular due the credit for them is due to Yakima Canutt, the legendary former stuntman turned second unit director, who directed them.

KID FOR TWO FARTHINGS, A   *DVD*

1955 91m c   Comedy/Fantasy   ★★★★
Big Ben/London Films   (U.K.)

Celia Johnson (*Joanne*), Diana Dors (*Sonia*), David Kossoff (*Kandinsky*), Joe Robinson (*Sam*), Jonathan Ashmore (*Joe*), Brenda de Banzie ("*Lady*" *Ruby*), Vera Day (*Mimi*), Primo Carnera (*Python Macklin*), Sydney Tafler (*Mme. Rita*), Sidney James (*Ice Berg*)

p, Carol Reed; d, Carol Reed; w, Wolf Mankowitz (based on his novel); ph, Ted Scaife (Eastmancolor); ed, Bert Bates; m, Benjamin Frankel; art d, Wilfred Shingleton; cos, Anna Duse

An absolutely charming comedy-fantasy set against the Jewish tradesmen's life in London's Petticoat Lane. Based on the novel by Mankowitz, it's the story of a young boy, Joe (Ashmore), who has been told stories about a unicorn by tailor Kadinsky (Kossoff). When the boy buys a goat with only one horn, he is convinced that he has purchased a unicorn, because "magical" things begin to happen to the denizens of the area.

Kadinsky has one great desire—to own his own steam press. Sonia (Dors) is a buxom blonde who has been waiting for many years to marry muscular Sam (Robinson). She gets her wish when he enters the ring and wins enough money for them to wed. Celia Johnson plays Joanne, Joe's mother, but she doesn't have enough to do to merit her casting. Tafler, a terrific comic actor (MAKE MINE MINK), is again shown to good advantage as a storekeeper, and Canadian character actor Lou Jacobi makes one of his earliest appearances as a wrestling promoter. Naturally, all of the miracles are logically explained, but, to the boy, it's the unicorn that has brought all the happiness to Petticoat Lane.

This is a delightful film, and Reed, working for the first time in color, shows how well he deals with children. He used this ability before in THE FALLEN IDOL and later with the musical version of OLIVER!.

KID FROM SPAIN, THE

1932 118m bw   Musical/Comedy   ★★★★
Goldwyn   (U.S.)

Eddie Cantor (*Eddie Williams*), Lyda Roberti (*Rosalie*), Robert Young (*Ricardo*), Ruth Hall (*Anita Gomez*), John Miljan (*Pancho*), Noah Beery Sr. (*Alonzo Gomez*), J. Carrol Naish (*Pedro*), Robert Emmett O'Connor (*Detective Crawford*), Stanley Fields (*Jose*), Paul Porcasi (*Gonzales, Border Guard*)

p, Samuel Goldwyn; d, Leo McCarey; w, William Anthony McGuire, Bert Kalmar, Harry Ruby; ph, Gregg Toland; ed, Stuart Heisler; art d, Richard Day; chor, Busby Berkeley; cos, Milo Anderson

A lavish musical vehicle for the immensely popular comic genius Eddie Cantor, THE KID FROM SPAIN is directed by the brilliant Leo McCarey (DUCK SOUP, THE AWFUL TRUTH, RUGGLES OF RED GAP, MAKE WAY FOR TOMORROW) and boasts choreography by the legendary Busby Berkeley just before he hit his hallucinatory stride

(42ND STREET, GOLD DIGGERS OF 1933, DAMES). This is Eddie Cantor at his best!

After being tossed out of school, Ricardo (Robert Young) invites his college roommate, Eddie (Eddie Cantor), to his home in Mexico. Their trip becomes a necessity when bank robbers mistake Eddie for their getaway driver, the only person who can identify them. Once they are south of the border, mistaken identity strikes again. This time Eddie is thought to be the offspring of a legendary matador and is forced into the bull ring, though Ricardo has arranged for him to face a tame animal that will stop its charge upon command. However, a rough character involved in one of the story's many subplots substitutes a considerably more docile bull and hilarity results as Eddie does his best not to get gored.

THE KID FROM SPAIN is chock-full of laughs and boasts some fine songs, written mostly by Bert Kalmar and Harry Ruby who co-wrote the screenplay.

KID GALAHAD

1937 101m bw   Sports   ★★★½
Warner Bros.   (U.S.)

Edward G. Robinson (*Nick Donati*), Bette Davis (*Louise "Fluff" Phillips*), Humphrey Bogart (*Turkey Morgan*), Wayne Morris (*Kid Galahad/Ward Guisenberry*), Jane Bryan (*Marie Donati*), Harry Carey (*Silver Jackson*), William Haade (*Chuck McGraw*), Soledad Jiminez (*Mrs. Donati*), Joe Cunningham (*Joe Taylor*), Ben Welden (*Buzz Stevens*)

p, Samuel Bischoff; d, Michael Curtiz; w, Seton I. Miller (based on the novel by Francis Wallace); ph, Tony Gaudio; ed, George Amy; m, Heinz Roemheld, Max Steiner; art d, Carl Jules Weyl; fx, James Gibbons, Edwin DuPar; cos, Orry-Kelly

Edward G. Robinson and Humphrey Bogart play rival fight managers in this memorable indictment of corruption in the boxing ring with Wayne Morris in the title role, the first of his three turns as a pugilist (THE KID COMES BACK and THE KID FROM KOKOMO).

When a bellhop (Morris) knocks out highly touted heavyweight Chuck McGraw (William Haade) in defense of the honor of "Fluff" Phillips (Bette Davis), she dubs him Kid Galahad. Her boyfriend, Nick Donati (Robinson), decides to make the young man into a prizefighter. Jealous because both Fluff and her sister appear interested in Kid, Nick arranges a bout with McGraw that he is so certain his fighter will lose that he assures the rival manager Turkey Morgan of the same. Of course, things don't work out as planned....

A solid story with good characterizations and sensational prizefight footage, KID GALAHAD was remade as THE WAGONS ROLL AT NIGHT, with the story switched to a circus, then made again as a fight film with Elvis Presley. To avoid confusion with the Presley movie, the title has been changed to THE BATTLING BELLHOP for television.

KIDNAPPED

1971 100m c   Adventure   ★★★
Omnibus   (U.K.)   G

Michael Caine (*Alan Breck*), Trevor Howard (*Lord Advocate Grant*), Jack Hawkins (*Capt. Hoseason*), Donald Pleasence (*Ebenezer Balfour*), Gordon Jackson (*Charles Stewart*), Vivien Heilbron (*Catriona Stewart*), Lawrence Douglas (*David Balfour*), Freddie Jones (*Cluny Macpherson*), Andrew McCulloch (*Andrew*), Eric Woodburn (*Doctor*)

p, Frederick H. Brogger; d, Delbert Mann; w, Jack Pulman (based on the novels *Kidnapped* and *Catriona* by Robert Louis Stevenson); ph, Paul Beeson (Panavision, Movielab Color); ed, Peter Boita; m, Roy Budd; art d, Alex Vetchinsky; fx, Cliff Culley; cos, Olga Lehmann

Originally released in 1938 with Warner Baxter and Freddie Bartholomew in the leads, KIDNAPPED was remade in 1948 with Roddy McDowall and Dan O'Herlihy, then again with James MacArthur and Peter Finch in 1960. This fourth version of Robert Louis Stevenson's novel was a rare, relatively classy project for American International Pictures (AIP), the prolific producer of "classic" teen-oriented drive-in fodder during the 1950s and 1960s. This screenplay offers the audience more bang for its buck by including material from Stevenson's less well known sequel, *Catriona*.

In the final years of the 18th century, the British are brutally ravaging the Scottish forces of the Jacobite Rebellion. David Balfour (Douglas) is an orphan boy who comes to the home of his wicked uncle, Ebenezer Balfour (Pleasence), unaware that he is actually the rightful heir to the family fortune. Ebenezer hires Captain Hoseason (Hawkins), a ruthless sea captain, to force the boy into service on a ship prior to selling him into slavery in the New World. On its way to the Carolinas, Hoseason's ship rams a small boat, sinking it and drowning every hand aboard save Alan Breck (Caine), a rebel on his way to France to raise money to continue the war against the Crown. Breck and young Balfour hit it off immediately and join forces to battle the cutthroat crew. However, a storm hits and the ship is wrecked. Here their high adventure begins in earnest.

Rather than use their well worn matte paintings, AIP splurged and went to England and Scotland to find the proper settings. The photography that resulted is splendid. After a decade of "Beach Party" films, AIP decided to remake classics and foisted some dreadful ones upon the public, WUTHERING HEIGHTS and JULIUS CAESAR among them. This is the best of the lot, although it has so much plot that it may be difficult for youngsters to follow. Caine shows his costume mettle in this role, a welcome change from the spies and cads he'd played until making KIDNAPPED. A little too much talk and not enough action, but it's still fun.

KIDS   DVD
1995   90m   c   Drama   ★★★
Independent Pictures/The Guys Upstairs   (U.S.)

Leo Fitzpatrick *(Telly)*, Justin Pierce *(Casper)*, Chloe Sevigny *(Jennie)*, Sarah Henderson *(Girl No. 1)*, Rosario Dawson *(Ruby)*, Harold Hunter *(Harold)*, Yakira Peguero *(Darcy)*, Joseph Knofelmacher *(Taxi Driver)*, Joseph Chan *(Ball Owner)*, Jonathan S. Kim *(Korean Guy)*

p, Cary Woods; d, Larry Clark; w, Harmony Korine (from an original story treatment by Larry Clark, Jim Lewis, Leo Fitzpatrick, and Justin Pierce); ph, Eric Alan Edwards; ed, Chris Tellefsen; m, Lou Barlow, John Davis; prod d, Kevin Thompson; cos, Kim Druce

Though it promised to be 1995's most scandalous indie release, this edgy, downbeat film emerged as little more than REEFER MADNESS for the Age of AIDS. Disney sought to hide its financial interest in KIDS by forcing its subsidiary, Miramax, to release the film under a corporate pseudonym, but it needn't have bothered. Director Larry Clark, famous for his arty, voyeuristic still photos of adolescents, cleverly seeds his titillating subject matter—teen sex and drug abuse—with enough fear, loathing, and cautionary finger-wagging to keep the most reactionary would-be censors at bay.

KIDS follows a crowd of bored, unblushingly aimless New York teenagers through a day of hanging out, getting stoned, kicking ass, and having sex; each of these activities is depicted in sometimes excruciating *verite* detail. The narrative center and moral focus of the piece is Telly (Leo Fitzpatrick), a thoroughgoing scumbag with a taste for deflowering and abandoning girls. When one of his conquests, Jennie (Chloe Sevigny), discovers she's HIV-positive, she resolves to find him before he passes on the virus to another innocent girl.

The screenplay, by 21-year-old skateboard enthusiast Harmony Korine, pays apparently clever—though possibly unwitting—homage to Arthur Schnitzler's classic *Reigen*, which follows the liaisons of a daisy-chain of sex partners. Unlike Schnitzler, however, Korine fails to root his characters in a plausible social context: these kids may be going nowhere, but that's no excuse for neglecting to tell us where they come from. Anyone who has grown up in New York City will detect something irredeemably bogus in the way Korine's characters mingle and match, regardless of class, race, ethicity, or neighborhood loyalties. Clark's visually trendy rendering of events is generally effective but eventually wears out its welcome: one yearns for a simple, steady tripod shot and release from the tangential glances at homeless people that suggest a Profound Statement in the making.

KIKA   DVD
1993   115m   c   Comedy/Drama   ★★
El Deseo/CiBy 2000   (Spain/France)   NC-17

Veronica Forque *(Kika)*, Peter Coyote *(Nicholas)*, Victoria Abril *(Andrea Scarface)*, Alex Casanovas *(Ramon)*, Rossy DePalma *(Juana)*, Santiago Lajustica *(Pablo)*, Anabel Alonso *(Amparo)*, Bibi Andersen *(Susana)*, Jesus Bonilla *(Policia One)*, Karra Elejalde *(Policia Two)*

d, Pedro Almodovar; w, Pedro Almodovar; ph, Alfredo Mayo; ed, Pepe Salcedo; cos, Jose Maria Cossia, Gianni Versace

Pedro Almodovar upholds his reputation for controversy with this candy-colored burlesque. Unfortunately, Almodovar's peculiar vision is more repellent than risque here, particularly in his farcical depiction of rape.

Kika (Veronica Forque) is a flirtatious make-up artist who gets involved with several odd characters in modern-day Madrid, including Nicholas (Peter Coyote), a penniless American writer whose wife has just died under suspicious circumstances, and his stepson Ramon (Alex Casanovas), who literally rises from the dead while Kika prepares him for his funeral. After Ramon's "resurrection," he and Kika move in together. Complications include Ramon's sexual quirks; their lesbian maid, Juana (Rossy de Palma), who has a crush on Kika; Juana's mentally retarded, sex-mad, ex-porno star brother Pablo (Santiago Lajustica), who rapes Kika; Andrea Scarface (Victoria Abril), host of the tabloid TV show "Today's Worst," who shows a videotape of Kika's ordeal on her program; and the fact that Kika is having an affair with Nicholas, who has a very scary secret life.

Despite the presence of some talented and charismatic actresses, KIKA is much closer in spirit to Almodovar's more disturbing recent films (TIE ME UP! TIE ME DOWN! 1989, HIGH HEELS 1991) than WOMEN ON THE VERGE OF A NERVOUS BREAKDOWN (1987), the witty ensemble comedy that put him on the international map. Almodovar's color design is as bright as ever, but his vision is at its ugliest, and many viewers may be put off by his freewheeling, screwball approach to violence against women. That KIKA isn't thoroughly offensive is a tribute to the cast, especially Forque and the striking Abril, a vision in Gaultier and Versace.

KILL BILL: VOL. 1   DVD
2003   96m   c/bw Action/Martial Arts   ★★★½
Super Cool ManChu/A Band Apart/Miramax   (U.S.)   R

Uma Thurman *(The Bride/Black Mamba)*, David Carradine *(Bill)*, Lucy Liu *(O-Ren Ishii/Cottonmouth)*, Daryl Hannah *(Elle Driver/California Mountain Snake)*, Vivica A. Fox *(Vernita Green/Copperhead)*, Michael Madsen *(Budd/Sidewinder)*, Michael Parks *(Sheriff)*, Sonny Chiba *(Hattori Hanzo)*, Chiaki Kuriyama *(Go Go Yubari)*, Julie Dreyfus *(Sofie Fatale)*

p, Lawrence Bender; d, Quentin Tarantino; w, Quentin Tarantino; ph, Robert Richardson; ed, Sally Menke; m, RZA; prod d, Yohei

Tanada, David Wasco; art d, Daniel Bradford; fx, Don Greenberg, Jason Gustafson; cos, Kumiko Ogawa, Catherine Marie Thomas; anim, Production I.G.

Quentin Tarantino's feverish homage to the cherished exploitation experiences of his youth may be the world's first movie-as-mix tape. Not a slapdash party tape with a bunch of popular stuff strung carelessly together, but a loving compendium of Proustian images and melodies, the more obscure the better, meticulously juxtaposed and segued into each other so they evoke an integrated memory of endless pulp highs savored in the smoky haze of grindhouses and darkened basements. If your sensibilities are in line with Tarantino's, the result is sheer sleaze Nirvana.

In Vol. 1, a professional assassin, code-named Black Mamba (Uma Thurman), is attacked on her wedding day, and her unborn child, wedding guests, and sundry bystanders murdered. The killers are the Bride's sisters in slaughter, fellow members of DiVAS (the Deadly Viper Assassins Squad—any resemblance to PULP FICTION's "Fox Force Five" is no doubt intentional): Elle Driver, aka California Mountain Snake (Daryl Hannah); Vernita Green, aka Copperhead (Vivica A. Fox); and O-Ren Ishii, aka Cottonmouth (Lucy Liu), aided by ex-viper Budd (Michael Madsen). All answer to Bill (David Carradine), who personally delivers the coup de grace: a bullet to the bloody bride's head. But the Bride doesn't die, and Bill calls off a second assassination attempt at her hospital bedside, where she lies comatose. Cut to four years later: The Bride awakens, thirsting for revenge. She makes a list, formulates a plan, and gets to work. In the film's lightly fractured chronology, she first takes on her second target, Copperhead, whom she surprises in her suburban Pasadena living room. Then it's back one step: After a stop over in Okinawa to persuade a legendary sword master ('70s kung-fu star Sonny Chiba) to make one last lethal blade, the Bride proceeds to Tokyo, where Cottonmouth has risen to rule Tokyo's seething underworld. At the House of Blue Leaves, a gleaming restaurant/nightclub complex whose glass dance floor, shoji-screens, graceful staircases, and serene garden cry out to be spattered with enough blood to paint Hell itself red, the Bride and Cottonmouth's minions face off.

Tarantino's movie madeleines include yakuza epics, spaghetti Westerns, anime, chop-socky pictures, Italian gialli, euro-sexploitation, and TV shows of the 1960s and '70s. His epic reworking of their lurid conventions proved so long that it was divided into two parts, and this one ends on a hell of a cliffhanger.

KILL BILL: VOL. 2

2004 137m   c/bw Crime/Action/Martial Arts ★★★★
A Band Apart/Super Cool ManChu/Miramax   R
(U.S.)

Uma Thurman (Beatrix Kiddo/The Bride/Black Mamba), David Carradine (Bill/Snake Charmer), Michael Madsen (Budd/Sidewinder), Daryl Hannah (Elle Driver/California Mountain Snake), Gordon Liu (Pai Mei), Michael Parks (Esteban Vihaio), Perla Haney-Jardine (B.B.), Chris Nelson (Tommy Plympton), Bo Svenson (Reverend Harmony), Jeannie Epper (Mrs. Harmony)

p, Lawrence Bender; d, Quentin Tarantino; w, Quentin Tarantino (based on the character of The Bride, created by Q and U); ph, Robert Richardson; ed, Sally Menke; m, Robert Rodriguez, The RZA; prod d, Cao Jui Ping, David Wasco; art d, Daniel Bradford, Liu Lu Yi; fx, Jason Gustafson, Corey Pritchett; cos, Kumiko Ogawa, Thomas

Less relentlessly action-packed than its predecessor, Quentin Tarantino's follow-up to KILL BILL: VOL. 1 slows down to let the story breathe without losing the energy that keeps it hurtling towards its appointed end: the showdown between the blood-spattered Bride (Uma Thurman) and the man who very nearly killed her—Bill (David Carradine), her former boss and lover.

Having thus far slain two of the five assassins responsible for the Texas church bloodbath that left her comatose and her groom-to-be (Chris Nelson) dead, the Bride—who here reclaims her name, Beatrix Kiddo—moves on to her next target, Bill's younger brother, Budd (Michael Madsen). Liquor-pickled, mean as a toad, and living near Barstow, CA, Budd gets the better of Beatrix, buries her alive, and arranges to sell her priceless samurai sword to one-eyed hit woman Elle Driver (Daryl Hannah), the fourth church assassin. Beatrix's underground imprisonment triggers a flashback to her apprenticeship under imperious, white-bearded martial-arts master Pai Mei (Gordon Liu), whose harsh training gave her the skills to survive almost anything—even interment. With Budd and Elle in her dirt-caked sights, Beatrix prepares to take on her final and most dangerous target.

Tarantino maintains a flawless balance between flat-out action, quirky dialogue, stylish homages to the glistening shadows of film-noir thrillers, the sun-baked brutality of Westerns (American and Italian), the ritualistic rhythms of Shaw Brothers martial-arts pictures from the 1970s, and quietly dramatic moments, shifting between them with quicksilver facility. The more intense your own relationship with movies, the harder it is to resist this masterful compendium of movie-made dreams. Tarantino reinvigorates the exploitation icons of his youth while synthesizing the vivid movie-going experiences of his cherished memories.

KILLER OF SHEEP

1978 80m   bw   Drama/Comedy   ★★★★★
(U.S.)

Henry Gayle Sanders (Stan), Kaycee Moore (Stan's Wife), Charles Bracy (Bracy), Angela Burnett (Stan's Daughter), Eugene Cherry (Eugene), Jack Drummond (Stan's Son)

p, Charles Burnett; d, Charles Burnett; w, Charles Burnett; ph, Charles Burnett; ed, Charles Burnett

Milieu is the main character in Charles Burnett's KILLER OF SHEEP, an essentially plotless look at everyday life in a semi-suburban black neighborhood. The film is probably the most perceptive and poetic study ever done of Americans existing one level above poverty. Produced for a mere $10,000 with an amateur cast, it was one of fewer than 100 pictures proclaimed "national treasures" by the National Film Registry of the Library of Congress in 1990.

Stan (Henry Gayle Sanders), a slaughterhouse worker, complains to a friend about his hard life. When his son (Jack Drummond) persists in teasing his sister (Angela Burnett), he chases the boy out of the house. Stan's wife (Kaycee Moore) attempts to talk to him about his increasing melancholy and lethargy, but he is unresponsive. Two of Stan's friends try to convince him to join them in a murder plot. He refuses and his wife, who has overheard, berates Stan's friends. Stan and his friend, Eugene (Eugene Cherry), visit a man with an old car motor for sale. Minutes after they purchase it, it falls out of the back of Eugene's pickup and is ruined. Stan and his wife share a romantic dance in their parlor but, when she initiates further intimacy, he does not respond and leaves her unhappily alone.

Burnett filmed KILLER OF SHEEP in Watts—the mostly black, largely poor area of Los Angeles where he grew up—and populated it with friends and acquaintances. The movie, which served as his master's thesis at UCLA, took five years to complete. It is a great film and a unique one. Rarely on the screen has authenticity been so artistic, or (relentless) irony so free of cynicism. The squalid settings, gritty black-and-white cinematography, and innate modesty of Burnett's sensibility and temperance of his voice tend at first to mask his enormous gifts. Burnett's overall reluctance to play on audience sympathy does not, however, prevent him from framing many affecting images. KILLER OF SHEEP is everything an independent film should be: artistically ambitious yet accessible; narrowly focused yet suggestive of larger ramifications; and free of obligation to formula, genre, or the star system. Brilliantly conceived, imaginatively structured, superbly written, stylishly composed and photographed, and very often wryly funny, KILLER OF SHEEP lives up to its official designation as a national treasure.

KILLER, THE *DVD*
(DIE XUE SHUANG XIONG)
1989 110m   c   Action/Crime   ★★★★
Film Workshop/Golden Princess/Magnum
(Hong Kong)

Chow Yun-Fat *(Jeffrey Chow)*, Sally Yeh *(Jennie)*, Danny Lee *(Detective "Eagle" Lee)*, Kenneth Tsang *(Sergeant Randy Chung)*, Chu Kong *(Sydney Fung)*, Lam Chung *(Willie Tsang)*, Shing Fui-on *(Johnny Wang)*, Ye Rongzu *(Tony Weng)*, Yi Fanwei *(Frankie Feng)*, Huang Guangliang *(Wong Tong)*

p, Tsui Hark; d, John Woo; w, John Woo; ph, Wong Wing Hang, Peter Pau; ed, Fan Kung-ming; m, Lowell Lowe; art d, Luk Man-wah; cos, Shirley Chan

In the world of John Woo's over-the-top action movies, it seems there's no problem that can't be solved by a hail of bullets. Don't be fooled; THE KILLER is far more than the sum of its plot elements.

Jeffrey Chow (Chow Yun-Fat) is a professional killer with his own code of ethics and a lethal two-handed draw. Detective "Eagle" Lee (Danny Lee) is a cop at odds with the system: he'd rather get the scum off the streets than play departmental politics. Sydney Fung (Chu Kong), a hit man past his prime, is Jeff's only friend. Jennie (Sally Yeh) is a nightclub singer caught in the crossfire and blinded when Jeff slaughters a room full of gangsters. Guilt-stricken, Jeff befriends and then falls in love with the blind woman. But when Sydney hires him to kill Tony Weng (Ye Rongzu)—the one last job that will allow him to leave the life of a killer forever—the hit doesn't go off as cleanly as it should, and Lee vows to hunt him down, using Jennie as bait.

THE KILLER rings a genuinely delirious set of changes on American movie themes, careening between brutality and mawkish sentiment without missing a beat. In the days before Quentin Tarantino brought HK stylings to the American screen, Western audiences were almost literally stunned by the extravagance of this film: the insistent visual and narrative symmetry, the barely repressed homoeroticism, the pathetic comedy of blind Jennie—unaware of the gunplay going on around her—trying to serve tea. One moment Woo's heroes are .44 magnum dervishes, the next they're spinning some outrageous fiction about childhood friendship and their nicknames for one another—"Mickey Mouse" and "Dumbo."

And the bullets ... the bullets. They fly freely at the drop of a hat, splatter bad guys all over the walls while missing the protagonists (special credit to the sightless Jennie, who shows a particular flare for dodging speeding projectiles), and generally make the world go round. For Western viewers unfamiliar with Hong Kong gangster films, there's no better introduction.

KILLERS, THE *DVD*
1946 102m   bw   Crime   ★★★★★
Universal   (U.S.)

Burt Lancaster *(Swede)*, Ava Gardner *(Kitty Collins)*, Edmond O'Brien *(Jim Reardon)*, Albert Dekker *(Big Jim Colfax)*, Sam Levene *(Lt. Sam Lubinsky)*, Virginia Christine *(Lilly Lubinsky)*, John Miljan *(Jake)*, Vince Barnett *(Charleston)*, Charles D. Brown *(Packy Robinson)*, Donald MacBride *(Kenyon)*

p, Mark Hellinger; d, Robert Siodmak; w, Anthony Veiller, John Huston (based on the story by Ernest Hemingway); ph, Elwood Bredell; ed, Arthur Hilton; m, Miklos Rozsa; art d, Jack Otterson, Martin Obzina; fx, David S. Horsley; cos, Vera West

AAN Best Director: Robert Siodmak; *AAN Best Screenplay:* Anthony Veiller; *AAN Best Film Editing:* Arthur Hilton; *AAN Best Score (Drama or Comedy):* Miklos Rozsa

The first Universal production supervised by Hellinger, a one-time reporter turned film producer, this definitive film noir is at least as powerful as his earlier crime movies, THE ROARING TWENTIES and HIGH SIERRA. THE KILLERS, which features a now famous musical score (later used in the "Dragnet" TV series) by Miklos Rozsa, is also notable as Burt Lancaster's film debut. The ace crime director Siodmak uses the bare bones of Hemingway's terse story to build a taut and fascinating tale of murder, robbery, and betrayal. It also features one of the genre's most celebrated femme fatales.

It opens with the killers of the Hemingway story (Charles McGraw and William Conrad) entering the diner in search of the Swede (Lancaster). They have a murder contract to fulfill, they learn that he will soon be coming in for dinner. Nick Adams (Phil Brown) overhears the killer's intent and runs to a boarding house to warn the Swede. He listens, but remains indifferently on his bed, explaining simply "I did something wrong...once." With that he quietly awaits his fate. The Hemingway story ends about there, but this is only the beginning of the film. Edmond O'Brien is Jim Reardon, an energetic insurance investigator whose company has to pay off on the Swede's death. By interviewing the Swede's associates, Rearden begins the laborious process of reconstructing the dead man's turbulent life, a process we see through a series of extended flashbacks.

We first see him as a young boxer who gets thrust into the posh and corrupt world of organized crime, overlorded by boss Big Jim Colfax (Dekker). He becomes enamored of the sultry Kitty Collins (Gardner), Colfax's girlfriend. She entices the big, handsome boxer with the promise that she will leave the boss for him if he helps the gang in an elaborate armored car robbery. Kitty and the Swede would then take the loot, double-cross Big Jim, and flee to a life of their own. This sounds too good to be true. It is.

The cast is excellent and Siodmak's direction is hard-edged and moody. Lancaster's personality amazed viewers seeing him for the first time, and he soon reached star status with BRUTE FORCE, I WALK ALONE, ALL MY SONS and other heavyweight films. Lancaster, a former circus acrobat, began his career here at age 32 but looked much younger. THE KILLERS was also the first important dramatic role for Gardner. Hemingway admired Gardner's portrayal of the eternal vixen and they became lifelong friends. She appeared in other Hemingway vehicles, notably THE SNOWS OF KILIMANJARO and THE SUN ALSO RISES.

KILLERS, THE *DVD*
1964 93m   c   Crime   ★★★
Revue   (U.S.)

Lee Marvin *(Charlie)*, Angie Dickinson *(Sheila Farr)*, John Cassavetes *(Johnny North)*, Ronald Reagan *(Browning)*, Clu Gulager *(Lee)*, Claude Akins *(Earl Sylvester)*, Norman Fell *(Mickey)*, Virginia Christine *(Miss Watson)*, Don Haggerty *(Mail Truck Driver)*, Robert Phillips *(George)*

p, Don Siegel; d, Don Siegel; w, Gene L. Coon (based on the story by Ernest Hemingway); ph, Richard L. Rawlings (Eastmancolor); ed, Richard Belding; m, John Williams; art d, Frank Arrigo, George Chan, George O'Connell; cos, Helen Colvig

Hit men Charlie (Marvin) and Lee (Gulager) are ordered to go to a school for the blind and kill Johnny North

(Cassavetes), one of the teachers there, who puts up no resistance. They wonder why he accepted his death so passively and who ordered him killed. The killers connect him to an armored car heist several years before from which the money was never recovered. They learn that North was a race car driver in love with Sheila Farr (Dickinson), the mistress of crime czar Browning (Reagan). She had persuaded him to drive the getaway car in the armored car job and they planned to double-cross Browning. But things did not work out that way. As they learn more about the story of the man they killed, the killers develop their own interest in its ultimate outcome.

This was Reagan's final film, and the only one in which he's the villain. THE KILLERS was originally produced for TV by NBC but censors determined it was too violent for that medium, so it was released in theaters. Reagan was reluctant to play the heavy, but the head of Universal at the time, Reagan's former agent, talked him into accepting the part, a decision Reagan still regrets. Though the film does not stand up to the 1946 version with Burt Lancaster, it has its own pleasures, including Marvin's rather likable role of an assassin, the exciting robbery sequence, and, of course, the villainous Reagan getting his just desserts. Two years later he was elected governor of California. And the rest is history.

KILLER'S KISS
1955 67m   bw   Thriller   ★★★½
Minotaur   (U.S.)

Frank Silvera (*Vincent Rapallo*), Jamie Smith (*Davy Gordon*), Irene Kane (*Gloria Price*), Jerry Jarret (*Albert, the Fight Manager*), Mike Dana, Felice Orlandi, Ralph Roberts, Phil Stevenson (*Gangsters*), Julius Adelman (*Owner of the Mannequin Factory*), David Vaughan

p, Stanley Kubrick, Morris Bousel; d, Stanley Kubrick; w, Stanley Kubrick, Howard Sackler (based on a story by Kubrick); ph, Stanley Kubrick; ed, Stanley Kubrick; m, Gerald Fried; chor, David Vaughan

The second film directed by future master filmmaker Stanley Kubrick, KILLER'S KISS is no one's idea of a great film but it displays much evidence of future brilliance. The story is nothing more than B-movie film noir fodder, but some of the images and set pieces are indelible.

Davy Gordon (Smith) is a second-rate prizefighter who gets romantically involved with Gloria Price (Kane), a young dancer who lives across the courtyard in his apartment building. Returning home one night after another lost fight, he sees Price fending off a rapist. The assailant is Vincent Rapallo (Silvera), Price's boss at the nightclub where she dances. Gordon rescues her and they decide to flee the city. But Rapallo plans a murderous revenge...

This modest thriller was financed for $75,000 by various friends and relatives of the neophyte filmmaker. He served not only as director, writer and producer but also filmed and edited the project. Though the screenplay is undistinguished (and gives no hint of what Kubrick's future ability as a writer), he makes some interesting choices as a director.

The vivid flashbacks and surrealistic nightmare sequences are memorable. The nightmares are represented on negative film stock, an interesting and effective choice. Other idiosyncratic touches include the disorienting contrast created by showing a bloody boxing match on a television screen while an equally violent near-rape and struggle occurs between the nominal viewers, and the surreal effect achieved by using the dismembered limbs of female mannequins as weapons during a brutal fight sequence in a factory.

All in all, it's hardly Kubrick's best work, but is a revealing early look at a visual style that soon ripened to maturity to produce such film classics as PATHS OF GLORY, SPARTACUS, DR. STRANGELOVE, 2001: A SPACE ODYSSEY, and A CLOCKWORK ORANGE.

This film was also the inspiration for Matthew Chapman's film, STRANGER'S KISS.

KILLING, THE   DVD
1956 83m   bw   Crime   ★★★★½
UA   (U.S.)

Sterling Hayden (*Johnny Clay*), Coleen Gray (*Fay*), Vince Edwards (*Val Cannon*), Jay C. Flippen (*Marvin Unger*), Marie Windsor (*Sherry Peatty*), Ted de Corsia (*Randy Kennan*), Elisha Cook Jr. (*George Peatty*), Joe Sawyer (*Mike O'Reilly*), Timothy Carey (*Nikki Arane*), Jay Adler (*Leo*)

p, James B. Harris; d, Stanley Kubrick; w, Stanley Kubrick, Jim Thompson (based on the novel *Clean Break* by Lionel White); ph, Lucien Ballard; ed, Betty Steinberg; m, Gerald Fried; art d, Ruth Sobotka Kubrick; cos, Rudy Harrington

Hardboiled early Kubrick. This lean, mean genre film is similar in mood and structure to John Huston's earlier THE ASPHALT JUNGLE, but many of Kubrick's characteristic obsessions are already firmly in place: fatally flawed humans, complicated interlocking timetables and meticulous plans gone awry.

Johnny Clay (Hayden) is an ex-con who tells his childhood sweetheart, Fay (Gray), that he and a few others are going to make a "big score" that will be his last caper. During a race at the local racetrack he intends to rob the money room where the betting take is kept, while Nikki Arane (Carey), a professional killer, shoots one of the horses on the far turn to create a diversion. Clay assembles a group of associates for the job, each with some problem that is getting too big for him to handle: Marvin Unger (Flippen), a retired friend; Randy Kennan (de Corsia), a cop who owes the syndicate money; Mike O'Reilly (Sawyer), a bartender at the racetrack who needs money for his sick wife; and George Peatty (Cook), a cashier at the track with a money-grubbing wife (Windsor). They are all ordinary men "with a touch of larceny in their souls." Everything is planned down to the smallest detail but things go terribly wrong.

THE KILLING brought Kubrick to the attention of the industry as a major directorial talent even though this film was produced on a small budget of $320,000—and it shows. The sets are like cardboard but Kubrick emphasizes that fact, panning his camera from one room to another, showing partitions, devising every conceivable angle from which to shoot, so that the space in which his actors move appears as it really is, confining, cramped, and claustrophobic, reflecting the attitudes of his characters. The film's semi-documentary feel is only enhanced by its meticulous intersecting flashback structure. Time becomes a palpable presence in this fatalistic film.

Hayden gives a stoical top drawer performance as the nominal leader of this unprofessional gang of thieves. Cook gives one of the best performances of his career as the henpecked little man who suffers an avalanche of insults from his wretched wife, Windsor, whose own performance is spectacular.

KILLING FIELDS, THE   DVD
1984 141m   c   Drama/War   ★★★½
Enigma/Goldcrest   (U.K.)   R

Sam Waterston (*Sydney Schanberg*), Haing S. Ngor (*Dith Pran*), John Malkovich (*Al Rockoff*), Julian Sands (*Jon Swain*), Craig T. Nelson (*Military Attache*), Spalding Gray (*U.S. Consul*), Bill Paterson (*Dr. Macentire*), Athol Fugard (*Dr. Sundesval*), Graham Kennedy (*Dougal*), Katherine Krapum Chey (*Ser Moeun*)

p, David Puttnam; d, Roland Joffe; w, Bruce Robinson (based on the magazine article "The Death and Life of Dith Pran," by Sydney Schanberg); ph, Chris Menges; ed, Jim Clark; m, Mike Oldfield; prod d, Roy Walker; art d, Roger Murray Leach, Steve Spence; fx, Fred Cramer; cos, Judy Moorcroft

AAN Best Picture; AAN Best Actor: Sam Waterston; AA Best Supporting Actor: Haing S. Ngor; AAN Best Director: Roland Joffe; AAN Best Adapted Screenplay: Bruce Robinson; AA Best Cinematography: Chris Menges; AA Best Film Editing: Jim Clark

A deeply moving film, THE KILLING FIELDS is the somewhat-fictionalized story of New York Times reporter Sydney Schanberg (Sam Waterston) and his efforts to find his friend Dith Pran (Haing S. Ngor) after the Cambodian translator falls into the hands of the brutal Khmer Rouge. Although Dith's family is evacuated with the last U.S. personnel to leave Phnom Penh, Schanberg persuades his translator to remain behind with him; and when Khmer Rouge troops enter the city, Dith convinces them that Schanberg and his photographer (John Malkovich) are French.

Regrettably, Schanberg is unable to return the favor later, and Dith is sent off to a rural reeducation camp, which he barely survives but eventually escapes. While undertaking the arduous journey to safety, he comes across the horrifying remains of some of the three million people who died at the hands of the Khmer Rouge. Meanwhile, racked with guilt, Schanberg, who has received a Pulitzer Prize for "international reporting at great risk," does everything he can to locate his friend.

THE KILLING FIELDS wisely emphasizes the human element of its story, concentrating on Schanberg and Dith's friendship, and lets the political situation speak for itself. Haing S. Ngor, the Cambodian physician whose real-life experiences were similar to those of the character he plays, gives a sincere, heartrending performance that is the film's emotional core. Although Waterston is less effective, he too contributes a believable performance, as does Malkovich in an impressive film debut. Aided by Chris Menges' spectacular Oscar winning cinematography, director Roland Joffe's first feature is a significant achievement, its sequences unfolding with precision as the emotions mount.

KIND HEARTS AND CORONETS
1949   105m   bw   Comedy   ★★★★★
Ealing   (U.K.)

Dennis Price (Louis Mazzini), Valerie Hobson (Edith D'Ascoyne), Joan Greenwood (Sibella), Alec Guinness (Duke/Banker/ Parson etc.), Audrey Fildes (Mama), Miles Malleson (The Hangman), Clive Morton (Prison Governor), John Penrose (Lionel), Cecil Ramage (Crown Counsel), Hugh Griffith (Lord High Steward)

p, Michael Balcon; d, Robert Hamer; w, Robert Hamer, John Dighton (based on a novel by Roy Horniman); ph, Douglas Slocombe; ed, Peter Tanner; m, Wolfgang Amadeus Mozart ("Don Giovanni"); art d, William Kellner

Coming on the heels of GREAT EXPECTATIONS and OLIVER TWIST, this was the film that made Alec Guinness an international star. Although Dennis Price has the largest single role in the picture (and plays it beautifully), Guinness took the lion's share of the credit for its success with a tour de force performance as no less than eight characters, all members of the same family. A black comedy about mass murder, KIND HEARTS AND CORONETS is one of the British film industry's funniest movies, as well as one of the most memorable and notorious.

The action is set around 1900. Price is in line to a dukedom, but is treated as a pariah because of his mother's unfortunate marriage. Seething with class resentment, he decides to remove all the obstacles in his way. While conducting an affair with the married Greenwood, he begins knocking off his relatives in various fanciful ways. Matters are complicated when he falls in love with Hobson, the widow of one of his victims. But after Price ascends to the dukedom and marries Hobson, fate catches up: he's arrested for a murder he did not commit.

The film is full of bright dialogue and quotable quotes ("Revenge is the dish which people of taste prefer to eat cold!").

Robert Hamer (who also directed) and John Dighton loosely based the story on Roy Horniman's turn-of-the-century novel Israel Rank, dispensing with all but the core of the book to write the sharp screenplay. The result, KIND HEARTS AND CORONETS, is one of those films that can be seen repeatedly and still offer surprises. As a combination of rollicking black humor and satirical pokes at the English upper crust, nothing else comes close.

KIND OF LOVING, A
1962   112m   bw   Drama   ★★★★
Vic/Waterhall (U.K.)

Alan Bates (Vic Brown), June Ritchie (Ingrid Rothwell), Thora Hird (Mrs. Rothwell), Bert Palmer (Mr. Brown), Gwen Nelson (Mrs. Brown), Malcolm Patton (Jim Brown), Pat Keen (Christine), David Mahlowe (David), Jack Smethurst (Conroy), James Bolam (Jeff)

p, Joseph Janni; d, John Schlesinger; w, Willis Hall, Keith Waterhouse (based on the novel by Stan Barstow); ph, Denys Coop; ed, Roger Cherrill; m, Ron Grainer; art d, Ray Simm; cos, Laura Nightingale

A kind of marvelous. One of the greatest achievements of the marriage between "angry young man" drama and the Free Cinema movement in Britain in the early 1960s, this was Schlesinger's first feature after a successful sojourn in commercials.

Bates stars as Vic Brown, a draftsman in a Lancashire factory attracted to Ingrid Rothwell (Ritchie), a typist at the plant. They sleep together at her place when her mother (Hird) is out of town and though Ingrid falls hard for Vic, he soon loses interest in her. Her pregnancy, however, leads to marriage and life with the domineering, snobbish Mrs. Rothwell. After Ingrid has a miscarriage Vic regrets having said "I do" and goes off on a bender. The film comes to its sober conclusion as the confused young couple sort through their relationship and wonder if "a kind of loving" is possible.

It's not much of a story when summarized, but that's part of the film's beauty, and the script and direction elevate this film far beyond the norm. Shot almost like a documentary, this low-key production reveals, as few have, the power of realism as a style.

Other than Bates, who was fairly recognizable to film audiences, many of the actors were newcomers with little or no film experience. This lack of movie stars works to the film's advantage, as Bates and Ritchie are simply superb as a young pair who act first and think later. Schlesinger is unafraid to expose the unsympathetic qualities of his characters, and the result is a remarkably rounded drama.

That seasoned veteran Thora Hird is at or near her greatest, and the casting throughout is well-nigh perfect. There's not a false note in the picture, and Schlesinger's supple control and Waterhouse and Hall's moving screenplay deserve much of the credit. Despite the grimy surroundings and downbeat theme, A KIND OF LOVING is filled with humor, insight and intelligence which make it an unjustly overlooked landmark in British cinema.

KING AND COUNTRY
1964   86m   bw   War   ★★★★½
BHE   (U.K.)

Dirk Bogarde (Capt. Hargreaves), Tom Courtenay (Pvt. Arthur Hamp), Leo McKern (Capt. O'Sullivan), Barry Foster (Lt. Webb), James Villiers (Capt. Midgley), Peter Copley (Colonel), Barry Justice (Lt. Prescott), Vivian Matalon (Padre), Jeremy Spenser (Pvt. Sparrow), James Hunter (Pvt. Sykes)

p, Joseph Losey, Norman Priggen; d, Joseph Losey; w, Evan Jones (based on the play Hamp by John Wilson, from an episode in the novel Return to the Wood by James Lansdale Hodson); ph,

Denys Coop; ed, Reginald Mills; m, Larry Adler; prod d, Richard MacDonald; art d, Peter Mullins; cos, Roy Ponting

This brutally frank, thoughtful anti-war tract contains no battle scenes and little gunfire. Bogarde is a British captain assigned to defend a slow-witted soldier, Courtenay, who has been accused of desertion. Highly educated and a strict military disciplinarian, Bogarde approaches this assignment with distaste. Consequently, he accepts his superior's expedient suggestion that he ignore Courtenay's shell-shocked state and push for a quick conviction. While interviewing his client, Bogarde learns that Courtenay enlisted in the army on a dare from friends. Three years later, the uneducated soldier—having learned of his wife's infidelity and emerging from a battle as the sole survivor of his unit—falls victim to what we now call "post traumatic stress syndrome." Fed up and very very tired, Courtenay simply wanted to "go for a walk." Twenty four hours later, he's still walking along the road when he's taken into custody. During the testimony Bogarde begins to feel sympathy for the obviously sincere and somewhat confused Courtenay. For the first time in his military career, Bogarde begins to question the army's methods and attitudes toward its men.

KING AND COUNTRY is a grim indictment of the arrogant, simple-minded mentality of the men who send their fellow citizens off to war. A good army is driven by discipline and devotion to duty, but director Losey shows us that things are not that simple. Bogarde's character is a cold, unblinking automaton, and therefore quite successful in the military. His interviews with Courtenay change all that. KING AND COUNTRY is an extremely claustrophobic film that takes place in dark, dirty, rat-infested interiors; shot mostly in long, deep-focus takes, they effectively portray the situation of all concerned as both physically and morally cramped. Tom Courtenay won the best actor award at the Venice film festival for his performance.

KING AND I, THE   DVD
1956 133m c   Musical   ★★★★
Fox   (U.S.)   G

Deborah Kerr *(Anna Leonowens)*, Yul Brynner *(The King)*, Rita Moreno *(Tuptim)*, Martin Benson *(Kralahome)*, Terry Saunders *(Lady Thiang)*, Rex Thompson *(Louis Leonowens)*, Carlos Rivas *(Lun Tha)*, Patrick Adiarte *(Prince Chulalongkorn)*, Alan Mowbray *(British Ambassador)*, Geoffrey Toone *(Ramsay)*

p, Charles Brackett; d, Walter Lang; w, Ernest Lehman (based on the musical by Oscar Hammerstein II and Richard Rodgers, from the book *Anna and The King of Siam* by Margaret Landon); ph, Leon Shamroy (CinemaScope, DeLuxe Color); ed, Robert Simpson; m, Richard Rodgers; art d, Lyle Wheeler, John De Cuir; chor, Jerome Robbins; cos, Irene Sharaff

AAN Best Picture; AA Best Actor: Yul Brynner; *AAN Best Actress:* Deborah Kerr; *AAN Best Director:* Walter Lang; *AAN Best Color Cinematography:* Leon Shamroy; *AA Best Score (Musical):* Alfred Newman, Ken Darby; *AA Best Art Direction-Set Decoration (Color):* Lyle R. Wheeler, John DeCuir, Walter M. Scott, Paul S. Fox; *AA Best Costume Design (Color):* Irene Sharaff; *AA Best Sound Recording:* Carl Faulkner

Starring Yul Brynner in the part he seemed born to play, this is a fine if slightly stage-bound example of the 1950s Hollywood musical spectacular.

Deborah Kerr is an English schoolteacher who journeys to Siam with her son, Thompson. She has been hired by the king (Brynner) to teach his many children about the world outside their kingdom. Arrogant and chauvinistic, the King is very comfortable as the unchallenged ruler of his land. Kerr herself is a very strong woman, and it isn't long before the two are at odds, mainly because Brynner is stunned by her unwillingness to bend to his every whim. In a series of vignettes, Kerr is shown teaching the children, dealing with problems within the household (one of which involves persuading Brynner to let Moreno, one of his wives, leave

because she loves another), and verbally sparring with the king. Eventually, Kerr wins Brynner's respect and his love.

Even without the music, this well-written story would be a splendid entertainment. But it's the music, that wonderful score written by Rodgers and Hammerstein, that makes this movie as beloved as it is. Kerr's voice was looped by that most ubiquitous of song loopers, Marni Nixon (wife of music composer Ernest Gold), who did the singing for, among others, Audrey Hepburn in MY FAIR LADY and Natalie Wood in WEST SIDE STORY. Brynner, of course, is marvelous in the role of the supreme ruler who slowly comes to realize he's behind the times. He won an Oscar for his portrayal, and continued to do the play on the stage. At the time of his death in 1985, he had played the king in more than 4,000 performances. The screenplay by Ernest Lehman, who went on to write the adaptation of Rogers and Hammerstein's THE SOUND OF MUSIC, is faithful to the play, and even improves on it somewhat.

KING ARTHUR   DVD
2004 130m c   Historical/Adventure/War   ★★
Jerry Bruckheimer Films/Touchstone   (U.S.)   PG-13

Clive Owen *(Arthur)*, Ioan Gruffudd *(Lancelot)*, Mads Mikkelsen *(Tristan)*, Joel Edgerton *(Gawain)*, Hugh Dancy *(Galahad)*, Ray Winstone *(Bors)*, Ray Stevenson *(Dagonet)*, Keira Knightley *(Guinevere)*, Stephen Dillane *(Merlin)*, Stellan Skarsgard *(Cerdic)*

p, Jerry Bruckheimer; d, Antoine Fuqua; w, David Franzoni; ph, Slawomir Idziak; ed, Conrad Buff, Jamie Pearson; m, Hans Zimmer; prod d, Dan Weil; art d, Anna Rackard; fx, Neil Corbould, Matt Johnson, Corina Rosca; cos, Penny Rose

Imagine a tale of King Arthur that tosses out Camelot, the Holy Grail, and everything else the average person knows or cares about Arthur and his knights. In its place: Some dodgy history involving a shadowy Roman commander named Lucius Artorius Castus and his men, bound to defend Roman interests in ancient Britain against native Picts and invading Saxons.

The brooding Artorius, widely known as Arthur (Clive Owen), leads a small band of warriors whose skill and ferocity is already the stuff of legend. His knights—Lancelot (Ioan Gruffudd), Tristan (Mads Mikkelsen), Gawain (Joel Edgerton), Galahad (Hugh Dancy), Bors (Ray Winstone), and Dagonet (Ray Stevenson)—who were all conscripted as children in their native Sarmatia, are looking forward to going home after 15 years of indentured service to Rome when Arthur is handed orders to rescue a Roman family whose estate lies directly in the path of the invading Saxon hordes. Torn between national and personal loyalty, Arthur leads his men on a mission that requires they elude guerilla leader Merlin's (Stephen Dillane) Pictish warriors on the way in and outrun the pillaging Saxons, commanded by brutal father-and-son warlords Cerdic (Stellan Skarsgard) and Cynric (Til Schweiger), on the way out. Arthur comes away stripped of his faith in Rome but enfolded in the love of Pictish warrior princess Guinevere (Keira Knightley).

Written by GLADIATOR's David Franzoni and directed by Antoine Fuqua, this gloomy action picture probably presents a relatively accurate picture of fifth-century life and death (mostly the latter), but it's hard to see the point in cobbling together scraps of legend and historical fact into a story this generic. Next to the grubby grandeur of John Boorman's visionary EXCALIBUR, this stunted epic looks very shabby indeed.

KING KONG
1933 100m bw   Science Fiction/   ★★★★½
Adventure/Fantasy
RKO   (U.S.)

Fay Wray *(Ann Darrow)*, Robert Armstrong *(Carl Denham)*, Bruce Cabot *(John Driscoll)*, Frank Reicher *(Capt. Englehorn)*, Sam

Hardy *(Charles Weston)*, Noble Johnson *(Native Chief)*, Steve Clemente *(Witch King)*, James Flavin *(2nd Mate Briggs)*, Victor Wong *(Charley)*, Paul Porcasi *(Socrates)*

p, Merian C. Cooper, Ernest B. Schoedsack; d, Merian C. Cooper, Ernest B. Schoedsack; w, James Ashmore Creelman, Ruth Rose (based on a story by Cooper and Edgar Wallace); ph, Eddie Linden, Vernon Walker, J.O. Taylor; ed, Ted Cheesman; m, Max Steiner; art d, Carroll Clark, Al Herman, Van Nest Polglase; fx, Willis O'Brien, E.B. Gibson, Marcel Delgado, Fred Reese, Orville Goldner, Carroll L. Shepphird, Mario Larrinaga, Byron L. Crabbe

The ultimate monster movie and one of the grandest and most beloved adventure films ever made, KING KONG is a film that has given us one of the most enduring icons of American popular culture—a massively destructive but curiously sympathetic giant gorilla whose rampage through New York City suggests, on a psychological level, the re-emergence of repressed desire. While Kong is, in most scenes, only an 18-inch studio model, the stop motion special effects are so intelligently accomplished and lovingly detailed that the animated gorilla often appears more expressive than the human actors.

Hollywood filmmaker Carl Denham (Robert Armstrong) takes starlet Ann Darrow (Fay Wray) to a mysterious prehistoric island in search of the legendary King Kong, a giant ape worshiped as a god by the local natives. They find the giant beast and it falls in love with Ann. Denham manages to capture the monster and bring it back to New York City for display, but Kong breaks loose and wreaks havoc on Manhattan in his search for his beloved Ann.

As a monster, Kong is akin to Boris Karloff's interpretation of the Frankenstein monster—more victim than victimizer. Of course, Kong was a fearful monster who killed with abandon and could destroy entire cities given a chance, but the beast had desires, a temper, needs and fears, and could feel emotions that audiences to this day identify with. No man in an ape suit could convey such a complex variety of emotions—only a fine actor or a master in the art of stop-motion animation, such as Willis O'Brien, who was able to create one of the cinema's most unique and memorable characters from an inanimate 18-inch stop-motion model.

On its initial release, at the height of the Great Depression, KING KONG grossed $1,761,000 and by itself saved the studio that produced it from bankruptcy. In 1938, the studio decided to re-release its classic, but took several steps to tone it down. The film had been made before 1934 when the Production Code began to be vigorously enforced. In accordance with the revised rules of the game, cut were the scenes of Kong chewing and crushing human beings. Gone was the scene in which a curious Kong strips Fay Wray of her clothing. In fact, RKO made the new release prints several shades darker in an effort to tone down the incredible detail of O'Brien's work (dying dinosaurs bleeding, etc.) that made everything seem so realistic.

This travesty practically obliterated the steps O'Brien took to ensure that his creations would *live* onscreen. Generations of moviegoers and television watchers were thus denied the true, uncut brilliance of the vision of Merian C. Cooper, Ernest B. Schoedsack, and O'Brien, until recently, when restored prints of KING KONG began to circulate both in revival houses and on home video. It's probably best, for your viewing pleasure if not for your conscience, if you don't think too hard about the racist subtext.

KING LEAR

1987 90m c Drama/Experimental ★★★½
Cannon (U.S./France)

Burgess Meredith *(Don Learo)*, Peter Sellars *(William Shakespeare, Jr., V)*, Molly Ringwald *(Cordelia)*, Jean-Luc

Godard *(Professor)*, Woody Allen *(Mr. Alien)*, Norman Mailer *(Himself)*, Kate Mailer *(Herself)*, Leos Carax *(Edgar)*

p, Menahem Golan, Yoram Globus; d, Jean-Luc Godard; w, Jean-Luc Godard (based on the play by William Shakespeare); ph, Sophie Maintigneux

It should come as no surprise that in this film version of Shakespeare's play, director Jean-Luc Godard shows very little concern for plot, or that—as with every addition to the Godard canon—KING LEAR further considers his previous ideas, preoccupations, and experiments. Though many will cry foul at this adaptation of Shakespeare, KING LEAR, in an odd sense, does more with the original than any number of faithful, literary adaptations by allowing the material to transcend its medium and find new power in a modern time. As usual, Godard is also interested in self-consciously exploring his own position as a filmmaker.

The film opens with Godard and producer Menahem Golem discussing the making of the film, and throughout we see shots of famous deceased directors. The rest is full of audacious experiments in sound, and bizarre casting with lots of established, movie star types (the weirdest of all being Molly Ringwald). Godard casts himself, in Rastafarian dreadlocks as the Fool in this often heady convergence of high camp, solemn philosophy, Fellini's 8 1/2, and someone's drug trip. A challenge, as with all Godard, but not quite his most rewarding one.

KING OF COMEDY, THE *DVD*

1983 108m c Comedy/Drama ★★★★½
20th Century Fox (U.S.) PG

Robert De Niro *(Rupert Pupkin)*, Jerry Lewis *(Jerry Langford)*, Diahnne Abbott *(Rita)*, Sandra Bernhard *(Masha)*, Ed Herlihy *(Himself)*, Louis Brown *(Bandleader)*, Whitey Ryan *(Stage Door Guard)*, Doc Lawless *(Chauffeur)*, Marta Heflin *(Young Girl)*, Katherine Wallach

p, Arnon Milchan; d, Martin Scorsese; w, Paul Zimmerman; ph, Fred Schuler (Deluxe Color); ed, Thelma Schoonmaker; m, Robbie Robertson; prod d, Boris Leven; art d, Edward Pisoni, Lawrence Miller; cos, Richard Bruno

Martin Scorsese and Robert De Niro must be the most celebrated director/star collaborators in recent American film history. Together they have produced some of the most powerful films of the last several decades—MEAN STREETS, TAXI DRIVER, RAGING BULL, GOODFELLAS—but here they tried something a little different and the result is a chilling black comedy.

Robert De Niro is tragic, goofy and crazy as Rupert Pupkin, a grown man working as a messenger and living in his parents' basement. (Scorsese's own mother is the off-screen voice of the unseen Mrs. Pupkin.) Pupkin is a Times Square hangabout who dogs celebrities for autographs but imagines himself the greatest comic in the world, patterning himself on his hero, funnyman talk-show host Jerry Langford (Jerry Lewis in a part written for the erstwhile King of Late Night, Johnny Carson). His dream is that he will appear on Langford's show, perform his comedy routine, and then take his rightful place among the stars. He'll have none of that nonsense about learning his craft and working his way up the ladder of success; he wants it *now*.

At the beginning of the film, Pupkin ingratiates himself with Langford by helping him fend off some particularly manic autograph seekers. Slipping into the car with Langford, he introduces himself as a yet-undiscovered great comedian who has written some terrific material. Initially Langford encourages him, but eventually Pupkin becomes a major nuisance. At first he hangs around the network offices for a followup meeting until he must be physically thrown out. Eventually he works up to calling on Mr. Langford at his fabulous country retreat. He resorts, at last, to even more drastic measures to get his big break on television.

De Niro gives a miraculous character performance, much different from the intense brooding loners for which he is renowned. He seems to disappear into this oddball, somewhat repulsive, but ultimately rather touching character. Sandra Bernhard, in her film debut, is nearly as memorable as Rupert's outrageous partner in crime. As a thoroughly demented, poor little rich girl who yearns to physically possess her favorite celebrity, Bernhard is simultaneously frightening, unconventionally sexy and *very* funny. THE KING OF COMEDY was a huge flop upon its release. Let's hope that future generations will hail it as the classic it truly is.

KING OF HEARTS   DVD
(LE ROI DE COEUR)
1966 100m c   Comedy/Drama/War   ★★★½
Artistes Associes/Montoro/Fildebroc   (France/Italy)

Alan Bates *(Pvt. Charles Plumpick)*, Pierre Brasseur *(Gen. Geranium)*, Jean-Claude Brialy *(The Duke—Le Duc de Trefle)*, Genevieve Bujold *(Coquelicot)*, Adolfo Celi *(Col. Alexander MacBibenbrook)*, Micheline Presle *(Mme. Eglantine)*, Francoise Christophe *(The Duchess)*, Julien Guiomar *(Bishop Daisy—Monseigneur Marguerite)*, Michel Serrault *(The Crazy Barber)*, Marc Dudicourt *(Lt. Hamburger)*

p, Philippe de Broca; d, Philippe de Broca; w, Daniel Boulanger (based on an idea by Maurice Bessy); ph, Pierre Lhomme (Techniscope, Deluxe Color); ed, Francoise Javet; m, Georges Delerue; art d, Francois de Lamothe; cos, Jacques Fonteray

Breathing new life into old themes, Philippe de Broca's charming antiwar fable KING OF HEARTS has been a perennial favorite on college campuses since it first reached the screen at the height of the Vietnam War.

Set during WWI, the occupying Germans retreat from the town of Marville, France, but not before leaving behind a time bomb. The fleeing townspeople tell the approaching British forces about the hidden explosives, and Pvt. Charles Plumpick (Bates, quite appealing), a poetry-loving Scotsman, is dispatched to locate the bomb. To avoid the German rear guard, Plumpick ducks into Marville's insane asylum, and the inmates hail him as the "King of Hearts" before retaking the town and resuming their former lives in a decidedly loony fashion.

While trying to find and defuse the bomb, Plumpick comes to love the crazy citizens, especially Coquelicot (Bujold). In time, the Germans and British clash in Marville, littering the town with bodies, and, when the townspeople return, Plumpick is left with a choice: go back to soldiering or join the "crazy" folks in the asylum. The film's last shot is justifiably famous.

In addition to its strong antiwar message, KING OF HEARTS ponders the old question of who's crazier, the people who accept life's brutality or those who reject it. Some have said that de Broca states his case with a heavy hand—and he does—but for those willing to open themselves to a lighthearted treatment of this all-too-serious subject, KING OF HEARTS will be both touching and life-affirming.

KING OF KINGS   DVD
1961 168m c   Religious/Biography   ★★★½
MGM   (U.S.)

Jeffrey Hunter *(Jesus Christ)*, Siobhan McKenna *(Mary)*, Hurd Hatfield *(Pontius Pilate)*, Ron Randell *(Lucius, the Centurion)*, Viveca Lindfors *(Claudia)*, Rita Gam *(Herodias)*, Carmen Sevilla *(Mary Magdalene)*, Brigid Bazlen *(Salome)*, Harry Guardino *(Barabbas)*, Rip Torn *(Judas)*

p, Samuel Bronston; d, Nicholas Ray; w, Philip Yordan; ph, Franz Planer, Milton Krasner, Manuel Berenguer (Technirama 70, Technicolor); ed, Harold F. Kress, Renee Lichtig; m, Miklos Rozsa; fx, Alex Weldon, Lee LeBlanc; chor, Betty Utey; cos, Georges Wakhevitch

This excellent biblical epic was produced by the legendary Samuel Bronston and directed with a skillful mix of spiritual reverence and cinematic imagination by Nicholas Ray. The film covers the 33 years from Jesus Christ's birth in Bethlehem through the Crucifixion, Resurrection and Ascension. Included are His relationship with John, the 40 days in the desert, the choosing of the Apostles, the Sermon on the Mount, and Judas's betrayal at the Passover seder that was Jesus's Last Supper.

Although Ray Bradbury is not credited, he reportedly wrote the narration spoken by Orson Welles, whose incredible voice and delivery would add dignity and import to dirty limericks. Jeffrey Hunter, not really a major actor, is much more effective than one would expect as Jesus, and Robert Ryan is excellent as John. Hurd Hatfield, though, who sadly never recovered from his initial amazing impression in THE PICTURE OF DORIAN GRAY, goes a bit over the top as Pilate. Other outstanding performances are contributed by Royal Dano, Harry Guardino, Viveca Lindfors and Rip Torn.

KING OF KINGS is an epic of considerable scope, filled with broad vistas, yet there are enough intimate moments to give audience a chance to engage with the characters rather than just admire their pontificating. This is a film where people sweat and labor, and the film, though hardly great, is much better for it. Credit reasonable and restrained writing by Yordan and Ray's sense of judgment for this one.

KING OF MARVIN GARDENS, THE   DVD
1972 103m c   Drama   ★★½
BBS   (U.S.)   R

Jack Nicholson *(David Staebler)*, Bruce Dern *(Jason Staebler)*, Ellen Burstyn *(Sally)*, Julia Robinson *(Jessica)*, Scatman Crothers *(Lewis)*, Charles Lavine *(Grandfather)*, Arnold Williams *(Rosko)*, John Ryan *(Surtees)*, Sully Boyar *(Lebowitz)*, Josh Mostel *(Frank)*

p, Bob Rafelson; d, Bob Rafelson; w, Jacob Brackman (based on a story by Jacob Brackman and Bob Rafelson); ph, Laszlo Kovacs (Eastmancolor); ed, John F. Link II; art d, Toby Rafelson; cos, Tony Scarano

Alternately dreary and fascinating, THE KING OF MARVIN GARDENS is half of a terrific film, but director Rafelson didn't know which half. After the success of FIVE EASY PIECES, Rafelson attempted to create something as different as possible, but his quest for uniqueness is what did him in.

Nicholson plays David Staebler, a long-winded FM talk jockey on a Philadelphia radio station. Instead of playing records, he waxes on about his brother Jason (Dern) and the things they did as children. He dubs Jason "The King of Marvin Gardens," in reference to the Monopoly board game landmark and the actual place in Atlantic City. David goes back to Atlantic City to visit Jason, now working for Lewis (Crothers), head of a black crime syndicate.

Jason is in jail on a "grand theft auto" charge and is released on bail. He and David have a happy reunion, and Jason introduces his baby brother to Sally (Burstyn), a fading ex-beauty queen, and her stepdaughter (Robinson). Jason tells David of his pipe dream to buy a small island near Hawaii and the others, humoring him, help him stage a beauty contest spoof. Things get hairy when David realizes Jason intends to use Lewis' money to buy his dream island.

Much of the film has been deliberately confused (or so it seems) by Rafelson and Brackman in order to flatten the crease between fantasy and reality. For all its faults, THE KING OF MARVIN GARDENS has some merit and many of the individual scenes linger in the memory. It appeared to be a melange of the 1960s mentality of FIVE EASY PIECES with a 1940s-type plot of irony and surprise. The weakest part of the film was the repetitious, indulgent dialogue credited to Brackman, but one wonders how much of that was in the script and how much Rafelson and his actors improvised. The film is a fairly daring if rather pretentious attempt at originality, but this type of intimate narrative generally requires that one be given the pleasure of caring about the characters.

KING OF NEW YORK   _DVD_
1990   103m   c   Crime   ★★★
Augusto Caminito   (Italy/U.S.)   R

Christopher Walken (Frank White), David Caruso (Dennis Gilley), Laurence Fishburne, billed as Larry Fishburne (Jimmy Jump), Victor Argo (Roy Bishop), Wesley Snipes (Thomas Flannigan), Janet Julian (Jennifer Poe), Joey Chin (Larry Wong), Giancarlo Esposito (Lance), Paul Calderon (Joey Dalesio), Steve Buscemi

p, Mary Kane; d, Abel Ferrara; w, Nicholas St. John; ph, Bojan Bazelli (Duart Color); ed, Anthony Redman; m, Joe Delia; prod d, Alex Tavoularis; art d, Stephanie Ziemer; fx, Matt Vogel; cos, Carol Ramsey

Frank White (Walken), a middle-aged drug lord, is released from prison to find that the streets of New York are tougher and less forgiving than they were when he went in. Still, his gang remains loyal, and his enemies—police and thieves alike—are as hostile as ever. Frank, though, has changed, and decides to make a positive mark on society. Countless hurdles, however, stand in the way of his civic-minded ambitions, which revolve around raising the money needed to keep a public hospital open in a poverty-stricken neighborhood. For starters, he has made a bad name for himself in virtually every ethnic enclave in the city. Nevertheless, White decides to team up with Lance Wong (Chin), a young Chinatown dealer who has a huge shipment of drugs to move. Wong's lack of altruism ("If I wanted socialized medicine, I'd have stayed in the Peking province") is a problem, as is the hostility of the Mafia, which is horrified by White's interracial operation. Further complicating White's efforts are some frustrated Brooklyn cops willing to use any means necessary to put an end to White's plans. Hot-headed Dennis Gilley (Caruso), in particular, persuades his fellow officers that the system favors the criminal, and that if anything is to be done about White, it won't be done by the book. Doomed from the start, White's plan precipitates a wave of violence.

Ferrara and St. John's vision of New York is jittery, complex, and defined by juxtapositions of wealth and poverty, legal and illegal commerce, politics and crime, business and recreation that are so extreme as to verge on the ludicrous. Their New York is the biggest, glossiest, most high-tech banana republic conceivable, a jungle of steel and concrete animated by atavistic rhythms and primitive, clannish conceptions of loyalty. Ferrara's great gift as a director is his ferocious sense of place: New York's boroughs, ethnic neighborhoods, subways, hotels, landmarks, bars and fast-food joints are all convincingly rendered here.

KING OF THE KHYBER RIFLES   _DVD_
1953   100m   c   Adventure   ★★★½
Fox   (U.S.)

Tyrone Power (Capt. Alan King), Terry Moore (Susan Maitland), Michael Rennie (Brig. Gen. Maitland), John Justin (Lt. Geoffrey Heath), Guy Rolfe (Karram Khan), Richard Stapley (Lt. Ben Baird), Murray Matheson (Maj. Ian MacAllister), Frank De Kova (Ali Nur), Argentina Brunetti (Lali), Sujata (Native Dancer)

p, Frank P. Rosenberg; d, Henry King; w, Ivan Goff, Ben Roberts (based on a story by Harry Kleiner from the novel by Talbot Mundy); ph, Leon Shamroy (CinemaScope, Technicolor); ed, Barbara McLean; m, Bernard Herrmann; art d, Lyle Wheeler, Maurice Ransford; fx, Ray Kellogg; chor, Asoka; cos, Travilla

This rousing adventure, a remake of John Ford's THE BLACK WATCH, was given the full treatment by Fox, which made this early CinemaScope epic its major Christmas release. Power stars as Capt. Alan King, a half-caste who leads a supply column to the British outpost at Peshawar, India. On the trail his unit is ambushed by rebellious Afridi tribesmen led by Karram Khan (Rolfe), a childhood friend of King's. The soldiers fend off the attack and make it to Peshawar where they are greeted by garrison commander Maitland (Rennie) and his daughter Susan (Moore). Alan and Susan are mutually turned on, leading to a rivalry with Alan's roomie, Lt. Geoffrey Heath (Justin).

Heath's attempt to spread bigotry amidst the officers by revealing King as a half-caste doesn't cut much professional mustard with Maitland, but it does make him pull a Romeo and Juliet on Susan. Alan's helping to save Susan from kidnappers only increases their hormone flow, however, and, on an endorphin high, King decides to infiltrate Khan's ranks and kill his former friend.

Ace director Henry King, once praised by Eisenstein himself and whose work resembles that of John Ford, has been sadly neglected by film historians obsessed by Ford. KING OF THE KHYBER RIFLES is a marvelously entertaining film helmed with energy and flair. Power was getting a little long in the tooth to be playing these roles, and he's not completely convincing as a half-caste, but he still performs with likable dash. Rolfe is properly menacing as the villainous Khan, and Rennie is properly proper as the British general. Largely shot on a California backlot, KING has good second-unit Himalayan footage to enhance the film's look. The bigotry angle, though not really explored in depth, is one of the more interesting aspects of this enjoyable adventure yarn.

KING SOLOMON'S MINES   _DVD_
1937   80m   bw   Adventure   ★★★½
Gaumont   (U.K.)

Paul Robeson (Umbopa), Cedric Hardwicke (Allan Quartermaine), Roland Young (Cmdr. Good), John Loder (Henry Curtis), Anna Lee (Kathy O'Brien), Sydney Fairbrother (Gagool), Majabalo Hiubi (Kapsie), Ecce Homo Toto (Infadoos), Robert Adams (Twala), Frederick Leister (Wholesaler)

d, Robert Stevenson; w, A.R. Rawlinson, Charles Bennett, Ralph Spence (based on the novel by H. Rider Haggard); ph, Bernard Knowles

Memorable version of H. Rider Haggard's oft-filmed novel which boasts superior production values and an excellent performance from Robeson. Spunky Irishwoman Kathy O'Brien (Lee) becomes determined to search for her father, who has disappeared deep in the African jungles while searching for the fabled diamond cache known as King Solomon's Mines. She is accompanied by three explorers (Hardwicke, Young, and Loder) and is guided through the treacherous territory by dignified African native Umbopa (Robeson). After hacking their way through desert and jungle, the small party finally arrives at an encampment of natives who look to the white explorers as gods. The tribe is run by an evil king who had stolen the throne from Umbopa years ago with the help of the witch Gagool (Fairbrother). Sensing a threat to their reign, the king and Gagool plot to kill the newcomers. The explorers manage to defend themselves, though, by capitalizing on a soon-to-arrive solar eclipse to prove that their magic is more powerful than Gagool's. Refusing to give up, the deposed king leads an attack by rival warriors. A final battle, the discovery of the mine and an ill-timed volcano bring the story to its thundering close.

Robeson almost singlehandedly undermines the racism in this classic adventure tale. It's a shame he had to go to England to become a movie star and even then (with occasional exceptions like PROUD VALLEY) he was generally cast as semi-articulate but sweet African natives. In this respect his very American singing interludes throw the entire film out of kilter, but he's so good that one really doesn't care.

He, Hardwicke, Fairbrother and Young are the standouts in KING SOLOMON'S MINES, which does less well by its romantic lead roles. Kathy and Henry are not choice parts, and the generally reliable Loder and the less-than-reliable Lee don't come off so well. Their love scenes tend to put a damper on the film between action highlights. The script is decent and director Stevenson shows the promise he would later (sometimes) get to display in Hollywood.

KING SOLOMON'S MINES 📀

1950 102m c   Adventure   ★★★★
MGM   (U.S.)

Deborah Kerr *(Elizabeth Curtis)*, Stewart Granger *(Allan Quartermain)*, Richard Carlson *(John Goode)*, Hugo Haas *(Van Brun)*, Lowell Gilmore *(Eric Masters)*, Kimursi *(Khiva)*, Siriaque *(Umbopa)*, Sekaryongo *(Chief Gagool)*, Baziga *(King Twala)*, Munto Anampio *(Chief Bilu)*

p, Sam Zimbalist; d, Compton Bennett, Andrew Marton; w, Helen Deutsch (based on the novel by H. Rider Haggard); ph, Robert Surtees (Technicolor); ed, Ralph E. Winters, Conrad A. Nervig; art d, Cedric Gibbons, Conrad A. Nervig; cos, Walter Plunkett

AAN Best Picture; AA Best Color Cinematography: Robert Surtees; *AA Best Film Editing:* Ralph E. Winters, Conrad A. Nervig

For those who love thrilling, large-scale adventure films loaded with action and exotic scenery, KING SOLOMON'S MINES is your cup of colonialist tea. MGM spent $3.5 million—a fortune in those days—in producing this highly engaging old-fashioned entertainment.

Great white hunter Allan Quartermain (Granger) is hired by the beautiful Elizabeth (Kerr) and her brother (Carlson) to help find Elizabeth's husband, who disappeared while searching for the fabled diamond mines of King Solomon. Their party goes through swamps and forests, over mountains and deserts, and flees nasty natives and stampeding animals in their search.

One of the most majestically filmed adventure tales ever put on celluloid, the film copped cinematographer Surtees a deserved Oscar for his efforts. The production went first to Nairobi and then, via specially built trucks and airplanes, to Tanganyika and the Belgian Congo, covering more than 14,000 miles and contending with temperatures soaring between 140 and 152 degrees and a wide variety of exotic diseases, snakes and flies. The footage of African natives (e.g. a Watusi dance) is fascinating and persuasive, and some efforts were made to portray the dignity of African tribal life. The imperialism of it all might get you hot under the collar, but don't despair entirely—the Africans are the most interesting characters in the film.

To be fair, the Hollywoodians are pretty decent and throw themselves into the bracing if silly spirit of the whole enterprise. Granger isn't sexy enough but he *is* stalwart, and Kerr expertly plays another one of those prim but horny types she was assigned to do every so often. So much excess quality footage of Africa was left over that MGM went on a recurrent diet of jungle epics, using the stuff in, among others, WATUSI, TARZAN THE APE MAN, DRUMS OF AFRICA, TRADER HORN, and even the 1977 remake of KING SOLOMON'S MINES.

KINGDOM, THE

(RIGET)
1994 271m c   Drama/Horror   ★★★★
Zentropa Entertainment/Danmarks Radio/Swedish   R
Television/Westdeutscher Rundfunk/ARTE/The
Coproduction Office   (Denmark)

Ernst-Hugo Jaregard *(Stig Helmer)*, Kirsten Rolffes *(Mrs. Drusse)*, Ghita Norby *(Rigmor)*, Soren Pilmark *(Krogen)*, Holger Juul Hansen *(Dr. Moesgaard)*, Annevig Schelde Ebbe *(Mary)*, Jens Okking *(Bulder)*, Otto Brandenburg *(Porter Hansen)*, Baard Owe *(Bondo)*, Solbjorg Hojfeldt *(Camilla)*

p, Ole Reim; d, Lars Von Trier; w, Lars von Trier, Tomas Gislason (from a story by Lars von Trier and Niels Vorsel); ph, Eric Kress; ed, Jacob Thuesen, Molly Marlene Stensgaard; m, Joachim Holbek; art d, Jette Lehmann; fx, Niels Skovgaard, Niels Fly

Made for Danish television, THE KINGDOM is four episodes of an entertainingly cracked medical soap opera-*cum*-ghost story, strung together and released in the U.S. as a theatrical film. The closest thing to it in recent memory is the David Lynch-produced television series "Twin Peaks," but THE KINGDOM works as a theatrical release, despite the segment breaks, episodic story development, and wildly unresolved cliff-hanger ending.

The Kingdom is the name of a huge, crumbling hospital, built on sinister marshland and home to a diverse and eccentric crew of doctors and patients. It's also the backdrop for an immensely complex storyline involving, *inter alia*, ghostly little girls, doomed romance, haunted ambulances, exorcism, medical malpractice, mongoloid seers, demon dogs, severed heads in lockers, and unearthly pregnancy.

Prior to THE KINGDOM, director Lars Von Trier (ZENTROPA) had distinguished himself primarily for his flamboyant visual style and singular humorlessness. So the great and pleasant surprise of THE KINGDOM is how blackly funny it is. At the same time Von Trier manages to work up some real scares: a little girl's first appearance, crouched in a high corner of the elevator shaft and ringing a tiny bell is chilling, as is the scene in which a medium questions a newly dead friend by having her make the buzzing fluorescent lights dim—once for yes, twice for no. The 271-minute running time, so daunting when spelled out—four-and-a-half hours!—seems like nothing in the unfolding.

KINGDOM OF HEAVEN 📀

2005 145m c   Historical/War/Adventure   ★★★
Scott Free Productions/Kanzaman/20th Century Fox/   R
20th Century Fox   (U.S./U.K./Spain)

Orlando Bloom *(Balian)*, Liam Neeson *(Godfrey)*, David Thewlis *(Hospitaler)*, Jeremy Irons *(Tiberias)*, Edward Norton *(King Baldwin)*, Brendan Gleeson *(Reynald)*, Eva Green *(Sibylla)*, Ghassan Massoud *(Saladin)*, Velibor Topic *(Almaric)*, Iain Glen *(Richard Coeur de Lion)*

p, Ridley Scott; d, Ridley Scott; w, William Monahan; ph, John Mathieson; ed, Dody Dorn; m, Harry Gregson-Williams; prod d, Arthur Max; art d, Marco Trentini; fx, Neil Corbould, Rick Leary (CG), Mark Meddings, Wesley Sewell; cos, Janty Yates

Ridley Scott's grand historical spectacle refracts contemporary Middle Eastern conflicts through the medieval Crusades (1095-1291) that mired Muslims, Christians, and Jews in a complex stew of lofty religious fervor and earthly greed.

France, 1184: Noble knight Godfrey of Ibelin (Liam Neeson) invites his illegitimate son, blacksmith Balian (Orlando Bloom), to accompany him to Jerusalem. Embroiled in a two-century war between Christians and Muslims, Jerusalem is the center of a brave new world where a man may shuck off hidebound European social structures and live up to his own potential. Balian's subsequent journey of self-reinvention gets a jump start when he inherits his father's title, holdings, and position. A man of conscience like his late father, Balian supports benevolent Christian King Baldwin IV (Edward Norton), a leper who opened the city to all faiths and maintains a fragile truce with Muslim leader Saladin (Ghassan Massoud), and Baldwin's right hand, principled warrior Tiberias (Jeremy Irons). But their efforts to maintain peace are undermined by rapacious Templar knights, led by unrepentant rape-and-pillager Reynald de Chatillon (Brendan Gleeson) and Guy de Lusignan (Marton Csokas), whose loveless marriage to Baldwin's sister, Sibylla (Eva Green), places him in the direct line of succession for the throne of Jerusalem.

Taking movies to task for playing fast and loose with history is a pedant's game; that William Monahan's screenplay shuffles events and chronology is a given. Scott's skill at handling of action sequences is thrilling, but Bloom lacks the gravity and raw charisma his role demands and robs the film of narrative urgency. And given that it's rooted in the infinitely complex political machinations that kept the Holy Land in constant turmoil, the story would actually have benefited from *more* talk.

KINGS OF THE ROAD
(IM LAUF DER ZEIT)
1976   176m   bw   Drama   ★★★★★
Filmverlag der Autoren   (West Germany)

Rudiger Vogler *(Bruno)*, Hanns Zischler *(Robert)*, Lisa Kreuzer *(Cashier)*, Rudolf Schuendler *(Robert's Father)*, Marquard Bohm *(Man Who Lost His Wife)*

p, Wim Wenders; d, Wim Wenders; w, Wim Wenders; ph, Robby Muller, Martin Schafer, Peter Przygodda; m, Axel Linstadt

One of the seminal films of New German cinema, KINGS OF THE ROAD is, along with WINGS OF DESIRE, one of Wim Wenders' greatest achievements to date. The ultimate road movie, this lengthy but never dull picture traces the small adventures of two men as they wander along the back roads of Germany, moving from one small town to the next.

One morning Bruno (Vogler), a motion-picture-projector repairman who lives in his van, sees a Volkswagen plunge off a dock and into the Elbe River, a natural border between East and West Germany. Out of the water comes Robert (Zischler), a linguist who has just made a half-hearted suicide attempt. Robert accepts a ride from Bruno—and, as they travel across the country on Bruno's repair route, a strong friendship develops. The two drink, meet people, wander the streets, and sing along to American songs, especially Roger Miller's "King of the Road."

The story is simple and told in the main without much dialogue (Wenders and crew set out with an itinerary but no script), and the core of the film eschews narrative. Instead, as the translated title tells us, it is "the course of time" that holds Wenders' interest. The changes that occur throughout history (symbolized by crumbling small-town movie houses) are the film's central concern and justify its length. Scenes are filmed in real time, as we watch the characters shave, wash, think, talk, and even defecate. This last moment is something that you not only don't mind, you find it entirely fitting amid the ordinariness of it all.

KINGS OF THE ROAD becomes an even more revealing entry in Wenders' canon when one views it in light of WINGS OF DESIRE. Both films examine the walls that exist between people, between past and present, and between East and West Germany. Both films also tellingly highlight the imbrication of American pop culture on European sensibilities. No reference to this film should fail to mention the power of the naturally lit, black-and-white images beautifully captured by Robby Muller. A terrific and thoughtful film.

KINGS ROW
1942   127m   bw   Drama   ★★★★½
Warner Bros.   (U.S.)

Ann Sheridan *(Randy Monoghan)*, Robert Cummings *(Parris Mitchell)*, Ronald Reagan *(Drake McHugh)*, Betty Field *(Cassandra Tower)*, Charles Coburn *(Dr. Henry Gordon)*, Claude Rains *(Dr. Alexander Tower)*, Judith Anderson *(Mrs. Harriet Gordon)*, Nancy Coleman *(Louise Gordon)*, Kaaren Verne *(Elise Sandor)*, Maria Ouspenskaya *(Mme. Von Eln)*

p, David Lewis; d, Sam Wood; w, Casey Robinson (based on the novel by Henry Bellamann); ph, James Wong Howe; ed, Ralph Dawson; m, Erich Wolfgang Korngold; prod d, William Cameron Menzies; art d, Carl Jules Weyl

AAN Best B/W Cinematography: James Wong Howe

"Where's the rest of me?" Too bad Ronnie never found the answer. Containing what is easily the future President's finest performance, KINGS ROW was a startling film for its day, portraying a small town not with the poignancy and little joys of Thorton Wilder's *Our Town*, but rather in grim, often tragic tones.

The film begins with its main characters as children. Playful Drake, tomboyish Randy and uppity Louise are among the friends of the sensitive Parris. He, meanwhile, befriends the strange, lonely Cassandra, but her psychiatrist father, Dr. Tower (Rains) soon removes her from school to be tutored at home. We advance in time to the grown Parris (Cummings), now a brilliant medical student who studies with Dr. Tower and still sees the increasingly quirky Cassandra (Field) occasionally. The feisty Randy loves both Parris and the rakish Drake (Reagan), but Louise (Coleman) remains sheltered by her strict parents.

Trouble brews when Louise becomes jealous of Randy's involvement with Drake, and Cassandra begins to go off the deep end and wants to go to Vienna with Parris. Ultimately, two very different fathers, the kindly Dr. Tower and Louise's avaricious dad, Dr. Gordon (Coburn), take brutal action in their misguided attempts to protect their daughters.

KINGS ROW remains one of director Wood's finest films, but one wonders how much he relied on his ace support. Robinson did a fine job of adapting Bellamann's rich novel, even if he cut out a death from cancer, deleted a mercy killing, and toned down the narrative's homosexual angle. Korngold's rich score is haunting and the detailed sets by Menzies quite stunning. Howe's gorgeous cinematography, meanwhile, maintains in deep focus many layers of drama, as befits this brooding tapestry. An uneven film in spots, but one of the most memorable melodramas of its day, compelling and unusual for early WWII.

KINSEY
2004   118m   c   Drama/Biography   📀
Qwerty Films/N1 European Film Produktions/   ★★★
American Zoetrope/Pretty Pictures   (U.S.)   R

Liam Neeson *(Alfred Kinsey)*, Laura Linney *(Clara McMillen)*, Chris O'Donnell *(Wardell Pomeroy)*, Peter Sarsgaard *(Clyde Martin)*, Timothy Hutton *(Paul Gebhard)*, John Lithgow *(Alfred Seguine Kinsey)*, Oliver Platt *(Herman Wells)*, Tim Curry *(Thurman Rice)*, Dylan Baker *(Alan Gregg)*, Julianne Nicholson *(Alice Martin)*

p, Gail Mutrux; d, Bill Condon; w, Bill Condon; ph, Frederick Elmes; ed, Virginia Katz; m, Carter Burwell; prod d, Richard Sherman; art d, Nicholas Lundy; fx, Connie Brink, Marlo Pabon; cos, Bruce Finlayson

AAN Best Supporting Actress: Laura Linney

While Bill Condon's excellent GODS AND MONSTERS vividly captured the essence of acclaimed horror director James Whale by focusing on one period in his life, this intelligently directed and superbly acted film chronicles the bulk of notorious sex researcher Alfred Kinsey's experiences but barely scratches the surface of his personality.

The film begins with Kinsey's childhood and his strained relationship with his religious father (John Lithgow). Rebelling against his family's pious ways, the adult Kinsey (Liam Neeson) embraces the secular world of science, assumes a professorship at Indiana University, and marries pretty student Clara (Laura Linney). Problems in the bedroom force them to consult a doctor, and Kinsey realizes that many young couples know little about sex. He proposes a course in basic sex education to the university's new president (Oliver Platt), who surprises everyone by agreeing. Positive response to the class spurs Kinsey to explore the subject in greater depth. His goal: to present the world with the first comprehensive study of human sexuality. He and his research team, including his lover, Clyde Martin (Peter Sarsgaard), interview thousands of people across the country about their sexual experiences. The initial results are published in 1948 to great acclaim and even greater controversy.

Like RAY, this film is driven by a powerful central performance—Neeson disappears into his role, appearing meeker and more vulnerable than ever before. Linney and Sarsgaard also contribute strong work and Condon gives each the opportunity to shine. But it's a shame that the script doesn't push the actors further; while touching upon Kinsey's unorthodox strategies, Condon omits some of the more distasteful details about his methods and subjects that came to light in the years since his work was first published.

KIRIKOU AND THE SORCERESS 📀
(KIRIKOU ET LA SORCIERE)
1998 74m c Children's/Animated/Adventure ★★★★
Les Armateurs/Odec Kid Cartooons/Monipoly/
Trans Europe Film/Studio O/France 3 Cinema/RTBF
Telefilms/Exposure (France/Belgium/Luxembourg)

VOICES OF: Theo Sebeko *(Kirikou)*, Antoinette Kellermann *(Karaba)*, Kombisile Sangweni *(The Mother)*, Mabuto Sithole *(The Old Man/Viellard)*, Fezele Mpeka *(Uncle)*

p, Didier Brunner, Jacques Vercruyssen, Paul Thiltges; d, Michel Ocelot; w, Michel Ocelot; ph, Daniel Borenstein; ed, Dominique Lefever; m, Youssou N'Dour; prod d, Thierry Million; anim, Inga Riba, Rija Studio, Exist Studio, Les Armateurs, Tiramisu

The perfect corrective for kids weaned on Disney's TARZAN and THE LION KING: an animated tale set in Africa whose central characters are actually *Africans*, not singing animals. That the film, adapted from a West African folktale by French filmmaker Michel Ocelot, is smart, funny, and stunningly designed is a bonus.

No sooner is precocious Kirikou born (he *demands* from within his mother's womb to be brought into the world) than he's out the door to join his uncle in battling Karaba, the wicked sorceress who's dried up the village spring and eaten nearly all its men. Dripping with gold and so wicked no vegetation can survive her approach, the fabulously fierce Karaba lives in a huge hut surrounded by her army of robotic fetish dolls. But they're no match for pint-size Kirikou; the fleet-footed infant outsmarts the sorceress at every turn, and is the only villager wise enough to ask the crucial question: *why* is Karaba so mean and evil?

A huge hit in France, this charming and wildly entertaining film originally came under fire when prudish distributors objected to Ocelot's frank treatment of female nudity (he resis-

ted suggestions that he paint bras on the naturally attired West African women). So if discreet, non-gratuitous nudity isn't an issue, you're in for a real treat. Ocelot forgoes the razzle-dazzle of 3D, computer-generated animation and turns instead to West African painting, sculpture, and fabric for layout, character design, and the film's gorgeous color palette. Best of all, Ocelot offers up an authentic African soundtrack by the great Senegalese pop star Youssou N'Dour instead of the overblown song stylings of Elton John or Phil Collins.

KISS BEFORE DYING, A 📀
1956 94m c Mystery ★★★
UA (U.S.)

Robert Wagner *(Bud Corliss)*, Jeffrey Hunter *(Gordon Grant)*, Virginia Leith *(Ellen Kingship)*, Joanne Woodward *(Dorothy Kingship)*, Mary Astor *(Mrs. Corliss)*, George Macready *(Leo Kingship)*, Robert Quarry *(Dwight Powell)*, Howard Petrie *(Chesser)*, Bill Walker *(Butler)*, Mollie McCart *(Annabelle)*

p, Robert L. Jacks; d, Gerd Oswald; w, Lawrence Roman (based on the novel by Ira Levin); ph, Lucien Ballard (CinemaScope, DeLuxe Color); ed, George Gittens; m, Lionel Newman; art d, Addison Hehr; cos, Henry Helfman, Evelyn Carruth

Wagner plays Bud Corliss, a money-hungry youth who kills his girlfriend Dorothy (Woodward), when her pregnancy threatens his chances of being accepted by her wealthy family. Her sister Ellen (Leith) refuses to believe the police report that the death was a suicide, and does some investigating on her own. She runs into Bud, ignorant of his relationship with Dorothy, and a romance between the two begins. When Ellen discovers Bud's involvement with her sister, the stage is set for the final showdown. An excellent screenplay (unoriginal but full of tension), subtle direction by the overlooked and underutilized Oswald, and good photography help gloss over any weaknesses in the performances.

KISS ME DEADLY 📀
1955 105m bw Crime ★★★★★
Parklane (U.S.)

Ralph Meeker *(Mike Hammer)*, Albert Dekker *(Dr. Soberin)*, Paul Stewart *(Carl Evello)*, Maxine Cooper *(Velda)*, Gaby Rodgers *(Gabrielle/Lily Carver)*, Wesley Addy *(Pat Chambers)*, Juano Hernandez *(Eddie Yeager)*, Nick Dennis *(Nick)*, Cloris Leachman *(Christina Bailey/Berga Torn)*, Marian Carr *(Friday)*

p, Robert Aldrich; d, Robert Aldrich; w, A.I. Bezzerides (based on the novel by Mickey Spillane); ph, Ernest Laszlo; ed, Michael Luciano; m, Frank DeVol; art d, William Glasgow

Private eye Mike Hammer (Meeker) is driving his convertible on a dark highway when he sees the almost naked Christina Bailey (Leachman) running down the middle of the road. He picks her up, but is soon forced off the road. Hammer is knocked unconscious, and Christina is killed. Both of them are put back in his car, which is then pushed off a cliff. Surviving, Hammer investigates, his curiosity aroused by an FBI warning to stay away. He finds Christina's roommate (Rodgers) and also meets a powerful gangster (Stewart) whose strings are being pulled by a mysterious higher power. Hammer knows he's on to something when his mechanic friend (Dennis) is killed and his secretary (Cooper) kidnapped. Hammer himself is kidnapped but manages to escape, killing his tormentors. He eventually figures out that Christina swallowed a key that will lead to the "great Whatsit." Convincing a morgue attendant (by slamming the man's fingers in a drawer) to give him the key, Hammer later uses similar charm at a health club to acquire the box the key opens. In the end, we meet the chief villain, see another side to the mysterious roommate, and discover the contents of the box. The results are, to put it mildly, explosive.

One of the most brutal films ever made, KISS ME DEADLY enjoys a huge cult following. There's not a single really likable character to be found; everyone wants something, and the neanderthal Hammer barely gives people a chance to say no before he starts beating them up. Aldrich's direction heightens the script's misanthropy, shooting with extreme close-ups and at disorienting angles. Christina's murder is achieved with a pair of pliers, and all we see are a pair of bare legs dangling in midair. The murder of the mechanic is similarly jarring, the camera swooping in on his screaming face as a set of hydraulic jacks do their work. Hammer himself is knocked out no less than six times, only to strut down those mean streets yet again. Aldrich was so concerned about possible reactions to all the violence that he wrote a defense of the film in the *New York Herald Tribune*.

KISS ME DEADLY is shot in an unforgettably harsh fashion, visually underlining the paranoia and existential funk of the film noir world view as few other films have done. Aldrich's greatest directorial effort, this important film takes a number of noir elements to their most nihilistic extremes, leaving us in the violent, atomically threatened world we encounter upon leaving the theater.

KISS ME KATE

DVD

1953 109m c   Musical/Comedy   ★★★★
MGM   (U.S.)

Kathryn Grayson (*Lilli Vanessi/Katherine*), Howard Keel (*Fred Graham/Petruchio*), Ann Miller (*Lois Lane/Bianca*), Tommy Rall (*Bill Calhoun/Lucentio*), Bobby Van (*Gremio*), Keenan Wynn (*Lippy*), James Whitmore (*Slug*), Kurt Kasznar (*Baptista*), Bob Fosse (*Hortensio*), Ron Randell (*Cole Porter*)

p, Jack Cummings; d, George Sidney; w, Dorothy Kingsley (based on the play by Cole Porter, Sam Spewack, Bella Spewack, from the play *The Taming of the Shrew* by William Shakespeare); ph, Charles Rosher (3-D, Ansco Color); ed, Ralph E. Winters; art d, Cedric Gibbons, Urie McCleary; fx, Warren Newcombe; chor, Hermes Pan; cos, Walter Plunkett

AAN Best Score (Musical): Andre Previn, Saul Chaplin

KISS ME KATE is almost, but not quite, a classic cinematic version of the hit Broadway musical. Filmed in 3-D, it was largely released "flat" when the 3-D craze began to wane. Boasting an intelligent and highly amusing book, this tunefest features parallel tales of a musical production of *The Taming of the Shrew* and simultaneously occurring events in the lives of its cast.

Actor-director Fred Graham (Keel) and Cole Porter (Randell) are working together to musicalize the Bard's comedy, and both feel that the only woman to play the shrew Katherine is Fred's ex-wife, Lilli Vanessi (Grayson). Trouble brews when Fred's current flame, Lois Lane (Miller), is set to play Bianca, Katherine's younger sister. Fred, playing Petruchio, enjoys needling his ex, while Lois' dancing partner (Rall) turns out to be a compulsive gambler who has signed Fred's name on an IOU for several thousand dollars. On opening night, two gangsters (Wynn and Whitmore) arrive to collect the debt; how this overlaps with Fred and Lilli's love-hate affair insures plenty of comic bickering until the finale.

KISS ME KATE makes for delightful entertainment, though it does have its drawbacks. Among them is director Sidney, as smooth and professional as ever, but still lacking real flair and imagination. The same might be said for Grayson, who is at or near her best here. Admittedly, Hollywood didn't really have any operetta stars then who could both hit high C and eat the camera whole. Keel, ever

a braggadocio, is fun; his best song is "Where Is the Life That Late I Led?" Miller is in great form, too, her loud charm quite amusing. She sparkles in one of her patented pneumatic tap numbers, absolutely blazing away with "Too Darn Hot." Much of the later dancing, though, is of the Gene Kelly/Bob Fosse type and it does tax her range, limiting her to high kicks and lots of spins. Rall and Randell are appealing, too, though the latter is a very whitewashed version of what we *know* the real Cole Porter was like.

Actually, since we brought up Bob Fosse, we should note that he is one of the onstage dancers. He enters (literally) with a screech and later does a backflip, effortlessly upstaging the struggling Bobby Van. (Look for a pre-*Pajama Game* Carol Haney, too.) The score, of course, is witty and tuneful, and one just waits for each classic to come bouncing along in this extremely enjoyable if less than brilliant musical.

KISS OF DEATH

1947 98m   bw Crime   ★★★★½
Fox   (U.S.)

Victor Mature (*Nick Bianco*), Brian Donlevy (*D'Angelo*), Coleen Gray (*Nettie*), Richard Widmark (*Tom Udo*), Karl Malden (*Sgt. William Cullen*), Taylor Holmes (*Earl Howser*), Howard Smith (*Warden*), Anthony Ross (*Williams*), Mildred Dunnock (*Ma Rizzo*), Millard Mitchell (*Max Schulte*)

p, Fred Kohlmar; d, Henry Hathaway; w, Ben Hecht, Charles Lederer (based on a story by Eleazar Lipsky); ph, Norbert Brodine; ed, J. Watson Webb; m, David Buttolph; art d, Lyle Wheeler, Leland Fuller; fx, Fred Sersen; cos, Charles LeMaire

AAN Best Supporting Actor: Richard Widmark; *AAN Best Original Story:* Eleazar Lipsky

A hard-hitting, often frightening crime drama from the Hecht-Lederer typewriter, KISS OF DEATH has a grimly realistic look and feel, mostly because expert helmsman Hathaway insisted upon shooting the whole film in New York. The movie pulls no punches as it represents life on the seamy side of the street. It also introduced an electric personality to the screen, Richard Widmark, in an unforgettable role. Narrating the film is Nettie (Gray), second wife of Nick Bianco (Mature). Recounting his tough life, she tells how he is the one member of a gang who was caught robbing a jewelry store at Christmastime. The gang's crooked lawyer (Holmes) lies to him assuring him that his family will be looked after. In prison, Nick learns that his first wife has committed suicide out of poverty and that his two little girls have been placed in an orphanage. In a rage, he makes a deal with district attorney D'Angelo (Donlevy): in exchange for his parole, he will inform on his old gang. D'Angelo particularly wants to send sadistic gang boss Tommy Udo (Widmark) to prison. Nick ingratiates himself with the perverted murderer, listening to his big talk and going with him to bars and bordellos. Meanwhile, Nick falls for and marries Nettie, moving his family into a new home. When Nick's cover is blown and D'Angelo forces him to testify against Tommy, Nick becomes a marked man. Unable to stand waiting, Nick decides to push Udo to the point of murder.

Hathaway's New York locations give KISS OF DEATH a style reminiscent of other crime films employing a documentary-like approach, including CALL NORTHSIDE 777 and THE NAKED CITY. Mature is exceptional as the reluctant squealer, Gray appealingly low-key as his wife, and Donlevy solid as the crusading attorney. Widmark, however, with his maniacal eyes, falsetto baby talk, and hyena-like laughter, really captured the public's imagination with his riveting performance. KISS OF DEATH features the famous scene where Udo murders a wheelchair-bound old woman by pushing her down a flight of stairs. An overnight sensation, Widmark was signed to a long-term contract by Fox. The Hecht-Lederer script is taut and clever, more literate than many gangster films, with well-developed characters and a starkly believable plot line. The story was later used for the shlock cult film THE FIEND WHO WALKED THE WEST.

KISS OF DEATH

1995 101m c Crime/Drama ★★★½
20th Century Fox (U.S.) R

DVD

David Caruso *(Jimmy Kilmartin)*, Samuel L. Jackson *(Calvin)*, Nicolas Cage *(Little Junior)*, Helen Hunt *(Bev)*, Kathryn Erbe *(Rosie)*, Stanley Tucci *(Frank Zioli)*, Michael Rapaport *(Ronnie)*, Ving Rhames *(Omar)*, Philip Baker Hall *(Big Junior)*, Anthony Heald *(Jack Gold)*

p, Barbet Schroeder, Susan Hoffman; d, Barbet Schroeder; w, Richard Price (based on the 1947 screenplay by Ben Hecht and Charles Lederer from a story by Eleazar Lipsky); ph, Luciano Tovoli; ed, Lee Percy; m, Trevor Jones; prod d, Mel Bourne; fx, Steve Kirshoff; cos, Theadora Van Runkle

Loosely based on the 1947 film of the same name, this solid crime drama marks TV star David Caruso's big-screen debut in a leading role, though Nicolas Cage dominates the proceedings as an eccentric crime lord.

Caruso plays smalltime ex-con Jimmy Kilmartin, a family man who, despite his best efforts to go straight, is drawn into the world of volatile, asthmatic Junior Brown (Cage). Part monster, part cornball New Age philosopher, the pumped-up, track-suited Brown runs the criminal empire bequeathed him by his dad from a strip club in Queens. While serving a second prison term following a bungled car theft operation, Jimmy is approached by the D.A. (Stanley Tucci) and a hard-nosed police detective (Samuel L. Jackson), who persuade him to infiltrate Junior's gang. When the Feds get involved, Jimmy realizes that he's become a pawn in an extremely dangerous game.

KISS OF DEATH has the right tone for this noir-ish examination of petty criminals and their world: Barbet Schroeder has shot much of it at night, using auto junkyards and other unglamorous locales, and screenwriter Richard Price has a well-known flair for grungy atmosphere. As Junior (a character only vaguely suggested by Richard Widmark's fiendish turn in the original), Cage dispenses with his customary mumbling lethargy to give an electric performance, alternately menacing and pitiable.

KISS OF THE SPIDER WOMAN

1985 119m c/bw Prison ★★★★
HB (U.S./Brazil) R

William Hurt *(Luis Molina)*, Raul Julia *(Valentin Arregui)*, Sonia Braga *(Leni Lamaison/Marta/Spider Woman)*, Jose Lewgoy *(Warden)*, Milton Goncalves *(Pedro)*, Miriam Pires *(Mother)*, Nuno Leal Maia *(Gabriel)*, Fernando Torres *(Americo)*, Patricio Bisso *(Greta)*, Herson Capri *(Werner)*

p, David Weisman; d, Hector Babenco; w, Leonard Schrader (based on the novel by Manuel Puig); ph, Rodolfo Sanchez (MGM Color); ed, Mauro Alice, Lee Percy; m, John Neschling, Wally Badarou; art d, Clovis Bueno; cos, Patricio Bisso

AAN Best Picture; AA Best Actor: William Hurt; AAN Best Director: Hector Babenco; AAN Best Adapted Screenplay: Leonard Schrader

Based on Manuel Puig's novel of the same name, KISS OF THE SPIDER WOMAN treats its unusual premise with an often lyrical grace. In a South American country, Luis Molina, a flamboyant gay man jailed for taking liberties with a minor,

shares a cell with Valentin Arregui (Julia), a political prisoner. Though the revolutionary initially dislikes Luis, he is gradually drawn in by the latter's retelling of films, including a Nazi propaganda piece about a cabaret singer, and a B picture featuring the "Spider Woman" (both "starring" Braga).

The two men develop a deep friendship wherein Luis learns the importance of political convictions and Valentin discovers the power of fantasy. He becomes able to withstand the tortures he endures by dreaming of his lover outside (Braga again). Luis falls in love with his cellmate and, shortly before Luis's release, Valentin agree to share a night of lovemaking with his smitten friend. Luis soon returns the favor by getting involved in Valentin's dangerous political efforts on the outside.

Hurt does a fine job with this difficult role, even if a self-conscious quality not entirely befitting the character does creep in; he seems to want to go out of his way to make it a showy performance, but he deserves credit for pursuing the challenge. Julia, while admittedly on much safer ground, really gives the performance to watch, however. His tenderness is as compelling as his rage, and he never strikes a false note. The impact of the entire film rests on the relationship these actors construct, and both Hurt and Julia succeed brilliantly.

Braga does a good job differentiating among her essentially thankless roles, but she's not entirely into the camp spirit of the movie sequences. Babenco's fine direction is a masterwork of detailed camera choreography, and the films-within-a-film episodes aptly complement the prisoners's relationship.

KITTY FOYLE

1940 105m bw Drama ★★★★
RKO (U.S.)

Ginger Rogers *(Kitty Foyle)*, Dennis Morgan *(Wyn Strafford)*, James Craig *(Mark)*, Eduardo Ciannelli *(Giono)*, Ernest Cossart *(Pop)*, Gladys Cooper *(Mrs. Strafford)*, Odette Myrtil *(Delphine Detaille)*, Mary Treen *(Pat)*, K.T. Stevens *(Molly)*, Walter Kingsford *(Mr. Kennett)*

p, David Hempstead; d, Sam Wood; w, Dalton Trumbo, Donald Ogden Stewart (based on the novel by Christopher Morley); ph, Robert de Grasse; ed, Henry Berman; m, Roy Webb; art d, Van Nest Polglase, Mark-Lee Kirk; fx, Vernon L. Walker; cos, Renie

AAN Best Picture; AA Best Actress: Ginger Rogers; AAN Best Director: Sam Wood; AAN Best Screenplay: Dalton Trumbo; AAN Best Sound Recording: John Aalberg

In a dramatic role right after the Astaire years, Ginger Rogers proved yet again that she had more than enough star quality herself to carry major films. A minor classic and a very typical "woman's picture" of its day, KITTY FOYLE details its feisty heroine's romances with two men. Wyn (Morgan) is the embodiment of the society scions Kitty has watched entering Philadelphia's classiest ball every year. The two fall in love when she becomes his secretary, but his social obligations continually tear them apart, even to the point where he marries another woman. Kitty later begins a sincere if casual romance with Mark (Craig), a struggling young doctor. Eventually accepting his marriage proposal, Kitty has a big choice to make when Wyn sweeps back into her life.

Highly sentimental, KITTY FOYLE features typically variable direction by Wood and includes an unnecessary prologue showing how the treatment of women supposedly changed through the years. Despite these drawbacks, this film makes no apologies for being a romantic tearjerker. The humor and warmth are real, and the film maintains admirable restraint even amid Kitty's most sorrowful travails. Best of all, Rogers offers a performance of considerable dexterity and poignancy. This proletariat Cinderella is a showcase part and she makes the most of it, whether wisecracking with her cronies or during a very cheap first date with Mark, telling off

Wyn's snobbish family in fine style, or in her several moving encounters with children. Rogers's Oscar win has always been slightly controversial, given the stiff competition that year (Bette Davis, Katharine Hepburn, Joan Fontaine and Martha Scott). If, however, one considers her equally fine work in the same year's excellent but controversial PRIMROSE PATH and realizes that Academy Awards are often given for a good *year's* work, then maybe it's entirely fitting to say that Ginger Rogers *was* the Best Actress of 1940.

KLUTE

	DVD
1971 114m c Crime	★★★★
Warner Bros. (U.S.)	R

Jane Fonda *(Bree Daniels)*, Donald Sutherland *(John Klute)*, Charles Cioffi *(Peter Cable)*, Roy Scheider *(Frank Ligourin)*, Dorothy Tristan *(Arlyn Page)*, Rita Gam *(Trina)*, Vivian Nathan *(Psychiatrist)*, Nathan George *(Lt. Trask)*, Morris Strassberg *(Mr. Goldfarb)*, Jean Stapleton *(Goldfarb's Secretary)*

p, Alan J. Pakula, David Lang; d, Alan J. Pakula; w, Andy Lewis, Dave Lewis; ph, Gordon Willis (Panavision, Technicolor); ed, Carl Lerner; m, Michael Small; art d, George Jenkins; cos, Ann Roth

AA Best Actress: Jane Fonda; *AAN Best Original Story and Screenplay:* Andy Lewis, Dave Lewis

Along with BARBARELLA and THEY SHOOT HORSES, DON'T THEY?, one of the best things the highly variable Jane Fonda has ever done.

When a research scientist turns up missing, his best friend, John Klute (Sutherland), a small-town police detective, goes to New York City in search of Bree Daniels (Fonda), a prostitute to whom the missing man had written letters. Bree, who is trying to switch professions, tells Klute that she has been getting threatening phone calls from a violent former client who she also thinks has been following her. In the process of his investigation, Klute falls for Bree, though she has difficulty returning his affection. After another prostitute who had contact with the sadistic caller is murdered, Bree finds herself alone in a dark warehouse in the exciting finale.

The film's predictable plotting is not its strong point, nor is Pakula's uneven direction. The strictly thriller aspects of the film vary from the artfully constructed to the showy but shallow. It's as if Pakula feels compelled to indulge all the conventions of the genre, but without quite knowing why. On the other hand, he does ably highlight some of the more provocative and complex aspects of Andy and Dave Lewis's often fine screenplay. We see Bree calmly look at her watch while simulating passionate sex, and she develops a sentimental attachment to the lonely old man who simply likes to look at her nude. Bree can, with perfect professionalism, explain that certain sex acts will cost clients more, but she also cowers from an awareness of her own vulnerability and realizes the painful contradictions in her life.

Sutherland is either an excellent sounding board for this nuanced portrait or he's a big zero, probably both. Fonda, however, transcends her limitations, making the most of her often forced quality as an actress. Bree emerges as likably strong yet dangerously weak, refreshingly intelligent yet searching and confused.

KNACK ... AND HOW TO GET IT, THE

	DVD
1965 84m bw Comedy	★★★★
Woodfall (U.K.)	

Rita Tushingham *(Nancy Jones)*, Ray Brooks *(Tolen)*, Michael Crawford *(Colin)*, Donal Donnelly *(Tom)*, William Dexter *(Dress Shop Owner)*, Charles Dyer *(Man in Photo Booth)*, Margot Thomas *(Female Teacher)*, John Bluthal *(Father)*, Wensley Pithey *(Teacher)*, Helen Lennox *(Blonde in Photo Booth)*

p, Oscar Lewenstein; d, Richard Lester; w, Charles Wood (from the play by Ann Jellicoe); ph, David Watkin; ed, Anthony Gibbs; m, John Barry; art d, Assheton Gorton; cos, Jocelyn Rickards

Director Lester continued to defy convention as he had with A HARD DAY'S NIGHT in this, his follow-up feature. The style is extremely fast paced; the characters are nonstop talkers who move about incessantly. Essentially created in the cutting room, Lester's films rely upon techniques which have been commonly employed throughout commercial film history, but which are combined in a unusual and flamboyant, if not always successful manner.

Tolen's (Brooks) luck with women ("the knack") baffles his schoolteacher landlord Colin (Crawford). This resident stud takes the eager but shy man under his wing and advises him to buy a new brass bed. After finding an appropriate model, they roll it through London streets to their digs, causing traffic jams and general hysteria. Along the way, they meet Nancy (Tushingham), who is new to London and is trying to find a place to stay. She accompanies them on their trek home, and Colin gets a yen for her. Back at the boarding house, however, Tolen takes control and runs off with her on his motorbike. Colin follows in hot pursuit, only to find the couple in a park, where Nancy is loudly accusing Tolen of rape. Losing his patience with this unusually (but justifiably) uncooperative woman, Tolen makes room for Colin.

The characters are deliberately little more than cardboard types. They talk all the time, but never say much of anything. They do, however, convey quite a bit of personality, which can be attributed to Lester's not over-dramatizing any situations and his reliance upon semi-improvisational material. Such an endlessly tricksy style does miss occasionally, but what often emerges is a genuinely energetic celebration of 1960s youth. A film of sunshiny, horny dreams and determinedly chic comic anarchy, this manic display remains a zingy if slightly dated adaptation of Ann Jellicoe's fascinating original play.

KNIFE IN THE HEAD

(MESSER IM KOPF)

1978 113m c Drama/Thriller/Political	★★★★
Biskop Film/Hallelujah-Film (West Germany)	

Bruno Ganz *(Dr. Berthold Hoffmann)*, Angela Winkler *(Ann Hoffmann)*, Hans Christian Blech *(Scholz)*, Udo Samel *(Schurig)*, Eike Gallwitz *(Dr. Groeske)*, Carla Egerer *(Nurse Angelika Mueller)*, Gabriele Dossi *(Nurse Emmilie)*, Hans Fuchs *(Head Doctor)*, Erich Kleiber *(Herr Arnold)*

p, Eberhard Junkersdorf; d, Reinhard Hauff; w, Peter Schneider; ph, Frank Bruhne

A dark, ambiguous political thriller reflecting the paranoia of Germany's Baader-Meinhof era. Bruno Ganz, in a moving and meticulously conceived performance, plays an apolitical scientist who is shot in the head during a clash between leftist students and a quasi-totalitarian police force. His tortuous recovery from aphasia figures both an Oedipal journey and a search for political certainty. Angela Winkler (THE TIN DRUM) is a standout as Ganz's chilly, faithless wife. Director Hauff's vision of an alienated, ultra-modern Germany is well served by Frank Bruhne's cool cinematography.

KNIFE IN THE WATER

(NOZ W WODZIE)

	DVD
1962 94m bw Thriller/Drama	★★★★½
Film Polski (Poland)	

Leon Niemczyk *(Andrzej)*, Jolanta Umecka *(Christine)*, Zygmunt Malanowicz *(The Young Man)*

p, Stanislaw Zylewicz; d, Roman Polanski; w, Roman Polanski, Jerzy Skolimowski, Jakub Goldberg; ph, Jerzy Lipman; m, Krzysztof Komeda

---

AAN Best Foreign Language Film

Roman Polanski's first feature immediately established him as a filmmaker to be reckoned with, winning top honors at the Venice Film Festival, a Best Foreign Film Oscar nomination, and a place on the cover of *Time* in conjunction with the first New York Film Festival. Polanski's career-long fascination with human cruelty and violence is already evident, as is his intense interest in exploring the complex tensions involved in close relations.

When Andrzej (Niemczyk), a successful sportswriter on holiday with his wife, Christine (Umecka), picks up a hitch-hiker (Malanowicz), the couple asks the young man (name-less throughout) to join them on a short boating excursion. Jealous of the blonde boy's youth and looks, Andrzej boasts of his physical prowess, faulting his guest's inexperience at sea. Tension between the men intensifies, with the pocket knife that represents the hitchhiker's particular skills lending a con-tinual suggestion of violence and sexuality to the goings-on. Things eventually do get violent.

Filmed in black and white, this film is extremely assured, concise, and telling in its characterizations. KNIFE IN THE WATER is also notable in the career of another Polish film-maker, coscenarist Jerzy Skolimowski, who had already begun to direct, but emerged internationally in 1982 with the offbeat MOONLIGHTING. Some would argue that KNIFE IN THE WATER is a more interesting movie than any Polanski made in the west after leaving his native land. Brilliantly told and well-acted, Polanski's half tongue-in-cheek, lugubrious and sinister filmic style seemed quite refreshing at the time.

KNIGHT WITHOUT ARMOR

1937 107m bw Adventure/Romance ★★★★
Korda/London Films (U.K.)

Marlene Dietrich *(Alexandra Vladinoff)*, Robert Donat *(Ainsley Fothergill)*, Irene Vanbrugh *(Duchess of Zorin)*, Herbert Lomas *(Gen. Gregor Vladinoff)*, Austin Trevor *(Col. Adraxine)*, Basil Gill *(Axelstein)*, John Clements *(Poushkoff)*, Miles Malleson *(Drunken Soldier)*, Hay Petrie *(Station Master)*, David Tree *(Alexis Maronin)*

p, Alexander Korda; d, Jacques Feyder; w, Lajos Biro, Arthur Wimperis, Frances Marion (based on the novel *Without Armour* by James Hilton); ph, Harry Stradling, Bernard Browne, Jack Cardiff; ed, William Hornbeck, A.W. Watkins; m, Miklos Rozsa; fx, Ned Mann; cos, G.K. Benda

---

"Knight Without Asthma" is what the "gwamowous Miss Dietwich" dubbed costar Wobert Donat upon his return to the set after a particularly nasty bout with chronic asthma. For a time the powers that be considered replacing him, but luckily Dietrich fought to keep Donat. It's a good thing, too, because their teamwork is one of the highlights of this lavish, under-rated spectacle.

About to be kicked out of Czarist Russia for writing an article critical of the state, Britisher Ainsley Fothergill (Donat) manages to stay when he is engaged as a spy for his native country. Investigating young radicals trying to overthrow the Czar, he meets one involved in a plot to kill General Gregor Vladinoff (Lomas), father of the Countess Alexandra (Dietrich). Fothergill is arrested along with others connected with the attempt, and spends years languishing in prison until he is set free by the Russian Revolution. He later meets up with the Countess, whose estate has been overrun and who has been taken prisoner herself. Ordered to escort her to Petrograd to stand trial, Fothergill reveals his identity to Alexandra and proceeds to help her escape. The two find an

unlikely ally in the form of Poushkoff (Clements, an appeal-ing actor) and must use disguises and their wits to make their way to safety.

KNIGHT WITHOUT ARMOR boasts grand period sets by Lazare Meerson and a thunderous, majestic Rosza score that captures the spirit of the stirring and cataclysmic events onscreen. Dietrich looks lovely and her performance is gener-ally quite good, even if she is tousled and dirtied up in only the most decorative manner possible amidst the fires of revolu-tion. Once described as having sex without gender, the incred-ible Marlene spans quite a sexual gamut in this film. One scene offers striking quasi-nudity as the Countess races across the lawn of her estate in a diaphanous white robe upon dis-covering that she has been abandoned by her servants. Not long afterward, though, she must masquerade as a Cossack during an escape and the Androgyne of the Ages gets to strut her stuff once more. Donat is in fine form, too, full of dash but avoiding the impulse to be too precious.

KNIGHT'S TALE, A

2001 130m c Adventure/Romance ★★½
Escape Artists/Finestkind Productions (U.S.) PG-13

Heath Ledger *(William)*, Rufus Sewell *(Count Adhemar)*, Shanynn Sossamon *(Jocelyn)*, Paul Bettany *(Chaucer)*, Laura Fraser *(Kate)*, Mark Addy *(Roland)*, Alan Tudyk *(Wat)*, Berenice Bejo *(Christiana)*, Scott Handy *(Germaine)*, James Purefoy *(Colville)*

p, Brian Helgeland, Todd Black, Tim Van Rellim; d, Brian Helgeland; w, Brian Helgeland; ph, Richard Greatrex; ed, Kevin Stitt; m, Carter Burwell; prod d, Tony Burrough; art d, John Hill; fx, Tim Burke, Terry Glass; cos, Caroline Harris

---

A 14th-century comic fairy tale about an ambitious young peasant who proves that aristocracy comes from the heart, not the bloodline.

Low-born squire William Thatcher (Heath Ledger) dares to impersonate his late master, an itinerant knight, at a regional tournament in France. The penalties for pretending to be of noble blood are stiff, but without the prize money, William and fellow squires Roland (Mark Addy) and Wat (Alan Tudyk) will starve. After he wins, William wants to compete further; there's money to be made, and the trio soon encounter another travel-er who can help them over the biggest obstacle to success. Aspiring writer Geoffrey Chaucer (Paul Bettany) can forge patents of nobility, and humble William is soon competing as Sir Ulrich von Lichtenstein, winning tourneys and the heart of noble lady Jocelyn (Shannyn Sossamon). Only dastardly Count Adhemar (Rufus Sewell) stands between William and his belief that with enough courage, "a man can change his stars."

Writer-director Brian Helgeland's intention seems to have been to revitalize the medieval epic with flagrant anachronisms, imagining a Middle Age world in which high-born ladies dress like 21st century runway models and armor-ers sign their work with a symbol that looks suspiciously like the Nike swoosh. The whole thing is goosed up with bom-bastic contemporary tunes: Tournaments are fought to Queen's arena rock standard "We Are the Champions," aris-tocrats boogie to Bowie's "Golden Years," and William trains to War's "Low Rider." A workable, if limited, conceit, this brazen mix of old and new is undermined by the predictable story, shallow characterizations, and a dopey sense of humor that evokes MONTY PYTHON AND THE HOLY GRAIL without actually being especially funny.

KNOCK ON ANY DOOR

1949 100m bw Crime ★★★½
Santana (U.S.)

Humphrey Bogart *(Andrew Morton)*, John Derek *(Nick Romano)*, George Macready *(District Attorney Kerman)*, Allene Roberts

(Emma), Susan Perry *(Adele)*, Mickey Knox *(Vito)*, Barry Kelley *(Judge Drake)*, Dooley Wilson *(Piano Player)*, Cara Williams *(Nelly)*, Jimmy Conlin *(Kid Fingers)*

p, Robert Lord; d, Nicholas Ray; w, Daniel Taradash, John Monks Jr. (based on the novel by Willard Motley); ph, Burnett Guffey; ed, Viola Lawrence; m, George Antheil; art d, Robert Peterson; cos, Jean Louis

"Live fast, die young, and have a good-looking corpse." This hard-hitting crime melodrama offers excellent direction from the always interesting Nicholas Ray and a fine performance from Bogart as Andrew Morton a crusading attorney.

Morton's latest crusade involves saving Nick Romano *(Derek)*, an embittered slum youth, from the electric chair. Piecing together the young man's story in flashback, Morton describes Nick's crooked early life and his brief happiness with Emma (Roberts). Already having difficulty holding down a job, Nick really cracks when Emma tells him she's pregnant. His return to thievery gets worse after Emma commits suicide, and Nick's crime spree climaxes with his murder of a policeman. An expert liar who makes the most of his boyish good looks, Nick has convinced Morton of his innocence, only to crack when district attorney Kerman (Macready) asks about Emma.

Ray really makes us feel the oppressive filth and poverty of slum life, conjuring considerable sympathy for the distinctly dislikable Nick Romano. A problem even he couldn't surmount, however, was John Derek. Making his film debut here, pretty boy Derek constructs his dull performance with scissors, cardboard and library paste. The role could have ignited the screen, but Derek's high-school histrionics make for a pretty wet blanket. Bogart, on the other hand, does quite well, even if principled attorney Morton recalls the actor's fledgling days in MARKED WOMAN more than any of the classic Bogie roles. Straightforward virtue was never his strong suit, but Bogart nevertheless does a great job with his long climactic courtroom speech.

Not as memorable as Bogart's other collaboration with director Ray, the haunting IN A LONELY PLACE, this film still makes for absorbing viewing. Sequel: LET NO MAN WRITE MY EPITAPH.

KNOCK ON WOOD

1954 103m c Spy/Thriller/Comedy ★★★
Dena (U.S.)

Danny Kaye *(Jerry)*, Mai Zetterling *(Ilse Nordstrom)*, Torin Thatcher *(Langston)*, David Burns *(Marty Brown)*, Leon Askin *(Gromeck)*, Abner Biberman *(Papinek)*, Gavin Gordon *(Car Salesman)*, Otto Waldis *(Brodnik)*, Steven Geray *(Dr. Kreuger)*, Diana Adams *(Princess)*

p, Norman Panama, Melvin Frank; d, Norman Panama, Melvin Frank; w, Norman Panama, Melvin Frank; ph, Daniel Fapp (Technicolor); ed, Alma Macrorie; chor, Michael Kidd

AAN Best Story and Screenplay: Norman Panama, Melvin Frank

An often funny, sight gag variation on Hitchcock's "wrong man" thrillers. Danny Kaye plays Jerry, a ventriloquist with a dummy that talks when he doesn't want it to and insults the customers. His manager (Burns) suggests he see a psychiatrist (Zetterling). Meanwhile, the the plans for a new weapon have been stolen and two rival groups are after them. The blueprints are placed in, you guessed it, the dummy. The spies begin chasing Jerry all over creation and that's where most of the comedy happens.

The entire premise is all an excuse for several of Kaye's best comic set pieces, including his dancing with a Russian ballet troupe to avoid being found by the spies. (Alfred Hitchcock did something similar in THE 39

STEPS when Robert Donat steps in front of a political rally and masquerades as a speaker while the spies look on.) The chase also leads Kaye into a convention of Irishmen, where he sings "The Drastic, Livid History of Monahan O'Han," penned by Kaye's wife, the writer, Sylvia Fine. The versatile Kaye gets the chance to wear several disguises, to sing a few tunes (including a nice ballad "All About You"), and, in general, to do what Danny Kaye does best. It's just that sometimes he's more manic than funny and he often doesn't know when to quit.

KNUTE ROCKNE—ALL AMERICAN

1940 98m bw Biography/Sports ★★½
Warner Bros. (U.S.)

Pat O'Brien *(Knute Rockne)*, Gale Page *(Bonnie Skiles Rockne)*, Ronald Reagan *(George Gipp)*, Donald Crisp *(Father John Callahan)*, Albert Basserman *(Father Julius Nieuwland)*, John Litel *(Committee Chairman)*, Henry O'Neill *(Doctor)*, Owen Davis Jr. *(Gus Dorais)*, John Qualen *(Lars Knutson Rockne)*, Dorothy Tree *(Martha Rockne)*

p, Robert Fellows; d, Lloyd Bacon; w, Robert Buckner (based on the private papers of Mrs. Knute Rockne); ph, Tony Gaudio; ed, Ralph Dawson; m, Ray Heindorf; art d, Robert Haas; fx, Byron Haskin, Rex Wimpy; cos, Milo Anderson

Corn doesn't grow any higher than this male bonding tribute to testosterone. Pat O'Brien gives a gung-ho performance as the great Notre Dame football coach Knute Rockne in this bland biography that features Reagan as Rockne's most famous player, George Gipp. The film follows Rockne from his Norwegian immigrant beginnings through his playing days at Notre Dame (when he helped invent the forward pass) and on to his glory days as head coach at his alma mater. With the support of Father Callahan (Donald Crisp), Rockne rises from assistant coach and chemistry teacher to the top spot, and revolutionizes the game as he turns out winning team after winning team, blessed with great players like the "Four Horsemen" and Gipp, who dies young of pneumonia and provides the inspiration for Rockne's famed "win one for the Gipper" pep talk. Along the way, Rockne even finds time to romance and marry Bonnie Skilles (Gale Page). Four of Rockne's contemporaries play themselves—the grandfather of all coaches, Amos Alonzo Stagg, Howard Jones of USC, William Spaulding, and "Pop" Warner—and much of the football action is culled from newsreel footage. For legal reasons, some of the big scenes—such as the pep talk O'Brien gives in the locker room and the "for the Gipper" speech are missing on television. But it's all there in the home video, sitting in the cobwebs on your video store shelf.

KOLYA

DVD
1996 112m c Drama ★★★★
Portobello Productions/Biograf Jan Sverak Pictures (France/Czech Republic/U.K.)

Zdenek Sverak *(Frantisek Louka)*, Andrej Chalimon *(Kolya)*, Libuse Safrankova *(Klara)*, Ondrez Vetchy *(Mr. Broz)*, Stella Zazvorkova *(Mother)*, Ladislav Smoljak *(Mr. Houdek)*, Irena Livanova *(Nadezda)*, Lilian Mankina *(Aunt Tamara)*, Petra Spalova *(Pasha)*, Nella Boudova *(Mrs. Brozova)*

p, Eric Abraham, Jan Sverak; d, Jan Sverak; w, Zdenek Sverak (based on a story by Pavel Taussig); ph, Vladimir Smutny; ed, Alois Fisarek; m, Ondrej Soukup; prod d, Milos Kohout; cos, Katerina Holla

AA Best Foreign Language Film

Winner of the Academy Award for Best Foreign Language Film, this delicate Czech film reveals the changing political landscape of Eastern Europe through a simple tale of a Czech bachelor and the Russian child he is forced to care for.

1988, one year before the fall of Communism in Czechoslovakia. Frantisek Louka (Zdenek Sverak), an aging bachelor cellist who has lost his position in the Czech Philharmonic, resigns himself to his new job playing at funerals, passing his days making time with an assortment of women. In need of money, he enters into a paper marriage with Nadezda (Irena Livanova), a young Russian woman. Nadezda soon flees to Germany, leaving her five-year-old son Kolya (beautifully played by young Andrej Chalimon) in the care of her mother. When the grandmother dies, Louka is forced to take in the boy. At first the little Russian—who cannot comprehend the animosity he inspires in the Czechs—is an albatross for Louka, but Kolya ultimately challenges his new guardian to reconsider his anti-Soviet attitude.

Eastern European cinema, with its long struggle to maneuver around state-controlled film censorship, has developed into a rare art form. Political bondage has helped the best Czech filmmakers to learn to convey the nuances of political and ideological struggle in complex, indirect terms. Directed by Jan Sverak and written by his father Zdenek Sverak, who also plays the lead role, KOLYA combines pathos, predicament, and wit in the way that has come to define the Czech cinema of such figures as Milos Forman and Jiri Menzel. The Sveraks use human terms to show the decline of Soviet power and the emotional vertigo that ensues when a recognizable enemy is removed.

KRAMER VS. KRAMER

1979 105m c Drama ★★★★
Columbia (U.S.) PG   📀

Dustin Hoffman (Ted Kramer), Meryl Streep (Joanna Kramer), Jane Alexander (Margaret Phelps), Justin Henry (Billy Kramer), Howard Duff (John Shaunessy), George Coe (Jim O'Connor), JoBeth Williams (Phyllis Bernard), Bill Moor (Gressen), Howland Chamberlin (Judge Atkins), Jack Ramage (Spencer)

p, Stanley R. Jaffe; d, Robert Benton; w, Robert Benton (based on the novel by Avery Corman); ph, Nestor Almendros (Panavision, Technicolor); ed, Jerry Greenberg; m, Henry Purcell, Antonio Vivaldi; prod d, Paul Sylbert; cos, Ruth Morley

---

AA Best Picture; AA Best Actor: Dustin Hoffman; AAN Best Supporting Actor: Justin Henry; AA Best Supporting Actress: Meryl Streep; AAN Best Supporting Actress: Jane Alexander; AA Best Director: Robert Benton; AA Best Adapted Screenplay: Robert Benton; AAN Best Cinematography: Nestor Almendros; AAN Best Film Editing: Jerry Greenberg

---

For weepie fans, a high class divorce, finely played. KRAMER VS. KRAMER is, essentially, a television movie that was raised into the feature category by the excellence of the execution. With Robert Reed in the Hoffman role and Suzanne Pleshette as his wife, it would have been a typical CBS entry.

Based on a novel by Avery Corman, the story takes place in New York City and shows Streep, an independent woman, leaving husband Hoffman, an art director in an ad agency, for no other reason than that she wants to "find herself." Hoffman is left to care for their young son, Henry. The extra strain of having to be both father and mother to Henry causes Hoffman to make some mistakes at work and lose a major account, which results in his getting fired. On top of that, Streep surfaces and is suing for custody of the child she's abandoned. Streep now has an excellent job and can afford day care for Henry, so she wants him back.

It's the old wash, but so well done that we can overlook Benton's manipulations of our emotions and let our feelings flow. Movies about divorce and the wrenching apart of families have been part of the motion picture scene since the

silents. They will always work, however, if the writing is honest and if the acting is sincere.

KUNDUN

1997 128m c Biography/Drama/Religious ★★★½   📀
Cappa/De Fina Productions/Touchstone Pictures PG-13
(U.S.)

Tenzin Thuthob Tsarong (Adult Dalai Lama), Gyurme Tethong (Dalai Lama—Age 12), Tulku Jamyang Kunga Tenzin (Dalai Lama—Age Five), Tenzin Yeshi Paichang (Dalai Lama—Age Two), Tencho Gyalpo (Dalai Lama's Mother), Tsewang Migyur Khangsar (Dalai Lama's Father), Geshi Yeshi Gyatso (Lama of Sera), Sonam Phuntsok (Reting Rinpoche), Lobsang Samten (Master of the Kitchen), Robert Lin (Chairman Mao)

p, Barbara De Fina; d, Martin Scorsese; w, Melissa Mathison; ph, Roger Deakins; ed, Thelma Schoonmaker; m, Philip Glass; prod d, Dante Ferretti; art d, Alan Tomkins; fx, Kevin Hannigan, Renato Agostini; cos, Dante Ferretti

---

AAN Best Art Direction: Dante Ferretti, Francesca Lo Schiavo; AAN Best Cinematography: Roger Deakins; AAN Best Original Dramatic Score: Philip Glass; AAN Best Costume Design: Dante Ferretti

---

Martin Scorsese's KUNDUN is a visually stunning but dramatically conventional biography of the 14th Dalai Lama.

In 1937 Tibet, a young boy named Tenzin Gyatso (Tenzin Yenshi Paichang) is found by a group of monks who determine the boy to be the 14th reincarnation of the Buddha—the Dalai Lama—who is destined to become the spiritual and political leader of Tibet. Tenzin is sent to a monastery where he is trained in Buddhist philosophy and its central tenet of nonviolence. Following WWII, China begins a campaign to convince the world that Tibet is one of its territories, and soon after Chairman Mao (Robert Lin) seizes power in 1949, China invades. At the age of 18, the Dalai Lama (Tenzin Thutob Tsarong) is enthroned, but is soon forced to leave his palace after clashing with Chinese generals. A futile meeting with Chairman Mao amid the slaughter of innocent Tibetans by Chinese soldiers is followed by several attempts on the Dalai Lama's life. In 1959, he finally agrees to leave his country for a life of exile in India.

Despite the apparent incongruity of Scorsese, the director of such hard-edged films as RAGING BULL and GOODFELLAS, making a film about the serene Dalai Lama, the match is really somewhat natural. There has always been a strong religious strain running through his more personal films, and one of the key themes of KUNDUN (which is what Tibetans call the Dalai Lama, meaning "Ocean of Wisdom") is violence. But ultimately, like all of Scorsese's films, the real subject is cinema itself and the transcendent power of the image. And therein lies KUNDUN's strength, as well as its weakness: what one recalls are not the film's philosophical or political messages, wrapped in Melissa Mathison's fairly prosaic screenplay, but rather its sensuous flow of ravishing images.

KUNG FU HUSTLE

(GONG FU)   📀
2004 99m c Action/Comedy/Martial Arts ★★★
Columbia Pictures Film Production/Beijing Film Studio R
of China Film Group Corporation/The Stars
Overseas Ltd. (China/Hong Kong)

Stephen Chow (Sing), Yuen Wah (Landlord), Yuen Qiu (Landlady), Chan Kwok Kwan (Brother Sum), Leung Siu Lung (The Beast), Dong Zhi Hua (Donut), Chiu Chi Ling (Tailor), Xing Yu (Coolie), Lam Tze Chung (Sing's Sidekick), Jia kang Xi (Harpist No.1)

p, Stephen Chow, Chui Po Chu, Jeff Lau; d, Stephen Chow; w, Chan Man Keung, Stephen Chow, Lola Huo, Tsang Kan Cheong;

ph, Poon Hang Sang; ed, Angie Lam; m, Raymond Wong; prod d, Oliver Wong; art d, Second Chan; fx, Frankie Chung; chor, Yuen Wo Ping (action); cos, Shirley Chan

A giant leap forward in Stephen Chow's ongoing assault on Jackie Chan's status as reigning clown-master of martial-arts mayhem, this extravagantly nutty crime comedy is a work of some kind of genius: an East-West blend of Looney Toons pratfalls, computer-assisted fight choreography, Shaw Brothers allusions, and sheer insanity set in '40s Shanghai.

Pretending to be foot soldiers of the hatchet-wielding criminal Axe Gang, wastrel Sing (Chow) and his nameless sidekick (Lam Tze Chung) try to scam the downtrodden residents of Pig Sty Alley, who live in fear of their cheap, slovenly Landlady (Yuen Qiu) and her scrawny pervert of a husband (Yuen Wah). But the Alley's fawning Donut (Dong Zhi Hua), fey Tailor (Chiu Chi Ling), and meek Coolie (Xing Yu) aren't the pathetic losers they appear; they're semi-retired kung-fu fighters who reveal themselves after Sing's bumbling brings the wrath of the real Axe Gang upon their humble neighborhood. Thoroughly humiliated by seeing his best killers routed by a bunch of slum dwellers, head Axe man Brother Sum (Chan Kwok Kwan) sends the second-best killers in China (Jia kang Xi, Fung Hak On) to avenge this disgrace; the greatest, the Beast (Leung Siu Lung), is unavailable because his dedication to martial arts drove him insane. But Brother Sum's hitmen only flush out an even greater pair of martial-arts masters hiding in the Alley. So Sum turns to Sing, who's willing to do anything to be a real gangster, to break the Beast out of the nuthouse.

You don't have to be a kung-fu freak to revel in the film's energetic silliness, but it helps. Chow's loving pastiche-parody is as thick with movie-buff stuff as Quentin Tarantino's KILL BILL pictures, and if that's all too geekily esoteric, there's plenty of slapstick that requires no explanation at all.

KURT AND COURTNEY [DVD]
1998 95m c Documentary ★★★
Strength Ltd. (U.K.)

Kurt Cobain, Courtney Love, Hank Harrison, El Duce, Dylan Carlson, Tom Grant, Alan Bowman, The Dwarves

p, Tine Van Den Brande, Michael D'Acosta; d, Nick Broomfield; ph, Joan Churchill, Alex Vendor; ed, Mark Atkins; m, David Bergeaud

Coasting on an oil slick of hype generated by grunge-girl diva Courtney Love's attempts to suppress it, UK shockumentarian Nick Broomfield's investigation into the death of rock idol Kurt Cobain exudes a near-irresistible freak-show fascination. Needless to say, Love comes off badly: Broomfield never succeeds in interviewing her at any length, but compiles a disturbing record of her harassment and intimidation of journalists she can't control, in light of which the hypocrisy of her carefully scripted remarks at an American Civil Liberties Union function is simply mindboggling. But for all the conspiratorial talk, evidence that Love had anything to do with her husband's apparent suicide by shotgun just isn't there. Broomfield, who has in recent years made high-profile sleaze his beat, turns over rocks in Seattle, Portland, and Los Angeles and uncovers a sorry cross-section of fringe-dwelling lowlifes, including Cobain's strung-out "best friend" Dylan Carlson; Amy, who bears a startling resemblance to Love before her glammed-up Hollywood makeover and claims she shot up with Kurt and Courtney; Love's opportunistic father, Hank Harrison, whose book suggests that his daughter killed Cobain because he was going to divorce her; a young nanny who heard "too much will talk" during her stint at the Cobain household; an obsessed private investigator who's bankrupted himself trying to prove that Cobain's death was murder; a former punk singer, one of Love's exes, who claims pathet-

ically that she pushed him so hard he gave up music; a pair of inept, self-proclaimed stalkerazzi who promise to help Broomfield ambush Love; and El Duce, a bloated, drunken excuse for a thrash-rocker who insists that she once offered him $50,000 to whack her husband. They're not a persuasive bunch. Cobain's first girlfriend, and his sentimental but wholly sympathetic Aunt Mary—who fostered his early interest in music—are pretty much the only people who don't come off as opportunistic, bottom-feeding losers.

KWAIDAN [DVD]
(KAIDAN)
1964 125m c Horror ★★★★
Toho (Japan)

Rentaro Mikuni (Samurai), Michiyo Aratama (1st Wife), Misako Watanabe (2nd Wife), Katsuo Nakamura (Hoichi), Ganjiro Nakamura (Head Priest), Takashi Shimura (Priest), Joichi Hayashi (Yoshitsune), Ganemon Nakamura (Kannai), Noboru Nakaya (Heinai), Tetsuro Tamba

d, Masaki Kobayashi; w, Yoko Mizuki (based on the stories of Lafcadio Hearn); ph, Yoshio Miyajima (Tohoscope, Eastmancolor); m, Toru Takemitsu; art d, Shigemasa Toda

AAN Best Foreign Language Film

Four short supernatural stories based on the tales of Lafcadio Hearn, an American who settled in Japan in 1890 and eventually became a citizen of that country, comprise KWAIDAN. Directed with an eerie visual sense by Masaki Kobayashi and containing some spectacular art direction by Shigemasa Toda, the stories each involve an encounter with a ghost—in Hearn's tales a supernatural being who appears to be corporeal but is actually one of the dear departed left to wander aimlessly through the real world. "Black Hair" is the tale of a samurai (Rentaro Mikuni) who returns to the wife he deserted years before and, after sleeping with her, discovers her skeletal remains and long black tresses in his bed. "The Woman of the Snow" is a story cut from the U.S. release about a young woodcutter (Tatsuya Nakadai) saved from death by a mysterious snow maiden who swears to kill him should he ever reveal what has occurred. "Hoichi, the Earless" is about a blind musician (Katsuo Nakamura) whose ears are cut off as he sings at the request of a samurai ghost. "In a Cup of Tea" features a guard (Ganemon Nakamura) who sees a samurai's face in his teacup and absorbs the ghost's soul into his body after drinking the tea. A celebration of the marvelous from director Kobayashi, KWAIDAN's haunting poetry is conveyed not only in its beautiful color images, but also through the chilling soundtrack.

L

L-SHAPED ROOM, THE
1962 142m bw Drama ★★★★
Romulus (U.K.)

Leslie Caron (Jane Fosset), Anthony Booth (Youth in Street), Avis Bunnage (Doris), Patricia Phoenix (Sonia), Verity Edmett (Jane II), Tom Bell (Toby), Cicely Courtneidge (Mavis), Harry Locke (News Agent), Ellen Dryden (Girl in News Agent's), Emlyn Williams (Dr. Weaver)

p, James Woolf, Richard Attenborough; d, Bryan Forbes; w, Bryan Forbes (based on the novel by Lynne Reid Banks); ph, Douglas Slocombe; ed, Anthony Harvey; m, John Barry; art d, Ray Simm; cos, Beatrice Dawson

AAN Best Actress: Leslie Caron

An excellent, albeit talky, drama with enough comedy to leaven the heaviness. Caron is a French woman in her late twenties who departs her home in the provinces and moves to London. She gets pregnant but, rather than have an abortion, she decides to have the baby after meeting a money-hungry gynecologist (Williams) in Harley Street. By this time, she's moved to a sleazy boarding house in Notting Hill Gate and occupies the small L-shaped room of the title.

The house is filled with characters, and she soon falls for Bell, an out-of-work writer. Since everyone in the small hotel knows everyone else, Caron and Bell's affair is the main topic of conversation, and the tenants are thrilled by what's transpiring. The other people who live there, actresses, hookers, et al., are sentimental about the love that's flourishing, but Bell's best friend, Brock Peters, is incensed. He's a jazz musician with a conservative streak, and when he learns that Caron is pregnant, he tells Bell in an attempt to split the two.

Bell is angered and leaves Caron, who responds by taking some "abortion pills" given to her by Courtneidge, an aging actress who occupies a room below Caron's. The pills fail to work and Caron is actually relieved. Bell returns but cannot accept the fact that Caron is having someone else's baby. Caron goes to the hospital to have the child, and Bell arrives with a copy of a story he's written about their situation. It's called "The L-Shaped Room." Caron returns to France and leaves the story in Bell's room with a note attached to it saying, "It's a lovely story but it has no end." That's basically what's wrong with the movie, though Forbes and co. do a good job of making these characters sympathetic and involving.

LA BALANCE

DVD

1982 102m c Crime ★★★
Ariane/Spectrafilm/A2 (France) R

Nathalie Baye *(Nicole)*, Philippe Leotard *(Dede)*, Richard Berry *(Palouzi)*, Christophe Malavoy *(Tintin)*, Jean-Paul Connart *(Le Belge)*, Bernard Freyd *(Le Capitaine)*, Albert Dray *(Carlini)*, Florent Pagny *(Simoni)*, Jean-Daniel Laval *(Arnaud)*, Luc-Antoine Diquero *(Picard)*

p, Georges Dancigers, Alexandre Mnouchkine; d, Bob Swaim; w, Bob Swaim, M. Fabiani; ph, Bernard Zitzermann (Eastmancolor); ed, Françoise Javet; m, Roland Bocquet; art d, Eric Moulard; cos, Catherine Meurisse

American expatriate director Bob Swaim puts a decidedly Parisian spin on Hollywood gangster conventions. One-time mobster Dede (Philippe Leotard) and prostitute Nicole (Nathalie Baye) play a power game with sleazy cops who are pressuring them to turn snitch. The couple are trying to live quietly on the money she earns from the street, but cop Palouzi (Richard Berry) is less concerned with their struggles than he is with busting a crime ring headed by a former associate of Dede's. If Dede cooperates, the police will leave him and Nicole alone. Unfortunately for Dede, he doesn't like the idea of being a stoolie or winding up dead. There are some nice moments here—the colorful opening sequence and an unlikely traffic jam shootout that results in a cop's Walkman stopping a bullet—but it all adds up to reasonably stylish pulp without much thought behind it. Warmly received by French audiences, LA BALANCE garnered a number of Cesars, including one for Best Picture.

LA BAMBA

DVD

1987 108m c Biography ★★½
New Visions (U.S.) PG-13

Lou Diamond Phillips *(Ritchie Valens)*, Esai Morales *(Bob Morales)*, Rosana DeSoto *(Connie Valenzuela)*, Elizabeth Pena *(Rosie Morales)*, Danielle von Zerneck *(Donna Ludwig)*, Joe Pantoliano *(Bob Keene)*, Rick Dees *(Ted Quillin)*, Marshall Crenshaw *(Buddy Holly)*, Howard Huntsberry *(Jackie Wilson)*, Brian Setzer *(Eddie Cochran)*

p, Taylor Hackford, Bill Borden; d, Luis Valdez; w, Luis Valdez; ph, Adam Greenberg (Deluxe Color); ed, Sheldon Kahn, Don Bruchu; m, Carlos Santana, Miles Goodman; prod d, Vincent Cresciman; cos, Sylvia Vega-Vasquez

Cliched melodrama about rock 'n' roll pioneer Ritchie Valens, notable as one of the first Mexican-Americans to achieve pop stardom. Beginning with his teenage days as a poor barrio resident in California, the film follows Valens (Lou Diamond Phillips) as he meets Donna Ludwig (Danielle von Zerneck), the love of his life and later the inspiration for his song "Donna," while living with his adoring mother (Rosana De Soto) and irresponsible, violent half-brother, Bob (Esai Morales). Ritchie's natural talent soon makes him the star of the small band he's joined, though his personal popularity causes friction with his jealous sibling. Soon, a record producer spots Ritchie, leading to his recording "Donna" and "La Bamba," which top the charts. At the peak of success, Valens loses his life in the plane crash made famous by Don McLean as "The Day the Music Died." The film is rich with period flavor, and Phillips is superb as Valens, but the rags-to-riches story (even if true) is maudlin and overfamiliar. Los Lobos does an excellent job of re-creating Valens' tunes and Carlos Santana provides a top-notch score.

LA BETE HUMAINE

1938 105m bw Drama ★★★½
Paris (France)

Jean Gabin *(Jacques Lantier)*, Simone Simon *(Severine)*, Fernand Ledoux *(Roubaud, Severine's Husband)*, Julien Carette *(Pecqueux)*, Blanchette Brunoy *(Flore)*, Jean Renoir *(Cabuche, the Poacher)*, Gerard Landry *(Dauvergne's Son)*, Jenny Helia *(Philomene)*, Colette Regis *(Victoire)*, Jacques Berlioz *(Grand-Morin)*

p, Robert Hakim, Raymond Hakim; d, Jean Renoir; w, Jean Renoir (based on the novel by Emile Zola); ph, Curt Courant; ed, Marguerite Renoir, Suzanne de Troeye; m, Joseph Kosma

Locomotive engineer Jacques Lantier (Jean Gabin) is infatuated with Severin (Simone Simon), the beautiful but dangerous young wife of assistant stationmaster Roubaud (Fernand Ledoux). When Roubaud learns that Severin secured his job by sleeping with his superior, he goes mad with jealousy. With the aid of Severin, he kills his superior, an act blamed on an innocent poacher but witnessed by Lantier. Roubaud then sends his wife to Lantier as a means of ensuring the engineer's silence. Again Severin's bedroom prowess secures a lover's loyalty, resulting in a romance between the pair, whereupon Severin tries to persuade Lantier to kill Roubaud.

Based on the novel by Emile Zola (whose *Nana* was also adapted by Jean Renoir in 1926), LA BETE HUMAINE features one of Jean Gabin's greatest performances—one with even more force than the locomotive he powers. The catlike Simon is perfect as the persuasive beauty who drives both of the men in her life to their destructive deeds, her unattainable love their tragic downfall. This picture was remade by Fritz Lang as HUMAN DESIRE, Lang's second remake of a Renoir film. The first was SCARLET STREET, a remake of LA CHIENNE.

LA CAGE AUX FOLLES

1978 103m c Comedy **DVD**
Artistes/Da.Ma. (France/Italy) ★★★½
R

Ugo Tognazzi *(Renato)*, Michel Serrault *(Albin/"Zaza")*, Michel Galabru *(Charrier)*, Claire Maurier *(Simone)*, Remi Laurent *(Laurent)*, Benny Luke *(Jacob)*, Carmen Scarpitta *(Madame Charrier)*, Luisa Maneri *(Andrea)*

p, Marcello Danon; d, Edouard Molinaro; w, Marcello Danon, Edouard Molinaro, Francis Veber, Jean Poiret (based on his play); ph, Armando Nannuzzi (Eastmancolor); ed, Robert Isnardon, Monique Isnardon; m, Ennio Morricone; art d, Mario Garbuglia; cos, Piero Tosi, Ambra Danon

AAN Best Director: Edouard Molinaro; *AAN Best Adapted Screenplay:* Francis Veber (Screenplay), Edouard Molinaro (Screenplay), Marcello Danon (Screenplay), Jean Poiret (Screenplay); *AAN Best Costume Design:* Piero Tosi, Ambra Danon

In less assured hands, this could have wound up as a disaster, but director Edouard Molinaro was skillfully able to film the long-running play and wring every drop of humor from it. Renato (Ugo Tognazzi) and Albin (Michel Serrault) have been lovers for more than 20 years. Albin is the lead "drag queen" of La Cage aux Folles, a Saint-Tropez nightclub, and Renato, the more masculine of the two, runs the day-to-day operations of the boite. Many years before, Renato stepped out of his gay lifestyle long enough to father Laurent (Remi Laurent) in a one-night stand, and since then both men have raised the boy. Now, Laurent comes home from college with the news that he is engaged to Andrea (Luisa Maneri), whose father, Charrier (Michel Galabru), is the secretary of the blue-nosed Union of Moral Order. As a result, Laurent has lied about his parentage and told his future father-in-law that his father is a cultural attache. From this set-up alone, one can guess that the situations that follow—revolving around Charrier's meeting with Renato—lead to some riotous results. Despite the apparent risk of making a movie with two gay leads, LA CAGE AUX FOLLES is basically an old-fashioned bedroom farce—and tamer than most, at that. Nonetheless, it was a huge international hit, spawning a pair of dreadful sequels and a fabulously successful stage musical.

LA COLLECTIONNEUSE

1967 88m c Drama **DVD**
Losange/Rome Paris (France) ★★★

Patrick Bauchau *(Adrien)*, Haydee Politoff *(Haydee)*, Daniel Pommereulle *(Daniel)*, Alain Jouffroy *(Writer)*, Mijanou Bardot *(Carole)*, Eugene Archer *(Sam)*, Annik Morice *(Carole's Friend)*, Denis Berry *(Charlie)*, Brian Belshaw *(Haydee's Lover)*, Donald Cammell *(Boy At St. Tropez)*

p, Georges Beauregard, Barbet Schroeder; d, Eric Rohmer; w, Eric Rohmer, Patrick Bauchau, Haydee Politoff, Daniel Pommereulle; ph, Nestor Almendros (Eastmancolor); ed, Jackie Raynal; m, Blossom Toes, Giorgio Gomelsky

This film is the third in a series by Rohmer, "Six Moral Tales." Adrien (Bachau) is the handsome young man faced with the problem of whether to sleep with Haydee (Politoff), the pretty temptress who is staying at the same boarding house during his vacation in St. Tropez. Listening to her carry on with a number of different men, he attempts to purify himself, avoiding sex and other pleasurable pursuits.

The figure of Woman here provides a vehicle for Rohmer to question notions of moral correctness. The narrative structure follows a pattern that resembles Rohmer's other films, a presentation of a threatened moral stance in which the male always opts out of taking chances for a more secure existence. Bauchau could be criticized for being

much too haughty and self-possessed to be very likable, but he is otherwise a perfect subject for Rohmer's experiment. The beautiful temptress played by Politoff is not really required to do much beyond looking nice; the camera does all the work. Almendros captures the beauty of Politoff and the scenery with an acute sense of detail. COLLECTIONEUSE was released belatedly in the U.S. following the tremendous success of MY NIGHT AT MAUD'S, the fourth entry in Romer's series.

L.A. CONFIDENTIAL

1997 137m c Crime/Thriller/Drama **DVD**
Regency Enterprises/Arnon Milchan/ ★★★★
David L. Wolper (U.S.) R

Kevin Spacey *(Jack Vincennes)*, Russell Crowe *(Bud White)*, Guy Pearce *(Ed Exley)*, James Cromwell *(Dudley Smith)*, Kim Basinger *(Lynn Bracken)*, Danny DeVito *(Sid Hudgens)*, David Strathairn *(Pierce Patchett)*, Ron Rifkin *(District Attorney Ellis Loew)*, Matt McCoy *('Badge of Honor' Star Brett Chase)*, Paul Guilfoyle *(Mickey Cohen)*

p, Curtis Hanson, Arnon Milchan, Michael Nathanson; d, Curtis Hanson; w, Brian Helgeland, Curtis Hanson (based on the book by James Ellroy); ph, Dante Spinotti; ed, Peter Honess; m, Jerry Goldsmith; prod d, Jeannine Oppewall; art d, Bill Arnold; fx, Eric Rylander, Richard Stutsman; cos, Ruth Myers

AA Best Supporting Actress: Kim Basinger; *AA Best Adapted Screenplay:* Curtis Hanson, Brian Helgeland; *AAN Best Picture*; *AAN Best Director:* Curtis Hanson; *AAN Best Art Direction:* Jeannine Oppewall, Jay R. Hart; *AAN Best Cinematography:* Dante Spinotti; *AAN Best Sound:* Andy Nelson, Anna Behlmer, Kirk Francis; *AAN Best Original Dramatic Score:* Jerry Goldsmith; *AAN Best Film Editing:* Peter Honess

Nothing in writer-director Curtis Hanson's resume of entertaining, if somewhat workmanlike, films (THE HAND THAT ROCKS THE CRADLE) hinted at what he accomplished with L.A. CONFIDENTIAL, an intricate story of crime and corruption in 1950s Hollywood.

The paths of three very different Los Angeles police officers—Edmund Exley (Guy Pearce), Jack Vincennes (Kevin Spacey), and Bud White (Russell Crowe)—cross initially when a police department Christmas party turns into a drunken riot. Their destinies become intertwined again when six people are murdered in a diner, an incident the papers dub the "Nite Owl Massacre." Eager to bring this case to swift resolution, the police apprehend a trio of young black men. Still, the cops suspect there is more to the Nite Owl case, and each begins his own line of investigation. Though the three men act independently, their investigations inexorably draw together as one name continues to crop up: veteran cop Dudley Smith (James Cromwell), who, it turns out, stole several hundred thousand dollars worth of heroin in a drug bust and then orchestrated the Nite Owl Massacre in an effort to cover his tracks.

Above all, L.A. CONFIDENTIAL is a tour de force of adaptation: writer Brian Helgeland and co-scripter Hanson won an Oscar for their work, paring James Ellroy's sprawling, epic novel into a tightly-wound, concise, and clear suspense story. The audience's ability to navigate the twisty plot of L.A. CONFIDENTIAL is aided by the sheer conviction of its three principal actors; for her part, Oscar winner Kim Basinger gives an adequate and ultimately forgettable performance. Though it was often likened to CHINATOWN (1974) by fawning critics, it should be noted that L.A. CONFIDENTIAL is not even a true film noir. Though it swims in the kind of seediness and corruption typical of many noir classics, it lacks the elements so crucial to true film noir: the morally ambiguous hero, the duplicitous femme fatale, the absence of ethical surety in the protagonists' actions. Noir or not, though, L.A. CONFIDENTIAL is one of the most solid dramas to come out of Hollywood in many years.

LA DOLCE VITA

1960 180m bw Drama
Riama/Pathe/Gray   (Italy/France)

DVD
★★★½

Marcello Mastroianni *(Marcello Rubini)*, Anita Ekberg *(Sylvia)*, Anouk Aimee *(Maddalena)*, Yvonne Furneaux *(Emma)*, Magali Noel *(Fanny)*, Alain Cuny *(Steiner)*, Nadia Gray *(Nadia)*, Lex Barker *(Robert)*, Annibale Ninchi *(Marcello's Father)*, Walter Santesso *(Paparazzo)*

p, Giuseppe Amato, Angelo Rizzoli; d, Federico Fellini; w, Federico Fellini, Ennio Flaiano, Tullio Pinelli, Brunello Rondi (based on a story by Federico Fellini, Ennio Flaiano, Tullio Pinelli); ph, Otello Martelli (Totalscope); ed, Leo Catozzo; m, Nino Rota; art d, Piero Gherardi; cos, Piero Gherardi

AAN Best Director: Federico Fellini; *AAN Best Original Story and Screenplay:* Federico Fellini, Tullio Pinelli, Ennio Flaiano, Brunello Rondi; *AAN Best Art Direction-Set Decoration (B/W):* Piero Gherardi; *AA Best Costume Design (B/W):* Piero Gherardi

After what we've seen of decadence during the past three decades or so, LA DOLCE VITA now seems tame, but people wasting time in nightclubs, dancing in the fountains of Rome, and just generally hanging out seemed a bit of a shock in 1960.

The picture begins as Romans are shocked by seeing a large statue of Jesus being carried over the city by a helicopter. Following in a second chopper is Mastroianni, a gossip writer for the local scandal sheets. He aspires to serious writing but never gets beyond what he churns out for *lire*. While visiting a local nightspot, Mastroianni meets Aimee, a wealthy heiress suffering from a huge case of ennui. Everything bores her, and she is constantly on the lookout for new thrills. Together, they pick up hooker Moneta and spend the night as a *menage a trois* in the prostitute's room. When Mastroianni gets home, he finds his regular mistress, Furneaux, has taken an overdose of sleeping pills. He rushes her to the hospital, where he is assured that she'll recover, then races off to cover the arrival of Hollywood starlet Ekberg at the airport. He is soon infatuated with the buxom blonde and takes her for a tour around his Rome, including all the usual spots—Trevi, St. Peter's, the Caracalla Baths, etc. The tour is interrupted violently when Mastroianni is attacked by Ekberg's fiance Barker (who was her husband in real life). Things continue in this mode as Mastroianni takes in a fake vision of the Blessed Virgin by two young children, a visit from his quiet-living father, an infatuation with an innocent young waitress, etc. His crisis about the meaninglessness of his life comes to a head when Cuny, a bohemian intellectual whom he idolizes and envies, inexplicably commits suicide and takes the lives of his two children. True to the spirit of the film, Mastroianni still fails to act on his feelings, continuing with his hollow, glamorous life.

Episodic yet engrossing, LA DOLCE VITA is still worth a look, primarily for the window it offers onto the early days of the jet-set lifestyle. After nearly three hours, though, Fellini's relentlessly enigmatic, non-committal approach leaves you wishing for something more than poignant imagery and moody, self-obsessed characters.

LA FEMME INFIDELE

1969 98m   c   Thriller
Les Films La Boetie/Cinegai   (France/Italy)

DVD
★★★★
R

Stephane Audran *(Helene Desvallees)*, Michel Bouquet *(Charles Desvallees)*, Maurice Ronet *(Victor Pegala)*, Serge Bento *(Bignon)*, Michel Duchaussoy *(Police Officer Duval)*, Guy Marly *(Police Officer Gobet)*, Stephane Di Napoli *(Michel Desvallees)*,

Louise Chevalier *(Maid)*, Louise Rioton *(Mother-in-Law)*, Henri Marteau *(Paul)*

p, Andre Genoves; d, Claude Chabrol; w, Claude Chabrol; ph, Jean Rabier (Eastmancolor); ed, Jacques Gaillard; m, Pierre Jansen; art d, Guy Littaye; cos, Maurice Albray

Michel Bouquet and Stephane Audran give superb performances in Claude Chabrol's LA FEMME INFIDELE, a gripping and stylishly made suspense tale.

Charles Desvallees (Michel Bouquet), a wealthy, mild-mannered insurance broker suspects that his wife Helene (Stephane Audran) is cheating on him. The detective reports that Helene spends her afternoons in the apartment of a divorced writer named Victor Pegala (Maurice Ronet). Charles visits Victor and sees Helene s cigarette lighter, and so questions him. As Victor starts to brag about their affair, Charles picks up a statuette and hits him over the head with it, killing him. He then calmly cleans up the blood, puts Victor's corpse into a sack and dumps it into a pond, then returns home to his son's birthday party. Helene is mystified by her lover's disappearance, but when the police interrogate her, she lies about their relationship. Subsequently, Helene finds a picture of Victor in Charles's coat pocket that would incriminate him in Victor's murder, but instead of informing the police, she burns it. Ironically, Helene develops a new-found love and respect for Charles, although neither of them lets the other know what they've done.

LA FEMME INFIDELE is arguably the best of Chabrol's superb, Hitchcockian studies of guilt, love, and murder among the French elite. His masterful, elegantly detached direction and trenchant psychological insight create ate moments of almost unbearable tension and suspense, aided by Jean Rabier's subtly sinister camera movements. Michel Bouquet and Stephane Audran (who was Chabrol's real-life wife at the time), give perhaps the finest performances of their careers. The two stars perfectly capture the deluded sensibility of their privileged characters in a satirical way without resorting to ridicule. Chabrol has stated that he makes films about the bourgeoisie because "I am one myself—I know them and I hate them, especially their extraordinary egoism." In Charles and Helene's complacent world of decorum and insincere emotions, nothing must be allowed to intrude to upset the balance and niceties of daily life, even murder.

LA FEMME NIKITA

(NIKITA)

1990 115m   c   Action/Drama
Films du Loup/Cecchi Gori Group/Tiger
Cinematografica/Gaumont Production   (France/Italy)

DVD
★★★
R

Anne Parillaud *(Nikita)*, Jean-Hugues Anglade *(Marco)*, Tcheky Karyo *(Bob)*, Jeanne Moreau *(Amande)*, Jean Reno *(Nikita's Partner)*, Jean Bouise *(Cabinet Chief)*, Philippe DuJanerand *(Ambassador)*, Roland Blanche *(Police Investigator)*, Phillipe Leroy-Beaulieu *(Commander Grossman)*, Marc Duret *(Rico)*

d, Luc Besson; w, Luc Besson; ph, Thierry Arbogast; ed, Olivier Mauffroy; m, Eric Serra; prod d, Dan Weil

A high-gloss thriller from director-writer Luc Besson about the transformation of a sociopathic punk into a beautiful, enigmatic spy.

After casually shooting a policeman during a bungled robbery attempt, Nikita (Parillaud) is tried and sentenced to death. Her nihilism lands her the chance to forego her sentence, in return for agreeing to work as an undercover government agent/hit-person. During several years of training in a mysterious high-tech compound, Nikita begins by exuding attitude—i.e. biting the ear of her karate instructor—but finally shapes up as an operative and is "released" into the world for a series of sleek, if farfetched assignments.

In the tradition of NOTORIOUS and DISHONORED, LA FEMME NIKITA features a morally questionable beauty burnished by a master spy, only to be converted from the secret trade by both a lover and the harsher elements of spycraft. LA FEMME NIKITA has far less substance than either of those films, offering little in the way of character development or verisimilitude. We are never given a rationale for Nikita's missions, and the screenplay never even begins to explain her behavior. Jeanne Moreau's cameo as a woman who instructs our heroine in the art of femininity borders on the ludicrous. For fans of Besson (SUBWAY, THE BIG BLUE), though, that's hardly the point. The director has turned out a supremely slick piece of entertainment where style triumphs over substance. The beautiful Parillaud leads us on a high-tech rollercoaster ride which, if you don't mind the stylized ultra-violence and throwaway plot, can be a lot of fun.

LA GUERRE EST FINIE   **DVD**
(KRIGETAR SLUT)
1966   121m   bw   Drama   ★★★★
Sofracima/Europa   (France/Sweden)

Yves Montand (Diego), Ingrid Thulin (Marianne), Genevieve Bujold (Nadine Sallanches), Jean Daste (Chief), Jorge Semprun (Narrator), Dominique Rozan (Jude), Jean-Francois Remi (Juan), Marie Mergey (Madame Lopez), Jacques Wallet (CRS Policeman), Michel Piccoli (1st Customs Inspector)

p, Catherine Winter, Gisele Rebillon; d, Alain Resnais; w, Jorge Semprun; ph, Sacha Vierny; ed, Eric Pluet; m, Giovanni Fusco; cos, Marie Martine

AAN Best Original Story and Screenplay: Jorge Semprun

Montand is Diego, a longtime revolutionary who lives in Paris. He has been active against the Spanish government and is now returning from Madrid carrying a false passport. The Guardia Civil stops him at the border and tries to determine his real identity, but a call to his Paris phone number turns up Nadine (Bujold), a student in the revolutionary movement who corroborates his papers. Diego returns to Paris to learn that his pals have been captured in Madrid and that his local contact, Juan (Remi), went back to Spain at the same time he was returning to France. Diego wants to help Juan, but has difficulties enlisting any aid for the mission.

He turns briefly to Nadine for love, but soon goes back to his former mistress Marianne (Thulin), a divorcee who is raising a son on her own. Diego still yearns to go to Madrid to aid the cause, but others in his group forbid their well-known colleague from going and send another (Jean Bouise) in his place. Diego must also contend with the plans of Nadine and her student comrades to terrorize tourists in Spain in order to publicize their political beliefs. Ultimately, though, Diego does head for Madrid, where things go awry almost instantly.

This picture has more tension than action, which is typical of director Resnais, who gave us the endlessly teasing LAST YEAR AT MARIENBAD. Filmed in and around Paris, LA GUERRE EST FINIE never did much at the box office and sank into the sunset all too quickly. Not Resnais' greatest effort, but a provocative portrait of political rebels and a challenging anti-war film just the same.

LA MARSEILLAISE
1938   130m   bw   Historical/War   ★★★½
La Marseillaise Society   (France)

Pierre Renoir (Louis XVI), Lise Delamare (Marie Antoinette), Leon Larive (Picard), William Haguet (La Rochefoucald-Liancourt), Louis Jouvet (Roederer), Aime Clariond (M. de Saint-Laurent), Maurice Escande (Le Seigneur du Village), Andre Zibral (M. de Saint Merri), Andrex (Arnaud), Ardisson (Bomier)

d, Jean Renoir; w, Jean Renoir, Carl Koch, N. Martel Dreyfus, Mme. Jean-Paul Dreyfus; ph, Jean Bourgoin, Alain Douarinou, Jean-Marie Maillols, Jean-Paul Alphen, J. Louis; ed, Marguerite Renoir, Marthe Huguet; m, Lalande, Gretry, Jean-Philippe Rameau, Johann Sebastian Bach, Wolfgang Amadeus Mozart, Rouget de l'Isle, Joseph Kosma, Sauveplane; cos, Granier Chanel

LA MARSEILLAISE is essentially a grand march from Marseilles to Paris, contrasting the lives of the commoners with those of the aristocracy. It tells the story of a battalion of 500 volunteers who arrive in time to capture the Tuilleries, leading to the publication of the Brunswick Manifesto and the overthrow of the monarchy of Louis XVI. With this march, of course, came "La Marseillaise," sung energetically here by the peasants—first as a quiet melody and later as an anthem. Jean Renoir does what he does best in providing a naturalistic, nearly documentary portrayal of the characters. In one sense, LA MARSEILLAISE is something of a Western, its march like the progress of a wagon train. Released on the heels of the brilliant GRAND ILLUSION, it's reception suffered from the belief that a director can't make two masterpieces in a row.

LA NOTTE   **DVD**
1961   122m   bw   Drama   ★★★
Nepi/Silver/Sofitedip   (France/Italy)

Marcello Mastroianni (Giovanni), Jeanne Moreau (Lidia), Monica Vitti (Valentina Gherardini), Bernhard Wicki (Tommaso), Maria Pia Luzi (Patient), Rosy Mazzacurati (Resy), Guido A. Marsan (Fanti), Gitt Magrini (Signora Gherardini), Vincenzo Corbella (Gherardini), Giorgio Negro (Roberto)

p, Emanuele Cassuto; d, Michelangelo Antonioni; w, Michelangelo Antonioni, Tonino Guerra, Ennio Flaiano (based on a story by Michelangelo Antonioni); ph, Gianni Di Venanzo; ed, Eraldo Da Roma; m, Giorgio Gaslini

Marcello Mastroianni and Jeanne Moreau play husband and wife in Antonioni's study of emptiness and sterility in modern life and relationships.

It opens with their visit to a hospitalized friend dying of cancer. They are on their way to a party for the publication of Giovanni's (Mastroianni) new novel, but the celebration is cut short when Lidia (Moreau) informs him, en route, that she disgusts her and she no longer wants to live with him. She leaves the party and wanders the barren streets for the remainder of the night, while Giovanni chases after Valentina (Vitti), the young daughter of an industrialist who has offered him a job. When Lidia and Giovanni confront one another at home later, the news of a friend's death that night draws them together once again.

Much of Antonioni's greatness is evident in this picture—the seemingly hopeless relationship between a man and a woman, the overwhelming environment which is devoid of emotion, and the quietly observant camerawork. But at the same time Antonioni is sometimes painfully obvious with his use of symbolism. One of the film's major faults lies in its casting of Mastroianni, who simply doesn't fit his role. This problematic film serves more as a transition for Antonioni than anything else, and seems to make even less sense when screened without having seen his previous film, the masterful L'AVVENTURA.

LA NUIT DE VARENNES
1982   135m   c   Historical/Comedy   ★★★★
Gaumont/Columbia   (France/Italy)   R

Marcello Mastroianni (Casanova), Jean-Louis Barrault (Nicolas Edme Restif), Hanna Schygulla (Countess Sophie de la Borde), Harvey Keitel (Thomas Paine), Jean-Claude Brialy (M. Jacob),

Daniel Gelin *(De Wendel)*, Jean-Louis Trintignant *(M. Sauce)*, Michel Piccoli *(King Louis XVI)*, Eleonore Hirt *(Queen Marie-Antoinette)*, Andrea Ferreol *(Mme. Adelaide Gagnon)*

p, Renzo Rossellini; d, Ettore Scola; w, Ettore Scola, Sergio Amidei; ph, Armando Nannuzzi; ed, Raimondo Crociani; m, Armando Travajoi; art d, Dante Ferretti; cos, Gabriella Pescucci

This fine, often bizarre, historical drama begins with a basis in fact and runs wild with imaginative possibilities. King Louis XVI (Michel Piccoli) and his queen (Eleonore Hirt) flee Paris for the safety of Varennes at the height of the French Revolution. Close behind in a pursuing coach, bickering about life and politics, are Casanova (Marcello Mastroianni, in an excellent performance) and American revolutionary Thomas Paine (Harvey Keitel). All the while, the revolution spreads like wildfire. As with other recent films by Italian director Ettore Scola—LE BAL, MACARONI, THE FAMILY—the exploration of the past becomes a vehicle for understanding today's problems and those of the future.

Besides the benefits of the lush photography and elegant costumes, Scola again works with an excellent cast that reads as a virtual Who's Who of European cinema, including Jean-Louis Barrault, Hanna Schygulla, Jean-Claude Brialy, Jean-Louis Trintignant, Andrea Ferreol and Daniel Gelin. A feast of a film in many ways.

LA RONDE
1950 93m   bw   Drama   ★★★★★
Societe des Films Sacha Gordine   (France)

Anton Walbrook *(Master of Ceremonies)*, Simone Signoret *(Leocadie—the Prostitute)*, Serge Reggiani *(Franz—the Soldier)*, Simone Simon *(Marie—the Chambermaid)*, Daniel Gelin *(Alfred—the Young Man)*, Danielle Darrieux *(Emma Breitkopf—the Married Lady)*, Fernand Gravety *(Charles—the Husband)*, Odette Joyeux *(The Grisette)*, Jean-Louis Barrault *(Robert Kuhlenkampf—the Poet)*, Isa Miranda *(The Actress)*

p, Sacha Gordine; d, Max Ophuls; w, Max Ophuls, Jacques Natanson (based on the play *Der Reigen* by Arthur Schnitzler); ph, Christian Matras; ed, Leonide Azar, S. Rondeau; m, Oscar Straus; art d, Marpaux, M. Frederix, Jean d'Eaubonne; cos, Georges Annenkov

AAN Best Screenplay: Jacques Natanson, Max Ophuls; *AAN Best Art Direction-Set Decoration (B/W):* D'Eaubonne (Art Direction)

Released in Paris in 1950, LA RONDE, though quickly hailed as one of Max Ophuls' greatest achievements, was kept from U.S. shores for four years thanks to a judgment of "immoral" by the New York State censorship board. A merry-go-round of romance is detailed in episodic fashion as characters drift from sequence to sequence, switching lovers as they go.

A young prostitute (Signoret) meets a soldier (Reggiani), who leaves her for a maid (Simon). The maid, however, soon meets another (Gelin), who seduces a wealthy married woman (Darrieux), whose husband is involved with a young worker (Joyeux). This woman in turn loves a poet (Barrault) in love with an actress (Miranda). The actress, however, loves an officer (Philipe). Love comes around full circle when he calls on the prostitute from the first episode. Each segment is delightfully introduced by a master of ceremonies (Walbrook), who appears with the metaphorical carousel in each of his scenes.

Originally Ophuls had planned to adapt a novel by Balzac with Greta Garbo in a lead role, but instead he turned his attentions to the heralded Arthur Schnitzler play, which in his hands emphasized the follies of love over the concerns about syphillis the play explored. One of four masterworks Ophuls dashed off in the 1950s before his untimely death, LA RONDE explores his recurrent obsession with circles to dizzying effect. The humor is beguiling, the satire on target, Ophuls legendary camerawork is in fine and restless form, and the acting of a very high order.

Signoret is particularly good, but stealing the show, unexpectedly, is the marvelous Walbrook. Indulging the gentle sentiment of the whole undertaking to just the right degree, he is dapper and alert. The moment where one story is interrupted as he quickly reassembles the broken film is perfection. You're not likely to forget Walbrook's song—a round, of course.

L.A. STORY   *DVD*
1991 95m   c   Comedy/Romance   ★★½
Carolco/IndieProd Company/L.A. Films   PG-13
(U.S.)

Steve Martin *(Harris K. Telemacher)*, Victoria Tennant *(Sara)*, Richard E. Grant *(Roland)*, Marilu Henner *(Trudi)*, Sarah Jessica Parker *(SanDeE*)*, Susan Forristal *(Ariel)*, Kevin Pollak *(Frank Swan)*, Sam McMurray *(Morris Frost)*, Patrick Stewart *(Maitre d' at l'Idiot)*, Andrew Amador *(Male News Reporter)*

p, Daniel Melnick, Michael Rachmil; d, Mick Jackson; w, Steve Martin (from his story); ph, Andrew Dunn; ed, Richard A. Harris; m, Peter Melnick; prod d, Lawrence Miller; art d, Charles Breen; cos, Rudy Dillon

In its dream-like sweetness and fairy tale romanticism, L.A. STORY resembles another film written by and starring Steve Martin, ROXANNE. But the comic romance that was that film's *raison d'etre* is not much in evidence here.

The film unfolds from the clear-eyed gaze of Harris K. Telemacher (Martin), who immediately reveals his peculiar malaise by confiding to us: "I was deeply unhappy but I didn't know it because I was happy all the time." As a TV news program's wacky weekend weatherman, Telemacher predicts the predictable, propagating a heaven-on-earth Los Angeles of perfect sunshine and a perpetual temperature of 72 degrees. But pockets of unease quietly begin to undermine his complacency, culminating in an outdoor luncheon with his testy girlfriend Trudi (Henner) and a group of shallow acquaintances. Arriving late is unconventional British reporter Sara (Tennant), to whom Harris is curiously attracted. Shortly afterward, Harris has an epiphany on the Los Angeles Freeway, and his life is turned upside down.

In L.A. STORY, the romance assumes a supporting role beside the mystical, apocalyptic aura evoked by the city itself. The characters in the film have no past, no future, and are in the grip of the off-balance life of L.A. Unlike Woody Allen's New York City, which becomes a staging area for character angst and transformation, Martin's L.A. stifles the characters, and neither they, screenwriter Martin or director Jackson seem to be aware of it. Instead, Harris and Sara find themselves put through the paces of a Spielbergian fantasy landscape as they gaze upward at the divine white aura of a Hollywood sign before the final clinch. And it is a sad loss, for the filmmakers squandered the opportunity to produce a satiric West Coast MANHATTAN.

LA STRADA   *DVD*
1954 115m   bw   Drama   ★★★★★
Trans-Lux   (Italy)

Giulietta Masina *(Gelsomina)*, Anthony Quinn *(Zampano)*, Richard Basehart *(Matto "The Fool")*, Aldo Silvani *(Columbiani)*, Marcella Rovere *(La Vedova)*, Livia Venturini *(La Suorina)*, Gustavo Giorgi, Kamadeva Yami, Mario Passante, Anna Primula

p, Carlo Ponti, Dino De Laurentiis; d, Federico Fellini; w, Federico Fellini, Tullio Pinelli, Ennio Flaiano (based on a story by Federico

Fellini and Tullio Pinelli); ph, Otello Martelli; ed, Leo Catozzo, Lina Caterini; m, Nino Rota; art d, Mario Ravasco, E. Cervelli

AA Best Foreign Language Film ; AAN Best Original Screenplay: Federico Fellini, Tullio Pinelli

Federico Fellini was at the top of his form here, as was his wife and frequent star, Giulietta Masina, whose pantomime in LA STRADA caused her to be dubbed a female Chaplin. She *is* marvelous.

Zampano (Anthony Quinn), a traveling strongman, "buys" the dim-witted but pure of heart Gelsomina (Masina) to help him with his act. The two travel together, with her beating the drum and playing a trumpet to herald his act, and serving as his mistress and slave. Eventually, the pair join a tiny circus and meet il Matto ("The Fool," played by Richard Basehart), a clown and high-wire artist who treats Gelsomina kindly. When the ethereal Fool is accidentally killed by the brutish Zampano, she is devastated and suffers an emotional breakdown, and the strongman abandons her. Many years later, still traveling, Zampano learns of Gelsomina's fate and belatedly realizes his need for her.

Perhaps the simplest and certainly one of the most powerful of Fellini's films, LA STRADA established his international fame while marking a distinct break from neorealism in its poetic, deeply personal imagery (especially the "Felliniesque" circus motif), and religious symbolism. While Masina's unforgettable performance, perfectly combining comedy and pathos, caused the greatest stir, Quinn and Basehart are also excellent, and Nino Rota's music became famous worldwide.

LA TERRA TREMA
1947 160m bw Drama   *DVD* ★★★★★
Universalia   (Italy)

Luchino Visconti, Antonio Pietrangeli *(Narrators)*, Antonio Arcidiacono

p, Salvo D'Angelo; d, Luchino Visconti; w, Luchino Visconti (based on the novel *I Malavoglia* by Giovanni Verga); ph, G.R. Aldo; ed, Mario Serandrei

With a lyrical, even operatic quality that subtly combines photographic beauty with the cruel plight of its subjects, LA TERRA TREMA is one of the greatest films to emerge from the Italian neorealist movement.

Set in Aci-Trezza, a small Sicilian fishing village, with the entire cast consisting of locals—their weather-beaten faces lending a sense of realism—the film involves the villagers' victimization by the entrepreneurs who control the fishing market. One young man, 'Ntoni (Antonio Arcidiacono), returns home from WWII convinced that the villagers need no longer be subject to such unfairness, that by pulling together they can alter the system and eventually overcome their imposed poverty.

LA TERRA TREMA is a powerful picture that exposes the injustice inherent in a society where the privileged are allowed to ride roughshod over their inferiors. Despite its social import, the film was a terrible failure at the Italian theaters. Its historical significance, however, is immense. The use of non-professional actors, deep-focus cinematography, natural light, and direct sound recording, while rarely seen in Italian films of the day, were all integral to LA TERRA TREMA—products undoubtedly of Visconti's work with Jean Renoir.

Serving as assistant directors on this picture were Francesco Rosi and Franco Zeffirelli, both of whom would eventually become leading directors. LA TERRA TREMA today stands as one of the most brilliant combinations of the realistic with the stylized that Visconti ever achieved.

LA TRAVIATA
1982 105m c Opera   *DVD* ★★★★
Accent/RA-1   (Italy)   G

Teresa Stratas *(Violetta Valery)*, Placido Domingo *(Alfredo Germont)*, Cornell MacNeil *(Giorgio Germont)*, Alan Monk *(Baron)*, Axelle Gall *(Flora Betvoix)*, Pina Cei *(Annina)*, Maurizio Barbacini *(Gastone)*, Robert Sommer *(Doctor Grenvil)*, Ricardo Oneto *(Marquis d'Obigny)*, Luciano Brizi *(Giuseppe)*

p, Tarak Ben Ammar; d, Franco Zeffirelli; w, Franco Zeffirelli (based on the libretto by Francesco Maria Piave from the novel *The Lady of the Camelias* by Alexandre Dumas); ph, Ennio Guarnieri; ed, Peter Taylor, Franca Sylvi; m, Giuseppe Verdi; prod d, Franco Zeffirelli; art d, Gianni Quaranta; chor, Alberto Testa; cos, Piero Tosi

AAN Best Art Direction-Set Decoration: Franco Zeffirelli (Art Direction), Gianni Quaranta (Set Decoration); *AAN Best Costume Design:* Piero Tosi

Franco Zeffirelli's version of the classic Verdi opera stars Teresa Stratas as Violetta and Placido Domingo as her lover, Alfredo. Zeffirelli outdoes himself this time, offering no less than one of cinema's finest opera adaptations. LA TRAVIATA boasts not only the presence of Domingo and the electrifying Stratas but some truly amazing camerawork. The camera dollies, zooms, cranes and pans relentlessly showcase the gigantic, elaborately constructed set. Indeed, cinematographer Ennio Guarnieri and art designer Gianni Quaranta have joined forces with Zeffirelli to present a feast for the eyes—a worthy accompaniment to the brilliant score.

LABYRINTH
1986 101m c Science Fiction/Children's/Fantasy   *DVD* ★★★½
Tri-Star   (U.S.)   PG

David Bowie *(Jareth)*, Jennifer Connelly *(Sarah)*, Toby Froud *(Toby)*, Shelley Thompson *(Stepmother)*, Christopher Malcolm *(Father)*, Natalie Finland *(Fairy)*, Shari Weiser *(Hoggle)*, Rob Mills *(Ludo)*, David Barclay *(Didymus)*, Karen Prell *(The Worm/Junk Lady)*

p, Eric Rattray; d, Jim Henson; w, Terry Jones (based on a story by Dennis Less, Henson); ph, Alex Thomson; ed, John Grover; m, Trevor Jones; prod d, Elliot Scott; art d, Roger Cain, Peter Howitt, Michael White, Terry Ackland-Snow; fx, George Gibbs; chor, Cheryl McFadden, Charles Augins, Michael Moschen; cos, Brian Froud, Ellis Flyte

Muppet creator Jim Henson, who previously directed THE DARK CRYSTAL, special-effects master George Lucas, screenwriter Terry Jones (of Monty Python fame), and rock star-actor David Bowie combined their talents to produce this fantasy reminiscent of THE WIZARD OF OZ, ALICE IN WONDERLAND and Maurice Sendak's "Outside over There." While baby-sitting, Sarah (Connelly), a suburban teenager, lets her imagination run wild and goes on a magical adventure to rescue her brother from Jareth (Bowie), the goblin king, who is holding the boy in his castle on the other side of an intricate maze. Along the way she meets an array of charming creatures and overcomes great danger, as well as Jareth's deceptions, to learn that the surest route to her brother is both simple and direct.

The finest work that the late Henson had yet produced, LABYRINTH packs enough surprises to captivate an audience of children and provides enough wisecracking to keep adults laughing. Besides acting in the role of the goblin king, Bowie (who was chosen for the role from a group of rock stars that included Mick Jagger, Sting and Michael Jackson) composed and performed a number of songs for the film.

LABYRINTH OF PASSION
(LABERINTO DE PASIONES)
1982 100m c   Comedy   ★★★★
Alphaville   (Spain)

Cecilia Roth *(Sexilia)*, Luis Ciges *(Her Father)*, Imanol Arias *(Riza Niro)*, Antonio Banderas *(Sadeq)*, Helga Line *(Toraya)*, Marta Fernandez-Muro *(Queti)*, Angel Alcazar *(Eusebio)*, Agustin Almodovar *(Hassan)*, Pedro Almodovar *(Performer)*

d, Pedro Almodovar; w, Pedro Almodovar; ph, Angel L. Fernandez; ed, Jose Salcedo; prod d, Pedro Almodovar

Made in 1982, but released in the U.S. in 1990 following the success of WOMEN ON THE VERGE OF A NERVOUS BREAKDOWN, Pedro Almodovar's LABYRINTH OF PASSION is a screwball sex comedy set in a world of unorthodox and baroquely intertwined personal relationships in Madrid. Predicated on mistaken identity and misinterpreted motives, the plot is a tangle that defies simple summary.

Among the some 50 characters is Sexilia (Cecilia Roth), "Sexi" for short, a carefree, heliophobic nymphomaniac whose father (Luis Ciges) is a repressed, world-famous fertility specialist. Hoping to exorcise her fear of sunlight, Sexi consults a therapist, who announces that Sexi's trouble is incestuous attraction to her father. The therapist then confesses her own determination to seduce the fertility expert, whose patients include the manipulative, aristocratic Toraya (Helga Line). Toraya, in turn, has designs on Riza Niro (Imanol Arias), the gay son of the deposed ruler of the Arab nation of Tyran. Riza, who just wants to cruise the Spanish bars and docks incognito, has difficulty maintaining a low profile. Scandal sheets speculate about his activities, revolutionary student terrorists hope to kidnap him, and Toraya is determined to find and seduce him as part of a plot to avenge herself on his father. Blithely unaware of these goings-on, Riza meets Sexi in a discotheque, and they fall head over heels for one another. Needless to say, the course of their love—true though it is—does not run smooth.

What gives the film its revolutionary twist is the breadth of its definition of love. LABYRINTH OF PASSION's sexual landscape is a virtual catalogue of erotic possibility, a pop paean to a multiplicity of forms and desires. Old and young, fat and thin, beautiful and homely pair off and break up according to the whims of outrageous fortune, paying little, if any, attention to conventional notions of appropriate coupling. And in the end, all's well that ends well—an optimistic message delivered with sophisticated, satirical bite.

LACOMBE, LUCIEN
1974 141m c   Drama/War   ★★★★
Fox   (U.S.)   R

Pierre Blaise *(Lucien)*, Aurore Clement *(France)*, Holger Lowenadler *(Albert Horn)*, Therese Gieshe *(Bella Horn)*, Stephane Bouy *(Jean Bernard)*, Loumi Iacobesco *(Betty Beaulieu)*, Rene Bouloc *(Faure)*, Pierre Decazes *(Aubert)*, Jean Rougerie *(Tonin)*, Gilberte Rivet *(Mme. Lacombe)*

p, Louis Malle; d, Louis Malle; w, Louis Malle, Patrick Modiano; ph, Tonino Delli Colli (Eastmancolor); ed, Suzanne Baron; m, Django Reinhardt, Andre Claveau, Irene de Trebert; art d, Ghislain Uhry

AAN Best Foreign Language Film

A masterful job. Director Louis Malle directs his intellectual focus at the Occupation this time around. Blaise plays Lucien, a young farm boy who tries to join the French Resistance but is rejected because of his youth. The Gestapo, however, is happy to have him and treats the boy royally, supplying him with liquor and anything else he requests. He then makes the mistake of falling in love with a Jewish girl, France (Clement), resulting in her father's deportation. With France and her mother in tow, Lucien sets out for Spain with the Resistance out to kill him.

LACOMBE, LUCIEN represents a turn for the better for Malle, whose sometimes tends to shroud audience sympathy in underdeveloped intellectualizing. Much of Malle's motivation came from his own experiences growing up in France during the German Occupation. Even so, his fellow countrymen did not care very much for this cutting portrayal of the Resistance. Their vocal indictments inspired Malle to migrate to America, where he made such films as ATLANTIC CITY and PRETTY BABY. A great score by Reinhardt helps flesh out this moving, carefully handled film.

LADDER 49
2004 105m c   Action/Thriller/Drama   ★★½
Touchstone/Beacon Pictures/Casey Silver   PG-13
Productions/Fantail Films   (U.S.)

Joaquin Phoenix *(Jack Morrison)*, John Travolta *(Captain Mike Kennedy)*, Jacinda Barrett *(Linda Morrison)*, Robert Patrick *(Lenny Richter)*, Morris Chestnut *(Tommy Drake)*, Billy Burke *(Dennis Gauquin)*, Balthazar Getty *(Ray Gauquin)*, Tim Guinee *(Tony Corrigan)*, Kevin Chapman *(Frank McKinney)*, Jay Hernandez *(Keith Perez)*

p, Casey Silver; d, Jay Russell; w, Lewis Colick; ph, James L. Carter; ed, Bud Smith, Scott Smith; m, William Ross; prod d, Tony Burrough; art d, Gregory Bolton, Kevin Constant; fx, Peter Donen, Larry Fioritto; cos, Elizabeth Shelton

Though handsomely mounted, this mass of firefighter cliches swings wildly between heartstring-tugging melodrama, testosterone-fueled action, and buddy comedy, weighed down by too many predictable twists and storytelling contrivances.

After a valiant effort to save a civilian from a blazing warehouse, Baltimore firefighter Jack Morrison (Joaquin Phoenix) finds himself trapped inside the crumbling cement building. As Capt. Mike Kennedy (John Travolta) directs rescue efforts outside, Jack reminisces about the highlights of his career and life. He starts with his first day on the job, when Mike, his new boss and mentor, welcomed him with an elaborate initiation prank. Jack soon develops a strong bond with Mike and the rest of the hardworking men who fight fires from Engine 33, as well as their companion search-and-rescue squad on Ladder 49. He becomes especially close to thoughtful family man Tommy Drake (Morris Chestnut) and laid-back ladies' man Dennis Gauquin (Billy Burke). Jack marries Linda (Jacinda Barrett), the dream girl he meets at a grocery store, and as their responsibilities grow, both become ever more aware of the costly risks of his honorable job, a point brought home vividly when a member of Jack's close-knit firehouse family dies in the line of duty.

Director Jay Russell does a tremendous job creating vivid, claustrophobic scenes of burning buildings, and makes an admirable effort to show the camaraderie that unites the firefighters. But too many solid supporting actors are given too little to do, their underwritten characters forgotten as soon as they're off-screen. A surprisingly toned-down Travolta and a beefed-up Phoenix are well cast, but the film falters when Jack and Linda's relationship is pushed to the forefront.

LADY AND THE TRAMP
1955 75m c   Animated   ★★★★
Walt Disney Productions   (U.S.)   G

VOICES OF: Peggy Lee *(Darling/Peg/Si/Am)*, Barbara Luddy *(Lady)*, Larry Roberts *(Tramp)*, Bill Thompson *(Jock/Bull/Dachsie)*, Bill Baucon *(Trusty)*, Stan Freberg *(Beaver)*, Verna Felton *(Aunt Sarah)*, Alan Reed *(Boris)*, George Givot *(Tony)*, Dal McKennon *(Toughy/Professor)*

p, Walt Disney; d, Hamilton Luske, Clyde Geronimi, Wilfred Jackson; w, Erdman Penner, Joe Rinaldi, Ralph Wright, Don DaGradi (based on the novel by Ward Greene); ed, Donald Halliday; m, Oliver Wallace; anim, Milt Kahl, Franklin Thomas, Oliver M. Johnston, John Lounsbery, Wolfgang Reitherman, Eric Larson, Hal King, Les Clark

This animated Disney classic tells the tale of Lady, a prim and proper cocker spaniel who falls in love with Tramp, a ragged mutt. When Lady runs away from her owner and is pursued by tough dogs in a bad neighborhood, Tramp rescues her. The two dogs spend a night on the town, which includes the memorable spaghetti-eating scene in which both Lady and Tramp eat the same strand, their mouths drawn closer and closer until at last they kiss. Lady is furious with Tramp when they end up in the pound after being caught raiding a chicken coup, but by the finale they are happily raising their own litter of pups. Disney's first CinemaScope cartoon, LADY AND THE TRAMP cost $4,000,000 and took three years to complete, but it grossed over $25,000,000, making more money than any other film from the 1950s except THE TEN COMMANDMENTS and BEN-HUR.

LADY EVE, THE   *DVD*
1941 97m   bw   Comedy/Romance   ★★★★★
Paramount   (U.S.)

Barbara Stanwyck (Jean Harrington), Henry Fonda (Charles Pike), Charles Coburn ("Colonel" Harry Harrington), Eugene Pallette (Mr. Pike), William Demarest (Muggsy-Ambrose Murgatroyd), Eric Blore (Sir Alfred McGlennan Keith), Melville Cooper (Gerald), Martha O'Driscoll (Martha), Janet Beecher (Mrs. Pike), Robert Greig (Burrows)

p, Paul Jones; d, Preston Sturges; w, Preston Sturges (based on the story "The Faithful Heart" by Monckton Hoffe); ph, Victor Milner; ed, Stuart Gilmore; art d, Hans Dreier, Ernst Fegte; cos, Edith Head

AAN Best Original Story: Monckton Hoffe

Sturges's chic, sly little masterpiece of comic seduction. Fonda, who is the son of a wealthy brewer (Pallette, whose slogan is "Pike's Pale, the Ale That Won for Yale"), is a rather shy and backward young man whose main interest is in snakes. As the film opens, he has just spent a year with a scientific expedition on the Amazon, looking for undiscovered species of reptiles. He and his bodyguard, Demarest, board a ship in the Atlantic which will take them back to New York. Of course, Fonda, being young, handsome, and the heir to a vast fortune, attracts the attention of virtually every female on the ship, but he shows no interest in the opposite sex.

Also on board is a team of card sharps, father and daughter Stanwyck and Coburn, and Cooper, posing as their butler. They figure Fonda would make an excellent pigeon, and Stanwyck conspires to gain his trust, which she does. Fonda is quickly smitten with her, and sits down to play some cards with her and her father. He considers himself to be quite the card player, but is embarrassed when he wins $600 from these nice people. Of course, he's only being set up to lose, but before the cons can reel in their prey, they hit a snag. Stanwyck has genuinely fallen in love with the man, much to the disgust of her associates.

THE LADY EVE is one of Sturges' best romantic comedies, with just the right blend of satire and slapstick, the laughs coming mostly from his clever, often inspired comedic lines. His direction is flawless, and the cast, from stars to stock players, performs beautifully. Stanwyck, is particular, is an effortless comedienne. She pitches much of her performance into a kind of hushed, urgent, intimate whisper. When she talks to Fonda, she's constantly toying with him, touching him like a fetish, and she's always in his face, often looking at his lips. Then out snakes a sexy leg—a very sexy leg—and over he topples. There's an unparalleled moment early on, when she narrates his movements, taking his part and every woman's who attempts to

trap him in conversation, while watching the action backwards in her compact mirror. It's a daring, roguish display of her talent; one can't imagine any comedienne—even Colbert or Russell—bringing it off as she does. Sturges, who began as a contract scriptwriter for Paramount, promised Stanwyck that he would write a great comedy for her some day, and she got it.

LADY FROM SHANGHAI, THE   *DVD*
1948 87m   bw   Crime   ★★★★½
Columbia   (U.S.)

Rita Hayworth (Elsa Bannister), Orson Welles (Michael O'Hara), Everett Sloane (Arthur Bannister), Glenn Anders (George Grisby), Ted de Corsia (Sidney Broome), Erskine Sanford (Judge), Gus Schilling (Goldie), Carl Frank (District Attorney), Lou Merrill (Jake), Evelyn Ellis (Bessie)

p, Orson Welles; d, Orson Welles; w, Orson Welles (based on the novel by [Raymond] Sherwood King); ph, Charles Lawton Jr.; ed, Viola Lawrence; m, Heinz Roemheld; art d, Stephen Goosson, Sturges Carne; fx, Lawrence Butler; cos, Jean Louis

This remarkably inventive if decidedly confusing film noir stars Welles as a wandering Irishman named Michael O'Hara. One evening he saves Elsa Bannister (Hayworth) from a couple of thugs and, as a result, she is drawn to him like a shark to a swimmer. Her husband, famed lawyer Arthur Bannister (Sloane), offers to hire O'Hara as a deckhand for an upcoming cruise. O'Hara—who begins the film by saying, "When I start out to make a fool of myself, there's very little can stop me!"—accepts the offer, trying not to succumb to Elsa's advances along the way. Pretty soon O'Hara is on his way to making an A-1 fool out of himself, entering into an agreement with Bannister's goony, sweat-stained friend George Grisby (Anders), who offers O'Hara a sum of money to stage Grisby's own murder. When things start to misfire, O'Hara becomes, in fatalistic noir fashion, a puppet under the reckless control of everyone around him.

Replete with humorous self-deprecating narration, marvelous performances, and typically Wellesian visuals, THE LADY FROM SHANGHAI dazzles as much as it obfuscates. The most amazing visual effect is the climactic Crazy House/Hall of Mirrors location, which is a wonder of surrealistic set design. With its complex and occasionally incoherent narrative, the film will stump many of those viewers who think they can easily decipher a mystery. Fans of Rita Hayworth, then Welles's wife, were shocked—as was studio mogul Harry Cohn—when they saw her long, luxuriant russet hair cut into a blonde bob. The yacht on which the characters sail belonged to Welles's friend Errol Flynn, and it is Flynn (unseen) who is sailing the vessel during the trip. An uneven film, perhaps, but one which only seems to improve with age.

LADY IN THE DARK
1944 100m   c   Musical   ★★★
Paramount   (U.S.)

Ginger Rogers (Liza Elliott), Ray Milland (Charley Johnson), Jon Hall (Randy Curtis), Warner Baxter (Kendall Nesbitt), Barry Sullivan (Dr. Brooks), Mischa Auer (Russell Paxton), Mary Philips (Maggie Grant), Phyllis Brooks (Allison DuBois), Edward Fielding (Dr. Carlton), Don Loper (Adams)

p, Richard Blumenthal; d, Mitchell Leisen; w, Frances Goodrich, Albert Hackett (based on the play by Moss Hart, Kurt Weill, Ira Gershwin); ph, Ray Rennahan, Farciot Edouart (Technicolor); ed, Alma Macrorie; m, Robert Emmett Dolan; art d, Hans Dreier, Raoul Pene du Bois; fx, Gordon Jennings, Paul K. Lerpae; chor, Billy Daniels, Don Loper; cos, Edith Head, Mitchell Leisen, Babs Wilomez, Raoul Pene Du Bois

AAN Best Color Cinematography: Ray Rennahan; *AAN Best Score (Musical):* Robert Emmett Dolan; *AAN Best Interior Decoration (Color):* Hans Dreier (Art Direction), Raoul Pene DuBois (Art Direction), Ray Moyer (Interior Decoration)

LADY IN THE DARK seemed like a breakthrough on Broadway, where it featured Danny Kaye and Victor Mature in support of Gertrude Lawrence. Unfortunately, none of these suitably cast players made it to the screen version, and the loss is evident. Also regrettable is the excising of several wonderful Weill-Gershwin tunes from the play in favor of new songs that don't enhance the plot. As if all this weren't enough, even the original's book doesn't seem quite as good as its reputation would suggest.

Ginger Rogers (in her first color film) is Liza Elliott, a magazine editor who's on the verge of a nervous breakdown, partly because she has too many men in her life. She seeks help from a psychiatrist (Sullivan), and her sessions with him and some dream sequences provide the material for the film's production numbers. Vying for Liza's attention and threatening her job security are Charley Johnson (Milland), the advertising manager for her magazine; recently divorced Kendall Nesbitt (Baxter); and handsome hunk Randy Curtis (Hall).

This expensive film made a lot of money upon its 1944 release, when audiences were clamoring for something light to relieve wartime anxieties. The story was unusual then, dealing as it did with Liza's position in a high-pressured man's world, her precarious emotional state (presented in Freudian terms that were still fairly novel for most moviegoers), and her inability to make a decision. It's all lavishly presented with glamorous style, but it's almost as if director Leisen cared more about the look of the film than its content.

Rogers has a good (if too distantly filmed) dance number with Don Loper, and she does a fine job singing the amusing "The Saga of Jenny," but her performance is uneven. The same goes for most of the cast, and even the storyline, missing the crucial song "My Ship" (from the heroine's childhood), seems a little out of kilter in retrospect. The result is a glitzy but superficial marriage of musical comedy and pop psychology.

LADY IN THE LAKE

1947   105m   bw   Mystery   ★★★½
MGM   (U.S.)

Robert Montgomery *(Philip Marlowe)*, Lloyd Nolan *(Lt. DeGarmot)*, Audrey Totter *(Adrienne Fromsett)*, Tom Tully *(Capt. Kane)*, Leon Ames *(Derace Kingsby)*, Jayne Meadows *(Mildred Havelend)*, Morris Ankrum *(Eugene Grayson)*, Lila Leeds *(Receptionist)*, Richard Simmons *(Chris Lavery)*, Ellen Ross *(Elevator Girl)*

p, George Haight; d, Robert Montgomery; w, Steve Fisher, Raymond Chandler (based on the novel by Chandler, uncredited); ph, Paul C. Vogel; ed, Gene Ruggiero; m, David Snell; art d, Cedric Gibbons, Preston Ames; fx, A. Arnold Gillespie; cos, Irene

"YOU accept an invitation to a blonde's apartment! YOU get socked in the jaw by a murder suspect!" That's how ads promoted this inventive if not entirely successful film noir, the first to employ a subjective camera. Under star Montgomery's direction, the viewer is in the film, so to speak, with all the action and characters addressing the camera, which tells the story from the point of view of Raymond Chandler's incorruptible private eye, Philip Marlowe.

The film opens as Marlowe begins to relate the "Lady in the Lake" caper. The subjective camera takes over, the story unfolding in flashback. Tired of sleuthing for a living, Marlowe has taken up writing and produced a number of detective stories that he has submitted to Kingsby Publications. Having read his most recent story, editor Adrienne Fromsett (Totter) asks that he come to see her. When he arrives in the magazine office, Marlowe learns that Adrienne is not really interested in his

story; instead she plans to wed Kingsby (Ames), and she wants the detective to find his missing wife so she can have her man. The first step in Marlowe's investigation is a visit to Lavery (Simmons), a wealthy, musclebound gigolo. At first, Montgomery is welcomed by the handsome young rake, but when the detective asks one sensitive question too many, he is suddenly punched silly.

Marlowe wakes up in the Bay City jail, where Lt. DeGarmot (Nolan) tells him that he was picked up for drunk driving. Marlowe claims that he was framed—averring that he was knocked out and had booze poured over him before he was thrown into his car, which was then sent careening down the street. Marlowe returns to Adrienne's office and informs her that he's dropping the case. Then comes a report that the wife of the caretaker of Kingsby's retreat at Little Fawn Lake has been murdered, her body found floating in the lake. Believing that the caretaker's wife was murdered by Kingsby's wife, Adrienne asks Marlowe to prove her theory so that the wife can be prosecuted for murder. The more Marlowe discovers about the lady in the lake, the more determined he is to stay with the case.

The cast is uniformly good, with Totter and Nolan real standouts. Appearing onscreen only in the introduction and conclusion (or when Marlowe looks into a mirror), Montgomery has deliberately and effectively soured his prewar playboy image. Yet Chandler not only disliked Montgomery's performance but hated the film itself, perhaps because of the hard time he had attempting to adapt his novel. (This was the only time Chandler was ever paid to create a screenplay from one of his original works.)

LADY IN WHITE

1988   112m   c   Thriller   ★★★★
New Century (U.S.)   PG-13

Lukas Haas *(Frankie Scarlatti)*, Len Cariou *(Phil)*, Alex Rocco *(Angelo Scarlatti)*, Katherine Helmond *(Amanda)*, Jason Presson *(Geno Scarlatti)*, Renata Vanni *(Mama Assunta)*, Angelo Bertolini *(Papa Charlie)*, Jared Rushton *(Donald)*, Gregory Levinson *(Louie)*, Joelle Jacob *(Melissa)*

p, Andrew G. La Marca, Frank LaLoggia; d, Frank LaLoggia; w, Frank LaLoggia; ph, Russell Carpenter (Deluxe Color); ed, Steve Mann; m, Frank LaLoggia; prod d, Richard K. Hummel; fx, Image Engineering, Fantasy II Film Effects; cos, Jacqueline Saint Anne

Independent filmmaker Frank LaLoggia's (FEAR NO EVIL) long-awaited second feature is an impressive, if overly ambitious, semiautobiographical ghost story that rejects gore in favor of genuine gothic chills.

Surprisingly rich in character, period, and place, LADY IN WHITE begins on Halloween, 1962, as the youngest son of a widower (Alex Rocco), young Frankie (Lukas Haas), is locked in the school cloakroom by pranksters who leave him there for the night. Resigned to his fate, Frankie climbs up on the top shelf and tries to get some sleep. Suddenly he is awakened by the ghost of a little girl (Joelle Jacob) about his age who was murdered in the cloakroom many years before. To his horror, Frankie watches as the murder of the child is reenacted before his eyes. Then, a real man, whose face is obscured, enters the cloakroom. It's the killer, and he has returned to the scene of the crime to remove the girl's hair clip, which fell down the heating duct during the murder so many years before (the school plans to install a new heater the very next day). Unfortunately for Frankie, the intruder notices the boy and tries to strangle him. Frankie survives the attack, and the police soon after arrest a drunken janitor and charge him with the attempted murder of Frankie, suspecting him of being the child killer who has plagued the town for several years. Frankie knows the man is innocent and sets out to find the real killer with the help of the little girl's ghost.

An intensely personal film, LADY IN WHITE is an incredibly ambitious low-budget effort that attempts to combine a good ghost story with a childhood reminiscence about growing up during the early 1960s. Fortunately, LaLoggia pulls off this unlikely combination, although his narrative is a bit too diffuse at times. Instead of using encounters with ghosts to escape the realities of everyday life, LaLoggia's film is firmly rooted in the real world—child murders, racism, and cruelty share the spotlight here. LaLoggia shares his unique vision with the viewer through an imaginative and innovative visual style that flows skillfully from traditional naturalism into surreal dreamlike fantasies and back again without ever seeming gratuitous or clumsy. A remarkable film.

LADY SINGS THE BLUES

1972 144m c   Biography/Musical   ★★★
Motown/Weston/Furie   (U.S.)   R

Diana Ross (Billie Holiday), Billy Dee Williams (Louis McKay), Richard Pryor (Piano Man), James Callahan (Reg Hanley), Paul Hampton (Harry), Sid Melton (Jerry), Virginia Capers (Mama Holiday), Yvonne Fair (Yvonne), Scatman Crothers (Big Ben), Robert L. Gordy (Hawk)

p, Jay Weston, James S. White; d, Sidney J. Furie; w, Terence McCloy, Chris Clark, Suzanne De Passe (based on the book by Billie Holiday, William Dufty); ph, John A. Alonzo (Panavision, Eastmancolor); ed, Argyle Nelson; m, Michel Legrand; prod d, Carl Anderson; cos, Bob Mackie, Ray Aghayan, Norma Koch

AAN Best Actress: Diana Ross; AAN Best Original Story and Screenplay: Terence McCloy, Chris Clark, Suzanne DePasse; AAN Best Song Score: Gil Askey (Adaptation); AAN Best Art Direction-Set Decoration: Carl Anderson (Art Direction), Reg Allen (Set Decoration); AAN Best Costume Design: Bob Mackie, Ray Aghayan, Norma Koch

View this film about Billie Holiday as a completely fictional story, and you'll enjoy it far more than you would otherwise. Ostensibly based on Holiday's autobiography, LADY SINGS THE BLUES begins in the early 1930s in Baltimore, where the teenaged Billie (Diana Ross) is raped and then sent to New York to stay with a friend of her mother's. In Harlem she works first as a maid, and later as a whore, in a brothel. With the encouragement of the brothel's "piano man" (Richard Pryor), she begins singing professionally and eventually becomes the lover of gambler Louis McKay (Billy Dee Williams)—actually Holiday's third husband but the sole romantic interest in the film.

"Lady Day's" inimitable style begins to win her notice on the club circuit, and she is invited to tour the South with a band led by white musicians. On tour she's devastated by racist treatment and turns to drugs, becoming an addict—a habit which threatens both her professional and personal success. Things get worse when her mother dies, and Holiday enters a sanitarium in an attempt to get clean. Although she later begins a new life with McKay, her triumph is short-lived, and the film closes by glancing over her remaining, troubled days until her death at age 44.

Perhaps because Holiday's true life story is so well documented, the filmmakers felt they had to alter the facts in order to interest audiences. The dramatized results angered many; jazz critic Leonard Feather, for one, noted that the film made no mention of Lester Young, Jimmy Monroe (to whom Holiday was married), John Hammond, Benny Goodman, Count Basie, Artie Shaw and Teddy Wilson—all important associations for Holiday during the period covered in the film. Taken as pure fiction, however, LADY SINGS THE BLUES is an overdirected but fairly watchable movie, aided by a good if not quite good enough performance by Ross in her dramatic screen debut. Ross's renderings of Holiday's songs, however, are travesties.

LADY VANISHES, THE   **DVD**

1938 97m   bw   Mystery/Spy   ★★★★★
Gaumont   (U.K.)

Margaret Lockwood (Iris Henderson), Michael Redgrave (Gilbert Redman), Paul Lukas (Dr. Hartz), Dame May Whitty (Miss Froy), Cecil Parker (Eric Todhunter), Linden Travers (Margaret Todhunter), Mary Clare (Baroness), Naunton Wayne (Caldicott), Basil Radford (Charters), Emile Boreo (Hotel Manager)

p, Edward Black; d, Alfred Hitchcock; w, Alma Reville, Sidney Gilliat, Frank Launder (based on the novel The Wheel Spins by Ethel Lina White); ph, Jack Cox; ed, Alfred Roome, R.E. Dearing; m, Louis Levy

Flabbergasting peak suspense, civilized but breathlessly fast. This is one of Hitchcock's finest British films, a classic mystery that manages to combine humor with a genuine sense of menace—not to mention the kinds of characters that everyone dreams of meeting on a Central European train journey.

The film is set into motion when a seemingly innocuous old woman, Miss Froy (Whitty), disappears while on board a train bound for England. An acquaintance, Iris (Lockwood), becomes concerned and sets out to find her. Despite the fact that there are only so many places to hide on a speeding train, Whitty cannot be found. Even more mysteriously, no one else seems convinced that she ever really existed. Each time that Lockwood thinks she has proof of what happened, that proof itself evaporates; and each time she begins to doubt her own memory, some objective fact re-alerts her suspicions. After a series of ingenious developments, Lockwood finally uncovers the truth with the help of music scholar Gilbert (Redgrave).

THE LADY VANISHES begins slowly but picks up speed as it goes along, finally steaming toward a suspenseful denouement. The film was extremely popular in the U.S. and laid the tracks for the great British director's new career in Hollywood. After striking a deal with David O. Selznick, Hitchcock completed one more British picture, JAMAICA INN, and began a love affair with America, returning to England just once more, some 30 years later, for FRENZY.

LADYHAWKE   **DVD**

1985 121m   c   Fantasy/Adventure   ★★★½
Warner Bros. (U.S.)   PG-13

Matthew Broderick (Phillipe Gaston), Rutger Hauer (Navarre), Michelle Pfeiffer (Isabeau), Leo McKern (Imperius), John Wood (Bishop), Ken Hutchison (Marquet), Alfred Molina (Cezar), Loris Loddi (Jehan), Alessandro Serra (Mr. Pitou), Charles Borromel (Insane Prisoner)

p, Richard Donner, Lauren Shuler; d, Richard Donner; w, Edward Khmara, Michael Thomas, Tom Mankiewicz (based on a story by Edward Khmara); ph, Vittorio Storaro (Technovision, Technicolor); ed, Stuart Baird; m, Andrew Powell; prod d, Wolf Kroeger; art d, Giovanni Natalucci, Ken Court; fx, John Richardson; cos, Nana Cecchi

AAN Best Sound: Les Fresholtz, Dick Alexander, Vern Poore, Bud Alper; AAN Best Sound Effects Editing: Bob Henderson, Alan Murray

Phillipe (Matthew Broderick), a pickpocket in 13th-century France, is thrown into a dungeon, but escapes and tries to elude the palace guards in the thick of a nearby forest. Rescued by Navarre (Rutger Hauer), a mysterious knight, Phillipe is eager to be on his way, but the knight refuses to set him free, eventually filling him in on his secret. Navarre, the former chief guard for an evil bishop (John Wood), was involved in a romance with the bishop's mistress Isabeau (Michelle Pfeiffer). When the bishop learned of the affair, he appealed to the gods and had the lovers cursed. As a result the two take on different forms—Navarre, a wolf by night, and

Isabeau, a hawk by day—never again able to embrace each other as humans.

Majestically photographed, LADYHAWKE is a joy to look at, employing some beautiful techniques to capture the transformations. Unfortunately, the synthesized soundtrack is drastically out of place and out of character. Hauer, playing a more gentle role than usual, is excellent, but Pfeiffer, who looks stunning, isn't given much to do. While not without faults, LADYHAWKE is much more striking than many of Donner's other films. A poetic, mythic tale of impossible love that was one of the overlooked films of 1985.

LADYKILLERS, THE   DVD

1955   96m   c   Comedy/Crime   ★★★★½
Ealing   (U.K.)

Alec Guinness *(Professor Marcus)*, Cecil Parker *(The Mayor)*, Herbert Lom *(Louis)*, Peter Sellers *(Harry)*, Danny Green *(One-Round)*, Jack Warner *(Police Superintendent)*, Katie Johnson *(Mrs. Wilberforce)*, Philip Stainton *(Police Sergeant)*, Frankie Howerd *(Barrow Boy)*, Fred Griffiths *(The Junkman)*

p, Seth Holt; d, Alexander Mackendrick; w, William Rose (based on his story); ph, Otto Heller (Technicolor); ed, Jack Harris; m, Tristram Cary; art d, Jim Morahan

AAN Best Original Screenplay: William Rose

The last of the comedies produced by the Ealing Studios, and one of the finest, with a supremely dark tone which makes a climactic series of murders as hilarious as they are grotesque.

THE LADYKILLERS pits an implacably dotty landlady (Katie Johnson) against a criminal gang which includes Alec Guinness, as a "mastermind" with hideous teeth; Cecil Parker, as a bumbling military type; Herbert Lom, as an American-style gangster; Peter Sellers, as an inept teddy boy; and Danny Green, as a kind-hearted thug. The gang are using Johnson's house as a base from which to plan an elaborate robbery, but their combined talents evaporate in the face of their landlady's blithe command of her own, idiosyncratic world. In one scene, they are forced to halt their attempted getaway in order to take tea with Johnson and her friends and join in a sing-song around the harmonium!

THE LADYKILLERS was the last comedy produced by Ealing, which was in the process of closing down at the time of the film's release in 1955. Johnson, who was to die two years later, won a British Film Academy Award for her role. Shortly after the film's completion, director Mackendrick left England for the U.S., where he scored another triumph with SWEET SMELL OF SUCCESS.

LAGAAN: ONCE UPON A TIME IN INDIA   DVD

2001   225m   c   Musical/Sports/Romance   ★★★★
Aamir Khan Productions   (India)   PG

Aamir Khan *(Bhuvan)*, Gracy Singh *(Gauri)*, Rachel Shelley *(Elizabeth Russell)*, Paul Blackthorne *(Capt. Andrew Russell)*, Suhasini Mulay *(Yashodamai)*, Kulbhushan Kharbanda *(Rajah Puran Singh)*, Raghuveer Yadav *(Bhura)*, Rajendra Gupta *(Mukhiya)*, Rajesh Vivek *(Guran)*, Sri Vallabh Vyas *(Ishwar)*

p, Aamir Khan; d, Ashutosh Gowariker; w, Ashutosh Gowariker, Kumar Dave, Sanjay Dayma (based on a story by Ashutosh Gowariker); ph, Anil Mehta; ed, Ballu Saluja; m, Padmashree A.R. Rahman; prod d, Nitin Chandrakant Desai; fx, Western Outdoor; chor, Ganesh Hegde ("Mitwa"), CHOR Raju Hkan ("Ghanan," "Chale Chalo" and "O Paalanhaare"), Saroj Khan ("Radha Kaisa na Jale"), Terence Lewis ("Waltz for a Romance"), Vaibhavi Merchant ("O Rey Chhori"); cos, Bhanu Athaiya

AAN Best Foreign Language Film

Unbeatable entertainment from India, and proof that the often derided Bollywood film industry is entirely capable of beating Hollywood at its own game.

The year is 1893, and the farmers of the central Indian village of Champener are chafing under a stiff, British-imposed "lagaan," or land tax. Each year, the raja of every province in British India collects a portion of each farmer's harvest in exchange for the British cantonment's ongoing protection against attacks by neighboring rulers. This year, however, a terrible drought produced a paltry harvest, but instead of mercy, dastardly Captain Russell (Paul Blackthorne) shows only malicious caprice: He threatens to double the lagaan, unless the village takes him up on an unusual wager. Russell proposes a game of cricket between his officers and 11 of the village's men. If they win, Champener and every other village in the province will be exempt from the tax for three years. If they lose, the village will have to pay a triple lagaan. Aware that his fellow farmers have little chance of paying any lagaan at all, young Bhuvan (Bollywood superstar Aamir Khan) steps forward and agrees to the three-day match, despite the howls of protest from the other villagers, who've never so much as *seen* a game of cricket, let alone played one.

Like much Bollywood product, director Ashutosh Gowariker's stunningly choreographed, four-hour musical is a fascinating mix of Hollywood genres and tropes. But rather than looking West for thematic inspiration, Gowariker turns to his country's own turbulent history: The plot may be straight out of the Hollywood formula file and the character types, but the story of 19th-century India's struggles against the forces of imperialism is entirely its own.

L'AGE D'OR   DVD

1930   60m   bw   Drama   ★★★★★
Corinth   (France)

Lya Lys *(The Woman)*, Gaston Modot *(The Man)*, Max Ernst *(Bandit Chief)*, Pierre Prevert *(Bandit)*, Caridad de Laberdesque, Lionel Salem, Madame Noizet, Jose Artigas, Jacques Brunius

p, Le Vicomte de Noailles; d, Luis Bunuel; w, Luis Bunuel, Salvador Dali; ph, Albert Duverger; ed, Luis Bunuel; m, Richard Wagner, Felix Mendelssohn, Ludwig van Beethoven, Claude Debussy

One of the most controversial films of all time, L'AGE D'OR is a surreal inquiry into the traditions and standards of modern culture that have kept true passion and instinct from being freely expressed.

Modot and Lys, simply called the Man and the Woman, are the lovers who allow nothing to prevent them from demonstrating their feelings for each other. They want to make love, but must first overcome a number of seemingly insurmountable obstacles: the church, bourgeois social etiquette, and their own psychological handicaps. This love is demonstrated through surreal images that are both hilarious (a cow lying on a bed, a frustrated man kicking a socialite's obnoxious poodle into the air) and disturbing (a helpless boy being brutally shot to death), but the overall impact suggests love's transcendent power.

L'AGE D'OR, like many other surrealist and Dadaist works, is more than a piece of art—it is a manifesto. It is not an entertainment but a display of the iconoclasm, rage, wit and passion which Bunuel, Salvador Dali and their contemporaries wanted humanity to embrace. L'AGE D'OR is full of incredible moments: the opening documentary on the savagery of scorpions, Lys obsessively sucking the toes of a statue, the pompous clerics on the rocks. The accompanying program for the film read, "It is LOVE that brings about the transition from pessimism to action: Love, denounced in the bourgeois demonology as the root of all evil. For love demands the sacrifice of every other value: status, family, and honor."

During one of the film's initial showings in Paris, a minor riot broke out as people destroyed paintings by such artists as Man Ray, Max Ernst and Dali. L'AGE D'OR was subsequently banned and became the subject of heated debate in both left- and right-wing newspapers. Although Dali was involved, this film more properly belongs to Bunuel. Many of the themes appearing in his later works are evident here for the first time, though less tempered with his later occasional gentleness.

LAMERICA   DVD
1994 120m   c   Drama/Political   ★★★★
Cecchi Gori Group/Tiger Cinematografica/
Arena Films/Alia Film   (Italy/France)

Enrico Lo Verso *(Gino)*, Michele Placido *(Fiore)*, Carmelo Di Mazzarelli *(Spiro)*, Piro Milkani *(Selimi)*, Elida Janushi *(Selimi's Cousin)*, Sefer Pema *(Prison Warden)*, Nikolin Elezi *(Boy Who Dies)*, Artan Marina *(Ismail)*, Besim Kurti *(Policeman)*, Esmerald Ara *(Little Girl)*

p, Mario Cecchi Gori, Vittorio Cecchi Gori; d, Gianni Amelio; w, Gianni Amelio, Andrea Porporati, Alessandro Sermoneta; ph, Luca Bigazzi; m, Simona Paggi; m, Franco Piersanti; prod d, Giuseppe M. Gaudino, Nicola Rubertelli; cos, Liliana Sotira, Claudia Tenaglia

LAMERICA is a boldly chilling portrait of post-Communist Europe in moral eclipse, directed with passion and singular grace by Italian Gianni Amelio (STOLEN CHILDREN).

A pair of cynical Italian capitalists, Gino and Fiore (Enrico Lo Verso and Michele Placido) need an Albanian—*any* Albanian—to serve as front man for a business scheme. They find him in Spiro (Carmelo Di Mazzarelli), an addled old man who has spent 50 years in a Communist prison. When Spiro disappears, Gino sets out in pursuit across the nightmarish landscape of contemporary Albania. Amelio's genuinely moving film deservedly won the European Felix Award and Italy's equivalent of the Oscar (it was also the Italian entry for the 1995 Academy Awards). Its near-hallucinatory portrayal of the chaotic plight of Albania in the grip of a singularly ruthless brand of capitalism is trenchant and unforgettable. LAMERICA's central theme, however, is the timeless hope of the migrant—a dubious dream of spiritual renewal in a real or imagined "Lamerica." Beautifully structured despite an episodic plot, the film is also brilliantly acted, especially by Lo Verso, one of the most gifted actors of his generation.

LANCELOT OF THE LAKE   DVD
(LE GRAAL)
1974 80m   c   Historical/Drama   ★★★★
Mara-Films/Laser Productions/ORTF/Gerico Sound (France)

Luc Simon *(Lancelot)*, Laura Duke Condominas *(Queen Guinevere)*, Humbert Balsan *(Gawain)*, Vladimir Antolek-Oresek *(King Arthur)*, Patrick Bernard *(Modrick)*, Arthur De Montalambert *(Lionel)*

p, Jean-Pierre Rassam, Jean Yanne, Francois Rochas; d, Robert Bresson; w, Robert Bresson; ph, Pasqualino de Santis (Eastmancolor); ed, Germaine Lamy; m, Philippe Sarde; prod d, Pierre Charbonnier; cos, Gres

In 1974, the most austere of the major filmmakers, Robert Bresson, released his version of the tale of Lancelot and Guinevere. Not surprisingly, Bresson's stripped-to-the-bone adaptation eschews the traditionally heroic, spectacular, fabulous, and exaltedly romantic aspects of the legendary saga in order to lay bare the confusion and pain within the human soul.

The knights of the round table have returned empty-handed from their quest for the Holy Grail. Lancelot (Luc Simon) the knight and young Queen Guinevere (Laura Duke Condominas) continue to carry on a clandestine affair behind the back of King Arthur (Vladimir Antolek-Oresek). Urged by Arthur to cultivate the friendship of the other nights, Lancelot offers his hand to the devious Modrick (Patrick Bernard) but is rebuffed. Gawain (Humbert Balsan), Arthur's nephew, urges his friend and ally to fight Modrick, but Lancelot declines, even though he is told that the other knights are shifting their allegiance from him to Modrick. Though he announces that he will not participate in an upcoming tournament, Lancelot appears there in disguise, and proceeds to win the jousting events. En route to the contest, Modrick tells Arthur that Guinevere and Lancelot are lovers. After Lancelot, wounded from the jousts, disappears into the forest, the other knights presume he is dead. Guinevere, however, believes that her lover is alive and will return to rescue her, possibly from execution as an adulteress.

Bresson's unrelenting minimalism carries over into every aspect of the production, most conspicuously in the flat, emotionless line readings of his amateur performers, the profusion of low-angled shots, and a modest soundtrack, heightened by the almost total absence of background music. This is one of the few film of its kind that never stoops to vulgarity and refuses to honor the genre's most cherished supposition: that all medieval people were animals. Though unwilling to render his characters as superhuman or godlike, Bresson never wallows in the mud he photographs. In exchange for all the pomp and pageantry of the old tradition and the phlegm and flatulence of the new tradition (pioneered by Monty Python), Bresson has given moviegoers something more valuable: a sober rendition of an oft told tale, freshened and renewed by the unique, almost aberrant sensibility of its narrator.

LAND BEFORE TIME, THE   DVD
1988 70m   c   Animated/Children's   ★★★½
Sullivan-Bluth/Amblin   (U.S.)   G

VOICES OF: Pat Hingle *(Narrator/Rooter)*, Helen Shaver *(Littlefoot's Mother)*, Gabriel Damon *(Littlefoot)*, Candice Houston *(Cera)*, Burker Barnes *(Daddy Topps)*, Judith Barsi *(Ducky)*, Will Ryan *(Petrie)*

p, Don Bluth, Gary Goldman, John Pomeroy; d, Don Bluth; w, Stu Krieger (based on a story by Judy Freudberg, Tony Geiss); ed, Dan Molina, John K. Carr; m, James Horner; prod d, Don Bluth; fx, D.A. Lanpher; anim, John Pomeroy, Linda Miller, Ralph Zondag, Dan Kuenster, Lorna Pomeroy, Dick Zondag

In THE LAND BEFORE TIME, created under the tutelage of George Lucas and Steven Spielberg, Don Bluth capitalizes on the renewed interest in dinosaurs among children, setting his tale millions of years ago and creating what has been called a prehistoric BAMBI.

An orphaned brontosaurus named Littlefoot (voiced by Gabriel Damon) is forced to make his way through desolation in order to find the Great Valley, which is lush and green but very far away. Joining Littlefoot on his adventure are a feisty baby triceratops named Cera (Candice Houston); a restless, chatty anatosaurus named Ducky (Judith Barsi); a pterodactyl named Petrie (Will Ryan); and a mute, dull-witted stegosaurus named Spike. A gorgeous production from beginning to end, THE LAND BEFORE TIME contains all the essential elements missing from most of Disney's recent efforts. Bluth, a former Disney animator, understands that the greatest Disney films take us on an emotional journey in which all our hopes and fears are played out in a vivid fantasy world where anything can happen. THE LAND BEFORE TIME continues that great tradition.

LARA CROFT: TOMB RAIDER

2001 105m c Action/Adventure **DVD**
Mutual Film Company/Paramount ★★½
(U.S./U.K./Germany) PG-13

Angelina Jolie *(Lady Lara Croft)*, Iain Glen *(Manfred Powell)*, Jon Voight *(Lord Croft)*, Noah Taylor *(Bryce)*, Daniel Craig *(Alex West)*, Christopher Barrie *(Hillary)*, Julian Rhind-Tutt *(Mr. Pimms)*, Leslie Phillips *(Wilson)*, Richard Johnson *(Distinguished Gentleman)*, Robert Phillips *(Assault Team Leader)*

p, Lawrence Gordon, Lloyd Levin, Colin Wilson; d, Simon West; w, Patrick Masset, John Zinman, Simon West (based on a story by Sara B. Cooper, Mike Werb, and Michael Colleary, based on the EIDOS Interactive game series developed Core Design); ph, Peter Menzies; ed, Dallas S. Puett, Glen Scantlebury; m, Graeme Revell; prod d, Kirk M. Petrucelli; art d, Dave Allday, David Lee, Jim Morahan, Su Whitaker; fx, Steve Begg, Chris Courbald; cos, Lindy Hemming

An action-packed crowd-pleaser whose appeal rests primarily on the supple shoulders of Angelina Jolie as the flesh-and-blood embodiment of video game pin-up Lara Croft.

Lara, an archeologically inclined English heiress, sharpens her martial skills by sparring with a computer-controlled robot designed by her trusty associate, Bryce (Noah Taylor). Elsewhere in the world, sleek schemer Manfred Powell (Iain Glen) and his effete sidekick (Julian Rhind-Tutt) are looking for a mysterious key that will unlock some ancient mystery that undoubtedly bodes ill for the rest of the planet. Meanwhile, Lara has a dream about her late father (Jon Voight, Jolie's real-life dad) that leads her to a strange clock hidden within the Croft mansion. The clock and the key are one and the same, and Powell's thugs steal it. Lara in turn pursues Powell and his crew—which includes her ex-boyfriend, Alex Cross (Daniel Craig)—to Cambodia's Angor Wat temple and gives them a taste of their own medicine. With time running out and the plot thickening, Lara and Powell face off over possession of an artifact that confers power over time itself.

Lara Croft, heroine of the phenomenally successful "Tomb Raider" series of interactive video games, has been uncharitably (but not inaccurately) described as Indiana Jones with booty, and comparisons with RAIDERS OF THE LOST ARK are inevitable (there's even a nod to RAIDERS's signature gag when Lara coolly plugs a sword-twirling monster), but not especially enlightening. Yes, RAIDERS is wittier, but this film hardly aspires to wit. It's all about action and ogling—Jolie's boobs, butt and thighs get so much screen time they deserve their own credits.

L'ARGENT

1983 90m c Crime **DVD**
Marion's/FR3/EOS (France/Switzerland) ★★★★★

Christian Patey *(Yvon Targe)*, Sylvie van den Elsen *(Old Woman)*, Michel Briguet *(The Woman's Father)*, Caroline Lang *(Elise Targe)*, Vincent Risterucci *(Lucien)*, Beatrice Tabourin *(Woman Photographer)*, Didier Baussy *(Man Photographer)*, Marc Ernest Fourneau *(Norbert)*, Brune Lapeyre *(Martial)*, Andre Cler *(Norbert's Father)*

p, Jean-Marc Henchoz; d, Robert Bresson; w, Robert Bresson (based on the story "The False Note" by Leo Tolstoy); ph, Emmanuel Machuel, Pasqualino De Santis; ed, Jean Francois Naudon; m, Johann Sebastian Bach; art d, Pierre Guffroy; cos, Monique Dury

Writer-director Robert Bresson's 13th film in 40 years, L'ARGENT is, like so many of his other films, a work of true cinematic genius that stands head and shoulders above most other pictures and seems to defy critical judgment. L'ARGENT begins with young schoolboy Norbert's (Marc Ernest Fourneau) trying unsuccessfully to get money from his parents. An enterprising classmate gives him some counterfeit bills, which Norbert passes on to a worker in a photographic shop. The shop owner (Didier Baussy) is determined to get rid of the phony bills and palms them off to an unsuspecting deliveryman (Christian Patey), who innocently pays a cafe bill with the forged notes and is promptly arrested. The schoolboy's mother pays the shop owner to keep silent about her son's involvement. Throughout the first half-hour of the film (before we are certain that Patey is the leading player), money is the central character. It changes hands from one person to another in extreme close-ups and carries us from one scene to the next, one location to the next. The bills are recognizable, whereas the people passing them are not. The power of money and the effects of one person's impositions upon another eventually lead the feckless deliveryman along an increasingly harrowing life's path to the film's stunning conclusion. Bresson justly won acclaim for this piercing film from the Cannes Film Festival, which voted him Best Director.

LASSIE COME HOME

1943 90m c Adventure/Children's **DVD**
MGM (U.S.) ★★★★

Roddy McDowall *(Joe Carraclough)*, Donald Crisp *(Sam Carraclough)*, Edmund Gwenn *(Rowlie)*, Dame May Whitty *(Dolly)*, Nigel Bruce *(Duke of Rudling)*, Elsa Lanchester *(Mrs. Carraclough)*, Elizabeth Taylor *(Priscilla)*, J. Pat O'Malley *(Hynes)*, Ben Webster *(Dan'l Fadden)*, Alec Craig *(Snickers)*

p, Samuel Marx; d, Fred M. Wilcox; w, Hugo Butler (based on the novel by Eric Knight); ph, Leonard Smith (Technicolor); ed, Ben Lewis; m, Daniele Amfitheatrof; art d, Cedric Gibbons, Paul Groesse; fx, Warren Newcombe

AAN Best Color Cinematography: Leonard Smith

This low-budget effort wasn't expected to do much at the box office, but moviegoers fell in love with the title collie, and many sequels, a radio program, and a long-running TV show followed. In Yorkshire in the dark days after WWI, young Joe Carraclough (Roddy McDowall) is forced to give up Lassie when his parents (Donald Crisp and Elsa Lanchester) can no longer afford to keep the dog. After escaping once from her new owner, the Duke of Rudling (Nigel Bruce), Lassie is taken by him to Scotland, and, freed by the duke's sympathetic granddaughter (Elizabeth Taylor), makes a long, eventful journey back to Joe.

This Lassie, actually a male dog named Pal, was bought for $10 by trainer Rudd Weatherwax, who had worked for MGM training animals for PECK'S BAD BOY and THE CHAMP. The studio wanted a female dog and Weatherwax was chosen to find a good one, but when shooting began the female shed heavily and was replaced by Pal. Contrary to popular belief, this was not Taylor's first film. She had been signed to a brief contract by Universal and appeared in THERE'S ONE BORN EVERY MINUTE the year before. Even more than costar Roddy McDowall, the seductive Taylor has that uncanny quality some child actors possess of looking and sometimes acting quite like an adult, even at a pre-adolescent age. The presence of these kids, and that of the well-trained pooch, quite upstage the endearing and highly professional actors surrounding them. Still, this film is a fairly well-balanced effort, and if you're in the mood for an evening of obvious sentiment, this boy-and-his-dog film works quite well.

LAST ACTION HERO

1993 122m c   Action/Adventure/Comedy   **DVD** ★★
Steve Roth Productions/Columbia   (U.S.)   PG-13

Arnold Schwarzenegger *(Sergeant Jack Slater)*, Austin O'Brien *(Danny Madigan)*, Mercedes Ruehl *(Ilene Madigan)*, Bridgette Wilson *(Whitney/Meredith)*, Charles Dance *(Benedict)*, Tom Noonan *(Ripper)*, Robert Prosky *(Nick)*, F. Murray Abraham *(John Practice)*, Art Carney *(Frank)*, Frank McRae *(Dekker)*

p, Steve Roth, John McTiernan; d, John McTiernan; w, Zak Penn, Adam Leff, Shane Black, David Arnott, William Goldman (from the story by Penn and Leff); ph, Dean Semler, David B. Nowell; ed, John Wright, Frank J. Urioste, Richard A. Harris; m, Michael Kamen; prod d, Eugenio Zanetti; art d, Marek Dobrowolski, Rick Heinrichs, John Wright Stevens; fx, Tommy Fisher, John Sullivan, Neil Krepela, Gene Warren Jr., Kevin O'Neil; cos, Gloria Gresham

Forget JURASSIC PARK. If you're fascinated by life-forms destined for extinction, look no further than Arnold Schwarzenegger, as presented in LAST ACTION HERO.

HERO claims to be a gentle, playful parody of the action/adventure genre, but comes off as a mercenary attempt to cash in on summer moviegoing habits. Action films pull in large audiences, mostly comprised of young men; non-violent films clean up in the family market. How to combine the two? Make an action movie in which the violence has no edge, since it takes place in a fictional world, and team your macho star with a young, fatherless child (Austin O'Brien) and a struggling single mom (Mercedes Ruehl).

If this sounds like naked calculation, it is. LAST ACTION HERO is a marketing idea with no real film to back it up. The central premise—that people can cross over from the real world into the world of moviedom and back—is borrowed from PURPLE ROSE OF CAIRO and mercilessly flogged to death. The relentless in-jokes and filmic references suggest, not a joyful homage to earlier movie feats, but a self-congratulatory smugness. Mr. O'Brien is an almost entirely charmless young man, but at least he's human; Schwarzenegger's performance, on the other hand, could easily have been computer-generated. Perhaps one day it will be.

The final irony is that HERO fails to parody a form that has already become a parody of itself. Without even meaning to, LETHAL WEAPON 3 or CLIFFHANGER generate bigger laughs than this clunking, joyless monolith of a movie.

LAST DAYS OF CHEZ NOUS, THE

1993 96m   c   Drama   ★★★
Jan Chapman Productions   (Australia)   R

Lisa Harrow *(Beth)*, Bruno Ganz *(J.P.)*, Kerry Fox *(Vicki)*, Miranda Otto *(Annie)*, Kiri Paramore *(Tim)*, Bill Hunter *(Beth's Father)*, Lex Marinos *(Angelo)*, Mickey Camilleri *(Sally)*, Lynne Murphy *(Beth's Mother)*, Clair Haywood *(Janet)*

p, Jan Chapman; d, Gillian Armstrong; w, Helen Garner; ph, Geoffrey Simpson; ed, Nicholas Beauman; m, Paul Grabowsky; prod d, Janet Patterson; cos, Janet Patterson

Australian director Gillian Armstrong (MY BRILLIANT CAREER) offers up an exquisite entertainment about a family upset by the return of a prodigal sister.

A novelist, Beth (Lisa Harrow) is accused by her effete French husband JP (Bruno Ganz) of viewing the world through rose-colored glasses in her work, evidenced in an over-tidiness in her novel's resolutions. Recovering from a failed relationship that has left her pregnant and alone, Beth's younger sister Vicki (Kerry Fox) at first irritates JP with her slovenliness and refusal to perform household duties. Shortly after helping her younger sister obtain an abortion that further upsets her emotional equilibrium, Beth takes her crusty, disagreeable father (Bill Hunter) on an extended motoring vacation through the outback. JP's efforts to comfort Vicki lead to an affair that escalates into a seri-

ous relationship, and threatens the delicate emotional connections betwene all the family members.

It's not surprising that Hollywood never quite figured out what to do with Gillian Armstrong: in CHEZ NOUS the accents are thick, crucial dialog is sometimes tossed away and there's no conventional "spine" to the story. There is a sense throughout CHEZ NOUS of the family as a state of contained anarchy that could also describe the film itself. Yet something is always happening, from the foreground to the edges of the screen, to the extent that you can literally blink and miss something important. The result feels oddly and warmly familiar throughout, and if it's sometimes baffling and annoying, it deserves to be cherished over the course of repeated viewings.

LAST DAYS OF DISCO, THE

1998 112m   c   Drama/Comedy   **DVD** ★★½
Westerly Films/Castle Rock (U.S.)   R

Chloe Sevigny *(Alice Kinnon)*, Kate Beckinsale *(Charlotte Pingress)*, Chris Eigeman *(Des McGrath)*, MacKenzie Astin *(Jimmy Steinway)*, Matt Keeslar *(Josh Neff)*, Matt Ross, billed as Matthew Rose *(Dan Powers)*, Tara Subkoff *(Holly)*, Burr Steers *(Van)*, David Thornton *(Bernie Rafferty)*, Jaid Barrymore *(Francesca—"Tiger Lady")*

p, Whit Stillman; d, Whit Stillman; w, Whit Stillman; ph, John Thomas; ed, Andrew Hafitz, Jay Pires; m, Mark Suozzo; prod d, Ginger Tougas; art d, Molly Mikula; fx, Todd R. Wolfeil; cos, Sarah Edwards

Early '80s nostalgia from the perspective of the tragically unhip. Writer-director Whit Stillman's chronicle of the boogie-oogie-oogie era bypasses supermodels and scene-makers in favor of the often humiliating experiences of expensively educated WASPs whose pedigrees count for everything on the job market and nothing behind the velvet ropes.

At the story's center are a pair mismatched Manhattan roommates: bitchy Charlotte (Kate Beckinsale) and sweet Alice (Chloe Sevigny), privileged girls with good haircuts, low-level publishing jobs, and a three-way share in a rundown railroad apartment. Around them buzz a swarm of square-jawed guys they knew from college—God forbid they should meet anyone *new* in a city of eight million—all of whom have come to New York to start their inevitable climb up the ladder of success. The exception to the upwardly mobile mass migration is Des (Chris Eigeman), the college screwup whom fate has deposited near the apex of the nightlife food chain. A bouncer at a trendy club (Studio 54 in all but name), he's their all-access pass to the disco Eden of drugs, dancing, and untrammeled sex, from which the whole uptight lot of them live in fear of being expelled.

The conclusion of a trilogy that started with METROPOLITAN and BARCELONA (though it feels as though it should be in the middle, especially when people start talking about taking jobs in Spain), Stillman's newest look at the lifestyles of the sheltered and parentally subsidized relies as heavily as the earlier installments on a brand of brittle, pseudo-sophisticated chatter (spare us, please, from sociological analyses of *Lady and the Tramp*) that sounds particularly artificial when delivered in a disco inferno. And the bloom is off his self-important preppies: it's one thing to think the world revolves around you when you're a teen, quite another when you're a young adult. But the soundtrack will delight anyone whose blood still stirs at the strains of "I'm Coming Out," "Le Freak," or "Doctor's Orders."

LAST DETAIL, THE

1973 103m   c   Drama   **DVD** ★★★★
Columbia   (U.S.)   R

Jack Nicholson *(Buddusky SM1)*, Otis Young *(Mulhall GM1)*, Randy Quaid *(Meadows SN)*, Clifton James *(Chief Master-at-Arms)*,

Michael Moriarty *(Marine Duty Officer)*, Carol Kane *(Young Whore)*, Luana Anders *(Donna)*, Kathleen Miller *(Kathleen)*, Nancy Allen *(Nancy)*, Gerry Salsberg *(Henry)*

p, Gerald Ayres; d, Hal Ashby; w, Robert Towne (based on the novel by Darryl Ponicsan); ph, Michael Chapman (Metrocolor); ed, Robert C. Jones; m, Johnny Mandel; prod d, Michael Haller; cos, Ted Parvin

AAN Best Actor: Jack Nicholson; *AAN Best Supporting Actor:* Randy Quaid; *AAN Best Adapted Screenplay:* Robert Towne

A grim yet very touching portrait of a trip taken by three men, one of whom is to lose his freedom by journey's end. Two career sailors, Nicholson and Young, are randomly selected to escort Quaid from their West Virginia base to a prison in Massachusetts. Quaid was caught stealing from the polio charity box; since that was the favorite charity of the admiral's wife, he is sentenced to eight years in jail, or a year for every five dollars. Nicholson and Young got a lot more than they bargained for when they were assigned this detail. At first, they think it's just another shore leave with liberty to be enjoyed and lots of carousing. The two hardened sailors are soon won over, however, by Quaid's bumbling ways and the difficulty of his plight. This causes them to take a paternal attitude toward him as they travel from one dim location to another. Only the characters in the film look alive, as everywhere they go appears to have been filtered by pale grays and yellows. Nicholson and Young try to show Quaid a good time before his long stay in the brig. They encounter Anders, who brings them to a Nicheren Shoshu meeting where religious zealots (including Gilda Radner before she became a TV star) chant "Nam-Myoho-Renge-Kyo" and dance happily in their scented environment. Anders next takes Quaid to her room when she learns of his bleak future and tells him that she's going to do something that will be very important. The naive Quaid thinks she's about to seduce him; instead, she begins to chant, which confuses him at first, then leads to a poignant scene later. Nicholson and Young can't make any time with Anders's pals, so it's off to another adventure—this time to a brothel where they offer Quaid a good time with Kane, which they'll pay for. Quaid unsuccessfully tries to escape (while chanting the liturgy Anders taught him), but after an agonizing chase across a frozen park, Nicholson and Young capture him and deliver him to prison. We get the feeling that Nicholson and Young, if their naval careers did not depend on it, would have taken off with Quaid. They try hard not to be emotional as Quaid is escorted up a small staircase to the room where he will spend the rest of his youth.

THE LAST DETAIL is a gritty look at the military life and the people who are attracted to it. It is dark in its message and gray to the eye. Locations are all washed out as though there were a thin membrane of filth spread across everything except the leads, who pop out colorfully like three strawberries in a bowl of Cream of Wheat. This is Nicholson's best work since FIVE EASY PIECES, perhaps because his character seems to be an extension of that film's Bobby DuPea. Ashby's direction is superlative, as is his use of music to help secure the mood. Ashby was able to get Nicholson's least-mannered performance in many a day, after bombs with THE KING OF MARVIN GARDENS; A SAFE PLACE; and DRIVE, HE SAID. Ponicsan also wrote the naval-based novel, *Cinderella Liberty*, which was made into a film the same year. THE LAST DETAIL won no Oscars but did get nominations for Quaid, Nicholson (who lost to Jack Lemmon for SAVE THE TIGER), and Robert Towne for his screenplay.

LAST EMPEROR, THE 📀
(MODAI HUANGDI)
1987 219m c   Historical/Biography   ★★★★½
Columbia   (Italy/U.S./China)   PG-13

John Lone *(Aisin-Gioro "Henry" Pu Yi as an Adult)*, Joan Chen *(Wan Jung, "Elizabeth")*, Peter O'Toole *(Reginald Johnston)*, Ying Ruocheng *(The Governor)*, Victor Wong *(Chen Pao Shen)*, Dennis Dun *(Big Li)*, Ryuichi Sakamoto *(Masahiko Amakasu)*, Maggie Han *(Eastern Jewel)*, Ric Young *(Interrogator)*, Wu Jun Mei *(Wen Hsiu)*

p, Jeremy Thomas; d, Bernardo Bertolucci; w, Mark Peploe, Bernardo Bertolucci, Enzo Ungari (based on *From Emperor To Citizen*, the autobiography of Pu Yi); ph, Vittorio Storaro (Technovision, Technicolor); ed, Gabriella Cristiani; m, Ryuichi Sakamoto, David Byrne, Cong Su; prod d, Ferdinando Scarfiotti; art d, Gianni Giovagnoni, Gianni Silvestri, Maria Teresa Barbasso; fx, Gianetto De Rossi, Fabrizio Martinelli; cos, James Acheson

AA Best Picture; AA Best Director: Bernardo Bertolucci; *AA Best Adapted Screenplay:* Mark Peploe, Bernardo Bertolucci; *AA Best Cinematography:* Vittorio Storaro; *AA Best Film Editing:* Gabriella Cristiani; *AA Best Original Score:* Ryuichi Sakamoto, David Byrne, Cong Su; *AA Best Art Direction-Set Decoration:* Ferdinando Scarfiotti (Art Direction), Bruno Cesari (Set Decoration); *AA Best Costume Design:* James Acheson; *AA Best Sound:* Bill Rowe, Ivan Sharrock

Originally released in 1987 shorn of a full hour of footage, this fascinating but ultimately passive pageant—in keeping with its protagonist, Aisin-Gioro "Henry" Pu Yi, tha last emperor of China and a man more acted upon than active—contains some of Italian director Bernardo Bertolucci's most sumptuous visuals. This grand and powerful biography begins in 1908 when, at the age of three, Pu Yi was named emperor of China and follows him through a tumultuous life inextricably intertwined with the history of modern-day China, one that that ended with the once-coddled emperor working quietly as a gardener at Peking's Botanical Gardens. The restored version of the film was completely re-edited by Bertolucci himself.

Told in an intricate flashback/flashforward narrative that uses Pu Yi's communist "remolding" period as its fulcrum, the film opens in 1950 as Pu Yi, and thousands of others, are returned to their now-communist homeland to face rehabilitation. From that point the story moves to Pu Yi's childhood, his imprisonment in the Forbidden City, his term as Japan's puppet emperor of Manchukuo, and his release into the population of China in 1959. Combining the command of the historical epic he displayed in 1900 with the political intrigue and melodrama of THE CONFORMIST, Bertolucci has, in THE LAST EMPEROR, constructed a beautiful film about the transformation of both a man and a country. A storyteller and not a historian, Bertolucci offers two tales in THE LAST EMPEROR—that of China's change, told through a selective sampling of events; and that of Pu Yi's change, told with an emphasis on myth rather than on fact. Moreover, Vittorio Storaro's carefully constructed lighting schemes and moving camera are unmatched by any cinematographer working today. Lone, as the adult Pu Yi, is wholly credible, and Wu Tao, as the adolescent Pu Yi, is every bit his equal. Both actors convey the emperor's innocence, ignorance, and veiled sadistic streak. Chen demonstrates her skill by playing both a radiant teen bride and a rotting opium addict. O'Toole shows more restraint than usual and simply becomes his character, as if he, like Reginald Johnston, would have made an excellent tutor for the emperor. Also worthy of note is the film's score, which combines lush romanticism with traditional Chinese melodies and was written chiefly by Ryuichi Sakamoto (who also scored MERRY CHRISTMAS, MR. LAWRENCE) and David Byrne (of Talking Heads fame). How we wish the film had used a more red-blooded attack on its commentary on blue-blooded privilege.

LAST EXIT TO BROOKLYN
1989 102m c   Drama   ★★★½
Neue Constantin   (West Germany)

Stephen Lang *(Harry Black)*, Jennifer Jason Leigh *(Tralala)*, Burt Young *(Big Joe)*, Peter Dobson *(Vinnie)*, Jerry Orbach *(Boyce)*, Stephen Baldwin *(Sal)*, Jason Andrews *(Tony)*, James Lorenz *(Freddy)*, Maia Danziger *(Mary Black)*, Cameron Johann *(Spook)*

p, Bernd Eichinger; d, Uli Edel; w, Desmond Nakano (based on the novel by Hubert Selby Jr.); ph, Stefan Czapsky; ed, Peter Przygodda; m, Mark Knopfler; art d, Mark Haack; cos, Carol Oditz

Red Hook, Brooklyn, 1952: Korea-bound conscripts, sadistic teenage gangs, and despondent strikers eke out their desolate existences amidst a frenzied mixture of prostitutes, psychos, winos, and junkies. Based on a collection of short stories by Hubert Selby Jr., which unleashed a storm of controversy upon their publication in 1964, German director Uli Edel's film is a relentlessly bleak account of life in the neighborhood during a brief period in the summer of '52.

The stories of a cross-section of characters is recounted in episodic fashion. Tralala (Jennifer Jason Leigh) is a prostitute who picks up tricks in sleazy bars and lures them to rubble-strewn vacant lots where they are mugged by ex-convict Vinnie (Peter Dobson) and his gang of thugs. Harry (Stephen Lang) is in charge of the local strike office, enjoying his position of power, but troubled by his awakening homosexuality. Georgette (Alexis Arquette) is an effeminate, tormented gay who lusts after Vinnie. Big Joe (Burt Young) is a striking worker who is upset over the pregnancy of his unmarried daughter Donna (Ricki Lake), while his motorcycle-obsessed son Spook (Cameron Johann) pines for Tralala.

In blending the personal worlds of these characters into a complete cosmology of the abyss, director Uli Edel (CHRISTIANE F.) and scriptwriter Desmond Nakano have transformed Selby's episodic book into an aesthetic whole that is greater than the sum of its parts. Moreover, Edel's and Nakano's efforts are just part of what was clearly the engaged teamwork of a group of gifted people committed to doing justice to Selby's uncompromising vision. Lang and, especially, Jason Leigh, are standouts in a terrific ensemble cast.

LAST HOUSE ON THE LEFT, THE   DVD
1972 91m c   Horror/Crime   ★★★½
Sean S. Cunningham Productions/Lobster (U.S.)   R

David Hess, billed as David A. Hess *(Krug)*, Lucy Grantham *(Phyllis)*, Sandra Cassel *(Mari Collingwood)*, Marc Sheffler *(Junior)*, Jeramie Rain *(Sadie)*, Fred Lincoln *(Weasel)*, Gaylord St. James *(Dr. Collingwood)*, Cynthia Carr *(Mrs. Collingwood)*, Ada Washington *(Truck Driver)*

p, Sean S. Cunningham; d, Wes Craven; w, Wes Craven; ph, Victor Hurwitz (Movielab color); ed, Wes Craven; m, Steve Chapin, David Hess

An ugly, disturbing, passionately conceived cult favorite, LAST HOUSE ON THE LEFT is much more complex (albeit crudely made) than its controversial reputation would suggest. Loosely based on Ingmar Bergman's THE VIRGIN SPRING, Wes Craven's film depicts the atrocities committed by a makeshift family of rootless criminals who kidnap, rape, and murder two teenaged girls on their way to a rock concert. The convicts then make their way through the dense New Jersey woods and take refuge with a suburban couple, posing as a family whose car has broken down. Little do the killers know that the house they have picked for their refuge is owned by Dr. and Mrs. Collingwood, the parents of one of their victims. After discovering the truth, the nice middle-class couple exact savage revenge on the killers.

Expertly made on a tiny budget, this drive-in exploitation flick decisively transcends its genre. The extremely graphic violence is never played for thrills; indeed, Craven has said he wanted to resensitize Americans to the reality of violence in the wake of the Vietnam war. Craven—who would go on to polish his themes in the slicker THE HILLS HAVE EYES—never for a moment allows the viewer to sympathize with the killers, but he does provide a window of understanding into how seemingly senseless acts of violence occur. The killers initially toy with the girls, as if playing a game; but when the game gets out of hand and the girls wind up dead, the killers look at their corpses with saddened confusion, like children who have broken a favorite doll. Some have seen the film as a critique of the nuclear family, exploring the threat of patriarchal violence that lies beneath traditional structures of domestic authority. Undeniably, the good Dr. Collingwood's behavior, from his surreptitious appraisal of his daughter's figure to his spectacularly gory revenge, is hardly a model of benign fatherhood.

LAST METRO, THE   DVD
(LE DERNIER METRO)
1980 133m c   War/Romance   ★★★½
Carrosse/TF-1   (France)   R

Catherine Deneuve *(Marion Steiner)*, Gerard Depardieu *(Bernard Granger)*, Jean Poiret *(Jean-Loup Cottins)*, Heinz Bennent *(Lucas Steiner)*, Andrea Ferreol *(Arlette Guillaume)*, Paulette Dubost *(Germaine Fabre)*, Sabine Haudepin *(Nadine Marsac)*, Jean-Louis Richard *(Daxiat)*, Maurice Risch *(Raymond, the Stage Manager)*, Marcel Berbert *(Merlin)*

d, Francois Truffaut; w, Francois Truffaut, Suzanne Schiffman, Jean-Claude Grumberg (based on a story by Truffaut, Schiffman); ph, Nestor Almendros; ed, Martine Barraque; m, Georges Delerue; art d, Jean-Pierre Kohut-Svelko; cos, Lisele Roos

AAN Best Foreign Language Film

Truffaut's oblique, microcosmic look at the German occupation of France is set almost entirely in a theater building. Marion Steiner (Deneuve, in an arresting performance) is the wife of top stage director Lucas Steiner (Bennent), who is forced to go underground in order to avoid Nazi persecution. Instead of fleeing Paris, Lucas hides in the cellar of the theater, eavesdropping on the rehearsals of his new play, which costars Marion and Bernard Granger (Depardieu). Time passes and the lives of the theater personnel become strained, particulary as Marion and Bernard try to resist a growing mutual attraction.

Politics and romance are placed on parallel tracks in this film through the figure of Marion, who tries to remain as loyal to her husband as she is to her countrymen. Often scolded for not addressing political issues in his pictures, director Francois Truffaut finally found a suitable vehicle in THE LAST METRO, which filters the Nazi occupation through a love story and recognizes the complexities of the situation with a dual, on- and off-stage ending. Truffaut's vision of 1940s Paris is more influenced by mythicized images of the city in films of the period than by historical reality, but the social commentary is vivid nonetheless.

LAST MOVIE, THE   ★★½
1971 108m c   Drama
Universal   (U.S.)   R

Julie Adams *(Mrs. Anderson)*, Dennis Hopper *(Kansas)*, Daniel Ades *(Thomas Mercado)*, Rod Cameron *(Pat)*, John Alderman *(Jonathan)*, Michael Anderson Jr. *(Mayor's Son)*, Rich Aguilar *(Gaffer)*, Donna Baccala *(Miss Anderson)*, Tom Baker *(Member of Billy's Gang)*, Toni Basil *(Rose)*

p, Paul Lewis; d, Dennis Hopper; w, Stewart Stern (based on a story by Dennis Hopper and Stewart Stern); ph, Laszlo Kovacs (Technicolor); ed, Dennis Hopper, David Berlatsky, Antranig Mahakian; m, Kris Kristofferson, John Buck Wilkin, Chabuca Granda, Severn Darden, The Villagers of Chinchero, Peru; art d, Leon Ericksen; fx, Milt Rice; cos, Jerry Alpert

After the success of EASY RIDER, Dennis Hopper was given $1 million by Universal to make a film, and came back with more than 40 hours of footage. His final cut, after more than a year of editing, was incomprehensible to the studio and to most of the people who saw the film, except for those at the Venice Film Festival, who gave it an award. Take a look at the cast list and you'll see that Hopper called in many of his pals to do cameos, but all that talent couldn't help. The picture is supposedly based on some experiences Hopper had while filming THE SONS OF KATIE ELDER in Mexico. He'd hoped to shoot this in Mexico but was refused, so he took the entire company to Peru. The movie begins at the end, flashes back to the beginning, and winds up somewhere in the middle. Hopper plays Kansas, a movie stunt man who stays behind on a film location after the company has moved off. He takes up with a local whore (Stella Garcia) then goes off to find gold with his friend Neville (Don Gordon) who, inexplicably, commits suicide. The local priest (Tomas Milian), meanwhile, makes trouble by blaming movies for the introduction of death and destruction to his naive villagers. Kansas is adopted by the local Peruvian Indians who have made some abandoned movie equipment part of their religion. In the end, the Indians plan to crucify Kansas as they have cast him as Billy The Kid in their production.

THE LAST MOVIE is filled with such distancing devices as blank frames and inserts that read "Scene Missing." It is also overly pretentious. Cinematographer Kovacs can usually make anything look good, but he comes a cropper in this case. Hopper, to this day, thinks that his film is a masterpiece, and while the film's self-conscious play with the medium of filmmaking does generate some interest, there probably aren't many people out there who agree with the director's evaluation.

LAST OF SHEILA, THE

1973 120m c Mystery ★★★½
Warner Bros. (U.S.) PG

Richard Benjamin (Tom), Dyan Cannon (Christine), James Coburn (Clinton), Joan Hackett (Lee), James Mason (Philip), Ian McShane (Anthony), Raquel Welch (Alice), Yvonne Romain (Sheila), Pierro Rosso (Vittorio), Serge Citon (Guido)

p, Herbert Ross; d, Herbert Ross; w, Anthony Perkins, Stephen Sondheim; ph, Gerry Turpin (Technicolor); ed, Edward Warschilka; m, Billy Goldenberg; prod d, Ken Adam; art d, Tony Roman

THE LAST OF SHEILA is a superb murder mystery and something of a curio in film history, thanks to a script (by Anthony Perkins and Stephen Sondheim) that is written in the style of a British crossword puzzle. A wealthy Hollywood producer (Coburn) whose wife was killed by a hit-and-run driver at a party a year before, invites six people, all suspects, to his yacht in the south of France, hoping to uncover the culprit. He engages the six—a failed screenwriter (Benjamin); his rich, neurotic wife (Hackett); a movie star (Welch); her manager-husband (McShane); an aging film director (Mason); and a high-powered agent (Cannon)—in a psychological game designed to provoke the murderer into revealing his or her identity. The producer actually succeeds in getting murdered himself, and another death follows before the mystery is solved. If you enjoy puns, anagrams, and wordplay, you will find THE LAST OF SHEILA a positive Joycean delight. Listen for Bette Midler singing "Friends" on the soundtrack.

LAST OF THE MOHICANS, THE

1936 91m bw Historical/Adventure/War ★★★★
Small (U.S.)

Randolph Scott (Hawkeye), Binnie Barnes (Alice Munro), Heather Angel (Cora Munro), Hugh Buckler (Col. Munro), Henry Wilcoxon (Maj. Duncan Heyward), Bruce Cabot (Magua), Robert Barrat (Chingachgook), Philip Reed (Uncas), Willard Robertson (Capt. Winthrop), Frank McGlynn Sr. (David Gamut)

p, Edward Small, Harry M. Goetz; d, George B. Seitz; w, Philip Dunne, John Balderston, Paul Perez, Daniel Moore (based on the novel by James Fenimore Cooper); ph, Robert Planck; ed, Jack Dennis, Harry Marker; art d, John DuCasse Schulze; cos, Franc Smith

AAN Best Assistant Director: Clem Beauchamp

Arguably the finest film version of James Fenimore Cooper's classic adventure tale, THE LAST OF THE MOHICANS benefits from fine performances by Randolph Scott as Hawkeye, Henry Wilcoxon as Maj. Duncan Heyward, and Bruce Cabot as the vicious, lascivious Huron Indian, Magua, one of the most hateful roles in film history. During the height of the French and Indian War, Hawkeye escorts Maj. Heyward, Alice (Binnie Barnes), and Cora Munro (Heather Angel), the daughters of the commander of Ft. William Henry, through hostile lines., accompanied by Chingachgook (Robert Barrat) and his son, Uncas (Philip Reed), who are the last survivors of the Mohican tribe, wiped out by the French-allied Hurons. During the course of their dangerous trek to the fort, Alice becomes enamored of Hawkeye, Cora and Uncas fall in love, and Magua makes life miserable for everyone. Before Chingachgook sends Magua to the happy hunting ground, the sadistic Huron brings about the deaths of both Cora and Uncas. What's more, the British are routed at Ft. William Henry and Hawkeye is taken prisoner and tied to a stake by the Hurons before Maj. Heyward comes to his rescue.

Packed with excitement and well-staged battle scenes, this superbly crafted adventure film was masterfully directed by George B. Seitz and magnificently lensed in California's High Sierras by Robert Planck. Cooper's famous tale has been brought to the screen a number of times (including two 1911 one-reelers; Maurice Tourneur and Clarence Brown's smashing 1922 feature-length silent with Wallace Beery as Magua; a ten-chapter 1924 serial version called LEATHERSTOCKING; Mascot Films's 1932 12-chapter serial with Harry Carey; and a 1947 Columbia version, THE LAST OF THE REDMEN, starring Jon Hall, Evelyn Ankers, and Buster Crabbe as Uncas), but none of these other versions matches the scope and wonderful performances of this extraordinary film. The film earned an Oscar nomination for Clem Beauchamp for Best Assistant Director, losing to Jack Sullivan for THE CHARGE OF THE LIGHT BRIGADE.

LAST OF THE MOHICANS, THE

1992 122m c Action/Adventure/Historical ★★★
Forward Pass Productions/Fox (U.S.) R

Daniel Day-Lewis (Nathaniel Poe/Hawkeye), Madeleine Stowe (Cora Munro), Russell Means (Chingachgook), Eric Schweig (Uncas), Jodhi May (Alice Munro), Steven Waddington (Major Duncan Heyward), Wes Studi (Magua), Maurice Roeves (Colonel Munro), Patrice Chereau (General Montcalm), Edward Blatchford (Jack Winthrop)

p, Michael Mann, Hunt Lowry; d, Michael Mann; w, Michael Mann, Christopher Crowe, Philip Dunne (from his screenplay, based on the adaptations by John L. Balderston, Paul Perez and Daniel Moore of the novel by James Fenimore Cooper); ph, Dante Spinotti; ed, Dov Hoenig, Arthur Schmidt; m, Trevor Jones,

Randy Edelman; prod d, Wolf Kroeger; art d, Richard Holland, Robert Guerra

AA Best Sound: Chris Jenkins, Doug Hemphill, Mark Smith, Simon Kaye

Michael Mann's version of the creaky Fenimore Cooper classic takes place in a wilderness America circa 1757, where British colonists in New York state have become pawns in a power struggle between England and France during the French and Indian War. The principal characters are Hawkeye (Day-Lewis), a frontier woodsman more at home with his adopted Mohican father, Chingachgook (Native American activist Russell Means), and brother, Uncas (Eric Schweig), than the white British colonials; Cora (Madeleine Stowe) and Alice Munro (Jodhi May), comely daughters of a British colonel (Maurice Roeves); the insufferable Major Duncan Heyward (Steven Waddington), who has set his sights on marrying Cora; and the hateful Huron brave Magua (Wes Studi), who has sworn revenge on Munro for the Colonel's earlier anti-Indian exploits.

Mann, best known for TV's "Miami Vice," here eschews his customary hip, urban locales in favor of the breathtaking colonial wilderness. THE LAST OF THE MOHICANS offers some of the most spectacular landscapes ever seen on screen, as well as some lavish, if confusingly staged, battle scenes. Given the two-dimensionality of the characters, the performances are all creditable, with Daniel Day-Lewis making a successful leap from art-house favorite to running, jumping, shooting box-office hero. Thanks to a hackneyed screenplay that also makes the historical background seem very confusing, these formulaic characters never stray too far from expectations, and indulge in dialogue that occasionally verges on self-parody ("What are you looking at, Sir?" "I'm looking at you, Miss"). Mann, however, successfully overcomes the weak script by dint of sheer directorial bravura, delivering Fenimore Cooper into the 1990s with roaring cannons and whizzing tomahawks.

LAST ORDERS   *DVD*
2001 110m c   Drama   ★★★★
Scala Productions/Winchester Films (U.K./Germany) R

Michael Caine *(Jack Dodds)*, Tom Courtenay *(Vic Tucker)*, David Hemmings *(Lenny)*, Bob Hoskins *(Ray Johnson)*, Helen Mirren *(Amy Dodds)*, Ray Winstone *(Vince Dodds/Vincent Ian Pritchett)*, JJ Feild *(Young Jack)*, Cameron Fitch *(Young Vic)*, Nolan Hemmings *(Young Lenny)*, Kelly Reilly *(Young Amy)*

p, Elisabeth Robinson, Fred Schepisi; d, Fred Schepisi; w, Fred Schepisi (based on the novel by Graham Swift); ph, Brian Tufano; ed, Kate Williams; m, Paul Grabowsky; prod d, Tim Harvey; art d, Paul Cross; fx, Stuart Brisdon, United Special Effects, Lailey SFX; cos, Jill Taylor

The cast is a *Who's Who* of great English actors, but the real star of writer-director Fred Schepisi's winning dramatic comedy is the screenplay, brilliantly adapted from Graham Swift's multi-character novel about a group of men entrusted with the grim task of scattering their friend's ashes in the sea.

The deceased is Jack Dodds (played in flashbacks by Michael Caine), an all-around good-time Charlie and the proprietor of Dodds & Son, Family Butcher. Dodds' son, tanned and nattily dressed Vince (Ray Winstone), however, wants no part of the family business; he's done quite well for himself as a used car salesman. So well, in fact, that when Jack suddenly finds himself in the hospital, dying and deeply in debt, he turns to Vince for a loan. Jack then gives the money to his Army buddy, Ray (Bob Hoskins), and asks him to bet it on a horse of his choosing. Once Jack dies, Ray, who has long been in love with Jack's wife, Amy (Helen Mirren), learns that he's to perform one last favor for his old friend. He, along with

Vince and their friends Lenny (David Hemmings) and Vic (Tom Courtenay), are to drive Jack's ashes from London to Margate, the seaside resort town where Jack and Amy once spent a happy holiday, and sprinkle them off the pier.

Jack's last orders are the catalyst for a sentimental but emotionally complex journey by four old friends who nevertheless harbor secrets and deep resentments. Given the number of characters involved and the fact that the film flashes back and forth over a 40-year period, it's amazing how beautifully the film flows. Credit goes to the sharp writing, excellent casting and Kate Williams's fluid editing.

LAST PICTURE SHOW, THE   *DVD*
1971 118m bw Drama   ★★★★½
BBS   (U.S.)   R

Timothy Bottoms *(Sonny Crawford)*, Jeff Bridges *(Duane Jackson)*, Cybill Shepherd *(Jacy Farrow)*, Ben Johnson *(Sam the Lion)*, Cloris Leachman *(Ruth Popper)*, Ellen Burstyn *(Lois Farrow)*, Eileen Brennan *(Genevieve)*, Clu Gulager *(Abilene)*, Sam Bottoms *(Billy)*, Sharon Taggart *(Charlene Duggs)*

p, Stephen Friedman; d, Peter Bogdanovich; w, Peter Bogdanovich, Larry McMurtry (based on the novel by McMurtry); ph, Robert Surtees; ed, Donn Cambern; prod d, Polly Platt; art d, Walter Scott Herndon

AAN Best Picture; AA Best Supporting Actor: Ben Johnson; *AAN Best Supporting Actor:* Jeff Bridges; *AA Best Supporting Actress:* Cloris Leachman; *AAN Best Supporting Actress:* Ellen Burstyn; *AAN Best Director:* Peter Bogdanovich; *AAN Best Adapted Screenplay:* Larry McMurtry, Peter Bogdanovich; *AAN Best Cinematography:* Robert Surtees

Bogdanovich's finest effort; bleak and beguiling. None of his other films ranks with THE LAST PICTURE SHOW when it comes to dramatic flair and authenticity. He seems comfortable doing period pieces, but, in this, his second feature (preceded by TARGETS), he captures the era so accurately that the viewer can feel the hopelessness of living in a dying Texas town. Bridges and Timothy Bottoms are the stars of the lackluster local high school football team. Bridges is the aggressive one, and Timothy Bottoms provides the contrasting sensitivity; they are best friends. The story unfolds seamlessly, detailing relationships in a small town. Sam Bottoms is a retarded boy (he got the part after he showed up to watch brother Tim's first day of shooting) who is the butt of cruel jokes by the denizens of the cafe-pool hall-theater owned by Johnson, a one-time cowboy who seems to be every boy's idol and surrogate father. Tim Bottoms takes up the cudgel as Sam Bottom's protector and is soon befriended, then bedded by Leachman, the lonely wife of the school's basketball coach, Thurman. The affair continues for most of the picture, heating up and cooling down a few times. To keep it up, Tim Bottoms ceases dating his regular girl friend, Taggart. Bridges continues dating his girl, Shepherd, but is not happy about her self-centered behavior. She attends a nude bathing party in order to meet the rich Brockette. Her mother, Burstyn, wants her daughter to marry well. Brockette rejects Shepherd because he doesn't want to be bothered with a virgin. Bridges and Tim Bottoms take a short and wild trip to Mexico, and when they return they are saddened to learn that Johnson has died.

THE LAST PICTURE SHOW is a refreshing look backward. While others were outfoxing themselves with multiscreen techniques, Bogdanovich made a movie that could have been shot years before and the result was critically and financially rewarding. The director is an admirer of Ford and Hawks and this is a homage to their styles, as opposed to the kind of ripoffs Colin Higgins and Brian De Palma have done with Hitchcock. The only element that separates this from an early film is the use of frontal nudity and the frank treatment accorded the adult themes. Bogdanovich was hailed as another Orson Welles (another of the director's mentors and friends). This episodic, human story lives and breathes with more power than any Darth Vader or Rocky. There was a time when Bogdanovich considered Jimmy Stewart, among others, for a part in the film. However, he wisely opted against using established stars. Johnson and Leachman each won Oscars, and the entire cast is quite fine (especially Ellen Burstyn, seen here like she's never been, before or since). Look for "Magnum's" John Hillerman in a small role as a teacher. THE LAST PICTURE SHOW could have been a tawdry, sleazy soap opera, but the 31-year-old former film critic kept a light, compassionate touch that elevated the story and presented it as a slice of a life that has all but disappeared.

LAST RESORT

2000 75m c Comedy/Drama ★★★★
BBC Films (U.K.)

Dina Korzun (Tanya), Artiom Strelnikov (Artiom), Paddy Considine (Alfie), Lindsey Honey (Les), Perry Benson (Immigration Officer), Katie Drinkwater (Katie), Dave Bean (Frank), Adrian Scarborough (Council Official), David Auker (2nd Council Official), Bruce Byron (Police Officer)

p, Ruth Caleb; d, Paul Pawlikowski; w, Paul Pawlikowski, Rowan Joffe; ph, Ryszard Lenczewski; ed, David Charap; m, Max de Wardener, Rowan Oliver; prod d, Tom Bowyer; cos, Julian Day

No plot description can really do this sweet, melancholy comedy justice. It's ineffable charm lies entirely in the delivery.

Tanya (Dina Korzun), an attractive Russian immigrant, and her young son, Artiom (Artiom Strelnikov), arrive at London's Stansted Airport expecting to begin a new life with Tanya's British "fiance." When he fails to meet them, Tanya panics and impulsively claims political asylum. She and Artiom are whisked off to Stonehaven, a desolate seaside resort that's seen better days; it now functions primarily as a holding area for refugees waiting for their asylum applications to be processed—a wait that can last anywhere from 12 to 16 months. Stonehaven has also become a refuge for assorted Brits who have fallen through the cracks—guys like Alfie (Paddy Considine), an ex-boxer who sells phone cards and cigarettes from his post at the Dreamland arcade. Housed in a grim cinderblock tower overlooking a cheerless amusement park on what feels like the edge of the world, Tanya wants nothing more than to leave; Alfie, who's fallen in love with the Russian beauty, would like her to stay.

Earlier in his career, Polish writer-director Paul Pawlikowski mostly made documentaries, and he approaches feature filmmaking with a verite camera style and no real script. With just a bare plot outline in mind, he picks a locale and allows the story to emerge through his actors and their reactions to the environment. The strategy works beautifully here. The forlorn, dreamlike aura of Stonehaven—actually Margate, a locale already rich in cinematic associations, thanks to Lindsay Anderson's landmark documentary O DREAMLAND—suffuses the characters, while their own dislocation adds to the town's sense of timeless limbo.

LAST SAMURAI, THE

2003 135m c Action/Adventure/Historical/War ★★★
Radar Pictures/Bedford Falls Company/ R
Cruise-Wagner Productions

Tom Cruise (Nathan Algren), Timothy Spall (Simon Graham), Ken Watanabe (Katsumoto), Billy Connolly (Zebulon Gant), Tony Goldwyn (Colonel Bagley), Hiroyuki Sanada (Ujio), Koyuki (Taka), Sosuke Ikematsu (Higen), Aoi Minato (Magojiro), Shichinosuke Nakamura (Emperor Meiji)

p, Tom Cruise, Tom Engleman, Marshall Herskovitz, Scott Kroopf, Paula Wagner, Edward Zwick; d, Edward Zwick; w, Marshall Herskovitz, John Logan, Edward Zwick (from a story by John Logan); ph, John Toll; ed, Victor du Bois, Steven Rosenblum; m, Hans Zimmer; prod d, Lilly Kilvert; art d, Chris Burian-Mohr, Jess Gonchor, Kim Sinclair; fx, Romulo Adriano Jr., Paul Lombardi, Jeffrey A. Okun; cos, Ngila Dickson

AAN Best Art Direction: Lilly Kilvert (art direction), Gretchen Rau (set decoration); AAN Best Sound Mixing: Andy Nelson, Anna Behlmer, Jeff Wexler; AAN Best Costume Design: Ngila Dickson; AAN Best Supporting Actor: Ken Watanabe

For all the epic visual, Edward Zwick's 19th-century drama of a disillusioned American war hero who finds redemption in the way of the samurai is hamstrung by Hollywood conventions.

1876: Haunted by his part in the slaughter of innocent Native Americans, alcoholic former war hero Captain Nathan Algren (Tom Cruise) is shilling for the Winchester rifle company when an old army buddy, Zebulon Gant (Billy Connolly), approaches him about a better gig. The Japanese government is hiring American military experts to train the imperial army in the ways of modern warfare, and paying handsomely. Despite the fact that taking the job means working with craven Colonel Bagley (Tony Goldwyn), whom he despises, Algren accepts. Once in Japan, Algren realizes the dimensions of the game in which he's become a pawn. Nominally governed by a teenage emperor (Shichinosuke Nakamura), Japan is divided between imperial advisors who favor all things new and Western and those who, like samurai Katsumoto (the charismatic Ken Watanabe), counsel respect for feudal traditions. Algren is forced to face Katsumoto's warriors before his troops are ready and is taken prisoner; Katsumoto spares Algren's life so he can learn about his opponents, but it's Algren who gets the real education.

If ever a film cried out for Akira Kurosawa's pragmatic bleakness, it's this high-minded yet simplistic story of courage and spiritual redemption. Unwilling to offend, Zwick whitewashes a culture in which brutality and contemplative beauty were inextricably intertwined and, afraid to alienate audiences, he shies away from the story's logical downbeat conclusion. Cruise gives a thoroughly respectable performance, but he can't make a symbol of the failures of Western capitalist thinking into a truly convincing character.

LAST SEDUCTION, THE

1994 110m c Thriller ★★★½
Oakwood Films Inc./DBA Kroy Pictures Inc. R
(U.S.)

Linda Fiorentino (Bridget Gregory), Peter Berg (Mike Swale), J.T. Walsh (Frank Griffith), Bill Nunn (Harlan), Bill Pullman (Clay Gregory), Jack Shearer (Public Defender), Michael Raysses (Phone Sales Rep), Zack Phifer (Gas Station Attendant), Brien Varady (Chris), Donna Wilson (Stacy)

p, Jonathan Shestak; d, John Dahl; w, Steve Barancik; ph, Jeff Jur; ed, Eric L. Beason; m, Joseph Vitarelli; prod d, Linda Pearl; art d, Dina Lipton; fx, John Hartigan; cos, Terry Dresbach

An updated noir thriller that decisively puts the *fatale* back into *femme fatale*, THE LAST SEDUCTION is a dark, expertly contrived display of paranoid nastiness; it's so gleefully mean that only the most tender-hearted viewer could resist going along for the ride.

Ambitious Bridget Gregory (Linda Fiorentino) and her malleable husband Clay (Bill Pullman), a doctor, have just pulled off a drug deal that's left them with $700,000, which Clay intends to use to pay off his gambling debts. While Clay's in the shower, she coolly takes the money and runs, ending up in a friendly little town called Beston. There she sizes up local stud Mike (Peter Berg) in a bar and, having deemed him adequate to her purposes, rocks his world and sets about guaranteeing her future with deadly precision.

Released theatrically after limited airings on the HBO cable channel, John Dahl's THE LAST SEDUCTION joined a growing handful of films—including Tamra Davis's GUN-CRAZY and Dahl's previous picture, RED ROCK WEST (both 1993)—to have transcended the stigma attached to made-for-TV movies. Unlike such bloated erotic thrillers as BASIC INSTINCT, which wallow in their own excesses, THE LAST SEDUCTION gets straight to the cold heart of classic noir: life is a stacked deck and only the most twisted, cunning, and ruthless stand a chance of survival. Jeffrey Jur's photography is excellent, dark and smoky at night, crisp and misleadingly clear during the day, and the production design is a marvel of smoky bars and bland suburban houses. But what really makes THE LAST SEDUCTION cook is the performances, especially Linda Fiorentino's praying-mantis-in-lace turn as the amoral Bridget. Though the film made many critics' Ten Best lists and Fiorentino was frequently singled out as an Oscar candidate, THE LAST SEDUCTION could not be included on Academy Awards nomination ballots because it debuted on television.

LAST STARFIGHTER, THE 📀

| 1984 | 101m | c | Science Fiction | ★★★½ |
| Lorimar | (U.S.) | | | PG |

Lance Guest (Alex Rogan), Dan O'Herlihy (Grig), Catherine Mary Stewart (Maggie Gordon), Barbara Bosson (Jane Rogan), Norman Snow (Xur), Robert Preston (Centauri), Kay E. Kuter (Enduran), Chris Hebert (Louis Rogan), Dan Mason (Lord Kril), John O'Leary (Rylan Bursar)

p, Gary Adelson, Edward O. DeNault; d, Nick Castle; w, Jonathan Betuel; ph, King Baggot (Panavison, Technicolor); ed, C. Timothy O'Meara; m, Craig Safan; prod d, Ron Cobb; art d, James D. Bissell; fx, Kevin Pike; cos, Robert Fletcher

This very good science fiction film has young Alex Rogan (Lance Guest) stuck in a trailer park in California with his mother (Barbara Bosson) and little brother (Chris Hebert). He longs to leave with his girlfriend Maggie (Catherine Mary Stewart). His only solace is a video game, "Starfighter," at which he breaks the record one evening. Later that night Centauri (Robert Preston) shows up, introduces himself as the inventor of the game, and asks Alex to climb into his unusual car to discuss a business proposition. Within minutes the bewildered youth finds himself hurtling through space to a strange planet, where he's given a uniform and is put into a room with a lot of strange-looking aliens for a briefing on the evil Kodan forces, under the traitor Xur, who are attacking the Star League. It finally dawns on Alex that he's being asked to be a real starfighter. Clever, exciting, and fun, THE LAST STARFIGHTER boasts good performances by Guest and Preston, and a literate, funny script that highlights the real story: not the space war that only Guest can win but the difficulty of leaving home, family, and security for a totally new life when the opportunity presents itself. The special effects, computer-generated rather than STAR WARS-type models, work rather well, giving the film an odd but effective look.

LAST TANGO IN PARIS 📀
(L'ULTIMO TANGO A PARIGI)

| 1972 | 129m | c | Drama/Erotic | ★★★★ |
| PEA/Les Artistes Associes | | (France/Italy) | | X |

Marlon Brando (Paul), Maria Schneider (Jeanne), Jean-Pierre Leaud (Tom), Massimo Girotti (Marcel), Maria Michi (Rosa's Mother), Veronica Lazare (Rosa), Gitt Magrini (Jeanne's Mother), Darling Legitimus (Concierge),

Catherine Sola (TV Script Girl), Mauro Marchetti (TV Cameraman)

p, Alberto Grimaldi; d, Bernardo Bertolucci; w, Bernardo Bertolucci, Franco Arcalli, Agnes Varda (based on a story by Bertolucci); ph, Vittorio Storaro; ed, Franco Arcalli; m, Gato Barbieri; prod d, Ferdinando Scarfiotti; cos, Gitt Magrini

AAN Best Actor: Marlon Brando; AAN Best Director: Bernardo Bertolucci

Shattering social and sexual conventions, LAST TANGO IN PARIS stands as one of Bernardo Bertolucci's finer achievements. Marlon Brando plays Paul, a confused middle-aged American living in Paris whose wife has just, inexplicably, committed suicide. Paul is obsessed with the thought that his wife's death, and her whole life, is a mystery to him. He knew nothing about her, and nothing of the secret affair she carried on for years with Marcel (Massimo Girotti).

Maria Schneider plays Jeanne, a 20-year-old from a wealthy Parisian family who is engaged to Tom (Jean-Pierre Leaud), a New Wave filmmaker who documents his fiancee's life in an attempt to discover the truth about her. While hunting for an apartment, Jeanne meets Paul. Moments later, the two strangers are making passionate love on the floor of the empty apartment. When they meet again, it is under Paul's ground rules: "You and I are going to meet here without knowing anything that goes on outside here. We are going to forget everything we knew—everything." If the psychosexual dynamics and existential maunderings of the screenplay are sometimes less than plausible, the remaining elements are perfectly synthesized in this landmark erotic film—Bertolucci's direction; the raw, brave performances of Brando and Schneider; Storaro's lush camerawork. Not to be missed.

LAST TEMPTATION OF CHRIST, THE 📀

| 1988 | 164m | c | Religious | ★★★★ |
| Cineplex Odeon | | (U.S.) | | R |

Willem Dafoe (Jesus Christ), Harvey Keitel (Judas Iscariot), Barbara Hershey (Mary Magdalene), Harry Dean Stanton (Saul/Paul), David Bowie (Pontius Pilate), Verna Bloom (Mary, Mother of Jesus), Andre Gregory (John the Baptist), Juliette Caton (Girl Angel), Roberts Blossom (Aged Master), Irvin Kershner (Zebedee)

p, Barbara De Fina; d, Martin Scorsese; w, Paul Schrader (based on the novel by Nikos Kazantzakis); ph, Michael Ballhaus (Technicolor); ed, Thelma Schoonmaker; m, Peter Gabriel; fx, Gino Galliano, Iginio Fiorentini; chor, Lahcen Zinoune

AAN Best Director: Martin Scorsese

Martin Scorsese's adaptation of Nikos Kazantzakis's controversial novel The Last Temptation of Christ seeks to emphasize the human aspects of Jesus Christ, a figure described in the Bible as both fully God and fully man. The film opens with the carpenter Jesus of Nazareth (Willem Dafoe) making crosses upon which the Romans crucify rebellious Jews; it closes with the controversial last-temptation sequence, depicting the human love and gratifications Jesus sacrificed to fulfill his destiny as the savior of humankind. Between these powerful and affecting scenes is a fresh and vivid retelling of the Gospel's familiar events—the assembly of the disciples, the miracles, and so forth. Striving for historical accuracy, Scorsese presents Jerusalem as a flat, arid, harsh land suffering under the oppressive thumb of Roman rule. Cinematographer Michael Ballhaus's and production designer John Beard's evocative vision of the Holy Land combines with Peter Gabriel's musical score (derived mostly from traditional and contemporary Arabic rhythms) to vividly convey Christ's world and time—and it is not the lush, picturesque, sanitized Hollywood version popularized by Cecil B. DeMille. Powerful, haunting, and at times very moving, THE

LAST TEMPTATION OF CHRIST presents its account of the events and conflicts of Christ's life with a depth of dramatized feeling and motivation that renders them freshly compelling.

LAST TIME I SAW PARIS, THE   DVD
1954 116m c   Romance   ★★★½
MGM   (U.S.)

Elizabeth Taylor *(Helen Ellsworth)*, Van Johnson *(Charles Wills)*, Walter Pidgeon *(James Ellsworth)*, Donna Reed *(Marie Ellsworth)*, Eva Gabor *(Lorraine Quarl)*, Kurt Kasznar *(Maurice)*, George Dolenz *(Claude Matine)*, Roger Moore *(Paul)*, Sandy Descher *(Vicki)*, Celia Lovsky *(Mama)*

p, Jack Cummings; d, Richard Brooks; w, Richard Brooks, Julius J. Epstein, Philip G. Epstein (based on the story, "Babylon Revisited," by F. Scott Fitzgerald); ph, Joseph Ruttenberg (Technicolor); ed, John Dunning; m, Conrad Salinger; art d, Cedric Gibbons, Randall Duell; fx, A. Arnold Gillespie; cos, Helen Rose

F. Scott Fitzgerald's tragic love story was brought to the screen with surprising vitality under Brooks' expert hand. He drew fine performances from Taylor, Johnson, and others in a sumptuous MGM production that captured the flavor of expatriate life in the City of Light. While Fitzgerald set his poignant tale in the 1920s, this film begins just after WWII; Johnson is a GI with literary ambitions who goes to Paris and meets the wealthy Taylor. They fall in love and he settles down there, attempting to write his first novel. All goes well for a while until failure to sell his writing causes Johnson to turn to the bottle. His excessive drinking soon causes the couple to argue and Taylor to be accidentally locked out of their Parisian quarters during a rainstorm. She catches pneumonia and later dies. Their child is raised by Taylor's sister, Reed, who has always disapproved of Johnson. He returns to the U.S. and becomes a successful novelist. Once back in Paris (which is how the film opens, with the Johnson-Taylor love story shown in flashback), Johnson begs for custody of his little girl. Reed relents at the last moment, and the child is reunited with her reformed father.

Taylor was never more lovely and turns in a superior performance as the star-crossed lady in love with Johnson. Johnson, who also turns in a good effort, although he's a bit glib in spots, was first teamed with Taylor in 1950 in THE BIG HANGOVER and got top billing. With THE LAST TIME I SAW PARIS, Taylor received the top slot because she had become one of the big box-office draws for MGM. Producer Lester Cowan had originally purchased the rights from Fitzgerald to this story for $3,000, intending to film it as a Mary Pickford vehicle in the 1920s for Goldwyn. Cowan sold the story to Paramount for a Gregory Peck–William Wyler production that fell through. But MGM purchased the rights from Paramount specifically for Taylor, assigning the clever Epstein twins to write a sparkling script that kept the flavor, if not the brilliance, of Fitzgerald's story intact. MGM shot two weeks on location in Paris and on the Riviera, mostly at Cannes, producing the balance of the film on the Culver City lot.

LAST WALTZ, THE   DVD
1978 117m c   Documentary   ★★★★
Last Waltz Productions   (U.S.)   PG

Rich Danko, Levon Helm, Garth Hudson, Richard Manuel, Robbie Robertson, Bob Dylan, Ronnie Hawkins, Neil Young, Joni Mitchell, The Staples

p, Robbie Robertson; d, Martin Scorsese; ph, Michael Chapman, Laszlo Kovacs, Vilmos Zsigmond, David Myers, Bobby Byrne, Michael Watkins, Hiro Narita; ed, Yeu-Bun Yee; m, Jan Roblee; prod d, Boris Leven; cos, Richard La Motte (supervisor)

Martin Scorsese combines his twin passions for movies and rock 'n' roll in this stylish mix of interviews, studio-shot production numbers, and expertly filmed footage of The Band's 1976 farewell concert.

After an on-screen message that reads "This Film Should Be Played Loud," The Band performs "Don't Do It," and Robbie Robertson, the group's leader, tells director-interviewer Martin Scorsese why they're calling it quits after 16 years on the road. The group is then seen at their farewell concert, given at San Francisco's Winterland Arena on Thanksgiving, performing such Band classics as "Up On Cripple Creek" and "The Night They Drove Old Dixie Down." Joining them onstage and back in the studio are Ronnie Hawkins, Joni Mitchell, Neil Young, The Staples, Emmylou Harris, Eric Clapton, Van Morrison, Muddy Waters, and many others. Bob Dylan does three songs, including the grand finale, "I Shall Be Released," for which the previous performers come back onstage, joined by Ringo Starr and Ron Wood.

Following the financial disaster of his first big-budget Hollywood production, NEW YORK NEW YORK, Scorsese returned to his early roots (he had been an editor on WOODSTOCK), and sought refuge in assembling The Band's concert footage. THE LAST WALTZ has much in common with NEW YORK NEW YORK, most notably in the clash of styles which represent Scorsese's two poles of cinematic influence: raw, Cassavetes-like intimacy (the candid interviews with The Band); and flamboyant, Visconti-Minnelli-Powell-like mise-en-scene (the concert and soundstage footage). While it certainly helps to be a fan of The Band, it's not essential in order to appreciate the film's eloquent accomplishments. From a technical perspective, it's undoubtedly the most impressive and authentic concert film ever made.

LAST WAVE, THE   DVD
1977 106m c   Thriller   ★★★★
Ayer/South Australian/Australian Film Commission   PG
(Australia)

Richard Chamberlain *(David Burton)*, Olivia Hamnett *(Anne Burton)*, David Gulpilil *(Chris Lee)*, Frederick Parslow *(Rev. Burton)*, Vivean Gray *(Dr. Whitburn)*, Nanjiwarra Amagula *(Charlie)*, Walter Amagula *(Gerry Lee)*, Roy Bara *(Larry)*, Cedric Lalara *(Lindsey)*, Morris Lalara *(Jacko)*

p, Hal McElroy, James McElroy; d, Peter Weir; w, Peter Weir, Tony Morphett, Peter Popescu; ph, Russell Boyd (Artlab Color); ed, Max Lemon; m, Charles Wain; art d, Neil Angwin; fx, Neil Angwin, Monty Fieguth; cos, Annie Bleakley

A powerful, yet subtle, picture from Australian director Weir, who has demonstrated quite a flair for mystical themes. Like his earlier work, PICNIC AT HANGING ROCK, this picture involves inexplicable events and their connection with the aboriginal world and the ancient Australian landscape. The picture opens as a raging thunderstorm from a clear blue sky drenches a small desert settlement, and then flashes quickly to Sydney, which is also in the midst of a torrential downpour. A voice over the radio unconvincingly attempts to explain the phenomenon as a reaction to cold winds from the Antarctic. An earlier shot of an aborigine painting on a cave wall lets the viewer know there is something at work here that transcends scientific explanation, setting the mood for the rest of the film. The contrast between the Western viewpoint, which attributes geophysical results to scientific reason, and the aboriginal perspective of a cosmos beyond the grasp of conscious thought, creates a tension that is carried throughout the film. Chamberlain plays a Sydney lawyer who becomes involved in defending a group of aborigines accused of murder (despite his lack of experience with both aborigines and criminal law).

Weir does a fine job of weaving real events with dream sequences, as well as capturing the aboriginal perspective—this is one of few films that does not portray the aborigines as a defeated people, entirely subjugated by white settlers. Chamberlain is convincing as a wealthy lawyer and family man who becomes possessed by a vision beyond his grasp. Although the plot falters in a few instances, it maintains a high level of overall suspense.

LAST YEAR AT MARIENBAD   *DVD*
(L'ANNEE DERNIERE A MARIENBAD)
1961 94m bw Drama   ★★★★★
Terra/Cormoran/Precitel/Como/Tamara/Silver-Cineriz
(France/Italy)

Delphine Seyrig (A/Woman), Giorgio Albertazzi (X/Stranger), Sacha Pitoeff (M/Escort/Husband), Francoise Bertin, Luce Garcia-Ville, Helena Kornel, Francois Spira, Karin Toeche-Mittler, Pierre Barbaud, Wilhelm von Deek

p, Pierre Courau, Raymond Froment; d, Alain Resnais; w, Alain Robbe-Grillet; ph, Sacha Vierny (Dyaliscope); ed, Henri Colpi; Jasmine Chasney; m, Francis Seyrig; art d, Jacques Saulnier; cos, Bernard Evein, Chanel

AAN Best Original Story and Screenplay: Alain Robbe-Grillet

The cinematic equivalent of the *nouveau roman* ("new novel") and a true landmark in film history. One of the most formally inventive of all feature films, LAST YEAR AT MARIENBAD stretches the limits of film language to the extreme. Scripted by Robbe-Grillet, the movie introduces us to four main characters—A (Seyrig), a lovely, well-dressed woman; X (Albertazzi), a handsome stranger; M (Pitoeff), a man who might be A's husband; and a luxurious estate (important enough to be considered a character) with long, sterile hallways and perfectly manicured grounds. The "plot," if you can call it one, focuses on X's attempt to convince A that they met, possibly last year, at a resort hotel, perhaps in Marienbad, where she may have promised to run away with him this year. A, however, has no recollection of the meeting…or else is being coy…or dares not recognize X…or whatever you care to make of it. The viewer is kept in perpetual doubt as to whether the meeting ever took place, whether it has not yet taken place, or whether it's a hopeful fantasy X has made up. Frustrated? You should be.

LAST YEAR AT MARIENBAD was hailed as a masterpiece at the time of its release, largely thanks to Robbe-Grillet and director Resnais's manipulation of time—past, present, and future—in relation to the subjective realities of the film's characters. Easy to read as a parody of Hollywood love triangles, MARIENBAD also mocks classical cinema's tendency to be redundant by repeating lines, indeed entire scenes, over and over again. All the characters are flat, often nothing but statues in a well-kept mausoleum. This is precisely how they appear in the film's most famous shot, in which the tiny figures amid the large sculpture garden cast shadows, but the starkly groomed bushes do not. A true cinematic puzzle, stunningly shot, MARIENBAD decenters the human subject from its place of primacy in most narrative cinema, and the result is a provocative study of alienation.

L'ATALANTE   *DVD*
(LE CHALAND QUI PASSE)
1934 89m bw Romance/Drama/Comedy   ★★★★★
J.L. Nounez (France)

Michel Simon (Pere Jules), Jean Daste (Jean), Dita Parlo (Juliette), Gilles Margaritis (Peddler), Louis Lefebvre (Cabin Boy), Fanny Clar (Juliette's Mother), Raphael Diligent, billed as Raya

Diligent (Juliette's Father—a Bargeman), Maurice Gilles (Barge Owner), Rene Bleck (Best Man), Charles Goldblatt (Thief)

p, Jacques-Louis Nouenz; d, Jean Vigo; w, Jean Vigo, Blaise Cendrars, Albert Riera (based on a scenario by R. de Guichen); ph, Boris Kaufman, Louis Berger; ed, Louis Chavance; m, Maurice Jaubert; prod d, Francis Jourdain

Jean Vigo's poetic tale centers on Jean (Daste), captain of the barge L'Atalante, who marries Juliette (Parlo), a young woman from the country. (The early scenes leading up to and including their wedding are marvelous.) Bored with life on the barge, Juliette longs to see the bright lights of Paris. Jean finally gives in to his wife's request and takes her to a Paris cabaret, where a peddler flirts with the young woman. The next day, an angry and jealous Jean leaves the ship without his wife. She is visited by the peddler, who entertains her and then is promptly thrown off the barge upon Jean's return. Juliette then sneaks off to Paris, and Jean purposefully sets sail without her, leaving his penniless wife to take a job in town. The film then concentrates on the lovers' pain before L'Atalante again sails on.

Vigo made only four films (A PROPOS DE NICE, TARIS CHAMPION DE NATATION, ZERO DE CONDUITE, and L'ATALANTE) before his untimely death at age 29. In L'ATALANTE, he treats his simple story both realistically and surrealistically, combining and contrasting styles. Thus, in one scene, Jean dives into the water and sees an image of a smiling Juliette swimming in her wedding gown; in another, a seaman played by Michel Simon (in possibly the greatest role of his distinguished career) displays his odd collection of curios, including a pair of severed hands in a jar. (Surrealist poet Jacques Prevert and his brother, filmmaker Pierre, also make cameo appearances.) L'ATALANTE was poorly received at its initial 1934 screening, prompting its distributors to insert a popular song and re-edit nearly all the scenes. The result was a box-office disaster, and three weeks later Vigo was dead.

Years later, a complete version was finally constructed thanks to the Cinematheque Francais and Henri Langlois. Less iconoclastic and experimental than his earlier films, L'ATALANTE is nonetheless brilliantly idiosyncratic and insightful, the warmest film of this great director's career.

LATE AUTUMN
(AKIBIYORI)
1960 127m c Drama   ★★★
New Yorker (Japan)

Setsuko Hara (The Mother), Yoko Tsukasa (The Daughter), Chishu Ryu (The Uncle), Mariko Okada (The Daughter's Friend), Keiji Sada (The Young Man)

d, Yasujiro Ozu; w, Kogo Noda, Yasujiro Ozu; ph, Yuharu Atsuta (Agfacolor); m, Takanobu Saito; art d, Tatsuo Hamada

One of the final efforts from one of the great masters of Japanese cinema, LATE AUTUMN was originally made in 1960 but not brought to the U.S. until ten years after Ozu's death. Tsukasa plays the daughter of Hara, a recently widowed woman who finds that her late husband's friends are taking an extreme interest in seeing her remarried. Hara herself is not so keen on walking down the aisle quite yet, something that shocks men raised in a tradition that has little place for an unattached woman. Eventually Hara does agree to marry, out of a desire to please the insistent elders, but her ideas of marriage still seem quite obscure to the traditionalists.

Ozu made 54 films in his long career, most marked by a subtle, distinctive directorial style featuring a stationary camera placed only a few feet above the floor. The latter portion of his career saw Ozu extremely concerned about the effects of Westernization upon traditional Japan; in LATE AUTUMN this is reflected in the consternation caused in the elders by Hara's "unorthodox" views.

LATE GEORGE APLEY, THE

1947 93m bw Comedy ★★★★
Fox (U.S.)

Ronald Colman (George Apley), Peggy Cummins (Eleanor Apley), Vanessa Brown (Agnes), Richard Haydn (Horatio Willing), Charles Russell (Howard Boulder), Richard Ney (John Apley), Percy Waram (Roger Newcombe), Mildred Natwick (Amelia Newcombe), Edna Best (Catherine Apley), Nydia Westman (Jane Willing)

p, Fred Kohlmar; d, Joseph L. Mankiewicz; w, Philip Dunne (based on the novel by John P. Marquand and the play by Marquand and George S. Kaufman); ph, Joseph La Shelle; ed, James B. Clark; m, Cyril J. Mockridge; art d, James Basevi, J. Russell Spencer; fx, Fred Sersen; cos, Rene Hubert

After a couple of whopping flops, Colman made it clear that he would only accept the very best material and was not about to make more than one film per year. His desire for quality was more than fulfilled by THE LATE GEORGE APLEY, which had first been a best-selling Pulitzer Prize-winning novel, then was adapted into a play. Colman is Apley, a man who believes his beloved Boston to be the hub of the universe. Moreover, he is convinced that any place not within 10 miles of Beacon Hill is savage as Borneo. Colman demands that his son, Ney, attend Harvard and that his daughter, Cummins, only marry a man who has grown up within earshot of the Charles Street Church. But as fate would have it, Ney falls for Brown, a girl from Worcester, and Cummins begins dating a Yalie (perish the thought!). What's a Brahmin to do? The situation is not hopeless, though, as Cummins's boyfriend, Russell, does show some signs of culture by regularly quoting Emerson, Colman's favorite author. Still, Colman forbids Ney to marry his love and by film's end, it seems likely that Ney will wind up like his father, watching birds and upholding all the moral standards that their ancestors handed down.

There are some similarities between this film and LIFE WITH FATHER in that the central characters in both stories are concerned with the status quo. However, Colman's Apley is basically a sympathetic character underneath all his surface bluster, while William Powell's Clarence Day is more or less the same on the inside as he is on the outside. Moreover, unlike Day, George Apley also demonstrates some openness to change. Reputedly, author Marquand pictured no one but Colman in the role of Apley, and the English actor—who had no problem slipping into the highbrow, quasi-English accent of the Back Bay—gives a wonderful performance. Cummins, another English import in her first American film, is also excellent, and Ney contributes some of his best work. Natwick and Best score in supporting roles, and Haydn is superb as a prissy Boston type. Mankiewicz, who had been known primarily as a writer and producer before directing DRAGONWYCK, handles the directional chores with aplomb and keeps the comedy coming with regularity. Bostonians, notoriously putoff by attempts to spoof them, flocked to the theaters to see THE LATE GEORGE APLEY and laughed their heads off.

LATE SHOW, THE

1977 94m c Crime 📀
Lion's Gate (U.S.) ★★★½ PG

Art Carney (Ira Wells), Lily Tomlin (Margo Sperling), Bill Macy (Charlie Hatter), Eugene Roche (Ron Birdwell), Joanna Cassidy (Laura Birdwell), John Considine (Lamar), Ruth Nelson (Mrs. Schmidt), John Davey (Sgt. Dayton), Howard Duff (Harry Regan)

p, Robert Altman; d, Robert Benton; w, Robert Benton; ph, Charles Rosher Jr.; ed, Lou Lombardo, Peter Appleton; m, Ken Wannberg

AAN Best Original Screenplay: Robert Benton (Story)

This fine, overlooked film stars Carney as Ira Wells, an aging private eye whose former partner, Harry Regan (Duff), is murdered while tracking down a missing cat for Margo Sperling (Tomlin). A sometime dealer in stolen goods, she suspects her pet has been nabbed by an associate whom she's failed to pay. At the urging of Charlie Hatter (Macy), Ira picks up where Regan left off, and he and Margo do a Nick and Nora Charles number as they piece together the complex clues that lead to the cat and climax of this intriguing mystery. Along the way, Margo begins to find herself attracted to Ira, but he doesn't return her affection—at least at first.

THE LATE SHOW was director Benton's second outing, and he showed immense sensitivity and the ability to spin a good yarn. Tomlin, in her second film after NASHVILLE, and Carney, in his return to the screen after his Oscar-winning performance in HARRY AND TONTO, work wonderfully together. Carney's portrayal of a man whose body is beginning to betray him but whose spirit won't throw in the towel is nothing short of elegant.

LAUGHTER

1930 85m bw Comedy/Drama ★★★½
Paramount (U.S.)

Fredric March (Paul Lockridge), Nancy Carroll (Peggy Gibson), Frank Morgan (C. Mortimer Gibson), Glenn Anders (Ralph Le Saint), Diane Ellis (Marjorie Gibson), Leonard Carey (Benham), Ollie Burgoyne (Pearl)

d, Harry d'Abbadie D'Arrast; w, Donald Ogden Stewart (based on a story by Douglas Doty, Harry d'Abbadie D'Arrast); ph, George Folsey; ed, Helene Turner

AAN Best Writing (Original Story): Harry d'Abbadie D'Arrast, Douglas Doty, Donald Ogden Stewart

Absolutely enchanting, and an important precursor to the romantic comedies of the 1930s. Director and cowriter Harry d'Abbadie D'Arrast had a brief film career that included a stint with Charlie Chaplin, but had he done nothing but work on LAUGHTER, his place in film history would be secure. This undated film is ahead of its time in content and style. Nancy Carroll is Peggy, a Follies dancer surrounded by amorous stage-door Johnnies. When she falls for wealthy C. Mortimer Gibson (Morgan) Peggy gives up all her old suitors, including Paul (March), a free-spirited composer who travels to Paris to forget his rejection. Neglected by her business-obsessed husband, Peggy occasionally revisits her bohemian past when she drops in on another former beau, Ralph (Anders), a Greenwich Village sculptor. She also befriends her stepdaughter Marjorie (Ellis), who is close to her own age. Trouble begins when Paul returns from Paris and when Ralph woos Marjorie because he can't have Peggy.

LAUGHTER could have been as soapy as a tubful of Tide, but d'Abbadie D'Arrast lends his fast-paced comedy-drama the deft sophisticated touch that would become Ernst Lubitsch's trademark. The characters relate to each other in a moving, adult, intimate manner, and even the film's melodramatic moments are beautifully underplayed. The script crackles with wit, and Carroll (the real centerpiece here), March and Morgan lead a cast shimmering with conviction.

LAURA

1944 88m bw Mystery 📀
Fox (U.S.) ★★★★★

Gene Tierney (Laura Hunt), Dana Andrews (Mark McPherson), Clifton Webb (Waldo Lydecker), Vincent Price (Shelby Carpenter),

Judith Anderson (*Ann Treadwell*), Dorothy Adams (*Bessie Clary*), James Flavin (*McAvity*), Clyde Fillmore (*Bullitt*), Ralph Dunn (*Fred Callahan*), Grant Mitchell (*Corey*)

p, Otto Preminger; d, Otto Preminger; w, Jay Dratler, Samuel Hoffenstein, Elizabeth Reinhardt, Ring Lardner Jr., Jerry Cady (based on the novel by Vera Caspary); ph, Joseph La Shelle; ed, Louis Loeffler; m, David Raksin; prod d, Thomas Little, Paul S. Fox; art d, Lyle Wheeler, Leland Fuller; fx, Fred Sersen; cos, Bonnie Cashin

AAN Best Supporting Actor: Clifton Webb; AAN Best Director: Otto Preminger; AAN Best Screenplay: Jay Dratler, Samuel Hoffenstein, Betty Reinhardt; AA Best B/W Cinematography: Joseph LaShelle; AAN Best Interior Decoration (B/W): Lyle Wheeler, Leland Fuller, Thomas Little

The sleekest of *noirs*, the chicest of murders, and deliciously twisted—the detective is a necrophilliac, two of the title character's suitors seem gay, and the Laura all the men are vying for is a corpse with no face. Indeed LAURA, goes the genre one further by taking apart the conventions, then putting them back together, and diving wholeheartedly into them for the finale—a cocktail party denouement to name the killer.

LAURA, based on the novel by Vera Caspary, revolves around the murder of the title character (Tierney)—a shotgun blast completely obliterating the corpse's once-lovely face. Homicide detective Mark McPherson (Andrews) has a trio of suspects—newspaper critic Waldo Lydecker (Webb), who "created" Laura; playboy/parasite and fiance Shelby Carpenter (Price); and Anne Treadwell (Anderson), Laura's socialite aunt who has been carrying on with Shelby. Just as Mark is beginning to fall in love with a vision of the deceased woman—in the form of an oil portrait—in walks the *real* Laura . . .

LAURA is a truly haunting study of obsession, with suitably poignant music provided by David Raksin (lyrics by Johnny Mercer). Originally, Otto Preminger was assigned only as producer, with studio chieftain Darryl Zanuck offering the directing chore to Rouben Mamoulian. Part of the way into production, however, Zanuck fired Mamoulian and handed the reins over to Preminger. Preminger reshot Mamoulian's footage, replaced cinematographer Lucian Ballard with Joseph La Shelle (who won an Academy Award), and scrapped the Mamoulian costumes and sets—including a portrait of Laura which Mamoulian's wife had painted.

LAVENDER HILL MOB, THE   DVD
1951 82m   bw   Crime/Comedy   ★★★★
Ealing   (U.K.)

Alec Guinness (*Henry Holland*), Stanley Holloway (*Pendlebury*), Sidney James (*Lackery*), Alfie Bass (*Shorty*), Marjorie Fielding (*Mrs. Chalk*), John Gregson (*Farrow*), Edie Martin (*Miss Evesham*), Clive Morton (*Station Sergeant*), Ronald Adam (*Turner*), Sydney Tafler (*Clayton*)

p, Michael Balcon; d, Charles Crichton; w, T.E.B. Clarke; ph, Douglas Slocombe; ed, Seth Holt; m, Georges Auric; art d, William Kellner; fx, Sydney Pearson; cos, Anthony Mendleson

AAN Best Actor: Alec Guinness; AA Best Story and Screenplay: T.E.B. Clarke

A hilarious tongue-in-cheek crime comedy, one of the finest to come out of the Ealing Studios during their most prolific years. Guinness stars as a mild-mannered transporter of gold bullion who, after 20 years of faithful service, blithely decides to steal one million pounds' worth. He enlists Holloway, an old pal who is a paperweight manufacturer and a bit of a sculptor. They team up with James and Bass, two cockney professional crooks, and the scheme is launched. After a successful hijack, they melt down their booty, mold it into small, souvenir

Eiffel Towers, and ship it off to Paris. Guinness and Holloway follow the gold, only to learn that six of the Eiffel Towers have been purchased by a group of daytripping English schoolgirls. Much hilarity follows, including a superlative chase scene in which Guinness and Holloway, driving a stolen police car, thwart their pursuers by issuing contradictory messages over the police radio, which ends by broadcasting "Old MacDonald Had a Farm" to all cars! The film had begun, however, with Guinness telling this story to a man in a swank Rio restaurant. The camera returns there for the conclusion, and we see that Guinness is not only having a drink with the other chap—he's handcuffed to him.

Guinness is winning as the last man on earth you'd suspect of being a criminal (he was nominated for an Oscar but lost to Gary Cooper, for HIGH NOON). Clarke's screenplay quite rightly won the award. Many of England's best comic actors are seen in small roles, including Sidney Tafler, Peter Bull, and John Gregson. In a tiny role, you may notice James Fox (brother of Edward), still being billed as William. And in the opening sequence, Guinness hands a cute young woman some money and tells her to buy a little gift. You'll have to look fast to recognize Audrey Hepburn as the little girl.

L'AVVENTURA   DVD
1960 143m   bw   Drama   ★★★★
Cino del Duca/Produzioni Cinematografiche Europee/Societe Cinematographique Lyre   (Italy/France)

Monica Vitti (*Claudia*), Gabriele Ferzetti (*Sandro*), Lea Massari (*Anna*), Dominique Blanchar (*Giulia*), James Addams (*Corrado*), Renzo Ricci (*Anna's Father*), Esmeralda Ruspoli (*Princess Patrizia*), Lelio Luttazzi (*Raimondo*), Dorothy De Poliolo (*Gloria Perkins*), Giovanni Petrucci (*Young Prince Geoffredo*)

p, Amato Pennasilico; d, Michelangelo Antonioni; w, Michelangelo Antonioni, Elio Bartolini, Tonino Guerra (based on a story by Michelangelo Antonioni); ph, Aldo Scavarda; ed, Eraldo da Roma; m, Giovanni Fusco; art d, Piero Poletto; cos, Adriana Berselli

The title translates as "The Adventure" and this *is* an adventure, if you're willing to take it. A group of wealthy Italians goes yachting to a rocky island near Sicily. After arriving, they notice that Anna (Massari) is missing, and everyone searches for her amidst the endless crevices and wave-battered cliffs. Her best friend, Claudia (Vitti), teams with Anna's lover, Sandro (Ferzetti), in the search, which is eventually abandoned in the hope that Anna simply left the island. Inquiries are made in town as to her whereabouts, and several people claim to have seen her. In the process, Sandro becomes increasingly involved with Claudia, who becomes his lover and substitute for Anna.

L'AVVENTURA is one of Antonioni's finest films, and a landmark in the devlopment of cinematic narrative. The seemingly pressing question raised by the film's opening—"What happened to Anna?"—becomes increasingly irrelevant as we learn that there is no "adventure" of this type, just a shifting, unsettling meditation on contemporary alienation and the opacity of all human relationships. The acting is appropriately minimalist and the blank-faced, passive Vitti is marvelouly Garboesque in the role that deservedly made her an international star. One character will be in deep focus at the "back" of the image, seemingly ready to call out to the person in the foreground, but communication is all but impossible. Even sex is a feeble attempt to escape the oddly charged ennui of this milieu. As with all Antonioni, the cinematography and composition are unsurpassed. He scatters his existential characters over the landscape, brilliantly emphasizing empty space over the trappings of plot. Photographed largely outdoors, shooting took months to complete and sent the original production company, Imeria, into debt. Cino Del Duca came to Antonioni's aid and filming continued, though many of the summer shots actually took place in the winter. Some four months later, the Cannes Film Festival audience greeted the picture with an unparalleled assault of hisses and boos. Several months later, though, L'AVVENTURA set box-office records in Paris; by the time it hit America, it had received a "condemned" rating from the National League of Decency—always a good sign.

LAW OF DESIRE
(LA LEY DEL DESEO)
1987 100m c   Comedy   ★★★½
El Deseo/Laurenfilm   (Spain)

Eusebio Poncela *(Pablo Quintero)*, Carmen Maura *(Tina Quintero)*, Antonio Banderas *(Antonio Benitez)*, Miguel Molina *(Juan Bermudez)*, Manuela Velasco *(Ada, Child)*, Bibi Andersen *(Ada, Mother)*, Fernando Guillen *(Inspector)*, Nacho Martinez *(Dr. Martin)*, Helga Line *(Antonio's Mother)*, Fernando G. Cuervo *(Policeman, Child)*

p, Miguel Angel Perez Campos; d, Pedro Almodovar; w, Pedro Almodovar; ph, Angel Luis Fernandez (Eastmancolor); ed, Jose Salcedo; m, Igor Stravinsky, Dmitri Shostakovich; cos, Jose M. Cossio

Spain's acclaimed director, Pedro Almodovar, who scored a huge international success with WOMEN ON THE VERGE OF A NERVOUS BREAKDOWN, has stated he wants to reach audiences through "their hearts, their minds, and their genitals." In LAW OF DESIRE, he more than fulfills this challenge, offering an exhilarating romp detailing the erotic adventures of Pablo (Eusebio Poncela), a gay filmmaker; his bisexual lover, Juan (Miguel Molina); his transsexual "sister," Tina (Carmen Maura), the mother of a teenager fathered by her when "she" was a "he"; and Antonio (Antonio Banderas), who becomes involved with both Pablo and Tina as the story accelerates to its tragic finale.

No one can accuse Almodovar of bashfulness. LAW OF DESIRE works overtime, piling one eccentric plot element atop another…and it works. Flashy? Yes. Vulgar? Yes. Impassioned? Thanks to the wonderful Maura and Banderas, definitely. In this, his seventh feature, Almodovar reveals himself to be a supremely stylish and self-assured filmmaker, one of the bright lights of international cinema.

LAWRENCE OF ARABIA   DVD
1962 220m c   Biography/Adventure/War ★★★★★
Horizon   (U.K.)

Peter O'Toole *(T.E. Lawrence)*, Alec Guinness *(Prince Feisal)*, Anthony Quinn *(Auda Abu Tayi)*, Jack Hawkins *(Gen. Allenby)*, Jose Ferrer *(Turkish Bey)*, Anthony Quayle *(Col. Harry Brighton)*, Claude Rains *(Mr. Dryden)*, Arthur Kennedy *(Jackson Bentley)*, Donald Wolfit *(Gen. Murray)*, Omar Sharif *(Sherif Ali Ibn El Kharish)*

p, Sam Spiegel, David Lean; d, David Lean; w, Robert Bolt, Michael Wilson (based on *The Seven Pillars of Wisdom* by T.E. Lawrence); ph, Freddie Young; ed, Anne V. Coates; m, Maurice Jarre; prod d, John Box; art d, John Stoll; cos, Phyllis Dalton

AA Best Picture; AAN Best Actor: Peter O'Toole; *AAN Best Supporting Actor:* Omar Sharif; *AA Best Director:* David Lean; *AAN Best Adapted Screenplay:* Robert Bolt; *AA Best Color Cinematography:* Fred A. Young; *AA Best Film Editing:* Anne Coates; *AA Best Original Score:* Maurice Jarre; *AA Best Art Direction-Set Decoration (Color):* John Box, John Stoll, Dario Simoni; *AA Best Sound:* John Cox

David Lean's splendid biography of the enigmatic T.E. Lawrence paints a complex portrait of the desert-loving Englishman who united Arab tribes in battle against the Ottoman Turks during WWI. At the center of Lean's superbly sun-drenched, 70mm canvas is Peter O'Toole's eccentric but magnificent portrayal of the erudite, Oxford-educated lieutenant, who wangles an assignment as an observer with Prince Feisal (Alec Guinness), the leader of the Arab revolt against the Turks. Feisal is resigned to allowing his tribal army to become just another branch of the British forces, but the messianic Lawrence, determined to prevent the Arabs from falling under British colonial domination, undertakes a military miracle. He, Sherif Ali (Omar Sharif)—whom Lean introduces as a tiny dot on the desert horizon that steadily enlarges, in one of the film's most striking scenes—and 50 men traverse the "uncrossable" Nefud Desert; join forces with their traditional tribal enemies, led by Auda Abu Tayi (Anthony Quinn); and rout the Turks at the strategic port city of Aqaba. Given the go-ahead by Gen. Allenby (Jack Hawkins), worshiped by the Arabs he has brought together, and cloaked in their flowing white robes, "El Aurens" leads the Arabs in a brutal guerrilla war that is as much about establishing Arab sovereignty as it is about defeating the Turks. His thrilling exploits are glorified by the Lowell Thomas-like American journalist Jackson Bentley (Arthur Kennedy). In time, however, Lawrence's legions dwindle, he begins to revel sadistically in violence, his grand attempt at overseeing the formation of a united Arab Council in Damascus collapses, and he returns to Britain exhausted. Lean's film is best appreciated on the big screen, and in 1989 a carefully restored version of LAWRENCE was released that reinstated 20 minutes cut for the original roadshow release and another 15 minutes trimmed when it was rereleased in 1970. Moreover, Lean and his original editor, Anne V. Coates, were finally given the chance to do a "fine cut" on the film, now 216 memorable minutes long.

LAWS OF GRAVITY
1992 100m c   Drama   ★★★½
Meistrich Corporation   (U.S.)   R

Peter Greene *(Jimmy)*, Edie Falco *(Denise)*, Paul Schulzie *(Frankie)*, Tony Fernandez *(Tommy)*, James McCauley *(Kenny)*, Anibal Lierras *(Ray)*, Miguel Sierra *(Vasquez)*, Adam Trese *(Jon)*, Arabella Field *(Celia)*, Saul Stein *(Sal)*

p, Larry Meistrich, Bob Gosse; d, Nick Gomez; w, Nick Gomez; ph, Jean DeSegonzac; ed, Tom McArdle; prod d, Monica Bretherton

A gritty take on the day-to-day life of petty thugs on the mean streets of Brooklyn, LAWS OF GRAVITY captures this violent and volatile world without without being exploitative or sensationalist.

Jimmy (Peter Greene) and his lifelong friend Jon (Adam Trese) are two neighborhood punks who spend their days stealing, fighting and hanging out. Jimmy, at least, is in a stable domestic relationship with Denise (Edie Falco), and is beginning to question his lot in life; Jon, a few years younger, runs on a very short fuse and is only one step ahead of the police, who have issued a summons for his arrest; this doesn't stop him from picking fights with virtually anyone who looks in the direction of his girlfriend Celia (Arabella Field). The endless cycle of stealing, brawling and drinking takes on new dimensions when another local, Frankie (Paul Schultzie), returns home from Florida. A sociopath with boy-next-door looks, Frankie has brought with him a cache of stolen handguns which he convinces Jon and Jimmy to help him "move." The presence of the weapons only serves to escalate the tensions within the group, leading to an appropriately violent conclusion.

LAWS OF GRAVITY's shoestring budget (reputedly only $38,000) forced some interesting choices on writer-director Nick Gomez. The use of a hand-held camera (masterfully employed by Jean De Segonzac); and frequent lack of master shots, gives the film a compelling *cinema verite* feel. This is complemented by the improvisational quality of the dialogue and the realistically drawn characters. Gomez's keen eye for casting is one of the film's strongest attributes,

with an entire group of virtual unknowns turning in uniformly credible performances.

LE BEAU MARIAGE

1982 97m c Drama/Comedy ★★★★

Losanger/Carosse (France) PG

Beatrice Romand (Sabine), Andre Dussollier (Edmond), Feodor
Atkine (Simon), Huguette Faget (Antique Dealer), Arielle
Dombasle (Clarisse), Thamila Mezbah (Mother), Sophie Renoir
(Lise), Herve Duhamel (Frederic), Pascal Greggory (Nicolas),
Virginie Thevenet (The Bride)

p, Margaret Menogoz; d, Eric Rohmer; w, Eric Rohmer; ph,
Bernard Lutic, Romain Winding, Nicolas Brunet; ed, Cecile
Decugis, Lisa Heredia; m, Ronan Gure, Simon Des Innocents

The second installment in Eric Rohmer's "Comedies and
Proverbs" series, LE BEAU MARIAGE is the charming tale
of Sabine (Beatrice Romand), a university student with a Paris
flat who decides one day, quite arbitrarily, to get married. All
she is lacking is a husband, a minor detail. She leaves her
painter boyfriend, quits her antique-store job, and begins pursuing Edmond (Andre Dussollier), a busy lawyer who is
friendly to Sabine but clearly not interested in romancing her.
This thoroughly enjoyable picture is carried by the spunky,
idiosyncratic performance of Romand, who appeared 12
years earlier in Rohmer's "Moral Tale," CLAIRE'S KNEE.
Two of her costars in this film would also be rewarded with
lead roles in subsequent Rohmer films—Arielle Dombasle,
who appears in PAULINE AT THE BEACH, and Sophie
Renoir (cast here as Romand's pesty little sister), who stars in
Rohmer's final "Comedies and Proverbs" entry,
BOYFRIENDS AND GIRLFRIENDS. There's also a fine
synthesized pop score that you may find yourself humming
long after the film's end. In French with English subtitles.

LE BEAU SERGE

1958 97m bw Drama ★★★½

United Motion Picture (France)

Gerard Blain (Serge), Jean-Claude Brialy (Francois), Bernadette
Lafont (Marie), Edmond Beauchamp (Glomaud), Michele Meritz
(Yvonne), Jeanne Perez, Claude Cerval, Andre Dino

d, Claude Chabrol; w, Claude Chabrol; ph, Henri Decae; ed,
Jacques Gaillard; m, Emile Delpierre

Generally considered the film that put the French New Wave
in the history books (though Jacques Rivette's PARIS
BELONGS TO US was the first to go into production), LE
BEAU SERGE received overwhelming critical approval of its
use of non-professional actors, raw black-and-white photography (masterfully executed by Henri Decae), and personal
vision. It is the tale of two old friends, Francois (Jean-Claude
Brialy), a city dweller who returns to the provincial French village of his childhood, and Serge (Gerard Blain), a successful
architect-turned-drunkard. After the birth of a malformed son,
Serge's life and marriage go into a tailspin as he collapses
under the weight of tremendous guilt. Unfortunately, the film
is cluttered with Catholicism, which director Claude Chabrol
had the good sense to deemphasize as his career developed.
Though highly acclaimed, LE BEAU SERGE was quickly
overshadowed by the subsequent success of Francois
Truffaut's 400 BLOWS, Jean-Luc Godard's BREATHLESS,
and Alain Resnais's HIROSHIMA MON AMOUR. LES
COUSINS, a companion piece to LE BEAU SERGE that
also starred Brialy and Blain, appeared the following year to
an equally enthusiastic reception.

LE BOUCHER

1969 93m c Thriller **DVD** ★★★★

La Boetie/Euro Intl. (France/Italy) GP

Stephane Audran (Helene), Jean Yanne (Popaul), Antonio
Passalia (Angelo), Mario Beccaria (Leon Hamel), Pasquale
Ferone (Pere Cahrpy), Roger Rudel (Police Inspector
Grumbach), William Guerault (Charles)

p, Andre Genoves; d, Claude Chabrol; w, Claude Chabrol; ph,
Jean Rabier (Eastmancolor); ed, Jacques Gaillard; m, Pierre
Jansen; cos, Joseph Poulard

A calculated, slow-paced thriller set in the French countryside, where schoolteacher Audran begins a new assignment.
She is soon romanced by the village butcher, Yanne, though
she seems more concerned with her schoolchildren than with
finding a lover. In the meantime, the village is stricken with
random murders. Audran finds herself directly involved
when a young girl's body is found near the schoolyard.
During a school outing, she and the children take a lunch
break and eat their sandwiches outdoors. One girl, who is sitting next to a cliff, suddenly finds blood dripping onto her
bread. Above her is discovered yet another butchered body.
Audran's suspicions are raised when she finds Yanne's cigarette lighter next to the body, but the clever, deranged killer is
one step ahead of her and buys an identical lighter. By the
finale, Audran's concern has turned into deadly fear as she
barricades herself inside her house.
    LE BOUCHER is a compelling psychological thriller
that occasionally gets bogged down and fails to reach the level
of suspense that could have been achieved. Like the psychopathic killer of little girls in Fritz Lang's M, Yanne's character
is presented in a manner which is calculated to stir a measure
of audience sympathy: he is a man with good qualities who is
unable to help himself. Audran, the real-life wife of director
Chabrol and star of three of his films, gives a compelling performance, but she is simply too sophisticated to come across
as a country schoolteacher.

LE GAI SAVOIR

1968 95m c Drama ★★★★

O.R.T.F./Anouchka/Bavaria Atelier (France)

Juliet Berto (Patricia Lumumba), Jean-Pierre Leaud (Emile
Rousseau)

d, Jean-Luc Godard; w, Jean-Luc Godard (based on "Emile" by
Jean Jacques Rousseau); ph, Georges Leclerc (Eastmancolor);
ed, Germaine Cohen

A fascinating film from the master of cinematic discourse,
Jean-Luc Godard, in which he makes a profound attempt to
dissolve narrative structure to its most basic elements: sound
and image. Commissioned by the French government as a television adaptation of Jean Jacques Rousseau's "Emile," LE
GAI SAVOIR instead turned out to be a study of language, or,
more precisely, film language. It is completely absent of plot
and leaves Berto and Leaud (two of the most prominent acting figures in the French New Wave) sitting in the black void
of a sound stage, lit only by a single light. Not surprisingly the
French government was furious with Godard for his failure to
deliver an "acceptable" movie and refused to televise it, allowing him to buy back the rights. What results is a wealth of philosophy relating to Godard's radical thoughts on filmmaking,
delivered in the form of a conversation between Leaud and
Berto. Intercut with their thoughts are some compelling word
association tests which further exemplify Godard's love of
language. It's no CASABLANCA, but for those with adventurous tastes and an interest in questioning the status quo, LE
GAI SAVOIR's language deserves the same consideration as
the literature of such contemporaries as Jean-Paul Sartre.

LE PETIT THEATRE DE JEAN RENOIR

1969 100m c Drama ★★★★
Son et Lumiere/ORTF (France)

THE LAST NEW YEAR'S EVE: Nino Fornicola *(The Bum)*, Minny Monti *(The Female Bum)*, Roger Trapp *(Max Vialle)*, Roland Martin, Frederic Santaya, Pierre Gulda, THE ELECTRIC FLOOR WAXER: Marguerite Cassan *(Isabelle)*, Pierre Olaf *(The Husband)*, Jacques Dynam *(The 2nd Husband)*, Jean-Louis Tristan *(Agent)*

p, Pierre Long; d, Jean Renoir; w, Jean Renoir; ph, Georges Leclerc (Eastmancolor); ed, Genevieve Winding; m, Joseph Kosma, Jean Wiener; prod d, Gilbert Margerie

An exceptional coda to the long and magnificent career of Renoir, which sums up his world in a personal manner. Divided into four parts, each introduced by the charming 75-year-old director himself, the picture moves from the artificially theatrical to the naturally realistic. The first episode, "The Last New Year's Eve," has Fornicola, a ragged and seemingly lonely bum, standing outside the window of an upper-class restaurant. One of the rich people inside pays to have the bum watch them eat from the outside. Of course, the diners lose their appetites, and as a consolation they have the food given to the bum. One of the rich women also gives her coat to the man. He is then seen returning to his riverside shelter, where he is greeted by his equally ragged wife. Together, during the night, they peacefully die. The segment was shot entirely on a stage, with Renoir paying homage in his narration to Hans Christian Andersen. The second episode, "The Electric Floor Waxer," is an odd little piece for those familiar with Renoir (and for anyone else, for that matter). Based on an earlier project, "It's Revolution," this tale is a satirical opera complete with singing choruses of office workers rising up from the lower depths of the Metro station. They sing repetitive refrains about their offices and their jobs. One woman (Cassan) goes through life obsessed with giving the floor a good waxing, causing heartache among her successive husbands. Dynam, her second, finally saves Cassan from waxing by throwing the vibrating, whirling machine out the window. As it crashes to the ground below, Cassan leaps from the window to join her electric lover. The third episode is hardly an episode at all; in one long dolly in-dolly out Jeanne Moreau sings a little tune called "When Love Dies" (Oscar Cremieux). It is included, as Renoir puts it, to "take us for a little while outside our century of sleazy progress." The fourth episode, "The King of Yvetot," is the most purely realistic, shot entirely on location. At the introduction Renoir shows us his little theater (a miniature model of a stage) and briefly explains the sport of petanque, the values and the rules of this game. He takes a tiny metal ball and rolls it along the little stage, and with one quick edit, we are transported into the world of cinema as a large petanque ball rolls along the ground. An old man is seen playing, then his young wife, and then her younger lover. The conflicts of this triangle are resolved peacefully and with respect to set morals in a final game of petanque, which Renoir "firmly believes to be an instrument of peace." The film's finale is also the end of Renoir's little theater; the members of the cast come out for a closing bow. The actors thank us for watching, and we cannot help but feel thanks for Renoir's humble presentation. What way could be more appropriate for one of filmdom's greatest directors (and probably the greatest in Europe) to wrap up his truly profound career? Originally made for French television in 1969.

LE SAMOURAI

1967 101m c Crime ★★★★
Filmel/CICC/Fida Cinematografica (France/Italy) PG

Alain Delon *(Jef Costello)*, Nathalie Delon *(Jan Lagrange)*, Francois Perier *(The Inspector)*, Cathy Rosier *(Valerie)*, Jacques Leroy *(The Gunman)*, Jean-Pierre Posier *(Olivier Rey)*, Catherine Jourdan *(Hat-Check Girl)*, Michel Boisrond *(Wiener)*, Robert Favart *(Barman)*, Andre Salgues *(Garage Man)*

p, Jean-Pierre Melville; d, Jean-Pierre Melville; w, Jean-Pierre Melville (based on the novel *The Ronin* by Joan McLeod); ph, Henri Decae, Jean Charvein; ed, Monique Bonnot, Yolande Maurette; m, Francois de Roubaix; art d, Francois de Lamothe

Alain Delon stars as a hyper-cool hit man in what is perhaps filmmaker Jean-Pierre Melville's definitive take on American gangster films.

Professional contract killer Jef Costello (Alain Delon) is hired to kill a nightclub proprietor. Costello carries out the killing but is spotted leaving the murdered man's office by the club's pianist, Valerie (Cathy Rosier). He is subsequently arrested and put in a lineup, but Valerie inexplicably refuses to identify him. Meanwhile, the mysterious men who hired Costello decide that he must be eliminated, and when he's released by the police and goes to a rendezvous for his payoff, a gunman (Jacques Leroy) shoots him, but only wounds him. After nursing his wounds, Costello goes back to the nightclub and asks Valerie why she didn't turn him in, but she won't tell him. On further investigation, Costello finds out the name of Valerie's true boss and the identity of his next target: Valerie.

While not necessarily Melville's best film, LE SAMOURAI is probably the most accessible and quintessential of all his existential re-imaginings of American crime films, and quite possibly his ultimate statement on solitude and the ethos of crime. Delon has one of his great roles here as the perfect embodiment of Melville's archetypal trench-coated, fedora-wearing anti-hero, whose blankly handsome face masks a surfeit of feelings. Besides being a marvelous character study, the film is also a painstaking crime procedural (much like THE ASPHALT JUNGLE, one of Melville's favorite films), as it contrasts the devious actions of the police with Costello's similarly ritualistic behavior. The film's influence on modern crime films is immense, from the costumes to the cinematography, most especially those of John Woo (who once called it "the closest thing to a perfect movie that I have ever seen"), and whose THE KILLER (1989) paid it homage with its nightclub milieu and cool, emotionless hitman named Jeff.

LEADBELLY

1976 126m c Musical/Biography ★★★½
Paramount (U.S.) PG

Roger E. Mosley *(Huddie Ledbetter)*, Paul Benjamin *(Wes Ledbetter)*, Madge Sinclair *(Miss Eula)*, Alan Manson *(Prison Chief Guard)*, Albert Hall *(Dicklicker)*, Art Evans *(Blind Lemon Jefferson)*, James E. Brodhead *(John Lomax)*, John Henry Faulk *(Governor Neff)*, Vivian Bonnell *(Old Lady)*, Dana Manno *(Margaret Judd)*

p, Marc Merson; d, Gordon Parks Sr.; w, Ernest Kinoy; ph, Bruce Surtees (Eastmancolor); ed, Harry Howard; m, Fred Karlin; prod d, Robert Boyle

Fine biopic of famed black blues/folk singer Huddie Ledbetter, known as Leadbelly, who wrote or adapted such classics as "Goodnight, Irene," "The Midnight Special," "Rock Island Line," and "The Bourgeois Blues." Ledbetter's hard life is related in flashback from his early teens to his last term in prison (he also served twice on chain gangs). The film shows how he he was victimized by racism but does not minimize the complexity of his erratic personality—often manifested in outbursts of violence. Though several of his songs are rendered well here by HiTide Harris, backed by Sonny Terry, Brownie McGhee, David Cohen, and Dick Rosmini, LEADBELLY focuses less on the man's musical artistry than one would wish. Still, this is a very informative film, beautifully photographed by Bruce Surtees, with fine performances by almost everyone in the cast, especially Robert E. Mosley in the title role.

LEAGUE OF EXTRAORDINARY GENTLEMEN, THE `DVD`
2003 112m c   Action/Fantasy/Adventure   ★
MediaStream III/Don Murphy   PG-13
Productions/20th Century Fox   (U.S./Germany)

Sean Connery (Allan Quatermain), Naseeruddin Shah (Captain Nemo), Peta Wilson (Mina Harker), Tony Curran (Rodney Skinner), Shane West (Tom Sawyer), Stuart Townsend (Dorian Gray), Jason Flemyng (Henry Jekyll/Edward Hyde), Richard Roxburgh (M), David Hemmings (Nigel), Max Ryan (Dante)

p, Trevor Albert, Don Murphy; d, Stephen Norrington; w, James Dale Robinson (based on the comic books by Alan Moore and Kevin O'Neill); ph, Dan Laustsen; ed, Paul Rubell; m, Trevor Jones; prod d, Carol Spier; art d, Elinor Rose Galbraith, Jindrich Koci, James McAteer, Marco Bittner Rosser, James F. Truesdale; fx, Tim Alexander, Terry Glass, David Goldberg, Industrial Light & Magic, Janek Sirrs, Thomas J. Smith, Dana Hunter Suddath, John E. Sullivan; cos, Jacqueline West

Bloated and incoherent, this big-budget adaptation of Alan Moore's brilliant graphic novel jettisons the clever amalgamation of 19th-century pulp fictions in favor of 21st-century Hollywood action formulas. The product of this reverse alchemy is numbingly ordinary.

London, 1899: Acting on behalf of Her Majesty's government, the mysterious M (Richard Roxburgh) assembles a group of peculiar and uniquely talented individuals: aging African adventurer Allan Quatermain (Sean Connery); shape-shifter Dr. Henry Jekyll (Jason Flemyng); immortal dandy Dorian Gray (Stuart Townsend); invisible cut purse Rodney Skinner (Tony Curran); enigmatic submariner Captain Nemo (Naseeruddin Shah); vampire Mina Harker (Peta Wilson); and American detective Tom Sawyer (Shane West). Their mission: to go to Venice, where a top-secret summit of world leaders is convening to avert a world war, and protect them from the nefarious Fantom, who seems determined to fan the flames of international conflict for his own benefit.

The issue isn't that screenwriter James Dale Robinson and director Stephen Norrington made radical changes to Moore's intensely literary, densely allusive work of steam-punk metafiction in the name of making it palatable to people who don't even read comic books, let alone 19th-century novels; it's that they turned an engaging story filled with flawed, complicated characters into a series of CGI-heavy action set pieces, each duller than the one before, and flattened the extraordinary personalities into one-note caricatures. For a big-budget effects extravaganza, the CGI is surprisingly unconvincing, and much of the production design leaves a less than wondrous impression. The League's custom-designed car—a sort of 19th-century Batmobile—looks simply ridiculous, and the first appearance of Nemo's submarine, the scimitar-like Nautilus, is a terrible disappointment.

LEARNING TREE, THE
1969 107m c   Drama   ★★★
Winger Enterprises   (U.S.)   M

Kyle Johnson (Newt Winger), Alex Clarke (Marcus Savage), Estelle Evans (Sarah Winger), Dana Elcar (Sheriff Kirby), Mira Waters (Arcella Jefferson), Joel Fluellen (Uncle Rob), Malcolm Atterbury (Silas Newhall), Richard Ward (Booker Savage), Russell Thorson (Judge Cavanaugh), Peggy Rea (Miss McClintock)

p, Gordon Parks Sr.; d, Gordon Parks Sr.; w, Gordon Parks (based on his novel); ph, Burnett Guffey (Panavision, Technicolor); ed, George Rohrs; m, Gordon Parks; art d, Edward Engoron; fx, Albert Whitlock

Undoubtedly the biggest surprise among the first 25 films selected in 1989 for inclusion in the National Film Registry, this visually beautiful and moving, if somewhat melodramatic, story of a black teenager growing up in Kansas in the 1920s was the first feature film by a black director to be financed by a major Hollywood studio. Gordon Parks directed, produced, wrote, and composed the score of this adaptation of his 1963 semi-autobiographical novel after a highly successful career as an acclaimed photojournalist.

Essentially a coming-of-age tale, the film focuses on small-town Kansas denizen Newt Winger (Johnson). Newt is shown learning about sex (from a prostitute) and death, encountering the latter after discovering the corpse of a black gambler who was murdered by the local sheriff, Kirby (Elcar). Newt's nemesis is Marcus Savage (Clarke), an embittered young man saddled with an absent mother and a negligent, angry father. Newt, by contrast, is supported by his hard-working, understanding mother (Evans), who has kept her son on the square despite the hardships and racism he must face. Newt's resolve is tested when Newt experiences heartbreak and later witnesses the murder of his benign white employer Kiner (George Mitchell) by Marcus's father (Ward) and a white drunkard (Atterbury).

In tracing the encounters that make up Newt's moral and practical education, Parks depicts the ambiguous racial attitudes of blacks and whites in the Kansas town with an ironic complexity rarely found in earlier films about racism. The film is far more complex than Parks's strikingly different second feature, SHAFT, the hugely successful, angry, urban action film that set the tone for the 1970s blaxploitation movies. THE LEARNING TREE's potential openness to criticism as a naive, old-fashioned tale is made greater by its sentimental characterizations, occasional sermonizing, and leisurely pace. On the other hand, Parks and cinematographer Guffey, who filmed on location in the director's native Fort Scott, beautifully capture the feel of 1920s Kansas, and Johnson's performance (if none of the others) is very fine.

LEATHER BOYS, THE `DVD`
1963 108m bw   Drama   ★★★
Raymond Stross   (U.K.)

Rita Tushingham (Dot), Colin Campbell (Reggie), Dudley Sutton (Pete), Gladys Henson (Gran), Avice Landone (Reggie's Mother), Lockwood West (Reggie's Father), Betty Marsden (Dot's Mother), Martin Matthews (Uncle Arthur), Johnny Briggs (Boy Friend), James Chase (Les)

p, Raymond Stross; d, Sidney J. Furie; w, Gillian Freeman (based on the novel by Eliot George); ph, Gerald Gibbs (CinemaScope); ed, Reginald Beck; m, Bill McGuffie; art d, Arthur Lawson

Dot (Tushingham) marries motorcycle buff Reggie (Campbell) to escape from her parents, but the relationship never gets off the ground. She doesn't do any housework, and only cooks cans of beans. Reggie moves out and goes to live with his friend Pete (Sutton), whom Reggie begins to suspect is gay. He moves back when he hears that Dot is pregnant but discovers that she's sleeping with another man. He and Pete decide to run off to sea, but a few realities about their relationship must be settled first. Not the greatest of Britain's "angry young man" films of the period, but it benefits from good acting. Furie's evocation of "kitchen sink" realism and an attempt to be adult about hasty marriages and gay themes.

LEAVING LAS VEGAS `DVD`
1995 112m c   Drama   ★★★
United Artists/Lumiere Pictures   (U.S.)   R

Nicolas Cage (Ben Sanderson), Elisabeth Shue (Sera), Julian Sands (Yuri), Richard Lewis (Peter), Valeria Golino (Terri), Steven Weber (Marc Nussbaum), Kim Adams (Sheila), Emily Procter

(Debbie), Graham Beckel *(L.A. Bartender)*, R. Lee Ermey *(Conventioneer)*

p, Lila Cazes, Annie Stewart; d, Mike Figgis; w, Mike Figgis (based on the novel by John O'Brien); ph, Declan Quinn; ed, John Smith; m, Mike Figgis; prod d, Waldemar Kalinowski; art d, Barry M. Kingston; fx, William Harrison; cos, Laura Goldsmith, Vivienne Westwood

AA Best Actor: Nicolas Cage; *AAN Best Actress:* Elisabeth Shue; *AAN Best Director:* Mike Figgis; *AAN Best Adapted Screenplay:* Mike Figgis

One of the most highly praised films of 1995, LEAVING LAS VEGAS is as obsessive, but not so well written, as LAST TANGO IN PARIS or JULES AND JIM, films that are also far more cinematically imaginative. The critical consensus on Mike Figgis's romantic downer hinged on its universal theme—"It's about unconditional love, don't you see?"—suggesting that certain overwhelmed critics really should get out more, and not just to the movies.

When we first meet Ben (Nicolas Cage), he's careening through the aisles of a liquor store, blissfully filling up his cart with bottles. Ben is systematically divesting himself of everything most people care about—his family, his possessions, his job—and intends to blow his severance pay on a final, fatal alcoholic binge in Las Vegas. While driving drunkenly along the Strip, he meets clean-scrubbed prostitute Sera (Elisabeth Shue), takes her back to his room and promptly passes out. This, perhaps needless to say, is only the beginning of a beautiful and damned relationship.

Figgis gives the film his trademark velvet-noir look—a remarkable, if not necessarily laudable achievement, given that it was shot for a pittance on Super 16 film—which belies the grittily nihilistic, verite intentions he professed. The busy jazz score was composed by Renaissance Man Figgis, and features the distinctive and wholly inappropriate vocal stylings of Sting. Cage, who has proved an effective comedian in RAISING ARIZONA, MOONSTRUCK, and VAMPIRE'S KISS, won an Academy Award for his monotonously doomed performance. His weird, San Fernando Valley-boy inflections merely emphasize the thudding banality of Figgis's would-be mordant lines, like "I kept running out of booze, and the store would be closed because I kept forgetting to look at my watch." Shue works like the dickens, but she's never convincing as a streetwalker: her Sera is too perfectly groomed, aerobicized, and dressed. What draws her to Ben is, like his inner torment, a complete mystery.

LEFT-HANDED GUN, THE

1958 102m bw Biography/Western ★★★½
Warner Bros. (U.S.)

Paul Newman *(Billy Bonney)*, Lita Milan *(Celsa)*, John Dehner *(Pat Garrett)*, Hurd Hatfield *(Moultrie)*, James Congdon *(Charlie Boudre)*, James Best *(Tom Folliard)*, Colin Keith-Johnston *(Tunstall)*, John Dierkes *(McSween)*, Robert Anderson *(Hill)*, Wally Brown *(Moon)*

p, Fred Coe; d, Arthur Penn; w, Leslie Stevens (based on the teleplay "The Death of Billy the Kid" by Gore Vidal); ph, Peverell Marley; ed, Folmar Blangsted; m, Alexander Courage; art d, Art Loel; cos, Marjorie Best

A good but disturbing psychological western, well directed by Penn and acted in a strangely fascinating style by Newman. Penn demythologizes Billy the Kid, and Newman plays him more honestly than anyone else ever has. He was a slow-witted illiterate with a streak of sadistic bloodlust in him, fiercely loyal to his few friends and deadly to all who became his enemy. Newman is nothing but a western guttersnipe until John Tunstall (Keith-Johnston), a kindly rancher whom Billy

had known in real life, treats him with understanding. Newman reacts as would any loveless human, becoming fanatically devoted to the rancher. When the unarmed Keith-Johnston is shot to death by a deputy and three others in a range war, Newman and his equally empty-headed saddlemates, Best and Congdon, track down the killers and murder them one by one. Pat Garrett (Dehner), the famous lawman who was the harsh, real-life father figure for Billy, vows revenge on the Kid after Newman kills one of the guests—the last of the foursome sought for Keith-Johnston's death—at Dehner's wedding party. Newman is arrested and jailed, but he escapes, murdering his guards in the process. The relentless Dehner then tracks him down and kills the unarmed outlaw with a single shot. Flitting in and out of Newman's life is a neurotic pulp writer, Hatfield, who creates the myth of Billy the Kid and then condemns the outlaw for not living up to his lies. This first film by director Penn stems from Gore Vidal's wacky, self-serving teleplay, "The Death of Billy the Kid," which was helmed by Penn for TV in 1955. Penn toned down Vidal's portrait of the Kid as a rampant homosexual which reflected the author's interests perhaps more than the facts of history. Newman, as he had in SOMEBODY UP THERE LIKES ME, took a role here which was originally coveted by James Dean, who died prematurely in a car accident, but he does a masterful job in portraying the ruthless killer whose reputation existed only beyond the grave.

LEGALLY BLONDE

DVD

2001 96m c Comedy ★★★½
Marc Platt Productions/MGM (U.S.) PG-13

Reese Witherspoon *(Elle Woods)*, Luke Wilson *(Emmett Rochmond)*, Selma Blair *(Vivian Kensington)*, Matthew Davis *(Warner Huntington)*, Victor Garber *(Professor Callahan)*, Jennifer Coolidge *(Paulette)*, Holland Taylor *(Professor Stromwell)*, Ali Larter *(Brooke Taylor Windham)*, Jessica Cauffiel *(Margot)*, Alanna Ubach *(Serena)*

p, Ric Kidney, Marc Platt; d, Robert Luketic; w, Karen McCullah Lutz, Kirsten Smith (based on the book by Amanda Brown); ph, Anthony B. Richmond; ed, Anita Brandt-Burgoyne, Grath Craven; m, Rolfe Kent; prod d, Melissa Stewart; art d, Daniel Bradford; fx, Dave Kelsey; chor, Toni Basi; cos, Carbonell, Sophie de Rakoff

Featherweight but eminently likeable fluff that serves as a perfect vehicle for Reese Witherspoon's considerable comedic talents.

The slim chance of being accepted to *any* law school, let alone Harvard, doesn't dissuade CULA senior Elle Woods (Witherspoon) from applying. Elle, whose signature color is pink, turns her baby blues towards Cambridge right after her snooty-but-cute Harvard-bound boyfriend, Warner (Matthew Davis), breaks up with her. Warner has political aspirations and tells Elle that he needs a wife who's a "Jackie," not a "Marilyn." Devastated, Elle decides to prove to Warner that she's got what it takes to be the kind of brainy wife he wants. Thanks to a surprisingly decent score on the LSATs—and an admissions video directed by a Coppola—Elle beats the unlikely odds, bamboozles the Harvard admissions panel, and gets in. Staying in, she soon learns, won't be so easy.

Making this kind of comedy work is a lot harder than it looks. Witherspoon, who's already demonstrated an admirable range in such diverse films as FREEWAY, PLEASANTVILLE, and ELECTION, takes what could have been a one-note character and lends her surprising depth; there's a real person under all that lip gloss, and she's adorable.

LEGENDS OF THE FALL

1994 133m c Western/Historical/Drama ★★½
TriStar (U.S.) R

Brad Pitt *(Tristan Ludlow)*, Anthony Hopkins *(Colonel William Ludlow)*, Aidan Quinn *(Alfred Ludlow)*, Julia Ormond *(Susannah Finncannon)*, Henry Thomas *(Samuel Ludlow)*, Karina Lombard *(Isabel Two)*, Tantoo Cardinal *(Pet)*, Gordon Tootoosis *(One Stab)*, Paul Desmond *(Decker)*, Christina Pickles *(Isabel)*

p, Edward Zwick, Bill Wittliff, Marshall Herskovitz; d, Edward Zwick; w, Susan Shilliday, Bill Wittliff (based on the novella by Jim Harrison); ph, John Toll; ed, Steven Rosenblum; m, James Horner; prod d, Lilly Kilvert; art d, Rick Roberts, Andrew Precht; fx, Mike Vezina; cos, Deborah Scott

AA Best Cinematography: John Toll; *AAN Best Art Direction-Set Decoration:* Lilly Kilvert, Dorree Cooper; *AAN Best Sound:* Paul Massey, David Campbell, Christopher David, Douglas Ganton

The golden shadows of the waning Old West are thrown across the big screen with full reverential treatment in this solid, unsurprising rendition of Jim Harrison's widely praised novella. Director Edward Zwick manages the requisite epic sweep, and most of the performances are on the money, but LEGENDS OF THE FALL succeeded at the box office largely thanks to freshly-minted screen superstar Brad Pitt.

Colonel Ludlow (Anthony Hopkins), an ex-cavalry officer living in the Montana wilderness, is left to raise three sons by himself when his wife leaves for the winter and never returns. The oldest, Alfred (Aidan Quinn), is sensible, with a head for business and politics. Hotheaded Samuel (Henry Thomas), the youngest, is always ready to subscribe to the latest political enthusiasm. The Colonel reserves a special fondness for the middle son, Tristan (Pitt). When Samuel returns from college with his fiancee, Susannah (Julia Ormond), all the men are smitten, stumbling over one another to teach her how to ride, rope, and shoot. But the close-knit family soon disintegrates, sundered by romantic rivalry and the outbreak of WWI.

Although Zwick's grand, even monumental, presentation is reminiscent of his Civil War opus GLORY, the picture belongs to the golden-maned Pitt, who is afforded no less than three princely entrances on horseback. A performer with more charisma than intelligence, he nevertheless easily dominates the ensemble and, with a big assist from Oscar-winning cinematographer John Toll, sometimes casts such a saintly, beatific sheen over the proceedings that he seems to glow from within. Newcomer Julia Ormond hits her mark as the sort of storybook British beauty for whom civilizations topple.

LEMONY SNICKET'S A SERIES OF UNFORTUNATE EVENTS

2004 107m c Fantasy/Adventure ★★★½
Nickelodeon Movies/Scott Rudin Productions/ PG
DreamWorks/Paramount (U.S.)

Jim Carrey *(Count Olaf)*, Meryl Streep *(Aunt Josephine)*, Jude Law *(Voice of Lemony Snicket)*, Emily Browning *(Violet Baudelaire)*, Liam Aiken *(Klaus Baudelaire)*, Kara Hoffman *(Sunny)*, Shelby Hoffman *(Sunny)*, Timothy Spall *(Mr. Poe)*, Billy Connolly *(Uncle Monty)*, Catherine O'Hara *(Justice Strauss)*

p, Laurie MacDonald, Walter Parkes, Jim Van Wyck; d, Brad Silberling; w, Robert Gordon (based on the books *The Bad Beginning*, *The Reptile Room*, and *The Wide Window* by Daniel Handler, aka Lemony Snicket); ph, Emmanuel Lubezki; ed, Michael Kahn; m, Thomas Newman; prod d, Rick Heinrichs; art d, John Dexter; fx, Stefen Fangmeier, Industrial Light & Magic, Michael Lantieri, Tom Peitzman; cos, Colleen Atwood; anim, Colin Brady

AAN Best Art Direction: Rick Heinrichs (art direction), Cheryl Carasik (set decoration)

Based on Daniel Handler's first three Lemony Snicket novels, this stylized gothic fairy tale unfolds in a flawlessly designed Dickensian once-upon-a-time world that's been retrofitted with gee-whiz modern conveniences.

There was once a most fortunate group of children named Baudelaire. Brilliant Violet (Emily Browning), 14, possessed a prodigious capacity for inventing useful things from everyday objects. Her younger brother, Klaus (Liam Aiken), read voraciously and retained every word. Their baby sister, Sunny (Kara and Shelby Hoffman), had a fine set of new teeth and used them to bite things with vigor and tenacity. Their charmed existence, however, ended the day a fire of highly suspicious origin killed their doting parents, destroyed their home, and left the children adrift with only a well-intentioned if useless lawyer, Mr. Poe (Timothy Spall), for protection. Poe places the children with a distant relative, master thespian Count Olaf (Jim Carrey), who intends to kill them for their large inheritance. The resourceful orphans stymie his every homicidal effort, but even after they're placed with new guardians—first Uncle Monty (Billy Connolly), a connoisseur of rare and exotic reptiles, and then Aunt Josephine (Meryl Streep), a once bold adventuress reduced to quivering for fear of uncommon household accidents—Olaf pursues them, hiding his wicked intentions behind ingenious disguises.

So much of the movie is pitch-perfect that it's a sorrowful responsibility to report that Carrey's relentless showboating is almost its undoing. A skilled and versatile mimic of enviable physical grace and flexibility, Carrey cannot resist the temptation to overdo, and his star wattage is such that no one is empowered to take him aside and insist that even when playing an evil hambone, less is truly more.

L'ENNUI

1998 120m c Drama ★★★½
Gemini Films/IMA Films/Canal Plus/CNC
(France) R

Charles Berling *(Martin)*, Sophie Guillemin *(Cecilia)*, Arielle Dombasle *(Sophie)*, Robert Kramer *(Meyers)*, Alice Grey *(Cecilia's Mother)*, Maurice Antoni *(Cecilia's Father)*, Tom Ouedraogo

p, Paulo Branco; d, Cedric Kahn; w, Cedric Kahn, Laurence Ferreira Barbosa (based on the novel *La Noia* by Alberto Moravia); ph, Pascal Marti; ed, Yann Dedet; prod d, Francois Abelanet; cos, Francoise Clavel

Reckless lust burns a hole through the life of a high-strung philosophy professor in this adaptation of Italian novelist Alberto Moravia's withering examination of sexual cruelty sans kinky thrills.

Glib intellectual Martin (Charles Berling) is an emotional wreck, recently separated from his wife (Arielle Dombasle) and given to wandering the Parisian streets by night. He impulsively follows a dazed-looking fellow—an unsuccessful painter named Meyers (Robert Kramer)—whom he spots arguing with a young girl on the street, and strikes up a conversation. Three days later, having learned that Meyers has died in flagrante, Martin meets the 17-year-old model whose nude image fills every corner of Meyers's shabby studio. Stolid and unnervingly impassive, Cecilia (Sophie Guillemin) exerts some hard-to-define hold over Martin; he badgers her about Meyers's obsession but never notices that he himself has fallen under her spell until it's too late. Completely baffled by his own behavior, Martin proceeds to make a shambles of his life. He abandons the book he's writing, alienates his friends, and completely debases himself, spying on the girl and insinuating himself into the bosom of her sad family. Cecilia, meanwhile, accepts everything with the same infuriating indifference.

Director Cedric Kahn's essay in anti-eroticism is both explicit and exhaustingly talky. But its evocation of the corrosive power of desire creeps up on you; just as you're about to dismiss the whole thing as those overanalytical French talking the subject to death, the movie catches you with a creepy sucker punch.

LENNY

1974 111m bw Biography   **DVD**
UA (U.S.)   ★★★
R

Dustin Hoffman *(Lenny Bruce)*, Valerie Perrine *(Honey Bruce)*, Jan Miner *(Sally Marr)*, Stanley Beck *(Artie Silver)*, Gary Morton *(Sherman Hart)*, Rashel Novikoff *(Aunt Mema)*, Guy Rennie *(Jack Goldstein)*, Frankie Man *(Baltimore Strip Club MC)*, Mark Harris *(San Francisco Defense Attorney)*, Lee Sandman *(San Francisco Judge)*

p, Marvin Worth; d, Bob Fosse; w, Julian Barry (based on the play by Julian Barry); ph, Bruce Surtees; ed, Alan Heim; prod d, Joel Schiller; cos, Albert Wolsky

AAN Best Picture; AAN Best Actor: Dustin Hoffman; AAN Best Actress: Valerie Perrine; AAN Best Director: Bob Fosse; AAN Best Adapted Screenplay: Julian Barry; AAN Best Cinematography: Bruce Surtees

Harsh, funny, grim, and, like all Bob Fosse's films, primarily concerned with the intersection of life and showbiz. Fosse's followup to the masterly CABARET, LENNY proves that it's not easy to be ahead of your time. By today's standards, much of what Lenny Bruce said on stage would be unremarkable, and it's still debatable whether the comedian was crushed for his irrepressible foul mouth or his subversive (if not exactly profound) social commentary. Either way, his customary mode of agonized self-analysis was irresistible to director Fosse, who was to use similar techniques in filming the story of his own life, ALL THAT JAZZ.

The film begins with Lenny's courtship of his wife Honey (Perrine), a stripper with a surprising amount of class and smarts (at least as Perrine plays her). His overpowering love for Honey suggests a problem with his personality: he never seems to know how to let go of anything. On the brink of mainstream success, he refuses, literally, to clean up his act, resulting in a series of arrests for obscenity; a heroin addiction brings further trouble with the law. He becomes preoccupied with his legal battles and begins to see himself as a martyr for artistic freedom. Finally, his obsession with death overrides all others.

A series of flashbacks prompted by pseudo-*verite* interviews (conducted by an unseen Fosse), LENNY is structured like a patchwork quilt a la CITIZEN KANE. Perrine, never considered much of an actress before this movie, is quite solid as Honey, as is Miner in a rendition of Bruce's actress-manager mom Sally Marr. Hoffman, generally successful in abrasive roles, never loses one's sympathy here, and is especially good in the courtroom scenes. Towards the end, one wonders whether the film's sexual and thanatological obsessions have more to do with Bruce or with Fosse (the *menage-a-trois* scene, for instance, has no known basis in the comedian's life, but it was familiar territory for the director). In ALL THAT JAZZ, Fosse's alter ego is shown editing a film very much like LENNY; it features Cliff Gorman as a death-obsessed comedian. Gorman had played Lenny Bruce on Broadway; his role in ALL THAT JAZZ was Fosse's apology for failing to use him in LENNY. Visually striking, due mostly to Surtees' beautifully shaded black-and-white cinematography.

LEOPARD, THE

DVD

(IL GATTOPARDO)
1963 165m c   Historical   ★★★★½
Titanus (Italy)   PG

Burt Lancaster *(Prince Don Fabrizio Salina)*, Alain Delon *(Tancredi)*, Claudia Cardinale *(Angelica Sedara/Bertiana)*, Rina Morelli *(Maria Stella)*, Paolo Stoppa *(Don Calogero Sedara)*, Romolo Valli *(Father Pirrone)*, Lucilla Morlacchi *(Concetta)*, Serge Reggiani *(Don Ciccio Turneo)*, Ida Galli *(Carolina)*, Ottavia Piccolo *(Caterina)*

p, Goffredo Lombardo; d, Luchino Visconti; w, Luchino Visconti, Suso Cecchi D'Amico, Pasquale Festa Campanile, Enrico Medioli, Massimo Franciosa (based on the novel *Il Gattopardo* by Giuseppe Tomasi di Lampedusa); ph, Giuseppe Rotunno (CinemaScope, DeLuxe Color); ed, Mario Serandrei; m, Nino Rota, Giuseppe Verdi; art d, Mario Garbuglia; cos, Piero Tosi, Reanda, Sartoria Safas

AAN Best Costume Design (Color): Piero Tosi

Superb, sumptuous epic based on Guiseppe di Lampedusa's novel about the decline of the Italian aristocracy and the rise to power of the bourgeoisie. Financed by 20th Century Fox and released to critical acclaim in Europe, THE LEOPARD was butchered for its initial, inauspicious U.S. release, finally earning the acclaim it deserved when a restored version was presented in 1983.

Burt Lancaster plays an elderly prince struggling to come to terms with the rapidly changing Italian social structure of the 1860s. He arranges for his nephew, Tancredi (Alain Delon), to marry Angela (Claudia Cardinale), the daughter of a rich merchant, in an attempt to shore up his status and lifestyle and, during a nearly hour long ball scene with which the film closes, ruminates on his own past and present as well as that of his social class.

This is a gorgeous, fascinating account of the interplay between the personal and the social, directed with the kind of insight that only an aristocrat turned Marxist like Visconti could afford. (Lancaster claimed that he actually based his performance on Visconti's character.) The ball scene, at which the aristocrats come to accept that power has passed into the hands of the nouveaux riches, is justly regarded as one of the finest set pieces in film history. THE LEOPARD took the Golden Palm as Best Film at Cannes.

LES BICHES

DVD

1968 104m c   Drama   ★★★½
Boetie/Alexandra (Italy/France)   R

Stephane Audran *(Frederique)*, Jacqueline Sassard *(Why)*, Jean-Louis Trintignant *(Paul Thomas)*, Nane Germon *(Violetta)*, Serge Bento *(Bookseller)*, Dominique Zardi *(Riais)*, Henri Attal *(Robeque)*, Claude Chabrol *(Filmmaker)*, Henri Frances

p, Andre Genoves; d, Claude Chabrol; w, Paul Gegauff, Claude Chabrol; ph, Jean Rabier (Eastmancolor); ed, Jacques Gaillard; m, Pierre Jansen; cos, Maurice Albray

Claude Chabrol's suspenseful and erotic story of two lesbian lovers—Frederique (Stephane Audran), a wealthy and elegant woman, and Why (Jaqueline Sassard), a young bohemian who earns a living making charcoal drawings on the sidewalks of Paris. Frederique, who has already seduced Why and dragged her off to a lovely St. Tropez villa, upsets the balance when she next seduces architect Paul (Jean-Louis Trintignant). Why loves them both and cannot bear the thought of being left behind when Frederique and Paul run off to Paris together. One of the few Chabrol films available on videotape (under the title BAD GIRLS), LES BICHES features the director's favorite lead actress, Audran (then his wife), in yet another situation of suspense that, while

Hitchcockian at its root, is pure Chabrol. The setup is a familiar one—a love triangle—but Chabrol's delicate treatment and highly controlled direction make this one of his finest efforts.

LES ENFANTS TERRIBLES

1950 107m bw Drama   ★★★
Melville   (France)

Nicole Stephane *(Elisabeth)*, Edouard Dermit *(Paul)*, Jacques Bernard *(Gerard)*, Renee Cosima *(Dargelos/Agathe)*, Roger Gaillard *(Gerard's Uncle)*, Melvyn Martin *(Michael)*, Maurice Revel *(Doctor)*, Adeline Aucoc *(Mariette)*, Maria Cyliakus *(The Mother)*, Jean-Marie Robain *(Headmaster)*

p, Jean-Pierre Melville; d, Jean-Pierre Melville; w, Jean-Pierre Melville, Jean Cocteau (based on the novel by Jean Cocteau); ph, Henri Decae; ed, Monique Bonnot; m, Johann Sebastian Bach, Antonio Vivaldi

Two seemingly disparate filmmakers—Jean-Pierre Melville, best known for his dark black-and-white ventures into the criminal underworld, and Jean Cocteau, the poet of the mythical underworld—came together to bring Cocteau's celebrated play of love, death, and incest to the screen. Paul (Edouard Dermit), a young Parisian, is severely injured when hit by a snowball thrown by Dargelos (Renee Cosima), the school bully whom he idolizes. He is cared for by his sister Elisabeth (Nicole Stephane), with whom he shares a bedroom, though both are in their teens. The near-incestuous pair are brought closer together by the death of their ailing mother and are joined by Paul's friend Gerard (Jacques Bernard), who is infatuated with Elisabeth. The trio eventually becomes a quartet when Paul meets his sister's friend Agathe (Cosima, in a dual, cross-gender role). As the relationships intertwine, Elisabeth is forced to admit her attraction to her brother. Melville, who was given the chance to direct this prestigious property after Cocteau saw one of his early 16mm films, shot LES ENFANTS TERRIBLES in his own apartment, which he rented with the intention of using it as a location. The film also unmistakably bears Cocteau's stamp, and he even directed one scene (at the beach) when Melville fell ill.

LES GIRLS

1957 114m c Musical/Comedy   📀 ★★★
MGM   (U.S.)

Gene Kelly *(Barry Nichols)*, Mitzi Gaynor *(Joy Henderson)*, Kay Kendall *(Lady Wren)*, Taina Elg *(Angele Ducros)*, Jacques Bergerac *(Pierre Ducros)*, Leslie Phillips *(Sir Gerald Wren)*, Henry Daniell *(Judge)*, Patrick Macnee, billed as Patrick MacNee *(Sir Percy)*, Stephen Vercoe *(Mr. Outward)*, Philip Tonge *(Associate Judge)*

p, Sol C. Siegel; d, George Cukor; w, John Patrick (based on a story by Vera Caspary); ph, Robert Surtees (CinemaScope, Metrocolor); ed, Ferris Webster; m, Cole Porter; art d, William A. Horning, Gene Allen; chor, Jack Cole; cos, Orry-Kelly

AAN Best Art Direction-Set Decoration: William A. Horning, Gene Allen, Edwin B. Willis, Richard Pefferle; *AA Best Costume Design:* Orry-Kelly; *AAN Best Sound:* Dr. Wesley C. Miller

Attempting to carry on the tradition of their great musicals of the 1930s and '40s, MGM released this relatively minor effort employing some of the studio's finest creative talents in 1957. Barry (Gene Kelly), Angele (Taina Elg), Joy (Mitzi Gaynor), and Sybil (Kay Kendall) are the former members of "Barry Nichols and Les Girls," a popular European cabaret act. Years after the group has dissolved, Sybil, now Lady Wren, publishes her all-too-candid recollections of what went on romantically behind the scenes among Barry and his partners. Angele is outraged by the revelations and sues Sybil for defamation of character, the case is tried in court, and the picture becomes a musical RASHOMON, with each of the principals telling the story of the act as they remember it—none lying, but all recalling matters very differently. Not surprisingly, Barry (now married to Joy) gives the key testimony, and the picture ends with resumed good relations among the group, after all have had their say and a host of musical numbers have been performed. The script is more complicated than witty and can't sustain what's meant to be a breezy paean to the great MGM musicals; Kelly (in his last MGM appearance before THAT'S ENTERTAINMENT) never quite musters the energy needed for his role; and Cole Porter's last Hollywood score is not one of his best. LES GIRLS's failure to make big money signaled the end of the "original musical" for Hollywood. The tunes include a delicious satire of Brando's THE WILD ONE entitled "Why Am I So Gone (About That Gal)?"

LES MISERABLES

1935 108m bw Drama   ★★★★
20th Century   (U.S.)

Fredric March *(Jean Valjean)*, Charles Laughton *(Javert)*, Cedric Hardwicke *(Bishop Bienvenu)*, Rochelle Hudson *(Big Cosette)*, Marilyn Knowlden *(Little Cosette)*, Frances Drake *(Eponine)*, John Beal *(Marius)*, Jessie Ralph *(Mme. Magloire)*, Florence Eldridge *(Fantine)*, Ferdinand Gottschalk *(Thenardier)*

p, Darryl F. Zanuck; d, Richard Boleslawski; w, W.P. Lipscomb (based on the novel by Victor Hugo); ph, Gregg Toland; ed, Barbara McLean

AAN Best Picture; AAN Best Cinematography: Gregg Toland; *AAN Best Assistant Director:* Eric Stacey; *AAN Best Film Editing:* Barbara McLean

Fredric March gives a superb performance as the sensitive, persecuted Jean Valjean who steals a loaf of bread to survive, is captured, and given ten years' hard labor. When he finally escapes the prison galley, March is a hardbitten, unsympathetic character, all compassion hammered out of him by the rigors of confinement. He is taken in by Bishop Bienvenu, played by Cedric Hardwicke, who refuses to prosecute him for stealing two silver candlesticks. Through Hardwicke's kindness and understanding, March regains his sensitive nature and is reformed. He builds a new life for himself under an assumed name and adopts a young child as his own. He becomes a well-to-do businessman, and, moving to another town, becomes so widely liked and respected that he is elected mayor, an office which helps him devote his life to benefiting others. Charles Laughton, as Javert, the town's chief of police, is a cold, unimpassioned official, single-minded in his view that the law is to be upheld and enforced at all costs, with no mercy shown to anyone committing the slightest infraction. Laughton and March clash repeatedly over the interpretation of the law, and the policeman becomes incensed when March intercedes on behalf of a social pariah (Florence Eldridge, March's real-life wife). One day March sees a villager trapped beneath a heavy wagon, and, with what seems to be superhuman strength, he puts his back to the wagon and lifts it so the man can be saved. Laughton watches this feat and is reminded of a galley prisoner he once encountered. He investigates March's past and identifies March as Jean Valjean, the wanted criminal. He is then confused when another prisoner is found, a mindless inmate who amazingly resembles March and who claims to be Jean Valjean. The impostor is put on trial, but the honorable March (who plays both parts) admits that he is the real Jean Valjean. Before he can be jailed, he again escapes with his daughter (Frances Drake) to Paris where he assumes yet another identity.

This lavish production is full of meticulous detail, and, with the exception of the ending, faithful to Victor Hugo's novel. (Valjean dies in the original tale.) Richard

Boleslawski (RASPUTIN AND THE EMPRESS, THE PAINTED VEIL), a largely forgotten director today, was masterful in his handling of LES MISERABLES, adhering closely to Hugo's scenes and working diligently from W.P. Lipscomb's compact 108-minute script, which is literate and moving. March gives one of his greatest performances as the hunted victim Jean Valjean, far superior to the rendering of the character in a French version in 1936, or in the crude 1918 silent version (also made by Fox, and starring William Farnum). The film was remade in 1952 with Michael Rennie as Jean Valjean and Robert Newton as Javert, the policeman, but this later version is a pale imitation of the 1935 classic. A number of other actors, including Richard Jordan in a British remake of the film in 1979, portrayed Hugo's great fictional character. But no one has ever approached March's profound performance.

LES MISERABLES

1998 129m c Historical/Drama **DVD**
Mandalay Entertainment/Sarah Radclyffe PG-13
Productions/James Gorman Productions (U.S.)

★★½

Liam Neeson *(Valjean)*, Geoffrey Rush *(Javert)*, Uma Thurman *(Fantine)*, Claire Danes *(Cosette)*, Hans Matheson *(Marius)*, Reine Brynolfsson *(Captain Beauvais)*, Peter Vaughan *(Bishop)*, Christopher Adamson *(Bertin)*, Tim Barlow *(Lafitte)*, Timothy Bateson *(Banker)*

p, Sarah Radclyffe, James Gorman; d, Bille August; w, Rafael Yglesias (based on the novel by Victor Hugo); ph, Jorgen Persson; ed, Janus Billeskov-Jansen; m, Basil Poledouris; prod d, Anna Asp; art d, Peter Grant; fx, Terry Glass, Jaroslav Stolba; cos, Gabriella Pescucci

An honorable and well-acted version of Victor Hugo's classic book bag-buster (*not* the musical), a sprawling melodrama whose prodigious length and scope have bedeviled all previous adaptations and hang heavily over this one as well.

Rafael Yglesias' screenplay pares down the novel's subplots to concentrate on the iconic story of convict Jean Valjean (Liam Neeson), condemned to 20 years of back- and spirit-breaking incarceration for a minor crime and persecuted by the implacable Inspector Javert (Geoffrey Rush). Illiterate and brutalized by his sentence, Valjean is paroled but can't find work because his papers brand him a thief. An elderly cleric's act of charity allows Valjean to make a fresh start in Vigau, and in 10 years he rises from laborer to factory owner, establishing such a reputation as a fair employer and pious citizen that the townspeople virtually force him to become mayor. He also cares for Fantine (Uma Thurman), a prostitute supporting an illegitimate child, and promises that he'll raise her daughter Cosette (Claire Danes). But cruel coincidence brings Valjean to Javert's attention, and the policeman dedicates himself to proving that the mayor and the convict who broke parole a decade earlier are the same man.

The fact is, there's too much of *Les Miserables* to fit into a feature running time, even a longish 129 minutes. But pruning back the story necessitates a series of choppy transitions of the "Ten years later…" variety. If ever a novel cried out for miniseries treatment, it's this one. The film's performances are its greatest asset: Neeson's Valjean is a self-made man of honor who must be ever on guard against the return of the beast within, while Rush plays Javert as a religious zealot whose god is the law. Though the words "filthy rags" must loom large in any discussion of Thurman's wardrobe as the bedraggled Fantine, the urge to make them bust-baring appears to have been irresistible.

LES PARENTS TERRIBLES

1948 105m bw Drama ★★★★
Ariane (France)

Jean Marais *(Michel)*, Yvonne de Bray *(Yvonne-Sophie)*, Gabrielle Dorziat *(Aunt Leo)*, Marcel Andre *(Georges)*, Josette Day *(Madeleine)*, Jean Cocteau *(Narrator)*

d, Jean Cocteau; w, Jean Cocteau (based on the play by Jean Cocteau); ph, Michel Kelber; ed, Jacqueline Sadoul; m, Georges Auric; art d, Christian Berard, Guy de Gastyne

Cocteau's brilliant domestic drama which many, including Cocteau himself, consider to be his greatest achievement. Based on his stage play (performed ten years earlier with much the same cast) it casts de Bray as the dangerously possessive mother who is wed to Andre, a weak and defeated man. De Bray opposes the marriage of her young son Marais to the beautiful Day. It turns out that Day is the mistress of Andre, who happens to be the object of Marais's aunt's (Dorziat's) desires. When the tangled affairs come into the open, de Bray commits suicide, unable to accept the loss of her magnetic hold over her family. Set in only two locations—de Bray's family's apartment and Day's apartment—the film is, as Cocteau said, a record "of the acting of an incomparable cast." Georges Auric's score is a prime example of sound in perfect unity with the picture. A far-inferior remake, INTIMATE RELATIONS, was released in Britain in 1953. Various lengths exist, with both a 98m and 86m cut being shown in the U.S.

LESS THAN ZERO

1987 96m c Drama **DVD**
Fox (U.S.) ★½
R

Andrew McCarthy *(Clay Easton)*, Jami Gertz *(Blair)*, Robert Downey Jr. *(Julian Wells)*, James Spader *(Rip)*, Tony Bill *(Bradford Easton)*, Nicholas Pryor *(Benjamin Wells)*, Donna Mitchell *(Elaine Easton)*, Michael Bowen *(Hop)*, Sarah Buxton *(Markie)*, Lisanne Falk *(Patti)*

p, Jon Avnet, Jordan Kerner, Marvin Worth; d, Marek Kanievska; w, Harley Peyton (based on the novel by Bret Easton Ellis); ph, Edward Lachman (Deluxe Color); ed, Peter E. Berger, Michael Tronick; m, Thomas Newman, Rick Rubin; prod d, Barbara Ling; art d, Stephen Rice; cos, Richard Hornung

Loosely based on the novel by Bret Easton Ellis, LESS THAN ZERO refuses to take the risks necessary to capture the keen social observation of the book. Clay Easton (Andrew McCarthy), a college freshman, returns home to Los Angeles for the Christmas holidays, largely because Blair (Jami Gertz), his old girlfriend, has requested it. Blair and Julian Wells (Robert Downey, Jr.), a former high-school buddy of Clay, have become an item, and now Blair wants Clay to save Julian from the downward spiral of his drug abuse. Julian is being harassed and forced to prostitute himself by the drug dealer (James Spader) to whom he owes $50,000. The filmmakers apparently felt there were no sympathetic characters in the novel, but in sanitizing and simplifying Ellis' downbeat story, transforming it into a relatively conventional love story and a didactic tragedy, they have diluted the disturbing social reality of the novel. The saving grace of LESS THAN ZERO is Downey, who gives an inspired performance. He makes his character a convincing lost cause, one the audience would rather see see saved. Gertz's performance is uneven, and McCarthy, an actor of limited range, brings what little he can to his role.

LETHAL WEAPON

1987 110m c Action/Adventure/Comedy ★★★½
Warner Bros. (U.S.) R

Mel Gibson *(Martin Riggs)*, Danny Glover *(Roger Murtaugh)*, Gary Busey *(Joshua)*, Mitchell Ryan *(The General)*, Tom Atkins *(Michael Hunsaker)*, Darlene Love *(Trish Murtaugh)*, Traci Wolfe *(Rianne Murtaugh)*, Jackie Swanson *(Amanda Hunsaker)*, Damon Hines *(Nick Murtaugh)*, Ebonie Smith *(Carrie Murtaugh)*

p, Richard Donner, Joel Silver; d, Richard Donner; w, Shane Black; ph, Stephen Goldblatt (Technicolor); ed, Stuart Baird; m, Michael Kamen, Eric Clapton; prod d, J. Michael Riva; fx, Chuck Gaspar; cos, Mary Malin

AAN Best Sound: Les Fresholtz, Dick Alexander, Vern Poore, Bill Nelson

It's drugs again, this time in southern California with cop partners Mel Gibson and Danny Glover chasing sleazy dope dealers in a nonstop crime actioner. Roger Murtaugh (Glover), who is about to turn 50, exercises the kind of life-preserving caution that Martin Riggs (Gibson) has discarded. Riggs's wife has been killed in an accident, and he doesn't care whether he lives or dies, just so long as he can take all the bad guys with him. Murtaugh has a hard time surviving with such a self-destructive partner as they investigate "The General" (Mitchell Ryan), head of an extensive drug smuggling operation. The acceleration of this film, which has a brisk pace at the start, is dizzying at the finale and is accomplished mostly through fantastic editing. It's an effective if not obvious ploy to blind the viewer to the fact that there is not much plot or character development in the predictable script. Gibson is truly frightening as the cop about to go into orbit, and Glover is a standout as the down-to-earth lawman with very much to lose. Director Richard Donner, whose previous efforts include the first SUPERMAN and LADYHAWKE, had another hit with LETHAL WEAPON, which grossed more than $60 million at the box office within three months after its release. At last count, the number of sequels was up to three.

LETHAL WEAPON 2

1989 113m c Comedy/Action/Adventure ★★★
Silver (U.S.) R

Mel Gibson *(Martin Riggs)*, Danny Glover *(Roger Murtaugh)*, Joe Pesci *(Leo Getz)*, Joss Ackland *(Arjen Rudd)*, Derrick O'Connor *(Pieter Vorstedt)*, Patsy Kensit *(Rika van den Haas)*, Darlene Love *(Trish Murtaugh)*, Traci Wolfe *(Rianne Murtaugh)*, Steve Kahan *(Capt. Murphy)*, Mark Rolston *(Hans)*

p, Richard Donner, Joel Silver, Steve Perry, Jennie Lew Tugend; d, Richard Donner; w, Jeffrey Boam (based on a story by Shane Black, Warren Murphy and on the characters created by Black); ph, Stephen Goldblatt (Panavision, Technicolor); ed, Stuart Baird; m, Michael Kamen, Eric Clapton, David Sanborn; prod d, J. Michael Riva; art d, Virginia Randolph, Richard Berger; cos, Barry Delaney

AAN Best Sound Effects Editing: Robert Henderson, Alan Robert Murray

A sequel that stands on its own, LETHAL WEAPON 2 is a well-crafted, rousingly fast-paced action thriller with a first-rate cast. Los Angeles cops Roger Murtaugh (Danny Glover) and Martin Riggs (Mel Gibson) are in hot pursuit of a red BMW as the film gets off to a fender-bending start. After much property destruction, the cops capture the red car, but lose the driver. However, they discover a fortune in South African gold Krugerrands in the trunk. Determined to keep the two hyperactive cops out of further high-priced mayhem, their superior puts them in charge of guarding a government witness in a drug-money laundering case. But when the witness (Joe Pesci) reveals he was laundering for

South Africans, Murtaugh and Riggs spring back into action. Those stopping to think about such things may find more than a few holes in LETHAL WEAPON 2's plot. But to question is to quibble in this case; LETHAL WEAPON 2's pluses easily outweigh its minuses. If anything, Gibson and Glover are even better here than they were the first time out. Jeffrey Boam's script polishes and improves their characters. Returning director Richard Donner seems to have smoothed over the few stylistic rough edges remaining from the earlier film to deliver here two hours of pure, breathless, high-impact entertainment.

LETHAL WEAPON 3

1992 118m c Action/Comedy/Crime ★★
Warner Bros./Silver Pictures (U.S.) R

Mel Gibson *(Martin Riggs)*, Danny Glover *(Roger Murtaugh)*, Joe Pesci *(Leo Getz)*, Rene Russo *(Lorna Cole)*, Stuart Wilson *(Jack Travis)*, Stephen Kahan *(Captain Murphy)*, Darlene Love *(Trish Murtaugh)*, Traci Wolfe *(Rianne Murtaugh)*, Damon Hines *(Nick Murtaugh)*, Ebonie Smith *(Carrie Murtaugh)*

p, Richard Donner, Joel Silver; d, Richard Donner; w, Jeffrey Boam, Robert Mark Kamen (from the story by Boam based on the characters created by Shane Black); ph, Jan De Bont; ed, Robert Brown, Battle Davis; m, Michael Kamen, Eric Clapton, David Sanborn; prod d, James Spencer; art d, Greg Papalia

More of the same, but it's now so far removed from any sense of reality, and done with such ham-fisted insistence, it's become a clumsy parody of itself. Ingredients: a "plot" about a bad ex-cop (Stuart Wilson) who's trafficking arms; a beautiful female detective (Rene Russo) whose kick-boxing prowess saves Riggs's heart; and Joe Pesci, who seems to have been asked by director Richard Donner to parody his already farcical performance in WEAPON 2. Murtaugh is not the only one who is "too old for this s…"

LETHAL WEAPON 4

1998 123m c Crime/Comedy/Action ★
Silver Pictures/Shuler Donner/Donner Productions/ R
Warner Bros. (U.S.)

Mel Gibson *(Det. Martin Riggs)*, Danny Glover *(Det. Roger Murtaugh)*, Joe Pesci *(Leo Getz)*, Rene Russo *(Lorna Cole)*, Chris Rock *(Lee Butters)*, Jet Li *(Wah Sing Ku)*, Steve Kahan *(Capt. Ed Murphy)*, Kim Chan *(Uncle Benny)*, Darlene Love *(Trish Murtaugh)*, Traci Wolfe *(Rianne)*

p, Joel Silver, Richard Donner; d, Richard Donner; w, Channing Gibson (from a story by Jonathan Lemkin, Alfred Gough, and Miles Millar; based on characters created by Shane Black); ph, Andrzej Bartkowiak; ed, Frank J. Urioste, Dallas Puett; m, Michael Kamen, Eric Clapton, David Sanborn; prod d, J. Michael Riva; art d, Richard Mays; fx, Matt Sweeney; cos, Ha Nguyen

"I'm too old for this shit," declares loose cannon Martin Riggs (Mel Gibson), and he's not the only one.

Cynical and contemptuous of its audience, this lazy sequel oozes an insufferable air of self-satisfaction. The actors choke with laughter at their own cleverness and high-salaried camaraderie, but what about the rest of us—especially those who can't be bought off with regularly spaced explosions and car crashes? Characters are so minimally drawn that unless you've seen at least one of the previous films, you'll have no idea what they mean to one another or why they behave the way they do. The mix of low laughs and brutal violence is jarring.

The plot, concocted by at least five writers, is a slapdash collection of situations and premises: Lorna (Rene Russo) is pregnant with Riggs's baby. Murtaugh (Danny Glover) is suspected of being on the take. Murtaugh's pregnant daughter, Rianne (Traci Wolfe), is secretly married to sharp-dressing

Detective Butters (Chris Rock) but doesn't dare tell Dad because he never wanted her to marry a cop. Riggs, Murtaugh, and old pal Leo (Joe Pesci) bumble into the path of a freighter transporting illegal Chinese immigrants, and Murtaugh rescues the frightened Hong family, taking them home like a litter of stray puppies in a cardboard box. It all has something to do with counterfeiting, triads, and modern-day slavery. Hong Kong action star Jet Li is reduced to playing an inscrutable Oriental sadist, and for all the Murtaugh-Riggs friendship, casual racism abounds in the form of "flied lice" cracks and "Confucius say"-style insults. Crude homophobia fuels the running gag that Murtaugh thinks Butters is gay, tainting with homosexual innuendo the younger man's efforts to curry favor with his unwitting father-in-law. Are you laughing yet? Someone is—all the way to the bank.

LETTER, THE
1940 95m bw Drama
Warner Bros. (U.S.)

Bette Davis (Leslie Crosbie), Herbert Marshall (Robert Crosbie), James Stephenson (Howard Joyce), Gale Sondergaard (Mrs. Hammond), Bruce Lester (John Withers), Elizabeth Inglis (Adele Ainsworth), Cecil Kellaway (Prescott), Victor Sen Yung (Ong Chi Seng), Doris Lloyd (Mrs. Cooper), Willie Fung (Chung Hi)

p, Robert Lord; d, William Wyler; w, Howard Koch (based on the story by W. Somerset Maugham); ph, Tony Gaudio; ed, George Amy; m, Max Steiner; art d, Carl Jules Weyl; cos, Orry-Kelly

AAN Best Picture; AAN Best Actress: Bette Davis; AAN Best Supporting Actor: James Stephenson; AAN Best Director: William Wyler; AAN Best B/W Cinematography: Gaetano Gaudio; AAN Best Film Editing: Warren Low; AAN Best Original Score: Max Steiner

As THE LETTER opens, David Newell visits Davis's Malayan rubber plantation while her husband, Marshall, is away on business. Davis shoots him to death, and later claims that Newell, an old family friend, tried to attack her and that she killed him in self-defense. Marshall, ever faithful, believes her absolutely and asks Stephenson, a respected lawyer, to defend her. Stephenson then receives word that Newell's Eurasian widow, Sondergaard, has in her possession a letter Davis wrote to Newell, asking him to come to visit her at the plantation on the night he was killed. When confronted with this information, Davis coldly admits that she murdered Newell and that he was her lover. Taking pity on her, Stephenson agrees to buy the letter for $10,000—Sondergaard's blackmail price—telling Marshall there will be some extra expenses in preparing Davis's case, but not how much money is involved. Sondergaard insists that she will not turn the letter over unless Davis claims it personally, leading to a dramatic scene in which Davis must kneel at her feet to pick up the incriminating document. After Davis is deemed innocent of the murder charge in court and returns home to Marshall, the husband discovers that all his savings have been spent to buy the letter and demands to be told what it contains. Davis admits everything, but the always forgiving Marshall—now an emotional shambles—tells her he loves her still. As Davis walks into the garden, Sondergaard appears with a henchman and stabs Davis to death. Police stop them when they try to flee.

Though W. Somerset Maugham's story could easily have been filmed as a turgid melodrama, director William Wyler's magnificent handling of the material and Bette Davis's taut and calculated performance converted it into enduring cinematic art. THE LETTER is as good today as it seemed upon its first release. Though Davis's strong performance is the film's center, Herbert Marshall (who had played the lover in an earlier version of the story) is excellent as the long-suffering husband, and James Stephenson actually manages to steal scenes from his costars as the honest lawyer who puts his career in jeopardy for a friend. Jack Warner asked Wyler to test Stephenson for the role, but when Wyler (to his own surprise)

recognized the superiority of Stephenson's acting and cast him, the unpredictable Warner balked at the move, worrying about the stock player's lack of name recognition. Wyler insisted upon keeping Stephenson, putting him in the odd position of having to fight to cast an actor Warner had originally suggested.

LETTER FROM AN UNKNOWN WOMAN
1948 86m bw Drama ★★★★★
Rampart (U.S.)

Joan Fontaine (Lisa Berndle), Louis Jourdan (Stefan Brand), Mady Christians (Frau Berndle), Marcel Journet (Johann Stauffer), John Good (Lt. Leopold von Kaltnegger), Leo B. Pessin (Stefan, Jr.), Art Smith (John), Carol Yorke (Marie), Howard Freeman (Herr Kastner), Erskine Sanford (Porter)

p, John Houseman; d, Max Ophuls; w, Howard Koch (based on the novel Brief Einer Unbekannten by Stefan Zweig); ph, Franz Planer; ed, Ted J. Kent; m, Daniele Amfitheatrof; art d, Alexander Golitzen; cos, Travis Banton

An intense and lush romantic film made by the incomparable Ophuls during his often trying sojourn in America in the WWII and immediate postwar years. Fontaine plays Lisa, who has a brief encounter with and falls for her pianist neighbor Stefan (Jourdan). As he heads off on a concert tour, Stefan promises to return for her, but that doesn't happen. Lisa holds out as long as possible but is forced to marry another man when she discovers that she's pregnant with Stefan's child. She meets the pianist some time later, but he doesn't remember her and sets about seducing her all over again. The story is told in flashbacks as Stefan reads a letter from Lisa as she is suffering from typhus, and he finally learns her entire story.

The first film from the production company formed by Fontaine and William Dozier, LETTER FROM AN UNKNOWN WOMAN has an unusually persuasive Continental look to it. Its lyrical, sweet sadness and incredibly lovely mise en scene are typical of Ophuls at his best. His meaningful, highly deliberate camera wanderings beautifully capture the sorrows of Lisa's entrapment by cultural norms. The direction and Koch's well-judged screenplay admirably manage to retain an ironic edge despite the potent romanticism of it all. Fontaine has never looked lovelier and gives what is probably the greatest performance of her career. The dashing and persuasive Jourdan and a fine cast ably support her, as does the incredible camerawork of regular Ophuls collaborator Franz Planer. Although CAUGHT and THE RECKLESS MOMENT are films of considerable merit, LETTER is almost certainly Ophuls' greatest American film. Watching it is like finding a locket you thought you had lost, one which contains the picture of someone who once broke your heart.

LETTER TO THREE WIVES, A
1949 103m bw Drama ★★★★
Fox (U.S.)

Jeanne Crain (Deborah Bishop), Linda Darnell (Lora May Hollingsway), Ann Sothern (Rita Phipps), Kirk Douglas (George Phipps), Paul Douglas (Porter Hollingsway), Barbara Lawrence (Babe), Jeffrey Lynn (Brad Bishop), Connie Gilchrist (Mrs. Finney), Florence Bates (Mrs. Manleigh), Hobart Cavanaugh (Mr. Manleigh)

p, Sol C. Siegel; d, Joseph L. Mankiewicz; w, Joseph L. Mankiewicz, Vera Caspary (based on the novel by John Klempner); ph, Arthur Miller; ed, J. Watson Webb; m, Alfred Newman; art d, Lyle Wheeler, J. Russell Spencer; fx, Fred Sersen; cos, Kay Nelson

AAN Best Picture, AA Best Director: Joseph L. Mankiewicz; *AA Best Screenplay:* Joseph L. Mankiewicz

Delicious bites of suburbia, with lucious Darnell a surprising prize plum. This ingeniously constructed film is one of the finest movies ever made about marriage. It focuses on the doubts, fears and recriminations of three lovely wives who believe they are soon to lose their husbands to another woman. Crain, Darnell, and Sothern are about to leave on a boat trip along the Hudson River, escorting a group of youngsters, when a messenger delivers a letter to each of them, all from the same woman, Addie Ross, never shown and played only as an off-screen voice by Holm. Holm has written the same message to all three wives; she has run off with *one* of their husbands but she does not mention which one, leaving them to figure out who has lost out, and subjecting all three to subtle emotional torture. The three wives live in comfortable homes in the Hudson Valley and have ostensibly happy marriages, but the letters cause them to frantically review their relationships.

The acting of the six leading players here is outstanding, with the aforementioned Darnell in particular giving the finest performance of her career (in the film's best sketch) as the supposedly hardhearted lady with only wealth on her mind (Top line—when Thelma Ritter cracks Darnell should dress up, wear beads, Linda retorts, "What I got don't need beads!"). Both Douglases, Ann Southern, the Gilchrist and Ritter team, Florence Bates and Jeanne Crain all rise to the occasion. The sharp piquancy of the dialog earned Mankiewicz an Oscar for his script, another for his deft direction. Originally, Zanuck wanted Ernst Lubitsch to direct the film, and gave producer Siegel a fight before he would accept Mankiewicz. The film was a landmark achievement for Mankiewicz, who, on the strength of it, became the darling of the Fox lot, earning profound resentment from Zanuck. Years later, Zanuck blamed Mankiewicz personally for almost destroying Fox with his hugely expensive production of CLEOPATRA.

LIANNA

1983 110m c Drama   *DVD*
Winwood   (U.S.)   ★★★   R

Linda Griffiths *(Lianna)*, Jane Hallaren *(Ruth)*, Jon DeVries *(Dick)*, Jo Henderson *(Sandy)*, Jessica MacDonald *(Theda)*, Jesse Solomon *(Spencer)*, John Sayles *(Jerry)*, Stephen Mendillo *(Bob)*, Betsy Julia Robinson *(Cindy)*, Nancy Mette *(Kim)*

p, Jeffrey Nelson, Maggie Renzi; d, John Sayles; w, John Sayles; ph, Austin de Besche (DuArt Color); ed, John Sayles; m, Mason Daring; art d, Jeanne McDonnell; chor, Marta Renzi; cos, Louise Martinez

Lianna (Linda Griffiths) is the unsure wife of a domineering college professor (Jon DeVries). He ridicules her decision to return to school, but she continues to pursue her degree anyway. Ruth (Jane Hallaren), one of her teachers, helps Lianna to cope with her internal struggles. The two women gradually grow closer until their friendship blossoms into a love affair. This is a restrained and caring film that never lapses into preachiness about its lesbian theme. Director-writer John Sayles was noted for writing such films as THE HOWLING and ALLIGATOR, so he could finance his own independent features. The direction and dialog appear completely natural, allowing the characters to tell the story; not a moment in the film seems false or contrived. The two female leads give sensitive performances, and DeVries handles his character's sexual confusions and anger convincingly. There are some technical problems, symptomatic of a low budget, but they don't much hamper this otherwise fine and intelligently told story.

LIAR LIAR

1997 86m c Comedy   *DVD*
Imagine Entertainment   (U.S.)   ★★★   PG-13

Jim Carrey *(Fletcher Reede)*, Maura Tierney *(Audrey Reede)*, Jennifer Tilly *(Samantha Cole)*, Swoosie Kurtz *(Dana Appleton)*, Amanda Donohoe *(Miranda)*, Jason Bernard *(Judge Marshall Stevens)*, Mitchell Ryan *(Mr. Allan)*, Anne Haney *(Greta)*, Justin Cooper *(Max Reede)*, Cary Elwes *(Jerry)*

p, Brian Grazer; d, Tom Shadyac; w, Paul Guay, Stephen Mazur; ph, Russell Boyd; ed, Don Zimmerman; m, John Debney, James Newton Howard; prod d, Linda DeScenna; art d, Richard A. Toyon; fx, Burt Dalton, Jon Farhat; cos, Judy L. Ruskin

A sickly, soft-swirl confection of low laughs and smarmy sentiment, this message comedy returns Jim Carrey to the form his fans know and love: a one-man whirlwind of pratfalls, silly faces, rude sounds, and anarchic *epater le bourgeoisie* schtick. And there's an important lesson in there, too: nothing in this crazy old world is more important than a little boy's love for his dad.

Lies are the air workaholic lawyer Fletcher Reede (Carey) breathes, both on the job and off. His ex-wife (Maura Tierney) is sick to death of him, and his adoring son Max (Justin Cooper) lives in a state of perpetual disappointment. When Fletcher breaks his promise to attend the child's 5th birthday party, Max makes a special birthday wish: that Fletcher will have to tell the truth for 24 hours. Wacky complications ensue, as Fletcher tells the whole truth and nothing but to family, acquaintances, and colleagues in the office and—even worse—the courtroom.

You'd be wrong to imagine that just because this movie's premise involves words, it is a verbal comedy: compulsive truth-teller Carrey spends most of his time mugging, contorting himself, and quite literally bouncing off walls. The evidence is irrefutable—he is the modern-day Jerry Lewis, a creepy blend of the infantile, the manic, and the deeply hostile. Fans put off by THE CABLE GUY's edgy shifts of tone should be mollified by this picture's consistent self-satisfaction: it is simultaneously all touchy-feely about the beauty of paternal love and contemptuous of women, who are all frumps, sex bombs, martyrs, bitches, and ugly cows who say stupid things like "Real beauty comes from the inside."

LIBELED LADY

1936 98m bw Comedy   *DVD*
MGM   (U.S.)   ★★★★

William Powell *(Bill Chandler)*, Myrna Loy *(Connie Allenbury)*, Jean Harlow *(Gladys Benton)*, Spencer Tracy *(Warren Haggerty)*, Walter Connolly *(James B. Allenbury)*, Charley Grapewin *(Hollis Bane)*, Cora Witherspoon *(Mrs. Burns-Norvell)*, E.E. Clive *(Evans, the Fishing Instructor)*, Bunny Beatty *(Babs Burns-Norvell)*, Otto Yamaoka *(Ching)*

p, Lawrence Weingarten; d, Jack Conway; w, Maurine Watkins, Howard Emmett Rogers, George Oppenheimer (based on a story by Wallace Sullivan); ph, Norbert Brodine; ed, Frederick Y. Smith; m, William Axt; art d, Cedric Gibbons, William A. Horning; cos, Dolly Tree

AAN Best Picture

A sparkler from the days when they knew how to do screwball comedy. Tracy plays Warren Haggerty, the managing editor of a newspaper which erroneously prints a story saying that wealthy Connie Allenbury (Loy) is busy nabbing another woman's husband, a British peer. She sues the paper for $5 million. Warren is about to marry Gladys Benton (Harlow), a woman he's left at the altar several times. Now the festivities have to be postponed once again, because Warren must get to the bottom of the story and defuse the lawsuit which could cost him his job. He hires Bill Chandler (Powell), a former co-worker who doesn't like him but needs a job. The task is to marry Gladys (in name only), thus clearing the way for Bill to woo Connie. If that works, Gladys can sue the heiress for alienation of affection, and then agree to drop that suit if Connie drops hers. What goes wrong in all this confusion is that Connie isn't entirely crazy about being used like this and Bill and Connie really do start falling in love. (What else would you expect from William Powell and Myrna Loy?) The complications are fast and furious before the expected two-pair finale.

LIBELED LADY combines the talents of four first-rate farceurs with a crackling script and ace direction. They all have a chance to shine, but we give the slightest of edges to Harlow, who shifts into high wisecracking gear for this one. Don't try to make any sense of the plot; you'll find yourself following its daffy logic just fine. Simply relax and enjoy the merry meanderings of a cast that seemed to be having a bang-up time making this movie. The laughs come rolling off the screen in just about every sequence, but Powell's attempt at fishing and the "bride kisses the best man" bit at one wedding are two highlights. Jack Conway, a good director of many fine films, isn't quite a Leo McCarey or a Howard Hawks, and this film doesn't quite equal THE AWFUL TRUTH or BRINGING UP BABY. Still, LIBELED LADY stands as one of the better "screwball" comedies of the 1930s. It earned an Academy Award nomination for Best Picture, but lost to THE GREAT ZIEGFELD.

LIFE
1999 105m c   Comedy   ★★★
Imagine Entertainment/Universal   (U.S.)   R

Eddie Murphy (Rayford Gibson), Martin Lawrence (Claude Banks), Obba Babtunde (Willie Long), Nick Cassavetes (Sgt. Dillard), Anthony Anderson (Cookie), Barry "Shabaka" Henley (Pokerface), Brent Jennings (Hoppin' Bob), Bernie Mac (Jangle Leg), Miguel A. Nunez Jr. (Biscuit), Michael "Bear" Taliferro (Goldmouth)

p, Brian Grazer, Eddie Murphy; d, Ted Demme; w, Robert Ramsey, Matthew Stone; ph, Geoffrey Simpson; ed, Jeffrey Wolf; m, Wyclef Jean; prod d, Dan Bishop; art d, Jeff Knipp; fx, Dan Sudick; cos, Lucy Corrigan

AAN Best Makeup: Rick Baker

Two sharp-dressed, Northern black men traveling through the violently segregated American South of 1932 are arrested by a bigoted white sheriff, falsely accused of murder, and sentenced to life in the state prison. A racially charged social drama? Heck no—it's an Eddie Murphy comedy.

Ray (Murphy), a motor-mouthed, would-be Harlem player, and Claude (Martin Lawrence), a mild-mannered bank teller, travel down to rural Mississippi to clear their debt to a dangerous Harlem club owner by driving a truckload of bootleg liquor back to New York. But no sooner do they make the pickup than Ray loses all their money to a cardsharp named Winston Hancock (Clarence Williams III), whose freshly murdered corpse the pair literally stumble upon minutes later in a dark alley. Ray and Claude are arrested by the town's nasty sheriff (Ned Vaughn), and in the time it takes an all-white jury to say "guilty," they've traded in their suits for stripes and are sent to spend the rest of their lives doing hard labor in the Mississippi State Prison.

It's hard to imagine a less appropriate setting for a buddy comedy than the notorious Southern prison system of the '30s. But Murphy (who has a couple of great, apparently improvised moments) and an uncharacteristically restrained Lawrence are a solid team, and Ted Demme's sympathetic direction allows them to draw as much humor out of the dismal situation as they can. And from the look of things, prison doesn't seem to be such

a bad place after all: there's plenty of time for baseball and barbecues, and while such minor infractions as attempted escapes and impregnating the lieutenant's lily-white daughter are certainly frowned upon, they go pretty much unpunished. The overall effect of Demme's film is a little like experiencing Nazi prison camps through reruns of Hogan's Heroes, right down to some bona fide laughs.

LIFE AND DEATH OF COLONEL BLIMP, THE   DVD
1943 163m c   Drama/War   ★★★★½
The Archers   (U.K.)

Roger Livesey (Clive Candy), Deborah Kerr (Edith Hunter/Barbara Wynne/Johnny Cannon), Anton Walbrook (Theo Kretschmar-Schuldorff), Roland Culver (Col. Betteridge), James McKechnie (Spud Wilson), Albert Lieven (Von Ritter), Arthur Wontner (Embassy Counsellor), David Hutcheson (Hoppy), Ursula Jeans (Frau von Kalteneck), John Laurie (Murdoch)

p, Michael Powell, Emeric Pressburger; d, Michael Powell; w, Michael Powell, Emeric Pressburger; ph, Jack Cardiff, Georges Perinal (Technicolor); ed, John Seabourne; m, Allan Gray

One of the most celebrated films from the extraordinary director-writer partnership of Michael Powell and Emeric Pressburger, THE LIFE AND DEATH OF COLONEL BLIMP is a warm and wise work that displays extraordinary generosity of spirit. It tells the story of Clive Candy (Roger Livesey), a stuffy British soldier whose life is shown in episodes that range from 1902, when he had a dashing career as a young officer in the Boer War, to 1943, when he creaks crankily about in the London blitz, remembering his lost youth and loves. Not at all a war film in any conventional sense, but a character study that lingers with the viewer long after it's over.

Roger Livesey ably portrays a character with a long and complex life as he is transformed by time and experience from the dashing young firebrand of the 1890s to the anachronistic old codger of the World War II era. The great old British warrior virtues of fair play and chivalry become quaint and inappropriate when faced with the modern horrors of war. Deborah Kerr is a joy to watch as she plays three different roles from different eras in the great man's life. Anton Walbrook (who would be even better a few years later in Powell and Pressburger's THE RED SHOES) is splendid as Theo Kretschmar-Schuldorff, the charming Prussian officer whom Clive fights in a duel and who far exceeds the young Briton in sensitivity and understanding.

The title comes from the satiric character created by cartoonist David Low in the London Evening Standard, by which members of Britain's pompous and stiff military upper-crust came to be known as "Colonel Blimps." Churchill illegally prohibited the film's exportation for two years, citing its portrayal of a Colonel Blimp as "detrimental to the morale of the Army." Refusing to heed the advice of the Ministry of Information (which felt his position would do more harm than good), Churchill lifted the ban only after the film became such a smash commercial hit in England that its export could no longer be thwarted. Initially released in America in a butchered 93-minute version, the film was restored to its full length in 1986 by Britain's National Film Archive.

LIFE AND NOTHING BUT   DVD
(LA VIE EST RIEN D'AUTRE)
1989 135m c   Drama   ★★★½
Hachette Premiere/Little Bear/A2   (France)   PG

Philippe Noiret (Maj. Dellaplanne), Sabine Azema (Irene de Courtil), Pascale Vignal (Alice), Maurice Barrier (Mercadot), Francois Perrot (Perrin), Jean-Pol Dubois (Andre), Daniel Russo (Lt. Trevise), Michel Duchaussoy (Gen. Villerieux), Arlette Gilbert (Valentine), Louis Lyonnet (Valentin)

p, Rene Cleitman, Albert Prevost; d, Bertrand Tavernier; w, Bertrand Tavernier, Jean Cosmos; ph, Bruno de Keyzer (Eastmancolor); ed, Armand Psenny; m, Oswald d'Andrea; prod d, Guy-Claude Francois; cos, Jacqueline Moreau

A compelling successor to such antiwar movies as Stanley Kubrick's PATHS OF GLORY and Lewis Milestone's ALL QUIET ON THE WESTERN FRONT, focusing, like these earlier films, on WWI. Instead of detailing the ongoing carnage of life in the trenches, however, Tavernier paints a grim portrait of devastation after the fact. The year is 1920 (almost two years after the Armistice), and the massive task of counting corpses and identifying the missing among the French soldiers remains. Supervising these efforts is Major Dellaplane (Noiret), a career soldier obsessed with detail who turns his responsibility into a personal crusade to justify the sacrifice made by the dead men, believing that by naming the unidentified and humanizing the statistics, he can somehow make sense of the horror that has occurred. Dellaplane's quest to tie up war's loose ends is interwoven with the tale of another officer's mission to locate a suitable unknown soldier for ceremonial enshrinement in the Arc de Triomphe, and with vignettes concerning families seeking information about the fate of loved ones.

Cowritten by Tavernier and Jean Cosmos (a playwright and TV scenarist making his screenwriting debut), LIFE AND NOTHING BUT is a carefully wrought drama about the emotionally shell-shocked survivors of WWI. Somber, handsome, exquisitely produced, with a towering performance by Noiret in what is reportedly his 100th screen role, Tavernier's elegy strikes no false notes. With an extraordinary talent for conveying the bustle of life amidst the stasis of death, Tavernier employs his sweeping camera and his skill in relating characters to their widescreen environment to create an unforgettable *mise-en-scene*. Despite its brilliant technical accomplishment and its seamless blend of gallows humor and intriguing drama, however, Tavernier's examination of lives held in check by the fortunes of war lacks the full-throttle emotionalism that might have made it a classic pacifist epic. Visually, Tavernier's work with the superb de Keyzer couldn't be improved upon (as in the haunting final shot), but one does wish it were a little less calculated, a little more reckless.

LIFE AQUATIC WITH STEVE ZISSOU, THE
DVD
2004 118m c   Comedy/Drama   ★★
American Empirical Pictures/Scott Rudin   R
Productions/Touchstone   (U.S.)

Bill Murray *(Steve Zissou)*, Owen Wilson *(Ned Plimpton)*, Cate Blanchett *(Jane Winslett-Richardson)*, Anjelica Huston *(Eleanor Zissou)*, Willem Dafoe *(Klaus Daimler)*, Jeff Goldblum *(Alistair Hennessey)*, Noah Taylor *(Vladimir Wolodarsky)*, Bud Cort *(Bill Ubell)*, Seu Jorge *(Pele dos Santos)*, Seymour Cassel *(Esteban du Plantier)*

p, Wes Anderson, Barry Mendel, Scott Rudin; d, Wes Anderson; w, Wes Anderson, Noah Baumbach; ph, Robert Yeoman; ed, David Moritz; m, Mark Mothersbaugh; prod d, Mark Friedberg; art d, Stefano Maria Ortolani; fx, Daniel Acon, Renato Agostini, Walt Conti (animatronic), Jeremy Dawson, Gray Marshall; cos, Milena Canonero; anim, Henry Selick

A pure product of the "isn't it ironic" generation, filmmaker Wes Anderson's sensibilities are steeped in received experience absorbed through a pop-culture filter of movies, TV, comic books, and classic *New Yorker* fiction. His resulting inclination towards precious observational humor and arch homage produces too-clever-by-half films full of glittering details sprinkled over a fundamental hollowness.

Grizzled celebrity naturalist Steve Zissou (Bill Murray) is drifting unhappily into middle-aged irrelevance, still grinding out installments of his once popular series of armchair adven-

ture films, "The Life Aquatic With Steve Zissou." His intrepid "Team Zissou" (which includes Willem Dafoe, Noah Taylor, and Seu Jorge) is still loyal, but they're reeling from the loss of senior team member Esteban du Plantier (Seymour Cassel) to a giant jaguar shark that just might be the pot-addled Zissou's very own white whale. Zissou's boat and his marriage to brainy, beautiful Eleanor (Anjelica Huston) are both deteriorating, and Eleanor's ex-husband, lean, mean, grant-seeking machine Alistair Hennessey (Jeff Goldblum), is diverting Zissou's funding. Courtly Kentucky Air pilot Ned Plimpton (Owen Wilson), who might be Zissou's son, wants to get to know his dad, and pregnant journalist Jane Winslett-Richardson (Cate Blanchett) is writing a warts-and-all piece for "Oceanographic Explorer" magazine. Zissou's quest for the jaguar shark is mostly an excuse for self-consciously quirky character bits, occasionally interrupted by trumped-up complications. Pirates, anyone?

Stranded awkwardly between the heartfelt and the put-on, as though Anderson couldn't bear to finger the heartstrings without appending a juvenile *gotcha!* to every emotional moment, the film isn't even so cool it hurts. It's so cool all the life has drained away, leaving nothing behind but a faint whiff of attitude.

LIFE BEGINS FOR ANDY HARDY
1941 100m bw Drama   ★★★½
MGM   (U.S.)

Mickey Rooney *(Andy Hardy)*, Lewis Stone *(Judge Hardy)*, Judy Garland *(Betsy Booth)*, Fay Holden *(Mrs. Hardy)*, Ann Rutherford *(Polly Benedict)*, Sara Haden *(Aunt Milly)*, Patricia Dane *(Jennitt Hicks)*, Ray McDonald *(Jimmy Frobisher)*, George Breakston *(Beezy)*, Pierre Watkin *(Dr. Waggoner)*

d, George B. Seitz; w, Agnes Christine Johnston (based on characters created by Aurania Rouyerol); ph, Lester White; ed, Elmo Veron; art d, Cedric Gibbons; cos, Robert Kalloch

A serious departure in MGM's highly successful "Andy Hardy" series finds Rooney as the prodigal. The recent high school graduate has a heart-to-heart discussion with his father, Stone, about his future. Not wanting to follow immediately in his father's footsteps, Rooney's ambition is to go off to New York and "find himself." Though they don't agree with him, the Hardys let their son go off to New York City. There he joins his long-suffering friend Garland (in her third and last film in the "Hardy" series, though she continued to work onscreen with Rooney in other films). After much difficulty, Rooney finds a job as an office boy for the paltry sum of $10 a week. He meets McDonald, a struggling dancer, and sneaks the penniless, homeless young man into his hotel room. But Rooney is startled one evening when he comes home to find his new friend dead of a heart attack. He gets a loan on his jalopy so McDonald can have a decent funeral rather than a pauper's grave. Rooney has befriended Dane, an older divorcee—the receptionist in his employer's office—who invites the young man up to her apartment for an evening. The offer is tempting, but Rooney's homespun value system—along with the arrival of his father in the big city—cause him to decline. Looking over the events that have happened since his arrival in New York, Rooney decides that his home town and college are his real future and he returns to Carvel with Stone. Though the critics attacked the film as too much of a departure from the "Andy Hardy" series's normal vein, this is a fine addition. Rooney and Garland both show great maturity with their characters. Garland is a fine counterbalance for Rooney, constantly watching over him like a loving mother and calling his father when things look dark. Though she truly wants to be in love with him, she can circumvent her feelings to help the skittish young man when he really needs her. The National Legion of Decency surprised everyone in the film world by rating this film A-2, an objectional film for children. They felt that Rooney's heart-to-heart talks with Stone were too "daring" for children, to say nothing of his scenes with Dane.

LIFE IS BEAUTIFUL   DVD
(LA VITA E BELLA)
1997 114m c   Comedy/Drama   ★★½
Melampo Cinematografica (Italy)   PG-13

Roberto Benigni (Guido Orefice), Nicoletta Braschi (Dora), Giorgio Cantarini (Giosue), Giustino Durano (Uncle), Sergio Bustric (Ferruccio Orefice), Marisa Paredes (Dora's Mother), Horst Buchholz (Dr. Lessing), Lydia Alfonsi (Guicciardini), Giuliana Lojodice (Didactic Principal), Amerigo Fontani (Rodolfo)

p, Gianluigi Braschi, Elda Ferri; d, Roberto Benigni; w, Roberto Benigni, Vincenzo Cerami; ph, Tonino Delli Colli; ed, Simona Paggi; m, Nicola Piovani; prod d, Danilo Donati; cos, Danilo Donati

AA Best Actor: Roberto Benigni; AA Best Foreign Language Film; AA Best Original Dramatic Score: Nicola Piovani; AAN Best Picture; AAN Best Director: Roberto Benigni; AAN Best Original Screenplay: Vincenzo Cerami, Roberto Benigni; AAN Best Film Editing: Simona Paggi

Italian comedian Roberto Benigni's World War II-era farce is a tough proposition: the first half is standard Benigni burlesque, complete with witty visual gags and rapid-fire repartee. The rest is set in a concentration camp, and its tragicomic inventions feel somewhat forced.

Arezzo, Italy, 1939. Puerile but good-hearted Guido Orefice (Benigni), an Italian Jew who dreams of opening a bookstore, gets a job at a fancy hotel through his uncle Eliseo (Giustino Durano). While applying for a permit, he has a disastrous encounter with officious local Fascist Rodolfo (Amerigo Fontani), who's in love with the beautiful Dora (Nicoletta Braschi). Guido keeps bumping into Dora—literally—and enchants her with his romantic inventions, and the two eventually wed amid a growing tide of anti-Semitism. Several years later, Guido and Dora have a small son, Giosue (Giorgio Cantarini). Their lives are circumscribed by anti-Jewish laws, but Guido manages to laugh matters off, until the town's Jews—Giosue, Eliseo, and himself included—are rounded up and put on a train bound for a concentration camp.

It may be folly to expect brutal realism, but Benigni's imperviousness toward real human suffering is a questionable tactic: when Giosue asks if it's true that the Germans make soap and buttons out of the prisoners, Guido starts riffing on the idea's preposterousness, plucking off shirt buttons he dubs "Antonio" and "Paolo." The laughs are nervous at best. Benigni wants to tell a poignant fable rooted in the love between a father and son, but everything hinges on whether one finds his gags inspired or tasteless. Humor can only save some of us.

LIFE IS SWEET
1991 102m c   Drama/Comedy   ★★★½
Thin Man Films (U.K.)

Alison Steadman (Wendy), Jim Broadbent (Andy), Timothy Spall (Aubrey), Claire Skinner (Natalie), Jane Horrocks (Nicola), David Thewlis (Nicola's Lover), Moya Brady (Paula), Stephen Rea (Patsy), David Neilson (Steve), Jack Thorpe Baker (Nigel)

d, Mike Leigh; w, Mike Leigh; ph, Dick Pope; ed, John Gregory; m, Rachel Portman; prod d, Alison Chitty; art d, Sophie Becher; cos, Lindy Hemming

Between HIGH HOPES (1988), a grimly humorous portrait of Thatcherite London, and the apocalyptic NAKED (1993), came this sometimes unsettling but essentially sweet-tempered feature from acclaimed British director Mike Leigh.

The film concerns a lower-middle-class family of more or less lovable eccentrics living in outer London. The woman of the house, Wendy (Alison Steadman), is perpetually busy and compulsively optimistic. Her husband, Andy (Jim Broadbent), is a chef employed in a large institutional kitchen. He's a laid-back sort, inclined to tinker but never completing any of his initially ambitious projects. Wendy and Andy have twin daughters, Natalie (Claire Skinner) and Nicola (Jane Horrocks). Natalie is quiet, subdued and focused, an apprentice plumber. The bulimic Nicola, by contrast, is a sullen university dropout intent on letting everyone within earshot know how awful life is and how much she hates living.

While hardly plot-driven, LIFE IS SWEET has its share of small events: Andy, intent on finally becoming his own boss, unwisely purchases a dilapidated mobile food stand; Nicola's disgusted lover (David Thewlis, soon to become famous as NAKED's mad anti-hero) walks out on her; Natalie quietly makes plans for a trip to America; Aubrey (Timothy Spall), a farcically drawn friend of the family, makes last-minute preparations for the opening of his small restaurant; Andy suffers an accident at work which, if only temporarily, brings the family together.

A creative force on London's fringe theater scene since the 1960s, Mike Leigh made his feature directorial debut with the acclaimed BLEAK MOMENTS in 1971. This was followed by a 17-year hiatus, during which Leigh focused on TV and stage work, notably Abigail's Party and the BBC tele-movies HARD LABOUR, HOME SWEET HOME and FOUR DAYS IN JULY. While not to everyone's taste, Leigh's films have been hailed as a kind of "neo-Marxist Dickens." Not surprisingly, his forte is chronicling, with grace and economy, the vicissitudes of daily life among Britain's downtrodden. The well-rounded characters who populate his films stem from extensive one-on-one collaborations with his actors, followed by group improv sessions from which his precisely structured scripts emerge.

LIFE OF EMILE ZOLA, THE   DVD
1937 123m bw Biography   ★★★★½
Warner Bros. (U.S.)

Paul Muni (Emile Zola), Gale Sondergaard (Lucie Dreyfus), Joseph Schildkraut (Capt. Alfred Dreyfus), Gloria Holden (Alexandrine Zola), Donald Crisp (Maitre Labori), Erin O'Brien-Moore (Nana), John Litel (Charpentier), Henry O'Neill (Col. Picquart), Morris Carnovsky (Anatole France), Louis Calhern (Maj. Dort)

p, Henry Blanke; d, William Dieterle; w, Norman Reilly Raine, Heinz Herald, Geza Herczeg (based on the story by Heinz Herald and Geza Herczeg); ph, Tony Gaudio; ed, Warren Low; m, Max Steiner; art d, Anton Grot; cos, Milo Anderson, Ali Hubert

AA Best Picture; AAN Best Actor: Paul Muni; AA Best Supporting Actor: Joseph Schildkraut; AAN Best Director: William Dieterle; AA Best Screenplay: Heinz Herald, Geza Herczeg, Norman Reilly Raine; AAN Best Original Story: Heinz Herald, Geza Herczeg; AAN Best Score: Warner Bros Studio Music Department, Leo Forbstein (Dept. Head); AAN Best Interior Decoration: Anton Grot; AAN Best Sound Recording: Nathan Levinson; AAN Best Assistant Director: Russ Saunders

Along with George Arliss, Paul Muni was Hollywood's designated portrayer of Great Men. He appeared as Louis Pasteur (an Oscar-winning role), as Benito Juarez, as French explorer Pierre Radisson, as Chopin's teacher Joseph Elsner, and as Napoleon and Schubert (among others) in SEVEN FACES. So it's no surprise to find him playing Emile Zola—and wonderfully—in this fine film. Literate and powerful, THE LIFE OF EMILE ZOLA was a huge box-office success, although its subject matter—the French novelist's part in the Dreyfus Affair—hardly seemed promising in that regard. The film introduces an anguished Zola censured by the French government and public for his frank treatment of squalid life and social problems in his novel *Nana* (based on his own experiences with a prostitute, played by O'Brien-Moore). As time passes, though, he is increasingly heralded as France's greatest writer and as the champion of those who cannot speak for themselves during France's Second Empire. Zola's greatest challenge comes when he fights for the freedom of the framed Jewish officer Alfred Dreyfus (Schildkraut). Pen in hand, Zola writes, "J'accuse…"

The film's script was originally shown to Ernst Lubitsch at Paramount, who liked it but felt he had no actor in his stable who could do justice to the main character. He generously passed it on to producer Henry Blanke of Warners, which had the services of Muni, Lubitsch's choice for the part. As on so many other occasions, Lubitsch was right; Muni triumphs completely in this demanding role. As was his custom, Muni steeped himself in his character, reading all of Zola's works, extensively researching the Dreyfus case, and attempting many different makeup variations before settling on his final choice. The other actors are equally fine, with Holden in particular a warm glow as Zola's wife. It's nice to see Sondergaard in a rare sympathetic part and, as her husband, the center of the controversy, Schildkraut rivals Muni in effectiveness. Scene after scene of the nervous and later numbed Dreyfus being stripped of his honor haunt this film and Schildkraut was the only possible choice for the year's Supporting Actor Oscar. The movie itself, though it deviates from the facts a bit, is basically faithful to history and well scripted, without extraneous characters or plot lines. The period details are all authentic, with no expense spared to recreate the settings. Director Dieterle, one of Hollywood's best, handles the script beautifully, especially in the brilliant courtroom scenes, and the anti-Semitic nature of Dreyfus's persecution is also conveyed potently, though circumspectly. (We never hear the word *Jew.*) Skip the 1958 remake, I ACCUSE.

LIFE ON A STRING

(BIAN ZOU BIAN CHANG)
1992 110m c Drama ★★★
Serene Productions/Pandora Film/Beijing Film Studio/China Film/Diva Film
(China/U.K./Germany)

Liu Zhongyuan *(The Saint),* Huang Lei *(Shitou),* Xu Qing *(Lanxiu),* Ma Ling *(Noodleshop Owner's Wife),* Zhang Zhenguan, Yao Jingou

p, Don Ranvaud; d, Chen Kaige; w, Chen Kaige (from the short story by Shi Tiesheng); ph, Gu Changwei; ed, Pei Xiaonan; m, Qu Xiaosong; art d, Shao Ruigang

A film—at least ostensibly—about blindness, LIFE ON A STRING contains some of the most stunning images in recent screen history, beautifully capturing the thundering waterfalls, sparkling mountain ranges and mistfallen crags of China's Shaanxi Province.

The setting is feudal China, where a sightless old musician, known simply as the Saint (Liu Zhongyuan), wanders purposefully with his young, equally blind apprentice, Shitou (Huang Lei). As a youth the Saint was disciple to Grand Master, who told him that if he spent his days in ceaseless practice on the *sanxian* (a long-necked banjo), his blindness would end. All the Saint had to do was break 1,000 strings in the course of playing. That task has consumed 60 years, and the count has reached the 990s. Meanwhile, Shitou yearns for earthier pleasures, mainly in the form of a peasant girl named Lanxiu (Xu Qing). The Saint disapproves, but is ultimately forced to reconsider his own, unquestioning faith in the rigid moral code by which he has lived.

LIFE ON A STRING presents itself as an epic fable whose precise moral has been lost to the ages, allowing many meanings to be read into its dense spectacle. Kaige composes each frame with an artisan's care. He restricts his camera movements to slow, formal pans and lengthy takes that slow down the narrative, but impart a mythic quality to the material. Most impressive is a lyrical series of long shots in which the Saint stops a war between two clans by hobbling into the midst of opposing armies and singing about peace and brotherhood. As the legendary minstrel's frail voice fills the soundtrack, the warriors unite around him to form a single, mighty procession. Though at times ponderous and obscure, LIFE ON A STRING leaves a lasting impression on the eye.

LIFE WITH FATHER

1947 118m c Comedy ★★★★
Warner Bros. (U.S.)

William Powell *(Clarence Day),* Irene Dunne *(Vinnie Day),* Elizabeth Taylor *(Mary),* Edmund Gwenn *(Rev. Dr. Lloyd),* ZaSu Pitts *(Cora),* James Lydon *(Clarence),* Emma Dunn *(Margaret),* Moroni Olsen *(Dr. Humphries),* Elisabeth Risdon *(Mrs. Whitehead),* Derek Scott *(Harlan)*

p, Robert Buckner; d, Michael Curtiz; w, Donald Ogden Stewart (based on the play by Howard Lindsay, Russel Crouse and the book by Clarence Day Jr.); ph, Peverell Marley, William V. Skall (Technicolor); ed, George Amy; m, Max Steiner; art d, Robert Haas; fx, Ray Foster, William McGann; cos, Milo Anderson

AAN Best Actor: William Powell; *AAN Best Color Cinematography:* Peverell Marley, William V. Skall; *AAN Best Score (Drama or Comedy):* Max Steiner; *AAN Best Art Direction-Set Decoration (Color):* Robert M Haas (Art Direction), George James Hopkins (Set Decoration)

Based on an autobiographical book by Clarence Day, Jr., and a play that ran for 3,224 performances on Broadway (a total that was eclipsed only by "Fiddler on the Roof"), LIFE WITH FATHER is a son's fond remembrance of his Victorian youth spent in the home of his authoritarian but lovable father (William Powell). There's really not much of a plot, just a lot of alternately quiet and raucous moments of love and laughter as the family goes about its urban, urbane life. Irene Dunne, playing the mother of the red-headed Day clan, is frequently rankled by Father's sexist ways, but, like the rest of the family, she loves dear old Dad anyway.

Powell is nothing less than magnificent as the mustached philosophizing patriarch, and Dunne casts a warm glow beside him. Elizabeth Taylor, Martin Milner, Jimmy Lydon, and Edmund Gwenn all contribute strong supporting performances; Michael Curtiz (CASABLANCA; YANKEE DOODLE DANDY; THE ADVENTURES OF ROBIN HOOD) provides his usual sure-handed direction. There was an attempt at a sequel, LIFE WITH MOTHER, but it doesn't hold a candle to this. Day's story also inspired a brief TV series in 1955. Look for a very young and beautiful Arlene Dahl in a scene at Delmonico's Restaurant. Older TV fans will also recognize singer Russell Arms as the stock quotation operator.

LIFEBOAT

1944 96m bw Drama/War ★★★★½
Fox (U.S.)

Tallulah Bankhead *(Connie Porter),* William Bendix *(Gus),* Walter Slezak *(The German),* Mary Anderson *(Alice),* John Hodiak *(Kovak),* Henry Hull *(Rittenhouse),* Heather Angel *(Mrs. Higgins),* Hume Cronyn *(Stanley Garrett),* Canada Lee *(Joe),* William Yetter Jr. *(German Sailor)*

p, Kenneth MacGowan; d, Alfred Hitchcock; w, Jo Swerling (based on the story by John Steinbeck); ph, Glen MacWilliams; ed, Dorothy Spencer; m, Hugo Friedhofer; art d, James Basevi, Maurice Ransford; fx, Fred Sersen

AAN Best Director: Alfred Hitchcock; *AAN Best Original Story:* John Steinbeck; *AAN Best B/W Cinematography:* Glen MacWilliams

Alfred Hitchcock's taut wartime thriller concerns a handful of survivors who climb into a lifeboat after their ship is torpedoed by a German U-boat. The captain (Walter Slezak) of the U-boat, which has also sunk, swims to the already crowded boat and is taken aboard by the kind-hearted survivors. Since he is the only man capable of handling the craft in rough weather and navigating it to a safe harbor, he is elected helmsman. The survivors are an odd lot—fashion writer Connie Porter (Tallulah Bankhead), industrial tycoon Rittenhouse (Henry Hull), socially conscious seaman Kovak (John Hodiak), wounded stoker Gus (William Bendix), meek radio operator Stanley Garrett (Hume Cronyn), bewildered nurse Alice (Mary Anderson), a mother in shock (Heather Angel), cradling her child who had just died, and black steward Joe (Canada Lee). Slowly, and with insidious cleverness, the German steers a course not for land, but to a secret rendezvous with a German mother ship. The entire cast is superb, but the standouts are Bankhead, as the spoiled, wealthy dilettante writer whose expensive furs and jewelry are worth more to her than the lives of her fellow survivors, and Bendix, as the compassionate but not-too-bright stoker whose gangrenous leg poses a threat to his dreams of returning home to dance with his sweetheart. John Steinbeck, on whose original story the film was based, was first assigned to pen the script, but reportedly felt too restricted by the film's single set (the lifeboat). Jo Swerling eventually wrote the script, but, as was customary with Hitchcock, the talented Ben Hecht was brought in at the last moment to tighten up scenes and sharpen dialogue.

LIGHT THAT FAILED, THE
1939 97m   bw Drama   ★★★★
Paramount   (U.S.)

Ronald Colman *(Dick Heldar)*, Walter Huston *(Terpenhow)*, Muriel Angelus *(Maisie)*, Ida Lupino *(Bessie Broke)*, Dudley Digges *(The Nilghai)*, Ernest Cossart *(Beeton)*, Ferike Boros *(Mme. Binat)*, Pedro de Cordoba *(M. Binat)*, Colin Tapley *(Gardner)*, Fay Helm *(Red-Haired Girl)*

p, William A. Wellman; d, William A. Wellman; w, Robert Carson (based on the novel by Rudyard Kipling); ph, Theodor Sparkuhl; ed, Thomas Scott; m, Victor Young; art d, Hans Dreier, Robert Odell

This tragic Kipling tale, from his first novel, displays Wellman's consummate directorial skills in following the story faithfully, unlike earlier versions in which sugar-coated endings are supplied. Colman is a gifted artist who receives a sabre cut during a battle. He returns to England where he becomes a famous painter; his masterpiece is a portrait of a London prostitute, Lupino. She is driven half-mad with desire for him, a part so intensely played that it brought her to stardom. Realizing that her station in life will prevent her from ever having him, she viciously destroys the painting. The old wound has caused him to slowly go blind. In a shattering scene, Colman proudly displays the portrait to his devoted friend Huston, not realizing that Lupino has slashed it. His sight almost gone, Colman bids goodbye to his childhood sweetheart and returns to the Sudan with friend Huston. At the first sound of battle, Colman begs Huston to put him into the fight, and he is sent blindly charging on his white stallion to his death. This moving, haunting film reinforces Kipling's love of honor, male friendship, and nobility of spirit. Wellman handles the story and gaslight era with great care, developing his characters with incisive scenes. This was no easy task for Wellman since he and Colman argued throughout the film, the director refusing Colman's perfectionist demands for endless takes and ignoring the actor's insistence that Vivien Leigh play the slatternly Bessie. Lupino got that emotion-charged part by barging into Wellman's office to tell

him that no other woman in the world could play Bessie as well as she and providing an impromptu interpretation right then and there. She got the role, and audiences around the world were stunned by her marvelous portrayal. Of Colman, the director would later comment: "Ronald Colman and Wellman, an odd combination to say the least. He didn't like me; I didn't like him—the only two things we agreed fully on. [He has] the most beautiful voice in the whole motion picture business."

LIKE WATER FOR CHOCOLATE   *DVD*
(COMO AGUA PARA CHOCOLATE)
1992 114m   c   Drama/Romance/Fantasy   ★★★½
Arau Films International/Mexican National
Council for Culture and the Arts/Mexican
Institute of Cinematography (Mexico)

Marco Leonardi *(Pedro Muzquiz)*, Lumi Cavazos *(Tita de la Garza)*, Regina Torne *(Mama Elena)*, Mario Ivan Martinez *(John Brown)*, Ada Carrasco *(Nacha)*, Yareli Arizmendi *(Rosaura)*, Claudette Maille *(Gertrudis)*, Pilar Aranda *(Chencha)*, Farnesio DiBernal *(Priest)*, Joaquin Garrido *(Sergeant Trevino)*

p, Alfonso Arau; d, Alfonso Arau; w, Laura Esquivel (from her Novel); ph, Emmanuel Lubezki, Steve Bernstein; ed, Carlos Bolado, Francisco Chiu; m, Leo Brower; art d, Marco Antonio Arteaga, Mauricio DeAguinaco, Denise Pizzini; fx, Raul Falomir; chor, Farnesio DeBernal

Alfonso Arau's LIKE WATER FOR CHOCOLATE proved a tremendous hit with American movie audiences, becoming the highest-grossing foreign-language feature ever released in the U.S.

Mexico, 1910. Tita (Lumi Cavazos) lives cursed by a cruel family tradition; as the youngest daughter, she is to take care of Mama Elena (Regina Torne) in her old age, and is forbidden to wed. Tita falls in love with Pedro (Marco Leonardi), and when Mama Elena refuses to let them marry, he agrees to take older daughter Rosaura's (Yareli Arizmendi) hand, thinking he will at least be close to his true love. Forced to bake their wedding cake, Tita moistens the cake batter with her heartbroken tears. Upon eating the cake, the wedding guests are overcome with an unbearable sadness and begin uncontrollably crying and throwing up. Thus begins Tita's special magic with food; resigned to her fate as family cook, she will impart her feelings to the dishes she prepares, with results that range from amusing to truly shocking.

An adult fairy tale, LIKE WATER FOR CHOCOLATE has evil family members, a prince charming, numerous trials, and a happy ending—sort of. It proved an international breakthrough for Arau, a character actor and filmmaker who previously specialized in political comedies. The real auteur of the piece, though, is novelist Laura Esquivel, a writer in the magic realist tradition, and her screenplay largely succeeds in translating the appeal of her book to the screen. Though one wonders if Arau couldn't have found more visual parallels for Esquivel's narrative, overall the film is a witty, charming diversion that struck a chord with audiences.

LILI
1953 81m   c   Drama   ★★★½
MGM (U.S.)

Leslie Caron *(Lili Daurier)*, Mel Ferrer *(Paul Berthalet)*, Jean-Pierre Aumont *(Marc)*, Zsa Zsa Gabor *(Rosalie)*, Kurt Kasznar *(Jacquot)*, Amanda Blake *(Peach Lips)*, Alex Gerry *(Proprietor)*, Ralph Dumke *(M. Corvier)*, Wilton Graff *(M. Tonit)*, George Baxter *(M. Enrique)*

p, Edwin H. Knopf; d, Charles Walters; w, Helen Deutsch (based on the story by Paul Gallico); ph, Robert Planck (Technicolor); ed, Ferris Webster; m, Bronislau Kaper; art d, Cedric Gibbons, Paul

Groesse; fx, Warren Newcombe; chor, Charles Walters, Dorothy Jarnac; cos, Mary Ann Nyberg

AAN Best Actress: Leslie Caron; *AAN Best Director:* Charles Walters; *AAN Best Screenplay:* Helen Deutsch; *AAN Best Color Cinematography:* Robert Planck; *AA Best Score (Drama or Comedy):* Bronislau Kaper; *AAN Best Art Direction-Set Decoration (Color):* Cedric Gibbons, Paul Groesse, Edwin B. Willis, Arthur Krams

Leslie Caron plays the title role in this charming film. Sixteen-year-old Lili Daurier runs off to work as a waitress with a carnival and falls in love with Marc (Jean Pierre Aumont), a magician who is more amused by the young innocent than anything else. Fired for paying too much attention to Marc, Lili is comforted by a group of puppets operated by Paul Berthalet (Mel Ferrer), a bitter ex-dancer crippled by a war injury. Though Paul is insanely jealous of Lili's affection for Marc, he is only able to show his tender side through his puppets (in the film's nicest moment, as Lili and the dancing figures sing the famous "Hi-Lili, Hi-Lo"), and Lili thinks of him as a cruel man. When Lili learns that Rosalie (Zsa Zsa Gabor, in a surprisingly good performance) is Marc's wife as well as his assistant, she packs her bags to leave, but love wins out in the end, though it's not the magician who has the final trick up his sleeve. Caron is wonderful as Lili, Ferrer and Aumont provide handsome support, and the whole look of the film is just right. LILI was the basis for a hit Broadway musical in 1961 called "Carnival," with Anna Maria Alberghetti in the Caron role.

LILI MARLEEN

| 1981 | 120m | c | Drama/War | ★★ |
| Roxy/CIP/Rialto | | (West Germany) | | R |

Hanna Schygulla *(Wilkie Bunterberg)*, Giancarlo Giannini *(Robert Mendelsson)*, Mel Ferrer *(David Mendelsson)*, Karl-Heinz von Hassel *(Henkel)*, Christine Kaufmann *(Miriam)*, Hark Bohm *(Tascher)*, Karin Baal *(Anna Lederer)*, Udo Kier *(Drewitz)*, Erik Schumann *(Von Strehlow)*, Gottfried John *(Aaron)*

p, Luggi Waldleitner, Enzo Peri; d, Rainer Werner Fassbinder; w, Manfred Purzer, Joshua Sinclair, Rainer Werner Fassbinder (based on the song by Lale Andersen); ph, Xaver Schwarzenberger; ed, Franz Walsch, Juliane Lorenz; m, Peer Raben; prod d, Rolf Zehetbauer; art d, Herbert Stravel; fx, Joachim Schulz; chor, Dr. Dieter Gackstetter; cos, Barbara Baum

Fassbinder was surely one of the world's most prolific filmmakers, producing an enormous body of work before his early death, which ironically occurred as he was editing film. With such a large output there were bound to be a few pictures that fell short of the director's normally high quality, LILI MARLEEN being an example. "The story of a song!" claimed the advertising copy, which is more or less truth in advertising. "Lili Marleen" was a song made famous in Germany by Lale Andersen and later Marlene Dietrich. It was very popular with the German forces during WWII. However, Fassbinder's film has little to do with the true story of the song. The film opens in 1938 with the lovely and accomplished Schygulla, a cabaret singer in Zurich. She discovers that boyfriend Giannini, a Swiss Jew, is not only a musical composer but also a member of the underground resistance movement. During a trip to Germany, her song becomes a hit, and no less than the Fuhrer himself wants to meet her. She becomes a big star, while Giannini's father blocks her return to Switzerland. Giannini sneaks into Berlin and meets once more with his now-famous lover. She becomes blacklisted and is forced to leave the country while Giannini is arrested. After the war, they meet once more, but he is now married and well on his way to success. Though Fassbinder's camerawork is excellent, including some allusions to the famous German studio UFA, his themes are never really developed. The political and social messages so often found in his work give way to more melodramatic

storytelling. Schygulla, who is usually a shining performer, is spotty here. Her singing makes one wonder how the song got to be such a hit.

LILIES OF THE FIELD   DVD

| 1963 | 94m | bw | Drama | ★★★½ |
| Rainbow | | (U.S.) | | |

Sidney Poitier *(Homer Smith)*, Lilia Skala *(Mother Maria)*, Lisa Mann *(Sister Gertrude)*, Isa Crino *(Sister Agnes)*, Francesca Jarvis *(Sister Albertine)*, Pamela Branch *(Sister Elizabeth)*, Stanley Adams *(Juan)*, Dan Frazer *(Father Murphy)*, Ralph Nelson *(Mr. Ashton)*

p, Ralph Nelson; d, Ralph Nelson; w, James Poe (based on the novel by William E. Barrett); ph, Ernest Haller; ed, John McCafferty; m, Jerry Goldsmith

AAN Best Picture; AA Best Actor: Sidney Poitier; *AAN Best Supporting Actress:* Lilia Skala; *AAN Best Adapted Screenplay:* James Poe; *AAN Best B/W Cinematography:* Ernest Haller

LILIES OF THE FIELD is a "feel-good" movie that blazed new trails in the motion picture world. Not that it had any particular special effects or innovations in movies. It had no spectacular action or dance sequences and surely no violence. But it was a trendsetter in that it marked the first time that the Academy of Motion Picture Arts and Sciences ever awarded an Oscar to a black actor, Poitier. Poitier is an ex-GI roaming around the Southwest, taking odd jobs and seeing what there is to see when he stops at a small farm to refill his car radiator. The farm is run by five German nuns who immediately set upon him to help them with their manual labors. They are new to these shores and don't speak much English but the Mother Superior, Skala, convinces Poitier to stay a while and help work the farm that was willed to them. He fixes their leaky roof and they send up prayers in honor of the man whom "God has sent." Now, Skala asks if he will stay on to help with some other chores. Poitier is a little tired of his aimless wanderings and not much convincing is necessary, even though they prevail on him to do a major project—the building of a chapel. Poitier agrees, as long as they will supply the needed materials. He teams up with Nelson (doing double chores as director and actor), a contractor, and they start to build the chapel. Meanwhile, he donates his small salary back to the nuns to buy food and spends his spare time teaching them how to speak English. When building materials for the chapel run out, Poitier disappears and the nuns think he's abandoned them, but he returns a few weeks later to complete the job he started for the nuns he has come to love. Now, however, he is finally assisted by the local townspeople who refused to help him the first time around. On the night before the sanctification of the chapel, Poitier leaves with as little fanfare as when he first arrived. This was a small, low-budget picture that went straight for the heart and succeeded critically as well as financially.

LILO & STITCH   DVD

| 2002 | 87m | c | Animated/Children's/Comedy | ★★★ |
| Walt Disney Pictures | | (U.S.) | | PG |

VOICES OF: Daveigh Chase *(Lilo)*, Chris Sanders, billed as Christopher Michael Sanders *(Stitch)*, Tia Carrere *(Nani)*, David Ogden Stiers *(Jumba)*, Kevin McDonald *(Pleakley)*, Ving Rhames *(Cobra Bubbles)*, Zoe Caldwell *(Grand Councilwoman)*, Jason Scott Lee *(David Kawena)*, Kevin Michael Richardson *(Captain Gantu)*, Susan Hegarty *(Rescue Lady)*

p, Clark Spencer; d, Dean Deblois, Chris Sanders; w, Dean DeBlois, Chris Sanders; ed, Darren Holmes; m, Alan Silvestri; prod d, Paul Felix; art d, Ric Sluiter; fx, Joseph F. Gilland; anim,

Ruben A. Aquino, Rob Bekuhrs, Bolhem Bouchiba, Philip S. Boyd, Arden Chan, Andreas Deja, Jeff Dutton, Eric Guaglione, Byron Howard, Alex Kupershmidt, Christine Lawrence-Finney, Stephane Sainte Foi, Robert E. Stanton

After the astounding success of such computer-generated features as TOY STORY and MONSTERS, INC., Disney takes a giant step back into making animated movies the old-fashioned way—by hand, in two dimensions, and one frame at a time. But beautiful illustrations and watercolor back-grounds can't save this well-meaning kid flick from a disap-pointing story.

Somewhere in the far reaches of the galaxy, Dr. Jumba (voice of David Odgen Stiers) has been accused by the Galactic Federation of illegal genetic experimentation. His project is a nasty piece of work he calls Experiment 626 (Chris Sanders), a smart, spiny, six-armed little *thing* that's extraordi-narily bad tempered and virtually indestructible. Jumba is found guilty, but before 626 can be banished to a desert aster-oid, he commandeers a police cruiser and lands on the island of Kauai, Hawaii, where he's mistaken for an ugly dog. 626 is renamed "Stitch" and adopted by Lilo (Daveigh Chase), a lonely six-year-old orphan who's being raised—with difficul-ty—by her older sister, Nani (Tia Carrere). Lilo makes allowances for Stitch's destructive behavior (she herself has been known to bite) and is determined to turn him into a respectable pet. Meanwhile, a hulking social worker named Cobra Bubbles (Ving Rhames) has already warned Nani that if she doesn't get her act together, he'll have to put Lilo in fos-ter care. The last thing Nani needs is a tiny Terminator destroy-ing her house.

The film is full of refreshing tweaks: The characters real-ly look like native Hawaiians, and the soundtrack is thankful-ly free of the usual Randy Newman-style goop. But the touching story of Nani's stuggle to keep her small family together—Nani is essentially a single teenage mom—soon gives way to a series of loud, anime-inspired chase scenes that, frankly, go nowhere.

LIMELIGHT   DVD
1952 145m bw Drama/Comedy   ★★★★
Chaplin   (U.S.)   G

Charles Chaplin *(Calvero)*, Claire Bloom *(Terry, a Ballet Dancer)*, Sydney Chaplin *(Neville, a Composer)*, Andre Eglevsky *(Harlequin)*, Melissa Hayden *(Columbine)*, Charles Chaplin Jr., Wheeler Dryden *(Clowns)*, Nigel Bruce *(Postant, an Impresario)*, Norman Lloyd *(Stage Manager)*, Buster Keaton *(Piano Accompanist)*

p, Charles Chaplin; d, Charles Chaplin; w, Charles Chaplin; ph, Karl Struss; ed, Joe Inge; m, Charles Chaplin; art d, Eugene Laurie; chor, Charles Chaplin, Andre Eglevsky, Melissa Hayden

AA Best Original Dramatic Score: Charles Chaplin, Raymond Rasch, Larry Russell

Chaplin, as usual, is the whole show, superb in this swansong statement about his own career and the old-style entertainment he best represented. He is a one-time great of the British music halls at the turn of the century (which is exactly where Chaplin himself began), who finds a young dancer, Bloom, depressed over setbacks, attempting suicide in their cheap boarding house. He takes her in, nurses her back to health, and supports her efforts to become a success. As her star rises, his fades, but he bows out with magnificent aplomb in the place he most loves, the theater. Chaplin plays comic and dramatic scenes with great skill. He is simply wonderful in his pantomime rou-tines, particularly so when he tames a flea and when he imag-ines himself a great lion tamer. Chaplin is a delight as he teaches Bloom his "laughter therapy." He ends his career— and his life—with a hilarious routine with the great comic

Keaton, collapsing from exhaustion, falling into the orchestra pit and getting wedged in a large drum, commenting: "Ladies and gentlemen, I would like to say something, but I am stuck." He dies happy, believing that Bloom is in love, not with him, but with a young composer, played by Chaplin's real-life son, Sydney. Other children, from his marriage with Oona O'Neill (daughter of the great American playwright), appear as street urchins. The overlong film is extraordinary in that Chaplin produced, directed, wrote the script, and helped compose the haunting, Oscar winning score (In an unusual occurance, the composers won the Award, not in 1952, but in 1972, which was the first year the picture was ever shown in a Los Angeles theatre). The film's main love theme, "Eternally," became a popular ballad. LIMELIGHT is a direct comment on Chaplin's own fabulous career, one which saw the triumph and decline of physical comedy. He had fallen out of favor with a public that believed him to be a wild-eyed leftist radi-cal, if not an outright communist, and LIMELIGHT suffered as a result, yielding little profit at the box office. LIMELIGHT pays homage to a past in which simple, nuance-free entertain-ment gave joy and laughter to millions. Bloom, at age 19, became an overnight star with her appearance in the film. (She had debuted in THE BLIND GODDESS at age 16.) She later recalled in her memoirs, *Limelight and After:* "Chaplin was the most exacting director, not because he expected you to produce wonders on your own, but because he expected you to follow unquestioningly his every instruction. I was sur-prised at how old-fashioned much of what he prescribed seemed—rather theatrical effects that I didn't associate with the modern cinema."

LIMEY, THE   DVD
1999 89m c Crime/Drama   ★★★½
Artisan Pictures   (U.S.)   R

Terence Stamp *(Wilson)*, Lesley Ann Warren *(Elaine)*, Luis Guzman *(Ed)*, Barry Newman *(Avery)*, Joe Dallesandro *(Uncle John)*, Nicky Katt *(Stacy)*, Peter Fonda *(Valentine)*, Amelia Heinle *(Adhara)*, Melissa George *(Jennifer)*, William Lucking *(Warehouse Foreman)*

p, John Hardy, Scott Kramer; d, Steven Soderbergh; w, Lem Dobbs; ph, Ed Lachman; ed, Sarah Flack; m, Cliff Martinez; prod d, Gary Frutkoff; fx, Kevin Hannigan; cos, Louise Frogley

Its cool, sleekly beautiful surface lying lightly over a story boiling with casual cruelty and festering unhappiness, this intelligent, oddly aloof thriller is a worthy follow-up to direc-tor Steven Soderbergh's OUT OF SIGHT.

English hard case Wilson (Terence Stamp) is a man pro-foundly out of his element. A career criminal who's just been released from prison, he's come to Los Angeles to investigate the death of his estranged daughter, Jennifer (Melissa George). Thinking it the decent thing to do, Jennifer's friend Ed (Luis Guzman) sent the still imprisoned Wilson a newspaper clip-ping about the auto accident that took Jennifer's life. But the brooding, congenitally suspicious Wilson convinces himself that her death was murder and ropes Ed into his single-mind-ed quest to find out who's responsible and make him—or them—pay. The trail leads to Jennifer's much older boyfriend, Valentine (Peter Fonda), a hugely successful record producer whose dark secrets are laid bare by Wilson's relentless and increasingly brutal search for the truth.

Woven into this fairly straightforward revenge story is the gradual disclosure of Wilson's relationship with Jennifer, and the film's stroke of genius is its use of clips from Ken Loach's 1968 film POOR COW, in which Stamp played a gentle, feckless young thief. The juxtaposition of that 20-year-old footage with Stamp's beautifully shaded portrayal of an older, embittered man looking to justify his misspent life by avenging the daughter he drove away is simply heartbreaking.

LION IN WINTER, THE
DVD
1968 134m c Historical ★★★★
Haworth (U.K.) PG

Peter O'Toole *(King Henry II)*, Katharine Hepburn *(Queen Eleanor of Aquitaine)*, Jane Merrow *(Princess Alais)*, John Castle *(Prince Geoffrey)*, Timothy Dalton *(King Philip of France)*, Anthony Hopkins *(Prince Richard the Lion-Hearted)*, Nigel Stock *(William Marshall)*, Nigel Terry *(Prince John)*, Kenneth Griffith *(Strolling Player)*, O.Z. Whitehead *(Bishop of Durham)*

p, Martin Poll; d, Anthony Harvey; w, James Goldman (based on the play by Goldman); ph, Douglas Slocombe (Panavision, Eastmancolor); ed, John Bloom; m, John Barry; art d, Peter Murton, Gilbert Margerie; cos, Margaret Furse

AAN Best Picture; AAN Best Actor: Peter O'Toole; AA Best Actress: Katharine Hepburn; AAN Best Director: Anthony Harvey; AA Best Adapted Screenplay: James Goldman; AA Best Original Score (Not a Musical): John Barry; AAN Best Costume Design: Margaret Furse

O'Toole, the all-powerful Henry II, summons his politically ambitious family to a reunion in 1183. This includes his wife, Hepburn, whom he has kept in a remote castle to keep her from meddling with his empire. His three sons—all coveting his wide kingdom—Castle, Terry, and Hopkins are also present, along with O'Toole's mistress Merrow and her brother Dalton, playing King Philip of France. The members of this tempestuous family jockey for position and brutally squabble among each other, rekindling every injury suffered and adding new, Homeric insults to their already bruised reputations.

Hepburn is simply wonderful as the scheming and shrewd Eleanor of Aquitaine. Her verbal duels with the equally impressive O'Toole (here playing a man of 50 behind a beard and heavy makeup) are spellbinding. Hepburn won her third Oscar for this superlative performance, becoming the first actress in history to do so (her previous Oscars were for MORNING GLORY and GUESS WHO'S COMING TO DINNER). O'Toole holds his own with the magnificent Hepburn in a witty, literate, and inventive script. The claim that costume dramas are never successful was mightily disproved by this film, which enjoyed a booming box-office business and the wide respect of the public. Shot on location in Ireland, Wales, and France.

LION KING, THE
DVD
1994 87m c Animated/Children's/Musical ★★★
Walt Disney Productions (U.S.) G

VOICES OF: Jonathan Taylor Thomas *(Young Simba)*, Matthew Broderick *(Adult Simba)*, James Earl Jones *(Mufasa)*, Jeremy Irons *(Scar)*, Moira Kelly *(Adult Nala)*, Niketa Calame *(Young Nala)*, Ernie Sabella *(Pumbaa)*, Nathan Lane *(Timon)*, Robert Guillaume *(Rafiki)*, Rowan Atkinson *(Zazu)*

p, Don Hahn; d, Roger Allers, Robert Minkoff; w, Irene Mecchi, Jonathan Roberts, Linda Woolverton; ed, Tom Finan, John Carnochan, Lisa M. Smith, Ivan Bilancio, Beth Stegmaier, Kat Connolly; m, Hans Zimmer; prod d, Chris Sanders; art d, Andy Gaskill; fx, Scott Santoro, Jeff Dutton

AA Best Original Score: Hans Zimmer; AA Best Original Song: "Can You Feel the Love Tonight"; Elton John (Music), Tim Rice (Lyrics); AAN Best Original Song: "Circle of Life"; Elton John (Music), Tim Rice (Lyrics); AAN Best Original Song: "Hakuna Matata"; Elton John (Music), Tim Rice (Lyrics)

The 1994 installment in a series of animated musical blockbusters from Disney, THE LION KING boasts animation as spectacular as any the studio has ever produced, and earned an extraordinary $300 million-plus at the box office. However, this tale of a lion cub's coming of age in the African veldt offers a less memorable song score than did the previous hits, and a hasty, unsatisfying dramatic resolution.

As son and heir of the Lion King Mufasa (voice of James Earl Jones), young Simba (Jonathan Taylor Thomas) expects to inherit dominion over the jungle kingdom called Prideland. But the machinations of Mufasa's jealous brother, Scar (Jeremy Irons), result in Simba's banishment. Near death from exhaustion in the desert, Simba is rescued by Timon (Nathan Lane), a meerkat, and Pumbaa (Ernie Sabella), a warthog, who take him to a jungle paradise, where they sing the praises of "Hakuna Matata" (a carefree life). With their advice and assistance, Simba grows to maturity and prepares to confront Scar and reclaim his throne.

An "original" story—reportedly devised by then-production head Jeffrey Katzenberg—THE LION KING obviously draws on several previous Disney hits. The real inspiration for the film's oddly anachronistic story line, however, seems to lie in Shakespeare's histories; in particular, the extended meditation on the nature and responsibilities of kingship found in *Henry V* and the two parts of *Henry IV*. Like many recent Hollywood epics of fatherhood (FIELD OF DREAMS, LEGENDS OF THE FALL), THE LION KING makes the most sense as an attempted redemption of patriarchy—a call upon contemporary males to resume their "natural" role as all-wise, all-powerful guarantors of the social order.

The film has some of Disney's most spectacular animation yet—particularly in the wildebeest stampede—and strong vocal performances, especially by skilled Broadway comedian Nathan Lane. However, it suffers from a curiously undeveloped story line: the climactic confrontation with Scar has few surprises and is disposed of rather quickly in the final minutes of the film. The events leading up to it, however, are well-told, exciting, and suspenseful, set against a series of exquisitely detailed background tapestries.

LIQUID SKY
DVD
1982 118m c Science Fiction ★★★½
Z Films (U.S.) R

Anne Carlisle *(Margaret/Jimmy)*, Paula Sheppard *(Adrian)*, Susan Doukas *(Sylvia)*, Otto von Wernherr *(Johann)*, Bob Brady *(Owen)*, Elaine C. Grove *(Katherine)*, Stanley Knapp *(Paul)*, Lloyd Ziff *(Lester)*, Harry Lum *(Deliveryman)*, Roy MacArthur *(Jack)*

p, Slava Tsukerman; d, Slava Tsukerman; w, Slava Tsukerman, Anne Carlisle, Nina V. Kerova; ph, Yuri Neyman (TVC Color); ed, Sharyn L. Ross; m, Slava Tsukerman, Brenda I. Hutchinson, Clive Smith; prod d, Marina Levikova; fx, Yuri Neyman; cos, Marina Levikova

Outrageous fun, this film is New Wave chic, satire, self-parody, science fiction, and certainly one of the more accessible independent features ever made. Aliens are after the heroin-like substance produced by the human brain at the point of orgasm. Anne Carlisle, who cowrote the screenplay, plays a lesbian punk model *and* a male homosexual punk model. As a woman, Carlisle discovers a special sexual power. At orgasm she can make her lover disappear into thin air, courtesy of some wonderful special effects. A subplot involves Otto von Wernherr, a government scientist investigating the UFO on Carlisle's roof. He holes up across the street in the apartment of a horny and hysterically funny socialite, Susan Doukas, whose vocal expressions of frustration he balances with a great low-key performance. This offbeat film was directed by Slava Tsukerman, a classically trained Soviet-born filmmaker. His observations of modern America, as well as the beautiful New York City photography, are right on the money. LIQUID SKY won a cult following shortly after its release.

LIST OF ADRIAN MESSENGER, THE

1963 98m bw Mystery ★★★½
Universal (U.S.)

George C. Scott (*Anthony Gethryn*), Dana Wynter (*Lady Jocelyn Brutenholm*), Clive Brook (*Marquis of Gleneyre*), Gladys Cooper (*Mrs. Karoudjian*), Herbert Marshall (*Sir Wilfred Lucas*), Jacques Roux (*Raoul le Borg*), John Merivale (*Adrian Messenger*), Marcel Dalio (*Anton Karoudjian*), Bernard Archard (*Inspector Pike*), Walter Huston (*Derek*)

p, Edward Lewis; d, John Huston; w, Anthony Veiller (based on the novel by Philip MacDonald); ph, Joseph MacDonald; ed, Terry Morse, Hugh S. Fowler; m, Jerry Goldsmith; art d, Alexander Golitzen, Stephen Grimes, George Webb

This convoluted but absorbing mystery begins when Anthony Gethryn (Scott), a retired British colonel, is given a list of 11 names by his friend Adrian Messenger (Merivale) and asked to check on the whereabouts of those on the list. When Messenger's plane blows up, Gethryn looks into the fates of those on the list and discovers that all have met a similar end. Gethryn also learns that the killer is a master of disguises—adopting a new identity for every victim—that all the victims were POWs in Burma during WWII, and that they all knew the identity of the traitor in their midst. John Huston directs this film with calculating care, setting up a number of red herrings who are all played by superstars in disguise, including Robert Mitchum, Frank Sinatra, Burt Lancaster, Kirk Douglas, Tony Curtis, and even Huston himself. It was all eerily effective and provided many a scary moment. Location shooting was conducted in Ireland.

LITTLE BIG MAN

1970 147m c Western/War ★★★★½
National General (U.S.) PG

Dustin Hoffman (*Jack Crabb*), Faye Dunaway (*Mrs. Pendrake*), Martin Balsam (*Allardyce T. Merriweather*), Richard Mulligan (*Gen. George A. Custer*), Chief Dan George (*Old Lodge Skins*), Jeff Corey (*Wild Bill Hickok*), Aimee Eccles (*Sunshine*), Kelly Jean Peters (*Olga*), Carol Androsky (*Caroline*), Robert Little Star (*Little Horse*)

p, Stuart Millar; d, Arthur Penn; w, Calder Willingham (based on the novel by Thomas Berger); ph, Harry Stradling Jr. (Panavision, Technicolor); ed, Dede Allen; m, John Hammond; prod d, Dean Tavoularis; art d, Angelo Graham; fx, Dick Smith, Logan Frazee; cos, Dorothy Jeakins

AAN Best Supporting Actor: Chief Dan George

One of the most unconventional westerns ever made. This startling (if occasionally heavy-handed) revisionist tale is recounted in flashback by 121-year-old Jack Crabb (Dustin Hoffman), who claims to be the only survivor of the massacre at the Little Big Horn. As a boy, Jack is taken in by Cheyenne Indians and raised by Old Lodge Skins (Chief Dan George), but later he protests that he is white when his tribe is attacked by the cavalry, beginning a pattern of cultural fence-hopping that dominates the rest of his life. Over the course of a century or so, Jack earns the name Little Big Man for his bravery in battle; is taken in by a preacher and his randy wife (Faye Dunaway); becomes both an assistant to a cure-all-peddling drummer (Martin Balsam) and a less-than-successful gunfighter; nearly dies when Custer (Richard Mulligan) and his troops attack his tribe at the Washita River; turns to alcohol; and guides the Seventh Cavalry into the Little Big Horn massacre.

Shot twenty years before Kevin Costner's smugly pro-Indian DANCES WITH WOLVES, Arthur Penn's epic western brilliantly retells American history from the viewpoint of its victims. Based on the Thomas Berger novel, LITTLE BIG MAN retains much of Berger's wit but invests the material with a passionate indignation inspired by Vietnam—a quality most obvious in the film's recreation of the Washita massacre, with its unmistakable overtones of My Lai (note Penn's use of Asian-American extras in this scene). Even with Vietnam fast receding from the national consciousness, Penn's movie remains fascinating; cultural studies types will note its handling of, *inter alia*, racial/cultural identity (Crabb defines himself as Indian or white as convenience dictates, but he can't control how others define *him*) and the ideology of the American past (compare Penn's treatment of the traditional "captivity narrative" with THE SEARCHERS).

Hoffman is uncharacteristically charming in a demanding role; the supporting cast is uniformly excellent, particularly Chief Dan George as a befuddled patriarch who takes the supernatural as a matter of course. Like all wide-screen westerns, the film loses a lot on television.

LITTLE CAESAR

1931 80m bw Crime ★★★★
First National (U.S.)

Edward G. Robinson (*Cesare Enrico Bandello/"Little Caesar"*), Douglas Fairbanks Jr. (*Joe Massara*), Glenda Farrell (*Olga Strassoff*), William Collier Jr. (*Tony Passa*), Ralph Ince (*Diamond Pete Montana*), George E. Stone (*Otero*), Thomas Jackson (*Lt. Tom Flaherty*), Stanley Fields (*Sam Vettori*), Armand Kaliz (*DeVoss*), Sidney Blackmer (*The Big Boy*)

p, Hal B. Wallis (uncredited); d, Mervyn LeRoy; w, Robert N. Lee, Darryl F. Zanuck (uncredited), Francis Edwards Faragoh (uncredited), Robert Lord (based on the novel by W.R. Burnett); ph, Tony Gaudio; ed, Ray Curtiss; art d, Anton Grot; cos, Earl Luick

AAN Best Writing (Adaptation): Francis Faragoh, Robert N. Lee

LITTLE CAESAR now seems a bit dated and inelegant, but it is an indisputable landmark. Though not the first gangster film, it spawned the immensely popular gangster cycle of the 1930s and launched the career of one of the greatest icons of the genre—Edward G. Robinson. This tough film still packs a considerable wallop largely due to the mesmerizing performance of Robinson as the thoroughly vicious Rico Bandello.

Rico Bandello is a dedicated killer and thief right from the opening scene. He disappears into a gas station and, after a flash of gunfire, emerges with the money from the till. His driver, Joe Massara (Douglas Fairbanks, Jr.), nervously wheels the coupe into the darkness. Later, Rico and Joe are in a diner, ordering "spaghetti and coffee for two," telegraphing their ethnicity to the audience. After reading in the newspaper about underworld big shots, Rico informs Joe of his ambition to become a rackets czar. He declares that he's not "just another mug." Rico is a man with a mission. He quickly goes about making his criminal dreams come true.

LITTLE CAESAR was one of the first sound films to portray the American gangster outside of prison walls, coming after such early prison stories as THE LAST MILE, THE BIG HOUSE, and NUMBERED MEN. Robinson's character is as ruthless as Al Capone, the real-life gangster upon whom Chicago author W.R. Burnett based the novel from which the film is adapted. Made for a then-hefty $700,000, the film was a box-office smash and typecast Robinson in the role of the gangster. Given free rein by Zanuck, director Mervyn LeRoy produced a fast-paced film that kept up with its lightning-fast star. Oddly, LITTLE CAESAR contains a minimum of explicit violence, although murderous intent is always lurking in Robinson's menacing face. The 37-year-old Robinson was not new to films; he had been acting in movies since 1923, though he was largely unnoticed. Wallis assigned Robinson the lead, but the sensitive actor found it difficult to adjust to the role of the killer, blinking wildly every time he had to fire a gun. LeRoy solved the problem by affixing little transparent bands of tape to Robinson's upper eyelids, so that when he did blast away, his eyes remained wide open; this trick had the added benefit of giving Robinson an even more menacing, heartless appearance.

LITTLE DORRIT

1988 360m c Comedy/Drama ★★★★
Sands/Cannon (U.K.) G

Alec Guinness *(William Dorrit)*, Derek Jacobi *(Arthur Clennam)*, Cyril Cusack *(Frederick Dorrit)*, Sarah Pickering *(Little Dorrit)*, Joan Greenwood *(Mrs. Clennam)*, Max Wall *(Flintwinch)*, Amelda Brown *(Fanny Dorrit)*, Daniel Chatto *(Tip Dorrit)*, Miriam Margolyes *(Flora Finching)*, Bill Fraser *(Mr. Casby)*

p, John Brabourne, Richard Goodwin; d, Christine Edzard; w, Christine Edzard (based on the novel by Charles Dickens); ph, Bruno de Keyzer (Technicolor); ed, Olivier Stockman, Fraser Maclean; m, Giuseppe Verdi; cos, Barbara Sonnex, Judith Loom, Joyce Carter, Jackie Smith, Sally Neale, Claudie Gastine, Danielle Garderes

AAN Best Supporting Actor: Alec Guinness; *AAN Best Adapted Screenplay:* Christine Edzard (screenplay)

Little Dorrit is one of Charles Dickens's greatest and least-read novels, and this massive, six-hour version by director-screenwriter Christine Edzard, essentially faithful to the work, is one of the finest of all Dickens screen adaptations. The film plays in two three-hour parts. Part I, "Nobody's Fault" (Dickens' original title), is told from the point of view of Jacobi, a middle-aged bachelor returning home to London after 20 years in China. Jacobi becomes interested in the case of Guinness, a man who has been locked in a debtors' prison for the last 25 years, and in his daughter, Pickering, a seamstress who works for Jacobi's forbidding mother. Impressed by their sad story, Jacobi sets out to help the man and his daughter to reclaim a fortune. Part II, "Little Dorrit's Story," told from the seamstress's point of view, begins with her birth in prison and follows her as she assumes the role of mother to her selfish family. When Jacobi arrives in England, she falls in love with him, though she knows he loves another. LITTLE DORRIT is *one* film in two feature-length parts. Part II is necessarily the stronger, developing themes and filling out the plot, but the two halves are interdependent. In Edzard's version, Dickens' Little Dorrit character takes on a much more forceful consciousness; she becomes, in a sense, the Dickensian conscience provided by the novel's third-person narration. Boasting a 211-member cast, LITTLE DORRIT is packed with fine performances—and best of all is veteran Dickensian Alec Guinness (GREAT EXPECTATIONS, OLIVER TWIST, SCROOGE).

LITTLE FOXES, THE

1941 .115m bw Drama **DVD** ★★★½
RKO (U.S.)

Bette Davis *(Regina Hubbard Giddens)*, Herbert Marshall *(Horace Giddens)*, Teresa Wright *(Alexandra Giddens)*, Richard Carlson *(David Hewitt)*, Patricia Collinge *(Birdie Hubbard)*, Dan Duryea *(Leo Hubbard)*, Charles Dingle *(Ben Hubbard)*, Carl Benton Reid *(Oscar Hubbard)*, Jessie Grayson *(Addie)*, John Marriott *(Cal)*

p, Samuel Goldwyn; d, William Wyler; w, Lillian Hellman, Arthur Kober, Dorothy Parker, Alan Campbell (based on a play by Lillian Hellman); ph, Gregg Toland; ed, Daniel Mandell; m, Meredith Willson; art d, Stephen Goosson; cos, Orry-Kelly

AAN Best Picture; AAN Best Actress: Bette Davis; *AAN Best Supporting Actress:* Patricia Collinge; *AAN Best Supporting Actress:* Teresa Wright; *AAN Best Director:* William Wyler; *AAN Best Screenplay:* Lillian Hellman; *AAN Best Film Editing:* Daniel Mandell; *AAN Best Score (Drama):* Meredith Willson; *AAN Best Interior Decoration (B/W):* Stephen Goosson (Art Direction), Howard Bristol (Interior Decoration)

Time has proven Bette Davis right—no one could top Tallulah Bankhead's Broadway portrayal of the vituperative Regina Giddens, the central figure of Lillian Hellman's now creaking, but still compelling Deep South potboiler. During filming, William Wyler was often heard to say, "We'll have to get Bankhead." Would that he had. Davis, in an impulsive stampede to make the role her own, took an opposite track to the character. Or perhaps Wyler did; every Davis bio tells it differently. Either way, it's wrong. In her rice powder, with her mouth drawn into a tiny, hard line (it makes her look more beaked and birdlike than ever) she loses the hothouse-flower sensuality that Bankhead brought to her manipulations. And it was precisely *that* certain quality that justified Regina's ability to manipulate men to high heaven in the turn of the century South.

FOXES tells the story of the Hubbards (whose exploits are also detailed in ANOTHER PART OF THE FOREST, 1948, from Hellman's prequel), as greedy a bunch as ever drank mint juleps. Regina's brothers (Dingle and Reid) ask her to persuade her husband Horace (Marshall) to supply the rest of the cash they need to build a cotton mill. Milking her position for all the leverage possible, Regina sends her daughter (Wright) to fetch Horace, recovering from a heart attack at a Baltimore sanitarium. The weakened man, however, proves a bigger hurdle than anyone had bargained for.

This is the third and last time Davis worked with Wyler, following the triumphs of JEZEBEL and THE LETTER. The furious battles enacted by the two on FOXES are Hollywood legend—a sad farewell to a legendary collaboration. Perhaps the rest of the principals didn't cotton to Davis's tantrums (having grown accustomed to Bankhead's); except for Wright, in her film debut, they look like wolves successfully moving in on her acting territory. Collinge, in fact, almost steals the movie. The other newcomer, Duryea, does move in; it's overkill that needed slapping down.

We are not, however, discounting FOXES's impressive technical achievement. Many of the sequences directed by Wyler and shot by cinematographer Toland (famed for his deep-focus work in CITIZEN KANE) have been hailed by film scholars, especially during the memorable murder scene (featuring Davis's Kabuki look). Orry-Kelly's costumes for Davis are either great or wrong. Somehow FOXES feels embalmed instead of lived; still we enjoy the drama done aloud.

LITTLE GIRL WHO LIVES DOWN THE LANE, THE

1976 91m c Thriller ★★★½
Rank (Canada) PG

Jodie Foster *(Rynn Jacobs)*, Martin Sheen *(Frank Hallet)*, Alexis Smith *(Mrs. Hallet)*, Mort Shuman *(Officer Miglioriti)*, Scott Jacoby *(Mario Podesta)*, Clesson Goodhue *(Bank Manager)*, Hubert Noel, Jacques Famery *(Bank Clerks)*, Mary Morter, Judie Wildman *(Tellers)*

p, Zev Braun; d, Nicolas Gessner; w, Laird Koenig (based on novel by Koenig); ph, Rene Verzier (Panavision); ed, Yves Langlois; m, Christian Gaubert; art d, Robert Prevost; cos, Denis Sperdouklis, Valentino

This Canadian-made film, a star vehicle for the then 13-year-old Jodie Foster, is a disturbing, wonderfully acted, well-scripted, and suspenseful study of a murderous 13-year-old girl, Rynn (Foster). Living alone in her father's home, Rynn makes up stories that her father is away when in fact he is dead. She handles the bills, the upkeep, and her own survival, admirably putting into practice what her father taught her. When a snooping neighbor makes a nuisance of herself, Rynn knocks her down the stairs. Matter-of-factly, Rynn lets the cellar door close and gets back to her work. Soon the creepy Frank (Martin Sheen) is making a pest of himself, wanting both answers to his suspicions and Rynn's barely pubescent body. Meanwhile, Rynn becomes genuinely attracted to Mario (Scott Jacoby), a youngster her own age. Frank, knowing that something is odd about Rynn's situation, presses her for answers about her father, his insistence threatening to ruin the private, self-sustaining, child-as-adult world she has created with Mario. This leads to a fatal game of cat-and-mouse between Rynn and Frank. Tautly directed by Nicolas Gessner, the film is a showcase for the young Foster and she does not disappoint, turning in a slyly nuanced performance that is downright creepy and at the same time oddly innocent.

LITTLE MERMAID, THE   📀

1989 82m c   Animated/Children's/Musical ★★★
Walt Disney Productions/Silver Screen Partners IV   G
(U.S.)

VOICES OF: Rene Auberjonois (Louis), Christopher Daniel Barnes (Eric), Jodi Benson (Ariel), Pat Carroll (Ursula), Paddi Edwards (Flotsam & Jetsam), Buddy Hackett (Scuttle), Jason Marin (Flounder), Kenneth Mars (King Triton), Edie McClurg (Carlotta), Will Ryan (Seahorse)

p, Howard Ashman, John Musker; d, John Musker, Ron Clements; w, John Musker, Ron Clements (based on the fairy tale by Hans Christian Andersen); ed, Mark Hester, John Carnochan; m, Robby Merkin, Alan Menken; prod d, Maureen Donley; art d, Michael A. Peraza Jr., Donald A. Towns; fx, Mark Dindal (visual effects supervisor); anim, Mark Henn, Glen Keane, Duncan Marjoribanks, Ruben Aquino, Andreas Deja, Matthew O'Callaghan

AA Best Original Score: Alan Menken; AA Best Original Song: "Kiss the Girl"; Alan Menken (Music), Howard Ashman (Lyrics); AAN Best Original Song: "Under the Sea"; Alan Menken (Music), Howard Ashman (Lyrics)

Disney's 28th feature-length cartoon, very loosely based on the Hans Christian Andersen fairy tale and featuring an Oscar-winning score by Alan Menkin, was a box-office smash that helped usher in a new era of top-flight feature animation.

Princess Ariel lives in Mermaid City with her father, King Triton. Ariel is fascinated by human beings. Attracted by a fireworks display on a ship, Ariel sneaks aboard and falls in love at first sight with the handsome Prince Eric. When a violent storm destroys the ship, Ariel saves Eric's life, and he is smitten with her beautiful singing voice. Mermaid City's court composer, a crab named Sebastian, accidentally tells King Triton that Ariel is in love with a human, and Triton destroys all of her human possessions and forbids her to see Eric again. An evil sea witch named Ursula, who has been banished by Triton, lures Ariel into a deal whereby she will be given human form, but will have to give Ursula her voice in return. If, after three days, Ariel cannot get Eric to bestow upon her a kiss, she will belong to Ursula.

THE LITTLE MERMAID was the first of Disney's new generation of animated musical features (which would be quickly followed by BEAUTY AND THE BEAST and others) that marked a return to the studio's former glory days, at least in the eyes of the public and most critics. The film features some undeniably impressive animation, particularly in the frightening scenes at

which Disney artists have always excelled at—the violent storms filled with swirling winds, lightning, and crashing waves. But just as undeniably, it also suffers from overly broad and juvenile humor, some sappy songs, and the "wide-eyed human" syndrome, wherein all the humans have huge saucer-eyes and the same constantly startled expression. Eric looks like a hunky fashion model, while Ariel is drawn as a big-haired, denatured Barbie doll, despite her hourglass figure and skimpy seashell brassiere. As usual with Disney, the nonhumans are much more interesting, and the various undersea creatures are quite amusing and very well-drawn, as is the whole underwater milieu. Overall, it's an enjoyable film, thankfully free of the computerized look of later Disney cartoons, but it really can't compare to the real Disney classics (which appealed equally to both kids and adults).

LITTLE OTIK   📀

(OTESANEK)
2000 127m c   Comedy/Horror   ★★★½
Athanor Film Production Co./Illuminations
Films/FilmFour/Barrandov Biografia/Helena
Uldrichova/Knoviz   (Czech Republic/U.K./Japan)

Veronika Zilkova (Bozena Horakova), Jan Hartl (Karel Horak), Jaroslava Kretschmerova (Mrs. Stadlerova), Pavel Novy (Franisek Stadler), Kristina Adamcova (Alzbetka), Dagmar Stribrna (Mrs. Spravcova, the Caretaker), Zdenek Kozak (Mr. Zlabek), Gustav Vondracek (Mladek, the Postman), Arnost Goldflam (Gynaecologist), Jitka Smutna (Bulankova, the Social Worker)

p, Jaromir Kallista; d, Jan Svankmajer; w, Jan Svankmajer; ph, Juraj Galvanek; ed, Marie Zemanova; art d, Jan Svankmajer, Eva Svankmajerova; fx, Pavel Spatny, Martin Stejskal; cos, Miroslava Gailova, Katerina Rudova, Katerina Stejskalova, Jan Svankmajer, Eva Svankmajerova; anim, Bedrich Glaser, Martin Kublak

For sheer perversity, Jan Svankmajer's CONSPIRATORS OF PLEASURE is a tough act to follow. But the renowned animator did it with this wickedly funny, deeply disturbing, live-action retelling of an old Czech folktale.

Bozena Horakova (Veronika Zilkova) and her husband Karel Horak (Jan Hartl) have been desperately trying to have a baby, but to no avail. One weekend at their country house, Karel tries to cheer up his deeply depressed wife with a little joke: he digs up a knotty stump, shapes its roots into arms and legs, coats it with varnish, and offers it to Bozena. She's ecstatic. Believing it to be a real baby, she plunges little "Otik" into a bassinet, powders his bottom, and dresses him in booties and a bonnet. Nine months later, Karel returns home to find the "baby" actually suckling at his wife's breast; like Pinocchio, the stump has somehow come to life, and it's hungry. When the food doesn't come fast enough, Otik, who is growing at an alarming rate, fillets the family cat. When the postman goes missing, the Horaks realize they have a serious problem on their hands.

The film touches on so many fears—from a primal discomfort over where babies come from to the terror of an all-consuming baby that literally feeds off its mother—that it's hard to isolate exactly what makes Svankmajer's nightmarish comedy so horrifying. Perhaps it's simply the recognition that we're all slaves to our desires. Like the obsessed fetishists of CONSPIRATORS, Svankmajer's characters are consumed by their own appetites—rapacious cravings for sex, alcohol and, most revoltingly, food. Gooey porridges and slimy stews are slurped with such revolting abandon that Otik's voracious flesh eating pales in comparison.

LITTLE PRINCESS, A

1995 97m c Children's/Drama   **★★★**
Baltimore Pictures/Mark Johnson Productions   G
(U.S.)

Eleanor Bron *(Miss Minchin)*, Liam Cunningham *(Captain Crewe/Prince Rama)*, Liesel Matthews *(Sara Crewe)*, Rusty Schwimmer *(Amelia Minchin)*, Arthur Malet *(Charles Randolph)*, Vanessa Lee Chester *(Becky)*, Errol Sitahal *(Ram Dass)*, Heather DeLoach *(Ermengarde)*, Taylor Fry *(Lavinia)*, Darcie Bradford *(Jesse)*

p, Mark Johnson; d, Alfonso Cuaron; w, Richard LaGravenese, Elizabeth Chandler (based on the novel *Sara Crewe* by Frances Hodgson Burnett); ph, Emmanuel Lubezki; ed, Steven Weisberg; m, Patrick Doyle; prod d, Bo Welch; art d, Tom Duffield; fx, Alan E. Lorimer; cos, Judianna Makovsky

AAN Best Art Direction-Set Decoration: Bo Welch (art direction), Cheryl Carasik (set decoration); *AAN Best Cinematography:* Emmanuel Lubezki

This new version of Frances Hodgson Burnett's children's classic boasts first-rate production values and a political sensitivity befitting the '90s, but it doesn't quite capture the magic of the 1939 Shirley Temple vehicle.

1914, Simla, India: Imaginative 10-year-old Sara Crewe (Liesel Matthews) lives with her wealthy, widowed father (Liam Cunningham), a British Army captain. Sara enjoys her life in exotic India, but the coming of the Great War destroys the tranquillity of Sara's life. Her father must rejoin his regiment, and places Sara in Miss Minchin's School for Girls in New York City. Stern headmistress Miss Minchin (Eleanor Bron) hates the girl, and when Sara's father is reported killed in battle, she launches a campaign to crush Sara's resilient spirit.

A LITTLE PRINCESS is adapted respectably by screenwriters Richard LaGravenese and Elizabeth Chandler, meticulously produced, opulently designed—particularly in the colorful fantasy sequences—elegantly photographed by cinematographer Emmanuel Lubezki and adequately (in the case of Eleanor Bron, more than adequately) acted. While Shirley Temple is a more appealing youngster than newcomer Liesel Matthews, Matthews is both sassy and unabashedly emotional. And though the new LITTLE PRINCESS is a far darker affair than the 1939 version, Mexican-born director Alfonso Cuaron doesn't make it anywhere near as drab and moody as Agnieszka Holland's more artistically and commercially successful THE SECRET GARDEN.

LITTLE ROMANCE, A

1979 108m c Romance/Comedy   **★★★★**
Pan Arts/Trinacra (U.S./France)   PG

Laurence Olivier *(Julius)*, Diane Lane *(Lauren)*, Thelonious Bernard *(Daniel)*, Arthur Hill *(Richard King)*, Sally Kellerman *(Kay King)*, Broderick Crawford *(Brod)*, David Dukes *(George de Marco)*, Andrew Duncan *(Bob Duryea)*, Claudette Sutherland *(Janet Duryea)*, Graham Fletcher-Cook *(Londet)*

p, Robert L. Crawford, Yves Rousset-Rouard; d, George Roy Hill; w, Allan Burns (based on the novel *E=MC, Mon Amour* by Patrick Cauvin); ph, Pierre-William Glenn (Panavision, Technicolor); ed, William Reynolds; m, Georges Delerue; prod d, Henry Bumstead; art d, Francois de Lamothe; cos, Rosine Delamare

AAN Best Adapted Screenplay: Allan Burns; *AA Best Original Score:* Georges Delerue

Completely charming, this teenage romantic comedy tells the innocent tale of a pair of 13-year-olds who fall in love in Paris. Lauren (Diane Lane) is living in Paris with her understanding stepfather (Arthur Hill) and her floozy mother (Sally Kellerman). While visiting the set of a movie production, Lauren meets Daniel (Thelonious Bernard), a lower-class youngster with a system for playing the horses and a fascination with both Robert Redford and Humphrey Bogart. Daniel becomes "Bogie" to Lauren's "Bacall," and before long they've fallen for each other in the most innocent of ways. Their attachment strengthens when they discover they both have extremely high IQs and interests in philosophy, qualities that usually embarrass them. Their adventures begin when they meet Julius (Laurence Olivier), a friendly old scoundrel who informs them of an age-old romantic legend: If two lovers kiss under Venice's Bridge of Sighs in a gondola at sunset when the bells toll, their love will last forever. The two youngsters are determined to try out the legend for themselves, but they cannot travel without a guardian and must bring along Julius, who isn't quite what he appears to be. This sweet and innocent movie about teen romance won't fail to bring a tear and a smile in its heart-tugging finale. Delerue's score is lovely.

LITTLE SHOP OF HORRORS

1986 88m c Comedy/Horror/Musical   **★★★**
Warner Bros. (U.S.)   PG-13

Rick Moranis *(Seymour Krelboin)*, Ellen Greene *(Audrey)*, Vincent Gardenia *(Mushnik)*, Steve Martin *(Orin Scrivello)*, Tichina Arnold *(Crystal)*, Tisha Campbell *(Chiffon)*, Michelle Weeks *(Ronette)*, James Belushi *(Patrick Martin)*, John Candy *(Wink Wilkinson)*, Christopher Guest *(1st Customer)*

p, David Geffen; d, Frank Oz; w, Howard Ashman (based on the musical stage play by Howard Ashman); ph, Robert Paynter (Panavision, Technicolor); ed, John Jympson; m, Alan Menken, Miles Goodman; prod d, Roy Walker; art d, Steve Spence; fx, Bran Ferren; chor, Pat Garrett; cos, Marit Allen

AAN Best Original Song: "Mean Green Mother from Outer Space"; Alan Menken (Music), Howard Ashman (Lyrics); *AAN Best Visual Effects:* Lyle Conway, Bran Ferren, Martin Gutteridge

This is the multimillion-dollar movie version of the off-Broadway musical, which was based in turn on an old movie conceived and shot in a matter of days by Roger Corman. Although the plots (in which a carnivorous plant feeds on human flesh, causing its creator to kill to satisfy it) are virtually identical, much of the edge was taken off of the material in its transition from screen to stage to screen. The killer plant has been transformed into a being from outer space (rather than a warped hybrid created by the dimwitted Seymour in his basement). Big-budget and bloated, the film has none of the shabby charm of Corman's effort and is memorable only for a couple of decent tunes, a parade of star cameos, some impressive special effects, and a wonderful performance from Greene as Audrey. Conway's special effects involved several generations of Audrey II, from a potted plant to a mammoth 12.5-foot-tall creature that takes over the entire florist shop. It weighed, at the close, more than 2,000 pounds and used almost 12 miles of cable. The most remarkable aspect of the device were the lips, perfectly in sync with the singing and dialogue. Although an impressive technical achievement, the film itself is a rather overblown and overhyped affair—which, for all its expensive excess, fails to recapture the spirit of the original.

LITTLE SHOP OF HORRORS, THE

1961 70m bw Comedy/Horror
Filmgroup (U.S.)

Jonathan Haze *(Seymour Krelboin)*, Jackie Joseph *(Audrey)*, Mel Welles *(Gravis Mushnick)*, Jack Nicholson *(Wilbur Force)*, Dick

Miller *(Fouch)*, Myrtle Vail *(Winifred Krelboin)*, Laiola Wendorf *(Mrs. Shiva)*

p, Roger Corman; d, Roger Corman; w, Charles B. Griffith; ph, Arch R. Dalzell; ed, Marshall Neilan Jr.; m, Fred Katz; art d, Daniel Haller

This is the ultimate Roger Corman super-low-budget cult favorite, also one of the funniest black comedies ever made. The plot details the sorry existence of a dim-witted schlepp, Haze, who works in Welles's Skid Row flower shop. To impress his girl, Joseph, Haze invents a flower he names Audrey, Jr. Soon the plant is all the rage among botanists. The only problem is that the little flower needs human blood to grow. After discovering this gruesome detail, and the fact that the plant can talk (when it's hungry it yells, "Feed me!"), Haze becomes slowly possessed by the flora and commits several murders in order to stop his plant's tummy from growling. With these feedings comes the plant's rapid growth; it soon overgrows the whole flower shop while bellowing "Feeeed meee!" in a monstrously loud and obnoxious voice. Poor Haze finds he can no longer handle his creation. While its story doesn't make for very funny reading, THE LITTLE SHOP OF HORRORS is a hilarious (and yes, quite silly) film filled to the brim with enough little vignettes and character quirks to sustain laughter throughout its brief 70-minute running time. Shot in two days by Corman, who was challenged by a studio employee to come up with a script and shoot a movie in the brief time remaining before the storefront set was torn down (it had been left standing from another production), THE LITTLE SHOP OF HORRORS is surprisingly well shot and performed. Corman contacted screenwriter Chuck Griffith from his other camp hit, A BUCKET OF BLOOD, and together they hacked out the killer plant story in less than a week. Aided by on-the-set inspiration, Corman, his crew, and the cast (including a very young Jack Nicholson in a side-splitting cameo as a masochistic dental patient begging for more pain) threw together a small masterpiece of taut, economical filmmaking. The story was revived in the 1980s as a very successful Off-Broadway musical, and a film version of the musical was released in 1986.

LITTLE WOMEN 📀
1933 117m bw Drama ★★★★½
RKO (U.S.)

Katharine Hepburn *(Jo)*, Joan Bennett *(Amy)*, Paul Lukas *(Prof. Fritz Bhaer)*, Edna May Oliver *(Aunt March)*, Jean Parker *(Beth)*, Frances Dee *(Meg)*, Henry Stephenson *(Mr. Laurence)*, Douglass Montgomery *(Laurie)*, John Lodge *(Brooke)*, Spring Byington *(Marmee)*

p, Kenneth MacGowan; d, George Cukor; w, Sarah Y. Mason, Victor Heerman (based on the novel by Louisa May Alcott); ph, Henry Gerrard; ed, Jack Kitchin; m, Max Steiner; art d, Van Nest Polglase; fx, Harry Redmond; cos, Walter Plunkett

AAN Best Picture; AAN Best Director: George Cukor; AA Best Writing (Adaptation): Victor Heerman, Sarah Y. Mason

This unabashedly sentimental adaptation of Louisa May Alcott's novel remains, to this day, an example of Hollywood's best filmmaking, as it tells the captivating Civil War-era story of four independent New England sisters—Jo (Katharine Hepburn), Amy (Joan Bennett), Meg (Frances Dee), and Beth (Jean Parker) March. Jo, who wants to leave home and become a writer, stays on for the good of the family, but when Meg plans to marry, Jo leaves for New York, fearing that the family will disintegrate. There she meets a professor who helps her with both her anger and her writing. Meanwhile, Amy falls in love with and marries Jo's old sweetheart (Douglass

Montgomery). Beth, however, is dying, and Jo returns to be with her during her last days.

Sarah Mason and Victor Heerman's script called for great production values, and RKO provided them, foreshadowing David O. Selznick's opulent treatment of life on the Southern side of the Civil War, GONE WITH THE WIND. The sets, costumes, lighting, and direction by George Cukor all contribute greatly to this magnificent film, but the performances, especially Hepburn's, are what make the simple story so moving. There are laughs and tears aplenty in this movie, which presents a slice of American history in a way that children will find palatable. Released during the depths of the Depression, LITTLE WOMEN buoyed Americans' spirits. It still does.

LITTLE WOMEN 📀
1994 115m c Drama/Historical/Romance ★★★½
Di Novi Pictures/Columbia (U.S.) PG

Winona Ryder *(Jo March)*, Susan Sarandon *(Marmee March)*, Gabriel Byrne *(Professor Friedrich Baer)*, Eric Stoltz *(John Brooke)*, Samantha Mathis *(Amy as 16-Year-Old)*, Trini Alvarado *(Meg)*, Kirsten Dunst *(Amy as 12-Year-Old)*, Claire Danes *(Beth)*, Christian Bale *(Laurie)*, Mary Wickes *(Aunt March)*

p, Denise DiNovi; d, Gillian Armstrong; w, Robin Swicord (based on the novel by Louisa May Alcott); ph, Geoffrey Simpson; ed, Nicholas Beauman; m, Thomas Newman; prod d, Jan Roelfs; art d, Richard Hudolin; cos, Colleen Atwood

AAN Best Actress: Winona Ryder; AAN Best Costume Design: Colleen Atwood; AAN Best Original Score: Thomas Newman

Director Gillian Armstrong's feminist spin on classic material retains the moving humanity of Louisa May Alcott's novel while reworking it with welcome freshness.

LITTLE WOMEN introduces us to the March family, a struggling, close-knit clan living in Concord, Massachusetts, at the time of the Civil War. The eldest daughter, Meg (Trini Alvarado), is pretty, conventional, and vain. Jo (Winona Ryder) is a hot-tempered tomboy who chafes against Victorian restraints on young women and dreams of a great literary career. Beth (Claire Danes) is musical and pathologically shy, a saint on earth. Amy (Kirsten Dunst, then Samantha Mathis) is artistic and amusingly selfish. Their beloved Marmee (Susan Sarandon) is the anchor that stabilizes the family while her husband is away fighting in the Civil War. The Marches have seen better days financially, but the spirit and invention of the girls are unquenchable as they struggle towards adulthood and overcome their individual weaknesses.

Robin Swicord's screenplay adaptation is very free, adding details of Alcott's life to the familiar events of the novel. At times, the overriding political correctness is a bit heavy-handed (one doesn't recall the Marches being *quite* so taken up with the cause of the "blacks," as they are anachronistically referred to here, or with women's suffrage). Quibbles aside, Armstrong can only be praised for her firm control over the material, steadfast refusal to slip into bathos, and acute visual and emotional sense. The strength of her vision overrides some acting weaknesses as well as the superfluous revisionism; visually, it is easily one of the most beautiful movies of the year. Geoffrey Simpson's camera records the four seasons with remarkable vividness, and the production is appropriately rich, full of dark wood surfaces, comforting quilts, and gleaming cook pots and china.

LIVE FLESH   **DVD**
(CARNE TREMULA)
1997   101m   c   Drama   ★★★½
CiBy 2000/France 3/El Deseo S.A./Goldwyn Films   R
(Spain/France)

Javier Bardem *(David)*, Francesca Neri *(Elena)*, Liberto Rabal *(Victor Plaza)*, Angela Molina *(Clara)*, Jose Sancho *(Sancho)*, Pilar Bardem, Penelope Cruz, Alex Angulo

d, Pedro Almodovar; w, Pedro Almodovar (based on the novel by Ruth Rendell); ph, Affonso Beato; ed, Jose Salcedo; m, Alberto Iglesias; art d, Antxon Gomez; fx, Molina; cos, Jose M. De Cossio

Using a tricky Ruth Rendell novel as his source, director Pedro Almodovar returns to form with LIVE FLESH, his best film in some time. The story of an ex-con's new lease on life contains many memorable moments.

In 1990, an impulsive young man, Victor (Liberto Rabal), has a crush on a drug addict named Elena (Francesca Neri). When Victor shows up at Elena's apartment uninvited, Elena furiously tries to throw him out. Their loud fight attracts the attention of two police officers, David (Javier Bardem) and Sancho (Jose Sancho). In a struggle, David is accidentally shot and Victor goes to prison for the crime. While in prison, Victor discovers that Elena is drug-free and married to David, who is confined to a wheelchair. Upon his release from prison, Victor vows to break up the union. Yet, before he meets up with Elena again, he begins an affair with Clara (Angela Molina), who happens to be the sex-starved wife of Sancho, David's ex-partner.

After a series of disappointments, including KIKA, Almodovar's LIVE FLESH reminds us that the Spanish director has talent beyond a colorful design sense. For the most part, Almodovar invests all his characters with strength, humor, pathos, and enough dramatic dimension to make the odd twists and turns of Rendell's plot seem almost plausible. As with nearly all Almodovar films, the visuals provide a sensual delight, although LIVE FLESH is pointedly more baroque (and Bunuel-esque) than usual. As with the better Almodovar films, the acting ensemble displays the flair of a great repertory company—no one hits a false note. Whether or not a British mystery writer was the inspiration, LIVE FLESH marks a high point of inventive filmmaking in an up-and-down director's career.

LIVES OF A BENGAL LANCER, THE   **DVD**
1935   109m   bw   Adventure/War   ★★★★
Paramount   (U.S.)

Gary Cooper *(Lt. Alan McGregor)*, Franchot Tone *(Lt. John Forsythe)*, Richard Cromwell *(Lt. Donald Stone)*, Guy Standing *(Col. Stone)*, C. Aubrey Smith *(Maj. Hamilton)*, Monte Blue *(Hamzulia Khan)*, Kathleen Burke *(Tania Volkanskaya)*, Colin Tapley *(Lt. Barrett)*, Douglas Dumbrille *(Mohammed Khan)*, Akim Tamiroff *(Emir)*

p, Louis D. Lighton; d, Henry Hathaway; w, Waldemar Young, John Balderston, Achmed Abdullah, Grover Jones, William Slavens McNutt (based on the novel by Maj. Francis Yeats-Brown); ph, Charles Lang, Ernest B. Schoedsack; ed, Ellsworth Hoagland; m, Milan Roder; art d, Hans Dreier, Roland Anderson; chor, LeRoy Prinz; cos, Travis Banton

AA Best Assistant Director: Clem Beauchamp, Paul Wing; *AAN Best Picture; AAN Best Director:* Henry Hathaway; *AAN Best Screenplay:* Achmed Abdullah, John L. Balderston, Grover Jones, William Slavens McNutt, Waldemar Young; *AAN Best Film Editing:* Ellsworth Hoagland; *AAN Best Interior Decoration:* Hans Dreier,

Roland Anderson (Art Direction); *AAN Best Sound Recording:* Franklin Hansen

Set in northwest India, this rousing adventure film was hailed by many as the greatest war movie ever made at the time of its release. Under Henry Hathaway's adroit direction, Gary Cooper stars as 41st Bengal Lancers member Lt. McGregor, a seasoned frontier fighter who doesn't hesitate to speak his mind or violate orders—a man first and a soldier second. His commanding officer, Col. Stone (Sir Guy Standing), is his very opposite, a total military man who will soon be retiring. In order to keep alive the name of Stone in the regiment, a fellow officer, Maj. Hamilton (C. Aubrey Smith), has Stone's son (Richard Cromwell) transferred into the unit, along with another new officer, Lt. Forsythe (Franchot Tone). The two new arrivals get a quick initiation, as Col. Stone and British intelligence try to prevent a planned Indian uprising by blocking a local chieftain's attempt to steal two million rounds of ammunition from the friendly Emir of Gopal (Akim Tamiroff).

The script is filled with plenty of humor and builds two strong, honest friendships—McGregor and Forsythe have a great buddy rapport while the cold and stubborn Col. Stone opens up to his cub soldier son. The Indian atmosphere is lovingly captured by Hathaway's direction (his love of the exotic appears to have been heavily influenced by his association with Josef von Sternberg) and by Charles Lang and Ernest B. Schoedsack's photography (incorporating some stock footage previously shot by Schoedsack). While the glorification of British imperialism hangs over the picture, the portrayal of the Indians is fortunately less offensive than in other Hollywood films such as 1939's GUNGA DIN.

LIVING DAYLIGHTS, THE   **DVD**
1987   130m   c   Spy   ★★★½
Eon/UA   (U.K.)   PG

Timothy Dalton *(James Bond)*, Maryam D'Abo *(Kara Malovy)*, Jeroen Krabbe *(Gen. Georgi Koskov)*, Joe Don Baker *(Brad Whitaker)*, John Rhys-Davies *(Gen. Leonid Pushkin)*, Art Malik *(Kamran Shah)*, Andreas Wisniewski *(Necros)*, Thomas Wheatley *(Saunders)*, Desmond Llewelyn *(Q)*, Robert Brown *(M)*

p, Albert R. Broccoli, Michael G. Wilson; d, John Glen; w, Richard Maibaum, Michael G. Wilson (based on a story by Ian Fleming); ph, Alec Mills (Panavision, Technicolor); ed, John Grover, Peter Davies; m, John Barry; prod d, Peter Lamont; art d, Terry Ackland-Snow; fx, John Richardson; cos, Emma Porteous

Celebrating the 25th year of the Bond series, THE LIVING DAYLIGHTS introduces the fourth actor to take on the role of 007, Timothy Dalton, a 40-year-old veteran of the English stage whose Bond is more human and serious than that of the wry Sean Connery and the droll Roger Moore. Scripters Richard Maibaum and Michael G. Wilson have also shifted the emphasis away from glitz and gadgetry and back to the business of spying. Bond is sent to Czechoslovakia to assist with the defection of Gen. Georgi Koskov (Jeroen Krabbe), a KGB higher-up, whose escape is accomplished in a specially designed vehicle that whisks him through the trans-Siberian natural gas pipeline to Austria. Meanwhile, Bond falls for the beautiful Kara Malovy (Maryam d'Abo), a cellist who is a victim of KGB intrigue, and later he helps her make a breathtaking escape, ultimately using her priceless cello as a sled. Once in the West, Koskov is seemingly abducted by the KGB, but Bond suspects otherwise and eventually learns that the Soviet is in cahoots with Brad Whitaker (Joe Don Baker), a psychopathic American arms dealer who, unlike the standard Bond villain, is interested in becoming fabulously wealthy but not in ruling the world. Bond's danger-filled attempts to put an end to Whitaker's scheming take him and Kara from Vienna to Tangier and eventually into the middle of the war in Afghanistan. Made for $30 million, this feast for the eyes has more action than any of the other Bond films and is certainly one of the best of them. Dalton is an engaging Bond, d'Abo is coolly alluring, and Krabbe is the epitome of the double-dealing spy master. Only Baker disappoints, hamming up his villain. Director John Glen is an old hand at James Bond films, having worked on three other 007 movies. He knows this popular spy well and does him great service in this well-paced film.

LOCAL HERO 📀

1983 111m c   Comedy   ★★★★½
Enigma/Goldcrest   (U.K.)   PG

Burt Lancaster *(Happer)*, Peter Riegert *(Mac)*, Fulton Mackay *(Ben)*, Denis Lawson *(Urquhart)*, Norman Chancer *(Moritz)*, Peter Capaldi *(Oldsen)*, Rikki Fulton *(Geddes)*, Alex Norton *(Watt)*, Jenny Seagrove *(Marina)*, Jennifer Black *(Stella)*

p, David Puttnam; d, Bill Forsyth; w, Bill Forsyth; ph, Chris Menges; ed, Michael Bradsell; m, Mark Knopfler; prod d, Roger Murray-Leach; art d, Richard James, Adrienne Atkinson, Frank Walsh, Ian Watson; fx, Wally Veevers

Charming, whimsical, and practically perfect, LOCAL HERO reminds us of the great pleasures that British comedy used to routinely provide. This is the greatest Ealing comedy never made: a quirky character comedy with a skillful use of location that is sweetly reminiscent of WHISKEY GALORE!. A discerning eye may even spot a wee bit of the magical Powell-Pressburger ethos as expressed in I KNOW WHERE I'M GOING. However the offbeat sensibility on display here is ultimately distinctively that of Scottish filmmaker Bill Forsyth (GREGORY'S GIRL, THAT SINKING FEELING, COMFORT AND JOY, HOUSEKEEPING).

Burt Lancaster gets star billing as the loony head of a huge oil company in Texas, a tycoon so ambivalent about his success that he has a psychiatrist (Norman Chancer) come in regularly and insult him. Bored with business success, astronomy has become his great passion. The true protagonist of the film is Mac (Peter Riegert), an ambitious young executive of the oil company, who is dispatched to Scotland to buy an entire town so the company can drill for North Sea oil. An important side mission is to keep watching the sky for anything interesting. The utterly charming remote little coastal town is largely controlled by Urquhart (Dennis Lawson), a sharp but good-natured lawyer-innkeeper. Victor (Christopher Rozycki), a Soviet trawler captain, makes regular stops at the village, where Urquhart conducts sundry investments for him in real estate and securities. The obvious plot turn would be to show the Americans as nasty and rapacious, but it turns out that the Scots would be only too happy to depart the area if the price were right. Throughout the film, nothing is quite what it seems to Mac, and the denouement is wonderfully unexpected.

The Scottish landscape is gorgeous, soothing, and handsomely shot. The casting, down to the smallest role, is just right. Lancaster gives one of his best performances in a parody of the role he's played straight so many times before—the blustering industrial mogul. Scottish writer-director Bill Forsyth has outdone himself with this funny, touching, and original film. Don't miss this magical treat. (Incidentally this film served as a MAJOR source of inspiration for the hit CBS television series, "Northern Exposure.")

LOCK, STOCK AND TWO SMOKING BARRELS 📀

1998 106m c   Crime/Thriller   ★★★★
Ska Productions/HandMade Films/The Steve Tisch   R
Company/Vaughn Productions   (U.K./U.S.)

Jason Flemyng *(Tom)*, Dexter Fletcher *(Soap)*, Nick Moran *(Eddie)*, Jason Statham *(Bacon)*, Steven Mackintosh *(Winston)*, Nicolas Rowe *(J)*, Nick Marq *(Charles)*, Charles Forbes *(Willie)*, Vinnie Jones *(Big Chris)*, Lenny McLean *(Barry the Baptist)*

p, Matthew Vaughn; d, Guy Ritchie; w, Guy Ritchie; ph, Tim Maurice-Jones; ed, Niven Howie; m, David A. Hughes, John Murphy; prod d, Iain Andrews, Eve Mavrakis; fx, Ken Lailey; cos, Stephanie Collie

Irreverent, violent, and wickedly clever, this smart-mouthed crime picture concerns four nice lads who get into some bad company and must get themselves out before things get really ugly.

Cardsharp Eddie (Nick Moran) wheedles his way into a high stakes game run by porn peddler and all-around petty villain Hatchet Harry (P.H. Moriarty), thinking he can turn his wad of cash stake into some really big money. But the game's rigged, and Eddie walks away owing Harry much, much more; if he doesn't pay up in a week, Harry's gangsters will take Eddie's dad's *(Sting)* pub in lieu of the loot. Oh, and three-quarters of the original stake belonged to Eddie's pals Tom (Jason Flemyng), Bacon (Jason Statham), and Soap (Dexter Fletcher), who can ill-afford to lose that kind of money. Fortunately, the flat next door to Eddie's houses four extravagantly loud thieves, and the walls are *very* thin: so Eddie knows the blundering baddies have a big score in the works, and ripping them off to appease Hatchet Harry seems a reasonable way out of the mess. Naturally, it's not as easy as all that.

This larky, self-aware crime picture has Tarantino-esque written all over it. But in this case that's not a bad thing: first-time writer-director Guy Ritchie appears to have been paying attention to what made RESERVOIR DOGS work, rather than coming away convinced that the formula for success begins and ends with pop-culture allusions and scarcely digested homages to classic crime films. Consequently, his film has both characters and a story, complicated by a slew of carefully worked out subplots involving boneheaded burglars, antique shotguns, yuppie hydroponic dope farmers, Jamaican drug dealers, and multiple gangs of hard cases with blood in their eyes. And oh, that cliffhanger ending....

LODGER, THE

1944 84m bw   Thriller   ★★★★
Fox   (U.S.)

Merle Oberon *(Kitty)*, George Sanders *(John Garrick)*, Laird Cregar *(The Lodger)*, Cedric Hardwicke *(Robert Burton)*, Sara Allgood *(Ellen)*, Aubrey Mather *(Supt. Sutherland)*, Queenie Leonard *(Daisy)*, David Clyde *(Sgt. Bates)*, Helena Pickard *(Anne Rowley)*, Lumsden Hare *(Dr. Sheridan)*

p, Robert Bassler; d, John Brahm; w, Barre Lyndon (based on the novel by Marie Belloc Lowndes); ph, Lucien Ballard; ed, J. Watson Webb; m, Hugo Friedhofer; art d, James Basevi, John Ewing; fx, Fred Sersen; chor, Kenny Williams

Cregar is absolutely chilling in this Jack the Ripper tale, perhaps the best film made about Bloody Jack. THE LODGER's re-creation of Victorian London is soaked with fog, with cobblestones sweating and gaslights flickering as blood-chilling screams pierce the night air and a dark figure goes running. Oberon is a beautiful singer whose parents, Allgood and Hardwicke, rent a room to Cregar. The mysterious lodger tells them he won't be joining them for breakfast, lunch, or dinner, because he works at night. During the night, Cregar slips out into the fog carrying a little black bag; in the early hours, he can be heard pacing back and forth in his rooms—which are always kept locked, and where he performs what he terms "experiments." Cregar eyes Oberon and fences with her friend Sanders, a Scotland Yard inspector developing new criminology techniques, but, in the end, he cannot resist killing the lovely Oberon, as he has killed so many others. Before he can murder her, however, the police and Sanders interrupt the attack and chase Cregar wildly through a theater. Trapped like a bear, salivating and maniacal, Cregar hurls himself through a huge window and into the Thames to drown rather than surrender.

This ending is not in keeping with that of the film's source material, the superlative novel written by Marie Belloc Lowndes. In addition, THE LODGER, unlike the novel, leaves no doubt that Cregar's character is Jack the Ripper. The huge actor is superb in this grand *film noir*; he and Sanders would almost repeat their parts in the similar HANGOVER SQUARE, also directed by John Brahm. (Only 28 at the time, Cregar longed to be a matinee idol and, shortly after the release of this film, went on a crash water diet and literally starved himself to death.) THE LODGER remakes the Alfred Hitchcock silent film starring Ivor Novello, and is probably better. Brahm's directs with a taut rein, the script is brilliant, the photography by Lucien Ballard (Oberon's husband-to-be) is a marvel of fluid action, and the whole is mightily enhanced by Hugo Friedhofer's strange and unnerving score.

LOLA   📀
(DONNA DI VITA)
1961 90m   bw   Drama   ★★★
Rome-Paris-Euro Intl.   (France/Italy)

Anouk Aimee *(Lola)*, Marc Michel *(Roland)*, Elina Labourdette *(Mme. Desnoyers)*, Alan Scott *(Frankie)*, Annie Duperoux *(Cecile)*, Jacques Harden *(Michel)*, Margo Lion *(Jeanne, Michel's Mother)*, Catherine Lutz *(Claire, the Waitress)*, Corinne Marchand *(Daisy)*, Yvette Anziani *(Mme. Frederique)*

p, Carlo Ponti, Georges de Beauregard; d, Jacques Demy; w, Jacques Demy; ph, Raoul Coutard (Franscope); ed, Anne-Marie Cotret, Monique Teisseire; m, Michel Legrand, Johann Sebastian Bach, Wolfgang Amadeus Mozart, Carl Maria von Weber; art d, Bernard Evein

Free-flowing debut feature from French director Jacques Demy who, with his wife, director Agnes Varda, flourished during the New Wave. Because of its abundance of sweeping camera movement (superbly engineered by Raoul Coutard), the film has often been called a musical without music. (Demy would later go to Hollywood and make a real musical with Gene Kelly.) Aimee plays the title role, a cabaret singer who awaits the return of Harden, her husband who has been away for seven years. In the meantime she has a few affairs, her strongest affections going to childhood friend Michel. Michel has dreams of settling down with Aimee, but those are shattered when Harden returns and sweeps Aimee away in his glaring white Cadillac. The picture is filled with cinematic allusions (a fondness of French New Wave directors) to Robert Bresson, Gary Cooper, Max Ophuls (especially his camerawork), and Josef von Sternberg. Demy received a helping hand from Jean-Luc Godard, who offered his talents as a production consultant.

LOLA MONTES   📀
1955 110m   c   Drama   ★★★★★
Gamma/Florida/Union   (France/West Germany)

Martine Carol *(Lola Montes)*, Peter Ustinov *(Circus Master)*, Anton Walbrook *(Ludwig I, King of Bavaria)*, Ivan Desny *(Lt. James)*, Will Quadflieg *(Franz Liszt)*, Oskar Werner *(Student)*, Lise Delamare *(Mrs. Craigie)*, Henri Guisol *(Maurice)*, Paulette Dubost *(Josephine)*, Helena Manson *(James' Sister)*

d, Max Ophuls; w, Max Ophuls, Jacques Natanson, Franz Geiger, Annette Wademant (based on the unpublished novel *La Vie Extraordinaire de Lola Montes* by Cecil Saint-Laurent); ph, Christian Matras (CinemaScope, Eastmancolor); ed, Madeleine Gug; m, Georges Auric; art d, Jean d'Eaubonne, Willy Schatz; cos, Georges Annenkov, Marcel Escoffier

Andrew Sarris in 1963 dubbed this film the greatest ever made, and although he's noted for his quirky opinions, he's no fool. A masterpiece, LOLA MONTES is certainly director Max Ophuls' greatest achievement. In flashback, we take a fascinating look at the life of the passionate yet oddly passive title character (Carol, more perfect in the part than she could possibly have fathomed). Introduced by a New Orleans circus master (Ustinov), the aging Lola answers (or has answered for her) personal questions from the audience for a small fee. The ringmaster tells of her many romances throughout Europe, including one with Franz Liszt (Quadflieg) and another with the king of Bavaria (Walbrook). In the last scene, Lola (who throughout has been made to perform various acts like a well-trained seal) stands atop a high platform, preparing for a dangerous jump. Her health is as precarious as her position, yet the ringmaster removes the safety net. The finale is unforgettable.

Along with Michael Powell's BLACK NARCISSUS, this is one of the most gorgeous films ever shot in color. Eastmancolor generally pales beside Technicolor; leave it to Ophuls to make the most of it. Ditto the use of CinemaScope, which Ophuls didn't want and tried to negate by using pillars and curtains at the edges of the frame. The effect is to frame the whole affair as a performance, and Ophuls' innate visual flair makes shot after shot (e.g. the descending chandeliers at the opening) a stunning use of widescreen. He even knows when to ditch both resources, as Lola's most intimate moments are signaled with a ghostly blue monochrome and a tight closeup with most of the frame in black. His customary genius with the camera has rarely been on better display, as he dizzyingly dollies 360 degrees around the trapped, immobile Lola while the exploitative ringmaster spins her platform. Never cutting when camera movement will do, Ophuls tilts, tracks and cranes magnificently, embodying Lola's flashback motto, "For me, life is movement." By contrast, the overwhelmingly cluttered *mise en scene* of the circus all but smothers the degraded courtesan.

Carol doesn't appear young enough as the teen-aged Lola nor does she look really ravaged at the finale, but her masklike quality allows Ophuls a great chance to project, indulging the French fondness for casting Woman *as* Cinema. Wolbrook is quietly heartrending as the aging monarch, and Werner, as a young student and sex interlude for Lola, displays the promise he would later fulfill so well. Top honors, though, go to the magnificent Ustinov, who, two Oscars elsewhere notwithstanding, has never done anything better. Both heartless and tender to Lola, abusive and always on the verge of falling in love, his rueful expression and biting wit speak volumes that otherwise never surface. A film whose power is in the image itself, the endlessly amazing LOLA MONTES explores the magic (and the cost) of illusion as few films have ever done.

LOLITA   📀
1962 152m   bw   Drama   ★★★★
Seven Arts/A.A./Anya/Trans World   (U.S./U.K.)

James Mason *(Humbert Humbert)*, Sue Lyon *(Lolita Haze)*, Shelley Winters *(Charlotte Haze)*, Peter Sellers *(Clare Quilty)*, Marianne Stone *(Vivian Darkbloom)*, Diana Decker *(Jean Farlow)*, Jerry Stovin *(John Farlow)*, Gary Cockrell *(Dick)*, Suzanne Gibbs *(Mona Farlow)*, Roberta Shore *(Lorna)* p, James B. Harris; d, Stanley Kubrick; w, Vladimir Nabokov (based on the novel by Nabokov); ph, Oswald Morris; ed, Anthony Harvey; m, Nelson Riddle; art d, Bill Andrews; cos, Gene Coffin

AAN Best Adapted Screenplay: Vladimir Nabokov

A fascinating if problematic early film from Stanley Kubrick, perhaps the most obsessive of the great auteurs of the 1960s, made just on the cusp of a run of cinematic masterpieces. Here Vladimir Nabokov adapts his own controversial satirical novel about the obsessive love a British middle aged professor develops for a 12-year-old girl. While the novel outraged many bluenoses, the film advances the age of the "nymphet" to about 15 thereby neutralizing much of of the controversy. It's quite long—too long—possibly as a result of having Nabokov do his own screen adaptation. Nabokov's novels are so intensely concerned with language that one would expect that they would be particularly difficult to translate to the screen. LOLITA, a great grey comedy of the 1950s, succeeds in carefully setting up and knocking down the shibboleths of the silent generation.

James Mason is the smitten professor, Humbert Humbert, in love with the American girl, Lolita (Sue Lyon). Shelly Winters is the vulgar mother with misguided intellectual aspirations who is attracted to Humbert. The ever resourceful Peter Sellers, with a great American accent and a succession of disguises, is a standout as Quilty. The scene in which he explains himself to Mason is a small masterpiece of the acting art. Mason and Winters are less showy but equally impressive while the young Lyon, sadly, is only barely adequate.

The film is not particularly shocking or titillating; the most erotic scene in the film is a pedicure. Kubrick exhibited great subtlety (he had to, or they'd have given this one a hard time in the theaters)—perhaps too much subtlety. The script was nominated for an Oscar.

LOLITA

1997 137m c Romance/Drama ★★★
Lolita Productions/Chargeurs Productions R
(U.S./France) DVD

Jeremy Irons *(Humbert Humbert)*, Melanie Griffith *(Charlotte Haze)*, Frank Langella *(Clare Quilty)*, Dominique Swain *(Lolita Haze)*, Suzanne Shepherd *(Miss Pratt)*, Keith Reddin *(Reverend Rigger)*, Erin J. Dean *(Mona)*, Joan Glover *(Miss LeBone)*, Pat P. Perkins *(Louise)*, Ed Grady *(Doctor Melnick)*

p, Mario Kassar, Joel B. Michaels; d, Adrian Lyne; w, Stephen Schiff, Harold Pinter, James Dearden (based on the novel by Vladimir Nabokov); ph, Howard Atherton; ed, Julie Monroe, David Brenner; m, Ennio Morricone; prod d, Jon Hutman; art d, W. Steven Graham; fx, Jeffrey A. Okun, Joseph Mercurio; cos, Judianna Makovsky

It's all but impossible not to see Adrian Lyne's film of Vladimir Nabokov's 1955 novel through a scrim of fevered controversy. But on its own merits it's really no more shocking than 1992's THE LOVER (based on the autobiographical novel by Marguerite Duras), a strikingly similar mix of softcore imagery and pedigreed philosophy from the boudoir.

Initially unhampered by the stringent mores that forced Stanley Kubrick and Nabokov himself—he scripted the 1962 LOLITA—to dance around the particulars of European aesthete Humbert Humbert's obsession with gum-snapping American jailbait Dolores "Lolita" Hayes, Lyne and his screenwriter are extremely faithful to the events of Nabokov's novel, and try to salvage fragments of its shimmering language in the form of voice-overs. Lyne's direction is sometimes overblown—debauched playwright Clare Quilty's (Frank Langella) appearance amid the pale fire of exploding bug-zappers really is a bit much—and the unfortu-

nate fact is that the novel is one long tease, an intricate, seductive game in which words are as important as deeds. The tricky beauty of Humbert's telling—a gossamer thing of lies and evasions and self-justifying spin—is inevitably lost when the tale is brought to life in the all-too-solid flesh of actors, no matter how perfectly cast. That said, Lyne scored a perfect Humbert in the wearily handsome Jeremy Irons, who trails a whiff of corruption picked up from roles in films like DAMAGE, REVERSAL OF FORTUNE, and DEAD RINGERS. Equally flawless is Dominique Swain, unnervingly seductive and conniving in some scenes, childishly coarse in others. Peter Sellers fans may miss his blackly comic Quilty, but Langella's reptilian interpretation nails the character's true monstrousness. Melanie Griffith strikes the only false note, capturing the vulgarity of Lolita's blowsy mother but missing her self-deluded vulnerability.

LONE STAR

1996 138m c Drama ★★★★
Rio Dulce, Inc./Castle Rock Entertainment (U.S.) R DVD

Chris Cooper *(Sam Deeds)*, Elizabeth Pena *(Pilar Cruz)*, Joe Morton *(Delmore Payne)*, Miriam Colon *(Mercedes Cruz)*, Clifton James *(Mayor Hollis Pogue)*, Kris Kristofferson *(Sheriff Charley Wade)*, Ron Canada *(Otis Payne)*, Matthew McConaughey *(Buddy Deeds)*, Frances McDormand *(Bunny)*, Eddie Robinson *(Chet Payne)*

p, R. Paul Miller, Maggie Renzi; d, John Sayles; w, John Sayles; ph, Stuart Dryburgh; ed, John Sayles; m, Mason Daring; prod d, Dan Bishop; art d, Kyler Black; fx, Jack Bennett; cos, Shay Cunliffe

AAN Best Original Screenplay: John Sayles

From stubbornly independent writer/director John Sayles, an attempted Great American Epic that falls only slightly short of its immoderate ambitions.

Nearly 40 years after the mysterious disappearance of brutal Sheriff Charley Wade (Kris Kristofferson), his skeletal remains are unearthed outside the tiny border town of Frontera, Texas. Rio County's latest sheriff, Sam Deeds (Chris Cooper), begins to suspect not only that Wade was murdered, but also that he died at the hands of the late Sheriff Buddy Deeds (Matthew McConaughey), a local hero and Sam's own father. This Oedipal mystery serves as the pretext for a much broader investigation of the substance of the American past. In what is easily his most accomplished film to date, Sayles aims to show how authority uses history to construct the borders that separate countries, communities, and individuals. The film stumbles a bit towards the end (some deeply rooted conflicts are implausibly resolved), but terrific performances from a large cast—particularly Elizabeth Pena as Sam's childhood sweetheart—smooth over the rough spots.

LONELINESS OF THE LONG DISTANCE RUNNER, THE

1962 104m bw Drama ★★★★
Woodfall/Bryanston/Seven Arts (U.K.)

Tom Courtenay *(Colin Smith)*, Michael Redgrave *(The Governor)*, Avis Bunnage *(Mrs. Smith)*, Peter Madden *(Mr. Smith)*, James Bolam *(Mike)*, Julia Foster *(Gladys)*, Topsy Jane *(Audrey)*, Dervis Ward *(Detective)*, Raymond Dyer *(Gordon)*, Alec McCowen *(Brown)*

p, Tony Richardson; d, Tony Richardson; w, Alan Sillitoe (based on his story); ph, Walter Lassally; ed, Anthony Gibbs; m, John Addison; prod d, Ralph Brinton; art d, Ted Marshall; cos, Sophie Harris

It was considered chic among cinephiles in the 1960s to denigrate British stage and film director Tony Richardson, but on balance he was responsible for as many important British films in these years as anyone else. One of the best of the British Angry Young Man films, THE LONELINESS OF THE LONG DISTANCE RUNNER concerns Courtenay, an ill-educated youth who is sentenced to a reformatory after robbing a bakery. The borstal's governor, Redgrave, a great believer in the rehabilitative powers of sports, is delighted to learn that Courtenay is a natural distance runner and encourages him to train for a big meet with a local public school, promising him special privileges in exchange for a victory. Most of the film is taken up with Courtenay's training, during which he flashes back to the events and relationships that have brought him to this point in his life. When the big race finally arrives, Courtenay easily outclasses his competitors, but at the finish line he shocks the governor with an unexpected act of defiance. Adapted by Alan Sillitoe from his own short story and masterfully directed by Richardson, this poignant film was also the auspicious film debut of Courtenay, whose excellent performance earned him the British Academy's Most Promising Newcomer award.

LONELY ARE THE BRAVE
1962 107m bw Western ★★★★
Universal (U.S.)

Kirk Douglas (*Jack Burns*), Gena Rowlands (*Jerri Bondi*), Walter Matthau (*Sheriff Johnson*), Michael Kane (*Paul Bondi*), Carroll O'Connor (*Hinton*), William Schallert (*Harry*), Karl Swenson (*Rev. Hoskins*), George Kennedy (*Guitierrez*), Dan Sheridan (*Deputy Glynn*), Bill Raisch (*"One Arm"*)

p, Edward Lewis; d, David Miller; w, Dalton Trumbo (based on the novel *Brave Cowboy* by Edward Abbey); ph, Philip Lathrop (Panavision); ed, Leon Barsha, Edward Mann; m, Jerry Goldsmith; art d, Alexander Golitzen, Robert E. Smith

Dalton Trumbo wrote this elegy to the western. Kirk Douglas gives one of his finest performances as an out-of-place cowboy in the modern west—almost like a time traveller. The theme of the film is eloquently set up by the opening of the film in which we see Douglas reclining beneath a clear and spacious western sky. The peace and quiet is suddenly disrupted by the sound of a jet plane passing overhead. This brings a wry smile to the old cowboy's face. He rides his horse into Albuquerque to visit friends Kane and Rowlands. Rowlands tells him that her husband has been jailed for helping Mexicans enter the U.S. illegally. Douglas starts a brawl in a saloon to get put into jail; there Douglas offers his friend Kane help in breaking out, but Kane tells Douglas that he wants to serve his brief time, intends to play out his hand with the law, and refuses to become a fugitive. Douglas is hurt but undaunted. He breaks out himself and heads for the hills, pursued by the compassionate technocratic sheriff Matthau and a posse.

Douglas is superb as the cowboy who will not yield to the modern world. Miller's direction is excellent, this being the finest film in his generally ineven career. Matthau is also convincing as the understanding sheriff who tries his best to capture a man he does not want to see locked up. Lathrop's sharp black-and-white photography and Goldsmith's evocative score add measurably to this outstanding production. There is one particularly memorable scene as Douglas and his good old horse attempt to cross a busy highway with the eighteen wheelers barrelling by. It will stay with you forever.

LONG DAY CLOSES, THE
1992 82m c Biography/Drama ★★★★
British Film Institute/Film Four International PG
(U.K.)

Marjorie Yates (*Mother*), Leigh McCormack (*Bud*), Anthony Watson (*Kevin*), Nick Lamont (*John*), Ayse Owens (*Helen*), Tina

Malone (*Edna*), Jimmy Wilde (*Curly*), Robin Polley (*Mr. Nicholls*), Peter Ivatts (*Mr. Bushell*), Joy Blakeman (*Frances*)

p, Olivia Stewart; d, Terence Davies; w, Terence Davies; ph, Michael Coulter; ed, William Diver; m, Bob Last, Robert Lockhart; prod d, Christopher Hobbs; art d, Kave Naylor; cos, Monica Howe

THE LONG DAY CLOSES vividly demonstrates the redemptive power of alternative modes of cinematic storytelling, even as it celebrates the glories of classical Hollywood movies.

Without a plot in any conventional sense, or traditionally articulated characters, this resonant slice of British family life in the '50s is infinitely more affecting than most conventional domestic dramas. Ironically, the film achieves some of its most sublime effects while depicting its young protagonist listening to American pop songs, watching his family taking part in group singalongs at the local pub, and—most importantly—in rapt contemplation of movies. The filmmaker's alter ego is the fey, lonely Bud (Leigh McCormack), an 11-year-old boy whose drab life is immeasurably more enriched by going to the movies than by attending school or church. Rarely has the mere act of spectatorship been so convincingly rendered as to suggest spiritual transfiguration.

Director Terence Davies effectively evokes the sounds and textures of post-WWII working-class life in England's Liverpool. At times, looking at THE LONG DAY CLOSES feels like leafing through someone else's old family album—indeed, much of the striking imagery has the quality of period photographs. This is due to an expressive deployment of long and often static takes, shadowy sculptural lighting, and a rich yet muted color scheme that suggests old three-strip Technicolor. Both this film and Davies's DISTANT VOICES, STILL LIVES are loosely autobiographical: whereas the earlier film was a very dark, impressionistic chronicle of Davies' family life in the '40s, before his birth and during his early childhood, the more sanguine follow-up covers the quiet period in the mid-'50s when he became a dedicated moviegoer.

LONG DAY'S JOURNEY INTO NIGHT
DVD
1962 174m bw Drama ★★★★★
Landau (U.S.)

Katharine Hepburn (*Mary Tyrone*), Ralph Richardson (*James Tyrone, Sr.*), Jason Robards Jr. (*James Tyrone, Jr.*), Dean Stockwell (*Edmund Tyrone*), Jeanne Barr (*Cathleen*)

p, Ely Landau, Jack J. Dreyfus Jr.; d, Sidney Lumet; w, Eugene O'Neill (based on his play); ph, Boris Kaufman; ed, Ralph Rosenblum; m, Andre Previn; prod d, Richard Sylbert; art d, Richard Sylbert; cos, Motley

AAN Best Actress: Katharine Hepburn

O'Neill's greatest play is brought to the screen with an overpowering wealth of talent: Hepburn, Richardson, and Robards give magnificent, once-in-a-lifetime performances as members of the doomed Tyrone family. The playwright described his autobiographical work as "a play of old sorrow, written in tears and blood."

The setting is one long, long day and night in the year 1912 at the Tyrone summer home in New London, Connecticut. The stingy senior Tyrone, James (Richardson), an impoverished youth turned fine Shakespearean actor, has spent years playing the same role over and over again in a commercial play simply for the money. His wife Mary (Hepburn) has just returned from a sanitarium. She is all lady, an Irish Catholic with strong moral principles, but she is also strangely withdrawn, partly as a result of the drug addiction which began when she was treated by cheap quack doctors. Elder son Jamie (Robards) has attempted to follow his father into the acting profession but, failing miserably, takes solace in drink, becoming a cynic who would rather destroy all around him than show his true feelings. Younger son Edmund (Stockwell), a budding writer, is recovering from tuberculosis and has spent time in a second-rate institution that his tightwad father sent him to in order to save money. As the day wears on, painful truths and long-buried resentments overwhelm them all.

Of the cast, Hepburn takes it. Where she takes it is in her transistion points, from girlish coquette remembering her apple-blossom youth to maddened dope fiend, from loving mother to mindless creature groping for identity. This is where Hepburn departed once and for all from delicious comedienne into legendary tragedienne. Richardson's performance is just right: his spareness as an actor incredibly personifies a miser. For once the camera captures Robards's wildness, his lunging danger, before alcohol crabbed him into permanent grit. There's nothing wrong with Stockwell's performance. It's just that we know he's O'Neill, a heavy task for a young actor. Obviously, it's a part for an older performer who looks younger. We can't help but brood that Montgomery Clift was too prematurely old and ruined for the role.

The screen version followed the superb play almost word for word. According to O'Neill's will, the play was not to be produced until 25 years after his death in 1951, but his widow, Carlotta, only waited until 1956 to let it be staged with Fredric March, Florence Eldridge, Robards and Bradford Dillman. Make sure you see the uncut 174-minute film, and not the shortened 136-minute version.

LONG GOOD FRIDAY, THE
1980 105m c   Crime/Drama   ★★★½
Calendar/Black Lion   (U.K.)   R

Bob Hoskins *(Harold)*, Helen Mirren *(Victoria)*, Eddie Constantine *(Charlie)*, Dave King *(Parky)*, Bryan Marshall *(Harris)*, George Coulouris *(Gus)*, Derek Thompson *(Jeff)*, Pierce Brosnan *(1st Irishman)*, Charles Cork *(Eric)*, Billy Cornelius *(Pete)*

p, Barry Hanson; d, John Mackenzie; w, Barrie Keeffe; ph, Phil Meheux; ed, Mike Taylor; m, Francis Monkman; art d, Vic Symonds

A smooth and efficient film about some pretty rough characters, THE LONG GOOD FRIDAY deserves its status as a modern-day crime classic. Though not quite in the league of some other entries in the genre, the story of a crime boss and people out to get him delivers the expected goods.

On "Good Friday" in early 1980s London, Harold (Bob Hoskins) learns that an unknown rival gang is killing off his henchmen. Harold fears less about his safety and more about his honor, however, and seeks to find out the culprit behind the murder of his men. Harold is especially eager to secure a deal with Charlie (Eddie Constantine), a Mafia don visiting from New Jersey, and worries that the murders will scare the money-man away. Harold and his men interrogate a number of underworld suspects, but they get few leads to the identity of the killers. After a near-fatal bomb attack on his American visitors, Harold steps up the pressure on his suspects to talk. Meanwhile, Harold's wife, Victoria (Helen Mirren), entertains Charlie and his lawyer at a restaurant, where they threaten to pull out of the deal unless she tells them what is going on. They then give Harold 24 hours to solve the mystery and stop the murders.

THE LONG GOOD FRIDAY compares well to the American gangster films of the 1930s (SCARFACE, LITTLE CAESAR), which also documented the way tough, fearless working-class thugs could rise and fall as infamous criminals. Screenwriter's Barrie Keeffe's well-rounded, almost Shakespearean, characters serve the genre well, his plot gets involved but not overly perplexing, and John Mackenzie's direction possesses a sure touch. In some ways, THE LONG GOOD FRIDAY presages Peter Greenaway's extraordinary THE COOK, THE THIEF, HIS WIFE AND HER LOVER (1989), which also starred Helen Mirren as a criminal's trophy

wife (or "moll"). Both films suggest a criticism of Margaret Thatcher's *nouveau riche* world order. Unfortunately, THE LONG GOOD FRIDAY makes Harold's antihero a bit too cuddly and likable to compete with the thoroughly reprehensible thief (Michael Gambon) in the Greenaway picture. Thus, THE LONG GOOD FRIDAY stops short of brilliant revisionism, but acquits itself admirably in most other ways.

LONG GOODBYE, THE   DVD
1973 112m c   Crime   ★★★★
UA   (U.S.)   R

Elliott Gould *(Philip Marlowe)*, Nina Van Pallandt *(Eileen Wade)*, Sterling Hayden *(Roger Wade)*, Mark Rydell *(Marty Augustine)*, Henry Gibson *(Dr. Verringer)*, David Arkin *(Harry)*, Jim Bouton *(Terry Lennox)*, Warren Berlinger *(Morgan)*, Jo Ann Brody *(Jo Ann Eggenweiler)*, Jack Knight *(Hood)*

p, Jerry Bick; d, Robert Altman; w, Leigh Brackett (based on the novel by Raymond Chandler); ph, Vilmos Zsigmond (PanaVision, Technicolor); ed, Lou Lombardo; m, John Williams; cos, Kent James, Marjorie Wahl

The detective film to end all detective films. Director Robert Altman offended the fans of Raymond Chandler's Philip Marlowe character by completely subverting the role here. Elliott Gould plays the usually hard-boiled detective as something of a well-meaning bumbler, and while it may not be Chandler, it is a moody and entertaining film. The film is set in Los Angeles where Gould's troubles begin when he gives his friend, Bouton (a former baseball pitcher), a ride to Tijuana. Upon his return, he learns that Bouton is wanted by police for the brutal murder of his wife. Convinced of his friend's innocence, Gould begins his own investigation of the crime. His inquiry first leads him to the beautiful Van Pallandt, with whom Bouton was having an affair. Her husband, Hayden, is a once-successful author who is suffering a severe case of writer's block, which has turned him into an alcohlic. Somewhat batty and insanely jealous regarding his wife, Hayden becomes Gould's prime suspect in the killing. Fueling his suspicion is the bizarre relationship Hayden has with the sinister Gibson, an alleged psychologist who has been treating him. The case is complicated further by vicious hood Rydell, to whom Boulton owed a large amount of cash. Rydell is certain Gould has the cash and goes to great lengths to show the detective he better fork it over if he does have it. As Gould sifts through the clues, he is sure he has solved the case—but his instincts are wrong, and the trail leads to a suprising and somewhat improbable conclusion.

Certainly Gould shatters the Marlowe mold in this film, playing the detective as a wisecracking, disheveled eccentric, much the same character he portrayed in other Altman films, M*A*S*H and CALIFORNIA SPLIT. From that viewpoint, Chandler's fans had reason to be upset, but Altman's approach to the film noir crime drama is not without its good points. Gould's persona is an amusing counterpoint to the traditional tough-guy detective who always knew exactly what to say and do and who never ran across a situation he couldn't handle. Gould's Marlowe is an often bewildered investigator, who nevertheless maintains the character's strong sense of morality in the midst of a cruel world. Look for Arnold Schwarzenegger (billed as "Arnold Strong") in a small role as one of Rydell's hoods.

LONG, HOT SUMMER, THE   DVD
1958 115m c   Drama   ★★★★
Fox   (U.S.)

Paul Newman *(Ben Quick)*, Joanne Woodward *(Clara Varner)*, Anthony Franciosa *(Jody Varner)*, Orson Welles *(Will Varner)*, Lee Remick *(Eula Varner)*, Angela Lansbury *(Minnie Littlejohn)*,

Richard Anderson (*Alan Stewart*), Sarah Marshall (*Agnes Stewart*), Mabel Albertson (*Mrs. Stewart*), J. Pat O'Malley (*Ratliff*)

p, Jerry Wald; d, Martin Ritt; w, Irving Ravetch, Harriet Frank Jr. (based on "Barn Burning," "Spotted Horses," and the novel *The Hamlet* by William Faulkner); ph, Joseph La Shelle (CinemaScope, DeLuxe Color); ed, Louis Loeffler; m, Alex North; art d, Lyle Wheeler, Maurice Ransford; fx, L.B. Abbott; cos, Adele Palmer

Filmmakers have often found it difficult to bring William Faulkner's dense novels to the screen, but here director Martin Ritt and writers Harriet Frank, Jr. and Irving Ravetch opted for a less-than-faithful adaptation of the author's work, and the results were excellent.

Newman plays a Mississippi man with a bad temper who drifts into a small town. He goes to work for Welles, a wealthy landowner, who likes the young man's toughness. He decides Newman would be better suited to running his empire than his weak son (Franciosa) and tries to marry off the newcomer to his resentful daughter (Woodward). Franciosa reacts murderously.

The pairing of Newman, on loan from Warner Bros., and Fox's rising star Woodward, was pure magic. She had already won an Oscar for her work in THE THREE FACES OF EVE, while Newman had impressed in films such as THE LEFT-HANDED GUN and SOMEBODY UP THERE LIKES ME, but wasn't quite a star yet. With this film and CAT ON A HOT TIN ROOF (for which he received his first Oscar nomination, also released in 1958), Newman quickly became one of Hollywood's hottest stars. There was plenty of electricity on the screen in his scenes with Woodward, and, evidently, off screen too, as they were married in 1958. Only 42 at the time, Welles looked much older and, though he overplays the role at times, was well cast as the tyrannical landowner. In fact, the whole cast is worthy of praise. Lansbury, who *always* played characters much older than she was, is delightful as Welles's mistress, tossing off many of the film's best lines. Franciosa had the year before been nominated for a Best Actor Oscar for his role in A HATFUL OF RAIN and again received good notices here. However, his film career stalled, and he moved into television, starring in such series as "Valentine's Day" and "The Name of the Game." The script is literate, sharp, and humorous. Ritt and screenwriters Ravetch and Frank would team two more times with Newman, first for HUD, one of Newman's best films, and again for HOMBRE.

LONG RIDERS, THE

1980 99m c Western ★★★★
UA (U.S.) R

David Carradine (*Cole Younger*), Keith Carradine (*Jim Younger*), Robert Carradine (*Bob Younger*), James Keach (*Jesse James*), Stacy Keach (*Frank James*), Dennis Quaid (*Ed Miller*), Randy Quaid (*Clell Miller*), Kevin Brophy (*John Younger*), Harry Carey Jr. (*George Arthur*), Christopher Guest (*Charlie Ford*)

p, Tim Zinnemann; d, Walter Hill; w, Bill Bryden, Steven Phillip Smith, James Keach, Stacy Keach; ph, Ric Waite (Technicolor); ed, David Holden; m, Ry Cooder; prod d, Jack T. Collis; art d, Peter Romero; chor, Katina Sawidis; cos, Bobbie Mannix

THE LONG RIDERS is a superb, nitty-gritty retelling of the story of the James-Younger gang, the most notorious American bandits of the 19th century. In a unique bit of casting, the Younger, James, Miller, and Ford brothers are played by the brothers Carradine, Keach, Quaid, and Guest. The film opens with the band led by Jesse James (James Keach) and Cole Younger (David Carradine) robbing a bank. In episodic fashion, it then follows the various gang members as they go their separate ways, reuniting later for a disastrous attempt to

rob a bank in Northfield, Minnesota. THE LONG RIDERS is one of the last great westerns made in America, directed tautly by Walter Hill from an excellent, well-researched script. The cinematography by Ric Waite is magnificent, the period is beautifully captured, and Ry Cooder's outstanding score nicely incorporates folk music of the era. The whole feeling of this film is one of antiquity, an atmosphere marvelously created by Hill and enhanced by a superb cast. James Keach realistically plays Jesse James; Stacy Keach is perfect as the puzzled, puritanical, but loyal Frank; David Carradine is excellent as the confident, bold Cole Younger; Keith and Robert Carradine are very good as the other Younger brothers; and Nicholas and Christopher Guest epitomize the treacherous Ford siblings. Though THE LONG RIDERS does not spare the violence, this is a must for any adult western fan.

LONG VOYAGE HOME, THE

1940 105m bw Drama ★★★★★
Argosy (U.S.)

John Wayne (*Ole Olsen*), Thomas Mitchell (*Aloysius Driscoll*), Ian Hunter (*Smitty*), Barry Fitzgerald (*Cocky*), Wilfrid Lawson (*Captain*), Mildred Natwick (*Freda*), John Qualen (*Axel Swanson*), Ward Bond (*Yank*), Joe Sawyer (*Davis*), Arthur Shields (*Donkeyman*)

p, Walter Wanger; d, John Ford; w, Dudley Nichols (based on the plays "The Moon of the Caribbees," "In the Zone," "Bound East for Cardiff," "The Long Voyage Home," by Eugene O'Neill); ph, Gregg Toland; ed, Sherman Todd; m, Richard Hageman; art d, James Basevi; fx, Ray Binger, R.T. Layton

AAN Best Picture; AAN Best Screenplay: Dudley Nichols; *AAN Best B/W Cinematography:* Gregg Toland; *AAN Best Film Editing:* Sherman Todd; *AAN Best Original Score:* Richard Hageman; *AAN Best Special Effects:* R. T. Layton (Photographic), R. O. Binger (Photographic), Thomas T. Moulton (Sound)

Based on four one-act plays by Eugene O'Neill, THE LONG VOYAGE HOME is a powerful saga of merchant seamen, their hardscrabble lives, and their hopes for the future. Ford's film is a magnificent portrayal of the struggle not only to survive, but also to remain civilized, during the early days of WWII. As the film opens, the crew of the tramp freighter SS *Glencairn* is enjoying a last night of liberty on a Caribbean island, attending a party that ends in a brawl before they stagger back to the freighter. Among the crew is Ole Olsen (Wayne), a good-hearted young Swede who only wants to make enough money to settle down with his family on a small farm, and Smitty (Hunter), who doesn't participate in the drunken on-shore revels and whose painful secret causes suspicion among the crew. In Baltimore, the ship takes on a load of dynamite to be delivered to England, and the film details the hazards of raging storms, German fighter planes, and scheming barroom wharf rats. Though several are killed, the men eventually pull together to help one crew member escape a life at sea.

THE LONG VOYAGE HOME is a Ford masterwork—grim, touching, and startlingly well-photographed. Toland's high contrast lighting and shot compositions cast a vivid aura over both sea and land. As Wayne told biographer Maurice Zolotow, "Usually it would be Mr. Ford who helped the cinematographer get his compositions for maximum effect…but in this case it was Gregg Toland who helped Mr. Ford. LONG VOYAGE is about as beautifully photographed a movie as there ever has been."

Wayne himself initially resisted Ford's instruction that he play his character with a Swedish accent, fearing he would appear comic. But he had actress Osa Massen (who was Danish) help him with the accent, and when he first employed it he was congratulated by Ford for getting it right. His work as a naive, simple but not simple-minded man is surprisingly reserved and very effective, not dominating the action the way he usually did. Mitchell, Bond, Fitzgerald, and Qualen are wonderful as various old salts, and Hunter is moving as the tortured seaman who has ruined his life on land. There is a pervasive air of gloom about THE LONG VOYAGE HOME: death lurks on land and at sea, and though the seamen yearn for their long-lost homes, most of them know that they will sail on until they are buried beneath the waves. THE LONG VOYAGE HOME was playwright O'Neill's favorite film; Ford gave him a print of it and he and he ran it over and over again until he wore it out.

LONGEST DAY, THE

DVD
1962 180m bw War   ★★★★
Fox   (U.S.)   G

John Wayne *(Col. Benjamin Vandervoort)*, Robert Mitchum *(Brig. Gen. Norman Cota)*, Henry Fonda *(Brig. Gen. Theodore Roosevelt)*, Robert Ryan *(Brig. Gen. James Gavin)*, Rod Steiger *(Destroyer Commander)*, Robert Wagner, Fabian, Paul Anka, Tommy Sands *(U.S. Rangers)*, Richard Beymer *(Schultz)*

p, Darryl F. Zanuck; d, Andrew Marton, Ken Annakin, Bernhard Wicki, Gerd Oswald; w, Cornelius Ryan, Romain Gary, James Jones, David Pursall, Jack Seddon (based on the novel by Cornelius Ryan); ph, Jean Bourgoin, Henri Persin, Walter Wottitz, Guy Tabary; ed, Samuel E. Beetley; m, Maurice Jarre; art d, Ted Haworth, Leon Barsacq, Vincent Korda; fx, Karl Helmer, Karl Baumgartner, Augie Lohman, Robert MacDonald, Alex Weldon

AAN Best Picture; AA Best B/W Cinematography: Jean Bourgoin, Walter Wottitz; *AAN Best Film Editing:* Samuel E. Beetley; *AAN Best Art Direction-Set Decoration (B/W):* Ted Haworth, Leon Barsacq, Vincent Korda, Gabriel Bechir; *AA Best Special Effects:* Robert MacDonald (Visual), Jacques Maumont (Audible)

One of the most ambitious war films ever undertaken, this star-studded depiction of the D-Day invasion was long the pet project of Fox Studios boss Darryl Zanuck, who spared no expense in bringing THE LONGEST DAY breathtaking scope and authenticity, going so far as to insist that the shooting be done only in weather conditions that matched those of the actual event. Based on Cornelius Ryan's compilation of interviews with D-Day survivors, the film is presented in three segments, the first detailing the Allied preparation for the invasion and the wait for the weather to break; the second re-creating the movement of the massive armada across the English Channel and the preliminary, behind-the-lines sallies of paratroops and glider-transported commandos; and the last depicting the assaults on the Normandy beaches. Intercut with the portrayal of the Allied side of the momentous invasion is the German (subtitled) response, including the report to headquarters of the first German officer to spot the armada: "Those thousands of ships you say the Allies don't have—well, they have them!" The work of three credited directors (reportedly, Zanuck helmed all the American and British interiors himself) and no less than eight cameramen, THE LONGEST DAY is visually stunning—its extraordinary camera movement and Cinemascope photography brilliantly augmenting the meticulously reenacted battle scenes. The only thing bigger than the film's scope are its stars, including John Wayne (who received $250,000 for four days' work) as Lt. Col. Benjamin Vandervoort of the 82nd Paratroop Division; Henry Fonda as Brig. Gen. Theodore Roosevelt, Jr.; Robert Mitchum as Brig. Gen. Norman Cota, who finally moves his hard-pressed men off bloody Omaha Beach, where they are being slaughtered by German crossfire; Red Buttons as a paratrooper; Rod Steiger as the captain of one of the armada ships; Peter Lawford as the flamboyant commando leader Lord Lovat (who was present at the shoot); Richard Burton as a wounded pilot; and Curt Jurgens as German general Blumentritt. Made for $10

million, this magnificent film was the most expensive black-and-white production to its date.

LONGEST YARD, THE

DVD
1974 121m c   Sports/Comedy   ★★★½
Paramount   (U.S.)   R

Burt Reynolds *(Paul Crewe)*, Eddie Albert *(Warden Hazen)*, Ed Lauter *(Capt. Knauer)*, Michael Conrad *(Nate Scarboro)*, James Hampton *(Caretaker)*, Harry Caesar *(Granville)*, John Steadman *(Pop)*, Charles Tyner *(Unger)*, Mike Henry *(Rassmeusen)*, Bernadette Peters *(Warden's Secretary)*

p, Albert S. Ruddy; d, Robert Aldrich; w, Tracy Keenan Wynn (based on a story by Ruddy); ph, Joseph Biroc (Technicolor); ed, Michael Luciano, Frank Capacchione, Allan Jacobs, George Hively; m, Frank DeVol; prod d, James Vance

AAN Best Film Editing: Michael Luciano

Part prison film, part football film, this violent but outstanding comedy-drama by gifted action director Robert Aldrich (KISS ME DEADLY, THE DIRTY DOZEN) explores the brutality inherent in both the American penal system and football. Burt Reynolds gives one of his best performances as Paul Crewe, a former pro who tires of being a kept man, steals his lover's car, and ends up in the prison ruled by Warden Hazen (Eddie Albert). Hazen compels Crewe to put together a team of prisoners to face the crack guard team, offering him parole in exchange for a lopsided loss. Crewe assembles the "Mean Machine" and then does his best to throw the game (which takes up 47 minutes of screen time), leaving it early with an "injury" but returning later to lead the Machine's comeback when the guards' savageness continues unabated. Deftly employing split-screen and slow-motion techniques, Aldrich makes the most of Tracy Keenan Wynn's incisive script, aided by fine cinematography and tight Oscar-nominated editing. Both sides of the line of scrimmage feature former gridiron stars: the guards boast one-time Viking quarterback Joe Kapp and Packer Hall of Famer Ray Nitschke, while among the prisoners are Ernie Wheelwright, Pervis Atkins, and the University of Washington's legendary QB Sonny Sixkiller. No stranger to football himself, Reynolds, an All-Southern Conference halfback at Florida State, also played a pigskin hero in SEMI-TOUGH.

LOOK BACK IN ANGER

DVD
1959 115m bw Drama   ★★★
Pathe/Associated British   (U.K.)

Richard Burton *(Jimmy Porter)*, Claire Bloom *(Helena Charles)*, Mary Ure *(Alison Porter)*, Edith Evans *(Mrs. Tanner)*, Gary Raymond *(Cliff Lewis)*, Glen Byam Shaw *(Cpl. Redfern)*, Phyllis Neilson-Terry *(Mrs. Redfern)*, Donald Pleasence *(Hurst)*, Jane Eccles *(Miss Drury)*, S.P. Kapoor *(Kapoor)*

p, Harry Saltzman; d, Tony Richardson; w, Nigel Kneale, John Osborne (based on the play by Osborne); ph, Oswald Morris; ed, Richard Best; m, Chris Barber; art d, Peter Glazier; cos, Jocelyn Richards

In the late 1950s and early 1960s, several films by "Angry Young Men" were written and produced. Osborne, a forerunner of the genre, wrote the play on which this film is based and which had enormous success in London and New York. This lensing was faithful to the original, but it lost a bit in the translation from the intimacy of the stage to the screen. Canadian Harry Saltzman, who made his fortune in England, produced the picture before he decided to make films that had more commercial possibilities (i.e., the James Bond series which he did with Albert Broccoli). He is to be congratulated for taking a chance with an iffy property. Burton, in a no-holds-barred performance, is a university-educated malcontent who currently earns his keep by running a candy stall in a large market run by Pleasence, in yet another of his fine roles. Burton seems to love his wife, Ure, but can't help verbally mistreating her. (She repeats the part she played on the stage. This was one of her very few film appearances. She had been married to playwright Osborne, then married playwright-actor Robert Shaw. She died at 42 after mixing whiskey with barbiturates.) Ure takes about as much as anyone can stand, then leaves Burton when her best friend, Bloom, persuades her that she must to save her sanity. Burton is now alone, with nobody to insult, and he takes up with Bloom, a woman he has despised for most of the first few reels. Ure has been pregnant all along but didn't tell Burton. When she loses the baby, she returns to Burton, and Bloom figures it's time for her to leave. Evans is a sweet old lady who helps Burton set up his business, and Kapoor has a few good scenes as an Indian trader, but most of the picture belongs to Burton's bravura performance.

The major problem of the picture is that Osborne seems to have concocted the slight plot for one reason only: to vent his spleen against the church, society, the rich, the government, and whatever irked him at the time. The dialogue at times is endless and much too flip in the wrong situations. It's as though the author attempted to be a modern-day Oscar Wilde, but with a social conscience, and his message is heard loud, clear, and far too often. Although Burton has the range to be kind, funny, earthy, noble, and passionate, he is given little opportunity to get beyond letting that memorable voice of his bellow and roar. Still, for all the obvious drawbacks, LOOK BACK IN ANGER should be seen by anyone who is interested in learning about the England of that era. Burton had been making films for ten years and had starred as Alexander in ALEXANDER THE GREAT and as Edwin Booth in PRINCE OF PLAYERS. This seamy role, however, was the one that brought him to the attention of many who thought that he could act only when dressed in Biblical clothes, as in THE ROBE, or in doublet and hose. He was only 34 at the time this was made, but the ravages of high living were already beginning to show on his rugged Welsh face.

LOOK WHO'S TALKING

1989 93m c Comedy

Tri-Star (U.S.)

DVD ★★★ PG-13

John Travolta (James), Kirstie Alley (Mollie), Olympia Dukakis (Rosie), George Segal (Albert), Abe Vigoda (Grandpa), Bruce Willis (Voice of Mikey), Twink Caplan (Rona), Jason Schaller, Jaryd Waterhouse, Jacob Haines

p, Jonathan D. Krane; d, Amy Heckerling; w, Amy Heckerling; ph, Thomas Del Ruth (AlphaCine Color); ed, Debra Chiate; m, David Kitay; art d, Reuben Freed; chor, Mary Ann Kellogg; cos, Molly Maginnis

The voice of Bruce Willis is the "who" in LOOK WHO'S TALKING, a mildly amusing comedy buoyed by a voiceover gimmick. With trademark irony, Willis supplies dialogue for an infant, whose jaundiced view of the adult word provides the laughs. Mollie (Kirstie Alley) is an accountant who's been sleeping with Albert (George Segal), a married client who can't bring himself to leave his wife. Even Mollie's pregnancy doesn't change his mind. But when Mollie goes into labor, she meets an interesting taxi driver (John Travolta).

Writer-director Amy Heckerling takes a clever idea and conveys it superbly. The voiceover works well because the filmmakers use the device for all it's worth, with Willis providing a voice for the child when it's a sperm, a fetus, and a baby. With his sarcastic delivery, Willis has the ideal voice for

the part. Alley and Travolta are affable enough, but the story itself is ordinary and merely passes time. Thanks to the ingenious voiceover, however, LOOK WHO'S TALKING is a genial, entertaining film, the enormous popularity of which led to two more mediocre installments, in 1990 and 1993.

LOOKING FOR MR. GOODBAR

1977 135m c Drama

Paramount (U.S.)

★★½ R

Diane Keaton (Theresa Dunn), Tuesday Weld (Katherine Dunn), William Atherton (James Morrissey), Richard Kiley (Mr. Dunn), Richard Gere (Tony Lopanto), Alan Feinstein (Professor Engle), Tom Berenger (Gary Cooper White), Priscilla Pointer (Mrs. Dunn), Laurie Prange (Brigid Dunn), Joel Fabiani (Barney)

p, Freddie Fields; d, Richard Brooks; w, Richard Brooks (based on the novel by Judith Rosner); ph, William A. Fraker (Panavision, Metrocolor); ed, George Grenville; m, Artie Kane; art d, Edward Carfagno; cos, Jodie Tillen

AAN Best Supporting Actress: Tuesday Weld; *AAN Best Cinematography:* William A Fraker

Brooks, hardly a great director, doesn't quite pull off this adaptation of the Rossner novel. Keaton is a repressed teacher of deaf-and-dumb children who lives under the thumb of her macho father, Kiley, and her let's-make-everything-nice mother, Pointer. She would love to be free of them, so she sets out to find "Mr. Right" but in all the wrong places. She haunts the singles bars and goes on a sexual voyage, sleeping with Atherton, a befuddled, sweet guy who loves her; Gere, a stud with sadistic tendencies that thrill her; and finally, Berenger, the insane bisexual who eventually takes her life. Keaton is shown existing in two worlds: the safety of school and home versus the madcap life of the swingers who stay up late, drowning their loneliness in stingers and sex. This is the other side of Hoffman and Farrow's JOHN AND MARY; we kept looking hard at the bar scenes to see if Dustin and Mia were in the background. There are many erotic scenes, but they are handled fairly well. Imagine Brian De Palma with the same script, and you'll realize how disgusting it could have been. Feinstein is excellent as Keaton's first lover, and Weld is sensational as Keaton's slightly dippy sister who is happy following whatever trend is au courant. LOOKING FOR MR. GOODBAR made lots of money and showed that Keaton, who had just scored in ANNIE HALL, could get out from under Woody Allen's wing and be a star on her own. An added plus is the score by Artie Kane, which evokes the solitude of living in a city with millions of people but still not having anyone with whom to really talk.

LORD JIM

1965 154m c Adventure

Columbia (U.K.)

DVD ★★★★

Peter O'Toole (Lord Jim), James Mason (Gentleman Brown), Curt Jurgens (Cornelius), Eli Wallach (The General), Jack Hawkins (Marlow), Paul Lukas (Stein), Akim Tamiroff (Schomberg), Daliah Lavi (The Girl), Ichizo Itami (Waris), Tatsuo Saito (Chief Du-Ramin)

p, Richard Brooks; d, Richard Brooks; w, Richard Brooks (based on the novel by Joseph Conrad); ph, Freddie Young (Super Panavision, Technicolor); ed, Alan Osbiston; m, Bronislau Kaper; prod d, Geoffrey Drake; art d, Bill Hutchinson, Ernest Archer; fx, Cliff Richardson; cos, Phyllis Dalton

This stunningly exotic film of Conrad's classic features O'Toole in the title role. He serves an apprenticeship at sea under the protective eye of Hawkins and later graduates to first officer of a tramp liner, the *Patna*, which carries religious passengers on an awful passage in which the ship is mercilessly lashed by a hurricane. In a moment of desperation, the idealistic O'Toole abandons the ship and leaves its passengers to their fate. The craft survives, although many of its passengers are drowned, and O'Toole loses his license and sinks into waterfront obscurity. To redeem himself, O'Toole agrees to take a shipment of dynamite from Lukas and deliver it to a tribe of natives in uncharted territory. The tribe is in bondage to oppressive warlord Wallach. Surviving ambushes and treachery from his own crew members, O'Toole manages to get the explosives to the settlement and hide the barrels, exploding one to make Wallach and his henchmen believe that the entire shipment has been destroyed. Wallach captures O'Toole and tortures him, but native girl Lavi helps him escape. He joins the natives and organizes an attack on the fortress, a seesaw battle that finally sees O'Toole and the natives triumph and Wallach killed. Jurgens, however, escapes to join river pirate Mason, and they muster their forces to return to the fortress to obtain Wallach's fabulous cache of jewels stolen from the natives. O'Toole greets the thieves with a cannon shot that decimates them, but the son of the native chief is killed in the encounter and, to make up for the death, O'Toole nobly sacrifices his own life at the finish. Beautifully photographed by Young and tightly directed by Brooks, LORD JIM is moving and suspenseful. Shot on location in Cambodia and Hong Kong.

LORD LOVE A DUCK   📀

1966 105m bw Comedy   ★★★
Charleston   (U.S.)

Roddy McDowall (Alan "Mollymauk" Musgrave), Tuesday Weld (Barbara Ann Greene), Lola Albright (Marie Green), Martin West (Bob Barnard), Ruth Gordon (Stella Barnard), Harvey Korman (Weldon Emmett), Sarah Marshall (Miss Schwartz), Lynn Carey (Sally Grace), Max Showalter, billed as Casey Adams (Howard Greene), Donald Murphy (Phil Neuhauser)

p, George Axelrod; d, George Axelrod; w, George Axelrod, Larry H. Johnson (based on a novel by Al Hine); ph, Daniel Fapp; ed, William Lyon; m, Neal Hefti; art d, Malcolm Brown; fx, Herman Townsley; cos, Paula Giokaris

A wacky satire/black comedy with high school senior McDowall helping schoolmate Weld get whatever she desires. McDowall's IQ is so high he knows what everyone wants before they speak. He gets Weld into the sorority of her choice and ensures she will get good grades by getting her a secretarial job with the high school principal, Korman. She meets West, a rich college senior, at a sex seminar at a drive-in church. Weld is tested for a beach party movie with West's help, but problems arise when West's mother, Gordon, doesn't approve of Weld. McDowall fixes that by introducing Gordon to booze. Weld's mother, Albright, kills herself when she thinks she has ruined her daughter's relationship and life. Weld and West marry and he becomes a marriage counselor. When he objects to his wife's movie career, McDowall decides to get rid of him. His attempts fail until he runs him over at the high school graduation with a bulldozer (killing everyone on the speaker's platform as well). The film is told in flashback with McDowall in the prison psychiatric wing telling his story to a tape recorder. Directed by the man who wrote THE SEVEN YEAR ITCH and WILL SUCCESS SPOIL ROCK HUNTER?

LORD OF THE FLIES   📀

1963 90m bw Science Fiction/Drama   ★★½
Allen/Hogdon/Two Arts   (U.K.)

James Aubrey (Ralph), Tom Chapin (Jack), Hugh Edwards (Piggy), Roger Elwin (Roger), Tom Gaman (Simon), The Surtees Twins (Sam and Eric), Roger Allen, David Brunjes, Peter Davy, Kent Fletcher

p, Lewis Allen; d, Peter Brook; w, Peter Brook (based on the novel by William Golding); ph, Tom Hollyman; ed, Peter Brook, Gerald Feil, Jean-Claude Lubtchansky; m, Raymond Leppard

Swat! A disappointing rendition of the Golding novel, routinely directed by Brook. With a war about to erupt, a plane carrying some wealthy British schoolboys is flown to the supposed safety of the South Pacific. The plane crashes on a remote island (the film was shot in Puerto Rico and Vieques in the Caribbean), none of the adults makes it to shore, and forty boys are left to fend for themselves. Since you all read the book in high school, you know that the boys split into two gangs and quickly descend to superstitious rituals and murder. Golding's haunting ruminations about the fine line between civilization and savagery are not done justice here. There are some vicious highlights, but the acting is wildly variable, and the film manages to be both overwrought and dull.

LORD OF THE RINGS: 📀
THE FELLOWSHIP OF THE RING, THE

2001 178m c   Fantasy/Adventure   ★★★★
Saul Zaentz Company/Wingnut Films/New Line   PG-13
(U.S./New Zealand)

Elijah Wood (Frodo Baggins), Ian McKellen (Gandalf), Viggo Mortensen (Aragorn—Strider), Sean Astin (Samwise "Sam" Gamgee), John Rhys-Davies (Gimli), Billy Boyd (Peregrin "Pippin" Took), Orlando Bloom (Legolas Greenleaf), Ian Holm (Bilbo Baggins), Sean Bean (Boromir), Christopher Lee (Saruman)

p, Peter Jackson, Barrie M. Osborne, Tim Sanders, Fran Walsh; d, Peter Jackson; w, Philippa Boyens, Peter Jackson, Fran Walsh (based on the novel by J.R.R. Tolkien); ph, Andrew Lesnie; ed, John Gilbert; m, Howard Shore; prod d, Grant Major; art d, Peter Jo Bleakley, Phil Ivey, Rob Outterside, Mark Robins; fx, Stephen Ingram, Jim Rygiel, Randall William Cook, Richard Taylor, Weta Digital; cos, Ngila Dickson, Richard Taylor

AA Best Cinematography: Andrew Lesnie; AA Best Makeup: Peter Owen, Richard Taylor; AA Best Original Score: Howard Shore; AA Best Visual Effects: Jim Rygiel, Randall William Cook, Richard Taylor; AAN Best Picture; AAN Best Supporting Actor: Ian McKellen; AAN Best Director: Peter Jackson; AAN Best Costume Design: Ngila Dickson, Richard Taylor; AAN Best Film Editing: John Gilbert; AAN Best Original Song: "May It Be Me"; Enya, Nicky Ryan, Roma Ryan; AAN Best Sound: Christopher Boyes, Michael Semanick, Gethin Creagh, Hammond Peek; AAN Best Adapted Screenplay: Fran Walsh, Philippa Boyens, Peter Jackson; AAN Best Art Direction: Grant Major, Dan Hennah

Devotees will surely quibble while others will staunchly resist anything involving elves, but New Zealand director Peter Jackson has taken the first volume of J.R.R. Tolkien's mythical beast and wrestled it into solid entertainment.

In the mystical land of Middle Earth, a variety of beings co-exist in relative harmony. There are diminutive hobbits; powerful forest elves; belligerent, cave-dwelling dwarves; and an assortment of humans. But there are also sinister forces, concentrated in the region of Mordor. In the legendary past, a ring was forged by the dark lord Sauron; its evil power helped his armies win a series of bloody battles, but a coalition of elves and human warriors defeated him. A human king captured the ring, but gave in to its malevolent allure and refused to destroy it. Lost for many lifetimes, the ring found its way into the gentle hands of hobbit Bilbo Baggins (Ian Holm), where it lay dormant. Bilbo is advised by wizard Gandalf (Ian McKellen) to pass it on to his nephew, Frodo Baggins (Elijah Wood). Gandalf, who knows evil is afoot, entrusts Frodo with the task of transporting it to Mount Doom, where it can be destroyed. Frodo's companions in this momentous journey include three stout-hearted hobbits (Sean Astin, Dominic Monaghan, Billy Boyd); a dwarf (John Rhys-Davies); an elfin archer (Orlando Bloom); a human warrior (Sean Bean), and an exiled king (Viggo Mortensen). Arrayed against them are scary mounted spectres, a nasty wizard (Christopher Lee), and—most frightening of all—their own worst impulses, which the ring magnifies and exploits.

Hokum? Yes, but it's top-of-the-line hokum; Tolkien knew his classic heroic quests and understood the heart of their enduring power. Jackson's film is richly imagined, cast with master thespians and youthful talents, and able to evoke an almost palpable sense of the will to power trapped within the ring. Without this, the entire enterprise would be pretty but precious drivel.

LORD OF THE RINGS: THE RETURN OF THE KING, THE 🖪 DVD

2003 210m c Fantasy/Adventure ★★★★
WingNut Films/Saul Zaentz Company/New Line R
(U.S./New Zealand)

Elijah Wood (*Frodo Baggins*), Ian McKellen (*Gandalf*), Liv Tyler (*Arwen*), Viggo Mortensen (*Aragorn*), Orlando Bloom (*Legolas*), Andy Serkis (*Gollum/Smeagol*), Sean Astin (*Samwise Gamgee*), Sean Bean (*Boromir*), John Rhys-Davies (*Gimli*), Bernard Hill (*King Theoden of Rohan*)

p, Peter Jackson, Barrie M. Osborne, Fran Walsh; d, Peter Jackson; w, Philippa Boyens, Peter Jackson (based on the novel by J.R.R. Tolkien); ph, Andrew Lesnie; ed, Jamie Selkirk; m, Howard Shore; prod d, Grant Major; art d, Grant Major, Dan Hennah; fx, Randall William Cook, Alex Funke, Joe Letteri, Jim Rygiel (visual effects), Richard Taylor; cos, Ngila Dickson, Richard Taylor

AA Best Picture; AA Best Director: Peter Jackson; *AA Best Adapted Screenplay:* Fran Walsh, Philippa Boyens, Peter Jackson; *AA Best Art Direction:* Grant Major (art direction), Dan Hennah (set decoration), Alan Lee (set decoration); *AA Best Sound Mixing:* Christopher Boyes, Michael Semanick, Michael Hedges, Hammond Peek; *AA Best Original Score:* Howard Shore; *AA Best Original Song:* "Into the West"; Fran Walsh, Howard Shore, Annie Lennox; *AA Best Costume Design:* Ngila Dickson, Richard Taylor; *AA Best Editing:* Jamie Selkirk; *AA Best Makeup:* Richard Taylor, Peter King; *AA Best Visual Effects:* Jim Rygiel, Joe Letteri, Randall William Cook, Alex Funke

The marathon conclusion to Peter Jackson's epic adaptation of J.R.R. Tolkien's fantasy trilogy is, like its predecessors, a spectacle of the first order. The balance of its 210-minute running time is weighted in favor of breathtaking battle sequences, but THE FELLOWSHIP OF THE RING and THE TWO TOWERS laid a firm foundation for the relationships that bind and divide the characters, and it's hard to imagine anyone going into this film without having seen its predecessors.

The fellowship of humans and fantastic beings dedicated to ridding Middle Earth of the ring of power forged by the Dark Lord Sauron has been sundered. Human prince Boromir (Sean Bean) is dead, and gentle hobbits Frodo (Elijah Wood) and Sam (Sean Astin) are making their painful way to the blasted land of Mordor, where the ring was forged and where it can be destroyed. Their guide, the cringing, duplicitous Gollum (Andy Serkis), has kept his promise to lead them safely through dangerous lands, but Sam suspects the creature is plotting against them. Wizard Gandalf (Ian McKellen), elfin archer Legolas (Orlando Bloom), belligerent dwarf Gimli (John Rhys-Davies), and dispossessed king Aragorn (Viggo Mortensen), meanwhile, are recovering in Rohan, where King Theoden (Bernard Hill) has just led his people to victory against an army of mutants, beasts and monsters at Helm's Deep. But Aragorn

must unite the diverse people of Middle Earth against Mordor if its dark forces are to be beaten back.

Jackson wraps up the strands of Tolkien's complicated story with alacrity, and despite its length, the film starts feeling long only at the end—or, more correctly, ends. Serious fans of the novels will be prepared for the serial codicils, but the uninitiated are likely to think the film is over several times before it actually is.

LORD OF THE RINGS: THE TWO TOWERS, THE 🖪 DVD

2002 170m c Fantasy/Adventure ★★★½
Saul Zaentz Company/WingNut Films/Lord PG-13
Zweite Productions/New Line
(U.S./New Zealand/Germany)

Elijah Wood (*Frodo Baggins*), Sean Astin (*Samwise "Sam" Gamgee*), Ian McKellen (*Gandalf*), Viggo Mortensen (*Aragorn*), Orlando Bloom (*Legolas*), Andy Serkis (*Voice of Gollum*), Billy Boyd (*Pippin*), Dominic Monaghan (*Merry*), Miranda Otto (*Eowyn*), Christopher Lee (*Saruman*)

p, Peter Jackson, Barrie M. Osborne, Fran Walsh; d, Peter Jackson; w, Philippa Boyens, Peter Jackson, Stephen Sinclair, Fran Walsh (based on the novel by J.R.R. Tolkien); ph, Andrew Lesnie; ed, Michael Horton, Jabez Olssen; m, Howard Shore; prod d, Grant Major; art d, Peter Joe Bleakley, Dan Hennah, Phil Ivey, Rob Otterside, Mark Robins, Alan Lee; fx, Jim Rygiel, Joe Letteri, Randall William Cook, Alex Funke, Richard Taylor; cos, Ngila Dickson, Richard Taylor

AA Best Sound Editing: Ethan Van der Ryn, Michael Hopkins; *AA Best Visual Effects:* Jim Rygiel, Joe Letteri, Randall William Cook, Alex Funke; *AAN Best Picture; AAN Best Art Direction:* Grant Major (Art Direction), Dan Hennah (Set Decoration), Alan Lee (Set Decoration); *AAN Best Film Editing:* Michael Horton; *AAN Best Sound:* Christopher Boyes, Michael Semanick, Michael Hedges, Hammond Peek

Picking up directly where THE LORD OF THE RINGS: THE FELLOWSHIP OF THE RING left off, this dark sequel plunges the band of hobbits, humans, dwarves, and elves assembled in the first film into a hellish landscape of war and waste.

Plucky hobbits Frodo (Elijah Wood) and Sam (Sean Astin) are traipsing towards the dark kingdom of Mordor, where Frodo must destroy the malevolent ring of power in the burning maw of Mount Doom before it falls into evil hands. The scrawny, desiccated Gollum (an amazing computer-generated creation, voiced by Andy Serkis), who once possessed the ring agrees to lead them. Meanwhile, fellow hobbits Merry (Dominic Monaghan) and Pippin (Billy Boyd) remain prisoners of the fearsome Uruk-hai, unnatural warrior beasts created by the wicked wizard Saruman (Christopher Lee) to destroy all human life in Middle-Earth. And in yet another location, warrior Aragorn (Viggo Mortensen) and his companions, Gimli (John Rhys-Davies) and Legolas (Orlando Bloom), are en route to the kingdom of Rohan, which lies directly in the path of the massive Uruk-hai army. Aided by the wizard Gandalf (Ian McKellen), now white-haired but otherwise unscathed by his apparently fatal encounter with a fire beast in the previous film, they join forces with King Theoden (Bernard Hill) to stop the Uruk-hai in their scaly-clawed tracks.

While the first film in Peter Jackson's epic adaptation of J.R.R. Tolkien's trilogy was weighted in favor of establishing characters, this second installment is heavy on battle sequences, which will thrill some viewers more than others. Several significant characters from the first film make token appearances, while many new players are added, including no-nonsense princess Eowyn (Miranda Otto), who might be a new love interest for Aragorn were it not for the fact that romantic love in Tolkien's tales is so often unrequited.

LORDS OF FLATBUSH, THE

DVD

1974 86m c Drama
Columbia (U.S.)

★★★
PG

Perry King *(Chico)*, Sylvester Stallone *(Stanley Rosiello)*, Henry Winkler *(Butchey Weinstein)*, Paul Mace *(Wimpy Murgalo)*, Susan Blakely *(Jane Bradshaw)*, Maria Smith *(Frannie Malincanico)*, Renee Paris *(Annie Yuckamanelli)*, Paul Jabara *(Crazy Cohen)*, Bruce Reed *(Mike)*, Frank Steifel *(Arnie)*

p, Stephen Verona; d, Stephen Verona, Martin Davidson; w, Stephen Verona, Martin Davidson, Gayle Gleckler, Sylvester Stallone; ph, Joseph Mangine, Edward Lachman (Technicolor); ed, Stan Siegel, Muffie Meyer; m, Joe Brooks, Paul Jabara, Joseph Nicholas; art d, Glenda Miller

Anyone who grew up in the Brooklyn of the 1950s will recognize the essential honesty of this picture, but it might as well be taking place in Korea for everyone else. The rambling movie with a good mix of drama and comedy served to introduce several actors who went on to much greater fame in other movies. The Lords of Flatbush is the name of a tough street gang but not one of those groups that pillage and vandalize. Rather, it is a social club, one of thousands that once were found in Brooklyn. (The small area of Coney Island alone had at least a dozen, including The Mariners, The Acwans [*A Club without a Name* acronym], the Emanons [*Nonames* backwards], et al). Stallone and King are best pals in Brooklyn's Flatbush area (and is there an uglier name for a neighborhood?). Codirector Verona must like the area because he used it for BRIGHTON BEACH. Stallone gets his girlfriend, Smith, pregnant and then takes her to a local jewelry shop to buy a ring. King's girlfriend is Blakely (while she was still "Susie" and not Susan), but she eventually dumps him. Several small but compelling incidents serve truly to represent life in Brooklyn. The film is a character piece that wanders from place to place with no single impetus, although one gets the feeling that this technique is intentional. The actors who distinguished themselves later include Blakely; Winkler ("Happy Days"); Armand Assante (I, THE JURY); Ray Sharkey (THE IDOLMAKER); Dolph Sweet ("Gimme a Break"); Jabara (who became a songwriter and won an Oscar); and, of course, Stallone, who was making his leading-man debut after an unbilled bit in Woody Allen's BANANAS and a few roles in films that will never reach a Saturday matinee for kids. Codirector Verona eventually became one of the prime movers of music video as well as a best-selling artist in his own right. Brooks did the music with some help from Nicholas and Jabara. Brooks will be best remembered (or forgotten) for scripting, producing, directing, and writing the song for YOU LIGHT UP MY LIFE.

LORENZO'S OIL

DVD

1992 135m c Drama
Kennedy-Miller Productions (U.S.)

★★★½
PG-13

Nick Nolte *(Augusto Odone)*, Susan Sarandon *(Michaela Odone)*, Peter Ustinov *(Professor Nikolais)*, Zack O'Malley Greenburg *(Lorenzo)*, Kathleen Wilhoite *(Deirdre Murphy)*, Gerry Bamman *(Doctor Judalon)*, Margo Martindale *(Wendy Gimble)*, James Rebhorn *(Ellard Muscatine)*, Ann Hearn *(Loretta Muscatine)*, Maduka Steady *(Omouri)*

p, George Miller, Doug Mitchell; d, George Miller; w, George Miller, Nick Enright; ph, John Seale; ed, Richard Francis-Bruce, Marcus D'Arcy, Lee Smith; prod d, Kristi Zea; art d, Dennis Bradford; cos, Colleen Atwood

AAN Best Actress: Susan Sarandon; *AAN Best Original Screenplay:* George Miller

An unusual piece of work that combines almost thriller-style suspense with an intelligent, neo-documentary approach to its harrowing subject.

The film is based on the true story of Augusto and Michaela Odone (Nick Nolte and Susan Sarandon), whose five-year-old outside, Lorenzo, is diagnosed as having a rare, fatal disease that is literally eating away his brain. Rather than accept the medical verdict, Lorenzo's parents become amateur research scientists, devoting their lives to finding a way of keeping him alive.

The film's highest achievement is its honest, uncompromising presentation of unconditional love. In the later stages of Lorenzo's disease, when he seems to have lost any grip on the world outside, Augusto hesitantly suggests that his son may no longer have a "soul": his brain has deteriorated so far that he is no longer capable of thought or emotion. Isn't there a point, we ask ourselves, when a person ceases to be a person, and we should stop feeling for them as we once did? For Lorenzo's mother, the question does not even bear consideration. She condemns anyone who fails to share her zeal to some lower moral plane, banishing not only two capable nurses, but her own sister, from the house when they question the unqualified ardor of her crusade.

Sarandon makes Mrs. Odone compelling, yet largely unsympathetic. We don't just applaud as she and her husband take on, and defeat, the bureaucracy of the medical establishment; we also recoil from her pious, pedantic self-righteousness. It's a brave, complex performance, and the centerpiece of an emotionally searing film.

LOS OLVIDADOS

1950 88m bw Drama
Tepeyac (Mexico)

★★★★★

Estela Inda *(The Mother)*, Alfonso Mejia *(Pedro)*, Roberto Cobo *(Jaibo)*, Jesus Navarro *(The Lost Boy)*, Miguel Inclan *(The Blind Man)*, Alma Fuentas *(The Young Girl)*, Francisco Jambrino *(The Principal)*, Hector Portillo, Salvador Quiros, Victor Manuel Mendoza

p, Oscar Dancigers; d, Luis Bunuel; w, Luis Bunuel, Luis Alcoriza; ph, Gabriel Figueroa; ed, Carlos Savage; m, Gustavo Pittaluga

After a strange interlude of nearly two decades of critical obscurity, one of the great masters of the cinema returned to the public eye with this gripping combination of gritty realism and disorienting surrealism. Set in the slums of Mexico City, this is Luis Bunuel's brutally clear-eyed account of "The Forgotten Ones," the reckless youth whose dismal marginal existence has become a deadly web from which they cannot extract themselves. Bunuel adopts many of the trappings of the popular form of the liberal social problem drama to tell his story but his goals are different. Rather than blaming all of the misery of these young people on their grim social conditions, he utilizes surrealism to expose the psychological underpinnings of their condition as he zeroes in on their dreams and sexuality. The result is a film that is realistic yet dreamy, heartrendingly sad yet subversively funny. There are no easy heroes or villains in this tough film. Bunuel also deftly avoids the sentimentalism that often afflicts this form.

At the film's core is the relationship between Pedro (Alfonso Mejia) and Jaibo (Roberto Cobo), two youths who live in Mexico's most disease-ridden urban slum. Jaibo, the older of the two, is already set in his ways, his selfish, vicious nature leading him to take advantage of those less fortunate than himself. As the film opens, he has just been released from jail and immediately returns to take control of the gang of boys who hang out in the streets and commit senseless acts of violence—not for money but for the pleasure of seeing the less fortunate suffer. The boy most eager to follow and please Jaibo is the childlike Pedro, whose innocent eyes reveal a spark of goodness lacking in the others.

The roots of this film extend back to LAS HURDES, Bunuel's devastating (yet also peversely amusing) 1932 documentary about the wretched living conditions in Spain's poorest region. There is also a vigorous nod to the Italian neo-realists; LOS OLVIDADOS is, as celebrated French critic Andre Bazin called it, "a film that lashes the mind like a red-hot iron and leaves one's conscience no opportunity for rest." Rarely have such squalor and savagery been displayed so unsentimentally, for Bunuel, who has a deep love for his characters, refuses to judge or pity them. Bunuel was named Best Director at the 1951 Cannes Film Festival, an award richly deserved.

LOST HIGHWAY

1997 135m c Horror/Crime/Drama ★★★½
Lost Highway Productions/Asymmetrical Features/ R
CiBy 2000 (U.S./France)

Bill Pullman *(Fred Madison)*, Patricia Arquette *(Renee Madison/Alice Wakefield)*, Balthazar Getty *(Pete Dayton)*, Robert Blake *(Mystery Man)*, Natasha Gregson Wagner *(Sheila)*, Robert Loggia *(Mr. Eddy/Dick Laurent)*, Gary Busey *(Bill Dayton)*, Richard Pryor *(Arnie)*, John Roselius *(Al)*, Lou Eppolito *(Ed)*

p, Deepak Nayar, Tom Sternberg, Mary Sweeney; d, David Lynch; w, David Lynch, Barry Gifford; ph, Peter Deming; ed, Mary Sweeney; m, Angelo Badalamenti, Barry Adamson; prod d, Patricia Norris; fx, Ann Kroeber-Splet (sound effects); cos, Patricia Norris

A lavishly beautiful, eerily violent, feature-length "Twilight Zone" episode, filtered—not entirely successfully—though the sensibilities of director David Lynch and his WILD AT HEART collaborator, Barry Gifford.

Sax player Fred Madison (Bill Pullman) and his slinky, auburn-tressed wife Renee (Patricia Arquette) are stalked by a video camera-carrying creepy-crawler who prowls through their house and films them in their sleep, then deposits the tapes on their doorstep. All very mysterious—until Madison gets sent to death row for killing Renee and changes inexplicably into someone named Pete Dayton (Balthazar Getty). Pete begins an affair with noir-ish, blue-nailed gangster's slut Alice Wakefield (Arquette again), and the whole thing spins off into some sort of chic, "isn't this *decadent?*" spookshow. This time, it's not the Devil who's in the details (he's prowling around in the person of Robert Blake in chalky, CABARET-era Joel Grey whiteface): it's the fun. Lovecraftian shadows on the wall; NATURAL BORN KILLERS-style montages, featuring shock-rockers Marilyn Manson and Twiggy Ramirez writhing in the neon slime; a just-plain-horrifying cameo by the wheelchair-bound Richard Pryor; the late Jack Nance; John Waters's gutter-diva Mink Stole; and tattooed rock-boy Henry Rollins. The look is to die for and the soundtrack is drop-dead cool, but there's something distastefully synthetic (as well as a bit sophomoric) about the proceedings. As to the story, it goes off-road the moment Pullman is transformed into the sullen Getty and it never comes back. Ultimately it's hypnotic but frustrating, much like Lynch's previous feature, TWIN PEAKS: FIRE WALK WITH ME.

LOST HONOR OF KATHARINA BLUM, THE

(DIE VERLORENE EHRE DER KATHARINA BLUM)
1975 104m c Drama ★★★★
Orion/WDR/Bioskop/Paramount (West Germany) R

Angela Winkler *(Katharina Blum)*, Mario Adorf *(Beizmenne)*, Dieter Laser *(Werner Toetgess)*, Heinz Bennent *(Dr. Blorna)*, Hannelore Hoger *(Trude Blorna)*, Harald Kuhlmann *(Moeding)*, Karl Heinz Vosgerau *(Alois Straubleder)*, Jurgen Prochnow *(Ludwig Goetten)*, Rolf Becker *(Hach)*, Regine Lutz *(Else Woltersheim)*

p, Eberhard Junkersdorf; d, Volker Schlondorff, Margarethe von Trotta; w, Volker Schlondorff, Margarethe von Trotta (based on the novel by Heinrich Boll); ph, Jost Vacano (Eastmancolor); ed, Peter Przygodda; m, Hans Werner Henze

Codirected by Volker Schlondorff and Margarethe von Trotta, this adaptation of the Heinrich Boll novel capably depicts the author's themes and structure on-screen. The title character (Angela Winkler), a housekeeper and model citizen, suddenly finds herself the victim of an unorthodox police investigation and media assault after a brief affair with a bank-robbing anarchist (Jurgen Prochnow) who is wanted by the police. Before her troubles began, Katharina had been respected by her employers, the Blornas (Heinz Bennent and Hannelore Holger), for her efficiency, and by her friends for her level head. Her calm and uneventful life is made a shambles when she's taken into custody, and becomes the target of a ruthless reporter (Dieter Laser) who stops at nothing (including a grueling interview with her dying mother) to dig up dirt, and labels Katharina a Communist conspirator. The story unfolds as a series of small revelations about the suspect, providing various conflicting viewpoints of her character. While this method may be too cold and distancing to evoke much audience empathy, it is effective in creating the oppressive atmosphere the story requires. Winkler's performance is equally cool, as a woman who seems incapable of revealing her emotions. An Americanized made-for-TV version, THE LOST HONOR OF KATHRYN BECK, appeared in 1984 starring Marlo Thomas and Kris Kristofferson.

LOST HORIZON

1937 138m bw Science Fiction/ ★★★★
Fantasy/Adventure
Columbia (U.S.)

Ronald Colman *(Robert Conway)*, Jane Wyatt *(Sondra)*, Edward Everett Horton *(Alexander P. Lovett)*, John Howard *(George Conway)*, Thomas Mitchell *(Henry Barnard)*, Margo *(Maria)*, Isabel Jewell *(Gloria Stone)*, H.B. Warner *(Chang)*, Sam Jaffe *(High Lama)*, Hugh Buckler *(Lord Gainsford)*

p, Frank Capra; d, Frank Capra; w, Robert Riskin (based on the novel by James Hilton); ph, Joseph Walker; ed, Gene Havlick, Gene Milford; m, Dimitri Tiomkin; art d, Stephen Goosson; fx, Roy Davidson; Ganahl Carson; cos, Ernest Dryden

AAN Best Picture; AAN Best Supporting Actor: H.B. Warner; AA Best Film Editing: Gene Havlick, Gene Milford; AAN Best Score: Columbia Studio Music Department, Morris Stoloff (Dept. Head); AA Best Interior Decoration: Stephen Goosson; AAN Best Sound Recording: John Livadary; AAN Best Assistant Director: C.C. Coleman Jr.

Frank Capra's classic romantic fantasy leaves the standard "Capraesque" middle-class milieu of most of his most beloved masterpieces for a vividly realized world of strange adventure and fantasy. Faithfully adapted from James Hilton's popular novel, the film opens as Robert Conway (Colman), a gallant but world-weary British diplomat, author and Far Eastern historian, comes to the aid of some refugees from a

Chinese revolution. The group takes off in a small passenger plane, the motley collection including Conway's younger, impressionable brother (Howard); a swindler on the lam (Mitchell); a tubercular prostitute (Jewell); and a fussy, fossil-hunting scientist (Horton). Conway notices that the plane is not headed for safety but climbing into the snow-topped Himalayas and into Tibet, "the Roof of the World." Moreover, the passengers discover that the pilot is not the European they had believed him to be, but an Asian. The plane crashes and the passengers struggle out of it, but awaiting them is the beautiful, snowless, sun-filled world known as the Valley of the Blue Moon, looking down upon the majestic landscapes that make up the lamasery of Shangri-La. Taken to a magnificent structure and given luxurious rooms, the Europeans soon discover the marvelous tranquility of this hidden, unknown land where nothing is known of greed, war, hatred or crime.

LOST HORIZON came to epitomize its audience's image of Utopia. Capra's paradise on earth—with its pure air, bright sun and untroubled centuries of blissful life—became so entrenched in the public imagination that *Shangri-La* became a household word. Though Hilton wrote the novel (published in 1933) in six weeks, Capra took two years to transfer the tale to celluloid. The magnificent Shangri-La set constructed by art designer Stephen Goosson was the largest ever built in Hollywood. For two months, 150 workmen labored to build the 1,000-foot-long, 500-foot-wide lamasery, with its deep flights of marbled stairs and huge patio, broad terraces, rich gardens, lily-coated pools, and main building influenced by art deco and Frank Lloyd Wright. Little Columbia Studios and its tough boss, Harry Cohn, staggered under the burden of the film's $2.5 million cost, which amounted to half of the company's entire yearly budget.

All of the painstaking care Capra took with LOST HORIZON shows; the film is directed with swift pace, inventive shots, and splendid acting. Capra was at a high point in his career. Two reels were eliminated after a problematic preview screening. LOST HORIZON was released in a cut version at 118 minutes to universal applause. Columbia had itself a box-office blockbuster which returned many millions to its depleted coffers and remained popular in re-release for decades. Everything about LOST HORIZON reflects quality work, from Robert Riskin's bright and literate script to Dimitri Tiomkin's stirring music, the outstanding special effects and Joseph Walker's evocative soft-focus photography.

LOST IN AMERICA

1985 91m c Comedy 📀 ★★½
Geffen (U.S.) R

Albert Brooks (*David Howard*), Julie Hagerty (*Linda Howard*), Tom Tarpey (*Brad Tooley*), Gary K. Marshall (*Casino Manager*), Maggie Roswell (*Patty*), Ernie Brown (*Pharmacist*), Art Frankel (*Employment Agent*), Joey Coleman (*Skippy*), Donald Gibb (*Ex-Convict*), Sylvia Farrel (*Receptionist*)

p, Marty Katz; d, Albert Brooks; w, Albert Brooks, Monica Johnson; ph, Eric Saarinen (Technicolor); ed, David Finfer; m, Arthur B. Rubinstein; prod d, Richard Sawyer; fx, Richard Albain Jr.; cos, Cynthia Bales

Just when it seemed Albert Brooks had gotten his creative energies under control, along comes this intermittently funny, often overdone comedy that could have been a classic. Brooks is an ad man expecting to get a senior VP stripe. His main worries are how to furnish the new $450,000 house he is about to occupy and how to satisfy his wife, Julie Hagerty, who is complaining that she is bored with the regimentation of their lives. Brooks is shocked when his boss tells him the veep job has gone to someone else and that Brooks will, instead, be transferred to New York. Brooks storms out of the office and then persuades Hagerty to quit her job. They have no children, and they have money saved up; this is their chance to do what everyone wants

to do, get lost in America and have a grand time. They sell everything, buy a huge motor home, and leave. It would be a perfect trip except that they get romantically remarried in Las Vegas, and that is the beginning of the end. If a moral exists here, it's that you can't win. Brooks and Hagerty are excellent, and it's good to see Brooks giving someone else a few moments on the screen. Somewhere, underneath all of the indulgence, beats the heart of a filmmaker.

LOST IN TRANSLATION

2003 105m c Romance/Comedy 📀 ★★★½
Tohokushinsha/American Zoetrope/Elemental Films R
(U.S.)

Bill Murray (*Bob Harris*), Scarlett Johansson (*Charlotte*), Giovanni Ribisi (*John*), Anna Faris (*Kelly*), Akiko Takeshita (*Ms. Kawasaki*), Catherine Lambert (*Jazz Singer*)

p, Sofia Coppola, Ross Katz; d, Sofia Coppola; w, Sofia Coppola; ph, Lance Acord; ed, Sarah Flack; m, Brian Reitzell, Kevin Shields; prod d, K.K. Barrett, Anne Ross; art d, Mayumi Tomita; cos, Nancy Steiner

AAN Best Picture; AA Best Original Screenplay: Sofia Coppola; AAN Best Actor: Bill Murray; AAN Best Director: Sofia Coppola

Lightweight and a bit of a let-down, Sofia Coppola's follow-up to the marvelous VIRGIN SUICIDES is a gently nuanced, two-character comedy revolving around the unlikely romance of an older, disaffected actor and an aimless young woman, set almost entirely in Tokyo's Park Hyatt Hotel.

Like many other American celebrities who slip off to foreign countries to appear in commercials they hope will never be seen at home, middle-aged movie star Bob Harris (Bill Murray) arrives in Tokyo to star in an ad campaign for Suntory whisky. Jet-lagged and depressed over where his career has taken him—he knows he should be home appearing in plays rather than collecting a $2 million paycheck for a few days of easy, albeit humiliating, work—Bob spends his downtime in his room, fielding faxes and FedEx packages from his wife, or in the hotel bar, throwing back drinks and avoiding fans. Insomnia, culture shock, and Tokyo's disorienting riot of sounds and images—a few of them his own—only exacerbate Bob's alienation. Twenty-two-year-old Yale grad Charlotte (Scarlett Johansson) is facing a life crisis of her own in the hermetically sealed rooms of the Park Hyatt. Left alone by her husband, John (Giovanni Ribisi), a celebrity photographer who's off on assignment, Charlotte listens to self-help CDs and wonders what she should be doing with her life. Charlotte can't sleep either, and also finds Tokyo a bewildering experience. She meets Bob in the safety of the hotel bar, and despite their differences, their mutual isolation and the odd, artificial circumstances of hotel life draw them together and a tentative romance begins.

Johansson is a wonderfully talented young actress, and Coppola allows Murray to improvise on top of his more serious, RUSHMORE persona. But the film never really transcends its simple situation and seems oddly unembarrassed by its provincial attitude towards a foreign culture. Coppola shows us Japan solely through the eyes of her characters, who see the Japanese as cartoonishly infantile, infatuated with asinine TV shows, karaoke and silly video games. It can be funny, but the humor is too often based in stereotypical perceptions of Asians (they're short, laughably polite, and eat weird food), and Coppola shamelessly invites us to laugh along with Murray's character, who, believe it or not, thinks it's hilarious when his hosts get their "r"s and "l"s switched.

LOST PATROL, THE

1934 74m bw War ★★★½
RKO (U.S.)

Victor McLaglen (The Sergeant), Boris Karloff (Sanders), Wallace Ford (Morelli), Reginald Denny (George Brown), J.M. Kerrigan (Quincannon), Billy Bevan (Herbert Hale), Alan Hale (Cook), Brandon Hurst (Bell), Douglas Walton (Pearson), Sammy Stein (Abelson)

p, Cliff Reid; d, John Ford; w, Dudley Nichols, Garrett Fort (based on the novel Patrol by Philip MacDonald); ph, Harold Wenstrom; ed, Paul Weatherwax; m, Max Steiner; art d, Van Nest Polglase, Sidney Ullman

AAN Best Score: RKO Radio Studio Music Department, Max Steiner (Dept. Head)

A strange and fascinating film, John Ford's THE LOST PATROL gives a sense of impending doom from frame to frame, but is nevertheless an absorbing adventure drama. The story concerns a British cavalry patrol in the Mesopotamian desert during WWI. A single shot rings out and their leader, an officer, falls dead from his horse, his face buried in the sand. With him goes the knowledge of their mission's purpose and even the direction in which the patrol is traveling. The unnamed sergeant (Victor McLaglen) who takes over finds nothing in the officer's map case to indicate where they are, and tells his men that the officer kept everything in his head. He leads the group to an oasis, but the men find themselves under occasional sniper fire from the Arabs who have surrounded them and lie in wait, out of sight in the stretching dunes. The soldiers—except for the sergeant—never see the Arabs, and this insidious enemy takes on an almost mythic character as, one by one, the British are picked off until only the sergeant, Morelli (Wallace Ford), and Sanders (Boris Karloff) are left, desperately trying to stay alive. Shot on location in the desert around Yuma, Arizona, THE LOST PATROL is a much superior remake of a like-titled 1929 British silent film that featured Agnew McMaster in Karloff's role and Cyril McLaglen, Victor's brother, as the sergeant.

LOST WEEKEND, THE

1945 101m bw Drama ★★★★½
Paramount (U.S.)

Ray Milland (Don Birnam), Jane Wyman (Helen St. James), Phillip Terry (Nick Birnam), Howard da Silva (Nat the Bartender), Doris Dowling (Gloria), Frank Faylen (Bim), Mary Young (Mrs. Deveridge), Anita Sharp Bolster (Mrs. Foley), Lilian Fontaine (Mrs. St. James), Lewis L. Russell (Charles St. James)

p, Charles Brackett; d, Billy Wilder; w, Charles Brackett, Billy Wilder (based on the novel by Charles R. Jackson); ph, John Seitz; ed, Doane Harrison; m, Miklos Rozsa, Giuseppe Verdi; art d, Hans Dreier, Earl Hedrick; fx, Gordon Jennings; cos, Edith Head

AA Best Picture; AA Best Actor: Ray Milland; AA Best Director: Billy Wilder; AA Best Screenplay: Charles Brackett, Billy Wilder; AAN Best B/W Cinematography: John F. Seitz; AAN Best Film Editing: Doane Herrison; AAN Best Score (Drama or Comedy): Miklos Rozsa

One of the most justly celebrated "problem films" of the 1940s. Though hailed in its time as a great advance in screen seriousness, this film just barely missed being shelved. The script by the noted team of Wilder and Brackett is dispassionate and unrelenting but also occasionally poetic. The film's emotional power is greatly abetted by Seitz's evocative black-and-white cinematography, ranging from unvarnished realism to delirious Expressionism. Finally, Milland's virtuoso work as the hopeless alcoholic is surprising, shocking and utterly riveting.

Don (Milland) is a struggling writer who waters down his writer's block with booze. The film opens with the camera zooming through the window of a New York apartment building which Don shares with his responsible brother Nick (Terry, Mr. Joan Crawford No. 3), who is about to go away for the weekend. Nick is somewhat worried about leaving his brother alone, but Don assures him that he will be settling down to do some serious writing. It's all downhill from there.

THE LAST WEEKEND is candid and brilliantly conceived from shot to shot. Wilder builds his film slowly and utilizes low-key lighting and deep-focus photography to emphasize objects that suggest the menace of alcohol, with scenes photographed through shot-glasses and bottles. A likable lead of light comedy and romance, Milland initially felt unequipped to handle such a serious role, but his wife encouraged him to try it. He was also encouraged by the fact that Wilder and Brackett had never had a flop. Faylen, though only onscreen for a few moments, makes an indelible impact as a bitchy male nurse in the sanitarium. Wyman forever escaped dumb blonde roles with her work here, and da Silva is excellent as a conscientious bartender.

Oddly, Paramount executives took one look at the finished film and told Wilder they were seriously considering not releasing it. They had received an avalanche of protest from temperance advocates who felt the film would encourage drinking. Powerful lobbyists for the liquor industry offered as much as $5 million for the negative of the film so it could be destroyed. But, at Wilder's urgings, Paramount released the film on a limited engagement in New York City, and the critics fell all over themselves praising it. It eventually became one of Paramount's biggest hits of 1945.

LOST WORLD: JURASSIC PARK, THE 📀

1997 134m c Action/Fantasy/Adventure ★★★½
Amblin Entertainment/Universal (U.S.) PG-13

Jeff Goldblum (Dr. Ian Malcolm), Julianne Moore (Dr. Sarah Harding), Pete Postlethwaite (Roland Tembo), Arliss Howard (Peter Ludlow), Richard Attenborough (John Hammond), Vince Vaughn (Nick Van Owen), Vanessa Lee Chester (Kelly Curtis), Peter Stormare (Dieter Stark), Harvey Jason (Ajay Sidhu), Richard Schiff (Eddie Carr)

p, Gerald R. Molen, Colin Wilson; d, Steven Spielberg; w, David Koepp (based on the novel The Lost World, by Michael Crichton); ph, Janusz Kaminski; ed, Michael Kahn; m, John Williams; prod d, Rick Carter; art d, Jim Teegarden, Lauren Polizzi, Paul Sonski; fx, Dennis Muren (full motion dinosaurs), Stan Winston (live action dinosaurs), Michael Lantieri (dinosaur effects), Ned Gorman (visual effects producer), Industrial Light & Magic, Kevin Rafferty (CG supervisor), Vicki L. Engel (senior effects coordinator), Randal M. Dutra; cos, Sue Moore (supervisor)

AAN Best Visual Effects: Dennis Muren, Stan Winston, Randal M. Dutra, Michael Lantieri

"It always starts this way," mutters Dr. Ian Malcolm (Jeff Goldblum) darkly, as his companions ooh and ahh at the sight of real live dinosaurs, "Then there's running and there's screaming." THE LOST WORLD gets right to the running and the screaming.

Twinkly-eyed old capitalist John Hammond (Richard Attenborough) summons Malcolm to tell him that, contrary to what he may have thought, the dinosaurs aren't all dead. There's another island, and—miracle of miracles—nature has found a way around that inbred lysine deficiency that was supposed to ground the genetically engineered colossi. Hammond has sent Malcolm's girlfriend (Julianne Moore) to see how they're doing, and would like Malcolm to take a small crew to check up on her. But Hammond's renegade relative, Peter Ludlow (Arliss Howard), is planning a corporate killing and has brought his own band of mercenaries, led by Great White Hunter Roland Tembo (Pete Postlethwaite), to round up some dinos. Naturally, it all goes terribly, terribly wrong.

The sequel features many more dinosaurs than the first film, and most of its narrative effort is channeled into getting the cast into the proper place from which to be plucked by one scaly set of jaws after another. To that end, seasoned hunters must venture far, far from the group to urinate and, after explaining how the Tyrannosaurus Rex can pick up a scent 10 miles away, brilliant scientists must then traipse through the jungle wearing clothing saturated with blood. "That is the worst idea ever in the sorry history of bad ideas," Malcolm says only once, but the sentiment hangs over many plot developments—not the least of which is the plan to take a very large prehistoric predator to California. Didn't *any* of these guys see KING KONG? A second sequel, JURASSIC PARK III, hit theaters in the summer of 2001.

LOVE ACTUALLY   DVD

2003   128m   c   Romance/Comedy   ★★★½
Working Title Films/DNA Films/StudioCanal   R
(U.K./U.S./France)

Alan Rickman *(Harry)*, Bill Nighy *(Billy Mack)*, Colin Firth *(Jamie)*, Emma Thompson *(Karen)*, Hugh Grant *(David, The Prime Minister)*, Laura Linney *(Sarah)*, Liam Neeson *(Daniel)*, Martine McCutcheon *(Natalie)*, Keira Knightley *(Juliet)*, Rodrigo Santoro *(Karl)*

p, Tim Bevan, Eric Fellner, Duncan Kenworthy; d, Richard Curtis; w, Richard Curtis; ph, Michael Coulter; ed, Nick Moore; m, Craig Armstrong; prod d, Jim Clay; art d, Rod McLean, Justin Warburton-Brown; fx, Richard Conway; cos, Joanna Johnston

You could take the measure of this ensemble film by its weakest elements, but why be churlish? A cast of fine actors commit their considerable talents to a sharply crafted series of interconnected stories that illustrate love in all its forms.

The newly elected prime minister (Hugh Grant) falls in love with Natalie (Martine McCutcheon), a slightly plump girl at the bottom rung of 10 Downing Street's household staff. Blissful newlyweds Peter (Chiwetel Ejiofor) and Juliet (Keira Knightley) can't figure out why Peter's best friend, artist Mark (Andrew Lincoln), treats Juliet like sour milk. Cuckolded during Peter and Juliet's wedding, mystery novelist Jamie (Colin Firth) falls for the Portuguese cleaning lady (Lucia Moniz) at his French retreat. Mark's friend Mia (Heike Makatsch) is hell-bent on seducing her boss, Harry (Alan Rickman), and sees the company Christmas party as the perfect opportunity. Harry's wife, Karen (Emma Thompson), the PM's sister, suspects their marriage is cooling. Harry encourages employee Sarah (Laura Linney), who's been nursing a crush on handsome officemate Karl (Rodrigo Santoro), to make a move, but she puts her demanding, mentally ill brother first. Newly widowed Daniel (Liam Neeson), Karen's best friend, tries to help his 11-year-old stepson, Sam (Thomas Sangster), navigate the choppy waters of puppy love. And the background to all their entanglements is forgotten '70s pop star Billy Mack's (Bill Nighy) comeback bid, which involves reworking a treacly love song into an even sappier Christmas song.

Sentimental? To be sure. Contrived? That too. Overstuffed? Indeed. But FOUR WEDDINGS AND A FUNERAL screenwriter Richard Curtis's directing debut is frequently funny, generally fizzy, and occasionally piercingly perceptive about the price love exacts. And it gives underrated character actor Nighy the role of a lifetime in the self-centered and secretly sentimental Mack, which alone is reason to celebrate.

LOVE AFFAIR   DVD

1939   87m   bw   Comedy/Romance   ★★★★
RKO   (U.S.)

Irene Dunne *(Terry McKay)*, Charles Boyer *(Michel Marnet)*, Maria Ouspenskaya *(Grandmother Janou)*, Lee Bowman *(Kenneth Bradley)*, Astrid Allwyn *(Lois Clarke)*, Maurice Moscovich *(Maurice Cobert)*, Scotty Beckett *(Boy on Ship)*, Bess Flowers, Harold Miller *(Couple on Deck)*, Joan Leslie *(Autograph Seeker)*

p, Leo McCarey; d, Leo McCarey; w, Delmer Daves, Donald Ogden Stewart (based on a story by McCarey, Daves, Mildred Cram); ph, Rudolph Mate; ed, Edward Dmytryk, George Hively; m, Roy Webb; art d, Van Nest Polglase, Al Herman; fx, Vernon L. Walker; cos, Howard Greer, Edward Stevenson

AAN Best Picture; AAN Best Actress: Irene Dunne; *AAN Best Supporting Actress:* Maria Ouspenskaya; *AAN Best Original Story:* Mildred Cram, Leo McCarey; *AAN Best Song:* "Wishing"; Buddy De Sylva (Music & Lyrics); *AAN Best Interior Decoration:* Van Nest Polglase (Art Direction), Al Herman (Art Direction)

A superb romance, the film deftly mixes humor with pathos and passion, and takes us on an emotional voyage that never fails to please. Michel (Boyer) is engaged to Lois (Allwyn), and Terry (Dunne) is engaged to Ken (Bowman) when the two meet onboard ship, but their mutual attraction is instant. The two flirt, but soon realize that this is not merely a shipboard fling; there is much more to their feelings about each other. They resolve to meet in six months at the top of the Empire State Building if they still feel the same way about each other. Tragedy strikes Terry on her way to meet Michel, but don't worry—"wishing will make it so."

There are many wonderful moments in the picture, both comedic and touching. As the couple takes its leave of Michel's grandmother (the magnificent Ouspenskaya), Terry suddenly rushes back to embrace the old woman, and Michel can't help but fall in love with her. As the "other man" and "other woman," Bowman and Allwyn are refreshingly adult and sympathetic, and Boyer and Dunne play beautifully together. The first half of the picture is breezy, witty and chic, but, while the second has a decidedly more serious tone, we never have the feeling that they are divided. Reportedly, the writers were scripting new pages every day. If that's true, more power to director McCarey who brought spontaneity rather than jumpiness to his direction. Look for veteran TV actor Gerald Mohr in a tiny extra bit and Joan Leslie, in her fourth film, at the age of 14. Decently remade as AN AFFAIR TO REMEMBER, with Deborah Kerr and Cary Grant.

LOVE AND DEATH   DVD

1975   85m   c   Comedy/War   ★★★★
UA   (U.S.)   PG

Woody Allen *(Boris Dimitrovich Grushenko)*, Diane Keaton *(Sonja)*, Georges Adet *(Old Nehamkin)*, Frank Adu *(Drill Sergeant)*, Edmond Ardisson *(Priest)*, Feodor Atkine *(Mikhail)*, Albert Augier *(Waiter)*, Yves Barsacq *(Rimsky)*, Lloyd Battista *(Don Francisco)*, Jack Berard *(Gen. Lecoq)*

p, Charles H. Joffe; d, Woody Allen; w, Woody Allen; ph, Ghislain Cloquet (Deluxe Color); ed, Ralph Rosenblum, Ron Kalish; m, Sergei Prokofiev; art d, Willy Holt; fx, Kit West; cos, Gladys De Segonzac

LOVE AND DEATH, Woody Allen's hilarious satire of classic Russian literature, might properly be described as Tolstoy meets the Marx Bros., as he and Diane Keaton get caught up in an uproariously funny plot to assassinate Napoleon in 1812.

In 19th-century Russia, Boris Grushenko (Woody Allen) falls in love with his beautiful cousin Sonja (Diane Keaton), but she's in love with his brother Ivan (Henry Czarniak). When Ivan announces his engagement to another woman, Sonja marries an elderly herring merchant, and Boris reluctantly joins the Russian army to fight Napoleon. Boris becomes an accidental hero after hiding in a cannon which destroys the enemy camp. Meanwhile, Sonja's husband dies and Boris proposes to her. Sonja accepts, believing Boris will surely be killed in an upcoming duel, but he survives and the two are married. Sonja eventually comes to love Boris, but when Napoleon again invades Russia, Sonja talks Boris into assassinating him. Disguised as the Spanish ambassador and his sister, Sonja and Boris manage to arrange an audience with Napoleon (James Tolkan), but are unaware that he is actually a double who has been substituted to protect the real Emperor.

LOVE AND DEATH was the first film which truly marked Woody Allen's growth from a stand-up comic and talented, but amateur, filmmaker, to a mature and original comedic director. It was a transitional film, coming between earlier shtick-filled movies such as BANANAS (1971) and his later, adult-oriented ones like ANNIE HALL (1977) and MANHATTAN (1979). LOVE AND DEATH successfully synthesizes Allen's penchant for inspired lunatic gags with his desire to broaden the scope of his films, by parodying the entire school of gloomy and portentous Russian novels with sophisticated wit and style. He also mixes in some priceless Groucho-esque wisecracks, along with other artistic and cultural references, including homages to Sergei Eisenstein (utilizing Prokofiev's score from ALEXANDER NEVSKY; quoting an image from THE BATTLESHIP POTEMKIN), and the Bob Hope costume-drama parodies which Allen has acknowledged as inspiration (particularly MONSIEUR BEAUCAIRE). Technically, the film is one of Allen's most accomplished, handsomely filmed in Hungary and France by Ghislain Cloquet (who had shot a number of Robert Bresson's films), which helps make the hysterical anachronistic sight gags stand out even more.

LOVE AND DEATH ON LONG ISLAND   📀

1998 93m   c   Drama/Comedy   ★★★
Skyline/Imagex   (U.K./Canada)   R

John Hurt *(Giles De'Ath)*, Jason Priestley *(Ronnie Bostock)*, Fiona Loewi *(Audrey)*, Sheila Hancock *(Mrs. Barker)*, Maury Chaykin *(Irving Buckmuller)*, Gawn Grainger *(Henry)*, Elizabeth Quinn *(Mrs. Reed)*, Linda Busby *(Mrs. Abbott)*, Bill Leadbitter *(Eldridge)*, Ann Reid *(Maureen)*

p, Steve Clark-Hall, Christopher Zimmer; d, Richard Kwietniowski; w, Richard Kwietniowski (from the novel by Gilbert Adair); ph, Oliver Curtis; ed, Susan Shipton; m, The Insects, Richard Grassby-Lewis; prod d, David McHenry; cos, Andrea Galer

Death in Venice on Long Island's East End.

Reclusive English widower Giles De'Ath (John Hurt)—that's DAY-ath, thank you—a poetry scholar, has spent his life immersed in the 19th century: televisions, answering machines, microwave ovens, and faxes are to him like science-fiction marvels of tomorrow. Caught one day in a sudden downpour, De'Ath ventures into the local cinema where a nice, arty E.M. Forster movie is playing. But fate directs him to the wrong theater, and he instead sees "Hotpants College II," whereupon the veil is lifted from his eyes. In the amiable person of American teen idol Ronnie Bostock (Jason Priestly), De'Ath sees a contemporary embodiment of the Romantic ideals to which he's devoted his life. He examines Bostock's oeuvre as he would the poetry of Rimbaud or Baudelaire, then heads for Long Island in hopes of meeting the man himself.

No question, the conceit is more than a little precious. And the true nature of De'Ath's interest in the virile Ronnie Bostock is obvious to viewers long before it's clear to either

man, resulting in a very high squirm factor. But the interactions between the raspy-voiced Hurt and various shallowly cheerful Americans are genuinely charming and dynamic: the mailman, taxi drivers, the proprietor of local dive *Chez D'Irv*, and motel owners all take him at face value, accepting his eccentricities as without malice, and indeed they are. Former *Beverly Hills, 90210* heartthrob Jason Priestley acquits himself quite respectably, and not just because he's mostly called upon to play a callow actor of no conspicuous talent. He resists the impulse to overplay when he's meant to be acting badly, and in his key scene with Hurt he manages to evoke a series of genuinely complex emotions.

LOVE CRAZY

1941 97m   bw   Comedy   ★★★★
MGM   (U.S.)

William Powell *(Steven Ireland)*, Myrna Loy *(Susan Ireland)*, Gail Patrick *(Isobel Grayson)*, Jack Carson *(Ward Willoughby)*, Florence Bates *(Mrs. Cooper)*, Sidney Blackmer *(George Hennie)*, Vladimir Sokoloff *(Dr. Klugle)*, Kathleen Lockhart *(Mrs. Bristol)*, Sig Rumann *(Dr. Wuthering)*, Donald MacBride *("Pinky" Grayson)*

p, Pandro S. Berman; d, Jack Conway; w, William Ludwig, Charles Lederer, David Hertz (based on a story by David Hertz, William Ludwig); ph, Ray June; ed, Ben Lewis; m, David Snell; art d, Cedric Gibbons

William Powell and Myrna Loy, who made over a dozen films together (six as the "Thin Man" characters Nick and Nora Charles), are romantically teamed again in this breakneck farce. This time, they're a happily married couple about to celebrate their fourth wedding anniversary. Unfortunately, their domestic tranquility is shattered when Loy's battleaxe mother (Bates) arrives for a visit, sprains an ankle, and extends her stay a lot longer than had been anticipated. Mother dearest soon misconstrues a conversation between her son-in-law and an old flame (Patrick), the perfect wife wants a divorce, and hubby must do anything he can—from pretending to be insane to dressing up as his own sister—to hang onto his marriage.

Featuring several superb set pieces and a great supporting cast, LOVE CRAZY has more slapstick than the verbal wit that usually characterized Powell and Loy's films, but there is also enough raillery to satisfy lovers of sophisticated dialogue. As usual Loy and Powell play beautifully together, and Powell is hilarious in drag. The final scene, with Loy and her "sister-in-law" about to go to bed together, is amusingly contemporary in its humor.

LOVE IS THE DEVIL: STUDY FOR A PORTRAIT OF   📀
FRANCIS BACON

1998 90m   c   Biography/Drama   ★★★½
BBC Films/British Film Institute/BBC Films/Premiere   R
Heure/Uplink/Arts Council of England/Partners in
Crime/State .   (U.K.)

Derek Jacobi *(Francis Bacon)*, Daniel Craig *(George Dyer)*, Tilda Swinton *(Muriel Belcher)*, Anne Lambton *(Isabel Rawsthorne)*, Adrian Scarborough *(Daniel Farson)*, Karl Johnson *(John Deakin)*, Annabel Brooks *(Henrietta Moraes)*, Richard Newbold *(Blonde Billy)*, Ariel De Ravenel *(French Official)*, Tallulah *(Ian Board)*

p, Chiara Menage; d, John Maybury; w, John Maybury; ph, John Mathieson; ed, Daniel Goddard; m, Ryuichi Sakamoto; prod d, Alan MacDonald; art d, Christina Moore; fx, Alan Church, Simon Giles; cos, Annie Symons

It's not a pretty picture, but painter Francis Bacon—who depicted the human form as distorted lumps of flesh, tooth, bone, and gristle—was never very interested in pretty. In this brilliant, stylistic tour de force, writer-director John Maybury offers a scathing portrait of the tormented artist, designed in the style of Bacon's own grotesque visions.

The film focuses on Bacon's life during the 1960s, and the years he spent with George Dyer, an ex-con who served as model, lover, and deeply troubled muse. Francis (Derek Jacobi, bearing a striking resemblance to the real-life Bacon) first meets George (Daniel Craig) when the would-be burglar tumbles down the rabbit hole of the artist's own private hell: intending to rob the place, George comes through the skylight of Francis's London studio. He winds up spending the next seven years by Francis's side, much to the savage amusement of the artist's pub-crawling art-world cronies, including photographer John Deakin (Karl Johnson) and Muriel Belcher (a fully transformed Tilda Swinton), the caustic proprietor of the Colony Room, one of Bacon's haunts. But George is prey to demons of his own—terrifying nightmares, debilitating paranoia, and an uncontrollable death wish—and as Francis continues to gain international acclaim, George begins to unravel.

Maybury's film is a harrowing examination of artistic and emotional interdependency, and he's unsparing in his depiction of Bacon as heartlessly self-serving, dishing up all the lurid details of the artist's masochistic sexual obsessions. But Maybury steers clear of facile psychologizing, offering instead Bacon at work amid the legendary chaos of his studio, slashing at his canvases with brushes, hands, and even a garbage can lid. Jacobi's and Craig's performances are both gut-wrenching and startlingly raw, and the whole film, thanks in large part to John Mathieson's inspired cinematography, has the frightening look of a Bacon canvas come to life.

LOVE JONES   📀DVD
1997 109m c   Romance/Comedy   ★★★
Jones Motion Picture Company/Addis-Wechsler   R
and Associates/New Line   (U.S.)

Larenz Tate (Darius Lovehall), Nia Long (Nina Mosley), Isaiah Washington (Savon Garrison), Lisa Nicole Carson (Josie Nichols), Khalil Kain (Marvin Cox), Leonard Roberts (Eddie Coles), Bernadette L. Clarke (Sheila Downes), Bill Bellamy (Hollywood), Cerall Duncan (Troy Garrison), David Nisbet (Publisher)

p, Nick Wechsler, Jeremiah Samuels; d, Theodore Witcher; w, Theodore Witcher; ph, Ernest Holzman; ed, Maysie Hoy; m, Darryl Jones; prod d, Roger Fortune; art d, Cydney Harris; fx, Sam Barkan; cos, Shawn Barton

In this romantic comedy, writer-director Theodore Witcher elects to trade glib one-liners and contrived situations for real discussions about love and relationships, and the ways in which people can sometimes find both in spite of themselves.

After Darius Lovehall (Larenz Tate) and Nina Mosley (Nia Long) meet at a Chicago jazz club, they embark on a bumpy relationship that is initially based on their undeniable sexual attraction. Nina decides to go back with her ex-fiancee, Marvin (Khalil Kain), in order to be sure of her feelings. In the meantime, Darius initiates a shallow relationship during Nina's absence. It doesn't take long for Nina to remember why her engagement to Marvin fell apart, and she soon returns to Darius only to find him with another woman. Feeling betrayed, Nina reluctantly accepts a date offer from one of Darius's friends, Hollywood (Bill Bellamy). 'Wood, however, is just interested in showing up Darius. Nina quickly dumps 'Wood and ends up trying it again with Darius. By basing this second attempt on love rather than sex, their relationship begins to grow in a whole different direction, but their future together contains at least one more breakup...

Though not entirely free of the clichés common to romantic comedies, LOVE JONES separates itself from the pack by concentrating on the kind of real issues that people often put between themselves and happiness. Director Witcher assembles a fine cast of supporting characters including Bellamy,

Isaiah Washington, and Lisa Nicole Carson, that help these scenes work. Unfortunately, the main plot thread—Darius and Nina—is not nearly as interesting as the conversations and musings encountered along the way. Still, the film is a fresh and mature look at modern relationships.

LOVE ME OR LEAVE ME   📀DVD
1955 122m c   Musical/Biography   ★★★★
MGM   (U.S.)

Doris Day (Ruth Etting), James Cagney (Martin "The Gimp" Snyder), Cameron Mitchell (Johnny Alderman), Robert Keith (Bernard V. Loomis), Tom Tully (Frobisher), Harry Bellaver (Georgie), Richard Gaines (Paul Hunter), Peter Leeds (Fred Taylor), Claude Stroud (Eddie Fulton), Audrey Young (Jingle Girl)

p, Joe Pasternak; d, Charles Vidor; w, Daniel Fuchs, Isobel Lennart (based on the story by Fuchs); ph, Arthur E. Arling (Eastmancolor, Cinemascope); ed, Ralph E. Winters; m, Percy Faith (for Doris Day); art d, Cedric Gibbons, Urie McCleary; fx, Warren Newcombe; chor, Alex Romero; cos, Helen Rose

AAN Best Actor: James Cagney; AA Best Motion Picture Story: Daniel Fuchs; AAN Best Screenplay: Daniel Fuchs, Isobel Lennart; AAN Best Score (Musical): Percy Faith, George Stoll; AAN Best Song: "I'll Never Stop Loving You"; Nicholas Brodszky (Music), Sammy Cahn (Lyrics); AAN Best Sound Recording: Wesley C. Miller

Unlike many musical bios of the day, LOVE ME OR LEAVE ME provides a hard-edged love story, augmented with Jazz Age tunes, chronicling the life and times of Prohibition-era torch singer Ruth Etting. This was a once-in-a-lifetime role for Doris Day, who is terrific as Etting in a part unlike any other she played, calling for her to be alternately sizzling in performance and naive offstage. James Cagney is equally sensational as Marty "The Gimp" Snyder, the ruthless gangster who was her Svengali, and normally lightweight Cameron Mitchell excels as Harry Myrl Alderman (called Johnny in the film), Etting's true love. Snyder, a powerful Chicago racketeer, sees Etting at a dime-a-dance club. She wants to be a singer, so Marty pushes the owner into giving her a small singing bit. Club pianist Alderman helps her develop her talents, and, with Snyder's aid, Etting eventually becomes a headliner, going on to radio and a spot in the Ziegfeld Follies in New York. When Etting grows increasingly independent of Snyder, however, he tears up her Ziegfeld contract and takes her on tour, then to movie stardom in Hollywood. There, Alderman resumes subtly courting her, but Snyder has manipulated her into marrying him, and Etting takes to drink over having to live with a man she does not love.

The chemistry between Cagney and Day is electric, Charles Vidor's direction is lively and inventive, and the overall production lavishly and accurately reproduces the 1920s era. The Jazz Age music is outstanding, superbly performed by Day. (Our favorite? "Ten Cents a Dance.") MGM paid $50,000 for the song rights alone, as well as hefty sums to Etting, Alderman, and Snyder for the rights to film their lives. Etting later noted that "they took a lot of liberties with my life, but I guess they usually do with that kind of thing." Metro made back the money upon the film's release, however, when it was enthusiastically received by both critics and audiences.

LOVE ME TONIGHT   📀DVD
(MAREZ-MOI CE SOIR!)
1932 104m bw   Musical/Comedy   ★★★★★
Paramount   (U.S.)

Maurice Chevalier (Maurice Courtelin), Jeanette MacDonald (Princess Jeanette), Charlie Ruggles (Vicomte Gilbert de Vareze), Charles Butterworth (Count de Savignac), Myrna Loy (Countess Vantine), C. Aubrey Smith (The Duke), Elizabeth Patterson, Ethel

Griffies, Blanche Frederici *(Aunts)*, Joseph Cawthorn *(Dr. Armand de Fontinac)*

p, Rouben Mamoulian; d, Rouben Mamoulian; w, Samuel Hoffenstein, Waldemar Young, George Marion Jr. (based on the play "Tailor in the Chateau" by Leopold Marchand, Paul Armont); ph, Victor Milner; ed, William Shea; art d, Hans Dreier; cos, Edith Head, Travis Banton

Love it forever. Along with SWING TIME and perhaps one of Busby Berkeley's best, this film stands as the greatest musical of the 1930s and one of the finest ever. Although the film seems very much in a Lubitsch vein, Rouben Mamoulian directed it, and he is perhaps most responsible for its stunning appeal. His earliest period in film (1929-34) was certainly his greatest and in this film he displays such audacity in playing with sound and image that it's no wonder he frightened everyone in Hollywood.

The tale of a romance between Princess Jeanette (MacDonald) and Maurice the tailor (Chevalier), LOVE ME TONIGHT is effervescent frippery to be sure, but it's so inventive as to be downright eerie. The slow-motion retreat from the lovers' cottage still astounds and Jeanette's final ride on horseback to stop a train is dramatically quite striking. One is not likely to forget the dark shadows of Chevalier's "I'm an Apache" number or the cutting and framing of both the title duet and the witty "The Son of a Gun Is Nothing But a Tailor." Jeanette's three worrisome aunts could almost be comic variants of the witches in MACBETH and, at one point, they sound like a kennel in an uproar. The film mocks those very conventions the genre employs, from the famous traveling rendition of "Isn't It Romantic?" to the sudden thud of a ladder which ends Jeanette's balcony reverie.

The cast, too, is quite remarkable, and they make the most of the saucy pre-Code antics. Ruggles's mad dash in his underwear and Butterworth's "I fell flat on my flute" demonstrate comic diffidence of the highest caliber. In what is almost certainly her most memorable role before achieving stardom, Loy plies her smooth comic touch and gets to add a naughtiness she usually wasn't allowed later. Her man-crazy Vantine displays a freshness partly inspired by Mamoulian and Loy's creating the part as they went along. When someone is ill and she is asked, "Could you go for a doctor?" she instantly replies, "Oh, yes, send him in." The starring duo, meanwhile, enjoy one of their greatest partnerings here. Though we like some of her later films with Nelson Eddy, the genial, risque tension between Chevalier and MacDonald works as deliciously as vodka in orange juice. MacDonald is not sufficiently appreciated for her wonderful comic flair and Mamoulian is bold enough to simply toss off her spirited rendition of "Lover" in long shot, knowing that her play with both an uncooperative horse and the ending of the verses will be funnier that way. She matches the winking Frenchman innuendo for innuendo and her carefully stylized, sexy performance fits perfectly within the film's magnificent sense of hypberbole. Finally, the incomparable Chevalier knows exactly what he's up to as well here. Not conventional leading man material, he's both beautifully tongue-in-cheek and utterly sincere. His naughtiness avoids the puerile and the nasty, yet he can get more out of his signature song "Mimi" than any lyricist can write.

LOVE ON THE RUN   📀
(L'AMOUR EN FUITE)
1979 94m   c   Drama/Comedy   ★★★½
Carosse   (France)   PG

Jean-Pierre Leaud *(Antoine Doinel)*, Marie-France Pisier *(Colette)*, Claude Jade *(Christine)*, Dani *(Liliane)*, Dorothee *(Sabine)*, Rosy Varte *(Colette's Mother)*, Marie Henriau *(Divorce Judge)*, Daniel Mesguich *(Xavier the Librarian)*,

Julien Bertheau *(M. Lucien)*, Jean-Pierre Ducos *(Christine's Lawyer)*

d, Francois Truffaut; w, Francois Truffaut, Marie-France Pisier, Jean Aurel, Suzanne Schiffman; ph, Nestor Almendros; ed, Martine Barraque; m, Georges Delerue; art d, Jean-Pierre Kohut-Svelko

LOVE ON THE RUN is the fifth and final entry in Francois Truffaut's "Antoine Doinel" series, which began in 1959 with THE 400 BLOWS. By now the young, unpredictable Antoine (Jean-Pierre Leaud) has grown into a man of 34, able to reminisce about his past loves and put them into his new book. The picture opens with the unshaven Antoine and his newest love, Sabine (Dorothee, in a wonderful debut performance), awakening to a sunny morning—the morning that he is to get a divorce from his wife, Christine (Claude Jade, from 1971's BED AND BOARD). Before the day is over Antoine also encounters his first love, Colette (Marie-France Pisier, who appeared years before in Truffaut's episode of LOVE AT TWENTY). There is actually very little in LOVE ON THE RUN that resembles a story. Its chief purpose is simply to look back at the women Antoine has loved. Like so many of Truffaut's characters, Antoine is obsessed with the desire to love, and here he tells how he found a ripped-up, discarded picture of Sabine in a phone booth and set out to find her. In the process, clips are shown from THE 400 BLOWS; LOVE AT TWENTY; STOLEN KISSES; and BED AND BOARD, amounting to an overview of the life of Doinel (as well as those of both Leaud and Truffaut). For those who haven't seen any of the previous "Doinel" pictures, LOVE ON THE RUN will probably be a difficult picture to sit through, but for those who have followed the growth of these characters, the film is a true charmer. In keeping with other Truffaut films, LOVE ON THE RUN includes a superb score from Georges Delerue and a perfectly hummable title song from Alain Souchon.

LOVE PARADE, THE
(PARADE D'AMOUR)
1929 107m   bw   Musical/Comedy   ★★★½
Paramount   (U.S.)

Maurice Chevalier *(Count Alfred Renard)*, Jeanette MacDonald *(Queen Louise)*, Lupino Lane *(Jacques)*, Lillian Roth *(Lulu)*, Edgar Norton *(Major Domo)*, Lionel Belmore *(Prime Minister)*, Albert Roccardi *(Foreign Minister)*, Carl Stockdale *(Admiral)*, Eugene Pallette *(Minister of War)*, E.H. Calvert *(Sylvanian Ambassador)*

p, Ernst Lubitsch; d, Ernst Lubitsch; w, Ernest Vajda, Guy Bolton (based on the play "The Prince Consort" by Leon Xanrof, Jules Chancel); ph, Victor Milner; ed, Merrill White; art d, Hans Dreier

AAN Outstanding Production: ; *AAN Best Actor:* Maurice Chevalier; *AAN Best Director:* Ernst Lubitsch; *AAN Best Cinematography:* Victor Milner; *AAN Best Interior Decoration:* Hans Dreier (Art Direction); *AAN Best Sound Recording:* Franklin Hansen

Students of film lore will find much to enjoy in THE LOVE PARADE. It was Ernst Lubitsch's first sound film, Jeanette MacDonald's debut, Maurice Chevalier's second picture, and the first of three that the director made with these leads. (The others were ONE HOUR WITH YOU, THE MERRY WIDOW.) The featherweight story takes place in mythical Sylvania, where Queen Louise (MacDonald) is desperately lonely for male companionship. Count Alfred Renard (Chevalier), her emissary to France, has been cavorting so conspicuously that she has recalled him to Sylvania. Summoned to Louise's bedchamber so she can check out what endears him to so many women, Alfred is quickly wedded to his Queen. Problems arise when the chauvinistic Count finds his role as consort intolerable, and the battle for the throne is on.

Lubitsch adapted to the requirements of sound film with ease, and the execution of the frail plot is insouciant and bubbly. The film's sexual politics are typical of its era, though a great deal of satiric ribbing takes place before the inevitable finale. The film differed from the many backstage musicals of the day in that its musical numbers advanced, rather than stopped, the action. Chevalier and MacDonald, both expert at risque material, play beautifully together, and are in fine voice as well. Their singing highlights include his "Paris, Stay the Same" and the amusing soliloquy "Nobody's Using It Now" and her rendition of "Dream Lover." The priceless Lupino Lane and Lillian Roth steal many scenes as palace servants, and team up for the delightful "Let's Be Common." Look for the scene where Chevalier ends up showing his "collection" of guns and garters.

LOVE STORY

1970 99m c Romance   *DVD*
Paramount (U.S.)   ★★
                                        GP

Ali MacGraw *(Jenny Cavilleri)*, Ryan O'Neal *(Oliver Barrett IV)*, Ray Milland *(Oliver Barrett III)*, Katharine Balfour *(Mrs. Oliver Barrett III)*, John Marley *(Phil Cavilleri)*, Russell Nype *(Dean Thompson)*, Sydney Walker *(Dr. Shapely)*, Robert Modica *(Dr. Addison)*, Walker Daniels *(Ray)*, Tommy Lee Jones *(Hank)*

p, Howard G. Minsky; d, Arthur Hiller; w, Erich Segal (based on the novel by Erich Segal); ph, Dick Kratina (Movielab Color); ed, Robert C. Jones; m, Francis Lai; art d, Robert Gundlach; cos, Alice Manougian Martin, Pearl Somner

AAN Best Picture; AAN Best Actor: Ryan O'Neal; *AAN Best Actress:* Ali MacGraw; *AAN Best Supporting Actor:* John Marley; *AAN Best Director:* Arthur Hiller; *AAN Best Original Story and Screenplay:* Erich Segal; *AA Best Original Score:* Francis Lai

"Love means never having to say you're sorry" was the catch phrase that helped make this a huge grosser, but we're sorry anyone ever fell in love with this script. LOVE STORY is actually better than Segal's previously released best-seller (written from his screenplay in order to promote the film). But then that's not saying much.

Wistful Oliver (O'Neal) is at Harvard (of course) in his final pre-law year, when he meets and falls for tragic Jenny (MacGraw), a music student at Radcliffe (where else?). She's a rude mite from a lower-class family, and he is one of the Boston Brahmins. You can guess the rest. O'Neal and MacGraw go together like applesauce spread on sandpaper, and the rest of the cast (except John Marley) comes across as a series of caricatures. Milland, in particular, as Oliver's snotty father, acts like a billiard ball in a business suit. By the time O'Neal gets around to intoning the famous tag line, you'll be so sick of hearing Francis Lai's love theme that you'll want to strangle the projectionist. Too bad MacGraw's already bitten the dust. Paging DARK VICTORY.

LOVE STREAMS

1984 141m c Drama   ★★★★
MGM (U.S.)   PG-13

Gena Rowlands *(Sarah Lawson)*, John Cassavetes *(Robert Harmon)*, Diahnne Abbott *(Susan)*, Seymour Cassel *(Jack Lawson)*, Margaret Abbott *(Margarita)*, Jakob Shaw *(Albie Swanson)*, Michele Conway *(Agnes Swanson)*, Eddy Donno *(Stepfather Swanson)*, Joan Foley *(Judge Dunbar)*, Al Ruban *(Milton Kravitz)*

p, Menahem Golan, Yoram Globus; d, John Cassavetes; w, Ted Allan, John Cassavetes (based on the play by Allan); ph, Al Ruban (Metrocolor); ed, George Villasenor; m, Bo Harwood; art d, Phedon Papamichael; cos, Jennifer Smith-Ashley

With Israeli filmmakers Golan and Globus watching over him, director John Cassavetes was guilty of less self-indulgence than usual, and the result is one of his best movies ever. Appearing for the first time in a movie that he also directed, Cassavetes and real-life spouse Gena Rowlands team up as a brother and sister, Robert Harmon and Sarah Lawson. The screen exudes their intensity; and despite their apparently different personalities, a oneness of spirit unites them. Robert is a well-known author, who is researching a book on prostitution and becomes the den father to some lively ladies of the evening. His research takes him on nightly forays to the underbelly of town. Sarah is a delicate creature in the throes of a divorce and custody battle against her husband, Jack (Seymour Cassel). The intercutting of the two stories contrasts the tawdriness of Robert's life to the exemplariness of Sarah's. For half the movie we see their separate lives and wonder when and if they will get together. Rowlands is wonderfully convincing in her many opportunities to play unusual scenes. Cassavetes also has his moments. More an amalgam of telling bits and pieces than a real story, this movie (like so many of Cassavetes' works) goes on too long. This time, however, it all seems to work.

LOVE WITH THE PROPER STRANGER

1963 102m bw Comedy/Drama   ★★★★
Boardwalk/Rona (U.S.)

Natalie Wood *(Angie Rossini)*, Steve McQueen *(Rocky Papasano)*, Edie Adams *(Barbie, Barbara of Seville)*, Herschel Bernardi *(Dominick Rossini)*, Tom Bosley *(Anthony Colombo)*, Harvey Lembeck *(Julio Rossini)*, Penny Santon *(Mama Rossini)*, Virginia Vincent *(Anna)*, Nick Alexander *(Guido Rossini)*, Augusta Ciolli *(Mrs. Papasano)*

p, Alan J. Pakula; d, Robert Mulligan; w, Arnold Schulman; ph, Milton Krasner; ed, Aaron Stell; m, Elmer Bernstein; art d, Hal Pereira, Roland Anderson; cos, Edith Head

AAN Best Actress: Natalie Wood; *AAN Best Original Story and Screenplay:* Arnold Schulman; *AAN Best B/W Cinematography:* Milton Krasner; *AAN Best Art Direction-Set Decoration (B/W):* Hal Pereira (Art Direction), Roland Anderson (Art Direction), Sam Comer (Set Decoration), Grace Gregory (Set Decoration); *AAN Best Costume Design (B/W):* Edith Head

Wood plays a sort of female Marty in this role that netted the actress her third Oscar nomination. She is a quiet, well-brought-up Italian girl in a situation that is more than she can handle. She is so quiet, well-brought-up, and Italian, in fact, that it's hard to imagine how she got into this mess! How does a sweet, traditional type manage to find herself pregnant after a one-night stand with McQueen? And what do you do when the father-to-be has a girlfriend and the expectant mother's unknowing family keep pushing her to marry another man?

The theme of unmarried pregnancy had been seen often before (e.g., in BLUE DENIM) but was not usually handled so deftly as in this picture, which not only dares to deal with the subject of abortion but has lots of down-to-earth, Italian humor from Bosley, Lembeck, and Bernardi. Adams is outstanding as McQueen's stripper girlfriend. She always had a way with comedy and showed it early when playing the foil for her genius husband, Ernie Kovacs. In small roles, look for Richard Mulligan, Arlene Golonka, Vic Tayback, and Richard Dysart, all of whom later achieved success on TV. Not perfect, but touching and adult; with fine work from the two leads, this is one of Mulligan's better films.

LOVED ONE, THE
1965 116m bw Comedy ★★★★
MGM (U.S.)

Robert Morse (Dennis Barlow), Jonathan Winters (Wilbur Glenworthy/Harry Glenworthy), Anjanette Comer (Aimee Thanatogenos), Rod Steiger (Mr. Joyboy), Dana Andrews (Gen. Brinkman), Milton Berle (Mr. Kenton), James Coburn (Immigration Officer), John Gielgud (Sir Francis Hinsley), Tab Hunter (Guide), Margaret Leighton (Mrs. Kenton)

p, John Calley, Haskell Wexler; d, Tony Richardson; w, Terry Southern, Christopher Isherwood (based on the novel by Evelyn Waugh); ph, Haskell Wexler; ed, Anthony Gibbs; m, John Addison; prod d, Rouben Ter-Arutunian; art d, Sydney Z. Litwack; fx, Geza Gaspar; cos, Nat Tolmach, Rouben Ter-Arutunian, James Kelly, Marie T. Harris

This spoof of morticians and funerals captures much of the macabre hilarity in the Waugh novel but failed to impress critics at the time of release. It often sinks into broad burlesque due to Southern and Isherwood's heavy-handed script, but the laughs are still there. Morse, a naive, rather gawky character from England, visits his uncle, Gielgud, an aging, fussy art director living in a dilapidated Hollywood mansion. When his studio fires him, Gielgud hangs himself. Robert Morley, head of the British community of Hollywood talent, arrives and instructs Morse to arrange to have Gielgud buried at Whispering Glades Memorial Park (the real-life Forest Lawn), the most resplendent funeral grounds in America, run by Winters. In the process of contacting morticians, Morse obtains a job at a pet cemetery run by Winters' twin brother (also played by Winters), and the various schemes, scams, and lack of concern by morticians for both humans and pets are revealed in all their callous glories. A host of bizarre characters then parade through Morse's life, including Comer, a sultry, naive beauty he covets and who is lusted after by Winters (the one running the high-class mortuary) and Steiger, a crackpot cosmetologist who works with her. Comer is repelled by Steiger's obese and gluttonous mother and is almost won over by Morse who reads poetry (stolen from Steiger) to her. Then Comer's ideals are smashed by Winters, head of Whispering Glades, when he tries to seduce her, and she commits suicide by injecting herself with embalming fluid. A further plot develops when Morse discovers that Winters, in collusion with Andrews, an Air Force general, plans to get rid of all the bodies on his property by sending them into space, so he can transform his cemetery into a luxurious spa for retirees, making even more millions. He is foiled by Morse who replaces the body of a dead astronaut, the first to be shot into space, with Comer's comely corpse. Having exposed Winters and sent him to ruin, Morse returns to England to try to forget his morbid, morose, and strange experience in America. Morse is unappealing, but the supporting players, especially Winters, and bits performed by Stander, Coburn, and Hunter are very funny.

LOVERS, THE
(LES AMANTS)
1959 90m bw Drama ★★★
Nouvelle Editions des Films (France)

Jeanne Moreau (Jeanne Tournier), Alain Cuny (Henri Tournier), Jean-Marc Bory (Bernard Dubois-Lambert), Judith Magre (Maggy Thiebaut-Leroy), Jose-Luis de Vilallonga (Raoul Flores), Gaston Modot (Coudray), Patricia Garcin (Catherine, Jeanne's Daughter), Claude Mansard (Marcelot), Georgette Lobbe (Marthe)

d, Louis Malle; w, Louis Malle, Louise de Vilmorin (based on the novel Point de Lendemain by Dominique Vivant); ph, Henri Decae (Dyaliscope); ed, Leonide Azar; m, Johannes Brahms, Alain de Rosnay; prod d, Bernard Evein, Jacques Saulnier

Notorious for its extended seminude love-making scene when first released in 1959, Louis Malle's THE LOVERS seems tame today when compared with average "R" rated films of the decades following it. The film tells the simple tale of Moreau, a bored mother and wife, who meets, falls in love with, and sleeps with young archaeologist Bory—all in the course of one evening. The next morning she abandons her family and runs off with her new lover to an uncertain future. The film was vastly overrated due to the censorship it incurred overseas and in the U.S. (A suburban Cleveland theater manager was prosecuted for showing an obscene film. The case went to the Supreme Court and was eventually thrown out.) The film is a solid but not great examination of female mid-life crisis, with Moreau in typically fine form.

LOVERS AND OTHER STRANGERS
1970 104m c Comedy ★★★½
ABC (U.S.) R

Gig Young (Hal Henderson), Bea Arthur (Bea Vecchio), Bonnie Bedelia (Susan Henderson), Anne Jackson (Cathy), Harry Guardino (Johnny), Michael Brandon (Mike Vecchio), Richard Castellano (Frank Vecchio), Bob Dishy (Jerry), Marian Hailey (Brenda), Joseph Hindy (Richie)

p, David Susskind; d, Cy Howard; w, Renee Taylor, Joseph Bologna, David Zelag Goodman (based on the play by Joseph Bologna, Renee Taylor); ph, Andrew Laszlo (Metrocolor); ed, David Bretherton, Sidney Katz; m, Fred Karlin; prod d, Ben Edwards; cos, Albert Wolsky

AAN Best Supporting Actor: Richard Castellano; AAN Best Adapted Screenplay: Renee Taylor, Joseph Bologna, David Zelag Goodman; AA Best Original Song: "For All We Know"; Fred Karlin (Music), Robb Royer (Lyrics), James Griffin (Lyrics), Arthur James (Lyrics)

A well-done, multifaceted comedy containing several romantic vignettes that take place before and during the wedding of a young couple, Brandon and Bedelia, who have decided to marry after living together for a year and a half. Though both the couple's families are thrilled, the tension and excitement leading up to the wedding and the wedding itself bring out many family squabbles heretofore repressed. Castellano is wonderful (it was his first major role and led to his being cast as a major character in THE GODFATHER) as the groom's father, whose happiness is disturbed by the news that his other son, Hindy, is considering divorcing his wife, Diane Keaton (this was also Keaton's first major role). On the other side of the family, Young, the rich, strict Irish-Catholic father of the bride, finds himself trapped by his longtime mistress, Jackson, who suddenly decides to force him into choosing between her and his wife. Meanwhile, Anne Meara, the bride's sister, is going through the collapse of her marriage because her husband, Guardino, has become more interested in television than sex. The evening before the wedding, Brandon and Bedelia arrange a blind date between her cousin, Hailey, and one of the ushers, Dishy. Dishy, hoping to score with Hailey, finds his efforts at seduction frustrated by the girl's nonstop chatter. The next day all the emotional turmoil works itself out and the wedding proceeds smoothly. LOVERS AND OTHER STRANGERS is a charming, hilarious film that skillfully balances the many divergent storylines into a fascinating, entertaining whole. Well cast (a fine example of ensemble acting), and well paced, it holds up to several viewings. For some mysterious reason the MPAA gave the film an undue "R" rating, but any nudity or foul language is not to be found, and the sexual aspects of the story are handled tastefully. Songs were performed by Country Coalition and Larry Meredith. "For All We Know" won the Oscar for Best Song.

LOVES OF A BLONDE

DVD

(LASKY JEDNE PLAVOVLASKY)
1965 88m bw Comedy ★★★½
Barrandov/Ceskoslovensky (Czechoslovakia)

Hana Brejchova *(Andula)*, Vladimir Pucholt *(Milda)*, Vladimir Mensik *(Vacovsky)*, Ivan Kheil *(Manas)*, Jiri Hruby *(Burda)*, Milada Jezkova *(Milda's Mother)*, Josef Sebanek *(Milda's Father)*, Marie Salacova *(Marie)*, Jana Novakova *(Jana)*, Jana Crkalova *(Jaruska)*

d, Milos Forman; w, Jaroslav Papousek, Ivan Passer, Milos Forman, Vaclav Sasek; ph, Miroslav Ondricek; ed, Miroslav Hajek; m, Evzen Illin; art d, Karel Cerny

AAN Best Foreign Language Film

This charming and frequently touching romantic comedy, directed by Milos Forman, concerns a young woman, Brejchova, who works in a shoe factory and dreams of love. Dissatisfied with the men in her town, she is forced to suffer the attentions of Blazejovsky, an ardent admirer, but less than what she perceives to be her ideal man. When a dance is held in honor of soldiers stationed in the town, Brejchova looks forward to meeting a handsome military man. To her disappointment, however, the soldiers all turn out to be middle-aged reserves, so she sets her sights on the piano player, Pucholt. After some uneasy introductions, Brejchova spends the night with Pucholt. Now in love, she travels to his parents' home in Prague, where her stay is anything but blissful. An international success, LOVES OF A BLONDE was an important film not only in the career of Forman (who would go to America and direct ONE FLEW OVER THE CUCKOO'S NEST), but also as one of the films (along with THE SHOP ON MAIN STREET and CLOSELY WATCHED TRAINS) that helped give Czech cinema worldwide attention. It received an Oscar nomination for Best Foreign Film, but lost to A MAN AND A WOMAN.

LUCAS

DVD

1986 104m c Comedy/Drama ★★★
Lawrence Gordon (U.S.) PG-13

Corey Haim *(Lucas Blye)*, Kerri Green *(Maggie)*, Charlie Sheen *(Cappie Roew)*, Courtney Thorne-Smith *(Alise)*, Winona Ryder *(Rina)*, Thomas E. Hodges *(Bruno)*, Ciro Poppiti *(Ben)*, Guy Boyd *(Coach)*, Jeremy Piven *(Spike)*, Kevin Gerard Wixted *(Tonto)*

p, David Nicksay; d, David Seltzer; w, David Seltzer; ph, Reynaldo Villalobos (Panavision, DeLuxe Color); ed, Priscilla Nedd; m, Dave Grusin; art d, James J. Murakami; cos, Molly Maginnis

After years of sophomoric teenage sex comedies, along came LUCAS, a film that deals with real problems of adolescent love. The title character (Corey Haim) is a 13-year-old eccentric who likes bugs and classical music. Being a short, four-eyed intellectual to boot, he is the victim of all the high school bullies. Offended by the teenage social system that rewards people (especially football players and their cheerleader acolytes) for their physical prowess, Lucas spots the lovely 16-year-old Maggie (Kerri Green). They become friends, and Lucas falls in love with her. His ideal is threatened, however, by Maggie's attraction to Cappie Roew (Charlie Sheen), a handsome football player. Worse, she decides to become a cheerleader. LUCAS, the directorial debut of Seltzer, has more honest teenage scenes than all of John Hughes's films combined. Seltzer's characters are real; and Haim, Green, and Sheen play them wonderfully. As a result LUCAS is not just a film for teenagers but for anyone who has ever been a teenager. The film's greatest fault is its reliance on football heroics at the end; after such wonderfully developed relationships, it is a shame to see LUCAS take a cheap turn.

LUMUMBA

DVD

2000 115m c Biography/Political/Thriller ★★★★
Entre chien et loup/Essential Filmproduktion GmbH/JBA Productions/Radio-television Belge Francofone/Velvet S.A./Arte France Cinema (France/Belgium/Haiti/Germany)

Eriq Ebouaney *(Patrice Lumumba)*, Alex Descas *(Joseph Mobutu)*, Theophile Moussa Sowie *(Maurice Mpolo)*, Maka Kotto *(Joseph Kasa Vubu)*, Dieudonne Kabongo *(Godefroid Munungo)*, Pascal N'Zonzi *(Moise Tshombe)*, Andre Debaar *(Walter J. Ganshof Van der Meersch)*, Cheik Doukoure *(Joseph Okito)*, Oumar Diop Makena *(Thomas Kanza)*, Mariam Kaba *(Pauline Lumumba)*

d, Raoul Peck; w, Pascal Bonitzer, Raoul Peck; ph, Bernard Lutic; ed, Jacques Comets; m, Jean-Claude Petit; prod d, Denis Renault; art d, Andre Fonsny; cos, Charlotte David

In his brief but incandescent heyday, Congolese revolutionary Patrice Lumumba was called "the Elvis Presley of Africa," though Malcolm X is the more apt comparison. The charismatic Lumumba was unyieldingly dedicated to helping his country forge a post-colonial identity and in 1960 became his country's first independently elected prime minister. In less than a year, he was brutally assassinated.

Inspired by recent revelations about Lumumba's death, Haitian filmmaker Raoul Peck dramatizes his life and times and posits an anti-Lumumba conspiracy that unites the CIA, disgruntled Belgian authorities, and power-hungry local leaders. 1958: Lumumba (Eriq Ebouaney) founds the Mouvement National Congolais party, using his position as a traveling salesman for a Belgian beer company to rally grassroots support. A year later, Belgium announces a plan to give the Congo its freedom over the course of five years; Congolese nationalists see a plot to rig elections and guarantee long-term political loyalty to Belgium. The next year, MNC candidates sweep the elections, and Prime Minister Lumumba and the more moderate President Joseph Kasa Vubu (Maka Kotto) are charged with governing a country that is descending into chaos. Belgian troops are sent in to "help" maintain order, the UN refuses to intervene, and Lumumba appeals to the Soviet Union for aid, panicking anti-communists in Europe and the U.S. Kasa Vubu dismisses Lumumba, and he is quickly betrayed and murdered.

Driven by a fiery, fiercely controlled performance from Ebouaney, Peck's film—which has been compared to Oliver Stone's JFK for its revisionist take on an assassination that became a nation's defining moment—is utterly enthralling even for viewers unfamiliar with the Congo's complicated political history.

LUST FOR LIFE

1956 122m c Biography ★★★★½
MGM (U.S.)

Kirk Douglas *(Vincent Van Gogh)*, Anthony Quinn *(Paul Gauguin)*, James Donald *(Theo Van Gogh)*, Pamela Brown *(Christine)*, Everett Sloane *(Dr. Gachet)*, Niall MacGinnis *(Roulin)*, Noel Purcell *(Anton Mauve)*, Henry Daniell *(Theodorus Van Gogh)*, Madge Kennedy *(Anna Cornelia Van Gogh)*, Jill Bennett *(Willemien)*

p, John Houseman; d, Vincente Minnelli; w, Norman Corwin (based on the novel by Irving Stone); ph, Freddie Young, Russell Harlan (CinemaScope, Metrocolor, Ansco Color); ed, Adrienne Fazan; m, Miklos Rozsa; art d, Cedric Gibbons, Hans Peters, Preston Ames; cos, Walter Plunkett

AAN Best Actor: Kirk Douglas; *AA Best Supporting Actor:* Anthony Quinn; *AAN Best Adapted Screenplay:* Norman Corwin; *AAN Best Art Direction-Set Decoration (Color):* Cedric Gibbons, Hans Peters, Preston Ames, Edwin B. Willis, Keogh Gleason

Lust for Life was optioned by MGM in 1947, but it took almost nine years before the studio finally filmed Irving Stone's immensely popular fictionalized biography of Vincent Van Gogh.

The Dutch painter (Douglas) leaves Holland to give religious instruction to coal miners in a Belgian province in 1878. Censured by his superiors in the church, he denounces them as hypocrites, abandons his evangelical activities, and suffers an emotional and physical decline. Found living in squalor by his art-dealer brother, Theo (Donald), Van Gogh is persuaded to return to Holland and recuperate, but his burgeoning interest in painting upsets the whole household, and his sister asks him to leave. In the Hague, Douglas sets up house with a prostitute (Brown) who becomes his model and mistress. After the death of their father, Van Gogh joins Theo in Paris, and meets the great artists of the Impressionist movement, befriending Paul Gauguin (Quinn). Gauguin is nearly as eccentric as Van Gogh, but the Dutchman's volatile nature endangers his closest friendship yet and precipitates another decline.

LUST FOR LIFE tells a tragic story, but the portrait of Van Gogh's uncompromised genius is also inspiring. Douglas gives an appropriately fiery star turn as Van Gogh, delivering some of the best work of his career. With typical dedication, Douglas even went so far as to take extensive painting lessons for the role. Quinn, in a relatively small part, is also excellent as the moody Gauguin, who attempts to befriend his fellow genius. Director Vincente Minnelli also searched out surviving contemporaries of the great artist, visited locales when Van Gogh lived and worked, and managed to film 200 of the painter's masterworks (located around the world) without subjecting them to the dangers of standard movie lighting.

LUSTY MEN, THE
1952   113m   bw   Sports/Western   ★★★★
RKO   (U.S.)

Susan Hayward *(Louise Merritt)*, Robert Mitchum *(Jeff McCloud)*, Arthur Kennedy *(Wes Merritt)*, Arthur Hunnicutt *(Booker Davis)*, Frank Faylen *(Al Dawson)*, Walter Coy *(Buster Burgess)*, Carol Nugent *(Rusty Davis)*, Maria Hart *(Rosemary Maddox)*, Lorna Thayer *(Grace Burgess)*, Burt Mustin *(Jeremiah)*

p, Jerry Wald, Norman Krasna; d, Nicholas Ray; w, Horace McCoy, David Dortort (based on a story by Claude Stanush); ph, Lee Garmes; ed, Ralph Dawson; m, Roy Webb; art d, Albert S. D'Agostino, Alfred Herman; cos, Michael Woulfe

Director Nicholas Ray was a master of the offbeat film, and this brilliant contemporary western, easily the best movie ever made about rodeo (see also JUNIOR BONNER, J.W. COOP and RODEO), is no exception. Washed-up rodeo champion Jeff McCloud (Robert Mitchum) takes a job on the ranch of Wes and Louise Merritt (Arthur Kennedy and Susan Hayward), and, with his guidance, Wes becomes a rodeo star. Meanwhile, Louise leads on the infatuated Jeff to insure his continued training of her husband, but, when Wes gets too big for his britches, Jeff goes head to swelled head with him in rodeo competition, with tragic results. THE LUSTY MEN is full of action and dangerous stunts, photographed beautifully by master cinematographer Lee Garmes. Ray's direction is superb, and all three leads give bravura performances. Based on a *Life* magazine story by Claude Stanush and coscripted by cowboy David Dortort, its screenplay presents classical situations, full of poetry and destiny. In his search for realism, Ray took his cameras on location, filming rodeos in Tucson, Arizona, Spokane, Washington, Pendleton, Oregon, and Livermore, California, using a host of real rodeo stars such as Gerald Roberts, Jerry Ambler, and Les Sanborn.

M

M   📀
(MÖRDER UNTER UNS)
1931   117m   bw   Crime/Horror   ★★★★★
Nero   (Germany)

Peter Lorre *(Franz Becker)*, Otto Wernicke *(Inspector Karl Lohmann)*, Gustaf Gründgens *(Schraenker)*, Theo Lingen *(Bauernfaenger)*, Theodor Loos *(Police Commissioner Groeber)*, Georg John *(Blind Peddler)*, Ellen Widmann *(Mme. Becker)*, Inge Landgut *(Elsie)*, Ernst Stahl-Nachbaur *(Police Chief)*, Paul Kemp *(Pickpocket)*

p, Seymour Nebenzal; d, Fritz Lang; w, Fritz Lang, Thea von Harbou, Paul Falkenberg, Adolf Jansen, Karl Vash (based on an article by Egon Jacobson); ph, Fritz Arno Wagner, Gustav Rathje; ed, Paul Falkenberg; m, Edvard Grieg (abstract from "Peer Gynt"); art d, Emil Hasler, Karl Vollbrecht

Fritz Lang's first sound film, his most chilling and provocative work, features Peter Lorre's greatest performance as a child molester and murderer. As the film opens, Berlin is gripped by terror: a child molester is killing little girls, while the police's frantic search has so far turned up no clues to his identity. Frenzied citizens inform on their neighbors; police raids net scores of criminals, but none that can be linked to the killings. To stop this trend, the underworld's leading members resolve to catch the killer themselves, ordering the criminal community to find the murderer and bring him to a tribunal—and the trap to catch the desperate man is set in thrilling motion. Lang tells his grim tale in murky, expressive shadow, and (keeping the murders offscreen) achieves chilling effects through brilliant cinematic strategies: distorted camera angles; expressive shadows; innovative use of sound; and meticulously designed claustrophobic sets. Lang succeeds in conveying the increasing frenzy of various strata of Berlin life as he cross-cuts between wildly different environments to suggest their mutual fear. One particularly interesting and effective manuever was Lang's decision to visually link the police search for the killer with that of the criminals, thereby suggesting a parallel between the two. Lang also makes inspired use of the city of Berlin, its antiquity and squalor, to suggest a deep-seated corruption.

While M offers a truly creepy image of its psychopathic killer, it is all the more effective for its psychological subtlety as it conveys his guilt, despair and compulsiveness. At that point in his life, Lorre was a rather roly-poly fellow; his plump child-like features add a poignancy and pathos to the character. The child murderer appears to be a child himself. Lorre was so effective in this role that he would be cast as grotesque psychopaths for the bulk of his long career.

MACBETH   📀
1971   140m   c   Drama   ★★★★
Playboy   (U.K.)   R

Jon Finch *(Macbeth)*, Francesca Annis *(Lady Macbeth)*, Martin Shaw *(Banquo)*, Nicholas Selby *(Duncan)*, John Stride *(Ross)*, Stephen Chase *(Malcolm)*, Paul Shelley *(Donalbain)*, Terence Bayler *(Macduff)*, Andrew Laurence *(Lennox)*, Frank Wylie *(Mentieth)*

p, Andrew Braunsberg, Roman Polanski; d, Roman Polanski; w, Roman Polanski, Kenneth Tynan (based on the play by William Shakespeare); ph, Gilbert Taylor (Todd AO 35, Technicolor); ed, Alastair McIntyre; m, The Third Ear Band; prod d, Wilfred

Shingleton; art d, Fred Carter; fx, Ted Samuels; chor, Sally Gilpin; cos, Anthony Mendleson

Roman Polanski's controversial version of the classic Shakespeare play casts Jon Finch and Francesca Annis as the murderously obsessed couple who utilize witchcraft and prophecies as stepping stones to power. Polanski's first film after the murder of his wife, Sharon Tate, by the Manson family, this graphically violent MACBETH could be read as an attempt to exorcise real-life demons. In any case, this version, if not the best Shakespearean adaptation, is certainly the most inspired in its recreation of the cold barbaric spirit of the play's original setting. The vulgarity and gore on the screen is neither exploitative nor irresponsible, but a thoughtful interpretation that is less beholden to conventional theatrical techniques of the time. In accordance with this approach, Polanski elicited naturalistic understated performances from his actors which bolstered the play's realism while bringing the poetry down to earth. Some would argue he brought it too far down.

While Annis's nude sleepwalking scene has been criticized as evidence of Playboy Enterprises' involvement (in fact, the script was written before Playboy agreed to produce the film), it is true to the period. The project was originally offered to Allied Artists and then to Universal but both deals fell through. *Playboy* publisher Hugh Hefner, who was anxious to diversify into film production, felt this would be an ideal project for the growing Playboy Enterprises. However it turned out to be his first major failure. Polanski originally intended to cast Tuesday Weld as Lady Macbeth, but she declined after learning about the nude scene. Photographed in Wales during incessant downpours and fog, the picture was completed way behind schedule and lost about $3.5 million dollars. The original cut received an "X" rating.

MACHINIST, THE
DVD
(EL MAQUINISTA)
2004 102m c Thriller ★★★
Filmax Entertainment/Canal +/Castelao Productions/ R
ICAA ICF (Spain)

Christian Bale *(Trevor Reznik)*, Jennifer Jason Leigh *(Stevie)*, Aitana Sanchez-Gijon *(Marie)*, John Sharian *(Ivan)*, Michael Ironside *(Miller)*, Larry Gilliard *(Jackson)*, Reg E. Cathey *(Jones)*, Anna Massey *(Mrs. Shrike)*, Matthew Romero *(Nicholas)*, Robert Long *(Supervisor Furman)*

p, Julio Fernandez; d, Brad Anderson; w, Scott Kosar; ph, Xavi Gimenez; ed, Luis de la Madrid; m, Roque Banos; prod d, Alain Bainez; fx, Laura Maynade, Raul Romanillos, Jaume Vilaseca; cos, Maribel Perez

Ultimately, there's less than meets the eye to Brad Anderson and Scott Kosar's "Twilight Zone" tale of mental disintegration. The film's persuasively doom-haunted atmosphere, however, and star Christian Bale's astonishing transformation into an emaciated walking skeleton (he lost nearly a third of his normal body weight before starting the film) are luridly hypnotic.

Afflicted by insomnia and shedding weight daily, machine operator Trevor Reznik (Christian Bale) is gradually drifting into a murky, waking-dream state in which everything seems both hazily unreal and too vivid to bear. Trent's eyes are retreating back into their sunken sockets, his clothes hang from his gaunt frame, and he's haunted by paranoid suspicions that may not be entirely baseless; after all, someone *is* leaving neatly pencilled games of hangman around Trent's gloomy apartment. Trent's nosy landlady, Mrs. Shrike (Anna Massey), thinks he's losing his grip, while lightly battered hooker Stevie (Jennifer Jason Leigh) sees a fixer-upper worthy of her heart of gold. Tormented by creepy new colleague Ivan (John Sharian) and shunned by the rest of his co-workers after an accident costs drill-press operator Miller (Michael Ironside) his arm,

Trent grows increasingly introverted. He finds refuge at an all-night airport diner, drinking coffee and not eating the pie served up by sweet-natured waitress Marie (Aitana Sanchez-Gijon). Trent's jittery obsessions have sent poisonous tendrils of mistrust into every corner of his ever-diminishing world, and Marie's sunny optimism can't keep his demons at bay.

The film's middle third is a repetitive slog, but Anderson and cinematographer Xavi Gimenez whip up a fog of atmosphere that goes a long way toward obscuring the material's fundamental slenderness. Anderson is a master of detail, but his film's punch line isn't really good enough to justify Bale's nauseating physical transformation. But really, what could?

MACOMBER AFFAIR, THE
1947 89m bw Adventure ★★★½
UA (U.S.)

Gregory Peck *(Robert Wilson)*, Robert Preston *(Francis Macomber)*, Joan Bennett *(Margaret Macomber)*, Reginald Denny *(Capt. Smollet)*, Carl Harbord *(Coroner)*, Earl Smith *(Kongoni)*, Jean Gillie *(Aimee)*, Vernon Downing *(Reporter Logan)*, Frederic Worlock *(Clerk)*, Hassan Said *(Abdullah)*

p, Benedict Bogeaus, Casey Robinson; d, Zoltan Korda; w, Casey Robinson, Seymour Bennett, Frank Arnold (based on the story "The Short Happy Life of Francis Macomber" by Ernest Hemingway); ph, Osmond Borradaile, John Wilcox, Freddie Francis, Karl Struss; ed, Jack Wheeler, George Feld; m, Miklos Rozsa; art d, Erno Metzner; cos, Greta, Jerry Bos

The tough, uncompromising Hemingway story "The Short Happy Life of Francis Macomber" (a title too long for any marquee) was brought to the screen with vitality and invention by the eccentric and talented Zoltan Korda, brother of mogul Alexander, and the result was surprisingly effective. Peck, Preston and Bennett had more to do with that than the script. Preston is Macomber, a wealthy playboy who, with wife Margaret (Bennett) at his side, hires great white hunter Robert Wilson (Peck) to guide them to the African hunting grounds. Margaret has little or no respect for her husband, knowing that he is a weak-willed character with no courage at all, and she makes a play for Robert, whose honor will not permit him to dally with a married woman. At first, Macomber shows his yellow streak on the dangerous safari, but he gradually discovers his courage. In a final hunt, he refuses to run from a charging animal but, before he can bring it down, he is shot by Margaret, who claims she was trying to save his life. She is later tried for murder and acquitted, the jury deciding that the shooting was accidental. The budding romance of Robert and Margaret, however, must still be dealt with.

Peck later stated that everyone in the production had a hand in adjusting the story to make it acceptable to the censor. Hemingway, who had been paid $80,000 for the story, refused to help, ignoring cables for ideas from the studio. The script, though considerably changed from the original story, still retains the direct style Hemingway made so famous. Except for background footage shot in Africa, this was filmed mostly on Hollywood soundstages, with the hunting scenes staged in the northern part of Baja, California. Despite the compromises and problems which plagued the production (including an ongoing debate about what to name the film) the result is a tense and provocatively adult piece, its often steamy material suitably underplayed by the talented star trio.

MAD DOG AND GLORY
DVD
1993 97m c Drama/Romance ★★★
Mad Dog Productions/Scorsese Productions/ R
Universal (U.S.)

Robert De Niro *(Wayne "Mad Dog" Dobie)*, Uma Thurman *(Glory)*, Bill Murray *(Frank Milo)*, David Caruso *(Mike)*, Mike Starr *(Harold)*,

Tom Towles (*Andrew*), Kathy Baker (*Lee*), Derek Anunciation (*Shooter*), Doug Hara (*Driver*), Evan Lionel (*Dealer in Car*)

p, Barbara DeFina, Martin Scorsese; d, John McNaughton; w, Richard Price; ph, Robby Muller; ed, Craig McKay, Elena Maganini; m, Elmer Bernstein; prod d, David Chapman; art d, Mark Haack; fx, Edward Drohan; cos, Rita Ryack

---

MAD DOG AND GLORY is an edgy romantic drama that never quite jells, but has enough moments of humor and/or charm to make it worth seeing.

The most intriguing aspect of this story—about a shy cop who is "given" a young woman for a week as a reward for saving a mobster's life—is the reverse casting. Robert De Niro, celebrated for a string of violent, volatile types in films from TAXI DRIVER to CAPE FEAR, plays the timid, ineffectual cop; Bill Murray, not exactly known for his hard-man roles, plays the mafioso—albeit a wise-cracking mafioso who moonlights as a stand-up comic. In a slightly more predictable assignment, Uma Thurman plays the lovely young barmaid over whom the two men eventually come to blows.

MAD DOG is stylishly shot and comes with some great macho confrontation scenes, courtesy of screenwriter Richard Price (SEA OF LOVE, THE COLOR OF MONEY). These are handled with humor, as well as real menace, by De Niro's partner (David Caruso, before he became America's first officially hunky redhead as the star of TV's "NYPD Blue") and Murray's lumbering henchman (Mike Starr). Good supporting players, though, tend to draw attention to what's wrong with the leads. De Niro's mumbling, inarticulate delivery is too close to the actor's real-life persona to really qualify as a performance, and Murray can't make the funny/sinister combination work. His comic schtick undercuts the power of his threats ("Have you ever heard of botulism? We can kill her with soup!"), while his nastiness makes it hard to laugh at some of the gags.

MAD LOVE
1935   83m   bw   Horror   ★★★★½
MGM   (U.S.)

Peter Lorre (*Dr. Gogol*), Colin Clive (*Stephen Orlac*), Frances Drake (*Yvonne Orlac*), Ted Healy (*Reagan*), Edward Brophy (*Rollo*), Sara Haden (*Marie*), Henry Kolker (*Prefect Rosset*), May Beatty (*Francoise*), Keye Luke (*Dr. Wong*), Isabel Jewell (*Marianne*)

p, John W. Considine Jr.; d, Karl Freund; w, Guy Endore, P.J. Wolfson, John Balderston (based on the novel *Les Mains d'Orlac* by Maurice Renard); ph, Chester Lyons, Gregg Toland; ed, Hugh Wynn; m, Dimitri Tiomkin

---

Mad about it. Combining Grand Guignol, surrealism and comedy to great effect, MAD LOVE remains to this day a chilling film. Peter Lorre is Gogol, a doctor who adores Yvonne Orlac (Drake), star of the Parisian Horror Theatre. Although she rebuffs him, Gogol buys a life-size replica of Yvonne that stood in the theater's lobby, harboring a secret wish that perhaps he can bring it to life as Pygmalion did Galatea. Yvonne's husband (Clive), a famous pianist, loses his hands in a railway accident; she goes to Gogol, a brilliant surgeon, and pleads with him to help. The love-crazed doctor grafts the hands of Reagan (Brophy), a recently executed knife-wielding murderer, onto Orlac's stumps. The initially grateful patient finds, though, that while he can't play the piano, he can throw knives only too well. When Gogol kills Orlac's stepfather, the mad doctor brainwashes Orlac into thinking that he did it. Things get even eerier when the dead Reagan ostensibly shows up, claiming that Gogol has sewn his head back on and that he wants his hands back! The truth behind this, as well as how Orlac's new hands ironically help him save his wife from Gogol's clutches, make for an improbable but brilliantly fitting climax.

Three excellent, distinctive cameramen were employed on the film, and the results show it. Director Karl Freund had been behind the lens on many films, and his bringing in Gregg Toland and Chester Lyons adds to the rich mixture of stark semi-Expressionism and dreamy near-surrealism that marks this film. One memorable shot shows Lorre's shaved head half in bright light and half in dark shadow, a striking visual rendering of his psychotic state. Casting the likable Brophy as the killer was admittedly a mistake, although it may have been done because Brophy was the only actor around who somewhat resembled the odd-looking Lorre and was about the same diminutive size. The comic relief by Ted Healy (who used to headline with The Three Stooges) is sometimes unwelcome as it takes too much edge off the film's scare tactics. At other points, though, it provided a much-needed punctuation to the ever-building suspense. Lorre, meanwhile, gives a top-notch performance in his well-written role. His doctor is no mad scientist of the Lugosi-Karloff school, but a man driven crazy by his lust. His character displays recognizable motivations throughout, no matter how bizarre his activities. Though the film is really Lorre's show, Colin Clive deserves praise for pulling off nervousness as few actors can, and Frances Drake brings serenity and vulnerability to the part of the heroine. A film which had a palpable influence on CITIZEN KANE (which Toland shot), MAD LOVE stands today as one of the most compelling horror films of its time.

MAD MAX   [DVD]
1979   90m   c   Action/Science Fiction   ★★★½
Mad Max   (Australia)   R

Mel Gibson (*Max*), Joanne Samuel (*Jessie*), Hugh Keays-Byrne (*the Toecutter*), Steve Bisley (*Jim Goose*), Roger Ward (*Fifi Macaffee*), Vincent Gil (*Nightrider*), Tim Burns (*Johnny the Boy*), Geoff Parry (*Bubba Zanetti*), Paul Johnstone (*Cundalini*), John Ley (*Charlie*)

p, Byron Kennedy; d, George Miller; w, George Miller, James McCausland (based on a story by George Miller, Byron Kennedy); ph, David Eggby (Todd-AO 35); ed, Tony Paterson, Clifford Hayes; m, Brian May; art d, Jon Dowding; fx, Chris Murray; cos, Clare Griffin

---

Australia exported this creative, original, exciting, low-budget genre landmark which gave the young Mel Gibson his first starring role. Set in the near future, MAD MAX presents a society descending into chaos. The forces of law and order are barely holding their own. The highways are terrorized by packs of lunatic speed demons. Gibson plays Max, a good cop who's fed up with his job. After chasing crazed criminals for years and seeing so many of his buddies killed in action, he just wants to retire and spend the rest of his days with his wife and child. His chief tries to bribe him with a new, faster police car ("the last of the V-8s"). He attempts to flatter him by telling him that he's the last of the heroes but Max isn't buying. The boss tells him to take a vacation and he does. Spending an idyllic week with his family on the beach, he decides to put away his badge and uniform for good. But this is not to be. A psychotic gang of road rats kills Gibson's wife and child in revenge for the death of one of their members. Left with nothing to live for, Gibson turns avenger, dons his black leather uniform, fuels up his V-8, and hits the road.

Though the plot is that of a simple revenge western, director George Miller infuses the film with a kinetic combination of visual style, amazing stunt work, creative costume design, and eccentric, detailed characterizations that practically jump out of the screen and grab the viewer by the throat. Miller, whose inspiration was comic books, serials, and B westerns, has created some of the most stunning car-chase/crash-and-burn scenes ever put on film. At this point in his career, Miller is a filmmaker who seems to have just discovered the exciting possibilities of composition, camera movement, and editing, and uses them to their most powerful effect, bringing movement back to the movies. Done independently with a laughably small budget (Miller edited most of the film in his bedroom), MAD MAX went on to make more money in Australia than George Lucas's STAR WARS. The American distributors, however, didn't quite know what to do with the film and stupidly dubbed lousy American-sounding voices over the Australians'. An even better sequel, THE ROAD WARRIOR (MAD MAX II in Australia), followed, and a third film, MAD MAX BEYOND THUNDERDOME, was released four years later.

MAD WEDNESDAY

1950 79m bw Comedy *DVD* ★★★½
California (U.S.)

Harold Lloyd *(Harold Diddlebock)*, Frances Ramsden *(Miss Otis)*, Jimmy Conlin *(Wormy)*, Raymond Walburn *(E.J. Waggleberry)*, Edgar Kennedy *(Jake, the Bartender)*, Arline Judge *(Manicurist)*, Franklin Pangborn *(Formfit Franklin)*, Lionel Stander *(Max)*, Margaret Hamilton *(Flora)*, Alan Bridge *(Wild Bill Hitchcock)*

p, Howard Hughes; d, Preston Sturges; w, Preston Sturges; ph, Robert Pittack; ed, Thomas Neff; m, Werner R. Heymann, Harry Rosenthal; art d, Robert Usher; fx, John P. Fulton

Far from Sturges's best, but intermittently hilarious. The film follows Harold Diddlebock, hero of Lloyd's classic silent THE FRESHMAN, into middle age. Harold is now a frumpy, office-bound bookkeeper with his glory days behind him. Fired from his job after two decades of toil, he goes on a drunken spree, and, in as unlikely a series of events as you'll ever see, wakes up the owner of a moth-eaten and bankrupt circus. Eventually Lloyd winds up reprising the silent comedy scene from SAFETY LAST for which he is perhaps most famous—hanging from a tall building, this time with a huge lion menacing him.

The idea of combining comic aces Lloyd and Sturges sounds highly promising, but both men's careers were on the wane, and the effort they make to milk laughs sometimes shows a bit too much. MAD WEDNESDAY was financed by, of all people, Howard Hughes, a man not usually known for his sense of humor. It includes several excellent character bits by some of Hollywood's best second bananas: Kennedy (master of the slow burn), Stander (who left movies for years due to Red-baiting, then came back as a TV star), Hamilton (the ultimate witch), and Pangborn, who elevated prissiness to an art form. If you can hang on through the long, dead scenes and wait for Lloyd to get going, you'll probably end up satisfied by at least some of the frantic slapstick which transpires. As with many films Hughes made, several versions of this film exist, the 89-minute version going under the title of THE SIN OF HAROLD DIDDLEBOCK.

MADAME CURIE

1943 124m bw Biography ★★★★
MGM (U.S.)

Greer Garson *(Mme. Marie Curie)*, Walter Pidgeon *(Pierre Curie)*, Robert Walker *(David LeGros)*, Dame May Whitty *(Mme. Eugene Curie)*, Henry Travers *(Eugene Curie)*, C. Aubrey Smith *(Lord Kelvin)*, Albert Basserman *(Prof. Jean Perot)*, Victor Francen *(President of University)*, Reginald Owen *(Dr. Henri Becquerel)*, Van Johnson *(Reporter)*

p, Sidney Franklin; d, Mervyn LeRoy; w, Paul Osborn, Paul H. Rameau (based on the book by Eve Curie); ph, Joseph Ruttenberg; ed, Harold F. Kress; m, Herbert Stothart; art d, Cedric Gibbons, Paul Groesse; fx, Warren Newcombe; cos, Irene Sharaff, Gile Steele

AAN Best Picture; AAN Best Actor: Walter Pidgeon; AAN Best Actress: Greer Garson; AAN Best B/W Cinematography: Joseph Ruttenberg; AAN Best Score (Drama or Comedy): Herbert Stothart; AAN Best Interior Decoration (B/W): Cedric Gibbons, Paul Groesse, Edwin B. Willis, Hugh Hunt; AAN Best Sound Recording: Douglas Shearer

This fine film stirs the heart and stays closer to the facts of its subject's life than might be expected for its time. Greer Garson plays Marie, a Polish student studying in Paris near the turn of the century, who shares a lab with scientist Pierre Curie (Walter Pidgeon). The shy Pierre grows not only to respect Marie's scientific knowledge, but also falls in love with her, and the two soon marry. Together they observe the odd behavior of certain samples of pitchblende, eventually leading, after five years of study, to Marie's discovery of radium. Years pass as the Curies struggle to continue financing their work, until finally they extract one decigram of radium from thousands of pounds of pitchblende. The breakthrough makes the couple famous, but tragedy awaits them as well.

MADAME CURIE maintains its dignity throughout and, if this occasionally weighs down the picture a bit, it also lends a certain low-key intensity to scientific research which proves quite gripping. Garson and Pidgeon are fully into the spirit of the film, and their teaming here is much more satisfying than in the more acclaimed MRS. MINIVER.

MADAME ROSA

(LA VIE DEVANT SOI)
1977 105m c Drama ★★★½
Lira (France) PG

Simone Signoret *(Mme. Rosa)*, Claude Dauphin *(Dr. Katz)*, Samy Ben Youb *(Mohammed "Momo")*, Gabriel Jabbour *(Mr. Hamil)*, Michal Bat Adam *(Nadine)*, Constantin Costa-Gavras *(Ramon)*, Stella Anicette *(Mme. Lola)*, Bernard Lajarrige *(Mr. Charmette)*, Mohammed Zineth *(Kadir Youssef)*, Genevieve Fontanel *(Maryse)*

p, Jean Bolary; d, Moshe Mizrahi; w, Moshe Mizrahi (based on the novel *Momo* by Romain Gary); ph, Nestor Almendros (Eastmancolor); ed, Sophie Coussein; m, Philippe Sarde, Dabket Loubna

AA Best Foreign Language Film

An aging survivor of Auschwitz, Madame Rosa (Simone Signoret) is a Parisian ex-streetwalker who cares for prostitutes' children in the city's poor Arab-Jewish section. Although she is slowly losing her memory, she is still able to care for her charges, especially Momo (Samy Ben Youb), an unruly Arab Muslim boy who, although he tends to be rebellious, reciprocates her love. When Madame Rosa has delusions that the Gestapo is coming for her and makes the boy promise to hide her, he does so, sending a doctor away and maintaining that the dying woman has gone to Israel.

MADAME ROSA handles its underlying conflicts—between Arabs and Jews, between Nazis and Jews—well, and explores its mixed racial and cultural milieu with grace, sensitivity, and subtlety. The film is the first pairing of director-writer Moshe Mizrahi, a Moroccan-born Israeli, and the great Simone Signoret, who won a Cesar for her marvelous and unglamorous performance here. The two would team again for the bittersweet 1981 drama I SENT A LETTER TO MY LOVE. Film director Costa-Gavras has a supporting role.

MADAME SOUSATZKA

1988 122m c Drama ★★★
Sousatzka/Cineplex Odeon (U.K.) PG-13

Shirley MacLaine *(Mme. Irina Sousatzka)*, Navin Chowdhry *(Manek Sen)*, Peggy Ashcroft *(Lady Emily)*, Twiggy *(Jenny)*, Shabana Azmi *(Sushila Sen)*, Leigh Lawson *(Ronnie Blum)*, Lee Montague *(Vincent Pick)*, Robert Rietty *(Leo Milev)*, Jeremy Sinden *(Woodford)*, Roger Hammond *(Lefranc)*

p, Robin Dalton; d, John Schlesinger; w, Ruth Prawer Jhabvala, John Schlesinger (based on a novel by Bernice Rubens); ph, Nat Crosby (Rank color); ed, Peter Honess; m, Gerald Gouriet; prod d, Luciana Arrighi; cos, Amy Roberts

A fiery, autocratic piano teacher, Madame Sousatzka (Shirley MacLaine) has spent the last 30 years living in a London boardinghouse when she meets Manek Sen (Navin Chowdhry), a gifted 15-year-old Indian pianist. She believes she can turn him into a brilliant musician, starting from scratch and molding him into a new whole. "I teach not only how to play the piano, but how to live," she claims. MADAME SOUSATZKA features a cast good enough to sidestep being sunk by the film's pedestrian script and direction. Five years after her Oscar-winning performance in TERMS OF ENDEARMENT, MacLaine attempts to deliver another tour de force here, and while she's often quite good, too often the showiness of her star turn sabotages the sentiment. Newcomer Chowdhry turns in a strong, believable performance as the musical prodigy on the verge of a major breakthrough. The movie's chief fault is its uninspired handling of the classic themes of change versus tradition, commerce versus art, and the general destruction of history and values. MADAME SOUSATZKA is not the great or important film that it tries to be; rather, it is a warm and touching human drama, made so by the often exceptional acting.

MADELINE
1998 89m c Children's/Comedy/Adventure ★★½ **DVD**
Jaffilms/Madeline Films/Columbia TriStar (U.S.) PG

Frances McDormand *(Miss Clavel)*, Nigel Hawthorne *(Lord Covington)*, Hatty Jones *(Madeline)*, Ben Daniels *(Leopold—the Tutor)*, Stephane Audran *(Lady Covington)*, Arturo Venegas *(Mr. Spanish Ambassador)*, Katia Caballero *(Mrs. Spanish Ambassador)*, Chantal Neuwirth *(Helene—the Cook)*, Kristian De La Osa *(Pepito)*, Clare Thomas *(Aggie)*

p, Stanley Jaffe, Allyn Stewart, Saul Cooper, Pancho Kohner; d, Daisy von Scherler Mayer; w, Mark Levin, Jennifer Flackett (from a story by Mark Levin, Jennifer Flackett and Malia Scotch Marmo; based on characters from the children's books by Ludwig Bemelmans; ph, Pierre Aim; ed, Jeffrey Wolf; m, Michel LeGrand; prod d, Hugo Luczyc-Wyhowski; art d, Bertrand Clercq-Roques, Gerard Drolon, Rebecca Holmes; fx, Graham Longhurst, Graham Hills; cos, Michael Clancy

This tolerable kiddie entertainment, adapted from Ludwig Bemelmans' beloved series of books, falls somewhere between the genteel charm of the original and the crude, anarchic humor of contemporary children's comedy at its dopiest.

Madeline (Hatty Jones), as legions of little girls, their mothers, and their mother's mothers already know, is a pint-sized Parisian orphan. She and 11 other, identically dressed little girls board at a Catholic school run by the firm but loving Miss Clavel (Frances McDormand), whose sixth sense for impending disaster serves her well, particularly when it comes to the fearless Madeline. In due course Madeline is stricken with appendicitis, tumbles into the Seine, gets herself kidnapped along with the Spanish ambassador's son Pepito (Kristian De La Osa)—a "bad hat" if ever there was one—and conspires with the rest of the girls to help save their school from being sold by its curmudgeonly owner (Nigel Hawthorne).

Director Daisy von Scherler Mayer scored a modest success with her first film, PARTY GIRL, then blew it on her second, the crude, raucous WOO. Here she shuffles together four of Bemelmans' six Madeline stories and deals a messy hand. The result is fast-paced, uneven, and occasionally aggravating. But pumpkin-faced Jones is awfully cute, McDormand and Hawthorne manage to maintain their dignity, and the bold, primary-color scheme captures some of the spirit of the book's illustrations. And there are worse role models than Madeline:

she's confident, brave, and able to leap any obstacle with a single, well-aimed "pooh-pooh." If your kids are old enough to request HARRIET THE SPY by name, you may want to surprise them with this film as well.

MADIGAN
1968 101m c Crime ★★★½ **DVD**
Universal (U.S.)

Richard Widmark *(Detective Daniel Madigan)*, Henry Fonda *(Commissioner Anthony X. Russell)*, Inger Stevens *(Julia Madigan)*, Harry Guardino *(Detective Rocco Bonaro)*, James Whitmore *(Chief Inspector Charles Kane)*, Susan Clark *(Tricia Bentley)*, Michael Dunn *(Midget Castiglione)*, Steve Ihnat *(Barney Benesch)*, Don Stroud *(Hughie)*, Sheree North *(Jonesy)*

p, Frank P. Rosenberg; d, Don Siegel; w, Howard Rodman, Abraham Polonsky, Harry Kleiner (based on the novel *The Commissioner* by Richard Dougherty); ph, Russell Metty (Techniscope, Technicolor); ed, Milton Shifman; m, Don Costa; art d, Alexander Golitzen, George Webb

Action-packed cops-and-robbers film cowritten by longtime television vet Howard Rodman, who evidently didn't like the way it turned out (he used his pseudonym, Henri Simoun). In the Spanish Harlem section of Manhattan, detectives Madigan and Bonaro (Widmark and Guardino) arrest Barney Benesch (Ihnat), a wanted hoodlum who is hiding out in a tacky flat to avoid an indictment by the Brooklyn courts. Benesch is in bed with a naked woman when they break in, which distracts the two cops from their quarry long enough for him to pull a gun on them and escape. Police commissioner Russell (Fonda) dresses the two men down for allowing Benesch to get away in such an inglorious manner and gives them 72 hours to nail the killer. Russell has a lot of other woes as well: he's having an affair with a married woman (Clark), his colleague (Whitmore) has accepted bribes to keep a brothel operating, and he must contend with a black minister (St. Jacques) whose activist son was badly beaten by racist cops. Aggravating this hornet's nest for Madigan is his socialite wife (Stevens), who urges him to give up his career in law enforcement.

Very documentarian in approach, MADIGAN successfully reworks standard genre material into a realistic, hard-hitting portrait which deliberately sticks pins in the police department hierarchy. Writer Polonsky had been blacklisted in the 1950s and his partner Rodman kept his status active with a local construction union even while working in the Hollywood community. The acting is good throughout, with many fine character sketches of urban types.

MADNESS OF KING GEORGE, THE
1994 107m c Historical/Drama ★★★½ **DVD**
Samuel Goldwyn Company/Channel Four/
Close Call Films (U.K./U.S.)

Nigel Hawthorne *(King George III)*, Helen Mirren *(Queen Charlotte)*, Amanda Donohoe *(Lady Pembroke)*, Rupert Everett *(The Prince of Wales)*, Rupert Graves *(Greville)*, Ian Holm *(Willis)*, Julian Wadham *(Prime Minister Pitt)*, Anthony Calf *(Fitzroy)*, John Wood *(Thurlow)*, Jim Carter *(Fox)*

p, Stephen Evans, David Parfitt; d, Nicholas Hytner; w, Alan Bennett (based on his play *The Madness of George III*); ph, Andrew Dunn; ed, Tariq Anwar; m, George Fenton; prod d, Ken Adam; art d, Martin Childs; cos, Mark Thompson

AA Best Art Direction-Set Decoration: Ken Adam, Carolyn Scott; *AAN Best Actor:* Nigel Hawthorne; *AAN Best Supporting Actress:* Helen Mirren; *AAN Best Adapted Screenplay:* Alan Bennett

Adapted by screenwriter Alan Bennett from his play, THE MADNESS OF KING GEORGE recounts a remarkable episode in the life of George III, who in 1788 experienced temporary insanity as a result of a metabolic imbalance known as porphyria. Despite an Oscar-nominated performance by Nigel Hawthorne, Bennett's theatrical triumph proves curiously flat on the screen.

England is in political turmoil: the unpopular King George III (Nigel Hawthorne) has antagonized his dissolute son, the Prince of Wales (Rupert Everett), while Prime Minister Pitt (Julian Wadham) is in the midst of a power struggle with Whig leader Fox (Jim Carter). Meanwhile, George's behavior is becoming increasingly erratic. Doctors are called in to treat him and the robust, roaringly confident monarch soon becomes a babbling, foul-mouthed, hyperactive mess. Then Queen Charlotte (Helen Mirren) learns of Dr. Willis (Ian Holm), whose innovative methods have proven remarkably successful in curing madness. With Pitt's help, she arranges to have George treated by the decidedly independent physician.

Acclaimed stage director Nicholas Hytner was obviously determined to make his cinematic debut a memorable one. He doesn't just open up the play; he scatters it across sun-drenched country fields, seemingly all of London, and every nook and cranny of the royal residence. Despite the talents involved, however, the effect is surprisingly static and unexciting, probably because the source material is the kind of talky *tour de force* that is best carried off on the stage. Even so, Hawthorne's performance is tremendously intelligent and affecting. He manages to strike a difficult and necessary balance between comedy and pathos throughout, energetically attacking Bennett's best scenes, in which the spectacularly vulgar symptoms of the King's condition subvert the bloodless, artificial refinement of aristocratic manners.

MAEDCHEN IN UNIFORM

1931 110m bw Drama ★★★★★
Deutsch/Gemeinschaft (Germany)

Emilia Unda *(The Principal)*, Dorothea Wieck *(Fraulein von Bernburg)*, Hedwig Schlichter *(Fraulein von Kesten)*, Hertha Thiele *(Manuela von Meinhardie)*, Ellen Schwannecke *(Ilse von Westhagen)*

p, Carl Froehlich; d, Leontine Sagan; w, Christa Winsloe, F.D. Andam (based on the play "Gestern und Heute" by Christa Winsloe)

Late Weimar Germany produced a number of fine anti-authoritarian films, perhaps the best of which was MAEDCHEN IN UNIFORM, the story of a girl's struggles within the rigid discipline of a boarding school for daughters of poor military officers. New student Manuela (Thiele) is homesick, introspective, and alienated. The headmistress (Unda) disapproves of such individualism, and rules her students with the proto-Nazi dictum: "Through discipline and hunger, hunger and discipline, we shall rise again." Manuela becomes attached to one teacher (Wieck), who sees in the sensitive new student a reflection of her former, nonconformist self. But Manuela's dependence on her mentor grows into obsessive love, testing the headmistress' tolerance.

Though MAEDCHEN IN UNIFORM's symbolism can seem heavy-handed (like Murnau's THE LAST LAUGH, it invests much in the uniform as an image of German social consciousness), this film displays remarkable emotional, narrative, and visual assurance. It is particularly insightful in its treatment of female bonding, lesbian love, and the perverse interplay of sexuality and power. Written (by Christa Winsloe and F.D. Andam, from the former's play) and directed (Leontine Sagan) by women, with an all-female cast, MAEDCHEN IN UNIFORM suggested for future generations of aspiring women filmmakers the cinematic potential of a woman's point of view.

MAGIC BOX, THE

1951 118m c Biography ★★★★
Festival (U.K.)

Renee Asherson *(Miss Tagg)*, Richard Attenborough *(Jack Carter)*, Robert Beatty *(Lord Beaverbrook)*, Martin Boddey *(Sitter in Bath Studio)*, Edward Chapman *(Father in Family Group)*, John Charlesworth *(Graham Friese-Greene)*, Maurice Colbourne *(Bride's Father at Wedding)*, Roland Culver *(1st Company Promoter)*, John Howard Davies *(Maurice Friese-Greene)*, Michael Denison *(Connaught Rooms Reporter)*

p, Ronald Neame; d, John Boulting; w, Eric Ambler (based on the book *Friese-Greene, Close-Up of an Inventor* by Ray Allister); ph, Jack Cardiff (Technicolor); ed, Richard Best; m, William Alwyn; prod d, John Bryan; art d, Hopewell Ash; cos, Julia Squire

Nearly every actor who ever appeared in British movies worked in this feature. Robert Donat plays William Friese-Greene, the pioneer who patented the first motion picture camera. The film shows his beginnings as a photographer's assistant and his days as a society lenser in London, spending all his resources on his new invention (patented two years before Edison's). His first wife (Maria Schell) shares his triumphs while his second wife (Margaret Johnston) shares his failures. In between, viewers are treated to the sight of at least 50 of England's finest actors, all playing tiny bits. (Laurence Olivier, for example, is quite amusing as a police officer who is an early witness to the moving pictures.) Friese-Greene is hardly remembered now and had already been dead more than 30 years when THE MAGIC BOX was made, but the filmmakers' conviction that his story should be told convinced all of the actors (who agreed to alphabetical billing) to devote their talents to this good-looking, well-directed film. Donat is excellent, holding his own among the industry's finest.

MAGICIAN, THE

(ANSIKTET)
1958 102m bw Drama ★★★★½
Svensk (Sweden)

Max von Sydow *(Vogler)*, Ingrid Thulin *(Manda Aman)*, Gunnar Bjornstrand *(Vergerus)*, Naima Wifstrand *(Grandmother)*, Bengt Ekerot *(Spegel)*, Bibi Andersson *(Sara)*, Gertrud Fridh *(Ottilia)*, Lars Ekborg *(Simson)*, Toivo Pawlo *(Starbeck)*, Erland Josephson *(Egerman)*

d, Ingmar Bergman; w, Ingmar Bergman; ph, Gunnar Fischer, Rolf Halmquist; ed, Oscar Rosander; m, Erik Nordgren; art d, P.A. Lundgren

In THE MAGICIAN, Ingmar Bergman takes two favorite motifs—masks and magic—and explores them on a number of different levels. Albert Emanuel Vogler (Max von Sydow), a 19-century magician, brings a troupe of traveling illusionists to a small Swedish town where the people don't believe in magic. Led by Vogler, the troupe proceeds to play with the townspeople's minds, and director Bergman, in turn, makes imaginative use of editing, lighting, and special effects to toy with audience expectations. Things are never quite what they seem, either narratively or cinematically. The film's mysterious nature is further enhanced by the dark, rich, gothic look of Bergman's *mise-en-scene*. Though at times the story is overwhelmed by its theme and symbols (especially in its final third), THE MAGICIAN is still fascinating, presenting a myriad of challenging ideas about magic, reality, and the nature of film itself. The acting, as is typical of Bergman, is exceptionally good, with Bjornstrand a standout. The video-cassette is available in both dubbed and subtitled (Swedish into English) versions.

MAGNIFICENT AMBERSONS, THE
DVD
★★★★★

1942 88m bw Drama
Mercury Theatre (U.S.)

Joseph Cotten *(Eugene Morgan)*, Dolores Costello *(Isabel Amberson Minafer)*, Anne Baxter *(Lucy Morgan)*, Tim Holt *(George Amberson Minafer)*, Agnes Moorehead *(Fanny Amberson)*, Ray Collins *(Jack Amberson)*, Richard Bennett *(Maj. Amberson)*, Erskine Sanford *(Benson)*, J. Louis Johnson *(Sam the Butler)*, Donald Dillaway *(Wilbur Minafer)*

p, Orson Welles; d, Orson Welles, Freddie Fleck, Robert Wise; w, Orson Welles (based on the novel by Booth Tarkington); ph, Stanley Cortez, Russell Metty, Harry Wild; ed, Robert Wise, Jack Moss, Mark Robson; m, Bernard Herrmann, Roy Webb; art d, Mark-Lee Kirk; fx, Vernon L. Walker; cos, Edward Stevenson

AAN Best Picture; AAN Best Supporting Actress: Agnes Moorehead; *AAN Best B/W Cinematography:* Stanley Cortez; *AAN Best Interior Decoration (B/W):* Albert S. D'Agostino, Al Fields, Darrell Silvera

Though mutilated by studio cuts and misunderstood at the time of its release, THE MAGNIFICENT AMBERSONS, based on the Tarkington novel and set during the twilight of the 19th century, remains Welles's second great masterpiece.

Young George Amberson (Holt), the spoiled, insufferable scion of the wealthy Amberson family, is first seen, to the consternation of his neighbors, whipping his buggy horse through the streets of Indianapolis. Eugene Morgan (Cotten) is a struggling inventor who loves George's mother Isabel (Costello), but loses her to the wealthy Wilbur Minafer (Dillaway). After an absence of several years, Eugene returns, now successful, having invented an automobile, an instrument of the future that many of the old school find repulsive, especially the haughty George. Wilbur dies, and Eugene, a widower with an attractive daughter, Lucy (Baxter), attempts to rekindle his love affair with Isabel, but George interferes. This affects not only George's romance with Lucy, but also the fading Amberson fortunes.

Though more controlled, subtle and cinematically exciting than CITIZEN KANE, Welles's earlier masterpiece, it's a wonder that AMBERSONS survived at all. Alarmed by the negative reaction at the film's premiere, RKO president George Schaefer instructed then-editor Robert Wise to shorten the film drastically. Welles had already cut it from 148 minutes to 131, but Wise hacked it down to 88, and a more optimistic ending was tacked on by a nameless studio writer and directed by Freddie Fleck. This presumptuous, dictatorial savaging of the film, according to Welles, destroyed "the whole heart of the picture, really." Luckily, that's not quite true.

The film is so rich in innovative technique that it takes several viewings to note even the most essential elements. The "Welles sound" permeates every frame, with overlapping dialogue and a subtle control of volume and texture giving a natural feel to the words spoken (sometimes improvised in group scenes) and sounds heard. In crowd scenes he allows a host of gossips to function as a Greek chorus in estimating the worth of the Amberson and Morgan families. At times the voices of the characters boom and bellow, while, at others, they are so hushed as to be barely discernible.

Many of the ideas initally used in CITIZEN KANE are refined in AMBERSONS, showing in split-second frames his people reflected in mirrors, highly glossed furniture, sometimes in a glare of light, most in half-shadow, as if the blackness of time were shutting out the light of the living. Through his great visual gifts, Welles was able to express the true nature of the characters through their actions: Fanny (Moorehead, in the performance of a lifetime) peering over a railing to eavesdrop on those far below; George methodically spooning down strawberry shortcake in the famous kitchen scene, indifferently listening to Aunt Fanny pour out her

heart; a stunned Eugene at the front door of the Amberson mansion, which has been closed in his face by George, who stands behind the frosted glass panes; a dark shot of the dying, incoherent Major (Bennett); Fanny slumping against a long-unused heater ("It's not hot!").

The look of AMBERSONS was modeled on the low-key lighting used by photographers at the turn-of-the-century, and Cortez's deep-focus lensing is arresting, dwelling upon scenes only Welles could have framed—notably, ten-minute soliloquies saved from tedium by the unique framing. Dolly and truck shots keep the film fluid, and some crane shots capture the changing architecture from Victorian to modern, from resplendent to mundane, as Welles eloquently shows the passing of an age.

MAGNIFICENT OBSESSION
DVD
★★★½

1954 107m c Drama
Universal (U.S.)

Jane Wyman *(Helen Phillips)*, Rock Hudson *(Bob Merrick)*, Barbara Rush *(Joyce Phillips)*, Agnes Moorehead *(Nancy Ashford)*, Otto Kruger *(Rudolph)*, Gregg Palmer *(Tom Masterson)*, Sara Shane *(Valerie)*, Paul Cavanagh *(Dr. Giraud)*, Judy Nugent *(Judy)*, George Lynn *(Williams)*

p, Ross Hunter; d, Douglas Sirk; w, Robert Blees, Wells Root (based on the novel by Lloyd C. Douglas and the screenplay by Sarah Y. Mason, Finley Peter Dunne, Jr., Victor Heerman); ph, Russell Metty (Technicolor); ed, Milton Carruth; m, Frank Skinner; art d, Bernard Herzbrun, Emrich Nicholson; fx, David S. Harsley; cos, Bill Thomas

AAN Best Actress: Jane Wyman

Not quite as heart-wrenching as the original version, this remake is still pretty good and does benefit from being filmed in color. Wyman is Helen Phillips, a blind woman, and Hudson is Bob Merrick, the cad who becomes her savior. Merrick is partly responsible for the accidental death of Helen's husband, a man who was revered in the community as a combination of Dr. Kildare, Ben Casey, and every other angel of mercy ever seen. After the doctor's demise, Bob attempts to apologize, and Helen, avoiding him, is blinded in an accident. With Rudolph (Kruger), a friend of the late, great physician, egging him on, Bob forsakes his wastrel ways and decides to dedicate himself to medicine. Without revealing his true identity, he contacts Helen, and their relationship soon becomes a loving one. When she finds out who he is, she departs. Much later, though, Bob is given an incredible opportunity to save Helen and redeem himself for his past peccadilloes.

A film requiring as many Kleenex as you can spare, this unabashed appeal to the tear ducts does not fail in its efforts. Director Douglas Sirk made only a few more films before retiring to Munich in 1959, just before he turned 60. He brings to this effort the same combination of overblown, indulgent melodramatics and distanced perspective which would mark his masterpiece, IMITATION OF LIFE. Notable also as the film which really put Rock Hudson on top and gave the first inklings that he might be able to act if sufficiently prodded, MAGNIFICENT OBSESSION really relies on Wyman's womanly, Oscar-nominated assurance to put this stuff over.

MAGNIFICENT SEVEN, THE
DVD
★★★★

1960 128m c Western
Mirisch/Alpha (U.S.)
R

Yul Brynner *(Chris)*, Eli Wallach *(Calvera)*, Steve McQueen *(Vin)*, Horst Buchholz *(Chico)*, Charles Bronson *(O'Reilly)*, Robert Vaughn *(Lee)*, Brad Dexter *(Harry Luck)*, James Coburn *(Britt)*, Vladimir Sokoloff *(Old Man)*, Rosenda Monteros *(Petra)*

p, John Sturges; d, John Sturges; w, William Roberts, Walter Newman, Walter Bernstein (based on THE SEVEN SAMURAI); ph, Charles Lang (Panavision, DeLuxe Color); ed, Ferris Webster; m, Elmer Bernstein; art d, Edward Fitzgerald; fx, Milt Rice

AAN Best Score (Drama or Comedy): Elmer Bernstein

Very nearly a classic, this Americanization of Akira Kurosawa's THE SEVEN SAMURAI does a good job of mirroring the major themes and attitudes of the original while re-creating that monumental film in an occidental setting. However, Sturges's film fails to present its heroes with the style, grace, and dignity that Kurosawa accords his samurai warriors. Nevertheless THE MAGNIFICENT SEVEN is an excellent film and deserves the accolades it has received through the years. A small Mexican village is pillaged regularly by Wallach and his cutthroats. The quaking townsfolk don't have the courage to take on Wallach and his desperadoes so they decide to hire seven of the toughest hombres on that side of the Rio Grande: Brynner, McQueen, Bronson, Vaughn, Dexter, Coburn, and Buchholz. The Seven train the fearful townspeople to fight alongside them and set a trap for the wily Wallach and his group.

There's not a weak performance in the film but that's to be expected with this cast, although Brynner, who had already won an Oscar for THE KING AND I, was the only "name" at the time the film was made. Although Coburn has little dialogue, his presence is strongly felt. It wouldn't be long before screenwriters were giving him plenty to say. In fact, the only member of the Seven who didn't rise in the acting ranks after this film was Dexter, who made a few more movies, then retired from the biz.

Sturges's direction is the key to the film's quality. Just as he did in BAD DAY AT BLACK ROCK and THE GREAT ESCAPE, Sturges assembled a superb cast and skillfully put them through their paces. Bernstein's score also plays a major role in the film's success, and his main theme became an even more familiar part of American popular culture as the signature music for Marlboro cigarettes. The film spawned a number of sequels: RETURN OF THE MAGNIFICENT SEVEN; GUNS OF THE MAGNIFICENT SEVEN; and THE MAGNIFICENT SEVEN RIDE. Perhaps the ultimate testimony to the excellence of THE MAGNIFICENT SEVEN is the sword that Kurosawa presented to Sturges after seeing the film.

MAGNOLIA
DVD
1999 188m c   Drama   ★★★★
Joanne Selar/Ghoulardi Film/New Line Cinema   R
(U.S.)

Julianne Moore *(Linda Partridge)*, William H. Macy *(Quiz Kid Donnie Smith)*, John C. Reilly *(Jim Kurring)*, Tom Cruise *(Frank T.J. Mackey)*, Philip Baker Hall *(Jimmy Gator)*, Philip Seymour Hoffman *(Phil Parma)*, Jason Robards *(Earl Partridge)*, Alfred Molina *(Solomon Solomon)*, Melora Walters *(Claudia Wilson Gator)*, Michael Bowen *(Rick Spector)*

p, Joanne Sellar; d, Paul Thomas Anderson; w, Paul Thomas Anderson; ph, Robert Elswit; ed, Dylan Tichenor; prod d, William Arnold; art d, David Nakabayashi; fx, Lou Carlucci, F/X Concepts, Joe Letteri, Joseph Grossberg, Dan Rebert, Steve Johnson's XFX Group; cos, Mark Bridges; anim, Colin Brady, John Zdankiewicz

AAN Best Supporting Actor: Tom Cruise; *AAN Best Original Screenplay:* Paul Thomas Anderson; *AAN Best Original Song:* "Save Me"; Aimee Mann

A sprawling, leisurely film that recalls Robert Altman's NASHVILLE in both idiosyncrasy and emotional depth as it strolls through the lives of several unhappy Angelenos. They include spiritually conflicted Linda (Julianne Moore), trophy wife of dying TV mogul Earl Partridge (Jason Robards); Earl's home-care nurse Phil Parma (Philip Seymour Hoffman); and Earl's estranged son, misogynistic

motivational speaker Frank Mackey (Tom Cruise), who changed his name in an attempt to bury his family past. Child prodigy Stanley Spector (Jeremy Blackman) is cleaning up on a quiz show called "What Do Kids Know?" but can't seem to please his dad (Michael Bowen), a failed actor. Host Jimmy Gator (Philip Baker Hall) is trying to reconcile with his coke-addict daughter (Melora Walters), who's caught the eye of a lovelorn cop (John C. Reilly) under unlikely circumstances. And Donnie Smith (William H. Macy), one-time "What Do Kids Know?" star, is broke and about to be fired from his menial job.

Writer-director P.T. Anderson strikes a near flawless balance between looseness and structure, and indulges the occasional flight of cinematic fancy without undermining the movie's emotional integrity. He opens with a series of *Believe It Or Not?* oddities, setting up the movie's off-kilter tone and preoccupation with coincidence, and slyly foreshadowing its bizarre climax. The virtuoso sequence in which he cuts to each character crooning a snippet of Aimee Mann's mournful "Wise Up," one picking up where the previous one leaves off, is a haunting metaphor for the connections that underlie their apparent isolation. But most important, Anderson gives his cast the room to deliver phenomenal performances; he even harnesses Tom Cruise's superstar presence, channeling it into the glossy, charismatic image of loathsome but pitiable Frank Mackey. And don't ignore the biblical citation (Exodus 8:2) that hovers around the edges of several scenes; it's not there for nothing.

MAID IN MANHATTAN
DVD
2002 105m c   Romance/Comedy   ★½
Red Om/Revolution Studios/Hughes   PG-13
Entertainment/Shoelace Productions   (U.S.)

Jennifer Lopez *(Marisa Ventura)*, Ralph Fiennes *(Christopher Marshall)*, Natasha Richardson *(Caroline Lane)*, Stanley Tucci *(Jerry Siegel)*, Tyler Garcia Posey *(Ty Ventura)*, Frances Conroy *(Paula Burns)*, Chris Eigeman *(John Bextrum)*, Marissa Matrone *(Stephanie Kehoe)*, Priscilla Lopez *(Veronica Ventura)*, Bob Hoskins *(Lionel Bloch)*

p, Elaine Goldsmith-Thomas, Paul Schiff, Deborah Schindler; d, Wayne Wang; w, Kevin Wade (based on a story by Edmond Dantes); ph, Karl Walter Lindenlaub; ed, Craig McKay; m, Alan Silvestri; prod d, Jane Musky; art d, Patricia Woodbridge; fx, J.C. Brotherhood, Sarah Coatts; cos, Albert Wolsky

If this lame Cinderella story—apparently the result of an unholy tryst between PRETTY WOMAN and WORKING GIRL—had an original idea in its head, it would swiftly die of loneliness.

Harried single mom Marisa Ventura (Jennifer Lopez), a struggling housekeeper at Manhattan's posh Beresford Hotel, first lays eyes on her Prince Charming in the unlikeliest of places: the bathroom of one of the Beresford's lavish suites, where good-looking senatorial candidate Christopher Marshall (Ralph Fiennes) is relieving himself, not noticing that Marisa's still cleaning. After a romantic setup like that, only a churl would doubt that the duo, despite the differences in their social status, are destined to fall in love. And so, Marisa dons a $5,000 Dolce & Gabbana outfit belonging to well-heeled guest Caroline Lane (Natasha Richardson), who has her own aspirations regarding the charismatic pol, and a short time later Marisa and the Kennedy-esque Marshall are enjoying a romantic walk in Central Park, with paparazzi nipping at their heels. Marshall still has no idea Marisa is a hotel maid, of course, and the rest of the film is a series of increasingly implausible complications. Eventually, the truth comes out. Marshall decides that love conquers all, the couple becomes the toast of the media, and all loose ends are tidied up with the depressing inevitability of bad art.

To say that the film isn't enjoyable would be an overstatement; a good time can be had counting the number of reassuringly stock characters it offers up. They include the treacherous rich bitch (Richardson); the wise-beyond-his-years 10-year-old (Tyler Garcia Posey) who conspires to bring the couple together; Marisa's salty-tongued, heart-of-gold best friend (Marissa Matrone); and the head butler (Bob Hoskins), who never loses his dignity or forgets his class. Most viewers should be able to find their favorite archetype.

MAJESTIC, THE   DVD

2001   153m   c   Drama   ★★
Castle Rock Entertainment/Village Roadshow   PG
Pictures/NPV Entertainment/Darkwoods
Productions   (U.S.)

Jim Carrey *(Peter Appleton/Luke Trimble)*, Martin Landau *(Harry Trimble)*, Laurie Holden *(Adele Stanton)*, Allen Garfield *(Leo Kubelsky)*, Amanda Detmer *(Sandra Sinclair)*, Bob Balaban *(Majority Counsel Elvin Clyde)*, Brent Briscoe *(Sheriff Cecil Coleman)*, Jeffrey DeMunn *(Ernie Cole)*, Hal Holbrook *(Congressman Doyle)*, Matt Damon *(Voice of Luke Trimble—uncredited)*

p, Frank Darabont; d, Frank Darabont; w, Michael Sloane; ph, David Tattersall; ed, Jim Page; m, Mark Isham; prod d, Gregory Melton; art d, Tom Walsh; fx, Charles Gibson, Darrell Pritchett, Industrial Light & Magic, Pacific Title and Art; cos, Karyn Wagner

A heartwarming melodrama pickled in calculatedly old-fashioned quaintness.

It's 1951, and Hollywood screenwriter Peter Appleton (Jim Carrey) is on a roll. His "Sand Pirates of the Sahara" just opened, and he has a starlet girlfriend, a snazzy car, and a studio contract. Then it all comes tumbling down: Appleton's accused of communist sympathies and warned that HUAC is about to subpoena him. Inebriated and miserable, he drunkenly drives his car off a bridge, smacking his head on a pylon. When Appleton awakes, he's on a beach not far from the small coastal town of Lawson, without the faintest idea who he is or how he got there. But the people of Lawson, who lost 62 young men in the war, think Appleton resembles local hero Luke Trimble, missing and presumed dead after the Normandy invasion. Luke's grieving father, Harry (Martin Landau), embraces Appleton as his long-lost son, and others follow his lead—including Luke's girlfriend, Adele (Laurie Holden). Why wouldn't they want to believe in a miracle that's brought one lost Lawson son home? The rejuvenated Harry even makes the symbolically freighted decision to reopen the town's sadly deteriorated motion picture palace, the Majestic. Meanwhile, the FBI is hot on his trail. What will shatter the idyll first—the arrival of the G-Men, or the return of Appleton's memory?

Screenwriter Michael Sloane and director Frank Darabont seem to have conceived this nostalgic tear-jerker in the tradition of HAIL THE CONQUERING HERO, without noticing that Preston Sturges's response to small-town patriotism was an astringent shot of satire. That Carrey, who's a bit old for the part, always seems one facial muscle away from a smirk doesn't help matters.

MAJOR AND THE MINOR, THE

1942   100m   bw   Comedy   ★★★★½
Paramount   (U.S.)

Ginger Rogers *(Susan Applegate)*, Ray Milland *(Maj. Kirby)*, Rita Johnson *(Pamela Hill)*, Robert Benchley *(Mr. Osborne)*, Diana Lynn *(Lucy Hill)*, Edward Fielding *(Col. Hill)*, Frankie Thomas *(Cadet Osborne)*, Raymond Roe *(Cadet Wigton)*, Charles Smith *(Cadet Korner)*, Larry Nunn *(Cadet Babcock)*

p, Arthur Hornblow Jr.; d, Billy Wilder; w, Billy Wilder, Charles Brackett (based on the play "Connie Goes Home" by Edward Childs Carpenter and the story "Sunny Goes Home" by Fannie Kilbourne); ph, Leo Tover; ed, Doane Harrison; m, Robert Emmett Dolan; art d, Hans Dreier, Roland Anderson; cos, Edith Head

The LOLITA of the 1940s, and just as sexy. A sparkling farce that marked Wilder's American directorial debut after years of writing witty screenplays for other directors, THE MAJOR AND THE MINOR sails along breezily from its very first scenes until its romantic ending. The scintillating dialogue is very risque and punches out the laughs in rapid-fire succession. Ginger Rogers plays Susan, a working girl who has had it with New York and is eager to return home to the Midwest. When she finds that prices have gone up at the train station, the budget-conscious Susan dresses up as a child and manages to get on for half-fare. ("She looks kind of filled out for twelve," notes one of the lunkheaded conductors.) Caught smoking on board, Susan takes refuge with Maj. Kirby (Milland), en route to a military academy. The major and his cadets are soon at a loss to understand their attraction to such a young girl.

Algonquin Round Table member Robert Benchley is his terrifically wry self in the early scenes. Rogers gives him a hilarious egg shampoo and he also gets the film's most famous line, "Why don't you step out of that wet coat and into a dry martini?" Milland, too, is excellent in a successful invasion of Cary Grant territory. The film, though, really belongs to Rogers, giving one of her greatest performances in a role you can't imagine any other actress pulling off. She seemed to have inherited Mary Pickford's gift for playing children without seeming too ridiculous or coy—except here Wilder takes it one better. Relying on Rogers's formidable talent for mimicry, he has her playing someone who plays someone. Almost as wonderful is Lynn, her pert wisecracking almost an adolescent version of Rogers's style. Featuring the famous "Maginot Line" sequence, THE MAJOR AND THE MINOR retains its sharpness even amidst today's rather more heavy-handed approaches to sex farce. Wilder was a great director from the start, and Ginger proves that she'd have her place in the pantheon even if she'd never even heard of Fred Astaire. Dully remade as YOU'RE NEVER TOO YOUNG.

MAJOR BARBARA   ★★★★½

1941   121m   bw   Comedy
Pascal/Rank   (U.K.)

Wendy Hiller *(Maj. Barbara Undershaft)*, Rex Harrison *(Adolphus Cusins)*, Robert Morley *(Andrew Undershaft)*, Emlyn Williams *(Snobby Price)*, Robert Newton *(Bill Walker)*, Sybil Thorndike *(The General)*, Deborah Kerr *(Jenny Hill)*, David Tree *(Charles Lomax)*, Penelope-Dudley Ward *(Sarah Undershaft)*, Marie Lohr *(Lady Brittomart)*

p, Gabriel Pascal; d, Gabriel Pascal, Harold French, David Lean; w, Anatole de Grunwald, George Bernard Shaw (based on his play); ph, Ronald Neame; ed, Charles Frend; m, William Walton; prod d, Vincent Korda

What price salvation? One of Shaw's most amusing comedies, excitingly performed by a brilliant cast, though Shaw's monologues sometimes get boggy with verbiage and the direction (largely by Pascal) isn't very spritely. Hiller plays the idealistic title character, a major in the Salvation Army who despises her munitions magnate father (Morley). Adolphus Cusins (Harrison), a young professor of Greek history and literature, is hopelessly in love with the major, but she's too busy saving souls. Pop Undershaft believes that benevolent industrial management, not charity and moral uplift, is the way to help the poor. He sets out to show that intellectual Cusins and spiritual Barbara can both be bought, with surprising consequences.

Shaw's 1905 social comedy was brought to the screen by Pascal, who had talked the curmudgeonly playwright into allowing him in 1938 to film (with great success) PYG-MALION, starring Hiller and Leslie Howard. MAJOR BARBARA, however, was not as well received by audiences, who found it too sophisticated and couldn't relate to its eccentric Fabian socialism. The cast is uniformly marvelous, with the dry radiance of Hiller (reminiscent of Katharine Hepburn's, but uniquely her own) firing scene after scene. Harrison has a great way with flip dialogue, yet still manages to convey his passion for Barbara. Newton is delightfully wicked as a money-grubbing slum dweller. The rest of the cast reads like a who's who of British character actors; they keep the rather stodgy, unimaginative direction constantly on the go. Special mention must go to the touching Kerr, just starting her career, and the wonderful Morley. (You almost have to look twice to recognize him behind that beard.) The 32-year-old actor is not only convincing as the father of the 28-year-old Hiller but also a worthy and likable mouthpiece for many of Shaw's ideas. Valuable as a fine performance of an important and delightful play, MAJOR BARBARA makes for bracingly intelligent cinema.

MAKE WAY FOR TOMORROW
1937 91m   bw   Drama   ★★★★
Paramount   (U.S.)

Victor Moore (*Barkley Cooper*), Beulah Bondi (*Lucy Cooper*), Fay Bainter (*Anita Cooper*), Thomas Mitchell (*George Cooper*), Porter Hall (*Harvey Chase*), Barbara Read (*Rhoda Cooper*), Maurice Moscovich (*Max Rubens*), Elisabeth Risdon (*Cora Payne*), Minna Gombell (*Nellie Chase*), Ray Mayer (*Robert Cooper*)

p, Leo McCarey; d, Leo McCarey; w, Vina Delmar (based on the novel *The Years Are So Long* by Josephine Lawrence and the play by Helen Leary, Nolan Leary); ph, William Mellor; ed, LeRoy Stone; m, Victor Young, George Antheil; art d, Hans Dreier, Bernard Herzbrun; fx, Gordon Jennings

---

MAKE WAY FOR TOMORROW is a melancholy tear-jerker that, amazingly, never once goes over the edge into false or maudlin sentimentality. But a sensitive script and flawless acting and direction didn't help at the box office; the issue of "what to do with the old folks" was not attractive to audiences still suffering the aftermath of the Depression. Give Paramount credit, however, for making the film, and Leo McCarey credit for the same skill with sentiment that distinguished GOING MY WAY and LOVE AFFAIR. Victor Moore and Beulah Bondi play Barkley and Lucy Cooper, a poor elderly couple whose home is being taken away. None of their children has the space or the wherewithal to take in both parents, so the couple must be split up. Several scenes depict the difficulties which arise in both houses. In the end, the couple share a beautifully restrained, realistic and moving farewell at the railway station from which they embarked on their honeymoon decades ago.

Stage and screen comedian Moore was already 60 when he accepted this unaccustomed dramatic role, and he was simply brilliant. Bondi was only 46, but Wally Westmore's makeup convinces the eye that she is two decades older. Critics loved it, and MAKE WAY FOR TOMORROW made many of the Best Film lists, although it was nominated for no awards by the Oscar crowd. Thomas Mitchell, as a son, and Fay Bainter as his wife were both just 16 years younger than Moore, although no one noticed. Bring several hankies for this one. The one song, "Make Way For Tomorrow," had about as much acceptance as the film.

MALA NOCHE
1985 78m   c/bw   Drama   ★★★★
Northern Film   (U.S.)

Tim Strecter (*Walt Curtis*), Doug Cooeyate (*Johnny*), Ray Monge (*Roberto Pepper*), Nyla McCarthy (*Betty*)

p, Gus Van Sant; d, Gus Van Sant; w, Gus Van Sant (based on the novella by Walt Curtis); ph, John Campbell; ed, Gus Van Sant; m, Creighton Lindsay, Karen Kitchen, Peter Daamaan

---

The often maddening perversity of love and desire is captured most effectively in director Gus Van Sant's MALA NOCHE, which was released theatrically after DRUGSTORE COW-BOY proved one of the year's biggest independent successes.

Shot in 1985 on a miniscule budget, this gritty, poetic 16mm feature concerns Walt Curtis (Tim Streeter), an amiable skid-row liquor-store clerk in Portland, Oregon, who falls madly in love with 18-year-old Johnny (Doug Cooeyate), an illegal Mexican immigrant. When Johnny turns out to be much more interested in Walt's sister, Betty (Nyla McCarthy), than he is in Walt, the rejected suitor settles for the more amenable, if less desirable, Roberto (Ray Monge).

The fluidly imaginative technique that Van Sant displayed in DRUGSTORE COWBOY is much in evidence in this earlier feature—the highly graphic, grainy black-and-white camera-work making ingenious use of partly blacked out frames, vertiginous angles, tight close-ups, and time-lapse photography. Van Sant's frequently astonishing script is funny and passionate, his editing savvy, and his choice of music perfect as he freely and unapologetically celebrates Walt's love of Mexican boys.

MALCOLM X   *DVD*
1992 201m   c   Biography/Historical/Drama ★★★★
40 Acres and a Mule Filmworks/Marvin Worth   PG-13
Productions   (U.S.)

Denzel Washington (*Malcolm X*), Angela Bassett (*Betty Shabazz*), Albert Hall (*Baines*), Al Freeman Jr. (*Elijah Muhammad*), Delroy Lindo (*West Indian Archie*), Spike Lee (*Shorty*), Theresa Randle (*Laura*), Kate Vernon (*Sophia*), Lonette McKee (*Louise Little*), Tommy Hollis (*Earl Little*)

p, Marvin Worth, Spike Lee; d, Spike Lee; w, Spike Lee, Arnold Perl, James Baldwin; ph, Ernest Dickerson; ed, Barry Alexander Brown; m, Terence Blanchard; prod d, Wynn Thomas; art d, Tom Warren; fx, Randall Balsmeyer, Steven Kirshoff; chor, Otis Sallid; cos, Ruth Carter

---

AAN Best Actor: Denzel Washington; *AAN Best Costume Design:* Ruth E. Carter

---

MALCOLM X opens with a pair of intercut, highly polemical images: the notorious video footage of unarmed black motorist Rodney King being beaten by white L.A. policemen; and an American flag burning down into the shape of an "X." Yet this is one of only a few times in the film where director Spike Lee wears his politics on his sleeve. Lee's biography of the slain civil rights leader treats Malcolm, not as a political rallying point, but as a fully rounded individual whose life defies reduction to symbolic status. The movie begins during WWII, when Malcolm Little (Denzel Washington) and his friend Shorty (Lee) are hustlers in Boston's Black Roxbury section. We then follow Malcolm's progress as he joins a numbers gang in Harlem; ends up in Charleston State Prison, where fellow inmate Baines (Albert Hall) introduces him to the Islamic religion and the teachings of Elijah Muhammad (Al Freeman, Jr.); adopts the name Malcolm X; meets Elijah Muhammad and becomes a spokesman for the Nation of Islam; marries Betty Shabazz (Angela Bassett), a Muslim nurse; has his differences with

the Nation crystallized by a pilgrimage to Mecca; and is finally assassinated, presumably by members of the Nation.

It is Lee's willingness to present all sides of Malcolm's
character that makes MALCOLM X so persuasive as a biography. Paradoxically, though, this evenhandedness occasionally seems to blunt the film's power; the anger that drove DO
THE RIGHT THING is reduced here. There is no denying,
however, the passion in Denzel Washington's performance, a
superlative job of acting that transcends impersonation.
Washington impressively brings across Malcolm's power as
an orator, whether he's making a fiery outdoor speech to
black followers or calmly, forcefully addressing a white col-
legiate audience. The rest of the cast is equally fine, particularly Al Freeman, Jr., who does just as persuasive a job of
portraying the aging Elijah Muhammad. Lee keeps the film
moving at a clip; although it feels long, it's never boring.

MALE ANIMAL, THE
1942 101m bw Comedy ★★★★
Warner Bros.   (U.S.)

Henry Fonda (Tommy Turner), Olivia de Havilland (Ellen Turner),
Joan Leslie (Patricia Stanley), Jack Carson (Joe Ferguson),
Eugene Pallette (Ed Keller), Herbert Anderson (Michael Barnes),
Hattie McDaniel (Cleota), Ivan Simpson (Dr. Damon), Don
DeFore (Wally), Jean Ames ("Hot Garters" Garner)

p, Wolfgang Reinhardt; d, Elliott Nugent; w, Julius J. Epstein, Philip
G. Epstein, Stephen Morehouse Avery (based on the play by
James Thurber, Elliott Nugent); ph, Arthur Edeson; ed, Thomas
Richards; m, Heinz Roemheld

Charming adaptation of the comic play by Thurber and
Nugent (who also directed the film) about a stuffy midwestern college professor who plans to read a letter written by
Vanzetti (of Sacco and Vanzetti infamy) to his students. The
trustees, lead by Pallette, say that Fonda will be fired if he
dares read the missive that was penned a few days before the
alleged anarchists were executed. At the same time, Carson
arrives in town. He's an old flame of Fonda's wife, de
Havilland, and she is, once again, taken by his dubious charm.
Carson has come home for "the big game," and Fonda thinks
he's just a big, beefy bore. Anderson is the editor of the school
paper who writes an editorial in which he applauds Fonda for
his decision to read the controversial letter. The editorial also
states that the school seems to have a bias against liberal teachers. Simpson, the dean, is irate and warns Fonda that his job is
in jeopardy. Matters come to a head when de Havilland suggests that Fonda forget about reading the letter. He refuses and
cites the First Amendment. She gets angry, they quarrel, and
she exits to join Carson at a cocktail party. Fonda and
Anderson meet and get drunk together, and this infusion of
whiskey courage causes Fonda to say he will never let his wife
be stolen by another man. When Carson and de Havilland
return to the Fonda home, they find Fonda smashed so badly
that he attempts to fight the bigger Carson and only manages
to knock himself unconscious. Carson lifts Fonda, puts him to
bed, and realizes that he may be in the middle of a separation.
Although he likes de Havilland, that's as far as it goes; there's
no way that he is about to steal her away. On the following day,
Fonda reads the letter in the school auditorium. He's slightly
hung over from the drinking the night before, and, as he reads
the real letter, the trustees and other members of the faculty
relax visibly when they hear it. The letter contains no politics
whatsoever; in fact, it's a lovely plea that calls for humanity to
understand. Tears are seen at the corners of some eyes, and de
Havilland and Fonda are reunited.

Director Nugent not only cowrote the play, he also
starred in it on Broadway. He insisted that Fonda was the only
person who could do it justice on screen. The remake, SHE'S
WORKING HER WAY THROUGH COLLEGE, was terri-

ble. Fonda eventually played it on the stage in the 1950s,
when he accepted an offer from his onetime stock company
to do the role. (One of the supporting parts in this stage version was essayed by an up-and-coming actress who had a
hugging relationship with Fonda. It was his daughter, Jane.)
In small roles, note Gig Young, David Willock, and Audra
Lindley as students, as well as Raymond Bailey and William
Hopper as reporters.

MALTESE FALCON, THE
1941 100m bw Mystery DVD ★★★★★
Warner Bros.   (U.S.)

Humphrey Bogart (Sam Spade), Mary Astor (Brigid
O'Shaughnessy), Gladys George (Iva Archer), Peter Lorre (Joel
Cairo), Barton MacLane (Detective Lt. Dundy), Lee Patrick (Effie
Perine), Sydney Greenstreet (Kasper Gutman the Fat Man),
Ward Bond (Detective Tom Polhaus), Jerome Cowan (Miles
Archer), Elisha Cook Jr. (Wilmer Cook)

p, Henry Blanke; d, John Huston; w, John Huston (based on the
novel by Dashiell Hammett); ph, Arthur Edeson; ed, Thomas
Richards; m, Adolph Deutsch; art d, Robert Haas; cos, Orry-Kelly

AAN Best Picture; AAN Best Supporting Actor: Sydney
Greenstreet; AAN Best Screenplay: John Huston

A rare bird, the prized one and only. This third film version of
the Dashiell Hammett novel was propelled into the ranks of
popular classic by a stunning directorial debut from screenwriter John Huston. This was also Bogart's big chance as a
star/leading man and he is peerless as private eye Sam Spade,
a cynical rebel-hero entangled in a mass of hissing vipers.

While trying to investigate the murder of his partner,
Miles Archer (Cowan), Spade finds himself surrounded by a
number of eccentric characters: the mysterious Brigid
O'Shaughnessy (Astor), the effeminate Joel Cairo (Lorre), the
huge Kasper Gutman (Greenstreet), and Gutman's psychotic
gunsel Wilmer (Cook)—all greedily fighting for possession of
a statue of a falcon containing priceless jewels. From the
superb casting (it was the 61-year-old Greenstreet's film
debut) to the textbook perfect direction, every aspect of THE
MALTESE FALCON revealed the surprisingly assured hand
of its novice director. A seminal moment in the development
of what would come to be known as film noir, Huston's faithful adaptation helped establish the cynicism, corruption, and
moral ambiguity that would mark the genre, while his visuals—although not nearly as dark as what would follow—
showed a cramped, stifling, claustrophobic world from which
there was no escape. Huston has a field day laughing at greedy
corruption and treating the plot with amused insolence; often
it's funny to us, too. Lorre's gardenia-scented little crook versus Cook's would-be tough guy, obsequious sugar daddy (to
Cook) Greenstreet meeting Bogie's snarls—these make us
laugh. Mary Astor has one howler bit when she kicks Lorre,
but otherwise she embodies the plot's dark, bottomless center.
Piling lie on top of lie, Astor's portrayal keeps us guessing
right up to the end. Gladys George is the classic noir widow—
you've seen this bit parodied countless times—here's the real
thing. Ditto Patrick's doggedly devoted secretary (it's nice to
see her playing a dame that's not cheap for once). And that's
Walter Huston, John's distinguished father, who delivers the
bird to Bogie.

MAMMA ROMA
1962 110m bw Drama DVD ★★★★
Arco Film   (Italy)

Anna Magnani (Mamma Roma), Ettore Garofolo (Ettore), Franco
Citti (Carmine), Silvana Corsini (Bruna), Luisa Loiano

(Blancofiore), Paolo Volponi *(Priest),* Luciano Gonini *(Zacaria),* Vittorio La Paglia *(Signor Pellissier),* Piero Morgia *(Piero)*

p, Alfredo Bini; d, Pier Paolo Pasolini; w, Pier Paolo Pasolini; ph, Tonino delli Colli; ed, Nino Baragli; m, Carlo Rustichelli

Pasolini's second film after ACCATTONE (1961) stars Magnani as a prostitute who tries to start a new life. She and her son (Garofolo) move to a different part of town where she tries to make a living legitimately, but her past keeps popping up. She is eventually forced to occasionally go back to the red-light district when money becomes scarce. Her son becomes a thief and soon things go from bad to worse for the pair.

The mood of this film is grim throughout and lingers long after the closing credits roll. Bolstered by yet another power-house performance from Magnani, MAMMA ROMA is strongly realistic and remains one of Pasolini's most accessible if not most important films.

MAN AND A WOMAN, A *DVD*
(UN HOMME ET UNE FEMME)
1966 102m c/bw Drama   ★★★½
Films 13   (France)

Anouk Aimee *(Anne Gauthier),* Jean-Louis Trintignant *(Jean-Louis Duroc),* Pierre Barouh *(Pierre Gauthier),* Valerie Lagrange *(Valerie Duroc),* Simone Paris *(Head Mistress),* Antoine Sire *(Antoine Duroc),* Souad Amidou *(Francoise Gauthier),* Yane Barry *(Mistress of Jean-Louis),* Paul Le Person *(Garage Man),* Henri Chemin *(Jean-Louis' Codriver)*

p, Claude Lelouch; d, Claude Lelouch; w, Claude Lelouch, Pierre Uytterhoeven (based on a story by Claude Lelouch); ph, Claude Lelouch (Eastmancolor); ed, Claude Lelouch, G. Boisser, Claude Barrois; m, Francis Lai; art d, Robert Luchaire

AA Best Foreign Language Film ; AAN Best Actress: Anouk Aimee; *AAN Best Director:* Claude Lelouche; *AA Best Original Story and Screenplay:* Claude Lelouche, Pierre Uytterhoeven

Effusively romantic, visually stunning, slightly bland. A MAN AND A WOMAN has been condemned by some as an exercise in style for style's sake and by others for its lack of emotional complexity. Yet for many viewers this Claude Lelouch-directed film is as magical a love story as any brought to the screen. Widowed film studio script girl Anne Gauthier (Aimee, lovely) and auto racer Jean-Louis Duroc (Trintignant), whose wife has committed suicide, meet at the boarding school attended by his son and her daughter. When Jean-Louis gives Anne a ride back to Paris, friendship and then love blossom, though the specter of her much-loved late husband confuses their romance. At one point it looks like the end, but Lelouch still has a dazzling scene on the beach at Deauville up his sleeve.

Pulling out all the stops, Lelouch employs a wide variety of filmmaking techniques (swirling cameras, slow motion, switches from color to black and white, flashforwards and flashbacks) to tell his simple but effective love story. Although not the equal of the work of Lelouch's French contemporaries, A MAN AND A WOMAN demonstrated that a wide American audience was interested in stylish films, provided their stories hit home.

MAN ESCAPED, A *DVD*
(UN CONDAMNE A MORT S'EST ECHAPPE)
1956 102m bw Drama   ★★★★★
Gaumont   (France)

Francois Leterrier *(Lt. Fontaine),* Charles Le Clainche *(Francois Jost),* Roland Monod *(De Leiris the Pastor),* Maurice Beerblock *(Blanchet),* Jacques Ertaud *(Orsini),* Roger Treherne *(Terry),* Jean-Paul Delhumeau *(Hebrard),* Jean-Philippe Delamare

(Prisoner No. 110), Jacques Oerlemans *(Chief Warder),* Klaus Detlef Grevenhorst *(German Intelligence Officer)*

p, Jean Thuillier, Alain Poire; d, Robert Bresson; w, Robert Bresson (based on articles by Andre Devigny); ph, L.H. Burel; ed, Raymond Lamy; m, Wolfgang Amadeus Mozart ("Kyrie" from "Mass in C Minor"); art d, Pierre Charbonnier

One of the most important films from a cinema giant. The very spare plot features Leterrier playing a Resistance hero captured by the Nazis and imprisoned in Fort Montluc. Most of the film shows him and his cellmate (Le Clainche) attempting to successfully scale the prison walls and escape. Based on a published account of Andre Devigny, a Resistance fighter who was sentenced to be executed in 1943, A MAN ESCAPED is one of Bresson's finest works, particularly notable for his creative use of sound. Even after the success of THE DIARY OF A COUNTRY PRIEST, Bresson had to wait five years to get this project underway. The two films have in common a faith in God which is made most obvious in this picture's alternate title, THE WIND BLOWETH WHERE IT LISTETH, and in the music (Mozart's "Mass in C Minor"). As in many of Bresson's films, the cast is made up of non-professionals such as Leterrier, a philosophy graduate and a lieutenant in the military. Bresson's experience as a POW at the start of WWII, Devigny's contribution as a technical adviser, and the use of his actual cell for the location make for an grippingly authentic and detailed account. In an unanimous decision, Bresson received the "Best Director" prize from the Cannes Film Festival in 1957 for this film. In a surprisingly similar, but less successful manner, Don Siegel detailed a prison break in ESCAPE FROM ALCATRAZ, with Clint Eastwood in the starring role.

MAN FACING SOUTHEAST
(HOMBRE MIRANDO AL SUDESTE)
1986 105m c   Science Fiction/Drama ★★★★½
Cinequanon (Argentina)   R

Lorenzo Quinteros *(Dr. Dennis),* Hugo Soto *(Rantes),* Ines Vernengo *(Beatriz),* Cristina Scaramuzza *(Nurse),* Rubens W. Correa *(Dr. Prieto),* David Edery, Rodolfo Rodas, Jean Pierre Requeraz

p, Lujan Pflaum; d, Eliseo Subiela; w, Eliseo Subiela; ph, Ricardo de Angelis; ed, Luis Cesar D'Angiolillo; m, Pedro Aznar; art d, Abel Facello

Argentine director Eliseo Subiela takes an allegorical approach to the story of Christ in this enigmatic parable. A jaded mental asylum psychiatrist, Dr. Dennis (Lorenzo Quinteros), becomes fascinated with Rantes (Hugo Soto), who suddenly appears in his ward. Upon questioning, Rantes explains he is a holographic being from another planet, which transmits to him from the southeast. As the two men grow closer, it begins to appear that Rantes' mission is something beyond an intergalactic visit; eventually, his inexplicable influence on the other patients incurs the displeasure of authorities who demand that Dennis take severe measures to counteract his friend and patient's delirium.

Writer-director Subiela incorporates a wide variety of influences to create a fascinating, multifaceted work of art. The reworking of the Gospels is evident, but the biblical references are a basis for convincing contemporary characters and open questions, with the film clearly participating in and reconsidering the mystical tradition in Latin American literature. Subiela also incorporates a variety of references to paintings in the film's design. Soto's performance is remarkable, with Quinteros proving an excellent counterpart. Their natural, often affectionate, and unique relationship becomes the heart of this profound and highly personal film.

MAN FOR ALL SEASONS, A

1966 120m c Drama
Highland (U.K.)
★★★★

Paul Scofield *(Sir Thomas More)*, Wendy Hiller *(Alice More)*, Leo McKern *(Thomas Cromwell)*, Robert Shaw *(King Henry VIII)*, Orson Welles *(Cardinal Wolsey)*, Susannah York *(Margaret More)*, Nigel Davenport *(Duke of Norfolk)*, John Hurt *(Richard Rich)*, Corin Redgrave *(William Roper)*, Colin Blakely *(Matthew)*

p, Fred Zinnemann; d, Fred Zinnemann; w, Robert Bolt, Constance Willis (based on the play by Robert Bolt); ph, Ted Moore (Technicolor); ed, Ralph Kemplen; m, Georges Delerue; prod d, John Box; art d, Terence Marsh; cos, Elizabeth Haffenden, Joan Bridge

AA Best Picture; AA Best Actor: Paul Scofield; AAN Best Supporting Actor: Robert Shaw; AAN Best Supporting Actress: Wendy Hiller; AA Best Director: Fred Zinnemann; AA Best Adapted Screenplay: Robert Bolt; AA Best Color Cinematography: Ted Moore; AA Best Costume Design (Color): Elizabeth Haffenden, Joan Bridge

This adaptation of Robert Bolt's hit play proved to be both prestigious and commercial. Studio executives were unsure whether folks would turn out for the story of Sir Thomas More, a Catholic statesman in England who rebelled against Henry VIII's self-proclaimed status as the head of the Church of England and paid for his beliefs with his life.

More (Scofield) is appointed to succeed Cardinal Wolsey (Welles) as Lord Chancellor. He comes to grips with Shaw, as Henry VIII, who wants to divorce his barren wife and take a new bride. Henry needs a male heir, but Rome (for reasons both political and spiritual) won't grant an annulment. Henry breaks with the Pope, declaring himself spiritual ruler of the new Church of England, and demands More's endorsement. More is torn between loyalty to his monarch and concern for his immortal soul; a lawyer, he at first hopes to survive through ethical hairsplitting. But the king's rage, and the machinations of Thomas Cromwell (Leo McKern) force his hand.

Scofield is magnificent in his first major film role; Shaw stands out as an energetic, youthfully impetuous Henry. Director Zinnemann never allows his primarily stage-trained actors to indulge in theatrical over-emoting. This absorbing film features inventive camerawork and superior production values. Winner of six Oscars, the film won the exact same awards (and Best British Film as well) from the British Film Academy.

MAN FROM LARAMIE, THE

1955 104m c Western
Columbia (U.S.)
★★★★

James Stewart *(Will Lockhart)*, Arthur Kennedy *(Vic Hansbro)*, Donald Crisp *(Alec Waggoman)*, Cathy O'Donnell *(Barbara Waggoman)*, Alex Nicol *(Dave Waggoman)*, Aline MacMahon *(Kate Canaday)*, Wallace Ford *(Charley O'Leary)*, Jack Elam *(Chris Boldt)*, John War Eagle *(Frank Darrah)*, James Millican *(Tom Quigby)*

p, William Goetz; d, Anthony Mann; w, Philip Yordan, Frank Burt (based on a *Saturday Evening Post* story by Thomas T. Flynn); ph, Charles Lang (Technicolor); ed, William Lyon; m, George Duning; art d, Cary Odell

Mann's westerns revitalized the genre in the 1950s because they were derived from classic struggles inspired by such works as the Bible and Shakespeare. His westerns weren't just action-packed chases; they were adult dramas which illustrated the psychological and moral dilemmas regarding the family, hatred, revenge, the land, and the nature of savagery versus civilization. In addition to being skillfully shot,

acted, and scripted, Mann's westerns have an intelligence and a brutal conviction which compares well even with those by John Ford.

Will Lockhart (Stewart) leaves his home in Laramie, Wyoming, on a mission to find the men responsible for selling automatic rifles to the Apaches who killed his brother. He enters the town of Coronado, New Mexico, and soon learns that most of the territory is ruled by Alec Waggoman (Crisp), a megalomaniacal rancher who has been waging war against rival female rancher Kate Canaday (MacMahon). The aging Waggoman must decide whether to leave his empire to his smart adopted son and ranch foreman Vic (Kennedy) or his crazed, vicious blood heir Dave (Nicol). While digging for clues, Will comes between not only rival ranchers but also rival sons. Nobody gets out unscathed.

At the time of his death in 1967, director Mann had announced his plan to adapt Shakespeare's King Lear as a western (much the same way Japanese director Akira Kurosawa did with RAN). One can see that THE MAN FROM LARAMIE was something of a dress rehearsal for this project. Crisp, as Lear, frets over the continuation of his empire and is blind to the fact that it is Kennedy who loves him most. His guilt over his ruthless life (and having turned his former lover into an enemy) cloud his mind and move him to make bad decisions that ensure his downfall. Violent but compelling stuff.

MAN FROM SNOWY RIVER, THE

1982 102m c Western/Adventure
Hoyts/Cambridge (Australia)
★★★
R

Kirk Douglas *(Harrison/Spur)*, Jack Thompson *(Clancy)*, Tom Burlinson *(Jim Craig)*, Terence Donovan *(Henry Craig)*, Tommy Dysart *(Mountain Man)*, Bruce Kerr *(Man in Street)*, David Bradshaw *(A. B. "Banjo" Paterson)*, Sigrid Thornton *(Jessica)*, Tony Bonner *(Kane)*, June Jago *(Mrs. Bailey)*

p, Geoff Burrowes; d, George Miller; w, John Dixon, Fred Cullen (based on the poem by A.B. "Banjo" Paterson); ph, Keith Wagstaff (Panavision, Eastmancolor); ed, Adrian Carr; m, Bruce Rowland; art d, Leslie Binns; cos, Robin Hall

Kirk Douglas plays two brothers, the one, Harrison, an aristocratic landowner, the other, Spur, a one-legged, scraggly prospector. The pair experience a falling out, though this is not addressed until the latter half of the picture. More important than the plot are the characters of the brothers. The film was one of Australia's top-grossing pictures, though the producers took a chance in casting an American in the roles. (Robert Mitchum and Burt Lancaster also were considered.) A fine directorial debut from George Miller, who, not surprisingly, tends to be confused with the director of MAD MAX and THE ROAD WARRIOR, also named George Miller.

MAN HUNT

1941 105m bw Spy
Fox (U.S.)
★★★★½

Walter Pidgeon *(Capt. Thorndike)*, Joan Bennett *(Jerry)*, George Sanders *(Quive-Smith)*, John Carradine *(Mr. Jones)*, Roddy McDowall *(Vaner the Cabin Boy)*, Ludwig Stossel *(Doctor)*, Heather Thatcher *(Lady Risborough)*, Frederic Worlock *(Lord Risborough)*, Roger Imhof *(Capt. Jensen)*, Egon Brecher *(Whiskers)*

p, Kenneth MacGowan; d, Fritz Lang; w, Dudley Nichols (based on the novel *Rogue Male* by Geoffrey Household); ph, Arthur Miller; ed, Allen McNeil; m, Alfred Newman; art d, Richard Day, Wiard Ihnen; cos, Travis Banton

One of the best-loved of Lang's spy dramas, MAN HUNT is a superbly exciting, tightly constructed picture which stars

Pidgeon, terrific as Thorndike, a big-game hunter in the Bavarian Alps who accidentally discovers that he has a chance to assassinate Hitler. Apprehended by Gestapo leader Quive-Smith (Sanders), he refuses to sign a confession and is beaten and left for dead. With the help of a friendly youngster (McDowall), Thorndike stows away on a Danish steamer. Also on board, however, is the mysterious, umbrella-wielding Mr. Jones (Carradine), who has Thorndike's passport and has taken his identity. Befriended by a friendly cockney prostitute (Bennett, rarely better) in London, Thorndike eventually has a memorable showdown with Jones in a subway tunnel. Our dashing hero isn't out of danger yet, though; Quive-Smith threatens as well, and it's up to a hatpin to save the day.

Based on the best-selling novel, *Rogue Male*, MAN HUNT was scripted by the immensely talented Dudley Nichols and intended as a John Ford picture. Ford, however, disliked the subject matter and the film was offered, by Darryl Zanuck, to Lang. Lang encountered, as he often did, some problems on the set involving both the Hays Code and budget constraints by Zanuck. A great lover of complex female characters, Lang had cast Bennett as a compassionate woman who happened to be a prostitute. The Hays Code, however, which would just as soon have denied the existence of prostitution, required some rewrites. According to Lang, "We had to prominently show a sewing machine in her apartment; thus she was not a whore, she was a 'seamstress.' Talk about authenticity!" Most objectionable to Zanuck was the parting scene between Pidgeon and Bennett which was to take place on London Bridge. Zanuck was distressed by the fact that a "decent" girl had to play the whore in front of the man she loved, and so refused to allow any money in the budget for this essential scene. As Lang tells it, he, cinematographer Miller and unit manager Benny Silvi found a single bridge railing in the props department. Two were needed, however, so Lang spent $40 to have a second one constructed. Without the aid of studio workers (whose unions would not allow such defiance), the threesome stole into the studio at four a.m. They painted the backdrop, hung light bulbs in a manner of diminishing perspective to create depth, and then obscured the whole thing in a blanket of fog. The result was a beautifully atmospheric set.

MAN IN LOVE, A

(UN HOMME AMOUREUX)
1987 108m c Romance
Camera One/Alexandre/JMS (France)
★★★½
R

Greta Scacchi *(Jane Steiner)*, Peter Coyote *(Steve Elliott)*, Peter Riegert *(Michael Pozner)*, Claudia Cardinale *(Julia Steiner)*, John Berry Jr. *(Harry Steiner)*, Vincent Lindon *(Bruno Schlosser)*, Jamie Lee Curtis *(Susan Elliott)*, Jean Pigozzi *(Dante Pizani)*, Elia Katz *(Sam)*, Constantin Alexandrov *(De Vitta)*

p, Marjorie Israel, Armand Barbault, Roberto Guissani; d, Diane Kurys; w, Diane Kurys, Olivier Schatzky, Israel Horovitz; ph, Bernard Zitzermann (Eastmancolor); ed, Joele Van Effenterre; m, Georges Delerue; art d, Dean Tavoularis; cos, Brigitte Nierhaus

A MAN IN LOVE is romantic melodrama on a grand, international scale. Set mostly in Italy's Cinecitta film studio, it stars Peter Coyote as Steve Elliott, a temperamental American actor playing the lead in a film biography of Cesare Pavese, the Italian Communist writer who committed suicide in 1950 at age 41. The film's stereotypically obsessive director (Jean Pigozzi) has cast a relatively unknown English-speaking actress, Jane Steiner (Greta Scacchi), in a minor role as one of the many women Pavese loved, and her first visit to the set results in an explosive confrontation with the difficult star, offering a hint of things to come. An unpredictable, sexually charged romance develops between the two actors both on-and offscreen, putting Steve's acting ability and his feelings for his wife (Jamie Lee Curtis) to the test. Diane Kurys's first film in English transcends borders. Displaying remarkable adroitness, she interweaves various lan-

guages and locales, shows her characters to be a unique group of people involved in a fiction-making process that overlaps with and confuses real life, and maintains a complex plot in which the simple act of choosing a supporting actress nearly sinks the film-within-the-film and upsets two relationships. Badly underrated by critics, especially in comparison with Kurys's ENTRE NOUS, A MAN IN LOVE firmly establishes that Kurys is one of the most compelling filmmakers to emerge from France in recent years.

MAN IN THE GRAY FLANNEL SUIT, THE

1956 152m c Drama
Fox (U.S.)
★★★

Gregory Peck *(Tom Rath)*, Jennifer Jones *(Betsy Rath)*, Fredric March *(Ralph Hopkins)*, Marisa Pavan *(Maria)*, Ann Harding *(Mrs. Hopkins)*, Lee J. Cobb *(Judge Bernstein)*, Keenan Wynn *(Caesar Gardella)*, Gene Lockhart *(Hawthorne)*, Gigi Perreau *(Susan Hopkins)*, Portland Mason *(Janie)*

p, Darryl F. Zanuck; d, Nunnally Johnson; w, Nunnally Johnson (based on the novel by Sloan Wilson); ph, Charles Clarke (CinemaScope, DeLuxe Color); ed, Dorothy Spencer; m, Bernard Herrmann; art d, Lyle Wheeler, Jack Martin Smith; fx, Ray Kellogg; cos, Charles LeMaire

Middle-class middle-America... the inside story? Hardly, but nonetheless a surprisingly engrossing, if shallow and overlong, Hollywood vision of 1950s thirtysomethings, with Peck turning in a dignified title role.

Tom Rath has a $10K mortgage, three brats, and psycho-Betsy (Jones). Fun. He also has bad memories of WWII, where he knifed a German during a freezing winter for his coat, had a fling with wistful peasant Maria (Pavan), and threw a grenade which accidentally killed his best friend. Oops. Acquiring a new, lucrative position writing speeches for avuncular company president Ralph (March), Tom must choose between working overtime on the job or on his relationship with psycho-Betsy. Hmm. And what about his grandmother's estate? And that kid he fathered during the war? My! Don't worry—Lee J. Cobb is on hand to tell us at the finale that "God's in His heaven and all's right with the world." Whew.

Totally hollow trash, with a hysteria-prone Jennifer Jones displaying an odd crease down the middle of her face. So slickly dished up, though, you can feel yourself sliding around on the sofa. Nice to see Ann Harding.

MAN IN THE IRON MASK, THE

1939 110m bw Historical/Adventure
UA (U.S.)
★★★★

Louis Hayward *(Louis XIV/Philippe)*, Joan Bennett *(Maria Theresa)*, Warren William *(D'Artagnan)*, Joseph Schildkraut *(Fouquet)*, Alan Hale *(Porthos)*, Miles Mander *(Aramis)*, Bert Roach *(Athos)*, Walter Kingsford *(Colbert)*, Marion Martin *(Mlle. de la Valliere)*, Montagu Love *(Spanish Ambassador)*

p, Edward Small; d, James Whale; w, George Bruce (based on the novel by Alexandre Dumas); ph, Robert Planck; ed, Grant Whytock; m, Lucien Moraweck; art d, John DuCasse Schulze; fx, Howard Anderson

AAN Best Original Score: Lud Gluskin, Lucien Moraweck

James Whale's high quality version of Dumas's classic tale of twin brothers, one the king of France and the other a prisoner at Isle St. Marguerite (Hayward, very fine in a dual role). William, as musketeer D'Artagnan, comes to the aid of the imprisoned brother, who is mercilessly forced to wear an iron mask to prevent anyone from realizing he is heir to the throne. Whale directed this elaborately costumed adventure with the greatest of verve and flair, though his career came to a halt in 1941. (Aging and frail, the master director committed suicide

16 years later.) This film also marked the first screen appearance of Peter Cushing.

MAN IN THE WHITE SUIT, THE
1951 85m bw Comedy **DVD** ★★★★★
Ealing (U.K.)

Alec Guinness (Sidney Stratton), Joan Greenwood (Daphne Birnley), Cecil Parker (Alan Birnley), Michael Gough (Michael Corland), Ernest Thesiger (Sir John Kierlaw), Howard Marion-Crawford (Cranford), Duncan Lamont (Harry), Henry Mollison (Hoskins), Vida Hope (Bertha), Patric Doonan (Frank)

p, Michael Balcon; d, Alexander Mackendrick; w, Roger MacDougall, John Dighton, Alexander Mackendrick (based on the play by Roger MacDougall); ph, Douglas Slocombe; ed, Bernard Gribble; m, Benjamin Frankel; art d, Jim Morahan; fx, Sydney Pearson, Geoffrey Dickinson; cos, Anthony Mendleson

AAN Best Screenplay: Roger MacDougall, John Dighton, Alexander Mackendrick

A sharp satirical comedy about the social contradictions of technology, THE MAN IN THE WHITE SUIT offers a tour de force by master comic Guinness. He plays Sidney Stratton, an eccentric inventor believed crazy by most except for Daphne Birnley (Greenwood), daughter of a millionaire textile king (Parker). Stratton manages to finagle access to Birnley's elaborate development laboratory, supplied with all the chemicals and equipment he requires. Although Birnley and his associates have to deal with lab explosions and the eerie gurgling of Stratton's setup, Sidney eventually comes through, creating a fabric that never wears out and which repels dirt completely. He fashions a pristine white suit of the material and is as first hailed as a genius. Soon enough, though, the problems with the miracle material become evident. Labor dislikes poor Sidney because they'll all be put out of work once people buy enough of these wonder suits, and management changes its attitudes when they realize they'll be put out of business by Sidney's new fashion line. Although the two opposing forces do seem to get the better of Sidney in the memorable finale, his last-second knowing smile suggests an even greater discovery just around the corner.

THE MAN IN THE WHITE SUIT, besides offering consistent humor and often hilarious scenes, is another minor masterpiece of acting on Guinness' part: he shows marvelous restraint that gives way to brief hysteria, emphasizing again the versatility of this astounding actor. Greenwood, meanwhile, with her striking eyes, haughty yet vaguely haunted manner and that one-of-a-kind voice, is at her peak, parrying comic thrusts with great aplomb. The reliable Parker shines yet again as the worried capitalist and, on the proletarian side, the forceful Hope and the adorable Edie Martin are especially outstanding. Special mention should also be made of Thesiger, that unique comic talent from several James Whale masterworks of the 1930s. He is wonderful here as the decrepit but all-powerful industrial czar who decrees Sidney's fate for the sake of business. In addition to the laughs, this film also indicts the ruthless and manipulative ways of businessmen. The acerbic social criticism lacing the film, however, does not exclude union representatives either, and the result is an intelligently rounded satire. Mackendrick's formidable gifts as both director and screenwriter are on vivid display here.

MAN OF A THOUSAND FACES
1957 122m bw Biography **DVD** ★★★½
Universal (U.S.)

James Cagney (Lon Chaney), Dorothy Malone (Cleva Creighton Chaney), Jane Greer (Hazel Bennet), Marjorie Rambeau (Gert), Jim Backus (Clarence Logan), Robert Evans (Irving Thalberg), Celia Lovsky (Mrs. Chaney), Jeanne Cagney (Carrie Chaney), Jack Albertson (Dr. J. Wilson Shields), Roger Smith (Creighton Chaney at Age 21)

p, Robert Arthur; d, Joseph Pevney; w, R. Wright Campbell, Ivan Goff, Ben Roberts (based on a story by Ralph Wheelright); ph, Russell Metty; ed, Ted J. Kent; m, Frank Skinner; art d, Alexander Golitzen, Eric Orbom; fx, Clifford Stine; cos, Bill Thomas

AAN Best Original Story and Screenplay: Ralph Wheelright, R. Wright Campbell, Ivan Goff, Ben Roberts

Few silent screen stars approached the status of Lon Chaney. A makeup genius, he was the heart of horror during the 1920s, and Cagney's respectful rendering of this great artist is spectacular. Born the son of deaf-mute parents, Chaney becomes a successful vaudeville entertainer, creating many distinctive characters through inventive makeup and skilled mime. He meets and marries beautiful but neurotic fellow performer Cleva Creighton (melodramatic Malone) but when he introduces her to his parents, she becomes hysterical at the thought that their children might be born with congenital deafness. When baby Creighton (later Lon Chaney Jr.) is born without these afflictions, all seems well until Cleva begins to resent her husband's popularity. She abandons her family, whereupon Chaney goes to Hollywood and, in true movie bio fashion, works his way up to film star status. He also marries the supportive Hazel Bennet (Greer, good but a trifle wasted) and Chaney's compelling characterizations in THE PHANTOM OF THE OPERA and THE HUNCHBACK OF NOTRE DAME thrill his ever-growing following. But, as might be expected, Cleva returns to the scene, threatening the relationship between Chaney and his now-grown son (Smith).

Cagney is riveting as Chaney (who died in 1930 at the age of 47), enacting the many great roles the silent star made famous in startling cameo performances. Many of Chaney's makeup secrets died with him, but experts Bud Westmore and Jack Kevan did a good job in coming close.

Lovsky is excellent as Chaney's mother, but newcomer Evans is unconvincing as MGM mogul Irving Thalberg. Thalberg's widow, retired film star Norma Shearer, did a good job in picking a handsome young man who resembled her "boy genius" husband, but that does not an actor make. Ironically, Evans later became a real-life mogul, heading Paramount from 1966 to 1976. Smith, playing the 21-year-old Creighton Chaney, is rather stoical, suggesting little of Chaney Jr's anguish.

MAN OF FLOWERS
1984 91m c Drama **DVD** ★★★½
Flowers (Australia)

Norman Kaye (Charles Bremer), Alyson Best (Lisa), Chris Haywood (David), Sara Walker (Jane), Julia Blake (Art Teacher), Bob Ellis (Psychiatrist), Barry Dickins (Postman), Patrick Cook (Coppershop Man), Victoria Eagger (Angela), Werner Herzog (Father)

p, Jane Ballantyne, Paul Cox; d, Paul Cox; w, Paul Cox, Bob Ellis; ph, Yuri Sokol (Fujicolor); ed, Tim Lewis; m, Gaetano Donizetti; art d, Asher Bilu; cos, Lirit Bilu

Charles Bremer (Norman Kaye) is a sexually repressed, middle-aged artist who sublimates his desires into paintings of flowers and impassioned organ playing. He hires artist's model Lisa (Alyson Best) for $100 a week to come to his house and take off her clothes for him on a makeshift altar while he plays "The Love Duet" from Donizetti's "Lucia di Lammermoor," after which he rushes to church and vents his emotions on a pipe organ. Charles finally goes to a psychiatrist, who, in the tradition of movie shrinks, is kinkier than his patients.

An interesting, sometimes funny film about loneliness and emotional isolation, MAN OF FLOWERS boasts a literate script, a lush, sensual texture and, best of all, a silent cameo by German director Werner Herzog as Bremer's domineering father.

MAN OF IRON   DVD
(CZLOWIEK Z ZELAZA)
1980 140m c   Historical   ★★★★
Film Polski/Film Unit X   (Poland)   PG

Jerzy Radziwilowicz (Tomczyk), Krystyna Janda (Agnieszka), Marian Opania (Winkiel), Irene Byrska (Anna Hulewicz' Mother), Boguslaw Linda (Radio-TV Technician Dzidek), Wieslawa Kosmalska (Anna), Andrzej Seweryn (Capt. Wirski), Krzysztof Janczar (Kryszka), Boguslaw Sobczuk (TV Editor), Franciszek Trzeciak (Badecki)

d, Andrzej Wajda; w, Aleksander Scibor-Rylski; ph, Edward Klosinski; Janusz Kalicinski; ed, Halina Prugar; m, Andrzej Korzynski; art d, Allan Starski, Maja Chrolowska; cos, Wieslawa Starska

AAN Best Foreign Language Film

Andrzej Wajda's sequel to MAN OF MARBLE uses the same scriptwriter and leading players and again traces its story through interviews. This film is a realistic portrayal of Gdansk from the student reform movement of 1968 to the Solidarity strikes in 1980. Strike leader Tomczyk (Jerzy Radziwilowicz) is harassed by the government and by a journalist (Marian Opania). The latter conducts a smear campaign against the young labor activist, but his own loyalties are tested during the strike. Wajda's superb amalgam of fictional characters and historical fact not only entertains but also documents a tense period in Polish history. Solidarity leader Walesa is among the real-life figures who appear. Made under intense political pressure shortly before an authoritarian crackdown, MAN OF IRON was finished only hours before its premiere at the Cannes Film Festival, where it won top honors.

MAN OF MARBLE   DVD
(CZLOWIEK Z MARMURU)
1977 160m c/bw Drama/Political   ★★★½
Enterprise de Realization/Zespoly Filmowe
Unit "X"   (Poland)

Krystyna Janda (Agnieszka), Jerzy Radziwilowicz (Mateusz Birkut/Maciek Tomczyk), Tadeusz Lomnicki (Jerzy Burski), Jacek Lomnicki (Young Burski), Krystyna Zachwatowicz (Hanka Tomcyzka), Michal Tarkowski (Wincenty Witek), Piotr Cieslak (Michalak), Wieslaw Wojcik (Secretary Jodia), Boguslaw Sobczuk (Agnieszka's Producer), Leonard Zajaczkowski (Leonard Frybos—Cameraman)

p, Jerzy Radziwilowicz, Krystyna Janda; d, Andrzej Wajda; w, Aleksander Scibor-Rylski; ph, Edward Klosinski (Eastmancolor); ed, Halina Pugarowa, Maria Kaliniciska; m, Andrzej Korzynski; prod d, Allan Starski; art d, Wojciech Majda, Maria Osiecka-Kuminek; cos, Lidia Rzeszewska, Wieslawa Konopelska

A fine example of political art. The events which culminated in the workers' revolt and eventual martial law crackdown in Poland in 1982 are foreshadowed by one of Poland's highest-ranking directors in this black satire. Director Wajda follows film student Janda who wants to make a documentary about a former worker as her graduation requirement. Radziwilowicz is to be her subject, a man who had been lauded for his brick-laying skills before vanishing into total obscurity. Previously the subject of a film that showed what a great worker he was, Radziwilowicz became something of a star. But when he began believing the publicity himself and started interfering in worker politics, the government quick-

ly stifled him, disgracing his name, and banishing him into historical obscurity. This is the story Janda discovers through interviews with Radziwilowicz's contemporaries and family and through old newsreels. Using an expository style similar to that of CITIZEN KANE, Wajda has fashioned a sophisticated indictment of Poland's communist regime, with all of its warts clearly exposed. Wajda followed this with MAN OF IRON, using similar storytelling methods to portray the rise of Poland's Solidarity movement and its leader Lech Walesa.

MAN OF THE WEST
1958 100m c   Western   ★★★★★
UA   (U.S.)

Gary Cooper (Link Jones), Julie London (Billie Ellis), Lee J. Cobb (Dock Tobin), Arthur O'Connell (Sam Beasley), Jack Lord (Coaley), John Dehner (Claude), Royal Dano (Trout), Bob Wilke (Ponch), Jack Williams (Alcutt), Guy Wilkerson (Conductor)

p, Walter M. Mirisch; d, Anthony Mann; w, Reginald Rose (based on the novel The Border Jumpers by Will C. Brown); ph, Ernest Haller (CinemaScope, DeLuxe Color); ed, Richard Heermance; m, Leigh Harline; art d, Hilyard Brown; cos, Yvonne Wood

Mann's last western, and his most disturbing foray into the genre. Working here with Cooper instead of Jimmy Stewart, Mann again tells a tale of Shakespearean proportions in which complicated men struggle against their own worst instincts. The film opens as Link (Cooper), a seemingly guileless Texas bumpkin, leaves his wife and children and boards a train to hire a schoolteacher from Fort Worth. Enlisted by con man Sam Beasley (O'Connell) to scam Link, saloon singer Billie Ellis (London) almost succeeds when the psychotic Tobin gang holds up the train. Stranded, Link leads Billie and Beasley to the Tobins's nearby cabin, where it is revealed that he is a former gang member and nephew of its leader (Cobb). While Uncle Dock is happy to see his former right-hand man, his cousins are less than thrilled by his presence but more than thrilled by Billie's. Plans to rob a bank in a former boomtown turned ghost town spearhead family rivalries and the ugly nature of Link's past.

As in Mann's other westerns, there is an air of epic tragedy to MAN OF THE WEST. Link's accidental reentry into the gang causes his base instincts to once again boil to the surface after years of conformity, but, better than the rest of the gang, he realizes that a way of life is passing. In some ways it is Dock rather than Link who plays the title character. Mann's heroes and villains do not wear white and black hats to separate good from evil; they are real people who suffer from anxiety, guilt, hatred, and doubt. Some succumb to lust, others to change, but a few achieve a transcendent grace. Excellent acting all around (even if casting the decade-older Cooper as Cobb's nephew doesn't quite wash), with a gun battle between Cooper and Dehner and a different sort of encounter between Cooper and London as highlights.

MAN ON FIRE   DVD
2004 145m c   Thriller/Action/Crime   ★★½
Fox 2000 Pictures/New Regency Pictures/Regency
Enterprises/Scott Free Productions   (U.S./U.K.) R

Denzel Washington (John Creasy), Dakota Fanning (Lupita "Pita" Martin Ramos), Marc Antony (Samuel Martin Ramos), Radha Mitchell (Lisa Martin Ramos), Christopher Walken (Rayburn), Giancarlo Giannini (Manzano), Rachel Ticotin (Mariana), Jesus Ochoa (Fuentes), Mickey Rourke (Jordan Kalfus), Angelina Pelaez (Sister Anna)

p, Lucas Foster, Conrad Hool, Lance Hool, Arnon Milchan, Tony Scott; d, Tony Scott; w, Brian Helgeland (based on the novel by A.J. Quinnell); ph, Paul Cameron; ed, Christian Wagner; m, Harry

Gregson-Williams; prod d, Benjamin Fernandez, Chris Seagers; art d, Hector Romero; fx, Jesus G. Duran; cos, Louise Frogley, Lucinda Syson, Manuel Teil

"He's an artist of death," says former mercenary Rayburn (Christopher Walken) of his friend John Creasy (Denzel Washington), "and he's about to paint his masterpiece." Only Walken can say that much without sounding like a complete ass, and he's on shaky ground in director Tony Scott's gloomy story of righteous retribution.

Guilt-ridden, alcoholic former U.S. military operative Creasy drifts to crime-ridden Mexico City to visit Rayburn, who has forged a new life pandering to the fears of foreign business people. Rayburn introduces Creasy to high-strung Mexican businessman Sammy Ramos (Marc Antony) and his steely American wife (Radha Mitchell), who need a bodyguard for their nine-year-old daughter, Pita (Dakota Fanning). Tormented and suicidal, Creasy is an uneasy fit for a job that's equal parts junkyard dog and babysitter to an inquisitive, lonely girl, but Pita soon warms his frozen heart. So when kidnappers do come, Creasy nearly dies trying to protect Pita. Having failed, he reverts to soulless-killing-machine mode and resolves to track down and do away with every single person who had anything to do with the child's abduction, no matter where the trail of greed and perfidy leads.

Transplanting pseudonymous novelist A.J. Quinnell's story from Italy to Mexico has the unintentional effect of playing into prejudices about Latin corruption, and Scott can't leave a thematic underpinning under anything. He swaddles this fundamentally straightforward revenge story in a jumble of bleary freeze-frames, random changes of color saturation and film stock, jump cuts, and stuttering montages. In the end, Scott cares too much about style to let the festering ugliness of true vigilantism stain his carefully art-directed mise-en-scene.

MAN ON THE EIFFEL TOWER, THE [DVD]

1949 97m c Mystery ★★★★
RKO (U.S.)

Charles Laughton (Inspector Maigret), Franchot Tone (Radek), Burgess Meredith (Huertin), Robert Hutton (Bill Kirby), Jean Wallace (Edna Wallace), Patricia Roc (Helen Kirby), Belita (Gisella), George Thorpe (Cornelieu), William Phipps (Janvier), William Cottrell (Moers)

p, Irving Allen; d, Burgess Meredith; w, Harry Brown (based on the story "A Battle of Nerves" by Georges Simenon); ph, Stanley Cortez (Ansco Color); ed, Louis Sackin; m, Michel Michelet; art d, Rene Renoux

Georges Simenon's famous sleuth, Inspector Maigret, was never better enacted than by the shrewd, slow, and sure Charles Laughton, who pursues a thrill killer-for-hire in this superb film noir production. The nephew of a rich woman hires Radek (Tone) to kill his aunt, and Maigret investigates. After dismissing a blind knife-grinder (Meredith, who also directed) as too obvious a suspect, Maigret unearths Tone, a psychopathic murderer who enjoys killing and baiting the police. Cop and killer play an intense cat-and-mouse game until one of them finally cracks under the psychological strain, with a superb chase up the Eiffel Tower as the exciting finale. The acting is outstanding in this film, and Franchot Tone actually overcomes Laughton's masterful mannerisms in their scenes together. Burgess Meredith both adroitly performs his red-herring role and directs with a sure hand. The lensing by Stanley Cortez, in rich Ansco color, lovingly shows a majestic Paris while sharply capturing the thrilling story. Michelet's score is also exceptional.

MAN ON THE FLYING TRAPEZE, THE

1935 65m bw Comedy ★★★★
Paramount (U.S.)

W.C. Fields (Ambrose Wolfinger), Mary Brian (Hope Wolfinger), Kathleen Howard (Leona Wolfinger), Grady Sutton (Claude Neselrode), Vera Lewis (Mrs. Cordelia Neselrode), Lucien Littlefield (Mr. Peabody), Oscar Apfel (President Malloy), Lew Kelly (Adolph Berg), Tammany Young ("Willie" the Weasel), Walter Brennan ("Legs" Garnett)

p, William LeBaron; d, Clyde Bruckman; w, Ray Harris, Sam Hardy, Jack Cunningham, Bobby Vernon (based on a story by Sam Hardy and Charles Bogle); ph, Alfred Gilks; ed, Richard Currier

There's no circus, no flying trapeze, but lots of laughs generated by the myriad frustrations and barely controlled rage of "the man" in this great W.C. Fields vehicle. A deft sketch of the potentially nightmarish qualities of small town America, it still has an edge.

Ambrose Wolfinger (Fields) dawdles over brushing his teeth and gargling in the bathroom until his shrewish wife, Leona (Howard) complains about the noise. Trundling to bed, he falls asleep snoring, only to be awakened when his wife improbably hears sounds of burglars singing. Gun in hand, Wolfinger creeps out of his bedroom to investigate, but the weapon accidentally discharges, bringing his horrendous mother-in-law, Mrs. Cordelia Neselrode (Lewis), and sponging stepson Claude (Sutton), on the run. Fortunately Wolfinger's good-hearted daughter, Hope (Brian) also appears to offer moral support. Wolfinger finds that two burglars "Legs" Garnett (Brennan) and "Willie" the Weasel (Young) have broken into his barrel of applejack whiskey. Soon they are all drinking and singing together. Ambrose Wolfinger's rebellion against the demands of his overbearing family and dead-end job has just begun.

One of Fields's most entertaining movies, THE MAN ON THE FLYING TRAPEZE features a series of ordinary mishaps that escalate into hilarious physical disasters. Directed by Clyde Bruckman (who worked on Buster Keaton's classic THE GENERAL), the film is more than a showcase for its star. Kathleen Howard, a former Metropolitan Opera singer and fashion writer, was Fields's favorite on-screen wife, and he never tired of telling reporters what an accomplished actress she was. Brian, Fields's neighbor, was no longer a star, but she was still charming. Less well known that IT'S A GIFT or THE BANK DICK, this is still an excellent comic outing. Check out that filing system!

MAN ON THE MOON [DVD]

1999 118m c Biography/Drama ★★½
Jersey Films/Cinehaus/Mutual Film Company/ R
Universal (U.S.)

Jim Carrey (Andy Kaufman/Tony Clifton), Danny DeVito (George Shapiro), Courtney Love (Lynne Margulies), Paul Giamatti (Bob Zmuda/Tony Clifton), George Shapiro (Mr. Besserman), Tom Dreesen (Wiseass Comic), Richard Belzer (Himself), Dr. Isadore Rosenfeld (ABC Executive), Vincent Schiavelli (Maynard Smith), Gerry Robert Byrne (Taxi AD/Stage Manager)

p, Danny DeVito, Michael Shamberg, Stacey Sher; d, Milos Forman; w, Scott Alexander, Larry Karaszewski; ph, Anastas Michos; ed, Christopher Tellefsen, Lynzee Klingman, Adam Boome; m, R.E.M.; prod d, Patrizia Von Brandenstein; art d, James Truesdale; fx, Larry Fioritto; chor, Jaymi Marshall; cos, Jeffrey Kurland

Jim Carrey's impersonation of late comedian Andy Kaufman is remarkable, but it never transcends impersonation to become a full-fleshed performance. Similarly, Milos Forman's film is a series of incredible simulations that never quite cohere into a movie.

Following a perfunctory prologue featuring little Andy performing for his younger sister, the movie fast-forwards to the '70s, where Kaufman is doing a similar act, baffling customers who don't see the humor in a guy badgering them to sing along with children's songs. But he's spotted by manager George Shapiro (Danny DeVito, Kaufman's "Taxi" co-star) and the career peaks and valleys soon follow: Kaufman invents the foreign man who mangles jokes and impersonations before doing a spot-on Elvis; lip-syncs the *Mighty Mouse* theme; becomes "Taxi"'s breakout star; sabotages his TV career by acting up on "Saturday Night Live" and its short-lived competitor "Fridays"; denies that he's obnoxious lounge singer "Tony Clifton"; reinvents himself as an odious professional wrestler who specializes in grappling with women; performs at Carnegie Hall; gets cancer.

The cancer turns out *not* to be Kaufman's latest stunt, though even today there are people who aren't entirely convinced it wasn't a hoax. Kaufman fans may get a nostalgic kick out of the faithful re-creations of his confrontational pranks and put-ons, but there's not much in the way of insight into what made Kaufman tick, which is generally acknowledged as a flaw in biopics. It could be argued that Kaufman channeled his life into his personas, which he frequently kept up offstage, but that's a specious argument. Staging "Kaufman-mania" on the big screen is what it is; pretending there really was no one behind the curtain is a copout.

MAN WHO CAME TO DINNER, THE

1942 112m bw Comedy
Warner Bros. (U.S.)
★★★★

Bette Davis *(Maggie Cutler)*, Ann Sheridan *(Lorraine Sheldon)*, Monty Woolley *(Sheridan Whiteside)*, Richard Travis *(Bert Jefferson)*, Jimmy Durante *(Banjo)*, Reginald Gardiner *(Beverly Carlton)*, Billie Burke *(Mrs. Stanley)*, Elisabeth Fraser *(June Stanley)*, Grant Mitchell *(Ernest Stanley)*, George Barbier *(Dr. Bradley)*

p, Jerry Wald, Jack Saper; d, William Keighley; w, Julius J. Epstein, Philip G. Epstein (based on the play by George S. Kaufman, Moss Hart); ph, Tony Gaudio; ed, Jack Killifer; m, Frederick Hollander; art d, Robert Haas; cos, Orry-Kelly

This hit Broadway comedy became a comparably popular film thanks to a smart adaptation, strong performances, and the fortunate retention of the play's star, Monty Woolley. The celebrated John Barrymore had been slated for the role but he had trouble with the dialogue. Luckily, another genuine movie star—Bette Davis—was eager to take a secondary role in this fanciful account of some thinly veiled real celebrities in an unlikely situation. Theater critics Alexander Woollcott, Harpo Marx and Noel Coward were among the brainy wits who met regularly at the Algonquin Hotel to exchange witticisms over lunch. Resourceful playwrights George S. Kaufman and Moss Hart utilized what they knew of the lunchers, placed them in a "fish out of water" setting, and crafted a funny, acerbic play and film.

Sheridan Whiteside (Woolley as Woollcott), a popular acid-tongued radio host, is traveling cross-country on a lecture tour with Maggie Cutler (Davis), his tolerant secretary. They stop in a small town in Ohio and accept a dinner invitation from Mr. and Mrs. Ernest Stanley (Mitchell and Burke), a prominent local family. Whiteside slips on a patch of ice in front of the Stanley house and gets carried inside spewing insults and threats of lawsuits. The Stanleys—who embody the kind of old-fashioned Middle American values that the intellectual Whiteside abhors—are terrified by the prospect of scandal, so they do their best to keep their "guest from hell" comfortable while he throws their household into chaos, advising the Stanley children to flee the social constraints of Ohio. The plot thickens when Maggie falls for

local newsman-playwright Bert Jefferson (Travis). Fearing that he may lose his loyal employee, Whiteside schemes to break up the relationship.

Cynically witty lines, top-notch characterizations (Ann Sheridan is a delight), and welcome guest appearances by Jimmy Durante (as a Harpo Marx figure) and Reginald Gardner (doing a take on Noel Coward) make for classic comedy.

MAN WHO FELL TO EARTH, THE

1976 140m c Science Fiction ★★★½
Cinema 5 (U.K.) R

David Bowie *(Thomas Jerome Newton)*, Rip Torn *(Nathan Bryce)*, Candy Clark *(Mary-Lou)*, Buck Henry *(Oliver Farnsworth)*, Bernie Casey *(Peters)*, Jackson D. Kane *(Prof. Canutti)*, Rick Riccardo *(Trevor)*, Tony Mascia *(Arthur)*, Linda Hutton *(Elaine)*, Hilary Holland *(Jill)*

p, Michael Deeley, Barry Spikings; d, Nicolas Roeg; w, Paul Mayersberg (based on the novel by Walter Tevis); ph, Anthony B. Richmond (Panavision); ed, Graeme Clifford; fx, Paul Ellenshaw

Nicolas Roeg's cult classic about an alien (Bowie) who arrives on Earth in search of water for his drought-stricken planet, where his wife and children are dying of thirst. The alien takes the name of Thomas Jerome Newton, arrives at the office of patent attorney Farnsworth (Buck Henry), and offers him a number of innovative designs with which they can make a great deal of money—enough for Newton to build a vehicle that will return him to his home planet. Newton and Farnsworth are soon running a huge financial empire, but Newton's plans are threatened both by an inquisitive chemistry professor (Rip Torn), and by his own descent into earthly ways.

Roeg began his career as a cameraman (he worked second-unit on LAWRENCE OF ARABIA) and progressed to become a director of photography (THE MASQUE OF THE RED DEATH, A FUNNY THING HAPPENED ON THE WAY TO THE FORUM, FAHRENHEIT 451). Here, he has come up with some memorable imagery, as well as coaxing a suitably enigmatic performance out of Bowie. Originally released at 140 minutes, the U.S. distributor, Cinema 5, edited the film down to versions of 117, 120, and 125 minutes, before restoring it to its original length in 1980.

MAN WHO KNEW TOO MUCH, THE

1934 75m bw Mystery ★★★★
Gaumont (U.K.)

Leslie Banks *(Bob Lawrence)*, Edna Best *(Jill Lawrence)*, Peter Lorre *(Abbott)*, Frank Vosper *(Ramon Levine)*, Hugh Wakefield *(Clive)*, Nova Pilbeam *(Betty Lawrence)*, Pierre Fresnay *(Louis Bernard)*, Cicely Oates *(Nurse Agnes)*, D.A. Clarke-Smith *(Binstead)*, George Curzon *(Gibson)*

p, Michael Balcon; d, Alfred Hitchcock; w, A.R. Rawlinson, Charles Bennett, D.B. Wyndham-Lewis, Emlyn Williams, Edwin Greenwood (based on a story by Charles Bennett and D.B. Wyndham-Lewis); ph, Curt Courant; ed, Hugh Stewart; m, Arthur Benjamin; art d, Alfred Junge, Peter Proud

Married couple Bob and Jill Lawrence (Banks and Best) are vacationing in Switzerland with daughter Betty (Pilbeam), when Louis Bernard (Fresnay), a Frenchman who befriends them, is found murdered. Before dying, however, Louis Bernard whispers a secret—that a diplomat will be assassinated at great embarrassment to the British government. To keep Bob's lips sealed, Betty is kidnapped—to be held until after the assassination by hired killer Abbott (Lorre), scheduled to take place during a concert at London's Albert Hall. Bob must follow his duty as a

Englishman and prevent the assassination, but at the same time he must do all in his power to insure the safety of his child. It is in this film that Hitchcock showed his development of a theme he would repeat in films to come—the innocent victim suddenly caught up in a terrifying situation with apparently no way out, coupled with breathless chases in popular public places. This was Lorre's first English-speaking part; he had been brought to England at Hitchcock's request after the director saw him in Fritz Lang's impressive M. Hitchcock, who was not known to favor child actors, got along so well with the young Pilbeam that he gave her her first adult leading role in his film YOUNG AND INNOCENT, three years later.

MAN WHO KNEW TOO MUCH, THE

1956 120m c   Mystery   ★★★★
Paramount   (U.S.)   PG

James Stewart (*Dr. Ben McKenna*), Doris Day (*Jo McKenna*), Brenda de Banzie (*Mrs. Drayton*), Bernard Miles (*Mr. Drayton*), Ralph Truman (*Buchanan*), Daniel Gelin (*Louis Bernard*), Mogens Wieth (*Ambassador*), Alan Mowbray (*Val Parnell*), Hillary Brooke (*Jan Peterson*), Christopher Olsen (*Hank McKenna*)

p, Alfred Hitchcock; d, Alfred Hitchcock; w, John Michael Hayes, Angus Macphail (based on a story by Charles Bennett, D.B. Wyndham-Lewis); ph, Richard Mueller (VistaVision, Technicolor); ed, George Tomasini; m, Bernard Herrmann; art d, Hal Pereira, Henry Bumstead; fx, John P. Fulton; cos, Edith Head

AA Best Song: "Whatever Will Be, Will Be (Que Sera, Sera)"; Jay Livingston, Ray Evans

The original version of this film so appealed to Hitchcock that he felt it could take a remake and survive. He also believed that he could improve upon it—an opinion open to debate. Though the director altered some locales (Switzerland became Morocco), he kept the original story fairly much intact, enhanced the production values, and added 45 minutes to its running time. Dr. Ben and Jo McKenna (Stewart and Day) are sweetly innocent and unsuspecting tourists whose vacation in French Morocco turns into a nightmare. Traveling with their son Hank (Olsen) they are enjoying their holiday when they meet Mr. and Mrs. Drayton (Miles and de Banzie), a friendly British couple, and Louis Bernard (Gelin), a suspicious but friendly Frenchman. Later, while Ben and Jo are shopping in the bazaar, an Arab runs frantically up to them, having been stabbed in the back. Ben grabs the man as he falls and finds, to his horror, that it is Louis Bernard in disguise. Before he dies, Louis Bernard whispers something to Ben, thereby tossing him into a tangle of international intrigue that only he can unravel. Though there is obviously more polish and a lavish budget in this remake, the 1956 version of THE MAN WHO KNEW TOO MUCH has no more or less impact than the first version. Again, Hitchcock's scenes are beautifully framed and tautly directed—especially the double climax of the assassination attempt at the Albert Hall and the Embassy search for the kidnapped Hank. Day delivers a song, "Que Sera, Sera," which became a smash hit. Hitchcock makes his customary cameo, as does his composer Bernard Herrmann.

MAN WHO LOVED WOMEN, THE

(L'HOMME QUI AIMAIT LES FEMMES)
1977 119m c   Drama/Comedy   ★★★
Carrosse/Artistes   (France)

Charles Denner (*Bertrand Morane*), Brigitte Fossey (*Genevieve Bigey*), Nelly Borgeaud (*Delphine Grezel*), Leslie Caron (*Vera*), Genevieve Fontanel (*Helene*), Nathalie Baye (*Martine Desdoits*),

Sabine Glaser (*Bernadette*), Valerie Bonnier (*Fabienne*), Martine Chassing (*Denise*), Roselyne Puyo (*Nicole*)

d, Francois Truffaut; w, Francois Truffaut, Michel Fermaud, Suzanne Schiffman; ph, Nestor Almendros; ed, Martine Barraque; m, Maurice Jaubert

Truffaut's swiftly paced, light-hearted exercise concerns a man whose very existence is devoted to women—a man perhaps not unlike Truffaut himself. Denner is the amorous title male, a well-off researcher who is surely one of the most woman-crazy men ever to appear on film. He can't keep his mind off women; a mere glance at one femme dressed in black silk stockings sends him on a long journey toward love. All the while that Denner chases skirts, he remains charming and innocent, never believing he is doing anything wrong or harmful. Unlike those men who abuse women, Denner adores them—all of them. THE MAN WHO LOVED WOMEN is filled with Truffaut's ironic sense of humor, always charming, and never in any way offending. As in all of Truffaut's romantic comedies, what appears as flippant and sugary is actually a cover for some very complex statements about the nature of love, Truffaut himself, and the cinema. In this sense THE MAN WHO LOVED WOMEN can be viewed, along with THE STORY OF ADELE H. and THE GREEN ROOM, as part of a trilogy about unrequited love and frustrating obsessions. A Hollywood remake of this film appeared in 1983, directed by Blake Edwards and starring Burt Reynolds.

MAN WHO SHOT LIBERTY VALANCE, THE

1962 123m bw   Western   ★★★½
Ford   (U.S.)

James Stewart (*Ransom Stoddard*), John Wayne (*Tom Doniphon*), Vera Miles (*Hallie Stoddard*), Lee Marvin (*Liberty Valance*), Edmond O'Brien (*Dutton Peabody*), Andy Devine (*Link Appleyard*), Ken Murray (*Doc Willoughby*), John Carradine (*Maj. Cassius Starbuckle*), Jeanette Nolan (*Nora Ericson*), John Qualen (*Peter Ericson*)

p, Willis Goldbeck; d, John Ford; w, Willis Goldbeck, James Warner Bellah (based on a story by Dorothy M. Johnson); ph, William Clothier; ed, Otho Lovering; m, Cyril J. Mockridge, Alfred Newman; art d, Hal Pereira, Eddie Imazu; cos, Edith Head

AAN Best Costume Design (B/W): Edith Head

A solid, if overrated, Ford western, one with its share of cliches and predictability. It's still fascinating to watch Wayne and Stewart deal with hellion Marvin in a changing West. The movie opens after the story is all over, when Sen. Ransom Stoddard (Stewart) and his wife (Miles) return to the western town of Shinbone in 1910. They have unexpectedly come to the funeral of Tom Doniphon (Wayne), which piques the interest of a local reporter. Ransom begins to tell how he came to know Tom, as the movie flashes back to Shinbone's wild and woolly days. A fledgling lawyer, Ransom must contend with local nasty Liberty Valance (Marvin). He is waylaid by Valance and his men just as he enters the territory; working for a group of powerful businessmen, they believe he is an agitator for statehood, exactly what the powerful locals don't want. Beaten up and left for dead by Valance, Ransom is found by Tom, who takes him to town, helps him find work, and supports his eventual bid for elected office. He even tries to teach the awkward lawyer the art of gunfighting, because Valance must still be dealt with. The truth behind the killing of the no-good varmint gradually comes out, but, as the reporter notes: "It ain't news. This is the West. When the legend becomes the fact, print the legend."

Starkly photographed and often heavily screened for nighttime shots, Ford's picture of the West here is a gloomy one, often pitch black when the only thing that comes out of it is the beastly Marvin. Many cliches and stereotypes people the film; the crusading newspaper editor, for example, had been used in many an earlier western, notably DODGE CITY. Oddly Ford, the master of great western exterior scenes, shot the entire film on two Paramount sound stages. Auteur critics have found much worth in this elegiac film, though in some ways it revisits the themes of Ford's earlier FORT APACHE. The movie is certainly above average, thanks to the performances by Stewart and Wayne, but Marvin is so flamboyant a badman that he is simply a caricature, even more so than in his outlandish Oscar-winning turn in CAT BALLOU.

MAN WHO WASN'T THERE, THE 📀

2001 116m bw Crime/Thriller ★★½
Working Title Productions/Mike Zoss R
Productions/Gramercy Pictures (U.S.)

Billy Bob Thornton (*Ed Crane*), Frances McDormand (*Doris Crane*), James Gandolfini (*Big Dave Nirdlinger*), Michael Badalucco (*Frank*), Katherine Borowitz (*Ann Nirdlinger*), Jon Polito (*Creighton Tolliver*), Scarlett Johansson (*Birdy Abundas*), Richard Jenkins (*Walter Abundas*), Tony Shalhoub (*Freddy Riedenschneider*), Christopher Kriesa (*Persky*)

p, Ethan Coen; d, Joel Coen; w, Joel Coen, Ethan Coen; ph, Roger Deakins; ed, Joel Coen, Ethan Coen, Tricia Cooke; m, Carter Burwell; prod d, Dennis Gassner; art d, Chris Gorak; fx, Peter Chesney, MVFX Los Angeles, Janek Sirrs; cos, Mary Zophres

AAN Best Cinematographer: Roger Deakins

A ravishingly beautiful film noir pastiche from the Coen brothers that draws on a classic noir twist: a hapless schmoe gets away with one misdeed but winds up paying for another.

The year is 1949. Ed Crane (Billy Bob Thornton) is a small-town barber, a terse loner married to flirtatious chippie Doris (Frances McDormand) and working in his chatty brother-in-law Frank's (Michael Badalucco) Santa Rosa clip shop. Doris is a bookkeeper at Nirdlinger's, the high-end local department store, and Ed is pretty sure there's more than business going on between his wife and her boss, Big Dave Nirdlinger (James Gandolfini), a glad-handing blowhard who landed his swanky position by marrying tight-lipped heiress Ann Nirdlinger (Katherine Borowitz). Ed sees a way out when he meets Creighton Tolliver (Jon Polito), an oily stranger who's peddling a investment scheme involving dry cleaning. To come up with the $10,000 ante, Ed writes a blackmail note to Big Dave, threatening to expose his affair. To Ed's amazement, Big Dave coughs up the dough, but the pay-off has a few unforseen consequences. Suffice it to say that one act of malfeasance follows another, and someone winds up dead.

Filmed in luminous B&W by Roger Deakins, this somber yet smirking pastiche is so glitteringly gorgeous you want to suck it up through a straw. It's a revelation to see how ruggedly handsome Thornton looks in shades of gray; in certain shots it's hard not to think of Gary Cooper and Humphrey Bogart. But for all its fancy narrative footwork, the film is only clever in a "name *this* homage" kind of way, and fundamentally heartless and hollow.

MAN WHO WOULD BE KING, THE 📀

1975 129m c Adventure ★★★★
Allied Artists (U.K.) PG

Sean Connery (*Daniel Dravot*), Michael Caine (*Peachy Carnehan*), Christopher Plummer (*Rudyard Kipling*), Saeed Jaffrey (*Billy Fish*), Karroum Ben Bouih (*Kafu-Selim*), Jack May (*District Commissioner*), Doghmi Larbi (*Ootah*), Shakira Caine (*Roxanne*), Mohammed Shamsi (*Babu*), Paul Antrim (*Mulvaney*)

p, John Foreman; d, John Huston; w, John Huston, Gladys Hill (based on the story by Rudyard Kipling); ph, Oswald Morris (Panavision, Technicolor); ed, Russell Lloyd; m, Maurice Jarre; prod d, Alexander Trauner; art d, Tony Inglis; cos, Edith Head

AAN Best Adapted Screenplay: John Huston, Gladys Hill; *AAN Best Film Editing:* Russell Lloyd; *AAN Best Art Direction-Set Decoration:* Alexander Trauner, Tony Inglis, Peter James; *AAN Best Costume Design:* Edith Head

This is writer-director John Huston's dream project for decades. He originally wanted to film the Rudyard Kipling short story in the 1940s with Clark Gable and Humphrey Bogart. Later he envisioned Richard Burton and Peter O'Toole. However, the long wait paid off: Michael Caine, Sean Connery, and Christopher Plummer deliver outstanding performances in a classic adventure that delivers thrills even as it meditates on issues of power and imperialism.

Kipling (Plummer) is working in his office in Lahore, India when an aged beggar enters and begins to spin an amazing tale that fascinates the writer. We flashback to Kipling's office many years earlier when a young, vibrant, if somewhat boorish Peachy Carnehan (Caine) and his dashing friend Daniel Dravot (Connery) ask the writer to witness some "official" document. Stationed in India, these British army officers have been supplementing their salaries with various scams. Down on their luck after squandering their money on vice, they have concocted a new scheme: they will sojourn into the hills of Kafiristan (a province in eastern Afghanistan now called Nuristan) where they will set themselves up as rulers. Intrigued by these brazen soldiers-of-fortune, Kipling secures them an appointment with the District Commissioner (May). However the official sees their true colors and sends them packing. Dravot and Carnehan endure assorted hardships as they trek through the storied Khyber Pass, and although Dravot gets mistaken for a god at one point, things don't quite work out as planned.

This is a grand adventure tale that does not stint on characterization. Connery and Caine join the ranks of Huston's classic overachievers, most notably Bogart's Fred C. Dobbs in THE TREASURE OF SIERRA MADRE. Caine may have gone a wee bit over-the-top but that helped the audience distinguish between the the natures of the two men. The film was shot on location in Morocco because of the costs and dangers of working in Afghanistan. Unfortunately, the score by the celebrated Jarre (LAWRENCE OF ARABIA) failed to match the evocative power of the setting. However these are minor flaws in a delightful and memorable film.

MAN WITH THE GOLDEN ARM, THE 📀

1955 119m bw Drama ★★★½
Carlyle (U.S.)

Frank Sinatra (*Frankie Machine*), Kim Novak (*Molly*), Eleanor Parker (*Zosch Machine*), Arnold Stang (*Sparrow*), Darren McGavin (*Louie*), Robert Strauss (*Schwiefka*), George Mathews (*Williams*), John Conte (*Drunky*), Doro Merande (*Vi*), George E. Stone (*Sam Markette*)

p, Otto Preminger; d, Otto Preminger; w, Walter Newman, Lewis Meltzer (based on the novel by Nelson Algren); ph, Sam Leavitt; ed, Louis Loeffler; m, Elmer Bernstein; prod d, Joseph C. Wright; cos, Mary Ann Nyberg

AAN Best Actor: Frank Sinatra; *AAN Best Score (Drama or Comedy):* Elmer Bernstein; *AAN Best Art Direction-Set Decoration (B/W):* Joseph C. Wright, Darrell Silvera

Otto Preminger defied the Code with this pioneering look at drug addiction, featuring a stylish rendering of the post-war hipster milieu, a crisp jazz soundtrack, and a remarkable Sinatra.

Crooked card dealer Frankie Machine (Sinatra), a junkie trying to stay clean, is back in town after six months in rehab. He wants to try his luck as a jazz drummer, but his resentful, crippled wife Zosch (Parker) demands that he return to his old job. Frankie later falls hard for B-girl Molly (Novak), and pursues his musical dreams in secret at her place. Finally securing an audition, he attempts to leave his old racket, but his boss (Strauss) prevails upon him to handle one last rigged marathon poker game. Professional and personal tensions only make the recurring offers of a drug pusher (McGavin) more tempting.

To some extent, Preminger's slickness clashes with the gritty realism of the screenplay, based on Nelson Algren's best-selling novel. Stang, in a rare dramatic outing for a man who usually played the comic flunky (beginning with Henry Morgan's radio show in the 1940s), is a standout as Frankie's slightly retarded pal. The typically stiff Novak has little to do except look pretty and act concerned, while the over-the-top Parker never hits the right mix of self-hatred and pity. Sinatra, by contrast, is superb, especially in a harrowing withdrawal scene. It's his movie... all the way.

MAN WITH TWO BRAINS, THE 📀

1983	93m	c	Science Fiction/Comedy	★★★½
Aspen	(U.S.)			R

Steve Martin (Dr. Michael Hfuhruhurr), Kathleen Turner (Dolores Benedict), Paul Benedict (Butler), David Warner (Dr. Necessiter), Richard Brestoff (Dr. Pasteur), James Cromwell (Realtor), George Furth (Timon), Peter Hobbs (Dr. Brandon), Earl Boen (Dr. Conrad), Bernie Hern (Gun Seller)

p, David V. Picker, William E. McEuen; d, Carl Reiner; w, Carl Reiner, Steve Martin, George Gipe; ph, Michael Chapman (Technicolor); ed, Bud Molin; m, Joel Goldsmith; prod d, Polly Platt; art d, Mark Mansbridge; fx, Allen Hall, Clay Pinney, Robert Willard; cos, Kevin Brennan

Following their triumphant parody of film noir, DEAD MEN DON'T WEAR PLAID (1982), comedian Steve Martin and director Carl Reiner took on the mad-scientist films of the 1940s, with hilarious results. Dr. Michael Hfuhruhurr (Martin), a famed neurosurgeon, travels to Vienna with his beautiful-but-frigid wife, Dolores (deliciously vixenish Kathleen Turner), in an attempt to revive their romance. There he meets fellow scientist Dr. Alfred Necessiter (David Warner), who has devised a method to keep disembodied brains alive. Hfuhruhurr begins to communicate telepathically with a brain in a jar; the brain is that of a sweet, sympathetic woman (the voice of Sissy Spacek) with whom he falls hopelessly in love. Desperate to consummate his love, Hfuhruhurr decides to plant the brain in the body of a beautiful woman—but where to find a fresh corpse? Enter the dreaded Elevator Killer.

Carl Reiner, once known chiefly as Mel Brooks' second banana, has stepped in to fill a gap that opened when the formerly able Brooks lost his comic touch. THE MAN WITH TWO BRAINS, which never ceases to amuse, is at its best when most outrageous—as when Hfuhruhurr and his beloved brain enjoy their first kiss (he applies a pair of wax lips to the jar), or when Martin mimes the effects of prolonged sexual abstinence—and wait till you find out who the Elevator Killer is!

MAN WITHOUT A PAST, THE 📀

2002	97m	c	Drama	★★★★
Pyramide Productions/Eila Werning/				PG-13
Pandora Film Produktion/Sputnik/YLE TV1/				
Bavaria Film	(Finland/France/Germany)			

Markku Peltola (M), Kati Outinen (Irma), Juhani Niemela (Nieminen), Kaija Pakarinen (Kaisa Nieminen), Sakari Kuosmanen (Anttila), Annikki Tahti (Flea Market Manageress), Anneli Sauli (Bar Owner), Elina Salo (Shipyard Clerk), Outi Maenpaa (Bank Clerk), Esko Nikkari (Bank Robber)

p, Aki Kaurismaki; d, Aki Kaurismaki; w, Aki Kaurismaki; ph, Timo Salminen; ed, Timo Linnasalo; prod d, Markku Patila, Jukka Salmi; cos, Outi Herjupatana

This warm and utterly beguiling fable about a man who loses everything only to discover that he never needed much in the first place won the 2002 Cannes Grand Prix. It's the second installment in Finnish director Aki Kaurismaki's projected "Finland Trilogy"; DRIFTING CLOUDS was the first.

M (Markku Peltola) dozes off on a Helsinki park bench, only to be awoken by a trio of thugs who beat him, steal his money, and toss his wallet—identity papers and all—into a trash can. M is declared dead at the hospital, but as soon as he's left alone, he springs back to life and walks out into the night, reborn but with no recollection of his name or past life. The following morning, kind-hearted night watchman Nieminen (Juhani Niemela) finds M unconscious down by the waterfront and takes him back to the rusted metal cargo container in which Nieminen and his wife, Kaisa (Kaija Pakarinen), live as squatters. They nurse M back to health and even arrange for him to rent his own container from officious security guard Anttila (Sakari Kuosmanen), who isn't above exploiting the homeless of Helsinki's waterfront. At a Salvation Army soup kitchen, M meets and quickly falls in love with Irma (Kati Outinen), a lonely Army soldier who helps M find work and, eventually, romance.

Like many of Kaurismaki's color features, the film has an almost plastic texture, and the story, with its deep sentiment and intimations of divine grace, leaves itself wide open to snarky irony. But Kaurismaki grounds the film in the very real poverty of his characters, and every beat of its huge heart is sincere. Kaurismaki's toe-tapping soundtrack features the gone-but-not-entirely-forgotten British beat combo, the Renegades. They were big in Finland.

MANCHURIAN CANDIDATE, THE 📀

1962	126m	bw	Political/Thriller	★★★★½
MC/Essex	(U.S.)			

Frank Sinatra (Bennett Marco), Laurence Harvey (Raymond Shaw), Janet Leigh (Rosie), Angela Lansbury (Raymond's Mother), Henry Silva (Chunjim), James Gregory (Sen. John Iselin), Leslie Parrish (Jocie Jordon), John McGiver (Sen. Thomas Jordon), Khigh Dhiegh (Yen Lo), James Edwards (Cpl. Melvin)

p, George Axelrod, John Frankenheimer; d, John Frankenheimer; w, George Axelrod (based on the novel by Richard Condon); ph, Lionel Lindon; ed, Ferris Webster; m, David Amram; prod d, Richard Sylbert; art d, Richard Sylbert, Philip Jefferies; fx, Paul Pollard; cos, Moss Mabry

AAN Best Supporting Actress: Angela Lansbury; AAN Best Film Editing: Ferris Webster

A nerve-beating masterpiece, and more timely now than then. Frankenheimer's tightrope walk between campy political satire and suspense is flawlessly rendered. Based on Richard Condon's paranoid novel.

Harvey returns from the Korean War a superhero and holder of the Congressional Medal of Honor, but those in his platoon—including his own commanding officer, Sinatra—are vague about what Harvey actually did to win the medal. When Sinatra begins to have recurring nightmares about Korea, he decides to investigate. Piece by sinister piece, Sinatra and others put the story together. It turns out that the entire platoon was captured by North Koreans and brainwashed to think Harvey was a hero when, in truth, he had been programmed as a killer. But whom is he to kill? Upon his return from service Harvey leaves his overly protective mother (Lansbury) and her husband (Gregory), a right-wing senator. Harvey goes to work as a journalist, but when his control contacts him with the code, he kills without mercy or memory; a liberal columnist-publisher is his first victim. Harvey, now married, is next sent to kill his own wife and his father-in-law, a liberal senator. Sinatra discovers the truth: Harvey's controller is Lansbury, the top Communist spy in the U.S. She orders her robotlike son to kill the presidential nominee; her husband, who is the vice-presidential running mate, will then take control of the White House. Can Sinatra foil the plot?

THE MANCHURIAN CANDIDATE takes aim at both the Left and the Right, rendering them both dangerous fraternal twins—an outrageous, terrifying premise to contend with. The entire cast is first-rate. This is Harvey's best work—for once the unlovable quality he built a career on emerges sympathetically. But it is Angela Lansbury's incestuous, power-mad mother who makes your blood run cold. This was the peak of the first part of her career, which depended upon these hardbitten kind of characters. Forget Hitchcock—here's the monster mother of all time. THE MANCHURIAN CANDIDATE is political fiction—we hope—at its finest, certainly at its most forceful on the screen. It earned distinction as one of the first of a genre that mixed reality, symbolism, and the fantastic, alternating caprice and grim fact so that the view is jarred from one scene to the next as it would be riding on a speeding train constantly being rerouted. Have a wild ride.

MANCHURIAN CANDIDATE, THE   DVD

2004   130m   c   Thriller   ★★★★
Clinca Estetico/Scott Rudin/Tina Sinatra Productions   R
(U.S.)

Denzel Washington *(Ben Marco)*, Meryl Streep *(Eleanor Shaw)*, Liev Schreiber *(Raymond Shaw)*, Jeffrey Wright *(Al Melvin)*, Kimberly Elise *(Rosie)*, Jon Voight *(Senator Thomas Jordan)*, Ted Levine *(Colonel Howard)*, Miguel Ferrer *(Colonel Garret)*, Bruno Ganz *(Delp)*, Tom Stechschulte *(Robert Arthur)*

p, Jonathan Demme, Ilona Herzberg, Scott Rudin, Tina Sinatra; d, Jonathan Demme; w, Daniel Pyne, Dean Georgaris (based on the 1962 screenplay by George Axelrod, adapted from the novel by Richard Condon); ph, Tak Fujimoto; ed, Carol Littleton, Craig McKay; m, Rachel Portman; prod d, Kristi Zea; art d, Teresa Carriker-Thayer; fx, Susie Brubaker, Richard Malzahn, Toby Wilkins; cos, Albert Wolsky

John Frankenheimer's THE MANCHURIAN CANDIDATE (1962) is a near-perfect adaptation of Richard Condon's 1959 novel, but Jonathan Demme's retooling is a timely and thought-provoking film in its own right.

Kuwait, 1991: Capt. Bennett Marco (Denzel Washington), Sgt. Raymond Shaw (Liev Schreiber), and their platoon are MIA for three days. All but two of the men later make their way back to safety, and Shaw is awarded the Congressional Medal of Honor. In the present day, Marco, now a major, is tormented by grotesque nightmares, while Shaw, the wealthy son of the powerful U.S. senator Eleanor Prentiss Shaw (Meryl Streep), has forged a brilliant post-military career. Two events force Marco's longtime obsession with Shaw to new heights: he has an unsettling run-in with a seriously disturbed member of their old platoon (Jeffrey Wright), and presidential candidate Robert Arthur (Tom Stechschulte) nominates Congressman Shaw as his vice presidential running mate in place of presumptive candidate Sen. Thomas Jordan (Jon Voight). Convinced that he and Shaw underwent some experience in Kuwait not reflected in the official story, the increasingly jittery Marco makes repeated attempts to speak with Shaw, attempts that look alarmingly like stalking and undermine what little credibility he has left.

Demme and screenwriters Daniel Pyne and Dean Georgaris preserve the essence of Condon's novel while doing some canny updating, conflating two characters into Streep's monstrous mother figure and, more importantly, replacing the Cold War-era Communist cabal that inspired the title with a multinational corporation called Manchurian Global. The result suggests the icy PARALLAX VIEW by way of JACOB'S LADDER, and, tellingly, in a story driven by questions of loyalty and allegiance, no candidate is identified by party. It's a bipartisan nightmare from which no one escapes unscathed.

MANDABI   DVD

(LE MONDAT)
1968   90m   c   Comedy   ★★★½
Domireve/Comptoir Francais   (France/Senegal)

Mamadou Gueye *(Ibrahim Dieng)*, Ynousse N'Diaye *(1st Wife)*, Issa Niang *(2nd Wife)*, Serigne N'Diayes *(Imam)*, Serigne Sow *(Maissa)*, Moustapha Toure *(Shopkeeper)*, Farba Sarr *(Businessman)*, Moudoun Faye *(Mailman)*, Moussa Diouf *(Nephew)*, Christophe M'Doulabia *(Water Seller)*

p, Jean Maumy; d, Ousmane Sembene; w, Ousmane Sembene (based on a story by L.S. Senghor); ph, Paul Soulignac (Eastmancolor); ed, Gil Kikoine

A breakthrough film for Sembene, Africa's best-known filmmaker. Ibrahim Dieng (Gueye) tries to cash a money order from his nephew, but finds he can't because he doesn't have an identity card. He can't get an identity card without a birth certificate, and he can't get a certificate without a photograph. Everywhere he goes he must have something else—either identification or money. After a series of setbacks, Ibrahim realizes his nephew is ripping him off.

A keen satire, MANDABI is not only Sembene's first comedy and first film in color, but also his first in Wolof, the language spoken by most Senegalese people. Its critique of a postcolonial state is much more narrowly focused than those of his earlier short films, and, as the first Senegalese film to be distributed commercially in Senegal, it more than got its point across. Because he is speaking to his own people, it's not Sembene's most accessible work, but it was still a hit at the 1969 New York Film Festival. Look for the director in a cameo appearance as a public scribe.

MANHATTAN   DVD

1979   96m   bw   Comedy/Romance   ★★★★½
UA   (U.S.)   R

Woody Allen *(Isaac Davis)*, Diane Keaton *(Mary Wilke)*, Michael Murphy *(Yale)*, Mariel Hemingway *(Tracy)*, Meryl Streep *(Jill)*, Anne Byrne *(Emily)*, Karen Ludwig *(Connie)*, Michael O'Donoghue *(Dennis)*, Victor Truro, Tisa Farrow

p, Charles H. Joffe; d, Woody Allen; w, Woody Allen, Marshall Brickman; ph, Gordon Willis (Panavision); ed, Susan E. Morse; m, George Gershwin; prod d, Mel Bourne; cos, Albert Wolsky, Ralph Lauren

AAN Best Supporting Actress: Mariel Hemingway; AAN Best Original Screenplay: Woody Allen, Marshall Brickman

Deft comedy set in a neurotic town. People may argue about the relative merits of ANNIE HALL (which took Oscars for Best Picture, Direction, Actress, and Screenplay) vis-a-vis MANHATTAN, which won nothing but is a better and more fully realized film. By this time Allen had forsworn the glib one-liner and spent more time developing well-rounded characters. Allen is Isaac, a well-known TV scribe fed up with the medium who wants to use his talent to amuse in another fashion. He knows how to make people laugh, but can he move them? Isaac sometimes lives with teenaged drama student Tracy (Hemingway), but feelings of guilt over their age difference lead him to try to end their relationship. He commiserates with best friend Yale (Murphy), who is cheating on his own wife Emily (Byrne) with Mary (Keaton). Yale introduces Isaac to Mary, and though he finds her annoying and aggressive, Isaac is also fascinated by her. He comes to realize that her pseudo-intellectual behavior is all a sham and that she's actually a lovely person playing the role of a "Manhattanite" a bit too well. Before Isaac begins having an affair with Mary himself, though, he must deal with his lesbian ex-wife's (Streep) book about their marriage and divorce entitled *Marriage, Divorce, and Selfhood.* Isaac tries to persuade her not to publish it, but she does and it's a huge hit; everyone in America now knows how weird Isaac is.

MANHATTAN is funny, though not as funny as some of Allen's earlier work. But it makes his earlier films seem shallow by comparison. Gershwin's music is the perfect accompaniment for the film. Gordon Willis' beautiful black-and-white cinematography reflects a sweet nostalgic sadness in keeping with both Isaac's gloom and Allen's romance with New York. Among the actors, MANHATTAN is stolen, rather surprisingly, by the appealing and assured Hemingway. In a small role, note Wallace Shawn, who has since distinguished himself as a writer for the stage and screen (MY DINNER WITH ANDRE) as well as an actor in several other films (ATLANTIC CITY). The producers petitioned to change the "R" rating to a "PG" but were turned down, mostly because of the content concerning the older man and the teenage girl.

MANHATTAN MELODRAMA
1934 93m bw Crime ★★★★
Cosmpolitan (U.S.)

Clark Gable (*Blackie Gallagher*), William Powell (*Jim Wade*), Myrna Loy (*Eleanor*), Leo Carrillo (*Father Joe*), Nat Pendleton (*Spud*), George Sidney (*Poppa Rosen*), Isabel Jewell (*Anabelle*), Muriel Evans (*Tootsie Malone*), Claudelle Kaye (*Miss Adams*), Frank Conroy (*Blackie's Attorney*)

p, David O. Selznick; d, W.S. Van Dyke II; w, Oliver H.P. Garrett, Joseph L. Mankiewicz (based on the story "Three Men" by Arthur Caesar); ph, James Wong Howe; ed, Ben Lewis; art d, Cedric Gibbons, Joseph C. Wright; fx, Slavko Vorkapich; cos, Dolly Tree

AA Best Writing (Original Story): Arthur Caesar

A splendid example of 1930s hardboiled melodrama, notable historically for two very different reasons: it marked the first of 14 pairings of the legendary team of William Powell and Myrna Loy, and it also reportedly marked legendary gangster John Dillinger for death—literally. A big Myrna Loy fan, Dillinger sneaked into the Biograph Theatre on July 22, 1934 to watch her in this film. He was spotted, the police were called, and he was gunned down after the picture was over.

Two boys (played by Jimmy Butler and a pre-stardom Mickey Rooney) are saved from a fire on a tour boat which claims the lives of their parents. Taken in by the kindly Jewish merchant Papa Rosen (Sidney), the boys become fast pals even though Jim (Butler) is upstanding and studious and Blackie (Rooney) regularly cuts school to shoot craps. Years later, Blackie (Gable) has, as might be expected, become New York's biggest gambler and racketeer and Jim (Powell) has, as might be expected, become a crusading prosecuting attorney for the Big Apple. Loy enters the picture as Blackie's girlfriend Eleanor, an educated woman who doesn't believe her man is really bad at heart. Will Blackie end up going to the electric chair for murder? Will Jim end up in the governor's mansion? Will Eleanor end up in Jim's arms? Considering all the THIN MAN movies that followed, it's not hard to answer the third question, but the twisty variations wreaked on the admittedly unoriginal plot premise make the ride worthwhile.

Director W.S. ("Woody") Van Dyke II directs with all the breezy assurance which distinguished so many of his films, and the screenplay by Garrett and Mankiewicz is full

of tasty one-liners. Gable (as the most sympathetic crook imaginable) and Powell (virtue never looked so good) perform the male-bonding routine with gusto, and Loy has great rapport with both her co-stars. (Don't forget that she made seven films with Gable.) The plot would go on to inspire such other well-remembered efforts as ANGELS WITH DIRTY FACES, but this early rendition is still well worth catching.

MANHATTAN MURDER MYSTERY
1993 108m c Comedy/Crime ★★½
Manhattan Productions (U.S.) PG

Woody Allen (*Larry Lipton*), Diane Keaton (*Carol Lipton*), Alan Alda (*Ted*), Anjelica Huston (*Marcia Fox*), Jerry Adler (*Paul House*), Lynn Cohen (*Lillian House*), Ron Rifkin (*Sy*), Joy Behar (*Marilyn*), William Addy (*Jack the Super*), John Doumanian (*Neighbor*)

p, Robert Greenhut; d, Woody Allen; w, Woody Allen, Marshall Brickman; ph, Carlo Di Palma; ed, Susan E. Morse; prod d, Santo Loquasto; art d, Speed Hopkins; cos, Jeffrey Kurland

Woody Allen's first film following the tabloid scandals that emerged during the breakup of his relationship with Mia Farrow, MANHATTAN MURDER MYSTERY is a light confection, whipped up from bits of old movies and toothless domestic banter.

Larry and Carol Lipton (Allen, Diane Keaton) are middle-aged New Yorkers whose lives are too good to be true and too dull to be fiction. He's a book editor and she's thinking about opening a restaurant. Larry is deflecting the advances of exotic writer Marcia Fox (Anjelica Huston), while Carol flirts half-heartedly with longtime friend Ted (Alan Alda). The death of an elderly neighbor, Lillian House (Lynn Cohen), provides the excitement Carol has been yearning for: she suspects Paul House (Jerry Adler) of murder, drawing Ted, Marcia, and even the skeptical Larry into her clumsy snooping. The mystery is resolved in a climax lifted straight from Orson Welles' THE LADY FROM SHANGHAI.

Though MANHATTAN MURDER MYSTERY seems intended as a straightforward comedy, a frothy homage to old movies featuring amateur sleuths and clever repartee, its tone is surprisingly curdled; when Larry mutters that there's nothing wrong with Carol that Prozac and a whack with a polo mallet wouldn't cure, the remark feels too sour for the situation. The film's nervous, gritty style is woefully out of sync with its broadly whimsical tone. Woody Allen is an acquired taste, and MANHATTAN MURDER MYSTERY is a movie for his steadfast fans only.

MANHUNTER

1986 119m c Crime/Thriller ★★★
DEG (U.S.) R

William Petersen (*Will Graham*), Kim Greist (*Molly Graham*), Joan Allen (*Reba*), Brian Cox (*Dr. Lektor*), Dennis Farina (*Jack Crawford*), Stephen Lang (*Freddie Lounds*), Tom Noonan (*Francis Dollarhyde*), David Seaman (*Kevin Graham*), Benjamin Hendrickson (*Dr. Chilton*), Michael Talbott (*Geehan*)

p, Richard Roth; d, Michael Mann; w, Michael Mann (based on the book *Red Dragon* by Thomas Harris); ph, Dante Spinotti (Technicolor); ed, Dov Hoenig; m, The Reds, Michel Rubini; prod d, Mel Bourne; art d, Jack Blackman; fx, Joseph DiGaetano II; cos, Colleen Atwood

A grim stylish thriller from the creator of television's "Miami Vice." Based on Thomas Harris's gripping novel *Red Dragon*, MANHUNTER introduces us to the Behavioral Science Unit of the FBI and its top agent, Will Graham (William Petersen). The secret of Graham's success is his uncanny ability to duplicate the twisted thought processes of serial killers and thereby predict their actions. Brought out of early retirement by his friend and colleague Jack (Dennis Farina), Graham launches an investigation of a serial killer who operates on a "lunar cycle," killing entire families only when the moon is full. Graham's peculiar talent of adopting a criminal's mindset extracts a heavy emotional toll and nearly destroyed him on his last case when he captured Dr. Hannibal Lektor (Brian Cox), a brilliant psychiatrist turned brutal killer. Lektor is in prison and though Graham clearly still fears him, he visits him in an effort to get insights on his new case. He only succeeds in putting himself and his family in great danger.

Writer-director Michael Mann wrote a superior script and assembled an incredible cast for MANHUNTER making one of the most underrated outstanding thrillers of the 1980s. Mann knows how to construct an intense movie. As in his earlier THIEF, he presents the viewer with a fascinating amount of procedural detail—both law-enforcement and criminal. Petersen is superb as the obsessive investigator who risks madness each time he takes on a case, and Tom Noonan is absolutely chilling as the psycho killer. Cox is also frightening as the complex Lektor, a character who would be memorably embodied by Anthony Hopkins in Jonathan Demme's adaptation of Harris's quasi-sequel, THE SILENCE OF THE LAMBS (where the doctor's name is spelled "Lecter," as it is in the novels).

MANON OF THE SPRING 📀
(MANON DES SOURCES)
1986   113m   c   Drama   ★★★½
Renn/RAI-TV/DEG/A2   (France)   R

Yves Montand (Cesar "Le Papet" Soubeyran), Daniel Auteuil (Ugolin Soubeyran), Emmanuelle Beart (Manon Cadoret), Hyppolite Girardot (Bernard Olivier), Elisabeth Depardieu (Aimee Cadoret), Gabriel Bacquier (Victor), Armand Meffre (Philoxene), Andre Dupon (Pamphile), Pierre Nougaro (Casimir), Jean Maurel (Anglade)

p, Pierre Grunstein; d, Claude Berri; w, Claude Berri, Gerard Brach (based on the novel by Marcel Pagnol); ph, Bruno Nuytten (Technovision, Eastmancolor); ed, Genevieve Louveau, Herve de Luze; m, Jean-Claude Petit, Giuseppe Verdi; prod d, Bernard Vezat; cos, Sylvie Gautrelet

The continuation of JEAN DE FLORETTE resumes the story and follows its characters to their fates. Ten years have passed, and Manon (played by newcomer Emmanuelle Beart), the daughter of the hunchbacked farmer Jean (Gerard Depardieu in Part I), has grown into a beautiful young shepherdess who tends her flock deep in the hills of Provence. In the years since Jean's death, Le Papet (Yves Montand) and his nephew, Ugolin (Daniel Auteuil), have worked Jean's land into a profitable carnation farm by unplugging the underground spring they had kept secret from the hardworking farmer. Ugolin's vibrant red carnations now blossom in full glory, enabling him to save a small fortune. Le Papet, now old and withered, pushes his nephew toward marriage. Unless Ugolin takes a wife and begins a family, the name of Soubeyran (once the most powerful family in the region) will cease to exist. Ugolin, however, has no desire to marry—until, one day, he sees Manon bathing in a small spring and falls instantly in love.

Like its predecessor, MANON OF THE SPRING is filled with marvelous photography, gorgeous rolling landscapes, and spectacular performances. While Part I favors Depardieu's character and his struggles against both man and nature, Part II concentrates on the tragic end of Montand and his final reconciliation with the higher forces of fate. Montand, always brilliant, turns in a performance that ranks

with his best work; Auteuil is also excellent as the manipulated young fool. Beart, while easy on the eyes, is given very little to do besides play the object of desire. This is an admirable though traditional piece of entertainment. MANON surpasses JEAN DE FLORETTE in its portrayal of the villagers, a necessary element virtually absent from the earlier picture. Together JEAN DE FLORETTE and MANON OF THE SPRING earned a total of eight Cesars (the French Oscar): Best Film, Best Director, Best Actor (Auteuil), Best Actress, Best Screenplay, Best Score, Best Cinematography, and Best Sound (Pierre Gamet, Dominique Hennequin).

MAN'S FAVORITE SPORT? 📀
1964   120m   c   Comedy   ★★½
Universal   (U.S.)

Rock Hudson (Roger Willoughby), Paula Prentiss (Abigail Page), Maria Perschy (Isolde "Easy" Mueller), Charlene Holt (Tex Connors), John McGiver (William Cadwalader), Roscoe Karns (Maj. Phipps), Forrest Lewis (Skaggs), Regis Toomey (Bagley), Norman Alden (John Screaming Eagle), Don Allen (Tom)

p, Howard Hawks; d, Howard Hawks; w, John Fenton Murray, Steve McNeil (based on the story "The Girl Who Almost Got Away" by Pat Frank); ph, Russell Harlan (Technicolor); ed, Stuart Gilmore; m, Henry Mancini; art d, Alexander Golitzen, Tambi Larsen; fx, Ben McMahon; cos, Edith Head

Director-producer Hawks here returned to the comic formulas that worked so well for him in BRINGING UP BABY and I WAS A MALE WAR BRIDE but achieved only limited success. Cary Grant had been able to carry the earlier films with a characteristic charm that leading man Hudson was unable to match. Hudson is the star fishing-supplies salesman of a large sporting goods store, but he knows nothing about fishing. Publicity agent Prentiss convinces Hudson's boss, McGiver, that Hudson should enter a fishing contest. With a little luck and assistance from a bear, Hudson wins. Acknowledging that his win is a fluke, he forfeits the prize and subsequently gets fired. In the end, Hudson gets his job back and lands Prentiss as well. Hawks delivers his usual heavy-handed direction, but the film's premise is too flimsy to spread over two hours. The script is marred by tired comic routines and slow pacing. The cast, though, with the exception of Hudson, offers very good performances—Prentiss in particular.

MAN'S HOPE
(SIERRA DE TERUEL)
1947   78m   bw   War   ★★★★
Lopert   (Spain)

Majuto (Capt. Munoz), Nicolas Rodriguez (Pilot Marquez), Jose Lado (The Peasant)

p, Andre Malraux; d, Andre Malraux; w, Andre Malraux (based on the novel Espoir by Andre Malraux); ph, Louis Page; m, Darius Milhaud

This film was shot in Spain during the Spanish Civil War and later smuggled into Occupied France, where screening was postponed until after the Liberation. As a result, it was eight years before the public was allowed to view MAN'S HOPE. When the film finally was screened, it received the Louis Delluc Award, one of the highest honors the French could bestow on a film. In adapting his own novel for the screen, Andre Malraux creates a powerful, sweepingly realistic film through the use of actual combat footage. The story focuses on a Loyalist air squadron's attempt to destroy a bridge. To succeed, the Loyalists must neutralize a new airfield. The only one who can locate the field is a peasant who can't read a map, so he is taken along on the air raid. Although the narrative structure of MAN'S HOPE is unconventional and the film is otherwise flawed, these problems pale next to the overwhelming realism of Malraux's depiction of life during wartime.

MANSFIELD PARK

DVD

1999 110m c Historical/Romance/Drama ★★★
BBC Films/HAL Films/Miramax (U.K.) PG-13

Frances O'Connor *(Fanny Price)*, Embeth Davidtz *(Mary Crawford)*, Jonny Lee Miller *(Edmond Bertram)*, Alessandro Nivola *(Henry Crawford)*, Harold Pinter *(Sir Thomas Bertram)*, Lindsay Duncan *(Lady Bertram/Mrs. Price)*, Victoria Hamilton *(Maria Bertram)*, Justine Waddell *(Julia Bertram)*, James Purefoy *(Tom Bertram)*, Hannah Taylor Gordon *(Young Fanny)*

p, Sarah Curtis; d, Patricia Rozema; w, Patricia Rozema (based on the novel by Jane Austen, and on her letters and early journals); ph, Michael Coulter; ed, Martin Walsh; m, Lesley Barber; prod d, Christopher Hobbs; art d, Andrew Munro; fx, Richard Ven Den Berg, Evolution FX; cos, Andrea Galer

Austen purists may gag, but director Patricia Rozema has managed to transform Jane Austen's problematic novel into an engaging bit of entertainment.

As an act of mercy, 10-year-old Fanny Price (Hannah Taylor Gordon) is taken from her family's squalid Portsmouth home and brought to live at Mansfield Park, the sprawling country estate of her wealthy uncle and aunt, Lord and Lady Bertram (Harold Pinter, Lindsay Duncan). Fanny is raised as the proverbial poor stepchild, overshadowed by her privileged cousins: Tom (James Purefoy), the heir to his father's property, including a sugar plantation in Antigua; sensitive younger brother Edmond (Jonny Lee Miller), who plans to become a cleric; and the shallow and spoiled Misses Bertram, Maria (Victoria Hamilton) and Julia (Justine Waddell). As the years pass, it becomes clear that Edmond and the nowgrown Fanny (Frances O'Connor) are an ideal match, but simple matters are complicated with the arrival of the Crawfords, the half-brother and -sister of the parson's wife. Edmond is captivated by the sharp and sophisticated Mary Crawford (Embeth Davidtz); her brother Henry (Alessandro Nivola), meanwhile, is bent on seducing the young ladies of Mansfield Park, Fanny included.

Rozema has solved the "problem" of Austen's novel by consulting the author's own letters and journals, transforming the priggish Fanny into, well, Jane Austen. Rozema squeezes in a little raunchy sex and lends her interpretation critical cachet by reading the novel in terms of English imperialism. Genteel life at Mansfield Park is explicitly grounded in the suffering of Antiguan slaves, and the business of Sir Thomas Bertram includes torture and rape. It's heavy-handed and not entirely original (Rozema owes a great, unacknowledged debt to critic Edward Said), but it's interesting nonetheless. Whatever havoc it happens to wreak in terms of characterization (where, exactly, does a rapist fit into a happy ending?) is smoothed over by the sterling cast.

MARATHON MAN

DVD

1976 125m c Spy/Thriller/War ★★★★
Paramount (U.S.) R

Dustin Hoffman *(Babe Levy)*, Laurence Olivier *(Szell)*, Roy Scheider *(Doc Levy)*, William Devane *(Janeway)*, Marthe Keller *(Elsa)*, Fritz Weaver *(Prof. Biesenthal)*, Richard Bright *(Karl)*, Marc Lawrence *(Erhard)*, Allen Joseph *(Babe's Father)*, Tito Goya *(Melendez)*

p, Robert Evans, Sidney Beckerman; d, John Schlesinger; w, William Goldman (based on his novel); ph, Conrad Hall (Metrocolor); ed, Jim Clark; m, Michael Small; prod d, Richard MacDonald; art d, Jack DeShields; fx, Richard E. Johnson, Dick Smith, Charles Spurgeon; cos, Robert de Mora

AAN Best Supporting Actor: Laurence Olivier

A truly harrowing film, MARATHON MAN is a clever series of accidents that produce a nightmare thriller with an unrelenting attack on the viewer's nerves. Babe Levy (Dustin Hoffman), a Columbia University graduate student who runs whenever possible, dreaming of the Olympic marathon, is haunted by the memory of his father's suicide, brought about by the McCarthy witchhunts. Babe's brother, Doc (Roy Scheider), an American secret agent, helps sneak Szell (Laurence Olivier), an old Nazi, into the U.S. from South America. Szell's brother, who has watched over a fortune in jewels taken from Jewish concentration camp victims, has died, and Szell has come to New York to collect the booty. After killing Doc, Szell uses the tools of his dentist's trade to torture Babe for information the student doesn't possess. Putting his marathon training to use, Babe escapes Szell, and eventually the pursuer becomes the pursued. Hoffman is excellent as the crazed Szell's victim, and Olivier is the essence of evil, his sadistic acts so expertly enacted that the film has a deeply disturbing quality. John Schlesinger's direction is highly stylized and more than effective, jammed with action and offering unforgettably terrifying scenes. Scheider is good as the errant older brother, and William Devane is his usual tricky self as the double-dealing intelligence chief. William Goldman's script, based on his novel, is morally confused but literate and full of surprises.

MARIA FULL OF GRACE

DVD

2004 101m c Drama ★★★½
Journeyman Pictures/Altercine/Tucan Producciones/ R
HBO Films (U.S.)

Catalina Sandino Moreno *(Maria)*, Yenny Paola Vega *(Blanca)*, Virgina Ariza *(Juana)*, Johanna Andrea Mora *(Diana)*, Wilson Guerrero *(Juan)*, John Alex Toro *(Franklin)*, Guilied Lopez *(Lucy)*, Patricia Rae *(Carla)*, Fernando Velasquez *(Pablo)*, Orlando Tobon *(Don Fernando)*

p, Paul Mezey; d, Joshua Marston; w, Joshua Marston; ph, Jim Denault; ed, Anne McCabe, Lee Percy; m, Leonardo Heiblum, Jacobo Lieberman; prod d, Debbie DeVilla, Monica Marulanda; art d, Yann Blanc; cos, Sarah Beers, Lauren Press

AAN Best Actress: Catalina Sandino Moreno

American writer-director Joshua Marston's debut feature is a low-key, affecting portrait of a teenager trying to escape her family's relentless poverty by working as a mule, smuggling drugs internally out of Colombia into the United States.

Seventeen-year-old Maria (Catalina Sandino Moreno) lives in an impoverished backwater not far from Bogota and, like virtually every other employed adult in the town, supports her mother (Virginia Ariza), sister (Johanna Andrea Mora), and infant nephew by working at the local flower factory. The newly pregnant Maria nevertheless quits after a humiliating run-in with her demeaning supervisor and unwilling to marry her boyfriend, Juan (Wilson Guerrero), Maria decides to hitch a ride to Bogota and see if she can find house-cleaning work. Handsome acquaintance Franklin (Jhon Alex Toro), however, has a better suggestion. His friend Javier (Jaime Osorio Gomez) pays handsomely for couriers to transport film from Colombia to New York City. Maria knows perfectly well what "film" means, but a single trip would pay more than she could earn in years of stripping flowers. Tutored by veteran mule Lucy (Giulied Lopez), Maria and her less-resilient best friend, Blanca (Yenny Paola Vega), ingest several dozen kumquat-sized pellets of cocaine apiece and board a plane to New Jersey, thinking the worst is over. It isn't.

Rather than aspire to the epic scale of TRAFFIC, Marston keeps his focus small and avoids sensationalizing, stereotyping, or sentimentalizing his characters. Moreno's subtly calibrated mix of intelligence, naivete, rebelliousness, and practicality produces an unforgettable protagonist. Maria doesn't embody Colombia's drug industry; she's just a girl burdened with adult responsibilities and facing a painfully circumscribed future who enters the lowest level of the multinational drug business and pays dearly for the opportunities it provides.

MARIANNE AND JULIANE
(DIE BLEIERNE ZEIT)

1981 103m c   Drama/Political   ★★★½
Bioskop Film/Sender Fries   (West Germany)

Jutta Lampe (Juliane), Barbara Sukowa (Marianne), Rudiger Vogler (Wolfgang), Doris Schade (Mother), Verenice Rudolph (Sabine), Luc Bondy (Werner), Franz Rudnick (Father), Julia Biedermann (Marianne—Age 16), Ina Robinski (Juliane—Age 17), Patrick Estrada-Pox (Jan—Age 10)

p, Eberhard Junkersdorf; d, Margarethe von Trotta; w, Margarethe von Trotta; ph, Franz Rath; ed, Dagmar Hirtz; m, Nicolas Economou; art d, Barbara Kloth; cos, Monica Hasse, Jorge Jara

Rigorously composed and devoid of easy sentiment, MARIANNE AND JULIANE may be director Margarethe von Trotta's most accessible film. It chronicles the lives of two German sisters for whom character truly is destiny.

Marianne (Barbara Sukowa), radicalized by the events of the mid-70s, joins a terrorist cell and asks sister Juliane (Jutta Lampe) to adopt her four-year-old son. Because of commitments to her lover Wolfgang (Rudiger Vogler) and to her writing career, Juliane reluctantly refuses, and her decision has terrible results: Marianne's ex-husband kills himself and the boy becomes a ward of the state. When the steely Marianne reappears with two comrades, she not only uses Juliane as a convenience but also disparages her lifestyle and part-time activism. While Juliane questions the government in print, militant Marianne attacks it through commando crimes, including bank robbery. Later, when Marianne dies mysteriously in jail, Juliane is overwhelmed with guilt and sets out to prove that her sister was officially silenced.

During the shooting of the movie GERMANY IN AUTUMN, director von Trotta met magazine editor Christine Ensslin, whose sister Gudrun died in Stammheim Prison under suspicious circumstances in 1977. Von Trotta's film uses this footnote to German history as a springboard for meditations on feminism, political activism, jingoism, and family psychology. It's a kind of treatise on the roots of political conscience, but the human element never suffers: the sisters' love-hate relationship is delineated with singular eloquence and subtlety. The film played briefly in U.S. art houses under the title THE GERMAN SISTERS.

MARIE

1985 112m c   Biography/Political   ★★★½
DEG   (U.S.)   PG-13

Sissy Spacek (Marie Ragghianti), Jeff Daniels (Eddie Sisk), Keith Szarabajka (Kevin McCormack), Morgan Freeman (Charles Traughber), Lisa Banes (Toni Greer), Fred Thompson (Himself), Trey Wilson (FBI Agent), John Collum (Deputy Attorney General), Don Hood (Gov. Blanton), Graham Beckel (Charlie Benson)

p, Frank Capra Jr.; d, Roger Donaldson; w, John Briley (based on the book Marie, A True Story by Peter Maas); ph, Chris Menges

(Joe Dunton Camera, Technicolor); ed, Neil Travis; m, Francis Lai; art d, Ron Foreman; cos, Joe I. Tompkins

The true story of Marie Ragghianti, a woman who fought corruption in Tennessee, is a powerful film from a book by Peter Maas with a screenplay by Oscar-winner John Briley and a first U.S. assignment for New Zealand director Roger Donaldson. Marie (Sissy Spacek) leaves home in 1968 after being brutalized by her husband. A mother of three, she must struggle as she stays at her mother's home, works as a waitress, and puts herself through Vanderbilt University. An old pal, Eddie Sisk (Jeff Daniels), helps her get a job with the state. He's the governor's legal counsel and not without power in the hierarchy, so her job as extradition director is an excellent first rung for her. It's not long before she rises in the state bureaucracy and becomes a member of the parole board and finally the chairperson of that board. It's not too long before Marie realizes that the governor (Don Hood) is using his influence to get some powerful criminals released. The movie could have become a cliched investigatory picture, as did so many after Watergate. Director Donaldson keeps matters moving. Spacek is superb and so is Daniels, unaccustomed as he is to the villain's role. But the acting surprise is the work of Fred Thompson, playing himself as the real-life attorney who handled the case for Marie Ragghianti.

MARIE ANTOINETTE

1938 160m bw Biography/Historical/Romance ★★★★
MGM   (U.S.)

Norma Shearer (Marie Antoinette), Tyrone Power (Count Axel de Fersen), John Barrymore (King Louis XV), Gladys George (Mme. Du Barry), Robert Morley (King Louis XVI), Anita Louise (Princess DeLamballe), Joseph Schildkraut (Duke of Orleans), Henry Stephenson (Count Mercey), Reginald Gardiner (Artois), Peter Bull (Garnin)

p, Hunt Stromberg; d, W.S. Van Dyke II, Julien Duvivier (uncredited); w, Claudine West, Donald Ogden Stewart, Ernest Vajda, F. Scott Fitzgerald (based on a book by Stefan Zweig); ph, William Daniels; ed, Robert J. Kern; m, Herbert Stothart; art d, Cedric Gibbons, William A. Horning; fx, Slavko Vorkapich; chor, Albertina Rasch; cos, Adrian, Gile Steele

AAN Best Actress: Norma Shearer; AAN Best Supporting Actor: Robert Morley; AAN Best Score: Herbert Stothart; AAN Best Interior Decoration: Cedric Gibbons

Although it has its admirers, this lengthy but consistently gripping film remains an underrated biopic done in the grand Hollywood manner. It's also an eerily apt showcase for Norma Shearer, and along with PRIVATE LIVES, SMILIN' THROUGH and THE WOMEN, stands as one of the best things she ever did. Shearer, long MGM's queen, was on the verge of a decline, like Marie's, linked to her husband's death. True, Marie Antoinette was executed and Shearer lost interest in her career and retired a wealthy woman, but the parallels between the lives of the two women permeate the film. Planned as early as 1933 by Shearer's husband, "boy genius" Irving Thalberg, but halted in 1936 when he died, it's amazing just how well the project turned out.

Marie is married off to Louis Auguste (Morley), heir to the throne, by her mother, Empress of Austria (Alma Kruger), but is repelled by her first meeting with the dullwitted, unattractive Dauphin. (Shearer and Morley share an excellent scene as Louis hints at his impotence—an adult, well-handled scene for the Hollywood of the day.) Further distressing Marie are the sneering, sickly King Louis XV and his conspiratorial mistress, Mme. Du Barry (George). Du Barry, feeling threatened by the future queen, forms intrigues against her, and Marie quickly becomes a pariah at court. She takes Orleans's (Schildkraut) advice and gains solace from fast living, beginning an affair with Count Axel de Fersen (Power). Marie is almost sent back to Austria in disgrace after humiliating the bitchy Du Barry at a ball, but the king dies suddenly and Marie becomes Queen. Fersen tells her that her duties must come before their love, and he sails off to America. Marie develops an affectionate relationship with Louis, who also gathers his wits enough to produce two children. Orleans, however, who had denied Marie help at her low ebb, is now an outcast at court and incites the people to revolt. The guillotine beckons.

After Thalberg's death, MGM mogul Louis B. Mayer tried to make a flat settlement with his estate. Shearer, however, held the studio to an agreement giving Thalberg's estate a percentage of all the profits MGM had made since its 1924 consolidation. The handling of MARIE ANTOINETTE ended up being not only an attempt to control costs on one of the studio's priciest pictures ever, but also perhaps a subtle revenge on the victorious Shearer. Mayer replaced original director Sidney Franklin with Woody Van Dyke, a no-nonsense helmsman who didn't cotton to La Norma's requests for more takes.

Gibbons's magnificent sets, crammed with authentic French antiques, outdid Versailles, and costumers Adrian and Steele used 500 yards of silk on one of Shearer's gowns alone. Daniels's camerawork is exceptional, and Van Dyke makes this long film move like a short one. The flash of Barrymore and Schildkraut (with a great makeup job) steals many scenes, but top supporting honors go to the gifted Morley, who somehow lost an Oscar to Walter Brennan in KENTUCKY. Above all, though, the film showcases the regal qualities fans loved in La Norma. While some scenes show her fluttering or hamming it up a bit much, there's a lot of excellent stuff here, especially as Marie awaits death. The overall result is ornate and satisfying, typical of MGM at its production zenith.

MARIUS   📀

1931   103m   bw   Drama   ★★★★
Joinville/Paramount   (France)

Raimu (Cesar Olivier), Orane Demazis (Fanny), Pierre Fresnay (Marius), Fernand Charpin (Honore Panisse), Alida Rouffe (Honorine Cabanis), Robert Vattier (Mon. Brun), Paul Dullac (Felix Escartefigue), Alexandre Mihalesco (Piquoiseau), Edouard Delmont (2nd Mate), Milly Mathis (Aunt Claudine Foulon)

p, Marcel Pagnol; d, Alexander Korda; w, Marcel Pagnol (based on the play by Marcel Pagnol); ph, Ted Pahle; ed, Roger Mercanton; m, Francis Gromon; prod d, Alfred Junge, Vincent Korda

Faithfully adapted from the enormously popular (over 1,000 performances) stage play by Marcel Pagnol, MARIUS was the first in a trilogy of films evoking, in richly sentimental and gently satirical style, waterfront life in Marseilles in the late 1920s and early '30s. Though still open to the criticism leveled at the time, that this was little more than canned theater, it's vastly enjoyable nonetheless, with the great Raimu stealing the show in the role (reprised from the stage version) of cafe owner Cesar. Cesar's son Marius (Pierre Fresnay) works at his father's Bar de la Marine and loves fish-stall worker Fanny (Orane Demazis), Pagnol's longtime companion and leading lady) just a little less than he does the sea. Cesar spends most of his time in amiably idle conversation with his patrons—the wealthy Panisse (Fernand Charpin), ferry captain Felix Escartefigue (Paul Dullac), and customs inspector Brun (Robert Vattier). When the elderly Panisse asks for Fanny's hand, she sees this as her opportunity to work on Marius' jealousy and force him to choose her over a life at sea, but she finally acknowledges the greater power of his wanderlust in a hugely touching gesture of self-denial. The joys of MARIUS are the joys of the stage play—a fantastic cast, many drawn,

like Raimu, from the Marseilles music hall; authentic, unpretentious dialogue peppered with richly provincial idioms; and fully realized, un-glamorous characters drawn with loving detail. Director Alexander Korda brought relatively little of his own to this screen adaptation; writer/producer Pagnol watched the proceedings carefully, hired Marc Allegret to direct the same cast in the next installment, FANNY, and took over the reigns himself for CESAR. This last was an oddity, in that the film preceded the stage play, but entirely in line with Pagnol's belief that the theater was dead and that talking pictures represented a new pinnacle of dramatic art.

MARK OF ZORRO, THE   📀

1940   93m   bw   Adventure   ★★★★
Fox   (U.S.)

Tyrone Power (Zorro/Don Diego Vega), Linda Darnell (Lolita Quintero), Basil Rathbone (Capt. Esteban Pasquale), Gale Sondergaard (Inez Quintero), Eugene Pallette (Fra Felipe), J. Edward Bromberg (Don Luis Quintero), Montagu Love (Don Alejandro Vega), Janet Beecher (Senora Isabella Vega), Robert Lowery (Rodrigo), Chris-Pin Martin (Turnkey)

p, Raymond Griffith; d, Rouben Mamoulian; w, John Taintor Foote, Garrett Fort, Bess Meredyth (based on the novel The Curse of Capistrano by Johnston McCulley); ph, Arthur Miller; ed, Robert Bischoff; m, Alfred Newman; art d, Richard Day, Joseph C. Wright; cos, Travis Banton

AAN Best Original Score: Alfred Newman

A smashing remake of the Douglas Fairbanks silent swashbuckler, this remarkable action film owes everything to inventive director Mamoulian. This was Fox's answer to Warner's THE ADVENTURES OF ROBIN HOOD, with some of THE SCARLET PIMPERNEL thrown in for good measure.

In a role that perfectly combines his feyness and machismo, Power is marvelous as the fop by day and brave avenger by night. Returning to 19th-century Los Angeles, Don Diego (Power) finds that his father Don Alejandro (Love) has been replaced as governor by the slimy Don Luis Quintero (Bromberg) and the cruel Capt. Pasquale (Rathbone). Shortly after the mincing Don Diego has convinced the powers that be that he's nothing to worry about, the dashing, heroic but mysterious Zorro begins righting wrongs left and right, leaving his mark (literally) on everything... and everyone. Who says the pen is mightier than the sword?

Power cuts a stylish and convincing Zorro, vigorously playing the brilliant swordsman, although his more strenuous routines are performed by stunt double Albert Cavens. Mamoulian cleverly cuts in and out of his terse scenes to suggest more action than really occurs. The final deadly confrontation between Rathbone and Power is a thrilling duel no less exciting than the final contretemps between Errol Flynn and Rathbone in THE ADVENTURES OF ROBIN HOOD. Rathbone is terrific as the villain, always fondling his sword, prepared at any moment to draw blood for sport or sadistic amusement. "Most men have objects they play with," Rathbone remarks in one scene. "Churchmen have their beads; I toy with a sword." Love is as sturdy as ever, the paunchy Bromberg and the sleek Sondergaard are a delight as the sleazy rulers, and the unique Palette gets to reprise his performance as Friar Tuck from ROBIN HOOD. Darnell doesn't get to do much more than glow in soft focus, but she does show lush promise beneath the prim dictates of her role.

Skilled swordsman Rathbone paid Power a supreme compliment: "Power was the most agile man with a sword I've ever faced before a camera. Tyrone could have fenced Errol Flynn into a cocked hat." There have been other Zorros, of course. Yakima Canutt, the great stuntman, played the role in 1937 in ZORRO RIDES AGAIN; Frank Langella had a swipe at the part in a middling 1974 TV-movie; and George

Hamilton overplayed the double-sided nature of the tale's hero to the point of cheap homophobic caricature in ZORRO, THE GAY BLADE. But none would ever equal Power. He looked and acted like a man who could, with bold acts and brave heart, change the course of history. And, of course, for the burgeoning coffers of Fox, he did.

MARNIE
DVD

1964 120m c   Thriller/Romance   ★★★★
Universal   (U.S.)   PG

Tippi Hedren (Marnie Edgar), Sean Connery (Mark Rutland), Diane Baker (Lil Mainwaring), Martin Gabel (Sidney Strutt), Louise Latham (Bernice Edgar), Bob Sweeney (Cousin Bob), Milton Selzer (Man at the Track), Alan Napier (Mr. Rutland), Henry Beckman (1st Detective), Edith Evanson (Rita)

p, Alfred Hitchcock; d, Alfred Hitchcock; w, Jay Presson Allen (based on the novel by Winston Graham); ph, Robert Burks (Technicolor); ed, George Tomasini; m, Bernard Herrmann; prod d, Robert Boyle; cos, Edith Head

Hitchcock's most liberated and poetic film, MARNIE is a masterpiece of psychological mystery that encompasses all of the director's obsessions—the unleashing of suppressed female sexuality, duplicitous personalities and false identities, childhood trauma leading to a disturbed and warped reality in adulthood, and the director's own love of cool-looking blondes and "pure cinema." Its characters are possessed by psychological demons similar to those in VERTIGO or PSYCHO. Hedren plays a kleptomaniac whose compulsion to steal springs from her need to be loved. Using various identities and disguises, she moves from one job to the next, each time running off with a cache of cash and leaving behind no clues. Connery, a business associate of one of Marnie's previous victims, recognizes Marnie when she comes to work for him, and confronts her with his information. Rather than turn her in, however, Mark blackmails her into marriage—discovering their deep-seated fears of men, sex, thunderstorms, and the color red. Met with a less-than-enthusiastic response, MARNIE was one of Hitchcock's 1960s films (THE BIRDS, TORN CURTAIN, and TOPAZ were the others) that raised suspicions among some critics of the master's having lost his touch, unable to adjust to the times. In retrospect, MARNIE emerges as prime Hitchcock—its tone and subtext as revealing as that of VERTIGO, although more desperate and disquieting (perhaps because of Hitchcock's deep obsession with Hedren during production). Of interest is Hitchcock's uncharacteristic use of a technique that makes the audience actually *feel* Hedren's traumas. Seeing Hedren against abstract backdrops and "poor" rear-screen projections makes her world seem disturbingly unreal. The ever-changing weather conditions, in which thunderstorms conveniently brew and night changes rapidly to day, and the use of a few frames of red shock the audience into experiencing Hedren's fear (a technique Hitchcock had attempted as early as 1935 in SECRET AGENT).

MARRIAGE OF MARIA BRAUN, THE
DVD

(DIE EHE DER MARIA BRAUN)

1978 120m c   Drama/War   ★★★★
Albatros/Trio/Westdeutscher/Autoren   R
(West Germany)

Hanna Schygulla (Maria Braun), Klaus Lowitsch (Hermann Braun), Ivan Desny (Oswald), Gottfried John (Willi), Gisela Uhlen (Mother), Gunter Lamprecht (Hans), Hark Bohm (Senkenberg), George Byrd (Bill), Elisabeth Trissenaar (Betti), Rainer Werner Fassbinder (Peddler)

p, Michael Fengler; d, Rainer Werner Fassbinder; w, Peter Marthesheimer, Pia Frohlich, Rainer Werner Fassbinder (based on an idea by Rainer Werner Fassbinder); ph, Michael Ballhaus

(Fujicolor); ed, Juliane Lorenz, Franz Walsch; m, Peer Raben; art d, Norbert Scherer, Helga Ballhaus, Claud Kottmann, Georg Borgel; cos, Barbara Baum, Susi Reichel, George Kuhn, Ingeborg Proller

She eludes you, even if she does start—and finish—with a bang. The first in Rainer Werner Fassbinder's trilogy about women in post-WWII Germany (followed by VERONIKA VOSS and LOLA), this was also the film that solidified Fassbinder's reputation abroad and in Germany. In the opening sequence, a German city is being torn apart by Allied bombs while Maria (Hanna Schygulla) and her soldier fiance, Hermann Braun (Klaus Lowitsch), are getting married. Immediately afterwards, the new husband is sent to the Russian front, leaving Maria with her mother and sister, impoverished and waiting for her husband, visiting the train station every day with the hope of hearing news about him. After receiving word that he has died, Maria takes work as a barmaid in a cafe that caters to American soldiers. There she meets Bill (George Byrd), a hefty black soldier who, despite the fact the they can barely converse, becomes her lover. Just when she has nearly forgotten about her husband, however, the starving and emasculated Hermann turns up while Maria and Bill are beginning to make love. The highly stylized, deliberate structure of THE MARRIAGE OF MARIA BRAUN owes much to such Douglas Sirk 1950s Hollywood melodramas as IMITATION OF LIFE and WRITTEN ON THE WIND. For both Sirk and Fassbinder, the director remains distanced from the heartwrenching dramatics of the story in order to comment on certain societal ills, but Fassbinder is even further removed from his material—a product of the alienation prominent in a postwar Germany striving to rebuild itself into an industrial power, yet failing to account for the human bonds that make a society healthy. The effect is one of helplessness; we can only watch as the beautiful, young Maria Braun places herself in an emotional vacuum. Schygulla is quite powerful in perhaps the best role of her career, remaining cold and aloof, yet evoking a strong sense of pity. Though THE MARRIAGE OF MARIA BRAUN is not always an easy film to understand, the stark atmosphere, icy performances, and poignant revelations make it one of the most important films to emerge from Germany in the 1970s, and one of Fassbinder's best.

MARRIED TO THE MOB
DVD

1988 103m c   Comedy/Crime   ★★★½
Mysterious Arts   (U.S.)   R

Michelle Pfeiffer (Angela Demarco), Matthew Modine (Mike Downey), Dean Stockwell (Tony "The Tiger" Russo), Mercedes Ruehl (Connie Russo), Oliver Platt (Ed Benitez), Alec Baldwin (Frank "The Cucumber" DeMarco), Anthony J. Nici (Joey DeMarco), Sister Carol East (Rita Harcourt), Paul Lazar (Tommy Boyle), Trey Wilson (Franklin)

p, Kenneth Utt, Edward Saxon; d, Jonathan Demme; w, Barry Strugatz, Mark R. Burns; ph, Tak Fujimoto (Duart Color); ed, Craig McKay; m, David Byrne; prod d, Kristi Zea; fx, Efex Specialists, Inc.; cos, Colleen Atwood

AAN Best Supporting Actor: Dean Stockwell

A pleasant trifle. Lacking the disturbing edge of director Demme's previous effort SOMETHING WILD, MARRIED TO THE MOB is a gangster film with a twist and the idiosyncratic Demme touch. There is plenty to amuse and delight here, including fine performances from Michelle Pfeiffer, Matthew Modine, and Dean Stockwell.

The movie begins on Long Island, where the homes are full of gilded Mediterranean furniture, the men dress in pinstriped suits, and the women spend most of their time getting their hair teased at the local beauty salon. Angela DeMarco (Pfeiffer), wife of up-and-coming hit man Frank "The Cucumber" DeMarco (Alec Baldwin), is tired of the criminal mentality of everyone around her and wants out. After Frank is caught by his boss, Mafia don Tony "The Tiger" Russo (Stockwell), with the boss's mistress and "iced," a couple of FBI agents (Modine and Oliver Platt) assume that Angela and Tony are lovers. Angela packs up with her son (Anthony J. Nici) and moves into a seedy apartment on Manhattan's Lower East Side, only to have the Feds follow and keep her embroiled in the mob's doings. Of course, romance eventually blooms between Angela and agent Mike Downey (Modine).

The wonderfully tacky production design by Kristi Zea, the bizarre costumes by Colleen Atwood, the clash of musical styles in the score by David Byrne, and the eccentric performances of the entire cast combine to create a dizzying array of forces swirling around Pfeiffer. She plays her part fairly straight, thus making everyone else seem that much more bizarre. Stockwell in particular is wonderful as the tyrannical hood. This was the last film appearance for veteran character actor Joe Spinell (TAXI DRIVER, ROCKY, NIGHT SHIFT), who has a small role as one of Stockwell's henchmen. He appeared in 40 films in the '70s and '80s before his death in 1989.

MARRIED WOMAN, THE

(UNE FEMME MARIEE)
1964 94m bw Drama ★★★★★
Anouchka/Orsay (France)

Macha Meril (Charlotte), Bernard Noel (Robert, the Lover), Philippe Leroy (Pierre, the Husband), Rita Maiden (Mme. Celine), Margaret Le Van, Veronique Duval (Girls in Swimming Pool), Chris Tophe (Nicolas), Georges Liron (The Physician), Roger Leenhardt (Himself), Jean-Luc Godard (Narrator)

d, Jean-Luc Godard; w, Jean-Luc Godard; ph, Raoul Coutard; ed, Agnes Guillemot, Francoise Collin; m, Claude Nougaro; art d, Henri Nogaret; cos, Laurence Clairval

Meril plays a Parisian housewife with both an airline pilot husband (Leroy) and a lover (Noel). When she becomes pregnant, she realizes either man could be the father. She debates whether she should stay with her husband or leave him for her lover; she gets no help from either in making her decision.

Subtitled "Fragments of a film made in 1964," THE MARRIED WOMAN is a fragmented, distanced film that dissects Meril's character and morally situates her between the two men in her life. Even at the film's opening, Meril is represented as a disembodied figure—in separate shots we are shown, against a white bed sheet, her hands, legs, feet, torso. Taking place over a 24-hour period, even THE MARRIED WOMAN's time frame is cut apart into almost Resnaisian divisions. Heavily under the influence of Brecht, director Jean-Luc Godard makes brilliant use of the written word, magazine advertisements and billboards, allusions to other artists (Racine, Apollinaire, Hitchcock, Resnais, Beethoven), visual references to film technique (the use of negative film images), and interviews in a *cinema-verite* mode. The result is one of his most important and provocative dissections of modern life.

MARS ATTACKS!

1996 105m c Science Fiction/Comedy ★★★
Warner Bros. (U.S.) PG-13

Jack Nicholson (President James Dale/Art Land), Glenn Close (First Lady Marsha Dale), Annette Bening (Mrs. Barbara Land), Pierce Brosnan (Professor Donald Kessler), Danny DeVito (Rude Gambler), Martin Short (Press Secretary Jerry Ross), Sarah Jessica Parker (Nathalie Lake), Michael J. Fox (Jason Stone), Rod Steiger (General Decker), Tom Jones (Himself)

p, Tim Burton, Larry Franco; d, Tim Burton; w, Jonathan Gems (from his story, based on the Topps trading-card series); ph, Peter Suschitzky; ed, Christopher Lebenzon; m, Danny Elfman; prod d, Wynn Thomas; art d, John Dexter; fx, Michael Lantieri, James Mitchell (visual effects supervisor), Industrial Light & Magic, Warner Digital Studios; cos, Colleen Atwood

A childlike sense of malicious fun pervades MARS ATTACKS!, a film inspired by an infamous set of Topps trading cards so graphically violent for their era (1962) that protests from parents caused them to be withdrawn.

After a televised message from the Martian Ambassador is interpreted to have a friendly tone, the shallow but telegenic President of the United States (Jack Nicholson) schedules an event to welcome them. Unfortunately, the Martian soldiers open fire and kill dozens of humans. The Martian Ambassador sends a formal apology to the President, who schedules a second meeting in Congress. Once again, the Martians kill dozens of the assembled and kidnap key Presidential advisor Donald Kessler (Pierce Brosnan), who winds up having an unusual flirtation on their spaceship with another kidnapped Earthling, vain TV news anchor Nathalie Lake (Sarah Jessica Parker). With major U.S. cities in ruin and the Martians on the warpath, certain heroes begin to emerge: an alienated Kansas teen (Lukas Haas); an ex-heavyweight champion (Jim Brown); a spacey follower of New Age philosophy (Annette Bening); and singer Tom Jones (playing himself) are among them.

MARS ATTACKS! stands as one of the better contemporary evocations of the low-budget alien invasion movies of the 1950s. Burton's affection for those films is apparent as this one bounces quickly and energetically from location to location. Several of the leads give wonderful performances, including Nicholson, Bening, Brown, Pam Grier, and gawky Haas, who functions well as Burton's ever-present misfit-protagonist. But despite the notable cast, it's the Martians who steal the show. These small, computer-generated creatures provoke laughs as they chatter and waddle along. Any time the film seems in danger of becoming irretrievably cute, however, Burton returns to the element that made the "Mars Attacks" cards so controversial (and attractive to youngsters)—violence and gore with no apologies.

MARTIN

1978 95m c Horror ★★★★
Laurel (U.S.) R

John Amplas (Martin), Lincoln Maazel (Cuda), Christine Forrest (Christina), Elayne Nadeau (Mrs. Santini), Tom Savini (Arthur), Sarah Venable (Housewife Victim), Fran Middleton (Train Victim), Al Levitsky (Lewis)

p, Richard P. Rubinstein; d, George Romero; w, George Romero; ph, Michael Gornick; ed, George Romero; m, Donald Rubinstein; fx, Tom Savini

Considered by many to be George Romero's greatest work, MARTIN is a shocking, thoughtful reworking of the vampire myth set in a dying American steel town. Martin (John Amplas) is a shy, alienated 17-year-old who thinks he may be a vampire—a theory which seems to be confirmed by the opening scene. Aboard a Pittsburgh-bound train, Martin waylays a female passenger, injects her with sodium pentothal, and, while she is in a stupor, violates her. Lacking fangs, he then cuts her wrist with a razor blade and drinks her blood. (The gruesomely realistic special makeup effects are by Tom Savini, here working on the first of his many films for Romero.) When Martin arrives in Pittsburgh, he is confronted with his elderly Old World cousin, Tata Cuda (Lincoln Maazel), a religious zealot who is convinced the boy is an 84-year-old vampire, the product of a family curse. Calling Martin "Nosferatu," Tata Cuda is determined both to save the boy's soul and to destroy him. Martin has no friends in his new life; he only gets to experience a sense of community by becoming a regular caller to a radio talk show. He spills his guts (figuratively) over the air but the host assumes he's just another colorful kook. However Martin becomes popular and earns a playful nickname: "The Count."

Writer-director Romero leaves Martin's true status up in the air. At times the boy is convinced that he is the monster Tata Cuda believes him to be, seeing himself in sepia flash-backs as a Count Dracula-like vampire eluding angry vil-lagers. Other times he seems able to differentiate fantasy from reality, as when he tells his grandfather "There's no magic." For the most part, Martin is shown to be a severely troubled teenager with deadly psychosexual problems, a nightmare version of the kid next door whose only way of relating to attractive women is by drinking their blood. At times, Martin's condition is compared to drug addiction, though the horror of vampirism is shown to pale by comparison to the brutality of a police raid on a den of drug dealers.

Combining the well-worn elements of countless horror films with the harsh realities of life in a depressed contemporary industrial city, Romero creates a resonant, multifaceted, and, at times, surprisingly lyrical film that works both as insightful social commentary and as a fascinating rumination on the con-ventions of the genre. Well worth a look for anyone with even a passing interest in horror, and essential viewing for serious fright fans. Romero himself appears as a priest and Savini plays the fiance of Martin's cousin.

MARTY   📀
1955 91m   bw   Drama   ★★★★
UA   (U.S.)

Ernest Borgnine (Marty), Betsy Blair (Clara), Esther Minciotti (Mrs. Pilletti), Karen Steele (Virginia), Jerry Paris (Thomas), Frank Sutton (Ralph), Walter Kelley (the Kid), Robin Morse (Joe), Augusta Ciolli (Catherine), Joe Mantell (Angie)

p, Harold Hecht; d, Delbert Mann; w, Paddy Chayefsky (based on a television play by Chayefsky); ph, Joseph La Shelle; ed, Alan Crosland Jr.; m, Roy Webb; art d, Ted Haworth, Walter M. Simonds; cos, Norma

AA Best Picture; AA Best Actor: Ernest Borgnine; AAN Best Supporting Actor: Joe Mantell; AAN Best Supporting Actress: Betsy Blair; AA Best Director: Delbert Mann; AA Best Screenplay: Paddy Chayefsky; AAN Best B/W Cinematography: Joseph LaShelle; AAN Best Art Direction-Set Decoration (B/W): Edward S. Haworth, Walter Simonds, Robert Priestley

Dowdy but winning and poignant, and Ernie's Oscar. Borgnine is a burly, lonely, good-natured man living with his mother, with no prospects for any other kind of future. The heavy-set Bronx butcher lives in a small world populated by his Italian relatives and fast-aging male friends, chiefly Mantell. When Borgnine and Mantell meet after work, they stand about mind-lessly thinking of ways to fill their lives with something inter-esting to do. Their soon predictable, groping interchange never varies: "So, what do you wanna do tonight, Marty?" "I dunno, Angie. What do you wanna do?" At home, Borgnine is totally dominated by his love-smothering mother, Minciotti, who fusses and worries over him. When Borgnine attempts to step outside of his world he's roundly rejected as a bumbling, unat-tractive person. He attends a dance with Mantell and others and tries to pick up some girls but strikes out. Then he spots home-ly Blair, a schoolteacher whose life is excruciatingly similar to his, dull, hopeless, inching into loveless middle-age. Borgnine asks Blair to dance, and not long afterward they begin to date. But Borgnine runs into a brick wall when he introduces Blair to his mother and male friends. His pals call her a "dog," and Minciotti is downright hostile to her, considering Blair a threat

to her life with her son. Borgnine, not a courageous man, backs away from Blair. He doesn't call her as he promised, leaving her to sit miserably at home alone watching TV, while he ago-nizes over ignoring the woman he has grown to love.

MARTY, coming in the mid-1950s, in an era of epics and extravagant films designed to stifle upstart television, was all the more startling in that it was a movie expanded from an orig-inal television drama (with Rod Steiger in the lead), written brilliantly by Chayefsky, one of the leaders of what came to be known as "kitchen sink" or "clothesline" dramas. Besides Borgnine, Oscars also went to Chayefsky for Best Screenplay and to Mann for Best Direction, and it was named Best Picture.

Before doing this film Borgnine was nothing more than an uninteresting heavy. But here he showed the world the great depths of his own character. Mantell also gives a solid per-formance as the pal addicted to the more bloody passages of Mickey Spillane, constantly asserting: "Boy, he sure can write." Blair is less effective, and Minciotti is not much more than a prop mother. UA executives were not enthusiastic about the production and almost cancelled the movie; they, along with the rest of Hollywood's elite, were amazed at the movie's uni-versal success, and MARTY soon set a trend toward the small-budgeted, prosaic films to come.

MARY POPPINS   📀
1964 140m   c   Musical/Comedy   ★★★★
Walt Disney Productions   (U.S.)

Julie Andrews (Mary Poppins), Dick Van Dyke (Bert/Mr. Dawes, Sr.), David Tomlinson (Mr. Banks), Glynis Johns (Mrs. Banks), Hermione Baddeley (Ellen), Reta Shaw (Mrs. Brill), Karen Dotrice (Jane Banks), Matthew Garber (Michael Banks), Elsa Lanchester (Katie Nanna), Arthur Treacher (Constable Jones)

p, Walt Disney, Bill Walsh; d, Robert Stevenson; w, Bill Walsh, Don DaGradi (based on the *Mary Poppins* books by P.L. Travers); ph, Edward Colman (Technicolor); ed, Cotton Warburton; m, Irwin Kostal; art d, Carroll Clark, William H. Tuntke; fx, Peter Ellenshaw, Eustace Lycett, Robert A. Mattey; chor, Marc Breaux, Dee Dee Wood; cos, Tony Walton; anim, Milt Kahl, Oliver M. Johnston Jr., John Lounsbery, Hal Ambro, Franklin Thomas, Ward Kimball, Eric Larson, Cliff Nordberg, Hamilton Luske

AAN Best Picture; AA Best Actress: Julie Andrews; AAN Best Director: Robert Stevenson; AAN Best Adapted Screenplay: Bill Walsh, Don DaGradi; AAN Best Color Cinematography: Edward Colman; AA Best Film Editing: Cotton Warburton; AA Best Original Score: Richard M. Sherman, Robert B. Sherman; AAN Best Adapted Score: Irwin Kostal; AA Best Song: "Chim Chim Cher-ee"; Richard M. Sherman (Music & Lyrics), Robert B. Sherman (Music & Lyrics); AAN Best Art Direction-Set Decoration (Color): Carroll Clark, William H. Tuntke, Emile Kuri, Hal Gausman; AAN Best Costume Design (Color): Tony Walton; AAN Best Sound: Robert O. Cook; AA Best Special Visual Effects: Peter Ellenshaw, Hamilton Luske, Eustace Lycett

One of the greatest children's films ever, MARY POPPINS is as perfect and inventive a musical as anyone could see, with a timeless story, strong performances, a flawless blend of live action and animation, wonderful songs, and a sterling script with all the charm of the P.L. Travers books upon which it is based. The film begins when a remote father and mother (Tomlinson and Johns) decide to advertise for a nanny to care for their rowdy children, Michael and Jane Banks (Garber and Dotrice). The children write their own ad, and when their father tears it up and burns it in the fireplace, the pieces miraculously reassemble and go up the flue. Next day, Mary Poppins (Andrews) appears, gliding down from on high with an umbrella as her parachute. This is no ordinary nanny, the children soon learn, as she leads them on a series of delightful escapades, all the while teaching them lessons in proper behavior. Among the wonderful new friends Mary introduces the children to are Bert the chimney sweep (Van Dyke). He accompanies them on holiday to a world inhabited by animated penguins, who serve them tea on a carousel having strangely willful horses, and Uncle Albert (Wynn), whose infectious laughter leads to strange consequences. In retrospect, we consider Andrews a trifle young for the role; she lacks the wisdom of, say, an Irene Dunne, our ideal vision of the role. Look for the magnificent Jane Darwell, as the Bird Lady, in her final role. The movie won Academy Awards for Best Actress, Best Film Editing, Best Original Score, Best Song, and Best Special Visual Effect. MARY POPPINS was producer Walt Disney's crowning achievement in a career that had earned him more Oscars than anyone else. The memorable songs by Disney writers Richard and Robert Sherman include "Supercalifragilisticexpialidocious," "Chim Chim Cher-ee," and "A Spoonful of Sugar."

MASCULINE FEMININE
(MASCULIN FEMININ)
1966 103m bw Drama ★★★★
Anouchka/Argos/Svensk/Sandrews (France/Sweden)

Jean-Pierre Leaud (Paul), Chantal Goya (Madeleine), Marlene Jobert (Elisabeth), Michel Deborb (Robert), Catherine Duport (Catherine), Eva-Britt Strandberg (Lavinia), Birger Malmsten (Actor), Elsa Leroy (Miss 19), Francoise Hardy (Woman with the American Officer), Chantal Darget (Woman on Metro)

d, Jean-Luc Godard; w, Jean-Luc Godard (based on the stories "The Signal" and "Paul's Mistress" by Guy de Maupassant); ph, Willy Kurant; ed, Agnes Guillemot, Marguerite Renoir; m, Francis Lai, Jean-Jacques Debout

Jean-Luc Godard visited the world of young folk to create his most humane film. This is Godard's fifteen-point inquiry into the generation he refers to as the "children of Marx and Coca-Cola," the 1960s youth culture. Paul (Jean-Pierre Leaud), a confused young romantic in search of perfect love, meets pop singer Madeleine (Chantal Goya) in a cafe and eventually moves in with her. Paul copes with his changing views by taking a job for a market research firm, gathering data, and interviewing people (including a young woman voted "Miss Nineteen"). While Madeleine pursues her career, Paul tries to coexist with her and her two roommates, Elisabeth and Catherine (Marlene Jobert and Catherine-Isabelle Duport). Leaud's character—practically an extension of the Antoine Doinel character he played for Francois Truffaut (he even adopts the name Doinel at one point in the film)—wants to live for love, but the ideal becomes problematic in a detached and increasingly consumer-oriented society.

With MASCULINE FEMININE, Godard began a string of increasingly political pictures, leading eventually to his self-imposed exile from commercial cinema. His interest in the synthesis of fiction and documentary is already in full evidence here, with long static shots of people being interviewed included as a means of bringing to the screen an everyday chronicle of Parisian youth in the winter of 1965. (Contrary to the director's intentions, the picture was banned in France for those under 18.) Charming, innovative, provocative, and prophetic, MASCULINE FEMININE is a Godard film that even appeals to people who think they don't like Godard films. One of Godard's masterpieces.

M*A*S*H
DVD
1970 116m c Comedy/War ★★★★½
Aspen (U.S.) R

Donald Sutherland (Hawkeye Pierce), Elliott Gould (Trapper John McIntyre), Tom Skerritt (Duke Forrest), Sally Kellerman (Maj. Hot Lips Houlihan), Robert Duvall (Maj. Frank Burns), Jo Ann Pflug (Lt. Hot Dish), Rene Auberjonois (Dago Red), Roger Bowen (Col. Henry Blake), Gary Burghoff (Radar O'Reilly), David Arkin (Sgt. Major Vollmer)

p, Ingo Preminger; d, Robert Altman; w, Ring Lardner Jr. (based on the novel by Richard Hooker); ph, Harold Stine (Panavision, Deluxe Color); ed, Danford B. Greene; m, Johnny Mandel; art d, Jack Martin Smith, Arthur Lonergan; fx, L.B. Abbott, Art Cruickshank

AAN Best Picture; AAN Best Supporting Actress: Sally Kellerman; AAN Best Director: Robert Altman; AA Best Adapted Screenplay: Ring Lardner Jr.; AAN Best Film Editing: Danford B. Greene

Set during the Korean War but made at the height of the war in Vietnam, Robert Altman's exceptional antiwar comedy-drama follows the fortunes of a MASH (Mobile Army Surgical Hospital) unit. Hawkeye Pierce (Sutherland), Trapper John (Gould), and Duke Forrest (Skerritt) are the martini-swilling, prank-playing, but compassionate and capable battlefield surgeons who make life miserable for chief nurse Hot Lips Houlihan (Kellerman) and fellow surgeon Maj. Frank Burns (Duvall), a by-the-book prig. Among the terrible trio's shenanigans are the broadcast of a Burns-Houlihan lovemaking session over the camp public address system and the collapse of the women's shower to reveal the naked Maj. Houlihan. At the root of all this foolishness, however, is the attempt to mitigate the otherwise overwhelming bleakness of the war, to distract the doctors and nurses from the terrible waste of life they witness. The film's climactic football game, one of Hollywood's funniest (featuring a number of onetime pro players), pits the MASH unit against a crack team brought in by a general who has been investigating the unit.

Clever camera setups, Altman's patented overlapping dialogue, wonderful sight gags and situations, and universally fine ensemble performances combine to make this one the most enjoyable war-themed films ever. What makes M*A*S*H so extraordinary, however, is that beyond its hilarious antics and rich characters, the film offers a poignant portrait of the madness of war. This film was Altman's first major hit; the strength of this film made his subsequent career over the next decade possible.

MASK OF DIMITRIOS, THE
1944 95m bw Crime/Spy ★★★★★
Warner Bros. (U.S.)

Sydney Greenstreet (Mr. Peters), Zachary Scott (Dimitrios), Faye Emerson (Irana Preveza), Peter Lorre (Cornelius Latimer Leyden), George Tobias (Fedor Muishkin), Victor Francen (Wladislaw Grodek), Steven Geray (Bulic), Florence Bates (Mme. Chavez), Eduardo Ciannelli (Marukakis), Kurt Katch (Col. Haki)

p, Henry Blanke; d, Jean Negulesco; w, Frank Gruber (based on the novel A Coffin For Dimitrios by Eric Ambler); ph, Arthur Edeson; ed, Frederick Richards; m, Adolph Deutsch; art d, Ted Smith

One of the great film noir classics to come out of the 1940s, THE MASK OF DIMITRIOS boasts no superstars, just uniformly fine talents, a terrific script full of subtle intrigue and surprises, and Negulesco's exciting direction. It's an edge-of-the-seater all the way.

Peter Lorre is Leyden, a Dutch mystery writer vacationing in Istanbul. At a party he meets one of his most ardent fans, Col. Haki (Kurt Katch), head of the secret police, who tells him that the body of arch criminal Dimitrios Makropoulous (Zachary Scott), has washed up on the nearby beach, murdered, stabbed to death. What fascinates Leyden is Haki's obsession with Makropoulos, a man who practiced "murder, treason, and betrayal" as a way of life. After a visit to the morgue to view the body, Leyden decides to write a novel about the sinister man and begins to delve into his past. What he encounters is a heady, complexly plotted brew of blackmail, seduction, spy intrigues, assassination and suicide.

Other than Ambler's American title for his novel and the fact that the mystery-detective writer is English rather than Dutch (an attempt to explain Lorre's slight accent), almost nothing was changed from the original novel. Ambler's despicable antihero is most certainly based upon the early career of one of the world's greatest intriguers, billionaire munitions king Basil Zaharoff. Though Lorre performs one of his few sympathetic roles with fascinating aplomb, Greenstreet, whom Lorre affectionately called "the old man" after they had become close friends while making THE MALTESE FALCON, dominates their scenes together. The entire film fits with the murky intrigue of the era, its stylized sets, low-key lighting, and a literate, witty script working to enchance the wonderful character actors in their segmented roles. Francen is particularly effective as the suave master spy, and impressive, handsome newcomer Scott is a properly loathsome creature without remorse or compassion for his myriad victims. Emerson, as a deserted tart, is also very good, as is Geray as a hapless, trusting government clerk. This film, under Negulesco's superb guidance, remains a superlative espionage yarn that artfully blends fact with fiction.

MASK OF ZORRO, THE   *DVD*

1998 136m c Action/Adventure/Romance ★★★½
Amblin Entertainment/Columbia TriStar (U.S.) PG-13

Antonio Banderas (Alejandro Murrieta/Zorro), Anthony Hopkins (Zorro/Don Diego de la Vega), Catherine Zeta-Jones (Elena), Stuart Wilson (Don Rafael Montero), Matthew Letscher, billed as Matt Letscher (Captain Harrison Love), Maury Chaykin (Prison Warden), Tony Amendola (Don Luiz), Pedro Armendariz (Don Pedro), L.Q. Jones (Three-Fingered Jack), William Marquez (Fray Felipe)

p, Doug Claybourne, David Foster; d, Martin Campbell; w, Ted Elliott, Terry Rossio, John Eskow; ph, Phil Meheux; ed, Thom Noble; m, James Horner; prod d, Cecilia Montiel; art d, Michael Atwell; fx, Rocky Gehr, John Stears, Laurencio Cordero; cos, Graciela Mazon

AAN Best Sound: Kevin O'Connell, Greg P. Russell, Pud Cusack;
AAN Best Sound Effects Editing: David McMoyler

Dashing *caballeros* in gleaming black-leather boots, cracking their bullwhips, flashing their swords and smoking disdainfully slim cigars: if stars Anthony Hopkins and Antonio Banderas had succumbed to the temptation to camp it up, this would be THE PHANTOM all over again. But the Tonys swash their buckles straight—OK, with just the slightest hint of knowing smiles—and the result is old-fashioned fun that goes down as smoothly as a vintage cocktail.

The year is 1821, and the people of Alta California are caught in the war between Mexican revolutionary Santa Ana and the forces of Spanish oppression, embodied in brutal governor Don Rafael Montero (Stuart Smith). Their one hope: the avenger named Zorro (Spanish for "fox"), who cuts a dashing figure in his black mask and cape while fighting for justice and the rights of the poor and defenseless. The man behind the mask is aristocratic Don Diego de la Vega (Hopkins), whom Montero ferrets out and imprisons; his wife is killed and his infant daughter Elena kidnapped to be raised as Montero's own child. Twenty years later, Elena is a beautiful and spirited young woman (Catherine Zeta-Jones), Montero has hatched a new plan to exploit Alta California to his own ends, and Don Diego has escaped and is training a successor, the bandit Alejandro Murrieta (Banderas), who has his own unfinished business with Montero's minions.

Rakishly handsome and a natural-born charmer, Banderas wears Zorro's slightly fetishistic getup with such graceful delight that the slate is wiped clean of such travesties as ZORRO, THE GAY BLADE. But the movie's secret weapon is Hopkins, whose Don Diego is a grizzled bon vivant who can still break a lady's heart as smoothly as he can extinguish candles with his whip.

MASK, THE   *DVD*

1994 101m c Comedy/Action ★★½
New Line/Dark Horse Entertainment (U.S.) PG-13

Jim Carrey (Stanley Ipkiss/The Mask), Cameron Diaz (Tina Carlyle), Peter Riegert (Lieutenant Kellaway), Peter Greene (Dorian Tyrel), Amy Yasbeck (Peggy Brandt), Richard Jeni (Charlie Shumacher), Orestes Matacena (Niko), Tim Bagley (Irv), Nancy Fish (Mrs. Peeman), Johnny Williams (Burt)

p, Bob Engelman; d, Chuck Russell; w, Mike Werb (from a story by Michael Fallon and Mark Verheiden based on the Dark Horse Comics strip); ph, John R. Leonetti; ed, Arthur Coburn; m, Randy Edelman; prod d, Craig Stearns; art d, Randy Moore; fx, Scott Squires, Steve Williams, Tom Bertino, Jon Farhat, Robert Staad, Dream Quest Images, Industrial Light & Magic; chor, Jerry Evans; cos, Ha Nguyen

AAN Best Visual Effects: Scott Squires, Steve Williams, Tom Bertino, John Farhat

THE MASK, a live-action cartoon featuring a thoroughly unrestrained performance by Jim Carrey, has a story so slight that it wouldn't be worth telling if it weren't tricked out with the best special effects money can buy, at least in 1994. The effects are show-stopping, but the film's hollowness makes the overall result curiously depressing.

Nebbishy bank clerk Stanley Ipkiss (Jim Carrey) is one of life's perpetual losers. The highlight of his day comes when curvaceous bombshell Tina Carlyle (Cameron Diaz) wants to open a bank account, and declares that only Stanley's help will do. Unbeknownst to him, she's the girlfriend of brutal gangster Dorian Tyrel (Peter Greene), and she's only cuddling up to Stanley so she can secretly photograph the bank's vault. Everything changes when Stanley fishes a funny-looking mask out of the river. When he puts it on, he's transformed into a cackling lime green id in a canary zoot suit, a living cartoon who can go anywhere, do anything, suffer any punishment, and pop up unharmed. Stanley Ipkiss has become The Mask.

There's no denying that THE MASK's special effects are spectacular and lavish; there's scarcely a scene in which something eye-popping (once, literally) is happening, and those few moments of quiet are strangely dead. It's a pachinko machine of a movie: lights flash, bells ring, buzzers buzz, and things spin all over the place, but to no apparent end. Though the story has a certain universal appeal—who hasn't felt like a useless jerk and wished to wake up capable of anything?—the execution is oddly sour and distasteful. Nevertheless, presumably on the basis of Jim Carrey's appeal, the film was a smash success; the combined domestic grosses of THE MASK, ACE VENTURA, and DUMB AND DUMBER made Carrey the second biggest star attraction of 1994, just behind Tom Hanks.

MASQUE OF THE RED DEATH, THE   *DVD*

1964 86m c Horror ★★★★
Alta Vista/Anglo-Amalgamated (U.S./U.K.)

Vincent Price (Prince Prospero), Hazel Court (Juliana), Jane Asher (Francesca), David Weston (Gino), Patrick Magee (Alfredo), Nigel Green (Ludovico), Skip Martin (Hop Toad), John Westbrook (Man in Red), Gaye Brown (Senora Escobar), Julian Burton (Senor Veronese)

p, Roger Corman; d, Roger Corman; w, Charles Beaumont, R. Wright Campbell (based on "The Masque of the Red Death" and "Hop-Frog, or the Eight Chained Orang-outangs" by Edgar Allan Poe); ph, Nicolas Roeg (Panavision/Pathecolor);

ed, Ann Chegwidden; m, David Lee; prod d, Daniel Haller; art d, Robert Jones; fx, George Blackwell; chor, Jack Carter; cos, Laura Nightingale

One of the best and most ambitious of the Roger Corman Edgar Allan Poe series, this is a colorful symphony of the macabre loosely based on two Poe stories. It boasts a magnificent performance from the always wonderful (and often hammy) Vincent Price. Price is Prince Prospero, a 12th-century Italian despot who lives for his one true love… Satan! After jailing two locals, Ludovico (Nigel Green) and Gino (David Weston) for defying his harsh tax laws, Prospero meets the beautiful Francesca (Jane Asher), daughter of Ludovico and the fiancee of Gino. She comes to him to plead for mercy. Prospero tells her that only one will be spared and toys with her emotions for his private amusement. When Prospero learns that the Red Death is sweeping the village, he locks himself and his followers in his castle where they continue their decadent parties. Soon a mysterious figure dressed in red robes arrives but he bides his time outside the castle, playing solitaire in the graveyard.

Weird and extremely downbeat, this is Corman's most sustained attempt at producing an Art Film. It even self-consciously echoes the work of Ingmar Bergman and Luis Bunuel—two directors Corman greatly admires. Best of all, however, is Price's inspired performance as the wicked Prospero. While Corman may veer dangerously close to pretention, his crisp staging and confident visual style keep the film from collapsing under its own weight.

MASTER AND COMMANDER: **DVD**
THE FAR SIDE OF THE WORLD

2003 138m c   Historical/Adventure   ★★★½
Samuel Goldwyn Films/Universal/Miramax   PG-13
(U.S.)

Russell Crowe *(Captain Jack Aubrey)*, Paul Bettany *(Dr. Stephen Maturin)*, James D'Arcy *(1st Lt. Thomas Pullings)*, Edward Woodall *(2nd Lt. William Mowett)*, Chris Larkin *(Captain Howard, Royal Marines)*, Max Pirkis *(Blakeney)*, Jack Randall *(Boyle)*, Max Benitez *(Calamy)*, Lee Ingleby *(Hollom)*, Richard Pates *(Williamson)*

p, Samuel Goldwyn Jr., Duncan Henderson, Peter Weir; d, Peter Weir; w, Peter Weir, John Collee (based on the novels *Master and Commander* and *The Far Side of the World* by Patrick O'Brian); ph, Russell Boyd; ed, Lee Smith; m, Iva Davies, Christopher Gordon, Richard Tognetti; prod d, William Sandell; art d, Bruce Crone, Mark Mansbridge; fx, Stefen Fangmeier, Nathan McGuiness, Daniel Sudick; cos, Wendy Stites

AA Best Sound Editing: Richard King; *AA Best Cinematography:* Russell Boyd; *AAN Best Picture:* Peter Weir; *AAN Best Director:* Peter Weir; *AAN Best Sound Mixing:* Paul Massey, D.M. Hemphill, Arthur Rochester; *AAN Best Art Direction:* William Sandell, Robert Gould; *AAN Best Costume Design:* Wendy Stites; *AAN Best Editing:* Lee Smith; *AAN Best Makeup:* Edouard Henriques III, Yolanda Toussieng; *AAN Best Visual Effects:* Dan Sudick, Stefen Fangmeier, Nathan McGuiness, Robert Stromberg

There's no need to be a fan of Patrick O'Brian's 20 Aubrey/Maturin novels to enjoy Peter Weir's adaptation of the first and tenth entries in the series. O'Brian's books have been called Tom Clancy thrillers for history buffs, but for all the minutiae of 19th-century warships and naval strategy, their heart lies in the complex friendship between Captain "Lucky Jack" Aubrey (Russell Crowe) and ship physician Stephen Maturin (Paul Bettany).

It's 1805, two years after the start of the Napoleonic wars: Aubrey, longtime commander of the HMS Surprise, is cruising along Brazil's eastern coast when he receives orders to stop the French warship Acheron from extending hostilities into the Pacific. The catch: The Acheron is newer, faster,

better-armored and equipped with 44 cannons of greater range than the venerable Surprise's 28; taking her will have to be a victory of skill and cunning over brute military strength. The adversaries are almost immediately launched into pitched battle. The Acheron melts out of the fog and gives the Surprise and her crew a brutal beating from which only Aubrey's experience enables them to escape—the crippled Surprise is literally towed by crewmen in lifeboats to safety in a fog bank.

Weir establishes character with exceptional dexterity; within minutes a good dozen individuals who will play featured parts in the story have emerged from the crowd. The film's overall momentum comes from Aubrey's decision to pursue the Acheron when a more temperate officer would have taken his battered ship and crew home. But its drama comes from relationships between the officers and crew, crammed together under circumstances Samuel Johnson famously described as like prison, "with the added danger of drowning." Morale erodes when a well-liked seaman is swept overboard and Aubrey must let him drown rather than endanger the ship. Suspicion grows that insecure midshipman Hollom (Lee Ingleby) is a "Jonah"—a jinx. And 13-year-old Lord Blakeney (Max Pirkis) is entrusted to Aubrey by his father; the youngster loses both an arm and his scarcely older best friend, rises to Aubrey's carefully timed offers of additional responsibility and develops an interest in Maturin's passion, the study of natural history. With the exception of a brief sequence on the Galapagos Islands, the entire film takes place aboard the ship, and Weir's greatest accomplishment may be that it never feels claustrophobic.

MATA HARI

1931 91m bw   Romance/Biography/Spy   ★★★½
MGM   (U.S.)

Greta Garbo *(Mata Hari)*, Ramon Novarro *(Lt. Alexis Rosanoff)*, Lionel Barrymore *(Gen. Serge Shubin)*, Lewis Stone *(Andriani)*, C. Henry Gordon *(Dubois)*, Karen Morley *(Carlotta)*, Alec B. Francis *(Caron)*, Blanche Frederici *(Sister Angelica)*, Edmund Breese *(Warden)*, Helen Jerome Eddy *(Sister Genevieve)*

p, Irving Thalberg; d, George Fitzmaurice; w, Benjamin Glazer, Leo Birinski, Doris Anderson, Gilbert Emery; ph, William Daniels; ed, Frank Sullivan

The subject of Mata Hari, the WWI Javanese-Dutch spy, was not new to film, but when Garbo agreed to play the role of the beautiful exotic dancer who traded sex for secrets, it was not only news but also cause for MGM to produce a lavish and memorable film. We first see the German spy in Paris, posing as a dancer. Her spymaster, Stone, directs her to intercept certain Russian messages involving Allied troop movements. For some time Garbo has been having an affair with Barrymore, an indiscreet general, but she meets Novarro, a lowly lieutenant, and truly falls in love with him. Then she learns that Novarro has the messages she is seeking and she betrays her love for him to serve her country, taking him to bed while her associates copy his messages. Barrymore learns of the tryst and explodes, threatening to turn Garbo in as an agent and implicate Novarro. To save herself and her unwitting lover, Garbo shoots and kills Barrymore. When Novarro begins to seek out Barrymore, Garbo compels him to leave. The pilot flies to Russia where he is shot down and blinded. Learning of this, Garbo follows her passion rather than her military orders and goes to Novarro to tell him of her devotion to him. Stone orders an agent to kill her, but the man is foiled by local police. Garbo is then unmasked and brought to trial.

Garbo is stunning, full of her special mystique as the exotic dancer-spy, in one scene wearing a revealing costume and snaking her body around a lascivious-looking, many-armed statue in an odd interpretive dance. Fitzmaurice directs with great style here and makes the most of the lavish production techniques available to him. Both Garbo and Novarro had accents that later caused some critics to sneer, particularly at one of Novarro's lines which sounded like "What's the mata, Mata?" Of course, little shown here is based on real events. The historical figure, Gertrud Margarete Zelle MacLeod (1876-1917), danced in Paris and stole secrets from the French for the Germans, low-level secrets at that, until she was uncovered as a spy and shot, not in Russia, but at Saint-Lazare in France on October 15, 1917.

MATCH FACTORY GIRL, THE
(TULITIKKUTEHTAAN TYTTO)
1990　70m　c　Drama/Comedy　★★★½
Villealfa/Svenska Filminstitutet　(Finland/Sweden)

Kati Outinen *(Iris)*, Elina Salo *(Iris's Mother)*, Esko Nikkari *(Iris's Stepfather)*, Vesa Vierikko *(Man in Dancehall)*, Reijo Taipale *(Singer)*, Silu Seppala *(Brother)*, Outi Maenpaa *(Workmate)*, Marja Packalen *(Doctor)*, Richard Reitinger *(Man in Bar)*, Helga Viljanen *(Office Employee)*

p, Aki Kaurismaki; d, Aki Kaurismaki; w, Aki Kaurismaki; ph, Timo Salminen; ed, Aki Kaurismaki; cos, Tuula Hilkamo

A darkly humorous fable, THE MATCH FACTORY GIRL chronicles, in extreme minimalist fashion, the transformation of an ugly duckling into a killer tigress. Utilizing perhaps only a half-dozen lines of dialogue, Finnish filmmaker Aki Kaurismaki relies instead on the lyrics of about a dozen songs to comment on the action. Like some industrial documentary, the film opens with close-ups of the machinery used in making wooden matches, from the skinning of a section of tree trunk to the packaging and labeling of the bundles. Iris (Kati Outinen) has the deadeningly routine job of making sure the labels are properly stuck to the cartons. Her home life is as dreary as her job, since she lives in a shabby apartment with her mother (Elina Salo) and stepfather (Esko Nikkari), whom she supports with her meager earnings. All this changes when, one pay day, Iris sees and buys a red floral print dress; the dress helps her attract a middle-class man (Vesa Vierikko) who, after a one-night stand, wants nothing more to do with her. His callous response when Iris later finds out she is pregnant moves her to exact a deadly, deadpan revenge on him and everyone else who has contributed to the unleavened misery of her existence.

The final installment in Kaurismaki's acclaimed "proletarian trilogy" (the others being SHADOWS IN PARADISE and ARIEL), THE MATCH FACTORY GIRL is a wondrous antidote to the sentimentality of most mainstream films. Kaurismaki's presentation of Helsinki is characteristically grim and anonymous, either modern and bare or old and shabby. The director, writer, producer and editor of the film, Kaurismaki has described it both as his "revenge on Robert Bresson" as well as a "piece of junk." He has also stated that he is not interested in middle-class family values, but in "losers."

MATCHSTICK MEN　DVD
2003　115m　c　Crime/Comedy/Drama　★★★½
Imagemovers Productions/Scott Free
Productions/Rickshaw Productions/LivePlanet
　　　　PG-13
　　　　(U.S.)

Nicolas Cage *(Roy Waller)*, Alison Lohman *(Angela)*, Sam Rockwell *(Frank)*, Bruce McGill *(Chuck Frechette)*, Bruce Altman *(Dr. Klein)*, Jenny O'Hara *(Mrs. Schaffer)*, Steve Eastin *(Mr. Schaffer)*, Beth Grant *(Laundry Lady)*, Sheila Kennedy *(Kathy)*, Fran Kranz *(Slacker Boyfriend)*

p, Sean Bailey, Ted Griffin, Jack Rapke, Ridley Scott, Steve Starkey; d, Ridley Scott; w, Nicholas Griffin, Ted Griffin (based on the book by Eric Garcia); ph, Jack Mathieson; ed, Dody Dorn; m, Hans Zimmer; prod d, Tom Foden; art d, Michael Manson; fx, Marty Bresin, Roy Savoy, Sony Pictures Imageworks; cos, Michael Kaplan

Based on the novel by Eric Garcia, Ridley Scott's ode to the conflicting allure of fatherhood and short cons is a breezy crime picture with an unforced sentimental underbelly.

Middle-aged Roy Waller (Nicolas Cage) and his younger protege, Frank (Sam Rockwell), specialize in quick, uncomplicated cons. Roy is almost pathologically cautious and has amassed a substantial nest egg; he also has a severe case of obsessive-compulsive disorder. Frank is a reckless spendthrift, but when Roy's shady shrink decamps without notice and leaves Roy without medication, Frank recommends a psychiatrist who once treated a relative. Dr. Klein (Bruce Altman) gets Roy talking about how he never knew whether his pregnant former wife bore his child, and Roy persuades Klein to call his ex. She wants no part of him, but his 14-year-old skateboarding daughter, Angela (Alison Lohman), does, and within days of their first meeting she turns up on his doorstep. Angela is intrigued by her dad's dishonest profession—so intrigued that she bullies him into teaching her the tricks of the trade. Frank, meanwhile, has found the perfect mark for a complicated con, a greedy jerk named Chuck Frechette (Bruce McGill), and Roy agrees reluctantly to break his "no long cons" rule and fleece Frechette.

The complicated family and criminal machinations resolve themselves in a whiplash-inducing twist, but the plot is firmly anchored by three engrossing performances. Cage's mannerisms are tailor-made for the role of Roy, and Rockwell slimes easily through Frank's heartless intrigues; the surprise is relative newcomer Lohman, who effortlessly holds her own against seasoned attention-grabbers. The soundtrack, which relies heavily on melancholy Sinatra standards like "The Good Life" and "Summer Wind," casts perfectly modulated warning shadows over the film's light, bright look.

MATEWAN　DVD
1987　132m　c　Drama　★★★★
Red Dog　(U.S.)　　　PG-13

Chris Cooper *(Joe Kenehan)*, Will Oldham *(Danny Radnor)*, Jace Alexander *(Hillard)*, Ken Jenkins *(Sephus Purcell)*, Bob Gunton *(C.E. Lively)*, Gary McCleery *(Ludie)*, Kevin Tighe *(Hickey)*, Gordon Clapp *(Griggs)*, Mary McDonnell *(Elma Radnor)*, James Earl Jones *("Few Clothes" Johnson)*

p, Peggy Rajski, Maggie Renzi; d, John Sayles; w, John Sayles; ph, Haskell Wexler; ed, Sonya Polonsky; m, Mason Daring; prod d, Nora Chavooshian; art d, Dan Bishop; cos, Cynthia Flynt

AAN Best Cinematography: Haskell Wexler

Made for $4 million but looking as if it cost three times that, this is an excellent offering from one of America's best-known independent filmmakers, John Sayles (THE BROTHER FROM ANOTHER PLANET; EIGHT MEN OUT). As the film opens, Danny Radnor (Will Oldham), a 15-year-old coal miner, spreads the news that the Stone Mountain Coal Company of Matewan, West Virginia, has decided to lower the tonnage rate paid the miners—again. A strike is called. Joe Kenehan (Chris Cooper), a pacifist and former Wobbly, is sent by the United Mine Workers to coordinate the action and to keep it from becoming violent; however, a group of Italian immigrants continues to work, as do the black miners whom the company has brought from Alabama. A battle seems inevitable; but slowly the three factions grow into a community, and the strike spreads like wildfire. In MATEWAN Sayles captures the feel of a 1930s Popular Front film but grounds it in the complex reality of a world that refuses to present easy choices. With Oscar winner Haskell Wexler acting as cinematographer, MATEWAN is beautifully shot, and there is not a weak performance in the film. Jones is a tower of dignity; Cooper is the epitome of quiet strength; and Oldham glows with the passion of a zealot, first for God, then for the union.

MATINEE 📀

1993 98m c Comedy/Drama/Science Fiction ★★★
Renfield/Matinee Inc./Falcon Film Finance Ltd./   PG
Pandora Cinema   (U.S.)

John Goodman *(Lawrence Woolsey)*, Cathy Moriarty *(Ruth Corday)*, Simon Fenton *(Gene Loomis)*, Omri Katz *(Stan)*, Lisa Jakub *(Sandra)*, Kellie Martin *(Sherry)*, Jesse Lee *(Dennis Loomis)*, Lucinda Jenney *(Anne Loomis)*, James Villemaire *(Harvey Starkweather)*, Robert Picardo *(Howard the Theater Manager)*

p, Michael Finnell; d, Joe Dante; w, Charlie Haas (from a story by Charlie Haas and Jerico Stone); ph, John Hora; ed, Marshall Harvey; m, Jerry Goldsmith; prod d, Steven Legler; art d, Nanci B. Roberts; fx, Dennis Michelson; cos, Isis Mussenden

A genuine love for B cinema informs all the work of director Joe Dante, from his own Roger Corman-produced cheapies through the GREMLINS films. This affection finds its purest expression in MATINEE, an affectionate homage to the "creature features" of the '50s and '60s.

The story is set in Key West, Florida, in October 1962, just before and during the Cuban missile crisis. Teenager Gene Loomis (Simon Fenton) lives with his mother (Lucinda Jenney) and brother Dennis (Jesse Lee) on a Naval base; his dad is serving on one of the U.S. ships blockading Cuba. Mass destruction looms, but Gene's preoccupied with the imminent arrival in town of his idol, horror filmmaker Lawrence Woolsey (John Goodman). A master showman, Woolsey plans to hold a preview in Key West of his new chiller, MANT ("Half Man, Half Ant, All Terror!"), in Atomo-Vision and Rumble-Rama.

MATINEE succeeds above all as an enjoyable tribute to the monster movies of yesteryear, not only in the way its young characters are enthralled by the promise of MANT's terrors, but in the clips of MANT itself that appear throughout the film. Cast with numerous (sadly uncredited) '50s creature-feature veterans like Kenneth Tobey and William Schallert, MANT is a perfect evocation of those cheesy science fiction thrillers in which atomic radiation turned humans into insectoid mutants. MATINEE has a surfeit of characters and climaxes, but these are compensated by many great moments and a terrific central theme: the juxtaposition of the real-life terrors of the Cold War with the cinematic horrors that reduced the nuclear threat to something outlandish and thus safely entertaining.

MATRIX, THE 📀

1999 120m c Science Fiction/Action/Thriller ★★★½
Village Roadshow Film/Silver Pictures   (U.S.)   R

Keanu Reeves *(Thomas A. Anderson/Neo)*, Laurence Fishburne *(Morpheus)*, Carrie-Anne Moss *(Trinity)*, Joe Pantoliano *(Cypher/Mr. Regan)*, Hugo Weaving *(Agent Smith)*, Belinda Mcclory *(Switch)*, Julian Arahanga *(Apoc)*, Marcus Chong *(Tank)*, Robert Taylor *(Agent Jones)*, Matt Doran *(Mouse)*

p, Joel Silver; d, Larry Wachowski, Andy Wachowski; w, Larry Wachowski, Andy Wachowski; ph, Bill Pope; ed, Zach Staenberg; m, Don Davis; prod d, Owen Paterson; fx, John Gaeta, Janek Sirrs, Steve Courtley, Jon Thum; cos, Kym Barrett

AA Best Sound: John Reitz, Gregg Rudloff, David Campbell, David Lee; *AA Best Sound Effects Editing:* Dane A. Davis; *AA Best Film Editing:* Zach Staenberg; *AA Best Visual Effects:* John Gaeta, Janek Sirrs, Steve Courtley, Jon Thum

Remember the Chinese philosopher who, upon waking from a vivid dream, wondered whether he was a man who had dreamed he was a butterfly or a butterfly dreaming that he was a man? Even if you don't, you can bet your life the Wachowski brothers, Larry and Andy, do.

The time is somewhere in the near future, and corporate drone Neo (Keanu Reeves), a computer programmer, is convinced there's something more to life than his humdrum existence. He's right, but not at all in the way he thinks. His enlightenment begins with a telephone call from Morpheus (Laurence Fishburne), who possesses an uncanny ability to predict what's going to happen just before it does and warns that Neo is in grave danger. Neo is baffled and scared, especially after he's arrested by a batch of goons in black and subjected to a terrifying interrogation. When he wakes up the next day, he has just about got himself convinced it was all a dream—okay, one hell of a nightmare—when unimpeachable evidence proves that it wasn't.

To say much more would be unfair to the Wachowskis' through-the-looking-glass plot, which manages to work surprisingly well on a number of levels: as a dystopian sci-fi thriller, as a brilliant excuse for the film's lavish and hyperkinetic fight scenes, and as a pretty compelling call to the dead-above-the-eyeballs masses to unite and cast off their chains. The Wachowskis come out of comics, and their achingly stupid script for ASSASSINS personifies every dire stereotype about comic-book-trained writers. But this dazzling pop allegory is steeped in a dark, pulpy sensibility that transcends nostalgic pastiche and stands firmly on its own merits. And it doesn't hurt that the latex-and-shades-clad cast looks good enough to eat.

MATRIX RELOADED, THE 📀

2003 138m c Science Fiction/Action/Martial Arts ★★★
NVP Entertainment/Silver Pictures/Village   R
Roadshow/Warner Bros.   (U.S.)

Keanu Reeves *(Neo)*, Laurence Fishburne *(Morpheus)*, Carrie-Anne Moss *(Trinity)*, Hugo Weaving *(Agent Smith)*, Jada Pinkett, billed as Jada Pinkett Smith *(Niobe)*, Monica Bellucci *(Persephone)*, Lambert Wilson *(Merovingian)*, Randall Duk Kim *(Keymaker)*, Harry Lennix *(Commander Lock)*, Neil Rayment *(Albino Twin)*

p, Joel Silver; d, Andy Wachowski, Larry Wachowski; w, Andy Wachowski, Larry Wachowski; ph, Bill Pope; ed, Zach Staenberg; m, Don Davis; prod d, Owen Paterson; art d, Hugh Bateup; fx, Steve Courtley, Hans Metz, John DesJardin, John Gaeta, Clay Pinney, Dan Glass, Janek Sirrs; chor, Yuen Wo Ping (fights); cos, Kym Barrett

The second installment in the Wachowski brothers' sci-fi trilogy does its damnedest to live up to the mind-boggling success of THE MATRIX, but the original film's disquieting appeal gets lost in the hurly-burly. Now that everyone knows what the Matrix is, something needs to take the place of its mystery. Unfortunately, nothing does.

The story picks up where the first film left off. Neo (Keanu Reeves) continues to develop his virtual-reality defying abilities, and Morpheus (Laurence Fishburne) persists in his belief that Neo is the prophesied messiah who will lead the human race out of bondage to the parasitic machines. Meanwhile, the machines have launched an all-out attack against Zion, the human citadel where the enlightened who've awakened from their womb-like prisons cluster. Morpheus butts heads with Commander Lock (Harry Lennix) over how best to defend Zion, but the real conflict is rooted in the fact that both have loved fierce fighter Niobe (Jada Pinkett Smith). Meanwhile, Neo is haunted by dreams of his lover Trinity (Carrie-Anne Moss) dying in the Matrix. The fetish-clad freedom fighters return to the Matrix to find the Keymaker (Randall Duk Kim), who can open the door to the uber-program's mainframe and permit them to destroy it forever. Standing between them and success is an array of adversaries, including dozens of versions of Agent Smith (Hugo Weaving) and a pair of dreadlocked albino twins (Neil and Adrian Rayment), literal ghosts in the machine.

The characters are embedded in a now-familiar grab bag of religious, mythological, and pop-culture references, but the allusions are overshadowed by the fists and feet of fury. More comic book-like and less intriguing than the original, the film's punch-drunk cyber-mysticism still has a dark allure that sets it far apart from juvenile, STAR WARS-style space opera.

MATRIX REVOLUTIONS, THE   DVD

2003 129m c Science Fiction/Action/Martial Arts ★★★
Silver Pictures Productions/NPV Entertainment/   R
Village Roadshow   (U.S.)

Keanu Reeves (Neo), Carrie-Anne Moss (Trinity), Laurence Fishburne (Morpheus), Nona Gaye (Zee), Clayton Watson (The Kid), Hugo Weaving (Agent Smith), Ian Bliss (Bane), Mary Alice (The Oracle), Jada Pinkett, billed as Jada Pinkett Smith (Niobe), Monica Bellucci (Persephone)

p, Joel Silver; d, Larry Wachowski, Andy Wachowski; w, Larry Wachowski, Andy Wachowski; ph, Bill Pope; ed, Zach Staenberg; m, Don Davis; prod d, Owen Paterson; art d, Jules Cook, Catherine Mansill, Charlie Revai; fx, Danielle Costa, Steve Courtley, John Des Jardin, Joen Gaeta, Dan Glass; chor, Yuen Wo Ping (martial arts); cos, Kym Barrett

The conclusion to the Wachowski brothers' Matrix trilogy picks up exactly where THE MATRIX RELOADED left off and, like RELOADED, it neither works as a stand-alone film nor captures the thrilling sense of somber, pulpy mystery that made THE MATRIX so compelling. Nevertheless, it brings the saga to a satisfying close, and relies less on clumps of pop-mystical cyber gobbledy-gook and more on the powerful emotional bonds that bind Neo (Keanu Reeves), Trinity (Carrie-Anne Moss), Morpheus (Laurence Fishburne), Niobe (Jada Pinkett Smith), Link (Harold Perrineau), and Zee (Nona Gaye).

The story begins with both Neo and Bane (Ian Bliss), who was possessed by Agent Smith (Hugo Weaving) and committed an act of vicious treachery at the end of the previous film, comatose in the hovercraft Mjolnir, whose doctor (Essie Davis) is deeply puzzled by Neo's brainwaves: They look exactly like the brainwaves of someone who's jacked into the Matrix. Even though logic dictates that Neo can't be in the Matrix, Trinity and Morpheus set out to find him there, facing down the treacherous Merovingian (Lambert Wilson)—whose lovely wife, Persephone (Monica Bellucci), is reduced to the most fleetingly glimpsed of decorative elements—and bring Neo back as Bane awakens, claiming to remember nothing of the cataclysmic events that preceded his coma. The Agent Smiths, meanwhile, are multiplying in such numbers that they threaten not only human infiltrators of the Matrix but the very infrastructure of the machine world, and Commander Lock (Harry Lennix) mobilizes Zion for all-out war as the machine drillers approach, trailed by a swarm of lethal sentinels of biblical proportions. Advised one last time by the Oracle in her new "shell" (Mary Alice, replacing the late Gloria Foster), Neo, accompanied by the eternally loyal Trinity, chooses what appears to be a suicide mission using Niobe's ship, while she pilots the remaining working vessel back to beleaguered Zion.

The nondenominational, pop religious elements that underlie the first two films come into full flower here. But

every airy-fairy, spoken-word aria about fate and destiny is balanced by a pitched battle between machines and humans strapped into mechanical APUs (armored personnel units that look uncannily like ALIENS' dock-loaders, which in turn pay homage to the comic art machines of Jack Kirby). The Matrix trilogy is, ultimately, less than the sum of its parts, but its best moments are high water marks in modern-day movie mythology. On a historical note, MATRIX REVOLUTIONS was the first film ever to open simultaneously worldwide on 10,013 screens in more than 50 countries and 43 languages, ranging from Mandarin to Turkish; the first showings in various countries ranged from 6 am in Los Angeles to 11 pm in Tokyo.

MAURICE   DVD

1987 140m c Drama   ★★½
Cinecom/Merchant Ivory/Film Four   (U.K.)   R

James Wilby (Maurice Hall), Hugh Grant (Clive Durham), Rupert Graves (Alec Scudder), Denholm Elliott (Dr. Barry), Simon Callow (Mr. Ducie), Billie Whitelaw (Mrs. Hall), Ben Kingsley (Lasker-Jones), Judy Parfitt (Mrs. Durham), Phoebe Nicholls (Anne Durham), Mark Tandy (Risley)

p, Ismail Merchant; d, James Ivory; w, Kit Hesketh-Harvey, James Ivory (based on the novel by E.M. Forster); ph, Pierre Lhomme (Technicolor); ed, Katherine Wenning; m, Richard Robbins; prod d, Brian Ackland-Snow; art d, Peter James; cos, Jenny Beavan, John Bright

AAN Best Costume Design: Jenny Beavan, John Bright

Following the enormous success of A ROOM WITH A VIEW, the producer-director team of Ismail Merchant and James Ivory undertook another E.M. Forster adaptation, MAURICE, the story of a young man's homosexual awakening. Maurice Hall (James Wilby) is a wide-eyed Cambridge underclassman in 1910 where his elder classmates espouse the glories of classical civilization. Maurice and Clive Durham (Hugh Grant), an aristocratic music student, grow increasingly closer, until one day Clive tells Maurice that he loves him. Confused, Maurice initially rebuffs him and then confesses his love, too, and attempts to consummate it physically. This time Clive is reticent. They remain in love but do not become lovers. As time passes, Maurice attempts to put his desires behind him. In the Merchant-Ivory tradition, MAURICE captures the look and spirit of Edwardian England in exquisite detail. At its best, the film is moving and thought-provoking, but at other moments it is unintentionally silly. It is not the story but the telling of it that is the problem; at 140 minutes, MAURICE simply goes on too long. Nonetheless, the performances are generally convincing. Nominated by the Academy for Best Costume Design.

MAYERLING

1936 96m bw Historical/Romance   ★★★★★
Concordea   (France)

Charles Boyer (Archduke Rudolph of Austria), Danielle Darrieux (Marie Vetsera), Suzy Prim (Countess Larisch), Jean Dax (Emperor Franz Joseph), Gabrielle Dorziat (Empress Elizabeth), Jean Debucourt (Count Taafe), Marthe Regnier (Baroness Vetsera/Helene), Yolande Laffon (Stephanie), Vladimir Sokoloff (Chief of Police), Andre Dubosc (Loschek, the Valet)

d, Anatole Litvak; w, Joseph Kessel, Irma Von Cube (based on the novel Idyl's End by Claude Anet); ph, Armand Thirard; ed, Henri Rust; m, Arthur Honegger

MAYERLING is one of the greatest love stories ever brought to the screen, the bittersweet, painfully poignant romance between the star-crossed Crown Prince Rudolph of Austria and his adoring mistress, Marie Vetsera. Charles Boyer, in a riveting performance, is Rudolph, son of the powerful Franz Joseph, Emperor of Austria-Hungary. A free spirit who associates with radicals and gypsies, Rudolph is also a prisoner of his royal blood. Everywhere there are court spies assigned to track and trail the errant heir to the throne. Eluding his followers at a fair, he meets 17-year-old Marie Vetsera (Danielle Darrieux), and it's love at first sight, although Marie has no idea that he is the prince as the couple enjoys such little pleasures as tossing rings around a swan's neck and watching a puppet show. The following night, Marie attends the opera and is startled to see the handsome young man from the fair sitting in the royal box. Though she comes from an aristocratic family, she has no hope of reaching so high. Instead, Rudolph reaches out to her, meeting secretly with the beautiful young woman. Only in Marie's presence does Rudolph find joy and peace; she responds to him with an innocence he has never encountered. When their liaison is discovered, however, the lovers must depart to a country hunting lodge from which they will never return. Based on fact, this story of an impossible love is told on a grand, exquisite scale by Anatole Litvak, and represents one of the high points of the director's spotty career. Filled with dreamy dissolves and fluid, nearly waltzlike camera movements, the film is a brilliant technical achievement, further enhanced by the wonderful performances of the two leads—the debonair Boyer and the ravishing Darrieux, who was then just 21 years old.

MAYTIME

1937 132m bw Romance/Musical ★★★★½
MGM (U.S.)

Jeanette MacDonald *(Marcia Morney/Miss Morrison)*, Nelson Eddy *(Paul Allison)*, John Barrymore *(Nicolai Nazaroff)*, Herman Bing *(August Archipenko)*, Tom Brown *(Kip Stuart)*, Lynne Carver *(Barbara Roberts)*, Rafaela Ottiano *(Ellen)*, Charles Judels *(Cabby)*, Paul Porcasi *(Composer Trentini)*, Sig Rumann *(Fanchon)*

p, Hunt Stromberg; d, Robert Z. Leonard; w, Noel Langley (based on the operetta by Rida Johnson Young, Sigmund Romberg); ph, Oliver T. Marsh; ed, Conrad A. Nervig; art d, Cedric Gibbons, Frederic Hope; chor, William von Wymetal, Val Raset; cos, Adrian

AAN Best Score: Metro-Goldwyn-Mayer Studio Music Department, Nat W. Finston (Dept. Head); *AAN Best Sound Recording:* Douglas Shearer

A very fragile lace valentine, admittedly, but performed with the conviction and style to make it work. Based on a Sigmund Romberg-Rida Johnson Young operetta that was so popular that two productions of it ran simultaneously on Broadway in 1917, MAYTIME returned its $1.5 million price tag five times en route to becoming the 1937 box-office champion. The third Nelson Eddy-Jeanette MacDonald pairing, it was also reputedly the actress's personal favorite, because the famed duo had so much more to do than sing and were finally able to prove their depth as actors. At a May Day celebration in 1906, Miss Morrison (MacDonald), an aged woman, meets Kip (Brown), whose fiancee, Barbara (Carver), yearns for a singing career. The elderly woman explains that she was once a famous opera star, and the film flashes back to France, 1865, where Marcia Mornay (MacDonald) accepts a marriage proposal from Nicolai Nazaroff (Barrymore, very potent here), the architect of her success. Later, she is swept off her feet by Paul Allison (Eddy), a handsome young American singer, but remains true to her promise to marry Nazaroff. Several years pass, and when Marcia and Paul costar in an American production, their love is rekindled. What advice will Miss Morrison give to Kip and Barbara? Get ready for the umpteenth reprise of "Will You Remember?"

Perhaps MAYTIME's most intriguing sidelight is the faked opera "Czaritza," written from Tchaikovsky music with French lyrics by Giles Guilbert, created in the tradition of such other great phony movie operas as CITIZEN KANE's "Salammbo," and CHARLIE CHAN AT THE OPERA's "Carnival." The staging is surprisingly intense, as is the entire film.

MCCABE AND MRS. MILLER

1971 121m c Western ★★★★½
Robert Altman-David Foster Productions (U.S.) R

Warren Beatty *(John McCabe)*, Rene Auberjonois *(Paddy Sheehan)*, John Schuck *(Smalley)*, Bert Remsen *(Bart Coyle)*, Keith Carradine *(Cowboy)*, Julie Christie *(Constance Miller)*, William Devane *(The Lawyer)*, Corey Fischer *(Mr. Elliott)*, Shelley Duvall *(Ida Coyle)*, Michael Murphy *(Sears)*

p, David Foster, Mitchell Brower; d, Robert Altman; w, Robert Altman, Brian McKay (based on the novel *McCabe* by Edmund Naughton); ph, Vilmos Zsigmond (Panavision, Technicolor); ed, Louis Lombardo; m, Leonard Cohen; prod d, Leon Ericksen; art d, Philip Thomas, Albert J. Locatelli; fx, Marcel Vercoutere; cos, Ilse Richter

AAN Best Actress: Julie Christie

A grim and dirty slice of bleak frontier life rendered with extraordinary beauty. Robert Altman cast a decidedly deglamourized Warren Beatty and Julie Christie together with his stock company in this richly textured anti-Western, with the stated intent of destroying "the myths of heroism in the Old West." The result is an atmospheric and resonant exploration of a small northwestern settlement in the middle of winter, with Christie as the thoroughly modern madam of a bordello and Beatty as the smaller-than-life hero.

Shortly after the turn of the century McCabe (Beatty), a man with a mysterious past, rides into a raw snow-covered northwestern wilderness settlement called Presbyterian Church. Here he gambles his way to some winnings and then establishes the community's first whorehouse. Initially a slapdash collection of tents, it becomes a smoothly running business when the feisty Mrs. Miller (Christie) comes aboard as the madam and chief prostitute. She uses McCabe's money to construct a whorehouse that becomes the communal center of the growing town. Miners pour into the brothel-bathhouse, and McCabe's success does not go unnoticed by the region's mining operators, who offer him $6,250 to sell out. McCabe, a business neophyte grown cocky with commercial triumph, refuses their offer. He's holding out for $15,000. Mrs. Miller warns her smart-talking partner that the company employs hired guns to get its way but he intends to settle before things reach that state. This turns out to be a tragic miscalculation.

MCCABE AND MRS. MILLER is a sad and beautiful film that sides with the losers and dreamers. Beatty, in a courageous anti-star turn, is bearded, blustery and ignorant, but ultimately endearing. Christie is at least as good as the tough-talking, opium-smoking lady from the Continent who's smart enough to know the real score. Altman makes extensive and effective use of Leonard Cohen's haunting ballads throughout the film and Vilmos Zsigmond provides sublime muted images of icy landscapes and warm interiors. Christie received a Best Actress Oscar nomination, but she lost to Jane Fonda for KLUTE. Not an easy film to watch, but undoubtedly a great one.

MEAN GIRLS

2004 97m c Comedy ★★★
M.G. Films/Broadway Video/Paramount (U.S.) PG-13

Lindsay Lohan *(Cady Heron)*, Rachel McAdams *(Regina George)*, Lacey Chabert *(Gretchen Weiners)*, Amanda Seyfried

(Karen Smith), Tina Fey *(Ms. Norbury)*, Lizzy Caplan *(Janis Ian)*, Daniel Franzese *(Damian)*, Tim Meadows *(Mr. Duvall)*, Ana Gasteyer *(Cady's Mom)*, Jonathan Bennett *(Aaron Samuels)*

p, Lorne Michaels; d, Mark Waters; w, Tina Fey (based on the book *Queen Bees & Wannabes* by Rosalind Wiseman); ph, Daryn Okada; ed, Wendy Greene Bricmont; m, Rolfe Kent; prod d, Cary White; art d, Brandt Gordon; fx, Rob Sanderson; chor, Donna Feore; cos, Mary Jane Fort

"Saturday Night Live" head writer Tina Fey takes on high-school cliques in her first feature script, which combines wicked humor and terrifying, real-life examples of bad behavior culled from Rosalind Wiseman's nonfiction bestseller *Queen Bees & Wannabes.*

Raised in Africa and home-schooled by her zoologist parents (Neil Flynn, Ana Gasteyer), Cady Heron (Lindsay Lohan) has trouble adapting to the fiercely stratified world of North Shore High School. She quickly sees the parallels between her fellow teens' behavior and the dynamics of a wilderness watering hole. The school "art freaks," Janis (Lizzy Caplan) and Damien (Daniel Franzese), clue her in to the subtleties of teen society, with special emphasis on the ways of their archenemies, the brutally superficial popular girls collectively known as the Plastics. The uber-teens—mega-rich Gretchen Weiners (Lacey Chabert), brainless Karen Smith (Amanda Seyfried), and queen bee Regina George (Rachel McAdams)—invite Cady to have lunch with them on a trial basis, and offer a crash course in girl-world mores: you can only wear a ponytail once a week, gossip contributions to their bitchy "burn book" are mandatory and, above all, ex-boyfriends are off-limits to friends. And that's a problem, since Cady has already developed a major crush on Aaron (Jonathan Bennett), who happens to have once been Regina's boyfriend.

A truly vicious mainstream black comedy about high-school violence and bullying like HEATHERS would be a hard sell in the post-Columbine era, but Fey's screenplay goes as far as it can, and director Mark Waters (whose brother, Daniel, wrote HEATHERS) strikes a carefully calibrated balance between the film's darkly malicious sense of humor and its pastel sets and costumes. Lohan thrives in her fish-out-of-water-turned-piranha role, and the mean girls are impressively mean.

MEAN STREETS *DVD*
1973 110m c Crime ★★★★½
TPS (U.S.) R

Harvey Keitel *(Charlie)*, Robert De Niro *(Johnny Boy)*, Amy Robinson *(Teresa)*, David Proval *(Tony)*, Richard Romanus *(Michael)*, Cesare Danova *(Giovanni)*, Victor Argo *(Mario)*, George Memmoli *(Joey Catucci)*, Lenny Scaletta *(Jimmy)*, Jeannie Bell *(Diane)*

p, Jonathan T. Taplin; d, Martin Scorsese; w, Martin Scorsese, Mardik Martin; ph, Kent Wakeford (Technicolor); ed, Sidney Levin

After making the interesting WHO'S THAT KNOCKING AT MY DOOR? and working for Roger Corman on BOXCAR BERTHA, Scorsese exploded onto the scene with this remarkable low-budgeter about the lives of small-time hoods in New York's Little Italy. The film centers on four guys who aspire to hit it big in business or crime. Tony (Proval), the big friendly one, runs the neighborhood bar; Mike (Romanus) likes to rip off naive teenagers from Brooklyn; Johnny Boy (De Niro) has a penchant for blowing up mailboxes and borrowing money from loan sharks he never intends to repay; and Charlie (Keitel), nephew of the local mafia boss (Danova), wants nothing more than to run his own restaurant. Charlie is torn between the life of the streets and the life his uncle can give him. He is also deeply religious, patterning himself after St. Francis of Assisi—testing his faith and seeking penitence for his sins on the streets. This testing takes the form of trying to "save"

Johnny Boy and being kind to his crazed pal's epileptic sister Teresa (Robinson), neither of whom his uncle likes.

MEAN STREETS is a brilliantly made film—terrifically acted, sharply photographed and crisply edited. Stand-out moments include an extended fight scene in a pool hall (the fight starts amusingly enough, over someone being called a "mook"—the guys aren't quite sure what it means, but they fight anyway), in which Scorsese uses long takes to emphasize the chaos and a wild tracking shot to follow a pair fighting throughout the room. Other highlights include Charlie's drunk scene at a party; the guys at a movie theater watching THE SEARCHERS; Johnny Boy shooting a gun from a roof; and the scene when Teresa has an epileptic fit and Charlie chooses to chase after Johnny instead of staying with his girlfriend (he leaves her in the care of an elderly woman played by Scorsese's mother). The hilarious scene in which Charlie and Johnny Boy argue about Johnny Boy's debts in the backroom of a bar (a scene that was improvised) is alone worth the price of admission.

MEDIUM COOL *DVD*
1969 110m c Political ★★★½
H and J (U.S.) R

Robert Forster *(John Cassellis)*, Verna Bloom *(Eileen Horton)*, Peter Bonerz *(Gus)*, Marianna Hill *(Ruth)*, Harold Blankenship *(Harold Horton)*, Sid McCoy *(Frank Baker)*, Christine Bergstrom *(Dede)*, Robert McAndrew *(Pennybaker)*, William Sickinger *(News Director Karlin)*, Beverly Younger *(Rich Lady)*

p, Jerrold Wexler, Haskell Wexler, Tully Friedman; d, Haskell Wexler; w, Haskell Wexler (based on the novel *The Concrete Wilderness* by Jack Couffer); ph, Haskell Wexler (Technicolor); ed, Verna Fields; m, Mike Bloomfield; art d, Leon Ericksen

This minor classic from the '60s time capsule is a self-conscious essay on the meaning of the media and the nature of political commitment. During the summer of 1968, with anti-war sentiment growing daily, a host of hippies, Yippies, and other countercultural types descended on Chicago for the Democratic Convention, an event marked by all-out battles between police and demonstrators in parks and on the streets. Celebrated left-wing cinematographer Haskell Wexler directed much of MEDIUM COOL while on location there, blending documentary footage with a fictional narrative.

John (Robert Forster) is a television cameraman, Gus (Peter Bonerz) his soundman, Eileen (Verna Bloom) a poor woman from the Kentucky hills who has recently moved to Chicago with her son, Harold (Harold Blankenship). John is initially presented as the archetypal artist divorced from society ("God, I love to shoot film"), but gradually becomes involved in the political process through his growing relationship with Eileen and Harold. Everything comes to a sticky end reminiscent of the finale of Godard's CONTEMPT. Finally, a very solemn-looking Wexler literally turns his camera on us: we're responsible, too, for what we've just seen on screen.

The noted photographer of such films as THE THOMAS CROWN AFFAIR and IN THE HEAT OF THE NIGHT, Wexler took on directorial duties for the first time here, something he would not do again until 1985's LATINO. Interestingly, it's Wexler's skills as a visual storyteller that give MEDIUM COOL its lasting power. While the more explicitly political scenes—any, in fact, that feature substantial dialogue—seem awkward and dated, the long, impressionistic sequences in which Wexler establishes character and locale almost exclusively with image and sound are hauntingly effective. One scene in particular, in which John and a girlfriend lounge, then romp around his spacious apartment, is as exhilarating a piece of camerawork as any we've seen.

MEET JOE BLACK
1998 174m c Romance/Fantasy/Drama ★★½
City Light Films/Universal (U.S.) PG-13

Brad Pitt *(Joe Black/Young Man in Coffee Shop)*, Anthony Hopkins *(William Parrish)*, Claire Forlani *(Susan Parrish)*, Jake Weber *(Drew)*, Marcia Gay Harden *(Allison)*, Jeffrey Tambor *(Quince)*, David S. Howard *(Eddie Sloane)*, Lois Kelly-Miller *(Jamaican Woman)*, Jahnni St. John *(Jamaican Woman's Daughter)*, Richard Clarke *(Butler)*

p, Martin Brest; d, Martin Brest; w, Bo Goldman, Kevin Wade, Jeff Reno, Ron Osborne (suggested by the play *Death Takes a Holiday* written by Alberto Casella and adapted by Walter Ferris, and the screenplay by Maxwell Anderson, Gladys Lehman); ph, Emmanuel Lubezki; ed, Joe Hutshing, Michael Tronick; m, Thomas Newman; prod d, Dante Ferretti; art d, Bob Guerra; fx, Connie Brink; cos, Aude Bronson-Howard, David Robinson

The 1934 film DEATH TAKES A HOLIDAY, this film's loose inspiration, is most fondly remembered by people who haven't actually seen it. It's a classic clunker in which Frederic March's painfully uncharismatic Death-made-flesh spends a long 79 minutes with a villa full of privileged flibbertigibbets. By comparison, three hours of Brad Pitt sparking with Claire Forlani fairly fly past, though for all its epic length the story is dead simple.

Tired of being greeted with wailing and gnashing of teeth, Death appropriates the body of a handsome youth (Pitt) who has just been run down by a car, and invites himself to stay with filthy-rich media mogul William Parrish (Anthony Hopkins), who happens to be a helluva nice, life-affirming guy. Death's house gift: as long as Parrish keeps him entertained, he'll let Parrish hang onto his mortal coil. Death adopts the transparent moniker "Joe Black" and discovers the joys of peanut butter, sharp clothes, and love with Parrish's gravely beautiful daughter (Susan), a fledgling doctor.

Make no mistake: this is a world-class chick flick that rests—sometimes more easily than others—on Pitt's golden shoulders. Death's first appearance, behind a pane of rippled glass in Parrish's study, is a stunner: Pitt's image is eerily distorted and genuinely mysterious. But he mostly stands around looking boyishly cute, which he does far better than anything else that's asked of him: the scenes in which Death trades homespun metaphysical chitchat with a dying Caribbean woman (who sees straight through his toy-boy disguise) in a lilting Jamaican patois is positively painful. And not to get too nitpicky, but what's up with all the other folks whose final exits are back-burnered while Death samples the lifestyle of the rich and famous? It doesn't pay to look too closely at this sumptuous fantasy, but if you're in the right mood, it's very warm and fizzy indeed.

MEET JOHN DOE
1941 135m bw Political ★★★★
Warner Bros. (U.S.)

Gary Cooper *("John Doe"/Long John Willoughby)*, Barbara Stanwyck *(Ann Mitchell)*, Edward Arnold *(D.B. Norton)*, Walter Brennan *(Colonel)*, James Gleason *(Henry Connell)*, Spring Byington *(Mrs. Mitchell)*, Gene Lockhart *(Mayor Lovett)*, Rod La Rocque *(Ted Sheldon)*, Irving Bacon *(Beany)*, Regis Toomey *(Bert Hansen)*

p, Frank Capra; d, Frank Capra; w, Robert Riskin (based on a story "The Life and Death of John Doe" by Robert Presnell, Richard Connell); ph, George Barnes; ed, Daniel Mandell; m, Dimitri Tiomkin; art d, Stephen Goosson; fx, Jack Cosgrove; cos, Natalie Visart

AAN Best Original Story: Richard Connell, Robert Presnell

Dark, oddball Capra, but a worthwhile watch with a tail ending wagging the dog. The film opens as Stanwyck, a struggling journalist, is fired from her job when a new managing editor, Gleason, takes over her newspaper. She angrily writes her last piece about a mythical idealist she calls John Doe and through him rants about the little guy being punished and mistreated by tycoons, moguls, magnates and captains of industry. To make good his protest, Doe states, in Stanwyck's fabricated letter to the paper, that he will leap off the top of City Hall on Christmas Eve. The public response is enormous, and Gleason demands that Stanwyck turn over the letter she has received from this so-called John Doe. She confesses that there is no letter, that she made up the whole story. But then, to keep the job she values above all else, Stanwyck suggests they find a phony hero from the ranks of the great unemployed and continue the story to sell more papers. When another paper jeeringly labels the story a fraud, Gleason, to save his newspaper's image, orders Stanwyck to pick out a stewbum and make him into her real-life John Doe. Enter Gary Cooper as Long John Willoughby, a onetime minor league pitcher with a bad arm and a shortage of cash.

MEET JOHN DOE was Capra's first independent film production done away from his home studio, Columbia, and beyond the tyrannical reach of its boss, Harry Cohn. It's basically an attack on the fascist elements then in America, notably the pro-Nazi German-American Bund. Capra wanted to warn Americans about the powerful fascist influences in their midst and did so mightily with this film. Though MEET JOHN DOE reportedly profited Capra and Riskin's independent company $900,000 on its initial release, Capra later reported that the tax bite was so heavy that he dissolved the company after a few months. So great had Capra's reputation become that all the leading players in MEET JOHN DOE agreed to do the film without reading the script.

MEET ME IN ST. LOUIS
1944 113m c Musical ★★★★★
MGM (U.S.)

Judy Garland *(Esther Smith)*, Margaret O'Brien *("Tootie" Smith)*, Mary Astor *(Mrs. Anne Smith)*, Lucille Bremer *(Rose Smith)*, June Lockhart *(Lucille Ballard)*, Tom Drake *(John Truett)*, Marjorie Main *(Katie)*, Harry Davenport *(Grandpa)*, Leon Ames *(Mr. Alonzo Smith)*, Hank Daniels *(Lon Smith, Jr.)*

p, Arthur Freed; d, Vincente Minnelli; w, Irving Brecher, Fred Finklehoffe (based on the stories by Sally Benson); ph, George Folsey (Technicolor); ed, Albert Akst; art d, Cedric Gibbons, Lemuel Ayers; chor, Charles Walters; cos, Irene Sharaff

AAN Best Screenplay: Irving Brecher, Fred F. Finkelhoffe; *AAN Best Color Cinematography:* George Folsey; *AAN Best Score (Musical):* Georgie Stoll; *AAN Best Song:* "The Trolley Song"; Ralph Blane (Music & Lyrics), Hugh Martin (Music & Lyrics)

A Valentine to the good old days, and all they stood for. Near-peak Judy Garland under the stylish direction of her future husband, Vincente Minnelli, in this wonderful period musical. It opens in 1903 in St. Louis, where Alonzo Smith (Leon Ames), a well-to-do businessman, lives with his wife (Mary Astor), daughters (Garland, Lucille Bremer, Joan Carroll, and Margaret O'Brien), son (Hank Daniels), capricious Grandpa (Harry Davenport), and maid (Marjorie Main). Daughter Rose (Bremer) is courted by one beau at home and corresponds with another away at college, while Esther (Garland) becomes engaged to the new boy next door. Little sisters Agnes (Joan Carroll) and Tootie (Margaret O'Brien) represent the timeless mischief of childhood. Trouble arises when Alonzo is promoted and ordered to New York, a move no one in the family wants to make.

This is a peerless portrayal of America at the turn of the century and one family's struggles to deal with progress, symbolized by the 1904 World's Fair in St. Louis (beautifully re-created for the film). Minnelli proves his eye for detail and captures the era and its values in richly colored, gentle images, displaying a startling balance of emotions from scene to scene, song to song. Among the songs included in this triumph of Americana are "The Boy Next Door," "Meet Me in St. Louis," the marvelous production number "The Trolley Song," and Garland's evergreen "Have Yourself a Merry Little Christmas." An almost unbeatable musical. Note Garland's beauty in this film: a tribute to the overhaul given her by Dottie Pondell, whose services Garland had snatched from under the noses of every major star in Hollywood, upon the death of Carole Lombard.

MEET THE FOCKERS

2004 100m c Comedy   **DVD** ★★
DreamWorks/Tribeca Productions/   PG-13
Everyman Pictures/Universal (U.S.)

Robert De Niro (Jack Byrnes), Ben Stiller (Greg Focker), Dustin Hoffman (Bernie Focker), Barbra Streisand (Roz Focker), Blythe Danner (Dina Byrnes), Teri Polo (Pam Byrnes), Owen Wilson (Kevin Rawley), Spencer Pickren (Little Jack), Bradley Pickren (Little Jack), Alanna Ubach (Isabel)

p, Robert De Niro, Jay Roach, Jane Rosenthal; d, Jay Roach; w, Jim Herzfeld, John Hamburg (from a story by Jim Herzfeld and Marc Hyman); ph, John Schwartzman; ed, Alan Baumgarten, Lee Haxall, Jon Poll; m, Randy Newman; prod d, Rusty Smith; art d, Andrew Neskoromny; fx, David D. Johnson, Clay Pinney; cos, Carol Ramsey

The inevitable follow-up to successful comedy-of-discomfort MEET THE PARENTS delivers fewer laughs than its predecessor, which leaves too much time in which to ponder what a sad spectacle it really is: two professionals in their 30s reduced to childish squirming and whining by their overbearing parents.

Engaged for two years, male nurse Greg Focker (Ben Stiller) and schoolteacher Pam Byrnes (Teri Polo) can't set a wedding date until Greg screws up the nerve to introduce frosty WASPs Jack and Dina Byrnes (Robert De Niro, Blythe Danner) to his uninhibited Jewish parents, Bernie and Roz (Dustin Hoffman, Barbra Streisand). Complicating matters are former CIA bigwig Jack's pathological devotion to honesty and the fact that Greg hasn't been entirely forthcoming about his family. Strictly speaking, they *are* a lawyer and a doctor, but Bernie abandoned his practice to be a househusband and therapist Roz specializes in geriatric sexuality. They're frank, spontaneous, and touchy-feely; the Byrnes are conservative, straight-laced control freaks. Within hours of the Byrneses' arrival chez Focker, they've learned that Greg slept in his parents' bed until he was 12, amassed a formidable collection of seventh-place ribbons, and lost his virginity to the family's super-sexy Latin housekeeper, Isabel (Alanna Ubach). It's a wonder Greg can still conceive of getting married at all.

Essentially a big-screen variation on the series "Dharma & Greg," the film surrenders to sitcom rhythms, ensuring that the quiet character moments that redeemed MEET THE PARENTS are sacrificed to a rigid setup/payoff structure. Danner, whose Dina actually resembles a human being, would be its saving grace if her gracefully controlled performance weren't lost in a sea of braying caricatures.

MEET THE PARENTS

2000 108m c Comedy   **DVD** ★★★
Nancy Tenebaum Films/Tribeca   PG-13
Productions/DreamWorks/Universal (U.S.)

Robert De Niro (Jack Byrnes), Ben Stiller (Greg Focker), Teri Polo (Pam Byrnes), Blythe Danner (Dina Byrnes), Nicole Dehuff (Debbie Byrnes), Jon Abrahams (Denny Byrnes), Tom McCarthy (Bob Banks), Phyllis George

(Linda Banks), James Rebhorn (Larry Banks), Owen Wilson (Kevin Rawley)

p, Nancy Tenenbaum, Jane Rosenthal, Robert De Niro, Jay Roach; d, Jay Roach; w, Jim Herzfeld, John Hamburg (from a story by Greg Glienna and Mary Ruth Clarke); ph, Peter James; ed, Jon Poll; m, Randy Newman; prod d, Rusty James; art d, John Kasarda; fx, Jonathan C. Brotherhood, David D. Johnson; cos, Daniel Orlandi

AAN Best Original Song: "A Fool in Love"; Randy Newman

A comedy of escalating discomfort in which a hapless shlub digs himself into a bottomless pit by trying to impress his girlfriend's family.

Male nurse Greg Focker (Ben Stiller) is ready to pop the question to girlfriend Pam Byrnes (Teri Polo), but her dear daddy (Robert De Niro), a retired horticulturist, has some old-fashioned ideas about manners and manhood. So Pam and Greg make a weekend pilgrimage to the Byrnes homestead in WASPy Oyster Bay, Long Island. Greg gets off on the wrong foot with Mr. Byrnes and never recovers; his carefully chosen gift, a rare orchid bulb, falls flat. The cork from Greg's conciliatory bottle of champagne nails the ornamental urn containing the ashes of Grandma Byrnes, which wind up being defiled on the dining-room floor by the family cat. Little white lies mushroom into ghastly whoppers. And Pam lets Greg in on a family secret: her dad was never really a horticulturist, but a psychological profiler for the CIA. And so the weekend goes, from bad to worse to mortifying.

On the plus side, the gross-out factor is surprisingly low, and the combination of Stiller and De Niro is inspired; no father could be more formidable, no prospective son-in-law better equipped to squirm. But the movie's humor consists of an odd mix of organic laughs rooted in Greg's exaggerated but nevertheless recognizable situation and frat-boy yucks at the expense of his last name and profession. If only there were more of the kind of nuttiness that places Jewish Greg in competition with Pam's old flame (Owen Wilson)—a goy who took up woodworking because Jesus was a carpenter—and less feline potty humor.

MELINDA AND MELINDA

2005 99m c Comedy/Drama   **DVD** ★★½
Gravier (U.S.)   PG-13

Radha Mitchell (Melinda), Chloe Sevigny (Laurel), Jonny Lee Miller (Lee), Chiwetel Ejiofor (Ellis), Brooke Smith (Cassie), Zak Orth (Peter), Will Ferrell (Hobie), Amanda Peet (Susan), Larry Pine (Max), Wallace Shawn (Sy)

p, Letty Aronson; d, Woody Allen; w, Woody Allen; ph, Vilmos Zsigmond; ed, Alisa Lepselter; prod d, Santo Loquasto; art d, Tom Warren; fx, John Ottesen; cos, Judy Ruskin Howell

To say this slight experiment in story spinning is Woody Allen's best film in years isn't saying much when it's up against the dire likes of ANYTHING ELSE and HOLLYWOOD ENDING.

Over a rainy-night dinner at a trendy New York bistro, successful playwrights Max (Larry Pine) and Sy (Wallace Shawn) test their opposing notions of the human condition by playing a little game. Each will take the same story elements and, according to his disposition, turn them into a fleshed-out narrative. Max, the tragedian, imagines a bedraggled Melinda (Radha Mitchell) bursting in on a downtown dinner party hosted by her chic high-school best friend, Laurel (Chloe Sevigny), and her underemployed actor husband, Lee (Jonny Lee Miller). Fresh from a suicide attempt prompted by the loss of her children in a vicious custody suit, the pill-popping Melinda moves into the spare room and puts a heavy strain on Laurel and Lee's already shaky marriage. As comic writer Sy tells it, perky Melinda (Mitchell again) crashes the dinner party given by her Upper East Side neighbors, independent filmmaker Susan (Amanda

Peet) and her nebbishy husband, Hobie (Will Ferrell). This Melinda promptly throws up an overdose of sleeping pills, and she's back on her feet in no time. As the stories progress, both Melindas fall in love, and both married couples are sundered by furtive love triangles, but the stories also diverge. One drags Melinda deeper into a psychological mire, while the other sends her skipping into a whirlwind of silly misunderstandings.

Mitchell is terrific as both Melindas, but ultimately, this witty narrative sport sounds better than it plays. It's all very well to say that laughter and tears are just a heartbeat apart, but both variations on Melinda's story bear the unmistakable mark of Allen's morose sensibilities. In the end they both feel muddy and unfocused rather than delightfully ambiguous.

MELO

1986 110m c Romance ★★★★★
MK2/CNC/A2 (France)

Sabine Azema (Romaine Belcroix), Pierre Arditi (Pierre Belcroix), Andre Dussollier (Marcel Blanc), Fanny Ardant (Christiane Levesque), Jacques Dacqmine (Dr. Remy), Hubert Gignoux (Priest), Catherine Arditi (Yvonne)

p, Marin Karmitz; d, Alain Resnais; w, Alain Resnais (based on the play "Melo" by Henri Bernstein); ph, Charlie Van Damme (Agfa-Gevaert Color); ed, Albert Jurgenson; m, Johannes Brahms, Johann Sebastian Bach, Philippe Gerard; prod d, Jacques Saulnier; cos, Catherine Leterrier

Since his brilliant HIROSHIMA, MON AMOUR, Alain Resnais's experiments with nonlinear structure and the relationship between memory and the past have placed him among the ranks of the greatest directors. In light of these experiments, MELO comes as a shock, a traditionally constructed linear narrative adapted from a 1929 Parisian stage melodrama written by Henry Bernstein. Deceptively simple in appearance, MELO is the story of two musicians, Marcel Blanc and Pierre Belcroix (Andre Dussollier and Pierre Arditi), whose friendship dates back to their days at the conservatory. Marcel has gone on to international fame as a soloist while Pierre has settled down in a Parisian suburb to lead a simple life with his wife, Romaine (Sabine Azema). After a quiet evening of drink and reminiscence, Marcel and Romaine begin a passionate affair. Romaine plots to gradually poison the unsuspecting and good-natured Pierre. Masterfully directed, MELO is both an entertaining romantic melodrama and an extension of Resnais's ideas about memory and imagination, reality and fiction. As in HIROSHIMA, MON AMOUR, Resnais gives us characters whose present is haunted by the past. Only rarely is a film this simple *and* this complex.

MELVIN AND HOWARD

1980 93m c Biography/Comedy ★★★½
Universal (U.S.) R

Jason Robards Jr. (Howard Hughes), Paul LeMat (Melvin Dummar), Elizabeth Cheshire (Darcy Dummar), Mary Steenburgen (Lynda Dummar), Chip Taylor (Clark Taylor), Melvin E. Dummar (Bus Depot Counterman), Michael J. Pollard (Little Red), Denise Galik (Lucy), Gloria Grahame (Mrs. Sisk), Pamela Reed (Bonnie Dummar)

p, Art Linson, Don Phillips; d, Jonathan Demme; w, Bo Goldman; ph, Tak Fujimoto (Technicolor); ed, Craig McKay; m, Bruce Langhorne; prod d, Toby Rafelson; art d, Richard Sawyer

AAN Best Supporting Actor: Jason Robards; *AA Best Supporting Actress:* Mary Steenburgen; *AA Best Original Screenplay:* Bo Goldman

After churning out CAGED HEAT and CRAZY MAMA for Roger Corman's New World Pictures, Jonathan Demme (STOP MAKING SENSE, SOMETHING WILD, THE SILENCE OF THE LAMBS) finally broke through the ranks of B-movie directors with this pungent fable about the elusiveness of the American Dream.

Based on a real-life incident, Melvin Dummar (Paul LeMat) is an amiable milkman and perpetual also-ran who, while driving along a lonesome stretch of Nevada highway early one morning, picks up a grizzled tramp (Jason Robards) headed for Las Vegas. He's nice to the eccentric codger, who claims to be Howard Hughes, and even gives him two bits at the end of the ride.

Melvin quickly dismisses the incident and goes about his life, remarrying his ex-wife, Lynda (Mary Steenburgen), and chasing success with typically poor results. Even when Lynda wins $10,000 tap dancing to the Rolling Stones's "Satisfaction" on a television game show, the Dummars are unable to turn the situation to their advantage. Life remains a struggle for the embattled couple until Melvin discovers that the bum he befriended earlier really was Howard Hughes—and that the recently deceased billionaire has made him the beneficiary of $156 million via the so-called Mormon will.

Like the earlier, underrated HANDLE WITH CARE, Demme displays an affinity for Preston Sturges-like tales that portray a system which places a premium on material success, but MELVIN AND HOWARD never quite lives up to its satiric or dramatic potential, suffering from a somewhat sidelong approach to Melvin's odyssey that renders the film more engaging than truly compelling.

MEMBER OF THE WEDDING, THE

1952 91m bw Drama ★★★
Columbia (U.S.)

Ethel Waters (Berenice Sadie Brown), Julie Harris (Frankie Addams), Brandon de Wilde (John Henry), Arthur Franz (Jarvis), Nancy Gates (Janice), William Hansen (Mr. Addams), James Edwards (Honey Camden Brown), Harry Bolden (T. T. Williams), Dickie Moore (Soldier), Danny Mummert (Barney MacKean)

p, Stanley Kramer; d, Fred Zinnemann; w, Edna Anhalt, Edward Anhalt (based on the novel and play by Carson McCullers); ph, Hal Mohr; ed, Harry Gerstad, William Lyon; m, Alex North; prod d, Rudolph Sternad; art d, Cary Odell

AAN Best Actress: Julie Harris

An overly static adaptation of Carson McCullers' 1950 Broadway hit about the end of adolescence, saved by the playwright's dialogue; the presence of Ethel Waters; and the work of veteran photographer Hal Mohr, who lovingly captures life in a sleepy Georgia town.

The then 26-year-old Julie Harris plays Frankie, a motherless 12-year-old tomboy who imagines herself a member of her brother's wedding party, then tries to tag along for the honeymoon. Dejected at being refused, she runs away, but returns home after a brush with a drunken soldier. It's the beginning of the end of her childhood, as well as of the two relationships that have defined her life thus far: with Berenice (Waters), her cook and ersatz mother; and with her much put-upon playmate and cousin, John Henry (Brandon de Wilde).

Zinnemann's distant, respectful direction fails, unsurprisingly, to capture the ironies and complexities of his source material. MEMBER was still, nonetheless, considered confusing to audiences, with many allegedly thinking Frankie was a boy until the end of the film. In an effort to address complaints that it was "slow-moving," Columbia cut about 20 minutes of footage, restoring it some twenty years later. Cameraman Mohr, approaching the end of his long career, had previously shot such films as THE JAZZ SINGER, THE WEDDING MARCH, A MIDSUMMER NIGHT'S

DREAM, and RANCHO NOTORIOUS. Five people from the award-winning theater production (Harris, Waters, de Wilde, Hansen, and Bolden) reprise their roles here. Harris had become a star with the Broadway show, and cemented her rise with an Oscar nomination for the film; de Wilde had made his debut in the play, becoming the first child actor to win Broadway's prestigious Donaldson Award in the process, and would become an Oscar-nominated star the following year in George Stevens' SHANE.

MEMENTO
2001 113m c Thriller ★★★★½
Newmarket Films/Summit Entertainment/Team R
Todd/I Remember Productions (U.S.)

DVD

Guy Pearce *(Leonard Shelly)*, Carrie-Anne Moss *(Natalie)*, Joe Pantoliano *(Teddy)*, Mark Boone *(Burt)*, Stephen Tobolowsky *(Sammy Jankis)*, Jorja Fox *(Leonard's Wife)*, Harriet Sansom Harris *(Mrs. Jankis)*, Cullum Keith Rennie *(Dodd)*, Larry Holden *(Jimmy Grantz)*, Russ Fega *(Waiter)*

p, Suzanne Todd, Jennifer Todd; d, Christopher Nolan; w, Christopher Nolan (based on a short story by Jonathan Nolan); ph, Wally Pfister; ed, Dody Dorn; m, David Julyan; prod d, Patti Podesta; fx, Andrew Sebok; cos, Cindy Evans

AAN Best Film Editing: Dody Dorn; *AAN Best Original Screenplay:* Christopher Nolan

An ingeniously convoluted tour-de-force, this tale of amnesia, murder, and revenge is told entirely in reverse chronological order. It begins at the end, and ends at the very beginning.
    Leonard Shelby (Guy Pearce) is living in a cheap L.A. motel room, but drives a Jaguar; he's wearing an expensive suit and seems to have a lot of cash, but doesn't work. And he's as much a mystery to himself as he is to the viewer: Leonard lives in the moment, not because he wants to, but because a terrible act of violence has destroyed his ability to form new memories. Despite this apparently insurmountable handicap, he's set himself the task of finding the man who raped and murdered his wife. He takes Polaroids so he can identify people and scrawls reminders on the back so he knows what to think; he writes notes to himself and has tattooed his flesh with the things he must under no circumstances forget. His only "friends" are Teddy (Joe Pantoliano), whose photo warns that he can't be trusted, and Natalie (Carrie-Anne Moss); her Polaroid says she'll help Leonard out of pity. Bit by agonizing bit, Leonard pieces together the truth, but it flows through his memory like water. And each time he goes to the well, what comes up is slightly changed.
    The viewer is in a similar predicament. Since writer-director Christopher Nolan's philosophical puzzle unfolds in reverse—each successive scene of the film is actually the preceding scene of the story—we are, in effect, also deprived of "memories"; we may be aware of what comes next, but not what has already happened. We're put in the uncomfortable position of knowing a *little* more than Leonard, but not enough to know what he should be doing about it.

MEN, THE
1950 85m bw Drama/War ★★★★
Kramer (U.S.)

Marlon Brando *(Ken)*, Teresa Wright *(Ellen)*, Everett Sloane *(Dr. Brock)*, Jack Webb *(Norm)*, Everett Erdman *(Leo)*, Arthur Jurado *(Angel)*, Virginia Farmer *(Nurse Robbins)*, Dorothy Tree *(Ellen's Mother)*, Howard St. John *(Ellen's Father)*, Nita Hunter *(Dolores)*

p, Stanley Kramer; d, Fred Zinnemann; w, Carl Foreman; ph, Robert de Grasse; ed, Harry Gerstad; m, Dimitri Tiomkin; prod d, Rudolph Sternad

AAN Best Story and Screenplay: Carl Foreman

This was Marlon Brando's film debut and, as such, set standards not only for his fellow actors but for himself. Brando gives a tremendous performance as Ken, a WWII veteran who has been left a paraplegic as a result of a sniper's bullet in the lower back. In the hospital, Ken is angry, resentful, and uncooperative with his doctors and nurses. His girlfriend, Ellen (Teresa Wright), visits him, but the embittered Ken turns her away. Dr. Brock (Everett Sloane) slowly breaks through Ken's mental wall, however, convincing him to begin his exercise program, through which Ken strengthens his upper torso, later learning to expertly manipulate his wheelchair and to drive a specially equipped auto. Ellen will not give up on him and soon Ken agrees to marry her, but despite the progress he has made, the vet is still consumed with doubt, anger, and self-pity. Producer Stanley Kramer earlier produced such message-filled films as CHAMPION and HOME OF THE BRAVE, the first concerning the corruption of the blood sport of prizefighting, the second dealing with racism and bigotry. Here Kramer, aided by the steady direction of Fred Zinnemann, studies the adjustment of severely wounded men with little hope of complete recovery. Zinnemann rarely steps over the line into mawkishness or bathos, and Carl Foreman's witty, sensitive script was the reason Brando agreed to step off the stage to appear in this film. Brando worked hard at his role, actually moving into a 32-bed ward with real paraplegics and observing their day-to-day agonies, research that resulted in a finely nuanced performance.

MEN...
(MANNER)
1985 99m c Comedy ★★★½
Olga/Second German TV (West Germany)

Heiner Lauterbach *(Julius Armbrust)*, Uwe Ochsenknecht *(Stefan Lachner)*, Ulrike Kriener *(Paula Armbrust)*, Janna Marangosoff *(Angelika)*, Marie-Charlott Schuler *(Marita Strass)*, Dietmar Bar *(Lothar)*, Edith Volkmann *(Frau Lennert)*

d, Doris Dorrie; w, Doris Dorrie; ph, Helge Weindler; ed, Jorg Neumann; m, Claus Bantzer

Taking an age-old situation and turning it on its head, this wonderful farce is brimming with unique twists, wit, and style. Julius Armbrust (Heiner Lauterbach) is an advertising executive about to celebrate his 12th year of wedded bliss with wife Paula (Ulrike Kriener). His world suddenly falls apart, however, when he discovers she has been cheating on him with Stefan Lachner (Uwe Ochsenknecht), a young, long-haired bohemian who meanders about town on his bicycle. Julius decides on revenge, not through blackmail or murder but in a manner he knows will bring Paula back to him. After ingratiating himself with Stefan on the sly, Julius begins work on his scheme, transforming Paula's artist-lover into a carbon copy of himself. MEN is a sharp satire, playing off gender roles and male bonding with some real insight. Made by female director Doris Dorrie, the film wisely carries no obtrusive social message that might undermine the wonderful humor. Dorrie does rely rather heavily on slapstick (there is a silly bit involving a gorilla suit), but fortunately her inventive storytelling overcomes the film's lesser elements. Shot in 25 days on a budget of only $360,000, MEN grossed in excess of $15 million in international box-office receipts.

MEN IN BLACK   DVD

1997 98m c   Science Fiction/Action/Comedy ★★★½
Amblin Entertainment/MacDonald/Parkes (U.S.)   PG-13

Tommy Lee Jones *(Agent K)*, Will Smith *(Agent J)*, Linda Fiorentino *(Dr. Laurel Weaver)*, Vincent D'Onofrio *(Edgar)*, Rip Torn *(Agent Zed)*, Tony Shalhoub *(Jeebs)*, Siobhan Fallon *(Beatrice)*, Mike Nussbaum *(Gentle Rosenberg)*, Jon Gries *(Van Driver)*, Sergio Calderon *(Jose)*

p, Walter F. Parkes, Laurie MacDonald; d, Barry Sonnenfeld; w, Ed Solomon (based on the Malibu Comic, "The Men in Black," by Lowell Cunningham); ph, Don Peterman; ed, Jim Miller; m, Danny Elfman; prod d, Bo Welch; art d, Thomas Duffield; fx, Peter M. Chesney, Kyle Ross Collinsworth, Eric Brevig, Industrial Light & Magic, K.N.B. EFX Group, ME*FX, XFX; cos, Mary E. Vogt

AA Best Makeup: Rick Baker, David LeRoy Anderson; *AAN Best Art Direction:* Bo Welch, Cheryl Carasik; *AAN Best Original Musical or Comedy Score:* Danny Elfman

GHOSTBUSTERS meets "The X-Files." Slick, directed with all the considerable panache Barry Sonnenfeld (THE ADDAMS FAMILY) can muster, and very clever in a deeply shallow sort of way, this sci-fi action comedy posits that all those paranoid UFO nuts babbling about the government sending mysterious "Men in Black" to cover up evidence of alien visitations are right on the money.

Since the late 1950s, displaced BEMs have been taking on human form and quietly settling into new lives, mostly alongside the rest of the huddled masses yearning to breathe free in New York City. "It's like Casablanca," says MIB Agent K (Tommy Lee Jones), the old alien hand, "but without the Nazis." The shadowy Men in Black license and monitor the intergalactic out-of-towners, and take care of any bad apples from outer space who try to spoil it for everyone else. Following his longtime partner's retirement, K teams up with hotshot new kid Agent J (Will Smith) to stop an alien assassin (Vincent D'Onofrio) who's hell-bent on starting an interstellar war that will spell bad times for this island Earth.

Extravagant special effects notwithstanding, this is really a triumph of casting: the aplomb with which Jones plays wry straight man to Smith's street-smart wiseacre is terrifically enjoyable. Ed Solomon's script (based on the *Men in Black* comic-book series) offers deadpan riffs on everything from the 1963 World's Fair, supermarket tabloids, and Dennis Rodman to velcro and microwaves (products of alien technology, don't you know), and Smith and Jones work them for all they're worth.

MEN IN BLACK II   DVD

2002 88m c   Science Fiction/Action/Comedy ★★
Amblin Entertainment/MacDonald/Parkes   PG-13
Productions/Columbia   (U.S.)

Tommy Lee Jones *(Kay)*, Will Smith *(Jay)*, Rip Torn *(Zed)*, Lara Flynn Boyle *(Serleena)*, Johnny Knoxville *(Scrad/Charlie)*, Rosario Dawson *(Laura Vasquez)*, Tony Shalhoub *(Jeebs)*, Patrick Warburton *(Agent Tee)*, Jack Kehler *(Ben)*, David Cross *(Newton)*

p, Laurie MacDonald, Walter F. Parkes; d, Barry Sonnenfeld; w, Barry Fanaro, Robert Gordon (from a story by Robert Gordon, based on the Malibu Comic by Lowell Cunningham); ph, Greg Gardiner; ed, Richard Pearson, Steven Weisberg; m, Danny Elfman; prod d, Bo Welch; art d, Alec Hammond, Sean Haworth, Tom Wilkins; fx, John Berton, Thomas L. Fisher, Industrial Light & Magic, John Richardson (creatures); cos, Mary E. Vogt; anim, Tom Bertino

A five-years-in-the-making sequel that slavishly duplicates all the identifiable elements that made MEN IN BLACK a smart-alecky hit, leeching every drop of spontaneity from the material in the process.

The film gets off to a bang-up start with Agent J (Will Smith) teaching a rowdy alien super-worm that's terrorizing New York City subway riders to act right or get smacked right, but the first *real* order of business is retrieving the formidable Agent K (Tommy Lee Jones) from retirement. It seems sexy alien super-bitch Serleena (Lara Flynn Boyle), whose fingertips sprout masses of writhing tentacles at the slightest provocation, is fully prepared to destroy Earth in her pursuit of some extraterrestrial thingamajig know as the "Light of Zartha." Since Agent K was in charge of the original Light of Zartha case, his expertise is sorely needed. K now runs a rinky-dink post office in Truro, MA; his memory of countless close encounters of the icky kind has been wiped clean by the MiB agency's nifty neuralizer. Unfortunately, K can't remember where the Light is hidden, even after he's been de-neuralized. Good thing he left himself a series of clever clues that have the reunited partners rushing around Manhattan like campers on a cosmic scavenger hunt, trying desperately to beat Serleena to the prize.

Rip Torn and Tony Shalhoub reprise their roles from the first film, while Johnny Knoxville, of MTV's "Jackass," plays an alien with two heads and half a brain. Screenwriter Robert Gordon's credits include the surprisingly clever sci-fi spoof GALAXY QUEST, but he couldn't overcome the fundamental problem with this material: you've seen it before. To his eternal credit, Jones gives his considerable all, while Smith just bops along, lobbing gags and grinning at the special effects.

MENACE II SOCIETY   DVD

1993 90m c   Crime/Drama   ★★★
New Line   (U.S.)   R

Tyrin Turner *(Caine)*, Larenz Tate *(O-Dog)*, Samuel L. Jackson *(Tat Lawson)*, Glenn Plummer *(Pernell)*, Khandi Alexander *(Karen Lawson)*, Jada Pinkett *(Ronnie)*, Vonte Sweet *(Sharif)*, Bill Duke *(Detective)*, Charles S. Dutton *(Mr. Butler)*, June Kyoko-Lu *(Grocery Store Woman)*

p, Darin Scott; d, Allen Hughes, Albert Hughes; w, Tyger Williams (from a story by Williams and Allen and Albert Hughes); ph, Lisa Rinzler; ed, Christopher Koefoed; m, QD III; prod d, Penny Barrett; fx, Frank Ceglia; cos, Sylvia Vega-Vasquez

An impressive first feature from the 21-year-old twin brother directing team of Albert and Allen Hughes, MENACE II SOCIETY is a gritty, uncompromising take on life in the Watts section of Los Angeles. MENACE chronicles the short, hopeless life of Caine (Tyrin Turner), a small-time drug dealer with a vague, barely articulated desire to escape his surroundings. The son of a dealer (Samuel L. Jackson) and an addict, both now dead, Tyrin's hope of escape is thwarted by a culture in which macho one-upmanship, combined with a liberal supply of guns, makes life little more than a cycle of revenge killings.

Although MENACE has invited comparisons to BOYZ N THE HOOD, it's not as good a film as John Singleton's breakthrough hit. It's edgier and savvier, and probably achieves a more accurate feel for life in a gun-crazy urban crucible. But it lacks the vision, and the fully defined characters, of BOYZ. Tyrin never becomes more than the sum of his conflicting impulses—he's a composite sample of a social group rather than a fully-fledged individual. The story, too, tries to cover too many bases, finally abandoning its urgent, streetwise edge in favor of B-movie melodrama. Nonetheless, MENACE is a compelling, visceral piece of work. Its most disturbing subplot—in which Tyrin's friend O-Dog (Larenz Tate) shoots a Korean store owner, and then watches the act over and over on the videotape taken from the store's security camera—has a horrifying, unforgettable ring of truth.

MEPHISTO 📀
1981   144m   c   War/Drama   ★★★★
Mafilm/Objectiv/Manfred Durniok/Analysis
(Hungary/West Germany)

Klaus Maria Brandauer *(Hendrik Hofgen)*, Krystyna Janda *(Barbara Bruckner)*, Ildiko Bansagi *(Nicoletta Von Niebuhr)*, Karin Boyd *(Juliette Martens)*, Rolf Hoppe *(The General)*, Christine Harbort *(Lotte Lindenthal)*, Gyorgy Cserhalmi *(Hans Miklas)*, Christiane Graskoff *(Cesar Von Muck)*, Peter Andorai *(Otto Ulrichs)*, Ildiko Kishonti *(Dora Martin)*

p, Manfred Durniok; d, Istvan Szabo; w, Istvan Szabo, Peter Dobai (based on the novel by Klaus Mann); ph, Lajos Koltai (Eastmancolor); ed, Zsuzsa Csakany; m, Zdenko Tamassy; art d, Jozsef Romvari

AA Best Foreign Language Film

The winner of 1981's Academy Award for Best Foreign Language Film, MEPHISTO is an inspired update of the Faust legend featuring a tour de force performance by Klaus Maria Brandauer. Critically acclaimed stage actor Hendrik Hofgen (Brandauer) tires of the "entertaining" theatrical forms and attempts something more revolutionary, more Brechtian. Despite his ground-breaking ideas, he does not rise to fame—they cannot even spell his name correctly on posters. Desperate, Hendrik sells his soul—not to the Devil, but to the Nazis—his desire for fame more urgent than his hatred of the oppressor. It is only later, after he is indebted to the Third Reich, that he realizes his mistake. Based on a novel by Klaus Mann (son of Thomas) and exquisitely photographed, MEPHISTO bubbles over with the energy of Brandauer's bravura performance, which quickly attracted the attention of Hollywood. Brandauer and director Istvan Szabo would team again to make COLONEL REDL and HANUSSEN.

MERRY CHRISTMAS, MR. LAWRENCE 📀
1983   124m   c   Prison/War   ★★★★
Recorded Picture/Cineventure TV/Asashi/Oshima
(U.K./Japan)   R

David Bowie *(Celliers)*, Tom Conti *(Col. John Lawrence)*, Ryuichi Sakamoto *(Capt. Yoni)*, Takeshi Kitano, billed as Takeshi *(Sgt. Hara)*, Jack Thompson *(Hicksley-Ellis)*, Johnny Okura *(Kanemoto)*, Alistair Browning *(DeJong)*, James Malcolm *(Celliers' Brother)*, Christopher Brown *(Celliers at Age 12)*, Yuya Uchida

p, Jeremy Thomas; d, Nagisa Oshima; w, Nagisa Oshima, Paul Mayersberg (based on the novel *The Seed and the Sower* by Laurens Van Der Post); ph, Toichiro Narushima (Eastmancolor); ed, Tomoyo Oshima; m, Ryuichi Sakamoto; prod d, Shigemasa Toda; art d, Andrew Sanders

Japanese director Nagisa Oshima's first film in English stars Tom Conti as the title character, a British colonel in a Japanese-run POW camp during WWII.
     Colonel Lawrence is an astute observer of the cultural codes of his captors and even forms a friendship of sorts with one Japanese officer (Takeshi). He is also witness to the strange dynamics between new camp commandant Yoni (Ryuichi Sakamoto) and a new prisoner, Jack Celliers (David Bowie), with whom Lawrence served in Libya. Yoni is fascinated by Celliers, and plans to make him the prisoners' CO, replacing Hicksley-Ellis (Jack Thompson).
     Oshima's ambitious film is not without faults, but these are overshadowed by its emotional power. Many of the characters' actions and impulses are apparently contradictory, but their motivation can generally be found buried in Oshima's complex story. (The Yoni-Celliers relationship, which needs greater development, is a notable exception). Fine performances by Conti, Takeshi (brilliant in his first dramatic role), Sakamoto (a

Japanese pop star in his film acting debut who also contributed the memorable score), and Bowie enhance this provocative film.

MERRY WAR, A 📀
1997   101m   c   Comedy/Drama/Romance   ★★★
Aspidistra Productions, Ltd./United British Artists/   R
John Wolstenholme Film and TV Entertainment
(U.K.)

Richard E. Grant *(Gordon Comstock)*, Helena Bonham Carter *(Rosemary)*, Jim Carter *(Erskine)*, Harriet Walter *(Julia Comstock)*, Lill Roughley *(Mrs. Trilling)*, Julian Wadham *(Ravelston)*, Lesley Vickerage *(Hermoine)*, John Clegg *(McKechnie)*, Barbara Leigh Hunt *(Mrs. Wisebeach)*, Grant Parsons *(Beautiful Young Man)*

p, Peter Shaw; d, Robert Bierman; w, Alan Plater (based on the novel *Keep the Aspidistra Flying* by George Orwell); ph, Giles Nuttgens; ed, Bill Wright; prod d, Sarah Greenwood; art d, Philip Robinson; cos, James Keast

An intermittently amusing but always thoughtful adaptation of George Orwell's autobiographical novel, *Keep the Aspidistra Flying.*
     Richard E. Grant stars as Gordon Comstock, a would-be poet who supports himself as a copywriter in 1930s London. When Comstock's first book of poetry receives a good review in the *Times Literary Supplement,* he decides to cast off the trappings of what he considers to be his predictable life (job, marriage, etc.) to become a full-time poet and free man. Comstock's subsequent free-fall into penury and degradation (remember that Orwell's nonfiction works include the terrifying *Down and Out in Paris and London*) is, fortunately, leavened with humor. Comstock isn't the most sympathetic of protagonists: he leaches money from his hardworking spinster sister Julia (Harriet Walter), and treats both his upper-class publisher, Ravelston (Julian Wadham), and his devoted girlfriend, Rosemary (Helena Bonham Carter), exceedingly badly, spurning them viciously whenever they try to pull him back into the safety of the middle-class fold.
     Grant, who first gained notice as the noisy heroes of Bruce Robinson's WITHNAIL AND I and HOW TO GET AHEAD IN ADVERTISING, was clearly born to play Gordon Comstock. He's perfectly cast (as is Bonham Carter), and Orwell's rants and whines about poverty and the bitter pills life forces one to swallow will no doubt continue to resonate with modern audiences. Less convincing, however faithful to the novel, is the ending and Comstock's embrace of that emblem of bourgeois conformity and staple of overstuffed parlors, the humble aspidistra plant.

MERRY WIDOW, THE
1934   99m   bw   Musical/Comedy   ★★★★★
MGM   (U.S.)

Maurice Chevalier *(Prince Danilo)*, Jeanette MacDonald *(Sonia)*, Edward Everett Horton *(Ambassador Popoff)*, Una Merkel *(Queen Dolores)*, George Barbier *(King Achmed)*, Minna Gombell *(Marcelle)*, Ruth Channing *(Lulu)*, Sterling Holloway *(Mischka)*, Henry Armetta *(Turk)*, Barbara Leonard *(Maid)*

p, Irving Thalberg; d, Ernst Lubitsch; w, Samson Raphaelson, Ernest Vajda (based on the operetta "Die Lustige Witwe" by Franz Lehar, Victor Leon, Leo Stein); ph, Oliver T. Marsh; ed, Frances Marsh; m, Franz Lehar; art d, Cedric Gibbons, Frederic Hope; chor, Albertina Rasch; cos, Adrian, Ali Hubert

AA Best Interior Decoration: Cedric Gibbons (Art Direction), Frederic Hope (Art Direction)

One of the greatest of the screen operettas. After a smashing debut in Austria, Franz Lehár's operetta "The Merry Widow" was brought to the U.S. in 1907, became a silent two-reeler in 1912, then, in 1925, Erich von Stroheim directed Mae Murray and John Gilbert in an opulent, controversial version in which Clark Gable appeared as an extra. This version, however, is by far the best of the lot. Jeanette MacDonald, at the peak of her career, is Sonia, an immensely wealthy widow whose spending keeps the small country of Marshovia afloat economically. When she decides to move to Paris to find a suitable husband, the king (George Barbier) dispatches Danilo (Maurice Chevalier), whom he has caught dallying with Queen Dolores (Una Merkel), to the City of Light to woo the widow and bring her home. Failing to recognize Sonia in a cafe, Danilo falls in love with her, then tries to persuade her that his affection is real when she learns the nature of his mission. Unable to convince her, Danilo is called back to Marshovia and put on trial; however, Sonia becomes the star witness for the defense, the two are trapped in a jail cell, and matters end happily and romantically.

The best musical helmed by the great Ernst Lubitsch, THE MERRY WIDOW is frothy, funny, and tuneful from start to finish. MacDonald more than holds her own in the comedy department, snapping off lines with Carole Lombard-like expertise. Star Chevalier had played with newcomer MacDonald at Paramount, and though he reputedly never liked her, their pairing here is near perfection. The dancing, choreographed by Albertina Rasch, is as good as it comes and the huge waltz in the embassy ball ranks among the best large ensemble pieces ever filmed. Enjoy the opening sequence where Marshovia is found on the map or the "There's a limit to every widow" scene. "The Merry Widow" is one of 30 operettas penned by Lehar, and here his music was given new lyrics by Lorenz Hart, Gus Kahn, and an uncredited Richard Rodgers.

METALLICA: SOME KIND OF MONSTER   DVD

2004   139m   c   Documentary   ★★★½
Third Eye Motion Picture Company/@radical.media productions   (U.S.)

James Hetfield, Lars Ulrich, Kirk Hammett, Robert Trujillo, Jason Newsted, Dave Mustaine, Bob Rock, Phil Towle, Torben Ulrich

p, Bruce Sinofsky; d, Joe Berlinger; w, Rachel Dawson; ed, Bob Richman, Doug Abel, M. Watanabe Milmore; m, David Zieff

Documentary filmmakers Bruce Sinofsky and Joe Berlinger signed on to make a promotional film about the creation of Metallica's first studio album in six years. Before the film and the album—2003's "St. Anger"—were finished, Berlinger and Sinofsky had amassed 1600 hours worth of Sturm und Drang. The project that metastasized into a highly personal, two-year slog through the aging rockers' personal and professional travails, starting with longtime bassist Jason Newsted's abrupt departure, despite the efforts of $40,000-per-month therapist/performance-enhancement coach Phil Towle to keep the band together. Towle, whose lucrative specialty is helping people who can't stand the sight of each other get along on the job, stayed to help the remaining three band members through the process of writing and recording their next album. A few months into the first round of riffing and soul searching, lead singer James Hetfield, who co-founded Metallica with drummer Lars Ulrich in 1981, stormed out of therapy and vanished into what became a year's worth of rehab. Hetfield returns, newly fluent in recovery-speak; Ulrich crusades against Napster, alienating fans; Towle gets his walking papers for starting to behave as though he's *in* the band, not working for the band. Ulrich and Hetfield supply the fireworks; lead guitarist Kirk Hammett worries; former lead guitarist Dave Mustaine, whom Hammett replaced after Mustaine was fired in 1983, has a sullen heart-to-heart with Ulrich; wives, children, and various relatives wander in and out. The resulting film is a mesmerizing spectacle that reveals little about the creative process and lots about Ulrich and Hetfield's personal mess, which is much the same mess other people tackle with fewer resources and no fanfare.

METROPOLITAN

1990   98m   c   Comedy   ★★★★
Westerly Film   (U.S.)   PG-13

Carolyn Farina *(Audrey Rouget)*, Edward Clements *(Tom Townsend)*, Chris Eigeman, billed as Christopher Eigeman *(Nick Smith)*, Taylor Nichols *(Charlie Black)*, Allison Rutledge-Parisi *(Jane Clarke)*, Dylan Hundley *(Sally Fowler)*, Isabel Gillies *(Cynthia McClean)*, Bryan Leder *(Fred Neff)*, Will Kempe *(Rick Von Sloneker)*, Elizabeth Thompson *(Serena Slocum)*

p, Whit Stillman, Brian Greenbaum, Peter Wentworth; d, Whit Stillman; w, Whit Stillman; ph, John Thomas; ed, Chris Tellefsen; m, Mark Suozzo; cos, Mary Jane Fort

AAN Best Original Screenplay: Whit Stillman

Thanks to taut direction, urbane writing and beguiling performances by a number of new actors, the young, privileged Manhattanites at the heart of this film are surprisingly disarming.

It's the Christmas season in Manhattan, and our principal characters are swallowed up in the heady round of debutante balls and swank receptions. One snowy eve, this determinedly proper crew, led by the arrogantly dissolute Nick (Christopher Eigeman), receives a new member, Tom Townsend (Edward Clements), from truly alien territory—the West Side. Although sweet young thing Audrey (Carolyn Farina) is infatuated with Tom, he is still weathering the after-effects of a fatal crush on the notorious heartbreaker Serena Slocum (Elizabeth Thompson). Also threatening the welfare and happiness of the clique is Nick's special enemy, Rick von Sloneker (Will Kempe), a pony-tailed Lothario over whom an alarming number of debs have committed suicide. The film climaxes with a pursuit and rescue of virtue in Southampton and ends on a sweet note of comradeship.

Exhibiting a prodigy's control over his cleverly devised material, Whit Stillman has made an updated drawing-room comedy that takes place largely at deb-party postmortems, with the characters endlessly jawing about honor and position. Surprisingly, the film is so adroitly written and played that there is nothing claustrophobic about the proceedings—who wants to leave the room with such stimulating talk going on? The film is a party-night dream vision of New York, with roots in Astaire-Rogers musicals, screwball comedies, and Woody Allen films. Nick emerges as the most engaging of METROPOLITAN's characters, with his easy hypocrisy in carnal matters and propensity for spreading scandalous stories about his rivals; Eigeman delivers his lines with aplomb worthy of Clifton Webb or George Sanders. Stillman is a careful observer with an obvious love of language, and his wonderful, fresh cast handles the script with ease, conveying just the right measure of deadpan, *jejune* super-seriousness.

MIAMI BLUES

1990   97m   c   Crime/Thriller   ★★★
Tristes Tropiques   (U.S.)   R

Fred Ward *(Sgt. Hoke Moseley)*, Alec Baldwin *(Frederick J. "Junior" Frenger)*, Jennifer Jason Leigh *(Susie "Pepper" Waggoner)*, Nora Dunn *(Ellita Sanchez)*, Obba Babatunde *(Blink Willie)*, Charles Napier *(Sgt. Bill Henderson)*, Shirley Stoler *(Edie Wulgemuth)*, Paul Gleason *(Sgt. Frank Lackley)*, Gary Goetzman *(Hotel Desk Manager)*, Ron Bozman *(Senor Lerner)* p, Jonathan Demme, Gary Goetzman; d, George Armitage; w, George Armitage (based on the novel *Miami Blues* by Charles Willeford); ph, Tak Fujimoto; ed, Craig McKay; prod d, Maher Ahmad

---

Frederick Frenger, Jr. (Baldwin), an amoral killer fresh out of prison, arrives in Miami with a dead man's wallet and an impractical urge to remake his life along more prosaic lines. In the airport he is annoyed by a Hare Krishna, whose finger he breaks out of instinctive viciousness, shocking the weak-hearted religious zealot to death. When Frenger checks into a hotel, he sends for a hooker. Pepper (Leigh), the naive young woman who answers the summons, harbors a secret wish to be an ordinary housewife. And the two see in each other an opportunity to live out their fantasies of conventionality. It's not to be.

MIAMI BLUES toys with hard-boiled crime-film cliches and keeps the viewer constantly off balance. The plot is minimal, and no attempt is made to explain the psychology of the sociopath who murders casually and yet yearns for the security of middle-class life. But the movie's details are fascinating and often surprising. Director Armitage, a Roger Corman protege, exposes a collection of idiosyncratic characters to Florida's hot sun and the effect is startling.

MIAMI BLUES suffers from a number of basic structural problems. Awkwardly paced, it alternates sharp, compact scenes with aimless ones that advance neither the plot nor develop the characters. Moreover, the characters never deviate far from their initial notes. In a slam-bang action picture in which something is blown up every ten minutes, these would be minor complaints, but MIAMI BLUES's overt quirkiness promises more without delivering. Often on the verge of wearing out its welcome, MIAMI BLUES is nevertheless redeemed by its offbeat, sporadic, intense set pieces.

MICHAEL   **DVD**
1996 105m c   Fantasy/Comedy/Drama   ★★★
Alphaville Productions/Turner Pictures   (U.S.)   PG

John Travolta *(Michael)*, William Hurt *(Frank Quinlan)*, Andie MacDowell *(Dorothy Winters)*, Robert Pastorelli *(Huey Driscoll)*, Jean Stapleton *(Pansy Milbank)*, Bob Hoskins *(Vartan Malt)*, Teri Garr *(Judge Esther Newberg)*, Wallace Langham *(Bruce Craddock)*, Joey Lauren Adams *(Anita)*, Carla Gugino *(Bride)*

p, Sean Daniel, Nora Ephron, James Jacks; d, Nora Ephron; w, Nora Ephron, Delia Ephron, Pete Dexter, Jim Quinlan; ph, John Lindley; ed, Geraldine Peroni; m, Randy Newman; prod d, Dan Davis; art d, James Tocci; fx, David Blitstein; cos, Elizabeth McBride

---

John Travolta's charms carry MICHAEL, a comedy-fantasy about a naughty angel and the three jaded humans he helps during a Midwestern road trip. This New Age WIZARD OF OZ fable contains some pleasant moments, but also a few awkward ones.

Michael (Travolta) is a lewd, crude, and heaven-sent angel whose miraculous assistance to an Iowa motel owner, Pansy (Jean Stapleton), inspires the elderly woman to write to Frank Quinlan (William Hurt), the lead reporter at a Chicago tabloid. Frank travels to Iowa with angel "expert" Dorothy Winters (Andie MacDowell) and Huey Driscoll (Robert Pastorelli), another reporter. Each believes the angel story is phony—that is, until they arrive at the motel and meet Michael, with his huge wings and slovenly appearance.

While angel movies may go way back to such classics as ANGEL ON MY SHOULDER, IT'S A WONDERFUL LIFE, and THE BISHOP'S WIFE, what makes MICHAEL unique is the appearance of a good angel who's not a saint, and Travolta makes Michael a perfectly raunchy one. But director Nora Ephron seems more interested in funny or touching bits than in making sense of the whole, and that keeps MICHAEL from achieving any great heights. Ephron makes some of the same mistakes that kept her SLEEPLESS IN SEATTLE so

uncomfortably calculated: too many cute moments, too much music bridging the scenes and montages of a bumpy plot. But how can anyone be unkind to a movie about angels and the power of believing? So accept MICHAEL the movie like Michael the angel, flaws and all.

MICHAEL COLLINS   **DVD**
1996 117m c   Biography   ★★½
Evergreen Entertainment/Geffen Pictures   (U.S./U.K.)   R

Liam Neeson *(Michael Collins)*, Aidan Quinn *(Harry Boland)*, Stephen Rea *(Ned Broy)*, Alan Rickman *(Eamon De Valera)*, Julia Roberts *(Kitty Kiernan)*, Charles Dance *(Soames)*, Ian Hart *(Joe O'Reilly)*, Richard Ingram *(British Officer)*, John Kenny *(Patrick Pearse)*, Roman McCairbe *(Thomas McDonagh)*

p, Stephen Woolley; d, Neil Jordan; w, Neil Jordan; ph, Chris Menges; ed, J. Patrick Duffner, Tony Lawson; m, Elliot Goldenthal; prod d, Anthony Pratt; art d, Arden Gantly, Jonathan McKinstry, Cliff Robinson; fx, Yves De Bono, Gerry Johnston; cos, Sandy Powell

AAN Best Cinematography: Chris Menges; *AAN Best Original Dramatic Score:* Elliot Goldenthal

---

Clearly a labor of love, Irish writer-director Neil Jordan's biography of Michael Collins is an admirable tribute to his country's beloved patriot that sometimes verges on hagiography.

Arrested after the brutally suppressed Easter Uprising of 1916, Irishmen Michael Collins (Liam Neeson), Harry Boland (Aidan Quinn), and Eamon De Valera (Alan Rickman) are released from jail two years later. The three men come into escalating conflict in pursuit of the common goal of an independent Irish republic. While organizing his fellow guerrilla warriors, Collins becomes intrigued with Boland's girlfriend, Kitty Kiernan (Julia Roberts), and they become intimate after "Dev" and Boland go to America to drum up support for the movement. When they return, Dev sends Collins to represent the Irish in negotiations with the British over a peace settlement. Collins returns with a treaty establishing the Irish Free State, a government which is independent but still answerable to the King. Dev is furious over the compromise. Joined by Boland, he vows to fight Collins, sparking a civil war in Ireland.

History can be messy, particularly when it's the history of a man to whom, it can (and will) be argued, the words *terrorist* and *freedom fighter* are equally applicable. Jordan cannily sidesteps the troubling issue by presenting Collins as the hero of what amounts to a briskly paced, beautifully executed espionage thriller—complete with daring escapes, exploding cars, and a beautiful woman (Roberts). Neeson has the charisma needed to portray Collins, and Rickman has rarely been better. But while the film is unflinching in its depiction of the brutality of both the English and the Irish, Jordan pointedly dissociates his hero from any actual ugliness. He may have been the architect, but Collins is never shown with blood on his hands.

MIDNIGHT
1939 94m   bw   Comedy   ★★★★★
Paramount   (U.S.)

Claudette Colbert *(Eve Peabody/"Baroness Czerny")*, Don Ameche *(Tibor Czerny)*, John Barrymore *(George Flammarion)*, Francis Lederer *(Jacques Picot)*, Mary Astor *(Helene Flammarion)*, Elaine Barrie *(Simone)*, Hedda Hopper *(Stephanie)*, Rex O'Malley *(Marcel)*, Monty Woolley *(Judge)*, Armand Kaliz *(Lebon)*

p, Arthur Hornblow Jr.; d, Mitchell Leisen; w, Charles Brackett, Billy Wilder (based on a story by Edwin Justus Mayer, Franz Shulz); ph, Charles Lang; ed, Doane Harrison; m, Frederick

Hollander; art d, Hans Dreier, Robert Usher; fx, Farciot Edouart; cos, Irene

An extremely witty, well-paced comedy which plays beautifully today. The story is set in Paris where Colbert is a struggling showgirl. Wealthy Barrymore believes gigolo Lederer is paying too much attention to his wife Astor, so he hires Colbert to keep Lederer occupied. Ameche plays a taxi driver who has fallen in love with Colbert. When the group goes to Barrymore's chateau in Versailles, Colbert is constantly in danger of being exposed, and the plot is further complicated when Ameche arrives, posing as her husband. Colbert was never better; ditto most of the cast. Leisen's direction (along with KITTY his finest effort) and the cynical Brackett and Wilder script complete one of the masterworks of '30s romantic comedy.

MIDNIGHT CLEAR, A   *DVD*
1992 107m c War/Drama   ★★★½
A&M Films/Tamrose Productions/Beacon   R
Communications (U.S.)

Peter Berg *(Bud Miller)*, Kevin Dillon *(Mel Avakian)*, Arye Gross *(Stan Shutzer)*, Ethan Hawke *(Will Knott)*, Gary Sinise *("Mother" Wilkins)*, Frank Whaley *("Father" Mundy)*, John C. McGinley *(Major Griffin)*, Larry Joshua *(Lieutenant Ware)*, Curt Lowens *(German Soldier)*, Rachel Griffin *(Janice)*

p, Bill Borden, Dale Pollock; d, Keith Gordon; w, Keith Gordon (from the novel by William Wharton); ph, Tom Richmond; ed, Donald Brochu; m, Mark Isham; prod d, David Nichols; art d, David Lubin; cos, Barbara Tfank

Like all the best war movies, A MIDNIGHT CLEAR looks at its subject on a human scale, bringing home the tragedy of armed conflict by showing its effects on a small group of individuals. Made with intelligence and wit, the film combines moments of lyrical beauty with a bitterly ironic sense of the absurdity of war. Adapted from William Wharton's autobiographical novel by actor-turned-director Keith Gordon (THE CHOCOLATE WAR), A MIDNIGHT CLEAR follows the misadventures of an infantry intelligence patrol somewhere in the Ardennes forest in 1944. Selected for reconnaissance work because of their high I.Q. ratings ("I guess if we're intelligent, we must be good at intelligence"), the group includes Will Knott (Ethan Hawke), a newly promoted sergeant who just can't get around to sewing on his stripes; "Mother" Wilkins (Gary Sinise), named for his attempts to enforce neatness among the squad members; "Father" Mundy (Frank Whaley), a former seminarian; and Mel Avakian (Kevin Dillon), the group's most—perhaps only—competent soldier. Shortly before Christmas, the group is sent by their sadistic commanding officer to commandeer an abandoned house and use it as a lookout to report on enemy troop movements. They do encounter some Germans, but of the kind that shatter their preconceptions about the "enemy." These Germans shout goodnight messages to their American counterparts, attack them with snowballs rather than bullets, and end up exchanging gifts with them around a makeshift Christmas tree. When these peaceful overtures end in bloodshed the effect is doubly moving, since we have come to know those on both sides as real people.

Though it hits an occasional false note, A MIDNIGHT CLEAR is well written and sensitively directed. The pristine, snowbound setting gives the film a still, other-worldly quality, and makes for some arresting images, particularly that of a German and an American corpse frozen in a posthumous embrace.

MIDNIGHT COWBOY   *DVD*
1969 119m c Drama   ★★★★
UA (U.S.)   R

Dustin Hoffman *(Enrico "Ratso" Rizzo)*, Jon Voight *(Joe Buck)*, Sylvia Miles *(Cass)*, John McGiver *(Mr. O'Daniel)*, Brenda Vaccaro *(Shirley)*, Barnard Hughes *(Towny)*, Ruth White *(Sally Buck)*, Jennifer Salt *(Annie)*, Gil Rankin *(Woodsy Niles)*, Gary Owens

p, Jerome Hellman; d, John Schlesinger; w, Waldo Salt (based on the novel by James Leo Herlihy); ph, Adam Holender (DeLuxe Color); ed, Hugh A. Robertson; m, John Barry; prod d, John Robert Lloyd; fx, Dick Smith; cos, Ann Roth

AA Best Picture; AAN Best Actor: Dustin Hoffman; *AAN Best Actor:* Jon Voight; *AAN Best Supporting Actress:* Sylvia Miles; *AA Best Director:* John Schlesinger; *AA Best Adapted Screenplay:* Waldo Salt; *AAN Best Film Editing:* Hugh A. Robertson

MIDNIGHT COWBOY was the only "X"-rated picture ever to win an Oscar as Best Picture. The rating was later changed to an "R" and, by today's standards, might almost be considered a "PG-13." The film presents New York at its seamiest and, though it includes one very funny parody of a bohemian party, it's mostly pretty downbeat stuff.

Joe Buck (Voight), a restless dishwasher in a tiny Texas burg, is convinced that he can use his sexual prowess to satisfy all of the rich New York women who don't know what real loving is like. He bids farewell to his Lone Star pals (including Salt, the screenwriter's daughter) and heads for the Big Apple. Arriving in New York, he picks up and beds down with a blowsy blonde (Miles), but she doesn't have any money. Soon, tubercular street hustler "Ratso" Rizzo (Hoffman) convinces Joe that what he needs is a manager. Although Joe isn't crazy about having to service a closeted gay Christian (McGiver), he and Rizzo soon become as close as George and Lenny in OF MICE AND MEN, talking about how they're going to move to Florida once they've hit it big.

After the success of THE GRADUATE and the disaster of MADIGAN'S MILLIONS, Hoffman was very picky about his roles and refused several parts that were not unlike the young man who was seduced by Mrs. Robinson. He wanted a part that was unique, and certainly found it in the role of Rizzo. Voight had appeared on Broadway in "The Sound of Music" and a couple of forgettable films (HOUR OF THE GUN, FEARLESS FRANK, OUT OF IT) before achieving acclaim with this role. Talented Englishman Schlesinger had an unerring eye for capturing the grimy reality of New York, even if his directorial style is more jittery than is really necessary. In a small role as one of the partygoers, notice songwriter Paul Jabara, who later won an Oscar for "Last Dance" for the forgettable THANK GOD IT'S FRIDAY. Good work by jazz harmonicist Jean "Toots" Theilemans helps the mood immensely. Several songs provided background, and one of them—"Everybody's Talking" (Fred Neil, sung by Harry Nilsson)—was a hit.

MIDNIGHT EXPRESS   *DVD*
1978 120m c Prison/Biography   ★★★★
Casablanca (U.K.)   R

Brad Davis *(Billy Hayes)*, Randy Quaid *(Jimmy Booth)*, Bo Hopkins *(Tex)*, John Hurt *(Max)*, Paul Smith *(Hamidou)*, Mike Kellin *(Mr. Hayes)*, Norbert Weisser *(Erich)*, Irene Miracle *(Susan)*, Paolo Bonacelli *(Rifki)*, Michael Ensign *(Stanley Daniels)*

p, David Puttnam, Alan Marshall; d, Alan Parker; w, Oliver Stone (based on the book by Billy Hayes, William Hoffer); ph, Michael Seresin (Eastmancolor); ed, Gerry Hambling; m, Giorgio Moroder; prod d, Geoffrey Kirkland; art d, Evan Hercules; cos, Milena Canonero, Bobby Lavender

AAN Best Picture; AAN Best Supporting Actor: John Hurt; AAN Best Director: Alan Parker; AA Best Adapted Screenplay: Oliver Stone; AAN Best Film Editing: Gerry Hambling; AA Best Original Score: Giorgio Moroder

Riveting from the word go. The acting is superb, the direction is excellent, and Moroder's score is exhilarating. Based on the true life story of Billy Hayes (who later became an actor), it begins as he (played by Davis) and girlfriend Susan (Miracle) are about to leave for home after a trip to Turkey. On the alert for drug smugglers, officials at the airport catch Hayes with blocks of hashish taped to his body. In a brilliantly tense scene he is herded at gunpoint to a room where he is stripped and interrogated, then taken to a fierce Turkish prison. Here comfort means a night when someone isn't brutally raped or beaten. Hayes meets many of the other inmates, including a few Westerners in there for the same drug raps: American Jimmy (Quaid), Englishman Max (Hurt), and Scandinavian Erich (Weisser), a gay man with whom Hayes has a brief sexual liason. Billy's father (Kellin) attempts to get his son out of jail, but the Turkish legal system is bent on making him an example to other potential smugglers. In a sensational courtroom scene Hayes berates his captors with an obscene lambasting of the judges, most of whom don't speak English and have no idea what he's saying. He is sentenced to more years than he thought he'd get and, once remanded to the jail, makes plans to take the "midnight express," i.e. escape.

All the performances are top-notch. Quaid's portrayal of the slightly deranged American is outstanding; Hurt, as the addicted Englishman, is a study in understatement; Weisser is totally believable; and Smith must rank a close second to Hume Cronyn's Captain Munsey in BRUTE FORCE for sheer evil in a prison official. But the standout is Davis, who is given the task of displaying just about every emotion known to man. MIDNIGHT EXPRESS is occasionally a bit too stylish for its own good, something that may have been an indulgence on the part of director Parker. He is nonetheless, a talent to be reckoned with, and both he and editor Hambling won British Film Academy Awards for their work.

MIDNIGHT IN THE GARDEN OF GOOD AND EVIL   *DVD*
1997 155m   c   Crime/Drama   ★★½
Malpaso/Silver Pictures   (U.S.)   R

Kevin Spacey *(Jim Williams)*, John Cusack *(John Kelso)*, Jack Thompson *(Sonny Seiler)*, Jude Law *(Billy Hanson)*, The Lady Chablis *(Chablis Deveau)*, Alison Eastwood *(Mandy Nichols)*, Irma P. Hall *(Minerva)*, Paul Hipp *(Joe Odom)*, Dorothy Loudon *(Serena Dawes)*, Anne Haney *(Margaret Williams)*

p, Clint Eastwood; d, Clint Eastwood; w, John Lee Hancock (based on the novel by John Berendt); ph, Jack N. Green; ed, Joel Cox; m, Lennie Niehaus; prod d, Henry Bumstead; art d, Jack G. Taylor Jr., James J. Murakami; fx, Joe Pancake, Steve Riley, Industrial Light & Magic

Long, lumpy, and sadly charmless, Clint Eastwood's adaptation of John Berendt's nonfiction portrait of Savannah, GA, refracted through the prism of a scandalous true-crime story, tramples all over the silkily seductive voice that made the bestselling book so compulsively readable.

In order to compress and give linear structure to Berendt's loosely connected web of gossip, screenwriter Lee Hancock invented the character of writer John Kelso (John Cusack), who's sent to Savannah to cover the lavish annual Christmas soiree of wealthy, homosexual antiques dealer Jim Williams (Kevin Spacey). After the party, Williams shoots his lover, volatile hustler Billy Hanson (Jude Law)—characterized by one local harpy as "a good time that had not yet been had by all"—and claims it was in self-defense. Kelso decides to hang around and see if there's a book in the

trial, the better to serve as the audience's guide through a gallery of hothouse personalities as bizarrely warped as wax figures in some eccentric house of horrors.

Cusack, who's apparently meant to be from New York, spends most of the film with his tiny mouth hanging open in an unlikely comic-book expression of shock at the baroque goings-on. The Southern Gothic material is all in Berendt's eerily haunting book, but onscreen his cast of fascinating eccentrics quickly descends into pointless grotesquerie, in part because time constraints force most of them into walk-on parts. The film's unquestioned star is transvestite performer The Lady Chablis, a pivotal figure in Berendt's book who plays herself in the film and is an absolutely riveting—if not altogether likable—example of what it means to turn life into performance.

MIDNIGHT RUN   *DVD*
1988 122m   c   Comedy/Crime   ★★★½
City Lights   (U.S.)   R

Robert De Niro *(Jack Walsh)*, Charles Grodin *(Jonathan Mardukas)*, Yaphet Kotto *(Alonzo Mosely)*, John Ashton *(Marvin Dorfler)*, Dennis Farina *(Jimmy Serrano)*, Joe Pantoliano *(Eddie Moscone)*, Richard Foronjy *(Tony Darvo)*, Robert Miranda *(Joey)*, Jack Kehoe *(Jerry Geisler)*, Wendy Phillips *(Gail)*

p, Martin Brest; d, Martin Brest; w, George Gallo; ph, Donald Thorin (Astro Color, Metrocolor); ed, Billy Weber, Chris Lebenzon, Michael Tronick; m, Danny Elfman; prod d, Angelo Graham; fx, Roy Arbogast; cos, Gloria Gresham

A thoroughly engaging action film, MIDNIGHT RUN boasts a superb cast that transforms its rather mundane story line into something memorable, funny, and moving. Tough, foul-mouthed bounty hunter Jack Walsh (Robert De Niro) is hired by bail bondsman Eddie Moscone (Joe Pantoliano) to bring back Mafia accountant Jonathan Mardukas (Charles Grodin), who has embezzled $15 million from the Los Angeles mob, given the money to charity, and skipped bail. In an extended cross-country chase, Walsh, flat broke, drags Mardukas on board nearly every modern mode of transportation available in an effort to avoid their pursuers and get back to L.A. so Walsh can collect his money. As the plot takes a series of complicated twists and turns, the two men's personalities and relationship develop. BEVERLY HILLS COP director Martin Brest has allowed the actors to improvise, and their resulting interaction is more realistic, funny, and surprising than that of any buddy film released in the last several years. The characters in MIDNIGHT RUN feel real—not only as if they existed before we met them, but also as if they will continue after the movie ends.

MIDSUMMER NIGHT'S DREAM, A
1935 132m   bw   Fantasy/Comedy   ★★★
Warner Bros.   (U.S.)

James Cagney *(Bottom)*, Dick Powell *(Lysander)*, Joe E. Brown *(Flute)*, Jean Muir *(Helena)*, Hugh Herbert *(Snout)*, Ian Hunter *(Theseus)*, Frank McHugh *(Quince)*, Victor Jory *(Oberon)*, Olivia de Havilland *(Hermia)*, Ross Alexander *(Demetrius)*

p, Max Reinhardt; d, Max Reinhardt, William Dieterle; w, Charles Kenyon, Mary C. McCall Jr. (based on the play by William Shakespeare); ph, Hal Mohr; ed, Ralph Dawson; m, Felix Mendelssohn; art d, Anton Grot; fx, Fred Jackman, Byron Haskin, H.F. Koenekamp; chor, Bronislava Nijinska, Nini Theilade; cos, Max Ree

AAN Best Picture; AA Best Cinematography: Hal Mohr; AA Best Film Editing: Ralph Dawson

Cigar-chomping Jack Warner does Shakespeare? What fools these mortals be! Theatrical genius Max Reinhardt had successfully staged the play in Europe and felt that A MID-SUMMER NIGHT'S DREAM was ideal for film, because the fairy sequences offered the proper magic for celluloid. Reinhardt, though, had no idea how to shoot this masterpiece, and blurry rushes of several forest scenes suggested that entrusting him with $1.5 million was unwise. So experienced Hollywood man Dieterle and a new cinematographer were added; Hal Mohr's lensing of the film (the only time a write-in ever won an Oscar) turned out to be its one real triumph. Years later, Powell would claim that he never really understood his lines. While such a remark may be after-the-fact cynicism, it does speak to the generally strained acting from a cast of Hollywoodians unschooled in blank verse. Above all else, this play needs inspiration to fly; the acting *must* be daringly effortless, clownishly gossamer, and if there's one thing Cagney and pals are not, it's gossamer. One would think that de Havilland, who had played Hermia onstage, would steal it, but she's too new to films to have refined her technique, and her emoting seems as heavy as everyone else's. Rooney is one of the few who really looks like he's having fun, but he's having *too* much fun and it begins to grate. (Life imitates art: the high-flying youngster broke his leg tobogganing during a production break and had to be wheeled around on an unseen bicycle for much of the shoot.) Cagney, Muir and Brown have their moments, but only Hunter and a few others with classical backgrounds work against the private school class play feel to the film. Typical Warners touch: the delicate original ballet sequences by Bronislava Nijinska and Nini Theilade (the lead ballerina in the film) were cut and re-choreographed in the Busby Berkeley mold.

MIDWINTER'S TALE, A
1995 98m bw Comedy ★★★
Midwinter Films/Kenneth Branagh Limited (U.K.) R

Richard Briers (*Henry Wakefield*), Hetta Charnley (*Molly*), Joan Collins (*Margaretta D'Arcy*), Nicholas Farrell (*Tom Newman*), Mark Hadfield (*Vernon Spatch*), Gerard Horan (*Carnforth Greville*), Celia Imrie (*Fadge*), Michael Maloney (*Joe Harper*), Jennifer Saunders (*Nancy Crawford*), Julia Sawalha (*Nina*)

p, David Barron; d, Kenneth Branagh; w, Kenneth Branagh; ph, Roger Lanser; ed, Neil Farrell; m, Jimmy Yuill; prod d, Tim Harvey; cos, Caroline Harris

Kenneth Branagh has written and directed, but chosen not to star in this cozy variation on the old "Brotherhood of Actors/Thespian Happy Families" theme.

Struggling actor Joe Harper (Michael Maloney) is determined to direct and star in a production of *Hamlet*. With the reluctant help of his more commercially minded agent, Margaretta D'Arcy (Joan Collins), he puts together the most motley crew imaginable. Air-headed Nina (Julia Sawalha) is to be his Ophelia; veteran hack Henry (Richard Briers) is Claudius; intense Method monster Tom (Nicholas Farrel) essays a myriad of roles, including Laertes and Fortinbras; drunken, lovable Carnforth (Gerard Horan) is Rosencranz and Guildenstern; and campy Terry du Bois (John Sessions) will do Gertrude … in drag. On a shoestring budget, they descend upon a small English village and begin rehearsals in the local church. The characters, of course, bring their own considerable personal agendas with them, and the rehearsal process is marked by all manner of fits, starts, and stormy blow-ups.

Branagh's way with comedic direction could best be described as unsubtle. His love for the profession of acting is, however, always evident as the performers are given every opportunity to shine, some more so than others. Briers makes a funny old curmudgeon, and Collins is cheekily assured as a hustling ten-percenter, yakking numbers on a cell phone while keeping her own figure in tip-top shape on an exercise machine. There's nothing really new or inordinately hilarious in the cartoonish black-and-white proceedings, but Branagh directs at a whiz-bang pace that keeps this likeable comedy bumping along over the script's many weak spots, clunky punchlines, and cliches.

MIGHTY APHRODITE
DVD
1995 95m c Comedy ★★★
Sweetland Films (U.S.) R

Woody Allen (*Lenny*), Helena Bonham Carter (*Amanda*), F. Murray Abraham (*Leader*), Claire Bloom (*Amanda's Mother*), Olympia Dukakis (*Jocasta*), Michael Rapaport (*Kevin*), Mira Sorvino (*Linda Ash*), David Ogden Stiers (*Laius*), Jack Warden (*Tiresias*), Peter Weller (*Jerry Bender*)

p, Robert Greenhut; d, Woody Allen; w, Woody Allen; ph, Carlo Di Palma; ed, Susan E. Morse; m, Dick Hyman; prod d, Santo Loquasto; art d, Tom Warren; chor, Graciela Daniele; cos, Jeffrey Kurland

AA Best Supporting Actress: Mira Sorvino; *AAN Best Original Screenplay:* Woody Allen

In MIGHTY APHRODITE, a nerd's revenge fantasy—yet again—from putative genius Woody Allen, our hero pits his romantic sensibilities against feckless women and crass consumerism. Yet again. And lest we forget how *serious* he is deep down, he gives us a Greek chorus.

We know they're The Chorus because they look like tag-sale statuary (if you can overlook the distinctly post-Classical schnozzes sported by F. Murray Abraham and Olympia Dukakis), and they mill around in a boulder-strewn sandpit spouting strophes— or what might pass for strophes in the Borscht Belt. Meanwhile, pity poor Lenny (Allen). He's not a writer but a *sports*writer. And a scrawny one who just happens to be followed around by this Greek chorus that comments on his disagreeable life. Tragedy and humiliation lurk down every alley. His marriage is coming apart. But when his wife, Amanda (Helena Bonham Caretr), isn't preoccupied with the blandishments of suave artmeister Jerry (Peter Weller), she demands a baby. A baby! Lenny doesn't want a baby. They're both too busy to deal with a pregnancy. And when Amanda suggests adoption, Lenny's offended. Nevertheless, he relents, and years later goes in search of the baby's mother, whom he finds in the person of hooker and occasional porno star Linda Ash, aka Judy Cum, a latter-day Irma La Douce played by Mira Sorvino.

The good news is that MIGHTY APHRODITE comes alive when Sorvino is onscreen. Her Linda is the largest cute woman on Earth, a six-foot Minnie Mouse with a closetful of wigs and high heels who voices her comic suspicions about Lenny in a voice that sounds like it was dubbed by Kukla. The bad news? As Woody/Lenny dallies with this conspicuously younger woman, making his case for dumb, beautiful, and innocent, it's impossible not to remember details of Allen's private life that we'd all rather forget. Though he'd done two films since the Mia/Soon Yi fiasco, only now has the production cycle caught up with Woody's world. Inevitably, this movie plays like an invitation to hear the story, *his* way.

MIGHTY JOE YOUNG
1949 94m bw Adventure/Fantasy ★★
Arko (U.S.)

Terry Moore (*Jill Young*), Ben Johnson (*Gregg*), Robert Armstrong (*Max O'Hara*), Frank McHugh (*Windy*), Douglas Fowley (*Jones*), Denis Green (*Crawford*), Paul Guilfoyle (*Smith*), Nestor Paiva (*Brown*), Regis Toomey (*John Young*), Lora Lee Michel (*Jill as a Girl*)

p, John Ford, Merian C. Cooper; d, Ernest B. Schoedsack; w, Ruth Rose (based on a story by Merian C. Cooper); ph, J. Roy Hunt; ed, Ted Cheesman; fx, Willis O'Brien, Ray Harryhausen, Harold Stine, Bert Willis, Linwood Dunn, Pete Peterson, George Lofgren, Marcel Delgado, Fitch Fulton; cos, Adele Balkan

AA Best Special Effects

Though produced by the same people responsible for the classic KING KONG, MIGHTY JOE YOUNG is a pale imitation. Moore lives in the jungles of Africa and raises Mighty Joe, an extremely large gorilla. Up pops Broadway producer Armstrong (a star in KING KONG), who is looking for a "knock 'em dead" act for his new nightclub in Hollywood. Armstrong and his bunch bring Moore and Joe to the "City of Dreams" and build an act around the beast. As part of the act, Moore plays "Beautiful Dreamer" on a piano while the gorilla holds her above her head, and is pitted against 10 wrestlers in a game of tug o' war. Some drunk patrons give Joe some drinks, which spurs him to go on a rampage. The gorilla makes up for his folly, however, by rescuing children from a burning orphanage. He then goes back to live peacefully in Africa. While the nightclub sequence is great camp and the Oscar-winning special effects by Willis O'Brien (KING KONG) and Ray Harryhausen are top-notch, the film doesn't capture the magic of KING KONG. The orphanage fire had originally been tinted.

MIGHTY WIND, A

2003 100m c Comedy/Musical ★★★½
Castle Rock Entertainment (U.S.) PG-13

Bob Balaban *(Jonathan Steinbloom)*, Michael McKean *(Jerry Palter)*, Catherine O'Hara *(Mickey Crabbe)*, Harry Shearer *(Mark Shubb)*, Eugene Levy *(Mitch Cohen)*, Ed Begley Jr. *(Lars Olfen)*, Jennifer Coolidge *(Amber Cole)*, Paul Dooley *(George Menschell)*, Christopher Guest *(Alan Barrows)*, John Michael Higgins *(Terry Bohner)*

p, Karen Murphy; d, Christopher Guest; w, Christopher Guest, Eugene Levy; ph, Arlene Donnelly Nelson; ed, Robert Leighton; m, Jeffrey C.J. Vanston; prod d, Joseph T. Garrity; art d, Pat Tagliaferro; fx, Christopher Walkowiak; cos, Durinda Wood

AAN Best Original Song: "A Kiss at the End of the Rainbow"; Michael McKean; Annette O'Toole

Christopher Guest does for folk music what THIS IS SPINAL TAP did for heavy metal in this affectionate send up of the early-'60s "folk revival" and its attendant boomer nostalgia. And like SPINAL TAP (which Guest co-wrote), you don't need to know the music to get the joke.

Culled from many hours of material improvised along a scripted outline, the film covers two weeks in the life of Jonathan Steinbloom (Bob Balaban) as he scrambles to organize a memorial concert for his late father, beloved folk-music producer Irv Steinbloom. Jonathan reunites the Folksmen (SPINAL TAP-sters Guest, Michael McKean and Harry Shearer) and the romantic-couple balladeers Mitch & Mickey (Eugene Levy, Catherine O'Hara), and calls in the New Main Street Singers, the sort of smiling, overly upbeat group in matching sweatervests that might still be playing state fairs.

As in his BEST IN SHOW and WAITING FOR GUFF-MAN, Guest and his actors so fully empathize with the world he's gently parodying that it's sometimes hard to tell it from the actual thing. Here, too, they zero in on aficionados' quirks and the music's conventions with hilarious accuracy, from the naively sincere proclamations of peace, love, and working-man authenticity to the homogenized packaging of folk-pop. Yet even the most self-absorbed characters here are never pathetic, and the movie's climax is genuinely and unexpectedly touching. The songs, too, are great—some are exaggerately precious, others could have come right off albums of the era.

MIKEY AND NICKY

1976 119m c Drama ★★½
Paramount (U.S.) R

Peter Falk *(Mikey)*, John Cassavetes *(Nicky)*, Ned Beatty *(Kinney)*, Rose Arrick *(Annie)*, Carol Grace *(Nell)*, William Hickey *(Sid Fine)*, Sanford Meisner *(Dave Resnick)*, Joyce Van Patten *(Jan)*, M. Emmet Walsh *(Bus Driver)*, Sy Travers *(Hotel Clerk)*

p, Michael Hausman; d, Elaine May; w, Elaine May; ph, Victor J. Kemper (Panavision, Movielab Color); ed, John Carter, Sheldon Kahn; m, Johann Strauss; prod d, Paul Sylbert

There is much to enjoy in this movie, but just as much to yawn over. One has the feeling that this was a play that was never produced on stage but went directly to the screen from the typewriter. Since so much of it is dialogue with very little cinematic action, it just feels stagebound. Cassavetes and Falk are two small-time thugs who have been friends since their youth. Cassavetes is going to be killed by Beatty, the unlikely hit man in the service of boss Meisner (who was just about everyone's acting coach in New York at one time). Cassavetes gets in touch with Falk after trying to get help from his estranged wife, Van Patten, and his current amour, Grace. Falk is apparently going to help Cassavetes get away from the potential assassin, though we are often struck by Falk's words and actions and not sure if he is friend or foe. Some very touching scenes punctuate the camaraderie, but the film is essentially far too long, self-indulgent, and talky to elicit much emotional response. It's a character study that would be at home in an East Village theater. It's hard to say where the script ends and the improvisation begins, as in so many of Cassavetes' films. The executive producer was veteran TV executive Bud Austin, who had run Paramount Television before moving into feature production. Very foul language and some painful sequences make this hardly fit for anyone with a priggish attitude. This was the third film directed by May and the most experimental. Her first two were A NEW LEAF (which she also wrote and costarred in) and THE HEARTBREAK KID, with a script by Neil Simon and some terrific performances by Jeannie Berlin, Charles Grodin, and Cybill Shepherd.

MILDRED PIERCE

1945 111m bw Drama ★★★★★
Warner Bros. (U.S.)

Joan Crawford *(Mildred Pierce)*, Jack Carson *(Wally Fay)*, Zachary Scott *(Monte Beragon)*, Eve Arden *(Ida)*, Ann Blyth *(Veda Pierce)*, Bruce Bennett *(Bert Pierce)*, George Tobias *(Mr. Chris)*, Lee Patrick *(Maggie Binderhof)*, Moroni Olsen *(Inspector Peterson)*, Jo Ann Marlowe *(Kay Pierce)*

p, Jerry Wald; d, Michael Curtiz; w, Ranald MacDougall (based on the novel by James M. Cain); ph, Ernest Haller; ed, David Weisbart; m, Max Steiner; art d, Anton Grot; fx, Willard Van Enger; cos, Milo Anderson

AAN Best Picture; AA Best Actress: Joan Crawford; *AAN Best Supporting Actress:* Eve Arden; *AAN Best Supporting Actress:* Ann Blyth; *AAN Best Screenplay:* Ranald MacDougall; *AAN Best B/W Cinematography:* Ernest Haller

Impeccable, bleak gloss, with the supreme Crawford engineering the greatest comeback of them all. MILDRED PIERCE is one of the finest noir soap operas ever, with the queen of pathos shouldering the storm alone; her efforts snagged the golden statuette as 1945's Best Actress. To begin with, MILDRED was leftovers: Barbara Stanwyck, Bette Davis and Ann Sheridan turned down the role, but producer Wald gambled on MGM-bounced Crawford, and the film swept the box offices, returning $5 million to Warners and putting Crawford back on top as the hottest star in town.

Mildred's marriage to Bert (Bennett) has gone sour. While she dotes on their two daughters, chiefly the older Veda (Blyth), Bert finds pleasant company with Mrs. Biederhof (Patrick). Leaving Bert, Mildred finds work as a waitress to misguidedly keep the vicious, snobbish Veda in fancy duds. Ever ambitious, Mildred slaves her way up to a chain of successful restaurants and takes up with classy playboy Monte Beragon (Scott). She mistakenly weds him, and he goes through her fortune like a plague of locusts. The crushing blow comes when Mildred learns that Monte has been having an affair with Veda behind her back.

Everything about MILDRED PIERCE is first-rate, from stellar production values to Curtiz's marvelously paced direction, which refuses to allow sentiment to rule the story. The MacDougall script, adapted from Cain's terse novel, is adult and literate, with plenty of sharp dialogue. The Curtiz string-pulling is greatly aided by Grot's imposing sets, Haller's moody photography and Steiner's haunting score. Bravely cresting the waves of disaster is a mature Crawford in a real tour de force, defying the industry to write her off as washed up. She's matched every slap of the way by Blyth, here giving the performance of *her* career.

The support in MILDRED is, without exception, expertly handled. Scott is an exceptionally attractive snake and Arden turned in a definitive job as Crawford's wise-cracking pal. Two peak scenes among aficionados of Saint Joan: Veda smacks Mildred; Mildred calls the police. Unforgettable.

MILKY WAY, THE
(LA VIA LATTEA)
1969 105m c   Religious   ★★★½
Greenwich/Fraia   (France/Italy)   PG

Paul Frankeur *(Pierre)*, Laurent Terzieff *(Jean)*, Alain Cuny *(Man with Cape)*, Edith Scob *(Virgin Mary)*, Bernard Verley *(Jesus)*, Francois Maistre *(French Priest)*, Claude Cerval *(Brigadier)*, Muni *(Mother Superior)*, Julien Bertheau *(Maitre d'Hotel)*, Ellen Bahl *(Mme. Garnier)*

p, Serge Silberman; d, Luis Bunuel; w, Luis Bunuel, Jean-Claude Carriere; ph, Christian Matras (Eastmancolor); ed, Louisette Hautecoeur; m, Luis Bunuel; art d, Pierre Guffroy; cos, Jacqueline Guyot, Francoise Tournafond

The most overtly religious film in Luis Bunuel's *oeuvre*, THE MILKY WAY is an allegorical journey through the history of Catholicism that follows a pair of travelers—the somewhat pious Pierre (Paul Frankeur) and the younger, more skeptical Jean (Laurent Terzieff)—as they undertake a pilgrimage across Spain to the tomb of Saint James. En route, they meet any number of religious figures, including a caped, God-like figure (Alain Cuny) with a midget, the Virgin Mary (Edith Scob), Jesus (Bernard Verley), a bishop (Jean-Claude Carriere, Bunuel's screenwriting collaborator), a sadistic Marquis (Michel Piccoli), a prostitute (Delphine Seyrig), and even the Devil (Pierre Clementi). This comical film will make any viewer question his beliefs—from religious fanatic to rabid atheist. While it may seem strange that Bunuel, a lifetime surrealist and professed atheist, would produce such a work, the filmmaker remarked in his autobiography, *My Last Sigh*, that THE MILKY WAY "evokes the search for truth, as well as the necessity of abandoning it as soon as you've found it." If that doesn't shed some light on Bunuel's intent, then perhaps his most famously ambiguous statement will: "Thank God I'm an atheist."

MILLER'S CROSSING
1990 115m c   Crime   ★★★½
Circle Films/Ted and Jim Pedas-Ben   R
Berenholtz-Bill Durkin   (U.S.)

Gabriel Byrne *(Tom Reagan)*, Marcia Gay Harden *(Verna)*, John Turturro *(Bernie Bernbaum)*, Jon Polito *(Johnny Caspar)*, J.E. Freeman *(Eddie Dane)*, Albert Finney *(Leo)*, Mike Starr *(Frankie)*, Al Mancini *(Tic-Tac)*, Richard Woods *(Mayor Dale Levander)*, Thomas Toner *(O'Doole)*

p, Ethan Coen; d, Joel Coen; w, Joel Coen, Ethan Coen; ph, Barry Sonnenfeld (Duart Color); ed, Michael R. Miller; m, Carter Burwell; prod d, Dennis Gassner; art d, Leslie McDonald; fx, Image Engineering, Peter Chesney; cos, Richard Hornung

Guns, booze, fast women—timeworn gangster film cliches given a fresh twist in this, the third offering from Joel and Ethan Coen. A gang war is brewing in the anonymous town run by Leo (Finney), a tough but sentimental Irishman, and his acerbic right-hand man, Tom Reagan (Byrne). The Italians are the new kids on the block, and they're sensitive about it. Johnny Caspar (Polito) is particularly thin-skinned, and he's mad as hell because small-time chiseler Bernie Bernbaum (Turturro) is cutting in on his gambling action. Caspar wants Bernie murdered, but Leo won't hear of it; he's promised Bernie's tough-as-nails sister, Verna (Harden), that he'll look out for her brother. Verna is the love of Leo's life, but she's also sleeping with Tom. Meanwhile, Tom, a drinker and gambler, is deeply in debt to his bookie, who's putting the screws to him. When Leo and Tom have a falling out over Verna, Tom offers his services to Caspar. Forced to prove his loyalty by killing Bernie, Tom fakes the murder, only to have Bernie turn around and attempt to blackmail him.

Surprisingly, the Coens resisted the Hollywood dictum that the protagonist must be sympathetic. Byrne's Tom is a man of principles—smart, loyal and willing to gratify his own ambitions through Leo. But he's also a drunk and a gambler. What's more, he sleeps with Verna and murders her brother. Tom has his reasons, and they're quite reasonable, but what's remarkable is that the Coens trust their audience to understand him.

While BLOOD SIMPLE paid homage to film noir, and RAISING ARIZONA put a wacky, post-modernist spin on the screwball comedy, MILLER'S CROSSING attempts to both sum up, and revivify, the gangster genre. It takes place in an artificial world constructed largely from the mythology of other movies, and, though it's both seamless and stylish, some find it a little too self-conscious for its own good.

MILLION, THE
(LE MILLION)
1931 83m bw Comedy   ★★★★★
Tobis   (France)

Annabella *(Beatrice)*, Rene Lefevre *(Michel)*, Paul Olivier *("Father Tulipe" Crochard, a Gangster)*, Louis Allibert *(Prosper)*, Constantin Stroesco *(Sopranelli)*, Odette Talazac *(La Chanteuse)*, Vanda Greville *(Vanda)*, Raymond Cordy *(Taxi Driver)*

d, Rene Clair; w, Rene Clair (based on a musical play by Georges Berr, M. Guillemaud); ph, Georges Perinal, Georges Raulet; m, Armand Bernard, Philippe Pares, Georges Van Parys; art d, Lazare Meerson

Perhaps Rene Clair's most appealing film, and an extremely inventive one in the bargain. One of the string of superb films this fine French director made in the 1920s and 1930s, this is a nonstop comic chase through a studio set of Paris (designed by Clair's collaborator Lazare Meerson) to find a winning lottery ticket left in the pocket of a discarded jacket. Generally considered Clair's masterpiece (though A NOUS LA LIBERTE also has its supporters), the film is a sustained comic delight. As in the previous UNDER THE ROOFS OF PARIS and his subsequent A NOUS LA LIBERTE, Clair creates a wholly original world of song and sound that completely defies realism. He also manages quite a few satiric touches which belie his background in the Surrealist and Dada movements of the 1920s. Although such uses of sound effects as the noise of a football game dubbed in over one particularly frantic chase have since been repeated, they still enchant today. The camerawork too, is amazingly supple for a period in which bulky sound recording devices turned so many films into stagy bores, and the story simply floats along as a result. Annabella and Rene Lefevre are immensely winning in the leading roles, and are backed by a solid supporting cast. One of the truly great early sound films, it was an international success with both critics and public.

MILLION DOLLAR BABY *DVD*

2004 132m   c   Sports/Drama   ★★★★
Lakeshore Entertainment/Malapaso/Ruddy Morgan   PG-13
Productions/Warner Bros.   (U.S.)

Clint Eastwood (Frankie Dunn), Hilary Swank (Maggie Fitzgerald), Morgan Freeman (Eddie "Scrap-Iron" Dupris), Jay Baruchel (Danger Barch), Mike Colter (Big Willie Little), Lucia Rijker (Billie "The Blue Bear"), Brian O'Byrne (Father Horvak), Anthony Mackie (Shawrelle Berry), Margo Martindale (Earline Fitzgerald), Riki Lindhome (Mardell Fitzgerald)

p, Clint Eastwood, Paul Haggis, Tom Rosenberg, Albert S. Ruddy; d, Clint Eastwood; w, Paul Haggis (based upon stories from Rope Burns by F.X. Toole); ph, Tom Stern; ed, Joel Cox; m, Clint Eastwood; prod d, Henry Bumstead; art d, Jack G. Taylor Jr.; fx, Steven Riley; cos, Deborah Hopper

AA Best Picture; AA Best Actress: Hilary Swank; AA Best Director: Clint Eastwood; AAN Best Actor: Clint Eastwood; AAN Best Adapted Screenplay: Paul Haggis; AAN Best Film Editing: Joel Cox

Adapted from F.X. Toole's collection Rope Burns: Stories from the Corner, Clint Eastwood's story of loss and deliverance is a fine, understated piece of storytelling but be warned: Eastwood has a third-act sucker punch in reserve.

Frankie Dunn (Eastwood) has spent his whole life around the ring, first as a cut man then as a trainer, manager and owner of a run-down Los Angeles gym. Deeply estranged from his only daughter, Frankie has only one real relationship, with former boxer Eddie "Scrap Iron" Dupris (Morgan Freeman). Frankie has just lost protege Big Willie Little (Mike Colter) to a slicker manager when 31-year-old Ozark Mountain girl Maggie Fitzgerald (Hilary Swank) starts badgering him to train her. All her life, Maggie has doggedly pursued a single idea about how to better her circumstances, but she's stuck on the bottom rung of a punishing sport, rudderless and so grindingly poor she scavenges table scraps while waitressing. Frankie wants no part of Maggie, but she wears him down and he takes her farther than she could ever have dreamed, at which point their story takes a turn that could have been absurdly sentimental were it not handled with such solid, matter-of-fact craftsmanship and the occasional flash of grace.

The film isn't flawless; a subplot involving scrawny, mentally challenged Danger Barch (Jay Baruchel), whose delusions can only survive in the fragile sanctuary of Frankie's gym, is heavy-handed and unnecessary. But overall it's a minor misstep in a film that transforms formulaic elements into such authentically resonant drama. Even Scrap's voice-over, which at first feels like an unsubtle shortcut to Frankie's history and inner life, is eventually placed in a bracingly poignant light.

MILLIONS *DVD*

2004 97m   c   Comedy/Drama/Crime   ★★★½
UK Film Council/BBC Films/Mission Pictures/   PG
Inside Track/Pathe Pictures/Ingenious Media   (U.S./U.K.)

Alex Etel (Damian), Lewis McGibbon (Anthony), James Nesbitt (Ronnie), Daisy Donovan (Dorothy), Christopher Fulford (The Poor Man), Pearce Quigley (Community Policeman), Jane Hogarth (Mum), Alun Armstrong (St. Peter), Enzo Cilenti (St. Francis), Nasser Memarzia (St. Joseph)

p, Graham Broadbent, Andrew Hauptman, Damian Jones; d, Danny Boyle; w, Frank Cottrell Boyce; ph, Anthony Dod Mantle; ed, Chris Gill; m, John Murphy; prod d, Mark Tildesley; art d, Mark Digby; fx, Peter Bach, Richard Conway, Evan Green-Hughes, Mark White, Nigel Williamson; cos, Susannah Buxton

UK director Danny Boyle turns his talents to an unabashed family film, though fans will detect an echo of his ferocious SHALLOW GRAVE. Screenwriter Frank Cottrell Boyce's altogether gentler story, however, allows goodness to trump greed when unexpected riches drop into the lap of motherless seven-year-old Damian Cunningham (Alex Etel).

Damian's grieving father (James Nesbitt) has just moved Damian and his brother, nine-year-old Anthony (Lewis McGibbon), to suburban Manchester in hopes of making a fresh start. Pragmatic Anthony slyly parlays his mom's death into gifts of goodies from sympathetic adults, while the dreamy Damian retreats into the lives of the saints, who become as vividly real to him as his neighbors and classmates. In Damian's off-kilter imagination, Saints Clare (Kathryn Pogson), Francis (Enzo Cilenti), Nicholas (Harry Kirkham), and even St. Peter (Alun Armstrong) himself are as imperfect and accessible as anyone else. When a gym bag stuffed with cash crashes into his makeshift clubhouse shortly before Christmas, Damian naturally presumes it's divine intervention. Anthony tries to figure out how best to spend the loot before England converts to the euro and all that lovely money becomes nothing but worthless paper. The arrival of a menacing stranger (Christopher Fulford) adds a note of danger and sets in motion the film's satisfying climax.

Boyle's flamboyant style is evident in the film's handling of Damian's rich inner life, from the quirky saints with their bobbing halos to his fantasy of being rocketed to Africa in his cardboard clubhouse. But this cheeky fable rests on the slender shoulders of Etel and McGibbon, and the lovely, natural performances Boyle elicits from them are the film's real miracle.

MIN AND BILL

1930 66m   bw   Drama/Comedy   ★★★★
MGM   (U.S.)

Marie Dressler (Min Divot), Wallace Beery (Bill), Dorothy Jordan (Nancy Smith), Marjorie Rambeau (Bella Pringle), Donald Dillaway (Dick Cameron), DeWitt Jennings (Groot), Russell Hopton (Alec Johnson), Frank McGlynn Sr. (Mr. Southard), Gretta Gould (Mrs. Southard), Jack Pennick (Merchant Seaman)

d, George Hill; w, Frances Marion, Marion Jackson (based on the novel Dark Star by Lorna Moon); ph, Harold Wenstrom; ed, Basil Wrangell; art d, Cedric Gibbons; cos, Rene Hubert

AA Best Actress: Marie Dressler

One of the most unlikely romantic duos ever to stroll across a screen was the pairing of 62-year-old bulldog Marie Dressler and big-bellied, 55-year-old Wallace Beery. Yet they made such a lovable couple in MIN AND BILL that they were teamed again in TUGBOAT ANNIE in 1933. Although MIN AND BILL is a heartfelt drama, most viewers recall its hilarious comedy sequences and the noisy relationship between Min (Dressler) and Bill (Beery). Min is the rough-and-tumble owner of a cheap waterfront hotel on the California coast; Bill is the local fisherman who is the object of her affections when she isn't doting on Nancy (Jordan), a sweet young girl whose mother deserted her several years previously. Nevertheless truant officers want Nancy living in a better environment and attending school regularly. Furthermore, local prohibition officers have been observing the cafe and appear ready to close it up. In a tearful scene, Nancy reluctantly leaves Min to live with the school's principal (McGlynn) and his wife (Gould). To make matters worse, Nancy's drunken, slatternly mother (Rambeau) appears on the scene, threatening Nancy's chance at happiness with the wealthy Dick Cameron Dillaway, in his film debut). Min to the rescue.

A legendary star of the stage and vaudeville, Dressler watched her silent screen stardom of the 1910s wane until she made a triumphant return in ANNA CHRISTIE earlier in 1930. As a result of her immense popular success in MIN AND BILL and half a dozen follow-up vehicles, she was to spend her last years as MGM's (indeed, the industry's) biggest star before her death from cancer in 1934. She'd still make any list of the ten most huggable stars in film history.

MINISTRY OF FEAR

1945 84m bw Mystery/Spy ★★★★
Paramount (U.S.)

Ray Milland (Stephen Neale), Marjorie Reynolds (Carla Hilfe), Carl Esmond (Willi Hilfe), Hillary Brooke (Mrs. Bellane), Percy Waram (Inspector Prentice), Dan Duryea (Cost/Travers), Alan Napier (Dr. Forrester), Erskine Sanford (Mr. Rennit), Thomas Louden (Mr. Newland), Aminta Dyne (1st Mrs. Bellaire)

p, Seton I. Miller; d, Fritz Lang; w, Seton I. Miller (based on the novel by Graham Greene); ph, Henry Sharp; ed, Archie Marshek; m, Victor Young; art d, Hans Dreier, Hal Pereira

Uncertainty and fear of the unknown are the hallmarks of this classic film noir by master director Lang, which, until the last revelation, is guaranteed to puzzle and chill the viewer. The suspense in this thriller is terrific as Lang, ever the careful craftsman, shows only what is necessary to the confusing plot. The low-key lighting and Sharp's moody cinematography are perfectly suited to the film's elaborate, Kafkaesque approach wherein shadow, silence and normally pedestrian movements, taken out of context, take on an air of evil and doom. Milland gives a spellbinding performance as a man who, ostensibly having murdered his wife, is released from an insane asylum after two years. She was ill, and he brought poison home to perform euthanasia but could not bring himself to go through with it; while his back was turned she took the fatal dose and he was convicted nevertheless. The terrors of the asylum, though, are nothing compared to the Nazi spies of the wartime England into which Milland steps. Lang, screenwriter-producer Seton Miller and Graham Greene (author of the source novel) have in store for Milland (and us) a succession of sinister seances, sinister suits, sinister scissors, sinister blind men and, best of all, a sinister cake. Eat at your own delicious risk.

MINNIE AND MOSKOWITZ   𝗗𝗩𝗗

1971 114m c Romance/Comedy/Drama ★★★½
Universal (U.S.) PG

Gena Rowlands (Minnie Moore), Seymour Cassel (Seymour Moskowitz), Val Avery (Zelmo Swift), Tim Carey (Morgan Morgan), Katherine Cassavetes (Sheba Moskowitz), Elizabeth Deering (Girl), Elsie Ames (Florence), Lady Rowlands (Georgia Moore), Holly Near (Irish), Judith Roberts (Wife)

p, Al Ruban; d, John Cassavetes; w, John Cassavetes; ph, Arthur J. Ornitz, Alric Edens, Michael D. Margulies (Technicolor); ed, Robert Heffernan, Frederic Knudtson; cos, Helen Colvig

Having provided a starring vehicle for himself and colleagues Peter Falk and Ben Gazzara in 1970's HUSBANDS, director John Cassavetes showcased both his talented wife, Gena Rowlands, and frequent collaborator Seymour Cassel in MINNIE AND MOSKOWITZ the following year.

Minnie Moore (Rowlands) is a lonely former prom queen who's about to turn 40. She's been having an unsatisfactory affair with Jim (John Cassavetes), a married man, and spends the rest of her spare time with Florence (Elsie Ames), her best friend and movie-going companion. Jim is cruel to Minnie, but she puts up with it until Jim's wife threatens suicide and he's forced to end the affair. They meet for a last time at the museum where Minnie works; he's brought his two kids with him, at the request of his wife, to corroborate the cessation of the affair.

Minnie, lonely and desperate for male companionship, accepts a blind date with Zelmo Swift (Val Avery), a noisy boor who never once notices Minnie's delicate condition. They have lunch at a restaurant, and Zelmo proposes marriage but Minnie, realizing that he's mentally unbalanced, demurs and tries to get away. In the parking lot Zelmo begins to harass Minnie, but this is witnessed by Seymour Moskowitz (Cassel), a thirtyish, aging hippy and parking lot attendant, who comes to her rescue. He gets Zelmo out of the picture, then gets Minnie into his pickup truck and rides away with her. In less than a minute, Moskowitz decides that he is madly in love with Minnie. She leaps out of the pickup truck, but Moskowitz follows her until she agrees to go on a date.

For 35 years, John Cassavetes held a unique position in American film, maintaining dual careers as a highly regarded actor in mainstream features and as a director of independent films which themselves explored the art of acting. With MINNIE AND MOSKOWITZ, Cassavetes took a break from the decidedly somber mood of FACES and HUSBANDS, and produced the most accessible, and endearing example of his very exceptional art.

MINORITY REPORT   𝗗𝗩𝗗

2002 144m c Science Fiction ★★★★
DreamWorks SKG/Amblin Entertainment/Cruise/ PG-13
Wagner/Blue Tulip/Ronald Shusett/Gary Goldman
(U.S.)

Tom Cruise (Chief Paul Anderton), Colin Farrell (Danny Witwer), Samantha Morton (Agatha), Max von Sydow (Director Lamar Burgess), Kathryn Morris (Lara Clarke), Tim Blake Nelson (Gideon), Peter Stormare (Dr. Solomon Eddie), Lois Smith (Dr. Iris Hineman), Steve Harris (Jad), Mike Binder (Leo Crow)

p, Bonnie Curtis, Jan De Bont, Gerald R. Molen, Walter F. Parkes; d, Steven Spielberg; w, Scott Frank, Jon Cohen (based on the short story by Philip K. Dick); ph, Janusz Kaminski; ed, Michael Kahn; m, John Williams; prod d, Alex McDowell; art d, Ramsey Avery, Chris Gorak, Leslie McDonald, Seth Reed; fx, Mark Russell, Michael Lantieri, Scott Farrar, Dana Friedman, Henry LaBounta, Nathan McGuiness, Industrial Light & Magic, PDI/DreamWorks, Asylum Visual Effects; cos, Deborah L. Scott

This downbeat follow-up to the equally dark and thoughtful A.I. ARTIFICIAL INTELLIGENCE strongly suggests that Steven Spielberg is intent on putting grown-up metaphysics back into science fiction, a genre he's long been accused of infantilizing.

The year is 2054, and premeditated murder has been all but eliminated from the nation's capital. The secret weapon: Three genetically mutated clairvoyants, or "Pre-Cogs," who witness murders *before* they occur. Doped into a perpetual dream state, the Pre-Cogs are the telepathic brain of the DC Precrime Division headed by John Anderton (Tom Cruise), a true believer whose enthusiasm for the project is fueled by a personal tragedy: six years earlier, his young son was abducted and presumably killed. Once a crime is "witnessed," the Pre-Cogs produce the names of both perpetrator and victim; Anderton and his team interpret the Pre-Cogs' recorded visions for clues as to when and where the crime will occur, then dispatch a response team to arrest the murderer-to-be. Anderton undergoes a crisis of faith when the Pre-Cogs finger him as a future killer. Convinced there's a glitch in the system, Anderton tracks down the scientist (Lois Smith) who nurtured the Pre-Cogs. She clues him into the existence of the "Minority Report," one Pre-Cog's alternate, but equally valid, version of the future that contradicts the other two and is therefore suppressed. The Minority Report stands as Anderton's only hope, but what it suggests—that the truth depends on what you're looking at—brings his entire belief system crashing down.

Released not long after terrorist attacks on the U.S. resulted in the granting of unprecedented powers to its Justice Department, this sober and prescient film raises a number of important questions about how much we're willing to sacrifice in the name of public safety. In this particular vision of the future, the world is "safer," but it's also soulless and inhumane. Spielberg, meanwhile, gets something from Cruise that not even Stanley Kubrick could manage: a truly great performance.

MIRACLE   *DVD*
2004 127m c Sports/Drama   ★★★½
Pop Pop Productions/Touchstone/Mayhem   PG
Pictures/Walt Disney Pictures   (U.S.)

Kurt Russell *(Herb Brooks)*, Patricia Clarkson *(Patti Brooks)*, Noah Emmerich *(Craig Patrick)*, Sean McCann *(Walter Bush)*, Kenneth Welsh *(Doc Nagobads)*, Eddie Cahill *(Jim Craig)*, Patrick O'Brien Dempsey *(Mike Eruzione)*, Michael Mantenuto *(Jack O'Callahan)*, Nathan West *(Rob McClanahan)*, Kenneth Mitchell *(Ralph Cox)*

p, Mark Ciardi, Gordon Gray; d, Gavin O'Connor; w, Eric Guggenheim; ph, Daniel Stoloff; ed, John Gilroy; m, Mark Isham; prod d, John Willett; art d, Ross Dempster; fx, Alex Burdett, Mitch Drain; cos, Tom Bronson

Nearly a quarter century after the underdog U.S. hockey team trounced their Russian counterparts at the 1980 Lake Placid Winter Olympics, director Gavin O'Connor ensures that this stirring story is still both engaging and relevant.

At a time when professional athletes were barred from competing in the Olympic Games, hockey coach Herb Brooks (Kurt Russell) searches for 20 top U.S. amateurs. He recruits a group of young, eager faces—mean age: 21—and works them hard, ignoring the doubts of his employers, who question his unorthodox training methods and choice of unconventional players. Meanwhile, Brooks neglects his family, especially his supportive but frustrated wife, Patti (Patricia Clarkson), who suspects Brooks' determination is just his way of compensating for having been cut from the previous gold-medal-winning hockey team just days before the 1960 Olympics began. As the naysayers continue to weigh in, Brooks pushes his little-team-that-could forward, and within six months, he has them ready to face their competition. Their subsequent legendary gold-medal run leads sportscaster Al Michaels (appearing as himself) to pose the now famous question, "Do you believe in miracles?"

While its outcome shouldn't come as a surprise to anyone who lived through it, this heartwarming film effectively brings the story behind the memories to life. Set against the backdrop

of America's political struggles with the Soviet Union, a gas crisis, and a worsening hostage situation in Iran, it might also serve as a history lesson for younger viewers. Russell deftly evokes Brooks' unflappable dedication, but the real stars are the kinetic hockey scenes and O'Connor's detailed re-creations of all the action on the ice.

MIRACLE IN MILAN
(MIRACOLO A MILANO)
1951 100m bw Fantasy   ★★★★
ENIC   (Italy)

Branduani Gianni *(Little Toto at Age 11)*, Francesco Golisano *(Good Toto)*, Paolo Stoppa *(Bad Rappi)*, Emma Gramatica *(Old Lolatta)*, Guglielmo Barnabo *(Mobbi, the Rich Man)*, Brunella Bovo *(Little Edvige)*, Anna Carena *(Signora Marta Altezzosa)*, Alba Arnova *(The Statue)*, Flora Cambi *(Unhappy Sweetheart)*, Virgilio Riento *(Sergeant)*

p, Vittorio De Sica; d, Vittorio De Sica; w, Cesare Zavattini, Vittorio De Sica, Suso Cecchi D'Amico, Mario Chiari, Adolfo Franci (based on the story "Toto Il Buono" by Cesare Zavattini); ph, Aldo Graziati; ed, Eraldo Da Roma; m, Alessandro Cicognini; art d, Guido Fiorini; fx, Ned Mann

The writing-directing team of Cesare Zavattini and Vittorio De Sica produced this picture shortly after they received international acclaim for THE BICYCLE THIEF. Though not as popular as that masterwork, MIRACLE IN MILAN is an equally touching look into human nature that concentrates on the plight of the poor in post-WWII Italy. The story is essentially a fairy tale, packed with a strong moral implications. The Good Toto (Francesco Golisano), a young orphan, finds refuge in a colony of beggars and helps to organize them, generating happiness among the otherwise distressed members of the group. When a wealthy landowner decides to kick the beggars off his land, Toto is given a magic dove by a fairy. Not only are the landowner's attempts thwarted, but the magical powers of the dove also allow Toto to grant wishes to the beggars. Unable to deny them anything, he grants their greedy requests, until eventually the dove is stolen. As in other neo-realist films, the performers in MIRACLE IN MILAN are a combination of professional actors and actual denizens of the street, and all the players give realistic and humane portrayals. De Sica handles his fantastic material subtly and with simplicity, yielding an original mix of sharp satire and poetic fable that extended the limits of the neo-realist style.

MIRACLE OF MORGAN'S CREEK, THE
1944 99m bw Comedy   ★★★★★
Paramount   (U.S.)

Eddie Bracken *(Norval Jones)*, Betty Hutton *(Trudy Kockenlocker)*, Diana Lynn *(Emmy Kockenlocker)*, William Demarest *(Officer Kockenlocker)*, Brian Donlevy *(Governor McGinty)*, Akim Tamiroff *(The Boss)*, Porter Hall *(Justice of the Peace)*, Emory Parnell *(Mr. Tuerck)*, Alan Bridge *(Mr. Johnson)*, Julius Tannen *(Mr. Rafferty)*

p, Preston Sturges; d, Preston Sturges; w, Preston Sturges; ph, John Seitz; ed, Stuart Gilmore; m, Leo Shuken, Charles Bradshaw; art d, Hans Dreier, Ernst Fegte; cos, Edith Head

AAN Best Original Screenplay: Preston Sturges

Miraculously mad masterpiece. The marvel of THE MIRACLE OF MORGAN'S CREEK is how the film ever got made in the first place. This onslaught against American morals in small towns, against the wartime romances of servicemen, against just about everything that the country held sacred during WWII was reckless, exaggerated, and very funny. Sturges was at his irreverent best with his screenplay and direction of this most unlikely story. Hutton is Trudy

Kockenlocker, a man-crazy blonde who lives with her bitchy sister Emmy (Lynn) and her policeman father (Demarest). She gets drunk during one wild, passionate night with a soldier, whom she thinks she may have married, and becomes pregnant. The soldier, who she recalls is named something like "Ratsky-Watsky," vanishes, and since being pregnant in a small town without being married is the worst thing that can happen in a girl's life, Trudy's sometime male clerk boyfriend Norval (Bracken) is tapped to be the father of her child. In one mix-up after another, Novral winds up being sought by authorities for impersonating a soldier, forgery, corrupting the morals of a minor, kidnapping and robbery. It looks bad for the young couple, and the only thing that can save them is a miracle. It does.

Every role is handled with deftness, and Sturges even gets in a few holdovers from an earlier success, THE GREAT McGINTY, by having Brian Donlevy and Akim Tamiroff stop by for a few well-chosen words. The idea of having squeaky-clean Hutton shown as a (shudder) girl with loose morals was a sensation that somehow eluded the censor's scissors. Some say that the plot managed to escape snipping because the picture was so funny that no one could take it seriously, but the truth is that this movie kept a tight grip on reality and that's what made it so hilarious. The manic Hutton, always an acquired taste, here gets a hilarious part that requires the frantic energy of a whirling dervish on speed. She was never better, and the same goes for the nervous Bracken, the grouchy Demarest and the wisecracking Lynn. Sturges, having begun his uninterrupted string of comic masterpieces in 1940 with MCGINTY, reached a peak in satirical zaniness with this one. Remade (sort of) in 1958 as ROCK-A-BYE BABY.

MIRACLE ON 34TH STREET
1947 96m bw Fantasy
Fox (U.S.) ★★★½

Maureen O'Hara *(Doris Walker)*, John Payne *(Fred Gailey)*, Edmund Gwenn *(Kris Kringle)*, Gene Lockhart *(Judge Henry X. Harper)*, Natalie Wood *(Susan Walker)*, Porter Hall *(Mr. Sawyer)*, William Frawley *(Charles Halloran)*, Jerome Cowan *(Thomas Mara)*, Philip Tonge *(Mr. Shellhammer)*, James Seay *(Dr. Pierce)*

p, William Perlberg; d, George Seaton; w, George Seaton (based on a story by Valentine Davies); ph, Charles Clarke, Lloyd Ahern; ed, Robert Simpson; m, Cyril J. Mockridge; art d, Richard Day, Richard Irvine; fx, Fred Sersen

AAN Best Picture; AA Best Supporting Actor: Edmund Gwenn; AA Best Original Story: Valentine Davies; AA Best Screenplay: George Seaton

A touch labored but lovable. THE MIRACLE ON 34TH STREET opens during Manhattan's Christmas Parade as Macy's executive Doris Walker (Maureen O'Hara) finds the Santa Claus for the store float so drunk he can't stand up. Chiding Doris for employing such a derelict is a kindly, white-bearded man who, when she asks his name, tells her it's "Kris Kringle." Ignoring this, she pleads with him to replace the drunk, and he proves such a crowd-pleaser that she hires him as Macy's resident Santa for the holiday rush. This sets in motion a series of events in which Kris touches the lives of many, teaching them a lot about faith and the true meaning of Christmas. Among those touched are Doris; her sophisticated little girl, Susan (Natalie Wood), who thinks the very idea of Santa Claus is ridiculous, Doris's suitor Fred Gailey (John Payne), and dozens of Macy's customers who are pleasantly surprised when Kris directs them to competitors to get the gifts they seek. Unfortunately all are not smitten with this kindly man, particularly the store's amateur psychologist whose contention that Kris is unbalanced leads to a trial in which the court must decide the weighty matter of whether or not there

is a Santa Claus. Gwenn won an Oscar for his role, and for many, his charming, endearing performance has been identified with the spirit of the Christmas season ever since the completion of this sentimental production. Wood is wonderful in MIRACLE; it's interesting to ponder what happened along the way to transform her into a usually synthetic actress.

MIRACLE WOMAN, THE
1931 90m bw Religious
Columbia (U.S.) ★★★½

Barbara Stanwyck *(Florence "Faith" Fallon)*, David Manners *(John Carson)*, Sam Hardy *(Bob Hornsby)*, Beryl Mercer *(Mrs. Higgins)*, Russell Hopton *(Sam Welford)*, Charles Middleton *(Simpson)*, Eddie Boland *(Collins)*, Thelma Hill *(Gussie)*, Aileen Carlyle *(Violet)*, Al Stewart *(Brown)*

p, Harry Cohn; d, Frank Capra; w, Dorothy Howell, Jo Swerling (based on the play "Bless You Sister" by John Meehan, Robert Riskin); ph, Joseph Walker; ed, Maurice Wright; art d, Max Parker

The subject of phony evangelists is a tricky one, entailing the risk of offending believers. Barbara Stanwyck is convincing as the daughter of a pastor who has just been discharged from his parish and, as a result, has died of a broken heart. Stanwyck goes in front of the congregation and delivers a stinging denunciation of their hypocrisy. Sam Hardy, a two-bit promoter and con man, realizing that Stanwyck is mighty handy with her mouth, talks her into becoming an evangelist. Soon she is one of the most important pulpit pounders in the land, and, caught up in the furor of phony cripples "healed" and testifying to the pigeons, Stanwyck is too successful to stop. David Manners, a blind ex-pilot who is about to kill himself by leaping out a window, hears Stanwyck preaching on the radio and decides that she might be able to cure him. He goes to the tent and volunteers to step inside a lion's cage. His faith brings him closer to Stanwyck, and she is soon in love with him. Russell Hopton, the press agent for the group, wants a larger piece of the spoils, but Hardy won't hear of it and knocks Hopton off. Helped by his love for Stanwyck, Manners overcomes his shyness enough to declare himself through his ventriloquist's dummy. When Hardy sees that Manners and Stanwyck are getting close, he arranges a trip to the Holy Land to get her away from the blind lad. Stanwyck is beginning to understand that her faith healing is a lot of nonsense and that the people whom she has really healed just needed something—anything—to believe in. All of her ravings don't help Manners recover his sight. (To the credit of the authors and director, there is no miracle recovery for the blind man.) Hardy sets the tent ablaze as Stanwyck is about to confess to all that she is a sham. Later Stanwyck, who has become a member of the Salvation Army, receives a wire from Manners, opening the possibility that the two young people will get together. Riskin, who became Frank Capra's favorite screenwriter, went on to write such classics as IT HAPPENED ONE NIGHT, MR. DEEDS GOES TO TOWN, LOST HORIZON, YOU CAN'T TAKE IT WITH YOU and and MEET JOHN DOE. THE MIRACLE WOMAN was an expensive film for its day, and every penny shows on the screen. There's hardly a wasted word or frame of film in the movie. It is a fine film, although it would have been even better had Capra and the writers had the freedom to attack their subject with sabers instead of pins.

MIRACLE WORKER, THE
1962 106m bw Biography
Playfilms (U.S.)   ★★★★½

Anne Bancroft *(Annie Sullivan)*, Patty Duke *(Helen Keller)*, Victor Jory *(Capt. Keller)*, Inga Swenson *(Kate Keller)*, Andrew Prine

(James Keller), Kathleen Corneygs *(Aunt Ev)*, Beah Richards *(Viney)*, Jack Hollander *(Mr. Anagnos)*, Peggy Burke *(Helen at Age Seven)*, Mindy Sherwood *(Helen at Age Five)*

p, Fred Coe; d, Arthur Penn; w, William Gibson (based on the play by William Gibson and the book *The Story of My Life* by Helen Keller); ph, Ernesto Caparros; ed, Aram Avakian; m, Laurence Rosenthal; art d, George Jenkins, Mel Bourne; cos, Ruth Morley

AA Best Actress: Anne Bancroft; *AA Best Supporting Actress:* Patty Duke; *AAN Best Director:* Arthur Penn; *AAN Best Adapted Screenplay:* William Gibson; *AAN Best Costume Design (B/W):* Ruth Morley

Excellent work, with Arthur Penn repeating his Broadway triumph directing Duke and Bancroft, the two stage leads. This remarkable story of Helen Keller began as a book, then became a William Gibson play that premiered on Broadway in 1959. When the time came to make the film, Penn, Gibson, and producer Coe insisted that Bancroft and Duke be retained, with resulting Oscars for both stars. Duke had riveted Broadway audiences with the role and, at age 16, became the youngest recipient of the Best Supporting Actress Oscar. (In 1973, Tatum O'Neal eclipsed her by winning the award at age 10 for PAPER MOON.)

THE MIRACLE WORKER is a powerful picture, even as the credits roll. Keller (Duke) is groping, lost and angry in her silent world when Annie Sullivan (Bancroft) arrives in Tuscumbia, Alabama, on a mission to teach the girl how to communicate through sign language. The task seems impossible, since Helen is blind as well as deaf. Annie, we learn, was blind at birth and still must wear very thick glasses in order to see images. Her own life had been brutalized by many years in institutions and the loss of the one person she cared about, a crippled brother who died young. Bancroft senses that the only way she can make any progress with Duke is to separate the child from her doting mother, Swenson, and her overbearing father, Jory.

The film is a harrowing, painfully honest, sometimes violent journey, astonishingly acted and rendered. Penn and cinematographer Caparros use short dissolves to great advantage, and Rosenthal's score heightens every nuance of the drama. The interiors were shot in New York and the exteriors in New Jersey, which doubled for Alabama. The eight-minute sequence featuring a physical fight between Bancroft and Duke as the teacher attempts to teach the pupil some manners stands as one of the most electrifying and honest ever committed to film.

MISERY [DVD]
1990 107m c Horror ★★★
Castle Rock/Nelson (U.S.) R

James Caan *(Paul Sheldon)*, Kathy Bates *(Annie Wilkes)*, Richard Farnsworth *(Buster, Sheriff)*, Frances Sternhagen *(Virginia)*, Lauren Bacall *(Marcia Sindell)*, Graham Jarvis *(Libby)*, Jerry Potter *(Pete)*, Thomas Brunelle Tom Brunelle *(Anchorman)*, June Christopher *(Anchorwoman)*, Wendy Bowers *(Waitress)*

p, Rob Reiner, Andrew Scheinman, Steve Nicolaides, Jeffrey Stott; d, Rob Reiner; w, William Goldman (based on the novel by Stephen King); ph, Barry Sonnenfeld; ed, Robert Leighton; m, Marc Shaiman; prod d, Norman Garwood; art d, Mark Mansbridge; fx, Phil Cory, K.N.B. EFX Group; cos, Gloria Gresham

AA Best Actress: Kathy Bates

In the "Kill the Bitch" tradition of FATAL ATTRACTION, this adaptation of Stephen King's misogynist fable about a "serious" (male) author trapped by his own "frivolous" (female) commercial creation isn't quite satisfying either as a flat-out horror screamer or a psychological thriller.

Paul Sheldon (Caan), the creator of the fabulously successful romance-novel heroine Misery Chastain, has a fan in Annie Wilkes (Bates) who is willing to die for him. The trouble is, after she discovers Sheldon has killed off his series of "Misery" novels in order to write "serious" fiction, Annie wants to take him with her.

Director Rob Reiner is clearly more comfortable with the humor and humanity than the gory horror in King's grisly tale. William Goldman's script is similarly at its strongest early on when Sheldon faces off in a test of artistic mettle against Wilkes, the toughest editor of his life. When the horror comes, it feels forced and derivative. The climactic battle between Sheldon and Annie degenerates into yet another recycling of the unkillable movie killer gimmick of "Friday the 13th." Ironically, it is Bates's Oscar-winning work that subverts MISERY as a horror tale. She gives the role a subtle mixture of wit, energy, and psychological realism that undermines the pat, bloodthirsty resolution.

MISFITS, THE [DVD]
1961 124m bw Western ★★★½
Seven Arts (U.S.)

Clark Gable *(Gay Langland)*, Marilyn Monroe *(Roslyn Taber)*, Montgomery Clift *(Perce Howland)*, Thelma Ritter *(Isabelle Steers)*, Eli Wallach *(Guido)*, James Barton *(Old Man in the Bar)*, Estelle Winwood *(Church Lady)*, Kevin McCarthy *(Raymond Taber)*, Denis Shaw *(Young Boy in Bar)*, Philip Mitchell *(Charles Steers)*

p, Frank E. Taylor; d, John Huston; w, Arthur Miller; ph, Russell Metty; ed, George Tomasini; m, Alex North; art d, Stephen Grimes, William Newberry; fx, Cline Jones; cos, Jesse Munden

A disturbing but captivating film about modern cowboys who have lost their purpose in a world that has robbed them of the West into which they were born. THE MISFITS was Gable's and Monroe's last film. Whether or not the strenuous stunts and bronc-busting feats he performed killed Gable is still in debate, but he certainly gave one of the finest performances of his career for the fade-out.

Gay (Gable) and sidekicks Guido (Wallach) and Perce (Clift) are cowboys without saddles, driving a pickup about the West in search of odd jobs. Their talk is laced with thin bravado, and they have more of the past to discuss than the future. In Reno, they meet recently divorced blond voluptuary Roslyn Taber (Monroe), who has left her successful businessman husband. She is a one-time stripper who is seeking truth and a meaningful relationship with anyone who can relate to her idealistic notions. Gay is twice Roslyn's age, has no noble purpose, and intends to round up "misfit" horses, those wild mustangs too small for rodeo or ranch work, so they can be ground up for dog food. They tentatively begin a romance, but these "misfits" have a few things to prove to themselves and to each other first.

This is an awkward film, even though it has many fine moments, most of them Gable's—when he gets drunk and begins calling for his long-lost children, his spirited horsebreaking scenes (he did not employ a double), and some of his nostalgic scenes with Monroe. Gable had his misgivings about what he called the "arty" qualities of Miller's script, but he eventually did more with his introspective role than the playwright could have expected. Monroe has her moments (e.g. screaming in the middle of the desert while she watches Gay and his buddies fighting one particularly spirited mustang), but is often weak and directionless in her part. She tries adopting Actor's Studio methods and deadpanning her scenes while belying her altruistic lines with a jiggling, tight-skirted image. Miller's presence at the on-location scenes in Reno and Dayton, Nevada, undoubtedly inhibited director Huston, who fails to develop anyone's character except Gable's. Huston could not control Monroe, who was taking various drugs and seemed to be on the verge of a nervous breakdown; when she did show up for work, she couldn't remember her lines without heavy coaching. Somewhat surprisingly, Gable treated her and the similarly distraught, alcoholic Clift with great consideration and kindness. He got on less well with Wallach, though, regularly referring to the "boiled ham" he planned to have for lunch, while the studious, showy Method actor would retort, "Hey, king, can you lower my taxes?" The film was finally completed on November 24, 1960, eight days after Gable's death from a heart attack and several months before his fifth wife Kay gave birth to his only child. Monroe's death from a sleeping-pill overdose would soon follow, and Clift would be dead within five years as well. Many have called this film a brilliant mood piece of a dying Old West; that doesn't make it a masterpiece, but the ghosts of its cast do still haunt one's viewing experience.

MISHIMA

1985 120m c Biography ★★★½
Zoetrope/Filmlink/Lucasfilm (U.S.) R

Ken Ogata (Yukio Mishima), Masayuki Shionoya (Morita), Hiroshi Mikami (Cadet No. 1), Junya Fukuda (Cadet No. 2), Shigeto Tachihara (Cadet No. 3), Junkichi Orimoto (Gen. Mashita), Eimei Exumi (Ichigaya Aide-de-Camp), Minoru Hodaka (Ichigaya Colonel), Go Riju (Mishima, Age 18–19), Yuki Nagahara (Mishima, Age Five)

p, Mata Yamamoto, Tom Luddy; d, Paul Schrader; w, Paul Schrader, Leonard Schrader (conceived in collaboration with Jun Shiragi, literary executor of the Mishima estate); ph, John Bailey (Technicolor); ed, Michael Chandler, Tomoyo Oshima; m, Philip Glass; prod d, Eiko Ishioka; art d, Kazuo Takenaka; cos, Etsuko Yagyu

"Never in physical action had I discovered the chilling satisfaction of words. Never in words had I experienced the hot darkness of action. Somewhere there must be a higher principle which reconciles art and action. That principle, it occurred to me, was death." These words, written by Japanese author Yukio Mishima and spoken in a voice-over narration by Roy Scheider, eloquently state what writer-director Paul Schrader tried to convey in this ambitious, unique undertaking. Though MISHIMA contains much biographical material, it doesn't claim to be a definitive biography of the controversial writer. Instead, the film concentrates on Mishima's art, attempting to piece together a complicated puzzle by examining his work and its relation to his personal obsessions. Perhaps Japan's best-known author, Mishima wrote 35 novels, 25 plays, 200 short stories, and eight volumes of essays before his ritual suicide at age 45. One of his driving concerns was his perception of Japan's post-WWII rejection of its rich history of tradition, ritual, honor, and religion in favor of the Western world's pursuit of money. He formed his own private army, called the Shield Society, whose purpose was to restore Japan to the emperor. Schrader approaches his subject with taste and intelligence, juxtaposing Mishima's suicide with flashbacks from his life and dramatizations of his novels Temple of the Golden Pavilion, Kyoko's House, and Runaway Horses. Separated into four chapters ("Beauty," "Art," "Action," and "Harmony of Pen and Sword"), the film skillfully integrates the novels and real events, slowly dissecting Mishima's obsessions. MISHIMA's most stunning aspect is the visual style employed in the dramatizations of the novels. With colorful, theatrical sets by famed Japanese designer Eiko Ishioka, the sequences are quite unique and impressive in their own right, and the entire film is photographed beautifully by John Bailey. The visuals are enhanced by Philip Glass's haunting score.

MISSING

1982 122m c Drama/War ★★★★
Polygram (U.S.) PG

Jack Lemmon (Ed Horman), Sissy Spacek (Beth Horman), Melanie Mayron (Terry Simon), John Shea (Charles Horman), Charles Cioffi (Capt. Ray Tower), David Clennon (Consul Phil Putnam), Richard Venture (U.S. Ambassador), Jerry Hardin (Col.

Sean Patrick), Richard Bradford (Carter Babcock), Joe Regalbuto (Frank Teruggi)

p, Edward Lewis, Mildred Lewis; d, Constantin Costa-Gavras; w, Donald Stewart, Constantin Costa-Gavras (based on The Execution of Charles Horman by Thomas Hauser); ph, Ricardo Aronovich (Technicolor); ed, Francoise Bonnot; m, Vangelis; prod d, Peter Jamison; art d, Agustin Ytuarte, Luceoro Isaac; fx, Albert Whitlock; cos, Joe I. Tompkins

AAN Best Picture; AAN Best Actor: Jack Lemmon; AAN Best Actress: Sissy Spacek; AA Best Adapted Screenplay: Constantin Costa-Gavras, Donald Stewart

With MISSING, Costa-Gavras (Z; STATE OF SEIGE; THE CONFESSION), one of cinema's most political filmmakers, turned his attention to the alleged U.S. involvement in the coup that led to the death of socialist Chilean president Salvador Allende in 1973. Based on Thomas Hauser's The Execution of Charles Horman, Costa-Gavras's first Hollywood-produced film presents an only slightly fictionalized account of the disappearance of American expatriate writer Charles Horman (John Shea) in Santiago (though neither the city nor Chile are ever mentioned) just after a military coup. His wife, Beth (Sissy Spacek), and his conservative father, Ed (Jack Lemmon), who has traveled from the U.S., become a political odd couple as they search for Charles, growing closer as they run into the official stonewalling of American embassy and Chilean authorities who insist there is no trace of Charles. Costa-Gavras pulled no few punches in this powerful, provocative thriller that then-Secretary of State Alexander Haig felt compelled to issue categorical denials of the film's allegations. Few films fuse the personal and the political as successfully as MISSING, and Lemmon and Spacek bring tremendous feeling to their portrayals. Though Costa-Gavras clearly has a political axe to grind, he manages to do so without haranguing the viewer, keeping the film's focus on his characters and masterfully building tension as the story moves toward its stinging resolution.

MISSION, THE

1986 126m c Historical ★★★
Enigma/Goldcrest/Kingsmere (U.K.) PG

Robert De Niro (Mendoza), Jeremy Irons (Gabriel), Ray McAnally (Altamirano), Liam Neeson (Fielding), Aidan Quinn (Felipe), Ronald Pickup (Hontar), Charles Low (Cabeza), Cherie Lunghi (Carlotta), Bercelio Moya (Indian Boy), Sigifredo Ismare (Witch Doctor)

p, Fernando Ghia, David Puttnam; d, Roland Joffe; w, Robert Bolt; ph, Chris Menges (JDC Widescreen, Rank Color); ed, Jim Clark; m, Ennio Morricone; prod d, Stuart Craig; art d, George Richardson, John King; fx, Peter Hutchinson; cos, Enrico Sabbatini

AAN Best Picture; AAN Best Director: Roland Joffe; AA Best Cinematography: Chris Menges; AAN Best Film Editing: Jim Clark; AAN Best Original Score: Ennio Morricone; AAN Best Art Direction-Set Decoration: Stuart Craig, Jack Stephens; AAN Best Costume Design: Enrico Sabbatini

In South America, circa 1750, Gabriel (Irons) is a Jesuit priest sent to build a mission for the Guarani Indians. There he encounters Mendoza (De Niro), a ruthless slave trader who kills several Guaranis and captures many more, taking them back to town as slaves. Mendoza also kills his handsome young brother Felipe (Quinn) in a duel over Mendoza's fiancee, but because he is an aristocrat, he isn't punished for his crime. But the slave trader has a conscience and feels that he must do penance; accordingly, Gabriel arranges for Mendoza to join him back at the mission where Mendoza committed so many sins. In time, the mission faces serious trouble, brought on by a dispute among Spain, Portugal, and the Church. Ambitious, moving, and visually stunning, THE MISSION falls right in step with other high-quality British historical epics, but also fails to escape the pitfalls that typically plague such projects. While an impressive production, THE MISSION tries to do so much that little is explored fully. Irons's character is really more an icon than a man, as is De Niro's. Perhaps most distressing is the fact that THE MISSION is yet another film made by Europeans or Americans that, while sympathetic to the plight of South American Indians, portrays them as an indistinguishable mass of childlike innocents just waiting to be exploited by outsiders.

MISSION: IMPOSSIBLE DVD
1996 110m c Thriller/Spy/Action ★★★
CW Productions/Paramount British Pictures (U.S.) PG-13

Tom Cruise (Ethan Hunt), Jon Voight (Jim Phelps), Emmanuelle Beart (Claire), Henry Czerny (Kittridge), Jean Reno (Krieger), Ving Rhames (Luther), Kristin Scott Thomas, billed as Kristin Scott-Thomas (Sarah Davies), Vanessa Redgrave (Max), Emilio Estevez (Jack Harmon—uncredited), Dale Dye (Frank Barnes)

p, Tom Cruise, Paula Wagner; d, Brian De Palma; w, David Koepp, Robert Towne (from a story by David Koepp and Steven Zaillian, based on the television series created by Bruce Geller); ph, Stephen H. Burum; ed, Paul Hirsch; m, Danny Elfman, Lalo Schifrin; prod d, Norman Reynolds; art d, Frederick Hole; fx, John Knoll, Richard Yuricich, Lyn Nicholson, Industrial Light & Magic; cos, Penny Rose

Brian De Palma's eagerly awaited big-screen adaptation of the classic TV series is a gutsy attempt to reconfigure the timeworn espionage formula. Although this presold blockbuster is far from a complete success on De Palma's terms—it doesn't subvert the genre but gives it a surprisingly gentle goose—it's a nimble, expertly contrived summer entertainment that doesn't insult the intelligence.

Tom Cruise stars as Ethan Hunt, member of the elite Impossible Mission Force led by grizzled patriarch Jim Phelps (Jon Voight). After most of his team is ruthlessly sacrificed during what turns out to be a decoy operation, Hunt turns renegade. He assembles his own crack but highly suspect team of fellow "disavowed" agents (Ving Rhames and Jean Reno) and goes after a mysterious arms dealer called Max (Vanessa Redgrave).

De Palma and screenwriters David Koepp and Robert Towne boldly reduce much of what made the series so popular (gadgets, international supervillains, even the conceit of the seemingly impossible mission) down to a bare minimum. The result is a gracefully plotted spy film in the classic mode, with just enough self-consciousness to keep things interesting.

The pleasures of MISSION: IMPOSSIBLE are mostly conventional—star/producer Cruise reportedly kept his adventurous director on a short leash—but there are moments when De Palma's distinctive obsessions and lyrical sensibility shine through. A parallel between spycraft and stagecraft is cleverly sustained throughout, and the elaborately imagined scenes of video surveillance are in keeping with the director's celebrated critique of vision, technology, and power.

MISSION: IMPOSSIBLE II DVD
2000 130m c Action/Spy ★★★
Paramount/Cruise-Wagner (U.S.) PG-13

Tom Cruise (Ethan Hunt), Dougray Scott (Sean Ambrose), Thandie Newton (Nyah Hall), Ving Rhames (Luther Stickell), Richard Roxburgh (Hugh Stamp), Anthony Hopkins (Mission Commander—uncredited), John Polson (Billy Baird), Brendan Gleeson (McCloy), Rade Sherbedgia (Dr. Nekhorvich), William R. Mapother (Wallis)

p, Tom Cruise, Paula Wagner; d, John Woo; w, Brannon Braga, Ronald D. Moore, Michael Towne, David Marconi, William Goldman, Robert Towne (based on the television series Mission: Impossible by Bruce Geller); ph, Jeffrey L. Kimball, Phil Pastuhov; ed, Christian Wagner, Steven Kemper; m, Hans Zimmer, Lalo Schifrin; prod d, Thomas E. Sanders; art d, Dan Dorrance; fx,

Bruce Steinheimer, Janek Sirrs (Digital), Richard Yuricich (Visual), Andrew Eio (Computer & Video), Henry L. Labounta (Visual), Pacific Data Images (Visual), Cinesite, Manex Visual Effects, Double Negative; chor, Antonio Vargas; cos, Lizzy Gardiner

Yes, it's a hit machine, a blockbuster by the numbers. But it's sharper, less reverential, and generally better than MISSION: IMPOSSIBLE. John Woo's stylish sequel is a globe-trotting, action-packed espionage romp in the style of James Bond films before they degenerated into smirking, bloated spectacles.

Rogue IMF agent Sean Ambrose (Dougray Scott) and his crew have hijacked both a lethal, man-made virus named Chimera and its antidote, and they're ransoming them off to the highest bidder. Ethan Hunt's (Tom Cruise) mission is to recover the doomsday bug with the help of Nyah Hall (Thandie Newton), a stunner of the glamorous, international felon variety. The reason for her mandatory inclusion—which Hunt only learns after he's fallen for her considerable charms—is that she's Ambrose's ex and is thus ideally suited to insinuate herself back into his confidence. Computer whiz Luther Stickell (Ving Rhames) handles all the hacking, and the action comes complete with vehicular pursuits, cunning masquerades, spectacular shootouts, and clever gadgetry.

Woo, late of the no-holds-barred, Hong Kong school of movie mayhem, is a singularly graceful filmmaker, a true believer in the power of elegant stunt choreography and the allure of the human face. That's not to say that this picture lacks spectacular CGI effects, only that Woo doesn't worship at their altar. There's a bit of leaden dialogue and overstated imagery, and a lot of wildly improbable plotting, but it doesn't matter; this is top-of-the-line disposable entertainment. An uncredited Anthony Hopkins appears as the new head of the IMF, and he gets the film's best line, spoken to a reluctant Hunt: "Well, it isn't Mission: Difficult, is it?" Touche!

MISSISSIPPI BURNING DVD
1988 128m c Historical ★★
Frederick Zollo (U.S.) R

Gene Hackman (Rupert Anderson), Willem Dafoe (Alan Ward), Frances McDormand (Mrs. Pell), Brad Dourif (Deputy Pell), R. Lee Ermey, billed as Lee Ermey (Mayor Tilman), Gailard Sartain (Sheriff Stuckey), Stephen Tobolowsky (Townley), Michael Rooker (Frank Bailey), Pruitt Taylor Vince (Lester Cowens), Badja Djola (Agent Monk)

p, Frederick Zollo, Robert F. Colesberry; d, Alan Parker; w, Chris Gerolmo; ph, Peter Biziou (Duart Color); ed, Gerry Hambling; m, Trevor Jones; prod d, Geoffrey Kirkland, Philip Harrison; fx, Stan Parks; cos, Aude Bronson Howard

AAN Best Picture; AAN Best Actor: Gene Hackman; AAN Best Supporting Actress: Frances McDormand; AAN Best Director: Alan Parker; AA Best Cinematography: Peter Biziou; AAN Best Film Editing: Gerry Hambling; AAN Best Sound: Robert Litt, Elliot Tyson, Richard C. Kline, Danny Michael

Using the shocking murders of three civil rights workers by the Ku Klux Klan in Mississippi on June 21, 1964, as its inspiration, MISSISSIPPI BURNING presents a grotesquely fictionalized version of the events and turns them into another cop-buddy movie. Alan Ward and Rupert Anderson (Dafoe and Hackman) are two very different FBI agents sent to Mississippi to investigate the disappearance of the young men. Ward is morally outraged by the racism he finds in the South and is determined to do something about it, while Anderson wanders the streets like a good ol' boy, chatting with the townsfolk to ferret out clues. MISSISSIPPI BURNING is visually splendid. From the sets, costumes, props, and Mississippi locations to the gorgeous cinematography of Peter Biziou, director Parker and his crew have created a film that is unquestionably watchable. As a history lesson, however, it's laughable: the FBI were far from heroes to civil rights activists, and insofar as the struggle succeeded, it was because American blacks took their own destiny in hand, not because they were rescued by paternalistic white authority figures.

MISSISSIPPI MASALA 〇 DVD
1992　118m　c　　Drama/Romance　　★★★½
Mira Nair Films/SCS Films/Palace Pictures/　　R
Film Four International　　(U.S./U.K.)

Denzel Washington (Demetrius), Sarita Choudhury (Mina), Roshan Seth (Jay), Sharmila Tagore (Kinnu), Charles S. Dutton (Tyrone), Joe Seneca (Williben), Ranjit Chowdhry (Anil), Mohan Gokhale (Pontiac), Mohan Agashe (Kanti Napkin), Tico Wells (Dexter)

p, Michael Nozik, Mira Nair; d, Mira Nair; w, Sooni Taraporevala; ph, Edward Lachman; ed, Roberto Silvi; m, L. Subramaniam; prod d, Mitch Epstein; art d, Jefferson Sage; cos, Hope Hanafin

"Masala" refers to a mix of varied spices, and one of the strengths of MISSISSIPPI MASALA is its own collection of colorful characters. While its ostensible focus is on an interracial romance, the film's dramatic scope is wide enough to encompass not only those around the couple, and their reactions to the affair, but the events and forces that led to their coming together in the first place. The lovers are Demetrius (Denzel Washington), a young black man who runs a carpet-cleaning business in Mississippi, and Mina (Sarita Choudhury), whose parents Jay (Roshan Seth) and Kinnu (Sharmila Tagore) run a local liquor store. (Like many of their friends, Mina and her family are Indians who were expelled from Uganda in 1972 by Idi Amin.) After Mina accidentally crashes a car into Demetrius's truck, the two become attracted to each other and begin a romance that stirs the ire of Mina's family.

Indian director Mira Nair, a Harvard graduate and former documentarian (INDIA CABARET) whose first narrative feature, SALAAM BOMBAY!, received widespread acclaim, does a fine job of exploring the complex relations at play here. Sooni Taraporevala's screenplay avoids easy polemics about race, and is as much about the outside forces and past events that influence the central love affair as it is about the affair itself.

In one of his first true romantic leads, Washington proves immensely charming as a man who resists, without being blind to, the social pressures working against the affair. Newcomer Choudhury is excellent as the rebellious Mina, effectively playing the nonconformist side of her character without ever losing sympathy. There's real romantic chemistry between the two, and their love scene in a Biloxi motel room generates real heat without indulging in the sultry silliness of so many recent "erotic" dramas.

MISSISSIPPI MERMAID 〇 DVD
(LA SIRENE DU MISSISSIPPI)
1969　123m　c　　Mystery　　★★★½
Carrosse/Artistes/Delphos　　(France/Italy)　　GP

Jean-Paul Belmondo (Louis Mahe), Catherine Deneuve (Julie Roussel/Marion), Michel Bouquet (Comolli), Nelly Borgeaud (Berthe Roussel), Marcel Berbert (Jardine), Martine Ferriere (Landlady), Roland Thenot (Richard), Yves Drouhet

p, Marcel Berbert; d, Francois Truffaut; w, Francois Truffaut (based on the novel Waltz into Darkness by Cornell Woolrich); ph, Denys Clerval (Dyaliscope, DeLuxe Color); ed, Agnes Guillemot; m, Antoine Duhamel; art d, Claude Pignot

Belmondo is a millionaire tobacco planter who becomes engaged to Deneuve through a personal column. He is taken by her beauty and they soon marry, but she leaves with his bank account. He hires a private detective to track her down, but eventually discovers her himself, or so he thinks. The girl

he finds is not his wife, but bears an uncanny resemblance to her (not surprising, since Deneuve plays both roles). Eventually Belmondo learns that his new companion is trying to kill him. As he is about to be poisoned, he professes his love for Deneuve, who promptly knocks the cup from his hand and shamefully vows to love him forever. This is Truffaut's most successful attempt to blend a complex, Hitchcockian genre film with his own personality. It was also his first chance to work with superstars, ensuring success at the box office. The film is full of references to cinema—a clip from LA MARSEILLAISE (the picture is dedicated to Jean Renoir, whose film LA CARROSSE D'OR [THE GOLDEN COACH] was the inspiration for the name of Truffaut's production company), and homages to Humphrey Bogart, Nick Ray, Honore de Balzac, Jean Cocteau, and a Cahiers Du Cinema editor who bore the same name as this film's detective, Comolli.

MISSOURI BREAKS, THE
1976　126m　c　　Western　　★★★
UA　(U.S.)　　PG

Marlon Brando (Lee Clayton), Jack Nicholson (Tom Logan), Randy Quaid (Little Tod), Kathleen Lloyd (Jane Braxton), Frederic Forrest (Cary), Harry Dean Stanton (Calvin), John McLiam (David Braxton), John Ryan (Si), Sam Gilman (Hank Rate), Steve Franken (Lonesome Kid)

p, Elliott Kastner, Robert M. Sherman; d, Arthur Penn; w, Thomas McGuane; ph, Michael Butler (DeLuxe Color); ed, Jerry Greenberg, Stephen A. Rotter, Dede Allen; m, John Williams; prod d, Albert Brenner; art d, Steve Berger; cos, Patricia Norris

In the 1970s westerns started to become a little weird, and this one was downright eccentric, although Brando, as a nutty gunfighter, and Nicholson, as a leader of rustlers, are fascinating to watch, if not believable in their disjointed roles. The film opens as a rustler, on ranch baron McLiam's orders, is hanged, no little example for Nicholson, who heads a gang of vicious horse thieves. The hanged man, Hunter Von Leer, was Nicholson's friend, and Nicholson intends to avenge the death; but he falls for Lloyd, daughter of the cattle baron, and somehow is persuaded to settle down to the mundane chores of farming, much to the disgust of his gang. The rustlers carry on without Nicholson's help, raiding McLiam's herds and driving the cattle baron half crazy. He sends for a top gun bounty hunter, Brando, who turns out to be the most unpredictable and outright strangest creature to ever visit a western movie. To capture one outlaw he takes to wearing a bonnet and dress, and when Nicholson goes to kill him he finds Brando taking a bubble bath, a sight that so jars him that he misses his opportunity to kill him. Brando continues his rampage, destroying all the rustlers except Nicholson, who manages to finish off the weirdo in the end. The whole thing, script, acting, and especially Penn's heavy-handed direction, is bizarre. Yet there's a perverse joy in watching Brando and Nicholson try to compete with each other in mugging, switching accents, and mannerisms that could only be found elsewhere in institutions like the Bellevue Insane Asylum. The erratic and exotic behavior of the stars is infectious, with Quaid, Forrest, Stanton, and others mimicking them with slavish devotion.

MR. BLANDINGS BUILDS HIS DREAM HOUSE 〇 DVD
1948　94m　bw　Comedy　　★★★½
RKO　(U.S.)

Cary Grant (Jim Blandings), Myrna Loy (Muriel Blandings), Melvyn Douglas (Bill Cole), Reginald Denny (Simms), Sharyn Moffett (Joan Blandings), Connie Marshall (Betsy Blandings), Louise Beavers (Gussie), Harry Shannon (W.D. Tesander), Ian Wolfe (Smith), Tito Vuolo (Mr. Zucca)

p, Norman Panama, Melvin Frank; d, H.C. Potter; w, Norman Panama, Melvin Frank (based on the novel by Eric Hodgins); ph, James Wong Howe; ed, Harry Marker; m, Leigh Harline; art d, Albert S. D'Agostino, Carroll Clark; fx, Russell A. Cully; cos, Robert Kalloch

Nice and easy. The novel upon which this film was based was very funny and timely. This movie suffered a bit in the translation to the screen, but it still had more than enough humor to make it a hit. This was the third duet for Grant and Loy, and a triangular plot-turn with Douglas was written in to add some spice. Jim and Muriel Blandings are married Manhattanites who must give up their apartment and find new lodgings for themselves and their daughters (Moffett and Marshall). Jim in particular is seduced by the dream of owning a suburban home in the greenery of the country. Dreaming, though, is much easier than building.

Timely in 1948 in light of postwar housing problems, BLANDINGS survives now primarily by the grace of its cast. Loy proves that she didn't need William Powell to be the "perfect wife," and she has two wonderful moments telling off her jealous husband and explaining the color scheme for her house to a laconic painter. Grant handles more of the film's farcical elements, yet he still retains the warm sophistication he's so justly famous for. Douglas is as wry as ever, and the fine supporting cast includes gems from Denny and Shannon. There's little originality here—gags are borrowed from radio's "Fibber McGee and Molly," and much here would be reprised on TV's "Green Acres," but serve up the "Wham" anyway, Gussie!

MR. DEEDS GOES TO TOWN   DVD
1936 115m bw Comedy   ★★★★★
Columbia   (U.S.)

Gary Cooper (Longfellow Deeds), Jean Arthur (Babe Bennett), George Bancroft (MacWade), Lionel Stander (Cornelius Cobb), Douglas Dumbrille (John Cedar), Raymond Walburn (Walter), Margaret Matzenauer (Madame Pomponi), H.B. Warner (Judge Walker), Warren Hymer (Bodyguard), Muriel Evans (Theresa)

p, Frank Capra; d, Frank Capra; w, Robert Riskin (based on the story "Opera Hat" by Clarence Budington Kelland); ph, Joseph Walker; ed, Gene Havlick; art d, Stephen Goosson; fx, Roy Davidson; cos, Samuel Lange

AAN Best Picture; AAN Best Actor: Gary Cooper; *AA Best Director:* Frank Capra; *AAN Best Screenplay:* Robert Riskin; *AAN Best Sound Recording:* John Livadary

Peak inspired lunacy, especially in the courtroom. Here is a shamelessly simple story with a populist point of view, but it is handled with such charm and charisma and acted so well by Cooper and Arthur that it became another Frank Capra classic. Cooper, a rural rube from Vermont, inherits his uncle's vast fortune and becomes national news overnight. The whole town turns out at the train station to see Cooper, tuba player and poet, off to New York, where he will assume the responsibilities of his uncle's business and move into an enormous mansion. But cynical news editor George Bancroft does not fall for Cooper's image of a simple, honest man. Bancroft assigns Arthur to interview Cooper, with explicit instructions not to spare the ridicule, but the aggressive reporter cannot corral Cooper. When she fakes a faint in front of his residence, the gallant Cooper picks her up and takes care of her. She tells him she's unemployed, and then begins wheedling him for information.

Capra directs flawlessly as he captures the prosaic character of Longfellow Deeds; Cooper is tailor-made for the role, natural and authentic. Both he and Arthur remained favorites of Capra, who would use Cooper again in MEET JOHN DOE, Arthur in YOU CAN'T TAKE IT WITH YOU,

and MR. SMITH GOES TO WASHINGTON. Capra never had any doubt in casting Cooper for the role of Longfellow Deeds—his first and only choice—but he was in a quandary over the female lead until he spotted Arthur in a minor western. The director was at his high-water mark at Columbia, allowed by Columbia studio chief Harry Cohn to function as he pleased without front office interference. Capra insisted that only Cooper play the lead in the film, causing the production to be delayed for six months while Cooper fulfilled other duties and costing Columbia $100,000. Cohn did not want any more postponements so he okayed Arthur and the production got under way. Arthur literally shook with nerves before each scene, believing she could not pull it off. Yet she was an original in front of the cameras.

The supporting cast is extraordinary, notably Dumbrille, Bancroft, and that venerable character player Warner, who had appeared in many a Capra film and played Christ in DeMille's classic KING OF KINGS. The film achieved immense popularity and gleaned a fortune for Columbia chiefly because of the gangling, rumpled, taciturn Cooper, who was one of the most durable film stars in history and ranked in the top-10 list for 15 years. In 1939 he made almost $500,000, making him the highest paid American actor that year, and would earn more than $10 million throughout his long career.

MR. HOLLAND'S OPUS   DVD
1995 142m c   Drama   ★★
Interscope Communications/The Charlie   PG
Mopic Company   (U.S.)

Richard Dreyfuss (Glenn Holland), Glenne Headly (Iris Holland), Jay Thomas (Bill Meister), Olympia Dukakis (Principal Jacobs), William H. Macy, billed as W.H. Macy (Vice Principal Wolters), Alicia Witt (Gertrude Lang), Terrence Howard (Louis Russ), Damon Whitaker (Bobby Tidd), Jean Louisa Kelly (Rowena Morgan), Alexandra Boyd (Sarah Olmstead)

p, Ted Field, Michael Nolin, Robert W. Cort; d, Stephen Herek; w, Patrick Sheane Duncan; ph, Oliver Wood; ed, Trudy Ship; m, Michael Kamen; prod d, David Nichols; art d, Dina Lipton; fx, Bob Riggs; chor, Bruce McDonald; cos, Aggie Guerard Rodgers

AAN Best Actor: Richard Dreyfuss

MR. HOLLAND'S OPUS wants desperately to be the baby boomer IT'S A WONDERFUL LIFE. It's too bad that position is already held by FORREST GUMP.

In 1964, Glenn Holland (Richard Dreyfuss) becomes a high school music teacher. He intends the job to be temporary, just something to pay the bills until his "real" career as a composer takes off. Holland discovers his gift for teaching and the positive impact the act of learning has on a child's self-esteem. Pretty soon, Mr. Holland is organizing a marching band, and his wife Iris (Glenne Headly) is pregnant. In a tragic twist, their son, Cole, is born deaf. Suddenly, it's 1980 and Mr. Holland is deciding whether or not to accompany his star pupil, beautiful ingenue Rowena Morgan (Jean Louisa Kelly), to New York where she wants to pursue a career on Broadway. Mr. Holland considers the notion, but decides not to. In the meantime, his troubled relationship with his son seems to be reaching a head.

MR. HOLLAND'S OPUS is a real tearjerker, but when the tears come, you feel like a jerk. Patrick Sheane Duncan's script is a formula of connect-the-dots cloying moments, and Stephen Herek directs it with all the push-button manipulation and ham-fisted subtlety he brought to THE MIGHTY DUCKS. They should at least be ashamed of the mawkish use of John Lennon's music and memory. Dreyfuss gives a very able performance as the earnest Every-ham, for which he received a Best Actor Oscar nomination.

MR. HULOT'S HOLIDAY
DVD
(LES VACANCES DE MONSIEUR HULOT)
1953 85m bw Comedy ★★★★½
Cady/Gaumont (France)

Jacques Tati (Mr. Hulot), Nathalie Pascaud (Martine), Louis Perrault (Fred), Michelle Rolla (The Aunt), Andre Dubois (Commandant), Suzy Willy (Commandant's Wife), Valentine Camax (Englishwoman), Lucien Fregis (Hotel Proprietor), Marguerite Gerard (Strolling Woman), Rene Lacourt (Strolling Man)

p, Jacques Tati, Fred Orain; d, Jacques Tati; w, Jacques Tati, Henri Marquet, Pierre Aubert, Jacques Lagrange; ph, Jacques Mercanton, Jean Mousselle; ed, Suzanne Baron, Charles Bretoneiche, Jacques Grassi; m, Alain Romans; prod d, Henri Schmitt; art d, R. Brian Court, Henri Schmitt

AAN Best Story and Screenplay: Jacques Tati, Henri Marquet

Director Jacques Tati turned his attention to those French who wrongly believe that a coastal holiday will be a time of rest and relaxation with this delightful film. Featuring the first appearance of M. Hulot (played by Tati himself, in the tradition of the great silent comedians), MR. HULOT'S HOLIDAY takes place at a coastal resort in Brittany. Chaos seems to follow Hulot wherever he goes, but he somehow makes it through life without ever really noticing. Like all vacationers, Hulot (and director Tati) spends a great deal of time observing other vacationers. There is the comely Martine (Nathalie Pascaud), whom Hulot would like to get to know better, but is too shy to confront directly; the workaholic businessman (Jean-Pierre Zola, later seen in MY UNCLE) who cannot stop to relax; the burly British old maid (Valentine Camax); the besieged waiter (Raymond Carl); the former military man who still thinks he's leading a battalion (Andre Dubois); the beachcombing couple (Rene Lacourt and Marguerite Gerard), and countless other unidentified persons who are equally important to the scenery. There is no plot (as the prologue warns us), only a seemingly endless stream of events—with and without Hulot—that carry the film through to the end. With very little dialogue and a creative use of sound, Tati (the actor and director) gives us an entirely new way of looking at a very familiar landscape.

MISTER ROBERTS
DVD
1955 123m c War/Comedy/Drama ★★½
Orange (U.S.)

Henry Fonda (Lt. Doug Roberts), James Cagney (Captain), Jack Lemmon (Ens. Frank Thurlowe Pulver), William Powell (Doc), Ward Bond (C.P.O. Dowdy), Betsy Palmer (Lt. Ann Girard), Philip Carey (Mannion), Nick Adams (Reber), Harry Carey Jr. (Stefanowski), Ken Curtis (Dolan)

p, Leland Hayward; d, John Ford, Mervyn LeRoy; w, Joshua Logan, Frank S. Nugent (based on the play by Logan and Thomas Heggen and the novel by Heggen); ph, Winton C. Hoch (CinemaScope, WarnerColor); ed, Jack Murray; m, Franz Waxman; art d, Art Loel; cos, Moss Mabry

AAN Best Picture; AA Best Supporting Actor: Jack Lemmon; AAN Best Sound Recording: William A. Mueller

Mister Nowhere. This stodgy film version of the famous Broadway success was one performance too many. Hank Fonda plays the title role of the cargo officer dying to leave his supply ship for the glories of battle like a wounded spaniel, all sad eyes and monotoned whining. James Cagney, as the megalomaniacal captain with the palm tree, acts like something out of a cartoon. The Tasmanian Devil is much funnier, folks. William Powell is good, but he doesn't have much to do as the sympathetic ship's doctor. That leaves it up to Jack Lemmon, in his film debut as Ensign

Pulver, to pump some life—and some humor—into this baby. To his immense credit, he does it. Oscar voters, with their usual inferiority complex about theater, probably felt they had to give this heavy, dull film some kind of honor, and they were so grateful for the Lemmon-fresh pledge that they voted for him lock, stock and barrel. John Ford began the film, came to blows (literally) with Fonda, who had played the role about a million times on stage and didn't want to change a thing, and then suffered a gall-bladder attack. Mervyn LeRoy, way past his peak as a director, took over for a time, and even Josh Logan, who helmed the Broadway production, directed some scenes. The behind-the-scenes tinkering shows.

MR. SMITH GOES TO WASHINGTON
DVD
1939 125m bw Political ★★★★★
Columbia (U.S.)

Jean Arthur (Saunders), James Stewart (Jefferson Smith), Claude Rains (Sen. Joseph Paine), Edward Arnold (Jim Taylor), Guy Kibbee (Gov. Hubert Hopper), Thomas Mitchell (Diz Moore), Eugene Pallette (Chick McGann), Beulah Bondi (Ma Smith), H.B. Warner (Sen. Fuller), Harry Carey (President of the Senate)

p, Frank Capra; d, Frank Capra; w, Sidney Buchman (based on the novel The Gentleman from Montana by Lewis R. Foster); ph, Joseph Walker; ed, Gene Havlick, Al Clark; m, Dimitri Tiomkin; art d, Lionel Banks; cos, Robert Kalloch

AAN Best Picture; AAN Best Actor: James Stewart; AAN Best Supporting Actor: Harry Carey; AAN Best Supporting Actor: Claude Rains; AAN Best Director: Frank Capra; AA Best Original Story: Lewis R. Foster; AAN Best Screenplay: Sidney Buchman; AAN Best Film Editing: Gene Havlick, Al Clark; AAN Best Score: Dimitri Tiomkin; AAN Best Interior Decoration: Lionel Banks; AAN Best Sound Recording: John Livadary

Stellar Capra-corn Americana. This great film works on the premise that all that is necessary for evil to triumph is the inaction of good men. Against this danger, director Frank Capra shows a naive everyman to be the true guardian of democratic ideals. James Stewart gives the performance that made him a star as Jefferson Smith, an innocent bumpkin selected by cynical politicians to replace a recently deceased senator in the belief that he can be manipulated by the state's esteemed senior senator, Joseph Paine (Claude Rains). Smith sets off for Washington full of ideals and dreams of working with his idol, Paine, little realizing that he is expected to be a rubber stamp for a crooked scheme to finance a new dam that will profit only Paine and his cronies. The Washington press immediately sizes Smith up as a gullible novice, getting him off to a rocky start, but his idealism captivates Saunders (Jean Arthur), his cynical new secretary. Saunders proves to be a valuable mentor as the innocent Smith slowly comes to realize that his altruistic view of the world doesn't necessarily jibe with reality, and he sets out to expose those who make a mockery of the country he loves so dearly.

While MR. SMITH GOES TO WASHINGTON is the most moral of films, it is so artfully filled with real emotion that it never becomes heavy-handed. Capra supervised every element of the production and used a variety of techniques to accelerate the story line without disrupting it, making every move by every player meaningful and illustrating his credo of "one man, one film." This inspiring masterpiece received 11 Oscar nominations but won only for Best Original Story. Stewart is tops and the rest of the much-loved cast, featuring such familiar veterans as Thomas Mitchell, Edward Arnold, William Demarest and especially Harry Carey, provides unforgettable support.

MIXED BLOOD
1984 98m c Drama ★★★½
Sef Satellite (U.S.)

Marilia Pera *(Rita La Punta)*, Richard Ulacia *(Thiago)*, Linda Kerridge *(Carol)*, Geraldine Smith *(Toni)*, Angel David *(Juan the Bullet)*, Ulrich Berr *(The German)*, Marcelino Rivera *(Hector)*, Rodney Harvey *(Jose)*, Ignazio Spalla *(Commanche)*, Carol Jean Lewis *(Woman Cop)*

p, Antoine Gannage, Steven Fierberg; d, Paul Morrissey; w, Paul Morrissey, Alan Browne; ph, Stefan Zapasnik (Eastmancolor); ed, Scott Vickrey; m, Andy Hernandez; art d, Stephen McCabe

An engaging mix of off-the-wall black humor and obdurate violence presents Rita La Punta (Marilia Pera), a Brazilian woman running a drug-pushing outfit in New York City's Lower East Side. Her gang consists of neighborhood teenagers, whom she sincerely loves as her own, living in a squalid apartment. When her gang intercepts a shipment intended for a rival group, a 14-year-old is tossed off a rooftop in retaliation. Instead of intimidating Rita, the action results in an all-out war between her gang and the rival group. Pera's performance is wacky and believable. This is a story steeped in violence, which happens as casually and frequently as spitting on a sidewalk. Unlike director Paul Morrissey's films for Andy Warhol or some of his 1970s underground work, this is not a comic gorefest. Despite the often-hysterical proceedings, the work is steadfastly rooted in realism. It captures the heart and soul of a neighborhood in one of the more unique slice-of-life pictures in a long time.

MO' BETTER BLUES
1990 127m c Comedy/Drama ★★★½
40 Acres and a Mule Filmworks (U.S.) R

Denzel Washington *(Bleek Gilliam)*, Spike Lee *(Giant)*, Wesley Snipes *(Shadow Henderson)*, Giancarlo Esposito *(Left Hand Lacey)*, Robin Harris *(Butterbean Jones)*, Joie Lee *(Indigo Downes)*, Bill Nunn *(Bottom Hammer)*, John Turturro *(Moe Flatbush)*, Dick Anthony Williams *(Big Stop Gilliam)*, Cynda Williams *(Clarke Bentancourt)*

p, Spike Lee; d, Spike Lee; w, Spike Lee; ph, Ernest Dickerson (Duart Color); ed, Sam Pollard; m, Bill Lee; prod d, Wynn Thomas; art d, Pam E. Stephens; fx, Tom Newton, Tom Brumberger; cos, Ruth Carter

After making the powerful and important DO THE RIGHT THING, Spike Lee took a break from controversial social issues and brought a quieter, more introspective work to the screen in MO' BETTER BLUES, a funny, moody jazz picture that focuses more on relationships and character.

The film follows Bleek Gilliam (Denzel Washington), a popular and talented jazz trumpeter whose life—both personally and professionally—is about to come to a turning point. The women in Bleek's life are Indigo (Joie Lee, the director's sister), a schoolteacher who genuinely loves Bleek and feels a great need for stability in their relationship, and Clarke (newcomer Cynda Williams), an aspiring singer who also cares for Bleek a great deal and who wants to be included in his band. Self-centered Bleek won't even consider Clarke's talents, and he refuses to commit to Indigo. He tells Clarke that "everything else [in life] is secondary" to his music, and this single-mindedness eventually costs him the love of both women.

MO' BETTER BLUES is a very entertaining film. Full of wonderful music, grand visuals, and melodramatic plot twists, the movie is laced with very funny moments, as well as interesting insights into the world of jazz and the plight of the dedicated musician. A lot goes on in the plot, but the pacing is agreeably zippy and the characters are fleshed out in enthrallingly complex fashion. Lee has again created a fun

film to watch that is also an insightful presentation of a specifically African-American milieu.

MOBY DICK
1956 116m c Adventure ★★★½
Moulin (U.K.)

Gregory Peck *(Capt. Ahab)*, Richard Basehart *(Ishmael)*, Leo Genn *(Starbuck)*, Harry Andrews *(Stubb)*, Bernard Miles *(Manxman)*, Orson Welles *(Father Mapple)*, Mervyn Johns *(Peleg)*, Noel Purcell *(Carpenter)*, Frederick Ledebur *(Queequeg)*, James Robertson Justice *(Capt. Boomer)*

p, John Huston, Vaughan N. Dean; d, John Huston; w, John Huston, Ray Bradbury (based on the novel by Herman Melville); ph, Oswald Morris (Technicolor); ed, Russell Lloyd; m, Philip Stainton; art d, Ralph Brinton, Stephen Grimes; fx, Gus Lohman; cos, Elizabeth Haffenden

Not too sea-worthy. John Huston gives a passionate and faithful rendering of Herman Melville's novel in MOBY DICK, aided by a stellar cast. The film opens as a man (Richard Basehart) enters the whaling town of New Bedford in 1840, and, in voiceover, makes the famous declaration "Call me Ishmael." He signs on board the *Pequod*, commanded by peg-legged Capt. Ahab (Gregory Peck). Once under way, the wild-eyed, stony, horribly scarred Ahab assembles his crew to tell them that this will be no routine whaling expedition but a mission of vengeance against the great white whale Moby Dick, which tore off his leg and scarred him for life. He whips them into a frenzy, and when Moby Dick is finally sighted, the crew is as obsessed with killing it as Ahab is. Filmed at considerable danger to cast and crew, MOBY DICK, under Huston's strong direction, is one of the most historically authentic, visually stunning, and powerful adventures ever made. Inevitably, many critics disagreed with Huston's interpretation of Melville's classic. Two fishbones to pick: Peck and Genn's miscasting. But there's Welles in rare form, fine whaling scenes, the first glimpse of Moby Dick, good use of color (akin to old whaling prints) and a literate adaptation by Ray Bradbury. When MOBY is good, it's a whale of a time. Huston received the New York Film Critics Best Director Award.

MODERN ROMANCE
1981 93m c Comedy ★★★★
Columbia (U.S.) R

Albert Brooks *(Robert Cole)*, Kathryn Harrold *(Mary Harvard)*, Tyann Means *(Waitress)*, Bruno Kirby *(Jay)*, Jane Hallaren *(Ellen)*, Karen Chandler *(Neighbor)*, Dennis Kort *(Health Food Salesman)*, Bob Einstein *(Sporting Goods Salesman)*, Virginia Feingold *(Bank Receptionist)*, Thelma Leeds *(Mother)*

p, Andrew Scheinman, Martin Shafer; d, Albert Brooks; w, Albert Brooks, Monica Johnson; ph, Eric Saarinen (Metrocolor); ed, David Finfer; m, Lance Rubin; prod d, Edward Richardson

Albert Brooks directed, cowrote, and stars in this brilliantly funny and at times uncomfortably perceptive comedy. Brooks plays Robert, a film editor trapped in an on-again, off-again relationship with Mary (Kathryn Harrold). After breaking up (again) with Mary, Robert is torn between freedom and love. Attempting to forget her, he invests hundreds of dollars in jogging clothes and vitamins, ventures into the L.A. singles scene (pre-AIDS), mopes, and buries himself in his work (editing a really bad science fiction film for an exploitation studio). None of it works, and soon he's pursuing Mary again in the hope of winning her back—which he does, until anxiety, paranoia, and doubt return to threaten the relationship once again. In addition to being one of the most realistic, insightful romantic comedies ever made, MODERN ROMANCE also offers a detailed and uproarious glimpse into the technical side of the movie business. A progressive, innovative comic filmmaker, Brooks began to find the large audience he deserves with LOST IN AMERICA.

MODERN TIMES

1936 85m bw Comedy
Chaplin (U.S.)

DVD
★★★★★

Charles Chaplin *(A Worker)*, Paulette Goddard *(Gamine)*, Henry Bergman *(Cafe Owner)*, Tiny Sandford *(Big Bill/Worker)*, Chester Conklin *(Mechanic)*, Hank Mann, Louis Natheaux *(Burglars)*, Stanley Blystone *(Sheriff Couler)*, Allan Garcia *(Company Boss)*, Sammy Stein *(Foreman)*

p, Charles Chaplin; d, Charles Chaplin; w, Charles Chaplin; ph, Roland Totheroh, Ira Morgan; m, Charles Chaplin; art d, Charles D. Hall, J. Russell Spencer

Charlie Chaplin's sentimental but keenly satirical swipe at the mechanization of everyday life is by consensus the last of the great silent features. Talkies were predominant in Hollywood as early as 1929, but this 1936 film reflects (and thematizes) Chaplin's resistance to change—though we do hear his voice for the first time during a nonsense song.

As with most Chaplin, MODERN TIMES proceeds as a loosely linked series of comic and/or melodramatic set-pieces. (One critic of the time complained that the film is really a quartet of two-reelers strung together: "The Shop," "The Jailbird," "The Watchman," and "The Singing Waiter.") The film follows Chaplin's familiar tramp persona through a day at the factory (the feeding machine experiment and Charlie's work-induced twitches are highlights), his accidental arrest (and jailhouse encounter with cocaine) when he's labeled a Communist, a stint working at an emporium (where he again displays the remarkable skating prowess he had first revealed in THE RINK twenty years earlier), and a brief engagement as a waiter, during which he's called upon suddenly to perform a song. Along the way he picks up and romances Paulette Goddard's impoverished waif. The narrative culminates in the famous final image of Chaplin and Goddard on the road together, facing an uncertain future with unquenchable optimism.

Despite its loose-knit structure, this remarkable picture—three years in the making—presents a powerful and coherent indictment of the mechanized workplace and the post-Ford "industrialization" of everyday life. At the same time, MODERN TIMES stands as one of Chaplin's most perfectly balanced mixtures of humor and pathos. The gags are impeccably timed and beautifully edited, and Chaplin's scenes with Paulette Goddard, in particular, glow with warmth. (Part of their chemistry doubtless stemmed from their offscreen love; she was Chaplin's third wife.)

The loving care that went into every detail of this film is evident, from Chaplin's own musical score to his makeshift sound effects (e.g., blowing bubbles in a pail of water to simulate a rumbling stomach). Chaplin would continue to delight audiences with his later movies, but all of them featured recorded dialogue—after this one, the master of mime was forced to adapt to modern times.

MODERNS, THE

1988 126m c Drama
Nelson Entertainment/Alive Films (U.S.)

DVD
★★★★
R

Keith Carradine *(Nick Hart)*, Linda Fiorentino *(Rachel Stone)*, Genevieve Bujold *(Libby Valentin)*, Geraldine Chaplin *(Nathalie de Ville)*, Wallace Shawn *(Oiseau)*, John Lone *(Bertram Stone)*, Kevin J. O'Connor *(Ernest Hemingway)*, Elsa Raven *(Gertrude Stein)*, Ali Giron *(Alice B. Toklas)*, Charl Elie Couture *(Charley)*

p, Carolyn Pfeiffer, David Blocker; d, Alan Rudolph; w, Alan Rudolph, Jon Bradshaw; ph, Toyomichi Kurita (CFI color); ed, Debra T. Smith, Scott Brock; m, Mark Isham; prod d, Steven Legler; cos, Renee April

With THE MODERNS, visionary Alan Rudolph completed his long-standing project about the spirit of Paris in the 1920s. Nick Hart (Carradine) is an American who earns a living as an illustrator, though his heart lies in painting. Into Hart's favorite cafe walks Stone (Lone), a proud American businessman who has amassed a fortune in the prophylactic business and who now wants to buy the best collection of modern art in Paris. With Stone is his wife, Rachel (Fiorentino) who, unknown to Stone, had a few years earlier married (and never divorced) Hart. It's not long before Hart and Stone are embroiled in a brutal struggle for art and romance. Displaying a vision of the world uniquely his own, Rudolph has succeeded in making a very modern period film that can be viewed as a documentary—not of an actual time or place, but of a feeling. Better than any piece of newsreel footage or recorded documents, THE MODERNS re-creates the spirit of Paris in the 1920s, a spirit that is the most important aspect of that era and the essence of all art of that period.

MOGAMBO

1953 115m c Adventure/Romance
MGM (U.S.)

★★★★

Clark Gable *(Victor Marswell)*, Ava Gardner *(Eloise Y. Kelly)*, Grace Kelly *(Linda Nordley)*, Donald Sinden *(Donald Nordley)*, Philip Stainton *(John Brown Pryce)*, Eric Pohlmann *(Leon Boltchak)*, Laurence Naismith *(Skipper)*, Denis O'Dea *(Father Josef)*, Asa Etula *(Young Native Girl)*

p, Sam Zimbalist; d, John Ford; w, John Lee Mahin (based on the play "Red Dust" by Wilson Collison); ph, Robert Surtees, Freddie Young (Technicolor); ed, Frank Clarke; art d, Alfred Junge; cos, Helen Rose

AAN Best Actress: Ava Gardner; *AAN Best Supporting Actress:* Grace Kelly

An action-packed remake of RED DUST (1932), this is an oddity in the Ford canon, lacking his stock company and many of the themes that make up his unmistakable signature.

Showgirl Eloise "Honey Bear" Kelly (Gardner), waiting for a steamer in the African jungle, meets safari leader Victor Marswell (Gable, reprising his earlier role). Sex and love follow, but when anthropologist Donald Nordley (Sinden) and his prim but horny wife Linda (Kelly) arrive, Marswell decides to apply his blowtorch to her iceberg. This not only distresses Honey Bear, but may also prove deadly for one third of the love triangle.

MOGAMBO lacks the engaging rauchiness of the superior RED DUST and the wild banter between Gable and his ideal co-star Jean Harlow. Here the verbal sparring goes on between Gardner and Kelly, while Gable wisely replaces his young buck of yore with a more weatherbeaten bwana. Ford provides action all the way, trekking his cameras through Kenya, Tanganyika, and Uganda. There are scenes, reminiscent of Ford's westerns, in which he visually exploits the lavish African landscape.

Kelly, teetering on the brink of major stardom, is quite effective as the repressed wife, and Gardner gives one of the most appealing, relaxed performances of her career. MGM had wanted to get rid of the high-priced Gable for some time, and he subsequently left the studio after completing his next film, BETRAYED. MOGAMBO, however, proved such a bonanza (returning almost $5 million on its initial release) that MGM soon regretted its decision.

MOMMIE DEAREST

1981 129m c Biography ★★½
Paramount (U.S.) PG

Faye Dunaway (*Joan Crawford*), Diana Scarwid (*Christina Crawford as an Adult*), Steve Forrest (*Greg Savitt*), Howard da Silva (*Louis B. Mayer*), Mara Hobel (*Christina as a Child*), Rutanya Alda (*Carol Ann*), Harry Goz (*Al Steele*), Michael Edwards (*Ted Gelber*), Jocelyn Brando (*Barbara Bennett*), Priscilla Pointer (*Mrs. Chadwick*)

p, Frank Yablans; d, Frank Perry; w, Frank Yablans, Frank Perry, Tracy Hotchner, Robert Getchell (based on the book by Christina Crawford); ph, Paul Lohmann (Metrocolor); ed, Peter E. Berger; m, Henry Mancini; prod d, Bill Malley; art d, Harold Michelson; cos, Irene Sharaff

"No wire hangers—ever!" That this apparently banal phrase has now achieved something like immortality is a reflection of the unbridled extravagance of Faye Dunaway's performance in MOMMIE DEAREST—every line, every glance, every Crawford-esque tic and mannerism is greeted by howls of gleeful recognition among camp cognoscenti. Joan Crawford (Dunaway, in a remarkable makeup job) comes off as a cartoon monster in this over-the-top biopic, which blithely mixes fact, legend, and—especially—elements of Crawford's unique screen persona. The film begins in 1939, when Crawford, already a huge star but unhappy and childless, decides to adopt two children. It ends with her death, when the grown-up kids are left out of her will. A neurotic, driven perfectionist, Crawford takes her frustrations out on her children—especially the rebellious Christina (Mara Hobel as a child, Diana Scarwid as an adult)—who are instructed to call her "Mommie Dearest." Largely from Christina's viewpoint, we see Crawford's succession of lovers and husbands, career ups and downs (mainly downs), fantastic egotism, and dependence on and abusiveness toward her children—especially the infamous scene in which she punishes Christina for using wire clothes hangers instead of wooden ones. Based on the best-selling expose by the real Christina Crawford, MOMMIE DEAREST did poorly upon initial release but has since picked up a dedicated cult following. Needless to say, a number of biographical facts (Crawford actually adopted four children) are ignored by the screenplay.

MON ONCLE D'AMERIQUE

(LES SOMNAMBULES)
1980 125m c Drama/Romance ★★★★½
Andrea/TF-1 (France) PG

Gerard Depardieu (*Rene Ragueneau*), Nicole Garcia (*Janine Garnier*), Roger Pierre (*Jean Le Gall*), Nelly Borgeaud (*Arlette Le Gall*), Marie Dubois (*Therese Ragueneau*), Pierre Arditi (*Zambeaux*), Gerard Darrieu (*Leon Veestrate*), Philippe Laudenbach (*Michel Aubert*), Alexandre Rignault (*Jean's Grandfather*), Guillaume Boisseau (*Jean as a Child*)

p, Philippe Dussart; d, Alain Resnais; w, Jean Gruault (based on the works of Prof. Henri Laborit); ph, Sacha Vierny (Eastmancolor); ed, Albert Jurgenson; m, Arie Dzierlatka

AAN Best Original Screenplay: Jean Gruault

Director Alain Resnais connects three "case histories" in MON ONCLE D'AMERIQUE, on odd, intellectually stimulating film that takes chances with narrative as it also works as a philosophical essay.

MON ONCLE D'AMERIQUE employs the scientific theories of Henri Laborit to explain the actions of three disparate characters, Jean, Janine and Rene, who are first introduced in broad sketches. Jean Le Gall (Roger Pierre), a government official and family man, falls for Janine Garnier (Nicole Garcia) an actress, who later changes her career and links up Rene Ragueneau (Gerard Depardieu) a textile plant manager and family man.

MON ONCLE D'AMERIQUE presents an unusual narrative structure in that the three main characters are only completely linked by the last reel and even then only tenuously. With a nod to Balzac, Resnais and screenwriter Jean Gruault seems to be in sync with nouvelle vague "brother," Jean-Luc Godard, whose concurrent 1980 "comeback" film, EVERY MAN FOR HIMSELF uses a similar device. MON ONCLE D'AMERIQUE punctuates the three characters' stories with Dr. Laborit's narration, which comments on brain functioning, the nervous system, and behavior types, in theories that sound like a blend of Freud, Piaget, and Noam Chomsky.

Beyond the structure, however, MON ONCLE D'AMERIQUE is less artistically adventurous than earlier Resnais work (HIROSHIMA MON AMOUR, LAST YEAR AT MARIENBAD), where even his great cinematographer, Sacha Vierny, shoots in a comparatively conventional manner. Still, MON ONCLE D'AMERIQUE neatly fits into the Resnais ouevre. By establishing a near-Proustian concern for memory and the impact of social conditions on human behavior (ending with images of a war-torn city that go far outside the "story"), Resnais makes a moving and lasting, if downbeat, statement.

MONA LISA

1986 104m c Crime ★★★½
Palace (U.K.) R

Bob Hoskins (*George*), Cathy Tyson (*Simone*), Michael Caine (*Mortwell*), Clarke Peters (*Anderson*), Kate Hardie (*Cathy*), Robbie Coltrane (*Thomas*), Zoe Nathenson (*Jeannie*), Sammi Davies (*May*), Rod Bedall (*Terry*), Joe Brown (*Dudley*)

p, Stephen Woolley, Patrick Cassavetti; d, Neil Jordan; w, Neil Jordan, David Leland; ph, Roger Pratt (Technicolor); ed, Lesley Walker; m, Michael Kamen; prod d, Jamie Leonard; art d, Gemma Jackson; cos, Louise Frogley

AAN Best Actor: Bob Hoskins

Irish director Neil Jordan (THE CRYING GAME) showed early promise with this "Hollywood-ready" blend of slick visual style and fairly standard genre narrative. MONA LISA has the quality of an outstanding audition.

George (Bob Hoskins), a recently released convict, has just served a seven-year sentence after taking the fall for his mob boss, Mortwell (Michael Caine). Looking to collect his due, George meets with Mortwell and is informed that he's been assigned a job chauffeuring a high-class black call girl, Simone (Cathy Tyson). George and Simone take an intense dislike to each other at first, but gradually their relationship warms up. Nearly every night, Simone has George drive her through an area where the streetwalkers gather to ply their trade. Here Simone searches for her only friend, Cathy (Kate Hardie), a 15-year-old woman who once worked for the same pimp (Clarke Peters). Eventually George agrees to descend into the underworld to bring back the young woman, a plot device in the grand tradition of TAXI DRIVER and HARDCORE.

Hoskins is tremendous, giving a sensitive, multi-faceted performance that infuses the film with an inner life. Tyson is perfect as Simone, bringing an enigmatic and exotic air to the role that captures the essence of the title. The ever-reliable Caine is good as the sometimes charming villain. The plot's similarity to Martin Scorsese's TAXI DRIVER is not lost on director Jordan, who quotes the earlier film several times. The film often is charming and distinctively offbeat, particularly in scenes featuring the delightful Robby Coltrane as Thomas, George's gentle giant of a roommate. MONA LISA is a detailed, thoughtful film that sensitively explores the emotions within its seedy, exploitative milieu.

MONA LISA SMILE
DVD
2003 117m c Drama ★★½
Revolution Studios/Red Om Films/Columbia PG-13
(U.S.)

Julia Roberts (Katherine Watson), Kirsten Dunst (Betty Warren), Julia Stiles (Joan Brandwyn), Maggie Gyllenhaal (Giselle Levy), Ginnifer Goodwin (Constance Baker), Dominic West (Bill Dunbar), Juliet Stevenson (Amanda Armstrong), John Slattery (Paul Moore), Marcia Gay Harden (Nancy Abbey), Topher Grace (Tommy Donegal)

p, Elaine Goldsmith-Thomas, Paul Schiff, Deborah Schindler; d, Mike Newell; w, Lawrence Konner, Mark Rosenthal; ph, Anastas N. Michos; ed, Mick Audsley; m, Rachel Portman; prod d, Jane Musky; art d, Patricia Woodbridge; fx, J.C. Brotherhood; cos, Michael Dennison

A rebellious art-history teacher tries to shake up her conformist students at Wellesley College in the mid-1950s, only to find that most have their eyes on graduating with an "Mrs. Degree."

California bohemian Katherine Watson (Julia Roberts) comes to chilly, East Coast Wellesley armed with boxes of slides and the conviction that today's best and brightest women should be tomorrow's leaders, not their wives. Katherine's proto-feminist ideas don't sit well with the powerful old-girl alumni association, but Katherine eventually wins over most of the students, including primly brilliant Joan Brandwyn (Julia Stiles), forward-thinking Giselle Levy (Maggie Gyllenhaal), and insecure Connie Baker (Ginnifer Goodwin), the plump duckling surrounded by swans. But holdout Betty Warren (Kirsten Dunst), bullied by her battle-ax of a mother (Donna Mitchell) into mimicking her own unyielding attitudes, writes bitter editorials for the school paper that give the alumni ammunition against the "subversive" Katherine.

Inspired by an article about Hillary Rodham Clinton's Wellesley experiences during the 1960s, screenwriters Lawrence Konner and Mark Rosenthal stepped back a generation to craft this formulaic coming-of-age story about young women trapped between postwar social backlash and the feminist revolution to come. The burden of invigorating this derivative story rests uneasily on the shoulders of Julia Roberts, who's incapable of playing anything but a variation on her thoroughly modern self. From her speech patterns to her body language, Roberts's performance is wrong for the period—even for a free-thinking character like Katherine—and she can't overcome a script that hands Katherine improbably easy victories and sugar-coated defeats that aren't really defeats at all.

MONKEY BUSINESS
DVD
1931 77m bw Comedy ★★★★
Paramount (U.S.)

Groucho Marx (Groucho), Harpo Marx (Harpo), Chico Marx (Chico), Zeppo Marx (Zeppo), Thelma Todd (Lucille), Tom Kennedy (Gibson), Ruth Hall (Mary Helton), Rockliffe Fellowes (Joe Helton), Harry Woods ("Alky" Briggs), Ben Taggart (Capt. Corcoran)

d, Norman Z. McLeod; w, Arthur Sheekman (based on a story by S.J. Perelman, W.B. Johnstone, Roland Pertwee); ph, Arthur Todd

One of the Marx Brothers' funniest films, MONKEY BUSINESS was their first to be written directly for the screen and is noticeably less stagy than earlier efforts. The boys have stowed away on an ocean liner and race from stateroom to stateroom in order to keep from being clapped in the brig. Harpo gets involved with a Punch and Judy show and delights all of the kids on the vessel (as well as all the adults in the audience). The Marxes become embroiled with Fellowes and Woods, a pair of well-dressed and well-heeled gangsters. Hall, the daughter of a hoodlum, is kidnapped and winds up in a barn after being at a

masquerade ball. In the finale, Zeppo, the "straight" brother, goes after the tough hoodlum, while Groucho leaps from one bale of hay to another, offering one-liners as punctuation to the punches. Things slow down a bit when Chico tickles the ivories and Harpo plucks the harp. Thelma Todd handles the female ingenue work well enough and dances the tango well with Groucho. All members of the supporting cast are as effective as they can be in the midst of the comedic cyclone.

MONSIEUR HIRE
1989 81m c Thriller ★★★★
Cinea/Hachette/FR3 (France)

Michel Blanc (M. Hire), Sandrine Bonnaire (Alice), Luc Thuillier (Emile), Andre Wilms (Inspector)

p, Philippe Carcassonne, Rene Cleitman; d, Patrice Leconte; w, Patrice Leconte, Patrick Dewolf (based on the novel Les Fiancailles de Monsieur Hire by Georges Simenon); ph, Denis Lenoir; ed, Joelle Hache; m, Michael Nyman

A superb thriller containing the ugliest portrait of French provincialism since Henri-Georges Clouzot's LE CORBEAU, Patrice Leconte's MONSIEUR HIRE is set in a Parisian suburb in which conformity reigns supreme. Based on the Georges Simenon novel that also inspired Julien Duvivier's PANIQUE, MONSIEUR HIRE is a penetrating psychological portrait of a love-starved outsider who, by the film's end, arouses the audience's protective instincts. When a young girl is murdered, a dogged police investigator (Wilms) immediately suspects Hire (Blanc), a loner distrusted and hated by his neighbors. Tormented by children who play vicious pranks on him, Hire is hounded mercilessly by the detective. Hire resembles his tormentor in that he is an ever-vigilant soul, if in a less acceptable form—for the outcast is a voyeur who spies on Alice (Bonnaire), the woman has moved in across the way. Eventually, Alice spots her secret admirer and, surprisingly, pays him a visit rather than reporting him to the police. An uninhibited free spirit, she is drawn to Hire and allows him to share the simple pleasures of his life with her. Despite continual harassment from the detective, Hire even makes plans to move to Switzerland with Alice, who, unfortunately, has a ne'er-do-well boyfriend (Thuillier). The denouement provides a heartrending exploration of duplicity and betrayal, with a particularly effective freeze-frame halting the action just before it flows into the twist ending.

Rather than jazz up the suspense through the conventional device of cross-cutting, director Leconte works within the frame to create a sense of inexorable doom. MONSIEUR HIRE doesn't move at a fast clip; instead, it involves the viewer in a downward spiral by making us co-voyeurs with the title character, whose life has been a study in self-protective detachment. The audience is implicated in this point of view, eyeing Bonnaire hungrily through her window as Leconte's camera pulls back to an over-the-shoulder shot of Blanc doing the same. In another dazzling, sexually provocative sequence that puts the same motif to very different purposes, the film cuts from an over-the-shoulder shot of Bonnaire watching Thuillier as he enjoys a brutal boxing match to a shot of Blanc fondling her.

Anchored by a haunting performance from Blanc as the voyeur who throws years of self-control to the winds, MONSIEUR HIRE is a study of blindness on two levels: that of prejudice and that of love. As a result of this blindness, both the deceiver and the deceived become victims of fate in this icily compelling film.

MONSIEUR VERDOUX
DVD
1947 102m bw Crime ★★★★
Chaplin (U.S.)

Charles Chaplin (Henri Verdoux/Varney/Bonheur/Floray/Narrator), Mady Correll (Mona Verdoux, His Wife), Allison

Roddan (Peter Verdoux, Their Son), Robert Lewis (Maurice Bottello), Audrey Betz (Martha Bottello), Martha Raye (Annabella Bonheur), Ada May (Annette, Her Maid), Isobel Elsom (Marie Grosnay), Marjorie Bennett (Marie's Maid), Margaret Hoffman (Lydia Floray)

p, Charles Chaplin; d, Charles Chaplin; w, Charles Chaplin (based on an idea by Orson Welles); ph, Roland Totheroh, Curt Courant, Wallace Chewing; ed, Willard Nico; m, Charles Chaplin; art d, John Beckman

AAN Best Original Screenplay: Charles Chaplin

Chaplin, that master comedian, cannot seem to decide here which way to go, either into straight drama or farcical crime, but his black humor is in force nevertheless and he has produced a compelling film about the notorious Landru, better known as "Bluebeard." Instead of WWI—when Landru was busy wooing and murdering scores of women, mostly rich spinsters bereft of the males who had gone to fight at the front—Chaplin sets his tale during the late 1930s, when France was on the brink of war with Germany. Though happily married, with a young son, Chaplin feels the need to murder after losing his bank-clerk job. To support his family he romances rich widows and women with savings and is quickly supplied with a countless stream of victims. Raye is exceptional as the one woman who proves his nemesis, and Chaplin is mesmerizing as the droll little methodical killer who becomes especially eccentric and scary when being tried for mass murder. Chaplin attempts to lift this depressing little film out of the pitch darkness of nightmare with little touches that sometimes fail to amuse. He falls into a lake and is rescued by his intended drowning victim; his little boy pulls a cat's tail and he wonders where the child learned such cruelty. Little of it is funny, even though the great silent comedian subtitled this effort "A Comedy of Murders." Had Chaplin played the role straight rather than reaching too far for empathy and some bizarre black laughs, it might have been a minor masterpiece. As it is, MONSIEUR VERDOUX is a curiosity with flashes of brilliance, but definitely not one of Chaplin's best. Later Chaplin stated that he made this film to protest the A-bomb. The film was utterly rejected by audiences worldwide when released, although it has gained some critical admirers and cult status since.

MONSOON WEDDING   DVD
2001 114m c   Comedy/Romance/Drama   ★★★½
IFC Productions/Key Films/Pandora Films/Paradis   R
Films/Mirabai Films   (U.S./Italy/Germany)

Naseeruddin Shah (Lalit Verma), Lillete Dubey (Pimmi Verma), Shefali Shetty (Ria Verma), Vijay Raaz (P.K. Dube), Tilotama Shome (Alice), Vasundhara Das (Aditi Verma), Parvin Dabas (Hemant Rai), Sameer Arya (Vikram Mehta), Rajat Kapoor (Tej Puri), Kemaya Kidwai (Aliya Verma)

p, Caroline Baron, Mira Nair; d, Mira Nair; w, Sabrina Dhawan; ph, Declan Quinn; ed, Allyson C. Johnson; m, Mychael Danna; prod d, Stephanie Carroll; art d, Sunil Chhabra; chor, Farah Khan; cos, Arjun Bhasin

Director Mira Nair's love letter to family, weddings, and India revolves around the elaborate nuptials of two young professionals, each with one foot planted in tradition and the other in the modern, globalized world.

Aditi Verma (Vasundhara Das) is in love with already married television personality Vikram Mehta (Sameer Arya) but allows her parents, Lalit (Naseeruddin Shah) and Pimmi (Lillete Dubey), to arrange a match with Hemant Rai (Parvin Dabas), an engineer who lives in Houston, TX. Soon the Verma and Rai families are up to their *bindis* in wedding preparations. Lalit hires planner P.K. Dube (Vijay Raaz) to handle the endless details while Pimmi entertains the dozens

of relatives converging on New Delhi from all over the world. Meanwhile, Aditi gets cold feet and, ignoring the good advice of her cousin Ria (Shefali Shetty), sneaks off for a disastrous assignation with Vikram. As the wedding approaches, emotions run high: Lalit worries about money, unaware that Aditi is about to confess her indiscretions to Hemant, possibly scuttling the wedding, and Ria must decide whether to explain her dismay that jovial Uncle Tej (Rajat Kapoor) has singled out little cousin Aliya (Kemaya Kidwai) for his special attentions.

Punjabi weddings are notorious for their lavishness, and Nair's intoxicating soap opera revels in the sights and sounds of this clamorous family ritual. Her style is a canny combination of contemporary realism—cinematographer Declan Quinn's hand-held camera glides among the participants like a nameless partygoer—and glossy Bollywood cliches. The subplot involving Dube's romance with the Vermas' shy young maid (Tilotama Shome) is the stuff of pulp romance, and Nair even manages to get in a dance number and a wet sari scene before the festivities are over.

MONSTER   DVD
2003 111m c   Crime/Drama/Biography   ★★★½
Media 8 Entertainment/DEJ Productions/K/W   R
Productions/Denver & Delilah Films/   (U.S./Germany)
VIP Medienfonds 2/MDP Filmproduktion

Charlize Theron (Aileen Wuornos), Christina Ricci (Selby Wall), Bruce Dern (Thomas), Scott Wilson (Horton—Last John), Pruitt Taylor Vince (Gene—Stuttering John), Lee Tergesen (Vincent Corey), Annie Corley (Donna Tentler), Marco St. John (Evan), Bubba Baker (Cubby), Marc Macaulay (Will Grueser)

p, Mark Damon, Donald Kushner, Clark Peterson, Charlize Theron, Brad Wyman; d, Patty Jenkins; w, Patty Jenkins; ph, Steven Bernstein; ed, Arthur Coburn, Jane Kurson; m, BT; prod d, Edward T. McAvoy; art d, Orvis Rigsby; fx, Phillip Beck; cos, Rhona Meyers

AA Best Actress: Charlize Theron

Former model Charlize Theron undergoes a remarkable physical transformation to play real-life serial murderess Aileen Wuornos in first-time feature filmmaker Patty Jenkins's gritty chronicle of a violent life on the fringes.

Broke and disillusioned, Wuornos (Theron), a 33-year-old drifter and highway prostitute, meets Midwestern misfit Selby Wall (Christina Ricci) in a Florida gay bar. Initially unreceptive to Selby's advances, Aileen warms up to the younger woman, and the needy Selby and the emotionally battered Aileen soon enter into a whirlwind romance. Unbeknownst to Selby, Aileen soon commits her first murder, turning the tables on a sadistic john. The two women drift from cheap motels to inexpensive apartments, drinking, squabbling, and making up; Aileen kills more men, apparently convinced that they're about to attack her. Always volatile, Aileen becomes increasingly belligerent, flouting rules in bars and diners, picking fights, and isolating the couple even from the drifters and fringe-dwellers whose paths overlap theirs. Aileen's only friend is alienated Vietnam veteran Thomas (Bruce Dern); her outbursts ensure that Selby never makes any of her own.

Though not entirely sympathetic towards Wuornos, Jenkins's film fleshes out the monstrous image Wuornos herself helped create with her foul-mouthed, confrontational flare-ups. But the real heavy lifting falls to Theron, who's unrecognizable under dental prostheses, weathered-skin makeup, and some extra 25 pounds of weight. In her hands what might have been an extreme-acting stunt is instead an abrasive study in bitter, lethal desperation; Wuornos knows she's beaten, but she isn't going to give them—whoever "they" are—the satisfaction of seeing her go down. Ricci's less flashy characterization of the immature Selby is equally skilled and meshes seamlessly with Theron's uncompromising performance.

MONSTER'S BALL

2001 108m c Drama   **★★★**
Lee Daniels Entertainment/Lions Gate Films (U.S.) R

Billy Bob Thornton *(Hank Grotowski)*, Halle Berry *(Leticia Musgrove)*, Peter Boyle *(Buck Grotowski)*, Heath Ledger *(Sonny Grotowski)*, Sean Combs *(Lawrence Musgrove)*, Mos Def *(Ryrus Cooper)*, Coronji Calhoun *(Tyrell Musgrove)*, Taylor Simpson *(Lucille)*, Gabrielle Witcher *(Betty)*, Amber Rules *(Vera)*

p, Lee Daniels; d, Marc Foster; w, Milo Addica, Will Rokos; ph, Roberto Schaefer; ed, Matt Chesse; m, Thad Spencer, Chris Beaty, Richard Werbowenko; prod d, Monroe Kelly; art d, Leonard Spears; cos, Frank Fleming

AA Best Actress: Halle Berry; *AAN Best Original Screenplay:* Milo Addica, Will Rokos

A somber meditation on racism and family pathology, anchored by a powerful, Academy Award-winning performance from Halle Berry, the first African American woman ever to win an Oscar in the Best Actress category.

Ailing Southern patriarch Buck Grotowski (Peter Boyle) has bequeathed his middle-aged son, Hank (Billy Bob Thornton), and Hank's son, Sonny (Heath Ledger), two legacies: loyalty to the Georgia Department of Corrections and racism. But Sonny, who's recently joined Hank's death-row team, refuses to embrace his forefather's prejudices; he's formed a quiet but intense bond with a condemned black inmate, Lawrence Musgrove (Sean "Puffy" Combs), and during Musgrove's traditional last walk, Sonny loses his composure and vomits. Hank later responds with a torrent of verbal abuse, and Sonny retaliates by shooting himself in front of his father and grandfather. Meanwhile, Musgrove's widow, Leticia (Halle Berry), is in her own family hell. She's broke and emotionally exhausted in the wake of her husband's death, and often directs her frustration at her obese 10-year-old son, Tyrell (Coronji Calhoun). Hank and Leticia meet accidentally and form an awkward, prickly relationship whose potential to liberate them both is overshadowed by Hank's participation in Musgrove's execution—a subject he can't bring himself to broach.

Will Rokos and Milo Addica's script kicked around Hollywood for the better part of six years, attracting talent as diverse as Robert De Niro and Oliver Stone before finally being made by sophomore director Marc Forster. The significance of certain peripheral details isn't always clear: Forster is clearly working a heavy-duty prison metaphor, but how much should we make of the fact that Hank likes his coffee black and his ice cream chocolate? Elliptical character development, meanwhile, sometimes renders the actors' work opaque; restraint is an underpracticed virtue, but it too can be taken to excess.

MONSTERS, INC.

2001 88m c Children's/Animated/Fantasy **★★½**
Walt Disney Pictures/Pixar Animation Studios G
(U.S.)

VOICES OF: John Goodman *(James P. "Sulley" Sullivan)*, Billy Crystal *(Mike Wazowski)*, Mary Gibbs *(Boo)*, Steve Buscemi *(Randall Boggs)*, James Coburn *(Henry J. Waternoose)*, Jennifer Tilly *(Celia)*, Bob Paterson *(Roz)*, John Ratzenberger *(Yeti)*, Frank Oz *(Fungus)*, Daniel Gerson *(Needleman/Smitty)*

p, Darla K. Anderson; d, Pete Docter, Lee Unkrich (co-director), David Silverman (co-director); w, Andrew Stanton, Daniel Gerson (based on an original story by Pete Docter, Jill Culton, Jeff Pidgeon, and Ralph Eggleston); ed, Jim Stewart; m, Randy Newman; prod d,

Harley Jessup, Bob Pauley; art d, Tia W. Kratter, Dominique Louis; fx, Michael Fong, Galyn Susman; anim, Scott Clark, Sarah Jo Helton, Glenn McQueen, Rich Quade, Doug Sweetland

AA Best Original Song: "If I Didn't Have You"; Randy Newman; *AAN Best Animated Feature Film; AAN Best Sound Editing:* Gary Rydstrom, Michael Silvers

An inspired premise—the childhood monster in the closet is just an everyday Joe with a job to do—is buried in a bland, carelessly plotted computer-generated feature from the Pixar Animation Studios.

In the other dimensional city of Monstropolis, the privately owned power company Monsters, Incorporated, keeps things running off of a suitably monstrous energy source: children's screams. The idea is simple. A "scarer" passes through a set of interdimensional closet doors and into the bedroom of an unsuspecting child, whose frightened yells are then captured and converted into electricity. The company's top scarer is the hulking and hairy but really quite easygoing monster James P. "Sulley" Sullivan (voice of John Goodman); his motor-mouthed best friend, Mike Wazowski (Billy Crystal), a walking, green-skinned eyeball, serves as his trusty scare assistant. The irony is that they're really more frightened of the children: Monsters are taught that all humans are toxic, though some, including company owner Henry J. Waternoose (James Coburn) and Sulley's evil rival, Randall Boggs (Steve Buscemi), know it's not true. Blackouts threaten as today's kids prove ever harder to scare, but Monstropolis faces an even graver crisis when a precocious, babbling toddler named Boo (Mary Gibbs) follows Sulley back to his world.

No reason is ever given as to why the generally decent, hardworking monsters are being lied to, and it's exactly this kind of general disregard for story details that mars this often cute, mildly funny film. All this might have been mitigated by great dialogue, but lines fall flat, and the relationships and conversations among adult characters are straight out of 1950s sitcoms. Now that's scary.

MONTE CARLO

1930 90m bw Musical/Comedy   **★★★★**
Paramount (U.S.)

Jack Buchanan *(Count Rudolph Falliere)*, Jeanette MacDonald *(Countess Vera von Conti)*, ZaSu Pitts *(Maria, Vera's Maid)*, Claud Allister *(Prince Otto von Seibenheim)*, Lionel Belmore *(Duke Gustave von Seibenheim, His Father)*, Tyler Brooke *(Armand, Rudolph's Friend)*, John Roche *(Paul, the "Real" Hairdresser)*, Albert Conti *(Prince Otto's Companion/M.C.)*, Helen Garden *("Lady Mary" in Stage Opera)*, Donald Novis *("M. Beaucaire" in Stage Opera)*

p, Ernst Lubitsch; d, Ernst Lubitsch; w, Ernest Vajda, Vincent Lawrence (based on the play *The Blue Coast* by Hans Muller and the novelette "Monsieur Beaucaire" by Booth Tarkington and Evelyn Sutherland); ph, Victor Milner; ed, Merrill White; m, Richard Whiting, W. Franke Harling; cos, Travis Banton

MONTE CARLO did much to advance the role of the sound film, still very much in its infancy when this musical comedy was made in 1929. The immensely talented Ernst Lubitsch was able to so integrate the fluid cinematic techniques he'd used in silents with the new-found discovery of sound that the outcome here is delightful. On the verge of marrying a prince (Claude Allister), countess Jeanette MacDonald dumps the Teutonic twit and boards the "Blue Express" train for Monte Carlo. In Monaco, with little money left, MacDonald checks into a posh hotel, and is spotted immediately in the casino by a wealthy count (Buchanan) who believes that touching MacDonald's golden tresses will bring him good luck. But when Buchanan strokes MacDonald's hair, it's the countess who begins winning magically, and, not knowing the count's true station in life, she hires him as her hairdresser-chauffeur-valet. Playing along just to be close to her, Buchanan calls MacDonald nightly, and, without identifying himself, sings his love for her. As her money again begins to run out and she is forced to reconsider marrying Allister, MacDonald grows increasingly frustrated. While attending "Monsieur Beaucaire" (an opera about a gentleman who poses as a commoner to be near the woman he loves), MacDonald spots Buchanan in a box seat and realizes that he is anything but common. When she confronts him, Buchanan admits that he is also the mysterious caller, and the two live happily and wealthily forever. Very sweet but not too much so, MONTE CARLO is a charming musical comedy generously blessed with the famous Lubitsch touch. MacDonald looks ravishing and is in wonderful voice; her comic skills are also on prominent display here, especially when she frizzes her hair in frustration. Costar Buchanan, who wasn't give the chance to transfer his legendary stage charisma to the screen often enough, fares less well. (He wouldn't appear in another American feature until THE BAND WAGON [1953].) Musical selections include: "Day of Days," "Give Me a Moment, Please," "This is Something New to Me," "Women, Just Women," "She'll Love Me and Like It," "Always in All Ways."

MONTY PYTHON AND THE HOLY GRAIL   DVD
1975   89m   c   Historical/Comedy   ★★★★
Python   (U.K.)   PG

Graham Chapman (King Arthur/Hiccoughing Guard/Three-Headed Knight), John Cleese (Second Soldier with a Keen Interest in Birds/Large Man with Dead Body/Black Knight/Mr. Newt, a Village Blacksmith Interested in Burning Witches/A Quite Extraordinarily Rude Frenchman/Tim the Wizard/Sir Lancelot), Terry Gilliam (Patsy/Arthur's Trusty Steed/The Green Knight/Soothsayer/Bridgekeeper/Sir Gawain, the First to be Killed by the Rabbit), Eric Idle (The Dead Collector/Mr. Blint, a Village Ne'er-Do-Well Very Keen on Burning Witches/Sir Robin/The Guard Who Doesn't Hiccough but Tries to Get Things Straight/Concorde, Sir Lancelot's Trusty Steed/Roger the Shrubber, a shrubber/Broth), Neil Innes (The First Self-Destructive Monk/Robin's Least Favourite Minstrel/The Page Crushed by a Rabbit/The Owner of a Duck), Terry Jones (Dennis's Mother/Sir Bedevere/Three-Headed Knight/Prince Herbert), Michael Palin (1st Soldier with a Keen Interest in Birds/Dennis/Mr. Duck, a Village Carpenter Who Is Almost Keener Than Anyone Else to Burn Witches/Three-Headed Knight/Sir Galahad/King of Swamp Castle/Brother Maynard's Roommate), Connie Booth (The Witch), Carol Cleveland (Zoot and Dingo), Bee Duffell (Old Crone to Whom King Arthur Said "Ni—")

p, Mark Forstater; d, Terry Gilliam, Terry Jones; w, Graham Chapman, John Cleese, Terry Gilliam, Eric Idle, Terry Jones, Michael Palin; ph, Terry Bedford; ed, John Hackney; m, Neil Innes, De Wolfe; prod d, Roy Smith

A zany, hysterically funny, and sometimes brilliant if sometimes sophomoric send-up of every medieval movie ever made, brought to you by the wacky six-member cast of BBC-television's "Monty Python's Flying Circus." Superior to their first film, AND NOW FOR SOMETHING COMPLETELY DIFFERENT (which was only a series of their televison vignettes released for the theaters), HOLY GRAIL is told in a straight (well all right, fairly straight) narrative structure that follows King Arthur (Chapman) and his knights in their search for the legendary Holy Grail. What transpires in the next 90 minutes is nearly impossible to describe to those unfamiliar with the lunacy of the Python bunch (the six male actors play nearly all the parts, including women's roles), but some of the highlights are well worth mentioning (this film must be seen to be understood). Due to the lack of horses in the kingdom

(and a low budget), Chapman and his knights are followed throughout the movie by their servants, who smack two coconuts together to simulate the sound of hoofbeats. One of Chapman's first battles is against the Black Knight (Cleese), who refuses to let the king pass. A reluctant Chapman is then forced to cut the man limb from limb until all that is left of Cleese is a torso that yells at the King to come back and fight like a man. Meanwhile, Sir Lancelot (once again Cleese) rushes into a castle and hacks up several wedding guests in a bloody frenzy in an attempt to rescue an effeminate prince who really doesn't need to be rescued. After Cleese calms down and surveys the carnage, he manages a feeble, "I just get carried away" as an apology. Of course, every fan of this film has his favorite moment (the Trojan Rabbit, the Knights Who Say "Ni," Robin and his Minstrels, the killer rabbit, the Holy Hand Grenade and the crazed bridgekeeper). But, all the insanity finally leads to a climactic battle scene populated with hundreds of costumed extras, which is stopped before it really gets started by a few carloads of policemen who interrupt the shooting and grab the camera. Not only is HOLY GRAIL a strange, occasionally sidesplitting film, but it paints a grubby, muddy, and vile portrait of life in the middle ages. The set design and visual style are detailed and rich, lending such credence to the film that at the end, when modern-day police arrive to break things up, it is a real shock. A must see.

MONTY PYTHON'S LIFE OF BRIAN   DVD
1979   93m   c   Religious/Comedy   ★★★★
Warner Bros./Orion   (U.K.)   R

Terry Jones (The Virgin Mandy/The Mother of Brian, a Ratbag/Colin/Simon the Holy Man/Saintly Passer-By), Graham Chapman (1st Wise Man/Brian Called Brian/Biggus Dickus), Michael Palin (2nd Wise Man/Mr. Big Nose/Francis a Revolutionary/Mrs. A. Who Casts the Second Stone/Ex-leper/Ben, an Ancient Prisoner/Pontius Pilate, Roman Governor/A Boring Prophet/Eddie/Nisus Wettus), John Cleese (3rd Wise Man/Reg, Leader of the Judean People's Front/Jewish Official at the Stoning/Centurion of the Yard/Deadly Dirk/Arthur), Kenneth Colley (Jesus the Christ), Gwen Taylor (Mrs. Big Nose/Woman with Sick Donkey/Young Girl), Eric Idle (Mr. Cheeky/Stan Called Loretta, a Confused Revolutionary/Harry the Haggler, Beard and Stone Salesman/Culprit Woman, Who Casts the First Stone/Intensely Dull Youth/Otto, the Nazarene Jailer's Assistant/Mr. Frisbee III), Terence Bayler (Gregory/Revolutionaries and Masked Commandos/Dennis), Carol Cleveland (Mrs. Gregory/Elsie), Charles McKeown (Man Further Forward/Revolutionaries and Masked Commandos/Roman Soldier Stig/Giggling Guard/A False Prophet/Blind Man)

p, John Goldstone; d, Terry Jones; w, Graham Chapman, John Cleese, Terry Gilliam, Eric Idle, Terry Jones, Michael Palin; ph, Peter Biziou; ed, Julian Doyle; m, Geoffrey Burgon, Andre Jacquemin, David Howman, Eric Idle; art d, Roger Christian; cos, Hazel Pethig, Charles Knode; anim, Terry Gilliam

Of all the feature films concocted by the British comedy troupe "Monty Python's Flying Circus," LIFE OF BRIAN is their most sustained effort, with a truly linear plot line. While it may lack the sheer comic anarchy of their other work, it is probably their funniest collective effort. In Judea, a mother tends her newborn infant. Three wise men come to herald his birth and then find out that they want the manger next door. This is the birthplace of one Brian Cohen, not Jesus Christ.

Forward to the year 33 AD. Brian joins the People's Front of Judea, a small group of would-be terrorists. Brian aids a PFJ plot to kidnap the wife of Pontius Pilate (Michael Palin), the Roman governor of Jerusalem. But inside Pilate's house, the PFJ run into another terrorist group with the same plan, and all are captured by Roman guards while squabbling among themselves. Brian escapes and hides from the soldiers by posing as a streetcorner preacher, extemporizing a sermon that is derided by his audience of jaded Messiah-seekers. As soon as he attempts to leave, however, he attracts followers, and the more he runs, the more they're persuaded that he is the true Messiah.

The Pythons spent rather a lot of time denying that LIFE OF BRIAN was blasphemous, which it clearly is not (though that didn't stop pickets and calls for bans across the U.S. and Great Britain—mostly from people who hadn't seen the film). Aside from such usual Python subjects of mirth as pompous public officials, men dressed as women, and do-gooders who spend too much time arguing parliamentary procedure ever to accomplish anything, the main subject of satire here is not religion but religious fanaticism. And even that is of a fairly inoffensive variety, making fun of those who just want to have a formula for behavior so that they don't have to bother thinking for themselves. Watch for a quick cameo by George Harrison, who funded LIFE OF BRIAN so the story goes, because he figured it was the only way he would ever get to see another Python movie.

MONTY PYTHON'S THE MEANING OF LIFE   *DVD*

1983 107m c   Comedy   ★★★
Celandine/Python   (U.K.)   R

Graham Chapman, John Cleese, Terry Gilliam, Eric Idle, Terry Jones, Michael Palin, Carol Cleveland, Judy Loe, Simon Jones, Andrew MacLachlan

p, John Goldstone; d, Terry Jones; w, Graham Chapman, John Cleese, Terry Gilliam, Eric Idle, Terry Jones, Michael Palin; ph, Peter Hannan (Technicolor); ed, Julian Doyle; m, Eric Idle, John Du Prez; prod d, Harry Lange; art d, Richard Dawking; chor, Arlene Phillips; cos, James Acheson; anim, Terry Gilliam

For their fourth film, the "Monty Python" troupe reverted to the vignette structure used in their first (and weakest) feature, AND NOW FOR SOMETHING COMPLETELY DIFFERENT. While the sketches are loosely structured to convey elements of life (e.g., birth, education, sex, food, the military, and death), the film is uneven and disconnected. It gets off to a promising start with a marvelous pre-credit sequence depicting a British financial building being raided by swashbuckling pirates and turned (literally) into a giant ship. Many of the sketches show the Pythons' deranged, offbeat humor at its best, but the film begins to pale long before the end and relies on some revolting bits such as a "live" organ transplant and the spectacular (and graphic) explosion of an obese glutton. This is definitely not for anyone with delicate sensibilities.

MOON AND SIXPENCE, THE

1942 89m c/bw Drama   ★★★★
UA   (U.S.)

George Sanders (*Charles Strickland*), Herbert Marshall (*Geoffrey Wolfe*), Steven Geray (*Dirk Stroeve*), Doris Dudley (*Blanche Stroeve*), Eric Blore (*Capt. Nichols*), Albert Basserman (*Doctor Coutras*), Molly Lamont (*Mrs. Strickland*), Elena Verdugo (*Ata*), Florence Bates (*Tiara Johnson*), Heather Thatcher (*Rose Waterford*)

p, David L. Loew; d, Albert Lewin; w, Albert Lewin (based on a novel by W. Somerset Maugham); ph, John Seitz; ed, Richard L. Van Enger; m, Dimitri Tiomkin; prod d, Gordon Willis; art d, F. Paul Sylos

AAN Best Score (Drama or Comedy): Dimitri Tiomkin

Though Marshall is the svelte-voiced narrator of this riveting story, it is Sanders as heartless artist Charles Strickland who makes this film a standout. He is a broker who decides to discard his career to take up his passion, painting. To that end he

convinces Dirk Stroeve (Geray), a successful but mediocre painter, to aid him in developing his art and, during the process, when Stroeve takes Strickland into his home as a protege, the cad seduces Stroeve's wife. Strickland's friend Geoffrey (Marshall) later finds the rake in Tahiti, where Strickland comes to grips with his own personality and discovers his great talent, producing masterpieces until his tragic death.

The Maugham story on which this film is based unabashedly profiles the profligate career of the great Paul Gauguin, and Sanders plays this introspective, cruel-streaked genius to the hilt. Lewin's direction is terse, swift, and often magnificent as he chronicles Strickland's meteoric career and love life, the best part of the film being that set in the tropics toward the end. Here a sepia tone is employed to capture some of the illustrative flavor of the paintings shown and, near the finale, employs color to potent effect. Seitz's camerawork is terrific and the supporting cast, especially Geray and Blore, as a drunkard, is excellent.

MOON IN THE GUTTER, THE

(LA LUNE DANS LE CANIVEAU)
1983 126m c   Drama   ★★★
TF-1/Opera/SFPC/Gaumont (France/Italy)   R

Gerard Depardieu (*Gerard*), Nastassja Kinski, billed as Nastassia Kinski (*Loretta*), Victoria Abril (*Bella*), Vittorio Mezzogiorno (*Newton Channing*), Dominique Pinon (*Frank*), Bertice Reading (*Lola*), Gabriel Monnet (*Tom*), Milena Vukotic (*Frieda*), Bernard Farcy (*Jesus*), Anne-Marie Coffinet (*Dora*)

p, Lise Fayolle; d, Jean-Jacques Beineix; w, Jean-Jacques Beineix, Olivier Mergault (based on the novel by David Goodis); ph, Philippe Rousselot, Dominique Brenguier (Panavision, Eastmancolor); ed, Monique Prim, Yves Deschamps; m, Gabriel Yared; prod d, Hilton McConnico, Sandro dell'Orco, Angelo Santucci, Bernard Vezat; cos, Claire Fraisse

Jean-Jacques Beineix's follow-up to DIVA is an obscure, poetic, dreamlike mystery based on a novel by cult favorite David Goodis. This visually awe-inspiring production tells the story of Gerard (Gerard Depardieu), a riverfront dock worker tormented by the need to find out who raped his sister, causing her to commit suicide while lying in a gutter. During his search, Gerard becomes attracted to Loretta (Nastassia Kinski), the stunning mystery woman who cruises the waterfront in her blazing red convertible. The billboard in front of Gerard's house reads "Try Another World," and that is precisely what he decides to do. Where DIVA overpowered with bright romanticism, MOON IN THE GUTTER stuns with obsession. The script is often embarrassingly indulgent, but, for every failed line, action, and camera swirl, there is another that is astoundingly effective.

MOON IS BLUE, THE

1953 99m bw Comedy   ★★
UA   (U.S.)

William Holden (*Donald Gresham*), David Niven (*David Slater*), Maggie McNamara (*Patty O'Neill*), Tom Tully (*Michael O'Neill*), Dawn Addams (*Cynthia Slater*), Fortunio Bonanova (*Television Announcer*), Gregory Ratoff (*Taxi Driver*), Hardy Kruger (*Sightseer*), Johanna Matz (*His Wife*)

p, Otto Preminger, F. Hugh Herbert; d, Otto Preminger; w, F. Hugh Herbert (based on his play); ph, Ernest Laszlo; ed, Ronald Sinclair, Otto Ludwig; m, Herschel Burke Gilbert; prod d, Nicolai Remisoff; cos, Don Loper

AAN Best Actress: Maggie McNamara; *AAN Best Film Editing:* Otto Ludwig; *AAN Best Song:* "The Moon is Blue"; Herschel Burke Gilbert (Music), Sylvia Fine (Lyrics)

No one today is likely to mistake this smarmy little sex farce for a good film, but it is significant historically as one of the nails in the coffin of Hollywood's self-imposed Production Code. Otto Preminger, an Austrian bull running amuck in the china shop of Hollywood censorship, refused to take the words "virgin," "pregnant," "mistress," and "seduction" out of his script, based on a popular Broadway farce. The film was released without the MPAA seal of approval, and was a solid box office success. The rest, as they say, is history.

The story—which hinges on whether a thirty-something architect (William Holden) or a forty-something roue (David Niven) will get a twenty-something virgin (Maggie McNamara) into bed—follows a painfully predictable line. Holden and Niven are fine, but McNamara, a rather amateurish performer here making her film debut, comes across like a recent drop-out from the Audrey Hepburn Spirited Gamine Academy. (She would act in only three more films before her suicide in 1978.) Luckily, the scene in the taxi where some of the "dirty" words are used comes fairly early on, so you can skip the rest and just read about it in some film history text. Try watching TROUBLE IN PARADISE or THE MAJOR AND THE MINOR instead.

MOONLIGHT MILE 📀

2002   117m   c   Drama   ★★★
Hyde Park Entertainment//Punch Productions/   PG-13
Reveal Entertainment/Gran Via Productions/
Touchstone   (U.S.)

Jake Gyllenhaal *(Joe Nast)*, Dustin Hoffman *(Ben Floss)*, Susan Sarandon *(JoJo Floss)*, Holly Hunter *(Asst. D.A. Mona Camp)*, Ellen Pompeo *(Bertie Knox)*, Richard T. Jones *(Ty)*, Allan Corduner *(Stan Michaels)*, Dabney Coleman *(Mlke Mulcahey)*, Aleksia Landeau *(Cheryl)*, Mary Ellen Trainor *(Mrs. Meyerson)*

p, Mark Johnson, Brad Silberling; d, Brad Silberling; w, Brad Silberling; ph, Phedon Papamichael; ed, Lisa Zeno Churgin; m, Mark Isham; prod d, Missy Stewart; art d, Mark Worthington; fx, Thomas P. Ryba; cos, Mary Zophres

An occasionally surreal meditation on coping with loss, and a love story with a dark side the size of Montana. However you categorize writer-director Brad Silberling's wry, often funny picture, it's clear that he's come a long way since the child-friendly haunts of his 1995 feature debut, CASPER.

Set in New England in the early '70s, the film revolves around young Joe Nast (the appealingly hangdog Jake Gyllenhaal), who has taken to hanging around his fiancée's family home after her apparently random murder and grieving with her parents, likeable but feckless real-estate salesman Ben Floss (Dustin Hoffman) and his artsy, plainspoken soulmate, JoJo (Susan Sarandon). Joe and the family are also involved with the local district attorney (Holly Hunter), who's attempting to put the killer away on their behalf. Before much progress is made, however, Joe has a meet-cute with the town's part-time postmaster, Bertie Knox (Ellen Pompeo), and against his better judgment starts to fall in love with her. Obviously, the potential for guilt on Joe's part is enormous, and in a jolting second-act plot turn we learn that Joe is carrying even more than the audience suspects.

Silberling, who lost his girlfriend, actress Rebecca Schaeffer (of TV's "My Sister Sam"), to a stalker's bullet in 1989, uses disturbing dream sequences to illustrate Joe's inner turmoil and includes a genuinely funny subplot involving one of Ben's potential business partners (Dabney Coleman), who, in a clever homage to THE GRADUATE, extols the virtues of plastics. There's no denying that it's all a bit of a downer—even though it ends happily—but Silberling's script is a feast for the talented cast, and the acting is, without exception, first-rate.

MOONLIGHTING

1982   97m   c   Drama   ★★★★
Miracle   (U.K.)   PG

Jeremy Irons *(Nowak)*, Eugene Lipinski *(Banaszak)*, Jiri Stanislav *(Wolski)*, Eugeniusz Hackiewicz *(Kudaj)*, Dorothy Zienciowska *(Lot Airline Girl)*, Edward Arthur *(Immigration Officer)*, Denis Holmes *(Neighbor)*, Renu Setna *(Junk Shop Owner)*, David Calder *(Supermarket Manager)*, Judy Gridley *(Supermarket Supervisor)*

p, Mark Shivas; d, Jerzy Skolimowski; w, Jerzy Skolimowski, Boleslaw Sulik, Barry Vince, Danuta Witold Stok; ph, Tony Pierce-Roberts; ed, Barrie Vince; m, Stanley Myers, Hans Zimmer; prod d, Tony Woollard; cos, Jane Robinson

One month after martial law was declared in Poland in the wake of the Solidarity uprising, Jerzy Skolimowski began work on this political allegory about a group of four Polish workers in London. Led by the only English speaker among them, their foreman, Nowak (Jeremy Irons), the group arrives to renovate a flat for their Polish boss. Working illegally at what by English standards are cut rates, they must live on the site under uncomfortable living arrangements. When Soviet troops roll into Warsaw, Nowak learns of the events, but, driven by private anxieties and determined to avoid dissent, schemes to conceal the news from his men. As budgetary and scheduling pressures mount, he must take increasingly drastic and draconian measures to do so. MOONLIGHTING contains no manifestos or crude symbols. Its politics are almost entirely limned in the actions and thoughts of Nowak, who is beautifully portrayed by Irons in the performance that made him one of the most respected actors of the decade. The better-educated and more highly paid Nowak is sympathetically characterized even as he mirrors the actions of the Polish authorities, cutting off his men's access to information and family ties, the workers' hierarchy (including the bosses back home) serving as a microcosm of Polish society. Director-cowriter Skolimowski never fails to truly dramatize his themes, however—creating that rarity, a "political film" that is also deeply personal, true to life, and morally and emotionally complex.

MOONRAKER 📀

1979   126m   c   Spy/Adventure   ★★½
UA   (U.K.)   PG

Roger Moore *(James Bond)*, Lois Chiles *(Holly Goodhead)*, Michel Lonsdale *(Drax)*, Richard Kiel *(Jaws)*, Corinne Clery *(Corinne Dufour)*, Bernard Lee *("M")*, Geoffrey Keen *(Frederick Gray)*, Desmond Llewelyn *("Q")*, Lois Maxwell *(Miss Moneypenny)*, Emily Bolton *(Manuela)*

p, Albert R. Broccoli; d, Lewis Gilbert; w, Christopher Wood (based on the novel by Ian Fleming); ph, Jean Tournier (Panavision); ed, John Glen; m, John Barry; prod d, Ken Adam; art d, Max Douy, Charles Bishop; fx, Derek Meddings, John Evans, John Richardson; cos, Jacques Fonteray

AAN Best Visual Effects: Derek Meddings, Paul Wilson, John Evans

A space-age James Bond (Moore) pursues evil to the final frontier in this big-budget entry that cost as much as the first eight Bond films put together. Bond is assigned to search for a missing space shuttle, and along the way he discovers a plot by Drax (Lonsdale) to take over the world by replacing its population with the super race he has bred in the huge space station to which Bond comes for their final battle. Richard Kiel, a dentist's dream, repeats his role from THE SPY WHO LOVED ME as the indestructible, steel-toothed Jaws. Lois Chiles plays the mandatory Bond love interest, and the film marks the last appearance of Lee as M. The gadgets are up to the usual Bond standards, but fancy effects do not a movie make, and 007 is less satisfying floating around in space than when his feet are more or less firmly planted on the ground. John Barry and Hal David collaborated on the theme song, which was sung by Shirley Bassey.

MOONSTRUCK
1987 102m c   Romance/Comedy   ★★★★
MGM (U.S.)   PG

Cher (*Loretta Castorini*), Nicolas Cage (*Ronny Cammareri*), Vincent Gardenia (*Cosmo Castorini*), Olympia Dukakis (*Rose Castorini*), Danny Aiello (*Johnny Cammareri*), Julie Bovasso (*Rita Cappomaggi*), John Mahoney (*Perry*), Louis Guss (*Raymond Cappomaggi*), Feodor Chaliapin Jr. (*Loretta's Grandfather*), Anita Gillette (*Mona*)

p, Patrick Palmer, Norman Jewison; d, Norman Jewison; w, John Patrick Shanley; ph, David Watkin; ed, Lou Lombardo; m, Dick Hyman; prod d, Philip Rosenberg; chor, Lofti Travolta

AAN Best Picture; AA Best Actress: Cher; *AAN Best Supporting Actor:* Vincent Gardenia; *AA Best Supporting Actress:* Olympia Dukakis; *AAN Best Director:* Norman Jewison; *AA Best Original Screenplay:* John Patrick Shanley

Oscar-nominated for Best Picture in 1987, this delightful romantic comedy directed by Norman Jewison and deftly scripted by John Patrick Shanley features excellent ensemble performances and an acting tour de force from Cher. A 38-year-old widow, Loretta Castorini (Cher), works as a book-keeper and lives in Brooklyn with her very Italian-American family: her father, Cosmo (Vincent Gardenia), a prosperous plumber; her mother, Rose (Olympia Dukakis); and her grandfather (Feodor Chaliapin). Her longtime boyfriend, Johnny Cammareri (Danny Aiello), proposes to her; although not passionately in love with him, she accepts. However, Johnny must travel to his mother's deathbed in Sicily before the wedding. Meanwhile, Loretta meets Ronny (Nicolas Cage), Johnny's brother, to whom Johnny hasn't spoken in five years, and they are instantly attracted to each other. MOONSTRUCK brilliantly captures its Italian-American milieu. Director Jewison and screenwriter Shanley have fashioned a charming, funny tale of infidelity and transcendent love whose cultural setting provides both content and context. A symbol of the undeniable power and unpredictability of passionate love, the moon that glows magically over the Manhattan skyline as the events in the film transpire is there not only for Cher and Cage but also for Gardenia and Dukakis. Cher turns in an outstanding performance that deservedly won her an Academy Award for Best Actress. Although Cage stumbles at points, the supporting performances are all superb and wonderfully nuanced. The moon and the whole of the film are beautifully photographed by Oscar winner David Watkin. Simply stated, it is difficult not to be swept up by this charming picture.

MORGAN!
1966 97m bw Comedy/Drama   ★★★
Quintra (U.K.)

Vanessa Redgrave (*Leonie Delt*), David Warner (*Morgan Delt*), Robert Stephens (*Charles Napier*), Irene Handl (*Mrs. Delt*), Newton Blick (*Mr. Henderson*), Nan Munro (*Mrs. Henderson*), Bernard Bresslaw (*Policeman*), Arthur Mullard (*Wally*), Graham Crowden (*Counsel*), Peter Cellier (*2nd Counsel*)

p, Leon Clore; d, Karel Reisz; w, David Mercer (based on the television play "A Suitable Case for Treatment" by David Mercer); ph, Larry Pizer, Gerry Turpin; ed, Victor Proctor, Tom Priestley; m, John Dankworth; art d, Philip Harrison

AAN Best Actress: Vanessa Redgrave; *AAN Best Costume Design (B/W):* Jocelyn Rickards

In the late 1950s and early 1960s, British films were densely populated with angry young men. In MORGAN! the young man is not only angry, he's crazier than a bedbug in Bedlam. By altering the nature of the role from the original TV play, the creators of this film seem to be saying that anything is possible if the leading character is deranged. With that premise, all normalcy is tossed out the window and we are asked to accept the lead as he is, crazy or not. By today's standards, this picture is somewhat dated. The technique often overwhelms the story, with innumerable slow-motion shots, freeze frames, and surrealistic scenes.

Warner is Morgan, a London artist married to Leonie (Redgrave), a woman considerably above his working-class standing. He spends his time daydreaming about swinging through the jungle, which understandably alienates his spouse. (Clips of KING KONG and TARZAN movies are used in the dream sequences.) Leonie secures a divorce, and Morgan, who was supposedly in Greece, shows up on the day it is to be granted. He wants her back and is upset at her plans to marry a priggish art dealer (Stephens) closer to her own social status. Morgan's crazed attempts to win Leonie back involve, among other things, bombs, skeletons, kidnapping, and gorilla suits. A Mona Lisa smile from Leonie and a hammer and sickle motif end the film on an enigmatic note.

The director's attempt to blend reality and fantasy is sometimes successful, but the humor is strained as a result and doesn't always work. It's a bizarre film, too heavy in places and not light enough in others. The picture was released in England as MORGAN: A SUITABLE CASE FOR TREATMENT. Czech director Reisz has made some fascinating films, especially SATURDAY NIGHT AND SUNDAY MORNING. Here, however, he tries so hard to be interesting that the effort shows in every frame.

MORNING GLORY
1933 74m bw Drama   ★★★
RKO (U.S.)

Katharine Hepburn (*Ada Love/"Eva Lovelace"*), Douglas Fairbanks Jr. (*Joseph Sheridan*), Adolphe Menjou (*Louis Easton*), Mary Duncan (*Rita Vernon*), C. Aubrey Smith (*Robert Harley Hedges*), Don Alvarado (*Pepe Velez, the Gigolo*), Fred Santley (*Will Seymour*), Richard Carle (*Henry Lawrence*), Tyler Brooke (*Charles Van Dusen*), Geneva Mitchell (*Gwendolyn Hall*)

p, Pandro S. Berman; d, Lowell Sherman; w, Howard J. Green (based on a play by Zoe Akins); ph, Bert Glennon; ed, William Hamilton; m, Max Steiner; art d, Van Nest Polglase, Charles Kirk; cos, Walter Plunkett

AA Best Actress: Katharine Hepburn

Hepburn received her first Oscar nomination for this, her third film, won the Oscar for her role, and was three times as good as the picture itself. The story paralleled Hepburn's own real-life experience so there was an undeniable streak of reality in her performance. Hepburn leaves a tiny burg in New England. She enters New York City as stagestruck as is humanly possible, but she soon learns that there are a lot of worms in the Big Apple and it's not the most hospitable place to seek fame and fortune. She encounters veteran actor Smith, who has been around since stages were lit by candles, and he takes an interest in her, teaches her a few tricks about acting, and squires her to the right parties. He brings her to a cocktail bash tossed by Duncan, a successful actress and neurotic woman in the Margo Channing (Bette Davis's role in ALL ABOUT EVE) mold. Hepburn hasn't eaten anything so she gets very drunk on champagne and performs two Shakespearean soliloquies for the sake of the startled party-goers. Later, Hepburn takes up with slick Menjou, a manager, then tosses him aside in favor of young playwright Fairbanks, who has written a new show that Duncan is to star in. When the actress goes off the deep end and leaves the show on opening night, guess who steps in, does the role, and is an overnight sensation?

By the story outline, it's easy to see where ALL ABOUT EVE got some of its characters and inspiration. The young actress, the older and temperamental star, the playwright, the manager should be evident. The picture was remade as STAGE STRUCK with Susan Strasberg as the aspiring hopeful and Henry Fonda and Christopher Plummer as the men in her life. That film was not as successful as this one, which was raised in entertainment value by Hepburn's glowing performance. By 1933, the combination of backstage manipulations and overnight success was already a cliché that had been covered many times before. Merian C. Cooper served as the executive producer, and if that seems familiar, it's because he was also responsible for such films as THE FOUR FEATHERS, KING KONG, FORT APACHE, MIGHTY JOE YOUNG, THE QUIET MAN, and many more.

MOROCCO

1930 90m   bw   Romance/War   ★★★★
Paramount   (U.S.)

Gary Cooper (*Tom Brown*), Marlene Dietrich (*Amy Jolly*), Adolphe Menjou (*Mons. Le Bessiere*), Ullrich Haupt (*Adjutant Caesar*), Juliette Compton (*Anna Dolores*), Francis McDonald (*Cpl. Tatoche*), Albert Conti (*Col. Quinnevieres*), Eve Southern (*Mme. Caesar*), Michael Visaroff (*Barratire*), Paul Porcasi (*Lo Tinto*)

p, Hector Turnbull; d, Josef von Sternberg; w, Jules Furthman (based on the novel *Amy Jolly* by Benno Vigny); ph, Lee Garmes, Lucien Ballard; ed, S.K. Winston; m, Karl Hajos; art d, Hans Dreier; cos, Travis Banton

AAN Best Actress: Marlene Dietrich; *AAN Best Director:* Josef Von Sternberg; *AAN Best Cinematography:* Lee Garmes; *AAN Best Interior Decoration:* Hans Dreier (Art Direction)

Marlene Dietrich's first American film is an atmospheric tale of love during wartime, exquisitely directed by Josef von Sternberg. Amy Jolly (Dietrich), a German singer, arrives in North Africa and is hired as the lead act in a cabaret frequented by members of the Foreign Legion. Pursued by Le Bessier (Adolphe Menjou), a worldly gentleman, she finds herself attracted to handsome Legionnaire Tom Brown (Gary Cooper), who ultimately tests the strength of her love.

Like many of Sternberg's most memorable films, MOROCCO is an intelligently observed, passionately realized story of sexual obsession, slim on plot but heavy on atmosphere. Don't look for realism here: it's a sumptuous, overheated Orientalist fantasy peopled with characters (especially Dietrich) who couldn't exist anywhere in the real world, let alone in a Moroccan desert city. MOROCCO would go a long way toward establishing Dietrich's unique star persona (THE BLUE ANGEL was held back from the U.S. market until this Americanized Dietrich could be presented). Camera wizard Lee Garmes was ordered by Sternberg to shoot Dietrich only from one side (an idea borrowed from Garbo films). But Dietrich's comparatively irregular features presented special problems. Garmes compensated with what he called "north light," positioning the key above her and slightly forward. It hollowed her cheeks, shadowed her heavy eyelids, and masked the dimensions of her wide nose. Dietrich was thrilled with the effect; she would insist on similar lighting in movies, public appearances, and photo shoots for the length of her career.

Sternberg and Cooper didn't get along well, and the star resented the director's use of German on the set. Sternberg retaliated by blocking scenes so that Dietrich stands above Cooper, and he's forced to look up to her. Perhaps because of Cooper's mood of angry resignation, he delivers a fey, inadvertently effective performance. His effete mannerisms—tuck-

ing a rose behind his ear, smoking with a limp wrist, kissing behind a fan—create a satisfying contrast with Dietrich's androgyny (which is most apparent when she kisses a woman on the mouth in a nightclub scene).

MORTAL THOUGHTS

1991 104m   c   Mystery   ★★★
New Visions Entertainment/Polar Entertainment   R
Corporation/Rufglen Films   (U.S.)

Demi Moore (*Cynthia Kellogg*), Glenne Headly (*Joyce Urbanski*), Bruce Willis (*James Urbanski*), John Pankow (*Arthur Kellogg*), Harvey Keitel (*Detective John Woods*), Billie Neal (*Detective Linda Nealon*), Frank Vincent (*Dominic Marino*), Karen Shallo (*Gloria Urbanski*), Crystal Field (*Jeanette Marino*), Maryanne Leone (*Aunt Rita*)

p, John Fiedler, Mark Tarlov; d, Alan Rudolph; w, Claude Kerven, William Reilly; ph, Elliot Davis; ed, Tom Walls; m, Mark Isham; prod d, Howard Cummings; art d, Robert K. Shaw Jr.; cos, Hope Hanafin

Directed by Robert Altman protege Alan Rudolph (WELCOME TO L.A., CHOOSE ME, THE MODERNS), MORTAL THOUGHTS is a low-key thriller revolving around the friendship of two women, a friendship that—one suspects—is the most important relationship in either of their lives.

When we first see Cynthia Kellogg (Demi Moore), she's confessing to police detectives John Woods (Harvey Keitel) and Linda Nealon (Billie Neal)—and a video camera. Her story begins with the wedding of her best friend Joyce (Glenne Headly) to handsome, loutish James Urbanski (Bruce Willis). Joyce and Cynthia work together at Joyce's beauty salon, Clip 'n' Dye, in Bayonne, New Jersey, and as Cynthia describes countless ugly incidents the viewer begins to suspect the reason she's sitting in a police station. A messy murder, and an inept coverup, follow in due course.

While not entirely successful, MORTAL THOUGHTS is surprisingly compelling. Headly and Moore go all-out with their working-girl mannerisms, but their friendship rings true and their ill-considered decisions are made strangely believable by their desperation. As the loathsome James, Bruce Willis is flawlessly cast; he's a smug, self-absorbed bully whose twin interests seem to be brutalizing Joyce and Cynthia, pleading with the latter to show him her breasts long past the point where anyone would excuse it as a joke. He's monstrous enough that anyone can see why either woman could kill him, but radiates enough lumpen charm that one can also imagine why Joyce married him in the first place.

MORVERN CALLAR

2002 97m   c   Drama   ★★★★
Morvern Callar Productions/Alliance Atlantis/BBC
Films/Film Council/Scottish Screen/Glasgow Film
Fund/Company Pictures   (U.K./Canada)

Samantha Morton (*Morvern Callar*), Kathleen McDermott (*Lanna*), Linda McGuire (*Vanessa*), Ruby Milton (*Couris Jean*), Dolly Wells (*Susan*), Jim Wilson (*Tom Boddington*), Dan Cadan (*Dazzer*), Carolyn Calder (*Tequila Sheila*), Raife Patrick Burchell (*Boy in Room 1022*), Steven Cardwell (*Welcoming Courier*)

p, George Faber, Charles Pattinson, Robyn Slovo; d, Lynne Ramsay; w, Liana Dognini, Lynne Ramsay (based on the novel by Alan Warner); ph, Alwin Kuchler; ed, Lucia Zucchetti; m,; prod d, Jane Morton; art d, Philip Barber; fx, Simon Frame; cos, Sarah Blenkinsop

Exceeding the high expectations set by her superb debut, 1999's grim but gripping RATCATCHER, Scottish director Lynne

Ramsay's second feature is an extraordinary adaptation of Alan Warner's acclaimed novel.

Morvern Callar (Samantha Morton), a twentysomething supermarket cashier in a remote Highland town, finds an awful surprise under her Christmas tree: the corpse of her boyfriend, aspiring novelist James. His suicide note bequeaths to Morvern the manuscript of his unpublished novel and invites her to help herself to his bank account. Grief-stricken and dazed, Morvern disposes of James's body without notifying anyone of his death, then puts her own name on his manuscript before shipping it off to a London publisher. She then empties James's account and leaves the damp murk of the Scottish Highlands for the sun and sand of Spain, treating herself and her best friend Lanna (newcomer Kathleen McDermott) to two weeks at a rowdy Youth Med resort on the Costa del Sol.

Warner's novel is a fragmented chronicle of events told entirely from Morvern's deadpan, affectless perspective. Ramsay, who co-wrote the screenplay with Liana Dognini, boldly decided to pass on the obvious choice of a voice-over narration and instead tells the story through Alwin Kuchler's intimate cinematography and Morton's remarkable face. With very little written dialogue at her disposal, Morton is able to convey not only Morvern's shock, grief, and eventual liberation through dire circumstances, but the disquieting blankness that's essential to her character. Astonishingly, McDermott, who has never acted before (she was busy pursuing a career as a barber before being discovered on a Glasgow street), manages to keep up with her every step of the way.

MOSCOW ON THE HUDSON 📀

1984 115m c Comedy/Drama ★★★½
Columbia (U.S.) R

Robin Williams (*Vladimir Ivanoff*), Maria Conchita Alonso (*Lucia Lombardo*), Cleavant Derricks (*Lionel Witherspoon*), Alejandro Rey (*Orlando Ramirez*), Savely Kramarov (*Boris*), Elya Baskin (*Anatoly*), Oleg Rudnik (*Yury*), Alexander Beniaminov (*Vladimir's Grandfather*), Ludmila Kramarevsky (*Vladimir's Mother*), Ivo Vrzal (*Vladimir's Father*)

p, Paul Mazursky; d, Paul Mazursky; w, Paul Mazursky, Leon Capetanos; ph, Don McAlpine (Metrocolor); ed, Richard Halsey; m, David McHugh; prod d, Pato Guzman; art d, Michael Molly, Peter Rothe; cos, Albert Wolsky

A loving, dramatic comedy that resembles early Frank Capra in its patriotism and sentiment, this movie just misses on several levels but has enough humor to make you smile and enough corn to warm anyone's heart. Vladimir Ivanoff (Robin Williams) is a saxophonist with a Russian circus visiting the U.S. on a tour. Just before leaving New York, Vladimir is in Manhattan's trendiest department store, Bloomingdale's, when he makes the decision to defect. He races around the store, chased by KGB men, and hides under a counter handled by Lucia Lombardo (Maria Conchita Alonso). After the cops come in and Vladimir tells them he's defecting, he is taken to Harlem by security guard Lionel Witherspoon (Cleavant Derricks), whose family welcomes him. It isn't long before Vladimir and Lucia are an item, and she tries to help him get official status in the U.S. through an immigration attorney (Alejandro Rey). There is no great story to speak of, just the adjustments Vladimir must make to become an American.

MOSQUITO COAST, THE 📀

1986 117m c Adventure ★★★½
Warner Bros. (U.S.) R

Harrison Ford (*Allie Fox*), Helen Mirren (*Mother*), River Phoenix (*Charlie*), Jadrien Steele (*Jerry*), Hilary Gordon (*April*), Rebecca Gordon (*Clover*), Jason Alexander (*Clerk*), Dick O'Neill (*Mr. Polski*), Alice Sneed (*Mrs. Polski*), Tiger Haynes (*Mr. Semper*)

p, Jerome Hellman; d, Peter Weir; w, Paul Schrader (based on the novel by Paul Theroux); ph, John Seale (Technicolor); ed, Thom Noble; m, Maurice Jarre; prod d, John Stoddart; art d, John Wingrove; fx, Larry Cavanaugh; cos, Gary Jones

A courageous and serious film that explores the limits of the mythic American virtues of persistence, inventiveness, and rugged individualism. Allie Fox (Harrison Ford) is an eccentric inventor, a wildly optimistic can-do kind of guy. Disgusted with what he perceives to be a dying America, Fox takes his wife (Helen Mirren) and four children, including 15-year-old Charlie (River Phoenix), to an unsettled area near Honduras called the Mosquito Coast. Fox buys the deed to an isolated town that turns out to be nothing but a few shacks and a handful of residents. But he mercilessly pushes his family, the locals, and himself, driven by an obsessive desire to recreate society along Utopian lines. His dream world is shaken when three gun-toting terrorists show up. Unfortunately, as Fox's dreams and sanity begin to fall apart, so does the film, but it's memorable and intense up to that point. Schrader's screenplay, based on an allegorical novel by Paul Theroux, suggests that the very qualities that allow people and nations to achieve greatness may also plant the seeds of future destruction.

MOST DANGEROUS GAME, THE 📀

1932 63m bw Thriller/Adventure ★★★½
RKO (U.S.)

Joel McCrea (*Bob Rainsford*), Fay Wray (*Eve Trowbridge*), Leslie Banks (*Count Zaroff*), Robert Armstrong (*Martin Trowbridge*), Steve Clemente, Noble Johnson (*Tartar Servants*), Hale Hamilton

p, Merian C. Cooper, Ernest B. Schoedsack; d, Ernest B. Schoedsack, Irving Pichel; w, James Ashmore Creelman (based on a story by Richard Connell); ph, Henry Gerrard; ed, Archie Marshek; m, Max Steiner

This is a grim and morose film with strong undertones of sadism and, toward the end, brutality. It is also a genuinely frightening film involving Banks as a mad Russian count who lords over a mist-enshrouded island and waits like a vicious spider for wayward ships to wreck themselves on the dangerous reefs surrounding his sinister domain. One of the sinking ships delivers up flotsam in the form of McCrea, Wray, and Armstrong, who are, at first, warmly welcomed to Banks's lavish estate. But slowly, as Banks describes his passion for hunting the wild beasts on the island, he begins to finger a scar on his forehead, one caused by a lion. Before they can realize their horrible situation, the shipwrecked survivors are compelled to flee into the thorny wilderness of the island with their host hunting them as he would animals, armed with bow and arrows, to give them a sporting chance. With Banks are his henchmen, and a pack of the most vicious dogs ever unleashed in any film. Directors Schoedsack and Pichel dwell on the hunt, showing the victims fleeing madly through the brush and forests, narrowly missing death at the claws of wild animals or plunging into bottomless gorges. The hounds are shown in quick close-ups that are terrifyingly abrupt, and telescopic shots cutting from the hunter to the hunted heighten the tension. Banks is relentless in his pursuit, crazily blowing his hunting horn and drawing his bow with an accuracy that proves deadly. He finally meets the grim fate he has designed for the others, plunging to his death while his own bloodthirsty hounds close in on him. There are wonderful atmospherics to this film—the count's looming, black castle, the primeval forests of the island—the same kind of environment producers Cooper and Schoedsack would create for their horror masterpiece, KING KONG, a year later. The studio thought that showing some decapitated heads, victims of Banks's unnatural hunts, might upset viewers, so these scenes were later cut. Wray, Armstrong, and Steiner, who composed the eerie score, would all be effectively used in KING KONG. The dark theme of this movie would be employed in countless films to come, as well as in radio and television programs. RKO would remake this film as A GAME OF DEATH and United Artists would explore the idea in RUN FOR THE SUN.

MOST TERRIBLE TIME IN MY LIFE, THE
(WAGA JINSEI SAIAKU NO TOKI)
1993 92m bw Crime/Thriller ★★★★
For Life Records/Film Detective Office/Shutter Pictures (Japan/Taiwan)

Masatoshi Nagase *(Maiku Hama)*, Yang Haitin *(Yang Haitin)*, Hou De Jian *(Hou De Jian)*, Shiro Sano *(Kanno)*, Kiyotaka Nanbara *(Hoshino)*, Xiu Jian, Akaji Maro *(Detective Nakayama)*, Shinya Tsukamoto *(Yamaguchi)*, Joe Shishido *(Joe Shishido)*, Yu Wei Yen

p, Shunsuke Koga, Kaizo Hayashi, Yu Wei Yen; d, Kaizo Hayashi; w, Daisuke Tengan, Kaizo Hayahsi; ph, Yuichi Nagata; ed, Nobuko Tomita; m, Meyna Co.; prod d, Takeo Kimura; cos, Masae Miyamoto

Far more than just another cheeky homage to film noir—specifically Mickey Spillane's tough-guy detective thrillers—this black-and-white beauty from Japanese director Kaizo Hayashi succeeds entirely on its own terms.

Maiku Hama (Masatoshi Nagase) is a Yokohama private detective who specializes in finding missing Chinese and Korean immigrants. One afternoon at a local mahjong parlor, Maiku rescues a young Taiwanese waiter named Yang (Yang Haitin) from a knife-wielding bully; in return, Yang hires Maiku to help find his missing brother. Maiku takes the case without realizing the Pandora's box he's about to pop open. Yang's brother is really a ruthless hit man who has defected from the Taiwanese Mafia and has joined the Black Dogs, a new and particularly brutal Japanese gang made up of naturalized immigrants. And Yang isn't just a smiling waiter; he's been sent to Japan to assassinate his brother, a killing that will inevitably spark a deadly gang war.

Hayashi and cinematographer Yuichi Nagata have gotten the hard-boiled feel exactly right, while thankfully dispensing with the nasty misogyny that spoils Spillane's books. That said, it's still full of sadistic, Spillane-style violence: Maiku loses a finger within the film's first five minutes, and an unfortunate *yakuza* loses four of *his* digits 10 minutes later. But for all the references and po-mo nods, there's an honest element of tragedy to the tale, and the film has something serious to say about assimilation among people to whom heritage once meant something. The film was a huge success in Japan, spawning two sequels and making private investigation a popular career choice.

MOTHER AND THE WHORE, THE
(LA MAMAN ET LA PUTAIN)
1973 210m bw Drama ★★★★
Losange/Elite/Cine Qua Non/Simar/V-M (France)

Bernadette Lafont *(Marie)*, Jean-Pierre Leaud *(Alexandre)*, Francoise Lebrun *(Veronika)*, Isabelle Weingarten *(Gilberte)*, Jacques Renard *(Friend)*, Jean-Noel Picq, Jessa Darrieux, Marinka Matuszewski, Genevieve Mnich, Berthe Grandval

p, Pierre Cottrell; d, Jean Eustache; w, Jean Eustache; ph, Pierre Lhomme, Jacques Renard, Michel Cenet; ed, Jean Eustache, Denise de Casabianca

If any film signified that the French New Wave had come to an end, it was THE MOTHER AND THE WHORE, a grueling three-and-a-half-hour study that may be one of the more enlightening works the cinema has ever produced. Set against a background of Paris cafes and tiny one-room apartments, it traces the amorous adventures of Alexandre (Jean-Pierre Leaud), an irresponsible young man who pretends to be a leftist intellectual. He is really little more than a victim of the post-war existentialist thought that paved the way for the materialistic attitudes of the early 1970s and a generation filled with empty ideals. One morning, Alexandre feels an extraordinary need to marry. Leaving the small flat he shares with Marie (Bernadette Lafont), his lover and willing meal ticket, he sets out to pop the question to his old girlfriend. Alexandre brings the girl to a cafe where he engages in a long pseudo-intellectual monologue while asking for her hand. She flatly refuses, responding, "What novel are you being a character in?" (Alexandre characteristically perceives himself in such terms.) Later that same day, he passes by a cafe where he spots the vampirish looking Veronika (Francoise Lebrun) staring at him. He gets her phone number and agrees to meet her later. After several failed attempts to meet her, the two eventually arrange to meet at a cafe. Veronika works as a nurse, a job that allows her enough money to pay for her dingy room, to buy pretty clothes, and to keep herself numbed with alcohol. Other than this, the only thing that interests her is sex, and she has no qualms about sleeping with any passing stranger. Alexandre and Veronika start a shaky affair that consists mainly of meeting in cafes and long monologues on Alexandre's part. To Veronika, he has become much more than her usual casual fling. She even calls him while he is spending the evening with Marie, then sleeps with both of them. Marie attempts suicide, and the tension created by the triangle continually mounts until a gruesome climax in which Veronika, who has seemed aloof and unaffected to this point, delivers a tear-filled soliloquy revealing her self-perception as a sexual object. Alexandre follows her to her room and asks her to marry him. She accepts while vomiting into a bucket which he holds.

Prior to THE MOTHER AND THE WHORE, director Eustache had worked as an assistant for New Wave directors, most notably Jean-Luc Godard. (He even appeared briefly in WEEKEND.) His first two solo efforts were medium-length features that were of some interest, but this picture proved he was a perceptive filmmaker. However, Eustache's career was very short. After THE MOTHER AND THE WHORE won both the Grand Prix and the International Critics Award at Cannes, he made only one more feature before his suicide in 1980. THE MOTHER AND THE WHORE captures a sense of realism rare in any type of film, bringing us deep beneath the surface of the characters' exteriors.

MOTHER INDIA
🅓🅥🅓
1957 152m c Drama ★★★½
Mehboob Productions Ltd. (India)

Nargis Dutt *(Radha)*, Sunil Dutt *(Birju)*, Raj Kumar *(Shamulu)*

p, Mehboob Khan; d, Mehboob Khan; w, V. Mirza, Ali Raza; m, Naushad; prod d, V.H. Palnitkar

AAN Best Foreign Language Film

The most popular film in Indian history—it's said to have been playing somewhere in the country every day since its release. This epic melodrama is so widely known and deeply revered that Indira Gandhi used the title on election posters and campaigned with star Nargis Dutt at her side. Radha (Nargis) is a rural matriarch who loses her husband (Raj Kumar) after a farming accident. With her sons, she struggles to survive despite the machinations of a singularly villainous landlord. When wayward son Birju (Sunil Dutt) becomes an outlaw, Radha must act to restore order to the community.

Director Mehboob Khan's very Indian brand of Marxism is unmistakably represented by his production company's logo, which combines the hammer and sickle with the symbol denoting "Om." The film is unmistakably left-leaning but curiously compromised—after it makes about as strong a case for killing the local *zamindar* (landlord) as could be imagined, it suggests that actually doing so would be a violation of *dharma* (order, propriety). Salvation lies not in violence but in adherence to the traditional values embodied in the archetypal mother figure, unforgettably played by Nargis Dutt. For Nargis, who had earlier specialized in urban sophisticates (AWAARA), the peasant Radha was a marked departure; it nevertheless became the definitive role of her career. Having conducted a notorious affair with Raj Kapoor (India's greatest star and a formidable director), she soon married co-star Sunil Dutt and settled down, redeeming herself in the eyes of the Indian public. Their son, musclebound Sunjay Dutt, became India's leading action star during the 1980s.

MOTORCYCLE DIARIES, THE

2004 126m c Biography/Drama ★★★½
South Fork Pictures/Tu Vas Voir Productions/FilmFour/ R
BD Cine/Senator Film Produktion/Southfork Pictures
(U.S./Argentina/U.K.)

Gael Garcia Bernal *(Ernesto Guevara de la Serna)*, Rodrigo de la Serna *(Alberto Granado)*, Mia Maestro *(Chichina Ferreyra)*, Mercedes Moran *(Celia de la Serna)*, Jean-Pierre Noher *(Ernesto Guevara Lynch)*, Lucas Oro *(Roberto Guevara)*, Marina Glezer *(Celita Guevara)*, Sofia Bertolotto *(Ana Maria Guevara)*, Franco Solazzi *(Juan Martin Guevara)*, Ricardo Diaz Mourelle *(Uncle Jorge)*

p, Michael Nozik, Edgard Tenembaum, Karen Tenkhoff; d, Walter Salles; w, Jose Rivera (based on the books *The Motorcycle Diaries* by Ernesto "Che" Guevara and *Traveling with Che Guevara* by Alberto Granado); ph, Eric Gautier; ed, Daniel Rezende; m, Gustavo Santaolalla; prod d, Carlos Conti; art d, Coca Oderigo, Laruent Ott, Maria Eugenia Sueiro; fx, Georges Demetrau; cos, Beatriz Di Benedetto, Marisa Urruti

AA Best Original Song: "Al Otro Lado Del Rio"; Jorge Drexler (music, lyrics); *AAN Best Adapted Screenplay:* Jose Rivera

Based in part on Ernesto "Che" Guevara's journal of his 1952 expedition through South America, this slightly fictionalized adventure dramatizes the journey that helped turn a restless young medical student into one of the 20th century's most romantic revolutionary figures.

Buenos Aires, 1952: With only a year remaining before he gets his medical degree, 23-year-old Ernesto Guevara de la Serna (Gael Garcia Bernal) and his friend, 29-year-old Alberto Granado (Rodrigo de la Serna), decide it's time to pack up Alberto's dilapidated 1939 Norton 500 motorbike—nicknamed "La Poderosa," or "The Mighty One"—bid farewell to their families, and hit the road. Like an Argentine Kerouac and Cassady, Ernesto and Alberto hope to discover the America that lies outside their comfortable lives, but what they experience—the majesty of the land and the extreme poverty of its indigenous peoples—will change their lives forever. The route: a four-month, 8,000-km trek through Argentina, Chile, Peru, Colombia, Venezuela, and, hopefully, Miami, where Ernesto has promised to buy his beautiful, aristocratic girlfriend (Mia Maestro) a bathing suit. That is if the unreliable and poorly balanced La Poderosa doesn't kill them first.

Director Walter Salles's adaptation is more serious and far less picaresque than Che's own account, and Salles often resorts to obvious juxtapositions and heavily metaphoric action to foreshadow Ernesto's future. The film works best when it doesn't try so hard, when Salles simply allows his excellent actors and his beautiful images to work their magic. Salles—who used the terrain of his native Brazil to such good effect in CENTRAL STATION and BEHIND THE SUN—and his brilliant cinematographer, Eric Gautier, capture the breathtaking variety of the Latin American landscape.

MOULIN ROUGE

2001 135m c Musical/Romance ★★★
Bazmark (U.S.) PG-13

Nicole Kidman *(Satine)*, Ewan McGregor *(Christian)*, John Leguizamo *(Toulouse Lautrec)*, Jim Broadbent *(Zidler)*, Richard Roxburgh *(Duke of Worcester)*, Garry McDonald *(The Doctor)*, Jacek Koman *(The Unconscious Argentinian)*, Matthew Whittet *(Satie)*, Kerry Walker *(Marie)*, Caroline O'Connor *(Nini Legs in the Air)*

p, Martin Brown, Fred Baron, Baz Luhrmann; d, Baz Luhrmann; w, Baz Luhrmann, Craig Pearce; ph, Donald M. McAlpine; ed, Jill Bilcock; m, Craig Armstrong; prod d, Catherine Martin; art d, Ian Gracie; fx, Chris Godfrey; chor, John O'Connell; cos, Catherine Martin, Angus Strathie

AA Best Art Direction: Catherine Martin, Brigitte Broch; *AA Best Costume Design:* Catherine Martin, Angus Strathie; *AAN Best Picture*; *AAN Best Actress:* Nicole Kidman; *AAN Best Cinematography:* Donald M. McAlpine; *AAN Best Film Editing:* Jill Bilcock; *AAN Best Makeup:* Maurizio Silvi, Aldo Signoretti; *AAN Best Sound:* Andy Nelson, Anna Behlmer, Roger Savage, Guntis Sics

Baz Luhrmann learned all the wrong lessons from dissident movie musicals like CABARET, filling dance sequences with fragmented, Fosse-esque shots of body parts without carrying the movement across the cuts. But he can roll together can-can dancers, "Lady Marmalade," top-hatted toffs, "Smells Like Teen Spirit," and "Diamonds Are a Girl's Best Friend" (with just a flash of "Material Girl") into an intoxicating, flagrantly anachronistic confection.

Montmartre, 1899. Into this hotbed of vice and absinthe-fueled creativity comes Christian (Ewan MacGregor), a straight-laced naif who dreams of love and literature. He finds kindred souls in the "Children of the Revolution," a loose-knit bohemian brigade dedicated to freedom, truth, beauty, and, above all, love. Their ringleader, lisping artist Toulouse-Lautrec (John Leguizamo), gets Christian a job writing an ill-defined show called "Spectacular Spectacular" for the dance hall cum brothel called the Moulin Rouge, and introduces him to exquisite, consumptive courtesan Satine (Kidman). Satine and Christian fall in love, but her favors are promised to the wealthy duke (Richard Roxburgh) who's underwriting both "Spectacular Spectacular" and the Moulin Rouge's conversion into a legitimate theater, where Satine hopes to become a respected actress like Sarah Bernhardt.

This cliched romantic triangle is simply a framework on which to hang glittering production design and gloriously excessive musical numbers. Who but Luhrman would have imagined the Police's "Roxanne" as a brutal tango pantomime? When the Duke declares petulantly, "I don't care about your silly dogma!" it's hard not to hear Luhrman's voice rejecting the stripped-down aesthetics of Dogme95 filmmakers. His belief in glorious artifice is so complete it feels like heresy to wince at his movie's frequent tumbles into pedestrian vulgarity.

MOULIN ROUGE

1952 123m c Biography ★★★★
Romulus (U.K.)

Jose Ferrer *(Henri de Toulouse-Lautrec/The Comte de Toulouse-Lautrec)*, Colette Marchand *(Marie Charlet)*, Suzanne Flon *(Myriamme Hayem)*, Zsa Zsa Gabor *(Jane Avril)*, Katherine Kath *(La Goulue)*, Claude Nollier *(Countess de Toulouse-Lautrec)*, Muriel Smith *(Aicha)*, Georges Lannes *(Patou)*, Walter Crisham *(Valentin Dessosse)*, Mary Clare *(Mme. Loubet)*

p, John Huston; d, John Huston; w, Anthony Veiller, John Huston (based on the novel by Pierre La Mure); ph, Oswald Morris (Technicolor); ed, Ralph Kemplen; m, Georges Auric; art d, Paul Sheriff; cos, Marcel Vertes, Juliaes Squire, Schiaparelli

AAN Best Picture; AAN Best Actor: Jose Ferrer; AAN Best Supporting Actress: Colette Marchand; AAN Best Director: John Huston; AAN Best Film Editing: Ralph Kemplen; AA Best Art Direction-Set Decoration (Color): Paul Sheriff, Marcel Vertes; AA Best Costume Design (Color): Marcel Vertes

Jose Ferrer made his mark with portrayals of real, or famous fictional, characters (CYRANO DE BERGERAC, the Dauphin in JOAN OF ARC); his role here can be seen as a combination of the two, since Huston's treatment of the life of artist Toulouse-Lautrec takes many liberties with the truth. Nonetheless, Ferrer does a fine job of limming the deformed (a childhood illness caused his legs to stop growing) artist, playing most of the film on his knees. MOULIN ROUGE was filmed in France and England and had a few interesting people in small roles. Look hard for horrormeisters Christopher Lee and Peter Cushing, as well as a young Tutte Lemkow (British choreographer/actor who was the Fiddler in FIDDLER ON THE ROOF). The first 25 minutes of the movie are outstanding, with a cancan sequence setting the tone for what is to come. This and other dance sequences completely eclipse similar scenes in Jean Renoir's FRENCH CANCAN and Walter Lang's CAN CAN.

MOUSE THAT ROARED, THE

1959 83m c Comedy/War **DVD** ★★★★
Open Road (U.K.)

Peter Sellers *(Tully Bascombe/Grand Duchess Gloriana XII/Prime Minister Count Mountjoy)*, Jean Seberg *(Helen)*, David Kossoff *(Prof. Kokintz)*, William Hartnell *(Will)*, Timothy Bateson *(Roger)*, MacDonald Parke *(Snippet)*, Monty Landis *(Cobbley)*, Leo McKern *(Benter)*, Harold Kasket *(Pedro)*, Colin Gordon *(BBC Announcer)*

p, Jon Penington, Walter Shenson; d, Jack Arnold; w, Roger MacDougall, Stanley Mann (based on the novel *The Wrath of the Grapes* by Leonard Wibberley); ph, John Wilcox (Eastmancolor); ed, Raymond Poulton; m, Edwin Astley; art d, Geoffrey Drake; cos, Anthony Mendleson

THE MOUSE THAT ROARED is the outlandish, sidesplitting tale of the fortunes of the Duchy of Grand Fenwick, a mythical land on the verge of bankruptcy because its one export, a fine wine, has been copied and undercut by a U.S. company. Grand Fenwick's prime minister (Peter Sellers) and female monarch (Sellers again) cook up a scheme to solve the problem: they will declare war on the States, lose immediately, then get back in the black with all the aid that the U.S. usually bestows upon its beaten foes. They send out an "army" of 20, clad in armor and carrying bows and arrows, led by Tully Bascombe (Sellers once more). Of course, the arrival of these ragtag warriors in New York leads to a series of very funny situations, including the group's inadvertent acquisition of the "Q-bomb," a weapon that makes them a genuine threat. In the meantime, Bascombe meets and falls in love with Helen (Jean Seberg), the daughter of a scientist. Besides the wonderful Sellers, there are fine performances from all, especially Leo McKern as the pompous leader of Grand Fenwick's "loyal opposition." An inferior sequel, MOUSE ON THE MOON, was directed by Richard Lester.

MOVIE MOVIE

1978 105m c/bw Comedy ★★★★
Warner Bros. (U.S.) PG

George C. Scott *(Gloves Malloy/Spats Baxter)*, Trish Van Devere *(Betsy McGuire/Isobel Stuart)*, Red Buttons *(Peanuts/Jinks Murphy)*, Eli Wallach *(Vince Marlowe/Pop)*, Jocelyn Brando *(Mama Popchik/Mrs. Updike)*, Barry Bostwick *(Johnny Danko/Dick Cummings)*, Art Carney *(Dr. Blaine/Dr. Bowers)*, DYNAMITE HANDS: Harry Hamlin *(Joey Popchik)*, Ann Reinking *(Troubles Moran)*, Michael Kidd *(Pop Popchik)*

p, Stanley Donen; d, Stanley Donen; w, Larry Gelbart, Sheldon Keller; ph, Bruce Surtees, Charles Rosher Jr.; ed, George Hively; m, Ralph Burns, Buster Davis; art d, Jack Fisk; chor, Michael Kidd; cos, Patty Norris

Two movies in one (hence the title), with many of the same actors appearing in both halves, this funny Stanley Donen-directed sendup of film cliches takes an affectionate look at an era when lawmen were "coppers" and people could say "swell" without smirking. Shot in both black-and-white and color, it is intended as a whole evening of entertainment and includes a coming-attractions trailer for "Zero Hour," a war movie that obviously was never made. After a George Burns prolog we plunge into the first movie, "Dynamite Hands," which parodies 1930s fight films, following the fortunes of a poor law student, Harry Hamlin, who takes to the ring to pay for an operation to save his sister's eyesight, then completes his studies to use the legal system to get even with a crooked promoter. In "Baxter's Beauties of 1933," which obviously was inspired by 42ND STREET, George C. Scott is a Flo Ziegfeld type who is trying to put on a big show. You know the story: An unknown girl gets the chance to star when the leading lady breaks her leg. Trish Van Devere (Scott's real-life wife) is the leading lady, Rebecca York is the ingenue, and Barry Bostwick is her beau. Choreographer Michael Kidd effects a passable imitation of Busby Berkeley, despite a small budget for chorines and cameras. The satire gets a bit heavy at times, and you have to know a lot about the movies upon which this is based to glean the most out of the humor; still, there's lots of nostalgic fun here and the tunes and cast are exceptional, even when removed from their satirical context.

MRS. BROWN

1997 103m c Drama/Historical **DVD** ★★½
WGBH Boston/Ecosse Films/Irish Screen/Mobile PG
Masterpiece Theater/BBC Scotland (U.K./Ireland)

Judi Dench *(Queen Victoria)*, Billy Connolly *(John Brown)*, Geoffrey Palmer *(Henry Ponsonby)*, Antony Sher *(Disraeli)*, Gerard Butler *(Archie Brown)*, Richard Pasco *(Doctor Jenner)*, David Westhead *(Bertie—Prince of Wales)*, Bridget McConnel *(Lady Ely)*, Georgie Glen *(Lady Churchill)*, Catherine O'Donnell *(Lady In Waiting)*

p, Sarah Curtis; d, John Madden; w, Jeremy Brock (from an idea by George Rosie); ph, Richard Greatrex; ed, Robin Sales; m, Stephen Warbeck; prod d, Martin Childs; art d, Charlotte Watts; fx, Tony Harding; cos, Deirdre Clancy

AAN Best Actress: Judi Dench; AAN Best Makeup: Lisa Westcott, Veronica Brebner, Beverley Binda

A beautifully acted but poorly paced tale for the kilts-and-corsets crowd, MRS. BROWN is based on Queen Victoria's little-known relationship with gruff and willful Scottish servant John Brown.

In 1864, three years after the death of her husband, Albert, Queen Victoria (Judi Dench) is still so overcome with grief that she has sequestered herself on the Isle of Wight, ignoring her official duties while surrounded by a staff who barely breathe for fear of upsetting her. As a reminder of her husband, she sends for John Brown (Billy Connolly), a stableman from the Balmoral Castle in Scotland whom Albert held in high esteem. Brown's earthy sensibilities immediately irk the queen's staff, especially Sir Henry (Geoffrey Palmer) and her son, the Prince of Wales (David Westhead). But his insistence on plain speaking helps draw Victoria out, and she comes to rely on Brown, even as society gossips begin to refer to Her Majesty as "Mrs. Brown."

Connolly is suitably forceful as the brash and stubborn Brown, and Dench does a remarkable job of uncovering a surprising vulnerability in the remote and disconsolate Queen.

But the real scene-stealer is Antony Sher as the eloquent and notoriously manipulative statesman Benjamin Disraeli. It's a shame, then, to see such great performances trapped in a film that's otherwise dramatically moribund. Director John Madden handles the central drama in what's now the stereotypically Merchant-Ivory mode of British self-restraint, while efforts to invigorate the story with court intrigue are transparent and unconvincing.

MRS. DALLOWAY
DVD
1997 97m c Drama ★★★½
Mrs. D Productions/Bergen Film PG-13
(U.K./Netherlands)

Vanessa Redgrave (*Mrs. Clarissa Dalloway*), Natascha McElhone (*Young Clarissa*), Rupert Graves (*Septimus Warren Smith*), Michael Kitchen (*Peter Walsh*), Alan Cox (*Young Peter*), Sarah Badel (*Sally Seton—Lady Rosseter*), Lena Headey (*Young Sally*), John Standing (*Richard Dalloway*), Robert Portal (*Young Richard*), Oliver Ford Davies (*Hugh Whitbread*)

p, Lisa Katselas Pare, Stephen Bayly; d, Marleen Gorris; w, Eileen Atkins (based on the novel by Virginia Woolf); ph, Sue Gibson; ed, Michiel Reichwein; m, Ilona Sekacz; prod d, David Richens; art d, Alison Wratten, Nik Callan; fx, John Horton; cos, Judy Pepperdine

A surprisingly supple adaptation of Virginia Woolf's dense stream-of-consciousness novel from the director of the Academy Award-winning ANTONIA'S LINE.

The action is confined to one hot summer day in 1923, as middle-aged English matron Clarissa Dalloway (Vanessa Redgrave) prepares to give a party and finds herself haunted by thoughts of old friends and lovers. Frequent flashbacks bridge the present and the past, specifically the summer three decades earlier when young Clarissa's (Natascha McElhone) fateful choices—chief among them her decision to marry staid future politician Richard Dalloway (Robert Portal/John Standing), rather than impulsive Peter Walsh (Alan Cox/Peter Kitchen)—set her on the path that made her the woman she is. Also on Clarissa's mind is her intensely romantic friendship with bold, charismatic Sally Seton (Lena Headey/Sarah Badel), a far more rebellious young woman than Clarissa could ever have been.

Though often read as an indictment of the English class system, *Mrs. Dalloway* is primarily a character study. Clarissa Dalloway is an extremely subtle character, an intelligent and fundamentally decent woman whose horizons have been progressively circumscribed by class conventions, social mores, and a certain fragility of character that inclines her to conform rather than rebel. Her energies are eventually absorbed entirely by the superficial pursuit of hosting parties.

Given that Woolf's novel is to all appearances the most unsuitable novel in the world for adaptation to the screen—it's all thought and no action—director Marleen Gorris and actress turned screenwriter Eileen Atkins have done an astonishing job. But the film rests on the shoulders of Redgrave and McElhone, who together create a quietly heartbreaking portrait of a deeply contradictory character who's simultaneously contented and restless, brittle and resilient, timid and impulsive, high-strung and surprisingly steadfast. Sure, the pace is stately and there are awkward moments, but overall it's a remarkable and moving achievement.

MRS. DOUBTFIRE
DVD
1993 120m c Comedy/Drama ★★½
Blue Wolf Productions/Fox (U.S.) PG-13

Robin Williams (*Daniel Hillard/Mrs. Iphegenia Doubtfire*), Sally Field (*Miranda Hillard*), Pierce Brosnan (*Stu*), Harvey Fierstein (*Frank*), Polly Holliday (*Gloria*), Lisa Jakub (*Lydia Hillard*), Matthew Lawrence (*Chris Hillard*), Mara Wilson (*Natalie Hillard*), Robert Prosky (*Mr. Lundy*), Anne Haney (*Mrs. Sellner*)

p, Marsha Garces Williams, Robin Williams, Mark Radcliffe; d, Chris Columbus; w, Randi Mayem Singer, Leslie Dixon (from the novel *Alias Madame Doubtfire* by Anne Fine); ph, Donald McAlpine; ed, Raja Gosnell, Alexandra Fitzpatrick; m, Howard Shore; prod d, Angelo Graham; art d, W. Steven Graham; fx, John McLeod; cos, Marit Allen

AA Best Makeup: Greg Cannom, Ve Neill, Yolanda Toussieng

The first film, to our knowledge, to propose cross-dressing as a form of marriage therapy, MRS. DOUBTFIRE became one of the biggest hits of 1993, grossing over $220 million at the U.S. box office.

Daniel Hillard (Robin Williams) is a San Francisco voice-over artist whose "principles" (read—New Age posturing) and "love of life" (read—infuriating childishness) prevent him from holding down a job. Daniel's naive exuberance makes him a hit with his kids, but has exhausted the patience of his wife (Sally Field), who sues for divorce and gets custody of the beloved children. In his desperation to spend more time with the extra-cute youngsters, Daniel does what any red-blooded male in his position would do: he impersonates a British nanny and lands a job taking care of his own offspring.

The manifold problems of MRS. DOUBTFIRE are hardly worth listing. Daniel is so hopelessly immature, and played with such puppy-dog overkill by Williams, that it's impossible to root for him—until you meet his wife, whom Sally Field makes even less appealing. But once Williams gets into costume and can hide—as he did in ALADDIN—behind an artfully constructed facade, he becomes hugely entertaining. He's still one of the funniest performers around, and when he gets on a roll—even if it's a sub-standard TOOTSIE role—you just don't want him to get off.

MRS. MINIVER
DVD
1942 134m bw Drama/War ★★★
MGM (U.S.)

Greer Garson (*Mrs. Kay Miniver*), Walter Pidgeon (*Clem Miniver*), Teresa Wright (*Carol Beldon*), Dame May Whitty (*Lady Beldon*), Henry Travers (*Mr. Ballard*), Reginald Owen (*Foley*), Miles Mander (*German Agent's Voice*), Henry Wilcoxon (*Vicar*), Richard Ney (*Vin Miniver*), Clare Sandars (*Judy Miniver*)

p, Sidney Franklin; d, William Wyler; w, Arthur Wimperis, George Froeschel, James Hilton, Claudine West (based on the novel by Jan Struther); ph, Joseph Ruttenberg; ed, Harold F. Kress; m, Herbert Stothart; art d, Cedric Gibbons, Urie McCleary; fx, A. Arnold Gillespie, Warren Newcombe; cos, Robert Kalloch

AA Best Picture; AAN Best Actor: Walter Pidgeon; *AA Best Actress:* Greer Garson; *AAN Best Supporting Actor:* Henry Travers; *AA Best Supporting Actress:* Teresa Wright; *AAN Best Supporting Actress:* May Whitty; *AA Best Director:* William Wyler; *AA Best Screenplay:* George Froeschel, James Hilton, Claudine West, Arthur Wimperis; *AA Best B/W Cinematography:* Joseph Ruttenberg; *AAN Best Film Editing:* Harold F. Kress; *AAN Best Sound Recording:* Douglas Shearer; *AAN Best Special Effects:* A. Arnold Gillespie (Photographic), Warren Newcombe (Photographic), Douglas Shearer (Sound)

Frightfully nice, it's like war at teatime. MRS. MINIVER tells of the British people's will to survive the German bombing raids and fight to the end for their own human dignity. Director William Wyler achieves his goal by concentrating on the inhabitants of the country village of Belham, especially the middle-class Miniver family—lovely Kay Miniver (Greer Garson), gallant husband Clem (Walter Pidgeon), brave eldest son Vin (Richard Ney) and adorable younger children Toby and Judy (Christopher Severn and Clare Sandars). As the country slips into war, Vin falls in love with noble Carol (Teresa Wright), the teenage daughter of crotchety village matriarch Lady Beldon (Dame May Whitty). As romance grows and the village prepares for its annual flower-growing competition, German bombs begin to decimate the once-peaceful countryside and a downed German aviator seeks refuge with the Minivers. Villagers die, the Miniver home is bombed, and the church is reduced to rubble, but the people's spirit is strengthened when the vicar (Henry Wilcoxon) delivers a powerful speech, and the flower show goes on.

When Winston Churchill saw the film, he maintained that MRS. MINIVER would prove more valuable than the combined efforts of six divisions. At Oscar time, this heavy-handed film was named Best Picture; statuettes were also given to Garson, Wyler, Wright, cinematographer Ruttenberg and the screenwriters. Garson gave the longest (five 1/2 minute) speech in Oscar history; never mind she didn't deserve the award. Ponder her as an actress: totally ordinary, though lovely. Just when you've settled into that opinion, she does something brilliant. Resigned to being wrong, you watch as she settles back into self-satisfied mediocrity. Did that. Quite right. Lovely.

MULAN   DVD
1998 86m   c   Animated/Children's/Musical   ★★★★
Walt Disney   (U.S.)   G

VOICES OF: Ming-Na Wen (Mulan), Lea Salonga (Mulan—Singing), Eddie Murphy (Mushu), B.D. Wong (Captain Li Shang), Donny Osmond (Captain Li Shang—Singing), Harvey Fierstein (Yao), Jerry Tondo (Chien-Po), Gedde Watanabe (Ling), James Hong (Chi Fu), Miguel Ferrer (Shan-Yu)

p, Pam Coats; d, Barry Cook, Tony Bancroft; w, Rita Hsiao, Jodi Ann Johnson, Alan Ormsby (from a story by Chris Sanders); m, Jerry Goldsmith; prod d, Ric Sluiter, Hans Bacher; anim, Ruben Aquino (supervisor), Dan Haskett, Mark Henn, Press Romanillos, Barry Temple, Alex Kupershmidt, Broose Johnson, Aaron Blaise, Jefrey Varab, Joe Haider

AAN Best Original Musical or Comedy Score: Matthew Wilder, David Zippel, Jerry Goldsmith

The folks at Disney prove that clothes—and little else—make a man, and do so with extraordinary style. This wonderful adaptation of a 2,000-year-old Chinese poem about a young woman who cross-dresses her way into China's imperial army stands alongside some of the studio's finest achievements.

Intelligent and fiercely independent, Mulan (voiced by Ming-Na Wen) runs afoul of social expectations that a woman will be always obedient and duty-bound to her husband. Her parents are starting to doubt that they'll ever arrange a marriage for her that will bring honor to the family, and Mulan knows that the person they want her to be and the person she really is are entirely different. But when the brutal Hun leader Shan-Yu (Miguel Ferrer) storms the Great Wall of China and Mulan's ailing father is drafted into the imperial army, she finds another way to honor her ancestors: knowing that her father is too sick to serve, she cuts her hair, steals his armor and shows up for basic training disguised as a man—a heroic deception, but one punishable by death.

The film succeeds on just about every level. The animation is gorgeous, simple but drawn with a lushness reminiscent of BAMBI: the opening shot of the Great Wall and the central battle sequence are truly breathtaking, and the animators do wonderful things with smoke and reflections. The script is razor-sharp and the comic relief—mostly provided by Mulan's pip-squeak of a guardian dragon (voiced with gusto by Eddie Murphy)—is actually very funny. The generally undistinguished songs are the weak link, but even they are crafted with a knowing, almost camp wink that's totally in keeping with the subtext of the film: "I'll Make a Man Out of You" could be a Village People original.

MULHOLLAND DR.   DVD
2001 146m   c   Crime/Drama/Mystery   ★★★★
Asymmetrical Productions/Studio Canal/   R
Les Films Alain Sarde/The Picture Factory
(U.S./France)

Justin Theroux (Adam Kesher), Naomi Watts (Betty Elms/Diane Selwyn), Laura Harring, billed as Laura Elena Harring (Rita/Camilla Rhodes), Ann Miller (Coco Lenoix), Dan Hedaya (Vincenzo Castigliane), Mark Pellegrino (Joe), Robert Forster (Detective Harry McKnight), Brent Briscoe (Detective Domgaard), Katharine Towne (Cynthia), Lee Grant (Louise Bonner)

p, Neal Edelstein, Tony Krantz, Michael Polaire, Alain Sarde, Mary Sweeney; d, David Lynch; w, David Lynch; ph, Peter Deming; ed, Mary Sweeney; m, Angelo Badalamenti; prod d, Jack Fisk; art d, Peter Jamison; fx, Scott Billups, Gary D'Amico, Electric Sandbox; cos, Amy Stofsky

AAN Best Director: David Lynch

In a strange reversal of fortune that totally befits this sexy nocturne's vision of Hollywood as a shadow world of unknowable evil, David Lynch's ninth feature film began life as a rejected TV pilot, then took a circuitous road to the big screen. And that's exactly where it belongs. A mysterious, self-reflexive ode to the dream factory, it's one of Lynch's most satisfying films.

Bubbling with the blend of nervous excitement and naive confidence that is the exclusive property of starry-eyed movie ingenues, blond Betty Elms (Naomi Watts) bounces off a plane at LAX, ready to make it big in pictures. Betty checks into her vacationing Aunt Ruth's Hollywood garden apartment but finds it already occupied by a mysterious, raven-haired amnesiac (Laura Elena Harring), the sole survivor of a triple-car pileup the night before. She calls herself Rita but has no solid clues as to her identity other than a purse full of cash, a strange blue key, and a fleeting memory of where she was at the time of the crash: Mulholland Drive. Sensing adventure, Betty channels her inner Nancy Drew ("It'll be just like the movies!") and, with Rita's help, sets out to solve this little mystery herself.

There's a related subplot involving a young director (Justin Theroux) who encounters malignant forces while recasting the female lead in his latest film, but just as everything starts pulling together, it all blows apart; the film's final half hour is a spine-tingling sequence of mystifying events that invites a number of interpretations. For a movie that seems to be all about casting and recasting, identities lost and found, and role-playing and replaying, this celluloid Mobius strip makes a strange sort of sense. But in once again reasserting his position as the master of unease—all those slow, sensual dissolves and creeping point-of-view shots that reveal nothing—Lynch ultimately shuts the puzzle box tight and keeps its secrets to himself.

MUMMY, THE   DVD
1932 72m   bw   Horror   ★★★★★
Universal   (U.S.)

Boris Karloff (Im-Ho-Tep/Ardeth Bey), Zita Johann (Helen Grosvenor/Princess Anck-es-en-Amon), David Manners (Frank Whemple), Edward Van Sloan (Professor Muller), A.S. Byron (Sir Joseph Whemple), Bramwell Fletcher (Norton), Noble Johnson (the Nubian), Leonard Mudie (Professor Pearson), Katherine Byron (Frau Muller), Eddie Kane (Doctor)

p, Carl Laemmle Jr.; d, Karl Freund; w, John Balderston (based on a story by Nina Wilcox Putnam, Richard Schayer); ph, Charles Stumar; ed, Milton Carruth; art d, Willy Pogany; fx, John P. Fulton

Absolutely marvelous. Following his triumph as the monster in FRANKENSTEIN, Boris Karloff created yet another unforgettable horror character with the help of makeup man Jack Pierce. THE MUMMY opens at an Egyptian archeological dig in 1921 as a group of scientists examine their most recent finding—a sarcophagus in an unmarked grave. The coffin in which the mummy rests has been stripped of all religious markings that would have ensured an afterlife for the deceased, proof that the 3700-year-old corpse was buried in disgrace. Interred with the mummy is a large box upon which is written a warning to those who would dare open it—this, however, is a horror movie, and were no one to open the box we would never be treated to Karloff's magnificent wrappings. THE MUMMY was the directorial debut of the brilliant German cinematographer, Freund, who had photographed such classic German silents as THE LAST LAUGH; VARIETY; and METROPOLIS, as well as DRACULA in the U.S. Though THE MUMMY is not an overtly terrifying film (with the exception of the mummy's revival at the beginning), Freund creates an uneasy atmosphere of dread and foreboding. His camera is remarkably mobile, with impressive tracking and crane shots that float through the action, creating an eerie mood. Although made during a time when many films suffered from a lack of music, THE MUMMY has a full score, an effectively muted collection of themes perfectly suited to the carefully paced, mystical feel of the film. Though the technical credits are excellent, it is Karloff who carries the day. Makeup genius Pierce once again molded his magic to the actor, and the combination of linen, fuller's earth, and clay used to create the recently discovered mummy took over eight hours a day to apply. The effect is startling, though Karloff only appears as the mummy briefly. Perhaps more impressive is the more subtle makeup Pierce created for Karloff in his reincarnated state. The mass of delicate wrinkles on Karloff's face and hands, combined with the actor's deliberately gentle, flowing movements, creates a being who looks as if he may fall apart at any moment. It is a tribute to Karloff's immense skill that he can lend dignity and conviction to such a role. The supporting roles are also well-handled, with Johann making an appealingly offbeat heroine and Van Sloan crusading against yet another movie monster. The relationship between Karloff's mummy and Johann, whom he believes to be the reincarnation of his lost love, lends the film conviction and a certain pathos amidst the horror. The re-creation of the days of the pharaohs is also quite effective, and the scene wherein Karloff is wrapped alive, eyes going wider as his mouth is covered, is unforgettable. One of the rare horror films to somehow include a touch of the poetic, this stately yet brilliantly absorbing work still works beautifully today. Four inferior, shlocky sequels followed: THE MUMMY'S HAND; THE MUMMY'S TOMB; THE MUMMY'S GHOST; and THE MUMMY'S CURSE. Hammer Films of England revived the series beginning with THE MUMMY in 1959.

MUMMY, THE 📀
1959 86m c Horror ★★★
Hammer (U.K.)

Peter Cushing (John Banning), Christopher Lee (Kharis, the Mummy), Yvonne Furneaux (Isobel Banning/Princess Ananka), Eddie Byrne (Inspector Mulrooney), Felix Aylmer (Stephen Banning), Raymond Huntley (Joseph Whemple), George Pastell (Mehemet, Priest), John Stuart (Coroner), Harold Goodwin (Pat), Denis Shaw (Mike)

p, Michael Carreras; d, Terence Fisher; w, Jimmy Sangster (based on the screenplays "The Mummy" by Nina Wilcox Putnam, and "The Mummy's Tomb" by Griffin Jay); ph, Jack Asher (Technicolor); ed, James Needs, Alfred Cox; m, Franz Reizenstein; prod d, Bernard Robinson; art d, Bernard Robinson

Doesn't come unravelled. This lively Hammer reworking of the classic mummy material stars Peter Cushing as John Banning, one of three British archaeologists who desecrate the tomb of an Egyptian princess, awakening Kharis (Lee), her mummified lover, who was buried alive with the princess when she died. Kharis follows the archaeologists back to England and is about to kill Banning when he sees his victim's beautiful wife, Isobel (Furneaux), the spitting image of Kharis's lover, Princess Ananka. Stylishly directed by Terence Fisher (the action scenes, in particular, are breathtakingly choreographed), THE MUMMY features a surprisingly energetic performance from Christopher Lee, whose mummy moves swiftly and with strength, unlike his slow, shuffling 1940s predecessors. By playing the Mummy, Lee completed something of a trilogy of terror, having already starred as Frankenstein's Monster and Dracula. This remake really can't compare with the 1932 original and Lee is given no chance to flesh out his character in the haunting manner that Boris Karloff did, but for fairly standardized movie horror, this flick isn't half bad.

MUMMY, THE 📀
1999 120m c Adventure/Horror/Thriller ★★★
Alphaville Productions/Universal (U.S.) PG-13

Brendan Fraser (Rick O'Connell), Rachel Weisz (Evelyn), John Hannah (Jonathan), Kevin J. O'Connor (Beni), Arnold Vosloo (Imhotep), Jonathan Hyde (Egyptologist), Oded Fehr (Ardeth Bay), Omid Djalili (Warden), Erick Avari (Curator), Aharon Ipale (Pharoah Seti)

p, James Jacks, Sean Daniel; d, Stephen Sommers; w, Stephen Sommers; ph, Adrian Biddle; ed, Bob Ducsay; prod d, Allan Cameron; art d, Tony Reading, Giles Masters, Clifford Robinson, Peter Russell; fx, Patricia Carr; cos, John Bloomfield

AAN Best Sound: Leslie Shatz, Chris Carpenter, Rick Kline, Chris Munro

A mummy movie for the video-game generation, this boys' own adventure deals decisively with the conceptual absurdity that undermines many older variations on the theme: since reanimated mummies shuffle along at the speed of your arthritic grandpa, why didn't all those terrified Egyptologists, treasure hunters, and reincarnations of long-dead Egyptian princesses just run a little faster?

This new mummy, Imhotep (Arnold Vosloo, assisted by extensive computer-generated effects), is no schlub in moldering bandages: he's a rag-clad Terminator who turns himself into sandstorms, visits the plagues of Egypt upon his enemies, commands flesh-eating scarab beetles, and regains human form by sucking the very life from those who desecrated his tomb. Why a 3000-year-old Egyptian priest would summon up plagues originally visited upon Pharaoh by the God of the Israelites is a bit puzzling, but hey—he's spent a long time seething in that sarcophagus, so who knows what he's been thinking? Boris Karloff's gloomy Imhotep (in the 1932 original) may have been a more elegant creation, but this year's model kicks some serious ass. The movie's other stroke of inspiration is to graft the mummy onto a RAIDERS OF THE LOST ARK-style adventure in which a charming American adventurer (Brendan Fraser) and a lovely lady Egyptologist (Rachel Weisz) go searching for the legendary Egyptian city of the dead and find themselves battling hoards of baddies at regular intervals.

The razzle-dazzle factor is high, and many viewers won't mind that it's all rather hollow, formulaic stuff any more than they'll be troubled by the offhanded treatment of Arabs as buffoons, exotics, and verminous riff-raff (it's one thing to set a movie in 1926, and another to appropriate the era's insidious racism). In all, it's the quintessential summer movie: noisy, spectacular, and disposable. An equally popular sequel, THE MUMMY RETURNS, followed in 2001.

MUPPET MOVIE, THE
1979 98m c Musical/Children's **DVD**
ITC (U.K.) ★★★
G

GUEST STARS: Charles Durning (Doc Hopper), Austin Pendleton (Max), Scott Walker (Frog Killer), Mel Brooks (Prof. Krassman), Carol Kane (Miss.), MUPPET PERFORMERS: Jim Henson (Kermit the Frog/Rowlf/Dr. Teeth/Waldorf), Frank Oz (Miss Piggy/Fozzie Bear/Animal/Sam the Eagle), Jerry Nelson (Floyd Pepper/Crazy Harry/Robin the Frog/Lew Zealand), Richard Hunt (Scooter/Statler/Janice/Sweetums/Beaker), Dave Goelz (The Great Gonzo/Zoot/Dr. Bunsen Honeydew)

p, Jim Henson; d, James Frawley; w, Jerry Juhl, Jack Burns; ph, Isidore Mankofsky (CFI color); ed, Christopher Greenbury; m, Paul Williams; prod d, Joel Schiller; art d, Les Gobruegge; cos, Calista Hendrickson (Muppets), Gwen Capetanos

AAN Best Song Score: Paul Williams, Kenny Ascher; *AAN Best Original Song:* "The Rainbow Connection"; Paul Williams (Music & Lyrics), Kenny Ascher (Music & Lyrics)

This charming children's film was the first to star the successful television puppets (two sequels followed). The loose plot follows Kermit the Frog and Fozzie Bear as they travel cross-country on their way to fame and fortune in Hollywood. On the road they pick up a variety of passengers (muppet and human) and sing a dozen songs. The special effects are handled very well; highlights feature Kermit riding a bicycle and rowing a boat. Cute without being insipid, funny without being childish, THE MUPPET MOVIE contains enough magic to please all ages.

MURDER
1930 92m bw Mystery **DVD**
British Intl. (U.K.) ★★★★

Herbert Marshall (Sir John Menier), Norah Baring (Diana Baring), Phyllis Konstam (Dulcie Markham), Edward Chapman (Ted Markham), Miles Mander (Gordon Druce), Esme Percy (Handel Fane), Donald Calthrop (Ion Stewart), Amy Brandon Thomas (Defence), Marie Wright (Miss Mitcham), Hannah Jones (Mrs. Didsome)

p, John Maxwell; d, Alfred Hitchcock; w, Alma Reville, Walter C. Mycroft, Alfred Hitchcock (based on the novel and play Enter Sir John by Clemence Dane and Helen Simpson); ph, Jack Cox; ed, Emile De Ruelle, Rene Harrison; m, John Reynders; art d, John Mead

An atypical Hitchcock film which depends on the element of surprise rather than his usual building of suspense. Diana (Baring), a young actress, is accused of killing one of her friends, tried, and sentenced to death by a jury. Jury member Sir John Menier (Marshall), an actor-manager and gentleman knight, remains unconvinced of her guilt and makes an attempt to locate the actual murderer. Visually astonishing, MURDER also makes creative use of sound by recording a character's spoken thoughts on the soundtrack. While the innocent person accused became a staple of Hitchcock's later films, the director would expand on this idea of theatricality in his mystery STAGE FRIGHT. Hitchcock also directed a German version of MURDER, entitled MARY, starring Alfred Abel.

MURDER BY DEATH
1976 94m c Mystery/Comedy **DVD**
Rastar (U.S.) ★★★
PG

Eileen Brennan (Tess Skeffington), Truman Capote (Lionel Twain), James Coco (Milo Perrier), Peter Falk (Sam Diamond), Alec Guinness (Butler Bensonumum), Elsa Lanchester (Jessica Marbles), David Niven (Dick Charleston), Peter Sellers (Sidney Wang), Maggie Smith (Dora Charleston), Nancy Walker (Yetta the Maid)

p, Ray Stark; d, Robert Moore; w, Neil Simon; ph, David M. Walsh (Panavision); ed, Margaret Booth, John F. Burnett; m, Dave Grusin; prod d, Stephen Grimes; art d, Harry Kemm; fx, Augie Lohman; cos, Ann Roth

This spoof of the great fictional-film detectives offers consistently funny scenes sparked by Falk, Niven, Sellers, and Guinness. Wealthy Lionel Twain (Capote, in his film debut), invites the world's greatest detectives to his eerie castle-like home. These counterparts to Miss Marple, Nick and Nora Charles, Sam Spade, Hercule Poirot, and Charlie Chan, tumble and fumble into the dungeonlike fortress full tilt and off tilt. They soon discover that Twain is holding them prisoner in a home suddenly covered with bars and steel doors, rooms that lead nowhere and everywhere, leaving them with the clue that a murder is about to be committed by one among them. Falk is terrific as the fiercely posturing Humphrey Bogart-Sam Spade prototype, with the other leading players not far behind him in a race for the insane asylum. Capote is so bad an actor that he's funny, which may or may not be the point. Producer Ray Stark, director Moore, screenwriter Neil Simon, and stars Falk, Coco, and Brennan teamed again two years later in the less successful parody THE CHEAP DETECTIVE.

MURDER, HE SAYS
1945 91m bw Comedy ★★★★
Paramount (U.S.)

Fred MacMurray (Pete Marshall), Helen Walker (Claire Mathews), Marjorie Main (Mamie Johnson), Jean Heather (Elany Fleagle), Porter Hall (Mr. Johnson), Peter Whitney (Mert Fleagle/Bert Fleagle), Mabel Paige (Grandma Fleagle), Barbara Pepper (Bonnie Fleagle), Walter Baldwin (Vic Hardy), James Flavin (Police Officer)

p, E.D. Leshin; d, George Marshall; w, Lou Breslow (based on a story by Jack Moffitt); ph, Theodor Sparkuhl; ed, LeRoy Stone; m, Robert Emmett Dolan; art d, Hans Dreier, William Flannery; fx, Gordon Jennings, Paul K. Lerpae

It's goodbye to logic and sanity in this one, a zany laugh riot in which MacMurray shines as a statistics-gathering insurance salesman in the Ozarks who must deal with hillbilly mentality and crazy twin killers, both played brilliantly by Whitney. MacMurray discovers, much to his chagrin, that the only sane person in the entire community is Walker, who is trying to vindicate her father, wrongly imprisoned for a robbery committed by female bandit Pepper. Meanwhile the Fleagle family members, who would just as soon kill a stranger as say hello, are frantically searching for Pepper's hidden $70,000 in stolen loot. "Ma" Main, doing something like her Ma Kettle routine but with sinister overtones, is splendid as she confuses MacMurray, already perplexed, in his quest for statistics. Further complicating matters is Pepper, who gets out of prison and is now looking to pick up her buried money. The chases—awkward, narrow escapes by MacMurray and Walker—are, granted, larded with slapstick, but the antics are so zany and Marshall's clever direction so swift that the laughs are delivered rapid-fire. A truly hilarious, fun-filled movie in the then-popular vein of the fatal farce (epitomized in ARSENIC AND

OLD LACE). MacMurray is in his element here and is nothing less than terrific.

MURDER, MY SWEET

DVD
★★★★½

1945 95m bw Mystery
RKO (U.S.)

Dick Powell (*Philip Marlowe*), Claire Trevor (*Velma/Mrs. Grayle*), Anne Shirley (*Ann*), Otto Kruger (*Amthor*), Mike Mazurki (*Moose Malloy*), Miles Mander (*Mr. Grayle*), Douglas Walton (*Marriott*), Don Douglas (*Lt. Randall*), Ralf Harolde (*Dr. Sonderborg*), Esther Howard (*Mrs. Florian*)

p, Adrian Scott; d, Edward Dmytryk; w, John Paxton (based on the novel *Farewell, My Lovely* by Raymond Chandler); ph, Harry Wild; ed, Joseph Noriega; m, Roy Webb; art d, Albert S. D'Agostino, Carroll Clark; fx, Vernon L. Walker; cos, Edward Stevenson

Near perfect, my sweet. Hard-boiled detective Philip Marlowe (Powell) is hired by ex-con Moose Malloy (Mazurki) to find his missing girlfriend Velma. Shortly thereafter, Marlowe is hired by socialite Mrs. Grayle (Trevor) to find a valuable jade necklace that has been stolen from her. Dividing his time between the seedy underworld and the ritzy digs of the upper class, Marlowe finds blackmail, doublecrosses, corruption, and murder on both sides of the tracks. Much to Marlowe's surprise, both cases dovetail into one. Considered one of the quintessential film noir films, this tough, sardonic, and unusually witty film brought one-time movie crooner Powell back from the brink of career catastrophe and made him a superstar. Not even Humphrey Bogart's portrayal of Marlowe in THE BIG SLEEP could match Powell's portrayal of the down-and-out gumshoe. Director Edward Dmytryk uses every cinematic trick in the book here, creating a truly bleak and disorienting netherworld populated by a variety of sordid characters. Here's Mazurki's best in his catalogue of hoods, our fave Shirley performance, but it's Miss Trevor who rises to the top, like a dangerous cup of posioned cream, viewing after viewing.

MURDER ON THE ORIENT EXPRESS

DVD
★★★½
PG

1974 128m c Mystery
Paramount (U.K.)

Albert Finney (*Hercule Poirot*), Lauren Bacall (*Mrs. Hubbard*), Martin Balsam (*Bianchi*), Ingrid Bergman (*Greta Ohlsson*), Jacqueline Bisset (*Countess Andrenyi*), Jean-Pierre Cassel (*Pierre Paul Michel*), Sean Connery (*Col. Arbuthnot*), John Gielgud (*Beddoes*), Wendy Hiller (*Princess Dragomiroff*), Anthony Perkins (*Hector McQueen*)

p, John Brabourne, Richard Goodwin; d, Sidney Lumet; w, Paul Dehn (based on the novel by Agatha Christie); ph, Geoffrey Unsworth (Panavision, Technicolor); ed, Anne V. Coates; m, Richard Rodney Bennett; prod d, Tony Walton; art d, Jack Stephens; cos, Tony Walton

AAN Best Actor: Albert Finney; AA Best Supporting Actress: Ingrid Bergman; AAN Best Adapted Screenplay: Paul Dehn; AAN Best Cinematography: Geoffrey Unsworth; AAN Best Original Dramatic Score: Richard Rodney Bennett; AAN Best Costume Design: Tony Walton

Elegant and stylish in the best Agatha Christie tradition—a thoroughly entertaining if poky whodunit. Hercule Poirot (a showy Finney) is aboard the luxurious Orient Express in 1934, traveling across Asia and Europe to Paris. When an American financier (Richard Widmark) is found dead—stabbed a dozen times—Poirot is prevailed upon by railway executive Bianchi (Balsam) to solve the case. Through an elaborate re-creation of the crime, he does just that. For years Christie refused to have this story filmed, but MURDER ON THE ORIENT EXPRESS was worth the wait. Even Ingrid

knew she didn't deserve her supporting Oscar, but she is fine, and sentimental Academy members slept well that night. Very enjoyable, but frankly, too many stars for its own good.

MURIEL

(MURIEL, OU LE TEMPS D'UN RETOUR)
★★★★★

1963 115m c Drama
Argos/Alpha/Eclair/Pleiade/Dear (France/Italy)

Delphine Seyrig (*Helene*), Jean-Pierre Kerien (*Alphonse*), Nita Klein (*Francoise*), Jean-Baptiste Thierree (*Bernard*), Claude Sainval (*de Smoke*), Laurence Badie (*Claudie*), Jean Champion (*Ernest*), Jean Daste (*The Goat Man*), Martine Vatel (*Marie-Dominique*), Philippe Laudenbach (*Robert*)

p, Anatole Dauman; d, Alain Resnais; w, Jean Cayrol (based on the story by Cayrol); ph, Sacha Vierny (Eastmancolor); ed, Kenout Peltier, Eric Pluet, Claudine Merlin; m, Hans Werner Henze; art d, Jacques Saulnier

Alain Resnais's third feature and first color film once again concerns memory. Helene (Delphine Seyrig) is a widow who sells antiques from her Boulogne-sur-Mer apartment. She shares the place with her eccentric filmmaker stepson, Bernard (Jean-Baptiste Thierree), a 22-month veteran of the Algerian War, during which he took part in the torture and murder of a young woman named Muriel. Bernard is haunted by the memory of Muriel, spending much time watching a grainy 8mm film of her and filming the surroundings in his neighborhood. He talks of Muriel to Helene, who assumes the woman is a girl friend she has yet to meet. Helene, meanwhile, is reunited with a past lover, Alphonse (Jean-Pierre Kerien), another veteran of Algeria, but they cannot recapture what they once had, if they had anything at all. Alphonse arrives at Helene's with his mistress, Francoise (Nita Klein), whom he introduces as his niece. While Helene, her present lover, de Smoke (Claude Sainval), and Alphonse try to sort out their emotions, Francoise shows an attraction to Bernard, who is involved with Marie-Dominique (Martine Vatel). MURIEL marked the second time Resnais worked with screenwriter Jean Cayrol, who previously contributed the commentary for Resnais's short documentary masterpiece NIGHT AND FOG. Their collaboration here produced a technical and thematic masterpiece that makes brilliant and confounding use of montage, sound construction, overlapping dialogue, and color photography. With MURIEL, Resnais' true filmmaking style had finally begun to emerge, employing characters who are real people (not named after cities or designated by letters) with memories that cut deeply into their personalities and relationships. The videotape is in French with English subtitles, though in most of the washed-out prints of the film the reportedly excellent use of color is hardly evident.

MURMUR OF THE HEART

(LE SOUFFLE AU COEUR)
★★★★

1971 118m c Drama/Comedy
Nouvelles Editions/Marianne/Vides/Franz Seitz
(France/Italy/West Germany)

Lea Massari (*Clara Chevalier*), Benoit Ferreux (*Laurent Chevalier*), Daniel Gelin (*the Father*), Marc Winocourt (*Marc*), Fabien Ferreux (*Thomas*), Michel Lonsdale (*Father Henri*), Ave Ninchi (*Augusta*), Gila von Weitershausen (*Freda*), Micheline Bona (*Aunt Claudine*), Henri Poirier (*Uncle Leonce*)

p, Vincent Malle, Claude Nedjar; d, Louis Malle; w, Louis Malle; ph, Ricardo Aronovich (Eastmancolor); ed, Suzanne Baron; m, Charlie Parker, Sidney Bechet, Gaston Freche, Henri Renaud; art d, Jean-Jacques Caziot, Philippe Turlure

AAN Best Original Story and Screenplay: Louis Malle

Of all the French New Wave directors, Malle has proved the most versatile and accessible. He isn't afraid to handle delicate issues and he approaches his subjects with sensitivity and wit. Incest, perhaps the most unspeakable of all taboos, was the subject of MURMUR OF THE HEART. Malle's comic take makes for a wonderful, tender film which accurately portrays all the joys and agonies of adolescent sexuality. Ferreux is Laurent, the 14-year-old son of a French gynecologist. His mother Clara (Massari), who had married his father when she was 16, is a kindred spirit and his closest confidante. Laurent's older brothers take him to a prostitute for his first sexual experience, but the drunken boys interrupt the tentative beginnings. Laurent later contracts scarlet fever, which leaves him with a heart murmur, and his mother takes him to a health health spa to recuperate. Mother and son are both rejected by prospective lovers at a Bastille Day celebration and somehow turn to each other, with surprising results.

MURMUR is a film alive with energy. One never forgets those terrible moments of early adolescence, and this film recaptures the feelings with honesty, humor and sensitivity. Backed by a wonderful jazz score, the drama is made believable by its characters. Massari and Ferreux have a marvelous chemistry that makes their relationship honest and understandable. Their lovemaking is treated in a subtle manner; Malle never dwells upon it, nor does he make it seem like a moment of depraved abandon. Instead, this is a special moment for two people who cannot explain their actions to outsiders. Rather than create a paean to incest, Malle has created a song of life.

MUSIC BOX

1989 124m c Drama 🅓🆅🅓
Carolco (U.S.) ★★★★
PG-13

Jessica Lange (*Ann Talbot*), Armin Mueller-Stahl (*Michael Laszlo*), Frederic Forrest (*Jack Burke*), Lukas Haas (*Michael "Mikey" Talbot*), Donald Moffat (*Harry Talbot*), Michael Rooker (*Karchy Laszlo*), Cheryl Lynn Bruce (*Georgine Wheeler*), Mari Torocsik (*Magda Zoldan*), J.S. Block (*Judge Erwin Silver*), Sol Frieder (*Istvan Boday*)

p, Irwin Winkler; d, Constantin Costa-Gavras; w, Joe Eszterhas; ph, Patrick Blossier; ed, Joele Van Effenterre; m, Philippe Sarde; prod d, Jeannine Claudia Oppewall; art d, Bill Arnold; chor, Eva Nemeth, Karoly Nemeth; cos, Rita Salazar

AAN Best Actress: Jessica Lange

As with BETRAYED, critics took director Costa-Gavras to task for not approaching the subject of MUSIC BOX (the prosecution of WWII Nazi war criminals residing in the U.S.) with more passion. Yet, what MUSIC BOX arguably loses by keeping its emotions reined in is more than made up for by a deliberately detailed, deeply disturbing realism. Jessica Lange plays Ann Talbot, the troubled attorney who helps her father, Michael Laszlo, played by Armin Mueller-Stahl, with what she first assumes to be a case of mistaken identity. A Hungarian immigrant after the war, Mueller-Stahl claimed on his application for citizenship to have been a farmer. After decades of raising a family in America on a steelworker's pay, Mueller-Stahl is now faced with deportation on the nominal charge of having lied about his former occupation. In fact, he is being sent back to Hungary to be tried for wartime atrocities he is accused of committing as part of that country's Nazi collaborationist police force. He admits to having been with the police but claims innocence on the atrocity charges, saying he left the force in reaction to the very brutality of which he is accused. Up against badgering prosecutor Forrest, who is fueled by righteous rage, Lange is nevertheless able to puncture the testimony of key government witnesses. Masterfully she then builds her own case, presenting the deportation as a revenge-motivated sham orchestrated by the Hungarian communist government against Mueller-Stahl for his disruption of a cultural exchange with the U.S. several years earlier. While preparing her case, though, she discovers a series of large payments—Mueller-Stahl dismisses them as loans—to a fellow immigrant subsequently killed in a hit-and-run accident. As she investigates these irregularities, she is forced to reevaluate the very foundations of her belief in herself and her family.

Throughout the film, Costa-Gavras chooses not to chastise or harangue. There is nothing shrill about his style here, nor about the performances he elicits from the uniformly excellent cast he has assembled. Rather, MUSIC BOX conveys a feeling of sadness and dread over American innocence, so easily turned to willful ignorance. Costa-Gavras defines Ann Talbot's dilemma as one shared by the nation.

MUSIC MAN, THE

1962 151m c Musical 🅓🆅🅓
Warner Bros. (U.S.) ★★★★

Robert Preston (*Harold Hill*), Shirley Jones (*Marian Paroo*), Buddy Hackett (*Marcellus Washburn*), Hermione Gingold (*Eulalie MacKechnie Shinn*), Paul Ford (*Mayor Shinn*), Ewart Dunlop, Oliver Hix, Jacey Squires, Olin Britt (*The Buffalo Bills*), Pert Kelton (*Mrs. Paroo*)

p, Morton Da Costa; d, Morton Da Costa; w, Marion Hargrove (based on the musical by Meredith Willson, Franklyn Lacey); ph, Robert Burks (Technirama, Technicolor); ed, William Ziegler; m, Meredith Willson; art d, Paul Groesse; chor, Onna White, Tom Panko

AAN Best Picture; AAN Best Film Editing: William Ziegler; *AA Best Adapted Score:* Ray Heindorf; *AAN Best Art Direction-Set Decoration (Color):* Paul Groesse, George James Hopkins; *AAN Best Costume Design:* Dorothy Jeakins; *AAN Best Sound:* George R. Groves

A nostalgic mix of corn, laughs, exuberance, and infectious songs. Robert Preston reprises his greatest Broadway role as Prof. Harold Hill, a traveling salesman/con man who arrives in River City, Iowa, in 1912 and persuades its citizens that the town is headed for moral ruin because of its new pool room. The way to keep the town youth from being corrupted is to start a band, says Hill, adding that he will sell the instruments and teach the kids how to play. His real plan is to take the money and run before the instruments arrive. Prim librarian Marian Paroo (Jones) questions Hill's credentials, but he sells her on his revolutionary "Think System," by which all one has to do is think a tune to be able to play it. As he attempts to swindle the townsfolk, Hill alternately charms and exasperates the mayor (Ford), his wife (Gingold), and the members of the town council (played by the barbershop quartet, the Buffalo Bills, who provide some delightful musical interludes).

Preston is a true joy in this film, perhaps as ideally suited for the role as Yul Brynner was for the King of Siam. Though the charming rogue has long been a staple in the entertainment world, few played the role as engagingly as Preston does here. The other performances are notable, particularly the lovely Jones, the delightful Gingold and Ford, and little, lisping Ron Howard. Splendid, but this is, and will always be, Preston's picture. Absurdly, he didn't even get a *nomination* for Best Actor, though the film was cited, losing to LAWRENCE OF ARABIA. Meredith Willson's songs, which are among the best ever to grace a musical production, include "Till There Was You" and the stirring "76 Trombones," which provides the unforgettable climax.

MUSIC ROOM, THE
(JALSAGHAR)
1958 95m bw Drama ★★★★½
Edward Harrison (India)

Chhabi Biswas *(Huzur Biswambhar Roy)*, Padma Devi *(His Wife)*, Pinaki Sen Gupta *(Khoka, His Son)*, Tulsi Lahari *(Manager of Roy's Estate)*, Kali Sarkar *(Roy's Servant)*, Ganga Pada Basu *(Mahim Ganguly)*, Akhtari Bai, Salamat Khan *(Singers)*, Roshan Kumari *(Kathak Dancer)*, Pratap Mukhopdhya

p, Satyajit Ray; d, Satyajit Ray; w, Satyajit Ray (based on a novel by Tarashankar Banerjee); ph, Subrata Mitra; ed, Dulal Dutta; m, Dakhin Mohan Takhur, Asis Kumar, Robin Majumder; art d, Bansi Chandragupta

One of Satyajit Ray's finest works, THE MUSIC ROOM is also one of the most meditative and lyrical. Its basic concern is the demise of an aristocratic household led by Biswas. Feeling a growing resentment toward his neighbors' elaborate parties, Biswas decides to hold his own and sells his wife's jewels to finance it. Shortly afterward his wife and son die at sea during a thunderstorm, which sends Biswas into seclusion. Four years later, when his neighbor plans a party in his newly built music room, Biswas decides to have his own party. He scrounges together all the money he has left and throws an elegant party. He loses his sanity, however, and takes off on his son's horse. He is thrown from the animal and dies in the arms of his servants. Beautifully photographed, THE MUSIC ROOM is a fine example of Ray's directorial mastery. Released in India in 1958, shortly before the completion of his Apu trilogy.

MUTE WITNESS
1995 90m c Thriller/Mystery/Drama ★★★
Comet Films/Avrora Media/Cobblestone Pictures/ R
Patmos Films (Germany/U.K./Russia)

Marina Sudina *(Billy Hughes)*, Fay Ripley *(Karen Hughes)*, Evan Richards *(Andy Clarke)*, Oleg Jankowski *(Larsen)*, Igor Volkov *(Arkadi)*, Sergei Karlenkov *(Lyosha)*, Alexander Buriev *(Strohbecker)*, Alec Guinness *(The Reaper)*, Alexander Piatov *(Wartschuk)*, Nikoai Pastuhov *(Janitor)*

p, Alexander Buchman, Norbert Soentgen, Anthony Waller; d, Anthony Waller; w, Anthony Waller; ph, Egon Werdin; ed, Peter Adam; m, Wilbert Hirsch; prod d, Matthias Kammermeier; art d, Barbara Becker; fx, Victor Orlov, Pavel Terchov, Christian Burgdorff, Opitical Arts; cos, Svetlana Luzanova

After a great start, this offbeat, self-referential genre picture begins to lose steam, but it's still a promising feature debut for writer-director Anthony Waller.

Andy (Evan Richards), a cocky American director, is shooting a film in Russia on antiquated sound stages with a local cast and crew. One night after shooting, Billy (Marina Sudina), a mute special effects artist, goes back to the studio to retrieve a needed prop and stumbles upon two crew members making a porn movie. As Billy watches, the movie abruptly becomes a snuff film when the unsuspecting actress is murdered on camera. A careless move on Billy's part alerts the murderers to her presence, and they chase her through the winding corridors and basement tunnels. Billy is rescued by Andy and his girlfriend and the police are called, but the two crew members insist that they were just testing some special effects. Billy is unable to produce any hard evidence that a murder has occurred. Only enigmatic Inspector Larsen (Oleg Jankowski) seems to be on Billy's side. Or is he?

An entertaining thriller about innocents abroad, MUTE WITNESS keenly pays homage to the conventions of the thriller genre, but eventually trips over its own cleverness. The nail-biting first half applies frightening twists to a cliched situa-

tion—a girl trapped in a scary place filled with dangerous people. The film owes quite a bit to Robert Siodmak's THE SPIRAL STAIRCASE, as well as the many Hitchcock nail-biters in which nightmarish foreigners menace fresh-faced Americans. Sudina's Billy is a spunky and resourceful heroine, but the twists and turns of her predicament ultimately become too implausible.

MUTINY ON THE BOUNTY
1935 132m bw Adventure ★★★★★
MGM (U.S.)

Charles Laughton *(Capt. William Bligh)*, Clark Gable *(1st Mate Fletcher Christian)*, Franchot Tone *(Roger Byam)*, Herbert Mundin *(Smith)*, Eddie Quillan *(Ellison)*, Dudley Digges *(Bacchus)*, Donald Crisp *(Burkitt)*, Henry Stephenson *(Sir Joseph Banks)*, Francis Lister *(Capt. Nelson)*, Spring Byington *(Mrs. Byam)*

p, Irving Thalberg; d, Frank Lloyd; w, Talbot Jennings, Jules Furthman, Carey Wilson (based on the novels *Mutiny On The Bounty* and *Men Against the Sea* by Charles Nordhoff, James Norman Hall); ph, Arthur Edeson; ed, Margaret Booth; m, Herbert Stothart; art d, Cedric Gibbons, Arnold Gillespie

AA Best Picture; AAN Best Actor: Clark Gable; *AAN Best Actor:* Charles Laughton; *AAN Best Actor:* Franchot Tone; *AAN Best Director:* Frank Lloyd; *AAN Best Screenplay:* Jules Furthman, Talbot Jennings, Carey Wilson; *AAN Best Film Editing:* Margaret Booth; *AAN Best Score:* Metro-Goldwyn-Mayer Music Department, Nat W. Finston (Dept. Head)

A bounty for viewers. Few adventures can approach MUTINY ON THE BOUNTY for its action-filled dramatization of good vs. evil. 1935's top grosser, the film confirmed Gable as Hollywood's biggest male star and gave Laughton the most famous role of his career. The film's basis in fact only adds sweep to this bracing saga of a 1788 ship mutiny.

The film opens as the Bounty gracefully sets sail from Portsmouth, England to Tahiti to gather breadfruit trees. Shipboard life, though, soon hits rough seas as conflicts arise between the vicious, bullying Capt. Bligh (Laughton) and his courageous first mate, Fletcher Christian (Gable), with idealistic midshipman Roger Byam (Tone) caught in the middle. The stay in Tahiti proves to be a momentary respite, even though Bligh seethes over Christian's romance with the island chief's daughter (Movita Castaneda). On the homeward voyage, Bligh becomes even more barbaric, and it's only a matter of time before Christian takes action.

Expertly crafted and brilliantly acted, MUTINY ON THE BOUNTY is one of the most durable and engrossing adventure films ever made. For the first and only time in motion-picture history, three actors from the same film—Gable, Laughton, and Tone—were nominated for Oscars in the Best Actor division. Lloyd's direction captures the exotic South Sea island of Tahiti and the rigors of the hard-scrabble voyage and gives the cast its full head (Digges is especially good). Gable, in splendid form, was originally afraid of wearing breeches and a small ponytail, and he also thought his American accent would stand out too much. (If anything, it works by contributing to a certain xenophobia in his struggles against the unhandsome and genuinely British Laughton.) His Christian is full of integrity and courage, and is even surprisingly tender in the oddly bisexual edge of the film's Tahiti scenes. The superb Laughton, meanwhile, relishing his self-righteous villainy, gave impersonators a lifetime of work uttering "Mr. Christian, come here!" Tone, an underrated actor, is also sturdy, and gets to strut his stuff in the courtroom finale. Although the production of the film was dogged by backstage sniping, scripting problems, expensive location footage ruined by tropical humidity, and the loss of $50K worth of equipment, you'd never know it to look at the result.

The film was remade under the same title in 1962. Trevor Howard was a compelling Bligh, but Marlon Brando's weird attempt to turn Christian into an effeminate fop could have made the film a camp classic if only he weren't so serious about it. As it is, his grand experiment entirely sabotages the film. 1984, meanwhile, brought us THE BOUNTY. Anthony Hopkins aimed for a more complex Bligh, but Mel Gibson was extremely bland and the undertaking entirely lacked the epic scope that made the 1935 version so bracing.

MY ARCHITECT ⊙DVD

2003 116m c/bw Biography/Documentary ★★★★
HBO/Cinemax Documentary Films (U.S.)

Nathaniel Kahn, Harriet Pattison, Anne Tyng, Philip Johnson, I.M. Pei, Robert Boudreau, Vincent Scully, Edmund Bacon, Frank O. Gehry, Sue Ann Kahn

p, Susan Rose Behr, Nathaniel Kahn; d, Nathaniel Kahn; w, Nathaniel Kahn; ph, Bob Richman; ed, Sabine Krayenbuhl; m, Joseph Vitarelli

AAN Best Documentary Feature

Much more than a profile of architect Louis I. Kahn, this touching documentary by his son, Nathaniel Kahn, is many things at once: a fascinating biography, a provocative disquisition on the relevance of architecture and, above all, the record of a son's poignant search for the meaning of "family" and for a father he scarcely knew in the architectural wonders he left behind.

On March 17, 1974, while passing through New York City alone, Louis Kahn suffered a fatal heart attack in the men's room at midtown Manhattan's busy Pennsylvania Station. His body lay unclaimed at the city morgue for three days. What wasn't widely known at the time was that in addition to his wife, Esther, and their daughter, Sue Ann, Kahn was survived by two mistresses, Harriet Pattison and Anne Tyng, and their two children. All three families lived within miles of each other in suburban Philadelphia, but their paths never crossed until the funeral. Twenty-five years later, Pattison's son, Nathaniel, felt it was time to confront his father by visiting Kahn's buildings. That journey, which took Nathaniel from Kahn's childhood home in Philadelphia to Bangladesh, where Kahn's last great work was completed after his death, serves as the basis for this extraordinary film.

The film's recurring motif is that of a small boy standing before Kahn's creations, each as timeless and eternal as the ancient monuments that inspired them. But the image that really touches the heart is the sight of Nathaniel rollerblading across the concrete courtyard of the Salk Institute—a child at play within the austere embrace of his father's legacy. In searching for Louis Kahn through his art, Nathaniel Kahn created a work of art of his own.

MY BEAUTIFUL LAUNDRETTE ⊙DVD

1985 93m c Drama ★★★★
Working Title/SAF/Channel 4 (U.K.) R

Daniel Day-Lewis, billed as Daniel Day Lewis *(Johnny)*, Saeed Jaffrey *(Nasser)*, Roshan Seth *(Papa)*, Gordon Warnecke *(Omar)*, Shirley Ann Field *(Rachel)*, Rita Wolf *(Tania)*, Richard Graham *(Genghis)*, Winston Graham, Dudley Thomas *(Jamaicans)*, Derrick Branche *(Salim)*

p, Sarah Radclyffe, Tim Bevan; d, Stephen Frears; w, Hanif Kureishi; ph, Oliver Stapleton; ed, Mick Audsley; m, Ludus Tonalis; prod d, Hugo Luczyc-Whyhowski; cos, Lindy Hemming

AAN Best Original Screenplay: Hanif Kureishi

An offbeat winner. Director Stephen Frears and screenwriter Hanif Kureishi have fashioned a wonderfully fresh examination of the political and racial climate of Margaret Thatcher's Britain.

Omar (Gordon Warnecke) is a young Pakistani living in London with his father (Roshan Seth), a drunk who was previously one of Pakistan's leading intellectuals. When Papa asks his brother Nasser (Saeed Jaffrey), an underworld crime boss, to find work for Omar, Nasser makes him the manager of a run-down laundrette, and Omar enterprisingly employs Johnny (Daniel Day Lewis), a London street punk and boyhood friend whom he has not seen since Johnny joined a fascist group. In addition to becoming work partners, Omar and Johnny also become lovers. In the meantime, Johnny's friends have turned against him, baffled by his devotion to the "Pakis." Kureishi has come up with at least a half-dozen complex characters whose lives are brilliantly woven together in the film's relatively short 93 minutes. Amidst all the conflicts of racism, sexuality, bigotry, violence, and politics, MY BEAUTIFUL LAUNDRETTE still manages to be humorous and entertaining, largely because of Frears's skill as a director and marvelous performances all round. Beautifully handled, warmly intelligent and insightful, extremely entertaining.

MY BEST FRIEND'S WEDDING ⊙DVD

1997 105m c Romance/Comedy ★★★
Predawn Productions/Zucker Brother Productions/ PG-13
TriStar (U.S.)

Julia Roberts *(Julianne Potter)*, Dermot Mulroney *(Michael O'Neal)*, Cameron Diaz *(Kimmy Wallace)*, Rupert Everett *(George Downes)*, Philip Bosco *(Walter Wallace)*, M. Emmet Walsh *(Papa Joe O'Neal)*, Rachel Griffiths *(Samantha Newhouse)*, Carrie Preston *(Amanda Newhouse)*, Susan Sullivan *(Isabelle Wallace)*, Chris Masterson *(Scott O'Neal)*

p, Jerry Zucker, Ronald Bass; d, P.J. Hogan; w, Ronald Bass; ph, Laszlo Kovacs; ed, Garth Craven, Lisa Fruchtman; m, James Newton Howard; prod d, Richard Sylbert; art d, Karen Fletcher Trujillo; fx, Tom Ryba; cos, Jeffrey Kurland

AAN Best Original Musical or Comedy Score: James Newton Howard

Australian director P.J. Hogan's big-budget follow-up to MURIEL'S WEDDING recycles many of the same elements, including karaoke bars, vulgar outfits, and mean-spirited satirical jabs at its main characters.

As her 28th birthday approaches, cranky food critic Julianne (Julia Roberts) remembers the deal she made with best-buddy Michael (Dermot Mulroney): they once vowed that if neither had married by the age of 28, he'd propose. But when the phone call comes, it's worse than she had imagined. Michael has fallen in love with someone else—Kimmy (Cameron Diaz), a blonde, seemingly perfect being who's younger, richer, and a lot nicer than Julianne. With only four days to go before the nuptials, Julianne decides to put a stop to the wedding by whatever means necessary, and marry Michael herself.

Though atypical in that our gal is forced to fight dirty for her man, this Roberts vehicle is still a first-class showcase for her blinding smile, cascading locks, and amiably klutzy mannerisms. But its revelations are Diaz and Rupert Everett, who plays Roberts' editor: Her Kimmy is all insouciance and honest ditziness, while he—the exceedingly suave and witty voice of reason—gives a modern spin to the classic role of romantic confidant. Every time Everett walks into frame, you can't help but think how much better a movie this would be if there were only more of him in it. As in his first film, Hogan relies too heavily on pop kitsch to establish mood and ironic counterpoint, replacing the synthetic sounds of ABBA with the smooth ditties of Burt Bacharach and Hal David.

MY BIG FAT GREEK WEDDING *DVD*

2002 95m c Romance/Comedy ★★★½
Gold Circle Films/Home Box Office/MPH PG
Entertainment/Playtone Films (U.S./Canada)

Nia Vardalos (*Toula Portokalos*), John Corbett (*Ian Miller*), Michael Constantine (*Gus Portokalos*), Lainie Kazan (*Maria Portokalos*), Andrea Martin (*Aunt Voula*), Joey Fatone (*Angelo*), Christina Eleusiniotis (*Toula at Age Six*), Kaylee Vieira (*Schoolgirl*), John Kalangis (*Greek Teacher*), Marita Zouravlioff (*Toula at Age 12*)

p, Gary Goetzman, Tom Hanks, Rita Wilson; d, Joel Zwick; w, Nia Vardalos (based on her play); ph, Jeffrey Jur; ed, Mia Goldman; m, Alexander Janko, Chris Wilson; prod d, Gregory Keen; art d, Kei Ng; fx, Martin Malivoire; cos, Michael Clancy

AAN Best Original Screenplay: Nia Vardalos

Second City veteran Nia Vardalos expanded her one-woman show about life as a not-so-traditional daughter in a very traditional Greek-American family into a feature-length film, and the result is a rare delight: a romantic comedy that's both deeply romantic and very funny.

Vardalos plays Toula, the frumpy 30-year-old daughter of Gus Portokalos (Michael Constantine), the extremely proud, extremely stubborn owner of Chicago's Dancing Zorba's Diner, and the somewhat more understanding Maria (Lainie Kazan). Toula works as a seating hostess at Zorba's and still lives in the house she grew up in, the one with the Greek flag emblazoned on the garage door and the occasional goat-roasting-on-a-spit on the front lawn. Gus worries that Toula will never find a nice Greek man to marry and wants to send her back to Greece to find a husband. But Toula has a better idea about her future: she wants to go back to school. So over Gus's objections, Toula enrolls in a few classes, gives herself a makeover, and even meets a Prince Charming, Ian Miller (John Corbett). He, true to storybook form, immediately falls in love with her and proposes. Toula accepts and together they face Gus, who's furious and hurt that any daughter of his would marry a *xeno*—a foreigner.

It's obvious from the title where it all ends up, so there are really no unexpected twists to the tale. What *is* surprising is how poignant it all turns out to be. Funny without ever making fun, Vardalos mixes elements of ethnic stand-up, Cinderella romance, and "Bridget Loves Bernie"-style situation comedy, all grounded in something very real: the tension between Gus and Toula. And that's what gives this already bighearted film its soul.

MY BODYGUARD *DVD*

1980 96m c Drama ★★★★
20th Century Fox (U.S.) PG

Chris Makepeace (*Clifford*), Adam Baldwin (*Linderman*), Matt Dillon (*Moody*), Paul Quandt (*Carson*), Joan Cusack (*Shelley*), Dean R. Miller (*Hightower*), Tim Reyna (*Koontz*), Richard Bradley (*Dubrow*), Denise Baske (*Leilani*), Hank Salas (*Mike*)

p, Don Devlin; d, Tony Bill; w, Alan Ormsby; ph, Michael D. Margulies (CFI Color); ed, Stu Linder; m, Dave Grusin; prod d, Jackson DeGovia

This is essentially a tale of revenge, but not along the lines of some mindless vigilante movie; this is revenge with intelligence and sensitivity. Young Makepeace moves to Chicago with his motel manager father, Mull, and grandmother, Ruth Gordon (doing her wisecracking, randy old lady bit). His new high school is ruled by Dillon, who extorts money from classmates ostensibly so they won't be pummeled by Baldwin, a huge, reclusive hulk whom everyone fears. Makepeace tries to befriend Baldwin and finds him to be a very troubled young man. This is a heartwarming film, superbly directed by ex-actor

Tony Bill. Makepeace is excellent as the slight protagonist, and Baldwin is perfect as the brooding, misunderstood mammoth. Dave Grusin's score adds immeasurably to the tone.

MY BRILLIANT CAREER *DVD*

1979 98m c Drama ★★★★
New South Wales/GUO/Analysis (Australia) G

Judy Davis (*Sybylla Melvyn*), Sam Neill (*Harry Beecham*), Wendy Hughes (*Aunt Helen*), Robert Grubb (*Frank Hawdon*), Max Cullen (*Mr. McSwat*), Patricia Kennedy (*Aunt Gussie*), Aileen Britton (*Grandma Bossier*), Peter Whitford (*Uncle Julius*), Carole Skinner (*Mrs. McSwat*), Alan Hopgood (*Father*)

p, Margaret Fink; d, Gillian Armstrong; w, Eleanor Witcombe (based on the novel by Miles Franklin); ph, Don McAlpine (Eastmancolor); ed, Nicholas Beauman; m, Nathan Waks; prod d, Luciana Arrighi; cos, Anna Senior

AAN Best Costume Design: Anna Senior

Late in the 19th century in the Australian outback everyone in a small farming community knows his or her place and what is expected. All except Sybylla Melvyn (Judy Davis), that is, a headstrong young woman who wants a career—an idea that shocks her family and friends. Resisting the rigid codes of society and the marriage proposal of a wealthy man, Harry Beecham (Sam Neill, in a fine portrayal), Sybylla plows ahead with pluck and charm.

Davis gives a lively and humanistic performance, and the direction by Gillian Armstrong (MRS. SOFFEL, HIGH TIDE), in her feature debut, matches her heroine's character: strong, with a good sense of wanting to get something done and then doing it. The *mise-en-scène* is well composed, and the story is well told in this wonderful Australian work. Based on a true story, MY BRILLIANT CAREER was one of the key films in the resurgence of Australian cinema in the late 1970s and early '80s.

MY COUSIN VINNY *DVD*

1992 119m c Comedy ★★★
Palo Vista Productions/Peter V. MillerInvestment R
Corporation (U.S.)

Joe Pesci (*Vincent La Guardia Gambino*), Ralph Macchio (*Bill Gambini*), Marisa Tomei (*Mona Lisa Vito*), Mitchell Whitfield (*Stan Rothenstein*), Fred Gwynne (*Judge Chamberlain Haller*), Lane Smith (*Jim Trotter, III*), Austin Pendleton (*John Gibbons*), Bruce McGill (*Sheriff Farley*), Maury Chaykin (*Sam Tipton*), Pauline Meyers (*Constance Riley*)

p, Dale Launer, Paul Schiff; d, Jonathan Lynn; w, Dale Launer; ph, Peter Deming; ed, Tony Lombardo; m, Randy Edelman; prod d, Victoria Paul; art d, Randall Schmook, Michael Rizzo; cos, Carol Wood

AA Best Supporting Actress: Marisa Tomei

Clocking in at just under two hours, MY COUSIN VINNY moves at an extremely leisurely pace for a Hollywood farce. But that's just one indication of what makes this appealingly quirky comedy stand apart from more run-of-the-mill fare. Driving across the country on their way to college, Bill Gambini and Stan Rothenstein (Ralph Macchio and Mitchell Whitfield) are arrested in Alabama. Thinking they've been accused of shoplifting, they sign confessions, only to discover they've been charged with murder. Enter Bill's cousin, Vincent La Guardia Gambino (Joe Pesci), a lawyer who graduated from law school six years earlier but who only passed the bar exam six weeks ago and has never been in a courtroom. Up against a curmudgeonly judge, Chamberlain Haller (Fred Gwynne), and a wily district attorney, Jim Trotter, III (Lane Smith), Vinny rises to the occasion, with the unexpected help of his leggy girlfriend Mona Lisa Vito (Marisa Tomei), a self-taught automotive expert.

Joe Pesci projects a surprising depth here, shrewdly bringing down his usual cartoonish Brooklyn bravado a few notches. The film also benefits from a well-crafted plot, courtesy of screenwriter and co-producer Dale Launer (RUTHLESS PEOPLE, DIRTY ROTTEN SCOUNDRELS), that puts a fresh twist on stock situations and characters.

The film's cast is a comfortable ensemble of reliable veterans like Gwynne and McGill, underrated performers like Macchio and at least one hot newcomer in Tomei, an accomplished comedienne with intelligence and talent to match her knockout looks. British director Jonathan Lynn (NUNS ON THE RUN) keeps planting unexpected grace notes along the way, making this a rare comedy that never quite wears out its welcome.

MY DARLING CLEMENTINE

1946 97m bw Western 📀

Fox (U.S.) ★★★★★

Henry Fonda *(Wyatt Earp)*, Linda Darnell *(Chihuahua)*, Victor Mature *(Doc Holliday)*, Walter Brennan *(Old Man Clanton)*, Tim Holt *(Virgil Earp)*, Cathy Downs *(Clementine)*, Ward Bond *(Morgan Earp)*, Alan Mowbray *(Granville Thorndyke)*, John Ireland *(Billy Clanton)*, Roy Roberts *(Mayor)*

p, Samuel G. Engel; d, John Ford; w, Samuel G. Engel, Winston Miller (based on a story by Sam Hellman from the novel *Wyatt Earp, Frontier Marshall* by Stuart N. Lake); ph, Joseph MacDonald; ed, Dorothy Spencer; m, Cyril J. Mockridge, David Buttolph; art d, James Basevi, Lyle Wheeler; fx, Fred Sersen; cos, Rene Hubert

Perhaps the best orchestrated western of all time, courtesy of the modest Mr. Ford. No western figure inspired more cinematic lore than the indomitable Wyatt Earp, and Fonda, back from WWII, gives a definitive portrayal of the famous frontier lawman.

Earp and his brothers (Bond, Holt and Don Garner) have driven their cattle to the outskirts of rough-and-tumble Tombstone, Arizona. Coming upon their campsite is Old Man Clanton (Brennan), who offers the Earps a cut-rate price for their herd. Wyatt rejects the offer and heads into town, leaving his youngest brother as watchman. In Tombstone Earp manages to rid the town of a bothersome drunken Indian, and the grateful townsfolk offer him the job of sheriff. He doesn't accept the position until he discovers the Clantons have stolen his cattle and killed his brother. Then it's time for the remaining Earps to strap on their guns, shore up Wyatt's mysterious, alcoholic friend Doc Holliday (Mature), and head for the OK Corral.

Dramatic and brooding, with shadows at night and blinding light at day under a sky that never ends, MY DARLING CLEMENTINE doesn't follow history exactly, but Ford is much more concerned with the myth of the West. The scene where Wyatt brings harmony to Tombstone by eliminating the disruptive element—notably, a Native American—is almost a prototypical expression of the genre's obsession with the formation of community. The most famous scene in this regard, however, is the dance at the church-founding social, where Wyatt and Clementine (Downs) walk down the street like it was a wedding aisle. Fonda was rarely better, his Midwest accent and measured delivery perfect for the part. His chair-balancing makes wonderful use of his lanky body, and his deliberately stiff but gracefully folksy dance with Clementine is a brilliant bit of acting. The often underrated Mature is also outstanding, acting out the tormented Holliday with amazing passion and restraint. Darnell's luscious noir persona is effective, even if she is too glamorized and seems about as Latina as "My Wild Irish Rose." Downs, meanwhile, cast as a refined parallel to Darnell, isn't much of an actress, but then this isn't

much of a part; schoolteacher Clementine is less a character than the embodiment of civilization from the East, and the ingenue fills the bill admirably. Finally, Brennan, downright chilling as Clanton, will make you forget every rerun of "The Real McCoys" you ever watched.

As with other Ford films, there is no sustained score; Newman merely provides haunting little variations of the title song on a harmonica, and other western ballads on fiddles or guitars as needed. The script is lean and tight, and MacDonald's startling photography, under the Master's guidance, provides graphics so sweeping that the whole of the West seems bounded by the frame.

Many other films about Wyatt Earp have been made: LAW AND ORDER with Walter Huston; two films named FRONTIER MARSHAL with George O'Brien and Randolph Scott in the role; TOMBSTONE, THE TOWN TOO TOUGH TO DIE with Richard Dix; WICHITA with Joel McCrea; GUNFIGHT AT THE O.K. CORRAL with Burt Lancaster; HOUR OF THE GUN with James Garner; and DOC with Harris Yulin. This, however, is the definitive rendering, if only for the sequence at the church dance. If that scene doesn't either give you chills or make you cry, see your doctor immediately.

MY DINNER WITH ANDRE

1981 110m c Docudrama 📀

Andre (U.S.) ★★★

PG

Wallace Shawn *(Wally)*, Andre Gregory *(Andre)*, Jean Lenauer *(Waiter)*, Roy Butler *(Bartender)*

p, George W. George, Beverly Karp; d, Louis Malle; w, Wallace Shawn, Andre Gregory; ph, Jeri Sopanen (Movielab Color); ed, Suzanne Baron; m, Allen Shawn; prod d, David Mitchell; art d, Stephen McCabe; cos, Jeffrey Ullman

Louis Malle's somewhat overrated MY DINNER WITH ANDRE is a filmed conversation between two friends, and whether you find the movie profound, pretentious, or entertaining will depend on how interesting you find the talk.

The main speaker is real-life theater director and playwright Andre Gregory, a seeker after enlightenment who details his occasionally bizarre quest as he dines with an old, very different friend (real-life actor/playwright Wallace Shawn) whom he hasn't seen in a long time. Wally is more concerned with creature comforts than with quixotic spiritual searches and serves as Andre's philosophical foil as the two men talk and eat (in real time) at a fancy New York restaurant.

Although Malle provided the minimal direction, the film really belongs to Shawn and Gregory, who also cowrote the script.

MY FAIR LADY

1964 170m c Musical/Comedy 📀

Warner Bros. (U.S.) ★★

Audrey Hepburn *(Eliza Doolittle)*, Rex Harrison *(Prof. Henry Higgins)*, Stanley Holloway *(Alfred P. Doolittle)*, Wilfrid Hyde-White *(Col. Hugh Pickering)*, Gladys Cooper *(Mrs. Higgins)*, Jeremy Brett *(Freddy Eynsford-Hill)*, Theodore Bikel *(Zoltan Karpathy)*, Isobel Elsom *(Mrs. Eynsford-Hill)*, Mona Washbourne *(Mrs. Pearce)*, John Alderson *(Jamie)*

p, Jack L. Warner; d, George Cukor; w, Alan Jay Lerner (based on a musical play by Alan Jay Lerner, Frederick Loewe and the play *Pygmalion* by George Bernard Shaw); ph, Harry Stradling (Super Panavision 70, Technicolor); ed, William Ziegler; m, Frederick Loewe; prod d, Cecil Beaton; art d, Gene Allen; chor, Hermes Pan; cos, Cecil Beaton

AA Best Picture; AA Best Actor: Rex Harrison; *AAN Best Supporting Actor:* Stanley Holloway; *AAN Best Supporting Actress:*

Gladys Cooper; *AA Best Director:* George Cukor; *AAN Best Adapted Screenplay:* Alan Jay Lerner; *AA Best Cinematography:* Harry Stradling; *AAN Best Film Editing:* William Ziegler; *AA Best Adapted Score:* Andre Previn; *AA Best Art Direction-Set Decoration (Color):* Gene Allen, Cecil Beaton, George James Hopkins; *AA Best Costume Design (Color):* Cecil Beaton; *AA Best Sound:* George R. Groves

Just fairly fair; call it the revenge of Mary Poppins. Audrey's effortless swan can't redeem the fact that she's a Givenchy mannequin picturesquely dusted with Jack Warner's cigar ashes, when we meet her "playing" an ugly duckling. Hepburn specialized in Cinderella variations (ROMAN HOLIDAY, SABRINA) but was getting too mature, too sophisticated to play the waif bit without outside plot stimuli (danger—CHARADE, broken heart—BREAKFAST AT TIFFANY'S, etc.). Anyway, Shaw's original Eliza is not quite as waifish as she is raffish. Hepburn can't summon up the guts to guttersnipe, and when she opens her mouth wide to presumably sing (dubbed by Marni Nixon, who deserves a special Oscar for all the stars she made look good) like she's never even seen a singer in her entire life, it's a shock and a laugh at the same time.

Otherwise, the Lerner and Loewe musical emerges as an overly long, sometimes enjoyable dinosaur. Perhaps there is truthfully no way to liberate Shaw—his writing is heavy, obtuse. Adding wonderful songs ("On the Street Where You Live," "I Could Have Danced All Night," "Get Me to the Church on Time") only makes it come up heavily trimmed, like a fancy Christmas turkey. The film makes you feel bloated and tired. But it made a fortune at the box office and undeservedly took Oscars in almost every category—with the exception of Best Actress, which ironically went to MARY POPPINS's Julie Andrews, who was Harrison's fair lady on Broadway.

Henry Higgins (Harrison) bets fellow linguist Col. Hugh Pickering (Hyde-White) that he can turn Cockney flower girl Eliza Doolittle (Hepburn) into a lady with elocution so pure no one will suspect her origins. She is, of course, a huge success at a fancy ball, but Higgins has a few lessons in humanity to learn from his "creation."

Yes, Harrison is mechanically expert, like a graduate with honors from the Lord Olivier School of Going through the Motions (we think, belatedly, we'd have preferred original choice Cary Grant opposite Andrews). But film always pointed up his hatefulness. It's hard not to think of dead Carole Landis lying on her bathroom floor when he waxes sentimental. Frankly, we hate this damned thing.

MY FAVORITE BLONDE
DVD
★★★½
1942 78m bw Spy/Comedy
Paramount (U.S.)

Bob Hope (*Larry Haines*), Madeleine Carroll (*Karen Bentley*), Gale Sondergaard (*Mme. Stephanie Runick*), George Zucco (*Dr. Hugo Streger*), Lionel Royce (*Karl*), Walter Kingsford (*Dr. Faber*), Victor Varconi (*Miller*), Otto Reichow (*Lanz*), Charles Cane (*Turk O'Flaherty*), Crane Whitley (*Ulrich*)

p, Paul Jones; d, Sidney Lanfield; w, Don Hartman, Frank Butler (based on a story by Melvin Frank and Norman Panama); ph, William Mellor; ed, William O'Shea; m, David Buttolph; art d, Hans Dreier, Robert Usher

Carroll is a beautiful spy who posesses plans involving the shipment of war planes to England and is being chased by Nazis who want the plans for themselves. While in New York, she escapes from them by ducking into a small dressing room at a theater. Coincidentally this is the dressing room of Hope, a wisecracking ladies' man who's preparing his performing penguin for its debut. Without much pleading, the lovely Carroll convinces Hope to aid her escape. From there it's a comic cross-country chase with lots of disguises and silliness.

Hope is wonderful, with something smart to say no matter what the situation. His smug behavior is very funny (far and away superior to anything he ever did in the television work that made him rich) and the pacing is as good as it usually is in these Hope comedies. His old partner from the ROAD films, the wonderfully laid back Bing Crosby, makes a cameo (as he so often did in Hope's solo comedies) as a man giving the two travelers directions. "No, it can't be," mutters Hope after the benefactor leaves. Some good fun, but the poor penguin is treated like a toy rather than an animal. Penguins are inherently funny animals (as television's "Monty Python's Flying Circus" proved time and again), and there was no need for the knockabout treatment of the bird.

MY FAVORITE BRUNETTE
DVD
★★★★
1947 87m bw Mystery/Comedy
Paramount (U.S.)

Bob Hope (*Ronnie Jackson*), Dorothy Lamour (*Carlotta Montay*), Peter Lorre (*Kismet*), Lon Chaney Jr. (*Willie*), Charles Dingle (*Maj. Simon Montague*), Reginald Denny (*James Collins*), Frank Puglia (*Baron Montay*), Ann Doran (*Miss Rogers*), Willard Robertson (*Prison Warden*), Jack LaRue (*Tony*)

p, Daniel Dare; d, Elliott Nugent; w, Edmund Beloin, Jack Rose; ph, Lionel Lindon; ed, Ellsworth Hoagland; m, Robert Emmett Dolan; art d, Hans Dreier, Earl Hedrick; fx, Gordon Jennings; cos, Edith Head

In what ranks as one of his best comedies, Hope plays a harried baby photographer who is asked by his private-eye pal to watch his detective business for a few days while he goes on vacation. Hope agrees and finds himself getting involved with a lot more than watching dust settle. Believing Hope to be the real private eye, Lamour hires him to search for her uncle, a wealthy baron who has vanished, and gives the dubious detective a map, warning him to guard it with his life. Hope goes off to the palatial estate of a former associate of the missing man, Dingle, who introduces Hope to a wheelchair-bound man who is supposedly Lamour's uncle. Hoyt, a doctor who is present, insists that Lamour has a few screws loose. Hope is just about convinced of the veracity of Dingle and Hoyt's story until he is about to leave and spots the "disabled" baron walking about. When Hope snaps a quick picture, Dingle gets one of his crazed henchmen (Lorre in a wonderful self-parody) to knock out Hope and recover the film. In an effort to determine the importance of the map, Hope and Lamour pay a visit to the geologist who drew it, but Lorre has killed him, framing Hope for the murder. Minutes before Hope is to be executed, fresh evidence is discovered by Lamour, and the executioner, furious that his day has been ruined, takes off his hood and reveals himself to be none other than Hope's offscreen and sometimes onscreen) pal Bing Crosby. "Boy," says Hope as he turns to the camera, "he'll take any kind of a part!" This is a classic Hope film, with one gag following another in rapid succession. Particularly good is Lorre, who was known at this stage in his career for doing films that approached this genre seriously. And Chaney's characterization of a dumb sanitarium guard so tough he cracks walnuts with his eyelids is great fun. Alan Ladd is equally amusing in his cameo role of the vacationing detective.

MY FAVORITE WIFE
DVD
★★★★
1940 88m bw Comedy
RKO (U.S.)

Irene Dunne (*Ellen Arden*), Cary Grant (*Nick Arden*), Randolph Scott (*Stephen Burkett*), Gail Patrick (*Bianca*), Ann Shoemaker (*Ma*), Scotty Beckett (*Tim Arden*), Mary Lou Harrington (*Chinch Arden*), Donald MacBride (*Hotel Clerk*), Hugh O'Connell (*Johnson*), Granville Bates (*Judge*)

p, Leo McCarey; d, Garson Kanin; w, Sam Spewack, Bella Spewack (based on a story by Leo McCarey, Sam Spewack, and Bella Spewack); ph, Rudolph Mate; ed, Robert Wise; m, Roy Webb; art d, Van Nest Polglase, Mark-Lee Kirk; cos, Howard Greer

---

AAN Best Original Story: Leo McCarey, Bella Spewack, Samuel Spewack; AAN Best Original Score: Roy Webb; AAN Best Interior Decoration (B/W): Van Nest Polglase, Mark-Lee Kirk

---

After Grant and Dunne made such a success of THE AWFUL TRUTH, they were reteamed for this up-to-date version of the "Enoch Arden" story. Producer McCarey was supposed to direct, but he had a terrible auto accident just before shooting, so Kanin was handed the task and came through with a fast-moving, often amusing film.

You all know the story. Ellen (Dunne), shipwrecked for seven years, returns to discover that her husband Nick (Grant) has just had her declared legally dead and has married Bianca (Patrick). Ellen wants her man back and proceeds to make him jealous over Stephen (Scott), the man she was shipwrecked with all those years. Meanwhile, Bianca is getting mentally disturbed. Love will find a way.

Lots of laughs for the first three-quarters of the film but then it peters out for the expected finale. A scene-stealing Bates helps out, though. Remade, not as well, as MOVE OVER, DARLING, which starred Doris Day and James Garner in the Dunne and Grant roles.

MY FAVORITE YEAR

1982 92m c Comedy ★★★★
Brooksfilms (U.S.) PG

Peter O'Toole (Alan Swann), Mark Linn-Baker (Benjy Stone), Jessica Harper (K.C. Downing), Joseph Bologna (King Kaiser), Bill Macy (Sy Benson), Lainie Kazan (Belle Carroca), Anne DeSalvo (Alice Miller), Basil Hoffman (Herb Lee), Lou Jacobi (Uncle Morty), Adolph Green (Leo Silver)

p, Michael Gruskoff; d, Richard Benjamin; w, Norman Steinberg, Dennis Palumbo (based on a story by Dennis Palumbo); ph, Gerald Hirschfeld (Metrocolor); ed, Richard Chew; m, Ralph Burns; prod d, Charles Rosen; cos, May Routh

---

AAN Best Actor: Peter O'Toole

A delightful film presenting a poignant portrait of television in the early 1950s. Benjy Stone (Mark Linn-Baker) is a fledgling writer for a live comedy television show hosted by zany, tough, yet soft-hearted King Kaiser (Joseph Bologna). Benjy is assigned to chaperone the unpredictable, boozing, onetime Hollywood swashbuckler Alan Swann (Peter O'Toole), who is to appear on television in a Kaiser skit. Arriving in Manhattan drunk and uncontrollable, Swann begins to lead Stone in a wild night of revelry, and over the next several days, the famous guest is involved in a series of escapades. On the show itself he staggers about with the near-DTs, forgetting his lines and getting into a fight with a bunch of union goons invading the set over Kaiser's past insults. O'Toole is superb as the former matinee idol, and Bologna is outstanding as the brusque and brawling comic. Linn-Baker, who would later go on to his own television series in 1986, is excellent, playing out a real-life incident where novice comedy writer Mel Brooks was assigned to chaperone the colorful Errol Flynn before he appeared on Sid Caesar's "Your Show of Shows." Cameron Mitchell plays a union crime boss with lead-foot accuracy and deadpan deadliness. Richard Benjamin's direction surprisingly provides a dizzy pace and inventive set-ups, aided greatly by cinematographer Gerald Hirschfeld and editor Richard Chew.

MY FIRST WIFE

1984 96m c Drama ★★★★
Dofine (Australia)

John Hargreaves (John), Wendy Hughes (Helen), Lucy Angwin (Lucy), David Cameron (Tom), Julia Blake (Kirstin), Anna Jemison (Hilary), Charles Tingwell (Helen's Mother), Robin Lovejoy (John's Father), Lucy Uralov (John's Mother), Xenia Groutas (John's Sister)

p, Paul Cox, Jane Ballantyne; d, Paul Cox; w, Paul Cox, Bob Ellis; ph, Yuri Sokol; ed, Tim Lewis; prod d, Santhana Naidu; art d, Asher Bilu

---

Cox, a Dutch-born director working in Australia, took the pain of his own divorce and turned it into an honest cinematic account of the end of a marriage, exposing painfully raw nerve endings with care and compassion. Hargreaves is a disc jockey for a classical music station, working also on his own musical compositions. Hughes, his wife, is sick of being ignored while her husband devotes himself to his work, and subsequently she begins a most indiscreet affair. Only Hargreaves is unaware of what is really happening, but eventually he learns the truth and separates from Hughes. Hargreaves refuses to tell his parents, who disapproved of the marriage in the first place. Lovejoy, Hargreaves's Russian emigrant father, is dying, and though his own marriage was far from happy, he lectures his son on the importance of matrimony. Hargreaves gives an emotional performance, a man who has no understanding of what is happening to his life. The cold indifference he displays toward Hughes early in the story is a sad but accurate portrait of a man for whom work means everything. Cox presents his story without redemption at the conclusion, leaving characters in pain and confusion. Though a bleak view of life, this is a frank and compelling film. MY FIRST WIFE was submitted as an Australian entry to the Venice Film Festival, but surprisingly it was rejected by this prestigious gathering. The film garnered three Australian Film Awards—Best Actor for Hargreaves, Best Director for Cox, and Best Original Screenplay for Cox and Ellis.

MY FRIEND FLICKA

1943 89m c Children's ★★★★
Fox (U.S.)

Roddy McDowall (Ken McLaughlin), Preston Foster (Rob McLaughlin), Rita Johnson (Nell), James Bell (Gus), Jeff Corey (Tim Murphy), Diana Hale (Hildy), Arthur Loft (Charley Sargent), Jimmy Aubrey

p, Ralph Dietrich; d, Harold Schuster; w, Lillie Hayward, Francis Edwards Faragoh (based on the novel by Mary O'Hara); ph, Dewey Wrigley (Technicolor); ed, Robert Fritch; m, Alfred Newman; art d, Richard Day, Chester Gore; cos, Herschel

---

A wonderful film, beautifully photographed and sensitively told. McDowall is a young boy who longs for a colt of his own. His rancher father finally gives in and is displeased when the boy chooses the foal from an unruly mare. But through painstaking work by McDowall, the colt is trained and nurtured, eventually growing to become a fine mare and a loyal companion. The performances and direction are as fine as they come. The humanistic qualities within the film come through well, without being the least bit overbearing or overly sentimental. The color photography is wonderful, capturing all the grandeur of the Rocky Mountains. Perfect for the whole family. A sequel was made with almost the same cast: THUNDERHEAD, SON OF FLICKA. Later a series on television.

MY LEFT FOOT

DVD

1989 98m c Biography ★★★★½

Granada (Ireland) R

Daniel Day-Lewis *(Christy Brown)*, Ray McAnally *(Mr. Brown)*, Brenda Fricker *(Mrs. Brown)*, Ruth McCabe *(Mary Carr)*, Fiona Shaw *(Dr. Eileen Cole)*, Eanna MacLiam *(Old Benny)*, Alison Whelan *(Old Sheila)*, Declan Croghan *(Old Tom)*, Hugh O'Conor *(Young Christy)*, Cyril Cusack *(Lord Castlewelland)*

p, Noel Pearson; d, Jim Sheridan; w, Shane Connaughton, Jim Sheridan (based on the book by Christy Brown); ph, Jack Conroy (Technicolor); ed, J. Patrick Duffner; m, Elmer Bernstein; prod d, Austin Spriggs; cos, Joan Bergin

AAN Best Picture; AA Best Actor: Daniel Day-Lewis; *AA Best Supporting Actress:* Brenda Fricker; *AAN Best Director:* Jim Sheridan; *AAN Best Adapted Screenplay:* Jim Sheridan, Shane Connaughton

Thank god, an insolent hoof. Stories about people overcoming devastating handicaps have long been grist for the filmmaker's mill. The title of this screen adaptation of Christy Brown's best-selling autobiography refers to the only limb over which Brown, crippled since birth by a severe case of cerebral palsy, ever had any control. Daniel Day-Lewis plays the acclaimed Irish-born artist and author, as the film intercuts flashbacks of his formative years with scenes at a stately Dublin home in 1959. There, the wheelchair-bound Brown, guest of honor at a benefit dinner for a cerebral palsy foundation, first meets Mary (Ruth McCabe), a young nurse assigned to care for him for the evening. Presented with a copy of Brown's book, Mary leafs through its pages, and the author's life is re-created on the screen, beginning with his early years as the ninth of 13 surviving children (out of 22) in a close-knit, working-class Irish Catholic family. That MY LEFT FOOT succeeds as well as it does is in large part due to a superb supporting cast and the virtuoso performances of Hugh O'Conor and Day-Lewis, who play Brown as child and adult, respectively. Undoubtedly, MY LEFT FOOT begs comparison with GABY, A TRUE STORY, the depiction of another cerebral palsy victim. Indeed, the films are like two sides of the same coin. While the less satisfying GABY focuses on the dour aspects of its subject's plight, the better-scripted, more entertaining MY LEFT FOOT is filled with wit and unselfconscious humor. To Brown's credit, his portrayal is unerringly tough, sometimes surprisingly sensual. It keeps FOOT from maudlin static. A rich cinematic experience, this uplifting British production will leave you in awe of the extraordinary Christy Brown.

MY LIFE AS A DOG

DVD

(MITT LIV SOM HUND)

1985 101m c Comedy/Drama ★★★½

AB/Svensk (Sweden) PG-13

Anton Glanzelius *(Ingemar Johansson)*, Anki Liden *(His Mother)*, Tomas von Bromssen *(Uncle Gunnar)*, Manfred Serner *(Erik)*, Melinda Kinnaman *(Saga)*, Ing-Marie Carlsson *(Berit)*, Kicki Rundgren *(Aunt Ulla)*, Lennart Hjulstrom *(Konstnaren)*, Leif Erickson *(Farbor Sandberg)*, Christina Carlwind *(Fru Sandberg)*

p, Waldemar Bergendahl; d, Lasse Hallstrom; w, Lasse Hallstrom, Reidar Jonsson, Brasse Brannstrom, Per Berglund (based on the novel by Jonsson); ph, Jorgen Persson, Rolf Lindstrom (Fujicolor); ed, Christer Furubrand, Susanne Linnman; m, Bjorn Isfalt; art d, Lasse Westfelt; cos, Inger Pehrsson, Susanne Falck

AAN Best Director: Lasse Hallstrom; *AAN Best Adapted Screenplay:* Lasse Hallstrom, Reidar Jonsson, Brasse Brannstrom, Per Berglund

This critically acclaimed Swedish film, which also won kudos for its talented star, Anton Glanzelius, is a tragicomic, sensitive portrayal of adolescence set in 1959. The film centers on 12-year-old Ingemar Johansson (Glanzelius), who lives with his abusive brother (Manfred Serner) and terminally ill mother (Anki Liden). He is not discouraged, however—sure, he has it bad, but not as bad as Laika, the Soviet spacedog who starved to death while in orbit and whose fate haunts the boy. Ingemar's life has begun to spin out of control, and, like Laika, there's little he can do to stop it. When Ingemar is sent away for the summer to stay with relations, he meets a menage of eccentric—and sexually intimidating—villagers; eventually, these experiences give him a sustaining inner strength. Writer-director Lasse Hallstrom's tale is an episodic rite of passage, a story in which the emotions are touching but never sappy, the main character has the integrity and complexity of a real child with real troubles, and the glimpses of village life are rich and engaging. Not just another charming film about growing up, but an expertly directed tale that takes a small, simple subject and colors it with invention and inspiration.

MY LIFE TO LIVE

DVD

(VIVRE SA VIE)

1962 85m bw Drama ★★★★★

Pleiade (France)

Anna Karina *(Nana)*, Sady Rebbot *(Raoul)*, Andre Labarthe *(Paul)*, Guylaine Schlumberger *(Yvette)*, Gerard Hoffman *(the Cook)*, Monique Messine *(Elizabeth)*, Paul Pavel *(A Journalist)*, Dimitri Dineff *(A Youth)*, Peter Kassowitz *(A Young Man)*, Eric Schlumberger *(Luigi)*

p, Pierre Braunberger; d, Jean-Luc Godard; w, Jean-Luc Godard; ph, Raoul Coutard; ed, Agnes Guillemot; m, Michel Legrand

An early stunner from Jean-Luc Godard and one of the seminal films of the French New Wave. The filmmaker's fourth feature stars his then-wife, Anna Karina, as Nana, a Parisian sales clerk who, after separating from her husband, Paul (Labarthe), tries to make it as an actress. After seeing Dreyer's silent classic THE PASSION OF JOAN OF ARC, she abandons the idea and turns to prostitution. The film is divided into 12 tableaux, which take place in cafes, in a record store, at a police station, and on the streets of Paris. The scenes and the issues raised range from prostitution (with quoted facts and figures on the subject) to experiments with narration and autobiographical elements (Godard narrating, Karina starring). In Godard's typically dense and provocative style, we also have many allusions to films and literature (Renoir's NANA, Zola's *Nana*, Truffaut's JULES AND JIM, Dreyer and Falconetti, and Edgar Allen Poe's "The Oval Portrait"), as well as an absorbing discussion on linguistic philosophy with Brice Parain.

Through this complex and intriguing network we have an abundance of humor and many uniquely touching vignettes. Karina is considerably more at home in front of the camera than in her earlier films, and Godard has by this point clearly learned how to bring out the very best that's in her. MY LIFE TO LIVE represents an interesting mix of those facets Godard has explored more individually in his earlier films—the genre elements of BREATHLESS, the politics of LE PETIT SOLDAT, and the narrative experimentation of A WOMAN IS A WOMAN. Technically MY LIFE TO LIVE was (and perhaps still is) far ahead of its time, knocking down the traditional walls of sound recording. Godard refused to mix the sound in the studio (except for Michel Legrand's barely used score), instead applying the same rule for sound and image—to capture them directly—and amended his "jump-cut" style of editing by allowing shots to last from six to eight minutes as the camera wandered through the set. MY LIFE TO LIVE also contains one of Godard's greatest and most personal scenes—a reading of Charles Baudelaire's translation of "The Oval Portrait," the story of an artist whose wife dies just as he finishes her portrait. Although Godard does not play Nana's lover in this scene, he does provide the character's voice. As we hear Godard reading Poe's words, we see the face of his wife, Anna Karina as Nana, and realize that, like Poe, Godard is painting a portrait of his wife. The finale is memorable and puts a suitable spin on this early mix of cinematic experimentation and the sociological concerns which would continue to distinguish's this great filmmaker's work as the decade progressed.

MY LITTLE CHICKADEE
DVD

1940 83m bw Comedy/Western ★★½
Universal (U.S.)

W.C. Fields *(Cuthbert J. Twillie)*, Mae West *(Flower Belle Lee)*, Joseph Calleia *(Jeff Badger)*, Dick Foran *(Wayne Carter)*, Margaret Hamilton *(Mrs. Gideon)*, George Moran *(Clarence)*, Si Jenks *(Deputy)*, Gene Austin *(Himself)*, Russell Hall *(Candy)*, Otto Heimel *(Coco)*

p, Lester Cowan; d, Edward F. Cline; w, Mae West, W.C. Fields; ph, Joseph Valentine; ed, Edward Curtiss; m, Frank Skinner; art d, Jack Otterson; cos, Vera West

Neither the best of the West nor the lillies of the Fields. Teaming Mae and W.C. in a Wild West spoof seemed inspired, and the marquee values brought plenty of people to the box office, but the film plays like two middling star vehicles uneasily spliced together.

Flower Belle (West), a woman whose corsets are tighter than her morals, is thrown out of town by righteous townsfolk after she's romanced by a masked bandit. On board a train, she's courted by snake oil salesman Cuthbert J. Twillie (Fields) and marries him to gain respectability while she continues searching for her lover's identity.

Mutual admirers Fields and West interact fairly well in their occasional scenes together, but her diamond-bright polish and his ambling, martini-fueled improvisations don't entirely mix. We don't have Abbott and Costello or Laurel and Hardy here, but rather two comics used to toplining alone. (It was cute, though, to end the film with his inviting her to "come up and see me sometime" and her responding, "Yeah, I'll do that, my little chickadee.") West parries both saloon owner Jeff Badger (Calleia) and crusading newspaperman Wayne Carter (Foran) with ease, and has a real comic highlight when she takes over a classroom for an indisposed teacher, but Fields comes off rather better. (The quality of his work was rarely affected by the quality of the film as a whole.) His attempts to get into Flower Belle's bed are hilarious, and the poker scene in the bar is a classic if only for the moment when Fuzzy Knight asks, "Is this a game of chance?" and Fields replies, "Not the way I play it."

MY MAN GODFREY
DVD

1936 94m bw Comedy ★★★★½
Universal (U.S.)

William Powell *(Godfrey Parke)*, Carole Lombard *(Irene Bullock)*, Alice Brady *(Angelica Bullock)*, Eugene Pallette *(Alexander Bullock)*, Gail Patrick *(Cornelia Bullock)*, Alan Mowbray *(Tommy Gray)*, Jean Dixon *(Molly, Maid)*, Mischa Auer *(Carlo)*, Robert Light *(Faithful George)*, Pat Flaherty *(Mike)*

p, Gregory La Cava; d, Gregory La Cava; w, Morrie Ryskind, Eric Hatch, Gregory La Cava (based on the story "1101 Park Avenue" by Eric Hatch); ph, Ted Tetzlaff; ed, Ted J. Kent; m, Charles Previn; art d, Charles D. Hall; cos, Brymer, Travis Banton

AAN Best Actor: William Powell; AAN Best Actress: Carole Lombard; AAN Best Supporting Actor: Mischa Auer; AAN Best Supporting Actress: Alice Brady; AAN Best Director: Gregory Lacava; AAN Best Screenplay: Eric Hatch, Morris Ryskind

A silvery romp. The flaw is that it never delivers on the satire it starts with, dissolving into Cinderella fantasy along the way. But the leads are so impeccable that the seam never shows and the greatly underrated La Cava directs with precision. Of all the great comediennes, Lombard's innocently unflappable center was unique. She's like an eternal playmate—a quality only Harlow shared. It's a pity the two never played sisters.

Anyway, MY MAN GODFREY is comedy with a social conscience, although the message's subtlety has to be unearthed from all the humor. The flaky, endearing Irene Bullock (Lombard) and the dark, calculating Cornelia (Patrick) are two Park Avenue brats in the midst of a scavenger hunt party. Among other items on their list is a "forgotten man" from one of Manhattan's hobo jungles. Irene for once bests her snobbish sister when she convinces down-and-out Godfrey (Powell) to come back to the party with her. Godfrey, however, turns out to be more than the Bullock family ever bargained for when when Irene hires him as butler.

The rich are made to look very foolish and the poor appear very noble in this film, something that Depression audiences must have appreciated. Two years later, a film inspired by this one, MERRILY WE LIVE, was released, but it and the flat 1957 remake of MY MAN GODFREY were inferior attempts at recreating the chemistry of this film. Powell and Lombard, married in 1931 and divorced in 1933, were still friendly enough to make a marvelous onscreen team. One of the better, if not the best, of the famous screwball comedies of the era, GODFREY stands as an excellent example of witty scripting, direction, and editing. With Eugene Palette (growling some of the best lines, and certainly one of the strangest, funniest men ever), Alice Brady (great in these dithery roles), and Mischa Auer (in his famous monkey imitation) among the congress of nitwits. Look fast—there's Janie Wyman in the party scene.

MY NAME IS IVAN
(IVANOVO DETSTVO)

1962 97m bw Drama/War ★★★★
Mosfilm (U.S.S.R.)

Kolya Burlyayev *(Ivan)*, Valentin Zubkov *(Capt. Kholin)*, Ye. Zharikov *(Lt. Galtsev)*, S. Krylov *(Cpl. Katasonych)*, Nikolai Grinko *(Col. Gryaznov)*, D. Milyutenko *(Old Man)*, V. Malyavina *(Masha)*, I. Tarkovskaya *(Ivan's Mother)*, Andrei Konchalovsky, Ivan Savkin

d, Andrei Tarkovsky; w, Vladimir Osipovich Bogomolov, Mikhail Papava (based on the short story "Ivan" by Vladimir Osipovich Bogomolov); ph, Vadim Yusov; ed, L. Feyginova; m, Vyacheslav Ovchinnikov; art d, Ye. Chernyayaev; fx, V. Sevostyanov, S. Mukhin

This first feature from Soviet director Andrei Tarkovsky, an intense cinematic poem about war and childhood, presents the most horrific account of war's ravaging effect on a child's innocence since Roberto Rossellini's GERMANY, YEAR ZERO. Like Rossellini's Edmund, Tarkovsky's Ivan (Kolya Burlyayev) is a 12-year-old man/boy who has known little else but war—war that has forced him to become an adult and (in the irony of the actual translated title) robbed him of his childhood. When first seen, Ivan might be assumed to be an average youngster until he is shown trekking, neck-deep, through a murky swamp. This swamp is at the enemy's front line, to which Ivan, a member of a WWII Russian military intelligence unit, has been sent to gather information on troop movements. Ivan has only a cause and a country; his town has been overrun by the Germans, his father murdered, his mother shot and killed, his sister blown apart by a bomb. Although his superiors are pleased with his efforts, they protectively transfer him to the rear, but Ivan rebels at this and is allowed to go on one more mission. Much more than a war film about a young boy, MY NAME IS IVAN is a pure film experience. Tarkovsky fills the frame with beautiful images composed in extreme high, low, or tilted angles; uses an unpredictable editing style that alternates between rapid, jarring cuts and carefully composed long takes; employs a stark black-and-white contrast, which often turns natural scenery into abstract imagery; and constructs a soundtrack that is as inventive as his visuals. Complementing Tarkovsky's vision is the performance of Burlyayev, whose face expresses both determination and tenderness. Highly praised upon its release—it won awards at the Venice Film Festival for Best Film, Director, and Actor—MY NAME IS IVAN has found a new audience with the rising international recognition of Tarkovsky.

MY NAME IS JOE

1998 105m c   Drama   ★★★
Westdeutscher Rundfunk/Tornasol Films/Degeto   R
Film/Channel Four Films/Scottish Arts Council
National Lottery Fund/Road Movies Vierte Produktionen/
Filmstiftung NRW/BIM Distribuzione/Diaphana
Distribution/Alta Films/Glasgow Film Fund/La Sept
Cinema/ARD/Arte/Parallax Pictures
(Germany/U.K./France/Italy/Spain)

Louise Goodall (Sarah Downie), Peter Mullan (Joe Kavanagh), David McKay (Liam), Anne-Marie Kennedy (Sabine), David Hayman (McGowan), Gary Lewis (Shanks), Lorraine McIntosh (Maggie), Scott Hannah (Scott), David Peacock (Hooligan), Gordon McMurray (Scrag)

p, Rebecca O'Brien; d, Ken Loach; w, Paul Laverty; ph, Barry Ackroyd; ed, Jonathan Morris; m, George Fenton; prod d, Martin Johnson; art d, Fergus Clegg; cos, Rhona Russell

Ken Loach, Britain's last crusading leftist film director, returns to his particular brand of social realism with this tale of a recovering alcoholic and general do-gooder whose best intentions jeopardize his opportunity to find love with a social worker.

Joe (Peter Mullan, who won the Best Actor prize at Cannes) hit bottom long ago and has spent the better part of a decade crawling back up. He's on the dole, lives in a decrepit Glasgow neighborhood dominated by crumbling concrete public housing, and passes the time coaching a group of raucous youths in their weekly football matches. It's a bleak world, and Loach never hesitates to turn the bleak Glaswegian light on these sickly complexioned Scots and their vacant, drug-addled stares. While picking up Liam (David McKay), of his soccer lads, Joe meets children's health visitor Sarah (Louise Goodall), who's checking up on Liam's kid. After an acerbic exchange, Joe runs into Sarah again and winds up offering to wallpaper her apartment. He gets ratted out for working while collecting unemployment benefits, but Sarah saves his hide by writing the authorities and insisting that she didn't pay for Joe's work. The episode perfectly encapsulates Loach's ongoing social concerns, from his ambivalence toward government intervention to all manner of subtle class issues. The fledgling couple's problems are compounded by Joe's desire to help Liam when Liam's partner Sabine (Anne-Marie Kennedy) starts turning tricks to support her heroin addiction. The charismatic Joe sticks out among this scowling bunch by virtue of the glimmer in his eye, which grows stronger as his relationship with the somewhat self-righteous Sarah deepens. This is familiar and predictable territory for Loach, but Mullan's complex performance makes us care about the inevitable hard knocks and ambiguous moral questions his character navigates. Forget the popcorn—pass the vodka.

MY NIGHT AT MAUD'S   DVD
(MA NUIT CHEZ MAUD)
1969 105m bw   Drama/Romance   ★★★★
F.F.P./Losange/Carrosse/Renn/Deux   GP
Mondes/Gueville/Simar/Pleiade   (France)

Jean-Louis Trintignant (Jean-Louis), Francoise Fabian (Maud), Marie-Christine Barrault (Francoise), Antoine Vitez (Vidal), Leonide Kogan (Concert Violinist), Anne Dubot (Blonde Friend), Guy Leger (Preacher), Marie Becker (Marie, Maud's Daughter), Marie-Claude Rauzier (Student)

p, Pierre Cottrell; d, Eric Rohmer; w, Eric Rohmer; ph, Nestor Almendros; ed, Cecile Decugis; art d, Nicole Rachline

AAN Best Foreign Language Film ; AAN Best Original Story and Screenplay: Eric Rohmer

Tantalizingly witty, beautifully shot. The fourth of Eric Rohmer's "Six Moral Tales," MY NIGHT AT MAUD'S stars Jean-Louis Trintignant as Jean-Louis, a devout Catholic in love with Francoise (Marie-Christine Barrault), a pretty student he sees in church but is too shy to approach. When Jean-Louis runs into Vidal (Antoine Vitez), an old friend, Vidal invites him to dinner at the home of his bohemian lover, Maud (Francoise Fabian). There, Maud, Vidal, a Marxist professor, and Jean-Louis become involved in a lively conversation about the philosophy of Pascal and freedom of choice. In light of the bad snowstorm outside and the heavy drinking inside, Jean-Louis is persuaded to stay overnight at Maud's, but despite his hostess's advances does not make love to her. Later, he finally meets, and then marries, Francoise, only to find years later that she is the former mistress of Maud's husband. As in all of Rohmer's films, there is little "action" in MY NIGHT AT MAUD'S, but there is a great deal of intelligent and fascinating conversation as the characters question, expose, and explain their motivations and feelings (hence the "morality" of the tale). In Jean-Louis's case, his belief in premarital chastity is at issue. Photographed in black-and-white by Nestor Almendros, the film nicely captures the snowbound mood of the Christmas season, and the ensemble acting is excellent. The film was nominated for Best Foreign-Language Film and Best Original Screenplay Oscars, and won the New York Film Critics Best Screenwriting award.

MY OWN PRIVATE IDAHO   DVD
1991 102m c   Drama   ★★★★
Idaho Productions   (U.S.)   R

River Phoenix (Mike Waters), Keanu Reeves (Scott Favor), James Russo (Richard Waters), William Richert (Bob Pigeon), Rodney Harvey (Gary), Chiara Caselli (Carmella), Michael Parker (Digger), Jessie Thomas (Denise), Flea (Budd), Grace Zabriskie (Alena)

p, Laurie Parker; d, Gus Van Sant; w, Gus Van Sant; ph, Eric Alan Edwards, John Campbell; ed, Curtiss Clayton; prod d, David Brisbin; art d, Kenneth A. Hardy; cos, Beatrix Aruna Pasztor

A genuinely poetic voice is heard in MY OWN PRIVATE IDAHO. Taking the form of a road movie, blended with elements borrowed from the two parts of Shakespeare's Henry IV, the film chronicles the misadventures of Mike Waters (River Phoenix), a lonesome young hustler who suffers from narcolepsy—he passes out at stressful moments and must literally depend on strangers to protect him. After one such fit at the opening of the film, Mike awakens in a Seattle flophouse, being fellated by a balding, overweight john. Later, he's picked up and taken to the home of a rich matron, where he meets Scott Favor (Keanu Reeves), the rebellious son of the mayor of Portland. After Mike has another fit, Scott carries him to a safe place to sleep it off. The next day Mike meets Hans (Udo Kier), a rich German, falls asleep again, and ends up in Portland with Scott. Led by the Falstaffian Bob Pigeon (William Richert), Mike, Scott and several other hustlers take over a derelict building, only to be cleared out by a police raid. The police are searching for Bob, but they also let Scott know that he must go to see his disapproving father, which he does before setting off with Mike on a motorbike to look for Mike's mother. The search takes them to Idaho, Snake River, and Italy, before the two return to the West Coast to fulfill their very different destinies.

Van Sant (MALA NOCHE, DRUGSTORE COWBOY) combines a realistic grasp of the underside of urban life with a visual sense that is by turns playful and elegiac. In one scene, a group of real-life hustlers exchange stories in a dingy coffee bar, with the director perfectly capturing the aimlessness and pathos which pervade their lives. In a more light-hearted set piece, the covers of a rack of gay porn magazines come to life with pop-art brio (a similar sensibility is evident in the screens of bright, '60s colors which divide up the film's sections.) Perhaps most memorably, Waters's narcoleptic trances are accompanied by fleeting images of extraordinary beauty: leaping fish in a silver stream; a lonely road; a bank of quickly moving clouds; a wooden house falling from the heavens.

Van Sant's attempt to impose a Shakesperean conceit on his material is much less successful. Though Richert brings an enjoyable Falstaffian swagger to the *Henry IV* sequences, most of the other actors seem ill at ease with Van Sant's self-consciously theatrical blend of Shakesperean dialogue and contemporary street slang. All these sequences pale in comparison to the understated pathos of the quiet scenes. In the most moving of these—a nighttime, roadside confession by Mike of his love for Scott—Van Sant casts a gently hypnotic spell that is not easily forgotten.

MY PAL TRIGGER
1946 79m bw Western ★★★½
Republic (U.S.)

Roy Rogers (*Roy Rogers*), George "Gabby" Hayes (*Gabby Kendrick*), Dale Evans (*Susan*), Jack Holt (*Brett Scoville*), LeRoy Mason (*Carson*), Roy Barcroft (*Hunter*), Sam Flint (*Sheriff*), Kenne Duncan (*Croupier*), Ralph Sanford (*Auctioneer*), Francis McDonald (*Storekeeper*)

p, Armand Schaefer; d, Frank McDonald; w, Jack Townley, John K. Butler (based on a story by Paul Gangelin); ph, William Bradford; ed, Harry Keller; art d, Gano Chittenden; fx, Howard Lydecker, Theodore Lydecker

---

Roy Rogers named this as his favorite of all his films, and one can see why. It's well plotted, with lively direction and much better camera work than most of the Singing Cowboy's films. Rogers plays a horse trader planning to mate a prize mare with a stallion belonging to his pal Gabby Kendrick (Gabby Hayes). A gambler (Jack Holt) with similar plans for his own mare tries to steal the stallion, which escapes and mates with Rogers's mare. When the gambler catches up to the horse, he shoots it. Rogers is blamed, but he and his now-pregnant mare escape capture and leave town, with Roy determined to return to clear his name and unmask the real villain. This is the quintessential Rogers film, with some fine acting (undoubtedly some of the best the genre would produce) and, of course, musical numbers by the Sons of the Pioneers and duets by Rogers and Dale Evans.

MY SON THE FANATIC
1998 86m c Comedy/Drama ★★★
BBC/UGC DA International/Zephyr Films/Arts R
Council of England (U.K.)

Om Puri (*Parvez*), Rachel Griffiths (*Bettina*), Stellan Skarsgard (*Shitz*), Akbar Kurtha (*Farid*), Gopi Desai (*Minoo*), Harish Patel (*Fizzy*), Sarah Jane Potts (*Madelaine*), Judi Jones (*Mrs. Fingerhut*), Geoffrey Bateman (*Chief Inspector Fingerhut*), Bernard Wrigley (*Drunk Man*)

p, Chris Curling; d, Udayan Prasad; w, Hanif Kureishi; ph, Alan Almond; ed, David Gamble; m, Stephen Warbeck; prod d, Grenville Horner; art d, Colin Blaymires, Sara Kane; fx, Ian Rowley, Steve Breheney, Dougie Robson; cos, Mary-Jane Reyner

---

This charming film about cross-cultural assimilation and inter-generational struggle in contemporary England may not live up to its brilliant opening scene, but it's a winner nonetheless.

Parvez (Om Puri), a Pakistani taxi driver who's engaged in offhanded pimping in a bleak Northern English town, ambles into a middle-age crisis that finds him falling in love with gentle prostitute Bettina (Rachel Griffiths) and increasingly estranged from his dutiful wife Minoo (Gopi Desai) and strident son Farid (Akbar Kurtha). Farid, engaged to the daughter of a local constable and headed to university, veers off the path of assimilation after experiencing the casual racism of the girl's parents. He's the first to realize that the family's 25 years in England hasn't assured them of acceptance, and this drives him back to core Muslim values and a rebellion against his father's largely atheistic attitude. When German businessman Shitz (Stellan Skarsgard) gets into Parvaz's cab preaching the religion of unbridled hedonism, his stable life of whiskey and Louis Armstrong tunes begins to unravel.

You may not know Indian actor Puri, but you should; his performance here is outstanding. His Parvez is a man full of contradictions, simultaneously whimsical and crotchety. He convincingly conveys Parvez's impossible position, wedged between an unrecoverable past and a rapidly changing present; between his son's hostile fundamentalism and his burgeoning love for Bettina. Oscar nominee Griffiths brings surprising credibility to her hooker-with-a-heart-of-gold role. Hanif Kureishi's screenplay does overplay schisms and character quirks for the sake of clarity and laughs, but director Udayan Prasad's warm-hearted handling of thorny family dynamics is truly accomplished without ever going soft.

MY 20TH CENTURY
1989 104m bw Comedy/Drama ★★★★
Mafilm/Friedlander/ICAIC (Hungary/Canada)

Dorotha Segda (*Dora/Lili/Mother*), Oleg Jankowski (*Z*), Peter Andorai (*Thomas Alva Edison*), Gabor Mathe (*X*), Paulus Manker (*Weininger*), Gyula Kery, Andrei Schwartz, Sandor Tery, Sandor Czvetko, Endre Koronszi

d, Ildiko Enyedi; w, Ildiko Enyedi; ph, Tibor Mathe; ed, Maria Rigo; m, Laszlo Vidovszky; prod d, Zoltan Labas; cos, Agnes Gyarmathy

---

Filmed in shimmering black and white that suggests a fairy tale, this film has such breathtaking visuals it makes one mourn that black-and-white cinematography has fallen into disfavor. This is a dazzling celebration of feminism, mechanical progress, unbreakable familial ties, and early 20th century history. Despite the occasionally slack pace, it is a magical achievement that creates its own universe.

Taking the form of a fable, the film outlines a world of unlimited possibilities. In Hungary in 1880, identical twin girls are separated while selling matches. The different paths of the girls, Lili and Dora (both played by Segda) unwind over many years before they serendipitously cross once more. Aglow with fervor, Lili has become a radical determined to free the masses, while Dora leans toward the pleasures of the flesh. To his total confusion, a man known as Z (Jankowski) meets both women while traveling on the Orient Express, believing them to be one fascinating creature. Intercut with this dual romance are depictions of technological breakthroughs of the time, including the tale of a laboratory dog who outsmarts his scientist keepers, and commentary by Thomas Alva Edison (Andorai). Somehow this fanciful comedy of errors seems to be a logical extension of the progress-driven world in the early 1900s; the characters exist in a shining new world where anything can happen. Since creativity charges the air, the ingenuity of the characters in getting themselves out of scrapes seems only natural. At the film's climax, Lili (en route to eliminate the minister of the interior) encounters her long-lost sister in a hall of mirrors, where the women effect a liberating union.

In his debut film, director Enyedi dexterously unfolds a fanciful tale layered with whimsical and historical segments that touch tangentially on the main storyline. Never tied to a linear structure, it is full of delightful asides, such as the story of the monkey whose naivete about human beings lands him in captivity. The best way to enjoy MY 20TH CENTURY is to approach it as a fantastic cavalcade in which human truths are revealed by accident. Despite the fact that the characters wander through a technological wonderland, the most magical proposition of the film lies not in inventiveness but in the capacity of the spirit to reinvent itself. A liberating experience from a filmmaking visionary.

MY UNCLE 🅳🆅🅳
(MON ONCLE)
1958 110m c Comedy ★★★★
Specta/Gray/Alter/Cady (France)

Jacques Tati (M. Hulot), Jean-Pierre Zola (M. Arpel), Adrienne Servantie (Mme. Arpel), Alain Becourt (Gerald Arpel), Lucien Fregis (M. Pichard), Betty Schneider (Betty, Landlord's Daughter), Yvonne Arnaud (Georgette, Arpel's Maid), Dominique Marie (Neighbor), J.F. Martial (Walter), Andre Dino (Sweep)

p, Jacques Tati; d, Jacques Tati; w, Jacques Tati, Jacques Lagrange, Jean L'Hote; ph, Jean Bourgoin (Eastmancolor); ed, Suzanne Baron; m, Franck Barcellini, Alain Romans; art d, Henri Schmitt, Pierre Etaix

AA Best Foreign Language Film

Tati followed MR. HULOT'S HOLIDAY with this impressive satire on modern gadgetry and the people who devote their lives to technological convenience. Tati has described his own comedy as "laughter born of a certain fundamental absurdity. Some things are not funny of themselves but become so on being dissected." It is this quality that Tati's films share with such satires as Rene Clair's A NOUS LA LIBERTE, Charles Chaplin's MODERN TIMES, and even Albert Brooks's LOST IN AMERICA. Tati again casts himself as Hulot, a lanky fellow with a raincoat and umbrella who stumbles through life. Content to live in his neglected quarters, Hulot is in direct contrast to the very modern Arpels, comprising his sister (Servantie), brother-in-law (Zola), and nephew, Gerald (Alain Becourt). The Arpels live in a modernized, desensitized suburb, their angular house hidden from the street by a clanging gate, and fronted by a fountain with an obscene metal fish spurting water from its mouth. Inside are gadgets meant to save time but which only waste it—and make noise. Hulot's humble, simple life attracts young Gerald, whose playfulness has no place in the modern world.

Less a condemnation of technology than of its worshippers, MY UNCLE is simultaneously entertaining, intelligent, and technically inventive. It makes vivid use of saturated color schemes and contains some truly great shots which suggest that the house has a life of its own, as when the Arpels walk back and forth before their round bedroom windows, giving the impression from the outside that the house is rolling its eyes.

MYSTERIOUS DR. FU MANCHU, THE
1929 80m bw Mystery ★★★
Paramount (U.S.)

Warner Oland (Dr. Fu Manchu), Jean Arthur (Lia Eltham), Neil Hamilton (Dr. Jack Petrie), O.P. Heggie (Nayland Smith), William Austin (Sylvester Wadsworth), Claude King (Sir John Petrie), Charles Stevenson (Gen. Petrie), Noble Johnson (Li Po), Evelyn Selbie (Fai Lu), Charles Giblyn (Weymouth)

d, Rowland V. Lee; w, Florence Ryerson, Lloyd Corrigan (based on the story by Sax Rohmer); ph, Harry Fischbeck; ed, George Nichols Jr.

The first of the popular Sax Rohmer (Arthur Sarsfield Ward) mystery novels to be made into a talking feature is a fairly good job, reaching the same level of chilling suspense as the novels and later radio shows. Benevolent looking, overweight Oland (known for his renditions of Charlie Chan) is the evil green-eyed Chinese doctor bent on revenge against the British officer who commanded forces during the Boxer rebellion. It was during this time that Oland's wife and son were killed, warping the doctor's mind to the extent that all he can think about is vengeance. To assist him, he uses the daughter of an English official killed during the Rebellion. The girl is put into a trance and forced to do Oland's dirty work. After having killed several of the British officers he is after, Oland then attempts to gain vengeance against King and son Hamilton. But before this can happen, Scotland Yard is aware of Oland's pattern, and warns King before he meets with a disastrous end. Oland is quite convincing in the title role that would later be shared by such greats as Boris Karloff and Christopher Lee. The eerie atmosphere and steadily building suspense make this early entry in the series as frightening as those made in the 1960s.

MYSTERY OF THE WAX MUSEUM, THE
1933 73m c Horror ★★★★
Warner Bros. (U.S.)

Lionel Atwill (Ivan Igor), Fay Wray (Charlotte Duncan), Glenda Farrell (Florence Dempsey), Frank McHugh (Jim), Gavin Gordon (Harold Winton), Edwin Maxwell (Joe Worth), Holmes Herbert (Dr. Rasmussen), Arthur Edmund Carewe (Sparrow), Allen Vincent (Ralph Burton), Monica Bannister (Joan Gale)

p, Henry Blanke; d, Michael Curtiz; w, Don Mullaly, Carl Erickson (based on a play by Charles Belden); ph, Ray Rennahan (Technicolor); ed, George Amy; art d, Anton Grot

Lionel Atwill and Fay Wray are teamed here for the second time in a Michael Curtiz-directed, Warner Brothers-produced two-strip Technicolor horror film (their first pairing was in DR. X in 1932). The film opens in London, in 1921, as the brilliant sculptor Ivan Igor (Atwill) is hard at work on his latest creation, surrounded by beautiful wax sculptures of female historical figures. Having eschewed the more sensational—and, therefore, more lucrative—figures of killers like Jack the Ripper in favor of these beautiful creations, Ivan finds his wax museum on the brink of bankruptcy. A fight over finances between Ivan and his partner, Joe Worth (Edwin Maxwell), results in the museum's destruction by fire, the "death" of the wax figures, and Ivan's near death. The scene then shifts to New York City, 1933, where the grey-haired Ivan is confined to a wheelchair, his hands crippled from the fire. When a wealthy socialite dies and her corpse is stolen from the morgue, tough-talking female reporter Florence Dempsey (Glenda Farrell) investigates the case. The strange disappearance of the corpse coincides suspiciously with Ivan's preparation for the opening of his new museum, in which the wax beauties have a remarkably lifelike appearance.

Feared to be lost for many years, MYSTERY OF THE WAX MUSEUM gained a mighty reputation when film historians' memories of the movie were jogged by the 1953 3-D remake, HOUSE OF WAX. When a print of the original film surfaced in the late 1960s, however, many critics were disappointed with it, shrugging it off as a silly mystery picture, though their initial reaction was entirely unfounded. An amazing film filled with stunning sets (by Anton Grot), exceptional moments, and perhaps Atwill's greatest performance, THE MYSTERY OF THE WAX MUSEUM is also a very adult film that deals explicitly with drug addiction, necrophilia, and insanity. Notable for its wonderful use of color, it was also one of the first horror films to be set in the everyday reality of modern-day New York and not in a mystical foreign land.

MYSTERY TRAIN
DVD

1989 113m c Comedy ★★★½

MTI (U.S.) R

Masatoshi Nagase *(Jun)*, Youki Kudoh *(Mitzuko)*, Screamin' Jay Hawkins *(Night Clerk)*, Cinque Lee *(Bellboy)*, Nicoletta Braschi *(Luisa)*, Elizabeth Bracco *(Dee Dee)*, Sy Richardson *(News Vendor)*, Tom Noonan *(Man in Diner)*, Stephen Jones *(The Ghost)*, Rufus Thomas *(Man in Station)*

p, Jim Stark; d, Jim Jarmusch; w, Jim Jarmusch; ph, Robby Muller; ed, Melody London; m, John Lurie; prod d, Dan Bishop; cos, Carol Wood

New York-based filmmaker Jim Jarmusch continues his deadpan Cook's Tour of America with MYSTERY TRAIN, a trio of tangentially related stories set in Memphis, Tennessee.

All three tales center on the run-down Arcade Hotel, where every room is a shrine to Memphis's favorite son, Elvis Aron Presley. A candidate for the wrecking ball, the Arcade is staffed by two dedicated souls (legendary rhythm & blues performer Screamin' Jay Hawkins and Cinque Lee, Spike's younger brother) who seem to have no existence beyond the front desk. As the film's first episode, "Far from Yokohama," opens, Jun (Masatoshi Nagase) and Mitzuko (Youki Kudoh), two teenaged devotees of American culture, check into the Arcade, where they argue over rock 'n' roll favorites, make love, listen to Elvis on the hotel radio, and remain undisturbed by everything that occurs—even the gunshot they hear near checkout time. The Arcade also plays host to Luisa (Nicoletta Braschi), an Italian woman visiting the States to bring her dead husband home to Italy. The focus of the second episode, "A Ghost," Luisa is harassed by a low-life who promises her she will be visited by visions of Elvis. The third episode, "Lost in Space," involves Dee Dee (Elizabeth Bracco), her alcohol-crazed lover (Joe Strummer), her nervous-wreck brother (Steve Buscemi), and their fast-talking pal (Rick Aviles) as they get involved in a shooting. At checkout time, all the characters go their separate ways.

As with STRANGER THAN PARADISE and DOWN BY LAW, Jarmusch focuses his offbeat sensibility on urban iconoclasts, small-town oddballs, and bewildered strangers. Not surprisingly, MYSTERY TRAIN will work best for those who share Jarmusch's fondness for America's pop culture junkyard; he's a true original, but Jarmusch's originality lies in a quirky viewpoint that may leave some audience members cold. Others who abandon themselves to his deadpan drollery and Robby Muller's witty cinematography, which makes squalor look festive, will be rewarded with a cockeyed valentine to the cradle of rock 'n' roll.

MYSTIC RIVER
DVD

2003 137m c Crime/Mystery/Drama ★★★½

Village Roadshow/NPV Entertainment (U.S.) R

Sean Penn *(Jimmy Markum)*, Tim Robbins *(Dave Boyle)*, Kevin Bacon *(Sean Devine)*, Laurence Fishburne *(Whitey Powers)*, Marcia Gay Harden *(Celeste Boyle)*, Laura Linney *(Annabeth Markum)*, Kevin Chapman *(Val Savage)*, Adam Nelson *(Nick Savage)*, Emmy Rossum *(Katie)*, Cameron Bowen *(Young Dave)*

p, Clint Eastwood, Judie G. Hoyt, Robert Lorenz; d, Clint Eastwood; w, Brian Helgeland (based on the novel by Dennis Lehane); ph, Tom Stern; ed, Joel Cox; m, Clint Eastwood; prod d, Henry Bumstead; art d, Jack G. Taylor Jr.; fx, H. Barclay Aaris, Steve Riley; cos, Deborah Hopper

AA Best Actor: Sean Penn; AA Best Supporting Actor: Tim Robbins; AAN Best Adapted Screenplay: Brian Helgeland; AAN Best Director: Clint Eastwood; AAN Best Supporting Actress: Marcia Gay Harden; AAN Best Picture

The shadows seethe with violence, guilt, secrets, and regret in the down-at-the-heels, working-class Boston neighborhood where this melancholy tale of murder—physical and spiritual—unfolds.

A brief prologue set in 1975 establishes the friendship between three neighborhood 11-year-olds, cocky and perpetually defiant Jimmy Marcum, tough but sensible Sean Devine, and wide-eyed, deferential Dave Boyle. Two men claiming to be police officers catch the youngsters in an act of minor vandalism, but only Dave, the natural-born victim, is bullied into their car. He returns four days later, abused and traumatized, and the lives of all three boys are forever changed. Some three decades later, Dave (Tim Robbins) and Jimmy (Sean Penn) still live in the old neighborhood. Jimmy's wild streak sent him to prison, but after losing his first wife to cancer while inside, he straightened up to raise their daughter, Katie (Emmy Rossum), now 19 and the apple of his eye. Remarried and still the cock of the walk, Jimmy has two more little girls with the steely Annabeth (Laura Linney). Annabeth's less resilient cousin, Celeste (Marcia Gay Harden), married Dave, who seems to be sinking under the weight of his inner demons, barely able to hold it together for the sake of their small son. Tragedy brings Sean (Kevin Bacon), now a state policeman, back: Katie is found beaten and shot to death in a state park, and Sean and his partner (Laurence Fishburne) are assigned to the crime. The volatile Jimmy immediately launches his own personal inquiry, and official and unofficial suspicions soon dovetail on Dave, who's acting oddly even for him and tells everyone a different story about why his hand looks as though he punched it through a wall. The burden of suspicion lies most heavily on Celeste, who knows what no one else does: Dave came home agitated and covered with blood the night Katie died.

Haunted by the resigned face of a child looking through the rear window of a car as it vanishes into moral darkness, Clint Eastwood's adaptation of Dennis Lehane's literary thriller is suffused with a sense of sadness for opportunities missed and wrong turns taken. If he were a more subtle director, it would be a great film; as it is, it's an extremely good one, anchored by the subtly devastating performances of Penn, Robbins, and Bacon. The supporting cast is equally good, and blue collar Boston's mean streets take on a beaten-down life of their own.

N

NAKED
1993 131m c Drama ★★★★
Thin Man Films/British Screen/First Independent/
Channel Four (U.K.)

David Thewlis (*Johnny*), Katrin Cartlidge (*Sophie*), Greg Cruttwell (*Jeremy*), Lesley Sharp (*Louise*), Claire Skinner (*Sandra*), Peter Wight (*Brian*), Elizabeth Berrington (*Giselle*), Ewen Bremner (*Archie*), Deborah MacLaren (*Woman In Window*), Carolina Giametto (*Masseuse*)

p, Simon Channing-Williams; d, Mike Leigh; w, Mike Leigh; ph, Dick Pope; ed, John Gregory; m, Andrew Dickinson; prod d, Alison Chitty; art d, Eve Stewart; cos, Lindy Hemming

Blackly funny and corrosively sad, Mike Leigh's NAKED is a rambling portrait of a young man flying apart at a breakneck pace. Like Leigh's earlier films, which include HIGH HOPES (1988) and LIFE IS SWEET (1991), NAKED is an artfully unpolished, ensemble portrait of a group of people who are resolutely undistinguished, if not exactly ordinary.

The film opens on a violent sexual encounter in a Manchester alley. Rape? Consensual rough sex? A casual pickup gone awry? It's impossible to tell, but Johnny (David Thewlis)—who's ferociously clever, cruelly funny, and passably attractive—steals a car and flees to London, where he looks up his old girlfriend, Louise (Lesley Sharp); seduces her drugged-out roommate, Sophie (Katrin Cartlidge); and wreaks havoc on the lives of everyone he meets. Meanwhile, sleek, disdainful, and apparently wealthy Jeremy (Greg Crutwell) rapes and terrorizes various women, including Sophie. Their paths eventually cross, during a very dark night of the soul.

NAKED's greatest accomplishment is that one is forced to empathize with Johnny, however loathsome his behavior. His wit is unfailingly mean, his intelligence without direction or purpose. He feels cheated—by women, by England, by the world, by God—and retaliates by humiliating everyone within range, by any means necessary. He's sexually vicious and practices conversation as a blood sport. His imagination is gridlocked with apocalyptic fantasies drawn from the Bible, the prophecies of Nostradamus, James Gleick's *Chaos*, and the tabloids.

Working from a script developed out of improvisations with the cast, Leigh has created one of the most abrasive—and articulate—characters in recent screen history. His work is triumphantly matched by that of Thewlis, with both director and actor taking awards at the 1993 Cannes festival, and Thewlis picking up a raft of prizes in the U.S.

NAKED CITY, THE
1948 96m bw Crime ★★★★
Universal (U.S.)

Barry Fitzgerald (*Lt. Dan Muldoon*), Howard Duff (*Frank Niles*), Dorothy Hart (*Ruth Morrison*), Don Taylor (*Jimmy Halloran*), Ted de Corsia (*Garzah*), House Jameson (*Dr. Stoneman*), Anne Sargent (*Mrs. Halloran*), Adelaide Klein (*Mrs. Batory*), Grover Burgess (*Mr. Batory*), Tom Pedi (*Detective Perelli*)

p, Mark Hellinger; d, Jules Dassin; w, Albert Maltz, Malvin Wald (based on a story by Malvin Wald); ph, William Daniels; ed, Paul Weatherwax; m, Miklos Rozsa, Frank Skinner; art d, John DeCuir; cos, Grace Houston

AAN Best Motion Picture Story: Malvin Wald; *AA Best B/W Cinematography:* William H. Daniels; *AA Best Film Editing:* Paul Weatherwax

This superlative film set the pattern for myriad documentary-type dramas to come. Its producer, Hellinger, patterned the tale after the tabloid newspaper stories he wrote in his youth, and he narrates the picture with the same kind of terse but poignant vitality that was the hallmark of his sensational prose. Though basically a crime story—with, oddly, only character actor Fitzgerald as its star—the film is also a romance with the city itself, one where Hellinger embraces soiled urchins and immaculate society ladies with equal passion. The story opens with the bathtub murder of a beautiful blonde playgirl. The police are left with no clues. Fitzgerald and his brash young assistant, Taylor, are assigned the case and spend most of their time running down weak leads that reveal nothing. In the process, the routine of their lives is detailed, as the various suspects and would-be witnesses who make up much of the story are presented. Fitzgerald, a cop for 30 years, is relentless in his pursuit of criminals. Taylor, who lives in a modest home and kisses his wife good-bye every morning on his way to headquarters, tries to please his superiors and cover up his lack of experience, but he slowly learns the wily ways of the cop under Fitzgerald's expert tutelage.

Shot completely on location in New York City, THE NAKED CITY chronicles the grim urban landscape and depicts its everyday life and citizens, embracing swank Fifth Avenue, Broadway, kids playing hop-skip-and-jump in the streets, straphangers en route to work and back on the crowded subways. More than 100 locations were employed, with the brilliant cameraman Daniels shooting most of his scenes from inside a van parked along the streets, using a one-way mirror and tinted windows so that passers-by were oblivious to the camera's presence. In the late 1950s and early '60s, a long-running ABC TV series used this film's title to show the "slice-of-life" style of drama the original film typified, and also employed Hellinger's postscript in this, his last feature production, a line which became a household phrase: "There are eight million stories in the naked city. This has been one of them."

NAKED GUN: FROM THE FILES OF POLICE SQUAD!, THE
1988 85m c Comedy ★★★½
Paramount (U.S.) PG-13

Leslie Nielsen (*Lt. Frank Drebin*), George Kennedy (*Capt. Ed Hocken*), Priscilla Presley (*Jane Spencer*), Ricardo Montalban (*Vincent Ludwig*), O.J. Simpson (*Nordberg*), Nancy Marchand (*Mayor*), John Houseman (*Driving Instructor*), Reggie Jackson (*Right Fielder*), Jeannette Charles (*Queen Elizabeth II*), Curt Gowdy

p, Robert K. Weiss; d, David Zucker; w, Jerry Zucker, Jim Abrahams, David Zucker, Pat Proft; ph, Robert Stevens (Technicolor); ed, Michael Jablow; m, Ira Newborn; prod d, John J. Lloyd; cos, Mary Vogt

The Zucker, Abrahams, and Zucker writing-directing team, who made a huge splash with AIRPLANE!, based THE NAKED GUN on their hilarious but short-lived TV show "Police Squad." Leslie Nielsen reprises his role as bumbling police lieutenant Frank Drebin, who becomes embroiled in a case involving suave heroin smuggler Vincent Ludwig (Ricardo Montalban). Drebin falls for Ludwig's assistant, Jane (Priscilla Presley), who is just as dim and clumsy as he is. Meanwhile, Drebin's boss (George Kennedy) learns that there will be an assassination attempt on Queen Elizabeth (played by look-alike Jeannette Charles) during her visit to Los Angeles.

Merely recounting the plot of any ZAZ comedy utterly fails to convey the lunacy and, believe it or not, charm of the production. From the inspired opening credit sequence, in which a camera mounted behind the flashing light of a police car drives down city streets, through a car wash, into a building, down a corridor, and finally into a women's locker room; to the sight of the villain falling off a tier at a ballpark and being crushed by a bus, a steamroller, and then a marching band, THE NAKED GUN is a continuous stream of verbal and visual gags that come so fast, you don't have time to realize how bad/old/corny they are.

NAKED LUNCH
1991 115m   c   Science Fiction/Fantasy/Drama ★★★
Naked Lunch Productions/Recorded Picture Co.   R
(U.K./Canada)

Peter Weller *(William Lee)*, Judy Davis *(Joan Frost/Joan Lee)*, Ian Holm *(Tom Frost)*, Julian Sands *(Yves Cloquet)*, Roy Scheider *(Dr. Benway)*, Monique Mercure *(Fadela)*, Nicholas Campbell *(Hank)*, Michael Zelniker *(Martin)*, Robert A. Silverman *(Hans)*, Joseph Scorsiani *(Kiki)*

p, Jeremy Thomas; d, David Cronenberg; w, David Cronenberg (from the novel by William S. Burroughs); ph, Peter Suschitzky; ed, Ronald Sanders; m, Howard Shore; prod d, Carol Spier; art d, James McAteer; fx, Chris Walas Inc; cos, Denise Cronenberg

A grotesquely humorous concoction, cooked up by Canadian director David Cronenberg with a little help from America's favorite underground novelist, William Burroughs. The Burroughs novel from which the movie is adapted is nearly devoid of narrative, but Cronenberg has sidestepped this problem by making a film *about* the writing of *Naked Lunch*. The movie combines elements from Burroughs's life—particularly the accidental shooting of his wife during a drunken game of "William Tell"—with scenes from several of his books to tell the story of his transformation into a writer. It opens in New York City in the early 1950s, where Burroughs's alter ego, Bill Lee (Peter Weller), is working as an exterminator. His problems begin when his wife, Joan (Judy Davis), turns him on to the narcotic qualities of the bug powder he uses. Under the influence of the powder, Lee hallucinates his way into an alternative realm where he is a secret agent for a ring of giant, infinitely disgusting beetles. The bugs instruct him to kill his wife and go to Interzone, a fictional city loosely modeled on Tangiers. There, Lee encounters an assortment of literary types and other shady characters, has conversations with typewriters which metamorphose into—you guessed it—giant bugs, and indulges in some exotic, mind-altering substances.

The result is a hallucinatory, often stomach-turning take on the bohemian life that incorporates loosely drawn portraits of Burroughs's contemporaries—Jack Kerouac, Allen Ginsberg, Paul and Jane Bowles—as well as conjuring up the nightmares of drug addiction and the excruciatingly painful process of writing itself. The director has come up with some of his most imaginative—and unpalatable—images to date, ranging from two-foot beetles which speak through sphincter-like openings in their backs, to giant, rubbery creatures which secrete a sticky, narcotic fluid from—ahem—organs that sprout from their heads. A treat for Cronenberg fans, though this could hardly be called a gripping, or emotionally involving, story; you're more likely to need a can of bug spray than a hanky.

NAKED PREY, THE
1966 96m   c   Adventure   ★★★½
Theodora/Sven Persson   (U.S./South Africa)

Cornel Wilde *(Man)*, Gert Van den Bergh *(2nd Man)*, Ken Gampu *(Warrior Leader)*, Patrick Mynhardt *(Safari Overseer)*, Bella Randels *(Little Girl)*, Jose Sithole, Richard Mashiya, Eric Sabela, Joe Diaminl, Frank Mdhluli

p, Cornel Wilde; d, Cornel Wilde; w, Clint Johnston, Donald A. Peters; ph, H.A.R. Thomson (Panavision, Eastmancolor); ed, Roger Cherrill; cos, Freda Thompson

AAN Best Original Story and Screenplay: Clint Johnston, Don Peters

An early cinema staple, the chase film, is resurrected, pure and simple, by star-producer-director Cornel Wilde. He plays a tour guide in the South African bush near the end of the 19th century, leading several men on an ivory hunting expedition. Despite his warnings, the party offends local tribesmen. Bad move. Ambushed, the men are taken back to the tribesmen's village for ritual torture and execution. (One especially horrifying, unforgettable image has a victim encased in clay except for a breathing tube, being roasted alive on a spit.) The guide, for whom the natives presumably have some respect, is offered "The Chance of the Lion." Stripped naked, he is given a head start of a few hundred yards. Then six warriors, each of whom has killed ten lions, set out to hunt him down, and the chase is on.

Wilde's fifth directorial outing was easily his best, tautly constructed and rapidly paced. (Fewer than 15 minutes pass between the credits and the start of Wilde's race for life.) His habit of beginning or ending scenes with shots of animal predators snaring their prey is obvious and becomes rather tiresome, but some of the imagery, such as a bird being caught or one frog devouring another, is extraordinary. The film is nothing but an extremely vivid and suspenseful chase, so pared down that there's absolutely no characterization whatsoever—let alone consideration of the environmental or racial issues and attitudes on rampant display here. Thank heavens for those white redcoats, right?

NAKED SPUR, THE
1953 91m   c   Western   ★★★★
MGM   (U.S.)

James Stewart *(Howard Kemp)*, Janet Leigh *(Lina Patch)*, Robert Ryan *(Ben Vandergroat)*, Ralph Meeker *(Roy Anderson)*, Millard Mitchell *(Jesse Tate)*

p, William H. Wright; d, Anthony Mann; w, Sam Rolfe, Harold Jack Bloom; ph, William Mellor (Technicolor); ed, George White; m, Bronislau Kaper; art d, Cedric Gibbons, Malcolm Brown

AAN Best Story and Screenplay: Sam Rolfe, Harold Jack Bloom

Another superb western from director Anthony Mann who, along with Budd Boetticher, created an outstanding series of engrossing, thoughtful, and challenging films that helped keep the genre fresh and vital during the 1950s. Stewart is excellent as Howard Kemp, the obsessed, disillusioned Civil War veteran who returns home to find he has lost his land. To raise the money needed to regain his land, Kemp decides to become a bounty hunter and enters the Colorado Territory in search of escaped killer Ben Vandergroat (Robert Ryan), who has a $5,000 reward on his head. Vandergroat is accompanied by Lina Patch (Janet Leigh), a lonely young woman who wants to escape to California. While searching for Vandergroat, Kemp picks up a pair of companions; Jesse Tate (Millard Mitchell), a grizzled prospector, and Roy Anderson (Ralph Meeker), a dishonorably discharged Union soldier. The two drifters believe Kemp to be a lawman and agree to help him capture Vandergroat; they corner the fugitive, together with Patch, on a rugged hillside and take them prisoner. When they learn that Kemp is a mere bounty hunter, however, they demand an equal share of the reward. Kemp refuses, and Vandergroat sees a chance to escape, via a clever campaign to pit the men against each other during the seven-day trip through dangerous Indian territory back to Abilene.

NAKED SPUR is a superb, tautly directed western in which Mann's protagonists, once again, allow the desire for vengeance to consume their inherent qualities of honor and decency. The journey becomes a process of near-religious revelation that finally allows one of them to achieve a bitterly earned state of grace.

NAME OF THE ROSE, THE
1986 130m c Mystery ★★★
Bernd Eichinger/Bernd Schaefers/Neue R
Constantin/Cristaldifilm/Ariane (U.S.)

Sean Connery *(William of Baskerville)*, F. Murray Abraham *(Bernardo Gui)*, Christian Slater *(Adso of Melk)*, Elya Baskin *(Severinus)*, Feodor Chaliapin Jr. *(Jorge de Burgos)*, William Hickey *(Ubertino de Casale)*, Michel Lonsdale *(The Abbot)*, Ron Perlman *(Salvatore)*, Volker Prechtel *(Malachia)*, Helmut Qualtinger *(Remigio de Varagine)*

p, Bernd Eichinger; d, Jean-Jacques Annaud; w, Andrew Birkin, Gerard Brach, Howard Franklin, Alain Godard; ph, Tonino Delli Colli (Technicolor); ed, Jane Seitz; m, James Horner; prod d, Dante Ferretti; art d, Giorgio Giovannini, Rainer Schaper; fx, Adriano Pischiutta; cos, Gabriella Pescucci

Based on the witty, flashily erudite first novel by Italian semiotician and journalist Umberto Eco, this medieval murder mystery is a little slow-moving but ultimately rewarding. At an Italian monastery in 1327, the Franciscans, who live in religious poverty, and the Dominicans, who enjoy a life of luxury, meet to debate whether the Catholic church should be in the business of accruing wealth. William of Baskerville (Connery), a brilliant English monk (whose Holmesian manner is reinforced by his name, taken from *The Hound of the Baskervilles*), and his teenage novice, Adso of Melk (Slater), arrive early, and when murders begin occurring, the abbot (Lonsdale) requests that they begin an investigation. But even as William begins looking into the matter, the murders continue, seemingly following the prophecy of the Apocalypse. The more rational clues lead to the monastery's extraordinary library, but before the Englishman can find the truth, the Dominicans and, most important, his old rival Bernardo Gui (Abraham), the Inquisitor, arrive and matters become even more complicated as Gui sees the Devil's hand in the murders. Gifted cinematographer Tonino Delli Colli has given the film an appropriately dark look, and the many odd-looking monks appear as if they have stepped from the set of a Fellini picture. Much of the $18 million production was shot at Kloster Eberbach, a 12th-century monastery near Frankfurt, West Germany.

NAPOLEON DYNAMITE
2004 86m c Comedy ★★★½
Access Films/MTV Films/Fox Searchlight (U.S.) PG

Jon Heder *(Napoleon Dynamite)*, Jon Gries *(Uncle Rico)*, Aaron Ruell *(Kip)*, Efren Ramirez *(Pedro)*, Diedrich Bader *(Rex)*, Tina Majorino *(Deb)*, Sandy Martin *(Grandma)*, Haylie Duff *(Summer)*, Trevor Snarr *(Don)*, Shondrella Avery *(LaFawnduh)*

p, Jeremy Coon, Sean C. Covel, Chris Wyatt; d, Jared Hess; w, Jared Hess, Jerusha Hess; ph, Munn Powell; ed, Jeremy Coon; m, John Swihart; prod d, Cory Lorenzen; art d, Curt Jenson; cos, Jerusha Hess

Dynamite is right: Writer-director Jared Hess and his wife and co-writer, Jerusha Hess, may have little previous filmmaking experience, but like their titular hero, they've got "skills." Their first feature is one of the most original and quirkily endearing debuts since Wes Anderson's BOTTLE ROCKET.

Awkward, imperfectly socialized teenager Napoleon Dynamite (Jon Heder) lives with his grandmother (Sandy Martin) and even geekier older brother, Kip (Aaron Ruell), in a small ranch house in Preston, ID. With his waistband hiked high above his hips and pant legs tucked into his moon boots,

Napoleon is every dork who's ever been pounded by a dodgeball or shoved into his locker. And like so many before him, Napoleon has compensated by developing a belligerent self-confidence in the strangest things; he's particularly proud of his ability to draw and is convinced that his doodles of dragons and ligers will help him score chicks. Napoleon has his eye on Deb (Tina Majorino), an easily overlooked classmate who's saving for college by shooting glamour portraits of Preston locals in her parents' house. Before Napoleon can make his move, she's swiped out from under him by Pedro (Efren Ramirez), the blank-faced new kid in school who has become Napoleon's friend by default. Napoleon can handle the disappointment, but he can't deal with sleazy Uncle Rico (Jon Gries), who moves into Napoleon's house after Grandma is injured. A former high-school football semistar, Uncle Rico hopes to make it rich peddling plastic container sets and herbal breast enhancers. Kip partners up with Rico, but Napoleon just wants him out of the house.

Imagine a drier, funnier WELCOME TO THE DOLLHOUSE minus the cruelty, and you'd have a pretty close approximation of this totally unexpected delight. Both Hesses and a surprisingly large number of their very talented cast and crew are graduates of Brigham Young University's film program; could BYU be tomorrow's NYU?

NARC
2002 102m c/bw Crime/Drama ★★★½
Tiara Blu/Cruise-Wagner/Splendid Pictures/Emmett R
Furla Films/Julius R. Nasso/Lions Gate Films/
Paramount (U.S.)

Jason Patric *(Nick Tellis)*, Ray Liotta *(Lt. Henry Oak)*, Anne Openshaw *(Katherine Calvess)*, Chi McBride *(Capt. Cheevers)*, Busta Rhymes *(Darnell "Big D Love" Beery)*, Richard Chevolleau *(Latroy Steeds)*, Alan Van Sprang *(Michael Calvess)*, John Ortiz *(Octavio Ruiz)*, Thomas Patrice *(Officer Marcotte)*, Dan Leis *(Elvin Dowd)*

p, Michelle Grace, Ray Liotta, Diane Nabatoff, Julius R. Nasso; d, Joe Carnahan; w, Joe Carnahan; ph, Alex Nepomniaschy; ed, John Gilroy; m, Cliff Martinez; prod d, Greg Beale, Taavo Soodor; art d, Greg Beale; fx, John LaForet; cos, Gersha Phillips

Familiar story, electrifying execution.

Detroit narcotics cop Nick Tellis (Jason Patric) is working deep undercover when a bust goes bad and he accidentally shoots a pregnant bystander. The subsequent departmental investigation reveals that while fraternizing with junkies and dealers, Tellis picked up a nasty drug habit. He's unceremoniously suspended and spends 18 months cleaning up, rebuilding his sorely stressed marriage, and trying to figure out what to do with the rest of his life. Then he's offered a chance for reinstatement, complete with guarantee of a desk job safely out of harm's (and temptation's) way, if Tellis will apply his street smarts to the recent murder of fellow undercover cop Michael Calvess (Alan Van Sprang). He must also work with Calvess's partner, veteran detective Henry Oak (Ray Liotta), an old-school proponent of brass-knuckle policing. Oak doesn't trust Tellis, and Tellis doesn't much care for Oak, but they share a common goal, and the inevitable grudging friendship develops. That fledgling bond is sorely tested when Tellis assembles the evidence and realizes Oak clearly knows more than he's telling.

Writer-director Joe Carnahan's second feature was, he says, inspired by Errol Morris's deeply subjective documentary THE THIN BLUE LINE, about the fatal shooting of a Dallas police officer in 1976. Carnahan was evidently less influenced by the facts of the case than by Morris's attempts to wrest a definitive version of events from a thicket of contradictory reports. But the film also owes a powerful stylistic debt of tone and style to bitter, '70s police thrillers like REPORT TO THE COMMISSIONER; its shattered, chilly look embodies the bleak brutality and casual corruption of Tellis's crumbling world.

NARROW MARGIN, THE

1952 71m bw Thriller *DVD*
RKO (U.S.) ★★★

Charles McGraw *(Walter Brown)*, Marie Windsor *(Mrs. Neall)*, Jacqueline White *(Ann Sinclair)*, Gordon Gebert *(Tommy Sinclair)*, Queenie Leonard *(Mrs. Troll)*, David Clarke *(Kemp)*, Peter Virgo *(Densel)*, Don Beddoe *(Gus Forbes)*, Paul Maxey *(Jennings)*, Harry Harvey *(Train Conductor)*

p, Stanley Rubin; d, Richard Fleischer; w, Earl Fenton (based on a story by Martin Goldsmith, Jack Leonard); ph, George E. Diskant; ed, Robert Swink; art d, Albert S. D'Agostino, Jack Okey

AAN Best Motion Picture Story: Martin Goldsmith, Jack Leonard

A competent B movie from RKO that takes place almost entirely on board a train from Chicago to Los Angeles. Walter Brown (McGraw) is a hard-boiled detective who, with his partner, Gus Forbes (Beddoe), is assigned to escort a racketeer's widow (Windsor) to a West Coast court where she will give testimony before a grand jury. However, three thugs aboard the train are trying to shut her up—permanently. Unfortunately for the gang members, they do not know what the widow looks like, so they bump off anyone they suspect might be their quarry. While far from a masterpiece, THE NARROW MARGIN is a well-executed programmer that turned a fantastic profit for RKO, considering its meager $230,000 budget. Audiences loved the film—thrilling at the plot twists, the characters, and the trick train photography—making it into one of the studio's most profitable B movies.

NASHVILLE

1975 159m c Drama *DVD*
Paramount (U.S.) ★★★★★
R

David Arkin *(Norman Chauffeur)*, Barbara Baxley *(Lady Pearl)*, Ned Beatty *(Delbert Reese)*, Karen Black *(Connie White)*, Ronee Blakley *(Barbara Jean)*, Lily Tomlin *(Linnea Reese)*, Timothy Brown *(Tommy Brown)*, Keith Carradine *(Tom Frank)*, Geraldine Chaplin *(Opal)*, Robert DoQui *(Wade)*

p, Robert Altman; d, Robert Altman; w, Joan Tewkesbury; ph, Paul Lohmann (Panavision, Metrocolor); ed, Sidney Levin, Dennis M. Hill; m, Richard Baskin

AAN Best Picture; AAN Best Supporting Actress: Ronee Blakely; *AAN Best Supporting Actress:* Lily Tomlin; *AAN Best Director:* Robert Altman; *AA Best Original Song:* "I'm Easy"; Keith Carradine (Music & Lyrics)

Robert Altman's triumph; one of the best American movies of the '70s and one of the most complex, expertly constructed narratives ever. Sprawling over two and one-half hours and never flagging, it successfully introduces and exposes 24 different characters, brilliantly critiquing the country music industry as a microcosm of American society.

NASHVILLE's songs, many of them written by the actors, are more integral to the storyline than is usually the case but, even if you do not cotton to country sounds, the effect is still overwhelming. Altman cuts back and forth between the characters with such aplomb that the audience never loses track of the narrative, which all takes place on one climactic weekend in the Country Music Capital of America. A huge music festival is taking place in Nashville, and at the same time a political rally is slated to promote the candidacy of the never-seen presidential hopeful Hal Phillip Walker, who leads

a new entity known as the Replacement Party. Though Walker's politics are not deeply plumbed, he sounds vaguely like George Wallace did when he was running on his third-party ticket. Walker's aides, Michael Murphy and Beatty, know what kind of people the candidate appeals to, and they prevail upon several of the top country music singers to help their cause. Henry Gibson, playing a veteran performer who appears to be patterned after Hank Snow, is the *eminence grise* whom most of the younger performers venerate. Despite his down-home smile as he sings, Gibson is a mean, rotten, self-serving man who would sell his mother for a gold record. Also in the top echelon is Blakley, a country music queen and authentic folk artist (said to be based on Loretta Lynn, who was angry about it) who has just recovered from a mental breakdown and is teetering on the edge of another. The festival has attracted singers from all over the country, each hoping to have a moment in the sun, be discovered, and take a place in the country pantheon. Carradine is one of a trio of folk singers. He's nothing more than skin stretched over lechery and is currently sleeping with partner Allan Nicholl's wife, Cristina Raines. That doesn't stop him from plucking favors from Lily Tomlin, Beatty's neglected wife, and Chaplin, an hilariously irritating BBC correspondent who is covering the festival for the listeners in the British Isles. Blakley's first concert is a flop, as she can't handle appearing in front of a crowd after such a long layoff, and her husband-manager, Allan Garfield, tells the annoyed assemblage that she will give them all a free concert in a couple of days to make up for this one—and to keep her crown from being stolen by Karen Black, doing a poisonous turn as a combo Tammy Wynette-Lynn Anderson. Beatty comes to Blakley and Garfield and asks her to appear for Walker at the rally, and she agrees. Beatty and Murphy stage a small fund-raising stag party and hire waitress Gwen Welles to sing, knowing she's so desperate for fame that they can force her to strip. (The leering men at the stag were actually played by some members of the Nashville Chamber of Commerce, and they turned in a totally convincing performance.) After she finishes, Beatty vainly attempts to bed Welles. On the day of the rally, David Hayward, whom we've seen flit in and out of the film carrying a violin case, comes to the stage and shoots Gibson and Blakley after their singing has stopped the show.

There are other rich characterizations: Barbara Harris, a dearranged white trash runaway out for her big break; Baxley, as Johnson's longtime cynical, bullshit mistress; Keenan Wynn as a Bible Belt family man, with Duvall as an eternal groupie; Tim Brown (magnificently playing a character based on Charlie Pride) is the black singer who has crossed over to become a success in the white world; Scott Glenn is the faithful puppy-dog serviceman who is entranced by Blakley; Jeff Goldblum is the local freak; Arkin as a chauffeur who witnesses everything; and David Peel is Gibson's son, a boy who does whatever his father asks and hates every minute of it. On top of all that, Elliott Gould and Julie Christie come in to do cameos as themselves, two movie stars tub-thumping a new project.

Amazingly, the movie was shot for about $2 million in less than 45 days, with much of the dialogue improvised by the performers.

NATIONAL LAMPOON'S ANIMAL HOUSE

1978 109m c Comedy *DVD*
Universal (U.S.) ★★★½
R

John Belushi *(John "Bluto" Blutarsky)*, Tim Matheson *(Eric "Otter" Stratton)*, Peter Riegert *(Donald "Boon" Schoenstein)*, John Vernon *(Dean Vernon Wormer)*, Tom Hulce *(Larry "Pinto" Kroger)*, Cesare Danova *(Mayor Carmine DePasto)*, Mary Louise Weller *(Mandy Pepperidge)*, Stephen Furst *(Kent "Flounder" Dorfman)*, James Daughton *(Greg Marmalard)*, Bruce McGill *(Daniel "D-Day" Simpson)* p, Matty Simmons, Ivan Reitman; d, John Landis; w, Harold Ramis, Douglas Kenney, Chris Miller; ph, Charles Correll (Panavision, Technicolor); ed, George Folsey Jr.; m, Elmer Bernstein; art d, John Lloyd; fx, Henry Millar; cos, Deborah Nadoolman

Rude, rough, tasteless, but often hilarious, this movie was a huge hit with young audiences and grossed more than $80 million. Supposedly based on the actual college experiences of the screenwriters (specifically Miller's year at Dartmouth), it served to introduce to films the anarchistic talents of Belushi as he played off the fine work by Hulce, Matheson, and others. The story takes place in the early 1960s, before the Vietnam War had heated up. Hulce and the rotund Furst attempt to join fraternities on their Faber College campus, but they are turned away and wind up at Delta House, a pigsty where they are welcomed by Matheson. The school's dean, Vernon, is keeping an eye on this particular house because its boozing members all have rotten grades and break nearly every school edict with their raucous "toga parties," in which the revelers dress up in bed sheets. Vernon, who would like to shut down the place, enlists Daughton, the head of the conservative Omega House, in his scheme, but he hasn't bargained on the tenacity, ingenuity, and unbelievably gross taste of his targets. This was the first of those crazy-college-antics films and remains, in most ways, the best.

NATIONAL TREASURE 📀

2004 126m c Action/Adventure/Crime ★★
Walt Disney Pictures/Jerry Bruckheimer Films PG
(U.S.)

Nicolas Cage (Benjamin Franklin Gates), Diane Kruger (Abigail Chase), Justin Bartha (Riley Poole), Sean Bean (Ian Howe), Jon Voight (Patrick Gates), Harvey Keitel (Agent Sadusky), Christopher Plummer (John Adams Gates), David Dayan Fisher (Shaw), Stewart Finlay-McLennan (Powell), Oleg Taktarov (Shippen)

p, Jerry Bruckheimer, Jon Turteltaub; d, John Turteltaub; w, Jim Kouf, Cormac Wibberley, Marianne Wibberley (based on a story by Jim Kouf, Oren Aviv, and Charles Segars); ph, Caleb Deschanel; ed, William Goldenberg; m, Trevor Rabin; prod d, Norris Spencer; art d, Geoff Hubbard, Larry Hubbs; fx, Mitchell S. Drain, Nathan McGuinness, Katrissa Peterson, Marc Varisco; cos, Judianna Makovsky

Less entertaining than flat-out exhausting, this frantic treasure-hunt movie is so determined to hold your attention that it unleashes a hailstorm of breakneck chases, wild leaps of logic, and cliff hangers that would have seemed hackneyed in the days of Polly Pureheart and Snidely Whiplash serials.

As an impressionable child, Benjamin Franklin Gates (Nicolas Cage) learned from his grandfather (Christopher Plummer) their family's unique and thrilling history. Six generations earlier, stable boy Thomas Gates (Jason Earles) was entrusted with the cryptic words "The truth lies with Charlotte" by the last surviving signer of the Declaration of Independence. This clue, declares grandpa, is a link in a chain that ends with the fabulous treasure of the Templar Knights, which made its way to the New World. Ben's father (Jon Voight) believes it's all a hoax, but Ben embraces the family legacy and makes his way to the Arctic Circle, where he hopes to uncover the frozen wreck of a ship: the long-lost Charlotte. Accompanied by computer geek Riley (Justin Bartha) and shady adventurer Ian Howe (Sean Bean), he finds not treasure, but another clue that suggests there's an invisible map on the back of the Declaration of Independence. Ian's response—that they need to steal the heavily guarded document—kicks off a race against time to locate historical artifacts and decipher their arcane mysteries.

Apparently conceived as a family-friendly variation on The Da Vinci Code, the film unfolds like one of those mind-numbing video games that claim to be educational because they incorporate historical trivia into their repetitive "solve clue/acquire object/advance to next level" format. Full of centuries-old devices in mind-bogglingly good working order and academics with the stamina of Olympic-caliber athletes, it's a silly, stupendously artificial enterprise.

NATIONAL VELVET 📀

1944 125m c Drama ★★★★
MGM (U.S.)

Mickey Rooney (Mi Taylor), Donald Crisp (Mr. Brown), Elizabeth Taylor (Velvet Brown), Anne Revere (Mrs. Brown), Angela Lansbury (Edwina Brown), Juanita Quigley (Malvolia Brown), Jackie "Butch" Jenkins (Donald Brown), Reginald Owen (Farmer Ede), Terry Kilburn (Ted), Alec Craig (Tim)

p, Pandro S. Berman; d, Clarence Brown; w, Theodore Reeves, Helen Deutsch (based on the novel by Enid Bagnold); ph, Leonard Smith (Technicolor); ed, Robert J. Kern; m, Herbert Stothart; art d, Cedric Gibbons, Urie McCleary; fx, Warren Newcombe; cos, Irene

AA Best Supporting Actress: Anne Revere; AAN Best Director: Clarence Brown; AAN Best Color Cinematography: Leonard Smith; AA Best Film Editing: Robert J. Kern; AAN Best Interior Decoration (Color): Cedric Gibbons, Urie McCleary, Edwin B. Willis, Mildred Griffiths

Perhaps the only time Elizabeth Taylor's costar matched her visual scene stealing. He's a horse, albeit a gelding. One of MGM's most beloved films, NATIONAL VELVET was the picture that made a star out of Taylor. The place is Sussex, England, where radiant Velvet Brown (Taylor) wins a horse that she names Pie and plans to enter in the Grand National. With the help of Mi Taylor (Rooney) she begins to rigorously train the animal, though she hasn't the money to enter the National. But Velvet's mother (Anne Revere) has been saving money she won as a young girl by swimming the English Channel, and she parts with it so Velvet can enter the race. Velvet, Mi and the horse then go off on their adventurous quest for the Grand National title. The movie features one of the best horse racing sequences ever filmed, as well as a host of winning performances. Although Taylor had already made her mark in four films, this was the one that really thrust her into the spotlight. Surprisingly she was not the first choice for the role, as Katharine Hepburn, Shirley Temple, and Margaret Sullavan were all candidates to play it. Angela Lansbury finally got one young role that wasn't opportunistic—here she's dreamy and romantic—English peaches and cream. And Jackie "Butch" Jenkins is an outstanding little brother, so ugly his cuteness makes you smile even hours after the movie. The film was remade as INTERNATIONAL VELVET starring Tatum O'Neal, and we grow ashen whenever we think of it.

NATURAL, THE 📀

1984 134m c Sports ★★★
Natural (U.S.) PG

Robert Redford (Roy Hobbs), Robert Duvall (Max Mercy), Glenn Close (Iris), Kim Basinger (Memo Paris), Wilford Brimley (Pop Fisher), Barbara Hershey (Harriet Bird), Robert Prosky (The Judge), Richard Farnsworth (Red Blow), Joe Don Baker (The Whammer), John Finnegan (Sam Simpson)

p, Mark Johnson; d, Barry Levinson; w, Roger Towne, Phil Dusenberry (based on the novel by Bernard Malamud); ph, Caleb Deschanel (Technicolor); ed, Stu Linder; m, Randy Newman; prod d, Angelo Graham, Mel Bourne; art d, James J. Murakami, Speed Hopkins; fx, Roger Hensen; cos, Bernie Pollack, Gloria Gresham

AAN Best Supporting Actress: Glenn Close; AAN Best Cinematography: Caleb Deschanel; AAN Best Original Score:

Randy Newman; *AAN Best Art Direction-Set Decoration:* Angelo Graham, Mel Bourne, James J. Murakami, Speed Hopkins, Bruce Weintraub

---

Transforming Bernard Malamud's fabulist first novel into a mythical morality play, THE NATURAL follows the fortunes of Roy Hobbs (Robert Redford) as the 19-year-old farm boy makes his way to try out with the Cubs. En route, he wins a bet by striking out the Whammer (Joe Don Baker), a slugger of Ruthian proportions, proving greatness is in his future. But in Chicago, a mysterious woman (Barbara Hershey) lures Roy to her hotel room and shoots him with a silver bullet. Fifteen years later, in 1939, Roy joins the hapless New York Knights and literally knocks the cover off the ball, leading the team back into contention. The Knights' owner (Robert Prosky), who is betting against his own team, sends Roy a beautiful temptress (Kim Basinger) so that he falls into a terrible slump, but his virtuous former girlfriend (Glenn Close) appears to revive his hitting. Without using his familiar "Wonderboy" bat for the big game, Roy still blasts an awe-inspiring home run into the lights, setting off a magical shower of fireworks to the strains of Randy Newman's evocative score. Somewhat overly sentimental, lacking the novel's subtlety, and less interesting when the action leaves the ball park, Barry Levinson's beautifully shot film is nonetheless a charming fairy tale. Redford, who played baseball at the University of Colorado, gives an appropriately iconic performance as Roy Hobbs—part Shoeless Joe Jackson (EIGHT MEN OUT), part Joe Hardy (DAMN YANKEES)—and the supporting roles are also well handled, especially Wilford Brimley as the manager. Filmed partly in Buffalo's War Memorial Stadium, a minor league park built in the 1930s, THE NATURAL also offers an appearance by "Super" Joe Charboneau, who had his own miracle season with the Cleveland Indians before disappearing from the big leagues.

NATURAL BORN KILLERS

1994 120m c   Action/Thriller ★★★
New Regency Productions/Ixtlan Productions/   R
Alcor Films/J.D. Productions   (U.S.)

Woody Harrelson *(Mickey Knox)*, Juliette Lewis *(Mallory Knox)*, Robert Downey Jr. *(Wayne Gale)*, Tommy Lee Jones *(Dwight McClusky)*, Tom Sizemore *(Jack Scagnetti)*, Rodney Dangerfield *(Mallory's Dad)*, Russell Means *(Old Indian)*, Edie McClurg *(Mallory's Mom)*, Balthazar Getty *(Gas Station Attendant)*, Joe Grifasi *(Duncan Homolka)*

p, Jane Hamsher, Don Murphy, Clayton Townsend; d, Oliver Stone; w, David Veloz, Richard Rutowski, Oliver Stone (from a story by Quentin Tarantino); ph, Robert Richardson; ed, Hank Corwin, Brian Berdan; m, Trent Reznor; prod d, Victor Kempster; art d, Alan Tomkins, Margery Zweizig; fx, Matt Sweeney, Steve Luport, Frank L. Pope, James Schwalm, Lucinda Strub, Rebecca Marie; cos, Richard Hornung; anim, Mike Smith

---

Wildly unconventional, corrosively satirical, savagely violent and vulgar, NATURAL BORN KILLERS is more self-consciously radical (in form, if not necessarily in content) than any other major studio release in recent memory. If it isn't the masterpiece it aspires to be—director Oliver Stone lacks, and may never attain, the kind of intellectual acuity that most of us still expect from artists—it's unquestionably a watershed.

Woody Harrelson and Juliette Lewis play Mickey and Mallory Knox, a post-utopian Bonnie and Clyde on a cross-country killing spree. If Bonnie and Clyde liked to think of themselves as Depression-era Robin Hoods, Mickey and Mallory have no such illusions—as a TV psychiatrist (Steven Wright) observes: "They know the difference between right and wrong. They just don't give a damn." On their way to racking up 52 victims, the couple become inter-

national celebrities, thanks mostly to the attentions of a lurid TV tabloid show hosted by the unapologetically venal Wayne Gale (Robert Downey, Jr.). After a series of increasingly hallucinatory adventures on the road, Mickey and Mallory are apprehended and imprisoned. Nothing, however, can stand in the way of true love (or Nielsen ratings): while deranged Warden McClusky (Tommy Lee Jones) schemes to have the Knoxes murdered, Mickey plots escape, using a live interview with Wayne Gale as a pretext for inciting an apocalyptic prison riot.

This astonishingly violent, technically brilliant satire of televisual culture baffled critics at the time of its release—as did A CLOCKWORK ORANGE 23 years earlier—and its indecorous brand of humor will strike many as insolent, even repellent. Stone, in a smart recovery from the disastrous HEAVEN AND EARTH, has wisely let his obsession with "significance" yield to his instinctive feel for pulp. Paradoxically, the result may be his most significant film. Accessing some of the farthest reaches of previously marginalized culture—direct-to-video splatter, cyberpunk, S&M, *anime*, serial killer fandom—NBK decisively wrenches mainstream cinema into the anarchic realm of post-modern pop.

NAUGHTY MARIETTA

1935 106m bw Musical   ★★★★
MGM   (U.S.)

Jeanette MacDonald *(Princess Marie de Namours de la Bonfain, "Marietta Franini")*, Nelson Eddy *(Capt. Richard Warrington)*, Frank Morgan *(Governor Gaspard d'Annard)*, Elsa Lanchester *(Mme. d'Annard)*, Douglas Dumbrille *(Prince de Namours de la Bonfain)*, Joseph Cawthorn *(Herr Schuman)*, Cecilia Parker *(Julie)*, Walter Kingsford *(Don Carlos de Braganza)*, Greta Meyer *(Frau Schuman)*, Akim Tamiroff *(Rudolpho, Puppet Master)*

p, Hunt Stromberg; d, W.S. Van Dyke II; w, John Lee Mahin, Frances Goodrich, Albert Hackett (based on the operetta by Victor Herbert, Rida Johnson Young); ph, William Daniels; ed, Blanche Sewell; art d, Cedric Gibbons; cos, Adrian

AAN Best Picture; AA Best Sound Recording: Douglas Shearer

Nelson Eddy made his full-fledged debut in this, the first of eight films in which he costarred with Jeanette MacDonald. Rita Johnson Young and Victor Herbert's hoary operetta was dusted off, given a new screenplay, new lyrics by Gus Kahn, and the result was a neatly paced (by "One-Take" Woodie Van Dyke) Best Picture nominee that only slightly belies its stage origins. Fleeing an arranged marriage to a Spanish grandee (Walter Kingsford), French princess Marie de Namours de la Bonfain (MacDonald) switches places with her maid and boards a ship bound for Louisana, where its female passengers are to become colonial brides. En route the ship is attacked by pirates, but the women are soon rescued by a group of soldiers led by Capt. Richard Warrington (Eddy), with whom the princess, now calling herself Marietta, falls in love. In New Orleans, she continues to conceal her identity, avoiding marriage by claiming to be a woman of ill repute. Eventually Capt. Warrington comes to the realization that he is in love with Marietta, but several hurdles stand in the way of their happiness, including arrest and the appearance of the princess' father (Douglas Dumbrille), who is determined to take his daughter back to her marital obligations in France. A much underrated if not great film, NAUGHTY MARIETTA features some particulary amusing supporting work by Harold Huber and Edward Brophy. Eddy is actually much better than most would have it, and his singing *is* quite stirring. MacDonald, though, is really the one in excellent form here, whether blasting the lengthy final high C of the "Italian Street Song" right in Nelson Eddy's face or doing an hilarious impersonation of a gluttonous, bespectacled woman on board the ship. One should admit, though, that the film isn't nearly as good as some of her others, most notably THE MERRY WIDOW, where her comedic talents are in full bloom.

NAVIGATOR, THE

DVD

1988 92m c/bw Adventure/Fantasy ★★½
Arenafilm/Film Investment Group PG
(New Zealand)

Bruce Lyons (Connor), Chris Haywood (Arno), Hamish McFarlane (Griffin), Marshall Napier (Searle), Noel Appleby (Ulf), Paul Livingston (Martin), Sarah Pierse (Linnet), Mark Wheatley (Tog 1), Tony Herbert (Tog 2), Jessica Cardiff-Smith (Esme)

p, John Maynard, Gary Hannam; d, Vincent Ward; w, Vincent Ward, Kely Lyons, Geoff Chapple; ph, Geoffrey Simpson; ed, John Scott; m, Davood A. Tabrizi; prod d, Sally Campbell; art d, Mike Becroft; cos, Glenys Jackson

THE NAVIGATOR is a singular experience, a time-warp, Chinese-box puzzle of a film that bespeaks the obsessed vision of its writer-director Vincent Ward. It begins in 1348 in Cumbria, England, where a psychic young boy, Griffin (Hamish McFarlane), dreams of a way to save his village from the advancing black plague. He leads his brother (Bruce Lyons) and four other men on a tunnelling expedition that somehow transports them to present-day New Zealand, and presents them with a chance to ward off the plague. But Griffin has also foreseen that, along the way, one of their number will be betrayed and another will die.

Ward has constructed a haunting fable that only occasionally lapses into self-parody, a la Monty Python. THE NAVIGATOR is certainly visually stylish, and employs a battery of cinematic effects—the mixed use of black and white with color, time-lapse views of clouds scampering across ominous skies, dizzying tracking shots up spiral staircases, etc. Worth a look.

NEAR DARK

DVD

1987 95m c Horror ★★★½
F/M (U.S.) R

Adrian Pasdar (Caleb), Jenny Wright (Mae), Lance Henriksen (Jesse), Bill Paxton (Severen), Jenette Goldstein (Diamondback), Tim Thomerson (Loy), Joshua Miller (Homer), Marcie Leeds (Sarah), Kenny Call (Deputy Sheriff), Ed Corbett (Ticket Seller)

p, Steven-Charles Jaffe, Eric Red; d, Kathryn Bigelow; w, Eric Red, Kathryn Bigelow; ph, Adam Greenberg (CFI Color); ed, Howard Smith; m, Tangerine Dream; prod d, Stephen Altman; art d, Dian Perryman; fx, Steve Galich, Dale Martin; cos, Joseph Porro

An auspicious solo directing debut from Kathryn Bigelow, NEAR DARK combines such diverse genres as horror, western, crime, and romance into what may be the first vampire road movie.

Set in the contemporary American Southwest, the film begins as Caleb (Adrian Pasdar), a bored farm boy, spots the beguiling Mae (Jenny Wright) at his usual Friday night hangout. By the break of dawn, Caleb has been bitten in the neck by Mae and befriended by a bizarre "family" of vampires—led by Jesse (Lance Henriksen), undead since before the Civil War—who travel across the country in a Winnebago. To his horror, Caleb learns that he has been "nipped" (i.e., he's almost a full-fledged vampire), and to graduate he must kill and drink blood. Sensing that Mae is in love with the boy, Jesse gives Caleb a week to perform his first kill.

Although several movie genres are represented here, NEAR DARK is most obviously based on Nicholas Ray's feature debut, THEY LIVE BY NIGHT (Bigelow's characters literally *must* live by night). Both films focus on a young couple desperately in love but trapped in a lifestyle they detest

by their surrogate families (bank robbers and vampires, respectively). Bigelow, who codirected THE LOVELESS with Monty Montgomery in 1982, and coscreenwriter Eric Red (THE HITCHER) demonstrate a keen understanding of the history of American cinema and create a unique film that explores the conventions of the vampire movie while moving it from dank European castles to modern-day Southwestern America. Bigelow sees the vampire (the word is never used in the film) as a nomadic outlaw, much like the fabled gunslingers of the Old West or the bands of bank robbers that roved the landscape during the Depression.

NEGOTIATOR, THE

DVD

1998 135m c Action/Thriller/Crime ★★★½
New Regency/Mandeville (U.S.) R

Samuel L. Jackson (Danny Roman), Kevin Spacey (Chris Sabian), David Morse (Commander Adam Beck), Ron Rifkin (Commander Grant Frost), John Spencer (Chief Al Travis), Regina Taylor (Karen Roman), J.T. Walsh (Inspector Terence Niebaum), Siobhan Fallon (Maggie), Paul Giamatti (Rudy), Bruce Beatty (Markus)

p, Arnon Milchan, David Hoberman; d, F. Gary Gray; w, James De Monaco, Kevin Fox; ph, Russell Carpenter; ed, Christian Adam Wagner; m, Graeme Revell; prod d, Holger Gross; art d, Kevin Ishioka; cos, Francine Jamison-Tanchuk

This taut crime thriller rests on two shrewd, perfectly modulated performances, and is a welcome antidote to brainless action extravaganzas in which the mayhem is the message.

Chicago negotiator Danny Roman (Samuel L. Jackson) is a bit of a cowboy, but he's also a peerless handler of life-or-death hostage situations. Over the course of a few awful days, his life is shattered: his partner, who's uncovered evidence of corruption among their ranks, is killed. Danny, who's on the board of the police pension fund, is accused of siphoning off money and committing murder to cover up the theft. Realizing that he's being expertly railroaded and hoping a little crisis might shake loose the perps behind the frame-up, Danny takes hostages, including fellow officers Niebaum (J.T. Walsh) and Frost (Ron Rifkin). He also demands an impartial negotiator from another precinct, the methodical Chris Sabian (Kevin Spacey).

Without demeaning director F. Gary Gray, who made the potentially tacky material of SET IT OFF crackle, the pairing of Spacey and Jackson is what makes this high-concept thriller work. Extraordinarily talented actors without being stars, they both embrace deeply flawed characters and wield words like weapons: think of Jackson's diner speech in PULP FICTION, or Spacey's serenely dishonest patter in THE USUAL SUSPECTS and L.A. CONFIDENTIAL, and try to imagine other actors making all those words work. Better, imagine Sylvester Stallone in Jackson's part—it was offered to him—and factor in that most of the scenes between the negotiators are played out over the phone. That's not to say the movie is all talk and no action: there are guns and gadgets, and a few set pieces to get the blood pumping. But the action isn't intelligence-insulting, and the thrills are mostly psychological. What a welcome change of pace.

NETWORK

DVD

1976 120m c Drama ★★★★
MGM (U.S.) R

Faye Dunaway (Diana Christensen), William Holden (Max Schumacher), Peter Finch (Howard Beale), Robert Duvall (Frank Hackett), Wesley Addy (Nelson Chaney), Ned Beatty (Arthur Jensen), Arthur Burghardt (Great Ahmed Kahn), Bill Burrows (TV Director), John Carpenter (George Bosch), Jordan Charney (Harry Hunter) p, Howard Gottfried; d, Sidney Lumet; w, Paddy Chayefsky; ph, Owen Roizman (Panavision, Metrocolor); ed, Alan Heim; m, Elliot Lawrence; prod d, Philip Rosenberg; cos, Theoni V. Aldredge

---

AAN Best Picture; AA Best Actor: Peter Finch; *AAN Best Actor:* William Holden; *AA Best Actress:* Faye Dunaway; *AAN Best Supporting Actor:* Ned Beatty; *AA Best Supporting Actress:* Beatrice Straight; *AAN Best Director:* Sidney Lumet; *AA Best Original Screenplay:* Paddy Chayefsky; *AAN Best Cinematography:* Owen Roizman; *AAN Best Film Editing:* Alan Heim

Paddy Chayefsky takes on television (his first true love), with somewhat self-congratulatory ardor.

Finch, a veteran newsman for the mythical United Broadcasting System, is sent over the mental edge when he is told that he will be fired after a quarter of a century on the air. He can't handle the situation and tells his audience that he intends to commit suicide on his final broadcast the following week. Ratings go straight through the roof, and his fan mail comes in by the carload. On the night he plans to put a gun to his head, Finch relents, apologizes to the millions watching (it's his largest audience ever), and stands up like an electronic Messiah to shout "go to your nearest window and yell as loud as you can, 'I'm mad as hell and I'm not going to take it anymore!'" His audience does just that. Dunaway, a programming executive at UBS, knows how to exploit this, so she signs Finch to a weekly show in which he can let it all hang out. This idea is opposed by Holden, the man in charge of network news and an old pal of Finch. He can see that Finch is on the edge of insanity and he can't stand the thought of the news being used to further ratings. Dunaway's bosses like the idea and fire Holden for his disagreement. Finch's program, a melange of various items, goes on and is a smash hit. Dunaway, now a star at the network, has other innovations in mind. She intends doing a show about urban guerrillas, but instead of hiring actors, she wants the terrorists to play themselves. Holden and Dunaway meet again and are soon involved; Holden then leaves his wife, Straight, in the most moving (and least gimmicky) scene in the film, as he tells her why he is departing.

NETWORK gives us several superb scenes, including one in which the communist guerrillas' lawyers argue with the network's representatives over the ancillary rights and syndication money that will accrue from their show. There's an amazing display of acting talent, even though director Lumet doesn't quite tie all the strands together. Finch's spouting *is* impressive, but we prefer Holden's sardonic edge, even if his big speeches seem the most predictably written. For Dunaway fans, there are some great moments: Faye zipping up her briefcase in a manic state, and that rattling teacup. With her strangely undersized mouth of yellow baby teeth, she's a believable media carnivore.

NEVER ON SUNDAY 📀
(POTE TIN KYRIAKI)
1960 97m bw Comedy/Drama ★★★
Melina (Greece)

Melina Mercouri *(Ilya)*, Jules Dassin *(Homer)*, George Foundas *(Tonio)*, Titos Vandis *(Jorgo)*, Mitsos Liguisos *(The Captain)*, Despo Diamantidou *(Despo)*, Dimos Starenios *(Poubelle)*, Dimitris Papamichael *(A Sailor)*, Alexis Salomos *(Noface)*

p, Jules Dassin; d, Jules Dassin; w, Jules Dassin; ph, Jacques Natteau; ed, Roger Dwyre; m, Manos Hadjidakis; cos, Denny Vachlioti

---

AAN Best Actress: Melina Mercouri; *AAN Best Director:* Jules Dassin; *AAN Best Original Story and Screenplay:* Jules Dassin; *AA Best Song:* "Never on Sunday"; Manos Hadjidakis; *AAN Best Costume Design (B/W):* Denny Vachlioti

Filmed in Greece for a pittance (under $200,000), this colorful art-house comedy broke through to the mainstream market and made a ton of money. NEVER ON SUNDAY is the brainchild of Jules Dassin, an American writer-director who ran afoul of Red-baiters in the 1950s and had to go to Europe to earn a living. He helmed RIFIFI, then went to Greece, where he met and married Melina Mercouri, NEVER ON SUNDAY's star. Although the film is a standard "hooker with a heart of gold" story, audiences were very much taken with its unfamiliar locale. Dassin not only wrote, produced, and directed, but also costarred as Homer, a tweedy American Grecophile who comes to Piraeus and encounters the local peasantry, who are slightly taken aback by his open ways. Homer loves Greece and everything about it. He soon meets Ilya (Mercouri), a prostitute who takes pride in her work and sees nothing immoral about the way she earns her living. Ilya takes customers six days a week and reserves Sunday for seeing the great Greek plays, none of which she actually comprehends. Homer intends to reform Ilya, but old habits are hard to break. Most of the dialogue is in English with a few speeches in Greek with titles.

NEVER SAY NEVER AGAIN 📀
1960 137m c Spy ★★½
Woodcote/Taliafilm (U.K.) PG

Sean Connery *(James Bond)*, Klaus Maria Brandauer *(Largo)*, Max von Sydow *(Blofeld)*, Barbara Carrera *(Fatima Blush)*, Kim Basinger *(Domino)*, Bernie Casey *(Felix Leiter)*, Alec McCowen *(Q/Algy)*, Edward Fox *(M)*, Pamela Salem *(Miss Moneypenny)*, Valerie Leon *(Lady in Bahamas)*

p, Jack Schwartzman; d, Irvin Kershner; w, Lorenzo Semple Jr. (based on a story by Kevin McClory, Jack Whittingham and Ian Fleming); ph, Douglas Slocombe (Panavision, Technicolor); ed, Robert Lawrence, Ian Crafford; m, Michel Legrand; prod d, Philip Harrison, Stephen Grimes; art d, Leslie Dilley, Michael White, Roy Stannard; fx, David Dryer, Ian Wingrove; cos, Charles Knode

---

Sean Connery returns to action after a 12-year absence from his role as 007. The title is based on his comment that he would never do a James Bond film again following DIAMONDS ARE FOREVER. Basically a remake of THUNDERBALL, the film opens with an aging Bond trying to get back in shape at a special clinic. When SPECTRE psycho Largo (Brandauer) hijacks a couple of American cruise missiles, Bond is assigned the case. Fatima Blush (Carrera), a gorgeous but deadly SPECTRE agent, does her best to bring an end to Bond's illustrious career, but, surviving the requisite high-speed chase, he eventually catches up with Largo and his beautiful companion Domino (Basinger) on the villain's yacht. Connery delivers his usual charming performance, and Brandauer (MEPHISTO, OUT OF AFRICA) makes a great Bond villain. Gone is the excessive gadgetry that mars Bond films, and, as a result, the characters are more prominent and colorful. This was director Irvin Kershner's first film following the huge success of THE EMPIRE STRIKES BACK. Lani Hall croons the title song, written by Alan and Marilyn Bergman.

NEVERENDING STORY, THE 📀
(DIE UNENDLICHE GESCHICHTE)
1984 94m c Fantasy/Science Fiction ★★★½
Neve Constantin/WDR (West Germany) PG

Barret Oliver *(Bastian)*, Gerald McRaney *(Bastian's Father)*, Drum Garrett, Darryl Cooksey, Nicholas Gilbert *(Bullies)*, Thomas Hill *(Koreander)*, Deep Roy *(Teeny Weeny)*, Tilo Pruckner *(Night Hob)*, Moses Gunn *(Cairon)*, Noah Hathaway *(Atreyu)*

p, Bernd Eichinger, Dieter Geissler; d, Wolfgang Petersen; w, Wolfgang Petersen, Herman Weigel (based on the novel by

Michael Ende); ph, Jost Vacano (Technivision, Technicolor); ed, Jane Seitz; m, Klaus Doldinger, Giorgio Moroder; prod d, Rolf Zehetbauer; art d, Gotz Weidner, Herbert Strabel, Johann Iwan Kot; fx, Brian Johnson; cos, Diemut Remy; anim, Steve Archer

Only a certified grump could dislike this engaging fantasy that wends its way into the imagination and is a delight on most levels. Bastian (Barret Oliver) is a troubled lad who has just lost his mother. He lives with his father (Gerald McRaney), who lectures Bastian about the boy's penchant for daydreaming. The lad has to fend off school bullies and is having difficulty adjusting to being motherless. One day, instead of going to school, he wanders into a weird bookstore and borrows a book called *The Neverending Story*. As Bastian turns the pages, the story comes to life. A childlike empress (Tami Stronach), who is not well, lives in a land called "Fantasia" and fears that it will be taken over if she dies. So she sends Atreyu (Noah Hathaway), a young warrior, off to find a cure for her lingering illness. What menaces Fantasia is a plague of "nothing": when the inhabitants of Earth lose hope and forget their aspirations, Fantasia is due to crumble as a direct result. Atreyu's voyage is fraught with peril, and he meets a cast of fantastic characters. Bastian is so enthralled by the story that he is plunged into it as a character. Made on a budget of more than $27 million, the film features state-of-the-art puppetry, animation, opticals, and makeup. THE NEVERENDING STORY owes much to ALICE IN WONDERLAND and THE DAY THE EARTH STOOD STILL in some sequences, but director Wolfgang Petersen combines the elements into a charming film that is excellent for children and won't put any adults to sleep, either.

NEW AGE, THE
1994   110m   c   Comedy/Drama   ★★★★
Ixtlan Productions/Addis-Wechsler/Regency   R
Enterprises/Alcor Films   (U.S.)

Peter Weller *(Peter Witner)*, Judy Davis *(Katherine Witner)*, Patrick Bauchau *(Jean Levy)*, Rachel Rosenthal *(Sarah Friedberg)*, Adam West *(Jeff Witner)*, Paula Marshall *(Alison Gale)*, Bruce Ramsay *(Misha)*, Tanya Pohlkotte *(Bettina)*, Susan Traylor *(Ellen Saltonstall)*, Corbin Bernsen *(Kevin Bulasky)*

p, Keith Addis, Nick Wechsler; d, Michael Tolkin; w, Michael Tolkin; ph, John J. Campbell; ed, Suzanne Fenn; m, Mark Mothersbaugh; prod d, Robin Standefer; art d, Kenneth A. Hardy; cos, Richard Shissler

Michael Tolkin's THE NEW AGE is something new, a comedy of horrors that's brittle, hypnotically hip, and so cool it almost freezes the audience out. It's like an update of Preston Sturges's THE PALM BEACH STORY in which the enviable rich people are no longer daffy eccentrics but energy vampires who feed off each other.

In the midst of the 1990-91 recession, L.A. literary agent Peter (Peter Weller) impulsively decides to find his bliss. He contemptuously walks out on his boss Kevin (Corbin Bernsen), without regard for the needs of his high-strung wife Katherine (Judy Davis), a graphic designer who is facing an exodus of clients. Primed by an assortment of gurus who flit through their social set, Peter and Katherine imprudently decide to invest in their own upscale clothing store, Hip-ocracy. Thereafter, the couple must undergo the kinds of humiliation, large and small, from which people of their class were well insulated in the glory days of American capitalism.

Michael Tolkin sets a difficult task for himself with THE NEW AGE: to satirize the tenets of New Age philosophizing while mustering the requisite sympathy for two fantastically overprivileged lost souls. The film suggests that West Coast swamis-for-hire have twisted legitimate spiritual quests into a religion of success in which the mantra is "Gimme!" As in THE RAPTURE, Tolkin treats a recognizable assortment of

fanatics and frauds with a certain sympathy (in an interview about THE RAPTURE's apocalyptic Christians, he asked seriously, "What if they're right?"); as a result, the comedy is overwhelmed with pain and bitterness.

NEW LEAF, A
1971   102m   c   Comedy   ★★★
Howard W. Koch/Hillard Elkins   (U.S.)   G

Walter Matthau *(Henry Graham)*, Elaine May *(Henrietta Lowell)*, Jack Weston *(Andrew McPherson)*, George Rose *(Harold Henry, Graham's Butler)*, William Redfield *(Beckett)*, James Coco *(Uncle Harry)*, Graham Jarvis *(Bo)*, Doris Roberts *(Mrs. Traggert)*, Rose Arrick *(Gloria Cunliffe)*, Renee Taylor *(Sally Hart)*

p, Joe Manduke; d, Elaine May; w, Elaine May (based on the short story "The Green Heart" by Jack Ritchie); ph, Gayne Rescher (Movielab Color); ed, Fredric Steinkamp, Don Guidice; prod d, Richard Fried; art d, Warren Clymer; cos, Anthea Sylbert

An often funny film that might have been funnier had anyone seen the original version. May, tripling as star, writer, and director, attempted to have her credits removed from the picture since, after the studio recut it, she felt that it did not reflect her work. In her version Henry Graham (Matthau) gets away with two murders. Another lost scene showed Henrietta (May) fantasizing herself as a sexy woman men cannot resist. The film May handed in ran over 180 minutes, and since this one is only 102 minutes, we can only guess what was excised. Nevertheless, and despite her rancor, the picture was delightful and did well with critics and audiences alike.

Graham is a ne'er-do-well who has exhausted the huge trust fund he was left at his father's death. Understandably shaken, Graham decides to follow the solution proposed by his live-in man (Rose): marry a rich woman. Borrowing some money from his hated uncle (Coco), he eventually sets his sights on the ungainly and myopic Henrietta, a botanist who is heir to a huge fortune. After marrying her, Graham plans to kill Henrietta when they make her yearly trip to the mountains. Before that, though, he must deal with Henrietta's crooked lawyer (Weston) and servant (Roberts). Will love ever find a way?

In some ways a throwback to the screwball comedies of the 1930s, A NEW LEAF often recalls several of them in its satire, inventiveness and wit. There is no music credit; the score of OH DAD, POOR DAD, MAMA'S HUNG YOU IN THE CLOSET AND I'M FEELIN' SO SAD was transferred, almost entirely, to this movie. That score was written by Neal Hefti and works better here than it did there.

NEW YORK, NEW YORK   📀
1977   155m   c   Musical   ★★★½
UA   (U.S.)   PG

Robert De Niro *(Jimmy Doyle)*, Liza Minnelli *(Francine Evans)*, Lionel Stander *(Tony Harwell)*, Mary Kay Place *(Bernice)*, George Memmoli *(Nicky)*, Murray Moston *(Horace Morris)*, Barry Primus *(Paul Wilson)*, Georgie Auld *(Frankie Harte)*, Dick Miller *(Palm Club Owner)*, Leonard Gaines *(Artie Kirks)*

p, Irwin Winkler, Robert Chartoff; d, Martin Scorsese; w, Earl Mac Rauch, Mardik Martin (based on a story by Rauch); ph, Laszlo Kovacs (Panavision, Deluxe Color); ed, Irving Lerner, Marcia Lucas, Tom Rolf, Bert Lovitt, David Ramirez; m, Ralph Burns; prod d, Boris Leven; art d, Harry Kemm; fx, Richard Albain; chor, Ron Field; cos, Theadora Van Runkle

Martin Scorsese's attempt at making an old-fashioned musical, NEW YORK, NEW YORK never found much of an audience, but remains a visually fascinating rumination on the genre.

New York City. 1945. USO singer Francine Evans (Liza Minnelli) and aspiring sax player Jimmy Doyle (Robert De

Niro) meet cute during the V-J Day revelry, audition for a job together, and later end up in the employ of big band leader Frankie Harte (Georgie Auld, who dubbed De Niro's sax playing), falling deeply in love and marrying. Jimmy eventually takes over Harte's band, and when Francine returns to New York to have their baby, he becomes involved with her replacement singer (Mary Kay Place). Francine and Jimmy have a son, but in time their marriage disintegrates as Francine becomes a hit recording artist (singing the kind of tunes her husband despises) and film star, while Jimmy turns to jazz and later opens his own club, en route to the film's distinctly downbeat ending.

NEW YORK, NEW YORK cost almost $9 million, and it's uneven in spots—the result of being drastically edited from its original four-hour length (among the slashes was the 12-minute, $300,000 "Happy Endings" production number, later reinserted for the film's 1981 re-release). Nevertheless, the film is a treat for the ears as well as the eyes. De Niro gives an outstanding performance, masterfully conveying Jimmy's vanity, selfishness, and egotism. Minnelli is nothing less than brilliant, more than deserving of an Oscar nomination that never came her way. Place (THE BIG CHILL, television's "Mary Hartman, Mary Hartman") got her first big break here, and longtime Roger Corman favorite Miller, comic Gaines, and rotund Memmoli all contribute fine work.

NEXT STOP, GREENWICH VILLAGE

1976   111m   c   Comedy   ★★★★
Fox   (U.S.)   R

Lenny Baker (*Larry Lapinsky*), Shelley Winters (*Mrs. Lapinsky*), Ellen Greene (*Sarah*), Lois Smith (*Anita*), Christopher Walken (*Robert*), Dori Brenner (*Connie*), Antonio Fargas (*Bernstein*), Lou Jacobi (*Herb*), Mike Kellin (*Mr. Lapinsky*), Michael Egan (*Herbert*)

p, Paul Mazursky, Tony Ray; d, Paul Mazursky; w, Paul Mazursky; ph, Arthur J. Ornitz (Deluxe Color); ed, Richard Halsey; m, Bill Conti; prod d, Philip Rosenberg; cos, Albert Wolsky

Anyone who spent time in New York's Greenwich Village in the early 1950s will attest to the accuracy of this wonderful, nostalgic look at that era. It's essentially Mazursky's own story, and he manages to capture the time and the people with a loving touch. Baker is the young man who graduates from Brooklyn College in 1953 and makes the decision to leave his family, Kellin and Winters, and switch boroughs to Manhattan. Winters, the ultimate Jewish mother, is totally against it, but he leaves anyway and takes up residence in the Village, where he takes a job at a health food place, then starts his acting lessons with Egan, a proponent of the "Method." He is soon part of "the scene," and his pals include nutty Brenner (who later married Andre Previn and became an important songwriter); Smith, who is always teetering on the brink of suicide; Walken, the WASPish poet who speaks in epigrams; and Fargas, a black homosexual with a Jewish name. The tight-knit group members are symbiotic and help each other when needed, so when Smith tries suicide, they pour coffee into her. When Baker's sweetheart, Greene, becomes pregnant they arrange an abortion. Baker is out of money and due to be tossed out of his apartment, so the others stage a "rent party" to raise the cash. Baker learns that a major studio wants to cast some juvenile delinquents and he hopes to get one of the parts. (In real life, Mazursky was in THE BLACKBOARD JUNGLE as "Stoker.") Winters and Kellin come to see how Baker is living, and Winters is shocked when she learns that Baker and Greene are sleeping together. Before she can faint, Kellin takes Winters home to Brooklyn. The group is saddened to learn that Smith's customary suicide attempt worked this time, and they share their grief with each other. Baker gets a chance at the role, then Greene announces that she is going off to Mexico with Walken, Fargas, and Brenner. Baker and Greene make love for the last time and she takes this opportunity to

inform him that she is also Walken's lover. An argument erupts as Winters and Kellin enter the apartment surreptitiously. Greene leaves, and Baker understands that this part of his life is now finished. Baker bids his pals farewell, goes to his job, and gets the call about the role. He is to report to Hollywood within the week. At the last supper with Winters and Kellin, she reminds him to never forget where he came from.

Baker was simply marvelous in the leading role. He went on to play in the Broadway hit musical, "I Love My Wife," before dying of cancer. Mazursky's real acting career began in Stanley Kubrick's first feature, FEAR AND DESIRE, which was followed by THE BLACKBOARD JUNGLE. Co-producer Tony Ray, director Nicholas Ray's son, later married his father's ex-wife, Gloria Grahame. In a small role, look for Jeff Goldblum. Conti's music is outstanding and evokes the period without parodying it.

NIAGARA   DVD

1953   92m   c   Thriller   ★★★★
Fox   (U.S.)

Marilyn Monroe (*Rose Loomis*), Joseph Cotten (*George Loomis*), Jean Peters (*Polly Cutler*), Max Showalter, billed as Casey Adams (*Ray Cutler*), Denis O'Dea (*Inspector Sharkey*), Richard Allan (*Patrick*), Don Wilson (*Mr. Kettering*), Lurene Tuttle (*Mrs. Kettering*), Russell Collins (*Mr. Qua*), Will Wright (*Boatman*)

p, Charles Brackett; d, Henry Hathaway; w, Charles Brackett, Walter Reisch, Richard Breen; ph, Joseph MacDonald (Technicolor); ed, Barbara McLean; m, Sol Kaplan; art d, Lyle Wheeler, Maurice Ransford; fx, Ray Kellogg; cos, Dorothy Jeakins

Everyone's honeymoon haven at one time, Niagara Falls, is the deceptive setting for this offbeat, absorbing film with bowstring-tight direction from Hathaway and superb performances from Cotten as a jealous husband and Monroe as his neurotic wife. Newlyweds Peters and Adams arrive at their Niagara honeymoon cottage and meet another couple, Cotten and Monroe. Monroe, from the beginning, confides about her husband being considerably older than she; he is depressed, and has just been released from a mental institution. Peters later sees Monroe kissing a young man, Allan, and learns that the couple plans to murder Cotten.

The film is breathtakingly photographed, in lurid Technicolor that heightens the sensual energy of the Monroe persona. Jean Peters is lovely and effective in a difficult part; the script calls for her to be in Monroe's shadow, yet she's the stronger of the two. Cotten makes a marvelous antihero, and Richard Allan's dark, macho seductiveness makes an exciting contrast to Monroe.

NICHOLAS AND ALEXANDRA   DVD

1971   183m   c   Biography/War   ★★★½
Horizon   (U.K.)   GP

Michael Jayston (*Nicholas II*), Janet Suzman (*Alexandra*), Roderic Noble (*Alexis*), Ania Marson (*Olga*), Lynne Frederick (*Tatiana*), Candace Glendenning (*Marie*), Fiona Fullerton (*Anastasia*), Harry Andrews (*Grand Duke Nicholas*), Irene Worth (*the Queen Mother*), Tom Baker (*Rasputin*)

p, Sam Spiegel; d, Franklin J. Schaffner; w, James Goldman, Edward Bond (based on a book by Robert K. Massie); ph, Freddie Young (Panavision, Eastmancolor); ed, Ernest Walter; m, Richard Rodney Bennett; prod d, John Box; art d, Jack Maxsted, Ernest Archer, Gil Parrondo; fx, Eddie Fowlie; cos, Yvonne Blake, Antonio Castillo

AAN Best Picture, AAN Best Actress: Janet Suzman; AAN Best Cinematography: Freddie Young; AAN Best Original Dramatic Score: Richard Rodney Bennett; AA Best Art Direction-Set Decoration:

John Box, Ernest Archer, Jack Maxsted, Gil Parrondo, Vernon Dixon; *AA Best Costume Design:* Yvonne Blake, Antonio Castillo

This lavish, overlong production chronicles the downfall of the last Russian czar Nicholas II (Michael Jayston), and his wife Alexandra (Janet Suzman). The film concentrates on their troubled family life, especially the affliction of their only son, Alexis (Roderic Noble), with hemophilia. Nicholas's preoccupation with this tragedy influences state decisions and increases his disengagement from his starving people, while Alexandra falls completely under the influence of the profligate peasant monk Rasputin (Tom Baker), believing that his mystic powers can heal her son. Rasputin's power increases in the Imperial Court despite Nicholas's weak efforts to maintain authority; meanwhile, hundreds are slaughtered at the Winter Palace, fueling Lenin (Michael Bryant) and Trotsky's (Brian Cox) crusade to overthrow "Bloody Nicholas." As the tide of assassination and unrest rises, an ill-prepared Russia suffers terrible losses in WWI, setting the stage for revolution in 1917 and the execution of the deposed czar and family in July 1918. While it remains a treat for the eyes, NICHOLAS AND ALEXANDRA attempts to tell too much. Its overview of more than two decades of tumultuous, epochal history develops few of its famous figures beyond caricature (although Baker, of "Dr. Who" fame, plays Rasputin with flamboyance and verve), and the failure to bring Nicholas and Alexandra to life—despite the script's intimate and sympathetic treatment of the pair—is especially critical. Shot on location in Spain and Yugoslavia, the film won Oscars for Best Art Direction, Set Decoration, and Costumes. It was also nominated for Best Picture (losing to THE FRENCH CONNECTION), Best Actress (Suzman, who lost to Jane Fonda for KLUTE), Best Score, and Best Cinematography.

NICHOLAS NICKLEBY 📀

2002 132m c Drama ★★★
Cloud Nine Films/Hart-Sharp PG
Entertainment/IMF/Meespierson Film/
VCL Communications/MGM/UA
(U.S./U.K./Germany)

Charlie Hunnam *(Nicholas Nickleby)*, Christopher Plummer *(Ralph Nickleby)*, Jim Broadbent *(Wackford Squeers)*, Juliet Stevenson *(Mrs. Squeers)*, Anne Hathaway *(Madeline Bray)*, Jamie Bell *(Smike)*, Edward Fox *(Sir Mulberry Hawk)*, Romola Garai *(Kate Nickleby)*, Stella Gonet *(Mrs. Nickleby)*, Andrew Havill *(Mr. Nickleby)*

p, John N. Hart, Jeffrey Sharp, Simon Channing Williams; d, Douglas McGrath; w, Douglas McGrath (based on the novel *The Life and Adventures of Nicholas Nickleby* by Charles Dickens); ph, Dick Pope; ed, Lesley Walker; m, Rachel Portman; prod d, Eve Stewart; art d, Andrew Grant; fx, Simon Carr; cos, Ruth Myers

If Charles Dickens's 800-page novel absolutely must be shoehorned into a two-hour feature film, this is undoubtedly one way to go: strip the story down to its barest essentials and fill the inevitable gaps with as many colorful cameos as time permits.

Nicholas Nickleby is born into a loving family in the pastoral heart of the Devonshire countryside, but his childhood happiness is short-lived. His father (Andrew Havill) first loses the family savings, then suffers the further misfortune of dying. Nineteen-year-old Nicholas (Charlie Hunnam), his sister, Kate (Romola Garai), and their mother (Stella Gonet) are now entirely dependent on the slender mercy of Nicholas's villainous Uncle Ralph (Christopher Plummer, at his slithery best), who secures his nephew a position in the hinterlands of Yorkshire at a wretched school for poor boys run by the sadistic, one-eyed schoolmaster Wackford Squeers (a wonderfully

loathsome Jim Broadbent) and his equally cruel wife (Juliet Stevenson). Nicholas befriends young Smike (BILLY ELLIOT's Jamie Bell), a good-natured soul crippled by countless beatings, and is so appalled by the abuse he sees around him that he makes a daring escape. Meanwhile, back in London, Uncle Ralph intends to marry Kate off to an aging bounder (Edward Fox) in exchange for an outstanding debt.

Writer-director Douglas McGrath (EMMA) has managed to trim nearly all the novel's subplots and secondary characters without losing its original shape. There's still a bit of romance (Anne Hathaway plays Nicholas's love interest), as well a good deal of comedy—courtesy of Nathan Lane, Alan Cumming, and Barry Humphries (a.k.a. Dame Edna Everage) as members of an absurd theatrical troupe who try to pull Nicholas into their ranks—and it all goes down rather smoothly.

NIGHT AND THE CITY 📀

1950 95m bw Crime ★★★★
Fox (U.K.)

Richard Widmark *(Harry Fabian)*, Gene Tierney *(Mary Bristol)*, Googie Withers *(Helen Nosseross)*, Hugh Marlowe *(Adam Dunn)*, Francis L. Sullivan *(Phil Nosseross)*, Herbert Lom *(Kristo)*, Stanislaus Zbyszko *(Gregorius)*, Mike Mazurki *(Strangler)*, Charles Farrell *(Beer)*, Ada Reeve *(Molly)*

p, Samuel G. Engel; d, Jules Dassin; w, Jo Eisinger (based on the novel by Gerald Kersh); ph, Mutz Greenbaum; ed, Nick De Maggio, Sidney Stone; m, Franz Waxman; art d, C.P. Norman; cos, Oleg Cassini, Margaret Furse

A dark, brooding *noir*, with Widmark riveting as a hustling promoter who sinks into the quagmire of his own ambitions. The film is set in London, where Widmark works for the obese Sullivan, owner of a sleazy dive. Widmark steers suckers to the joint on the promise of witnessing some racy shows, but it's all pretty tame stuff—even the very proper Tierney sings there, she being a disapproving girlfriend of wily Widmark. Tierney keeps after Widmark to get a decent job, but the con is in his blood and he is obsessed with developing a big money scheme. He overhears famed wrestler Zbyszko talking to his protege Ken Richmond in a huge sports arena owned by Zbyszko's son, Lom. Before Widmark is thrown out of the arena for hustling customers to Sullivan's club, he learns that Zbyszko is disgusted by the fake wrestling matches his son offers to the public. Zbyszko believes that only his traditional Greco-Roman wrestling is a pure sport. Widmark later goes to Zbyszko and cons him into believing that he will promote the long-neglected Greco-Roman wrestling and bring it back to the popularity it once enjoyed. The legendary wrestler agrees to lend his name to the enterprise, which incenses the powerful Lom, who threatens to kill Widmark if he misuses Lom's father. On the other hand, if he truly promotes Greco-Roman wrestling, Lom tells Widmark, he can go ahead....

NIGHT AND THE CITY is an uncompromising, exciting, anxiety-inducing film that is seen entirely through Widmark's desperate viewpoint. Director Dassin relentlessly displays London without charm and grace, showing only the seamy side where Widmark and his kind live out their unscrupulous lives without thought of love or compassion. Everything is cold and calculating, one character greedily using another for human control. The world Widmark desires to enter is that controlled by the Loms and Sullivans—who belong to a very exclusive club. They are as crooked and immoral as Widmark, but they have the money and the connections, and Widmark only aspires to be a loftier version of his own venal self. Despite the feeling of lonely helplessness that pervades the film, the story proceeds at such a frenetic pace that it's utterly captivating. Widmark's performance is nothing short of remarkable. Greene's camerawork is exceptional, as is

Waxman's score. The wrestling scene between Zbyszko, a former heavyweight wrestling champion, and Mazurki is one of the most heart-pounding matches ever filmed. Remade, with mixed results, in 1992.

NIGHT AT THE OPERA, A   DVD
1935 90m   bw   Comedy   ★★★★
MGM   (U.S.)

Groucho Marx *(Otis B. Driftwood)*, Chico Marx *(Fiorello)*, Harpo Marx *(Tomasso)*, Kitty Carlisle *(Rosa Castaldi)*, Allan Jones *(Riccardo Baroni)*, Walter Woolf King *(Rodolfo Lassparri)*, Sig Rumann *(Herman Gottlieb)*, Margaret Dumont *(Mrs. Claypool)*, Edward Keane *(Captain)*, Robert Emmett O'Connor *(Detective Henderson)*

p, Irving Thalberg; d, Sam Wood; w, George S. Kaufman, Morrie Ryskind, Al Boasberg, Bert Kalmar, Harry Ruby (based on a story by James Kevin McGuinness); ed, Merritt Gerstad; ed, William LeVanway; m, Herbert Stothart; art d, Cedric Gibbons, Ben Carre; chor, Chester Hale; cos, Dolly Tree

The Marx Brothers' most popular film and Groucho's favorite, before MGM queered their joyful anarchy. (Groucho must have loved the money which started rolling in; actually, the Marx Bros. were far more at home at Paramount.) Groucho, Chico, and Harpo join forces to disrupt the stuffy world of opera by wreaking havoc on the music, stage, and audience. Otis B. Driftwood (Groucho) tries to con rich Mrs. Claypool (Margaret Dumont, in fabulous form) into investing her money in an opera company, while Tomasso (Harpo) and Fiorello (Chico) join the fray and take it upon themselves to help advance the careers of two struggling young singers, Allan Jones and Kitty Carlisle—both begging for a stagehand to drop twin sandbags and kill the misery they subject an audience to. OPERA is their first at MGM, in case you hadn't guessed, after being dropped by Paramount and the first without Zeppo. Producer Irving Thalberg had faith in them but thought their films for Paramount lacked cohesive stories and enough time to work out the routines, so he prevailed upon them to take a 50-minute precis of the best scenes on the road. They toured four cities with writers George S. Kaufman and Morrie Ryskind in the audience for 24 days and polished the gags until they were ready to film. The result was a huge success and the picture was a hit. Today it is fondly remembered for such classic comedy bits as Groucho and Chico drafting a contract, the stateroom scene, and the hilarious climax where the brothers make a shambles of "Il Trovatore." Sans DUCK SOUP, we'll watch this any day.

'NIGHT, MOTHER
1986 96m   c   Drama   ★★★½
Universal   (U.S.)   PG-13

Sissy Spacek *(Jessie Cates)*, Anne Bancroft *(Thelma Cates)*, Ed Berke *(Dawson Cates)*, Carol Robbins *(Loretta Cates)*, Jennifer Roosendahl *(Melodie Cates)*, Michael Kenworthy *(Kenny Cates)*, Sari Walker *(Agnes Fletcher)*

p, Aaron Spelling, Alan Greisman; d, Tom Moore; w, Marsha Norman (based on her play); ph, Stephen Katz (Deluxe Color); ed, Suzanne Pettit; m, David Shire; prod d, Jackson DeGovia; art d, John R. Jensen; cos, Robert Blackman

Deceptively complex, this adaptation of the 1983 Pulitzer Prize winner hews closely to the grim line of the stage play and seldom compromises. It's early evening in a small house in the Midwest. Jessie Cates (Sissy Spacek), a woman in her late 30s, is going about what seems to be a normal routine, as though she is about to take a trip. She cleans the refrigerator, cancels the newspaper delivery, packs and labels her clothes for the Salvation Army, and does a few other chores. After 10 minutes

or so have elapsed, she tells her mother (Anne Bancroft) that she is going to kill herself later that evening. Jessie is an epileptic; she has an ex-husband and a son who is on his way to becoming a criminal. The only person she ever loved, her father, has died and now she is living with her mother. Her life has spun out of control and she is apparently exercising her only remaining option by ending it. Director Tom Moore, who also directed the play, makes a fairly good debut in a difficult task. Spacek and Bancroft have the only speaking roles, but brief glimpses of some of the other family members are provided in an effort to keep the picture from seeming totally stagebound, which it is. Marsha Norman's script had many levels, switching sympathies for both actresses at the turn of a phrase. It is to her credit that it works.

NIGHT MOVES   DVD
1975 100m   c   Mystery   ★★★½
Hiller/Layton   (U.S.)   R

Gene Hackman *(Harry Moseby)*, Susan Clark *(Ellen Moseby)*, Edward Binns *(Ziegler)*, Harris Yulin *(Marty Heller)*, Kenneth Mars *(Nick)*, Janet Ward *(Arlene Iverson)*, James Woods *(Quentin)*, Anthony Costello *(Mary Ellman)*, John Crawford *(Tom Iverson)*, Melanie Griffith *(Delly Grastner)*

p, Robert M. Sherman; d, Arthur Penn; w, Alan Sharp; ph, Bruce Surtees (Technicolor); ed, Dede Allen; m, Michael Small; prod d, George Jenkins; fx, Marcel Vercoutere, Joe Day; cos, Rita Riggs

This excellent contemporary noir features some of the best work of both director Arthur Penn and actor Gene Hackman. Hackman is a small-time private eye working in Los Angeles. Fading movie actress Ward hires him to find Griffith, her wild teenage daughter who has run off to the Florida Keys to be with her stepfather, Crawford, and his mistress, Warren. Hackman finds the girl easily and returns her to her mother, but the next day she is killed in an accident while filming a stunt for a movie. After watching footage of the accident, Hackman becomes convinced Griffith was murdered, and the clues lead him back to the Florida Keys. Although the mystery itself is at times confusing and ultimately pointless, NIGHT MOVES is wholly engrossing and thematically rich, with much material reflecting the disillusionment of post-Watergate America. In particular, Penn and screenwriter Sharp are out to revise the mythos of the private eye; here, no longer a Chandleresque knight-errant, he's an impotent anachronism—by the time he solves the mystery it's too late to do anything about it. The last shot, with Hackman circling aimlessly in a boat called the "Point of View," says it all. The film marked the feature debut of 17-year-old Melanie Griffith. Especially interesting when viewed as a forerunner to Francis Coppola's THE CONVERSATION, also starring Hackman as a character named Harry.

NIGHT MUST FALL
1937 117m   bw   Thriller   ★★★★
MGM   (U.S.)

Robert Montgomery *(Danny)*, Rosalind Russell *(Olivia)*, Dame May Whitty *(Mrs. Bransom)*, Alan Marshal *(Justin)*, Merle Tottenham *(Dora)*, Kathleen Harrison *(Mrs. Terence)*, Matthew Boulton *(Belsize)*, Eily Malyon *(Nurse)*, E.E. Clive *(Guide)*, Beryl Mercer *(Saleslady)*

p, Hunt Stromberg; d, Richard Thorpe; w, John Van Druten (based on a play by Emlyn Williams); ph, Ray June; ed, Robert J. Kern; m, Edward Ward; art d, Cedric Gibbons; cos, Dolly Tree

AAN Best Actor: Robert Montgomery; *AAN Best Supporting Actress:* May Whitty

Due primarily to an amazing performance by Robert Montgomery, this superb, nerve-tingling thriller improves on Emlyn Williams's already shocking stage hit. Whitty is a fussy, domineering grande dame living in a cottage in Essex, England, with niece Russell and several cowed servants. Just after Russell and Whitty hear that a "very flashy" woman guest in a nearby inn has vanished, Montgomery appears, claiming that he has been working as a page boy at the inn but is now looking for a new job. Montgomery brings with him a heavy hatbox that he places in a closet after being hired as a handyman by the wheelchair-bound Whitty. He waits hand and foot upon her, flattering Whitty at every opportunity, but exchanges barbs with Russell, who distrusts him. When asked about the missing woman, Montgomery describes her in chilling detail, revealing his psychopathic personality and further arousing Russell's suspicion.

NIGHT MUST FALL is directed with great care by Richard Thorpe, who evokes every bit of suspense intended by playwright Williams (who played the role of the killer on stage, though not nearly as subtly as Montgomery does). Producer Hunt Stromberg saw the play in London and insisted on making it into a film. Although MGM boss Louis B. Mayer thought it was an awful idea, he reluctantly agreed to allow Stromberg, his most successful producer, to undertake the project. Mayer was outraged when Stromberg cast Montgomery, the popular star of frothy MGM comedies, in the role of the killer, but the critical and popular success of the film proved him wrong. The film was remade by the studio nearly 20 years later, starring Albert Finney, Susan Hampshire, and Mona Washbourne, but the remake lacked the tautness and dramatic impact of the original.

NIGHT OF THE HUNTER, THE
1955 93m bw Thriller
UA (U.S.)

Robert Mitchum *(Preacher Harry Powell)*, Shelley Winters *(Willa Harper)*, Lillian Gish *(Rachel)*, Evelyn Varden *(Icey Spoon)*, Peter Graves *(Ben Harper)*, Billy Chapin *(John)*, Sally Jane Bruce *(Pearl)*, James Gleason *(Birdie)*, Don Beddoe *(Walt Spoon)*, Gloria Castillo *(Ruby)*

p, Paul Gregory; d, Charles Laughton; w, James Agee (based on the novel by Davis Grubb); ph, Stanley Cortez; ed, Robert Golden; m, Walter Schumann; art d, Hilyard Brown; fx, Jack Rabin, Louis DeWitt; cos, Jerry Bos

Actor Charles Laughton's only directorial effort is a brilliantly eerie tale of religious madness, greed, innocence, and murder set in the rural Ohio River Basin during the Great Depression. Harry Powell (Mitchum), a psychopathic preacher with the word "Love" tattooed on the fingers of his right hand and "Hate" tattooed on the left, is driven by repressed sexual desires to murder women. While in jail for driving a stolen car, Powell meets young Ben Harper (Graves), a bank robber condemned to death for killing a man during a heist. Powell is certain Harper has stashed the loot ($10,000) from the robbery somewhere, but is unable to get Harper to reveal where. Powell is released shortly after Harper is executed, and the mad preacher tracks down his cellmate's widow, Willa (Winters). Powell soon persuades the idiotic Willa to marry him—much to the dismay of her son, John (Chapin), who senses what the preacher is really after and knows that the money is hidden inside one of the dolls of his sister, Pearl (Bruce). Powell soon becomes frustrated with the ignorant Willa and murders her, turning his attention to the children. John and Pearl take the doll and flee into the countryside with the murderous Powell always one step behind them.

Working from a script by James Agee (THE AFRICAN QUEEN), Laughton created what he called "a nightmarish sort of Mother Goose tale," employing an eclectic mix of visu-

al styles (German expressionism, D.W. Griffith) to convey both the horror of Powell's quest and the idyllic flight of the children to the safety of the farm of an old spinster (Gish). In addition to Stanley Cortez's stunning cinematography, the film boasts Robert Mitchum's greatest performance—a chilling essay that would unfortunately typecast him for much of his career. Beautiful, haunting, poetic, and intensely personal, THE NIGHT OF THE HUNTER is a unique, terrifying masterpiece. The adaptation of the Davis Grubb novel was the last film work by James Agee. Audiences didn't know *what* to make of this one; it bombed, and the great Laughton never directed again.

NIGHT OF THE IGUANA, THE
1964 125m bw Drama ★★½
Seven Arts (U.S.)

Richard Burton *(Rev. T. Lawrence Shannon)*, Ava Gardner *(Maxine Faulk)*, Deborah Kerr *(Hannah Jelkes)*, Sue Lyon *(Charlotte Goodall)*, James Ward *(Hank Prosner)*, Grayson Hall *(Judith Fellowes)*, Cyril Delevanti *(Nonno)*, Mary Boylan *(Miss Peebles)*, Gladys Hill *(Miss Dexter)*, Billie Matticks *(Miss Throxton)*

p, Ray Stark; d, John Huston; w, Anthony Veiller, John Huston (based on the play by Tennessee Williams); ph, Gabriel Figueroa (CinemaScope); ed, Ralph Kemplen; m, Benjamin Frankel; art d, Stephen Grimes; cos, Dorothy Jeakins

AAN Best Supporting Actress: Grayson Hall; *AAN Best B/W Cinematography:* Gabriel Figueroa; *AAN Best Art Direction-Set Decoration (B/W):* Stephen Grimes; *AA Best Costume Design (B/W):* Dorothy Jeakins

Based on the Williams play that won the New York Drama Critics Award for 1961-62, THE NIGHT OF THE IGUANA is alternately fascinating and boring. It served to put the sleepy little village of Puerto Vallarta on the Mexican vacation map, and visitors to the town are still shown the rotting sets for the movie as part of their "official" tour. Burton is a defrocked Episcopalian priest who now earns his living as a tour guide. He's taking a group of schoolteachers around. Lyon, the junior member of the group, finds him attractive, so he squires her to his ratty hotel room, where they are discovered by Hall. The older woman threatens to have him sacked for his dalliance with Lyon unless he ceases. The group are supposed to be quartered in a plush inn, but Burton takes them to a run-down place owned by friend Gardner, who has just been widowed. The teachers balk, but they are stranded while Burton tinkers with their bus and must now remain at the seedy hotel. Burton falls ill with fever and tells Gardner that Hall means to have him fired, so Gardner won't let Hall use the phone to call Burton's employers. Kerr, a poor artist, and her grandfather, Delevanti, a poorer poet, have been working their way across Mexico by selling her sketches and arranging readings by him, and they arrive at the hotel broke. Ward, the tour's bus driver, soon becomes Lyon's suitor. He repairs the bus and leaves, as tour leader, with the teachers. Kerr, Burton, Delevanti, and Gardner remain at the hotel, and Kerr and Burton become friends. But Burton's mind seems to be on the verge of crumbling. Gardner loves Burton although she sees that his existence might be better served by Kerr and offers her hotel to the two of them. Meanwhile Delevanti, who has been working on the same poem for 20 years, finally finishes it and dies. Kerr leaves, after burying her grandfather, and Burton and Gardner stay on at the shuttered hostelry as the picture ends. We're never certain whether Hall's jealousy of the relationship, if it can be called that, between Lyon and Burton, stems from her attraction to Burton or to Lyon. Gardner is depicted as an aging nymphomaniac, whose two hotel boys, Fidelman Duryan and Roberto Leyva, meet a number of her needs.

The offscreen conduct of cast and crew was almost as weird as the film itself. Burton's wife, Elizabeth Taylor, was on hand throughout the filming, sticking like glue to Burton's side, reportedly to make sure her husband's eyes didn't turn too far in Gardner's direction. Gardner, on the other hand, spent most of her time driving a sports car wildly through the surf along the beach. Director Huston cultivated paranoia by providing guns for the leading players with which to protect themselves from unknown dangers. Lyon, who began her career as the title character in LOLITA, was making her second film appearance chaperoned by her mother. Her movie life was, at best, erratic (TONY ROME, SEVEN WOMEN, etc.), and she later retired to become a teacher in Los Angeles. The iguana mentioned in the title refers to a long lizard that can be seen roaming the streets and hotels of Puerto Vallarta—and looks far more ferocious than it is.

NIGHT OF THE LIVING DEAD DVD
1968 90m bw Horror ★★★★
Image Ten (U.S.)

Judith O'Dea *(Barbara)*, Russell Streiner *(Johnny)*, Duane Jones *(Ben)*, Karl Hardman *(Harry Cooper)*, Keith Wayne *(Tom)*, Judith Ridley *(Judy)*, Marilyn Eastman *(Helen Cooper)*, Kyra Schon *(Karen)*, Bill Heinzman, Charles Craig

p, Russell Streiner, Karl Hardman; d, George Romero; w, John A. Russo (based on a story by Romero); ph, George Romero; ed, George Romero; prod d, Vincent Survinski; fx, Regis Survinski, Tony Pantanello

Pittsburgh-based industrial filmmaker George Romero gathered together a loyal cast and youthful crew from the local talent, scrounged up enough money to shoot on weekends, and made motion picture history. The first truly modern horror movie, NIGHT OF THE LIVING DEAD is the most influential work to emerge in the genre since PSYCHO. Despite mostly unprofessional acting, near nonexistent production values, homemade special effects, and cheap grainy black-and-white film stock, the film is a triumph. It's also a sign of its times—the era of the Vietnam War abroad and social upheaval at home—in which good does not triumph over evil, and likable people die just as brutally and unexpectedly as the despicable ones. The violence, which was extreme in its day, reflects the horrors Americans were seeing each night on the evening news, and patriarchal values and institutions are depicted in a critical manner. The horror movie would never be the same again.

Barbara (O'Dea) and her brother, Johnny (Streiner), have driven many miles at the behest of their mother to honor their dead father by placing a wreath on his grave. Neither is enthusiastic about the annual task. Johnny reminisces about how he used to frighten his sister when they were children. "They're coming to get you, Barbara!" he intones ominously in his best Boris Karloff fashion. Though now grown up and ostensibly too mature to be affected by such juvenile scare tactics, Barbara is still unnerved by her brother's creepy performance. Johnny sees an odd-looking fellow lurching unsteadily in the distance. "Look, there's one of them now!" The fun and games abruptly stop, however, when the weird man savagely grabs Barbara. Johnny leaps to his sister's defence but he's knocked down by the maniac. His head strikes a tombstone, apparently killing him. Barbara races for her life back to the car, leaps in, and discovers that the keys are in Johnny's pocket. The maniac bangs on the windows, desperate to get at her. Barbara releases the emergency brake and the car rolls down a hill away from her clumsy pursuer. She gets out and runs to an old farmhouse where she is soon joined by Ben (Jones), a young black man. Ben informs Barbara that the recently dead have been returning to life to eat the living. He sets

about fortifying the house by nailing boards over doors and windows, without much help from Barbara, who has gone into a semi-catatonic state.

Thus the stage is set for one of the most nightmarish films ever made, and one that's still hard to laugh off today. Things get a bit talky once all the characters gather in the farmhouse, but NIGHT OF THE LIVING DEAD grips in the manner of a good "Twilight Zone" episode. Produced for less than $150,000, the film was booked in a haphazard manner—rejected by Columbia because it wasn't in color and by American International Pictures because it had no romance and a downbeat ending—and turned up at kiddie matinees, scaring the daylights out of unprepared youngsters. NIGHT OF THE LIVING DEAD then found its niche on the midnight movie circuit and went on to become one of the most successful independent films of all time. Romero made two (far bloodier) sequels, DAWN OF THE DEAD and DAY OF THE DEAD; all three movies are essential viewing for horror fans.

NIGHT OF THE SHOOTING STARS, THE DVD
1981 106m c Drama/War ★★★
RAI-TV/Ager/Premier (Italy) R

Omero Antonutti *(Galvano)*, Margarita Lozano *(Concetta)*, Claudio Bigagli *(Corrado)*, Massimo Bonetti *(Nicole)*, Norma Martelli *(Ivana)*, Enrica Maria Modugno *(Mara)*, Sabina Vannucchi *(Rosanna)*, Dario Cantarelli *(Priest)*, Sergio Dagliana *(Olinto)*, Giuseppe Furia *(Requiem)*

p, Giuliani G. De Negri; d, Paolo Taviani, Vittorio Taviani; w, Vittorio Taviani, Paolo Taviani, Giuliani G. De Negri, Tonino Guerra; ph, Franco Di Giacomo (Agfacolor); ed, Roberto Perpignani; m, Nicola Piovani; art d, Gianni Sbarra

On the night of San Lorenzo (a magical evening during which many Europeans believe wishes may become fulfilled), a shooting star darts across the sky, sending a grown woman into a recollection of her childhood. As the star passes her window, she relates the events that took place in her small town during the last days of WWII: With the advancing Allies pushing the last remnants of the German army out of Italy, the Nazis enact sick and desperate revenge on the Italian civilians, staging vicious attacks on the old men, women, and children left in the villages. The members of the small town of San Miniato are divided in their opinions as to whether to remain in their village and risk dealing with the Germans, or to attempt traveling across the back roads, dodging attacks from sadistic Blackshirts, in an effort to meet the advancing Allies. One group made up of various segments of the town's population sets out on the journey, with all the old prohibitions breaking down as the people pull together in an effort to survive. An elderly peasant man with natural leadership ability is chosen to guide the group to safety. Despite a few voices of dissent, the old man brings ingenuity to his assignment and keeps the group's spirits up by showing a humane concern for all and encouraging them to watch out for one another. During the journey, he develops a romantic relationship with an aristocratic woman who has always admired him but could never let him know because of their difference in class. Once he has guided the group out of danger, however, the townspeople immediately resume the societal roles that previously divided them. The Taviani brothers, who gained international attention with 1977 Cannes Film Festival Golden Palm winner PADRE PADRONE, approached this film in much the same way as they did their earlier effort—using an imaginative combination of events and showing them as remembered by the narrator as she reminisces about the magical moments of her childhood—and came up with a dazzling, immensely popular film that earned them the Special Jury Prize at Cannes.

NIGHT ON EARTH

1992 130m c   Drama/Comedy   ★★★
Locus Solus/Black Snake Productions   (U.S.)   R

Gena Rowlands *(Victoria Snelling)*, Winona Ryder *(Corky)*, Armin Mueller-Stahl *(Helmut Grokenberger)*, Giancarlo Esposito *(YoYo)*, Rosie Perez *(Angela)*, Isaach de Bankole *(Driver)*, Beatrice Dalle *(Blind Woman)*, Roberto Benigni *(Gino)*, Paolo Bonacelli *(Priest)*, Matti Pellonpaa *(Mika)*

p, Jim Jarmusch; d, Jim Jarmusch; w, Jim Jarmusch; ph, Frederick Elmes; ed, Jay Rabinowitz; m, Tom Waits; cos, Magda Bava, Claire Fraisse, Alexandra Welker, Gordon Barbara

This global shaggy-dog story is director/writer/producer Jim Jarmusch's most accessible work to date. The film comprises five segments, each of which is set in a taxi, that take place simultaneously at different points around the globe. Starring a very cool collection of international actors, and directed by the king of the American alternative movie scene, these funny yet poignant stories could be described as joined at the hip.

    NIGHT ON EARTH begins at sunset on a winter's day in L.A., and then moves through nighttime in New York, Paris, Rome, and finally Helsinki, where the sun is rising as the last section comes to an end. The basic connection is the relationship between driver and passenger that each story explores, though the segments are also linked in other, less obvious, ways. As with the best short stories, the segments are less about plot—very little actually *happens*—than they are about character, dialogue, and mood. Jarmusch is a master of all these elements, and clearly has an intuitive rapport with his cast. The best of the actors—Giancarlo Esposito and Armin Mueller-Stahl in New York, Isaach de Bankole and Beatrice Dalle in Paris, Roberto Benigni in Rome, and Matti Pellonpaa in Helsinki—bring the proceedings to three-dimensional life, mining the script for laughs and even coaxing social and political overtones from Jarmusch's minimalist writing. On a purely visual level, the casting choices are inspired. De Bankole, as a brusque, defensive Ivory Coast native transplanted to Paris, has a face that radiates sullen pride; and Pellonpaa, who subdues a cabful of Helsinki drunks with a story that moves the film from comedy into elegy, has a hang-dog expression that cannot be rivalled. All this is perfectly complemented by the director's moody evocation of the five night-shrouded urban settings. The film's only low points come courtesy of Winona Ryder, who unforgivably mugs her way through the glib first segment; and Rosie Perez, whose high-pitched whining in the New York section reminds you what it's like to be trapped in a cab with a driver who won't shut up.

NIGHT TO REMEMBER, A   *DVD*

1958 123m bw Disaster   ★★★★
Rank (U.K.)

Kenneth More *(Herbert Lightoller)*, Ronald Allen *(Clarke)*, Robert Ayres *(Peuchen)*, Honor Blackman *(Mrs. Lucas)*, Anthony Bushell *(Capt. Rostron)*, John Cairney *(Murphy)*, Jill Dixon *(Mrs. Clarke)*, Jane Downs *(Mrs. Lightoller)*, James Dyrenforth *(Col. Gracie)*, Michael Goodliffe *(Thomas Andrews)*

p, William McQuitty; d, Roy Ward Baker; w, Eric Ambler (based on the book by Walter Lord); ph, Geoffrey Unsworth; ed, Sidney Hayers; m, William Alwyn; art d, Alex Vetchinsky; cos, Yvonne Caffin

A NIGHT TO REMEMBER treats in brilliant, semi-documentary style the night of April 14, 1912, when the lux-

ury liner *Titanic* struck an iceberg and sank, taking 1,513 passengers and crew members (out of a total complement of 2,224 on board) to the bottom of the ocean on the fifth day of her maiden voyage from Southampton to New York. Although Kenneth More is ostensibly the star, this multi-layered production boasts more than 200 speaking parts. Sticking pretty closely to the facts, Baker and Ambler have constructed a startling drama, uncluttered by fictional sub-plots. Made for a mere $1,680,000, A NIGHT TO REMEMBER looks much more expensive, with superb costumes and sets. Though far superior to Fox's TITANIC of 1953, this critically acclaimed film met with only lukewarm box-office support.

NIGHT TRAIN TO MUNICH   *DVD*

1940 90m bw Spy/War   ★★★★
Gaumont (U.K.)

Margaret Lockwood *(Anna Bomasch)*, Rex Harrison *(Gus Bennett)*, Paul Henreid *(Karl Marsen)*, Basil Radford *(Charters)*, Naunton Wayne *(Caldicott)*, James Harcourt *(Axel Bomasch)*, Felix Aylmer *(Dr. John Fredericks)*, Wyndham Goldie *(Dryton)*, Roland Culver *(Roberts)*, Eliot Makeham *(Schwab)*

p, Edward Black; d, Carol Reed; w, Sydney Gilliat, Frank Launder (based on a story by Gordon Wellesley); ph, Otto Kanturek; ed, R.E. Dearing; art d, Alex Vetchinsky

AAN Best Original Story: Gordon Wellesley

One of the finest spy films ever, NIGHT TRAIN reflects the immense talents of its brilliant director, Carol Reed, and of scripters Frank Launder and Sydney Gilliat. After Hitler's conquest of Czechoslovakia, Anna Bomasch (Margaret Lockwood) is arrested. Her father, Axel (James Harcourt), who possesses technical information the Nazis want, has fled to England, but Anna is interred in a concentration camp. There, she meets Karl Marsen (Paul Henreid), with whom she manages to escape to England, and in London she contacts music hall performer Gus Bennett (Rex Harrison)—who is actually a British secret agent—to get in touch with her father. In short order the Bomasches, duped by Marsen—who is himself a Gestapo plant—are taken to Germany, where the Nazis threaten Anna to secure Axel's cooperation. Bennett follows, infiltrates the Naval Ministry in Berlin, and discovers that the Bomasches are on the night train to Munich. With the help of two comedic cricketers played by Naunton Wayne and Basil Radford (who performed the same service in Alfred Hitchcock's THE LADY VANISHES), Bennett boards the train and is able to free father and daughter, leading to the trio's final flight to Switzerland, with Marsen and the SS in hot pursuit. Though action-packed with one harrowing scene after another, the film is not broadly played, and Reed employs subtlety over bravado. Its portrayal of the Germans, too, is fairly balanced, without the propagandistic characterizations that would mark films made later in the war. Harrison is perfect as the daring, suave British spy; Lockwood is fine as his love interest; and Henried is appropriately subtle as the deceiving Marsen in this gripping, razor-edged melodrama that mounts to a stunning climax.

NIGHTHAWKS   *DVD*

1981 99m c   Crime   ★★★½
Universal (U.S.)   R

Sylvester Stallone *(Deke DaSilva)*, Billy Dee Williams *(Matthew Fox)*, Lindsay Wagner *(Irene)*, Persis Khambatta *(Shakka)*, Nigel Davenport *(Peter Hartman)*, Rutger Hauer *(Wulfgar)*, Hilarie

Thompson *(Pam)*, Joe Spinell *(Lt. Munafo)*, Walter Mathews *(Commissioner)*, E. Brian Dean *(Sergeant)*

p, Martin Poll; d, Bruce Malmuth; w, David Shaber (based on a story by David Shaber and Paul Sylbert); ph, James A. Contner (Technicolor); ed, Christopher Holmes; m, Keith Emerson; prod d, Peter Larkin; fx, Ed Drohan, Walter Tatro, Dick Smith, Nick Allder; cos, Robert DeMora, John Falabella

---

Deke DaSilva (Sylvester Stallone) and Matthew Fox (Billy Dee Williams) are New York cops assigned to track down terrorist Wulfgar (Rutger Hauer). In London, Wulfgar planted a bomb in a London department store, killing several children and incurring the wrath of terrorist leaders. He resumes his career with financing from Shakka (Persis Khambatta). Soon DaSilva and Wulfgar are engaged in a violent battle of wits, while DaSilva struggles to save his marriage to Irene (Lindsay Wagner). This very effective thriller features a chilling performance by Hauer as the emotionless killing machine. Stallone and Williams are also credible, and the film makes good use of its New York locations.

NIGHTMARE ALLEY   📀

1947 111m bw Crime   ★★★★
Fox   (U.S.)

Tyrone Power *(Stanton Carlisle)*, Joan Blondell *(Zeena)*, Coleen Gray *(Molly)*, Helen Walker *(Dr. Lilith Ritter)*, Taylor Holmes *(Ezra Grindle)*, Mike Mazurki *(Bruno)*, Ian Keith *(Pete)*, Julia Dean *(Mrs. Peabody)*, James Flavin *(Clem Hoatley)*, Roy Roberts *(McGraw)*

p, George Jessel; d, Edmund Goulding; w, Jules Furthman (based on the novel by William Lindsay Gresham); ph, Lee Garmes; ed, Barbara McLean; m, Cyril J. Mockridge; art d, Lyle Wheeler, J. Russell Spencer; fx, Fred Sersen; cos, Bonnie Cashin

Power is simply terrific as Stanton Carlisle, a sideshow hustler who makes it to the big time through underhanded methods that ultimately bring about his horrific ruination. Carlisle gets a menial job with a cheap carnival and becomes fascinated with a mind-reading act performed by Pete and Zeena (Keith and Blondell). Becoming the show's barker, Carlisle entices carnival patrons to another attraction as well: an illegal geek show featuring a "half-man, half-beast" who works in a pit and bites the heads off live chickens. Here the geek is a fallen carney performer, a dipsomaniac who conducts his ghastly routines so he can be paid off with a quart of booze each evening. In no time, Carlisle is made a part of the mind-reading act; plying Pete with friendship and liquor, he later replaces the older man in the act after accidentally giving him some poisonous wood alcohol. Carlisle then seduces Zeena into recreating with him a more spectacular version of the act which relies on a secret word code which enables the spiritualist to discern the questions Carlisle has gathered from patrons in the audience. Molly (Gray), a pretty sideshow artist, falls for Carlisle, who, incurring the wrath of the carnival people, marries the girl and moves to Chicago. A successful nightclub artist there, he fascinates Lilith (Walker), a sultry psychologist who agrees to give him confidential information about her wealthy clients in return for a substantial cut of the take. Molly, however, finds it increasingly hard to bilk people, and Lilith discovers some damning information about Carlisle from Zeena.

Although it could not include all the terrifying detail of Gresham's shocking novel, Furthman's script potently reveals the sleazy world of the spiritual con artist. Carefully constructing Power's rise and fall, director Goulding is merciless in his inspection of a character who is rotten through and through.

Power, who had Fox buy the rights of the novel for him, gives the performance of his career, proving that he was not merely a matinee idol but a player who could dig deep inside himself and produce a memorable and telling characterization. Goulding was then Power's favorite director; they had worked together in the worthy 1946 adaptation of Somerset Maugham's THE RAZOR'S EDGE. Goulding was noted for eliciting excellent performances from his actors, as he did in GRAND HOTEL, DARK VICTORY, THE GREAT LIE, and CLAUDIA.

Walker is a standout as the cold-blooded psychologist and Blondell excels as the frowzy but calculating spritualist, the essence of cheapness. Gray is also fine as the stupid but loving wife who can forgive any crime. Mockridge's score is eerie and perfectly suited to the shadowy images captured in Garmes's photography.

NIGHTMARE ON ELM STREET, A   📀

1984 91m c Horror   ★★★½
New Line   (U.S.)   R

John Saxon *(Lt. Thompson)*, Ronee Blakley *(Marge Thompson)*, Heather Langenkamp *(Nancy Thompson)*, Amanda Wyss *(Tina Gray)*, Nick Corri *(Rod Lane)*, Johnny Depp *(Glen Lantz)*, Robert Englund *(Fred Krueger)*, Charles Fleischer *(Dr. King)*, Joseph Whipp *(Sgt. Parker)*, Mimi Meyer-Craven *(Nurse)*

p, Robert Shaye, Sara Risher; d, Wes Craven; w, Wes Craven; ph, Jacques Haitkin (Deluxe Color); ed, Rick Shaine; m, Charles Bernstein; prod d, Gregg Fonseca; fx, Jim Doyle; cos, Dana Lyman

"One, two; Freddy's comin' for you/Three, four; better lock your door/Five, six; grab your crucifix/Seven, eight; gonna stay up late/Nine, ten; never sleep again."

A NIGHTMARE ON ELM STREET, one of the most intelligent and terrifying horror films of the 1980s, begins and ends with this haunting children's song. This was the film that introduced the world to Freddy Krueger, the horribly scarred man with the ragged slouch hat, dirty red-and-green striped sweater, and metal gloves with knives at the tips. Freddy (Robert Englund), a genius of a monster who exists in his victims' dreams and preys on them in the vulnerability of sleep, has returned to the town where years before he was burnt alive as a child killer by locals who took the law into their own hands. Now he's back to take revenge on their kids. In an era in which the horror film has become little more than a mindless exercise in gratuitous high-tech bloodletting, A NIGHTMARE ON ELM STREET (like most of Wes Craven's films) brought some hope to those concerned about the fate of the genre. This movie intelligently probes into the audience's terror of nightmares and combines it with another horrific element—the very real fear of killers in one's own neighborhood. The teenagers in the film, who are paying for the sins of their parents, are not simply fodder for the special-effects crew but have distinct personalities and are independent and intelligent. The initial success of the movie was based on the audience's insecurity: we are never sure whether the characters are dreaming because the line between nightmare and reality is blurred, and, as a result, the terror is almost nonstop. The success of the sequels, while still based in the dream-versus-reality premise, has become increasingly dependent on the heroic pose of Freddy Krueger, played with energy and humor by Robert Englund.

NIGHTS OF CABIRIA   📀

(LE NOTTI DI CABIRIA)
1957 110m bw Drama   ★★★★
De Laurentiis Cinematografica/Les Films Marceau
(Italy/France)

Giulietta Masina *(Cabiria)*, Francois Perier *(Oscar D'Onofrio—Accountant)*, Amedeo Nazzari *(Alberto Lazzari—Movie Star)*,

Aldo Silvana *(Hypnotist)*, Franca Marzi *(Wanda—Cabiria's Friend)*, Dorian Gray *(Jessy—Lazzari's Girlfriend)*, Mario Passante *(Cripple in the "Miracle" Sequence)*, Pina Gualandri *(Matilda the Prostitute)*, Polidor *(The Monk)*, Ennio Girolami

p, Dino De Laurentiis; d, Federico Fellini; w, Federico Fellini, Ennio Flaiano, Tullio Pinelli, Pier Paolo Pasolini; ph, Aldo Tonti, Otello Martelli; ed, Leo Catozzo; m, Nino Rota; art d, Piero Gherardi; cos, Piero Gherardi

AA Best Foreign Language Film

Giulietta Masina's finest hour, and perhaps husband Federico Fellini's as well. NIGHTS OF CABIRIA lacks the lyrical simplicity that made LA STRADA such a magical experience, but is an impressive enough display of Fellini's fascinating visual style to have warranted the Academy Award for Best Foreign-Language Film. Set in a district on the outskirts of Rome, the film focuses on Cabiria (Masina), a near-perfect embodiment of the prostitute with a heart of gold. She's the type who understands misfortune to be part and parcel of life, but never loses faith in the value of life itself. When misfortune does come her way, Cabiria shrugs it off and continues walking the streets for money. A handsome movie star picks her up during a brawl with his girlfriend. He takes her to his fabulous home, but quickly discards her when he is through with her services. Eventually someone does fall in love with Cabiria—the shy and withdrawn Oscar D'Onofrio (Francois Perier)—or at least she believes this to be the case. Perhaps the most difficult aspect of NIGHTS OF CABIRIA is accepting Masina as a prostitute: this sweet and naive-looking woman, who stole audiences' hearts with her childlike innocence in LA STRADA, isn't at all typical of women selling themselves on the streets, but does express the dismal point that fate makes no exceptions. Her Cabiria is a sucker for a sob story, and this very flaw gives her a saving grace. As in the majority of Fellini's films, the emphasis here is on visual elements rather than on straight narrative form, relying on small details and eccentricities to breathe life into Cabiria. The film was the basis for the Broadway and film version of *Sweet Charity*.

NINE TO FIVE   DVD
1980 110m c   Comedy   ★★★
IPC   (U.S.)   PG

Jane Fonda *(Judy Bernly)*, Lily Tomlin *(Violet Newstead)*, Dolly Parton *(Doralee Rhodes)*, Dabney Coleman *(Franklin Hart, Jr.)*, Sterling Hayden *(Tinsworthy)*, Elizabeth Wilson *(Roz)*, Henry Jones *(Hinkle)*, Lawrence Pressman *(Dick)*, Marian Mercer *(Missy Hart)*, Ren Woods *(Barbara)*

p, Bruce Gilbert; d, Colin Higgins; w, Colin Higgins, Patricia Resnick (based on a story by Patricia Resnick); ph, Reynaldo Villalobos (Deluxe Color); ed, Pembroke J. Herring; m, Charles Fox; prod d, Dean Edward Mitzner; art d, Jack G. Taylor Jr.; fx, Chuck Gaspar, Matt Sweeney; cos, Ann Roth

AAN Best Original Song: "9 to 5"; Dolly Parton (Music & Lyrics)

Recently divorced Jane Fonda takes an office job and soon becomes pals with fellow secretaries Dolly Parton (in a sensational movie debut) and Lily Tomlin. Their boss is male chauvinist Dabney Coleman, who is trying to land Parton in bed. While smoking dope one night the women hatch a plan to take revenge on their cruel boss. Lots of laughs, little sense, and pure fantasy. Produced by Fonda's company, NINE TO FIVE is an amusing way to spend 110 minutes, but hardly memorable. Later made into a short-lived TV series. The title song received an Oscar nomination.

1918   DVD
1985 91m   c   Drama   ★★★½
Guadalupe (U.S.)

William Converse-Roberts *(Horace Robedaux)*, Hallie Foote *(Elizabeth Robedaux)*, Rochelle Oliver *(Mrs. Vaughn)*, Michael Higgens *(Mr. Vaughn)*, Matthew Broderick *(Brother)*, Jeanne McCarthy *(Bessie)*, Bill McGhee *(Sam)*, L.T. Felty *(Mr. Thatcher)*, Horton Foote Jr. *(Jessie)*, Tom Murrel *(Stanley)*

p, Lillian V. Foote, Ross Milloy; d, Ken Harrison; w, Horton Foote (based on his play); ph, George Tirl (Duart Color); ed, Leon Seith; art d, Michael O'Sullivan; cos, Van Broughton Ramsey

This thoughtful and carefully detailed story examines life on the WWI homefront in a rural Texas town that, in its own way, is forever changed by the war's far-reaching effects. Horace (William Converse-Roberts) and Elizabeth Robedaux (Hallie Foote) are a young married couple with an eight-month-old daughter. Their home, where much of the film's action takes place, has been paid for by Elizabeth's wealthy parents (Michael Higgins, Rochelle Oliver), who exert a domineering influence over the two. Horace has claimed he would fight in the war if he could be assured his wife and baby would be properly taken care of. His father-in-law promises to care for the family and leaves Horace no excuse. Elizabeth is furious with her husband and father, but matters take a sudden turn when the flu epidemic sweeps the country. 1918 is a multilayered work that delves deeply into the complexities of its characters and how they cope with the encroaching specter of death both at home and abroad. Foote gives a strong central performance that anchors the film with honest, deeply felt emotions. The screenplay, by her father, Horton Foote, is based on family experiences. The direction by Ken Harrison is thoughtful, allowing the events to unfold naturally in long takes. The small moments of everyday life are as prominent as the war in Europe, an important factor 1918 reflects with care and intelligence, complemented by its exact period detail.

1984   DVD
1984 117m c   Drama/Science Fiction ★★★
Umbrella/Rosenblum/Virgin (U.K.)   R

John Hurt *(Winston Smith)*, Richard Burton *(O'Brien)*, Suzanna Hamilton *(Julia)*, Cyril Cusack *(Charrington)*, Gregor Fisher *(Parsons)*, James Walker *(Syme)*, Andrew Wilde *(Tillotson)*, David Trevena *(Tillotson's Friend)*, David Cann *(Martin)*, Anthony Benson *(Jones)*

p, Simon Perry; d, Michael Radford; w, Michael Radford, Jonathan Gems (based on the novel by George Orwell); ph, Roger Deakins (Eastmancolor); ed, Tom Priestley; m, The Eurythmics, Dominic Muldowney; prod d, Allan Cameron; art d, Martyn Hebert, Grant Hicks; cos, Emma Porteous

In this admirable attempt at bringing George Orwell's classic novel to the screen, director Michael Radford is perhaps too faithful to his source material. This is the well-known story of Winston Smith (John Hurt), a citizen of Oceania whose job it is to rewrite history for Big Brother, the autocratic symbol of a repressive regime that has forbidden such things as freedom of thought and expression—including sex. Winston becomes involved in an illict love affair with Julia (Suzanna Hamilton), a young woman who works in the Ministry of Truth. Unfortunately for Winston, a high-ranking member of the government, O'Brien (Richard Burton), who has looked upon him as a protege, discovers the rebellion. Orwell wrote his novel in 1948, and his vision of the future is unrelentingly bleak. Radford chooses to present a view of the future as it might have looked to Orwell in 1948. This is not a future made up of colorful blinking lights and high-tech manufacturing; it is a gray, dull, stark, depressing world possessed of little visual stimulation. The performances in the film are excellent, and its look is entirely appropriate and mesmerizing—but only for a while. The basic flaw in 1984 is that it is just too painful, too depressing, and too slow to watch.

1900

(NOVECENTO)

1976 245m c   Drama/Historical   ★★½
TCF/PEA/Artistes Associes/Artemis   (Italy)   R

Burt Lancaster *(Alfredo Berlinghieri—the Grandfather)*, Romolo Valli *(Giovanni)*, Anna-Maria Gherardi *(Eleonora)*, Laura Betti *(Regina)*, Robert De Niro *(Alfredo Berlinghieri— the Grandson)*, Paolo Pavesi *(Alfredo as a Child)*, Dominique Sanda *(Ada)*, Sterling Hayden *(Leo Dalco)*, Gerard Depardieu *(Olmo Dalco)*, Roberto Maccanti *(Olmo as a Child)*

p, Alberto Grimaldi; d, Bernardo Bertolucci; w, Franco Arcalli, Bernardo Bertolucci, Giuseppe Bertolucci; ph, Vittorio Storaro (Technicolor); ed, Franco Arcalli; m, Ennio Morricone; art d, Ezio Frigerio; cos, Gitt Magrini

Like a delicious pasta salad, ruined with intermittent slabs of Velveeta cheese. It's the portable Bernardo Bertolucci film, but it's too heavy to lift. The director wanted to make a collective-memory, "popular" film— there's no denying some brilliant, definitive moments in this left-wing homage to peasant life—if that's your thing. But somewhere Bertolucci got popular culture confused with pulp. Sometimes, this looks like animated Harold Robbins.

1900 captures everything that characterizes the director: his concern with the class dialectic and the battle between Marxism and Fascism, his painterly images of Italy, his historical scope, and his "divided hero" (to borrow a phrase from critic Robin Wood). While it may be a masterpiece at its original length of 320 minutes, 1900's American, British, and videocassette release is a shortened, somewhat erratic 245-minute version. The plot is about as grand and baroque as one can get, entailing the history of the Italian people and politics in the first half of the 1900s, from the organization of the peasant class to the rise of socialism to the fall of Fascism. This political dialectic is personified in Bertolucci's two central characters (the "divided hero"), Alfredo (Robert De Niro), born into a bourgeois clan of landowners, and Olmo (Gerard Depardieu), born into a peasant family, who share the same birthday, January 27, 1901 (the day Verdi died, another point of homage). Although they grow up the best of friends, their friendship turns into a love/hate relationship. As an adult, the weak Alfredo is put in charge of his family's property but is merely a puppet controlled by his evil foreman, Attila (Donald Sutherland), while the Marxist Olmo becomes a leading union organizer. Even in its shortened version, 1900 is an achievement of considerable genius, directed by Bertolucci but made possible by the combined efforts of collaborator-cinematographer Vittorio Storaro, composer Ennio Morricone, art director Enzo Frigerio, costumer Gitt Magrini, and a phenomenal cast that includes an international Who's Who of performers. But if this were an American work would we be so impressed?

NINOTCHKA

1939 110m bw Comedy   ★★★★★
MGM   (U.S.)

Greta Garbo *(Lena Yakushova, "Ninotchka")*, Melvyn Douglas *(Count Leon Dolga)*, Ina Claire *(Grand Duchess Swana)*, Sig Rumann *(Michael Ironoff)*, Felix Bressart *(Buljanoff)*, Alexander Granach *(Kopalski)*, Bela Lugosi *(Commissar Razinin)*, Gregory Gaye *(Count Alexis Rakonin)*, Richard Carle *(Vaston)*, Edwin Maxwell *(Mercier)*

p, Ernst Lubitsch; d, Ernst Lubitsch; w, Charles Brackett, Billy Wilder, Walter Reisch (based on a story by Melchior Lengyel); ph, William Daniels; ed, Gene Ruggiero; m, Werner R. Heymann; art d, Cedric Gibbons, Randall Duell; cos, Adrian

AAN Best Picture; AAN Best Actress: Greta Garbo; AAN Best Original Story: Melchior Lengyel; AAN Best Screenplay: Charles Brackett, Walter Reisch, Billy Wilder

Garbo laughs. So read the advertising for the star's first outright comedy, and it brilliantly sums up the appeal of this remarkable film. Director Ernst Lubitsch has the actress gracefully step down from her pedestal as the stern Communist who warms to the appeal of Paris champagne and playboy Melvyn Douglas. Combining farce, romance and satire, yet still maintaining moments of that soaring Garbo intensity, NINOTCHKA is special indeed.

When three Soviet emissaries (Bressart, Rumann, Granach, whose work could not possibly be bettered) arrive in Paris on a mission, it's not long before Paris arrives on them instead. And so, super efficient Comrade Ninotchka (Garbo) appears to retrieve jewelry in the possession of the former Grand Duchess Swana (Claire). It is the Soviet government's contention that the property of the aristocrats properly belongs to the people. The two women's tussle over the goods becomes complicated, however, when Swana's swain Leon (Douglas) becomes infatuated with the frosty commissar.

Many of Garbo's films rely on her presence alone for their appeal. That's not the case here. Working from a brittle, witty script by no less than Wilder, Brackett, and Reisch, the gifted Lubitsch brings his patented "touch" to scene after scene. From the bumbling emissaries' arithmetic about ringing for hotel maids to Ninotchka's hilarious "execution scene" the film bubbles merrily throughout. Garbo rarely had a paramour as adroit as Douglas, who wears a dinner jacket with the flair of Astaire and the polish of Powell. He plays the gushy romantic dialogue early on with the perfect combination of conviction and playfulness, and one of the film's beauties is watching Garbo shift gears into this mode herself. The lovely scene in a cafe where Douglas cracks Ninotchka up only when he falls off his chair remains a highlight of both film comedy and screen romance.

An adroit satire of both Communism and capitalism, NINOTCHKA still manages a healthy heartiness and a sweet sadness. Its success inspired pallid imitations from COMRADE X with Lamarr and Gable to THE IRON PETTICOAT with Hepburn and Hope. A musical remake, SILK STOCKINGS, featured some good Fred Astaire-Cyd Charisse dancing and a show-stealing turn by Janis Paige, but had little sparkle and even less depth. Garbo would attempt, but fail, to repeat this film's magic with her next, TWO-FACED WOMAN, with George Cukor (at one point slated for NINOTCHKA) directing.

NIXON

1995 190m c/bw   Drama/Biography/Political ★★½
Cinergi Productions/Illusion Entertainment   R
Group/Hollywood Pictures   (U.S.)

Anthony Hopkins *(Richard M. Nixon)*, Joan Allen *(Pat Nixon)*, Powers Boothe *(Alexander Haig)*, Ed Harris *(E. Howard Hunt)*, Bob Hoskins *(J. Edgar Hoover)*, E.G. Marshall *(John Mitchell)*, David Paymer *(Ron Ziegler)*, David Hyde Pierce *(John Dean)*, Paul Sorvino *(Henry Kissinger)*, Mary Steenburgen *(Hannah Nixon)*

p, Clayton Townsend, Oliver Stone, Andrew G. Vajna; d, Oliver Stone; w, Stephen J. Rivele, Christopher Wilkinson, Oliver Stone; ph, Robert Richardson; ed, Brian Berdan, Hank Corwin; m, John Williams; prod d, Victor Kempster; art d, Donald Woodruff, Richard Mays, Margery Zweizig; fx, F. Lee Stone, Peter Kuran, Christer Hokanson, Chris Loudon; cos, Richard Hornung

AAN Best Actor: Anthony Hopkins; *AAN Best Supporting Actress:* Joan Allen; *AAN Best Original Screenplay:* Stephen J. Rivele, Christopher Wilkinson, Oliver Stone; *AAN Best Dramatic Score:* John Williams

A lurching, addlebrained biopic that lacks even the crackpot energy of JFK, Oliver Stone's NIXON struggles to invest its nakedly venal subject with tragic dignity.

Even more than NATURAL BORN KILLERS, it's offered as a Big Statement: We're meant to see Nixon as a flawed but quintessentially *American* figure, to understand (and rationalize) his criminal foibles as a disturbing reflection of our own dark side. What's *really* disturbing—if not precisely surprising—is how closely Stone identifies with his brooding, paranoid antihero. Anthony Hopkins, miscast in the title role, gives the kind of self-consciously hammy performance that automatically qualifies for an Oscar nomination; Joan Allen is a one-dimensional Pat.

One's appreciation of the screenplay (by Stephen J. Rivele, Christopher Wilkinson, and Stone) will probably depend on one's familiarity with real events. Opening and closing on the ill-starred President's "final days," NIXON loops back and forth through well-trodden historical ground (the Checkers speech, the Nixon-Kennedy debates, the Hiss case, etc.), semi-factual elaborations of little-known events (Nixon's strict Quaker upbringing in Whittier, California, his marital woes), and outright fabrications (a sinister meeting with Hoover at the racetrack, a blackmail attempt by an imaginary Texas power broker played by Larry Hagman, TV's J.R. Ewing). All of it is refracted through Stone's peculiar penchant for seeing diabolical connections everywhere. In this case, a link is made between Nixon's supposed involvement in the Bay of Pigs invasion and his ultimate vulnerability to the "military-industrial complex." Ironically, the film posits a nutty theory of the Kennedy assassination that is completely inconsistent with the equally nutty theory offered in Stone's JFK.

NO GREATER GLORY

1934 117m bw Drama   ★★★★
Columbia   (U.S.)

George Breakston *(Nemecsek)*, Jimmy Butler *(Boka)*, Jackie Searl *(Gereb)*, Frankie Darro *(Feri Ats)*, Donald Haines *(Csonakos)*, Rolf Ernest *(Ferdie Pasztor)*, Julius Molnar *(Henry Pasztor)*, Wesley Giraud *(Kolnay)*, Beaudine Anderson *(Csele)*, Bruce Line *(Richter)*

d, Frank Borzage; w, Jo Swerling (based on the novel *The Paul Street Boys* by Ferenc Molnar); ph, Joseph August; ed, Viola Lawrence

This is a fine and honest film with excellent performances by its youthful cast. George Breakston plays a frail youngster

who idolizes gang leader Jimmy Butler. The gang is modeled after an army, complete with uniforms and a flag. Breakston's ill health makes him something of an outcast, but he is allowed to join up as a private, the only enlisted soldier in an army otherwise composed of officers. Butler despises him for his weakness, but Breakston cannot see this, so great is his admiration and his need to belong. When their flag is stolen by a rival gang of older boys called "The Red Shirts," Breakston takes it upon himself to retrieve the banner. He invades the enemy camp in a driving rain and confronts their leader Frankie Darro, who repeatedly shoves the younger boy's head under water. Darro cannot break the boy's spirit and gradually comes to respect his pluck. Breakston catches pneumonia and is forced to remain in bed but, when he learns that Butler's gang is taking on the Red Shirts, he sneaks off to join the battle. The excitement is too much for him and he dies fighting for his cause. Butler, realizing the true meaning of strength and courage, tearfully watches as Breakston's mother carries away the limp body of her son.

Breakston is all heart and innocent emotion, the epitome of admiring, loyal youth. Butler, whose career was tragically cut short by his death in World War II, is equally fine. His portrayal of the handsome, serious-minded idol is believable and moving. This film also serves as an allegory of the futility of war and what it does to the best of men. The film is based on an autobiographical novel by noted Hungarian playwright Ferenc Molnar. Sensitive adaptation and direction bring out the honesty and spirit of the book.

NO MAN'S LAND

2001 98m   c   War   ★★★★
Counihan Villiers Productions/Fabrica Cinema/   R
Man's Films/Noe Productions/Studio Maj/Casablanca
(Bosnia-Herzegovina/Belgium/France/Italy/U.K.)

Branko Djuric *(Tchiki)*, Rene Bitorajac *(Nino)*, Filip Sovagovic *(Tsera)*, Georges Siatidis *(Marchand)*, Serge-Henri Valcke *(Dubois)*, Sacha Kremer *(Michel)*, Simon Callow *(Soft)*, Alain Eloy *(Pierre)*, Katrin Cartlidge *(Jane Livingstone)*, Tanja Ribic *(Martha)*

p, Marc Baschet, Frederique Dumas-Zajdela, Cedomir Kolar; d, Danis Tanovic; w, Danis Tanovic; ph, Walther Vanden Ende; ed, Francesca Calvelli; m, Danis Tanovic; fx, Jean-Claude Calais, Olivier De Laveleye, Marie Pierre Franck, Darko Njavro, Pierrot Planckaert; cos, Zvonka Makuc

AA Best Foreign Language Film

The winner of the 2001 Best Foreign Film is a bare-knuckled, absurdly comic, and at times unbearably tense look back at the madness of the Balkan conflict.

Bosnia, 1993: A lost Bosnian relief squad awakes to find itself mere yards from the Serbian front line. Most of the squad is killed in the ensuing melee, but a shell from a Serbian tank blows Tchiki (Branko Djuric), a scruffy soldier in a Rolling Stones T-shirt, into the temporary safety of an abandoned trench in the no man's land separating the Serbian and Bosnian fronts. A Serb commander orders Nino (Rene Bitorajac), an inexperienced recruit, and an older officer to search for survivors. Once inside the trench, the officer has an idea: he takes an American-made "bouncing" mine and buries it under the body of Tsera (Filip Sovagovic), one of Tchiki's fallen comrades. Now if anyone moves the body, the mine will detonate. No sooner is this nasty booby trap rigged than Tchiki bursts out of hiding, killing the older Serb but only wounding Nino. They quickly fall to bickering over which side started the war, but soon have a far more pressing problem on their hands: Tsera is still very much alive, but if he moves even the slightest bit, he'll blow them all to pieces.

Other films have used the classic stalemate situation to express the no-win absurdity of the Bosnian war, but writer-director Danis Tanovic casts a wider net, taking to task the United Nations Protection Force for its "neutrality" and international media vultures for their by-any-means-necessary approach to newsgathering. The film, which start's out like HELL IN THE PACIFIC, unexpectedly becomes ACE IN THE HOLE and ends on a cruel, cynical note that would surely make Billy Wilder snort with approval.

NO TIME FOR SERGEANTS

1958 111m bw Comedy   ★★★½
Warner Bros.   (U.S.)

Andy Griffith (Will Stockdale), Myron McCormick (Sgt. King), Nick Adams (Ben Whitledge), Murray Hamilton (Irvin Blanchard), Howard Smith (Gen. Bush), Will Hutchins (Lt. Bridges), Sydney Smith (Gen. Pollard), James Millhollin (Psychiatrist), Don Knotts (Manual Dexterity Corporal), Jean Willes (WAF Captain)

p, Mervyn LeRoy; d, Mervyn LeRoy; w, John Lee Mahin (based on the play by Ira Levin from the novel by Mac Hyman); ph, Harold Rosson; ed, William Ziegler; m, Ray Heindorf; art d, Malcolm Brown; fx, Louis Lichtenfield

Mac Hyman's hilarious novel, which then became a TV special, which then became a Broadway smash (script by Ira Levin), now comes to the screen with all of the fun intact. Andy Griffith played the role on TV and the stage and gets his chance to show how humorous he is in this, his second film, after a sensational debut in A FACE IN THE CROWD. He's a Georgia backwoods boy who is inducted into the peacetime Air Force when his country sends him "Greetings." His sergeant is McCormick (also repeating his Broadway role), a man who thinks that being in the service is a fine way to spend one's life, as long as nobody creates a ruckus. But that's exactly what Griffith does, as his warm naivete and questioning ways throw a monkey wrench into the sedate peacetime service. It's an episodic farce with one bright scene after another and some terrific acting by everyone. Griffith is sent to psychiatrist Millhollin and totally confounds the doctor. After he and Adams fall out of a plane and are posted as "missing, presumed dead," they turn up at their own funeral in a scene reminiscent of Mark Twain's *Tom Sawyer*.

The film is clearly the inspiration for TV's much cruder "Gomer Pyle." Note Don Knotts and veteran Benny Baker in small roles, as well as a man who went on to star in TV's M*A*S*H after he changed his name from Jameel Farah to Jamie Farr.

NO WAY OUT   DVD

1987 114m c   Crime/Thriller   ★★★
Neufeld, Ziskin, Garland   (U.S.)   R

Kevin Costner (Lt. Cmdr. Tom Farrell), Gene Hackman (David Brice), Sean Young (Susan Atwell), Will Patton (Scott Pritchard), Howard Duff (Sen. Willy Duvall), George Dzundza (Dr. Sam Hesselman), Jason Bernard (Maj. Donovan), Iman (Nina Beka), Fred Dalton Thompson (Marshall), Leon Russom (Kevin O'Brien)

p, Laura Ziskin, Robert Garland; d, Roger Donaldson; w, Robert Garland (based on the novel The Big Clock by Kenneth Fearing); ph, John Alcott (Metrocolor); ed, Neil Travis; m, Maurice Jarre; prod d, J. Dennis Washington, Kai Hawkins; art d, Anthony Brockliss; fx, Jack Monroe, Terry Frazee, Ken Durey

Kevin Costner displays some charisma, for once, in a twisty, stylish espionage thriller. Tom Farrell (Costner) is a Naval officer working in the Pentagon who discovers that his lover, Susan (Young), is also the mistress of his boss, Secretary of Defense Brice (Hackman). When Brice arrives unexpectedly at Susan's lavish duplex, Tom sneaks out a side door, and although Brice sees Tom in the dark street outside, he cannot identify him. Brice then explodes

with jealousy, and he and Susan get into a fierce argument that leads to Susan's accidental fall over a railing to her death. A shaken Brice returns to his offices in the Pentagon and there seeks the help of another aide, the ruthlessly ambitious Scott Prichard (Patton), who goes to Susan's duplex, wipes away fingerprints, and removes all traces of his boss. Next, to throw off investigators, he introduces a theory that the killer is a KGB mole long rumored to be operating in the Pentagon. Ironically, Tom, who knows that Brice is the real culprit, is then put in charge of ferreting out the fictitious enemy agent. A worthy remake of the film noir classic THE BIG CLOCK, NO WAY OUT adds, among other things, a delightfully subversive twist ending. Good performances from a strong cast.

NOBODY'S FOOL   DVD

1994 110m c   Drama   ★★★½
Skillet Pictures/Scott Rudin Productions/Cinehaus   R
(U.S.)

Paul Newman (Donald "Sully" Sullivan), Jessica Tandy (Miss Beryl), Bruce Willis (Carl Roebuck), Melanie Griffith (Toby Roebuck), Dylan Walsh (Peter), Pruitt Taylor Vince (Rub Squeers), Gene Saks (Wirf), Josef Sommer (Clive Peoples, Jr.), Philip Seymour Hoffman (Officer Raymer), Philip Bosco (Judge Flatt)

p, Scott Rudin, Arlene Donovan; d, Robert Benton; w, Robert Benton (based on the novel by Richard Russo); ph, John Bailey; ed, John Bloom; m, Howard Shore; prod d, David Gropman; art d, Dan Davis; fx, Tom Ryba; cos, Joseph G. Aulisi

AAN Best Actor: Paul Newman; AAN Best Adapted Screenplay: Robert Benton

This thoughtful character study of an aging misfit was such a welcome rarity in 1990s Hollywood that it was perhaps overpraised on release; still, Paul Newman's Oscar-nominated performance and Robert Benton's solid, unobtrusive direction combine to create a resonant if unsurprising meditation on growing old in America.

Sixty years old, unemployable, and alone, Donald "Sully" Sullivan (Newman) has spent the better part of his life shirking responsibility in weather-beaten North Bath, New York. Having walked out on his family years before, Sully leads a dead-end existence, drinking, playing cards with his buddy Rub (Pruitt Taylor Vince), and renting a room in the house of his old schoolteacher, Miss Beryl (Jessica Tandy). Sully supports himself by doing periodic construction work for hard-headed Carl Roebuck (Bruce Willis), while pursuing a fruitless lawsuit against his boss for a partially disabling knee injury. Sully seems comfortable with his long, downward spiral, but when his estranged son Peter (Dylan Walsh) and his family come to town for Thanksgiving, he's forced to confront issues that he's long repressed.

Newman's performance is more than the stock collection of curmudgeonly tics that we've come to expect from major stars playing older men; he manages to suggest a great deal more about Sully's past foibles and present-day class resentments than is contained in Robert Benton's episodic script, based on the novel by Richard Russo. Willis and Griffith are both surprisingly good, and John Bailey's camera turns a ramshackle neighborhood of Poughkeepsie (standing in for the fictional town) into something close to a character in itself. NOBODY'S FOOL is to be commended just for acknowledging the existence of old age in the context of youth-obsessed pop culture; more importantly, the film is refreshingly frank about the everyday struggles of many senior citizens in an era of fractured families and a disappearing social safety net.

NONE BUT THE LONELY HEART

1944 113m bw Drama ★★★★
RKO (U.S.)

Cary Grant *(Ernie Mott)*, Ethel Barrymore *(Ma Mott)*, Barry Fitzgerald *(Twite)*, June Duprez *(Ada)*, Jane Wyatt *(Aggie Hunter)*, George Coulouris *(Jim Mordiney)*, Dan Duryea *(Lew Tate)*, Konstantin Shayne *(Ike Weber)*, Eva Leonard Boyne *(Ma Chalmers)*, Morton Lowry *(Taz)*

p, David Hempstead; d, Clifford Odets; w, Clifford Odets (based on the novel by Richard Llewellyn); ph, George Barnes; ed, Roland Gross; m, Hanns Eisler; prod d, Mordecai Gorelik; art d, Albert S. D'Agostino, Jack Okey; fx, Vernon L. Walker; cos, Renie

AAN Best Actor: Cary Grant; *AA Best Supporting Actress:* Ethel Barrymore; *AAN Best Film Editing:* Roland Gross; *AAN Best Score (Drama or Comedy):* C. Bakaleinikoff, Hanns Eisler

This was a daring and inventive film in its day, and Grant, playing the dedicated outsider, and Barrymore, as his cockney mother, are superb. The time is just prior to WWII and the place is Whitechapel in the East End of London. Through these mean streets wanders Grant, a shiftless but lighthearted young man whose mother, Barrymore, runs a dingy second-hand furniture store. Grant and his mother exchange barbs whenever they meet; however, Grant is seldom home to occupy his room above the store. Instead, he vagabonds his way through the area, cadging cigarettes and food from friendly shopkeepers who have known him since boyhood. Particularly concerned about Grant and protective of his mother is the local pawnbroker, Shayne, who dispenses wisdom and wit, as does family friend Fitzgerald, a drifter. Though cellist Wyatt is in love with Grant, he forsakes her for sultry Duprez, the divorced wife of British underworld leader Coulouris. The gangster persuades Grant to join his band of thieves, knowing that Grant will spend his ill-gotten gain on the high-living Duprez.

Odets's powerful script and direction do well by the Llewellyn novel, and the film is uncompromising in its portrayal of slum life. NONE BUT THE LONELY HEART was not a box-office winner, but has remained a critical favorite, boosted by a dedicated cast. To get Barrymore into the film during its hurried production schedule, RKO paid the expenses of closing the long-running play "The Corn Is Green," in which the actress was starring.

NORMA RAE

1979 110m c Drama ★★★★
Fox (U.S.) PG

Sally Field *(Norma Rae)*, Beau Bridges *(Sonny)*, Ron Leibman *(Reuben)*, Pat Hingle *(Vernon)*, Barbara Baxley *(Leona)*, Gail Strickland *(Bonnie Mae)*, Morgan Paull *(Wayne Billings)*, Robert Broyles *(Sam Bolen)*, John Calvin *(Ellis Harper)*, Booth Colman *(Dr. Watson)*

p, Tamara Asseyev, Alexandra Rose; d, Martin Ritt; w, Irving Ravetch, Harriet Frank Jr.; ph, John A. Alonzo (Panavision, Deluxe Color); ed, Sidney Levin; m, David Shire; prod d, Walter Scott Herndon; art d, Tracy Bousman

AAN Best Picture; AA Best Actress: Sally Field; *AAN Best Adapted Screenplay:* Irving Ravetch, Harriet Frank, Jr.; *AA Best Original Song:* "It Goes Like It Goes"; David Shire (Music), Norman Gimbel (Lyrics)

Sally Field won her first Oscar for her performance in the title role, a complex portrayal of an working-class southern woman who matures into a complete person when she is faced with labor woes and must grow up or fall by the wayside. Field is one of many overworked and underpaid workers at a cotton mill where management doesn't seem to realize that the days of slavery are over. Her father, Hingle, dies for lack of proper medical attention, while her mother, Baxley, is rapidly going deaf from the incessant din of the factory's equipment. The place is functioning without a union, and when New York labor organizer Leibman arrives to establish one, the workers fear for their jobs. When Field and Leibman first meet, his aggressive personality irritates her, while her lack of ambition does the same to him; but as the film progresses, so does their mutual respect. A divorced woman with two children (one of whom is illegitimate), Field marries Bridges, who becomes jealous of her relationship with Leibman once she decides to to join the union organizer in his efforts to unite the workers. Field begins undermining management from within and eventually manages to rally the workers into a strike. Production at the mill ceases, and management must capitulate in order to keep production rolling.

The simple story is enlivened by an intelligent, compassionate screenplay, whose sole deficiency is that it makes no attempt to represent the management point of view. Field's performance is flawless. Audiences thronged to see NORMA RAE, which made more money than just about any other union movie with the possible exception of ON THE WATERFRONT. (NORMA RAE grossed well over $10 million on initial release.) The film's technical excellence is at least partly due to director Ritt's using the same crew he used on many of his films about the south; Alonzo, Levin, and Herndon have a history of working well with each other and with Ritt.

NORTH BY NORTHWEST

1959 136m c Spy ★★★★
MGM (U.S.)

Cary Grant *(Roger O. Thornhill)*, Eva Marie Saint *(Eve Kendall)*, James Mason *(Phillip Vandamm)*, Jessie Royce Landis *(Clara Thornhill)*, Leo G. Carroll *(Professor)*, Philip Ober *(Lester Townsend)*, Josephine Hutchinson *(Handsome Woman)*, Martin Landau *(Leonard)*, Adam Williams *(Valerian)*, Edward Platt *(Victor Larrabee)*

p, Alfred Hitchcock; d, Alfred Hitchcock; w, Ernest Lehman; ph, Robert Burks (VistaVision, Technicolor); ed, George Tomasini; m, Bernard Herrmann; prod d, Robert Boyle; art d, William A. Horning, Merrill Pye; fx, A. Arnold Gillespie, Lee LeBlanc

AAN Best Original Story and Screenplay: Ernest Lehman; *AAN Best Film Editing:* George Tomasini; *AAN Best Art Direction-Set Decoration (Color):* William A. Horning, Robert Boyle, Merrill Pye, Henry Grace, Frank McKelvy

One of Hitchcock's most famous films, NORTH BY NORTHWEST has everything—thrills, suspense, mystery, and black humor, as well as dark undertones of sexual exploitation and covert political machination. Roger Thornhill (Grant, in perennially spectacular form) is a successful advertising executive in New York City who is lunching with mother (Landis, the exact same age as Grant) at Plaza Hotel's Oak Room when he answers the wrong page, one for a George Kaplan, and is mistaken for Kaplan. It becomes an identity which Thornhill cannot shake and one that drags him across the country in the face of death with the pretty Eve Kendall (a rather wooden Saint) at his side. The great suspense director was at his most entertaining, creating a helter skelter action film where the hero is propelled from one breathless situation to the next. It is filled with classic scenes—the two most memorable being the crop-dusting sequence in which Thornhill is terrorized by an aerial menace, and the chase across the face of Mt. Rushmore. The title of the film paraphrases *Hamlet*: "I am but mad north-northwest; when the wind is southerly I know a hawk from a handsaw," an implication that neither Thornhill, Hitchcock, nor Hamlet is mad. Although NORTH BY NORTHWEST is available on video and DVD, no small screen viewing can match the

Technicolor, VistaVision experience of seeing this one in the theater. With James Mason, a study in velvet villany, but looking dowdy for once, next to Grant, and Landau as a chillingly effeminate gunsel.

NORTH DALLAS FORTY   DVD
1979 119m c   Sports   ★★★½
Paramount   (U.S.)   R

Nick Nolte *(Phillip Elliott)*, Mac Davis *(Maxwell)*, Charles Durning *(Coach Johnson)*, Dayle Haddon *(Charlotte)*, Bo Svenson *(Jo Bob Priddy)*, Steve Forrest *(Conrad Hunter)*, G.D. Spradlin *(B.A. Strothers)*, Dabney Coleman *(Emmett)*, Savannah Smith *(Joanne)*, Marshall Colt *(Art Hartman)*

p, Frank Yablans; d, Ted Kotcheff; w, Frank Yablans, Ted Kotcheff, Peter Gent (based on the novel by Gent); ph, Paul Lohmann (Panavision, Metrocolor); ed, Jay Kamen; m, John Scott; prod d, Alfred Sweeney; cos, Dorothy Jeakins

Pro football fans may be disillusioned by this excellent, honest, and often brutal expose of the play-for-pay game. Phillip Elliott (Nick Nolte) is a veteran pass-catcher for the North Dallas Bulls, who bear a strong resemblance to the Dallas Cowboys—not surprising given that the film is based on a novel by former Cowboy wide receiver Pete Gent. The coaches (G.D. Spradlin and Charles Durning) and team owner (Steve Forrest) feel the fiercely independent Elliott has an attitude problem because of his blatant cynicism and his awareness of how he and his teammates are constantly being manipulated by management. Cast aside after being callously used to motivate a fellow player, the receiver comes to realize there is more to life than football, but that he loves the game just the same. Country singer Mac Davis, making his film debut, is quite good as the quarterback who is Elliott's best friend and knows how to play the game both on and off the field and Bo Svenson is effective as a big, dumb defensive lineman. The National Football League refused to help with the production of this film in any way, so the action is kept to a minimum (though what *is* shown is brutal), but the locker room atmosphere and the off-the-field drama smack of authenticity in NORTH DALLAS FORTY, as telling a depiction of pro football as any to be found. Note the presence of one-time Oakland Raider behemoth John Matuszak, who went on to appear in films such as CAVEMAN and THE GOONIES before his death in 1989.

NORTHWEST PASSAGE
1940 125m c   Adventure   ★★★★★
MGM   (U.S.)

Spencer Tracy *(Maj. Robert Rogers)*, Robert Young *(Langdon Towne)*, Walter Brennan *(Hunk Marriner)*, Ruth Hussey *(Elizabeth Browne)*, Nat Pendleton *(Capt. Huff)*, Louis Hector *(Rev. Browne)*, Robert Barrat *(Humphrey Towne)*, Lumsden Hare *(Gen. Amherst)*, Donald MacBride *(Sgt. McNott)*, Isabel Jewell *(Jennie Coit)*

p, Hunt Stromberg; d, King Vidor, Jack Conway (uncredited); w, Laurence Stallings, Talbot Jennings (based on the novel by Kenneth Roberts); ph, Sidney Wagner, William V. Skall (Technicolor); ed, Conrad A. Nervig; m, Herbert Stothart; art d, Cedric Gibbons, Malcolm Brown

AAN Best Cinematography: Sidney Wagner, William V. Skall

One of the greatest adventure films of all time, this Vidor classic owes much of its success to the rugged Tracy, who plays celebrated Indian fighter Robert Rogers, leader of Rogers' Rangers. Tracy is earthy and eloquent as the frontier leader who knows no fear in a wilderness rife with terror and bloodshed. Set in 1759, the film opens with talented artist Young arriving home in Portsmouth, New Hampshire, to sheepishly

explain to his family that he has been expelled from Harvard because of the snide political comments he has inserted into his cartoons. Naturally, his criticism is aimed at the British, which alienates fiancee Hussey's Tory family. Young and his roughneck sidekick, Brennan, get drunk in a pub one night and tell off Hussey's stuffed-shirt father, Hector. As a result, Young's arrest is ordered, but he and Brennan escape into the wilderness, later stopping at a wayside inn, where they meet Tracy. After a night of hard drinking, Young and Brennan wake up outside the military post at Crown Point, headquarters of Tracy's rangers. Tracy entices Young to join the Rangers as a mapmaker, and Brennan tags along. Soon Young and Brennan are boating along with hundreds of other leather-clad veterans of many an Indian war. Their goal is St. Francis, the headquarters of the vicious, French-backed Abenaki tribe, which has conducted bloody raids into colonial territory under British control.

Based on Kenneth Roberts's well-researched novel about Rogers's exploits, NORTHWEST PASSAGE is a rousing adventure all the way, full of thundering action. Its depiction of the colonial era is amazingly convincing, thanks to the perfectionist techniques of director Vidor, who went at the $2 million production with the vigor and relentless energy of Robert Rogers himself. In fact, Vidor, who began working on the film with an incomplete script (new portions of which were flown daily to the production's Idaho location), believed that he was shooting a prologue for a film that would also include Rogers's search for the Northwest Passage. However, producer Hunt Stromberg and MGM decided to confine the film to Rogers's adventures during the Indian Wars, bringing Jack Conway in to shoot an ending to the film while Vidor was in New York. To make his "prologue," Vidor took his almost all-male cast into the wilds of Idaho, around Lake Payette, which resembled the New England terrain of 200 years earlier.

In his first Technicolor film, Vidor made good use of the lush locations; Wagner and Skall's cinematography is absolutely breathtaking, capturing the rich blues of the lakes and the deep greens of the forests (although they had some trouble with the colors of the ranger costumes, until special dyes were ordered to tone down the kelly green hues). The film is marred only by its racism, pretty virulent even by Hollywood standards.

NOSFERATU, THE VAMPIRE   DVD
(NOSFERATU, PHANTOM DER NACHT)
1978 107m c   Horror   ★★★
Fox   (France/West Germany)   PG

Klaus Kinski *(Count Dracula)*, Isabelle Adjani *(Lucy Harker)*, Bruno Ganz *(Jonathan Harker)*, Roland Topor *(Renfield)*, Walter Ladengast *(Dr. Van Helsing)*, Dan Van Husen *(Warden)*, Jan Groth *(Harbormaster)*, Carsten Bodinus *(Schrader)*, Martje Grohmann *(Mina)*, Rijk de Gooyer *(Town Official)*

p, Werner Herzog; d, Werner Herzog; w, Werner Herzog (based on the novel *Dracula* by Bram Stoker and the film script NOSFERATU by Henrik Galeen); ph, Jorg Schmidt-Reitwein (Eastmancolor); ed, Beate Mainka-Jellinghaus; m, Popol Vuh, Florian Fricke, Richard Wagner, Charles Gounod; prod d, Henning von Gierke, Ulrich Bergfelder; art d, Henning von Gierke; fx, Cornelius Siegel; cos, Gloria Storch

After capturing the attention of American critics and public with ambitious, unique, and powerful films, German director Werner Herzog remade what he considers to be the most visionary and important of all German films, F.W. Murnau's 1922 silent masterpiece, NOSFERATU. Held together by the sheer power of Klaus Kinski's performance as the vampire, NOSFERATU, THE VAMPIRE evokes several scenes (practically shot-for-shot) from the Murnau classic while slightly altering some of the original's thematic structures. In

Murnau's film, the vampire is pure evil invading a small German community (Herzog feels that the 1922 film adumbrated the rise of Nazism in Germany). Herzog's vampire is much more sympathetic. An outcast from society (as are all of Herzog's protagonists), Kinski's Nosferatu longs for contact, acceptance, and even love from the humans who fear and revile him. Sadly, his curse and death's-head appearance forever prevent this. The vampire's undead state and need for blood seem to be presented as a horrible, irreversible *disease*, rather than an inherently evil harbinger of hell. While this isn't exactly an innovation in the development of the horror film (Tod Browning's DRACULA, 1931, starring Bela Lugosi, had moments of pathos, as does George Romero's MARTIN), Herzog and Kinski succeed here because they convey a sense of pity for a creature so visually repulsive it's hard to look at him.

As with most of Herzog's films, the story behind the production is almost more interesting than the film itself. Unable to shoot in Bremen, as Murnau did in 1922, Herzog prepared to settle for the Dutch town of Delft. Still bitter over their occupation by the Nazis during WWII, the citizens of Delft were less than enthusiastic about this small army of German filmmakers invading their town. When Herzog announced his plan to release 11,000 rats into the streets of Delft for the scene in which Nosferatu arrives (the director wanted grey rats but could only obtain white ones, which his crew painted grey), the Delft *burgermeister* categorically refused and told the apparently insane German that his town had just spent months clearing the canals of their own home-grown rats and had no intention of reinfesting the area with laboratory rats from Hungary. Nonplussed, Herzog moved his rats to a more accommodating city, Schiedam, where he was allowed to shoot, albeit on a smaller scale.

NOSTALGHIA

DVD
★★★★

1983 120m   c/bw Drama

Sovin/RAI-TV/Opera   (U.S.S.R./Italy)

Oleg Yankovsky (*Andre Gortchakov*), Domiziana Giordano (*Eugenia*), Erland Josephson (*Domenico*), Patrizia Terreno (*Gortchakov's Wife*), Delia Boccardo (*Domenico's Wife*), Laura De Marchi (*Chambermaid*), Milena Vukotic (*Civil Servant*), Alberto Canepa (*Farmer*)

d, Andrei Tarkovsky; w, Andrei Tarkovsky, Tonino Guerra; ph, Giuseppe Lanci (Technicolor); ed, Amedeo Salfa, Erminia Marani; m, Ludwig van Beethoven, Giuseppe Verdi; prod d, Andrea Grisanti; fx, Paolo Ricci; cos, Lina Nerli Taviani

A meditative film by visionary Soviet filmmaker Tarkovsky that lures viewers into its mysterious, mystical world and completely envelops them for a two-hour stretch. Yankovsky is a Soviet architecture professor who travels to northern Italy's Tuscan Hills to research an exiled 18th-century Russian composer who committed suicide there. Away from his homeland, Yankovsky becomes nostalgic suffering with his unfulfilled desire to return to a home that is out of reach. The melancholy Yankovsky becomes involved with Giordano, his volatile, strong-minded interpreter. Their relationshop, however, is never consummated and gradually deteriorates. Their romance is strained even further by Yankovsky's growing friendship with Josephson, a batty Italian professor who years ago locked his family inside their house and awaited Armageddon—for seven years. Josephson proves too much for Giordano, who makes plans to return to her lover in Rome. Yankovsky finds Josephson living among the rain-soaked ruins of a 16th-century spa. In this ancient crumbling structure is a large, placid mineral bath that Josephson unsuccessfully tries to wade across (its waters are chest-high) while holding a lit candle. His crazy belief is that to save mankind he must cross the bath without letting the candle flame extinguish.

Having once again failed, Josephson makes a public proclamation. He climbs atop Michelangelo's statue of Marcus Aurelius in Rome, plays Beethoven's "Ode to Joy" on a portable turntable, and shouts prophetic doomsday messages to those who'll listen. At the same time, Yankovsky has taken up Josephson's plight to cross the bath. His first two attempts fail, each time the candle flame flickering out in the swirling drafts of hot air. Back atop the statue, Josephson soaks himself with kerosene and sets himself ablaze. As he burns to death, Yankovsky completes a successful trip across the waters. The candle burns, but Yankovsky's energy is extinguished. Struggling at the water's edge to stay alive, Yankovsky envisions his homeland as the snow covers its grassy hills.

The final sequence of NOSTALGHIA is one of the most captivating ever put on film. The viewer becomes completely swept away by Tarkovsky's world where the elements reign supreme—fire and water are everywhere. The atmosphere Tarkovsky creates is one of constantly dripping water, unsettling mists, and dew seeping through the eternally damp walls. Coupled with these memorable visuals is a remarkable highlighting of sounds (a job admirably performed by Remo Ugolinelli) such as the echoing drip of water or the swirling of the drafts. NOSTALGHIA is not a film for everyone—if it is fast-paced action you desire, then you will quickly be snoring. Instead of excitement, the feeling one gets after seeing NOSTALGHIA is one of utter relaxation that makes us long for the world we left behind in the theater.

NOTEBOOK, THE

DVD

2004 121m   c   Romance/Drama   ★★½

Gran Via Productions   (U.S.)   PG-13

Ryan Gosling (*Noah*), Rachel McAdams (*Allie*), James Garner (*Duke*), Gena Rowlands (*Allie Calhoun*), James Marsden (*Lon Hammond*), Sam Shepard (*Frank Calhoun*), David Thornton (*John Hamilton*), Joan Allen (*Anne Hamilton*), Kevin Connolly (*Fin*), Tim Ivey (*Rower*)

p, Lynn Harris, Mark Johnson; d, Nick Cassavetes; w, Jeremy Leven, Jan Sardi (based on the novel by Nicholas Sparks, adapted by Jan Sardi); ph, Robert Fraisse; ed, Alan Heim; m, Aaron Zigman; prod d, Sarah Knowles; art d, Scott Ritenour; fx, David Dryer, Bob Shelley; cos, Karyn Wagner

Nicholas Sparks fans can breathe easy: Director Nick Cassavetes' adaptation of Sparks' best-selling tearjerker retains the mushy sentimentality that readers loved.

In the present day, an older gentleman named Duke (James Garner) regularly visits senile Allie (Gena Rowlands, Cassavetes' mother) in her hospital room and regales her with a romantic tale that he reads from a well-worn notebook. In the 1940s, spirited, college-bound Allie Hamilton (Rachel McAdams) and her wealthy, class-conscious family are summering in small-town Seabrook, NC. She winds up falling madly in love with handsome Noah Calhoun (Ryan Gosling), who works at the local lumberyard, and they spend the lazy summer days imagining the future. The idyll comes to an abrupt end when Allie's normally doting father (David Thornton) and stern, ambitious mother (Joan Allen) learn that their little girl is dallying with a working-class boy and ship her off to Sarah Lawrence. Brokenhearted Noah writes daily, but Mrs. Hamilton intercepts the letters, and after a year without word from his beloved, Noah enlists in the military. Noah and Allie meet again years later, but everything has changed: Allie is now engaged to be married to handsome, upper-class war veteran Lon (James Marsden). Back in the present, the elderly listener—who has a feeling she's heard this story before—wonders which worthy young man Allie ultimately chose, and who this Duke fellow really is.

Cassavetes' film is lovely to look at and unusually well acted, but his wholehearted embrace of saccharine melodrama and tendency to let scenes ramble make for some slow going. That said, relative newcomer McAdams (best known for comedies like THE HOT CHICK and MEAN GIRLS) is outstanding in this period role and has genuine chemistry with brooding, puppy-dog-eyed Gosling.

NOTHING BUT A MAN
DVD
1964 95m bw Drama ★★★
Du Art (U.S.)

Ivan Dixon (*Duff Anderson*), Abbey Lincoln (*Josie Dawson*), Gloria Foster (*Lee*), Julius Harris (*Will Anderson*), Martin Priest (*Driver*), Leonard Parker (*Frankie*), Yaphet Kotto (*Jocko*), Stanley Greene (*Rev. Dawson*), Helen Lounck (*Effie Simms*), Helene Arrindell (*Doris*)

p, Robert Young, Michael Roemer, Robert Rubin; d, Michael Roemer; w, Michael Roemer, Robert Malcolm Young; ph, Robert Young; ed, Luke Bennett; prod d, William Rhodes; cos, Nancy Ruffing

A well-intentioned, independently made film describing the life of a black man in the 1960s South. Basically, all the title character (Dixon) wants to do is live simply. While working for the railroad in Alabama, he falls in love with Lincoln, the daughter of the minister (Greene). Greene does not like Dixon, so the couple goes to Birmingham to see Dixon's father, a dying alcoholic. Dixon also visits his illegitimate son, who has been abandoned by his mother and left in the care of a woman not related to him. Lincoln wants to marry, but Dixon does not want to assume the responsibility. The couple finally weds, and Dixon gets a job at the town sawmill. When he won't ingratiate himself to his racist white employers, he is fired and labeled a troublemaker. He then finds work at a gas station but is still harassed by the townspeople. After beating and berating his wife, out of frustration, he returns to Birmingham to watch his father die. Facing the situation is a step toward manhood, and he begins to come to terms with his responsibilities. He gets his son and goes back to Lincoln to try to live in peace and dignity. The film garnered a great deal of praise, at the time of its release, for its realistic recounting of the life of a black laborer in the South and for refusing to sentimentalize the subject matter.

NOTHING SACRED
DVD
1937 75m c Comedy ★★★★★
Selznick (U.S.)

Carole Lombard (*Hazel Flagg*), Fredric March (*Wally Cook*), Charles Winninger (*Dr. Enoch Downer*), Walter Connolly (*Oliver Stone*), Sig Rumann (*Dr. Emile Egglehoffer*), Frank Fay (*MC*), Maxie Rosenbloom (*Max Levinsky*), Margaret Hamilton (*Drug Store Lady*), Troy Brown (*Ernest Walker*), Olin Howlin (*Baggage Man*)

p, David O. Selznick; d, William A. Wellman; w, Ben Hecht, Ring Lardner Jr., Budd Schulberg (based on the story "Letter to the Editor" by James H. Street); ph, W. Howard Greene (Technicolor); ed, Hal C. Kern, James E. Newcom; m, Oscar Levant; art d, Lyle Wheeler; fx, Jack Cosgrove; cos, Travis Banton, Walter Plunkett

A marvelous black comedy full of wit and journalistic wisdom in the grand and capricious style of Hecht (who co-authored, with Charles MacArthur, THE FRONT PAGE), this film is all the more stunning thanks to the outrageous and hilarious performance of super comedienne Lombard. This was one of the first of the screwball comedies, a classic of the genre which is just as funny today as when it was first filmed.

March is an ambitious newsman who gets into big trouble when he tries to pass off a black New Yorker as the "Sultan of Marzipan," a potentate who is about to donate $500,000 to establish an art institute (the man is actually penniless and doesn't know Marzipan from Manhattan). When Connolly, the editor of March's sensation-seeking tabloid, finds out about the impersonation, he becomes livid and demotes March to writing obituaries. Meanwhile, Lombard, a working girl in Warsaw, Vermont, who longs to visit New York City, is routinely examined by her less than competent doctor, Winninger; the bumbling doctor sadly tells Lombard that she has radium poisoning and has not much longer to live. News of this tragedy reaches March and he sets out to write a great sob story, but by the time he reaches Lombard, Winninger has changed his diagnosis: Lombard is as healthy as can be. March won't hear of it; he has a great story and refuses to allow the truth to ruin his fabulous tale. He persuades Lombard to go through with the charade, promising that she will not only see New York but will enter the great city in style. She agrees, and by the time March begins grinding out the tragedy in daily installments in his paper, New York is weeping loudly.

Hecht had a great deal of fun writing NOTHING SACRED for the screen, plucking the background from his own newspaper experiences. The fake sultan, for instance, was based upon a prank Hecht himself had concocted, one in which his eccentric poet friend Maxwell Bodenheim, then unknown, pretended to be a foreign potentate visiting Chicago where Hecht was working as a spectacular journalist. Lombard is wonderfully funny here, playing a role that was made for her madcap talent, and March, recognized as a great dramatic player, showed a considerable flair for comedy.

NOTORIOUS
DVD
1946 101m bw Thriller/Spy ★★★★★
RKO (U.S.)

Cary Grant (*Devlin*), Ingrid Bergman (*Alicia Huberman*), Claude Rains (*Alexander Sebastian*), Louis Calhern (*Paul Prescott*), Mme. Konstantin (*Mme. Sebastian*), Reinhold Schunzel (*Dr. Anderson*), Moroni Olsen (*Walter Beardsley*), Ivan Triesault (*Eric Mathis*), Alexis Minotis (*Joseph*), Wally Brown (*Mr. Hopkins*)

p, Alfred Hitchcock; d, Alfred Hitchcock; w, Ben Hecht; ph, Ted Tetzlaff; ed, Theron Warth; m, Roy Webb; art d, Albert S. D'Agostino, Carroll Clark; fx, Vernon L. Walker, Paul Eagler; cos, Edith Head

AAN Best Supporting Actor: Claude Rains; *AAN Best Original Screenplay:* Ben Hecht

This brilliant Hitchcock offering combines romance, suspense, and international intrigue with unforgettable performances from Grant and Bergman. The thriller trappings are merely trim: what's really at hand is a twisted love affair between Grant and Bergman that hints at sadomasochism. He's untrusting, passive, and unsympathetic; she's shady, aggressive, and alcoholic. It's a dangerous chocolate box of poisoned candy, Hitchcock's ode to the dementia of passion. Dig in.

Alicia Huberman (Bergman), the daughter of a convicted Nazi spy, has an international jet set reputation as a playgirl, causing American agent Devlin (Grant) to fall in love with her. Devlin, in an effort to uncover a Nazi plot, enlists Alicia's aid in Rio de Janeiro. They contact Nazi agent Alexander Sebastian (Rains), whom Alicia must eventually marry. Meanwhile, Devlin and she must discover how the Sebastian plot is being engineered.

With the blistering onscreen romance between Grant and Bergman—two of the most popular stars in Hollywood—and the creation of one of Hitchcock's greatest "MacGuffins"—the secret uranium shipments—NOTORIOUS emerges as one of Hitchcock's most masterful and sophisticated efforts. The passionate kissing scene in which the lovers devour one another instead of their chicken dinner still retains all of its power. Ingrid Bergman was certainly never sexier: here's the woman who scandalized America with her torrid, extramarital affair. Next to the protagonists, Rains's expert villany is mama's boyism gone awry. And no wonder. With Mme. Leopoldine Konstantin chomping cigars, Hitch really flails away at motherhood. The camera swoons right along with us in a dizzying manner. Best shot: the key. You can't miss it.

NOTTING HILL **DVD**

1999 123m c   Comedy/Romance   ★★★½
PolyGram Films/Working Title Films/Notting   PG-13
Hill Pictures/Duncan Kenworthy Productions (U.S.)

Julia Roberts *(Anna Scott)*, Hugh Grant *(William Thacker)*, Hugh Bonneville *(Bernie)*, Emma Chambers *(Honey)*, Rhys Ifans *(Spike)*, Tim McInnerny *(Max)*, Gina McKee *(Bella)*, Richard McCabe *(Tony)*, James Dreyfus *(Martin)*, Dylan Moran *(Rufus the Chef)*

p, Duncan Kenworthy; d, Roger Michell; w, Richard Curtis; ph, Michael Coulter; ed, Nick Moore; m, Trevor Jones; prod d, Stuart Craig; art d, Andrew Ackland-Snow, David Allday; cos, Shuna Harwood

Julia Roberts flashes her megawatt smile, Hugh Grant does his patented dithering English fellow bit and they're just as cute as two buttons in this winning romantic comedy.

Anna Scott (Roberts) is a lanky, high-maintenance Hollywood movie star, while William Thacker (Grant) is the self-deprecating owner of a less-than-successful London shop. Anna wanders in looking to buy a book, and a bit of contrived romantic comedy nonsense later, she's agreeing to be William's date for a little birthday dinner for his flighty sister (Emma Chambers). It all goes so swimmingly that disappointment must inevitably follow, and does. But the movie has faith in true love even when the characters don't, so no one needs to worry that it's going to do something horribly modern and leave the made-for-each-other cutie-pies pining for what might have been.

Roberts fans will, of course, be delighted to see her in a role that plays to all her strengths—fresh-faced looks, charming gangliness, an air of infinite approachability—and neatly sidesteps her glaring inability to act by having her more or less play herself. But the filmmakers—several of whom helped concoct FOUR WEDDINGS AND A FUNERAL, which cast Grant opposite another long-legged American to stunningly successful effect—also beef up the cast with actors who can take a nicely written supporting role and make it into a small gem, which means the world to moviegoers who aren't entirely in thrall to the pretty woman's charms.

NOWHERE IN AFRICA **DVD**
(NIRGENDWO IN AFRIKA)
2001 138m c   Drama   ★★★½
MTM Medien & Television Munchen/Constantin Film Produktion/Bavaria Film/Media Cooperation One (Germany)

Juliane Kohler *(Jettel Redlich)*, Merab Ninidze *(Walter Redlich)*, Matthias Habich *(Susskind)*, Sidede Onyulo *(Owuor)*, Lea Kurka *(Young Regina)*, Karoline Eckertz *(Older Regina)*, Gerd Heinz *(Max)*, Hildegard Schmahl *(Ina)*, Maritta Horwarth *(Liesel)*, Regine Zimmermann *(Kathe)*

p, Peter Herrmann; d, Caroline Link; w, Caroline Link (based on the novel by Stefanie Zweig); ph, Gernot Roll; ed, Patricia Rommel; m, Niki Reiser, Jochen Schmidt-Hambrock; prod d, Susann Bieling, Uwe Szielasko; cos, Barbara Grupp

AA Best Foreign Language Film

Of all the places European Jews found safe haven during the dark years of Hitler's Holocaust, few could have been further

afield than Kenya. But that's exactly where six-year-old Stefanie Zweig and her parents wound up. This beautiful and engaging film from German director Caroline Link is based on Zweig's autobiographical novel, in which young Regina Redlich and her family abandon their comfortable, middle-class lives in Silesia for the desert wilds of Africa.

Rongai, Kenya, 1938: Regina's father, Walter (Merab Ninidze), a Jewish attorney prohibited from practicing law by the Nazis, lies deathly ill with malaria on the British-owned cattle farm where he works as a caretaker. Walter is cared for by Owuor (Sidede Onyulo), a native Kenyan who serves as the farm's cook; by the time five-year-old Regina (Lea Kurka) and her mother, Jettel (Juliane Kohler), arrive, Walter has regained his strength. Regina adores the desert and she and Owuar become close friends, but pampered Jettel is appalled by the tiny house and the drought-stricken conditions. Life is made marginally easier with the help of Susskind (Matthias Habich), a fellow Jewish refugee, and when the rains finally come, the farm flourishes. Storm clouds of a different sort, however, are gathering over Europe, as radio reports and letters from home bear witness to the growing nightmare that is destroying all those the Redlichs left behind.

True to the voice of Zweig's novel, the film is told through the eyes of Regina, but it's really Jettel's story; she's the one who learns to confront her own prejudices and embrace her new home with open arms. Beautifully shot on location in Kenya and filled with touching, almost magical moments, Link's film won the 2002 Academy Award for Best Foreign Language Film.

NOW, VOYAGER **DVD**
1942 117m bw Drama   ★★★★
Warner Bros. (U.S.)

Bette Davis *(Charlotte Vale)*, Paul Henreid *(Jerry D. Durrance)*, Claude Rains *(Dr. Jaquith)*, Gladys Cooper *(Mrs. Henry Windle Vale)*, Bonita Granville *(June Vale)*, John Loder *(Elliott Livingston)*, Ilka Chase *(Lisa Vale)*, Lee Patrick *("Deb" McIntyre)*, James Rennie *(Frank McIntyre)*, Charles Drake *(Leslie Trotter)*

p, Hal B. Wallis; d, Irving Rapper; w, Casey Robinson (based on the novel by Olive Higgins Prouty); ph, Sol Polito; ed, Warren Low; m, Max Steiner; art d, Robert Haas; fx, Willard Van Enger; cos, Orry-Kelly

AAN Best Actress: Bette Davis; *AAN Best Supporting Actress:* Gladys Cooper; *AA Best Score (Drama or Comedy):* Max Steiner

Now, Bette: A glittering, slushy take on the ugly duckling transformation. It's Olive Higgins Prouty, at it again (she also penned *Stella Dallas*, the durable soap opera from which three films, including the Barbara Stanwyck classic, were made), with a title lifted from Walt Whitman's *Leaves of Grass*, a conceit enough to raise a dead poet. Irving Rapper directs as if he wants to stay out of the way of Davis and Cooper—perfectly understandable.

As usual, Davis has to overplay her hand at Jekyll/Hyde transformation. Beforehand, she's got unplucked eyebrows like last spring's dead caterpillars, hair like a mudpuddle with a net over it, and glasses and shoes borrowed from the first continental congress. It sets a satisfyingly camp feeling of self-sacrifice over the entire proceedings. Later she *is* artfully styled; you have the feeling Davis is shedding her own New England repression, which is exactly what she means for you to feel.

Davis plays the dowdy, frustrated daughter of Cooper, with whom she lives in their oppressive Boston mansion. Davis is close to a nervous breakdown because she can't get any love from Cooper, who also forces her to dress "sensibly." Chase, Davis's sister-in-law, worries about Davis's mental condition and enlists the services of famed psychiatrist Rains, who sees that Davis is near collapse and recommends that she leave her lonely home and take refuge at his sanitarium. There, Davis begins a regimen that begins to restore her mental and physical health; she drops pounds and gains confidence daily, transforming into a self-assured swan within three months (a feat none of us can seem to master so quickly). At Rains's suggestion, Davis boards a liner for South America. On the cruise, she meets Henreid, whose wife pretends to be in bad health to keep her unhappy husband from ending their marriage. On a stopover in Rio, Davis and Henreid enjoy a wonderful day and night together, then wake up to discover that their ship has already left the port. They stay in Rio for a few days and Davis experiences passionate love for the first time in her life, although she understands from the start that Henreid will never leave his wife.

Though VOYAGER is best remembered for the scene in which Henreid lights two cigarettes simultaneously and then hands one to Davis, this pleasurable, popular tearjerker is Davis's show all the way. She claimed to have worked extensively on the screenplay, deleting some of Casey Robinson's hard work in favor of Prouty's original words. Cooper is an excellent choice for the matriarchal dowager; Davis always stood in awe (or angry envy) of stage actors, and their scenes have a weight the rest of the picture lacks. Henreid and Rains, both great friends of Davis's (and supposedly Rains was a lover) contribute smooth work. The marvelous Ilka Chase is wasted here, and Bonita Granville is grating. The Polito camerawork finally settles down to Davis-devotion and Steiner's Oscar-winning score clings to her like flypaper. It's Grade-A schlock, but not without depth: critics have detected feminist overtones in this movie, one in which men prove eminently dispensable in the quest for happiness.

NUMBER TWO
(NUMERO DEUX)
1975 88m c Drama ★★★★
Sonimage/Bela (France)

Sandrine Battistella *(Wife)*, Pierre Dudry *(Husband)*, Alexandre Rignault *(Grandpa)*, Rachel Stefanopoli *(Grandma)*

d, Jean-Luc Godard; w, Jean-Luc Godard

Announced by Godard as a remake of BREATHLESS (a ploy to get financing), this video project has almost nothing to do with his 1959 masterpiece. Battistella and Dudry are a dissatisfied couple who suffer from physical ailments. Battistella is stricken with chronic constipation, and her husband is unable to perform sexually. They teach their children about sex by showing them, and the grandparents, naked, speak directly to the camera. As Richard Roud writes, "although NUMERO DEUX is a frustrating film about frustration, a constipated film about constipation, it is not entirely without a sense of hope." Shot on videotape (and later transferred to film), the majority of the picture uses only a portion of the screen, usually the upper-left and the lower-right portions. The finish, however, relieves the tension by opening up the entire screen. To further his interests in video, Godard built a studio in Grenoble where his tape experiments for French television continued until 1980 with the release of EVERY MAN FOR HIMSELF, marking his much-awaited return to commercial filmmaking and international distribution. An audacious film.

NUN'S STORY, THE
1959 149m c Religious/Biography ★★★★
Warner Bros. (U.S.)

Audrey Hepburn *(Sister Luke/Gabrielle Van Der Mal)*, Peter Finch *(Dr. Fortunati)*, Edith Evans *(Mother Emmanuel Superior General)*, Peggy Ashcroft *(Mother Mathilde)*, Dean Jagger *(Dr.*

Van Der Mal), Mildred Dunnock *(Sister Margharita)*, Beatrice Straight *(Mother Christophe)*, Patricia Collinge *(Sister William)*, Eva Kotthaus *(Sister Marie)*, Ruth White *(Mother Marcella)*

p, Henry Blanke; d, Fred Zinnemann; w, Robert Anderson (based on the book by Kathryn C. Hulme); ph, Franz Planer (Technicolor); ed, Walter Thompson; m, Franz Waxman; art d, Alexander Trauner; cos, Marjorie Best

AAN Best Picture; AAN Best Actress: Audrey Hepburn; *AAN Best Director:* Fred Zinnemann; *AAN Best Adapted Screenplay:* Robert Anderson; *AAN Best Color Cinematography:* Franz Planer; *AAN Best Film Editing:* Walter Thompson; *AAN Best Score (Drama or Comedy):* Franz Waxman; *AAN Best Sound:* George R. Groves

A superbly restrained piece of filmmaking, with Zinnemann directing in simple, unadorned style and Hepburn giving a truly radiant performance. Hepburn is the daughter of Belgian surgeon Jagger, and she has the desire to become a nursing nun in the Congo, which was still overseen by Belgium at the time, several years prior to WWII. After experiencing the rigors of a convent, Hepburn goes off to a school where she learns tropical medicine. Her desire to go to the Congo is sidetracked when she is first assigned to a mental hospital in Belgium, where she is almost killed by a maniacal patient whom she thought she could handle. Eventually, she travels to the Congo, where she is disappointed by her assignment. She'd hoped to do her nursing with natives, but is sent, instead, to a hospital for Europeans where she meets crusty Finch, a dedicated surgeon who has no room in his life for women or religion and devotes himself to medicine. Hepburn understands that she must shed her old ways and plunges into her work. Assigned to escort a Belgian official back to the motherland, she arrives there just as the war is beginning. When Jagger is killed by Nazis as he's helping refugees escape, she realizes that she is incapable of keeping her dispassionate attitude and that she must leave the convent in order to fight against the oppressors.

This was perhaps the only movie from this studio (Warners) in which there was no music over the final titles. No one could decide if Waxman should write an upbeat or a downbeat theme because the choice would imply an editorial decision on the part of the filmmakers, something that Zinnemann zealously and successfully avoided all the way through. Jack Warner fought against that viewpoint, but Zinnemann prevailed, and the end credits are accompanied by silence. Assistant director Piero Mussetta used 70 members of Rome's Royal Opera Ballet to stage a sequence in which nuns are involved in various rituals. That sequence should be viewed by every film student as an exercise in how to handle a large group. It's hard to believe that this rare and moving film did not win one single Oscar of the six for which it was nominated; most went to BEN-HUR, with the others going to Simone Signoret and the screenplay for ROOM AT THE TOP.

NUTS
1987 116m c Drama ★★½
Barwood (U.S.) R

Barbra Streisand *(Claudia Draper)*, Richard Dreyfuss *(Aaron Levinsky)*, Maureen Stapleton *(Rose Kirk, Claudia's Mother)*, Karl Malden *(Arthur Kirk)*, Eli Wallach *(Dr. Herbert A. Morrison, Psychiatrist)*, Robert Webber *(Francis MacMillan, Prosecuting Attorney)*, James Whitmore *(Judge Stanley Murdoch)*, Leslie Nielsen *(Allen Green)*, William Prince *(Clarence Middleton)*, Dakin Matthews

p, Barbra Streisand; d, Martin Ritt; w, Tom Topor, Darryl Ponicsan, Alvin Sargent (based on the play by Topor); ph, Andrzej Bartkowiak (Technicolor); ed, Sidney Levin; m, Barbra Streisand; prod d, Joel Schiller; art d, Eric Orbom; cos, Joe I. Tompkins

Claudia Draper (Barbra Streisand) is a high-priced prostitute. She has been arrested for killing one of her johns (Leslie Nielsen), and her erratic behavior and frequent outbursts would lead one to believe she is crazy. Her mother (Maureen Stapleton) and stepfather (Karl Malden) have conspired with their attorney (William Prince) to have Claudia committed to a mental institution rather than have her go on trial for manslaughter. Claudia knows that if she is committed, she may never get out of her hospital gown. She wants a sanity hearing and wishes to stand trial, believing she can prove the killing was in self-defense. After Claudia physically attacks her parents' attorney, he immediately asks to be taken off the case. A hapless public defender, Aaron Levinsky (Richard Dreyfuss), is given the task of dealing with the wild woman. There are holes galore in the script. As a story, it's thin. As cinema, it's static. There is enough in all the performances to make it a diversion, but little more. For a fleeting moment, there is just a scintilla of attraction between Dreyfuss and Streisand; but that's tossed aside in favor of the bare-bones plot. Although he costars, Dreyfuss has fashioned more of a Best Supporting Actor performance and seems happy to stand outside the glow of Streisand's histrionics. Despite all of her emoting, the picture seldom catches fire. All of the secondary roles are well cast, and Martin Ritt's direction is as good as it can be, considering the script's limitations.

NUTTY PROFESSOR, THE
1963   107m   c   Comedy   ★★★
Paramount   (U.S.)

Jerry Lewis (*Prof. Julius Ferris Kelp/Buddy Love*), Stella Stevens (*Stella Purdy*), Del Moore (*Dr. Hamius R. Warfield*), Kathleen Freeman (*Millie Lemmon*), Med Flory, Skip Ward, Norman Alden (*Football Players*), Howard Morris (*Father Kelp*), Elvia Allman (*Mother Kelp*), Milton Frome (*Dr. Leevee*)

p, Jerry Lewis, Ernest D. Glucksman; d, Jerry Lewis; w, Jerry Lewis, Bill Richmond (based on a story by Lewis); ph, W. Wallace Kelley (Technicolor); ed, John Woodcock; m, Walter Scharf; art d, Hal Pereira, Walter Tyler; fx, Paul K. Lerpae; cos, Edith Head

Jerry Lewis's best film stars the often moronic comic as Julius F. Kelp, a bumbling professor of chemistry at a small college who falls hopelessly in love with one of his more popular students, Stella Purdy (Stella Stevens). Seeking to improve his looks, Kelp whips up a chemical potion and is transformed into an overbearing and obnoxious but dashing singer who calls himself Buddy Love. Though totally conceited, Buddy Love (Lewis in a dual role) succeeds in winning over Stella. Unfortunately, his formula has a way of wearing off at the wrong times. Although only tangentially related to horror films, THE NUTTY PROFESSOR can be seen as a strange companion piece to the *Dr. Jekyll and Mr. Hyde* films, in which the dark, menacing side of an otherwise harmless character seeps through to the forefront. Much has been made of Buddy Love's resemblance to Lewis's former partner, Dean Martin, but the person Love really resembles is the pompous, self-important and bitter Jerry Lewis of talk shows and telethons.

NUTTY PROFESSOR, THE
1996   95m   c   Comedy   ★★½
Imagine Entertainment   (U.S.)   PG-13

Eddie Murphy (*Sherman Klump/Buddy Love/Lance Perkins/Papa Klump/Mama Klump/Grandma Klump/Ernie Klump*), Jada Pinkett (*Carla Purty*), James Coburn (*Harlan Hartley*), Larry Miller (*Dean Richmond*), Dave Chappelle (*Reggie Warrington*), John Ales (*Jason*), Patricia Wilson (*Dean's Secretary*), Jamal Mixon (*Ernie Clump, Jr.*), Nichole McAuley (*Fit Woman*), Hamilton Von Watts (*Health Instructor*)

p, Brian Grazer, Russell Simmons; d, Tom Shadyac; w, David Sheffield, Barry W. Blaustein, Tom Shadyac, Steve Oedekerk (based on the motion picture written by Jerry Lewis and Bill Richmond); ph, Julio Macat; ed, Don Zimmerman; m, David Newman; prod d, William A. Elliott; art d, Greg Papalia; fx, Jon Farhat, Burt Dalton; cos, Ha Nguyen

AA Best Makeup: Rick Baker, David Leroy Anderson

Eddie Murphy devised this comeback for himself using a remake of Jerry Lewis's classic THE NUTTY PROFESSOR, but it fails to match the original.

Sherman Klump (Eddie Murphy), a kindly overweight science teacher, conducts extra-curricular weight-loss experiments on lab hamsters. Carla (Jada Pinkett), a new grad student, takes a liking to the misunderstood professor, and agrees to a date. Sherman's efforts to lose weight are futile, and his date goes from bad (as his family, all played by Murphy, trade insults over dinner) to worse (a nightclub comic pokes fun at Sherman's size). In desperation, Sherman decides to test his hamster formula on himself, and transforms, temporarily, into the lean, dashing "Buddy Love" (Murphy again). Carla finds Buddy attractive, but is put off by his mean streak. At a ritzy party for Harlan Hartley (James Coburn), a wealthy college donor, Sherman and his alter ego reveal themselves at the same time, astonishing the crowd. Sherman thinks that his days are numbered, but Hartley is so impressed by the experiment, that he insists Sherman continue his work for the school. Sherman (sans Buddy) also finds Carla proudly waiting for him on the dance floor.

This remake strains a little too hard for laughs with excessive, occasionally grotesque special effects. Neither Murphy nor director Tom Shadyac succeed in duplicating the brilliant way the Lewis film played with the two sides of Lewis's public persona—introverted nerd and extroverted lounge lizard. Murphy simply cannot pull off the sensitive scenes convincingly, because his characters have always been based on his jovial, devilish personality. Murphy does shows signs of his old comic skill as Buddy becomes increasingly deranged, but this NUTTY PROFESSOR is generally just mean-spirited and depressing.

O

O BROTHER, WHERE ART THOU?
2000   93m   c   Comedy   ★★★
Studio Canal/Working Title/Touchstone/Universal   PG-13
(U.S.)

George Clooney (*Ulysses Everett McGill*), John Turturro (*Pete*), Tim Blake Nelson (*Delmar*), John Goodman (*Big Dan Teague*), Holly Hunter (*Penny Wharvey*), Chris Thomas King (*Tommy Johnson*), Charles Durning (*Pappy O'Daniel*), Del Pentecoste (*Junior O'Daniel*), Michael Badalucco (*George Babyface Nelson*), Lee Weaver (*Blind Seer*)

p, Ethan Coen; d, Joel Coen; w, Ethan Coen, Joel Coen (based upon *The Odyssey* by Homer); ph, Roger Deakins; ed, Roderick Jaynes, Tricia Cooke; m, T Bone Burnett; prod d, Dennis Gassner; art d, Richard Johnson; fx, Peter Chesney; cos, Mary Zophres

AAN Best Cinematography: Roger Deakins; *AAN Best Adapted Screenplay:* Joel Coen, Ethan Coen

Tinged with Joel and Ethan Coen's trademark snooty hijinks, this mild-mannered comedy about three convicts who flee a Mississippi chain gang in hopes of recovering some stolen loot is actually quite a charmer.

Pencil-moustached, pomaded sharpie Ulysses Everett McGill (George Clooney), buried the swag in a place that's about to be flooded as part of a federal hydroelectric project, so Everett and his slack-jawed cohorts, the simple-minded Delmar (Tim Blake Nelson) and hot-tempered Pete (John Turturro) have only a few days to recover their prize. Along the way, they're advised by a blind prophet (Lee Weaver) and taken in by a treacherous cyclops (John Goodman, as a one-eyed bible salesman) and some seductive sirens (Mia Tate, Musetta Vander, Christy Taylor), singing their treacherous hearts out from a rock in a creek. The ex-cons also fall in with neurotic gangster Babyface Nelson (Michael Badalucco), and run afoul of local politicians (Charles Durning, Wayne Duvall) and the KKK, whose broadly comic antics make for the film's most uncomfortable moments.

The title is taken from Preston Sturges' satire SULLI-VAN'S TRAVELS; "O Brother, Where Art Thou?" is the problem picture an earnest Hollywood director wants to make before he logs some time on a chain gang and learns that sometimes desperate people need fluffy pictures like "So Long, Sarong." But the Coens' story is loosely adapted from Homer's *Odyssey*, with emphasis on the loosely. Often clever but fundamentally shallow, this shaggy-dog story is greatly enriched by its extraordinary bluegrass soundtrack, supervised by T Bone Burnett and performed by a phenomenal collection of artists.

O LUCKY MAN!

1973   186m   c   Comedy   ★★★★
Memorial/Sam   (U.K.)   R

Malcolm McDowell *(Mick Travis)*, Ralph Richardson *(Monty/Sir James Burgess)*, Rachel Roberts *(Gloria Rowe/Mme. Paillard/Mrs. Richards)*, Arthur Lowe *(Mr. Duff/Charlie Johnson/Dr. Munda)*, Helen Mirren *(Patricia Burgess)*, Dandy Nichols *(Tea Lady/Neighbor)*, Mona Washbourne *(Sister Hallett/Usher/Neighbor)*, Michael Medwin *(Army Captain/Power Station Technician/Duke of Belminster)*, Mary McLeod *(Mrs. Ball/Vicar's Wife/Salvation Army Woman)*, Vivian Pickles *(Welfare Lady)*

p, Michael Medwin, Lindsay Anderson; d, Lindsay Anderson; w, David Sherwin (based on an idea by Malcolm McDowell); ph, Miroslav Ondricek (Technicolor); ed, David Gladwell, Tom Priestley; m, Alan Price; prod d, Jocelyn Herbert; art d, Alan Withy; fx, John Stears; cos, Elsa Fennell

Bizarre, loosely conceived sequel to IF..., in which Malcolm McDowell again plays Mick Travis, now a Candide-like coffee salesman bent on achieving corporate success. Travis's Kafkaesque, state-of-the-nation odyssey takes in a businessmen's sex club; a military camp where he's arrested and tortured; a medical research center where experiments include attaching a human head to a pig's body; an affair with the hippie daughter (Helen Mirren) of a corrupt industrialist (Ralph Richardson); and a scheme involving the sale of Napalm to an African nation that lands Travis in prison.

A variety of framing and distancing devices give a determinedly modernist dimension to Travis's blackly humorous adventures: his travels are punctuated by musical interludes, courtesy of Alan Price, that provide a neo-Brechtian commentary on the action; scenes are divided by blackouts that highlight the episodic nature of the proceedings; members of Anderson's informal repertory company each play several different roles; and Travis's exploits end with him being selected to play the lead role in the film we have just seen. A lucky man, indeed.

O. HENRY'S FULL HOUSE

1952   117m   bw   Comedy/Drama   ★★★½
Fox   (U.S.)

Jeanne Crain *(Della)*, Farley Granger *(Jim)*, Anne Baxter *(Joanna)*, Jean Peters *(Susan)*, Charles Laughton *(Soapy)*, Marilyn Monroe *(Streetwalker)*, David Wayne *(Horace)*, Richard Widmark *(Johnny Kernan)*, Fred Allen *(Sam)*, Oscar Levant *(Bill)*

p, Andre Hakim; d, Henry Hathaway, Henry Koster, Henry King, Howard Hawks, Jean Negulesco; w, Lamar Trotti, Richard Breen, Ben Roberts, Ivan Goff, Walter Bullock, Nunnally Johnson (based on the stories by O. Henry); ph, Lloyd Ahern, Lucien Ballard, Joseph MacDonald, Milton Krasner; ed, Nick De Maggio, Barbara McLean, William B. Murphy; m, Alfred Newman; art d, Lyle Wheeler, Chester Gore, Joseph C. Wright, Irving Richard, Addison Hehr

This hearty and entertaining compendium of O. Henry's best stories features some energetic performances and, in a few cases, marvelous direction. The first tale, "The Cop and the Anthem," is about a haughty tramp who, with the onset of winter, tries to get arrested so he can enjoy the warmth of a jail cell. But, try as he might, he simply cannot offend the law. "The Clarion Call" is a terse slice of life in which a decent cop must arrest an old friend. In "The Last Leaf," a dying woman watches autumn leaves wither, and comes to believe that when the last leaf blows away, she, too, will die. Winter comes and the leaves vanish, one by one, until a single leaf remains, stubbornly clinging to the wall and giving the woman hope. There's a laugh a minute in "The Ransom of Red Chief," the story of a boy so bad that his parents couldn't care less when he's kidnapped. The rowdy kid makes life so miserable for his abductors that *they* bribe the parents to take the insufferable brat back. In the famous "The Gift of the Magi," a pair of impoverished young newlyweds sacrifice their most cherished possessions to buy each other Christmas gifts. The direction and writing in all these sequences are good, and the entire film is a great treat, enhanced by John Steinbeck's narration—an homage to the mysterious O. Henry.

OBJECT OF MY AFFECTION, THE   📀

1998   111m   c   Romance/Comedy   ★★★½
Laurence Mark Productions/20th Century Fox   R
(U.S.)

Jennifer Aniston *(Nina)*, Paul Rudd *(George Hanson)*, Tim Daly *(Dr. Robert Joely)*, Alan Alda *(Sidney Miller)*, Nigel Hawthorne *(Rodney Fraser)*, John Pankow *(Vince McBride)*, Kali Rocha *(Melissa Marx)*, Lena Cardwell, Natalie B. Kikkenborg *(Girls at Community Center)*, Lauren Varija Pratt *(Sally Miller)*

p, Laurence Mark; d, Nicholas Hytner; w, Wendy Wasserstein (based on the novel by Stephen McCauley); ph, Oliver Stapleton; ed, Tariq Anwar; m, George Fenton; prod d, Jane Musky; art d, Patricia Woodbridge; cos, John Dunn

Witty and charming, this romantic comedy about a heterosexual woman who falls for a gay man explores the often hazy border between friendship and love.

Social worker Nina (Jennifer Aniston) and grade-school teacher George (Paul Rudd) meet at a swank dinner party thrown by Nina's sister Constance (Allison Jenney) and Constance's husband, Sidney (Alan Alda), and the two immediately hit it off. Nina's been dating an overbearing Legal Aid lawyer (John Pankow) to whom she can't quite commit, and George has just been unceremoniously dumped by his boyfriend (Tim Daly), and the way is paved for the pair to become roommates. The unlikely couple quickly become fast friends and are soon taking dance lessons and looking, well, amazingly cute together. Nina begins to fall in love, and after learning that she's pregnant, considers asking George to raise the child with her. But George's gayness is one thing that isn't so easily overcome, either by sheer force of affection or desire.

What makes this movie so refreshing is that George's sexuality is mostly undiluted by Hollywood standards: he even gets to have a boyfriend of his own. Director Nicholas Hytner's commitment to telling this story and allowing us to know all the characters—not just the leads—is evident; the supporting players are more than two-dimensional backup for George and Nina. Playwright Wendy Wasserstein, who has done a fine job adapting Stephen McCauley's novel, hands the film's best lines to Nigel Hawthorne (star of Hytner's MADNESS OF KING GEORGE), perfectly cast as a waspish theater critic. You come away with a sense of filmmakers and actors working in harmony as they delve into the heart of relationships between friends and lovers, finding, as Shakespeare wrote, that "Friendship is constant in all other things/Save in the office and affairs of love."

OBJECTIVE, BURMA! 📀
1945 142m bw War ★★★★
Warner Bros. (U.S.)

Errol Flynn *(Maj. Nelson)*, James Brown *(Sgt. Treacy)*, William Prince *(Lt. Sid Jacobs)*, George Tobias *(Gabby Gordon)*, Henry Hull *(Mark Williams)*, Warner Anderson *(Col. Carter)*, John Alvin *(Hogan)*, Mark Stevens *(Lt. Barker)*, Richard Erdman *(Nebraska Hooper)*, Anthony Caruso *(Miggleori)*

p, Jerry Wald; d, Raoul Walsh; w, Ranald MacDougall, Lester Cole (based on a story by Alvah Bessie); ph, James Wong Howe; ed, George Amy; m, Franz Waxman; art d, Ted Smith; fx, Edwin DuPar

AAN Best Original Story: Alvah Bessie; *AAN Best Film Editing:* George Amy; *AAN Best Score (Drama or Comedy):* Franz Waxman

This is one of the finest WWII films made during the war, and Errol Flynn, discarding his usual impudent and pranksterish style, is terrific as the straightforward and very human leader of 50 American paratroops who drop behind enemy lines to destroy a Japanese radar station. The commandos complete their mission successfully, but while waiting to rendezvous with the rescue planes they are attacked by a force of Japanese and have to fight their way out of the Burmese jungle on foot. Flynn gives one of his most convincing and powerful performances, and Raoul Walsh's direction is nothing less than excellent, with the great action director maintaining a harrowing pace, providing a wealth of interesting military detail, and delivering one thrilling scene after another. Alvah Bessie, who would later become one of the "Hollywood Ten" writers indicted by HUAC, provided the engrossing story, marked by its relative lack of patriotic speechifying and some marvelously entertaining banter between the experienced commandos. Exceptional, too, is the dynamic, masterful score by Franz Waxman, which fits the mood and menace of the mysterious jungle and incorporates the sounds of wild animals and exotic birds. James Wong Howe's splendid photography, with its naturalistic lighting, lends a great deal of authenticity to the jungle scenes, especially when one considers that the film was shot almost entirely on the "Lucky" Baldwin Santa Anita ranch outside Pasadena. The film received rave reviews and heavy box-office support in the U.S., but when OBJECTIVE, BURMA! was released in England, the British press exploded, claiming that the film minimized the efforts of the British in Burma by giving the impression that an American commando team liberated the area by themselves. The film was banned in Britain until 1952, when prints were reissued with a prologue extolling the British contribution to the campaign.

OCEAN'S ELEVEN 📀
2001 116m c Crime ★★★½
Village Roadshow/NPV Entertainment/Jerry PG-13
Weintraub Productions/Section Eight Productions
(U.S.)

George Clooney *(Danny Ocean)*, Matt Damon *(Linus Caldwell)*, Andy Garcia *(Terry Benedict)*, Brad Pitt *(Rusty Ryan)*, Julia Roberts *(Tess Ocean)*, Casey Affleck *(Virgil Malloy)*, Scott Caan *(Turk Malloy)*, Don Cheadle *(Basher Tarr—uncredited)*, Elliott Gould *(Reuben Tishkoff)*, Bernie Mac *(Frank Catton)*

p, Jerry Weintraub; d, Steven Soderbergh; w, Ted Griffin (based on the screenplay by Harry Brown and Charles Lederer, and a story by George Clayton Johnson and Jack Golden Russell); ph, Steven Soderbergh; ed, Stephen Mirrione; m, David Holmes; prod d, Philip Messina; art d, Keith P. Cunningham; fx, Kevin Hannigan; cos, Jeffrey Kurland

A genial, personality-driven heist comedy, based on the 1960 rat-pack escapade, that wants nothing more than to entertain.

Con man Danny Ocean (George Clooney), the sort of smooth operator who gets sprung from jail in a tuxedo, is fresh out of the joint and already setting up a new scam. And it's a doozy: he plans to rob the vault that houses hundreds of millions of dollars in cash for *three* glittering Las Vegas casinos. They're all owned by a notoriously security-conscious thug named Terry Benedict (Andy Garcia), who's dating a leggy beauty named Tess (Julia Roberts) who just happens to be Danny's ex-wife. Danny quickly assembles a crew from the rogues' gallery of friends: card sharp Ryan (Brad Pitt), pickpocket Linus Caldwell (Matt Damon), cockney explosives specialist Basher Tarr (Don Cheadle), crooked casino dealer Frank Catton (Bernie Mac), drivers and all-purpose chameleons Virgil and Turk Malloy (Casey Affleck, Scott Caan), surveillance geek Dell (Eddie Jemison), and veteran flimflam man Saul Bloom (Carl Reiner).

Like the original OCEAN'S ELEVEN—whose cult-classic status is entirely due to the combined appeal of Frank Sinatra, Dean Martin, Sammy Davis Jr., and Peter Lawford—the film's main attraction is the easy banter between the stars, who appear to be having the time of their lives. At the same time, it's also one of those rare movies in which it doesn't feel as though the fun is being had at the viewer's expense. Director Steven Soderbergh is one of the few contemporary filmmakers who really knows how to use movie stars. Not one of the megawatt cast is asked to do anything except turn on that larger-than-life glow, and they respond by sparkling brilliantly.

OCEAN'S TWELVE 📀
2004 125m c Crime/Comedy ★★
Warner Bros./Village Roadshow Pictures/Section PG-13
EightProductions/Jerry Weintraub Productions
(U.S./Australia)

George Clooney *(Danny Ocean)*, Brad Pitt *(Rusty Ryan)*, Matt Damon *(Linus Caldwell)*, Bernie Mac *(Frank Catton)*, Don Cheadle *(Basher Tarr)*, Catherine Zeta-Jones *(Isabel Lahiri)*, Julia Roberts *(Tess Ocean)*, Andy Garcia *(Terry Benedict)*, Scott Caan *(Turk Malloy)*, Casey Affleck *(Virgil Malloy)*

p, Jerry Weintraub; d, Steven Soderbergh; w, George Nolfi (based on characters created by George Clayton Jackson and Jack Golden Russell); ph, Steven Soderbergh; ed, Stephen Mirrione; m, David Holmes; prod d, Philip Messina; art d, Tony Fanning; fx, Kevin Hannigan, Thomas J. Smith; cos, Milena Canonero

Driven by director Steven Soderbergh's hankering to shoot in Europe and the fortuitous discovery of an existing George Nolfi screenplay called "Honor Among Thieves"—suitable for reconfiguring to accommodate the sprawling OCEAN'S

ELEVEN cast—this lackluster sequel was surely much more fun to make than it is to watch.

Three years after Danny Ocean (George Clooney) and his 10 accomplices split the $160 million jackpot they stole from casino owner Terry Benedict (Andy Garcia), each gets a visit from the still seething Benedict, who wants his money back, with interest, in two weeks. So the crew—Rusty Ryan (Brad Pitt), Linus Caldwell (Matt Damon), Basher Tarr (Don Cheadle), Frank Catton (Bernie Mac), bickering brothers Turk and Virgil Malloy (Scott Caan, Casey Affleck), Saul Bloom (Carl Reiner), Reuben Tishkoff (Elliott Gould), Livingston Dell (Eddie Jemison), and Yen (Shaobo Qin)—reassemble to formulate a plan. The titular twelfth is Tess (Julia Roberts), whom Ocean won back from Benedict in ELEVEN. They're all still too hot to pull off another major heist in the U.S., so they invade Europe, crossing paths with colorful supporting characters until the plot threads involving Rusty's ex, a comely Europol agent (Catherine Zeta-Jones), and a vainglorious bandit (Vincent Cassell) converge.

The biggest disappointment about this halfhearted follow-up is that while in OCEAN'S ELEVEN every member of the crew was an indispensable cog in the casino heist, here more than half are reduced to glorified cameos. The proceedings are no less plausible than the average heist picture, but they're soured by the smug vibe of "Isn't it great to be gallivanting around Europe on Warner Bros.' dime pretending you're working because you deign to step in front of a camera and crack wise with your friends?"

ODD COUPLE, THE 📀

1968 105m c Comedy ★★★½
Paramount (U.S.) G

Jack Lemmon *(Felix Ungar)*, Walter Matthau *(Oscar Madison)*, John Fiedler *(Vinnie)*, Herb Edelman *(Murray)*, David Sheiner *(Roy)*, Larry Haines *(Speed)*, Monica Evans *(Cecily)*, Carole Shelley *(Gwendolyn)*, Iris Adrian *(Waitress)*, Heywood Hale Broun *(Sportswriter)*

p, Howard W. Koch; d, Gene Saks; w, Neil Simon (based on the play by Simon); ph, Robert B. Hauser (Panavision, Technicolor); ed, Frank Bracht; m, Neal Hefti; art d, Hal Pereira, Walter Tyler; fx, Paul K. Lerpae; cos, Jack Bear

AAN Best Adapted Screenplay: Neil Simon; *AAN Best Film Editing:* Frank Bracht

A film adaptation of a Neil Simon play, which means that it resembles an old, Manhattan-set syndicated sitcom. Gene Saks directing, which means that it looks like neither he nor the cast ever left the theater. The good news is that, as sitcom-style theater goes, THE ODD COUPLE is often highly amusing, with Lemmon and Matthau ideally cast as prissy neatnik and unmitigated slob. You all know the plot—both men have botched their marriages and try living together without killing each other. With gay domestic partnerships increasingly visible on the American family landscape, this film gingerly dancing around its own queerness does seem either ahead of its time or rather dated, but even if you take your Simon straight, so to speak, he does have a fairly good ear for a wisecrack, and the supporting cast is thankfully expert. The plot, nothing more than a premise based on Simon's real-life brother, Danny, goes nowhere, but then it's not really supposed to. Of course, if you don't feel like renting this video sitcom, you can always watch the actual sitcom with Tony Randall and Jack Klugman, still a big success in syndication. It's the same damn thing.

ODD MAN OUT 📀

1947 116m bw Drama ★★★★★
Two Cities (U.K.)

James Mason *(Johnny McQueen)*, Robert Newton *(Lukey)*, Kathleen Ryan *(Kathleen)*, Robert Beatty *(Dennis)*, William Hartnell *(Barman)*, F.J. McCormick *(Shell)*, Fay Compton *(Rosie)*, Beryl Measor *(Maudie)*, Cyril Cusack *(Pat)*, Dan O'Herlihy *(Nolan)*

p, Carol Reed; d, Carol Reed; w, F.L. Green, R.C. Sherriff (based on the novel by F.L. Green); ph, Robert Krasker; ed, Fergus McDonell; m, William Alwyn; prod d, Roger Furse; art d, Ralph Brinton; fx, Stanley Grant, Bill Warrington

AAN Best Film Editing: Fergus McDonell

Reed, one of Britain's finest directors, made his name with this haunting, lyrical masterpiece about a doomed fugitive. In perhaps the greatest performance of his illustrious career, Mason plays Johnny, an IRA leader who breaks out of jail and then plans a payroll holdup of a mill in Belfast to fund his underground operations. Though he abhors violence, Johnny accidentally kills a man during the holdup, and is himself critically wounded. Left behind by the panicky driver of the getaway car, Johnny stumbles away, descending into a nightmare as he becomes more and more delirious from his wound. He is harbored by a bunch of strange people who either want to help him or sell him to the British authorities. Sweetheart Kathleen (Ryan) and Johnny's IRA pals are in the meantime searching frantically for him. The man is hidden in deserted buildings and even in a junkyard bathtub for a while. On another occasion, two spinsters take him in, serve him tea, and then discover he is wounded, bandaging him before he departs. He finally falls into the clutches of an eccentric painter (Newton), who wants to catch the look of death in Johnny's eyes before it's too late. Struggling free from this madman, Johnny makes his way toward the docks in a final desperate effort to escape. Kathleen finally finds him there, but so do the police. The finale is very powerful.

Mason's performance as the dying fugitive, enhanced by that unique voice, is nothing less than great. Johnny's escalating pain, his lingering pride and the desperate look he gives an uncomprehending child searching for a ball are searingly intense. Ryan, who debuted here, never had the chance to impact like this again, and marvelous performances are contributed by Cusack and O'Herlihy as Mason's chief lieutenants. The fascinating McCormick steals most of his scenes as a rag-picking bum who hides Johnny, and Newton positively gorges himself on the scenery in a wild portrait of the artist as a crazed man.

Early on, Reed, aided by Krasker's gritty cinematography, establishes a deeply somber mood in this modern odyssey to doom and death in an uncaring world. Each frame is another lethal step for Johnny as Reed poetically captures his last moments on earth. The plot and character development are touchingly constructed and enhanced by a magnificent score by Alwyn. Though Mason is initially presented as a culprit, his agonizing plight slowly transfigures him into a Christ-like figure. Visually reminiscent of John Ford's THE INFORMER, ODD MAN OUT also shares thematic concerns with Ford's THE FUGITIVE, insofar as both films depict an intolerable fate for a man who is basically decent but is condemned for his own altruistic beliefs. A great work of art, ODD MAN OUT is a painting on celluloid, evoking the best canvases of Goya and Velasquez. (Check out the weird shot of what manifests itself in Johnny's beer bubbles.) Although it was not popular at the box office, the film quickly won worldwide plaudits and established Reed as a great director.

ODDS AGAINST TOMORROW

1959 95m bw Crime

Harbel (U.S.)

DVD

★★★★

Harry Belafonte (Johnny Ingram), Robert Ryan (Earl Slater), Shelley Winters (Lorry), Ed Begley (Dave Burke), Gloria Grahame (Helen), Will Kuluva (Bacco), Richard Bright (Coco), Lew Gallo (Moriarity), Fred J. Scollay (Cannoy), Carmen de Lavallade (Kitty)

p, Robert Wise; d, Robert Wise; w, Abraham Polonsky, Nelson Gidding (based on the novel by William P. McGivern); ph, Joseph Brun; ed, Dede Allen; m, John Lewis; art d, Leo Kerz; cos, Anna Hill Johnstone

A crackling crime caper that includes an overlay of racial tension, ODDS AGAINST TOMORROW was the first film out of Belafonte's own producing entity and proved that he wasn't just another pretty face and froggy voice. Robert Ryan, who was a liberal in real life, plays a psychotic racist similiar to the anti-Semitic character he played in CROSSFIRE. Belafonte is a gambling junkie, a man whose love for the horses has caused his marriage to fall apart. He's a childish nightclub singer and is now in danger from the harassment of Kuluva, a gay gangster in the employ of the people who hold Belafonte's IOUs. Ryan is an ex-con looking for a big score and Begley is a former cop who has been cashiered from the force for illegal dealings. This unlikely trio unite to rob an upstate New York bank of $150,000. Belafonte desperately needs his share of the swag to call off Kuluva, who is now threatening to kill Belafonte's wife and daughter. Ryan is married to Winters, though dallying with Grahame, who gets vicarious thrills before they make love when she pleads with Ryan to tell her how it feels to murder someone. Ryan's anti-black feelings are overcome by Begley and the robbery takes place. But everything goes awry. A gas station jockey spots Ryan. Belafonte witnesses an accident and must give his version of the incident; then he switches places with the food delivery man who brings the bank's night workers their refreshments. The regular guy shows up and so do the cops. Begley is shot, and when he can't get the getaway car's keys to his buddies, he takes his own life, rather than suffer the ignominy of arrest. Ryan and Belafonte escape and flee to an oil storage area not unlike the one in the final scenes of WHITE HEAT.

This is a fine slice of noir that didn't get the box-office attention it deserved. It features a terrific jazz score by John Lewis, pianist for the Modern Jazz Quartet, and, in small roles, Cicely Tyson, Wayne Rogers, and Zohra Lampert. Blacklisted scripter Abraham Polonsky was omitted from the credits in favor of a front, John O. Killens. In 1996, the Writer's Guild of America officially restored Polonsky's credit.

OF HUMAN BONDAGE

1934 83m bw Drama

RKO (U.S.)

DVD

★★★★

Leslie Howard (Philip Carey), Bette Davis (Mildred Rogers), Frances Dee (Sally Athelny), Reginald Owen (Thorpe Athelny), Reginald Denny (Harry Griffiths), Kay Johnson (Norah), Alan Hale (Emil Miller), Reginald Sheffield (Dunsford), Desmond Roberts (Dr. Jacobs), Tempe Pigott (Landlady)

p, Pandro S. Berman; d, John Cromwell; w, Lester Cohen (based on the novel by W. Somerset Maugham); ph, Henry Gerrard; ed, William Morgan; m, Max Steiner; art d, Van Nest Polglase, Carroll Clark; fx, Vernon L. Walker; cos, Walter Plunkett

Cautious adaptation of Somerset Maugham's tragic tale features the electric performance by Bette Davis that made her a star. Today, it looks a trifle much, but given time and circumstance—the stylized acting of the early sound era, and her desire to be noticed—it's a blistering job.

Club-footed Philip Carey (Howard) studies painting in Paris but realizes that his work will never be more than sec-ond-rate, so he returns to England and begins to study medicine. Davis is Mildred, a blond tart whom he meets in the restaurant where she works as a waitress. She manipulates his affection cruelly, but even though she later breaks off the relationship to marry Emil Miller (Hale) and he takes solace with sympathetic Norah (Johnson), Philip can only think of Mildred. When a pregnant Mildred returns after Emil has abandoned her, Philip takes her in, but she runs away again, this time with Philip's friend Harry (Denny). And yet she returns one last time...

Thanks to wonderful performances by the leads, this version of the Maugham story is certainly the finest. Howard's quiet, studied performance is just right. Davis came by her role the hard way. After RKO acquired the novel for production, studio executives were shocked to learn that none of their leading ladies wanted the part of the sluttish Mildred. Katharine Hepburn, Ann Harding, and Irene Dunne all rejected the role. Davis, however, was languishing in unimportant roles at Warners, and she began to lobby Jack Warner to loan her to RKO for the part. The actress threw herself into the role, adopting a Cockney accent which she refused to discard when off-camera. She even supervised her own makeup so that it would convey Mildred's decline from syphilis. Davis's natural tendency to slouch worked very well for Mildred; within a few years that tendency would be gone for good. She was profoundly disappointed when she failed to receive an Oscar nomination as Best Actress, but this film was her watershed picture.

OF MICE AND MEN

1939 107m bw Drama

Hal Roach (U.S.)

DVD

★★★★

Burgess Meredith (George), Betty Field (Mae), Lon Chaney Jr. (Lennie), Charles Bickford (Slim), Roman Bohnen (Candy), Bob Steele (Curley), Noah Beery Jr. (Whit), Oscar O'Shea (Jackson), Granville Bates (Carlson), Leigh Whipper (Crooks)

p, Lewis Milestone; d, Lewis Milestone; w, Eugene Solow (based on the novel by John Steinbeck); ph, Norbert Brodine; ed, Bert Jordan; m, Aaron Copland; art d, Nicolai Remisoff; fx, Roy Seawright

AAN Best Picture; AAN Best Original Score: Aaron Copland; AAN Best Score: Aaron Copland; AAN Best Sound Recording: Elmer Raguse

John Steinbeck's moving, powerful story of two ranch hands trying to find a safe haven in a hostile world comes to the screen with penetrating compassion under the deft hand of director Milestone. The huge, childlike, slightly retarded Lennie (Chaney) and the sharp, protective George (Meredith) wander the rural West, looking for work during the Great Depression. Hired as hands at a ranch, they fantasize about owning a farm themselves one day, where George will be in charge and Lennie can tend to the small, furry, barnyard animals. Lennie, unfortunately, can't always control his passions, or the tremendous strength with which he can act on them. When the ranch owner's vicious son Curley (Steele) begins browbeating the men too much, the trouble begins. Things get even worse when Curley's bored, flirtatious wife (Field) begins toying with the baffled Lennie, and George realizes he must do something about his friend.

Though grim and offbeat, OF MICE AND MEN is a noble morality tale that can be appreciated for its simplicity. The acting is faultless and Copland's score is magnificent. Hollywood censorship deserves at least a modest amount of praise for not completely eviscerating a powerfully adult story. This was Chaney's finest performance ever; equally impressive are Meredith, Bickford, Field, Bohnen (in an especially moving turn as the pathetic Candy), and B-film cowboy star Steele. Remade by clumsier hands, and with too much gloss, in 1992.

OFFICER AND A GENTLEMAN, AN

DVD

1982 126m c   Romance/War   ★★★½
Lorimar   (U.S.)   R

Richard Gere (Zack Mayo), Debra Winger (Paula Pokrifki), David Keith (Sid Worley), Robert Loggia (Byron Mayo), Lisa Blount (Lynette Pomeroy), Lisa Eilbacher (Casey Seeger), Louis Gossett Jr. (Sgt. Emil Foley), Tony Plana (Emiliano Della Serra), Harold Sylvester (Perryman), David Caruso (Topper Daniels)

p, Martin Elfand; d, Taylor Hackford; w, Douglas Day Stewart; ph, Donald Thorin (Metrocolor); ed, Peter Zinner; m, Jack Nitzsche; prod d, Philip Jefferies; art d, John V. Cartwright

AAN Best Actress: Debra Winger; AAN Best Supporting Actor: Louis Gossett, Jr.; AAN Best Original Screenplay: Douglas Day Stewart; AAN Best Film Editing: Peter Zinner; AAN Best Original Score: Jack Nitzsche; AA Best Original Song: "Up Where We Belong"; Jack Nitzsche (Music), Buffy Sainte-Marie (Music), Will Jennings (Lyrics)

Lou Gossett, Jr., won a much-deserved Best Supporting Actor Oscar for his stellar portrayal of a drill instructor in this story of determination and love set against the backdrop of a Naval Aviation Officer Candidate School. Richard Gere plays Zack Mayo, a would-be flyer with a tough-luck background who, like his classmates, must survive the rigors of training under draconian Marine sergeant Emil Foley (Gossett) before moving on to flight school. Sgt. Foley singles out Zack for special derision, and though he pushes his charge to the limit, the feisty Zack refuses to give up, eventually tangling with the DI in martial-arts battle. Meanwhile, Zack and classmate Sid Worley (David Keith), the film's tragic figure, become involved with a couple of local girls, millworkers Paula Pokrifki (Debra Winger), who received a Best Actress nomination for her fine performance) and Lynette Pomeroy (Lisa Blount). Paula becomes convinced that Zack is like all the other officer candidates who do their training, take advantage of local women, and then disappear forever once they've earned their white uniform. Douglas Day Stewart's Oscar-nominated screenplay is generally involving (if a little over-heated), but it is ultimately compromised by its sexism, particularly in the finale, which leaves Paula with only one hope for happiness—to be carried off by a dashing knight. Nonetheless, the performances are uniformly strong, with Gere offering some of his best work—though it pales in comparison with Gossett's tour de force as the tough, principled Sgt. Foley, which he patterned after real-life army DI Bill Dower (familiar to some from his appearances in Miller Lite commercials). The film's memorable theme song, "Up Where We Belong" (sung by Joe Cocker and Jennifer Warnes), also won an Academy Award.

OFFICIAL STORY, THE

DVD

(LA HISTORIA OFICIAL)
1985 112m c   Drama   ★★★½
Historias Cine   (Argentina)

Hector Alterio (Roberto), Norma Aleandro (Alicia), Chela Ruiz (Sara), Chunchuna Villafane (Ana), Hugo Arana (Enrique), Patricio Contreras (Benitez), Guillermo Battaglia (Jose), Maria-Luisa Robledo (Nata), Jorge Petraglia (Macci), Analia Castro (Gaby)

p, Marcelo Pineyro; d, Luis Puenzo; w, Luis Puenzo, Aida Bortnik; ph, Felix Monti; ed, Juan Carlos Macias; m, Atilio Stampone; prod d, Abel Facello; art d, Abel Facello; cos, Tiky Garcia Estevez

AA Best Foreign Language Film ; AAN Best Original Screenplay: Luis Puenzo, Aida Bortnik

The first important film to emerge from Argentina after the fall of its military regime, THE OFFICIAL STORY is a deeply moving drama examining one of the saddest chapters in that country's history. The tranquil lives of Alicia (Norma Aleandro), a history professor; her husband, Roberto (Hector Alterio), a high-powered businessman; and their five-year-old daughter, Gaby (Analia Castro), are thrown into turmoil when an old friend who was tortured and exiled by the military reveals that, under the junta, babies were taken from political prisoners and sold to well-connected adoptive parents. Realizing that Gaby may be one of these children, Alicia begins to investigate her daughter's background and meets Sara (Chela Ruiz), one of the women who march each day at the Plaza de Mayo to protest the disappearance of loved ones in the junta's "dirty war." Coming to grips with her political naivete, Alicia confronts Roberto, who proves to be deeply involved with the reprehensible junta. An impressive feature debut by Luis Puenzo, who invests his scenes with tremendous emotional impact, THE OFFICIAL STORY won the 1986 Oscar for Best Foreign-Language Film. Poignantly political, its power derives from the depiction of the junta's tragic effect on individual lives. The screenplay was written with Aleandro (a political exile who returned to her native Argentina after the change of government) in mind, and she delivers a tour de force performance that won her the Best Actress Award at Cannes. Originally, Puenzo intended to shoot the film in secret, using hidden 16mm cameras, but the junta was voted out of office just after cowriter Aida Bortnik completed the screenplay.

OH! WHAT A LOVELY WAR

1969 144m c   War/Musical   ★★★½
Accord   (U.K.)   G

Ralph Richardson (Sir Edward Grey), Meriel Forbes (Lady Grey), Wensley Pithey (Archduke Franz Ferdinand), Ruth Kettlewell (Duchess Sophie), Ian Holm (President Poincare), John Gielgud (Count Berchtold), Kenneth More (Kaiser Wilhelm II), John Clements (Gen. von Moltke), Paul Daneman (Czar Nicholas II), Pamela Abbott (Czarina)

p, Brian Duffy, Richard Attenborough, Len Deighton (uncredited); d, Richard Attenborough; w, Len Deighton (based on Joan Littlewood's stage production of Charles Chilton's play The Long, Long Trail); ph, Gerry Turpin (Panavision, Technicolor); ed, Kevin Connor; m, Alfred Ralston; prod d, Don Ashton; art d, Harry White; fx, Ron Ballanger; chor, Eleanor Fazan; cos, Anthony Mendleson

Richard Attenborough's directorial debut is a sprawling, highly stylized musical satire of WWI featuring some of Britain's very finest actors—Ralph Richardson, Laurence Olivier, Michael Redgrave, John Mills, Jack Hawkins, Ian Holm, and Vanessa Redgrave among them. After an opening that finds Europe's heads of state choosing up sides when Archduke Franz Ferdinand is killed during a royal photo session, OH! WHAT A LOVELY WAR traces WWI through a series of surreal set pieces, alternating between the front lines in France and the English homefront, where generals and diplomats conduct a distant war that is actually waged by the young and poor. In particular, the film focuses on the Smith family, whose sons, seduced into the service in the carnival atmosphere of Brighton, all end up dying for their country. Meanwhile, the sacrifices of the British aristocracy, as embodied by Eleanor (Susannah York) and Stephen (Dirk Bogarde), are limited to boycotting German wine. Against a backdrop that includes flashing neon messages and a cricket scoreboard that keeps tally of the war's casualties, a series of musical numbers from 1914-18 are performed and given a distinctly antiwar slant that won considerable support from the British Left for this film and its inspiration, Joan Littlewood's 1963 stage adaptation of Charles Chilton's radio play "The Long, Long Trail." The rights to the play were purchased by producer Brian Duffy and novelist Len Deighton, the latter of whom had his name taken off the film before its release because of differences with Attenborough.

OH, WHAT A LOVELY WAR is not a flawless film but is thoughtful and enthralling.

OKLAHOMA! 📀

1955 145m c Western/Musical ★★★
Magna (U.S.) G

Gordon MacRae *(Curly)*, Gloria Grahame *(Ado Annie)*, Gene Nelson *(Will Parker)*, Charlotte Greenwood *(Aunt Eller)*, Shirley Jones *(Laurey)*, Eddie Albert *(Ali Hakim)*, James Whitmore *(Carnes)*, Rod Steiger *(Jud Fry)*, Barbara Lawrence *(Gertie)*, Jay C. Flippen *(Skidmore)*

p, Arthur Hornblow Jr.; d, Fred Zinnemann; w, Sonya Levien, William Ludwig (based on the musical by Richard Rodgers, Oscar Hammerstein II, from the play *Green Grow the Lilacs* by Lynn Riggs); ph, Robert Surtees (Todd-AO, Eastmancolor); ed, Gene Ruggiero; m, Richard Rodgers; prod d, Oliver Smith; art d, Joseph C. Wright; chor, Agnes De Mille; cos, Orry-Kelly, Motley

AAN Best Color Cinematography: Robert Surtees; AAN Best Film Editing: Gene Ruggiero, George Boemler; AA Best Score (Musical): Robert Russell Bennett, Jay Blackton, Adolph Deutsch; AA Best Sound Recording: Fred Hynes

Watch it for the songs. A paean to Oklahoma's "Sooner" pioneers, it's a watchable, if hardly terrific, rendering of an innovative Broadway landmark. Boys (MacRae and Nelson) meet girls (Jones and Grahame); boys almost lose girls, all complicated by the villainous Jud Fry (Steiger, in a ridiculously hammy, off-key performance as the farmhand-from-hell). Although the score is, by now, deeply embedded in the minds of anyone who has ears, it gets spirited renditions here that are worth listening to. MacRae, in the best-remembered role of his career, gets the film off to a wonderful start with "Oh, What a Beautiful Morning." A very young Jones also makes a nice impression and became an instant star (though her film career never did take root), and Grahame, Greenwood, Albert and Lawrence have fun with their parts as well. In the Dream Ballet, choreographer Agnes DeMille followed what she did onstage and replaced non-dancing Jones and MacRae with Bambi Lynn and James Mitchell, respectively, thus unfortunately encouraging filmmakers to cast movie stars without musical comedy talent in adaptations of Broadway shows. OKLAHOMA! was actually shot outside of Nogales, Arizona, where the cast and crew put in nearly eight months of work, delayed by flash floods, one of which washed away a car containing a week's worth of film. Easy come, easy go.

OLD DARK HOUSE, THE 📀

1932 70m bw Horror ★★★★
Universal (U.S.)

Boris Karloff *(Morgan)*, Melvyn Douglas *(Roger Penderell)*, Charles Laughton *(Sir William Porterhouse)*, Gloria Stuart *(Margaret Waverton)*, Lilian Bond *(Gladys DuCane)*, Ernest Thesiger *(Horace Femm)*, Eva Moore *(Rebecca Femm)*, Raymond Massey *(Philip Waverton)*, Brember Wills *(Saul Femm)*, Elspeth Dudgeon *(Sir Roderick Femm)*

p, Carl Laemmle Jr.; d, James Whale; w, Benn W. Levy, R.C. Sherriff (based on the novel *Benighted* by J.B. Priestley); ph, Arthur Edeson; ed, Clarence Kolster; art d, Charles D. Hall; fx, John P. Fulton

"No beds! They can't have beds!" A uniquely bizarre, wonderfully funny and exciting haunted house film with an all-star cast directed by the brilliant James Whale. Loosely based on J.B. Priestley's novel *Benighted*, the story has a group of stranded travelers forced to seek refuge at the strange house of the Femm family. Philip Waverton (Massey), his wife Margaret (Stuart) and their friend Roger Penderell (Douglas) arrive first. Inside lurks a "home" presided over by the 102-year-old bedridden patriarch Sir Roderick (Elspeth Dudgeon, an actress billed in the credits as "John Dudgeon" and brilliant in the role). Also featured are his atheist son Horace (Thesiger), his religious fanatic daughter Rebecca (Moore), and their older brother Saul (Wills), a crazed pyromaniac kept locked in his room upstairs. Hovering around the action is the house's hulking, mute, scarred, and slightly psychotic butler Morgan (Karloff, in his first starring role). Two more stranded travelers, Sir William Porterhouse (Laughton) and his "companion" Gladys DuCane (Bond), arrive soon after, and then the fun starts. The horrors here are not supernatural and arise solely from the madnesses of the Femm household, particularly when Morgan gets drunk and lets Saul loose. The suspense builds incredibly in the final showdown between Penderell and the mad Saul.

Handled in the uniquely theatrical manner that makes James Whale's work instantly recognizable, THE OLD DARK HOUSE is nonetheless never "stagy," benefitting as it does from Edeson's wonderful camerawork. The first glimpse of the foreboding house is still among the best of its kind, and the lighting of the stark indoor sets quite stunning. The marvelous screenplay is full of memorable bits, such as the harsh Rebecca's retelling of past family debaucheries or Saul's genuinely creepy conversation with Penderell near the end. The dialogue is often hilarious, but it takes a cast as brilliant as this one to make the most of it. Massey's early speech about the water trickling down his neck or his remarks about seeing the house ("Perhaps it might be wiser to push on") are beautifully handled. With his typically demonstrative aplomb, Whale gives us these moments *as* we see an extreme close-up of Massey's neck or just after the house stands illuminated by flashes of lightning. Douglas can shift from glib wisecracks to a warm and touching romance with Bond in moments, and she and Stuart are appealing leading ladies here. Laughton affects a marvelous Lancashire accent as a hearty, bluff man, and yet he can also touch the heart when speaking about his deceased wife. Karloff may not speak here but his acting is as effective as ever and he and Wills demonstrate a remarkable rapport together. His final embrace of the crazed man is unexpectedly powerful. If we had to reserve top honors, though, they would have to go to Thesiger and Moore, whose work is absolutely flawless. When Eva Moore eats her dinner at warp speed or Ernest Thesiger makes "Have a potato" a classic highlight of a film, you know you're in the presence of rare talents.

As historian William K. Everson has noted, former stage actor and director Whale knows how to emphasize an actor's entrances and exits, or to delay them as needed (as in the case of Saul). His striking flair for composition and editing works an audience over thoroughly, and he adds to the film's impact by deliberately playing with the buildup of suspense. Brilliantly performed, staged and timed, a sly parody on the English household, THE OLD DARK HOUSE stands alongside THE BRIDE OF FRANKENSTEIN and ONE MORE RIVER as one of Whale's most sublime achievements.

OLD MAN AND THE SEA, THE 📀

1958 86m c Drama ★★★
Warner Bros. (U.S.)

Spencer Tracy *(The Old Man)*, Felipe Pazos *(The Boy)*, Harry Bellaver *(Martin)*, Don Diamond, Don Blackman, Joey Ray, Richard Alameda, Tony Rosa, Carlos Rivera, Robert Alderette

p, Leland Hayward; d, John Sturges; w, Peter Viertel (based on the novella by Ernest Hemingway); ph, James Wong Howe, Floyd Crosby, Tom Tutwiler, Lamar Boren; ed, Arthur Schmidt; m, Dimitri Tiomkin; art d, Art Loel, Edward Carrere; fx, Arthur S. Rhoades

AAN Best Actor: Spencer Tracy; *AAN Best Color Cinematography:* James Wong Howe; *AA Best Score (Drama or Comedy):* Dimitri Tiomkin

Years before A RIVER RUNS THROUGH IT, the original fish story. This was a near-impossible film to make, but Warner Bros. and Sturges tackled the job sensibly and, with Tracy in bravura form, it came off surprisingly well. Tracy plays a semi-literate Cuban fisherman whose pedantic efforts to practice his trade only cause snickers of derision from his community. Regarded as a fool, he only receives respect from the small boy (Pazos) who brings him coffee every morning. Most of the film is Tracy alone onscreen, as he goes head to head with a gigantic marlin, which, if landed, would be the catch of a lifetime. The struggle and its outcome form a story of irony, achievement and sadness, a battle of man vs. both the elements and his own pride.

THE OLD MAN AND THE SEA is an allegorical tale providing Tracy with a worthy one-man show, and his work has a powerful impact laced with humor and an overwhelming sense of stoic heroism. (Unlike his Portuguese fisherman in CAPTAINS COURAGEOUS, however, Tracy here does not attempt any kind of accent, which does stand out a bit in his scenes with the rest of the cast.) Sturges's direction, given the confining nature of the settings, is masterful, and the cinematography headed by Howe and pieced together by many others is sometimes stunning. (The contribution of much of the footage by many sources, however, has a tendency to present alternating and inconsistent color patterns from scene to scene.)

Attempts to film on location encountered problems; landing an actual marlin proved impossible; and Hayward fired original director Fred Zinneman over, among other things, disagreements about the script. Eventually, much of the film was shot (using a rubber fish) in a huge water tank at Warner Bros. Although Tracy would state that "This is for the birds" during the painfully protracted shoot, his disillusionment doesn't affect his performance, and he received kudos from most of the critics. One exception was Hemingway, who grouched that the film looked like the work of "a rich, fat actor."

OLD SCHOOL   *DVD*
2003 91m   c   Comedy   ★★½
Montecito Pictures   (U.S.)   R

Luke Wilson *(Mitch)*, Will Ferrell *(Frank)*, Vince Vaughn *(Beanie)*, Jeremy Piven *(Pritchard)*, Ellen Pompeo *(Nicole)*, Juliette Lewis *(Heidi)*, Leah Remini *(Lara)*, Perrey Reeves *(Marissa)*, Craig Kilborn *(Mark)*, Elisha Cuthbert *(Darcie)*

p, Daniel Goldberg, Joe Medjuck, Todd Phillips; d, Todd Phillips; w, Scot Armstrong, Todd Phillips (from a story by Court Crandall, Todd Phillips, and Scot Armstrong); ph, Mark Irwin; ed, Michael Jablow; m, Theodore Shapiro; prod d, Clark Hunter; art d, Max Biscoe; fx, William Aldridge; cos, Nancy Fisher

Writer-director Todd Phillips (ROAD TRIP) once again brings his brand of adolescent humor to bear on the world of college life, and whether you view that as a blessing or a curse is simply a matter of personal taste.

After conservative Mitch (Luke Wilson) returns from a business trip to find live-in girlfriend Heidi (Juliette Lewis) in the middle of a kinky sex act, he moves into a rambling house situated on the outskirts of the local college campus. Mitch's rowdy best friends—newlywed Frank (Will Ferrell) and married-with-children Beanie (Vince Vaughn)—convince Mitch to throw a housewarming party, and things inevitably get out of hand, infuriating college dean Pritchard (Jeremy Piven), whom Mitch and his pals used to torment mercilessly back in high school. Pritchard rezones the property so Mitch can now be evicted, but the clever trio find a loophole: they recruit a

motley pack of pledges and turn the house into the new home of the honorary Lambda Epsilon Omega fraternity. Everything's great until fraternity life starts to interfere with Frank's marriage and Mitch's fledgling relationship with Nicole (Ellen Pompeo), whom he's had a crush on since high school. Outsmarted by three stooges, Pritchard is now on a rampage to shut the house down.

Phillips's testosterone-driven romp was clearly inspired by classic lowbrow college comedies like ANIMAL HOUSE and REVENGE OF THE NERDS and, not surprisingly, its talented female cast is left with little to do. But the frat brothers have some surprisingly touching moments, and their diverse but perfectly matched personalities generate a fairly steady stream of laugh-out-loud moments. Now if only those gross-out moments—particularly the one in which a streaking Ferrell bares a bit too much of his bottom—didn't drag on so long.

OLD YELLER   *DVD*
1957 83m   c   Children's/Drama   ★★★½
Walt Disney Productions   (U.S.)   G

Dorothy McGuire *(Katie Coates)*, Fess Parker *(Jim Coates)*, Tommy Kirk *(Travis Coates)*, Kevin Corcoran *(Arliss Coates)*, Jeff York *(Bud Searcy)*, Beverly Washburn *(Lisbeth Searcy)*, Chuck Connors *(Burn Sanderson)*, Spike the Dog *(Old Yeller)*

p, Walt Disney; d, Robert Stevenson; w, Fred Gipson, William Tunberg (based on the novel by Fred Gipson); ph, Charles P. Boyle (Technicolor); ed, Stanley Johnson; m, Oliver Wallace; art d, Carroll Clark; cos, Chuck Keehne, Gertrude Casey

Set in Texas in 1869, Disney Studios' first and best attempt at a boy-and-his-dog film tells the story of a farm family whose head, Jim Coates (Fess Parker), must go on a cattle drive for three months, leaving his 15-year-old son, Travis (Tommy Kirk), in charge. When Travis's younger brother, Arliss (Kevin Corcoran), finds a stray yellow dog and decides to adopt him, Travis is frustrated by this breach of his authority. But his mother (Dorothy McGuire) approves of the dog's presence and reminds Travis that his little brother is lonely. Soon the dog, Old Yeller, has won the hearts of the whole family. Their attachment to the dog will serve as a test for their strength and love in this powerful and moving film. Sequel: SAVAGE SAM.

OLDBOY   *DVD*
2004 120m   c   Thriller   ★★★★
ShowEast/Egg Films   (South Korea)   R

Choi Min-sik *(Oh Daesu)*, Yoo Ji-Tae *(Lee Woo-jin)*, Gang Hye-jung *(Mido)*, Chi Dae-han *(No Joo-hwan)*, Oh Dal-su *(Park Cheol-woong)*, Kim Byoung-ok *(Mr. Han)*, Lee Seung-shin *(Yoo Hyung-ja)*, Yoon Jin-seo *(Lee Soo-ah)*, Lee Dae-yun *(Beggar)*, Oh Gwang-rok *(Suicidal Man)*

p, Kim Dong-joo; d, Park Chan-wook; w, Hwang Jo-yun, Lim Joon-hyung, Park Chan-wook (based on an original story by Garon Tsuchiya and Nobuaki Minegishi); ph, Jung Jung-hoon; ed, Kim Sang-bum; m, Cho Young-wuk, Lee Ji-soo, Shim Hyun-jung; prod d, Yoo Seong-hee; fx, Lee Jun-hyung, Lee Jung-soo; cos, Cho Sang-kyung

Korean director Park Chan-wook's controversial Cannes Film Festival Grand Prix winner is a revenge fable wrapped in a strange romance and embedded in a mystery. Brutal, bizarre, and utterly absorbing, it begins as pudgy, obnoxious every-loser Oh Daesu (Choi Min-sik) makes an ass of himself in a police station holding area. Detained for public drunkenness on his daughter's birthday, the feathery costume wings he bought as a last-minute gift still in their paper bag, he's eventually bailed out by a friend. But as the friend makes a phone call, Daesu simply vanishes from the busy, rain-soaked Seoul street. He wakes up in a seedy, windowless hotel room with a steel door, held by unseen captors who refuse to tell him where he is, why he's there, or when, if ever, he'll be allowed to leave. His only diversions are his daily meals of fried dumplings and television, from which he learns that his wife has been murdered and he's the chief suspect. His mind clouded by forcibly administered drugs and solitude, Daesu tries to kill himself but is cruelly revived. He gradually adapts to his Kafkaesque predicament, scribbling in notebooks and transforming himself into a lean, scruffy bruiser with the wherewithal to begin plotting his escape. And then, as suddenly as he was locked up, Daesu is released. He wakes up in a suitcase on a grassy high-rise rooftop, 15 years after he was incarcerated, burning with the desire to find his daughter and exact revenge on the person or persons who imprisoned him. He makes his way to a restaurant and orders "something alive," faints while swallowing a squirming octopus (the sequence that separates fans from detractors), and wakes up in the shabby apartment of pretty, alienated sushi chef Mido (Gang Hyejung), who falls in with his bleak quest. But Daesu's tormentor is still toying with him, challenging him to figure out in five days what he did to deserve his extravagant punishment. If he fails, his tormentor will kill every woman Daesu cares about. Like Park's earlier SYMPATHY FOR MR. VENGEANCE, Daesu's odyssey is structured as an escalating series of outrages, preposterous contrivances both tightly plotted and utterly logical within the feverish, ruthless world Park evokes. This is absolutely not a film for all tastes, but it's a masterpiece of pitiless power whose audacious, ambiguous climax strikes a note of insane romanticism as haunting as it is perverse.

OLIVER!

1968 153m c Musical **★★★★**
Warwick/Romulus (U.K.) G

Ron Moody *(Fagin)*, Shani Wallis *(Nancy)*, Oliver Reed *(Bill Sikes)*, Harry Secombe *(Mr. Bumble)*, Mark Lester *(Oliver Twist)*, Jack Wild *(The Artful Dodger)*, Hugh Griffith *(The Magistrate)*, Joseph O'Conor *(Mr. Brownlow)*, Peggy Mount *(Widow Corney)*, Leonard Rossiter *(Mr. Sowerberry)*

p, John Woolf; d, Carol Reed; w, Vernon Harris (based on the play by Lionel Bart from the novel *Oliver Twist* by Charles Dickens); ph, Oswald Morris (Panavision, Technicolor); ed, Ralph Kemplen; m, Lionel Bart; prod d, John Box; art d, Terence Marsh; fx, Allan Bryce; chor, Onna White; cos, Phyllis Dalton

AA Best Picture; AAN Best Actor: Ron Moody; *AAN Best Supporting Actor:* Jack Wild; *AA Best Director:* Carol Reed; *AAN Best Adapted Screenplay:* Vernon Harris; *AAN Best Cinematography:* Oswald Morris; *AAN Best Film Editing:* Ralph Kemplen; *AA Best Score (Musical):* John Green; *AA Best Art Direction-Set Decoration:* John Box, Terence Marsh, Vernon Dixon, Ken Muggleston; *AAN Best Costume Design:* Phyllis Dalton; *AA Best Sound:* Shepperton Studio Sound Department

Sweetened Dickens, a contradiction in kind. If the works of Charles Dickens have their moments of sentiment, they're well-earned, thanks to the savagry and deprivation abundant in the master storyteller's plots. Here, Carol Reed tries to balance the story elements by rendering the story as a fable; the moments of tenderness are intellectualized. Given that *Oliver!* could easily get that perfunctory cuteness that packs the matinees with old ladies, it's a wise move. But being English himself and probably knowing Dickens better than we do, why didn't Carol Reed restore the Dickensian flavor that could give OLIVER! some bite? OLIVER! is the familiar story of young Oliver Twist (strongly played by Mark Lester), an orphan who prefers life on the streets to the hard labor of a foster family or life in a vile orphanage. One day he meets another street urchin, the Artful Dodger (Jack Wild, in an equally strong performance), who tells him of a group of young hooligans that will consider him "part of the family." All Oliver has to do is

learn to pickpocket and give his earnings to Fagin (Ron Moody), the crusty criminal gang leader; in return he'll have a "family" and a place to stay.

OLIVER! is better than most screen musicals of the 1960s, a period when oversized, poorly rendered songfests virtually killed the genre. The score, while hardly immortal, is well served by the actors and Oliver Reed for once found a character he could sink his loathsome self into.

OLIVER TWIST

1948 105m bw Drama **★★★★½** DVD
Cineguild (U.K.)

Robert Newton *(Bill Sikes)*, Alec Guinness *(Fagin)*, Kay Walsh *(Nancy)*, Francis L. Sullivan *(Mr. Bumble)*, Henry Stephenson *(Mr. Brownlow)*, Mary Clare *(Mrs. Corney)*, John Howard Davies *(Oliver Twist)*, Josephine Stuart *(Oliver's Mother)*, Henry Edwards *(Police Official)*, Ralph Truman *(Monks)*

p, Ronald Neame, Anthony Havelock-Allan; d, David Lean; w, David Lean, Stanley Haynes (based on the novel by Charles Dickens); ph, Guy Green; ed, Jack Harris; m, Arnold Bax; fx, Joan Suttie, Stanley Grant; cos, Margaret Furse

David Lean's version of Charles Dickens's *Oliver Twist* is not as enthralling as his GREAT EXPECTATIONS, but it is a fine film in its own right. This time Alec Guinness (EXPECTATIONS was his first film) plays Fagin, Anthony Newley is the Artful Dodger, and the then-unknown and now-forgotten John Howard Davies is Oliver Twist. (Actually, some may recognize Davies as the British television producer responsible for "Monty Python's Flying Circus" and "Fawlty Towers.") Guinness's performance ran into some trouble from Jewish pressure groups—seven minutes of his performance was excised—and the film finally entered the country in 1951. Many of the novel's characters have been excised or compressed to fit the time frame of the film, but only the most die-hard Dickensians will protest. The sets are as much a part of the story as the dialogue, and set designer John Bryan's work is effectively photographed by Guy Green. All the acting is first-rate, and there is not a false note from the cast.

OMEN, THE

1976 111m c Horror **★★★** DVD
Fox (U.S.) R

Gregory Peck *(Robert Thorn)*, Lee Remick *(Katherine Thorn)*, David Warner *(Jennings)*, Billie Whitelaw *(Mrs. Baylock)*, Leo McKern *(Bugenhagen)*, Harvey Stevens *(Damien)*, Patrick Troughton *(Father Brennan)*, Martin Benson *(Father Spiletto)*, Anthony Nicholls *(Dr. Becker)*, Holly Palance *(Young Nanny)*

p, Harvey Bernhard; d, Richard Donner; w, David Seltzer; ph, Gilbert Taylor (Panavision, DeLuxe Color); ed, Stuart Baird; m, Jerry Goldsmith; art d, Carmen Dillon; fx, John Richardson

AA Best Original Score: Jerry Goldsmith; *AAN Best Original Song:* "Ave Satani"; Jerry Goldsmith (Music & Lyrics)

This silly and bloody, but at times very effective, horror film takes THE EXORCIST one step further by concentrating, not on possession by the Devil, but on the Antichrist himself. Robert Thorn (Gregory Peck) is a highly respected American ambassador to England whose wife, Katherine (Lee Remick), gives birth to a stillborn child. Thorn is encouraged by a priest to switch his dead child with the living baby of a mother who died during childbirth. Five years later, strange things begin happening in the Thorn household, all of which can be traced to their boy, Damien (Harvey Stevens), who, unbeknownst to his surrogate parents, is the Antichrist. Regardless of its rather questionable premise, execution (unintentionally funny dialogue abounds), or taste, THE OMEN is a fairly entertaining horror picture that made an obscene amount of money and spawned two sequels, DAMIEN—OMEN II and THE FINAL CONFLICT, neither of which was very good. The films were originally conceived as four parts, tracing Damien's rise to power from his childhood through adulthood and eventually to Armageddon, but patron interest slacked off considerably after the second film, forcing the producers to cut the saga short at three.

ON GOLDEN POND
1981 109m c Comedy/Drama ★★★½
ITC/IPC/AFD/Universal (U.S.) PG

Katharine Hepburn *(Ethel Thayer)*, Henry Fonda *(Norman Thayer, Jr.)*, Jane Fonda *(Chelsea Thayer Wayne)*, Doug McKeon *(Billy Ray)*, Dabney Coleman *(Bill Ray)*, William Lanteau *(Charlie Martin)*, Christopher Rydell *(Sumner Todd)*

p, Bruce Gilbert; d, Mark Rydell; w, Ernest Thompson (based on his play); ph, Billy Williams; ed, Robert Wolfe; m, Dave Grusin; prod d, Stephen Grimes; cos, Dorothy Jeakins

AAN Best Picture; AA Best Actor: Henry Fonda; *AA Best Actress:* Katharine Hepburn; *AAN Best Supporting Actress:* Jane Fonda; *AAN Best Director:* Mark Rydell; *AA Best Adapted Screenplay:* Ernest Thompson; *AAN Best Cinematography:* Billy Williams; *AAN Best Film Editing:* Robert L. Wolfe; *AAN Best Original Score:* Dave Grusin; *AAN Best Sound:* Richard Portman, David Ronne

Retired professor Norman Thayer, Jr. (Henry Fonda), and his wife Ethel (Katharine Hepburn) are spending the summer at their New England cottage, just as they have done for nearly 50 years. The Thayers' daughter Chelsea (Jane Fonda) arrives at the cottage with her fiance Bill Ray (Dabney Coleman) and Billy (Doug McKeon), his son from a previous marriage. They plan for Billy to stay at the cottage while Jane Fonda and Coleman head for a summer in Europe. The gruff Norman and the irritating Billy are immediately at odds—much as the father and daughter have always been. The two come to a better understanding of one another over the course of the summer, however, while Fonda also tries to come to terms with his mortality. A beautifully photographed movie filled with poignancy, humor, and (of course) some superb acting. Henry Fonda was 75 when this picture was made and must have known he didn't have much time. There could have been no finer final curtain for him than this.

ON HER MAJESTY'S SECRET SERVICE
1969 140m c Spy ★★★½
UA (U.K.) M

George Lazenby *(James Bond)*, Diana Rigg *(Tracy Draco)*, Telly Savalas *(Ernst Stavro Blofeld)*, Ilse Steppat *(Irma Bunt)*, Gabriele Ferzetti *(Marc Ange Draco)*, Yuri Borienko *(Gruenther)*, Bernard Horsfall *(Campbell)*, George Baker *(Sir Hilary Bray)*, Bernard Lee *("M")*, Lois Maxwell *(Miss Moneypenny)*

p, Albert R. Broccoli, Harry Saltzman; d, Peter Hunt; w, Richard Maibaum, Simon Raven (based on the novel by Ian Fleming); ph, Michael Reed, Egil Woxholt, Roy Ford, John Jordan, Willy Bogner, Alex Barbey, Ken Higgins (Panavision, Technicolor); ed, John Glen; m, John Barry; prod d, Syd Cain; art d, Robert Laing; fx, John Stears; cos, Marjorie Cornelius

This might have been the best of the James Bond series if it had starred Sean Connery instead of Australian model George Lazenby, whom the producers grabbed after a frantic talent search when Connery turned down the role. When Bond is ordered to cease his pursuit of old nemesis Blofeld (played by Savalas this time), 007 turns in his license to kill and returns to Portugal to pick up the trail. There he falls for Tracy (Rigg), the ravishing daughter of Draco (Ferzetti), an

organized crime kingpin. Draco helps Bond locate the Swiss mountaintop stronghold from which Blofeld plans to engineer universal sterilization unless he is granted a title of nobility and amnesty for his past crimes. After rescuing Tracy from Blofeld's clutches and seemingly doing away with him once and for all, Bond marries her and they *almost* live happily ever after. Based on one of the best of Ian Fleming's Bond novels, ON HER MAJESTY'S SECRET SERVICE benefited from an extremely well-written script that finally revealed a bit more of Bond's character. Lazenby, however, had no previous acting experience, and his lackadaisical performance limits the whole production, yet it still manages to remain one of the more entertaining Bond films.

ON THE BEACH
1959 133m bw Science Fiction/Drama/War ★★½
Kramer (U.S.)

Gregory Peck *(Dwight Towers)*, Ava Gardner *(Moira Davidson)*, Fred Astaire *(Julian Osborn)*, Anthony Perkins *(Peter Holmes)*, Donna Anderson *(Mary Holmes)*, John Tate *(Adm. Bridie)*, Lola Brooks *(Lt. Hosgood)*, John Meillon *(Swain)*, Lou Vernon *(Davidson)*, Guy Doleman *(Farrel)*

p, Stanley Kramer; d, Stanley Kramer; w, John Paxton, James Lee Barrett (based on the novel by Nevil Shute); ph, Giuseppe Rotunno, Daniel Fapp; ed, Frederic Knudtson; m, Ernest Gold; prod d, Rudolph Sternad; art d, Fernando Carrere; fx, Lee Zavitz; cos, Joe King, Fontana Sisters

AAN Best Film Editing: Frederic Knudtson; *AAN Best Score (Drama or Comedy):* Ernest Gold

Based on Nevil Shute's popular novel, this flawed but moving end-of-the-world drama is set in Australia in 1964, after nuclear war has eliminated life in the northern hemisphere. While the folks down under await the nuclear fallout that will eventually kill them, the U.S. *Sawfish*, a submarine commanded by Dwight Towers (Gregory Peck), ventures to California, only to learn that the radio signal still being transmitted from San Diego is being produced by a soda bottle—everyone at home is dead (dramatically reinforced by some extraordinary shots of a deserted San Francisco). Back in Australia, the principal characters deal with their imminent deaths in their own way: scientist Julian Osborn (Fred Astaire) enters and wins an auto race, then asphyxiates himself; Australian naval officer Peter Holmes (Anthony Perkins) and his wife, Mary (Donna Anderson), take their child's and their own lives; good-time girl Moira Davidson (Ava Gardner) tries to drink her fears away, then falls for Towers, who eventually returns with his crew to the U.S. to die at home. Produced and directed by Stanley Kramer, this unremittingly bleak message film was intended to have a big impact and premiered simultaneously in 18 cities on all seven continents. And though it occasionally goes over the top with its melodrama and lacks some technical credibility, ON THE BEACH remains a powerful, well-acted, deftly photographed film in the tradition of THE WORLD, THE FLESH AND THE DEVIL; FAIL SAFE; DR. STRANGELOVE; and TESTAMENT. Its effective use of "Waltzing Matilda" also contributed to making that most Australian of songs a hit in the U.S.

ON THE TOWN
1949 98m c Musical ★★★★
MGM (U.S.)

Gene Kelly *(Gabey)*, Frank Sinatra *(Chip)*, Betty Garrett *(Brunhilde Esterhazy)*, Ann Miller *(Claire Huddesen)*, Jules Munshin *(Ozzie)*, Vera-Ellen *(Ivy Smith)*, Florence Bates *(Mme.*

Dilyovska), Alice Pearce *(Lucy Shmeeler)*, George Meader *(Professor)*, Bern Hoffman *(Worker)*

p, Arthur Freed; d, Gene Kelly, Stanley Donen; w, Adolph Green, Betty Comden (based on the musical play by Comden, Green and Leonard Bernstein, from the ballet *Fancy Free* by Jerome Robbins); ph, Harold Rosson (Technicolor); ed, Ralph E. Winters; m, Leonard Bernstein, Roger Edens, Saul Chaplin, Conrad Salinger; art d, Cedric Gibbons, Jack Martin Smith; fx, Warren Newcombe; chor, Gene Kelly, Stanley Donen; cos, Helen Rose

AA Best Score (Musical): Roger Edens, Lennie Hayton

Just a trifle forced, like Gene Kelly. And stolen by a tapping whirlwind named Annie Miller, flying through the Museum of Natural History in a blaze of green gingham. But New York City never looked more beautiful or exciting on screen than in ON THE TOWN, a breakthrough film that, for the first time, took the musical out of the claustrophobic sound stages and onto the streets for on-location shooting. Perfectly fusing story, songs, and dances, with no production number staged merely for its own sake, ON THE TOWN is so energetic and vital that the screen barely contains it; the actors seem ready to leap off and dance up the aisles. The slim story follows sailors Gabey (Gene Kelly), Chip (Frank Sinatra), and Ozzie (Jules Munshin) during their 24-hour pass in New York. In the subway, they note the picture of this month's "Miss Turnstiles," with whom Gabey is especially taken; later they meet Miss Turnstiles—one Ivy Smith (Vera-Ellen)—in the flesh, but she vanishes into the rush-hour crowd. Chasing after her, they enlist the help of cabbie Brunhilde Esterhazy (Betty Garrett), who takes a fancy to Chip. Continuing their search, they meet anthropologist Claire Huddesen (Ann Miller), who sets her sights on Ozzie. The group splits into three units—Brunhilde and Chip, Claire and Ozzie, and Gabey—to look for Ivy, agreeing to meet on the Empire State Building's observation deck that night. After a day of romantic adventures and misadventures, they rendezvous at the appointed site, Gabey squiring Ivy, whom he mistakenly believes to be a big star in her position as Miss Turnstiles. By the time she gets around to telling him she's really just a no-name dancer from a tiny town (as it happens, the same tiny town *he's* from), it makes no difference to the smitten Gabey, and, after a run-in with the cops that forces the gobs to pretend they're girls, they return to their ship exactly 24 hours from the time they left.

Loius B. Mayer didn't want the film to go on location, while Kelly wanted to shoot the entire picture in New York, leading to a compromise in which Kelly was allowed one frantic week of location shooting, filming the Bronx, the Battery, Coney Island, Brooklyn, the Empire State Building, Times Square, the Statue of Liberty, Fifth Avenue, Radio City, the Bronx Zoo, Central Park, Carnegie Hall, the subway, Wall Street, Grant's Tomb, and the Brooklyn Navy Yard. Perhaps it was the short shooting schedule that contributed to the frantic pace of the film, a jampacked tour without a wasted second. There may have been better songs and even better performances in other musicals, but for effervescent energy nothing has yet come close to the joyous, influential ON THE TOWN. One quibble: Leonard Bernstein's innovative Broadway score is here diminished by Hollywood-style orchestration and much tinkering.

ON THE WATERFRONT
1954 108m bw Drama **DVD**
Columbia (U.S.) ★★★★½

Marlon Brando *(Terry Malloy)*, Karl Malden *(Father Barry)*, Lee J. Cobb *(Johnny Friendly)*, Rod Steiger *(Charley Malloy)*, Pat Henning *("Kayo" Dugan)*, Eva Marie Saint *(Edie Doyle)*, Leif Erickson *(Glover)*, James Westerfield *(Big Mac)*, Tony Galento *(Truck)*, Tami Mauriello *(Tillio)*

p, Sam Spiegel; d, Elia Kazan; w, Budd Schulberg (based on a story suggested by a series of articles by Malcolm Johnson); ph, Boris Kaufman; ed, Gene Milford; m, Leonard Bernstein; art d, Richard Day; cos, Anna Hill Johnstone

AA Best Picture; AA Best Actor: Marlon Brando; *AAN Best Supporting Actor:* Lee J. Cobb; *AAN Best Supporting Actor:* Karl Malden; *AAN Best Supporting Actor:* Rod Steiger; *AA Best Supporting Actress:* Eva Marie Saint; *AA Best Director:* Elia Kazan; *AA Best Story and Screenplay:* Budd Schulberg; *AA Best B/W Cinematography:* Boris Kaufman; *AA Best Film Editing:* Gene Milford; *AAN Best Score (Drama or Comedy):* Leonard Bernstein; *AA Best Art Direction-Set Decoration (B/W):* Richard Day

A *tour de force* for director Elia Kazan, star Marlon Brando and, perhaps above all, cinematographer Boris Kaufman. ON THE WATERFRONT is a gritty, no-holds-barred drama about the corruption-glutted New York docks and the dock workers' excruciating struggle to make a living under the control of corrupt unions. Cobb is gangster union boss Johnny Friendly, and Steiger his crooked lawyer, Charley Malloy. Charley's brother, Terry (Brando), a former boxer, hangs around the docks and runs errands for Johnny, who gives handouts to those who do his bidding. Already a has-been as a young man, Terry keeps pigeons on a rooftop and dreams about his days as a promising fighter. Johnny tells Terry to ask a truculent union worker who is holed up in his apartment to meet him on the roof of his tenement. The worker shows up, and two of Johnny's goons push him off to his death as Terry watches in shock. Later, Terry tells some of Johnny's other thugs, "I thought they were only gonna lean on him a little," to which Truck (onetime heavyweight boxer "Two-ton" Tony Galento) replies, "The canary could sing but he couldn't fly!" Terry later meets Edie (Saint), the murdered man's sister, and begins to feel responsible for the death. She introduces him to Father Barry (Malden), who tells Terry that the dead man was killed because he was going to expose Johnny and his henchmen. The priest then exhorts Terry to provide the crime commission with information that will smash the dock racketeers.

Brando is spectacular as the ex-fighter who finds his conscience and risks his life for his newfound principles. The realistic dialogue is poetic in its simplicity, and the seedy tenements and clammy docks are strikingly captured. Kazan sets every scene with menace and suspense, evoking a pitiless world where tough hope is requisite for survival. Cobb is a great villain, exercising his power with a payoff, a sneering smile, and a booming voice, and his goons are really frightening characters, many of them former real-life boxers with faces scarred by years in the ring. Saint is an island of sanity and decency, but the attempt to use Malden as a symbol of good in a troubled world is awfully pat. The film is a draining experience from beginning to end, relentless in its portrayal of inhumanity. And it is all the more grim and hard-hitting because of the steel-gray look of cinematographer Kaufman's startling, neo-documentary approach.

A controversial film of its time because of its violence, raw language (at one point Terry tells the priest to "go to hell"), and its daring in representing labor unions in a negative light, WATERFRONT enjoyed a surprising box office success to match its critical acclaim, taking in $9.5 million on a $900,000 investment.

ONCE UPON A TIME IN AMERICA
1984 227m c Crime **DVD**
Ladd (U.S.) ★★★★
R

Robert De Niro *(Noodles)*, James Woods *(Max)*, Elizabeth McGovern *(Deborah)*, Treat Williams *(Jimmy O'Donnell)*, Tuesday Weld *(Carol)*, Burt Young *(Joe)*, Joe Pesci *(Frankie)*, Danny Aiello *(Police Chief Aiello)*, Bill Forsythe *(Cockeye)*, James Hayden *(Patsy)*

p, Arnon Milchan; d, Sergio Leone; w, Leo Benvenuti, Piero De Bernardi, Enrico Medioli, Franco Arcalli, Franco Ferrini, Sergio Leone, Stuart Kaminsky (based on the novel *The Hoods* by Harry Grey); ph, Tonino Delli Colli (Technicolor); ed, Nino Baragli; m, Ennio Morricone; art d, Carlo Simi, James Singelis; cos, Gabriella Pescucci, Nino Baragli

Italian director Sergio Leone returned to the screen after a 12-year absence, and the result is this ambitious, sprawling, insightful, frustrating, and ultimately challenging gangster film. Its structure is incredibly complex, flashing back and forth from the '20s to the '30s, to the '60s, basically following a group of Jewish boys who meet in the 1920s on Manhattan's Lower East Side. The story concentrates on the mercurial, borderline psychotic Max (James Woods) and Noodles (Robert De Niro), who has loved Deborah (Elizabeth McGovern) since they were children. The gang is virtually destroyed in 1933, but Noodles escapes and goes into hiding for 35 years, returning to New York in 1968 after receiving a mystifying letter. Though it's a confusing movie that has sparked debate and criticism, ONCE UPON A TIME IN AMERICA is visually stunning, rich in detail, and filled with outstanding performances.

ONCE UPON A TIME IN CHINA 📀
(HUANG FEIHONG)
1991 112m c   Action/Historical/Martial Arts ★★★★
Film Workshop   (Hong Kong)

Jet Li *(Wong Fei-hung)*, Yuen Biao *(Leung Foon)*, Jacky Cheung *(Buck Teeth Sol)*, Rosamund Kwan *(Aunt Yee)*, Kent Cheng *(Porky Lang)*, Wu Ma

p, Raymond Chow; d, Tsui Hark; w, Tsui Hark, Yuen Kai-chi, Leung Yiu-ming, Tang Pik-yin; ph, David Chung, Bill Wong, Arthur Wong, Ardy Lam, Chan Tung-chuen, Wilson Chan; ed, Mak Chisin; m, James Wong; prod d, Lau Man-hung; art d, Yee Chung-man; cos, Yu Ka-on

Tsui Hark's ONCE UPON A TIME IN CHINA is a truly dazzling achievement, even measured against Tsui's own considerable accomplishments and the hyperbolic standards of Hong Kong filmmaking, where riotous visual excess and surreal cross-cultural appropriations are the norm.

The year is 1875. Master Wong Fei-hung (Jet Li), a Confucian bone setter and righteous martial artist, establishes a clinic in Canton province and takes on several apprentices, including the comic Porky Lang (Kent Cheng) and Buck Teeth Sol (Jacky Cheung). Also in the mix is beautiful Aunt Yee (Rosamund Kwan), who has returned to China after many years abroad, bringing with her some strange and modern ideas. When Wong's clinic is burned down, he and his companions set out to right the many wrongs they see around them. A rival kung-fu master, divorced from the spiritual component of his training, forces Wong to engage in a series of spectacular showdowns, but the real villain is creeping Westernization, embodied in the American soldiers who encourage opium addiction and coerce poor peasants to sail for America, where they'll wind up virtual slaves to the railroad barons.

For fans of Hong Kong films, Tsui Hark is a superstar on the level of a Steven Spielberg or George Lucas. Born in Vietnam and trained at the University of Texas, he has written, directed, and produced dozens of the most striking Hong Kong movies never seen in U.S. theaters. The adventures of Master Wong are a longtime staple of Hong Kong genre cinema, so for Chinese viewers ONCE UPON A TIME IN CHINA is a revisionist exercise in the vein of YOUNG GUNS: the characters, settings, and situations are familiar, but they're all delivered with a distinctly contemporary twist. The title, with its knowing nod to Sergio Leone's remaking of American national fables, ONCE UPON A TIME IN THE

WEST, is the tip-off that Tsui's aim is to dust off old genre conventions and present them, refreshed and revitalized, to a new generation of movie buffs.

ONCE UPON A TIME IN CHINA is a virtual non-stop festival of kung-fu display. Battles are staged in spectacular locales: at the opera, where the bad guys hide beneath brilliant traditional costumes and make-up; in a bizarrely out-of-place European-style restaurant; and in an enemy fortress full of ladders, which are deployed to astonishing effect. The action is lightning-fast (though it shows few signs of the overcranking that Hong Kong pictures often use to up the ante) and balletically staged, living up to the choreographic potential often claimed—but seldom truly realized—for martial arts pictures by their highbrow admirers.

ONCE UPON A TIME IN MEXICO 📀
2003 98m c   Action/Crime ★★★
Troublemaker Studios/Miramax/Columbia   (U.S.)   R

Antonio Banderas *(El Mariachi)*, Salma Hayek *(Carolina)*, Johnny Depp *(Agent Sands)*, Mickey Rourke *(Billy Chambers)*, Eva Mendes *(Ajedrez)*, Danny Trejo *(Cucoy)*, Enrique Iglesias *(Lorenzo)*, Marco Leonardi *(Fideo)*, Cheech Marin *(Belini)*, Ruben Blades *(Jorge—FBI)*

p, Elizabeth Avellan, Carlos Gallardo, Robert Rodriguez; d, Robert Rodriguez; w, Robert Rodriguez; ph, Robert Rodriguez; ed, Robert Rodriguez; m, Robert Rodriguez; prod d, Robert Rodriguez; art d, Melo Hinojosa; fx, Keefe Boerner, Sergio Jara, Daniel Leduc, Mike Reedy, Robert Rodriguez; cos, Graciela Mazon

The spirit of Sergio Leone haunts Robert Rodriguez's ambitious second sequel to his micro-budget EL MARIACHI, in which the mariachi with no name (Antonio Banderas) is enmeshed in a plot to kill Mexico's president (Pedro Armendariz).

Since the deaths of his beloved Carolina (Salma Hayek)—whose heart the mariachi stole from vicious General Marquez (Gerardo Virgil)—and their child, El Mariachi has retreated into self-imposed seclusion. Marquez now works for drug lord Barillo (Willem Dafoe) and is spearheading the presidential assassination plot. Deeply dirty CIA agent Sands (Johnny Depp) enlists the aid of mercenary thug Cucoy (Danny Trejo) to press-gang "El" into a plot to prevent Marquez from assuming power once the president is dead. Sands similarly recruits retired FBI agent Jorge (Ruben Blades), who decides that the weak link in Barillo's organization is fugitive American goon Billy (Mickey Rourke). Sands also conspires with beautiful but corrupt Mexican fed Ajedrez (Eva Mendes), while El Mariachi enlists the help of fellow gun slinging musicians Lorenzo (Enrique Iglesias) and Fideo (Marco Leonardi). Bullets fly, traitors betray their accomplices, and Sands, his eyes gouged out by one of his many crooked confederates, becomes a blind gunman led by a child (Tony Valdes)—a conceit worthy of the most grotesque Italian Western.

If not quite a one-man show, Rodriguez's mini-epic is something close to it; he wrote, directed, produced, scored, edited, designed the production, and did many of the special effects. Fortunately, he resisted the temptation to star, since Banderas inhabits the role of the mariachi with a feral grace. Hayek makes the most of what is essentially a long cameo role, and the cult-fave supporting players revel in their small but juicy parts; even Rourke's Chihuahua is a runny-eyed scene stealer.

ONCE UPON A TIME IN THE WEST 📀
1969 165m c   Western ★★★★★
Rafran/San Marco   (U.S./Italy)   PG

Henry Fonda *(Frank)*, Claudia Cardinale *(Jill McBain)*, Jason Robards Jr. *(Cheyenne)*, Charles Bronson *(The Man*

"Harmonica"), Frank Wolff (Brett McBain), Gabriele Ferzetti (Morton), Keenan Wynn (Sheriff), Paolo Stoppa (Sam), Marco Zuanelli (Wobbles), Lionel Stander (Barman)

p, Fulvio Morsella; d, Sergio Leone; w, Sergio Leone, Sergio Donati (based on a story by Dario Argento, Bernardo Bertolucci, Leone); ph, Tonino Delli Colli (Techniscope, Technicolor); ed, Nino Baragli; m, Ennio Morricone; art d, Carlo Simi; cos, Carlo Simi

---

Sergio Leone's masterpiece. In ONCE UPON A TIME IN THE WEST, Leone pulls together all the themes, characterizations, visuals, humor, and musical experiments of the three "Dollars" films and comes up with a true epic western. It is a stunning, operatic film of breadth, detail, and stature that deserves to be considered among the greatest westerns ever made. Although the original release in America was a severely edited version (Paramount wanted to cram an extra show in every night to sell more popcorn), the film was rereleased, uncut, in 1984. (The videotape version is also uncut.) ONCE UPON A TIME IN THE WEST's credit sequence is perhaps one of the most famous in cinema history. It unfolds slowly, deliberately, as Leone lingers on the strange behavior of Frank's (Fonda) three hired killers (two of whom are Jack Elam and Woody Strode in unforgettable cameos) who await the arrival of a train carrying "the Man" (Bronson), a stranger who has asked for an audience with Frank. The perfectly realized details—water dripping on Strode's bald head, Elam trying to shoo a pesky fly, and the third gang member cracking his knuckles—brings the scene immediately to life and create an almost unbearable sense of anticipation. It doesn't let up from there.

A series of galvanizing confrontations and shootouts built around a landowning whore-turned-widow (Cardinale), a scheming railroad magnate (Ferzetti), and the Man's mysterious reason for stalking the cold-blooded Frank, ONCE UPON A TIME IN THE WEST is often mesmerizing cinema. Casting baby blue-eyed, open-faced Fonda, with that underlying edge of hardness which Leone loved in Fonda's John Ford films, as a ruthless killer was a stroke of genius. His best bits: Frank's murder of a little boy, and the finale with the harmonica. Another major distinction is Morricone's brilliant score, featuring distinct themes for each of the four main characters (tuneless harmonica for Bronson, biting electric guitar for Fonda, humorous banjo for Robards's charming outlaw, and a lush, romantic score for Cardinale). What is really striking, though, is that Morricone based his composition on the script rather than shot footage, and Leone had his cast adapt their body rhythms to the score. The paths Leone was struggling to develop in his previous three westerns finally merge and take shape here. Called a "dance of death" by some critics who picked up on the strange relationship between the music and the actors, the film is an operatic eulogy for the western hero.

ONCE WERE WARRIORS
1994 99m c Drama *DVD* ★★★
Communicado/New Zealand Film Commission/ R
Avalon Studios/New Zealand On Air
(New Zealand)

Rena Owen (Beth Heke), Temuera Morrison (Jake Heke), Mamaengaroa Kerr-Bell (Grace Heke), Julian Arahanga (Nig Heke), Taungaroa Emile (Boogie Heke), Rachael Morris Jr. (Polly Heke), Joseph Kairau (Huata Heke), Cliff Curtis, billed as Clifford Curtis (Bully), Pete Smith (Dooley), George Henare (Bennett)

p, Robin Scholes; d, Lee Tamahori; w, Riwia Brown (based on the novel by Alan Duff); ph, Stuart Dryburgh; ed, Michael Horton; m, Murray Grindlay, Murray McNabb; prod d, Michael Kane; art d, Shayne Radford; cos, Michael Kane

---

A huge hit in New Zealand, where it surpassed JURASSIC PARK's box-office take, ONCE WERE WARRIORS is a fairly conventional look at lives blighted by poverty and cultural disenfranchisement. Still, it's hard-hitting stuff, and a welcome antidote to the sentimentalized picture of the Maoris—New Zealand's indigenous people—in 1993's THE PIANO.

The film opens with an image of New Zealand countryside that seems too placid and beautiful to be true. It is: the shot widens, and we're looking at a billboard in the middle of a squalid slum inhabited by urbanized Maoris. Proud, stubborn Beth Heke (Rena Owen) is making the best of a bad marriage to sexy, brutal ne'er-do-well Jake (Temuera Morrison). They have five children, no car, and a rundown house in a shabby neighborhood; what passes for fun is pub crawling and marathon drinking parties that frequently end in violence. When Jake loses his job and goes on the dole, their fragile family disintegrates with terrifying speed. Jake beats Beth, eldest son Nig (Julian Arahanga) joins a brutal gang, and adolescent Boogie (Taungaroa Emile) is placed in a group home for troubled boys. Thirteen-year-old Grace (Mamaengaroa Kerr-Bell), a shy dreamer, tries to shield her younger siblings from the chaos around them, but herself becomes its victim.

There's little new here, but uniformly powerful performances (especially Owen's) give the tale unexpected power and depth, and the exotic details—like the elaborate tribal tattoos worn by Nig's gang, or the Maori chants Boogie learns in reform school—make the Heke family's descent into misery seem fresher than it otherwise might.

ONE-EYED JACKS
1961 141m c Western *DVD* ★★★½
Pennebaker (U.S.)

Marlon Brando (Rio), Karl Malden (Dad Longworth), Katy Jurado (Maria), Pina Pellicer (Louisa), Slim Pickens (Lon), Ben Johnson (Bob Amory), Sam Gilman (Harvey), Larry Duran (Modesto), Timothy Carey (Howard Tetley), Miriam Colon (Redhead)

p, Frank P. Rosenberg; d, Marlon Brando; w, Guy Trosper, Calder Willingham (based on the novel The Authentic Death of Hendry Jones by Charles Neider); ph, Charles Lang (VistaVision, Technicolor); ed, Archie Marshek; m, Hugo Friedhofer; art d, Hal Pereira, Joseph MacMillan Johnson; fx, John P. Fulton, Farciot Edouart; chor, Josephine Earl; cos, Yvonne Wood

---

AAN Best Color Cinematography: Charles Lang Jr.

Make room for Marlon. This offbeat, indulgent western, the only film directed by La Marlon, is almost as strange as his later THE MISSOURI BREAKS, but it does pack a wallop for patient viewers. Rio (Brando) and Dad (Malden) are bandits who rob a Mexican bank in 1880 but end up having to share a horse during their getaway. Realizing that they cannot outdistance the posse on one horse, Rio sends Dad off to find a second mount while he holds off the posse. Dad, however, gives up trying to find another horse, and rides off with the loot. Rio is of course caught when his ammo runs out, and goes to prison. Breaking out after five years of brutal treatment, Rio eventually meets Dad again, still a nasty and deceptive man but now sheriff of a small town, with a wife (Jurado) and stepdaughter (Pellicer). It's not Father's Day, folks—Dad knows he's in trouble, so he takes steps to protect himself against the vengeful Rio.

Brando took over the film from Stanley Kubrick after the two disagreed on character development. The story draws heavily upon the legend of Billy the Kid (the father-son relationship between Malden and Brando is almost identical to that between lawman Pat Garrett and the outlaw William Bonney; the escape from jail and the abusive guard are obviously drawn from the Kid's own experiences). It is also fraught with too many pensive moments in which Brando, obviously in love with his own performance, broods and ponders. The painfully exacting star took all the time in the world behind the camera as well, spending six months shooting a film scheduled for two, exposing over a million feet of film. Marshek and others edited the film down to 141 minutes but it was still overlong, with scenes that played up Brando's martyr-like character (the whipping scene is almost a duplication of the Crucifixion). Lang's photography of the spectacular Monterey Peninsula, the windswept, ocean-lapped coast and rocky coastline, is outstanding, and Brando's performance, weird or not, is dynamic and intriguing. Malden is a classic study in guile, but the talented Jurado is unfortunately only a prop, and Pellicer is unconvincing as the naive girl. (This was Pellicer's only U.S. film; after a short-lived career in Mexican pictures, she committed suicide at the age of 24.) Costing over $6 million (with an original budget of only $1.8 million), it only returned $4.3 million. This tale of basic revenge shows man as vile and contemptuous of his fellow man, a view repeatedly seen through the eyes of the often smug but never boring Brando.

ONE FALSE MOVE
1992   105m   c   Crime/Drama   ★★★★
IRS Media   (U.S.)   R

Cynda Williams (*Fantasia/Lila*), Bill Paxton (*Dale "Hurricane" Dixon*), Billy Bob Thornton (*Ray Malcolm*), Jim Metzler (*Dud Cole*), Michael Beach (*Pluto*), Earl Billings (*McFeely*), Natalie Canerday (*Cherylann*)

p, Jesse Beaton, Ben Myron; d, Carl Franklin; w, Billy Bob Thornton, Tom Epperson; ph, James L. Carter; ed, Carole Kravitz; m, Peter Haycock, Derek Holt; prod d, Gary T. New; art d, Dana Torrey; cos, Ron Leamon

A superbly understated thriller from director Carl Franklin, an AFI graduate whose previous work was limited to Roger Corman outings like NOWHERE TO RUN and FULL FATHOM FIVE. ONE FALSE MOVE opens in suburban Los Angeles with the brutal murder of several family members and friends as part of a cash and cocaine robbery. The culprits are an interracial trio made up of a sadistic redneck sociopath, Ray Malcolm (Billy Bob Thornton, who co-wrote the screenplay); Pluto (Michael Beach), a would-be criminal genius who has a mean way with a knife; and Fantasia (Cynda Williams), the femme fatale who set up the slaughter. Piecing together accounts provided by neighbors with voices recorded on a videocam, L.A. cops Cole and McFeely (Jim Metzler and Earl Billings) identify Pluto and Ray, both ex-cons, and discover they're on their way to Star City, Arkansas, where Ray has an uncle. (In fact, the trio's plan is to go to Houston, convert the coke into cash, and then pass through Star City so that Fantasia can see her baby boy.) As Ray, Pluto, and Fantasia wend their way through the Southwest on a road trip that becomes increasingly fraught and futile, Cole and McFeely go to Star City, where they team up with local sheriff Dale "Hurricane" Dixon (Bill Paxton) to wait for the killers.

ONE FALSE MOVE is a finely observed character study punctuated by some highly suspenseful, and sometimes grisly, confrontations. Franklin gives a low-key, realistic feel to the criminals' travels, throwing in docudrama-style titles to show which towns they're driving through. The killer trio's road experiences are intercut with the L.A. cops' almost vacation-like stay in Star City, where Dixon amuses the big-city boys with his puppyish enthusiasm and aspirations to join the L.A. force. The cast is uniformly first rate, with Paxton an immensely charming small-town hero, Metzler suggesting a youthful Gig Young, and Beach and Thornton a memorably evil duo.

ONE FLEW OVER THE CUCKOO'S NEST
1975   129m   c   Drama   ★★★★
Fantasy   (U.S.)   R

Jack Nicholson (*Randle Patrick McMurphy*), Louise Fletcher (*Nurse Mildred Ratched*), William Redfield (*Harding*), Michael Berryman (*Ellis*), Brad Dourif (*Billy Bibbit*), Peter Brocco (*Col. Matterson*), Dean R. Brooks (*Dr. John Spivey*), Alonzo Brown (*Miller*), Scatman Crothers (*Turkle*), Mwako Cumbuka (*Warren*)

p, Saul Zaentz, Michael Douglas; d, Milos Forman; w, Lawrence Hauben, Bo Goldman (based on the novel by Ken Kesey and the play by Dale Wasserman); ph, Haskell Wexler, William A. Fraker, Bill Butler (DeLuxe Color); ed, Richard Chew, Lynzee Klingman, Sheldon Kahn; m, Jack Nitzsche; prod d, Paul Sylbert; art d, Edwin O'Donovan; cos, Aggie Guerard Rodgers

AA Best Picture; AA Best Actor: Jack Nicholson; *AAN Best Actress:* Louise Fletcher; *AAN Best Supporting Actor:* Brad Dourif; *AA Best Director:* Milos Forman; *AA Best Adapted Screenplay:* Lawrence Hauben, Bo Goldman; *AAN Best Cinematography:* Haskell Wexler, Bill Butler; *AAN Best Film Editing:* Richard Chew, Lynzee Klingman, Sheldon Kahn; *AAN Best Original Score:* Jack Nitzsche

Ken Kesey's grim satire of institutionalized authority, bracingly filmed by Milos Forman. This romp through a microcosmic lunatic ward with an energetic, wisecracking Nicholson turns unforgettably ugly at the end.

Doing time on a prison farm, Nicholson gets out of work detail and escapes the rigors of prison life by pretending to be crazy. Shipped to a mental asylum, he becomes the prisoner of a much more hateful system, presided over by a quietly sadistic head nurse, Fletcher. To his amazement Nicholson finds his fellow inmates are "no crazier than any other SOB on the street." To bring life to the dead atmosphere, Nicholson introduces card games (with pornographically illustrated cards), organizes basketball games, and even conducts a field trip for his fellow inmates, but at every turn Fletcher is there to administer punishment, attempting to break Nicholson's spirit. After Nicholson smuggles two floozies into the ward for an evening of booze and sex, Fletcher determines to squelch his rebellion—by any means necessary.

Jarring and electrifying drama, ONE FLEW OVER THE CUCKOO'S NEST is consummately acted by a talented ensemble including several future stars. Nicholson is at his peak; Fletcher's characteristic rigidity works well here. Actor Kirk Douglas acquired the rights to Wasserman's play (based on Kesey's novel) and had a great success with it on Broadway in the 1960s; by the time the film was made, he was too old to play the lead and turned the property over to his son Michael, who brought in Forman as director. This picture marked the screen debuts of gigantic Cree Indian painter Will Sampson, Brad Dourif, and Christopher Lloyd, and of Brooks (who was superintendent of the Damasch State Mental Hospital in Salem, Oregon, where the picture was filmed). Danny DeVito had acted on screen, but was almost unknown. Tom McCall, a former Oregon governor, plays a news commentator.

ONE HOUR PHOTO
2002   98m   c   Thriller   ★★★½
Catch 23 Entertainment/Killer Films/Laughlin   R
Park Pictures   (U.S.)

Robin Williams (*Seymour "Sy" Parrish*), Connie Nielsen (*Nina Yorkin*), Michael Vartan (*Will Yorkin*), Dylan Smith (*Jakob "Jake" Yorkin*), Eriq La Salle (*Det. James Van Der Zee*), Erin Daniels (*Maya Burson*), Paul Hansen Kim (*Yoshi Araki*), Lee Garlington (*Waitress*), Gary Cole (*Bill Owens*), Marion Calvert (*Mrs. Von Unwerth*) p, Pamela Koffler, Christine Vachon, Stan Wlodkowski; d, Mark Romanek; w, Mark Romanek; ph, Jeff Cronenweth; ed, Jeffrey Ford; m, Reinhold Heil, Johnny Klimek; prod d, Tom Foden; art d, Michael Manson; fx, David Peterson; cos, Arianne Phillips

The gradual build-up to the final moments of this smart and deeply unsettling psychological thriller from ace music video director Mark Romanek is so good that the actual denouement comes as something of a disappointment.

For the past 11 years, Seymour "Sy" Parrish (a perfectly creepy Robin Williams) has been manning the one-hour photo counter at the local SavMart, and it's a job he takes very seriously. Sy knows just how important photos are, especially to lonely voyeurs like himself who value the glimpses snapshots can offer into happier lives. Over the years, Sy has grown extremely fond of Nina Yorkin (Connie Nielsen) and her nine-year-old son, Jake (Dylan Smith). For each roll Nina drops off, Sy processes two sets of prints—one for the Yorkins, one for himself—and dreams of somehow worming his way into the bosom of this lovely family. But no one ever takes pictures of the bad times, and the Yorkins aren't nearly as happy as their 4 x 6 glossies suggest. Nina feels her husband, Will (Michael Vartan), is emotionally neglectful; he accuses her of living beyond their means. When "Uncle Sy" processes a roll of film that suddenly exposes the lie behind the Yorkins' picture-perfect life, he springs into action with a sense of purpose that's truly chilling. Like Michael Mann's MANHUNTER, the film probes the modern fear that we inadvertently leave the door to our private lives wide open all the time, and there's no telling who's going to walk in. Romanek's smart script is filled with interesting observations about photos and the people who take them; too bad that he feels compelled to end this uncommonly complex thriller with such a simplistic, pop-psych explanation.

ONE HUNDRED AND ONE DALMATIANS
1961 79m c Children's/Animated ★★★½
Walt Disney Productions (U.S.) G

VOICES OF: Rod Taylor (Pongo), Lisa Davis (Anita), Cate Bauer (Perdita), Ben Wright (Roger Radcliff), Frederic Worlock (Horace), J. Pat O'Malley (Jasper/Miscellaneous Dogs), Betty Lou Gerson (Cruella De Vil/Miss Birdwell), Martha Wentworth (Nani/Goose/Cow), Tom Conway (Collie), George Pelling (Great Dane)

p, Walt Disney; d, Wolfgang Reitherman, Hamilton Luske, Clyde Geronimi; w, Bill Peet (based on a book by Dodie Smith); ed, Donald Halliday, Roy M. Brewer Jr.; m, George Bruns; prod d, Ken Anderson; art d, Ken Anderson; anim, Milt Kahl, Marc Davis, Oliver M. Johnston Jr., Franklin Thomas, John Lounsbery, Eric Larson, Hal King, Cliff Nordberg, Eric Cleworth, Art Stevens, Hal Ambro, Bill Keil, Dick Lucas, Les Clark, Blaine Gibson, John Sibley, Julius Svendsen

Three hundred artists worked on this project for three years and came up with one of the best feature cartoons ever produced by Disney Studios. The story, a romance with an interesting detective twist, is combined with exquisite caricatures of both humans and dogs. The plot revolves around a dog, Pongo, and his master, Roger, who fall for Anita and her dog, Perdita. Roger and Anita marry, allowing Pongo and Perdita to be together and produce a litter of 15 Dalmatian puppies. Wicked Cruella De Vil is overly persistent in her desire to have all 15 puppies, but Roger refuses her, prompting the wealthy woman to hire a pair of cockney crooks to steal the pups. Roger and Anita try everything to locate them, but to no avail, so Pongo resorts to the "twilight bark," a system of dog signals that locates the puppies in a deserted mansion on the outskirts of London. Pongo, assisted by a dog named the Colonel, a horse, and a cat, then sets out to rescue the puppies, discovering in the process a total of 99 Dalmatians that the evil Cruella has gathered to make herself a rare coat. Throughout the story are subtle visual elements creating an atmosphere that transcends mere cartoon reality. The characters are also evocatively voiced by a cast that includes Rod Taylor as Pongo. For fun, note the physical resemblance between many of the dogs and their masters.

101 DALMATIANS DVD
1996 103m c Children's/Comedy ★★★
Great Oaks Entertainment/Walt Disney Pictures G
(U.S.)

Glenn Close (Cruella DeVil), Jeff Daniels (Roger), Joely Richardson (Anita), Joan Plowright (Nanny), Hugh Laurie (Jasper), Mark Williams (Horace), John Shrapnel (Skinner), Tim McInnerny (Alonzo), Hugh Fraser (Frederick), Zohren Weiss (Herbert)

p, John Hughes, Ricardo Mestres; d, Stephen Herek; w, John Hughes (based on the novel The One Hundred and One Dalmatians by Dodie Smith); ph, Adrian Biddle; ed, Trudy Ship; m, Michael Kamen; prod d, Assheton Gorton; art d, Alan Tomkins, John Ralph; fx, Michael Owens, Chrissie England, George Gibbs, Industrial Light & Magic, Jim Henson's Creature Shop; cos, Anthony Powell, Rosemary Burrows

This live-action remake of one of Disney's best, most commercially successful animated features is long and loud, but short on any real wit or charm.

Anita (Joely Richardson) is a put-upon fashion designer working for Queen Bitch of London, Cruella DeVil (Glenn Close). She suffers the insults of her boss-from-hell as well as her very un-p.c. fashion ideas involving the use of furs from various endangered species. One day in the park, she meets Roger (Jeff Daniels), a video game designer. Actually, it's their pet dalmatians, Pongo and Perdy, who begin the introductions, by falling instantly in love. The human owners immediately follow suit and are married. It is not long before the patter of little feet is heard, belonging to the amazing litter of 15 puppies which Perdy bestows on them. Cruella unfortunately learns of this blessed event and becomes obsessed with turning them all into the coat of her dreams.

The dogs Pongo and Perdy give by far the best performances in the film. Hack Disney house director Stephen Herek (THE MIGHTY DUCKS, MR. HOLLAND'S OPUS) leaves no antic stone unturned, lavishing them with closeups in which they run the gamut of emotions, from the elation of first love to blissful parenthood to childless sorrow. The humans fare decidedly less well than the dogs. Daniels could have given this performance in his sleep, and Richardson manages to give a slight impression of charm in her seriously undeveloped role. And Close, of course, has a field day: in her chiaroscuro hair and gaudy-baroque Anthony Powell ensembles, she's a visual joke that wears progressively thinner with her every cackling, snorting scene.

ONE HUNDRED MEN AND A GIRL DVD
1937 85m bw Musical ★★★★
Universal (U.S.)

Deanna Durbin (Patricia Cardwell), Leopold Stokowski (Himself), Adolphe Menjou (John Cardwell), Alice Brady (Mrs. Frost), Eugene Pallette (John R. Frost), Mischa Auer (Michael Borodoff), Billy Gilbert (Garage Owner), Alma Kruger (Mrs. Tyler), Jack Smart (Marshall, the Doorman), Jed Prouty (Tommy Bitters)

p, Joe Pasternak; d, Henry Koster; w, Bruce Manning, Charles Kenyon, James Mulhauser, Hans Kraly (based on a story by Hans Kraly); ph, Joseph Valentine; ed, Bernard W. Burton

AAN Best Picture; AAN Best Original Story: Hans Kraly; AAN Best Film Editing: Bernard W. Burton; AA Best Score: Universal Studio Music Department, Charles Previn (Dept. Head); AAN Best Sound Recording: Homer Tasker

Charming, still. There are many child stars who have been horrors to work with, but that was not the case with Deanna Durbin, who was surely one of the most agreeable tykes ever to don greasepaint. She began her career with Judy Garland in an MGM short, EVERY SUNDAY, but the studio dropped her and kept Garland. It wasn't that her voice wasn't resonant; it was merely that the studio felt there was only room for one teen singer (BIG mistake) and opted for Judy. Durbin was signed by Universal, cast in THREE SMART GIRLS, and did so well that they top-lined her in this one, which turned out to be a box-office winner that took the studio from the brink of bankruptcy. Menjou is a trombonist without a place to blow. His problem is shared by many of his musician friends, so our perky heroine forms an orchestra and convinces the eminent Leopold Stokowski to conduct it in concert. The orchestra is a hit and all ends well.

Many of Durbin's films (and Durbin herself) have been long underrated as being just too sweet for words, but this is hardly the case, partly because Durbin herself adds such an agreeable touch of spunk and spice to her standard "nice girl" roles. Her first ten films for Universal play delightfully today. ONE HUNDRED MEN AND A GIRL, for instance, is smoothly entertaining from start to finish, with an excellent mix of classical and pop music. The music includes selections from Liszt, Verdi, Wagner, Tschaikovsky and Mozart as well as tunes like "It's Raining Sunbeams" and "A Heart That's Free."

ONE OF OUR AIRCRAFT IS MISSING

1941   90m   bw   War   ★★★½
Archers/British National   (U.K.)

Godfrey Tearle (Sir George Corbett), Eric Portman (Tom Earnshaw), Hugh Williams (Frank Shelley), Bernard Miles (Geoff Hickman), Hugh Burden (John Glyn Haggard), Emrys Jones (Bob Ashley), Googie Withers (Jo de Vries), Pamela Brown (Else Meertens), Joyce Redman (Jet van Dieren), Hay Petrie (Burgomeister)

p, Michael Powell, Emeric Pressburger; d, Michael Powell, Emeric Pressburger; w, Michael Powell, Emeric Pressburger; ph, Ronald Neame; ed, David Lean; art d, David Rawnsley; fx, Ronald Neame

AAN Best Original Screenplay: Michael Powell, Emeric Pressburger; AAN Best Special Effects: Ronald Neame (Photographic), C.C. Stevens (Sound)

During WWII, squadrons of heavy Wellington bombers take off from Britain at dusk and cross the English Channel for a raid on Stuttgart. On the return flight, six crewmen on one plane are forced to bail out over German-occupied Holland. Some Dutch children help them evade a German patrol; then, disguised, they are aided by an underground network that enables them to reach the coast and to return to Britain in a small boat. Almost immediately after being reunited with their squadron they are back in the air, flying even more dangerous missions into Germany. The second Michael Powell-Emeric Pressburger collaboration (the first on which Pressburger was codirector), this film does not reach the heights of their previous, similarly plotted picture, THE INVADERS. The best sequences are the opening ones, precisely detailing the raid as the men concentrate on their duties, adjusting instruments while their planes shake under the anti-aircraft fire all around them. The performances—of the stiff-upper-lip variety—are all good, especially Godfrey Tearle's as the aircraft commander, Googie Withers's as an important link in the chain of rescuers, and Scottish character actor Hay Petrie's as an apoplectic burgomeister. The film's worth as a propaganda piece was considerable, but too many long-winded speeches about people uniting to fight the Germans date the film somewhat now.

ONE TRUE THING   DVD

1998   127m   c   Drama   ★★★½
Ufland Productions/Monarch Pictures/Diamond   R
Heart Productions/Universal   (U.S.)

Meryl Streep (Kate Gulden), Renee Zellweger (Ellen Gulden), William Hurt (George Gulden), Tom Everett Scott (Brian Gulden), Lauren Graham (Jules), Nicky Katt (Jordan Belzer), James Eckhouse (District Attorney), Patrick Breen (Mr. Tweedy), Gerrit Graham (Oliver Most), David Byron (Senator Sullivan)

p, Harry Ufland, Jesse Beaton; d, Carl Franklin; w, Carl Franklin, Karen Croner (based on the novel by Anna Quindlen); ph, Declan Quinn; ed, Carole Kravetz; m, Cliff Eidelman; prod d, Paul Peters; art d, Jefferson Sage; cos, Donna Zakowska

AAN Best Actress: Meryl Streep

Even apparently happy families are often unhappy in their own ways, and beneath the Martha Stewart-like perfection of the Gulden household lies a hornet's nest of conflicting desires, suppressed anger, and fragile alliances.

George Gulden (William Hurt) is a professor of literature and a critically acclaimed essayist, adored by his ambitious daughter, Ellen (Renee Zellweger), a journalist, and resented by his son, Brian (Tom Everett Scott), whose gifts are athletic rather than intellectual. Kate (Meryl Streep) is the happy homemaker they all treat with just a touch of condescension until she becomes ill with cancer. George browbeats Ellen into coming home to care for her mother—God forbid that he should scale back his class load, or that Brian should leave the classes he's secretly flunking. Ellen inevitably comes to realize that it's Kate who, through her drive, intelligence, and considerable skills channeled into running a household and caring for her selfish husband, has permitted the rest of the family to pursue their own lives and think they're somehow more accomplished than she.

There are no particularly new insights here, but many painfully sharp observations about the way children and parents see each other through distorting webs of expectation and assumptions formed somewhere in the distant past. It's all told in flashback as Ellen is questioned about Kate's death, because small-town gossip has raised the specter of assisted suicide. The framing story is pointless and almost insulting, even though it is part of former New York Times columnist Anna Quindlen's novel. In fact, it's been scaled back for the film, which rests firmly on the shoulders of Streep and, to a lesser degree, Zellweger. Their fine performances, and Carl Franklin's understated direction, keep the tears and life-affirming revelations from ever congealing into chicken shmaltz for the soul.

ONE, TWO, THREE   DVD

1961   115m   bw   Comedy   ★★★½
Mirisch/Pyramid   (U.S./West Germany)

James Cagney (C.R. MacNamara), Horst Buchholz (Otto Ludwig Piffl), Pamela Tiffin (Scarlett Hazeltine), Arlene Francis (Phyllis MacNamara), Lilo Pulver (Ingeborg), Howard St. John (Hazeltine), Hanns Lothar (Schlemmer), Lois Bolton (Mrs. Hazeltine), Leon Askin (Peripetchikoff), Peter Capell (Mishkin)

p, Billy Wilder; d, Billy Wilder; w, Billy Wilder, I.A.L. Diamond (based on the play Egy, Ketto, Harom by Ferenc Molnar); ph, Daniel Fapp (Panavision); ed, Daniel Mandell; m, Andre Previn; art d, Alexander Trauner; fx, Milt Rice

AAN Best B/W Cinematography: Daniel L. Fapp

James Cagney left the movie business for more than 20 years after finishing his role in ONE, TWO, THREE and it's no wonder; he needed at least that much time to rest up after the fastest-moving comedy made in the 1960s, and surely one of the funniest. This film begins at mach one and gets somewhere near the speed of light by the time it finishes. As a matter of fact, it's often too furiously quick for its own good as the dialogue comes at the ears with Uzi-like speed. Cagney is the fast-talking, hard-driving, self-made man who heads up Coca-Cola's bottling interests in Germany. His attitude is similar to the man who once ran General Motors and said, "What's good for General Motors is good for America." And since there is nothing in Europe more American than Coca-Cola, Cagney is determined to bring it to everyone with two lips and a gullet. Cagney would like to become chief of all the European operations and is working toward that end when Tiffin, the teenage daughter of St. John—one of the heavyweights at Coca-Cola's Georgia headquarters—arrives, and Cagney has to baby-sit her for two weeks as she makes her way through a tour of the Continent. Cagney does his best to squire the dippy Tiffin, in the hope that his behavior will get him his desired promotion, but things go awry when she falls hard for Buchholz, a dedicated East Berlin Communist hippy. Cagney learns that St. John is coming to Germany at the same time he discovers Tiffin has married Buchholz. He plants a copy of that most capitalistic of papers, *The Wall Street Journal*, on Buchholz, figuring the youth will be clapped in irons and an annulment can be secured. Then he learns that Tiffin is expecting Buchholz's baby, so he has to get the kid out of jail and train him to be a capitalist in order to make him a suitable son-in-law for St. John. Cagney successfully springs Buchholz, spends a few bucks to purchase a royal title for him, and gives him a crash course in American business. Buchholz impresses St. John so much that the pleased father-in-law hands the plum job of running Europe to his new relation, the father of his unborn grandchild. Cagney winds up going back to Atlanta with wife Francis. He did his job too well and lost the promotion he'd hoped for.

Cagney plays this part with such verve and energy that he seems to be a much younger man than he was (62) and even appears to be a new actor eager to impress the studio with his abilities. But that was always the way Cagney played things—to the hilt. Many of the jokes were taken right from the period's headlines and were already dated by the time the film was released. It was based on a one-act play by the master farceur Molnar and expanded beautifully by Wilder and Diamond. Filmed on location in West Berlin and at the studios in Munich (where Wilder had been before the war), it won no awards except the laughter of those who saw it. Fapp got an Oscar nomination for his cinematography. Previn's score was perfect, and the use of several old ditties was excellent, including "Yes, We Have No Bananas" (Frank Silver, Irving Cohn). It would be better to watch this alone as the sound of chuckling in a theater will drown out many of the clever lines.

ONION FIELD, THE
1979 122m c Crime ★★★
Avco Embassy (U.S.) R

John Savage *(Karl Hettinger)*, James Woods *(Greg Powell)*, Franklyn Seales *(Jimmy Smith)*, Ted Danson *(Ian Campbell)*, Ronny Cox *(Pierce Brooks)*, David Huffman *(District Attorney Phil Halpin)*, Christopher Lloyd *(Jailhouse Lawyer)*, Diane Hull *(Helen Hettinger)*, Priscilla Pointer *(Chrissie Campbell)*, Beege Barkett *(Greg's Woman)*

p, Walter Coblenz; d, Harold Becker; w, Joseph Wambaugh (based on the book by Wambaugh); ph, Charles Rosher Jr.; ed, John W. Wheeler; m, Eumir Deodato; prod d, Brian Eatwell

After having some of his earlier works unacceptably altered, Wambaugh decided to write the screenplay himself for this version of his true story about two Los Angeles cops and the killers of one of them. Danson and Savage, a pair of plain-

clothes officers working the Hollywood beat, go after two lowlifes in a car, Woods and Seales, and are shocked when a gun is put in their faces. The cops are disarmed, kidnapped, and taken to a field some distance from Los Angeles where Danson is assassinated. Savage gets away, and with his accurate description the killers are soon nabbed. The rest of the picture concerns the judicial system and how it favors the felon over the victim. Both killers are willing to cooperate in return for a deal from the DA's office, and each claims it was the other who pulled the trigger on Danson. Meanwhile, Savage is so wracked with guilt for his partner's death that he begins to break down mentally. An authentic look at police work (and that is where it shines), the picture gets confused in the court scenes and can't sustain the power of its opening sequences. Good acting and careful direction by Becker make it worth seeing, but the violence and the language may be too graphic for some tastes. Although Wambaugh himself was a cop with the Los Angeles Police Department, he had technical assistance on this from Richard Falk. Advice on courtroom procedures came from Phillip Halpin and Dino Fulgoni, who were portrayed by Huffman and Pataki. The crime took place in 1963 and Smith (Seales) was released in the 1980s, over strenuous objections.

ONLY ANGELS HAVE WINGS
1939 121m bw Drama ★★★★
Columbia (U.S.)

Cary Grant *(Geoff Carter)*, Jean Arthur *(Bonnie Lee)*, Richard Barthelmess *(Bat McPherson)*, Rita Hayworth *(Judith McPherson)*, Thomas Mitchell *(Kid Dabb)*, Sig Rumann *(Dutchman)*, Victor Kilian *(Sparks)*, John Carroll *(Gent Shelton)*, Allyn Joslyn *(Les Peters)*, Don "Red" Barry *(Tex Gordon)*

p, Howard Hawks; d, Howard Hawks; w, William Rankin (uncredited), Eleanore Griffin (uncredited), Jules Furthman (based on a story by Howard Hawks); ph, Joseph Walker, Elmer Dyer; ed, Viola Lawrence; m, Dimitri Tiomkin, Manuel Maciste, M.W. Stoloff; art d, Lionel Banks; fx, Roy Davidson, Edwin C. Hahn; cos, Robert Kalloch

AAN Best B/W Cinematography: Joseph Walker; *AAN Best Special Effects:* Roy Davidson (Photographic), Edwin C. Hahn (Sound)

An amazing adventure film in which the adventure is primarily confined to a shabby saloon, this Grant-Arthur vehicle clearly bears the mark of director Howard Hawks. Grant, the head of a broken-down air freight company, sends courageous pilots over the treacherous Andes Mountains in Peru. Arthur becomes involved with one such pilot, Noah Beery, Jr., then quickly switches her attention to the hardboiled Grant. Several other pilots (Joslyn, Carroll, and Barry) are much taken with Arthur, but she only has eyes for the all-business Grant, who fails to return her affection. Enter Barthelmess, a pilot who tarnished his reputation in an accident years earlier in which another flier was killed. The guilt-ridden Barthelmess is washed up as a pilot, but Grant gives him a job anyway. Hayworth, Barthelmess's sexy, cuckolding wife, tries to seduce Grant and almost succeeds before Grant realizes he really loves the smart-talking Arthur. Although the other pilots have made a pariah of Barthelmess, he proves that he's made of courageous stuff by volunteering to take on the most hazardous missions. Meanwhile, Mitchell—an elderly pilot who acts as surrogate father to Grant and whose brother was killed in the accident that ruined Barthelmess's reputation—is losing his sight but won't admit it. Grant keeps him on the ground to protect him. But when Grant prepares to undertake a dangerous flight himself, Mitchell goes in his place.

ONLY ANGELS HAVE WINGS is a powerful character study, and director Hawks and his fine, predominantly male cast carefully develop the personalities of an interesting collection of characters. Though much of the dialogue is predictable, the story is strong, the acting is outstanding, and

Hawks's cameras move with fluid grace through the confining sets.

Rita Hayworth gives a notable performance as a vamp, and supporting players Allyn Joslyn and John Carroll are jaded, sardonic live wires. Richard Barthelmess, as the film's most complex character, plays his role stoically, failing to invest his washed-up flier with the necessary emotional depth. This was an important comeback attempt for Barthelmess, who had experienced lean years since his days as a silent screen star. Regrettably, the meaty part he was given was left on the kitchen table, half-eaten, and Barthelmess never again appeared in a major film as a lead. The special effects, particularly the fine aerial sequences, earned Roy Davidson and Edwin C. Hahn an Oscar nomination in a category recognized for the first time by the Academy. The film was also nominated for Best Black-and-White Cinematography.

OPEN CITY   *DVD*
(ROMA, CITTA APERTA)
1945 105m bw War/Drama   ★★★★
Excelsa (Italy)

Anna Magnani *(Pina)*, Aldo Fabrizi *(Don Pietro Pellegrini)*, Marcell Pagliero *(Giorgio Manfredi)*, Maria Michi *(Marina)*, Harry Feist *(Maj. Bergmann)*, Francesco Grandjacquet *(Francesco)*, Giovanna Galletti *(Ingrid)*, Vito Annichiarico *(Marcello Pina's Son)*, Carla Revere *(Lauretta)*, Nando Bruno *(Agostino)*

p, Roberto Rossellini; d, Roberto Rossellini; w, Sergio Amidei, Federico Fellini, Roberto Rossellini (based on a story by Amidei and Alberto Consiglio); ph, Ubaldo Arata; m, Renzo Rossellini

AAN Best Screenplay: Federico Fellini, Sergio Amidei

In its time, OPEN CITY was an innovative fusion of documentary and melodrama. Filmed on the streets, without the use of sound recorders (dialogue was dubbed in later), during the months just after the Allies liberated Italy from the grip of Fascism, the film has the appearance of a documentary. The actors, except for Anna Magnani (then a sometime dance-hall girl), were all nonprofessionals. The backgrounds were not constructions on a Cinecitta lot, but actual apartments, shops, and streets—a change for those used to sets and costumes. Set in Rome, 1943-44, the story brings together two enemy forces—the Communists and the Catholics—and unites them in the fight for their country's liberation. Manfredi (Marcello Pagliero) is a Resistance leader wanted by the Germans who must deliver some money to his compatriots. Hiding out in the apartment block of Francesco (Francesco Grandjacquet) and his pregnant fiancee, Pina (Magnani), Manfredi plans to let a Catholic priest, Don Pietro (Aldo Fabrizi), make the delivery. When their building is raided, Francesco is arrested and hauled away. Pino chases after him, screaming, and is gunned down in the middle of the street. Manfredi takes refuge in the apartment of his mistress, Marina (Maria Michi). She's a drug addict who, unknown to him, snitches for her dealer, an outrageous lesbian Gestapo agent (Giovanna Galletti). As excellent as OPEN CITY is, it has often been criticized for its simplistic moral scheme and emotional manipulation. Renzo Rossellini's score and various comic contrivances, for instance, don't jibe with the supposedly objective aims of neorealist cinema. Most videotape copies offer prints of mediocre quality and often unreadable subtitles.

OPEN RANGE   *DVD*
2003 139m c Western   ★★★
Cobalt Media Group/Touchstone/   R
Beacon Pictures/Tig Productions   (U.S.)

Robert Duvall *(Boss Spearman)*, Kevin Costner *(Charley Waite)*, Annette Bening *(Sue Barlow)*, Michael Gambon *(Denton Baxter)*, Michael Jeter *(Percy)*, Diego Luna *(Button)*, James Russo *(Sheriff Poole)*, Abraham Benrubi *(Mose)*, Dean McDermott *(Doc Barlow)*, Kim Coates *(Butler)*

p, Kevin Costner, Jake Eberts, David Valdes; d, Kevin Costner; w, Craig Storper (based on the novel *The Open Range Men* by Lauran Paine); ph, James Muro; ed, Michael J. Duthie, Miklos Wright; m, Michael Kamen; prod d, Gae Buckley; art d, Gary Myers; fx, David J. Negron Jr., Neil Trifunovich; cos, John Bloomfield

A leisurely elegy for the American West with "Kevin Costner's Unforgiven" written all over it. That's not inherently a bad thing, but the big drawback is that actor-turned-director Costner is no Clint Eastwood.

The western frontier, 1882: Grizzled Boss Spearman (Robert Duvall) is a land-poor cattle owner who grazes his stock on the wide-open range. Boss's second-in-command, Charley Waite (Costner), doesn't talk much but knows everything worth knowing about working cattle and living off the land. Chubby, perpetually optimistic Mose (Abraham Benrubi) and callow Button (Diego Luna), the closest thing Boss has to a son, are the younger hands. Boss's crew inevitably runs afoul of brutal Denton Baxter (Michael Gambon), who owns the land they're camped on, the nearby town of Harmonville, and local sheriff Poole (James Russo), and is willing to discourage free-grazers by any means necessary. His men kill Mose, wound Button, and try to scatter Boss's herd. Provoked, Charley and Boss leave Button with Harmonville's doctor (Dean McDermott) and his spinster sister, Sue (Annette Bening), and prepare to exact frontier justice.

Based on Lauran Paine's novel *The Open Range Men*, this spare story of the changing West is handsome and deeply respectful; it's also too long and handles certain cliches clumsily, guaranteeing laughter at the wrong moments. But the extended, HIGH NOON-style shootout is suitably brutal, chaotic, and messy, and extending the sequence to include its grim, sad aftermath was an intelligent touch. The movie's real trouble is that Costner's performance as an aging cowboy doesn't resonate as did western-veteran Eastwood's, and while Costner the actor clearly imagines himself the Gary Cooper of the 21st century, he's got a crude sentimental streak that Costner the director fails to curtail.

OPEN WATER   *DVD*
2004 79m c Thriller   ★★★½
Plunge Pictures (U.S.)   R

Blanchard Ryan *(Susan)*, Daniel Travis *(Daniel)*, Saul Stein *(Seth)*, Estelle Lau *(Estelle)*, Michael E. Williamson *(Davis)*, Cristina Zenarro *(Linda)*, John Charles *(Junior)*

p, Laura Lau; d, Chris Kentis; w, Chris Kentis; ph, Chris Kentis, Laura Lau; ed, Chris Kentis; m, Graeme Revell

Neither a BLAIR WITCH PROJECT-like spook show nor a thrill ride a la JAWS, Chris Kentis's second film, an ingenious triumph of imagination over budget, is a modest psychological thriller that plucks a primal nerve—the fear of being abandoned, helpless, and forgotten.

Inspired by the 1998 disappearance of divers Tom and Eileen Lonergan off the coast of Australia, Kentis follows harried couple Susan and Daniel (Blanchard Ryan and Daniel Travis) as they depart for a hastily arranged Caribbean vacation and book a spot on a rinky-dink dive boat, which chugs out to sea with a full load of tourists. While the others stick together underwater, Daniel and Susan, experienced divers, strike out on their own. When they surface some 45 minutes later, they can't find the boat. Their first thought is that they've come up at the wrong spot; their second is that the boat has indeed left without them, but will return as soon as someone realizes they're two passengers short. The remainder of the film's brief but anxiety-provoking duration charts Susan and Daniel's waterlogged ordeal of jellyfish, barracuda, thirst, cold, anger, exhaustion, and sharks.

Lacking money for elaborate special effects, Kentis and his producer-wife, Laura Lau, hit on an elegant solution: real sharks, nature's natural heavies. The film's dispassionate examination of the shifts in Susan and Daniel's relationship as they drift from irritation to barely suppressed panic is at least as nerve-wracking, and breathless stories about the film's $130,000 budget, you-are-there digital cinematography, and canny casting (Ryan and Travis are a couple in real life) skip over Kentis's boldest decision: making his protagonists a little unlikable. Susan and Daniel are standoffish and full of themselves, but their comeuppance escalates well beyond a good slap in the ego.

OPERATION PETTICOAT
DVD

1959 124m c   Comedy/War   ★★★½
Granarte   (U.S.)

Cary Grant *(Adm. Matt Sherman)*, Tony Curtis *(Lt. Nick Holden)*, Joan O'Brien *(Lt. Dolores Crandall)*, Dina Merrill *(Lt. Barbara Duran)*, Arthur O'Connell *(Sam Tostin)*, Dick Sargent *(Stovall)*, Virginia Gregg *(Maj. Edna Hayward)*, Robert F. Simon *(Capt. J.B. Henderson)*, Robert Gist *(Watson)*

p, Robert Arthur; d, Blake Edwards; w, Stanley Shapiro, Maurice Richlin (based on a story by Paul King, Joseph Stone); ph, Russell Harlan, Clifford Stine (Eastmancolor); ed, Ted J. Kent, Frank Gross; m, David Rose; art d, Alexander Golitzen, Robert E. Smith; cos, Bill Thomas

AAN Best Original Story and Screenplay: Paul King, Joseph Stone, Stanley Shapiro, Maurice Richlin

After the end of WWII, Adm. Matt Sherman (Cary Grant) reads over his log from the USS *Sea Tiger*, the submarine he captains. Sherman is about to turn over the command of the sub to Lt. Nick Holden (Tony Curtis), who is assigned to squire it until it is destroyed and replaced by a nuclear vessel. The movie unwinds in flashback as Sherman recalls some of the events in the sub's life—particularly how that life was renewed when he became determined to raise the *Sea Tiger* in the wake of an attack on Manila Bay. It's December 1941 and, with help from Holden, who secures the supplies and gear to help restore the badly damaged sub, Sherman and his crew take to the waters. Along the way, they are joined by five stranded nurses, a couple of Filipino families, and a goat. The sailors ferry them out of harm's way, especially enjoying the presence of the nurses—a chesty bunch who always seem to be passing the hot young sailors in the sub's very narrow corridors. They also paint the sub pink. There's not much story to speak of, and the jokes are more than a bit sexist, but the gags are bright and Blake Edwards's direction adroit enough to make OPERATION PETTICOAT an enjoyable time. A TV series was later attempted, but never came close to the energy of the movie.

OPPOSITE OF SEX, THE
DVD

1998 105m c   Comedy/Drama   ★★★★
Original Voices   (U.S.)   R

Christina Ricci *(Dedee Truitt)*, Martin Donovan *(Bill Truitt)*, Lisa Kudrow *(Lucia Dalury)*, Lyle Lovett *(Sheriff Carl Tippett)*, Johnny Galecki *(Jason Bock)*, Ivan Sergei *(Matt Mateo)*, William Scott Lee *(Randy)*, Megan Blake *(Bobette)*, Colin Ferguson *(Tom Dalury)*, Dan Bucatinsky *(Timothy)*

p, David Kirkpatrick, Michael Besman; d, Don Roos; w, Don Roos; ph, Hubert Taczanowski; ed, David Codron; m, Mason Daring; prod d, Michael Clausen; cos, Peter Mitchell

Batten down the hatches: Hurricane Dedee is coming! Fresh, sharp, and very funny, this vicious comedy of sexual manners is driven by the selfish whims of Dedee Truitt (Christina Ricci), an underage strumpet who runs away from home and blows the quiet life of her half-brother Bill (Martin Donovan) right to hell.

Indiana high-school teacher Bill is still in mourning for his longtime lover who died of AIDS, but lives with hunky new boyfriend Matt (Ivan Sergei), a none-too-bright stud muffin who works at the local copy shop. Bill's best friend Lucia (Lisa Kudrow) takes an instant dislike to Dedee, who in short order lives up to Lucia's worst expectations: she seduces Matt, announces that she's pregnant, and hits the road with $10,000 of Bill's money and his late lover's ashes. And as if that's not bad enough, Jason (Johnny Galecki), Matt's ex, decides in a fit of pique to accuse Bill of having molested him when he was still a student.

The wonder of it all is how bitterly funny the complications are, especially as filtered through Dedee's monstrously self-centered voice-over. Vulgar, bigoted, and knowing beyond her years, Dedee isn't exactly lovable, but you've got to admire her spunk. Ricci, who has the ripely lush figure of a young Elizabeth Taylor topped by a thatch of bleached-blond straw, is by turns adorable, infuriating, and oddly vulnerable (though she'd slap you for saying so). Making his directing debut, screenwriter Don Roos (SINGLE WHITE FEMALE, BOYS ON THE SIDE) coaxes assured performances from his talented cast and maintains a fast and furious pace that really does recall classic screwball comedies.

ORCHESTRA WIVES

1942 98m   bw   Musical   ★★★★
Fox   (U.S.)

George Montgomery *(Bill Abbott)*, Ann Rutherford *(Connie)*, Glenn Miller *(Gene Morrison)*, Cesar Romero *(Sinjin)*, Lynn Bari *(Jaynie)*, Carole Landis *(Natalie)*, Virginia Gilmore *(Elsie)*, Mary Beth Hughes *(Caroline)*, Brothers Nicholas *(Specialty)*, Tamara Geva *(Mrs. Beck)*

p, William LeBaron; d, Archie Mayo; w, Karl Tunberg, Darrell Ware (based on a story by James Prindle); ph, Lucien Ballard; ed, Robert Bischoff; art d, Richard Day, Joseph C. Wright

AAN Best Song: "I've Got a Gal in Kalamazoo"; Harry Warren (Music), Mack Gordon (Lyrics)

Among the many cinematic looks behind the scenes in the 1940s, ORCHESTRA WIVES may be the finest example of the genre, due in great part to the presence of Glenn Miller (in his final appearance before his ill-fated flight over the English Channel). The plot concerns Connie (Ann Rutherford), the new wife of trumpeter Bill Abbott (George Montgomery). Connie accompanies Bill as he tours with Gene Morrison's (Miller) orchestra; meanwhile, the other wives cattily speculate as to how long the union can last, especially considering sensuous band singer Jaynie's (Lynn Bari, whose singing is dubbed by Pat Friday) fondness for other women's men. Sure enough, Jaynie sets her sights on Bill, and the sniping among the wives nearly breaks up the band, but all ends happily as the ensemble's dapper pianist (Cesar Romero) manages to keep both the newlyweds and the orchestra together. The picture swings with Miller music from start to finish, with songs provided by those aces of movie tunes, Harry Warren and Mack Gordon.

ORDET

1955 123m bw Drama/Religious ★★★★
Palladium (Denmark)

Henrik Malberg *(Morten Borgen)*, Emil Hass Christensen *(Mikkel Borgen)*, Preben Lerdorff-Rye *(Johannes Borgen)*, Cay Kristiansen *(Anders Borgen)*, Birgitte Federspiel *(Inger—Mikkel's Wife)*, Ejner Federspiel *(Peter Skraedder)*, Ove Rud *(Vicar)*, Ann Elisabeth Hansen *(Maren—Mikkel Borgen's Daughter)*, Susanne Rud *(Lilleinger—Mikkel Borgen's Daughter)*, Gerda Nielsen *(Anne Skraedder)*

p, Carl-Theodor Dreyer; d, Carl-Theodor Dreyer; w, Carl-Theodor Dreyer (based on the play by Kaj Munk); ph, Henning Bendtsen; ed, Carl-Theodor Dreyer, Edith Schussel; m, Poul Schierbeck; art d, Erik Aaes

Based on the play by Kaj Munk, this inspirational drama focuses on one of director Dreyer's favorite themes, the conflict between institutional religion and personal faith.

Set in a staunchly God-fearing Danish village, ORDET tells the story of Morten Borgen (Malberg) and his three sons. Mikkel (Christensen) is filled with religious doubt. Anders (Kristiansen), meanwhile, is involved in a romance complicated by differences of faith. The central character, Johannes (Lerdorff-Rye), has the biggest problem of all: He believes he is Christ and his extreme faith is viewed as madness. Things change when he is visited by the Holy Spirit and Mikkel's wife is resurrected at her funeral.

Although any plot summary of ORDET would border on the ludicrous, the film is nothing of the kind. This is an overwhelming emotional and intellectual experience, thanks both to its subject matter and its austere yet potent presentation. Dreyer's rigorously spare visual style (the film contains only 114 shots in 126 minutes) perfectly conveys his metaphysical themes and creates a meditative and genuinely inspirational mood. Not to be missed, certainly by anyone who loved his great THE PASSION OF JOAN OF ARC.

ORDINARY PEOPLE

1980 124m c Drama ★★★½
Wildwood (U.S.) R

Donald Sutherland *(Calvin)*, Mary Tyler Moore *(Beth)*, Judd Hirsch *(Berger)*, Timothy Hutton *(Conrad)*, M. Emmet Walsh *(Swim Coach)*, Elizabeth McGovern *(Jeannine)*, Dinah Manoff *(Karen)*, Fredric Lehne *(Lazenby)*, James B. Sikking *(Ray)*, Basil Hoffman *(Sloan)*

p, Ronald L. Schwary; d, Robert Redford; w, Alvin Sargent (based on the novel by Judith Guest); ph, John Bailey (Technicolor); ed, Jeff Kanew; art d, Phillip Bennett, Michael Riva; cos, Bernie Pollack

AA Best Picture; AAN Best Actress: Mary Tyler Moore; *AA Best Supporting Actor:* Timothy Hutton; *AAN Best Supporting Actor:* Judd Hirsch; *AA Best Director:* Robert Redford; *AA Best Adapted Screenplay:* Alvin Sargent

Robert Redford chose to adapt Judith Guest's novel as his first directorial effort, with impressive results. Timothy Hutton (son of actor Jim Hutton) also debuts here, as Conrad, a potentially suicidal teen who is consumed with guilt over the drowning death of his brother (Doebler), compounded by the resentment his mother (Moore, in an astounding performance that made a dramatic departure from her clean-cut image) directs at him for having survived. As tensions mount, Conrad's father (Sutherland) becomes increasingly distanced from his wife and depressed by his inability to communicate with, let alone restore, his family. After a friend (Manoff) kills herself, Conrad is able to

achieve a breakthrough with his psychiatrist (Hirsch), deciding he wants to live.

Although the story is admittedly slight, Redford demonstrates a tremendous understanding of his subjects, wealthy white suburbanites who struggle to conceal the rage and fear that eats away at them. His quiet, gentle direction is epitomized in memorably painful moments, such as the famous photo scene, when the squelched feelings threaten to explode. Several times, the film escapes easy resolutions, hanging on difficult moments longer than expected and refusing to slide into artificial closure. The script, which has the difficult task of illustrating the inner lives of essentially inarticulate people, is strongest in its characterization of the mother, whose own misery is withheld until Moore's heartbreaking final sequence (her own son died around the time of this production).

Redford was rewarded, not only with critical praise and a huge box-office hit, but with a surprising slew of Oscars, including Best Picture (beating out the infinitely more deserving RAGING BULL). Nonetheless, it would be eight years before he would direct again (THE MILAGRO BEANFIELD WAR), and he has yet to equal the sure touch and depth of insight shown in this film (with the possible exception of QUIZ SHOW, which is better directed but less emotionally resonant).

ORLANDO

1993 92m c Drama/Historical ★★½
Adventure Pictures/Lenfilm/Spectator Entertainment PG-13
International/Sigma Films/Mikado Film/Rio Film
(U.K./Netherlands/Italy/France)

Tilda Swinton *(Orlando)*, Billy Zane *(Shelmerdine)*, Lothaire Bluteau *(The Khan)*, John Wood *(Archduke Harry)*, Charlotte Valandrey *(Sasha)*, Heathcote Williams *(Nick Greene/Publisher)*, Quentin Crisp *(Queen Elizabeth I)*, Peter Eyre *(Mr. Pope)*, Thom Hoffman *(William of Orange)*, Kathryn Hunter *(Countess)*

p, Christopher Sheppard; d, Sally Potter; w, Sally Potter (from the novel by Virginia Woolf); ph, Alexei Rodionov; ed, Herve Schneid; art d, Michael Buchanan, Michael Howells, Stanislav Romanovsky, Igor Gulyenko; fx, Effects Associates; chor, Jacky Lansley

AAN Best Art Direction-Set Decoration: Jan Roeles, Ben Van Os; *AAN Best Costume Design:* Sandy Powell

Suffocatingly beautiful, ORLANDO is a precious trifle whose literary pedigree intimidated audiences into ignoring its sublime silliness. It's visually intoxicating, with its lavish ruffs and furbelows, stately homes and manicured gardens, jewels and silks and elaborately curled hair, but there's less to ORLANDO than meets the eye.

Based on the 1928 novel by Virginia Woolf, ORLANDO opens in 17th century London. Orlando (Tilda Swinton) is an aristocratic youth, androgynous in the fashion of the time and gravely determined to translate life, of which he knows little, into art, of which he knows even less. Orlando captures the fancy of aging Queen Elizabeth I (Quentin Crisp), a crone who orders him not to grow old or wither. Orlando obeys, inexplicably remaining fresh-cheeked as centuries slip past. A romantic to his core, Orlando suffers mightily his unrequited love for the enchanting Russian princess Sasha (Charlotte Valandrey); when she proves false, he seeks out an extended term as England's ambassador to Arabia. One day, Orlando falls into a deep sleep and, when he awakens days later, has undergone a miraculous sex change. Orlando's adventures continue, and she spends the ensuing centuries refusing to behave differently simply because she's now a woman.

ORLANDO is undeniably ravishing, and its politics are almost suspiciously in tune with the times. But beneath the glittering surface is precious little substance: this is a date movie for aspiring intellectuals, a source of smug satisfaction at having chosen to see a thought-provoking movie, unspoiled by the realization that there isn't much to think about.

ORPHANS

1987 115m c   Drama   ★★★★
Lorimar   (U.S.)   R

Albert Finney *(Harold)*, Matthew Modine *(Treat)*, Kevin Anderson *(Phillip)*, John Kellogg *(Barney)*, Anthony Heald *(Man in Park)*, Novella Nelson *(Mattie)*, Elizabeth Parrish *(Rich Woman)*, B. Constance Barry *(Lady in Crosswalk)*, Frank Ferrara *(Cab Driver)*, Clifford Fearl *(Doorman)*

p, Alan J. Pakula, Susan Solt; d, Alan J. Pakula; w, Lyle Kessler (based on the play by Lyle Kessler); ph, Don McAlpine (Technicolor); ed, Evan Lottman; m, Michael Small; prod d, George Jenkins; art d, John J. Moore; chor, Lynnette Barkley; cos, John Boxer

After the dismal failure of 1986's DREAM LOVER, director Alan J. Pakula returned to top form with the screen version of the popular 1985 Lyle Kessler play *Orphans*. Basically a three-man show, ORPHANS deals with a pair of orphaned brothers, Treat (Matthew Modine) and Phillip (Kevin Anderson), who live in a dilapidated old house in a seedy part of Newark, New Jersey. Treat, a potentially dangerous petty thief, is the dominant sibling. Fearing that he will lose his brother just as he lost his parents, Treat keeps Phillip imprisoned in his own home. Harold (Albert Finney) is brought home by Treat as a potential kidnapping victim, but he quickly begins to take control of the situation. It's not often that a play can survive the transition from stage to screen without suffering some loss. ORPHANS, however, does. Kessler (who wrote both the stage play and the screenplay) worked his claustrophobic, prisonlike setting to the film's advantage. More important to the success of ORPHANS is the brilliant acting by all three leads. Finney turns in a spectacular performance. Modine displays another facet of his acting ability as the violent, emotionally confused Treat. Anderson, whose image changes as his character becomes readied for the outside world, keeps pace with (and often surpasses) his costars. Part fairy tale and part heightened reality, ORPHANS manages to strike an emotional chord with almost everyone who sees it.

ORPHANS

                                         DVD
1999 95m   c   Comedy/Drama   ★★★½
Antonine Greenbridge/Channel Four   (U.K.)

Gary Lewis *(Thomas)*, Douglas Henshall *(Michael)*, Rosemarie Stevenson *(Sheila)*, Stephen McCole *(John)*, Frank Gallagher *(Tanga)*, Alex Norton *(Hanson)*, Laura O'Donnell *(Carole)*, Dave Anderson *(Uncle Ian)*, Malcom Shields *(DD Duncan)*, John Comerford *(Ed)*

p, Frances Higson; d, Peter Mullan; w, Peter Mullan; ph, Grant Scott Cameron; ed, Colin Monie; m, Craig Armstrong; prod d, Campbell Gordon; art d, Frances Connell; fx, Stuart Brisdon, Roy Field (Visual); cos, Lynn Aitken

This brisk and bloody black comedy, written and directed by Scottish actor Peter Mullan (MY NAME IS JOE), follows four grown Glaswegian siblings as they journey through the longest night of their lives.

On the eve of their mother's funeral, the Flynn orphans—Thomas (Gary Lewis), Michael (Douglas Henshall), Sheila (Rosemarie Stevenson) and John (Stephen McCole)—gather at a local pub to raise a glass to the dear departed. When Thomas is heckled during a teary rendition of "The Air That I

Breathe," Michael explodes, rushing to his brother's defense and getting stabbed for his trouble. Michael refuses to go to the hospital until the next morning—he wants to go to work first and claim workman's comp—and wanders into the night, slowly bleeding to death. John vows revenge on Michael's attacker while Thomas, the eldest, retreats into his misguided, self-righteous devotion to his mother. He returns to the church for an all-night vigil with the wheelchair-bound Sheila, who soon wants to go home and leaves in a snit. After smashing a statue of the Virgin Mary, her wheelchair breaks down on a dark and lonely street. As the long night wears on, Glasgow braces itself for a gale-force windstorm that seems to bring out the very worst in each of the motherless Flynns.

Mullan's film is filled with some marvelously funny bits, including a bilious pub owner who holds patrons prisoner in his storeroom. But it's neither the humor nor the strong undercurrent of barely controlled mayhem that stays with you; Mullan's emotional uppercut is as powerful and unexpected as anything else in the film.

ORPHEUS
                                         DVD
(OPRHEE)
1949 112m   bw   Fantasy   ★★★★½
Andre Paulve   (France)

Jean Marais *(Orpheus)*, Maria Casares *(The Princess)*, Marie Dea *(Eurydice)*, Francois Perier *(Heurtebise)*, Juliette Greco *(Aglaonice)*, Edouard Dermit *(Cegeste)*, Henri Cremieux *(Friend in Cafe)*, Pierre Bertin *(Police Commissioner)*, Roger Blin *(Writer)*, Jacques Varennes

p, Emil Darbon; d, Jean Cocteau; w, Jean Cocteau (based on the play by Jean Cocteau); ph, Nicolas Hayer; ed, Jacqueline Sadoul; m, Georges Auric, Christophe Willibald Gluck; art d, Jean d'Eaubonne

A compelling cinematic allegory from one of the great artists of the twentieth century, ORPHEUS is the perfect example of magical filmmaking. Updating the Greek myth and adding an autobiographical element—the story is now set in in contemporary Paris—Cocteau casts his longtime companion Jean Marais as Orpheus, a famous poet married to Eurydice (Marie Dea). When a fellow poet, the handsome young Cegeste (Edouard Dermit), is hit by a passing motorcyclist in front of a popular cafe, Orpheus is invited by an elegant and mysterious Princess (Maria Casares) to accompany her and the dead poet to her chalet. There, the Princess brings Cegeste "back to life" (by ingeniously running the film backwards for that one shot, Cocteau was able to perform such magic) and disappears through a liquescent mirror into the Underworld. Later, after being chauffeured home by the Princess's servant, the angel Heurtebise (Francois Perier), Orpheus devotes himself to his poetry, scribbling down indecipherable messages transmitted to him over a car radio. He ignores everything but the radio and fails to even notice when Eurydice is killed. Heurtebise, who has fallen in love with Eurydice during Orpheus's preoccupation with poetry, comes to suspect that the Princess overstepped her authority as an Angel of Death by killing Eurydice in order to make room for herself in Orpheus's life. Together, Heurtebise and Orpheus pass through the mirror and journey into the Underworld to find the Princess and Eurydice.

Awarded the top prize at the 1950 Venice Film Festival, ORPHEUS was instantly heralded as a masterpiece. It was blessed with perfect casting (though Cocteau had considered both Greta Garbo and Marlene Dietrich for Casares's role), photographic innovation, indelible imagery and an exceptional score by Georges Auric. The film is as much about the creative process as it is about death, but even those who miss its many meanings will still be hypnotized by its style and beauty. As with all Cocteau's films, the written word cannot adequately describe the visual sensations he creates, sensations that do not diminish with the passage of time.

OSCAR AND LUCINDA

1997 120m c Historical/Romance/Drama ★★★½
Dalton Films/Meridian Films/Artisan Films/ R
Fox Searchlight (Australia)

Ralph Fiennes *(Oscar Hopkins)*, Cate Blanchett *(Lucinda Leplastrier)*, Ciaran Hinds *(Reverend Dennis Hasset)*, Tom Wilkinson *(Hugh Stratton)*, Clive Russell *(Theophilus)*, Richard Roxburgh *(Mr. Jeffris)*, Bille Brown *(Percy Smith)*, Josephine Byrnes *(Miriam Chadwick)*, Barnaby Kay *(Wardley-Fish)*, Barry Otto *(Jimmy D'Abbs)*

p, Robin Dalton, Timothy White; d, Gillian Armstrong; w, Laura Jones (based on the novel by Peter Carey); ph, Geoffrey Simpson; ed, Nicholas Beauman; m, Thomas Newman; prod d, Luciana Arrighi; art d, John Ralph, Paul Ghiradani; fx, Joss Williams; cos, Janet Patterson

AAN Best Costume Design: Janet Patterson

A passionate romance between a gangly minister and a strong-willed heiress played out against the backdrop of the 19th-century Australian Outback... are we in bodice-ripping territory here? The answer is firmly no. Adapted from the Booker Prize-winning novel by Peter Carey, this off-kilter epic revolves around the near-romance of Oscar Hopkins (Ralph Fiennes) and Lucinda Leplastrier (Cate Blanchett), but takes eccentric detours into gambling addiction, the genocidal displacement of Australian aborigines by European settlers, and the arcane world of glass production. The son of a Protestant minister (Clive Russell) so doctrinaire that his followers consider the celebration of Christmas a popish blasphemy, young Oscar scandalizes his father by adopting the Anglican faith. As a young man, the physically awkward, socially unschooled Oscar discovers a gift for gambling that marks him further as an outcast and a sinner, even though he gives his winnings to the poor. Bloomer-clad Lucinda, meanwhile, is a feminist before her time. Intelligent, impetuous, and fiercely independent, she uses her substantial inheritance to buy a glass factory and throws herself into the minutiae of the business, assuaging her loneliness by playing cards and dice. Gambling brings Oscar and Lucinda together, but their relationship is cemented by a mad plan to build a glass church and deliver it to the god-forsaken Outback town of Bellingen.

Richly imagined and resolutely unpredictable, this dark and profoundly optimistic paean to passion—for glass, for horses, for the thrill of the moment after a coin is flipped but before it falls—is held together by Gillian Armstrong's solid direction and by strong, if occasionally strident, performances from Fiennes and Blanchett.

OSSESSIONE

1942 112m bw Drama ★★★½
ICI Roma (Italy)

Clara Calamai *(Giovanna)*, Massimo Girotti *(Gino)*, Juan De Landa *(The Husband)*, Elia Marcuzzo *(Lo Spagnuolo)*, Dhia Cristani *(Anita)*, Vittorio Duse *(The Lorry Driver)*, Michele Riccardini, Michele Sakara

p, Libero Solaroli; d, Luchino Visconti; w, Mario Alicata, Antonio Pietrangeli, Gianni Puccini, Giuseppe De Santis, Luchino Visconti (based on the novel *The Postman Always Rings Twice* by James M. Cain); ph, Aldo Tonti, Domenico Scala; ed, Mario Serandrei; m, Giuseppe Rosati; art d, Gino Rosati

The first directorial effort in the brilliant, though sporadic, career of Luchino Visconti was made in 1942 but not shown in the U.S. until 1959 because of copyright problems. Based

on the James M. Cain novel *The Postman Always Rings Twice,* the film is a sizzling love story set against a background of murder and adultery along the backroads of the Italian countryside. The nomadic Gino (Massimo Girotti), a man living under the illusion that attachments only act as a hindrance, happens upon the roadside inn run by Giovanna (Clara Calamai) and her older, grotesque-looking husband (Juan de Landa). One look at this couple tells their entire story: she is young, beautiful, and full of passion, married to a man unequal to her in all areas except one—money. Giovanna soon takes a romantic interest in the visitor, discovering the spark that never ignited with her husband. It's a potentially murderous situation.

Despite its exquisitely hardboiled source material and film noir plot, OSSESSIONE is often cited as the first harbinger of neorealism. The film was shot in the Italian countryside (as opposed to the studios—a technique favored by Jean Renoir, with whom Visconti apprenticed) and showed the Italian people living in their natural environs. Because the Fascist government of 1942 had complete control over film production in Italy, Visconti had to have his script okayed before shooting. The government saw nothing wrong with the script he presented, but was quite shocked with the final product, which displayed an Italy in contrast to the stylized depiction common to Italian films of the time. Fearful of political overtones, the government temporarily shelved the film, only to put it back into circulation after Mussolini saw and enjoyed it. As a portrayal of the conflict between moral conscience and uncontrollable passion, between the need to maintain a secure existence and the desire to remain free of any confining forces, OSSESSIONE is a powerful statement, and a remarkable first film from Visconti.

OTHELLO

1952 90m bw Drama ★★★½
Mercury (U.S./France/Italy)

Orson Welles *(Othello)*, Michael MacLiammoir *(Iago)*, Suzanne Cloutier *(Desdemona)*, Robert Coote *(Roderigo)*, Hilton Edwards *(Brabantio)*, Michael Laurence *(Cassio)*, Fay Compton *(Emilia)*, Nicholas Bruce *(Lodovico)*, Jean Davis *(Montano)*, Doris Dowling *(Bianca)*

p, Orson Welles; d, Orson Welles; w, Orson Welles (based on the play by William Shakespeare); ph, Anchisi Brizzi, G.R. Aldo, Georges Fanto, Oberdan Trojani, Alverto Fusi; ed, Jean Sacha, John Shepridge, Renzo Lucidi, William Morton; m, Angelo Francesco Lavagnino, Alberto Barberis; art d, Alexander Trauner; cos, Maria De Matteis

Orson Welles's version of the Shakespearean tragedy, with the director also turning in a magnificent performance as the title character. Though he had spent only three weeks shooting his MACBETH, Welles devoted four years to this picture, a production that proceeded by fits and starts as he struggled to scrape together cash from various sources. (As part of his fund-raising efforts, Welles did acting duties in Henry King's PRINCE OF FOXES, Henry Hathaway's THE BLACK ROSE, and Carol Reed's THE THIRD MAN.) Though the final result cannot disguise its on-again, off-again production history—sloppy sound synchronization, cutaways to hide absent actors, lines dubbed by performers other than those onscreen—it nonetheless stands as an important part of the Welles canon, and one of the finest screen adaptations of Shakespeare. The text of the original play has been slashed to its bare bones, with bravura cinematography and editing also helping make this a taut, visceral experience. Michael MacLiammoir, an old Abbey Theatre friend of Welles's, makes a truly devious and convincing Iago, and Suzanne Cloutier is a serenely beautiful Desdemona. OTHELLO co-won the Best Feature Film prize at Cannes in 1952, but enjoyed little commercial success in the U.S. at the time. A partially restored version was released to considerable critical acclaim in 1992.

OTHERS, THE *DVD*
(LOS OTROS)
2001 104m c Horror ★★½
Cruise-Wagner Productions/Sogecine/Las PG-13
Producciones del Escorpion/Miramax International/
Le Studio Canal Plus/Dimension Films (U.S./Spain)

Nicole Kidman (Grace), Fionnula Flanagan (Mrs. Bertha Mills), Christopher Eccleston (Charles), Alakina Mann (Anne), James Bentley (Nicholas), Eric Sykes (Mr. Edmund Tuttle), Elaine Cassidy (Lydia), Renee Asherson (Old Lady), Gordon Reid (Assistant), Keith Allen (Mr. Marlish)

p, Fernando Bovaira, Jose Luis Cuerda, Sunmin Park; d, Alejandro Amenabar; w, Alejandro Amenabar; ph, Javier Aguirresarobe; ed, Nacho Ruiz Capillas; m, Alejandro Amenabar; prod d, Benjamin Fernandez; fx, Felix Berges, Derek Langley, Daiquiri/Telson (digital); cos, Sonia Grande

A high-strung woman, an isolated estate, two precocious children.... You could be forgiven for thinking this derivative but carefully crafted chiller is mining the same psychological territory as Henry James's classic tale *The Turn of the Screw.* It's not, and while Spanish writer-director Alejandro Amenabar works up some spooky atmosphere, his script hinges on a surprisingly obvious twist.

Jersey, the Channel Islands, 1945: Grace (Nicole Kidman) is raising her young daughter, Anne (Alakina Mann), and son, Nicholas (James Bentley), in a gloomy mansion while awaiting the return of her soldier husband, Charles (Christopher Eccleston). The war is over but there's been no word of him, and all the servants have just up and left. Before Grace can even place a "help wanted" ad in the local paper, three new applicants appear out of the murky fog: middle-aged Mrs. Mills (Fionnula Flanagan), mute Lydia (Elaine Cassidy), and elderly Mr. Tuttle (Eric Sykes). Grace hires them but explains that certain rules must be strictly followed, because her children are allergic to sunlight: curtains must always be drawn and doors locked. The servants soon discover that the shadows hold secrets. Little Anne claims she sees mysterious strangers, and Grace hears mysterious thuds and thumps from supposedly empty rooms. But there's also something odd about the servants; could they be trying to drive Grace insane, or worse, might there be something supernatural about *them*?

Amenabar's attempt to tell a classic uncanny tale, in which goosebumps take precedence over special effects, is commendable. But the fact that the big surprise is so obvious makes the deliberate pacing seem painfully slow, and Kidman's prissy accent and tight-lipped performance are more than a little grating.

OUR LADY OF THE ASSASSINS *DVD*
(LA VIRGEN DE LOS SICARIOS)
2000 101m c Drama ★★★½
Le Studio Canal/Les Films du Losange/Vertigo R
Films/Tucan Producciones Cinematograficas Ltda
(Colombia/France/Spain)

German Jaramillo (Fernando), Anderson Ballesteros (Alexis), Juan David Restrepo (Wilmar), Manuel Busquets (Alfonso), Wilmar Agudelo (Child Sniffing Glue), Juan Carlos Alvarez (4x4 Thief), Jairo Alzate (Taxi Driver Santo Domingo), Zulma Arango (Waitress), Jose Luis Bedoya (Taxi Sabaneta 1), Cenobia Cano (Alexis's Mother)

p, Jaime Osorio Gomez, Margaret Menegoz, Barbet Schroeder; d, Barbet Schroeder; w, Fernando Vallejo (based on his novel La

Virgen de Los Sicarios); ph, Rodrigo Lalinde; ed, Elsa Vasquez; m, Jorge Arriagada; prod d, Jose Gabriel Sanchez, Monica Marulanda; fx, Miguel Angel Guzman, Libar Neira; cos, Maria Ines Abad, Mercedes Caicedo, Monica Marulanda

A postcard from hell. Director Barbet Schroeder steps away from the glossy, unsatisfying studio fare he's been turning out for the past few years for this breathless adaptation of Fernando Vallejo's ferociously sardonic novel.

After a 30-year absence, Fernando (German Jaramillo), Colombia's foremost grammarian and an inveterate lover of much younger men, returns to his hometown of Medellin to die. Colombia's second-largest city is now overrun by gangs of teenage hit men, the living remnants of the cocaine empire once lorded over by the late Pablo Escobar. With little left to do but squabble over territory, they ride around the city on motorbikes, shooting each other and innocent bystanders in an ever-escalating series of revenge killings. Ironically, it's one of these young hit men, Alexis (Anderson Ballesteros), who gives the grammarian a reason to live. Fernando meets Alexis at the home of a friend, and the pair is soon spending days strolling the streets of the city, dodging bullets, stepping over corpses, visiting churches. Buoyed by love but sobered by the inevitable fact that somewhere in Medellin there's a bullet with Alexis's name scrawled on it, the older man imparts his bitter wisdom to a youth who, despite his tender years, has seen more death than most men see in their entire lives.

Schroeder and screenwriter Vallejo have toned down the novel's surreal violence and rendered the action at once more realistic and more horrifying. Shot on high-definition video on the streets of Medellin—often under the threat of real-life violence from genuine hit men—Schroeder made the wise decision to use actual street toughs in his cast. Surely no actor could capture the mixture of youthful innocence and deadly experience that haunts the eyes of these young men.

OUR MAN FLINT *DVD*
1966 107m c Comedy/Spy ★★★
Fox (U.S.)

James Coburn (Derek Flint), Lee J. Cobb (Cramden), Gila Golan (Gila), Edward Mulhare (Malcolm Rodney), Benson Fong (Dr. Schneider), Shelby Grant (Leslie), Sigrid Valdis (Anna), Gianna Serra (Gina), Helen Funai (Sakito), Michael St. Clair (Gruber)

p, Saul David; d, Daniel Mann; w, Hal Fimberg, Ben Starr (based on a story by Fimberg); ph, Daniel Fapp (CinemaScope, DeLuxe Color); ed, William Reynolds; m, Jerry Goldsmith; art d, Jack Martin Smith, Ed Graves; fx, L.B. Abbott; cos, Ray Aghayan

James Coburn's first starring role casts him as Derek Flint, a suave 007-type secret agent with Zonal Organization World Intelligence, or Z.O.W.I.E. Flint, who's proficient in everything from martial arts to speaking dolphin and, of course, women, is called in to put a stop to GALAXY, a secret organization led by an evil tycoon (Edward Mulhare) seeking to dominate the world via weather control. Flint sets out with his cigarette lighter, which has some 83 uses, and locates the three scientists who have masterminded the plot. He goes head-to-head with a dangerous beauty (Gila Golan), sent to assassinate his boss (Lee J. Cobb), and he's later captured by the evil GALAXY, but fear not; Flint manages to escape and save the planet. The script is loaded with holes and the direction is tired, but the film is still one of the better Bond spoofs. Jerry Goldsmith's swinging score helps, and the decor—particularly Flint's remote control bachelor pad—served as a bottomless well of inspiration for the enormously popular AUSTIN POWERS series some 30 years later. Coburn returned for IN LIKE FLINT, the 1967 sequel.

OUR MAN IN HAVANA

1959 111m bw Comedy ★★★★
Kingsmead (U.K.)

Burl Ives (*Dr. Hasselbacher*), Alec Guinness (*Jim Wormold*), Burl Ives (*Dr. Hasselbacher*), Maureen O'Hara (*Beatrice Severn*), Ernie Kovacs (*Capt. Segura*), Noel Coward (*Hawthorne*), Ralph Richardson ("*C*"), Jo Morrow (*Milly Wormold*), Paul Rogers (*Hubert Carter*), Gregoire Aslan (*Cifuentes*)

p, Carol Reed; d, Carol Reed; w, Graham Greene (based on his novel); ph, Oswald Morris (CinemaScope); ed, Bert Bates; m, Hermanos Deniz; art d, John Box; cos, Phyllis Dalton

As hilarious as it is absurd, this droll comedy about spies in Cuba stars the prodigiously talented Guinness. The real world of espionage is ridiculous enough, but director Reed manages to make it seem even sillier by putting an innocuous vacuum cleaner salesman (Guinness) in the the middle of all the clandestine goings-on. Guinness, the owner of a small store in Havana, is approached by Coward, a master spy who enlists him as an agent. Realizing he will be making good money for every tidbit of information he passes along to headquarters in London, and wanting that money to be able to buy the good things in life for his daughter (Morrow), but knowing there is no real information to gather, Guinness begins to invent information. Kovacs, the reportedly brutal chief of police, who has cast a covetous eye on Morrow, gets reports that Guinness has been acting in a furtive manner. Kovacs spies on Guinness, while Guinness spies on Kovacs, and the whole affair begins to expand crazily. However, the intrigue ceases to be phony when Guinness is forced to dispatch a very real enemy. Nevertheless, Guinness eventually has to admit to the fabricated nature of the information he has been providing to British intelligence, and he is ordered back to London, where he meets an unexpected fate. Mixing subtle comedy with sinister consequences, OUR MAN IN HAVANA is probably Guinness' drollest film. Guinness is superb as the greedy but imaginative shop owner, but Kovacs, as the posturing police chief, and Coward, as the British master spy, steal the film, which was shot in Havana shortly after the Cuban Revolution.

OUR RELATIONS

1936 65m bw Comedy ★★★★
Stan Laurel/Hal Roach (U.S.)

Stan Laurel (*Himself/Alfie Laurel*), Oliver Hardy (*Himself/Bert Hardy*), Sidney Toler (*Captain of the S.S. Periwinkle*), Alan Hale (*Joe Groagan, the Waiter*), Daphne Pollard (*Mrs. Daphne Hardy*), Betty Healy (*Mrs. Betty Laurel*), Iris Adrian (*Alice, the Beer Garden Girl*), Lona Andre (*Lily, the Other Cafe Girl*), James Finlayson (*Finn, the Chief Engineer*), Arthur Housman (*Inebriated Stroller*)

p, Stan Laurel, L.A. French; d, Harry Lachman; w, Richard Connell, Felix Adler, Charles Rogers, Jack Jevne (based on the short story "The Money Box" by William Jacobs); ph, Rudolph Mate; ed, Bert Jordan; m, LeRoy Shield; art d, Arthur I. Royce, William Stevens; fx, Roy Seawright

Perhaps the best Laurel and Hardy feature, OUR RELATIONS marked Stan Laurel's first credit as a producer, and he does an excellent job in this elaborate picture that owes a great deal to Shakespeare's "Comedy Of Errors." Stan and Ollie, sailors on shore leave, have a valuable diamond ring to deliver. Knowing that in the past they've spent all their money while on liberty, they give their cash to Sidney Toler, their captain, telling him to hold it in safekeeping and not to return it until after their ship has sailed. The town they are visiting is the same place where their twin brothers now live in domestic harmony with their henpecking wives, Daphne Pollard and Betty Healy. Stan and Ollie meet two girls, Iris Adrian and Lona Andre, in a local waterfront dive, while nearby, their twins are quaffing beer with their mates

in another tavern. Need we say that the duos are soon mixed? The diamond ring turns up missing, and when Stan and Ollie can't locate the jewel, gangsters Ralf Harolde and Noel Madison trap the pair in cement blocks and leave them on a pier where they will soon fall into the water. Naturally, it all comes together in the end with the right husbands re-matched with the correct wives and the twins reunited after a long separation. Several funny scenes include Laurel and Hardy attempting to convince Toler to give them back their money; a set-piece in a hotel room where they have been placed without clothing; and their difficulty (as the married men) to make beer-hall owner Alan Hale, Sr., understand that they had not been there earlier with Adrian and Andre. Amidst all the fun, there is real danger to the boys when they come up against the villains. This was the first and only time they worked with director Harry Lachman, who was not known for his comedic skills. (His most famous feature was DANTE'S INFERNO, 1935; he also did a couple of CHARLIE CHAN films.) He seems to just turn on Rudolphe Mate's camera and let the boys have their way with the humor. A standout comedy role was played by Arthur Housman as a drunk, and Stanley Sandford, one of the wharf rats, was appearing in his final film of the 23 he made with Laurel and Hardy. In one of her first roles, Iris Adrian was developing the character she would play for the next several decades, the brash blonde with a heart of gold. Despite the excellence of this film, other Laurel and Hardy movies are better remembered.

OUR TOWN

1940 90m bw Drama ★★★★
Principal Artists (U.S.)

Frank Craven (*Mr. Morgan, the Narrator*), William Holden (*George Gibbs*), Martha Scott (*Emily Webb*), Fay Bainter (*Mrs. Gibbs*), Beulah Bondi (*Mrs. Webb*), Thomas Mitchell (*Dr. Gibbs*), Guy Kibbee (*Editor Webb*), Stuart Erwin (*Howie Newsome*), Philip Wood (*Simon Stinson*), Doro Merande (*Mrs. Soames*)

p, Sol Lesser; d, Sam Wood; w, Thornton Wilder, Frank Craven, Harry Chandlee (based on the play by Thornton Wilder); ph, Bert Glennon; ed, Sherman Todd; m, Aaron Copland; prod d, William Cameron Menzies, Harry Horner; art d, Lewis J. Rachmil

AAN Best Picture; AAN Best Actress: Martha Scott; *AAN Best Original Score:* Aaron Copland; *AAN Best Interior Decoration (B/W):* Lewis J. Rachmil; *AAN Best Sound Recording:* Thomas Moulton

Sam Wood directed this version of Thorton Wilder's Pulitzer Prize-winning play about the multiple relationships among the folks in a small New England town. The "our town" genre—studies of the relationships that mold a community—became a welcome staple of the movies. Wilder must be given credit for establishing such an important form.

Our Town is brought to the screen with wonderful characterizations by an inspired cast. Small-town America is typified by Craven, the down-home narrator who profiles the lives of citizens of Grover's Corners. Scott is the idealistic but hard-working daughter of the local newspaper editor, and Holden is the son of the local physician who falls in love with Scott, goes through a difficult courtship, and finally wins her hand in marriage. Life in this quaint small town is shown in three periods—1901, 1904, and 1913—with the attention basically focused upon two families, those of Holden and Scott. The result is a moving portrait of small-town America before WWII.

Remaining faithful to Wilder's script, director Wood skillfully conveys the laughter, love, and pain in the lives of Wilder's heartwarming characters. And the techniques Wood employs to tell their stories are marvelous to behold: a dazzling series of dissolves, evocative lighting, and montages that effectively capture the flavor of the periods depicted. Scott, appearing in her first film, is splendid, as is Holden. Mitchell as the physician, Kibbee as the editor, and their wives, played by Bainter and Bondi, all provide sturdy supporting performances. Wood's outstanding direction is enhanced by a stirring score by Copland and lovely sets by Menzies, who is a genius at capturing any locale.

OUR VINES HAVE TENDER GRAPES
1945 105m bw Drama ★★★★
MGM (U.S.)

Edward G. Robinson *(Martinius Jacobson)*, Margaret O'Brien *(Selma Jacobson)*, James Craig *(Nels Halverson)*, Agnes Moorehead *(Bruna Jacobson)*, Jackie "Butch" Jenkins *(Arnold Hanson)*, Morris Carnovsky *(Bjorn Bjornson)*, Frances Gifford *(Viola Johnson)*, Sara Haden *(Mrs. Bjornson)*, Louis Jean Heydt *(Mr. Faraassen)*, Francis Pierlot *(Minister)*

p, Robert Sisk; d, Roy Rowland; w, Dalton Trumbo (based on the novel *For Our Vines Have Tender Grapes* by George Victor Martin); ph, Robert Surtees; ed, Ralph E. Winters; m, Bronislau Kaper; art d, Cedric Gibbons, Edward Carfagno; fx, A. Arnold Gillespie, Danny Hall; cos, Irene, Kay Carter

Few films touch the heart so deeply as this one and fewer still present such moving performances.

Robinson is terrific as a Wisconsin farmer who takes very seriously the raising of his daughter, O'Brien. When attractive Gifford arrives in Benson Junction to teach school, a great deal of excitement ensues, particularly over the way in which handsome town newspaper editor Craig is drawn to her. Craig is called to serve in WWII and asks Gifford to wait for him, but she cannot make such a commitment. Robinson is disraught later when O'Brien and her cousin, Jenkins, disappear. The children are found alive but soaking wet in a bathtub that has taken them on a perilous journey through the swollen waters of a nearby stream. The event that brings the whole town together and convinces Gifford that there is a lot to be said for the "boring" small town is a tragedy: a neighbor's farm is struck by lightning and the resultant fire wipes him out. O'Brien is the first to offer help, in the form of her prize calf; her father and the rest of the townspeople follow in quick succession.

Supporting Robinson with marvelous performances are O'Brien, who furthered her juvenile career in films mightily with this entry, as did Jenkins, one of Louis B. Mayer's favorite child actors. Moorehead is excellent and sports a mild Norwegian accent in an underplayed part, and Morris, as the retarded neighbor who dies, displays fine talent. Released just after V-J Day, OUR VINES HAVE TENDER GRAPES was written with great care by the talented Trumbo, whom Robinson had earlier befriended (he was later criticized for this friendship by citizens siding with HUAC during the Sen. Joseph McCarthy era, when Trumbo was part of the "Hollywood Ten").

OUT OF AFRICA
1985 150m c Romance ★★½
Universal (U.S.) PG

Meryl Streep *(Karen Blixen-Finecke)*, Robert Redford *(Denys Finch Hatton)*, Klaus Maria Brandauer *(Baron Bror Blixen-Finecke)*, Michael Kitchen *(Berkeley)*, Malick Bowens *(Farah)*, Joseph Thiaka *(Kamante)*, Stephen Kinyanjui *(Kinanjui)*, Michael Gough *(Delamere)*, Suzanna Hamilton *(Felicity)*, Rachel Kempson *(Lady Belfield)*

p, Sydney Pollack; d, Sydney Pollack; w, Kurt Luedtke (based on *Out of Africa* and other writings by Isak Dinesen, *Isak Dinesen: The Life of a Storyteller* by Judith Thurman, and *Silence Will Speak* by Errol Trzebinski); ph, David Watkin (Technovision, Rank Color); ed, Fredric Steinkamp, William Steinkamp, Pembroke J. Herring, Sheldon Kahn; m, John Barry, Wolfgang Amadeus

Mozart; prod d, Stephen Grimes; art d, Herbert Westbrook, Colin Grimes, Clifford Robinson; fx, David Harris; cos, Milena Canonero

AA Best Picture; AAN Best Actress: Meryl Streep; *AAN Best Supporting Actor:* Klaus Maria Brandauer; *AA Best Director:* Sydney Pollack; *AA Best Adapted Screenplay:* Kurt Luedtke; *AA Best Cinematography:* David Watkin; *AAN Best Film Editing:* Fredric Steinkamp, William Stienkamp, Pembroke Herring, Sheldon Kahn; *AA Best Original Score:* John Barry; *AAN Best Art Direction-Set Decoration:* Stephen Grimes, Josie MacAvin; *AAN Best Costume Design:* Milena Canonero; *AA Best Sound:* Chris Jenkins, Gary Alexander, Larry Stensvold, Peter Handford

There was very little to begin with here—a delicate, lyrical, autobiographical tale written by an austere, refined woman who brought an opera glass instead of a microscope to her life. The author, Isak Dinesen, recounts the tale of lost loves and old imperial Africa. Karen (Meryl Streep) is the well-born woman who marries Baron Bror Blixen-Finecke (Klaus Maria Brandauer), a playboy who bestows a title upon her, promises her eternal bliss on an African plantation in 1914, and then leaves her alone to run things. Bror is nothing more than a drinker, spendthrift, and womanizer. Denys Finch Hatton (Robert Redford) is an enigmatic white hunter who falls in love with the plantation-bound Karen.

Streep, affecting the most inarticulate and cumbersome accent in any film within the last three decades, strives a little too mightily to bring reason and substance to a role that has neither. Streep's performances started becoming strangled by her highly deliberate technique as early as THE FRENCH LIEUTENANT'S WOMAN, and in this one she's so rarefied as to leave one completely cold. Redford, meanwhile, is at once too old, not in the least British (which wouldn't have been so bad if manic Meryl hadn't attempted to be *so* Danish), and obviously quite bored. To make up for the lack of real story here, director Sydney Pollack shoots endless travelogue footage in soft light and pleasing colors. The movie is not drama and far from a compelling romance. Needless to say, the prestige and technical polish on display here were enough to win this flick a passel of Oscars.

OUT OF SIGHT
1998 129m c Crime/Romance/Comedy ★★★½
Jersey Films/Universal (U.S.) R

George Clooney *(Jack Foley)*, Jennifer Lopez *(Karen Sisco)*, Ving Rhames *(Buddy Bragg)*, Don Cheadle *(Maurice (Snoopy) Miller)*, Dennis Farina *(Marshall Sisco)*, Albert Brooks *(Richard Ripley)*, Michael Keaton *(Ray Nicolette—Uncredited)*, Samuel L. Jackson *(Hejira—Uncredited)*, Jim Robinson *(Bank Employee)*, Elgin Marlow *(Bank Customer)*

p, Danny DeVito, Michael Shambert, Stacey Sher; d, Steven Soderbergh; w, Scott Frank (based on the novel by Elmore Leonard); ph, Elliot Davis; ed, Anne V. Coates; m, Cliff Martinez; prod d, Gary Frutkoff; art d, Phil Messina; fx, Carol Lynn Wenger, Cliff Wenger; cos, Betsy Heimann

AAN Best Adapted Screenplay: Scott Frank; *AAN Best Film Editing:* Anne V. Coates

Faintly melancholy and alluringly fatalistic, this dark, mercurial romance passing as a crime thriller is sly, entertaining, and very sexy.

Jack Foley (George Clooney) is a lifelong crook who specializes in talking bank clerks out of large sums of money. Karen Sisco (Jennifer Lopez) is a cocksure, Florida-based federal marshal who adores her dad (Dennis Farina), guns, and unsuitable men; her current squeeze is grandstanding FBI agent Ray Nicolette (Michael Keaton, doing an uncredited reprise of his JACKIE BROWN role), who's both married and a dope. Jack and Karen meet when she accidentally interrupts his jailbreak, and she winds up sharing a couple of hours with Jack in the trunk of his partner Buddy's (Ving Rhames) getaway car. During the cramped, sexually fraught trip in the trunk, Jack and Karen reluctantly fall for one another. (Perhaps it really is all about propinquity, as poor, neglected Zelda Gillis used to tell Dobie Gillis.) Even after she escapes, Karen fantasizes dreamily about Jack; he's doing the same, while he and Buddy plan to rob a smug Detroit financial whiz (Albert Brooks) who keeps millions in uncut diamonds in his house.

Elmore Leonard's huge collection of sharply drawn unsavory characters is perfectly cast, from the leads to a bevy of supporting (but emphatically not lesser) lights, including Steve Zahn as a chatty jail house hanger-on; Don Cheadle as psycho boxing buff Snoopy Miller; Nancy Allen as a beleaguered victim of his gang; Luis Guzman as a prison hardcase; Catherine Keener as Foley's flaky ex-wife; and an uncredited Samuel L. Jackson as a prison-bound con whose interests dovetail serendipitously with Foley's. Steven Soderbergh's stylish direction conjures an authentic and understated '70s vibe, striking an apparently effortless balance between grit and glamour.

OUT OF THE PAST

1947 97m   bw   Mystery   **DVD**
RKO   (U.S.)   ★★★★★

Robert Mitchum (*Jeff Bailey*), Jane Greer (*Kathie Moffett*), Kirk Douglas (*Whit Sterling*), Rhonda Fleming (*Meta Carson*), Richard Webb (*Jim*), Steve Brodie (*Fisher*), Virginia Huston (*Ann*), Paul Valentine (*Joe*), Dickie Moore (*The Kid*), Ken Niles (*Eels*)

p, Warren Duff; d, Jacques Tourneur; w, James M. Cain (uncredited), Frank Fenton (uncredited), Geoffrey Homes (based on the novel Build My Gallows High by Geoffrey Homes); ph, Nicholas Musuraca; ed, Samuel E. Beetley; m, Roy Webb; art d, Albert S. D'Agostino, Jack Okey; fx, Russell A. Cully; cos, Edward Stevenson

This quintessential film noir catapulted contract player Robert Mitchum into superstardom and set the standard for the genre for years to come. Boasting a typically confusing and convoluted plot line, the film follows laconic private eye Jeff Bailey (Mitchum) as he is lured into a fateful quagmire when hired by notorious gangster Whit Sterling (Douglas) to find his mistress, Kathie Moffett (Greer), who shot him and ran off with $40,000. Jeff traces Kathie to Mexico, but when he meets the seductive *femme fatale* he falls in love with her and willingly becomes involved in an increasingly complicated web of double-crosses, blackmail, and murder. Directed with supreme skill by Jacques Tourneur (CAT PEOPLE, I WALKED WITH A ZOMBIE) and brilliantly photographed by Nicholas Musuraca, this is an unrelentingly gloomy film set in a dark world of greed and deceit where love is just another device to ensnare the gullible. It was here that Mitchum created what became his iconographic screen persona: the droopy-eyed cynic who accepts fate with a studied nonchalance. Jane Greer is equally superb, perfecting the role of the *femme fatale* with a combination of erotic fire and cool detachment. Her first appearance in the film—cutting a sultry silhouette as she enters a dark cantina from the bright white outdoors—is one of the great entrances in film history. A seminal genre film, certainly among the greatest whose influence is still felt today, OUT OF THE PAST was remade as the distinctly inferior AGAINST ALL ODDS.

OUT OF TIME

2003 114m   c   Crime/Thriller   ★★
Monarch Pictures/Original Film/MGM   (U.S.)   PG-13

Denzel Washington (*Matt Lee Whitlock*), Eva Mendes (*Alex Diaz Whitlock*), Sanaa Lathan (*Ann Merai Harrison*), Dean Cain (*Chris Harrison*), John Billingsley (*Chae*), Robert Baker (*Tony Dalton*), Alex Carter (*Cabot*), Antoni Corone (*Deputy Baste*), Terry Loughlin (*Agent Stark*), Nora Dunn (*Dr. Donovan*) James Murtaugh (*Dr. Frieland*)

p, Jesse B'Franklin, Neal H. Mortiz; d, Carl Franklin; w, David Collard; ph, Theo van de Sande; ed, Carole Kravetz Aykanian; m, Graeme Revell; prod d, Paul Peters; art d, Gary Kosko; fx, Kevin Harris; cos, Sharen Davis

Slick but ludicrously contrived, Carl Franklin's noir-inflected thriller is an exercise in putting a poor jerk in a bad situation and tightening the screws until he sweats blood.

Police Chief Matt Lee Whitlock (Denzel Washington) is a big fish in the very small pond of Banyan Key, FL, where crime is mostly a matter of rowdy drunks and petty robbery. That said, Matt recently participated in a substantial drug bust, which is why there's nearly $500,000 in shrink-wrapped cash languishing in his evidence lock up. Unhappily separated from his wife, Alex (Eva Mendes), a detective with the Miami Police Department, Matt is sneaking around with his high-school sweetheart, Ann (Sanaa Lathan), who's miserably married to an abusive ex-quarterback (Dean Cain). Ann also has terminal cancer, so Matt violates every law and principle governing his profession and gives her the confiscated drug money for an experimental treatment in Switzerland. When arson and a double murder intrude upon this volatile situation, Matt's complacent cheating blows up in his face. Alex is sent to head up the investigating task force and if Matt's sneaking around comes to light, he'll be the obvious suspect.

Matt's desperate scramble to hobble the official investigation while conducting his own—the same suspense structure that drives Kenneth Fearing's celebrated 1946 pulp novel, *The Big Clock*—propels the plot's many twists and turns. David Collard's preposterous script relies heavily on fortuitous coincidence and thoroughly stupid behavior. That this atmospheric time-waster works at all is almost entirely due to Washington's performance, which in turn owes a great deal to Franklin's light touch with actors. Under Franklin's assured direction, Washington shakes off the dreary gravity he so often affects, letting his sly natural charisma shine through.

OUT-OF-TOWNERS, THE

1970 98m   c   Comedy   **DVD**
Jalem   (U.S.)   ★★★½
                                                         G

Jack Lemmon (*George Kellerman*), Sandy Dennis (*Gwen Kellerman*), Milt Kamen (*Counterman*), Sandy Baron (*TV Man*), Anne Meara (*Woman in Police Station*), Robert Nichols (*Man in Airplane*), Ann Prentiss (*Airline Stewardess*), Ron Carey (*Boston Cab Driver*), Philip Bruns (*Officer Meyers*), Graham Jarvis (*Murray*)

p, Paul Nathan; d, Arthur Hiller; w, Neil Simon; ph, Andrew Laszlo (Movielab Color); ed, Fred Chulack; m, Quincy Jones; art d, Charles Bailey, Walter Tyler; cos, Forrest T. Butler, Grace Harris

If playwriting success were gauged solely on money in the bank, Neil Simon would likely be tops in his field; having brought laughter to so many, he probably deserves that status. In his script for THE OUT-OF-TOWNERS, he mines gold from a field that had been virtually tapped out. Lemmon is an Ohio businessman on his way to New York with his wife, Dennis, to talk about taking a job in the Big Apple. Anticipating dining in one Manhattan's fine restaurants, they refuse an in-flight meal. Their intention is to sup, check into a good hotel, have the appointment the following morning, and return to Dayton. But things don't work out the way they were planned. The plane cannot land in New York because of fog, so it's shunted to Boston. In Beantown, Lemmon and Dennis learn that their luggage is missing;

then they have to take a crowded, foodless train to New York. Arriving in a driving rainstorm, they learn that the city has been crippled by a number of strikes, including walkouts by the transit workers and the garbage collectors. They walk a distance to the Waldorf only to learn that the hotel has cancelled their reservation. Jarvis, an apparently sweet man, says he can find them a room; instead, he steals all of their money. With no cash, they decide to try the police, who tell them they can be put up at a local armory for the night. On their way there, the police car is hijacked by crooks, and Lemmon and Dennis are tossed out in Central Park, where they spend the night. The next morning, Lemmon is taken to be a rapist by two joggers, who beat him up. Then he is chased by a police officer on a horse who thinks Lemmon is a child molester. In an attempt to get to his interview, Lemmon hitches a ride in the car of a Cuban official, Carlos Montalban, but the auto is sidetracked by angry anti-Castro demonstrators. When he finally gets to his appointment, Lemmon looks seedy and totally unpresentable, but the company offers him the job anyway. Lemmon decides that New York is no place for him and Dennis, and he turns the job down, preferring to stay in quiet, tranquil Ohio.

While it's implausible that all of these mishaps would befall a couple in 24 hours, none of these occurrences is beyond the realm of belief, and Simon has cleverly strung them together in one of his best screenplays. Director Hiller happily keeps Dennis' quirky mannerisms to a minimum and lets Lemmon do his thing (and a wonderful thing it is), with all secondary roles well cast. The picture did well at the box office and enhanced Lemmon's reputation as one of Hollywood's finest comedic actors. Many of Simon's plays have not transferred well to the screen (with the notable exceptions of THE ODD COUPLE and BAREFOOT IN THE PARK), perhaps because he writes differently for the stage. But when Simon has written directly for the screen, he has done much better, as he did with this film, THE GOODBYE GIRL, and THE HEARTBREAK KID.

OUTLAW, THE
1943 126m bw Western
Hughes   (U.S.)

DVD
★

Jack Beutel (*Billy the Kid*), Jane Russell (*Rio*), Thomas Mitchell (*Pat Garrett*), Walter Huston (*Doc Holliday*), Mimi Aguglia (*Guadalupe*), Joe Sawyer (*Charley*), Gene Rizzi (*Stranger*), Frank Darien (*Shorty*), Pat West (*Bartender*), Carl Stockdale (*Minister*)

p, Howard Hughes; d, Howard Hughes, Howard Hawks; w, Jules Furthman; ph, Gregg Toland; ed, Otho Lovering, Wallace Grissell; art d, Perry Ferguson; fx, Roy Davidson

Shabby, contrived, cornball western, but a marvelous curiosity. The movie as such is forgettable, but Howard Hughes's cynically brilliant commodification of Jane Russell's bosom was a triumph of Hollywood marketing and a harbinger of things to come. THE OUTLAW is a very loose retelling of the legend of Billy The Kid (Jack Beutel), with Walter Huston as Doc Holliday and Thomas Mitchell as lawman Pat Garrett. When the devastating Rio (Russell) enters the picture, old friends Billy and Doc are soon at each other's throats.

Hughes hired Howard Hawks to direct, nagged him to distraction, then took over the reins himself, presiding over the set with a demented attention to detail. Despite the best efforts of cameraman Gregg Toland, the resulting film is static and amateurish; the publicity campaign surrounding its release, however, was a masterpiece. Armed with stills of 19-year-old Russell revealing a remarkable decolletage (while stooping to pick up a pair of milk pails!), Hughes spent tens of thousands of dollars purposely to agitate the censor and arouse public indignation. He released the film in San Francisco in 1943 after United Artists refused to distribute it; it was quickly closed down by civic groups (which is just what he wanted).

Meanwhile, legendary publicist Russell Birdwell leased thousands of billboards from coast to coast for three years, plastering a suggestive photo of the scantily clad Russell reclining on a bed of hay, gun in hand. By 1946, when Hughes finally released the film, audiences flocked to theaters, hoping to answer the question splashed across every newspaper ad: "What are the two reasons for Jane Russell's rise to stardom?"

OUTLAW JOSEY WALES, THE
1976 135m c   Western
Malpaso   (U.S.)

DVD
★★★★
R

Clint Eastwood (*Josey Wales*), Chief Dan George (*Lone Watie*), Sondra Locke (*Laura Lee*), Bill McKinney (*Terrill*), John Vernon (*Fletcher*), Paula Trueman (*Grandma Sarah*), Sam Bottoms (*Jamie*), Geraldine Kearns (*Little Moonlight*), Woodrow Parfrey (*Carpetbagger*), Joyce Jameson (*Rose*)

p, Robert Daley; d, Clint Eastwood; w, Philip Kaufman, Sonia Chernus (based on the book *Gone to Texas* by Forrest Carter); ph, Bruce Surtees (Panavision, DeLuxe Color); ed, Ferris Webster; m, Jerry Fielding; prod d, Tambi Larsen

AAN Best Original Score: Jerry Fielding

An underrated early directorial effort by Clint Eastwood. The film opens as Union guerillas known as "redlegs" destroy the home and family of Missouri farmer Josey Wales (Eastwood). He joins up with Confederate soldiers to get his revenge, and, after years of battle, refuses to surrender to Terrill (McKinney), the man responsible for his family's death. He even rescues Jamie (Bottoms), a wounded young rebel, from the Union soldiers, who send Terrill and the reluctant Fletcher (Vernon) after them. Josey and Jamie next pick up two Cherokees (George and Kearns), a stray dog, and, after rescuing them from Comanches, an elderly woman (Trueman) and her granddaughter (Locke). The old woman is so grateful that she offers to let Josey and his ragtag bunch live at the farmhouse her son built. Josey manages to make peace with the Comanches, but the Union soldiers are another story.

Whereas Eastwood's homage to director Sergio Leone, HIGH PLAINS DRIFTER, was bleak from start to finish, THE OUTLAW JOSEY WALES begins with life (Eastwood and his family) and ends with life (the communal family). In between is a long period of healing and rebuilding wherein Eastwood re-examines the "man with no name" screen persona he developed with Leone. THE OUTLAW JOSEY WALES is a cautiously optimistic epic, deeply rooted in the history of America. Wales, despite his efforts, is not a loner. Instead of surrendering and assimilating into the "rebuilt" post-war society full of carpetbaggers, Klansmen, and dishonor, Wales and his group create their own society, steeped in honor, mutual respect and love. Bolstered by Surtees's magnificent cinematography, Fielding's fine score and an excellent supporting cast highlighted by the scene-stealing dry wit of Chief Dan George, JOSEY WALES affirms life and community with bracing conviction.

OUTSIDERS, THE
1983 91m c   Drama
Zoetrope   (U.S.)

DVD
★★★
PG

Matt Dillon (*Dallas Winston*), Ralph Macchio (*Johnny Cade*), C. Thomas Howell (*Ponyboy Curtis*), Patrick Swayze (*Darrel Curtis*), Rob Lowe (*Sodapop Curtis*), Emilio Estevez (*Two-Bit Matthews*), Tom Cruise (*Steve Randle*), Glenn Withrow (*Tim Shephard*), Diane Lane (*Cherry Valance*), Leif Garrett (*Bob Sheldon*)

p, Fred Roos, Gray Frederickson; d, Francis Ford Coppola; w, Kathleen Rowell (based on the novel by S.E. Hinton); ph, Stephen H. Burum (Panavision, Technicolor); ed, Anne Goursaud; m, Carmine Coppola; prod d, Dean Tavoularis; cos, Marge Bowers

In the early 1980s, after his "Godfather" films (1972, 1974) and APOCALYPSE NOW (1979), works of epic scale, Francis Ford Coppola began choosing small projects and blowing them up to preposterous proportions. Such is the case with THE OUTSIDERS, an awkward, splashy melo based on a popular teenage novel by S.E. Hinton (who makes a cameo appearance here as a nurse). Set in Oklahoma of the 1950s, the story hinges on a conflict between the "greasers"—leather-clad poor kids with Elvis-style pompadours—and their affluent high school classmates, the "Socs." Dallas Winston (Matt Dillon) leads his rebellious buddies on a succession of typical teenage adventures, but when two fellow gang members (Ralph Macchio and C. Thomas Howell) have a run-in with their rivals, events take a violent turn. Charismatic Dillon, a believable J.D., gets solid support from a cast that went on to populate some of the better youth pictures in years to come. The fault lies in Coppola's unduly reverent approach to a sudsy story. Sometimes laughably, the movie attempts to evoke REBEL WITHOUT A CAUSE, but it lacks the emotional conviction and psychological insight of Nicholas Ray's classic work. Nevertheless, Coppola's grandiose vision pays off in some stunning camerawork, and a barely repressed homoeroticism sometimes strikes sparks.

OVER THE EDGE

1979 95m c Drama   ★★★½
Orion (U.S.)   PG

Michael Kramer (Carl), Pamela Ludwig (Cory), Matt Dillon (Richie), Vincent Spano (Mark), Tom Fergus (Claude), Harry Northrup (Doberman), Andy Romano (Fred Willat), Ellen Geer (Sandra Willat), Richard Jamison (Cole), Julia Pomeroy (Julia)

p, George Litto; d, Jonathan Kaplan; w, Charlie Haas, Tim Hunter; ph, Andrew Davis; ed, Robert Bargere; m, Sol Kaplan; prod d, James William Newport; fx, Richard E. Johnson

IF… comes to suburbia. In a Californian prefab community, teenagers are bored silly; the developers, in their haste to make a buck, have failed to make any provision for the needs of young people. They turn for entertainment to the Big Three: sex, drugs, and rock 'n' roll. Carl (Michael Kramer) is harassed by the local cop, who likes to shake down kids for drugs. Receiving no support from his boosterish parents, he begins to hang out with Richie (Matt Dillon, in his film debut), a local hood who carries a pistol. Deadly violence, and an invigorating all-out assault on the high school building, ensue. With OVER THE EDGE, director Jonathan Kaplan (THE ACCUSED, HEART LIKE A WHEEL) graduated from exploitation films to shoot a memorably offbeat teen rebellion picture. Perceptive, kinetic, and believable, with a vigorous rock score featuring The Ramones and Cheap Trick.

OX-BOW INCIDENT, THE   DVD
1943 75m bw Western   ★★★★★
Fox (U.S.)

Henry Fonda (Gil Carter), Dana Andrews (Donald Martin), Mary Beth Hughes (Rose Mapen), Anthony Quinn (Juan Martines), William Eythe (Gerald Tetley), Harry Morgan, billed as Henry Morgan (Art Croft), Jane Darwell (Ma Grier), Matt Briggs (Judge Daniel Tyler), Harry Davenport (Arthur Davies), Frank Conroy (Maj. Tetley)

p, Lamar Trotti; d, William A. Wellman; w, Lamar Trotti (based on the novel by Walter Van Tilburg Clark); ph, Arthur Miller; ed, Allen McNeil; m, Cyril J. Mockridge; art d, Richard Day, James Basevi; cos, Earl Luick

AAN Best Picture

The finest indictment of lynching ever made, and we're not forgetting LeRoy's THEY WON'T FORGET or Lang's FURY either. THE OX-BOW INCIDENT is a powerful portrait of mob violence that rises to the level of tragedy.

Fonda and Morgan play two travelers who ride into Bridger's Wells, Nevada, a dying town, and head for the local saloon after finishing a cattle drive. Soon thereafter someone races in to announce that a popular local rancher has been shot by rustlers. Although a storekeeper (Davenport) cautions against rash action in the absence of the local sheriff, many locals form a posse anyway. Under the leadership of a pompous ex-Confederate officer (Conroy) who suddenly appears in his old Civil War uniform, the posse rides off. The strangers join the posse largely to keep the townspeople from unfairly suspecting them.

The posse eventually finds three exhausted homesteaders (Andrews, Quinn and Francis Ford) and, although the evidence against them is largely circumstantial, they are convicted of the crime on the spot. The three are given no real trial, just enough time to write farewell letters to loved ones and to "make their peace with God." The men, are of course, innocent, and the memorable finale has Fonda reading aloud the letter Andrews wrote to his family.

Fonda gives a compassionate performance; good work is also done by Darwell, Davenport, Hurst, and Conroy. Quinn only has a small role as one of the victims, but he is terrific as the indignant lynch candidate who is about to be hanged, not for past crimes, but for something he did not do. Wellman's direction of this superb cast is nothing less than awesome; he coaxes subtle performances from some of his players, properly bombastic renderings from others. In keeping with its somber subject matter, the whole film has a gritty, worn-out look, right down to the threadbare costumes on the actors. Much of the credit for the film's tone is due to Miller's outstanding photography, supported by a downbeat score from Mockridge. Although scenes at the beginning and the end of the film offer realistic-looking western exteriors, Wellman insisted that the bulk of the film be shot on a set with painted backdrops, mostly since the bulk of the story occurs at night. On the set he could better control the nuances of lighting he wanted. Some critics complained about the "claustrophobic" look and feel of the picture because of its set-bound image, but it is exactly that atmosphere that helps to create the mood of pervasive doom and maniacal intent of the two dozen "average citizens" to commit a capital crime.

P

PACIFIER, THE   DVD
2005 95m c Comedy   ★★
Walt Disney Pictures/Spyglass Entertainment/   PG
Birnbaum/Barber Productions (U.S./Canada)

Vin Diesel (Shane Wolfe), Lauren Graham (Principal Claire Fletcher), Faith Ford (Julie Plummer), Brittany Snow (Zoe), Max Thieriot (Seth), Chris Potter (Capt. Bill Fawcett), Carol Kane (Helga), Brad Garrett (Vice-Principal Murney), Morgan York (Lulu), Keegan Hoover (Peter)

p, Gary Barber, Roger Birnbaum, Jonathan Glickman; d, Adam Shankman; w, Robert Ben Garant, Thomas Lennon; ph, Peter James; ed, Christopher Greenbury; m, John Debney; prod d,

Linda DeScenna; art d, Arv Grewal; fx, Colin Chilvers, Tony Kenny, Paula Nederman; cos, Kirston Mann

The easily entertained may be mollified by this unimaginative variation on KINDERGARTEN COP, but anyone expecting more than formulaic pabulum will feel a temper tantrum coming on.

Assigned to coordinate a mid-ocean rescue operation, no-nonsense Navy S.E.A.L. Shane Wolfe (Vin Diesel) takes a bullet for government security expert Howard Plummer (Tate Donovan), but fails to save Plummer's life. Two months later, Wolfe is back on his feet and assigned to protect the Plummer kids while their grieving mom, Julie (Faith Ford), retrieves the contents of her late husband's Swiss safe-deposit box, which his commanding officer (Chris Potter) hopes will include the secrets of his clandestine satellite program, GHOST. The house is sheer chaos, and the kids (Brittany Snow, Max Thieriot, Morgan York, Keegan and Logan Hoover, Bo and Luke Vink) are classic comedy types. The Plummers already have a nanny, the high-strung Helga (Carol Kane), so Shane assumes he's on straightforward security detail. He tries to rein in the out-of-control youngsters, but his cold, efficient approach only makes them hate him. When Helga abandons her post and Julie's overseas trip is extended, Shane is left to shape up and protect the Plummer crew with a little guidance from conveniently attractive Principal Claire Fletcher (Lauren Graham).

Diesel is fine, if a bit bland, as Shane, upon whom every movie cliché of child-oriented torture for childless adults is visited: He changes diapers, does silly dances, becomes the repeat victim of the teenagers' pranks, and is even forced to lead a Brownie-like troop. Most of the occasional chuckles are provided by the spunky York, who really gives Diesel a run for his money.

PADRE PADRONE   DVD
1977 114m c   Drama   ★★★½
Radio Italiano   (Italy)

Omero Antonutti *(Gavino's Father)*, Saverio Marconi *(Gavino)*, Marcella Michelangeli *(Gavino's Mother)*, Fabrizio Forte *(Gavino as a Child)*, Marino Cenna *(Servant/Shepherd)*, Stanko Molnar *(Sebastiano)*, Nanni Moretti *(Cesare)*

p, Giuliani G. De Negri; d, Paolo Taviani, Vittorio Taviani; w, Vittorio Taviani, Paolo Taviani (based on a book by Gavino Ledda); ph, Mario Masini (Eastmancolor); ed, Roberto Perpignani; m, Egisto Macchi; art d, Gianni Sbarra

This is the simple story of a boy's growth into manhood under the despotism of his father. At age six, Gavino (played as a child by Fabrizio Forte) is pulled out of school and taken by his father (Omero Antonutti) into the mountains to become a shepherd. His father tries to control his son's life in every respect, with a comportment bordering on the sadistic. As he grows to manhood, Gavino (played as a young man by Saverio Marconi) begins to discover things for himself and rebel against his father's authority, eventually escaping from the patriarch's rule but encountering his changed father one last time in the film's denouement. Originally filmed by the Taviani brothers for Italian television, PADRE PADRONE is a fine example of a strong ensemble telling a story naturally, without intrusion by the directors. Using both professional actors and untrained locals from the Sardinian countryside, this story of the virtual imprisonment of young Sardinians by the sheep and pastures of their land unfolds simply and yet with great power. The winner of the grand prize at the Cannes Film Festival of 1977, the tale is based in truth: the real-life Gavino underwent similar experiences before escaping at age 20, going on to become a linguistics professor, and writing a book about his experiences.

PAISAN   DVD
(PAISA)
1946 120m bw War   ★★★★★
Organizational Films/Foreign Film   (Italy)

Carmela Sazio *(Carmela)*, Robert Van Loon *(Joe)*, Alfonsino Pasca *(Boy)*, Maria Michi *(Francesca)*, Renzo Avanzo *(Massimo)*, Harriet White *(Harriet)*, Dotts Johnson *(MP)*, William Tubbs *(Capt. Bill Martin)*, Dale Edmonds *(Dale)*, Carlo Piscane *(Peasant in Sicily Story)*

p, Roberto Rossellini, Rod E. Geiger, Mario Conti; d, Roberto Rossellini; w, Sergio Amidei, Federico Fellini, Roberto Rossellini, Annalena Limentani (based on stories by Victor Haines, Marcello Pagliero, Amidei, Fellini, Rossellini, Klaus Mann, Vasco Pratolini); ph, Otello Martelli; ed, Eraldo Da Roma; m, Renzo Rossellini

AAN Best Story and Screenplay: Alfred Hayes, Federico Fellini, Sergio Amidei, Marcello Pagliero, Roberto Rossellini

PAISAN, perhaps Rossellini's greatest achievement, is one of those rare segmented films that never loses steam as it moves through six chronologically ordered sequences beginning with the Allied invasion of Sicily in 1943 and concluding with liberation in 1945. In addition to moving across time, the film transports the viewer northward throughout Italy, each episode observing a slice of regional life. In the first, a New Jersey soldier (Van Loon) gets the job of guarding a young Sicilian woman (Sazio) who refuses to say anything or betray any emotion. The story details his attempts to win her over with no knowledge of Italian. In Naples, meanwhile, a black MP (Johnson) falls into a drunken sleep and has his shoes stolen by a street urchin. He finds the boy living in a cavern with a horde of homeless Neapolitans and decides that others need his shoes more than he. In the Roman tale, an American soldier (Gar Moore) meets Francesca (Michi), a streetwalker. He drunkenly reminisces about a woman he met as his tank rolled into the city. Francesca recognizes him—she was that woman, but he is too drunk to know it. On to Florence, where an American nurse (White) and an Italian partisan (Gigi Gori) scramble through German lines in a suspenseful episode which shows that John Sturges has nothing on Rossellini. In the fifth episode, three army chaplains (Catholic, Protestant, and Jewish) have an amusing yet telling ecumenical encounter with Franciscan monks at a rural monastery. And the final episode brings action: a shootout with the Germans against a group of OSS and British. The shot with the baby is stunning.

A film unlike any other the world had seen, PAISAN is OPEN CITY without the melodrama. Rossellini doesn't have De Sica's ability to coax brilliant dramatic performances out of nonprofessionals, yet there's an amazing honesty about the actors' sometimes awkward presence in this film. Despite the film's slice-of-life approach, it is anything but a flat, uninvolving newsreel. Rossellini in fact uses newsreel techniques precisely to point out the propaganda inherent in their purportedly "objective" style. PAISAN is instead a wartime portrait full of humor, pathos, romance, tension, and warmth. Handled in a seemingly direct manner, free of ornamental flourishes, PAISAN highlights the power of the neorealist style better than almost any other film.

PAJAMA GAME, THE   DVD
1957 101m c   Musical   ★★★★
Warner Bros. (U.S.)

Doris Day *(Kate "Babe" Williams)*, John Raitt *(Sid Sorokin)*, Carol Haney *(Gladys Hotchkiss)*, Eddie Foy Jr. *(Vernon Hines)*, Reta Shaw *(Mabel)*, Barbara Nichols *(Poopsie)*, Thelma Pelish *(Mae)*, Jack Straw *(Prez)*, Ralph Dunn *(Hasler)*, Owen Martin *(Max)*

p, George Abbott, Stanley Donen; d, George Abbott, Stanley Donen; w, George Abbott, Richard Bissell (based on the Broadway musical by Bissell, Abbott and the novel *Seven and a*

Half Cents by Bissell); ph, Harry Stradling (Warner Color); ed, William Ziegler; art d, Malcolm Bert; chor, Bob Fosse; cos, William, Jean Eckart

A terrific movie comes out of this simple idea: Katie "Babe" Williams (Doris Day) works in a pajama factory. She and her coworkers want a 7.5-cent raise, but management refuses, so she leads a grievance committee and takes their complaints to shop superintendent Sid Sorokin (John Raitt), spoiling the whole movement when she falls in love. Day is an utter delight in the role, funny and intelligent even in pajamas, and the choreography by Bob Fosse is energetic. The dancing isn't just left to the actors, however; the camera moves are carefully planned to give the hoofing the best look possible, and the inventive pans and tracking shots seem wonderfully natural and add to the fun. The camera even serves as an additional dance partner, doing a unique, comic tango with Carol Haney. This is a movie that knows how to move! Codirectors George Abbott and Stanley Donen lift the film from its Broadway roots to produce a cinematic musical that everyone will enjoy, with a smash-hit score. Excellent second banana work from Haney, Eddie Foy, Jr., Barbara Nichols, and Thelma Pelish.

PAKEEZAH

1971 175m c Drama/Musical ★★★★½
Mahal Pictures (India)

Meena Kumari *(Sahebjan/Nargis)*, Ashok Kumar *(Shahabuddin)*, Raj Kumar *(Salim)*, Veena *(Nawabjan)*, Pratima Devi, Altaf, Parveen Paul, Lotan, Chandabai, Meenakshi

p, Kamal Amrohi; d, Kamal Amrohi; w, Kamal Amrohi; ph, Joseph Wirsching; m, Naushad, Ghulam Mohammed; prod d, Guari Shankar; cos, Meena Kumari

A passionate, opulent Indian melodama, far removed from the rarefied aesthetics of Satyajit Ray. Arguably the greatest achievement of Hindi popular cinema, Kamal Amrohi's tribute to his ill-starred wife, Meena Kumari (who died of drink shortly after the film's release), rivals Sirk and Minnelli in its quasi-feminist subversion of melodramatic norms. Kumari plays the title character, a Muslim courtesan who longs for escape from a Lucknow brothel; Raj Kumar is the wealthy young man who loves her, to the horror of his parents. In keeping with the conventions of Indian commercial films, the narrative proceeds at a leisurely pace and pauses frequently for song and dance sequences (which are uniformly enchanting); it builds powerfully, however, and climaxes in a moment of unforgettable hysteria as a barefoot Kumari dances on broken glass at Kumar's wedding to another woman.

Due to financial and marital problems, as well as Kumari's declining health, PAKEEZAH was filmed intermittently over nearly a decade; fortunately, it was shot roughly in sequence, and the marked deterioration of Kumari's beauty over time only reinforces the tragic quality of her portrayal. The soundtrack songs, performed by Mohammed Rafi and Lata Mangeshkar (who holds a place in the *Guinness Book of World Records* for having recorded more songs than anyone else in history), are considered classics in India and sound lovely even to untrained Western ears. While PAKEEZAH was enthusiastically received by British critics and audiences after its London premiere, it has been neglected in recent years; filmmaker/critic Peter Wollen, however, named it as one of the ten best movies ever made in the 1992 "Sight and Sound" poll.

PAL JOEY

1957 111m c Musical/Comedy 📀
Essex/George Sidney (U.S.) ★★★★

Rita Hayworth *(Vera Simpson)*, Frank Sinatra *(Joey Evans)*, Kim Novak *(Linda English)*, Barbara Nichols *(Gladys)*, Bobby

Sherwood *(Ned Galvin)*, Hank Henry *(Mike Miggins)*, Elizabeth Patterson *(Mrs. Casey)*, Robin Morse *(Bartender)*, Frank Wilcox *(Col. Langley)*, Pierre Watkin *(Mr. Forsythe)*

p, Fred Kohlmar; d, George Sidney; w, Dorothy Kingsley (based on the *New Yorker* stories by John O'Hara, the musical play by O'Hara, Richard Rodgers, Lorenz Hart); ph, Harold Lipstein (Technicolor); ed, Viola Lawrence, Jerome Thoms; m, Nelson Riddle; art d, Walter Holscher; chor, Hermes Pan; cos, Jean Louis

AAN Best Film Editing: Viola Lawrence, Jerome Thoms; *AAN Best Art Direction-Set Decoration:* Walter Holscher, William Kiernan, Louis Diage; *AAN Best Costume Design:* Jean Louis; *AAN Best Sound:* John P. Livadary

PAL JOEY's original source was John O'Hara's series of fictional "letters," published in the *New Yorker*, from a mythical dancer who signed all the missives, "Your Pal Joey." O'Hara was approached by producer George Abbott, who talked him into adapting the stories into a book for a musical. Rodgers and Hart came aboard and the play was a success, with sensational, sexy tunes. In this bowdlerized film adaptation, Joey is not a dancer but a singer. Sinatra does a bang-up job as Joey, a saloon singer who arrives in San Francisco with a gleam in his eye, a tuxedo in his suitcase, and not a penny in his pocket. He gets a job at a nightclub, and soon has his way with most of the club chorines, the hold-out being Linda (Kim Novak), a sweet ingenue. When Joey and the band (led by real-life bandleader Bobby Sherwood) are booked for a private soiree at the posh home of wealthy widow Vera (Rita Hayworth), Joey recognizes her as a former stripper. Vera has eyes for Joey, who is himself rapidly falling for Linda, and decides to finance him in his own nightspot, the Chez Joey. Noting, however, that there is more between Joey and Linda than a professional relationship, she holds back the money and tells Joey he cannot open the club if Linda remains with the establishment. Turning over a new leaf, erstwhile heel Joey won't give in, but Linda begs Vera to go ahead with the deal. Vera says she'll do so if Linda will get lost, and offers to end Joey's years of poverty by marrying him, a tempting prospect—but Joey makes the right choice. Some of Rodgers and Hart's best songs ever are in this score, including Sinatra's classic rendition of "The Lady Is a Tramp." (Novak and Hayworth's singing voices are dubbed.) Add gorgeous costumes, excellent choreography by Hermes Pan, and snappy direction by George Sidney to the tunes and what you have is a don't-miss picture.

PALE RIDER

1985 115m c Western 📀
Malpaso (U.S.) ★★★½
R

Clint Eastwood *(Preacher)*, Michael Moriarty *(Hull Barret)*, Carrie Snodgress *(Sarah Wheeler)*, Christopher Penn *(Josh LaHood)*, Richard Dysart *(Coy LaHood)*, Sydney Penny *(Megan Wheeler)*, Richard Kiel *(Club)*, Doug McGrath *(Spider Conway)*, John Russell *(Stockburn)*, Charles Hallahan *(McGill)*

p, Clint Eastwood; d, Clint Eastwood; w, Michael Butler, Dennis Shryack; ph, Bruce Surtees (Panavision, Technicolor); ed, Joel Cox; m, Lennie Niehaus; prod d, Edward Carfagno; fx, Chuck Gaspar; cos, Glenn Wright

The quiet calm of a beautiful autumn day is broken by the thundering sound of hooves coming down the hillside. A cadre of men employed by powerful strip-miner Coy LaHood (Richard Dysart) rides into a small mining encampment and begins shooting up the place. One of the terrorists kills the dog of young Megan Wheeler's (Sydney Penny). As Megan buries her pet, she says a prayer, begging the Lord to send someone to defend them. Later Megan sits with her widowed mother (Carrie Snodgress) and reads from the

Bible: "And I saw, and behold, a pale horse, and its rider's name was death, and hell followed him." Then a lone horseman (Clint Eastwood), dressed as a preacher, rides into camp. From its breathtaking opening, PALE RIDER heralds the return of the western. Although PALE RIDER is definitely a step down from producer-director Eastwood's masterpiece, THE OUTLAW JOSEY WALES and even from HIGH PLAINS DRIFTER (which it most resembles), it had been so long since a quality western had hit America's screens that it appears as if Eastwood purposely set out to remind audiences of all the elements that make the genre work. Eastwood has a deep love and understanding for the genre, and it shows in every frame of PALE RIDER. The supernatural elements of the story are incidental and handled in a restrained, subtle manner that does not distract from the story but enhances it, bringing another dimension to the oft-told tale. Eastwood the director has delivered a thought-provoking, well-crafted western.

PALINDROMES

DVD

2005 100m c Drama ★★
Extra Large Pictures (U.S.) R

Ellen Barkin *(Joyce Victor)*, Jennifer Jason Leigh *(Mark Aviva)*, Matthew Faber *(Mark Wiener)*, Emani Sledge *(Dawn Aviva)*, Valerie Shusterov *(Judah Aviva)*, Hannah Freiman *(Henry Aviva)*, Will Denton *(Huckleberry Aviva)*, Rachel Corr *(Henrietta Aviva)*, Sharon Wilkins *(Mama Sunshine Aviva)*, Stephen Adly Guirgis *(Joe/Earl/Bob)*

p, Mike S. Ryan, Derrick Tseng; d, Todd Solondz; w, Todd Solondz; ph, Tom Richmond; ed, Mollie Goldstein, Messman; m, Nathan Larson; prod d, Dave Doernberg; cos, Victoria Farrell

Were it not for the casting gimmick—two adult women, four teenage girls, and one girlish boy, all of various shapes, sizes and colors, play the same put-upon, 12-year-old—Todd Solondz' sour, mean-spirited tale would be nothing more than a pallid retread of the Marquis de Sade's *Justine*.

The travails of little Aviva Victor (six-year-old Emani Sledge) begin at the funeral of her unloved cousin, Dawn Weiner. Aviva fears that she's somehow like the suicidal Dawn, though her mother (Ellen Barkin), assures her she isn't. A few years later, 12-year-old Aviva (Valerie Shusterov), possessed by baby love, becomes pregnant. Her mother bullies her into an abortion which, unbeknownst to Aviva (Hannah Freiman) goes badly. Aviva (Rachel Corr) runs away and, after a predatory truck driver (playwright Stephen Adly Guirgis) abandons her at a roadside motel, she (Will Denton) climbs into a child's toy boat, floats dreamily down a brook, and is found on the shore. Another edition of Aviva (Sharon Wilkins) is taken in by Christian crusader Mama Sunshine (Debra Monk) and her husband (Walter Bobbie), who've opened their hearts and homes to a throng of special-needs children while helping plot the murder of abortionists.

Few filmmakers can rival Solondz' willingness to charge in where others fear to tread, but you have to wonder why he bothered dragging a tabula rasa like Aviva through a bleak landscape of suicide, murder, pedophilia, and sociopathic selfishness just so her cousin, accused child molester Mark (Matthew Faber, reprising his DOLLHOUSE role), can tell her that no matter how we change superficially, we stay the same under the skin. Even for a thin, curdled fable like this one, that's a half-hearted excuse for a moral.

PALM BEACH STORY, THE

DVD

1942 90m bw Comedy ★★★★
Paramount (U.S.)

Claudette Colbert *(Gerry Jeffers)*, Joel McCrea *(Tom Jeffers)*, Mary Astor *(Princess Centimillia)*, Rudy Vallee *(J.D. Hackensacker III)*, Sig Arno *(Toto)*, Robert Warwick *(Mr. Hinch)*, Arthur Stuart

Hull *(Mr. Osmond)*, Torben Meyer *(Dr. Kluck)*, Jimmy Conlin *(Mr. Asweld)*, Victor Potel *(Mr. McKeewie)*

p, Paul Jones; d, Preston Sturges; w, Preston Sturges; ph, Victor Milner; ed, Stuart Gilmore; m, Victor Young; art d, Hans Dreier, Ernst Fegte; cos, Irene

Preston Sturges at full tilt, with Claudette Colbert and Joel McCrea, Rudy Vallee, and Mary Astor. Joel is a crazy young architect who has dreams of building a magnificent airport. Claudette is his adoring wife who, in search of investment money for her beloved's dreams, runs away to Palm Beach with the Ale and Quail Club and meets Rudy, the incredibly normal zillionaire J.D. Hackensacker III, who of course falls in love with her. Rudy's sister, Mary, falls for Joel. In the end all's set right again and each Jack has his Jill. It's hard to describe Sturges' special brand of comedy. Perhaps it's realistic farce. He takes a perfectly natural action and lets it run on just too long to the point of slight but affectionate absurdity.

McCrea and Sturges had just come off the wonderful SULLIVAN'S TRAVELS, which took telling aim at Hollywood. They teamed again to snipe at the idle rich with this hysterically funny fairy tale. Colbert was never lovelier or more energetic than she is here, blithely delivering Sturges's sophisticated dialogue. Vallee is delightful as the somewhat naive and eccentric billionaire, carefully cataloging every cent he spends. As his sister, Astor is wickedly caustic, especially when dealing with her incomprehensible lover, Arno. As in SULLIVAN'S TRAVELS, McCrea is well-cast, adeptly playing off the film's wild collection of characters. All the other roles are carefully cast and virtually anyone who walks on screen delivers a memorable witticism. Though this film may lack the satirical bite of Sturges's great comedies such as SULLIVAN'S TRAVELS or MIRACLE AT MORGAN'S CREEK, it remains a delight.

PANIC IN NEEDLE PARK, THE

1971 110m c Drama ★★
Dunne/Didion/Dunne (U.S.) R

Al Pacino *(Bobby)*, Kitty Winn *(Helen)*, Alan Vint *(Hotchner)*, Richard Bright *(Hank)*, Kiel Martin *(Chico)*, Michael McClanathan *(Sonny)*, Warren Finnerty *(Sammy)*, Marcia Jean Kurtz *(Marcie)*, Raul Julia *(Marco)*, Angie Ortega *(Irene)*

p, Dominick Dunne; d, Jerry Schatzberg; w, Joan Didion, John Gregory Dunne (based on the book by James Mills); ph, Adam Holender (DeLuxe Color); ed, Evan Lottman; art d, Murray P. Stern; cos, Jo Ynocencio

Al Pacino tries hard in his first starring role, but even his considerable talents can't breath life into this dreary, exploitative, and ultimately distasteful look at young heroin addicts in New York City. Helen (Kitty Winn), a pregnant girl from the Midwest, arrives in New York City for an abortion. While recovering at the apartment of her former lover (Raul Julia), she takes up with Bobby (Pacino), a young, heroin-addicted dope dealer. Helen is soon sharing his habit, and the pursuit of heroin becomes an all-consuming obsession. In order to pay for his drugs and hopefully marry Helen, Bobby agrees to help his brother Hank (Richard Bright) knock over a warehouse, but Bobby gets caught and is sent to prison. By the time he's released, Helen has taken up with Hank and has turned to prostitution to finance her heroin habit. Supposedly a no-holds-barred look at the seamy heroin subculture, THE PANIC IN NEEDLE PARK is really little more than a boring romance between two dullards intercut with close-ups of filthy needles being jabbed into scarred veins. Director Jerry Schatzberg and writers Joan Didion and John Gregory Dunne attempt to show the horrors of drug abuse by plunging the film into the sleazy underworld and letting the camera linger on the degradation, but the characters are never fully developed. The viewer is naturally repulsed, but a deeper level of understanding is never achieved. It becomes the cinematic equivalent of a yellow journalism expose: all sensation, but little content.

PANIC ROOM
1973 108m c Thriller   **DVD** ★★★
Hofflund/Polone Productions/Indelible Pictures   R
(U.S.)

Jodie Foster (Meg Altman), Kristen Stewart (Sarah Altman), Forest Whitaker (Burnham), Dwight Yoakam (Raoul), Jared Leto (Junior), Patrick Bauchau (Stephan Altman), Ann Magnuson (Lydia Lynch), Ian Buchanan (Evan Kurlander), Paul Schulze (Officer Keeney), Nicole Kidman (Voice of Stephan's Girlfriend—uncredited)

p, Cean Chaffin, Judy Hofflund, David Koepp, Gavin Polone; d, David Fincher; w, David Koepp; ph, Conrad W. Hall, Darius Khondji; ed, James Haygood, Angus Wall; m, Howard Shore; prod d, Arthur Max; art d, Keith Neely, James E. Tocci; fx, Kevin Tod Haug, Joseph Viskocil, BUF, Toybox; cos, Michael Kaplan

A well-crafted exercise in urban paranoia that's so controlled it never achieves the reckless, visceral immediacy its subject matter demands.

Newly divorced Meg Altman (Jodie Foster) and her diabetic daughter, Sarah (Kristen Stewart), move into a spectacularly spacious townhouse on Manhattan's Upper West Side. It's something of a bargain and even comes complete with a "panic room," a fortified safe harbor equipped with video monitors, a separate phone line and all the conveniences of a fallout shelter. Meg can't imagine needing such a thing, but the very night she and Sarah move in, three intruders—Junior (Jared Leto), Burnham (Forest Whitaker) and Raoul (Dwight Yoakam)—invade the house and refuse to leave, even after mother and daughter are safe inside the panic room. What the bad guys want is in the panic room, and they're not leaving without it.

Though the action is largely confined to a single location and shot in the sweaty shades of sickly gray-green that director David Fincher and cinematographer Darius Khondji first concocted for SE7EN, the film is surprisingly kinetic: Fincher's camera is constantly panning through floors, diving into holes and entwining itself with tangles of wiring. It's intelligently scripted by David Koepp, and the shifting alliances between the intruders are deftly sketched. But overall, this claustrophobic thriller suffers from the one-two punch of megastar casting and contemporary mainstream spinelessness. However skillfully the twists and turns are constructed, it's hard to get really worked up about Meg and Sarah's plight because Hollywood movies don't seriously abuse the A-list likes of Jodie Foster. The menace is cerebral rather than gut-wrenching, more to be admired than endured.

PAPER CHASE, THE
1973 112m c Comedy/Drama   **DVD** ★★½
Fox (U.S.)   PG

Timothy Bottoms (Hart), Lindsay Wagner (Susan Kingsfield), John Houseman (Prof. Kingsfield), Graham Beckel (Ford), Edward Herrmann (Anderson), Bob Lydiard (O'Connor), Craig Richard Nelson (Bell), James Naughton (Kevin), Regina Baff (Asheley), David Clennon (Toombs)

p, Robert C. Thompson, Rodrick Paul; d, James Bridges; w, James Bridges (based on the novel by John Jay Osborn Jr.); ph, Gordon Willis (Panavision, DeLuxe Color); ed, Walter Thompson; m, John Williams; art d, George Jenkins

AA Best Supporting Actor: John Houseman; AAN Best Adapted Screenplay: James Bridges; AAN Best Sound: Donald O. Mitchell, Lawrence O. Jost

John Houseman had already distinguished himself as a writer (JANE EYRE), a producer (EXECUTIVE SUITE, THE BAD AND THE BEAUTIFUL) and the story editor of CITIZEN KANE before winning the Best Supporting Actor Oscar for this, his second role. Bottoms is a Minnesota-bred law student who comes to Harvard and the lecture hall of Houseman, an instructor who seemingly takes great pleasure in puncturing his students' egos. Bottoms falls in love with Wagner. Essentially, this is a military school plot with a change of venue. Bridges secured an Oscar nomination for his adaptation of the novel, and the film was also nominated for Best Sound.

PAPER MOON
1973 102m bw Comedy/Drama   **DVD** ★★★½
Saticoy (U.S.)   PG

Ryan O'Neal (Moses Pray), Tatum O'Neal (Addie Loggins), Madeline Kahn (Trixie Delight), John Hillerman (Sheriff Hardin/Jess Hardin), P.J. Johnson (Imogene), Jessie Lee Fulton (Miss Ollie), James N. Harrell (Minister), Lila Water (Minister's Wife), Noble Willingham (Mr. Robertson), Bob Young (Gas Station Attendant)

p, Peter Bogdanovich; d, Peter Bogdanovich; w, Alvin Sargent (based on the novel Addie Pray by Joe David Brown); ph, Laszlo Kovacs; ed, Verna Fields; prod d, Polly Platt; fx, Jack Harmon; cos, Pat Kelly, Sandra Stewart

AA Best Supporting Actress: Tatum O'Neal; AAN Best Supporting Actress: Madeline Kahn; AAN Best Adapted Screenplay: Alvin Sargent; AAN Best Sound: Richard Portman, Les Fresholtz

Bogdanovich's warmest film, featuring charming performances from real-life father and daughter Ryan and Tatum O'Neal. Driving a Model-T roadster in the Depression year of 1936, O'Neal stops to pay his respects at the funeral of one of his former girlfriends. Neighbors explain that the woman's death has left an "adorable" nine-year-old daughter an orphan and beg him to take the child to relatives in St. Joseph, Missouri. O'Neal takes Tatum O'Neal along with him and almost instantly regrets his generosity. The little girl smokes, swears, and exhibits altogether unchildlike behavior. After taking sly vengeance on the brother of the man who caused the death of Tatum's mother in a car accident, defrauding him of $200, O'Neal buys a new car and then takes Tatum to a train station, buying her a ticket for St. Joseph. Rather than get on the train, she creates a scene in the station restaurant, screaming that O'Neal owes her $200. Since he got it from the family that inadvertently caused her mother's death, she asserts, it is therefore her rightful inheritance—and he's probably her father to boot. O'Neal gives in and takes her along on his roadway adventures through Kansas and Missouri, where he works a variety of con games on the gullible rurals.

PAPER MOON offers brilliant, bittersweet images and an entertaining story. The O'Neals are excellent, but Madeline Kahn almost steals the film in a small turn as a travelling floozy. Bogdanovich's direction is fast, furious, and full of fun. As with THE LAST PICTURE SHOW, the director opted for black-and-white cinematography (beautifully done by Kovacs) in a world swimming in color celluloid, to achieve an historical feel. "I have more affection, more affinity for the past," Bogdanovich later stated. "Since I am more interested in it, it comes easier for me." This was Tatum O'Neal's film debut, and no one would ever forget it, especially Tatum O'Neal, who won a Best Supporting Actress Oscar for her performance (over costar Kahn). For Bogdanovich, the grown-up little girl provided "one of the most miserable experiences of my life." The picture was filmed on location near Hays, Kansas, and St. Joseph, Missouri. The highly effective musical backdrop for the picture is a procession of period tunes from the record collection of Rudi Fehr.

PAPILLON

DVD
★★★★

1973 150m c Prison

Corona/General Production (U.S.) PG

Steve McQueen *(Henri Charriere Papillon)*, Dustin Hoffman *(Louis Dega)*, Victor Jory *(Indian Chief)*, Don Gordon *(Julot)*, Anthony Zerbe *(Toussaint Leper Colony Chief)*, Robert Deman *(Maturette)*, Woodrow Parfrey *(Clusoit)*, Bill Mumy *(Lariot)*, George Coulouris *(Dr. Chatal)*, Ratna Assan *(Zoraima)*

p, Robert Dorfmann, Franklin J. Schaffner; d, Franklin J. Schaffner; w, Dalton Trumbo, Lorenzo Semple Jr. (based on the autobiographical novel by Henri Charriere); ph, Fred Koenekamp (Panavision, Technicolor); ed, Robert Swink; m, Jerry Goldsmith; prod d, Tony Masters; art d, Jack Maxsted; cos, Anthony Powell

AAN Best Original Dramatic Score: Jerry Goldsmith

A grim, authentically brutal film about the escape of notorious French felon Henri "Papillon" Charriere (Steve McQueen) from the supposedly inescapable prison fortress of Devil's Island. The story begins in the streets of Marseilles in the 1930s, with French soldiers escorting a large group of prisoners to the docks. Among them are McQueen, a convicted murderer, and Hoffman, a big-time stock swindler who still has a lot of money hidden. During the ensuing voyage, a couple of brutal murderers attempt to kill Hoffman but McQueen saves him. Once in Cayenne McQueen thinks only about escape. He attacks a guard who abuses Hoffman, and makes a break, only to be later recaptured. McQueen spends most of his time in solitary confinement for repeated escape attempts. Here he staves off starvation, madness, and disease while his body deteriorates. He and William Smithers, the commandant of the solitary confinement compound, engage in a contest of wills and slowly age together, their hair turning white over the years. Finally returned to the main prison, McQueen is received warmly by Hoffman, who is now living a (relatively) cushy life, paying off the guards and the warden for favorable treatment. Hoffman tries to persuade McQueen to serve out his time and wait for parole, but eventually joins him in an escape attempt just as harrowing as life on the inside.

PAPILLON was produced with consummate technical skill and offers brilliant acting by McQueen and Hoffman. Schaffner, who expertly captured the gritty story of PATTON, does not flinch from showing every conceivable horror of the French penal system. Excellent supporting performances are provided by Zerbe, as the compassionate leader of a leper colony, Jory, as a stoic Indian chief, and Coulouris, as a venal prison doctor. Even scriptwriter Trumbo, who had become a cult figure by the time of this film, gets into the act, appearing as the commandant of the penal colony at the beginning of the film. Shot on location in Spain and Jamaica, PAPILLON was costly, but earned $22 million in its U.S. release. PAPILLON was originally rated R by the MPAA for its extreme violence, but Allied Artists appealed and the rating was changed to PG.

PARALLAX VIEW, THE

DVD
★★★½

1974 102m c Thriller

Paramount (U.S.) R

Warren Beatty *(Joseph Frady)*, Hume Cronyn *(Editor Edgar Rintels)*, William Daniels *(Austin Tucker)*, Paula Prentiss *(Lee Carter)*, Kelly Thordsen *(Sheriff L.D.)*, Earl Hindman *(Deputy Red)*, Chuck Waters *(Busboy-Assassin)*, Bill Joyce *(Sen. Carroll)*, Bettie Johnson *(Mrs. Carroll)*, Bill McKinney *(Art, an Assassin)*

p, Alan J. Pakula; d, Alan J. Pakula; w, David Giler, Lorenzo Semple Jr. (based on the novel by Loren Singer); ph, Gordon Willis (Panavision, Technicolor); ed, John W. Wheeler; m, Michael Small; prod d, George Jenkins; art d, George Jenkins; cos, Frank Thompson

A popular senator is shot by a waiter at the Seattle Space Needle. Three years later Lee (Prentiss), a television reporter who was on the scene, goes to newspaper reporter Joe Frady (Beatty) frightened for her life. Assassination witnesses have been systematically killed, she says, and Lee knows that she's next. Frady discounts her fears as irrational paranoia, but after her supposed suicide, doubt creeps into his mind. He begins investigating the story and uncovers a huge conspiracy involving the mysterious "Parallax Corporation," a secret company that recruits assassins to eliminate troublemakers on their "list." Alan J. Pakula's taut direction maintains a neat balance between the real and the perceived; things are not what they appear to be. He presents disorienting shots and editing patterns with characters often filmed behind glass or curtains, allowing only a partial look at the whole scene. The most compelling aspects are of course the political and historical overtones. The fictional assassination was a deliberate attempt to suggest a possible explanation for the John F. Kennedy assassination. Using historical parallels (the photographs implying a second gunman at Dallas; the fact that many of the assassination witnesses died mysteriously in the years following 1963), Pakula created a possible, though fictional, explanation in a film steeped in American symbolism. The film was released in June 1974, after the studio had let the controversial work sit for several months. This is one of the best political thrillers of the 1970s.

PARDON MON AFFAIRE

(UN ELEPHANT CA TROMPE ENORMEMENT)

★★★½

1977 105m c Comedy/Romance

Gaumont/La Gueville (France) PG

Jean Rochefort *(Etienne)*, Claude Brasseur *(Daniel)*, Guy Bedos *(Simon)*, Victor Lanoux *(Bouly)*, Daniele Delorme *(Marthe)*, Anny Duperey *(Charlotte)*, Martine Sarcey *(Esperanza)*, Marthe Villalonga *(Mouchy)*

p, Alain Poire, Yves Robert; d, Yves Robert; w, Jean-Loup Dabadie (based on the story by Robert, Dabadie); ph, Rene Mathelin; ed, Gerard Pollicand; m, Vladimir Cosma

Yves Robert, the director responsible for THE TALL BLONDE MAN WITH ONE BLACK SHOE and its sequel, struck again with this pleasant, enjoyable mixture of comedy and drama about husbands and their affairs. Etienne (Jean Rochefort) is a Parisian civil servant who, while in his company parking lot, gazes at the bright red dress of a pretty young woman (Anny Duperey) as it is blown up above her waist by a rush of air. Although he is happily married to Marthe (Daniele Delorme, wife of director Robert) and has never even thought of having an affair, Etienne becomes enamored of this mystery woman. In the meantime, he and his three best friends witness the result of years of dalliances when one of them, Bouly (Victor Lanoux), comes home one day to find that his wife has left him, taking along his children and every last possession. Robert successfully creates a number of believable characters with honest emotions and places them in lightly humorous situations, and the result falls somewhere between broad comedy (one memorable scene has a character pretending to be blind and causing havoc in an elegant restaurant) and heartfelt drama (Bouly's reaction to his wife's departure), as if Robert was attempting a farcical French version of John Cassavetes's HUSBANDS. Many of the same names reunited for the less successful sequel, PARDON MON AFFAIRE, TOO! Remade in Hollywood as THE WOMAN IN RED.

PARENT TRAP, THE

1998 124m c Comedy *DVD*
Stansbury Productions/Meyers/Shyer/Walt ★★★
Disney Pictures (U.S.) PG

Lindsay Lohan *(Hallie Parker/Annie James)*, Dennis Quaid *(Nick Parker)*, Natasha Richardson *(Elizabeth James)*, Elaine Hendrix *(Meredith Blake)*, Lisa Ann Walter *(Chessy)*, Simon Kunz *(Martin)*, Polly Holliday *(Marva Kulp Sr.)*, Ronnie Stevens *(Grandfather)*, Maggie Wheeler *(Marva Kulp Jr.)*, Joanna Barnes *(Vicki)*

p, Charles Shyer; d, Nancy Meyers; w, David Swift, Nancy Meyers, Charles Shyer (based on the novel *Das Doppelte Lottchen* by Erich Kastner); ph, Dean Cundey; ed, Stephen A. Rotter; m, Alan Silvestri; prod d, Dean Tavoularis; art d, Alex Tavoularis; fx, Cliff Wenger, Jim Rygiel; cos, Penny Rose

An amiable kid-flick with a potentially troublesome premise—that clever youngsters can reunite their divorced parents if they try hard enough—this remake of the 1961 Disney favorite (itself a remake of the 1953 British film TWICE UPON A TIME, based on a German novel) is a bubbly, girl-power romp.

Eleven-year-olds Hallie Parker and Annie James (both played by Lindsay Lohan) meet at summer camp and hate each other on sight: identical freckled, red-haired looks aside, the girls at first seem to have nothing in common. Tomboy Hallie lives in Northern California with her dad (Dennis Quaid), who runs a vineyard; slightly stuck-up Annie lives in London with her mom (Natasha Richardson), the kind of swanky wedding-dress designer whose creations are modeled by Vendela. That they're actually twins separated at birth explains their common allergies, tastes (peanut butter and Oreos), and skills (fencing and poker-playing chief among them), and the girls quickly cook up a plan to bring their perfect-for-each-other parents back together. The complication: a peroxided vixen named Meredith (Elaine Hendrix), who's got her jungle-red claws deep into Dad and wants to hear wedding bells ringing in two weeks' time.

Nancy Meyers and Charles Shyer, the husband-and-wife team who updated FATHER OF THE BRIDE (1991), perform a similar face-lift on the original PARENT TRAP, making the girls younger, the beloved mom more independent (and English), the gold digger an opportunistic career woman (a *publicist,* if you please) rather than a spoiled deb, and cooking up a rather unlikely romance between Annie's prissy butler (Simon Kunz) and Hallie's earthy housekeeper (Lisa Ann Walter). The technology for twinning a single young actress is considerably more seamless than it was in 1961, and Lohan is a perky charmer.

PARENTHOOD

1989 124m c Comedy *DVD*
Imagine (U.S.) ★★★½
  PG-13

Steve Martin *(Gil Buckman)*, Tom Hulce *(Larry Buckman)*, Rick Moranis *(Nathan)*, Jason Robards Jr. *(Frank Buckman)*, Martha Plimpton *(Julie)*, Mary Steenburgen *(Karen Buckman)*, Dianne Wiest *(Helen)*, Keanu Reeves *(Tod)*, Harley Kozak *(Susan)*, Leaf Phoenix *(Garry)*

p, Brian Grazer; d, Ron Howard; w, Lowell Ganz, Babaloo Mandel (based on a story by Lowell Ganz, Babaloo Mandel, Ron Howard); ph, Don McAlpine (Deluxe Color); ed, Michael Hill, Dan Hanley; m, Randy Newman; prod d, Todd Hallowell; art d, Christopher Nowak; cos, Ruth Morley

AAN Best Supporting Actress: Dianne Wiest; *AAN Best Original Song:* "I Love to See You Smile"; Randy Newman (Music & Lyrics)

Occasionally corny, yet thoroughly entertaining, PARENTHOOD is a movie by, for, and about parents. Four generations

are portrayed by an all-star cast, delivering a lesson in child-rearing worthy of Dr. Spock. Jason Robards plays Frank, the head of the Buckman clan. Gil (Steve Martin), Helen (Dianne Wiest), Susan (Harley Kozak), and Larry (Tom Hulce) are his children; all of them have kids of their own. Gil tries to balance his career with being the attentive father Frank never was; divorcee Helen has her hands full with son Garry (Leaf Phoenix), who is badly in need of a male role model, rebellious teenage daughter Julie (Martha Plimpton), and burn-out son-in-law Tod (Keanu Reeves). Susan does her best to give her toddler a childhood while husband Nathan (Rick Moranis) has the precocious kid studying karate, long division, and Kafka. With his own illegitimate son in tow, prodigal son Larry has returned home deeply in debt to some very rough customers. All of these situations get worse before they get better, but by film's end the family is closer than ever. PARENTHOOD's coscreenwriters Ron Howard, Lowell Ganz, and Babaloo Mandell—the fathers of 14 children in all—have produced a funny, poignant script with very contemporary humor. It is the acting, though, that shines brightest in the movie. Rarely has such a formidable array of talent been assembled for one film, and theirs is truly an ensemble effort. While PARENTHOOD crosses the border into schmaltz a number of times, the movie runs the gamut of realistic emotions, and one scene or another is bound to hit home with the parents who see the film.

PARIS BELONGS TO US

(PARIS NOUS APPARTIENT)
1960 120m bw Mystery ★★★
Ajym/Carrosse (France)

Betty Schneider *(Anne Goupil)*, Gianni Esposito *(Gerard Lenz)*, Francoise Prevost *(Terry Yok)*, Daniel Crohem *(Philip Kaufman)*, Francois Maistre *(Pierre Goupil)*, Jean-Claude Brialy *(Jean Marc)*, Jean-Marie Robain *(De Georges)*, Brigitte Juslin, Noelle Leiris, Monique Le Poirier

p, Roland Nonin; d, Jacques Rivette; w, Jacques Rivette, Jean Gruault; ph, Charles Bitsch; ed, Denise de Casabianca; m, Philippe Arthuys

Schneider, after overhearing a discussion on the suicide of a young Spaniard, is compelled to learn why the youth's life ended so tragically. She gets involved with Esposito, a theater director, and takes a part in his production of Shakespeare's "Pericles." She becomes worried for Esposito's life when he tells her that the Spaniard was part of a worldwide conspiracy and that he is targeted for murder by the same organization. She also meets Crohem, an American victim of McCarthyism, who is responsible for informing the Spaniard and Esposito of the organization. Eventually it is revealed that Crohem made the whole thing up, but not before Esposito's paranoia gets the better of him and he commits suicide.

Along with Claude Chabrol's LE BEAU SERGE, this first feature by Jacques Rivette kindled the flame that became known as the French New Wave. Production began in the early summer of 1958 with money borrowed from the magazine Rivette (and his New Wave counterparts) worked for, *Cahiers du Cinema.* Technicians, actors, and lab fees were all on credit, with no money exchanged until the film's release in 1960. Without so much as a car, Rivette and his entourage of film enthusiasts worked whenever they could, spending Sundays trying to raise enough money to begin filming again on Mondays. With the help of Chabrol and Truffaut, whose first films were already receiving acclaim at the Cannes Film Festival, PARIS was finally released—a stepping stone toward French cinema's rebirth.

PARIS, TEXAS

1984 150m c Drama 📀 ★★★★
Road Movies/Argos/Westdeutscher/ R
Channel 4/Pro-Ject (France/West Germany)

Harry Dean Stanton *(Travis Clay Henderson)*, Nastassja Kinski, billed as Nastassia Kinski *(Jane)*, Dean Stockwell *(Walt Henderson)*, Aurore Clement *(Anne)*, Hunter Carson *(Hunter)*, Bernhard Wicki *(Dr. Ulmer)*, Viva Auder *(Woman on TV)*, Socorro Valdez *(Carmelita)*, Tommy Farrell *(Screaming Man)*, John Lurie *(Slater)*

p, Don Guest; d, Wim Wenders; w, Sam Shepard (based on a story adapted by L.M. Kit Carson); ph, Robby Muller; ed, Peter Pryzgodda; m, Ry Cooder; art d, Kate Altman; cos, Birgitta Bjerke

Epic but intimate, PARIS, TEXAS combines the European sensibility of director Wim Wenders with the expansive locations of the American West.

Amid the desert and brilliant sky of Big Bend, Texas, Travis Clay Henderson (Harry Dean Stanton) aimlessly wanders under the boiling sun. He stops in a tavern and promptly collapses, awakening in the care of a German doctor (Bernhard Wicki). Assuming the catatonic Travis is mute, the doctor calls a number in his wallet and reaches Travis's brother, Walt (Dean Stockwell), who lives in Los Angeles with his French wife (Aurore Clement) and Hunter (Hunter Carson), Travis's seven-year-old son by his estranged wife, Jane (Nastassia Kinski). It turns out Travis has been missing and assumed dead for four years. Walt brings him back to L.A. for a reunion with Hunter, who subsequently joins his father on a quixotic quest for family, true love, and Jane.

PARIS, TEXAS features neither sweeping themes, grandiose sets, nor a cast of thousands, but from its opening shots one senses its uniquely epic quality. The vast landscapes recall those of John Ford, but instead of John Wayne it's Stanton who wanders across the frame, a modern American father in suit and tie, displaced, aimless, and emotionally dead, on an odyssey to find himself. He knows where he began—in Paris, Texas—but not where he is going. Although based on stories by Sam Shepard, the film's vision of America is wholly that of Wenders, a German director deeply fascinated by Americana. As the title suggests, Wenders' America is a by-product of the European imagination.

Superbly scripted, the film features wonderful performances from all its major players. Equally brilliant, especially in a film that emphasizes script and character, is the cinematography by Robby Muller, perfectly capturing the notion of "America." A final factor in PARIS, TEXAS's success is the remarkably haunting score by blues musician Ry Cooder.

PARTING GLANCES

1986 90m c Drama 📀 ★★★
Rondo (U.S.)

Richard Ganoung *(Michael)*, John Bolger *(Robert)*, Steve Buscemi *(Nick)*, Adam Nathan *(Peter)*, Kathy Kinney *(Joan)*, Patrick Tull *(Cecil)*, Yolande Bavan *(Betty)*, Richard Wall *(Douglas)*, Jim Selfe *(Douglas' Sidekick)*, Kristin Moneagle *(Sarah)*

p, Yoram Mandel, Arthur Silverman; d, Bill Sherwood; w, Bill Sherwood; ph, Jacek Laskus (DuArt Color); ed, Bill Sherwood; prod d, John Loggia; art d, Daniel Haughey, Mark Sweeney; cos, Sylvia Heisel

Unlike several major studio productions, in which homosexuality is used either as an issue or as comic relief, PARTING GLANCES takes an inside look at New York's gay community. The pain and joys of love, unspoken cultural rules, and the specter of AIDS are all dealt with in an energetic manner that balances the story's varying shades of emotion.

Michael (Richard Ganoung) is a pleasant young man about to end a six-year relationship with his live-in lover, Robert (John Bolger). Robert is preparing to leave for Africa, ostensibly to accept an employment opportunity, but also to give himself a little breathing room from Michael's steady companionship. Before going to a dinner to be hosted by Robert's boss, Cecil (Patrick Tull), and his wife, Michael drops by the apartment of Nick (Steve Buscemi), a cynical New Wave musician who is dying of AIDS. Later, as the evening of farewells continues, Michael becomes more despondent.

The plot is fairly simple, but the affection displayed by PARTING GLANCES's marvelous ensemble makes these everyday events something more than commonplace. At the center of it all is Ganoung, who handles his key role well. Buscemi's performance as the dying musician is another standout. Writer-director Bill Sherwood shows marvelous talent in his feature debut. He deals with touchy issues in a forthright manner and doesn't allow these events to unfold without a well-aimed sense of humor. Sadly, Sherwood himself succumbed to AIDS complications in early 1990.

PASSAGE TO INDIA, A

1984 163m c Drama 📀 ★★★½
John Heyman/Edward Sands/HBO (U.K.) PG

Judy Davis *(Adela Quested)*, Victor Banerjee *(Dr. Aziz)*, Peggy Ashcroft *(Mrs. Moore)*, James Fox *(Richard Fielding)*, Alec Guinness *(Godbole)*, Nigel Havers *(Ronny Heaslop)*, Richard Wilson *(Turton)*, Antonia Pemberton *(Mrs. Turton)*, Michael Culver *(McBryde)*, Art Malik *(Mahmoud Ali)*

p, John Brabourne, Richard Goodwin; d, David Lean; w, David Lean (based on the play by Santha Rama Rau and the novel by E.M. Forster); ph, Ernest Day (Metrocolor); ed, David Lean; m, Maurice Jarre; prod d, John Box; art d, Leslie Tomkins, Clifford Robinson, Ram Yedekar, Herbert Westbrook; cos, Judy Moorcroft

AAN Best Picture; AAN Best Actress: Judy Davis; AA Best Supporting Actress: Peggy Ashcroft; AAN Best Director: David Lean; AAN Best Adapted Screenplay: David Lean; AAN Best Cinematography: Ernest Day; AAN Best Film Editing: David Lean; AA Best Original Score: Maurice Jarre; AAN Best Art Direction-Set Decoration: John Box, Leslie Tomkins, Hugh Scaife; AAN Best Costume Design: Judy Moorcroft; AAN Best Sound: Graham V. Hartstone, Nicolas LeMessurier, Michael A. Carter, John Mitchell

At 75, David Lean, whose epics THE BRIDGE ON THE RIVER KWAI, LAWRENCE OF ARABIA, and DOCTOR ZHIVAGO garnered 19 Oscars, returned to work after a 14-year absence with this adaptation of the E.M. Forster novel about sexual repression and racial prejudice in 1924 India. Set in the fictional town of Chandrapore, the story concerns Adela Quested (Judy Davis) who has settled in India and is to marry Ronny Heaslop (Nigel Havers), a town magistrate. She is befriended by the charming Dr. Aziz (Victor Banerjee), but it's a friendship that ultimately leads to tragedy. Lean does an excellent job of conveying the repressive nature of British society captured in the novel. Although the story makes for a movie that is often slow going, it is also a beautiful and evocative film fueled by an excellent performance from Davis and Peggy Ashcroft.

PASSAGE TO MARSEILLE

1944 110m bw Drama/War ★★★½
Warner Bros. (U.S.)

Humphrey Bogart *(Matrac)*, Claude Rains *(Capt. Freycinet)*, Michele Morgan *(Paula)*, Philip Dorn *(Renault)*, Sydney Greenstreet *(Maj. Duval)*, Peter Lorre *(Marius)*, George Tobias *(Petit)*, Victor Francen *(Capt. Patain Malo)*, Helmut Dantine *(Garou)*, John Loder *(Manning)*

p, Hal B. Wallis; d, Michael Curtiz; w, Casey Robinson, John C. Moffitt (based on the novel *Men Without a Country* by Charles Nordhoff, James Norman Hall); ph, James Wong Howe; ed, Owen Marks; m, Max Steiner; art d, Carl Jules Weyl; fx, Jack Cosgrove, Edwin DuPar, Byron Haskin, Roy Davidson, Rex Wimpy; cos, Leah Rhodes

With adventurer Humphrey Bogart as his lead, director Michael Curtiz here offers a slam-bang action film, one with a tricky plot whose narrative unfolds through a complicated series of flashbacks-within-flashbacks and flash forwards, but that is nevertheless exciting and absorbing all the way. A group of prisoners who have escaped the dreaded prison at Cayenne in French Guiana are picked up by a passing French freighter, commanded by Malo (Victor Francen), who is loyal to Free France but who hides his sympathies from the fascistic Maj. Duval (Sydney Greenstreet), a French officer sympathetic to the Vichy government. The rescued men claim they are survivors of a torpedoed ship, but eventually their true identities are learned. They are Matrac (Bogart), a French journalist who opposed the Nazi takeover of his country from within, and his criminal comrades Marius (Peter Lorre), Garou (Helmut Dantine), Renault (Philip Dorn), and Petit (George Tobias). All are loyal to the Free French, and when Maj. Duval plans to turn the ship over to the Vichy government, Matrac and his comrades fight to keep the ship from the clutches of the collaborators. Although Curtiz draws superb performances from his great cast, many of whom (Bogart, Lorre, Greenstreet, Dantine, Claude Rains, Corinna Mura, and Louis Mercier) appeared in Warner Bros.' recent smash hit CASABLANCA, which was also directed by Curtiz, the story is more than a little confusing because of the unwieldy flashbacks used to tell the tale. Yet the great action director packs the film with marvelous adventure and exciting scenes, not to mention stirring patriotism. Warners attempted to time PASSAGE TO MARSEILLE's release to coincide with what the studio thought would be the invasion of southern France, but when this failed to take place the film was distributed without an international news event to boost the production (as had been the case with CASABLANCA, released just after American troops landed in Africa and Allied leaders met in that African city for top-level conferences). James Wong Howe's gritty photography helps set the mood, and Max Steiner's music dynamically establishes patriotic fervor.

PASSENGER, THE

1975 123m c   Drama   ★★★★
CIC/Concordia/C.I.P.I./Champion   (Italy)   PG

Jack Nicholson *(David Locke)*, Maria Schneider *(Girl)*, Jenny Runacre *(Rachel Locke)*, Ian Hendry *(Martin Knight)*, Steven Berkoff *(Stephen)*, Ambroise Bia *(Achebe)*, Jose Maria Caffarel *(Hotel Keeper)*, James Campbell *(Witch Doctor)*, Manfred Spies *(German Stranger)*, Jean Baptiste Tiemele *(Murderer)*

p, Carlo Ponti; d, Michelangelo Antonioni; w, Mark Peploe, Peter Wollen, Michelangelo Antonioni (based on a story by Peploe); ph, Luciano Tovoli (Metrocolor); ed, Franco Arcalli, Michaelangelo Antonioni; art d, Piero Poletto; cos, Louise Stjernsward

In this visually stunning adventure David Locke (Jack Nicholson) is a reporter sent to northern Africa on a mission to interview a band of guerrillas. After a battle with a Jeep that refuses to travel through sand, Locke winds up in a blisteringly hot, rundown hotel. There he is confused with another hotel guest, Robertson (Chuck Mulvehill), to whom he bears a striking resemblance. When he discovers Robertson dead in his room, Locke is presented with a perfect opportunity to escape his hell of a life. He switches passport photos and personal belongings and places the corpse in his own room. Looking through "his" daily planner, he finds a number of women's names and various appointments. Curious, he decides to keep

a rendezvous and discovers that Robertson was a gun runner who supplied foreign governments with plans and documents. In the meantime he meets an enigmatic young woman (Maria Schneider) to whom he is magnetically drawn, causing him to ignore and avoid the efforts of his wife and best friend to locate him. THE PASSENGER could probably be analyzed until the end of time, each viewing uncovering a different path to understanding the film as a whole. What is more interesting than the "whys" and "hows" of the plot however, are the "where" and "when." Locke and the girl are very much a part of their environment, whether it's the sandy wastelands of northern Africa or the exquisitely organic Gaudi architecture of Barcelona. The girl has no history—she just is—a state of being to which Locke also aspires.

PASSION FISH   DVD

1992 136m c   Drama/Romance   ★★★½
Atchafalaya Films Inc./Esperanza Productions   R
(U.S.)

Mary McDonnell *(Mary-Alice Culhane)*, Alfre Woodard *(Chantelle)*, David Strathairn *(Rennie)*, Vondie Curtis Hall, billed as Vondie Curtis-Hall *(Sugar LeDoux)*, Angela Bassett *(Dawn/Rhonda)*, Lenore Banks *(Nurse Quick)*, William Mahoney *(Max)*, Nelle Stokes *(1st Therapist)*, Brett Ardoin *(2nd Therapist)*, Michael Mantell *(Dr. Kline)*

p, Sarah Green, Maggie Renzi; d, John Sayles; w, John Sayles; ph, Roger Deakins; ed, John Sayles; m, Mason Daring; prod d, Dan Bishop, Dianna Freas; cos, Cynthia Flynt

AAN Best Actress: Mary McDonnell; *AAN Best Original Screenplay:* John Sayles

After attempting historical dramas and multi-character urban sagas, John Sayles returns here to the kind of small, intimate film with which he first established his reputation.

PASSION FISH opens on a typically vivid Sayles image: soap opera actress Mary-Alice Culhane (Mary McDonnell) lying immobile in a hospital bed, watching herself walking and talking on TV. The nurse tells her she's been paralyzed from the waist down in a traffic accident (she was on her way to have her legs waxed), but her fear and anger have immobilized her as well: she refuses to participate in her physical therapy, and drowns her sorrows in endless TV watching and drinking. Moving back to her Louisiana Bayou hometown, Mary-Alice goes through a succession of caretakers ranging from Russian authoritarians to biker chicks. The last hope for this self-proclaimed "bitch on wheels" is the quiet Chantelle (Alfre Woodard), who needs the job badly enough that she can't quit, but refuses to indulge Mary-Alice's tantrums. Both women, it turns out, are trying to start over in life, grappling with new identities and responsibilities, and their isolated situation, as well as the subtle magic of the bayou, soon begins to change them.

Never maudlin, and never opting for big dramatic climaxes, PASSION FISH succeeds most of the time, thanks to a typically deft Sayles screenplay and two fine, understated performances from McDonnell and Woodard. For viewers willing to accomodate themselves to its rhythms, which are as unhurried as its bayou setting, Sayles has cooked up an affecting story, one that takes the audience on a slow ride into the swampland with two of its denizens, trying to redefine themselves in the second act of their lives.

PASSION OF ANNA, THE   DVD
(EN PASSION)
1969 100m c   Drama   ★★★
Cinematograph   (Sweden)   R

Liv Ullmann *(Anna Fromm)*, Bibi Andersson *(Eva Vergerus)*, Max von Sydow *(Andreas Winkelman)*, Erland Josephson *(Elis*

Vergerus), Erik Hell *(Johan Andersson)*, Sigge Furst *(Verner)*, Svea Holst *(Verner's Wife)*, Annika Kronberg *(Katarina)*, Hjordis Pettersson *(Johan's Sister)*, Lars-Owe Carlberg

d, Ingmar Bergman; w, Ingmar Bergman; ph, Sven Nykvist (Eastmancolor); ed, Siv Kanalv; prod d, P.A. Lundgren; fx, Ulf Nordholm; cos, Mago

---

Max von Sydow, an ex-convict who lives alone in an island farmhouse, is visited one day by the crippled Ullmann, who requests to use the phone. Ullmann soon leaves, but forgets to take her purse with her. Von Sydow looks through it, finds her name, address, and a letter from her husband which discusses their unhappy marriage. He returns the purse and is introduced to Josephson and Andersson, friends of Ullmann's. Eventually Ullmann moves into von Sydow's farmhouse. Tensions between the two begin to rise, partially due to reports of a crazed murderer who is on the loose. In a fit of anger, von Sydow goes after Ullmann with an ax. Later, the *real* maniac strikes at von Sydow's farm, setting his barn on fire. Ullmann rescues von Sydow from the scene of the blaze, and drives frantically down the road. Von Sydow accuses Ullmann of trying to kill him, perhaps as she killed her husband and son years earlier in the auto accident that left her crippled. Hailed by many as a masterpiece, THE PASSION OF ANNA (only Bergman's second film in color) employs some interesting techniques, such as interviews with each of the four main actors and also sheds some light on many of the baroque mannerisms and symbols that have come to be associated with Bergman. It still contains, however, that element of coldness which has turned many viewers against Bergman. Filmed on the island of Faro, a one-time home for Bergman.

PASSION OF THE CHRIST, THE   *DVD*
2004   127m   c   Religious/Drama   ★★★
Icon Productions   (U.S.)   R

James Caviezel *(Jesus)*, Maia Morgenstern *(Mary)*, Monica Bellucci *(Mary Magdalene)*, Mattia Sbragia *(Caiphas, the High Priest)*, Hristo Naumov Shopov *(Pontius Pilate)*, Claudia Gerini *(Claudia Procles, Pilate's Wife)*, Luca Lionello *(Judas Iscariot)*, Sergio Rubini *(Dismas)*, Toni Bertorelli *(Annas)*, Roberto Bestazzoni *(Malchus)*

p, Bruce Davey, Mel Gibson, Stephen McEveety; d, Mel Gibson; w, Benedict Fitzgerald, Mel Gibson; ph, Caleb Deschanel; ed, John Wright; m, John Debney; prod d, Francesco Frigeri; fx, Ted Rae, Daniel Acon, Renato Agostini, Marcus Andexler; cos, Maurizio Millenotti

---

Vivid and controversial, Mel Gibson's gore-spattered, self-financed celebration of the suffering and death of Jesus (James Caviezel) is inseparable from the bitter debate it engendered, rooted in issues of scriptural fidelity, explicit violence, and anti-Semitic stereotypes. A product of both its time and producer/director/co-writer Gibson's particular beliefs—conservative Catholic—this chronicle of Jesus' last 12 hours is deeply invested in the same spectacle of redemptive agony that drives the excruciating conclusion of BRAVEHEART.

It begins with Jesus praying in the fog-shrouded garden of Gethsemane that God spare him the martyr's death to which he was born while steeling himself for its brutal rigors. As a spookily androgynous Satan (Rosalinda Celentano) whispers diabolical blandishments, traitorous disciple Judas Iscariot (Luca Lionello) betrays Jesus to the Jewish religious authorities, who revile his teachings as blasphemous. Jesus rejects Satan, surrenders dutifully to the temple guards, and the relentless march to Golgotha begins, with stops at the austere chambers of Roman governor Pilate (Hristo Naumov Shopov), and ultimately, the trial by rabble that condemns Jesus.

Unlike most previous films about Jesus, Gibson's narrowly focused account is unconcerned with catering to the casually curious—the dialogue is in Latin and Aramaic—or witnessing to the unenlightened. It preaches squarely to the converted, assuming its target audience is familiar with both the teachings and dramatis personae of the New Testament. An efficient if unsubtle director, Gibson's vision of ancient Judea is a whirl of grotesques—Jewish and Roman—whose spiritual bankruptcy is written on their twisted faces; make no mistake, they're all in desperate need of salvation. He largely absolves Pilate, whom history remembers as a brutal tyrant, and comes down hard on the Jewish authorities with a spiritual fiefdom to preserve. Caviezel may have been cast for his martyr's mien, but it's the face of Maia Morgenstern's stoic, grief-stricken Mary that will linger long after the bloodbath has run its course.

PASSPORT TO PIMLICO   *DVD*
1949   84m   bw   Comedy   ★★★
Ealing/Eagle-Lion   (U.K.)

Stanley Holloway *(Arthur Pemberton)*, Hermione Baddeley *(Eddie Randall)*, Margaret Rutherford *(Prof. Hatton-Jones)*, Paul Dupuis *(Duke of Burgundy)*, Basil Radford *(Gregg)*, Naunton Wayne *(Straker)*, Jane Hylton *(Molly)*, Raymond Huntley *(Mr. Wix)*, Betty Warren *(Connie Pemberton)*, Barbara Murray *(Shirley Pemberton)*

p, Michael Balcon; d, Henry Cornelius; w, T.E.B. Clarke; ph, Lionel Barnes, Cecil Cooney; ed, Michael Truman; m, Georges Auric; art d, Roy Oxley; cos, Anthony Mendleson

---

AAN Best Story and Screenplay: T.E.B. Clarke

A light British comedy about an unexploded bomb that suddenly goes off and unearths documents stating that part of London belongs to Burgundy, France. Halloway becomes the head of the new government; new borders are drawn and new customs barriers are put into effect. A fresh comedy with some well-aimed satirical arrows from producer Balcon's Ealing Studios, famous for their sophisticated, irreverent comedies.

PAT AND MIKE   *DVD*
1952   95m   bw   Comedy/Romance   ★★★★½
MGM   (U.S.)

Spencer Tracy *(Mike Conovan)*, Katharine Hepburn *(Pat Pemberton)*, Aldo Ray *(Davie Hucko)*, William Ching *(Collier Weld)*, Sammy White *(Barney Grau)*, George Mathews *(Spec Cauley)*, Loring Smith *(Mr. Beminger)*, Phyllis Povah *(Mrs. Beminger)*, Charles Bronson, billed as Charles Buchinsky *(Hank Tasling)*, Frank Richards *(Sam Garsell)*

p, Lawrence Weingarten; d, George Cukor; w, Ruth Gordon, Garson Kanin; ph, William Daniels; ed, George Boemler; m, David Raksin; art d, Cedric Gibbons, Urie McCleary; fx, Warren Newcombe; cos, Orry-Kelly

---

AAN Best Story and Screenplay: Ruth Gordon, Garson Kanin

After playing a sports-hating character 10 years earlier in WOMAN OF THE YEAR, Katharine Hepburn essays the role of an all-around athlete not unlike the great Babe Didrikson Zaharias (who plays herself here) in this marvelous romantic comedy, which paired her again with real-life companion Spencer Tracy. Pat (Hepburn), a perky PE instructor at a southern California college and gifted athlete, falls apart whenever her professor fiance, Collier (William Ching), comes to watch her compete. Mike (Tracy), a somewhat shady sports promoter, recognizes her talent and persuades her to turn pro. Despite his unsuccessful attempt to get her to throw a match, she begins winning golf and tennis tournaments under his guidance, and gradually they fall for each other. What did you expect? Still, the point isn't what happens, but how it happens, and under the direction of George Cukor—working from the script by Garson Kanin and Ruth Gordon—Tracy and Hepburn turn in unforgettable performances. Shot mostly at the Riviera Country Club in Pacific Palisades, PAT AND MIKE gave Hepburn an opportunity to display her authentic athletic ability amidst a cast that included pro golfers Helen Dettweiler and Betty Hicks, as well as tennis professionals Don Budge and Pancho Gonzales. Chuck Connors, on loan from his job as the Triple A Los Angeles Angels's first sacker, makes his film debut as a police captain. Oscar nominated for Best Screenplay.

PAT GARRETT AND BILLY THE KID

1973 106m c Western ★★★½
Gordon Carroll/Sam Peckinpah (U.S.) R

James Coburn *(Pat Garrett)*, Kris Kristofferson *(Billy the Kid)*, Bob Dylan *(Alias)*, Jason Robards Jr. *(Gov. Lew Wallace)*, Richard Jaeckel *(Sheriff Kip McKinney)*, Katy Jurado *(Mrs. Baker)*, Slim Pickens *(Sheriff Baker)*, Chill Wills *(Lemuel)*, John Beck *(Poe)*, Rita Coolidge *(Maria)*

p, Gordon Carroll; d, Sam Peckinpah; w, Rudy Wurlitzer; ph, John Coquillon (Panavision, Metrocolor); ed, Roger Spottiswoode, Garth Craven, Robert Wolfe, Richard Halsey, David Berlatsky, Tony De Zarraga; m, Bob Dylan; art d, Ted Haworth; fx, Augie Lohman

After director Sam Peckinpah handed in his final cut of PAT GARRETT AND BILLY THE KID, which he considered his finest film, the hierarchy at MGM saw fit to radically reedit it. The approximately 15 minutes cut from the film so drastically altered Peckinpah's structure and pacing that the incensed director tried to get his name removed from the credits. A restored version of Peckinpah's original film was given a very limited rerelease in 1990, but the initial-release version remains the one that most viewers will be able to see and it is a very choppy affair.

James Coburn is Pat Garrett; Kris Kristofferson is Billy the Kid. Feeling that the time has come for him to settle down, aging desperado Garrett switches sides of the law and puts on a badge; he is assigned to hunt down his old friend Billy. Apprehended and sentenced to hang, Billy shoots his way out of jail and hits the trail, accompanied by a former printer, Alias (Bob Dylan, who contributed the film's score). Back in New Mexico, Billy puts a gang together. Meanwhile, Garrett hires Alamosa Bill (Jack Elam), another former criminal, to help him, and the territorial governor, Lew Wallace (Jason Robards), engages Poe (John Beck) to bring Billy to justice. The manhunt begins.

Among the important scenes cut from the initial release of film was an epilogue that reveals Garrett to have been killed by the same man who ordered the outlaw-turned-lawman to shoot Billy. A prologue was also cut, as were a scene between Garrett and his wife, and the roles of Barry Sullivan, Elisha Cook, Jr., and Dub Taylor. Indeed, at those moments when the film begins to hit its stride, awkward edits undermine its development. Nevertheless the film is visually stunning, and Peckinpah makes great use of his Durango, Mexico, locations. He and screenwriter Rudy Wurlitzer (TWO-LANE BLACKTOP; WALKER) also make cameo appearances.

PATHER PANCHALI

1955 112m bw Drama DVD
West Bengal Government (India) ★★★★★

Kanu Banerjee *(Harihar the Father)*, Karuna Banerjee *(Sarbajaya the Mother)*, Subir Banerjee *(Apu)*, Runki Banerjee *(Durga as a child)*, Uma Das Gupta *(Durga as a young girl)*, Chunibala Devi *(Indirthakrun the Old Aunt)*, Reba Devi *(Mrs. Mookerjee)*, Rama

Gangopadhaya *(Ranu Mookerjee)*, Tulshi Chakraborty *(Schoolmaster)*, Harimoran Nag *(Doctor)*

p, Satyajit Ray; d, Satyajit Ray; w, Satyajit Ray (based on the novel by Bibhutibhusan Bandopadhaya); ph, Subrata Mitra; ed, Dulal Dutta; m, Ravi Shankar; art d, Banshi Chandragupta

Satyajit Ray's debut film, and the first installment in his "Apu Trilogy," quietly and intently studies a family living in the grip of poverty in a Bengal village. This was the first film of a great body of work characterized by visual beauty, humor, and emotional generosity, and announced the arrival of a major new director on the world scene, as well as the debut of Indian cinema in the West.

The father, a struggling writer, sets off to seek his fortune in the city, leaving his wife to take care of the children and an elderly aunt. Mere survival is a struggle for the poor family and the mother worries about how much the old lady eats. What follows is a series of perfectly ordinary events with a cumulative emotional power which may make some western viewers forever question the way Hollywood tells our stories. It's a powerful, unforgettable experience to watch characters whose lives are so different from our own, but whose concerns are ultimately universal. The remaining two films of the trilogy, APARAJITO and THE WORLD OF APU, follow the son, Apu (here played by Subir Banerjee), into manhood and fatherhood.

Commissioned in 1945 to illustrate a children's version of the popular novel *Pather Panchali*, Ray became interested in bringing the novel to the screen, even though he had no previous film experience (nor did most of his crew). The production began sporadically on weekends, and was often interrupted by cash shortages before the Bengal government helped finish the picture. Like all Ray's best films, PATHER PANCHALI is influenced by the work of Jean Renoir (Ray visited the set of THE RIVER during its production in India) and of the Italian neorealists.

PATHS OF GLORY

1957 86m bw War DVD
Bryna (U.S.) ★★★★★

Kirk Douglas *(Col. Dax)*, Ralph Meeker *(Cpl. Paris)*, Adolphe Menjou *(Gen. Broulard)*, George Macready *(Gen. Mireau)*, Wayne Morris *(Lt. Roget)*, Richard Anderson *(Maj. Saint-Auban)*, Joseph Turkel *(Pvt. Arnoud)*, Timothy Carey *(Pvt. Ferol)*, Peter Capell *(Col. Judge)*, Susanne Christian *(The German Girl)*

p, James B. Harris; d, Stanley Kubrick; w, Stanley Kubrick, Calder Willingham, Jim Thompson (based on the novel by Humphrey Cobb); ph, Georg Krause; ed, Eva Kroll; m, Gerald Fried; art d, Ludwig Reiber

Stanley Kubrick's first great film established the epic style that has served him so well since. This is a harrowing and still very effective antiwar film that ranks with Lewis Milestone's epic ALL QUIET ON THE WESTERN FRONT in its power. The split between officers and men has never been so sharply delineated. The film was banned in France when it first appeared for eighteen years because of its anti-militarist stance.

Col. Dax (Kirk Douglas) is the commander of the battle-decimated 701st Infantry Regiment of the French Army during WWI, dug in along the Western Front in a brutally stalemated war. It is 1916, and the Allies have been struggling to overcome an equally determined German war machine for two years. Dax's hope that his regiment will be relieved from front-line duty is destroyed when corps commander Gen. Broulard (Adolphe Menjou) orders Gen. Mireau (George Macready), the divisional general in charge, to make an all-out attack against an impregnable German position nicknamed "the

Ant Hill." The battle scenes showing the suicidal attack on the Ant Hill are devastating and brutally authentic, the barrage through which Dax leads his men (Kubrick's camera moving inexorably through the carnage) is a hurricane of death. Three soldiers are selected to be court-martialed unjustly to serve as scapegoats for the military humiliation. Dax is the officer charged with their defense but the powers-that-be confound his efforts.

This is a director's film: Kubrick profiles naked power and the effects thereof with a visual excitement seldom seen on the screen; his attitude toward the actions he portrays is always felt. One particularly striking and effective strategy is the tendency to utilize mesmerizing but inhuman tracking shots for the trenches and battlegrounds while using elegant circling camera movements for the comfortable surroundings of the officers' chateau.

Though its condemnation of war is overwhelming, PATHS OF GLORY offers more optimism than is usual for the pessimistic Kubrick. The film may be read as a testament to human courage, compassion, and spirit that battles valiantly for survival despite the efforts of tyrants to vanquish principle and humanity.

PATRIOT GAMES

1992 113m c Thriller/Action ★★½

Neufeld/Rehme Productions/Paramount (U.S.) R

Harrison Ford (*Jack Ryan*), Anne Archer (*Dr. Cathy Ryan*), Patrick Bergin (*Kevin O'Donnell*), Sean Bean (*Sean Miller*), Thora Birch (*Sally Ryan*), James Fox (*Lord Holmes*), Samuel L. Jackson (*Robby Jackson*), Polly Walker (*Annette*), James Earl Jones (*Admiral James Greer*), Richard Harris (*Paddy O'Neil*)

p, Mace Neufeld, Robert Rehme; d, Phillip Noyce; w, W. Peter Iliff, Donald Stewart (from the novel by Tom Clancy); ph, Donald McAlpine; ed, Neil Travis, William Hoy; m, James Horner; prod d, Joseph Nemec III; art d, Joseph P. Lucky; cos, Norma Moriceau

---

PATRIOT GAMES is a stolid, reactionary thriller in which the good old nuclear family becomes the last line of defense against that favorite action-movie staple, a group of international terrorists. In this wooden adaptation of Tom Clancy's best-seller, Harrison Ford plays Jack Ryan, an ex-C.I.A. analyst who single-handedly foils an I.R.A. kidnap attempt while on vacation in London. Ryan kills one of the terrorists, which makes the young man's elder brother, Sean Miller (Sean Bean), *really* mad—so mad, he spends the rest of the movie either scowling moodily into the distance, or trying to do away with Ryan and his family. Just in case there were any doubt about how bad the bad guys are, it's explained to us that Miller and his colleagues are not part of the regular I.R.A., but of an "ultraviolent" fringe group. The good guys, on the other hand, are a picture-perfect WASP family portrayed with all the depth and sincerity of an L.L. Bean catalog. Ryan is a reluctant hero who, when asked why he intervened in the kidnap attempt, looks brave and earnest and says, "I just couldn't stand by and watch those people get killed." His devoted wife Cathy (Anne Archer) is a brilliant eye surgeon who sails blithely into the operating room, performs a minor medical miracle, and then skips out in time to pick up her precocious daughter from school.

The action scenes in PATRIOT GAMES are handled efficiently, if unremarkably, by director Phillip Noyce (DEAD CALM), and a little extra color is provided by some good supporting players, particularly James Fox and Samuel L. Jackson. Our favorite parts, though, were the moments of unintentional humor, mostly courtesy of Ms. Archer. Her insufferably goody-goody performance makes you wish Glenn Close would show up brandishing a kitchen knife.

PATRIOT, THE

2000 158m c Historical/War/Drama ★★½

Mutual Film/Centropolis/Columbia Pictures R
(U.S.)

Mel Gibson (*Benjamin Martin*), Heath Ledger (*Gabriel Martin*), Joely Richardson (*Charlotte Selton*), Jason Isaacs (*Col. William Tavington*), Chris Cooper (*Col. Harry Burwell*), Tcheky Karyo (*Jean Villeneuve*), Rene Auberjonois (*Rev. Oliver*), Lisa Brenner (*Anne Howard*), Tom Wilkinson (*Gen. Cornwallis*), Donal Logue (*Dan Scott*)

p, Dean Devlin, Mark Gordon, Gary Levinsohn; d, Roland Emmerich; w, Robert Rodat; ph, Caleb Deschanel; ed, David Brenner; m, John Williams; prod d, Kirk M. Petruccelli; art d, Barry Chusid; fx, Stuart Robertson, Glenn R. Karpf, Centropolis, Thomas Dadras, Conny Fauser, Magicmove/Magicon Miniature FX, Joachim Gruninger; cos, Deborah L. Scott

---

AAN Best Cinematography: Caleb Deschanel; *AAN Best Sound:* Kevin O'Connell, Greg P. Russell, Lee Orloff; *AAN Best Original Score:* John Williams

---

You didn't read this in your history book, but if Mel Gibson hadn't taught guerilla warfare to the rebellious colonials, there might not be an American republic. Star power like Gibson's isn't easily subsumed into character, and that you never lose sight of the fact that you're watching a huge star swanning around in old-fashioned clothes seriously undermines this epic's powerful historical underpinnings.

The year is 1776. Revolution is in the air, and all Benjamin Martin (Gibson)—South Carolina landowner, respected veteran, and father of seven motherless children—wants is to keep his head and those of his teenage sons down. Martin is haunted by his memories of the brutal French and Indian War, and what he learned about war's ability to unleash the beast within. But his idealistic son Gabriel (Heath Ledger) enlists in the Continental Army, and soon Martin is back on the field, reluctantly commanding a ragtag militia with more heart than English General Cornwallis's (Tom Wilkinson) entire army. Outmanned and outgunned, the rebels use surprise, misdirection, and the people's support to undermine the redcoats. But can they withstand sadistic Colonel Tavington's (Jason Isaacs) bloody reprisals against their families?

Though a step up, prestige-wise, from GODZILLA and INDEPENDENCE DAY, this project in no way exploits director Roland Emmerich's strengths. His pulp sensibility made INDEPENDENCE DAY a cotton-candy blast, but reduces what may well have been a complex and thoughtful screenplay by SAVING PRIVATE RYAN's Robert Rodat into a shameless knockoff of UNFORGIVEN. The film is undeniably handsome, but no cliché is left unturned, right down to the spray of toy soldiers falling from a dead child's hand.

PATTERNS

1956 83m bw Drama ★★★★

UA (U.S.)

Van Heflin (*Fred Staples*), Everett Sloane (*Walter Ramsey*), Ed Begley (*William Briggs*), Beatrice Straight (*Nancy Staples*), Elizabeth Wilson (*Marge Fleming*), Joanna Roos (*Miss Lanier*), Eleni Kiamos (*Sylvia Trammel*), Shirley Standlee (*Miss Hill*), Ronnie Welsh Jr. (*Paul Briggs*), Sally Gracie (*Ann*)

p, Michael Myerberg; d, Fielder Cook; w, Rod Serling (based on his television play); ph, Boris Kaufman; ed, David Kummins, Carl Lerner; art d, Richard Sylbert; cos, Mary Merrill

---

There wasn't one note of music in PATTERNS, and the absence wasn't felt; Serling's words had a music of their own. It began as a television play for the "Kraft Theatre" and, like MARTY and other TV plays, it was turned into a film. The limited use of film technique (much of the movie takes place in the offices of a huge conglomerate and it is basically an interior story) does not work against this film since the characters are so fascinating and the performances are universally superior. Heflin is brought in from Ohio to serve at a company's New York office. The boss of all bosses is Sloane, a ruthless company man who runs the firm like a tyrant. Begley is an executive who has seen better days and is being eased out by Sloane, who intends Heflin to be Begley's replacement. There is no room in Sloane's mind for old loyalties, and the company's interests must be above all feelings. Heflin truly likes Begley, who is always excusing Sloane's behavior and shrugging off the boss's insults. There are a few cutaways as Heflin discusses matters with his wife, Straight, but most of the action is strictly in the "executive suite," which was the name of a movie not unlike this one. Anyone who has ever worked in a large company will recognize the people and the situations depicted in the screenplay, but some of the Machiavellian tactics may be lost on others. Brilliantly directed by another TV veteran, Cook, this picture did not garner any awards and didn't do much business, which was a shame. Sloane's work as the corporation chief is sensational, a portrait of a driven man who rules his roost like an emperor. Begley, who came out of radio, where he appeared in more than 10,000 programs, was one of the most versatile actors in show business and proved so when he played the William Jennings Bryan role in Broadway's "Inherit the Wind" for more than 700 performances, then turned around and did Clarence Darrow after Paul Muni left the show.

PATTON
1970 170m c War/Biography ★★★★½ 🖭
Fox (U.S.) PG

George C. Scott *(Gen. George S. Patton Jr.)*, Karl Malden *(Gen. Omar N. Bradley)*, Michael Bates *(Field Marshal Sir Bernard Law Montgomery)*, Edward Binns *(Maj. Gen. Walter Bedell Smith)*, Lawrence Dobkin *(Col. Gaston Bell)*, John Doucette *(Maj. Gen. Lucian K. Truscott)*, James Edwards *(Sgt. William George Meeks)*, Frank Latimore *(Lt. Col. Henry Davenport)*, Richard Munch *(Col. Gen. Alfred Jodl)*, Morgan Paull *(Capt. Richard N. Jenson)*

p, Frank McCarthy, Frank Caffey; d, Franklin J. Schaffner; w, Francis Ford Coppola, Edmund H. North (based on the books *Patton: Ordeal and Triumph* by Ladislas Farago and *A Soldier's Story* by Gen. Omar N. Bradley); ph, Fred Koenekamp (Dimension 150, CinemaScope, Deluxe Color); ed, Hugh S. Fowler; m, Jerry Goldsmith; art d, Urie McCleary, Gil Parrondo; fx, L.B. Abbott, Art Cruickshank

AA Best Picture; AA Best Actor: George C. Scott; *AA Best Director:* Franklin J. Schaffner; *AA Best Original Story and Screenplay:* Francis Ford Coppola, Edmund H. North; *AAN Best Cinematography:* Fred Koenekamp; *AA Best Film Editing:* Hugh S. Fowler; *AAN Best Original Score:* Jerry Goldsmith; *AA Best Art Direction-Set Decoration:* Urie McCleary, Gil Parrondo, Antonio Mateos, Pierre-Louis Thevenet; *AA Best Sound:* Douglas Williams, Don Bassman; *AAN Best Special Visual Effects:* Alex Weldon

What PATHS OF GLORY attempted to show about the relationships between officers and men of the first World War, PATTON in part attempts to do for the second. Patton, of course, is best remembered as the general who slapped a soldier. But George C. Scott, under the direction of Franklin Schaffner, creates a much more colorful and ambiguous portrait. This WWII spectacle is immense but Scott's virtuoso performance looms larger than any of its battles. His characterization can appeal to both hawks and doves; it can appreciated either as a critique or a paean. He's insensitive to his men's plight on some occasions, gentle as a loving father on others. Patton's eccentricity may very well have been an important ingredient of victory. PATTON is a war movie of unusual depth and a landmark in screen biographies.

Beginning with a classic six-minute speech by Patton about the fighting spirit of Americans, the film traces the legendary WWII exploits of "Old Blood and Guts" from his defeat of Rommel's *Afrika Korps* at El Guettar to the invasion of Sicily, during which he disobeys orders and beats rival Field Marshal Montgomery (Michael Bates) to Messina. We also see his loss of command for slapping a battle-fatigued soldier because he has been hospitalized but has no wounds. Then, after sitting out D-Day as a decoy, Patton is given command of the 3rd Army, winning one mighty battle after another with his armored troops and eventually speeding to the rescue of the encircled 101st Airborne Division at Bastogne, ending Hitler's last great counteroffensive in the Battle of the Bulge. Following the war, Patton is sent into involuntary retirement after his highly vocal criticism of the Soviet Union, and the film ends with his farewell to his faithful staff.

Scott won a richly deserved Academy Award (which he refused) for his performance. Sturdy support is provided by Karl Malden as Gen. Omar Bradley, Edward Binns as Maj. Gen. Walter Bedell Smith, John Doucette as Maj. Gen. Lucian K. Truscott, and Bates as Montgomery. Franklin J. Schaffner's direction is majestic particularly in his masterful handling of complex battle scenes; shot in 70-millimeter, Dimension 150, these broad, impersonal spectacles have a macabre beauty that gives the viewer a serene God's-eye-view of modern warfare. Fox hoped to duplicate the success of its black-and-white blockbuster, THE LONGEST DAY, by spending a fortune on this spectacular film, which was shot on location in England, Spain, Morocco, and Greece.

PAULIE
1998 105m c Children's/Comedy/Fantasy ★★★½ 🖭
Mutual Film Company/DreamWorks SKG PG
(U.S.)

Gena Rowlands *(Ivy)*, Tony Shalhoub *(Misha)*, Cheech Marin *(Ignacio)*, Bruce Davison *(Dr. Reingold)*, Trini Alvarado *(Adult Marie)*, Jay Mohr *(Voice of Paulie/Benny)*, Buddy Hackett *(Artie)*, Hallie Kate Eisenberg *(Marie)*, Matt Craven *(Warren Alweather)*, Tia Texada *(Ruby/Voice of Lupe)*

p, Mark Gordon, Gary Levinsohn, Allison Lyon Segan; d, John Roberts; w, Laurie Craig; ph, Tony Pierce-Roberts; ed, Bruce Cannon; m, John Debney; prod d, Dennis Washington; art d, Tom Taylor; fx, David Kelsey, Michael "Tony" Meagher, Charles Linehan, Stan Winston; cos, Mary Zophres

Though not quite as perfectly pitched as BABE, to which comparisons are inevitable, this superior children's movie about a vocally gifted parrot named Paulie (voice of Jay Mohr) aims for the same emotional richness.

The love of Paulie's life is a sweetly grave little girl named Marie (Hallie Kate Eisenberg), whose parents give Pauie away because they think Marie's attachment to her pet is stifling her development. But Paulie isn't so easily cast off: he devotes himself to finding Marie, even after her family moves across the U.S., and along the way falls in with a variety of human companions. There's pawnshop owner Artie (Buddy Hackett), and aging widow Ivy (Gena Rowlands), who drives Paulie halfway to California in a rattletrap Winnebago before she's sidelined by failing sight. There's Ignacio (Cheech Marin), who owns a taco stand and a small flock of trained parrots, and there's Benny (Jay Mohr), a petty thief whose criminal exploits land Paulie where we first meet him: in a cage.

Paulie's adventures, some of them very amusing, are driven by his loyalty to Marie, and while the movie's tone is generally upbeat, it doesn't shy away from the sadness that's an inevitable part of life. The main draw is, of course, chattering Paulie, and the mix of real birds and special effects is seamlessly convincing. But the above-average human cast keeps the special-effects wizardry in the background, where it belongs. The story is rooted in real feelings and relationships, and parents will find as much to enjoy as children.

PAULINE AT THE BEACH   *DVD*
(PAULINE A LA PLAGE)
1983 94m c Drama/Comedy   ★★★½
Losange/Ariane (France)   R

Amanda Langlet *(Pauline)*, Arielle Dombasle *(Marion)*, Pascal Greggory *(Pierre)*, Feodor Atkine *(Henry)*, Simon de la Brosse *(Sylvain)*, Rosette *(Louisette)*

p, Margaret Menegoz; d, Eric Rohmer; w, Eric Rohmer; ph, Nestor Almendros; ed, Cecile Decugis; m, Jean-Louis Valero

For the third in Eric Rohmer's series of "Comedies and Proverbs," the director shifts from Paris to the coast of Normandy. Pauline (Amanda Langlet) is a teenager on vacation with her older, recently divorced cousin, Marion (Arielle Dombasle). They become involved with three men during a beachside vacation. Marion carries on with a writer, Henry (Feodor Atkine), and tries to ignore the advances of an old friend, Pierre (Pascal Greggory), while Pauline meets a boy her own age, Sylvain (Simon De La Brosse), and has her first sexual experiences. This film is close in spirit to the work of Jean Renoir. Rohmer confines much of it to the beach and a vacation home, turning his directorial attention to the interplay among the five main characters as they move in and out of rooms, spied through windows and doors and forced to become masters of romantic deception. Instead of characteristically following one determined individual, Rohmer intertwines his characters and lets their paths overlap. Pauline, though singled out in the title, tends to function more as an observer caught in the whirlwind of love and romance. Rohmer was named Best Director at the Berlin Film Festival for PAULINE.

PAWNBROKER, THE   *DVD*
1965 114m bw Drama/War   ★★★★
Landau/Unger/Pawnbroker (U.S.)

Rod Steiger *(Sol Nazerman)*, Geraldine Fitzgerald *(Marilyn Birchfield)*, Brock Peters *(Rodriguez)*, Jaime Sanchez *(Jesus Ortiz)*, Thelma Oliver *(Ortiz's Girl)*, Marketa Kimbrel *(Tessie)*, Baruch Lumet *(Mendel)*, Juano Hernandez *(Mr. Smith)*, Linda Geiser *(Ruth Nazerman)*, Nancy R. Pollock *(Bertha)*

p, Roger Lewis, Philip Langner; d, Sidney Lumet; w, David Friedkin, Morton Fine (based on the novel by Edward Lewis Wallant); ph, Boris Kaufman; ed, Ralph Rosenblum; m, Quincy Jones; art d, Richard Sylbert; cos, Anna Hill Johnstone

AAN Best Actor: Rod Steiger

Although there have been numerous films about the post-Vietnam era and the war's psychological aftereffects on the soldier returning home, very few pictures have dealt with the similar predicament of those who lived through WWII (or WWI, for that matter). THE PAWNBROKER, one of the seminal American films of the 1960s, focuses on Sol Nazerman (Rod Steiger), a middle-aged concentration camp survivor who lost his entire family to the Nazis and now runs a pawnshop in Harlem. That he remained alive is a source of bewilderment and pain. He lost faith in God and man; he is emotionless and totally removed from the world that surrounds his run-down shop. Shop assistant Jesus Ortiz (Jaime Sanchez) and social worker Marilyn Birchfield (Geraldine Fitzgerald) try to get through Sol's icy exterior, but to no avail.

Instead, Sol becomes increasingly cruel and offensive. Meanwhile, he conducts an affair with Tessie (Marketa Kimbrell), a fellow camp survivor whose husband was a victim of Nazi atrocities.

Directed by Sidney Lumet in a gritty, raw style that was fashionable at the time, THE PAWNBROKER is memorable today for its innovative use of flashbacks—in this case quick cuts lasting only a fraction of a second—to represent the disturbing, unrelenting flashes of Sol's memory. Also unforgettable is Steiger's towering performance as the volatile survivor, a powder keg of hateful remembrances. The soundtrack was composed by Quincy Jones.

PEARL HARBOR   *DVD*
2001 170m c War/Action/Drama   ★★½
Jerry Bruckheimer Films/Touchstone Pictures   PG-13
(U.S.)

Ben Affleck *(Rafe McCawley)*, Josh Hartnett *(Danny Walker)*, Kate Beckinsale *(Evelyn Johnson)*, Cuba Gooding Jr. *(Doris "Dorie" Miller)*, Alec Baldwin *(Colonel Jimmy Doolittle)*, William Lee Scott *(Billy)*, Greg Zola *(Anthony R. Fusco)*, Ewen Bremner *(Red)*, James King *(Betty)*, Catherine Kellner *(Barbara)*

p, Michael Bay, Jerry Bruckheimer; d, Michael Bay; w, Randall Wallace; ph, John Schwartzman; ed, Roger Barton, Mark Goldblatt, Chris Lebenzon, Steven Rosenblum; m, Hans Zimmer; prod d, Nigel Phelps; art d, Jon Billington, William Ladd Skinner; fx, Eric Brevig, John Frazier, Ed Hirsh, Ben Snow; cos, Michael Kaplan

AA Best Sound Editing: George Watters II, Christopher Boyes; *AAN Best Original Song:* "There You'll Be"; Diane Warren; *AAN Best Visual Effects:* Eric Brevig, John Frazier, Ed Hirsh, Ben Snow

Michael Bay's epic take on the bombing of Pearl Harbor is thirty-five minutes of pure spectacle bracketed by 90 minutes of wartime-romance cliches and a cynical attempt to get some rah-rah into a climax that's otherwise one hell of a downer. The film ends not with the immediate aftermath of the attack, but with the first U.S. retaliatory strike against Japan.

Tennessee, 1923. Country lads Danny and Rafe dream of flying and swear eternal friendship. Eighteen years later, Rafe (Ben Affleck) has matured into an effortless charmer and earned his wings with the U.S. Army Air Corps. But while Europe is already at war, the U.S. remains neutral, so Rafe volunteers for England's Eagle Squadron. He leaves behind Evelyn (Kate Beckinsale), the Navy nurse he loves, and fellow pilot Danny (Josh Hartnett), both of whom are shipped off to cushy berths in Hawaii. Circumstances conspire to spawn a classic romantic triangle in which no one's the bad guy, played out against the bloody events of December 7, 1941. This is Hollywood history at its glossiest, and while it's visually engaging, Rafe, Danny, and Evelyn are never more than one-dimensional—and they're the fleshed-out characters. Clearly, neither screenwriter Randall Wallace nor director Michael Bay ever met a cliché he didn't embrace. The film abounds with green recruits who remind seasoned officers of themselves as youngsters, dying men asking if they're going to make it, and wee dogs escaping what appears to be certain death. Like the epic TORA! TORA! TORA! (1970), it works up slowly to the attack, but it's less concerned with the minutia of military and diplomatic machinations and mistakes than the romantic travails of attractive young people whose petty problems truly don't amount to a hill of beans.

PEDESTRIAN, THE
(DER FUSSGANGER)
1974 97m c Drama/War ★★★½
Cinerama (West Germany) PG

Gustav Rudolf Sellner *(Heinz Alfred Giese)*, Ruth Hausmeister *(Inge Maria Giese)*, Maximilian Schell *(Andreas Giese)*, Manuel Sellner *(Hubert Giese)*, Elsa Wagner *(Elsa Giese)*, Dagmar Hirtz *(Elke Giese)*, Michael Weinert *(Michael Giese)*, Peter Hall *(Rudolf Hartmann)*, Alexander May *(Alexander Markowitz)*, Christian Kohlund *(Erwin Gotz)*

p, Maximilian Schell, Zev Braun; d, Maximilian Schell; w, Maximilian Schell; ph, Wolfgang Treu, Klaus Koenig (Eastmancolor); ed, Dagmar Hirtz; m, Manos Hadjidakis

AAN Best Foreign Language Film

A powerful and revealing film about death, guilt, and Germany's involvement in wartime atrocities, THE PEDESTRIAN focuses on an aging industrialist, Heinz Alfred Giese (Gustav Rudolf Sellner), who prefers not to remember the events of WWII. In fact, he prefers to be involved with life as little as possible. Since the death of his son Andreas (Maximilian Schell) in an auto accident in which Giese was driving (resulting in the loss of his license, hence the title), his whole life has centered around his grandson, Hubert (Manuel Sellner). Although Giese would rather forget his past, Alexander Markowitz (Alexander May), the senior editor of a newspaper, begins a probe into Giese's involvement in the massacre of a Greek village. With the help of two witnesses—a survivor of the attack (Fani Fotinou) and a former German soldier (Walter von Varndal)—Markowitz discovers that Giese was involved in the massacre and could have prevented it. When the story is printed, Giese becomes the target of moral outrage and violence. This strong indictment of his generation's complacency is especially damning because its villain is not a monster but a well-respected businessman and a loving grandfather. Produced, directed, and written by Maximilian Schell, THE PEDESTRIAN received a Golden Globe award for Best Film and an Oscar nomination for Best Foreign Film.

PEE-WEE'S BIG ADVENTURE 📀
1985 90m c Comedy ★★★½
Aspen/Shapiro (U.S.) PG

Pee-wee Herman *(Himself)*, Elizabeth Daily *(Dottie)*, Mark Holton *(Francis)*, Diane Salinger *(Simone)*, Judd Omen *(Mickey)*, Irving Hellman *(Neighbor)*, Monty Landis, billed as Monte Landis *(Mario)*, Damon Martin *(Chip)*, David Glasser, Gregory Brown

p, Robert Shapiro, Richard Gilbert Abramson; d, Tim Burton; w, Phil Hartman, Paul Reubens, Michael Varhol; ph, Victor J. Kemper (Technicolor); ed, Billy Weber; m, Danny Elfman; prod d, David L. Snyder; fx, Chuck Gaspar; cos, Aggie Guerard Rodgers; anim, Rich Heinrichs

Pee-wee Herman is not like the other boys. "I'm a loner... a rebel," he announces to his would-be girlfriend. He's a comic rebel without a pause. Inspired lunacy, PEE-WEE'S BIG ADVENTURE is one of the most inventive films in recent memory. This clever and wholly original work incorporates a wide variety of cinematic tools with a fresh and unique sense of style. Pee-wee Herman, a creation of writer-comedian Paul Reubens, is a great comic creation on a par with Chaplin's Little Tramp. Somewhat reminiscent of the most popular Jerry Lewis screen persona, Pee-wee is a magical, happy-go-lucky, occasionally mischievous little boy living in an adult body. What makes this seemingly moronic character work on an intelligent level is the cartoonlike environment he inhabits. In both structure and content, PEE-WEE'S BIG ADVENTURE

often resembles a Warner Bros. cartoon. Like those classic animations, this film thrives on easily identifiable characterizations, simple plot motivations, throwaway gags, and an often surreal sense of logic, all mixed together with talent and ingenuity. The story gets started when the pride and joy of Pee-wee's life, his shiny red bicycle, is stolen. The police are of no help, so a crazed Pee-wee consults a fraudulent fortuneteller who tells him his bike is in the basement of the Alamo in Texas. Naturally, Pee-wee takes to the road.

The episodic plot is a perfect format for Reuben's comedy. For many this character was rather hard to take prior to this marvelous movie. In his nightclub act and numerous appearances on "Late Night with David Letterman," Pee-wee was a bit too disturbingly manic, regressive, and grotesquely fey for some genteel sensibilities. He's just as frenetic and sexually ambiguous here but he is so thoroughly contextualized within his own beautifully realized world that he allows even the most traditional among us to get the joke. The smart and wacky script by Rubens and Phil Hartman (of television's "Saturday Night Live" and "The Simpsons") is given added vibrance by director Tim Burton (BEETLEJUICE, BATMAN, EDWARD SCISSORHANDS, and FRANKENWEENIE). Burton's background as a Disney animator is perfect for the film; he gives PEE-WEE'S BIG ADVENTURE a wonderfully cartoonish look through design, lighting, and camera angles. Two stars were born with the release of this film—one in front of the camera and one behind it. One could also make a case for a third star here: Soundtrack composer Danny Elfman from the rock group Oingo Bongo provides a witty and manic score that bolsters every scene.

PEEPING TOM 📀
1960 109m c Thriller ★★★★★
Anglo-Amalgamated (U.K.)

Karl Boehm *(Mark Lewis)*, Moira Shearer *(Vivian)*, Anna Massey *(Helen Stephens)*, Maxine Audley *(Mrs. Stephens)*, Esmond Knight *(Arthur Baden)*, Bartlett Mullins *(Mr. Peters)*, Shirley Ann Field *(Diane Ashley)*, Michael Goodliffe *(Don Jarvis)*, Brenda Bruce *(Dora)*, Martin Miller *(Dr. Rosan)*

p, Michael Powell; d, Michael Powell; w, Leo Marks; ph, Otto Heller (Eastmancolor); ed, Noreen Ackland; m, Brian Easdale; art d, Arthur Lawrence; chor, Wally Stott

With its incredibly complex structure—which implicates the audience in the central character's crimes—PEEPING TOM is a remarkable examination of the psychology of filmmaking and film viewing, and one of the most disturbing films ever made.

Mark Lewis (Boehm), a focus-puller at a film studio, works part-time at a corner cigar store taking pornographic photos of women. One night, he approaches a prostitute on the street, goes to her apartment, and murders her while filming the event.

Mark rents out most of the house he owns, and a young tenant named Helen (Anna Massey) takes a liking to her landlord. When he screens movies of himself as a young boy, Helen is horrified by scenes of Mark's father (Michael Powell), a quack psychologist, tormenting the boy—part of the psychologist's studies in fear, Mark explains.

A dancer working at the film studio (Moira Shearer) is the next victim of Mark's grisly obsession. Increasingly attracted to Helen, he tries to repress his cinematic obsession by leaving his camera at home when they go out, but his perverted impulses begin to get the best of him.

Michael Powell, who, along with partner Emeric Pressburger, was one of the cornerstones of the British film industry during the 1940s, was vilified by the British press following PEEPING TOM's release in 1960. The director of THE LIFE AND DEATH OF COLONEL BLIMP,

STAIRWAY TO HEAVEN, BLACK NARCISSUS, and THE RED SHOES had made a rich and provocative psychological horror film, but critics in his homeland found it completely repugnant. The film was quickly butchered by the studio and was shown briefly in U.S. second-run houses. It wasn't until 1979, however, that a restored version was released due to the efforts of director Martin Scorsese, a devout fan of the picture. Sadly, Powell's career never recovered from the critical attacks, and he made only a handful of features and shorts before his death in 1990.

PEGGY SUE GOT MARRIED   DVD
1986 104m c   Fantasy/Comedy   ★★★
Rastar   (U.S.)   PG-13

Kathleen Turner (Peggy Sue), Nicolas Cage (Charlie Bodell), Barry Miller (Richard Norvik), Catherine Hicks (Carol Heath), Joan Allen (Maddy Nagle), Kevin J. O'Connor (Michael Fitzsimmons), Barbara Harris (Evelyn Kelcher), Don Murray (Jack Kelcher), Maureen O'Sullivan (Elizabeth Alvorg), Leon Ames (Barney Alvorg)

p, Paul R. Gurian; d, Francis Ford Coppola; w, Jerry Leichtling, Arlene Sarner; ph, Jordan Cronenweth (Deluxe Color); ed, Barry Malkin; m, John Barry; prod d, Dean Tavoularis; art d, Alex Tavoularis; cos, Theodora Van Runkle

AAN Best Actress: Kathleen Turner; AAN Best Cinematography: Jordan Cronenweth; AAN Best Costume Design: Theodora Van Runkle

A bittersweet cross between OUR TOWN and IT'S A WONDERFUL LIFE, PEGGY SUE GOT MARRIED tells the poignant story of Peggy Sue Bodell (Kathleen Turner). She's a 43-year-old housewife on the verge of a divorce from Charlie (Nicholas Cage), an obnoxious philanderer who is locally famous for his tacky TV commercials for his retail appliance business. Peggy Sue squeezes into her old prom dress and goes to her 25th high school reunion to meet all her old friends from James Buchanan High. Subsequently named queen of the reunion, she ascends the podium to accept her crown, and passes out. Tossed into a time warp, she awakens in 1960, a 43-year-old consciousness in an ostensibly 17-year-old body. This feat requires a suspension of disbelief on the part of the audience but Turner pulls it off admirably. The film asks a powerful question: If we had a chance to go back and do it all again, would we do it the same way? Or would we rewrite our lives to create a new outcome?

Released the year after BACK TO THE FUTURE, there were inevitable comparisons. However, PEGGY SUE GOT MARRIED is a more grown up and fatalistic film (even if it is ultimately inferior) that eschews cartoonish exaggeration for a more realistic approach to its subject matter. The film features good acting from almost everyone, the one notable exception being the annoying Cage who adopts a grating constricted voice for the role. The movie has many lovely moments and just as many dead spots, but its strengths make this atypical film from Francis Coppola a worthwhile viewing experience.

PEKING OPERA BLUES   DVD
(DAO MA DAN)
1986 104m c   Martial Arts/Comedy   ★★★★
Cinema City   (Hong Kong)

Harkitte Lin, billed as Lin Ching-hsia, Sally Yeh, Cherie Chung, Mark Cheng, Ling Pak-hoi, Wu Ma, Leong Po Chih, Ku Feng, Li Hai Sheng, Kenneth Tsang

p, Tsui Hark, Claudie Chung; d, Tsui Hark; w, To Kwok-wai; ph, Poon Hang-sang; ed, David Wu; m, James Wong; art d, Vincent Wai, Ho Kim-sing, Leung Chi-hing; fx, Cinefex Workshop; chor, Ching Sui-tung; cos, Ng Po-ling

A delightfully frenetic comedy-adventure, PEKING OPERA BLUES serves as a terrific introduction to the energetic popular cinema of Hong Kong. Set in China circa 1913, the fast-paced and complicated story centers on three young women from different social classes who become embroiled in a revolutionary plot to overthrow the military government. Surprisingly, one of the key players in the revolution is the beautiful Brigitte Lin (aka Lin Ching-hsia), the daughter of China's most powerful general. She and a male accomplice are ordered to steal some secret documents from her father's safe. Through a series of slapstick circumstances, a winsome but dim-witted street performer, a disaffected soldier, and the attractive daughter of the local opera house owner become involved in the plot and wind up comrades of the revolutionaries. Together, the five do battle with the army, the generals, and the secret police, with most of the zany action revolving around the colorful opera house. After a series of nonstop seductions, disguises, gunfights, kung-fu skirmishes, gymnastics, chases, double crosses, separations and reunions, the heroes succeed in getting the valued documents to the revolutionary leaders. The film ends with the five on horseback vowing to meet again someday before going their separate ways.

In an era in which most American films are either lifeless bores or cynical exercises in mass marketing (or both), PEKING OPERA BLUES is a welcome burst of manic energy that never fails to please. The skillful combination of breathtaking action and slapstick comedy in this film is nearly indescribable. Martial arts coordinator Ching Sui Tung's innovative choreography of the film's numerous action scenes is superb and the cast boasts three of Hong Kong's most popular actresses—Brigitte Lin, Cherie Chung, and Sally Yeh. They make a splendidly vivacious team and their ensemble comedic timing is flawless. Tsui Hark directs with a verve and style little seen on American screens and, while he always entertains, he also slips in some genuinely touching scenes and social observations.

A massive box-office hit in Hong Kong, the film proved popular with festival audiences in Europe and North America, who discovered that Hong Kong cinema had come a long way since the martial arts cheapies of the early 1970s.

PELICAN BRIEF, THE   DVD
1993 140m c   Thriller   ★★
Warner Bros./Pakula Productions   (U.S.)   PG-13

Julia Roberts (Darby Shaw), Denzel Washington (Gray Grantham), Sam Shepard (Thomas Callahan), John Heard (Gavin Verheek), Tony Goldwyn (Fletcher Coal), James B. Sikking (FBI Director F. Denton Voyles), William Atherton (Bob Gminski), Robert Culp (President of the United States), Stanley Tucci (Khamel), Hume Cronyn (Justice Abraham Rosenberg)

p, Alan J. Pakula, Pieter Jan Brugge; d, Alan J. Pakula; w, Alan J. Pakula (from the novel by John Grisham); ph, Stephen Goldblatt; ed, Tom Rolf, Trudy Ship; m, James Horner; prod d, Philip Rosenberg; art d, Robert Guerra; fx, Connie Brink, Lynda Lemon, John Nelson; cos, Albert Wolsky

In this slow, talky adaptation of John Grisham's best-seller, Alan Pakula—director of subtle and suspenseful thrillers like KLUTE and ALL THE PRESIDENT'S MEN—is undone by the stubborn shortcomings of his source material. Grisham's ramshackle plot has no suspense, yields no surprises, and demands almost constant explanations to get to its ending.

The plot is set in motion by the baffling murders of two Supreme Court justices, a curmudgeonly liberal (Hume Cronyn) and a closeted Republican homosexual (Ralph Cosham); all they have in common is a pro-environment inclination. Spirited and beautiful law student Darby Shaw (Julia

Roberts) puts together a brief theorizing that the culprit could be a shadowy oil millionaire determined to tap a billion-dollar oil reserve in the fragile Louisiana bayou habitat of the endangered brown pelican. Her lover (Sam Shepard) shows the brief to a friend in the FBI, Verheek (John Heard), and suddenly Darby is the most hunted woman in America. *Washington Herald* reporter Gray Grantham (Denzel Washington) becomes her ally as she seeks to evade her shadowy pursuers and find out the truth behind a scandal that reaches to the highest levels of government.

THE PELICAN BRIEF is a shallow bore. Grisham's characters are rudimentary, and both Roberts and Washington are stiff and over-earnest. Normally, the bad guys could be relied upon to enliven the action, but THE PELICAN BRIEF's creepy oilman has only one scene in the book and none in the screen version, which may be the most realistic aspect of the film—in real life, bad guys almost invariably appear only in the damage they do. In the movies, however, staying true to life makes for a long and trying evening.

PELLE THE CONQUEROR   📀
(PELLE EROVRAREN)
1987 160m c Drama   ★★★
Svensk/Danish Film Institute/Swedish Film)   PG-13
Institute/DRTV/SID   (Denmark/Sweden

Max von Sydow *(Pappa Lasse)*, Pelle Hvenegaard *(Pelle, His Son)*, Erik Paaske *(Farm Foreman)*, Bjorn Granath *(Farmhand Erik)*, Axel Strobye *(Kongstrup)*, Astrid Villaume *(Mrs. Kongstrup)*, Troels Asmussen *(Rud)*, John Wittig *(Schoolteacher)*, Anne Lise Hirsch Bjerrum *(Karna)*, Sofie Grabol *(Miss Sine)*

p, Per Holst; d, Bille August; w, Bille August (based on volume one of a novel by Martin Andersen Nexo); ph, Jorgen Persson (Fujicolor); ed, Janus Billeskov Jansen; m, Stefan Nilsson; prod d, Anna Asp; cos, Kicki Ilander, Gitte Kolvig, Birthe Qualmann

AA Best Foreign Language Film ; *AAN Best Actor:* Max Von Sydow

Bille August, the director of TWIST AND SHOUT (1986), the most commercially successful Danish film ever, followed that teen drama with this Swedish-Danish coproduction set in the 1890s and starring Max von Sydow as an impoverished Swedish widower who moves to Bornholm, a Danish island in the Baltic, hoping to improve his lot in life. He takes along his seven-year-old son, Hvenegaard, but instead of finding a better life, they are reduced to virtual slavery. A grim story of deprived and depraved humanity unfolds, focusing on both the oppressed and the oppressors. An Oscar winner for Best Foreign Film, this is an often brutal tale which is boosted by a powerful performance from Von Sydow.

PENNIES FROM HEAVEN   📀
1936 80m bw Musical   ★★★
Columbia   (U.S.)

Bing Crosby *(Larry)*, Madge Evans *(Susan)*, Edith Fellows *(Patsy)*, Donald Meek *(Gramps)*, John Gallaudet *(Hart)*, Louis Armstrong *(Henry)*, Tom Dugan *(Crowbar)*, Nana Bryant *(Miss Howard)*, Charles Wilson *(Warden)*, Harry Tyler *(Concessionaire)*

p, Emanuel Cohen; d, Norman Z. McLeod; w, Jo Swerling (based on the story "The Peacock's Feather" by Katherine Leslie Moore); ph, Robert Pittack; ed, John Rawlins; m, Arthur Johnston; art d, Stephen Goosson

AAN Best Song: "Pennies From Heaven"; Arthur Johnston (Music), Johnny Burke (Lyrics)

An amusing musical, notable mainly for its fine selection of songs, including the Academy Award-nominated title tune penned by Johnny Burke and Arthur Johnston. The film opens

with Crosby serving a jail sentence for smuggling (for which he has been wrongly convicted). Before he is released he is given a note by a murderer who is about to meet his end in the gas chamber. The killer's note contains the name and address of his victim's relatives. As a final request, he asks Crosby to locate the relatives and move them into his abandoned family estate. Crosby finds the relatives—a 10-year-old girl, Fellows, and her grandfather, Meek—living in squalor. At Crosby's urging, Fellows and Meek pack their bags and head for their new home, only to find that it looks haunted. To make the place more inviting, Crosby comes up with the idea of turning it into a restaurant called the Haunted House Cafe. To draw the crowds he croons a number of Johnston and Burke tunes, with the title tune being nominated for an Oscar for Best Song. Other numbers include "One, Two, Button Your Shoe," "So Do I," "Let's Call a Heart a Heart," "Now I've Got Some Dreaming to Do," "What This Country Needs," and "Skeleton in the Closet."

PEOPLE VS. LARRY FLYNT, THE   📀
1996 130m c Biography   ★★★½
Phoenix Pictures/Ixtlan Productions   (U.S.)   R

Woody Harrelson *(Larry Flynt)*, Courtney Love *(Althea Leasure)*, Edward Norton *(Isaacman)*, Brett Harrelson *(Jimmy Flynt)*, Miles Chapin *(Miles)*, Donna Hanover *(Ruth Carter Stapleton)*, James Cromwell *(Charles Keating)*, Crispin Glover *(Arlo)*, Vincent Schiavelli *(Chester)*, James Carville *(Simon Leis)*

p, Oliver Stone, Janet Yang, Michael Hausman; d, Milos Forman; w, Scott Alexander, Larry Karaszewski; ph, Philippe Rousselot; ed, Christopher Tellefsen; m, Thomas Newman; prod d, Patrizia Von Brandenstein; art d, James Nezda, Shawn Hausman; fx, Rodman Kiser; cos, Theodor Pistek, Arianne Phillips

AAN Best Actor: Woody Harrelson; *AAN Best Director:* Milos Forman

A warm, fuzzy movie for armchair liberals, THE PEOPLE VS. LARRY FLYNT whitewashes the life of the infamous pornographer for the benefit of viewers who are all for the First Amendment—so long as it doesn't protect anything too unpleasant.

In 1972, Larry Flynt (Woody Harrelson), is running a string of Cincinnati strip clubs when he hits on the idea of publishing a newsletter featuring nude photographs of his strippers. The idea is a big success, largely because the pictures are substantially more explicit that those found in mainstream men's magazines like *Playboy*. Expanded to magazine format, *Hustler* becomes a huge hit. Aided by his wife and business partner Althea (Courtney Love), a former stripper, Flynt becomes a wealthy man by testing the limits of obscenity and good taste. But as the national mood of the late 1970s grows more conservative, the relentlessly provocative Flynt becomes the object of numerous obscenity lawsuits.

You'd be hard-pressed to find another biopic that whitewashes its subject so thoroughly as THE PEOPLE VS. LARRY FLYNT. Director Milos Forman would like you to believe that Flynt's vulgar catalogue of racism, sexism, and anything else that might be construed as offensive is simply a more honest variation on *Playboy*. Of course, we expect controversial subjects to be watered down in mass-market films, but in a film whose purpose is to salute our Constitutional right to free speech, the contents of *Hustler* properly are an issue: the filmmakers' argument is seriously compromised by their failure to trust their audience with the knowledge of what kind of material that right protects. Despite lacking the courage of its convictions, THE PEOPLE VS. LARRY FLYNT is generally an intelligent and entertaining film. Harrelson's good-ol'-boy raunchiness is amusing, and singer Courtney Love gives an astonishingly good performance in her first substantial film role.

PEOPLE WILL TALK

DVD
★★★★

1951 110m bw Comedy
Fox (U.S.)

Cary Grant *(Dr. Noah Praetorius)*, Jeanne Crain *(Annabel Higgins)*, Finlay Currie *(Shunderson)*, Hume Cronyn *(Prof. Elwell)*, Walter Slezak *(Prof. Barker)*, Sidney Blackmer *(Arthur Higgins)*, Basil Ruysdael *(Dean Lyman Brockwell)*, Katherine Locke *(Miss James)*, Will Wright *(John Higgins)*, Margaret Hamilton *(Miss Pickett)*

p, Darryl F. Zanuck; d, Joseph L. Mankiewicz; w, Joseph L. Mankiewicz (based on the play "Dr. Praetorius" by Curt Goetz); ph, Milton Krasner; ed, Barbara McLean; m, Johannes Brahms, Richard Wagner; art d, Lyle Wheeler, George W. Davis; fx, Fred Sersen; cos, Charles LeMaire

Joseph L. Mankiewicz had just won two Oscars for ALL ABOUT EVE (writing, directing) and the year before that two more for the same tasks on A LETTER TO THREE WIVES. He took on a big challenge here, adapting Curt Goetz's play, "Dr. Praetorius," making it into an odd amalgam of wit, satire, high drama, and glistening dialog. Grant is an early crusader in the medical profession who thinks that the mind can cure just as well, if not better, than massive doses of medicine. He believes in treating the patient rather than the disease, a practice that delights his charges but horrifies his colleagues, who are far more traditional and hidebound in their diagnoses. Grant is teaching at a medical school and living what is thought to be a strange life. His servant and best friend is Currie, a murderer who has been sent to jail twice. His other friend is Slezak, a rotund scientist who loves model trains and knockwurst, not necessarily in that order. Grant's enemy at the school is Cronyn, a sourpuss anatomy instructor who feels more at home dissecting corpses than talking to humans. One day, while Grant is teaching his students, Crain, an aspiring young doctor, faints during the lecture. Grant is soon aware that she's newly pregnant, and when she tries to kill herself, he says that his first diagnosis was wrong, then marries her. Crain's father is Blackmer, a drunk and a loser, but a man with what Tennessee Williams called "the charm of the defeated." In between his classes, Grant conducts the school's orchestra in Wagner and Brahms. Out of spite, Cronyn contacts the dean, Ruysdael, and brings up a few interesting things about Grant's medical background, obliging Grant to defend himself to the school's board of directors. He explains his philosophy of medicine and eventually wins over the listeners. While all this is going on, Grant is spending his time at home convincing Crain that he really does love her and didn't marry her out of pity for her plight. The designation "sophisticated" applies well to PEOPLE WILL TALK, and Grant gives one of his best performances, a carefully controlled job of acting that never becomes farce. The movie is mature and frank, and Mankiewicz uses the opportunity to take a few potshots at academic hypocrisy.

PEPE LE MOKO

DVD
★★★★½

1937 90m bw Crime/Romance
Hakim/Paris (France)

Jean Gabin *(Pepe le Moko)*, Mireille Balin *(Gaby Gould)*, Line Noro *(Ines)*, Lucas Gridoux *(Inspector Slimane)*, Gabriel Gabrio *(Carlos)*, Fernand Charpin *(Regis)*, Saturnin Fabre *(Grandfather)*, Gilbert Gil *(Pierrot)*, Roger Legris *(Max)*, Gaston Modot *(Jimmy)*

p, Robert Hakim, Raymond Hakim; d, Julien Duvivier; w, Julien Duvivier, Henri Jeanson, Henri La Barthe, Jacques Constant (based on the book by Henri La Barthe); ph, Jules Kruger, Marc Fossard; ed, Marguerite Beauge; m, Vincent Scotto, Mohamed Yguerbouchen; prod d, Jacques Krauss

Based on the life of a real criminal who hid in the Casbah under the protection of his pals, PEPE LE MOKO stars Jean Gabin as the title thief, brigand, and charmer, who has surrounded himself with loyal gang members and keeps them in line through the sheer force of his personality, never resorting to violence. Tired of life with his moll, Ines (Line Noro), and of being on the run, Pepe yearns for his old days in Paris. He falls in love with a gorgeous tourist, Gaby Gould (Mireille Balin), but in the process lets his guard down and gives Algerian police inspector Slimane (Lucas Gridoux) the opportunity to finally nab him.

PEPE LE MOKO owes a thematic and stylistic debt to the early Hollywood gangster films, most notably Howard Hawks' SCARFACE, but director Julien Duvivier took the conventional mix of love and bullets and made it into dark poetry. Indeed this film is cited as a prime example of the Poetic Realism movement in France. The camera undulates through dingy realistic sets cloaked in deep shadow. The performances are so naturalistic that the actors don't seem to be acting, and the lack of sentimentality deserves special praise.

The film's success and the universality of its themes can be attested to by the fact that a Hollywood version, ALGIERS, was made immediately after PEPE LE MOKO and released in the States before the original could be imported. Charles Boyer turned the part of Pepe down when it was offered by Duvivier, then starred in the U.S. version when Gabin refused to make the trip to Hollywood, explaining that he, like French wine, "didn't travel well." When WW II started, the French government banned the film as too depressing and demoralizing, especially since the news from the front was also bleak. The Germans took over and their puppet government retained the ban, but the moment the war ended, PEPE LE MOKO was again shown and hailed as a classic.

PEPPERMINT SODA
(DIABOLO MENTHE)

★★★½

1977 97m c Drama/Comedy
Alma/Alexandre/Gaumont (France) PG

Eleonore Klarwein *(Anne Weber)*, Odile Michel *(Frederique Weber)*, Coralie Clement *(Perrine Jacquet)*, Marie Veronique Maurin *(Muriel Gazau)*, Valerie Stano *(Martine Dubreuil)*, Anne Guillard *(Sylvie Le Garrec)*, Corinne Dacla *(Pascal Carimil)*, Veronique Vernon *(Evelyne Delacroix)*, Francoise Berlin *(Mlle. Sassy)*, Arlette Bonnard *(Mme. Poliakoff)*

d, Diane Kurys; w, Diane Kurys; ph, Philippe Rousselot (Eastmancolor); ed, Joele Van Effenterre; m, Yves Simon

A thoroughly charming picture which brings to life the loves and fears of two teenaged sisters. Kurys marks her directing debut with a semi-autobiographical story starring Klarwein as the 13-year-old Anne (Kurys's age in 1963—the setting of the film) and Michel as her 15-year-old sibling. Living with their divorced mother, Ferjac, the girls discover and talk about the things that interest teenage girls—boys, sex, school, and politics (they *are* French). Lacking a boyfriend, Klarwein steams open her older sister's love letters from *her* boyfriend. Klarwein's confused reaction to men is further illustrated by her dislike for her mother's boyfriend. It is only from her father that she gets what she wants (a ski trip), but not until she shows her disapproval at his leaving home.

A sensitive portrayal of teens which compares with Truffaut's Antoine Doinel series (THE 400 BLOWS through LOVE ON THE RUN) and George Roy Hill's A LITTLE ROMANCE. Kurys continued exploring her growing years with ENTRE NOUS and C'EST LA VIE. For the curious, the film's title refers to an "adult" drink that Klarwein nearly gets a chance to taste.

PERFECT STORM, THE
2000 129m c   Adventure/Drama   **DVD** ★★★
Baltimore/Spring Creek/Radiant/Warner Bros.   PG-13
(U.S.)

George Clooney *(Captain Billy Tyne)*, Mark Wahlberg *(Bobby Shatford)*, Diane Lane *(Christina "Chris" Cotter)*, John C. Reilly *(Dale "Murph" Murphy)*, William Fichtner *(David "Sully" Sullivan)*, Mary Elizabeth Mastrantonio *(Linda Greenlaw)*, Karen Allen *(Melissa Brown)*, Bob Gunton *(Alexander McAnally III)*, Christopher McDonald *(Todd Gross)*, John Hawkes *(Mike "Bugsy" Moran)*

p, Paula Weinstein, Wolfgang Petersen, Gail Katz; d, Wolfgang Petersen; w, Bo Goldman, William D. Wittliff, Jennifer Flackett, Mark Levin (based on the book *The Perfect Storm: A True Story of Men Against the Sea* by Sebastian Junger); ph, John Seale; ed, Richard Francis-Bruce; m, James Horner; prod d, William Sandell; art d, Bruce Crone; fx, John Frazier, Stefen Fangmeier, Habib Zargarpour, Walt Conti, Stephen Rosenbaum, Industrial Light & Magic; cos, Erica Edell Phillips

AAN Best Sound: John Reitz, Gregg Rudloff, David Campbell, Keith A. Wester; *AAN Best Visual Effects:* Stefen Fangmeier, Habib Zargarpour, John Frazier, Walt Conti

Wolfgang Petersen directed DAS BOOT. Sebastian Junger's nonfiction best-seller was riveting. The special effects are state of the art. So why is this account of the fate of the *Andrea Gail*, a fishing boat that vanished in the middle of the storm of the century, so oddly slapdash?

October 1991. The *Andrea Gail* leaves Gloucester, MA, manned by seasoned captain Billy Tyne (George Clooney) and his crew, including warring tough guys Murph (John C. Reilly) and Sully (William Fichtner), and rookie Bobby Shatford (Mark Wahlberg). Forced far afield by poor fishing, the crew has no idea that three weather systems are about to converge and unleash a tempest of unparalleled proportions.

Since the details of the *Andrea Gail*'s final hours are ultimately unknowable, journalist Junger cast a wide narrative net, interspersing interviews with survivors of the "perfect storm" with side trips into historic disasters at sea, the economics of commercial fishing, the physics of weather, and background on the *Andrea Gail*'s crew. Petersen also pursues several narrative threads, periodically cutting away to a foundering sailboat, Coast Guard rescuers, and the ordeal by waiting of family and friends ashore. But while books can digress at will, Hollywood films must move forward like sharks or die. Petersen's efforts to keep things moving are infelicitous: enthralling details are thrown overboard, Christopher MacDonald wallows in the role of a TV meteorologist, and James Horner's overbearing score labors to whip up emotion at every turn. The weather effects are stunning, several scenes do pack a powerful emotional wallop, and the downbeat conclusion is a bracing antidote to Hollywood's usual feel-good endings. But, overall, the book is a far more rewarding experience than the movie.

PERFECT WORLD, A
1993 130m c   Crime/Drama   **DVD** ★★½
Malpaso Productions   (U.S.)   PG-13

Kevin Costner *(Butch Haynes)*, Clint Eastwood *(Red Garnett)*, Laura Dern *(Sally Gerber)*, T.J. Lowther *(Phillip Perry)*, Keith Szarabajka *(Terry Pugh)*, Leo Burmester *(Tom Adler)*, Paul Hewitt *(Dick Scuttle)*, Bradley Whitford *(Bobby Lee)*, Ray McKinnon *(Bradley)*, Bruce McGill *(Paul Saunders)*

p, Mark Johnson, David Valdes; d, Clint Eastwood; w, John Lee Hancock; ph, Jack N. Green; ed, Joel Cox, Ron Spang; m, Lennie

Niehaus; prod d, Henry Bumstead; art d, Jack G. Taylor Jr.; fx, John Frazier, David Amborn, J.W. McCormick; cos, Erica Edell Phillips

In a perfect world, screenwriters would be forbidden from using cute pre-teens to make up for creaky plots; Clint Eastwood would stop churning out his patented over-the-hill-but-still-tough routine; and there would be an injunction against Kevin Costner doing death scenes, especially ones as long and meandering as a cross-Texas road trip.

A PERFECT WORLD starts out quite well, with Butch Haynes (Costner) and a companion breaking out of a Texas prison and, after a tense confrontation with a terrified family, making off with seven-year-old Phillip Perry (T.J. Lowther) as a hostage. Hot on their heels are an initially promising team that includes Eastwood, as grizzled Texas Ranger Red Garnett, and Laura Dern, as inexperienced but independent criminologist Sally Gerber.

You know things have started to go wrong when Butch, after getting rid of his fellow escapee, starts to shape up as the loving father figure that young Phillip has never had. As Butch and the boy's drive turns into one warm, fuzzy episode after another, the team that is pursuing them comes to a physical, and dramatic, halt. With their high-tech trailer stuck in a field, Garnett and his deputies can do nothing either to pursue Butch, or to develop the character relations set up earlier. Throw in a transformation scene in which Costner turns—with a supreme lack of conviction—into a psycho killer, and you have a movie experience that's a long, long way from perfect.

PERFORMANCE
1970 105m c   Drama   ★★★½
Goodtimes Enterprises   (U.K.)   R

James Fox *(Chas Devlin)*, Mick Jagger *(Turner)*, Anita Pallenberg *(Pherber)*, Michele Breton *(Lucy)*, Ann Sidney *(Dana)*, John Bindon *(Moody)*, Stanley Meadows *(Rosebloom)*, Allan Cuthbertson *(The Lawyer)*, Anthony Morton *(Dennis)*, Johnny Shannon *(Harry Flowers)*

p, Sanford Lieberson; d, Nicolas Roeg, Donald Cammell; w, Donald Cammell; ph, Nicolas Roeg; ed, Antony Gibbs, Brian Smedley-Aston; art d, John Clark

Visually dazzling, finely acted investigation into such diverse matters as identity, sexuality, violence, power, and underground culture in late 1960s London.

James Fox stars as Chas, a sadistic petty gangster who has trouble fitting in, even with his hoodlum cohorts. Chas gets into trouble with boss Harry Flowers (Johnny Shannon) after Chas carries out a murder for personal—as opposed to business—reasons, and hides out in the basement of "retired" rock star Turner (Mick Jagger) while he waits to skip the country. Turner has secluded himself in the house in order to lament the loss of his powers of "incantation," which seems primarily to mean that he indulges in a lot of drug-taking and sex with two female companions (Anita Pallenberg and Michele Breton). Soon, Turner senses a connection between Chas's brutally violent nature and his criminal "performances" and Turner's own dried-up creative powers, and he draws the young hood into his world. Introduced to hallucinogenic drugs, Chas begins wearing androgynous clothes and even admits he is sexually attracted by Turner, before the mob shows up again and things turn sour.

Uneven, dated, and—at least during the first half-hour—too frantically paced, PERFORMANCE is nevertheless a haunting meditation on human identity from co-directors Donald Cammel and Nicolas Roeg (Roeg had previously worked as a cinematographer on films including FAHRENHEIT 451 and FAR FROM THE MADDING CROWD). Questions of role-playing, imagery and individuality are explored in uniquely visual terms, particularly by the directors' intriguing use of mirror shots. Mick Jagger's performance is a pleasant surprise, and his presence in the film accounted for most of the limited commercial success it enjoyed at the time of its initial release. PERFORMANCE has since become a much-discussed cult classic. Originally released with an "X" rating in the U.S., the film was subsequently re-edited and re-catalogued as an "R."

PERSONA
1966 81m bw Drama   *DVD* ★★★★★
. Svensk (Sweden)

Bibi Andersson *(Nurse Alma)*, Liv Ullmann *(Actress Elisabeth Vogler)*, Gunnar Björnstrand *(Mr. Vogler)*, Margareta Krook *(Dr. Lakaren)*, Jorgen Lindstrom *(The Boy)*

p, Ingmar Bergman; d, Ingmar Bergman; w, Ingmar Bergman; ph, Sven Nykvist; ed, Ulla Ryghe; m, Lars-Johan Werle; prod d, Bibi Lindstrom; art d, Bibi Lindstrom; fx, Evald Andersson; cos, Mago

---

This is Ingmar Bergman's chaste exploration of psychosis. It's not a horror story but a poem, and remarkable for that. This is one of the director's masterworks. Opening with a sequence that includes a bare bulb projecting onto a screen, the countdown leader of the first reel, and short film clips from slapstick comedies and cartoons, Bergman reminds us that we are in the act of watching a film. Gradually, however, the story gets underway. Ullmann plays an actress who mysteriously stops speaking after a performance of "Electra" and is sent by a psychiatrist to a seaside cottage where she is looked after by nurse Andersson. Using light and shadow masterfully, Bergman and his cinematographer, Sven Nykvist, accentuate the resemblance between the two women, drawing the viewer into a psychodrama that is more the nurse's story than the patient's, as Andersson pours her soul out to the silent Ullmann. She gradually appears to be just as troubled as her patient, whose personality she seems to be assuming. The shot of their two faces merged near the end of the film is one of the great images of cinema.

PERSONA has variously been interpreted as an exploration of the role of the artist, an embodiment of the psychoanalytic process, and as a meditation on Bergman's favorite existential themes. In any case, it is a film of great emotional intensity that benefits from the superlative performances of Ullmann—who reacts only with facial and body gestures—and Andersson, who speaks for both of them as she slips into a kind of subtle madness.

PERSONAL BEST
1982 124m c Sports   ★★★
Geffen (U.S.)   R

Mariel Hemingway *(Chris Cahill)*, Scott Glenn *(Terry Tingloff)*, Patrice Donnelly *(Tory Skinner)*, Kenny Moore *(Denny Stites)*, Jim Moody *(Roscoe Travis)*, Kari Gosswiller *(Penny Brill)*, Jodi Anderson *(Nadia "Pooch" Anderson)*, Maren Seidler *(Tanya)*, Martha Watson *(Sheila)*, Emily Dole *(Maureen)*

p, Robert Towne; d, Robert Towne; w, Robert Towne; ph, Michael Chapman, Allan Gornick Jr. (Technicolor); ed, Ned Humphreys, Jere Huggins, Jacqueline Cambas, Walt Mulconery, Bud Smith; m, Jack Nitzsche, Jill Fraser; prod d, Ron Hobbs; fx, Dale Newkirk; cos, Linda Henrikson, Ron Heilman

---

Oscar-winning screenwriter Robert Towne (CHINATOWN; SHAMPOO) made his directorial debut with this uneven but affecting study of romantic and athletic commitment set against the background of women's track and field. At the 1976 Olympic trials, pentathlete Tory Skinner (onetime track star Patrice Donnelly in her film debut) and hurdler Chris Cahill (Mariel Hemingway) meet after the former

qualifies for the U.S. team, while the latter runs badly. The two become lovers, and Tory persuades her reluctant coach, Terry Tingloff (Scott Glenn), to allow Chris to train with her under his guidance. Eventually, Tingloff convinces Chris to train for the pentathlon, creating a rivalry between Chris and Tory that leads to the breakup of their relationship. Later, Chris falls for Denny (Kenny Moore), a onetime Olympic medalist in swimming; then, against Tingloff's wishes, Chris renews her friendship with Tory during the 1980 Olympic trials.

Although Towne's script is a little talky and heavy-handed, he nonetheless captures the essence of the competitive impulse, exploring both the "killer instinct" and the inner drive to compete only with oneself. The lesbian love story at the film's center is less well developed, but still engaging, its poignancy heightened by the well-cast Hemingway's understated performance. Visually, PERSONAL BEST is frequently interesting, if occasionally studied. Towne's over-reliance on slow motion ultimately undercuts the poetry of motion he seeks to convey, but his camera placement during the track and field action is almost always inventive, as is the film's editing. Moreover, PERSONAL BEST offers a detailed, believable insider's portrait of the world of track and field. This very different sports film isn't for everyone, but patient viewers should find many small pleasures in it. Olympic marathoner Frank Shorter and veteran sportscaster Charlie Jones provide the commentary during the Olympic trials.

PERSONAL VELOCITY
2002 85m c Drama   *DVD* ★★★½
IFC Productions/InDigEnt/Goldheart/   R
Blue Magic Pictures (U.S.)

Kyra Sedgwick *(Delia)*, Parker Posey *(Greta)*, Fairuza Balk *(Paula)*, John Ventimiglia *(Narrator)*, Tim Guinee *(Lee, Greta's Husband)*, Wallace Shawn *(Mr. Gelb)*, Lou Taylor Pucci *(Kevin, the Hitchhiker)*, Mara Hobel *(Fay)*, David Warshofsky *(Kurt Wurtzle)*, Joel de la Fuente *(Thavi Matola)*

p, Alexis Alexanian, Lemore Syvan, Gary Winick; d, Rebecca Miller; w, Rebecca Miller; ph, Ellen Kuras; ed, Sabine Hoffman; m, Michael Rohaytn; prod d, Judy Becker; cos, Marie Abma

---

Writer-director Rebecca Miller adapts three of her own short stories into a trio of tightly focused, beautifully acted half-hour films.

First up: Delia Shunt (Kyra Sedgwick), a married mother of three. Delia's power once lay in her sexuality, but she soon succumbed to the inertia that can result from raising three kids while standing by an abusive husband (David Warshofsky). One night after a bad beating, Delia runs away to the home of a high-school acquaintance (Mara Hobel). Now on her own, Delia must rediscover her power. Next is New York City book editor Greta Herskovitz (Parker Posey), whose sluggish career is given an unexpected jolt when a hot young novelist (Joel de la Fuente) personally requests she edit his new manuscript. No one's more surprised than Greta herself, whose ambition drained away years ago when she opted for a simple life with her mild-mannered husband, Lee (Tim Guinee). Now positioned to become one of the hottest young editors in the city, Greta realizes her old life is due for an overhaul. The last story concerns Paula (Fairuza Balk), a waitress who's nearly killed when a car swerves out of control and hits the man walking beside her, a stranger with whom she'd just switched places. Fleeing the scene in a panic, Paula jumps in her car and heads north, hoping to untangle this strange twist of fate while deciding what to do about the fact that she's pregnant.

Cinematographer Ellen Kuras shot all three films on video using a herky-jerky camera technique, and the effect is occasionally dizzying. All three actresses, however, are simply dazzling, particularly Balk, who's finally been given a part worthy of her considerable talents.

PETER PAN

DVD

1953 76m c Animated/Children's ★★★★
Walt Disney Productions (U.S.) G

VOICES OF: Bobby Driscoll (Peter Pan), Kathryn Beaumont (Wendy), Hans Conried (Capt. Hook/Mr. Darling), Bill Thompson (Mr. Smee), Heather Angel (Mrs. Darling), Paul Collins (Michael Darling), Tommy Luske (John), Candy Candido (Indian Chief), Tom Conway (Narrator)

p, Walt Disney; d, Hamilton Luske, Clyde Geronimi, Wilfred Jackson; w, Ted Sears, Bill Peet, Joe Rinaldi, Erdman Penner, Winston Hibler, Milt Banta, Ralph Wright (based on the play by James M. Barrie); m, Oliver Wallace, Edward Plumb; anim, Milt Kahl, Franklin Thomas, Wolfgang Reitherman, Ward Kimball, Eric Larson, Oliver M. Johnston, Marc Davis, John Lounsbery, Les Clark, Norman Ferguson

PETER PAN is a wonderful movie. Patriarch Mr. Darling (whose voice is provided by Hans Conried) is annoyed that daughter Wendy (voiced by Kathryn Beaumont) insists on telling stories to the other children about a mythical boy known as Peter Pan. When Mr. and Mrs. Darling leave for a night on the town, Peter Pan (voiced by Bobby Driscoll) and fairy sidekick Tinkerbell magically appear in Wendy's room. They all take a magical trip to Never Neverland, where they get involved in a series of adventures that include a confrontation with the evil Captain Hook (Conried, in a dual role). Lots of laughs, fabulous animation, and excellent voicing by the actors. The picture cost more than $4 million to make, a huge amount for a film in 1953. Lest you wonder why it came in so high, you should know that Disney filmed a live-action version of the movie first in order to give his artists something to base their sketches upon.

PETER PAN

DVD

2003 113m c Fantasy/Adventure/Children's ★★★
Revolution Studios/Columbia/Universal/ PG
Douglas Wick-Lucy Fisher Productions/
Allied Stars (U.S./U.K./Australia)

Jason Isaacs (Mr. Darling/Captain Hook), Jeremy Sumpter (Peter Pan), Rachel Hurd-Wood (Wendy Darling), Olivia Williams (Mrs. Darling), Ludivine Sagnier (Tinkerbell), Lynn Redgrave (Aunt Millicent), Geoffrey Palmer (Sir Edward Quiller Couch), Harry Newell (John Darling), Freddie Popplewell (Michael Darling), Carsen Gray (Tiger Lily)

p, Lucy Fisher, Patrick McCormick, Douglas Wick; d, P.J. Hogan; w, P.J. Hogan, Michael Goldberg (based on the original stage play and books by J.M. Barrie); ph, Donald M. McAlpine; ed, Garth Craven, Michael Kahn; m, James Newton Howard; prod d, Roger Ford; art d, Richard Hobbs, Michelle McGahey; fx, Bruce Bright, Scott Farrar, Dana Friedman, Clayton W. Pinney; cos, Janet Patterson; anim, Jenn Emberly

Simultaneously groundbreaking and remarkably faithful to J.M. Barrie's play, P.J. Hogan's version of the children's classic will forever be known as the one in which young Peter Pan was finally played by a real, live boy.

The story unfolds in a cozy vision of Victorian London, where the Darling family live in a cocoon of snug eccentricity. Mr. and Mrs. Darling (Jason Isaacs, Olivia Williams) have a dog for a nanny and indulge their children shamelessly, allowing tomboyish Wendy (Rachel Hurd-Wood) to romp with younger brothers John (Harry Newell) and Michael (Freddie Popplewell). Bold, quick-witted, and adventurous, the unflappable Wendy accepts Peter Pan's (Jeremy Sumpter) invitation to the magical world called Neverland without hesitation. There, the Darling siblings meet the Lost Boys, a gaggle of unruly, unkempt youngsters; capricious fairy Tinkerbell (Ludivine Sagnier), Peter's guardian sprite; a pod of eerie mermaids; plucky Princess Tiger Lily (Carsen Gray), and the fearsome pirate Captain Hook (Isaacs), who hates Peter and lives in terror of the gigantic crocodile that devoured one of his hands.

The film's special effects are state-of-the-art without being too obtrusive; even the Hong Kong-style wirework stays within the spirit of Barrie's play. Hogan and Michael Goldberg's screenplay brings up a sexual undercurrent understated enough not to clash with Barrie's essentially pre-sexual vision but sufficiently present to vividly clarify certain relationships, notably Tinkerbell's jealousy. Isaacs very nearly steals the show as the vain and spiteful but cruelly charismatic Hook; casting the same actor who plays Wendy's beloved, mild-mannered father lends his characterization an unsettling frisson that goes unremarked but not unnoticed. Sumpter is game as Peter, but there's something slightly forced about his boyish bravado. Perhaps the problem is simply that 21st-century adolescents aren't children.

PETRIFIED FOREST, THE

DVD

1936 83m bw Crime ★★★★
Warner Bros. (U.S.)

Leslie Howard (Alan Squier), Bette Davis (Gabrielle Maple), Genevieve Tobin (Mrs. Chisholm), Dick Foran (Boze Hertzlinger), Humphrey Bogart (Duke Mantee), Joe Sawyer (Jackie), Porter Hall (Jason Maple), Charley Grapewin (Gramp Maple), Paul Harvey (Mr. Chisholm), Eddie Acuff (Lineman)

p, Henry Blanke; d, Archie Mayo; w, Charles Kenyon, Delmer Daves (based on the play by Robert E. Sherwood); ph, Sol Polito; ed, Owen Marks; m, Bernhard Kaun; art d, John Hughes; fx, Warren Lynch, Fred Jackman, Willard Van Enger, cos, Orry-Kelly

One of the variants on the GRAND HOTEL theme halfway between the pleasant comings and goings at that hostelry and the screaming disasters of, say, THE POSEIDON ADVENTURE. This screen version of Robert E. Sherwood's smash play is handled with great care by director Archie Mayo and a sterling cast. This was the film that catapulted Humphrey Bogart to fame, but without Leslie Howard's insistence on Bogart for the part of Duke Mantee, Bogart might never have gotten his big movie break.

This film is really about the confrontation between intellectualism and brute force. Howard, an idealistic writer and world traveler who has grown weary of life's cruelties, finds himself penniless and hitchhiking through the Arizona desert. As he passes the renowned Petrified Forest, it occurs to him that he is like it, an ossified relic of the past. Stopping at a dilapidated service station restaurant run by grumpy Porter Hall, Howard meets and falls in love with poet Bette Davis, Hall's daughter. She dreams of studying in Paris. Dick Foran, a college halfback who pumps gas for Hall, is in love with Davis, and therefore jealous of Howard; but Howard assures him that he has little to worry about. When a rich couple, Paul Harvey and Genevieve Tobin, arrive at the station, Davis persuades them to take Howard along with them to California. After Howard departs, Hall, Davis, Foran, and Charley Grapewin, Hall's ancient father, hear on the radio that the ruthless gangster Duke Mantee and his henchmen, on the run after committing murders in Oklahoma, are headed into Arizona. On the road, Mantee (Bogart) and his gang are stalled by a broken down car. When Harvey's car comes along, they order the occupants out and drive off with the rich man's auto. Bogart then storms into Hall's service station cafe and holds everyone prisoner, waiting to join up with another carload of henchmen and his gun moll. When Howard, Harvey, Tobin, and their chauffeur, John Alexander, return to the cafe, Bogart holds them hostage as well. Howard challenges Bogart with words Bogart doesn't understand, calling the gangster "the last great apostle of rugged individualism." Howard makes a quiet pact with Bogart, requesting that Bogart shoot him before leaving.

Howard was born for the role of the fatalistic lover and lapsed idealist of THE PETRIFIED FOREST. He had played it to the hilt on Broadway, as did Bogart with the Mantee role in the 1935 stage play. But when it came to casting the film, Jack Warner wanted no part of Bogart, who had appeared in small roles in B films some years earlier. He selected Edward G. Robinson to play Duke Mantee. When Howard heard this, he went to Warner, telling him that if Bogart did not get the role of gangster, he (Howard) would drop out of the picture. Warner needed Howard, so he cast Bogart, who went on to become one of the studio's greatest stars. Bogart's gangster was clearly based on Public Enemy No. 1, John Dillinger (as was Sherwood's original character). Coincidentally, Bogart closely resembled Dillinger, and after studying films of the gangster to perfect his mannerisms, he was a sensation. Yet the Duke Mantee role was also a curse, typecasting Bogart for years to come in the ruthless gangster mold, until 1941 when he appeared as a sympathetic gangster in HIGH SIERRA and, in the same year, as Sam Spade in THE MALTESE FALCON. Davis, too, is outstanding as the culture-hungry girl who yearns to escape the desert and the ominous Petrified Forest. This success of this film would soon land her meatier roles. The film was remade as ESCAPE IN THE DESERT. In 1955, Bogart, Lauren Bacall, and Henry Fonda would reenact the original play in an excellent television production.

PETULIA

1968 105m c Drama/Comedy ★★★½
Petersham (U.S./U.K.) R

Julie Christie (Petulia Danner), George C. Scott (Archie Bollen), Richard Chamberlain (David Danner), Arthur Hill (Barney), Shirley Knight (Polo), Pippa Scott (May), Kathleen Widdoes (Wilma), Roger Bowen (Warren), Richard Dysart (Motel Receptionist), Ruth Kobart

p, Raymond Wagner; d, Richard Lester; w, Larry Marcus, Barbara Turner (based on the novel Me and the Arch Kook Petulia by John Haase); ph, Nicolas Roeg (Technicolor); ed, Anthony Gibbs; m, John Barry; prod d, Tony Walton; art d, Dean Tavoularis; cos, Tony Walton, Arlette Nastat

PETULIA was a transitional work for director Richard Lester, a cross between the jump-cutting gimmickry of his earlier films (A HARD DAY'S NIGHT, THE KNACK) and the more conventional storytelling of JUGGERNAUT and ROBIN AND MARIAN. Extravagantly praised by some critics and dismissed by others, it is nevertheless one of the best American films of the sixties (if largely by default). Archie Bollen (George C. Scott) meets Petulia Danner (Julie Christie) at a San Francisco charity function with counter-cultural pretensions (The Grateful Dead and Big Brother and the Holding Company provide the entertainment). Bollen doesn't know that Petulia recognizes him as the surgeon who operated on a young mexican boy whom she and her husband David (Richard Chamberlain) had befriended on a recent trip to Tijuana. David is an abusive husband who may have caused the boy's injuries. Through flashbacks, which come at a rate of maybe one every ten minutes, we see a large portion of the Tijuana trip, and the subsequent surgery in all its gory detail. Bollen, meanwhile, has his own problems. Divorced, his ex-wife has married a man he despises, and he spends most of his free time either on absurd "divorced Dad" excursions with his two sons (their trip to Alcatraz is a highlight), or trying to figure out exactly what Petulia means to him. PETULIA is both a finely observed comedy of manners set in the San Francisco of the late sixties, and an absorbing drama about abuse and betrayal. Nicholas Roeg did the cinematography.

PEYTON PLACE DVD

1957 162m c Drama ★★
Fox (U.S.)

Lana Turner (Constance MacKenzie), Hope Lange (Selena Cross), Lee Philips (Michael Rossi), Lloyd Nolan (Dr. Matthew Swain), Diane Varsi (Allison MacKenzie), Arthur Kennedy (Lucas Cross), Russ Tamblyn (Norman Page), Terry Moore (Betty Anderson), Barry Coe (Rodney Harrington), David Nelson (Ted Carter)

p, Jerry Wald; d, Mark Robson; w, John Michael Hayes (based on the novel by Grace Metalious); ph, William Mellor (CinemaScope, DeLuxe Color); ed, David Bretherton; m, Franz Waxman; art d, Lyle Wheeler, Jack Martin Smith; fx, L.B. Abbott; cos, Adele Palmer, Charles Le Maire

AAN Best Picture; AAN Best Actress: Lana Turner; AAN Best Supporting Actor: Arthur Kennedy; AAN Best Supporting Actor: Russ Tamblyn; AAN Best Supporting Actress: Hope Lange; AAN Best Supporting Actress: Diane Varsi; AAN Best Director: Mark Robson; AAN Best Adapted Screenplay: John Michael Hayes; AAN Best Cinematography: William Mellor

Tawdry potboiler based on one of the best-selling novels of all time. Not to be confused with the suggestive, subversive melodramas of Sirk and Minnelli, this is the kind of hypertensive trash that gives melodrama a bad name, cynically tempering its naughty bits with smug moralizing. The fact that the film won an "A" rating from the Catholic Legion of Decency, meaning it was deemed "acceptable to all," is a dead giveaway.

Into the small New England community of Peyton Place comes a new school principal (Philips), a hotshot Ph.D with "advanced" educational ideas. In no time at all, he meets Turner, a widow with a teenage daughter, Varsi. He's surprised when Turner spurns his amorous advances and he retaliates by sniping at her for the way she treats Varsi when the teen's birthday party turns into a petting fest. Wealthy Coe marries Moore, a sensuous young woman, despite his father's annoyance. Meanwhile, Varsi is having a sincere friendship with Tamblyn, whose mother, Erin O'Brien-Moore, is a domineering woman who resents his friendship with anyone. At the same time, Lange, the stepdaughter of the school's drunken caretaker, Kennedy, is raped by Kennedy, and she later kills him (accidentally, of course). The war begins, and the town's respectable veneer falls to pieces.

PHANTOM LADY

1944 87m bw Mystery ★★★★
Universal (U.S.)

Franchot Tone (Jack Marlow), Ella Raines (Carol "Kansas" Richman), Alan Curtis (Scott Henderson), Aurora Miranda (Estela Monteiro), Thomas Gomez (Inspector Burgess), Fay Helm (Ann Terry), Elisha Cook Jr. (Cliff March), Andrew Tombes (Bartender), Regis Toomey, Joseph Crehan (Detectives)

p, Joan Harrison; d, Robert Siodmak; w, Bernard C. Schoenfeld (based on the novel by Cornell Woolrich); ph, Elwood Bredell; ed, Arthur Hilton; m, H.J. Salter; art d, John B. Goodman, Robert Clatworthy; cos, Vera West, Kenneth Hopkins

A superb thriller, and the first American film by German director Siodmak to enjoy any significant success. Alan Curtis plays an innocent man accused of murdering his wife, with Ella Raines, as his secretary, and Thomas Gomez, as an off-duty copy, engaging in a search for the man's female alibi, a mysterious woman (Fay Helm) whose existence is denied by every witness. Adapted from a novel by Cornell Woolrich, with suitably Expressionistic camera angles and moody lighting.

PHANTOM OF LIBERTY, THE   DVD
(LE FANTOME DE LA LIBERTE)
1974 104m c   Comedy   ★★★★
Greenwich (France)   R

Jean-Claude Brialy *(M. Foucauld)*, Monica Vitti *(Mme. Foucauld)*, Milena Vukotic *(Receptionist)*, Michel Lonsdale *(Jean Bermans)*, Anne-Marie Deschott *(Edith Rosenblum)*, Michel Piccoli *(2nd Prefect of Police)*, Claude Pieplu *(Inspector)*, Paul Frankeur *(Innkeeper)*, Julien Bertheau *(1st Prefect of Police)*, Adriana Asti *(Woman in Black/Prefect's Sister)*

p, Serge Silberman; d, Luis Bunuel; w, Luis Bunuel, Jean-Claude Carriere; ph, Edmond Richard (Eastmancolor); ed, Helene Plemiannikov; art d, Pierre Guffroy; fx, Francois Sune; cos, Jacqueline Guyot

An uproarious summary of Luis Bunuel's surrealistic concerns in a collection of anecdotes starring Jean-Claude Brialy, Michel Piccoli, and Monica Vitti. THE PHANTOM OF LIBERTY jumps from place to place and time to time in a manner that follows the (il)logic of dreams. The film opens in the Napoleonic era with Spanish patriots urging on the firing squad that's about to execute them with shouts of things like "Down with Liberty!" and "Up with Chains!" Following this is a scene of a maid reading to a child the story we have just witnessed. Again the scene changes to show a man selling supposedly pornographic postcards that are actually shots of entirely non-pornographic French tourist attractions. A nurse then makes the mistake of wandering into a poker game played by a group of monks. A man with a rifle kills passers-by from the top of a Montparnasse building and is hailed as a hero. A missing girl helps the police fill out a report on her disappearance. And, in perhaps the most memorable sequence, a group of elegantly dressed dinner guests sit on toilet seats as they converse around a dining room table. They sheepishly request to be excused when hunger strikes and then creep off to a room containing a private little stall where they may dine.

This is a crazy, subversively funny film about convention-bound characters who have a hard time dealing with sexuality and freedom. It's heartening to see that Bunuel could still ruffle as many feathers at age 75 as he did in 1928 and 1930 with UN CHIEN ANDALOU and L'AGE D'OR.

PHANTOM OF THE OPERA, THE   DVD
1925 93m   c/bw   Horror   ★★★★
Universal (U.S.)

Lon Chaney *(The Phantom)*, Mary Philbin *(Christine Daae)*, Norman Kerry *(Raoul de Chagny)*, Snitz Edwards *(Florine Papillon)*, Gibson Gowland *(Simon)*, Edward Martindel *(Philippe de Chagny)*, Virginia Pearson *(Carlotta)*, Arthur Edmund Carewe *(Ledoux)*, Edith Yorke *(Mama Valerius)*, Anton Vaverka *(Prompter)*

p, Carl Laemmle; d, Rupert Julian, Edward Sedgwick, Ernst Laemmle (sound sequences); w, Raymond L. Schrock, Elliott Clawson, Tom Reed, Frank M. McCormack (based on the story "Le Fantome de l'Opera" by Gaston Leroux); ph, Virgil Miller, Milton Bridenbecker, Charles Van Enger; ed, Maurice Pivar; prod d, Charles D. Hall, Ben Carre

One of the most famous horror movies of all time, THE PHANTOM OF THE OPERA still manages to frighten after more than 60 years. The legendary Lon Chaney is magnificent as Erik, the horribly disfigured maniac composer known only as the "Phantom," who takes an interest in Christine (Mary Philbin), an understudy at the Paris Opera. Hidden in secret passages, he coaches her, perfecting her art until she is a star. Then he forces the company's leading soprano to step down by unleashing a series of horrors, including sending an enormous chandelier crashing down on the audience during a performance. Eventually the

masked Phantom lures Christine to his subterranean lair, where he professes his love for her. He also agrees to let her return to the stage on the condition that she break off her relationship with Raoul (Norman Kerry). Christine agrees, but once she is free rushes to her lover, and they make plans to flee to England following her performance. The Phantom overhears them, however, and kidnaps Christine. As he sits and plays his huge pipe organ, curiosity overwhelms Christine and she creeps up behind the Phantom and pulls off his mask, revealing the terrible skull-like visage beneath. Eventually, Raoul and a mysterious foreign agent set out to capture the Phantom, as does an enraged mob led by the brother of one of the Phantom's victims.

A much stronger film than THE HUNCHBACK OF NOTRE DAME (1923), THE PHANTOM OF THE OPERA further cemented Chaney's reputation as a superstar and made Universal synonymous with horror. From the point of view of the studio's management, however, THE PHANTOM OF THE OPERA was horrific in more ways than one, taking more than two years to reach the theaters after its initial completion in 1923. When it was originally previewed in California, critics told Carl Laemmle that he would have a turkey on his hands unless he offset the scary aspects with plenty of comedy relief, so the studio head brought in Chester Conklin from the Sennett lot and additional footage was shot. These additions, however, necessitated a new set of titles, and the expensive Walter Anthony was hired to provide them. When the picture, which Universal hoped would achieve "prestige" status, was then screened in San Francisco, the consensus was that it had some wonderful moments but failed to make sense. So the whole production was turned over to a new staff of title writers and editors who *really* tore it apart. Out came the comedy, as well as a whole subplot involving Ward Crane and a lot of sword play, until finally studio execs felt they had their "big picture." With its play of light and shadow, its secret passageways, masked ball (filmed in two-strip Technicolor), and the still-chilling unmasking scene, THE PHANTOM OF THE OPERA deserves its revered place in horror film history.

PHANTOM OF THE OPERA   DVD
1943 92m   c   Horror   ★★★
Universal (U.S.)

Nelson Eddy *(Anatole Garron)*, Susanna Foster *(Christine DuBois)*, Claude Rains *(Enrique Claudin)*, Edgar Barrier *(Inspector Raoul de Chagny)*, Leo Carrillo *(Signor Feretti)*, Jane Farrar *(Biancarolli)*, J. Edward Bromberg *(Amiot)*, Fritz Feld *(Lecours)*, Frank Puglia *(Villeneuve)*, Steven Geray *(Vercheres)*

p, George Waggner; d, Arthur Lubin; w, Eric Taylor, Hans Jacoby, Samuel Hoffenstein (based on the novel *Le Fantome de l'Opera* by Gaston Leroux); ph, Hal Mohr, W. Howard Greene (Technicolor); ed, Russell Schoengarth; m, Edward Ward (operatic score), George Waggner; art d, John B. Goodman, Alexander Golitzen; cos, Vera West

AA Best Color Cinematography: Hal Mohr, W. Howard Greene; *AAN Best Score (Musical):* Edward Ward; *AA Best Interior Decoration (Color):* Alexander Golitzen, John B. Goodman, Russell A. Gausman, Ira S. Webb; *AAN Best Sound Recording:* Bernard B. Brown

Universal Studios' elaborate and expensive remake of their classic 1925 silent horror film THE PHANTOM OF THE OPERA boasts fabulous sets, gorgeous costumes, and stunning Technicolor photography—but fails in the horror department, because of an excess of music and low comedy. Draining much of the fear, suspense, and mystery out of the original Gaston Leroux material, this remake posits Enrique Claudin (Claude Rains)—the future "Phantom"—as a somewhat frail, middle-aged violinist with the Paris Opera who is in love from afar with Christine DuBois (Susanna Foster), a pretty and talented singer in the chorus. Although Christine doesn't even know the violinist exists, Enrique devotes his entire life to her, sacrificing his musical future just to make her happy. Universal spent $1.5 million on PHANTOM OF THE OPERA and every dollar is on the screen. While the opera house set is the same one used in the original, many additional sets were constructed and dressed up with elaborate and expensive wares. Rains, who had just finished playing what would later become his best-remembered role—that of Capt. Louis Renault in CASABLANCA—managed to bring a sense of pathos and menace to the Phantom. The sparse and briefly seen makeup of the disfigured violinist is merely serviceable; wisely, no attempt was made to duplicate or surpass Lon Chaney's amazing visage in the original. While this version can be quite entertaining at times, it is frustrating that the horror elements are used merely as a plot device to propel the story along to the next elaborate opera scene—a structure that pleased neither horror fans nor opera buffs. PHANTOM OF THE OPERA won Oscars for Best Color Cinematography and Best Color Interior Decoration (John B. Goodman, Alexander Golitzen, R.A. Gausman, Ira S. Webb), receiving nominations for Best Sound Recording and Best Musical Score.

PHANTOM OF THE OPERA, THE

1962 84m c Horror ★★★
Hammer (U.K.)

Herbert Lom (The Phantom), Heather Sears (Christine Charles), Thorley Walters (Lattimer), Edward De Souza (Harry Hunter), Michael Gough (Lord Ambrose D'Arcy), Martin Miller (Rossi), Miles Malleson (Philosophical Cabby), Miriam Karlin (Charwoman), John Harvey (Vickers), Harold Goodwin (Bill)

p, Anthony Hinds; d, Terence Fisher; w, Anthony Hinds (based on a story by Gaston Leroux); ph, Arthur Grant (Technicolor); ed, Alfred Cox; m, Edwin Astley; prod d, Bernard Robinson; art d, Don Mingaye

Following successful reinterpretations of such horror film icons as Frankenstein, Dracula, the Mummy, and the Wolfman, Hammer Studios turned its attention to the classic tale of THE PHANTOM OF THE OPERA. Fully aware that its small-budget efforts would be closely compared with the two previous big-budget American versions (in 1925 starring Lon Chaney, Sr., and again in 1943 starring Claude Rains), Hammer bravely forged ahead and managed to produce a film that, while no classic, stands as a well-crafted thriller with some chilling, memorable moments. Shifting the action from Paris to London, the film tells the familiar story of a grotesquely disfigured composer who haunts an opera house and falls hopelessly in love with a beautiful singer.

Hammer's THE PHANTOM OF THE OPERA was originally to have starred the studio's favorite Dracula, Christopher Lee, but a last-minute switch was made in favor of Lom. While he could not hope to equal Chaney's classic tour-de-force or even Rains's memorable portrayal, Lom succeeded admirably in creating an alternately malevolent, sympathetic, and even tragic character. Hammer had hired professional maskmakers to create the phantom's mask, but they failed to come up with a suitable design. Director Fisher tried to shoot around Lom's masked scenes while awaiting the result of the maskmaker's work, but he finally grew impatient and had Hammer's makeup man, Roy Ashton, construct a crude mask out of cloth, tape, and gauze. The effect is perfect because the mask looks like something the Phantom would have made for himself while combing the dank sewers beneath the opera house. Despite the film's low budget, the production has the usual Hammer eye for detail and looks as if it had an expensive treatment. Gough turns in

his usual fine performance as the evil opera benefactor, while Sears (whose singing was dubbed by opera singer Pat Clark) and De Souza are serviceable as the standard heroine and hero.

PHANTOM TOLLBOOTH, THE

1970 90m c Animated/Children's/Fantasy ★★★½
MGM (U.S.) G

Butch Patrick (Milo), VOICES OF: Mel Blanc, Daws Butler, Candy Candido, Hans Conried, June Foray, Patti Gilbert, Shepard Menken, Cliff Norton, Larry Thor

p, Chuck Jones, Abe Levitow, Les Goldman; d, Chuck Jones, Abe Levitow, David Monahan; w, Chuck Jones, Sam Rosen (based on the book by Norton Juster); ph, Lester Shorr (Metrocolor); ed, Jim Faris; m, Dean Elliott; prod d, Maurice Noble; art d, George W. Davis, Charles K. Hagedon; anim, Irv Spence, Bill Littlejohn, Richard Thompson, Tom Ray, Philip Roman, Alan Zaslove, Edwin Aardal, Ed DeMattia, Xenia, Lloyd Vaughan, Carl Bell

This fine adaptation of the children's book by Norton Juster was Chuck Jones's and MGM's first animated feature. Butch Patrick stars (in the live-action sequences) as Milo, a bored youngster who cannot maintain an interest in anything. One day the "phantom tollbooth" appears in his bedroom and Milo drives his toy car into it. He is then transported through the magic of animation into a strange and wonderful world broken up into two camps, letters and numbers. Unfortunately, letters and numbers are at war with each other (each thinking they are more important to society), and Milo soon finds himself caught in the middle. Aided by a dog called Tock, Milo strives mightily to restore the land to peace, in a charming film that combines some fairly sophisticated ideas (demons from the "Mountains of Ignorance" cause much of the trouble, and Milo tries to restore "Rhyme and Reason" to the land) with cute and likable characters that are sure to grab a child's attention.

PHAR LAP

1983 107m c Sports ★★★½
Fox (Australia) PG

Tom Burlinson (Tommy Woodcock), Ron Leibman (Dave Davis), Martin Vaughan (Harry Telford), Judy Morris (Bea Davis), Celia De Burgh (Vi Telford), Richard Morgan ("Cashy" Martin), Robert Grubb (William Neilsen), Georgia Carr (Emma), James Steele (Jim Pike), Vincent Ball (Lachlan McKinnon)

p, John Sexton; d, Simon Wincer; w, David Williamson (based on the book The Phar Lap Story by Michael Wilkinson); ph, Russell Boyd (Panavision); ed, Tony Paterson; m, Bruce Rowland; prod d, Lawrence Eastwood; art d, David Bowden; cos, Anna Senior

Another story of a boy and his horse, this time a factual one set in Australia in the early 1930s. The film opens as the horse lies dying in a Mexican stable after winning the biggest race of its career, the Agua Caliente, in April 1932. The cause of Phar Lap's death goes unexplained, as it has to this day, although blame is clearly directed toward the gamblers who consistently lost money as the horse won race after race. From this point the narrative moves backward, showing how the young horse was purchased in New Zealand by Harry Telford (Martin Vaughan), a trainer whose experienced eye spots potential in the animal despite its lack of pedigree. His partner in the purchase is Dave Davis (Ron Leibman), a fast-talking American Jew who suffers greatly at the hands of anti-Semites in Australia as his horse triumphs over their horses. The horse is extremely skittish, though, and loses its first four races, even as Telford tries ever more brutal methods of snapping it into line. Finally Tommy Woodcock (Tom Burlinson), a stable boy, establishes a bond with the horse through kindness, and from that time on it wins every race. Phar Lap today is remembered in Australia in the same way as Man

O' War in the U.S. or Red Rum in Britain—as the greatest horse of its day and a symbol of national pride. Although the film plays a little too heavily on this patriotic theme, its simple boy-and-his-horse story is beautifully effective.

PHILADELPHIA
DVD
1993 119m c Drama ★★★
TriStar (U.S.) PG-13

Tom Hanks (Andrew Beckett), Denzel Washington (Joe Miller), Antonio Banderas (Miguel Alvarez), Ron Vawter (Bob Seidman), Joanne Woodward (Sarah Beckett), Jason Robards Jr., billed as Jason Robards (Charles Wheeler), Robert Ridgely (Walter Kenton), Paul Lazar (Dr Klenstein), Bradley Whitford (Jamey Collins), Tracey Walter (Librarian)

p, Edward Saxon, Jonathan Demme; d, Jonathan Demme; w, Ron Nyswaner; ph, Tak Fujimoto; ed, Craig McKay; m, Howard Shore; prod d, Kristi Zea; art d, Tim Galvin; cos, Colleen Atwood

AA Best Actor: Tom Hanks; AA Best Original Song: "Streets of Philadelphia"; Bruce Springsteen; AAN Best Original Song: "Philadelphia"; Neil Young; AAN Best Original Screenplay: Ron Nyswaner; AAN Best Makeup: Alan D'Angerio, Carl Fullerton

The first mainstream Hollywood film to deal with the subject of AIDS, and one of the few to feature gay characters in a serious dramatic context, PHILADELPHIA is highly competent and equally—if surprisingly—conventional.

Handsome, self-assured young corporate lawyer Andrew Beckett (Tom Hanks) is fired by his white-shoe Philadelphia firm when his sleek, self-satisfied employers—including Charles Wheeler (Jason Robards) and Bob Seidman (Ron Vawter)—discover that he's HIV positive. With the support of his family—especially his mother, Sarah (Joanne Woodward)—and his lover, Miguel (Antonio Banderas), Beckett sues. But the only lawyer who will take his case is local ambulance chaser Joe Miller (Denzel Washington), who's not sure he wants to be associated with a high profile case about homosexual prejudice.

PHILADELPHIA fails to create complex characters or finely nuanced drama, but it succeeds in its real goal: the education of an audience whose thinking about AIDS and gay life has been shaped by notions of perversion and divine retribution. Screenwriter Ron Nyswaner and director Jonathan Demme assemble a drama filled with familiar elements: the importance of family (and, especially, a mother's love for her children); the decent little man pitted against a smugly uncaring system; the mismatched legal team of affluent white suburbanite Beckett and struggling, black, city-bred Miller. Strong performances from Hanks and Washington are among the film's greatest assets. Doomsayers foretold that the movie would fail to find a mainstream audience and that this would insure the subject's relegation, once again, to the independent arena, but the dire predictions proved false.

PHILADELPHIA STORY, THE
DVD
1940 112m bw Comedy ★★★★
MGM (U.S.)

Cary Grant (C.K. Dexter Haven), Katharine Hepburn (Tracy Lord), James Stewart (Macauley Connor), Ruth Hussey (Elizabeth Imbrie), John Howard (George Kittredge), Roland Young (Uncle Willie), John Halliday (Seth Lord), Mary Nash (Margaret Lord), Virginia Weidler (Dinah Lord), Henry Daniell (Sidney Kidd)

p, Joseph L. Mankiewicz; d, George Cukor; w, Donald Ogden Stewart, Waldo Salt (based on the play by Philip Barry, uncredit-

ed); ph, Joseph Ruttenberg; ed, Frank Sullivan; m, Franz Waxman; art d, Cedric Gibbons, Wade B. Rubottom; cos, Adrian

AAN Best Picture; AA Best Actor: James Stewart; AAN Best Actress: Katharine Hepburn; AAN Best Supporting Actress: Ruth Hussey; AAN Best Director: George Cukor; AA Best Screenplay: Donald Ogden Stewart

George Cukor directed this classic comedy talkfest that offers special pleasures for fans of Katharine Hepburn, James Stewart, and Cary Grant. Tracy Lord (Hepburn), the daughter of a super-wealthy family living in a ritzy suburb of Philadelphia, is slated to marry George Kittredge (Howard), a stuffed-shirt coal company executive. Previously she had been married to C.K. Dexter Haven (Grant) in a stormy short-lived relationship that ended largely because Tracy couldn't deal with Dexter's drinking and irresponsible ways. As her wedding nears, Dexter shows up at the estate, ostensibly to attend the nuptials, but really to protect the reputation of his ex-in-laws. Dexter has learned that publisher Sidney Kidd (Daniell) plans to run an expose about Tracy's stagedoor Johnny father (Halliday), revealing in Spy magazine details of his chronic womanizing. To mollify the publisher, Dexter, who works for Kidd, arranges for the magazine's chief scandal reporter, Mike Conner (Stewart), and photographer Liz Imbrie (Hussey) to report on the wedding for the magazine. Mike has a healthy skepticism about the ways of the rich until he gets smitten by Tracy, who grows more unsure of her desires as her wedding nears. Indeed most of the major characters must decide whom they really love before the film is over. Of course, all must end happily even if unexpectedly.

With such a stellar cast, a fine director working in the type of picture he did best, and some genuinely witty dialogue, this film has all the ingredients for a great comedy. And it is great, though there have been many funnier comedies. The film has an unfortunate tendency to take itself too seriously for long stretches. Mike's shameless adoration of Tracy and the cloying speeches he's forced to deliver in her praise try our credulity and patience. A very strong case is being made here for the sheer irresistibility of the film's female star. The film also strenuously drives home the point that people born poor aren't necessarily noble while men born rich aren't necessarily cads. No need to stop the presses for this little news bulletin!

This was a project especially dear to Hepburn. Two years prior to the release of THE PHILADELPHIA STORY, Hepburn had been branded "box-office poison" by a leading exhibitor, thus prompting her to look for a Broadway show suitable for her talents. Playwright Barry wrote the role of Tracy expressly for Hepburn, who covered 25 percent of the play's cost and took no salary, shrewdly opting to take 45 percent of the considerable profits. Joseph Cotten played the Cary Grant role while Van Heflin originated Stewart's part. The cagey actress also purchased the film adaptation rights and eventually succeeded in getting Louis B. Mayer not only to pay her $250,000 for them but also won the right to select her own director, screenwriter, and costars. Grant accepted his role only on the proviso that he receive top billing, which he did. He then demanded a then-whopping salary of $137,000 and got it. (Grant later donated his entire salary from the film to the British War Relief Fun.)

The film became a box-office smash. It broke all records at Radio City Music Hall with a return of almost $600,000 in six weeks. Hepburn, who won the coveted New York Film Critics Award, lost the Oscar to Ginger Rogers for her role in KITTY FOYLE. The film was poorly remade as a musical, HIGH SOCIETY, in 1956, starring Bing Crosby, Frank Sinatra, and Grace Kelly.

PHONE BOOTH

DVD

2003 80m c Thriller

★★★

Zucker/Netter Production/Fox 2000 (U.S.) R

Colin Farrell *(Stu Shepard)*, Kiefer Sutherland *(The Caller)*, Forest Whitaker *(Captain Ramey)*, Radha Mitchell *(Kelly Shepard)*, Katie Holmes *(Pamela McFadden)*, Paula Jai Parker *(Felicia)*, Arian Ash *(Corky)*, Tia Texada *(Asia)*, John Enos III *(Leon)*, Keith Nobbs *(Adam)*

p, Gil Netter, David Zucker; d, Joel Schumacher; w, Larry Cohen; ph, Matthew Libatique; ed, Mark Stevens; m, Harry Gregson-Williams; prod d, Andrew Laws; art d, Martin Whist; fx, Jim Fredburg; cos, Daniel Orlandi

Screenwriter Larry Cohen, one of the most consistently subversive writer-directors of the 1970s, and director Joel Schumacher spin a classic, cautionary urban legend into a sharp little entertainment that ends right before the single-location gimmick wears thin.

Manhattan publicist Stu Shepard (Colin Farrell) works his cell phone within an inch of its life, buttering up deluded fame junkies and playing off media whores against each another, but he's got a standing date at the last phone booth in Manhattan, a battered cubicle on Eighth Avenue. The booth is where Stu calls his crush, Pam (Katie Holmes), so his wife, Kelly (Radha Mitchell), won't get suspicious when she checks the cell-phone bill. One afternoon he picks up the receiver to find a smooth-talking psycho (Kiefer Sutherland) on the other end, ready to play some head games. The caller tells Stu he has a high-powered rifle trained on the booth and he'll kill him if he hangs up. When low-life Leon (John Enos III) tries to bully Stu into relinquishing the booth, the caller shoots him. A phalanx of trigger-happy cops, who think Stu shot Leon, surround the booth with their guns at the ready. Sympathetic Captain Ramey (Forest Whitaker) tries to persuade him to hang up and leave the booth, but the sniper promises to kill Stu or someone else if he fails to stay on the line and do as he's told.

Postponed from its original 2002 release date because of a real-life sniper spree in the Washington DC-area, this small-scale thriller has the lean, slightly ragged feel of a '70s exploitation movie. The payoff doesn't quite equal the intensity of the spectacularly squirm-inducing premise, but Farrell takes his showboating star turn and runs with it.

PIANIST, THE

DVD

2002 148m c/bw Drama/War

★★★★

Agencja Produkcji Filmowej/Heritage Films/R.P. R

Productions/Runteam/Studio Babelsberg

(U.S./U.K./France/Poland/Germany)

Adrien Brody *(Wladyslaw Szpilman)*, Thomas Kretschmann *(Captain Wilm Hosenfeld)*, Frank Finlay *(The Father)*, Maureen Lipman *(The Mother)*, Emilia Fox *(Dorota)*, Ed Stoppard *(Henryk Szpilman)*, Julia Rayner *(Regina Szpilman)*, Jessica Kate Meyer *(Halina Szpilman)*, Ruth Platt *(Janina)*, Roy Smiles *(Itzak Heller)*

p, Robert Benmussa, Roman Polanski, Alain Sarde; d, Roman Polanski; w, Ronald Harwood (based on the autobiography of Wladyslaw Szpilman); ph, Pawel Edelman; ed, Hervè de Luze; m, Wojciech Kilar; prod d, Allan Starski; art d, Nenad Pecur; fx, Christian Kunstler, Alister Mazzotti, Hans Seck, Kazimierz Wroblewski; cos, Anna Sheppard

AA Best Actor: Adrien Brody; *AA Best Director:* Roman Polanski; *AA Best Adapted Screenplay:* Ronald Harwood; *AAN Best Picture; AAN Best Cinematography:* Pawel Edelman; *AAN Best Costume Design:* Anna Sheppard; *AAN Best Film Editing:* Hervè de Luze

After two decades of aborted projects and mediocre films, Roman Polanski returns to form with an adaptation of Polish pianist Wladyslaw Szpilman's autobiography, a powerful evocation of life in the Warsaw ghetto during the Nazi occupation.

Warsaw, 1939: Szpilman (Adrien Brody, in a career-defining performance) is playing Chopin for a live Polish radio broadcast when the Luftwaffe begins bombing Warsaw, heralding the beginning of a nightmare for Szpilman, his parents (Frank Finlay, Maureen Lipman), his two sisters (Jessica Kate Meyer, Julia Rayner), and his brother (Ed Stoppard). It all unfolds with frightening speed: the Nazis' entrance into Warsaw and the subsequent relocation of the city's 360,000 Jews into the newly established Jewish district, where disease, starvation, and Gestapo brutality would soon take their toll. Unlike the rest of his family, Szpilman manages to escape deportation to a concentration camp, his life saved by a hated Jewish collaborator (Roy Smiles). But left behind in the ghetto's nearly empty streets, Szpilman is just beginning his tour of hell among Warsaw's living dead.

An uncompromising vision that seems terrifyingly real—Polanski himself escaped the Krakow ghetto shortly before it was liquidated, while his family wound up in the camps—the film draws much of its dark power from the director's willingness to explore the absurd randomness of Szpilman's survival, and what fear and terror bred in the victims of unrelenting persecution. Many die heroically behind the brick walls of the ghetto, but not everyone acts nobly. Awarded the coveted Palme d'Or at the 2002 Cannes Film Festival, Polanski's film is an unqualified success both artistically and dramatically. Pawel Edelman's extraordinary cinematography captures the emptying of the ghetto and its haunting aftermath in what must surely rank among the most powerful sequences in recent cinema.

PIANO, THE

DVD

1993 120m c Drama/Historical

★★★★

Jan Chapman Productions/CiBy 2000 (New Zealand) R

Holly Hunter *(Ada McGrath)*, Sam Neill *(Stewart)*, Harvey Keitel *(George Baines)*, Anna Paquin *(Fiona McGrath)*, Kerry Walker *(Aunt Morag)*, Genevieve Lemon *(Nessie)*, Tungia Baker *(Hira)*, Ian Mune *(Reverend)*, Peter Dennett *(Head Seaman)*

p, Jan Chapman; d, Jane Campion; w, Jane Campion; ph, Stuart Dryburgh; ed, Veronika Jenet; m, Michael Nyman; prod d, Andrew McAlpine; cos, Janet Patterson

AA Best Actress: Holly Hunter; *AA Best Supporting Actress:* Anna Paquin; *AA Best Original Screenplay:* Jane Campion; *AAN Best Picture*Jan Chapman; *AAN Best Director:* Jane Campion; *AAN Best Cinematography:* Stuart Dryburgh; *AAN Best Costume Design:* Janet Patterson; *AAN Best Film Editing:* Veronika Jenet

A period love story with strange metaphysical inclinations, Jane Campion's THE PIANO garnered lavish—though not unanimous—critical acclaim and a raft of awards. This is a film of mysterious beauty and subtle passion, set in a past so alien it might as well be another galaxy and peopled with characters so odd it's hard to believe they're not real.

Ada (Holly Hunter), a 19th-century Scottish woman of formidable and eccentric intelligence who hasn't spoken since childhood, is sent with her gravely beautiful daughter Flora (Anna Paquin)—conceived out of wedlock and her mother's intermediary with the speaking world—to the wilds of New Zealand to marry Stewart (Sam Neill), a farmer whose spirit has been deformed by hardship and displaced decorum. Though speechless, Ada is a gifted pianist who plays with an intensity that simultaneously enthralls and frightens the average listener. Stewart refuses to have her piano hauled to his isolated farm, but Baines (Harvey Keitel), an uneducated Englishman gone native, buys the instrument and arranges for Ada to give him piano lessons in his hut. Their increasingly erotic liaison eventually transforms the lives of all concerned.

Though without explicit sex scenes, THE PIANO is intensely sensual—when Ada massages Stewart's bare flesh or plays for the naked Baines, the sexual charge is almost palpable—and Campion's eye is extraordinary. She searches out the detail that makes the image, and the image that tells the story more eloquently than words ever could. Her film is a compelling examination of the wondrously strange ways in which people treat one another, the poetically eccentric accommodations they make to life's incomprehensible cruelty and flashes of brilliant wonder.

PICKPOCKET

1959 75m bw Crime ★★★★
Lux (France)

Martin Lassalle (Michel), Marika Green (Jeanne), Pierre Leymarie (Jacques), Jean Pelegri (Police Inspector), Kassagi (Master Pickpocket), Pierre Etaix (Accomplice), Dolly Scal (Michel's Mother), Cesar Gattegno (Detective)

p, Agnes Delahaie; d, Robert Bresson; w, Robert Bresson (based on the novel Crime and Punishment by Feodor Dostoyevsky); ph, L.H. Burel; ed, Raymond Lamy; m, Jean-Baptiste Lully; art d, Pierre Charbonnier

Using Dostoyevsky's *Crime and Punishment* as a point of departure, director Bresson has created a wonderful study of a criminal on the road to redemption in PICKPOCKET (released in Paris in 1959). Lassalle stars as a lonely young man who resigns himself to the fate of becoming a pickpocket. An initial attempt is unsuccessful, and he is easily caught. It is during his arrest that Lassalle's consciousness is raised on the rights and wrongs of theft. When his sickly mother dies, Green and Leymarie, his two closest friends, offer advice and solace. Lassalle, however, chooses to return to crime, taking lessons from master pickpocket Kassagi. The police inspector observes Lassalle's criminal life but fails to arrest him, partly because of flimsy evidence and partly because he is intrigued with Lassalle's ideas. When Lassalle's partners in crime are arrested, the pickpocket flees France, leaving behind Green, who has by now fallen in love with him. When he returns years later he finds Green unmarried and with a child. Again he resorts to stealing and again he is caught. Green visits him in his cell, and for the first time he realizes that he loves her. In the memorable final moments, Green and Lassalle embrace through the bars of the cell as he tells her, "What a strange way I have traveled to find you at last." As Bresson has so often done in his films, PICKPOCKET details a man's struggle between his inner feelings and his attempt to survive in society. What separates PICKPOCKET from so many other films is Bresson's use of Lassalle's inner voice (which corresponds to the written words in his diary) as a narrative element. Those familiar with the work of screenwriter-director Paul Schrader will note a few similarities in style and thought, which comes as no surprise since Schrader wrote a book entitled *Transcendental Style on Film: Ozu, Bresson, and Dreyer*. Elements of TAXI DRIVER's narrative (voiceover and diary passages corresponding) are lifted from PICKPOCKET, as in the final line of AMERICAN GIGOLO. While Schrader's transcendental style has failed to achieve the status of Bresson or Ozu or Dreyer (TAXI DRIVER, his finest achievement, comes closest), he has, at least, brought an interesting philosophical element into American film.

PICKUP ON SOUTH STREET

1953 80m bw Crime/Spy **DVD**
Fox (U.S.) ★★★★

Richard Widmark (Skip McCoy), Jean Peters (Candy), Thelma Ritter (Moe), Murvyn Vye (Capt. Dan Tiger), Richard Kiley (Joey), Willis Bouchey (Zara), Milburn Stone (Winoki), Henry Slate (MacGregor), Jerry O'Sullivan (Enyart), Harry Carter (Dietrich),

p, Jules Schermer; d, Samuel Fuller; w, Samuel Fuller (based on the story "Blaze of Glory" by Dwight Taylor); ph, Joseph MacDonald; ed, Nick De Maggio; m, Leigh Harline; art d, Lyle Wheeler, George Patrick; fx, Ray Kellogg; cos, Travilla

AAN Best Supporting Actress: Thelma Ritter

A brutal melodrama set against a backdrop of New York's seedy underworld, PICKUP ON SOUTH STREET delves into the shadowy world of federal agents and communist spies.

Widmark is a petty crook, a three-time loser whose actions are motivated solely by greed. When he steals a wallet from the purse of Peters, he finds himself in deeper trouble than he ever imagined. Inside the wallet is top-secret microfilm that Peters is unwittingly transporting for her lover, Kiley, a communist spy she believes to be a patent lawyer. When Kiley discovers that the microfilm has been stolen, he demands that Peters find Widmark and get the film back. Also on Widmark's track are two federal agents who have been shadowing Peters. Both the agents and Peters get information on Widmark's whereabouts from Ritter, an aging ex-pickpocket who supplements her scant income from tie peddling by selling information on underworld criminals. Peters tries to use sex to get the microfilm from Widmark but fails. The agents appeal to Widmark's sense of patriotism, but this, too, fails since Widmark doesn't care about the effect of communism on the American way of life. With all the interest that has been shown in the microfilm, Widmark knows that it is worth a great deal of money, so he holds out for an offer from Kiley. By now Peters has fallen for Widmark, and has turned against Kiley, whom she sees as un-American. Kiley attempts to buy Widmark's address from Ritter, but she proudly refuses to sell to a communist—at any price. Enraged, Kiley kills Ritter. Widmark now has a reason to keep the microfilm out of Kiley's hands—not because Kiley is a communist but because the spy killed a friend of Widmark's. Kiley then returns to Peters (who by now has obtained the film) and mercilessly beats her when he learns of her part in the scheme. After discovering that some of the microfilm is missing and obtaining Widmark's waterfront address, Kiley pays the thief a visit. Widmark eludes Kiley and follows him to a subway station, where Widmark manages to steal back the microfilm. In retaliation for the death of Ritter and the attack on Peters, Widmark pounds Kiley into the pavement and turns him over to the federal agents. Only after Kiley is killed is it revealed that his contact is none other than the federal agent who has been heading up the search for the spy. Having assisted the feds, Widmark is left to finish his romance with Peters and to return to his gutter life.

This provocative film from Sam Fuller is is based on "Blaze of Glory," a straightforward story about drug pushers written by Dwight Taylor. Although this original story line was retained in the dubbed version of the film released in France under the title LA PORTE DE LA DROGUE, Fuller decided to politicize the American version of the film. Unfortunately, PICKUP ON SOUTH STREET has been viewed by some as rabidly anticommunist, an assessment that ignores the depth and complexity that Fuller brings to the film. Like so many of Fuller's heroes, Widmark's Skip McCoy fights to retain his individuality in the face of societal pressures. Yet McCoy doesn't foil the communist scheme because of his devotion to the American ideal but because Kiley, who just happens to be a communist spy, has done McCoy wrong. Both Widmark and Peters are superb, but it is Ritter, as the seedy but much-loved Moe, who gives the film its emotional punch, and her performance earned an Oscar nomination for Best Supporting Actress—something of an oddity for a Fuller-directed B movie.

PICNIC
1955 115m c Drama
Columbia (U.S.)

DVD
★★★★

William Holden (Hal Carter), Rosalind Russell (Rosemary Sydney), Kim Novak (Madge Owens), Betty Field (Flo Owens), Susan Strasberg (Millie Owens), Cliff Robertson (Alan), Arthur O'Connell (Howard Bevans), Verna Felton (Mrs. Helen Potts), Reta Shaw (Linda Sue Breckenridge), Nick Adams (Bomber)

p, Fred Kohlmar; d, Joshua Logan; w, Daniel Taradash (based on the play by William Inge); ph, James Wong Howe (CinemaScope, Technicolor); ed, Charles Nelson, William Lyon; m, George Duning; prod d, Jo Mielziner; art d, William Flannery; chor, Miriam Nelson; cos, Jean Louis

AAN Best Picture; AAN Best Supporting Actor: Arthur O'Connell; AAN Best Director: Joshua Logan; AA Best Film Editing: William A. Lyon, Charles Nelson; AAN Best Score (Drama or Comedy): George Duning; AA Best Art Direction-Set Decoration (Color): William Flannery, Jo Mielziner, Robert Priestley

Joshua Logan's faithful screen adaptation of William Inge's Pulitzer Prize-winning play about small-town America. PICNIC features a bravura performance by Holden as a drifter come to a small Kansas town just as the community is preparing to celebrate Labor Day. Seeking out old college friend Robertson in the hope of landing a job with Robertson's father, the richest man in the county, Holden is invited to join in the festivities. What's more, Robertson insists that Holden meet his fiancee, the beautiful Novak, and she and the drifter fall in love at first sight. Holden struts about the town flexing his muscles, and most of the local ladies, including Novak's naive younger sister, Strasberg, and schoolmarm Russell, fall for the handsome stranger. Holden brags about his adventures, and Russell gets drunk while admiring him, thrusting aside her reliable date, O'Connell, and losing control, ripping Holden's shirt right off his back in her seizure of lust. Along with this humiliation, Holden is forced into a fight with Robertson so that he beats up his old friend and then must run from the law, dragging Novak with him. He finally persuades her to return home, confessing that he's nothing but a bum and a liar. Novak does go home, and Holden exits the way he arrived, by hopping a freight train. Novak, however, realizes that her love for Holden is stronger than the security of home and she takes a bus heading in the same direction as the train, intending to catch up with the love of her life.

Holden is brilliant; Novak, in her first major role, was terrified of botching the job but performs admirably. The love scenes between the two have real fire, and the sequence showing their dance together is as sensual as any recorded on film. Hollywood lore has it that Holden didn't believe he was up to the famous slow dance with Novak. Logan, who rubbed every scene in the film to high gloss, took Holden to roadhouses and compelled him to dance with choreographer Nelson to jukebox songs until the actor was confident he could perform on the dance floor. Cinematographer Howe circled the two dancers with his camera, showing them mostly from the waist up, their eyes riveted to each other, capturing the love scene in one take. That scene became one of the most famous of the 1950s and it made "Moonglow" a sensational hit. The film was shot in Hutchinson, Kansas, and in Columbia's Burbank Studio.

PICNIC AT HANGING ROCK
1975 110m c Drama
Atlantic (Australia)

DVD
★★★½
PG

Rachel Roberts (Mrs. Appleyard), Dominic Guard (Michael Fitzhubert), Helen Morse (Dianne De Poiters), Jacki Weaver (Minnie), Vivean Gray (Miss Greta McGraw), Kirsty Child (Dora Lumley), Anne Louise Lambert, billed as Anne Lambert

(Miranda), Karen Robson (Irma), Jane Vallis (Marion), Christine Schuler (Edith Horton)

p, Jim McElroy, Hal McElroy; d, Peter Weir; w, Cliff Green (based on the novel by Joan Lindsay); ph, Russell Boyd (Eastmancolor); ed, Max Lemon; m, Bruce Smeaton; art d, David Copping; cos, Judy Dorsman

The critical recognition of Australia's film industry in the late 1970s can, to a large degree, be credited to the works of Peter Weir. After his first feature, THE CARS THAT ATE PARIS, films such as PICNIC AT HANGING ROCK and THE LAST WAVE exhibited a peculiar and fascinating mystical quality that revealed a distinctive sensibility. Unfortunately Weir's decidedly personal vision is often rather murky.

PICNIC AT HANGING ROCK recounts the strange story of three girls and a teacher from a Victoria finishing school who go missing from a school picnic while exploring nearby Hanging Rock on St. Valentine's Day, 1900. One of the girls, Edith (Christine Schuler), takes a nap and wakes to find that the other three, seemingly under a spell, have removed their shoes and stockings to climb higher. They vanish. The police are called in but they are unsuccessful in their search. A young Englishman conducts a search of his own with odd and inconclusive results.

An exceedingly beautiful film, PICNIC AT HANGING ROCK seems to aspire to be an existential thriller of some sort. At times the film seems to tread in BLACK NARCISSUS territory with its depiction of barely controlled sexual hysteria and its eccentric lyrical quality. It's all pretty overheated and underexplained but this arty, vague, and possibly supernatural movie lingers on in the memory.

PICTURE OF DORIAN GRAY, THE
1945 110m c/bw Horror
MGM (U.S.)

★★★½

George Sanders (Lord Henry Wotton), Hurd Hatfield (Dorian Gray), Donna Reed (Gladys Hallward), Angela Lansbury (Sybil Vane), Lowell Gilmore (Basil Hallward), Peter Lawford (David Stone), Richard Fraser (James Vane), Reginald Owen (Lord George Farmoor), Lydia Bilbrook (Mrs. Vane), Morton Lowry (Adrian Singleton)

p, Pandro S. Berman; d, Albert Lewin; w, Albert Lewin (based on the novel by Oscar Wilde); ph, Harry Stradling; ed, Ferris Webster; m, Herbert Stothart; art d, Cedric Gibbons, Hans Peters

AAN Best Supporting Actress: Angela Lansbury; AA Best B/W Cinematography: Harry Stradling; AAN Best Interior Decoration (B/W): Cedric Gibbons, Hans Peters, Edwin B. Willis, John Bonar, Hugh Hunt

This subtle and frightening adaptation of the classic Oscar Wilde novel allows the audience's imagination to do most of the scaring. Hurd Hatfield stars as the title character—a young aristocrat in 19th-century London whose gentle, angelic appearance is dangerously deceptive. Coaxed by the manipulative and hedonistic Lord Henry Wotton (George Sanders), Dorian grows as evil and scandalous as his mentor, becoming a philandering louse who entertains sadistic and perverse thoughts, alluding to (unseen) orgies and unspeakable evils. At the height of his vanity, Dorian has his portrait painted, and, in a Faustian pact, trades his soul for eternal youth. As a result, the portrait ages hideously, while Dorian's appearance never changes. In much the same manner as Val Lewton's horror films, THE PICTURE OF DORIAN GRAY frightens the audience by mere suggestion, without ever resorting to distracting visual representations of the horrible. All the infamy of Hatfield's character is implied, resulting in a building up of evil so horrible that it becomes unspeakable. The only visual shock the audience is subjected to is the portrait itself (which one never expects to see when it pops onto the screen in

Technicolor with a violent musical crash), painted in a brilliantly grotesque style by Ivan Albright. THE PICTURE OF DORIAN GRAY not only frightened many viewers, it also earned the respect of the Motion Picture Academy, which bestowed upon the film two Oscar nominations—one to Angela Lansbury (as Dorian's jilted fiancee) for Best Supporting Actress and another to Cedric Gibbons and Hans Peters for Best Black-and-White Art Direction—and one statuette for the deep-focus camerawork of Harry Stradling.

PIECES OF APRIL

2003 80m c Comedy/Drama ★★★
InDiGent Productions/IFC Productions/ PG-13
Kalkaska Productions (U.S.)

Katie Holmes (April Burns), Patricia Clarkson (Joy Burns), Oliver Platt (Jim Burns), Derek Luke (Bobby), Sean Hayes (Wayne), Alison Pill (Beth Burns), John Gallagher Jr. (Timmy Burns), Alice Drummond (Grandma Dottie), Lillias White (Evette), Isiah Whitlock Jr. (Eugene)

p, Alexis Alexanian, Holly Becker, John Lyons, Gary Winick; d, Peter Hedges; w, Peter Hedges; ph, Tami Reiker; ed, Mark Livolsi; m, Stephin Merritt; prod d, Rick Butler; art d, Shannon Robert Bowen, Aleta Shaffer; cos, Laura Bauer

AAN Best Supporting Actress: Patricia Clarkson

Former "Dawson's Creek" good girl Katie Holmes overhauls her squeaky-clean image with her surprising portrayal of April, the punky black sheep of the Burns family who's determined to fix Thanksgiving dinner for her family in her run-down New York City apartment.

Virtually estranged from her difficult mother, Joy (Patricia Clarkson), and her well-meaning father, Jim (Oliver Platt), April is now hoping to effect a reconciliation: Joy has been diagnosed with cancer and this Thanksgiving may be her last. Joy's certain that the dinner will end in disaster, but Jim is more optimistic; he thinks April might actually be getting herself together. She's found a new apartment and a boyfriend (Derek Luke), who seems willing to put up with her moods and abrasive personality. April knows there's a lot riding on this dinner, but just as she pops the turkey into the oven, she realizes that the appliance is broken. With no other recourse, she throws herself on the mercy of her neighbors, begging them the use of their oven for a few hours at a time. As April's family, including her eager-to-please sister (terrific newcomer Alison Pill), her shutterbug brother (John Gallagher Jr.), and their senile grandmother (Alice Drummond) make their way toward the city, the film's simple message takes shape: No one, not April nor the Pilgrims, can go it alone.

This gentle comedy marks the feature directing debut of writer Peter Hedges, and his lead character poses a unique challenge for an actor. With little else to do other than race from apartment to apartment with a half-cooked turkey, April must somehow emerge as a fully formed, sympathetic character. The charismatic Holmes is certainly a good actor, but this tricky part requires a great one.

PIERROT LE FOU

1965 110m c Crime/Romance ★★★★
Rome/Paris/SNC/DEG (France/Italy)

Jean-Paul Belmondo (Ferdinand Griffon, "Pierrot"), Anna Karina (Marianne Renoir), Dirk Sanders (Fred, Marianne's Brother), Raymond Devos (Man on the Pier), Graziella Galvani (Ferdinand's Wife), Roger Dutoit, Hans Meyer (Gangsters), Jimmy Karoubi (Dwarf), Krista Nell (Mme. Staquet), Pascal Aubier (2nd Brother)

p, Georges de Beauregard; d, Jean-Luc Godard; w, Jean-Luc Godard (based on the novel Obsession by Lionel White); ph,

Raoul Coutard (Techniscope, Eastmancolor); ed, Francoise Collin; m, Antoine Duhamel, Antonio Vivaldi; art d, Pierre Guffroy

Like BAND OF OUTSIDERS before it and the incomprehensible MADE IN USA afterward, Jean-Luc Godard's PIERROT LE FOU is based on a pulp detective novel, providing the filmmaker with a simple story on which to hang his personal, artistic and philosophical beliefs.

Ferdinand Griffon (Jean-Paul Belmondo) leaves behind his Parisian wife and child during a party and takes off on an adventure with Marianne Renoir (Anna Karina), the family baby-sitter with whom he had an affair five years earlier. The following morning a man is found in Marianne's apartment with scissors sticking out of his throat. They set out for the Riviera (heading south, as the characters in Godard's previous film, ALPHAVILLE, hoped to do) in the hope of locating Marianne's gunrunner brother. Ferdinand spends his time writing a journal, but Marianne grows increasingly impatient and gets herself involved once more in gangster activities. Again the result is a mobster—a dwarf—being found with scissors in his throat.

The pair is separated when Ferdinand is kidnapped and tortured by gangsters who are interested in finding Marianne. Ferdinand eventually meets up with her and learns that her brother is really her lover. A double cross follows, and Ferdinand ends up shooting them both. Having had enough of the adventure, Ferdinand phones his wife in Paris but cannot get through to her. He goes to the top of a hill, paints his face blue, ties red and yellow sticks of dynamite to his head, and lights the fuse.

PIERROT LE FOU was Godard's tenth film in six years (not including four sketches that he contributed to compilation films) and perhaps the first to contain all the elements that have been called "Godardian." He combined everything that came before—the romanticism of BREATHLESS, the inner monologue externalized in LE PETIT SOLDAT, the structural divison of MY LIFE TO LIVE, and the epic odyssey of CONTEMPT—with the linguistic diary format that would overpower some of his later films.

Working from the outline provided by Lionel White's novel Obsession, Godard was able to proceed without a script and create what he called "a completely spontaneous film." Spontaneous or not, PIERROT LE FOU is arguably one of the few Godard pictures to have the desired balance of romance, adventure, violence, and humor on one side, and philosophy, literary and cinematic allusion, and Brechtian distancing on the other.

The film was lensed quickly in May, June, and July 1965 and then edited even more rapidly for a showing at the Venice Film Festival at the end of August. Despite the mixed reaction that inevitably accompanies a new Godard film, it was soon elevated to the position of runner-up in the prestigious Sight and Sound poll of 1972.

PILLOW BOOK, THE

1996 126m c Erotic/Romance/Drama ★★½
Kasander/Wigman Productions/Woodline Films/ NC-17
Alpha Film/Channel Four Films/Canal Plus/Delux
Productions (U.K./Netherlands/France)

Vivian Wu (Nagiko Kiohara), Yoshi Oida (The Publisher), Ken Ogata (The Father), Ewan McGregor (Jerome), Hideko Yoshida (Sei Shonagon/The Aunt/The Maid), Judy Ongg (The Mother), Yutaka Honda (Hoki), Ken Mitsuishi (The Husband), Barbara Lott (Jerome's Mother), Miwako Kawai

p, Kees Kasander; d, Peter Greenaway; w, Peter Greenaway; ph, Sacha Vierny; ed, Chris Wyatt, Peter Greenaway; prod d, Wilbert van Dorp, Andree Putman, Emi Wada; art d, Koichi Hamamura, Vincent De Pater; cos, Dien van Straalen, Koji Tatsuno, Martin Margiela, Emi Wada

An excellent introduction to the films of Peter Greenaway, this seductive eye-candy masquerading as thought-provoking art cinema wears its brain on its sleeve, or—more accurately—its bare skin.

Nagiko (Vivian Wu)—namesake of Sei Shonagon, the author of a 10th-century collection of sensual writings called *The Pillow Book*—cherishes the memory of the birthday ritual devised by her father (Ken Ogata), a writer and skilled calligrapher who writes birthday greetings on her upturned face. As an adult, Nagiko finds the act of writing on the body suffused with erotic potential, and the scent of paper reminds her of human skin, an apparently quixotic detail that experienced viewers of Greenaway films will know can only have ominous significance. A series of unsatisfactory affairs with calligraphers behind her, she falls in love with bisexual translator Jerome (Ewan McGregor). He becomes her link to a publisher (Yoshi Oida) who once humiliated her father and against whom she plots an elaborate revenge.

With its attractive cast, beguiling score, and relatively straightforward narrative, this dark fable of letters and lust is one of Greenaway's most accessible works, although it retains the hallmarks of his earlier films: obsessions with ritual, with counting, with densely layered and embedded images, sex in conjunction with grotesque violence, and the transformation of life into literature. While undeniably exquisite, the entire enterprise carries a faint whiff of orientalism—naked Asian flesh (to be fair, McGregor, the only European with a significant role, bares all as well) and an obsession with mysterious Eastern arts—that's a bit troubling in so conspicuously learned an enterprise.

PILLOW TALK
1959 105m c   Comedy   ★★★½
Arwin   (U.S.)

Rock Hudson *(Brad Allen)*, Doris Day *(Jan Morrow)*, Tony Randall *(Jonathan Forbes)*, Thelma Ritter *(Alma)*, Nick Adams *(Tony Walters)*, Julia Meade *(Marie)*, Allen Jenkins *(Harry)*, Marcel Dalio *(Pierot)*, Lee Patrick *(Mrs. Walters)*, Mary McCarty *(Nurse Resnick)*

p, Ross Hunter, Martin Melcher; d, Michael Gordon; w, Stanley Shapiro, Maurice Richlin (based on a story by Russell Rouse, Clarence Greene); ph, Arthur E. Arling (CinemaScope, Eastmancolor); ed, Milton Carruth; m, Frank DeVol; art d, Alexander Golitzen, Richard H. Riedel; cos, Bill Thomas, Jean Louis

AAN Best Actress: Doris Day; AAN Best Supporting Actress: Thelma Ritter; AA Best Original Story and Screenplay: Russell Rouse, Clarence Greene, Stanley Shapiro, Maurice Richlin; AAN Best Score (Drama or Comedy): Frank DeVol; AAN Best Art Direction-Set Decoration (Color): Richard H. Riedel, Russell A. Gausman, Ruby R. Levitt

PILLOW TALK was the first of the witty, well-produced sex comedies featuring Day and Hudson. Hudson, a playboy songwriter, and Day, a successful, independent interior designer, learn to loathe each other when they are forced to share a party line during a Manhattan phone-line shortage. Day gets increasingly angry every time she tries to make a call and hears Hudson coming on to yet another unsuspecting woman he's trying to bed. After listening to enough of his suave baloney, Day begins causing trouble. Naturally, Hudson thinks she's an uptight old hag, and eventually they agree to take turns using the phone every half-hour. Coincidentally, Hudson's buddy, Randall, is in love with Day and the phone-sharers finally meet when Randall brings her to see the progress of a Broadway show he's funding and for which Hudson is writing the tunes. Surprised by Day's good looks, Hudson pretends to be a dopey Texan and begins to work his charms on her. Day quickly realizes who Hudson is and puts an end to the romance. Now hooked, Hudson seeks

advice from Day's maid, Ritter (who nearly steals the movie), and she suggests that Hudson let Day decorate his apartment. This ploy backfires, however, when the not-to-be-fooled Day gets her licks in by doing over Hudson's pad in a hideous manner. Frustrated because he can get her no other way, Hudson does some quick thinking and states that he hopes his apartment will be to her liking when they get married.

Though PILLOW TALK is silly and at times overly "cute," it was the first time Day was allowed to show a more sexually frank side to her character, and Hudson was able to prove he was more than just a good-looking hunk. The combination clicked, leaving the two among the most popular stars of the next five years. It was also among the bigger box-office successes of its day, taking in $7.5 million in domestic distribution.

PIMPERNEL SMITH
1941 100m bw Spy/War   ★★★½
British National   (U.K.)

Leslie Howard *(Prof. Horatio Smith)*, Francis L. Sullivan *(Gen. von Graum)*, Mary Morris *(Ludmilla Koslowski)*, Hugh McDermott *(David Maxwell)*, Raymond Huntley *(Marx)*, Manning Whiley *(Bertie Gregson)*, Peter Gawthorne *(Sidimir Koslowski)*, Allan Jeayes *(Dr. Beckendorf)*, Dennis Arundell *(Hoffman)*, Joan Kemp-Welch *(Teacher)*

p, Leslie Howard; d, Leslie Howard; w, Anatole de Grunwald, Roland Pertwee, Ian Dalrymple (based on a story by A.G. MacDonnell, Wolfgang Wilhelm); ph, Mutz Greenbaum; ed, Douglas Myers; m, John Greenwood

Leslie Howard more or less reprises his most famous swashbuckling role, that of THE SCARLET PIMPERNEL, as that tale of disguise and rescue is transplanted from Paris during the Reign of Terror to Germany under the Nazis. Prof. Horatio Smith (Howard), an absent-minded professor of archaeology, is supposedly involved in the search for Aryan artifacts near Switzerland, but secretly he runs refugees over the border to safety while disguising himself in a bewildering variety of get-ups. Meanwhile, Gen. von Graum (Francis L. Sullivan), a corpulent Gestapo officer, sets out to stop the elusive "Pimpernel." Eventually Smith's students figure out what their professor is up to and help him smuggle a large group of persecuted scientists across the border. Smith then goes back one more time, all the way to Berlin, to free Ludmilla Koslowski (Mary Morris), a young woman being held by the Gestapo. This was Howard's first solo directorial effort (he codirected PYGMALION earlier) and he does a creditable job, keeping the film moving with the right mixture of action and suave, stiff-upper-lip heroism; however, his relaxed acting and immensely likable screen presence are what carry the film.

PINK FLAMINGOS
1972 95m c   Comedy   ★★★½
Saliva Films   (U.S.)   NC-17

Divine *(Divine/Babs Johnson)*, David Lochary *(Raymond Marble)*, Mink Stole *(Connie Marble)*, Mary Vivian Pearce *(Cotton)*, Edith Massey *(Miss Edie)*, Danny Mills *(Crackers)*, Channing Wilroy *(Channing)*, Cookie Mueller *(Cookie)*, Paul Swift *(Egg Man)*, Susan Walsh *(Suzie—Blonde in Basement)*

p, John Waters; d, John Waters; w, John Waters; ph, John Waters; ed, John Waters; prod d, Vincent Peranio; art d, Vincent Peranio; cos, Van Smith

Billed as "the most disgusting picture of all time," this absolutely uninhibited exercise in scatology and low camp was the breakthrough film for Baltimore-based independent filmmaker John Waters, who later entered the commercial mainstream with such films as HAIRSPRAY and SERIAL MOM. The improbable star of this ultra-low budget cinematic gross-out is 300-pound transvestite Divine, whose willingness to do virtually anything in front of the camera, along with an undeniable screen presence, made PINK FLAMINGOS a favorite on the campus and midnight-movie circuits. Gleefully grotesque Babs Johnson (Divine) lives in a trailer park with her simpleminded son, Crackers (Danny Mills), and revolting Mama Edie (Edith Massey), who is obsessed with eggs. Everyone agrees that Babs is the "filthiest person in the world"; her status draws the envy of black-market baby farmers Raymond and Connie Marble (David Lochary and Mink Stole), who vow to "out-filthy" their rival. The resulting competition encompasses acts of arson, bestiality, cannibalism, castration and coprophagy. Waters's early films sought to explode the conventions of bourgeois taste, which he saw as fraudulent and oppressive; ironically, bourgeois taste now cheerfully embraces the sensibility (if not, perhaps, the explicit grossness) of PINK FLAMINGOS. To commemorate the film's 25th anniversary, Waters has prepared a special edition of his trash epic, which includes an addendum of never-before-seen footage and a commentary from the director himself.

PINK FLOYD—THE WALL

1982 99m c Musical **★★**
Tin Blue/Goldcrest (U.K.) R

Bob Geldof *(Pink)*, Christine Hargreaves *(Pink's Mother)*, James Laurenson *(Pink's Father)*, Eleanor David *(Pink's Wife)*, Kevin McKeon *(Young Pink)*, Bob Hoskins *(Rock 'n' Roll Manager)*, David Bingham *(Little Pink)*, Jenny Wright *(American Groupie)*, Alex McAvoy *(Teacher)*, Ellis Dale *(English Doctor)*

p, Alan Marshall; d, Alan Parker; w, Roger Waters (based on the album "The Wall" by Pink Floyd); ph, Peter Biziou (Metrocolor); ed, Gerry Hambling; prod d, Brian Morris; art d, Chris Burke, Clinton Cavers; fx, Martin Gutheridge, Graham Longhurst; anim, Gerald Scarfe

This overlong, tedious film based on the multimillion-selling record album by Pink Floyd stars Boomtown Rats singer and "Live Aid" organizer Bob Geldof as Pink, a successful, narcissistic, and wholly unsympathetic rock star on the verge of burnout. Driven to the edge by the news that his wife has left him for another man, Pink spirals into a neurotic conglomeration of flashbacks and fantasies detailing his life. A child of WWII, he grows up amidst the horrors and ruins of wartime Britain. Eventually he becomes a star singer, in the process discovering his power to manipulate a crowd for his own satisfaction (much as his own schoolteachers manipulated and dehumanized him when he was a boy). Cut off from human feeling, Pink slowly builds a wall around himself to deflect suffering. While the music may be interesting and effective on vinyl, on film it becomes repetitious and pretentious, despite director Alan Parker's flair for flashy visuals. Thematically the film is banal, and even its simple themes of alienation, loneliness, and paranoia are muddled and sapped of relevancy by the overblown treatment. Geldof is effective in the lead, and the animation sequences by political cartoonist Gerald Scarfe are interesting and well executed, though too long. Rabid Pink Floyd fans have supported this film enthusiastically since its inception and look upon it as one of the greatest rock 'n' roll films of all times (it isn't).

PINK NARCISSUS

1999 70m c Experimental/Erotic/Fantasy **★★★½**
(U.S.)

Bobby Kendall

d, James Bidgood; w, James Bidgood; ed, Martin Jay Sandoff; m, Gary Goch

Somewhere between Kenneth Anger's 1964 "Scorpio Rising" and the explicit gay porn that began appearing at the end of the '60s stands physique photographer-turned-filmmaker James Bidgood's nearly indescribable ode to male beauty.

A handsome, self-obsessed young hustler (Bobby Kendall) lolls about his pink and gold boudoir in various states of undress, gazing at his reflection, taking calls from clients, and dreaming himself into a series of erotic tableaux. He imagines himself a strutting matador battling a blond "bull" on a motorbike, then a harem boy entranced by a dancing slave. Suddenly the outside world, embodied in a nightmare vision of a Times Square crawling with freaks, midnight cowboys, and aging johns crashes in on his idylls.

Bidgood toiled over this mini-masterpiece for nearly seven years, until it was finally taken away by his more profit-minded investors. The film feels unfinished—it's full of sudden lurches and odd blanks—but that hardly detracts from its fascination. Part underground art film, part soft-core porn, the film marks a turning point, a moment when highly aestheticized erotica was about to give way to liberated but less imaginative hardcore. Bidgood's artistic sources are clear (Anger, Cocteau, Genet), but the film's fluid imagination and startling ingenuity are entirely his own. A delirious, decadent mix of baroque kitsch and real artistry, most of this ravishing film was shot on meticulously handmade sets in Bidgood's cramped New York City apartment. The artifice is amusing, but film is more than mere camp; Bidgood was an untrained but resourceful filmmaker who, in translating his fantasies to celluloid from scratch, happened upon the essential magic of filmmaking.

PINK PANTHER, THE

1964 113m c Comedy **★★★½**
Mirisch/G&E (U.S.)

David Niven *(Sir Charles Lytton)*, Peter Sellers *(Inspector Jacques Clouseau)*, Robert Wagner *(George Lytton)*, Capucine *(Simone Clouseau)*, Claudia Cardinale *(Princess Dala)*, Brenda de Banzie *(Angela Dunning)*, Fran Jeffries *(Greek "Cousin")*, Colin Gordon *(Tucker)*, John Le Mesurier *(Defense Attorney)*, James Lanphier *(Saloud)*

p, Martin Jurow; d, Blake Edwards; w, Blake Edwards, Maurice Richlin; ph, Philip Lathrop (Technirama, Technicolor); ed, Ralph E. Winters, Marshall M. Borden, David Zinnemann; m, Henry Mancini; art d, Fernando Carrere; fx, Lee Zavitz; chor, Hermes Pan; cos, Yves Saint-Laurent

AAN Best Original Score: Henry Mancini

Writer-director Blake Edwards hit paydirt with the character of Inspector Clouseau, a Tati-like police inspector in an overlarge trenchcoat who is sublimely indifferent to the physical realities that surround him. Peter Sellers brought magnificent life to the character and it lasted through a number of movies until Sellers' death. (Clouseau has occasionally been played by others, most recently by Italian comic Roberto Benigni.)

Niven, in a role not unlike his RAFFLES character (or the part played by Cary Grant in TO CATCH A THIEF almost a decade before), is a famous jewel thief who is suave beyond belief, fairly dripping with sophistication. He is vacationing at the Alpine resort of Cortina D'Ampezzo, where all the skiers are swathed in clothes by famous French designers. One of the guests is Cardinale, an Indian princess who owns the famous "Pink Panther" gem, a bauble of immeasurable value. Niven wants the jewel and will stop at nothing to get it. He has been the scourge of Interpol for the previous 15 years, as he's pulled off one daring robbery after another. All that time, Niven has been tailed by Sellers, a

French inspector, who also wants to nail Niven's female accomplice. The fact that Sellers can never seem to catch up with Niven must have something to do with the fact that his wife, Capucine, is Niven's lover and is therefore able to alert Niven before Sellers can nab him. Meanwhile, Niven's American-born nephew, Wagner, is being supported by his uncle under the pretext that he is a college student. Wagner seems, however, to have inherited a predisposition for his uncle's "occupation." Niven is moving in on Cardinale and the gem when Wagner arrives, also intent on purloining the "Panther."

Though he has less time on screen than the other principals, Sellers steals the film. The ensuing follow-up pictures proved his staying power. Gorgeous photography and sets, huge guffaws, and lots of fun. Mancini took an Oscar nomination and stuck around to do the music for several sequels.

PINK PANTHER STRIKES AGAIN, THE 📀
1976 103m c Comedy ★★★
Amjo (U.K.) PG

Peter Sellers *(Inspector Jacques Clouseau)*, Herbert Lom *(Ex-Chief Inspector Dreyfus)*, Colin Blakely *(Alex Drummond)*, Leonard Rossiter *(Quinlan)*, Lesley-Anne Down *(Olga)*, Burt Kwouk *(Kato)*, Andre Maranne *(Francois)*, Richard Vernon *(Dr. Hugo Fassbender)*, Michael Robbins *(Jarvis)*, Briony McRoberts *(Margo Fassbender)*

p, Blake Edwards; d, Blake Edwards; w, Blake Edwards, Frank Waldman; ph, Harry Waxman (Panavision, DeLuxe Color); ed, Alan Jones; m, Henry Mancini; prod d, Peter Mullins; art d, John Siddall; fx, Kit West

AAN Best Original Song: "Come to Me"; Henry Mancini (Music), Don Black (Lyrics)

Director Edwards and co-author Maurice Richlin created the Clouseau character in the first PINK PANTHER picture, and in 1974 THE RETURN OF THE PINK PANTHER took in huge amounts at the theaters. Consequently, this one was rushed out to take advantage of the wave, and it looks it. That's not to say that there aren't plenty of laughs in the picture, but it lacks a credible story, something that was present in the earlier ones. Lom, the head of the French police, has been driven mad by Sellers's behavior and is now incarcerated, with Sellers sitting in the chief's seat. Lom escapes, kidnaps scientist Vernon, who has invented a "death ray," and he threatens to use it to end the world unless the authorities see fit to turn over Sellers to Lom. Down plays a Soviet spy who is put on the case but defects, NINOTCHKA-style, because she falls in love with Sellers. There are some marvelous sight gags, but the film goes over the top into mindless farce at times, destroying much of the Chaplinesque believability that Sellers had earlier engendered.

PINKY
1949 102m bw Drama ★★★★
Fox (U.S.)

Jeanne Crain *(Pinky, Patricia Johnson)*, Ethel Barrymore *(Miss Em)*, Ethel Waters *(Granny Dysey Johnson)*, William Lundigan *(Dr. Thomas Adams)*, Basil Ruysdael *(Judge Walker)*, Kenny Washington *(Dr. Canady)*, Nina Mae McKinney *(Rozelia)*, Griff Barnett *(Dr. Joe McGill)*, Frederick O'Neal *(Jake Walters)*, Evelyn Varden *(Melba Wooley)*

p, Darryl F. Zanuck; d, Elia Kazan; w, Philip Dunne, Dudley Nichols (based on the novel *Quality* by Cid Ricketts Sumner); ph, Joseph MacDonald; ed, Harmon Jones; m, Alfred Newman; art d, Lyle Wheeler, J. Russell Spencer; cos, Charles LeMaire

AAN Best Actress: Jeanne Crain; *AAN Best Supporting Actress:* Ethel Barrymore; *AAN Best Supporting Actress:* Ethel Waters

Producer Darryl F. Zanuck, who had attacked anti-Semitism in GENTLEMAN'S AGREEMENT in 1947, tackled the subject of prejudice against African Americans in this film. Crain plays the eponymous Pinky (a term used in the black community to described those whose complexions are light enough that they can pass for white), a bright young woman who has been studying nursing at a school in New England. Lundigan, a white physician, would like to marry her, but Crain believes the interracial union could never work, suspects Lundigan of being more "tolerant" than committed, and is unwilling to be absorbed into the white world. Sadly, she leaves and returns to the southern town of her birth. Crain's grandmother, Waters, works for feisty dowager Barrymore, and when the old woman becomes ill, Crain becomes her nurse and stays on until her death. Barrymore leaves her estate to Crain, but her family contests the legacy because Crain is black, claiming that Crain exerted undue influence on the dying Barrymore. The dispute is taken to court, where Crain wins the estate. Afterwards, she turns it into a nursing home and school for blacks. Zanuck initially asked John Ford to direct PINKY, but he was reportedly relieved, nevertheless, when Ford (who didn't get along with actress Waters and felt little enthusiasm for the story) asked to be taken off the picture two weeks into shooting, since Zanuck had misgivings about Ford's ability to create credible black characters. After Ford's exit, Zanuck immediately called in Elia Kazan; eight weeks later the film was completed, Ford's footage totally scrapped. Today, PINKY is still remarkable for its sincerity and directness, especially when one considers its date of origin. This is a mature film, with great respect for the humanity of people who are able to transcend social barriers and care for one another. Crain, Waters, and Barrymore all received Oscar nominations for their performances.

PINOCCHIO 📀
1940 88m c Children's/Fantasy/Animated ★★★★★
Walt Disney Productions (U.S.)

VOICES OF: Dick Jones *(Pinocchio)*, Christian Rub *(Geppetto)*, Cliff Edwards *(Jiminy Cricket)*, Evelyn Venable *(The Blue Fairy)*, Walter Catlett *(J. Worthington Foulfellow)*, Frankie Darro *(Lampwick)*, Charles Judels *(Stromboli the Coachman)*, Don Brodie *(Barker)*

p, Walt Disney; d, Ben Sharpsteen, Hamilton Luske; w, Ted Sears, Otto Englander, Webb Smith, William Cottrell, Joseph Sabo, Erdman Penner, Aurelius Battaglia (based on the story by Carlo Collodi); m, Paul J. Smith; art d, Charles Philippi, Hugh Hennesy, Dick Kelsey, Terrell Stapp, John Hubley, Ken Anderson, Kendall O'Connor, Thor Putnam, McLaren Stewart, Al Zinnen; anim, John Lounsbery, Charles A. Nichols, Art Palmer, Fred Moore, Eric Larson, Milt Kahl, Ward Kimball, Franklin Thomas, Vladimir Tytla, Arthur Babbitt, Wolfgang Reitherman

AA Best Original Score: Leigh Harline, Paul J. Smith, Ned Washington; *AA Best Song:* "When You Wish Upon a Star"; Leigh Harline (Music), Ned Washington (Lyrics)

This was Disney's second full-length animated feature and it may well the greatest of the studio's cartoon classics.

A technical tour de force, PINOCCHIO was brilliantly crafted with an awesome attention to detail and verisimilitude. This film showcased all of Disney's innovative techniques when they were still fresh. The episodic story of the wooden puppet who earns real life by learning to be a good person was an unusual but inspired choice for adaptation. Emotionally rich, humorous, and periodically terrifying, the film offers images so startling and memorable that generations of children have been enthralled by it.

This timeless story focuses on a wooden puppet that wants nothing more than to be a real boy, a wish echoed by his creator, Geppetto. One night, the Blue Fairy descends from the skies and promises to turn Pinocchio into a flesh-and-blood little boy if he swears to be brave and unselfish and to learn right from wrong. The Blue Fairy even assigns Pinocchio a conscience, in the form of Jiminy Cricket. This is, of course, the film that features what would become the Disney theme song, "When You Wish upon a Star," sung by the inimitable Cliff Edwards, the voice of Jiminy Cricket. Pinocchio must undergo many harrowing life lessons before his dream comes true.

PINOCCHIO boasts the first extensive use of the Disney-developed multiplane camera. This allows for a convincing illusion that the animation camera is actually moving in three dimensions through different planes of action in the way a dolly or tracking shot functions in a live action film. The animators have further refined their animation of human figures which had still been a bit shaky in their first feature, SNOW WHITE. With both FANTASIA and PINOCCHIO in release in 1940, the future must have seemed bright and interesting at the Disney studios. Then came DUMBO, BAMBI, the studio strike, WWII, and a long stretch of declining success with animated features from which Disney was not able to recover artistically. Some would argue did this recovery finally occured with the release of THE LITTLE MERMAID but this film and BEAUTY AND THE BEAST were, at best, a return to form rather than new plateaus for the animated feature. See PINOCCHIO again and again. A marvel and a joy to behold, it's the real thing. It's the stuff that dreams—and nightmares—are made of.

PINOCCHIO

2002 105m c Children's/Fantasy
Melampo Cinematografica/Medusa Film/Cecchi
Gori Group (Italy)

DVD
★★
G

Roberto Benigni *(Pinocchio)*, Breckin Meyer *(Voice of Pinocchio)*, Nicoletta Braschi *(Blue Fairy)*, Glenn Close *(Voice of Blue Fairy)*, Mino Bellei *(Medoro)*, Eric Idle *(Voice of Medoro)*, Carlo Giuffrè *(Geppetto)*, David Suchet *(Voice of Geppetto/Narrator)*, Peppe Barra *(The Talking Cricket)*, John Cleese *(Voice of the Talking Cricket)*

p, Gianluigi Braschi, Nicoletta Braschi, Elda Ferri; d, Roberto Begnini; w, Roberto Benigni, Vincenzo Cerami (based on the book *L'Avventure di Pinocchio* by Carlo Collodi); ph, Dante Spinotti; ed, Simona Paggi; m, Nicola Piovani; prod d, Danilo Donati; art d, Maurizio Sabatini; fx, Maurizio Corridori, Rob Hodgson; cos, Danilo Donati

Roberto Benigni's fanciful adaptation of Carlo Collodi's classic tale of the naughty wooden puppet who dreams of becoming a real boy was a huge hit in its native Italy but suffers on these shores from poor English-language dubbing.

Benigni returned to Collodi's original material, so anyone weaned on Disney's 1940 animated classic may be surprised at just how bad a puppet Pinocchio is: He's lazy, he refuses to go to school, and he is an incorrigible liar whose nose grows with every falsehood. The moment penniless wood-carver Geppetto (Carlo Giuffre, with voice dubbed by David Suchet) is done whittling Pinocchio (Benigni, voice of Breckin Meyer) from an enchanted block of pine, the puppet is out the door and wreaking havoc in the village market. Pinocchio promises Geppetto he'll go to school, but the pursuit of fun and easy profit lead him astray. When the Talking Cricket (Peppe Barra, voice of John Cleese) tries to teach him the

value of obedience, Pinocchio attacks him with a hammer. Nor will he listen to the Blue Fairy (Benigni's wife, Nicoletta Braschi, voice of Glenn Close), even after she tells Pinocchio that he could one day become a real, live boy if he'd only learn to be good.

That Benigni, who turned 50 shortly after the film was finished, is too old to be playing a boy puppet is really beside the point; he's one Italian icon playing another, and physically, he's quite good. But there's no getting past the badly dubbed voice work of the English-speaking cast, and those old enough to read will be better off watching the subtitles on the original Italian version on the DVD.

PIRATE, THE

1948 102m c Musical
MGM (U.S.)

★★★½

Judy Garland *(Manuela)*, Gene Kelly *(Serafin)*, Walter Slezak *(Don Pedro Vargas)*, Gladys Cooper *(Aunt Inez)*, Reginald Owen *(The Advocate)*, George Zucco *(The Viceroy)*, The Nicholas Brothers *(Specialty Dancers)*, Lester Allen *(Uncle Capucho)*, Lola Deem *(Isabella)*, Ellen Ross *(Mercedes)*

p, Arthur Freed; d, Vincente Minnelli; w, Albert Hackett, Frances Goodrich, Joseph L. Mankiewicz (uncredited), Joseph Than, Lillian Braun, Anita Loos, Wilkie Mahoney (based on a play by S.N. Behrman); ph, Harry Stradling (Technicolor); ed, Blanche Sewell; m, Cole Porter; art d, Cedric Gibbons, Jack Martin Smith; chor, Robert Alton, Gene Kelly; cos, Tom Keogh, Barbara Karinska

AAN Best Score (Musical): Lennie Hayton

The story is wearisome and the acting fever-pitched, but the music and dancing in this colorful film are spectacular. The setting is the Caribbean Island of San Sebastian in the 1820s, where young Manuela (Judy Garland) fantasizes about the notorious pirate Macoco, better known as "Mack the Black," and Serafin (Gene Kelly), a strolling minstrel, tries to win her heart by impersonating him. Manuela discovers his fraud and a knock-down, drag-out fight between the fiery lovers takes place while they sing/shout Cole Porter's "Love of My Life." To his peril, Serafin learns that Don Pedro, Manuela's fiance by arrangement and mayor of the town, is *really* Macoco incognito; Manuela, however, has never known this and is by now hopelessly in love with the street performer. Eventually, she joins his troupe of players, ending the film with a reprise of "Be a Clown" in which Garland and Kelly sing and dance with several of their teeth blackened and big red noses gleaming. THE PIRATE is an old-fashioned lavish MGM musical, dripping with lush color and peppered with wonderful numbers. Little care is given to the script and the dramatics, but the film is a scenic treat, offering magnificent sets and a frenetic pace typical of director Vincente Minnelli (then Garland's husband). Filming was slowed down considerably by Garland's emotional illness; she was on the verge of a breakdown and delayed the proceedings with paranoiac attacks directed at Minnelli, Kelly, and Porter. A financial failure that cost MGM $3,768,000 and earned back only $2,290,000 in its initial release, THE PIRATE has earned a cult following, chiefly for its extravagant choreography, especially in the sweeping "Nina" and "Mack the Black" numbers, danced energetically by Kelly. A special treat is the appearance of the Nicholas Brothers, who dance with Kelly in the first "Be a Clown" number; they were edited out of this scene in southern theaters at the time of release.

PIRATES OF THE CARIBBEAN: THE CURSE OF THE BLACK PEARL **DVD**

2003 133m c Action/Adventure ★★½
Jerry Bruckheimer Films/Walt Disney Pictures PG-13
(U.S.)

Johnny Depp (Jack Sparrow), Geoffrey Rush (Barbossa), Orlando Bloom (Will Turner), Keira Knightley (Elizabeth Swann), Jack Davenport (Norrington), Jonathan Pryce (Governor Weatherby Swann), Lee Arenberg (Pintel), Mackenzie Crook (Ragetti), Damian O'Hare (Lt. Gillette), Giles New (Murtogg)

p, Jerry Bruckheimer; d, Gore Verbinski; w, Ted Elliott, Terry Rossio (from a screen story by Ted Elliott, Terry Rossio, Stuart Beattie and Jay Wolpert, based on Walt Disney's Pirates of the Caribbean theme-park ride); ph, Dariusz Wolski; ed, Stephen Rivkin, Arthur R. Schmidt, Craig Wood; m, Klaus Badelt; prod d, Brian Morris; art d, Derek R. Hill; fx, Danny Cangemi, Terry Frazee, John Knoll; cos, Penny Rose

AAN Best Actor: Johnny Depp; AAN Best Sound Mixing: Christopher Boyes, David Parker, David Campbell, Lee Orloff; AAN Best Sound Editing: Christopher Boyes, George Watters II; AAN Best Makeup: Ve Neill, Martin Samuel; AAN Best Visual Effects: John Knoll, Hal Hickel, Charles Gibson, Terry Frazee

This foolhardy, mega-budget Disney gamble comes close to besting the curse that has befallen every other recent attempt to revive the pirate movie: the first 20 minutes include a ripped corset, a daring escape and a sword fight full of derring-do. But the next two hours are only more of the same.

For nearly 10 years, the fearsome pirates of the *Black Pearl* have terrorized the Caribbean under a dire curse. After dumping their notorious captain, Jack Sparrow (a hilarious Johnny Depp), on a desert isle, the mutinous crew made off with a chest of Aztec gold. Unbeknownst to them, the coins were cursed, and ever since the men have been able to consume neither grub nor grog, and moonlight reveals what they've become: creepy, crumbling skeletons. To lift the whammy, the rotting rovers must return all 882 gold pieces to the chest, including the one that now hangs around the lovely neck of Elizabeth Swann (Keira Knightley), feisty daughter of Port Royal Governor Weatherby Swann (Jonathan Pryce). The pirates storm the island and snatch Elizabeth away, but they're pursued by her two devoted suitors: Elizabeth's dull fiance, Commodore Norrington (Jack Davenport), and her secret crush, humble blacksmith Will Turner (Orlando Bloom). Norrington has the British fleet at his disposal, but Turner must turn to the only person who can lead him to the *Black Pearl*: Jack Sparrow.

The action is fast, and the hokey-jokey script by SHREK scribes Ted Elliott and Terry Rossio squeezes in just about every convention of the genre. What else could they do? Unlike, say, Westerns, pirate movies don't really have much to say, nor do they revive them. Director Gore Verbinski delivers the best one can hope for: a cleverly nostalgic, high-tech copy of the real deal.

PIT AND THE PENDULUM, THE **DVD**

1961 85m c Horror ★★★½
Alta Vista (U.S.)

Vincent Price (Nicholas Medina), John Kerr (Francis Barnard), Barbara Steele (Elisabeth Barnard Medina), Luana Anders (Catherine Medina), Anthony Carbone (Dr. Charles Leon), Patrick Westwood (Maximillian the Butler), Lynn Bernay (Maria), Larry Turner (Nicholas as a Child), Mary Menzies (Isabella), Charles Victor (Bartolome)

p, Roger Corman; d, Roger Corman; w, Richard Matheson (based on a story by Edgar Allan Poe); ph, Floyd Crosby

(Panavision, Pathe Color); ed, Anthony Carras; m, Les Baxter; prod d, Daniel Haller; art d, Daniel Haller; fx, Pat Dinga; cos, Marjorie Corso

The second and one of the best films in Roger Corman's Edgar Allan Poe series stars Vincent Price as Nicholas Medina, owner of a large and spooky castle with an elaborate torture chamber built by his father during the Spanish Inquisition. Stricken with grief after the death of his wife, Elisabeth (Barbara Steele, in her American film debut), Nicholas becomes obsessed with the notion that he accidentally buried her alive. Elisabeth's brother, Francis Barnard (John Kerr), suspects foul play and travels to the castle looking for answers. He finds Nicholas slowly going mad and claiming to hear Elisabeth's voice calling to him. Eventually it is revealed that Elisabeth is not dead at all, but has conspired with her lover, family doctor Charles Leon (Anthony Carbone), to drive her husband insane. Corman brought in THE PIT AND THE PENDULUM on a 15-day shooting schedule, and the result is a very entertaining horror film with chills, humor, and a bravura performance by Price, who was just beginning to finely hone his wickedly delightful, villainous characters. Shot in lush and almost garish color by cinematographer Floyd Crosby (who also shot Corman's previous Poe film, THE HOUSE OF USHER), the picture includes some impressive techniques and camera movement. Screenwriter Richard Matheson did a fine job of adapting Poe's rather limited (for films) short story by saving the dungeon sequences for the climax and then creating a rather interesting plot line to lead up to it. One of Corman's best.

PIXOTE **DVD**

1981 127m c Drama/Crime/Prison ★★★★
HB/Embrafilme (Brazil)

Fernando Ramos da Silva (Pixote), Jorge Juliao (Lilica), Gilberto Moura (Dito), Edilson Lino (Chico), Zenildo Oliveira Santos (Fumaca), Claudio Bernardo (Garatao), Israel Feres David (Roberto Pie de Plata), Jose Nilson dos Santos (Diego), Marilia Pera (Sueli), Jardel Filho (Sapatos Brancos)

p, Paulo Francini, Jose Pinto; d, Hector Babenco; w, Hector Babenco, Jorge Duran (based on the novel A Infancia Dos Mortos by Jose Louzeiro); ph, Rodolfo Sanchez; ed, Luiz Elias; m, John Neschling; art d, Clovis Bueno; cos, Carminha Guarana

A grim, disturbing and engrossing portrait of children living in poverty on the streets of Sao Paulo, PIXOTE is one of the most powerful films ever made on the subject of urban degradation.

The story focuses on Pixote (da Silva), a boy abandoned by his parents, who becomes a streetwise pimp and eventually a murderer by the age of 10. The film depicts a life of unrelenting squalor and hopelessness, and director Babenco does not flinch from confronting his audience with the most grisly details of his subjects' lives: violence in the reformatory; an aborted baby in a bucket in a bathroom; the young hero suddenly reverting to infancy, suckling at the breast of a momentarily sympathetic prostitute.

PIXOTE draws on a tradition of films in which innocence is stripped from the young, from Rossellini's GERMANY YEAR ZERO to Truffaut's THE 400 BLOWS. In its combination of a documentary-like approach influenced by neorealism with a sometimes surreal visual sense, it clearly owes most to Bunuel's LOS OLVIDADOS. In fact, the director had originally intended to make a documentary and had completed 200 hours of interviews with reformatory children for this purpose. When he was denied further access to the reformatories, he turned to the streets and hired slum children to portray themselves, building scenes around improvisation workshops that allowed the youths to contribute their own experiences to the picture. In 1986, in a tragic and ironic coda to the making of the film, da Silva was killed in a shootout with police after allegedly resisting arrest for an assault.

PLACE IN THE SUN, A   📀

1951 122m bw Drama   ★★★★
Paramount   (U.S.)

Montgomery Clift (George Eastman), Elizabeth Taylor (Angela Vickers), Shelley Winters (Alice Tripp), Anne Revere (Hannah Eastman), Keefe Brasselle (Earl Eastman), Fred Clark (Bellows), Raymond Burr (Marlowe), Herbert Heyes (Charles Eastman), Shepperd Strudwick (Anthony Vickers), Frieda Inescort (Mrs. Vickers)

p, George Stevens; d, George Stevens; w, Michael Wilson, Harry Brown (based on the novel An American Tragedy by Theodore Dreiser and the play by Patrick Kearney); ph, William Mellor; ed, William Hornbeck; m, Franz Waxman; art d, Hans Dreier, Walter Tyler; fx, Gordon Jennings; cos, Edith Head

AAN Best Picture; AAN Best Actor: Montgomery Clift; AAN Best Actress: Shelley Winters; AA Best Director: George Stevens; AA Best Screenplay: Michael Wilson, Harry Brown; AA Best B/W Cinematography: William C. Mellor; AA Best Film Editing: William Hornbeck; AA Best Score (Drama or Comedy): Franz Waxman; AA Best Costume Design (B/W): Edith Head

A ponderous version of Dreiser's An American Tragedy, based on the real-life murder of Grace Brown by her social-climbing boyfriend Chester Gillette at Big Moose Lake, New York, in 1906. The film opens with Clift on a highway trying to hitch a ride. Taylor drives past him in a shiny sports car, beeps her horn in a flirtatious manner, and keeps going. Clift gapes after her, awed by her stunning beauty. When Clift arrives in the city looking for a job in his uncle's bathing-suit factory, he is amazed to discover that Taylor is his cousin. The uncle, Heyes, puts Clift to work in the factory, giving him a menial job, but providing the young man with the security Clift's doting mother, Revere, has prayed for. Clift looks from afar at the grand life style, the foreign cars, clothes, and the estate of Heyes and Taylor and, goaded by unbridled ambition, decides to reach upward. Meanwhile, he combats his loneliness by getting involved with Winters, who works in the factory. As his affair with Winters deepens, so does Clift's association with Heyes and his upper-crust family. Clift is invited to a party at Heyes's mansion where he meets and instantly falls in love with the ravishing Taylor, and she with him. In a whirlwind of torrid trysts, Clift and Taylor fall so deeply in love that they plan to wed. Clift is on the verge of elevating himself from the lower class into the ranks of the super rich, but Winters dashes his plans by telling Clift that she is pregnant and insisting that he marry her.

Dreiser's story was first filmed in 1931 by Josef von Sternberg in a much starker, more realistic manner. This version is almost cartoony by comparison, with Elizabeth Taylor, at the peak of her MGM-sorority loveliness, balanced against an unbelievably plain Shelley Winters. It's as if there were no middle ground in this small town, just extremes of wealth and poverty, beauty and drabness. Taylor was only 17 when Stevens cast her in her rich-girl role, but the studio tried to promote a romance between the young actress and Clift. The liaison didn't require much prompting; Clift fell in love with his leading lady and helped her through her most difficult scenes, with spellbinding results. Meanwhile, A PLACE IN THE SUN marked the beginning of Winters' journey from B-bombshell to character actress. Though Stevens at first refused to consider her for the role (he couldn't see beyond the brassy blondes she had played for years), she became indelibly linked to this part and was asked to play many similar types in the future. A PLACE IN THE SUN also marked the last screen appearance for Revere, who was branded a communist by the House Un-American Activities Committee and blacklisted.

PLACES IN THE HEART   📀

1984 112m c   Drama   ★★★½
Tri-Star   (U.S.)   PG

Sally Field (Edna Spalding), Lindsay Crouse (Margaret Lomax), Ed Harris (Wayne Lomax), Amy Madigan (Viola Kelsey), John Malkovich (Mr. Will), Danny Glover (Moze), Yankton Hatten (Frank), Gennie James (Possum), Lane Smith (Albert Denby), Terry O'Quinn (Buddy Kelsey)

p, Arlene Donovan; d, Robert Benton; w, Robert Benton; ph, Nestor Almendros (Technicolor); ed, Carol Littleton; m, John Kander, Howard Shore; prod d, Gene Callahan; art d, Sydney Z. Litwack; fx, Bran Ferren; cos, Ann Roth

AAN Best Picture; AA Best Actress: Sally Field; AAN Best Supporting Actor: John Malkovich; AAN Best Supporting Actress: Lindsay Crouse; AAN Best Director: Robert Benton; AA Best Original Screenplay: Robert Benton; AAN Best Costume Design: Ann Roth

Set in Texas in 1930, this film stars Sally Field as Edna Spalding, a mother of two whose lawman-husband has just been killed by a drunk. Near penniless, she is stunned to learn that the bank is about to foreclose on her property, which includes a 40-acre cotton field. Determined to keep her home, she decides to plant and harvest the cotton, though she's ill equipped to do so. She hires wandering laborer Moze (Danny Glover) to help and takes in blind boarder Mr. Will (John Malkovich) to generate some cash, and the little group struggles to make a go of it. Director Robert Benton (KRAMER VS. KRAMER) effectively re-creates depression-era Texas in this moving tale that landed the second Oscar for Field (her first came for NORMA RAE). Malkovich's terrific performance generated an Oscar nomination, while Benton was nominated for Best Director and Best Screenplay, winning the latter. The film was also nominated as Best Picture but lost to AMADEUS.

PLAN 9 FROM OUTER SPACE   📀

1959 79m   bw Science Fiction   ★★½
J. Edward Reynolds   (U.S.)

Gregory Walcott (Jeff Trent), Mona McKinnon (Paula Trent), Duke Moore (Lt. Harper), Tom Keene (Col. Tom Edwards), Vampira (The Ghoul Woman), Bela Lugosi (The Ghoul Man), Tor Johnson (Police Inspector Clay), Lyle Talbot (Gen. Roberts), Dudley Manlove (Eros), John Breckinridge (The Ruler)

p, Edward D. Wood Jr.; d, Edward D. Wood Jr.; w, Edward D. Wood Jr.; ph, William C. Thompson; ed, Edward D. Wood; m, Gordon Zahler

The cult reputation earned by Edward D. Wood Jr.'s bizarre sci-fi epic has been one of the film industry's strangest "success" stories. Using two minutes of footage Wood had shot featuring his friend Bela Lugosi that was to be used for a never-realized project (Lugosi died days later), the bargain-basement director, responsible for such other noteworthy oddities as GLEN OR GLENDA? (AKA: I CHANGED MY SEX), BRIDE OF THE MONSTER, and JAIL BAIT, put before the cameras "the sworn testimony of miserable souls who survived the ordeal of graverobbers from outer space!" This claim was intoned with all seriousness by the film's host and narrator, famed TV psychic (and close personal friend of the director) Criswell, whose impassioned prologue and epilogue to PLAN 9 FROM OUTER SPACE frame the fantastic tale of aliens using resurrected human zombies to conquer the earth. Alongside—or rather, as well as—Lugosi, the cast includes Vampira, a popular LA TV horror-show hostess; ex-wrestler Tor Johnson, a friend of Wood's; and Joanna Lee, who went on to become a highly successful TV scriptwriter.

PLAN 9 could be the movie for which the critical cliché "it's so bad, it's good" was coined. Voted "The Worst Film of All Time" in a readers' poll for the 1980 book *The Golden Turkey Awards*, Wood's *piece de resistance* so shamelessly ignores all the rules of filmmaking that it's impossible not to be impressed by the director's implacable indifference to "production values." For most of the film, Wood's wife's chiropractor stands in for Lugosi and, even though his face is always hidden by his Dracula cape, it's still obvious he's not the legendary horror star—the two men have entirely different builds. (Meanwhile, the real Lugosi footage, shot two years previously, is repeated over and over throughout the movie.) Some flying saucers seen attacking L.A. are, in fact, paper plates. In the cemetery scenes, a concrete floor is clearly visible under the "grass," as are some ratty-looking mattresses, there to cushion the fall of a woman who is dropped to the ground; it's obvious, too, that the tombstones are made out of cardboard. There are inexplicable shifts from day to night in the course of several scenes, and the same set of furniture appears in different rooms in Trent's house. Hardly THE REMAINS OF THE DAY, but some would claim it's more fun.

PLANES, TRAINS, AND AUTOMOBILES 📀
1987 93m c Comedy ★★★
Paramount (U.S.) R

Steve Martin *(Neal Page)*, John Candy *(Del Griffith)*, Laila Robins *(Susan Page)*, Michael McKean *(State Trooper)*, Kevin Bacon *(Taxi Racer)*, Dylan Baker *(Owen)*, Carol Bruce *(Joy Page)*, Olivia Burnette *(Marti)*, Diana Douglas *(Peg)*, William Windom *(Boss)*

p, John Hughes; d, John Hughes; w, John Hughes; ph, Don Peterman (Technicolor); ed, Paul Hirsch; m, Ira Newborn; prod d, John W. Corso; art d, Harold Michelson; cos, April Ferry

The guru of teenager movies, John Hughes, enters the world of adults with this seasonal comedy based on the horrors of transportation in America. Two days before Thanksgiving, yuppie marketing consultant Neal Page (Steve Martin) races from Manhattan to catch a plane home to Chicago, only to find that his flight has been delayed. Hours later, he boards the plane and ends up next to Del Griffith (John Candy), a huge slob wearing a polyester suit. When the flight is detoured to Wichita, it's just the beginning of Page's trip and his association with Griffith. With a concept as thin as this, PLANES, TRAINS AND AUTOMOBILES could have easily become a repetitious bore. Instead, producer-director-writer Hughes infuses his film with an appealing sense of sentiment and humanity—not to mention many hilarious scenes. Candy finally has a bravura role and proves himself to be not only a superb comedian but also a fine actor. Martin, in the less flamboyant of the two roles, is excellent as well. Hughes's insistence on cramming the film with a glut of pop songs (which in most cases do nothing to complement the action) is unfortunate.

PLANET OF THE APES 📀
1968 112m c Science Fiction ★★★★
Apjac (U.S.) G

Charlton Heston *(George Taylor)*, Roddy McDowall *(Cornelius)*, Kim Hunter *(Dr. Zira)*, Maurice Evans *(Dr. Zaius)*, James Whitmore *(President of the Assembly)*, James Daly *(Honorius)*, Linda Harrison *(Nova)*, Robert Gunner *(Landon)*, Lou Wagner *(Lucius)*, Woodrow Parfrey *(Maximus)*

p, Arthur P. Jacobs; d, Franklin J. Schaffner; w, Michael Wilson, Rod Serling (based on the novel *Monkey Planet* by Pierre Boulle); ph, Leon Shamroy (Panavision, Deluxe Color); ed, Hugh S. Fowler; m, Jerry Goldsmith; art d, Jack Martin Smith, William

Creber; fx, John Chambers, L.B. Abbott, Art Cruickshank, Emil Kosa Jr.; cos, Morton Haack

AAN Best Original Score (Not a Musical): Jerry Goldsmith; *AAN Best Costume Design:* Morton Haack

"Get your stinking paws off me, you damn dirty ape!" An outstanding science-fiction film that spawned four sequels, an animated cartoon series, a live-action TV series, bubble-gum cards, Halloween masks, and a rash of plastic models. Massive marketing notwithstanding, the original film is still quite an achievement. Heston plays the commander of a lengthy outer-space mission that is interrupted when the spaceship crashes on an unknown planet. He and two other survivors make their way through an arid wasteland into a lush forest where they observe what appears to be a tribe of Stone Age humans. A bizarre horn cries, and the sounds of hoof-beats and gunfire are heard, sending the savages running into the woods. The confused astronauts are shocked to see that the armed horsemen are actually gorillas wearing leather uniforms. Welcome to the planet of the apes, where they wear the clothes and do the talking, and we have reverted to our (natural?) savage state.

PLANET OF THE APES is a success on many levels, with a witty, intelligent script by Rod Serling and a suitably hot-tempered, athletic performance from Charlton Heston. Roddy McDowall and Kim Hunter are highly effective as a sympathetic ape scientist and doctor, respectively, with John Chambers's superb latex makeup allowing them a full range of expressive facial gestures. (Chambers won a special Oscar for his work.) None of the sequels (BENEATH THE PLANET OF THE APES, ESCAPE FROM THE PLANET OF THE APES, CONQUEST OF THE PLANET OF THE APES, BATTLE FOR THE PLANET OF THE APES) lived up to the original and, partly in reaction to all the marketing push, the "Apes" series eventually spiraled into self-parody.

PLANET OF THE APES 📀
2001 100m c Science Fiction/Action ★★½
Zanuck Company Productions/20th Century Fox PG-13
(U.S.)

Mark Wahlberg *(Captain Leo Davidson)*, Tim Roth *(Thade)*, Helena Bonham Carter *(Ari)*, Michael Clarke Duncan *(Attar)*, Paul Giamatti *(Limbo)*, Estella Warren *(Daena)*, Cary-Hiroyuki Tagawa *(Krull)*, David Warner *(Sandar)*, Kris Kristofferson *(Karubi)*, Charlton Heston *(Thade's Father—uncredited)*

p, Richard D. Zanuck; d, Tim Burton; w, Lawrence Konner, Mark Rosenthal, William Broyles Jr. (based on the novel by Pierre Boulle); ph, Philippe Rousselot; ed, Chris Lebenzon; m, Danny Elfman; prod d, Rick Heinrichs; art d, John Dexter, Sean Haworth, Philip Toolin; fx, Bill George, Christopher Raimo, Rick Baker (makeup); cos, Colleen Atwood

Rick Baker's ape suits are astonishing, and the cast of Tim Burton's "reimagining" of the 1968 sci-fi classic works overtime to strike a balance between a civilized demeanor and animal behavior, but the film is sorely deficient on the story front.

Space, 2029. When an exploratory shuttle manned by a trained chimp vanishes into what appears to be a wormhole, hotshot pilot Leo Davidson (Mark Wahlberg) disobeys orders and blasts off after him. After being buffeted by various visual effects, Davidson finds himself stranded on a planet where apes rule and savage humans are hunted, enslaved, and kept as pets. Davidson is rescued from captivity by sympathetic chimp Ari (Helena Bonham Carter), a human-rights activist with a powerful politico for a father (David Warner). Hard-line Homo sapiens hater General Thade (Tim Roth) has been fanning the flames of anti-human sentiment and is betting that Davidson's defiant behavior will tip the balance of popular opinion in favor of a military solution to the pesky people problem. Davidson wants only to get home, but finds himself cast in the role of savior to his oppressed fellow humans.

Whatever the faults of the first PLANET and its sequels, they were all *about* something. Burton's film is empty, if gorgeous, spectacle, and his decision to loose the tongues of the original ape planet's mute humans undermines the contrast that lies at the heart of the story's power: civilized apes vs. beast-like men. The remake does toss some sops to fans, and a pair of classic lines are revisited in very different contexts. A gorilla soldier howls, "Get your stinking hands off me, you damned dirty human," and a nearly unrecognizable Charlton Heston sputters "Damn them.... Damn them all to hell!"

PLATOON
1986 111m c War   ★★★★
Hemdale (U.S.)   R

Tom Berenger *(Sgt. Barnes)*, Willem Dafoe *(Sgt. Elias)*, Charlie Sheen *(Chris)*, Forest Whitaker *(Big Harold)*, Francesco Quinn *(Rhah)*, John C. McGinley *(Sgt. O'Neill)*, Richard Edson *(Sal)*, Kevin Dillon *(Bunny)*, Reggie Johnson *(Junior)*, Keith David *(King)*

p, Arnold Kopelson; d, Oliver Stone; w, Oliver Stone; ph, Robert Richardson; ed, Claire Simpson; m, Samuel Barber; prod d, Bruno Rubeo; art d, Rodel Cruz, Doris Sherman Williams; fx, Yves De Bono

AA Best Picture; AAN Best Supporting Actor: Tom Berenger; *AAN Best Supporting Actor:* Willem Dafoe; *AA Best Director:* Oliver Stone; *AAN Best Original Screenplay:* Oliver Stone; *AAN Best Cinematography:* Robert Richardson; *AA Best Film Editing:* Claire Simpson; *AA Best Sound:* John "Doc" Wilkinson, Richard Rogers, Charles "Bud" Grenzback, Simon Kaye

Chris (Charlie Sheen), a green recruit and child of privilege who dropped out of college and enlisted, finds himself in Vietnam as a member of a platoon divided against itself. On one side is Sgt. Barnes (Tom Berenger), a horribly scarred veteran of several tours of duty—a morally corrupt, remorseless killing machine. The men who follow him seek clear-cut solutions to the complicated realities they face. On the other side is veteran sergeant Elias (Willem Dafoe), who, though equally skilled in the ways of death, still retains some semblance of humanity and attempts to impose a sense of compassion and responsibility on his men. Chris is caught between these two in what he describes as a "battle for possession of my soul."

PLATOON is a shattering experience. Writer-director Stone, a Vietnam veteran, used his first-hand knowledge to create one of the most realistic war films ever made, one whose success lies in the mass of detail Stone brings to the screen, bombarding the senses with vivid sights and sounds that have the feel of actual experience. Stone captures the heat, the dampness, the bugs, the jungle rot, and, most important, the confusion and fear experienced by the average soldier. The men in PLATOON do perform heroic acts on occasion, but the heroism isn't motivated by love of country or idealism—it is motivated by pure terror, by desperation, by a desire to end the madness one way or another. Never before in a war film has stark terror among soldiers been such a tangible, motivating force. There is nothing appealing in Stone's war; it doesn't have a "recruitment flavor." However, while PLATOON has no equal when it comes to capturing the reality of the combat experience, it falters when Stone attempts to apply greater meaning to his vision. The film's battle between the forces of good and evil as represented by the two sergeants is heavy-handed, as is Sheen's totally unnecessary voice-over narration, which dilutes the power of Stone's visuals. On an incredibly low budget of $6.5 million, Stone brought his cast and crew to the Philippines and shot PLATOON in a swift 54 days. To everyone's surprise, the film was a massive hit with the critics and the public.

PLAY IT AGAIN, SAM
1972 85m c Comedy   ★★★½
Apjac/Rollins-Joffe (U.S.)   PG

Woody Allen *(Allan Felix)*, Diane Keaton *(Linda Christie)*, Tony Roberts *(Dick Christie)*, Jerry Lacy *(Humphrey Bogart)*, Susan Anspach *(Nancy Felix)*, Jennifer Salt *(Sharon)*, Joy Bang *(Julie)*, Viva *(Jennifer)*, Mari Fletcher *(Fantasy Sharon)*, Diana Davila *(Girl in Museum)*

p, Arthur P. Jacobs; d, Herbert Ross; w, Woody Allen (based on the play by Allen); ph, Owen Roizman (Technicolor); ed, Marion Rothman; m, Billy Goldenberg, Max Steiner; prod d, Ed Wittstein; cos, Anna Hill Johnstone

A true film buff's film about a film buff, Allan Felix (Allen), who is obsessed with CASABLANCA. The impish, neurotic Allan patterns his personality after Humphrey Bogart but has nothing of the actor's tough guy image. When Allan's wife (Anspach), leaves him she explains, "You're one of life's great watchers. I'm not like that, I'm a doer." While the distressed Allan laments over his lack of "cool," he is visited by Bogart (Lacy), who sits in a dark corner of the room, wearing his usual trenchcoat and smoking a cigarette. Bogart gives him advice: "Dames are simple. I never met one that didn't understand a slap in the mouth or a slug from a forty-five." To boost his spirits Allan's married friends, Linda (Diane Keaton) and Dick (Woody Allen good-luck charm Tony Roberts), try to fix him up with another woman. Their meddling and Allan's attempts to emulate his hero lead him into many failures and one undesired success in the game of love, but at least our hero gets to play a scene from CASABLANCA at the finale.

Based on Allen's Broadway play (Allen, Roberts, Keaton, and Lacy all appeared in the stage version, which opened on February 12th, 1969, and ran for 453 performances), PLAY IT AGAIN, SAM differs somewhat from Allen's earlier pictures. Allen handed over the directorial reins here to Herbert Ross, a craftsman, but a director who has no recognizable style of his own. What Ross brings to Allen's play is a sense of control and drama as opposed to the slapstick vignettes of TAKE THE MONEY AND RUN and BANANAS. Still, PLAY IT AGAIN, SAM is clearly Allen's film. (Atypical, however, for an Allen film is the location. A strike in New York caused filming to move to San Francisco.) Though his character is the typical neurotic Allen hero, he strikes a common chord with film audiences. What Allen hits on in PLAY IT AGAIN, SAM is a cultural phenomenon unique to the movie era—audiences living their lives as a movie. While not every audience can relate to the New York intellectual idiosyncracies of ANNIE HALL, they can relate on a gut emotional level to an average man idolizing a movie star. For film buffs, Allen has included countless film references (Erich von Stroheim, Francois Truffaut, Ida Lupino), film posters, and, of course, clips and music from CASABLANCA. Composer Goldenberg borrows heavily from the themes of Max Steiner, which are heard throughout, as is the unforgettable "As Time Goes By" and an Oscar Peterson composition titled "Blues for Allan Felix." Also deserving special mention is Lacy's flawless portrayal of Bogart, which consistently makes one feel as if Allen somehow got the real Bogart for this film.

PLAY MISTY FOR ME
1971 102m c Thriller   ★★★½
Malpaso (U.S.)   R

Clint Eastwood *(Dave Garver)*, Jessica Walter *(Evelyn Draper)*, Donna Mills *(Tobie Williams)*, John Larch *(Sgt. McCallum)*, Jack Ging *(Dr. Frank Dewan)*, Irene Hervey *(Madge Brenner)*, James McEachin *(Al Monte)*, Clarice Taylor *(Birdie)*, Don Siegel *(Murphy the Bartender)*, Duke Everts *(Jay Jay)* p, Robert Daley; d, Clint Eastwood; w, Jo Heims, Dean Riesner (based on a story by Jo Heims); ph, Bruce Surtees (Technicolor); ed, Carl Pingitore; m, Dee Barton; art d, Alexander Golitzen; cos, Helen Colvig, Brad Whitney

This was Clint Eastwood's directorial debut and it far surpasses other attempts in the genre, such as the popular FATAL ATTRACTION, for thrills, suspense, and insight into sexual obsession. Dave Garver (Eastwood) is a Carmel, California, disc jockey who gets a call every night from a mysterious woman listener who requests that he play the Erroll Garner classic "Misty." After breaking up with his girlfriend Tobie (Mills), Dave looks for action in the local bars and meets Evelyn (Walter), a rather high-strung but seductive woman who, he learns, is the mysterious voice that requests "Misty." The lustful pair adjourn to Evelyn's apartment and they sleep together with the understanding that it will be a one-night stand. Unfortunately for Dave, Evelyn is quite mad and absolutely refuses to leave him alone despite the fact that he has patched up his relationship with Tobie. Evelyn's jealous rage is at first suicidal, then quite murderous. A superior thriller, PLAY MISTY FOR ME proved that popular actor Eastwood could direct himself in a film, concentrate on every aspect of the production from the visuals to the performances, and complete the shooting ahead of schedule and under budget. What he delivered was an engrossing study of how loneliness and longing can be transformed into irrational rage after a thoughtless act of selfish indulgence. Much of the credit must go to Jessica Walter for her outstanding performance which somehow manages to be chilling while at the same time sympathetic.

PLAYER, THE   DVD
1992 123m c Comedy/Mystery   ★★★★
Avenue Entertainment/Spelling Entertainment   R
(U.S.)

Tim Robbins (Griffin Mill), Greta Scacchi (June Gudmundsdottir), Fred Ward (Walter Stuckel), Whoopi Goldberg (Detective Avery), Peter Gallagher (Larry Levy), Brion James (Joel Levison), Cynthia Stevenson (Bonnie Sherow), Vincent D'Onofrio (David Kahane), Dean Stockwell (Andy Civella), Richard E. Grant (Tom Oakley)

p, David Brown, Michael Tolkin, Nick Wechsler; d, Robert Altman; w, Michael Tolkin (from his novel); ph, Jean Lepine; ed, Geraldine Peroni, Maysie Hoy; m, Thomas Newman; prod d, Stephen Altman; art d, Jerry Fleming; cos, Alexander Julian

AAN Best Director: Robert Altman; AAN Best Adapted Screenplay: Michael Tolkin; AAN Best Film Editing: Geraldine Peroni

A hilarious and deftly convincing satire of contemporary Hollywood, courtesy of industry "bad boy" Robert Altman. Lighter in tone than classic exposes like THE BAD AND THE BEAUTIFUL, THE PLAYER sees Tinseltown as run by power brokers who are not so much ruthless as they are inept and insecure. The film's lackadaisical plot, about a production executive (Tim Robbins) who murders a writer (Vincent D'Onofrio), is really just an excuse for an Altmanesque tour of make-believe-land. Along the way, we encounter the dead man's girlfriend, a radiantly composed artist who never completes a painting (Greta Scacchi); an industry whiz-kid who gives great car-phone (Peter Gallagher); a veteran producer who drops Julia Roberts's name into every other sentence (Dean Stockwell); and a preening studio security chief who doesn't think twice about checking his reflection in the back of a coffee-spoon (Fred Ward). The daily rituals of a studio executive's life—speakerphone conferences, power lunches, private screenings—are portrayed with an authenticity reinforced by the presence of scores of real celebrities, playing themselves in cameo roles.

Among the film's choicer moments: Buck Henry (who wrote THE GRADUATE) pitching an idea for "The Graduate

2," in which a bed-ridden Mrs. Robinson would move in with Benjamin and Elaine; Whoopi Goldberg, playing a police detective, picking up an Oscar in a studio office and mimicking the speech which the real Goldberg gave after winning the award for GHOST; and the murdered writer's funeral, where the best tribute the dead man's friends can muster is to read aloud from the screenplay he was working on before he died ("Long, slow pan across room," etc.) Though it's a canny piece of work, THE PLAYER doesn't compare with Altman's multi-layered masterpiece, NASHVILLE. The earlier film made the world of country music a mirror for American society at large, using its immediate setting to address wider, more universal issues. THE PLAYER looks no further than Hollywood, perhaps because Hollywood is incapable of looking beyond itself.

PLAYTIME   DVD
1967 120m c Comedy   ★★★★½
Specta-Films (France)

Jacques Tati (M. Hulot), Barbara Dennek (Young Tourist), Jacqueline Lecomte (Her Friend), Leon Doyen (Porter), Georges Montant (M. Giffard), John Abbey (Mr. Lacs), Valerie Camille (Mr. Lacs's Secretary), Henri Piccoli (Important Gentleman), France Rumilly (Eyeglass Saleswoman), France Delahalle (Client at the Strand)

p, Rene Silvera; d, Jacques Tati; w, Jacques Tati, Jacques Lagrange, Art Buchwald; ph, Jean Badal, Andreas Winding (Eastmancolor); ed, Gerard Pollicand; m, Francis Lemarque, David Stein, James Campbell; prod d, Eugene Roman

Jacques Tati's familiar comic character, Monsieur Hulot, weaves his way through Tati's most ambitious and costly film, the award-winning PLAYTIME.

A group of American tourists arrive at Orly Airport, among them a pretty young woman named Barbara (Barbara Dennek). As a bus transports them to their hotel in Paris, M. Hulot (Jacques Tati) attempts to keep an appointment with M. Giffard (Georges Montant), who works in a large, ultramodern office building. That evening, Hulot runs into an old army buddy (Yves Barsacq) who invites him to his apartment, the residential equivalent of a display window in a department store. An elegant, new (but unfinished) supper club opens its doors for business. One of its customers is Barbara; another is Hulot. Havoc ensues as the management tries to accommodate a capacity turnout and, at the same time, complete construction of the club. Most of the clientele manage to have a splendid time nonetheless and at dawn, they move on to a local snack bar. Among them are Hulot and Barbara, who have paired off.

PLAYTIME was the most elaborate and ambitious film of Tati's career. It took 100 workers more than five months to build the movie's huge setting, an ultramodern mini-city which was nicknamed "Tati-ville" and became an actual tourist attraction until it was razed to make room for a highway. Initially released in 70mm and stereophonic sound, the three-hour-plus picture was gradually whittled down to less than half of its original length, but nothing could save it from commercial disaster. Nonetheless, Tati was enormously proud of PLAYTIME and, although it was not his final film, regarded it as the climactic work and crowning glory of his career.

The notion of technology developing beyond people's capacity to cope with it is a familiar one that has frequently been treated in films of science, horror, and strident satire. Tati alone chose to take the theme into the perennially unfashionable realm of benign comedy. His mechanical monsters are more annoying than harmful and the beings who control and are controlled by them are not villains and victims but, invariably, innocents as guileless as they are hapless.

PLAZA SUITE

1971 114m c Comedy   *DVD*
Paramount   (U.S.)   ★★★★
                                      GP

Walter Matthau *(Sam Nash/Jesse Kiplinger/Roy Hubley)*,
Maureen Stapleton *(Karen Nash)*, Jose Ocasio *(Waiter)*, Dan
Ferrone *(Bellhop)*, Louise Sorel *(Miss McCormack)*, Barbara
Harris *(Muriel Tate)*, Lee Grant *(Norma Hubley)*, Jenny Sullivan
(Mimsey Hubley), Tom Carey *(Borden Eisler)*

p, Howard W. Koch; d, Arthur Hiller; w, Neil Simon (based on the
play by Neil Simon); ph, Jack Marta (Technicolor); ed, Frank
Bracht; m, Maurice Jarre; art d, Arthur Lonergan; cos, Jack Bear

To his credit, Neil Simon never stops trying to expand. With
several solid successes in the comedy genre behind him, he
attempted something here that wasn't merely a pack of one-
liners but had an underlying pathos and humanity. George C.
Scott and Maureen Stapleton opened on Broadway in the
show, which ran more than 1,000 performances with Mike
Nichols directing. Stapleton returns to do one of the three
vignettes, as does Lee Grant, who did the Road Show version
playing another of the parts, and Barbara Harris in the middle
segment. Simon's plays are almost always one-set jobs, and
the task of adapting them for the screen is not an enviable one,
since movie fans will often carp that they are photographed
stage plays of people talking with no cinematic value. Since
this picture takes place in one suite at New York's Plaza Hotel,
its staginess was all the more evident. The only unifying force
in the trio of stories is Matthau in a tour-de-force job as three
very different men. There were to be four stories in the original, and the one that was dropped was used as the basis for
Simon's original screenplay of THE OUT-OF-TOWNERS.
Director Hiller had just come off LOVE STORY, and there
was some doubt as to whether he could direct a comedy.

The first segment has Matthau and Stapleton as a middle-
aged couple trying to revive their failing marriage in what they
believe is the same suite they occupied on their wedding night.
In the second segment, Matthau is a Hollywood producer who
attempts to seduce Harris with his endless store of motion picture anecdotes. The final, funniest sketch has Matthau driven
to distraction when his daughter locks herself in the bathroom
and refuses to come out for her wedding ceremony.

Of the female roles, Harris steals the picture. Critics
were divided in their assessment of PLAZA SUITE, but we
have to stand in the "pro" corner, although Simon has had
some terrible adaptations (STAR SPANGLED GIRL) and
even some bummer screenplays of his own, as in THE
SLUGGER'S WIFE.

PLEASANTVILLE

1998 116m c/bw Comedy/Drama   *DVD*
Larger Than Life Productions   (U.S.)   ★★★
                                        PG-13

Joan Allen *(Betty)*, William H. Macy *(George)*, Tobey Maguire
(David), Reese Witherspoon *(Jennifer)*, Jeff Daniels *(Mr.
Johnson)*, Don Knotts *(TV Repairman)*, J.T. Walsh *(Big Bob)*,
Natalie Ramsey *(Mary Sue)*, Kevin Connors *(Bud)*, Heather
McGill *(Girl in School Yard)*

p, Jon Kilik, Robert J. Degus, Steven Soderbergh, Gary Ross; d,
Gary Ross; w, Gary Ross; ph, John Lindley; ed, William
Goldenberg; m, Randy Newman; prod d, Jeannine Oppewall; art
d, Diane Wager; fx, Chris Watts (visual effects), Michael Southard
(color effects); cos, Judianna Makovsky

AAN Best Art Direction: Jeannine Oppewall, Jay Hart; *AAN Best
Costume Design:* Judianna Makovsky; *AAN Best Original
Dramatic Score:* Randy Newman

This flip side to the acclaimed TRUMAN SHOW is glossy,
high-concept Hollywood entertainment that uses special
effects to awaken the senses rather than numb them.

David (Tobey Maguire) is a nerdy high-school student
who finds refuge in reruns of the '50s sitcom "Pleasantville,"
a show whose black-and-white verities, close-knit families,
and predictable characters are a comforting alternative to the
anxieties of life in the '90s. With the help of an avuncular TV
repairman (Don Knotts) and a magic remote control, David
and his twin sister, Jennifer (Reese Witherspoon), are zapped
into the black-and-white world of "Pleasantville," where
they're forced to play perfect teens Bud and Mary Sue, children of George and Betty Parker (William H. Macy, Joan
Allen). David at first loves playing Bud: for once he knows
exactly what to say, and what happens next. Jennifer, on the
other hand, chafes under layers of underwear, poodle skirts,
and '50s social norms, and stirs up trouble when she introduces sex into the cheerfully repressed town. As the other
teens and a few open-minded adults follow her lead, color
begins to bleed into Pleasantville's monochromatic palette.
But as the town's conformist, TV-show reality begins to erode,
angry citizens, led by Mayor Big Bob (J.T. Walsh) begin
organizing a backlash campaign against the "coloreds."

The issues writer-director Gary Ross (who also scripted
BIG and DAVE) addresses in this high-tech fable—the
importance of diversity, tolerance, and the ongoing need to
question the status quo—are big ones, and not easily resolved
in under two hours: characters are left to speechify their way
to a denouement. But in using a cinematic development to
symbolize the cultural growth of a town that exists only on
celluloid, Ross has hit upon a stunning metaphor, and there
are several frissons when it all comes together—the sign in a
Pleasantville shop warning "No Coloreds" is chief among
them. There are also moments of pure, unbridled joy: the
teens tapping their toes to Buddy Holly's "Rave On," or the
town's soda jerk (Jeff Daniels) laying his black-and-white
eyes on Van Gogh's *Starry Night,* in glorious color for the
very first time.

PLEDGE, THE

2001 123m c Mystery   *DVD*
Morgan Creek Productions/Franchise Pictures/   ★★★½
Clyde Is Hungry Films   (U.S.)   R

Jack Nicholson *(Jerry Black)*, Robin Wright Penn *(Lori)*, Sam
Shepard *(Eric Pollack)*, Aaron Eckhart *(Stan Krolak)*, Vanessa
Redgrave *(Annalise Hansen)*, Michael O'Keefe *(Duane Larson)*,
Benicio Del Toro *(Toby Jay Wadenah)*, Harry Dean Stanton *(Floyd
Cage)*, Helen Mirren *(Doctor)*, Patricia Clarkson *(Margaret Larson)*

p, Michael Fitzgerald, Sean Penn; d, Sean Penn; w,
Jerzy Kromolowski, Mary Olson-Kromolowski (based on the book
by Friedrich Durrenmatt); ph, Chris Menges; ed, Jay Cassidy; m,
Hans Zimmer, Klaus Badelt; prod d, Bill Groom; art d, Helen
Jarvis; fx, David Gauthier; cos, Jill Ohanneson

If you're looking for quick thrills, look elsewhere. But if
you're in a patient mood and don't mind waiting a good two
hours to be reminded just how cruel fate can be, sit yourself
down. Sean Penn's adaptation of Friedrich Durrenmatt's
1958 meta-mystery about one man's pledge to capture a serial killer is smart, somber, characteristically understated, and
altogether chilling.

Detective Jerry Black (Jack Nicholson), an esteemed
Nevada homicide detective, sneaks out of his own retirement
party when a gruesome call comes in. The mutilated body of
an eight-year-old girl has been found in the deep, snowy
woods, and a mentally challenged Native American (Benicio
Del Toro) with a rap sheet was seen running from the crime
scene. Ambitious Detective Krolak (Aaron Eckhart) wrings a
barely coherent confession out of the suspect, but Black is
unconvinced. Bound by his promise to the dead girl's parents

(Patricia Clarkson, Michael O'Keefe) that he'll bring the killer to justice, but unable to convince his former colleagues that they've got the wrong guy, Black puts his retirement on hold and embarks on a dark journey that will ultimately leave him alone and stranded on the other side of sanity.

The plot creeps along at a deliberate pace and has more in common with Claude Chabrol's icy chillers than THE SILENCE OF THE LAMBS. But it's a rewarding experience. Black's incipient madness is inconsistently developed, but Nicholson is just fine, and his all-star supporting cast, including a seriously drabbed-down Robin Penn Wright, is even better. The film is short on action but heavy on ambiance, and the cumulative effect packs a whopper if you're willing to stop and think about it.

PLOUGHMAN'S LUNCH, THE

1983 107m c Drama ★★★★
Greenpoint (U.K.) R

Jonathan Pryce *(James Penfield)*, Tim Curry *(Jeremy Hancock)*, Rosemary Harris *(Ann Barrington)*, Frank Finlay *(Matthew Fox)*, Charlie Dore *(Susan Barrington)*, David De Keyser *(Gold)*, Nat Jackley *(Mr. Penfield)*, Bill Paterson *(Lecturer)*, William Maxwell, Paul Jesson

p, Simon Relph, Ann Scott; d, Richard Eyre; w, Ian McEwan; ph, Clive Tickner; ed, David Martin; m, Dominic Muldowney; prod d, Luciana Arrighi; art d, Michael Pickwoad; cos, Luciana Arrighi

BBC radio journalist and would-be historian James Penfield (Jonathan Pryce) is an unbridled opportunist and self-promoter. He is at work on a book about the 1956 Suez Canal crisis in which his aim is to interpret events in a politically popular manner that will enhance his career. He pursues television-documentary researcher Susan Barrington (Charlie Dore), mainly because her mother (Rosemary Harris) is an expert on Suez. As he gets more involved with these characters and his work, it becomes more difficult to determine just who is using whom. First-time director Richard Eyre has created a gripping film that honestly explores political morality in the 1980s. Pryce is superb as the self-interested corporate-social climber, and the entire film plays like THE GRADUATE stood on its head.

POCAHONTAS

1995 87m c Animated/Musical/Romance ★★★
Walt Disney (U.S.) G

VOICES OF: Irene Bedard *(Pocahontas—Speaking Voice)*, Judy Kuhn *(Pocahontas—Singing Voice)*, Mel Gibson *(Captain John Smith)*, Russell Means *(Chief Powhatan)*, David Ogden Stiers *(John Ratcliffe)*, Linda Hunt *(Grandmother Willow)*, Joe Baker *(Lon)*, Billy Connolly *(Ben)*, Christian Bale *(Thomas)*, John Kassir *(Meeko)*

p, James Pentecost; d, Mike Gabriel, Eric Goldberg; w, Carl Binder, Susannah Grant, Philip LaZebnik (from a story by Glen Keane, Joe Grant, Ralph Zondag, Burny Mattinson, Ed Gombert, Kaan Kaylon, Francis Glebas, Robert Gibbs, Bruce Morris, Todd Kurosawa, Duncan Majoribanks, and Chris Buck); ed, H. Lee Peterson; m, Alan Menken, Stephen Schwartz; art d, Michael Giaimo; anim, Glen Keane, John Pomeroy, Duncan Majoribanks, Ruben Aquino, Nik Ranieri, Dave Prulksma, Chris Buck, Ken Duncan

AA Best Musical or Comedy Score: Alan Menken, Stephen Schwartz; AA Best Original Song: "Colors of the Wind"; Alan Menken, Stephen Schwartz

Balancing historical revisionism on the one hand and a cherished story of early America on the other, POCAHONTAS is a candy-coated lesson in tolerance and the ennobling power of love. English adventurer John Smith (voiced by Mel Gibson) and his crew arrive in the New World in 1607, under the command of rapacious Governor Ratcliffe (David Ogden Stiers), who lusts for gold. Smith and Algonquian maiden Pocahontas (newcomer Irene Bedard) fall in love. Relations between the Native Americans and the settlers quickly deteriorate and war seems inevitable, but Pocahontas saves Smith's life and her selflessness shames everyone into doing the right thing.

POCAHONTAS breaks the Disney mold in several small but significant ways. Unlike generations of animated princesses, the capable Pocahontas doesn't waste much time waiting for her prince. She's too busy canoeing over waterfalls, harvesting corn, and chatting with a wise old tree spirit (Linda Hunt). It's also the first Disney film based on the life of a real person, though it's been widely criticized for the many liberties taken with historical fact. And it doesn't have a doggedly happy ending—the chaste lovers part at the end, returning to their own people rather than running off together to seek improbable bliss. Still, in many respects, POCAHONTAS embodies the Disney style flawlessly. It's technically polished, gently preachy, and a beautifully realized piece of feature-length animation. But it's visually subdued, all cool greens and blues, and the score is unusually bland: there's nothing here to match THE LION KING's toe-tapping "Hakuna Matata" number.

POCKETFUL OF MIRACLES

DVD
1961 136m c Crime/Comedy ★★★½
Franton (U.S.)

Glenn Ford *(Dave, the Dude, Conway)*, Bette Davis *(Apple Annie, "Mrs. E. Worthington Manville")*, Hope Lange *(Elizabeth "Queenie" Martin)*, Arthur O'Connell *(Count Alfonso Romero)*, Peter Falk *(Joy Boy)*, Thomas Mitchell *(Judge Henry G. Blake)*, Edward Everett Horton *(Hutchins, the Butler)*, Mickey Shaughnessy *(Junior)*, David Brian *(Governor)*, Sheldon Leonard *(Steve Darcey)*

p, Frank Capra; d, Frank Capra; w, Hal Kanter, Harry Tugend, Jimmy Cannon (based on the story "Madame La Gimp" by Damon Runyon and the screenplay LADY FOR A DAY by Robert Riskin); ph, Robert Bronner (Panavision, Technicolor); ed, Frank P. Keller; m, Walter Scharf, Peter Ilich Tchaikovsky; art d, Hal Pereira, Roland Anderson; fx, Farciot Edouart; chor, Nick Castle; cos, Edith Head, Walter Plunkett

AAN Best Supporting Actor: Peter Falk; AAN Best Song: "Pocketful of Miracles"; James Van Heusen (Music), Sammy Cahn (Lyrics); AAN Best Costume Design (Color): Edith Head, Walter Plunkett

This was Frank Capra's swan song as a producer-director, and although it was not well received upon initial release, it's still a good movie with some outstanding performances. New York gangster Dave "the Dude" Conway (Glenn Ford) is a superstitious type who believes he can't come to any harm as long as he continues to buy his daily apple from Apple Annie (Bette Davis), a drunken fruit vendor. In essence, Dave's belief is that "an apple a day keeps the Mafia away," and although his bodyguard, Joy Boy (Peter Falk), and chauffeur, Junior (Mickey Shaughnessy), think it's a lot of hooey, his girlfriend (Hope Lange) goes along with whatever Dave wants. When Apple Annie isn't at her usual street corner one morning, Dave goes looking for her. He finds her in deep depression because her daughter, Louise (Ann-Margret, in her first role), who thinks her mother is a wealthy matron, is coming to pay a visit. With Dave's help, Apple Annie is able to pull off her charade as "Mrs. E. Worthington Manville," even receiving help from the mayor, the governor, and a horde of real socialites. A remake of Capra's picture LADY FOR A DAY.

POINT BLANK
DVD
1967 92m c Crime ★★★★½
Bernard/Winkler (U.S.)

Lee Marvin *(Walker)*, Angie Dickinson *(Chris)*, Keenan Wynn *(Fairfax, "Yost")*, Carroll O'Connor *(Brewster)*, Lloyd Bochner *(Frederick Carter)*, Michael Strong *(Stegman)*, John Vernon *(Mal Reese)*, Sharon Acker *(Lynne)*, James B. Sikking *(Hired Gun)*, Sandra Warner *(Waitress)*

p, Judd Bernard, Robert Chartoff; d, John Boorman; w, Alexander Jacobs, David Newhouse, Rafe Newhouse (based on the novel *The Hunter* by Richard Stark *(aka* Donald E. Westlake)); ph, Philip Lathrop (Panavision, Metrocolor); ed, Henry Berman; m, Johnny Mandel; art d, George W. Davis, Albert Brenner; fx, Virgil Beck, J. McMillan Johnson; cos, Margo Weintz

The ultimate arty '60s thriller, and we mean that as a compliment. John Boorman's second film (after HAVING A WILD WEEKEND) and his first U.S. production, POINT BLANK layers some of the stylistic traits of the French New Wave onto a quintessentially American thriller. The result is a breathtakingly composed genre classic, and a surprisingly complex allegory of modern urban life.

After pulling off a successful heist from the mob, Walker (Lee Marvin) is double-crossed by his wife (Sharon Acker) and his partner-in-crime (John Vernon), who shoots him and leaves him for dead in a cell of the now-deserted Alcatraz prison. Walker survives, escapes, and moves to L.A. There, he begins a search for revenge (and for his share of the loot) that takes him through successively elevated ranks of an organized crime syndicate that is increasingly hard to distinguish from a legitimate business organization. After he tracks down his wife, she commits suicide; he is then aided in his quest by her sister, Chris (Angie Dickinson), and by a shadowy figure (Keenan Wynn) who steers Walker toward each fresh target with unerring accuracy.

A deceptively simple action film, POINT BLANK actually succeeds on many levels. As a thriller, it is fast, suspenseful, and peppered with the kind of brilliantly stylized violence now associated with Quentin Tarantino. On a purely visual level, it is an absolute treasure; Philip Lathrop's widescreen compositions continually make you want to stop the film to take in particular images, or re-run particularly impressive scenes: Walker fighting two hoods in a nightclub, against a swirling psychedelic backdrop, to the strains of the house R&B band; Chris futilely pounding Walker with her fists, until she sinks into a useless heap at his feet (he never flinches); Walker trashing a sports car just to intimidate his passenger.

Based on the novel by Richard Stark *(aka* Donald Westlake), POINT BLANK reaches beyond genre conventions to make pertinent social and existential observations. Its artsy effects (time lapses, echoing dialogue-flashbacks, etc.) suggest an alternative storyline, in which our hero dies in that opening scene, and the entire revenge plot is a dream/wish-fulfilment experienced in his last moments of consciousness. And Walker, anachronistically seeking retribution according to a code that seems outmoded in contemporary, corporate L.A., is a figure both brutal and poignant—a fully realized tragic hero.

POLAR EXPRESS, THE
DVD
2004 100m c Animated/Children's/Fantasy ★★½
Shangri-La Entertainment/Playtone/ImageMovers/ G
Golden Mean/Castle Rock Entertainment (U.S.)

Tom Hanks *(Hero Boy/Father/Conductor/Hobo/Scrooge/Santa)*, Daryl Sabara *(Voice of Hero Boy)*, Nona Gaye *(Hero Girl)*, Jimmy Bennett *(Voice of Lonely Boy)*, Michael Jeter *(Smokey/Steamer)*, Leslie Zemeckis *(Sister Sarah/Mother)*, Eddie Deezen *(Know-It-All)*, Peter Scolari *(Lonely Boy)*, Steven Tyler *(Elf Lieutenant/Elf Singer)*, Phil Fondacaro *(Elf)*

p, Gary Goetzman, Steve Starkey, William Teitler, Robert Zemeckis; d, Robert Zemeckis; w, William Broyles Jr. (based on the book by Chris Van Allsburg), Robert Zemeckis; ph, Don Burgess, Robert Presley; ed, R. Orlando Duenas, Jeremiah O'Driscoll; m, Alan Silvestri; prod d, Alan Silvestri, Rick Carter; art d, Doug Chiang; fx, Rob Bredow, Jerome Chen, Mark Lambert, Alberto Menache, Sean Phillips, Ken Ralston; chor, John Carrafa; cos, Joanna Johnston; anim, David Schaub

AAN Best Original Song: "Believe"; Glen Ballard, Alan Silvestri (music, lyrics); *AAN Best Sound Mixing:* Randy Thom, Tom Johnson, Dennis Sands, William B. Kaplan; *AAN Best Sound Editing:* Randy Thom, Dennis Leonard

Based on the award-winning book by Chris Van Allsburg, Robert Zemeckis's computer-animated feature is an extraordinary achievement, which isn't the same as being an extraordinary film. The screenplay overlays Van Allsburg's delicate, atmospheric conceit with irrelevant songs and frantic but meaningless action.

The adventure begins on a small-town Christmas Eve, where "Hero Boy" (voice of Daryl Sabara)—the children are all nameless—lies awake in bed, suspended between the desire to believe and the growing conviction that holiday magic is an invention of well-meaning grown-ups. While straining fruitlessly to hear the tinkle of Santa's sleigh bells, he hears something equally amazing: the huffing of a train—the Polar Express—coming to a halt in his front yard. Hero Boy is invited aboard by the genial but no-nonsense conductor (Tom Hanks, who was the motion-capture model for almost all the film's characters) and finds the train carrying several pajama-clad youngsters, including Hero Girl (Nona Gaye) and a self-centered Know-It-All (Eddie Deezen). It makes one last stop to pick up Lonely Boy (modeled on Peter Scolari, voiced by Jimmy Bennett), a child scarred by a lifetime of Christmas disappointments. The Express navigates dark tunnels, roller-coaster climbs, and a lake of dangerously thin ice before delivering the youngsters to the North Pole, where they're greeted by a benevolent Santa (Hanks).

Clearly designed to be an instant holiday classic, the film's tone alternates awkwardly between bittersweet childhood nostalgia and an aggressive cheer that smacks of trying much too hard to convince everyone they're having fun. Similarly, the film's look vacillates between breathtaking beauty and creepiness. Snow, steam, and the soft glow of lights have rarely been so beautifully realized, but the blank-eyed and rubbery-looking characters, computer-animated over footage of flesh-and-blood performers, are the stuff of nightmares, not dreams.

POLICE
1984 113m c Crime ★★★
TF1/Gaumont (France)

Gerard Depardieu *(Mangin)*, Sophie Marceau *(Noria)*, Richard Anconina *(Lambert)*, Pascale Rocard *(Marie Vedret)*, Sandrine Bonnaire *(Lydie)*, Franck Karoui *(Rene)*, Jonathan Leina *(Simon Slimane)*, Meaachou Bentahar *(Claude)*

p, Emmanuel Schlumberger; d, Maurice Pialat; w, Catherine Breillat, Sylvie Danton, Jacques Fieschi, Maurice Pialat (based on a story by Catherine Breillat); ph, Luciano Tovoli (Eastmancolor); ed, Yann Dedet; m, Henryk Mikolaj Gorecki; art d, Constantine Mejinsky; cos, Malika Brahim

A hard-bitten expose of the volatile Parisian criminal underworld, starring Gerard Depardieu as a brawny, animalistic cop who crosses over to the other side of the law when it suits him.

The film opens with a long, purposely tedious interrogation scene as Mangin (Depardieu) plays a game of cat-and-mouse with a nervous North African drug dealer. Mangin follows his leads to drug dealer Simon (Jonathan Leina), a Tunisian who has come to Paris with his many brothers and his streetwise, sensual teenage sister Noria (Sophie Marceau). Mangin nabs them both and throws them into jail. Upon her release, Noria contrives a clever plan to steal a cache of drug money, gradually luring Mangin into the scam.

If not wholly successful as a narrative, POLICE displays a welcome stylistic restraint. Director Pialat not only allows his actors the freedom of improvisation, but also avoids censoring their characters, passing no judgment on their moral qualities. Certain scenes drag, others are perhaps too diffuse and improvisatory. Depardieu is excellent, though his abrupt change from brute to sensitive lover is perhaps too conspicuous. Marceau proves her range by turning in a performance poles apart from her charming, dewy teenager in LA BOUM.

POLLOCK
2000 122m c Biography ★★½
Fred Berner Films/Zeke Productions/Brant-Allen Films R (U.S.)

Ed Harris (Jackson Pollock), Marcia Gay Harden (Lee Krasner), Amy Madigan (Peggy Guggenheim), Jennifer Connelly (Ruth Kligman), Jeffrey Tambor (Clement Greenberg), Bud Cort (Howard Putzel), John Heard (Tony Smith), Val Kilmer (Willem de Kooning), Stephanie Seymour (Helen Frankenthaler), Tom Bower (Dan Miller)

p, Fred Berner, Ed Harris, Jon Kilik, James Francis Trezza; d, Ed Harris; w, Barbara Turner, Susan J. Emshwiller (based on the book Jackson Pollock: An American Saga by Steven Naifeh and Gregory White Smith); ph, Lisa Rinzler; ed, Kathryn Himoff; m, Jeff Beal; prod d, Mark Friedberg; art d, Teresa Mastropierro, Peter Rogness; cos, David Robinson

AA Best Supporting Actress: Marcia Gay Harden; AAN Best Actor: Ed Harris

Awkwardly adapted from Steven Naifeh and Gregory White Smith's Pulitzer-Prize winning biography, Ed Harris's directing debut is a smart but disappointingly conventional portrait of an artist who had little use for convention.

New York, 1941. Pollock (Harris) is a starving New York City artist struggling against form and alcoholism when he first meets Lee Krasner (Marcia Gay Harden), the fellow painter who would eventually become his advocate, mouthpiece, and long-suffering wife. Krasner arranges a meeting with eccentric patron-of-the-arts Peggy Guggenheim (Amy Madigan), who then agrees to show Pollock in her new gallery. The exhibit is a success, but a real artistic breakthrough remains elusive. That comes six years later when Pollock, now living with Krasner on the eastern end of Long Island, NY, puts down the brush and picks up the paint, dripping and splashing it across the canvas in expressive tangles and arcs. Art critic Clement Greenberg (Jeffrey Tambor) anoints Pollock America's greatest living painter, and a profile in Life magazine catapults him to stardom. The action then jumps ahead ten years to find Pollock a blocked and bloated has-been, drinking himself to death, carrying on an affair with a much-younger woman (Jennifer Connelly), and making his wife's life a living hell.

Harris and Harden both approach greatness, but their performances are frustrated by the clumsy, self-conscious dialogue, and while Harris the director attempts to put Pollock's achievements in an art-historical context, his film opts for reproduction over insight. Unlike, say, John Maybury's portrait of Francis Bacon, LOVE IS THE DEVIL, Harris's film never really enters into the art or the

artist. The man remains hidden behind a scrim of alcohol and paint, much as he lived.

POLLYANNA
1960 134m c Comedy ★★★★
Walt Disney Productions (U.S.)

Hayley Mills (Pollyanna), Jane Wyman (Aunt Polly Harrington), Richard Egan (Dr. Edmund Chilton), Karl Malden (Reverend Paul Ford), Nancy Olson (Nancy Furman), Adolphe Menjou (Mr. Pendergast), Donald Crisp (Mayor Karl Warren), Agnes Moorehead (Mrs. Snow), Kevin Corcoran (Jimmy Bean), James Drury (George Dodds)

p, Walt Disney; d, David Swift; w, David Swift (based on the novel by Eleanor H. Porter); ph, Russell Harlan (Technicolor); ed, Frank Gross; m, Paul J. Smith; art d, Carroll Clark, Robert Clatworthy; fx, Ub Iwerks; cos, Walter Plunkett, Chuck Keehne, Gertrude Casey

Ever since Mary Pickford filmed the silent version of this book in 1920, the name "Pollyanna" has become English vernacular meaning someone who is a die-hard optimist. This time Pollyanna (Hayley Mills) is an orphan who comes to live with her Aunt Polly (Jane Wyman), a wealthy woman in a small 1912 town. The village is filled with nay-sayers and depressing townsfolk, but Pollyanna soon changes matters by always managing to find something good in every situation, seeing the bright side of even the blackest occurrences. Although the townspeople are initially reluctant to share in her optimism, they are eventually won over, even coming to Pollyanna's aid when she is temporarily paralyzed and can no longer find any good in life.

POLTERGEIST
1982 114m c Horror ★★
MGM-UA (U.S.) PG

Craig T. Nelson (Steve), JoBeth Williams (Diane), Beatrice Straight (Dr. Lesh), Dominique Dunne (Dana), Oliver Robins (Robbie), Heather O'Rourke (Carol Anne), Zelda Rubinstein (Tangina), Martin Casella (Marty), Richard Lawson (Ryan), Michael McManus (Tuthill)

p, Steven Spielberg, Frank Marshall; d, Tobe Hooper; w, Steven Spielberg, Michael Grais, Mark Victor; ph, Matthew F. Leonetti (Panavision, Metrocolor); ed, Michael Kahn; m, Jerry Goldsmith; prod d, James H. Spencer; cos, L.J. Mower

AAN Best Original Score: Jerry Goldsmith; AAN Best Visual Effects: Richard Edlund, Michael Wood, Bruce Nicholson; AAN Best Sound Effects Editing: Stephen Hunter Flick, Richard L Anderson

A vapid, silly horror movie with occasional moments of promise that ultimately fails due to an overdose of cuteness.

Steve and Diane (Craig T. Nelson and JoBeth Williams) are a happy suburban couple who suddenly find that their perfect house in the perfect neighborhood has begun acting funny, scaring their perfect children. They really sit up and take notice, however, when wide-eyed young daughter Carol Anne (Heather O'Rourke) becomes possessed by late-night television and gets sucked into limbo by God knows what. Enter clairvoyant Tangina (Zelda Rubinstein), who surmises that the subdivision was built on a sacred Indian burial ground and that the gods aren't happy. POLTERGEIST is frustrating because one gets a hint of what director Tobe Hooper really wanted to do, but it's obvious that he was restrained by producer Steven Spielberg. The problem is, some of the truly horrifying moments slip through the censorship cracks, scaring little kids (and their parents), leaving POLTERGEIST a very disjointed, uneven movie.

POOR COW

1967 101m c Drama ★★½
Vic/Fenchurch (U.K.)

Carol White *(Joy)*, Terence Stamp *(Dave)*, John Bindon *(Tom)*, Kate Williams *(Beryl)*, Queenie Watts *(Aunt Emm)*, Geraldine Sherman *(Trixie)*, James Beckett, Billy Murray *(Tom's Friends)*, Simon King *(Johnny, Age 1 1/2)*, Stevie King *(Johnny, Age Three)*

p, Joseph Janni; d, Ken Loach; w, Kenneth Loach, Nell Dunn (based on her novel); ph, Brian Probyn (Eastmancolor); ed, Roy Watts; m, Donovan; art d, Bernard Sarron

By-the-book British realism from often interesting director Ken Loach (RIFF-RAFF). Joy (Carol White), a lumpen Cockney housewife, suffers in a dingy London flat with her swinish husband (John Bindon), a petty thief; when he's sent to jail, she moves in with Dave (Terence Stamp), who's a criminal associate of her husband. Surprisingly, Dave turns out to be a gentle and caring man who treats Joy's son with affection; but their fleeting happiness ends when Dave is also arrested. On her own, Joy ekes out a living as a barmaid and sometime nude model, treating herself to an occasional affair. She begins divorce proceedings, but when her husband is released she resolves to patch things up for the benefit of their son. While the film deserves praise for its unusual sensitivity to a woman's point of view, it's earnest to a fault and sometimes painfully dreary.

PORGY AND BESS

1959 138m c Musical ★★★½
Goldwyn (U.S.)

Sidney Poitier *(Porgy)*, Dorothy Dandridge *(Bess)*, Sammy Davis Jr. *(Sportin' Life)*, Pearl Bailey *(Maria)*, Brock Peters *(Crown)*, Leslie Scott *(Jake)*, Diahann Carroll *(Clara)*, Ruth Attaway *(Serena)*, Clarence Muse *(Peter)*, Everdinne Wilson *(Annie)*

p, Samuel Goldwyn; d, Otto Preminger; w, N. Richard Nash (based on the operetta by George Gershwin, Ira Gershwin, DuBose Heyward, the play by DuBose Heyward, Dorothy Heyward, and the novel by DuBose Heyward); ph, Leon Shamroy (ToddAO/Technicolor); ed, Daniel Mandell; m, George Gershwin; prod d, Oliver Smith; art d, Serge Krizman, Joseph C. Wright; chor, Hermes Pan; cos, Irene Sharaff

AAN Best Color Cinematography: Leon Shamroy; *AA Best Score (Musical):* Andre Previn, Ken Darby; *AAN Best Costume Design (Color):* Irene Sharaff; *AAN Best Sound:* Gordon E. Sawyer, Fred Hynes

With a budget of over $6 million, why wasn't this classic American operetta a classic American movie? Perhaps the fault lies in Samuel Goldwyn's decision to fire director Rouben Mamoulian in favor of Otto Preminger—if anyone could muddle a great saga, it was Preminger. The crippled Porgy (Sidney Poitier) loves Bess (Dorothy Dandridge), a floozy adored by many men, including Crown (Brock Peters), a tough stevedore, and Sportin' Life (Sammy Davis, Jr.), who supplies her with heroin and who is always trying to take her away from life in Catfish Row. After Crown kills a man in an argument over a game of craps and must flee the police, Bess settles in with Porgy. When Crown returns, wanting Bess back, Porgy kills him in turn, then hides out, while Bess agrees to follow Sportin' Life to New York. Porgy comes back to Catfish Row, learns that she's left, and is determined to follow her as the film ends—a simple story carried into the stratosphere by the glorious music. Poitier, not yet a star, initially accepted the role of Porgy, then declined, reportedly because of feeling within the black community that the story was racist, until producer Goldwyn and Mamoulian again convinced him to do the project. His singing voice and

Dandridge's are dubbed; Davis, Pearl Bailey (as Maria), and Peters all do their own singing. (As Clara, Diahann Carroll, a wonderful nightclub singer lacking operatic range, also has her voice looped.) Shooting was delayed when fire decimated the Goldwyn lot, and in the month it took to rebuild everything, Goldwyn and Mamoulian began to have "creative differences." Thus Preminger was called in to replace Mamoulian, with rather heavy-handed results. The brilliant score by the Gershwins and DuBose Heyward, however, will last forever, while Preminger's veteran cameraman, Leon Shamroy, did a wonderful job and the art direction by Serge Krizman and Joseph Wright is sensational.

PORK CHOP HILL 🔲 DVD

1959 97m bw War ★★★★
Melville (U.S.)

Gregory Peck *(Lt. Clemons)*, Harry Guardino *(Forstman)*, Rip Torn *(Lt. Russell)*, George Peppard *(Fedderson)*, James Edwards *(Cpl. Jurgens)*, Bob Steele *(Kern)*, Woody Strode *(Franklin)*, George Shibata *(Lt. O'Hashi)*, Norman Fell *(Sgt. Coleman)*, Robert Blake *(Velie)*

p, Sy Bartlett; d, Lewis Milestone; w, James R. Webb (based on a story by S.L.A. Marshall); ph, Sam Leavitt; ed, George Boemler; m, Leonard Rosenman; prod d, Nicolai Remisoff; cos, Edward Armand

A grim, harrowing film detailing a single brutal Korean War battle, PORK CHOP HILL was directed by veteran helmsman Lewis Milestone and is the third entry in his informal trilogy devoted to 20th-century military conflict (ALL QUIET ON THE WESTERN FRONT was set during WWI, and A WALK IN THE SUN during WWII). Gregory Peck plays the commander of an Army company that is ordered to take Pork Chop Ridge, an inconsequential tactical objective. Compounding the seeming pointlessness of the assignment are the Panmunjom peace talks, which the troops believe may end the war at any minute, so that they are reluctant to participate in what may be its final battle. PORK CHOP HILL is an ode to the common American infantryman, soldiers who manage to retain their honor and dignity despite being ordered into an insane action by a top brass unwilling to lose face to the enemy, even though the conflict's end appears imminent. Peck is outstanding as the resolute but compassionate commander, and Rip Torn, Harry Guardino, Woody Strode, James Edwards (veteran of Sam Fuller's excellent Korean War film THE STEEL HELMET), and Robert Blake provide solid support. Moreover, Milestone employs his considerable technical skills to create an authentic and memorable cinematic experience, projecting a grim realistic air that captures the forlorn atmosphere of the meaningless mission. Sam Leavitt's photography is topnotch and depicts this heroic battle in such stark detail that the viewer can almost smell the acrid fumes of cordite and taste the dust blown from the dead ridge. This powerful movie and HAMBURGER HILL, which deals similarly with an assault during the Vietnam War, would make a very interesting double bill.

PORT OF SHADOWS 🔲 DVD

(QUAI DES BRUMES)
1938 91m bw Drama ★★★★
Gregor Rabinovitch (France)

Jean Gabin *(Jean)*, Michele Morgan *(Nelly)*, Michel Simon *(Zabel)*, Pierre Brasseur *(Lucien Laugardier)*, Robert Le Vigan *(Michel Krauss)*, Jenny Burnay *(Lucien's Friend)*, Marcel Peres *(Chauffeur)*, Rene Genin *(Doctor)*, Edouard Delmont *(Panama)*, Raymond Aimos *(Quart-Vittel)*

p, Gregor Rabinovitch; d, Marcel Carne; w, Jacques Prevert (based on the novel *Le Quai Des Brumes* by Pierre Mac Orlan); ph, Eugene Schuftan, Louis Page; ed, Rene Le Henaff; m, Maurice Jaubert; prod d, Alexander Trauner

This marvelous distillation of the prevailing mood in prewar France was the first feature to win critical acclaim for the directing-writing team of Marcel Carne and Jacques Prevert (who had collaborated on JENNY and BIZARRE, BIZARRE, and who would later create the beloved CHILDREN OF PARADISE). Gabin plays a deserter who comes to the port of Le Havre looking for passage to a distant country. In a local dive he becomes attracted to Morgan, ward of the owner of a shop that is a front for illicit dealing. When Gabin comes to Simon's shop to buy a gift for Morgan, the evil Simon promises Gabin a passport and money if he will kill one of Simon's enemies. Gabin refuses. But hope for Gabin's escape comes when visionary artist Le Vigan gives the deserter his own passport before walking out on the quay and drowning himself.

A classic of French poetic realism, PORT OF SHADOWS conveys a deeply fatalistic belief that humankind is at the mercy of malevolent fate, a message that is communicated both through the simple story line and through the superb fog-shrouded sets (the work of Alexander Trauner) and forbidding locations. Ironically, PORT OF SHADOWS was originally to have been a German production. Carne was introduced to the Mac Orlan novel on which the picture is loosely based by Raoul Ploquin, then head of French productions at UFA in Berlin. Nazi propaganda minister Josef Goebbels turned thumbs down on the project, however; he considered this story of a deserter to be decadent. The rights were sold to French producer Gregor Rabinovitch, who envisioned a lighter, happier film, and so quarreled constantly with Carne. Carne also had political problems within his own country, primarily with the French minister of war, who would not permit the word "deserter" to be used and insisted that Gabin's soldier's uniform be treated respectfully. As a result, writer Prevert was forced to deviate from the novel in almost every respect. Notably, in the book, Morgan's heroine is no tempest-tossed innocent; she is a prostitute who murders her pimp and ends up wealthy. Banned from being shown during the Nazi occupation of France.

PORTRAIT OF A LADY, THE
1996 144m c   Drama   ★★★½
Propaganda Films   (New Zealand/U.K./U.S.)   PG-13

Nicole Kidman *(Isabel Archer)*, John Malkovich *(Gilbert Osmond)*, Barbara Hershey *(Madame Serena Merle)*, Martin Donovan *(Ralph Touchett)*, Shelley Winters *(Mrs. Touchett)*, John Gielgud *(Mr. Touchett)*, Richard E. Grant *(Lord Warburton)*, Shelley Duvall *(Countess Gemini)*, Christian Bale *(Edward Rosier)*, Viggo Mortensen *(Caspar Goodwood)*

p, Monty Montgomery, Steve Golin; d, Jane Campion; w, Laura Jones (based on the novel by Henry James); ph, Stuart Dryburgh; ed, Veronika Jenet; m, Wojiech Kilar; prod d, Janet Patterson; art d, Martin Childs; cos, Janet Patterson

AAN Best Supporting Actress: Barbara Hershey; *AAN Best Costume Design:* Janet Patterson

Director Jane Campion's feminist intentions are clear in this adaptation of Henry James's classic novel. While it lacks the power and originality of her previous films, PORTRAIT offers much to be admired.

Isabel Archer (Nicole Kidman), a young American orphan, has come to live at the English estate of her wealthy aunt and uncle (John Gielgud and Shelley Winters) and their consumptive son, Ralph (Martin Donovan). An independently minded young woman, Isabel declines two attractive mar-

riage proposals. She instead finds inspiration in the worldly independence of a mysterious widow, Madame Merle (Barbara Hershey), and the two become fast friends. After her uncle dies, Isabel is bequeathed a surprisingly large fortune and she travels to Italy, where Madame Merle introduces her to Gilbert Osmond (John Malkovich). An American expatriate with exquisite taste but little money, Osmond seduces Isabel into marriage. Soon, however, Osmond lets his true nature be known, and Isabel's dream of independence becomes a nightmare of imprisonment.

Campion takes the title of James's novel fully to heart, offering up an enticing visual portrait of a woman constrained by the limits of a patriarchal society. Despite a few too many obvious visual metaphors, Campion takes some commendable risks, such as fantasy sequences and changes in film speed. Kidman's thoughtful portrayal has depth, but she's unable to measure up to the character's strength and intelligence. At this point in his career, Malkovich's villain feels cliched, but Hershey is a revelation: her complex portrayal of a ruthless woman torn between the need to provide for herself and a genuine horror at her own manipulations is both chilling and heartbreaking. Drawing parallels between the 19th century and the present, Campion creates her own portrait of modern femininity, while exposing the persistent social structures with which it is necessarily framed.

PORTRAIT OF JENNIE   DVD
1948 86m   c/bw   Romance   ★★★★
Vanguard   (U.S.)

Jennifer Jones *(Jennie Appleton)*, Joseph Cotten *(Eben Adams)*, Ethel Barrymore *(Miss Spinney)*, Cecil Kellaway *(Mr. Matthews)*, David Wayne *(Gus O'Toole)*, Albert Sharpe *(Mr. Moore)*, Florence Bates *(Mrs. Jekes the Landlady)*, Lillian Gish *(Mother Mary of Mercy)*, Henry Hull *(Eke)*, Esther Somers *(Mrs. Bunce)*

p, David O. Selznick; d, William Dieterle; w, Paul Osborn, Peter Berneis, Leonardo Bercovici (based on the novel by Robert Nathan); ph, Joseph August; ed, William Morgan; m, Dimitri Tiomkin; prod d, J. McMillan Johnson; art d, Joseph B. Platt; fx, Clarence Slifer, Paul Eagler, J. McMillan Johnson; cos, Lucinda Ballard, Anna Hill Johnstone

AAN Best B/W Cinematography: Joseph August; *AA Best Special Effects:* Paul Eagler (Visual), Joseph McMillan Johnson (Visual), Russell Shearman (Visual), Clarence Slifer (Visual), Charles Freeman (Audible), James G. Stewart (Audible)

An eerie love story, PORTRAIT OF JENNIE offers superb performances from Cotten, as a struggling painter, and Jones, as a girl from the past with whom he falls in love. It is 1932, the nadir of the Depression, and Cotten, a young painter who feels that his work lacks depth, sits glumly in New York City's Central Park, contemplating his not-so-bright future. A beautiful young girl, Jones, approaches him and begins to speak with him, using strange words that belong to a previous era, mentioning that she attends a convent school and that her parents are trapeze artists at Hammerstein's Opera House. She sings Cotten a haunting song, then disappears as abruptly as she appeared. Afterwards, Cotten struggles on with his art, encouraged by wealthy art dealer Barrymore, who takes a motherly interest in him, buying his water colors even though she knows they are poor, and suggesting that he try a new medium. Jones turns up periodically throughout that winter, while Cotten finds work painting a mural on the wall of an Irish saloon, a commission arranged by Cotten's good friend Wayne, a cab driver. Each time Jones reappears through the following spring and summer, she seems older by years, growing up from adolescence to young womanhood. Cotten asks her to sit for a portrait and finishes it just as she tells him she's about to graduate from college. When Barrymore and her associate, Kellaway, see the portrait of Jones, they hail it as a startling, innovative work by the hitherto unpromising Cotten that will surely establish his artistic reputation. Yet Cotten is haunted by Jones and begins to look into her background, discovering that her parents were killed in a high-wire accident. Moreover, he finds out from Gish, the mother superior at an all-girl college, that Jones was in fact killed during a hurricane in New England in the 1920s. Cotten refuses to believe that the girl he painted is a ghost, but on the eve of the hurricane's anniversary, he rushes to New England. There, Jones comes to him during a raging storm and tells him that their love will live across the barriers of time, then vanishes for good. Eventually, Cotten begins to doubt he ever really met the beautiful girl, but when he finds her scarf, he begins to believe that he will meet his true love again in the afterlife after all.

Dieterle's direction is sensitive and the sequences are wonderfully constructed, with no scene bruising the next. He draws forth stellar performances, especially from Cotten; Jones is seen too briefly, but projects a genuinely ethereal quality during her moments on the screen. August's photography is stunning, and Tiomkin's lyrical score, drawn from Claude Debussy's themes (principally "The Afternoon of a Faun") is highly memorable. The foreword of the film, written by Ben Hecht, sums up the story's effect: "Out of the shadows of knowledge, and out of a painting that hung on a museum wall, comes our story, the truth of which lies not on our screen but in your heart." (A similar story of love that crosses mortal boundaries is at the core of a Hecht romance of considerable note, MIRACLE IN THE RAIN.)

POSSESSION

DVD
2002 102m c   Drama   ★★
USA Films/Warner Bros./Baltimore/Spring Creek   PG-13
Productions/Contagious Films   (U.S./U.K.)

Gwyneth Paltrow (_Maud Bailey_), Aaron Eckhart (_Roland Michell_), Jeremy Northam (_Randolph Henry Ash_), Jennifer Ehle (_Christabel LaMotte_), Lena Headey (_Blanche Glover_), Holly Aird (_Ellen Ash_), Toby Stephens (_Fergus Wolfe_), Trevor Eve (_Cropper_), Tom Hickey (_Blackadder_), Graham Crowden (_Sir George_)

p, Barry Levinson, Paula Weinstein; d, Neil LaBute; w, David Henry Hwang, Laura Jones, Neil LaBute (based on the novel by A.S. Byatt); ph, Jean Yves Escoffier; ed, Claire Simpson; m, Gabriel Yared; prod d, Luciana Arrighi; art d, Paul Ghirardani, Andrew Sanders; fx, Paul Dunn, Wilma Dunn; cos, Jenny Beavan

A.S. Byatt's novel _Possession_ is a heady mix of poems, love letters, and diary entries—literary stuff that's always the first to go whenever a book is adapted for the screen. Unfortunately, as this thin and ill-conceived adaptation from director Neil LaBute demonstrates, that stuff is the lifeblood of Byatt's wonderful book.

Scruffy American academic Roland Michell (Aaron Eckhart) works as a research assistant to Professor Blackadder (Tom Hickey), one of the leading authorities on the 19th-century English poet Randolph Henry Ash. One afternoon in the London Library, Roland stumbles upon what appear to be early drafts of love letters written by Ash to the poet Christabel LaMotte. Proving that the two writers even knew each other would be a real coup; confirming that the very married Ash carried on a secret affair with LaMotte would make Roland's career. Roland nicks the letters and takes them to chilly LaMotte scholar Maud Bailey (Gwyneth Paltrow), who suggests a trip to the crumbling estate where LaMotte once lived. There Maud and Roland hit the jackpot when they uncover two hidden bundles of letters—the amorous correspondence between LaMotte and her lover, R.H. Ash. As Maud and Roland pore over the letters and attempt to reconstruct the clandestine affair, the film flashes back to the 19th century to find Ash (Jeremy

Northam) and LaMotte (Jennifer Ehle) overcoming their scruples and declaring their love. Our scholars inevitably follow suit.

It's hard to see what attracted the writer-director of YOUR FRIENDS & NEIGHBORS to Byatt's book; it's a bad fit all around. Paltrow tries to get into the swing of things, but she's too young, and Maud comes off as immature. Eckhart is even less persuasive. Gruff and unshaven, he crashes through it all like Indiana Jones out to prove that poesy ain't for pansies.

POSTCARDS FROM THE EDGE

DVD
1990 101m c   Comedy/Drama   ★★★
Columbia   (U.S.)   R

Meryl Streep (_Suzanne Vale_), Shirley MacLaine (_Doris Mann_), Dennis Quaid (_Jack Falkner_), Gene Hackman (_Lowell_), Richard Dreyfuss (_Dr. Frankenthal_), Rob Reiner (_Joe Pierce_), Mary Wickes (_Grandma_), Conrad Bain (_Grandpa_), Annette Bening (_Evelyn Ames_), Simon Callow (_Simon Asquith_)

p, Mike Nichols, John Calley; d, Mike Nichols; w, Carrie Fisher (based on her novel); ph, Michael Ballhaus (Technicolor); ed, Sam O'Steen; m, Carly Simon; prod d, Patrizia Von Brandenstein; art d, Kandy Stern; cos, Ann Roth

AAN Best Actress: Meryl Streep; _AAN Best Original Song:_ "I'm Checkin' Out"; Shel Silverstein

Adapted by Fisher from her first novel, POSTCARDS FROM THE EDGE is yet further proof that Hollywood makes its best films about what it knows best—making films in Hollywood. But while POSTCARDS is entertainingly observant of the filmmaking scene, too much time is taken up with the cliched mother-daughter drama at the film's core. Continuing in the dark comedy vein she began in SHE DEVIL, Streep, as actress Suzanne Vale, starts at rock bottom. Working on a film, Suzanne is so addled by a cocaine habit that her director, Lowell (Hackman), must threaten her life just to get her focused. When she overdoses on sedatives while in bed with Jack Falkner (Quaid), the womanizing producer anonymously wheels her into a hospital emergency room. There her stomach is pumped by a doctor (Dreyfuss) who later asks her out on a date. During her rehabilitation, Suzanne must contend with a therapist (CCH Pounder from BAGDAD CAFE) whose grab-bag of self-help slogans is enough to drive a patient back to drugs. Upon completing her clinical rehab, Suzanne finds she is only able to find work on a low-budget cop movie. She's also required to live with her domineering, alcoholic, entertainer-mom, Doris (MacLaine playing Debbie Reynolds), the too-obvious cause of Suzanne's problems.

Director Nichols and Fisher manage to slip a few provocative ideas in here. Notably, Suzanne's return to sobriety is hardly rewarding; instead it provides her with a new sensitivity to the apathy and treachery of agents, producers, directors, lovers, and, most importantly, her mother. Suzanne's personal struggle is also contrasted throughout with Doris's nonstop, unrepentant boozing. The film suggests that sedation is an almost reasonable response to such a crazy life. In the final analysis, POSTCARDS is a mixed bag. There are a number of entertaining moments; however, potentially rich characters and situations wither from lack of development for the sake of the central relationship, which is never wholly convincing.

POSTMAN ALWAYS RINGS TWICE, THE

DVD
1946 113m bw Crime   ★★★★
MGM   (U.S.)

Lana Turner (_Cora Smith_), John Garfield (_Frank Chambers_), Cecil Kellaway (_Nick Smith_), Hume Cronyn (_Arthur Keats_), Leon Ames (_Kyle Sackett_), Audrey Totter (_Madge Gorland_), Alan Reed (_Ezra_

Liam Kennedy), Jeff York *(Blair)*, Charles Williams *(Jimmie White)*, A. Cameron Grant *(Willie)*

p, Carey Wilson; d, Tay Garnett; w, Harry Ruskin, Niven Busch (based on the novel by James M. Cain); ph, Sidney Wagner; ed, George White; m, George Bassman; art d, Cedric Gibbons, Randall Duell; cos, Irene, Marion Herwood Keyes

The best version of James M. Cain's torrid, hard-hitting romance comes to startling life under Garnett's shrewd direction, surprisingly at MGM. The studio threw in the towel on Turner's sweet pants and let her turn on the blow-torch and expose the seething passions. Although 1946 cen-sors assured some downplaying of the heat between the leads, from the moment surly Garfield sees the "Man Wanted" sign, and Turner's lipstick rolls tauntingly across the floor, we know we're in for dangerous pulp romance. By the time the camera tilts from Turner's foot to the top of her white-hot visage, we know what the goods are and that Garfield's horny drifter is sold. If Turner is more girlish than Stanwyck in DOUBLE INDEMNITY, we also know it's a ruse she knows works with men.

Drifter Frank Chambers (Garfield) stops at a California roadside cafe owned by the amiable Nick Smith (Kellaway), who offers him a job as a handyman. Frank is disinclined toward such menial work until he catches a glimpse of Nick's siren wife, Cora (La Lana). He immediately takes the job and then begins making advances to a most receptive lady. The two become lovers ("Give me a kiss or I'll sock ya!") but what are they going to do about Nick?

Except for two scenes in which Turner wears black (one when she contemplates suicide and the other when she goes to her mother's funeral), the alluring platinum blond actress wears nothing but white in the film, further propelling her haughty phosphorescent steaminess: this angelically venal little trollop begged to be dirtied up. Though she is a *femme fatale* here, Turner is a softer, more emotionally vulnerable Lucrezia Borgia than her sisterly counterparts in other Cain stories. Even at the end she is seeking love, not revenge, telling Garfield after the murder that she wants "kisses that come from life, not death." So impressed was Cain with Turner's performance that he presented her with a leather-bound first edition of the novel, inscribing it, "For my dear Lana, thank you for giving a performance that was even finer than I expected."

The critical and public response to THE POSTMAN ALWAYS RINGS TWICE was enormous. Turner and Garfield won kudos from the critics, and the supporting play-ers, especially Ames and Cronyn, received plaudits. The studio announced in 1972 that it would remake this *film noir* classic, but delays in casting and directing stalled the production until 1980 when Bob Rafelson took over the chore of directing Jack Nicholson and Jessica Lange. The remake was much less sat-isfying and much more crudely sexual, with Nicholson rav-ishing Lange on the kitchen table. For all the '80s heaving and pawing, the 1946 version is far more suggestive.

POSTMAN, THE

(IL POSTINO)

1994 113m c   Comedy/Drama   ★★★½
Cecchi Gori Group/Tiger Cinematographica/   PG
Pentafilm/EsternoMediterraneo Film/Blue Dahlia
Productions/Canal Plus/K2T   (Italy/France/Belgium)

Massimo Troisi *(Mario Ruoppolo)*, Philippe Noiret *(Pablo Neruda)*, Maria Grazia Cucinotta *(Beatrice Russo)*, Linda Moretti *(Donna Rosa)*, Renato Scarpa *(Telegraph Operator)*, Anna Bonaiuto *(Matilde)*, Mariana Rigillo *(Di Cosimo)*, Bruno Alessandro *(Pablo Neruda's Voice)*, Sergio Solli, Carlo di Maio

p, Mario Cecchi Gori, Vittorio Cecchi Gori, Gaetano Daniele; d, Michael Radford; w, Anna Pavignano, Michael Radford, Furio Scarpelli, Giacomo Scarpelli, Massimo Troisi (from a story by Furio Scarpelli and Giacomo Scarpelli based on the novel *Burning Patience* by Antonio Skarmeta); ph, Franco Di Giacomo; ed, Roberto Perpignani; m, Luis Enrique Bacolov; prod d, Lorenzo Baraldi; cos, Gianni Gissi

AAN Best Picture; AAN Best Actor: Massimo Troisi; *AAN Best Director:* Michael Radford; *AAN Best Adapted Screenplay:* Anna Pavignano, Michael Radford, Furio Scarpelli, Giacomo Scarpelli, Massimo Troisi; *AA Best Dramatic Score:* Luis Enrique Bacolov

In 1952, exiled Chilean dissident and poet Pablo Neruda trav-eled to Europe, where a nervous, deeply anti-Marxist Italian government tried to kick him out, eventually depositing him on the isle of Capri. That a famous Communist should have found himself living in a rich man's villa, learning about life from the "simplest people in the world," is the arch conceit underlying this finely wrought film.

Massimo Troisi plays Mario Ruoppolo, a listless fellow who lives with his father in a tiny fishing village. Mario has never liked fishing, and at his father's urging he finally finds a job as a postman, working for the district's Postmaster (Renato Scarpa), a Marxist. His village has never before needed a post-man, but the arrival of Neruda (Philippe Noiret) has changed everything. To the shy Mario, Neruda is a charismatic but baf-fling figure. Only when Mario sets out to win the heart of his own Beatrice (Maria Grazia Cucinotta) does he begin to understand the real power of poetry.

Based on *Burning Patience* by Antonio Skarmeta, this film was a labor of love for Troisi, who sought Radford (1984, WHITE MISCHIEF) to direct and who shares a screenplay credit. The film has a gentle political edge, knocking Marxists and Christian Democrats with equal cheerfulness, and Troisi's self-deprecating humor, sly delivery, and melancholic charm are inimitable. Troisi, who suffered from a congenital heart defect, postponed surgery to complete the film, and died the day after shooting wrapped. The actor's fate hangs over every minute of THE POSTMAN (which he shot in small bursts, often an hour or less in a day), and necessarily frames the audi-ence's response. When, toward the end, Mario discovers that Neruda has forgotten all about him, he shrugs it off, saying he was a fool to expect more. It is impossible to be unmoved by a dying man's despairing assumption that nobody will remember him.

POWERPUFF GIRLS MOVIE, THE

DVD

2002 90m c   Animated/Children's/Adventure   ★★★
Cartoon Network/Warner Bros.   (U.S.)   PG

VOICES OF: Catherine Cavadini *(Blossom)*, Tara Strong *(Bubbles)*, E.G. Daily *(Buttercup)*, Roger L. Jackson *(Mojo Jojo)*, Tom Kenny *(Narrator/Mayor)*, Jennifer Hale *(Ms. Keane)*, Jennifer Martin *(Sara Bellum)*, Tom Kane *(Professor Utonium)*, Jeff Glen Bennett *(Ace/Big Billy/Grubber)*, Grey DeLisle *(Linda/Woman at Zoo)*

p, Donna Castricone; d, Craig McCracken; w, Charlie Bean, Lauren Faust, Craig McCracken, Paul Rudish, Don Shank (from a story by Charlie Bean, Lauren Faust, Craig McCracken, Amy Keating Rogers, Paul Rudish, and Don Shank); ed, Robert DeSales; m, James L. Venable; art d, Mike Moon; fx, John Dillon; anim, Genndy Tartakovsky, David Dunnet, Craig Kellman, Carey Yost

Rather than concocting a 90-minute mega-episode from the popular Cartoon Network series, the film's screenwriters—including "Powerpuff Girls" creator Craig McCracken—have opted for the prequel approach, showing how three precocious kindergartners became the cutest crime fighters in the known universe.

Professor Utonium (voice of Tom Kane) is tired of mis-creants running rampant in Townsville and is ready to do some-thing about it. Combining the classic ingredients sugar, spice, and everything nice, he'll create little girls capable of learning the difference between right and wrong. But an accident occurs, and a dash of toxic "Chemical X" gets into the mix. Instead of sweet, normal young ladies, Professor Utonium finds himself raising a trio of rambunctious hellions with laser-beam eyes and the ability to fly. The lasses emerge fully formed, and each has a distinct personality: Blossom (Catherine Cavadini) is the outspoken leader; Bubbles (Tara Strong) goes from giggles to tears at the drop of a hair clip; and Buttercup (E.G. Daily) has anger management issues. The girls befriend fellow outcast Mojo Jojo (Roger L. Jackson), but the diabolical primate tricks the girls into using their superpowers to further his evil plot to take over Townsville.

An entertaining romp that stays true to the material's television roots, this is a good starting point for viewers unfamiliar with the series, and the animation is first-rate. The action sequences are so dizzying that they make RUN LOLA RUN look as though it unfolds in slow motion, and the simian puns fly fast and furious. Adults will groan, but most kids in the movie's target age group won't even notice.

PRANCER

DVD
1989 103m c Drama ★★★½
Raffaella/Nelson/Cineplex Odeon (U.S.) G

Sam Elliott *(John Riggs)*, Rebecca Harrell *(Jessica Riggs)*, Cloris Leachman *(Mrs. McFarland)*, Rutanya Alda *(Aunt Sarah)*, John Joseph Duda *(Steve Riggs)*, Abe Vigoda *(Dr. Orel Benton)*, Michael Constantine *(Mr. Stewart/Santa)*, Ariana Richards *(Carol Wetherby)*, Mark Rolston *(Herb Drier)*, Johnny Galecki *(Billy Quinn)*

p, Raffaella De Laurentiis, Greg Taylor, Mike Petzold; d, John Hancock; w, Greg Taylor (based on his story); ph, Misha Suslov; ed, Dennis M. O'Connor; m, Maurice Jarre; prod d, Chester Kaczenski; art d, Marc Dabe; cos, Denny Burt

Plucky nine-year-old Jessica Riggs (Rebecca Harrell) resolutely believes in Santa Claus even though her schoolmates think she's a baby. When she finds Prancer, one of Saint Nick's famous reindeer, injured in nearby forest, Jessica secretly nurses the reindeer back to health, aided by an elderly veterinarian (Abe Vigoda). However, her attempts to help Prancer are complicated when she confides in a shopping-mall Santa (Michael Constantine), who spills the beans to the press, and by her father (Sam Elliott), who sells the reindeer to a merchant for use as part of a promotional stunt. When children's films are released for the holidays, one's heart sinks at the memory of such saccharine seasonal "gems" as SANTA CLAUS: THE MOVIE, and television's "It Came upon a Midnight Clear"; however, PRANCER marches to the beat of a different little drummer boy. Sensitively directed by John Hancock and filmed in the Indiana area where he grew up, the movie benefits from an authentic atmosphere, fleshed-out characters who behave as if they live in the real world, and an especially charming performance by Harrell. Good family films are as rare as flying reindeer, but PRANCER deserves to join the select ranks of those Christmas movies we return to again and again.

PREDATOR

DVD
1987 107m c Thriller/Science Fiction ★★★½
Gordon/Silver/Davis/American Entertainment R
Partners (U.S.)

Arnold Schwarzenegger *(Maj. Alan "Dutch" Schaefer)*, Carl Weathers *(Dillon)*, Elpidia Carrillo *(Anna)*, Bill Duke *(Mac)*, Jesse Ventura *(Sgt. Blain)*, Sonny Landham *(Billy)*, Richard Chaves *(Pancho)*, R.G. Armstrong *(Gen. Phillips)*, Shane Black *(Hawkins)*, Kevin Peter Hall *(Predator)*

p, Lawrence Gordon, Joel Silver, John Davis; d, John McTiernan; w, Jim Thomas, John Thomas; ph, Don McAlpine; ed, John F. Link II, Mark Helfrich; m, Alan Silvestri; prod d, John Vallone; art d, Frank Richwood, Jorge Saenz, John K. Reinhart Jr.; fx, Robert M. Greenberg, Richard Greenberg, Joel Hynek, Stuart Robertson, Dream Quest Images, Al Di Sarro, Laurencio Cordero, Stan Winston

AAN Best Visual Effects: Joel Hynek, Robert M. Greenberg, Richard Greenberg, Stan Winston

Crisply stylish and suspenseful, making brilliant use of optical special effects, PREDATOR is one of Schwarzenegger's best. Director McTiernan (DIE HARD) nimbly sustains suspense throughout this tale of a special forces platoon assigned to locate an unnamed menace lurking in the jungles of Central America. The film is one of the cleverest of the many action pictures that allegorize Vietnam—its hardbitten soldiers, ill used by a government that lies to them about the real nature of their mission, face an invisible enemy that picks them off using guerilla tactics. In the end, however, the creature proves curiously sympathetic, and its final confrontation with Major Dutch Schaefer (Schwarzenegger) has tragic overtones.

PRESIDENT'S ANALYST, THE

DVD
1967 103m c Spy/Comedy ★★★½
Panpiper (U.S.)

James Coburn *(Dr. Sidney Schaefer)*, Godfrey Cambridge *(Don Masters)*, Severn Darden *(Kropotkin)*, Joan Delaney *(Nan Butler)*, Pat Harrington Jr. *(Arlington Hewes)*, Barry Maguire *(Old Wrangler)*, Jill Banner *(Snow White)*, Eduard Franz *(Ethan Allan Cocket)*, Walter Burke *(Henry Lux)*, Will Geer *(Dr. Lee Evans)*

p, Stanley Rubin; d, Theodore J. Flicker; w, Theodore J. Flicker; ph, William A. Fraker (Panavision, Technicolor); ed, Stuart Pappe; m, Lalo Schifrin; prod d, Pato Guzman; art d, Hal Pereira, Al Roelofs; cos, Jack Bear

Though it's now somewhat dated, at the time of its release this picture was a mostly on-the-mark satire of American culture and international politics in the 1960s. Coburn plays a psychiatrist who serves his country as the analyst for the president of the United States. It isn't long before some in the government become concerned about what Coburn has learned in this position, and he's marked for assassination. However, other nations figure Coburn might be able to supply them with valuable information, and soon agents from around the globe are tracking the hapless psychiatrist. Among those in pursuit are American agent Cambridge, his longtime friend and adversary Russian agent Darden, and Arte Johnson and Martin Horsey as a couple of humorless "FBR" agents. Mindless bureaucracy, Cold War mentality, blind liberalism, and psychoanalysis are spoofed in this fast-paced comedy.

PRESUMED INNOCENT

DVD
1990 127m c Crime/Mystery ★★★½
Mirage (U.S.) R

Harrison Ford *(Rusty Sabich)*, Brian Dennehy *(Raymond Horgan)*, Raul Julia *(Sandy Stern)*, Bonnie Bedelia *(Barbara Sabich)*, Paul Winfield *(Judge Larren Lyttle)*, Greta Scacchi *(Carolyn Polhemus)*, John Spencer *(Detective Lipranzer)*, Joe Grifasi *(Tommy Molto)*, Tom Mardirosian *(Nico Della Guardia)*, Anna Maria Horsford *(Eugenia)*

p, Sydney Pollack, Mark Rosenberg; d, Alan J. Pakula; w, Frank Pierson, Alan J. Pakula (based on the novel by Scott Turow); ph, Gordon Willis (Du Art Color); ed, Evan Lottman; m, John Williams; prod d, George Jenkins; art d, Bob Guerra; fx, C5, Inc.; cos, John Boxer

If they gave an Oscar for the year's most claustrophobic film, PRESUMED INNOCENT could have won it in a walk. Everything about this film is as cramped, clenched, and constricted as Harrison Ford's face, which looks like a tightly balled-up fist here. However, Ford's perpetually coiled-up state also makes him a natural murder suspect in this adaptation of attorney Scott Turow's best-selling novel. Ford plays prosecuting attorney Rusty Sabich, the quintessential good soldier right down to his Roman Centurion haircut. But Sabich serves a degraded master, District Attorney Raymond Horgan (Brian Dennehy), a soured idealist whose principles have been compromised by years of deals made to keep the wheels of justice from grinding to a halt. As the film begins, Horgan is making a halfhearted run at re-election, but his campaign is fatally rocked by the sordid rape-murder of his star prosecutor in the sex-crimes division, the brilliant, beautiful, and ambitious Carolyn Polhemus (Scacchi). The list of suspects narrows to a single name when Sabich's fingerprints are found on a beer glass five feet from Polhemus' body and when tests reveal that the killer's blood type also matches that of Sabich, who had an affair with Polhemus that ended messily.

The solution to this whodunit will hardly surprise any of the millions who have read Turow's novel. However, neither the book nor the movie hinges on the killer's disclosure. Despite cinematographer Gordon Willis's penchant for underlit scenes of Sabich implausibly poring over legal documents in near-darkness, and Pakula's overemphasis on Sabich's weariness and dessication, PRESUMED INNOCENT is never less than engrossing.

PRETTY BABY
1978 109m c Drama ★★★½
Paramount (U.S.) **DVD** R

Keith Carradine *(E.J. Bellocq)*, Susan Sarandon *(Hattie)*, Brooke Shields *(Violet)*, Frances Faye *(Mme. Nell Livingston)*, Antonio Fargas *(Professor, Piano-Player)*, Gerrit Graham *(Highpockets)*, Mae Mercer *(Mama Mosebery)*, Diana Scarwid *(Frieda)*, Barbara Steele *(Josephine)*, Matthew Anton *(Red Top)*

p, Louis Malle; d, Louis Malle; w, Polly Platt (based on a story by Platt and Malle, from the book *Storyville, New Orleans: Being an Authentic Account of the Notorious Redlight District* by Al Rose); ph, Sven Nykvist (Metrocolor); ed, Suzanne Baron, Suzanne Fenn; prod d, Trevor Williams; fx, Maureen Lambray; cos, Mina Mittleman

AAN Best Song Score: Jerry Wexler

Beautifully shot and subtly rendered, but too slowly told for its ambiguities to really be effective. Violet (Brooke Shields) lives with her mother, Hattie (Susan Sarandon), a prostitute in 1917 New Orleans. Her touching innocence seems unaffected even when, at the age of twelve, her virginity is auctioned off for the princely sum of $400. After leaving the brothel to live for a while with photographer E.J. Bellocq (a real-life figure), Violet is eventually reunited with her mother, who has escaped the brothel for a more "respectable" life on the outside.

The strength of Malle's film lies in its simultaneous presentation of two viewpoints: that of Violet, whose sweetly innocent appreciation of her life is so convincing that we feel her entry into "civilized" society will be her downfall; and that of Bellocq, who sees the girl and her surroundings as both erotically compelling and artistically challenging. Cinematographer Nykvist does a superlative job of capturing this luxuriant world-unto-itself, but the pace is so slow that, by the end, we've given up caring about Malle's characters, let alone his critique of bourgeois morality.

PRETTY IN PINK
1986 96m c Comedy/Drama ★★★
Paramount (U.S.) **DVD** PG-13

Molly Ringwald *(Andie Walsh)*, Harry Dean Stanton *(Jack Walsh)*, Jon Cryer *(Phil "Duckie" Dale)*, Andrew McCarthy *(Blane McDonough)*, Annie Potts *(Iona)*, James Spader *(Steff McKee)*, Jim Haynie *(Donnelly)*, Alexa Kenin *(Jena)*, Kate Vernon *(Benny)*, Andrew Dice Clay *(Bouncer)*

p, Lauren Shuler; d, Howard Deutch; w, John Hughes; ph, Tak Fujimoto (Technicolor); ed, Richard Marks; m, Michael Gore; prod d, John W. Corso; chor, Kenny Ortega

Andie Walsh (Molly Ringwald) is a kid from the wrong side of the tracks. She's a self-confident high-school senior who dresses in handmade clothes, works in a record store, and lives in a modest home with her unemployed father (Harry Dean Stanton). Times are tough for Andie in school, where she and her friends are tormented by the wealthy students who make up the majority of the student body, and where her worst fear is that she won't get invited to the senior prom. Her best friend, "Duckie" (Jon Cryer), talks matter-of-factly with her father about marrying Andie, but he never thinks of taking her to the prom—a social event that most of the poor kids avoid. To her surprise, she is asked to go to the dance by the charming Blaine (Andrew McCarthy), who's not as snobbish as the rest of his elitist friends. As in all of John Hughes's films, PRETTY IN PINK touches a chord with today's teens (as well as anyone who has been that age), but at the same time seems to pander somewhat to the audience's expectations. Interestingly, however, the finest moments in PRETTY IN PINK come not from the script by Hughes, but from Howard Deutch's careful direction. While the script contains trite and unbelievable dialogue, the superbly convincing performances make up for these faults.

PRETTY POISON
1968 89m c Thriller ★★★½
Lawrence Turman/Molino (U.S.)

Anthony Perkins *(Dennis Pitt)*, Tuesday Weld *(Sue Ann Stepanek)*, Beverly Garland *(Mrs. Stepanek)*, John Randolph *(Azenauer)*, Dick O'Neill *(Bud Munsch)*, Clarice Blackburn *(Mrs. Bronson)*, Joe Bova *(Pete)*, Ken Kercheval *(Harry Jackson)*, Don Fellows *(Detective)*, Parker Fennelly *(Night Watchman)*

p, Marshal Backlar, Noel Black; d, Noel Black; w, Lorenzo Semple Jr. (based on the novel *She Let Him Continue* by Stephen Geller); ph, David Quaid (DeLuxe Color); ed, William Ziegler; m, Johnny Mandel; art d, Jack Martin Smith, Harold Michelson; fx, Ralph Winigar, Billy King; cos, Ann Roth

A fascinating thriller that was mostly ignored at the time of its release, this is a fine film with a terrific performance by Tuesday Weld. Perkins is again a mentally unstable young man. As a youth, after a fight with his aunt, he kills the woman by burning down her house, though he claims he didn't know she was inside. As the film opens, he's recently been released from prison and is being watched carefully by parole officer Randolph. He gets a job with a lumber company and meets Weld, a pert high-school student. To impress her, he tells her he's with the CIA and in town to investigate nasty business at the lumber company. The two soon begin a relationship, though Weld's domineering mother, Garland, thinks Perkins is a nut and tells her daughter to stay away from him. It isn't long before Perkins finds that Weld's sweet face hides a killer's psyche, and he finds himself caught in a murder wrap as he is cleverly manipulated by the calculating Weld. It's up to the wily Randolph to figure out what really happened. This was Noel Black's directorial debut, and he maintains a brisk pace and a necessary level of tension throughout. Perkins, of course, is fine in the kind of role he excels at, but it's Weld's performance that really makes the film something special. She is superb as the pretty young thing whose exterior cloaks an ice-cold killer. With this film and her fine performances in such movies as SOLDIER IN THE RAIN; THE CINCINNATI KID; and WHO'LL STOP THE RAIN?, she consistently proved herself to be an actress of depth who is much more than a pretty face and a silly name. The picture was made in Great Barrington, Massachusetts.

PRETTY WOMAN

1990 119m c   Comedy/Romance   ★★½
Silver Screen Partners/Touchstone   (U.S.)   R

Richard Gere *(Edward Lewis)*, Julia Roberts *(Vivian Ward)*, Ralph Bellamy *(James Morse)*, Jason Alexander *(Philip Stuckey)*, Laura San Giacomo *(Kit De Luca)*, Alex Hyde-White *(David Morse)*, Amy Yasbeck *(Elizabeth Stuckey)*, Elinor Donahue *(Bridget)*, Hector Elizondo *(Hotel Manager)*, Judith Baldwin *(Susan)*

p, Arnon Milchan, Steven Reuther; d, Garry Marshall; w, J.F. Lawton; ph, Charles Minsky; ed, Priscilla Nedd; m, James Newton Howard; prod d, Albert Brenner; art d, David M. Haber; fx, Gary Zink; cos, Marilyn Vance-Straker

AAN Best Actress: Julia Roberts

None too pretty. Director Garry Marshall, the sophisticated talent who gave the world "Laverne and Shirley," comes a cropper with this Happy Hooker harangue. Yes, Julia Roberts's goofy good looks and giggly charm have a certain glimmer about them, rather like expensively wrapped Christmas candy, but she's an actress of considerable shallowness. If anyone gets unwrapped in this film, it's Richard Gere, whose body is, interestingly enough, more on display than Roberts's or Laura San Giacomo's (who, by the way, gives the film's funniest performance). Maybe that's why some feminists liked the film—though most of them knew better. Otherwise, Gere's performance as a corporate takeover specialist who picks up a pneumatic fantasy whore is strictly paint-by-numbers. The silly script lurches from one jarring, implausible moment to another, and Marshall directs like he was wearing earplugs and boxing gloves on the set. OK, PRETTY WOMAN is supposed to be a fairy tale, but whose? Bound to offend prostitutes and millionaires everywhere, this flick is not the street-smart "Pygymalion" it desperately wants to be.

PRICK UP YOUR EARS

1987 111m c   Biography   ★★★½
Civilhand Zenith   (U.K.)   R

Gary Oldman *(Joe Orton)*, Alfred Molina *(Kenneth Halliwell)*, Vanessa Redgrave *(Peggy Ramsay)*, Wallace Shawn *(John Lahr)*, Lindsay Duncan *(Anthea Lahr)*, Julie Walters *(Elsie Orton)*, James Grant *(William Orton)*, Janet Dale *(Mrs. Sugden)*, Dave Atkins *(Mr. Sugden)*, Margaret Tyzack *(Mme. Lambert)*

p, Andrew Brown; d, Stephen Frears; w, Alan Bennett (based on the biography by John Lahr); ph, Oliver Stapleton (Eastmancolor); ed, Mick Audsley; m, Stanley Myers; prod d, Hugo Luczyc-Wyhowski; art d, Philip Elton; cos, Bob Ringwood

Stephen Frears's PRICK UP YOUR EARS chronicles the rise and tragic demise of Joe Orton, the gay playwright whose brief but dazzling career spawned the brilliant farces *Loot*, *Entertaining Mr. Sloan* and *What the Butler Saw* and made a lasting contribution to the English-language theater.

Born John Orton in Leicester, England, Orton died at age 34 in 1967 when his longtime lover, Kenneth Halliwell, crushed his skull with a hammer before downing two handfuls of Nembutal to take his own life. PRICK UP YOUR EARS opens with this grisly event, then unfolds in flashbacks as biographer John Lahr (Wallace Shawn) researches Orton's brief life.

This is director Frears's second film with an openly homosexual theme, the first being 1986's acclaimed MY BEAUTIFUL LAUNDRETTE, and he attempts to delve deeply into the relationship between the two protagonists.

In real life, however, Halliwell was not the bearish brute that Molina's physical presence indicates; those who knew him say that he had a certain charm of his own as well as a Svengali influence over Orton. Other than the unfortunate miscasting of Molina, an otherwise superb actor, and Wallace Shawn's grating performance, everyone else is right on the money. Oldman, fresh from his triumph as Sex Pistol Sid Vicious in SID AND NANCY, is the key and holds it all together.

PRIDE AND PREJUDICE

1940 117m   bw   Drama   ★★★★½
MGM   (U.S.)

Greer Garson *(Elizabeth Bennet)*, Laurence Olivier *(Mr. Darcy)*, Mary Boland *(Mrs. Bennet)*, Edna May Oliver *(Lady Catherine de Bourgh)*, Maureen O'Sullivan *(Jane Bennet)*, Ann Rutherford *(Lydia Bennet)*, Frieda Inescort *(Miss Caroline Bingley)*, Edmund Gwenn *(Mr. Bennet)*, Karen Morley *(Charlotte Lucas)*, Heather Angel *(Kitty Bennet)*

p, Hunt Stromberg; d, Robert Z. Leonard; w, Aldous Huxley, Jane Murfin (based on the play by Helen Jerome and the novel by Jane Austen); ph, Karl Freund; ed, Robert J. Kern; m, Herbert Stothart; art d, Cedric Gibbons, Paul Groesse; chor, Ernst Matray; cos, Adrian, Gile Steele

AA Best Interior Decoration (B/W): Cedric Gibbons, Paul Groesse

We may be prejudiced, but MGM can be proud. A remarkable example of Hollywood's not choking on the prestige adorning the filming of a classic, PRIDE AND PREJUDICE is an unusually successful adaptation of Jane Austen's most famous novel. Although the satire is slightly reduced and coarsened and the period advanced in order to use more flamboyant costumes, the spirit is entirely in keeping with Austen's sharp, witty portrait of rural 19th-century social mores. The film tells the familiar story of Mr. and Mrs. Bennet (Gwenn and Boland) and their five marriageable daughters. Jane (O'Sullivan) falls for the wealthy Mr. Bingley (Bruce Lester), but, unsure of her love and discouraged by his snooty sister (Inescort) and his haughty friend Mr. Darcy (Olivier), he leaves town without any promises. The middle daughter, Mary (Marsha Hunt) is goofy and bookish, the fourth child Kitty (Angel) insecure and suggestible and the youngest, Lydia (Rutherford), overly flirtatious. Troubles really brew when Lydia runs off with a caddish officer (Edward Ashley) and when Darcy, who feels himself too "proud" to fall for just any woman, flips for the second Bennet daughter, the independent Elizabeth (Garson). She, however, "prejudiced" against him because of his arrogance, will have none of him. Meanwhile, her mother plans for her to wed their foppish cousin, Mr. Collins (Melville Cooper).

The screenplay, by Aldous Huxley and old hand Jane Murfin, retains much of the novel's famous dialogue (e.g., the opening conversation between Mr. and Mrs. Bennet). They have also added a few scenes to "open up" the action a bit; our favorites are the hilarious carriage race and the enchanting archery lesson. The sets and costumes are lovingly rendered and the cinematography by Karl Freund evokes a glorious sense of period. PRIDE AND PREJUDICE represents the finest directorial work by MGM perennial Robert Z. Leonard. Liked by actors whom he indulged, Leonard generally crafts his work smoothly but it often lacks personality or imagination. Here, however, the pacing is perfect and the details just right. For personality, all one has to do is turn to that amazing cast. Garson never did anything better than her Elizabeth Bennet. Genteel but not precious, witty yet not forced, spirited but never vulgar, Garson's Elizabeth is an Austen heroine incarnate. Olivier, too, has rarely been better in a part requiring the passion of his Heathcliff from WUTHERING HEIGHTS but strapping it into the straitjacket of snobbery. As

Mr. Bennet, Gwenn makes a wonderfully wry and composed foil for his wife's antics, and Cooper rarely had the chance to huff and fluff quite so amusingly again.

PRIDE OF THE MARINES
1945 119m bw War   ★★★★
Warner Bros. (U.S.)

John Garfield *(Al Schmid)*, Eleanor Parker *(Ruth Hartley)*, Dane Clark *(Lee Diamond)*, John Ridgely *(Jim Merchant)*, Rosemary DeCamp *(Virginia Pfeiffer)*, Ann Doran *(Ella Merchant)*, Warren Douglas *(Kebabian)*, Don McGuire *(Irish)*, Tom D'Andrea *(Tom)*, Rory Mallinson *(Doctor)*

p, Jerry Wald; d, Delmer Daves; w, Albert Maltz, Marvin Borowsky (based on a story by Roger Butterfield); ph, Peverell Marley; ed, Owen Marks; m, Franz Waxman; art d, Leo K. Kuter; fx, L. Robert Burgs

AAN Best Screenplay: Albert Maltz

A grand and emotional study in heroism, PRIDE OF THE MARINES is a tour de force for rugged Garfield and a film that allowed director Daves to introduce some startling psychological techniques which made this film exceptional. Based on the true story of Al Schmid, the film shows us Garfield as a workingman in Philadelphia who courts and marries Parker on the eve of WW II. Garfield enlists in the Marines and is sent to Guadalcanal, where he and his small machine gun crew receive orders to be on the alert for a massive Japanese attack. With extraordinary heroism, they fend off the assault, but not before Garfield is blinded. Now, in readjusting to life and marriage without his sight, Garfield must display heroism of a different kind.

Garfield is brilliant in his portrayal of Schmid, and Daves's direction is superb, utilizing remarkable techniques such as double printings, negative images, and telescopic shots which all add to the eerie and unnerving experience Garfield is undergoing in his rehabilitation. The battle scenes in this film are some of the most harrowing ever shot. The idea for the film was largely Garfield's. He read an article about Schmid in *Life* magazine and contacted writer Maltz, suggesting a script be written about the man. Maltz had worked on the film DESTINATION TOKYO, also directed by Daves, and Garfield felt he would be the ideal writer to handle the project. Daves was brought into the project a short time later. This film, along with AIR FORCE and DESTINATION TOKYO, was one of Garfield's favorite films made at Warner Bros. PRIDE OF THE MARINES was a box office smash, released just as WWII came to a close, timed perfectly with the public's curiosity about rehabilitating a generation of wounded American servicemen. Co-author Maltz later became one of the "Hollywood Ten," and some of the dialogue in PRIDE OF THE MARINES was later recalled by the House Un-American Activities Committee, particularly those lines dealing with social consciousness and working class arguments (mostly expressed by Clark), as an example of communistic philosophy insidiously inserted into movies. The film nevertheless remains a deeply moving, sensitive production, and one of the finest war films ever made.

PRIDE OF THE YANKEES, THE
1942 127m bw Biography/Sports   ★★★★½
RKO (U.S.)

Gary Cooper *(Lou Gehrig)*, Teresa Wright *(Eleanor Gehrig)*, Walter Brennan *(Sam Blake)*, Dan Duryea *(Hank Hanneman)*, Babe Ruth *(Himself)*, Elsa Janssen *(Mom Gehrig)*, Ludwig Stossel *(Pop Gehrig)*, Virginia Gilmore *(Myra)*, Bill Dickey *(Himself)*, Ernie Adams *(Miller Huggins)*

p, Samuel Goldwyn; d, Sam Wood; w, Jo Swerling, Herman J. Mankiewicz (based on a story by Paul Gallico); ph, Rudolph Mate; ed, Daniel Mandell; m, Leigh Harline; prod d, William Cameron Menzies; art d, Perry Ferguson, McClure Capps; fx, Jack Cosgrove, Ray Binger; cos, Rene Hubert

AAN Best Picture; AAN Best Actor: Gary Cooper; *AAN Best Actress:* Teresa Wright; *AAN Best Original Story:* Paul Gallico; *AAN Best Screenplay:* Herman J. Mankiewicz, Jo Swerling; *AAN Best B/W Cinematography:* Rudolph Mate; *AA Best Film Editing:* Daniel Mandell; *AAN Best Score (Drama or Comedy):* Leigh Harline; *AAN Best Interior Decoration (B/W):* Perry Ferguson, Howard Bristol; *AAN Best Sound Recording:* Thomas Moulton; *AAN Best Special Effects:* Jack Cosgrove (Photographic), Ray Binger (Photographic), Thomas T. Moulton (Sound)

Eloquently written (by Herman Mankiewicz and Jo Swerling from a story by Paul Gallico), stunningly photographed, and directed with great sensitivity, THE PRIDE OF THE YANKEES is the sweet, sentimental, and utterly American story of Lou Gehrig, the "Iron Man" first baseman of the indefatigable New York Yankees of the 1920s and '30s. Gary Cooper is exceptional as Gehrig and Teresa Wright marvelous as his sweetheart (and later wife), Eleanor.

Gehrig leads the Yankees to the World Series, becoming one of the best ever to play the game, until, in 1939, he learns that he has a lethal neurological disease (amyotrophic lateral sclerosis, since known as Lou Gehrig's disease) and has only a short time to live. He retires from baseball and makes a dramatic farewell at Yankee Stadium (perhaps the most famous scene in any sports film), standing at home plate and stating, "Some people say I've had a bad break, but I consider myself to be the luckiest man on the face of the earth."

THE PRIDE OF THE YANKEES is the story of a simple man with extraordinary talent and a soaring spirit that made him the idol of every American schoolboy. Although the film keeps the on-field action to a minimum, Cooper, a righthander, spent many weeks under the tutelage of Lefty O'Doul learning to bunt and throw lefthanded like Gehrig. To complete the illusion, Cooper wore a uniform with the numbers reversed and ran to third base instead of first so that when the film was processed, in reverse, he would appear to be swinging from the left side of the plate. Among the real-life Bronx Bomber teammates who appear in the film are Babe Ruth, Bill Dickey, Mark Koenig, and Bob Meusel.

PRIMARY COLORS
1998 135m c   Political/Comedy/Drama   ★★★½
Mutual Film Co./Icarus Productions/Universal   R
(U.S.)

John Travolta *(Governor Jack Stanton)*, Emma Thompson *(Susan Stanton)*, Billy Bob Thornton *(Richard Jemmons)*, Adrian Lester *(Henry Burton)*, Kathy Bates *(Libby Holden)*, Maura Tierney *(Daisy)*, Larry Hagman *(Governor Fred Picker)*, Paul Guilfoyle *(Howard Ferguson)*, Caroline Aaron *(Lucille Kaufman)*, Rebecca Walker *(March Cunningham)*

p, Mike Nichols; d, Mike Nichols; w, Elaine May (based on the novel *Primary Colors: A Novel of Politics* by Anonymous, aka Joe Klein); ph, Michael Ballhaus; ed, Arthur Schmidt; m, Ry Cooder; prod d, Bo Welch; art d, Tom Duffield; fx, Alan Lorimer, Brad Kuehn, Cinesite; cos, Ann Roth

AAN Best Adapted Screenplay: Elaine May; *AAN Best Supporting Actress:* Kathy Bates

Streamlined by director Mike Nichols and screenwriter Elaine May, Joe Klein's sprawling, thinly veiled roman a clef about the 1992 Clinton presidential campaign becomes an intelligent and very funny satire about the bloody game of American politics.

In a media-driven world of sound bites and spin doctors, young and stubbornly idealistic Henry Burton (Adrian Lester) continues to believe in the possibility of a politician who actually cares about the American people. His hopes are pinned on Democratic Governor Jack Stanton (John Travolta), a deceptively laid-back good ol' boy from an unnamed Southern state, who's making a run for the White House alongside his equally ambitious wife, Susan (Emma Thompson). And Stanton just might make it, unless he's derailed by the storm of unsavory scandal—adultery, draft-dodging, pregnant teenage girls—that shadows his every step. Together with Stanton's campaign posse—which includes a redneck-and-proud-of-it political strategist (Billy Bob Thornton) and a barely sane, turbo-powered fixer (Kathy Bates)—Henry tries to pull his candidate through one of the strangest presidential campaigns in U.S. history.

The irony, of course, is that in the two years since Klein's novel was published, the sort of outrageous shenanigans that made *Primary Colors* a cause celebre have become real-life news. Nichols and May take the only smart approach possible, turning gossip into biting satire, focusing on the themes of honor and the price of leadership, and adding their own brand of humor that's sophisticated but never too highbrow. In the center of it all is Travolta, complete with raspy drawl, steely-eyed squint and a gut that can only come from donuts and baby-back ribs. It's a spot-on Clinton impersonation, tempered with enough smarts and compassion to boost it several notches above simple caricature.

PRIME CUT 📀
1972 88m c Crime ★★★
Cinema Center (U.S.) R

Lee Marvin *(Nick Devlin)*, Gene Hackman *("Mary Ann")*, Angel Tompkins *(Clarabelle)*, Gregory Walcott *(Weenie)*, Sissy Spacek *(Poppy)*, Janit Baldwin *(Violet)*, William Morey *(Shay)*, Clint Ellison *(Delaney)*, Howard Platt *(Shaughnessy)*, Les Lannom *(O'Brien)*

p, Joe Wizan; d, Michael Ritchie; w, Robert Dillon (based on a novel by Robert Dillon); ph, Gene Polito (Panavision, Technicolor); ed, Carl Pingitore; m, Lalo Schifrin; art d, Bill Malley; fx, Logan Frazee; cos, Patricia Norris

Hackman is a degenerate Kansas City cattleman who sells as many girls as he does cows. Chicago gangster Marvin is sent to teach him a lesson on behalf of factory owners who are fed up with Hackman's insolence. Some of the more interesting aspects of this violent film from director Michael Ritchie are an unlikely setting for a gangster film (a country fair), a wheatfield chase scene (a la NORTH BY NORTHWEST), and a switch in casting (Hackman playing the louse and Marvin playing the relatively good guy). Ritchie breaks tradition by portraying the rural population as far more despicable than the city folk, referring to Chicago as being "as peaceful as anyplace anywhere." Sissy Spacek makes her film debut as one of Hackman's commodities.

PRIME OF MISS JEAN BRODIE, THE 📀
1969 116m c Drama/Comedy ★★★★
Fox (U.K.) PG

Maggie Smith *(Jean Brodie)*, Robert Stephens *(Teddy Lloyd)*, Pamela Franklin *(Sandy)*, Gordon Jackson *(Gordon Lowther)*, Celia Johnson *(Miss MacKay)*, Diane Grayson *(Jenny)*, Jane Carr *(Mary McGregor)*, Shirley Steedman *(Monica)*, Lavinia Lang *(Emily Carstairs)*, Antoinette Biggerstaff *(Helen McPhee)*

p, Robert Fryer; d, Ronald Neame; w, Jay Presson Allen (based on the play by Allen from the novel by Muriel Spark); ph, Ted Moore (DeLuxe Color); ed, Norman Savage; m, Rod McKuen; prod d, John Howell; art d, Brian Herbert; cos, Elizabeth Haffenden, Joan Bridge

AA Best Actress: Maggie Smith; *AAN Best Original Song:* "Jean"; Rod McKuen (Music & Lyrics)

Prime, indeed. In the Edinburgh of 1932, Smith teaches in an upscale private girls' school. She inspires her students with her ideas on art, music, and politics—the latter based on romantic notions that lead her to express admiration for the *fascisti* in Italy. Smith has assembled a small coterie of adoring students—including Carr, Grayson and Franklin—who follow her around. She even arranges to take them with her on one of her occasional visits to the country home of Jackson, a fellow teacher who is more interested in her than she is in him. Actually, she is romantically involved with Stephens, another teacher and a sometime painter, whose jealousy she hopes Jackson's attentions will arouse. Stephens, however, a married Catholic with children, balks at breaking up his marriage to make a commitment to Smith. Dour headmistress Johnson, meanwhile, takes a dim view of Smith's influence and has her suspicions about the impropriety of the teacher's actions. Young follower Franklin, annoyed by Smith's evaluation of her as scholarly and practical—and of Grayson as a romantic beauty—determines to seduce Stephens away from Smith.

Celia Johnson makes a formidible adversary for Smith, and Smith's then-husband Stephens is dead-on right as the art professor. Pamela Franklin, accomplished and lovely, does the best she can with the film's most difficult plot-fulcrum role. The movie loses some steam when it turns to romantic melodrama, but Smith keeps you watching to see how she works with it. Work she does, managing at the same time to make her unique brand of magic look easy as breathing. The film is slightly marred by Rod McKuen's insufferable title song.

PRINCE AND THE PAUPER, THE 📀
1937 120m bw Adventure ★★★½
Warner Bros./First National (U.S.)

Errol Flynn *(Miles Hendon)*, Claude Rains *(Earl of Hertford)*, Henry Stephenson *(Duke of Norfolk)*, Barton MacLane *(John Canty)*, Billy Mauch *(Tom Canty)*, Bobby Mauch *(Prince Edward)*, Alan Hale *(Captain of the Guard)*, Eric Portman *(1st Lord)*, Montagu Love *(Henry VIII)*, Robert Warwick *(Lord Warwick)*

p, Robert Lord; d, William Keighley; w, Laird Doyle (based on the novel by Mark Twain and the play by Catherine Chishold Cushing); ph, Sol Polito; ed, Ralph Dawson; m, Erich Wolfgang Korngold; art d, Robert Haas; fx, Willard Van Enger, James Gibbons; cos, Milo Anderson

This Mark Twain doppelganger tale of rags and royalty in 16th-century England is sumptuously produced and full of high drama and adventure, with Errol Flynn swashbuckling between the precocious Mauch twins—Bill and Bobby. The look-alikes decide that they will switch roles as a lark, one being Prince Edward (later King Edward VI), the other a beggar boy. Despite the beggar boy's outlandish behavior in his new station, the royal court and advisors accept him as the heir to the throne. The true Edward, however, is submerged in low-life London and, when he decides he's had enough of the game, asserts that he is the real prince. Miles Hendon (Flynn), a soldier of fortune, meets the real Edward and is amused by his claims to the throne, thinking him mad until he begins to believe the emphatic urchin just as the impostor is about to be crowned king. Enemies at court send an assassin (Alan Hale) after the boy, but he is prevented from carrying out his evil task by Miles, who saves the real king-to-be at the last moment.

PRINCE AND THE SHOWGIRL, THE 📀
1957 117m c Comedy ★★★½
Marilyn Monroe/L.O.P. (U.K.)

Marilyn Monroe *(Elsie Marina)*, Laurence Olivier *(Charles)*, Sybil Thorndike *(Queen Dowager)*, Richard Wattis *(Northbrooke)*, Jeremy Spenser *(King Nicholas)*, Esmond Knight *(Hoffman)*, Paul

Hardwick *(Major Domo)*, Rosamund Greenwood *(Maud)*, Aubrey Dexter *(The Ambassador)*, Maxine Audley *(Lady Sunningdale)*

p, Laurence Olivier; d, Laurence Olivier; w, Terence Rattigan (based on the play *The Sleeping Prince* by Rattigan); ph, Jack Cardiff (Technicolor); ed, Jack Harris; m, Richard Addinsell; chor, William Chappell; cos, Beatrice Dawson

By combining the light comic skills of Monroe and the grand acting ability of Olivier, THE PRINCE AND THE SHOWGIRL manages to succeed not only as pleasant entertainment but also as a wonderful mixture of two very different screen personalities. It's 1911 in London, and Monroe plays a flighty American showgirl who catches the eye of the prince regent of Carpathia, Olivier, who is in town for the coronation of George V.

Produced and directed by Olivier and financed by Monroe's newly formed production company (she reportedly was to receive a phenomenal 75 percent of the profits), THE PRINCE AND THE SHOWGIRL shows both actors in fine form. Monroe—in this, her 25th picture—had turned 30 and was as beautiful as ever, delivering a comic performance which is among her very finest. Olivier had already familiarized himself with the role on the British stage in the Rattigan play "The Sleeping Prince," which costarred his miscast wife, Vivien Leigh. Initially Rattigan had expressed reservations about having an actor of Olivier's stature playing a character the author had envisioned as a mundane bureaucrat. But Rattigan needn't have worried; after much ballyhoo in the press, the play opened to rave reviews. What's more, the casting of Monroe in place of Leigh brought the film a remarkable balance between two of film's most arresting screen personalities.

PRINCE OF EGYPT, THE 📀
1998 93m c Religious/Children's/Animated ★★★½
Patchwork Productions/DreamWorks PG
Feature Animation (U.S.)

VOICES OF: Val Kilmer *(Moses/God))*, Sandra Bullock *(Miriam)*, Ralph Fiennes *(Rameses)*, Danny Glover *(Jethro)*, Jeff Goldblum *(Aaron)*, Steve Martin *(Hotep)*, Helen Mirren *(Queen)*, Michelle Pfeiffer *(Tzipporah)*, Martin Short *(Huy)*, Patrick Stewart *(Pharaoh Seti)*

p, Penney Finkelman Cox, Sandra Rabins; d, Brenda Chapman, Steve Hickner, Simon Wells; w, Philip LaZebnik; ed, Nick Fletcher; m, Hans Zimmer; prod d, Derek Gogol; art d, Kathy Alteri, Richard Chavez; fx, Don Paul, Dan Philips; anim, Kelly Asbury, Lorna Cook, Lorenzo E. Martinez

AA Best Original Song: "When You Believe"; Stephen Schwartz; *AAN Best Original Musical or Comedy Score:* Stephen Schwartz, Hans Zimmer

Neither a lackluster score nor the spotty attempts at comic relief really dull DreamWorks' first foray into Disney-land: this musical retelling of the Biblical story of Moses features a first-rate voice cast and state-of-the-art animation that's nothing short of miraculous. And thanks to a sharp, economical script, this lavish production also puts a fresh spin on a very old story.

Baby Moses, child of Hebrew slaves, is found floating down the Nile in a reed basket by the wife (voiced by Helen Mirren) of Pharaoh Seti (Patrick Stewart). Moses is raised as one of the royal household, ignorant of his Hebraic origins. When the adult Moses (Val Kilmer) is clued into his history by his real sister (Sandra Bullock), he's struck with newfound horror at the Egyptians' treatment of the Hebrews, and abandons the comforts of his foster family to wander the desert. Moses eventually takes a wife (Michelle Pfeiffer), hears the voice of God in a burning bush, and returns to Egypt to free his people.

The religious dimensions of the story take a back seat to the complicated relationship between Moses and Seti's son, prince of Egypt Rameses II (Ralph Fiennes). But even that rides shotgun to what any Biblical epic worth its pillar of salt is *really* all about: sheer spectacle. Awesome vistas worthy of David Lean, a breathtaking chariot race, swarms of locusts, a plague of frogs, a river of blood, and a genuinely creepy wraith that comes to claim the first born: it's all so brilliantly executed that parents of young impressionables should be forewarned. And if you think the parting of the Red Sea is something, just wait till it slams shut: it's enough to give Cecil B. DeMille a goosebump or two.

PRINCE OF FOXES
1949 107m bw Adventure/Historical ★★★★
Fox (U.S.)

Tyrone Power *(Andrea Corsini)*, Orson Welles *(Cesare Borgia)*, Wanda Hendrix *(Camilla Verano)*, Everett Sloane *(Mario Belli)*, Marina Berti *(Angela Borgia)*, Katina Paxinou *(Mona Zeppo Constanza)*, Felix Aylmer *(Count Marc Antonio Verano)*, Leslie Bradley *(Don Esteban)*, Joop van Hulzen *(D'Este)*, James Carney *(Alphonso D'Este)*

p, Sol C. Siegel; d, Henry King; w, Milton Krims (based on the novel by Samuel Shellabarger); ph, Leon Shamroy; ed, Barbara McLean; m, Alfred Newman; art d, Lyle Wheeler, Mark-Lee Kirk; fx, Fred Sersen; cos, Vittorio Nino Novarese

AAN Best B/W Cinematography: Leon Shamroy; *AAN Best Costume Design (B/W):* Vittorio Nino Novarese

Great adventure, a literate script, and fine performances combine in PRINCE OF FOXES to produce splendid entertainment, directed with marvelous briskness by Henry King. Set during the Italian Renaissance, the film opens with Welles, as the notorious Cesare Borgia, outlining his plans for the domination of Italy to his trusted aide, Power. Welles tells Power that the city-state cannot be taken of Ferrara by force, its fortress being too well-manned and well-defended by the Duke Alfonso D'Este (van Hulzen), cannon-maker extraordinaire. He assigns Power to persuade van Hulzen to marry Welles's sister, the scheming Lucrezia Borgia. This Power does, with considerable guile and brass, after which he is instructed by Welles to seduce the young Hendrix—wife of the elderly Aylmer, who presides over a neighboring duchy—and then to turn over Aylmer's mountain fortress to Welles. En route to Aylmer's duchy, Power, an aspiring painter, stops to visit his mentor, art dealer Eduardo Ciannelli, and arranges to have one of his own works on display when Hendrix inspects Ciannelli's collection. She spots Power's work and admires it, after which the artist makes a gift of it to her. Hendrix, in turn, invites Power to visit her and Aylmer. However, having thus inveigled his way into Aylmer's court, Power soon realizes that the old duke is an honorable, decent man whose deep love for Hendrix is more paternal than sexual, and he cannot bring himself to betray Hendrix and Aylmer's trust. Deciding he can no longer wait for Power to deliver the duchy, Welles orders his men to march against the mountain fortress. Power offers his sword to Aylmer and Hendrix, betraying his master to join in the heroic defense of the stronghold. Welles's troops eventually overcome the defenders, however, and Aylmer is dead by the time Hendrix and Power surrender the duchy. After Sloane, Power's erstwhile friend and advisor, reports to Welles that he has discovered that Power's mother (Paxinou) is a peasant, Welles realizes that his former aide, now his prisoner, has not only betrayed him but is not of noble birth, and allows Sloane to gouge out Power's eyes before a dinner party at which Hendrix begs for Power's life. However, Sloane has really crushed two grapes over Power's eyes and offered this gore up as the real thing, whispering to Power to scream in feigned pain. Power is led away, but soon organizes a plot to retake Citta del Monte and free Hendrix.

Beautifully photographed on location in Italy by cinematographer Leon Shamroy, this Fox production is both tasteful and lavish, with Power exceptional in his portrait of an ambitious but honorable Renaissance man. Unfortunately, the exquisite costuming suffers somewhat as a result of Fox's decision to shoot in black and white, even though King had begged for color. Welles, who makes a wholly sinister Cesare Borgia, took the role because he was desperately in need of cash to fuel his own projects. But he couldn't resist the urge to direct, and reportedly infuriated King when, during his scenes, he would upbraid his fellow actors for not reacting correctly to his evil, powerful character.

PRINCE OF THE CITY

1981 167m c   Crime   ★★★½
Orion   (U.S.)   R

Treat Williams *(Daniel Ciello)*, Jerry Orbach *(Gus Levy)*, Richard Foronjy *(Joe Marinaro)*, Don Billett *(Bill Mayo)*, Kenny Marino *(Dom Bando)*, Carmine Caridi *(Gino Mascone)*, Tony Page *(Raf Alvarez)*, Norman Parker *(Rick Cappalino)*, Paul Roebling *(Brooks Paige)*, Bob Balaban *(Santimassino)*

p, Burtt Harris; d, Sidney Lumet; w, Jay Presson Allen, Sidney Lumet (based on the book by Robert Daley); ph, Andrzej Bartkowiak (Technicolor); ed, John J. Fitzstephens; m, Paul Chihara; prod d, Tony Walton; art d, Edward Pisoni; cos, Anna Hill Johnstone

AAN Best Adapted Screenplay: Jay Presson Allen, Sidney Lumet

PRINCE OF THE CITY is an excellent, if overlong, fictional treatment of a true story, set in the 1960s. New York cop Daniel Ciello (Treat Williams) reluctantly turns informer on his pals and colleagues after being recruited by the U.S. Justice Department to expose police corruption, especially the involvement of the cops in the drug trade. Williams gives a fine performance, the rest of the cast is also excellent, and director Sidney Lumet's eye for detail is sure throughout this authentic look at the dirtier side of police work.

PRINCE OF TIDES, THE

1991 132m c   Drama/Romance   ★★½
Barwood Films/Longfellow Productions/   R
Columbia   (U.S.)

Nick Nolte *(Tom Wingo)*, Barbra Streisand *(Dr. Susan Lowenstein)*, Blythe Danner *(Sallie Wingo)*, Kate Nelligan *(Lila Wingo Newbury)*, Jeroen Krabbe *(Herbert Woodruff)*, Melinda Dillon *(Savannah Wingo)*, George Carlin *(Eddie Detreville)*, Jason Gould *(Bernard Woodruff)*, Brad Sullivan *(Henry Wingo)*, Maggie Collier *(Lucy Wingo)*

p, Barbra Streisand, Andrew Karsch; d, Barbra Streisand; w, Becky Johnston, Pat Conroy (from the novel by Conroy); ph, Stephen Goldblatt; ed, Don Zimmerman; m, James Newton Howard; prod d, Paul Sylbert; art d, W. Steven Graham; cos, Ruth Morley

AAN Best Picture; AAN Best Actor: Nick Nolte; *AAN Best Supporting Actress:* Kate Nelligan; *AAN Best Adapted Screenplay:* Pat Conroy, Becky Johnston; *AAN Best Cinematography:* Stephen Goldblatt; *AAN Best Original Score:* James Newton Howard; *AAN Best Art Direction-Set Decoration:* Paul Sylbert, Caryl Heller

Directed with loving care by Barbra Streisand, this adaptation of the best-seller also boasts a serious flaw: Streisand herself. Narrated by Tom Wingo (Nolte) in flashbacks intercut with present-day sequences, THE PRINCE OF TIDES tells the story of his family, a poor white clan from the South Carolina tidewater emotionally crippled by a never-talked-about event which took place during Tom's childhood. Only years later, following yet another suicide attempt by Tom's twin sister Savannah (Dillon), a Greenwich Village poet, is the family demon exorcised.

Savannah, who has lost her will to live, does not respond to therapy. At the request of Dr. Susan Lowenstein

(Streisand), Tom flies north to shed light on his sister's troubled psyche. Tom, too, has been left emotionally scarred by the mysterious childhood event. An unemployed high-school teacher and football coach, the father of three, he spends depressing days as house-husband to wife Sallie (Danner), a doctor who's thinking of leaving him for her lover. Over a six-week period with Dr. Susie, Tom explores the fragments of the Wingo past. His own confidence slowly returns—partly thanks to a soft-focus love affair with Dr. Sue, partly thanks to his successful coaching in football of her withdrawn, preppy son Bernard (Gould, Streisand's son by Elliott). What pigskin won't do for a guy.

Therapists will be scornful of Lowenstein's quick cure of the Wingo family trauma (i.e. remember the past, and all will be well), especially since she dispenses her expertise *gratis*—not to mention the fact that she tumbles into bed with her "client." Most moviegoers, though, are probably willing to let this slip by. What *doesn't* wash is La Strident's glamorous characterization of the sophisticated New York shrink. As star, director and co-producer, Streisand shifts the book's focus from the Wingo past to the Tom-Susan love affair. This could have worked had Streisand directed herself better—if, indeed, she had directed herself at all. Instead of a performance, we get smirks, poses, campy shots that linger on her outrageously long manicured fingernails, and radiant, cloying smiles. Streisand's inadequacies, though, are more than compensated for by Nolte's compelling Tom. He brings conviction and depth to the role, treading a fine line between self-pity and self-respect and exposing his frailties with a rare sensitivity. He also manages to keep a straight face during a scene where La Babs orders dinner in French—now *that's* acting.

PRINCESS BRIDE, THE   📀

1987 98m c   Adventure/Children's/Comedy   ★★★★
Act III   (U.S.)   PG

Cary Elwes *(Westley)*, Mandy Patinkin *(Inigo Montoya)*, Chris Sarandon *(Prince Humperdinck)*, Christopher Guest *(Count Rugen)*, Wallace Shawn *(Vizzini)*, Andre the Giant *(Fezzik)*, Fred Savage *(The Grandson)*, Robin Wright *(Buttercup, the Princess Bride)*, Peter Falk *(The Grandfather)*, Peter Cook *(The Impressive Clergyman)*

p, Arnold Scheinman, Rob Reiner; d, Rob Reiner; w, William Goldman (based on his novel); ph, Adrian Biddle (Deluxe Color); ed, Robert Leighton; m, Mark Knopfler; prod d, Norman Garwood; art d, Keith Pain, Richard Holland; fx, Nick Allder; cos, Phyllis Dalton

AAN Best Original Song: "Storybook Love"; Willy DeVille

A hilarious mixture of Errol Flynn swashbuckler and Monty Python send-up, THE PRINCESS BRIDE works as love story, as adventure, and as satire. In the framing story, a sick 10-year-old (Fred Savage) is visited by his grandfather (Peter Falk), who reads him *The Princess Bride*, a "kissing" story set in a medieval make-believe land. In it, the beautiful Buttercup (Robin Wright) reluctantly becomes engaged to a prince (Chris Sarandon) when her true love, Westley (Cary Elwes), disappears. Soon, however, she is kidnapped by a crafty Sicilian (Wallace Shawn) and his hirelings, Spanish swordsman Inigo Montoya (Mandy Patinkin) and gargantuan Fezzik (Andre the Giant). Buttercup is rescued by a mysterious man in black, who turns out to be Westley; but after surviving the Dreaded Fireswamp, they are apprehended by the prince. Buttercup agrees to marry the prince when he promises to free Westley, but the dashing lad is actually tortured to death—or is he? With the help of a wizened miracle maker (Billy Crystal), Inigo and Fezzik join forces with Westley to fight the forces of evil. With tongues in cheeks and hearts on sleeves, director Rob Reiner and scripter William Goldman create a dazzling adventure for younger viewers, while at the same time hilariously satirizing the same genre. Goldman's screenplay, adapted from his own novel, made the rounds for 14 years before finally making it to the screen. The wait was worth it. When it comes to pleasing both kids and adults, you can't do much better than THE PRINCESS BRIDE.

PRINCESS MONONOKE
(MONONOKE HIME)
1997 135m c Animated/Fantasy/Action ★★★½
Tokuma Shoten Publishing Company/Nippon PG-13
Television Network/Dentsu & Studio Ghibli
(Japan)

VOICES OF Claire Danes *(Princess Mononoke-San)*, Billy Crudup *(Ashitaka)*, Minnie Driver *(Lady Eboshi)*, Gillian Anderson *(Moro the Wolf)*, Jada Pinkett *(Otoki)*, Billy Bob Thornton *(Jog Boh the Monk)*, John DiMaggio *(Gonza)*, John DeMita *(Kohroku)*, Keith David *(Okkoto)*

p, Toshio Suzuki; d, Hayao Miyazaki; w, Neil Gaiman (based on the original Japanese screenplay and story by Hayao Miyazaki); ph, Atsushi Okui; ed, Hayao Miyazaki, Takeshi Seyama; m, Joe Hisaishi; anim, Hayao Miyazaki, Masahi Ando, Kitaro Kosakfa, Yoshifumi Kondo

Lavishly animated and painstakingly dubbed into English, this grand-scale Japanese adventure revolves around man's relationship with the natural world and the dire consequence of a life out of balance.

The story begins with a monstrous demon-boar heading straight for a small rural village; Prince Ashitaka (voiced by Billy Crudup) kills the beast but receives a poisonous, supernatural wound. The village wisewoman tells the prince that he must uncover the demon-boar's origins and may heal himself in the process. Ashitaka's travels take him to Irontown, whose smoking foundries have wounded the forest and earned overseer Lady Eboshi (Minnie Driver) the enmity of San (Claire Danes), the human daughter of a wolf goddess (Gillian Anderson). All-out war seems inevitable, and Ashitaka is torn between the cause of human progress, the rights of the forest spirits, and his growing love for San, the Princess Mononoke. Complicating matters further is a mercenary warrior (Billy Bob Thornton) determined to hunt down the Nightwalker, greatest of the animal gods.

Directed by revered Japanese animator Hayao Miyazaki (KIKI'S DELIVERY SERVICE) and scripted for U.S. release by cult comic book icon Neil Gaiman (*Sandman*), this melancholy epic blends mythological archetypes with timely ecological concerns. Its imagery is never less than breathtakingly beautiful, and it's occasionally truly awesome. Overall, the film deftly negotiates the line between accessibility and exoticism: the story's fairy-tale appeal is universal, but the animals are less sweetly anthropomorphized than their Disney cousins, and the clattering tree spirits—with their blank faces and child-ghost bodies—are truly eerie. Be warned: it's occasionally very violent and may be too intense for younger children.

PRISONER OF SHARK ISLAND, THE
1936 95m bw Prison/Biography ★★★★
Fox (U.S.)

Warner Baxter *(Dr. Samuel A. Mudd)*, Gloria Stuart *(Mrs. Peggy Mudd)*, Joyce Kay *(Marth Mudd)*, Claude Gillingwater *(Col. Jeremiah Dyer)*, Douglas Wood *(Gen. Ewing)*, Fred Kohler Jr. *(Sgt. Cooper)*, Harry Carey *(Commandant of Fort Jefferson "Shark Island")*, Paul Fix *(David Herold)*, John Carradine *(Sgt. Rankin)*, Francis McDonald *(John Wilkes Booth)*

p, Darryl F. Zanuck; d, John Ford; w, Nunnally Johnson (based on the life of Dr. Samuel A. Mudd); ph, Bert Glennon; ed, Jack Murray; art d, William Darling; cos, Gwen Wakeling

Warner Baxter is smashing as a doctor who treats the ankle of fugitive assassin John Wilkes Booth, played by Francis McDonald. Arrested shortly thereafter, Baxter is charged with being part of the conspiracy to murder President Abraham Lincoln. Dragged away from his wife, Gloria Stuart, and their small child, Baxter is convicted on scant evidence and sent to prison for life at Fort Jefferson on Shark Island in the Dry Tortugas. There he is considered, even by the black guards, to be a worthy "southern gentleman" doctor determined to care for prisoners and their captors alike when they fall sick. When a yellow fever epidemic breaks out, Baxter, risking his own life, saves the lives of many. For this heroic act, Baxter's case is reopened; exonerated of being part of the Lincoln conspiracy, he returns to his family. This based-on-fact story about the injustice meted out to one man is handled beautifully by director John Ford, whose cameras, under Bert Glennon's expert guidance, starkly depict the horrors of prison life. Baxter underplays his role superbly, eliciting viewer sympathy early on. Ford leaves no doubt as to the man's innocence by stating the facts of the case right at the beginning of the film. The good doctor's sympathies are revealed when Baxter, while treating Booth, refers to Abraham Lincoln as the only salvation Southerners can look to. There are some slight similarities between this film and I AM A FUGITIVE FROM A CHAIN GANG and LES MISERABLES, but THE PRISONER OF SHARK ISLAND is a distinctive Ford film with his imprint on every frame, offering a taut, believable script by Nunnally Johnson. Typical of the reverential Ford is the scene depicting the assassination. Frank McGlynn, who played Lincoln many times, is shown seated in his box; when the shot that ends his life rings out, only McGlynn's hand is shown slumping, then a quick full shot of the lifeless body dissolves into a magnificent portrait of the President.

PRISONER OF ZENDA, THE
1937 101m bw Romance/Adventure ★★★★★
Selznick (U.S.)

Ronald Colman *(Rudolph Rassendyl/King Rudolf V)*, Madeleine Carroll *(Princess Flavia)*, Douglas Fairbanks Jr. *(Rupert of Hentzau)*, Mary Astor *(Antoinette De Mauban)*, C. Aubrey Smith *(Col. Zapt)*, Raymond Massey *(Black Michael)*, David Niven *(Capt. Fritz von Tarlenheim)*, Eleanor Wesselhoeft *(Cook)*, Byron Foulger *(Johann)*, Montagu Love *(Detchard)*

p, David O. Selznick; d, John Cromwell, George Cukor, W.S. Van Dyke II (uncredited); w, John Balderston, Wells Root, Donald Ogden Stewart (based on the novel by Anthony Hope and the play by Edward Rose); ph, James Wong Howe; ed, Hal C. Kern, James E. Newcom; m, Alfred Newman; art d, Lyle Wheeler; fx, Jack Cosgrove; cos, Ernest Dryden

AAN Best Score: Selznick International Pictures Music Department, Alfred Newman (Dept. Head); *AAN Best Interior Decoration:* Lyle Wheeler

Hollywood movies don't get much classier. The great Anthony Hope adventure is adapted for the screen with loving loyalty to the story, and Cromwell's helmsmanship is decisive and full of affection for the tale.

Colman plays the doppelganger roles of Rudolph Rassendyl and Prince Rudolf of the mythical European kingdom of Ruritania. Rassendyl is spotted by Col. Zapt (Smith) and Capt. von Tarlenheim (Niven), aides to the Prince, and he ends up dining with his royal double who is, as it turns out, a distant cousin. The next morning, however, the Prince lies in a coma, having been drugged by a servant in the employ of the Prince's brother "Black" Michael (Massey) and his villainous cohort Rupert (Fairbanks). Zapt vows that Michael will never sit on the throne and presses Rudolph to substitute for the Prince, through the coronation if need be, until the real Prince recovers. Of course this not only entails weathering additional attempts on the future King Rudolf V's life, but also standing in for His Majesty in the business of love, convincing Princess Flavia (Carroll) that he is indeed her fiance.

Director Cromwell does a marvelous job in extracting great performances from his leading players, as well as carefully developing the Colman-Carroll romance, which is touched with gentility and poetic grace. Selznick was repeatedly warned not to revive this Ruritanian adventure, his advisors telling him that the production was doomed. Selznick, however, didn't listen, and he was proved right: the film was a smash, enhancing the careers of everyone involved.

Voted Hollywood's handsomest actor (at age 46) the same year that ZENDA appeared, Colman is the essence of gentlmanly dash. He is matched by a true Hollywood princess, Madeleine Carroll, in what she would later call her favorite role. In additon to their fine work, the film boasts flawless visual elegance thanks to Cromwell and ace cameraman Howe, the script by Balderston, Root, and Stewart is witty, literate, and lyrical, and Newman's sweeping, memorable score is one of that composer's finest.

PRIVATE BENJAMIN   📀DVD
1980 109m c   Comedy/War   ★★½
Warner Bros. (U.S.)   R

Goldie Hawn (Judy Benjamin), Eileen Brennan (Capt. Doreen Lewis), Armand Assante (Henri Tremont), Robert Webber (Col. Clay Thornbush), Sam Wanamaker (Teddy Benjamin), Barbara Barrie (Harriet Benjamin), Mary Kay Place (Pvt. Mary Lou Glass), Harry Dean Stanton (Sgt. Jim Ballard), Albert Brooks (Yale Goodman), Alan Oppenheimer (Rabbi)

p, Nancy Meyers, Charles Shyer, Harvey Miller; d, Howard Zieff; w, Nancy Meyers, Charles Shyer, Harvey Miller; ph, David M. Walsh (Technicolor); ed, Sheldon Kahn; m, Bill Conti; prod d, Robert Boyle; art d, Jeff Howard; fx, Robert Peterson; cos, Betsy Cox

AAN Best Actress: Goldie Hawn; AAN Best Supporting Actress: Eileen Brennan; AAN Best Original Screenplay: Nancy Meyers, Charles Shyer, Harvey Miller

Goldie Hawn brings that old standby, the service comedy, into the 1980s in this funny tale of a Jewish girl who decides to be all that she can be in the all-new Army. After her second husband (wonderfully played by Albert Brooks) dies while they are making love, Hawn enlists in the Army, much to the chagrin of her well-to-do parents, Sam Wanamaker and Barbara Barrie. The reality of Army life under demanding commanding officer Eileen Brennan turns out to be a far cry from Hawn's notion that she'll have her own room to decorate and the opportunity to visit exciting locales. The pampered Hawn's reactions to rigorous training exercises, her interactions with her superiors, and a not-quite-successful love affair with French physician Armand Assante while on duty in Europe inspire plenty of laughs. Hawn makes the most of the script, written by Nancy Meyers, Charles Shyer, and Harvey Miller, providing many funny moments in her performance. Brennan, as her lesbian-leaning CO, Robert Webber (as the unit commander) and Mary Kay Place (as Judy's sidekick) also provide strong support.

PRIVATE LIFE OF HENRY VIII, THE   📀DVD
1933 97m bw Biography   ★★★★
London Films (U.K.)

Charles Laughton (Henry VIII), Robert Donat (Thomas Culpepper), Lady Tree (Henry's Old Nurse), Binnie Barnes (Katherine Howard), Elsa Lanchester (Anne of Cleves), Merle Oberon (Anne Boleyn), Wendy Barrie (Jane Seymour), Everley Gregg (Catherine Parr), Franklin Dyall (Thomas Cromwell), Miles Mander (Wriothesley)

p, Alexander Korda, Ludovico Toeplitz; d, Alexander Korda; w, Lajos Biro, Arthur Wimperis; ph, Georges Perinal; ed, Harold Young, Stephen Harrison; m, Kurt Schroeder; art d, Vincent Korda; chor, Espinosa; cos, John Armstrong

AAN Best Picture; AA Best Actor: Charles Laughton

An admirable glutton. And a resurrection for England's film industry, with palms going to Korda, and French cinematograper Georges Perinal. Many costume epics were made in the silent years and some even touched upon the life of the monarch, but this is the one that will be remembered. Laughton's performance was outstanding and won the first Oscar ever for a British-made movie. Korda called upon his brother Vincent to be set designer and the nepotism was worthwhile, as Vincent managed to make this picture look far more expensive than the 60,000 pounds it cost to produce it in just five weeks. The attitude taken was to dispense with the public utterances and show the intimate side of the monarch, a technique Korda was to use again in the less fulfilling THE PRIVATE LIFE OF DON JUAN.

There is a great deal of humor in this picture, which details the life of Henry VIII and five of his six wives. The first wife, Catherine of Aragon, is dispensed with in a prologue that explains that she was far "too respectable to be included." Merle Oberon is Anne Boleyn, his first spouse pictured, who is soon beheaded after failing to give Henry a male heir. Wendy Barrie plays Jane Seymour and dies giving birth. Henry next marries Lanchester (Anne of Cleves), wearing an odd wig and doing her best to look terrible in order to justify the film's most famous line, uttered by Laughton with a regal sigh as he enters the bedroom, "The things I've done for England." Lanchester, using a German accent, is the only performer to come close to Laughton in scene-stealing, nearly swiping their sequences entirely. That marriage leads to divorce, and Henry next marries Binnie Barnes, who loses her head after losing her heart to Laughton's pal, Robert Donat. At the finale, after raving and roaring and ranting, eating like an animal, ruling his roost like a cock of the walk, Laughton is shown to be a tranquil, almost whipped man at the hands of his last mate, Everley Gregg, a sharp-faced shrew.

Laughton was only 33 at the time this film was made but already a veteran of nine movies and many stage productions. There are several standout scenes, not the least of which are the "eating" sequences with Laughton chewing on a chop, then tossing the remains over his shoulder. Actually, the eating bits are sexier than the bedroom scenes, and one wonders if Tony Richardson didn't study them for his directing of TOM JONES. Until this movie was released, there had been a mild recession in costume epics, but they came back with a flurry when the totals were in on the profits, about 10 times the cost. Korda's sets, which were poverty-stricken at best, were photographed so well by Perinal that no one realized how frail they were.

PRIVATE LIFE OF SHERLOCK HOLMES, THE   📀DVD
1970 125m c   Comedy/Mystery   ★★★½
Phalanx/Mirisch (U.S./U.K.)   GP

Robert Stephens (Sherlock Holmes), Colin Blakely (Dr. John H. Watson), Irene Handl (Mrs. Hudson), Stanley Holloway (1st Gravedigger), Christopher Lee (Mycroft Holmes), Genevieve Page (Gabrielle Valladon), Clive Revill (Rogozhin), Tamara Toumanova (Petrova), George Benson (Inspector Lestrade), Catherine Lacey (Old Lady)

p, Billy Wilder; d, Billy Wilder; w, Billy Wilder, I.A.L. Diamond (based on the characters created by Sir Arthur Conan Doyle); ph, Christopher Challis (Panavision, DeLuxe Color); ed, Ernest Walter; m, Miklos Rozsa; prod d, Alexander Trauner; art d, Tony Inglis; fx, Wally Veevers, Cliff Richardson; chor, David Blair; cos, Julie Harris

This unjustly forgotten Billy Wilder film takes on the much-loved character of Sherlock Holmes and attempts to humanize him by examining his vulnerabilities: his ambiguous sexuality and his cocaine addiction. Told via an unpublished manuscript by Dr. Watson (Blakely), the story begins with a bored, frustrated Sherlock Holmes (Stephens), who turns to cocaine between cases. One evening a beautiful Belgian woman, Gabrielle Valladon (Page), turns up at 221B Baker Street asking Holmes to find her missing husband. Although warned by his mysterious brother, Mycroft (Lee), to abandon the case, Holmes persists and the trail leads to Scotland's Loch Ness, where Holmes and Watson come face to face with the legendary monster. Although the film was cut by more than 30 minutes by United Artists, what is left of this satirical, intimate look at the revered character is intriguing and wholly entertaining. Nevertheless it it bombed at the box office. The sets were designed under the direction of Alexander Trauner, who re-created, in detail, the Victorian atmosphere of Holmes's London residence, including a massive back-lot reproduction of Baker Street. The score by Miklos Rozsa is one of his most impressive, and he can be seen conducting it during the ballet sequence. Robert Stephens is an excellent, never-before-seen Holmes, one with wild mood swings which veil his insecurities. Colin Blakely's Dr. Watson is loyal, humorous, and energetic, while Christopher Lee as Mycroft is excellent, making him the only actor in Holmes screen history to play both the detective (in the German-made SHERLOCK HOLMES AND THE NECKLACE OF DEATH) and his brother.

PRIVATE LIVES
1931 92m   bw   Comedy   ★★★★½
MGM   (U.S.)

Norma Shearer (*Amanda Chase Paynne*), Robert Montgomery (*Elyot Chase*), Reginald Denny (*Victor Paynne*), Una Merkel (*Sibyl Chase*), Jean Hersholt (*Oscar*), George Davis (*Bellboy*)

d, Sidney Franklin; w, Hans Kraly, Richard Schayer, Claudine West (based on the play by Noel Coward); ph, Ray Binger; ed, Conrad A. Nervig; art d, Cedric Gibbons; cos, Adrian

PRIVATE LIVES is one of those enduring scripts that can't be hurt, even by ordinary actors; in the case of this film, the acting is excellent, and the result is charming. Norma Shearer and Robert Montgomery play Amanda and Elyot, a once-married couple who have divorced and wed other mates. He's now married to Sibyl (Merkel) and she to Victor (Denny). Both Sibyl and Victor are conservative sorts, devoid of the joy and madness that once attracted Amanda and Elyot to one another. By a coincidence, both couples are honeymooning at the French hotel where Amanda and Elyot had spent their first two weeks of marriage years before. For a time we see the divorced pair struggling to show affection to their new spouses, a tall order when considering the surpassingly bland Sibyl and the stuffed-shirt Victor. Since their suites are next to each other, it isn't long before our fireball lovers meet on their balconies, at once delighted and stunned to see one another. In no time, the newlyweds are quarreling; the formerly-weds, convinced that they are still in love, leave their fresh spouses behind and go to a mountain chalet to have another honeymoon. Of course, their passion is as volatile as it ever was, and they are soon arguing viciously between romantic interludes. The words become blows, and when Sibyl and Victor finally catch up with the elopers they are in the midst of a battle royale. Amanda and Elyot reconcile with Victor and Sibyl, but when the latter two get into an argument over breakfast, the true lovers realize that even the most placid types get into scrapes. What the impish pair do and how the word "Sollochs" helps them make for an amusingly sweet finale.
   Noel Coward wrote and starred in PRIVATE LIVES onstage with Gertrude Lawrence in a 1930 London produc-

tion, then brought it to New York with Laurence Olivier and Jill Esmond in the secondary roles. Producer Irving Thalberg, Shearer's husband, made a film record of this production to aid cast and crew in bringing its unique flavor to the cinema. One of the film's joys is that it achieves a faithful reproduction of the original without seeming a mere copy. The actors don't convince as British (only Denny was), but that really doesn't matter. Shearer and Montgomery attack their roles with such zest and comic elan that we don't miss the spirits of Noel and Gertie hanging around. Opening up the play for a spot of mountain climbing (and a *very* pre-Code sleeping scene), director Franklin does a fine job in preventing his film from becoming stagy.

PRIZZI'S HONOR   DVD
1985 129m c   Romance/Comedy/Crime   ★★★★
ABC   (U.S.)   R

Jack Nicholson (*Charley Partanna*), Kathleen Turner (*Irene Walker*), Robert Loggia (*Eduardo Prizzi*), John Randolph (*Angelo "Pop" Partanna*), William Hickey (*Don Corrado Prizzi*), Lee Richardson (*Dominic Prizzi*), Michael Lombard (*Filargi "Finlay"*), Anjelica Huston (*Maerose Prizzi*), George Santopietro (*Plumber*), Lawrence Tierney (*Lt. Hanley*)

p, John Foreman; d, John Huston; w, Richard Condon, Janet Roach (based on the novel by Condon); ph, Andrzej Bartkowiak (Panavision, DeLuxe Color); ed, Rudi Fehr, Kaja Fehr; m, Alex North; prod d, J. Dennis Washington; art d, Michael Helmy, Tracy Bousman; fx, Connie Brink; cos, Donfeld

AAN Best Picture; AAN Best Actor: Jack Nicholson; AAN Best Supporting Actor: William Hickey; AA Best Supporting Actress: Anjelica Huston; AAN Best Director: John Huston; AAN Best Adapted Screenplay: Richard Condon, Janet Roach; AAN Best Film Editing: Rudi Fehr, Kaja Fehr; AAN Best Costume Design: Donfeld

Director John Huston, one-time master of film noir, returns to the form with a black comedy about the Mafia. The film benefits from some stellar performances from Jack Nicholson, Kathleen Turner, and William Hickey. This was the penultimate film from the ailing great director. It is also one of his best.
   Charley Partanna (Nicholson) is an aging dopey hit man who works for a powerful New York Mafia family. He spots luscious Irene Walker (Turner) at a gangster wedding and loses his heart. She's ostensibly a tax consultant living in Los Angeles, and soon Charley finds himself flying westward to court her. Then he discovers that she is really a hit woman for the mob. With this, at least, Charley can identify, but when he learns that Irene has cheated his own Mafia family—the Prizzis—out of a great sum of money, his loyalties are painfully divided. The finale is a shocker finish few viewers will ever forget. It's all good and funny in a cynical, bleak sort of way, reflecting the then 78-year-old Huston's perspective of the world. A lesser-known director might have been pilloried for bad taste. Huston was not only tolerated but cheered.
   The film received a host of Oscar nominations, including Best Picture, Best Actor (Nicholson), Best Supporting Actor (Hickey), Best Costume Design, Best Direction, Best Editing, and Best Screenplay from Another Medium (Richard Condon, Janet Roach). Anjelica Huston (the director's daughter) won an Oscar as Best Supporting Actress.

PRODUCERS, THE   DVD
1968 88m   c   Comedy   ★★★★
Springtime/Crossbow   (U.S.)

Zero Mostel (*Max Bialystock*), Gene Wilder (*Leo Bloom*), Dick Shawn (*Lorenzo St. Du Bois*), Kenneth Mars (*Franz Liebkind*), Estelle Winwood (*Old Lady*), Christopher Hewett (*Roger De Bris*),

Andreas Voutsinas *(Carmen Giya)*, Lee Meredith *(Ulla)*, Renee Taylor *(Eva Braun)*, Michael Davis *(Production Tenor)*

p, Sidney Glazier; d, Mel Brooks; w, Mel Brooks; ph, Joseph Coffey (Pathe Color); ed, Ralph Rosenblum; m, John Morris; art d, Charles Rosen; chor, Alan Johnson; cos, Gene Coffin

AAN Best Supporting Actor: Gene Wilder; *AA Best Original Story and Screenplay:* Mel Brooks

Mel Brooks's first and funniest, a spoof of Broadway theater that has earned a deservedly devoted cult following. Forewarned, though, is forearmed: Mostel, genius that he is, doesn't scale his performances down at all for film. The first half hour you feel you're in the presence of comedy's king. After that, you gradually begin to feel bludgeoned by shrill overkill.

Mostel is a down-and-out but still pompous theater producer who desperately wants to regain his former glory. Wilder is his new, meek accountant who finds his books an utter disaster. He tells Mostel that the only way he will ever recover is to produce an enormous hit or, he whimsically suggests, to collect a lot of money from investors for a play guaranteed to fail. That way Mostel could keep most of the investors' money. Mostel persuades Wilder not only to doctor the books but to become his partner in the production. They exhaust themselves soliciting and reading the worst scripts ever penned until they hit upon a play that is a surefire flop, "Springtime for Hitler," written by Mars, a Nazi fanatic living in Yorkville. Next, Mostel woos and wins the backing of every spinster in New York, taking in hundreds of thousands of dollars to back his doomed play. Although everything possible is done to make the play an unbearably tasteless flop, disaster strikes when it proves a smash hit.

THE PRODUCERS raised Mostel to new heights of zany appeal and made a star of Wilder, who proceeded to beat this kind of role into the ground in a series of subsequent films. Our favorite among the investors: Estelle Winwood, as "Touch Me, Feel Me"—she takes the material and runs with it. Highlights: the opening number, opening night; "I'm hysterical! I'm wet and I'm hysterical! I'm in *pain* and I'm wet and I'm hysterical!"

PROJECTIONIST, THE
1970 88m c Drama/Comedy ★★★½
Maglan (U.S.) PG

Chuck McCann *(Projectionist/Captain Flash)*, Ina Balin *(The Girl)*, Rodney Dangerfield *(Renaldi/The Bat)*, Jara Kohout *(Candy Man/Scientist)*, Harry Hurwitz *(Friendly Usher)*, Robert Staats *(TV Pitchman)*, Robert King *(Premiere Announcer)*, Stephen Phillips *(Minister)*, Clara Rosenthal *(Crazy Lady)*, Jacquelyn Glenn *(Nude on Bearskin)*

p, Harry Hurwitz; d, Harry Hurwitz; w, Harry Hurwitz; ph, Victor Petrashevic (Technicolor); ed, Harry Hurwitz; m, Igo Kantor, Erma E. Levin

Long before ZELIG, THE PURPLE ROSE OF CAIRO, and DEAD MEN DON'T WEAR PLAID, there was THE PROJECTIONIST, an innovative low-budget oddity with a cult following. McCann plays the title character, a lovable nebbish who sees himself as part of every movie he's ever seen, including newsreels. In the imaginary role of Captain Flash, fearless defender of the downtrodden, McCann does battle with the Bat, who is played in McCann's dreamworld by Dangerfield (in his film debut). When he meets Balin, she immediately becomes part of his cinematic fantasy, cast as an imperiled Pauline whom McCann must save with regularity from the clutches of Dangerfield. McCann's mind movies feature archival footage from CASABLANCA, GUNGA DIN, DAMES, FORT APACHE, THE BIRTH OF A NATION, and many other Hollywood classics.

PROOF
1992 86m c Drama ★★★½
House & Moorhouse Films (Australia) R

Hugo Weaving *(Martin)*, Genevieve Picot *(Celia)*, Russell Crowe *(Andy)*, Heather Mitchell *(Martin's Mother)*, Jeffrey Walker *(Young Martin)*, Daniel Pollock *(Gary—the Punk)*, Frank Gallacher *(Vet)*, Frankie J. Holden *(Brian—Policeman)*, Saskia Post *(Waitress)*, Belinda Davey *(Doctor)*

p, Lynda House; d, Jocelyn Moorhouse; w, Jocelyn Moorhouse; ph, Martin McGrath; ed, Ken Sallows; m, Not Drowning Waving; prod d, Patrick Reardon; cos, Cerri Barnett

Australian filmmaker Jocelyn Moorhouse made an auspicious debut with PROOF, a dry, dark comedy about a blind photographer and his efforts to find someone to trust. The disabled individual in question, Martin (Hugo Weaving), does little but walk his dog in the park and take pictures, using a modern auto-focus camera and aiming at sounds, or objects he feels with his hands. Since he can never see what he shoots, he needs someone to describe what he has photographed. Martin's housekeeper, Celia (Genevieve Picot), is an attractive but dour figure who has become obsessed with her employer, and is constantly trying to seduce him. The two are locked in battle, Martin despising Celia and she tormenting him in infinite, petty ways. A new factor enters the equation when Martin befriends Andy (Russell Crowe), a likable restaurant dishwasher.

PROOF unfolds with the clarity and purity of a fable. The metaphor of the blind photographer is an intriguing premise, and Moorhouse sustains it brilliantly as a way of commenting on the extent to which we all depend on those around us for confirmation of our own perceptions. For all its cerebral thematics, however, what is most remarkable about PROOF is how firmly and easily it stays on a human level. Moorhouse has written three full, rich characters who come vividly alive as acted by the excellent cast. Though the film is unabashedly unrealistic from the outset, it never for a moment feels contrived.

PROSPERO'S BOOKS
1991 120m c Drama/Fantasy ★★★
Allarts/Cinea/Camera One/Penta Film/Elsevier R
Vendex Film/Film Four International/VPRO
Television/Canal Plus/Nippon Hoso Kyokai
(U.K./Netherlands/France/Italy)

John Gielgud *(Prospero)*, Michael Clark *(Caliban)*, Michel Blanc *(Alonso)*, Erland Josephson *(Gonzalo)*, Isabelle Pasco *(Miranda)*, Tom Bell *(Antonio)*, Kenneth Cranham *(Sebastian)*, Mark Rylance *(Ferdinand)*, Gerard Thoolen *(Adrian)*, Pierre Bokma *(Francisco)*

p, Yoshinobu Numano, Katsufumi Nakamura; d, Peter Greenaway; w, Peter Greenaway (adapted from the play *The Tempest* by William Shakespeare); ph, Sacha Vierny; ed, Marina Bodbyl; m, Michael Nyman; prod d, Ben Van Os, Jan Roelfs

A loose, multi-layered deconstruction of Shakespeare's final play by Peter Greenaway, *enfant terrible* of the British arthouse scene. Beginning with its opening sequence of a urinating angel, PROSPERO'S BOOKS is a remarkable celebration of naked excess. Penises, especially, proliferate like so many pairs of socks dangling from a clothesline. It's Shakespeare's work, though certainly not as originally envisioned. The 86-year-old Gielgud gives an undeniably virtuoso performance as a most regal Prospero, master manipulator of people and events. Gielgud functions as a sort of onscreen chorus—an intermediary between the action and audience to give form and fabric to the film. Throughout, he also portrays the Bard who, like the veteran actor himself, is nearing the end of his long career. In a triple conceit of Greenaway's, we see Gielgud-Shakespeare-Prospero writing the play in elegant Elizabethan script. Concurrently, he conjures onscreen the images and characters he has just created on paper and recites all their dialogue. Their voices are dimly overlaid with his, as if by echo. Only at the film's very end, when Prospero has given up all thoughts of revenge and reconciled with his enemies, are the other characters allowed to speak for themselves in their own voices.

Gielgud breathes life into a difficult role and makes it look natural and easy. Richly garbed in embroidered cowl and cloak, looking like a cross between a Venetian doge and Dame Edith Sitwell, it's as if he were born to it. It was at Gielgud's suggestion that Greenaway undertook the project, designing the film for him in that role. Does it work? That depends on whether you find Greenaway's elaborate visual conceits and rarified narrative structures daring and liberating, or boringly self-indulgent.

PROVIDENCE
1977   104m   c   Drama   ★★★★
Action/SFP   (France/Switzerland)   R

John Gielgud *(Clive Langham)*, Dirk Bogarde *(Claude Langham)*, Ellen Burstyn *(Sonia Langham)*, David Warner *(Kevin Woodford)*, Elaine Stritch *(Helen Weiner/Molly Langham)*, Denis Lawson *(Dave Woodford)*, Cyril Luckham *(Dr. Mark Eddington)*, Kathryn Leigh-Scott *(Miss Boon)*, Milo Sperber *(Mr. Jenner)*, Anna Wing *(Karen)*

p, Yves Gasser, Yves Peyrot, Klaus Hellwig; d, Alain Resnais; w, David Mercer; ph, Ricardo Aronovich (Eastmancolor); ed, Albert Jurgenson; m, Miklos Rozsa; art d, Jacques Saulnier; cos, Catherine Leterrier, Yves Saint-Laurent, John Bates

Alain Resnais's PROVIDENCE is truly a breakthrough film, a provocative attempt to synthesize past and future, literature and cinema, into a disarming but totally compelling present tense.

The film takes place on the eve of the 78th birthday of Clive Langham (John Gielgud), a dying novelist. He lives alone in his country estate in Providence, Rhode Island, battling alcoholism, the memory of his dead wife, and a chronic rectal disorder. At night, he struggles to write what appears to be his last novel, basing the characters on his own children. In this malevolent fiction, his son, Claude (Dirk Bogarde), and daughter-in-law, Sonia (Ellen Burstyn), are unhappily married and constantly—if wittily—sparring. Another, illegitimate son, Kevin Woodford (David Warner) is a former soldier on trial, prosecuted by Claude, for killing an old man who turned into a werewolf. Claude is the prosecuting attorney, but the defendant is acquitted, and soon falls in love with Sonia. This, however, does not upset Claude as much as it disgusts him.

The increasingly inebriated Clive decides to give Claude a mistress, but the character he creates, Helen (Elaine Stritch), is the image of his dead wife—an older woman with a terminal disease, whom Clive continually mistakes for her prototype. As he labors to complete his retributive narrative, characters disintegrate further and further, delivering each other's dialogue and hopelessly confusing the story. Settings, too, change inexplicably. The next morning, Clive's children pay a birthday visit and prove a far cry from the ailing novelist's representations of them.

Director Alain Resnais—who collaborated with novelists Marguerite Duras in HIROSHIMA MON AMOUR, Alain Robbe-Grillet in LAST YEAR AT MARIENBAD, and Jorge Semprun in LA GUERRE EST FINIE—joined forces here with playwright David Mercer, best known for his *A Suitable Case for Treatment* (filmed by Karel Reisz as MORGAN!). PROVIDENCE should put those who attack Resnais for being pretentious and cold at ease, especially in light of Gielgud's virtuoso performance. Filled with brilliant wit, PROVIDENCE is a superb instance of inventive filmmaking with a comic touch and an intellectual theme.

PSYCHO
1960   109m   bw   Horror   ★★★★★
Universal   (U.S.)

Anthony Perkins *(Norman Bates)*, Janet Leigh *(Marion Crane)*, Vera Miles *(Lila Crane)*, John Gavin *(Sam Loomis)*, Martin Balsam *(Milton Arbogast)*, John McIntire *(Sheriff Chambers)*, Lurene Tuttle *(Mrs. Chambers)*, Simon Oakland *(Dr. Richmond)*, Frank Albertson *(Tom Cassidy)*, Patricia Hitchcock *(Caroline)*

p, Alfred Hitchcock; d, Alfred Hitchcock; w, Joseph Stefano (based on the novel by Robert Bloch); ph, John L. Russell Jr.; ed, George Tomasini; m, Bernard Herrmann; prod d, Joseph Hurley, Robert Clatworthy; fx, Clarence Champagne; cos, Helen Colvig

AAN Best Supporting Actress: Janet Leigh; *AAN Best Director:* Alfred Hitchcock; *AAN Best B/W Cinematography:* John L Russell; *AAN Best Art Direction-Set Decoration (B/W):* Joseph Hurley (Art Direction), Robert Clatworthy (Art Direction), George Milo (Set Decoration)

Perhaps no other film changed Hollywood's perception of the horror film so drastically as did PSYCHO. Nowadays, when any psychological thriller featuring a loony with a knife is designated "Hitchcockian" in some quarters, it's easy to forget just what a dramatic change of pace this was for Hitchcock. Though renowned for stories of murder, intrigue, and high adventure, Hitchcock's Hollywood films of the 1950s generally boasted top drawer production values, big stars, picturesque surroundings, and, more often than not, Technicolor. In comparison to the likes of, say, NORTH BY NORTHWEST, PSYCHO was intentionally sleazy and cheap both in look and subject matter.

The now familiar plot concerns Norman Bates (Anthony Perkins), a nervous, bird-like motel proprietor who lives under the domineering influence of his aged invalid mother. Norman takes care of Mother and, in return, she protects the disturbingly boyish man from temptation and corruption, particularly in the form of attractive single women who come to stay at the motel. Marion Crane (Janet Leigh) stops at the Bates Motel after impulsively fleeing from her workplace with a large sum of stolen money. She had hoped this cash would allow her married lover, Sam Loomis (John Gavin), to divorce his wife and marry her. After chatting with Norman, Marion appears to resolve to return the money. However Mother intervenes, leaving a bloody mess for Norman to clean up. After he's scrubbed down the bathroom, the dutiful son places the corpse in the trunk of Crane's rented car and sinks all the evidence in a nearby swamp. The situation gets tense for Norman when Marion's sister, Lila (Vera Miles), Marion's lover, Sam, and private investigator Milton Arbogast (Martin Balsam) arrive to ask some questions.

PSYCHO is not at all like the many movies that tried to imitate it. It's got a jet black sense of humor that becomes increasingly apparent upon repeated viewings and there's no doubt that it is masterful filmmaking. Hitchcock himself approached it almost as a technical joke: he wanted to see what would happen to audiences if you killed off the star in the first reel. The film is a textbook example of audience manipulation, as Hitchcock shifts our identification from character to character with the alacrity of a magician.

Inspired by the life of the demented, cannibalistic Wisconsin killer Ed Gein (whose gruesome acts would also inspire THE TEXAS CHAIN SAW MASSACRE and DERANGED), PSYCHO's importance to the horror genre cannot be overestimated. The influence comes not only from the Norman Bates character (who has since been reincarnated in a staggering variety of forms), but also from Hitchcock's use of pop psychological themes (the probable cause of the mayhem stems from the character's perverse familial and sexual history rather than an outside supernatural agency); Bernard Herrmann's famed all-string instruments score (his innovative nerveracking violin "screams" have been oft-mimicked); and new levels of screen violence. One intriguing difference between PSYCHO and the horror films of today is in the age of the characters. There isn't a teenager in sight in the Hitchcock classic—a revealing sign of the subsequent evolution of the genre *and* the downward shift in the age of moviegoing audiences.

PSYCHO

1998 110m c   Thriller/Horror/Drama   ★★½
Imagine/Universal   (U.S.)   R

Vince Vaughn (*Norman Bates*), Anne Heche (*Marion Crane*), Julianne Moore (*Lila Crane*), William H. Macy (*Milton Arbogast*), Viggo Mortensen (*Sam Loomis*), Robert Forster (*Dr. Simon*), Philip Baker Hall (*Sheriff Chambers*), Anne Haney (*Mrs. Chambers*), Chad Everett (*Tom Cassidy*), Rance Howard (*Mr. Lowery*)

p, Brian Grazer, Gus Van Sant; d, Gus Van Sant; w, Joseph Stefano (based on the novel by Robert Bloch); ph, Christopher Doyle; ed, Amy Duddleston; m, Bernard Herrmann; prod d, Tom Foden; art d, Carlos Barbosa; fx, Erick Brennan; cos, Beatrix Aruna Pasztor

Yes, the blood swirling down the drain *is* disgusting in color, as Hitchcock said it would be, though today's moviegoers won't flinch. Let's forgo the rant about creative bankruptcy and cinematic grave-robbing, however ghoulishly appropriate it may be. Gus Van Sant's "re-creation"—his term, and he insists—of the granddaddy of serial-killer shockers has a sharp young cast and glorious Deluxe color to recommend it. But its structure and dialogue are clearly of 1960, and what scared audiences then will almost certainly strike kids raised on the unholy trinity of Michael, Jason, and Freddy as quaint and slow.

In deference to the innocent few who don't know the big secret about Norman Bates (Vince Vaughn) and his mother, we'll keep the plot vague. Desperately in love with Sam (Viggo Mortensen), who won't marry her because he's crippled by family debt, Marion (Anne Heche) is presented with the opportunity to abscond with $400,000 and impulsively succumbs. She never makes it to Sam's place, and is last seen at the Bates Motel, which twitchy Norman runs while caring for his sick old mother.

Anthony Perkins so made the part of Norman his own that it haunted his career, but Vaughn acquits himself well, as do Heche, Mortensen, and Julianne Moore, who plays Marion's concerned sister Lila. If anything, Van Sant's supporting cast is actually better than the original, and for the most part Van Sant faithfully mimics Hitchcock's striking compositions and camera moves. He adds a couple of bizarre inserts (a bikinied girl and a cow on a highway, recalling MY OWN PRIVATE IDAHO) during the film's second murder scene, and they're simply baffling, though he also restores a couple of images—a fly buzzing around Sam and Marion's seedy hotel room, an overhead shot of a corpse draped crudely over the edge of a tub—originally lost to censorship and other considerations. But the upshot is that Van Sant's film feels as dated as Hitchcock's, and Hitchcock's has the better excuse.

PUBLIC ENEMY, THE

1931 83m bw Crime   ★★★★½
Warner Bros.   (U.S.)

James Cagney (*Tom Powers*), Jean Harlow (*Gwen Allen*), Edward Woods (*Matt Doyle*), Joan Blondell (*Mamie*), Beryl Mercer (*Ma Powers*), Donald Cook (*Mike Powers*), Mae Clarke (*Kitty*), Leslie Fenton (*Nails Nathan*), Robert Emmett O'Connor (*Paddy Ryan*), Murray Kinnell (*Putty Nose*)

p, Darryl F. Zanuck; d, William A. Wellman; w, Kubec Glasmon, John Bright, Harvey Thew (based on the original story *Beer and Blood* by John Bright); ph, Dev Jennings; ed, Ed McCormick; art d, Max Parker; cos, Earl Luick, Edward Stevenson

AAN Best Writing (Original Story): John Bright, Kubec Glasmon

Fascinating and brutally realistic, THE PUBLIC ENEMY, along with LITTLE CAESAR, BAD COMPANY, and SCARFACE, set the pattern for the gangster films of the 1930s. It also made a star of its volatile leading man, James Cagney, and confirmed director William Wellman as a major force in talkies.

The film opens with two young Irish boys, Tom (Frank Coghlan) and Matt (Frankie Darro), growing up in the shantytown South Side of Chicago, circa 1909, and learning a life of crime from Putty Nose (Kinnell), a fence. As adults, Tom (now played by Cagney) and Matt (Woods) move into robbery but, on a warehouse heist, a panicky Tom fires his gun needlessly and the police descend. Tom and Matt escape, but not before killing a cop. Putty Nose skips town, and the two young crooks move into bootlegging on the advice of Paddy Ryan (O'Connor). (In a scene which memorably uses the off-screen sound of a discordant piano, Matt and Tom square their accounts with Putty Nose.) Working for Nails Nathan (Fenton), the two are successful in their new racket, and move into an apartment with Mamie (Blondell) and Kitty (Clarke), two blondes they have picked up. Tom, the more nasty and aggressive of the two, continues to rise up in the gangster hierarchy, especially after Nails is killed in a freak accident by a horse. (So used to killing are Tom and Matt that they even execute the unfortunate animal.) The price of success, though, is great, as Tom's crusading brother Mike (Cook) prevents their mother (Mercer) from accepting the largesse of Tom's misdeeds. Even though Tom takes up with the seductive Gwen (Harlow), gang warfare takes its toll. The film's famous final shot, with "I'm Forever Blowing Bubbles" playing on a victrola, is still, even after exposure to today's graphic filmic violence, horrifying.

THE PUBLIC ENEMY is one of the most realistic gangster films ever produced. Wellman's direction is a frontal attack on the subject; other than handling a number of violent deaths offscreen, he spares no brutality of emotion, action, or thought in his grim portrayal of a lethal criminal. Cagney is *the* gangster of his day, cocky, tough as nails, and utterly without conscience, a character molded into evil by his environment. We see only the criminal world; the one cop shown in detail is Tom's father, a brute who walks around the house in half his uniform, communicating with his unruly child via a razor strop. Photographer Dev Jennings shot the film emphasizing sharp contrasts: glaring sunlit exteriors and grainy gray interiors that fade to black alleyways and gutters.

Tom's casual brutality scars the memory in shot after shot. The moment best remembered, of course, is the one in which Cagney smashes half a grapefruit in Clarke's face when she taunts him with the suggestion that maybe he's found a new lover. Everyone connected with this famous scene recalls it differently—whose idea it was, was Cagney really supposed to hit her, was Clarke prepared, etc. Whatever the case, Clarke is unfortunately remembered more for this small role than any other she played, and Cagney was for years to come offered a grapefruit whenever he entered a restaurant.

PULP FICTION

1994 154m c   Crime/Thriller   ★★★★
Jersey Films   (U.S.)   R

John Travolta (*Vincent Vega*), Samuel L. Jackson (*Jules Winfield*), Uma Thurman (*Mia Wallace*), Harvey Keitel (*The Wolf*), Tim Roth (*Pumpkin*), Amanda Plummer (*Honey Bunny*), Maria de

Medeiros *(Fabienne)*, Ving Rhames *(Marsellus Wallace)*, Eric Stoltz *(Lance)*, Rosanna Arquette *(Jody)*

p, Lawrence Bender; d, Quentin Tarantino; w, Quentin Tarantino, Roger Avary (based on stories by Quentin Tarantino and Roger Avary); ph, Andrzej Sekula; ed, Sally Menke; prod d, David Wasco; art d, Charles Collum; fx, Larry Fioritto; cos, Betsy Heimann

---

AA Best Original Screenplay: Quentin Tarantino, Roger Avary; *AAN Best Picture; AAN Best Actor:* John Travolta; *AAN Best Supporting Actor:* Samuel L. Jackson; *AAN Best Supporting Actress:* Uma Thurman; *AAN Best Director:* Quentin Tarantino; *AAN Best Film Editing:* Sally Menke

---

Witty, stylish, and romantic to its dark heart, PULP FICTION is a compulsively funny and strangely dreamy look at the criminals, hangers-on, and low-life scum who populate a glamorously sleazy Los Angeles of the mind.

After an introductory sequence featuring a pair of small-time holdup artists (Amanda Plummer and Tim Roth), we meet talkative hit men Jules Winfield (Samuel Jackson) and Vincent Vega (John Travolta), who are on their way to deal with some drug-dealing college kids who've made the mistake of trying to double-cross crime kingpin Marsellus (Ving Rhames). Their visit with the college boys takes a nasty turn after they find a briefcase—which emits a strange, radiant light—that Marsellus has sent them to retrieve. In the next episode, Vincent beards the boss's wife, Mia (Uma Thurman), through an evening on the town; their date turns ugly after she accidentally snorts an overdose of heroin. Lastly, we meet Butch (Bruce Willis), a nearly-washed up boxer who is being paid by Marsellus to take a dive in an upcoming fight. But Butch has other plans: he fights to win and then flees. By the end, all these seemingly disparate plot elements have been pulled together through a daring series of narrative somersaults.

Movie-mad writer-director Quentin Tarantino's second feature is a witty, violent, and unexpectedly redemptive tour-de-force. The movie skims along on a sea of lurid cliches, but these are twisted, transfigured, and given astonishingly fresh life: from the washed-up boxer and his French sex-kitten girlfriend, to the platform shoes enshrined on a hippie drug dealer's wall, to the mysterious suitcase whose glowing contents strike viewers dumb, PULP FICTION pays homage to its B-movie past while existing comfortably in its own perfectly realized world.

For all the violent action—and there's plenty—talk is paramount: the all-star cast is awash in words, endlessly debating such issues as whether a foot massage is tantamount to adultery or the relative filthiness of pigs and dogs, while beset by serial sex maniacs, contract gunmen, and bottom feeders of every stripe. No one and nothing is quite what it seems, from the billing and cooing couple of the opening sequence to the coolly professional killer who sees the light during a routine hit, to the raven-haired seductress whose evening out takes a sudden turn for the nightmarish. Yet PULP FICTION isn't all flash and chronological sleight-of-hand. It's driven by an astonishingly pure romantic impulse: it's filled with people who want to be saved, though most of them have no more idea about how to go about saving themselves than fish flopping around on the bottom of a boat. Without its commitment to an idea of salvation, PULP FICTION would be little more than a terrific parlor trick; with it, it's something far richer and more haunting.

PUMPKIN EATER, THE ★★★★
1964 118m bw Drama
Romulus (U.K.)

Anne Bancroft *(Jo Armitage)*, Peter Finch *(Jake Armitage)*, James Mason *(Bob Conway)*, Janine Gray *(Beth Conway)*, Cedric Hardwicke *(Mr. James, Jo's Father)*, Rosalind Atkinson *(Mrs. James, Jo's Mother)*, Alan Webb *(Mr. Armitage, Jake's*

Father), Richard Johnson *(Giles)*, Maggie Smith *(Philpot)*, Eric Porter *(Psychiatrist)*

p, James Woolf; d, Jack Clayton; w, Harold Pinter (based on the novel *The Pumpkin Eater* by Penelope Mortimer); ph, Oswald Morris; ed, James B. Clark; m, Georges Delerue; art d, Edward Marshall; cos, Motley

---

AAN Best Actress: Anne Bancroft

Bancroft, in an Oscar-nominated performance, plays a twice-married mother of six. She divorces her second husband (Johnson) and takes up with Finch, a highly successful screenwriter. The two marry; it seems like a perfect marriage until Bancroft realizes her philandering husband will never buckle down to her notions of marital fidelity. She gives birth to her seventh child and suffers a nervous breakdown. This, along with an encounter with an unbalanced woman at her hairdresser's, sends Bancroft to a psychiatrist (Porter). He is not much help. Bancroft's father dies, and she discovers that she is once more expecting a baby. She refuses to accompany Finch to a film location in Morocco but agrees to his arguments for sterilization. Later she runs into Mason, a man who once made a pass at her. Mason reveals that Finch has been having an affair with his wife (Gray), who is now expecting a child. In an ugly scene Bancroft confronts Finch and returns to Johnson. After she spends the night with her former husband, Johnson gets a phone call from old-friend Finch, whose father has just died. Bancroft goes to the funeral, but Finch pretends not to notice her. As she chases him, she slips and falls in the mud. Demoralized once more, she goes to their unfinished country house and spends the night alone. In the morning she wakes to the sound of her children as Finch leads them up a hill. Bancroft resigns herself to life, for good or ill, with the man. This is a fine film, encompassing the joys and tragedies of life: birth and death, marriage and divorce, love and hate. The leads give their characters life. They seem to be real people on the screen, not actors in a drama. Bancroft lends her role real depth, switching moods with eerie and wonderful believability. Mason, in a small supporting role, is nothing short of excellent. The script, by noted playwright Pinter, is complex and painful but often exhibits a good sense of the comic as well. The direction, slow and even-handed, allows the story to develop at its own pace, gradually building in speed as the story's intensity grows. This is a fine and sensitive work, a truthful portrait of human foibles and complexities. The film was charismatic character-actor Hardwicke's final one; he died the year of its release.

PUNCH-DRUNK LOVE 📀 ★★★½
2002 95m c Romance/Comedy R
Revolution Studios/New Line/JoAnne Sellar Productions/Ghoulardi Film Company (U.S.)

Adam Sandler *(Barry Egan)*, Emily Watson *(Lena Leonard)*, Philip Seymour Hoffman *(Dean Trumbell)*, Luis Guzman *(Lance)*, Mary Lynn Rajskub *(Elizabeth)*, Lisa Spector *(Susan)*, Julie Hermelin *(Kathleen)*, Karen Hermelin *(Anna)*, Hazel Mailloux *(Rhonda)*, Ashley Clark *("Georgia"—Phone Sex Sister)*

p, Paul Thomas Anderson, Daniel Lupi, JoAnne Sellar; d, Paul Thomas Anderson; w, Paul Thomas Anderson; ph, Robert Elswit; ed, Leslie Jones; m, Jon Brion; prod d, William Arnold; art d, Sue Chan; fx, Tim Alexander, Lou Carlucci, Industrial Light & Magic, Jeff Jarvis; cos, Mark Bridges

---

The strangest thing about this Paul-Thomas Anderson comedy is that it is based on a true story. In 1999, a California man noticed a mistake in a promotion run by Healthy Choice foods and earned over a million frequent flyer miles by sending in the UPC codes from some 12,000 cups of the company's pudding. Anderson figured the "pudding man" would make the perfect hero for his fourth feature, a dizzy romantic comedy with a touch of film noir.

Barry Egan (Adam Sandler) may run his own business selling junk like decorative plungers ("fungers"), and live alone in Sherman Oaks, Calif., but in many ways he's still an adolescent. He's too shy to meet girls, and the taunts of his seven harpy-like sisters can still send him into fits of rage. Barry's life changes dramatically one morning when he notices the flaw in the Healthy Choice promotional campaign and meets Lena (Emily Watson), who has secretly been sent by Barry's sister, Rhonda (Hazel Mailloux). That night, in a moment of weakness, Barry calls a phone-sex line and gives all of his personal information to a throaty voice named Georgia (Ashley Clark). But when he refuses to send her $750, four blond brothers dispatched by Georgia's sleazy boss (Philip Seymour Hoffman) soon arrive in Sherman Oaks. Desperate to shake them, Barry hits on a plan: Redeem thousands of cups of Healthy Choice pudding and fly to Lena in Hawaii.

Anderson has transformed Sandler's overworked manchild persona into something far more interesting: an emotionally disturbed adult whose immaturity hints at something a lot darker than Happy Gilmore. The film is really an old-fashioned romantic comedy, yet nothing about it is conventional. Robert Elswit's cinematography bends nearly every rule in the book, and the soundtrack purloins "He Needs Me" from Robert Altman's POPEYE—an appropriately loopy choice for a refreshingly unpredictable film.

PURPLE ROSE OF CAIRO, THE

1985   84m   c/bw   Comedy/Fantasy   [DVD]
Jack Rollins/Charles H. Joffe   (U.S.)   ★★★½
                                                         PG

Mia Farrow (Cecilia), Jeff Daniels (Tom Baxter/Gil Shepherd), Danny Aiello (Monk), Dianne Wiest (Emma), Van Johnson (Larry), Zoe Caldwell (The Countess), John Wood (Jason), Milo O'Shea (Fr. Donnelly), Deborah Rush (Rita), Irving Metzman (Theater Manager)

p, Robert Greenhut; d, Woody Allen; w, Woody Allen; ph, Gordon Willis (Deluxe Color); ed, Susan E. Morse; m, Dick Hyman; prod d, Stuart Wurtzel; art d, Edward Pisoni; cos, Jeffrey Kurland

AAN Best Original Screenplay: Woody Allen

The premise here is unique, but it wears thin after the first reel, even though director-writer Woody Allen strives mightily to keep things humming. Cecilia (Mia Farrow) is married to loutish, womanizing Monk (Danny Aiello) and lives a miserable life as a diner waitress. Her only escape from the woes of the depression is in the local movie house. Cecilia is particularly absorbed by a film (fictional) entitled "The Purple Rose of Cairo" starring a simon-pure hero (Jeff Daniels). She watches the same movie over and over, and then the miracle occurs. The hero suddenly faces the camera on-screen and begins to talk to Cecilia in the audience, then he startles the rest of the on-film actors by stepping out of the screen and into the theater, asking Cecilia to show him what real life is all about. He falls in love with her and she with him, but Monk and the Hollywood moguls are concerned. It's all a clever gimmick, of course, and Allen pulls it off well technically, but the story is as one-dimensional as the fictional Daniels. Where Allen succeeds is in his recreation of the old studio programmers of the 1930s, something he had done briefly before in ZELIG. Allen has done better than this, but THE PURPLE ROSE OF CAIRO is a sweet little film and an interesting diversion for his legion of followers.

PURSUED

1947   101m   bw   Mystery/Western   [DVD]
United States   (U.S.)   ★★★½

Teresa Wright (Thorley Callum), Robert Mitchum (Jeb Rand), Judith Anderson (Medora Callum), Dean Jagger (Grant Callum), Alan Hale (Jake Dingle), Harry Carey Jr. (Prentice McComber),

John Rodney (Adam Callum), Clifton Young (The Sergeant), Ernest Severn (Jeb, Age Eight), Charles Bates (Adam, Age 10)

p, Milton Sperling; d, Raoul Walsh; w, Niven Busch; ph, James Wong Howe; ed, Christian Nyby; m, Max Steiner; art d, Ted Smith; fx, William McGann, Willard Van Enger; cos, Leah Rhodes

An offbeat, film noir western/murder mystery which stars Robert Mitchum as Jeb Rand, a man pursued for his entire life by unseen (by him) assailants. Told in flashback, the film tells Jeb's story beginning when, as a young boy, his entire family was slaughtered—a vision that haunts him into adulthood. When the killers discover that Jeb was the only family member to survive, they vow to kill him too. He spends his life trying to find out who is responsible and why his adopted mother agreed to raise him. While not a mystery in the truest sense, PURSUED is one of darkest films ever made—one in which the main character spends his entire life (and the duration of the film) being victimized by everyone around him. Although some of the motives are made clear in an early scene, Mitchum's character knows nothing of the mysterious events which envelop him. It's not completely a western (it's merely a western location) and it's not completely a mystery, but it is a film which stretches the parameters of both genres.

PYGMALION

1938   96m   bw   Comedy   [DVD]
MGM   (U.K.)   ★★★★★

Leslie Howard (Prof. Henry Higgins), Wendy Hiller (Eliza Doolittle), Wilfrid Lawson (Alfred Doolittle), Marie Lohr (Mrs. Higgins), Scott Sunderland (Col. Pickering), Jean Cadell (Mrs. Pearce), David Tree (Freddy Eynsford-Hill), Everley Gregg (Mrs. Eynsford-Hill), Leueen MacGrath (Clara Eynsford-Hill), Esme Percy (Count Aristid Karpathy)

p, Gabriel Pascal; d, Anthony Asquith, Leslie Howard; w, George Bernard Shaw, W.P. Lipscomb, Cecil Lewis, Ian Dalrymple, Anthony Asquith (based on the play by George Bernard Shaw); ph, Harry Stradling; ed, David Lean; m, Arthur Honegger; art d, Laurence Irving; cos, Prof. Czettell, Worth, Schiaparelli

AAN Best Picture; AAN Best Actor: Leslie Howard; AAN Best Actress: Wendy Hiller; AA Best Screenplay: George Bernard Shaw, Ian Dalrymple, Cecil Lewis, W.P. Lipscomb

Shaw's magnificent comedy, a 1913 stage smash, was never better served than here, with Howard and Hiller perfectly matched as thoroughly mismatched lovers. Howard is Henry Higgins, a wealthy phonetics professor who encounters Cockney flower girl Eliza Doolittle (Hiller) and bets his friend Col. Pickering (Sunderland) that he can transform the uncouth and thick-accented woman ("a squashed cabbage leaf," he calls her) into a grand lady within three months. Eliza's hilarious lessons include speaking with marbles in her mouth to perfect her elocution. (When she swallows one, Higgins calmly notes, "That's all right. We have plenty more.") Eliza turns out to be a huge success at the ball, but what to do with her now?

The film, which Howard codirected with Asquith, is a delight from beginning to end. Hiller is splendid, making an amazing transformation from illiterate to lady. Eliza's first public test, when she takes tea with Henry's mother (Lohr, marvelous) is sidesplittingly funny. You may have tears in your eyes when Eliza goes on about her father's drinking and the fate of her deceased aunt's lovely straw hat. The curmudgeonly Shaw originally wanted Charles Laughton for Higgins, but Howard went way beyond the playwright's dour expectations, becoming the epitome of the intellectual tyrant. Sunderland is excellent as Pickering, and Lawson, as Doolittle the dustman, is stupendous. Lawson's speeches, along with other philosophical diatribes, were cut, despite producer Pascal's promises to Shaw; the playwright despised the interpolated "happy" ending, which was also used in the stage and screen versions of MY FAIR LADY.

Q

Q
1982 100m c Horror ★★★½
United Film Distribution (U.S.) R

Michael Moriarty (*Jimmy Quinn*), Candy Clark (*Joan*), David Carradine (*Detective Shepard*), Richard Roundtree (*Sgt. Powell*), James Dixon (*Lt. Murray*), Malachy McCourt (*Police Commissioner*), Fred J. Scollay (*Capt. Fletcher*), Peter Hock (*Detective Clifford*), Ron Cey (*Detective Hoberman*), Mary Louise Weller (*Mrs. Pauley*)

p, Larry Cohen; d, Larry Cohen; w, Larry Cohen; ph, Fred Murphy; ed, Armond Lebowitz; m, Robert O. Ragland; fx, Steve Neill, David Allen, Randall William Cook, Peter Kuran

Larry Cohen once again proves himself to be among the most creative, original, and intelligent American horror film directors in this bizarre masterwork, which successfully combines a *film noir* crime story with a good old-fashioned "giant monster" movie. Michael Moriarty turns in a brilliant performance as Jimmy Quinn, an ex-con, former junkie, and small-time hood looking to make one big score. After robbing a Manhattan diamond center, he hides out in the tower of the Chrysler Building and discovers a large hole in the dome of the structure, containing a huge nest with an equally large egg and several partially devoured human corpses. Meanwhile, the New York City police have been plagued by a bizarre string of deaths, and Detective Shepard (David Carradine) and Sgt. Powell (Richard Roundtree) have been investigating reports of people being snatched off rooftops. What all soon find out is that the Aztec god Quetzalcoatl, the winged serpent, is flying over Manhattan. Though Q's premise seems fairly silly (so does KING KONG's), Cohen's handling of the material is superior; he really convinces us that the idea of a giant bird living in a nest at the top of the Chrysler building isn't as implausible as it sounds. Cohen packs the film with stunning visuals and makes the most of New York City's architecture, capitalizing on its dozens of facades with birds and birdlike carvings. Q bombed at the box office because it was nearly impossible to package into a nice, simple ad campaign, but the film is a skillful combination of genres, sporting some fine acting and a literate, fascinating script with dashes of biting humor, that is well worth seeing.

Q&A
1990 134m c Crime/Drama ★★½
Regency International Pictures-Odyssey
Distributors Ltd. (U.S.) R

Nick Nolte (*Lt. Mike Brennan*), Timothy Hutton (*Al Reilly*), Armand Assante (*Bobby Texador*), Patrick O'Neal (*Kevin Quinn*), Lee Richardson (*Leo Bloomenfeld*), Luis Guzman (*Detective Luis Valentin*), Charles S. Dutton, billed as Charles Dutton (*Detective Sam Chapman*), Jenny Lumet (*Nancy Bosch*), Paul Calderon (*Roger Montalvo*), International Chrysis (*Jose Malpica*)

p, Arnon Milchan, Burtt Harris; d, Sidney Lumet; w, Sidney Lumet (based on the book by Edwin Torres); ph, Andrzej Bartkowiak (Technicolor); ed, Richard Cirincione; m, Ruben Blades; prod d, Philip Rosenberg; art d, Beth Kuhn; cos, Ann Roth, Neil Spisak

An attempt to return to the police corruption territory which had provided Lumet with two of his best films (SERPICO and PRINCE OF THE CITY), Q&A is a pungent, graphic drama sabotaged by a stupid romantic sub-plot, misjudged casting and a truly abysmal soundtrack. Hailed by his peers as one of the finest cops in New York, Lt. Mike Brennan (Nick Nolte) is, in fact, one of the dirtiest men on the force. In the film's opening scene, he kills an unarmed Latino drug dealer in cold blood, then plants a gun on him. When more officers arrive on the scene, Brennan claims he shot the dealer in self-defense. Still, this incident requires an investigation by the DA's office, and cop turned assistant DA Al Reilly (Timothy Hutton) is assigned to the case. This being Reilly's first investigation, chief of homicide Kevin Quinn (Patrick O'Neal) briefs him on how to go about it: Reilly will ask questions regarding the incident, a stenographer will record Brennan's answers (the Q&A of the title) and, after a few interviews with some witnesses, the whole matter will be neatly cleared up. In their initial meeting, Brennan explains his side of the story in suspiciously thorough detail; then Reilly learns his own former girlfriend, Nancy (Jenny Lumet, the director's daughter), is now romantically involved with Bobby Texador (Armand Assante), a drug dealer who is also a witness. The young assistant DA decides to launch a full investigation of this seemingly simple matter and events take a dangerous turn. The trail of corruption leads from drug dealers to Brennan and, ultimately, Quinn.

Q&A is authentic and uncompromising in its depiction of racism within the police force, probably coming closer to capturing the casually offensive repartee of New York cops than any other film. It also does a fine job of evoking Lumet's much-loved city, from smoky bars to cluttered station houses to opulent criminal hideaways. But while creating this dark, seedy world, Lumet overstuffs Q&A with plot. Providing little or no character motivation, he trivializes the film's central concerns (racism and corruption) with his banal, cliched treatment of the relationship between Riley and Nancy. Matters aren't helped by the fact that Hutton is miscast, while Jenny Lumet seems simply incapable of acting. Nolte, meanwhile, turns in a riveting performance, superbly aided and abetted by Luis Guzman and Charles Dutton as his initially loyal colleagues. The work of these three alone makes Q&A worth seeing, though you'll cringe every time the film's embarrassing theme song comes thudding over the soundtrack.

QUADROPHENIA
1979 120m c Drama ★★★★
Who Films (U.K.) R

Phil Daniels (*Jimmy Michael Cooper*), Mark Wingett (*Dave*), Philip Davis (*Chalky*), Leslie Ash (*Steph*), Garry Cooper (*Pete*), Toyah Wilcox (*Monkey*), Sting (*The Ace Face*), Trevor Laird (*Ferdy*), Gary Shail (*Spider*), Kate Williams (*Mrs. Cooper*)

p, Roy Baird, Bill Curbishley; d, Franc Roddam; w, Dave Humphries, Martin Stellman, Franc Roddam, Pete Townshend; ph, Brian Tufano; ed, Mike Taylor; m, The Who; prod d, Simon Holland; chor, Gillian Gregory

In 1964 London, Jimmy (Phil Daniels) and his pals are Mods, dividing their time between dancing and brawling with Rockers. QUADROPHENIA episodically depicts Jimmy's struggles with his seemingly empty existence, alleviated only by his relationships with his pals, most of whom are in the same grim boat. Adapted from a double album written by Pete Townshend and performed by the Who (who also acted as executive producers for the film), QUADROPHENIA is one of the best films about youth ever made, beautifully illustrating the frustrations of being young and bright but still having no future. First-time director Franc Roddam does a fine job with his young cast and his re-creation of period detail is nearly perfect. Daniels gives an amazing performance as the confused Jimmy, looking for an identity and coming literally to the brink of self-destruction—so intense and full of divergent emotions, he seems ready to explode at any moment.

QUARTET

1949 120m bw Drama/Comedy ★★★★
Gainsborough/Eagle-Lion/Rank (U.K.)

Basil Radford (*Henry Garnet*), Naunton Wayne (*Leslie*), Ian Fleming (*Ralph*), Jack Raine (*Thomas*), Angela Baddeley (*Mrs. Garnet*), James Robertson Justice (*Branksome*), Jack Watling (*Nicky*), Nigel Buchanan (*John*), Mai Zetterling (*Jeanne*), Dirk Bogarde (*George Bland*)

p, Antony Darnborough; d, Ken Annakin, Arthur Crabtree, Harold French, Ralph Smart; w, R.C. Sherriff (based on the stories of W. Somerset Maugham); ph, Ray Elton; ed, Charles Knott, Jean Baker; m, John Greenwood; art d, George Provis

Few segmented films are successful, generally because the sequences are not of consistent quality. In QUARTET, however, the wit and poignancy of the W. Somerset Maugham stories upon which the segments are based are in full force throughout, each tale holding its own in the hands of a different director and through the talents of the performers. In "The Facts of Life," the conservative Radford cautions his apparently naive son, Watling, to avoid gambling, lending money, or trusting women while on his tennis tour of Monte Carlo. Indeed, Watling does seems to be as gullible as they come, winning big at roulette only to be duped by an adventuress, Zetterling. But can he be so dumb? "The Alien Corn" stars Bogarde, in one of his early and most memorable roles, as an aspiring musician who is in love with Honor Blackman, but also obsessed with becoming a world-class talent. After studying for two years in Paris, he returns to England to be bluntly and cruelly informed by a famous composer that he will never make the grade. In "The Kite," George Cole is dominated by a shrewish mother, Baddeley, and marries the same kind of woman, Susan Shaw. But he escapes this cycle when Shaw destroys his prized kite. The final entry, "The Colonel's Lady," features Nora Swinburne as a woman who becomes famous after a collection of her love poems is published. Her husband, Cecil Parker, is driven to distraction by the fact that this sonnet sequence is addressed to a younger, dashing man. Unable to stand it any longer, he finally confronts his wife and demands to be told the identity of the young lover, with whom he suspects her of having an affair. All of these ironic tales are excellent, disproving the notion that segmented films cannot sustain interest. This one does it all the way.

QUEEN CHRISTINA

1933 97m bw Historical/Romance ★★★★★
MGM (U.S.)

Greta Garbo (*Queen Christina*), John Gilbert (*Don Antonio De la Prada*), Ian Keith (*Magnus*), Lewis Stone (*Chancellor Oxenstierna*), Elizabeth Young (*Ebba Sparre*), C. Aubrey Smith (*Aage*), Reginald Owen (*Prince Charles*), Georges Renavent (*French Ambassador*), Gustav von Seyffertitz (*General*), David Torrence (*Archbishop*)

p, Walter Wanger; d, Rouben Mamoulian; w, H.M. Harwood, Salka Viertel, S.N. Behrman (based on a story by Salka Viertel, Margaret R. Levino); ph, William Daniels; ed, Blanche Sewell; m, Herbert Stothart; art d, Alexander Toluboff, Edwin B. Willis; cos, Adrian

A revelation, wrung from the usual MGM Bio identikit, but given shape by Mamoulian's painterly eye, and immortality by Garbo's ability to transcend. Even when the script serves up great clumps of unleavened bread, Garbo imbues it with living emotion. Although the same cannot be said of still-handsome Gilbert's Spanish Ambassador, their love scenes

capture the depth of overwhelming emotion in an unparalleled, perfectly beautiful way. If some of Garbo's other performances have dated, this one documents her magical strangeness in a way that has stood the test of time.

Garbo's CHRISTINA is a decisive queen, ruling Sweden with wisdom and compassion. Her former lover, Magnus (Keith), attempts to arrange a marriage between Christina and a dashing prince, but she will have nothing to do with political unions. Then, while out riding, she encounters Don Antonio (Gilbert), the newly appointed ambassador from Spain. Intrigued by the gallant Spaniard, Christina decides to discover his real nature by disguising herself as a man. She goes to an inn where she knows Don Antonio is staying. She befriends her, and, unaware that she is a woman, invites Christina to spend the night in his room. She eventually reveals her identity and the two fall in love, spending two glorious days and nights together. Their idyll over, Christina returns to her court and receives Don Antonio officially, pretending she knows him only as an official representative of a foreign power. He is there, he informs her, to ask for her hand in marriage—for the king of Spain. She does not respond, but instead continues to meet him secretly. When the manipulative Magnus discovers their meetings, he rouses the public against Don Antonio, labeling him a trifling interloper.

In QUEEN CHRISTINA, Garbo had her way, making use of an iron-clad contract that paid her $250,000 a film, gave her the choice of director, cameraman, leading man, and, in fact, the entire cast, if she cared to select the extras. She had seen a young British actor, Laurence Olivier, in an Ann Harding vehicle, WESTWARD PASSAGE, and liked him. Olivier was signed to play the Spanish ambassador and came to the studio to rehearse with Garbo, at Mamoulian's suggestion. The rehearsal was a disaster, as Garbo froze up. Olivier was told to forget about appearing in a Garbo film, and Mamoulian immediately called Gilbert, asking him to help warm up the woman he had starred with in the heyday of the silent era. The effect he had on her was amazing. Still, the studio proposed other leading players, *anyone* but Gilbert, but Garbo refused anyone else. Much has been said about Garbo's magnanimous insistence that Gilbert, the fallen star, join her in a major film to rescue his almost lost career. She was reportedly no longer in love with him but was returning the favor he had extended to her at the beginning of *her* career, when he demanded she costar with him in the silent classic FLESH AND THE DEVIL. But not until Gilbert signed his contract to do QUEEN CHRISTINA did Mayer give up trying to replace him. Chief of production Irving Thalberg and Garbo hoped for a comeback for Gilbert, but even though he was touching in his role, the public was no longer interested, having bought the myth, sponsored by Mayer, about the actor's inadequacy in talkies.

QUEEN MARGOT
(LA REINE MARGOT)

1994 143m c Drama/Historical/Romance ★★★
Renn Productions/France 2 Cinema/Films Nef R
Filmproduktion/Wing RCS Films & TV
(France/Germany/Italy)

Isabelle Adjani (*Marguerite de Valois—the Queen Margot*), Vincent Perez (*Joseph de la Mole*), Virna Lisi (*Catherine de Medici*), Jean-Hugues Anglade (*Charles IX*), Daniel Auteuil (*Henri of Navarre*), Otto Tausig (*Mendes*), Thomas Kretschmann (*Nancay*), Pascal Greggory (*Duc d'Anjou*), Julien Rassam (*Alencon*), Jean-Claude Brialy (*Coligny*)

p, Claude Berri; d, Patrice Chereau; w, Patrice Chereau, Daniele Thompson (based on the novel by Alexander Dumas); ph, Philippe Rousselot; ed, Francois Gedigier, Helene Viard; m,

Goran Bregovic; prod d, Richard Peduzzi, Olivier Radot; fx, Georges Demetrau; cos, Moidele Bickel

AAN Best Costume Design: Moidele Bikel

A lavish historical spectacle, QUEEN MARGOT is the sort of film Hollywood never made, teeming with violence, sex, and colorful period accessories, all legitimized with a veneer of historical importance. It's sumptuous and entertaining, but keeping up with the huge cast and complicated plot is no easy task.

In 1572, during the reign of Catholic King Charles IX (Jean-Hugues Anglade), France is torn by religious strife: Protestants and Catholics vie for political control, and power-behind-the-throne Catherine de Medici (Virna Lisi) decides to placate the Protestants by wedding her daughter Marguerite de Valois (Isabelle Adjani), better known as Margot, to the Protestant Henri of Navarre (Daniel Auteuil). Their arranged marriage is the catalyst of a series of intrigues, massacres, and murders.

QUEEN MARGOT manages—though only barely—to survive the film's relentless focus on the basest aspects of life among the "silk-clad vultures" who were France's 16th-century elite. Most of the film veers between scenes of ghastly violence and scenes of steamy sex (in a curious nod to American conventions, the violence is extremely graphic, while the bedroom scenes involve no frontal nudity). Margot's relationship with her older brothers is unmistakably incestuous and, generally speaking, her carnal desires take precedence over all other concerns; when Protestant zealots refer to her as the Catholic whore, it's hard to take issue with their assessment.

Based on the historical novel by Alexandre Dumas, QUEEN MARGOT was directed with tremendous attention to visual detail by Patrice Chereau, whose background lies in theater and opera. In contrast to most Hollywood epics of this size and scope, the film wallows in the period's nasty details as lovingly as its sumptuous ones: it's filled with rich silks and lavishly embroidered fabrics, and they're all grimy.

QUEST FOR FIRE   DVD
1981 97m c   Adventure/Historical   ★★★
ICC/Cine-Trail/Belstar   (France/Canada)   R

Everett McGill (*Naoh Ulam Tribe Member*), Ron Perlman (*Amoukar Ulam Tribe Member*), Nameer El-Kadi (*Gaw Ulam Tribe Member*), Rae Dawn Chong (*Ika Ivaka Tribe Member*), Gary Schwartz, Frank Olivier Bonnet, Jean-Michel Kindt, Kurt Schiegl, Brian Gill, Terry Fitt

p, John Kemeny, Denis Heroux, Jacques Dorfmann, Vera Belmont; d, Jean-Jacques Annaud; w, Gerard Brach (based on the novel *La Guerre de Feu* by J.H. Rosny, Sr.); ph, Claude Agostini (Panavision, Bellevue-Pathe Color); ed, Yves Langlois; m, Philippe Sarde; prod d, Brian Morris, Guy Comtois; art d, Clinton Cavers; fx, Martin Malivoire; cos, John Hay, Penny Rose

AA Best Makeup: Sarah Monzani, Michele Burke

A fascinating look at what the life of early man may have been like, QUEST FOR FIRE stars Everett McGill, Ron Perlman, and Nameer El-Kadi as members of a prehistoric tribe, the Ulams, who are sent out to find fire after their only source is accidentally extinguished. They find another, barbarous tribe, the Ivakas, who to the amazement of the Ulams can create fire using flint and sticks. The three rescue Ika (Rae Dawn Chong) from the cruel Ivakas and take her along, with the secret of firestarting. The characters register humor, grief, happiness, anxiety, and other everyday emotions, creating realistic personalities that the audience can identify with. Desmond Morris, author of "The Naked Ape," created a body language

for the film based on actual simian gestures, while famed novelist Anthony Burgess created a primitive language. Although occasionally bleak, the film affords many pleasurable moments, showing early man learning to laugh and expressing delight and amazement at the sight of fire. The film received an Academy Award for Best Make-Up.

QUIET AMERICAN, THE   DVD
2002 101m c   Drama/Mystery   ★★★★
IMF/Mirage Enterprises/Saga Films (U.S./Germany)   R

Michael Caine (*Thomas Fowler*), Brendan Fraser (*Alden Pyle*), Do Thi Hai Yen (*Phuong*), Rade Sherbedgia (*Inspector Vigot*), Tzi Ma (*Hinh*), Robert Stanton (*Joe Tunney*), Holmes Osborne (*Bill Granger*), Ferdinand Hoang (*Mr. Muoi*), Pham Thi Mai Hoa (*Phuong's Sister*), Mathias Mlekuz (*French Captain*)

p, Staffan Ahrenberg, William Horberg; d, Phillip Noyce; w, Christopher Hampton, Robert Schenkkan (adapted from the novel by Graham Greene); ph, Christopher Doyle; ed, John Scott; m, Craig Armstrong; prod d, Roger Ford; art d, Ian Gracie; fx, Steve Courtley, Lisa Anne Morris; cos, Norma Moriceau

AAN Best Actor: Michael Caine

The second film version of Graham Greene's sad and prescient 1955 novel about American involvement in Vietnam hews far closer to the book than the first, preserving the sophisticated ambiguity of Greene's depiction of a tangled struggle for power played out on personal and political fronts.

French Indochina, 1952: In the rural north, the French colonial government is under siege by communist Vietminh guerillas. But the fighting hasn't reached Saigon, where veteran *London Times* journalist Thomas Fowler (Michael Caine) maintains a cozy routine and a 22-year-old mistress, Phuong (Do Thi Hai Yen). Fowler's idyll is interrupted by two arrivals: idealistic American doctor Alden Pyle (Brendan Fraser), who's attached to an official government aid mission, and a letter recalling Fowler to London. If Fowler goes home, he'll have to leave Phuong, and the fresh-faced Pyle seems awfully taken with her when they all have dinner together. In a last-ditch effort to prove that the *Times* needs a man in Indochina, Fowler undertakes a dangerous journey north, where French soldiers are blaming communists for massacring an entire village. The story buys Fowler a reprieve but further complicates his relationship with Pyle and Phuong.

The strengths of Greene's novel are well served by this quietly accomplished film, which, unlike the 1958 version, doesn't shy away from identifying Pyle's connection to the American government. As an account of the circumstances that lead to U.S. involvement in Vietnam, it's strikingly well observed; Greene was a journalist as well as a writer of fiction. And Caine's performance as Fowler, who soon abandons his commitment to impartial observation and becomes deeply involved with events beyond his control, is simply outstanding.

QUIET MAN, THE   DVD
1952 129m c   Romance/Comedy   ★★★★★
Argosy (U.S.)

John Wayne (*Sean Thornton*), Maureen O'Hara (*Mary Kate Danaher*), Barry Fitzgerald (*Michaeleen Flynn*), Ward Bond (*Fr. Peter Lonergan*), Victor McLaglen (*Red Will Danaher*), Mildred Natwick (*Mrs. Sarah Tillane*), Francis Ford (*Dan Tobin*), Eileen Crowe (*Mrs. Elizabeth Playfair*), May Craig (*Woman at Railway Station*), Arthur Shields (*Rev. Cyril Playfair*)

p, Merian C. Cooper, John Ford, Michael Killanin (uncredited); d, John Ford; w, Frank S. Nugent, Richard Llewellyn (based on the story by Maurice Walsh); ph, Winton C. Hoch, Archie Stout

(Technicolor); ed, Jack Murray; m, Victor Young; art d, Frank Hotaling; cos, Adele Palmer

AAN Best Picture; AAN Best Supporting Actor: Victor McLaglen; *AA Best Director:* John Ford; *AAN Best Screenplay:* Frank S. Nugent; *AA Best Color Cinematography:* Winton Hoch, Archie Stout; *AAN Best Art Direction-Set Decoration (Color):* Frank Hotaling, John McCarthy Jr., Charles Thompson; *AAN Best Sound Recording:* Daniel J. Bloomberg

Epic romantic comedy, but so thick on the blarney, that it helps to be Irish, at least to a degree. Otherwise, it may be hard to get a grasp on the turbulent traditions, fiesty sentimentality and burning coldness that exists in the Irish soul. That understood, cook a corned beef and invite the neighbors over.

THE QUIET MAN is Ford's sentimental journey into the past of his ancestral Ireland, a journey enacted by Ford's onscreen alter ego, John Wayne. The story begins in the 1920s, when American Sean Thornton (Wayne), a quiet fellow but a former boxer with a brutal past, arrives in Innisfree. He is met by the elfin, capricious Michaeleen Flynn (Fitzgerald), the village cabman. Sean is off to a little cottage—his birthplace, White O'Mornin'—which he has bought from a local widow (Natwick). En route, he sees in the distance a beautiful, red-haired woman framed by trees, a soft wind rippling her skirts and hair. She seems a vision of a lost world, and Wayne asks Flynn, "Is that real?" (Quips the cabbie, "Only a mirage brought on by your terrible thirst!") Wayne is really asking about the scene itself, rather than the lovely woman gracing it, and recalls his dead mother as she described Innisfree to him as a child. Arriving at his cottage, he tells Flynn, "I'm Sean Thornton and I was born in that little cottage. I'm home and home I'm going to stay." It's almost a declaration of war against the perils of the present in favor of the safety of the past.

In buying his land, Sean has alienated the richest, toughest man in the area, Red Will Danaher (McLaglen), who is doubly peeved over his being a "dirty Yank." Though his land looks fertile, Sean turns up nothing but rocks when he tries to plow it for planting. He battles the present for the illusion of the past at every turn, and is even upbraided for his romanticism when he proudly shows off his cottage to a neighbor, who inspects its thatched roof and immaculately painted walls, remarking that "It looks the way all Irish cottages should, and seldom do. And only an American would think of painting it emerald green." One day, Sean enters his cottage to find his neighbor Mary Kate (O'Hara) cleaning up for him, a gesture suggesting more than communal fellowship. Just as she is about to flee, Sean attempts to kiss her. She gives him a stiff-armed slap, but, before running off, encourages him with a kiss of her own. Later, Sean meets Red Will, Mary Kate's brutish brother, in the local pub. When Sean extends his hand, the powerful Irishman squeezes it with all his might and the ex-boxer responds with his own pressure, until both are wincing in pain.

Witnessing this first confrontation between the two giants is a group of locals—most of whom hate Red Will and side with Sean. Sean has already befriended Father Lonergan (Bond), though he goes out of his way to say nothing of his past. But the local Protestant clergyman (Shields) knows Sean's dark secret and tells him so privately. The minister, a onetime amateur boxer, has kept a scrapbook about boxers the world over and knows that "Trooper Thorn" retired after accidentally killing a man in the ring. Discredited, Sean moved with his prize money to Ireland to find the peace, happiness, and beauty of his boyhood. A memorable fight with Red Will, though, awaits the "quiet man."

A love story that packs a fearsome punch, THE QUIET MAN is a passionate, full-blooded film. Ford constructs the picture carefully, and lavishes the tale with some of the most visually extraordinary scenes ever filmed. Some of these, such as the idealistic vision of O'Hara in the glen herding her sheep,

are presented in muted, diffused tones that suggest an ethereal world—into which Wayne has barged. THE QUIET MAN is Ford's symbolic homecoming, in which he shapes his own longing and memories in the form of living, full-blooded characters, who are at the same time representative types. Wayne is Ford's youth; O'Hara his great love, as well as all the women of Ireland; McLaglen, the sentimental bully; Bond, the priest who would rather fish than pray, though fishing is also a form of prayer; Shields, the patient outsider; Natwick, the typical Irish widow; Fitzgerald, the local conscience and historian (he also delivers the film's best line after seeing the broken wedding bed: "Impetuous! Homeric!"). The wonderful performances by Ford's stock company in these roles help make THE QUIET MAN an utterly moving and fascinating portrait of rural life in Ireland.

QUILLS   DVD

2000 130m c   Drama   ★★★

Industry Entertainment/Walrus & Associates/   R
Hollywood Partners/Fox Searchlight (U.S./Germany)

Geoffrey Rush *(The Marquis de Sade),* Kate Winslet *(Madeleine),* Joaquin Phoenix *(Coulmier),* Michael Caine *(Dr. Royer-Collard),* Billie Whitelaw *(Madame LeClerc),* Patrick Malahide *(Delbene),* Amelia Warner *(Simone),* Jane Melelaus *(Renee Pelagie),* Stephen Moyer *(Prouix),* Tony Pritchard *(Valcour)*

p, Julia Chasman, Nick Wechsler, Peter Kaufman; d, Philip Kaufman; w, Doug Wright (based on the play by Doug Wright); ph, Rogier Stoffers; ed, Peter Boyle; m, Stephen Warbeck; prod d, Martin Childs; art d, Mark Raggett, Steven Lawrence; fx, Stuart Brisdon, Tim Field; cos, Jacqueline West

AAN Best Actor: Geoffrey Rush; *AAN Best Art Direction:* Martin Childs (Art Direction), Jill Quertier (Set Decoration); *AAN Best Costume Design:* Jacqueline West

Censorship, madness, social rebellion, and the power of art. With such heavy-duty topics in the mix, Philip Kaufman's impassioned adaptation of Doug Wright's 1995 play can't be accused of shallow sensationalism.

In 1807, the Marquis de Sade (Geoffrey Rush) is confined to the Charenton asylum for the insane, run by the gentle Abbe de Coulmier (Joaquin Phoenix). The abbe believes in treating madness through art and exercise, and encourages the Marquis to purge his mind of poison by committing his thoughts to paper. The Marquis, naturally, isn't the least bit interested in purging his poisons; instead, he pens stories of such extravagant obscenity they retain the power to shock a full two centuries later. With the help of free-spirited laundress Madeleine (Kate Winslet), the Marquis smuggles his writings to a publisher, and they cause such a scandal that Napoleon himself sends a new administrator, Dr. Royer-Collard (Michael Caine), to Charenton to break the spirit of the defiant Marquis.

Wright clearly wants his audience to see the battle over De Sade's pornographic imagination in light of ongoing cultural debates over obscenity, art, and censorship. Not surprisingly, he and Kaufman (never the most subtle of filmmakers) come down firmly on the side of free speech, healthy sexuality, and gentle treatment of the insane, and rail against pious hypocrisy, censorship, and erotic repression. As is often the case with Kaufman's films (see HENRY AND JUNE), there's lots of naughty sex (from a cheerful threesome to tormented necrophilia) presented in an extraordinarily unerotic fashion. Rush, however, is thoroughly delightful as the Marquis, who smirks and leers with unrepentant glee and retains a bizarre dignity *in extremis.*

QUILOMBO

1984 114m c Historical ★★★★
CDK (Brazil)

Antonio Pompeo *(Zumbi)*, Zeze Motta *(Dandara)*, Tony Tornado *(Ganga Zumba)*, Vera Fischer *(Ana de Ferro)*, Antonio Pitanga *(Acaiuba)*, Mauricio do Valle *(Domingos Jorge Velho)*, Daniel Filho *(Carrilho)*, Joao Nogueira *(Rufino)*, Jorge Coutinho *(Sale)*, Grande Otelo *(Baba)*

p, Augusto Arraes; d, Carlos Diegues; w, Carlos Diegues; ph, Lauro Escorel Filho; ed, Mair Tavares

This is a spectacular, brilliantly colored historical epic that explores the beginnings of Quilombo de Palmares, the Brazilian slave nation in the mid-1600s. Director Diegues described the nation as "the first democratic society that we know of in the Western hemisphere." The picture begins as the slaves revolt and violently murder their Portuguese owners. Taking to the forests of northeastern Brazil, the slaves form a nation, free from the oppression of slave owners. They are soon joined by other oppressed peoples such as Jews and poor white farmers. A government is created and a leader elected—Ganga Zumba, played by Tornado. The Portuguese, however, retaliate and attempt to conquer the nation. Diegues previously scored on American art-house screens with BYE BYE BRAZIL and XICA. Here, he successfully manages to mix history with folklore. Exquisitely photographed and lavishly produced, the film has a great deal of action, culminating with some intense battle sequences, but it often loses sight of its story. More than examining a historic period, QUILOMBO, like Diegues's other films, comments on the present state of Brazil as well as the nation's possible future.

QUIZ SHOW
DVD

1994 132m c Drama/Historical ★★★½
Baltimore Pictures/Dreyfuss-James Productions/ PG-13
Hollywood Pictures (U.S.)

John Turturro *(Herb Stempel)*, Rob Morrow *(Richard Goodwin)*, Ralph Fiennes *(Charles Van Doren)*, Paul Scofield *(Mark Van Doren)*, David Paymer *(Dan Enright)*, Hank Azaria *(Albert Freedman)*, Christopher McDonald *(Jack Barry)*, Johann Carlo *(Toby Stempel)*, Elizabeth Wilson *(Dorothy Van Doren)*, Allan Rich *(Robert Kintner)*

p, Robert Redford, Michael Jacobs, Julian Krainin, Michael Nozik; d, Robert Redford; w, Paul Attanasio (based on the book "Remembering America: A Voice From the Sixties" by Richard N. Goodwin); ph, Michael Ballhaus; ed, Stu Linder; m, Mark Isham; prod d, Jon Hutman; art d, Tim Galvin; cos, Kathy O'Rear

AAN Best Picture; AAN Best Supporting Actor: Paul Scofield; AAN Best Director: Robert Redford; AAN Best Adapted Screenplay: Paul Attanasio

A meditation on the loss of moral character in America, director Robert Redford's recounting of the 1950's quiz show scandals has much to recommend it, but fails to answer the $64,000 question—"so what?"

New York, 1957. Herb Stempel (John Turturro) is the reigning champion on "Twenty-One," one of the big-money quiz shows drawing huge new audiences to the fledgling medium of television. Stempel is seemingly unbeatable, but network and sponsor think he's a "schmuck with a face for radio," and they want him off the show. Enter Columbia professor Charles Van Doren (Ralph Fiennes), a handsome WASP with an impeccable intellectual pedigree. "Twenty-One" producer Dan Enright (David Paymer) convinces Van Doren to participate in a fraudulent scheme: in order to guarantee his continuing appearance on the show, he's supplied with the answers in advance.

Ironically, the scandal that threatened to bring down television served as the impetus for the three networks to take monopolistic control over the entire industry, from production to broadcast, ending TV's "Golden Age" and ushering in the so-called "Vast Wasteland" era of the '60s. QUIZ SHOW's success is likewise defined by its unintended consequences. It purports to reveal the genesis of a morally ambiguous culture that accepts, and even expects, deception. Assuming that's true, however, the contemporary mass audience, raised on televisual values and inured to fraudulence, will presumably shrug off Redford's charges with bemused apathy.

Formally, QUIZ SHOW deserves a great deal of praise. It's a blessedly old-fashioned, well-made and well-acted narrative; the scenes involving the Van Doren and Stempel families, and the show's producers, stand out, while Rob Morrow (as crusading attorney Richard Goodwin) makes an unnecessary meal out of his character's Boston accent.

QUO VADIS

1951 171m c Historical ★★★½
MGM (U.S.)

Robert Taylor *(Marcus Vinicius)*, Deborah Kerr *(Lygia)*, Leo Genn *(Petronius)*, Peter Ustinov *(Nero)*, Patricia Laffan *(Poppaea)*, Finlay Currie *(Peter)*, Abraham Sofaer *(Paul)*, Marina Berti *(Eunice)*, Buddy Baer *(Ursus)*, Felix Aylmer *(Plautius)*

p, Sam Zimbalist; d, Mervyn LeRoy; w, John Lee Mahin, S.N. Behrman, Sonya Levien (based on the novel by Henryk Sienkiewicz); ph, Robert Surtees, William V. Skall (Technicolor); ed, Ralph E. Winters; m, Miklos Rozsa; art d, William McCoy, Cedric Gibbons, Edward Carfagno; fx, Thomas Hayward, A. Arnold Gillespie, Donald Jarnhaus; chor, Madi Obolensky, Auriel Millos; cos, Herschel McCoy

AAN Best Picture; AAN Best Supporting Actor: Leo Genn; AAN Best Supporting Actor: Peter Ustinov; AAN Best Color Cinematography: Robert Surtees, William V. Skall; AAN Best Film Editing: Ralph E. Winters; AAN Best Score (Drama or Comedy): Miklos Rozsa; AAN Best Art Direction-Set Decoration (Color): William A. Horning, Cedric Gibbons, Edward C. Carfagno, Hugh Hunt; AAN Best Costume Design (Color): Herschel McCoy

One of MGM's biggest box-office hits, the epic QUO VADIS offers a spectacular cast to match its overwhelming production; there's plenty to enjoy, but don't look for greatness. Over it all looms a loony Ustinov as Emperor Nero, despite director LeRoy's best efforts to keep him from chewing the scenery as he enjoyably steals the show. Taylor is the nominal star, playing Marcus Vinicius, a Roman army commander who returns victorious to the Eternal City in the 1st century AD. After receiving a hero's welcome from the empress (Laffan), Marcus meets Lygia (Kerr), a hostage who is the Christian daughter of a defeated king. He lusts after her, but is put off by her oversized pal Ursus (the aptly named Baer), and further rejected by Lygia because he is a pagan. Angered, Marcus makes Lygia his slave, but is still unable to make her his mistress. How he manages forms the core of the story.

The acting is good, especially that of Kerr, Taylor, and Genn (as the gentle advisor to the emperor), but it's the wild Ustinov who scoops up every scene he's in, giving one of the most outlandish performances ever filmed. Ustinov tested for the role of the lyre-playing little arsonist in 1949, but the film was slow to develop. A year later, MGM wired Ustinov that they were still interested in him for the part but they were worried that he might be too young for the role. Ustinov wired back, "If you wait much longer I shall be too old. Nero died at thirty-one."

Shot in six months at a cost of almost $7 million, QUO VADIS gleaned $25 million in world rentals and became the second all-time grosser after GONE WITH THE WIND. It led the way for all those crazy religious epics which dominated popular postwar production: SALOME, IVANHOE, THE ROBE, DAVID AND BATHSHEBA, THE SILVER CHALICE, and BEN HUR, which would surpass its box-office take. Enhancing this epic's success was the fine score by Miklos Rozsa, who, along with MGM librarian George Schneider, located all the known instruments of the period and then, although no clear record of the era's music remained, pieced his score together through slave songs, Christian hymns, marches, and fanfares played on modern instruments (using the Scottish clarsach to approximate the sound of the ancient lyre, for example). QUO VADIS was nominated for eight Oscars, but the lions were passed over. Imagine that.

R

RABBIT-PROOF FENCE

2002 94m c Drama ★★★★
HanWay/Australian Film Finance Corp./Rubalara PG
Films/Olsen Levy Productions (Australia/U.K.)

Everlyn Sampi *(Molly Craig)*, Tianna Sansbury *(Daisy Craig)*, Laura Monaghan *(Gracie Fields)*, David Gulpilil *(Moodoo)*, Kenneth Branagh *(A.O. Neville)*, Myarn Lawford *(Molly's Grandmother)*, Deborah Mailman *(Mavis)*, Jason Clarke *(Constable Riggs)*, Ningali Lawford *(Molly's Mother)*, Garry McDonald *(Mr. Neal)*

p, Phillip Noyce, Christine Olsen, John Winter; d, Phillip Noyce; w, Christine Olsen (based on the book *Follow the Rabbit-Proof Fence*, by Doris Pilkington Garimara); ph, Christopher Doyle; ed, Veronika Jenet, John Scott; m, Peter Gabriel; prod d, Roger Ford; art d, Laurie Faen; cos, Roger Ford

Phillip Noyce's superb, heart-wrenching film tells the real-life tale of an incredible journey made by three young Australian girls who fell victim to a cruel government policy.

Beginning in the early 20th century, "half-caste" children—the offspring of aboriginal women and white, often migrant, men—were taken from their homes and "re-educated" to serve as domestic laborers. Many of their white fathers were workers on the rabbit-proof fence, an ambitious, 1,500-mile barrier designed to halt Australia's plague of crop-destroying rabbits. Along its route, depots were established where workers inevitably met aboriginal women. In 1931, 14-year-old Molly Craig (wonderfully played by young Everlyn Sampi), her eight-year-old sister, Daisy (Tianna Sansbury), and their 10-year-old cousin, Gracie Fields (Laura Monaghan), were taken from their families in the depot town of Jigalong and placed in the Moore River Native Settlement center some 1,200 miles away. Refusing to be separated from their mothers, the girls escaped and, with no supplies and only the rabbit-proof fence to guide them, began their remarkable cross-country odyssey home.

Noyce uses A.O. Neville (Kenneth Branagh), who, as Chief Protector of Aborigines in Western Australia, ordered the girls' relocation, to explicate the paternalistic assumptions about race that fueled a policy that was still in effect until the early 1970s. In tearing families apart, officials like Neville believed they were rescuing mixed-race children who, if

allowed to remain in the outback, would inevitably revert to their natural blackness. By ripping children from their mothers and forcing them into servitude, future generations could thus be "advanced" into whiteness. However appalling these notions may seem, the same self-serving attitudes underlay a number of official U.S. policies, including the placement of Native American children in Mission schools and the removal of thousands of Amerasian children from South Vietnam during 1975's "Operation Babylift."

RABID

1977 91m c Science Fiction/Horror ★★
Cinepix/Dibar (Canada) R

Marilyn Chambers *(Rose)*, Frank Moore *(Hart Read)*, Joe Silver *(Murray Cypher)*, Howard Ryshpan *(Dr. Dan Keloid)*, Patricia Gage *(Dr. Roxanne Keloid)*, Susan Roman *(Mindy Kent)*, Roger Periard *(Lloyd Walsh)*, Lynne Deragon *(Nurse Louise)*, Terry Schonblum *(Judy Glasberg)*, Victor Desy *(Claude LaPointe)*

p, John Dunning; d, David Cronenberg; w, David Cronenberg; ph, Rene Verzier (Panavision, Eastmancolor); ed, Jean LaFleur; art d, Claude Marchand; fx, Joe Blasco, Al Griswold; cos, Erla Gliserman

A virtual remake of THEY CAME FROM WITHIN, RABID finds director David Cronenberg more in control of his narrative and his visual style than in his previous films, but the results are still somewhat uneven. Once again Cronenberg explores sexually transmitted horror, but this time through none other than hardcore porno starlet Marilyn Chambers, who makes her legitimate debut here as Rose, a woman seriously injured in a motorcycle accident. A local plastic surgeon uses the opportunity to experiment with some new skin grafts he's been developing, but somehow the surgery goes awry and soon Rose sports a grotesque, phallus-like organ in her armpit that sucks blood out of her unsuspecting lovers (the original treatment of the film was entitled "Mosquito"). This soon leads to an epidemic that turns the citizens of Montreal into rabid, blood-seeking, sex-crazed monsters that drool green slime.

Once again, Cronenberg has made a rather frustrating film. Although RABID is full of interesting ideas, they are not particularly well developed or presented by Cronenberg's unfocused script. And while the film has an uneasy sense of humor, Cronenberg again overplays his most visceral sequences, including the well-shot but pointless car crash. As with THEY CAME FROM WITHIN, the performances are weak, and while Chambers does add some resonance to the film as a sexual icon, her acting ability is decidedly limited.

RACHEL, RACHEL

1968 101m c Drama ★★★½
Kayos (U.S.) R

Joanne Woodward *(Rachel Cameron)*, James Olson *(Nick Kazlik)*, Kate Harrington *(Mrs. Cameron)*, Estelle Parsons *(Calla Mackie)*, Donald Moffat *(Niall Cameron)*, Terry Kiser *(Preacher)*, Franco Corsaro *(Hector Jonas)*, Bernard Barrow *(Leighton Siddley)*, Geraldine Fitzgerald *(Rev. Wood)*, Nell Potts *(Rachel as a Child)*

p, Paul Newman; d, Paul Newman; w, Stewart Stern (based on the novel *A Jest of God* by Margaret Laurence); ph, Gayne Rescher (Technicolor); ed, Dede Allen; m, Jerome Moross, Erik Satie, Robert Schumann; art d, Robert Gundlach; cos, Domingo Rodriguez

AAN Best Picture; AAN Best Actress: Joanne Woodward; *AAN Best Supporting Actress:* Estelle Parsons; *AAN Best Adapted Screenplay:* Stewart Stern

Woodward, Parsons, Stern (screenwriter), and the picture itself were all nominated for Oscars, and Newman and

Woodward both won awards from the New York Film Critics. While other directors were impressing with their flash and technique in the 1960s, Newman chose to make a small, understated, and very sensitive film as his directorial debut. It was sometimes halting and quite spare, but the overall effect was excellent and business was meritorious, something no one expected. Newman had trouble securing the financing and was saved by then-production chief Ken Hyman, a man with some foresight who recognized the need for this kind of story. Shot on location at various Connecticut sites, the film was a departure for Woodward, who had been made into a glamour girl in her early years and resented it.

Woodward is a lonely, bored spinster who lives with her widowed mother, Harrington. Her best friend, Parsons, makes what has to be termed a "pass" at Woodward, who decides she had better find out what men are like before she falls into a homosexual pattern. Woodward is sexually naive, frustrated, and willing to learn, so when Olson, a childhood friend, comes back to the small town to visit his parents, she is easy for him to seduce.

The film's double-word title is made more intriguing because Newman uses his and Woodward's daughter, Nell Potts, as the young Rachel; and Woodward is occasionally replaced by Potts to indicate that the child in her still remains. In the final scene, for example, as Woodward climbs on the bus to Oregon, she waves farewell to Potts, finally bidding good-bye to the child she's been. In later years, a horde of "women's pictures" would appear, but this one was the first in the cycle and one of the best. It could have been a drab, weepy story, but Stern and Newman collaborated to make it an inspiring one that proves one is never too old to change one's life.

RACKET, THE
1951 88m bw Crime ★★★★
RKO (U.S.)

Robert Mitchum (Capt. McQuigg), Lizabeth Scott (Irene), Robert Ryan (Scanlon), William Talman (Johnson), Ray Collins (Welch), Joyce MacKenzie (Mary McQuigg), Robert Hutton (Ames), Virginia Huston (Lucy Johnson), William Conrad (Turck), Walter Sande (Delaney)

p, Edmund Grainger; d, John Cromwell, Nicholas Ray; w, William Wister Haines, W.R. Burnett (based on the play by Bartlett Cormack); ph, George E. Diskant; ed, Sherman Todd; m, Paul Sawtell, Roy Webb; art d, Albert S. D'Agostino, Jack Okey; cos, Michael Woulfe

This hard-hitting melodrama was the second film adaptation of Bartlett Cormack's popular 1920s play from Howard Hughes, who released a version in 1928 and updated the story here to tie it in with the then-controversial Kefauver crime hearings, which had captured the TV viewing audience of the day. Mitchum (in a switch from his usual casting) plays a tough, honest police captain in a midwestern city who, on the eve of an important election, battles to wrest control of the city's government from crime boss Ryan.

Director Cromwell does a fine job of keeping up a lightning pace here, and elicits a great performance from Ryan, who is truly sinister in his profile of the gang boss striving to change his unalterably violent character. Mitchum is solid if not enthusiastic in his role as an honest cop, and the rest of the cast (particularly Collins and Conrad) is excellent, though Scott, while appropriately sultry and attractive, is little more than window dressing in her role. After taking over RKO in 1948, Hughes immediately scheduled THE RACKET for production, banking on the success of the 1928 film version, though the remake is more faithful to Cormack's play (in which Cromwell had appeared as an actor). The city profiled, of course, is Chicago and its corrupt politics of the 1920s. Cromwell had been directing films on and off at

RKO since 1932; this picture marked his last such assignment for the studio.

RADIO DAYS
1987 85m c Comedy ★★★½
Orion (U.S.) PG

Woody Allen (Narrator), Seth Green (Little Joe), Julie Kavner (Mother), Michael Tucker (Father), Dianne Wiest (Aunt Bea), Josh Mostel (Uncle Abe), Renee Lippin (Aunt Ceil), William Magerman (Grandpa), Leah Carrey (Grandma), Joy Newman (Ruthie)

p, Robert Greenhut; d, Woody Allen; w, Woody Allen; ph, Carlo Di Palma (Duart Color); ed, Susan E. Morse; prod d, Santo Loquasto; art d, Speed Hopkins; cos, Jeffrey Kurland

AAN Best Original Screenplay: Woody Allen; AAN Best Art Direction-Set Decoration: Santo Loquasto, Carol Joffe, Les Bloom, George DeTitta Jr.

Writer-director Woody Allen draws on his own past in this nostalgic piece, cross-cutting between the Brooklyn of his youth, in this case the Rockaway area, and the uptown life being led by radio personalities. Allen gives us a typical yet intriguing family in Rockaway. Joe (Seth Green) is the youthful protagonist who lives with his parents (Julie Kavner and Michael Tucker), grandparents (Willian Magerman and Leah Carrey), maiden aunt Bea (Dianne Wiest), uncle Abe (Josh Mostel, son of Zero), Abe's wife Ceil (Renee Lippin), and their daughter Ruthie (Joy Newman). In voice-over, Allen (who doesn't appear in the film) relates stories about members of this household. While life goes on in Brooklyn, Allen intercuts stories about radio and its personalities, many of the tales focusing on Sally White (Mia Farrow), a cigarette girl with a dreadful "Noo Yawk" accent who dreams of radio stardom. If this summary sounds disjointed, so is the film. There is no real story, just a succession of funny and nostalgic interludes. Allen presents a host of anecdotes and remembrances of things past, but one wishes it could have been slightly more cohesive. One of the joys in this picture is the soundtrack of songs of the period that will delight anyone who lived in those radio days.

RAGING BULL
1980 129m c/bw Biography/Sports ★★★★★
UA (U.S.) R

Robert De Niro (Jake LaMotta), Cathy Moriarty (Vickie LaMotta), Joe Pesci (Joey), Frank Vincent (Salvy), Nicholas Colasanto (Tommy Como), Theresa Saldana (Lenore), Frank Adonis (Patsy), Mario Gallo (Mario), Frank Topham (Toppy/Handler), Lori Anne Flax (Irma)

p, Irwin Winkler, Robert Chartoff; d, Martin Scorsese; w, Paul Schrader, Mardik Martin (based on the book by Jake LaMotta with Joseph Carter, Peter Savage); ph, Michael Chapman (Technicolor); ed, Thelma Schoonmaker; prod d, Gene Rudolf; art d, Alan Manser, Kirk Axtell, Sheldon Haber

AAN Best Picture; AA Best Actor: Robert De Niro; AAN Best Supporting Actor: Joe Pesci; AAN Best Supporting Actress: Cathy Moriarty; AAN Best Director: Martin Scorsese; AAN Best Cinematography: Michael Chapman; AA Best Film Editing: Thelma Schoonmaker; AAN Best Sound: Donald O. Mitchell, Bill Nicholson, David J. Kimball, Les Lazarowitz

RAGING BULL is an uncompromisingly brutal and emotionally devastating movie based on the life of middleweight boxing champion Jake LaMotta. The film chronicles the life of the fighter from 1941 until the mid-1960s and is chiefly concerned with the irrational and violent LaMotta's struggle to find peace within himself. Loosely based on LaMotta's autobiography and filmed in gorgeous black and white, the story begins in 1941 and follows LaMotta (Robert De Niro), who is managed by his brother, Joey (Joe Pesci), as he pursues the middleweight championship. During his rise to the crown the hostile LaMotta is distracted by both the local mafia's efforts to control his career and his romance with 15-year-old Vickie (Cathy Moriarty). Eventually LaMotta divorces his first wife to marry Vickie, but the extremely paranoid and insanely jealous boxer abuses both his wife and his brother when he unjustly suspects them of wrongdoing. LaMotta eventually wins the championship (in a bout with Frenchman Marcel Cerdan), but quickly relinquishes it to his nemesis, Sugar Ray Robinson (Johnny Barnes), who defeated LaMotta five out of the six times they met. The collapse of his boxing career coincides with the destruction of his personal life, and, estranged from both his brother and his wife, the now-bloated boxer begins the long road back to personal salvation.

Fueled by Martin Scorsese's brilliant direction and a magnificent Oscar-winning performance by De Niro—who gained nearly 50 pounds to play the older, fatter LaMotta—RAGING BULL is one of the most powerful boxing films ever made. Often unpleasant and painful to watch, the film is a no-holds-barred look at a violent man in a brutal sport, in which, amazingly, the wholly unsympathetic LaMotta attains a state of grace at the end that is inspiring. As usual, the director is examining maleness in this film, and RAGING BULL has a way of zeroing in on masculine values and codes, and how they weigh men down. The film's senseless feel for violence forces you to consider its place in the male identity—it's easier for most men to retreat into than honest emotion. Many people feel BULL was the best movie of the '80s; like the decade, it leaves a sour taste that lingers long after.

RAGTIME

1981 155m c Historical ★★★
Sunley (U.S./U.K.) PG

James Cagney *(Police Commissioner Waldo)*, Brad Dourif *(Younger Brother)*, Moses Gunn *(Booker T. Washington)*, Elizabeth McGovern *(Evelyn Nesbit)*, Kenneth McMillan *(Willie Conklin)*, Pat O'Brien *(Delmas)*, Donald O'Connor *(Evelyn's Dance Teacher)*, James Olson *(Father)*, Mandy Patinkin *(Tateh)*, Howard E. Rollins Jr. *(Coalhouse Walker, Jr.)*

p, Dino De Laurentiis; d, Milos Forman; w, Michael Weller (based on the novel by E.L. Doctorow); ph, Miroslav Ondricek (Todd-AO, Technicolor); ed, Anne V. Coates, Anthony Gibbs, Stanley Warnow; m, Randy Newman; prod d, John Graysmark; art d, Patrizia von Brandenstein, Tony Reading; chor, Twyla Tharp; cos, Anna Hill Johnstone

AAN Best Supporting Actor: Howard E. Rollins Jr.; *AAN Best Supporting Actress:* Elizabeth McGovern; *AAN Best Adapted Screenplay:* Michael Weller; *AAN Best Cinematography:* Miroslav Ondricek; *AAN Best Original Score:* Randy Newman; *AAN Best Original Song:* "One More Hour"; Randy Newman (Music & Lyrics); *AAN Best Art Direction:* John Graysmark, Patrizia Von Brandenstein, Anthony Reading, George De Titta Sr. George De Titta Jr., Peter Howitt; *AAN Best Costume Design:* Anna Hill Johnstone

Although more than $32 million was pumped into this kaleidoscopic portrait of American life in 1906, RAGTIME is too long, too splintered in its characterizations, and too much of a good thing squeezed dry. The most impressive aspect of the film is the return, after a 20-year hiatus, of top-billed Cagney, at age 81, to play a feisty NYC police commissioner.

Based on Doctorow's novel, the film balances several themes and four families—one factual, three fictional. The most compelling story is that of the infamous Thaw-White murder case, in which mad millionaire Harry K. Thaw (Robert Joy) kills famed architect Stanford White (Norman Mailer) over the affections of Thaw's showgirl wife Evelyn Nesbit

(Elizabeth McGovern). This story was better told in THE GIRL IN THE RED VELVET SWING. A second plot line follows the disintegration of an upper-class American family led by Mary Steenburgen and James Olson; their complacency is disturbed by black ragtime artist Coalhouse Walker (Howard E. Rollins Jr.), who arrives to woo a pregnant young woman living in their home. Walker's sense of dignity turns to rage when he is abused by local racists; he gathers a band of revolutionaries who are joined by Steenburgen's younger brother (Dourif), a munitions expert. Another plotline follows starving immigrant artist Patinkin, who encounters Nesbit by chance and later sets off to make his fortune in Hollywood. An exploration of the down side of the American Dream, RAGTIME is not always convincing, and under Forman's occasionally heavy-handed direction, its performances are uneven. Ambitious, but only sporadically engaging.

RAIDERS OF THE LOST ARK

1981 115m c Adventure ★★★★½
Lucasfilm (U.S.) PG

Harrison Ford *(Indiana Jones)*, Karen Allen *(Marion Ravenwood)*, Paul Freeman *(Belloq)*, Ronald Lacey *(Toht)*, John Rhys-Davies *(Sallah)*, Denholm Elliott *(Brody)*, Wolf Kahler *(Dietrich)*, Anthony Higgins *(Gobler)*, Alfred Molina *(Satipo)*, Vic Tablian *(Barranca)*

p, Frank Marshall; d, Steven Spielberg; w, Lawrence Kasdan (based on a story by George Lucas, Philip Kaufman); ph, Douglas Slocombe, Paul Beeson (Panavision, Metrocolor); ed, Michael Kahn; m, John Williams; prod d, Norman Reynolds; art d, Leslie Dilley; fx, Richard Edlund, Kit West; cos, Deborah Nadoolman; anim, John Van Vliet, Kim Knowton, Garry Waller, Lording Doyle, Scott Caple, Judy Elkins, Sylvia Keuler, Scott Marshal

AAN Best Picture; AAN Best Director: Steven Spielberg; *AAN Best Cinematography:* Douglas Slocombe; *AA Best Film Editing:* Michael Kahn; *AAN Best Original Score:* John Williams; *AA Best Art Direction:* Norman Reynolds, Leslie Dilley, Michael Ford; *AA Best Sound:* Bill Varney, Steve Maslow, Gregg Landaker, Roy Charman; *AA Best Visual Effects:* Richard Edlund, Kit West, Bruce Nicholson, Joe Johnston

The 1930s-style adventure serial was never better served than in this spectacular cliffhanger to end all cliffhangers. Indeed RAIDERS OF THE LOST ARK totally transcends its modest source material. Packed with astounding action setpieces, this movie was crafted with such polish, humor, and elan that it became an instant classic. This was the film that Spielberg made while still smarting from the massive flop of 1941, his large-scale period slapstick comedy about invasion paranoia in southern California on the eve of WWII. Spielberg described it as "work for hire" for his old pal executive producer George Lucas, but it comes off as a labor of love.

Harrison Ford went stellar with this perfect portrayal of archaeologist Dr. Indiana Jones, a distinguished scholar who sheds his spectacles to live a life of high adventure outside of the classroom. Ford's performance is an underrated but remarkable achievement; he succeeds in fully embodying a comic-book style hero without ever descending into camp. It's a brilliantly stylized portrayal that is now burned into our pop-cultural memory.

Set in 1936, the film follows Jones on his U.S. intelligence mission to find the Ark of the Covenant, which reputedly still contains the Ten Commandments. The catch is that the Ark is also being sought by agents of Adolf Hitler, who resort to all manner of treachery to stop our hero. Aided by Marion Ravenwood (Karen Allen), his tough, beautiful, hard-drinking ex-flame, Indy escapes one outrageous life-threatening situation after another in the quest that takes him from Nepal to Cairo.

Most viewers are powerless to resist the kinetic pleasures of this endlessly inventive action adventure. Some naysayers have correctly pointed out that the film gave new life to late and unlamented racial stereotypes—cowering natives of color and all that—and that initially proto-feminist Marion is all-too-soon reduced to screeching for Indy to rescue her. It is difficult to resuscitate dead genres without bringing back their offensive aspects and assumptions, but RAIDERS OF THE LOST ARK could have been far worse on these counts. This is great filmmaking, warts and all.

The action, though fairly intense, is extremely witty and playful. The violent setpieces have the imaginatively stylized quality of the progressively escalating gags in a vintage 1940s Tex Avery cartoon. Spielberg demonstrates a delightfully oblique approach to action. He also has a sharp eye for simultaneous movement on several planes of action. The supporting performances are outstanding, as are the stuntwork and special effects. Shot in Hawaii, France, Tunisia, and at Elstree Studios in England—in just 73 days for $22.8 million—this perpetual motion machine has made more than $200 million and inspired two sequels (INDIANA JONES AND THE TEMPLE OF DOOM and INDIANA JONES AND THE LAST CRUSADE).

RAILWAY CHILDREN, THE 📀

1970	108m	c	Historical/Children's ★★★
EMI	(U.K.)		G

Dinah Sheridan (*Mother*), Bernard Cribbins (*Perks Railway Porter*), William Mervyn (*Old Gentleman*), Iain Cuthbertson (*Father*), Jenny Agutter (*Bobbie*), Sally Thomsett (*Phyllis*), Peter Bromilow (*Doctor*), Ann Lancaster (*Ruth*), Gary Warren (*Peter*), Gordon Whiting (*Russian*)

p, Robert Lynn; d, Lionel Jeffries; w, Lionel Jeffries (based on a novel by E. Nesbit); ph, Arthur Ibbetson (Technicolor); ed, Teddy Darvas; m, Johnny Douglas; art d, John Clark; fx, Pat Moore, John Richardson; cos, Elsa Fennell

An effective children's film set in Britain during the Edwardian period and starring Sheridan as the wife of a British Foreign Office employee who is falsely accused of treason and imprisoned. Forced by disgrace and lack of income to move from their lush surroundings to the Yorkshire moors, Sheridan sells the idea to her children as sort of a game (they "pretend" to be poor). The kids take to their new surroundings quickly, and it is only a matter of time until they have made new friends and sunk roots in the area. The village they now live in is located near a railway, and much of their play time is spent among the trains. Among their new friends is a wealthy resident of the area who volunteers to help them clear their father's name. Well acted, nicely scripted, and produced with the right amount of heart and sentiment.

RAIN MAN 📀

1988	128m	c	Drama ★★★½
Guber-Peters	(U.S.)		R

Dustin Hoffman (*Raymond Babbitt*), Tom Cruise (*Charlie Babbitt*), Valeria Golino (*Susanna*), Jerry Molen (*Dr. Bruner*), Jack Murdock (*John Mooney*), Michael Roberts (*Vern*), Ralph Seymour (*Lenny*), Lucinda Jenney (*Iris*), Bonnie Hunt (*Sally Dibbs*), Kim Robillard

p, Mark Johnson; d, Barry Levinson; w, Ronald Bass, Barry Morrow (based on a story by Morrow); ph, John Seale (DeLuxe Color); ed, Stu Linder; m, Hans Zimmer; prod d, Ida Random; cos, Bernie Pollack

AA Best Picture; AA Best Actor: Dustin Hoffman; *AA Best Director:* Barry Levinson; *AA Best Original Screenplay:* Ronald Bass, Barry Morrow; *AAN Best Cinematography:* John Seale; *AAN Best Film Editing:* Stu Linder; *AAN Best Original Score:* Hans Zimmer; *AAN Best Art Direction-Set Decoration:* Ida Random, Linda DeScenna

Well written, smartly directed, and sensitively performed, RAIN MAN depicts the one-sided relationship between two brothers, self-centered Los Angeles hustler Charlie Babbitt (Tom Cruise) and the older Raymond (Dustin Hoffman), an autistic resident of a home for the mentally disabled. Their father's estate, worth $3 million, has been left in trust to Raymond, and figuring he can force the trustee to turn over half of the inheritance, Charlie abducts Raymond and attempts to fly him back to Los Angeles. Raymond—an *idiot savant* who can cite airline crash statistics and other bizarre facts and figures in astounding detail—refuses to fly, however, forcing the pair to drive from Cincinnati to L.A. in their father's car. As they make their way across the country, the emotionally unreachable Raymond becomes the catalyst for Charlie's transformation from a self-absorbed character incapable of intimacy into a caring and sympathetic adult. RAIN MAN rises above the banality of its concept—another buddy movie crossbred with a road picture—to become a genuinely moving and intelligent look at what it means to be human. Hoffman delivers a magnificent stunt of a performance; Cruise brings depth and conviction to the emotional development of his character; and Valeria Golino (as Charlie's girlfriend) gives the film an extra spark.

RAIN PEOPLE, THE

1969	101m	c	Drama ★★★
Warner Bros.	(U.S.)		R

James Caan (*Jimmie "Killer" Kilgannon*), Shirley Knight (*Natalie Ravenna*), Robert Duvall (*Gordon*), Marya Zimmet (*Rosalie*), Tom Aldredge (*Mr. Alfred*), Laurie Crewes (*Ellen*), Andrew Duncan (*Artie*), Margaret Fairchild (*Marion*), Sally Gracie (*Beth*), Robert Modica (*Vinny Ravenna*)

p, Bart Patton, Ronald Colby; d, Francis Ford Coppola; w, Francis Ford Coppola (based on his story "Echoes"); ph, Wilmer C. Butler (Technicolor); ed, Blackie Malkin; m, Ronald Stein; art d, Leon Ericksen

This is one of those "better luck next time" pictures—and, of course, next time meant THE GODFATHER for Coppola. He'd already directed five films without much success: the vile little TONIGHT FOR SURE!, the disastrous FINIAN'S RAINBOW, and the unjustly overlooked THE TERROR, DEMENTIA 13, and YOU'RE A BIG BOY NOW. Although studios had some confidence in his writing ability, his directorial work was seriously in question. This odd odyssey was not a hit, even though over the years it has been regarded as one of Coppola's more personal pictures and has attained a limited following. Knight plays Natalie, a childless Long Island housewife married to a decent man, Vinny (Modica). She learns she's pregnant and can't decide what to do, so she bolts, calling her husband from time to time to apologize, to tell him of the baby and her thoughts on aborting it. Eager for sexual experience, Natalie picks up Jimmie (Caan), a brain-damaged former football player whose prospective job in West Virginia falls through when his former girlfriend's father (Duncan) sees Jimmie's current state. Traveling around with Jimmie through the South and Midwest, she eventually meets Gordon (Duvall), a widowed cop, when he pulls her over for speeding in Nebraska. Natalie begins a dalliance with Gordon, but her sexual and emotional odyssey ultimately results in a tragic conflict between the two men.

Too many flashbacks spoil the narrative, and Knight's character is confused, not very sympathetic, and not clearly motivated. Caan, who had played athletes in several films, is convincingly wooden here. Shot in Colorado, Tennessee, Nebraska, New York, and West Virginia, THE RAIN PEOPLE was was somewhat ahead of its time as a "feminist" movie (even if it does punish its heroine for her desires), predating STAND UP AND BE COUNTED and AN

UNMARRIED WOMAN in the 1970s. The title is from a line by Caan that is hardly right for the retarded youth— "The rain people are made of rain, and when they cry, they disappear altogether"—whatever that means. The movie races all over the place in a hurry to illuminate the "little people" who live in quiet desperation. It's a bit too noisy for that, and yet there is enough about it to warrant attention.

RAINING STONES

1993 90m c   Comedy/Drama   *DVD*

Parallax Pictures   (United Kingdom)   ★★★½

Bruce Jones *(Bob)*, Julie Brown *(Anne)*, Gemma Phoenix *(Coleen)*, Ricky Tomlinson *(Tommy)*, Tom Hickey *(Father Barry)*, Mike Fallon *(Jimmy)*, Jonathan James *(Tansey)*, Ronnie Ravey *(Butcher)*, Lee Brennan *(Irishman)*, Karen Henthorn *(Young Mother)*

p, Sally Hibbin; d, Ken Loach; w, Jim Allen; ph, Barry Ackroyd; ed, Jonathan Morris; m, Stewart Copeland; prod d, Martin Johnson; art d, Fergus Clegg

A bittersweet working-class comedy that resonates far beyond its immediate milieu, RAINING STONES may be Ken Loach's most approachable film and, ironically, his most slyly political.

Bob (Bruce Jones), wife Anne (Julie Brown), and daughter Coleen (Gemma Phoenix) live in Manchester, where jobs are scarce and Bob is reduced to sheep-rustling with best friend Tommy (Ricky Tomlinson) to make ends meet. Coleen's first Holy Communion is approaching and Bob can't afford to buy her a dress, so he embarks on some quick-money misadventures, often with Tommy in tow, which include drain-cleaning and robbing lawn turf from an absent homeowner. Bob's van is stolen and he borrows heavily from a loan shark, but money gets squandered in the pub almost as fast as it comes in. Soon, the loan shark turns violent, with Coleen's first Communion only days away. What's a father to do? "We start off with all these big ideas," observes Anne. "I'll live and die in this flat and nobody will even know."

RAINING STONES has a cumulative power that draws you into its bleak, but never humorless, world and produces some beautiful moments of recognition. Loach avoids pat answers and stereotypes, his apparent lack of style belying a sophisticated grasp of character development and episodic narrative drive. The naturalistic acting is uniformly excellent, in tune with Loach's uncompromising vision of a world in which an uncaring political/economic system turns decent, hard-working people into scavengers who will steal from one another. RAINING STONES ends on an upbeat note, but not until Loach has illuminated one family's struggle and despair.

RAINMAKER, THE

1956 121m c   Comedy   *DVD*

Paramount   (U.S.)   ★★★

Burt Lancaster *(Starbuck)*, Katharine Hepburn *(Lizzie Curry)*, Wendell Corey *(File)*, Lloyd Bridges *(Noah Curry)*, Earl Holliman *(Jim Curry)*, Cameron Prud'Homme *(H.C. Curry)*, Wallace Ford *(Sheriff Thomas)*, Yvonne Lime *(Snookie)*, Dottie Bee Baker *(Belinda)*, Dan White *(Deputy)*

p, Hal B. Wallis; d, Joseph Anthony; w, N. Richard Nash (based on the play by N. Richard Nash); ph, Charles Lang (VistaVision, Technicolor); ed, Warren Low; m, Alex North; art d, Hal Pereira, Walter Tyler; fx, John P. Fulton; cos, Edith Head

AAN Best Actress: Katharine Hepburn; *AAN Best Score (Drama or Comedy):* Alex North

THE MUSIC MAN may have owed something to this story, since both concern confidence men who come to small towns to peddle their scams, then fall for spinsters. Nash wrote the film as a television play then expanded it to work on the Broadway stage, where it ran 124 performances with Geraldine Page in the Hepburn role and Prud'Homme as her father, under the direction of Anthony, who also did this film and, later, the musical version, "110 in the Shade." Composer North garnered an Oscar nomination, as did Hepburn, her seventh. The main problem is that the film is far too talky, and the leads are somewhat grizzled for the situation. Hepburn is a hick-town spinster in an arid area of the Southwest. (She never really convinces anyone that she's a country girl because that New England accent and her flighty mannerisms constantly intrude.) Lancaster is a brash, lively con artist who comes to the burg claiming that he can bring rain to the drought-ravaged locale for the sum of $100. He is taken into Prud'Homme's house and allowed to live in one of the outbuildings. Hepburn's brothers are Bridges, who never quite buys Lancaster's spiel, and Holliman, an oafish young man who is wooing town beauty Lime. Once Lancaster is ensconced, he begins to change things around. Hepburn is being courted, albeit reluctantly, by the town's lawman, Corey, but he doesn't seem to be able to pop the question, and time is a-wasting in her old maid life. Lancaster convinces the plain Hepburn that she is gorgeous, and once she feels that's true, her attitude about herself begins to alter. She's been told for years by everyone, mostly her brother Bridges, that she is, at best, plain, but the intrusion of Lancaster works a minor miracle on her self-confidence. She now has a duo of suitors in Lancaster and Corey, who suddenly awakens to the fact that she is a terrific woman. At the end, there is a coincidental downpour, and Lancaster, it should go without saying, takes all the credit before departing for his next conquest. Behind him, he has left a changed woman, and his visit has been the most exciting thing to happen to the tiny village in its history. Lancaster does one of his ELMER GANTRY bravura performances and was a perfect selection, although a little timeworn at 43. Hepburn was pushing 50 and Corey was seven years younger. The difference in all their ages was revealed by the close-ups and worked against the believability of the story. Still, it's a pleasant movie with more than many laughs.

RAISE THE RED LANTERN

(DA HONG DENGLONG GAOGAO GUA)

1991 125m c   Drama   ★★★★★

Era International/Salon Productions/China Film   PG

Co-Production Corporation   (China/Hong Kong)

Gong Li *(Songlian)*, Ma Jingwu *(Master Chen Zuoqian)*, He Saife, billed as He Caifei *(Meishan)*, Cao Cuifeng *(Zhuoyun)*, Jin Shuyuan *(Yuru)*, Kong Lin *(Yan'er)*, Ding Weimin *(Mother Song)*, Cui Zhigang *(Doctor Gao)*, Chu Xiao *(Feipu)*, Cao Zhengyin *(Old Servant)*

p, Chiu Fu-sheng; d, Zhang Yimou; w, Ni Zhen (from the novel *Wives and Concubines* by Su Tong); ph, Zhao Fei; ed, Du Yuan; m, Zhao Jiping; art d, Cao Jiuping, Dong Huamiao; cos, Huang Lihua

AAN Best Foreign Language Film

A masterpiece. The historical dramas of Zhang Yimou, a master "Fifth Generation" filmmaker who emerged from the reopened Beijing Film Academy during the liberal climate of the early 1980s, resonate with subtexts of repression, resistance and retribution. Though Zhang's screenplay for RAISE THE RED LANTERN (based on the 1989 novel *Wives and Concubines* by Su Tong) got a stamp of approval from the Chinese censors, the finished production was banned at home while playing to great praise abroad.

Set in a wealthy 1920s Chinese household, the tale has the timeless quality of a fable, as a lovely 19-year-old named Songlian (Gong Li), forced to set aside her academic ambitions, resignedly sells herself to a rich man who already has three wives. "Let me be a concubine," she declares. "Isn't that a woman's fate?" Songlian arrives at the ancient, sprawling palace of Master Chen (Ma Jingwu), where she is welcomed as "Fourth Sister" in the aristocrat's harem. But beneath the polite surface boils a cauldron of intrigue and hatred, as rival wives scheme to win the Master's favor from day to day. As the freshest arrival, Songlian gets the most of Chen's sexual attentions, until he's dragged away by the complaints of wife number three, Meishan (He Caifei), a onetime opera star who now craves the spotlight at home. Songlian is comforted by Second Sister, Zhuoyun (Cao Cuifeng), a kind-looking matron who is later accurately described by Meishan as having the face of the Buddah and the heart of a scorpion.

Almost all of this superbly rendered tragedy takes place within the confines of the Master's vast estate, and Zhang Yimou uses a mostly stationary camera to frame the characters within careful compositions of doorways, portals, canopies and courtyards; the severe, rigid style effectively turns the sumptuous residence into a metaphorical prison compound. As bleak as the material sounds, there is a certain sardonic humor, mostly from the spirited Meishan and even the Master himself, who's absolutely baffled as to why his spouses seem so discontented.

This sumptuously shot $1 million production was financed by Taiwanese interests through a Hong Kong intermediary, and it was Hong Kong that submitted RAISE THE RED LANTERN as its official candidate for the 1992 Academy Award for best foreign language film, a move disapproved by Beijing.

RAISIN IN THE SUN, A

1961 127m bw Drama   DVD ★★★★
Paman/Doris   (U.S.)

Sidney Poitier *(Walter Lee Younger)*, Claudia McNeil *(Lena Younger)*, Ruby Dee *(Ruth Younger)*, Diana Sands *(Beneatha Younger)*, Ivan Dixon *(Asagai)*, John Fiedler *(Mark Lindner)*, Louis Gossett Jr. *(George Murchison)*, Stephen Perry *(Travis)*, Joel Fluellen *(Bobo)*, Roy E. Glenn Sr. *(Willie Harris)*

p, David Susskind, Philip Rose; d, Daniel Petrie; w, Lorraine Hansberry (based on the play by Lorraine Hansberry); ph, Charles Lawton Jr.; ed, William Lyon, Paul Weatherwax; m, Laurence Rosenthal; art d, Carl Anderson

---

Hansberry's lovely adaptation of her 1959 Broadway hit about a black family in financial straits reunites seven of the original cast in the film version.

McNeil is the matriarch of a family living in cramped quarters on Chicago's south side (where all the location shots were done). Her husband has just died and she receives a check for $10,000 from the insurance company, quite a sizeable sum at the time. McNeil wants to get out of the ghetto and buy a decent house, then use the rest of the windfall to put her daughter through med school. But Poitier, her angry, ambitious son, has other ideas.

The performances are uniformly excellent, with Poitier illuminating the limitations placed on black men in American society and McNeil handling the role of the matriarch with unflinching emotional honesty. Look for Gossett in a small part as a black youth fixated by WASP values. Since much of the action takes place in the tiny apartment, director Petrie had to pull out all the stops to keep it from being stage-bound, and, with the help of cinematographer Lawton, he succeeded.

RAISING ARIZONA

1987 94m c Comedy   DVD ★★★
Circle (U.S.)   PG-13

Nicolas Cage *(H.I. McDonnough)*, Holly Hunter *(Edwina)*, Trey Wilson *(Nathan Arizona, Sr.)*, John Goodman *(Gale)*, William Forsythe *(Evelle)*, Sam McMurray *(Glen)*, Frances McDormand *(Dot)*, Randall "Tex" Cobb *(Leonard Smalls)*, T.J. Kuhn *(Nathan Arizona, Jr.)*, Lynne Dumin Kitei *(Florence Arizona)*

p, Ethan Coen, Mark Silverman; d, Joel Coen; w, Ethan Coen, Joel Coen; ph, Barry Sonnenfeld (Duart Color); ed, Michael R. Miller; m, Carter Burwell; prod d, Jane Musky; art d, Harold Thrasher; cos, Richard Hornung

---

The promise that was evident in BLOOD SIMPLE, the Coen brothers' remarkably assured debut, is fulfilled in RAISING ARIZONA, an entertaining, energetic, and stylish comedy about a simple but loving couple who long to be parents.

H.I. "Hi" McDonnough (Nicholas Cage) is a hopelessly inept petty crook who attempts to go straight after he marries prison officer Edwina (Holly Hunter), and they settle down in a trailer in the middle of the Arizona desert. They long for a normal family life, but are childless and unable to adopt due to Hi's criminal past. When Hi and Edwina read that the wife of wealthy furniture dealer Nathan Arizona (Trey Wilson) has given birth to quintuplets, they decide to steal one for themselves.

RAISING ARIZONA is populated with excellent performances, especially from its two leads. Cage creates a homey and thoroughly likable character who earns the respect of the audience, but Hunter is the real surprise. Appearing in her first starring role, the stage veteran displays so much energy that she forces the audience to pay attention. The supporting cast is equally impressive, particularly John Goodman and William Forsythe as a couple of escaped convicts who pay a visit to their old friend Cage. Former professional boxer Randall "Tex" Cobb is also memorable as a thoroughly bizarre and very menacing bounty hunter.

RAMBLING ROSE

1991 112m c Drama/Romance/Comedy   DVD ★★★★
Carolco (U.S.)   R

Laura Dern *(Rose)*, Robert Duvall *(Daddy Hillyer)*, Diane Ladd *(Mother Hillyer)*, Lukas Haas *(Buddy Hillyer)*, John Heard *(Willcox "Buddy" Hillyer)*, Kevin Conway *(Doctor Martinson)*, Robert Burke *(Police Chief Dave Wilkie)*, Lisa Jakub *(Doll Hillyer)*, Evan Lockwood *(Waski Hillyer)*, Matt Sutherland *(Billy)*

p, Renny Harlin; d, Martha Coolidge; w, Calder Willingham (from his novel); ph, Johnny Jensen; ed, Steveny Cohen; m, Elmer Bernstein; prod d, John Vallone; art d, Christiaan Wagener; cos, Jane Robinson

---

AAN Best Actress: Laura Dern; AAN Best Supporting Actress: Diane Ladd

---

Directed by Martha Coolidge from a screenplay by Calder Willingham based on his autobiographical novel, RAMBLING ROSE is a humorous coming of age story with a barbed central message.

When Rose (Laura Dern) becomes part of the eccentric Hillyer household in 1935, she proves more of a disruptive element than anyone could have anticipated. A tall country girl with flowing golden hair, she quickly captivates the Hillyer children, especially 13-year-old Buddy (Lukas Haas). Rose, in turn, is awed by the genteel, learned Mother (Diane Ladd) and courtly Daddy (Robert Duvall). Rose's failing is that she ... rambles. Beautiful, naive, and sexually uninhibited, she has an overriding need for emotional—and physical—affection. As the narrator (an adult Buddy, played by John Heard) observes, the result is "one damnable commotion."

Coolidge does a supremely assured job of bringing the period to life, handling her story with a charm that does not blunt the edge of its message. Dern is impeccable as a heroine whose unbridled sexuality is matched by a complete lack of guile, and Robert Duvall is superb as a Southern gentleman completely nonplussed by the combination. Lukas Haas is winning, and Diane Ladd paints a finely observed portrait of a compassionate, intellectual Southern matron.

RAMBLING ROSE deals with cultural misogyny and sexual oppression in a human, comic way accessible to all. An intelligent screenplay, deft direction, and excellent production values make this a quietly compelling gem.

RAN

DVD

1985 160m c Historical/War ★★★★★
Herald Ace/Nippon Herald/Greenwich (France/Japan) R

Tatsuya Nakadai (Lord Hidetora Ichimonji), Akira Terao (Tarotakatora Ichimonji), Jinpachi Nezu (Jiromasatora Ichimonji), Daisuke Ryu (Saburonaotora Ichimonji), Mieko Harada (Lady Kaede), Yoshiko Miyazaki (Lady Sue), Kazuo Kato (Ikoma), Masayuki Yui (Tango), Peter (Kyoami), Hitoshi Ueki (Fujimaki)

p, Masato Hara, Serge Silberman; d, Akira Kurosawa; w, Akira Kurosawa, Hideo Oguni, Masato Ide (based on "King Lear" by William Shakespeare); ph, Takao Saito, Masaharu Ueda, Asakazu Nakai; ed, Akira Kurosawa; m, Toru Takemitsu; prod d, Yoshiro Muraki, Shinobu Muraki; art d, Yoshiro Muraki; cos, Emi Wada

AAN Best Director: Akira Kurosawa; AAN Best Cinematography: Takao Saito, Masaharu Ueda, Asakazu Nakai; AAN Best Art Direction-Set Decoration: Yoshiro Muraki, Shinobu Muraki; AA Best Costume Design: Emi Wada

At age 75, Akira Kurosawa, Japan's greatest living director, created one more magnificent work that will surely stand the test of time. In RAN, Kurosawa turned to Shakespeare for inspiration—as he had in THRONE OF BLOOD nearly 30 years before—and chose to film a Japanese adaptation of "King Lear." Set in 16th-century Japan, RAN (the Japanese character for fury, revolt, and madness—chaos) begins as Hidetora Ichimonji (Tatsuya Nakadai), an aging warlord who has acquired power through 50 years of ruthless bloodshed, announces his intention to divide his kingdom among his three sons, each of whom will live at one of three outlying castles. While the elder sons thank him for the honor, the youngest calls his father senile and mad, noting—prophetically—that it will only be a matter of time until the ambitious brothers begin battling for possession of the whole domain. In the process, Hidetora and his kingdom are consigned to a tragic and spectacular end. For more than 10 years, Kurosawa wanted desperately to make RAN, and, on the strength of KAGEMUSHA's success, he was finally able to obtain funding for this, the most expensive film ever made in Japan (though the $11 million budget is small by Hollywood standards). Partly shot at two of that country's most revered landmarks (the ancient castles at Himeji and Kumamoto; the third castle was constructed of plastic and wood on the slopes of Mount Fuji), RAN is a visually stunning epic, containing some of the most beautiful, colorful, breathtaking imagery ever committed to celluloid. As he grew older, Kurosawa began to shoot his films in a more traditionally Japanese style (static takes, little camera movement, no flamboyant editing). Here, especially in the battle scenes, he adopts a detached, impassive camera, heightening the tragedy by giving the audience a godlike but powerless perspective on all the madness and folly unfolding onscreen. At the same time, Kurosawa infuses the film with deep human emotion, aided by uniformly superb performances. The work of a mature artist in complete control of his medium, RAN is a true cinematic masterwork of sight, sound, intelligence, and—most important—passion.

RANCHO DELUXE

DVD

1975 93m c Western/Comedy ★★★½
UA (U.S.) R

Jeff Bridges (Jack McKee), Sam Waterston (Cecil Colson), Elizabeth Ashley (Cora Brown), Charlene Dallas (Laura Beige),

Clifton James (John Brown), Slim Pickens (Henry Beige), Harry Dean Stanton (Curt), Richard Bright (Burt), Patti D'Arbanville (Betty Fargo), Maggie Wellman (Mary Fargo)

p, Elliott Kastner; d, Frank Perry; w, Thomas McGuane; ph, William A. Fraker (DeLuxe Color); ed, Sidney Katz; m, Jimmy Buffett; art d, Michael Haller

Frank Perry's second comedy (after DIARY OF A MAD HOUSEWIFE) is an underrated anti-western about modern-day cattle rustlers. Jack McKee (Jeff Bridges) and Cecil Colson (Sam Waterston) ply their trade with chainsaws, high-powered rifles and a pick-up truck. When they steal a steer from the ranch of John Brown (Clifton James), a newcomer who sold a profitable restaurant business in Schenectady to make it as a cattle rancher in Montana, the adventure begins. Brown is so bored with his new life that the sleuthing associated with catching the two becomes an obsession. His ranch hands, (Harry Dean Stanton and Richard Bright), no dyed-in-the-wool cowpokes themselves, make a deal with McKee and Colson to relieve Brown of a large portion of his cattle, completely oblivious to the fact that the elderly 'detective' Henry Biege (Slim Pickens) that Brown has brought to the case and his 'niece', Laura (Charlene Dallas), are not nearly as incompetent as they seem. Scripted by novelist Thomas McGuane, RANCHO DELUXE is an often hilarious look at how the vast societal upheaval of the sixties and the creeping industrialization which began at the turn of the century were changing the face of the 'old west.'

RANCHO NOTORIOUS

1952 89m c Western ★★★★
Fidelity (U.S.)

Marlene Dietrich (Altar Keane), Arthur Kennedy (Vern Haskell), Mel Ferrer (Frenchy Fairmont), Lloyd Gough (Kinch), Gloria Henry (Beth), William Frawley (Baldy Gunder), Lisa Ferraday (Maxine), John Raven (Chuck-a-Luck Dealer), Jack Elam (Geary), George Reeves (Wilson)

p, Howard Welsch; d, Fritz Lang; w, Daniel Taradash (based on the story "Gunsight Whitman" by Sylvia Richards); ph, Hal Mohr (Technicolor); ed, Otto Ludwig; m, Emil Newman; prod d, Wiard Ihnen; cos, Joe King, Don Loper

The last of Fritz Lang's three westerns, following THE RETURN OF JESSE JAMES and WESTERN UNION, RANCHO NOTORIOUS is a bizarre, strangely poetic, and highly personal ballad of a man transformed by revenge. Kennedy plays cowhand Vern Haskell who, at the film's opening, is flirting with his fiancee (Henry), who works at the general store. Soon afterwards, two outlaws hold up the store, and when Vern returns, he learns that the woman "wasn't spared anything." Vern begins a quest for revenge and eventually finds one of the killers, shot in the back by the other. The man's last words point him toward a criminal hideout, a ranch run by former barroom singer Altar Keane (Dietrich). Insinuating himself into the gang holed up at Altar's place, Vern attempts to find out which man killed his fiancee.

RANCHO NOTORIOUS combines the quintessential Lang theme of a man ruled by fate with the generic elements of the western. Although set in the West, it is not a classic western in the style of John Ford. Whereas Ford, along with other western-movie pioneers, has a sense of American myth-making, Lang is still absorbed in his German heritage, with its external, physical representation of inner turmoil. Like Lang's hero in THE BIG HEAT, Vern is a basically good man turned inside out by thoughts of revenge. In both movies, fate leads a man to express his dark side, bringing tragedy to a femme fatale (Gloria Grahame in THE BIG HEAT, Dietrich here) in the process.

Lang's experience with RKO and notorious studio head Howard Hughes was far from happy. Even though Lang was to have been consulted before any reediting was undertaken, the film was recut under producer Welsch's orders. Lang also had troubles with Dietrich, here playing an aging woman for the first time. Like her Altar Keane character, Dietrich could not accept the effects of mortality, begging cameraman Mohr to make her look as lovely as he had for 1939's DESTRY RIDES AGAIN. Lang was no angel on the set, either; by the film's end he and Dietrich were not even speaking to each other.

None of those problems, however, appear to have affected the film. Dietrich's songs and performance are superb (especially fun is her first scene, in which she rides a man, as if on horseback, in a drunken barroom contest). Her portrayal of a woman torn between two men, and between youth and old age, is a revelation, and the rest of the cast, especially Kennedy, is similarly excellent. The garish color is oddly effective in conveying the sense of gloom which hangs over so many of Lang's films. Missing from the credits was actor Lloyd Gough who, because he refused to testify before the House Un-American Activities Committee, was blacklisted and had his name removed by Hughes.

RANDOM HARVEST
DVD
1942 125m bw Drama ★★★½
MGM (U.S.)

Ronald Colman *(Charles Rainier)*, Greer Garson *(Paula)*, Philip Dorn *(Dr. Jonathan Benet)*, Susan Peters *(Kitty)*, Reginald Owen *("Biffer")*, Edmund Gwenn *(Prime Minister)*, Henry Travers *(Dr. Sims)*, Margaret Wycherly *(Mrs. Deventer)*, Bramwell Fletcher *(Harrison)*, Arthur Margetson *(Chetwynd)*

p, Sidney Franklin; d, Mervyn LeRoy; w, Claudine West, George Froeschel, Arthur Wimperis (based on the novel by James Hilton); ph, Joseph Ruttenberg; ed, Harold F. Kress; m, Herbert Stothart; art d, Cedric Gibbons, Randall Duell; chor, Ernst Matray; cos, Robert Kalloch

AAN Best Picture; AAN Best Actor: Ronald Colman; *AAN Best Supporting Actress:* Susan Peters; *AAN Best Director:* Mervyn LeRoy; *AAN Best Screenplay:* George Froeschel, Claudine West, Arthur Wimperis; *AAN Best Score (Drama or Comedy):* Herbert Stothart; *AAN Best Interior Decoration (B/W):* Cedric Gibbons, Randall Duell, Edwin B. Willis, Jack D. Moore

Amnesia, that standard movie plot device, was never used better than in this filmed adaptation of James Hilton's popular 1940 novel. The setting is England, where WWI veteran Colman is hospitalized for shell shock, having lost his memory in battle. When the armistice is declared, Colman wanders out of the hospital during a joyous celebration and meets Garson, who takes him to a country village to help him put his life back together. Although Colman is unable to regain his memory, he builds a new identity and discovers he has a talent for writing. In time, he and Garson fall in love, marry, and have a child.

The idyll ends when Colman is hit by a car: the accident restores his old memories, but wipes out his last three years with Garson. He returns to his relatives and works in the family business. After much struggle, Garson locates her husband and gets a job as his secretary (on a psychiatrist's advice, she doesn't let on who she is). Colman has a new fiancee and is embarking on a political career. But since he still fails to recognize his ex-wife...

RANDOM HARVEST is a deeply moving film, marked by superb direction of its intricate story from Mervyn LeRoy, and by the strong performances of Colman and Garson (who's better here than she was in her Oscar-winning turn the same year in MRS. MINIVER). Their scenes together are sensitive and heartfelt, giv-

ing a depth to the implausible plot that allows the proceedings to transcend soap opera. Made at a cost of $2 million, RANDOM HARVEST brought in $4.5 million at the box office, made record receipts for Radio City Music Hall, and became one of the top 25 money-making films of its year. On the strength of its success, Colman won renewed respect in Hollywood and Garson's future at MGM was assured.

RASHOMON
DVD
1950 90m bw Drama ★★★★★
Daiei (Japan)

Toshiro Mifune *(Tajomaru)*, Machiko Kyo *(Masago)*, Masayuki Mori *(Takehiro)*, Takashi Shimura *(Firewood Dealer)*, Minoru Chiaki *(Priest)*, Kichijiro Ueda *(Commoner)*, Fumiko Homma *(Medium)*, Daisuke Kato *(Policeman)*

p, Jingo Minoura; d, Akira Kurosawa; w, Shinobu Hashimoto, Akira Kurosawa (based on the short story "Yabu no Naka" and the novel *Rasho-Mon* by Ryunosuke Akutagawa); ph, Kazuo Miyagawa; m, Fumio Hayasaka; art d, So Matsuyama

AAN Best Art Direction-Set Decoration (B/W): Matsuyama, H. Motsumoto

One of the most brilliantly constructed films of all time, RASHOMON is a monument to Akira Kurosawa's greatness, combining his well-known humanism with an experimental narrative style that has become a hallmark of film history. The central portion of the film revolves around four varying points of view of the rape of a woman and the death of her husband in a forest. Set in the 11th century, the film opens with a framing device, the conversation between three men—a woodcutter (Takashi Shimura), a priest (Minoru Chiaki), and a commoner (Kichijiro Ueda)—who have taken refuge from a rainstorm under the ruins of the stone Rashomon Gate. The priest relates the details of a trial he witnessed in a prison courtyard involving the rape of Masago (Machiko Kyo) and the murder of her samurai husband Takehiro (Masayuki Mori). As he explains, the audience is shown the four main defendants: Masago; the bandit Tajomaru (Toshiro Mifune); the spirit of Takehiro, which has been conjured by a medium; and the woodcutter, who admits that he witnessed the murder. Each of their viewpoints is depicted, the "truth" changing with each new defendant's explanation. Based on two short stories by Japanese author Ryunosuke Akutagawa ("In the Grove," the inspiration for the central crime story, and "Rashomon," the basis for the framing scenes), RASHOMON is a reflection of Kurosawa at his most Eisensteinian. Here he uses a juxtaposition of shots and a varying sequence of events to tell an essentially visual story. Although the film has been described by some as being about the search for truth, it is much more than that, as the framing story hints. Like the ruins of the Rashomon Gate (the film is after all named RASHOMON and not IN THE GROVE), the humanity Kurosawa depicts is crumbling and in danger of completely collapsing. While philosophers contend there are many truths, logic asserts there is only one, and, therefore, three of the four testifying characters in this film must be lying. Since Kurosawa's interests lie chiefly in human nature (and not philosophy or narrative structure), it follows that RASHOMON is not about truth but human fallibility, dishonesty, and selfishness. Like so many Kurosawa films, RASHOMON also contains some of the most amazing performances you are likely to find anywhere, especially that of the wildly fascinating Toshiro Mifune as the bandit. The videocassette is available in both dubbed and subtitled versions.

RASPUTIN AND THE EMPRESS

1932 135m bw Historical   ★★★★
MGM (U.S.)

John Barrymore *(Prince Paul Chegodieff)*, Ethel Barrymore *(Empress Alexandra)*, Lionel Barrymore *(Rasputin)*, Ralph Morgan *(Emperor Nikolai)*, Diana Wynyard *(Natasha)*, Tad Alexander *(Alexis)*, C. Henry Gordon *(Grand Duke Igor)*, Edward Arnold *(Doctor)*, Gustav von Seyffertitz *(Dr. Wolfe)*, Anne Shirley *(Anastasia)*

p, Bernard H. Hyman; d, Richard Boleslawski, Charles Brabin (uncredited); w, Charles MacArthur; ph, William Daniels; ed, Tom Held; m, Herbert Stothart; art d, Cedric Gibbons, Alexander Toluboff; cos, Adrian

---

AAN Best Writing (Original Story): Charles MacArthur

This excellent historical epic gathers the royal family of the American stage, the only film in which the three dynamic Barrymores appeared together. A feast for the eyes, it bids a lavish farewell to the Russian imperium. An even greater treat is to see the magnificent Barrymores vie with each other for every frame of this memorable film.

Starving peasants are in the streets and revolution is in the air, but the weak Czar Nicholas II (Ralph Morgan) and his strong-willed Czarina Alexandra (Ethel Barrymore) are preoccupied with the health of their son (Tad Alexander), a hemophiliac. When the boy suffers a fall, he begins to bleed to death and his doctors are helpless. The desperate Empress hears of a mystical holy man who may save the young prince and bids him to court. Rasputin (Lionel Barrymore) hypnotizes the child and appears to save him. Thereafter, Alexandra becomes devoted to the Mad Monk, who sees an opportunity to seize power. He uses Alexandra's dependency on him to assume authority and slowly begins to take control, naming his own graft-paying cronies to high office, stealing a fortune from the public treasury, and casting a covetous eye on the older royal daughters.

Director Boleslawsky moves things along at a fair clip, while Charles MacArthur's screenplay displays deep sympathy for the royal couple and their afflicted son, but shows the revolutionaries as unthinking brutes. Not surprisingly, this stance did not endear the film to Stalin; it was banned in the USSR. This was a pet project of MGM production chief Irving Thalberg, whose inspiration it was to star the three Barrymores in the lead roles. He had no trouble signing John and assigning Lionel, who was then an MGM contract player. But Ethel, a grand dame of Broadway theater, was a different matter. With a Broadway commitment looming, she agreed to play the Empress only if the Hollywood-based production could be completed in eight weeks. Thalberg agreed and Ethel traveled to the West Coast to join her brothers in their first effort together since they had appeared in *Camille* in Baltimore, circa 1916. True to her word, Ethel marched off the set at the end of her time as stipulated by her contract, leaving Boleslawsky (who had replaced Charles Brabin) to shoot around her.

RATCATCHER

1999 94m c Drama   *DVD*   ★★★½
Les Productions Lazennec/Studio Canal Plus/BBC Films/Arts Council of England/Holy Cow Films (U.K./France)

William Eadie *(James)*, Tommy Flanagan *(Da)*, Mandy Matthews *(Ma)*, Michelle Stewart *(Ellen)*, Lynne Ramsay Jr. *(Anne Marie)*, Leanne Mullen *(Magaret Anne)*, John Miller *(Kenny)*, Thomas McTaggert *(Ryan)*, Jackie Quinn *(Mrs. Quinn)*, James Ramsay *(Mr. Quinn)*

p, Gavin Emerson; d, Lynne Ramsay; w, Lynne Ramsay; ph, Alwin Kuchler; ed, Lucia Zucchetti; prod d, Jane Morton; art d, Robina Nicholson; fx, Steve Begg; cos, Gill Horn

---

It's an overwhelmingly dreary experience, but Scottish director Lynne Ramsay's debut feature is beautifully done and a worthy addition to the canon of youth *in extremis* films that includes THE 400 BLOWS and KES.

Glasgow, the not-too-distant past. A garbagemen's strike has entered its third month, and the run-down housing block where 12-year-old James Gillespie (William Eadie) lives with his family is brimming with rotting trash and crawling with rats. The neighborhood bullies pass the time either hunting vermin with sticks, cajoling 14-year-old Margaret Anne (Leanna Mullen) into having sex, or cruising the pestilent canal that runs behind the council flats. There, one rainy afternoon, something terrible happens. James and little Ryan Quinn (Thomas McTaggart) are horsing around in the canal's muddy water when Ryan accidentally drowns. Rather than run for help, James runs home and doesn't tell a soul, not even after Ryan's body is found. Haunted by his secret, James retreats into a fantasy of a happy life in one of the shiny new homes being built amid the rolling wheat fields that lie at the end of the local bus line.

For all its harsh realism, the film flows like a dream, albeit a highly unpleasant one. Ramsay has a strong stomach when it comes to squalor but also a keen eye for unexpected, heart-stopping imagery: a white mouse tied to a red balloon that's destined for the moon; a melting ice cream cone dripping with blood. She also has a way with young nonprofessionals. Young Eadie carries the entire film, and newcomer Mullen is a heartbreaker as a young girl who's popular with the all boys for all the wrong reasons.

RAW DEAL

1948 79m bw Crime   *DVD* ★★★
Reliance/Eagle-Lion (U.S.)

Dennis O'Keefe *(Joe Sullivan)*, Claire Trevor *(Pat)*, Marsha Hunt *(Ann Martin)*, John Ireland *(Fantail)*, Raymond Burr *(Rick Coyle)*, Curt Conway *(Spider)*, Chili Williams *(Marcy)*, Richard Fraser, Whit Bissell, Cliff Clark *(Men)*

p, Edward Small; d, Anthony Mann; w, Leopold Atlas, John C. Higgins (based on a story by Arnold B. Armstrong, Audrey Ashley); ph, John Alton; ed, Al DeGaetano; m, Paul Sawtell; art d, Edward L. Ilou; fx, George J. Teague

---

A hard-hitting gangster film with lots of action, good dialog, and fine performances by all, especially Trevor as a gun moll. O'Keefe is serving time for a crime of which he was innocent. His one-time associates arranged a frame, and O'Keefe is determined to get even with them when he breaks out of jail. With the aid of Trevor, his lover and pal, O'Keefe flees prison and is on his way to wreak revenge. While inside he was visited by Hunt, a social worker; he decides that she would be a good hostage in case the cops close in, so he kidnaps her. The three begin a trip to get Burr and his gang, the men responsible for O'Keefe's stint in prison. It isn't long before O'Keefe begins to fall for Hunt, much to the jealous consternation of Trevor, who has risked her life and her freedom for O'Keefe. Hunt, a heretofore legal and solid citizen, finds this all very exciting, and when O'Keefe has a battle with Ireland, one of the thugs, and loses, O'Keefe pleads with Hunt to save him, which she does by shooting Ireland in the back. Now she's a full part of the underworld. Hunt thinks she is in love with O'Keefe, but he wants her out of this hard life, so he temporarily sends her off while he goes to execute Burr—playing a pyromaniacal part in the best Laird Cregar style. O'Keefe bursts into the hideout as Burr is experimenting with some flames, and Burr shoots O'Keefe. Then the place goes up in a conflagration, and Burr leaps out the window to escape the heat and smoke and falls to his death. As

O'Keefe is dying from the gunshot wound, Hunt holds him in her arms, and Trevor watches. A *film noir* picture in the best tradition, with fast-paced direction by Mann and superior photography by Alton. Whit Bissell (still known at the time as "Whitner") does a small role as a hood.

RAY
DVD

2004 152m c Biography ★★★
Bristol Bay Productions/Anvil Films/ PG-13
Baldwin Entertainment/Universal (U.S.)

Jamie Foxx *(Ray Charles)*, Kerry Washington *(Della Bea Robinson)*, Regina King *(Margie Hendricks)*, Clifton Powell *(Jeff Brown)*, Harry Lennix *(Joe Adams)*, Bokeem Woodbine *(Fathead Newman)*, Aunjanue Ellis *(Mary Ann Fisher)*, Sharon Warren *(Aretha Robinson)*, C.J. Sanders *(Young Ray Robinson)*, Curtis Armstrong *(Ahmet Ertegun)*

p, Howard Baldwin, Karen Baldwin, Stuart Benjamin, Taylor Hackford; d, Taylor Hackford; w, James L. White (from a story by Taylor Hackford and James L. White); ph, Pawel Edelman; ed, Paul Hirsch; m, Craig Armstrong; prod d, Stephen Altman; art d, John E. Bucklin, Scott Plauche; fx, Chris Bailey, Robert H. Cooper, Jerry Pooler; cos, Sharen Davis

AA Best Actor: Jamie Foxx; *AA Best Sound Mixer:* Scott Millan, Greg Orloff, Bob Beemer, Steve Cantamessa; *AAN Best Picture*; *AAN Best Costume Design:* Sharen Davis; *AAN Best Director:* Taylor Hackford; *AAN Film Editing:* Paul Hirsch

There are two broad schools of biographical pictures: those that use their subjects to explore larger issues and those whose primary interest is recounting the person's life story. Taylor Hackford's entertaining but cursory film about musical legend Ray Charles fits squarely into the latter category.

It begins in 1948, as 17-year-old Ray Robinson (Jamie Foxx) stands at a bus stop, waiting for the Greyhound that will take him to Seattle, where a friend has promised him a tryout at a local watering hole. When the blind boy from Alabama first takes the stage the audience assumes it's a joke, but then he tears into a Nat King Cole number that silences the jeers. Ray becomes a fixture at the club and is soon noticed by a record producer, who signs him to a recording contract and puts him on the road with a traveling band. It's on one of these trips that Ray first experiments with heroin. Tired of touring, Ray moves to New York City and meets Atlantic Records executive Ahmet Ertegun (Curtis Armstrong), under whose influence Ray records the successful "I Got a Woman." From there, Ray produces a string of hits, but his offstage life isn't quite as rosy. Ray's constant touring puts a strain on his marriage to Della (Kerry Washington), as does his affair with backup singer Margie (Regina King). He's also haunted by memories of his difficult childhood.

At two-and-a-half hours, the movie could have used some trimming, but for the most part Ray's story is briskly told and Hackford deserves credit for not shying away from the darker aspects of Charles's life. Ultimately, the real reason to see the film is for Foxx's world-caliber performance. He doesn't just impersonate Charles, he actually seems to be channeling him.

RAZOR'S EDGE, THE
DVD

1946 146m bw Drama/War ★★★★
Fox (U.S.)

Tyrone Power *(Larry Darrell)*, Gene Tierney *(Isabel Bradley)*, John Payne *(Gray Maturin)*, Anne Baxter *(Sophie Nelson)*, Clifton Webb *(Elliott Templeton)*, Herbert Marshall *(Somerset Maugham)*, Lucile Watson *(Mrs. Louise Bradley)*, Frank Latimore *(Bob MacDonald)*, Elsa Lanchester *(Miss Keith)*, Fritz Kortner *(Kosti)*

p, Darryl F. Zanuck; d, Edmund Goulding; w, Lamar Trotti (based on the novel by W. Somerset Maugham); ph, Arthur Miller; ed, J.

Watson Webb; m, Alfred Newman; art d, Richard Day, Nathan Juran; fx, Fred Sersen; chor, Harry Pilcer; cos, Charles LeMaire, Oleg Cassini

AAN Best Picture; AAN Best Supporting Actor: Clifton Webb; *AA Best Supporting Actress:* Anne Baxter; *AAN Best Interior Decoration (B/W):* Richard Day, Nathan Juran, Thomas Little, Paul S. Fox

Larry Darrell (Tyrone Power) is an idealistic youth, a former WWI pilot whose experiences in battle have caused him to question the moral values and the very fiber of his society. Returning to Chicago, Larry disturbs his high-society fiancee, Isabel (Gene Tierney), with his inexplicable urge to seek out the real meaning of life. He balks at the thought of joining the social *creme de la creme*, and instead embarks on a quest to find intellectual and spiritual freedom, journeying to Paris and Nepal, where he finds an elderly Hindu mystic who brings peace to his troubled mind and spirit. Ten years later, Larry is reunited with Isabel and his former friends, all of whom have undergone various degrees of suffering—physically, emotionally, and financially. More melodrama and romance than war film, THE RAZOR'S EDGE—based on the classic novel by Somerset Maugham—depicts a generation of people affected by war, by the senselessness of battlefield deaths and war's constant reminders of mortality. The film examines the possible futility of life, including the certain futility of war, and provides an intelligent and thoughtful counterpoint to the many films that celebrate glory in battle.

RE-ANIMATOR
DVD

1985 86m c Horror ★★★
Re-Animated (U.S.)

Jeffrey Combs *(Herbert West)*, Bruce Abbott *(Dan Cain)*, Barbara Crampton *(Megan Halsey)*, David Gale *(Dr. Carl Hill)*, Robert Sampson *(Dean Halsey)*, Gerry Black *(Mace)*, Carolyn Purdy-Gordon *(Dr. Harrod)*, Peter Kent *(Melvin the Re-Animated)*, Barbara Pieters *(Nurse)*, Ian Patrick Williams *(Swiss Professor)*

p, Brian Yuzna; d, Stuart Gordon; w, Dennis Paoli, William J. Norris, Stuart Gordon (based on the story "Herbert West, The Re-Animator" by H.P. Lovecraft); ph, Mac Ahlberg (DeLuxe Color); ed, Lee Percy; m, Richard Band; art d, Robert Burns; fx, Anthony Doublin, John Naulin; cos, Robin Burton

H.P. Lovecraft, a Rhode Island native and recluse, wrote a large number of short stories, most of which were published only in lurid pulp magazines like *Weird Tales*. He has since been acclaimed as the most important and influential writer of horror and fantasy to appear post-Poe and pre-King. Several attempts to film Lovecraft's eerie tales of monsters and madness have been made, ranging from DIE, MONSTER, DIE to THE DUNWICH HORROR. While RE-ANIMATOR fails as a faithful adaptation of Lovecraft, it is an incredibly demented movie in its own right that combines a plethora of downright disgusting grand guignol with disturbing black humor. Herbert West (Jeffrey Combs) is an intense young med student determined to make a scientific breakthrough and bring the dead back to life. He works at home on mysterious experiments and finally, using the glowing green fluid he has developed, revivifies a dead cat. The next stop is the med school morgue, where Herbert reanimates a human corpse. Of course, this and every other cadaver he brings to life becomes a bit difficult to subdue. A major-league splatterfest, RE-ANIMATOR has a number of horrifying moments, made even more macabre by the grisly humor evident in almost every unforgettable scene (the most memorable and bizarre being the sex scene with a cadaver's detached head). Perhaps the film's only drawback is the somewhat arch self-consciousness of the performers, who are constantly winking at the viewer as the horrible is defused into the safely ludicrous. Director-coscreenwriter Stuart Gordon again turned his attention to Lovecraft in FROM BEYOND.

READ MY LIPS 📀
(SUR MES LÈVRES)
2001   119m   c   Crime/Thriller   ★★★½
Sedif/Cine B/Pathe Image/France 2 Cinema/Canal +
(France)

Vincent Cassel *(Paul Angeli)*, Emmanuelle Devos *(Carla Bhem)*, Olivier Gourmet *(Marchand)*, Olivier Perrier *(Masson)*, Olivia Bonamy *(Annie)*, Bernard Alane *(Morel)*, Cèline Samie *(Josie Marchand)*, Pierre Diot *(Keller)*, Franáois Loriquet *(Jean-Francois)*, Serge Boutleroff *(Mammouth)*

p, Philippe Carcassonne, Jean-Louis Livi; d, Jacques Audiard; w, Jacques Audiard, Tonino Benacquista; ph, Mathieu Vadepied; ed, Juliette Welfling; m, Alexandre Desplat; prod d, Michel Barthèlèmy; cos, Virginie Montel

A downtrodden, near-deaf office clerk and a not-too-bright ex-con join forces to beat the system, but that's not the half of this sly, sexy French thriller.

Shy, awkward Carla Bhem (Emmanuelle Devos), whose bulky hearing aids are hidden beneath her unkempt hair, is exploited at work and at home. Carla manages to get the go-ahead to hire an assistant, and she chooses Paul Angeli (Vincent Cassel), a rough-hewn hunk who's fresh out of jail and completely unqualified. She shows him the ropes, covers for him when his parole officer (Olivier Perrier) stops by, and even finds Paul a place to live. Carla is dismayed when Paul leaves the office to tend bar at a dive called Le Rubis, whose owner, small-time crook Marchand (Olivier Gourmet), is forcing him to pay off an old debt. After a couple of days on the job, Paul sees an opportunity to make a new start by ripping off his boss, but he needs Carla's help. Carla can read lips, and the roof of the club provides a clear view into Marchand's apartment. If Carla can tell him what Marchand is saying, Paul will know when to rob the place. Bound together by mutual need and an undercurrent of simmering desire, the odd couple dive headfirst into some very murky waters.

Hailed as "Hitchcockian," this clever and very satisfying crime picture is really more "Chabrolian." Co-writer and director Jacques Audiard is less interested in formal plotting and voyeuristic imagery than in his characters' tangled motives and twisted desires. Cassel is good as hard-luck case Paul, but Devos is extraordinary: Carla's incremental blossoming is both poignant and alarming; you're never quite sure what she might do next.

REAL LIFE 📀
1979   99m   c   Comedy   ★★★½
Paramount   (U.S.)   PG

Dick Haynes *(Harris)*, Albert Brooks *(Himself)*, Charles Grodin *(Warren Yeager)*, Frances Lee McCain *(Jeanette Yeager)*, Matthew Tobin *(Dr. Howard Hill)*, J.A. Preston *(Dr. Ted Cleary)*, Mort Lindsey *(Himself)*, Joseph Schaffler *(Paul)*, Phyllis Quinn *(Donna)*, James Ritz *(Jack)*

p, Penelope Spheeris; d, Albert Brooks; w, Albert Brooks, Monica Johnson, Harry Shearer; ph, Eric Saarinen (Panavision); ed, David Finfer; m, Mort Lindsey; art d, Linda Spheeris, Linda Marder

Comedian-filmmaker Albert Brooks established himself as a major force in film comedy with this devastating satire on the interplay between the media and "real life." Brooks plays someone not unlike himself, an obnoxious documentary

filmmaker who sets out to find a "typical American family" and then film their lives for a year. He chooses an Arizona clan headed by Charles Grodin and Frances Lee McCain, who are at first enchanted with their sudden fame. But things turn sour. Normal family problems are blown up by filmmaker Brooks into crises of disastrous proportions—McCain's trip to the gynecologist, for example, becomes an expose on her doctor. Eventually the family comes apart at the seams and members stop talking to each other. Brooks desperately tries to manipulate the family members so that they will do *something* in front of the cameras. Before long, he begins to lose his grip.

REAL LIFE was inspired by the PBS television documentary "An American Family," which followed the lives of the Loud family and serendipitously documented the couple's breakup and divorce. At the time of that program's airing, critics and psychologists debated whether the presence of cameras in the household contributed to the collapse of the family—whether the documentary merely *recorded* the events or helped to shape them. REAL LIFE delivers a pointed critique of the influence of media on our lives; it is also one of the funniest looks at filmmaking ever put on screen. With REAL LIFE, Brooks pushed his way into the forefront of American comedy. Subsequent films, including LOST IN AMERICA and DEFENDING YOUR LIFE, are as insightful and funny as his first.

REAR WINDOW 📀
1954   112m   c   Thriller   ★★★★★
Paramount   (U.S.)

James Stewart *(L.B. "Jeff" Jeffries)*, Grace Kelly *(Lisa Carol Fremont)*, Wendell Corey *(Detective Thomas J. Doyle)*, Thelma Ritter *(Stella)*, Raymond Burr *(Lars Thorwald)*, Judith Evelyn *(Miss Lonely Hearts)*, Ross Bagdasarian *(Songwriter)*, Georgine Darcy *(Miss Torso)*, Sara Berner *(Woman on Fire Escape)*, Frank Cady *(Fire Escape Man)*

p, Alfred Hitchcock; d, Alfred Hitchcock; w, John Michael Hayes (based on the story "It Had to Be Murder" by Cornell Woolrich); ph, Robert Burks (Technicolor); ed, George Tomasini; m, Franz Waxman; art d, Hal Pereira, Joseph MacMillan Johnson; fx, John P. Fulton; cos, Edith Head

AAN Best Director: Alfred Hitchcock; *AAN Best Screenplay:* John Michael Hayes; *AAN Best Color Cinematography:* Robert Burks; *AAN Best Sound Recording:* Loren L. Ryder

This much-loved Hitchcock picture, based on the Cornell Woolrich story "It Had to Be Murder," is a superb example of suspense filmmaking, especially when one considers the technical limitations of its single set. Magazine photographer Stewart has a broken leg and is confined to a wheelchair in his Greenwich Village apartment, where he has nothing to do but passively sit back and watch the mundane day-to-day activities that take place in the courtyard outside his rear apartment window. His neighbors are conspicuously unconscious of their own vulnerability to Stewart's constant gaze. He watches housewives, newlyweds (the only persons who actually draw the shades on *their* rear windows), a composer in a posh apartment, a lonely woman he dubs Miss Lonely Hearts, a Broadway ballerina, and, of particular interest, Lars Thorwald (Burr). After playing the voyeur for some time, Stewart begins to suspect that Thorwald has murdered his wife. Since Stewart is immobile, he enlists the aid of Kelly, a cool, blonde fashion model (here at her loveliest and most beguiling) who, because she is desperately in love with him, agrees to do his dangerous "legwork."

This, of all Hitchcock films, is an exercise in voyeurism, in which the audience has no choice but to assume the role of voyeur. It's like being Hitchcock for 112 minutes. "Look out the window, see things you shouldn't see," says Stewart's nurse Ritter, and look out the window the viewer does, having the same single and mounting terrifying perspective as does Stewart. One of the film's early ad campaigns read, "If you do not experience delicious terror when you see REAR WINDOW, then pinch yourself—you are most probably dead."

REBECCA
1940 130m bw Thriller ★★★★
Selznick (U.S.)
DVD

Laurence Olivier *(Maxim de Winter)*, Joan Fontaine *(Mrs. de Winter)*, George Sanders *(Jack Favell)*, Judith Anderson *(Mrs. Danvers)*, Nigel Bruce *(Maj. Giles Lacy)*, C. Aubrey Smith *(Col. Julyan)*, Reginald Denny *(Frank Crawley)*, Gladys Cooper *(Beatrice Lacy)*, Philip Winter *(Robert)*, Edward Fielding *(Frith)*

p, David O. Selznick; d, Alfred Hitchcock; w, Robert E. Sherwood, Joan Harrison (based on the novel by Daphne du Maurier, adapted by Philip MacDonald, Michael Hogan); ph, George Barnes; ed, James Newcom, Hal C. Kern; m, Franz Waxman; art d, Lyle Wheeler; fx, Jack Cosgrove

AA Best Picture; AAN Best Actor: Laurence Olivier; *AAN Best Actress:* Joan Fontaine; *AAN Best Supporting Actress:* Judith Anderson; *AAN Best Director:* Alfred Hitchcock; *AAN Best Screenplay:* Robert E. Sherwood, Joan Harrison; *AA Best B/W Cinematography:* George Barnes; *AAN Best Film Editing:* Hal C. Kern; *AAN Best Original Score:* Franz Waxman; *AAN Best Interior Decoration (B/W):* Lyle Wheeler; *AAN Best Special Effects:* Jack Cosgrove (Photographic), Arthur Johns (Sound)

A landmark: Hitchcock's Oscar, his first Hollywood film and his second Daphne du Maurier adaptation in a row (JAMAICA INN preceded). REBECCA is women's gothic melo-romance, but Hitchcock makes it a film about his distrust and dislike for women. He must have enjoyed a private chuckle over the women he knew would flood theaters to see it.

Fontaine stars as the unnamed narrator and shy, young, second wife of the urbane and handsome Maxim de Winter (Olivier). They meet and fall in love while vacationing on the Riviera. Following their quick marriage, they return to Maxim's vast English estate, Manderley. His wife is introduced to an army of servants who immediately, though subtly, display hostility toward her, as they all adored Rebecca, Maxim's first wife, whose death is shrouded in secrecy. As the servants become more hostile, the second wife grows more fearful, until she finally learns what happened to Rebecca. REBECCA was a prestige project for producer David O. Selznick, who was still coming down off the high of GONE WITH THE WIND. As with that 1939 classic, Selznick surrounded REBECCA with publicity including a massive talent hunt for this film's leads. Loretta Young, Margaret Sullavan, Olivia de Havilland, Vivien Leigh (Olivier's intended bride and GONE WITH THE WIND star), and Anne Baxter were all mentioned, but it was the 22-year-old Fontaine who was ultimately selected for the part.

Depending on your own feelings, you will find Fontaine either endearing or totally maddening. Whichever, she's right in the part; and Hitchcock's relentless camera seems to luxuriate in her emotional masochism. Olivier seems oddly out of command here—perhaps he and Welles should have switched off acting chores on REBECCA and JANE EYRE. The supporting roles are rendered quite well indeed. Anderson, Sanders, and Florence Bates all reveled in nasty roles; they look delighted sharpening their talons on Fontaine's little brown wren.

REBEL WITHOUT A CAUSE
1955 111m c Drama ★★★★
Warner Bros. (U.S.)
DVD

James Dean *(Jim)*, Natalie Wood *(Judy)*, Sal Mineo *(Plato)*, Jim Backus *(Jim's Father)*, Ann Doran *(Jim's Mother)*, Corey Allen

(Buzz), William Hopper *(Judy's Father)*, Rochelle Hudson *(Judy's Mother)*, Virginia Brissac *(Jim's Grandma)*, Nick Adams *(Moose)*

p, David Weisbart; d, Nicholas Ray; w, Stewart Stern (based on Irving Shulman's adaptation of "The Blind Run," a story by Dr. Robert M. Lindner); ph, Ernest Haller (CinemaScope, Warner Color); ed, William Ziegler; m, Leonard Rosenman; prod d, William Wallace; art d, Malcolm Bert; cos, Moss Mabry

AAN Best Supporting Actor: Sal Mineo; *AAN Best Supporting Actress:* Natalie Wood; *AAN Best Motion Picture Story:* Nicholas Ray

In this powerful study of juvenile violence, Dean is riveting as a teenager groping for love from a society he finds alien and oppressive. This film forever linked Dean to the restless 1950s generation; even though the indicted parents are caricatures, it's the best of its kind. Dean is Jim, a troublemaker who has caused his parents to move from one town to another before settling in L.A. Much of Jim's problem stems from the smothering but superficial love he receives from his domineering mother (Doran) and weak-willed father (Backus). Waiting at the police station after being picked up for being drunk and disorderly, he notices Judy (Wood), a girl taken in for walking the streets after curfew, and Plato (Mineo), a disturbed rich kid brought in for killing a litter of puppies. Entering his new high school the next day, Jim spots Judy and asks her for a date. She rejects him and drives off with her hot-rodding, black leather-jacketed boyfriend Buzz (Allen). Jim and Buzz later get into a knife fight, and Jim finally accepts Buzz's challenge in which both boys drive cars at breakneck speed to the edge of a cliff, diving out before they go over the edge. Whoever jumps out first is, of course, considered a coward. The game has surprising results.

The mundane plot is somehow made forceful in this directorial gem. Perfectionist director Ray spent hours researching hundreds of teenage police cases before filming. Transcending what might have been merely a teen exploitation film, REBEL draws heavily upon the presence of the intense and fascinating Dean. The young actor's appearance here electrified audiences, especially teenagers, who identified with this powerful symbol of their alienated generation. There is much of Marlon Brando's character from THE WILD ONE (1953), and critics accused Dean of mimicking Brando's brooding, mumbling delivery, but Dean was later recognized as an actor of singular stature. Wood and Mineo, although fine in their roles, serve mainly as dramatic foils for Dean's brooding. Many adults saw the film as promoting violence; with this picture the clean-cut juvenile ideal of yore moved into the adult world of film noir. Warners executives initially proposed, of all people, Tab Hunter and Jayne Mansfield (it would have been a classic, but of another kind). Ray, however, insisted upon Dean and Wood. He had been impressed by Dean's work in EAST OF EDEN, and drove the actor mercilessly on the set.

The tragedy of the film was relived offscreen, as all three principals died prematurely. Mineo was murdered in West Hollywood. He became one of the stars of a chic gay set and spent money crazily on clothes, fast cars, and even a $250,000 estate for his parents in Long Island. On the eve of the Academy Awards, he was so convinced that he would win for REBEL that he gave a party at which a huge banner was strung across the facade of his home reading: "Congratulations, Sal!" He didn't win, and the banner was yanked down and burned before dawn the next day. When Mineo was murdered in 1976, little was left of his fortune. On the wall, however, in an expensive frame, was a prized possession: a poster for REBEL WITHOUT A CAUSE ironically captioned: "Teenage terror torn from today's headlines."

Wood drowned in a still-mysterious accident while boating off Catalina Island with her husband, Robert Wagner, and Christopher Walken. Dean himself was killed in a perverse replay of the "chickie run" in REBEL, speeding at more than 100 mph in a racing car on a public highway in California.

Besides killing himself, he seriously injured two other people. Only two hours before his death, Dean was given a ticket for driving 75 mph in a 45 mph zone. "So what?" he responded, before gunning his car down the road toward doom.

RECRUIT, THE
DVD
2003 115m c   Spy/Thriller
★★★
Spyglass Entertainment/Touchstone   (U.S.)
PG-13

Al Pacino *(Walter Burke)*, Colin Farrell *(James Clayton)*, Bridget Moynahan *(Layla)*, Gabriel Macht *(Zack)*, Mike Realba *(Ronnie)*, Dom Fiore *(Instructor #1)*, Karl Pruner *(Dennis Slayne)*, Ron Lea *(Dell Rep—Bill Rudolph)*, Jeanie Calleja *(Co-Ed #1)*, Jessica Greco *(Brunette at Blue Ridge)*

p, Jeff Apple, Gary Barber, Roger Birnbaum; d, Roger Donaldson; w, Mitch Glazer, Roger Towne, Kurt Wimmer; ph, Stuart Dryburgh; ed, David Rosenbloom; m, Klaus Badelt; prod d, Andrew McAlpine; art d, Dennis Davenport; fx, Kaz Kobielski; cos, Beatrix Aruna Pasztor

Slick, spare, and coolly entertaining, even if there's less to the game than meets the eye.

MIT computer cryptography genius James Clayton (Colin Farrell) is a hotshot with a future and a flaw: the gaping hole in his psyche left by the mysterious death of his father, a globe-trotting Shell Oil executive. James tries to fill the space with two-fisted drinking and flashy feats of technical prowess, and his senior programming project has corporate recruiters scrambling to sign him up. James also proves dangerously vulnerable to surrogate father figures like enigmatic Walter Burke (Al Pacino), who offers James an interesting career alternative: espionage. Burke slyly implies that James's late father was with the Company, and James takes the bait. He enters CIA boot camp at "the Farm," an isolated facility in Langley, VA, where Burke teaches recruits to lie, cheat, and steal in the name of patriotism. James aces one test after another, strikes extracurricular sparks with sultry spy-to-be Layla (Bridget Moynahan), and appears headed for a bright future in black ops. But surprise, surprise: Nothing is what it seems, and James quickly finds himself enmeshed in a high-stakes game of deception.

Since THE DEVIL'S ADVOCATE, Pacino's performances all carry a whiff of sulfur, and his presence here ensures that the mephistophelean machinations appear more plausible than they otherwise might. And Farrell is up to balancing Pacino's bluster; he not only gives good glower, but he undermines it with a hint of unpredictable insecurity. Even conventional material can be galvanized by well-matched performers battling for the spotlight.

RED
DVD
(TROIS COULEURS: ROUGE)
1994 100m c   Drama
★★★★
Marin Karmitz Productions/Tor Film Studios/
R
CAB Productions   (France/Poland/Switzerland)

Irene Jacob *(Valentine)*, Jean-Louis Trintignant *(Judge Joseph Kern)*, Frederique Feder *(Karin)*, Jean-Pierre Lorit *(Auguste)*, Samuel Le Bihan *(The Photographer)*, Marion Stalens *(Veterinary Surgeon)*, Teco Celio *(Barman)*, Bernard Escalon *(Record Dealer)*, Jean Schlegel *(Neighbor)*, Elzbieta Jasinska *(Woman)*

p, Marin Karmitz, Gerard Ruey; d, Krzysztof Kieslowski; w, Krzysztof Kieslowski, Krzysztof Piesiewicz; ph, Piotr Sobocinski; ed, Jacques Witta; m, Zbigniew Preisner; prod d, Claude Lenoir; cos, Corinne Jorry

AAN Best Director: Krzysztof Kieslowski; *AAN Best Original Screenplay:* Krzysztof Piesiewicz, Krzysztof Kieslowski; *AAN Best Cinematography:* Piotr Sobocinski

RED, the final film in Krzysztof Kieslowski's THREE COLORS trilogy, shrewdly weaves together the disparate lead characters from all three films, while telling its own moving and clever tale.

RED takes place in contemporary Carouge, a suburb of Geneva, where several residents are united by fate. One night, a young model, Valentine (Irene Jacob), accidentally hits a dog while driving home from a fashion show. She takes the wounded animal to the home of its owner (Jean-Louis Trintignant), a reclusive retired judge who likes to spy on his neighbors by using an elaborate phone-tapping system. Meanwhile, one of the judge's neighbors and spying victims, weather forecaster Karin (Frederique Feder), cheats on her boyfriend, Auguste (Jean-Pierre Lorit), a Swiss law student.

Many film critics were shocked (and a few were skeptical) when the 53-year old Krzysztof Kieslowski announced at Cannes in 1993 that RED would be his final film. While RED lands tonally somewhere between the serious, enigmatic BLUE and the lighter but more eccentric WHITE, the three films together constitute a humanistic statement about the need for connection. In RED, Kieslowski underscores his theme with bold, often humorous cinematic brushstrokes that challenge the inherent sentimentality of the project.

RED is a superb European co-production, from the touching performances by Jacob and Trintignant, to the restless, roving camerawork by Piotr Sobocinski, to the stunning production design by Claude Lenoir. Academy rules disqualified it from competing for the Oscar for Best Foreign Language Film, since its multi-national participants did not meet country-of-origin guidelines (perhaps in reaction, Academy members awarded Kieslowski with a Best Director nomination).

RED BADGE OF COURAGE, THE
DVD
1951 69m bw War/Western
★★★★★
MGM   (U.S.)

Audie Murphy *(Henry Fleming the Youth)*, Bill Mauldin *(Tom Wilson the Loud Soldier)*, Douglas Dick *(Lieutenant)*, Royal Dano *(Tattered Man)*, John Dierkes *(Jim Conlin the Tall Soldier)*, Arthur Hunnicutt *(Bill Porter)*, Andy Devine *(Fat Soldier)*, Robert Easton *(Thompson)*, Smith Ballew *(Captain)*, Glenn Strange *(Colonel)*

p, Gottfried Reinhardt; d, John Huston; w, John Huston, Albert Band (based on the novel by Stephen Crane, adapted by Band); ph, Harold Rosson; ed, Ben Lewis; m, Bronislau Kaper; art d, Cedric Gibbons, Hans Peters

John Huston always insisted that this Civil War battle picture examining the fine line between cowardice and bravery, "could have been" his greatest film, and certainly it is among the director's best, despite the tampering of studio executives. Audie Murphy, the most decorated hero of WWII, *is* Henry Fleming, a youth who joins the Union army and grows restless waiting for the orders that will take him into battle. When news finally comes that his unit is to join others for an impending battle, he turns braggart. But faced with the enemy, Murphy runs in terror, only to confront his fear later and return to his unit for another battle. Huston's direction is vivid in every scene; the film's battle sequences, however, are its most impressive element. In more pensive moments, THE RED BADGE OF COURAGE is a moving study of Americans fighting Americans, and the reluctance many of them bring to this awful task. Much of the credit for the overall visual effect of the film goes to cameraman Harold Rosson, who lends it a gritty, hardscrabble feel, marvelously capturing the period. Huston left the production immediately after its completion to fly across the world to make THE AFRICAN QUEEN, leaving his film in the hands of studio chiefs who cut it as they saw fit. They removed much of the director's questioning of the necessity for warfare (unacceptable during the Cold War), adding narration by James Whitmore and reducing the running time to a scant 69 minutes. Because the film didn't play well with premiere audiences, MGM sent it out without fanfare, offering it as a second feature on double bills—hardly a way to recoup production costs. Audiences failed to identify with the film's grim realism and its mostly unknown cast, and the classic Crane story wasn't enough of a draw to insure box-office success. Huston maintained that the movie as he filmed it was one of his favorites, and in the 1970s an attempt was made to revive the uncut version. To Huston's knowledge, however, a print of his original cut no longer existed, so the idea was dropped.

RED DESERT   DVD
(IL DESERTO ROSSO)
1964 116m c   Drama   ★★★★★
Film Duemila/Federiz/Francoriz   (France/Italy)

Monica Vitti *(Giuliana)*, Richard Harris *(Corrado Zeller)*, Carlo Chionetti *(Ugo)*, Xenia Valderi *(Linda)*, Rita Renoir *(Emilia)*, Aldo Grotti *(Max)*, Valerio Baroleschi *(Valerio)*, Giuliano Missirini *(Workman)*, Lili Rheims *(Workman's Wife)*, Emanuela Paola Carboni *(Girl in Fable)*

p, Antonio Cervi; d, Michelangelo Antonioni; w, Michelangelo Antonioni, Tonino Guerra; ph, Carlo Di Palma (Eastmancolor); ed, Eraldo Da Roma; m, Giovanni Fusco, Vittorio Gelmetti; art d, Piero Poletto; fx, Franco Freda; cos, Gitt Magrini

A masterpiece of color cinematography, RED DESERT uses its carefully rendered color scheme to heighten the emotional impact of Michelangelo Antonioni's portrayal of the alienating effect of the modern world on one woman. Giuliana (an atypically brunette Monica Vitti in a marvelous performance) lives in the northern Italian town of Ravenna with her husband, Ugo (Carlo Chionetti), a factory engineer who fails to appreciate the depth of her despair, and with her young son, Valerio (Valerio Bartoleschi), upon whom she dotes. The city's grim industrial landscape weighs heavily on Giuliana. Corrado (Richard Harris), who has come to recruit workers for a South American project, is attracted to her and understands her depression, realizing that the auto accident ostensibly responsible for her malaise was really a suicide attempt. Giuliana's struggle to come to terms with her environment is not easily resolved. As the film ends and her son asks her why birds don't fly through the poisonous yellow smoke of factory, she is able to tell him it's "because they have learned to fly around it," illustrating the separate peace she must make with technology.

An extremely disturbing film, RED DESERT captures a rare beauty that extends the boundaries of film art in its use of color and setting. In attempting to depict Giuliana's perception of the destructive influence of technology on the natural environment, Antonioni went so far as to enhance the bleakness of his industrial wasteland by literally painting the marshlands gray, and Giuliana's sense of isolation is further reenforced by a frightening electronic soundtrack. Not an easy film to watch because of its very deliberate pacing, but well worth the effort.

RED DRAGON   DVD
2002 126m c   Thriller   ★★½
De Laurentiis Productions/MGM/Mikona   R
Productions/Universal   (U.S./Germany)

Anthony Hopkins *(Hannibal Lecter)*, Edward Norton *(Will Graham)*, Ralph Fiennes *(Francis Dolarhyde)*, Harvey Keitel *(Jack Crawford)*, Emily Watson *(Reba McClane)*, Mary-Louise Parker *(Molly Graham)*, Philip Seymour Hoffman *(Freddy Lounds)*, Anthony Heald *(Dr. Chilton)*, Ken Leung *(Lloyd Bowman)*, Frankie Faison *(Barney)*

p, Martha De Laurentiis, Dino De Laurentiis; d, Brett Ratner; w, Ted Tally (based on the novel by Thomas Harris); ph, Dante

Spinotti; ed, Mark Helfrich; m, Danny Elfman; prod d, Kristi Zea; art d, Steve Saklad; fx, Kenneth D. Papiot; cos, Betsy Heimann

A nearly scene-for-scene remake of Michael Mann's hypnotic MANHUNTER, this prequel to THE SILENCE OF THE LAMBS and HANNIBAL offers fans heaping helpings of Anthony Hopkins's popular serial-killer schtick.

FBI agent Will Graham (Edward Norton) has a gift for stalking psychopaths and has been consulting with psychiatrist, bon vivant, and gourmet cook Hannibal Lecter (Hopkins) on a particularly difficult case. When Will suddenly realizes Lecter himself is the killer, a struggle ensues, and both are grievously wounded. Lecter winds up in a maximum-security psychiatric hospital, while a mentally shaken Graham retires to Florida to live quietly with his wife, Molly (Mary-Louise Parker), and their small son. Flash-forward to the mid-'80s: Will is lured back into the game by his old boss, Jack Crawford (Harvey Keitel), who needs help finding the "Tooth Fairy," a savage killer who's murdering entire families on a monthly basis. As the pursuers ramp up their investigation, their prey (Ralph Fiennes) is sinking deeper into a swamp of murderous delusions. The link between the hunters and the hunted is Lecter, who's corresponding with the killer and playing head games with Graham.

Though Lecter is a minor character in the novel, screenwriter Ted Tally and director Brett Ratner beef up his role to obscene proportions. Who cares if Hopkins's overripe delivery and Grand Guignol tomfoolery turn Lecter's every insinuating remark into a laugh line? Fans eat it up, reveling in the ghoulish giggles. Though truer to the source in some details, this workmanlike version of Harris's 1981 novel never approaches the seductive spookiness of MANHUNTER, and without the top-notch cast it would be indistinguishable from hundreds of pedestrian serial-killer pictures that clog video store shelves.

RED RIVER   DVD
1948 125m   bw   Western   ★★★★★
UA   (U.S.)

John Wayne *(Tom Dunson)*, Montgomery Clift *(Matthew Garth)*, Joanne Dru *(Tess Millay)*, Walter Brennan *(Groot Nadine)*, Coleen Gray *(Fen)*, John Ireland *(Cherry Valance)*, Noah Beery Jr. *(Buster McGee)*, Harry Carey *(Mr. Millville)*, Harry Carey Jr. *(Dan Latimer)*, Paul Fix *(Teeler Yacy)*

p, Howard Hawks; d, Howard Hawks; w, Borden Chase, Charles Schnee (based on the novel *The Chisholm Trail* by Borden Chase); ph, Russell Harlan; ed, Christian Nyby; m, Dimitri Tiomkin; art d, John Datu Arensma; fx, Don Steward

AAN Best Motion Picture Story: Borden Chase; *AAN Best Film Editing:* Christian Nyby

There have been many classic westerns but this Hawks masterpiece certainly ranks among the best of the genre. Along with Ford's MY DARLING CLEMENTINE, it's probably the best of all the 1940s westerns—an unforgettable sweeping spectacle with the kind of grandeur few westerns achieved.

Wayne, as Tom Dunson, is shown as a young, determined man at the opening of RED RIVER, taking his wagon out of the line of a train heading west. He and his companion Groot (Brennan) intend to head south, toward Texas and the Red River, leaving behind Tom's sweetheart Fen (Gray). When Tom and Groot see black smoke trailing behind them in the distance, they know that Indians have attacked the wagon train, but the two men must soon deal with an attack on their own wagon. The next day they find young Matthew Garth (Micky Kuhn), a survivor from the wagon train massacre, and take him along on their journey to Texas. Dunson eventually lays claim to a substantial expanse of land, successfully defeating a wealthy Mexican who also claims the territory. Years pass, and Tom

Dunson owns a sprawling cattle empire. Matthew (now played by Clift) has fought in the Civil War and has returned to become Tom's right-hand man. Needing cash, Wayne decides to drive a herd of cattle north and sell them. But he doesn't take the advice of Matt's friend, hired gun Cherry Valance (Ireland), and pushes his herds through a painfully difficult route. Men start deserting him, but Tom mercilessly drives both his crew and his cattle on. Matthew is unable to confront his father figure for a long time, but an eventual showdown is inevitable.

Hawks fills every frame of this movie with action and drama. Borden Chase, author of the original novel, always resented the changes Hawks made to his story (especially the ending), but the plot and characterization are steady and strong nonetheless. Wayne gives a terrific performance, certainly one of the best of his career, and Clift matches him all the way, Matthew's sensitive but determined manner a perfect counterpoint to Dunson's ruthlessness. It was Hawks who insisted that the marvelous Brennan remove his false teeth for the running gag with Chief Yowlachie; at first the 42-year-old balked at the idea, but he quickly remembered that it was Hawks who had expanded his Oscar-winning role in COME AND GET IT. All of the supporting players, especially Ireland, Beery, the Careys, and Fix, are memorable, and Dru firmly joins the ranks of the strong women who invade a man's world in Hawks's films. Harlan's photography is stunning, sweeping through the horizonless plains and covering the vast territory the cowboys must travel in their odyssey: storms, rivers, canyons, distant buttes all encompassed beautifully. Matching the elegance of the cinematography is Tiomkin's stirring score.

At this point in his career, Hawks was already an established master of the directorial craft. His work had included comedies (HIS GIRL FRIDAY), war films (AIR FORCE), and mysteries (THE BIG SLEEP), all classics. This was his first western, and he quickly exhibited his mastery of that genre as well as he once again considered the status of the male hero and the bonding he makes with others in the name of professionalism. RED RIVER, which would gross almost $5 million in its initial release, was seen by the public and critics alike as a classic, and it remains so today.

RED ROCK WEST   DVD

1993 98m   c   Crime/Drama   ★★★½
Black Crow Productions/Propaganda Films   R
(U.S.)

Nicolas Cage (Michael Williams), Dennis Hopper (Lyle), Lara Flynn Boyle (Suzanne Brown), J.T. Walsh (Wayne Brown), Craig Reay (Jim), Vance Johnson (Mr. Johnson), Robert Apel (Howard), Bobby Joe McFadden (Old Man), Dale Gibson (Kurt), Ted Parks (Cashier)

p, Sigurjon Sighvatsson, Steve Golin; d, John Dahl; w, John Dahl, Rick Dahl; ph, Marc Reshovsky; ed, Scott Chestnut; m, William Olvis; prod d, Robert Pearson; art d, Don Diers; fx, Frank Ceglia; cos, Terry Dresbach

One of the more successful entries in the crowded ranks of early '90s neo-noir thrillers, RED ROCK WEST is the tale of a hapless drifter caught in a web of corruption in a remote western town. It offers suspense, wit, genuine surprises, and a trio of top-notch performances.

Hard-luck case Michael (Nicolas Cage) finds himself broke in the town of Red Rock, where bar owner Wayne Brown (J.T. Walsh) mistakes him for "Lyle from Dallas," whom he's hired for a job. Eager for work, Michael plays along with the misunderstanding, only to find out he's being offered $10,000 to murder Wayne's wife, Suzanne (Lara Flynn Boyle). Michael informs Suzanne of Wayne's intentions, whereupon she doubles the money offered if Michael will turn around and kill Wayne. Michael takes the money and tries to run, but finds himself trapped in the inevitable web of

violence, corruption, and double-dealing, which only gets worse when the real Lyle from Dallas (Dennis Hopper) arrives on the scene.

Released directly to video in 1993, RED ROCK WEST surfaced theatrically in 1994, thanks to the enthusiasm of one San Francisco exhibitor and a handful of critics. A cleverly plotted drama of infidelity, greed, and bad luck, it's truer to the spirit of classic film noir than many of the rival offerings released at about the same time (DREAM LOVER, CHINA MOON, etc.). Cage is the near-perfect embodiment of a modern-day noir hero and the rest of the cast is equally fine. There's hardly a false note in a script that stands out for its structure and consistency, and the story never stops twisting and turning. The result is stylish, suspenseful and satisfying.

RED SHOES, THE   DVD

1948 133m   c   Dance   ★★★★★
Archers   (U.K.)

Anton Walbrook (Boris Lermontov), Moira Shearer (Victoria Page), Marius Goring (Julian Craster), Leonide Massine (Grischa Ljubov), Robert Helpmann (Ivan Boleslawsky), Albert Basserman (Sergei Ratov), Esmond Knight (Livy), Ludmilla Tcherina (Irina Boronskaja), Jean Short (Terry), Gordon Littman (Ike)

p, Michael Powell, Emeric Pressburger; d, Michael Powell, Emeric Pressburger; w, Michael Powell, Emeric Pressburger, Keith Winter; ph, Jack Cardiff (Technicolor); ed, Reginald Mills; m, Brian Easdale; art d, Hein Heckroth, Arthur Lawson; chor, Robert Helpmann; cos, Hein Heckroth

AAN Best Picture; AAN Best Motion Picture Story: Emeric Pressburger; AAN Best Film Editing: Reginald Mills; AA Best Score (Drama or Comedy): Brian Easdale; AA Best Art Direction-Set Decoration (Color): Hein Heckroth, Arthur Lawson

Magical. Although THE RED SHOES is the ultimate ballet film, you don't have to be a balletomane to enjoy this backstage love story distinguished by glorious dancing, superb acting, and masterful direction. After the successful staging of a new ballet, impresario Boris Lermontov (Walbrook, obviously modeled on Serge Diaghilev) admits two new members to his company: Victoria Page (Shearer), a gifted young ballerina, and Julian Craster (Goring) an equally talented composer. After Julian acquits himself well as an arranger, Boris gives him a chance to collaborate on a new ballet, "The Red Shoes," with Victoria. A breathtaking 20-minute ballet based on Hans Christian Anderson's story about a pair of magical shoes that permit their wearer to dance gloriously but tragically prevent her from stopping, it brings great acclaim to both Julian and Victoria, who have fallen in love. When Julian leaves the company, Victoria follows, marrying him over the objections of the jealous Boris, who avers that she is ruining her brilliant future. Owning the rights to "The Red Shoes," Boris prevents her from dancing her greatest role until, much later, he gives her one more opportunity to perform in Monaco. Doing so, however, means she will miss the premiere of Julian's new work. The three principals confront one another just before the performance as the film builds to its memorable climax.

THE RED SHOES began as a Pressburger script commissioned by producer Alexander Korda for wife Merle Oberon, whose dancing was to have been done by a double. Pressburger and collaborator Powell then bought the script back from Korda and co-helmed this extraordinary tale of romance and artistic obsession. According to Lermontov, there is hardly the time to be both a ballerina and a loving wife. While some may quibble with this, the film's tension becomes such that you totally understand why dancing or composing becomes the most important thing in the world to those gifted and dedicated enough to do them. The parallels between Victoria's story and that of the ballet are obvious without being too heavy-handed. The ballet, meanwhile, is so engrossing that it flies breathlessly by. Full of audacious lighting, dance modernisms and swirling plastic, it is gloriously unafraid of its own pretensions. The always impassioned but usually more subdued Walbrook does a magnificent job essaying the driven impresario, and the unusual-looking Goring is convincing and compelling as well. Shearer, whose gorgeous red hair is beautifully rendered by Cardiff's opulent Technicolor photography, was a Sadler's Wells ballerina who proved to be a much better actress than anyone had dreamed. This bewitching performer covers the emotional gamut quite skillfully and would ever after be identified with this role. Praise should also go to the other dancers in the cast—Massine, Tcherina, and Helpmann (who also did the choreography). They all perform with great assurance and grace, onstage or off. The film's backstage detail remains intoxicating and when it comes to the more melodramatic aspects of the film, Powell and Pressburger let the naysayers be damned.

RED SORGHUM
(HONG GAOLIANG)
1987 91m   c   Drama   ★★★★
Xi'an   (China)

Gong Li (Nine, the Grandmother), Jiang Weng (Yu, the Grandfather), Jiu Ji (Their Son), Ji Cun Hua (Sanpao, the Bandit Chief), Teng Rujun (Luohan), Cui Cun-hua

d, Zhang Yimou; w, Chen Jianyu, Zhu Wei, Mu Yan; ph, Gu Changwei; ed, Du Yuan; m, Zhao Jiping; prod d, Yang Gang

A devastating first feature from Zhang Yimou, one of the "Fifth Generation" of Chinese filmmakers, previously known as the photographer of Chen Kaige's THE BIG PARADE and YELLOW EARTH and as the lead actor in Wu Tianming's OLD WELL. RED SORGHUM won the Golden Bear at the Berlin Film Festival and was acclaimed at the New York Film Festival, marking a new level of Western interest in Chinese cinema. The film opens in the 1930s, an unseen narrator informing us that this story is about his grandparents. The grandmother (Gong Li) is a pretty 18-year-old whose name means "Nine," called thus because she was the ninth child, born on the ninth day of the ninth month. Sold in exchange for a donkey, Nine is prepared for a wedding to a leprosy-infected winemaker. When her wedding party is attacked by a masked bandit, the bandit tries to rape the young woman, but the chair-bearers, led by the strong Yu (Jiang Weng), attack and kill him. Later, before the wedding, Nine and Yu make love in the sorghum fields, and the leprous winemaker is found murdered. Nine takes charge of the distillery, marries Yu and eventually has a son. China is in the midst of war, and invading Japanese soldiers have recruited the winemakers to trample the fields to make way for a new road. The Chinese are treated savagely by the Japanese; at the close, a solar eclipse turns the sky and the sorghum field a deep red.

Although the visual style of RED SORGHUM is one of resounding natural beauty—wide-screen horizon shots, flowing sorghum fields, heavenly sunsets—and the directorial style invokes myth and legend, the film does incorporate a certain level of realism. Shown in great detail are the distilling of the sorghum, the preparation of an ox-head meal at the butcher's, the trampling of the fields, and the bloody butchering of an ox during the Japanese attack—all of which contrast with the sense of fable Zhang Yimou creates. While the film essentially seems a sentimental ballad to the director's grandparents (and to their generation), RED SORGHUM is also a documentary on the color red—the red of sorghum, wine, a bridal robe, blood, the Communist victory, solar eclipses, and camera filters.

Some of RED SORGHUM's best moments come from the violent yoking together of moments of humor and pathos. The male bearers transporting the young bride-to-be, for example, sing a raucous, vulgar song and make her trip as bumpy as possible, while the poor Nine looks alter-

nately sick and suicidal. When the men hear her terrible sobbing from inside and realize their mistake, though, they carry on ceremoniously. Much of the film's humor comes from Jiang Weng, a large man, bare-chested and bald, who recalls some of Toshiro Mifune's clownish antics. Gong Li's character is equally compelling—a powerful, independent woman who drinks and works like a man but who has a coy, girlish sexuality.

REDS
1981 200m   c   Historical/Biography/War   ★★★½
Paramount   (U.S.)   PG

Warren Beatty (John Reed), Diane Keaton (Louise Bryant), Edward Herrmann (Max Eastman), Jerzy Kosinski (Grigory Zinoviev), Jack Nicholson (Eugene O'Neill), Paul Sorvino (Louis Fraina), Maureen Stapleton (Emma Goldman), Nicolas Coster (Paul Trullinger), M. Emmet Walsh (Speaker at the Liberal Club), Ian Wolfe (Mr. Partlow)

p, Warren Beatty; d, Warren Beatty; w, Warren Beatty, Trevor Griffiths; ph, Vittorio Storaro (Technicolor); ed, Dede Allen, Craig McKay; m, Stephen Sondheim, Dave Grusin; prod d, Richard Sylbert; art d, Simon Holland; cos, Shirley Russell

AAN Best Picture; AAN Best Actor: Warren Beatty; AAN Best Actress: Diane Keaton; AAN Best Supporting Actor: Jack Nicholson; AA Best Supporting Actress: Maureen Stapleton; AA Best Director: Warren Beatty; AAN Best Original Screenplay: Warren Beatty, Trevor Griffiths; AA Best Cinematography: Vittorio Storaro; AAN Best Film Editing: Dede Allen, Craig McKay; AAN Best Art Direction: Richard Sylbert, Michael Seirton; AAN Best Costume Design: Shirley Russell; AAN Best Sound: Dick Vorisek, Tom Fleischman, Simon Kaye

Produced, directed, and cowritten by Warren Beatty, who also stars as radical journalist John Reed, REDS is a sprawling yet highly personal epic. Focusing on Reed's tempestuous relationship with feminist Louise Bryant (Diane Keaton), the $45-million production also encompasses a capsule history of the American Left in the early 20th century and depicts the Russian Revolution, which Reed chronicled in Ten Days That Shook the World. Punctuated by the reminiscences of a number of Reed's real-life contemporaries (shot in stark black and white and unidentified, although they include Rebecca West, Henry Miller, and Hamilton Fish) the three-hour-plus marathon shifts the action among a variety of American locales and from the States to the Soviet Union. Among the larger-than-life figures given the personal treatment are Louise's one-time lover Eugene O'Neill (Jack Nicholson), Emma Goldman (magnificently portrayed by Maureen Stapleton, who won a Best Supporting Actress Oscar for her work), Communist party chief Grigory Zinoviev (novelist Jerzy Kosinski), and Max Eastman (Edward Herrmann). Beatty, has created a film of DOCTOR ZHIVAGO-like scope and majesty, yet REDS succeeds best in its smallest moments, focusing on the interaction among its carefully drawn characters. Keaton fails to bring the necessary depth to her portrayal and relies too much on her familiar, quirky film persona; but Beatty gives a highly nuanced, appropriately energized performance, and the supporting players are uniformly excellent. The film's chief attribute, however, is also one of its major flaws. In presenting an up-close, personal look at the lives of its famous figures—particularly Reed and Bryant in their love affair and marriage—the film sometimes gives short shrift to the world-shaking events that are its unique subject. Nonetheless, the brilliantly designed and photographed REDS is a beautiful, passionate film, both in its stunningly recreated action scenes and its quietest moments.

REMAINS OF THE DAY, THE 📀

1993 134m c Drama/Historical/Romance ★★★½
Merchant Ivory/Columbia (U.S.) PG

Anthony Hopkins *(Stevens)*, Emma Thompson *(Miss Kenton)*, James Fox *(Lord Darlington)*, Christopher Reeve *(Lewis)*, Peter Vaughan *(Father)*, Hugh Grant *(Cardinal)*, Michael Lonsdale *(Dupont D'Ivry)*, Tim Pigot-Smith *(Benn)*, John Haycraft *(Auctioneer)*, Caroline Hunt *(Landlady)*

p, Mike Nichols, John Calley, Ismail Merchant; d, James Ivory; w, Ruth Prawer Jhabvala (from the novel by Kazuo Ishiguro); ph, Tony Pierce-Roberts; ed, Andrew Marcus; m, Richard Robbins; prod d, Luciana Arrighi; art d, John Ralph; chor, Elizabeth Aldrich; cos, Jenny Beavan, John Bright, Cosprop

AAN Best Picture; AAN Best Actor: Anthony Hopkins; AAN Best Actress: Emma Thompson; AAN Best Director: James Ivory; AAN Best Original Score: Richard Robbins; AAN Best Adapted Screenplay: Ruth Prawer Jhabvala; AAN Best Art Direction-Set Decoration: Luciana Arrighi, Ian Whittaker; AAN Best Costume Design: Jenny Beavan, John Bright

THE REMAINS OF THE DAY is yet another quietly intense, dignified period drama from the producing-directing-writing team of Ismail Merchant, James Ivory, and Ruth Prawer Jhabvala. Though it offers a host of fine performances in a smoothly crafted, adult drama of unfulfilled love, it lacks the cumulative dramatic impact of the team's best work.

During the 1930s, Miss Kenton (Emma Thompson) is hired by Lord Darlington (James Fox), as is the elderly Stevens (Peter Vaughan), who has spent his life in service. Darlington's perfect butler, the younger Stevens (Anthony Hopkins), attempts to cover for his father's failing abilities, but Miss Kenton points out the dangers of the older man's continuing on. Stevens reacts with scorn, yet the repressed butler also begins to develop deeper feelings for Miss Kenton, as does she for him. Their painfully repressed relationship is played out against the backdrop of world affairs, as Darlington becomes involved with Nazism while trying to keep England out of WWII.

As with many of this team's other films, THE REMAINS OF THE DAY is intelligently and respectfully faithful to its prestigious source, in this case Kazuo Ishiguro's Booker Prize-winning novel. Though the film teeters dangerously close to what lurks just beyond the edge of many Merchant-Ivory productions—camp—its telling vignettes are adroitly sketched, Tony Pierce-Roberts's luscious cinematography is quietly expressive, and the acting lends freshness and urgency to a drama which could have been just so much highbrow soap.

REMBRANDT 📀

1936 84m bw Biography ★★★★
London Films (U.K.)

Charles Laughton *(Rembrandt van Rijn)*, Gertrude Lawrence *(Geertje Dirx)*, Elsa Lanchester *(Hendrickje Stoffels)*, Edward Chapman *(Fabrizius)*, Walter Hudd *(Banning Cocq)*, Roger Livesey *(Beggar Saul)*, John Bryning *(Titus van Rijn)*, Allan Jeayes *(Dr. Tulp)*, John Clements *(Gavaert Flink)*, Raymond Huntley *(Ludvig)*

p, Alexander Korda; d, Alexander Korda; w, Carl Zuckmayer, Lajos Biro, June Head, Arthur Wimperis; ph, Georges Perinal, Richard Angst; ed, William Hornbeck, Francis D. Lyon; m, Geoffrey Toye; prod d, Vincent Korda; fx, Ned Mann; cos, John Armstrong

This box-office failure wonderfully exposes the creative process of the artist and presents an unromanticized look at one of art's geniuses. The film confines itself to the final 27 years of the Dutchman's life, beginning shortly after the death of Rembrant's first wife, with Rembrandt, played by Charles

Laughton, busily at work on "The Night Watch." The men who appear in the famous painting, all of whom have paid a fee for the privilege of sitting for the master, are unhappy with the way they have been painted, but Rembrandt, true to his vision, will not allow them to criticize his work. With his first wife buried, he turns to the female closest to him, Geertje (Gertrude Lawrence), his housekeeper and sometime model, a vulgar woman he might never have noticed were he still happily married. The moment he begins his alliance with Geertje, things go rotten. First, he must sell his regal house and most of his assets in order to satisfy his outstanding bills. Then, when he turns his attentions to the maid, Hendrickje (Elsa Lanchester), Geertje leaves him. Hendrickje is soon pregnant, and they are married after she gives birth. When Hendrickje dies, Rembrandt becomes almost instantly old, a doddering old fool on the brink of total senility. Producer-director Alexander Korda, an art collector, teamed up with his brother in designing a marvelous "look" to the movie, each scene looking as though it were taken from one of Rembrandt's own paintings. Laughton did his research by traveling to Holland, studying the art and whatever biographical material he could lay hands on, then steeped himself in the information and entered into the persona of the painter, offering a superb, complex characterization that must rank among his best, and, perhaps, one of the best biographical roles in film history. Laughton dominated the film in the title role, as he'd done before in the roles of Henry, Nero, Javert, and Bligh. He was in every scene but one, giving such a restrained performance that audiences expecting his thespian fireworks were disappointed. That the movie was not a hit does not detract from the achievements of the Kordas, Laughton, and everyone associated with this tasteful, mostly accurate, and satisfying motion picture.

REMEMBER LAST NIGHT?

1935 81m bw Comedy/Mystery ★★★★
Universal (U.S.)

Edward Arnold *(Danny Harrison)*, Constance Cummings *(Carlotta Milburn)*, Sally Eilers *(Bette Huling)*, Robert Young *(Tony Milburn)*, Robert Armstrong *(Fred Flannagan)*, Reginald Denny *(Jack Whitridge)*, Monroe Owsley *(Billy Arliss)*, George Meeker *(Vic Huling)*, Edward Brophy *(Maxie)*, Jack LaRue *(Baptiste Bouclier)*

p, Carl Laemmle Jr.; d, James Whale; w, Doris Malloy, Harry Clork, Louise Henry, Dan Totheroh (based on the novel *Hangover Murders* by Adam Hobhouse); ph, Joseph Valentine; ed, Ted J. Kent

Effervescent, quirky comedy/whodunnit about a murder that takes place during a night of heavy drinking by a bunch of wealthy socialites, including Constance Cummings and Robert Young. It actually develops into a string of murders, all dealt with in sublimely light-hearted fashion. Edward Arnold plays a jovial detective who enlists the aid of a hypnotist (Gustav von Seyffertitz) to try and jog the memories of the hungover revellers; naturally enough, the hypnotist is himself dispatched just on the point of disclosure. This is screwball comedy-mystery at its strangest, with imaginatively outrageous gags, superb character players, and direction that perfectly blends parody and suspense. A film which neatly subverts the very conventions its genre employs, REMEMBER LAST NIGHT? was, not surprisingly, a cult favorite of the French New Wave.

REMEMBER THE NIGHT

1940 86m bw Comedy/Romance ★★★½
Paramount (U.S.)

Barbara Stanwyck *(Lee Leander)*, Fred MacMurray *(John Sargent)*, Beulah Bondi *(Mrs. Sargent)*, Elizabeth Patterson *(Aunt Emma)*, Willard Robertson *(Francis X. O'Leary)*, Sterling Holloway *(Willie)*, Charles Waldron *(Judge, New York)*, Paul Guilfoyle *(District Attorney)*, Charles Arnt *(Tom)*, John Wray *(Hank)* p, Mitchell Leisen; d, Mitchell Leisen; w, Preston Sturges; ph, Ted Tetzlaff; ed, Doane Harrison; m, Frederick Hollander; art d, Hans Dreier, Roland Anderson; cos, Edith Head

You'd have to be a grump not to like this funny, sentimental blend of pathos, drama and zaniness. It may have been former art director Leisen's best directorial effort, mainly due to the superior Sturges script. Sturges had a way with designing a picture so it could get right to the brink of syrup, then pull back with an hysterical comedy sequence. Conversely, just as the humor was about to disintegrate into chaotic slapstick, Sturges would throw a curve that put the story back onto a firm, dramatic footing. Stanwyck is a tough cookie with a shoplifting habit. Christmas is approaching and she decides to give herself a present, a bracelet of diamonds. She's caught by the security people and sent to jail to await trial. She's been in twice before for the same sort of crime and the judge decides to deal with her after the Christmas holidays. MacMurray is to prosecute her in his job as assistant district attorney. He's going home to Indiana for the holiday and when he learns that Stanwyck is also from the same state, he gets her out of jail in his custody. He takes her to her home, but her mother, Georgia Caine, wants nothing to do with her. MacMurray takes her to his home to meet his mother, Bondi, his aunt, Patterson, and their handyman, Holloway. Stanwyck has never been part of such a loving family and is struck by the closeness. She and MacMurray are soon in love but she holds back, fearing that it could never be permanent. She considers fleeing, then changes her mind and returns to New York for the trial. Her defense attorney, Robertson (who usually played the stern judge or vicious no-nonsense prosecutor) makes an impassioned and funny plea on Stanwyck's behalf, but that all goes out the window when she pleads guilty and accepts the brief jail term. It goes without saying that MacMurray will be waiting for her when she is released. It could have been maudlin and dreary in many other hands but Leisen and Sturges have made this a wonderful Yuletide movie that's good watching any time of year. Three songs: "Easy Living" (Ralph Rainger, Leo Robin, sung by Martha Mears in a nightclub sequence), "Back Home in Indiana" (James F. Hanely, Ballard MacDonald, performed by Mears and the King's Men), and "End of a Perfect Day" (Carrie Jacobs Band, sung by Holloway as Stanwyck plays the piano).

REPO MAN
1984 92m   c   Science Fiction/Comedy   ★★★½
Edge City   (U.S.)   R

Harry Dean Stanton (Bud), Emilio Estevez (Otto), Tracey Walter (Miller), Olivia Barash (Leila), Sy Richardson (Lite), Susan Barnes (Agent Rogers), Fox Harris (J. Frank Parnell), Tom Finnegan (Oly), Del Zamora (Lagarto), Eddie Velez (Napo)

p, Jonathan Wacks, Peter McCarthy; w, Alex Cox; d, Alex Cox; ph, Robby Muller (Deluxe Color); ed, Dennis Dolan; m, Tito Larriva, Steven Hufsteter; art d, J. Rae Fox, Lynda Burbank; fx, Robby Knott, Roger George; cos, Theda Deramus

The youth cult film of 1984, REPO MAN marked the auspicious debut of writer-director Alex Cox, born in Britain and educated as a lawyer at Oxford before relocating to Los Angeles to study at UCLA Film School on a Fulbright scholarship.

Otto (Emilio Estevez) is a disaffected youth in Los Angeles who loses his supermarket stock boy job as the film opens. He spends the night wandering through the punk underground before he encounters Bud (Harry Dean Stanton), who tells him that his wife left her car in a bad neighborhood and offers Otto $25 to drive it out for him. Otto accepts but is indignant when he learns that Bud lied to him and that he has just helped repossess a car. Later, however, he listens to offers of big money and sets off to learn the trade under Bud's tutelage. Meanwhile, a nuclear physicist (Fox Harris), who has

had himself lobotomized to stop guilt feelings about his work on the neutron bomb, has stolen something dangerous and glowing and put it in the trunk of his 1964 Chevy Malibu. A nuclear device of some sort? The decomposing body of an alien with spectacular powers? Several government agencies are after the car and offer a $20,000 reward for whoever finds it, a prize that makes it the most sought-after car in the city.

REPO MAN looks at the neon-lit, horizontal sprawl of Los Angeles in a way that no one had before, and a great deal of credit for the film's distinctive look goes to German cinematographer Robby Muller, who'd already distinguished himself via numerous collaborations with Wim Wenders. Cox's familiarity with the punk milieu is impressive, and he would continue in this vein for his follow-up, SID AND NANCY. The performances vary wildly in their quality, with Stanton and Estevez taking top honors and most of the other characters little more than cartoons. Still, REPO MAN is one of the most original films of recent memory, with an edge of black humor and punk sensibility—wickedly funny, ceaselessly inventive, and never boring.

REPULSION
1965 104m bw Horror   ★★★★★
Compton/Tekli   (U.K.)

Catherine Deneuve (Carol Ledoux), Ian Hendry (Michael), John Fraser (Colin), Patrick Wymark (Landlord), Yvonne Furneaux (Helen Ledoux), Renee Houston (Miss Balch), Helen Fraser (Bridget), Valerie Taylor (Mme. Denise), James Villiers (John), Hugh Futcher (Reggie)

p, Gene Gutowski; d, Roman Polanski; w, Roman Polanski, Gerard Brach, David Stone; ph, Gilbert Taylor; ed, Alastair McIntyre; m, Chico Hamilton; art d, Seamus Flannery

One of the most frightening and disturbing pictures ever made, REPULSION contains a scene in which a man's face is slashed with a razor until he dies, captured by Polanski's camera with a clinical expertise that pushes the viewer's nervous system to the edge. REPULSION has often been compared to PSYCHO, but Polanski's film, rather than presenting a portrait of a psychotic killer from outside, pulls the audience into the crazed individual's mind.

Deneuve plays a Belgian manicurist working in London and living in an apartment with her sister, Furneaux. She becomes increasingly unhinged, apparently due to her feelings about sex, which simultaneously repulses and attracts her, and about which she is constantly reminded by the presence of Furneaux's lover. When her sister goes on holiday, Deneuve is left to fend for herself and becomes the victim of terrifying, destructive hallucinations within the confines of the apartment. REPULSION tells a simple story, but Polanski turns it into something undeniably brilliant. The director-writer took great pains in creating the proper composition and details for his nightmarish black-and-white visuals, extracting maximum hallucinatory effect from the apartment set. A powerfully engrossing film that owes much to the realistic, nearly silent performance of Deneuve, REPULSION was Polanski's first English-language feature. The director makes a cameo appearance as a spoons player.

REQUIEM FOR A DREAM
2000 102m c Horror   ★★★
Artisan/Thousands Words/Truth and Soul Pictures/Sibling/Protozoa Productions/Bandeira Entertainment/Industry Entertainment   (U.S.)

Ellen Burstyn (Sara Goldfarb), Jared Leto (Harry Goldfarb), Jennifer Connelly (Marion Silver), Marlon Wayans (Tyrone C. Love), Christopher McDonald (Tappy Tibbons), Louise Lasser (Ada), Sean Gullette (Arnold the Shrink)

p, Eric Watson, Palmer West; d, Darren Aronofsky; w, Hubert Selby Jr., Darren Aronofsky (based on the novel by Hubert Selby Jr.); ph, Matthew Libatique; ed, Jay Rabinowitz; m, Clint Mansell; prod d, James Chinlund; fx, Amoeba Proteus; cos, Laura Jean Shannon

AAN Best Actress: Ellen Burstyn

Depending on your sensibilities, you'll find Darren Aronofsky's visually dazzling adaptation of Hubert Selby Jr.'s grueling 1978 novel either hard to take or hard to take seriously. In any event, it's a wild ride and a worthy entry in the hallowed canon of drugsploitation flicks that already includes REEFER MADNESS, THE TRIP, and THE ACID EATERS.

Set in and around the dying dreamland of Coney Island, the film follows four lost souls as they chase the vapor trails of their dreams into chemically induced perdition. A random telephone call leads sweet, zaftig Sara Goldfarb (Ellen Burstyn) to believe she's going to be on TV; wanting to drop a few pounds, she becomes hopelessly addicted to diet pills and quickly goes insane. Sara's son, Harry (Jared Leto), and his girlfriend, Marion (Jennifer Connelly), shoot heroin and fantasize about opening a clothing boutique. To bankroll their dream, Harry and junkie pal Tyrone (Marlon Wayans) score a quantity of near-pure smack, which they cut and distribute. But as the money rolls in, their habits increase, and when their source suddenly runs dry, Harry, Marion, and Tyrone find themselves in their own private drug hells.

With the same hyperinventiveness that made PI so dynamic, Aronofsky directs for maximum impact, using just about every known camera technique (and then some) to simulate the rush-and-crash of the drug experience. Not that Selby's already sensational material needs juicing up: His characters fall so far, so hard, and so fast that by the time the movie reaches its revolting climax—a veritable hallelujah chorus of degradation—it feels no more convincing than the fates of the hopped-up psychos from MARIHUANA: THE WEED WITH ROOTS IN HELL. Aronofsky has given us a well-acted, gorgeously overwrought and luridly entertaining exploitation flick; a midnight movie for future generations to chuckle through.

REQUIEM FOR A HEAVYWEIGHT   [DVD]
1962   85m   bw   Sports   ★★★½
Columbia   (U.S.)

Anthony Quinn *(Mountain Rivera)*, Jackie Gleason *(Maish Rennick)*, Mickey Rooney *(Army)*, Julie Harris *(Grace Miller)*, Stanley Adams *(Perelli)*, Madame Spivy *(Ma Greeny)*, Herbie Faye *(Bartender)*, Jack Dempsey *(Himself)*, Muhammad Ali, billed as Cassius Clay *(Ring Opponent)*, Steve Belloise *(Hotel Desk Clerk)*

p, David Susskind; d, Ralph Nelson; w, Rod Serling (based on his TV play); ph, Arthur J. Ornitz; ed, Carl Lerner; m, Laurence Rosenthal; art d, Burr Smidt; cos, John Boxer

Six years after Jack Palance brilliantly essayed the character of Mountain Rivera on television's "Playhouse 90," Anthony Quinn took on the role of the battered boxer for this big-screen adaptation of Rod Serling's Emmy-winning teleplay. As the film begins, Rivera, a veteran of 17 years in the ring, is beaten senseless by a younger, faster opponent (played by Cassius Clay, soon to be Muhammad Ali), going down for the count in the seventh round. His longtime manager, Gleason, who assured mobster Spivy that his fighter wouldn't last past the first few rounds, is given three weeks to compensate her for her betting losses—or else. Rivera has been told that he may go blind if he fights again, so he tries to get a job to come up with the money with the help of Harris, a caring employment counselor. Gleason, however, sabotages his interview for a position at a summer camp. Disappointed with Gleason but ever loyal, Rivera compromises his dignity by donning an Indian war bonnet and entering the professional wrestling ring to save his manager's life. Quinn,

Gleason, and Rooney, as Rivera's erstwhile trainer, turn in magnificent performances in this unforgettable drama of abiding friendship and the abuse of trust. However, director Ralph Nelson, who also helmed the original 1956 television production, asked that his name be removed from the credits when nonessential scenes that had been cut from the original release print were reinstated to make the feature longer. Although those scenes, which slow down the narrative, certainly work against the film, REQUIEM FOR A HEAVYWEIGHT remains a thoroughly engaging movie.

RESCUERS, THE   [DVD]
1977   76m   c   Animated/Children's   ★★★
Walt Disney Productions   (U.S.)   G

VOICES OF: Bob Newhart *(Bernard)*, Eva Gabor *(Miss Bianca)*, Geraldine Page *(Mme Medusa)*, Joe Flynn *(Mr. Snoops)*, Jeanette Nolan *(Ellie Mae)*, Pat Buttram *(Luke)*, Jim Jordan *(Orville)*, John McIntire *(Rufus)*, Michelle Stacy *(Penny)*, Bernard Fox *(Chairman)*

p, Wolfgang Reitherman; d, Wolfgang Reitherman, John Lounsbery, Art Stevens; w, Ken Anderson, Vance Gerry, Larry Clemmons, David Michener, Burny Mattinson, Frank Thomas, Fred Lucky, Ted Berman, Dick Sebast (based on the stories "The Rescuers" and "Miss Bianca" by Margery Sharp); ed, Jim Melton, Jim Koford; m, Artie Butler; art d, Don Griffith; anim, Oliver M. Johnston, Franklin Thomas, Milt Kahl, Don Bluth

AAN Best Original Song: "Someone's Waiting for You"; Sammy Fain (Music), Carol Connors (Lyrics), Ayn Robbins (Lyrics)

Four years in the making, costing nearly $8 million, THE RESCUERS is a beautifully animated film that showed Disney still knew a lot about making quality children's fare even as their track record was weakening. The story concerns two mice, Bernard and Miss Bianca (their voices provided by Newhart and Gabor), who set out to rescue a girl named Penny (Stacy) from the evil Mme Medusa (Page). The girl is held captive in a swamp, which offers the setting for some genuinely frightening action. Comic relief is provided by a bird named Orville, who transports the mice as they search for the girl. The voices are all well suited to the characters, and the film is a delight for children as well as adults who appreciate good animation and brisk storytelling.

RESERVOIR DOGS   [DVD]
1992   99m   c   Crime/Drama   ★★★★
Dog Eat Dog Productions   (U.S.)   R

Harvey Keitel *(Mr. White/Larry)*, Tim Roth *(Mr. Orange/Freddy)*, Michael Madsen *(Mr. Blonde/Vic)*, Christopher Penn *(Nice Guy/Eddie)*, Steve Buscemi *(Mr. Pink)*, Lawrence Tierney *(Joe Cabot)*, Randy Brooks *(Holdaway)*, Kirk Baltz *(Marvin Nash)*, Edward Bunker, billed as Eddie Bunker *(Mr. Blue)*, Quentin Tarantino *(Mr. Brown)*

p, Lawrence Bender; d, Quentin Tarantino; w, Quentin Tarantino; ph, Andrzej Sekula; ed, Sally Menke; m, Karyn Rachtman; prod d, David Wasco; cos, Betsy Heimann

RESERVOIR DOGS heralded the arrival of an extraordinary new talent leading a first-rate cast in one of 1992's most original releases. Most of the film deals with the aftermath of a jewelry heist gone awry. The protagonists are strangers who address each other using false names assigned by the heist's organizer, Joe Cabot (Lawrence Tierney). Wounded Mr. Orange (Tim Roth) is screaming and flailing in the back seat of a car driven by Mr. White (Harvey Keitel). They return to the gang rendezvous, an abandoned warehouse somewhere in Los Angeles, where they meet Mr. Pink (Steve Buscemi), who has escaped with the stolen diamonds. Convinced there is a traitor in their gang, Pink proposes to White that they simply leave Orange (who is, unbeknownst to them, an undercover cop) to die and split the jewels. Their deliberations are interrupted by Mr. Blonde (Michael Madsen), who has brought along a cop (Kirk Baltz) he took as a hostage. Later, "Nice Guy" Eddie (Christopher Penn) arrives, sent by his father, Cabot, to try and straighten out the mess. Things only get more complicated, however, leading to a climax that is both blood-soaked and, in its formal symmetry, darkly funny.

As in GLENGARRY GLEN ROSS, the actual heist in RESERVOIR DOGS is never seen. Instead, we get flashbacks that etch in the backgrounds of key players White, Orange, Blonde, Eddie and Joe. We also see bits and pieces of the post-heist chase that both punctuate the warehouse scenes with some tautly handled action and reveal further complications underpinning what's going on. RESERVOIR DOGS betrays the influence of Godard in the fragmentation of its narrative, which deconstructs the criminal subculture as a parody of "legitimate" capitalism. The film's look and themes also recall those of Howard Hawks. Avoiding artful, fussy compositions, Tarantino constructs much of RESERVOIR DOGS from simple medium-shot long takes. Tarantino also puts a post-modernist spin on the classic Hawksian theme of professionalism. The gangsters keep debating and defining the meaning of the term, while their actions undercut their words by proving these addled psychopaths to be anything but "professional." For Tarantino, the age of heroic competence is as dead as his characters are at the fadeout.

RETURN OF MARTIN GUERRE, THE 📀
(RETOUR DE MARTIN GUERRE, LE)
1982 111m c Historical ★★★½
La Societe Francaise/France Region 3/Marcel Dassault/Roissi/Palace (France)

Gerard Depardieu *(Martin Guerre)*, Bernard-Pierre Donnadieu *(Martin Guerre)*, Nathalie Baye *(Bertrande de Rols)*, Roger Planchon *(Jean de Coras)*, Maurice Jacquemont *(Judge Rieux)*, Isabelle Sadoyan *(Catherine Boere)*, Rose Thiery *(Raimonde de Rols)*, Maurice Barrier *(Pierre Guerre)*, Stephane Peau *(Young Martin)*, Sylvie Meda *(Young Bertrande)*

p, Daniel Vigne; d, Daniel Vigne; w, Daniel Vigne, Jean-Claude Carriere; ph, Andre Neau (Fujicolor); ed, Denise de Casabianca; m, Michel Portal; art d, Alain Negre; cos, Anne-Marie Marchand

AAN Best Costume Design: Anne-Marie Marchand

Set in 16th-century France, this engrossing period piece is based on existing records of an actual court case tried in a small village. Two youngsters, Martin Guerre and Bertrande de Rols, enter into a marriage of convenience at the behest of their peasant families. After a number of years, the strangely distant Martin disappears from the village, leaving behind his chaste, love-starved wife (Nathalie Baye). When Martin (Gerard Depardieu) returns, nine years later, he receives a warm welcome from the townsfolk and Bertrande, who has remained faithful to him. However, when Martin experiences occasional lapses of memory and fails to recognize faces, accusations fly—some of the villagers accusing him of being an impostor in the belief that the real Martin lost a leg in combat. Bertrande grows increasingly confused, at times defending her husband who has discovered a newfound affection for her, but on other occasions condemning him with her silence. The matter becomes even more confused when another man claiming to be Martin Guerre (Bernard Pierre Donnadieu) arrives in the village. One of the most successful art-house films of the 1980s, THE RETURN OF MARTIN GUERRE relies on two powerful performers—Depardieu, who is perfectly cast as the mysterious peasant, and Baye, whose demanding role calls for carefully measured silence and reserve. In his second cinematic outing, television

director Daniel Vigne realized that he need only stick to the original facts to create a captivating film. Anne-Marie Marchand's costumes received an Oscar nomination. The year 1993 saw the release of SOMMERSBY, a bloodless American remake of MARTIN GUERRE starring Richard Gere and Jodie Foster.

RETURN OF THE JEDI 📀
1983 133m c Science Fiction ★★★½
Lucasfilm (U.S.) PG

Mark Hamill *(Luke Skywalker)*, Harrison Ford *(Han Solo)*, Carrie Fisher *(Princess Leia Organa)*, Billy Dee Williams *(Lando Calrissian)*, Anthony Daniels *(C-3P0)*, Peter Mayhew *(Chewbacca)*, James Earl Jones *(Voice of Darth Vader)*, Alec Guinness *(Ben Obi-Wan Kenobi)*, Frank Oz *(Voice of Yoda)*, Ian McDiarmid *(Emperor Palpatine)*

p, Howard Kazanjian, Robert Watts, Jim Bloom; d, Richard Marquand; w, Lawrence Kasdan, George Lucas (based on a story by Lucas); ph, Alan Hume, Jack Lowin, James Glennon (Panavision, Rank Color); ed, Sean Barton, Marcia Lucas, Duwayne Dunham, Arthur Repola; m, John Williams; prod d, Norman Reynolds; art d, Fred Hole, James Schoppe, Joe Johnston; fx, Roy Arbogast, Kit West, Richard Edlund, Dennis Muren, Ken Ralston; chor, Gillian Gregory; cos, Aggie Guerard Rodgers, Nilo Rodis-Jamero; anim, James Keefer

AAN Best Original Score: John Williams; *AAN Best Art Direction-Set Decoration:* Norman Reynolds, Fred Hole, James Schoppe, Michael Ford; *AAN Best Sound:* Ben Burtt, Gary Summers, Randy Thom, Tony Dawe; *AAN Best Sound Effects Editing:* Ben Burtt; *AA Special Achievement Award—Visual Effects:* Richard Edlund, Dennis Muren, Ken Ralston, Phil Tippett

The first STAR WARS trilogy comes to an end with RETURN OF THE JEDI, technically the most sophisticated of the bunch, and a favorite among fans.

R2-D2 (Kenny Baker) and C-3P0 (Anthony Daniels) are sent to the palace of loathsome space gangster Jabba the Hutt to deliver a message from Luke (Mark Hamill), who asks that Jabba negotiate for the freedom of the imprisoned Han Solo (Harrison Ford). But the droids are also imprisoned, and soon Princess Leia (Carrie Fisher), Chewbacca (Peter Mayhew), Lando Calrissian (Billy Dee Williams), and Luke are all gathered in Jabba's lair. After a daring escape, Luke goes to consult with Yoda about his destiny. The dying Yoda (Frank Oz) confirms that Darth Vader (voiced by James Earl Jones) is indeed Luke's father, and reveals that Leia is his twin sister.

RETURN OF THE JEDI does not hold up particularly well independent of the preceding two films. Characterization here is a given: if you don't know who Luke, Leia, Solo, et al. are and what they mean to one another, you won't find out by watching this film. The dialogue is repetitive ("I won't give in to the dark side of the Force!" "You *will!*") and significant characters from earlier films—notably bounty hunter Boba Fett and Yoda—are dispatched without fanfare, and the whole business has a slightly rushed, perfunctory feel at the same time that it feels oddly attenuated. The chattering, spear-rattling, calculatedly adorable Ewoks, the furry inhabitants of the planet Endor, are unbearable—it's no wonder that cynical viewers cheer when one finally bites the dust. Still, the space battles are well-staged (the debt owed to JEDI by the far slicker INDEPENDENCE DAY is conspicuous) and various loose narrative threads are neatly pulled together.

RETURN OF THE PINK PANTHER, THE 📀
1975 115m c Mystery/Comedy ★★★½
UA (U.K.) PG

Peter Sellers *(Inspector Jacques Clouseau)*, Christopher Plummer *(Sir Charles Litton)*, Catherine Schell *(Claudine Litton)*, Herbert

Lom *(Chief Inspector Dreyfus)*, Peter Arne *(Col. Sharki)*, Burt Kwouk *(Cato)*, Andre Maranne *(Francois)*, Gregoire Aslan *(Chief of Police)*, Peter Jeffrey *(Gen. Wadafi)*, David Lodge *(Jean Duval)*

p, Blake Edwards; d, Blake Edwards; w, Frank Waldman, Blake Edwards; ph, Geoffrey Unsworth (Panavision, DeLuxe Color); ed, Tom Priestley; m, Henry Mancini; prod d, Peter Mullins; art d, Peter Mullins; fx, John Gant; cos, Bridget Sellers

This was the third in the "Pink Panther" series, which starred Sellers. Alan Arkin and director Bud Yorkin had attempted their version with INSPECTOR CLOUSEAU, but it couldn't compare to the comedy engendered by Sellers under Edwards's direction. This sequel took in more than $30 million and earned every cent. The famous diamond named in the title has been stolen from the museum where it had been residing for the past several years. Blame is laid at the feet of retired jewel thief Plummer (doing the David Niven role established in THE PINK PANTHER), though he is innocent. Plummer is married to Schell and is in danger of being arrested for a crime he didn't commit, so he must find out who the real crook is. Lom, again Sellers's boss, reluctantly gives Sellers the task of solving the crime. A series of sight gags and misplaced-word jokes follows, with Sellers playing off Aslan and Arne, two Middle Eastern cops; Victor Spinetti and Mike Grady, employees at a Gstaad resort; and all of the villains, led by Eric Pohlmann in an imitation of Sydney Greenstreet. The picture comes to life only when Sellers is onscreen, and the rest of the time it's just vamping. The locations were visually satisfying with scenes being shot at Gstaad, Switzerland, the French Riviera, Marrakesh, and Casablanca. The picture races along like a "Road Runner" cartoon with occasional stops to catch its breath. Try to see it on television in a room alone because the laughter in a full-theater audience might cause you to miss some good lines. Julie Andrews, who is Edwards's wife, did a small cameo as a chambermaid, but the scene was cut out in the final print. Edwards comes from directorial genes, as his grandfather, J. Gordon Edwards, was in charge of the lensing of many films.

RETURN OF THE SECAUCUS SEVEN   *DVD*
1980 110m c   Drama   ★★★½
Salsipuedes   (U.S.)   R

Mark Arnott *(Jeff)*, Gordon Clapp *(Chip)*, Maggie Cousineau *(Frances)*, Brian Johnston *(Norman Gaddis)*, Adam LeFevre *(J.T.)*, Bruce MacDonald *(Mike)*, Jean Passanante *(Irene)*, Maggie Renzi *(Kate)*, John Sayles *(Howie)*, David Strathairn *(Ron)*

p, William Aydelott, Jeffrey Nelson; d, John Sayles; w, John Sayles; ph, Austin de Besche (DuArt Color); ed, John Sayles; m, Mason Daring

After scripting low-budget horror films such as PIRANHA and BATTLE BEYOND THE STARS for Roger Corman, acclaimed novelist and short story writer John Sayles made an auspicious directorial debut with THE RETURN OF THE SECAUCUS SEVEN, a more authentic and charming portrait of the same territory explored in the glossier THE BIG CHILL.

In the late 1960s seven friends were arrested in Secaucus, New Jersey, on their way to a march on the Pentagon. Ten years after graduating from college, the forgotten "Secaucus Seven" and a few companions come together at the New Hampshire home of Mike (Bruce MacDonald) and Kate (Maggie Renzi, coproducer of LIANNA, THE BROTHER FROM ANOTHER PLANET, MATEWAN). Over the course of the few days they spend together, much is revealed about their past and present lives and romances.

Shot in 1978 on a miniscule budget (reportedly $40,000) and using inexperienced actors, Sayles succeeds in creating an intelligent and often compelling study of former 1960s political activists coming to grips with their lives. Though that's about all THE RETURN OF THE SECAUCUS

SEVEN offers, it is nevertheless an honest examination of the characters and their relationships. Fans of Sayles's work will note the presence of Gordon Clapp and David Strathairn, both of whom appear in the director's MATEWAN and EIGHT MEN OUT.

REVENGE OF THE NERDS   *DVD*
1984 90m c   Comedy   ★★★½
Interscope (U.S.)   R

Robert Carradine *(Lewis)*, Anthony Edwards *(Gilbert)*, Timothy Busfield *(Poindexter)*, Andrew Cassese *(Wormser)*, Curtis Armstrong *(Booger)*, Larry B. Scott *(Lamar)*, Brian Tochi *(Takashi)*, Julie Montgomery *(Betty)*, Michelle Meyrink *(Judy)*, Ted McGinley *(Stan)*

p, Ted Field, Peter Samuelson; d, Jeff Kanew; w, Steve Zacharias, Jeff Buhai (based on a story by Tim Metcalfe, Miguel Tejada-Flores, Zacharias, Buhai); ph, King Baggot (Deluxe Color); ed, Alan Balsam; m, Thomas Newman; prod d, James Schoppe; fx, Joe Unsinn; chor, Dorain Grusman; cos, Radford Polinsky, Deborah Hopper

This funny movie is about 10 rungs above the usual teenage-college films. Lewis (Robert Carradine) and Gilbert (Anthony Edwards) are the essential nerds, in that Gilbert is a shy computer genius and Lewis is a boy with an annoying laugh and a huge overbite. When they arrive at Adams College and try to join fraternities, they are turned aside as they are so nerdy. In desperation, they join with other nerds to start their own branch of Lambda Lambda Lambda, an all-black fraternity that is functioning on other campuses. All the while, they are being closely watched by the jock contingent led by Stan (Ted McGinley), who is also the chairman of the Greek council. The jocks begin to make life miserable for the nerds, but revenge is on its way. This picture is hipper than NATIONAL LAMPOON'S ANIMAL HOUSE; PORKY'S; and all of the other teenage films lumped together. It's engaging, hysterically funny at times, wildly satiric, and has fewer lapses of good taste than most.

REVERSAL OF FORTUNE   *DVD*
1990 120m c   Drama   ★★★★
Edward R. Pressman/Shochiku Fuji/Sovereign   R
(U.S.)

Jeremy Irons *(Claus von Bulow)*, Glenn Close *(Sunny von Bulow)*, Ron Silver *(Alan M. Dershowitz)*, Annabella Sciorra *(Carol)*, Uta Hagen *(Maria)*, Fisher Stevens *(David Marriott)*, Christine Baranski *(Andrea Reynolds)*, Mano Singh, Felicity Huffman, Alan Pottinger

p, Edward R. Pressman, Oliver Stone; d, Barbet Schroeder; w, Nicholas Kazan (based on the book by Alan Dershowitz); ph, Luciano Tovoli; ed, Lee Percy; m, Mark Isham; prod d, Mel Bourne; cos, Judianna Makovsky, Milena Canonero

AA Best Actor: Jeremy Irons; *AAN Best Director:* Barbet Schroeder; *AAN Best Adapted Screenplay:* Nicholas Kazan

A cool, quirky adaptation of lawyer Alan Dershowitz's book about his successful appeal of Claus von Bulow's conviction for the attempted murder of his wife, Martha "Sunny" von Bulow. Neither docudrama nor out-and-out fiction, REVERSAL OF FORTUNE is somewhere in between, a darkly humorous, determinedly ambiguous delight. Schroeder begins with Sunny (Glenn Close), who narrates the film from the vantage point of her "persistent vegetative state"—recalling William Holden's ghostly narration of SUNSET BOULEVARD. She summarizes the first murder trial, which ended with Claus (Jeremy Irons) convicted and released on bail pending appeal. The drama really begins when Claus approaches Harvard Law professor Dershowitz (Ron Silver) to handle the case. Dershowitz is initially reluctant to accept Claus—an arrogant, elitist, decadent multi-millionaire—as a client. Ultimately, though, he is caught up in the challenge of defending the indefensible. Working with a small army recruited from his classes, Dershowitz demolishes the prosecution case, which had Claus injecting Sunny with enough insulin to bring about her coma. After a second trial, Claus is acquitted. Did he do it? Shroeder isn't saying.

Irons's canny performance dominates the film. He plays the role with apparent frankness and dignity rather than melodramatic villainy, and Schroeder's camera frames him in isolation to convey his bleakness and solitude. Claus remains, above all, enigmatic. The movie finally "guesses" that Claus didn't mean to kill Sunny, and Sunny didn't necessarily mean to kill herself. In fact, the point of Scroeder's film is not "whodunit?," but the suggestion that, in the end, legal guilt and moral culpability are not the same thing at all. REVERSAL OF FORTUNE is one of those rare films that deals with class difference in supposedly classless America, which makes for an unusually provocative tragicomedy of (bad) manners.

RHAPSODY IN BLUE

1945 139m bw Musical/Biography ★★★½
Warner Bros. (U.S.)

Robert Alda (George Gershwin), Joan Leslie (Julie Adams), Alexis Smith (Christine Gilbert), Charles Coburn (Max Dreyfus), Julie Bishop (Lee Gershwin), Albert Basserman (Prof. Frank), Morris Carnovsky (Poppa Gershwin), Rosemary DeCamp (Momma Gershwin), Anne Brown (Bess), Herbert Rudley (Ira Gershwin)

p, Jesse L. Lasky; d, Irving Rapper; w, Howard Koch, Elliot Paul (based on a story by Sonya Levien); ph, Sol Polito; ed, Folmar Blangsted; m, George Gershwin; art d, John Hughes, Anton Grot; fx, Ray Davidson, Willard Vaneriger; chor, LeRoy Prinz

AAN Best Score (Musical): Ray Heindorf, Max Steiner; AAN Best Sound Recording: Nathan Levinson

George Gershwin died before he was 40, but his music continues to be a source of delight and inspiration. Like NIGHT AND DAY and WORDS AND MUSIC—film biographies about Cole Porter and Rogers and Hart, respectively—RHAPSODY IN BLUE has little to do with the *real* life of its subject, but, as is the case with those films, its subject's wonderful songs are the main attraction. In telling its story of the Gershwin Brothers' rise to fame from Manhattan's Lower East Side, RHAPSODY IN BLUE offers the usual scenes of song-plugging, struggle, failure, rehearsals, and backstage life; episodes in New York, London, and Paris; goes so far as to invent a character who never existed (played by Joan Leslie); and alters others to the point of laughability. In his second film, Robert Alda won't be confused for Laurence Olivier, but he does contribute a relatively convincing portrayal of George Gershwin, while Herbert Rudley, as Ira, looks very much like the master wordsmith at the same age and carries off his part well. There are many celebrity impersonations, as well as appearances by several stars playing themselves, but the film's best lines belong to Gershwin's good friend Oscar Levant (as himself), who contributes piano solos along with Ray Turner. Max Steiner did the musical adaptation with orchestrations by Ray Heindorf and Ferde Grofe, composer of the "Grand Canyon Suite." Given this lineup and Gershwins' timeless tunes, it would be possible to remove all the talk, leave the music, and still have a good movie; and, of course, in the age of remote-control "mute" buttons, that's an option.

RICHARD III

1955 158m c Historical/War ★★★½
Big Ben/London Films (U.K.)

Laurence Olivier (King Richard III), Ralph Richardson (Buckingham), Claire Bloom (Lady Anne), John Gielgud (Clarence), Cedric Hardwicke (King Edward IV), Mary Kerridge (Queen Elizabeth), Pamela Brown (Jane Shore), Alec Clunes (Hastings), Stanley Baker (Henry Tudor), Michael Gough (Dighton)

p, Laurence Olivier; d, Laurence Olivier, Anthony Bushell; w, Alan Dent, Laurence Olivier, Colley Cibber, David Garrick (based on the play by William Shakespeare); ph, Otto Heller (VistaVision, Technicolor); ed, Helga Cranston; m, William Walton; prod d, Roger Furse; art d, Carmen Dillon; fx, Wally Veevers; cos, H. Nathan, L. Nathan

AAN Best Actor: Laurence Olivier

Laurence Olivier's third Shakespeare film, after HENRY V and HAMLET, and in some ways the most suitable of the three for his rather cold talents. For once, Olivier finds a part in which he can fully exploit his chilly magnetism, and the viewer can only root for his vicious but charismatic cripple.

The picture begins with Richard, Duke of York (Olivier) enviously observing the coronation of Edward IV (Cedric Hardwicke)—the sun (son) of York that illuminates Richard's metaphorical winter of discontent. Richard sets about scheming for the throne, arranging the deaths of Clarence (John Gielgud) and Edward's young heirs, and incidentally seducing Lady Anne (Claire Bloom). After Edward's death, he becomes protector and then king, but must face the House of Tudor in a bloody battle at Bosworth Field.

The battle scene was the first shot (in Spain); during shooting Olivier was accidentally pierced by a bolt from the film's stunt archer that was supposed to hit the protected horse (an animal that had been trained to fall and play dead on command). Olivier continued the scene until a natural break in the action was called for, then asked for medical aid. (The limp he sports as Richard is real, a result of the accident.) It took three hours each day to put on Olivier's complex makeup—the same prosthetics he wore on stage, including a false nose, hunched back, false hand, and black pageboy wig.

RICHARD III was not a hit when it was released in England, so the producers made a unique deal with the NBC television network in the U.S. in which the networks acquired the rights to broadcast the film for the sum of $500,000 (in later years it was re-released to resounding success, and has been the most financially rewarding of Olivier's Shakespeare films).

This film lacks the cinematic boldness of Olivier's earlier screen Shakespeare; there's nothing here to match the gloomy *mise-en-scene* of HAMLET or the cocky theatrical conceits of HENRY V. But his riveting performance transcends his conventional directing and utterly dominates the movie. Indeed, this filmed record of Olivier's Richard has intimidated generations of actors—how can they hope to compete with an interpretation both so brilliant and so familiar to audiences?

Olivier and Alexander Korda had hoped to film a version of "Macbeth," with Vivien Leigh as Lady Macbeth, but Korda died a year after RICHARD III was made, and lack of interest in the project caused it to be tabled. The British Film Academy gave RICHARD III Best British Film, Best Film, and Best Actor awards.

RICHARD III
1995 104m c Drama/Historical/War ★★★½
Bayly/Pare Productions/United Artists/First Look   R
Pictures (U.K./U.S.)

Ian McKellen *(Richard III)*, Annette Bening *(Queen Elizabeth)*, Maggie Smith *(The Duchess of York)*, Nigel Hawthorne *(Clarence)*, John Wood *(King Edward IV)*, Robert Downey Jr. *(Earl Rivers)*, Kristin Scott Thomas *(Lady Anne)*, Jim Broadbent *(Buckingham)*, Jim Carter *(Lord Hastings)*, Bill Paterson *(Richard Ratcliffe)*

p, Lisa Katselas Pare, Stephen Bayly; d, Richard Loncraine; w, Ian McKellen, Richard Loncraine (adapted from the stage production by Richard Eyre, based on the play by William Shakespeare); ph, Peter Biziou; ed, Paul Green; m, Trevor Jones; prod d, Tony Burrough; art d, Choi Ho Man, Richard Bridgland; fx, John Evans; cos, Shuna Harwood

AAN Best Art Direction-Set Decoration: Tony Burrough; *AAN Best Costume Design:* Shuna Harwood

Ian McKellen's delightfully sinister portrait of a power-hungry sociopath highlights this oddly breezy adaptation of Shakespeare's play. This is a flawed and far from definitive rendering, but it is nonetheless dynamic and enjoyably revisionist.

McKellen and director-co-writer Richard Loncraine have completely re-envisioned the setting of the 1592 historical drama. The hunchbacked Duke of Gloucester still malevolently murders his family members one by one, climbing his way to the top to become King Richard III, but now his coup takes place among the aristocratic, pro-fascist Cliveden Set of the 1930s.

By reinventing the material in a timely and imaginative way, RICHARD III succeeds where other recent Shakespeare-on-film adaptations fail. This version brazenly moves around chunks of text, shifts the story to a more recent and comprehensible era, and irreverently spoofs the sacrosanct material. However, the film does not take its revisionist point quite far enough. The look is appropriately elegant, but only a few scenes stand out as truly eye-catching (e.g., a fascist rally shot like TRIUMPH OF THE WILL in three-strip Technicolor, Richard's fiery death scene). Moreover, the parallels between Richard's ascent and the rise of European fascism make for interesting allegory, but McKellen and Loncraine stop far short of driving the point home with reference to the present day.

McKellen's forceful and frighteningly funny performance is matched by Kristin Scott Thomas's mournful, masochistic Lady Anne. They are both well supported by Nigel Hawthorne, Maggie Smith, and Jim Broadbent in parts that amount to showy cameos. Far less successful are the performances by two American actors clearly added to the film for marquee value, Annette Bening and Robert Downey Jr.

RIDE THE HIGH COUNTRY
1962 94m c Western ★★★★★
MGM (U.S.)

Randolph Scott *(Gil Westrum)*, Joel McCrea *(Steve Judd)*, Mariette Hartley *(Elsa Knudsen)*, Ronald Starr *(Heck Longtree)*, R.G. Armstrong *(Joshua Knudsen)*, Edgar Buchanan *(Judge Tolliver)*, John Anderson *(Elder Hammond)*, L.Q. Jones *(Sylvus Hammond)*, Warren Oates *(Henry Hammond)*, James Drury *(Billy Hammond)*

p, Richard E. Lyons; d, Sam Peckinpah; w, N.B. Stone Jr.; ph, Lucien Ballard (CinemaScope, Metrocolor); ed, Frank Santillo; m, George Bassman; art d, George W. Davis, Leroy Coleman

A much-loved revisionist Western, director Peckinpah's second feature film proved to be a bittersweet swan song for the Old West and a classy farewell to the screen for actors Scott and—for some years—McCrea. Set at the turn of the century, the film opens in the town of Hornitos, which is in the midst of a celebration. Down the crowded main street rides Steve Judd (McCrea), an aging former lawman who has seen better days. He mistakenly thinks the cheers of the crowd are for him, but is abruptly reminded of the changing times when a car nearly runs him over. Steve has been hired to escort a gold shipment from the mining town of Coarse Gold back to a bank in Hornitos, but the banker is taken aback by his age. (An especially good scene has Steve reading over his contract in the bathroom so the banker can't see that he needs spectacles.) The old lawman is finally given the job, and he sets out to hire help for the trip. He runs into Gil Westrum (Scott), a fellow former lawman who has survived by dressing up as the dandified "Oregon Kid," selling out his former heroic image. Steve hires Gil and his young sidekick Heck Longtree (Starr), but Gil plans to steal the gold at the first opportunity.

In RIDE THE HIGH COUNTRY, director Peckinpah began what was to be an obsession with men who have lived past their era in history and find it difficult to adapt to changing times (THE WILD BUNCH; THE BALLAD OF CABLE HOGUE; and PAT GARRETT AND BILLY THE KID all share this theme). His two protagonists, in some ways mirror images of each other, are wracked with guilt for sometimes failing to live up to the standards they have set for themselves. What separates them, though, from the scoundrels they invariably encounter is a personal code of honor they both try to uphold. Eventually, these tortured souls attain a sort of grace because they do what it takes to regain their self-respect. Soon after producer Lyons talked McCrea and Scott into doing the film, McCrea—who had originally agreed to play the part of Gil Westrum, the lawman gone bad—felt uncomfortable with the role (he had never played a villain before, albeit, here, a sympathetic one) and asked Lyons if he could see how Scott felt about switching parts. Later that same afternoon, Lyons received a call from Scott who confessed that he was feeling insecure about his role and wondered if McCrea would mind a swap. Much to the actors' relief, the roles were switched. The only problem left was to decide who would receive top billing, but a public coin toss at the Brown Derby restaurant solved that one.

Shooting was planned on location at Mammoth Lake in the High Sierras, but after four days it began to snow, and cost-conscious MGM insisted the production be moved to a more workable area, using soap suds to simulate snow. Shooting was completed in an astounding 26 days, but a shake-up at MGM saw Peckinpah supporter Sol Siegel ousted and replaced by Joseph R. Vogel, who barred the director from the studio, forcing him to consult with editors and sound mixers by phone. The film was dumped onto the bottom half of double bills, but proved an astounding popular and critical success in Europe, winning First Prize at the Cannes Film Festival, the Grand Prize at the Brussels Film Festival (beating out Federico Fellini's 8 1/2), and the Silver Goddess from the Mexican Film Festival for Best Foreign Film. Peckinpah's attention to detail and character makes this film a multifaceted jewel to be studied and enjoyed again and again. The honest, subtle, and consummately skillful performances by Scott and McCrea and promising newcomer Mariette Hartley continue to draw viewers in.

RIDER ON THE RAIN
(LE PASSAGER DE LA PLUIE)
1970 119m c Thriller ★★★½
Greenwich/Medusa (France/Italy) GP

Marlene Jobert *(Melancolie "Mellie" Mau)*, Charles Bronson *(Col. Harry Dobbs)*, Annie Cordy *(Juliette)*, Jill Ireland *(Nicole)*, Gabriele Tinti *(Tony)*, Jean Gaven *(Toussaint)*, Marc Mazza *(The Stranger)*,

Corinne Marchand *(Tania)*, Jean Piat *(M. Armand)*, Marika Green *(Hostess at Tania's)*

p, Serge Silberman; d, Rene Clement; w, Sebastien Japrisot, Lorenzo Ventavoli; ph, Andreas Winding (Eastmancolor); ed, Francoise Javet; m, Francis Lai; art d, Pierre Guffroy; cos, Rosine Delamare

A young woman (Jobert) who lives in a small seaside resort in France happens to see a stranger exit from a bus; later, he seems to be following her. That evening the stranger breaks into Jobert's home after her husband has left. The stranger rapes Jobert; she kills him with a shotgun and disposes of the body in the ocean. After a few days the stranger's body washes up on the beach, making newspaper headlines. Jobert goes to a wedding reception and meets Bronson, an American who accuses her of murder—the victim, it seems, was a sex fiend who escaped from prison and stole $60,000 from the U.S. Army. Bronson demands that Jobert return an airline bag that held the money, but Jobert ignores his threats. The pursuit begins.

RIDER ON THE RAIN is a tightly plotted, well-executed thriller in which Bronson's three stock expressions are put to superb use by director Rene Clement. The locations, on the French coast and in Paris, are used effectively; combined with careful cinematography, the scenery adds greatly to the story's inherent tension. This stylish, Hitchcockian suspenser was filmed in French and dubbed into English for American distribution, but the dubbing was unusually well done. RIDER ON THE RAIN helped make Bronson a star in France, giving him the clout that eventually led to international fame.

RIDICULE   *DVD*
(LE RIDICULE)
1996 102m c Historical/Drama ★★★½
Epithete/Cinea/France 3 Cinema/Investimage 4/   R
Procirep/Gras Savoye (France)

Charles Berling *(Ponceludon de Malavoy)*, Jean Rochefort *(Marquis de Bellegarde)*, Fanny Ardant *(Madame de Blayac)*, Judith Godreche *(Mathilde de Bellegarde)*, Bernard Giraudeau *(Abbot de Vilecourt)*, Bernard Dheran *(Monsieur de Montalieri)*, Carlo Brandt *(Knight de Milletail)*, Jacques Mathou *(Abbot de l'Epee)*, Urbain Cancelier *(Louis XVI)*, Albert Delpy *(Baron de Gueret)*

p, Gilles Legrand, Frederic Brillion, Philippe Carcassonne; d, Patrice Leconte; w, Remi Waterhouse, Michel Fessler, Eric Vicaut; ph, Thierry Arbogast; ed, Joelle Hache; m, Antoine Duhamel; prod d, Ivan Maussion; cos, Christian Gasc

AAN Best Foreign Language Film

Thanks largely to a wonderfully literate script, RIDICULE is a flavorful divertissement which recalls the great French period films of yore. Somewhere, Guitry and Duvivier are smiling.

In the Versailles of Louis XVI, country aristocrat Ponceludon de Malavoy (Charles Berling) comes to court with the hope of pleading the cause of his disease-ridden people. He is taken under the wing of the Marquis de Bellegarde (Jean Rochefort), who agrees to coach Malavoy in the Byzantine ways of court etiquette and, above all, language. In a palace that worships a well-turned phrase, having a reputation for a sharp tongue is the only way of gaining access to the King. Fortunately, Malavoy (a natural wit) is a sensation. He allows himself to be seduced by the formidable Madame de Blayac (Fanny Ardant), but really loves the Marquis's independent daughter, Mathilde (Judith Godreche). While those around him rise and fall, Malavoy inches closer to an audience with the King, until a venom of a deadlier sort—jealousy—leads to his undoing.

Remi Waterhouse's lovingly crafted script is a highly inventive, wonderfully wicked bauble. The barbed repartee

flows like wine, and the battles of wits are as absorbing as any sports match. The bright, brainy cast revels in the rococo garb and effervescent dialogue. Berling is at once fresh, intelligent, and dashing, while Ardant is perfect as the brilliant Comtesse cum courtesan. Shot on the dream location of the gardens of Versailles, the production is handsome and, best of all, looks lived in. Anyone expecting a lavish spectacle on the order of MARIE ANTOINETTE (1938) or DANGEROUS LIAISONS (1988) will be disappointed by the relatively low-key but historically evocative decor.

RIFF-RAFF
1991 94m c Comedy/Drama/Political ★★★
Parallax Productions/Channel Four (U.K.)

Robert Carlyle *(Stevie)*, Emer McCourt *(Susan)*, Jimmy Coleman *(Shem)*, George Moss *(Mo)*, Ricky Tomlinson *(Larry)*, David Finch *(Kevin)*, Richard Belgrave *(Kojo)*, Ade Sapara *(Fiaman)*, Derek Young *(Desmonde)*, Bill Moores *(Smurph)*

p, Sally Hibbin; d, Ken Loach; w, Bill Jesse; ph, Barry Ackroyd; ed, Jonathan Morris; m, Stewart Copeland; prod d, Martin Johnson

Following a foray into commercial cinema with the political thriller HIDDEN AGENDA, British director Ken Loach returned to his roots in social realism with a bittersweet comedy-drama about London construction workers.

The film's slight plot focuses on Stevie (Robert Carlyle), who moves to London from his home in Glasgow, where he has served a prison term for theft. Stevie finds work with an unscrupulous building contractor whose disregard for safe working conditions is balanced by his willingness to hire laborers without checking their backgrounds or identities. This suits Stevie's colorful, polyglot co-workers, most of whom use false names in order to continue drawing welfare benefits.

Loach has made an insightful, quietly affecting study of people who, amidst the economic wreckage of post-Thatcherite Britain, have been reduced to outcasts in their own country—converting rundown buildings into condos for the rich, while having to break into abandoned buildings for homes of their own. Using a neo-documentary style and improvisational acting techniques, the director has brought emotional resonance and humor to a script by the late Bill Jesse, a struggling comedy writer and playwright who had been supporting himself as a construction laborer; he died shortly after the film's completion. The result is an aptly moving epitaph, mining both poignancy and humor from its ostensibly grim subject matter. This English-language film was released in a subtitled version in the U.S., which is a big help for American viewers attempting to unravel the crazy quilt of accents—Scottish, Liverpudlian, Cockney, African—that weave the story together.

RIFIFI   *DVD*
1954 117m bw Crime ★★★★★
Indus/Pathe/Prima (France)

Jean Servais *(Tony le Stephanois)*, Carl Mohner *(Jo Le Suedois)*, Robert Manuel *(Mario)*, Jules Dassin *(Cesar)*, Magali Noel *(Viviane)*, Marie Sabouret *(Mado)*, Janine Darcey *(Louise)*, Pierre Grasset *(Louis Grutter)*, Robert Hossein *(Remi Grutter)*, Marcel Lupovici *(Pierre Grutter)*

p, Rene G. Vuattoux; d, Jules Dassin; w, Jules Dassin, Rene Wheeler, Auguste Le Breton (based on the novel by Le Breton); ph, Philippe Agostini; ed, Roger Dwyre; m, Georges Auric; art d, Auguste Capelier

This landmark caper film shows the robbery of a Parisian jewelry store and the complications that follow for the thieves—mastermind Tony (Jean Servais), a recently released ex-con who may or may not have a terminal respiratory problem; Jo

(Carl Mohner), whom Tony served time to protect; safecracker Cesar (the film's director, Jules Dassin, acting under the pseudonym Perlo Vita); and Mario (Robert Manuel)—all of them surprisingly decent men. The film's centerpiece is a 28-minute sequence that captures the robbery itself in fascinating detail, employing neither dialogue nor music, allowing only the actual sounds of the thieves at work to be heard. Once the heist is accomplished, life doesn't get any easier for the crooks, as Tony's gangster rival (Marcel Lupovici) and cohorts get violently greedy after learning about the robbery through Cesar's indiscretion. The kidnapping of Jo's son and plenty of shooting follow before RIFIFI (French slang for "trouble") is over.

This was the second European-made film for writer-director-actor Dassin, an American who plied his trade abroad after the House Un-American Activities Committee made life difficult at home. Dassin, whose wonderful you-are-there direction won him a share of the Best Director award at Cannes, also manages to inject more than a little humor into this tension-filled genre classic, preceded by the likes of THE ASPHALT JUNGLE and followed by films like BIG DEAL ON MADONNA STREET and Dassin's own TOPKAPI.

RIGHT STUFF, THE
DVD
1983 192m c Biography ★★★★
Ladd Co. (U.S.) PG

Sam Shepard (*Chuck Yeager*), Scott Glenn (*Alan Shepard*), Ed Harris (*John Glenn*), Dennis Quaid (*Gordon Cooper*), Fred Ward (*Gus Grissom*), Barbara Hershey (*Glennis Yeager*), Kim Stanley (*Bancho Barnes*), Veronica Cartwright (*Betty Grissom*), Pamela Reed (*Trudy Cooper*), Scott Paulin (*Deke Slayton*)

p, Irwin Winkler, Robert Chartoff; d, Philip Kaufman; w, Philip Kaufman (based on the book by Tom Wolfe); ph, Caleb Deschanel (Technicolor); ed, Glenn Farr, Lisa Fruchtman, Stephen A. Rotter, Tom Rolf; m, Bill Conti; prod d, Geoffrey Kirkland; art d, Richard Lawrence, Stewart Campbell, Peter Romero; fx, Gary Gutierrez, Jordan Belson

AAN Best Picture; AAN Best Supporting Actor: Sam Shepard; AAN Best Cinematography: Caleb Deschanel; AA Best Film Editing: Glenn Farr, Lisa Fruchtman, Stephen A. Rotter, Douglas Stewart, Tom Rolf; AA Best Original Score: Bill Conti; AAN Best Art Direction-Set Decoration: Geoffrey Kirkland, Richard J. Lawrence, W. Stewart Campbell, Peter Romero, Pat Pending, George R. Nelson; AA Best Sound: Mark Berger, Tom Scott, Randy Thom, David MacMillan; AA Best Sound Effects Editing: Jay Boekelheide

Funny, trenchant account, based on Tom Wolfe's book, of the dawn of the space age, seen as both a shameless piece of media mythmaking, and as an act of genuine courage on the part of the first astronauts. The movie spans about 15 years, beginning with Chuck Yeager (Sam Shepard) breaking Mach 1, and concluding with a huge barbecue at the Astrodome at which President Johnson (Donald Moffat) hosts the astronauts. In between, it depicts their arduous training and complex personal lives, and the absurd lengths to which they have to go to satisfy the public's demand for real-life heroes. Director-writer Philip Kaufman's script brings a wealth of humor to a faithful retelling of the astronauts' fascinating stories, the actors fit smoothly into their roles and even physically resemble their characters, and the direction is well-paced and visually exciting.

RING
DVD
(RINGU)
1997 92m c Horror ★★★★
Kadokawa/Pony Canyon/Toho/Imagica/
Asmik-Ace/Omega Project (Japan)

Nanako Matsushima (*Reiko Asakawa*), Miki Nakatani (*Mai Takano*), Hiroyuki Sanada (*Ryuji Takayama*), Yuko Takeuchi

(*Tomoko Oishi*), Hitomi Sato (*Masami Kurahashi*), Yoichi Numata (*Takashi Yamamura*), Yutaka Matsushige (*Yoshino*), Katsumi Muramatsu (*Koichi Asakawa*), Rikiya Otaka (*Yoichi Asakawa, Reiko's Son*), Masako (*Shizuko Yamamura*)

p, Takashige Ichise, Shinya Kawai, Takenori Sento; d, Hideo Nakata; w, Hiroshi Takahashi (based on the novels by Koji Suzuki); ph, Junichiro Hayashi; ed, Nobuyuki Takahashi; m, Kinji Kawai; prod d, Iwao Saito; fx, Ko Kawabata, Hajime Matsumoto, Sei Yokoyama

A blockbuster in Japan, this restrained horror film crosses urban legend conventions with Chinese ghost story traditions, and the results are truly spooky.

It opens as high schooler Tomoko (Yuko Takeuchi) tells another girl the story of a cursed videotape. If you watch it, Tomoko says, you'll get a phone call shortly after; no one will be on the line, and you'll die exactly one week later. Having suitably scared her friend, Tomoko admits that she and three friends actually saw the tape while away for the weekend at a country inn in Yitou. Moments later, the phone rings, Tomoko is dead, and her friend has gone mad. Tomoko's aunt, Reiko Asakawa (Nanako Matsushima), a divorced TV reporter and mother of little Yoichi (Rikiya Otaka), investigates the tale of the tape and finds it widespread among local teenagers. She pursues the story to Yitou and sees the tape for herself: its grainy images include a woman combing her hair in front of a mirror, a well in the woods, and a newspaper article about a volcanic explosion 40 years earlier. The tape finishes, the phone rings, there's no one on the line.

Subtle and atmospheric, this eerie chiller builds to a truly disturbing climax that owes nothing to squishy special effects and much to carefully contrived atmosphere. The film was adapted from a 1991 novel by young-adult novelist Koji Suzuki—Japan's answer to Stephen King. The book was the first in a hugely popular series, and the film spawned both a sequel and a prequel, as well as a virtual remake from Korea entitled THE RING VIRUS.

RING, THE
DVD
2002 105m c Horror ★★★½
MacDonald-Parkes/Bender-Spink/DreamWorks PG-13
SKG (U.S.)

Naomi Watts (*Rachel Keller*), Martin Henderson (*Noah*), David Dorfman (*Aidan*), Brian Cox (*Richard Morgan*), Jane Alexander (*Dr. Grasnik*), Lindsay Frost (*Ruth*), Amber Tamblyn (*Katie*), Rachael Bella (*Becca*), Daveigh Chase (*Samara*), Shannon Cochran (*Anna Morgan*)

p, Laurie MacDonald, Walter F. Parkes; d, Gore Verbinski; w, Ehren Kruger (based on the novel *Ringu*, by Koji Suzuki, and the motion picture RING by The Ring/Spiral Production Group); ph, Bojan Bazelli; ed, Craig Wood; m, Hans Zimmer; prod d, Tom Duffield; art d, Patrick M. Sullivan Jr.; fx, Christopher Anderson, Burt Dalton, Charles Gibson, Jennifer Lee; cos, Julie Weiss

English-language remakes of successful foreign films are rarely a good idea, but Gore Verbinski's close do-over of Japan's phenomenally popular and absolutely terrifying RING is a shivery surprise.

It begins with the mysterious death of 16-year-old Seattle high-school student Katie (Amber Tamblyn), found in a closet with her face horribly contorted; whatever killed her also scared her friend Becca (Rachael Bella) right into a mental institution. When Katie's aunt, reporter Rachel (Naomi Watts), starts poking around, Katie's friends tell her about a cursed videotape that supposedly kills anyone who watches it. Once the tape is over, the phone rings, and a voice on the other end warns that the viewer has only seven more days to live. Rachel brushes it off as an urban legend, but the deeper she digs, the more sense it makes; how else to explain the fact that everyone who watched the tape with Katie died at exactly the same time? Rachel drives up to the lodge where the ill-fated teens spent the weekend before their deaths, and finds an unmarked videocassette in the front office. She pops it into the VCR and watches as bizarre images flicker across the screen. The tape abruptly ends and the phone rings; "Seven days," the voice whispers, and the countdown begins.

Watts does great work here, and the constant Seattle rain supplies an appropriately dank and airless mood. In simplifying the story, writer Ehren Kruger (SCREAM 3) has also added a number of creepy embellishments. The ending, however, is something of a disappointment. By toning down a final act of desperate cruelty, Kruger and Verbinski rob the finale of that resounding ring of doom—the stroke that ensured the original a permanent place under your skin.

RING TWO, THE　DVD
2005　111m　c　Horror　★★½
Benderspink/Vertigo Entertainment/Macari/　PG-13
Edelstein Films/MacDonald/Parkes Productions/
DreamWorks　(U.S.)

Naomi Watts (Rachel Keller), David Dorfman (Aidan Keller), Simon Baker (Max Rourke), Elizabeth Perkins (Dr. Emma Temple), Gary Cole (Martin Savide), Sissy Spacek (Evelyn), Ryan Merriman (Jake), Emily Vancamp (Emily), Kelly Overton (Betsy), Daveigh Chase (Samara)

p, Laurie MacDonald, Walter F. Parkes; d, Hideo Nakata; w, Ehren Kruger (based on the novel The Ring by Koji); ph, Gabriel Beristain; ed, Michael N. Knue; m, Henning Lohner, Martin Tillman; prod d, Jim Bissell; art d, Christa Munro; fx, Betsy Paterson, Peter Chesney; cos, Wendy Chuck

Director Hideo Nakata's RINGU (successfully remade in English as THE RING) unleashed "J-horror" on the West and paved the way for an invasion of grudges, fatal phone calls, and malevolent little girl ghosts. Nakata's RING TWO attempts to take the story in a different direction, but its focus on the relationship between protective Rachel Keller (Naomi Watts) and her imperiled son, Aidan (David Dorfman), is surprisingly dull.

Seattle newspaper reporter Rachel learned first-hand that the urban legend of the lethal videotape was more than just a spooky story. Having escaped from vicious ghost child Samara Morgan (Daveigh Chase), whose tormented spirit spawned the cursed videotape, Rachel and her nightmare-plagued son have relocated to sleepy small-town Astoria, OR. The news that one local teenager is dead under bizarre circumstances and another so traumatized she can't speak tips off Rachel that copies of the tape are still circulating. David falls ill, and Rachel quickly deduces that Samara is trying to possess her son. Unfortunately, Rachel's frantic efforts to drive Samara out look an awful lot like child abuse to her new neighbors. As David grows sicker and suspicions about Rachel's intentions taint her every effort to help him, she dives headlong into Samara's past in hopes of uncovering the roots of the child's supernatural malice.

Working from a screenplay by RING screenwriter Ehren Kruger, Nakata evokes a compelling sense of menace lurking beneath the surface of everyday life. But a little Keller-family Sturm und Drang goes a long way. Rachel's Nancy Drew-ing feels oddly perfunctory, and one-scene guest star Sissy Spacek packs enough genuine madness into her brief screen time to make the surrounding film feel like so much listless play-acting.

RING-A-DING RHYTHM
1962　73m　bw　Musical/Comedy　★★½
Amicus　(U.K.)

Helen Shapiro (Helen), Craig Douglas (Craig), Felix Felton (Mayor), Arthur Mullard (Police Chief), Timothy Bateson

(Coffeeshop Owner), Hugh Lloyd (Usher), Ronnie Stevens, Frank Thornton (TV Directors), Derek Nimmo (Head Waiter), Mario Fabrizi (Spaghetti Eater)

p, Richard Lester; d, Richard Lester; w, Milton Subotsky; ph, Gilbert Taylor; ed, Bill Lenny; m, Ken Thorne; prod d, Al Marcus; art d, Maurice Carter; cos, Gamp Ferris, Maude Churchill

Richard Lester's first feature proved to be an effective springboard for his highly stylized direction, employing techniques (unusual camera angles, quick cuts) that he polished further in the Beatles' A HARD DAY'S NIGHT. The plot here is not unlike a number of '50s films in which a town's upstanding citizens react vehemently to the corrupting spread of demon rock 'n' roll, forcing the kids to stand up for their rights. In this case, the mayor of an English town, Felton, goes so far as to take away one coffeeshop's license for having a jukebox. A pair of crafty local teens, Shapiro and Douglas, counterattack by trying to put together a festival that will demonstrate the merits of traditional jazz (then an important part of British counterculture) and rock 'n' roll, traveling to a London TV studio to try to persuade some big-name performers to appear. This plot gives Lester an opportunity to creatively showcase a number of pop, rock, and trad jazz stars, including Del Shannon, Chubby Checker, Gary "U.S." Bonds, Gene Vincent, Chris Barber's Jazz Band and the Temperance Seven.

RIO BRAVO　DVD
1959　141m　c　Western　★★★★
Armada　(U.S.)

John Wayne (John T. Chance), Dean Martin (Dude), Ricky Nelson (Colorado Ryan), Angie Dickinson (Feathers), Walter Brennan (Stumpy), Ward Bond (Pat Wheeler), John Russell (Nathan Burdette), Pedro Gonzalez-Gonzalez (Carlos), Estelita Rodriguez (Consuelo), Claude Akins (Joe Burdette)

p, Howard Hawks; d, Howard Hawks; w, Jules Furthman, Leigh Brackett (based on a story by Barbara Hawks McCampbell); ph, Russell Harlan (Technicolor); ed, Folmar Blangsted; m, Dimitri Tiomkin; art d, Leo K. Kuter; cos, Marjorie Best

Annoyed that the acclaimed and popular HIGH NOON portrayed a sheriff so afraid of his adversaries that he spends most of the movie asking the townsfolk for help, director Howard Hawks decided to make a filmed response, namely RIO BRAVO. A lengthy, leisurely paced film, RIO BRAVO is set in a small Texas border town, Rio Bravo, that is under the control of evil cattle baron Russell and his dim-witted brother, Akins. When Akins commits a murder, the sheriff (Wayne), throws him in jail to await the arrival of a U.S. Marshall. Russell lays seige to the jailhouse, and Wayne is forced to rely on the town drunk (Martin), a cranky old cripple (Brennan), and an untested young gunslinger (Nelson) for help.

With its simple plotline, familiar characters, songs, and frequent humor, RIO BRAVO is outstanding entertainment. However, the film has been overrated by some zealous critics, who either ignore its weak points or defend them as praiseworthy oddities. As enjoyable as the film is, it has flaws that prevent it from reaching the classic status of RED RIVER—particularly the casting. Pop star Ricky Nelson was cast on the basis of his great popularity with teenagers rather than because of any acting talent, a decision that ensured additional box office from young girls who wouldn't normally think of going to see a western. Despite his money-making potential, however, Nelson simply couldn't act, and Hawks must have known it. The singer is given the fewest lines possible for a third-billed actor, and he is physically restricted to the background or alongside the other leads. He is never given center stage alone—this is no Montgomery Clift (Wayne's costar in RED RIVER). Also somewhat weak is Angie Dickinson. While she is given all the right Hawksian dialog and her character is the quintessential Hawks woman, tough enough to stand up to any man who comes her way, she doesn't possess the spunkiness of a Jean Arthur or the sultriness of a Lauren Bacall. Wayne, however, turns in a fine performance (though not as good his work in RED RIVER), and Walter Brennan is superb as the grouchy, nasty old man who is undyingly loyal to his friends. The real revelation, however, is Dean Martin, in a part he obviously understood well. His role as the drunken deputy who redeems himself is crucial to the film, and the singer-actor handles his part with skill. Hawks enjoyed working with Martin, whom he found eager and willing to take direction.

RIO BRAVO was very successful commercially, and Hawks later used two variations of the story (with the same character types, similar situations, sometimes even the same sets) in his last two westerns, EL DORADO and RIO LOBO. All cowritten by Leigh Brackett, the films form a sort of informal trilogy, although they become successively weaker. Though Hawks was inspired to make RIO BRAVO as a rebuttal to HIGH NOON, his daughter, Barbara Hawks McCampbell, an aspiring writer, came up with the basic plotline that later became the film's climax—outlaws holed up in a house, while the heroes explode sticks of dynamite by shooting them like clay targets—and was paid and given screen credit for the story. Overall, RIO BRAVO is an excellent film featuring strong, proud, but very human characters who fight against their various handicaps and pull together to do a job and do it right. The people in RIO BRAVO have the same kind of deep affection and understanding for one another as do close family members who are not afraid to speak truthfully for fear of hurting each other's feelings, and it is that aspect of the film that is so appealing. Director John Carpenter's second feature, ASSAULT ON PRECINCT 13, is an updated remake of RIO BRAVO.

RIO GRANDE   📀
1950 105m bw   Western/War   ★★★★
Argosy   (U.S.)

John Wayne (Lt. Col. Kirby Yorke), Maureen O'Hara (Mrs. Kathleen Yorke), Ben Johnson (Trooper Tyree), Claude Jarman Jr. (Trooper Jeff Yorke), Harry Carey Jr. (Trooper Daniel "Sandy" Boone), Chill Wills (Dr. Wilkins), J. Carrol Naish (Gen. Philip Sheridan), Victor McLaglen (Sgt. Maj. Quincannon), Grant Withers (Deputy Marshal), Peter Ortiz (Capt. St. Jacques)

p, John Ford, Merian C. Cooper; d, John Ford; w, James Kevin McGuinness (based on the story "Mission with No Record" by James Warner Bellah); ph, Bert Glennon; ed, Jack Murray; m, Victor Young; art d, Frank Hotaling; fx, Howard Lydecker, Theodore Lydecker; cos, Adele Palmer

This fine portrait of the U.S. Cavalry was the third in John Ford's magnificent trilogy about the troopers of the Old West, following FORT APACHE and SHE WORE A YELLOW RIBBON. Lt. Col. Kirby Yorke (John Wayne) is a tough commanding officer at a remote cavalry post whose hard edge is softened when his only son, Jeff (Claude Jarman, Jr.), reports for duty. After dropping out of West Point, the shamed Jeff has enlisted in the Cavalry and now wants to prove himself to his father. Kirby is cool toward the boy, promising no favoritism, and explains what Army life is really about: "Put out of your mind any romantic ideas that it's a way of glory. It's a life of suffering and hardship, an uncompromising devotion to your oath and your duty." Jeff is taken under the wings of fun-loving troopers Tyree (Ben Johnson) and Boone (Harry Carey, Jr.), who keep an eye on the young man, and the arrival of Kathleen Yorke (Maureen O'Hara), Kirby's estranged wife and Jeff's mother, adds some tension to the scene. She is determined to buy back Jeff's enlistment, and in the process rekindles Kirby's love for her. An excellent post-Civil War tale with romance (Wayne and O'Hara), humor (Johnson, Carey, and Victor McLaglen), and music (a few

tunes by the Sons of the Pioneers), RIO GRANDE is one of Ford's great achievements. As in FORT APACHE and SHE WORE A YELLOW RIBBON, Ford creates a powerful portrait of the wild, remote Southwest during the Indian wars, presenting the traditions and exploits of the old cavalry in very realistic terms, showing them in action as tired, dirty, wounded men performing their assignments in pain and discomfort and emphasizing the real glory of these soldiers as typified by their leader Kirby. The director's camera angles, broadly encompassing whole lines of riding cavalrymen, accentuate their prosaic nobility and dedication to taming the frontier. Much of the score nicely supports the story, indicating the cavalrymen's Irish background and sentimentality, especially in the inclusion of the fine Sons of the Pioneers song "I'll Take You Home Again, Kathleen."

RIO LOBO   📀
1970 114m c   Western   ★½
Malabar/Cinema Center   (U.S.)   G

John Wayne (Col. Cord McNally), Jorge Rivero (Capt. Pierre Cordona), Jennifer O'Neill (Shasta Delaney), Jack Elam (Phillips), Victor French (Ketcham), Susana Dosamantes (Maria Carmen), Christopher Mitchum (Tuscarora), Mike Henry (Sheriff Tom Hendricks), David Huddleston (Dr. Jones), Bill Williams (Sheriff Pat Cronin)

p, Howard Hawks; d, Howard Hawks; w, Leigh Brackett, Burton Wohl (based on a story by Burton Wohl); ph, William Clothier (Technicolor); ed, John Woodcock; m, Jerry Goldsmith; prod d, Robert Smith; fx, A.D. Flowers, Cliff Wenger; cos, Luster Bayless, Ted Parvin

This is probably the hardest film to watch that either Howard Hawks or John Wayne ever took part in, surpassing even Wayne's early days in Republic's "Three Mesquiteer" series for forced acting and situations. The 1930s pictures are more forgivable because the budgets were limiting and the outings were approached routinely. But for such a refined director as Hawks to end his career on a note like this, having made some of the finest films in the history of American cinema, is an atrocity not worth the silver used in the negative. The story isn't so bad, taking place soon after the Civil War. Union captain Wayne teams up with two Confederate soldiers to track down the man responsible for stealing a shipment of gold. Their efforts land them in the middle of a town being terrorized by a crooked sheriff. Wayne and company put an end to the sheriff's tyranny by rallying the townspeople to stand up for their rights. Witty lines are injected that would normally provide a chuckle but are so poorly delivered here that veiwers are left sighing. The common Hawksian theme of male comradeship can be found in the relationship between Wayne and his Confederate cohorts, but the way Wayne and his supporting cast walk through their roles is ridiculous. Rivero and O'Neill face the Duke like beginning stars in the shadow of a great master, something Wayne is aware of and can't seem to shake. Only the performance of Elam remains lively, but it is the type of characterization he has done dozens of times. A sad finale to Hawks's magnificent career.

RISE OF LOUIS XIV, THE
(LA PRISE DE POUVOIR PAR LOUIS XIV)
1966 100m c   Biography   ★★★
O.R.T.F.   (France)   G

Jean-Marie Patte (King Louis XIV), Raymond Jourdan (Jean Baptiste Colbert), Silvagni (Cardinal Mazarin), Katherina Renn (Queen Anne of Austria), Dominique Vincent (Mme. du Plessis), Pierre Barrat (Nicolas Fouquet), Fernand Fabre (Michel Le Tellier), Francoise Ponty (Louise de la Valliere), Joelle Langeois (Marie Therese), Jacqueline Corot (Mme. Henrietta) d, Roberto Rossellini; w, Philippe Erlanger, Jean Gruault; ph, Georges Leclerc (Eastmancolor); ed, Armand Ridel; art d, Maurice Valay; cos, Christiane Coste

---

This is Roberto Rossellini's sparse, near-documentary look at the young Sun King (Jean-Marie Patte) and at how he codified and choreographed an empire, framing fashions to ensure absolute obedience. No detail of the artful young king's designs and graces—which culminated in the structured elegance of the court at Versailles—is too small to be captured by the camera, while the big events, the executions and rebellions, are, quite properly, trivialized. What won obeisance for playboy Louis was fashion, carefully crafted for conquest. Rossellini's pans and zooms follow these strategies of manners and mores intimately: Louis's dying mentor Mazarin (Silvagni) rouges his pallid cheeks prior to his audience with the young king; Louis demands more height to his wigs to enhance his stature and more lace to his jacket to gain attention; the king choreographs the rituals attendant on funerals, cabinet meetings, banquets. The complexities of Louis's life-structurings consolidate his previously shaky power—all eyes are on the young king, hoping to spot each new nuance, each fad-to-be—and intrigues and plots are forgotten in this atmosphere of utter attendance: the Sun King is all-powerful. A revival of sorts for Rossellini, this picture would set the standard for its genre, playing as important a part in film history as did his earliest Neo-Realist films. Like PAISAN, its predecessor of 20 years, the film is constructed of episodes, each giving the observer a chance to bear witness to a reality, a view of history not of battles and bravado, but of guile, manipulation, and role-playing charisma.

RISKY BUSINESS

1983 98m c Comedy ★★★½
Geffen (U.S.) R

Tom Cruise *(Joel)*, Rebecca De Mornay *(Lana)*, Joe Pantoliano *(Guido)*, Richard Masur *(Rutherford)*, Bronson Pinchot *(Barry)*, Curtis Armstrong *(Miles)*, Nicholas Pryor *(Joel's Father)*, Janet Carroll *(Joel's Mother)*, Shera Danese *(Vicki)*, Raphael Sbarge *(Glenn)*

p, Jon Avnet, Steve Tisch; d, Paul Brickman; w, Paul Brickman; ph, Reynaldo Villalobos (Technicolor); ed, Richard Chew; m, Tangerine Dream; prod d, William J. Cassidy; cos, Robert de Mora

---

One of the key films of the 1980s, and proof that a teen sex comedy could merit serious consideration. Smart, stylish, and cynical about the values of its time, this movie aspires to be THE GRADUATE for its generation and it comes pretty close. The affluent teenaged hero is poised on the brink of manhood, eager for the promised pleasures of maturity and fearful of the responsibilities. One wrong step could destroy a potentially bright future. The title refers to both sex and capitalist endeavor; RISKY BUSINESS documents a time in which everything has become a commodity.

Like Fellini's 8 1/2, RISKY BUSINESS begins with a revealing dream of its stymied protagonist. A steamy sexual encounter is nightmarishly transformed into a crucial college entrance examination to which Joel (Tom Cruise) has arrived too late: there will be no future for our young protagonist. Joel, we learn, lives in a fashionable Chicago suburb with his alarmingly straight parents (Nicholas Pryor and Janet Carroll). They go off on a trip leaving their outwardly model son in charge. His thoughts soon turn to sex and the "adult" ads in a local newspaper. After an unsettling initial encounter with a black transvestite, Joel is referred to the services of the spectacular Lana (Rebecca De Mornay), who visits his home and rocks his world. The morning after, the kittenish hooker surveys her upscale surroundings and proposes to Joel a plan that could net them a lot of money. She and her associates have something that the neighborhood boys want and Joel has an empty house where they can all gather. What sounds like a risky but

potentially profitable plan is complicated by the intervention of Guido the Killer Pimp (Joe Pantoliano) and the equally frightening interviewer from Princeton University, Mr. Rutherford (Richard Masur).

Cruise is likable and credible in the lead. His youthful nervousness and exuberance in the early part of the film—particularly his starmaking solo dance around the empty house—are joyous to behold. De Mornay is sexy and touching, and Bronson Pinchot and Curtis Armstrong are memorable in supporting roles. Paul Brickman does a slickly professional job directing his own darkly satirical screenplay and Tangerine Dream provide the dreamy electronic score.

RIVER, THE 🖵

1951 99m c Drama ★★★★★
Oriental-International Films/Theatre Guild (India)

Nora Swinburne *(The Mother)*, Esmond Knight *(The Father)*, Arthur Shields *(Mr. John)*, Thomas E. Breen *(Captain John)*, Radha Shri Ram *(Melanie)*, Suprova Mukerjee *(Nan)*, Patricia Walters *(Harriet)*, Adrienne Corri *(Valery)*, Richard Foster *(Bogey)*, Penelope Wilkinson *(Elizabeth)*

p, Kenneth McEldowney; d, Jean Renoir; w, Jean Renoir, Rumer Godden (based on the novel by Rumer Godden); ph, Claude Renoir, Ramananda Sen Gupta (Technicolor); ed, George Gale; m, M.A. Partha Sarathy; prod d, Eugene Lourie; art d, Bansi Chandragupta

---

Jean Renoir's first film in color, THE RIVER is an extraordinarily rich and almost therapeutically heartening movie about an English family living in Bengal. Part coming-of-age story, part empathetic travelogue, part philosophic poem, THE RIVER was cited by Renoir as "one film that corresponds almost exactly to my initial concept of it."

Harriet (Patricia Walters), a bright and sensitive adolescent, lives with her large family in a big house overlooking the Ganges River. One day, a handsome young American named Captain John (Thomas E. Breen) arrives at the home of his cousin, Mr. John (Arthur Shields), a widower who lives next door to Harriet's family. A somewhat mysterious and romantic figure who has lost a leg in the war, Captain John becomes the immediate object of new and unfamiliar longings in Harriet, in her only slightly older but considerably riper friend, Valery (Adrienne Corri), and, perhaps, in Mr. John's half-Indian daughter, Melanie (Radha Shri Ram), the least flighty of the three girls.

Before contracting to film THE RIVER, Renoir required producer Kenneth McEldowney, a Beverly Hills florist, to agree to four stipulations: (1) Renoir would be allowed to make a reconnaissance trip to India, all expenses paid; (2) he would write the script in collaboration with Rumer Godden, author of the source novel; (3) he would have final cut; and (4) the film would include no elephant hunt, a staple ingredient of English-language movies set in India. Rumer Godden's semi-autobiographical script (co-written with Renoir) for THE RIVER is superb. The visuals of Renoir and crew fully live up to the words of Godden. Dense with documentary and aesthetic asides but, amazingly, never sidetracked by them, Renoir's "mural" movie blesses its viewers with a multitude of riches and bonuses, including a series of mini-travelogues spotted throughout. THE RIVER is further graced by the presence of its three young leading ladies: Radha Shri Ram, a precociously, hauntingly grave beauty recruited from the world of Hindu dance; Adrienne Corri, a robust, red-headed nymph; and Patricia Walters as Harriet, a homely girl who yearns to be "outstandingly beautiful" and becomes so in her last onscreen moments with Captain John.

Anyone who still believes in family sentiment, but is disheartened by Hollywood's characteristically mawkish and insincere treatment of it, is urged to immediately take a voyage on Renoir's river.

RIVER RUNS THROUGH IT, A   *DVD*
1992 123m c   Drama   ★★½
The Big Sky Motion Picture Co./North Fork   PG
Motion Picture Company   (U.S.)

Craig Sheffer *(Norman MacLean)*, Brad Pitt *(Paul MacLean)*, Tom Skerritt *(Reverend MacLean)*, Brenda Blethyn *(Mrs. MacLean)*, Emily Lloyd *(Jesse Burns)*, Edie McClurg *(Mrs. Burns)*, Stephen Shellen *(Neal Burns)*, Joseph Gordon-Levitt *(Young Norman)*, Vann Gravage *(Young Paul)*, Robert Redford *(Narration)*

p, Patrick Markey, Robert Redford; d, Robert Redford; w, Richard Friedenberg (from the novella by Norman MacLean); ph, Philippe Rousselot; ed, Lynzee Klingman, Robert Estrin; m, Mark Isham; prod d, Jon Hutman; art d, Walter Martishius; cos, Bernie Pollack

AAN Best Adapted Screenplay: Richard Friedenberg; *AA Best Cinematography:* Philippe Rousselot; *AAN Best Original Score:* Mark Isham

Directed by Robert Redford, A RIVER RUNS THROUGH IT employs picture-postcard scenery as a backdrop for a mildly engaging family melodrama. Norman (Craig Sheffer) and Paul MacLean (Brad Pitt) grow up in a Montana town under the stern but loving guidance of their Presbyterian minister father, Reverend MacLean (Tom Skerritt), and soft-spoken mother (Brenda Blethyn). After school lessons, the Reverend lets the boys share his greatest passion—fly fishing. To the elder MacLean, the sport is almost a religion. Young Paul is continually rebelling against the Reverend, while Norman is the responsible son. When they grow up, Norman goes away to college and Paul stays in Montana, becoming a newspaper reporter. When Norman returns from college, he is disturbed by Paul's gambling, drinking and skirt-chasing, but can do little to stop his brother's downward spiral, which eventually leads to a tragic end. Meanwhile, Norman falls in love with Jesse Burns (Emily Lloyd), a flapper from an eccentric Methodist family.

Some 12 years after making his directorial debut with ORDINARY PEOPLE, Robert Redford once again turns his attention to the story of a family. His directorial style, however, involves little more than a tendency to use huge close-ups of every performer—particularly Sheffer and Pitt, who are continually shown looking at each other, even when they have nothing to say. While Redford centers on the actors, the screenplay wallows in cliches. Richard Friedenberg, who adapted Norman MacLean's autobiographical novella, does little to make this depiction of 1920s Montana fresh, and Norman's narration is chock-full of neo-philosophical platitudes: "Life is not a work of art," etc. Compounding the situation is the fact that fly fishing isn't the most visually dynamic of sports. Even set against the Sierra Club beauty of Redford's Montana, it's hard to get excited by fisherman casting their lines into the water.

RIVER'S EDGE   *DVD*
1987 99m c   Drama   ★★★½
Hemdale   (U.S.)   R

Crispin Glover *(Layne)*, Keanu Reeves *(Matt)*, Ione Skye, billed as Ione Skye Leitch *(Clarissa)*, Daniel Roebuck *(Samson "John" Tollette)*, Dennis Hopper *(Feck)*, Joshua Miller *(Tim)*, Roxana Zal *(Maggie)*, Josh Richman *(Tony)*, Phil Brock *(Mike)*, Tom Bower *(Bennett)*

p, Sarah Pillsbury, Midge Sanford, David Streit; d, Tim Hunter; w, Neal Jimenez; ph, Frederick Elmes (Metrocolor); ed, Howard

Smith, Sonya Sones; m, Jurgen Knieper; prod d, John Muto; art d, Mick Muhlfriedel; cos, Claudia Brown

One of the most haunting films of the 1980s, RIVER'S EDGE looks at a suburban, postpunk generation which has no causes, no morals, no feelings, and, worst of all, no future.

This controversial drama, based on a notorious 1981 murder case profiled in *Rolling Stone*, opens with John Tollette (Daniel Roebuck), a hulking teenager who strangles his girlfriend Jamie (Danyi Deats, in the ultimate thankless role) and then matter-of-factly tells his friends about it. Matt (Keanu Reeves) and Clarissa (Ione Skye), the murdered girl's best friend, are disturbed, but Layne (Crispin Glover), a speed freak, views the situation differently. In his eyes, Jamie was a friend, but now she's dead; John is also their friend, but he's still alive and needs their help. As tensions within the group escalate, John and Layne take refuge with Feck (Dennis Hopper), a burned-out biker from the 1960s who had killed his own beloved girlfriend and has now given his heart to a blow-up sex doll named Ellie.

RIVER'S EDGE owes its success, in large part, to Neal Jimenez's superb screenplay, which digs beneath the facades that contemporary teenagers hide behind and yields honest and complex portraits. This generation's postpunk worldview is rooted in nihilism, detachment, and fear of nuclear annihilation—nothing matters to them except friends, rock 'n' roll, and getting stoned.

RIVER'S EDGE also boasts the best cast of unknowns since Francis Ford Coppola's THE OUTSIDERS. Reeves and Skye are superb as the moral centers of the film, Roebuck is great as the killer, and the supporting performances are also impressive. Glover and Hopper go over the top and get away with it.

ROAD HOUSE
1948 95m   bw   Thriller   ★★★
Fox   (U.S.)

Ida Lupino *(Lily Stevens)*, Cornel Wilde *(Pete Morgan)*, Celeste Holm *(Susie Smith)*, Richard Widmark *(Jefty Robbins)*, O.Z. Whitehead *(Arthur)*, Robert Karnes *(Mike)*, George Andre Beranger *(Lefty)*, Ian MacDonald *(Police Captain)*, Grandon Rhodes *(Judge)*, Jack G. Lee *(Sam)*

p, Edward Chodorov; d, Jean Negulesco; w, Edward Chodorov (based on a story by Margaret Gruen, Oscar Saul); ph, Joseph La Shelle; ed, James B. Clark; m, Cyril J. Mockridge; art d, Lyle Wheeler, Maurice Ransford; fx, Fred Sersen; cos, Kay Nelson

A stylish and perverse film noir which stars Widmark as the owner of a roadhouse near the Canadian border and Wilde as his best friend and manager. When they hire Lupino as the joint's singer and piano player, the friendship takes a strange turn. Widmark becomes obsessed with Lupino, who in turn finds herself attracted to Wilde. Wilde, however, also the object of cashier Holm's desires, remains aloof. When Widmark goes away on a hunting trip, Wilde finally gives in to Lupino and the two become lovers. When Widmark returns and is told by Wilde of the new situation, Widmark's dark side comes to light. He stages a robbery which points to Wilde as the guilty party. Rather than watch the framed Wilde go to jail, however, he persuades the judge to release the "criminal" into his custody. Widmark's form of imprisonment is a psychological one—forcing Wilde to stay on at the roadhouse but keeping him from Lupino and, ultimately, his freedom. To further torment him, Widmark arranges for a trip to a lodge nestled in the woods, placing Wilde even closer to the border than before. Widmark hopes that his "prisoner" will make an attempt to escape across the border, thereby giving Widmark the chance to shoot him. Meantime, Holm, who has come along to the lodge, is still silently in love with Wilde. A chance finally comes to escape, and Wilde and

Lupino run off into the woods. Holm tries to warn them that Widmark is on their trail, hunting them with a psychotic vengeance, but in the process she is wounded by the crazed hunter. A battle follows between Widmark and Wilde. Lupino, determined to fight for her man, intervenes and guns down Widmark for the animal he is. A strong movie scattered with land mines of psychotic characters, ROAD HOUSE has a disturbing quality of psychological torture to it—a quality magnified by the claustrophobic atmosphere of the stylized diner and the false outdoors of the studio's sound stage. Wilde does fine as the victimized lover, Widmark plays his archetypal villain with his usual intensity, and Lupino is remarkable in her raw toughness. Holm, however, is the one who keeps ROAD HOUSE from going over the edge by playing a normal girl with a foothold on reality. Adding to the film's atmosphere is Lupino's delivery of a few bluesy numbers including "Again," (Dorcas Cochran, Lionel Newman), "One for My Baby" (Johnny Mercer, Harold Arlen), and "The Right Time."

ROAD TO MOROCCO

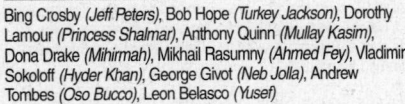

1942 83m bw Comedy/Musical ★★★★
Paramount (U.S.)

Bing Crosby *(Jeff Peters)*, Bob Hope *(Turkey Jackson)*, Dorothy Lamour *(Princess Shalmar)*, Anthony Quinn *(Mullay Kasim)*, Dona Drake *(Mihirmah)*, Mikhail Rasumny *(Ahmed Fey)*, Vladimir Sokoloff *(Hyder Khan)*, George Givot *(Neb Jolla)*, Andrew Tombes *(Oso Bucco)*, Leon Belasco *(Yusef)*

p, Paul Jones; d, David Butler; w, Frank Butler, Don Hartman; ph, William Mellor; ed, Irene Morra; art d, Hans Dreier, Robert Usher; chor, Paul Oscard; cos, Edith Head

AAN Best Original Screenplay: Frank Butler, Don Hartman; *AAN Best Sound Recording:* Loren Ryder

The third, and best, in the "Road" series, ROAD TO MOROCCO has everything going for it. Bob Hope and Bing Crosby were not yet tired of the formula, and their breezy acting wafts the picture along in a melange of gags, songs, thrills, and calculated absurdities. The duo had already sent up adventure movies in ROAD TO SINGAPORE and jungle films in ROAD TO ZANZIBAR—the next target was the Arabian Nights. Jeff Peters (Crosby) and Turkey Jackson (Hope) are the lone survivors of a Mediterranean shipwreck. They land on a beach, mount a passing camel, and go off toward Morocco, where they learn that things aren't swell. The area is parched, the people poor, and foreigners looked upon with scorn. The two are penniless and hungry when a local merchant offers Jeff money to sell Turkey into slavery as the personal plaything of Princess Shalmar (Dorothy Lamour). Jeff makes the deal, Turkey is forcibly removed to the palace, and life in Morocco gets increasingly difficult for everyone thereafter. The picture is filled with great gags and one-liners, including Hope's lament for the Oscar he might have won; the camel's complaint that "this is the screwiest picture I've ever been in!"; Hope's appearance in drag; and the backfire of the "patty cake" routine, after which it's remarked, "Hmmm. That gag sure got around." And there are countless more, delivered at a pace that never lets up.

ROAD TO PERDITION

2002 119m c Crime/Drama ★★★★
Zanuck Company/20th Century Fox/ R
DreamWorks SKG (U.S.)

Tom Hanks *(Michael Sullivan)*, Paul Newman *(John Rooney)*, Jude Law *(Maguire)*, Jennifer Jason Leigh *(Annie Sullivan)*, Stanley Tucci *(Frank Nitti)*, Daniel Craig *(Connor Rooney)*, Tyler Hoechlin *(Michael Sullivan Jr.)*, Liam Aiken *(Peter Sullivan)*, Ciaran Hinds *(Finn McGovern)*, Dylan Baker *(Alexander Rance)*

p, Sam Mendes, Richard D. Zanuck, Dean Zanuck; d, Sam Mendes; w, David Self (based on the graphic novel written by Max Allan Collins and illustrated by Richard Piers Rayner); ph, Conrad L. Hall; ed, Jill Bilcock; m, Thomas Newman; prod d, Dennis Gassner; art d, Richard L. Johnson; fx, Allen L. Hall, Michael J. McAlister, Cinesite; chor, Mark Howard, Harrison McEldowney; cos, Albert Wolsky

A professional killer, searching for the gunman who murdered his wife and child. A powerful robber baron, forced to make a choice of Old Testament proportions. A young boy, learning the true meaning of violence at his father's knee. Based on Max Allan Collins's graphic novel, Sam Mendes's majestic follow-up to AMERICAN BEAUTY has all the elements of a classic Western, done up in the somber, quasi-religious trappings of a Depression-era gangster film.

Rock Island, IL, 1931: Twelve-year-old Michael (Tyler Hoechlin) isn't exactly sure what his father (Tom Hanks) does for a living, but he knows he works for John Rooney (Paul Newman), the town patriarch and Capone-connected racketeer who virtually raised the elder Sullivan as one of his own. One night, Michael hides in the back seat when Sullivan and Rooney's son, Connor (Daniel Craig), take the car out on a job, and looks on as his father massacres a roomful of men. Connor catches Michael, and though the boy swears not to tell, it's not enough; Connor wants to hurt the man who usurped his rightful place in his father's heart. Sullivan returns home to find his wife (Jennifer Jason Leigh) and younger son (Liam Aiken) shot to death. The surviving Sullivans abandon their home and embark on a bloody, six-week crime spree across the dusty plains of the Midwest, eluding a vicious hit man (a truly twisted Jude Law) while trying to pressure Rooney into sacrificing his own son.

Collins rooted his novel in local Quad City legend, but modeled the central figures of father and son bound by violence on Kazuo Koike's manga epic *Lone Wolf and Cub.* This dark, almost mythic heart is what makes Mendes's film such an emotionally rich experience. It's ultimately not just about damnation and America's violent legacy, but the stuff of the great gangster films from SCARFACE to THE GODFATHER: family.

ROAD TO RIO

1947 100m bw Comedy/Musical ★★★½
Paramount (U.S.)

Bing Crosby *(Scat Sweeney)*, Bob Hope *(Hot Lips Barton)*, Dorothy Lamour *(Lucia Maria De Andrade)*, Gale Sondergaard *(Catherine Vail)*, Frank Faylen *(Trigger)*, Joseph Vitale *(Tony)*, Frank Puglia *(Rodrigues)*, Nestor Paiva *(Cardoso)*, Robert Barrat *(Johnson)*, Jerry Colonna *(Cavalry Captain)*

p, Daniel Dare; d, Norman Z. McLeod; w, Edmund Beloin, Jack Rose; ph, Ernest Laszlo; ed, Ellsworth Hoagland; art d, Hans Dreier, Earl Hedrick; fx, Gordon Jennings, Paul K. Lerpae; chor, Bernard Pearce, Billy Daniel; cos, Edith Head

AAN Best Score (Musical): Robert Emmett Dolan

The fifth "Road" picture was a more standard comedy than most of the others and paid off at the box office, becoming the top-grossing film of the year. Gone were the talking animals and some of the zany humor of the earlier entries. In their place was a more conventional story, *sans* Hollywood in-jokes, in which Hot Lips Barton (Bob Hope) and Scat Sweeney (Bing Crosby) are musicians who accidentally cause a fire at a carnival. To avoid being arrested for arson, they jump on an ocean liner headed for Rio and stow away. On the ship, they meet Lucia Maria De Andrade (Dorothy Lamour), who is friendly, then chilly, smiling, then frowning, so that the boys can't figure her out. Upon investigation, they discover she has been hypnotized by the evil Catherine Veil (Gale Sondergaard) and is to marry a man she doesn't love once they reach Rio. Of course, the pair decide they must interfere and prevent the marriage, going so far as to crash the wedding party dressed as a pirate (Crosby) and a Latin American bombshell (Hope in drag) in order to expose the hypnotist's deceit. Lots of laughs.

ROAD TO UTOPIA
DVD
1945 90m bw Comedy/Musical ★★★½
Paramount (U.S.)

Bing Crosby *(Duke Johnson/Junior Hooton)*, Bob Hope *(Chester Hooton)*, Dorothy Lamour *(Sal Van Hoyden)*, Hillary Brooke *(Kate)*, Douglas Dumbrille *(Ace Larson)*, Jack LaRue *(LeBec)*, Robert Barrat *(Sperry)*, Nestor Paiva *(McGurk)*, Robert Benchley *(Narrator)*, Will Wright *(Mr. Latimer)*

p, Paul Jones; d, Hal Walker; w, Norman Panama, Melvin Frank; ph, Lionel Lindon; ed, Stuart Gilmore; m, Leigh Harline; art d, Hans Dreier, Roland Anderson; fx, Farciot Edouart; chor, Danny Dare; cos, Edith Head; anim, Jerry Fairbanks

AAN Best Original Screenplay: Norman Panama, Melvin Frank

This addition to the "Road" series is told in flashback, as a wealthy couple, Chester Hooton (Bob Hope) and Sal Van Hoyden (Dorothy Lamour), recall how they got rich. They'd gained control of a Klondike gold mine but lost their best friend, Duke Johnson (Bing Crosby), in the process. While they reminisce, he suddenly pops in, very much alive. The three begin to talk about the old days, and the film goes back in time to show Chester and Duke as a couple of failed vaude-villians who try to make a shady deal in San Francisco and then must flee the city. They board a northbound ship and pur-loin the deed to a gold mine in Alaska from a pair of vicious murderers. Considering this theft and the fact that they are run-ning from the cops, the vaudevillians pretend to be the tough guys they just scammed. But, in keeping with tradition, the duo get in deep trouble and find themselves vying for the affections of Sal before the final credits roll. Lots of excellent gags punctuate the story, including one in which Hope and Crosby are in the boiler room of the steamer when a formally dressed gentleman walks in looking for a match. Hope and Crosby want to know if he's supposed to be in the movie, and the man replies with a shrug, "Nope, I'm taking a shortcut to stage 10." Once again, animals talk, sight gags abound, and the complementing temperaments of Hope and Crosby are mined to great advantage.

ROAD TO ZANZIBAR
DVD
1941 92m bw Comedy/Musical ★★★½
Paramount (U.S.)

Bing Crosby *(Chuck Reardon)*, Bob Hope *(Hubert "Fearless" Frazier)*, Dorothy Lamour *(Donna Latour)*, Una Merkel *(Julia Quimby)*, Eric Blore *(Charles Kimble)*, Iris Adrian *(French Soubrette in Cafe)*, Lionel Royce *(Mons. Lebec)*, Buck Woods *(Thonga)*, Leigh Whipper *(Scarface)*, Ernest Whitman *(Whiteface)*

p, Paul Jones; d, Victor Schertzinger; w, Frank Butler, Don Hartman (based on the story "Find Colonel Fawcett" by Don Hartman, Sy Bartlett); ph, Ted Tetzlaff; ed, Alma Macrorie; m, Victor Young; art d, Hans Dreier, Robert Usher; chor, LeRoy Prinz; cos, Edith Head

Tarzan movies had been around for years when ROAD TO ZANZIBAR, the second of the "Road" pictures, took the opportunity to satirize every jungle picture lensed up to that time. The script was funny, although much of the humor reportedly derived from on-set improvisations. Connivers Fearless Frazier (Bob Hope) and Chuck Reardon (Bing Crosby) must blow town because they sold a bogus diamond mine to Mons. Lebec (Lionel Royce), a criminal type who doesn't take well to being fleeced. Rather than face Lebec,

Chuck and Hubert (as Fearless is known) light out for Zanzibar, where they meet a pair of Brooklynite entertainers, Donna Latour (Dorothy Lamour) and Julia Quimby (Una Merkel), who are in Africa to find Donna's brother. The girls convince Chuck and Hubert to put up the money for a safari into the interior, but the boys soon realize that they've been duped. It's not Donna's brother they're after, but a British mil-lionaire she hopes to marry. Things only get worse after that, but that's as expected. The lyrics of "On the Road to Zanzibar" are banal compared to Sammy Cahn's words for "Road to Morocco," but it's a funny routine, with cannibals chanting a nonsense background.

ROAD WARRIOR, THE
DVD
1981 94m c Science Fiction/Action ★★★★
Warner Bros. (Australia) R

Mel Gibson *(Max)*, Bruce Spence *(Gyro Captain)*, Vernon Wells *(Wez)*, Emil Minty *(Feral Kid)*, Mike Preston *(Pappagallo)*, Kjell Nilsson *(Humungus)*, Virginia Hey *(Warrior Woman)*, Syd Heylen *(Curmudgeon)*, Moira Claux *(Big Rebecca)*, David Slingsby *(Quiet Man)*

p, Byron Kennedy; d, George Miller; w, Terry Hayes, George Miller, Brian Hannat; ph, Dean Semler (Panavision, Technicolor); ed, David Stiven, Tim Wellburn, Michael Chirgwin; m, Brian May; art d, Graham Walker; fx, Jeffrey Clifford, Kim Priest; cos, Norma Moriceau

Director George Miller, whose MAD MAX set new stan-dards of kinetic, visceral excitement, surpasses himself with the sequel. The film is set in a savage, post-apocalyptic world devoted solely to the pursuit of gasoline with which to fuel surviving vehicles. Max (Mel Gibson), whose wife and child were killed in the previous movie, has become an alienated drifter. He is led by the Gyro Captain (Bruce Spence) to a small oil refinery populated by the "good" people under the leadership of Pappagallo (Mike Preston). Their precious encampment is continuously besieged by an army of grotesque, nomadic desert rats led by a massive bodybuilder known as the Humungus (Kjell Nilsson), who wants their gasoline. In one of the most spectacular chase scenes ever put on film, Max and his comrades fight off a series of vicious high-speed attacks from a convoy of bizarre vehicles.

Miller brings every visual trick in the book into play, creating a stunningly detailed, vibrant new world that never ceases to amaze. He pulls all the fresh and original elements of MAD MAX together, and straightens out his earlier mud-dled narrative style into a strict linear plot that rips along at a breathtaking pace. In addition, THE ROAD WARRIOR has a connotative richness unusual for an action film, drawing equally on cinematic history (Max's relationship with The Feral Kid echoes SHANE), classical literature (the film is replete with references to the *Iliad*), and myth (Miller was a devotee of scholar-guru Joseph Campbell long before his work on myth and the heroic tradition became inescapably trendy during the late 1980s). Perhaps needless to say, this is the film that made Mel Gibson an international star.

ROARING TWENTIES, THE
DVD
1939 104m bw Crime ★★★★
Warner Bros. (U.S.)

James Cagney *(Eddie Bartlett)*, Priscilla Lane *(Jean Sherman)*, Humphrey Bogart *(George Hally)*, Jeffrey Lynn *(Lloyd Hart)*, Gladys George *(Panama Smith)*, Frank McHugh *(Danny Green)*, Paul Kelly *(Nick Brown)*, Elisabeth Risdon *(Mrs. Sherman)*, Edward Keane *(Pete Henderson)*, Joe Sawyer *(Sgt. Pete Jones)*

p, Samuel Bischoff; d, Raoul Walsh, Anatole Litvak; w, Jerry Wald, Richard Macaulay, Robert Rossen (based on a story by Mark

Hellinger); ph, Ernest Haller; ed, Jack Killifer; m, Heinz Roemheld, Ray Heindorf; art d, Max Parker; fx, Byron Haskin, Edwin DuPar; cos, Milo Anderson

A fitting finale to a decade of memorable gangster films. This slick, whirlwind-paced crime melodrama is another tour de force for James Cagney, making it a companion piece to ANGELS WITH DIRTY FACES. It was the brain-child of journalist-turned-producer Mark Hellinger, who assures audiences in voice-over during the opening credits that what they are about to see is based upon real people and events he covered as a newsman during the 1920s, when the gangster was king and Prohibition was nothing more than a bad law that elevated the gangster to his deadly throne.

The picture opens with three WWI doughboys, Eddie Bartlett (Cagney), George Hally (Bogart) and Lloyd Hart (Lynn) discussing their future plans in a bomb crater during a battle in France. Hart intends to become a lawyer, and Eddie plans on going back to repairing cabs, but Hally explains that he is determined to put his Army weapons training to good use. Back home, Eddie becomes a success-ful bootlegger, hires Hally away from a rival gin peddler, and employs Hart to handle legal affairs for the legit end of his business. When war breaks out between the rival gangs, Hally, tired of playing second fiddle, helps set Eddie up in a trap that backfires. Later, Hally decides to go after Hart, who is now a crusading attorney. Chorus girl Jean (Lane) begs Eddie for help, and the stage is set for a climactic confronta-tion between Cagney and Bogart. Viewers aren't likely to forget Cagney's walk down the street at the end of the film.

Walsh's direction of this third and last film in which Cagney and Bogart appeared together is awesomely swift, encompassing a decade in slick episodes, interspersed with newsreel footage of gangsters, rumrunning, and booze being made on an assembly line. Eddie is shown to be a good man ruined by the excesses of the times. Though he has gone bad, strains of decency are apparent in his relationship with Hart and Jean, and in his self-sacrificing attempt to save them from the violence of Hally.

Cagney gives a supercharged performance, particularly when he is down-and-out and acting the role of a drunk in a stupor. Bogart is icily sinister as a man devoid of human kind-ness or affection, while George is terrific as the loyal saloon gal who will go to the Devil for her man.

Cagney's role is based upon the spectacular rise and fall of New York gangster Larry Fay, a colorful and enigmatic underworld character who promoted the career of brassy nightclub singer Texas Guinan (the role model for Panama). Fay also reputedly provided the inspiration for F. Scott Fitzgerald's *The Great Gatsby*. This would be Cagney's last gangster film for a decade, until he took on the psychotic lead role in WHITE HEAT, working again with his good friend Walsh.

ROBE, THE
DVD
1953 135m c Religious ★★½
Fox (U.S.)

Richard Burton (*Marcellus Gallio*), Jean Simmons (*Diana*), Victor Mature (*Demetrius*), Michael Rennie (*Peter*), Jay Robinson (*Caligula*), Dean Jagger (*Justus*), Torin Thatcher (*Sen. Gallio*), Richard Boone (*Pilate*), Betta St. John (*Miriam*), Jeff Morrow (*Paulus*)

p, Frank Ross; d, Henry Koster; w, Albert Maltz (originally uncred-ited), Philip Dunne (based on the novel by Lloyd C. Douglas); Gina Kaus; ph, Leon Shamroy (CinemaScope, Technicolor); ed, Barbara McLean; m, Alfred Newman; art d, Lyle Wheeler, George W. Davis; fx, Ray Kellogg

AAN Best Picture; AAN Best Actor: Richard Burton; *AAN Best Color Cinematography:* Leon Shamroy; *AA Best Art Direction-Set Decoration (Color):* Lyle Wheeler, George W. Davis, Walter M. Scott, Paul S. Fox; *AA Best Costume Design (Color):* Charles LeMaire, Emile Santiago

Fighting for fashion, in widescreen no less. A heavy Biblical dirge, bulging with blandfilmitis bigbudgetitis, THE ROBE was the first film in CinemaScope, Hollywood's answer to the threat of TV. Audiences (primarily Catholic schoolchildren dragged kicking and screaming by their teachers) dutifully poured into theaters to watch orgy-weary Roman officer turned luminous Christian Richard Burton (very stiff in a part he considered prissy and silly) and his equally shiny and suf-fering co-star Jean Simmons (who deserves better) fight for a bolt of cloth that J.C. (and we don't mean Joan Crawford) wore before his death. Their opponent is evil emperor Caligula (Jay Robinson, in a flamboyant camp classic per-formance that must be seen to be believed). Luckily, Dick and Jean, who have an unfortunate date with death, have Demetrius (the Mature Vic, giving the film's best perform-ance) on their side. He rescues the rumpled but revered wrap just in time to tote it with him to the sequel, DEMETRIUS AND THE GLADIATORS, where he must face a more dan-gerous lioness than any Caligula ever kept penned up: Susie Hayward. Stick with THE TEN COMMANDMENTS, or try watching FELLINI SATYRICON instead.

ROBERTA
1935 105m bw Musical/Comedy ★★★★
RKO (U.S.)

Irene Dunne (*Stephanie*), Fred Astaire (*Huck Haines*), Ginger Rogers (*Countess Scharwenka/Lizzie Gatz*), Randolph Scott (*John Kent*), Helen Westley (*Roberta/Aunt Minnie*), Victor Varconi (*Ladislaw*), Claire Dodd (*Sophie*), Luis Alberni (*Voyda*), Ferdinand Munier (*Lord Delves*), Torben Meyer (*Albert*)

p, Pandro S. Berman; d, William A. Seiter; w, Jane Murfin, Sam Mintz, Allan Scott, Glenn Tryon (from the musical play *Roberta* by Jerome Kern and Otto Harbach based on the novel *Gowns By Roberta* by Alice Duer Miller); ph, Edward Cronjager; ed, William Hamilton; m, Jerome Kern; art d, Van Nest Polglase, Carroll Clark; chor, Fred Astaire, Hermes Pan; cos, Bernard Newman

AAN Best Song: "Lovely To Look At"; Jerome Kern (Music), Dorothy Fields (Lyrics), Jimmy McHugh (Lyrics)

The least-seen and appreciated of the magical Astaire-Rogers series at RKO, this now seems, along with TOP HAT and SWING TIME, one of the three wonder films of the series. Astaire and Rogers persistently upstage the romantic leads, Irene Dunne and Randolph Scott, and they simply fly, largely unburdened by the plot.

John Kent (Scott) is a former football star touring Europe with a swing band led by his pal Huck Haines (Astaire, in a role that combined those performed by Bob Hope and George Murphy in the Broadway original). In Paris they visit the salon of noted designer Mme. Roberta, actually John's Aunt Minnie (a marvelous Westley), where they encounter Stephanie (Dunne), a Russian princess employed there since the Revolution. They also meet Countess Scharwenka (Rogers), who, as with the other women, is not what she seems—she's an old girlfriend of Huck's using an aristocratic Polish stage name. John becomes involved with Stephanie, Huck and his old flame rekindle their passion, and together the four see to it that the fashion show goes on at the finale.

What's hung on this frivolous plot are some of Jerome Kern's most beautiful tunes and a set of dances that leave audi-ences waiting impatiently for the return of Astaire and Rogers. Thankfully they return frequently. "I'll Be Hard to Handle" remains one of their greatest ever, partly because it firmly establishes the personas of "Fred and Ginger" in the popular imagination. Astaire, a great light comedian, makes the most of his many savage wisecracks, and a hilarious Rogers steals practically every scene in which she appears. Astaire does one of his all-time greatest solos to "I Won't Dance," a brilliantly choreographed and performed routine. Two other brief duets, a touchingly simple yet dramatic romantic turn to "Smoke Gets in Your Eyes," and a blistering final recap of "I Won't Dance" make this film dancer-happy to the max.

ROBIN AND MARIAN
1976 106m c Romance/Adventure ★★★
Columbia (U.K.) PG

Sean Connery (*Robin Hood*), Audrey Hepburn (*Maid Marian*), Robert Shaw (*Sheriff of Nottingham*), Richard Harris (*King Richard*); Nicol Williamson (*Little John*), Denholm Elliott (*Will Scarlett*), Kenneth Haigh (*Sir Ranulf de Pudsey*), Ronnie Barker (*Friar Tuck*), Ian Holm (*King John*), Bill Maynard (*Mercadier*)

p, Denis O'Dell; d, Richard Lester; w, James Goldman; ph, David Watkin (Technicolor); ed, John Victor Smith; m, John Barry; prod d, Michael Stringer; art d, Gil Parrondo; fx, Eddie Fowlie; cos, Yvonne Blake

ROMEO AND JULIET for senior citizens. What might have been a wonderful movie is only so-so due to Lester's typically (but here unnecessarily) busy direction and a ponderous script by James Goldman, who had so much success with THE LION IN WINTER that some of his lines for this seem like bon mots he may have cut from that screenplay. Twenty years have passed since the bandit who robbed from the rich to give to the poor ran off to fight in the Crusades with his beloved king. He's now back, in the form of wizened Connery, and in the two decades since he left much has transpired. His love, Marian, is still a maid; she's become a nun, in fact. The king (Harris), meanwhile, has become a madman dedicated to amassing a fortune. The one thing remaining constant in Robin's life is that the sheriff of Nottingham (Shaw) is still eager to see him hang. Robin hooks up with some of the old gang (including Nicol Williamson, all wrong as Little John), kidnaps Marian and gets involved in some spirited adventures, climaxing with a long, cruel duel with the nasty sheriff.

The film's greatest asset is the teaming of Connery and Hepburn. Their more quiet and amusing moments together are as luminous as one would expect, and the coda is very touching indeed. Taken as a whole, ROBIN AND MARIAN is a spotty picture that's sometimes satirical, a trifle pretentious, occasionally exciting. If the powers that be had decided to shoot an all-out comedy that showed Connery creakily trying to recapture his old derring-do, it might have made more sense. Hepburn came back to movies after a nine-year absence to accept this role and had nothing but praise for Lester's quick direction. The trouble is that it's either too quick or too slow, and neither he nor the screenwriter achieve a supple balance between the rueful laughter of maturity and the depressing horrors of medieval bloodshed and old age. You just don't know where you stand with this one.

ROBIN HOOD: PRINCE OF THIEVES
1991 143m c Action/Adventure/Historical ★★½
Morgan Creek/Trilogy Entertainment Group PG-13
(U.S.)

Kevin Costner (*Robin of Locksley/Robin Hood*), Morgan Freeman (*Azeem*), Mary Elizabeth Mastrantonio (*Maid Marian*), Christian Slater (*Will Scarlett*), Alan Rickman (*Sheriff of Nottingham*), Geraldine McEwan (*Mortianna*), Michael McShane (*Friar Tuck*), Brian Blessed (*Lord Locksley*), Michael Wincott (*Guy of Gisborne*), Nick Brimble (*Little John*)

p, Richard B. Lewis, Pen Densham, John Watson; d, Kevin Reynolds; w, Pen Densham, John Watson (from the story by

Densham); ph, Doug Milsome; ed, Peter Boyle; m, Michael Kamen; prod d, John Graysmark; art d, Alan Tomkins, Fred Carter, John F. Ralph; cos, John Bloomfield

AAN Best Original Song: "(Everything I Do) I Do It for You"; Michael Kamen (Music), Bryan Adams (Lyrics), Robert John Lange (Lyrics)

One of 1991's biggest hits, for reasons increasingly obscure. Costner and company struggle desperately to make the Robin Hood legend relevant to contemporary audiences.

With the help of Azeem (Morgan Freeman), young nobleman Robin of Locksley (Kevin Costner) escapes from a Middle Eastern prison and makes his way home to England, where a rude surprise awaits him. His father has been murdered, King Richard is in exile, and Prince John has usurped the throne. Locally, the wicked Sheriff of Nottingham (Alan Rickman), has laid siege to the countryside. Robin gathers his merry men and fights back, pausing only for romance with the lovely, strong-willed Maid Marian (Mary Elizabeth Mastrantonio).

If nothing else, ROBIN HOOD: THE PRINCE OF THIEVES is resolutely politically correct, positing a feminist Marian, adding women to the band of merry men, and inventing the incongruous Azeem, a black Muslim. Costner's surprisingly portly Robin is less a dashing force of justice than a decent kind of guy forced by circumstance to do the right thing because the wrong thing—embodied in the flamboyantly wicked Sheriff of Nottingham—is so obviously unacceptable. He's a Robin Hood for an age when no one believes in heroes.

Director Kevin Reynolds (FANDANGO) has no flair for action: the climactic battle is so ineptly shot and edited that it is difficult to tell who is smiting whom. While Costner is lifeless and speaks strangely (he was said to have attempted a British accent, then abandoned it during shooting), Mastrantonio is an acceptably vivacious Marian. As the Sheriff of Nottingham, Alan Rickman, swaggering through his scenes in sinister black, hissing one-liners and basically acting up a storm, is so theatrically vile that he seems to be in another movie altogether; one can't help but think it's a more entertaining movie than ROBIN HOOD: PRINCE OF THIEVES.

ROBOCOP
1987 103m c Crime/Science Fiction ★★★½
Orion (U.S.) R

Peter Weller (*Alex J. Murphy/Robocop*), Nancy Allen (*Anne Lewis*), Ronny Cox (*Richard "Dick" Jones*), Kurtwood Smith (*Clarence J. Boddicker*), Miguel Ferrer (*Robert Morton*), Robert DoQui (*Sgt. Reed*), Dan O'Herlihy (*The Old Man*), Ray Wise (*Leon Nash*), Felton Perry (*Johnson*), Mario Machado

p, Arne L. Schmidt; d, Paul Verhoeven; w, Edward Neumeier, Michael Miner; ph, Jost Vacano (DuArt Color); ed, Frank J. Urioste; prod d, William Sandell; art d, Gayle Simon; fx, Dale Martin, Rob Bottin, Craig Davies, Peter Ronzani; cos, Erica Edell Phillips

AAN Best Film Editing: Frank J. Urioste; *AAN Best Sound:* Michael J. Kohut, Carlos DeLarios, Aaron Rochin, Robert Wald

A first-rate production full of nonstop action and inventive special effects but what truly makes ROBOCOP spellbinding is a superior script. Intelligent and satirical, it has the quality of cutting-edge British comic books such as the "Judge Dredd" series. Kudos to the screenwriting team of Michael Miner and Edward Neumeier.

It's the not-too-distant future in crime-ridden Old Detroit. A corporate conglomerate is running the city and, under the direction of Richard Jones (Ronny Cox), has developed a huge metal android to combat rampant street crime. When this creation demonstrates a murderous "glitch," Robert Morton

(Miguel Ferrer) sees an opportunity to advance his company position by building a better cop machine. He gets his chance when cop Alex Murphy (Peter Weller) is brutally killed by a gang of sadistic hoodlums. Murphy's body is reconstructed by technicians and dubbed RoboCop. It proves to be more than effective against street criminals thereby elevating Morton to top corporate management. This motivates the scheming Jones to make a pact with supervillain Boddicker (Kurtwood Smith) to destroy RoboCop.

Though extremely violent, ROBOCOP showcases an invigorating style even in its goriest scenes. Paul Verhoeven makes every scene sparkle with tilted angles, oddball twists, and special-effects wonders. ROBOCOP effectively conveys a combination of reality and fantasy in a hard-boiled world of humane robots and unfeeling humans.

ROBOTS

2005 89m c Animated/Comedy ★★★
Fox Animation Studios/Blue Sky Studios (U.S.) PG

VOICES OF: Ewan McGregor (Rodney Copperbottom), Robin Williams (Fender), Mel Brooks (Bigweld), Amanda Bynes (Piper), Greg Kinnear (Phineas T. Ratchet), Halle Berry (Cappy), Jennifer Coolidge (Aunt Fanny), Jim Broadbent (Madame Gasket), Stanley Tucci (Herb Copperbottom), Dianne Wiest (Mrs. Copperbottom)

p, Jerry Davis, Jonh C. Donkin, William Joyce; d, Chris Wedge, Carlos Saldanha (co-director); w, Lowell Ganz, David Lindsay-Abaire, Babaloo Mandel (from a story by David Lindsay-Abaire, Jim McClain, and Ron Mita); ed, John Carnochan; m, John Powell; prod d, William Joyce; art d, Steve Martino; fx, Kirk Garfield, Mike Gargiulo (CGI), Michael J. Travers (CGI); anim, James Bresnahan, Galen Tan Chu, Michael Thurmeier, David Torres

The mechanical script takes a while to get into gear, but this computer-generated "reach for the stars" story is a well-calibrated piece of entertainment.

When it comes to their "child," Rodney (Ewan McGregor), working-class robots Mr. and Mrs. Copperbottoms (Stanley Tucci, Dianne Wiest) couldn't be more proud: Rodney is far more than the sum of his spare parts. An aspiring inventor, Rodney idolizes self-made tycoon and TV personality Mr. Bigweld (Mel Brooks), whose motivational mantra, "You can shine no matter what you're made of!" encourages Rodney to leave cozy little Rivet Town for Robot City. He hopes to show Mr. Bigweld his not quite perfected Wonderbot, a helpful little teapot with stress-management issues, but disappointment awaits. After a wild, Rube Goldbergian train trip with motormouth Fender (Robin Williams), Rodney discovers that Bigweld has been ousted from Bigweld Industries by the super-shiny corporate tool Phineas T. Ratchet (Greg Kinnear). Ratchet has a cruel new motto—"Why be you, when you can be new?"—and big plans to sell expensive, full-body upgrades to rich robots and consign the rest to the scrap heap run by his mother, Madame Gasket (Jim Broadbent). Rodney is determined to return Mr. Bigweld from hiding, and dedicates himself to keeping out-of-date robots in good working order. Helped by Fender, Fender's little sister, Piper (Amanda Bynes), and Aunt Fanny (Jennifer Coolidge), who lends new meaning to the term "junk in the trunk," Rodney assembles a plan to thwart Ratchet's wicked scheme.

Directed by Chris Wedge (ICE AGE), this energetic, pun-laden feature abounds with meticulous visual details, from peeling coats of paint to the robotized *American Gothic* painting on Fender's wall. They add depth and texture to this brightly colored coming-of-age adventure and help flesh out the notion that not all tin men are heartless.

ROCCO AND HIS BROTHERS

(ROCCO ET SES FRERES)
1960 175m bw Drama ★★★★
Titanus/Marceau (France/Italy)

Alain Delon (Rocco Parondi), Renato Salvatori (Simone Parondi), Annie Girardot (Nadia), Katina Paxinou (Rosaria Parondi), Roger Hanin (Morini), Paolo Stoppa (Boxing Impresario), Suzy Delair (Luisa), Claudia Cardinale (Ginetta), Spiros Focas (Vincenzo Parondi), Max Cartier (Ciro Parondi)

p, Giuseppe Bordogni; d, Luchino Visconti; w, Luchino Visconti, Suso Cecchi D'Amico, Pasquale Festa Campanile, Massimo Franciosa, Enrico Medioli (based on the novel The Bridge of Ghisolfa by Giovanni Testori); ph, Giuseppe Rotunno; ed, Mario Serandrei; m, Nino Rota; art d, Mario Garbuglia; cos, Piero Tosi

Luchino Visconti's episodic prize-winning study of five brothers and their widowed mother transplanted from rural Sicily to industrial Milan in northern Italy is violent, deliberately operatic, and makes ambiguous social statements. The characters' relationships are explored over a period of 12 years, with concentration chiefly on Delon and Salvatori as they alternately enjoy and abuse the affections of Girardot, a prostitute who yearns to be free. She loves Delon, but he sacrifices her to the brutal Salvatori because the latter seems to have greater need of her love. Unable to return Salvatori's affection or to put up with his possessiveness, she returns to her former profession. Enraged, he stabs her to death (the 13 on-screen stabbings in European versions are cut to three for American audiences). ROCCO exists in a variety of running times. The American premiere audience found the 175-minute version overlong and began walking out before the film's final scene ended; but the raped 95-minute version should be avoided.

ROCK AROUND THE CLOCK

1956 77m bw Musical ★★★
Columbia (U.S.)

Bill Haley and the Comets, The Platters, Tony Martinez and His Band, Frankie Bell and His Bellboys (Themselves), Alan Freed (Himself), Johnnie Johnston (Steve Hollis), Alix Talton (Corinne Talbot), Lisa Gaye (Lisa Johns), John Archer (Mike Dennis), Henry Slate (Corny LaSalle)

p, Sam Katzman; d, Fred F. Sears; w, Robert E. Kent, James B. Gordon; ph, Benjamin Kline; ed, Saul A. Goodkind, Jack Ogilvie; art d, Paul Palmentola; chor, Earl Barton

The rock 'n' roll movie. Producer Sam Katzman and director Fred Sears again pooled their exploitative talents to deliver a film not so much *about* rock 'n' roll, but a film that *was* rock 'n' roll. The story is barely evident—legendary rock deejay Alan Freed discovers Bill Haley and the Comets in a mountain village and brings them back to New York, where they quickly become a musical phenomenon. Katzman was correct in assuming that if rock concerts could cause youth riots, so could a movie. In England, soon after a couple of screenings, young rockers were tearing up the seats and dancing up a storm. Of course all their moms and dads were bowled over with shock and banned the film from the theaters. Even now it can still make the feet move to the beat. Haley's tunes include "Razzle Dazzle," "Happy Baby," "See You Later, Alligator," "Rudy's Rock," and the greatest rocker of them all "Rock around the Clock." And then there's "The Great Pretender," "Only You" (The Platters), "Codfish and Potatoes," "Sad and Lonely," "Cuero," "Mambo Capri" (Tony Martinez), "Giddy Up, Ding Dong," and "We're Gonna Teach You to Rock" (Freddie Bell).

ROCK 'N' ROLL HIGH SCHOOL *DVD*

1979 93m c Musical/Comedy ★★★★
New World (U.S.) PG

P.J. Soles *(Riff Randell)*, Vincent Van Patten *(Tom Roberts)*, Clint Howard *(Eaglebauer)*, Dey Young *(Kate Rambeau)*, Mary Woronov *(Evelyn Togar)*, Dick Miller *(Police Chief Klein)*, Paul Bartel *(Mr. McGree)*, Alix Elias *(Coach Steroid)*, Don Steele *(Screamin' Steve Stevens)*, Loren Lester *(Fritz Hansel)*

p, Michael Finnell; d, Allan Arkush; w, Richard Whitley, Russ Dvonch, Joseph McBride (based on a story by Arkush, Joe Dante); ph, Dean Cundey (Metrocolor); ed, Larry Bock, Gail Werbin; m, The Ramones; art d, Marie Kordus; chor, Siana Lee Hall; cos, Jack Buehler

When tickets for an upcoming concert by her favorite rock band, the Ramones, go on sale, aspiring teenage songwriter Riff Randell (P.J. Soles) skips school to be the first in line, enraging Evelyn Togar (Mary Woronov), the no-nonsense principal of Vince Lombardi High School, who has dedicated herself to putting an end to her charges' obsession with rock 'n' roll. Aided by a couple of aggressive henchmen (Loren Lester and Daniel Davies), Togar does everything in her power to see that no backbeat bopping deters her students from their studies, including confiscating all of the Ramones' concert tickets Riff has purchased. Meanwhile, under the guidance of the school's resident operator, Eaglebauer (Clint Howard), Tom Roberts (Vince Van Patten), a handsome but hopelessly unhip football player, pursues Riff, while smart but not particularly sexy Kate Rambeau (Dey Young) tries to win Tom's affections. The action heats up—both in Tom's van and between Togar and the students—and after an attempted record burning, Riff, the kids, *and* the Ramones prove once again that winning isn't everything, it's the only thing, turning Lombardi High into Rock 'n' Roll High School. Written by Joe Dante and directed by Allan Arkush, this refreshingly wacky teenage film is filled with warped humor (including mice exploding to Ramones music), and makes wonderful use of the "so dumb they're smart" Ramones, who stepped to the fore when Cheap Trick backed out of the project. Nothing is taken seriously and nothing should be—it's only rock 'n' roll.

ROCKY *DVD*

1976 119m c Sports ★★★★
UA (U.S.) PG

Sylvester Stallone *(Rocky Balboa)*, Talia Shire *(Adrian)*, Burt Young *(Paulie)*, Carl Weathers *(Apollo Creed)*, Burgess Meredith *(Mickey)*, Thayer David *(Miles Jergens)*, Joe Spinell *(Tom Gazzo)*, Jimmy Gambina *(Mike)*, Bill Baldwin *(Fight Announcer)*, Aldo Silvani *(Cut Man)*

p, Irwin Winkler, Robert Chartoff; d, John G. Avildsen; w, Sylvester Stallone; ph, James Crabe (Technicolor); ed, Richard Halsey, Scott Conrad; m, Bill Conti; prod d, William J. Cassidy; art d, James H. Spencer; fx, Garrett Brown; chor, Sylvester Stallone; cos, Robert Cambel, Joanne Hutchinson

AA Best Picture; AAN Best Actor: Sylvester Stallone; *AAN Best Actress:* Talia Shire; *AAN Best Supporting Actor:* Burgess Meredith; *AAN Best Supporting Actor:* Burt Young; *AA Best Director:* John G. Avildsen; *AAN Best Original Screenplay:* Sylvester Stallone; *AA Best Film Editing:* Richard Halsey, Scott Conrad; *AAN Best Original Song:* "Gonna Fly Now"; Bill Conti (Music), Carol Connors (Lyrics), Ayn Robbins (Lyrics); *AAN Best Sound:* Harry Warren Tetrick, William McCaughey, Lyle Burbridge, Bud Alper

Better films have been made about the world of sports, but for many ROCKY is *the* sports movie. As drenched in sentiment as it is in sweat, as much love story as fight film, this classic tale of a tireless "bum" who makes good is one of the most uplifting films ever made. Set primarily in working-class Philadelphia, it follows the fortunes of Rocky Balboa (Sylvester Stallone), a 30-year-old club fighter who earns his living as a collections man for a loan shark. His boxing career has hit bottom, but Rocky's love life is looking up. He clumsily but endearingly woos Adrian (Talia Shire), the shy, repressed sister of Paulie (Burt Young), Rocky's friend who engineers their strange first date, and in no time, Rocky and Adrian are deeply in love. When a challenger's injury leaves the Ali-like world heavyweight champion Apollo Creed (ex-Oakland Raider linebacker Carl Weathers) without an opponent for his upcoming title defense, the boisterous champ decides to give a nobody a chance and chooses Rocky, "the Italian Stallion." Urged on by Mickey (Burgess Meredith), his crotchety old manager, and to the accompaniment of Bill Conti's rousing theme "Gonna Fly Now," Rocky undergoes grueling training for his title long shot: doing one-armed push-ups, pounding slabs of meat in a slaughterhouse freezer, making his now-famous run through the Philadelphia streets and up the steps of its art museum. Come fight time, Rocky wants only to go the distance with Creed, to prove he isn't "just another bum from the neighborhood." Surprising everyone, he gives Creed the fight of his life, narrowly losing a split decision. Amid the post-fight hubbub, Rocky and Adrian meet in a loving mid-ring clinch. Establishing a formula that would be duplicated over and over (especially in its own sequels—see ROCKY series), the film slowly draws the audience into Rocky's struggle, until his triumph becomes that of every "little guy" who's dreamed of making it big. Reminiscent of Marlon Brando's Terry Malloy (ON THE WATERFRONT) and Paul Newman's Rocky Graziano (SOMEBODY UP THERE LIKES ME), Stallone's Rocky is magnificent, mirroring the actor's own battle for Hollywood success. As a struggling actor and screenwriter known mainly for THE LORDS OF FLATBUSH, Stallone, inspired by New Jersey club boxer Chuck Wepner's courageous loss to Muhammad Ali (a 15th-round TKO), wrote ROCKY's screenplay in three days. Determined to star in it himself, he turned down a quarter-million-dollar offer for his script, won the part, and, under John Avildsen's Oscar-winning direction, gave the screen one of its most memorable characters. The fairy-tale championship match is generally well choreographed (by Stallone), and the training montage, in its originality, remains more gripping than the many glossier imitations it inspired. Expertly paced, benefiting from well-drawn characters and an evocative, often funny script, ROCKY simply pushes all the right buttons. Former heavyweight champ and Philly native Joe Frazier appears as himself.

ROCKY II *DVD*

1979 119m c Sports ★★★½
UA (U.S.) PG

Sylvester Stallone *(Rocky Balboa)*, Talia Shire *(Adrian)*, Burt Young *(Paulie)*, Carl Weathers *(Apollo Creed)*, Burgess Meredith *(Mickey)*, Tony Burton *(Apollo's Trainer)*, Joe Spinell *(Gazzo)*, Leonard Gaines *(Agent)*, Sylvia Meals *(Mary Anne Creed)*, Frank McRae *(Meat Foreman)*

p, Irwin Winkler, Robert Chartoff; d, Sylvester Stallone; w, Sylvester Stallone; ph, Bill Butler (Panavision, Technicolor); ed, Danford B. Greene, Stanford C. Allen, Janice Hampton, James Symons; m, Bill Conti; art d, Richard Berger; chor, Sylvester Stallone; cos, Tom Bronson, Sandra Berke

Considerably less satisfying than the original ROCKY, but head and shoulders above the later installments, ROCKY II picks up the saga of "the Italian Stallion" during the last two rounds of his gutsy loss to world champ Apollo Creed (Carl Weathers). After the bout, Rocky (Sylvester Stallone) and

Adrian (Talia Shire), his no-longer-mousy sweetheart, marry and use his fight purse to buy a car and condo. Soon Rocky learns that if he enters the ring again he runs the risk of being blinded in the eye he injured fighting Apollo. He does his best to provide for Adrian but is laid off by the slaughterhouse where he works with his brother-in-law, Paulie (Burt Young). Worried about the future—which is about to include a new baby—Rocky accepts a rematch with Apollo, who is anxious to prove Rocky's showing in their first bout was a fluke.

All the endearing characters from Part One are back, as is Bill Conti's familiar music—indeed, the sequel is a virtual remake of the original film. This time Stallone both wrote and directed the film, and though his handling of the actors and camera is less assured than John Avildsen's in ROCKY, he keeps things moving at a good pace and delivers another charming performance himself.

ROCKY HORROR PICTURE SHOW, THE *DVD*
1975 100m c   Comedy/Horror/Musical   ★★★
Adler/White (U.K.)   R

Tim Curry *(Dr. Frank N. Furter)*, Susan Sarandon *(Janet Weiss)*, Barry Bostwick *(Brad Majors)*, Richard O'Brien *(Riff Raff)*, Jonathan Adams *(Dr. Everett Scott)*, Nell Campbell, billed as Little Nell *(Columbia)*, Peter Hinwood *(Rocky Horror)*, Patricia Quinn *(Magenta)*, Meat Loaf, billed as Meatloaf *(Eddie)*, Charles Gray *(Criminologist)*

p, Michael White, John Goldstone; d, Jim Sharman; w, Jim Sharman, Richard O'Brien (based on the stage musical by O'Brien); ph, Peter Suschitzky (Eastmancolor); ed, Graeme Clifford; m, Richard O'Brien; prod d, Brian Thomson; art d, Terry Ackland Snow; fx, Wally Veevers; chor, David Toguri; cos, Sue Blane, Richard Pointing, Gillian Dods

This film has become the official definition of a cult movie— so much so that the audience watching (or more accurately, participating in) the picture is the most interesting element. What happens on the screen is secondary.

Based on a British musical stage play by O'Brien (who also appears in the film and wrote all the music), RHPS eventually made it to the screen with the help of Lou Adler and Michael White. After a short run in New York it closed, but soon was revived on the midnight circuit. It is the story of Brad and Janet (Bostwick and Sarandon) whose car breaks down during a rainstorm in Ohio. They look for shelter in a mansion, which turns out to be the residence of Dr. Frank N. Furter, wildly played by Curry. They soon find themselves in the middle of a convention of alien transsexuals from the planet Transsexual in the galaxy Transylvania. Curry is ready to reveal his Frankenstein-esque creation—a monster named Rocky who is to be the ultimate sexual male. What follows, in a nutshell, is sex, cannibalism (Meat Loaf is appropriately eaten), murder, seduction, more sex, people being turned into statues, RKO Radio Pictures being spoofed, and Brad and Janet (dammit!) escaping before everything is blown up. The film itself is a lot of fun—but the audience-participation phenomenon has turned it into a one-of-a-kind cinematic experience. SHOCK TREATMENT was a sequel of sorts.

ROGER DODGER *DVD*
2002 105m c   Comedy/Drama   ★★★★
Holedigger Films (U.S.)   R

Campbell Scott *(Roger Swanson)*, Jesse Eisenberg *(Nick)*, Isabella Rossellini *(Joyce)*, Elizabeth Berkley *(Andrea)*, Jennifer Beals *(Sophie)*, Mina Badie *(Donna)*, Ben Shenkman *(Donovan)*, Chris Stack *(Chris)*, Morena Baccarin *(Girl in Bar)*, Lisa Emery *(Woman in Bar)*

p, Anne Chaisson, Dylan Kidd, George Van Buskirk; d, Dylan Kidd; w, Dylan Kidd; ph, Joaquin Baca-Asay; ed, Andy Kier; m, Craig Wedren; prod d, Stephen Beatrice; art d, Dina Varano; cos, Amy Westcott

Campbell Scott's fiendishly mercurial performance as a razor-tongued womanizer is a revelation, but it's only one of this nimble film's pleasures. Dylan Kidd's lacerating dialogue is another, as is the astonishingly accomplished sense of mise-en-scène this writer-director demonstrates in his first feature.

Advertising copywriter Roger (Scott) has a dauntingly articulate theory about everything and knows that the real power of words is that people never expect them to hurt so much. He takes particular pleasure in turning his smug verbosity on women with the nerve to recognize a practiced line of pick-up patter when they hear it. Over the course of one long, harrowing evening of carousing, however, Roger's festering insecurities seep through his polished facade. The twin catalysts for this particular dark night of the libido are a crushing heave-ho from his girlfriend-boss, Joyce (Isabella Rossellini), and a visit from his teenage nephew, Nick (Jesse Eisenberg), a naive high school senior desperate to lose his virginity. Roger squires the youngster around town and instructs him in the tricks of the trade, slipping him into bars, parties, and, finally, one hellish whorehouse.

Scott is the film's excoriating center, but 18-year-old Eisenberg is the ballast that keeps it from lurching into Neil LaBute territory. His Nick is naive without being an idiot, and the youngster's admiration of Roger's slick moves is tempered by an innate understanding that if you spend your life running mind games on women, sooner or later you're going to get played. Kidd makes the most of strong supporting performances from Jennifer Beals and Elizabeth Berkley as a pair of prowling party girls who, like everything else in this bracingly smart movie, aren't what they at first appear.

ROLLERBALL *DVD*
1975 129m c   Sports/Science Fiction   ★★★
UA (U.S.)   R

James Caan *(Jonathan E.)*, John Houseman *(Bartholomew)*, Maud Adams *(Ella)*, John Beck *(Moonpie)*, Moses Gunn *(Cletus)*, Pamela Hensley *(Mackie)*, Barbara Trentham *(Daphne)*, Ralph Richardson *(Librarian)*, Shane Rimmer *(Team Executive)*, Alfred Thomas *(Team Trainer)*

p, Norman Jewison; d, Norman Jewison; w, William Harrison (based on his story "Rollerball Murders"); ph, Douglas Slocombe (Technicolor); ed, Anthony Gibbs; m, Andre Previn, Johann Sebastian Bach, Peter Ilich Tchaikovsky, Dmitri Shostakovich, Tomaso Albinoni; prod d, John Box; art d, Robert Laing; fx, Sass Bedig, John Richardson, Joe Fitt; cos, Julie Harris

It is the year 2018 and society is rid of war and poverty, and the only violence left is supplied by the corporation-controlled rollerball teams, who fight to the bloody finish with spikes and motorcycles in a sport combining roller derby, football, and hockey. When champion rollerball player Caan is asked to retire because the corporate executives who rule the world are fearful that he has become too popular with the masses, he fights the move. To get rid of him, the corporate executives decide to change the rollerball rules and make it a fight to the death. Produced and directed by Norman Jewison, this science-fiction film envisions a time when major corporations will control the populace by offering them a brutal and compelling entertainment to distract from the real social issues at hand and act as a funnel for their frustrations, hatred, and resentment. While the questions raised about the relationship between corporate power and sporting events are valid and intriguing, ROLLERBALL is, unfortunately, hopelessly heavy-handed and ponderous. From its gloomy and solemn air to the overbearing use of baroque music, the film is far too self-important for its own good. Luckily, the performances of Caan and Richardson are excellent, and the rollerball sequences are fast-paced and interesting.

ROLLING THUNDER

1977 99m c Drama/War ★★★
TBC Film (U.S.) R

William Devane *(Maj. Charles Rane)*, Tommy Lee Jones *(Johnny Vohden)*, Linda Haynes *(Linda Forchet)*, Lisa Richards *(Janet)*, Dabney Coleman *(Maxwell)*, Cassie Yates *(Candy)*, Lawrason Driscoll *(Cliff)*, Luke Askew *(Automatic Slim)*, James Victor *(Lopez)*, Jordan Gerler *(Mark)*

p, Norman T. Herman; d, John Flynn; w, Paul Schrader, Heywood Gould (from a story by Paul Schrader); ph, Jordan Cronenweth (Deluxe Color); ed, Frank P. Keller; m, Barry De Vorzon; art d, Steve Berger; fx, Richard Helmer

Hot on the heels of TAXI DRIVER came a new film penned by its prolific screenwriter (soon to be director), Paul Schrader, and shot on a shoestring by in Texas by director John Flynn. ROLLING THUNDER stars Devane (in a superb performance) as a Vietnam POW who, after years in captivity, is returned home along with cellmate Jones. Devane is given a hero's welcome by his little Texas town and presented with a small fortune in silver dollars—one for each day he was a prisoner. While all this attention is heartwarming, he has also come home to a wife who no longer loves him, a son who doesn't remember him, and a society that doesn't understand him. Emotionally deadened by his wartime experiences ("You learn to love the pain," the vet ominously tells his wife's lover), Devane only comes alive after his wife and son are killed by thieves who invade their home to steal the silver coins. The thugs try to torture information out of Devane by shoving his hand down a garbage disposal, but he refuses to break—a macho display that brings about his family's deaths. Fitted with a hook to replace his mangled hand, Devane, with the help of his former comrade Jones, goes to Mexico in search of vengeance. While ROLLING THUNDER suffers from Schrader's predictable obsessions with masculine ritual and gunplay, Devane and Jones enhance the material with their nuanced, sensitive portrayals of men who have lost their souls in another land. The scenes of their attempted readjustment are unforgettable, especially those in which the obviously tormented Jones rots away in the bosom of his stiflingly polite family, who refuse to discuss the war with him. Aside from TAXI DRIVER, this is probably the best of the shortlived Vietnam vet-as-vigilante subgenre, which also included GOOD GUYS WEAR BLACK (1979) and THE EXTERMINATOR (1980).

ROMAN HOLIDAY

DVD
1953 119m bw Romance/Comedy ★★★★
Paramount (U.S.)

Gregory Peck *(Joe Bradley)*, Audrey Hepburn *(Princess Anne)*, Eddie Albert *(Irving Radovich)*, Hartley Power *(Mr. Hennessy)*, Laura Solari *(Hennessy's Secretary)*, Harcourt Williams *(Ambassador)*, Margaret Rawlings *(Countess Vereberg)*, Tullio Carminati *(Gen. Provno)*, Paolo Carlini *(Mario Delani)*, Claudio Ermelli *(Giovanni)*

p, William Wyler; d, William Wyler; w, Ian McLellan Hunter, John Dighton (based on a story by Dalton Trumbo); ph, Franz Planer, Henri Alekan; ed, Robert Swink; m, Georges Auric; art d, Hal Pereira, Walter Tyler; cos, Edith Head

AAN Best Picture; AA Best Actress: Audrey Hepburn; *AAN Best Supporting Actor:* Eddie Albert; *AAN Best Director:* William Wyler; *AA Best Motion Picture Story:* Ian McLellan Hunter (Later accredited to Dalton Trumbo); *AAN Best Screenplay:* Ian McLellan Hunter, John Dighton; *AAN Best B/W Cinematography:* Frank Planer, Henry Alekan; *AAN Best Film Editing:* Robert Swink; *AAN Best Art Direction-Set Decoration (B/W):* Hal Pereira, Walter Tyler; *AA Best Costume Design (B/W):* Edith Head

Delicious, and delectable Audrey's Oscar-winning American debut. But not such a difficult feat with William Wyler backing you up. The secret is in the way Wyler, who had been away from comedy for about 18 years, builds an atmosphere of charm that leads us to her. And it didn't hurt Hepburn at all that she came along during a time when Monroe's sex doll influence had Hollywood brimming over with sex bombs from all over; or that Wyler cast her opposite dependable, protective Gregory Peck. The film gained 10 Academy Award nominations—amazing for a comedy—with Oscars awarded (beside Hepburn) to costumer Edith Head, and Ian McClellan Hunter for the film's story. Charming, wistful, and frothy, it earned strong receipts at the box office. Hepburn, who had previously appeared in six European movies and in "Gigi" on Broadway (selected for her role in that play by author Colette herself, who met the actress in the south of France and was immediately struck by her gamine beauty), ROMAN HOLIDAY auspiciously presents her. She *is* infectious as Anne, a princess on holiday in Rome, where her ever-present coterie includes Rawlings, her chaperon, and Carminati, an aide. Overprotected all her life, she hasn't the vaguest idea of what the world outside her castle and her small country is like. Now in her teenage years, she is beginning to rebel against the formality and constrictions of her royal position and, seeing her chance to see how the other half lives, escapes her claustrophobic entourage. While they conduct a frantic search for her, she falls asleep on a park bench and meets Peck, one of the many reporters who have been trying to interview the princess, who has hitherto been shielded from the world's press corps by her aides. Peck knows he has a major scoop in meeting Hepburn, but initially pretends not to know who she is, taking her on a sightseeing tour of Rome while Albert, a news photographer, secretly snaps pictures of her as she plays hookey. For 24 hours, Peck shows Hepburn the famous sights, as well as some that are less familiar, since it is necessary to evade the police who are looking everywhere for the missing princess. Peck takes her on a motorcycle, they go dancing, and the pair land in some minor scrapes; all the while, the hard-boiled reporter falls harder for the guileless, beautiful Hepburn.

The film also has enough adventure and excitement to satisfy, and the faintly bittersweet note of the ending is made deliciously palatable by its artistic rightness. ROMAN HOLIDAY inspired several imitations, but none came close to the charming insouciance of the original. Hunter, picking up his Oscar, was fronting for blacklisted Dalton Trumbo, who was awarded a posthumous statuette in 1993.

ROMAN SPRING OF MRS. STONE, THE

1961 103m c Drama ★★★½
Seven Arts/Anglo-Amalgamated (U.S./U.K.)

Vivien Leigh *(Karen Stone)*, Warren Beatty *(Pablo di Leo)*, Coral Browne *(Meg)*, Jill St. John *(Bingham)*, Lotte Lenya *(Contessa Magda Terribili-Gonzales)*, Jeremy Spenser *(Young Man)*, Stella Bonheur *(Mrs. Jamison-Walker)*, Josephine Brown *(Lucia)*, Peter Dyneley *(L. Greener)*, Carl Jaffe *(Baron)*

p, Louis de Rochemont; d, Jose Quintero; w, Gavin Lambert, Jan Read (based on the novel by Tennessee Williams); ph, Harry Waxman (Technicolor); ed, Ralph Kampeln; m, Richard Addinsell; prod d, Roger Furse; art d, Herbert Smith; cos, Pierre Balmain, Bumble Dawson

AAN Best Supporting Actress: Lotte Lenya

This picture grows better with age. Leigh was 48, and her husband, Olivier, had just left her for a younger woman. Beatty was 23, eager, ambitious, and sincerely wanting to change his image after SPLENDOR IN THE GRASS. Based on Tennessee Williams's only novel, the screenplay by Lambert became far more explicit in many ways than the subtle, short book. The film preserves many of Williams's bon mots, some of which went right over the heads of the movie's detractors.

Leigh is a fading actress who has just failed in a role more appropriate for a younger woman. She decides that it's time for a vacation in Europe. Her wealthy husband sickens and dies on the way to Italy, but she continues to Rome. When the widow admits to a friend (Browne) that she could use some male companionship, Browne sets her up with high-society pimp Lenya, who provides the widow with a handsome Italian boy (Beatty). Needless to say, Leigh falls in love, and heartbreak results.

The lines are pure Williams. When Lenya has a complaint, Leigh retorts: "The beautiful make their own laws." Beatty mentions a middle-aged woman he knows of who died in bed with her throat cut. Leigh, who has been concentrating on her card hand, looks up and says, "After three more years of this, assassination would be a convenience." Lenya is superb; the great German actress never had much success in U.S. movies, although she will always be remembered as the villainess in FROM RUSSIA WITH LOVE. The assistant director, who went on to great success, was Peter Yates.

ROMANCING THE STONE

1984 105m c Adventure/Romance ★★★½
Fox (U.S.) PG

Michael Douglas *(Jack Colton)*, Kathleen Turner *(Joan Wilder)*, Danny DeVito *(Ralph)*, Zack Norman *(Ira)*, Alfonso Arau *(Juan)*, Manuel Ojeda *(Zolo)*, Holland Taylor *(Gloria)*, Mary Ellen Trainor *(Elaine)*, Eve Smith *(Mrs. Irwin)*, Joe Nesnow *(Super)*

p, Michael Douglas; d, Robert Zemeckis; w, Diane Thomas; ph, Dean Cundey (Panavision, Deluxe Color); ed, Donn Cambern, Frank Morriss; m, Alan Silvestri; prod d, Lawrence G. Paull; art d, Augustin Ituarte; chor, Jeffrey Hornaday; cos, Marilyn Vance

AAN Best Film Editing: Donn Cambern, Frank Morriss

A rousing, old-fashioned romantic adventure about Joan Wilder (Kathleen Turner), an author of lusty, best-selling bodice-rippers whose own life is a colorless bore. The picture opens as a tearful Joan is completing her latest literary fantasy. She's snapped out of her reverie by the arrival of a strange package that contains some sort of treasure map pointing the way to a fabulous gemstone. Then follows a frantic phone call from her sister, who is being held captive by an evil art dealer, Ira (Zack Norman), and his snarling cousin, Ralph (Danny DeVito). Her sister's husband has disappeared in Colombia, and it was he who sent Joan the map. Ira and Ralph threaten to kill Joan's sister unless the treasure map is turned over to Ralph in Colombia. So timid Joan takes off for the jungles of South America only to discover that Zolo (Manuel Ojeda), a corrupt military official, is also after the map. Luckily, she is rescued by a handsome, American soldier-of-fortune, Jack Colton (Michael Douglas), and together they go after the treasure. ROMANCING THE STONE moves like lightning through its 105-minute running time, barely giving viewers a chance to catch their breath. Although comparisons with Steven Spielberg's RAIDERS OF THE LOST ARK are inevitable, it is the interplay between Turner and Douglas that gives the film its real charm. Norman and DeVito score strongly in roles that would have been played by Sydney Greenstreet and Peter Lorre 30 years ago, and the whole film has the feel of an old Warner Bros. thriller with broadly comic overtones. An inferior sequel, THE JEWEL OF THE NILE, was released the following year.

ROMANTIC ENGLISHWOMAN, THE

1975 115m c Comedy/Romance ★★★½
Dial/Meric/Matalon (U.K./France) R

Glenda Jackson *(Elizabeth Fielding)*, Michael Caine *(Lewis Fielding)*, Helmut Berger *(Thomas)*, Marcus Richardson *(David Fielding)*, Kate Nelligan *(Isabel)*, Rene Kolldehoff *(Herman)*, Michel Lonsdale *(Swan)*, Beatrice Romand *(Catherine)*, Anna Steele *(Annie)*, Nathalie Delon *(Miranda)*

p, Daniel M. Angel; d, Joseph Losey; w, Tom Stoppard, Thomas Wiseman (based on the novel by Wiseman); ph, Gerry Fisher (Eastmancolor); ed, Reginald Beck; m, Richard Hartley; art d, Richard MacDonald; cos, Ruth Myers

Caine is a successful writer whose imagination becomes increasingly vivid when his wife, Jackson, travels to Europe. Separated by hundreds of miles and angry emotions, Jackson forgets about her husband and becomes attracted to German drug-smuggler Berger. She returns home to Caine in Britain, and the pair invite Berger to stay with them. Caine is intent on having the fellow help do some writing, but instead finds him fondling his wife. Jackson runs away with Berger, but Caine pursues and retrieves his wife. This intelligent film (a comedy, of sorts) from Joseph Losey explores Luigi Pirandello's concept of characters being under control of the author.

ROMEO AND JULIET

1936 127m bw Romance/Historical ★★★★
MGM (U.S.)

Norma Shearer *(Juliet)*, Leslie Howard *(Romeo)*, Edna May Oliver *(Nurse to Juliet)*, John Barrymore *(Mercutio)*, C. Aubrey Smith *(Lord Capulet)*, Basil Rathbone *(Tybalt)*, Andy Devine *(Peter)*, Henry Kolker *(Friar Lawrence)*, Violet Kemble-Cooper *(Lady Capulet)*, Ralph Forbes *(Paris)*

p, Irving Thalberg; d, George Cukor; w, Talbot Jennings (based on the play by William Shakespeare); ph, William Daniels; ed, Margaret Booth; m, Herbert Stothart; art d, Cedric Gibbons; chor, Agnes De Mille; cos, Oliver Messel, Adrian

AAN Best Picture; AAN Best Actress: Norma Shearer; *AAN Best Supporting Actor:* Basil Rathbone; *AAN Best Interior Decoration:* Cedric Gibbons, Frederic Hope, Edwin B. Willis

MGM production chief and lover of the classics Irving Thalberg spared no expense in this excellent filming of Shakespeare's famous tragedy/romance, starring the queen of the MGM lot, Norma Shearer (Thalberg's wife) and the sensitive Leslie Howard. The eternal Romeo and Juliet story is here brought alive with verve and lavish, gorgeous production values. George Cukor was a good choice to direct this romance, able to communicate to his cast his own passion for the characters. Although Howard and Shearer are technically too old for their roles (the characters were teenagers), they perform splendidly, rendering their parts with great sensitivity. She flutters girlishly a bit too much early on and is not quite right in the balcony scene; her reading of the famous potion speech is, however, superb. Howard, more reticent than one would like, nonetheless performs with considerable grace. Shearer was 34 when she did the film; Howard was 46 and refused the part at first, saying that he was too old. Barrymore gives a spritely, compelling, if somewhat strange performance in the role of Mercutio, delivered with a slight Irish brogue. On the set, Barrymore vexed the gentle Cukor no end by inserting foul words into the beautiful Shakespearean lines. The rest of the cast is fine, and the film as a whole is rather better than some would have it.

ROMEO AND JULIET

1968 138m c   Historical/Romance   **DVD**

British Home Entertainment/Verona/DEG   ★★★★

(U.K./Italy)   PG

Olivia Hussey *(Juliet)*, Leonard Whiting *(Romeo)*, Milo O'Shea *(Friar Laurence)*, Murray Head *(The Chorus)*, Michael York *(Tybalt)*, John McEnery *(Mercutio)*, Pat Heywood *(The Nurse)*, Natasha Parry *(Lady Capulet)*, Robert Stephens *(Prince of Verona)*, Keith Skinner *(Balthazar)*

p, Anthony Havelock-Allan, John Brabourne; d, Franco Zeffirelli; w, Franco Zeffirelli, Masolino D'Amico, Franco Brusati (based on the play by William Shakespeare); ph, Pasqualino De Santis (Technicolor); ed, Reginald Mills; m, Nino Rota; prod d, Lorenzo Mongiardino; art d, Luciano Puccini, Emilio Carcano; cos, Danilo Donati

AAN Best Picture; AAN Best Director: Franco Zeffirelli; AA Best Cinematography: Pasqualino DeSantis; AA Best Costume Design: Danilo Donati

This beautiful version of the Veronese love story was by far the most successful at the box office, although Zeffirelli took a huge chance casting two unknowns in the leads. Whiting was 17 and Hussey was 15, the closest any screen actors have actually come to the ages of the characters. It's a visually stunning adaptation with much action, broad humor, and eroticism. The Italian director had made THE TAMING OF THE SHREW the year before with Elizabeth Taylor and Richard Burton. Although that film was not a big hit, his backers felt that his assured direction merited another attempt at Shakespeare, and the project was filmed in Tuscany at Pienza, Gubbio, Artena, and in the palace once owned by the Borgias. In order to take the onus off the relatively inexperienced leads, Zeffirelli trimmed some of the longer speeches, used reaction shots to break matters up, and gave the actors bits of business to do so they wouldn't seem like talking heads. That technique was successful, although both leads did betray their youth on several occasions. Major excisions in the text include, unforgivably, Juliet's potion speech. Laurence Olivier was around to lend his mellifluous voice as a narrator, a definite plus, but the director is the true star here as he gives us rousing crowd scenes, vicious fights, and a brief nude scene. The sets are magnificent, the supporting actors excellent, and the costumes attractive enough to warrant an Oscar for Donati, beating out another period piece that year, OLIVER!

RONIN

1998 121m c   Action/Spy/Thriller   **DVD**

FGM Entertainment/United Artists   (U.S.)   ★★★

R

Robert De Niro *(Sam)*, Jean Reno *(Vincent)*, Natascha McElhone *(Deirdre)*, Stellan Skarsgard *(Gregor)*, Jonathan Pryce *(Seamus O'Rourke)*, Sean Bean *(Spence)*, Skipp Sudduth *(Larry)*, Michael Lonsdale *(Jean-Pierre)*, Jan Triska *(Dapper Gent)*, Bernard Bloch *(Sergi)*

p, Frank Mancuso Jr.; d, John Frankenheimer; w, J.D. Zeik, David Mamet (based on the stort by J.D. Zeik); ph, Robert Fraisse; ed, Tony Gibbs; m, Elia Cmiral; prod d, Michael Hanan; art d, Gerard Viard; fx, Georges Demetrau; cos, May Routh

A throwback to morose, washed-out-looking, '70s thrillers (think THREE DAYS OF THE CONDOR, THE FRENCH CONNECTION and DAY OF THE JACKAL), by director John Frankenheimer, a veteran who's been there and done all that.

Five professional killers converge in Paris, summoned by the tight-lipped Deirdre (Natascha McElhone) who answers to the ruthless Seamus (Jonathan Pryce) and reveals only that she wants the men to steal a closely guarded metal briefcase. Jacks-

of-all-trades Sam and Vincent (Robert De Niro and Jean Reno) are, respectively, an American ex-CIA operative and a French coordinator of mysterious pedigree. Eastern European Gregor (Stellan Skarsgard) is a computer specialist. The Englishman Spence (Sean Bean) specializes in weapons, and Larry (Skip Sudduth), another American, is the driver. The mercenaries don't know what's in the briefcase, don't trust each other, and think Deirdre is in over her head. Deirdre is clearly troubled by the assignment, vicious Russian gangsters—led by the volatile Mikhi (Feodor Atkine)—are gumming up the works, and after one of the five betrays the rest, the mission dissolves into a bloody, vengeance-driven game of cat and mouse.

Frankenheimer pretty much ignores everything that's happened in the action and thriller genres since 1975, and mostly that's a good thing. It's a relief to see car chases that don't look like high-gloss bumper-car exhibitions, action sequences that aren't aquiver with ultrafast cuts, and professional killers who aren't wisecracking comedians. Frankenheimer, whose GRAND PRIX raised the bar for high-speed auto footage, delivers some brisk action sequences, but his real interest lies in the casually cruel compromises and betrayals that go with the mercenary territory. The question, of course, is whether contemporary thrill junkies can get past the fact that this somber tale delivers no knee-jerk adrenaline rush or cheap moral redemption to justify sitting through the nastiness.

ROOM AT THE TOP

1959 115m bw Drama   **DVD**

Romulus   (U.K.)   ★★★★½

Laurence Harvey *(Joe Lampton)*, Simone Signoret *(Alice Aisgill)*, Heather Sears *(Susan Brown)*, Donald Wolfit *(Mr. Brown)*, Ambrosine Phillpotts *(Mrs. Brown)*, Donald Houston *(Charles Soames)*, Raymond Huntley *(Mr. Hoylake)*, John Westbrook *(Jack Wales)*, Allan Cuthbertson *(George Aisgill)*, Mary Peach *(June Samson)*

p, John Woolf, James Woolf; d, Jack Clayton; w, Neil Paterson (based on the novel by John Braine); ph, Freddie Francis; ed, Ralph Kemplen; m, Mario Nascimbene; art d, Ralph Brinton

AAN Best Picture; AAN Best Actor: Laurence Harvey; AA Best Actress: Simone Signoret; AAN Best Supporting Actress: Hermione Baddeley; AAN Best Director: Jack Clayton; AA Best Adapted Screenplay: Neil Paterson

A ruthless indictment of the British class system, ROOM AT THE TOP is a hallmark, seminal film in the social realist British "kitchen sink" movement, which produced such movies as SATURDAY NIGHT AND SUNDAY MORNING, A TASTE OF HONEY, and THIS SPORTING LIFE. But ROOM set the trend and lured adults back into theaters in droves, thanks to its frank treatment of sexuality and the blaze of energy brought to it by the magnificence and suffering of the incomparable Signoret. You may not agree, but we think (because of *her*) it stands the test of time. Laurence Harvey, the film's ruthless anti-hero, hopes to gatecrash past his working-class origins. Arriving in a bleak Yorkshire industrial town, he secures a low-paying job as a government accountant, but soon realizes that professional skill won't bring social status. He sets his cap for Sears, the naive young daughter of millionaire industrialist Wolfit, who tries to break up the romance by shipping Sears off to the Continent. Harvey then begins an affair with Signoret, a married woman 10 years his senior. When Sears returns, love clashes with ambition.

Based on the "angry young man" novel by John Braine, ROOM AT THE TOP broke new ground in its realistic dialogue, sexual frankness (it received an X certificate in Britain), and bitter condemnation of provincialism and class-consciousness. Jack Clayton, who had previously directed only the mid-length THE BESPOKE OVERCOAT, was hailed as an important new voice in British cinema on its strength, while screenwriter Neil Paterson and Simone Signoret both won Oscars for their work. It also took Best Film and Best Foreign Actress (Signoret) British Film Academy awards, as well as another Best Actress for Signoret at Cannes. Among the supporting performers Wolfit and Phillpotts (as Harvey's wealthy future in-laws) are especially good. ROOM AT THE TOP memorably conveys the snobbery, poverty, desperation, and politics of class in provincial England. A sequel, LIFE AT THE TOP, also starred Harvey, but otherwise failed to live up to the standard of the original.

ROOM WITH A VIEW, A   📀

1985 115m c Comedy/Drama   ★★★★
Cinecom (U.K.)   PG-13

Maggie Smith *(Charlotte Bartlett)*, Helena Bonham Carter *(Lucy Honeychurch)*, Denholm Elliott *(Mr. Emerson)*, Julian Sands *(George Emerson)*, Daniel Day-Lewis, billed as Daniel Day Lewis *(Cecil Vyse)*, Simon Callow *(Rev. Beebe)*, Judi Dench *(Miss Lavish)*, Rosemary Leach *(Mrs. Honeychurch)*, Rupert Graves *(Freddy Honeychurch)*, Patrick Godfrey *(Mr. Eager)*

p, Ismail Merchant; d, James Ivory; w, Ruth Prawer Jhabvala (based on the novel by E.M. Forster); ph, Tony Pierce-Roberts; ed, Humphrey Dixon; m, Richard Robbins; prod d, Gianni Quaranta, Brian Ackland-Snow; cos, Jenny Beavan, John Bright

AAN Best Picture; AAN Best Supporting Actor: Denholm Elliott; AAN Best Supporting Actress: Maggie Smith; AAN Best Director: James Ivory; AA Best Adapted Screenplay: Ruth Prawer Jhabvala; AAN Best Cinematography: Tony Pierce-Roberts; AA Best Art Direction-Set Decoration: Gianni Quaranta, Brian Ackland-Snow, Brian Savegar, Elio Altramura; AA Best Costume Design: Jenny Beavan, John Bright

Made for only $3 million, this Merchant-Ivory production was nominated for eight Oscars and won three. The droll comedy of manners and morals begins in 1907, when Lucy Honeychurch (Helena Bonham Carter) goes off to Italy in the company of Charlotte Bartlett (Maggie Smith), her maiden cousin and spinster chaperone. They arrive in Florence and take up residence at the Pensione Bertolini, where they meet the charming Mr. Emerson (Denholm Elliott) and his son, George (Julian Sands). It's evident from the start that George finds Lucy pleasing to gaze upon, and on a visit to Fiesole, the town high above Florence, he takes the opportunity to kiss the young girl. Charlotte witnesses the kiss and insists they leave for England at once. Back in Surrey, where Lucy lives with her mother (Rosemary Leach) and ne'er-do-well brother, Freddy (Rupert Graves), Lucy settles into her relationship with Cecil (Daniel Day Lewis), the twit to whom she is engaged. But the Emersons move into a vacant villa in the area, and uninhibited passion again enters Lucy's safe world. It's hard to believe A ROOM WITH A VIEW cost so little; the costumes and sets are dazzling and the acting is superb—from two-time Oscar-winner Smith to the smallest role, there's not a false note.

ROPE   📀

1948 80m c Thriller   ★★★
Transatlantic (U.S.)

James Stewart *(Rupert Cadell)*, John Dall *(Shaw Brandon)*, Farley Granger *(Philip)*, Joan Chandler *(Janet Walker)*, Cedric Hardwicke *(Mr. David Kentley's Father)*, Constance Collier *(Mrs. Atwater)*, Edith Evanson *(Mrs. Wilson the Governess)*, Douglas Dick *(Kenneth Lawrence)*, Dick Hogan *(David Kentley)*

p, Sidney Bernstein, Alfred Hitchcock; d, Alfred Hitchcock; w, Arthur Laurents, Hume Cronyn, Ben Hecht (based on the play "Rope's End" by Patrick Hamilton); ph, Joseph Valentine, William

V. Skall (Technicolor); ed, William Ziegler; m, David Buttolph; art d, Perry Ferguson; cos, Adrian

Hitchcock's first film in color is famous for appearing to be one continuous take. It tells of two cocky young collegiates, Shaw and Philip (Dall and Granger), who murder a weak-willed friend, David (Hogan), simply for the thrill of it. Strangling their friend with rope, they stuff his corpse into an antique chest and then ready the apartment for a cocktail party. Among the guests are David's father (Hardwicke), his fiancee (Chandler), and Rupert Cadell (Stewart), a philosophy professor whose discussions of Nietzsche's "superman" theory have inspired the murderers. Shaw, the more arrogant of the two, insists that dinner be served from the chest and makes veiled references to the crime such as "I could kill you." Philip, on the other hand, reacts nervously to such purposely ironic comments. As time passes, the guests become concerned by David's absence and the increasingly morbid conversation.

Although the story of this verbose film is intriguing, it's not top-drawer Hitchcock. Like LIFEBOAT before it, ROPE is an experiment in overcoming technical restrictions—a task which always thrilled Hitchcock. Here, all of his energies go into technique, but, paradoxically, ROPE seems favorable to the actors because it plays like so much theater. The construction of ROPE is simple—eight 10-minute takes cut together (except for the opening and a few reverse-angle shots) to appear as one continuous shot. (Feature films generally have about 600 shots.) Since the maximum length of a reel of 35mm film is around 10 minutes, the reels were joined by stopping the camera behind a character with his back filling the entire frame. Not surprisingly, there were many other hurdles for Hitchcock and his crew to overcome. Ziegler's job was to choreograph the actors' movements with a small scale model of the set. Valentine's camera needed the freedom to travel through the set without crashing into things, so breakaway walls on rollers were built. A special camera dolly was invented (by head grip Morris Rosen) to allow for greater freedom of movement.

Valentine was only experienced with black-and-white photography, so he was unable to capture the color Hitchcock needed during sundown. Technicolor advisor Skall was brought in and, after Valentine left the production due to illness, reshot the final five reels. Special care was also taken on the New York City skyline; since the film took place in real time, night had to fall over the city. A set was built which encompassed 35 square miles of skyline, including such landmarks as the Empire State Building and the Chrysler Building. (The skyline included an ad for Reduco, featuring a before and after silhouette of Hitchcock—a gag also used in a newspaper in LIFEBOAT.) Correct cloud formations were even constructed from spun glass and chickenwire under the advice of a meteorologist.

Hitchcock later said, "I undertook ROPE as a stunt," and that's how it plays. Stewart seems uncomfortable playing an intellectual; his dull performance never displays the disturbance or authority that it needs. Dall and Granger, by contrast, are superb. Their characters and their thinly shrouded homosexuality were based on the murderous exploits of Richard Leopold and Nathan Loeb, wealthy Chicago teenagers who, in 1924, killed 14-year-old Bobbie Franks just to see if they could pull it off. Because of the homosexuality in ROPE, however discreet, the film was initially banned in Chicago (perhaps because it evoked memories of the real case), Spokane, Memphis, and Seattle, and was morally condemned in many other towns. Only after an "adults only" policy was enacted in Chicago, and the opening murder scene deleted in Sioux City, Iowa, could the film be shown in those cities. The Leopold/Loeb case also was the basis for SWOON, a stylish, if self-indulgent, 1992 feature by independent New York filmmaker Tom Kalin.

ROSE, THE

1979 134m c Musical

Fox (U.S.)

DVD ★★★

R

Bette Midler (Rose), Alan Bates (Rudge), Frederic Forrest (Dyer), Harry Dean Stanton (Billy Ray), Barry Primus (Dennis), David Keith (Mal), Sandra McCabe (Sarah), Will Hare (Mr. Leonard), Rudy Bond (Monty), Don Calfa (Don Frank)

p, Marvin Worth, Aaron Russo; d, Mark Rydell; w, Bo Goldman, Bill Kerby, Michael Cimino (based on the story by Kerby); ph, Vilmos Zsigmond (DeLuxe Color); ed, Robert Wolfe; m, Paul A. Rothchild; prod d, Richard MacDonald; art d, James Schoppe; chor, Toni Basil; cos, Theoni V. Aldredge

AAN Best Actress: Bette Midler; AAN Best Supporting Actor: Frederic Forrest; AAN Best Film Editing: Robert L. Wolfe, C. Timothy O'Meara; AAN Best Sound: Theodore Soderberg, Douglas Williams, Paul Wells, Jim Webb

Bette Midler turns in a magnificent performance as a dissipated, Janis Joplin-like rock singer. Exhausted from touring, Rose (Midler) tells her manager (Alan Bates) that she wants a year off to rest, and when he resists, the singer goes into a tailspin. One night she picks up Dyer (Frederic Forrest), a chauffeur, and embarks on the most fulfilling romance of her life. Dyer cannot deal with the penalties of fame that come with Rose's success, however, and eventually he leaves her to his music. A triumphant performance before a hometown audience turns out to be her last as the troubled singer resorts to a fatal combination of booze and drugs. Midler successfully brings her charged stage persona to the screen, presenting a convincing portrait of the backstage life of a rock 'n' roll performer. Forrest, as the chauffeur, and Harry Dean Stanton, in a cameo as a country singer, add an earthy contrast to the glamorous aspects of rock stardom. Only Bates is wasted in a relatively minor role as the manager whose hunger for success is greater than Rose can handle.

ROSE MARIE

1936 110m bw Musical/Comedy

MGM (U.S.)

★★★★½

Jeanette MacDonald (Marie de Flor), Nelson Eddy (Sgt. Bruce), James Stewart (John Flower), Reginald Owen (Myerson), George Regas (Boniface), Robert Greig (Cafe Manager), Una O'Connor (Anna), Jimmy Conlin (Joe the Piano Player), Lucien Littlefield (Storekeeper), Dorothy Gray (Edith)

p, Hunt Stromberg; d, W.S. Van Dyke II; w, Frances Goodrich, Albert Hackett, Alice Duer Miller (based on the operetta by Otto Harbach, Oscar Hammerstein II, Rudolf Friml, Herbert Stothart); ph, William Daniels; ed, Blanche Sewell; m, Rudolf Friml, Herbert Stothart; art d, Cedric Gibbons, Joseph C. Wright, Edwin B. Willis; chor, Chester Hale, William von Wymetal; cos, Adrian

Of all the Jeanette MacDonald-Nelson Eddy films, ROSE MARIE made the most money and is the best remembered. Grace Moore was to star but due to a schedule conflict, MacDonald, coming off her smash hit collaboration with Eddy, NAUGHTY MARIETTA, replaced her. As opera star Marie de Flor, she pleads with the Canadian priemer (Alan Mowbray) to release convicted bank robber John Flower (James Stewart, in his second film), but when he kills a man during a breakout, Marie leaves the opera (five acts of Charles Gounod's "Romeo et Juliette" amazingly compressed into roughly six minutes) and hires Boniface (George Regas), a half-breed guide, to take her into the wilderness in search of Flower. After Boniface double-crosses Marie, stealing all her money, she survives by becoming a saloon singer. Enter handsome Sgt. Bruce (Eddy) of the Mounties, whose mission it is to bring in Flower and who

falls for the lovely Marie, then learns of her connection with the escapee. However, a Mountie always gets his man, and so does Sgt. Bruce, though by film's end he's also gotten his woman. A few laughs, excellent singing, and gorgeous photography all contribute to making this a must-see for Eddy-MacDonald fans. Her opening impersonation of a pampered prima donna is hilarious, an ample reminder of MacDonald's formidable if not always utilized comic talents. Although composer Rudolf Friml is always remembered for ROSE MARIE, it was actually MGM musical director Herbert Stothart who wrote many of the tunes. Under no circumstances confuse this offering, retitled INDIAN LOVE CALL for television showings, with the remake, which is inferior, despite its wide-screen, color treatment.

ROSE TATTOO, THE

1955 117m bw Drama

Paramount (U.S.)

DVD ★★★★

Anna Magnani (Serafina Delle Rose), Burt Lancaster (Alvaro Mangiacavallo), Marisa Pavan (Rosa Delle Rose), Ben Cooper (Jack Hunter), Virginia Grey (Estelle Hohengarten), Jo Van Fleet (Bessie), Sandro Giglio (Father De Leo), Mimi Aguglia (Assunta), Florence Sundstrom (Flora), Dorrit Kelton (Schoolteacher)

p, Hal B. Wallis; d, Daniel Mann; w, Tennessee Williams, Hal Kanter (based on the play by Williams); ph, James Wong Howe (VistaVision); ed, Warren Low; m, Alex North; art d, Hal Pereira, Tambi Larsen; cos, Edith Head

AAN Best Picture; AA Best Actress: Anna Magnani; AAN Best Supporting Actress: Marisa Pavan; AA Best B/W Cinematography: James Wong Howe; AAN Best Film Editing: Warren Low; AAN Best Score (Drama or Comedy): Alex North; AA Best Art Direction-Set Decoration (B/W): Hal Pereira, Tambi Larsen, Sam Comer, Arthur Krams; AAN Best Costume Design (B/W): Edith Head

Tennessee Williams wrote "The Rose Tattoo" as a stage vehicle for Anna Magnani several years before this film appeared, but at that time she was still struggling with English and declined the role. Five years later, after a fairly successful run, Williams did the screenplay and Mann, the director of the stage production, handled the directing. Magnani, by this time, had more confidence in her command of the language (plus the safety afforded by retakes) and took the role, her first U.S. job. The result was a hit.

Magnani, a Sicilian-born widow with a 15-year-old daughter (Pavan) enounters Lancaster, a banana hauler like her late husband who (also like her husband) sports a rose tattoo on his chest, symbolizing virility. She's drawn to Lancaster but reveres her husband's memory so much that she holds her emotions in check—until she discovers the truth about her late spouse.

Magnani later appeared opposite Marlon Brando in THE FUGITIVE KIND, another Williams piece, but never came close in any of her other U.S. pictures to her dynamic performance here. North's excellent music helps the mood enormously. Pavan, the sister of the tragic Pier Angeli, later married Jean-Pierre Aumont.

ROSEMARY'S BABY

1968 136m c Horror

Paramount (U.S.)

DVD ★★★★

R

Mia Farrow (Rosemary Woodhouse), John Cassavetes (Guy Woodhouse), Ruth Gordon (Minnie Castevet), Sidney Blackmer (Roman Castevet), Maurice Evans (Hutch), Ralph Bellamy (Dr. Sapirstein), Victoria Vetri, billed as Angela Dorian (Terry Fionofffrio), Patsy Kelly (Laura-Louise), Elisha Cook Jr. (Mr. Nicklas), Charles Grodin (Dr. Hill) p, William Castle; d, Roman Polanski; w, Roman Polanski (based on the novel by Ira Levin); ph, William A. Fraker (Technicolor); ed, Sam O'Steen, Bob Wyman; m, Krzysztof Komeda; prod d, Richard Sylbert; art d, Joel Schiller; fx, Farciot Edouart; cos, Anthea Sylbert

---

AA Best Supporting Actress: Ruth Gordon; *AAN Best Adapted Screenplay:* Roman Polanski

---

Roman Polanski's first American movie and his second masterpiece of horror (REPULSION was released in 1965) is set under the sunny skies of modern-day New York City. There are no creepy characters and no eerie locations, just a happy young couple expecting their first child. Newlyweds Rosemary (Mia Farrow) and unemployed actor Gus (John Cassavetes) have just moved into their new apartment in a gothic Central Park building (shot in the famous Dakota, home of the late John Lennon). Their neighbors, the elderly Minnie (Ruth Gordon) and Roman Castevet (Sidney Blackmer), are friendly but a bit intrusive. Rosemary learns that she is pregnant but feels a strange sense of anxiety. She seems to remember a vague dream in which she was raped by a savage beast. She has mysterious scratches on her stomach. Her doctor prescribes a curious elixir. It's perhaps not surprising that Rosemary becomes fixated by the idea that she has been impregnated by Satan and is now carrying his unholy child in her womb while living among a coven of witches.

Truly frightening because so much of it is so plausible, ROSEMARY'S BABY is one of the finest examples of modern horror, a milestone in the evolution of the genre. Although the subject matter is ultimately supernatural, the treatment is very realistic. Perhaps the film's most disturbing aspect is that the fears and anxiety that Rosemary experiences initially seem like an understandable response for a neurasthenic young woman to have when an "alien" being is growing within her. The brilliance of the film is that it takes this realistic basis and builds upon it with supernatural metaphors that make pregnancy a rich and strange condition.

ROSETTA

1999 95m c Drama ★★★½
Les Films du Fleuve/RTBF/ARP Selection R
(Belgium/France)

Emilie Dequenne *(Rosetta)*, Fabrizio Rongione *(Riquet)*, Anne Yernaux *(The Mother)*, Olivier Gourmet *(The Boss)*, Bernard Marbaix *(The Campgrounds Manager)*, Frederic Bodson *(The Head of Personnel)*, Florian Delain *(The Boss's Son)*, Christiane Dorval *(First Saleswoman)*, Mireille Bailly *(Second Saleswoman)*, Thomas Gollas *(The Mother's Boyfriend)*

p, Luc Dardenne, Jean-Pierre Dardenne, Michele Petin, Laurent Petin; d, Luc Dardenne, Jean-Pierre Dardenne; w, Luc Dardenne, Jean-Pierre Dardenne; ph, Alain Marcoen; ed, Marie-Helene Dozo; art d, Igor Gabriel; cos, Monic Parelle

---

This bleak slice of realism from Belgian filmmakers Luc and Jean-Pierre Dardenne (LA PROMESSE), which won the *Palm d'Or* at the 1999 Cannes Film Festival, is a psychologically acute profile of one teenaged girl obsessed with leading what she thinks of as a normal life.

Seventeen-year-old Rosetta (Emilie Dequenne) and her mother live on the fringe of Belgian society in a seedy trailer park. Resourceful, determined, and proud, Rosetta is really the head of the household; she makes sure bills are paid and scolds her mother for her excessive drinking and her sleazy boyfriend. Rosetta poaches fish from a nearby river and resells the damaged clothes her mother repairs, but they're just scraping by. What she really wants is a steady job, the first step toward leading an ordinary life. An opportunity arises after Rosetta meets waffle-vendor Riquet (Fabrizio Rongione), who mistakes her occupation envy for something friendlier. He persuades his boss

to hire her, and, for a while, she's happy; Rosetta even lets down her guard long enough to smile. But when her new career-making waffles suddenly appears imperiled, Rosetta betrays the only source of kindness in her dreary life.

Dequenne is a startlingly physical actress—her debut performance here won her the Best Actress Award at Cannes—who lends Rosetta's anger and desperation a scrabbling, animalistic quality. Alain Marcoen's camera focuses so tightly on her that at times we only glimpse her immediate environment. What we do see is far more important: the effect that environment has on Rosetta. And in the complete absence of soundtrack music, Rosetta's every grunt and pant is amplified; her struggle and her despair become deafening.

ROUND MIDNIGHT
 📀
1986 133m c Drama ★★★★
PECF/Little Bear (France/U.S.) R

Dexter Gordon *(Dale Turner)*, Francois Cluzet *(Francis Borier)*, Gabrielle Haker *(Berangere)*, Sandra Reaves-Phillips *(Buttercup)*, Lonette McKee *(Darcey Leigh)*, Christine Pascal *(Sylvie)*, Herbie Hancock *(Eddie Wayne)*, Bobby Hutcherson *(Ace)*, Pierre Trabaud *(Francis's Father)*, Frederique Meininger *(Francis's Mother)*

p, Irwin Winkler; d, Bertrand Tavernier; w, Bertrand Tavernier, David Rayfiel (based on incidents in the lives of Francis Paudras and Bud Powell); ph, Bruno de Keyzer (Panavision, Eastmancolor); ed, Armand Psenny; m, Herbie Hancock; prod d, Alexander Trauner; art d, Pierre Duquesne; cos, Jacqueline Moreau

---

AAN Best Actor: Dexter Gordon; *AA Best Original Score:* Herbie Hancock

---

ROUND MIDNIGHT might easily be called the best jazz film ever made, and not only because, aside from 1988's BIRD, the competition is so weak. The film's quality lies not just in its vivid portrayal of the bebop milieu, but also in its sensitive examination of the turbulent forces within an artist compelled to create on a nightly basis, despite personal consequences. Dedicated to jazz greats Lester Young and Bud Powell, the film begins in 1959 as black bebop jazzman Dale Turner (Dexter Gordon), "the greatest tenor saxophone player in the world," leaves New York City for Paris. Alcoholic, ill, and apparently a former heroin addict, Turner plays nightly at Paris' famous Blue Note club to adoring fans, who appreciate his and his fellow expatriates' music. One of his most fervent admirers, Francis (Francois Cluzet), forms a close friendship with Turner, who moves in with him. Together the two try to bring Turner's self-destructive impulses under control, until Turner decides to risk a return to the U.S.. The irony of ROUND MIDNIGHT—a sadly familiar one recognized in the plot—is that it took a Frenchman, director-cowriter and jazz lover Betrand Tavernier, to make this most accurate and intelligent film about the distinctly American art of jazz. Casting musicians (including Wayne Shorter, Tony Williams, Ron Carter, and Herbie Hancock, who did the Oscar-winning score) as his actors and insisting that the music be recorded live on the set with cameras rolling, Tavernier captures the complex relations among the players at work; the process has never been shown so well in a narrative film. Turner (an amalgam of various figures, including Young, Powell, and Gordon himself) is brilliantly played by the great Gordon, who contributed much of the dialogue, suggested changes in the script, and eventually received a Best Actor Oscar nomination. The aging Gordon's playing is well below the standards of his prime, but the soundtrack became a best seller anyway.

ROXANNE
DVD

1987 107m c Comedy/Romance ★★★½
Columbia (U.S.) PG

Steve Martin *(Charlie "C.D." Bales)*, Daryl Hannah *(Roxanne Kowalski)*, Rick Rossovich *(Chris McDonell)*, Shelley Duvall *(Dixie)*, John Kapelos *(Chuck)*, Fred Willard *(Mayor Deebs)*, Max Alexander *(Dean)*, Michael J. Pollard *(Andy)*, Shandra Beri *(Sandy)*, Brian George *(Dr. David Schepisi)*

p, Michael Rachmil, Daniel Melnick; d, Fred Schepisi; w, Steve Martin (based on the play "Cyrano de Bergerac" by Edmond Rostand); ph, Ian Baker (Deluxe Color); ed, John Scott; m, Bruce Smeaton; prod d, Jackson DeGovia; art d, David Fischer; fx, Bill Orr; cos, Richard Bruno, Tish Monaghan

Unlike many of his comedic contemporaries, Steve Martin likes to take risks. Martin served as executive producer and wrote the screenplay for this modernization of Edmond Rostand's "Cyrano de Bergerac," which stars Martin as C.D. Bales, the fire chief in a small northwestern town, a much beloved and witty man who happens to have a huge nose. C.D. has hired Chris McDonell (Rick Rossovich), a handsome dimwit who knows his way around hoses but not around women. Roxanne Kowalski (Daryl Hannah) is an astronomer who has rented a local house for the summer, and in scant moments we see that C.D. is mad about Roxanne. But Roxanne gets a look at Chris and falls for him, whereupon Chris asks C.D. for help in wooing her. C.D. agrees, albeit reluctantly. Many wonderful jokes dot the picture, but it is, in essence, a love story and most satisfying in that respect. The bright, literate screenplay sometimes descends into slapstick but stays close enough to its source that it pays homage without sacrificing originality. Martin makes his character amiable and downright lovable; Hannah shows a fire she hadn't demonstrated in previous efforts. In an era when romance seems to have taken second place to sex, it's heartwarming to see a film like ROXANNE bring back the loveliness of love.

ROYAL FAMILY OF BROADWAY, THE

1930 68m bw Drama/Comedy ★★★★
Paramount (U.S.)

Ina Claire *(Julia Cavendish)*, Fredric March *(Tony Cavendish)*, Mary Brian *(Gwen Cavendish)*, Henrietta Crosman *(Fanny Cavendish)*, Charles Starrett *(Perry Stewart)*, Arnold Korff *(Oscar Wolff)*, Frank Conroy *(Gilbert Marshall)*, Royal C. Stout *(Joe)*, Elsie Edmond *(Della)*, Murray Alper *(McDermott)*

d, George Cukor, Cyril Gardner; w, Herman J. Mankiewicz, Gertrude Purcell (based on the play *The Royal Family* by George S. Kaufman and Edna Ferber); ph, George Folsey; ed, Edward Dmytryk

AAN Best Actor: Fredric March

When George S. Kaufman and Edna Ferber's thinly veiled parody of the acting Barrymores, "The Royal Family," opened in Los Angeles, Fredric March took on the role Otto Kruger had played on Broadway. Paramount studio bosses were so impressed by March's performance that they cast him in the lead in their film version of the play, THE ROYAL FAMILY OF BROADWAY (the name was changed to prevent confusion), and he responded by gaining an Oscar nomination and a huge following. Adapters Herman Mankiewicz and Gertrude Purcell wisely jettisoned some extraneous subplots and hammered out a tight script that George Cukor snappily directed, with assistance from Cyril Gardner.

Henrietta Crosman, matriarch of the famous acting Cavendishes, lives in a fabulous apartment and talks of her ancient theatrical triumphs. When son March arrives, he is not welcomed: by leaving the stage for the movies, he has incurred the wrath of the purists in the family. With March in the movies, daughter Ina Claire semi-retired, and a second daughter (Brian) unwilling to carry on the family tradition, Crosman accepts an offer to go on tour with a repertory company. The tour proves too much for her and she suffers a heart attack while performing. Her children must now decide whether to pick up the torch.

Even though March is on screen less than the other leads, his presence is extraordinarily powerful in the film's flashiest role. His impression of John Barrymore is nearly flawless, capturing every gesture, every raised eyebrow, every sneer perfectly. Although the film's humor is tempered by the drama of Crosman's demise, the screenwriters crafted her death so skillfully that even this heart-tugging scene has funny moments. A must-see for anyone who loves the theater, THE ROYAL FAMILY OF BROADWAY was edited by Edward Dmytryk, later the director of such films as THE JUGGLER, RAINTREE COUNTY, and WALK ON THE WILD SIDE.

ROYAL TENENBAUMS, THE
DVD

2001 110m c Comedy/Drama ★★★
American Empirical/Touchstone (U.S.) R

Gene Hackman *(Royal Tenenbaum)*, Anjelica Huston *(Etheline Tenenbaum)*, Ben Stiller *(Chas Tenenbaum)*, Gwyneth Paltrow *(Margot Helen Tenenbaum)*, Luke Wilson *(Richie Tenenbaum)*, Owen Wilson *(Eli Cash)*, Jonah Meyerson *(Uzi Tenenbaum)*, Grant Rosenmeyer *(Ari Tenenbaum)*, Bill Murray *(Raleigh St. Clair)*, Danny Glover *(Henry Sherman)*

p, Wes Anderson, Barry Mendel, Scott Rudin; d, Wes Anderson; w, Wes Anderson, Owen Wilson; ph, Robert D. Yeoman; ed, Dylan Tichenor; m, Mark Mothersbaugh; prod d, David Wasco; art d, Carl Sprague; fx, Bob Scupp; cos, Karen Patch

AAN Best Original Screenplay: Wes Anderson, Owen Wilson

Precociously glib but never less than engaging, Wes Anderson's oddball comedy of family manners chronicles the fortunes of the Tenenbaum siblings, three Manhattan prodigies who never fulfilled their potential.

It once seemed everything the young Tenenbaums touched turned to gold. Chas was a pint-sized financial whiz, Richie a tennis virtuoso, and adopted Margot a prize-winning playwright. Their childhood playmate, Eli was so desperate to bask in the Tenenbaums' aura that he virtually adopted himself into their ranks. The elder Tenenbaums, glad-handing scoundrel Royal (Gene Hackman) and quietly capable Etheline (Anjelica Huston), eventually separated; Etheline kept the family's shabbily genteel townhouse, and Royal moved into a hotel. Ironically, Eli (played as an adult by Owen Wilson) grew up to become a successful novelist, while the Tenenbaum children foundered. Now Chas (Ben Stiller), a recent widower and the father of two small boys (Grant Rosenmeyer, Jonah Meyerson), is having a nervous breakdown; Richie (Luke Wilson) is aimlessly cruising the world; and Margot (Gwyneth Paltrow) hasn't written in years. Unhappy and directionless, Chas and Margot retreat to the security of Mom's house. Richie returns to confront his unrequited love for Margot, and Royal comes home because he says he's dying and wants to make things right with his family before he goes.

The self-consciously loopy plot is mostly a showcase for the cast, and Hackman and Houston easily outshine the younger actors: Stiller's sputtering rage, Paltrow's goth-deb anomie, and the Wilsons' goofy antics are entertaining, but they're one-note characterizations. Anderson has said he took some of his inspiration from classic *New Yorker* fiction, and the film's studied eccentricities do indeed recall the magazine's more precious offerings.

ROYAL WEDDING

1951   93m   c   Musical/Comedy   ★★★★
MGM   (U.S.)

Fred Astaire *(Tom Bowen)*, Jane Powell *(Ellen Bowen)*, Peter Lawford *(Lord John Brindale)*, Sarah Churchill *(Anne Ashmond)*, Keenan Wynn *(Irving Klinger/Edgar Klinger)*, Albert Sharpe *(James Ashmond)*, Viola Roache *(Sarah Ashmond)*, Henri Letondal *(Purser)*, James Finlayson *(Cabby)*, Alex Frazer *(Chester)*

p, Arthur Freed; d, Stanley Donen; w, Alan Jay Lerner; ph, Robert Planck (Technicolor); ed, Albert Akst; art d, Cedric Gibbons, Jack Martin Smith; fx, Warren Newcombe; chor, Nick Castle

AAN Best Song: "Too Late Now"; Burton Lane (Music), Alan Jay Lerner (Lyrics)

On the eve of the royal wedding of then-Princess Elizabeth and Philip Mountbatten, an American brother and sister vaudeville act, Ellen (Jane Powell) and Tom Bowen (Fred Astaire), ventures to London to perform. There Tom falls in love with Anne Ashmond (Sarah Churchill, daughter of Sir Winston Churchill, making her only U.S. film appearance) a music hall dancer, while Ellen becomes involved with an English lord (Peter Lawford). The picture ends with couples married, after the usual misunderstandings and rocky romantic plot twists. That's about it for the story, but what shines here are the great songs by Alan Jay Lerner and Burton Lane (among them the Oscar-nominated "Too Late Now"), the singing, and the dancing, including two of the most spectacular Astaire routines ever devised. In the first, he dances with a hat rack that nearly comes alive as his partner; in the second and most celebrated, the legendary hoofer seems to be dancing on the walls and ceiling of a room—accomplished by building the room so it could be rotated at the same speed as the camera, with the camera operator strapped in and shooting upside down. Although Nick Castle is listed as choreographer, it seems likely that it was Astaire's genius that inspired these dazzling routines. When all is said and done, Stanley Donen's first solo directorial assignment, after his work with Gene Kelly, is a lovely bit of frou-frou.

RUGGLES OF RED GAP

1935   76m   bw   Comedy   ★★★★
Paramount   (U.S.)

Charles Laughton *(Marmaduke Ruggles)*, Mary Boland *(Effie Floud)*, Charlie Ruggles *(Egbert Floud)*, ZaSu Pitts *(Mrs. Judson)*, Roland Young *(George Van Bassingwell)*, Leila Hyams *(Nell Kenner)*, Maude Eburne *(Ma Pettingill)*, Lucien Littlefield *(Charles Belknap-Jackson)*, Leota Lorraine *(Mrs. Belknap-Jackson)*, James Burke *(Jeff Tuttle)*

p, Arthur Hornblow Jr.; d, Leo McCarey; w, Walter DeLeon, Harlan Thompson, Humphrey Pearson (based on the play and novel by Harry Leon Wilson); ph, Alfred Gilks; ed, Edward Dmytryk; m, Ralph Rainger, Sam Coslow; art d, Hans Dreier, Robert Odell; cos, Travis Banton

AAN Best Picture

RUGGLES OF RED GAP is one of the great comedies of all time, a wonderful source of pleasure. Charles Laughton is brilliantly cast as Marmaduke Ruggles, the ultimate valet. His aristocratic, impoverished English master (Roland Young) loses him in a poker game in Paris to a rough-and-ready visiting American rancher, played by actor Charlie Ruggles. Laughton, Ruggles, and one of Ruggles's buddies have a hysterically funny night on the town before Laughton packs up everything and goes to Red Gap, a brawling frontier town in the West. The locals there take Laughton for a British aristo-

crat, and he decides that since he is here in the land of the free, he no longer has to be an indentured servant. He falls for and marries ZaSu Pitts, and leaves Ruggles and his wife (Mary Boland) to open a restaurant with Pitts. Eventually, Young comes to visit the small town, meets Maude Eburne, falls in love with her, and decides to stay in Red Gap. Seventy-six fast-moving minutes directed with an eye toward huge laughs, RUGGLES OF RED GAP ends with a startling scene where the slightly tipsy Laughton recites Lincoln's "Gettysburg Address," his masterful reading and palpable sincerity overcoming the incongruity of the scene to win over on-screen listeners and generations of audiences.

Laughton had already shown himself to be a superb dramatic actor in MUTINY ON THE BOUNTY and HENRY VIII, but few knew that he could be funny as well as pompous, underplay as well as emote, and show a subtle comedic side, which he did masterfully in this film. The versatile Leo McCarey deftly directs the picture, making it one his best films. Harry Leon Wilson's 1915 novel was first done by Essanay as a silent starring Taylor Holmes in 1918, and again by Paramount in 1923, with a youthful Edward Everett Horton in the lead. The picture was remade as FANCY PANTS, starring Bob Hope, but the remake was a tepid imitation of McCarey's hilarious version.

RULES OF ATTRACTION, THE

2002   110m   c   Comedy/Drama   ★★★
Kingsgate Films   (U.S.)   R

James Van Der Beek *(Sean Bateman)*, Ian Somerhalder *(Paul Denton)*, Shannyn Sossamon *(Lauren Hynde)*, Jessica Biel *(Lara)*, Kip Pardue *(Victor)*, Thomas Ian Nicholas *(Mitchell)*, Kate Bosworth *(Kelly)*, Fred Savage *(Marc)*, Eric Stoltz *(Mr. Lance Lawson)*, Clifton Collins Jr. *(Rupert)*

p, Greg Shapiro; d, Roger Avary; w, Roger Avary (based on the novel by Bret Easton Ellis); ph, Robert Brinkman; ed, Sharon Rutter; m, tomandandy; prod d, Sharon Seymour; art d, Christopher Tandon; fx, Ron Bolanowski, Raymond McIntyre Jr.; cos, Louise Frogley

Further proving that so-so books often make better movies, writer-director Roger Avary pulls Bret Easton Ellis's second novel out of its sophomore slump and delivers a technically deft, sometimes bitterly funny look at sex, drugs, and synth-pop at a small New England college.

The center attraction is Sean Bateman (James Van Der Beek), a bed-hopping, drug-dealing senior at Camden College who owes quite a bit of money to a coke-crazed townie (Clifton Collins Jr.). Sean's been receiving anonymous mash notes from a secret admirer he suspects is Lauren Hynde (Shannyn Sossamon), a skateboarding coed who's somehow made it to college with her virginity intact. She's interested in Sean but pines for her "only slightly gay" boyfriend, Victor (Kip Pardue), a drama major who's off touring Europe. Paul Denton (Ian Somerhalder), Lauren's ex, on the other hand, is now entirely gay and has his sights set on Sean. Filled with coke, booze, and inexpressible feelings, none of these kids can connect; their interactions are defined by confused signals, unsigned letters, and misheard requests for more beer.

The film may ultimately leave you with the same empty feeling as Ellis's fiction, but it's often ingenious in its telling. The opening sequence, in which Avary introduces each of his characters, then sets the clock spinning backwards, is a thrilling tour de force, and Avary manages to make Ellis's vision of college as four wasted years of musical beds, drunken bacchanals, suicides, and overdoses (classes? what classes?) seem somewhat believable. It's like the negative reverse of "Dawson's Creek," an impression that's reinforced by the surprisingly successful casting of Van Der Beek as the scowling Sean, whose older sibling, the serial-killing Wall Street warrior Patrick Bateman, is the protagonist of Ellis's next novel, *American Psycho*.

RULES OF THE GAME
(LA REGLE DU JEU)
1939 110m bw Drama
Nouvelle Edition Francaise (France)

DVD

★★★★★

Marcel Dalio *(Robert de la Chesnaye)*, Nora Gregor *(Christine de la Chesnaye)*, Roland Toutain *(Andre Jurieu)*, Jean Renoir *(Octave)*, Mila Parely *(Genevieve de Marrast)*, Paulette Dubost *(Lisette)*, Gaston Modot *(Schumacher)*, Julien Carette *(Marceau)*, Odette Talazac *(Charlotte de la Plante)*, Pierre Magnier *(The General)*

d, Jean Renoir; w, Jean Renoir (in collaboration with Carl Koch, Camille Francois, and the cast); ph, Jean Bachelet, Jacques Lemare, Jean-Paul Alphen, Alan Renoir; ed, Marguerite Renoir, Marthe Huguet; m, Roger Desormieres, Camille Saint-Saens, Salabert, E. Rose, Vincent Scotto, Wolfgang Amadeus Mozart, Johann Strauss, Frederic Chopin, Monsigny, G. Claret, Camille Francois, Delonnel Garnier; art d, Eugene Lourie, Max Douy; cos, Coco Chanel

One of cinema's most monumental achievements, Renoir's RULES OF THE GAME passionately tackles the pre-WWII French class system, and succeeds in bringing forth the complexities and frailties underlying bourgeois civility. When aviator Andre Jurieu (Toutain) is met by his friend Octave (director Renoir) and ecstatic reporters after a record-setting flight, he tells the radio audience that he undertook the adventure for the love of a woman—who failed to greet him at the airport. This woman, Christine (Gregor), is in the meantime preparing for an evening out with her husband, Robert de la Chesnaye (Dalio), who knows of his wife's affair and doesn't want to lose her. Toward this end, he tries to end his relationship with his adoring mistress (Parely). Octave, the character with the clearest understanding of his environment, admits to Andre that he too cares for Christine (although, like the others, he has difficulty distinguishing love from "friendship"), and maintains that Andre will never win her because he doesn't heed "the rules" of society. Later the two are among the guests at a weekend shooting party at de la Chesnaye's country estate (a remarkably beautiful location evoking the works of the director's father, Auguste Renoir, and that is greatly enhanced by the gorgeous deep-focus photography). Everyone, servants included, brings along their own little drama, to be played out during and after the hunt—a brutal game complete with its own rigid rules threatening to spill over into the domestic, "civilized" sphere.

RULES OF THE GAME has a flavor like no other film, its tone covering farce, satire, and tragedy alike. Renoir extracts great power from sequences such as the slaughter of the rabbits, an act done with the utmost cool by the aristocrats partying in the country. Later Robert displays his latest mechanical toy for his guests, and a stunning dolly shot carries us into several planes of action, as seductions and murderous chases occur among both servants and masters. So many things here unfold with the beauty of inevitability (e.g. what Christine sees through a set of binoculars during the hunt) and yet the film breathes surprise, improvisation, reversal. No stone is left unturned as Renoir explores the follies of love, the contradictory class relations and the casual anti-Semitism inhabiting these barren people.

The acting is great, with Dalio and Carette giving perhaps the performances of their careers as the self-indulgent host and the hilarious and sneaky poacher of rabbits and wives alike. Toutain, Parely, and Modot, meanwhile, as would-be lover, mistress, and cuckold respectively, superbly cover a range of types frustrated by love. Dubost manages to be both very appealing and appropriately vague as the blithe and careless maid, and the actors embodying the guests and servants are perfectly cast. (Could Magnier's marvelously fading military man have inspired, if only by osmosis, Richard Bennett's character in THE MAGNIFICENT AMBERSONS?) Renoir, as the hapless, compassionate yet insightful friend to all, proves himself a terrific actor, leaving one to regret that he didn't act more often. His Octave, the most likable character in the film, is appropriately its emotional center. And finally Gregor (a real-life aristocrat and sometime actress who would commit suicide in the late 1940s), carefully coached by Renoir, gives perhaps her most impressive performance. Interested in her at the time, Renoir realizes her limitations and turns them into strengths. The Austrian actress's flawed French and slightly remote quality are well-nigh perfect for the role of an outsider tossed amidst a rampaging sea of desire.

The ending is one of incredible poignancy, and if anything brilliantly highlights the film's already intense reflexivity. A labor of love and passion, RULES OF THE GAME was borne of Renoir's discontent with the complacency of his French contemporaries as the country faced occupation. Relentlessly booed at its 1939 Paris premiere and banned by both the French and Vichy governments, the film is a classic example of audience revulsion to a perceptive critique of their world. Renoir aimed to create "an exact description of the bourgeoisie of our time" and he evidently struck a very raw nerve. It wasn't until 1959 that the film was restored to its nearly original form at 110 minutes. The Venice Film Festival premiere of the restored version quickly put the film onto nearly every list of greatest films ever made, a position it has justly retained. Alain Resnais considered this film the most overwhelming experience he had ever had at the cinema, and while those knowledgeable in French history may pick up on more, several viewings of this unique film (what it takes) will get you hooked too.

RULING CLASS, THE
1972 148m c Comedy
Keep (U.K.)

DVD

★★★½

R

Peter O'Toole *(Jack, 14th Earl of Gurney)*, Alastair Sim *(Bishop Lampton)*, Arthur Lowe *(Tucker)*, Harry Andrews *(13th Earl of Gurney)*, Coral Browne *(Lady Claire Gurney)*, Michael Bryant *(Dr. Herder)*, Nigel Green *(McKyle)*, William Mervyn *(Sir Charles Gurney)*, Carolyn Seymour *(Grace Shelley)*, James Villiers *(Dinsdale Gurney)*

p, Jules Buck, Jack Hawkins; d, Peter Medak; w, Peter Barnes (based on the play by Barnes); ph, Ken Hodges (DeLuxe Color); ed, Ray Lovejoy; m, John Cameron; prod d, Peter Murton; fx, Roy Whybrow; chor, Eleanor Fazan; cos, Ruth Myers

AAN Best Actor: Peter O'Toole

Overly long, controversial comedy with plenty of tragedy mixed in, this was adapted by the playwright, Peter Barnes, for the screen and might have benefitted from some disinterested pruning. It is nevertheless a vigorous, and sometimes wildly funny, assault on classbound British mores.

Andrews, a peer, accidentally loses his life while performing what seems to be a nightly ritual: he dons long underwear, a tutu, and a Napoleonic hat, puts a silken noose around his neck, and dangles contentedly. Peter O'Toole, the family lunatic, gets the peerage and estate; manservant Lowe gets 30,000 pounds; the rest of the family gets stiffed. The formerly servile Lowe begins spouting communist slogans, swilling booze, and telling the family exactly what he thinks of them. O'Toole returns from a mental institution dressed as Jesus Christ; he spends many hours on a huge cross in the living room and distributes wealth to the meek and downtrodden, infuriating the rest of the family. They decide they have only one means by which to rectify matters: have O'Toole sire a child, then toss him back into the looney bin so the family can assume control of the money by becoming the unborn child's guardians.

Hardly a segment of British society comes out of this film unscathed: the public school system, Parliament, snobbery, religion, homosexuals, servants, the upper classes, and just about everything else that can be decried. It's caustic and funny, but often goes too far and stays too long in making its points. O'Toole was nominated for an Oscar as the mad earl and bites off Barnes's speeches with Shavian diction. Lowe steals every scene he's in, while Sim's role as a doddering bishop is one of his best in a long career. A lot of money was spent on this movie, making it one of the best-produced British films of the year. Interiors were done at Twickenham with locations shot in Buckinghamshire, Lincolnshire, Surrey, Hampshire, and London.

RUMBLE FISH
1983 105m c/bw Drama ★★★★½
Zoetrope (U.S.) R

Matt Dillon *(Rusty James)*, Mickey Rourke *(Motorcycle Boy)*, Diane Lane *(Patty)*, Dennis Hopper *(Father)*, Diana Scarwid *(Cassandra)*, Vincent Spano *(Steve)*, Nicolas Cage *(Smokey)*, Christopher Penn *(B.J.)*, Laurence Fishburne, billed as Larry Fishburne *(Midget)*, William Smith *(Patterson)*

p, Fred Roos, Doug Claybourne; d, Francis Ford Coppola; w, S.E. Hinton, Francis Ford Coppola (based on a novel by S.E. Hinton); ph, Stephen H. Burum (Technicolor); ed, Barry Malkin; m, Stewart Copeland; prod d, Dean Tavoularis; chor, Michael Smuin; cos, Marge Bowers

If THE OUTSIDERS was a GODFATHER for teens, RUMBLE FISH was APOCALYPSE NOW. Filmed in dreamy black-and-white with an occasional dab of color, RUMBLE FISH is an unabashed art film. Deliriously expressionistic visually and aurally, it owes at least as much to the work of Jean Cocteau, Kenneth Anger, and F.W. Murnau as to the juvenile delinquent sagas of the 1950s. Set in Tulsa, Oklahoma, RUMBLE FISH tells of a somewhat slow-witted but charismatic teenager, Rusty James (Dillon), who idolizes his elder brother, the Motorcycle Boy (Rourke). The Motorcycle Boy has repudiated his gang-leader past and disapproves of Rusty's fighting but really has no practical advice to offer his sibling. He's intelligent enough to know that he has done nothing admirable to earn his local notoriety; he's just a very cool dude in a way that his hot-headed and increasingly dopey younger brother can never hope to match. Rusty, though, is too blinded by hero-worship and addled by injury-induced deliriums and booze to see things clearly. The person most annoyed by the former gang leader's lofty reputation is Officer Patterson (Smith) who ominously watches the Motorcycle Boy from behind his jet black shades.

Coppola has never made a more beautiful film. The rumble sequence alone is a rousingly choreographed frenzy that deserves to be studied by generations of film students. Hinton collaborated with the director in adapting her eccentric but profoundly moving novel for the screen. The resulting film is an amazingly sensitive recreation of the sensibility of the literary work. Burum's black-and-white cinematography utilizes deep focus and time-lapse effects to reflect the peculiar point-of-view of the protagonists. The fighting fish to which the title refers are in color though they float in a black-and-white pet shop window. The innovative score from Copeland (formerly drummer for The Police) plays a major part in creating mood, blending perfectly with Coppola's striking images. Often it sounds like ticking clocks, thereby heightening the sense that time is running out for these characters. Clocks are also a recurring visual motif.

RUMBLE FISH also contains some truly outstanding performances. Rourke gives what may be his most satisfying

performance as the impossibly cool Motorcycle Boy. One never knows whether he is truly insane, as several characters assert, or just suffers from what his father calls "acuteness of the senses." Dillon shines through with a heartbreaking portrayal of a vulnerable teen increasingly lost in a mental fog. Lane is quite touching and believable as Rusty's long-suffering girlfriend, and Spano shows great range in an atypical role as Rusty's nerdy pal. Hopper is likewise superb, his ravaged but still beautiful face suggesting a fallen angel.

This is not a film for all audiences; indeed it is difficult to imagine to what audience it is targeted. Some wags even had the temerity to christen this minor masterpiece as "Mumble Fish." Give it a try. It might change your life.

RUN LOLA RUN
(LOLA RENNT)
1998 87m c/bw Thriller/Drama ★★★★
Bavaria Film International/German Independents/ R
X-Film Creative Pool (Germany)

Franka Potente *(Lola)*, Moritz Bleibtreu *(Manni)*, Herbert Knaup *(Lola's Father)*, Armin Rohde *(Mr. Schuster)*, Joachim Krol *(Norbert von Au—Tramp)*, Nina Petri *(Mrs. Hanson)*, Heino Ferch

p, Stefan Arndt; d, Tom Tykwer; w, Tom Tykwer; ph, Frank Griebe; ed, Mathilde Bonnefoy, Tom Tykwer; m, Tom Tykwer, Johnny Klimek, Reinhold Heil; prod d, Alexander Manasse; cos, Monika Jacobs; anim, Gil Alkabetz

A blast. German writer-director Tom Tykwer tells one story three times, varying the outcome with each go-round: the constant is resourceful redhead Lola (Franka Potente), a scruffy beauty with a scream that shatters glass and a boyfriend named Manni (Moritz Bleibtreu), who's messed up a job for a small-time crime lord and better come up with a whole lot of money in 20 minutes or he's dead meat. Manni calls Lola, and Lola comes running—literally. She bolts out of the house and tears through the streets, nimble brain going as fast as her feet in search of some way out of what appears to be an impossible test of devotion.

Granted, this sounds like the same old reckless youth stuff, but it's not. First, it's unusually clever, colorful, and gleefully anarchic in its mix of color, B&W, animation, and other filmmaking tricks: Lola's random encounters with a mother pushing a baby carriage, for example, touch off a series of possible futures for the woman (which unfold through a rapid-fire series of stills), depending on whether they collide or Lola just sweeps past. And second, it *is* like a video game in which some cosmic cinematic reset button gets pushed every time the story paints itself into a corner, but it's not just some shallow exercise in smarty-pants film-geek bravado. The film's extra-special trick, the one that kicks in under your radar because it's so busy with all the flash, is that it makes you care deeply for Lola and Manni. Credit goes in large part to the radiant Potente, who's got an ocean of charisma under the tattoos and flame-colored hair, and Bleibtreu, who sneaks an endearing sweetness into Manni's slightly doltish manner. But Tykwer's script gives them the room to work: he's one to watch.

RUN SILENT, RUN DEEP
1958 93m bw War ★★★
Hecht/Hill/Lancaster (U.S.)

Clark Gable *(Cmdr. Richardson)*, Burt Lancaster *(Lt. Jim Bledsoe)*, Jack Warden *(Mueller)*, Brad Dexter *(Cartwright)*, Don Rickles *(Ruby)*, Nick Cravat *(Russo)*, Joe Maross *(Kohler)*, Mary LaRoche *(Laura)*, Eddie Foy III *(Larto)*, Rudy Bond *(Cullen)*

p, Harold Hecht; d, Robert Wise; w, John Gay (based on a novel by Cmdr. Edward L. Beach); ed, George Boemler; m, Franz Waxman; art d, Edward Carrere; fx, A. Arnold Gillespie

After his lucrative teaming with Gary Cooper in VERA CRUZ, Burt Lancaster and his partners, Harold Hecht and James Hill, decided to pair Lancaster with the fading but still popular Clark Gable. Gable plays Commander Richardson, the only survivor when the submarine he commands is sunk by a Japanese destroyer dubbed "Bongo Pete." Back at Pearl Harbor, he is given command of another submarine, the *Nerka*, but on it he encounters much dissension. Lt. Bledsoe (Lancaster), the sub's executive officer, is upset because he expected to get the command, and the crew refuses to trust a commander who is the sole survivor of a sunken vessel. Richardson battles frequently with Bledsoe, who is just short of mutinous, and drills the crew repeatedly in a tricky maneuver designed to torpedo "Bongo Pete" head on, an operation he calls the "down the throat shot." Ordered to stay well clear of Japan's dangerous Bongo Straits, the obsessed commander disobeys and pursues the destroyer. Gable, two years and three films away from death, is plainly too old for his role, but he makes the most of it with a very good performance. The entire film, in fact, is one of the better submarine dramas ever made, tense and claustrophobic, with a minimum of dalliances back at the base (in defiance of the Hollywood dictum that no movie without a love interest can succeed). On the set, things were rather tense, with Lancaster and his two partners arguing over the script, while Gable worried about what was going to happen to his character when the dust settled. Although reasonably successful at the box office, RUN SILENT, RUN DEEP was ultimately overshadowed by another film that put an old star and a new star in a submarine, OPERATION PETTICOAT, with Cary Grant and Tony Curtis.

RUNAWAY JURY   DVD

2003 127m c   Crime/Thriller   ★★★
Regency Enterprises/New Regency   PG-13
Productions   (U.S.)

John Cusack (*Nick Easter*), Gene Hackman (*Rankin Fitch*), Dustin Hoffman (*Wendall Rohr*), Rachel Weisz (*Marlee*), Bruce Davison (*Cable*), Bruce McGill (*Judge Harkin*), Jeremy Piven (*Lawrence Green*), Nick Searcy (*Doyle*), Joanna Going (*Celeste Wood*), Dylan McDermott (*Jacob Woods—uncredited*)

p, Gary Fleder, Christopher Mankiewicz, Arnon Milchan; d, Gary Fleder; w, Rick Cleveland, Brian Koppleman, David Levien, Matthew Chapman (based on the novel by John Grisham); ph, Robert Elswit; ed, William Steinkamp; m, Christopher Young; prod d, Nelson Coates; art d, Scott Plauche; fx, Robert H. Cooper; cos, Abigail Murray

"Trials are too important to be decided by juries," quips jury consultant extraordinaire Rankin Fitch (Gene Hackman), the man you want whispering in your attorney's ear when it's jury selection time.

Two years after a disgruntled day trader opened fire in an office full of former co-workers, laid-back New Orleans lawyer Wendall Rohr (Dustin Hoffman) is attempting the impossible: representing the young widow (Joanna Going) of a murdered broker (an uncredited Dylan McDermott) in her wrongful-death suit against the gun manufacturer. Knowing juries invariably side with the manufacturer, Rohr reluctantly hires jury consultant Lawrence Green (Jeremy Piven) to advise in juror selection. The defense, however, has sprung for a much bigger fish. Their consultant, the brilliant Fitch, uses undercover agents and high-tech surveillance equipment to gather all there is to know about the entire jury pool. It's not surprising that one prospective juror, shleppy video-game dealer Nick Easter (John Cusack), is beginning to suspect he's

being watched. Once the trial begins, both Rohr and Fitch are contacted by someone (Rachel Weisz) offering to sell the jury to the highest bidder, and it becomes clear to both sides that someone else entirely is pulling the strings.

There's not a whole lot of moral ambiguity in this entertaining tale of corruption and righteousness: the good are very good, and the bad are downright evil. The screenplay is based on one of John Grisham's best-selling novels, but surprisingly little of the film actually takes place in the courtroom—which, in a way, is exactly the point. Nevertheless, it's a clever legal thriller, and one that thankfully doesn't twist itself into knots of illogic trying to keep audiences off guard.

RUNAWAY TRAIN   DVD

1985 111m c   Prison/Thriller   ★★★½
Northbrook   (U.S.)   R

Jon Voight (*Manny*), Eric Roberts (*Buck*), Rebecca De Mornay (*Sara*), Kyle T. Heffner (*Frank Barstow*), John P. Ryan (*Ranken*), T.K. Carter (*Dave Prince*), Kenneth McMillan (*Eddie MacDonald*), Stacey Pickren (*Ruby*), Walter Wyatt (*Conlan*), Edward Bunker (*Jonah*)

p, Menahem Golan, Yoram Globus; d, Andrei Konchalovsky; w, Djordje Milicevic, Paul Zindel, Edward Bunker (based on the screenplay by Akira Kurosawa, Ryuzo Kikushima, Hideo Oguni); ph, Alan Hume (Rank Color); ed, Henry Richardson; m, Trevor Jones; prod d, Stephen Marsh; art d, Joseph T. Garrity; fx, Keith Richins, Rick H. Josephsen, Bob Riggs, Tassilo Baur, Ray Brown; cos, Katherine Dover

AAN Best Actor: Jon Voight; *AAN Best Supporting Actor:* Eric Roberts; *AAN Best Film Editing:* Henry Richardson

The action in this superlative film is relentless and gripping from beginning to end. Manny (Jon Voight) is a hard-as-nails prison inmate who, with vicious punk Buck (Eric Roberts), escapes from a brutal Alaskan prison. They emerge into a blizzard and grope their way toward the train tracks, clambering aboard a passing train. They are unaware that the engineer has just suffered a fatal heart attack. Frantic passenger Sara (Rebecca De Mornay), a railroad employee, encounters the hiding convicts and begs them to save the train and her. The tough cons make it to the engineer's cab, and then their brutal ordeal to stop this train begins—an exercise in raw courage and chilling perils that drives both convicts to the brink of madness. What's more, Ranken (John P. Ryan), the prison warden who has a long-standing vendetta with Manny, is after the train as well. Voight is powerful and absorbing, and Roberts gives a fascinating performance as his cretinous sidekick. This is the second American-made film by Russian director Andrei Konchalovsky, and he does an outstanding job with his material and actors. Based on an original screenplay by Japanese master Akira Kurosawa.

RUNNING ON EMPTY   DVD

1988 116m c   Drama   ★★★
Lorimar/Double Play   (U.S.)   PG-13

Christine Lahti (*Annie Pope*), River Phoenix (*Danny Pope*), Judd Hirsch (*Arthur Pope*), Martha Plimpton (*Lorna Phillips*), Ed Crowley (*Mr. Phillips*), L.M. Kit Carson (*Gus Winant*), Steven Hill (*Mr. Patterson*), Augusta Dabney (*Mrs. Patterson*), David Margulies (*Dr. Jonah Reiff*), Lynne Thigpen (*Contact at Eldridge St.*)

p, Amy Robinson, Griffin Dunne; d, Sidney Lumet; w, Naomi Foner; ph, Gerry Fisher (Technicolor); ed, Andrew Mondshein; m, Tony Mottola; prod d, Philip Rosenberg; cos, Anna Hill Johnstone

AAN Best Supporting Actor: River Phoenix; *AAN Best Original Screenplay:* Naomi Foner

Sidney Lumet fuses the personal with the political in RUN-
NING ON EMPTY, dramatizing the conflicts in a family on
the run from the FBI. Arthur and Annie Pope (Judd Hirsch and
Christine Lahti) are former student radicals who have been
underground for 15 years, moving from town to town with
their two children and changing identities whenever the law
begins to catch up. Their son, Danny (River Phoenix), a gifted musician, is ready to graduate from high school and is
being encouraged by his music teacher (Ed Crowley) to apply
to Julliard. To do so, however, Danny would have to produce
a transcript, which would mean leaving the underground and
separating permanently from his family. At the same time, the
boy falls in love with the music teacher's daughter, Lorna
(Martha Plimpton), further straining familial bonds. RUN-
NING ON EMPTY is about an age-old dilemma: the difficulties that arise when the time comes for children to leave the
nest. Lumet develops his story at a leisurely but effective pace,
allowing the dynamics of a family in transition—not the sudden appearance of the FBI or an action-paced chase—to give
the film its tension. Though Arthur and Annie are center stage
very nearly as much as Danny, RUNNING ON EMPTY is
Danny's story, seen from his perspective. Phoenix delivers a
convincing, serious performance, and the rest of the cast, save
for the miscast Hirsch, is also strong.

RUSH
   📀
1991 120m c Crime/Drama   ★★★
The Zanuck Company/MGM-Pathe   (U.S.)   R

Jason Patric (Jim Raynor), Jennifer Jason Leigh (Kristen Cates),
Sam Elliott (Larry Dodd), Max Perlich (Walker), Gregg Allman
(Will Gaines), Tony Frank (Chief Donald Nettle), William Sadler
(Monroe), Special K. McCray (Willie Red), Dennis Letts (Senior
District Attorney), Dennis Burkley (Motorcycle Guy)

p, Richard D. Zanuck; d, Lili Fini Zanuck; w, Pete Dexter (from the
novel by Kim Wozencraft); ph, Kenneth MacMillan; ed, Mark
Warner; m, Eric Clapton; prod d, Paul Sylbert; cos, Colleen Atwood

Producer-turned-director Lili Fini Zanuck and novelist-
screenwriter Pete Dexter have largely de-fanged ex-narcotics
cop Kim Wozencraft's semi-autobiographical thriller, turning
RUSH into a melodramatic, if gritty, Hollywood muddle.

    Jim Raynor (Jason Patric) is an undercover Texas cop
ordered to "sacrifice a virgin" by his supervisor, Larry Dodd
(Sam Elliott), as part of establishing a cover to bring down suspected big-time drug dealer Will Gaines (Gregg Allmann).
Over Dodd's objections, Raynor chooses fresh-scrubbed
police recruit Kristen Cates (Jennifer Jason Leigh).
Unbeknownst to Kristen, Raynor has already succumbed to
substance abuse and part of her own cover will include snorting, smoking or shooting up *anything* that is put in front of her
to establish her credibility on the street.

    Gutted of many of the novel's key ironies, the film version
of RUSH becomes a routine revenge melodrama in its final
moments. Zanuck and Dexter employ an elliptical narrative
style, stringing together vaguely connected scenes that nervously cut away before their full, depressing implications can
sink in. The result is a lack of any meaningful character development or narrative drive. Along the way, though, Patric and
Leigh do highly compelling work, and Zanuck does a fine job
of recreating the feel of a small Texas town in the age of
"Freebird," flared trousers, and Ford Impalas. As Gaines,
Gregg Allman is scary in a way that only aging rock stars can
be. Speaking of aging rock stars, Eric Clapton scored a huge
hit with the theme song, "Tears in Heaven."

RUSH HOUR
   📀
1998 94m c Action/Crime/Comedy   ★★½
New Line/Caravan   (U.S.)   PG-13

Jackie Chan (Lee), Chris Tucker (Carter), Tom Wilkinson
(Griffin/Juntao), Elizabeth Pena (Johnson), Tzi Ma (Consul Han),
Julia Hsu (Soo Yung), Ken Leung (Sang), Robert Littman (First
Caucasian), Michael Chow (Dinner Guest), Chris Penn (Clive)

p, Roger Brinbaum, Arthur Sarkissian, Jonathan Glickman; d,
Brett Ratner; w, Ross LaManna, Jim Kouf (based on the story by
Ross LaManna); ph, Adam Greenberg; ed, Mark Helfrich; m, Lalo
Schifrin; prod d, Robb Wilson King; art d, Thomas Fichter; fx,
Dennis King; cos, Sharen Davis

Brash, stupid, and surprisingly watchable. RUSH HOUR puts
just the slightest spin on the 48 HRS. formula, which throws
together a smart-mouthed African-American charmer and an
older, by-the-book authority figure so they can bicker, spar,
and solve crimes that more conventional law-enforcement
types can't crack.

    Here the straight man is martial-arts legend Jackie Chan,
playing Hong Kong cop Inspector Lee. He's summoned to
L.A. by his old pal Consul Han (Tzi Ma) to investigate the kidnapping of Han's young daughter, Soo Yung (Julia Hsu). But
the FBI doesn't want Lee's help, so they press-gang arrogant
LAPD screwup James Carter (Chris Tucker) into pretending
to work with him while actually keeping Lee out of the way.
Needless to say, neither Carter nor Lee is into this babysitting
gig, and after they're done playing adolescent tricks on each
other they get down to the business of finding Soo Yung.

    Now, the thing that made 48 HRS. such an exhilarating,
unpredictable ride was that it took all its elements seriously:
the crime stuff was tough and bloody, while the mismatched
buddy comedy was edgy and razor-sharp. Some 15 years
down the line, the formula has gotten soft: the crime story here
is lazily constructed, mostly an excuse for the give-and-take
between Tucker and Chan, which is shrill and raucous without being especially clever. That said, the movie skims along
at a pretty decent clip—though the climax comes about 15
minutes too late—and gives Chan (who's concentrating *very*
hard on his English-language lines) ample opportunity to
demonstrate both his trademark skills: lightning-fast martial-
arts action and graceful physical comedy. Tucker's one-note
shtick is abrasive—Carter is pompous, conceited, reckless, not
so bright, and a relentless hound dog—but he and Chan occasionally spark a genuine comic rapport. RUSH HOUR 2 followed in 2001.

RUSHMORE
   📀
1998 95m c Comedy/Drama   ★★★★
American Empirical/Touchstone Pictures   (U.S.)   R

Bill Murray (Mr. Blume), Olivia Williams (Miss Cross), Jason
Schwartzman (Max Fischer), Brian Cox (Dr. Guggenheim),
Seymour Cassel (Bert Fischer), Mason Gamble (Dirk Calloway),
Sara Tanaka (Margaret Yang), Stephen McCole (Magnus Buchan),
Luke Wilson (Dr. Peter Flynn), Deepak Pallana (Mr. Adams)

p, Barry Mendel, Paul Schiff; d, Wes Anderson; w, Wes Anderson,
Owen Wilson; ph, Robert Yeoman; ed, David Moritz; m, Mark
Mothersbaugh; prod d, David Wasco; art d, Andrew Laws; fx, Ron
Trost; cos, Karen Patch; anim, David Ridlen

Another quirky, hard-to-put-your-finger-on delight from the
creators of BOTTLE ROCKET.

    Geeky 15-year-old Max Fischer (Jason Schwartzman)
may be flunking school, but he's cornered the market on
extracurricular activities at snooty Rushmore Academy. The
consummate multi-tasker, Max embraces, ingests, conde-
scends, comprehends, and fails to comprehend with equal
ardor. Yet despite the scattered, frantic quality to Max's pursuit

of everything—staging elaborate plays based on seminal '70s films like SERPICO and APOCALYPSE NOW; engaging in endless activities, from model UN to calligraphy club—he's irresistible. Max hasn't had his first heartbreak, hasn't yet suffered any real adult disappointment, and doesn't know the meaning of passivity: he's bursting with a deep enthusiasm for life. Max is also bursting with love for first-grade teacher Miss Cross (Olivia Williams), whom, despite the serious age difference, he pursues with characteristic relentlessness. Max schemes to impress Miss Cross by building her an elaborate aquarium, but he needs steel tycoon and Rushmore benefactor Mr. Blume (Bill Murray) to foot the bill. Mr. Blume, tired of his family, his job, and life itself, likes having someone like Max around and lets the youngster go to town. As Max happily makes plans that eventually bring his two favorite people together, he never dreams that Miss Cross might find a more appropriate suitor in Mr. Blume.

Without being slavish, writer Owen Wilson and director Wes Anderson's subtle and witty script echoes the themes (and sometimes the look) of Hal Ashby's best films, including HAROLD AND MAUDE and BEING THERE. Anderson's *mise en scene*—heavy on the '70s influences and bolstered by the combination of Mark Mothersbaugh's excellent score and the British Invasion soundtrack—captures the wistful nature of Max's teenage tumult and outsider's ebullience. A rare comedy that keeps you thinking long after its plot machinations have played themselves out, this film is the exciting product of indescribably unique artists reaching the peak of their powers.

RUSSIA HOUSE, THE
1990 123m c   Romance/Spy   ★★★½
Pathe   (U.S.)   R

Sean Connery *(Barley Blair)*, Michelle Pfeiffer *(Katya)*, Roy Scheider *(Russell)*, James Fox *(Ned)*, John Mahoney *(Brady)*, Klaus Maria Brandauer *(Dante)*, Ken Russell *(Walter)*, J.T. Walsh *(Quinn)*, Michael Kitchen *(Clive)*, David Threlfall *(Wicklow)*

p, Fred Schepisi, Paul Maslansky; d, Fred Schepisi; w, Tom Stoppard (based on the novel by John Le Carre); ph, Ian Baker; ed, Peter Honess; m, Jerry Goldsmith; prod d, Richard MacDonald; cos, Ruth Myers

A finely crafted and beautifully acted adaptation of John Le Carre's glasnost-era spy thriller that never quite gets as gripping as it should. THE RUSSIA HOUSE was the first entirely U.S.-produced film to be substantially filmed on location in the Soviet Union, and director Fred Schepisi (PLENTY, ROXANNE) and his regular cinematographer Ian Baker make extensive—sometimes excessive—use of their marvelous settings. The film opens at a Moscow audio-book fair where a furtive Russian woman, Katya (Michelle Pfeiffer), is seeking a British publisher named Barley Blair. Katya has an important manuscript she wishes to deliver to Blair, but he has elected not to attend. Desperate, she enlists the aid of another exhibitor, Niki Landau (Nicholas Woodeson), imploring him to help her by smuggling the manuscript out of Moscow and giving it to Blair in London. Landau agrees to help, but when he arrives in London, he turns the manuscript over to British intelligence, who want to know more about the entire matter. Blair (Sean Connery) is found in Lisbon, where he indulges in his favorite activities: drinking and playing the saxophone in seedy jazz clubs. British intelligence agents Ned (James Fox) and Walter (played with expected flamboyance by director Ken Russell) want Blair to become involved in a plan to establish the identity of the author and, thereby, the credibility of the manuscript, but Blair is unwilling to cooperate. That is, until he sees a photograph of the beautiful Katya.

THE RUSSIA HOUSE is an occasionally profound study in miscommunication and misinterpretation, contrasting a jaded West, made complacent by its long history of freedom, with the East, passionate and sincere as it tests the bounds of that same freedom it is only beginning to taste. The plot turns

and diversions are superbly handled by the excellent cast. Connery is in top form as the apparent cynic who at his heart is a true romantic, while Pfeiffer is thoroughly credible as the idealistic Katya. Brandauer makes good use of his limited screen time, Fox is excellent as the intelligence professional who is wise enough to recognize the foibles of the game, and Scheider is convincing as a CIA man who is as much a politician as he is an expert on international intrigue.

RUSSIAN ARK   DVD
(RUSSKIJ KOVCHEG)
2002 96m c Experimental/Historical/Drama ★★★★
Egoli Tossell Film/Fora Film/Hermitage Bridge Studio (Russia)

Sergey Dreiden *(The Marquis)*, Maria Kuznetsova *(Catherine the Great)*, Leonid Mozgovoy *(The Spy)*, Mikhail Piotrovsky *(Himself)*, David Giorgobiani *(Orbeli)*, Maxim Sergeyev *(Peter the Great)*, Alexander Chaban *(Boris Piotrovsky)*, Lev Yeliseyev *(Himself)*, Oleg Khmelnitsky *(Himself)*, Alla Osipenko *(Herself)*

p, Andrey Deryabin, Jens Meurer, Karsten Stoter; d, Alexander Sokurov; w, Anatoly Nikiforov, Alexander Sokurov; ph, Tilman Buttner; m, Sergey Yevtushenko; art d, Natalia Kochergina, Yelena Zhukova; fx, Bettina Kuntzsch; chor, Galy Abaidulov; cos, Maria Grishanova

Alexander Sokurov's surprisingly accessible film is both a grand tour through three hundred years of Russian cultural identity and an astonishing technical accomplishment: The entire 96-minute cinematic fresco consists of a single, unedited Steadicam shot.

The setting is St. Petersburg's Hermitage museum, forever the jewel of Russian culture. As a repository of some of Europe's greatest masterpieces, it can also be read as a symbol of the cultural conflict at the heart of Russian identity. Our unseen narrator (voiced by Sokurov) awakens after some sort of accident to find himself back in Tsarist Russia. Confused, he joins a group of giddy partygoers as they sneak into the Hermitage through a series of passageways. Our narrator appears to be invisible to everyone except a 19th-century French marquis (Sergey Dreiden), a fellow time traveler. Around each corner, a different tableau unfolds, and it soon becomes clear that this is not only a trip through a magnificent space, but through time as well. Along the way, we encounter Peter the Great (Maxim Sergeyev), contemporary museum officials, Catherine the Great (Maria Kuznetsova), and the Romanovs, sitting down to what could be their final meal.

It's amazing that Sukarov and his superhuman camera operator, Tilman Buttner (RUN LOLA RUN), pulled this off at all; even the latest video technology at first proved inadequate. A brand-new hard drive, capable of recording up to 100 minutes of uncompressed images, needed to be developed before this amazing feat of timing and coordination could be attempted. The final effect, particularly the climactic ballroom sequence, is stunning: a haunting impression of the vast, unbroken synchronicity of time that must surely stand as one of the great achievements in the development of the movie medium.

RUTHLESS PEOPLE   DVD
1986 93m c   Comedy   ★★★½
Touchstone/Silver Screen Partners II   (U.S.)   R

Danny DeVito *(Sam Stone)*, Bette Midler *(Barbara Stone)*, Judge Reinhold *(Ken Kessler)*, Helen Slater *(Sandy Kessler)*, Anita Morris *(Carol)*, Bill Pullman *(Earl)*, William Schilling *(Police Commissioner)*, Art Evans *(Lt. Bender)*, Clarence Felder *(Lt. Walters)*, J.E. Freeman *(Bedroom Killer)*

p, Michael Peyser; d, Jim Abrahams, David Zucker, Jerry Zucker; w, Dale Launer; ph, Jan De Bont (DeLuxe Color); ed, Arthur

Schmidt; m, Michel Colombier; art d, Don Woodruff; cos, Rosanna Norton; anim, Sally Cruikshank

This is a wacky, tasteless, hilarious reworking of O. Henry's classic short story "The Ransom of Red Chief." The movie begins as millionaire garment manufacturer Sam Stone (Danny DeVito) is having dinner with Carol (Anita Morris), his sultry mistress. He is planning to murder Barbara (Bette Midler), his overweight and shrewish wife, unaware that Carol is cheating on him with her hunky, clunky beau, Earl (Bill Pullman). Before Sam can kill Barbara, however, she is kidnapped by a sweet young couple, Ken (Judge Reinhold) and Sandy (Helen Slater), who are seeking revenge against Sam for using an idea of Sandy's to make a fortune without paying her one cent in royalties. They tell Sam that Barbara will be tortured and killed if he breathes one word of the kidnapping to the police or the press. Naturally, Sam thinks his troubles are over, but he's wrong. Everyone in the movie seems to have a comic moment, because the laughs are piled on top of each other. Call it rude, crude, and lewd, but you also have to call it very funny.

RYAN'S DAUGHTER
1970 192m c Romance/War ★★½
Faraway (U.K.) R

Robert Mitchum (Charles Shaughnessy), Sarah Miles (Rosy Ryan), Trevor Howard (Father Collins), Christopher Jones (Randolph Doryan), John Mills (Michael), Leo McKern (Tom Ryan), Barry Foster (Tim O'Leary), Archie O'Sullivan (McCardle), Marie Kean (Mrs. McCardle), Evin Crowley (Moureen)

p, Anthony Havelock-Allan; d, David Lean; w, Robert Bolt; ph, Freddie Young (Super/Panavision, Metrocolor); ed, Norman Savage; m, Maurice Jarre; prod d, Stephen Grimes; art d, Roy Walker; fx, Robert MacDonald; cos, Jocelyn Rickards

AAN Best Actress: Sarah Miles; AA Best Supporting Actor: John Mills; AA Best Cinematography: Freddie Young; AAN Best Sound: Gordon K. McCallum, John Bramall

The best thing about this much-vaunted, overlong Irish epic love triangle is its gorgeous photography by Young. The rest is an expensive potboiler (costing more than $12 million) in which Mitchum saunters through his role as a schoolteacher, cuckolded by trampy wife Miles. The marriage between Miles, the daughter of saloon-keeper McKern, and Mitchum is passionless, the result of Mitchum's lack of interest in sex. Troubled by this absence of lovemaking, Miles consults the parish priest, Howard, who tells her that she should be thankful she's married to such a saint of a man. Then shell-shocked British officer Jones arrives, assigned to suppress associations between the IRA and German spies (it's 1916 and WWI is raging). Miles and Jones are much taken with each other and make wild love in empty buildings and open meadows. Halfwit Mills finds a button ripped off Jones' uniform during one of the love scenes between Miles and Jones and parades around the village square with it, offering it up as evidence against the sinful Miles. Mitchum does not respond to the resulting gossip, preferring to let the romance dissipate. IRA leader Foster then arrives with a boatload of guns sent by the Germans, but, believing the British will make fierce reprisals against the town, Mitchum informs on the gun-runners and the British swoop in. Believing that it was Miles who told her British lover about the weapons, the townspeople swarm into Mitchum's house, strip Miles, and shave her head. Knowing now that he has lost Miles, Jones blows himself up with a hand grenade. Miles and Mitchum pack their things and head for a new life in Dublin.

Directed by fine craftsman Lean, RYAN'S DAUGH-TER is self-indulgent and dull, a long-winded period piece that is so introspective that its love scenes, presented in a frenetic style, appear out of place. Miles is only vaguely interesting, Jones boring, and Mitchum so detached that he appears to be thinking about anything but this film. Only Mills, essaying the village idiot, provides a spark to an otherwise aimless and lifeless film. The whole thing is a great disappointment from a great director. Lean and Bolt—actress Miles' husband, and the director's frequent collaborator—spent five years making the picture, which was photographed on location on the Dingle Peninsula, Ireland's rainiest area. Cast and crew spent a full year there, once shooting only a minute of screen time in a 10-day period because of the awful weather.

S

SABOTAGE
1936 76m bw Thriller/Spy ★★★½
Gaumont (U.K.)

Sylvia Sidney (Sylvia Verloc), Oscar Homolka (Karl Verloc), John Loder (Sgt. Ted Spencer), Desmond Tester (Steve), Joyce Barbour (Renee), Matthew Boulton (Supt. Talbot), S.J. Warmington (Hollingshead), William Dewhurst (A.S. Chatman), Austin Trevor (Vladimir), Torin Thatcher (Yunct)

p, Michael Balcon, Ivor Montagu; d, Alfred Hitchcock; w, Charles Bennett, Ian Hay, Alma Reville, Helen Simpson, E.V.H. Emmett (based on the novel The Secret Agent by Joseph Conrad); ph, Bernard Knowles; ed, Charles Frend; m, Louis Levy

Terrorist Karl Verloc (Homolka) is engaged in a bombing spree in London using a trusting young boy Stevie (Tester), the little brother of his wife Sylvia (Sidney), to deliver the packages of destruction without knowing their contents. Meanwhile, neighborhood grocer Ted Spencer (Loder), actually an undercover Scotland Yard detective, is investigating Verloc's activities. A tense and chilling espionage picture, SABOTAGE contains one sequence that many consider among the director's most excruciatingly suspenseful; Hitchcock, however, later called it a mistake. While delivering a package containing a time bomb, the unknowing Stevie is delayed several times along the way, and ends up on a public bus which stops and starts in traffic as the bomb ticks away. In an interview with Truffaut years later, Hitchcock observed that "the boy was involved in a situation that got him too much sympathy from the audience, so that when the bomb exploded and he was killed, the public was resentful." Truffaut called the sequence a near abuse of cinematic power, and Hitchcock agreed, although his posture of repentance is difficult to reconcile with comparable cruelties in, for instance, PSYCHO and FRENZY. SABOTAGE was banned in several countries where censors viewed it as a handbook for terrorism. Based on a Joseph Conrad novel entitled The Secret Agent, the film's title was changed to SABOTAGE to avoid confusion with Hitchcock's previous picture SECRET AGENT. The confusion came later, however, in 1942, when Hitchcock directed SABOTEUR. If you're not confused yet, SABOTAGE was originally released in the U.S. as A WOMAN ALONE.

SABOTEUR

1942 108m bw Spy/War
Universal (U.S.)

DVD
★★★★

Priscilla Lane *(Patricia Martin)*, Robert Cummings *(Barry Kane)*, Otto Kruger *(Charles Tobin)*, Alan Baxter *(Freeman)*, Clem Bevans *(Neilson)*, Norman Lloyd *(Frank Fry)*, Alma Kruger *(Mrs. Henrietta Sutton)*, Vaughan Glaser *(Phillip Martin)*, Dorothy Peterson *(Mrs. Mason)*, Ian Wolfe *(Robert, the Butler)*

p, Frank Lloyd, Jack H. Skirball; d, Alfred Hitchcock; w, Peter Viertel, Joan Harrison, Dorothy Parker (based on an original story by Hitchcock); ph, Joseph Valentine; ed, Otto Ludwig; m, Charles Previn, Frank Skinner; art d, Jack Otterson

This film, Hitchcock's first contribution to wartime American propaganda, is as polished and suspenseful as any the great director would make. A forerunner to NORTH BY NORTH-WEST, SABOTEUR tells a similar story of an innocent man accused of murder and chasing a bunch of insidious spies across the country. Barry Kane (Robert Cummings) is a simple factory worker in an airplane plant whose best friend is killed in a fire. It turns out the extinguisher Kane handed him was filled with gasoline, engulfing his friend in flames before burning the whole factory. An investigation points to Kane as the saboteur, forcing him to flee across the country to find the real fifth columnist. Along the way he meets Pat Martin (Priscilla Lane), the only one who believes his story. SABOTEUR is no doubt best remembered for its harrowing Statue of Liberty (actually a Universal backlot) finale, in which Cummings chases his man to the Lady's torch. Hitchcock had originally hoped to cast Gary Cooper and Barbara Stanwyck in the leads, with Harry Carey, Sr., in the role of master spy Charles Tobin.

SABRINA

1954 112m bw Romance/Comedy
Paramount (U.S.)

DVD
★★★½

Humphrey Bogart *(Linus Larrabee)*, Audrey Hepburn *(Sabrina Fairchild)*, William Holden *(David Larrabee)*, Walter Hampden *(Oliver Larrabee)*, John Williams *(Thomas Fairchild)*, Martha Hyer *(Elizabeth Tyson)*, Joan Vohs *(Gretchen Van Horn)*, Marcel Dalio *(Baron)*, Marcel Hillaire *(The Professor)*, Nella Walker *(Maude Larrabee)*

p, Billy Wilder; d, Billy Wilder; w, Billy Wilder, Samuel Taylor, Ernest Lehman (based on the play *Sabrina Fair* by Taylor); ph, Charles Lang; ed, Arthur Schmidt; m, Frederick Hollander; art d, Hal Pereira, Walter Tyler; fx, John P. Fulton, Farciot Edouart; cos, Edith Head

AAN Best Actress: Audrey Hepburn; *AAN Best Director:* Billy Wilder; *AAN Best Screenplay:* Billy Wilder, Samuel Taylor, Ernest Lehman; *AAN Best B/W Cinematography:* Charles Lang, Jr.; *AAN Best Art Direction-Set Decoration (B/W):* Hal Pereira Walter Tyler, Sam Comer, Ray Moyer; *AA Best Costume Design (B/W):* Edith Head

Three recent Oscar winners and the sure guidance of Wilder helped make this familiar Cinderella story into something more than it might have been under other auspices. Holden was 36 at the time, a bit old for a dissolute playboy. Further, he is eclipsed by Bogart's performance as his older brother, an unaccustomed comedy role that showed Bogie could play for laughs as well as sneers. Wilder had already won an Oscar, and co-author Lehman was to be the recipient of the coveted statuette later, so this was a formidable team. The story isn't much, but it's the treatment and the witty dialogue that set it apart from the ordinary.

Holden and Bogart are the wealthy sons of Hampden and Walker. Holden lives for fast cars and faster women; Bogart is a hard-headed businessman. Also living on the estate are Williams, the chauffeur, and his impressionable daughter, Hepburn. She's mad about Holden, and attempts suicide when she realizes he's only toying with her. Williams sends her to France, where she is transformed into a sophisticated lady of fashion. In the U.S., Bogart seeks to enhance the family's wealth by marrying Holden off to heiress Hyer. Hepburn returns to Long Island, and once Holden gets a look at this new version, he falls for her. Hepburn is determined to win Holden, but Bogart and Hampden are determined to prevent the match. To take her mind off Holden, bachelor Bogart pretends to be courting her. The expected romantic complications follow.

A charming, if often-seen, tale, paced with alacrity by Wilder from the adaptation of Taylor's hit play which had starred Margaret Sullavan, SABRINA was a resounding hit at the box office and with the critics and proved that silk purses were still possible from less than perfect sources. Bogart had been making movies for more than two decades, but this was his first effort for Paramount. He and Wilder did not get along and had differing views of what was funny. Whoever won those battles will never be known, but the results were satisfying, as Bogart played drawing-room comedy with aplomb.

SACCO AND VANZETTI

(SACCO E VANZETTI)
1971 120m c Historical
Jolly/Unidis/Theatre Le Rex (Italy/France)

DVD
★★★
GP

Gian Maria Volonte *(Bartolomeo Vanzetti)*, Riccardo Cucciolla *(Nicola Sacco)*, Cyril Cusack *(Frederick Katzmann)*, Milo O'Shea *(Fred Moore)*, Geoffrey Keen *(Judge Webster Thayer)*, William Prince *(William Thompson)*, Rosanna Fratello *(Rosa Sacco)*, Claude Mann *(Journalist)*, Edward Jewesbury, Armenia Balducci

p, Arrigo Colombo, Giorgio Papi; d, Giuliano Montaldo; w, Giuliano Montaldo, Fabrizio Onofri, Ottavio Jemma; ph, Silvano Ippoliti (Technicolor); ed, Nino Baragli; m, Ennio Morricone; art d, Aurelio Crugnola; cos, Enrico Sabbatini

The American judicial system has a long and spotted history of convicting and executing those whose political views defy the status quo. One most notorious such trial was that of Sacco and Vanzetti, two Italian immigrants and admitted anarchists who were convicted and sent to the electric chair as a result of the 1920s red scare. This English-dubbed version of the tale accurately portrays the facts, with clear sympathy shown towards the two defendants. Cucciolla and Volonte (the latter from A FISTFUL OF DOLLARS and FOR A FEW DOL-LARS MORE) portray the duo, who are brought up on charges of murder when two employees of a shoe store are killed in a robbery. After a sham trial in which Cucciolla and Volonte are tried more for their politics than for the actual crime, they are found guilty and sentenced to death. The case causes worldwide commotion as literally thousands of people rally behind them over the course of the next six years. However, despite some evidence of their innocence, Cucciolla and Volonte are executed on August 23, 1927. Though overall an impressive and accurate retelling of this miscarriage of justice, the film is not without its faults. The major problem is length. Considering the scope of actual time and the myriad events that took place over those seven years, two hours is simply insufficient for the story. Worst of all is an annoying theme song by Joan Baez which is packed with such insincere (and ultimately condescending) lyrics as, "Here's to you, Sacco and Bart/Something, something forever in my heart." The film is at its strongest when allowed to simply speak for itself. This is a story fraught with natural emotion, portrayed with sincerity and genuine sympathy for its doomed protagonists. In the end,

SACCO AND VANZETTI becomes an eloquent portrait of two simple men swept up in the fury of political self-righteousness, a portrait which is not flattering to the American way of justice, to say the least.

SACRIFICE, THE
(OFFRET-SA CRIFICATIO)
1986 145m c Drama ★★★★
Swedish Film Institute/Argos/Film Four/ PG
Josephson & Nykvist/Swedish Television/SVT 2/
Sandrew/French Ministry of Culture (France/Sweden)

Erland Josephson (Alexander), Susan Fleetwood (Adelaide), Valerie Mairesse (Julia), Allan Edwall (Otto), Gudrun Gisladottir (Maria), Sven Wollter (Victor), Filippa Franzen (Marta), Tommy Kjellqvist (Little Man)

d, Andrei Tarkovsky; w, Andrei Tarkovsky; ph, Sven Nykvist (Eastmancolor); ed, Andrei Tarkovsky, Michal Leszczylowski; m, Johann Sebastian Bach, Watazumido Shuoo; art d, Anna Asp; fx, Svenska Stuntgruppen, Lars Hoglund, Lars Palmqvist, Richard Roberts, Johan Toren; cos, Inger Pehrsson

The final film from one of Russia's greatest filmmakers, Andrei Tarkovsky, was also his first to receive any widespread recognition in the U.S. Like all of Tarkovsky's work, it tackles complex themes and concerns that most directors would never approach. THE SACRIFICE is about a number of things, none obvious and none remaining wholly consistent from one viewing to the next; it is a poetic vision, filled with the symbolism peculiar to Tarkovsky's imagination. It is also a visually stunning, hauntingly beautiful, brilliant piece of art. THE SACRIFICE opens as Alexander (Erland Josephson) and his six-year-old son are busily planting a tree along the sandy, barren shore of the small island where the family is vacationing. During this vacation, it is announced on the radio that WWIII has begun—and the complete destruction of Europe by nuclear arms is certain. Later, when Alexander is alone, he gets down on his hands and knees to ask forgiveness from his creator, begging for the terrible events that are transpiring to be undone. He promises to do anything—give up all his possessions, even part with his son—if only things will be returned to normal. More than a beautiful film, THE SACRIFICE is a hopeful message to future generations to live in harmony with nature and with one another (which only gains in power by virtue of its dedication to the filmmaker's son). By December 29, 1986, less than a year after this movie was completed, Tarkovsky would fall victim to the cancer that he already knew would kill him. Aware that this would probably be his last film, Tarkovsky makes a conscious plea that we consider the damage done to the planet before it's too late, and seems to be saying that for all the modern world's astounding scientific progress, there is nothing to compensate for the loss of our spiritual essence—creating a dangerous gap between human consciousness and the natural world. While perhaps not the most typical of Tarkovsky's works, (the Swedish cast, Sven Nykvist's photography, and the Faro location occasionally lend it a Bergmanesque quality), THE SACRIFICE is a brilliant picture that should not be missed.

SADDEST MUSIC IN THE WORLD, THE
2004 99m c/bw Musical/Comedy/Drama ★★★½
Rhombus Media/Buffalo Gal Pictures/Ego Film Arts
(Canada)

Isabella Rossellini (Lady Port-Huntly), Mark McKinney (Chester Kent), Maria de Medeiros (Narcissa), Ross McMillan (Roderick/Gravillo), David Fox (Fyodor), Claude Dorge (Duncan), Darcy Fehr (Teddy), Erik J. Berg (Orphan)

p, Niv Fichman, Jody Shapiro; d, Guy Maddin; w, Guy Maddin, George Toles (based on an original screenplay by Kazuo Ishiguro); ph, Luc Montpellier; ed, David Wharnsby; m, Christopher Dedrick; prod d, Matthew Davies; cos, Meg McMillan

Another slice of bizarre, movie-mad brilliance from Winnipeg's Guy Maddin, and that's always cause for celebration.

It's 1933, and the Great Depression has hit Winnipeg so hard that the city has been voted the "world capital of sorrow." The only business that's booming is the brewery that's owned and operated by haughty beer baroness Lady Port-Huntly (Isabella Rossellini), a glamorous double-amputee who knows that the sadder people are, the more beer they'll drink. Lady Port-Huntly has devised a worldwide radio contest to determine which country produces the saddest music in the world. From the U.S. comes hard-hearted Chester Kent (Mark McKinney), a Winnipeg-born producer of musical spectaculars who was once Lady P.'s lover. Chester's father, Fyodor (David Fox), a WWI veteran whose unrequited love for the malt queen resulted in the loss of her legs, will be representing Canada. But neither father nor son anticipates the sudden reappearance of Chester's inconsolable brother, world-renowned cellist Roderick (Ross McMillan), who left home 10 years earlier. Roderick is searching for his long-gone wife, scatterbrained nympho Narcissa (Maria de Medeiros). Coincidentally, she now lives in Winnipeg and has been dating Chester. Once Narcissa takes the stage as the star of Chester's splashy, Broadway-style bid for the saddest music in the world, Roderick will realize the depths of his brother's perfidy.

This very odd but hugely enjoyable musical melodrama sounds like typical Maddin—Oedipal histrionics packaged like some forgotten Poverty Row programmer—but the original script was actually written by the famed Anglo-Japanese novelist Kazuo Ishiguro (Remains of the Day). Maddin, however, makes the material entirely his own, which is to say you won't see anything quite like it from any other filmmaker working today.

SAFE
1995 123m c Drama ★★★★
American Playhouse Theatrical Films/Chemical R
Films/Good Machine/Kardana/Channel Four Films (U.S.)

Julianne Moore (Carol White), Peter Friedman (Peter Dunning), Xander Berkeley (Greg White), Susan Norman (Linda), Kate McGregory Stewart (Claire), Mary Carver (Nell), Steven Gilborn (Dr. Hubbard), April Grace (Susan), Peter Crombie (Dr. Reynolds), Ronnie Farer (Barbara)

p, Christine Vachon, Lauren Zalaznick; d, Todd Haynes; w, Todd Haynes; ph, Alex Nepomniaschy; ed, James Lyons; m, Ed Tomney; prod d, David J. Bomba; art d, Anthony R. Stabley; cos, Nancy Steiner

Controversial, undeniably brilliant alternative filmmaker Todd Haynes (POISON, SUPERSTAR: THE KAREN CARPENTER STORY) reached the mainstream with this dreamy but tough-minded satire. It's about a fragile housewife (Julianne Moore) who develops a mysterious syndrome called Multiple Chemical Sensitivity—as one character puts it, she's "allergic to the 20th Century."

In the sterile landscape of California's San Fernando Valley, suburban homemaker Carol White (Moore, in a stunning performance) slowly discovers that she's allergic to her new sofa. Next, she has a terrifying choking attack caused by exhaust fumes on the freeway. Both Carol's husband Greg (Xander Berkeley) and her physician, Dr. Hubbard (Stephen Gilborn), dismiss the malady as emotional. But Carol continues to experience adverse reactions to everything from her hairspray to the food she eats. Desperate, Carol tries everything, winding up in a "wellness center" near Albuquerque, New Mexico. There, doctors, gurus, and assorted lost souls fail to halt Carol's inexorable retreat from reality.

SAFE sounds like a disease-of-the-week TV movie, but it transforms the formulaic material into something original and spellbinding. Much as Douglas Sirk and Rainer Werner Fassbinder reimagined the conventions of melodrama, director Todd Haynes—who was indeed inspired by a TV movie, THE BOY IN THE PLASTIC BUBBLE—turns the form on its head. Haynes keeps viewers at arm's-length through the cool detachment of his technique. Viewers unused to his elliptical style may have difficulty discerning his point of view (many experienced similar difficulties the previous year with Michael Tolkin's masterly THE NEW AGE), but few will fail to register his disdain for the overweening gurus who advise their clients that sick people are responsible for their own diseases.

SAHARA
1943 97m bw War   **DVD**
Columbia (U.S.)   ★★★★

Humphrey Bogart *(Sgt. Joe Gunn)*, Bruce Bennett *(Waco Hoyt)*, Lloyd Bridges *(Fred Clarkson)*, Rex Ingram *(Sgt. Tambul)*, J. Carrol Naish *(Giuseppe)*, Dan Duryea *(Jimmy Doyle)*, Richard Nugent *(Capt. Jason Halliday)*, Patrick O'Moore *(Ozzie Bates)*, Louis Mercier *(Jean Leroux)*, Carl Harbord *(Marty Williams)*

p, Harry Joe Brown; d, Zoltan Korda; w, John Howard Lawson, Zoltan Korda, James O'Hanlon (based on a story by Philip MacDonald); ph, Rudolph Mate; ed, Charles Nelson; m, Miklos Rozsa; art d, Lionel Banks, Eugene Lourie

AAN Best Supporting Actor: J Carrol Naish; *AAN Best B/W Cinematography:* Rudolph Mate; *AAN Best Sound Recording:* John Livadary

One of the most exciting and entertaining propaganda films to come out of WWII, SAHARA features Humphrey Bogart as Sgt. Joe Gunn, an American tank commander who, along with his crew (Bruce Bennett and Dan Duryea), is separated from his unit just after the fall of Tobruk. As the tank, nicknamed *Lulubelle*, slowly makes its way through the desert, Sgt. Gunn and his crew pick up a number of stragglers: several British soldiers (Patrick O'Moore, Lloyd Bridges, Richard Nugent, Carl Harbord), a Sudanese corporal (Rex Ingram) with an Italian prisoner (J. Carrol Naish) in tow, a Free Frenchman (Louis Mercier), a South African volunteer (Guy Kingsford), and a downed Nazi pilot (Kurt Kreuger). As the small rag-tag unit advances, the search for an oasis becomes their primary mission; however, they soon discover that a large German force in the area has the same objective. Blessed with a great cast and smart direction by Zoltan Korda, SAHARA remains one of the most appealing films of WWII. Although the constant speechifying, especially by Naish's repentant Italian, may strike some as passe and overbearing, the basic humanity of the entire affair is a pleasant change from the xenophobic posturing found in most films of the era. Sadly, scriptwriter John Howard Lawson's humane outlook would come back to haunt him when, in the 1950s, he became one of the Hollywood Ten. However, when McCarthyite government officials tried to pressure Columbia Pictures boss Harry Cohn into firing Lawson, he refused, much to his credit.

SALAAM BOMBAY!
1988 113m c Drama   ★★★★
Mirabai (India)

Shafiq Syed *(Krishna/Chaipau)*, Sarfuddin Qurrassi *(Koyla)*, Raju Barnad *(Keera)*, Raghubir Yadav *(Chillum)*, Nana Patekar *(Baba)*, Aneeta Kanwar *(Rekha)*, Hansa Vithal *(Manju)*, Mohanraj Babu *(Salim)*, Chandrashekhar Naidu *(Chungal)*, Ramesh Deshavani

p, Mira Nair; d, Mira Nair; w, Sooni Taraporevala (based on a story by Nair, Sooni Taraporevala); ph, Sandi Sissel; ed, Barry Alexander Brown; m, L. Subramaniam; prod d, Mitch Epstein

AAN Best Foreign Language Film

The breakthrough film for onetime documentarist Mira Nair (INDIA CABARET), who later entered the English-language mainstream with MISSISSIPPI MASALA. Nair leavens her story of a desperately impoverished 11-year-old (Shafiq Syed) with enough sentimentality to insure broad audience appeal.

Abandoned by his family, unable to read or write, unsure even of the name of his native village, the boy arrives in the Bombay slums where he hopes to raise enough money to return to his family. He makes a few rupees a day delivering tea, and in the process comes into contact with a variety of seedy characters: a pimp (Nana Patekar), his prostitute wife (Aneeta Kanwar), a drug-addicted pusher (Raghubir Yadav) who works for the pimp, the pimp's daughter (Hansa Vithal), and a naive peasant girl called "Sweet Sixteen" (Chanda Sharma), a prostitute-to-be whose virginity is being auctioned off to the highest bidder. As time wears on, however, the youngster's surrogate family collapses around him.

Shot in the slums of Bombay with child actors recruited by Nair from the street, SALAAM BOMBAY! is moving and well-crafted, but far from original. Like Satyajit Ray's early work, it is heavily indebted to the Italian neo-realist tradition and implicitly contemptuous of mainstream Indian cinema. Nair uses her characters' devotion to Bombay musicals to make a rather tired point about the contrast between their squalid lives and the fantasies purveyed by commercial cinema. In one place, this strategy notably backfires: when the protagonist and his friends visit the cinema, the clip we see them viewing—a comic dance number from MR. INDIA performed by Indian megastar Sridevi—is far more arresting than anything in SALAAM BOMBAY! Nair's film received the prestigious Camera d'Or for best first feature at the 1988 Cannes Film Festival.

SALO, OR THE 120 DAYS OF SODOM   **DVD**
(SALO, O LE 120 GIORNATE DI SODOMA)
1975 117m c Drama   ★★½
PEA/Les Productions Artistes Associes (Italy/France)

Paolo Bonacelli *(The Duke)*, Giorgio Cataldi *(The Monsignore)*, Uberto Paolo Quintavalle *(His Excellency)*, Aldo Velletti *(The President)*, Caterina Boratto *(Signora Castelli)*, Elso de Giorgi *(Signora Maggi)*, Helene Surgere *(Signora Vaccari)*, Sonia Saviange *(The Pianist)*, Ines Pellegrini *(Maid)*

p, Alberto Grimaldi; d, Pier Paolo Pasolini; w, Pier Paolo Pasolini (based on the novel *Les 120 Journees de Sodome* by the Marquis de Sade), Sergio Citti; ph, Tonino delli Colli; ed, Nino Baragli; m, Ennio Morricone; prod d, Dante Ferretti; art d, Dante Ferretti; cos, Danilo Donati

Uncompromisingly violent, apocalyptic, and repulsive, SALO is the last film directed by Pier Paolo Pasolini, who was beaten to death by a male prostitute shortly before its release. Very loosely based on Sade's notorious fantasy of consensual sexual cruelty, *Les 120 Journees de Sodome*, this brutally explicit film is set in 1944 during the waning days of Italian fascism. A cabal of four authority figures—a magistrate, a banker, a duke, and a monsignor—lures a group of young men and women to an isolated villa, where they are subjected to unrelenting, ritualistic torture. The director, a Marxist with anarchistic leanings, presumably means to allegorize the institutionalization of violence under late capitalism—"It is the first time I am making a film about the modern world," he said—while transgressing every conceivable convention of bourgeois taste. The result, despite moments of undeniably brilliant insight, is nearly unwatchable, extremely disturbing, and often literally nauseous.

SALOME'S LAST DANCE

DVD

1988 89m c Comedy/Religious ★★★½

Vestron (U.K.) R

Glenda Jackson (Herodias/Lady Alice), Stratford Johns (Herod/Alfred Taylor), Nickolas Grace (Oscar Wilde), Douglas Hodge (John the Baptist/Lord Alfred "Bosie" Douglas), Imogen Millais-Scott (Salome/Rose), Denis Ull (Tigellenus/Chilvers), Russell Lee Nash (Pageboy), Alfred Russell (Cappadodern), Ken Russell (Kenneth), David Doyle (A. Nabda)

p, Penny Corke, Robert Littman; d, Ken Russell; w, Ken Russell (based on the play Salome by Oscar Wilde); ph, Harvey Harrison (Technicolor); ed, Timothy Gee; chor, Arlene Phillips; cos, Michael Arrals

Ken Russell's most impressive offering in years presents Oscar Wilde's Salome as a play within a film. Wilde (Nickolas Grace) and his lover, Lord Alfred Douglas (Douglas Hodge), visit a local bordello, where a performance of his banned play Salome is to be staged. Playing Herod, the gluttonous king, is the bordello's proprietor (Stratford Johns). Other bordello residents fill out the remaining roles, including a Cockney servant girl (Imogen Millais-Scott) in the role of Salome, and Lord Alfred plays the prophet, John the Baptist. The play dramatizes an ancient biblical tale: Salome tries to seduce the imprisoned prophet and is repulsed. As a reward for performing the titillating "Dance of the Seven Veils" for her sexually besotted stepfather, Herod, she demands the prophet's head on a silver platter. The events that take place off the stage, however, are as important as what occurs on it. The play-within-a-film structure achieves a synthesis of real-life decadence, historical decadence, and that particular decadence that flowed from Wilde's pen. In an effort to stretch these boundaries even further, director Russell casts himself as a photographer who captures and frames the images, and as the stagehand who creates the sound effects—the aural counterpart to the imagemaker. Despite what are often called "excesses" in Russell's style, SALOME'S LAST DANCE is a film of emotional depth and warmth.

SALT OF THE EARTH

DVD

1954 94m bw Docudrama ★★★★

Intl. Union of Mine, Mill and Smelter Workers (U.S.)

Rosaura Revueltas (Esperanza Quintero), Will Geer (Sheriff), David Wolfe (Barton), Melvin Williams (Hartwell), David Sarvis (Alexander), Juan Chacon (Ramon Quintero), Henrietta Williams (Teresa Vidal), Ernest Velasquez (Charley Vidal), Angela Sanchez (Consuelo Ruiz), Joe T. Morales (Sal Ruiz)

p, Paul Jarrico, Sonja Dahl Biberman, Adolfo Barela; d, Herbert Biberman; w, Michael Wilson, Michael Biberman; ph, Leonard Stark, Stanley Meredith; ed, Ed Spiegel, Joan Laird; m, Sol Kaplan; prod d, Sonja Dahl Biberman, Adolfo Barela

Landmark semi-documentary account of a strike by Mexican-American mineworkers in the American Southwest which was released at the height of McCarthyism and led to the imprisonment and/or blacklisting of several of the key figures involved. This was one of the first films to deal with the rights of Chicanos and to depict women as playing a central role in the labor movement.

SALT OF THE EARTH was filmed using actual participants of the real-life struggle on which it is based (Chacon, a non-professional actor, does an amazing job in his real-life role). The film rises above the level of agitprop by avoiding sloganeering and using the real words of real people to tell its story. Its feminism, too, is real and unforced, with women simply being shown struggling alongside—and when necessary defying—their male counterparts.

Naturally a film with such liberal leanings became a source of controversy in the 1950s; SALT OF THE EARTH

was doubly cursed, for its content and its background. Producer Paul Jarrico had been banned from Hollywood, but this could not stop him. He joined with director Herbert Biberman, a member of the "Hollywood Ten," who had served a five-month prison sentence for being an uncooperative House Un-American Activities Committee (HUAC) witness. They wanted to create a film company which would give work to blacklisted members of the film industry. Their intent was to create stories, as the two wrote 20 years later, "drawn from the living experiences of people long ignored in Hollywood—the working men and women of America." As it turns out, this was their only production, made in association with the International Mine, Mill, and Smelter Workers. They were lucky to make the film at all; shortly after production began in early 1953 the pro-McCarthy establishment press sought to discredit the film and filmmakers. Hollywood actor Walter Pidgeon, then president of the Screen Actors Guild, upon receiving a letter from a New Mexico schoolteacher warning of "Hollywood Reds... shooting a feature-length anti-American racial-issue propaganda movie" alerted his contacts in government, ranging from members of HUAC to officials of the FBI and CIA. Donald Jackson, a member of HUAC, claimed he would do everything he could to prevent the screening of "this communist-made film," citing non-existent scenes as examples of the film's Red leanings. Even billionaire Howard Hughes, head of RKO, got on the bandwagon and came up with a plan to stop the film's processing and distribution. The local population near the shooting site also got into the act. Vigilante groups took action, picking fights with crew members and setting fire to real union headquarters. Local merchants refused to do business with anyone in the production. One group threatened to take out the company "in pine boxes," and finally the New Mexico State Police had to come in to protect the filmmakers.

Problems were compounded when Revueltas, a Mexican actress, was arrested by immigration officials for a minor passport violation. She returned to Mexico, and the film had to be completed with a double. Some of her scenes were also shot in her native country on the pretext of being test shots for a future production. (Sadly, the Red fever of this country spilled over into Mexico, and Revueltas was blacklisted there for her work in this film. The talented actress would never work again.) SALT OF THE EARTH enjoyed critical acclaim in Europe but, due to continued blacklisting, did not enjoy wide U.S. release until 1965, when it became a rallying point for the political activism of that decade.

SALVADOR

DVD

1986 123m c Drama/War ★★★★

Hemdale (U.K.) R

James Woods (Richard Boyle), James Belushi (Dr. Rock), Michael Murphy (Ambassador Thomas Kelly), John Savage (John Cassady), Elpidia Carrillo (Maria), Tony Plana (Maj. Max), Colby Chester (Jack Morgan), Cynthia Gibb (Cathy Moore), Will MacMillian (Col. Hyde), Valerie Wildman (Pauline Axelrod)

p, Gerald Green, Oliver Stone; d, Oliver Stone; w, Oliver Stone, Richard Boyle; ph, Robert Richardson; ed, Claire Simpson; m, Georges Delerue; prod d, Bruno Rubeo; art d, Melo Hinojosa; fx, Yves De Bono; cos, Kathryn Morrison

AAN Best Actor: James Woods; AAN Best Original Screenplay: Oliver Stone, Richard Boyle

Caustic, vivid, and without question the best major film about recent conflicts in Latin America. This often-overlooked Oliver Stone effort is in some ways better than his Oscar-winning Vietnam film PLATOON. Although there have been other major films dealing with conflict in Latin America (Chile in MISSING; Nicaragua in UNDER

FIRE), none has conveyed the chaos, tension, and fear within the region as convincingly as SALVADOR.

Based on the experiences of real-life journalist Richard Boyle, the film begins in 1980, as the unemployed veteran reporter (played brilliantly by James Woods) heads down to El Salvador with his buddy, Dr. Rock (James Belushi), an out-of-work disc jockey. Promising drink, drugs, and an endless supply of cheap whores, Boyle cons his friend into coming along to a place where he can make some quick money covering a "little guerrilla war." Once they cross the border, however, things begin to get dangerous as Boyle becomes embroiled in the devastating civil war.

Director Stone persuasively conveys the turmoil and horror of life in El Salvador; at the same time, he shows the rebirth of conscience in a cynical, self-absorbed journalist whose problems pale in comparison with the atrocities suffered by the Salvadoran people. Woods is superb, and it is a tribute to his considerable dramatic skill that he manages to elicit sympathy for a uniquely obnoxious character. But if Woods' performance is one of the most challenging and fascinating to hit the screen in some time, it is Stone's stinging portrayal of El Salvador that gives the film its disturbing tone. Limning the chaotic events of 1980-81, Stone recreates the confusion, terror, senselessness, and despair felt by Salvadorans, while jaded Americans—government, military, and press—blithely ignore the realities of the country's predicament. Stone's camera suggests photojournalism, always on the move, running, swirling, probing, trying to get as close as possible to the truth of the tragedy in El Salvador.

SALVATORE GIULIANO

1961   125m   bw   Biography/Crime   📀 DVD

Lux/Vides/Galatea   (Italy)   ★★★

Frank Wolff (Gaspare Pisciotta), Salvo Randone (President of Viterbo Assize Court), Federico Zardi (Pisciotta's Defense Counsel), Pietro Cammarata (Salvatore Giuliano), Fernando Cicero (Bandit), Sennuccio Benelli (Reporter), Bruno Ekmar (Spy), Max Cartier (Francesco), Giuseppe Calandra (Minor Official), Cosimo Torino (Frank Mannino)

p, Franco Cristaldi; d, Francesco Rosi; w, Francesco Rosi, Suso Cecchi D'Amico, Enzo Provenzale, Franco Solinas; ph, Gianni Di Venanzo; ed, Mario Serandrei; m, Piero Piccioni; art d, Sergio Canevari, Carlo Egidi; cos, Marilu Carteny

This film is based on the true story of Salvatore Giuliano, an important Sicilian Mafia chieftain who was found shot full of holes on July 5, 1950. The film opens with the bullet-ridden remains found in a sunny courtyard. After his wake and funeral begin, the mobster's career is portrayed in flashbacks. Cammarata is the gangster who becomes involved with some guerrilla activities in postwar Sicily. When the group breaks up, a number of his men continue to follow Cammarata as he stages a minor war against legal authorities. He has a group of peasants slaughtered at a Communist rally, which triggers violent confrontations between gangsters and the law. Slowly, his men grow disillusioned with him and they abandon the man. Wolff, Cammarata's second-in-command, also abandons his boss but, like many of the outlaws, is tried and thrown in jail. There, Wolff is poisoned by members of the Mafia, a group he joined after leaving Cammarata. This is an interesting gangster picture, made in the heart of the Mafia's birthplace. The use of camera technique is excellent, coupled with a strong sense of direction. The acting is equally good, making full use of the cast's respective talents. Non-professional actors, as well as professionals, were used with fine results. However, the film is severely hampered for American audiences by the confusing plot line that was clearly designed with more local audiences in mind. The political, historical, and social references are not always clear, which can be distracting, yet this still works and works well.

SAMMY AND ROSIE GET LAID

1987   100m   c   Drama   ★★★½

Cinecom/Film Four   (U.K.)   R

Shashi Kapoor (Rafi Rahman), Claire Bloom (Alice), Ayub Khan Din (Sammy), Frances Barber (Rosie Hobbs), Roland Gift (Danny/Victoria), Wendy Gazelle (Anna), Suzette Llewellyn (Vivia), Meera Syal (Rani), Badi Uzzaman (Ghost)

p, Tim Bevan, Sarah Radclyffe; d, Stephen Frears; w, Hanif Kureishi; ph, Oliver Stapleton; ed, Mick Audsley; m, Stanley Myers; prod d, Hugo Luczyc-Whyowski; cos, Barbara Kidd

Director Stephen Frears and screenwriter Hanif Kureishi, the team that produced the splendid MY BEAUTIFUL LAUNDRETTE, join forces again to provide a cynically humorous and apocalyptic portrait of life in Prime Minister Margaret Thatcher's England. Sammy (Ayub Khan Din) and Rosie (Frances Barber), a young interracial married couple, lead a bohemian existence in a marginal London neighborhood. Theirs is a relationship based on "freedom plus commitment," meaning that they sleep with whomever they want but still love each other. Into this genially amoral world comes Sammy's father, Rafi Rahman (Shashi Kapoor, a huge star in India), a charming rogue who has not seen his son in years. Having made a fortune in his murderous political dealings in Pakistan, Rafi has returned to transfer his wealth into his son's account on the condition that Sammy and Rosie buy a house in a respectable part of England and that they supply him with a grandson. Though he has blood on his own hands, Rafi is appalled by the violence, squalor, and social unrest. The beloved London of his youth has become a living hell in his eyes. Sammy and Rosie's friends disapprove of Rafi's political sins while he is revolted by their "perverted" sexuality and left wing views. Only the strikingly handsome mulatto street person named Danny (Roland Gift, lead singer for the Fine Young Cannibals)—but who prefers to be called "Victoria"—looks up to Rafi and follows him around town. However, before long, the charismatic scoundrel's old crimes come back to haunt him.

SAMMY AND ROSIE GET LAID is a biting satire that does its best to achieve screenwriter Kureishi's stated aim to "get as much filth and anarchy into the cinema as possible." In addition to literate hardhitting scripting and smooth direction, the movie is features excellent performances. However, this is a case where a film is simply too ambitious. Kureishi does an admirable job of juggling numerous balls in the air for the first half of the film—dealing with issues of politics, class, drugs, and interracial strife and attraction—but he becomes less graceful in the film's second half after a bravura triple split screen sex scene. Matters become increasingly contrived as the film collapses in exhaustion from thematic overload. Still it's a fairly impressive achievement as a whole.

SAMSON AND DELILAH

1949   131m   c   Religious   ★★★½

Paramount   (U.S.)

Hedy Lamarr (Delilah), Victor Mature (Samson), George Sanders (Saran of Gaza), Angela Lansbury (Semadar), Henry Wilcoxon (Ahtur), Olive Deering (Miriam), Fay Holden (Hazel), Julia Faye (Hisham), Russ Tamblyn (Saul), William Farnum (Tubal)

p, Cecil B. DeMille; d, Cecil B. DeMille; w, Vladimir Jabotinsky, Harold Lamb, Jesse Lasky Jr., Fredric M. Frank (based on the story in the Bible and the book Judge and Fool by Vladimir Jabotinsky); ph, Dewey Wrigley, George Barnes (Technicolor); ed, Anne Bauchens; m, Victor Young; art d, Hans Dreier, Walter Tyler;

fx, Gordon Jennings, Paul K. Lerpae, Devereaux Jennings; chor, Theodore Kosloff; cos, Edith Head, Gus Peters, Dorothy Jeakins, Gwen Wakeling, Elois Jenssen

AAN Best Color Cinematography: George Barnes; AAN Best Score (Drama or Comedy): Victor Young; AA Best Art Direction-Set Decoration (Color): Hans Dreier, Walter Tyler, Sam Comer, Ray Moyer; AA Best Costume Design (Color): Edith Head, Dorothy Jeakins, Elois Jenssen, Gile Steele, Gwen Wakeling; AAN Best Special Effects

Late but classic Cecil B. DeMille blockbuster, and one of the director's top money-makers, about biblical strong man Samson (Victor Mature), vanquished by the soft curves of the vixen Delilah (Hedy Lamarr).

SAMSON AND DELILAH was tried and true ground for the great DeMille, best remembered for his spectacular interpretations of the Bible (KING OF KINGS, SIGN OF THE CROSS, THE TEN COMMANDMENTS) and other extravagant historical recreations (CLEOPATRA, THE CRUSADES). Here DeMille, the master of the crowd scene, is in top form managing thousands of extras, particularly in the savage battle scenes in which Samson destroys the Philistine army with the jawbone of an ass. DeMille spent $3 million to film the Old Testament story, but the movie gained enormous and immediate returns, filling Paramount's coffers with more than $12 million from its initial release, the largest box-office take the studio had enjoyed to date.

SAN FRANCISCO

1936 115m bw Romance/Disaster ★★★★
MGM (U.S.)

Clark Gable (Blackie Norton), Jeanette MacDonald (Mary Blake), Spencer Tracy (Father Tim Mullin), Jack Holt (Jack Burley), Ted Healy (Matt), Margaret Irving (Della Bailey), Jessie Ralph (Maisie Burley), Harold Huber (Babe), Al Shean (Professor), William Ricciardi (Baldini)

p, John Emerson, Bernard H. Hyman; d, W.S. Van Dyke II, D.W. Griffith (uncredited); w, Anita Loos, Erich von Stroheim (based on a story by Robert E. Hopkins); ph, Oliver T. Marsh; ed, Tom Held; m, Edward Ward; art d, Cedric Gibbons, Arnold Gillespie, Harry McAfee; fx, A. Arnold Gillespie, James Basevi; chor, Val Raset; cos, Adrian

AAN Best Picture; AAN Best Actor: Spencer Tracy; AAN Best Director: W.S. Van Dyke; AAN Best Original Story: Robert Hopkins; AA Best Sound Recording: Douglas Shearer; AAN Best Assistant Director: Joseph Newman

This film left no doubt that MGM was the most formidable studio in Hollywood. Star power, a great, rowdy story, and one of the most awesome special effects sequences in the history of film made SAN FRANCISCO a blockbuster. The pairing of Gable and Tracy here is historic: Tracy envied Gable's roguish charm and romantic image; Gable thought Tracy the finest actor on screen.

Gable stars as the brassy, colorful boss of the infamous Paradise beer garden, who ensnares starving MacDonald into a contract singing for him, although she also gains fame with Nob Hill patrons of the San Francisco Opera and amazingly finds time to inspire churchgoers, trilling in priest Tracy's choir. Yes, Jeanette overdoes it a bit, and why not? She's The Belle of San Francisco. Until the special effects, this is a Lifetime Achievement period piece for McDonald, with the rough 'n' ready leads battling over her soul and other extremities. It almost holds the picture together while we're waiting for the Big Rumble.

And rumble it does: the great old historic sites of San Francisco are shown breaking to pieces under the strain of the tremendous earthquake. City Hall collapses, fountains disintegrate, and office and residential buildings sway and tumble as the quake grips the entire city. Everywhere people are looking for lost loved ones. A long view of the city shows widespread fires breaking out, and a series of quick shots show firemen helpless to combat them because the water mains are broken. A second tremor begins, and this time the very streets split. But when The King finds Jeanette, she's still in concert.

SAN FRANCISCO is the biggest film Van Dyke ever directed, a work he maintains at a fantastic pace, hustling along his actors to keep time with the gaudy, bawdy era he presented in the background. Although Van Dyke certainly earned the credit for his astounding, technically flawless film, his mentor and the father of American silent film (and creator of almost all the techniques used thereafter in the sound era), D.W. Griffith, appeared at MGM one day and Van Dyke asked "the master" if he cared to direct any of the scenes in the film. He did, but just which scene the great Griffith directed is still in debate. One report had it that he directed one of MacDonald's operatic scenes, another one of the mob scenes at the Paradise club. But it was also rumored that the he directed the gem of this golden film, the incredible 20-minute earthquake and fire sequence, or at least that portion which was not achieved by the special effects of Gillespie and the uncredited James Basevi.

Van Dyke did not forget others of the silent era and tried to put to work many of the silent stars who were then unemployed and suffering during that year of the Great Depression, including Flora Finch; one-time Vitagraph star Naomi Childers; Jean Acker, who had been Rudolph Valentino's first wife and a leading lady in her own right during the silent days; King Baggot and Rhea Mitchell, whom Van Dyke had directed in the 1918 silent film THE HAWK'S LAIR. Even silent film director Erich von Stroheim got into the act, writing some additional dialogue for Loos's script.

SAND PEBBLES, THE   DVD

1966 195m c Adventure/War ★★★★
Argyle/Solar (U.S.) M

Steve McQueen (Jake Holman), Richard Attenborough (Frenchy Burgoyne), Richard Crenna (Capt. Collins), Candice Bergen (Shirley Eckert), Marayat Andriane (Maily), Mako (Po-han), Larry Gates (Jameson), Charles Robinson (Ens. Bordelles), Simon Oakland (Stawski), Ford Rainey (Harris)

p, Robert Wise; d, Robert Wise; w, Robert Anderson (based on the novel by Richard McKenna); ph, Joseph MacDonald (Panavision, Deluxe Color); ed, William Reynolds; m, Jerry Goldsmith; prod d, Boris Leven; fx, Jerry Endler; cos, Renie

AAN Best Picture; AAN Best Actor: Steve McQueen; AAN Best Supporting Actor: Mako; AAN Best Color Cinematography: Joseph MacDonald; AAN Best Film Editing: William Reynolds; AAN Best Original Score: Jerry Goldsmith; AAN Best Art Direction-Set Decoration (Color): Boris Leven, Walter M. Scott, John Sturtevant, William Kiernan; AAN Best Sound: James P. Corcoran

A powerful and spectacular film, featuring Steve McQueen at his finest and director Robert Wise at his most persuasive, THE SAND PEBBLES is the panoramic story of a U.S. Navy gunboat cruising China's Yangtze River in 1926 amidst the Nationalist rebellion led by Chiang Kai-Shek. In an Oscar-nominated performance, McQueen plays Jake Holman, the lone wolf sailor who keeps the cranky engines of the USS San Pablo running while Collins (Richard Crenna), its captain, negotiates tricky political waters. Ordered to remain neutral in the Chinese conflict despite the abuse heaped on them, the crew, who call themselves the "Sand Pebbles," become restive. When Chinese authorities, anxious to create an international incident, frame Jake for the murder of the Chinese wife of a dead shipmate (Richard Attenborough), Collins refuses to hand over the engineer, though the crew is reluctant to back him up. However, when U.S. Marines land in Shanghai, the Sand Pebbles are finally given a chance to fight back, the gunboat battling its way through a blockade to evacuate American missionaries Jameson (Larry Gates), who resents the U.S. involvement in Chinese affairs, and Shirley Eckert (Candice Bergen), with whom Jake has fallen in love. The final rescue, like the rest of this long but involving film, is carefully unfolded by Wise, building in intensity towards a heroic but tragic conclusion. Released in 1966, THE SAND PEBBLES offered parallels to the controversial U.S. involvement then taking place in Vietnam. Although it has undergone several edits, THE SAND PEBBLES is available on videocassette at its original 195-minute running time.

SANDS OF IWO JIMA

1949 110m bw War   DVD
Republic   (U.S.)   ★★★★

John Wayne (Sgt. John M. Stryker), John Agar (Pfc. Peter Conway), Adele Mara (Allison Bromley), Forrest Tucker (Pfc. Al Thomas), Wally Cassell (Pfc. Benny Regazzi), James Brown (Pfc. Charlie Bass), Richard Webb (Pfc. Shipley), Arthur Franz (Cpl. Robert Dunne/Narrator), Julie Bishop (Mary), James Holden (Pfc. Soames)

p, Edmund Grainger; d, Allan Dwan; w, Harry Brown, James Edward Grant (based on a story by Brown); ph, Reggie Lanning; ed, Richard L. Van Enger; m, Victor Young; art d, James Sullivan

AAN Best Actor: John Wayne; AAN Best Motion Picture Story: Harry Brown; AAN Best Film Editing: Richard L. Van Enger; AAN Best Sound Recording: Republic Sound Department

Unlike John Wayne's many WWII films in which he singlehandedly destroys whole Japanese battalions, SANDS OF IWO JIMA presents him as a believable, vulnerable human being. Sgt. John M. Stryker (Wayne), a battle-toughened Marine, prepares a group of recruits for combat, driving them hard without worrying about making friends, although he is hurt when Pfc. Peter Conway (John Agar) hopes aloud that his newborn son won't be anything like Stryker. Later, in combat on Tarawa, Stryker's men grow furious with him when he refuses to rescue a Marine who has been separated from the squad, because to do so would give away their position. After Tarawa, they go to Hawaii for some R & R, where Stryker shows his heart of gold to a young mother forced into prostitution. The Marines' biggest test comes on Iwo Jima, and Stryker's men perform magnificently as they inch their way up Mt. Suribachi, but their leader is killed and Conway, now his disciple, must try to fill Stryker's big shoes. This is one of Wayne's finest performances, earning him an Oscar nomination. Directed with marvelous restraint by old hand Allan Dwan, SANDS OF IWO JIMA features appearances by three of the Marines who actually participated in the famous flag-raising on Mt. Suribachi—Ira Hayes, Rene Gagnon, and John Bradley.

SANSHO THE BAILIFF

(SANSHO DAIYUU)
1954 125m bw Drama
Daiei/Kyoto (Japan)   ★★★★★

Yoshiaki Hanayagi (Zushio), Kyoko Kagawa (Anju), Kinuyo Tanaka (Tamaki), Eitaro Shindo (Sansho), Akitake Kono (Taro), Masao Shimizu (Masauji Taira), Ken Mitsuda (Prime Minister Morozane Fujiwara), Chieko Naniwa (Ubatake), Kikue Mori (Priestess), Kazukimi Okuni (Norimura)

p, Masaichi Nagata; d, Kenji Mizoguchi; w, Yahiro Fuji, Yoshikata Yoda (based on the story "Sansho Daiyuu" by Ogai Mori); ph, Kazuo Miyagawa; ed, Mitsuji Miyata; m, Fumio Hayasaka, Kanahichi Odera, Tamekichi Mochizuki; art d, Kisaku Ito

A classic of Japanese and world cinema, SANSHO THE BAILIFF, set in the 11th century, tells the story of Zushio

(Yoshiaki Hanayagi) and his struggle within the limits of feudal society. The film begins as family members—mother Tamaki (Kinuyo Tanaka), sister Anju (Kyoko Kagawa), and Zushio—travel through the woods in search of their exiled patriarch. They are soon assaulted by kidnappers, and Tamaki is sold into prostitution and exiled to Sado Island, while the children are sold as slaves to a powerful and cruel bailiff, Sansho (Eitaro Shindo). Ten years pass, and Zushio has become as evil as Sansho, for whom he now works as an overseer at a labor compound. Haunted by thoughts of his dead father and his exiled mother, Zushio prepares his escape, planning to leave with Anju. She, however, in order to keep from burdening her brother or from revealing his whereabouts, drowns herself. When Zushio reaches his destination, Kyoto, he discovers that his father has become a folk hero immortalized in song. In recognition of his father's stature, Zushio is granted the post of governor, and he takes it upon himself to abolish slavery and to banish the bailiff from his land. Having performed his service to humanity, he resigns, resumes his search for his mother, and finds her, now blind, facing the sea. Perhaps Kenji Mizoguchi's greatest achievement, SANSHO THE BAILIFF is a visually mesmerizing picture that pays great and careful attention to the smallest details of nature and environment, highlighted by Mizoguchi's use of the long take and deep-focus shots. In an attempt to film life as he sees it, Mizoguchi and his cinematographer, Kazuo Miyagawa, capture images much as a painter might—using the entire palette of contrasts and colors to create a richly textured atmosphere. The film was not released in the U.S. until 1969.

SANTA CLAUSE, THE

1994 95m c Children's/Comedy/Fantasy   DVD
Outlaw Productions/Walt Disney Productions   ★★★½
(U.S.)   PG

Tim Allen (Scott Calvin), Judge Reinhold (Neal), Wendy Crewson (Laura), Eric Lloyd (Charlie), David Krumholtz (Bernard), Larry Brandenburg (Detective Nunzio), Mary Gross (Ms. Daniels), Paige Tamada (Elf—Judy), Peter Boyle (Mr. Whittle), Judith Scott (Susan)

p, Brian Reilly, Jeffrey Silver, Robert Newmyer; d, John Pasquin; w, Steve Rudnick, Leo Benvenuti; ph, Walt Lloyd; ed, Larry Bock; m, Michael Convertino; prod d, Carol Spier; art d, James McAteer; fx, John Sullivan, Buena Vista Visual Effects, Denise Davis; cos, Carol Ramsey

A tale of a suburban single father thrust into the role of St. Nick, THE SANTA CLAUSE offers a holiday-themed fantasy with appeal to both children and parents. It's an ideal debut vehicle for the talents of TV sitcom star Tim Allen ("Home Improvement").

When Santa Claus falls from a roof on the night before Christmas and sustains a fatal injury, the homeowner, divorced single father and toy company exec Scott Calvin (Tim Allen), has no choice but to don Santa's suit, hop into the sleigh, and continue Santa's rounds, accompanied by his young son Charlie (Eric Lloyd). When the job is done, Scott finds himself at the North Pole being lectured by head elf Bernard (David Krumholtz), who informs him that he has exactly eleven months to get his affairs in order and prepare for next Christmas. By putting on the red suit, Bernard explains, Scott activated the "Santa Clause," which makes him contractually bound to perform Santa's duties. To make matters worse, Scott's growing, Santa-esque eccentricities prompt his ex-wife to file for sole custody of Charlie.

With stronger emotional highs and lows, THE SANTA CLAUSE could have become a Christmas perennial on the order of IT'S A WONDERFUL LIFE or the original MIRACLE ON 34TH STREET. Unlike those earlier movies, the screenplay soft-pedals inherent domestic conflicts—e.g., the rivalry between Scott and his former wife's new husband over

Charlie's affections—that might have made the narrative more involving and resonant. Nevertheless, THE SANTA CLAUSE is a charming, if mild, fantasy, distinguished by a gentle directorial touch that strikes a deft balance between dramatic and fantastic elements. At the heart of the film are engaging performances by the two male leads—Allen, as the bewildered single father, and young Lloyd, who responds plausibly as a son whose father becomes a new man in his eyes overnight. While the film breaks no new ground, it offers the kind of simple, well-crafted, family entertainment that used to be a staple of the Disney studio. THE SANTA CLAUSE was the surprise hit of 1994, earning domestic grosses of more than $100 million.

SANTA CLAUSE 2, THE   *DVD*

2002 98m c Comedy/Fantasy ★★½
Boxing Cats Films/Outlaw Productions/Walt Disney   G
Pictures (U.S.)

Tim Allen *(Scott Calvin/Santa/Toy Santa)*, Elizabeth Mitchell *(Carol Newman)*, David Krumholtz *(Bernard)*, Eric Lloyd *(Charlie Calvin)*, Judge Reinhold *(Ned Miller)*, Wendy Crewson *(Laura Miller)*, Spencer Breslin *(Curtis)*, Liliana Mumy *(Lucy Miller)*, Danielle Woodman *(Abby)*, Art LaFleur *(Tooth Fairy)*

p, Bobby Newmyer, Brian Reilly, Jeffrey Silver; d, Michael Lembeck; w, Ken Daurio, Cinco Paul, Don Rhymer, Ed Decter (from a story by Leo Benvenuti and Steve Rudnick); ph, Adam Greenberg; ed, David Finfer; m, George S. Clinton; prod d, Tony Burrough; art d, Sandy Cochrane; fx, Brennan Doyle, John Gajdecki, Dean Lockwood, David Yrisarri; cos, Ingrid Ferrin

After a string of misses, comedian Tim Allen reprises his role as Santa Claus in this reasonably entertaining sequel to 1994's surprise family hit.

It's been nine years since former toy exec Scott Calvin (Allen) stepped into Santa's boots, and things have been going pretty well at the North Pole; in fact, the elves think Scott is the best Santa ever. Problems arise when Scott's son, Charlie (Eric Lloyd), now a rebellious teenager who lives with his mom (Wendy Crewson) and her new husband (Judge Reinhold), turns up in the naughty column of this year's "Naughty or Nice" list. Scott, meanwhile, is mysteriously de-Santafying, losing his bowl-full-of-jelly belly and white beard. Faithful assistant elf Bernard (David Krumholtz) discovers that, according to the "Mrs. Clause" in the Santa contract, if Scott doesn't get married before Christmas Eve, he'll stop being Santa forever. So Scott sets off for his former hometown, leaving a cloned Santa (Allen again) in his place. Scott meets and falls in love with pretty high-school principal Carol Newman (Elizabeth Mitchell), reconciles with his troubled son, and saves the North Pole from a hostile takeover by the increasingly authoritarian faux Santa.

Veteran sitcom director Michael Lembeck's film is geared towards undemanding youngsters and parents whose diminished expectations are such that their only hope is that the film doesn't become too dull or, worse, adorable. That their prayers are answered is mostly thanks to Allen, who's thoroughly likeable in an everyguy sort of way. The wonderfully imaginative, neo-Victorian art direction in the North Pole sequences is also an asset, and there's a very funny turn by Art LaFleur as the identity crisis-ridden Tooth Fairy.

SANTA FE TRAIL   *DVD*

1940 110m bw Historical/Adventure ★★★½
First National (U.S.)

Errol Flynn *(Jeb Stuart)*, Olivia de Havilland *(Kit Carson Holliday)*, Raymond Massey *(John Brown)*, Ronald Reagan *(George Armstrong Custer)*, Alan Hale *(Barefoot Brody)*, Guinn "Big Boy" Williams *(Tex Bell)*, Van Heflin *(Rader)*, Henry O'Neill *(Cyrus Holliday)*, William Lundigan *(Bob Holliday)*, John Litel *(Harlan)*,

p, Robert Fellows; d, Michael Curtiz; w, Robert Buckner; ph, Sol Polito; ed, George Amy; m, Max Steiner; art d, John Hughes; fx, Byron Haskin, H.F. Koenekamp; cos, Milo Anderson

Despite its misleading title, this roaring, action-packed film, directed with great vigor by Curtiz, is not a western and has little to do with the Santa Fe Trail. And though it purports to deal with a serious segment of American history, even that is inaccurate.

Flynn is his ever-dashing self as he appears at West Point, playing the southern-born J.E.B. Stuart, who later became the South's greatest cavalryman during the Civil War. He arrives, along with mule and dog, wearing an outlandish uniform of his own design which so confuses the sentinels at the post that they mistakenly call out an honor guard to salute what appears to be a high-ranking officer of a foreign power. This auspicious arrival is soon ended when it is learned that Flynn is nothing more than a new cadet reporting to the Point for training. Other than his academic studies, Flynn's real enemy at the Point is Heflin, a wild-eyed radical abolitionist who is out to change the class and caste system of America. He is a secret follower of the fanatic John Brown, and his political activities finally get Heflin cashiered from the Point. Flynn and his friends (Reagan, playing George Armstrong Custer; David Bruce, essaying Phil Sheridan; Wilcox, playing Longstreet; William Marshall, enacting the role of George Pickett; and George Haywood, playing John Hood) all graduate from the Point in 1854 and are assigned to a western post in Kansas where they must combat the illegal activities of the dreaded Brown, played by Massey. A travesty of history, SANTA FE TRAIL is nonetheless a rousing adventure yarn, offering a great romp for Flynn and providing a bevy of colorful characterizations. De Havilland is at her feisty, attractive best, while Reagan has the "best friend" role, losing her to the handsome Flynn. Massey, who overacts frantically as Brown, would play him again in SEVEN ANGRY MEN in 1955. The film's gratuitous patriotism is countered by the tentative sympathies Reagan and a few others utter on behalf of Massey, stating that he may be misdirected but that his ambition to free the slaves is a worthy one.

SANTA SANGRE

1989 124m c Horror/Thriller ★★★
Intersound (Italy/Spain) R

Axel Jodorowsky *(Fenix, Age 20)*, Blanca Guerra *(Concha)*, Guy Stockwell *(Orgo)*, Adan Jodorowsky *(Fenix, Age Eight)*, Thelma Tixou *(Tattooed Woman)*, Sabrina Dennison *(Alma)*, Faviola Elenka Tapia *(Young Alma)*

p, Claudio Argento; d, Alexandro Jodorowsky; w, Alexandro Jodorowsky, Roberto Leoni, Claudio Argento (based on a story by Alexandro Jodorowsky); ph, Daniele Nannunzi; ed, Mauro Bonanni; m, Simon Boswell; prod d, Alexandro Luna; cos, Tolita Figueroa

Alexandro Jodorowsky's first film after a 10-year hiatus, and only his third since his notorious 1971 surrealist western EL TOPO, SANTA SANGRE is at least a decade out of step. Despite the film's surrealist trappings, parody is at the heart of this effort.

After a brief opening scene involving a Christ-like nude perched on a tree limb in what appears to be the cell of a sanitarium, the film promptly flashes back to tell the story behind the young man's present state. As a youngster, Fenix (played as a child by Jodorowsky's son Adan, then as an adult by his elder son, Axel) is billed as the world's youngest magician. He performs his act for the Circus del Gringo, run by his womanizing father, Orgo (Guy Stockwell), and his mother, Concha (Blanca Guerra), a crazed religious fanatic. Concha, enraged by her husband's latest infidelity, attacks Orgo's genitals with acid. Orgo, a knife thrower, retaliates by slicing off Concha's arms before slitting his own throat. Back in the present, Fenix is coaxed into escaping from the sanitarium by the armless Concha. He becomes her vengeful "hands," both in a bizarre nightclub act and in an orgy of murder.

SANTA SANGRE could hardly be described as boring: gorgeously photographed and crammed with the startling imagery for which Jodorowsky is justly famed, it's never less than beautiful. Yet the film can't help but remain stubbornly earthbound because of its derivative, slasher-movie scenario, obviously the influence of producer Claudio Argento, the younger brother of splashy Italian horror director Dario Argento. Whether it would have been a better film had it been more purely Jodorowsky's work is debatable. Still, if Jodorowsky is not yet worthy of inclusion in the pantheon with Bunuel, he remains, nonetheless, in a class by himself. Although obviously not for every taste, SANTA SANGRE is a film that no adventurous moviegoer can afford to miss.

SATURDAY NIGHT AND SUNDAY MORNING DVD
1960 90m bw Drama ★★★★
Woodfall (U.K.)

Albert Finney (*Arthur Seaton*), Shirley Ann Field (*Doreen Gretton*), Rachel Roberts (*Brenda*), Hylda Baker (*Aunt Ada*), Norman Rossington (*Bert*), Bryan Pringle (*Jack*), Robert Cawdron (*Robboe*), Edna Morris (*Mrs. Bull*), Elsie Wagstaffe (*Mrs. Seaton*), Frank Pettitt (*Mr. Seaton*)

p, Tony Richardson; d, Karel Reisz; w, Alan Sillitoe (based on his novel); ph, Freddie Francis; ed, Seth Holt; m, John Dankworth; art d, Ted Marshall

In a scant 89 minutes, Sillitoe and Reisz create a world and immerse the viewer in it. This was 23-year-old Finney's first major film (he'd done a bit in THE ENTERTAINER earlier that year) and the resulting performance remains a fresh revelation. It's another of the "angry young men" pictures (e.g., ROOM AT THE TOP) and this is one that lingers. Sillitoe, who also wrote THE LONELINESS OF THE LONG DISTANCE RUNNER, adapted his own novel here with major results.

Finney is a lathe operator in a small town near Nottingham. He is a lively young man devoted to pleasure and thumbing his nose at authority. As he says, "All I want is a good time. The rest is propaganda." To that end, he spends his weekends boozing and brawling and bedding down any woman he can. He makes a good wage; he has plenty of discretionary money to spend. He hates his job but is willing to put in his week at the lathe in return for the fun he can have with his pay envelope. He's having an affair with Roberts, who is married to his fellow worker, Pringle. Finney enjoys the sexual liaisons with Roberts, but that's as far as he will go with her; she wants more. At the same time, Finney meets Field, a beautiful, old-fashioned young woman with strict morals. Finney finds himself falling in love with Field, but she won't sleep with him unless there is a commitment, something Finney cannot bear to make. Then Roberts announces that she's pregnant.

The story seems slim at best, but Reisz's sharp direction and the superb editing combine with Sillitoe's grasp of the argot to make this a compelling, if somewhat difficult to understand, movie. The accents in that area of England are almost impossible for U.S. ears (and even many London auricles) to fathom, so it had to be looped in places where the words blurred. Sillitoe, who used to work in a Midlands factory, captures the nuances perfectly in his script, and Reisz, who was in his early thirties at the time, does a smashing job in his first feature after having worked in the documentary field. Despite Finney's youth, he was already a veteran Shakespearean actor and had once taken over for Olivier when Sir Larry was felled by injury on the eve of a performance of

Coriolanus at Stratford. It was a sensational outing for Finney, and great things were in store. Roberts was excellent and her performance (not unlike that of Simone Signoret in ROOM AT THE TOP), like Finney's, was also honored with a BFA award. One of the best of the "kitchen sink" pictures of the era, SATURDAY NIGHT AND SUNDAY MORNING has more than its share of humor to temper the highly charged drama, and it stands out in every department—the sex is steamy, the language is raw, the emotions are strong. Still a must-watch.

SATURDAY NIGHT FEVER DVD
1977 119m c Drama ★★★★
Paramount (U.S.) R

John Travolta (*Tony Manero*), Karen Lynn Gorney (*Stephanie*), Barry Miller (*Bobby C.*), Joseph Call (*Joey*), Paul Pape (*Double J*), Donna Pescow (*Annette*), Bruce Ornstein (*Gus*), Julie Bovasso (*Flo*), Martin Shakar (*Frank*), Sam Coppola (*Fusco*)

p, Robert Stigwood; d, John Badham; w, Norman Wexler (based on the *New York* magazine article "Tribal Rites of the New Saturday Night" by Nik Cohn); ph, Ralf D. Bode (Panavision, Movielab Color); ed, David Rawlins; m, Barry Gibb, Robin Gibb, Maurice Gibb, David Shire; prod d, Charles Bailey; chor, Lester Wilson (Lorraine Fields); cos, Patrizia Von Brandenstein, Jennifer Nichols

AAN Best Actor: John Travolta

Reminiscent of both MARTY and SATURDAY NIGHT AND SUNDAY MORNING, this hugely popular picture and its even more popular soundtrack album (more than 27 million copies of which have been sold) raked in nearly $200 million. Moreover, John Travolta's heartfelt portrayal of Tony Manero, a directionless young clerk in a Brooklyn paint store, catapulted him to stardom. Refusing to compete with his seminarian brother (Martin Shakar) for his father's approval, Tony lives for the weekend, strutting his stuff on the disco dance floor with his girlfriend, Annette (Donna Pescow), whom he shuns after meeting Stephanie (Karen Lynn Gorney), an upwardly mobile, smart-stepping miss who becomes his partner for a big dance contest. Tony's tempestuous relationship with Stephanie, his desertion of Annette, and the pleasures and problems of his neighborhood buddies make up the rest of the film, which reaches its tragic climax in a scene at the Verrazano Bridge, where Bobby C. (Barry Miller), overcome with worries about the baby he has fathered out of wedlock, precariously scales the bridge.

The story here is really secondary to character and milieu, as director John Badham and his actors create a convincing portrait of frustrated 1970s working-class youth and the escape offered by the swirling lights and pulsing rhythms of the disco. Although technically not a musical—no one in the cast sings—this highly energized film has more songs than many musicals proper, most courtesy of the Bee Gees, who reached their creative and popular apex here. It also features some great dancing by Travolta, who made a triumphant critical comeback in 1994's PULP FICTION, during the same period that a '70s nostalgia boom turned SNF into a college cult favorite and the Bee Gees' "Tragedy" briefly re-appeared on the *Billboard* charts. The sequel, STAYING ALIVE, is nowhere near as involving.

SAVAGE NIGHTS
(LES NUITS FAUVES)
1993 126m c Erotic/Drama/Romance ★★★
Banfilm Ter/La Sept/Erre Produzioni/SNC (France/Italy)

Cyril Collard (*Jean*), Romane Bohringer (*Laura*), Carlos Lopez (*Samy*), Corine Blue (*Laura's Mother*), Claude Winter (*Jean's Mother*), Rene-Marc Bini (*Marc*), Maria Schneider (*Noria*),

Clementine Celarie *(Marianne)*, Laura Favali *(Karin)*, Denis D'Archangelo *(Cabaret Singer)*

p, Nella Banfi; d, Cyril Collard; w, Cyril Collard (based on his novel *Les Nuits' Fauves*); ph, Manuel Teran; ed, Lise Beaulieu; prod d, Jacky Macchi, Katja Kosenina; cos, Regine Arniaud

Coming on the heels of the sentimental PHILADELPHIA, it was predictable that SAVAGE NIGHTS would be heralded as a tough-minded AIDS movie—one that dares to address the complicity of some victims in the transmission of the disease. The film has a fascinating, trenchant first hour, collapses of its own weight before the end, and lingers like a bad dream—to its credit.

Jean (director Cyril Collard) is an HIV-positive, bisexual filmmaker who drowns his anxiety in passion. He auditions 17-year-old boutique clerk Laura (Romane Bohringer), who fails the screen test but becomes Jean's lover. Almost concurrently, Jean auditions and seduces Samy (Carlos Lopez), who hustles tricks at Mr. Andre's, a louche, anything-goes bordello. Despite developing KS lesions, Jean pursues Laura; at first she doesn't quibble over his admission of bisexuality. After he and Samy have a failed menage with a Swiss streetwalker, he confesses his health status to Laura, but she refuses to allow a condom to interfere with their passion.

This ambitious, passionate movie means to shock its audience. Collard, who was himself struggling with AIDS as he shot the film, may have regarded it as a final statement, and accordingly tried to make it as bold as possible—perhaps to a fault. Often his actors (including himself) project grand Parisian posturing rather than suffering, and Collard's screenplay lets Bohringer's character rant on to the point of irritation about what she will soon be missing (namely Collard—it's as though a Greek chorus were lamenting his charms). Nor does the film's golden, overly pretty cinematography do much to strengthen its story line.

NIGHTS swept France's Cesar Awards: Best Debut Film, Best Editing, Best Female Newcomer (Romane Bohringer), and Best Picture of the Year. Collard's death of AIDS complications at age 35, three days before the awards, added a mythic, poignant touch to NIGHTS' day in the sun.

SAVE THE TIGER
1973   100m   c   Drama   ★★★
Filmways/Jalem/Cirandinha (U.S.)   R

Jack Lemmon *(Harry Stoner)*, Jack Gilford *(Phil Greene)*, Laurie Heineman *(Myra the Hitchhiker)*, Norman Burton *(Fred Mirrell)*, Patricia Smith *(Janet Stoner)*, Thayer David *(Charlie Robbins)*, William Hansen *(Meyer)*, Harvey Jason *(Rico)*, Liv von Linden *(Ula)*, Lara Parker *(Margo the Prostitute)*

p, Steve Shagan; d, John G. Avildsen; w, Steve Shagan; ph, James Crabe (Movielab Color); ed, David Bretherton; m, Marvin Hamlisch; art d, Jack Collis

AA Best Actor: Jack Lemmon; *AAN Best Supporting Actor:* Jack Gilford; *AAN Best Original Story and Screenplay:* Steve Shagan

Director John Avildsen has a knack for using small budgets to make "big" movies. First it was JOE, then this film, then his triumph with ROCKY.

The action of SAVE THE TIGER takes place in about a day and a half in the life of a man who is trapped by his own indulgences. Business is rotten, and Lemmon, the managing partner of Capri Casuals, a Los Angeles garment manufacturing company, finds himself daydreaming about his youth. After a nightmare-filled night, he rises in his sumptuous Beverly Hills home; says goodbye to his wife, Smith, who is on her way to a relative's funeral; and gets into his Lincoln for the long drive downtown. On the street, he picks up Heineman, a liberated young woman who proposes that they go to bed together. Lemmon balks. At the office, he and partner Gilford try to figure a way out of their dire financial straits (they owe a bundle and there isn't a bank in town willing to give them a loan). Lemmon suggests torching the company's Long Beach warehouse to collect insurance money, but Gilford won't hear of it. When Burton, a conservative out-of-town client who lets his hair down in L.A., arrives to see the new line from Capri, Lemmon arranges for him to be entertained by call girl Parker. Later, in a porno movie house, Lemmon meets with David, who is willing to burn down the warehouse for a price. Outside the theater, Bif Elliott is raising funds to protect wildlife, particularly lions and tigers—hence the film's title. Things continue in this vein, with the increasingly pressured Lemmon eventually breaking down in front of the audience at a fashion show, convinced that the assembled clients are his dead comrades-in-arms from WWII.

SAVE THE TIGER is an uneven but engaging look at a man whose lust for success has bankrupted not only his company but his conscience. Yet despite his illegal and immoral practices, we are drawn to Lemmon's Harry Stoner.

SAVING PRIVATE RYAN   DVD
1998   170m   c   War/Drama   ★★★★
DreamWorks SKG/Mutual Film/Paramount   R
(U.S.)

Tom Hanks *(Captain Miller)*, Tom Sizemore *(Sergeant Horvath)*, Edward Burns *(Private Reiben)*, Barry Pepper *(Private Jackson)*, Adam Goldberg *(Private Mellish)*, Vin Diesel *(Private Caparzo)*, Giovanni Ribisi *(T/4 Medic Wade)*, Jeremy Davies *(Corporal Upham)*, Matt Damon *(Private Ryan)*, Ted Danson *(Captain Hamill)*

p, Steven Spielberg, Ian Bryce, Mark Gordon, Gary Levinsohn; d, Steven Spielberg; w, Robert Rodat; ph, Janusz Kaminski; ed, Michael Kahn; m, John Williams; prod d, Tom Sanders; art d, Daniel T. Dorrance, Ricky Eyres, Tom Brown, Chris Seagers, Alan Tomkins; fx, Neil Corbould, Carol McAulay; cos, Joanna Johnston

AA Best Director: Steven Spielberg; *AA Best Cinematography:* Janusz Kaminski; *AA Best Film Editing:* Michael Kahn; *AA Best Sound:* Gary Rydstrom, Gary Summers, Andy Nelson, Ronald Judkins; *AA Best Sound Effects Editing:* Gary Rydstrom, Richard Hymns; *AAN Best Picture:* AAN Best Actor: Tom Hanks; *AAN Best Original Screenplay:* Robert Rodat; *AAN Best Art Direction:* Tom Sanders, Lisa Dean Kavanaugh; *AAN Best Makeup:* Lois Burwell, Conor O'Sullivan, Daniel C. Striepeke; *AAN Best Original Dramatic Score:* John Williams

Does anyone still believe WWII was the good war, and that cynicism, spin control, and U.S. brutality were born in Vietnam? If so, Steven Spielberg's visceral re-creation of the Second World War experience will come as a shock: the film's battle scenes are anarchic, bloody, frenzied, and studded with atrocious acts. Screenwriter Robert Rodat's script (based loosely on an actual incident and heavily indebted to historian Stephen Ambrose), however, sticks to familiar ground.

Battle-scarred Captain Miller (Tom Hanks) is sent on a special mission to retrieve one Private Ryan (Matt Damon), a grunt who merits extra-heroic efforts because he's the sole survivor of four enlisted brothers, and his safe return is conceived as a home-front morale booster. Miller's hand-picked squadron is a checklist of war-movie types—hard-nosed sergeant (Tom Sizemore); decent private (Vin Diesel); Brooklyn wiseass (Edward Burns), introspective medic (Giovanni Ribisi); tough Jew (Adam Goldberg); pious Southern sharpshooter (Barry Pepper); and bookish corporal (Jeremy Davies) with no frontline experience—and their destinies follow a well-worn path. The exception is the GI who clings to the hope that war exposes the hidden strength in men, and instead has the worst wrenched out of him in a scene that elicits scattered applause but seems designed to evoke a mixture of pity and contempt.

The movie's greatest strength lies in phenomenal performances that reach from the leads right down to the smallest supporting roles: Hanks' affability is worked under Miller's hardened skin, and Damon gives Ryan a boyish determination as convincing as it is naive. Spielberg does some of his best work (the pointless present-day framing sequence notwithstanding), but follows in distinguished footsteps: among the films that shouldn't be lost in the rush to praise are Samuel Fuller's harrowing BIG RED ONE, whose credo—"the only glory in war is surviving"—could be this movie's own.

SAW
2004 100m c Horror **DVD**
Evolution Entertainment/Burg/Koules/Hoffman ★★★
Productions (U.S.) R

Leigh Whannell (Adam), Cary Elwes (Dr. Lawrence Gordon), Danny Glover (Detective Tapp), Ken Leung (Detective Steven Sing), Dina Meyer (Kerry), Mike Butters (Paul), Paul Gutrecht (Mark), Michael Emerson (Zep Hindle), Benito Martinez (Brett), Shawnee Smith (Amanda)

p, Mark Burg, Gregg Hoffman, Oren Koules; d, James Wan; w, Leigh Whannell (from a story by James Wan and Leigh Whannell); ph, David A. Armstrong; ed, Kevin Greutert; m, Charlie Clouser; prod d, Julie Berghoff; art d, Nanet Harty; fx, Tom Bellissimo; cos, Jennifer Soulages

James Wan's debut feature is a nasty bit of work, which isn't a criticism; that's exactly what he and co-writer Leigh Whannell had in mind.

Two strangers, middle-aged Dr. Lawrence Gordon (Cary Elwes) and seething slacker Adam (Whannell), awake at opposite ends of a large, dirty, industrial bathroom. Neither remembers how he got there. Each is chained by his ankle to a pipe. A man's corpse lies on the floor leaking blood, just out of reach, clutching a microcassette recorder and a gun. Lawrence and Adam soon discover that each of them has a personal message on the tape from a serial killer nicknamed "Jigsaw," who promises that unless one kills the other, both will die. Various objects and cryptic messages are concealed around the room, starting with a pair of hacksaws that won't cut metal but could make short work of flesh and bone.

Living up to a premise this warped is no mean feat, and Wan and Whannell don't entirely succeed. The film's fractured time structure is intriguing but verges on too tricky, and opening up the story beyond the bathroom dissipates a certain measure of sheer, claustrophobic suspense and admits what may be the worst performance of Danny Glover's career. As damaged, Jigsaw-obsessed Detective Tapp, he's as wooden as the Jeff Fahey caliber B-movie stalwarts you normally find in such roles. But opening the story out also clears the way for a series of elaborate set pieces illustrating the brilliantly cruel trials Jigsaw devises to test the mettle of his victims, all involving grotesque moral choices. Whannell is stiff and veteran actor Elwes is worse, but Wan's confident, stylish direction suggests that he's a genre filmmaker to watch.

SAY ANYTHING
1989 100m c Comedy/Drama **DVD**
Gracie/Cameron Crowe (U.S.) ★★★★
PG-13

John Cusack (Lloyd Dobler), Ione Skye (Diane Court), John Mahoney (James Court), Lili Taylor (Corey Flood), Amy Brooks (D.C.), Pamela Segall (Rebecca), Jason Gould (Mike Cameron), Loren Dean (Joe), Joan Cusack (Constance), Glenn Walker Harris Jr. (Jason)

p, Polly Platt; d, Cameron Crowe; w, Cameron Crowe; ph, Laszlo Kovacs (Deluxe Color); ed, Richard Marks; m, Richard Gibbs, Anne Dudley, Nancy Wilson; prod d, Mark Mansbridge; cos, Jane Ruhm

A far cry from the standard Hollywood teen romance, SAY ANYTHING is the extraordinary directorial debut of Cameron Crowe (who adapted his own novel for the hilariously inventive FAST TIMES AT RIDGEMONT HIGH). Set in Seattle, Crowe's wonderfully nuanced screenplay develops a complex triangular relationship involving a gifted and ambitious high-school graduate, Diane Court (Ione Skye), her doting father, James (John Mahoney), and Lloyd Dobler (John Cusack), the likable, underachieving classmate who falls for her. The relationship of father and daughter is tested when Diane is wooed by Lloyd, an Army brat who lives with his unmarried sister (real-life sibling Joan Cusack) and her young son (Daniel Will-Harris). His best friends, Corey and D.C. (Lili Taylor and Amy Brooks) know just how sensitive, creative, and loving Lloyd is. Diane, too, is won over by Lloyd's generosity of spirit, but her father wants nothing to stand in the way of her success, and pressures her to break up with Lloyd. Seldom have such complexity, emotional depth, honesty, and realism been invested in what is ostensibly a teen love story. Crowe's script is full of careful observations, and his camera unobtrusively serves the spot-on production design, the witty but believable dialog, and especially the outstanding performances by Skye (RIVER'S EDGE; A NIGHT IN THE LIFE OF JIMMY REARDON), Mahoney (MOONSTRUCK; SUSPECT; BETRAYAL), and Cusack, whose Lloyd Dobler is an exceedingly winning portrayal.

SAYONARA
1957 147m c War/Drama **DVD**
Goetz/Pennebaker (U.S.) ★★★★

Marlon Brando (Maj. Lloyd Gruver), Ricardo Montalban (Nakamura), Red Buttons (Joe Kelly), Patricia Owens (Eileen Webster), Martha Scott (Mrs. Webster), James Garner (Capt. Mike Bailey), Miiko Taka (Hana-ogi), Miyoshi Umeki (Katsumi), Kent Smith (Gen. Webster), Douglas Watson (Col. Craford)

p, William Goetz; d, Joshua Logan; w, Paul Osborn (based on the novel by James A. Michener); ph, Ellsworth Fredricks (Technirama, Technicolor); ed, Arthur Schmidt, Philip W. Anderson; m, Franz Waxman; art d, Ted Haworth; chor, LeRoy Prinz; cos, Norma Koch

AAN Best Picture; AAN Best Actor: Marlon Brando; AA Best Supporting Actor: Red Buttons; AA Best Supporting Actress: Miyoshi Umeki; AAN Best Director: Joshua Logan; AAN Best Adapted Screenplay: Paul Osborn; AAN Best Cinematography: Ellsworth Fredricks; AAN Best Film Editing: Arthur P. Schmidt, Philip W. Anderson; AA Best Art Direction-Set Decoration: Ted Haworth, Robert Priestley; AA Best Sound: George Groves

This beautifully photographed and often moving story of racial prejudice features Marlon Brando as Lloyd Gruver, an Army major reassigned to a Japanese air base in the midst of the Korean conflict. In Japan, Gruver sees the U.S. military's racism against the Japanese, which goes so far as to forbid servicemen from marrying Japanese women. Although at first indifferent to the situation, Gruver is forced to take a stand when his buddy Joe Kelly (Red Buttons) falls in love with a local woman, Katsumi (Miyoshi Umeki), and becomes determined to marry her, going over the heads of the military high command and petitioning Congress for permission. Sticking by his comrade, Gruver risks the wrath of his superiors when he agrees to be Kelly's best man at the ceremony. What's more, Gruver himself falls in love with a beautiful Japanese dancer, Hana-ogi (Miiko Taka), and finds himself in the same predicament as Kelly. SAYONARA is a sensitive work, sparing neither Americans nor Japanese in condemning prejudice. This updating of the "Madame Butterfly" theme is a powerful, well-told story, with a statement on racism that remains timeless. It was certainly topical: when filming began, in 1956, more than 10,000 American servicemen had defied extant regulations and married Japanese women (as the novel's author, James A. Michener, had done earlier). The film received 10 Academy Award nominations, including Best Picture (it lost to THE BRIDGE ON THE RIVER KWAI), Best Director, Best Actor (Brando lost to Alec Guinness for RIVER KWAI), Best Cinematography, Best Screenplay, and Best Editing. Oscars went to the film for Sound, Art Direction, and Set Decoration, as well as to Buttons and Umeki for their supporting performances.

SCANDAL

1989 114m c   Biography/Political   ★★★
Palace/British Screen   (U.K.)   R

John Hurt *(Stephen Ward)*, Joanne Whalley-Kilmer *(Christine Keeler)*, Bridget Fonda *(Mandy Rice-Davies)*, Ian McKellen *(John Profumo)*, Leslie Phillips *(Lord Astor)*, Britt Ekland *(Mariella Novotny)*, Roland Gift *(Johnnie Edgecombe)*, Jeroen Krabbe *(Eugene Ivanov)*, Daniel Massey *(Mervyn Griffith-Jones)*, Jean Alexander *(Mrs. Keeler)*

p, Stephen Woolley; d, Michael Caton-Jones; w, Michael Thomas; ph, Mike Molloy (Technicolor); ed, Angus Newton; m, Carl Davis; prod d, Simon Holland; art d, Chris Townsend; cos, Jane Robinson

Michael Caton-Jones's SCANDAL peeks under the bedsheets of Britain's ruling class with a rehashing of the Profumo Affair, the early '60s sex scandal that eventually toppled the Conservative Party from power. Minister of War John Profumo (Ian McKellan) is romantically linked to accused prostitute Christine Keeler (Joanne Whalley-Kilmer), who, as it happened, was also involved with Soviet attache Eugene Ivanov (Jeroen Krabbe), an alleged spy. Keeler met both men through Dr. Stephen Ward (John Hurt), a high-society osteopath. Meanwhile, teenage beauty Mandy Rice-Davies (Bridget Fonda), another Ward protegee, was bedhopping with the high and mighty of two continents, and the whole crew were reported to be frequent participants at extravagant orgies. Instead of sleaze, director Caton-Jones and screenwriter Michael Thomas deliver a vindication of the affair's chief scapegoats—Ward and Keeler—in the form of a two-hour nostalgia trip (complete with imitation Beatles), with some complex and powerful performances. The screen is filled with memorabilia of 1960s London: miniskirts, smoke-filled dens of West Indians, rows of tenements, opportunistic newsmen from tabloids. Overall, however, the direction is uninspired. One problem with SCANDAL is that, compared to scandals of the '80s, the Profumo affair is rather tame. If it's a poke at England's Conservatives you're looking for, the honest fiction of Mike Leigh's HIGH HOPES did more to make them bleed than the pointless fact of SCANDAL.

SCANNERS

1981 102m c   Horror   ★★★
Filmplan   (Canada)   R

Stephen Lack *(Cameron Vale)*, Jennifer O'Neill *(Kim)*, Patrick McGoohan *(Dr. Paul Ruth)*, Lawrence Dane *(Keller)*, Charles Shamata *(Gaudi)*, Adam Ludwig *(Crostic)*, Michael Ironside *(Darryl Revok)*, Victor Desy *(Dr. Gatineau)*, Mavor Moore *(Trevellyan)*, Robert Silverman *(Pierce)*

p, Claude Heroux; d, David Cronenberg; w, David Cronenberg; ph, Mark Irwin (CFI Color); ed, Ronald Sanders; m, Howard Shore; art d, Carol Spier; fx, Dick Smith, Gary Zeller, Henry Pierrig, Chris Walas

SCANNERS is a nifty science fiction comic-book of a movie that makes excellent use of its low budget and hastily-written script. The film boasts a few extraordinary set pieces and some inspiredly gory special effects, as well as some resonant visual metaphors for the telepathic condition.

Ephemerol, an experimental tranquilizer, was tested on pregnant women during the 1940s and produced some severe long range side effects. Before the drug was taken off the market, 236 babies were born to the women tested. They were found to possess the ability to read minds. Dubbed "scanners," these powerful telepaths spread out through North America for decades until many were sought and rounded up by two mysterious and competing corporations: Consec, headed by Dr. Paul Ruth (McGoohan), and Biocarbon Amalgamated, headed by the deadly Darryl Revok (Ironside), a scanner assassin. Cameron Vale (Lack) is a homeless drifter with the gift. He is abducted from the street and ends up in the healing hands of Dr. Ruth, who gives him medication that allows him to control his power. Vale is informed that Revok plans to take over the world with an army of evil scanners. He must link up with his farflung "brethren" so they can determine their own futures.

Notorious for the scene in which Ironside uses his awesome scanning power to literally explode the head of another man, SCANNERS is relatively conventional by Cronenberg standards—though wildly imaginative by normal ones. Despite the loose ends and inconsistencies, SCANNERS is a memorable and absorbing genre entertainment that has spawned several direct-to-video sequels. Cronenberg displays more confidence as a visual stylist here than in his previous films, but his storytelling abilities are not much in evidence. Matters aren't helped by Lack's weak lead performance, though his large, emotive eyes add poignance to his predicament. Fortunately McGoohan (of television's "Secret Agent" and "The Prisoner") is on hand to provide an eccentrically entertaining performance as the fatherly Dr. Ruth. Ironside is fantastic as the lethal Revok, helping make this a popular cult favorite.

SCARECROW

1973 112m c   Drama   ★★★
Warner Bros.   (U.S.)   R

Gene Hackman *(Max)*, Al Pacino *(Lion)*, Dorothy Tristan *(Coley)*, Ann Wedgeworth *(Frenchy)*, Richard Lynch *(Riley)*, Eileen Brennan *(Darlene)*, Penny Allen *(Annie)*, Richard Hackman *(Mickey)*, Al Cingolani *(Skipper)*, Rutanya Alda *(Woman in Camper)*

p, Robert M. Sherman; d, Jerry Schatzberg; w, Garry Michael White; ph, Vilmos Zsigmond (Panavision, Technicolor); ed, Evan Lottman; m, Fred Myrow; prod d, Albert Brenner; cos, Jo Ynocencio

This is a good look at a pair of losers that is a bit too episodic. Hackman has recently been released from San Quentin where he did some hard time for assault. He's on his way to Pittsburgh where he hopes to open a car wash on the modest savings he's accumulated. Pacino is a seaman who has just completed a voyage. The two men hit it off and decide to go east together. On the trip, they have adventures in bars, diners, and various residences belonging to former loves and old pals. As they near their destinations, Pacino becomes nervous about seeing his wife, Allen, whom he left while she was pregnant. Hackman does his best to encourage him, but Pacino is beginning to crumble. He's never seen his child, and, when he phones ahead to Detroit and talks to Allen (in a very sensitive portrayal), she lies, telling him that the child he'd thought she had was never born. She says she miscarried early and all of his trepidation about meeting his child was for naught. Pacino goes into a violent form of nervous breakdown. The final scenes show Hackman using his savings to pay for Pacino's hospital care, his hopes of opening his own business tossed aside in favor of helping his only friend. Hackman gives another splendid, compelling performance. Pacino's characterization is rather weak, however. His roles in DOG DAY AFTERNOON and THE GODFATHER are better indications of his talents. There are points where writer White has created unrealistic lines for Pacino instead of allowing the character to emerge subtly and become part of the story. Brennan does well as a barroom floozie, and Tristan scores as one of Hackman's ex-girlfriends. The picture looks wonderful and captures the grittiness of the road. Schatzberg had been a photographer and his collaboration with Zsigmond is fruitful in that respect for much of the film, though they are both occasionally guilty of gratuitous Hollywood gloss. The ending is not consistent with Hackman's behavior all the way through. Given the box office potency of the two stars, the receipts were disappointing, although the movie eventually did make a small profit. No four-letter word seems to have been omitted.

SCARFACE

1932 99m bw Biography/Crime ★★★★★
Caddo (U.S.)

Paul Muni *(Tony Camonte)*, Ann Dvorak *(Cesca Camonte)*, Karen Morley *(Poppy)*, Osgood Perkins *(Johnny Lovo)*, Boris Karloff *(Gaffney)*, George Raft *(Guino Rinaldo)*, Vince Barnett *(Angelo)*, C. Henry Gordon *(Inspector Guarino)*, Inez Palange *(Tony's Mother)*, Edwin Maxwell *(Commissioner)*

p, Howard Hughes; d, Howard Hawks; w, Ben Hecht, Seton I. Miller, John Lee Mahin, W.R. Burnett, Fred Pasley (based on the novel by Armitage Trail); ph, Lee Garmes (additional scenes for censor), L.W. O'Connell; ed, Edward Curtiss; m, Adolph Tandler, Gus Arnheim; prod d, Harry Olivier

One of Hawks's undisputed masterpieces, and a landmark in the screen depiction of gangsters. Though the gangster genre had recently exploded with LITTLE CAESAR and PUBLIC ENEMY, it was SCARFACE (a.k.a. "Scarface, the Shame of a Nation") that depicted the professional hood as a murderous beast. In earlier films of the genre, a great deal of attention was paid to developing the background of the criminal and placing the blame for his antisocial activities on his environment. But with SCARFACE, all of that was dispensed with to give audiences for the first time an adult, fully developed monster who thrived on murder and power.

The first scene of SCARFACE shows Tony Camonte (Muni) only in shadow, whistling a few bars of an Italian aria before shooting a victim and then walking calmly away. It's obvious that the career shown on screen is that of the notorious Al Capone. Tony is honestly portrayed as the typical gangster of the era; he is brutal, arrogant, and stupid (Truffaut said Hawks directed Muni to make him look and move like an ape; it's likely), a homicidal maniac who revels in gaudy clothes, fast cars, and machine guns, because their rapid fire allows him to kill more people at a single outing. (The number of deaths recorded in this ultra-violent film is 28, with many more reported as occurring off-camera.) But Tony is also insanely jealous of his slinky sister (Ann Dvorak), to the point where his feelings toward her are obliquely incestuous. Tony works for Johnny Lovo (Osgood Perkins), a more sophisticated and clever hoodlum who, in turn, is the chief lieutenant of Big Louis (Harry Vejar), the city's nominal crime boss. (Perkins's role is based on Johnny Torrio, the creator of organized crime in America, and Vejar is a duplicate of Chicago's old-time crime czar, Big Jim Colosimo.) Tony is arrested for the murder shown in the opening scene, but the mob lawyer soon has him freed on a special writ. Tony encourages Johnny to kill Louis since he won't take advantage of the new Prohibition law and go into bootlegging liquor. But when Johnny tells Tony to leave the North Side boss (Boris Karloff) alone, and especially after Tony meets Johnny's sexy mistress (Karen Morley), it's clear that Tony's tactics are only going to intensify.

SCARFACE was the most violent, bloody film the genre had seen. Hawks outdid himself, running his cameras with the action in vivid truck and dolly shots often missing from the static early talkies of the period. Note in particular how Hawks uses the symbol of an "X" to indicate death (the rafters of a ceiling, Karloff's bowling score, Raft's apartment number, etc.) Aiding the director was cameraman Lee Garmes, whose sharp contrasts created some of the starkest images ever captured on screen. Producer Howard Hughes spared no expense, but he also interfered with Hawks (as he did with other directors), insisting that Hawks present all decisions for his approval. In fact, the production was almost cancelled because of the incessant squabbling between the producer and director.

Little of the original novel was kept except for the title. Profiling the gangster and his tempestuous sister as modern-day Borgias was Hawks's idea, with the incest relationship brilliantly suggested as the emotional weakness that destroys the unthinking gangster. Hecht had been offered $20,000 by Hawks to write the script, but wanted instead $1,000 a day in cash—not a particularly advantageous deal since he finished the script in 11 days.

Muni is superb in his role of the maniac killer, and Morley is perfect as his ice-cool moll. Raft, meanwhile, with his tuxedo and pomaded hair parted in the middle, is also excellent as Muni's right-hand man, a killer who does Muni's bidding without question. Muni and Raft became stars overnight because of SCARFACE, and both received lucrative long-term Hollywood contracts.

SCARFACE

1983 170m c Crime ★★★★
Universal (U.S.) R

Al Pacino *(Tony Montana)*, Steven Bauer *(Manny Ray)*, Michelle Pfeiffer *(Elvira)*, Mary Elizabeth Mastrantonio *(Gina)*, Robert Loggia *(Frank Lopez)*, Miriam Colon *(Mama Montana)*, F. Murray Abraham *(Omar)*, Paul Shenar *(Alejandro Sosa)*, Harris Yulin *(Bernstein)*, Angel Salazar *(Chi Chi)*

p, Martin Bregman, Peter Saphier; d, Brian De Palma; w, Oliver Stone (based on the 1932 film script by Ben Hecht); ph, John A. Alonzo (Panavision, Technicolor); ed, Jerry Greenberg, David Ray; m, Giorgio Moroder; art d, Ed Richardson; fx, Ken Pepiot, Stan Parks; cos, Patricia Norris

A beautiful, at times poetic exercise in excess from Brian De Palma. Based on the classic 1932 gangster film of the same name, the screenplay (written by Oliver Stone) follows the plot of its source almost to the letter.

Two-bit Cuban hood Tony Montana (Pacino) lies his way into the U.S., where he and his friend Manny (Stephen Bauer) soon enter the world of crime. They murder a political figure for drug dealer Frank Lopez (Robert Loggia) to get their green cards and are soon on his payroll. Tony's elimination of rival Colombian drug dealers gives him a more prominent role in the organization. His duties include serving as chauffeur to Lopez's beautiful but cocaine-addicted wife, Elvira (Michelle Pfeiffer). Tony's other female obsession is his sister Gina (Mary Elizabeth Mastrantonio). Tony's feelings for his sister are a bit on the incestuous side, and he dominates the girl, refusing to let her date. After a bad business deal and an argument over Elvira, Lopez attempts to have Tony killed. After killing the assassins, Tony murders Lopez, marries Elvira, and becomes the most powerful drug lord in Florida. The problems really begin to multiply then: Manny secretly dates Gina (though warned not to), Elvira has become increasingly zombie-like, and Tony's money is not earning the interest it should be. Moreover, he also has become a selfish, paranoid drug addict.

Jammed with action sequences and unbearably tense moments, the film depicts the seediest aspects of the American underworld. Stone's screenplay twists gangster movie conventions, and De Palma demonstrates an unusual understanding of the genre. The latter's skill with the camera is certainly his strongest talent. Although not as flashy as some of his work (such as DRESSED TO KILL or CARRIE), it is a showboat of cinematic style (the most memorable composition is an overhead shot of Pacino soaking in an obscenely large bath tub). In addition to the high-octane action sequences, SCARFACE offers some excellent acting (especially from Loggia). An undeniably effective, visceral experience.

SCARLET EMPRESS, THE　DVD

1934　110m　bw　Biography/Historical　★★★★★
Paramount　(U.S.)

Marlene Dietrich *(Sophia Frederica)*, John Lodge *(Count Alexei)*, Sam Jaffe *(Grand Duke Peter)*, Louise Dresser *(Empress Elizabeth)*, Maria Sieber *(Sophia as a Child)*, C. Aubrey Smith *(Prince August)*, Ruthelma Stevens *(Countess Elizabeth)*, Olive Tell *(Princess Johanna)*, Gavin Gordon *(Gregory Orloff)*, Jameson Thomas *(Lt. Ostvyn)*

d, Josef von Sternberg; w, Manuel Komroff (based on the diary of Catherine the Great); ph, Bert Glennon; ed, Josef von Sternberg; m, Felix Mendelssohn, Peter Ilich Tchaikovsky, Richard Wagner, Josef von Sternberg; art d, Hans Dreier, Peter Ballbusch, Richard Kollorsz; fx, Gordon Jennings; cos, Travis Banton

For lovers of cinema, this film is practically a religious experience. Like Griffith's INTOLERANCE, Von Stroheim's GREED or Ophuls's LOLA MONTES, this is one of those masterpieces which contemporaries just couldn't grip. Josef von Sternberg's name was scarlet in Hollywood after he made this costly, indulgent box-office failure, but his work has been entirely vindicated by the passing of time. A highly romanticized rendering of the life of Catherine the Great, from her childhood through her arranged married to the half-witted Peter (Jaffe) and her later usurping of the throne of Russia, THE SCARLET EMPRESS represents Sternberg's ultimate recreation of a world from his own eccentric mind. Marlene Dietrich exists in this never-never-land like some incredible goddess who manifests various aspects of human personality and desire, from wide-eyed, open-mouthed innocence through cynical worldliness to political ambition. It's a real credit to Dietrich that she's both credible throughout these changes and ironically distanced in a way that she alone could pull off. The crazed intensity of the film pits her aggressive seduction of the entire Russian army versus Peter's rights as heir and his manic desires. Jaffe matches Dietrich in brilliance with his remarkable facial expressions, whispered lunacies and childishly temperamental displays. Stealing much of the film is Louise Dresser as the queen who regrets passing her throne onto Peter and who attempts to prime Catherine to be a baby machine. She plays the role like a pushy, middle-aged matchmaking mother from the windy Midwest, and it works beautifully. Also worthy of mention is the stunningly handsome John Lodge (who later gave up acting for politics) as the emissary who brings the young princess to the Russian court and later becomes her lover. Delivering his suggestive lines through clenched teeth, he makes an ideal object of desire in the lavish Russian court. As his large dark uniform covers the frame during one seduction of Catherine, we get a striking visual rendering of her initiation into court politics.

In terms of visuals, THE SCARLET EMPRESS is a symphony verging on insanity. From the cuckoo clock of the woman who exposes herself to the long roving shots surveying a grotesque wedding dinner, Sternberg paints a rich tapestry of decadence. Most memorable of all is the statuary of deformed gargoyles and slaughtered people decorating most of the palace. But it's not just the sets which tell the story here. The staging, frame composition and camera movement produce moments of great beauty as well. Consider the shot

showing a locket Catherine discards as it bounces down from one tree branch to another, or the scene where Catherine is being hairdressed and garbed for her wedding. Or, for a saucier moment, notice how Sternberg tilts his camera slightly after Peter strips one of Catherine's soldier lovers of his rank. As critic Charles Silver has noted, with the men's groins now in frame as well, we realize that the soldier wears other medals which distinguish him in the Russian court. Sternberg loves to clutter his frame, using veils, smoke and shadows to distance us from his characters. A portrait of Catherine lounging on her bed as she fingers a screen drawn around her focuses so intently on the netting that Catherine becomes an inscrutable blur enmeshed in her own reverie. Greatest of all, though, in their combination of photography, lights and editing, are three moments whose emotional impact comes from the filming and not the writing. As a child Catherine is told of the powers and horrors of ruling, and she envisions an incredible montage of torture scenes, climaxing with the unforgettable shot of a man being used as a clapper inside a giant bell. (The dissolve which links this scene to the next is unforgettable.) The finale, meanwhile, done largely without dialogue to the strains of the "The Ride of the Valkyries," builds great momentum as Catherine rides her horse up the palace steps to declare her ultimate triumph. But the scene of scenes is Catherine's wedding to Peter. A frame jammed with crosses; powerful cuts between the pleased Queen, the helpless emissary, the eccentric Peter and the desperate Catherine; the lingering, increasingly tight closeups of Dietrich behind yet another veil—what can one say? See this film on a large screen and in 35 mm if at all possible. The film does justice to the visual possibilities of cinema as few others have done, so do justice to the film when watching it.

SCARLET PIMPERNEL, THE　DVD

1935　85m　bw　Adventure　★★★★
London Films　(U.K.)

Leslie Howard *(Sir Percy Blakeney)*, Merle Oberon *(Lady Marguerite Blakeney)*, Raymond Massey *(Chauvelin)*, Nigel Bruce *(The Prince of Wales)*, Bramwell Fletcher *(The Priest)*, Anthony Bushell *(Sir Andrew Ffoulkes)*, Joan Gardner *(Suzanne de Tournay)*, Walter Rilla *(Armand St. Just)*, Mabel Terry-Lewis *(Countess de Tournay)*, O.B. Clarence *(Count de Tournay)*

p, Alexander Korda; d, Harold Young, Rowland V. Brown (uncredited), Alexander Korda (uncredited); w, S.N. Behrman, Robert E. Sherwood, Arthur Wimperis, Lajos Biro (based on the novel by Baroness Orczy); ph, Harold Rosson; ed, William Hornbeck; m, Arthur Benjamin; prod d, Vincent Korda; fx, Ned Mann; cos, John Armstrong, Oliver Messel

Classic Korda adventure. THE SCARLET PIMPERNEL is based on a romantic novel about deposed French aristocrats, written by the daughter of deposed Hungarian aristocrats; this powerful film secured lasting fame for Leslie Howard.

Sir Percy Blakeney (Howard) is a mild-mannered aristocrat in the court of the Prince of Wales. While large numbers of aristocrats in France are guillotined in the Reign of Terror, Blakeney loses the respect of his wife, Lady Marguerite (Merle Oberon), for being so ineffectual, and he in turn believes that she has been responsible for the arrest of some old friends of hers. Meanwhile, Robespierre (Ernest Milton) and the rest of the French revolutionary government are troubled by a series of daring rescues of condemned nobles, pulled off by the mysterious agency of a man who leaves behind him a small red flower—a pimpernel—for which he comes to be named. The Scarlet Pimpernel adopts a variety of disguises as he saves the gentry from the guillotine. Suspecting English involvement, the French send one of their most capable individuals, Chauvelin (Raymond Massey), to London, ostensibly to serve as ambassador, but really to discover the identity of the Pimpernel. Chauvelin persuades Lady Marguerite to help bait a trap for the Pimpernel, in return for the lives of her arrested friends.

Although directed by Harold Young, the film is much more the work of its producer, Alexander Korda, another transplanted Hungarian (Howard too, for that matter, was the son of Hungarian immigrants). The first director hired was Rowland Brown, director of QUICK MILLIONS, BLOOD MONEY, and author of several respected screenplays. He also had a reputation for getting fired, however, and on the first day of shooting he butted heads with Korda and lost. The producer took over directing for that day, hired Young the next day, and kept a tight rein on him throughout the production. Much of the film was shot outdoors, contrary to the general practice in England at the time. The impressive production resources of Korda's studio are very much in evidence. Korda imported Hal Rosson from Hollywood to shoot the film, and the cinematographer was ecstatic at the varied English skies. Howard gives a wonderful performance, languid and almost effeminate as Sir Percy, and richly deserving of his wife's contempt, but dashing and daring as the Pimpernel. He is supported by Massey in fine form as the villain, and Merle Oberon, as empty as ever.

The novel served as the basis of several silent films, and was remade in 1950 as THE ELUSIVE PIMPERNEL, with David Niven in the title role. The sequel suffers from having been originally shot as a musical; the way it's edited, you can see where the numbers were cut.

The best remembered thing about the original classic adventure is the little bit of doggerel that Howard makes up to throw off suspicion: "They seek him here, they seek him there / The Frenchies seek him everywhere / Is he in Heaven? Is he in Hell? / That damned elusive Pimpernel."

SCARLET STREET
1945 103m bw Crime **DVD**
Diana (U.S.) ★★★★★

Edward G. Robinson (*Christopher Cross*), Joan Bennett (*Kitty March*), Dan Duryea (*Johnny Prince*), Margaret Lindsay (*Millie*), Rosalind Ivan (*Adele Cross*), Jess Barker (*Janeway*), Arthur Loft (*Dellarowe*), Samuel S. Hinds (*Charles Pringle*), Vladimir Sokoloff (*Opo Lejon*), Charles Kemper (*Patcheye*)

p, Fritz Lang; d, Fritz Lang; w, Dudley Nichols (based on the novel and play *La Chienne* by Georges de la Fouchardiere, Mouezy-Eon); ph, Milton Krasner; ed, Arthur Hilton; m, H.J. Salter; art d, Alexander Golitzen, John B. Goodman; fx, John P. Fulton; cos, Travis Banton

Fritz Lang brings his eye for the bleak to this grim but brilliant noir (done before in a 1931 French film, LA CHIENNE, which featured Michel Simon and director Jean Renoir). Robinson, a cashier for a large New York city clothing retailer, spends his spare time painting. At a company banquet held in his honor for two decades of employment, he is characterized as one of those faceless people who make things tick but never receive their due, except at dinners like this. When Robinson leaves the party, he finds Bennett being attacked in the street. He fends off the mugger by using his umbrella as a saber and takes Bennett to have a quiet drink at a bar. Robinson finds this young woman fascinating and can't bear to tell her what he really does for a living, so he lies about it and lets her think he is a renowned artist. Robinson is married to Ivan, a shrewish woman who heckles him unmercifully for his lack of ambition. It isn't long before he thinks he is in love with Bennett, who continues to lead him on and doesn't make him aware of her relationship with Duryea, a hoodlum living on the edge of legality. Since they reckon that Robinson is a good mark, Bennett and Duryea conspire to have him rent a studio where he can meet Bennett for their trysts. Robinson does that and hauls several of his art works to the studio. Duryea brings in a profes-

sional critic, Barker, to look at the work; he is impressed. The cost of maintaining the separate residence is cutting into Robinson's savings, and he is at a loss to figure how to pay for his passion. Duryea removes Robinson's name from the art and puts Bennett's signature on the work. Robinson is annoyed at this, but when the pictures are acknowledged to be the work of a talented person, Robinson takes solace in the fact that someone appreciates him. Robinson begins to embezzle cash from his company, then learns that Ivan's first husband, long thought dead, is actually still alive. That means he can divorce Ivan and marry Bennett. When he races to the studio to tell Bennett the good news, he finds her and Duryea in each other's arms. He watches surreptitiously until Duryea exits, then walks in and has a confrontation with Bennett. When she taunts him with the news that he's been a patsy all along, he does something he (even more, perhaps, than Duryea) will regret the rest of his days.

One of the quintesstial expressions of the noir sensibility, SCARLET STREET does not flinch from the harsher aspects of its sordid story. Robinson, Bennett and Duryea are all in splendid form, and the incredible visuals entrap the feckless Robinson long before plot circumstances do. The paintings for the film were done by John Decker, the artist who palled around with such luminaries as Errol Flynn, John Barrymore, and W.C. Fields.

SCENES FROM A MARRIAGE
1973 168m c Drama **DVD**
Cinematograph (Sweden) ★★★
PG

Liv Ullmann (*Marianne*), Erland Josephson (*Johan*), Bibi Andersson (*Katarina*), Jan Malmsjo (*Peter*), Anita Wall (*Mrs. Palm*), Gunnel Lindblom (*Eva*), Barbro Hiort af Ornas (*Mrs. Jacobi*)

p, Ingmar Bergman; d, Ingmar Bergman; w, Ingmar Bergman; ph, Sven Nykvist (Eastmancolor); ed, Siv Lundgren; cos, Inger Pehrsson

One of the finest of Ingmar Bergman's late-period films, SCENES FROM A MARRIAGE was in its original form a six-episode, 300-minute Swedish television series; Bergman cut it for U.S. release. Here the director-writer again proves that he is one of film's best, and most theatrical, directors of actresses, giving the inimitable Ullmann a superb script that casts her in the role of an abandoned wife forced to deal with her weak husband Josephson's involvement with a younger woman. Filmed almost entirely in extreme close-ups by the masterful Sven Nykvist, Ullmann's face conveys a variety of expressions reminiscent of Renee Falconetti in Carl Dreyer's silent THE PASSION OF JOAN OF ARC. The film is not without its faults, especially a certain choppiness resulting from the paring of the television version. (Its made-for-television visual content, however, should be admirably suited to videocassette.) There is little plot to speak of—the film's chief force lying in its dramatization of marital trauma—but viewers will be deeply moved by the marvelous acting and the honesty of Bergman's screenplay.

SCENT OF A WOMAN
1992 157m c Drama **DVD**
City Light Films/Universal (U.S.) ★★★
R

Al Pacino (*Lt. Col. Frank Slade*), Chris O'Donnell (*Charlie Simms*), James Rebhorn (*Mr. Trask*), Gabrielle Anwar (*Donna*), Philip Seymour Hoffman, billed as Philip S. Hoffman (*George Willis Jr.*), Richard Venture (*W.R. Slade*), Bradley Whitford (*Randy*), Rochelle Oliver (*Gretchen*), Margaret Eginton (*Gail*), Tom Riis Farrell (*Garry*)

p, Martin Brest; d, Martin Brest; w, Bo Goldman (from the characters created by Ruggero Maccari and Dino Risi, from the novel *Il Buio e il Miele* by Giovanni Arpino); ph, Donald E. Thorin; ed, William Steinkamp, Michael Tronick, Harvey

Rosenstock; m, Thomas Newman; prod d, Angelo Graham; art d, W. Steven Graham; chor, Jerry Mitchell, Paul Pellicoro; cos, Aude Bronson-Howard

AAN Best Picture; AA Best Actor: Al Pacino; AAN Best Director: Martin Brest; AAN Best Adapted Screenplay: Bo Goldman

Thanks to a landmark performance by Al Pacino, SCENT OF A WOMAN is an agreeably watchable film. If they'd made it half an hour shorter and re-written the ending, it could have been a great one.

Pacino plays Frank Slade, a brilliant ex-Lieutenant Colonel whose career was cut short by a stupid accident. Now blind and embittered and living in New Hampshire with relatives, Slade has planned to exit this life in glorious style: after one last, hedonistic New York City weekend—the Waldorf, the Oak Room, etc.—he plans to don his dress blues for the last time and casually blow out his brains.

The unwitting accomplice to Slade's plan is Charlie Simms, (Chris O'Donnell), an earnest, hard-up scholarship student at nearby cradle of WASP manhood, Baird College. Charlie, who has problems of his own—he witnessed a student prank and is faced with expulsion unless he sneaks on the culprits—thinks he's going to earn $300 baby-sitting the abrasive Slade over Thanksgiving weekend. Instead, he finds himself on a whirlwind, induction-into-manhood tour of Manhattan.

Most of the adventures that befall Frank and Charlie are entirely unbelievable. Pacino inhabits the role with such passion and conviction, however, that we suspend our skepticism and delight in watching him dance a tango, test-drive a Ferrari or simply rail at his lot.

The dialogue ranges from the insightful to the crassly sentimental, and there's no dramatic structure to speak of. Nevertheless, Pacino, with commendable support from O'Donnell, makes us overlook these shortcomings—until the end, that is, when a hammy show-down at Baird College finally pushes the credibility meter off the scale.

SCHINDLER'S LIST   DVD

1993 185m c/bw Drama/Historical/War ★★★★★
Amblin/Universal (U.S.) R

Liam Neeson *(Oskar Schindler)*, Ben Kingsley *(Itzhak Stern)*, Ralph Fiennes *(Amon Goeth)*, Caroline Goodall *(Emilie Schindler)*, Jonathan Sagalle *(Poldek Pfefferberg)*, Embeth Davidtz *(Helen Hirsch)*, Andrzej Seweryn *(Julian Scherner)*, Norbert Weisser *(Albert Hujar)*, Elina Lowensohn *(Diana Reiter)*, Malgoscha Gebel *(Victoria Klonowska)*

p, Steven Spielberg, Gerald R. Molen, Branko Lustig; d, Steven Spielberg; w, Steve Zaillian (from the novel *Schindler's Ark* by Thomas Keneally); ph, Janusz Kaminski; ed, Michael Kahn, Bill Kimberlin; m, John Williams; prod d, Allan Starski; art d, Maciej Walczak, Ewa Tarnowska, Ryszard Melliwa, Grzegorz Piatkowski; fx, Bruce Minkus, Industrial Light & Magic, Steve Price; cos, Anna Biedrzycka-Sheppard

AA Best Picture; AA Best Director: Steven Spielberg; AA Best Cinematography: Janusz Kaminski; AA Best Adapted Screenplay: Steven Zaillian; AA Best Original Score: John Williams; AA Best Film Editing: Michael Kahn; AA Best Art Direction-Set Decoration: Ewa Braun, Allan Starski; AAN Best Actor: Liam Neeson; AAN Best Supporting Actor: Ralph Fiennes; AAN Best Costume Design: Anna Biedrzycka-Sheppard; AAN Best Sound: Andy Nelson, Steve Pederson, Scott Millan, Ron Judkins; AAN Best Makeup: Christina Smith, Matthew Mungle, Judith A. Cory

The seven Academy Awards and virtually unanimous acclaim accorded to SCHINDLER'S LIST were entirely merited. Director Steven Spielberg has achieved something close to the impossible—a morally serious, aesthetically stunning historical epic that is nonetheless readily accessible to a mass audience.

In 1941, the Jews of Nazi-occupied Kracow are dispossessed of their businesses and herded into a tiny, squalid ghetto. Small-time entrepreneur Oskar Schindler (Liam Neeson), a gentile, conceives of a get-rich-quick scheme that involves Itzhak Stern (Ben Kingsley), an accountant and member of the local *judenrat* (Jewish council), and an enamelware plant where cheap labor is supplied by ghetto Jews.

Stern sees a way to save Jewish lives: factory employees, classified as essential workers, are exempt from "resettlement" in concentration camps. Against his better judgment, Schindler looks the other way as Stern adds musicians, academics, rabbis, and cripples to the factory rolls. Within a year, the Final Solution is well underway, and a monstrous Nazi commandant, Amon Goeth (Ralph Fiennes), brutally liquidates the ghetto and ships surviving Jews to a forced labor camp. Schindler bribes the cynical Goeth to permit re-establishment of the factory within camp walls, and business continues more or less as before. But Schindler is changing, and at great risk to himself, he begins to take an active role in protecting his workers.

Though based on fact, SCHINDLER'S LIST is neither history, nor the "definitive" film version of the Holocaust some reviewers wanted it to be. It's an intensely personal meditation on the nature of heroism and moral choice, rendered on the kind of rich, dreamlike cinematic canvas that only Hollywood can realize. Far from a departure for Spielberg, SCHINDLER'S LIST is the fulfillment of his singular talent for achieving high seriousness—as with EMPIRE OF THE SUN—within and despite the constraints of corporate filmmaking.

SCHOOL FOR SCOUNDRELS

1960 94m bw Comedy ★★★★
Guardsman (U.K.)

Ian Carmichael *(Henry Palfrey)*, Terry-Thomas *(Raymond Delauney)*, Alastair Sim *(Stephen Potter)*, Janette Scott *(April Smith)*, Dennis Price *(Dunstan Dorchester)*, Peter Jones *(Dudley Dorchester)*, Edward Chapman *(Gloatbridge)*, John Le Mesurier *(Headwaiter)*, Irene Handl *(Mrs. Stringer)*, Kynaston Reeves *(General)*

p, Hal E. Chester, Douglas Rankin; d, Robert Hamer; w, Hal E. Chester, Patricia Moyes, Peter Ustinov (based on the books *Theory and Practice Gamesmanship, Same Some Notes on Lifemanship* and *Oneupmanship* by Stephen Potter); ph, Erwin Hillier; ed, Richard Best; m, John Addison; art d, Terence Verity

Reminiscent of HOW TO SUCCEED IN BUSINESS WITHOUT REALLY TRYING, this nonstop British comedy, subtitled "How to Win Without Cheating," is a delicious satire of self-improvement strategies. Henry Palfrey (Ian Carmichael) is one of life's real losers. He'd like to win the heart of April Smith (Janette Scott), but she's already spoken for by boorishly successful Raymond Delauney (Terry-Thomas). Determined to change his fortunes, Henry enrolls in the College of Lifesmanship, run by Stephen Potter (Alastair Sim). After immersing himself in such courses as "woomanship," "partymanship," and "oneupmanship," Henry returns to London to get the best of those who have taken advantage of him in the past, most notably—and hilariously—Delauney. Not surprisingly, Henry also ends up with April. Based on the satirical how-to-get-ahead books written by the real Stephen Potter, SCHOOL FOR SCOUNDRELS features a terrific cast of comic actors who play the whole affair straight, netting laugh after laugh.

SCHOOL OF ROCK

DVD

2003 108m c Comedy ★★★
MFP Munich Film Partners/New Century/ PG-13
Scott Rudin Productions/Paramount (U.S./Germany)

Jack Black *(Dewey Finn)*, Mike White *(Ned Schneebly)*, Joan Cusack *(Rosalie Mullins)*, Sarah Silverman *(Patty Di Marco)*, Joey Gaydos Jr. *(Zack)*, Miranda Cosgrove *(Summer Hathaway)*, Kevin Clark *(Freddy)*, Robert Tsai *(Lawrence)*, Maryam Hassan *(Tomika)*, Rebecca Brown *(Katie)*

p, Scott Rudin; d, Richard Linklater; w, Mike White; ph, Rogier Stoffers; ed, Sandra Adair; m, Randall Poster; prod d, Jeremy Conway; art d, Adam Scher; fx, John Sifanich; chor, Adesola Osakalumi; cos, Karen Patch

Director Richard Linklater and writer Mike White are both known independently for edgy comedies about social outsiders, so it's surprising and mildly disappointing that their joint efforts produced a light, mainstream comedy with a traditional story line and some catchy tunes.

Rock-and-roll dreamer Dewey Finn (Jack Black) is determined to lead his band, No Vacancy, to victory at an upcoming Battle of the Bands contest, but his onstage antics have so sorely tried his bandmates' patience that they've handed him his walking papers. Devastated, Dewey holes up with his friend Ned (Mike White) at his apartment, but Ned's girlfriend (Sarah Silverman) issues an ultimatum: Dewey must find employment or face eviction. Dewey scams one of Ned's substitute-teaching gigs at Horace Green prep school, and after catching a music class, Dewey comes up with a new plan to ace the Battle of the Bands: he'll bang together a new group out of these talented fifth-graders. Dewey begins adapting their musical abilities to his needs. String bass player Katie (Rebecca Brown) tries her hand at the electric version; classical pianist Lawrence (Robert Tsai) is cajoled into keyboards; Freddy (Kevin Clark) is easily persuaded to ditch homework for drums; and Zack (Joey Gaydos Jr.) trades his acoustic guitar for something with an amp. The ragtag group's most daunting challenge, however, is avoiding the watchful eye of uptight Principal Mullins (Joan Cusack).

Linklater and White showcase Black's sarcastic humor and musical talent in equal parts, and those who find his crass comedy painful in large doses should be warned that he's in nearly every scene. But the kids—most of them first-timers cast for natural charisma and musical ability—steal the show, and a talented supporting cast helps take the edge off Black's manic antics.

SCOOBY-DOO

DVD

2002 86m c Adventure/Mystery/Comedy ★★½
Mosaic Media Group/Atlas Entertainment/ PG
Hanna-Barbera Productions/Village Roadshow
Productions (U.S.)

Freddie Prinze Jr. *(Fred)*, Sarah Michelle Gellar *(Daphne)*, Matthew Lillard *(Shaggy)*, Linda Cardellini *(Velma)*, Scott Innes *(Voice of Scooby-Doo)*, Rowan Atkinson *(Emile Mondavarious)*, Isla Fisher *(Mary Jane)*, Miguel A. Nunez Jr. *(Voodoo Maestro)*, Steven Grives *(N'Goo Tuana)*, Sam Greco *(Zarkos)*

p, Chuck Roven, Richard Suckle; d, Raja Gosnell; w, James Gunn (from a Story by James Gunn and Craig Titley, based on characters created by Hanna-Barbera Productions); ph, David Eggby; ed, Kent Beyda; m, David Newman; prod d, Bill Boes; art d, Bill Booth, Donna Brown, Gabrielle Gliniak, Christian Wintter (Christian "Pipo" Wintter); fx, Peter Crosman; cos, Leesa Evans

As live-action adaptations of unabashedly dumb cartoons go, this is top of the line: the cast is appealing, the sets brightly colored, and the mystery as goofy as any featured in the many "Scooby-Doo" cartoons.

The movie opens as the ever-game members of Mystery, Inc.—vain Fred (a bleached Freddie Prinze Jr.), beautiful Daphne (Sarah Michelle Gellar), comic-relief Shaggy (Matthew Lillard), brilliant Velma (Linda Cardellini), and talking Great Dane Scooby—wrap up a typical "supernatural" mystery by revealing that the real culprit is the cranky old janitor. But when Fred once again takes credit for everything, Velma quits in a huff. The others follow suit, and Mystery, Inc. is no more. Two years later, each receives an invitation from amusement park magnate Emile Mondavarious (Rowan Atkinson) to solve a mystery plaguing his Spooky Island resort. College kids arrive filled with high spirits and leave as surly Stepford teens—what could be happening? The answer involves ectoplasm and a fiendish plan to revitalize ancient demons hell-bent on ruling the world.

The movie is aimed squarely at youngsters, so all you smart alecks looking for further proof that Shaggy is a pot head, Velma a lesbian, and Scrappy-Doo the product of an unnatural liaison will be sorely disappointed. The only sop to cynics lies in the indignities heaped on the oversized head of the much-hated Scrappy. On the plus side, the casting is just about flawless, and CGI Scooby is a marvel of modern special effects technology, even if the results are distinctly grotesque. A cartoon dog with freakish proportions and human expressions is awfully creepy when rendered in an essentially realistic style.

SCOUNDREL, THE

1935 76m bw Drama/Comedy ★★★★
Paramount (U.S.)

Noel Coward *(Anthony Mallare)*, Julie Haydon *(Cora Moore)*, Stanley Ridges *(Paul Decker)*, Rosita Moreno *(Carlotta)*, Martha Sleeper *(Julia Vivian)*, Hope Williams *(Margie)*, Ernest Cossart *(Jimmy Clay)*, Everley Gregg *(Mildred Langwiter)*, Eduardo Ciannelli *(Maurice Stern)*, Helen Strickland *(Mrs. Rollinson)*

p, Ben Hecht, Charles MacArthur; d, Ben Hecht, Charles MacArthur; w, Ben Hecht, Charles MacArthur; ph, Lee Garmes; ed, Arthur Ellis; art d, Walter E. Keller

AA Best Original Story: Ben Hecht, Charles MacArthur

This is a smart-set literati piece starring Noel Coward as a New York publisher who is a marionette master, pulling the strings of everyone around him while scattering *bons mots* like rose petals. He is a charming heel who loves 'em, leaves 'em, and remains the main topic of conversation at swank hotels, various watering spots, and brittle cocktail parties. Julie Haydon, a young author, is in love with Stanley Ridges, and Coward means to break them up and make her his own. Meanwhile, he meets his female counterpart in Hope Williams, who is just as world-weary, cynical, and cunning as he is. Coward gets aboard a Bermuda-bound flight which crashes, killing everyone aboard. But he gets a new lease on life and is allowed to return to this world, never to rest until he finds someone, anyone, who mourns his passing. In the end, Coward makes peace with his Maker and is allowed to have eternal salvation. The metaphysical conclusion left many in the audience wondering what it all meant, and some of the actors were mystified as well. The picture is mostly talk with very little action. Coming off their sensational debut as co-authors-directors-producers of CRIME WITHOUT PASSION, Ben Hecht and Charles MacArthur made the virtually unreleasable ONCE IN A BLUE MOON. (It was held for a year before it was let slip out.) They followed up with this movie, which must be one of the earliest existential films produced. Hecht and MacArthur were not true directors who knew how to make the screen dance with images, and their lack of expertise is evident throughout. Yet the wonderful words spoken by almost everyone in the cast keep the movie afloat. To star in their original work, which owes a bit to the Hecht novel *Fantazius Mallare* and to his well-known *A Jew In Love*, they chose Noel Coward, who was making his talking picture debut after having done a silent juvenile bit in Griffith's HEARTS OF THE WORLD in 1918. This movie was made at the Astoria, Long Island, lot and was a favorite of sophisticates, pseudo-sophisticates, and anyone who could recognize the real-life people upon whom the screenplay was based.

SCREAM 📀

1996 100m c Horror ★★★½
Wes Craven Films/Woods Entertainment/ R
Dimension (U.S.)

Neve Campbell *(Sidney)*, Drew Barrymore *(Casey)*, Skeet Ulrich *(Billy)*, Courteney Cox *(Gale Weathers)*, David Arquette *(Dewey)*, Rose McGowan *(Tatum)*, Matthew Lillard *(Stuart)*, Henry Winkler *(Principal Himbry)*, Lawrence Hecht *(Mr. Prescott)*, Jamie Kennedy *(Randy)*

p, Cary Woods, Cathy Konrad; d, Wes Craven; w, Kevin Williamson; ph, Mark Irwin; ed, Patrick Lussier; m, Marco Beltrami; prod d, Bruce Alan Miller; art d, David Lubin; fx, Frank Ceglia, Kamar Bitar (effects make-up); cos, Mathew Clayton Hooey, Gary J. Saldutti

Director Wes Craven continues his reign as one of horror's kingpins with this self-reflexive twist on "dead-teen" movies. The film mixes sly humor and grisly deaths into a tale that both updates and satirizes the slasher genre.

Small-town virgin Sidney Prescott (Neve Campbell) is being stalked by a masked psycho-killer who's already slaughtered two of her classmates and may have also murdered her mom—exactly one year earlier. Is it the video store geek (Jamie Kennedy)? Sidney's hunky and too-good-to-be-true boyfriend Billy (Skeet Ulrich)? Her dad (Lawrence Hecht), who's supposedly away on business but can't be located? Class weirdo Stuart (Matthew Lillard), who's dating Sidney's perky best friend (Rose McGowan)? The high-strung, teen-hating school principal (Henry Winkler)? Or could it be the janitor in the Freddy Krueger sweater?

Unlike most modern horror movies, which are little more than exploitation cash cows, director Craven and scriptwriter Kevin Williamson have created a surprisingly clever thriller, which embraces the genre even as it subverts it. It's fast-paced and complex enough to keep viewers guessing, and while never aiming for outright comedy, the in-jokes will get laughs from knowing viewers. Better still, in a change from the teen horror films of the '80s, the cast actually has an opportunity to act! Campbell is sympathetic as the emotionally abused (but strong-willed) heroine; McGowan is full of attitude and sex appeal, and Drew Barrymore's small but pivotal role sets the edgy tone for the entire film. But above all, this is Craven's show. He knows how to ladle on the thrills, get an audience to jump, or pull back for a laugh.

SCROOGE 📀

1970 118m c Fantasy/Musical ★★★½
Waterbury (U.K.) G

Albert Finney *(Ebenezer Scrooge)*, Alec Guinness *(Jacob Marley's Ghost)*, Edith Evans *(Ghost of Christmas Past)*, Kenneth More *(Ghost of Christmas Present)*, Laurence Naismith *(Fezziwig)*, Michael Medwin *(Nephew)*, David Collings *(Bob Cratchit)*, Anton Rodgers *(Tom Jenkins)*, Suzanne Neve *(Isabel)*, Frances Cuka *(Mrs. Cratchit)*

p, Robert H. Solo; d, Ronald Neame; w, Leslie Bricusse (based on the novel *A Christmas Carol* by Charles Dickens); ph, Oswald Morris (Panavision, Technicolor); ed, Peter Weatherley; m, Leslie Bricusse; prod d, Terence Marsh; art d, Robert Cartwright; fx, Wally Veevers, Jack Mills; cos, Margaret Furse

AAN Best Original Song Score: Leslie Bricusse (Music & Lyrics), Ian Fraser (Adaptation), Herbert W Spencer (Adaptation); *AAN Best Original Song:* "Thank You Very Much"; Leslie Bricusse (Music & Lyrics); *AAN Best Art Direction-Set Decoration:* Terry Marsh (Art Direction), Bob Cartwright (Art Direction), Pamela Cornell (Set Decoration); *AAN Best Costume Design:* Margaret Furse

At the center of this musical adaptation of Charles Dickens's *A Christmas Carol* is Albert Finney, singing, dancing, and "Bah, humbug"-ing his way through the familiar title role. Guiding him on his journey to moral reawakening are Edith Evans as the Ghost of Christmas Past, Kenneth More as the Ghost of Christmas Present, and Paddy Stone as the Ghost of Christmas Yet to Come. Director Ronald Neame's well-paced film captures the period beautifully, and the acting is superb, with Finney and Alec Guinness, as Marley's ghost, real standouts. Richard Harris was originally slated to star, then was replaced by Rex Harrison, who also dropped out, and Finney stepped in just three weeks before shooting began. SCROOGE received Oscar nominations for Best Song ("Thank You Very Much"), Best Art Direction, Best Score, and Best Costumes. If you like your Dickens set to music, this (like OLIVER!) is just the ticket; if you prefer the story played a little straighter, see A CHRISTMAS CAROL or the 1935 version of SCROOGE.

SEA HAWK, THE 📀

1940 126m bw Romance/Adventure/War ★★★★★
Warner Bros. (U.S.)

Errol Flynn *(Capt. Geoffrey Thorpe)*, Brenda Marshall *(Donna Maria Alvarez de Cordoba)*, Claude Rains *(Don Jose Alvarez de Cordoba)*, Flora Robson *(Queen Elizabeth)*, Donald Crisp *(Sir John Burleson)*, Henry Daniell *(Lord Wolfingham)*, Alan Hale *(Carl Pitt)*, Una O'Connor *(Martha)*, William Lundigan *(Danny Logan)*, James Stephenson *(Abbott)*

p, Henry Blanke; d, Michael Curtiz; w, Howard Koch, Seton I. Miller; ph, Sol Polito; ed, George Amy; m, Erich Wolfgang Korngold; art d, Anton Grot; fx, Byron Haskin, H.F. Koenekamp; cos, Orry-Kelly

AAN Best Score: Erich Wolfgang Korngold; *AAN Best Interior Decoration (B/W):* Anton Grot; *AAN Best Sound Recording:* Nathan Levinson; *AAN Best Special Effects:* Byron Haskin (Photographic), Nathan Levinson (Sound)

First class, rousing adventure with the inimitable Flynn swashing away, aided by top Curtiz direction and bracing Korngold score. Everything else clicks, too: the cinematography of Sol Polito, terrific Warners production values and a cast of character actors hard to match in any era.

As the film opens, Spain's King Philip II (Montagu Love) instructs his advisors to devise a plan to conquer England and continental Europe. To placate England's Queen Elizabeth (Flora Robson), he sends Don Jose Alvarez de Cordoba (Claude Rains), his crafty ambassador, to soothe the Virgin Queen's fears and disguise Spain's intentions. En route, the Spanish galleon carrying Don Jose and his niece, Donna Maria (Brenda Marshall), is sunk by a British ship commanded by Geoffrey Thorpe (Flynn). The dashing captain takes the indignant ambassador and Maria on board, bringing them safely to

England. Despite his fine manners, Thorpe is a dedicated "Sea Hawk," one of a half-dozen British sea captains who foresee war and have been raiding Spanish coastal forts and seizing Philip's treasures to fund a British fleet, all with Elizabeth's unofficial approval. Although Thorpe's gallantry soon wins over Maria, Don Jose intrigues to capture him in Panama, where Spanish forces waylay the Englishman.

Warners lavished a then-staggering $1.7 million on THE SEA HAWK, with gorgeous results. The 31-year-old Flynn, at the peak of his spectacular career, is magnificent in his swashbuckling role; Marshall was never more radiant; Rains is deliciously evil; and Robson makes a wonderfully witty and intelligent Elizabeth. Eschew shortened versions; you want all 127 minutes.

SEA INSIDE, THE
(MAR ADENTRO)
2004 125m c Drama ★★★½
Canal+/Eurimages/Eyescreen/Filmanova/ PG-13
Himenoptero/Lucky Red/Sociedad General de Cine/
Sogepaq/Television Espanola/UGC Images
(Spain/Italy/France)

Javier Bardem *(Ramon Sampedro)*, Belen Rueda *(Julia)*, Lola Duenas *(Rosa)*, Mabel Rivera *(Manuela)*, Celso Bugallo *(Jose)*, Clara Segura *(Gene)*, Joan Dalmau *(Joaquin)*, Alberto Jimenez *(German)*, Tamar Novas *(Javi)*, Francesc Garrido *(Marc)*

d, Alejandro Amenabar; w, Alejandro Amenabar, Mateo Gil; ph, Javier Aguirresarobe; ed, Alejandro Amenabar; m, Alejandro Amenabar; prod d, Benjamin Fernandez; art d, Benjamin Fernandez; cos, Sonia Grande

AA Best Foreign Language Film; AAN Best Makeup: Jo Allen, Manuel Garcia

In bringing the true story of Ramon Sampedro—a quadriplegic who waged a decades-long court battle for the right to die—to the big screen, Spanish director Alejandro Amenabar (THE OTHERS) has produced a classic melodrama, complete with a soaring score (composed, as always, by himself) and lots of tears.

Paralyzed from the waist down in a diving accident, Ramon (Javier Bardem) has seen his world shrink to the bedroom where he's cared for by his older brother, Jose (Celso Bugallo), sister-in-law Manuela (Mabel Rivera), elderly father, Joaquin (Joan Dalmau), and teenage nephew Javi (Tamar Novas). Ramon's upbeat, charismatic personality wins him a number of admirers, including lonely single mother Rosa (Lola Duenas), who falls in love with him. While Ramon seems happy, he wants the right to end his life. Suicide, however, is forbidden under Spanish law, and his repeated legal challenges have failed. Ramon has trouble finding a new lawyer until Julia (Belen Rueda) enters his life, prepared to take up the cause. They quickly forge a powerful bond that might have blossomed into romance were it not for Ramon's condition and the fact that Julia is married. Ramon now finds himself with two women for whom he cares deeply, and they in turn must decide whether they're capable of helping him carry out his wish to die.

Unlike Amenabar's previous films, which tinkered with the givens of their respective genres, this one hews closely to established conventions, and at times the ordinariness is disappointing. Nevertheless, Amenabar's clear-eyed direction ensures that it never becomes a cable-TV problem-of-the-week movie, and he's helped immeasurably by Bardem's masterful performance in an emotionally tricky role.

SEA OF LOVE
1989 113m c Mystery/Thriller ★★★½
Martin Bregman (U.S.) R

Al Pacino *(Frank Keller)*, Ellen Barkin *(Helen)*, John Goodman *(Sherman)*, Michael Rooker *(Terry)*, William Hickey *(Frank Keller, Sr.)*, Richard Jenkins *(Gruber)*, Paul Calderon *(Serafino)*, Gene Canfield *(Struk)*, Larry Joshua *(Dargan)*, John Spencer *(Lieutenant)*

p, Martin Bregman, Louis A. Stroller; d, Harold Becker; w, Richard Price; ph, Ronnie Taylor (Deluxe Color); ed, David Bretherton; m, Trevor Jones; prod d, John Jay Moore; cos, Betsy Cox

A thriller featuring a mysterious femme fatale, an involving plot, and some nice offbeat twists, SEA OF LOVE owes a good deal to Hitchcock, and to such recent efforts as FATAL ATTRACTION and JAGGED EDGE, though it can claim plenty of originality as well. Several men who have responded to the personals in a popular New York magazine have been found murdered in their beds. Twenty-year veteran cop Frank Keller (Al Pacino), a stressed-out borderline alcoholic, and Sherman (John Goodman), a jolly family man, team up to track the killer, planting an ad and "dating" the respondents. Breaking the first rule of investigation, Keller gets deeply involved with one respondent, a tough and savvy single mother (Ellen Barkin). He becomes caught in a web of infatuation and rough, steamy sex, despite signs that she might be the killer. Beyond its slight (though satisfying) plot, SEA OF LOVE's strength lies in the realism of its characterizations. Writer Richard Price is a master at contriving sympathetic, believable characters. His dialogue here, the skewed, elliptical jargon of urban social maneuvering, is dead on. Director Harold Becker (THE ONION FIELD; TAPS) skillfully and unobtrusively supports the drama with just the right lighting, details, and mood. Pacino gives perhaps his best film performance since DOG DAY AFTERNOON; Barkin matches him well as the hard-bitten, voraciously carnal suspect. SEA OF LOVE captures the emotional risk and false hope of the urban singles scene so accurately it's almost painful to watch.

SEA WOLF, THE
1941 100m bw Drama ★★★★
Warner Bros. (U.S.)

Edward G. Robinson *(Wolf Larsen)*, John Garfield *(George Leach)*, Ida Lupino *(Ruth Webster)*, Alexander Knox *(Humphrey Van Weyden)*, Gene Lockhart *(Dr. Louie Prescott)*, Barry Fitzgerald *(Cooky)*, Stanley Ridges *(Johnson)*, Francis McDonald *(Svenson)*, David Bruce *(Young Sailor)*, Howard da Silva *(Harrison)*

p, Henry Blanke; d, Michael Curtiz; w, Robert Rossen (based on the novel by Jack London); ph, Sol Polito; ed, George Amy; m, Erich Wolfgang Korngold; art d, Anton Grot; fx, Byron Haskin, H.F. Koenekamp

AAN Best Special Effects: Byron Haskin (Photographic), Nathan Levinson (Sound)

After a ferryboat capsizes in a fog-shrouded sea, the scavenger ship the *Ghost* picks up two survivors: Knox, an author and scholar, and the sad, sick Lupino. Captained by the brutal, callous Robinson—who rules his seagoing fiefdom both by physical might and strategic cunning—the *Ghost* is manned by shanghaied sailors who have been pressed into service with belaying pins and Mickey Finns in the old British way, except for Garfield, a surly young sailor who has signed on to escape the clutches of the law. Robinson refuses to take Knox and Lupino to shore. Instead, he presses them both into service, telling the reluctant but somewhat fascinated Knox, "You're soft, like a woman. This voyage ought to do you a lot of good." To humiliate the scholar, but also to gain his company—for the cruel captain is a secret intellectual who, when closeted in his cabin, reads poetry and philosophy—Robinson makes

Knox the cabin boy for the duration of the voyage. In this servitude, Knox functions as a captive intellectual audience of one for Robinson as the captain elucidates his Nietzschean superman theories. During one of these discourses, Robinson is suddenly seized with a headache that is literally blinding. He attempts to hide this fact, both because he despises weakness and because his condition threatens his absolute control over his crew. Robinson exerts authority over his men more in the manner of a chess master than a ship's master, manipulating them mentally, divining their weaknesses, and dividing them in order to conquer them. As his condition worsens, however, he becomes locked into a relationship of mutual dependence and fascination with Knox which becomes the ultimate test of each man's character.

THE SEA WOLF contains little of the prolixity of Jack London's philosophically oriented novel, yet it is true to the spirit of the book. The megalomania of the ship's master is wonderfully expressed in Edward G. Robinson's fine portrayal of the contemptuous captain. Alexander Knox's reserve makes a perfect foil for Robinson's sneering bombast; in his screen debut, this fine stage actor is beautifully restrained. Ida Lupino, in her role as a loser, gives one of her best screen performances; John Garfield is also fine as her masculine counterpart; and a laudable assemblage of Warner Bros. stock-company character actors ably supports the leads. Required to work a romance into London's all-male work to satisfy studio formula, screenwriter Robert Rossen did very well with the unenviable task. He added the characters played by Garfield and Lupino, which help flesh out the story, substituting for the novel's uncinematic dialogue. Warner's all-purpose director, Michael Curtiz, performed up to par, shooting all the seafaring scenes in studio tanks. THE SEA WOLF earned an Oscar nomination for Best Special Effects. Erich Wolfgang Korngold's score melds well with the excellent sound effects—the constant creaking of timbers under stress, the whipping of ratlines—that create the ambience of a ship at sea.

SEABISCUIT

2003 129m c Biography/Sports/Drama ★★★½
Universal/DreamWorks/Spyglass Entertainment/ PG-13
Larger Than Life Productions/Kennedy/Marshall
Productions (U.S.)

Tobey Maguire (Red Pollard), Jeff Bridges (Charles Howard), Chris Cooper (Tom Smith), Elizabeth Banks (Marcela Howard), William H. Macy ("Tick-Tock"McGlaughlin), Gary Stevens (George Woolf), Eddie Jones (Samuel Riddle), Kingston DuCoeur (Sam), Valerie Mahaffey (Annie Howard), Ed Lauter (Charles Strub)

p, Kathleen Kennedy, Frank Marshall, Gary Ross, Jane Sindell; d, Gary Ross; w, Gary Ross (based on the book by Laura Hillenbrand); ph, John Schwartzman; ed, William Goldenberg; m, Randy Newman; prod d, Robert Katz; art d, Andrew Neskoromny, Jeannine Oppewall; fx, Don Elliot, Richard Hoover, Michael Lantieri, Tom Phak; cos, Judianna Makovsky

ANN Best Picture; AAN Best Sound Mixing: Gary Ross; AAN Best Cinematography: John Schwartzman; AAN Best Sound Mixing: Andy Nelson, Anna Behlmer, Tod A. Maitland; AAN Best Costume Design: Judianna Makovsky; AAN Best Editing: William Goldenberg; AAN Best Art Direction: Jeannine Oppewall (art direction), Leslie Pope (set decoration)

Based on Laura Hillenbrand's nonfiction best seller, this solid, old-fashioned story of Seabiscuit, the unprepossessing horse that rose to the highest ranks of thoroughbred racing and enchanted Depression-era America, never quite achieves the significance to which it so desperately aspires.

Seabiscuit's saga is also the tale of three men: self-made automotive millionaire Charles Howard (Jeff Bridges), who bought the undistinguished three-year-old after the death of his son; horse whisperer Tom Smith (Chris Cooper), an old-time

man of the West; and world-class horseman Red Pollard (Tobey Maguire), a bare-knuckled boxer who was blind in one eye and beset by personal problems but who formed a winning bond with his temperamental mount. Howard chooses the eccentric, taciturn Smith as his trainer because his gut tells him Smith has a rare way with horses. Smith's gut tells him that the unlovely and underachieving Seabiscuit, a knock-kneed, scrub-tailed, undersized, bad-tempered beast, could be a champion, and that Pollard, a young man too tall and too troubled for professional racing, has the mettle to ride him to victory.

Director-screenwriter Gary Ross simplifies, streamlines and soft-pedals the complexities of the Seabiscuit saga, saddling it with syrupy voice-over narration and a painfully sentimental score. Such missteps might have sunk a less inherently gripping story, but Seabiscuit's tale is real-life inspirational drama at its purest. The movie's secret weapons are its stellar cast and its brilliantly shot racing sequences. They're heart-stoppingly suspenseful even when the outcome is a matter of record.

SEANCE ON A WET AFTERNOON   DVD

1964 115m bw Crime ★★★★
Beaver/Allied (U.K.)

Kim Stanley (Myra Savage), Richard Attenborough (Billy Savage), Mark Eden (Charles Clayton), Nanette Newman (Mrs. Clayton), Judith Donner (Amanda Clayton), Patrick Magee (Supt. Walsh), Gerald Sim (Sgt. Beedle), Margaret Lacey (Woman at 1st Seance), Maria Kazan (Other Woman at Seance), Lionel Gamlin (Man at Seances)

p, Richard Attenborough, Bryan Forbes; d, Bryan Forbes; w, Bryan Forbes (based on the novel by Mark McShane); ph, Gerry Turpin; ed, Derek York; m, John Barry; art d, Ray Simm

AAN Best Actress: Kim Stanley

In this eerie tale, Myra Savage (Kim Stanley), a medium, claims contact with "the other side" through her late son Arthur, a stillborn child whose death Myra cannot come to accept. Myra's husband, Billy (Richard Attenborough, the British actor who would later direct MAGIC, CRY FREEDOM and GANDHI), does his best to keep her happy, knowing well that she is walking a tightrope between insanity and rationality. He is a weak man and adores Myra, so he can deny her nothing. Myra would like some publicity for her flagging business, so she concocts a plan to have Billy kidnap a wealthy child and collect his ransom. Myra will then offer the services of her psychic powers to the bereaved family and, of course, "find" the child. An atmospheric film, SEANCE ON A WET AFTERNOON succeeds because of Bryan Forbes' excellent direction and the superb performances of both Kim Stanley (in a rare film appearance) and Attenborough (who also produced). While the film can be slow going in spots, Stanley's portrayal of the emotionally unfit Myra Savage is riveting as she gradually loses her grip on reality and slips into a dark psychological abyss.

SEARCH, THE

1948 105m bw Drama ★★★★
Prasens (U.S.)

Montgomery Clift (Ralph Stevenson), Aline MacMahon (Mrs. Murray), Jarmila Novotna (Mrs. Malik), Wendell Corey (Jerry Fisher), Ivan Jandl (Karel Malik), Mary Patton (Mrs. Fisher), Ewart G. Morrison (Mr. Crookes), William Rogers (Tom Fisher), Leopold Borkowski (Joel Makowsky), Claude Gambier (Raoul Dubois)

p, Lazar Wechsler; d, Fred Zinnemann; w, Richard Schweizer, David Wechsler, Paul Jarrico; ph, Emil Berna; ed, Hermann Haller; m, Robert Blum

AAN Best Actor: Montgomery Clift; AAN Best Director: Fred Zinnemann; AA Best Motion Picture Story: Richard Schweizer,

David Wechsler; *AAN Best Screenplay:* Richard Schweizer, David Wechsler

Clift was making his first movie, RED RIVER, when he was approached by Zinnemann to read the first draft of the script by Peter Viertel, and he liked it enough to commit to making THE SEARCH (which, as it turned out, was released before RED RIVER). When Swiss producer Wechsler hired his son to help rewrite the screenplay, Clift became angered and began to substitute his own words for those in the script. Attorneys were called in to mediate, and, in the end, the younger Wechsler and co-author Schweizer won an Oscar for a screenplay that contained many of Clift's words.

THE SEARCH begins in a camp for children who have been orphaned or displaced by WWII. Among them is Jandl, a traumatized nine-year-old Czech who hasn't seen his mother since he was torn from her arms at the age of five. Frightened, Jandl escapes from a Red Cross ambulance; soon, he's living like a frightened animal in the burnt-out houses of the city, foraging for food in trash cans. He is nearly starved when Clift, an American soldier, finds him and takes him home. Jandl is hostile, fearful, and makes attempts to leave, but Clift begins to convince the boy of his good intentions. Clift attempts to trace Jandl's history with the help of his pal Corey, but it's a brick wall. Meanwhile, Jandl's mother, Novotna, continues her search for the boy.

A rather saccharine ending mars the believablity of the plot, and audiences might have liked it better if Novotna's character were not so wonderful and Jandl had gotten a new lease on life by going to the U.S. with Clift. Zinnemann and Clift received Oscar nominations and Jandl won a special juvenile Oscar for his haunting portrayal of the tragic child. Jandl was discovered singing with a youth choir in Prague, and, after this picture, it was just assumed that he would stay in films, but his parents refused, and he disappeared from sight. Zinnemann had been with MGM, but they dropped his contract while he was shooting this film, so he signed with RKO. However, after the picture was released, Zinnemann's star again rose, so they re-signed him for a great deal more money. THE SEARCH was shot entirely in the American Occupied Zone of Germany, the first movie to be made there after the war. With THE SEARCH and RED RIVER released the same year, Clift became a huge star and was given a *Life* magazine cover. Only 27, he received $75,000 for this film. He brought along his friend and mentor, Mira Rostova, who stood behind the camera and gave her approval on each scene. Zinnemann objected to this, so she stayed away but spent almost every night before shooting going over each nuance of the next day's pages. Only four professional actors appeared in the movie: Clift, who was under contract to Howard Hawks; Corey, on loan from Hal Wallis; Novotna, an opera star at the Met; and MacMahon. The others were locals, and their unfamiliar presence lent an air of credibility to the project. This superior movie made the world aware of the plight of these children and money poured in to the UNRRA to help their plight.

SEARCHERS, THE

1956 119m c Western
Warner Bros. (U.S.)

📀
★★★★★

John Wayne *(Ethan Edwards),* Jeffrey Hunter *(Martin Pawley),* Vera Miles *(Laurie Jorgensen),* Ward Bond *(Capt. Rev. Samuel Clayton),* Natalie Wood *(Debbie Edwards),* John Qualen *(Lars Jorgensen),* Olive Carey *(Mrs. Jorgensen),* Henry Brandon *(Chief Scar),* Ken Curtis *(Charlie McCorry),* Harry Carey Jr. *(Brad Jorgensen)*

p, Merian C. Cooper, C.V. Whitney; d, John Ford; w, Frank S. Nugent (based on the novel by Alan LeMay); ph, Winton C. Hoch (VistaVision, Technicolor); ed, Jack Murray; m, Max Steiner; art d, Frank Hotaling, James Basevi; fx, George Brown; cos, Frank Beetson, Ann Peck

"What makes a man to wander?/What makes a man to roam?/What makes a man leave bed and board and turn his back on home?/Ride away, ride away, ride away."

This sad and beautiful song accompanies the opening credits of what may be the finest and most ambitious film from director John Ford, America's premier poet of the Western. Part of what makes this classic film so remarkable is that these questions are never answered directly—an oddity for a product of Hollywood where loose ends are rarely allowed. This is the ultimate cult film for the new Hollywood. It is quoted and alluded to in numerous films such as HARD-CORE, TAXI DRIVER, CLOSE ENCOUNTERS OF THE THIRD KIND, and STAR WARS.

As THE SEARCHERS begins, we hear the extraordinarily beautiful strains of Max Steiner's score over darkness. A cabin door opens to reveal the harsh beauty of the arid Monument Valley in the distance. The silhouette of a frontier woman moves into the doorway. Far beyond we see a tiny figure on horseback approaching. "Ethan?" queries the woman uncertainly. The figure dismounts and walks toward the house. The woman is Martha Edwards (Dorothy Jordan), the wife of Ethan's brother. She is joined on the porch by her husband, Aaron (Walter Coy), their teenaged daughter, Lucy (Pippa Scott), 10-year-old Debbie (Lana Wood), and teenaged Ben (Robert Lyden). Ethan's clothes are filthy and he wears a faded Confederate coat. The children chant "Uncle Ethan! Uncle Ethan!" Ethan Edwards has finally come home—three years after the end of the Civil War.

John Wayne gives the performance of his career as Ethan Edwards, one of the most intriguing characters the American cinema has given us. Ethan is a mysterious obsessive man who rides in from the wastelands of Monument Valley into a small frontier farm settled by his brother years earlier. He has been missing since the end of the Civil War in which he fought for the Confederacy. He never turned up at the surrender to give up his sword and saber. He is also inexplicably carrying a large quantity of gold and, in the words of the local captain of the Texas Rangers, Reverend Samuel Clayton (Ward Bond), Ethan "fits a lot of descriptions."

The last family member to arrive is Martin Pawley (Jeffrey Hunter). Now nearly grown, Martin was saved years ago by Ethan when his parents were slaughtered by Indians. Ethan left him in the care of Aaron, who has raised him as his own son, but because Martin is one-eighth Cherokee, Ethan now treats him as a boarder rather than as one of the family.

The tranquility of the Edwards' lives is shattered when the local Commanche tribe goes on the warpath. Most of the men are lured away from the farm and the Edwards' farm is attacked. Most of the family is brutally murdered and the two daughters are abducted. The men form a search party and go off in hot pursuit. The ravaged body of the older girl is found and buried while the search for Debbie continues. When the winter snows come, most of the men turn back. Ethan is undaunted by this temporary setback. He and Martin resolve to continue the search and they do—for seven years. As the months drag on, Martin is amazed by Ethan's knowledge of the Indians' ways and his ability to read their signs and speak their language, but comes to realize that his guide is also a fanatical racist who intends to kill Debbie when they find her because she has become a "squaw."

THE SEARCHERS is an extremely rich film that continues to reveal new nuances with each viewing. The genre's traditional opposition between "Civilization" and "Wilderness" has rarely been as powerfully represented dramatically or visually. Ethan sees himself as an agent of civilization but his skills ally him with the forces of wilderness. He can find nowhere where he can be at peace and accepted. His difficulty in accepting a Native American as part of his family mirrors America's tensions regarding civil rights and integration in the 1950s. In a genre that has often be justly condemned for its racism, THE SEARCHERS—while hardly politically correct by modern standards—was a major breakthrough for Ford, Wayne, and the genre. The traditional Western hero and the Cavalry is shown in an unusually critical light. Furthermore the Native American point of view is considered for a change. By balancing points of view, Ford deepens and informs our understanding of the story. Equally well managed is the film's balance of drama and humor. THE SEARCHERS is essentially a tragedy, and without its humorous passages the film would have been almost too grim to bear (as was Alan LeMay's novel). The humor grows out of and illuminates character; even the hard-driven Ethan reveals a sense of irony and wit.

Ford's poetic visual sensibility has never been more richly demonstrated. The film provides an opportunity for numerous striking portraits of John Wayne set against the western vistas in color and widescreen. If you had to pick an ultimate Western still, it would probably come from this film. THE SEARCHERS is also that rare sound film in which more is revealed through facial expression, physical stance, and subtle gesture than through dialogue. Deep and complex insights into characters are all beautifully conveyed by body language. All in all, this is about as good as Hollywood filmmaking gets. A deeply emotional experience that is also a grand entertainment, THE SEARCHERS is a true American masterpiece.

SEARCHING FOR BOBBY FISCHER

1993 110m c Drama
Paramount/Mirage Productions (U.S.) PG

Max Pomeranc (Josh Waitzkin), Joe Mantegna (Fred Waitzkin), Joan Allen (Bonnie Waitzkin), Ben Kingsley (Bruce Pandolfini), Laurence Fishburne (Vinnie), Michael Nirenberg (Jonathan Poe), Robert Stephens (Poe's Teacher), David Paymer (Kalev), William H. Macy (Tunafish Father), Dan Hedaya (Tournament Director)

p, Scott Rudin, William Horberg; d, Steve Zaillian; w, Steve Zaillian (from the book by Fred Waitzkin); ph, Conrad L. Hall; ed, Wayne Wahrman; m, James Horner; prod d, David Gropman; art d, Gregory Keen; cos, Julie Weiss

AAN Best Cinematography: Conrad L. Hall

A rare family film that's not afraid to inject conflict and complexity into its images of domestic happiness.

Based on the real-life story of chess prodigy Josh Waitzkin, SEARCHING begins with the seven-year-old boy (Max Pomeranc) becoming enthralled by the matches he sees being played in New York's Washington Square Park. Josh, it turns out, harbors a rare talent for the game and, encouraged by his sportswriter father (Joe Mantegna), begins to learn more about it from two markedly different teachers: Vinnie (Laurence Fishburne), a kind of chess bum who apparently lives in the park and plays with a fast, streetwise style; and Bruce Pandolfini (Ben Kingsley), a reclusive scholar with a purist intellectual approach. Josh soon becomes a chess star, moving some to compare him to the young Bobby Fischer. (Excerpts from Fischer's life are narrated in voice-over by Josh, providing a poignant parallel to his own story.) Success, however, brings the inevitable pitfalls. His father's support starts to look like obsession, causing friction within the family; and Josh's confidence and innocence are fractured by the appearance of a brilliant young rival.

Though SEARCHING finally ties up its loose ends a little too neatly, what comes before that is a joy; an engrossing, witty story about far more than chess, directed with a flawless eye for detail and superbly performed by some of the best actors around—including young Mr. Pomeranc.

SECONDS

1966 106m bw Mystery/Thriller ★★★★
Paramount (U.S.)

Rock Hudson (Antiochus "Tony" Wilson), Salome Jens (Nora Marcus), John Randolph (Arthur Hamilton), Will Geer (Old Man), Jeff Corey (Mr. Ruby), Richard Anderson (Dr. Innes), Murray Hamilton (Charlie Evans), Karl Swenson (Dr. Morris), Khigh Dhiegh (Davalo), Frances Reid (Emily Hamilton)

p, Edward Lewis; d, John Frankenheimer; w, Lewis John Carlino (based on the novel Seconds by David Ely); ph, James Wong Howe; ed, Ferris Webster, David Webster; m, Jerry Goldsmith; art d, Ted Haworth

AAN Best B/W Cinematography: James Wong Howe

Middle-aged New York businessman Arthur Hamilton (John Randolph) is blackmailed into accepting the services of a clandestine organization which provides paunchy middle-aged businessmen with new lives through plastic surgery, physical reconditioning and reckless career placement. The end result is that Arthur Hamilton is transformed into Tony Wilson (Rock Hudson), a swinging bachelor and abstract painter with a groovy pad by the California seashore, a girlfriend (Salome Jens), and a butler (Wesley Addy) who is unusually anxious for his boss to indulge in heavy partying activities. Unfortunately, Tony Wilson still acts a lot like Arthur Hamilton: he can't hold his liquor and he's afraid of girls. After hosting a disastrous cocktail party for some of his neighbors, Wilson is shipped back to corporate headquarters for some fine tuning. He's willing to give it another try and has some thoughtful suggestions for his next "placement" and for the future of the program. The Old Man (Will Geer), the founder of the organization that got him into this mess in the first place, is appreciative, but nonetheless has other ideas for the body of Tony Wilson and the soul of Arthur Hamilton.

SECONDS received mixed reviews, and was critically savaged at the Cannes Film Festival, but repeated showings on late night television have improved its reputation to the point where it is now considered a cult classic. The film features a surprisingly good performance by Rock Hudson, an impeccable supporting cast and stunning cinematography by screen veteran James Wong Howe.

SECRET AGENT

1936 83m bw Spy ★★★½
Gaumont (U.K.)

Madeleine Carroll (Elsa Carrington), John Gielgud (Edgar Brodie/Richard Ashenden), Peter Lorre (The General), Robert Young (Robert Marvin), Percy Marmont (Caypor), Florence Kahn (Mrs. Caypor), Lilli Palmer (Lilli), Charles Carson ("R"), Michel Saint-Denis (Coachman), Andreas Malandrinos (Manager)

p, Michael Balcon, Ivor Montagu; d, Alfred Hitchcock; w, Charles Bennett, Ian Hay, Jesse Lasky Jr., Alma Reville (based on the play by Campbell Dixon, from the stories "Triton" and "The Hairless Mexican" in the book Ashenden by W. Somerset Maugham); ph, Bernard Knowles; ed, Charles Frend; cos, Joe Strassner

One of a string of British espionage thrillers Hitchcock directed in the mid-1930s (THE 39 STEPS preceded it in 1935 and SABOTAGE followed in 1936), this one begins in England, 1916, with the funeral of war hero and famed novelist Edgar Brodie (Gielgud). The funeral is a ruse, however, with Brodie still very much alive and in the service of British Intelligence. He is given a new identity, Richard Ashenden, and sent to Switzerland to terminate an enemy agent—although no one knows the identity or description of the agent. Also assigned to the mission are agents Elsa Carrington (Carroll), who is undercover as Ashenden's wife, and The General (Lorre), a demented, sexually charged, professional killer, and together they chase through the Swiss Alps to carry out their operation. SECRET AGENT bursts with not-so-hidden sexual innuendos and a heavy dose of comic dialogue, as well as Lorre's unrestrained lunatic comic performance. Based on two Somerset Maugham stories (for the espionage angle) and a Campbell Dixon play (for the romance), SECRET AGENT did not perform at the box office as well as Hitchcock had hoped. Although the director has cited this film among his favorites, he felt that its fault was in having a main character with whom the audience could not identify. London-based animator Len Lye (who had, in 1934, invented a technique for painting directly on film) had created, for the climactic train crash scene, a piece of brightly colored film which was to make it appear as if the film itself had burst into flames. Proving too much of a distraction, the effect was eliminated in the film's preview screenings.

SECRET GARDEN, THE
1993 101m c Children's/Drama ★★★
American Zoetrope/Warner Bros. (U.S.) G

Kate Maberly *(Mary Lennox)*, Heydon Prowse *(Colin Craven)*, Andrew Knott *(Dickon)*, Maggie Smith *(Mrs. Medlock)*, Laura Crossley *(Martha)*, John Lynch *(Lord Craven)*, Walter Sparrow *(Ben Weatherstaff)*, Irene Jacob *(Mary's Mother/Lilias Craven)*, Frank Baker *(Government Official)*, Valerie Hill *(Cook)*

p, Fred Fuchs, Fred Roos, Tom Luddy; d, Agnieszka Holland; w, Caroline Thompson (from the novel by Frances Hodgson Burnett); ph, Roger Deakins; ed, Isabelle Lorente; prod d, Stuart Craig; art d, Peter Russell; fx, John Evans, Digby Milner, Peter Dawson, Peter Pickering, Simon Hewitt; cos, Marit Allen

Polish director Agnieszka Holland, who scored an art-house hit in the U.S. with EUROPA, EUROPA, deserved to find her way into the hearts of a larger audience with this reworking of Frances Hodgson Burnett's classic childrens' tale. Though it can get laborious, and produces the odd unintended chuckle, THE SECRET GARDEN is charming and sometimes chillingly authentic.

At the center of the film is young Mary Lennox, winningly played by English actress Kate Maberly in her feature debut. Orphaned by an earthquake in India, Mary is sent to a forbidding Gothic house in the north of England to be looked after by her widower uncle, Lord Craven (John Lynch). Since he wants nothing to do with her, she is effectively left in the charge of the dour, mean-spirited housekeeper, Mrs. Medlock (Maggie Smith). Things look rather grim until Mary discovers a garden that her aunt had tended and that Craven declared off-limits after her death, as well as a companion on each side of the great English class divide: Colin (Heydon Prowse), Craven's invalid son; and Dickon (Andrew Knott), a young, Yorkshire Dr. Dolittle who walks and talks with the animals.

While there's nothing subtle about the story's metaphors of growth and rebirth, Holland avoids cliches as deftly as she does the hero/villain syndrome. The dark, oppressive characters have reasons for being that way, and Mary and Colin can be just as obnoxious as they are sympathetic.

SECRET LIFE OF WALTER MITTY, THE
1947 105m c Fantasy/Comedy ★★★★
Goldwyn (U.S.)

Danny Kaye *(Walter Mitty)*, Virginia Mayo *(Rosalind van Hoorn)*, Boris Karloff *(Dr. Hugo Hollingshead)*, Fay Bainter *(Mrs. Mitty)*, Ann Rutherford *(Gertrude Griswold)*, Thurston Hall *(Bruce Pierce)*, Konstantin Shayne *(Peter van Hoorn)*, Florence Bates *(Mrs. Griswold)*, Gordon Jones *(Tubby Wadsworth)*, Reginald Denny *(RAF Colonel)*

p, Samuel Goldwyn; d, Norman Z. McLeod; w, Ken Englund, Everett Freeman (based on the story by James Thurber); ph, Lee Garmes (Technicolor); ed, Monica Collingwood; m, David Raksin;

art d, George Jenkins, Perry Ferguson; fx, John P. Fulton; cos, Irene Sharaff

Though James Thurber offered to give producer Sam Goldwyn $10,000 *not to* film his classic short story, the rights to which Goldwyn had purchased, THE SECRET LIFE OF WALTER MITTY is still an outstanding production and possibly Kaye's best film. Thurber's tale about a middle-aged man who escapes reality by imagining himself in all sorts of heroic situations doesn't lose much in the film adaptation.

Though it slips into slapstick toward the end, THE SECRET LIFE OF WALTER MITTY is enjoyable and presents more genuinely funny scenes than most comedies. Goldwyn sank more than $3 million into this sumptuous showcase for Kaye, parading his statuesque Goldwyn Girls through some of the star's big musical numbers. Mayo is alluring, Bainter is terrific as the overbearing mom, and Hall stands out as the ghoulish publisher. Without the aid of makeup, Karloff also does a great burlesque of himself as the monster from FRANKENSTEIN. And throughout the film there is that memorable sound of Kaye's imaginary life-saving machine—"pucketa, pucketa, pucketa."

SECRET OF NIMH, THE
1982 82m c Animated/Children's ★★★
MGM-UA (U.S.) G

VOICES OF: Derek Jacobi *(Nicodemus)*, Elizabeth Hartman *(Mrs. Brisby)*, Arthur Malet *(Ages)*, Dom DeLuise *(Jeremy)*, Hermione Baddeley *(Auntie Shrew)*, John Carradine *(Great Owl)*, Peter Strauss *(Justin)*, Paul Shenar *(Jennar)*, Tom Hattan *(Farmer Fitzgibbons)*, Shannen Doherty *(Teresa)*

p, Don Bluth, Gary Goldman, John Pomeroy; d, Don Bluth; w, Don Bluth, Gary Goldman, John Pomeroy, Will Finn (based on the novel *Mrs. Frisby and the Rats of N.I.M.H.* by Robert C. O'Brien); ph, Joe Jiuliano, Charles Warren, Jeff Mellquist (Technicolor); ed, Jeffrey Patch; m, Jerry Goldsmith; fx, D.A. Lanpher, Tom Hush

This superbly animated (but weakly scripted) tale was produced by Don Bluth, who left Disney Studios when he became dissatisfied with the quality of their animated films in the 1970s, taking a dozen of Disney's best animators with him. The result is a return to the lush, finely detailed animation seen in the best Disney features. This is the story of a mother mouse's desperate attempt to move her family to a new location before they are killed by the farmer who is soon to plow his field. Although hindered by her son's illness, the mother mouse gets help from some escaped laboratory rats with superior intelligence. Among the actors who lend their vocal talents to the proceedings are Dom DeLuise and the fine British stage actor Derek Jacobi.

SECRET OF ROAN INISH, THE
1995 102m c Fantasy/Romance/Children's ★★★½
Skerry Movies Corporation/Peter Newman PG
Productions (U.S.)

Jeni Courtney *(Fiona Coneelly)*, Mick Lally *(Hugh Coneelly)*, Eileen Colgan *(Tess Coneelly)*, Richard Sheridan *(Eamon)*, John Lynch *(Tadhg)*, Cillian Byrne *(Jamie)*, Susan Lynch *(Selkie Woman)*, Frankie McCafferty, Fergal McElheron, Brendan Conroy

p, Maggie Renzi, Sarah Green; d, John Sayles; w, John Sayles (based on the book *The Secret of Ron Mor Skerry* by Rosalie K. Fry); ph, Haskell Wexler; ed, John Sayles; m, Mason Daring; prod d, Adrian Smith; art d, Henry Harris; fx, Trevor Neighbour; cos, Consolata Boyle

A change of pace from filmmaker John Sayles, better known for realistic dramas, this is a lush, allegorical fairy tale filmed in Ireland. Darkly lyrical and imbued with a genuine sense of magic, ROAN INISH has the haunted quality of Irish folk music.

In late 1940s Ireland, an unemployed widower sends his young daughter, Fiona (Jeni Courtney), to live with her grandparents, Tess (Eileen Colgan) and Hugh Coneelly (Mick Lally), in a northwest coast fishing village. Hugh tells Fiona the story of how, years earlier, her baby brother, Jamie, was swept out to sea in his cradle, and Fiona becomes obsessed with finding the boy. Fiona's search begins on the nearby island of Roan Inish ("seal island"), where she soon finds herself on the trail of a mysterious half-human sea creature called the Selkie.

During the 1980s, John Sayles earned a reputation as a maker of serious, topical independent films about worthy subjects. Ironically, this seemingly innocuous children's fantasy is his most satisfying film to date. Thanks to his earnest, straightforward approach to unlikely material (the source is a 1957 novella, *Secret of the Ron Mor Skerry*, by Rosalie K. Fry), Sayles ends up tempering the excesses of what might have been sentimental blarney. Here, he creates a fresh, captivating mise-en-scene, simultaneously realistic and magical (Haskell Wexler's cinematography of the Irish locales is crucial here). A highlight is the Selkie myth, which is depicted with a refreshing minimum of camera tricks and special effects. Another great sequence is the Old Hollywood-style montage illustrating the children's rebuilding of the cottage on Roan Inish. In all, this is family entertainment in the best sense of the term.

SECRETS & LIES

1995 142m c   Drama   ★★★★½
CiBy 2000/Thin Man Films   (U.K.)   R

Timothy Spall *(Maurice)*, Phyllis Logan *(Monica)*, Brenda Blethyn *(Cynthia)*, Claire Rushbrook *(Roxanne)*, Marianne Jean-Baptiste *(Hortense)*, Elizabeth Berrington *(Jane)*, Michele Austin *(Dionne)*, Lee Ross *(Paul)*, Lesley Manville *(Social Worker)*, Ron Cook *(Stuart)*

p, Simon Channing-Williams; d, Mike Leigh; w, Mike Leigh; ph, Dick Pope; ed, John Gregory; m, Andrew Dickson; prod d, Alison Chitty, Georgina Lowe; cos, Maria Price

---

AAN Best Picture; AAN Best Actress: Brenda Blethyn; *AAN Best Supporting Actress:* Marianne Jean-Baptiste; *AAN Best Director:* Mike Leigh; *AAN Best Original Screenplay:* Mike Leigh

Winner of the Palme d'Or at Cannes, Mike Leigh's SECRETS & LIES is a fascinating, brilliantly acted slice-of-life drama.

After the death of her adoptive mother, Hortense (Marianne Jean-Baptiste), a young black woman living in London, learns that Cynthia (Brenda Blethyn), a white, middle-aged single parent, is her birth mother. When Hortense telephones her, Cynthia is initially shocked, but agrees to meet her at a coffeeshop. When they see each other, Cynthia assumes there has been a mistake, until she remembers having had a one-night stand with a black man. The two develop an understanding, and Cynthia decides to present Hortense to her family at the 21st birthday party of Roxanne (Claire Rushbrook), Cynthia's other daughter.

On paper, the plot of a Mike Leigh film often sounds like the stuff of TV soap opera, and that's especially true in the case of SECRETS & LIES. But where soaps breed familiarity over time, Leigh and his actors hone characters so sharply that viewers become as familiar with them over the running time of a film as they would with people they have known for years. Leigh's films are staged simply, not because of laziness or indifference, but because he has in every case found the best point from which to view the proceedings. SECRETS & LIES contains several long scenes shot in single takes that would be impossible for actors working under standard film-

ing conditions: the long take of Cynthia and Hortense at their first meeting is particularly astonishing. This scene alone is enough to merit the Best Actress Award Blethyn received at Cannes, as well as the Oscar nominations for both her and Jean-Baptiste. SECRETS & LIES may be a trifle long, but there isn't a moment that needs to be cut.

SECRETS OF WOMEN
(KVINNORS VANTAN)
1952 114m bw Drama/Comedy   ★★★½
Svensk   (Sweden)

Anita Bjork *(Rakel)*, Karl-Arne Holmsten *(Eugen Lobelius)*, Jarl Kulle *(Kaj)*, Maj-Britt Nilsson *(Marta)*, Eva Dahlbeck *(Karin)*, Gunnar Bjornstrand *(Fredrik Lobelius)*, Birger Malmsten *(Martin)*, Gerd Andersson *(Maj)*, Bjorn Bjelvenstam *(Henrik)*, Aino Taube *(Annette)*

p, Allan Ekelund; d, Ingmar Bergman; w, Ingmar Bergman; ph, Gunnar Fischer; ed, Oscar Rosander; m, Erik Nordgren; art d, Nils Svenwall

---

This mostly light-hearted comedy was written by Bergman during what he considered a dark time in his life—which seems strange, considering how much fun the film is. Divided into three parts, SECRETS OF WOMEN is told in flashback as the wives of the Lobelius brothers converse about past romantic experiences. The first section (based on a Bergman play) relates the tale of Rakel's (Anita Bjork) infidelity with an old lover, the second depicts Marta's (Maj-Britt Nilsson) Parisian affair and subsequent marriage to Martin (Birger Malmsten), and the last takes place in a broken elevator that strands Karin (Eva Dahlbeck) and husband Fredrik (Gunnar Bjornstrand). At the conclusion of these three stories, a fourth Lobelius wife (Aino Taube) decides to keep her story to herself. Although this is one of several well-received comedies that Bergman somewhat grudgingly turned out at the request of the Swedish film industry in the 1950s, it still shows a deliberate attempt on the director's part to advance his cinematic style. In the elevator sequence especially, Bergman, under the influence of Alfred Hitchcock, tried primarily to let images tell his story, keeping the dialogue to a minimum.

SECRETARY
2002 111m c   Comedy/Drama   ★★½
Double A Films/Slough Pond/TwoPound   R
Bag Productions   (U.S.)

James Spader *(E. Edward Grey)*, Maggie Gyllenhaal *(Lee Holloway)*, Jeremy Davies *(Peter)*, Lesley Ann Warren *(Joan Holloway)*, Stephen McHattie *(Burt Holloway)*, Patrick Bauchau *(Dr. Twardon)*, Jessica Tuck *(Tricia O'Connor)*, Oz Perkins *(Jonathan)*, Amy Locane *(Lee's Sister)*, Mary Joy *(Sylvia)*

p, Andrew Fierberg, Amy Hobby, Steven Shainberg; d, Steven Shainberg; w, Erin Cressida Wilson (based on the story by Mary Gaitskill, adapted by Steven Shainberg and Erin Cressida Wilson); ph, Steve Fierberg; ed, Pam Wise; m, Angelo Badalamenti; prod d, Amy Danger; art d, Nick Ralbovsky; fx, Randall Balsmeyer; cos, Marjorie Bowers

---

Before it devolves into a bizarre romantic comedy, Steven Shainberg's adaptation of Mary Gaitskill's harrowing short story about dominance, submission, and the twisted sexual dynamics of the workplace is a brilliantly played, deeply unsettling experience.

Lee Holloway (Maggie Gyllenhaal) is fresh out of the sanitarium but still unable to keep her obsessive compulsion to cut herself in check. Egged on by her coddling mother (Lesley Ann Warren), Lee takes a secretarial job at the offices of E. Edmund Grey, Esq. (James Spader), a damp and furtive lawyer. The mind games begin as soon as he notices the telltale pattern of tiny Band-Aids on the backs of Lee's thighs.

Mr. Grey sets out an assortment of bizarre and demeaning tasks for her to perform and asks Lee probing, inappropriate questions. And when Mr. Grey decides he can no longer tolerate the typos on Lee's documents, he bends her over his desk and administers a stern spanking that leaves Lee sore, humiliated, and disconcertingly aroused.

So far, so good. Shainberg gets right to the dark heart of Gaitskill's story with startling directness, and his two stars are so in synch it's like watching two psyches surgically exposed with a scalpel. And then it's as if another director stepped in for a game of cinematic exquisite corpse. Grey's assault on Lee turns into a moment of sexual liberation; she's a kinky girl, and her boss has only given her what she needed all along. When Mr. Grey's interest in his secretary flags, this once edgy film becomes a silly madcap comedy, spiced up by an air of naughty chic that's more John Willie than Mary Gaitskill.

SEDUCTION OF JOE TYNAN, THE

1979 107m c Political ★★★½
Universal (U.S.) R

Alan Alda (Joe Tynan), Barbara Harris (Ellie), Meryl Streep (Karen Traynor), Rip Torn (Sen. Kittner), Melvyn Douglas (Sen. Birney), Charles Kimbrough (Francis), Carrie Nye (Aldena Kittner), Michael Higgins (Sen. Pardew), Blanche Baker (Janet), Adam Ross (Paul Tynan)

p, Martin Bregman; d, Jerry Schatzberg; w, Alan Alda; ph, Adam Holender (Technicolor); ed, Evan Lottman; m, Bill Conti; art d, David Chapman; cos, Jo Ynocencio

A fine political drama with lots of comedy on the order of THE CANDIDATE, THE BEST MAN, and several others in the genre. Alda proved himself a good writer with this intelligent and observant screenplay loosely based on the supposed life of Ted Kennedy. The seduction of the title refers to the corrupting potential of political power. Alda is a liberal senator married to Harris, with two children, Ross and Baker. Harris hates being in the limelight, while Alda revels in it. His basically nice nature is seen to change as he rises higher in the national scene. He dallies with labor lawyer Streep but recognizes the affair as basically dishonest and returns to Harris. The performances are fine. Harris especially is sensational, conveying more with a look than many actresses can with 10 pages of dialogue. Torn is vigorous and compelling as a powerful lawmaker. Douglas, who made a career out of portraying public figures near the end of his life (he was the President's adviser in BEING THERE), is superb as a man who's seen his best days and is now looking forward bleakly to his last. The film delves beneath the phony smiles, hearty handshakes, and false sentiment that politics engenders. Viewers may never believe a candidate's speech again.

SEDUCTION OF MIMI, THE
(MIMI METALLURGICO FERITO NELL'ONORE) *DVD*
1972 92m c Drama ★★★½
Vera/Euro-International (Italy) R

Giancarlo Giannini (Carmelo "Mimi" Mardocheco), Mariangela Melato (Fiore), Agostina Belli (Rosalia), Elena Fiore (Signora Finocchiaro), Turi Ferro (Tricarico), Agostina Belli, Luigi Diberti, Tuccio Musumeci, Ignazio Pappalardo, Rosaria Rapisarda

p, Daniele Senatore, Romano Cardarelli; d, Lina Wertmuller; w, Lina Wertmuller; ph, Dario Di Palma; ed, Franco Fraticelli; m, Piero Piccioni

This early film by Lina Wertmuller earned her the Best Director prize at the Cannes Film Festival and stars Giancarlo Giannini as a Sicilian metallurgist named Mimi. After refusing to vote for the Mafia candidate in a local election, Mimi

loses his factory job and decides to head north for work. Although professing to be communist, he is eager to get rich, enjoy a life of luxury, and step on his fellow workers. Leaving behind his wife, Rosalia (Agostina Belli), whom he cruelly dominates and castigates for her infertility, Mimi finds work in Turin. There, he falls in love with Fiore (Mariangela Melato), a virgin anarchist who bears him a child. Mimi's idyllic life in the north is sabotaged, however, by the menacing Mafia-controlled authorities who transfer him back to Sicily. A clever examination of the bonds between sexual and political power, and the differences between the "civilized" northern Italians and the "barbaric" southerners, Wertmuller's film comes to life through Giannini's bravura performance; a macho brute and philistine, his Mimi is still a sympathetic character, more victim than victimizer. The videocassette is dubbed in English though, as in LOVE AND ANARCHY, the image appears to have been squeezed into the television format.

SEMI-TOUGH *DVD*
1977 108m c Comedy/Sports ★★★
UA (U.S.) R

Burt Reynolds (Billy Clyde Puckett), Kris Kristofferson (Shake Tiller), Jill Clayburgh (Barbara Jane Bookman), Robert Preston (Big Ed Bookman), Bert Convy (Friedrich Bismark), Roger E. Mosley (Puddin), Lotte Lenya (Clara Pelf), Richard Masur (Phillip Hooper), Carl Weathers (Dreamer Tatum), Brian Dennehy (T.J. Lambert)

p, David Merrick; d, Michael Ritchie; w, Walter Bernstein (based on the novel by Dan Jenkins); ph, Charles Rosher Jr.; ed, Richard A. Harris; m, Jerry Fielding; prod d, Walter Scott Herndon; cos, Theoni V. Aldredge

Set against the backdrop of professional football, SEMI-TOUGH is both a three-cornered romantic comedy and a scathing satire of self-help movements. Reynolds and Kristofferson are teammates on a fictitious Super Bowl-bound Miami football team owned by Preston, a recent convert to BEAT, the est-like way to a better life "gurued" by Convy. Recently returned from Africa, Preston's twice-divorced daughter, Clayburgh, reappraises her longtime friends, Reynolds and Kristofferson, and finds the latter, whom Convy has led to BEAT, not only a changed man but a suitable fiance. The trouble is Reynolds is in love with Clayburgh; however, being a resourceful guy, he manages to poke a hole in Convy's BEAT bubble, pull off some Super Bowl magic, and make sure that the right guy ends up with Preston's daughter. Based on a book by Dan Jenkins, SEMI-TOUGH is periodically funny and frequently on target in its satire, and it boasts a strong performance from Reynolds (who also starred in the football-themed THE LONGEST YARD). Jenkins's novel did not include the self-help lampooning, which was introduced into the story by screenwriter Bernstein at the insistence of director Ritchie (THE BAD NEWS BEARS; DOWNHILL RACER). Several sportscasters and former football players appear in the film in character or as themselves, including Joe Kapp, Carl Weathers (ROCKY), Paul Hornung, and Lindsay Nelson.

SENSE AND SENSIBILITY *DVD*
1995 135m c Drama/Romance ★★★½
Mirage Enterprises (U.S.) PG

Emma Thompson (Elinor Dashwood), Kate Winslet (Marianne Dashwood), Alan Rickman (Colonel Brandon), Hugh Grant (Edward Ferrars), Greg Wise (John Willoughby), Emilie Francois (Margaret Dashwood), Elizabeth Spriggs (Mrs. Jennings), Gemma Jones (Mrs. Dashwood), Harriet Walter (Fanny Dashwood), James Fleet (John Dashwood) p, Lindsay Doran; d, Ang Lee; w, Emma Thompson (based on the novel by Jane Austen); ph, Michael Coulter; ed, Tim Squyres; m, Patrick Doyle; prod d, Luciana Arrighi; art d, Philip Elton; fx, Ricky Farns, Randall Balsmeyer; cos, Jenny Beavan, John Bright

AAN Best Picture; AAN Best Supporting Actress: Kate Winslet; *AAN Best Actress:* Emma Thompson; *AA Best Adapted Screenplay:* Emma Thompson; *AAN Best Cinematography:* Michael Coulter; *AAN Best Costume Design:* Jenny Beavan, John Bright; *AAN Best Dramatic Score:* Patrick Doyle

To Hollywood's astonishment, SENSE AND SENSIBILI-TY was something very close to a blockbuster hit. First-time screenwriter Emma Thompson and director Ang Lee combined their talents for a graceful adaptation of Jane Austen's well-loved novel. If the result is not as sharp as Austen's prose, it is nonetheless as handsome and intelligent an adaptation as one could reasonably expect.

John Dashwood (James Fleet) inherits the entirety of his father's estate, Norland, since law does not permit his father to leave property to John's half-sisters. Prodded by his haughty wife Fanny (Harriet Walter), he minimizes his settlement on his stepmother and her daughters, and the couple moves into Norland. Mrs. Dashwood and her daughters—sensible Elinor (Emma Thompson), passionate Marianne (Kate Winslet), and young tomboy Margaret (Emilie Francois) prepare to vacate their home. Compelled by economics and convention, the three must begin a search for socially suitable husbands—happiness, of course, is only a secondary consideration.

Beautifully helmed by Lee, SENSE AND SENSIBILI-TY surprised many who saw the Taiwanese director as an odd choice for this comedy of 19th-century British manners. However, Lee's earlier works—e.g., THE WEDDING BANQUET and EAT DRINK MAN WOMAN—are not as far from Austen's worldview as it might seem. These are delicately wrought studies of social mores; especially where marriage is concerned, a highly structured society forces propriety and money to take precedence over love. Lee's frequently distanced framing works as a cinematic rendering of Austen's coolly ironic prose, and his camera angles and moving shots are splendid. Lee also elicits uniformly excellent performances from his cast, with Thompson and Winslet particularly fine. Thompson also deserves credit for a faithful, intelligent screenplay which never rushes through Austen's plot.

SEPARATE TABLES 📀
1958 98m bw Drama ★★★★½
Clifton/Joanna (U.S.)

Deborah Kerr (*Sibyl Railton-Bell*), Rita Hayworth (*Ann Shankland*), David Niven (*Maj. Pollack*), Wendy Hiller (*Miss Pat Cooper*), Burt Lancaster (*John Malcolm*), Gladys Cooper (*Mrs. Railton-Bell*), Cathleen Nesbitt (*Lady Matheson*), Felix Aylmer (*Mr. Fowler*), Rod Taylor (*Charles*), Audrey Dalton (*Jean*)

p, Harold Hecht; d, Delbert Mann; w, Terence Rattigan, John Gay (based on the play by Rattigan); ph, Charles Lang; ed, Marjorie Fowler, Charles Ennis; m, David Raksin; prod d, Harry Horner; art d, Edward Carrere; cos, Edith Head, Mary Grant

AAN Best Picture; AA Best Actor: David Niven; *AAN Best Actress:* Deborah Kerr; *AA Best Supporting Actress:* Wendy Hiller; *AAN Best Adapted Screenplay:* Terence Rattigan, John Gay; *AAN Best B/W Cinematography:* Charles Lang Jr.; *AAN Best Score (Drama or Comedy):* David Raksin

Superb drama, marred by an unexpected failure among the brilliant cast. It's Deborah Kerr, overacting a repressed spinster almost to the point of retardation. That Delbert Mann could pull such fine work from the rest of the ensemble makes the usually strong Kerr's performance all the more curious, for hers is a career built on underacting.

Terence Rattigan's original play consisted of two one-acts set in the same Bournemouth, England locale. It was a tour de force for Eric Portman and Margaret Leighton, who played it successfully in London, then in New York during the fall of 1956. Rattigan collaborated with John Gay to blend the two stories into one that used four leads instead of two. The title refers to the practice of seating solo guests at their own dining tables. The small hotel is at the seashore, and the dining room is filled with a host of lonely people. Niven is a very British retired major who waxes on about his experiences in the war's North African campaign, but his stories have the ring of prevarication about them. Cooper is a stern and forceful matriarch (a Cooper specialty; was anyone ever better at these roles?) with daughter, Kerr, a mousey spinster fascinated by Niven but far too shy to let him know. Hiller, who runs the hotel, devotes herself to the comfort of others. It distracts her from troubles with her lover, Lancaster, a reclusive American writer who drinks more than he creates and spends much of his time in his room (with his macho bluster, Lancaster brings a Hemingway feeling to the role). Aging socialite Hayworth, Lancaster's former wife, arrives unexpectedly at the hotel, and everyone's lives begin to unravel simultaneously.

This is adult, intelligent stuff, marvelously shaded by the amalgamation of talents. That Niven and Hiller are sublime is almost to be expected. But one watches Hayworth with genuine surprise, as the poignant divorcee watching her beauty slip away. This kind of part is usually the province of Englishwomen—Vivien Leigh, for example. It's the only strong mature role she ever got to play. Lancaster, cast against two women whose talents have an air of gentility, is able to tone down his trademark bravura. Besides Miss Kerr, wouldn't it have been lovely to have been spared Vic Damone's insistent croon over the opening credits?

SERGEANT YORK
1941 134m bw War/Biography ★★★★
Warner Bros. (U.S.)

Gary Cooper (*Alvin C. York*), Walter Brennan (*Pastor Rosier Pile*), Joan Leslie (*Gracie Williams*), George Tobias (*Michael T. "Pusher" Ross*), Stanley Ridges (*Maj. Buxton*), Margaret Wycherly (*Mother York*), Ward Bond (*Ike Botkin*), Noah Beery Jr. (*Buck Lipscomb*), June Lockhart (*Rose York*), Dickie Moore (*George York*)

p, Jesse L. Lasky, Hal B. Wallis; d, Howard Hawks; w, Abem Finkel, Harry Chandlee, Howard Koch, John Huston (based on *War Diary of Sergeant York* by Sam K. Cowan, *Sergeant York and His People* by Cowan, and *Sergeant York—Last of the Long Hunters* by Tom Skeyhill); ph, Sol Polito, Arthur Edeson (war sequences); ed, William Holmes; m, Max Steiner; art d, John Hughes

AAN Best Picture; AA Best Actor: Gary Cooper; *AAN Best Supporting Actor:* Walter Brennan; *AAN Best Supporting Actress:* Margaret Wycherly; *AAN Best Director:* Howard Hawks; *AAN Best Original Screenplay:* Harry Chandlee, Abem Finkel, John Huston, Howard Koch; *AAN Best B/W Cinematography:* Sol Polito; *AA Best Film Editing:* William Holmes; *AAN Best Score (Drama):* Max Steiner; *AAN Best Interior Decoration (B/W):* John Hughes, Fred MacLean; *AAN Best Sound Recording:* Nathan Levinson

Predictable, a trifle slow, but ultimately winning. Gary Cooper won his first Oscar for his strong portrayal here of WWI hero Alvin C. York, who single-handedly captured 132 German soldiers during the Meuse-Argonne offensive and became one of America's most decorated and beloved heroes. Beginning in 1916, Howard Hawks' masterfully directed film follows the man from the hills of East Tennessee as he falls in love with Gracie Williams (Joan Leslie) and struggles to hold onto his land. When lightning strikes his rifle, York views it a sign from

God and, becoming a pacifist, tries to avoid service in WWI. Eventually he does fight in France, however, and the rest is spectacular military history. Hawks brings the life of this incredible hero to the screen with forceful integrity, and Cooper is wonderful as the country fellow who gets religion and holds onto it, even through the nightmare of war. Technically, the film is faultless, with Hawks keeping his cameras fluid and employing Sol Polito's magnificent photographic skills at every turn.

Jesse Lasky, who saw York in the 1919 Armistice Day Parade, spent years trying to convince the modest Tennessean to allow his story to be filmed, finally winning York's approval provided that the proceeds go to charity and that Gary Cooper play him. At first Cooper refused, but he changed his mind after visiting York. Warner Bros. had hoped to have Michael Curtiz direct SERGEANT YORK, but Cooper wouldn't work with him, and when several others couldn't take the job, Hawks was hired, to the lasting pleasure of all who see this magnificent film. That's Robert Porterfield as Zeb Andrews; he established Barter Theater, Virginia's state theater, the oldest repertory still running in the United States.

SERPICO
DVD
1973 129m c Biography/Crime ★★★★
Artists Entertainment/DEG (U.S.) R

Al Pacino (Frank Serpico), Tony Roberts (Bob Blair), John Randolph (Chief Sidney Green), Jack Kehoe (Tom Keough), Biff McGuire (Capt. McClain), Barbara Eda-Young (Laurie), Cornelia Sharpe (Leslie), John Medici (Pasquale Serpico), Allan Rich (D.A. Tauber), Norman Ornellas (Rubello)

p, Martin Bregman; d, Sidney Lumet; w, Waldo Salt, Norman Wexler (based on the book by Peter Maas); ph, Arthur J. Ornitz (Technicolor); ed, Dede Allen, Richard Marks; m, Mikis Theodorakis; prod d, Charles Bailey; art d, Douglas Higgins; cos, Anna Hill Johnstone

AAN Best Actor: Al Pacino; AAN Best Adapted Screenplay: Waldo Salt, Wexler Norman

In 1970, police officer Frank Serpico electrified the Knapp Commission investigating the New York City Police Department by testifying that there were as many cops taking payoffs as there were crooks. Peter Maas's biography of Serpico formed the basis of the script by Waldo Salt (MIDNIGHT COWBOY) and Norman Wexler (SATURDAY NIGHT FEVER), and Al Pacino is the title character, an honest cop who refuses to go on the take.

Surrounded by corruption, Frank Serpico is distrusted and harrassed by fellow officers, who suspect him both for his honesty and for his countercultural lifestyle. When the double-dealing and persecution become too much, he tries to inform police commissioner White of the corruption within the department, but the response is discouraging. Frustrated, Serpico takes his story to the New York Times editors; the resultant scandal prompts the mayor to initiate a high-profile investigation. Serpico is called to testify, and now both cops and criminals are gunning for him.

All of the actors contribute excellent performances under the assured direction of Sidney Lumet, who replaced John Avildsen on the project. It's a particular pleasure to see Tony Roberts working in a film that wasn't directed by Woody Allen, and he is outstanding as Pacino's trusted pal. Oscar-winner F. Murray Abraham (AMADEUS), Mary Louise Weller (ANIMAL HOUSE), M. Emmet Walsh (STRAIGHT TIME), and Hank Garrett (THREE DAYS OF THE CONDOR) also appear in small but telling roles. But when all is said and done, Pacino is the riveting presence that makes the movie work and it is difficult to imagine any other actor in the part.

SERVANT, THE
DVD
1963 115m bw Drama ★★★½
Springbok (U.K.)

Dirk Bogarde (Hugo Barrett), Sarah Miles (Vera), Wendy Craig (Susan), James Fox (Tony), Catherine Lacey (Lady Mounset), Richard Vernon (Lord Mounset), Ann Firbank (Society Woman), Doris Knox (Older Woman), Patrick Magee (Bishop), Jill Melford (Younger Woman)

p, Joseph Losey, Norman Priggen; d, Joseph Losey; w, Harold Pinter (based on the novel by Robin Maugham); ph, Douglas Slocombe; ed, Reginald Mills; m, John Dankworth; prod d, Richard MacDonald; art d, Ted Clements; cos, Beatrice Dawson

Opaque but hypnotically absorbing allegory of power, exploitation, and sublimated sexuality in a class-based society. British screenwriter Harold Pinter and expatriate American director Joseph Losey (he'd run afoul of anti-Communist witch-hunters in the U.S.) married disparate sensibilities to tell the story of a dissipated Cockney servant (Dirk Bogarde) who trades roles with his master (James Fox), a classically effete aristocrat.

Although THE SERVANT's critical reputation has declined in recent years, it was initially received as an important, groundbreaking film, and won British Academy Awards for Best Actor (Bogarde), Most Promising Newcomer (Fox), and Best Cinematography (Douglas Slocombe, whose astonishing credit list encompasses over 70 films, including major works by Alexander Mackendrick, Roman Polanski, Steven Spielberg, John Huston, and Ken Russell). Pinter's adaptation of Robin Maugham's novel employs his customary strategies (e.g., fractured dialogue, cryptic silences, pregnant discussions of ostensible trivialities) but lacks the cockeyed humor of his best work for the stage. (Pinter appears in a cameo as a society man.) After working in major films throughout the '60s, Fox experienced a religious conversion in 1973 and retired from movies for several years. He is the younger brother of Edward Fox (DAY OF THE JACKAL, A BRIDGE TOO FAR), with whom he is often confused.

SET ME FREE
(EMPORTE-MOI)
1999 94m c Drama ★★★½
Cite-Amerique/Catpics/Haut et Court
(France/Canada/Switzerland)

Karine Vanasse (Hanna), Alexandre Merineau (Paul), Pascale Bussieres (The Mother), Miki Manojlovic (The Father), Charlotte Christeler (Laura), Nancy Huston (The Teacher), Monique Mercure (The Grandmother), Anne-Marie Cadieux (The Prostitute), Marie-Helene Gagnon (The Landlady), Sebastien Burns (Sebastien)

p, Lorraine Richard; d, Lea Pool; w, Lea Pool, Nancy Huston, Monique H. Messier, Isabelle Raynault; ph, Jeanne Lapoirie; ed, Michel Arcand; m, ECM; prod d, Serge Bureau; art d, Serge Bureau; cos, Michele Hamel

Spare and quietly heartbreaking, this French-Canadian feature uses a fine brush to depict a teenage girl in the midst of a quiet crisis.

The year is 1963, and 13-year-old Hanna Riel (Karine Vanasse) is in love with actress Anna Karina, the chic star of Jean-Luc Godard's VIVRE SA VIE. In Karina, Hanna sees a strong, independent woman who takes responsibility for her actions and accepts the consequences. Hanna's life, by contrast, is chaos and confusion; at an age when fitting in is everything, she feels like a perpetual outsider. Her parents are unmarried, her mother (Pascale Bussieres) is Catholic and her poet father (Miki Manojlovic) is Jewish, and they're desperately poor because her father can't hold a job and her mother must support the family on a seamstress's wages. Hanna is also baffled by love—she's only ever kissed her slightly older brother Paul (Alexandre Merineau) and her new friend Laura (Charlotte Christeler), who seems equally interested in both siblings—and she feels abandoned by her mother, who is slowly retreating into a cocoon of depression. Desperate for someone to emulate, Hanna transfers her adoration for Karina to her calmly intelligent schoolteacher (Nancy Huston), the first person she meets with anything approaching the actress's glamour.

Quebecois writer-director Lea Pool elicits beautifully complex performances from her cast, especially Vanasse, whom she often photographs floating underwater, suspended between two worlds. Rumor has it that Godard, with whom the clips from VIVRE SA VIE used in the film had to be cleared, took an avuncular interest in the film; though the polar opposite of his dazzling, self-referential works, it's every bit as assured.

SET-UP, THE DVD
1949 72m bw Sports ★★★★
RKO (U.S.)

Robert Ryan (Bill "Stoker" Thompson), Audrey Totter (Julie), George Tobias (Tiny), Alan Baxter (Little Boy), Wallace Ford (Gus), Percy Helton (Red), Hal Baylor, billed as Hal Fieberling (Tiger Nelson), Darryl Hickman (Shanley), Kenny O'Morrison (Moore), James Edwards (Luther Hawkins)

p, Richard Goldstone; d, Robert Wise; w, Art Cohn (based on the poem by Joseph Moncure March); ph, Milton Krasner; ed, Roland Gross; art d, Albert S. D'Agostino, Jack Okey

One of the most realistic and gripping boxing films ever made, THE SET-UP is a tautly constructed, emotionally charged examination of one night in the life of an aging boxer, Stoker Thompson (Robert Ryan). Played out in real time as 72 uninterrupted minutes of Stoker's life, the movie begins as a crowd gathers in front of the arena in anticipation of the evening's bouts. Although almost washed up, Stoker is convinced that if he can win that night's bout he'll be back on the road to the top, "just one punch away" from being able to collect a big purse, open his own tavern, and retire. Meanwhile, his seedy manager (George Tobias) has taken $50 from a hood in return for Stoker's throwing the fight. Since, as of late, Stoker has been getting knocked out regularly after the second round, the manager simply doesn't tell the fighter about the setup. Back in the locker room, Stoker watches as the fighters—ranging from fresh-out-of-high-school talent to punchy veterans—prepare for their bouts, while he awaits the fight of his life. THE SET-UP is an amazingly powerful film. Within a very simple format (the screenplay was based on a poem), director Robert Wise and his performers present a myriad of criticisms and emotions, making for one of the most brutal condemnations of boxing ever filmed. The fighting is shown as dehumanizing and cruel, the audience as a mass of animalistic maniacs who live vicariously through the boxers. Everyone, from trainers to promoters to gangsters, is a seedy, uneducated opportunist; only the fighters themselves are shown to have any self-respect. Ryan gives the best performance of his career as the quiet, inarticulate fighter who is determined to stick with the game because he feels that he's "just one punch away" from success. Ryan, who actually boxed for four years undefeated while at Dartmouth College, handles his role with great subtlety: always soft-spoken and sincere, Stoker clings to his simple beliefs and will take whatever punishment is necessary to retain his self-respect and dignity. The fight scenes in THE SET-UP are among the best ever filmed, surpassed only by those in Martin Scorsese's incredible RAGING BULL.

SEVEN DVD
1995 107m c Thriller/Crime/Action ★★★½
New Line (U.S.) R

Brad Pitt (Detective David Mills), Morgan Freeman (Lieutenant William Somerset), Gwyneth Paltrow (Tracy), Richard Roundtree (Talbot), John C. McGinley (California), Kevin Spacey (John Doe), John Cassini (Officer Davis), Peter Crombie (Dr. O'Neill), Reg E. Cathey (Dr. Santiago), Richard Portnow (Dr. Beardsley)

p, Arnold Kopelson, Phyllis Carlyle; d, David Fincher; w, Andrew Kevin Walker; ph, Darius Khondji; ed, Richard Francis-Bruce; m, Howard Shore; prod d, Arthur Max; art d, Gary Wissner; fx, Peter Albiez, Danny Cangemi, Greg Kimble, Tim Thompson; cos, Michael Kaplan

AAN Best Film Editing: Richard Francis-Bruce

Bleak and deeply serious, SEVEN forges the formulaic elements of dozens of lousy movies—mismatched cops, a serial killer, noir trappings—into a compelling one. As dark as an anvil and as subtle as a hammer, SEVEN gets the job done—it entertains, if you accept it on its own implacable terms.

The hard rain that pours down daily on the streets of the unnamed metropolis in which SEVEN is set isn't enough to wash the human filth off the streets. Having spent 34 years in the futile task of street cleaning, detective William Somerset (Morgan Freeman) is set to retire. He wants his last week to pass quietly, but he's charged with training his replacement, David Mills (Brad Pitt), an eager hotshot, new to the city. First thing Monday, they're faced with an unusual murder: an obese man has been force-fed spaghetti until he literally burst, and the word "GLUTTONY" was written in grease on the wall. As Somerset instantly realizes, they're on the trail of a serial slayer with a biblical bent: he's staging brilliantly sadistic murders that illustrate each of the Seven Deadly Sins. Greed follows, and the mismatched cops try desperately to identify the madman as he works his way through Sloth, Lust, Pride, and—in a startling conclusion—Envy and Wrath.

SEVEN is unnerving from the the opening credits, jarring graphics set to the electronic pulse of Nine Inch Nails' industrial rock. The stench and filth of the gluttony scene is tangible and nauseating. The sloth episode is horrific, and contains a sickening shock, while the rape-murder of lust is almost unimaginably gruesome. Director David Fincher assaults the audience relentlessly; his "Noir York" is a claustrophobic world, colored from a palette of stark grays and the occasional, dingy yellow. Fincher wants to immerse viewers in the rot of this world, and indict its (and our) malaise for the on-screen sins: the murderous John Doe is only a festering symptom.

SEVEN BEAUTIES DVD
(PASQUALINO SETTEBELLEZZE)
1976 115m c Comedy/Drama ★★★
Medusa (Italy) R

Giancarlo Giannini (Pasqualino Frafuso), Fernando Rey (Pedro), Shirley Stoler (Commandant), Elena Fiore (Concettina), Enzo Vitale (Don Raffaele), Mario Conti (Totonno), Piero Di Orio (Francesco), Ermelinda De Felice (Mother), Francesca Marciano (Carolina), Lucio Amelio (Lawyer)

p, Lina Wertmuller, Giancarlo Giannini, Arrigo Colombo; d, Lina Wertmuller; w, Lina Wertmuller; ph, Tonino Delli Colli (Eastmancolor); ed, Franco Fraticelli; m, Enzo Iannacci; art d, Enrico Job

AAN Best Actor: Giancarlo Giannini; AAN Best Director: Linda Wertmuller; AAN Best Original Screenplay: Linda Wertmuller; AAN Best Foreign Language Film

Memorable, but nasty. The grotesque casting, the surrealistic shooting, and the entire production make one think that

Federico Fellini was in charge. But it was Wertmuller who handled the writing and directing Giannini is a small-time crook in Naples during the dark days of WWII. He has seven ugly sisters, none of whom is ever likely to get married, and he is busily supporting them doing whatever he can do to keep their fat bodies and souls together. Giannini is subjected to the terrors of a German prison camp, where gross matron Shirley Stoler forces him to do unspeakable things to her body. In an all-out attempt to survive, Giannini does whatever it is that's necessary to keep from being killed and, finally, manages to live through the war. Wertmuller seems to be saying that Italians are a race willing to do anything to hang on; she strips them of pride and their natural dignity. Giannini's character is a facistic Little Tramp who swallows whatever bull is thrown at him. The picture made a lot of money, proving desensitized audiences were looking for goofball black comedy pratfalls, mixed in with a soupcon of peversion and cruelty. Things haven't changed much since then.

SEVEN BRIDES FOR SEVEN BROTHERS 📀

1954   102m   c   Musical   ★★★★½
MGM   (U.S.)   G

Jane Powell *(Milly)*, Howard Keel *(Adam Pontabee)*, Jeff Richards *(Benjamin Pontabee)*, Russ Tamblyn *(Gideon Pontabee)*, Tommy Rall *(Frank Pontabee)*, Howard Petrie *(Pete Perkins)*, Virginia Gibson *(Liza)*, Ian Wolfe *(Rev. Elcott)*, Marc Platt *(Daniel Pontabee)*, Matt Mattox *(Caleb Pontabee)*

p, Jack Cummings; d, Stanley Donen; w, Albert Hackett, Frances Goodrich, Dorothy Kingsley (based on the story "The Sobbin' Women" by Stephen Vincent Benet); ph, George Folsey (CinemaScope, Ansco Color); ed, Ralph E. Winters; art d, Cedric Gibbons, Urie McCleary; chor, Michael Kidd; cos, Walter Plunkett

AAN Best Picture; AAN Best Screenplay: Albert Hackett, Frances Goodrich, Dorothy Kingsley; AAN Best Color Cinematography: George Folsey; AAN Best Film Editing: Ralph E. Winters; AA Best Score (Musical): Adolph Deutsch, Saul Chaplin

Close to perfect. A magical blend of the right story, a great score, and the astonishing choreography of Michael Kidd, SEVEN BRIDES FOR SEVEN BROTHERS is one the big screen's most entertaining musicals. The action takes place in Oregon, where Adam (Howard Keel), the oldest of the Pontabee brothers, who live on a ranch high in the mountains, decides to find a bride. In town, he meets Milly (Jane Powell), a waitress, and woos, marries, and takes her back to the homestead, which is considerably less civilized than she'd expected. Soon Adam's brothers decide they, too, would like some female company, and, taking their inspiration from the story of the "Sobbin' Women" (Sabine women), they kidnap some local beauties, who have to winter at the ranch when an avalanche prevents the townspeople from rescuing them. Come spring, wedding bells ring for all. Based on Stephen Vincent Benet's "The Sobbin' Women," SEVEN BRIDES FOR SEVEN BROTHERS is a rollicking film with a breathless pace, well-defined characters, and incredible vitality under Stanley Donen's direction, marred marginally by an overlying patina of corny Americana. Adolph Deutsch and Saul Chaplin's scoring won an Oscar. The dynamo dancing is mostly due to the terrific male dancers, whose standouts include the barn-raising and the "Lonesome Polecat Lament" ballet. Keel and Powell have an adorable chemistry; neither would ever be this well-matched again, which reminds us we would have preferred Powell in for Kathryn Grayson in KISS ME, KATE. Look for ripe Julie Newmar (then Newmeyer) among the other brides, whom we always found sexier as a wild-maned brunette. The score is by Gene dePaul and Johnny Mercer.

SEVEN DAYS IN MAY 📀

1964   120m   bw   Thriller/Political/War   ★★★★
Seven Arts/Joel   (U.S.)

Burt Lancaster *(Gen. James M. Scott)*, Kirk Douglas *(Col. Martin "Jiggs" Casey)*, Fredric March *(President Jordan Lyman)*, Ava Gardner *(Eleanor Holbrook)*, Edmond O'Brien *(Sen. Raymond Clark)*, Martin Balsam *(Paul Girard)*, George Macready *(Christopher Todd)*, Whit Bissell *(Sen. Prentice)*, Hugh Marlowe *(Harold McPherson)*, Bart Burns *(Arthur Corwin)*

p, Edward Lewis; d, John Frankenheimer; w, Rod Serling (based on the novel by Fletcher Knebel, Charles Waldo Bailey II); ph, Ellsworth Fredricks; ed, Ferris Webster; m, Jerry Goldsmith; art d, Cary Odell

AAN Best Supporting Actor: Edmond O'Brien; AAN Best Art Direction-Set Decoration (B/W): Cary Odell, Edward G. Boyle

The surprising revelations of the Iran-Contra scandal have given new meaning to this gripping, well-acted political thriller based on Charles Waldo Bailey II's and Fletcher Knebel's 1962 best-seller. SEVEN DAYS IN MAY begins as the President of the United States, Jordan Lyman (Fredric March), signs a nuclear disarmament treaty with the Soviets, outraging the military establishment, particularly Gen. James M. Scott (Burt Lancaster), head of the Joint Chiefs of Staff, who conspires with other Joint Chiefs to stage a coup d'etat. His aide, Marine Col. "Jiggs" Casey (Kirk Douglas), stumbles onto evidence of the plot, including a secret Air Force base, and approaches the president. With only days left before the coup is to take place, Lyman swings into action, but trusted friends Sen. Raymond Clark (Edmond O'Brien) and Paul Girard (Martin Balsam), whom the president has sent to secure the proof needed to expose Scott and his cohorts, are captured and killed in a plane crash, respectively. Armed with incriminating letters from Scott's former mistress (Ava Gardner), Lyman confronts the general, and though the president cannot bring himself to use blackmail he eventually triumphs over Scott. Filmed in stark black and white, unraveling its complicated plot at a rapid clip, this exciting film from John Frankenheimer, the director of the similarly taut THE MANCHURIAN CANDIDATE, packs a grim warning about the military's potential abuse of power. Douglas, who, like Lancaster and March, contributes an outstanding performance, initiated the project after reading galleys of the novel. Given the enthusiastic cooperation of the Kennedy administration (though not of the Pentagon, whom the filmmakers understandably never approached), SEVEN DAYS IN MAY smacks of realism, from its skillfully realized sets to its wholly believable supporting performances by O'Brien, Balsam, and John Houseman. Sure to keep you on the edge of your seat.

7 FACES OF DR. LAO 📀

1964   100m   c   Science Fiction/Fantasy   ★★★½
Galaxy/Scarus   (U.S.)

Tony Randall *(Dr. Lao/Merlin the Magician/Pan/The Abominable Snowman/Medusa/The Giant Serpent/Apollonius of Tyana)*, Barbara Eden *(Angela Benedict)*, Arthur O'Connell *(Clint Stark)*, John Ericson *(Ed Cunningham)*, Noah Beery Jr. *(Tim Mitchell)*, Lee Patrick *(Mrs. Howard T. Cassan)*, Minerva Urecal *(Kate Lindquist)*, John Qualen *(Luther Lindquist)*, Frank Kreig *(Peter Ramsey)*, Peggy Rea *(Mrs. Peter Ramsey)*

p, George Pal; d, George Pal; w, Charles Beaumont (based on the novel *The Circus of Dr. Lao* by Charles G. Finney); ph, Robert Bronner (Metrocolor); ed, George Tomasini; m, Leigh Harline; art d, George W. Davis, Gabriel Scognamillo; fx, Paul Byrd, Wah Chang, Jim Danforth, Ralph Rodine, Robert R. Hoag

AAN Best Special Visual Effects: Jim Danforth

Set in the Old West, this is a wonderful fantasy from puppeteer George Pal, whose futurist fancies have delighted many. When Dr. Lao (Tony Randall), an Oriental magician, rides into Abalone with his strange circus, he finds the good citizens threatened by the land-grabbing activities of villainous Clint Stark (Arthur O'Connell). Calling upon his mysterious powers and the services of the bizarre characters who populate the strange circus (all played by Randall), Lao comes to the aid of the crusading young newspaper editor (John Ericson) who tries to prevent Stark's takeover of the town. In the film's most fantastic sequence, Lao's pet fish becomes a seven-headed monster to chase down one of Stark's henchmen. Randall gives a virtuoso multiple-character performance, and the special effects are dazzling, including a few scenes from Pal's ATLANTIS, THE LOST CONTINENT. Makeup man William Tuttle won the first of only two special Academy Awards for his work on this film—before the category was permanently established in 1981.

SEVEN LITTLE FOYS, THE   DVD
1955 95m   c   Musical/Biography   ★★★½
Paramount   (U.S.)

Bob Hope *(Eddie Foy)*, Milly Vitale *(Madeleine Morando)*, George Tobias *(Barney Green)*, Angela Clarke *(Clara)*, Herbert Heyes *(Judge)*, Richard Shannon *(Stage Manager)*, Billy Gray *(Brynie)*, Lee Erickson *(Charley)*, Paul De Rolf *(Richard Foy)*, Lydia Reed *(Mary Foy)*

p, Jack Rose; d, Melville Shavelson; w, Melville Shavelson, Jack Rose; ph, John F. Warren (VistaVision, Technicolor); ed, Ellsworth Hoagland; art d, Hal Pereira, John B. Goodman; chor, Nick Castle; cos, Edith Head

AAN Best Story and Screenplay: Melville Shavelson, Jack Rose

Funny and heartwarming, though a little on the cute side, this engaging musical biography of vaudevillian Eddie Foy, Sr. features a socko cameo by multitalented James Cagney, reprising his Oscar-winning role as George M. Cohan. Bob Hope plays Foy, who declares that he'll always do a "single," both onstage and in life, but who, in short order, is married and has seven kids. When his wife (Milly Vitale) dies, Foy has problems adjusting to single parenthood, but before long the kids are not only in the act, but stealing the show. With Eddie, Jr., Foy's real-life son, doing the narrating, we are taken through the various episodes of the family's life. The highlight of the film comes at a Friars Club dinner for Foy, when he and his great pal Cohan get on stage, throw some fast and furious jokes back and forth, and wind up in a splendid dance routine. Cagney reportedly did the role for no pay, even though he and Hope rehearsed their dancing for 10 days. A must see for Hope and Cagney fans.

SEVEN-PER-CENT SOLUTION, THE   DVD
1976 113m   c   Mystery   ★★★
Universal   (U.K.)   PG

Alan Arkin *(Sigmund Freud)*, Vanessa Redgrave *(Lola Deveraux)*, Robert Duvall *(Dr. Watson)*, Nicol Williamson *(Sherlock Holmes)*, Laurence Olivier *(Prof. Moriarty)*, Joel Grey *(Lowenstein)*, Samantha Eggar *(Mary Watson)*, Jeremy Kemp *(Baron von Leinsdorf)*, Charles Gray *(Mycroft Holmes)*, Georgia Brown *(Mrs. Freud)*

p, Herbert Ross; d, Herbert Ross; w, Nicholas Meyer (based on his novel); ph, Oswald Morris (Panavision, Technicolor); ed, Chris Barnes; m, John Addison; prod d, Ken Adam; art d, Peter Lamont; cos, Alan Barrett

AAN Best Adapted Screenplay: Nicholas Meyer; *AAN Best Costume Design:* Alan Barrett

A hit at the box office, this revisionist Sherlock Holmes film is based on the best seller by Nicholas Meyer and places a historical figure (Sigmund Freud) and a fictitious one (Sherlock Holmes) from the late 19th century together in a hypothetical situation. The result is a fascinating film that sees the loyal Dr. Watson (Duvall) scheme to trick his friend Holmes (Williamson) into seeking a cure for his cocaine addiction from the soon-to-be-famous Freud (Arkin). The criminologist and the psychologist come to respect each other's considerable deductive talents, and they team up to rescue one of Arkin's patients (Redgrave) who has been kidnapped. Williamson is a Holmes unlike any other, a man of genius but also a man tormented by things he cannot recall. His obsession with the completely innocent Professor Moriarty (Olivier) is actually a reaction to a long-buried secret in the sleuth's subconscious. Williamson's Holmes actually cries at one point, something Basil Rathbone would never have done. Duvall is a breath of fresh air as well; far from the Nigel Bruce bumbler, he is a capable man and a devoted friend. Production design is nothing short of marvelous, conveying the gentility of the late Victorian era in splendid detail. The music was originally to be composed by Bernard Herrmann, but he died before completing it and was replaced by John Addison. Stephen Sondheim, a mystery buff, contributed a witty saloon song.

SEVEN SAMURAI, THE   DVD
(SHICHININ NO SAMURAI)
1954 200m   bw   Drama   ★★★★★
Toho   (Japan)

Takashi Shimura *(Kambei)*, Toshiro Mifune *(Kikuchiyo)*, Yoshio Inaba *(Gorobei)*, Seiji Miyaguchi *(Kyuzo)*, Minoru Chiaki *(Heihachi)*, Daisuke Kato *(Shichiroji)*, Ko Kimura *(Katsushiro)*, Kuninori Kodo *(Gisaku)*, Kamatari Fujiwara *(Manzo)*, Yoshio Tsuchiya *(Rikichi)*

p, Shojiro Motoki; d, Akira Kurosawa; w, Shinobu Hashimoto, Hideo Oguni, Akira Kurosawa; ph, Asakazu Nakai; ed, Akira Kurosawa; m, Fumio Hayasaka; art d, So Matsuyama

AAN Best Art Direction-Set Decoration (B/W): Takashi Matsuyama (Art Direction); *AAN Best Costume Design (B/W):* Kohei Ezaki

Much imitated, still unsurpassed. By critical consensus one of the best movies ever made, THE SEVEN SAMURAI covers so much emotional, historical, and cinematic ground that that it demands to be viewed over and over again. Director Akira Kurosawa re-imagines the epic westerns of John Ford in a Japanese context, yielding an art-house action picture with cross-cultural appeal.

The film is set in the 1600s during the Sengoku era, when the once-powerful samurai were coming to the end of their rule. A small, unprotected village, which is regularly pillaged by murderous thieves, comes under the protection of a band of these samurai. Kambei (Takashi Shimura) is a veteran warrior who has fallen on hard times and who answers the villagers' appeal for help by gathering six comrades to help defend the town. (Each of the samurai is quickly limned to show us who they are, what they do, and whatever personal quirks they may have.) In return for three small meals daily, the men drill the town on how to fight, but the parties are battling for different reasons. The townspeople are desperate to keep their lives and property intact; the warriors are in it for honor alone. The last of the samurai to join is Kikuchiyo (Toshiro Mifune), a loudmouth who pretends that he is qualified but who is, in reality, a farmer's son who hopes to be accepted by the others. The 40 bandits arrive, and a huge battle takes place. In the end, only three of the warriors survive.

Akira Kurosawa's classic tells a simple tale, but one so rich with underlying meaning and cinematic technique that no synopsis can do justice to the film's power. Those viewers under the misconception that foreign films are boring should be thrilled by the staging of this film's brutal action sequences, such as the raid on the town, the violent hand-to-hand combat in the pouring rain, and the epic horseback battles. The action is never shown strictly for its own sake, however. All the characters are so carefully etched that we sincerely grieve when they are killed. One of the most successful of all Japanese films, and one of the most immediately accessible to English-speaking audiences.

SEVEN THIEVES
1960 102m bw Crime ★★★★
Fox (U.S.)

Rod Steiger *(Paul Mason)*, Edward G. Robinson *(Theo Wilkins)*, Joan Collins *(Melanie)*, Eli Wallach *(Poncho)*, Michael Dante *(Louis)*, Alexander Scourby *(Raymond Le May)*, Berry Kroeger *(Hugo Baumer)*, Sebastian Cabot *(Director of Casino)*, Marcel Hillaire *(Duc di Salins)*, John Beradino *(Chief of Detectives)*

p, Sydney Boehm; d, Henry Hathaway; w, Sydney Boehm (based on the novel *Lions at the Kill* by Max Catto); ph, Sam Leavitt (CinemaScope); ed, Dorothy Spencer; m, Dominic Frontiere; art d, Lyle Wheeler, John De Cuir; cos, Bill Thomas

AAN Best Costume Design (B/W): Bill Thomas

There have been many copies of RIFIFI since the early 1950s, some of which have been awful and some excellent. This film falls into the latter category. Robinson was beginning his fourth decade as a hoodlum star, and not many actors could play tough guys better than he could. This time he's a former scientist who realizes he doesn't have much time left and wants to commit the perfect crime. Robinson enlists six accomplices to help him carry out his plan. Prominent among them is Steiger, a recently released crook and old acquaintance of Robinson's. Meeting on the French Riviera, Robinson and Steiger spar verbally in a funny scene that shows both men jockeying for position. Once Steiger is committed to the project—the robbery of millions from the casino at Monte Carlo—the crew of criminals is rounded out by Collins, a sexpot chorine; Wallach, her boyfriend; Dante, a jumpy safecracker; Kroeger, an expert wheel man; and Scourby, the insider who works as the right-hand man to the boss of the casino, Cabot. The first half of the film is devoted to gathering the conspirators and planning the robbery. The second half depicts the robbery itself and the plot-twist ending. Collins supposedly seduces Scourby; Wallach fakes a suicide in the casino to divert the security guards. While this goes on, Steiger and Dante make their way to the rooms where the money is kept. The heist is successful, but the cash is in huge denominations that are registered, so the crooks can not do anything with their take. Robinson is so thrilled by having pulled off the job that his heart gives out, and when the other six realize that there is no way they can spend the money, they return it to the casino. The ending is a bit of a disappointment because the characters are so engaging that we want them to succeed, especially since they don't hurt or kill anyone. Until the conclusion, SEVEN THIEVES is a tight, taut, and superior heist film with well-drawn characters. Well-directed by Hathaway and beautifully photographed by Levitt, the film would have benefitted greatly by being shot in color. (It was nominated by the Academy for Best Costume Design for a black-and-white film.) Frontiere's score adds nicely to the tension. The chief of detectives was played by John Beradino, who went on to great success in "General Hospital" but whom sports fans may remember as being the light-hitting infielder for the St. Louis Browns.

SEVEN YEAR ITCH, THE
1955 105m c Comedy 📀 ★★★
Fox (U.S.)

Marilyn Monroe *(The Girl)*, Tom Ewell *(Richard Sherman)*, Evelyn Keyes *(Helen Sherman)*, Sonny Tufts *(Tom McKenzie)*, Robert Strauss *(Kruhulik)*, Oscar Homolka *(Dr. Brubaker)*, Marguerite Chapman *(Miss Morris)*, Victor Moore *(Plumber)*, Roxanne *(Elaine)*, Donald MacBride *(Mr. Brady)*

p, Charles K. Feldman; Billy Wilder; d, Billy Wilder; w, Billy Wilder, George Axelrod (based on the play by Axelrod); ph, Milton Krasner (CinemaScope, DeLuxe Color); ed, Hugh S. Fowler; m, Alfred Newman; art d, Lyle Wheeler, George W. Davis; fx, Ray Kellogg; cos, Travilla, Charles LeMaire

Entertaining Billy Wilder outing, adapted—and toned down—by George Axelrod from his hit Broadway play. This is probably Monroe's best known film, largely thanks to the scene in which a rush of air from a subway grating sends her skirt flying up around her shoulders.

Tom Ewell plays a book publisher who has been married for seven years, and who stays behind in Manhattan for the summer when his wife (Keyes) and son (Bernard) leave on vacation. Ewell's small building has an upstairs apartment which has been sublet to Monroe, a flighty commercial actress/model who becomes the object of his (mostly imaginary) amorous advances. Ewell's lively imagination sends him into flights of fancy involving both his conquest of Monroe, and the humiliation which would result from the exposure of his infidelity (Monroe appearing on a local TV show to openly discuss his proclivities, etc.). The picture ends with no adultery having been committed, except in Ewell's mind.

This was Monroe's 23rd movie and Ewell's eighth, since he broke in opposite Judy Holliday in ADAM'S RIB. Monroe was falling in and out of depression during filming, as her marriage to Yankee slugger Joe DiMaggio was ending. Oscar Homolka has a bit part as a psychiatrist.

SEVENTH SEAL, THE
(DET SJUNDE INSEGLET) 📀
1957 105m bw Drama ★★★★★
Svensk (Sweden)

Max von Sydow *(Antonius Block)*, Gunnar Bjornstrand *(Jons)*, Nils Poppe *(Jof)*, Bibi Andersson *(Mia)*, Bengt Ekerot *(Death)*, Ake Fridell *(Blacksmith Plog)*, Inga Gill *(Lisa)*, Maud Hansson *(Tyan)*, Gunnel Lindblom *(Girl)*, Inga Landgre *(Block's Wife)*

p, Allan Ekelund; d, Ingmar Bergman; w, Ingmar Bergman (based on his play "Tramalning"); ph, Gunnar Fischer; ed, Lennart Wallen; m, Erik Nordgren; fx, Evald Andersson; chor, Else Fischer; cos, Manne Lindholm

The film that gained Ingmar Bergman an international reputation, THE SEVENTH SEAL is an all-out religious allegory addressing that most-contemplated question, "Does God exist?" Set during a single day in the Middle Ages, the film concerns the philosophical quandary of a knight, Antonius Block (von Sydow), who returns from the Crusades to find his country at the mercy of plague and witchhunts. In the midst of his moral and religious confusion, Antonius is visited by Death (Ekerot), a black-cloaked figure who is ready to call the knight from this earth. Antonius strikes a deal with Death, winning a brief reprieve by inviting him to play a game of chess. Since Death apparently has a soft spot for chess, he agrees. Over the next several hours, Antonius is confronted by some who are unconvinced of God's existence (the Knight's agnostic squire, played by Bjornstrand) and some who are (a wandering band of performers). Who survives the plague and who doesn't propels the narrative; the issues, however, are what really matter here.

Long hailed as a masterpiece of cinema, the status of THE SEVENTH SEAL (and, more generally, Bergman's place in the pantheon of great filmmakers) has steadily declined over the years. Still, we must admit to really liking this one. It is most powerful on its first viewing, when the opening burst of light through the sky, the incredible parade of flagellants through the town, and the memorable finale with Death and his conquests have their greatest impact for a viewer. On later viewings the craft of the film remains bracing and its greater concerns stay provocative without becoming heavy-handed. Whatever one thinks of Bergman's philosophical debates on good and evil or God and the Devil, the film nevertheless deserves one's respect. As with so much of this filmmaker's cinema, the acting is of a very high order. Von Sydow's long face makes a perfect portrait of stoicism, and the incredibly versatile Bjornstrand scores again in a change of pace role. Poppe would never again achieve a performance quite as good as this one, his Jof a combination of artlessness and winning grace. Andersson and Lindblom are equally fine, and the details and dignity of the acting throughout render an incredibly effective sense of period. What's most important here is that THE SEVENTH SEAL, for all its downbeat aspects, is so gripping as to be entertaining in an enlightening way. Less austere and more visually striking than some of Bergman's later films.

SEVENTH VEIL, THE
1945 95m bw Drama   ★★★★
Theatrecraft/Ortus (U.K.)

James Mason (Nicholas), Ann Todd (Francesca Cunningham), Herbert Lom (Dr. Larson), Hugh McDermott (Peter Gay), Albert Lieven (Maxwell Leyden), Yvonne Owen (Susan Brook), David Horne (Dr. Kendal), Manning Whiley (Dr. Irving), Grace Allardyce (Nurse), Ernest Davies (Parker)

p, Sydney Box; d, Compton Bennett; w, Muriel Box, Sydney Box; ph, Reginald Wyer; ed, Gordon Hales; m, Benjamin Frankel; art d, James Carter; cos, Dorothy Sinclair

AA Best Original Screenplay: Muriel Box, Sydney Box

An intelligent and absorbing psychological drama that took the Oscar for Best Screenplay, THE SEVENTH VEIL was shot in under three months on a modest budget of less than 100,000 pounds and proved that a polished movie could be made for a reasonable price. Todd, in her best performance of an up-and-down career in which she never got the acclaim she deserved, is a concert pianist who suffers from fits of depression and attempts suicide. Her hands were once hurt in an accident and she fears that she will lose their use. The picture unreels in flashback as Todd checks into a mental hospital and puts herself in the care of psychiatrist Lom, who guides her through her past and lifts the veils of her memory. With the aid of drugs and hypnosis, Todd goes back to the time when she was brutally caned by a cruel headmistress the night before she was to take her final exams in music. The result was that she failed the test. Todd is an orphan put in the care of crippled and charismatic Mason, a bachelor who dedicates himself to cultivating her talents. When Todd attempts romance with bandleader McDermott, Mason takes her to Paris where she plays brilliantly and delights crowds and critics. Then she falls for Lieven, an artist; in an attempt to put an end to that attachment, Mason steals a car and crashes it with Todd inside; her hands are burned. Now that Todd has discovered why she feels the way she does, she becomes aware that her talent remains, and the recognition of her personal history causes her to race to the arms of the man she truly loves, Mason.

It's a complex picture that only skims the surface of mental illnes, but the attempt was admirable, if a bit simplistic. Still, for the time, praise must be given to the Boxes for their story and to former film editor Bennett for his direc-

tion. The producers showed it to audiences on a sneak-preview basis and let them decide the ending. At first, no one was quite sure how to conclude it. But when the cards came in, it was indicated that the audiences felt Todd should wind up with Mason, and so that is implied at the conclusion. Pianist Eileen Joyce did the solos for Todd. Two years before this, Todd electrified London with her stage work in "Lottie Dundass," in which she played opposite Sybil Thorndike. She began her professional career in 1931 in KEEPERS OF YOUTH and eventually became a producer and director of travel films. Czech-born Lom, who later was seen as Peter Sellers's boss in the "Pink Panther" films, was making his fifth film.

SEVENTH VICTIM, THE
1943 71m bw Horror   ★★★★
RKO (U.S.)

Tom Conway (Dr. Louis Judd), Kim Hunter (Mary Gibson), Jean Brooks (Jacqueline Gibson), Hugh Beaumont (Gregory Ward), Erford Gage (Jason Hoag), Isabel Jewell (Frances Fallon), Chef Milani (Mr. Romari), Marguerita Sylva (Mrs. Romari), Evelyn Brent (Natalie Cortez), Mary Newton (Mrs. Redi)

p, Val Lewton; d, Mark Robson; w, DeWitt Bodeen, Charles O'Neal; ph, Nicholas Musuraca; ed, John Lockert; m, Roy Webb; art d, Albert S. D'Agostino, Walter E. Keller; cos, Renie

"I runne to death and death meets me as fast/And all my pleasures are like yesterday." This epigraph from the first "Holy Sonnet" by John Donne sets the tone for what is perhaps producer Val Lewton's most personal film, and certainly one of his greatest. While very little in the way of horrific action takes place in THE SEVENTH VICTIM, the film has a haunting, lyrical, overwhelming sense of melancholy and despair to it—death is looked upon as a sweet release from the oppression of a cold, meaningless existence. Kim Hunter makes her film debut as Mary Gibson, an orphan attending a gloomy Catholic boarding school. Informed by the nuns that her older sister, Jacqueline (Jean Brooks), has disappeared and stopped sending tuition money, Mary is forced to go to New York City and find her. With the help of Jacqueline's husband, Gregory (Hugh Beaumont), Mary discovers that her sister has fallen in with a group of satanists who meet in secret and virtually control the lives of their members. No plot description can fully convey the uneasy sense of dread that pervades every frame of this film. Although Mark Robson, who made his directorial debut here, is no Jacques Tourneur, his direction is restrained and effective. Lewton ensured this by seeing to it that all the delicate nuances of mood and character were written into the screenplay. The film includes a number of unforgettable moments: the scene in which Mary persuades Jacqueline's landlord to open up her room—only to find a noose hanging from the ceiling and a chair placed beneath it, Mary watching in horror as the body of a murder victim is transported by its killers on the subway, a precursor to the shower scene in PSYCHO that must have been seen by Hitchcock, and the film's final moment—without a doubt the bleakest ending to any film ever made in Hollywood.

7TH VOYAGE OF SINBAD, THE   DVD
1958 87m c Science Fiction/Fantasy   ★★★½
Morningside (U.S.)

Kerwin Mathews (Capt. Sinbad), Kathryn Grant (Princess Parisa), Richard Eyer (Baronni the Genie), Torin Thatcher (Sokurah the Magician), Alec Mango (Caliph), Danny Green (Karim), Harold Kasket (Sultan), Alfred Brown (Harufa), Nana de Herrera (Sadi), Nino Falanga (Gaunt Sailor)

p, Charles H. Schneer; d, Nathan Juran; w, Ken Kolb; ph, Wilkie Cooper (Dynamation, Technicolor); ed, Edwin Bryant,

Jerome Thoms; m, Bernard Herrmann; art d, Gil Parrendo; fx, Ray Harryhausen

Stop-motion animation master Ray Harryhausen's first color film is also one of the greatest achievements in fantasy filmmaking since KING KONG. For the first time Harryhausen ventures into the realm of myth and legend (his previous films were the modern-day giant monster variety), resuscitating the Sinbad adventure, long thought to be box-office poison. The film opens as Sinbad (Kerwin Mathews) sails to Baghdad, accompanied by Princess Parisa (Kathryn Grant), his future bride. A violent storm blows the ship off course, and the travelers land on the island of Colossa, where they find the sorcerer Sokurah (Torin Thatcher) being chased by a monstrous cyclops from whom he has stolen a magic lamp. Sinbad fends off the cyclops, but only with help from the lamp's genie are they able to escape. During their retreat, the lamp falls into the sea and is recovered by the angry cyclops. Despite the sorcerer's pleas to return for the lamp, Sinbad sails for Baghdad. Sokurah, however, shrinks the princess to miniature size to force Sinbad to see things his way. The rest of the film is an assault of the visually fantastic: Sinbad and his crew battle a baby roc and its giant mother, another cyclops, a fire-breathing dragon, and in the most memorable scene of all, Sinbad has a thrilling sword fight with a living skeleton. Harryhausen would make more magic in such outstanding fantasy features as MYSTERIOUS ISLAND, JASON AND THE ARGONAUTS, and CLASH OF THE TITANS.

SEX, LIES, AND VIDEOTAPE

1989 101m c Drama 📀
Outlaw (U.S.) ★★★½
R

James Spader *(Graham Dalton)*, Andie MacDowell *(Ann Millaney)*, Peter Gallagher *(John Millaney)*, Laura San Giacomo *(Cynthia Bishop)*, Ron Vawter *(Therapist)*, Steven Brill *(Barfly)*, David Foil *(John's Colleague)*, Earl Taylor *(Landlord)*, Alexandra Root *(Girl on Tape)*

p, Robert Newmyer, John Hardy; d, Steven Soderbergh; w, Steven Soderbergh; ph, Walt Lloyd (CFI Color); m, Cliff Martinez; art d, Joanne Schmidt; cos, James Ryder

AAN Best Original Screenplay: Steven Soderbergh

Like its title, SEX, LIES, AND VIDEOTAPE sneaks by quietly, in subtle increments, gradually accumulating force. Graham Dalton (James Spader) arrives at the upscale home of his old college friend John Millaney (Peter Gallagher) and the friend's wife, Ann (Andie MacDowell). The two men have little in common any more: Graham is jobless and alienated; John is an aggressive yuppie attorney. He is also having an affair with his wife's sister, Cynthia (Laura San Giacomo), who's a trouble-maker. Graham and Ann become friendly, and he reveals that he is impotent. They have a falling out over his collection of videotapes, which contain conversations with women who've consented to speak intimately about sex before his camera. Then Cynthia pays him a visit and makes a tape, precipitating a series of emotional revelations. An unusually mature and self-assured fiction-feature debut for director Steven Soderbergh, SEX, LIES, AND VIDEOTAPE was the winner of the Cannes Film Festival's top prize, the Palme d'Or, scoring a rare double win when Spader was named Best Actor as well. Notwithstanding the fervency of its reception, this is a quiet film, relying on talk rather than scenes of sex or nudity to make its points, and in the process establishing a far more intimate tone than many more explicit pictures. Soderbergh coaxes remarkably well-nuanced performances from the four principals. Beautifully edited by Soderbergh, the film is evenly paced, its subtleties accreting slowly, and by the end it gathers powerful emotional momentum.

SEXY BEAST

2000 89m c Crime 📀
Recorded Picture Company/FilmFour/Fox ★★★½
Searchlight/KanZaman SA/Chronopolis Films R
(U.K./U.S./Spain)

Ray Winstone *(Gary Dove—"Gal")*, Ben Kingsley *(Don Logan)*, Ian McShane *(Teddy Bass)*, Amanda Redman *(DeeDee)*, Cavan Kendall *(Aitch)*, Julianne White *(Jackie)*, Alvaro Monje *(Enrique, the Kid)*, James Fox *(Harry)*, Robert Atiko *(Andy)*, Nieves del Amo Oruet *(Air Hostess)*

p, Jeremy Thomas; d, Jonathan Glazer; w, Louis Mellis, David Scinto; ph, Ivan Bird; ed, John Scott, Sam Sneade; m, Roque Banos; prod d, Jan Houllevigue; art d, James Alexander Hamilton, Steve Simmonds, Carlos Suarez Bodelon, Marcus Wookey; fx, Reyes Abades, The Computer Film Company, Tom Harris, Reyes Abades Efectos Especiales, Jason Troughton, Alan Whibley; cos, Louise Stjernsward

AAN Best Supporting Actor: Ben Kingsley

A color-saturated jolt of pure vicious energy, this darkly comic crime thriller has far more style than substance, but what style! Forget the story: the main event is the Mamet-esque battle of foul words between vintage hard case Ray Winstone and the seething sociopath played by Ben Kingsley.

Gary Dove (Winstone) is a laid-back English thug who's left behind a life of bad deeds for a cushy, take-it-as-it-comes retirement on the Costa del Sol with his former porn-star wife (Amanda Redman). Even when two friends (Cavan Kendall, Julianne White) show up quaking because gangster Don Logan (Ben Kingsley) has called looking for Gary, he remains calm. Whatever Don wants, Gary assures them, he'll just say no. Don, it turns out, is assembling a crew for a bank heist masterminded by oily boss-of-bosses Teddy Bass (Ian McShane), and Don wants Gary in. Gary says yes, but thanks to the film's disjointed time frame, which glides sinuously between flashbacks and the occasional dream sequence involving a deformed rabbit-beast, it's a while before we learn why Gary takes the gig, or why Don pulls a disappearing act that has the higher-ups in London asking a few pointed questions.

Unlike many music-video vets, director Jonathan Glazer knows when to get out of an actor's way. Viewers who still think of Kingsley as Gandhi are in for a particularly rude shock; his performance is by any standard a masterpiece of bubbling belligerence. The usually volatile Winstone is a slyly benevolent foil to his fury, and the supporting cast—including James Fox as a seamy aristocrat for whom slumming ends exceptionally badly—holds up its end with apparently effortless aplomb.

SHADOW OF A DOUBT

1943 108m bw Thriller 📀
Universal (U.S.) ★★★★½

Teresa Wright *(Young Charlie)*, Joseph Cotten *(Uncle Charlie)*, Macdonald Carey *(Jack Graham)*, Henry Travers *(Joseph Newton)*, Patricia Collinge *(Emma Newton)*, Hume Cronyn *(Herbie Hawkins)*, Edna May Wonacott *(Ann Newton)*, Wallace Ford *(Fred Saunders)*, Irving Bacon *(Station Master)*, Charles Bates *(Roger Newton)*

p, Jack H. Skirball; d, Alfred Hitchcock; w, Thornton Wilder, Sally Benson, Alma Reville (based on a story by Gordon McDonnell); ph, Joseph Valentine; ed, Milton Carruth; m, Dimitri Tiomkin; art d, John B. Goodman, Robert Boyle

AAN Best Original Story: Gordon McDonell

Deathly Americana; not as fun or spine-tingling as other Hitchcocks, but who's complaining? Hitch's favorite among his own films was based on the case of the real-life "Merry Widow Murderer," Earle Leonard Nelson, a mass strangler of the 1920s. The sly Hitchcock made this chiller all the more frightening by having his crafty homicidal maniac intrude into the tranquility of a warm, middle-class family living in a small town, deeply developing his characters and drawing from the soft-spoken Joseph Cotten one of the actor's most remarkable and fascinating performances.

At the beginning of the film, Charlie (Cotten) is shown wooing and then murdering a woman for her riches. He barely escapes the police and then boards a train, having wired his sister Emma (Collinge) in Santa Rosa, California, that he is coming for an extended stay with the only family he has. (On board the train, as a passenger in his cameo appearance, is director Hitchcock.) In Santa Rosa his niece, also named Charlie (Wright), is delighted to hear that her urbane, witty, and adventurous uncle will be visiting the family. She, her father (Travers), and her young brother and sister (Wonacott and Bates) greet Uncle Charlie at the train station, but are shocked to see him limping on a cane, being helped by porters. He claims to be ill, and the family quickly takes him home, where Emma pampers him. Charlie stops at a bank and makes a scene while depositing $40,000, but his strange behavior is explained as an idiosyncrasy by his adoring niece. Gradually, though, Charlie's past comes to town to haunt him, especially when a detective (Carey) shows up. Battling the thought that her beloved uncle could be the mass killer the detective has suggested he is, Charlie tries to get closer to her uncle, hoping to learn about his past and allay her fears.

This is Hitchcock's most penetrating analysis of a murderer—a masterful profile, aided by Cotten's superb performance, of a subtle killer who cannot escape his dark passions, despite a superior intellect. The film's construction is adroit and perfectly calculated, letting the viewer know early on just what kind of man Cotten really is, but providing tension through Cotten's devious charade as a gentle, kind man deserving of his family's love—a tension which fuels the chilling cat-and-mouse game between Cotten and Wright that provides the film's suspenseful center.

Hitchcock took his time in making SHADOW OF A DOUBT, and the care shows. The director got Thornton Wilder to write the screenplay, assuming that the playwright who created "Our Town" would be the perfect scenarist to bring the right kind of ambience and characterization to the film's small, close-knit Santa Rosa. After consulting briefly with Hitchcock, Wilder wandered about Hollywood with a notebook, writing bits and pieces of the screenplay when he could. He and the director took their time developing the intricate story, and Wilder had not finished the screenplay when he enlisted to serve in the Psychological Warfare Division of the Army. To finish the script, Hitchcock boarded a cross-country train to Florida (where Wilder was to begin his training) with the writer, and patiently sat in the next compartment as Wilder periodically emerged to give him another few pages of copy. The great playwright finished the last page of SHADOW OF A DOUBT just as the train was coming to his stop, and he used the train upon which he and Hitchcock traveled as his model in creating the setting for the gripping finale.

SHADOW OF THE VAMPIRE

2000 93m c Horror/Drama ★★★½
Saturn Films/Delux Productions/Metrodome Films/ R
BBC Films/Long Shot Films (U.S./U.K./Luxembourg)

John Malkovich *(F.W. Murnau)*, Willem Dafoe *(Max Schreck)*, Udo Kier *(Albin Grau)*, Cary Elwes *(Fritz Wagner)*, Catherine McCormack *(Greta Schroder)*, Eddie Izzard *(Gustav von Wangenheim)*, Aden Gillett *(Henrick Galeen)*, Ronan Vibert

(Wolfgang Muller), Ingeborga Dapkunaite *(Micheline)*, Nicholas Elliott *(Paul)*

p, Nicolas Cage, Jeff Levine; d, E. Elias Merhige; w, Steven Katz; ph, Lou Bogue; ed, Chris Wyatt; m, Dan Jones; prod d, Assheton Gorton; art d, Chris Bradley; cos, Caroline De Vivaise

AAN Best Supporting Actor: Willem Dafoe; *AAN Best Makeup:* Ann Buchanan, Amber Sibley

E. Elias Merhige's fantasia on the theme of NOSFERATU is a creepy, clever, film buff's delight.

The year is 1921, and flamboyant German filmmaker F.W. Murnau (John Malkovich) is making a vampire movie, an unauthorized version of Bram Stoker's *Dracula*. He's already shot interiors in a Berlin studio but now plans to take his cast and crew to a distant island location. Producer Albin Grau (Udo Kier) and scripter Henrick Galeen (Aden Gillett) think it's a waste of resources, but location shooting is the least of Murnau's startling innovations. He's cast a real vampire, teasingly named Max Schreck (Willem Dafoe), in the film's title role, though he assures everyone his gaunt, spooky star has merely been studying with some fellow named Stanislavsky, who encourages actors to immerse themselves in their roles. Hammy leading man Gustav Von Wangenheim (Eddie Izzard) thinks that's ridiculous, but the cast and crew accept that Herr Murnau is a visionary and indulge his eccentricities. Unfortunately, "Schreck" is having trouble keeping his bloodthirsty impulses in check and begins preying on the crew as he awaits the arrival of haughty star Greta (Catherine McCormack). She's the one the bloodsucker really wants, and once he has her, Murnau's tenuous control over the monster will be broken.

Classic horror buffs will delight in Steven Katz's knowing screenplay, which Merhige brings to the screen with equal parts solemnity and mordant humor. The performances are perfectly pitched—overwrought without being camp—and Dafoe's interpretation of the real Max Schreck's vampire is hypnotic. The transitions between clips from the real NOSFERATU and Merhige's recreation of the shooting of those same scenes is simply magical.

SHADOWS   DVD

1960 81m bw Drama ★★★★
Lion (U.S.)

Hugh Hurd *(Hugh)*, Lelia Goldoni *(Lelia)*, Ben Carruthers *(Ben)*, Anthony Ray *(Tony)*, Dennis Sallas *(Dennis)*, Tom Allen *(Tom)*, David Pokitillow *(David)*, Rupert Crosse *(Rupert)*, David Jones *(David)*, Pir Marini *(Pir)*

p, Maurice McEndree; d, John Cassavetes; ph, Erich Kollmar; ed, Maurice McEndree, Len Appelson; m, Charlie Mingus, Shifi Hadi

While on a radio talk show during the late 1950s, actor John Cassavetes casually mentioned his desire to film an improvisatory project and was soon surprised to receive public donations totaling nearly $20,000. Inspired, Cassavetes scraped together additional funds and, armed with a 16mm camera, he shot the powerful and moving SHADOWS, heralding a vital new era in independent American filmmaking.

Based on a series of improvisations created by members of the Variety Arts Studio, of which Cassavetes was the director, the film depicts the struggle of three black siblings to survive in the mean streets of Manhattan. Hugh (Hugh Hurd), the oldest and a would-be jazz musician, watches over Ben (Ben Carruthers) and Lelia (Lelia Goldoni), both of whom can, and do, pass for white. Darker-skinned than his younger siblings, Hugh has grown increasingly embittered due to the limited opportunities open to him; his artistic potential is being wasted in the dives and strip joints he's forced to play trumpet in just to survive.

Meanwhile, Lelia hooks up with the pretentious New York art crowd and moves among them, teasing and flirting. She has an affair with Tony (Anthony Ray), a young white man, and loses her virginity to him. However, when Tony learns that Lelia is a mulatto, he leaves her. Ben leads a carefree life, hanging out with his friends Tom (Tom Allen) and Dennis (Dennis Sallas), drinking, carousing and getting into trouble. One night the three young men become involved in a vicious street fight. By the film's end, Hugh grows more determined to win over one of the catatonic strip joint audiences, Lelia has taken refuge with friends, and Ben is abandoned by his buddies and left alone to lick his wounds.

Failing to interest American distributors—who, in addition to the obvious issue of content, were put off by the fact that the film was technically spotty and directed by a man heretofore known only as an actor—Cassavetes took SHADOWS to the 1960 Venice Film Festival, where it won the prestigious Critics Award. Shortly thereafter, the film was picked up for British distribution by Lion International. Finally, it made its way to the States and, to Hollywood's surprise, created a minor sensation.

Cassavetes was promptly hailed as a genius by critics and in no time began receiving offers to direct from major studios. The new director accepted Hollywood's embrace, but after making only two films (TOO LATE BLUES and A CHILD IS WAITING) he became frustrated by the limitations imposed on him by producers and returned to independent filmmaking, which allowed him complete control over his art.

While SHADOWS has become somewhat dated over the years and Cassavetes went on to greater heights as a filmmaker, its importance in the development of the American independent movement cannot be overstated, nor can the unique power it still retains. The film perfectly captured a specific time and place, illuminating simple truths regarding the human condition, while unveiling an important, powerful, and visionary new force in the American cinema.

SHAFT

1971 98m c Crime
Stirling Silliphant/Roger Lewis (U.S.)

DVD
★★★
R

Richard Roundtree *(John Shaft)*, Moses Gunn *(Bumpy Jonas)*, Charles Cioffi *(Lt. Vic Androzzi)*, Christopher St. John *(Ben Buford)*, Gwenn Mitchell *(Ellie Moore)*, Lawrence Pressman *(Sgt. Tom Hannon)*, Victor Arnold *(Charlie)*, Sherri Brewer *(Marcy)*, Rex Robbins *(Rollie)*, Camille Yarbrough *(Dina Greene)*

p, Joel Freeman; d, Gordon Parks Sr.; w, John D.F. Black, Ernest Tidyman (based on the novel by Tidyman); ph, Urs Furrer (Metrocolor); ed, Hugh A. Robertson; m, Isaac Hayes; art d, Emanuel Gerard; cos, Joseph Aulisi

AAN Best Original Dramatic Score: Isaac Hayes; *AA Best Original Song:* "Theme from Shaft"; Isaac Hayes (Music & Lyrics)

This was the second feature of the longtime still photographer Parks, in which he brought together talent for capturing an image and personal knowledge of life on the streets to create a hard-hitting action thriller. Roundtree plays a private detective hired by Harlem mobster Gunn to find his kidnapped daughter. This requires infiltrating the mob before finding the girl. St. John plays the black militant who assists Roundtree, and Cioffi is the cop who helps keep a gangland war from escalating. Although obvious racial tensions are created, these are kept under check by Parks, who concentrated on the humanistic elements in his character.

SHAKESPEARE IN LOVE

1998 120m c Comedy/Romance/Historical
United International Pictures (U.S.)

DVD
★★★★
R

Gwyneth Paltrow *(Viola De Lesseps)*, Joseph Fiennes *(Will Shakespeare)*, Colin Firth *(Lord Wessex)*, Geoffrey Rush *(Philip Henslowe)*, Judi Dench *(Queen Elizabeth)*, Tom Wilkinson *(Hugh Fennyman)*, Ben Affleck *(Ned Alleyn)*, Simon Callow *(Tilney, Master of the Revels)*, Jim Carter *(Ralph Bashford)*, Martin Clunes *(Richard Burbage)*

p, David Parfitt, Donna Gigliotti, Harvey Weinstein, Edward Zwick, Marc Norman; d, John Madden; w, Marc Norman, Tom Stoppard; ph, Richard Greatrex; ed, David Gamble; m, Stephen Warbeck; prod d, Martin Childs; art d, Steve Lawrence; fx, Stuart Brisdon; chor, Quinny Sacks; cos, Sandy Powell

AA Best Picture; AA Best Actress: Gwyneth Paltrow; *AA Best Supporting Actress:* Judi Dench; *AA Best Costume Design:* Sandy Powell; *AA Best Art Direction:* Martin Childs, Jill Quertier; *AA Best Original Musical or Comedy Score:* Stephen Warbeck; *AA Best Original Screenplay:* Marc Norman, Tom Stoppard; *AAN Best Supporting Actor:* Geoffrey Rush; *AAN Best Director:* John Madden; *AAN Best Cinematography:* Richard Greatrex; *AAN Best Film Editing:* David Gamble; *AAN Best Makeup:* Lisa Westcott, Veronica Brebner; *AAN Best Sound:* Robin O'Donoghue, Dominic Lester, Peter Glossop

A delightful, fast-paced, and entirely fictional imagining of Shakespeare's life during the writing of *Romeo and Juliet*. The screenplay by Tom Stoppard and Marc Norman brims with witticisms and is dedicated to having a rollicking good time while exploring the link between libido and creativity.

It's 1593, and scruffy but good-hearted theater owner Philip Henslowe (Geoffrey Rush) has commissioned the newest play by up-and-comer William Shakespeare (Joseph Fiennes). Unfortunately, young Will has also sold the idea to a rival theater company, and, more unfortunate still, all he has is the unpromising title *Romeo and Ethel, the Pirate's Daughter,* and a bad case of writer's block. At a ball, the lusty playwright meets the lovely Viola de Lesseps (Gwyneth Paltrow), a young noblewoman who, disguised as a boy, had just auditioned for and won the role of Romeo. Will eventually figures out that the object of his affection and his leading "man" are one and the same, but the course of true love does not run smooth. Viola's wealthy family plans to marry her off to the noble (if penniless) Lord Wessex (Colin Firth), and the doomed affair inspires Will to write the tragic *Romeo and Juliet,* which is just the sort of play commercially minded Henslowe *doesn't* want.

By dipping into the Bard's own bag of dramatic tricks—including mistaken identity and gender-bending—Norman and Stoppard celebrate Shakespeare while making him as accessible to contemporary audiences as he was to his own. In a particularly well-cast film that includes Judi Dench as Queen Elizabeth and Rupert Everett as rival Christopher Marlowe, Fiennes is a felicitous lead: he replaces the stodgy, historical image of the Bard of Avon with a youthful man bursting with creativity, snatching ideas from everywhere, and making them wonderfully his own. Henslowe may be onto something when he jokes that all audiences want is love and a bit with the dog, but this film delivers much, much more.

SHAKESPEARE WALLAH

1965 115m bw Drama
(India)

DVD
★★★

Shashi Kapoor *(Sanju)*, Felicity Kendal *(Lizzie Buckingham)*, Madhur Jaffrey *(Manjula)*, Geoffrey Kendal *(Mr. Tony Buckingham)*, Laura Liddell *(Mrs. Carla Buckingham)*, Utpal Dutt *(Maharaja)*, Praveen Paul *(Didi)*, Jim D. Tytler *(Bobby)*, Prayag Raaj *(Sharmaji)*, Pincho Kapoor *(Guptaji)*

p, Ismail Merchant; d, James Ivory; w, Ruth Prawer Jhabvala, James Ivory (based on a story by Jhabvala); ph, Subrata Mitra; ed, Amit Bose; m, Satyajit Ray

Diverting piece about a bedraggled theatrical troupe engaged in a valiant effort to keep the spirit of Shakespeare alive in post-Independence India. English actress Felicity Kendal stars, and much of the material is based on the experiences of her real-life theatrical family. Kendal gets involved in an interracial romance with a rich playboy (Shashi Kapoor); Madhur Jaffrey, an Indian actress also known for her books on Indian cuisine, turns in a colorful performance as a movie star. A wryly humorous film from the directing/producing/ writing team of James Ivory, Ismail Merchant and Ruth Prawer Jhabvala.

SHALL WE DANCE 🔲 DVD

1937 101m bw Romance/Musical/Comedy ★★★★
RKO (U.S.)

Fred Astaire *("Petrov"/Peter P. Peters)*, Ginger Rogers *(Linda Keene)*, Edward Everett Horton *(Jeffrey Baird)*, Eric Blore *(Cecil Flintridge)*, Jerome Cowan *(Arthur Mille—Linda's Manager)*, Ketti Gallian *(Lady Denise Tarrington)*, William Brisbane *(Jim Montgomery)*, Harriet Hoctor *(Harriet Hoctor)*, Ann Shoemaker *(Mrs. Fitzgerald)*, Ben Alexander *(Rooftop Bandleader)*

p, Pandro S. Berman; d, Mark Sandrich; w, Allan Scott, Ernest Pagano, P.J. Wolfson (based on the story "Watch Your Step" by Lee Loeb, Harold Buchman); ph, David Abel; ed, William Hamilton; m, George Gershwin; art d, Van Nest Polglase, Carroll Clark; fx, Vernon L. Walker; chor, Hermes Pan, Harry Losee; cos, Irene

AAN Best Song: "They Can't Take That Away From Me"; George Gershwin (Music), Ira Gershwin (Lyrics)

Shall we dance some more, please? For the seventh time in four years, Fred Astaire and Ginger Rogers team up for another frolicsome romp, though this effort doesn't amount to much more than a rehash of their previous films, replete with the usual romantic screw-ups, people pretending to be what they aren't, and too few stylized dances. Thank goodness for Astaire and Rogers and especially for a sensational Gershwin brothers score. Astaire is Petrov, a Russian ballet dancer; Rogers is Linda Keene, a high-powered musical-comedy star. To keep Linda from retiring to marry, Linda's agent (Cowan) suggests that she's already married to Petrov, to the surprise of the breathless press. Petrov and Linda ultimately decide to get married so they can get a very public divorce and clear the air, but true love does blossom amid the many plot complications.

SHALL WE DANCE might have made more of an impact on moviegoers, who, judging from the still huge but slowly declining boxoffice appeal of the Astaire-Rogers efforts, were growing tired of the formula. The film itself still has plenty of shine, but deficiencies exist. The peerless pair enjoy one of their best-ever tap duets with "They All Laughed," one which includes jokes, challenges, hard and soft tap, changes in tempo, a lovely merging of his ballet and her tap and a snappy close. But it's the only duet that measures up. Astaire and Rogers croon "Let's Call the Whole Thing Off" ("you say ee-ther, and I say eye-ther") quite agreeably, but neither quite pulls off the roller-skating routine which follows. Astaire's solo to "Slap That Bass" has some great moments and a blistering finale, but the fuel it provides really doesn't last. The finale, meanwhile, although it offers a clever resolution to the plot, seems more than a bit forced, with Rogers falling back in love with Astaire at the sight of duplicates of herself dancing onstage. The ballet surrounding this climax is a mess, with chorines and ballerinas ambling about in clumps, Astaire looking uncomfortable, and sideshow freak Harriet Hoctor bollixing any impact the number may have. A ballerina-cum-contortionist, Hoctor stops the show dead (and we mean *dead*) when she performs her signature move: kicking herself in the head while bent backwards like a human croquet wicket. Please be sure to share this moment with someone you love, for things like

this don't appear in films everyday. The supporting cast (except for the awkward Ketti Gallian) is as expert as it was in earlier RKO musicals, even if the hilarious and gifted duo of Horton and Blore really have to work overtime to put over some of the thin material. Although it didn't initially appear to be hit-laden, George and Ira Gershwin's unfailingly marvelous score ultimately produced a number of standards, including the haunting, Oscar-nominated "They Can't Take That Away From Me." (What a glorious romantic duet that song would have made for Fred and Ginger!) Maybe we've been harsh, because there's still plenty to enjoy in this typically exhilarating Astaire-Rogers effort, but the lack of invention and the slight dearth of dancing do make this a lesser entry in the duo's joint canon.

SHALL WE DANCE?

2004 106m c Romance/Comedy/Dance ★★★
Miramax (U.S.) PG-13

Richard Gere *(John Clark)*, Jennifer Lopez *(Paulina)*, Susan Sarandon *(Beverly Clark)*, Stanley Tucci *(Link Peterson)*, Bobby Cannavale *(Chic)*, Lisa Ann Walter *(Bobbie)*, Omar Benson Miller *(Vern)*, Anita Gillette *(Miss Mitzi)*, Richard Jenkins *(Detective)*, Tamara Hope *(Jenna Clark)*

p, Simon Fields; d, Peter Chelsom; w, Audrey Wells (based on the screenplay by Masayuki Suo); ph, John de Borman; ed, Charlie Ireland; m, Gabriel Yared; prod d, Caroline Hanania; art d, Sue Chan; chor, John O'Connell; cos, Sophie de Rakoff Carbonell

Director Peter Chelsom's remake of Masayuki Suo's quietly beautiful SHALL WE DANCE? is decidedly American—the women have more pizzazz and the men more humor—but it offers a surprisingly acceptable variation on a lovely theme.

Well-off attorney John Clark (Richard Gere) spends his dreary days drafting wills and his nights home alone; between her own job and playing chauffeur to their teenage daughter (Tamara Hope), John's wife, Beverly (Susan Sarandon), is often preoccupied. Night after night, John stares out the train window on his way home, catching regular glimpses of Paulina (Jennifer Lopez) sadly gazing at the night sky from the window of Miss Mitzi's Dance School. One Wednesday evening, John impulsively gets off the train and walks into Miss Mitzi's studio; the next thing he knows he's signed up for a weekly series of beginners' ballroom-dance lessons. Along with goofballs Chic (Bobby Cannavale) and Vern (Omar Benson Miller), John is soon blissfully practicing steps under Miss Mitzi's (Anita Gillette) tutelage. Feeling vaguely guilty about his newfound happiness away from his marriage, John decides to keep his new passion a secret. Not surprisingly, Beverly begins to suspect an affair—and hires a private detective (Richard Jenkins).

Gere is in fine form as a husband and father whose midlife malaise doesn't diminish his devotion to his family; it's refreshing to see a film in which the middle-aged crazies aren't resolved through a steamy affair with a hot younger woman. Sarandon, Cannavale, and Stanley Tucci—an inspired Latin dancer—claim their share of quirky and heartfelt moments. Only the expressionless Lopez, the film's ostensible star, seems to be struggling. Fortunately the script makes few demands on her limited talent.

SHALL GRAVE 🔲 DVD

1994 94m c Thriller/Crime ★★½
Figment Film/Film Four/Channel Four Films/ R
Glasgow Film Fund (U.K.)

Kerry Fox *(Juliet Miller)*, Christopher Eccleston *(David Stephens)*, Ewan McGregor *(Alex Law)*, Ken Stott *(Detective McCall)*, Keith Allen *(Hugo)*, John Bett *(Brian McKinley)*, Kenneth Bryans

(Senior Police Officer), Elspeth Cameron *(Elderly Woman)*, Jean Marie Coffey *(Goth)*, Tony Curran *(Salesman)*

p, Andrew Macdonald; d, Danny Boyle; w, John Hodge; ph, Brian Tufano; ed, Masahiro Hirakubo; m, Simon Boswell; prod d, Kave Quinn; art d, Zoe MacLeod; fx, Tony Steers; cos, Kate Carin

Wildly overpraised by critics in search of a new master of suspense, SHALLOW GRAVE has plenty of visual style but no soul. Three Edinburgh yuppies—Alex (Ewan McGregor), a journalist, David (Christopher Eccleston), an accountant, and Juliet (Kerry Fox), a doctor—are looking for a fourth tenant for their shared apartment. They agree on mysterious Hugo (Keith Allen), who dies of a drug overdose soon after, leaving behind a suitcase full of money. After some debate, the trio decide to slice up the corpse, bury it in the woods, and keep the cash. The scheme begins to unravel when two of Hugo's associates break into the apartment and viciously attack Juliet and Alex. Although David manages to kill the pair, it's only the beginning of the trio's troubles.

Even before its UK release, SHALLOW GRAVE was enthusiastically flacked by the British press, who hailed director Danny Boyle as a "British Quentin Tarantino." While Boyle's visual skill is evident, he lacks the vision and sense of structure that distinguish RESERVOIR DOGS and PULP FICTION; John Hodges's brittle dialogue, furthermore, doesn't come close to the loopy poetry of QT's best writing. Alex, David and Juliet are self-centered, obnoxious louts, the British equivalent of American yuppie scum: there's no possible way to empathize with them. As a result, the plentiful violence is more unpleasant than frightening, several potentially compelling scenes lose their resonance, and the gory, histrionic finale—evidently intended to play as black comedy—just feels excessive.

SHAME

DVD

(SKAMMEN)
1968 103m   bw   Drama   ★★★★½
Svensk   (Sweden)   R

Liv Ullmann *(Eva Rosenberg)*, Max von Sydow *(Jan Rosenberg)*, Gunnar Björnstrand *(Col. Jacobi)*, Sigge Furst *(Filip)*, Birgitta Valberg *(Mrs. Jacobi)*, Hans Alfredson *(Lobelius)*, Ingvar Kjellson *(Oswald)*, Raymond Lundberg *(Jacobi's Son)*, Frank Sundstrom *(Chief Interrogator)*, Willy Peters *(Elder Officer)*

d, Ingmar Bergman; w, Ingmar Bergman; ph, Sven Nykvist; ed, Ulla Ryghe; art d, P.A. Lundgren, Lennart Blomkvist; fx, Evald Andersson; cos, Mago

Ingmar Bergman's SHAME is a tremendously profound and unsettling film about the indignities of war. In remarkably subtle performances, Liv Ullmann and Max von Sydow play a middle-class couple whose bucolic existence is forever shattered by a mysterious civil war tearing across their homeland.

Former concert violinists Eva and Jan Rosenberg (Liv Ullmann, Max von Sydow) work and live on a small island, where they've escaped the war on the mainland. The apolitical Rosenbergs concern themselves only with selling the produce that they grow in their greenhouse. Despite ominous warnings of an impending invasion, the couple cling to their routine and ponder their future. Without warning, military warplanes fill the sky with explosions and gunfire while an officer warns Jan and Eva to evacuate immediately. Before they have a chance to start their car, Jan and Eva are ambushed by a film crew, who demand to know their political beliefs. Eva says that they have no interest in the war and the two are set free. Later, the Rosenbergs are arrested because of Eva's interview—which has been completely re-dubbed by a voice spouting revolutionary propaganda.

Considered by many critics to be one of Bergman's masterpieces, SHAME is certainly one of his most accessible. In the 1960s, Bergman moved to Faro, a small Swedish island in the Baltic where he also shot a series of daring and introspective films. In two of those "island" films—PERSONA (1966) and THE PASSION OF ANNA (1969)—he experimented with self-reflexive form and fragmented narratives using the bleak landscape as an existential purgatory where his characters were exiled. But with SHAME, Bergman felt compelled to make a non-political statement about the dehumanization of war as the conflict in Vietnam intensified.

SHAME's power is its simplicity. Cinematographer Sven Nykvist bathes the scenery in harsh sunlight, which gives the film an otherworldly and dreamlike glow. Longtime regulars Ullmann, von Sydow, and Gunnar Björnstrand embody their characters with a raw emotionalism that's upsetting and not always easy to watch. Bergman hardly shows any violence, yet his spare stylistic touches—phones and automobiles that fail to work, the sound of water lapping against a boat full of doomed passengers—brilliantly convey the horror of destruction and how the greater ideologies of politics don't matter when one is faced with survival and death.

SHAMPOO

DVD

1975 109m   c   Drama/Comedy   ★★★½
Columbia   (U.S.)   R

Warren Beatty *(George Roundy)*, Julie Christie *(Jackie Shawn)*, Goldie Hawn *(Jill)*, Lee Grant *(Felicia Carr)*, Jack Warden *(Lester Carr)*, Tony Bill *(Johnny Pope)*, Carrie Fisher *(Lorna Carr)*, Jay Robinson *(Norman)*, George Furth *(Mr. Pettis)*, Ann Weldon *(Mary)*

p, Warren Beatty; d, Hal Ashby; w, Robert Towne, Warren Beatty; ph, Laszlo Kovacs (Panavision, Technicolor); ed, Robert C. Jones; m, Paul Simon; prod d, Richard Sylbert; art d, Stewart Campbell; cos, Anthea Sylbert

AAN Best Supporting Actor: Jack Warden; *AA Best Supporting Actress:* Lee Grant; *AAN Best Original Screenplay:* Robert Towne, Warren Beatty; *AAN Best Art Direction-Set Decoration:* Richard Sylbert, W. Stewart Campbell, George Gaines

Satire of a satyr. Playing a Jay Sebring-like hairdresser/boy toy to the Beverly Hills elite, Beatty mercilessly lampoons his own offscreen image in a bumptious comedy of manners that turns persuasively sombre at the end. The events take place on Election Day, 1968, a date clearly chosen to signify the end of an era. Beatty is fooling around with Grant, an attractive married woman. Their coupling is interrupted by a phone call from Hawn, who represents the closest thing to a serious relationship Beatty can manage; he rushes over to her home and ends up spending the rest of the night with her. Later Beatty talks to a bank loan officer, hoping to get money to open his own hair salon. The loan officer thinks Beatty is a poor risk, and the angered hairdresser retaliates by screaming, "I've got the heads!"

Grant suggests Beatty approach her husband, Warden, for the money. Warden is sleeping with Christie, an old client/lover of Beatty's; he assumes Beatty is gay and doesn't catch on even when he finds his mistress and her lover virtually *in flagrante*. He agrees to consider Beatty's request, and asks Beatty to beard Christie at an election night party. Beatty reluctantly agrees, and the party proves to be a fiasco of drink, boorishness, and sexual betrayal.

Beatty, who produced SHAMPOO and cowrote the script (reportedly working for six years on it), was born to play the aimless, none-too-bright Don Juan. Hawn sums up his character nicely when she shouts at him: "You never stop moving! You never go anywhere!" The film's use of television election returns during the election night party is effective. History is in flux—with Nixon's election, the Swinging Sixties are definitively over—but the overprivileged party guests remain oblivious, caught up in the drama of their own sexual politics. The Beach Boys' popular song "Wouldn't It Be Nice" plays as the credits roll, a black-humored punch line to the film. Fisher made her film debut late as Grant's feisty daughter who seduces Beatty in record time. Reportedly Fisher's mother, Debbie Reynolds, was furious with her daughter for taking the part. SHAMPOO was an enormous success at the box office, taking in some $60 million during its initial release.

SHANE
1953 118m c Western   [DVD] ★★★★
Paramount (U.S.)

Alan Ladd (Shane), Jean Arthur (Marion Starrett), Van Heflin (Joe Starrett), Brandon de Wilde (Joey), Jack Palance (Wilson), Ben Johnson (Chris), Edgar Buchanan (Lewis), Emile Meyer (Ryker), Elisha Cook Jr. (Torrey), Douglas Spencer (Shipstead)

p, George Stevens; d, George Stevens; w, A.B. Guthrie Jr., Jack Sher (based on the novel by Jack Schaefer); ph, Loyal Griggs (Technicolor); ed, William Hornbeck, Tom McAdoo; m, Victor Young; art d, Hal Pereira, Walter Tyler; fx, Gordon Jennings; cos, Edith Head

AAN Best Picture; AAN Best Supporting Actor: Brandon DeWilde; AAN Best Supporting Actor: Jack Palance; AAN Best Director: George Stevens; AAN Best Screenplay: A.B. Guthrie Jr.; AA Best B/W Cinematography: Loyal Griggs

Self-important, overly solemn, middlingly paced—all harbingers of what would become Stevens's later style. It's the western styled as Arthurian legend, flawlessly cast, undeniably splendid. The thematic attempt really takes off when the Black Knight himself, Jack Palance, arrives, or when a dog mourns the passing of his master. And Brandon de Wilde had a very special line in children's roles—an ability to bring complexity and individual humor to the realm of childhood's longing. We love him very much.

SHANE stars Alan Ladd in the title role of the gunslinger who becomes a young boy's idol. Joe and Marion Starrett (Van Heflin and Jean Arthur) and their adventurous young son Joey (Brandon de Wilde) are struggling to survive on their Wyoming frontier homestead. One day, Shane (Alan Ladd) approaches on horseback and asks for water for himself and his mount. Joe obliges, and before long Shane is helping the family protect its land from villainous cattle baron Ryker (Emile Meyer). Shane stays on as a ranch hand and, in the process, becomes a friend and hero to young Joey. Shane's presence, however, proves to be too much of an obstacle for Ryker, and the inevitable showdown occurs. SHANE is a powerful drama in which the old West of gunslingers and cattle barons bows to the new era of the homesteader and the family. Ladd, who was never better as the doomed hero, and who gives one of the best performances ever seen in any western, knows he is a creature of the past and that he cannot escape his reputation as a hired gun. Although the film is often brutal, there is such a positive sense of morality displayed here that SHANE should be seen by the whole family. How many Academy members knew Paramount had sliced the top and bottom off Griggs's compositions, to accomodate the then-new, wide screen, and therefore had lost some of the color? Ladd learned a bitter lesson from SHANE. Then in the process of leaving Paramount for Warners, the former did no lobbying to earn him a Best Actor nomination. Yet the legacy of character he left behind gave this lonely, taciturn man immortality among children who see this movie.

SHANGHAI EXPRESS
1932 80m bw Drama   ★★★★
Paramount (U.S.)

Marlene Dietrich (Shanghai Lily), Clive Brook (Capt. Donald "Doc" Harvey), Anna May Wong (Hui Fei), Warner Oland (Henry Chang), Eugene Pallette (Sam Salt), Lawrence Grant (Rev. Carmichael), Louise Closser Hale (Mrs. Haggerty), Gustav von Seyffertitz (Eric Baum), Emile Chautard (Maj. Lenard), Claude King (Albright)

d, Josef von Sternberg; w, Jules Furthman (based on a story by Harry Hervey); ph, Lee Garmes; m, W. Franke Harling; art d, Hans Dreier; cos, Travis Banton

AAN Best Picture; AAN Best Director: Josef Von Sternberg; AA Best Cinematography: Lee Garmes

The fourth of the Josef von Sternberg-Marlene Dietrich collaborations (following THE BLUE ANGEL, MOROCCO, and DISHONORED), SHANGHAI EXPRESS is a mystical and exotic story of love and destruction, a film for which both star and director became legends. The film begins at the Peking Railroad as China's great train, the Shanghai Express, is being boarded and loaded with baggage. En route to Shanghai is a mixed assortment of characters, including Dietrich, a lady of questionable reputation known as "the White Flower of the Chinese coast;" Clive Brook, a British Medical Corps officer; Warner Oland, a shady half-caste merchant with a penchant for carrying a cane; and Anna Mae Wong, an American-bred Chinese prostitute with plans for starting anew in marriage. The time of the journey is one of great political unrest, with the possibility of bands of rebels attacking the train looming large. Before the train even leaves the station, arrests are made. Brook is surprised to find that he is traveling with Dietrich, a past love of his whom he deserted. Because of his constant work and busy schedule, he has never heard of her reputation as a glamorous prostitute and seductress. But he soon begins to understand Dietrich and the power she holds over men. In the meantime, it becomes clear to everyone on board that Oland is a rebel leader, desperate over the arrest of his aides. Along the way, Oland orders the train stopped at an old station that has been taken over for use as rebel headquarters, while he makes plans to take hostages from among his fellow first-class passengers. Oland, like Brook, is strongly attracted to the elusive Dietrich, but when the rebel leader asks Dietrich to be his mistress, she turns him down flat. But Oland pressures Dietrich by threatening to torture Brook. Only then—in order to save Brook—does Dietrich give in. Brook, however, is unaware of what she has done. Oland's fate is sealed, however, not by Dietrich or Brook, but by Wong, the prostitute in search of redemption, who has earlier been raped by the insatiable rebel leader. As Oland returns to his room, Wong stabs him to death, thereby freeing herself, the Shanghai Express, and the love between Dietrich and Brook.

Though von Sternberg insisted the film was based on a one-page treatment handed him by Harry Hervey, the story of THE SHANGHAI EXPRESS is clearly drawn from Guy de Maupassant's classic short story of a French prostitute during the Franco-Prussian war, "Boule de Suif." The final film, however, is all von Sternberg, his enigmatic creation, filling the screen with her stunning persona. Dietrich, as always, gave von Sternberg the exact performance he had envisioned, but feuds and hard feelings ran rampant between the director and the remainder of the cast. Von Sternberg was something of a tyrant on the set, and actors received the brunt of his wrath. Lending further credence to his tyrannical image on the set, von Sternberg, who had nearly lost his voice from shouting, dismissed a suggestion from Sam Jaffe to use a megaphone, instead hooking up a public address system. This enthusiasm and complete control over the production paid off for the director and for SHANGHAI EXPRESS come Oscar time. The film was nominated for Best Picture (losing to GRAND HOTEL), von Sternberg received a nomination for Best Director (his second in a row), and Lee Garmes walked away with a statuette for his cinematography.

SHANGHAI KNIGHTS   DVD

2003 97m c   Comedy/Western/Martial Arts   ★★
Spyglass Entertainment/Birnbaum-Barber   PG-13
Production/Jackie Chan Films/Touchstone   (U.S.)

Jackie Chan (Chon Wang), Owen Wilson (Roy O'Bannon), Aaron Johnson (Charlie), Thomas Fisher (Artie Doyle), Aidan Gillen (Rathbone), Fann Wong (Chon Lin), Donnie Yen (Wu Chan), Oliver Cotton (Jack the Ripper), Alison King (Prostitute), Gemma Jones (Queen Victoria)

p, Gary Barber, Roger Birnbaum, Jonathan Glickman; d, David Dobkin; w, Alfred Gough, Miles Millar (based on characters created by Alfred Gough and Miles Millar); ph, Adrian Biddle; ed, Malcolm Campbell; m, Randy Edelman; prod d, Allan Cameron; art d, Giles Master, Anthony Reading, Jaromir Svarc; fx, Nick Allder, Barbora Kolarova; chor, Jackie Chan (action); cos, Anna Sheppard

The inevitable sequel to the popular comedy-western-martial arts hybrid SHANGHAI NOON reunites East and West in 1887 London, faithfully re-creating the first film's mix of high-energy pratfalls, cultural misunderstandings, and self-referential gags.

Sheriff Chon Wang (Jackie Chan) is happily cleaning up Carson City, NV, when he gets a letter from his baby sister, Chon Lin (Fann Wong). Their father has been murdered, and the imperial seal of the Chinese emperor, which the Chon family has safeguarded for generations, is gone. Lin has followed the killer, Lord Rathbone (Aidan Gillen), to London and needs Wang's help avenging their father's death. Wang heads for New York, where his old partner Roy O'Bannon (Owen Wilson) now writes self-aggrandizing pulp novels, and together they stow away on a London-bound ship. Once in England, the mismatched friends cross paths with Queen Victoria (Gemma Jones), a Scotland Yard inspector named "Artie" Doyle (Thomas Fisher)—goofy Sherlock Holmes gags abound—and the wicked Rathbone, who's tenth in line for the British throne but has a plan to improve his odds. The womanizing O'Bannon falls for Wang's comely, high-kicking sister, while Wang kicks ass without really hurting anyone and is roundly defeated by the Queen's English.

Chan and Wilson have more effortless chemistry than the stars of most romantic comedies, and their banter is by far the best thing about this knockabout farce that's nowhere near as clever as it thinks it is. There are a couple of memorable comic moments, but most of the film's humor derives from smug anachronisms and jokes about bad English food, teeth, and weather that were old when Victoria was a girl.

SHANGHAI TRIAD   DVD

(YAO A YAO YAO DAO WAIPO QIAO)
1995 108m c   Drama/Crime   ★★★★
Shanghai Film Studios/Alpha Films/UGC Images/   R
La Sept   (China/France)

Gong Li (Bijou—Xiao Jinbao), Li Baotian (Tang, the Triad Boss), Wang Xiaoxiao (Shuisheng, the Boy), Li Xuejian (6th Uncle), Sun Chun (Song, Tang's No. 2), Fu Biao (Tang's No. 3), Chen Shu (Shi Ye), Liu Jiang (Fat Yu), Jiang Baoying (Cuihua, the Widow), Yang Qianquan (Ah Jiao)

p, Jean-Louis Piel; d, Zhang Yimou; w, Bi Feiyu (freely adapted from the novel Men Gui (Gang Law) by Li Xiao); ph, Lu Yue; ed, Du Yuan; m, Zhang Guangtian; prod d, Cao Jiuping; art d, Huang Xinming, Ma Yongming; chor, Wang Qing; cos, Tong Huamiao

AAN Best Cinematography: Lu Yue

This gorgeously appointed gangster picture, a departure for acclaimed Chinese art-house director Zhang Yimou, looks like a Hollywood genre movie—in fact, it looks a lot like BILLY BATHGATE. Here, however, the volatile gangster's moll (Gong Li) is moved—often literally—to center stage.

Zhang was criticized in the U.S. for making an apparently apolitical film, but political controversy nevertheless attended the 1995 New York Film Festival showing of SHANGHAI TRIAD. At the request of the Chinese Government—angered by another festival entry, Tiananmen Square massacre documentary THE GATE OF HEAVENLY PEACE—Zhang had to abandon his plans to attend the Festival. In addition, SHANGHAI TRIAD marked the apparent end of the long-time collaboration of Zhang and star Gong Li, which has often been compared to the intense professional and personal relationship between Josef von Sternberg and Marlene Dietrich. Gong had appeared in all seven of Zhang's features.

Simultaneously over- and underdressed in extravagant shades of red and gold, Gong Li is a star in the old-fashioned Hollywood sense: she's China's first screen diva, easily outshining the bravura gunplay and macho posturing of an essentially generic story line, about warring gangsters and their women in the Shanghai underworld of 1930. The film represents a retreat from the explicitly political concerns of TO LIVE (which landed the director in serious trouble with P.R.C. authorities), but there's a distinct satirical subtext underlying Zhang's Chinese Gangland, a place of limitless greed, self-destructive ritual and fatal hubris. Arguably, Zhang was up to something that in 1995 was far more dangerous than criticizing China's Maoist past—with necessary subtlety, he was contemplating its bleak capitalist future.

SHARK TALE   DVD

2004 93m c   Animated/Comedy   ★★
DreamWorks Animation   (U.S.)   PG

VOICES OF: Will Smith (Oscar), Robert De Niro (Don Lino), Renee Zellweger (Angie), Angelina Jolie (Lola), Jack Black (Lenny), Martin Scorsese (Sykes), Ziggy Marley (Ernie), Doug E. Doug (Bernie), Michael Imperioli (Frankie), Vincent Pastore (Luca)

p, Bill Damaschke, Janet Healy, Allison Lyon Segan; d, Eric Bergeron, Vivky Jenson, Rob Letterman; w, Rob Letterman, Michael J. Wilson; ed, John Venzon; m, Hans Zimmer; prod d, Daniel St. Pierre; art d, Seth Engstrom, Samuel Michlap; fx, Doug Cooper; anim, Ken Stuart Duncan, Lionel Gallat, Fabrice Joubert, Fabio Lignini, William Salazar

AAN Best Animated Feature

Though clearly designed to challenge the deep-sea supremacy of Pixar's FINDING NEMO, DreamWorks' gaudy, sadly debased spin on Kenneth Grahame's sly fairy tale "The Reluctant Dragon" is one soggy, charmless heap of chum.

In an underwater metropolis, small-fry Oscar (voice of Will Smith) dreams of the lush life but can barely hang on to his lowly job at the Whale Wash. In fact, were it not for pretty, levelheaded Angie (Renee Zellweger), Oscar would already have been tossed out on his tail fins for goofing off and borrowing against his salary to fund ill-conceived get-rich-quick schemes. Angie is secretly in love with Oscar, who's too self-centered to notice but happily accepts her financial help in repaying their excitable boss (Martin Scorsese). Oscar stupidly bets the money on a long shot at the sea-horse track, and just when it looks as though Oscar's luck has run out, he's mistakenly credited with having killed a vicious shark. Suddenly Oscar is a hero, rewarded with a deluxe apartment, public adulation, and the amorous attentions of glittering slutfish Lola (Angelina Jolie). Naturally, there's a downside to Oscar's good fortune: The dead shark's father, powerful crime lord Don Lino (Robert De Niro), vows vengeance. Oscar, however, finds an unlikely ally in Don Lino's other son, Lenny (Jack Black).

The script is an undeniably clever barrage of puns, in-jokes, and allusions to movies ranging from SCARFACE to JAWS, but like Oscar himself, it's more grating than endearing. For a hero, Oscar is an irritating, motor-mouthed hustler swimming in a sea of glossy urban stereotypes. He deserves a stinging comeuppance, not the rewards that drift his undeserving way, and for all the film's obvious moral lessons it winds up celebrating the shallow flash-and-trash values it pretends to mock.

SHATTERED GLASS
2003   103m   c   Drama   🅳🅥🅓
Baumgarten Merims Productions/   ★★★½
Forest Park Pictures/Cruise-Wagner   PG-13
Productions/Lions Gate Films   (U.S.)

Hayden Christensen (Stephen Glass), Peter Sarsgaard (Charles "Chuck" Lane), Chloe Sevigny (Caitlin Avey), Rosario Dawson (Andy Fox), Melanie Lynskey (Amy Brand), Hank Azaria (Michael Kelly), Steve Zahn (Adam Penenberg), Mark Blum (Lewis Estridge), Simone-Elise Girard (Catarina Bannier), Chad Donella (David Bach)

p, Craig Baumgarten, Tove Christensen, Gaye Hirsch, Adam Merims; d, Billy Ray; w, Billy Ray (based on the article by H.G. "Buzz" Bissinger); ph, Mandy Walker; ed, Jeffrey Ford; m, Mychael Danna; prod d, Francois Sequin; cos, Renee April

Several years before the "Blair Affair" rocked the New York Times, there was the case of Stephen Glass, one-time associate editor at the New Republic. Like Jayson Blair, Glass had also been caught cooking stories, but his fall from grace at TNR was even more spectacular.

This briskly told version of events is framed by an appearance by the 24-year-old Glass (Hayden Christensen) before a journalism class at his old high school. Hailed as a hometown hero, he attributes his success to his humility in a profession filled with egomaniacs. But as the film flashes back to the spring of 1998, we see that his meteoric rise also had a lot to do with the nature of his stories. Instead of boring old policy pieces, Glass's stories are filled with humor and colorful characters—stuff that's almost too good to be true. In "Hacker Heaven," he writes about a teenage hacker who'd been extorting money and cars from a large software firm. But when a reporter (Steve Zahn) from Forbes's new online publication warns TNR's editor, Chuck Lane (Peter Sarsgaard), that they'll be running a story about how very little of "Hacker Heaven" appears to be true, Glass's brilliant career comes to a screeching halt.

It's almost inconceivable that Glass could have gotten away with so much, but the movie makes a convincing case for how Glass used office politics, the good faith of his editors, and his own personal charisma to get away with some of the worst offenses a journalist could commit. While closely following the facts, the film unfolds like a thriller, and the acting is equally exciting.

SHAUN OF THE DEAD
2004   99m   c   Horror/Comedy   🅳🅥🅓
WT2 Productions/Big Talk Productions/   ★★★½
Working Title Films   (U.K.)   R

Simon Pegg (Shaun), Kate Ashfield (Liz), Nick Frost (Ed), Lucy Davis (Dianne), Dylan Moran (David), Bill Nighy (Philip), Penelope Wilton (Barbara), Jessica Stevenson (Yvonne), Nicola Cunningham (Mary), Peter Serafinowicz (Pete)

p, Nira Park; d, Edgar Wright; w, Simon Pegg, Edgar Wright; ph, David M. Dunlap; ed, Chris Dickens; m, Daniel Mudford, Pete Woodhead; prod d, Marcus Rowland; art d, Karen Wakefield; fx, Claudia Dehmel, Paul Dunn, Jeremy Hattingh; cos, Annie Hardinge

Dying is easy, comedy is hard, and combining the two is no joke. But just when it seemed there were no more changes to be wrung from zombie-movie conventions, along came first-time feature filmmakers Edgar Wright and Simon Pegg with this sharp, witty nightmare comedy that proves there's still life in the dead.

On Friday morning, 29-year-old London slacker Shaun (Pegg) is just another loser with a soul-sucking job and a berth in a shabby house with warring roommates, boorish best friend Ed (Nick Frost) and snooty yuppie Pete (Peter Serafinowicz). Shaun hates his stepfather (Bill Nighy) but feels guilty about neglecting his patient mother, Barbara (Penelope Wilton); meanwhile, his fed-up girlfriend, Liz (Kate Ashfield), has finally called it quits. Shrouded in petty misery, Shaun fails to take proper notice of the signs of an impending apocalypse, but by Saturday, even Shaun's and Ed's massive hangovers can't muffle the realization that something's gone terribly wrong with the world. The streets are eerily depopulated, the news is a blur of cannibal-zombie carnage, and there's a dead girl rooting around the back garden. Resolved to stop dithering and get his life together, Shaun commandeers Pete's car and, with Ed in tow, takes off on a mission. They'll rescue Barbara, pick up Liz, and hide out at their favorite pub, the Winchester. If you have to ride out a siege of the living dead, you might as well do it somewhere where they have liquor and snacks.

Directed by Wright and co-written by Wright and Pegg, veterans of the popular U.K. sitcom "Spaced," this darkly larky spin on George Romero's cannibal-zombie classics twists living-dead pictures and British romantic comedies with equal ferocity. Both genuinely funny and authentically horrifying, it puts the average horror comedy to shame.

SHAWSHANK REDEMPTION, THE
1994   142m   c   Prison/Drama   🅳🅥🅓
Columbia/Castle Rock   (U.S.)   ★★★½
                                               R

Tim Robbins (Andy Dufresne), Morgan Freeman (Ellis Boyd "Red" Redding), Bob Gunton (Warden Norton), William Sadler (Heywood), Clancy Brown (Captain Hadley), Gil Bellows (Tommy), Mark Rolston (Bogs Diamond), James Whitmore (Brooks Hatlen), Jeffrey DeMunn (1946 DA), Larry Brandenburg (Skeet)

p, Niki Marvin; d, Frank Darabont; w, Frank Darabont (based on the short story "Rita Hayworth and Shawshank Redemption" by Stephen King); ph, Roger Deakins; ed, Richard Francis-Bruce, David Johnson; m, Thomas Newman; prod d, Terence Marsh; art d, Peter Smith; cos, Elizabeth McBride

AAN Best Picture; AAN Best Actor: Morgan Freeman; AAN Best Adapted Screenplay: Frank Darabont; AAN Best Cinematography: Roger Deakins; AAN Best Film Editing: Richard Francis-Bruce; AAN Best Original Score: Thomas Newman; AAN Best Sound: Robert J. Litt, Elliot Tyson, Michael Herbick, Willie Burton

A "life-affirming" tale about life imprisonment, THE SHAWSHANK REDEMPTION is the kind of old-fashioned entertainment that is easily overvalued in an era of diminishing expectations. This reverent adaptation of an unremarkable 1982 Stephen King novella was received tepidly at the box office—due in part to advertising that offered no clue as to what the movie was about—but gained a remarkably enthusiastic following and surprised many by netting seven Oscar nominations.

In mid-1940s Maine, banker Andy Dufresne (Tim Robbins) is tried and convicted for the murder of his wife and her lover. He is sentenced to life at Shawshank prison, where he meets affable lifer Ellis Boyd "Red" Redding (Morgan Freeman), whose applications for parole are turned down on an annual basis. Known as one who can get things—for a price—Red secures for Andy a pinup of Rita Hayworth and a rock hammer to pursue his geological hobbies. Both items turn out to be crucial parts of a scheme that the mild-mannered banker nurses through years of painstaking preparation.

Whereas some Stephen King adapters have seemed intent on transcending or trashing their source material, writer-director Frank Darabont succeeds through fidelity to the text; the few deviations make this subdued male love story even more audience-friendly. The film benefits greatly from elegant cinematography by Roger Deakins and a poignant score by Thomas Newman. Freeman creates an endearing portrait of a decent man with a dark deed in his past, and Tim Robbins gives what may be his most accomplished portrayal. The excellent supporting cast includes James Whitmore, cute as the dickens as old-timer Brooks Hatlen, and William Sadler as a con who starts out scary and ends up lovable.

Which brings us to the film's greatest limitation: prison hasn't looked this inviting since 1940s Hollywood. Nothing seems to build character like a long stint at Shawshank, which on the whole seems not much worse than a downmarket summer camp. This makes for a crowd-pleasing story that has little to do with the messy complexities of reality.

SHE DONE HIM WRONG
1933 66m bw Comedy ★★★★½
Paramount (U.S.)

Mae West (Lady Lou), Cary Grant (Capt. Cummings), Owen Moore (Chick Clark), Gilbert Roland (Serge Stanieff), Noah Beery Sr. (Gus Jordan), David Landau (Dan Flynn), Rafaela Ottiano (Russian Rita), Dewey Robinson (Spider Kane), Rochelle Hudson (Sally Glynn), Tammany Young (Chuck Connors)

p, William Le Baron; d, Lowell Sherman; w, Mae West, Harvey Thew, John Bright (based on the play "Diamond Lil" by Mae West); ph, Charles Lang; ed, Al Hall; art d, Robert Usher; chor, Harold Hecht; cos, Edith Head

AAN Best Picture

Marvelously crude melodrama dished up with generous portions of undiluted West in her first starring vehicle. Re-creating her bediamonded demimonde, *Diamond Lil*, for the screen, she wriggles her way through some lowdown dirty blues ditties, seduces young Cary Grant's righteous Salvation Army crusader, kicks asses and takes names. Little-known director Lowell Sherman ably evokes the gaudy squalor of the Bowery at the turn of the century, and West establishes herself as a persona happiest squabbling among the chiselers and moneylenders.

West already reigned supreme on Broadway when Hollywood beckoned her at around age 40 (West was hazy about age) to support George Raft in NIGHT AFTER NIGHT. With SHE DONE HIM WRONG, West became an enormous star. She made 12 movies altogether, 10 of which she wrote either alone or with collaborators. Amazingly, SHE DONE HIM WRONG was shot in 18 days, plus one week of rehearsal, as West fiddled with the lines to mislead the censors.

West's Lou must rank as one of the first truly liberated women ever seen onscreen as she runs a Bowery saloon, fronting for owner Noah Beery, Sr. Cary Grant, a captain at the local mission, spends more than the usual amount of time in the bar in what seems to be an attempt to save her immortal soul; before long the buxom West is in love with the youthful Grant. Having been the mistress of Beery, who plies her with diamonds, West knows she's in trouble when her heart begins to obscure the glow of the gems. But Beery is discovered to be running a counterfeiting ring and, as a sideline, sending young

women to San Francisco to be pickpockets. Gilbert Roland and Rafaela Ottiano have been passing the bogus money that Beery needs to pay for West's diamonds. Then, in a jealous battle with West, Ottiano gets herself killed.

Remember what we said about crude melodrama? Scenes like the latter obviously recall the touring shows West herself must have seen growing up as a tyke in turn of the century Brooklyn. West's original character of Lil was derived from her mother, a former French corset model whose husband (West's Irish prizefighter father) referred to her affectionately as "Champagne Til." And some of Lil was undoubtedly West herself: as a child, West's mother spoiled her outrageously, always dressing her in minature versions of her own elaborate gowns. West never lost her taste for long skirts, fancy fabrics, wasp waists and cornucopic picture hats.

She had spotted Grant on the Paramount lot and asked to have him in the picture, a request that pleased director Lowell Sherman, who liked Grant's work with Marlene Dietrich in BLONDE VENUS. But West, who never saw other women's movies, didn't know that. Eyeing Grant up and down, West said to Sherman, "If he can talk, I'll take 'im." In the years to come, West always played variations on this "Diamond Lil" role in everything she did, tacking on other character names. West once asked, "Why should I go good, when I'm packin' 'em in 'cause I'm bad?"

SHE WORE A YELLOW RIBBON 📀 DVD
1949 103m c Western/War ★★★★
Argosy (U.S.)

John Wayne (Capt. Nathan Brittles), Joanne Dru (Olivia Dandridge), John Agar (Lt. Flint Cohill), Ben Johnson (Sgt. Tyree), Harry Carey Jr. (Lt. Ross Pennell), Victor McLaglen (Sgt. Quincannon), Mildred Natwick (Mrs. Abby Allshard), George O'Brien (Maj. Mack Allshard), Arthur Shields (Dr. O'Laughlin), Francis Ford (Barman)

p, John Ford, Merian C. Cooper; d, John Ford; w, Frank S. Nugent, Laurence Stallings (based on the stories "War Party" and "The Big Hunt" by James Warner Bellah); ph, Winton C. Hoch, Charles P. Boyle (Technicolor); ed, Jack Murray; m, Richard Hageman; art d, James Basevi; fx, Jack Cosgrove, Jack Caffee; cos, Michael Meyers, Ann Peck

AA Best Color Cinematography: Winton Hoch

The second film in John Ford's "Cavalry Trilogy" features John Wayne at his best and boasts some incredible, Oscar-winning Technicolor photography of Monument Valley. Capt. Nathan Brittles (Wayne) is a career officer in the U.S. Cavalry marking the final days before his forced retirement from the service. In the wake of the massacre of Custer and the Seventh Cavalry, the local Indians are becoming agitated, and, worse, confident. Brittles is assigned to escort two women (Joanne Dru and Mildred Natwick) from the fort to the stagecoach stop at Sudrow's Wells, but the Indians are on the warpath and there is little chance now to evacuate the women from the area. Wayne gives one of the finest performances of his career here, in the first serious role Ford gave him. (Wayne himself later said that Ford never respected him as an actor until he made RED RIVER.) As Capt. Brittles—the character a full generation older than the actor—Wayne is at his most human, a man who has made the Army his whole life, even sacrificing the lives of his family to its service, and now having to watch his Army career end on a note of failure. The passing of time is the film's recurring theme, suggested as Brittles arrives late with his troops, is forced to retire because of his age, leaves a dance to speak to his dead wife; even the inscription on the watch the troopers give him, "Lest we forget," plays on this theme of time lost and recalled. Ford's main inspiration for the film's scenic look was the western paintings of Frederic Remington. On the set, the director clashed with cinematographer Winton Hoch, a technical perfectionist who would endlessly fiddle with his camera while the cast baked in the sun. One day in the desert, when a line of threatening clouds darkened the horizon, indicating a thunderstorm, Hoch started to pack up his equipment. Ford ordered him to continue shooting, and Hoch did so, but filed an official protest with his union. The shot that emerged, of a fantastic purple sky with jagged streaks of lightning reaching toward earth in the distance, was breathtaking and helped Hoch win an Oscar for his work on the film. After decades of terribly washed-out color prints of SHE WORE A YELLOW RIBBON, the film has recently been restored to its original glory and may soon be available on home video in pristine condition.

SHENANDOAH
📀 DVD
1965 105m c War ★★★½
Universal (U.S.)

James Stewart (Charlie Anderson), Doug McClure (Sam), Glenn Corbett (Jacob Anderson), Patrick Wayne (James Anderson), Rosemary Forsyth (Jannie Anderson), Phillip Alford (Boy Anderson), Katharine Ross (Ann Anderson), Charles Robinson (Nathan Anderson), James McMullan (John Anderson), Tim McIntire (Henry Anderson)

p, Robert Arthur; d, Andrew V. McLaglen; w, James Lee Barrett; ph, William Clothier (Technicolor); ed, Otho Lovering; m, Frank Skinner; art d, Alexander Golitzen, Alfred Sweeney; cos, Rosemary Odell

AAN Best Sound: Waldon O. Watson

An offbeat performance from James Stewart as Virginia farmer Charlie Anderson makes SHENANDOAH an involving and entertaining look at one family's attempt to deal with the Civil War. A prosperous farmer with six sons and one daughter, Charlie is a widower whose wife died during the birth of Boy (Phillip Alford). Charlie, who is opposed to slavery, tries to maintain a neutral stance in the conflict between North and South. However, a number of events threaten to change his pacifist leanings: 16-year-old Boy is captured by Union soldiers; Confederate son-in-law Sam (Doug McClure) is called to duty; son James (Patrick Wayne) and his wife, Ann (Katharine Ross), are murdered by Confederate looters; and another son, Jacob (Glenn Corbett), is killed by a Confederate guardsman. Andrew V. McLaglen's excellent direction and carefully crafted battle scenes successfully combine with one of the best supporting casts you're likely to find outside of a John Ford film, including Harry Carey, Jr., Warren Oates, Strother Martin, Denver Pyle, George Kennedy, Paul Fix, and Bob Steele.

SHE'S ALL THAT
📀 DVD
1999 97m c Romance/Comedy ★★★
Tapestry Films/Miramax Films/FilmColony PG-13
(U.S.)

Freddie Prinze Jr. (Zack Siler), Rachael Leigh Cook (Laney Boggs), Matthew Lillard (Brock Hudson), Paul Walker (Dean Sampson), Jodi Lyn O'Keefe (Taylor Vaughn), Kevin Pollak (Wayne Boggs), Anna Paquin (MacKenzie Siler), Kieran Culkin (Simon Boggs), Elden Henson (Jesse Jackson), Usher Raymond (Campus D.J.)

p, Peter Abrams, Robert L. Levy, Richard N. Gladstein; d, Robert Iscove; w, R. Lee Fleming Jr.; ph, Francis Kenny; ed, Casey O. Rohrs; m, Stewart Copeland; prod d, Charles Breen; art d, Gary Diamond; chor, Adam Shankman; cos, Denise Wingate

In the grand tradition of CLUELESS—that ingenious reworking of Jane Austen's *Emma* as a high-school comedy of manners—comes this light, unassuming teen romance with an equally prestigious literary forebear: George Bernard Shaw's *Pygmalion.*

Zack Siler (Freddie Prinze Jr.) is a handsome high-school senior who seems to have it all: class president, captain of the soccer team, and boyfriend of Taylor Vaughn (Jodi Lyn O'Keefe), the most desirable girl in school and a shoo-in for prom queen. But when Taylor comes back from spring break on the arm of Brock Hudson (Matthew Lillard), the obnoxious star of cable TV's reality-based series "The Real World," a humiliated Zack sets out to prove that girls like Taylor really aren't so special. He bets his best friend Dean (Paul Walker) that, with the right hair, makeup, and clothes, *anyone* could be transformed into a queen by prom night, and dares Dean to give it his best shot. Dean finds their unsuspecting Eliza Doolittle in Laney Boggs (Rachael Leigh Cook), an intense, paint-splattered art student who's more concerned about riots in Mogadishu than popularity contests. Zack turns on the charm and gets to work, but the kicker, and what makes this first feature from TV director Robert Iscove so refreshing, is that Laney's nobody's fool: she's smart, socially conscious, and, even when Zack starts to fall for her for real (surprised?), stubbornly independent.

If you went to the movies at all during the early '80s, you'll probably experience a not altogether unpleasant sense of deja vu: there's the big second-act house-party scene, a poignant father-daughter heart-to-heart, the prom-night climax. It may not have the sharp wit and sparkling sophistication of CLUELESS—which admittedly raised the bar pretty high—but Iscove's film has its own brand of charm and is reasonable enough in its ambitions that it's awfully hard to resist.

SHE'S GOTTA HAVE IT
1986 84m c/bw Comedy/Drama ★★★
Spike Lee Joint/Forty Acres and a Mule (U.S.) R

Tracy Camila Johns (Nola Darling), Tommy Redmond Hicks (Jamie Overstreet), John Canada Terrell (Greer Childs), Spike Lee (Mars Blackmon), Raye Dowell (Opal Gilstrap), Joie Lee (Clorinda Bradford), Epatha Merkinson (Dr. Jamison), Bill Lee (Sonny Darling), Cheryl Burr (Ava), Aaron Dugger (Noble)

p, Shelton J. Lee; d, Spike Lee; w, Spike Lee; ph, Ernest Dickerson; ed, Spike Lee; m, Bill Lee; prod d, Wynn Thomas; art d, Ron Paley; cos, John Michael Reefer

Combining a lively, topical theme with stylish filmmaking techniques, NYU Film School alum Spike Lee won instant recognition for SHE'S GOTTA HAVE IT, his promising but flawed feature debut.

Nola Darling (Tracy Camila Johns) is a young, black Brooklyn woman whose bed is a shrine visited with great frequency by three very different boyfriends. She can't, however, pick the one she likes the best. First there's Jamie Overstreet (Tommy Redmond Hicks), a sensitive, well-mannered sort who smothers Nola with his overpossessiveness. Then there's Greer Childs (John Canada Terrell), a self-absorbed fashion model. The most likable character is the third beau, Mars Blackmon (director Lee), an unemployed bicycle messenger who always manages to make Nola—and audiences—laugh.

Combining humor, drama, and documentary techniques, Lee has created an energetic film that takes an unflinching look at modern sexuality—specifically black sexuality. The film is filled with scenes of the main characters speaking to the camera, commenting on the story and their rival characters—adding a sense of authenticity it might otherwise lack. Although the film's small budget and tight shooting schedule (lensed in 15 days on Super 16mm) is betrayed by sloppy editing, unpolished sound and an occasional flat performance, particularly Johns in the lead role, SHE'S GOTTA HAVE IT still bursts with the energy and technical command that have quickly established Lee as a major force in American cinema. The Mars Blackmon character lived on in a series of commercials for Nike sneakers shot by Lee.

SHINE
DVD
1996 105m c Drama ★★★½
Momentum Films (Australia/U.K.) PG-13

Geoffrey Rush *(David as an Adult)*, Armin Mueller-Stahl *(Peter)*, Lynn Redgrave *(Gillian)*, Noah Taylor *(David as a Young Man)*, John Gielgud *(Cecil Parkes)*, Alex Rafalowicz *(David as a Child)*, Googie Withers *(Katharine Susannah Prichard)*, Sonia Todd *(Sylvia)*, Nicholas Bell *(Ben Rosen)*

p, Jane Scott; d, Scott Hicks; w, Jan Sardi (from a story by Scott Hicks); ph, Geoffrey Simpson; ed, Pip Karmel; m, David Hirschfelder; prod d, Vicki Niehus; cos, Louise Wakefield

AA Best Actor: Geoffrey Rush; *AAN Best Picture; AAN Best Supporting Actor:* Armin Mueller-Stahl; *AAN Best Director:* Scott Hicks; *AAN Best Film Editing:* Pip Karmel; *AAN Best Original Dramatic Score:* David Hirschfelder; *AAN Best Original Screenplay:* Jan Sardi, Scott Hicks (story)

Based on the true story of David Helfgott, a gifted pianist whose troubled private life cut short a brilliant career, Scott Hicks's film is neither exploitative nor excessively sentimental, managing the difficult task of relating familiar screen material in a fresh way.

As a little boy, David (Alex Rafalowicz) is forced to learn piano by his domineering father, Peter (Armin Mueller-Stahl), a Holocaust survivor who was denied the opportunity to play music during his own upbringing. David shows great promise as a teenager and wins a scholarship to study in America, but a resentful Peter forbids him to leave home. Later, through the encouragement of an elderly writer, Katherine Susannah Prichard (Googie Withers), David defies his father and leaves to study at London's Royal College of Music. But his success there is matched by mounting pressures, and after Katherine dies, David suffers a nervous breakdown. After receiving electro-shock therapy, David is committed to an institution where he is forbidden to ever play the piano.

SHINE succeeds better than many other stories about artists overcoming adversity because it does not condescend to either the characters or the audience. David's jabbering adult self may be a bit annoying at first, but in the hands of Geoffrey Rush (whose performance as the adult David won him an Academy Award for Best Actor) he becomes a fully rounded character. Likewise, the father-son melodrama at the heart of the film resists becoming a simplistic power struggle. Rush is well-supported by the entire cast, particularly Mueller-Stahl, who turns in one of his best performances as the psychotic stage-father. SHINE's classical production will particularly thrill music lovers (most of the music is played by Helfgott himself), but the film's emotional force can be appreciated by all audiences.

SHINING, THE
DVD
1980 146m c Horror ★★★★
Warner Bros. (U.K.) R

Jack Nicholson *(Jack Torrance)*, Shelley Duvall *(Wendy Torrance)*, Danny Lloyd *(Danny)*, Scatman Crothers *(Halloran)*, Barry Nelson *(Ullman)*, Philip Stone *(Grady)*, Joseph Turkel *(Lloyd)*, Anne Jackson *(Doctor)*, Tony Burton *(Durkin)*, Lia Beldam *(Young Woman in Bathtub)*

p, Stanley Kubrick; d, Stanley Kubrick; w, Stanley Kubrick, Diane Johnson (based on the novel by Stephen King); ph, John Alcott; ed, Ray Lovejoy; m, Bela Bartok, Wendy Carlos, Rachel Elkind, Gyorgi Ligeti, Krzysztof Penderecki; prod d, Roy Walker; art d, Leslie Tomkins; cos, Milena Canonero

With remarkable visual panache and a keen sense of irony, Stanley Kubrick rehabilitates Stephen King's trashy, terrifying novel. Not a horror film in any traditional sense, but a perversely comic, occasionally frightening melodrama of intrafamilial rage, THE SHINING retains the Oedipal structure of King's narrative while running rings around its pulpy sensibility.

Jack Torrance (Nicholson) is a former schoolteacher hoping to find the solitude necessary to write a novel, so he accepts a position as the off-season caretaker of a Colorado resort, the Overlook Hotel. Because the winter storms are so fierce in this isolated mountain region, the hotel is often cut off from the rest of civilization. When he accepts the job, Jack is warned that the isolation can be devastating (some years earlier the caretaker axed his wife and two daughters to death). Jack and his wife, Wendy (Duvall), and their son, Danny (Lloyd), journey by car to the Overlook. Danny possesses the psychic gift that the hotel's chef (Crothers) calls "the shining"—he can "see" events from the future and the past. He can also project his thoughts into the minds of others. Danny senses something evil about the hotel and, while riding his bike through its labyrinthine halls, has visions of the carnage of past murders. His only playmate in this lonely environment is his "imaginary" friend, Tony. The emotionally vulnerable Jack—he's a recovering alcoholic with a history of violent episodes—is bedeviled by visions as well. Before long he begins to succumb to the hotel's supernatural forces and becomes possessed by thoughts of chopping up his family.

The film begins with astounding aerial footage of the Torrances' car driving through breathtaking mountain landscapes, accompanied by Wendy Carlos' mournful electronic score. There's also some impressive Steadicam work as the camera follows directly behind Danny, riding his Big Wheel bike through the winding corridors of the hotel. Cinematographer John Alcott (A CLOCKWORK ORANGE, BARRY LYNDON) does his usual outstanding job in each of these sequences. The film is rich thematically as well as visually—it's interesting to see how well the themes of the novel coincide with Kubrick's ongoing obsessions—but dramatically somewhat unsatisfying; it seems to have been conceived as a horror film for people who have lost patience with the genre. Duvall and Lloyd are excellent, while Nicholson's performance is over the top, complete with rolling eyes and hyperactive eyebrows. By the time of the climactic chase, he's lurching around like a cut-rate Quasimodo.

SHIP OF FOOLS
DVD
1965 148m bw Drama ★★★★
Columbia (U.S.)

Vivien Leigh *(Mary Treadwell)*, Simone Signoret *(La Condesa)*, Jose Ferrer *(Rieber)*, Lee Marvin *(Tenny)*, Oskar Werner *(Dr. Schumann)*, Elizabeth Ashley *(Jenny)*, George Segal *(David)*, Jose Greco *(Pepe)*, Michael Dunn *(Glocken)*, Charles Korvin *(Capt. Thiele)*

p, Stanley Kramer; d, Stanley Kramer; w, Abby Mann (based on the novel by Katherine Anne Porter); ph, Ernest Laszlo; ed, Robert C. Jones; m, Ernest Gold; prod d, Robert Clatworthy; fx, Albert Whitlock, Farciot Edouart, John Burke; cos, Bill Thomas, Jean Louis

AAN Best Picture; AAN Best Actor: Oskar Werner; *AAN Best Actress:* Simone Signoret; *AAN Best Supporting Actor:* Michael Dunn; *AAN Best Adapted Screenplay:* Abby Mann; *AA Best B/W Cinematography:* Ernest Laszlo; *AA Best Art Direction-Set Decoration (B/W):* Robert Clatworthy, Joseph Kish; *AAN Best Costume Design (B/W):* Bill Thomas, Jean Louis

GRAND HOTEL at sea. It's the early 1930s, and an ocean-liner peopled with a cross-section of society is leaving Vera Cruz for Bremerhaven. In the high class section are several well-to-do people, while steerage holds sugar workers returning to Spain after a season of work in Cuba. There are several wealthy Germans on the ship, and all are asked to sit at the captain's table save two—Heinz Ruhmann, a Jew, and Dunn, a dwarf. Werner, the ship's doctor and a man with a bad heart, makes time with Signoret, a Spaniard being deported for her political activities. Drunken satyr Marvin is a failed baseball player whose career went awry because he couldn't hit the outside curve ball. Also on the ship are unmarried lovers Segal and Ashley, flirtatious divorcee Leigh (in her last screen role), evangelist Wengraf, and dancer Greco. All of the above stories are interwoven, soap opera style, so we never follow any single story for any lengthy period of time. It's an adult picture with graphic language and important themes, the main one being Nazism. Superb acting in an Abby Mann script that seldom descends into bathos.

SHIPPING NEWS, THE
2001   117m   c   Drama   *DVD*
                                      ★★
Winkler Films   (U.S.)   R

Kevin Spacey *(Quoyle)*, Julianne Moore *(Wavey Prowse)*, Judi Dench *(Agnis Hamm)*, Cate Blanchett *(Petal Bear)*, Pete Postlethwaite *(Tert X. Card)*, Rhys Ifans *(Beaufield Nutbeem)*, Gordon Pinsent *(Billy Pretty)*, Scott Glenn *(Jack Buggit)*, Jason Behr *(Dennis Buggit)*, Alyssa Gainer *(Bunny)*

p, Leslie Holleran, Linda Goldstein Knowlton, Irwin Winkler; d, Lasse Hallstrom; w, Robert Nelson Jacobs (based on the novel by E. Annie Proulx); ph, Oliver Stapleton; ed, Andrew Mondshein; m, Christopher Young; prod d, David Gropman; art d, Karen Schulz Gropman, Peter Rogness; fx, Neil Trifunovich; cos, Renee Ehrlich Kalfus

Based on the Pulitzer Prize-winning novel by E. Annie Proulx, this drab drama charts one man's gradual awakening to the world's rich possibilities.

Thirty-six-year-old Quoyle (Kevin Spacey) has shambled through life unloved and unnoticed, doing dead-end jobs and haunted by memories of a joyless childhood. After his marriage to his relentlessly unfaithful wife (Cate Blanchett) finally falls apart and both of his estranged parents commit suicide, Quoyle agrees to take his daughter and move back to the family home in Killick-Claw, Newfoundland, with his flinty aunt Agnis (Judi Dench). Newfoundland comes as a shock to the newcomers: It's chilly in the summer, boats outnumber cars, and the ramshackle house at Quoyle Point creaks, leaks, and is literally lashed to the ground against the howling winds. Quoyle finds a job at the local paper and a friend—and perhaps more—in local schoolmistress Wavey Prowse (Julianne Moore), who's hiding her own secret sorrow. We, meanwhile, learn there's none so queer as Newfoundland folk: they eat squid burgers and seal-flipper pie, bear silly names, believe in visions, and have colorful histories, none more so than the Quoyles. Of course, the more Quoyle learns about his forebears the less he likes them, but that's all part of the process of learning to love himself.

Though generally well acted, this film has all the unfortunate earmarks of a "quality" adaptation of an acclaimed novel. It's crammed with characters who never quite amount to more than the sum of their eccentricities, embellished with exotic detail (like that seal-flipper pie), flashbacks (you can almost see the italics) and harshly beautiful vistas—the eye-candy equivalents of literary language. But everything has a fusty, embalmed quality; whatever gave the novel its vitality has been smothered.

SHOCK CORRIDOR
1963   101m   c/bw   Drama   *DVD*
                                      ★★★½
Allied Artists   (U.S.)

Peter Breck *(Johnny Barrett)*, Constance Towers *(Cathy)*, Gene Evans *(Boden)*, James Best *(Stuart)*, Hari Rhodes *(Trent)*, Larry Tucker *(Pagliacci)*, William Zuckert *(Swanee)*, Philip Ahn *(Dr. Fong)*, Neyle Morrow *(Psycho)*, John Matthews *(Dr. Cristo)*

p, Samuel Fuller; d, Samuel Fuller; w, Samuel Fuller (based on his scenario); ph, Stanley Cortez, Samuel Fuller (Technicolor); ed, Jerome Thoms; m, Paul Dunlap; art d, Eugene Lourie; fx, Charles Duncan, Lynn Dunn; chor, Jon Gregory; cos, Einar Bourman

Good example of Fuller's "tabloid" filmmaking style, displaying the contradictory politics and pugnacious visual style that earned him the label "American primitive."

A self-serving reporter (Breck) has himself confined to an asylum so he can uncover a murder and win a Pulitzer Prize. He is sucked into the maelstrom of the asylum, which is presented as a microcosm of contemporary society, and eventually loses his mind. Fuller plays cinematic bully here, forcefully confronting us with unpleasant characters and situations in a way that makes us rethink our preconceptions about insanity and civilization. The bravura camerawork, by Stanley Cortez, is a marvel. Original release prints included some color sequences the director had shot in Japan and Africa as early as 1955. Fuller followed this piece with what was probably one of his best works, THE NAKED KISS.

SHOCK TO THE SYSTEM, A
1990   91m   c   Comedy/Drama   *DVD*
                                      ★★★½
(U.S.)   R

Michael Caine *(Graham Marshall)*, Elizabeth McGovern *(Stella Anderson)*, Peter Riegert *(Robert Benham)*, Swoosie Kurtz *(Leslie Marshall)*, Will Patton *(Lt. Laker)*, Jenny Wright *(Melanie O'Connor)*, John McMartin *(George Brewster)*, Barbara Baxley *(Lillian)*, Haviland Morris *(Tara Liston)*, Philip Moon *(Henry Park)*

p, Patrick McCormick; d, Jan Egleson; w, Andrew Klavan (based on the novel by Simon Brett); ph, Paul Goldsmith; ed, Peter C. Frank, William Anderson; m, Gary Chang; prod d, Howard Cummings; art d, Robert K. Shaw Jr.; fx, Randall Balsmeyer; cos, John Dunn

A feel-good movie for anyone who's ever wanted to see yuppies burned, blown up, or dropped from the sky. Indefatigable Michael Caine plays Graham Marshall, an aging ad executive who is passed over for a promotion in favor of his nemesis within the department (Peter Riegert). Graham is already undergoing a mid-life crisis, and this professional setback sends him over the edge. But rather than suffering in silence or swallowing his pride, he takes matters into his own hands, determined to show the world just how bloodthirsty a shark he can be.

Once SHOCK puts its premise in place, there are few surprises as Graham—with a hilarious wave of his hand and a "Bippity, boppity, boo"—murderously removes one obstacle after another in his quest for success. Moreover, the film's venomous satire of corporate life is diluted by the hint of moral uplift in its resolution. But that doesn't dampen the delights of SHOCK, which lie not so much in the tale itself as in its telling.

SHOESHINE
(SCIUSCIA)
1946   93m   bw   Prison   ★★★½
Lopert   (Italy)

Rinaldo Smordoni *(Giuseppe)*, Franco Interlenghi *(Pasquale)*, Aniello Mele *(Raffaele)*, Bruno Ortensi *(Arcangeli)*, Pacifico Astrologo *(Vittorio)*, Francesco de Nicola *(Ciriola)*, Antonio Carlino *(L'Abruzzese)*, Enrico de Silva *(Giorgio)*, Antonio Lo Nigro *(Righetoo)*, Angelo D'Amico *(Siciliano)*

p, Paolo W. Tamburella; d, Vittorio De Sica; w, Cesare Zavattini, Sergio Amidei, Adolfo Franci, Cesare Viola, Vittorio De Sica (based on a story by Zavattini); ph, Anchise Brizzi; m, Alessandro Cicognini

AAN Best Original Screenplay: Sergio Amidei, Adolfo Franci, C G Viola, Cesare Zavattini

Along with THE BICYCLE THIEF and UMBERTO D, this film is one of the three neorealist masterpieces produced through the collaborative efforts of director Vittorio De Sica and screenwriter Cesare Zavattini. Like so many of the films of the neorealist movement, SHOESHINE is simply real life projected on a screen. After spying on a pair of shoeshine boys for a year in war-torn Rome, De Sica and Zavattini decided to bring their story to the screen with two nonprofessionals in the lead roles. Giuseppe (Rinaldo Smordoni) and Pasquale (Franco Interlenghi) are waifs who survive by harassing American soldiers—the only ones in postwar Italy with spare change—into spending a few lire to have their boots cleaned. Despite their bleak surroundings, these shoeshine boys still have innocent dreams and hopes, and, in fact, are saving their earnings to buy a handsome white horse. When Giuseppe's brother approaches them with a black market opportunity to make some quick money, they jump at the chance, buy their dream horse, and refuse to let it out of their sight, even going so far as to sleep in the stable with it. This brief moment in paradise is short-lived, however, and they are arrested, taken to a reformatory, and locked away. The longer they stay in their damp, vermin-infested cells, the more hardened the youngsters become. A powerful indictment of the Italian penal system and, on a larger scale, the brutal inevitability of the loss of innocence.

SHOOT THE PIANO PLAYER   **DVD**
(TIREZ SUR LE PIANISTE)
1960   80m   bw   Crime   ★★★★★
Pleiade   (France)

Charles Aznavour *(Charlie Kohler/Edouard Saroyan)*, Marie Dubois *(Lena)*, Nicole Berger *(Theresa)*, Michele Mercier *(Clarisse)*, Albert Remy *(Chico Saroyan)*, Jacques Aslanian *(Richard Saroyan)*, Richard Kanayan *(Fido Saroyan)*, Claude Mansard *(Momo)*, Daniel Boulanger *(Ernest)*, Serge Davri *(Plyne)*

p, Pierre Braunberger; d, Francois Truffaut; w, Francois Truffaut, Marcel Moussy (based on the novel *Down There* by David Goodis); ph, Raoul Coutard (Dyaliscope); ed, Cecile Decugis, Claudine Bouche; m, Georges Delerue; art d, Jacques Mely

A marvelously funny movie about sadness. For his follow-up to THE 400 BLOWS (1959), Francois Truffaut chose not to deliver another episode of his autobiography, nor to study childhood, but to pay homage to Hollywood gangster films. Deciding to adapt David Goodis's pulp novel *Down There*, Truffaut chose Charles Aznavour, one of France's most popular singers and songwriters, to play the role of Charlie Kohler, a honky-tonk cafe piano player who has given up his life as the famed concert pianist Edouard Saroyan. He becomes mixed up in the underworld affairs of his brother, Remy, and fears not only for his own safety, but for that of his adolescent brother, Kanayan. In the process he falls in love with Dubois but has trouble mustering the courage to court her. As he gets entangled deeper and deeper in the underworld and in romance, Aznavour reveals who he really is, how he got "down there," and why he doesn't ever want to go back.

    SHOOT THE PIANO PLAYER is a magnificent picture, not because of its debt to the gangster genre, but because of Truffaut's personal approach to that genre. Truffaut doesn't concern himself with plot mechanisms—since those have been provided for him countless times by Hollywood—but instead uses the conventions as a frame upon which to hang his own ideas (in much the same way the science-fiction genre served him in FAHRENHEIT 451), which burst out into all kinds of witty explorations. Said Truffaut, "The idea behind SHOOT THE PIANO PLAYER was to make a film without a subject, to express all I wanted to say about glory,

success, downfall, failure, women, and love by means of a detective story. It's a grab bag." More than anything, it is a collection of beautifully scripted and photographed moments, many of which do nothing to further the narrative, but give the film a soul. One such moment lasts only a split second: A heartless club owner swears that he is telling the truth and proclaims, "If I am lying, may my mother drop dead." At that instant, Truffaut cuts to a shot of a decrepit old woman dropping to the floor. The casting of Aznavour is brilliant, the actor combining the proper blend of cafe piano man and classical pianist—a figure who loses everything he has ever loved, except his music.

SHOOTING, THE   **DVD**
1971   82m   c   Western   ★★★★
Proteus/Favorite   (U.S.)   R

Jack Nicholson *(Billy Spear)*, Millie Perkins *(Woman)*, Warren Oates *(Willett Gashade)*, Will Hutchins *(Coley)*, B.J. Merholz *(Leland Drum)*, Guy El Tsosie *(Indian)*, Charles Eastman *(Bearded Man)*

p, Monte Hellman, Jack Nicholson; d, Monte Hellman; w, Adrien Joyce; ph, Gregory Sandor (DeLuxe Color); ed, Monte Hellman; m, Richard Markowitz

Moody, absurdist anti-Western from cult director Monte Hellman (TWO-LANE BLACKTOP), anchored by the charismatic presence of young Jack Nicholson. Warren Oates plays a bounty hunter on an existential quest for a man who may be his twin brother; he's joined by flirtatious Perkins, fatally naive Hutchins, and mysterious gunman Nicholson. A clash of wills in the vast desert leads to a violent, surrealistic confrontation.

    Minimal dialogue, spatial disorientation, and a tone of cynical revisionism characterize this little-known, strikingly unconventional film. Nicholson's minimalist performance is arresting, and Perkins (a minor starlet in the '50s) is good in her unusual role. THE SHOOTING was filmed simultaneously with the equally fascinating RIDE IN THE WHIRLWIND during a six-week period in 1965. Both films were produced on minuscule budgets by Nicholson and director Hellman, with an uncredited Roger Corman serving as executive producer. WHIRLWIND, whose sparse dialogue and bleak thematic material is strikingly similar, was scripted by Nicholson (THE SHOOTING was penned by Adrien Joyce, who later wrote FIVE EASY PIECES for Nicholson). Despite excellent reviews after screenings at the Montreal Film Festival and Cannes, no distributor would touch the film, and Nicholson was forced to sell the rights to a French producer who later went bankrupt. After sitting on the shelf for a few years, both films began to turn up on late-night TV, developing a word-of-mouth reputation that won them limited screenings after the success of EASY RIDER.

SHOOTIST, THE   **DVD**
1976   100m   c   Western   ★★★★
DEG   (U.S.)   PG

John Wayne *(John Bernard Books)*, Lauren Bacall *(Bond Rogers)*, Ron Howard *(Gillom Rogers)*, James Stewart *(Dr. Hostetler)*, Richard Boone *(Sweeney)*, Hugh O'Brian *(Pulford)*, Bill McKinney *(Cobb)*, Harry Morgan *(Marshall Thibido)*, John Carradine *(Beckum)*, Sheree North *(Serepta)*

p, M.J. Frankovich, William Self; d, Don Siegel; w, Miles Hood Swarthout, Scott Hale (based on the novel by Glendon Swarthout); ph, Bruce Surtees (Panavision, Technicolor); ed, Douglas Stewart; m, Elmer Bernstein; prod d, Robert Boyle; fx, Augie Lohman; cos, Moss Mabry, Luster Bayless, Edna Taylor

AAN Best Art Direction-Set Decoration: Robert F. Boyle, Arthur Jeph Parker

Eloquent last hurrah for a man who superseded mere movie-star status to become an icon of American culture, with Wayne playing aging, legendary gunfighter J.B. Brooks. Opening with a black-and-white montage of scenes from Wayne's earlier westerns, the film traces Brooks's career from 1871 to 1901, when THE SHOOTIST is set. As we move through scenes from RED RIVER, HONDO, RIO BRAVO and EL DORADO, Wayne ages before our eyes until he rides up before the camera and the film turns to color. During this sequence a voice-over spoken by Howard tells us that Wayne has killed 30 men in 30 years but was never an outlaw—he even spent time as a lawman. Wayne's credo: "I won't be wronged, I won't be insulted, and I won't be laid a hand on. I don't do these things to other people and I expect the same from them." Wayne rides into Carson City, Nevada, where he is informed by the doctor (James Stewart) that his cancer. The drama of his life's end is complicated by the presence of a beautiful widow, played by Lauren Bacall, and a host of young gunfighters looking to prove their worth by going up against him.

THE SHOOTIST is an uneven, elegiac tribute to a great career. The script leaves a lot to be desired, but is compensated for by some fine performances (especially Wayne's), Bruce Surtees' poignant cinematography, and Don Siegel's carefully paced direction.

SHOP AROUND THE CORNER, THE [DVD]

1940 97m bw Comedy/Romance ★★★★★
MGM (U.S.)

James Stewart *(Alfred Kralik)*, Margaret Sullavan *(Klara Novak)*, Frank Morgan *(Hugo Matuschek)*, Joseph Schildkraut *(Ferencz Vadas)*, Sara Haden *(Flora)*, Felix Bressart *(Pirovitch)*, William Tracy *(Pepi Katona)*, Inez Courtney *(Ilona)*, Charles Halton *(Detective)*, Charles Smith *(Rudy)*

p, Ernst Lubitsch; d, Ernst Lubitsch; w, Samson Raphaelson (based on the play "Parfumerie" by Nikolaus Laszlo); ph, William Daniels; ed, Gene Ruggiero; m, Werner R. Heymann; art d, Cedric Gibbons, Wade B. Rubottom

Delectable Hungarian pastry, served up by masters all around. This may be the best romantic comedy ever made. The great Ernst Lubitsch handles his "small" theme brilliantly, bringing the lives of everyday people to the screen as he had never done before.

In contrast to the glamorous heroes of other Lubitsch films, James Stewart's everyman sales clerk is as prosaic as they come. Working in a leather goods shop in Budapest, Stewart is the top clerk and a trusted friend of the owner, Morgan. Together, Morgan and Stewart head a tightly knit force of workers, all eager to please. Among them are Stewart's closest ally, Bressart, an aging clerk who leads a simple life and avoids confrontation; Schildkraut, a braggart who flashes his newly acquired wealth; and Tracy, an aspiring clerk who is constantly being bossed around. Trouble brews when the unemployed Sullavan enters the shop and begs Morgan to hire her as Christmas help. He rudely refuses; before she leaves, however, she impresses Morgan by selling a musical cigarette box to a fat woman for use as a candy box. Morgan gives her a job, much to Stewart's consternation.

But Stewart has another distraction, as he confides to Bressart: through a lonely-hearts ad, Stewart has met a wonderful girl, though he knows her only by her box number. After exchanging a number of increasingly romantic letters with the charming lady of Box 237, Stewart makes a date to meet her in the flesh. Sullavan is herself carrying on an epistolary romance with a man she's never met and whose name she doesn't know—Stewart, of course. While Sullavan and Stewart may love each other in their anonymous letters, however, they feel only an increasing mutual dislike at the shop.

While THE SHOP AROUND THE CORNER lacks the immediate impact of the more spectacular TO BE OR NOT TO BE or HEAVEN CAN WAIT, this late entry from Lubitsch touches viewers deeply. The director renders a broad array of characters and emotions with a delicacy unusual even for him. Lubitsch said of the film: "As for human comedy, I think I never was as good as in THE SHOP AROUND THE CORNER. Never did I make a picture in which the atmosphere and the characters were truer than in this picture."

The film features a James Stewart many of us have forgotten once existed—his touch is delicate and precise. He's perfectly matched by Sullavan, a forgotten genius who never gave a bad performance. SHOP was later turned into a musical for Judy Garland and Van Johnson, IN THE GOOD OLD SUMMERTIME—one of Garland's most formulaic efforts, and was also the basis for the popular 1998 Tom Hanks/Meg Ryan vehicle YOU'VE GOT MAIL.

SHOP ON MAIN STREET, THE [DVD]
(OBCHOD NA KORZE)
1964 128m bw War/Drama ★★★★★
Barrandov (Czechoslovakia)

Jozef Kroner *(Tono Brtko)*, Ida Kaminska *(Rozalie Lautmann)*, Hana Slivkova *(Evelina Brtko)*, Frantisek Zvarik *(Marcus Kolkotsky)*, Helena Zvarikov *(Rose Kolkotsky)*, Martin Holly *(Imro Kuchar)*, Martin Gregory *(Katz)*, Adam Matejka *(Piti Baci)*, Mikulas Ladizinsky *(Marian Peter)*, Eugen Senaj *(Blau)*

p, Jaromir Lukas, Jordan Balurov; d, Jan Kadar, Elmar Klos; w, Jan Kadar, Elmar Klos, Ladislav Grosman (based on the story "Obchod Na Korze" by Grosman); ph, Vladimir Novotny; ed, Jaromir Janacek, Diana Heringova; m, Zdenek Liska; art d, Karel Skvor

AA Best Foreign Language Film ; AAN Best Actress: Ida Kaminska

Among the most highly praised Eastern European films of the 1960s, THE SHOP ON MAIN STREET is a profoundly moving tragicomedy set against a WWII backdrop of racial hatred and fascism. Tono Brtko (Kroner) seemingly walks through life without any guiding morals or principles. He is content just to get by—though his domineering wife, Evelina (Slivkova), who longs for a more comfortable existence, tries to force him into working for her fascist brother-in-law, Marcus (Zvarik). One night Marcus brings news that Tono has been appointed Aryan comptroller of a Jewish button shop, a job that will bring money and status. Tono visits the shop the next day, informing the aged, frail, and rheumatic proprietress, Rozalie (Kaminska), that he is now in charge. She, however, too deaf to understand and too blind to read his authorization, begins bossing him around. Only later does Tono learn that the shop is completely bankrupt, and that the old woman is supported by her fellow Jewish merchants. He eventually agrees to the charade of working as Rozalie's assistant and forms a strong friendship with her that transcends racial, religious, and political divisions. But the Nazis soon appear, setting off a series of ironic—and highly dramatic—developments.

Codirected by the team of Kadar and Klos, THE SHOP ON MAIN STREET is a relatively straightforward narrative, without the stylistic virtuosity of so many other films by young Eastern European filmmakers. What the film lacks in flash, however, it makes up for in craftsmanship and intelligence. The acting is excellent throughout, and Kroner and Kaminska are both spellbinding. When Tono must decide between turning Rozalie over to the Nazis or trying to hide her, the film's careful buildup begins to pay off. When the elderly woman finally realizes what is happening around her and Tono desperately tries to shut her up, you may feel your guts wrenching in awe, terror and pity. Mixing a comic tone with a tragic subject, the film paints a uniquely vivid portrait of wartime persecution and enforces the view that the greatest, most inhumane of tragedies can strike anyone at any time.

SHORT CUTS

DVD

1993 189m c Drama ★★★½
Sandcastle 5/Avenue Pictures/Fine Line Features R
(U.S.)

Tim Robbins *(Gene Shepard)*, Tom Waits *(Earl Piggot)*, Lily Tomlin *(Doreen Piggot)*, Madeleine Stowe *(Sherri Shepard)*, Peter Gallagher *(Stormy Weathers)*, Anne Archer *(Claire Kane)*, Fred Ward *(Stuart Kane)*, Buck Henry *(Gordon Johnson)*, Andie MacDowell *(Ann Finnigan)*, Jack Lemmon *(Paul Finnegan)*

p, Robert Altman, Scott Bushnell; d, Robert Altman; w, Robert Altman, Frank Barhydt (from short stories and a poem by Raymond Carver); ph, Walt Lloyd; ed, Geraldine Peroni; m, Mark Isham; prod d, Stephen Altman; art d, Jerry Fleming; cos, John Hay

AAN Best Director: Robert Altman

With SHORT CUTS, director/co-screenwriter Robert Altman revisits the format of his 1975 masterpiece NASHVILLE, presenting a panorama of intertwined Southern California lives adapted from works by Raymond Carver. The result is quirky, sometimes brilliant, and mostly ice-cold.

Waitress Doreen (Lily Tomlin) is married to Earl (Tom Waits), a drunken lout who may have importuned to her daughter Honey (Lili Taylor). Honey's husband Bill (Robert Downey Jr.) is an aspiring makeup artist who pals around with Jerry (Chris Penn), who runs a pool maintenance service and is frustrated and disturbed by his wife Lois' (Jennifer Jason Leigh) career in phone sex. Claire (Anne Archer) and Stuart (Fred Ward) meet surgeon Ralph (Matthew Modine) and his painter wife Marian (Julianne Moore) at a concert featuring cellist Zoe Trainer (Lori Singer); the couples plan a barbecue, after Stuart takes a fishing trip during which he and his buddies discover a dead, naked woman in a stream. Marian's sister Sherri (Madeleine Stowe) decides to let her motorcycle cop husband Gene's (Tim Robbins) affair with Betty (Frances McDormand) play itself out. Betty's jealous, estranged husband, Stormy Weathers (Peter Gallagher), watches. Doreen runs over Casey Finnigan (Zane Cassidy), son of Ann (Andie MacDowell) and news anchor Howard (Bruce Davison). Their lives—and those of many others—overlap and intertwine, until an earthquake shakes up everyone and everything involved.

Altman's "Carver soup" didn't please all the author's admirers, many of whom felt that, by changing the locale and tone of Carver's stories and linking them to form an integrated web, the director had dispensed with exactly what was Carveresque about his source. It's hard not to be impressed, though, by Altman's narrative legerdemain—he sustains at least ten major stories, each of which has depth, definition, and dramatic interest—or the first-rate contributions of the players. The film is fascinating and complex, and benefits from a densely textured soundtrack that makes it as interesting to listen to as to watch.

SHORT FILM ABOUT KILLING, A

DVD

(KROTKI FILM O ZABIJANIU)
1987 85m c Drama/Political ★★★★
Polish Corporation for Film Production/Tor Film
Unit/Zespoly Filmowe/Telewizja Polska/Sender
Freies Berlin (Poland)

Miroslaw Baka *(Jacek Lazar—The Murderer)*, Krzysztof Globisz *(Piotr Balicki—The Lawyer)*, Peter Jan Tesarz *(Waldemar Rekowski—The Taxi Driver)*, Zbigniew Zapasiewicz *(Bar Examiner)*, Barbara Dziekan-Vajda *(Girl in Cinema Box Office)*, Aleksander

Bednarz *(Executioner)*, Jerzy Zass *(Court Official)*, Zdzislaw Tobiasz *(Judge)*, Artur Barcis *(Young Man)*, Krystyna Janda

p, Ryszard Chutkowski; d, Krzysztof Kieslowski; w, Krzysztof Kieslowski, Krzysztof Piesiewicz; ph, Slawomir Idziak; ed, Ewa Smal; m, Zbigniew Preisner; prod d, Halina Dobrowolska; art d, Grazyna Tkaczyk, Robert Czesak; cos, Malgorzata Obloza, Hanna Cwiklo

A SHORT FILM ABOUT KILLING is an expanded version of Episode Five of late director Krzysztof Kieslowski's DECALOGUE (1988), a ten-part series made for Polish television interpreting the themes of the biblical Ten Commandments in modern stories. This episode, focusing on the Fifth Commandment, brilliantly portrays the dynamics between killer, victim, and legal system.

Jacek (Miroslaw Baka) is a young thug from the countryside, unhappy and restless, who wanders the city aimlessly. Piotr (Krzysztof Globisz) is an idealistic law student who takes and passes his bar exams. Waldemar (Peter Jan Tesarz) is a simple taxi driver and a thoroughly unpleasant character. The film intercuts the lives of these three apparently unrelated figures throughout the course of the day in which their fates will intersect irretrievably. It is with apparent arbitrariness that Jacek finally hails one cab and not another, instructs the driver to take a desolate alternative route, and then brutally murders him. Jacek will be defended unsuccessfully by the young lawyer Piotr, given the death penalty, and hanged by the state.

The relative speed with which the film moves from the murder to capital punishment serves to highlight their moral equivalence. The long buildup that precedes the murders engenders no sympathy but rather adopts the cold perspective of a stranger. In this sense, Kieslowski relies entirely on the crimes themselves to reveal the meanings of the moral commandment. Released in Poland in 1988, this film preceded the success of Kieslowski's later French films, including THE DOUBLE LIFE OF VERONIQUE (1991) and the much acclaimed trilogy RED (1995), WHITE (1995), and BLUE (1995), which take up similar themes of contingency, fate, and coincidence surrounding and defining human action and responsibility.

SHOT IN THE DARK, A

DVD

1964 103m c Mystery/Comedy ★★★★
Mirisch/Geoffrey (U.S./U.K.)

Peter Sellers *(Inspector Jacques Clouseau)*, Elke Sommer *(Maria Gambrelli)*, George Sanders *(Benjamin Ballon)*, Herbert Lom *(Chief Inspector Charles Dreyfus)*, Tracy Reed *(Dominique Ballon)*, Graham Stark *(Hercule Lajoy)*, Andre Maranne *(Francois)*, Douglas Wilmer *(Henri Lafarge)*, Vanda Godsell *(Mme. Lafarge)*, Maurice Kaufmann *(Pierre)*

p, Blake Edwards; d, Blake Edwards; w, Blake Edwards, William Peter Blatty (based on plays by Harry Kurnitz, Marcel Achard); ph, Christopher Challis (Panavision, De Luxe Color); ed, Bert Bates; m, Henry Mancini; prod d, Michael Stringer; cos, Margaret Furse

This picture, the second in the Inspector Clouseau series starring Sellers, was drawn from a French play, "L'idiote," by Marcel Achard, which opened in Paris in the fall of 1960. About a year later Kurnitz presented his adaptation, "A Shot in the Dark," on Broadway, and it is from both these plays that the screenplay was fashioned. Sommer is a chambermaid, in the Parisian residence of Sanders and Reed, who has been accused of murdering her boyfriend. Sellers is mistakenly assigned to the case. His superior, Lom, would like to get him off it because he knows the havoc the man can wreak. ("Give me 10 men like Clouseau and I could destroy the world.") All the clues point to Sommer's guilt, but Sellers believes she is innocent.

The picture is filled with one sight gag after another, many familiar to anyone old enough to remember the glory days of silent comedy. The funniest sustained sequence occurs when Sellers attempts to bed down Sommer, and his aide (Burt Kwouk) leaps into the room ready to conduct the violent judo lesson that was to punctuate many of the later comedies. The original Achard-Kurnitz plays had the lead character a nutty judge, but that was altered in this screenplay to fit the character Sellers played in the first PINK PANTHER film. In the movies that followed, Lom continued as the boss, despite having murdered all of the victims in this one.

SHOUT, THE
1978 87m c Horror ★★★
Recorded Picture (U.K.) R

Alan Bates *(Crossley)*, Susannah York *(Rachel)*, John Hurt *(Anthony)*, Robert Stephens *(Medical Man)*, Tim Curry *(Robert)*, Julian Hough *(Vicar)*, Carol Drinkwater *(Wife)*, Nick Stringer *(Cobbler)*, John Rees *(Inspector)*, Susan Wooldridge *(Harriet)*

p, Jeremy Thomas; d, Jerzy Skolimowski; w, Michael Austin, Jerzy Skolimowski (based on a story by Robert Graves); ph, Mike Molloy; ed, Barrie Vince; m, Rupert Hine, Tony Banks, Michael Rutherford; art d, Simon Holland

THE SHOUT is a strange, disturbing, and elusive tale of a mental patient, Bates, who, having once lived with a tribe of Aborigines, has learned the secret of "the shout," which has the power to kill. Told in flashback during a cricket match that takes place on the grounds of a mental asylum, the film follows Bates's relationship with experimental composer Hurt and his wife, York. Bates moves in with the couple, and gradually his disturbing presence takes its toll. He tells the couple that he killed his own children, demonstrates his ability to kill with his shout, seduces York, and tries to destroy Hurt. Directed by Polish director Jerzy Skolimowski (MOONLIGHTING), THE SHOUT has a certain compelling element that both mystifies and involves the viewer, its unusual story told with equal amounts of obscurity and skill. It has no tidy conclusions or explanations, leaving the audience as baffled at the end as they were at the start, but the film is definitely worth experiencing. Tony Banks and Mike Rutherford of the rock group Genesis contributed to the electronic score, and ROCKY HORROR star Tim Curry has a supporting role.

SHOW BOAT
1936 110m bw Musical ★★★★½
Universal (U.S.)

Irene Dunne *(Magnolia Hawks)*, Allan Jones *(Gaylord Ravenal)*, Charles Winninger *(Capt. Andy Hawks)*, Helen Westley *(Parthy Hawks)*, Paul Robeson *(Joe)*, Helen Morgan *(Julie)*, Donald Cook *(Steve)*, Sammy White *(Frank Schultz)*, J. Farrell MacDonald *(Windy)*, Arthur Hohl *(Pete)*

p, Carl Laemmle Jr.; d, James Whale; w, Oscar Hammerstein II (based on the novel by Edna Ferber and the play by Hammerstein, Jerome Kern; ph, John Mescall; ed, Ted J. Kent, Bernard W. Burton; m, Jerome Kern, Oscar Hammerstein II; art d, Charles D. Hall; fx, John P. Fulton; chor, LeRoy Prinz; cos, Vera West, Doris Zinkeisen

This time around, Universal got it right. Carl Laemmle, Jr., whose father produced the 1929 version of SHOW BOAT that owed more to Edna Ferber's novel than to the 1927 Hammerstein and Kern musical, took over the reins here and the result is splendid. It's still the same romance between gambler Gaylord Ravenal (Jones) and Magnolia Hawks (Dunne), daughter of showboat captain Andy Hawks (Winninger). The stars of this mobile 19th century theatre, Julie (Morgan) and Steve (Cook), must leave the showboat when it is found out that Julie is half-black. Gaylord and Magnolia step in and play

their romance onstage and off, but an unlucky gambling streak spells trouble for the young couple.

SHOWBOAT's many-tiered plot is secondary to its extraordinary score, but it does make for some beguiling romance, delightful comedy and potent dramatics. Master director Whale, here essaying his first musical, does some typically marvelous things with the camera and *mise-en-scene* and gets wonderful performances from his cast. Many of them had essayed their roles previously onstage, so their dazzling assurance should come as no surprise. Dunne's lilting soprano does full justice to such favorites as "Make Believe" and "You Are Love" and she is sidesplittingly funny acting the role of a schoolteacher in a barnstorming melodrama aboard the showboat. It is fortunate that Winninger's legendary performance has been captured on film. His greatest moment comes when, with incredible dexterity and panache, he enacts the entire finale of a play before an audience. Jones, too, a likable actor-singer underused by Hollywood, does excellent work as a roguish but loving gambler. The rest of the supporting cast, including the ever-marvelous Westley and the one-and-only Hattie McDaniel, are in grand form, but Robeson and Morgan must be singled out for special praise. Robeson's immortal rendition of "Ol' Man River" is stunningly staged by Whale, as a 270 degree pan sweeps around him and the lyrics are enacted with Expressionistic vignettes. The film really suffers when Robeson is no longer around, but his presence haunts even the last reels. The same goes for Helen Morgan, whose decline at this point in her brief life and career is clearly apparent. She makes Julie almost unbearably poignant. Her tremulous voice and slight gestures convey volumes, and one is grateful when she briefly turns up again in Magnolia's life at just the right moment. When Morgan sings "Bill" (with that amazing close-up near the end), one feels privileged to witness one of the greatest filmed performances of a song in the history of cinema. If you doubt that two minutes of a woman singing can break your heart, guess again.

Universal really poured its money into this film, and it shows in Hall's lovely set designs, Mescall's sumptuous cinematography, and the actual riverboat built for the film. Whale's trademark theatricality lends itself perfectly to this film, and he plays the famous miscegenation scene for all it's worth. The film is only really flawed in the last third, as we are rushed into the 1930s while Magnolia's daughter becomes a stage star herself. It's quite improbable that Capt. Andy and Parthy would still be alive, and other contrivances mar the impact of what has come before.

SHOW BOAT
1951 107m c Musical DVD
MGM (U.S.) ★★★½

Kathryn Grayson *(Magnolia Hawks)*, Ava Gardner *(Julie LaVerne)*, Howard Keel *(Gaylord Ravenal)*, Joe E. Brown *(Capt. Andy Hawks)*, Marge Champion *(Ellie May Shipley)*, Gower Champion *(Frank Schultz)*, Robert Sterling *(Stephen Baker)*, Agnes Moorehead *(Parthy Hawks)*, Adele Jergens *(Cameo McQueen)*, William Warfield *(Joe)*

p, Arthur Freed; d, George Sidney; w, John Lee Mahin (uncredited), George Wells, Jack McGowan (based on the musical by Jerome Kern and Oscar Hammerstein II from the novel by Edna Ferber); ph, Charles Rosher (Technicolor); ed, John Dunning; m, Jerome Kern; art d, Cedric Gibbons, Jack Martin Smith; fx, Warren Newcombe, Peter Ballbusch; chor, Robert Alton; cos, Walter Plunkett

AAN Best Color Cinematography: Charles Rosher; *AAN Best Score (Musical):* Adolph Deutsch, Conrad Salinger

Greatly enhanced by its deft use of color, this third film version of Hammerstein and Kern's classic musical is nearly as good as the superlative second and much better than the lackluster first (1936 and 1929, respectively). Yet, as was the case with the 1936 version, the Motion Picture Academy barely acknowledged the film's excellence, nominating only Charles Rosher's cinematography and Adolph Deutsch and Conrad Salinger's musical direction. This time out the story is considerably altered and compressed, with Kathryn Grayson in the role of Magnolia and Ava Gardner as Julie, the much-wronged mulatto who helps save Magnolia's marriage to gambler-turned-entertainer Gaylord Ravenal (Howard Keel). The action is again played out on a Mississippi riverboat, *The Cotton Blossom*, piloted by Magnolia's father, Capt. Andy Hawks (Joe E. Brown, whom Edna Ferber reputedly had in mind when she created the character of Capt. Andy for the novel whence the musical sprang). Agnes Moorehead plays Capt. Andy's tough cookie spouse and Leif Erickson is the deckhand who reveals Julie's miscegenation to the authorities when she rebuffs his advances. After planning to shoot the film on location in Mississippi, MGM decided it would be more cost effective to keep the cast at home and, like the 1936 production, went to great lengths to create a realistic riverboat, constructing one from scratch that was over 170 feet long, nearly 60 feet high, and cost more than $125,000. Among the film's fine performances are those of Grayson, who had already played Magnolia in a segment of the fanciful biopic of Kern, TILL THE CLOUDS ROLL BY, and Gardner, who did her own singing but had her voice dubbed by Annette Warren after preview audiences reacted coolly to the beautiful leading lady's vocalizing. Although the film's musical numbers are almost entirely the Kern-Hammerstein originals, the finale, "After the Ball," was penned by Charles K. Harris, while P.G. Wodehouse and Guy Bolton wrote new lyrics for "Bill."

SHOWGIRLS

1995 131m c Erotic/Drama
Chargeurs/Carolco/Vegas Productions/
United Artists (U.S.)

DVD
★½
NC-17

Elizabeth Berkley (Nomi Malone), Kyle MacLachlan (Zack Carey), Gina Gershon (Cristal Connors), Glenn Plummer (James Smith), Robert Davi (Al Torres), Alan Rachins (Tony Moss), Gina Ravera (Molly Abrams), Lin Tucci (Henrietta Bazoom), Greg Travis (Phil Newkirk), Al Ruscio (Mr. Karlman)

p, Alan Marshall, Charles Evans; d, Paul Verhoeven; w, Joe Eszterhas; ph, Jost Vacano; ed, Mark Goldblatt, Mark Helfrich; m, David A. Stewart; prod d, Allan Cameron; art d, William F. O'Brien; fx, Burt Dalton, Special Effects Unlimited, Inc.; chor, Marguerite Pomerhn-Derricks; cos, Ellen Mirojnick

Perhaps *the* most hyped movie of 1995, SHOWGIRLS was Hollywood's first attempt to mass-market a film with an NC-17 rating. Its non-stop display of flesh and sleaze aside, the film is a cliched and coarsely-acted backstage drama whose only possible value lies in its camp posturing.

Brassy young Nomi Malone (Elizabeth Berkley) hitchhikes into Las Vegas determined to become a star showgirl. She is befriended by Molly (Gina Ravera), a young costumer, who invites Nomi to share her trailer. Nomi quickly begins clawing her way up the greased pole of the Vegas entertainment industry, first landing a job dancing in a sleazy topless club and later graduating to higher-paying, semi-private lap dances. After performing for hotel entertainment director Zack Carey (Kyle MacLachlan) and Stardust Hotel revue star Cristal Connors (Gina Gershon), Nomi wins an audition in front of a powerful producer and gets a shot at the topless big-time.

This colossal misfire from the writer-director team of Joe Eszterhas and Paul Verhoeven—the creators of BASIC INSTINCT—received the critical censure it so richly merited. Verhoeven claimed he intended to make a provocative movie revealing the harsh, corrupt side of the showgirl business and the glitzmeisters who run it. Instead, he produced an unpleasant gawk at the seamy facade and sleazy back rooms of topless Las Vegas. Eszterhas's story and characters are as superficial as the subject matter, turning the viewer into a voyeur. Berkley's wooden performance only accentuates the script's weaknesses. Her Nomi is witlessly unsympathetic—even in comparison with the despicable snakes who surround her.

SHREK

2001 89m c Animated/Comedy
PDI/DreamWorks (U.S.)

DVD
★★★★
PG

VOICES OF: Mike Myers (Shrek/Blind Mouse), Eddie Murphy (Donkey), Cameron Diaz (Princess Fiona), John Lithgow (Lord Farquaad), Vincent Cassel (Monsieur Hood), Peter Dennis (Ogre Hunter), Clive Pearse (Ogre Hunter), Jim Cummings (Captain of Guards), Bobby Block (Baby Bear), Chris Miller (Geppetto/Magic Mirror)

p, Jeffrey Katzenberg, Aron Warner, John H. Williams; d, Andrew Adamson, Vicky Jenson; w, Ted Elliott, Terry Rossio, Joe Stillman, Roger S.H. Schulman (based on the book Shrek! by William Steig); ed, Sim Evan-Jones; m, Harry Gregson-Williams, John Powell; prod d, James Hegedus; art d, Guillaume Aretos, Douglas Rogers; fx, Ken Bielenberg; cos, Isis Mussenden; anim, Tim Cheung, Paul Chung, Denis Couchon, Donnachada Daly, Raman Hui, James Satoru Strauss

AA Best Animated Feature Film: ; AAN Best Adapted Screenplay: Ted Elliott, Terry Rossio, Joe Stillman, Roger S.H. Schulman

This monstrously entertaining animated fairy tale marries state-of-the-art computer graphics with a rich, multilevel story for all ages. Very loosely based on the 1990 children's book by legendary *New Yorker* cartoonist William Steig, the film both honors and subverts classic storybook tales with a controlled explosion of pop-culture references.

Ogre Shrek (voiced by Mike Myers) is a green-skinned, incredible bulk who rids himself of torch-bearing villagers as much as by patronizing them as scaring them. Misanthropic but also misunderstood, the big grumbler is less than pleased when preening Prince Farquaad (John Lithgow) turns his beloved swamp into a refugee camp for resettled fairy-tale characters. Determined to sort it out, Shrek and his motor-mouthed sidekick, Donkey (Eddie Murphy), head to the nearby city of Duloc. They arrive just as Farquaad is about to select a knight to rescue one Princess Fiona (Cameron Diaz); Shrek, of course, reluctantly gets the gig.

Fast, irreverent, and magnificently animated with a degree of expressiveness and detail previously unseen in computer graphics, this adventure-comedy-romance succeeds in all three areas, despite a slight overabundance of gross-out humor early on. It should also be noted that while Murphy's talents make Donkey a hilarious character, he's essentially a throwback to the shameful "frightened darkie" stereotype of yore; you half expect him to blurt out, "Hooves, don't fail me now!" Equally bothersome is that for all the film's talk of tolerance over physical appearances, it relentlessly teases Farquaad for being short—an inexplicable bit of hypocrisy that leaves a sour aftertaste. In the works since 1994, the project was originally conceived as a stop-motion animated film starring the late Chris Farley and was reworked after his death in 1997.

SHREK 2

2004 93m c Animated/Comedy/Fantasy ★★★½
DreamWorks Productions/Pacific Data Images PG
(U.S.)

VOICES OF: Mike Myers (Shrek), Eddie Murphy (Donkey),
Cameron Diaz (Princess Fiona), Julie Andrews (Queen Lillian),
John Cleese (King Harold), Antonio Banderas (Puss in Boots),
Rupert Everett (Prince Charming), Jennifer Saunders (Fairy
Godmother), Aron Warner (Wolf), Kelly Asbury
(Page/Elf/Nobleman/Nobleman's Son)

p, David Lipman, Aron Warner, John H. Williams; d, Andrew
Adamson, Kelly Asbury, Conrad Vernon; w, Andrew Adamson, J.
David Stern, Joe Stillman, David N. Weiss (from a story by
Andrew Adamson, based on the book by William Steig); ed,
Michael Andrews, Sim Evan-Jones; m, Harry Gregson-Williams;
prod d, Guillaume Aretos; art d, Steve Pilcher; fx, Ken Bielenberg,
Philippe Gluckman; anim, James Baxter, Tim Cheung, Raman Hui

AAN Best Animated Feature; AAN Best Original Song:
"Accidentally in Love"; Adam Durtiz, Charles Gillingham, Jim
Boglios, David Immergluck, Matthew Malley, David Bryson (music),
Adam Duritz, Daniel Vickrey (lyrics)

Awash in pop-culture jokes that will fly over the heads of tots
and delight their parents, this vividly colored romp is a worthy
sequel to the 2001 Oscar winner.

Newlyweds Shrek (voice of Mike Myers) and his bride,
Princess Fiona (Cameron Diaz), return home from their honeymoon to find that Shrek's pal Donkey (Eddie Murphy) has
moved into their swamp shack because things aren't working
out with his fire-breathing dragon of a girlfriend. Before they
can give Donkey the boot, Fiona receives an invitation from
her parents, King Harold (John Cleese) and Queen Lillian
(Julie Andrews) of the kingdom of Far, Far Away, asking her
to visit so they can celebrate her nuptials in high style. But the
royals are in for a shock: They had no idea that their lovely
daughter had permanently assumed ogre form, and her new
husband isn't the princely fellow they'd hoped she'd marry.
Fiona's scheming Fairy Godmother (Jennifer Saunders),
meanwhile, is fuming because Fiona married some green
goon instead of her dimwitted but handsome son, Prince
Charming (Rupert Everett). Pressured by Fairy Godmother,
King Harold hires an assassin to eliminate Shrek. Fortunately,
the Zorro-inspired Puss in Boots (Antonio Banderas) not only
fails to rip Shrek to shreds with his razor-sharp claws but he
befriends his quarry, then joins forces with Shrek and Donkey
to stop the Fairy Godmother's meddling and win back Fiona
from the vapid prince.

The film's distinctive CGI animation is even more
detailed than the original, while the Disney needling has been
minimized. But there are still plenty of one-liners and gags to
go around and if Murphy's nonstop outrageousness occasionally makes Donkey seem like, well, an ass, Puss in Boots is a
natural-born star and Banderas' gravelly purr is as flawlessly
apt a piece of voice casting as anyone could desire.

SHY PEOPLE

1988 119m c Drama ★★★½
Golan-Globus (U.S.) R

Jill Clayburgh (Diana Sullivan), Barbara Hershey (Ruth Sullivan),
Martha Plimpton (Grace Sullivan), Merritt Butrick (Mike Sullivan),
John Philbin (Tommy Sullivan), Don Swayze (Mark Sullivan),
Pruitt Taylor Vince (Paul Sullivan), Mare Winningham (Candy),
Michael Audley (Louie), Brad Leland (Larry)

p, Menahem Golan, Yoram Globus; d, Andrei Konchalovsky; w,
Gerard Brach, Andrei Konchalovsky, Marjorie David (based on a

story by Konchalovsky); ph, Chris Menges (Rank color); ed, Alain
Jakubowicz; fx, Cal Acord

The fourth American film from Soviet emigre Andrei
Konchalovsky (MARIA'S LOVERS; RUNAWAY TRAIN;
and DUET FOR ONE preceded), SHY PEOPLE is about a
meeting of two people, and two worlds, who initially appear
to be diametrically opposed but who, we learn by the film's
end, have more in common than we imagined. The film opens
in Manhattan, where *Cosmopolitan* reporter Diana Sullivan
(Jill Clayburgh) lives with her teenaged coke-sniffing daughter, Grace (Martha Plimpton). At her editor's suggestion,
Diana has traced her own roots back to the Louisiana Bayou
and talks her bored daughter into accompanying her on a visit
to the relatives. As Diana and Grace reveal their urban depend-
encies, the Cajun cousins reveal their backwoods, superstitious ways. Ruth Sullivan (Barbara Hershey) informs her
guests that the family is watched over by her former husband,
the outlaw Joe, though he hasn't been seen for over 15 years.
The film is full of strange and wonderful events, and in the
course of the action the two women grow and change as a
result of their exposure to one another. As in his 1985 RUN-
AWAY TRAIN, Konchalovsky here presents powerful characterizations, beautiful imagery, and philosophical content as
entertainment that can appeal to the average filmgoer but that
also still has enough depth to stand up to critical analysis.

SID AND NANCY

1986 111m c Biography ★★★★
Zenith/Initial (U.K.) R

Gary Oldman (Sid Vicious), Chloe Webb (Nancy Spungen), Drew
Schofield (Johnny Rotten), David Hayman (Malcolm McLaren),
Debbie Bishop (Phoebe), Tony London (Steve), Perry Benson
(Paul), Anne Lambton (Linda), Kathy Burke (Brenda), Mark
Monero (Clive)

p, Eric Fellner; d, Alex Cox; w, Alex Cox, Abbe Wool; ph, Roger
Deakins; ed, David Martin; m, Pray for Rain, The Pogues, Joe
Strummer; prod d, Andrew McAlpine; art d, J. Rae Fox, Lynda
Burbank; cos, Cathy Cook, Theda De Ramus

The sordid, pathetic lives of Sex Pistols bassist Sid Vicious and
his groupie girlfriend Nancy Spungen might strike some as
unsuitable material for a movie romance, but British filmmaker Alex Cox brings their embattled relationship and tragic end to powerful cinematic life.

SID AND NANCY opens in 1978, as police arrive at
New York's Chelsea Hotel to find the body of Nancy (Chloe
Webb) in the couple's bathroom and zombie-like Sid (Gary
Oldman) staring at the wall and holding a knife. The film then
flashes back to 1977 when the couple first meet at the home
of Linda (Anne Lambton), a friend of Sid's and Johnny
Rotten's (Drew Schofield). Nancy is a loud, whining,
American rock 'n' roll groupie who's wound up in London at
the height of the punk rock movement. She's impressed when
she learns that Linda's guests are members of the infamous
Sex Pistols, the brainchild of young entrepreneur Malcolm
McLaren (David Hayman). (Sid, born John Ritchie, abandoned his role as drummer for the nascent Siouxsie and the
Banshees to replace original Sex Pistol bassist Glen Matlock.)
That night, she goes to hear the band, riding high on the British
charts with "God Save the Queen," their second single, and
later tries to seduce Rotten, but he declares sex "boring" and
leaves her to Vicious.

A few days later Sid spots Nancy in a pub and follows her
when she runs out yelling and crying; another rocker has
absconded with her heroin money. Angry and frustrated,
Spungen scrapes her knuckles on a brick wall. "That looks
like it hurts," Sid tells her sympathetically. "So does this," he
continues, and brutally slams his head into the brick wall, a
gesture which Nancy seems to understand and appreciate. Sid

then gives Nancy money to buy heroin for both of them; although she's already a full-blown junkie, Sid has never done hard drugs.

SID AND NANCY does not canonize Sid Vicious and Nancy Spungen, the Sex Pistols or the punk movement itself, nor does it glamorize the couple's horrible self-destruction. (Sid died of a heroin overdose on February 2, 1979, before his case could be tried.) Although Cox, abetted by co-screenwriter Abbe Wool, often displays a black, quirky sense of humor, the horror of drug addiction is always at the forefront and never made light of.

The performances of Oldman and Webb, both stage-trained veterans, are simply astonishing. SID AND NANCY will certainly be tough going for viewers unfamiliar with the punk movement and unprepared for the extraordinary amount of cynicism, ignorance, anger, and self-abuse that went hand-in-hand with it, but the film's value lies in its honest, unflinching gaze at a social phenomenon.

SIDEWAYS
2004 123m c Comedy ★★★★
Michael London Productions/Sideways Productions/ R
Fox Searchlight (U.S.)

Paul Giamatti *(Miles)*, Thomas Haden Church *(Jack)*, Virginia Madsen *(Maya)*, Sandra Oh *(Stephanie)*, Marylouise Burke *(Mile's Mother)*, Jessica Hecht *(Victoria)*, Missy Doty *(Cammi)*, MC Gainey *(Cammi's Husband)*, Alysia Reiner *(Christine Erganian)*, Shake Toukhmanian *(Mrs. Erganian)*

p, Michael London; d, Alexander Payne; w, Alexander Payne, Jim Taylor (based on the novel by Rex Pickett); ph, Phedon Papamichael; ed, Kevin Tent; m, Rolfe Kent; prod d, Jean Ann Stewart; art d, Timothy Kirkpatrick; fx, Terry Frazee; cos, Wendy Chuck

AA Best Adapted Screenplay: Alexander Payne, Jim Taylor; *AAN Best Picture; AAN Best Supporting Actor:* Thomas Haden Church; *AAN Best Supporting Actress:* Virginia Madsen; *AAN Best Director:* Alexander Payne

Nebraska-born auteur Alexander Payne trades the flat Midwestern settings of CITIZEN RUTH, ELECTION, and ABOUT SCHMIDT for the sun-kissed hills of California's wine country in this wry, observant buddy comedy.

At first glance, cynical, would-be writer Miles (Paul Giamatti) and his old college buddy Jack (Thomas Haden Church), a has-been TV actor, couldn't appear more different: Jack is handsome and outgoing, while Miles is a lumpy, depressed introvert. Nevertheless, their friendship has survived everything from career disappointment to Miles's failed marriage. Now Jack is about to take the plunge, and Miles proposes a weeklong vacation in wine country before the big day. A longtime oenophile, Miles pictures them golfing, relaxing and drinking wine. Jack soon reveals that he has his own agenda: He wants to enjoy a wild fling before settling into married life. On the second day of their grand adventure, Jack arranges a double date with Stephanie (Sandra Oh), a local wine pourer, and Maya (Virginia Madsen), a pretty waitress who works at Miles's favorite restaurant. While Jack and Stephanie leap into bed right away, Miles is more tentative in his pursuit of Maya, who has her own relationship demons.

All of Payne's films have been studies of human behavior but where ABOUT SCHMIDT painted its characters in broad, somewhat condescending strokes, these people are richer and more complex. It helps that the movie has been perfectly cast. This is easily Payne's funniest film to date, yet the comedy never undercuts the difficult emotions with which the characters are dealing. By the time they come to the end of the road, you know them intimately and are a little sorry to see them go.

SIEGE, THE
DVD
1998 124m c Drama/Political/Thriller ★★½
20th Century Fox/Lynda Obst/Edward Zwick R
(U.S.)

Denzel Washington *(Anthony "Hub" Hubbard)*, Annette Bening *(Elise Kraft/Sharon Bridger)*, Bruce Willis *(General William Devereaux)*, Tony Shalhoub *(Frank Haddad)*, Sami Bouajila *(Samir Nazhde)*, Ahmed Ben Larby *(Sheik Ahmed Bin Talal)*, Mosleh Mohamed *(Muezzin)*, Liana Pai *(Tina Osu)*, Mark Valley *(Mike Johanssen)*, Jack Gwaltney *(Fred Darius)*

p, Edward Zwick, Lynda Obst; d, Edward Zwick; w, Lawrence Wright, Menno Meyjes, Edward Zwick (based on a story by Lawrence Wright); ph, Roger Deakins; ed, Steven Rosenblum; m, Graeme Revell; prod d, Lily Kilvert; art d, Chris Shriver; fx, Paul Lombardi; cos, Ann Roth

In this sober cautionary tale masquerading as an action movie, resolutely ethical FBI agent Anthony Hubbard (Denzel Washington) finds himself at ground zero of an international disaster area.

A New York City bus is blown up by Islamic suicide bombers, and further violence is threatened unless one Sheik Ahmed Bin Talal (Ahmed Ben Larby)—whom the U.S. government won't even admit it's holding—is released. Hubbard's investigation attracts CIA case officer Elise Kraft (Annette Bening), who clearly knows more than she's sharing but has potentially useful connections to the Islamic underground in Brooklyn. Unfortunately, they're not good enough to prevent the bombing of a gala theater event, which incites public clamor for military intervention. Next thing you know, U.S. troops under the command of consummate company man Gen. Devereaux (Bruce Willis) are securing the Brooklyn Bridge, and Arab-Americans—including the teenage son of Hubbard's partner, Frank Haddad (Tony Shaloub)—are being herded into makeshift detention centers.

Clearly, director and cowriter Edward Zwick isn't interested in the cool accoutrements of high-tech espionage or the adrenaline-pumping spectacle of blowing things up. He's interested in how quickly frightened people will compromise their constitutional rights in the interests of safety, and the way the constant threat of random violence translates into the poisonous need to hate someone—just about anyone. (None of which has saved him from accusations of demonizing the Arab-American community). Unfortunately, Zwick frequently sacrifices dramatic urgency in the name of sobriety. That makes the inevitable high-voltage showdown between Hubbard and Devereaux—who, having been established as a pragmatic, if occasionally brutal military functionary, suddenly pulls a Captain Queeg—seem even more preposterously formulaic than it might in a less conspicuously unsensational movie.

SIGNS
DVD
2002 c Science Fiction ★★★
Blinding Edge Pictures/Kennedy/Marshall PG-13
Company/Spyglass Entertainment/Touchstone
(U.S.)

Mel Gibson *(Graham Hess)*, Joaquin Phoenix *(Merrill Hess)*, Patricia Kalember *(Colleen Hess)*, Cherry Jones *(Officer Caroline Paski)*, Rory Culkin *(Morgan Hess)*, Abigail Breslin *(Bo Hess)*

p, M. Night Shyamalan, Frank Marshall, Sam Mercer; d, M. Night Shyamalan; w, M. Night Shyamalan; ph, Tak Fujimoto; ed, Barbara Tulliver; m, James Newton Howard; prod d, Larry Fulton; art d, Keith Cunningham; fx, Stefen Fangmeier, Eric Brevig, Industrial Light & Magic; cos, Ann Roth

Downbeat family drama and supernatural menace converge in this low-voltage thriller from writer-director M. Night Shyamalan.

Recently widowed Episcopalian minister Graham Hess (Mel Gibson), who experienced a spiritual crisis when his wife died in a freak accident, must weather a dark night of the soul with only common sense to guide him. Without his faith, Graham is hard put to cope with the increasingly ominous phenomena that follow the mysterious appearance of giant crop circles in the corn field behind the farmhouse he shares with his youngsters, Morgan (Rory Culkin) and Bo (Abigail Breslin), and his younger brother, Merrill (Joachim Phoenix). The family dogs start behaving strangely, Graham and Merrill hear strange noises at night, and the news is filled with spooky reports—crop circles have suddenly appeared all over the world, followed by mysterious lights hovering over major cities. Are aliens preparing to invade Earth, or is there a more mundane explanation? Graham is determined not to panic the children or let himself succumb to irrational fears, but the isolated farmhouse feels less like a sanctuary and more like a trap as the days wear on and reports of strange sightings trickle in.

The film's tightly constructed conclusion is genuinely gripping, but like Shyamalan's earlier THE SIXTH SENSE and UNBREAKABLE, the movie takes its own sweet time getting there. The film's underlying themes dovetail efficiently with the action, but don't generate the emotional gut punch the movie needs; overall it feels padded and logy. The flashbacks that gradually reveal the exact circumstances of the late Mrs. Hess's (Patricia Kalember) demise don't actually add up to all that much, and the Hess brothers' obligatory character-revealing run-ins with colorful locals feel exactly that—obligatory.

SILENCE OF THE LAMBS, THE _DVD_

1991 118m c Thriller/Mystery/Horror ★★★★½
Strong Heart Productions/Orion (U.S.) R

Jodie Foster *(Clarice Starling)*, Anthony Hopkins *(Dr. Hannibal Lecter)*, Scott Glenn *(Jack Crawford)*, Ted Levine *(Jame Gumb)*, Anthony Heald *(Dr. Frederick Chilton)*, Brooke Smith *(Catherine Martin)*, Charles Napier *(Sergeant Boyle)*, Diane Baker *(Senator Ruth Martin)*, Kasi Lemmons *(Ardelia Mapp)*, Roger Corman *(FBI Director Hayden Burke)*

p, Edward Saxon, Kenneth Utt, Ron Bozman; d, Jonathan Demme; w, Ted Tally (from the novel by Thomas Harris); ph, Tak Fujimoto; ed, Craig McKay; m, Howard Shore; prod d, Kristi Zea; art d, Tim Galvin; fx, Dwight Benjamin-Creel; cos, Colleen Atwood

AA Best Picture; AA Best Actor: Anthony Hopkins; *AA Best Actress:* Jodie Foster; *AA Best Director:* Jonathan Demme; *AA Best Adapted Screenplay:* Ted Tally; *AAN Best Film Editing:* Craig McKay; *AAN Best Sound:* Tom Fleischman, Christopher Newman

One of the most talked-about movies of 1991, multiple Academy Award-winner THE SILENCE OF THE LAMBS was actually the second "Hannibal Lecter" film, Michael Mann having previously adapted the character from Thomas Harris's novel *Red Dragon* in 1986's MANHUNTER. But Jonathan Demme's taut thriller proved to have a much greater impact on the public imagination.

FBI trainee Clarice Starling (Jodie Foster) is recruited by the Bureau's behavioral sciences unit to help track down one serial killer by getting inside the head of another who's already behind bars—the notorious Hannibal "the Cannibal" Lecter (Anthony Hopkins), a brilliant but psychopathic psychiatrist. In a series of riveting interviews, Starling reveals personal details about her past to Lecter, in exchange for information that may snare "Buffalo Bill," the murderer who flays his female victims. Tensions escalate when Bill kidnaps the daughter of a U.S. senator and Lecter plots an escape.

While the suspenseful pursuit of the killer is handled well by Demme, the film's principle attraction stems not from the thrill of the hunt, but from the spellbinding skull sessions between Jodie Foster's heroine and Anthony Hopkins's brilliant, menacing villain. Hopkins plays the cannibalistic doctor with a quiet, controlled erudition, lacing his performance with moments of black humor. His Lecter is a sort of satanic Sherlock Holmes whose spasms of violence are all the more terrifying because they erupt from beneath such an intelligent and refined mask.

Although not as overwhelming, Foster's performance is equally impressive. Her strong-yet-vulnerable interpretation of the rookie FBI agent projects a quietly convincing feminism. Although she remains the pupil of the benign patriarch Crawford, Starling rises above the pettiness of her male colleagues. Despite the cinematic and dramatic triumphs of SILENCE OF THE LAMBS, the film's accomplishments cannot be endorsed without reservation. While behavioral scientists within the film offer much psychoanalytical reading of character, the movie itself fails to separate Buffalo Bill's sexual confusion from his homicidal psychopathy. While not central to the story, such a depiction threatens to demonize sexual ambiguity as criminal. Finally, while the amount of violence in this thriller is not unusual, the disturbingly bizarre nature of Lecter's face-eating cannibalism and the misogyny of Buffalo Bill's *modus operandi* may be sufficient reason for many would-be viewers to forego the film's gripping drama.

SILENT RUNNING _DVD_

1972 89m c Science Fiction ★★★½
Universal (U.S.) PG

Bruce Dern *(Freeman Lowell)*, Cliff Potts *(Wolf)*, Ron Rifkin *(Barker)*, Jesse Vint *(Keenan)*, Steven Brown, Mark Persons, Cheryl Sparks, Larry Whisenhunt *(Drones)*

p, Michael Gruskoff; d, Douglas Trumbull; w, Deric Washburn, Steven Bochco, Michael Cimino; ph, Charles F. Wheeler (Technicolor); ed, Aaron Stell; m, Peter Schickele; fx, Douglas Trumbull, John Dykstra, Richard Yuricich, Richard O. Helmer, James Rugg, Marlin Jones, Richard Helmer, Vernon Archer

In the year 2008, all of Earth's natural plant and animal life has been destroyed by nuclear forces. A group of space stations orbiting Saturn function as outer-space greenhouses, waiting for a time when the planet *may* again be able to support life. When the project is terminated and orders given for the greenhouses to be destroyed, Freeman Lowell (Bruce Dern) kills his three colleagues and takes off in one of the stations, to preserve the potential for life in some other place or time. Lowell is aided in his efforts by three cute robots, known as Huey, Louie and Dewey.

This was a directorial debut for Trumbull, who had previously worked with Stanley Kubrick on the special effects for 2001: A SPACE ODDYSSEY. Like that film, SILENT RUNNING concentrates heavily on special effects, resulting in some stunning imagery. Dern gives an engaging, against-type performance, though the script is stretched out very thin to support a feature-length film. The unusual score is by Peter Schickele, best known for his classical music parodies written under the pseudonym P.D.Q. Bach. Despite the presence of some very dated Joan Baez songs on the soundtrack, SILENT RUNNING has built up a deserved cult status over the years. The writing team of Washburn, Bochco, and Cimino would go on to make the Vietnam drama THE DEER HUNTER.

SILK STOCKINGS _DVD_

1957 117m c Musical/Comedy ★★★★
MGM (U.S.)

Fred Astaire *(Steve Canfield)*, Cyd Charisse *(Ninotchka)*, Janis Paige *(Peggy Dainton)*, Peter Lorre *(Brankov)*, Jules Munshin

(Bibinski), Joseph Buloff (Ivanov), George Tobias (Commissar Vassili Markovich), Wim Sonneveld (Peter Ilyitch Boroff), Belita (Dancer Vera), Ivan Triesault (Russian Embassy Official)

p, Arthur Freed; d, Rouben Mamoulian; w, Leonard Gershe, Harry Kurnitz (uncredited), Leonard Spigelgass (based on the musical play by George S. Kaufman, Leueen McGrath, Abe Burrows and the screenplay by Billy Wilder, Charles Brackett, Walter Reisch from Ninotchka by Melchior Lengyel); ph, Robert Bronner (CinemaScope, Metrocolor); ed, Harold F. Kress; m, Cole Porter; art d, William A. Horning, Randall Duell; chor, Hermes Pan, Eugene Loring; cos, Helen Rose

Great light entertainment that paid heavy dividends at the box office, SILK STOCKINGS is the delightful film version of the George S. Kaufman-Leueen McGrath-Abe Burrows-Cole Porter Broadway musical based on Ernst Lubitsch's classic screen comedy NINOTCHKA (1939). Fred Astaire is Hollywood film producer Steve Canfield, who comes to Paris to make a movie, meets touring Soviet composer Peter Ilyitch Boroff (Wim Sonneveld), and persuades him to remain in France to score his film, prompting Commissar Vassili Markovitch (George Tobias, who appeared in both the stage version and in NINOTCHKA) to dispatch of trio of underlings to retrieve the revered composer. In short order, Brankov (Peter Lorre, who is very funny but struggles vainly as a dancer), Bibinski (Jules Munshin), and Ivanov (Joseph Buloff) are contentedly indulging in the pleasures of life in the West. Ninotchka (Cyd Charisse, in the role Greta Garbo essayed so brilliantly), the exemplary Communist sent by Commissar Markovitch to retrieve the retrievers, is not so easily seduced by Western ways or by Steve, who falls in love with her. Despite Steve's marriage proposal, Ninotchka and the others return to the USSR; however, when Brankov, Bibinski, and Ivanov, sent again to Paris as representatives of the Soviet film industry, become partners in a nightclub with Steve, Ninotchka returns to collect her errant comrades, but this time love wins out. Hermes Pan oversaw Astaire's dancing, some of the last really dazzling terping he would do, while Eugene Loring handled the rest of the choreography. Charisse, a great dancer in her own right, gives a terrific performance (vocally looped by Carol Richards). Rouben Mamoulian's direction is brisk but not brilliant; Cole Porter's songs are witty, airy, and tuneful, though not as memorable as many of the renowned tunesmith's other works; and because the chemistry between Charisse and Astaire isn't the equal of that of Garbo and Melvyn Douglas, SILK STOCKINGS lacks NINOTCHKA's warmth. It does, however, have some wonderful musical moments and is the kind of picture that anyone of any age will enjoy.

SILKWOOD   📀
1983   131m   c   Biography   ★★★★
20th Century Fox   (U.S.)   R

Meryl Streep (Karen Silkwood), Kurt Russell (Drew Stephens), Cher (Dolly Pelliker), Craig T. Nelson (Winston), Diana Scarwid (Angela), Fred Ward (Morgan), Ron Silver (Paul Stone), Charles Hallahan (Earl Lapin), Josef Sommer (Max Richter), Sudie Bond (Thelma Rice)

p, Mike Nichols, Michael Hausman; d, Mike Nichols; w, Nora Ephron, Alice Arlen; ph, Miroslav Ondricek (Technicolor); ed, Sam O'Steen; m, Georges Delerue; prod d, Patrizia von Brandenstein; art d, Richard James; cos, Ann Roth

AAN Best Actress: Meryl Streep; *AAN Best Supporting Actress:* Cher; *AAN Best Director:* Mike Nichols; *AAN Best Original Screenplay:* Nora Ephron, Alice Arlen; *AAN Best Film Editing:* Sam O'Steen

Karen Silkwood, a worker at the Kerr-McGee nuclear materials plant in Cimarron, Oklahoma, died in 1974 in a suspect auto accident on her way to meet a *New York Times* reporter to present evidence she had gathered concerning safety violations at her workplace. Based on that story, SILKWOOD is a sensational expose of big business seen through the eyes of average working people. Meryl Streep, in another brilliant portrayal, is the title character, a tough, hard-drinking woman who lives with her boyfriend (Kurt Russell), and a lesbian friend (an engagingly low-key Cher). In the course of her dull, dangerous job at Kerr-McGee, Silkwood is repeatedly contaminated. She begins to suspect a management cover-up of safety measures violations at the plant, and undertakes to get proof of her suspicions for the union brass in Washington. Though her relationship with her boyfriend deteriorates as she plugs more and more of her energy into her spying, she gathers evidence that she intends to give to the reporter, and heads out for the meeting that never took place. The clear implication is that Silkwood was silenced to prevent her from making trouble for the plant. Mike Nichols, in his first venture into movies since THE FORTUNE (1975), elicited superlative performances from the actors, particularly Streep and stage veteran Sudi Bond.

SILVERADO   📀
1985   132m   c   Western   ★★½
Columbia   (U.S.)   PG-13

Kevin Kline (Paden), Scott Glenn (Emmett), Rosanna Arquette (Hannah), John Cleese (Sheriff Langston), Kevin Costner (Jake), Brian Dennehy (Cobb), Danny Glover (Mal), Jeff Goldblum (Slick), Linda Hunt (Stella), Raymond Baker (McKendrick)

p, Lawrence Kasdan; d, Lawrence Kasdan; w, Lawrence Kasdan, Mark Kasdan; ph, John Bailey (Super Techniscope, Technicolor); ed, Carol Littleton, Mia Goldman; m, Bruce Broughton; prod d, Ida Random; fx, Roy Arbogast; cos, Kristi Zea

AAN Best Original Score: Bruce Boughton; *AAN Best Sound:* Donald O. Mitchell, Rick Kline, Kevin O'Connell, David Ronne

Jammed with enough characters and plot elements to fill at least 10 films, SILVERADO is a big stampede of a movie with ideas and scenes thundering off in dozens of directions. Without things getting out of hand, the plot here sees four unlikely heros—Paden (Kevin Kline), Emmett (Scott Glenn), Jake (Kevin Costner), and Mal (Danny Glover)—team up to rescue the town of Silverado from nasty sheriff Cobb (Brian Dennehy) and his army of goons. The basics are simple enough and definitely the stuff of 1940s westerns, but then writer-director Lawrence Kasdan bloats the plot with dozens of side stories that, in painfully predictable detail, show how each of our heroes has a reason for being in Silverado and why they decide to stick their necks out. Though much of the running time is devoted to these expository passages, it's all very basic and shallow. Between the gratuitous climaxes that seem to occur every 10 minutes, Kasdan parades a myriad of stereotypes before us and never develops them (Rosanna Arquette as the pretty young widow; Jeff Goldblum as the slimy, dandified gambler; Linda Hunt as the tough saloon owner). In fact, he never really explores any of his characters but only provides them with enough motivation to justify the slaughter of dozens of people.

SIMPLE PLAN, A   📀
1998   120m   c   Thriller/Crime/Drama   ★★★½
Scott Rudin Productions/Mutual Film Co/   R
Paramount Pictures   (U.S.)

Bill Paxton (Hank Mitchell), Billy Bob Thornton (Jacob Mitchell), Bridget Fonda (Sarah Mitchell), Brent Briscoe (Lou Chambers),

Becky Ann Baker *(Nancy)*, Chelcie Ross *(Carl)*, Gary Cole *(Baxter)*, Jack Walsh *(Mr. Pederson)*, Bob Davis *(FBI Agent Renkins)*, Peter Syvertson *(FBI Agent Freemont)*

p, Adam Schroeder, James Jacks; d, Sam Raimi; w, Scott B. Smith, Susana Preston (based on the novel by Scott B. Smith); ph, Alar Kivilo; ed, Arthur Coburn, Eric Beason; m, Danny Elfman; prod d, Patrizia Von Brandenstein; art d, James Truesdale; fx, John Milinac; cos, Julie Weiss

AAN Best Supporting Actor: Billy Bob Thornton; *AAN Best Adapted Screenplay:* Scott B. Smith

What wouldn't you do for a third of $4.4 million, tax-free? Lie, steal, betray your friends and family, kill? That dilemma drives director Sam Raimi's cool, spare adaptation of novelist Scott B. Smith's darkly compelling page-turner.

Brothers Hank (Bill Paxton) and Jacob (Billy Bob Thornton) have grown apart since their childhood on a failing Midwestern farm. Hank went to college and got an accounting job, married pretty Sarah (Bridget Fonda), bought a small house, and has a baby on the way. Jacob, never the sharpest knife in the drawer, has lived down to the role of born loser: he drinks too much, fails any test of personal grooming you can imagine, lives in a shack, and pals around with Lou (Brent Briscoe), a surly, bellicose lump of seething class resentment. The three of them happen to be together when they stumble across a downed plane in the middle of some woods, a gym bag crammed with cash in the hold. The pilot is long dead and the money is obviously dirty, or so they tell themselves as they plot to keep these pennies from heaven. It goes without saying that the lure of free riches—and the infinite possibilities wealth promises—corrupts them all, and their downward spiral is like a slow-motion highway pileup: you might think you don't want to watch, but you can't tear your eyes away.

The spectacle of petty depravity played out against a white-on-white landscape recalls FARGO (Raimi and the Coen brothers are longtime friends and sometime collaborators), but Raimi abandons the ironic prankster mannerisms that make the EVIL DEAD pictures such a gas. Smith's bloody backwoods morality tale is played for pure tragedy, each character undone by his or her own inherent flaws. The result is a chilly blast from the cold, cold heart of darkness.

SIN OF MADELON CLAUDET, THE   DVD
1931 74m bw Drama   ★★★★
MGM (U.S.)

Helen Hayes *(Madelon Claudet)*, Lewis Stone *(Carlo Boretti)*, Neil Hamilton *(Larry)*, Robert Young *(Dr. Claudet)*, Cliff Edwards *(Victor)*, Jean Hersholt *(Dr. Dulac)*, Marie Prevost *(Rosalie)*, Karen Morley *(Alice)*, Charles Winninger *(Photographer)*, Alan Hale *(Hubert)*

d, Edgar Selwyn; w, Charles MacArthur (based on the play *The Lullaby* by Edward Knoblock); ph, Oliver T. Marsh; ed, Tom Held; art d, Cedric Gibbons

AA Best Actress: Helen Hayes

Helen Hayes made her sound-film debut in this well-acted soaper scripted by her husband, Charles MacArthur. Jean Hersholt narrates in flashback the story of Hayes, a French girl who falls in love with Neil Hamilton, an American artist. The two move in together without marrying, but their idyllic life is ruined when Hamilton leaves and marries another woman. Hayes then becomes involved with Lewis Stone, but, arrested on jewel theft charges, he kills himself rather than face the law; Hayes, charged as his accomplice, is sentenced to 10 years in prison. On her release, she becomes a streetwalker to support her illegitimate son, Robert Young, sending the money to Hersholt, a doctor tutoring Young in medicine. Young is suspicious about the money because of the irregular sums and sporadic deliveries; however, Hayes lies, telling Young the money is from the estate of his late mother. Eventually Young becomes a successful doctor, set-

ting Hayes up in a Parisian apartment. The film ends as Hersholt finishes his narration. He has been telling the story to Young's wife, a woman upset by Young's devotion to his career. She had been considering leaving him, but after hearing Hayes' story, the woman reconsiders.

Hayes won a well-deserved Oscar for this performance, taking her character from young girl to old woman with astonishing believability. The story piles twist upon emotional twist, coming close to self-parody, but audiences of the day loved the picture. The story had been made numerous times under the title MADAME X. Two silent versions were made in 1915 and 1920, while sound versions were made in 1929, 1937, 1948, 1960 (as THE TRIAL OF MADAME X), 1966, and 1981 as a television film.

SINCE YOU WENT AWAY   DVD
1944 172m bw War/Drama   ★★★★
UA (U.S.)

Claudette Colbert *(Anne Hilton)*, Jennifer Jones *(Jane)*, Shirley Temple *(Bridget "Brig" Hilton)*, Joseph Cotten *(Lt. Anthony Willett)*, Monty Woolley *(Col. Smollett)*, Robert Walker *(Cpl. William G. Smollett II)*, Lionel Barrymore *(Clergyman)*, Hattie McDaniel, Agnes Moorehead *(Emily Hawkins)*, Guy Madison *(Harold Smith)*

p, David O. Selznick; d, John Cromwell; w, David O. Selznick (based on the book *Together* by Margaret Buell Wilder, adaptation by Wilder); ph, Stanley Cortez, Lee Garmes, Jack Cosgrove; ed, Hal C. Kern, James E. Newcom, Don DiFaure, Arthur Fellows, Wayland M. Hendrys; m, Max Steiner, Louis Forbes; prod d, William L. Oereira; fx, Jack Cosgrove, Clarence Slifer; chor, Charles Walters

AAN Best Picture; AAN Best Actress: Claudette Colbert; *AAN Best Supporting Actor:* Monty Woolley; *AAN Best Supporting Actress:* Jennifer Jones; *AAN Best B/W Cinematography:* Stanley Cortez, Lee Garmes; *AA Best Film Editing:* James E. Newcom, Hal C. Kern; *AA Best Score (Drama or Comedy):* Max Steiner; *AAN Best Interior Decoration (B/W):* Mark-Lee Kirk, Victor A. Gangelin; *AAN Best Special Effects:* John R. Cosgrove (Photographic), Arthur Johns (Sound)

Focusing on the plight of those left behind when the soldiers went off to fight in WWII, SINCE YOU WENT AWAY was a smash hit with audiences on the home front, grossing well over $4 million at a time when movie ticket prices were as low as 25 cents. Based on a collection of letters written by Ohio newspaper columnist Margaret Buell Wilder to her husband fighting overseas, which Wilder first published in her column, then collected in a book, and finally rewrote as a screen story, SINCE YOU WENT AWAY is a long, episodic, but always interesting film scripted by producer David O. Selznick from Wilder's adaptation. The film focuses on the wartime life of Colbert and her two daughters (Jones and a teenaged Temple, the latter making her first screen appearance after a layoff of a couple of years) after Colbert's husband leaves his family and his job in the advertising business to go off to fight in the war. Jones is in love with a soldier—Walker, a corporal, who returns from the service to romance her. (Jones and Walker were married in real life at the time, and, though they divorced a year later, their off-screen love is still evident here). Also figuring in the proceedings are Cotten, a family friend and Navy lieutenant who lends his moral support to Colbert and never takes advantage of her loneliness; Wooley, Colbert's acerbic boarder, whose sarcasm provides the film's lighter moments; and Soda, the family's scene-stealing English bulldog.

SINCE YOU WENT AWAY unfolds its loosely structured story realistically—even the battle scenes lack the phony heroics common in WWII films—and the film's three hours pass quickly, sped by its interesting assortment of characters, touchingly portrayed by the cast, its well-written script by Selznick, and its high level of technical accomplishment.

SINGIN' IN THE RAIN

DVD

1952 103m c Musical ★★★★★
MGM (U.S.)

Gene Kelly *(Don Lockwood)*, Donald O'Connor *(Cosmo Brown)*, Debbie Reynolds *(Kathy Selden)*, Jean Hagen *(Lina Lamont)*, Millard Mitchell *(R.F. Simpson)*, Rita Moreno *(Zelda Zanders)*, Douglas Fowley *(Roscoe Dexter)*, Cyd Charisse *(Dancer)*, Madge Blake *(Dora Bailey)*, King Donovan *(Rod)*

p, Arthur Freed; d, Gene Kelly, Stanley Donen; w, Adolph Green, Betty Comden (suggested by the song "Singin' in the Rain"); ph, Harold Rosson (Technicolor); ed, Adrienne Fazan; m, Nacio Herb Brown; art d, Cedric Gibbons, Randall Duell; fx, Warren Newcombe, Irving G. Ries; cos, Walter Plunkett

AAN Best Supporting Actress: Jean Hagen; *AAN Best Score (Musical):* Lennie Hayton

Very likely the greatest musical MGM or anyone else ever produced, SINGIN' IN THE RAIN has everything—great songs, great dances, a wonderful, nostalgic story, and a dependable cast, although we're beginning to find Kelly and O'Connor a trifle overanimated in scenes they needn't be (but then whenever we see the talented yet obsequious Mr. Kelly play modest, we get a strange olfactory sensation—that of ham baking). It's admittedly directed (by Gene Kelly and Stanley Donen) with a dazzling pace equal to the speed-crazy era the film profiles, the Roaring Twenties. Asked to create a story that would tie together numbers from the best of MGM's musical output, many of which were penned by Nacio Herb Brown and Arthur Freed, screenwriters Adolph Green and Betty Comden found that some of the finest of those tunes appeared in films made during the transition from silents to talkies, and so they decided to focus their tale on that dynamic period when new stars replaced old; bright, shiny faces took the places of heavily rouged vamps and mascared lotharios.

As the film opens in 1927, dashing Don Lockwood (Kelly) and blonde bombshell Lina Lamont (Jean Hagen) are one of Hollywood's favorite romantic teams, though Lina mistakenly believes their on-screen love is for real. Don and his less famous former partner, song-and-dance man Cosmo Brown (Donald O'Connor), have worked their way to the top the hard way (vaudeville, stuntwork, etc.), and when THE JAZZ SINGER changes the cinematic rules, making a pleasant voice a necessity, Don is ready. Not so Lina, whose shrill voice makes a mockery of the musical their most recent film has been transformed into, despite the best efforts of a stuffy diction coach which are wonderfully lampooned by Don and Cosmo in "Moses Supposes" (written by Comden and Green and Roger Edens). Kathy Selden (Debbie Reynolds, who makes a great flapper—like UNSINKABLE MOLLY BROWN, here's a character with Reynolds's energy level), an aspiring "serious" actress whose life Don enters quite unexpectedly and with whom he falls in love, saves the film when her voice is dubbed for Lina's (ironically, Reynolds's own singing was looped by Betty Royce—her own voice hadn't much training yet). Although it seems at first that Kathy is destined to remain behind the scenes indefinitely, the film's ending sees to it that fair is fair as true love triumphs.

Contributing some of the most captivating choreography ever filmed, Kelly, more than anyone, is responsible for the delightful ambience of this spectacular musical. His *tour de force* dance to the classic title song (which first appeared in HOLLYWOOD REVUE OF 1929) alone makes the film a must-see; bounding through a rain-clogged street, swinging around a lamppost, splashing and jumping in joy over having fallen in love with Kathy, he creates one of the cinema's most unforgettable moments. Nearly as engaging are the hilarious, highly energized comic dance O'Connor performs with props and sets on a soundstage to "Make 'Em Laugh" and the marvelous "Broadway Ballet" sequence with a wonderful guest appearance by surly Cyd Charisse and her "crazy veil," a 25-foot long piece of white China silk that streamed about her, kept afloat by three airplane motors whirring off-camera. This sequence took a month to rehearse, two weeks to shoot, and cost $600,000, almost a fifth of the overall budget of this superlative musical, one of the most popular films ever. Look for Madge Blake as a saccharine sob sister columnist and Rita Moreno as a flapper actress.

SINGLE WHITE FEMALE

DVD

1992 107m c Thriller ★★½
SWF Productions/Guber-Peters R
Entertainment Company (U.S.)

Bridget Fonda *(Allison Jones)*, Jennifer Jason Leigh *(Hedra Carlson)*, Steven Weber *(Sam Rawson)*, Peter Friedman *(Graham Knox)*, Stephen Tobolowsky *(Mitchell Meyerson)*, Frances Bay *(Elderly Neighbor)*, Michele Farr *(Myerson's Assistant)*, Tara Karsian *(Mannish Applicant)*, Christiana Capetillo *(Exotic Applicant)*, Jessica Lundy *(Talkative Applicant)*

p, Barbet Schroeder; d, Barbet Schroeder; w, Don Roos (from the novel "SWF Seeks Same" by Jon Lutz); ph, Luciano Tovoli; ed, Lee Percy; m, Howard Shore; prod d, Milena Canonero; art d, P. Michael Johnston; cos, Milena Canonero

SINGLE WHITE FEMALE is a stylishly shot thriller with several hair-raising moments. Considering that it's directed by Barbet Schroeder and stars Bridget Fonda and Jennifer Jason Leigh, it's also a major disappointment. Fonda plays Alison Jones, a chic New Yorker who finds herself in need of a roommate after she kicks out her unfaithful boyfriend Sam (Steven Weber). Enter Hedra Carlson (Leigh), who seems like the perfect candidate. Waif-like and dowdy, Hedra helps Alison through her crisis, and obviously derives satisfaction from the fact that her new friend comes to depend on her for support. When Sam works his way back into Alison's life, Hedra's jealousy is so blatant and intense it prompts Alison into some amateur investigation. Surprise, surprise! Turns out Hedra is no bookish introvert, but a psycho intent on taking over her roommate's life. That's what you get for not checking references.

Like too many contemporary thrillers, SWF starts out with an intriguing psychological premise which it fails to develop. Hedra, we find out, is an identical twin who lost her sister at an early age and is compulsively seeking a replacement. Thus she begins to dress in clothes identical to Alison's and even gets her hair styled in the exact same fashion. When we cut to the chase, though, she behaves just like any other generic movie psycho, killing anyone who gets in her way and covering her tracks with professional efficiency. Despite the formidable talents of the two leads, SWF is resoundingly inauthentic—a particular disappointment given that Schroeder's earlier films, REVERSAL OF FORTUNE and BARFLY, were such keenly observed studies of different social milieus. What we see of Alison and Hedra's lives outside the apartment rings patently untrue, as does Alison's tolerance of her patently manipulative, unhinged roommate. Any single white female that gullible should seek professional help.

SINGLES

DVD

1992 99m c Romance/Comedy ★★★½
Warner Bros. (U.S.) PG-13

Bridget Fonda *(Janet Livermore)*, Campbell Scott *(Steve Dunne)*, Kyra Sedgwick *(Linda Powell)*, Sheila Kelley *(Debbie Hunt)*, Jim True *(David Bailey)*, Matt Dillon *(Cliff Poncier)*, Bill Pullman *(Dr. Jamison)*, James LeGros *(Andy)*, Devon Raymond *(Ruth)*, Camilo Gallardo *(Luiz)*

p, Richard Hashimoto, Cameron Crowe; d, Cameron Crowe; w, Cameron Crowe; ph, Ueli Steiger; ed, Richard Chew; m, Paul Westerberg; prod d, Stephen J. Lineweaver; art d, Mark Haack

Rolling Stone contributor turned writer-director Cameron Crowe pulled off a near-impossible feat with his first film, SAY ANYTHING: he made an intelligent, endearing, non-sappy teen romance. With his follow-up, SINGLES, Crowe ambitiously tackles the romantic lives of a group of twentysomething characters, as played out against an appealing Seattle backdrop. SINGLES is more a series of interlocking vignettes than a straightforward narrative; the film is divided into "chapters" and characters occasionally talk directly to the screen, to introduce themselves or comment on the action. The principals are Linda (Kyra Sedgwick), who works for an environmental agency, and Steve (Campbell Scott), an urban planner, who enjoy an idyllic love affair that gets complicated when Linda discovers she's pregnant. Steve's U-shaped singles apartment complex also houses Janet (Bridget Fonda) and Cliff (Matt Dillon), the clownish lead singer of grunge-metal band Citizen Dick (played by members of Seattle sensation Pearl Jam). Janet, Steve's trusted advisor on matters of the heart, is hung up on Cliff, but Cliff is more devoted to the band than to his quasi-girlfriend, and Janet makes several attempts to win him over before she finally breaks off the relationship.

SINGLES works because it gets so many details right: the discussions about how long to wait after a date before calling someone back, or the strategies people use to convince themselves someone is attracted to them, are skewered with amusing accuracy. Mercifully, Crowe hasn't added a syrupy orchestral score to cue the audience during emotional scenes. Instead, there's music from former Replacements front man Paul Westerberg and some of the Seattle bands who rose to national prominence in 1992: Alice in Chains, Soundgarden and many others. These angry, fiercely contemporary sounds act as an effective counterpoint to the characters' seemingly cool, collected psyches. SINGLES is funny and well-observed and, most notably, plays to its audience's intelligence rather than its libido.

SINK THE BISMARCK! **DVD**
1960 97m   bw War/Historical   ★★★★
Fox   (U.K.)

Kenneth More (Capt. Jonathan Shepard), Dana Wynter (Anne Davis), Carl Mohner (Capt. Lindemann), Laurence Naismith (First Sea Lord), Geoffrey Keen (A.C.N.S.), Karel Stepanek (Adm. Lutjens), Michael Hordern (Commander on King George), Maurice Denham (Cmdr. Richards), Michael Goodliffe (Capt. Banister), Esmond Knight (Captain, Prince of Wales)

p, John Brabourne; d, Lewis Gilbert; w, Edmund H. North (based on the book by C.S. Forester); ph, Christopher Challis (CinemaScope); ed, Peter Hunt; m, Clifton Parker; art d, Arthur Lawson; fx, Howard Lydecker, Bill Warrington

Screenwriter Edmund North knows how to write about war, as he proved with his Oscar-winning screenplay for PATTON. Here, he has fashioned a taut, tense wartime drama out of the real story of how the Germans' most powerful naval fighting machine was destroyed. The film starts with actual newsreel footage as the Bismarck is launched in Hamburg to the cheers of the Nazi chiefs in 1938. Flash ahead to 1941 and the War Room of the British Admiralty, where More, still stunned by the death of his wife in an air raid, begins to conduct the campaign to blow the German battleship out of the water. Wynter, a WREN (the British equivalent of a WAVE), is at More's side in the War Room. No sooner does More take over the job when word comes in that the Bismarck has left its hiding place and is now steaming toward the battle zone. More has to figure some way to make th most of his sparse fleet, and the news

is bad when the Bismarck sinks the Hood, one of Britain's best, then cripples the cruiser Prince of Wales. More's son is a gunner on the Ark Royal, a carrier More sends to fight the Bismarck. Rushing from Gibraltar, Ark Royal damages the behemoth enough to cause it to seek shelter on the French coast. Once the Bismarck is slowed down, the British ships King George V and Rodney are able to catch up with it and finally destroy it in a huge sea battle. The film is a marvel of intercutting, shifting repeatedly from More and Wynter in the War Room, to action aboard the German battleship, to all the other British ships as they begin to tighten the noose. More spends countless hours plotting the destruction of the Bismarck, grabbing a nap here and there, sharing his personal woes with Wynter, who is always at his side. Although there's a bit of caricature in the portrayal of the Germans, the film is still even-handed enough in its portrayal of the enemy that the villains remain interesting characters. Actual battle footage is combined with flawless miniature work by Howard Lydecker and Bill Harrington and the effect is stunningly convincing. SINK THE BISMARCK is a first-class war drama that ranks with IN WHICH WE SERVE and COCKLESHELL HEROES as examples of how to create excitement with a great script. The most impressive part of North's screenplay is that we are almost able to look inside More's head to see why he does what he does.

SISTER ACT **DVD**
1992 96m   c   Comedy/Musical   ★★½
Touchstone   (U.S.)   PG

Whoopi Goldberg (Deloris), Maggie Smith (Mother Superior), Kathy Najimy (Mary Patrick), Wendy Makkena (Mary Robert), Mary Wickes (Mary Lazarus), Harvey Keitel (Vince LaRocca), Bill Nunn (Eddie Souther), Robert Miranda (Joey), Richard Portnow (Willy), Ellen Albertini Dow

p, Teri Schwartz; d, Emile Ardolino; w, Paul Rudnick, Eleanor Bergstein, Jim Cash, Jack Epps Jr., Carrie Fisher, Robert Harling, Nancy Meyers; ph, Adam Greenberg; ed, Richard Halsey; m, Marc Shaiman; prod d, Jackson DeGovia; cos, Molly Maginnis

A tremendous commercial success, Touchstone's SISTER ACT is yet another Disney comedy that keeps threatening to get genuinely interesting, only to veer back into by-the-numbers banality. The main plot is triggered when Reno lounge singer Deloris (Whoopi Goldberg) walks in on her lover, thug Vince LaRocca (Harvey Keitel), killing an informer. Deciding her life expectancy would be severely limited otherwise, Deloris takes an offer from a cop, Eddie Souther (Bill Nunn), to go temporarily undercover until she can testify against LaRocca. Her new identity? A nun in a San Francisco convent presided over by a stern Mother Superior (Maggie Smith), the only person in the place who knows Deloris's true identity. Since Deloris makes an unconvincing holy sister, the Mother Superior strikes a bargain with her: she will confine herself to her room and come out only to coach the convent choir, an ensemble of jaw-dropping ineptness. Deloris soon turns the choir into a hymn-singing girl group whose repertoire includes pop classics like "My Guy" and "I Will Follow Him," reworked into religious anthems.

Though it was SISTER ACT's major selling point, the idea of hip, singing nuns bringing down the house wears thin quickly. Nonetheless, director Emile Ardolino (THREE MEN AND A LITTLE LADY, DIRTY DANCING) largely saves the day by coaxing winning performances from an excellent cast. Goldberg's work here never loses its edge or originality, allowing her to shine opposite Smith, who is so good that she barely seems to be acting. The supporting cast is consistently funny, from veteran performer Wickes to Kathy Najimy, whose maniacally sunny-spirited Sister Mary Patrick keeps threatening to steal the picture.

SISTERS OF THE GION
(GION NO SHIMAI)
1936 70m   bw   Drama   ★★★★
Daiichi Eiga   (Japan)

Isuzu Yamada *(Umekichi)*, Yoko Uemumura *(O-Mocha)*, Eitaro Shindo, Benkei Shiganoya, Namiko Kawahima, Fumio Okura, Taizo Fukami, Reido Aoi

p, Masaichi Nagata; d, Kenji Mizoguchi; w, Yoshikata Toda (based on a story by Mizoguchi); ph, Minoru Miki

This is one of two excellent films (the other being THE OSAKA ELEGY) that director Kenji Mizoguchi made in 1936. Both were made possible by Daiichi Eiga, the failing studio for whom the director was employed, which gave him complete control before it was shuttered. Like so many of Mizoguchi's works, SISTERS OF THE GION focuses on female characters, in this case two sisters, both of whom are geishas. Umekichi (Isuzu Yamada) is the elder, an experienced prostitute who has become romantically involved with one of her former clients, a bankrupt merchant. Omocha (Yoko Umemura), the younger sister, has different ideas about men and relationships. Having seen the way men treat women, especially her sister, she decides to take the upper hand, manipulating, and ultimately to destroying, a young kimono clerk. In a twist of fate that seems to suggest that gender roles are irreversible, both sisters are victimized by the film's end. This elegant, carefully directed tale shows Mizoguchi's early talents. He manages to elicit beautiful performances from his actresses, establishing himself as one of the great directors of women, and embarking on his career as the greatest cinematic interpreter of the lives of Japanese women. From SISTERS OF THE GION's very beginning, with its rollicking jazz score, Mizoguchi demonstrates his unique mastery of the film frame, moving through the expansive space of a merchant's home in which every last piece of furniture is auctioned off—a masculine material defeat that neatly contrasts with the female romantic defeat at the film's end. (In Japanese; English subtitles.)

SIX DEGREES OF SEPARATION
1993 102m c   Comedy/Drama   ★★★
MGM/New Regency Productions   (U.S.)   R

Stockard Channing *(Ouisa Kittredge)*, Will Smith *(Paul)*, Donald Sutherland *(Flan Kittredge)*, Ian McKellen *(Geoffrey)*, Mary Beth Hurt *(Kitty)*, Bruce Davison *(Larkin)*, Richard Masur *(Dr. Fine)*, Anthony Michael Hall *(Trent Conway)*, Heather Graham *(Elizabeth)*, Eric Thal *(Rick)*

p, Fred Schepisi, Arnon Milchan; d, Fred Schepisi; w, John Guare (from his play); ph, Ian Baker; ed, Peter Honess; m, Jerry Goldsmith; prod d, Patrizia Von Brandenstein; art d, Dennis Bradford; cos, Judianna Makovsky

AAN Best Actress: Stockard Channing

Witty, wordy, well-acted satire of contemporary class and race relations, based on John Guare's acclaimed stage play.

Art dealers Ouisa and Flan Kittredge (Stockard Channing, Donald Sutherland) are entertaining a rich South African business partner (Ian McKellen) in their posh Fifth Avenue apartment when a suave and personable young black man bursts in. Paul (Will Smith), who claims to be the son of Sidney Poitier and a college friend of the Kittredges' children, says he's been wounded by muggers. By the end of the evening he has charmed the initially suspicious Kittredges with his culinary and elocutionary talents—so much so that they invite him to stay the night. The next morning, however, they discover Paul in bed with a man he has picked up on the street and throw him out. But that's only the beginning of their involvement with this offbeat confidence man.

Channing holds this sometimes stagy movie together in the pivotal role of Ouisa, the Park Avenue matron who ultimately snaps when Paul makes her realize the ways in which her privileged status has isolated her from the rest of humanity. It is she who invokes the film's title, referring to an old conversational gambit to the effect that any two people in the world can be linked together by a chain of no more than six relationships. For a mainstream Hollywood production, the film is refreshingly frank about race and class in the U.S.; for a darker, more acerbic variation on the same theme, see Wendell B. Harris's brilliant CHAMELEON STREET (1991).

SIX IN PARIS
(PARIS VU PAR...)
1965 96m   c   Comedy/Drama   ★★★
Losange/Barbet Schroeder   (France)

SAINT-GERMAIN-DES-PRES: Barbara Wilkin *(Katherine)*, Jean-Francois Chappey *(Jean)*, Jean-Pierre Andreani *(Raymond)*, GARE DU NORD: Nadine Ballot *(Odile)*, Barbet Schroeder *(Jean-Pierre)*, Gilles Queant *(Stranger)*, RUE SAINT-DENIS: Micheline Dax *(Prostitute)*, Claude Melki *(Leon)*, PLACE DE L'ETOILE: Jean-Michel Rouziere *(Jean-Marc)*, Marcel Gallon *(Victim)*

p, Barbet Schroeder; d, Jean Douchet ("Saint-Germain-des-Pres"), Jean Rouch ("Gare du Nord"), Jean-Daniel Pollet ("Rue Saint-Denis"), Eric Rohmer ("Place de L'Etoile"), Jean-Luc Godard ("Montparnasse-Levallois"), Claude Chabrol ("La Muette"); w, Jean Douchet, Jean Rouch, Georges Keller, Jean-Daniel Pollet, Eric Rohmer, Jean-Luc Godard, Claude Chabrol; ph, Nestor Almendros, Etienne Becker, Alain Levent, Albert Maysles, Jean Rabier (Ektachrome); ed, Jackie Reynal; art d, Eliane Bonneau

This six-part compilation film, which opened in Paris in October 1965, is notable for the talent that worked on some of the segments; many of these directors, actors and cinematographers would go on to become central figures of the French New Wave.

In "Saint-Germain-des-Pres," Chappey brings American student Wilkin to his flat for the night. He gets rid of her the next day, announcing that he's flying to Mexico to join his father. Wilkin is later disillusioned when Chappey turns up as a model in her art class. She then allows Andreani to pick her up, only to discover that this boy had loaned his apartment to Chappey for the original affair. The photographer was Almendros, who became a celebrated cinematographer during the 1970s.

In "Gare du Nord," Ballot runs out on her husband (Schroeder) after a fight. She's almost run down by Queant, a handsome stranger in a fancy car. He says he's going to kill himself but will change his mind if Ballot goes away with him. She refuses, and he takes a plunge off a railway bridge.

"Rue Saint-Denis" depicts shy, young Melki bringing prostitute Dax back to his place for a night of fun. His incessant conversation leads to Dax's staying for dinner before they can get to bed.

"Place de l'Etoile," directed by Rohmer, has salesman Rouziere bumping into Gallon, a street person, on his way to work. He hits the poor man with his umbrella during the confrontation, and Gallon falls down. Rouziere is convinced he's killed the derelict and looks for news of his death in the papers. A few weeks later, he sees Gallon engaged in a similar argument with another person at the same place.

"Montparnasse-Levallois" was directed by the bad boy of the *Nouvelle Vague*, Godard, and photographed by noted American documentary filmmaker Maysles. This story has Joanna Shimkus serving as a lover for two men. She sends each a note telling the site of their respective rendezvous but panics when she thinks she mistakenly switched the notes. She goes to each lover to explain away her mistake and is surprised when each man throws her out, then realizes the mistake was all in her mind.

The last segment, "La Muette," was written and directed by Chabrol. He also plays a man who constantly fights with his wife (Stephane Audran) about money and who flirts with the housemaid. His son, tired of the noise, buys some earplugs for himself. The earplugs end up doing more harm than good when his mother falls down the stairs, and the boy doesn't hear her cry out for help.

SIXTEEN CANDLES   DVD
1984 93m c Comedy   ★★★
Channel (U.S.)   PG

Molly Ringwald *(Samantha)*, Justin Henry *(Mike Baker)*, Michael Schoeffling *(Jake)*, Haviland Morris *(Caroline)*, Gedde Watanabe *(Long Duk Dong)*, Anthony Michael Hall *(Ted, the Geek)*, Paul Dooley *(Jim Baker)*, Carlin Glynn *(Brenda Baker)*, Blanche Baker *(Ginny)*, Edward Andrews *(Howard)*

p, Hilton A. Green; d, John Hughes; w, John Hughes; ph, Bobby Byrne (Technicolor); ed, Edward Warschilka; m, Ira Newborn; prod d, John W. Corso; cos, Mark Peterson, Marla Denise Schlom

This funny, unpretentious film marked writer John Hughes's first time out as a director. The premise is ordinary, but the film is distinguished by funny gags and excellent performances by Molly Ringwald and Anthony Michael Hall. Samantha (Ringwald) is a high-school sophomore about to turn 16, and her life is dominated by her love for Jake (Michael Schoeffling), a senior and the school heartthrob. In turn, she is followed around by Ted (Hall), a younger boy who is acknowledged to be a nerd. Nothing seems to be going right for Samantha. Her older sister is about to be married, and her parents are overlooking Samantha's birthday, a major moment in her young life. Her grandparents move into her room, and her relationship with her smart-alecky brother (Justin Henry) gets tense. Simultaneously, Samantha has to be kind and caring to Long Duk Dong (Gedde Watanabe), a loony but sweet Japanese exchange student staying at her home. The situations are predictable, but Hughes saves them from being cliches with his attention to detail. Hall and Ringwald became part of the Hollywood "Brat Pack" with this film, and Hughes emerged as a hot director.

SIXTH SENSE, THE   DVD
1999 107m c Thriller/Horror   ★★
Spyglass Entertainment/Kennedy/Marshall Co./   PG-13
Nostalgia Films/Hollywood Pictures   (U.S.)

Bruce Willis *(Dr. Malcolm Crowe)*, Haley Joel Osment *(Cole Sear)*, Toni Collette *(Lynn Sear)*, Olivia Williams *(Anna Crowe)*, Trevor Morgan *(Tommy Tammisimo)*, Donnie Wahlberg *(Vincent Gray)*, Peter Tambakis *(Darren)*, Jeffrey Zubernis *(Bobby)*, Bruce Norris *(Stanley Cunningham)*, Glenn Fitzgerald *(Sean)*

p, Kathleen Kennedy, Frank Marshall, Barry Mendel; d, M. Night Shyamalan; w, M. Night Shyamalan; ph, Tak Fujimoto; ed, Andrew Mondshein; m, James Newton Howard; prod d, Larry Fulton; art d, Philip Messina; fx, Garry Elmendorf; cos, Joanna Johnston

AAN Best Picture; AAN Best Supporting Actor: Haley Joel Osment; *AAN Best Supporting Actress:* Toni Collette; *AAN Best Director:* M. Night Shyamalan; *AAN Best Film Editing:* Andrew Mondshein; *AAN Best Original Screenplay:* M. Night Shyamalan

Buried deep inside this ponderous, repetitive psychological thriller is a fantastic half-hour *Twilight Zone* episode. In its last minutes, the story takes a brilliant turn, one that comes as a total surprise but is, in retrospect, perfectly set up; certain scenes that seemed awkward or contrived suddenly come into focus and make perfect sense. But what you have to sit through to get to the payoff is simply torturous.

Successful Philadelphia-based child psychologist Malcolm Crowe (Bruce Willis) takes a body blow to the ego when a former patient (Donnie Wahlberg) breaks into his home, shoots him in the stomach, and then commits suicide, all the while cursing Crowe for having failed him. Months later, Crowe's recovered from his physical wounds, but he's subdued and insecure, and his marriage is disintegrating; he and wife Anna (Olivia Williams) seem to be living parallel lives, never really touching or speaking. Crowe sees the possibility of redemption in another troubled child, Cole Sear (Haley Joel Osment). The reclusive, isolated boy eventually confesses to Crowe that he sees ghosts.

Eventually is most certainly the word: it's a full hour before writer-director M. Night Shyamalan throws us the sop of conclusive evidence that this isn't a glum drama about child abuse and that, no, the kid's not imagining all that spooky stuff. Shyamalan seems to have a thing about withdrawn, misunderstood Catholic schoolboys tormented by deep thoughts and their shallow, silly peers; his last picture, WIDE AWAKE, took a lighter but no more compelling approach to the same subject. Speculating about a filmmaker's psychological hang-ups is a cheap shot, but hard to resist when he seems to be practicing filmmaking as therapy.

SKY CAPTAIN AND THE WORLD OF TOMORROW   DVD
2004 107m c Action/Science Fiction   ★★★★
Brooklyn Films/Natural Nylon Entertainment/Blue   PG
Flower Productions/Brooklyn Films II/Filmauro/
Rorschach-Blue Flower/Riffraff Films   (U.S./Italy/U.K.)

Gwyneth Paltrow *(Polly Perkins)*, Jude Law *(Joe Sullivan—"Sky Captain")*, Giovanni Ribisi *(Dex Dearborn)*, Michael Gambon *(Editor Paley)*, Bai Ling *(Mysterious Woman)*, Omid Djalili *(Kaji)*, Laurence Olivier *(Dr. Totenkopf)*, Angelina Jolie *(Capt. Franky Cook)*, Trevor Baxter *(Dr. Walter Jennings)*, Julian Curry *(Dr. Jorge Vargas)*

p, Jon Avnet, Sadie Frost, Jude Law, Marsha Oglesby; d, Kerry Conran; w, Kerry Conran; ph, Eric Adkins; ed, Sabrina Plisco; m, Edward Shearmur; prod d, Kevin Conran; art d, Kirsten Conran; fx, Tim Alexander, Jill Ambrosino, Scott E. Anderson, Greg Anderson, Mark Freund, Darin Hollings, Kenneth Nakada, David G. Santiago (CG), Ian Unterreiner; cos, Kevin Conran, Stella McCartney; anim, Robert Dressel, Steven F. Yamamoto

Set in an idealized 1930s that never existed outside the movies, first-time filmmaker Kerry Conran's rapturous homage to golden-age pulp fantasies is an extraordinary technical achievement: with the exception of the actors and certain props, every image was computer generated. But if it were only that, the film would be a soulless exercise in whiz-kid proficiency. Instead, it's like watching the movie that fired your childhood imagination and discovering that it's every bit as magical as you remembered.

Ace girl reporter Polly Perkins (Gwyneth Paltrow) is on the case of several missing scientists when an armada of flying robots invades New York, and a call goes out to fearless flyboy Joe Sullivan (Jude Law), aka "Sky Captain." Sullivan captures a robot and hauls it back to his island hideaway and hands it off to his trusty sidekick, Dex Dearborn (Giovanni Ribisi). Before all's right with the world again, Dex is kidnapped, Sullivan has gone *mano-a-mano* with a mysterious woman in black (Bai Ling), and Sullivan's globe-trotting quest for truth has narrowed to the search for Totenkopf, a scientific prodigy who turned his genius to evil ends. Accompanied by Polly and aided by no-nonsense secret agent Franky Cook (Angelina Jolie), Sullivan braves hostile terrain, duplicitous allies, killer machines, and Laurence Olivier, resurrected through the miracle of mechanical memory.

The cast plays their parts straight and snappy, surrendering modern-day mannerisms to the conventions of classic B-movie performance without looking camp. A glorious distillation of yesterday's tomorrows rendered in a soft, silvery palette that's more than black-and-white and less than living color, it's a dream of a movie from which a certain kind of movie lover will never want to awake.

SLACKER

1991 97m c Comedy ★★★½

Detour Filmproduction (U.S.) R

Richard Linklater *(Should Have Stayed at the Bus Station)*, Rudy Basquez *(Taxi Driver)*, Jean Caffeine *(Roadkill)*, Jan Hockey *(Jogger)*, Stephan Hockey *(Running Late)*, Mark James *(Hit-and-Run Son)*, Samuel Dietert *(Grocery Grabber of Death's Bounty)*, Bob Boyd *(Officer Bozzio)*, Terrence Kirk *(Officer Love)*, Keith McCormack *(Street Musician)*

p, Richard Linklater; d, Richard Linklater; w, Richard Linklater; ph, Lee Daniel; ed, Scott Rhodes; prod d, Deborah Pastor

An original, narratively innovative, low-budget film from the fringe, SLACKER is a perfectly plotless work that tracks incidental moments in the lives of some one hundred characters who have made the bohemian side of Austin, Texas, their hangout of choice.

Because it lacks any conventional storyline, or even a central character, SLACKER is impossible to synopsize or categorize. The film's organizing sensibility is perhaps best explained by director Richard Linklater himself, who appears onscreen in his film's opening scene. On his way into town, he free-associates to his cab driver: "You know in THE WIZARD OF OZ where Dorothy meets the Scarecrow ... and they think about going in all those directions and they end up going in that *one* direction? All those other directions, just because they thought about them, became separate realities ... entirely different movies." SLACKER consists of all those other different movies. Its camera follows one character, splinters off to follow another, then another, never spending more than a few minutes with any one and never returning to a place or person from preceding scenes.

The two forces that hold the film together are its clear sense of place (specifically Austin, more generally college towns) and its intimate knowledge of a certain character type: the "slacker." The term is slang that refers loosely to any number of young underemployed residents of college communities who either lack direction in life or choose an alternative direction. In an hour and a half we meet dozens of these street musicians, espresso czars, co-op kids, sidewalk psychics, paranoid hitchhikers, disgruntled grad students, cafe philosophers, anti-artists, petty thieves, anarchists, postmodernists, dropouts and freaks—slackers all.

While many appear to be lazy and indulgent drags on society, what emerges is a portrait of a collective of creative malcontents. In the clubs, coffeehouses, streets and unfurnished apartments near campus they each spin their idiosyncratic conspiracy theories about modern life, UFOs, Elvis, Madonna, George Bush, popular culture, JFK, Oswald, Marx and various forms of cosmic consciousness. Although there is little action as they practice the fine art of hanging out, their constant talk is full of energy, humor, eccentricity and a warped but discernable intelligence.

Produced on a budget of only $23,000, SLACKER became a surprise hit on the festival circuit. At age 29, director Richard Linklater obtained a major distribution deal from Orion Classics, which blew the original 16mm print up to 35mm and remixed its soundtrack. Such treatment was exceptional for a self-taught, first-time filmmaker who used mostly unpaid amateur talent to create an experiment in cinematic form. But the film's improvisatory, meandering style is actually carefully constructed.

SLAP SHOT

1977 123m c Sports ★★★

Universal (U.S.) R

Paul Newman *(Reggie Dunlop)*, Strother Martin *(Joe McGrath)*, Michael Ontkean *(Ned Braden)*, Jennifer Warren *(Francine Dunlop)*, Lindsay Crouse *(Lily Braden)*, Jerry Houser *("Killer" Carlson)*, Andrew Duncan *(Jimm Carr)*, Jeff Carlson *(Jeff Hanson)*, Steve Carlson *(Steve Hanson)*, David Hanson *(Jack Hanson)*

p, Robert J. Wunsch, Stephen Friedman; d, George Roy Hill; w, Nancy Dowd; ph, Victor J. Kemper (Panavision, Technicolor); ed, Dede Allen; m, Elmer Bernstein; art d, Henry Bumstead; cos, Tom Bronson

Funny, frank, and violent, George Roy Hill's absorbing film about minor league hockey offers a wonderful comic performance from Newman as the aging player-coach of the Charleston Chiefs. Mired in a long losing streak and deserted by their fans, the Chiefs learn that the franchise is to fold at the end of the season because the steel mill that employs most of their Pennsylvania town's populace is closing. Refusing to give up, Newman encourages his team in no-holds-barred play. Surprisingly, three recently acquired, bespectacled brothers (Carlson, Carlson, and Hanson) prove to be the ultimate monsters of high-sticking mayhem, leading the Chiefs to victory after violent victory and filling the stands. This doesn't sit well with leading scorer Ontkean, a Princeton grad committed to "old-fashioned" hockey. Meanwhile, Newman plants stories that the Chiefs' unknown owner is negotiating to sell the club and tries to reconcile with his beautician-wife, Warren. The team is destined to become a tax write-off, but with pride on the line, they take on a club composed of the league's roughest players for the championship—a game with a bizarre finish unlike that of any other sports film. Upon its release, SLAP SHOT gained instant notoriety for its locker-room language, which may offend some but is perfect for its milieu. In fact, screenwriter Dowd based the diction on tape recordings her brother, a minor league hockey player, made in the locker room and on the team bus. In addition to Newman's masterful work, the film includes excellent supporting performances by Martin as the Chiefs' general manager, Duncan as a sportscaster, and Crouse as Ontkean's most unhappy wife. The on-ice violence is hyperreal, the emotions believable, and the laughs plentiful in this slightly off-the-wall comedy.

SLEEPER

1973 88m c Science Fiction/Comedy ★★★½

Rollins-Joffe (U.S.) PG

Woody Allen *(Miles Monroe)*, Diane Keaton *(Luna Schlosser)*, John Beck *(Erno Windt)*, Marya Small *(Dr. Nero)*, Bartlett Robinson *(Dr. Orva)*, Mary Gregory *(Dr. Melik)*, Chris Forbes *(Rainer Krebs)*, Peter Hobbs *(Dr. Dean)*, Spencer Milligan *(Jeb Hrmthmg)*, Stanley Ralph Ross *(Sears Wiggles)*

p, Jack Grossberg; d, Woody Allen; w, Woody Allen, Marshall Brickman; ph, David M. Walsh; ed, Ralph Rosenblum; m, Woody Allen; prod d, Dale Hennesy; art d, Dianne Wager; fx, A.D. Flowers, Jerry Endler; cos, Joel Schumacher

Like most of Allen's movies, this one is better than the box-office receipts would indicate; it still looks good many years after it was shot. Allen never lets his actors see a full script while they are shooting, so no one, except Allen, knows what's happening in the film. Consequently, many of the performers were confused by their roles.

A Greenwich Village health food store owner who dabbles in Dixieland jazz, Allen reluctantly goes to the hospital for an ulcer operation in 1973. The operation fails, and the doctors quickly put him into the deep freeze. Two hundred years later, he awakens in a dystopian future presided over by a Big Brother-style leader. With Keaton, a writer of Rod McKuenesque verse, he sets out to overthrow the government.

There is one sight gag after another, in a physical, Buster Keaton-like fashion, and many barbs puncture contemporary targets. When someone asks what happened to Norman Mailer, Allen says that he donated his ego to science. The McDonald's signs show trillions of hamburgers sold, etc. SLEEPER is a highly inventive science fiction parody that is typical of Allen's tight, well-edited movies, which usually come in under 90 minutes. Costumes by Joel Schumacher are excellent; he later gave up sewing for writing (CAR WASH) and then directing.

SLEEPING BEAUTY
DVD
1959 75m c Children's/Animated ★★★½
Walt Disney Productions (U.S.) G

VOICES OF: Eleanor Audley (*Maleficent*), Verna Felton (*Flora*), Vera Vague, billed as Barbara Jo Allen (*Fauna*), Barbara Luddy (*Merryweather*), Taylor Holmes (*King Stefan*), Bill Thompson (*King Hubert*), Candy Candido (*Goons*), Mary Costa (*Princess Aurora*), Bill Shirley (*Prince Phillip*)

p, Walt Disney; d, Clyde Geronimi, Eric Larson, Wolfgang Reitherman, Les Clark; ed, Roy M. Brewer Jr., Donald Halliday; m, George Bruns (from Pyotr Illich Tchaikovsky's *Sleeping Beauty Ballet*); prod d, Donald Da Gradi, Ken Anderson; anim, Hal King, Hal Ambro, Don Lusk, Blaine Gibson, John Sibley, Bob Carson, Ken Hultgren, Harvey Toombs, Fred Kopietz, George Nicholas, Bob Youngquist, Eric Cleworth, Henry Tanous, John Kennedy, Ken O'Brien

AAN Best Score: George Bruns

One of the most ambitious projects ever undertaken by Disney, SLEEPING BEAUTY opens as the king and queen decide to throw a gala celebration announcing the birth of their daughter, Aurora, and her immediate betrothal to the infant Prince Phillip. Unfortunately, the overjoyed parents neglect to invite the evil fairy Maleficent, causing the angry denizen of the forest to place a curse on the infant girl that ensures she will prick her finger on a spindle upon her 16th birthday and die. The curse, however, is altered by a good fairy who changes the promise of death to sleep. Hoping to circumvent this prophecy, three good fairies named Flora, Fauna, and Merryweather take the baby into the forest where they can raise her away from the prying eyes of Maleficent. The fairies keep the girl's royal identity a secret from her, and she grows up to be a normal young woman. One day she meets Prince Phillip in the forest, and though both are unaware that they have been betrothed since birth, they fall in love. Tragedy soon strikes despite the three good fairies' precautions; on Aurora's 16th birthday the curse is fulfilled and she falls into a deep sleep which can only be broken by the kiss of a brave prince. This was the most expensive animated film to date, and every penny was on the screen. The attention to movement and detail is stunning, with multiple layers of action filling the frame. The highlight of the film, the fight with the dragon, is terrifying, exciting, and brilliantly executed, though some youngsters may find it a bit too scary.

SLEEPING CAR MURDER, THE
(COMPARTIMENT TUEURS)
1965 92m bw Mystery/Thriller ★★★½
PECF/Seven Arts (France)

Yves Montand (*Inspector Grazzi*), Simone Signoret (*Eliane Darres*), Pierre Mondy (*Commissioner*), Catherine Allegret

(*Bambi*), Pascale Roberts (*Georgette Thomas*), Jacques Perrin (*Daniel*), Michel Piccoli (*Cabourg*), Jean-Louis Trintignant (*Eric*), Charles Denner (*Bob*), Claude Mann (*Jean-Lou*)

p, Julien Derode; d, Constantin Costa-Gavras; w, Constantin Costa-Gavras, Sebastien Japrisot (based on the novel *Compartiment Tueurs* by Japrisot); ph, Jean Tournier; ed, Christian Gaudin; m, Michel Magne; art d, Rino Mondellini

Costa-Gavras (Z, STATE OF SIEGE, MISSING) made his directorial debut with this tightly constructed suspense thriller. Montand portrays a French police inspector investigating the murder of a woman who was sleeping in a lower berth on a moving train. Aided by his assistant Mann, Montand begins to track down all the passengers who were in the train compartment where the murder took place. Piccoli, an office worker who was on the train, volunteers information but afterward is found murdered. At the same time, two other passengers, Allegret and Perrin, attempt to avoid the police because the latter is a runaway who will be taken back to his parents if found. Perrin was hiding from the conductor in a berth and was aided by Allegret, a young woman traveling to a new job in Paris. After the murder, the pair stumble across the wallet of Signoret, an aging actress who also was a passenger on the train that night. They then go to her home to return it. Before knocking at her door, they notice she is being interrogated by Montand. Perrin and Allegret hide nearby and watch as a young man, Trintignant, slips out the back door of Signoret's house. During the interrogation, Signoret reveals that Perrin was hiding in an upper berth of the compartment. Soon after Montand leaves, Trintignant is murdered. Eventually, the police determine that Trintignant was Signoret's lover, and when interrogated, the young man provides an airtight alibi. Meanwhile, Perrin overhears a plot by two men to kill Allegret and he tells the girl to hide out in a hotel. The young runaway then goes to Montand and spills everything he knows. When the police arrive, they thwart the murder attempt on Allegret and capture Trintignant. The suspect reveals that he was only an accomplice; the real killer is Montand's assistant Mann, who masterminded the whole scheme in order to pilfer Signoret's large bank account. Trintignant then goes on to state that Mann is out in the streets of Paris now, seeking to kill Perrin. Montand immediately sets out after Mann and following a thrilling chase, he saves Perrin and captures the killer. THE SLEEPING CAR MURDERS was sort of a family affair for Montand and Signoret, who were married, and for the beautiful Allegret, who is Signoret's daughter by writer director Yves Allegret. While the subject matter of this film is less political than those he would go on to make, Costa-Gavras' taut direction, coupled with a superb cast of foreign actors, propels this somewhat impenetrable mystery along at breakneck speed. It is an intriguing, highly entertaining thriller.

SLEEPING WITH THE ENEMY
DVD
1991 99m c Thriller/Romance ★★★
Fox (U.S.) R

Julia Roberts (*Laura Burney/Sara Waters*), Patrick Bergin (*Martin Burney*), Kevin Anderson (*Ben Woodward*), Elizabeth Lawrence (*Chloe*), Kyle Secor (*Fleishman*), Claudette Nevins (*Dr. Rissner*), Tony Abatemarco (*Locke*), Marita Geraghty (*Julie*), Harley Venton (*Garber*), Nancy Fish (*Woman on Bus*)

p, Leonard Goldberg; d, Joseph Ruben; w, Ronald Bass (from the novel by Nancy Price); ph, John W Lindley; ed, George Bowers; m, Jerry Goldsmith; prod d, Doug Kraner; art d, Joseph P. Lucky; cos, Richard Hornung

With its timely theme of domestic violence, SLEEPING WITH THE ENEMY is both contemporary fairy tale and Hollywood hokum of the highest grade, its sturdy prototype the "woman's picture" of the '40s and '50s. A perfect young beauty named Laura (Julia Roberts) lives with her perfect businessman husband Martin Burney (Patrick Bergin) in their perfect high-tech home by the sea. Laura dutifully conforms to her husband's lifestyle, which is excruciatingly controlled and formal. He also beats her up periodically—a tasteful sadist. The high-tech home begins to resemble a prison tower and the handsome businessman an evil wizard. Laura, with her trailing red tresses, devises a way to escape her tormentor.

Laura seizes her opportunity during a stormy yacht excursion where she jumps into the ocean and fakes her own death. She settles in a baseball and apple pie North Carolina town and begins a new life as Sara Waters. She acquires a suitor (Kevin Anderson), a bearded natural-man drama instructor at the local college. They fall blandly in love. Meanwhile Martin has put two and two together and begins to track his wife down with a bitter vengeance.

SLEEPING WITH THE ENEMY teeters constantly on the verge of silliness but director Joseph Ruben keeps the cornball melodrama scaled down to a pleasant lull. Nothing is overplayed and there's an admirable restraint in the story telling. The scenes speed along at a confident pace. Everything is designed to show off the movie's best asset: Julia Roberts.

SLEEPLESS IN SEATTLE   DVD

1993   100m   c   Comedy/Drama/Romance   ★★★
Big Onion Productions/Gary Foster Productions/   PG
TriStar   (U.S.)

Tom Hanks *(Sam Baldwin)*, Meg Ryan *(Annie Reed)*, Bill Pullman *(Walter)*, Rosie O'Donnell *(Becky)*, Rob Reiner *(Jay)*, Rita Wilson *(Suzy)*, Gaby Hoffmann *(Jessica)*, Carey Lowell *(Maggie Baldwin)*, Ross Malinger *(Jonah Baldwin)*, Victor Garber *(Greg)*

p, Gary Foster; d, Nora Ephron; w, Nora Ephron, David S. Ward, Jeffrey Arch (from his story); ph, Sven Nykvist; ed, Robert Reitano; m, Marc Shaiman; prod d, Jeffrey Townsend; art d, Gershon Ginsburg, Charley Beal; fx, Bob Riggs, Rick Fichter; cos, Judy Ruskin

AAN Best Original Screenplay: Jeff Arch, Nora Ephron, David S. Ward; *AAN Best Original Song:* "A Wink and a Smile"; Marc Shaiman, Ramsey McLean

JOE VS. THE VOLCANO co-stars Tom Hanks and Meg Ryan are reunited by director/co-writer Nora Ephron in this equally whimsical, but far more successful, romantic comedy. Superbly acted, beautifully photographed, and resolutely warm and fuzzy, SLEEPLESS IN SEATTLE is a romantic treat.

Recent widower Sam Baldwin (Hanks), a Chicago architect, moves with his eight-year-old son Jonah (Ross Malinger) to Seattle, where he hopes to start fresh, though he's haunted by the memory of his wife, Maggie (Carey Lowell, seen in home movies, dreams, and flashbacks). One night, a desperate Jonah calls a nationwide radio psychologist to see if she can help Sam (whose depression has made him insomniac) find a new wife; Sam, whom the woman dubs "Sleepless in Seattle," is eventually drawn into the conversation.

Sam's call captures the fancy of women across the country; one of them, Annie Reed (Ryan), is a reporter for The Baltimore Sun who is about to be married to the likable-but-dull Walter (Bill Pullman). Annie becomes obsessed with "Sleepless" and, though the course of true love doesn't run smooth, SLEEPLESS IN SEATTLE will not disappoint the romantic at heart.

Despite the inherently downbeat nature of the story, Ephron keeps the movie light, a series of witty riffs on grief, loss, and desperation, loosely held together by a plot that delights in referencing a slew of older movies, particularly AN AFFAIR TO REMEMBER. For a film crafted from so seemingly delicate a conceit, SLEEPLESS has the sturdy feeling of something that will continue to find receptive—if lovesick—audiences for years to come.

SLEEPY HOLLOW   DVD

1999   111m   c   Horror   ★★★½
Mandalay Pictures/American Zoetrope/Paramount   R
Pictures/Scott Rudin Productions   (U.S.)

Johnny Depp *(Ichabod Crane)*, Christina Ricci *(Katrina Van Tassel)*, Casper Van Dien *(Brom Van Brunt)*, Miranda Richardson *(Lady Van Tassel)*, Michael Gambon *(Baltus Van Tassel)*, Marc Pickering *(Young Masbeth)*, Christopher Walken *(Headless Horseman)*, Michael Gough *(Hardenbrook)*, Christopher Lee *(Burgomaster)*, Jeffrey Jones *(Steenwyck)*

p, Scott Rudin, Adam Schroeder; d, Tim Burton; w, Andrew Kevin Walker (from a story by Kevin Yagher and Andrew Kevin Walker, based on the book *The Legend of Sleepy Hollow* by Washington Irving); ph, Emmanuel Lubezki; ed, Chris Lebenzon; m, Danny Elfman; prod d, Rick Heinrichs; art d, Ken Court, Jonh Dexter, Leslie Tomkins; fx, Theresa Corrao, Paddy Eason, Jim Mitchell, Industrial Light & Magic; cos, Colleen Atwood

AA Best Art Direction: Rick Heinrichs, Peter Young; *AAN Best Cinematography:* Emmanuel Lubezki; *AAN Best Costume Design:* Colleen Atwood

Roll over, Washington Irving. Tim Burton's stylish and very creepy homage to the Hammer horror films of the late '50s is also the most atmospheric piece of Grand Guignol gothic since Mario Bava's BLACK SUNDAY.

Ichabod Crane (Johnny Depp) is an early American New York City cop in dutch with the department because he prefers searching for clues using the latest in forensics to torturing suspects. As punishment, a nasty judge (Hammer star Christopher Lee) dispatches him upstate to investigate three mysterious decapitations. Once there, the fiercely rationalist Crane is disturbed to learn that the locals blame the deaths on the Headless Horseman, the ghost of a monstrous Hessian soldier (Christopher Walken at his feral best). Crane also discovers he's not much of a hero (he twitches and faints a lot) and begins to have troubling dreams, perhaps inspired by the beautiful Katrina (Christina Ricci), the witchy daughter of the village's richest citizen.

What follows—an extremely convoluted mystery rife with countless suspects and plot reversals—may be silly in the abstract, but Burton renders it with total conviction and a poet's eye, with woods that seem literally alive and a sensational showdown in a burning windmill a la FRANKENSTEIN. He also makes great use of a terrific cast—even the usually wooden Casper Van Dien seems to be in on the joke for a change—and in a particularly sly touch, he gives the various village bigwigs the corrupt, overfed look of characters in a Hogarth illustration. A triumph of genre filmmaking.

SLEUTH   DVD

1972   138m   c   Mystery   ★★★★
Palomar   (U.K.)   PG

Laurence Olivier *(Andrew Wyke)*, Michael Caine *(Milo Tindle)*, Alec Cawthorne *(Inspector Doppler)*, Margo Channing *(Marguerite)*, John Matthews *(Detective Sgt. Tarrant)*, Teddy Martin *(Police Constable Higgs)*

p, Morton Gottlieb; d, Joseph L. Mankiewicz; w, Anthony Shaffer (based on his play); ph, Oswald Morris (DeLuxe Color); ed, Richard Marden; m, John Addison; prod d, Ken Adam; art d, Peter Lamont; cos, John Furniss

AAN Best Actor: Michael Caine; *AAN Best Actor:* Laurence Olivier; *AAN Best Director:* Joseph L. Mankiewicz; *AAN Best Original Dramatic Score:* John Addison

This stylish, intelligent mystery is full of delightfully unexpected twists, and boasts extraordinary performances from Michael

Caine and Laurence Olivier. Caine, the owner of a chain of hair salons, is invited to the 16th-century country home of Olivier, a well-known detective novelist with a passion for elaborate games. Olivier reveals that he knows Caine is having an affair with his estranged wife, but instead of being angry, he is delighted and proposes a scheme that will profit both men. Olivier's idea is for Caine to put on a clown disguise and steal his wife's jewels, thereby allowing Olivier to collect the insurance money and Caine to fence the gems and support his lover in the style to which she is accustomed. The film goes through a number of shocking reversals on its way to the surprising but satisfying end. The script, written by Anthony Shaffer from his own stage play, is an actor's dream, and the two stars whip up their roles with relish, pulling the mystery back and forth in this deadly cat-and-mouse game. Director Joseph L. Mankiewicz was determined to keep the unusual nature of his mystery a secret to the audience throughout. Listed in the closing credits as playing Olivier's wife (who appears in the film only as a portrait on Olivier's wall for which actress Joan Woodward posed) is Margo Channing, which film buffs will recognize as the name of Bette Davis's famed character in Mankiewicz's classic film ALL ABOUT EVE.

SLIDING DOORS

DVD

1998 105m c   Romance/Drama/Fantasy   ★★½
Mirage Enterprises/InterMedia Film Equities/   R
Big Deal Pictures   (U.K./U.S.)

Gwyneth Paltrow (Helen), John Hannah (James), John Lynch (Gerry), Jeanne Tripplehorn (Lydia), Zara Turner (Anna), Douglas McFerran (Russell), Paul Brightwell (Clive), Nina Young (Claudia), Virginia McKenna (James' Mother), Kevin McNally (David)

p, William Horberg, Philippa Braithwaite, Sydney Pollack; d, Peter Howitt; w, Peter Howitt; ph, Remi Adefarasin; ed, John Smith; m, David Hirschfelder; prod d, Maria Djurkovic; art d, John Martyn; cos, Jill Taylor

---

Dithery, nattering, and a bit long for such a conspicuously airy trifle, this fanciful "what if" romance follows London press rep Helen Quilley (Gwyneth Paltrow) as she lives two overlapping lives.

Helen's futures begin diverging when she either does or does not miss the train home after being fired from her agency job. If Helen catches that train, she arrives home to find boyfriend Gerry (John Lynch) having ex-sex with his old girlfriend Lydia (Jeanne Tripplehorn): that's the future in which Helen gets a chic new blond 'do, washing that man right out of her hair. If she misses it, she gets mugged and taken to the hospital, a delay that allows Gerry's betrayal to go undetected—at least for the moment—and Helen's locks to remain a mousy brown (in this guise, Paltrow's resemblance to '70s sexploitation starlet Lynn Lowry is positively uncanny).

As a showcase for Paltrow (which is what double roles, not to mention those demanding accents, are all about) the film's a triumph: she gets to laugh, flirt, cry, scheme, take charge, take to her bed, get hammered, get motivated, and dress up in a variety of fabulous outfits. But unkind though it may be to say, Helen is a rather slight personality around which to spin such an elaborate narrative prank, and the supporting characters are strident one-note wonders: supportive, no-nonsense best friend Anna (Zara Turner); hysterical harpie Lydia; nice-guy James (John Hannah), the new boyfriend; and, of course, waffling jerk Gerry. In the end it all feels like much ado about nothing much.

SLING BLADE

DVD

1996 135m c   Drama   ★★★½
Shooting Gallery   (U.S.)   R

Billy Bob Thornton (Karl Childers), Dwight Yoakam (Doyle Hargraves), J.T. Walsh (Charles Bushman), John Ritter

(Vaughan Cunningham), Lucas Black (Frank Wheatley), Natalie Canerday (Linda Wheatley), James Hampton (Jerry Woolridge), Robert Duvall (Karl's Father), Rick Dial (Bill Cox), Brent Briscoe (Scooter Hodges)

p, Brandon Rosser, David L. Bushell; d, Billy Bob Thornton; w, Billy Bob Thornton (from his screenplay "Some Folks Call It a Sling Blade"); ph, Barry Markowitz; ed, Hughes Winborne; m, Daniel Lanois; prod d, Clark Hunter; cos, Douglas Hall

---

AA Best Adapted Screenplay: Billy Bob Thornton; AAN Best Actor: Billy Bob Thornton

---

A long, unusual, and compelling film. Written and directed by its star, Billy Bob Thornton, SLING BLADE concerns a mentally retarded man who experiences love and moral awakening despite his handicaps and memories of a horrifying childhood. Thornton's script garnered him a Best Adapted Screenplay Oscar.

In an Alabama mental institution, Karl Childers (Thornton) tells the story of how he killed both his mother and her young lover while they were having sex. Upon his release at the age of 37, Karl returns to his hometown, where he gets a job as a mechanic. He befriends a young boy, Frank (Lucas Black), whose widowed mother Linda (Natalie Canerday) allows Karl to stay with them. He is treated kindly by both Linda and her longtime friend Vaughan (John Ritter), but is ridiculed by Linda's abusive boyfriend, Doyle (Dwight Yoakam). Though Karl feels at home in his new surroundings, he is haunted by his violent past.

Thornton first introduced Karl Childers in a performance piece, then brought him to the screen the 1993 short film SOME FOLKS CALL IT A SLING BLADE. Thornton's inspired and humane performance earns his character great sympathy and respect, beginning with the movie's most powerful set piece: a long monologue in which Karl relates the key events of his traumatic childhood, his recitation underscored and enhanced by the slow, sad, portentous music of Daniel Lanois. Superbly photographed by Barry Markowitz in small-town Arkansas, SLING BLADE affords respect to both its characters and its viewers by telling its story in long, straightforward, and subtly absorbing takes. Despite a very minor slackening and softening of the plot in the last act, SLING BLADE is a moving, thought-provoking, and accomplished piece of filmmaking.

SLITHER

1973 97m   c   Crime/Comedy   ★★★
MGM   (U.S.)   PG

James Caan (Dick Kanipsia), Peter Boyle (Barry Fenaka), Sally Kellerman (Kitty Kopetzky), Louise Lasser (Mary Fenaka), Allen Garfield (Vincent J. Palmer), Richard B. Shull (Harry Moss), Alex Rocco (Man With Ice Cream), Alex Henteloff (Man at Phone Booth), Garry Goodrow (Man with Camera), Len Lesser (Jogger)

p, Jack Sher; d, Howard Zieff; w, W.D. Richter; ph, Laszlo Kovacs (Metrocolor); ed, David Bretherton; m, Tom McIntosh; art d, Dale Hennesy; fx, John Coles; cos, Lambert Marks, Janet Strong

---

A hip, eccentrically amusing road movie, SLITHER marked the debuts of director Zieff, a respected veteran of TV commercials who'd won every major advertising award, and screenwriter/associate producer Richter, who went on to become one of the most expensive, though not necessarily commercial, writers in the movie world.

Caan, just reclased from jail after serving time for grand theft auto, is hanging out with fellow parolee Shull when the latter is gunned down by snipers. With his final words, Shull tells Caan that he can have lots of money if he finds Boyle and mentions the name Garfield. Caan locates Boyle, who admits that he and the late Shull had stolen over $300,000 and given the money to investment counselor Garfield. Neither man trusted the other, so each had half of the information needed to get the cash. Caan, with Boyle and his wife (Lasser) and a kooky speed freak (Kellerman), hits the road in search of the cash. But a mysterious black van gives chase.

SLITHER features some very funny moments and benefits from fine editing by Bretherton and assured camera work by Kovacs. Zieff later made THE MAIN EVENT, HOUSE CALLS and HEARTS OF THE WEST.

SMALL CHANGE   DVD
(L'ARGENT DE POCHE)
1976 105m c   Drama/Comedy   ★★★★
Carrosse/Artistes   (France)   PG

Geory Desmouceaux *(Patrick)*, Philippe Goldman *(Julien)*, Claudio Deluca *(Mathieu Deluca)*, Franck Deluca *(Franck)*, Richard Golfier *(Richard)*, Laurent Devlaeminck *(Laurent Riffle)*, Bruno Staab *(Bruno Rouillard)*, Sebastien Marc *(Oscar)*, Sylvie Grezel *(Sylvie)*, Pascale Bruchon *(Martine)*

d, Francois Truffaut; w, Francois Truffaut, Suzanne Schiffman; ph, Pierre-William Glenn (Eastmancolor); ed, Yann Dedet; m, Maurice Jaubert; art d, Jean-Pierre Kohut-Svelko; cos, Monique Dury

Chiefly a collection of vignettes, this sentimental homage to children and their innocent ways focuses on two young boys, Patrick (Geory Desmouceaux) and Julien (Philippe Goldman). Patrick is a shy, slightly plump boy who looks after his paralyzed father and who is infatuated with a schoolmate's mother. His desire for romance is finally satisfied by the film's end, when he gets his first kiss from schoolgirl Martine (Pascale Bruchon). Julien's life is the polar opposite of Patrick's. Long-haired and neglected, he is a present-day "wild child" (see Truffaut's 1972 film, THE WILD CHILD) living in a hovel with his hateful mother and grandmother, who are not beyond physically abusing him. At the center of the children's lives is a schoolteacher (Jean-Francois Stevenin), a thoughtful, fatherly man who eventually becomes a parent himself. The film is filled with adorable youngsters: Sylvie, a seven-year-old with two pet fish and a fuzzy elephant purse that her parents won't let her bring to a restaurant; the Deluca brothers, who offer to play barber to save a classmate some money; and little Gregory, a mischievous tyke too charming to incur ire. Director Francois Truffaut worked his screenplay around the children, using them as his inspiration rather than forcing a script on them. The result is a collection of some of the most natural sequences ever filmed. Although the cast is made up of children, parents will appreciate SMALL CHANGE far more than kids will.

SMALL SOLDIERS   DVD
1998 105m c   Action/Fantasy   ★★★
Universal/DreamWorks SKG   (U.S.)   PG-13

Denis Leary *(Gil Mars)*, Kirsten Dunst *(Christy Fimple)*, Gregory Smith *(Alan Abernathy)*, Ann Magnuson *(Irene Abernathy)*, Phil Hartman *(Phil Fimple)*, David Cross *(Irwin Wayfair)*, Jay Mohr *(Larry Benson)*, Alexandra Wilson *(Ms. Kegel)*, Gregory Itzin *(Mr. Florens)*, Dick Miller *(Joe)*

p, Michael Finnell, Colin Wilson; d, Joe Dante; w, Gavin Scott, Adam Rifkin, Ted Elliott, Terry Rossio; ph, Jamie Anderson; ed, Marshall Harvey; m, Jerry Goldsmith; prod d, William Sandell; art d, Mark Mansbridge, Bradford Ricker; fx, Stan Winston, Leslie Barnett, Kenneth Pepiot, Erik Mattson, Alexandra Altrocchi, Amanda Montgomery, Michele Spina, Industrial Light & Magic; cos, Carole Brown-James; anim, David Andrews, Stefen Fangmeier

Feel a little queasy at the sight of row upon row of hypertrophic, armed-to-the-eyeballs action figures at the local toy shop? Well, check out Chip Hazard's dirty half-dozen and weep.

Driven by smart technology intended for military applications, Chip's commando squad is designed to destroy the gentle Gorgonites, toy soldiers whose fierce appearance belies their pacifist programming. "You put *munitions chips* in toys?" wails old-fashioned toy designer Irvin (David Cross) to the associate (Jay Mohr) who's done just that in hopes of impressing the rapacious mogul (Denis Leary) who's itching to shut down their outmoded little toy company. Two days before the plastic warriors go on sale officially, young Alan Abernathy (Gregory Smith) is left briefly in charge of his family's hippie-dippy toy store, The Inner Child, and persuades a shady delivery man (Dick Miller) to hand over one full set of each. They swiftly turn Alan's suburban neighborhood into a small-scale killing field littered with plastic limbs and wire guts. Pretty Christy (Kirsten Dunst) next door joins the fray when her frilly Gwendy-girl collection is transformed into a mutant doll squad guaranteed to traumatize anyone who's still getting over "The Twilight Zone"'s Talky Tina.

Back in GREMLINS territory, director Joe Dante keeps this hugely clever trifle—crammed with homage-heavy dialogue and lethal mini-military hardware imaginatively fashioned from household items—moving at a brisk clip. And the voice cast is a delight: macho men Tommy Lee Jones, Ernest Borgnine, Jim Brown, Bruce Dern, George Kennedy, and Clint Walker as the Commandos; Frank Langella, Christopher Guest, Michael McKean, and Harry Shearer as the Gorgonites; and Sarah Michelle Gellar and Christina Ricci as the grrrrl-y Gwendys.

SMASH PALACE   DVD
1981 108m c   Drama   ★★★½
Aardvark Films/New Zealand Film Commission   R
(New Zealand)

Bruno Lawrence *(Al Shaw)*, Anna Jemison *(Jacqui Shaw)*, Greer Robson *(Georgie Shaw)*, Keith Aberdein *(Ray Foley)*, Desmond Kelly *(Tiny)*, Lynn Robson *(Linda)*, Margaret Umbers *(Rose)*, Sean Duffy *(Frank)*, Bryan Johnson *(2nd Police Officer)*, Terence Donovan *(Traffic Officer)*

p, Roger Donaldson; d, Roger Donaldson; w, Roger Donaldson, Peter Hansard, Bruno Lawrence; ph, Graeme Cowley (Eastmancolor); ed, Michael Horton; m, Sharon O'Neill; art d, Reston Griffiths; cos, Annabel Blackett

Former racing champ Al Shaw (Bruno Lawrence) returns to his native New Zealand to take over his father's old auto junk shop. Accompanying him is his pregnant European wife, Jacqui (Anna Jemison), who through the years grows tired of her husband and goes to live with his best friend, police officer Ray Foley (Keith Aberdein). The crazed Shaw attempts reconciliation by kidnapping his daughter and running off into the bush, forcing a widespread hunt for the missing child. Although the plot is fairly thin, the concentration is on the characters and on the growing tension between the married couple. The result is a pointed look into the formation and dissolution of a relationship where neither person is to blame. Lawrence is outstanding as the self-absorbed man whose personality undergoes massive changes in the course of the film.

SMILE   DVD
1975 113m c   Comedy   ★★★★
UA (U.S.)   PG

Bruce Dern *("Big Bob" Freelander)*, Barbara Feldon *(Brenda DiCarlo)*, Michael Kidd *(Tommy French)*, Geoffrey Lewis *(Wilson Shears)*, Nicholas Pryor *(Andy DiCarlo)*, Colleen Camp *(Connie Thompson/"Miss Imperial County")*, Joan Prather *(Robin Gibson/"Miss Antelope Valley")*, Denise Nickerson *(Shirley*

Tolstoy/"Miss San Diego"), Annette O'Toole (Doria Houston/"Miss Anaheim"), Maria O'Brien (Maria Gonzales/"Miss Salinas")

p, Michael Ritchie; d, Michael Ritchie; w, Jerry Belson; ph, Conrad Hall (DeLuxe Color); ed, Richard A. Harris; m, Daniel Osborn, Leroy Holmes, Charles Chaplin; chor, Jim Bates; cos, Patricia Norris

Director Ritchie does a fine job handling a huge cast, with many first-timers, in this satirical glimpse of a real beauty pageant staged in Santa Rosa, California. The original script, written by TV veteran Belson, supplies plenty of laughs, but the picture has so many characters we never get to truly know any of them, and the result, while often hilarious, is ultimately skin-deep, just as the beauty contestants are. Dern is a mobile-home dealer in the town and the chief judge of the contest. His son, Eric Shea, is a pre-teener with an eye toward female flesh and money so he takes some surreptitious shots of the nude beauties and means to sell them to his pals. When that's discovered, father and son have to see a court-ordered psychiatrist, George Skaff, to allow the boy to go back to school. Kidd is a tired choreographer who has received this second-rate assignment and hopes it might lead to a rekindling of his flagging career. The president of the beauty pageant is Lewis, and the prudish female chief of the proceedings is Feldon, who is married to Pryor and is as cold as an Arctic night to him. Cutting between all of these people and the many contestants, Ritchie tries to give us a picture like NASHVILLE with multiple stories going at the same time. The final scenes were staged at the actual pageant, and no one, except Belson and Ritchie, knew the winner, so the conclusion seems realistic. The best of the beauty contestants is Prather, who has to alter her character from naive waif to win-at-any-cost contestant. Pryor eventually shoots her out of frustration, thus reducing the film's level to something near "Tom and Jerry." Before that, however, the picture is superior in many ways. In 1986 a stage musical based on the movie was being financed, with music by Marvin Hamlisch. The music for SMILE was based on Charles Chaplin's original song "Smile," which became a hit for Nat "King" Cole. Osborn's incidental music was appropriate, and some pop tunes by Neil Sedaka, Shirley and Lee, and the Beach Boys were also used. Like many of Ritchie's films, it was sharp but not good-natured, and people stayed away from it in droves. Most of the beauty contest participants were exactly that, and it's a tribute to Ritchie's ability with actors that he gets them to come off as nonactors, which is one of the most difficult things an actor can do.

SMILES OF A SUMMER NIGHT DVD
(SOMMARNATTENS LEENDE)
1955 108m bw Comedy ★★★★
Svensk (Sweden)

Ulla Jacobsson (Anne Egerman), Eva Dahlbeck (Desiree Armfeldt), Margit Carlqvist (Charlotte Malcolm), Harriet Andersson (Petra the Maid), Gunnar Bjornstrand (Fredrik Egerman), Jarl Kulle (Count Malcolm), Ake Fridell (Frid the Groom), Bjorn Bjelvenstam (Henrik Egerman), Naima Wifstrand (Mrs. Armfeldt), Gull Natrop (Malla)

p, Allan Ekelund; d, Ingmar Bergman; w, Ingmar Bergman; ph, Gunnar Fischer; ed, Oscar Rosander; m, Erik Nordgren; art d, P.A. Lundgren; cos, Mago

A heavenly boudoir farce, alternately sardonic to it's inhabitants, then surprisngly tender, this is easily Bergman's finest comedy.

SMILES OF A SUMMER NIGHT is set in turn-of-the-century Sweden and takes place primarily at an old country estate, where love permeates the summer air. As a result of the scheming of actress Desiree Armfeldt (Eva Dahlbeck), a group of former, present, and would-be lovers gathers at her mother's country home, including Desiree's one-time lover

Fredrik Egerman (Gunnar Bjornstrand); Anne (Ulla Jacobsson), his 20-year-old, still-virgin wife of two years; Fredrik's son, Henrik (Bjorn Bjelvenstam), a theology student a little younger than his stepmother; Desiree's current lover, Count Malcolm (Jarl Kulle); and his wife, Charlotte (Margit Carlqvist). In the course of this midsummer's eve, Anne runs off with her stepson, Fredrik rekindles his romance with Desiree, and Count Malcolm and Charlotte reconcile their marriage—while the maid, Petra (Harriet Andersson), literally rolls in the hay with a coachman.

SMILES OF A SUMMER NIGHT is erotic and lyrical, full of blithe spirits brilliantly evoked. Though Bergman's staging of the affair occasionally suggests a proscenium is just beyond the frame, the ensemble brings joyful veracity to the romantic complications and well-drawn characters. Influenced by Shakespeare's A Midsummer Night's Dream, Bergman's film provided the inspiration for the Broadway musical A Little Night Music and Woody Allen's A MIDSUMMER NIGHT'S SEX COMEDY.

SMILIN' THROUGH
1932 96m bw Drama ★★★★
MGM (U.S.)

Norma Shearer (Moonyean Clare/Kathleen), Fredric March (Kenneth Wayne/Jeremy Wayne), Leslie Howard (John Carteret), O.P. Heggie (Dr. Owen), Ralph Forbes (Willie Ainley), Beryl Mercer (Mrs. Crouch), Margaret Seddon (Ellen), Cora Sue Collins (Kathleen as a Child), Forrester Harvey (Orderly), David Torrence (Gardener)

d, Sidney Franklin; w, Ernest Vajda, Claudine West, Donald Ogden Stewart, James Bernard Fagan (based on the play by Jane Cowl, Jane Murfin, Langdon McCormick); ph, Lee Garmes; ed, Margaret Booth; art d, Cedric Gibbons; cos, Adrian

AAN Best Picture

Lovely, simply lovely. SMILIN' THROUGH was first a stage play, then a 1922 silent film starring Norma Talmadge. The story begins in England in 1868, on the day of Norma Shearer's wedding to Leslie Howard. Tragedy strikes during the ceremony, when Shearer's jealous suitor, Fredric March, shows up drunk and crazed. He pulls a pistol and fires at his rival, but the bullet hits Shearer. As she lies dying in Howard's arms, she promises him that she will always be near and that someday they will be reunited. March manages to escape and disappears. Howard spends the rest of his days as a lonely recluse grieving over his loss. Years pass, and Howard's loneliness is interrupted by the arrival of his young niece, who comes to live with the old man after her parents are drowned. One day the niece (played as an adult by Shearer) and a friend are caught in a rainstorm and seek shelter in an empty old house—the same house March had fled long ago. While exploring the place, Shearer meets March's son (also played by March), and there is an instant romantic attraction between the two. Shearer excitedly tells Howard of her discovery, but the old man angrily forbids her to see the son of the man who robbed him of his true love. Soon after, March goes to fight in WWI, and the ghost of the dead woman keeps returning to Howard to beg him to let the young lovers be united.

SMILIN' THROUGH is an example of romantic melodrama at its best. A hit at the box office, the film boasts a superb production and a strong cast who handle their roles with aplomb. La Norma was perhaps never better (and she never looked lovelier), and March, Howard, O.P. Heggie, and Ralph Forbes lend sterling support. One of those rare films whose gorgeous soft-focus look and dreamy, unashamed, sentimental romantic conviction suggests the best of Frank Borzage, SMILIN' THROUGH was remade by Borzage with less success in 1941, with Jeanette MacDonald, Gene Raymond and Brian Aherne.

SMILING LIEUTENANT, THE
1931 102m bw Musical/Comedy ★★★★½
Paramount (U.S.)

Maurice Chevalier *(Niki)*, Claudette Colbert *(Franzi)*, Miriam Hopkins *(Princess Anna)*, George Barbier *(King Adolf)*, Charlie Ruggles *(Max)*, Hugh O'Connell *(Orderly)*, Robert Strange *(Adjutant von Rockoff)*, Janet Reade *(Lily)*, Lon MacSunday *(Emperor)*, Elizabeth Patterson *(Baroness von Schwedel)*

p, Ernst Lubitsch; d, Ernst Lubitsch; w, Ernest Vajda, Samson Raphaelson, Ernst Lubitsch (based on the operetta *A Waltz Dream* by Leopold Jacobson and Felix Doermann, and the novel *Nux der Prinzgemahl* by Hans Muller); ph, George Folsey; ed, Merrill White; m, Oscar Straus; art d, Hans Dreier

AAN Best Picture

Only six years after the release of *EIN WALZERTRAUM*, the 1925 German silent based on the operetta inspired by Hans Muller's novel *Nux, der Prinzgemahl*, Ernst Lubitsch gathered Maurice Chevalier, Claudette Colbert and Miriam Hopkins, moved them into Paramount's Astoria, Long Island, studios, and made this musical as well as a French-language version, LE LIEUTENANT SOURIANT, with the same cast working from a new French script by Jacques Bataille-Henri. The delightful story is set in Vienna, where Niki (Chevalier), an officer of the Royal Guards, shares romance and an apartment with Franzi (Claudette Colbert), a violinist. During a state visit to the Austrian capital by King Adolf (George Barbier), his desperately plain daughter, Princess Anna (Miriam Hopkins), mistakenly believes that the smile Niki has intended for Franzi was actually directed in her royal direction, but is convinced the handsome soldier is only being kind. When Niki protests that he finds the princess attractive, she falls in love with him, and in no time, bound by his duty to his country, he finds himself married to her. Niki refuses to consummate their marriage, however—that is, until Franzi does a makeover job on Anna that sends the guardsman's head reeling.

The operetta plot bears little resemblance to reality, but the players are so good, the dialogue (by Lubitsch, Ernest Vajda and Samson Raphaelson) so witty, and the direction so skillful that no one minds the logic lapses. The music is delightful, and the songs include such bon-bons as "Spruce Up Your Lingerie." Made and released during the Depression, THE SMILING LIEUTENANT offered welcome escapism for a public reeling under too real economic woes. Colbert—warm, sweet, with touches of sadness—is in wonderful form, and proves to be a fine singer to boot. Hopkins, meanwhile, enjoyed her first major opportunity to display her considerable comic prowess as the princess in need of a makeover, and Chevalier is in his best and most typical form. This was the noted French entertainer's first work together with master director Lubitsch after their successful collaboration on THE LOVE PARADE two years earlier, and the result is an utterly charming film that was box-office hit.

SMOKE
DVD
1995 112m c Comedy/Drama ★★★½
Miramax/Nippon Film Development/Smoke R
Productions/Euro Space Productions/Interal
(U.S.)

Harvey Keitel *(Auggie Wren)*, William Hurt *(Paul Benjamin)*, Harold Perrineau, billed as Harold *(Thomas "Rashid" Cole)*, Forest Whitaker *(Cyrus Cole)*, Stockard Channing *(Ruby McNutt)*, Victor Argo *(Vinnie)*, Erica Gimpel *(Doreen Cole)*, Clarice Taylor *(Ethel)*, Ashley Judd *(Felicity)*, Malik Yoba *(The Creeper)*

p, Greg Johnson, Peter Newman, Hisami Kuriowa, Kenzo Horikoshi; d, Wayne Wang; w, Paul Auster (based on his story "Auggie Wren's Christmas Story"); ph, Adam Holender; ed, Maisie

Hoy; m, Rachel Portman; prod d, Kalina Ivanov; art d, Jeff McDonald; cos, Claudia Brown

Author Paul Auster (THE MUSIC OF CHANCE) teamed up with filmmaker Wayne Wang (CHAN IS MISSING) to create this novel excursion into storytelling.

Auggie Wren (Harvey Keitel) runs a cigar store in the Park Slope neighborhood of Brooklyn, where a colorful assortment of regular customers, including blocked novelist Paul Benjamin (William Hurt), hang out and spin philosophy while puffing on Panatelas. Paul still grieves for his wife, who was killed in a holdup, and dwells obsessively on the contingency of life. When Paul is saved from a hit-and-run collision by a young man who calls himself Rashid (Harold Perrineau Jr.), some elaborate—if not exactly earth-shattering—events ensue.

Forget the convolutions of the plot. In SMOKE, narrative is about fiction: invented selves and imagined histories, the lies we tell ourselves to make our lives bearable. Auster's script, which appropriately receives top billing, is unabashedly literary: instead of delivering conventional cross-talk, characters spin yarns or regale each other with elaborate fabrications and opinions. Most of these are refreshing and original enough to carry the film through narrative contrivances and unsubtle performances. Wang yields to both the writer and the actors throughout the film, noticeably asserting himself only in the doubled story at the film's conclusion. But his attention to detail is quietly omnipresent and extremely effective: the look, sound, and feel of the locations provide a palpable backdrop against which Auster paints his slightly surreal word pictures.

Wang and Auster enjoyed their collaboration so much that they made a second, improvised film on the same set, with many of the same actors, during the few days left after their main shoot wrapped. That film, BLUE IN THE FACE, was released shortly after SMOKE.

SMOKEY AND THE BANDIT
DVD
1977 96m c Comedy ★½
Rastar (U.S.) PG

Burt Reynolds *(Bandit)*, Jackie Gleason *(Sheriff Buford T. Justice)*, Sally Field *(Carrie)*, Jerry Reed *(Cledus Snow)*, Mike Henry *(Junior Justice)*, Paul Williams *(Little Enos Burdette)*, Pat McCormick *(Big Enos Burdette)*, Alfie Wise *(Traffic Jam Patrolman)*, George Reynolds *(Sheriff Branford)*, Macon McCalman *(Mr. B)*

p, Mort Engelberg; d, Hal Needham; w, James Lee Barrett, Charles Shyer, Alan Mandel (based on a story by Needham and Robert L. Levy); ph, Bobby Byrne (Panavision, Technicolor); ed, Walter Hannemann, Angelo Ross; m, Bill Justis, Jerry Reed; art d, Mark Mansbridge; fx, Art Brewer

AAN Best Film Editing: Walter Hannemann, Angelo Ross

The first in the series and the best of a lousy lot. Depending on whom you believe, the movie grossed anywhere between $40 million and $70 million; that must be some sort of new record for fooling the public. It was the first picture directed by Needham, one of the highest-paid stuntmen in movies, and is one long, stupid car chase punctuated by four-letter words in a live-action version of the "Roadrunner" cartoons.

The plot is premised on the fact that it once was illegal for Coors to sell their Colorado beer east of Texas unless a special permit was secured. McCormick and Williams play a father-son team of filthy-rich Texans who have a car entered in an Atlanta stock race, which they fully expect to win. In order to celebrate, they'd like to have enough Coors around for themselves and their guests, but the race is the following day and there doesn't seem to be any means to get the beer there in time. Reynolds makes an $80,000 wager that he can drive to

Texas and back in the needed 28 hours, and the obligatory chases and stunts ensue.

The stunts in SMOKEY are excellent but the comedy is numbing, and the acting is on a par with a junior high school production of *Our Town*. Even Gleason comes across badly, and that's a major feat. Adolph Coors and Sons must have been very happy to have a 97-minute commercial for their brew.

SNAKE PIT, THE   〈DVD〉
1948 108m bw Drama   ★★★½
Fox   (U.S.)

Olivia de Havilland (*Virginia Stuart Cunningham*), Mark Stevens (*Robert Cunningham*), Leo Genn (*Dr. Mark Kirk*), Celeste Holm (*Grace*), Glenn Langan (*Dr. Terry*), Helen Craig (*Miss Davis*), Leif Erickson (*Gordon*), Beulah Bondi (*Mrs. Greer*), Lee Patrick, Isabel Jewell

p, Anatole Litvak, Robert Bassler; d, Anatole Litvak; w, Frank Partos, Millen Brand (based on the novel by Mary Jane Ward); ph, Leo Tover; ed, Dorothy Spencer; m, Alfred Newman; art d, Lyle Wheeler, Joseph C. Wright; cos, Bonnie Cashin

AAN Best Picture; AAN Best Actress: Olivia DeHavilland; *AAN Best Director:* Anatole Litvak; *AAN Best Screenplay:* Frank Partos, Millen Brand; *AAN Best Score (Drama or Comedy):* Alfred Newman; *AA Best Sound Recording:* 20th Century Fox Sound Department

Produced under the aegis of 20th Century Fox studio head Darryl F. Zanuck, this remains one of the best screen explorations of mental illness and its treatment.

In a bravura performance, de Havilland is a disturbed young woman who is put into a mental institution by her husband, Stevens. While he loves his wife, he realizes that she needs more help than he can give her. Luckily, de Havilland's case comes to the attention of Genn, a patient, thoughtful, and caring doctor who devotes much of his time to her. Though the hospital is overcrowded and understaffed, Genn manages to concentrate on her case while desperately trying to keep his hospital from becoming the "snake pit" which most people believe mental institutions to be.

Though the portrayal of the causes and cures of mental illness remains Hollywood-simplistic here, THE SNAKE PIT was one of the first films to seriously examine the subject and treat it with—sometimes harrowing—realism. Producer-director Litvak saw the galley pages to Jane Ward's fictionalized autobiography and immediately paid $75,000 for the film rights. After trying to sell the idea to every other studio in town, Litvak went to his friend Zanuck as a last resort. (Fox rarely took on independent productions.) The studio head was a bit leery about the subject matter, but he felt that films should deal with important subjects, so he agreed to finance the project. Zanuck worked closely with Litvak to tighten the script so that its "suspense and urgency" would cause viewers to accept the more unpleasant passages. Litvak spent three months in preproduction researching mental facilities and procedures, and he required his cast and crew to accompany him. De Havilland gave a subtle, passionate performance and was deservedly nominated for a Best Actress Oscar (though she lost to Jane Wyman for JOHNNY BELINDA). THE SNAKE PIT turned out to be a critical and financial success for Zanuck, and the film called such attention to the treatment of mental illness that 26 states passed new legislation pertaining to procedures in state institutions.

SNAPPER, THE   〈DVD〉
1993 94m c Comedy/Drama   ★★★½
BBC Films (U.K.)   R

Tina Kellegher (*Sharon*), Colm Meaney (*Dessie*), Ruth McCabe (*Kay*), Colm O'Byrne (*Darren*), Eanna Macliam (*Craig*), Ciara

Duffy (*Kimberley*), Joanne Gerrard (*Lisa*), Peter Rowen (*Sonny*), Fionnula Murphy (*Jackie*), Pat Laffan (*George Burgess*)

p, Lynda Myles; d, Stephen Frears; w, Roddy Doyle (from his novel); ph, Oliver Stapleton; ed, Mick Audsley; prod d, Mark Geraghty; fx, Gerry Johnston; cos, Consolata Boyle

The amiable SNAPPER is a domestic comedy that never degenerates into sitcom platitudes, even though it was made for TV. Though the film has its share of brisk one-liners and contrived situations played for their obvious comic potential, its appealing mix of sweetness and grit, and ultimate reliance on character to carry the material, make it a pleasant surprise.

Young Sharon Curley (Tina Kellegher) is pregnant, unmarried, and determined to have her baby, the (whipper)snapper of the title. Her parents, Dessie (Colm Meaney) and Kay (Ruth McCabe), are less than thrilled but make the best of things. This becomes increasingly difficult when the rumor begins going about that the baby's father, whom Sharon steadfastly refuses to name, is middle-aged neighbor George Burgess (Pat Laffan). Sharon's situation becomes a local scandal and, as her pregnancy progresses, Sharon learns who her real friends are, forging a new relationship with her parents, particularly her father.

The transformation of gruff "man's man" Dessie into a working model of a sharing, caring new man provides THE SNAPPER with its narrative spine, and what could be an entirely contrived exercise becomes instead an engaging character study. Roddy Doyle, who adapted the screenplay from his own novel, also wrote Alan Parker's THE COMMITMENTS; THE SNAPPER is the second of three books dealing with the same neighborhood and overlapping characters. Well written and directed, THE SNAPPER celebrates common sense and human decency, qualities which triumph over prudishness and restrictive social mores.

SNOW WHITE AND THE SEVEN DWARFS   〈DVD〉
1937 83m c Children's/Animated   ★★★★★
Walt Disney Productions (U.S.)   G

VOICES OF: Adriana Caselotti (*Snow White*), Harry Stockwell (*Prince Charming*), Lucille La Verne (*The Queen*), Moroni Olsen (*Magic Mirror*), Billy Gilbert (*Sneezy*), Pinto Colvig (*Sleepy/Grumpy*), Otis Harlan (*Happy*), Scotty Mattraw (*Bashful*), Roy Atwell (*Doc*), Stuart Buchanan (*Humbert*)

p, Walt Disney; d, David Hand, Perce Pearce, Larry Morey, William Cottrell, Wilfred Jackson, Ben Sharpsteen; w, Ted Sears, Otto Englander, Earl Hurd, Dorothy Ann Blank, Richard Creedon, Dick Richard, Merrill De Maris, Webb Smith (based on the fairy tale by the Brothers Grimm); m, Frank Churchill, Leigh Harline, Paul J. Smith, Larry Morey; art d, Charles Philippi, Hugh Hennesy, Terrell Stapp, McLaren Stewart, Harold Miles, Tom Codrick, Gustaf Tenggren, Ken Anderson, Kendall O'Connor, Hazel Sewell; anim, Hamilton Luske, Vladimir Tytla, Fred Moore, Norman Ferguson

AAN Best Score: Walt Disney Studio Music Department, Liegh Harline (Dept. Head)

"The only film that made money in 1937 was SNOW WHITE AND THE SEVEN DWARFS," said Mae West. "And that would have made more money if they woulda let *me* play Snow White."

West wasn't far from wrong. Consider Snow White, living with seven devoted, worshipful little men. Obviously, Disney was as naive in ways as the children in his audiences. Maybe that's the secret to his animated successes, or one of them. SNOW WHITE softens the Grimms's fairytale, but then there are the sequences of terror. Timeless they are, and here Expressionistic. Indeed, Disney always seemed to pull the stops out for the moments evoking evil in his animated features. And for all the bird trills of Snow White (never again would Walt's heroine have such a fantasy singing voice, and for that reason, she's the favorite heroine of many animation *auteurs*; certainly, we could all agree she's the most surreal of the sisterhood), and the cuteness of the comic relief inspired by the little men, our nod goes to Eleanor Audley (who would supply the voice for all Disney's memorable villainesses through SLEEPING BEAUTY) and the animated rendering of the Wicked Queen. Did Mr. Disney and Mr. Hitchcock have more than love of terror in common?

Dubbed "Disney's Folly" by its detractors, this masterpiece was a personal success for Walt Disney—the fulfillment of his dream to pioneer animation of unimagined scope. The film opens on a storybook, and as "Some Day My Prince Will Come" plays in the background, the turning pages explain how the orphaned Snow White has been brought up as a servant of a wicked queen. The queen, an icily beautiful woman with piercing eyes, stands before her Magic Mirror and poses her vain, oft-asked question: "Mirror, mirror, on the wall, who is the fairest of them all?" She is shocked when the mirror gives an unexpected answer: "Snow White." The nasty queen then orders that the innocent young woman be killed. Snow White, however, has eight things going for her—Prince Charming and seven dwarfs named Doc, Happy, Sleepy, Sneezy, Bashful, Grumpy, and Dopey.

This is animation as it had never before been experienced. Disney wisely realized the film could only work if it was full of believable characters, and each personality is distinct, from the purity of Snow White to the absolute evil of the queen. This film classic also features some unforgettable songs, including "Whistle While You Work," "Heigh Ho" and "Some Day My Prince Will Come."

SNOWS OF KILIMANJARO, THE

DVD

1952 117m c Adventure ★★★½
Fox (U.S.)

Gregory Peck (*Harry*), Susan Hayward (*Helen*), Ava Gardner (*Cynthia*), Hildegarde Neff (*Countess Liz*), Leo G. Carroll (*Uncle Bill*), Torin Thatcher (*Johnson*), Ava Norring (*Beatrice*), Helene Stanley (*Connie*), Marcel Dalio (*Emile*), Vincente Gomez (*Guitarist*)

p, Darryl F. Zanuck; d, Henry King; w, Casey Robinson (based on the short story by Ernest Hemingway); ph, Leon Shamroy (Technicolor); ed, Barbara McLean; m, Bernard Herrmann; art d, Lyle Wheeler, John De Cuir; fx, Ray Kellogg; chor, Antonio Triana; cos, Charles LeMaire

AAN Best Color Cinematography: Leon Shamroy; AAN Best Art Direction-Set Decoration (Color): Lyle Wheeler, John DeCuir, Thomas Little, Paul F. Fox

One of the more successful attempts to bring Hemingway material to the screen, this story of a writer who has lost his intellectual and emotional bearings after enjoying early commercial success works splendidly under King's sure directorial hand, and is enacted with power and conviction by Peck. Scriptwriter Robinson expanded the original Hemingway story to incorporate several elements from the writer's own life and, despite some carping from Hemingway purists, the film was an immense box-office success.

As the story begins, Peck is shown half delirious with fever, lying on a cot in an African campsite, his leg infected with gangrene. A rich and popular author, he finds himself with little left to live for as he drifts in and out of consciousness, with his wealthy wife Hayward at his side. The writer thinks back on his colorful life, seeing himself at age 17 in the Midwest; as a young writer living in Paris and falling in love with Gardner, on whom he bases the heroine of his first novel; traveling around Africa oblivious to Gardner's pregnancy, which is terminated when she falls down a flight of stairs; finally being abandoned by Gardner in Spain, when she realizes he will never settle down with her; re-encountering her

during the Spanish Civil War but then being separated from her again; and finally marrying Hayward, whom he initially mistakes for Gardner when he is drunk one night in Paris. The movie ends with him coming to realize the depth of his love for Hayward, and vowing to return to serious work.

This beautifully photographed film, King's favorite, combines many Hemingway tales to make its point, and it features a magnificent score by Herrmann that captures all the exotic locales profiled. Gardner is excellent as the star-crossed lover, but Hayward has a part that is mostly lost inside the flashbacks featuring Gardner. Peck had played a Hemingway hero in THE MACOMBER AFFAIR five years earlier, portraying a white hunter in Africa, and that film had also been written by Robinson. Although the script for SNOWS OF KILIMANJARO is a seamless blend of Robinson's and Hemingway's style, Hemingway didn't like the film, calling Fox mogul Zanuck personally to say that it was a compilation of his stories and that it should have been called "the Snows of Zanuck."

SO PROUDLY WE HAIL

1943 126m bw War/Drama ★★★★
Paramount (U.S.)

Claudette Colbert (*Lt. Janet Davidson*), Paulette Goddard (*Lt. Joan O'Doul*), Veronica Lake (*Lt. Olivia D'Arcy*), George Reeves (*Lt. John Summers*), Barbara Britton (*Lt. Rosemary Larson*), Walter Abel (*Chaplain*), Sonny Tufts (*Kansas*), Mary Servoss (*Capt. "Ma" McGregor*), Ted Hecht (*Dr. Jose Bardia*), John Litel (*Dr. Harrison*)

p, Mark Sandrich; d, Mark Sandrich; w, Allan Scott; ph, Charles Lang; ed, Ellsworth Hoagland; m, Miklos Rozsa; art d, Hans Dreier, Earl Hedrick; fx, Gordon Jennings, Farciot Edouart, George Dutton

AAN Best Supporting Actress: Paulette Goddard; AAN Best Original Screenplay: Allan Scott; AAN Best Cinematography: Charles Lang; AAN Best Special Effects: Farciot Edouart (Photographic), Gordon Jennings (Photographic), George Dutton (Sound)

SO PROUDLY WE HAIL is a surprisingly unglamorous Hollywood depiction of the lives of three Army nurses (Goddard, Lake, and Colbert) who survive the battles at Bataan and Corregidor in WWII. The film begins as they arrive back home in the U.S., then relates their story in flashback, beginning in December 1941. After the attack on Pearl Harbor, the trio's Hawaii-bound ship is diverted to Bataan and finally to Corregidor. Along the way, the women witness the fighting at its most brutal, but also find time for relaxation and romance. Never, however, does SO PROUDLY WE HAIL succumb to pinup star glamour; rather, Mark Sandrich's direction and Allan Scott's screenplay concentrate on the ugly realities of war, the painful scenes including a sequence in which a mother stands by while her son's legs are amputated. All three leads are superbly cast in their nicely balanced characters. Colbert is the mother-hen nurse who avoids romance but eventually winds up married to Reeves; Lake fights a private battle against the Japanese, who killed her boyfriend at Pearl Harbor; and the showy Goddard evenly divides her time between the war and her romance with happy-go-lucky Kansas pal Tufts.

Because of the popularity of its stars, the patriotic spirit of the film, and the novelty of female combat nurses, SO PROUDLY WE HAIL made a sizable dent in the box office. The critics praised its authenticity, which Sandrich went to great lengths to achieve. Having read a news item about 10 nurses who escaped the fall of Corregidor in May 1942, Sandrich, together with Scott, tracked them down. He found one of them, Lt. Eunice Hatchitt, as a technical advisor and, after receiving permission from the government to tell the nurses' story, began filming. However, although certain to hit box-office gold with Paramount's Claudette Colbert, Veronica Lake, and Paulette Goddard as the stars, Sandrich was also destined to have a battle of egos on his hands. The feuding began when Goddard told a reporter that she preferred working with Lake because "after all, we are closer in age." Colbert was naturally upset at the implication that she was over the hill (and, in fact, Goddard was wrong—her own birth date is usually cited as 1911, making her seven years younger than Colbert and eight years older than Lake). There were also arguments over how they were photographed and rivalry over their respective technical skills. (Goddard and Lake were considered screen *personalities*, while only Colbert was viewed as an *actress*.) Often Sandrich would have to retake scenes many times to accommodate Lake's and Goddard's deficiencies, while Colbert needed no more than a couple of takes. Fans of Lake and her famous peek-a-boo hairstyle should be forewarned that she wears her hair short in this picture. Reportedly, the government asked that she not appear as a servicewoman with that hairstyle because there were a number of women factory workers whose long, Lake-inspired hair was getting tangled in the machinery.

SOBIBOR, OCT. 14, 1943, 4 PM
(SOBIBOR, 14 OCTOBRE 1943, 16 HEURES) ★★★★
2001 95m c/bw Documentary
France 2 Cinema/Les Films Aleph/Why Not Productions
(France)

Yehuda Lerner

d, Claude Lanzmann; ph, Caroline Champetier (1979), Dominique Chapuis (2001); ed, Chantal Hymans, Sabine Marnou

Claude Lanzmann's gripping documentary about the 1943 uprising at Poland's Sobibor death camp helps counter a troubling myth perpetuated by many Holocaust accounts: that Europe's Jews offered little or no resistance as they were led to the gas chambers, and were thus somehow collusive in their own deaths.

Lanzmann originally planned to include his interview with Yehuda Lerner, a key participant in the rebellion, in SHOAH, Lanzmann's epic documentary about the destruction of European Jewry. But the director rightly felt that Lerner's story attested to a "reappropriation of power and violence by the Jews" too important to be reduced to a mere moment in a nine-hour chronicle. This film is still very much of a piece with SHOAH, and the subject is presented in the same haunting manner. Instead of archival materials, Lanzmann opts for long takes of the locales as they appear today, eerily silent and disturbingly empty. He also maintains SHOAH's oral approach, allowing Lerner, who was 16 at the time of the uprising, to tell the entire story. Lerner begins with the emptying of the Warsaw ghetto and his separation from his family, then recounts his remarkable series of escapes from eight camps in six months, and ends with a detailed description of the ingenious plan to escape from Sobibor.

Lerner's words are triumphant and horrifying; the most disturbing moment comes when Lerner describes the honking of the hundreds of geese kept at Sobibor for the express purpose of drowning out the screams of dying Jews. And while he provides valuable insight into why the situation at Sobibor was more conducive to rebellion than that at other camps, he also describes an attitude of rebelliousness on the part of camp populations that strongly suggests that not all went gently elsewhere.

SOFT SKIN, THE *DVD*
(LA PEAU DOUCE)
1964 120m bw Drama ★★½
Carrosse/SEDIF (France)

Jean Desailly (*Pierre Lachenay*), Francoise Dorleac (*Nicole Chomette*), Nelly Benedetti (*Franca Lachenay*), Daniel Ceccaldi

(*Clement*), Laurence Badie (*Ingrid*), Jean Lanier (*Michel*), Paule Emanuele (*Odile*), Philippe Dumat (*Reims Cinema Manager*), Pierre Risch (*Canon*), Dominique Lacarriere (*Pierre's Secretary*)

d, Francois Truffaut; w, Francois Truffaut, Jean-Louis Richard; ph, Raoul Coutard; ed, Claudine Bouche; m, Georges Delerue; cos, Renee Rouzot

One of Truffaut's least successful, most derivative films, THE SOFT SKIN was a response to the resounding impact of JULES AND JIM. While the latter concentrates on love in the country, Truffaut's aim in THE SOFT SKIN was, as he put it, to create "a violent answer to JULES AND JIM. It's as though someone else had made JULES AND JIM … [THE SOFT SKIN shows] a truly modern love; it takes place in planes, in elevators; it has all the harassments of modern life." From its opening, THE SOFT SKIN surely does not seem like a Truffaut film. It is distant, restrained—as the title implies, a "surface" film in which emotions run only skin deep. The story concerns Desailly as Lachenay (named after Truffaut's friend), a literary critic with a wife (Benedetti) and a child, who falls in love with a stewardess (Dorleac) after a trip to Lisbon. Although THE SOFT SKIN is perhaps Truffaut's weakest film, it can also be considered his most daring. Rather than present a conventionally melodramatic love triangle, Truffaut chooses for his leading man a common, albiet somewhat bookish, individual (not nearly so romantic as the characters in the Balzac novels on which the critic is an authority). When fate intervenes and Pierre gets his beautiful dream girl, he begins his downward Hitchcockian spiral, an innocent caught up in a situation he cannot control. In THE SOFT SKIN Balzac (a personal favorite of Truffaut) meets Hitchcock, and the film frame becomes an arena in which Truffaut's two greatest influences do battle.

SOLARIS *DVD*
1972 165m c Science Fiction ★★★★
Mosfilm/Magna (U.S.S.R.) PG

Nathalie Bondarchuk (*Harey*), Yuri Yarvet (*Snaut*), Donatas Banionis (*Kris*), Anatoli Sonlonitsin (*Sartorius*), Vladislav Dvorjetzki (*Burton*), Nikolai Grinko (*Father*), Sos Sarkissian (*Gibarian*)

d, Andrei Tarkovsky; w, Andrei Tarkovsky, Friedrich Gorenstein (based on the novel by Stanislaw Lem); ph, Vadim Jusov (Sovcolor); m, Eduard Artemyer; art d, Mikhail Romadin

Perhaps the most accessible of Tarkovsky's films, certainly free of the overbearing portentousness that would mark later work like THE SACRIFICE. The story concerns a cosmonaut who travels to a distant space station on Solaris. No ordinary planet, Solaris is in fact a superintelligent being capable of giving material form to human desires. Slow, but ravishingly beautiful and charged with a real poignancy.

SOLARIS *DVD*
2002 100m c Science Fiction ★★½
Lightstorm Entertainment/20th Century Fox PG-13
(U.S.)

George Clooney (*Chris Kelvin*), Natascha McElhone (*Rheya*), Jeremy Davies (*Snow*), Viola Davis (*Gordon*), Ulrich Tukur (*Gibarian*), Shane Skelton (*Young Boy/Gibarian's Son*), John Cho (*Suited Professional #1*), Morgan Rusler (*Suited Professional #2*), Donna Kimball (*Mrs. Gibarian*), Michael Ensign (*Friend #1*)

p, James Cameron, Jon Landau, Rae Sanchini; d, Steven Soderbergh; w, Steven Soderbergh (based on the novel by Stanislaw Lem); ph, Steven Soderbergh; ed, Steven Soderbergh; m, Cliff Martinez; prod d, Philip Messina; art d, Steve Arnold, Keith P. Cunningham; fx, Brooke Breton, Werner Hahnlein, Kevin Hannigan; cos, Milena Canonero

Steven Soderbergh's determination to remake Andrei Tarkovsky's acclaimed 1972 sci-fi mindbender without compromising the story's philosophical underpinnings or the original's extraordinary aesthetics is a noble gesture, but the result is a big, beautiful bore.

Earth, sometime in the near future: Psychiatrist Chris Kelvin (George Clooney) is having difficulty recovering from the suicide of his beautiful but troubled wife, Rheya (Natascha McElhone). Kelvin is roused from his torpor by a desperate summons from his friend Dr. Gibarian (Ulrich Tukur), who's orbiting the violet, vaporous planet Solaris aboard a corporate-owned space station. Gibarian's vague transmission hints at weird happenings aboard ship; the crew have grown strange and fearful, and they refuse to leave the planet's orbit. By the time Kelvin arrives, Gibarian is in a body bag, and the only people left alive appear to be Snow (Jeremy Davies), a half-mad scientist; Dr. Gordon (Viola Davis), who won't leave her quarters; and, incongruously, a young boy (Shane Skelton). That night, Kelvin wakes to find his late wife lying alongside him, apparently alive and well and caressing his face. As Gordon explains, Rheya is a "gift" from Solaris, which seems capable of peering into the crew's hearts and making their deepest longing a flesh-and-blood reality.

Talk about a tough sell. Audiences expecting another video-game adaptation will be put off by the film's glacial pacing, while fans of super-cerebral sci-fi already consider Tarkovsky's adaptation of Stanislaw Lem's novel the greatest film ever made. Soderbergh's project is a deliberate throwback to a pre-STAR WARS age when science fiction was actually about something other than special effects and juvenile mythmaking. The irony is that for all its integrity, the film isn't as thought-provoking as Steven Spielberg's recent A.I.: ARTIFICIAL INTELLIGENCE or MINORITY REPORT, and nowhere near as entertaining.

SOLDIER OF ORANGE

1977 165m c War/Drama *DVD*
Rank (Netherlands) ★★★½
R

Rutger Hauer (*Erik*), Jeroen Krabbe (*Gus*), Peter Faber (*Will*), Derek De Lint (*Alex*), Eddy Habbema (*Robby*), Lex Van Delden (*Nico*), Edward Fox (*Col. Rafelli*), Belinda Meuldijk (*Esther*), Susan Penhaligon (*Susan*), Andrea Domburh (*Queen Wilhelmina*)

p, Rob Houwer; d, Paul Verhoeven; w, Paul Verhoeven, Gerard Soeteman, Kees Holierhoek (based on the autobiography of Erik Hazelhoff Roelfzema); ph, Jan De Bont, Jost Vacano (Eastmancolor); ed, Jane Speer; m, Rogier Van Otterloo; art d, Roland De Groot; cos, Elly Claus

Carefully crafted by veteran Dutch director Paul Verhoeven (ROBOCOP, THE FOURTH MAN), this WWII drama details the effects of Nazi occupation on a group of Dutch students. Erik (Rutger Hauer) is at first hesitant to join the resistance effort, but after escaping to England he becomes deeply involved, courageously transporting supplies to his comrades in Holland. After the war, he returns home to find that most of his fellow students and resistance fighters have been killed, including onetime student leader Gus (Jeroen Krabbe), while others have come through the war barely affected. An exceptional character study, SOLDIER OF ORANGE is also beautifully photographed by Jan De Bont—the shots of Hauer on the supply boat's windy prow as he travels between Britain and Holland linger long after the film is over. Verhoeven would again work with Krabbe and screenwriter Gerard Soeteman in his haunting THE FOURTH MAN.

SOLDIER'S STORY, A

1984 101m c Mystery *DVD*
Columbia (U.S.) ★★★½
PG

Howard E. Rollins Jr. (*Capt. Davenport*), Adolph Caesar (*Sgt. Waters*), Art Evans (*Pvt. Wilkie*), David Alan Grier (*Cpl. Cobb*), David Harris (*Pvt. Smalls*), Dennis Lipscomb (*Capt. Taylor*), Larry Riley (*C.J. Memphis*), Robert Townsend (*Cpl. Ellis*), Denzel Washington (*Pfc. Peterson*), William Allen Young (*Pvt. Henson*)

p, Norman Jewison, Ronald L. Schwary, Patrick Palmer; d, Norman Jewison; w, Charles Fuller (based on his stage play "A Soldier's Play"); ph, Russell Boyd (Metrocolor); ed, Mark Warner, Caroline Biggerstaff; m, Herbie Hancock; prod d, Walter Scott Herndon; cos, Chuck Velasco, Robert Stewart

AAN Best Picture; AAN Best Supporting Actor: Adolph Caesar; *AAN Best Adapted Screenplay:* Charles Fuller

Gripping, thanks to spotless direction and Rollins's inspired work, but nothing new to relay. Charles Fuller's powerful play (a Pulitzer Prize-winner, based on Melville's *Billy Budd*) was adapted by Fuller himself for the screen, and the power of the stage presentation is not diminished (which means it's not particularly cinematic, either).

The action takes place at Fort Neal, Louisiana, a base for black soldiers during WWII. Sgt. Waters (Adolph Caesar), a tough African-American topkick and manager of the baseball team, is coming back to the base drunk one night when he is shot to death by a .45-caliber weapon. That's the only clue to his death. Capt. Davenport (Howard E. Rollins, Jr.) is the black Army attorney who is sent to investigate the murder. The white officers on the base, as well as the black soldiers, are astounded at the choice, and Davenport finds that he's not getting any help in his search for the truth. Some of the black troops blame the Klan, while others suggest it might have been one of the white soldiers who rankled at Waters's attitude. A series of flashbacks establishes Waters and the relationship he had with all those around him as Davenport begins his interrogations. What makes this such a good film is the multilayered complexity of the script. Fuller has taken a basic Agatha Christie-type plot and bathed it in social issues; A SOLDIER'S STORY is an insightful period drama as well as a totally engaging character study. The picture does become a trifle talky at times, thus betraying its stage origin, but Fuller's words are almost always interesting and powerful and make worthwhile listening. Caesar's performance stands out. With the addition of two musical treats: "The St. Louis Blues March," one of our favorites, over the credits, and Patti Labelle in a cameo as Big Mary, wailing away and tearing down the house as usual.

SOLID GOLD CADILLAC, THE

1956 99m bw Comedy *DVD*
Columbia (U.S.) ★★★★

Judy Holliday (*Laura Partridge*), Paul Douglas (*Edward L. McKeever*), Fred Clark (*Clifford Snell*), John Williams (*John T. Blessington*), Hiram Sherman (*Harry Harkness*), Neva Patterson (*Amelia Shotgraven*), Ralph Dumke (*Warren Gillie*), Ray Collins (*Alfred Metcalfe*), Arthur O'Connell (*Jenkins*), Richard Deacon (*Williams*)

p, Fred Kohlmar; d, Richard Quine; w, Abe Burrows (based on the play by George S. Kaufman and Howard Teichmann); ph, Charles Lang; ed, Charles Nelson; m, Cyril J. Mockridge; art d, Ross Bellah; cos, Jean Louis

AAN Best Art Direction-Set Decoration (B/W): Ross Bellah, William R. Kiernan, Louis Diage; *AA Best Costume Design (B/W):* Jean Louis

A charming, often hysterically funny poke at big business, government, and the plight of the underdog. The script was by Abe Burrows, based on the hit Broadway play starring a much older Josephine Hull, written by Kaufman and Teichmann. Burrows would later be involved with another successful comedy on the same general subject entitled HOW TO SUCCEED IN BUSINESS WITHOUT REALLY TRYING. The original play was to have had a younger woman, but when Hull, who was so delicious in ARSENIC AND OLD LACE, became available, she was paged for the part. In the film Holliday has the role, and a love story was added to fill the romantic gaps. She plays her patented daffy blonde with a heart of gold who owns 10 shares in a massive company. The board of directors of the organization are a panel of stern-visaged prigs including Clark, Williams, Sherman, Collins, and Dumke. Holliday shows up at a stockholders meeting and protests some of the shenanigans of the board. At first, she is a mere fly in their gargantuan ointment, but her presence is duly noted by the press, and things begin to happen. The former head of the company is Douglas, a hard-driving tycoon who has given up his role as top man on that totem pole in order to donate his services to the government, for which he is functioning as a "dollar-a-year" man. Holliday meets the bombastic Douglas and enlists him in her quest to secure representation for the small stockholders. When Douglas learns that his former aides have stabbed him in the back in their running of the company he started and nurtured, he joins with Holliday to get proxy votes from all the little people and to regain his position with the firm. O'Connell is the "don't rock the boat" office manager who is Holliday's boss, and Patterson is the secretary who aids and abets Holliday's mischief. George Burns handles the narrating chores in the same way Fred Allen did it (pre-recorded) on Broadway. The narration provides a few funny lines and bridges some of the gaps. The title stems from Holliday's fervent wish to own a solid gold cadillac. At the film's conclusion, with Douglas and Holliday united and running the company, she gets her desire.

The humor in the screenplay seldom derives from one-liners. Rather, it is in the situations, the caricatures that are the targets for its darts, and the unflagging energy of Holliday and Douglas as two utterly different people who find love with each other and blend to defeat the pompous executives. Kaufman, who was known as the "Great Collaborator," wrote with more people than the average sit-com scribe. His partners included Moss Hart (YOU CAN'T TAKE IT WITH YOU, among others), Edna Ferber (THE ROYAL FAMILY OF BROADWAY), Marc Connelly (MERTON OF THE MOVIES), Morrie Ryskind (A NIGHT AT THE OPERA), and Ring Lardner, Sr.

SOME CAME RUNNING
1958 137m c Drama ★★★★
MGM (U.S.)

Frank Sinatra (Dave Hirsh), Dean Martin (Bama Dillert), Shirley MacLaine (Ginny Moorhead), Martha Hyer (Gwen French), Arthur Kennedy (Frank Hirsh), Nancy Gates (Edith Barclay), Leora Dana (Agnes Hirsh), Betty Lou Keim (Dawn Hirsh), Larry Gates (Prof Robert Haven French), Steven Peck (Raymond Lanchak)

p, Sol C. Siegel; d, Vincente Minnelli; w, John Patrick, Arthur Sheekman (based on the novel by James Jones); ph, William Daniels (CinemaScope, Metrocolor); ed, Adrienne Fazan; m, Elmer Bernstein; art d, William A. Horning, Urie McCleary; cos, Walter Plunkett

AAN Best Actress: Shirley MacLaine; AAN Best Supporting Actor: Arthur Kennedy; AAN Best Supporting Actress: Martha Hyer; AAN Best Song: "To Love and Be Loved"; James Van Heusen, Sammy Cahn; AAN Best Costume Design: Walter Plunkett

The protagonist of Jean-Luc Godard's CONTEMPT won't remove his hat, even in the bathtub, because he wants to look like Dean Martin in SOME CAME RUNNING—a nice index of the reverence with which Vincente Minnelli's eloquent, passionate melodramas were regarded by French New Wave critics, who saw in them an ironic encapsulization of American culture. Expertly condensed by studio hacks Sheekman and Patrick from a massive, windy best-seller by James Jones (From Here To Eternity), this film captures the disillusionment of returning WWII vets, and brilliantly addresses itself to many of the director's characteristic concerns—masculine fear of domestication and attendant resentment of women; the tensions of masculine friendship; women's complicity in their own oppression; the compromises demanded of artists functioning under capitalism.

As the film opens, unsuccessful novelist and WWII vet Sinatra returns to his home town of Parkman, Illinois, with a new manuscript under one arm and a charming floozy, MacLaine, draped over the other. Their appearance creates a minor sensation in the small town, in which, of course, superficial respectability masks a hotbed of corruption and sexual intrigue. Sinatra's brother is Kennedy, a rigid businessman married to Dana but having an affair with his assistant, Nancy Gates. Hyer teaches at the local college and finds Sinatra intriguing, but the jaded Sinatra is impatient with her refusal to sleep with him. He befriends Martin, an easygoing, superstitious gambler with whom he enjoys endless card games and drinking bouts. The two are casually contemptuous of MacLaine, who is sexually available and thus, to their minds, less desirable than the icy Hyer; MacLaine endures many cruelties out of love for Sinatra. Eventually, Sinatra's frustration with the town's ubiquitous hypocrisy boils over; his subsequent recklessness leads to tragedy.

SOME LIKE IT HOT
1959 120m bw Crime/Comedy ★★★★★ DVD
Ashton/Mirisch (U.S.)

Marilyn Monroe (Sugar Kane), Tony Curtis (Joe/Josephine), Jack Lemmon (Jerry/Daphne), George Raft (Spats Columbo), Pat O'Brien (Mulligan), Joe E. Brown (Osgood E. Fielding III), Nehemiah Persoff (Little Bonaparte), Joan Shawlee (Sweet Sue), Billy Gray (Sig Poliakoff), George E. Stone (Toothpick Charlie)

p, Billy Wilder; d, Billy Wilder; w, Billy Wilder, I.A.L. Diamond (based on Robert Thoeren and M. Logan's screenplay for the film FANFARES OF LOVE); ph, Charles Lang; ed, Arthur Schmidt; m, Adolph Deutsch; art d, Ted Haworth; cos, Orry-Kelly, Milt Rice

AAN Best Actor: Jack Lemmon; AAN Best Director: Billy Wilder; AAN Best Adapted Screenplay: Billy Wilder, I.A.L. Diamond; AAN Best B/W Cinematography: Charles Lang Jr.; AAN Best Art Direction-Set Decoration (B/W): Ted Haworth Edward G. Goyle; AA Best Costume Design (B/W): Orry-Kelly

Nobody's perfect—except Billy Wilder in top form. One of the most well-loved of Hollywood comedies, Wilder's masterly spoof of gangster films and gender roles revels in invention and effervescent high camp. It's February, 1929, and Joe (Tony Curtis) and Jerry (Jack Lemmon) are two unemployed musicians desperate for work. The pair accidentally witness the St. Valentine's Day Massacre, watching mobster Spats Columbo (George Raft) and his henchmen wipe out Toothpick Charlie (George E. Stone) and his gang. Forced to leave town in a hurry, Joe and Jerry take the first job they can get: playing in Sweet Sue's all-girl band. Dressing up as women, the two join the rest of the band on their train ride to Florida. Both Joe, who adopts Josephine as his nom de drag, and Jerry, who becomes Daphne, are thrown for a loop when they meet Sweet Sue's lead singer, the pneumatic Sugar Kane (Marilyn Monroe)—"jello on springs," says Jerry.

SOME LIKE IT HOT expands a one-joke premise with hysterical results, due in no small part to the contributions of the near-perfect ensemble, with each of the major characters shining like a perfect jewel. Lemmon and Curtis are marvelous as the men-turned-women, creating believable characters and generally eschewing the lower forms of camp. Monroe is at her best, delightfully spoofing her dizzy blonde image. Billy Wilder and I.A.L. Diamond's witty script is full of clever twists, throwing in unexpected turns at a frantic pace. The script was written with Lemmon in mind, but at one point Frank Sinatra was considered as a possible replacement. Fortunately, this alternative casting fell through when Monroe expressed interest in doing the film. Although Monroe's presence was welcomed, both cast and crew learned to regret it as she lived up to her reputation as a "difficult" performer, consistently showing up late, forgetting her lines, and spending endless time in her dressing room. Wilder took to writing her lines on furniture in the hope that it would help the legendary actress to get through her scenes, but even this drastic effort failed. What's more, the other actors resented Monroe's antics, and Curtis compared kissing her to kissing Hitler. Nevertheless, Monroe still demonstrates her marvelous comic touch and sings three songs: "I Wanna Be Loved By You," "Running Wild," and "I'm Through with Love."

Ironically, Monroe's constant absences led to the creation of the film's classic exit line. Knowing Monroe's unreliability, Wilder took to shooting around her. It was decided that the film would end on a closeup of Lemmon and Joe E. Brown, as Daphne/Jerry explains to the lovesick Osgood E. Fielding III why s/he can't marry him. "We wrote it the night before we had to shoot it," Diamond explained in an interview, "and I mentioned a line I'd considered using at some earlier point.... Billy said, 'Do you think it's strong enough for the tag of the picture?' And I said, 'I don't know.' But it was getting to be eleven o'clock at night, so we wrote it that way, and he said, 'Well, maybe we'll think of something better on the set.' Fortunately, we didn't think of anything better on the set."

Monroe, unpopular on the set, wasn't invited to the wrap party. But she may have had the last laugh since she received 10 percent of the film's gross; the film made over $8 million in its initial release and would make several million more over the next few years. Said Wilder after the difficult shoot: "You have to be orderly to shoot disorder; this was the best disorder we ever had."

SOMEBODY UP THERE LIKES ME

1956 113m bw Sports/Biography ★★★½
MGM (U.S.)

Paul Newman (Rocky Graziano), Pier Angeli (Norma), Everett Sloane (Irving Cohen), Eileen Heckart (Ma Barbella), Sal Mineo (Romolo), Harold J. Stone (Nick Barbella), Joseph Buloff (Benny), Sammy White (Whitey Bimstein), Arch Johnson (Heldon), Robert Lieb (Questioner)

p, Charles Schnee; d, Robert Wise; w, Ernest Lehman (based on the autobiography of Rocky Graziano written with Rowland Barber); ph, Joseph Ruttenberg; ed, Albert Akst; m, Bronislau Kaper; art d, Cedric Gibbons, Malcolm Brown

AA Best B/W Cinematography: Joseph Ruttenberg; AAN Best Film Editing: Albert Akst; AA Best Art Direction-Set Decoration (B/W): Cedric Gibbons, Malcolm Brown, Edwin B. Willis, Keogh Gleason

After pulling no punches in his brilliant study of the downside of professional boxing, THE SET-UP, director Robert Wise presents a much more upbeat picture of the fight game in this entertaining biography of one-time middleweight champion Rocky Graziano. Paul Newman plays the New York slum-bred fighter, the son of a boxer whose career was stifled by the bottle. In and out of trouble for most of his young life, Rocky drifts from petty crime to reform school, from a dishonorable discharge from the Army to Leavenworth Prison. In the joint, however, Rocky is encouraged to develop his boxing talents, and when he is released he is taken under the wing of small-time manager Irving Cohen (Everett Sloane). Under Cohen's guidance, Rocky begins winning fights, and it isn't until he meets and marries Norma (Pier Angeli) that Rocky becomes a big winner. In time, he battles Tony Zale (brilliantly boxed by Courtland Shepard) for the championship, losing their first fight, but taking the title in the second. Newman, who spent time with Graziano and observed his speech patterns, mannerisms, movements, and boxing style, worked himself into peak condition for the role, lifting weights and sparring with top professionals, and his portrayal of the scrappy, often tongue-tied, but wholly likable boxer is superb. Although the role was originally intended for James Dean, Newman makes it his own, delivering such memorable lines as "I'll drink from the bottle like the rest of the boys" when asked if he needs a cup to complete his boxing garb.

SOMEONE TO WATCH OVER ME

1987 106m c Thriller/Romance ★★★
Columbia (U.S.) R

Tom Berenger (Mike Keegan), Mimi Rogers (Claire Gregory), Lorraine Bracco (Ellie Keegan), Jerry Orbach (Lt. Garber), John Rubinstein (Neil Steinhart), Andreas Katsulas (Joey Venza), Tony DiBenedetto (T.J.), James Moriarty (Koontz), Mark Moses (Win Hockings), Daniel Hugh Kelly (Scotty)

p, Thierry de Ganay, Harold Schneider; d, Ridley Scott; w, Howard Franklin; ph, Steven Poster (Deluxe Color); ed, Claire Simpson; m, Michael Kamen; prod d, Jim Bissell; art d, Christopher Burian-Mohr, John J. Moore; cos, Colleen Atwood

Hot on the heels of FATAL ATTRACTION came SOMEONE TO WATCH OVER ME, another film about a happily married man who strays from the marital bed. Mike Keegan (Tom Berenger) is a New York police detective who lives in Queens with his ex-cop wife, Ellie (Lorraine Bracco), and their young son. When wealthy socialite Claire Gregory (Mimi Rogers) witnesses a murder, Keegan is assigned to protect her from the killer. Cold and aloof at first, Claire begins to warm to the handsome, shy, and somewhat dim-witted detective. Although SOMEONE TO WATCH OVER ME has some major problems with plot plausibility, its emphasis is properly on the people involved in the romantic triangle and not the machinations of a contrived story line. Much of the credit for what works in the film should go to the excellent cast. Berenger is superb, and Rogers proves here that she can handle a lead role with class and aplomb. Bracco, however, steals the picture with a refreshing energy and wit.

SOMETHING WILD

1986 113m c Drama/Comedy ★★★½
Religioso Primitiva (U.S.) R

Jeff Daniels (Charles Driggs), Melanie Griffith (Audrey Hankel), Ray Liotta (Ray Sinclair), Margaret Colin (Irene), Tracey Walter (The Country Squire), Dana Preu ("Peaches"), Jack Gilpin (Larry Dillman), Su Tissue (Peggy Dillman), Kristin Olsen (Tracy), John Sayles (Motorcycle Cop)

p, Jonathan Demme, Kenneth Utt; d, Jonathan Demme; w, E. Max Frye; ph, Tak Fujimoto (DuArt Color); ed, Craig McKay; m, John Cale, Laurie Anderson; prod d, Norma Moriceau; art d, Stephen J. Lineweaver

One bright Friday afternoon in lower Manhattan, Charles Driggs (Jeff Daniels), a successful young tax consultant, capriciously skips out of a tiny diner without paying his lunch check. Just outside, he is stopped by Audrey Hankel (Melanie Griffith), a Louise Brooks-clone in black wig and vaguely

African attire. She calls herself "Lulu," presumably a reference to Brooks' character in PANDORA'S BOX. She tells Charles that she saw him walk out on the check and threatens to turn him in. Declaring that Charles is actually a "closet rebel," she decides instead that he'd be game for a road trip. Before he knows what is happening, Charles finds himself in Audrey's convertible being driven to New Jersey. Through Audrey he is temporarily freed from his normal bourgeois restraints. They have a little adventure on the road as they engage in some petty theft, mildly kinky sex, and finally attend Audrey's high school reunion. This modern screwball comedy takes a frightening dark turn when they encounter Audrey's psychotic ex-husband, Ray (Ray Liotta), who has just gotten out of jail.

Since his early films, director Jonathan Demme has demonstrated a sharp eye for the American landscape and its people. With a keen wit and an optimistic compassion, Demme has creates vividly human characters whose quirks have the ring of truth about them. With a screenplay from first-time screenwriter E. Max Frye and superior performances from his principal cast, Demme has created a unique and likable film in SOMETHING WILD. John Cale and Laurie Anderson compiled the film's rousing rock soundtrack which features nearly 50 songs.

Some viewers were alarmed at the dark violent turn the story takes more than halfway through but close viewing reveals that the audience is subtely being prepared for this tonal shift from early on. This is a film that benefits greatly from a second screening. Demme keeps his quirky narrative twisting and turning so that the viewer can never predict what will happen next. He draws us in with humor and then grabs us by the throat, bringing us face-to-face with the failures of the American dream. A filmmaker with a small but devoted following, he would not have a major popular hit until the 1991 blockbuster, THE SILENCE OF THE LAMBS.

SOMETHING'S GOTTA GIVE　　　　**DVD**
2003　123m　c　　Comedy/Romance　　**★★½**
Waverly Films/Columbia　　(U.S.)　　　　PG-13

Jack Nicholson (*Harry Sanborn*), Diane Keaton (*Erica Barry*), Frances McDormand (*Zoe Barry*), Keanu Reeves (*Julian Mercer*), Amanda Peet (*Marin*), Jon Favreau (*Leo*), Paul Michael Glaser (*Dave*), Rachel Ticotin (*Dr. Martinez*), Marjie Gum (*Annie*), Kadee Strickland (*Kristen*)

p, Bruce A. Block, Nancy Meyers; d, Nancy Meyers; w, Nancy Meyers; ph, Michael Ballhaus; ed, Joe Hutshing; m, Hans Zimmer; prod d, Jon Hutman; art d, John Warnke; fx, Bruce A. Kuroyama, Scott Rader; cos, Suzanne McCabe

AAN Best Actress: Diane Keaton

It's a perfect example of strong casting improving weak material. Writer-director Nancy Meyers's formulaic romantic comedy about the turbulent love affair between a 63-year-old Lothario with a taste for younger women and a neurotic, 50-ish playwright would probably be as dull as it sounds if Jack Nicholson and Diane Keaton weren't playing the lovers.

Harry Sanborn (Nicholson) and his latest conquest, Marin Berry (Amanda Peet), are just about to get down to business at her house in the Hamptons when Marin's mom, Erica (Keaton), and aunt, Zoe (Frances McDormand), walk in. The four adults agree that no one should be forced to leave, but that evening Harry suffers a heart attack. His doctor, Julian Mercer (Keanu Reeves), insists he's not ready to return to the city, so over Erica's objections, Harry takes up residence in her house. And since Marin and Zoe have to go back to work, the two are stuck with each other. Things get off to a rocky start—particularly after Harry accidentally glimpses Erica naked—but the soon-to-be soul mates gradually grow on each other. At the

same time, Erica discovers she has another suitor in the handsome—and much younger—Dr. Mercer.

Though filled with elaborate contrivances, this gentle comedy shines when there are no plot twists or eccentric supporting characters in the way of Keaton's and Nicholson's characterizations of ordinary people tentatively exploring a new relationship. A whiz at crafting conventional Hollywood screenplays, Meyers's direction relies too heavily on close-ups and medium shots; there's no life to any of the images. Still, the film coasts along smoothly on the charisma of its stars, and if Keaton and Nicholson aren't the hottest screen couple going, they may be the most convincing.

SOMMERSBY　　　　　　　　　　**DVD**
1993　112m　c　　Drama/Historical/Romance　**★★★**
New Regency Films/Warner Bros.　(U.S.)　　PG-13

Richard Gere (*Jack*), Jodie Foster (*Laurel*), Lanny Flaherty (*Buck*), Wendell Wellman (*Travis*), Bill Pullman (*Orin*), Brett Kelley (*Little Rob*), William Windom (*Reverend Powell*), Clarice Taylor (*Esther*), James Earl Jones (*Judge Issacs*), Frankie Faison (*Joseph*)

p, Arnon Milchan, Steven Reuther; d, Jon Amiel; w, Nicholas Meyer, Sarah Kernochan (from story by Meyer and Anthony Shaffer based on the screenplay *Le Retour de Martin Guerre* by Daniel Vigne and Jean-Claude Carriere); ph, Philippe Rousselot; ed, Peter Boyle; m, Danny Elfman; prod d, Bruno Rubeo; art d, P. Michael Johnston; fx, Gregory S. Hull; chor, Colleen Kelly; cos, Marilyn Vance-Straker

Like BREATHLESS, THREE MEN AND A BABY and COUSINS, SOMMERSBY is a Hollywood remake of a successful French film, this time THE RETURN OF MARTIN GUERRE. With the setting switched from 16th-century France to post-civil war Tennessee, the story remains largely the same: a man returns home after an absence of several years to reclaim his wife and property, but is so changed as to arouse suspicions about his real identity.

As played by Richard Gere, Jack Sommersby seems transformed from a spoilt, mean-spirited landowner into a paragon of heroism and virtue. By day, he leads his wife (Jodie Foster) and tenants in an enlightened, profit-sharing scheme to bring prosperity back to his war-ravaged estate by growing tobacco; by night, he takes time out from reading Homer to his young son to single-handedly rout KKK gangs who beat up his emancipated black workers.

"Sommersby" is made with enough intelligence to overcome its credulity-straining premise, and handles its outdoor scenes with epic charm. It's fun to watch the farmers nurture their precious tobacco seed into full-grown plants, at one point fighting off an invasion of swollen, wormlike bugs. The worms are only slightly less appealing, however, than Richard Gere, whose facial expressions run the gamut from smug to smarmy. Gere's pairing opposite Jodie Foster is a fatal flaw here, with her self-contained performance reflecting his glib narcissism. Though it's billed as a romantic drama, SOMMERSBY is better at recreating a time and place than at sparking even the faintest glimmer of passion. On this particular tobacco farm, there's plenty to smoke, but no fire.

SON OF FRANKENSTEIN　　　　　　**DVD**
1939　95m　　bw　Horror　　　　　　**★★★★**
Universal　　(U.S.)

Basil Rathbone (*Baron Wolf von Frankenstein*), Boris Karloff (*The Monster*), Bela Lugosi (*Ygor*), Lionel Atwill (*Inspector Krogh*), Josephine Hutchinson (*Elsa von Frankenstein*), Donnie Dunagan (*Peter von Frankenstein*), Emma Dunn (*Amelia*), Edgar Norton (*Thomas Benson*), Perry Ivins (*Fritz*), Lawrence Grant (*Burgomaster*) p, Rowland V. Lee; d, Rowland V. Lee; w, Willis Cooper (based on characters created by Mary Shelley); ph, George Robinson; ed, Ted J. Kent; m, Frank Skinner; art d, Jack Otterson; fx, John P. Fulton; cos, Vera West

In the Universal "Frankenstein" series and the last feature film appearance by Boris Karloff as the monster, SON OF FRANKENSTEIN boasts some stunning set design by Russell Gausman, a good script, and a magnificent cast. Set 25 years after the end of BRIDE OF FRANKENSTEIN, the film begins as the late Baron von Frankenstein's son, Wolf (Basil Rathbone), returns to his homeland and receives a weak welcome from the burgomaster, who presents him with a box containing his father's papers. Once safe in his castle, Wolf is visited by Inspector Krogh (Lionel Atwill), who warns him that he is not welcomed by the villagers, who fear that he will continue his father's experiments. Wolf laughs off their suspicions, but the next day, while wandering the ruins of his father's laboratory, he meets Ygor (Bela Lugosi). The deceased Baron's assistant now hides among the ruins, guarding his "friend"—the comatose Frankenstein monster (Karloff) laid out on a slab, immobile, but very much alive. Wolf becomes obsessed with the idea of bringing the monster back to full power, then vindicating his father by teaching the creature to behave. SON OF FRANKENSTEIN is a rousing, memorable addition to the series, and features a collection of superb portrayals from Lugosi (who delivers the performance of his career and nearly steals the film), Rathbone (in a part originally planned for Peter Lorre), and Lionel Atwill (who milks his false arm for all it's worth), though Karloff is a bit of a disappointment—his beloved monster turned into little more than a mute robot. Dwight Frye, who had been Frankenstein's assistant in the first two films, unfortunately had his entire role as one of the villagers cut out. While the offbeat vision and humor of James Whale (the director of the first two FRANKENSTEIN films) are missing, Rowland Lee manages to create a memorable world all his own. The series would go downhill from here and end with a rousing parody of the whole genre in ABBOTT AND COSTELLO MEET FRANKENSTEIN.

SON OF PALEFACE

1952 95m c Western/Comedy Paramount (U.S.)
★★★½ [DVD]

Bob Hope (Junior), Jane Russell (Mike), Roy Rogers (Himself), Bill Williams (Kirk), Lloyd Corrigan (Doc Lovejoy), Paul E. Burns (Ebenezer Hawkins), Douglas Dumbrille (Sheriff McIntyre), Harry von Zell (Stoner), Iron Eyes Cody (Indian Chief), Wee Willie Davis (Blacksmith)

p, Robert L. Welch; d, Frank Tashlin; w, Frank Tashlin, Robert Welch, Joseph Quillan; ph, Harry Wild (Technicolor); ed, Eda Warren; m, Lyn Murray; art d, Hal Pereira, Roland Anderson; fx, Gordon Jennings, Paul K. Lerpae, Farciot Edouart; chor, Josephine Earl

AAN Best Song: "Am I in Love"; Jack Brooks

This very funny sequel to THE PALEFACE took four years to put on the screen while Hope made a few other pictures. This time, Hope plays his own son. The original character of the pioneer dentist was played by Hope, and now he comes back, again with Russell, as the Harvard graduate who goes west to claim the inheritance left by his father. Russell is a bandit who sings in a saloon known as "The Dirty Shame." Hope teams with Roy Rogers and Trigger the Horse (playing themselves) to nab a crook who has been robbing various gold shipments. They suspect that the criminal may be Russell. She thinks Rogers is a handsome guy and has the warms for him, but he would rather kiss his horse, so, rarity of rarities, Hope gets the girl.

SON OF PALEFACE is a satire of every cowboy cliché, with Hope getting the chance to rattle off one-liners while the action takes in Indian uprisings, lynch mobs, posses, ghost towns, mirages, deserts, quick-draws, saloon brawls—in other words, everything that John Wayne ever did for real. Tashlin was receiving his first directorial credit; he had co-directed THE LEMON DROP KID with Sid Lanfield but was not credited. He'd written THE PALEFACE and was rewarded with this assignment, a job he didn't muff. It's fast and witty, and all the rootin' tootin' shootin' cannot be taken seriously for a moment. Tashlin was a one-time cartoonist, and it shows as he sets up the scenes like animated sequences, much to the picture's benefit. In the original, Ray Evans and Jay Livingston wrote the Oscar tune "Buttons and Bows" and they wisely bring it back for another go-around with new lyrics, as sung by Hope, Rogers, and Russell.

Rogers had been the king of the small western movies for over a decade, but after this movie, began to limit his appearances. He did a small guest bit in ALIAS JESSE JAMES, then a role in MACKINTOSH AND T.J. Other than those, he spent most of his time tending his huge real estate investments which are worth over $100 million.

SONATINE

1994 94m c Crime/Drama/Comedy Bandai Visual/Shochiku Dai-Ichi Kogyo/Office Kitano/Right Vision (Japan)
★★★½ [DVD] R

Takeshi Kitano, billed as "Beat" Takeshi (Murakawa), Aya Kokumai (Miyuki—the Village Girl), Tetsu Watanabe (Uechi—the Okinawan Gangster), Masanobu Katsumura (Ryoji), Susumu Terajima, billed as Susumu Terashima (Ken), Ren Ohsugi (Katagiri), Tonbo Zushi (Kitajima), Kenichi Yajima (Takahashi), Eiji Minakata (The Hit Man)

p, Masayuki Mori, Hisao Nabeshima, Takio Yoshida, Ritta Saito; d, Takeshi Kitano; w, Takeshi Kitano; ph, Katsumi Yanagishima; ed, Takeshi Kitano; m, Joe Hisaishi; art d, Osamu Saseki

Where do old gangsters go to die? To the seaside, if one is to believe this bleakly pensive crime picture by Japanese cultural phenomenon "Beat" Takeshi Kitano.

Yakuza big man Kitajima (Tonbo Zushi) sends his trusted, middle-age underboss Murakawa (Kitano) to the resort town of Okinawa to settle some petty internecine warfare. Murakawa gathers up a bunch of young guns and does as he's told, but suspects there's more to the assignment than meets the eye. Is he being set up? After Murakawa and his henchmen are ambushed, they retreat to the beachfront home of a local yakuza and spend a few weirdly idyllic days horsing around by the sea, wondering when real life will intrude.

Hugely praised on its initial release, this 1993 Japanese film hit Western screens shortly after Kitano's more recent FIREWORKS. The difference in Kitano's appearance is shocking (SONATINE was shot before Kitano was nearly killed in a motorcycle accident, while FIREWORKS was made afterward), but his sly, acid-tipped sense of humor and melancholy twists on genre conventions remain the same. The picture's uneasy but perfectly calibrated mix of brutal violence and goofy humor is pure Kitano—the scene in which Murakawa and his henchmen play a variation on Rock'em Sock'em Robots with paper sumo wrestlers is just too bizarre—and its convulsively nihilistic ending is unforgettable.

SONG OF BERNADETTE, THE

1943 156m bw Religious/Biography Fox (U.S.)
★★★★ [DVD]

Jennifer Jones (Bernadette Soubirous), William Eythe (Antoine), Charles Bickford (Peyremaie), Vincent Price (Dutour), Lee J. Cobb (Dr. Dozous), Gladys Cooper (Sister Vauzous), Anne Revere

(Louise Soubirous), Roman Bohnen (Francois Soubirous), Mary Anderson (Jeanne Abadie), Patricia Morison (Empress Eugenie)

p, William Perlberg; d, Henry King; w, George Seaton (based on the novel by Franz Werfel); ph, Arthur Miller; ed, Barbara McLean; m, Alfred Newman; art d, James Basevi, William Darling; fx, Fred Sersen; cos, Rene Hubert

AAN Best Picture; AA Best Actress: Jennifer Jones; AAN Best Supporting Actor: Charles Bickford; AAN Best Supporting Actress: Gladys Cooper; AAN Best Supporting Actress: Anne Revere; AAN Best Director: Henry King; AAN Best Screenplay: George Seaton; AA Best B/W Cinematography: Arthur Miller; AAN Best Film Editing: Barbara McLean; AA Best Score (Drama or Comedy): Alfred Newman; AA Best Interior Decoration (B/W): James Basevi, William Darling, Thomas Little; AAN Best Sound Recording: E.H. Hansen

This film depicts the stirring true story of the woman who had a vision of the Virgin Mary in a grotto at Lourdes in 1858. Jennifer Jones is Bernadette Soubirous, a peasant girl whose family lives in the town jail because they have no place of their own. One morning, Bernadette is gathering sticks of wood near the grotto when she is visited by the Virgin (Linda Darnell). Bernadette is directed to dig at the grotto for a healing water with curative power for the lame and the halt. Everyone scoffs at her except her devout mother and, eventually, Peyremaie (Charles Bickford), a local priest. He helps her get into a convent, and, after many years of defending her vision, Bernadette is canonized by the Catholic Church. Since that time, millions have flocked to Lourdes to bathe in the Holy Water. Jones is touching in an Oscar-winning performance.

SONG OF THE SOUTH
1946 94m c Animated/Children's ★★★★
Walt Disney Productions (U.S.)

Ruth Warrick (Sally), Bobby Driscoll (Johnny), Luana Patten (Ginny), Lucile Watson (Grandmother), Hattie McDaniel (Aunt Tempy), Glenn Leedy (Toby), James Baskett (Uncle Remus), Nicodemus Stewart (Voice of Brer Bear), Johnny Lee (Voice of Brer Rabbit), George Nokes

p, Walt Disney; d, Harve Foster (live action), Wilfred Jackson (animated); w, Dalton Raymond, Morton Grant, Bill Peet, George Stallings, Ralph Wright, Maurice Rapf (based on Tales of Uncle Remus by Joel Chandler Harris); ph, Gregg Toland (Technicolor); ed, William Morgan; m, Daniele Amfitheatrof, Paul J. Smith; art d, Perry Ferguson; fx, Ub Iwerks; cos, Mary Wills; anim, Milt Kahl, Erick Larson, Oliver M. Johnston Jr., Les Clark, Marc Davis, John Lounsbery, Don Lusk, Tom Massey, Murray McClellan, Jack Campbell, Hal King, Harvey Toombs, Ken O'Brien, Al Coe, Hal Ambro, Cliff Nordberg, Rudy Larriva

AAN Best Score (Musical): Daniele Amfitheatrof, Paul J. Smith, Charles Wolcott; AA Best Song: "Zip-A-Dee-Doo-Dah"; Allie Wrubel (Music), Ray Gilbert (Lyrics)

This Disney charmer is also the studio's most controversial production. Set in the Reconstruction South, it stars Bobby Driscoll as Johnny, a white little boy who goes to live on his grandmother's plantation after his parents separate. Upset by things he can't understand, Johnny runs away and meets former slave Uncle Remus (James Baskett). Uncle Remus decides to trick Johnny into going home, telling the boy he would also like to run away, but must stop home for a few things. Uncle Remus packs, he tells Johnny a story, and the film moves into a marvelous combination of live action and animation in a bright cartoon setting in which Brer Rabbit, too, has an adventure while running away from home. SONG OF THE SOUTH's cartoon sequences are as fine as anything produced by the Disney animators. The live action projected into a cartoon setting transcends gimmickry, with the actors and

caricatures carefully matched within the frame. Baskett's excellent performance (for which he received an honorary Academy Award) makes the technique work that much better. The film's idyllic portrayal of the Reconstruction setting was controversial, however, particularly among black Americans. The NAACP and the National Urban League, among others, protested the stereotypes in the film, though Disney officials of course maintained the film was "a sincere effort to depict American folklore, to put the Uncle Remus stories into pictures." Included is the well-known song "Zip A Dee Doo Dah."

SONG TO REMEMBER, A
1945 113m c Musical/Biography ★★★½
Columbia (U.S.)

Paul Muni (Professor Joseph Elsner), Merle Oberon (George Sand), Cornel Wilde (Frederic Chopin), Stephen Bekassy (Franz Liszt), Nina Foch (Constantia), George Coulouris (Louis Pleyel), Sig Arno (Henri Dupont), Howard Freeman (Kalbrenner), George Macready (Alfred DeMusset), Claire DuBrey (Mme. Mercier)

p, Louis F. Edelman; d, Charles Vidor; w, Sidney Buchman (based on the story by Ernst Marischka); ph, Tony Gaudio, Allen Davey (Technicolor); ed, Charles Nelson; m, Miklos Rozsa; art d, Lionel Banks, Van Nest Polglase; cos, Walter Plunkett, Travis Banton

AAN Best Actor: Cornel Wilde; AAN Best Original Story: Ernst Marischka; AAN Best Color Cinematography: Tony Gaudio, Allen M. Davey; AAN Best Film Editing: Charles Nelson; AAN Best Score (Drama or Comedy): Miklos Rozsa, Morris Stoloff; AAN Best Sound Recording: John Livadary

As a fictional tale of a composer who gives his all for his music, this is a fine picture; as a biography, it bears as much resemblance to the truth as NIGHT AND DAY did to the life of Cole Porter. Nonetheless, Cornel Wilde earned an Oscar nomination for his convincing performance as Frederic Chopin, whom screenwriter Sidney Buchman presents as a revolutionary Polish patriot (though, in fact, his support of Polish nationalism was never so zealous). Top-billed Paul Muni, in his only Technicolor film, portrays Chopin's mentor Prof. Joseph Elsner, while Merle Oberon essays the role of novelist George Sand, whom the infatuated Chopin meets in Paris and follows to Majorca, where he becomes consumptive (the real-life relationship between Sand and Chopin was considerably less whirlwind, lasting some 10 years), resulting in his death when he refuses to cancel a concert tour whose proceeds are earmarked for the cause.

SONS AND LOVERS
1960 99m bw Drama ★★★½
Fox (U.K.)

Trevor Howard (Walter Morel), Dean Stockwell (Paul Morel), Wendy Hiller (Mrs. Morel), Mary Ure (Clara Dawes), Heather Sears (Miriam Lievers), William Lucas (William), Conrad Phillips (Baxter Dawes), Donald Pleasence (Pappleworth), Ernest Thesiger (Henry Hadlock), Rosalie Crutchley (Miriam's Mother)

p, Jerry Wald; d, Jack Cardiff; w, Gavin Lambert, T.E.B. Clarke (based on the novel by D.H. Lawrence); ph, Freddie Francis (CinemaScope); m, Mario Nascimbene; art d, Lionel Couch; cos, Margaret Furse

AAN Best Picture; AAN Best Actor: Trevor Howard; AAN Best Supporting Actress: Mary Ure; AAN Best Director: Jack Cardiff; AAN Best Adapted Screenplay: Gavin Lambert, T.E.B. Clarke; AA Best B/W Cinematography: Freddie Francis; AAN Best Art Direction-Set Decoration (B/W): Tom Morahan, Lionel Couch

They might well have titled this SON AND MOTHER, for the famous relationship between a mother and son is at the center of this respectful adaptation of Lawrence's autobiographical novel. A few characters have been altered and a sister has been dropped in the transition from print to the screen, but these changes hardly call attention to themselves.

The story is set in Nottingham, where Hiller and Howard have raised three sons on Howard's miner's wages. Hiller is a forceful woman who manages men like puppets. Stockwell is the sensitive son who longs to pursue a career as an artist in London. After romancing naive local lass Sears for a while, Stockwell takes up with an older woman, Ure, who is married to Phillips. Hiller puts an end to her son's relationship with Sears, and when Ure leaves her husband for Stockwell, Hiller is livid. Stockwell listens to his mother but knows he should follow his heart; however, he appears powerless to free himself of her grasp. No matter what he does or where he goes, Stockwell feels Hiller's presence. The love that Hiller should be giving her husband is, instead, showered upon Stockwell. When one of his brothers dies in a mining accident and the other goes off to London, Stockwell is forced to abandon his dreams in order to be near his bereaved mother. Hiller eventually dies, and Stockwell leaves for London, looking forward to a life away from the claustrophobic town, but we know that the specter of his dear mother will always be with him.

Many works have been written about the domination of sons by mothers, but few have come close to the insights of Lawrence's classic, and it is much to the film's credit that a great deal of its dialogue comes straight from the novel. The film's period details are excellent, and the direction by cinematographer-turned-director Cardiff (who photographed such films as THE RED SHOES, LEAVE HER TO HEAVEN and THE AFRICAN QUEEN) is first rate. All of the actors acquit themselves well, even in the most menial roles. Crutchley is exquisite as Sears' mother and veteran Thesiger (who, at 81, was making his penultimate film in a career that begain in 1918) is equally memorable. Cardiff's assistant on the film was Peter Yates, who later directed such films as BULLITT and BREAKING AWAY.

SON'S ROOM, THE 📀
(LA STANZA DEL FIGLIO)
2001 99m c Drama ★★★½
Sacher Film/Bac Films/Studiocanal/ R
Rai Cinema/Tele+/Parigi (Italy/France)

Nanni Moretti (Giovanni), Laura Morante (Paola), Jasmine Trinca (Irene), Giuseppe Sanfelice (Andrea), Sofia Vigliar (Arianna), Silvio Orlando (Oscar—Patient), Stefano Accorsi (Tommaso—Patient), Claudia Della Seta (Raffaella—Patient), Renato Scarpa (Headmaster), Roberto Nobile (Priest)

p, Angelo Barbagallo, Nanni Moretti; d, Nanni Moretti; w, Linda Ferri, Nanni Moretti, Heidrun Schleef (from a story by Nanni Moretti); ph, Giuseppe Lanci; ed, Esmeralda Calbria; m, Nicola Piovani; art d, Giancarlo Basili; fx, Studio A.M.; cos, Maria Rita Barbera

A major filmmaker in his native Italy, writer-director-star Nanni Moretti has been virtually ignored in the United States. Moretti's international profile, however, was raised considerably in 2001 when this film, his 11th feature, won the Palm d'Or at the Cannes Film Festival.

Moretti stars as Giovanni, a successful psychiatrist with a busy practice in the picturesque Northern Italian coastal town he and his family call home. Giovanni is happily married to beautiful book publisher Paola (Laura Morante) and shares what he considers a close relationship with his teenaged daughter Irene (Jasmine Trinca) and son Andrea (Giuseppe Sanfelice). Lately, however, there have been a few problems: Andrea and his friends have been accused of stealing a valuable fossil from his school. But nothing prepares Giovanni for the sudden tragedy that occurs one sunny Sunday afternoon. Called away from home by a desperate

client, Giovanni cancels his plans to go jogging with Andrea. Andrea instead goes scuba diving with friends, and drowns in an underwater cave. Plunged into unimaginable grief, Giovanni attempts to carry on with his life, but bereft of his objectivity, he finds he's no longer able to function as an analyst. Bereft of his son, he wonders whether he can continue to function as a father and husband.

It's tempting to compare Moretti's film with Todd Field's similarly themed IN THE BEDROOM, in which an apparently happy Maine family is destroyed by a son's sudden death. But where death in Field's film begets further violence, Moretti ultimately finds peace, and the rather banal revelation that life inevitably goes on comes as an effective spiritual balm. Occasionally melodramatic, the film is also extremely effective.

SOPHIE'S CHOICE 📀
1982 157m c Drama ★★★
ITC (U.S.) R

Meryl Streep (Sophie Zawistowska), Kevin Kline (Nathan Landau), Peter MacNicol (Stingo), Josef Sommer (Narrator), Rita Karin (Yetta Zimmerman), Stephen D. Newman (Larry), Greta Turken (Leslie Lapidus), Josh Mostel (Morris Fink), Marcell Rosenblatt (Astrid Weinstein), Moishe Rosenfeld (Moishe Rosenblum)

p, Alan J. Pakula, Keith Barish; d, Alan J. Pakula; w, Alan J. Pakula (based on the novel by William Styron) (Technicolor); ph, Nestor Almendros (Technicolor); ed, Evan Lottman; m, Marvin Hamlisch; prod d, George Jenkins; art d, John J. Moore; cos, Albert Wolsky

AA Best Actress: Meryl Streep; AAN Best Adapted Screenplay: Alan J. Pakula; AAN Best Cinematography: Nestor Almendros; AAN Best Original Score: Marvin Hamlisch; AAN Best Costume Design: Albert Wolsky

Meryl Streep essays another foreign accent in this overwrought melodrama. Adapted from William Styron's wildly ambitious semiautobiographical novel (its first line is "Call me Stingo"—get it?), the film follows Stingo (Peter MacNicol), a compone author who moves into a Brooklyn boarding house in 1947 and meets driven Nathan Landau (Kevin Kline) and mysterious Sophie Zawistowska (Meryl Streep), a Polish woman with a past. For most of the film one wonders what Sophie's "choice" is: is she to choose between Nathan and Stingo? But then the film flashes back to monochrome sepia to depict war, concentration camps, and the moment of revelation.

Competently directed by Pakula and featuring gorgeous cinematography by Almendros, SOPHIE'S CHOICE is an overlong, fairly schlocky film that takes itself very seriously. Streep emotes in customary fashion; Kline overacts wildly; MacNicol is charming in an unforgiving role.

SORROW AND THE PITY, THE 📀
1970 260m c/bw Documentary ★★★★½
Norddeutscher Rundfunk/Societe Suisse de
Radiodiffusion/Television Rencontre
(France/Switzerland/West Germany)

Pierre Mendes-France, Louis Grave, Alexis Grave, Helmuth Tausend, Marcel Verdier, Emanuel de la Vigier, Anthony Eden, Rene de Chambrun, Emile Caubaudon, Christian de la Maziere

d, Marcel Ophuls; w, Marcel Ophuls, Andre Harris; ph, Andre Gazut, Jurgen Thieme; ed, Claude Vaida

THE SORROW AND THE PITY, Marcel Ophuls' eye-opening documentary about French complicity in the Nazi Holocaust, has only grown in importance over the years, mainly because the subject matter has become increasingly remote to viewers. Though lengthy and obviously downbeat, the 1970 film should be a staple for all serious filmgoers.

Through newsreels and the interviews with those that fought on both sides, THE SORROW AND THE PITY tells the story of the German occupation of France, mainly in the town of Clermont-Ferrand, during WWII. In Part One, "The Collapse," several French, German, and British observers look back at the attack on France in June 1940. Part Two, "The Choice," details some of the incidents during the occupation and eventual liberation of Clermont-Ferrand.

THE SORROW AND THE PITY provides a refreshingly unemotional account of events during WWII in contrast to such romanticized Holocaust and war film stories that have aped the documentary form—including IS PARIS BURNING? (1966) and SCHINDLER'S LIST (1993). More in the tradition of Alain Resnais's NIGHT AND FOG (1955), THE SORROW AND THE PITY searches for the truth through straightforward fact-finding. But unlike the short (32-minute) Resnais documentary, THE SORROW AND THE PITY (at 260 minutes) emphasizes not the victims, but the perpetrators (Nazis and the French collaborators) who speak to Ophuls at length with openness and ease. (Combining the perspectives of both killers and survivors, Claude Lanzmann created the 9 1/2 hour SHOAH in 1984.) Ophuls, the son of director Max Ophuls, uses a form that is seemingly styleless, but really just as meticulous and carefully planned as anything his father might have made. The "talking head" format is deceptively simple and "balanced." But Ophuls brilliantly indicts the fascists interviewed with their own words, and contradicts their assertions with newsreel footage. In an opening sequence, Maurice Chevalier entertains German soldiers, but, in the closing sequence defends himself in a newsreel as having only entertained French POWs in Germany. Thus, the truth brings down this symbol of Gallic France for a devastating finale.

SORRY, WRONG NUMBER 💿
1948   89m   bw   Thriller   ★★★★
Paramount   (U.S.)

Barbara Stanwyck (Leona Stevenson), Burt Lancaster (Henry Stevenson), Ann Richards (Sally Lord Dodge), Wendell Corey (Dr. Alexander), Harold Vermilyea (Waldo Evans), Ed Begley (James Cotterell), Leif Erickson (Fred Lord), William Conrad (Morano), John Bromfield (Joe), Jimmy Hunt (Jimmy Lord)

p, Hal B. Wallis, Anatole Litvak; d, Anatole Litvak; w, Lucille Fletcher (based on her radio play); ph, Sol Polito; ed, Warren Low; m, Franz Waxman; art d, Hans Dreier, Earl Hedrick; fx, Gordon Jennings; cos, Edith Head

AAN Best Actress: Barbara Stanwyck

A gripping film version of the classic 22-minute radio play which was made famous by Agnes Moorehead in a tour-de-force performance in 1943. Because Moorehead was not a "star" in Hollywood, Barbara Stanwyck was given the role in the movie version and she made it her own. Leona Stevenson (Stanwyck) is a whining, domineering, paranoid, hypochondriac New York heiress who has developed a psychosomatic illness that has made her a bed-ridden invalid. She lives in a fancy apartment with her milquetoast husband Henry (Lancaster), her only contact with the outside world being the telephone. One evening, while trying to reach Henry at the office, she overhears two men confirming plans for a murder. She tries to contact the outside world—the police, the phone company, Henry—to warn them of the impending violence, but time is quickly running out and the hour of the murder is approaching. The film's title is also its last line of dialogue.

SORRY, WRONG NUMBER is a wonderful premise which made for a taut, fast-paced 22-minute radio play, but

at 89 minutes, much of them told in flashback, the suspense ebbs somewhat. Both Lancaster and Stanwyck are excellent.

SOUND OF MUSIC, THE 💿
1965   174m   c   Musical/Biography   ★★½
Fox   (U.S.)   G

Julie Andrews (Maria), Christopher Plummer (Capt. Von Trapp), Eleanor Parker (The Baroness), Richard Haydn (Max Detweiler), Peggy Wood (Mother Abbess), Charmian Carr (Liesl), Heather Menzies (Louisa), Nicholas Hammond (Friedrich), Duane Chase (Kurt), Angela Cartwright (Brigitta)

p, Robert Wise; d, Robert Wise; w, Ernest Lehman (based on the musical play by Richard Rodgers, Oscar Hammerstein II, Howard Lindsay, Russel Crouse); ph, Ted McCord (Todd-AO, DeLuxe Color); ed, William Reynolds; m, Richard Rodgers; prod d, Boris Leven; fx, L.B. Abbott, Emil Kosa Jr.; chor, Marc Breaux, Dee Dee Wood; cos, Dorothy Jeakins

AA Best Picture; AAN Best Actress: Julie Andrews; AAN Best Supporting Actress: Peggy Wood; AA Best Director: Robert Wise; AAN Best Color Cinematography: Ted McCord; AA Best Film Editing: William Reynolds; AA Best Adapted Score: Irwin Kostal; AAN Best Art Direction-Set Decoration (Color): Boris Leven, Walter M. Scott, Ruby Levitt; AAN Best Costume Design (Color): Dorothy Jeakins; AA Best Sound: James P. Corcoran, Fred Hynes

We'd give anything to be little Von Trapp children, living our lives in the confines of this film. We'd refuse to wear clothes made from curtains. We'd sing loudly (like off-key Ethel Mermans) when we were hiding from Nazis, and never compromise our talent to sing before Papa's guests. We'd snatch Eleanor Parker's Eva Gabor wig, moon nuns, and wet Julie's bed during "My Favorite Things." What fun we'd have. And make this travesty real. For despite the political danger, we know it's leading to music swells and Andrews's million-dollar wedding gown—enough to make Grace Kelly and Princess Di and Elizabeth Taylor slap their mothers. It's so perfectly contrived and mechanical and fresh as a daisy, it's infuriating. And only the sly, insistently subversive Christopher Plummer is on our side.

Maria (Julie Andrews) is a young postulant at a nunnery who quickly realizes that the cloister is not for her. Yet she still believes in the values espoused by the church, so she goes out into the world and radiantly attempts to bring what she's learned to the lay world. Soon Maria is hired by Austrian widower Capt. Von Trapp (Christopher Plummer) as a governess for his seven singing children. Noting that the children seem cowed by their disciplinarian father, she strives to open their lives to joy. They live in one of the most beautiful sections of the Alps, but only learn to appreciate the surrounding vistas when Maria, with her fresh outlook, shows them what they have. All that is soon threatened by Nazi rule in Austria, forcing the Von Trapps to flee while en route to Salzburg for a musical festival in which they are to perform. A staple of 1960s Hollywood films, THE SOUND OF MUSIC delivered an unforgettable Julie Andrews performance (simultaneously damning her career; we'd have preferred the more authentic Mary Martin), and presented a most postcard view of Austria. The songs are hard to forget—"The Sound of Music," "Do Re Mi," "My Favorite Things," "Edelweiss," "Climb Every Mountain," and our pick of the litter, "The Lonely Goatherd"—but we're trying. So you expected a *serious* review?

In a nutshell: lovely to look at, scripted competently, with a few chilling moments about the lurking Nazis. But Wise can't direct Plummer to play along. And who does Eleanor Parker think she is—Anne Baxter standing in for Joan Crawford?

SOUNDER

1972 105m c Drama   **DVD**
Radnitz/Mattel (U.S.)   ★★★½   G

Cicely Tyson *(Rebecca Morgan)*, Paul Winfield *(Nathan Lee Morgan)*, Kevin Hooks *(David Lee Morgan)*, Carmen Mathews *(Mrs. Boatwright)*, Taj Mahal *(Ike)*, James Best *(Sheriff Young)*, Yvonne Jarrell *(Josie Mae Morgan)*, Eric Hooks *(Earl Morgan)*, Sylvia Kuumba Williams *(Harriet)*, Janet MacLachlan *(Camille Johnson)*

p, Robert B. Radnitz; d, Martin Ritt; w, Lonne Elder III (based on a novel by William H. Armstrong); ph, John A. Alonzo (Panavision, DeLuxe Color); ed, Sidney Levin; m, Taj Mahal; prod d, Walter Scott Herndon; cos, Nedra Watt

AAN Best Picture; AAN Best Actor: Paul Winfield; AAN Best Actress: Cicely Tyson; AAN Best Adapted Screenplay: Lonne Elder III

Heartbreaking and intelligent, SOUNDER celebrates a family's dedication to each other through whatever travails befall them. In 1930s Louisiana, Nathan and Rebecca Morgan (Winfield and Tyson) are sharecroppers raising their three children and their dog, Sounder, as best they can in the poverty of the Depression. Nathan does the farming and hunts for game to feed his family. Rebecca takes in washing, and the trio of children take an equal part in doing the other tasks. Not much game is to be had, however, and when Nathan is arrested for stealing a ham, the family is torn apart. Rebecca and the children now begin a backbreaking schedule as they strive to work the land, make their quota, and keep body and soul together.

Adapted from a slim book that won the 1970 Newbery Award for children's literature, SOUNDER is one of the truest examples of a "family film" ever made and a triumph for all concerned. A sequel, SOUNDER, PART 2, followed in 1976, with Harold Sylvester and Ebony Wright taking over the roles played here by Winfield and Tyson.

SOUTH PACIFIC

1958 171m c Musical   **DVD**
South Pacific/Magna (U.S.)   ★★★½

Rossano Brazzi *(Emile De Becque)*, Mitzi Gaynor *(Nellie Forbush)*, John Kerr *(Lt. Cable)*, Ray Walston *(Luther Billis)*, Juanita Hall *(Bloody Mary)*, France Nuyen *(Liat)*, Russ Brown *(Capt. Brackett)*, Jack Mullaney *(Professor)*, Ken Clark *(Stewpot)*, Floyd Simmons *(Harbison)*

p, Buddy Adler; d, Joshua Logan; w, Paul Osborn (based on the play by Oscar Hammerstein II, Richard Rodgers, Logan, from the book *Tales of the South Pacific* by James A. Michener); ph, Leon Shamroy (Todd-AO, Technicolor); ed, Robert Simpson; art d, Lyle Wheeler, John DeCuir, Walter M. Scott, Paul S. Fox; fx, L.B. Abbott; chor, LeRoy Prinz; cos, Dorothy Jeakins

AAN Best Color Cinematography: Leon Shamroy; AAN Best Score (Musical): Alfred Newman, Ken Darby; AA Best Sound: Fred Hynes

SOUTH PACIFIC isn't the screen classic it should have been, but despite the fact that it pales in comparison with the long-running Rodgers and Hammerstein Broadway musical on which it is based, the film still stands up as terrific entertainment. Inspired by James Michener's book *Tales of the South Pacific*, both the stage musical and the movie were directed by Joshua Logan—not entirely a good thing, since he allows his actors to resort to stage techniques that aren't always suited to the close-up medium of film. Set on an island in (you guessed it) the South Pacific, the story concerns Nellie Forbush (Mitzi Gaynor), a midwestern nurse who falls in love with Emile De Becque (Rossano Brazzi), a widowed planter who is much

older, has children, and is set in his ways (shades of THE KING AND I). At the same time, Lt. Cable (John Kerr), a young Marine, falls for Liat (France Nuyen), a local native girl.

Ray Walston steals every scene in which he appears as a SeaBee conniver not unlike Sergeant Bilko, and Juanita Hall is wonderful as she repeats her stage role as Bloody Mary, though her singing is dubbed by Muriel Smith. Brazzi's voice work was provided by Giorgio Tozzi, and Bill Lee sang for Kerr, but Gaynor handled vocal chores herself. Made for $5 million, SOUTH PACIFIC was shot on location in Hawaii with a large cast that includes such names as Tom Laughlin (BILLY JACK), Ron Ely (TV's "Tarzan"), Doug McClure, and a non-speaking cameo by Joan Fontaine. Ultimately, though, it is the glorious Rodgers and Hammerstein songs that really distinguish the film.

SOUTH PARK: BIGGER, LONGER & UNCUT

1999 80m c Animated/Musical/Comedy   **DVD**
Scott Rudin Productions/Trey Parker/Matt Stone   ★★★
Productions/Paramount (U.S.)   R

VOICES OF: Trey Parker, Matt Stone, Mary Kay Bergman, Isaac Hayes *(Chef)*, Jesse Howell, Anthony Cross-Thomas, Francesca Clifford *(Ike)*, Bruce Howell *(Man In Theatre)*, Deb Adair *(Woman In Theatre)*, Jennifer Howell *(Bebe)*

p, Trey Parker, Matt Stone; d, Trey Parker; w, Trey Parker, Matt Stone, Pam Brady (based on the television series "South Park"); ed, John Venzon; m, Marc Shaiman; art d, J. C. Wegman; anim, Martin Cendreda, Toni Nugnes

AAN Best Original Song: "Blame Canada"; Marc Shaiman (music), Trey Parker (lyrics)

Is it the rudest, most offensive feature-length cartoon since FRITZ THE CAT, or a blistering satire on the effects of movies on our nation's children? It's both, actually, and also very funny.

As anyone who's ever seen the Comedy Central series on which the film is based already knows, Kyle, Stan, Kenny, and corpulent Cartman (all voiced by the show's creators, Matt Stone and Trey Parker) are four eight-year-olds who live in snowy South Park, CO, a "quiet little white-bread, red-neck mountain town," as the film's opening number (yes, it's a musical) proudly states. But all that is about to change: "Asses of Fire," an R-rated, feature-length cartoon based on a hit TV show (sound familiar?) and starring those flatulent Canadians, Terrance and Phillip, has come to town, exposing the innocent youth of South Park to a constant stream of toilet-humor and obscenities. Soon the playground is ringing with the sounds of tots spouting profanity, and a group of concerned South Park parents quickly forms to do what concerned-parent groups do best—look for someone to blame. In almost no time, war is declared on Canada, the entire Baldwin and Arquette clans are nuked, and Satan is preparing to claim dominion over the world of the living.

Often targeted as a prime offender in the ongoing debate over raunch in the media, "South Park" answers its critics with a double-barreled blast of offending material. Rarely has a single cartoon—or any movie, for that matter—featured as much profanity, violence, blasphemy, and deliberately offensive behavior, and the film suggests that to take any of it seriously would be to throw in your lot with the likes of M.A.C. (Mothers Against Canada) and risk inviting the apocalypse. Songs (written by Stone, Parker, and four-time Oscar nominee Marc Shaiman) include the hilarious Oscar and Hammerstein parody "It's Easy, Mmmkay," "What Would Brian Boitano Do?," and that old favorite, "Kyle's Mom's a Bitch." Brilliant, in its own twisted way.

SOUTHERN COMFORT

1981 100m c Drama/War ★★★½
Phoenix/Cinema Group (U.S.) R

Keith Carradine *(Spencer)*, Powers Boothe *(Hardin)*, Fred Ward *(Reece)*, Franklyn Seales *(Simms)*, T.K. Carter *(Cribbs)*, Lewis Smith *(Stuckey)*, Les Lannom *(Casper)*, Peter Coyote *(Poole)*, Carlos Brown *(Bowden)*, Brion James *(Trapper)*

p, David Giler; d, Walter Hill; w, Michael Kane, Walter Hill, David Giler; ph, Andrew Laszlo (Deluxe Color); ed, Freeman Davies; m, Ry Cooder; prod d, John Vallone

Arguably writer-director Walter Hill's best film to date, SOUTHERN COMFORT works both as a pure action film and as an extremely effective allegory of America's involvement in Vietnam. Vaguely reminiscent of John Boorman's DELIVERANCE, the film follows a group of National Guardsmen on maneuvers in the swamps of Louisiana. These weekend warriors, ill-equipped for their task, are given to horseplay and bickering. While out in the country, they "borrow" some canoes from local Cajuns, and soon find themselves pursued by the angry backwoodsmen. When one Guardsman (Lewis Smith) makes the mistake of shooting at the Cajuns, albeit with blanks, the enraged locals return the fire with real bullets, killing the detachment's commander (Peter Coyote), the only real soldier in the bunch. A deadly battle ensues as the Guardsmen attempt to escape from the swamp before more blood is shed. Unfamiliar with the terrain and extremely disorganized, the soldiers are no match for their pursuers. Tautly directed by Hill, superbly shot by Andrew Lazlo, and boasting an excellent score by Ry Cooder that incorporates authentic Cajun music, SOUTHERN COMFORT is a gripping, atmospheric, and disturbing film. Without straining to make his points, Hill evokes the American struggle in Southeast Asia by pitting a group of directionless recruits in unfamiliar terrain against enigmatic guerrillas. The director also considers the tensions that result when a diverse group of men is thrown together an extreme situation.

SOUTHERNER, THE

1945 91m bw Drama ★★★★½
UA (U.S.)

Zachary Scott *(Sam Tucker)*, Betty Field *(Nona Tucker)*, Beulah Bondi *(Granny Tucker)*, Bunny Sunshine, billed as Jean Vanderwilt *(Daisy Tucker)*, Jay Gilpin *(Jot Tucker)*, Percy Kilbride *(Harmie Jenkins)*, Blanche Yurka *(Ma Tucker)*, Charles Kemper *(Tim, the Narrator)*, J. Carrol Naish *(Henry Devers)*, Norman Lloyd *(Finlay Hewitt)*

p, David L. Loew, Robert Hakim; d, Jean Renoir; w, Jean Renoir, Hugo Butler, William Faulkner (uncredited), Nunnally Johnson (based on the novel *Hold Autumn in Your Hand* by George Sessions Perry); ph, Lucien Andriot; ed, Gregg Tallas; m, Werner Janssen

AAN Best Director: Jean Renoir; AAN Best Score (Drama or Comedy): Werner Janssen; AAN Best Sound Recording: Jack Whitney

A remarkably naturalistic portrayal of one family's struggle to start a farm in the South.

With the coming of autumn, Scott decides to work his own land. Though its appearance is off-putting, the land is workable. Scott comes into conflict with his neighbor Naish, an embittered man who cannot appreciate the success of his hard work without thinking about how it caused the deaths of his wife and child. When his crops cause him trouble and his boy becomes seriously ill, Scott appeals to Naish for much-needed milk; he is turned down cold. Kemper, a friend of Scott's from the city who has offered the farmer a factory job,

does all he can to help by buying the family a cow, thereby saving the boy's life. In the meantime, Scott's rivalry with Naish grows stronger when Naish's livestock are found in Scott's vegetable garden. Scott goes angrily to Naish's farm and a brawl begins between them, with Naish finally being thrown into the pig pen.

THE SOUTHERNER, Renoir's most critically respected American film, is a superb depiction, in spirit if not in historical authenticity, of the plight of the farmer. As with such great pictures as OUR DAILY BREAD, THE GRAPES OF WRATH and the brilliant government documentaries of Pare Lorentz to which THE SOUTHERNER is most similar (PLOW THAT BROKE THE PLAINS and THE RIVER), this picture makes characters of the land, the cotton, the plow, and the water, granting them the same importance as the actors. With the original Hugo Butler script (he later dropped out of the production, in reverence to Renoir who, Butler felt, could rewrite the script however he pleased) of the Perry novel *Hold Autumn in Your Hand*, Renoir and his producers, Loew and Hakim, were able to convince Hollywood to make their film. Nunnally Johnson and William Faulkner did uncredited work on the script.

SPANGLISH

2004 130m c Comedy ★★★
Gracie Films/Columbia (U.S.) PG-13

Adam Sandler *(John Clasky)*, Tea Leoni *(Deborah Clasky)*, Paz Vega *(Flor Moreno)*, Cloris Leachman *(Evelyn Norwich)*, Shelbie Bruce *(Cristina)*, Sarah Steele *(Bernice)*, Ian Hyland *(Georgie)*, Victoria Luna *(Cristina—Six-years-old)*, Cecilia Suarez *(Monica)*, Ricardo Molina *(Flor's Husband)*

p, Julie Ansell, James L. Brooks, Richard Sakai; d, James L. Brooks; w, James L. Brooks; ph, John Seale; ed, Richard Marks; m, Hans Zimmer; prod d, Ida Random; art d, Tom Reta; fx, Theresa Ellis, Tyler Foell, Eric Rylander; cos, Louise Mingenbach

Though the title would have been better suited to one of star Adam Sandler's trademark goofball comedies, writer-director James L. Brooks's serious comedy is closer in tone to his poignant AS GOOD AS IT GETS.

Hoping to spend more time with her young daughter, Cristina (Shelbie Bruce), beautiful Mexican single mother Flor (Paz Vega), quits her two jobs and takes a position as housekeeper for the Clasky family, whose lavish home in a gated community epitomizes a certain insular L.A. affluence. Celebrity chef John Clasky (Sandler) and his neurotic wife, Deborah (Tea Leoni) have two children—adorable but easily ignored Georgie (Ian Hyland) and overweight and socially awkward Bernice (Sarah Steele)—and Evelyn (Cloris Leachman), Deborah's livin-in, hard-drinking mother. Flor doesn't speak much English, but her bewilderment with the Claskys has nothing to do with language. While John is clearly devoted to his children, Deborah is so out of touch with her own flesh and blood that she humiliates Bernice by purchasing too-small clothes as a weight-loss incentive. Flor quietly begins tackling the problems she can fix, like altering Bernice's wardrobe to fit, but while John appreciates her efforts, a miscommunication with Deborah nearly gets Flor fired. When the Claskys decide to take a cottage in Malibu for the summer and ask Flor to move in, Flor worries that Deborah is having a bad influence on Cristina.

As the straight man to Leoni's often shrill and over-the-top character, Sandler gets a chance to demonstrate the range first revealed in PUNCH-DRUNK LOVE. The true stars, however, are newcomers Vega and Bruce; their touching mother-daughter relationship is the centerpiece of this surprisingly heartfelt tale.

SPANISH PRISONER, THE

DVD

1998 112m c Thriller/Drama/Mystery ★★½
Jean Doumanian Productions/Jasmine Productions PG
(U.S.)

Campbell Scott *(Joe Ross)*, Rebecca Pidgeon *(Susan Ricci)*, Steve Martin *(Jimmy Dell)*, Ben Gazzara *(Mr. Klein)*, Ricky Jay *(George Lang)*, Felicity Huffman *(Pat McCune)*, Richard L. Freidman, Jerry Graff, G. Roy Levin *(Businessmen)*, Hilary Hinckle *(Resort Concierge)*

p, Jean Doumanian; d, David Mamet; w, David Mamet; ph, Gabriel Beristain; ed, Barbara Tulliver; m, Carter Burwell; prod d, Tim Galvin; art d, Kathleen Rosen; cos, Susan Lyall

Call it "Office of Games." David Mamet returns to the same thematic soil he tilled in his first film: the art of the con and the seductive lure of perfectly executed deception.

Joe Ross (Campbell Scott) is a cog in the corporate machine, inventor of "The Process," which may make his company millions. Big boss Mr. Klein (Ben Gazzara) flies Ross to the Caribbean to tantalize deep-pocket investors, but Ross quickly begins to feel as though he's being cut out of the loop where it counts: the point at which the money will start rolling in. A disgruntled dupe looking for a hook to take, Ross is just waiting for the con man who'll reel him in, flopping and gasping. Is that man Jimmy Bell (Steve Martin)? Or is Bell the wealthy entrepreneur he appears to be, a man of the world who might be able to help Ross negotiate the shark-filled corporate waters? And what about Susan (Rebecca Pidgeon), the bright-eyed secretary with a sticky little crush on Ross? Is she the guileless waif she appears, or is there more to her as well?

It's funny how conventional Mamet's screenplay is. Cast differently and produced with the casually lavish gloss of, say, THE GAME, this intricate psychological thriller could be throwaway, adrenaline-driven Hollywood fare. But Mamet's intentions are different: he wants to make you think, but doesn't appear to care whether or not you feel. The result is hugely frustrating. The story works in that everything fits together, but the film feels hollow and unfinished, like a run-through for a movie rather than the movie itself.

SPARTACUS

DVD

1960 196m c Historical/War ★★★★½
Bryna (U.S.)

Kirk Douglas *(Spartacus)*, Laurence Olivier *(Marcus Licinius Crassus)*, Tony Curtis *(Antoninus)*, Jean Simmons *(Varinia)*, Charles Laughton *(Gracchus)*, Peter Ustinov *(Lentulus Batiatus)*, John Gavin *(Julius Caesar)*, Nina Foch *(Helena Glabrus)*, Herbert Lom *(Tigranes)*, John Ireland *(Crixus)*

p, Edward Lewis; d, Stanley Kubrick, Anthony Mann (uncredited); w, Dalton Trumbo (based on the novel by Howard Fast); ph, Russell Metty, Clifford Stine (Super Technirama-70, Technicolor); ed, Robert Lawrence, Robert Schulte, Fred Chulack; m, Alex North; prod d, Alexander Golitzen; art d, Eric Orbom; cos, Bill Thomas, Valles

AA Best Supporting Actor: Peter Ustinov; *AA Best Color Cinematography:* Russell Metty; *AAN Best Film Editing:* Robert Lawrence; *AAN Best Score (Drama or Comedy):* Alex North; *AA Best Art Direction-Set Decoration (Color):* Alexander Golitzen, Eric Orbom, Russell A. Gausman, Julia Heron; *AA Best Costume Design (Color):* Bill Thomas, Valles

Although this is the only one of Stanley Kubrick's pictures over which he did not have complete control (he was brought in by Kirk Douglas to direct when Anthony Mann was fired after the first week of shooting), SPARTACUS is still a remarkable epic—one of the greatest tales of the ancient world ever to hit the screen. It's especially strong,

and more typical of Kubrick, in the first half—before satire gives way to sentiment.

It tells the true story of a slave rebellion that panicked Rome for more than two years circa 73 BC, though some historical facts have been Hollywoodized (including Spartacus's demise—he was hacked to death in battle, not crucified). Spartacus (Douglas) is a rebellious Thracian slave purchased by Lentulus Batiatus (Peter Ustinov), the proprietor of a school for gladiators. Like his fellow trainees, he is rigorously trained in fighting skills in order to be profitably peddled to Roman coliseum owners. Discovering in himself and his fellow gladiators a spark of human dignity, Spartacus helps to lead a revolt and organize an army of slaves that will descend on Rome and liberate all oppressed men from the tyrannical rule of the patricians, specifically Marcus Crassus (Laurence Olivier). Also playing parts in this battle between free will and oppression are Gracchus (Charles Laughton), a senator engaged in a political power struggle with Crassus; Varinia (Jean Simmons), the beautiful slave and wife of Spartacus whom Crassus previously arranged to purchase; and young Julius Caesar (John Gavin), a student of Gracchus who later allies himself with Crassus.

More visually restrained than usual for Kubrick (the Technirama equipment made camera movement difficult), SPARTACUS instead concentrates on the *mise-en-scene*, most notably in the preparation of the massive final battle scene, as the various Roman military units position themselves like pieces on some gigantic chessboard. SPARTACUS today remains a stirring, intelligent comment on the spirit of revolt, largely due to Dalton Trumbo's literate and impassioned screenwriting (this was the blacklisted Trumbo's first screen credit in over a decade). Severely cut for its 1967 re-release, the film was largely restored in 1991. The restorers took advantage of this opportunity to insert some footage that was considered too suggestive for the film's initial release, a thinly-veiled attempted seduction of Curtis by Olivier. The soundtrack of this sequence had been lost and, since Olivier had recently died, his dialogue was indetectably redubbed by Anthony Hopkins.

SPEED

DVD

1994 115m c Action/Thriller ★★★½
Fox (U.S.) R

Keanu Reeves *(Jack Traven)*, Dennis Hopper *(Howard Payne)*, Sandra Bullock *(Annie)*, Joe Morton *(Captain McMahon)*, Jeff Daniels *(Harry)*, Alan Ruck *(Stephens)*, Glenn Plummer *(Jaguar Owner)*, Richard Lineback *(Norwood)*, Beth Grant *(Helen)*, Hawthorne James *(Sam)*

p, Mark Gordon; d, Jan De Bont; w, Graham Yost; ph, Andrzej Bartkowiak; ed, John Wright; m, Mark Mancina; prod d, Jack DeGovia; art d, John R. Jensen; fx, John Frazier, Boyd Shermis, Sony Pictures Imageworks; cos, Ellen Mirojnick

AA Best Sound: Gregg Landaker, Steve Maslow, Bob Beemer, David R.B. MacMillan; *AA Best Sound Effects Editing:* Stephen Hunter Flick; *AAN Best Film Editing:* John Wright

Acclaimed cinematographer Jan De Bont's directing debut is a mindless, implausible, and thoroughly gripping adventure movie. SPEED parlays its crackerjack premise into a satisfying but instantly forgettable rollercoaster ride of explosions, car crashes, and awesome hardware.

Jack Traven (Keanu Reeves) is an irreverent L.A. cop who insists on doing things his way; he and his partner Harry Temple (Jeff Daniels) specialize in defusing bombs. They rescue an elevator full of people from mad bomber-extortionist Howard Payne (Dennis Hopper), but their triumph turns sour when he returns with an even more audacious plan. There's a bomb on a city bus. Once the bus goes over 50mph, the bomb is armed. If it then drops below 50mph, it blows up. If any passengers are taken off, it blows up. If Payne doesn't get his $3.7 million ransom, it blows up. Jack must figure out how to rescue the commuters—including spunky Annie (Sandra Bullock), who takes over driving duty when the bus driver is shot—and get Payne, all before 11 a.m.

SPEED lives up to its title, delivering carefully crafted action/adventure thrills without ever breaking out of the genre rut. Though the film runs out of steam near the end, as long as the action stays on the bus, it's thrilling. De Bont deploys helicopters, motorcycles, police cars, and SWAT teams with aplomb; Reeves, except for the rare occasions when he's called upon to do more than flex his muscles or utter terse one-liners, makes an appealing action hero.

SPELLBOUND   DVD
1945   111m   bw   Thriller   ★★★★
Selznick/Vanguard   (U.S.)

Ingrid Bergman *(Dr. Constance Peterson)*, Gregory Peck *(John "J.B." Ballantine)*, Jean Acker *(Matron)*, Donald Curtis *(Harry)*, Rhonda Fleming *(Mary Carmichael)*, John Emery *(Dr. Fleurot)*, Leo G. Carroll *(Dr. Murchison)*, Norman Lloyd *(Garmes)*, Steven Geray *(Dr. Graff)*, Paul Harvey *(Dr. Hanish)*

p, David O. Selznick; d, Alfred Hitchcock; w, Ben Hecht, Angus Macphail (based on the novel *The House of Dr. Edwardes* by Francis Beeding [Hilary St. George Saunders, John Palmer]); ph, George Barnes, Rex Wimpy (uncredited); ed, William Ziegler, Hal C. Kern; m, Miklos Rozsa; art d, James Basevi; art d, John Ewing; fx, Jack Cosgrove; cos, Howard Greer

AAN Best Picture; AAN Best Supporting Actor: Michael Chekhov; AAN Best Director: Alfred Hitchcock; AAN Best B/W Cinematography: George Barnes; AA Best Score (Drama or Comedy): Miklos Rozsa; AAN Best Visual Effects: Jack Cosgrove

An intriguing Hitchcock thriller which probes the dark recesses of a man's mind through psychoanalytic treatment and the love of a woman. Dr. Edwardes (Peck), a young psychiatrist, begins a new assignment as the director of a modern mental asylum. His behavior, however, is rather strange and eccentric, causing Dr. Peterson (Bergman), a brilliant but emotionally icy doctor, to grow suspicious. When she discovers that the doctor's real initials are J.B., she doubts that he is really Dr. Edwardes. She wonders not only what happened to Dr. Edwardes, but who J.B. really is, thereby involving herself professionally and emotionally as she falls in love with J.B. while digging into his past.

Generated by David O. Selznick, who purchased the rights because of his keen interest in psychoanalysis, the film often gets bogged down in psychiatric and psychoanalytic jargon, but it is counterbalanced by the love story that develops between J.B. and Dr. Peterson. Depending on the viewer's preference, the breakthrough to J.B.'s mystery can be credited to one of two things: the success of modern psychiatry or the power of love. As Hitchcock describes it, the film is "a manhunt story wrapped up in pseudo-psychoanalysis." Although heavy on dialogue, it is not without some brilliant visual touches, most obviously the heralded dream sequence created by avant-garde artist Salvador Dali. In its original conception it was far longer and more complex than the two-minute sequence that finally appeared. It was to have run 22 minutes (much of which was actually shot but edited out) and included a disturbing sequence described by Hitchcock: "He [Dali] wanted a statue to crack like a shell falling apart, with ants crawling all over it, and underneath, there would be Ingrid Bergman, covered by ants! It just wasn't possible." As it happened, Hitchcock did not even shoot the dream sequence, returning instead to London. The brilliant visual stylist Josef von Sternberg was first considered as the director of the sequence, but William Cameron Menzies (THINGS TO COME) was finally chosen, though he later expressed dissatisfaction and asked that his name be removed from the credits.

SPELLBOUND   DVD
2003   97m   c   Documentary   ★★★★
HBO/Cinemax Documentary Films   (U.S.)   G

Harry Altman, Angela Arenivar, Ted Brigham, April Degideo, Neil Kadakia, Nupur Lala, Emily Stagg, Ashley White

p, Jeff Blitz, Ronnie Eisen, Sean Welch; d, Jeff Blitz; ph, Jeff Blitz; ed, Yana Gorskaya; m, Daniel Hulsizer

AAN Best Documentary Feature

An enthralling, even suspenseful documentary about spelling bees... yes, spelling bees. The spectacle of kids conquering freaky, tongue-twisting words really is thrilling.

First-time feature filmmakers Jeff Blitz and Sean Welch single out eight children from wildly different backgrounds and trace the paths that lead them to the 1999 Scripps Howard National Spelling Bee, a two-day event held annually in Washington, DC. Eligibility ends at the eighth grade and students can't be older than 16, but only 249 qualify to go to the Nationals and test their skills against words like *cephalgia*, *heuristic*, *cabotinage*, and *opsimath*. Neil, from San Clemente, CA, is the privileged child of ambitious Indian immigrants who've hired spelling coaches and language tutors. Perryton, TX, native Angela, by contrast, is a self-taught speller whose Mexican immigrant parents speak almost no English. Optimistic Ashley practices with Scrabble tiles in the apartment she shares with her single mother in a Washington, DC, housing project, while Ted, a friendly loner from rural Rolla, MO, actually prefers math. Nupur, from Tampa, FL, is calm and self-possessed; chatty, high-strung Harry, from Glen Rock, NJ, tells goofy jokes, and while neither Emily, from New Haven, CT, nor April, from Ambler, PA, thinks she can win, Emily is philosophical: the best thing about losing, she confides, would be tossing her word lists forever.

The filmmakers branch out to include interviews with previous winners, but the kids are the main event, and their stories are proof that real life rushes in where fiction fears to tread. What screenwriter would dare invent a spelling bee champ from a non-English-speaking family, have the child of Indian immigrants stumble on *Darjeeling* or the winner triumph on *logorrhea*?

SPETTERS   DVD
1980   109m   c   Drama   ★★★
VSE   (Netherlands)   R

Toon Agterberg *(Eve)*, Maarten Spanjer *(Hans)*, Hans Van Tongeren *(Reen)*, Marianne Boyer *(Maya)*, Renee Soutendijk *(Fientje)*, Jeroen Krabbe *(Henkhof)*, Rutger Hauer *(Witkamp)*, Peter Tuinman, Yvonne Valkenberg, Rudi Falkenhagen

p, Joop Van Den Ende; d, Paul Verhoeven; w, Gerard Soeteman; ph, Jost Vacano (Eastmancolor); ed, Ine Schenkkan; m, Ton Scherpenzeel; art d, Dick Schillemans, Peter Jasuai; cos, Yan Tax

A flashy, fast-paced drama, SPETTERS is the story of Dutch teenage motorcycle enthusiasts Eve (Toon Agterberg), Hans (Maarten Spanjer), and Reen (Hans Van Tongeren), all of whom dream of being as tough and successful as motorcycle champ Witkamp (Rutger Hauer). Their youthful rebellion ends tragically for both Reen, who is crippled in an accident, and Eve, who is raped, beaten, and killed by a gang of violent homosexuals. Providing a sexual outlet for the teenagers, and just about every other biker on the wharf, is Fientje (Renee Soutendijk), a conniving creature who runs a greasy spoon with her gay brother. SPETTERS is a violent, action-packed assault on the sensibilities of all but the most hardened filmgoers, not surprising given that it was directed by Paul Verhoeven, who would go on to score a major success in the U.S. with his ultraviolent ROBOCOP (1987). Here he demonstrates his penchant for startling visuals, explicit sex, and graphic violence, though his intelligent direction is anything but careless or irresponsible. The beautiful blonde Soutendijk and Jeroen Krabbe would later costar again in another Verhoeven film, THE FOURTH MAN.

SPICE WORLD

1998 93m   c   Musical/Comedy   **DVD**
Spice Girls/Fragile Films/PolyGram   ★★★
Filmed Entertainment   (U.K.)   PG

Melanie Brown, billed as Mel B (*Scary Spice*), Victoria Adams (*Posh Spice*), Melanie Chisholm, billed as Mel C (*Sporty Spice*), Emma Bunton (*Baby Spice*), Geri Halliwell (*Ginger Spice*), Richard E. Grant (*Clifford*), Elvis Costello (*Himself*), Jennifer Saunders (*Fashionable Woman*), Naoko Mori (*Nicola*), George Wendt (*Martin Barnfield—Film Producer*)

p, Uri Fruchtmann, Barnaby Thompson; d, Robert Spiers; w, Kim Fuller (based on an idea by the Spice Girls and Kim Fuller); ph, Clive Tickner; ed, Andrea MacArthur; m, Paul Hardcastle; prod d, Grenville Horner; art d, David Walley, Colin Blaymires; fx, Stuart Brisdon; cos, Kate Carin

Bright, bubbly, and clever in a silly sort of way, this candy-colored homage to the Pre-fab Five, the Spice Girls, takes its cue from A HARD DAY'S NIGHT and chronicles a manic day and a half in the lives of Baby (Emma Bunton), Scary (Melanie Brown), Sporty (Melanie Chisolm), Posh (Victoria Adams), and Ginger Spice (Geri Halliwell).

The outlandishly undercled girls ride their magic bus from photo sessions to rehearsals to command performances to press ops and parties, squealing and giggling all the way. Screenwriter Kim Fuller whips up a frothy series of blackout sketches (the girls take dance lessons from a military martinet, spend a night in a spooky house, have a close encounter with aliens), fantasy sequences (the girls as pregnant slatterns and silver-clad secret agents), musical interludes, and encounters with guest stars ranging from Jennifer Saunders to Elvis Costello. All of it is interspersed with a wafer-thin plot having to do with their pregnant friend Nicola (Naoko Mori); a pair of Hollywood hustlers (George Wendt, Mark McKinney) looking to make a Spice Girls movie; pushy, pretentious documentarian Piers Cutherton-Smythe (Alan Cumming); and big, bad tabloid press baron Kevin McMaxford's (Barry Humphries) nefarious plan to whip up anti-Spice backlash by hiring a guerilla paparazzo (Richard O'Brien) to catch them in compromising situations. Perpetually nervous manager Clifford (Richard E. Grant) frets while their coolly mysterious boss (Roger Moore), uttering solemn and incomprehensible aphorisms while stroking various small animals, pulls the strings behind the scenes. It's all pure, brainless fluff, but it's unpretentious and infectiously good-natured, and the song "Wannabe" is damnably catchy.

SPIDER

2002 98m   c   Drama/Mystery   **DVD**
Davis Films/Artists Independent Network/Capitol   ★★★½
Films/CBL/SpiderProductions/Spider Films/Odeon   R

Films/Media Suits/Grosvenor Park
(Canada/U.K./France/Japan)

Ralph Fiennes (*Dennis "Spider" Cleg*), Miranda Richardson (*Yvonne/Mrs. Cleg/Mrs. Wilkinson*), Gabriel Byrne (*Bill Cleg*), Lynn Redgrave (*Mrs. Wilkinson*), John Neville (*Terrence*), Bradley Hall (*Boy Spider*), Gary Reineke (*Freddy*), Philip Craig (*John*), Cliff Saunders (*Bob*), Tara Ellis (*Nora*)

p, Catherine Bailey, David Cronenberg, Samuel Hadida; d, David Cronenberg; w, Patrick McGrath (based on the novel by Patrick McGrath); ph, Peter Suschitzky; ed, Ronald Sanders; m, Howard Shore; prod d, Andrew Sanders; art d, Arvinder Grewal; fx, Alan Senior; cos, Denise Cronenberg

David Cronenberg's ruthlessly unsentimental adaptation of Patrick McGrath's 1990 novel entangles viewers in the skewed perceptions of Dennis "Spider" Cleg (Ralph Fiennes), until recently a 20-year resident of an English mental hospital.

Spider arrives in London wearing four shirts and a mucky overcoat, and moves into a run-down East End halfway house run by the starchy Mrs. Wilkinson (Lynn Redgrave). Overshadowed by a menacing gasworks, the residence is located around the corner from the row house where Spider grew up, and every moldering brick and paving stone is tainted with damp, disturbing memories. His story unfolds through darkly vivid flashbacks in which the adult Spider watches from the shadows while his younger self (Bradley Hall) skips inexorably toward his dreadful fate. Young Spider's parents, plumber Bill (Gabriel Byrne) and his primly coiffed wife (Miranda Richardson), appear happy enough, until Spider trails his father to the local pub and sees him flirting with Yvonne (also Richardson), a foul-mouthed tart. Bill and Yvonne tryst brutally in sheds and alleys, and their tawdry affair apparently culminates in the drunken murder of Spider's mother.

Brilliantly portrayed by a twitching, mumbling Fiennes, Spider is a mundane sort of madman, neither an uber-criminal like Hannibal Lecter nor a troubled genius whose beautiful mind must shine through layers of mental murk. Unlike some of Cronenberg's earlier films, which blossomed with spectacular grotesquerie, this film is the product of the director in miniaturist mode. Its minutely detailed revelations work their way under the skin like slivers of glass, chilled by the cold air you can almost feel whistling through the underpopulated streets, past scabrous wallpaper and frayed upholstery, right into Spider's clenched heart.

SPIDER-MAN

2002 121m   c   Action/Fantasy   **DVD**
Laura Ziskin Productions/Marvel Enterprises/   ★★★★
Columbia   (U.S.)   PG-13

Tobey Maguire (*Peter Parker/Spider-Man*), Willem Dafoe (*Norman Osborn/The Green Goblin*), Kirsten Dunst (*Mary Jane Watson*), James Franco (*Harry Osborn*), Cliff Robertson (*Ben Parker*), Rosemary Harris (*Aunt May Parker*), J.K. Simmons (*J. Jonah Jameson*), Joe Manganiello (*Flash Thompson*), Gerry Becker (*Maximillian Fargas*), Ted Raimi (*Hoffman*)

p, Ian Bryce, Laura Ziskin; d, Sam Raimi; w, David Koepp (based on the Marvel comic book by Stan Lee and Steve Ditko); ph, Don Burgess; ed, Arthur Coburn, Bob Murawski; m, Danny Elfman; prod d, Neil Spisak; art d, Steve Arnold; fx, Lydia Bottegoni, John Dykstra, John Frazier, Scott Stokdyk; cos, James Acheson

It took Spider-Man 40 years to make his movie debut, but this fast-paced entertainment is a surprisingly successful mix of spectacle and human-scale drama.

Orphaned high-school senior Peter Parker (Tobey Maguire) lives with his elderly Aunt May (Rosemary Harris)

and Uncle Ben (Cliff Robertson) in Queens, NY, loved at home but snubbed by his cooler peers. Peter nurses a hopeless crush on the vivacious girl next door, Mary Jane Watson (Kirsten Dunst), and pals around with poor little rich boy Harry Osborn (James Franco), son of ruthless industrialist Norman Osborn (Willem Dafoe). Then comes the moment that changes everything: Peter is bitten by a genetically jiggered super-spider and undergoes a painful but exhilarating physical transformation. His eyesight sharpens, he acquires a gym rat's physique overnight, and he finds he can extrude spider silk with the tensile strength of steel cable from his wrists. After Uncle Ben's death at the hands of a carjacker, who Peter could have apprehended earlier but didn't, the budding superhero realizes he must use his powers to defend the weak and helpless. This mission swiftly pits him against super-freak Green Goblin, Mr. Osborn's evil alter-ego.

Purists may quibble about tweaks to Spider-Man's original story, but director Sam Raimi and screenwriter David Koepp remain true to its soul. Beneath the spiffy costume, Peter Parker is a smart, geeky teen trying to reconcile his inner turmoil with complex moral responsibilities thrust upon him by unasked-for super-powers. Spider-Man paved the way for the outcast agonies of the X-Men, but Raimi has a lighter touch than X-MEN's Bryan Singer: Raimi keeps things moving and has a little fun with the self-dramatizing conventions of comic-book villainy.

SPIDER-MAN 2
2004 127m c   Action/Fantasy   ★★★★
Marvel Enterprises/Laura Ziskin Productions/   PG-13
Columbia   (U.S.)

Tobey Maguire (Peter Parker/Spider-Man), Kirsten Dunst (Mary Jane Watson), James Franco (Harry Osborn), Alfred Molina (Dr. Otto Octavius/Doc Ock), Rosemary Harris (Aunt May), J.K. Simmons (J. Jonah Jameson), Donna Murphy (Rosalie Octavius), Daniel Gillies (John Jameson), Dylan Baker (Dr. Curt Connors), Willem Dafoe (Norman Osborn)

p, Avi Arad, Laura Ziskin; d, Sam Raimi; w, Alvin Sargent (from a story by Alfred Gough, Miles Millar, and Michael Chabon, based on the Marvel comic book by Stan Lee and Steve Ditko); ph, Bill Pope; ed, Bob Murawski; m, Danny Elfman; prod d, Neil Spisak; fx, Steve Johnson, Greg Anderson, John Dykstra, Scott Stokdyk, Anthony LaMolinara, John Frazier; cos, James Acheson, Gary Jones

AA Best Visual Effects: John Dykstra, Scott Stokdyk, Anthony LaMolinara, John Frazier; AAN Best Sound Editing: Paul N.J. Ottosson; AAN Best Sound Mixing: Kevin O'Connell, Greg P. Russell, Jeffery J. Haboush, Joseph Geisinger

A rare sequel that actually improves on the original, this robust entertainment boasts intelligence and emotional impact belying conventional wisdom that summer movie spectaculars are by nature brainless nonsense and only a stupid snob would complain about their cynical insubstantiality.

When we last saw high-school science nerd Peter Parker (Tobey Maguire), he was coming to terms with the immense responsibilities that accompany his great powers. Two years later, his life is a mess. He still pines for pretty Mary Jane (Kirsten Dunst), now a successful actress, but knows that Spider-Man's girlfriend would always be in harm's way. Peter's once carefree best friend, Harry Osborn (James Franco), forced to take over the family firm, OsCorp, because Spider-Man killed his father (Willem Dafoe), is using alcohol to slake his all-consuming thirst for revenge. Peter's bereaved Aunt May (Rosemary Harris) is in danger of losing her home, and Peter is too broke to help; between delivering pizzas and fighting crime, Peter is falling behind in his studies at Columbia University. Tabloid editor J. Jonah Jameson (J.K. Simmons) continues crusading against Spider-Man, while his handsome son, astronaut John Jameson (Daniel Gillies), has

poached Mary Jane. And because things are always lightest just before the dark, Peter gets to meet and befriend his idol, the brilliant humanitarian scientist Otto Octavius (Alfred Molina), just before the inevitable freak accident that transforms gentle Octavius into villainous Doctor Octopus.

Director Sam Raimi and screenwriter Alvin Sargent understand that big emotions and strong performances trump stuff blowing up, and in a film filled with runaway trains, flying masonry, and glowing sci-fi machinery, the thread of tragic consequence pulsing through the extravagant set pieces elevates it from thrill ride to authentic popular myth.

SPIRAL STAIRCASE, THE   DVD
1946 83m   bw   Thriller   ★★★★★
RKO/Vanguard   (U.S.)

Dorothy McGuire (Helen Capel), George Brent (Prof. Warren), Ethel Barrymore (Mrs. Warren), Kent Smith (Dr. Parry), Rhonda Fleming (Blanche), Gordon Oliver (Steve Warren), Elsa Lanchester (Mrs. Oates), James Bell (Constable), Charles Wagenheim (Desk Clerk), Ellen Corby (Neighbor)

p, Dore Schary; d, Robert Siodmak; w, Mel Dinelli (based on the novel Some Must Watch by Ethel Lina White); ph, Nicholas Musuraca; ed, Harry Marker, Harry Gerstad; m, Roy Webb; art d, Albert S. D'Agostino, Jack Okey; fx, Vernon L. Walker

AAN Best Supporting Actress: Ethel Barrymore

The setting in this suspense-filled film is an old, dark Gothic mansion located in New England at the turn of the century. Young innocent Helen Capel (McGuire), long ago made mute due to a childhood trauma, is a servant for Mrs. Warren (Barrymore), a cantankerous, widowed invalid. The wealthy widow has two sons: one (Oliver), a hell-raiser, and the other (Brent), a gentle professor for whom Helen carries a secret torch. When three local girls—all physically handicapped—are murdered, everyone worries that Helen will be next. The tension builds as her suspicion of the killer's identity proves wrong and she is forced to confront the real madman.

Dorothy McGuire, one of the finest actresses of her day, gives a touching and totally convincing pantomime performance as the victimized mute in this prototype old-dark-house thriller. Not one thriller convention has been neglected in a picture that is virtually guaranteed to suffuse audiences with gooseflesh: creaking doors, wind-gusted curtains, flickering candles, cutaways to the menacing eyes of the unseen, unknown murdering maniac, every element of terror is in place. Director Robert Siodmak, a gifted craftsman noted for his expressionistic style, had made a number of atmospheric suspense films for Universal before joining with producer Dory Schary and RKO for this one. Ethel Barrymore, Elsa Lanchester, and George Brent all turn in brilliant performances. Author White's novel was substantially modified for the film; in the book, the menaced serving girl had been a cripple rather than a mute, and the setting was contemporary England. Dismally remade in Britain in 1975 under the direction of Peter Collinson.

SPIRIT OF ST. LOUIS, THE
1957 135m   c   Biography   ★★★½
Warner Bros.   (U.S.)

James Stewart (Charles A. Lindbergh), Murray Hamilton (Bud Gurney), Patricia Smith (Mirror Girl), Bartlett Robinson (B.F. Mahoney), Robert Cornthwaite (Knight), Sheila Bond (Model/Dancer), Marc Connelly (Father Hussman), Arthur Space (Donald Hall), Harlan Warde (Boedecker), Dabbs Greer (Goldsborough) p, Leland Hayward; d, Billy Wilder; w, Billy Wilder, Wendell Mayes, Charles Lederer (based on the book by Charles A. Lindbergh); ph, Robert Burks, Peverell Marley (CinemaScope, Warner Color); ed, Arthur Schmidt; m, Franz Waxman; art d, Art Loel; fx, H.F. Koenekamp, Louis Lichtenfield

AAN Best Special Effects: Louis Lichtenfield

Billy Wilder's re-creation of Charles A. Lindbergh's 1927 solo flight from New York to Paris is an intelligent piece, marked by James Stewart's strong performance as the brave pilot. The story, based on Lindbergh's autobiography, opens as Lindbergh is working as an airmail pilot. His flying goals go well beyond his mail route, however, and he begins to think about a solo voyage across the Atlantic, something no single pilot has ever accomplished. Lindbergh tries to find financial backers for his dream and, after much struggle, finds a willing group in St. Louis, Missouri. He has a special plane built for the trip, dubbing it *The Spirit of St. Louis* in honor of his backers. On the day he is to take off from New York, Lindbergh is forced to spend some time on the ground while waiting for the rain to stop and, in flashback, reflects on his career.

This is a well-told story, capturing the thoughts and feelings of a man alone under the most extraordinary conditions. Stewart is sincere and thoughtful in his depiction of the 1920s' greatest hero, and Wilder's direction shows the monotony of the flight while largely sidestepping the tedium which ever threatens to emerge. Perhaps the real star, though, is Waxman's marvelous score. The film gives a complete picture of Lindbergh, one that shows this dangerous journey to be the fulfillment of a devotion to and pure love of flying. The film was nominated for a Best Special Effects Oscar.

SPIRIT OF THE BEEHIVE, THE
(EL ESPIRITU DE LA COLMENA)
1973 98m c Drama ★★★★
Ellas Querejeta (Spain)

Ana Torrent *(Ana)*, Isabel Telleria *(Isabel)*, Fernando Fernan Gomez *(Fernando)*, Teresa Gimpera *(Teresa)*, Jose Villasante *(the Monster)*, Lally Soldavilla *(Milagros)*, Juan Margallo *(the Fugitive)*, Miguel Picazo *(the Doctor)*

p, Elias Querejeta; d, Victor Erice; w, Francisco J. Querejeta (based on an idea by Erice, Angel Fernandez Santos); ph, Luis Cuadrado (Eastmancolor); ed, Pablo del Amo; m, Luis de Pablo; art d, Adolfo Cofino

A haunting, atmospheric film that focuses on a young girl's obsession with the Frankenstein monster. Ana (the stunning Ana Torrent), a charming eight-year-old, lives in a Castillian village in 1940, just after the end of the Spanish Civil War. Although the village has been spared the destruction of battle, the after-effects of war are still felt, and the villagers buckle under Francoist repression. Ana's mother (Teresa Gimpera) shares a dream world with an imaginary lover; her father (Fernando Fernan Gomez) tends a beehive and ponders existence in an ongoing work he calls "The Spirit of the Beehive." After watching the 1931 James Whale-Boris Karloff version of FRANKENSTEIN, Ana begins to worry about the monster, and returns daily to the old house where her 10-year-old sister (Isabel Telleria) says he can be found. Eventually, an escaped convict becomes a surrogate for the monster, but though he is killed, Ana continues to cling to the idea that the monster's spirit exists, holding on to the power of imagination. Slow-moving but lyrical, Victor Erice's stunning feature-film directorial debut carefully re-creates the post-Civil War period, but much more is at work here than appears at first glance. SPIRIT OF THE BEEHIVE is a thought-provoking, highly symbolic work about the isolation engendered by Franco's stultifying reign, made by one of a generation of Spanish filmmakers forced to cloak their political messages in allegory.

SPIRITED AWAY 📀
(SEN TO CHIHIRO NO KAMIKAKUSHI)
2001 124m c Adventure/Animated/Fantasy ★★★★
Tokuma Shoten/Studio Ghibli/Nippon Television PG
Network/Dentsu/Buena Vista Home Entertainment/
Tohokushinsha Film/Mitsubishi (Japan/U.S.)

VOICES OF: Daveigh Chase *(Chihiro)*, Suzanne Pleshette *(Yubaba/Zeniba)*, Jason Marsden *(Haku)*, Susan Egan *(Lin)*, David Ogden Stiers *(Kamaji)*, Lauren Holly *(Chihiro's Mother)*, Michael Chiklis *(Chihiro's Father)*, John Ratzenberger *(Assistant Manager)*, Tara Strong *(Boh, the Baby)*, Mickie McGowan

p, Donald W. Ernst (U.S. production); d, Hayao Miyazaki, Kirk Wise (U.S. production); w, Cindy Davis Hewitt, Donald H. Hewitt (U.S. production); Hayao Miyazaki (from a story by Hayao Miyazaki); ed, Takeshi Seyama; m, Joe Hisaishi; art d, Youji Takeshige; anim, Masashi Ando, Megumi Kagawa, Kitaro Kosaka

AA Best Animated Feature Film

Filled with creatures both natural and otherwise, this magical animated feature from Japanese anime master Hayao Miyazaki has one hand in such family fare as his own MY NEIGHBOR TOTORO and the other in traditional Japanese ghost tales. Creating a rare story-world that allows for most anything to happen, Miyazaki again proves himself to be more genie than filmmaker.

Ten-year-old Chihiro (voice of Daveigh Chase) isn't too happy about moving to a new town, and her mood isn't helped when her father (Michael Chiklis) takes a wrong turn and winds up at what appears to be an abandoned theme park. Mom (Lauren Holly) and Dad chow down at the suspiciously well-stocked food stand, but the anxious Chihiro wisely demurs. Wandering across a nearby footbridge, she's suddenly confronted by Haku (Jason Marsden), a boy dressed in traditional garb who angrily tells her to leave. Startled, Chihiro rushes back to her parents, only to find them transformed into immense, grunting pigs. Haku helps the now parentless Chihiro find work in a spirit bathhouse where all manner of ghosts, goblins, and gods unlike any in Western tradition glide in to relax and socialize. So begins Chihiro's journey to childhood's end, as she learns courage, responsibility, and a sense of self.

While quickly and admirably dismissing the possibility that it's all just a dream, the film still possesses a dreamy soft-edged palette; the watercolor-inspired panoramas are, like the movie itself, serenely stunning. Understandably, the film became Japan's biggest box-office hit to date, surpassing James Cameron's TITANIC and eclipsing the record held for a time by Miyazaki's previous feature, PRINCESS MONONOKE.

SPLASH 📀
1984 111m c Fantasy/Comedy/Romance ★★★½
Touchstone (U.S.) PG

Tom Hanks *(Allen Bauer)*, Daryl Hannah *(Madison)*, Eugene Levy *(Walter Kornbluth)*, John Candy *(Freddie Bauer)*, Dody Goodman *(Mrs. Stimler)*, Shecky Greene *(Mr. Buyrite)*, Richard B. Shull *(Dr. Ross)*, Bobby Di Cicco *(Jerry)*, Howard Morris *(Dr. Zidell)*, Tony DiBenedetto *(Tim the Doorman)*

p, Brian Grazer; d, Ron Howard; w, Lowell Ganz, Babaloo Mandel, Bruce Jay Friedman (based on the story by Grazer, Friedman); ph, Don Peterman (Technicolor); ed, Dan Hanley, Michael Hill; m, Lee Holdridge; prod d, Jack T. Collis; art d, John B. Mansbridge; fx, Mitch Suskin; cos, May Routh, Charles De Muth, Jody Berke

AAN Best Original Screenplay: Lowell Ganz, Babaloo Mandel, Bruce Jay Friedman, Brian Grazer

An "alien" picture from an alien source (Disney with a new moniker), SPLASH, for all its nudity and hip humor, is a throwback to pictures of days past such as NEPTUNE'S DAUGHTER (1914) and MR. PEABODY AND THE MERMAID (1948). Nevertheless, young viewers who never heard of the aforementioned thought that this film was wildly creative and flocked to the theaters. The premise is simple: boy meets girl, boy falls for girl, but girl is not girl at all—she's a mermaid. Mermaid Madison (Daryl Hannah) meets Allen Bauer (Tom Hanks), a bright, young man who is a wholesale fruit and vegetable dealer in New York. Allen works with his brother, Freddie (John Candy), a smarmy playboy pudge. Madison is human when on dry land but the moment she is touched by saltwater, she reverts to her half-woman, half-fish form. Walter Kornbluth (Eugene Levy), a scientist who suspects that Madison is a mermaid, tracks her and Allen until he finally pours water on Madison, transforming her in front of hundreds on a New York street. Naturally, some mean government types get interested at this point. Director Ron Howard has a good sense of the whimsical, and his film is sweet and unpretentious, though somewhat ribald when one realizes the studio from whence it sprang.

SPLENDOR IN THE GRASS   DVD

1961 124m c   Drama   ★★★
NBI/Newton   (U.S.)

Natalie Wood (Wilma Dean Loomis), Warren Beatty (Bud Stamper), Pat Hingle (Ace Stamper), Audrey Christie (Mrs. Loomis), Barbara Loden (Ginny Stamper), Zohra Lampert (Angelina), Fred Stewart (Del Loomis), Joanna Roos (Mrs. Stamper), Jan Norris (Juanita Howard), Gary Lockwood (Toots)

p, Elia Kazan; d, Elia Kazan; w, William Inge; ph, Boris Kaufman (Technicolor); ed, Gene Milford; m, David Amram; art d, Richard Sylbert; chor, George Tapps; cos, Anna Hill Johnstone

AAN Best Actress: Natalie Wood; AA Best Original Story and Screenplay: William Inge

SPLENDOR IN THE GRASS has a few firsts attached to it. It was Beatty's debut in the movies; it was Inge's first work done specifically for the screen; and it was Kazan's first picture that failed to satisfy. A self-consciously Freudian melodrama of repressed sexuality and its consequences, the film takes place in 1925 in Kansas, where Inge grew up. Beatty and Wood are high schoolers who can't consummate their love due to social constraints. Their frustration is exacerbated by Wood's shrewish mom (Christie) and Beatty's rigid, unloving dad (Hingle); madness and heartbreak result.

The title comes from Wordsworth: "There's nothing can bring back the hour / Of splendor in the grass, of glory in the flower / We will grieve not, but rather find / Strength in what remains behind." What remains of interest after more than three decades is Zohra Lampert's excellent work in a small but crucial part, and a key role in the evolution of Beatty's star image. Beatty was in his early twenties and had just appeared in Inge's play "A Loss of Roses" in 1959, after having been discovered by Josh Logan and Inge while working in a small playhouse in New Jersey. Despite that play's failure, Inge was mesmerized by Beatty and wrote this screenplay for him. Later, he would adapt James Leo Herlihy's novel All Fall Down into a screenplay for Beatty after Beatty himself had impressed another epicene playwright, Tennessee Williams, sufficiently to get the plum role in THE ROMAN SPRING OF MRS. STONE. While making this film, Beatty began the off-screen amours that have since become legendary. Wood was married to Robert Wagner (the first time around) and she was the first of many who would fall for Beatty.

In small bits, note Phyllis Diller as Texas Guinan, Sandy Dennis in her first film, and Gary Lockwood in his third. Youth exploitation pictures were all the rage at the time, and while this is better than some in execution and intent, it's still exactly that.

SPONGEBOB SQUAREPANTS MOVIE, THE   DVD

2004 90m   c   Animated/Comedy/Children's ★★½
Nickelodeon Movies/United Plankton Pictures (U.S.) PG

VOICES OF: Tom Kenny (SpongeBob SquarePants/Narrator/Gary/Clay), Clancy Brown (Mr. Eugene H. Krabs), Rodger Bumpass (Squidward Tentacles/Fish #4), Bill Fagerbakke (Patrick Star/Fish #2/Chum Customer/Local Fish), Carolyn Lawrence (Sandy Cheeks), Douglas Lawrence (Sheldon J. Plankton/Larry the Lobster/Fish #7), Mary Jo Catlett (Mrs. Puff), Jill Talley (Karen the Computer/Old Lady), Alec Baldwin (Dennis), Scarlett Johansson (Mindy)

p, Stephen Hillenburg, Julia Pistor; d, Stephen Hillenburg; w, Derek Drymon, Tim Hill, Stephen Hillenburg, Kent Osborne, Aaron Springer, Paul Tibbitt (based on a story and the series created by Hillenburg); ph, Jerzy Zielinski; ed, Lynn Hobson; m, Gregor Narholz; prod d, Nick Jennings; fx, Brad Kuehn, Brain Tipton; cos, Terri Valazza; anim, Hoon Choi, Sherm Cohen, Yu Mun Jeong, Sang Kyun Shin, Alan Smart, Dong Kun Won, Hee Man Yang

If you already know the answer to the question "Who lives in a pineapple under the sea?" then this is your movie: a feature-length version of the double entendre-filled cartoon series about a loveable but nerdy sponge that's as popular with adults as tiny tots.

In the underwater world of Bikini Bottom, fry-cook SpongeBob (voice of Tom Kenny) dreams of managing the newest location of the Krusty Krab restaurant chain. Mr. Krabs (Clancy Brown), however, gives the job to SpongeBob's pessimistic neighbor, Squidward (Roger Bumpass). Devastated, SpongeBob grabs his best pal, Patrick (Bill Fagerbakke), and drowns his sorrows in ice cream. Meanwhile, Mr. Krabs' archrival, Plankton (Doug Lawrence), is furious that the Krusty Krab 2 opening is getting TV coverage while his restaurant, the Chum Bucket, has never had so much as a single customer. He conspires to steal the top-secret recipe for the popular Krabby Patty by swiping the treasured crown of King Neptune (Jeffery Tambor) and framing Mr. Krabs. At first everything goes according to plan: ignoring the counsel of his daughter, Mindy the Mermaid (Scarlett Johansson), Neptune demands that Mr. Krabs return the royal headgear. Good fellow that he is, SpongeBob swallows his pride and offers to help Mr. Krabs.

The film isn't as consistently funny as some of the 11-minute TV episodes, but creator/director Stephen Hillenburg keeps the film swimming along and only runs into rough water when certain gags go on far too long. Parents should be forewarned that the film earns its PG rating for some crude humor, but most of the "adult" jokes—like the self-mocking cameo by David Hasselhoff—will sail right over the heads of small fry.

SPY KIDS   DVD

2001 90m   c   Children's/Spy   ★★★½
Troublemaker Studios/Miramax   (U.S.)   PG

Antonio Banderas (Gregorio Cortez), Carla Gugino (Ingrid Cortez), Alexa Vega (Carmen Cortez), Daryl Sabara (Juni Cortez), Alan Cumming (Fegan Floop), Tony Shalhoub (Alexander Minion), Teri Hatcher (Mrs. Gradenko), Cheech Marin (Felix Gumm), Robert Patrick (Mr. Lisp), Danny Trejo (Isidor "Machete" Cortez) p, Elizabeth Avellan; d, Robert Rodriguez; w, Robert Rodriguez; ph, Guillermo Navarro; ed, Robert Rodriguez; m, John Debney, Danny Elfman, Gavin Greenway, Los Lobos, Heitor Pereira, Robert Rodriguez; prod d, Cary White; art d, Ed Vega; fx, Daniel LeDuc, Robert Rodriguez; cos, Deborah Everton

Robert Rodriguez brings the same ferocious energy that drove DESPERADO and FROM DUSK TILL DAWN to this gentler, but no less high-octane, escapade. The result is a kid's movie that truly can be enjoyed by teenagers and adults as well.

Adolescent Carmen's (Alexa Vega) favorite bedtime story is the one about the glamorous superspies who, assigned to kill each other, instead fall in love, marry, and retire from the whole dirty but exciting business. Little does she know it's the story of her own parents, Ingrid (Carla Gugino) and Gregorio (Antonio Banderas), whose surrender to domestic bliss is only occasionally tinged with nostalgia. They accept a job for old times' sake, leaving Carmen and her little brother, Juni (Daryl Sabara), with their "Uncle" Felix (Cheech Marin). Ingrid and Gregorio are captured, the Cortez home is invaded by mutant mercenaries, and the kids escape through a secret passageway to a high-tech mini-submarine. It's now up to Carmen and Juni to take on the villainous Fegan Floop (Alan Cumming), who's creating a lethal army of pint-sized robots who look just like the children of various world leaders. The cover for his nefarious operation? A surreal kid's TV show with a ghastly secret: Floop's dancing sidekicks, the "FloOglies," are really missing secret agents who've been mutated into whimsical monstrosities. Can the kids stop Floop, un-mutate the FloOglies, and rescue Mom and Dad?

Even more than vintage James Bond movies, Rodriguez's inspiration seems to have been European Bond knockoffs, in which style trumped substance and espionage conventions were subjugated to pop-art set design. The high-profile cast plays their roles with just the right mix of seriousness and tongue-in-cheek self-awareness.

SPY KIDS 2: THE ISLAND OF LOST DREAMS   **DVD**

2002   100m   c   Adventure/Spy/Comedy   ★★½
Troublemaker Studios/Dimension   (U.S.)   PG

Antonio Banderas (Gregorio Cortez), Carla Gugino (Ingrid Cortez), Alexa Vega (Carmen Cortez), Daryl Sabara (Juni Cortez), Steve Buscemi (Romero), Mike Judge (Donnagon Giggles), Matt O'Leary (Gary Giggles), Emily Osment (Gerti Giggles), Ricardo Montalban (Grandfather), Holland Taylor (Grandmother)

p, Elizabeth Avellan, Robert Rodriguez; d, Robert Rodriguez; w, Robert Rodriguez; ph, Robert Rodriguez; ed, Robert Rodriguez; m, John Frick, Robert Rodriguez; prod d, Robert Rodriguez; art d, John Frick, Ed Vega; fx, Keefe Boerner, Daniel Leduc, Darrell D. Pritchett, Corey Pritchett, Robert Rodriguez; cos, Graciela Mazon

If it were all as loud and ridiculous as its opening sequence, this sequel to the unexpectedly delightful SPY KIDS would be awful. Fortunately, it settles down when teenage Carmen Cortez (Alexa Vega) and her nine-year-old brother, Juni (Daryl Sabara), get to the titular island, a volcanic speck located in the Bermuda Triangle.

Carmen and Juni, the OSS school's most celebrated junior agents, are rudely eclipsed by bratty Gerti (Emily Osment) and Gary Giggles (Matt O'Leary) when the president's daughter (Taylor Momsen) needs rescuing at an extreme amusement park. Gary's dad, Donnagon Giggles (Mike Judge), is competing with Carmen's father, Gregorio (Antonio Banderas), for a big promotion at the agency. At a swanky soiree, Donnagon nabs the director's gig, and Gary gets Juni expelled. Meanwhile, at home, mom Ingrid (Carla Gugino) has acquiesced to a visit from her parents (Holland Taylor, Ricardo Montalban), both of whom are retired spies. Itching

to prove themselves, Carmen and Juni snatch a prime case out from under Gary and Gertie's noses and decamp for mysterious Ukata Island. Their gizmos disabled by the island's magnetic field, Carmen and Juni must rely on their wits to deal with a mad geneticist (Steve Buscemi) and his Ray Harryhausen-esque creations: slinky "slizzards," a monkey with spider legs, and a passel of pugnacious skeletons.

One of the charming things about the film is that it delivers its family-values message with considerable affection and utter conviction, even though the older Cortezes are reduced to minor supporting players. But the movie flaunts way too much CGI gadgetry—some of it inventive, much of it simply flashy in the worst kind of video-game way. The kids are nearly lost in the glitz.

SPY WHO CAME IN FROM THE COLD, THE   **DVD**

1965   112m   bw   Spy   ★★★★
Salem   (U.K.)

Richard Burton (Alec Leamas), Claire Bloom (Nan Perry), Oskar Werner (Fiedler), Peter Van Eyck (Hans-Dieter Mundt), Sam Wanamaker (Peters), George Voskovec (East German Defense Attorney), Rupert Davies (Smiley), Cyril Cusack (Control), Michael Hordern (Ashe), Robert Hardy (Carlton)

p, Martin Ritt; d, Martin Ritt; w, Paul Dehn, Guy Trosper (based on the novel by John Le Carre); ph, Oswald Morris; ed, Anthony Harvey; m, Sol Kaplan; prod d, Hal Pereira, Tambi Larsen; art d, Edward Marshall; cos, Motley

AAN Best Actor: Richard Burton; *AAN Best Art Direction-Set Decoration (B/W):* Hal Pereira, Tambi Larsen, Edward Marshall, Josie MacAvin

Gripping grit, with a perfect performance from Burton, before Liz and alcohol robbed him of his center.

Spying is a grim, desperate business that is at once boring and exciting, with dirty work behind the scenes and hardly any derring-do. This superb adaptation of John Le Carre's novel artfully conveys that sense. Audiences must have preferred the more glamorous spies like James Bond because this film, which was one of the best ever made on the subject, failed to gather much interest at the box office. Produced and directed by Martin Ritt in Ireland and England, with some second-unit lensing in Europe, the film stars Richard Burton as a burnt-out case, a man who is looking forward to getting out of the spy game and retiring from British Intelligence. Just before he is to leave, Burton is called back to London and put on the carpet. It seems that several of his sub-agents have been caught by Van Eyck, who is Burton's counterpart on the East Berlin side. Van Eyck is a former Nazi who has taken over as chief of operations for the Communists, and his handiwork is putting a crimp in the British operations. Since it is well known that Burton is tired of what he's doing, Burton's boss, Cusack, gives him his final assignment. He is to masquerade as a drunk who wants to defect to the East Germans. If it works and Burton gets inside the Communist operations, he can find out if there is a "mole" in their own organization as well as get the goods on what's happening inside the East German operation.

There are no gimmicks, no fast cars that turn into airplanes, no weapons that fire lasers, just a tense battle of wits shot in stark black and white. The title refers to the time when an outside spy has to "come in from the cold" and take a sedentary job as another spy's control or even some menial desk assignment until the mandatory age limit forces retirement. Only Graham Greene has come close to Le Carre in detailing the emotional drudgery of the espionage world.

SPY WHO LOVED ME, THE

1977 125m c Spy
Eon (U.K.)

DVD
★★
PG

Roger Moore *(James Bond)*, Barbara Bach *(Maj. Anya Amasova)*, Curt Jurgens *(Karl Stromberg)*, Richard Kiel *(Jaws)*, Caroline Munro *(Naomi)*, Walter Gotell *(Gen. Gogol)*, Geoffrey Keen *(Minister of Defense)*, Bernard Lee *("M")*, Shane Rimmer *(Capt. Carter)*, Bryan Marshall *(Commander Talbot)*

p, Albert R. Broccoli; d, Lewis Gilbert; w, Christopher Wood, Richard Maibaum (based on the novel by Ian Fleming); ph, Lamar Boren, Claude Renoir (Panavision, Eastmancolor); ed, John Glen; m, Marvin Hamlisch; prod d, Ken Adam; art d, Peter Lamont; fx, Derek Meddings, Alan Maley, John Evans; cos, Ronald Paterson

AAN Best Original Score: Marvin Hamlisch; *AAN Best Original Song:* "Nobody Does it Better"; Marvin Hamlisch (Music), Carole Bayer Sager (Lyrics); *AAN Best Art Direction-Set Decoration:* Ken Adam, Peter Lamont, Hugh Scaife

James Bond (Moore) teams with a beautiful Russian secret agent, Maj. Anya Amasova (Bach), to stop the Captain Nemo-esque Karl Stromberg (Jurgens) from using two stolen nuclear-armed submarines to destroy life on the Earth's surface so he can create an undersea kingdom. Stromberg dispatches seven-foot two-inch, steel-toothed Jaws (Kiel) to take Bond out of the picture, and 007 leads the indestructible behemoth on a globe-trotting chase.

As the Bond series moved deeper into the 1970s, the emphasis moved away from the inventive scripts that made the best Sean Connery films fine examples of the spy genre and toward the kind of feats of daring and visual spectacle that abound in THE SPY WHO LOVED ME. Take for example Bond's daring jump off a 90-foot cliff, a feat that ski jumper Rick Sylvester was paid $30,000 to accomplish and which took 10 days to shoot. The largest studio set to date was also built to house the submarines and for Stromberg's menacing headquarters, and shooting was done in Egypt, Sardinia, Malta, Scotland, Okinawa, Switzerland, and Nassau.

STAGE DOOR

1937 83m bw Comedy/Drama
RKO (U.S.)

DVD
★★★★★

Katharine Hepburn *(Terry Randall)*, Ginger Rogers *(Jean Maitland)*, Adolphe Menjou *(Anthony Powell)*, Gail Patrick *(Linda Shaw)*, Constance Collier *(Catherine Luther)*, Andrea Leeds *(Kaye Hamilton)*, Samuel S. Hinds *(Henry Sims)*, Lucille Ball *(Judy Canfield)*, Pierre Watkin *(Richard Carmichael)*, Franklin Pangborn *(Harcourt)*

p, Pandro S. Berman; d, Gregory La Cava; w, Morrie Ryskind, Anthony Veiller, Gregory La Cava (based on the play by Edna Ferber, George S. Kaufman); ph, Robert de Grasse; ed, William Hamilton; art d, Van Nest Polglase, Carroll Clark; cos, Muriel King

AAN Best Picture; AAN Best Supporting Actress: Andrea Leeds; *AAN Best Director:* Gregory Lacava; *AAN Best Screenplay:* Morris Ryskind, Anthony Veiller

A stellar cast, superb direction, and a screenplay even better than the stage play on which it was based, all add up to one of the best movies about show business—or about women living together—ever made. Hepburn is a wealthy debutante from an important family. She has come to New York to seek a career on the stage and, rather than take a Park Avenue apartment far removed from the mainstream, she checks into a theatrical boarding house for young, aspiring actresses. The luck of the draw puts her in a room with Rogers (in one of her finest performances), a sarcastic tough cookie who heckles everyone. The two of them are like flint and steel and are

close to hair-pulling on a few occasions. All the actresses in the boarding house spend most of their time discussing work, food, and potential husbands. But the ins and outs of their professional lives are central. Ball (who was appearing in her twenty-seventh movie at the age of 27) has been invited to dinner by some lumber barons from the Northwest and she asks Rogers to double date with her. Rogers has a short fuse, and there is no mistaking her likes and dislikes. Among the latter is Patrick, who is more of a mistress to Broadway producer Menjou than she is an actual working actress. Leeds hasn't worked for more than 12 months and she's trying to save some money, so she often foregoes meals. She thinks she may have a chance for the ingenue lead in a new play Menjou is planning, "Enchanted April." (The actual play shown was a rewrite of *The Lake*, a failed Hepburn vehicle that she starred in after making SPITFIRE.)

Rogers and Miller audition for Menjou with the Hal Borne-Mort Greene song "Put Your Heart Into Your Feet and Dance," and he is taken by them, especially by Rogers. He gets them a job at a nightspot in which he has a financial stake. Menjou asks Rogers for a date and she accepts—not that she finds the old lecher attractive, she just wants to make sure she and Miller get the dance job and she also wants to give the needle to Patrick. Soon Patrick is replaced by Rogers, and fumes about the turn of events. Leeds and Hepburn go together to audition for Menjou's play, but the reading is cancelled. Leeds faints from hunger in the reception area and Hepburn promptly tells Menjou off for the cavalier fashion in which he treats actors. Although he's in his office and apparently not busy, he is sending the actors away as a power play. Now attorney Watkin enters the picture, telling Menjou that a wealthy client, Hinds (who is Hepburn's father), will back Menjou's show if Hepburn is hired for the lead.

Directing his first film since MY MAN GODFREY, La Cava showed that he could handle a large group of actors as well as he could a straight two-lead comedy. So much work was done on the script that co-author of the play George S. Kaufman suggested waggishly that it should have been called "Screen Door." Legend has it that La Cava ordered the actresses to the studio for two weeks of rehearsal and familiarization with the boarding house set. Then he had a stenographer take their dialogue down as they sat around between rehearsals, and their words were incorporated into the script. The large cast includes Eve Arden (in her fourth film and already taking out a patent on her no-nonsense spinsters), Franklin Pangborn, Grady Sutton, and Jean Rouverol, who later became a well-known screenwriter with her husband, Hugo Butler. For years, impressions of Hepburn have used the line she speaks in while acting onstage: "The calla lillies are in bloom again." The best line in the film, though, is Rogers' marvelous barb to a friend over the phone when Gail Patrick enters the scene: "Hold on, gangrene just set in." The best prop, meanwhile, is the cat forever draped over Eve Arden's shoulders. A brilliant script and strong, realistic acting make this film a treat to the eyes and ears, and it affords the additional pleasure of seeing all those future stars like Ball, Miller, Arden, and Jack Carson in their early days.

STAGE DOOR CANTEEN

1943 132m bw Musical/War
UA (U.S.)

DVD
★★★★

Cheryl Walker *(Eileen)*, William Terry *(Ed "Dakota"Smith)*, Marjorie Riordan *(Jean Rule)*, Lon McCallister *("California")*, Margaret Early *(Ella Sue)*, Sunset Carson *("Texas")*, Dorothea Kent *(Mamie)*, Fred Brady *("Jersey" Wallace)*, Marion Shockley *(Lillian)*, Patrick O'Moore *(Australian)*

p, Sol Lesser; d, Frank Borzage; w, Delmer Daves; ph, Harry Wild; ed, Hal C. Kern; m, Freddie Rich; prod d, Harry Horner, Clem Beauchamp; art d, Hans Peters; cos, Albert Dano

AAN Best Score (Musical): Frederic E. Rich; *AAN Best Song:* "We Mustn't Say Goodbye"; James Monaco (Music), Al Dubin (Lyrics)

In this boy-meets-canteen-girl story set in a Stage Door Canteen in Manhattan, three enlisted men on a one-day pass in New York fall in love with three young hostesses at the canteen. The story is nothing special, but the cast is: everybody who was anybody at the time, from Katharine Hepburn to Johnny Weissmuller to Gypsy Rose Lee to violinist Yehudi Menuhin, makes an appearance. The story is a trifle, but you'll want to see this movie in its full 132 minutes to revel in the sight of its 65 guest stars, playing themselves and seeming to have more fun than they had playing characters. The American Theatre Wing operated several Stage Door Canteens, with the flagship location on West 44th Street in Manhattan, and 90 percent of the movie's profits went back to the Theatre Wing to help defray expenses for the venues. In WWII, officers went to the officer's clubs, but at the Stage Door Canteen, you had to be ranked below officer status to be admitted. Jammed from start to finish with stars, music, laughs, tears, and pure entertainment, STAGE DOOR CANTEEN casts Cheryl Walker as Eileen, a young hostess at the Canteen who falls for soldier Dakota Smith (William Terry), while Jean Rule (Marjorie Riordan) hits it off with California (Lon McCallister) and Mamie (Dorothea Kent) goes ga-ga for Texas (Michael Harrison, aka Sunset Carson). The three soldiers meet the three women at the Canteen while on a one-day pass in New York; when their ship is delayed, they spend another day, and another, until love is in full bloom, despite the prohibition against hostesses seeing servicemen outside of the Canteen. When the boys finally do go off to war, they know the girls will be waiting for them upon their return. That's about it for plot, but writer Delmer Daves and director Frank Borzage insert into the story a cavalcade of musical and comedy numbers and many cameo appearances. In the cameos, Katherine Cornell makes her only film appearance doing a snippet of "Romeo and Juliet," George Jessel reprises his famous phone call to "Mama," Harpo Marx runs around like a nut, George Raft is seen as a dishwasher, Lunt and Fontanne have an argument, and Paul Muni rehearses his new play. Fred Rich's score gained an Oscar nomination, as did Al Dubin and Jimmy Monaco for "We Mustn't Say Goodbye," sung by Lanny Ross.

STAGE FRIGHT

1950 111m bw Thriller 🄳🄫🄳 ★★★★
Warner Bros./First National   (U.K.)

Jane Wyman *(Eve Gill/Doris Tinsdale)*, Marlene Dietrich *(Charlotte Inwood)*, Michael Wilding *(Wilfrid O. "Ordinary" Smith)*, Richard Todd *(Jonathan Cooper)*, Alastair Sim *(Commodore Gill)*, Kay Walsh *(Nellie Goode)*, Sybil Thorndike *(Mrs. Gill)*, Miles Malleson *(Mr. Fortesque)*, Hector MacGregor *(Freddie Williams)*, Joyce Grenfell *("Lovely Ducks")*

p, Alfred Hitchcock; d, Alfred Hitchcock; w, Whitfield Cook, Alma Reville, James Bridie, Ranald MacDougall (based on the stories "Man Running" and "Outrun the Constable" by Selwyn Jepson, uncredited); ph, Wilkie Cooper; ed, E.B. Jarvis; m, Leighton Lucas; cos, Christian Dior, Milo Anderson

The standard British murder mystery is raised to a higher plateau by Hitchcock in STAGE FRIGHT, but still falters in comparison to the best of the master's works. Over the opening credits a theatrical safety curtain rises, revealing not a stage but London street life—the actual stage for Hitchcock's mystery. Eve Gill (Wyman) is an acting student at the Royal Academy of Dramatic Art (RADA) when she runs into a former boyfriend, Jonathan Cooper (Todd), who explains how his mistress, stage and singing star Charlotte Inwood (Dietrich, in marvelous form), came to him wearing a dress bloodied when she killed her husband. Because of his

involvement with the singer, Jonathan is suspected and must turn to Eve for help. The plot twists are many.

STAGE FRIGHT was far from being one of Hitchcock's most memorable or successful films, drawing criticism for both his provocative use of false flashbacks and the relative absence of any real threat of danger. Hitchcock's main interest in the film, and its most fascinating aspect today, is the concentration on acting and deception. Like MURDER in 1930 (and the same year's ALL ABOUT EVE), STAGE FRIGHT has an actress as the heroine. Here Eve gets her finest training not from RADA (where Hitchcock's daughter Patricia was enrolled, and where some of the film was photographed) but from real life. Her character's performance is not a simple one, forcing her to appear as something different to everyone—an actress, a maid, a Nancy Drew-type, and a newspaper reporter—with London serving as her stage, and death being her greatest fright. Shot at England's Elstree Studios, it was the last film Hitchcock shot in his home country until 1971 when he returned to film FRENZY. A special treat is Dietrich singing two of her standards: Cole Porter's "The Laziest Gal in Town" and Edith Piaf's "La Vie en Rose."

STAGECOACH

1939 97m bw Western 🄳🄫🄳 ★★★★★
UA   (U.S.)

Claire Trevor *(Dallas)*, John Wayne *(The Ringo Kid)*, John Carradine *(Hatfield)*, Thomas Mitchell *(Dr. Josiah Boone)*, Andy Devine *(Buck Rickabaugh)*, Donald Meek *(Mr. Samuel Peacock)*, Louise Platt *(Lucy Mallory)*, George Bancroft *(Sheriff Curly Wilcox)*, Berton Churchill *(Henry Gatewood)*, Tim Holt *(Lt. Blanchard)*

p, Walter Wanger; d, John Ford; w, Dudley Nichols (based on the short story "Stage to Lordsburg" by Ernest Haycox); ph, Bert Glennon; ed, Dorothy Spencer, Walter Reynolds; m, Richard Hageman, W. Franke Harling, Louis Gruenberg, Leo Shuken, John Leipold (adapted from 17 American folk tunes of the early 1880s); art d, Alexander Toluboff; fx, Ray Binger; cos, Walter Plunkett

AAN Best Picture; AA Best Supporting Actor: Thomas Mitchell; *AAN Best Director:* John Ford; *AAN Best B/W Cinematography:* Bert Glennon; *AAN Best Film Editing:* Otho Lovering, Dorothy Spencer; *AA Best Score:* Richard Hageman, Frank Harling, John Leipold, Leo Shuken; *AAN Best Interior Decoration:* Alexander Toluboff

The classic western, STAGECOACH is one of John Ford's greatest frontier epics. This western eclipsed all films in the genre that had gone before it, and so vastly influenced those that followed that its stamp can be found in most superior westerns made since Ford stepped into Monument Valley for the first time. Set in a landscape of endless horizons, STAGECOACH is a wonderful, broad portrait of pioneer life in the untamed Great Southwest, as well as an in-depth character study of eight people, all diverse in their pursuits and all traveling to separate fates on a journey packed with danger.

High peril is present from the first scenes, which depict Geronimo on the warpath and telegraph wires cut by raiding Apaches. Leaving the town of Tonto, New Mexico, by stagecoach are a motley bunch of Western types. Doc Boone (Mitchell) is a conniving drunkard, long ago kicked out of the medical profession for malpractice. Dallas (Trevor) is a prostitute whose sexual exploits have so unnerved the local women that they have banded together to oust her from their scandal-mongering society. Hatfield (Carradine), meanwhile, is a shady gambler with the manners of a southern gentleman, with his own mysterious reasons for leaving Tonto. He pretends, however, that his real motivation is to offer the withdrawn Lucy (Platt), who is pregnant and married to a cavalry officer, his "protection" as she travels to be with her husband. Henry Gatewood (Churchill), a pompous and demanding banker, gets aboard the coach carrying a small valise which is locked and which he will not let go of, while Samuel Peacock (Meek), a whiskey salesman, carries a sample case. These six strangers make up the passenger list, and riding on top on the driver's seat is Buck (Devine), a garrulous type with an aversion to Indians, and tough, gruff, but fair-minded Curly (Bancroft), a lawman riding "shotgun." Before they've been on the trail very long they pick up the Ringo Kid (Wayne, in a star-making performance), whose horse has gone lame. The stagecoach is set, so to speak, so bring on the adventure!

Ford had not directed a western in 13 years before making STAGECOACH, his previous film in the genre being THREE BAD MEN. This film came as a shock to the movie community, in that Ford was no longer thought of as a western director; now he had, almost out of the blue, produced the greatest western ever seen. He would later state that "STAGECOACH blazed the trail for the 'adult' western," but this discounted too many great silent films of the genre, including his own and those of William S. Hart, who made many "adult" westerns, such as HELL'S HINGES and TUMBLEWEEDS. But STAGECOACH was nonetheless an important, sterling prototype, with in-depth characters and allegorical themes running just beneath the surface of the plot. Moveover, Ford employs a dazzling array of technical skills in presenting this film, as well as framing each breathtaking scene as if it were a painting. The landscape of the awesome Monument Valley serves both as a backdrop and a constant reminder of the freedom of the frontier and the dangers inherent in enjoying that freedom. With its arid plains, 4,000 feet above sea level, and jutting buttes, some reaching 1,500 feet, Monument Valley still startles audiences of this film today. During the 1880s, stagecoaches had actually crossed this enormous valley, and Ford made excellent use of the old coach trails which are seen running through the broad expanses like old scars. Marvelously cast and acted, stunningly shot and featuring a beautifully effective musical score, the exciting STAGECOACH was poorly remade in 1966 with Alex Cord, Ann-Margret and Bing Crosby.

STAIRWAY TO HEAVEN

1946   104m   c/bw   Fantasy/Romance   ★★★★½

Archers/Independent Producers   (U.K.)

David Niven (Squadron Leader Peter D. Carter), Kim Hunter (June), Roger Livesey (Dr. Reeves), Robert Coote (Bob Trubshawe), Marius Goring (Conductor 71), Raymond Massey (Abraham Farlan), Kathleen Byron (An Angel), Richard Attenborough (English Pilot), Bonar Colleano (American Pilot), Joan Maude (Chief Recorder)

p, Michael Powell, Emeric Pressburger; d, Michael Powell, Emeric Pressburger; w, Michael Powell, Emeric Pressburger; ph, Jack Cardiff (Technicolor); ed, Reginald Mills; m, Allan Gray; prod d, Alfred Junge; art d, Arthur Lawson; fx, Douglas Woolsey, Henry Harris; cos, Hein Heckroth

Made by Powell and Pressburger at the instigation of the Ministry of Information to promote goodwill between Britain and the U.S., STAIRWAY TO HEAVEN achieves an almost impossible task—blending fantasy and reality with deftness and impeccable taste.

The plot concerns an RAF pilot, Niven, who is forced to bail out of his flaming plane as it is dropping out of the sky. With all his fellow crew members either dead or having parachuted to safety and his own chute riddled with bullet holes, Niven gets on the radio and shares what he believes to be his last words with an American WAC, Hunter. Niven, a poet, has a romantic conversation with Hunter and falls hopelessly in love with her voice. When he finally jumps for his life, he lands in the ocean and is washed safely ashore. By some fateful coincidence he meets Hunter and the pair fall in love. Although Niven appears to be healthy, he actually is suffering from brain damage and must undergo an operation.

Meanwhile, in heaven it is realized that a terrible mistake has been made, that Niven, who was scheduled to die, has somehow lived. This discovery is made by Heavenly Conductor Number 71, Goring, a Frenchman who was beheaded in his country's revolution. While Goring and his superiors debate Niven's fate, Niven argues that because of their mistake and because he has fallen in love with Hunter, he should be allowed to remain on Earth.

Shining with surrealistic cinematic bravura (the fantasy sequences were shot in black and white, the earthly ones in color), STAIRWAY TO HEAVEN is a marvel, with a notable contribution from production designer Junge. Most remarkable is his monumental stairway which reaches majestically into the heavens, peopled with a cast of history's dead. Niven and Livesey enjoy two of their finest roles, Hunter is warm and appealing, Goring a quirky delight, and such actors as Coote, Massey and Abraham Sofaer (as God, no less) are clearly having a blast. Chosen as the first of the Royal Command Film Performances, STAIRWAY TO HEAVEN garnered some critical acclaim in Britain but was generally attacked by stuffy detractors who felt it was anti-British. It received a far warmer welcome in the U.S.

STAKEOUT

1987   115m   c   Crime   ★★★½

Touchstone/Silver Screen Partners III   (U.S.)   R

Richard Dreyfuss (Chris Leece), Emilio Estevez (Bill Reimers), Madeleine Stowe (Maria McGuire), Aidan Quinn (Richard "Stick" Montgomery), Dan Lauria (Phil Coldshank), Forest Whitaker (Jack Pismo), Ian Tracey (Caylor Reese), Earl Billings (Capt. Giles), Jackson Davies (FBI Agent Lusk), J.J. Makaro

p, Jim Kouf, Cathleen Summers; d, John Badham; w, Jim Kouf; ph, John Seale (Deluxe Color); ed, Tom Rolf, Michael Ripps; m, Arthur B. Rubinstein; prod d, Philip Harrison; art d, Richard Hudolin, Michael Ritter

It doesn't matter that this film is a traditional cop vs. killer picture, since it is presented in very human terms and sparkles with top-flight performances from Richard Dreyfuss, Emilio Estevez, and Madeleine Stowe. Chris Leece (Dreyfuss) is a plainclothes detective on the Seattle police force, a man with a thankless job and an empty life until he and his partner, Bill Reimers (Estevez), are assigned to stake out the home of Maria McGuire (Stowe), the former girlfriend of escaped killer Stick Montgomery (Aidan Quinn). Chris meets Maria when he pretends to be a phone repairman and bugs her phones, and they are quickly attracted to each other. But fugitive Montgomery plans to retrieve not only the loot from his last job (hidden in Maria's apartment) but also his girl. STAKEOUT is a well-handled, quick-paced, and often funny film that accurately details the humdrum routine of police work. Director John Badham expertly mixes just the right amount of action with a very delightful romance. This movie marked a virtuoso return for Dreyfuss, who is captivating in his role.

STALAG 17

1953   120m   bw   Comedy/War   ★★★★½

Paramount   (U.S.)

William Holden (Sefton), Don Taylor (Lt. Dunbar), Otto Preminger (Oberst Von Scherbach), Robert Strauss ("Animal" Stosh), Harvey Lembeck (Harry), Richard Erdman (Hoffy), Peter Graves (Price), Neville Brand (Duke), Sig Rumann (Schultz), Michael Moore (Manfredi)

p, Billy Wilder; d, Billy Wilder; w, Billy Wilder, Edwin Blum (based on the play by Donald Bevan, Edmund Trzcinski); ph, Ernest

Laszlo; ed, Doane Harrison, George Tomasini; m, Franz Waxman; art d, Hal Pereira, Franz Bachelin; fx, Gordon Jennings

AA Best Actor: William Holden; *AAN Best Supporting Actor:* Robert Strauss; *AAN Best Director:* Billy Wilder

The trenchant trenches of a German POW camp, uneven but not without its gallows humor fascination. Made just eight years after the end of WWII, writer-director Wilder's classic black comedy is too cross-pollinated by slapstick Germans, who interfere with the abrasive edge of satirical statements on free enterprise and oppressed peoples banding together to become a variation on witch-hunting fascists. But the film did amazing things for Holden. Even in SUNSET BOULE-VARD he was transforming from the handsome juvenile lead of yore. His performance made him Bogie's successor to American Cynicism; without a doubt, Holden was one of the finest actors of his generation, thanks to his scrunched-face concentration which surprised you with its quick-change range. Holden plays Sefton, the glib loner whose scams and scheming make life in Stalag 17 bearable for him but incurs the wrath of his fellow POWs. Still, they willingly participate in the games and attractions (like observing female Russian prisoners through a telescope) he operates for fun and profit. When two prisoners are killed while trying to escape, the Americans come to believe an informer is in their midst, and suspicion falls on Sefton. Later, after the camp's sadistic commandant, Von Scherbach (brilliantly played by director Preminger, in a take on Stroheim in LA GRANDE ILLU-SION), learns how newcomer Dunbar (Don Taylor) managed to blow up a train, the POWs are certain Sefton is the rat and make life miserable for him.

Unlike previous POW films, Wilder and co-writer Edwin Blum's script, based on the play by Donald Bevan and Edmund Trzcinski, presents the prisoners not as paragons of patriotic virtue but as real, self-interested, bored soldiers trying to survive. Holden is magnificent as the heel-turned-hero, but STALAG 17 is full of wonderful, well-directed performances, including Sig Rumann as the barracks guard (the prototype for John Banner's Sgt. Schultz on "Hogan's Heroes," the long-running TV series inspired by the film); Gil Stratton, Jr., as Sefton's gopher; Harvey Lembeck and Robert Strauss as the barracks clowns; and real-life war hero Neville Brand. Peppered with Wilder's distinctive biting wit, STALAG 17 was justly a hit with the critics and at the box office.

STALKER

DVD

1979 161m c/bw Science Fiction ★★★½
Mosfilm Unit 2 (U.S.S.R.)

Aleksandr Kaidanovsky *(Stalker)*, Nikolai Grinko *(Professor)*, Anatoly Solonitsin *(Writer)*, Alisa Freindlikh *(Stalker's Wife)*, Natasha Abramova *("Monkey"—Stalker's Daughter)*, F. Yurna, E. Kostin, R. Rendi

p, Alexandra Demidova; d, Andrei Tarkovsky; w, Boris Strugatsky, Arkady Strugatsky (based on their novel *Roadside Picnic*); ph, Aleksandr Knyazhinsky; ed, L. Feiginovoi; m, Eduard Artemyev; prod d, Andrei Tarkovsky; art d, A. Merkulov; cos, N. Fominoi

Andrei Tarkovsky's STALKER is a metaphysical allegory in the guise of a sci-fi adventure, that like most of this visionary director's films, alternates between mesmerizing brilliance and intense boredom.

In a futuristic and desolate industrial wasteland, there exists a supernatural "Zone" which contains a miraculous "Room," where all of one's wishes will be granted. The Zone has been declared off limits, but unauthorized guides known as Stalkers still lead travellers inside. One such Stalker (Aleksandr Kaidanovsky) meets a Writer (Anatoly Solonitsin), and a Professor (Nikolai Grinko) who hire him to take them into the Zone, and the Stalker agrees to

do so, despite his wife's (Alisa Freindlikh) fears that he'll be imprisoned again. The Writer says he's going there because he's lost his inspiration and the Professor claims to be going for scientific reasons. The three men sneak past a police guard, then travel down railroad tracks until they reach the Zone. The men work their way through a complex tunnel system, and after emerging from the final tunnel, known as the "meat grinder," they reach the threshold of the mysterious Room.

STALKER is an impenetrable film about the inexplicable mysteries of the universe, that's open to myriad interpretations. Anyone looking for a typical sci-fi film will be sorely disappointed, for Tarkovsky merely uses the basic plot as a metaphor, with the trip to the Zone being a spiritual journey into the heart of one's soul. The Stalker, Writer, and Professor, represent Blind Faith, Jaded Art, and Amoral Science, respectively, and the characters spend most of the trip philosophizing. The methodical tracking shots and lumbering movements of the actors are so painfully slow that one feels the weight and gravity of each and every shot, but just when one is lulled into a narcotized state, Tarkovsky comes up with some stunning cinematic moments, such as the mystical framing scenes, where the earsplitting roar of a train shaking the Stalker's house is undercut by the soothing sound of Beethoven's "Ode to Joy." Tarkovsky was undoubtedly a serious artist, but his films operate on their own private wavelength of sometimes maddening deliberateness which can create a hypnotic and soporific effect simultaneously and STALKER certainly has its share of both, but it also has enough hauntingly beautiful images and profound ideas to linger in one's mind.

STAND AND DELIVER

DVD

1988 105m c Biography ★★★
American Playhouse (U.S.) PG

Edward James Olmos *(Jaime Escalante)*, Lou Diamond Phillips *(Angel)*, Rosana DeSoto *(Fabiola Escalante)*, Andy Garcia *(Ramirez)*, Ingrid Oliu *(Lupe)*, Karla Montana *(Claudia)*, Vanessa Marquez *(Ana)*, Mark Eliot *(Tito)*, Patrick Baca *(Javier)*, Will Gotay *(Pancho)*

p, Tom Musca; d, Ramon Menendez; w, Ramon Menendez, Tom Musca; ph, Tom Richmond (Foto-Kem Color); ed, Nancy Richardson; m, Craig Safan; cos, Kathryn Morrison

AAN Best Actor: Edward James Olmos

Another one of those teachers who uses entertainment to save young souls, this time in East Los Angeles. Based on a true story, the movie stars Edward James Olmos as Jaime Escalante, a math teacher at East L.A.'s Garfield High. Escalante's class is filled with kids who have no desire to learn—they come late to class, can't do multiplication, talk and eat in class, and live in fear of gang violence. Escalante, however, is no ordinary high school teacher—he's a Movie Teacher (cf. DEAD POET'S SOCIETY), so he wear costumes, engages in amateur theatrics (he dresses as a chef and violently slices up apples to illustrate the concept of fractions), and refers to his class as a "show." Gradually the students respond to his style. With his school facing a loss of accreditation, Escalante makes a radical request—to prepare his students for the Advanced Placement exams in Calculus. Carefully scripted and well acted, STAND AND DELIVER is sentimental and utterly predictable but better than many films of this kind. First-time director Ramon Menendez, a Cuban UCLA graduate, gives the charismatic Olmos a showcase.

STAND BY ME

DVD

1986 87m c Comedy ★★★½

Columbia (U.S.) R

Wil Wheaton *(Gordie Lachance)*, River Phoenix *(Chris Chambers)*, Corey Feldman *(Teddy Duchamp)*, Jerry O'Connell *(Vern Tessio)*, Richard Dreyfuss *(The Writer)*, Kiefer Sutherland *(Ace Merrill)*, Casey Siemaszko *(Billy Tessio)*, Gary Riley *(Charlie Hogan)*, Bradley Gregg *(Eyeball Chambers)*, Jason Oliver *(Vince Desjardins)*

p, Andrew Scheinman, Bruce A. Evans, Raynold Gideon; d, Rob Reiner; w, Raynold Gideon, Bruce A. Evans (based on the novella *The Body* by Stephen King); ph, Thomas Del Ruth (Panavision, Technicolor); ed, Robert Leighton; m, Jack Nitzsche; prod d, J. Dennis Washington; fx, Richard L. Thompson, Henry Millar; cos, Sue Moore

AAN Best Adapted Screenplay: Raynold Gideon, Bruce A. Evans

From the moment we hear the Ben E. King–Mike Stoller–Jerry Lieber hit "Stand By Me," we know we're in for a nostalgia trip, but STAND BY ME is a lot more than that. The picture is framed by the reminiscences of a writer (Richard Dreyfuss). Hearing about a friend's death, he recalls the summer of 1959, when he and his 12-year-old friends spent their time hanging around doing what boys do. Gordie (Wil Wheaton) is the writer as a youth, and he's joined by Chris (River Phoenix), a somewhat older kid who's considered bad because of his family, Teddy (Corey Feldman), an erratic boy whose father is in a mental hospital, and pudgy Vern (Jerry O'Connell). Vern hears his older brother (Casey Siemaszko) tell a pal that his gang found the body of a missing boy while they were out for a spin in a stolen car, and when he repeats the story to his own pals, they set out to find the body.

Directed by Rob Reiner from a semi-autobiographical Stephen King story, STAND BY ME is a sentimental film that works because of its unsentimental moments—in particular, its sometimes embarrassingly honest portrayal of what interests boys and how they talk about it. Reiner elicits some excellent performances from his young cast (River Phoenix is a standout) and Kiefer Sutherland is memorable as a menacing teen hood.

STANDING IN THE SHADOWS OF MOTOWN

DVD

2002 108m c/bw Documentary ★★★½

Rimshot Productions (U.S.) PG

Andre Braugher *(Narrator)*, The Funk Brothers: Jack "Black Jack" Ashford, Bob Babbitt, Johnny Griffith, Joe Hunter, Uriel Jones, Joe Messina, Eddie "Chank" Willis, Performers: Joan Osborne, Bootsy Collins

p, Paul Justman, Sandy Passman, Allan Slutsky; d, Paul Justman; w, Walter Dallas, Ntozake Shange (inspired by the book by Allan Slutsky); ph, Doug Milsome, Lon Stratton; ed, Anne Erikson; m, Mick Rossi, Alan Slutsky, Evan Solot; prod d, Rolfe Bergsman; art d, Amy Yaroch-Carroll; cos, Scarlett Jade

Motown's stable of '60s vocal stars like the Supremes, the Temptations, and Marvin Gaye all became household names, but few can say who actually played the music. The answer lies in Paul Justman's wonderfully warm tribute to Motown's Funk Brothers, a group of incredibly talented studio musicians who were the heart of the Motown Sound.

Justman relies mostly on extensive interviews with the surviving Brothers to tell their stories, many of which begin in the South before the promise of jobs in Detroit auto plants brought the musicians north. Most had roots in jazz, ensuring that their music always had that swing, and even after Berry Gordy had them laying down backing tracks in his Hitsville U.S.A. studio (vocal tracks were recorded separately), many

of the Brothers regularly hit the city's after-hours jazz clubs, working out risqué rhythms that soon found their way onto Motown recordings. The names may be virtually unknown, but the music they played is an essential part of the '60s: the galloping rhythm of "I'll Be There," the opening bars of "My Girl," the soaring key changes of "What Becomes of the Broken Hearted."

The Brothers maintain a gentlemanly decorum throughout the film; mention is made of the troubles that haunted genius bass player James Jamerson, who allegedly played the tricky bass line that drives Marvin Gaye's masterpiece "What's Goin' On" flat on his back and drunk as a skunk, but the dark side of the story is never really discussed. That said, the movie more than compensates with thrilling footage of a recent reunion concert in which the Funk Brothers, still in top form, back the likes of Bootsy Collins, Joan Osborne, and Chaka Kahn, playing their greatest hits and setting the record straight.

STANLEY AND LIVINGSTONE

1939 101m bw Biography/Adventure ★★★★

Fox (U.S.)

Spencer Tracy *(Henry M. Stanley)*, Nancy Kelly *(Eve Kingsley)*, Richard Greene *(Gareth Tyce)*, Walter Brennan *(Jeff Slocum)*, Charles Coburn *(Lord Tyce)*, Cedric Hardwicke *(Dr. David Livingstone)*, Henry Hull *(James Gordon Bennett)*, Henry Travers *(John Kingsley)*, Miles Mander *(Sir John Gresham)*, David Torrence *(Mr. Cranston)*

p, Kenneth MacGowan; d, Henry King; w, Philip Dunne, Julien Josephson (based on historical research and story outline by Hal Long, Sam Hellman); ph, George Barnes, Otto Brower; ed, Barbara McLean; m, Russell Bennett, David Buttolph, Louis Silvers, R.H. Bassett, Cyril J. Mockridge, Rudy Schrager; art d, William Darling, George Dudley; cos, Royer

An intelligent, if not strictly factual, retelling of the Stanley and Livingstone legend, this hardy adventure succeeds largely because of Henry King's graceful direction and Spencer Tracy's fine, subdued performance as American journalist Henry Stanley, who searches for the missing Dr. David Livingstone (Sir Cedric Hardwicke). The film opens as Stanley returns to New York after filing reports from the West. His editor next wants the reporter to head into the African jungle and find Livingstone, a Scottish missionary who has disappeared. Stanley accepts the assignment, taking along Jeff Slocum (Walter Brennan) to accompany him on the search. The trip proves full of dangers hidden within the jungle. Stanley comes down with jungle fever, yet will not let this stop the mission. Finally he encounters the missionary in a remote jungle settlement and utters the famous line, "Dr. Livingstone, I presume?"

Tracy gives a dignified portrait of a man who is profoundly changed as a result of his experience. The drama is well constructed, adroitly combining adventure with the humane values Livingstone espouses. The story is romanticized, with characters added to suit Hollywood conventions, and the truth about Stanley's life after his encounter with Livingstone fictionalized. Still, the final courtroom battle is a memorable one.

STAR!

DVD

1968 175m c Musical/Biography ★★★½

Fox (U.S.) G

Julie Andrews *(Gertrude Lawrence)*, Richard Crenna *(Richard Aldrich)*, Michael Craig *(Sir Anthony Spencer)*, Daniel Massey *(Noel Coward)*, Robert Reed *(Charles Fraser)*, Bruce Forsyth *(Arthur Lawrence)*, Beryl Reid *(Rose)*, John Collin *(Jack*

Roper), Alan Oppenheimer *(Andre Charlot),* Richard Karlan *(David Holtzman)*

p, Saul Chaplin; d, Robert Wise; w, William Fairchild; ph, Ernest Laszlo (Todd-AO, DeLuxe Color); ed, William Reynolds; prod d, Boris Leven; fx, L.B. Abbott, Art Cruickshank, Emil Kosa Jr.; chor, Michael Kidd; cos, Donald Brooks

AAN Best Supporting Actor: Daniel Massey; *AAN Best Cinematography:* Ernest Laszlo; *AAN Best Score (Musical):* Lennie Hayton; *AAN Best Original Song:* "Star!"; James Van Heusen (Music), Sammy Cahn (Lyrics); *AAN Best Art Direction-Set Decoration:* Boris Leven, Walter M. Scott, Howard Bristol; *AAN Best Costume Design:* Donald Brooks; *AAN Best Sound:* 20th Century Fox Studio Sound Department

Gertrude Lawrence was a huge star in England and on Broadway, but not in movies, and this cinematic biography left audiences wondering why Fox spent about $14 million to tell her story. Julie Andrews, on the other hand, was a huge marquee star after MARY POPPINS and THE SOUND OF MUSIC, and director Robert Wise and producer Saul Chaplin thought she would make a smashing Lawrence. Viewers disagreed, and the picture plummeted from its opening day. (It was re-released in a cut version, titled THOSE WERE THE HAPPY TIMES, a year later, but with no success either.) The film begins during WWII, as Lawrence, starring in the musical play *Lady in the Dark,* watches a newsreel about her own life. The film flashes back to 1915 in Clapham, England, when she leaves home to join her vaudevillian father (Bruce Forsyth), who is working in a run-down Brixton music hall. Gertrude decides to follow in her dad's footsteps and gets a job as a chorine in one of Andre Charlot's famous revues. Though Charlot (Alan Oppenheimer) is annoyed when she steals scenes and throws carefully rehearsed sketches out of whack, stage manager Jack Roper (John Collin) steps in and keeps her from getting fired. Jack and Gertrude marry but cannot agree on her role as a wife (he wants her to stay home; she wants to perform). After their daughter is born, Gertrude leaves. She becomes great friends with Noel Coward (Daniel Massey, who actually was Coward's godson), who uses his influence to get her a spot in Charlot's latest show, and she is instantly acclaimed as a new find after the opening in New York. Her career and romantic prospects soar, but her relationship with her neglected daughter (Jenny Agutter) is poor; moreover, she spends all her considerable earnings and overtaxes herself to pay her debts. After her success in Coward's *Tonight at 8:30,* she appears in *Susan and God,* showing she can play drama, then meets banker and theatrical dabbler Richard Aldrich (Richard Crenna) and appears in his staging of *Skylark.* Afterward, she moves on to *Lady in the Dark,* marries Aldrich, and is happy and fulfilled at last. There the picture ends, though in real life Lawrence lived another eight years and died at age 54. The movie lost millions, but it deserved a better fate for its enormous score, top-flight production, excellent choreography, and fine acting.

STAR 80

1983 102m c   Biography   ★★★★
Ladd/Warner Bros.   (U.S.)   R

Mariel Hemingway *(Dorothy Stratten),* Eric Roberts *(Paul Snider),* Cliff Robertson *(Hugh Hefner),* Carroll Baker *(Dorothy's Mother),* Roger Rees *(Aram Nicholas),* David Clennon *(Geb),* Josh Mostel *(Private Detective),* Lisa Gordon *(Eileen),* Sidney Miller *(Nightclub Owner),* Keith Hefner *(Photographer)*

p, Wolfgang Glattes, Kenneth Utt; d, Bob Fosse; w, Bob Fosse (based on "Death of a Playmate" by Teresa Carpenter); ph, Sven Nykvist (Technicolor); ed, Alan Heim; m, Ralph Burns; art d, Jack G. Taylor Jr., Michael Bolton; cos, Albert Wolsky

Brilliant and sickening. Bob Fosse's version of the short life and gory death of *Playboy* "Playmate of the Year" Dorothy Stratten focuses on the machinations and tacky ambitions of her boyfriend/murderer Paul Snider, hypnotically played by Eric Roberts. Stratten (Mariel Hemingway, who underwent breast augmentation for the role) is a shown as sweet small-town girl, easy prey for sleazy mediocrity Snider, who promises to make her a star. He marries her and brings her to Los Angeles, where she poses for *Playboy.* When she *does* become a star (a starlet, anyway—Stratten did an acceptable job in one film, Peter Bogdanovich's THEY ALL LAUGHED), she dumps Snider for the glitzy, cocaine-snorting Playboy mansion crowd, hangs out with Hef (Cliff Robertson), and has an affair with Aram Nicholas (a fictionalized Bogdanovich, played by Roger Rees). Snider reacts with murderous rage. Fosse's last film is a disturbing essay on sex, violence and showbiz in a world where attractive women function as tokens of exchange between men. A must-see that is guaranteed to ruin your day.

STAR IS BORN, A

1937 111m c   Drama   ★★★★½
Selznick   (U.S.)

Janet Gaynor *(Esther Blodgett/Vicki Lester),* Fredric March *(Norman Maine),* Adolphe Menjou *(Oliver Niles),* Andy Devine *(Danny McGuire),* May Robson *(Lettie),* Lionel Stander *(Libby),* Owen Moore *(Casey Burke),* Elizabeth Jenns *(Anita Regis),* J.C. Nugent *(Theodore Smythe),* Clara Blandick *(Aunt Mattie)*

p, David O. Selznick; d, William A. Wellman; w, Dorothy Parker, Alan Campbell, Robert Carson, David O. Selznick, William A. Wellman, Ring Lardner Jr., Budd Schulberg, John Lee Mahin (based on the story by Wellman, Carson) (Technicolor); ed, James E. Newcom; m, Max Steiner; art d, Lyle Wheeler; fx, Jack Cosgrove; cos, Omar Kiam

AAN Best Picture; AAN Best Actor: Fredric March; *AAN Best Actress:* Janet Gaynor; *AAN Best Director:* William Wellman; *AA Best Original Story:* William A. Wellman, Robert Carson; *AAN Best Screenplay:* Alan Campbell, Robert Carson, Dorothy Parker; *AAN Best Assistant Director:* Eric Stacey

March is a movie superstar whose heyday has slipped by, although he is still held in high esteem by his producer and studio head, Menjou. Everyone, except March, seems to know that he is losing popularity with the public and his films are seeing less and less box-office success. At a Hollywood party where he drinks too much, as usual, March meets and is attracted to Gaynor, who is serving sandwiches and, in his cups, he proposes to make her a star. She has been longing to become an actress and has been starving while waiting for Central Casting to call her for her big break. This call never comes, which annoys her boarding house owner, Kennedy, no end. March winds up breaking the dishes Gaynor is responsible for and charming her into leaving the party with him, later painting for her a life of splendor and happiness as a movie star, encouraging her to follow his lead. March persuades a reluctant Menjou to give Gaynor a screen test Impressed, Menjou decides to make her a star. March and Gaynor marry and, while her career accelerates, his takes a complete nose-dive. Soon he's the most unemployable actor in Hollywood, shamelessly getting drunk in public and embarrassing a wife who loves him in spite of himself.

A STAR IS BORN captures wonderfully the hustle of Hollywood, especially in scenes which show Gaynor being physically (and painfully) prepared for stardom by having her perfectly acceptable face redone by cosmetic experts, facial experts, eyebrow experts, hair stylists, and makeup magicians—these scenes lack the forced "let's kid Judy" energy of the 1954 version—they're colder. It profiles the behind-the-scenes machinations of stars and producers, and it shows that, however accidentally, a person of talent, sincerity, and good-heartedness sometimes slips through the corrosive Hollywood system to become a star. The film is marvelously constructed by Wellman, who elicited superb performances from his stars.

The dialogue created for this film is tough, and most of the words Stander is given to growl portray him and the many Hollywood types similar to his character as vindictive and ruthless, people without pity, charisma, or compassion. Even after March dies of drowning, Stander can only spit out vicious quips: "First drink of water he's had in 20 years, and then he had to get it by accident. How do you wire congratulations to the Pacific Ocean?" Producer Menjou is no less cynical when evaluating the movie-going public: "Fans will write to anyone for a picture. It only takes a three-cent stamp, and that makes pictures cheaper than wallpaper." Of course, much of this acid-dripping dialogue stemmed from the black humor for which "Algonquin Round Table" member Dorothy Parker was famous.

STAR IS BORN, A

1954 176m c Musical   DVD
Transcona   (U.S.)   ★★★★★
                        PG

Judy Garland (*Esther Blodgett/Vicki Lester*), James Mason (*Norman Maine*), Jack Carson (*Matt Libby*), Charles Bickford (*Oliver Niles*), Tommy Noonan (*Danny McGuire*), Lucy Marlow (*Lola Lavery*), Amanda Blake (*Susan Ettinger*), Irving Bacon (*Graves*), Hazel Shermet (*Libby's Secretary*), James Brown (*Glenn Williams*)

p, Sidney Luft; d, George Cukor; w, Moss Hart (based on the Dorothy Parker, Alan Campbell, Robert Carson screenplay from a story by William A. Wellman, Carson, based on the film WHAT PRICE HOLLYWOOD?); ph, Sam Leavitt (CinemaScope, Technicolor); ed, Folmar Blangsted, Craig Holt (reconstruction ed); m, Harold Arlen; prod d, Gene Allen; art d, Malcolm Bert; fx, H.F. Koenekamp; chor, Lize Bechtold Blyth, Eric Durst; cos, Jean Louis, Mary Ann Nyberg, Irene Sharaff

AAN Best Actor: James Mason; AAN Best Actress: Judy Garland; AAN Best Score (Musical): Ray Heindorf; AAN Best Song: "The Man That Got Away"; Harold Arlen (Music), Ira Gershwin (Lyrics); AAN Best Art Direction-Set Decoration (Color): Malcolm Bert, Gene Allen, Irene Sharaff, George James Hopkins; AAN Best Costume Design (Color): Jean Louis, Mary Ann Nyberg, Irene Sharaff

Judy Garland is at her peak, pulling out all the stops, daring the gods in this dark, weighty fable of the price one pays to be at the top. This version, directed by Cukor, is lent all manner of mythic significance by Garland, teetering on the abyss before the slide. There would be other triumphs in concert, but this is the peak of her film career. Here she finally exposed her powerful dramatic range, coupled with the magnificent singing voice that she pushed further than anyone could imagine. Her genius is attached to an uncomfortable, intense plot that allows reason for the tremulous mannerisms and bottomless, dark eyes.

The plot essentially follows that of the original 1936 film (directed by William Wellman and starring Janet Gaynor and Fredric March). A young singer (Garland) saves Norman Maine (James Mason), a star actor, from making a drunken fool of himself on stage. Later, a sober Norman hears her sing and decides to help this incredible talent get started in pictures. Eventually (after she changes her name from Esther Blodgett to Vicki Lester) he manages to get her the lead in a big musical. As Vicki's star rises, however, Norman's begins to fall. The two elope, but their happiness is short-lived, and Norman's drinking increases when he is cut by his studio. Frustrated by the fickleness of his public and "friends," he drunkenly interrupts the Oscar ceremonies where Vicki has won the award for Best Actress, humbly pleading for a job and accidentally slapping his wife during

the presentation ceremony. Despite all Vicki's attempts to find Norman work in Hollywood, his slide cannot be stopped by his wife's love.

Director George Cukor previously filmed the story as WHAT PRICE HOLLYWOOD? in 1932. Here he delivers a much more savage film, allowing moments and characters to speak for themselves in a way that give A STAR IS BORN that much more power. Garland is well matched by Mason, who imbues Norman's hellish descent with a deep sense of self-understanding, a dignified awareness of what is transpiring and ultimate acceptance of fate. And in the scenes of drunkenness, a threatening aura of danger that seems to give him an unhuman kind of vigor and strength. If Mason looks healthier than Garland sometimes, it works. Policing and caretaking an addict takes enormous energy; sometimes the toll is greater on the spouse than the addict themselves. Mason's work on STAR is the equal of any good performance you can name.

Harold Arlen and Ira Gershwin provided Garland with songs that would become standards in her concert repertoire, including the ten-ton torch song, "The Man That Got Away" (which earned an Oscar nomination for Best Song), rendered by Garland with incredible emotional power. Leonard Gershe's classic "Born in a Trunk" sequence is also one of Garland's finest moments, a near-autobiographical musical sequence that shows the star's rise, incorporating the songs "I'll Get By," "You Took Advantage of Me," "Black Bottom," "Peanut Vendor," "My Melancholy Baby," and "Swanee." After Garland's Oscar-nominated performance lost to Grace Kelly's amateur thesping in THE COUNTRY GIRL, many in Hollywood felt that she was being punished by her peers for her past troubles, and Groucho Marx sent a telegram to Garland saying that the loss "was the biggest robbery since Brink's."

Warners stupidly cut A STAR IS BORN considerably after its premiere, but Cukor's version was eventually partially restored through the reinsertion of recovered soundtrack with production stills and some alternate takes that had somehow survived, giving the film a continuity that unfeeling hands had removed. Seemingly vindicated, Cukor passed away the night before he was to see his restored film, which reopened in 1983 to enthusiastic crowds. George Hoyningen-Huene consulted on the color, which gives the film either somber depth or hysterical, raw splashes of color—it's exactly right. If this version is more closely aligned with showbiz tradition than the 1937 version, it works, largely because it underlines the Garland legend. With Jack Carson in a definitive role as a bastard press agent, and Lucy Marlow and Joan Shawlee as putrid starlet and columnist and Tommy Noonan, surprisingly effective as Garland's jazz musician pal, in the best role of his career.

STAR IS BORN, A

1976 140m c Musical   ★★★
Warner Bros.   (U.S.)   R

Barbra Streisand (*Esther Hoffman*), Kris Kristofferson (*John Norman Howard*), Gary Busey (*Bobby Ritchie*), Oliver Clark (*Gary Danziger*), Vanetta Fields, Clydie King (*The Oreos*), Marta Heflin (*Quentin*), M.G. Kelly (*Bebe Jesus*), Sally Kirkland (*Photographer*), Joanne Linville (*Freddie*)

p, Jon Peters; d, Frank Pierson; w, John Gregory Dunne, Joan Didion, Frank Pierson (based on a story by William A. Wellman, Robert Carson); ph, Robert Surtees (Panavision, Metrocolor); ed, Peter Zinner; m, Roger Kellaway; prod d, Polly Platt; art d, William M. Hiney; fx, Chuck Gaspar; chor, David Winters; cos, Shirley Strahm, Seth Banks

AAN Best Cinematography: Robert Surtees; AAN Best Song Score: Roger Kellaway; AA Best Original Song: "Evergreen (Love

Theme from A Star is Born)"; Barbra Streisand (Music), Paul Williams (Lyrics); AAN Best Sound: Robert Knudson, Dan Wallin, Robert Glass, Tom Overton

The fourth remake of this story, this is a fairly good, though overlong, film, executive-produced by Barbra Streisand and produced by her companion of the time, Jon Peters. Rock star John Norman Howard (Kris Kristofferson) takes solace in booze while his career slides. After a particularly embarrassing concert performance, the sullen star visits a nightclub where the interracial female singing trio "The Oreos" is performing. Impressed by the talents of Oreo Esther Hoffman (Streisand), John gets her an audition that leads to a recording contract. An album is released, Esther becomes a star, and she and John marry. But, as everyone watching expects, trouble looms in paradise as her career soars and his plummets. John ruins Esther's Grammy acceptance speech, staggering onstage to interrupt her triumph. Eventually he leaves her and dies in a car crash. The picture should have ended there; unfortunately, a lengthy coda follows, with Esther performing a concert dedicated to her late husband. Streisand fans will love this extra footage, but others will yawn. The songs, from several sources but mostly by Paul Williams and Kenny Ascher, range in quality from "Watch Closely Now" (a dreadful, interminable tune sung too often by Kristofferson) to "Evergreen," cowritten by Streisand and Williams. Director Frank Pierson clashed repeatedly with Streisand and later made some much-publicized charges blasting the star for megalomania.

STAR TREK II: THE WRATH OF KHAN   DVD
1982   113m   c   Science Fiction   ★★★½
Paramount   (U.S.)   PG

William Shatner (Adm. James T. Kirk), Leonard Nimoy (Mr. Spock), DeForest Kelley (Dr. Leonard "Bones" McCoy), Ricardo Montalban (Khan Noonian Singh), James Doohan (Chief Engineer Montgomery "Scotty" Scott), Walter Koenig (Chekov), George Takei (Sulu), Nichelle Nichols (Cmdr. Uhura), Bibi Besch (Dr. Carol Marcus), Merritt Butrick (David Marcus)

p, Robert Sallin; d, Nicholas Meyer; w, Jack B. Sowards (based on a story by Sowards and Harve Bennett and on the TV series "Star Trek"); ph, Gayne Rescher (Panavision, Movielab Color); ed, William Dornisch; m, James Horner; prod d, Joseph R. Jennings; art d, Michael Minor; fx, Bob Dawson, Ken Ralston, Jim Veilliux, Alan Howarth

Of the first three Trek films, #2 comes closest to the spirit of the TV series. It's conceived as a sequel to the "Space Seed" episode from the 1967 show, in which Kirk had banished the evil Khan (Ricardo Montalban) to the edge of the universe. Now Khan is back and looking for revenge, via a device capable of reversing creation. This is one of the most popular in the series, thanks to a high action quotient (including a tensely staged space battle), a suitably campy turn by Montalban, and the shock value of Spock's "death." There is some novelty value, too, in the focus on Kirk's family life back on Earth.

STAR TREK IV: THE VOYAGE HOME   DVD
1986   119m   c   Science Fiction   ★★★
Paramount   (U.S.)   PG

William Shatner (James T. Kirk), Leonard Nimoy (Mr. Spock), DeForest Kelley (Dr. Leonard "Bones" McCoy), James Doohan (Chief Engineer Montgomery "Scotty" Scott), George Takei (Sulu), Walter Koenig (Chekov), Nichelle Nichols (Cmdr. Uhura), Majel Barrett (Dr. Christine Chapel), Jane Wyatt (Amanda, Spock's Mother), Catherine Hicks (Dr. Gillian Taylor)

p, Harve Bennett; d, Leonard Nimoy; w, Harve Bennett, Steve Meerson, Peter Krikes, Nicholas Meyer (based on a story by

Leonard Nimoy, Harve Bennett, and the TV series created by Gene Roddenberry); ph, Don Peterman (Panavision, Technicolor); ed, Peter E. Berger; m, Leonard Rosenman; prod d, Jack T. Collis; art d, Joe Aubel, Pete Smith; fx, Michael Lantieri; cos, Robert Fletcher

AAN Best Cinematography: Don Peterman; AAN Best Original Score: Leonard Rosenman; AAN Best Sound: Terry Porter, Dave Hudson, Mel Metcalfe, Gene S. Cantamessa; AAN Best Sound Effects Editing: Mark Mangini

With directorial tongue firmly in cheek, Leonard Nimoy again takes the helm (he had begun his career with the lumbering third episode), in this environmentally-minded installment which sends our heroes back in time to 1986 San Francisco. Spock gives a Vulcan pinch to a punk, Kirk gets lost on a bus, and we learn the importance of saving the whales. (A huge space probe is threatening to destroy 23rd-century Earth unless a whale—by then extinct—can be found for it to "chat" with.) By far the silliest and most self-mocking of the series, with the interplay between Spock and Kirk veering somewhere between Hope and Crosby and Cheech and Chong, but also one of the most successful, grossing around $110 million.

STAR TREK: FIRST CONTACT   DVD
1996   105m   c   Science Fiction   ★★★
Rick Berman   (U.S.)   PG-13

Patrick Stewart (Captain Jean-Luc Picard), Jonathan Frakes (Commander William Riker), Brent Spiner (Lieutenant Commander Data), LeVar Burton (Lieutenant Commander Geordi La Forge), Michael Dorn (Lieutenant Commander Worf), Gates McFadden (Dr. Beverly Crusher), Marina Sirtis (Counselor Deanna Troi), Alfre Woodard (Lily Sloane), James Cromwell (Zefram Cochrane), Alice Krige (Borg Queen)

p, Rick Berman; d, Jonathan Frakes; w, Rick Berman, Brannon Braga, Ronald D. Moore (from a story by Rick Berman, Brannon Braga and Ronald D. Moore, based on characters created by Gene Rodenberry); ph, Matthew F. Leonetti; ed, John W. Wheeler; m, Jerry Goldsmith; prod d, Herman Zimmerman; art d, Ron Wilkinson; fx, Terry Frazee, Jeff Olson, Scott Rader, Adam Howard, Industrial Light & Magic; cos, Deborah Everton

AAN Best Makeup: Michael Westmore, Scott Wheeler, Jake Garber

The eighth film in the STAR TREK movie series, FIRST CONTACT continues the tradition of the even-numbered entries' superiority. It's the second STAR TREK movie to feature the cast of TV's "The Next Generation," and the first with no members of the original show's cast.

In the 24th century, Captain Jean-Luc Picard (Patrick Stewart) is breaking in a new Starship Enterprise when the Borg, a notoriously fearsome race of cyborgs, attack. Rather than fight fair, the Borg travel back to the 21st century to alter the course of human events to their advantage, and it's up to Picard and crew to stop them.

Saving the universe is small potatoes compared to the real mission assigned to Jonathan Frakes (who plays Commander William Riker and also directed), Stewart, and company. This installment's prime directive: Save the STAR TREK franchise! Without the popular cast of the original series or the guidance of the late Gene Roddenberry, the future looked uncertain. However, now free of the demands of "classic TREK" mythology, FIRST CONTACT demonstrates that Trek flicks can actually be decent films. The story line follows up on a popular "Next Generation" episode, in which Picard is captured and assimilated by the Borg. All the show's favorites—including Picard, Data (Brent Spiner), Deanna (Marina Sirtis), and Worf the Klingon (Michael Dorn)—reprise their roles. The film may be action-heavy, but it features a smartly-written script and, in a big departure from TREK tradition, camp-free acting. Stewart and Alice Krige, who stars as the dangerously seductive Borg Queen, both give performances of surprising depth.

STAR TREK: INSURRECTION
DVD
1998 103m c Science Fiction ★★★½
Rick Berman Production (U.S.) PG

Patrick Stewart *(Picard)*, Jonathan Frakes *(Riker)*, Brent Spiner *(Data)*, LeVar Burton *(Geordi)*, Michael Dorn *(Worf)*, Gates McFadden *(Beverly)*, Marina Sirtis *(Troi)*, F. Murray Abraham *(Ru'afo)*, Donna Murphy *(Anij)*, Anthony Zerbe *(Dougherty)*

p, Rick Berman; d, Jonathan Frakes; w, Michael Piller (based on "Star Trek" created by Gene Roddenberry); ph, Matthew F. Leonetti; ed, Peter E. Berger; m, Jerry Goldsmith; prod d, Herman Zimmerman; art d, Ron Wilkinson; fx, Terry Frazee; cos, Sanja Milkovic Hays

Director Jonathan Frakes breaks the curse of the odd-numbered *Star Trek* sequels with this ninth installment in the canon. It departs from many treasured traditions but borrowing from the classic Western premise of a small town's last stand against high-powered bullies.

On the idyllic Ba'ku homeworld, everyone is happy, buff, and beautiful, awash in their planet's flattering longitudinal light. Apparently under the influence of a flipped chip, android Lt. Cdr. Data (Brent Spiner) of the *Enterprise* takes a cultural survey team hostage, and Federation honchos want him deactivated. Enter Capt. Jean-Luc Picard (Patrick Stewart) and his crew, who free the hostages and clear the android's name. Mission accomplished, right? Not so fast: the Feds are allied with the Son'a, an aging race of ugly people who want the Ba'kus' eternal youth and beauty secret, which involves radiation emitted by their planet's rings. Picard uncovers a plan to exile the Ba'ku from their own world, forcing him to choose between disobeying a direct order and violating the sacred Prime Directive, which forbids interference in a culture's natural evolution.

Frakes proved his action-movie mettle with STAR TREK: FIRST CONTACT, and the *Next Generation* gang have relaxed into their roles: the sense that they're old friends who know each other's moods suffuses their scenes together. As Ru'afo, the Son'a leader whose toxic blood oozes from his leathery skin when he's angry, F. Murray Abraham supplies a baroquely icky counterpoint to all the bonhomie. The supporting characters get short shrift, casualties of an unusually heavy story load for a *Trek* movie, but it's an interesting tale, more accessible to non-Trekkers than previous entries.

STAR TREK: NEMESIS
DVD
2002 117m c Science Fiction ★★
Paramount (U.S.) PG-13

Patrick Stewart *(Jean-Luc Picard)*, Jonathan Frakes *(William Riker)*, Brent Spiner *(Data/B-4)*, LeVar Burton *(Geordi La Forge)*, Michael Dorn *(Worf)*, Marina Sirtis *(Deanna Troi)*, Gates McFadden *(Beverly Crusher)*, Tom Hardy *(Shinzon)*, Ron Perlman *(Viceroy)*, Kate Mulgrew *(Admiral Janeway)*

p, Rick Berman; d, Stuart Baird; w, John Logan (from a story by John Logan, Rick Berman, and Brent Spiner, based on the "Star Trek" TV series created by Gene Roddenberry); ph, Jeffrey L. Kimball; ed, Dallas Puett; m, Jerry Goldsmith; prod d, Herman Zimmerman; art d, Cherie Baker; fx, Terry Frazee, Mark O. Forker; cos, Bob Ringwood

It's dead, Jim. The tenth STAR TREK film sadly gives power to the premise that this beloved science-fiction franchise has collapsed into the black hole of its own mythology.

After the Romulan Imperial Senate falls victim to an act of sabotage, the action shifts to the wedding reception of Commander William Riker (Jonathan Frakes) and Counselor Deanna Troi (Marina Sirtis). The happy couple and the rest of TV's "Star Trek: The Next Generation" crew depart for Troi's home planet but make an unexpected stop on a barren world near the Romulan border when they pick up a signal from a previously unknown prototype of the android Data (Brent Spiner). When they arrive, they find the prototype's body parts scattered across the planet's surface. Back aboard the *Enterprise*, Captain Jean-Luc Picard (Patrick Stewart) gets a call from Admiral Janeway (Kate Mulgrew) that sends the ship on a diplomatic mission to Romulus, where Shinzon (Tom Hardy), a military leader from Romulus's warlike sister planet, Remus, has staged a coup. As the new praetor, the nefarious Shinzon assures Picard he wants peace with the Federation—and drops the bombshell that he's been cloned from Picard himself.

Plot points such as the threat of a Romulan countercoup and some unexplained telepathic nonsense involving Shinzon's viceroy (Ron Perlman) are raised and dropped, while the heavy-close-up hackwork of director Stuart Baird reveals that the intended primary market for the film is actually home video. Spectacle and special effects have saved equally bad movies in the past, but never one so hackneyed that there are virtually no surprises or suspense.

STAR WARS
DVD
1977 121m c Science Fiction ★★★★½
20th Century Fox (U.S.) PG

Mark Hamill *(Luke Skywalker)*, Harrison Ford *(Han Solo)*, Carrie Fisher *(Princess Leia Organa)*, Peter Cushing *(Grand Moff Tarkin)*, Alec Guinness *(Ben Obi-Wan Kenobi)*, Anthony Daniels *(C-3PO)*, Kenny Baker *(R2-D2)*, Peter Mayhew *(Chewbacca)*, David Prowse *(Darth Vader)*, James Earl Jones *(Voice of Darth Vader)*

p, Gary Kurtz; d, George Lucas; w, George Lucas; ph, Gilbert Taylor (Panavision, Technicolor); ed, Paul Hirsch, Marcia Lucas, Richard Chew; m, John Williams; prod d, Jonathan Barry; art d, Norman Reynolds, Leslie Dilley; fx, John Dykstra (effects photography supervisor), John Stears (special production and mechanical effects supervisor), Grant McCune (modelmaker supervisor), Robert Blalack (composite optical photography), Richard Edlund (miniature photography, optical effects), Les Bowie, Industrial Light & Magic; cos, John Mollo, Ron Beck; anim, Adam Beckett

AAN Best Picture; AAN Best Supporting Actor: Alec Guinness; *AAN Best Director:* George Lucas; *AAN Best Original Screenplay:* George Lucas; *AA Best Film Editing:* Marcia Lucas, Paul Hirsch, Richard Chew; *AA Best Original Score:* John Williams; *AA Best Art Direction-Set Decoration:* Jonathan Barry, Norman Reynolds, Leslie Dilley, Roger Christian; *AA Best Costume Design:* John Mollo; *AA Best Sound:* Don MacDougall, Ray West, Bob Minkler, Derek Ball; *AA Best Visual Effects:* John Stears, John Dykstra, Richard Edlund, Grant McCune, Robert Blalack; *AA Special Achievement Award—Sound Effects:* Benjamin Burtt Jr.

"A long time ago, in a galaxy far far away," reads the opening title of STAR WARS, introducing not only this one film but, in effect, a whole new wave in Hollywood filmmaking. From this point on, American films changed—for better or worse—as did audience expectations. STAR WARS left viewers craving more; "bigger and better" spectacles became the rage for years afterwards, although much that followed paled in comparison. It soon became common to hear even casual fans conversing about previously arcane special effects in a critical and knowledgeable manner.

There's no denying the appeal of this historic blockbuster. What's fascinating from a cinematic point of view is the magnificently derivative nature of the film. It's an enormous summary of characters, styles, and plot points that surveys 40 years of film history. There's probably not a frame in it that doesn't have some cinematic antecedent—Lucas quotes with such enthusiastic abandon that he doesn't balk at referencing even THE TRIUMPH OF THE WILL. This is not necessarily a criticism. STAR WARS brought back for a new generation many of the most attractive elements of studio-era moviemaking, and it did so in breathless anthology form. For some young filmgoers this film acted as a doorway to the glory of the movies.

STAR WARS presents a cast of characters who have become part of our collective consciousness: Mark Hamill is the callow youth Luke Skywalker; Harrison Ford is the rugged, roguish adventurer Han Solo; and Carrie Fisher is the lovely, spunky Princess Leia. Also along for the ride are a pair of adorable 'droids, R2-D2 (Kenny Baker) and C-3P0 (Anthony Daniels); Chewbacca (Peter Mayhew), the fierce, towering bearlike Wookie navigator who's really a softie at heart; and Obi-Wan Kenobi (Alec Guinness), the wise old hermit who is actually a great Jedi Master.

Luke is an "orphan" (see THE EMPIRE STRIKES BACK) living with his aunt and uncle on their farm on a dusty remote planet called Tatooine. He yearns for a life of high adventure. He wants to go offworld to join the academy like his friends, but his uncle needs help with the coming harvest. Meanwhile, the Imperial Senate has been disbanded and the galaxy has been taken over by the evil Emperor. The Empire's greatest weapon, the dreaded Death Star, is a huge globular craft able to disintegrate entire planets. This fearsome device is commanded by the sinister Grand Moff Tarkin (Peter Cushing) and his feared masked aide, Darth Vader (David Prowse, voiced by the uncredited James Earl Jones). Princess Leia acquires the plans for the craft and hides them in R2-D2, who is jettisoned in an escape pod with the fussy translator 'droid C-3P0. R2-D2 has been programmed to find Obi-Wan Kenobi, but first he ends up on the Skywalker farm. The little 'droid wanders off one night to fulfill his mission; Luke follows and meets old Ben Kenobi who offers to teach him the mysterious ways of the Force. The rest is movie history.

STAR WARS EPISODE I: THE PHANTOM MENACE 📀

1999 131m c Science Fiction/Adventure ★★★
JAK Productions Ltd./Lucasfilm Ltd. (U.S.) PG

Liam Neeson (Jedi Knight Qui-Gon Jinn), Ewan McGregor (Ben "Obi-Wan" Kenobi as a Young Man), Natalie Portman (Queen Padme Naberrie Amidala—Pricess Leia's Mother), Jake Lloyd (Anakin Skywalker—Young Darth Vader), Ian McDiarmid (Senator Palpatine), Pernilla August (Shmi Skywalker—Anakin's Mother), Ahmed Best (Jar Jar Binks), Frank Oz (Voice of Yoda), Samuel L. Jackson (Jedi Knight Mace Windu), Ray Park (Darth Maul)

p, Rick McCallum; d, George Lucas; w, George Lucas; ph, David Tattersall; ed, Paul Martin Smith; m, John Williams; prod d, Gavin Bocquet; art d, Phil Harvey; fx, Nick Dudman, Dennis Muren, Scott Squires, John Knoll, Rob Coleman; cos, Trisha Biggar; anim, Rob Coleman

AAN Best Sound: Gary Rydstrom, Tom Johnson, Shawn Murphy, John Midgley; AAN Best Sound Effects Editing: Ben Burtt, Tom Bellfort; AAN Best Visual Effects: John Knoll, Dennis Muren, Scott Squires, Rob Coleman

One of the most eagerly awaited films ever, EPISODE 1 is not the Second Coming, and it's not the end of cinema as we know it. It is a prequel that feels especially dependent on its sequels (made and unmade) for interest.

Set 30 years before the events that unfold in the much-loved STARS WARS trilogy, it chronicles the deprived childhood of Anakin Skywalker (Jake Lloyd), who grows up to be Darth Vader, and the travails of teen Queen Amidala (Natalie Portman) of Naboo, who must save her planet from destruction while weighed down by a series of brow-burdening head-dresses. In Amidala's corner: Jedi knights Qui-Gon Jinn

(Liam Neeson) and his cheeky apprentice Obi-Wan Kenobi (Ewan McGregor), who will, of course, mature into Luke Skywalker's wise mentor. Against her: devilish-looking Darth Maul (Ray Parks), a passel of toad-like aliens who take their marching orders from Maul's hooded boss, and the apparently benevolent Senator Palpatine (Ian McDiarmid), who must be two-faced scum because he's due to metamorphose somewhere down the line into the Emperor of the evil Empire.

There's plenty to look at: the movie's crammed with goofball aliens, futuristic hardware, and elaborate costumes, some of them truly stunning in their intricacy. The lumbering banality of the dialogue, ameliorated in places by the efforts of actors like Neeson and McGregor, is painful but hardly unexpected—the trilogy is full of wince-inducers. But it's a bit disturbing that along with the simplistic heroics of old-fashioned space operas, this film has also picked up their unexamined racism: why, for example, do the duplicitous toad aliens speak and dress like Chinese people? And how did comic-relief Jar Jar Binks (Ahmed Best), a lizard-like creature notable for his affable cowardice, come to sound Jamaican? It's a kiddie movie rejiggered for childish grown-ups, of whom there are enough to make it a hit. How such childishness has become a virtual secular religion is hard to imagine, and far beyond the scope of movie criticism.

STAR WARS EPISODE II: ATTACK OF THE CLONES 📀

2002 132m c Science Fiction/Adventure ★★½
JAK Productions Ltd./Lucasfilm Ltd. (U.S.) PG-13

Ewan McGregor (Obi-Wan Kenobi), Natalie Portman (Senator Padme Amidala), Hayden Christensen (Anakin Skywalker), Christopher Lee (Count Dooku/Darth Tyranus), Samuel L. Jackson (Jedi Knight Mace Windu), Frank Oz (Voice of Yoda), Ian McDiarmid (Supreme Chancellor Palpatine/Darth Sidious), Pernilla August (Shmi Skywalker), Temeura Morrison (Jango Fett), Jimmy Smits (Senator Bail Organa)

p, Rick McCallum; d, George Lucas; w, George Lucas, Jonathan Hales (based on a story by George Lucas); ph, David Tattersall; ed, Ben Burtt; m, John Williams; prod d, Gavin Bocquet; art d, Peter Russell (supervising); fx, Pablo Helman, Geoff Heron, John Knoll, Dennis Muren, Ben Snow, Dave Young, Industrial Light & Magic; cos, Trisha Biggar; anim, Rob Coleman

Set ten years after 1999's EPISODE I, this whiz-bang spectacle is a two-and-a-quarter hour cornucopia of aliens, hardware, and deep-space derring-do—it's got everything but the kitchen sink and credible characters. There's a great deal of plot—seceding planets, disgruntled miners, political intrigue—all subtly undermined by proper names that sound like baby talk: Naboo, Jar Jar, Boba, Windu, Dooku, Shmi. But what drives this second chapter in the beloved six-film saga (or more correctly, what *should* drive it) is the transformation of teenage Jedi-in-training Anakin Skywalker (Hayden Christensen) from an impulsive youth into the man who will be Darth Vader. Granted, Lucas is at a disadvantage: We've already seen episodes four, five, and six, so major plot developments have been robbed of any potential for suspense. No matter how much the dewy Padme Amidala (Natalie Portman), former child Queen of Naboo, loves Anakin, no matter how hard Jedi master Obi-Wan Kenobi (Ewan McGregor) tries to guide him away from his worst impulses, Anakin *will* surrender to the Force's dark side. That his destiny is preordained, however, is no excuse for a Cliff's Notes telling and carelessness with beloved characters. When Obi-Wan laments to Anakin, "Why do I get the feeling you'll be the death of me?" we should feel a portentous frisson. Instead, it's a laugh line, designed to elicit the same delight as the sight of wizened Yoda (voice of Frank Oz) picking up a lightsaber and strutting his stuff. And while it was always clear that Lucas cared more about special effects than acting, here his lack of interest has produced phenomenally wooden performances from newcomers and veterans alike. Only the imperious Christopher Lee, as baleful Count Dooku, emerges unscathed.

STAR WARS EPISODE III: REVENGE OF THE SITH

2005 140m c Science Fiction/Adventure ★★★½
Lucasfilm/JAK Productions (U.S.) PG-13

Ewan McGregor (Obi-Wan Kenobi), Natalie Portman (Padme), Hayden Christensen (Anakin Skywalker), Ian McDiarmid (Supreme Chancellor Palpatine), Samuel L. Jackson (Mace Windu), Jimmy Smits (Senator Bail Organa), Frank Oz (Yoda), Anthony Daniels (C-3PO), Christopher Lee (Count Dooku), Keisha Castle-Hughes (Queen of Naboo)

p, Rick McCallum; d, George Lucas; w, George Lucas; ph, David Tattersall; ed, Roger Barton, Ben Burtt; m, John Williams; prod d, Gavin Bocquet; art d, Ian Gracie, Phil Harvey, Peter Russell; fx, Dave Elsey (creatures), Roger Guyett, Industrial Light & Magic, John Knoll, David Young; cos, Trisha Biggar; anim, Rob Coleman

In the old-fashioned tradition of saving the best for last, George Lucas's last STAR WARS film is by far the best of the second trilogy and comes closest of all the installments to achieving the balance between sci-fi spectacle and mythic resonance to which Lucas aspired.

The film opens with the democratic galactic alliance in crisis, Supreme Chancellor Palpatine (Ian McDiarmid) consolidating his political capital, and Anakin Skywalker (Hayden Christensen) increasingly disenchanted with his Jedi masters. Palpatine's request that Anakin serve as his personal representative among the Jedi sets in motion the dark events that will bring forth sinister Darth Vader and the fascistic empire whose oppressive cloud hangs over STAR WARS EPISODE IV: A NEW HOPE. For viewers seeing the films in the order in which they were made (rather than in order of internal chronology), this chapter contains the fewest surprises. Knowing it's the bridge between CLONES and NEW HOPE means knowing everything that must happen. The Jedi, except for Obi-Wan Kenobi (Ewan McGregor) and Yoda (the voice of Frank Oz), will die; soon-to-be-Emperor Palpatine will reveal his true, evil colors; and Anakin will betray his principles and undergo the disfiguring transformation into Vader. Padme (Natalie Portman) will bear her twins, Luke and Leia, whom Yoda will send off to be raised in separate corners of the troubled universe.

There's no excuse for Lucas's utter indifference to nuance; unpersuasive performances and wooden dialogue mar much of the film. But the battle sequences and lightsaber duels are gripping, and for every scene that doesn't deliver the goods, another hums with surprising intensity. The STAR WARS films are glossy pulp fictions, but good pulp is as powerful a force as any in this world or any other, even those far, far away.

STARDUST MEMORIES

DVD
1980 90m bw Comedy ★★½
UA (U.S.) PG

Woody Allen (Sandy Bates), Charlotte Rampling (Dorrie), Jessica Harper (Daisy), Marie-Christine Barrault (Isobel), Tony Roberts (Tony), Daniel Stern (Actor), Amy Wright (Shelley), Helen Hanft (Vivian Orkin), John Rothman (Jack Abel), Anne DeSalvo (Sandy's Sister)

p, Robert Greenhut; d, Woody Allen; w, Woody Allen; ph, Gordon Willis; ed, Susan E. Morse; prod d, Santo Loquasto; art d, Michael Molly

After flirting with autobiography in a few films, Woody Allen dug directly into personal experience to fashion this tale. Allen plays a prominent comedian-turned-film-director who attends a weekend film seminar where he is surrounded by hordes of adoring critics and fans who mine his every word looking for profundity and hidden meanings. The usual Allen neuroses and problems with women are given an episodic treatment, with a number of jokes along the way, but the film has an underlying angry tone that Allen fails to blend successfully with the comedy. Allen is to be commended for broadening the psychology and themes of his films, but STARDUST MEMORIES remains a disappointing outing, despite its many laughs and inside jokes. (The head of United Artists, Andy Albeck, plays a film chief who is worried that his new movie has no laughs.)

STARGATE

DVD
1994 119m c Science Fiction/Adventure ★★★
Canal Plus/Centropolis Film/Carolco PG-13
(U.S./France)

Kurt Russell (Colonel Jonathan "Jack" O'Neil), James Spader (Dr. Daniel Jackson), Jaye Davidson (Ra), Viveca Lindfors (Catherine), Alexis Cruz (Skaara), Mili Avital (Sha'uri), Leon Rippy (General W.O. West), John Diehl (Lieutenant Kawalsky), Carlos Lauchu (Anubis), Djimon Hounsou, billed as Djimon (Horus)

p, Joel B. Michaels, Oliver Eberle, Dean Devlin; d, Roland Emmerich; w, Roland Emmerich, Dean Devlin; ph, Karl Walter Lindenlaub; ed, Michael J. Duthie, Derek Brechin; m, David Arnold; prod d, Holger Gross; art d, Peter Murton, Frank Bollinger, Mark Zuelzke; fx, Kit West; cos, Joseph Porro

Lavishly produced and designed, this science fiction epic became one of the biggest commercial hits of 1994, despite a second-hand storyline and ponderous tone that were pounced upon by most critics.

Nerdy Egyptologist Daniel Jackson (James Spader) is called upon to assist in a classified Air Force project near the great pyramid of Giza. The Feds suspect that a huge circular structure discovered near the pyramid is a "StarGate"—a teleportation device that links the earth with another site far off in the universe. Jackson deciphers the hieroglyphic code on the structure and, accompanied by a military team led by Colonel Jack O'Neil (Kurt Russell), embarks on a perilous journey to the unknown. They emerge into a bizarre desert civilization ruled by a Machiavellian tyrant (Jaye Davidson) who claims to be the sun god Ra.

This was an expensive film to make, and every penny spent is visible onscreen. It incorporates excellent special effects, burnished cinematography that gives the distant planet a convincing other-worldly aura, highly effective action sequences populated by legions of meticulously costumed extras, and towering sets of which Cecil B. DeMille would surely have been proud. Given these assets, STARGATE rides out the bumps in its fanciful story. The film handles its all-important human elements capably, and leavens its high-tech bravado with just the right amount of comic relief. Though overblown and overlong, it rewards viewers with meticulously designed thrills and conveys a genuine sense of wonder—no small feat in these times of post-modern cinematic ennui.

STARMAN

DVD
1984 115m c Science Fiction/Romance ★★★
Columbia (U.S.) PG

Jeff Bridges (Starman), Karen Allen (Jenny Hayden), Charles Martin Smith (Mark Shermin), Richard Jaeckel (George Fox),

Robert Phalen *(Maj. Bell)*, Tony Edwards *(Sgt. Lemon)*, John Walter Davis *(Brad Heinmuller)*, Ted White *(Deer Hunter)*, Dirk Blocker, M.C. Gainey *(Cops)*

p, Larry Franco; d, John Carpenter; w, Bruce A. Evans, Raynold Gideon; ph, Donald Morgan (Panavision, MGM Color); ed, Marion Rothman; m, Jack Nitzsche; prod d, Daniel Lomino; fx, Roy Arbogast, Bruce Nicholson, Michael McAlister; cos, Andy Hylton, Robin Bush

---

AAN Best Actor: Jeff Bridges

In this pleasant surprise from director John Carpenter, Jenny Hayden (Karen Allen) is a young Wisconsin widow still grieving over the loss of her husband. She spends her evenings looking through photo albums and watching home movies of their brief time together. One night, a bright blue light zooms from outer space and flies into Jenny's home. It hovers over the photo album and runs the home movies until it has assimilated enough characteristics of Earthlings to take on the shape of one—Jenny's dead husband. She is shocked and confused when confronted with this man who looks just like her late husband (Jeff Bridges). The alien manages to explain that he has come with greetings in return for the message Earth sent into space on *Voyager II*. His people have arranged for him to be picked up in the Arizona desert in a few days, and he forces Jenny to drive him there. Meanwhile, the government, represented by a National Security Council agent (Richard Jaeckel), is out to capture the alien in order to study him. Jenny's fear is eventually overcome by her compassion for the vulnerable being who is almost childlike in his sense of wonder about Earth and its inhabitants. Slowly, hesitantly, they fall in love, knowing that he must return to his planet or die. STARMAN is a wonderful film that combines science fiction, road movies, and romance into an engaging, very entertaining whole. While the plot may have some holes and the story may be a bit hard to swallow, the film works due to the performances by Bridges and Allen. Carpenter directs the film in a straightforward manner, and the brief forays into special effects and pyrotechnics are handled deftly without distracting from the basic story line. STARMAN is an enjoyable film filled with the kind of sensitivity, love, and humor seldom seen on today's screens.

STARS LOOK DOWN, THE
1939 104m bw Drama   ★★★★
Grand National   (U.K.)

Michael Redgrave *(David Fenwick)*, Margaret Lockwood *(Jenny Sunley)*, Emlyn Williams *(Joe Gowan)*, Nancy Price *(Martha Fenwick)*, Allan Jeayes *(Richard Barras)*, Edward Rigby *(Robert Fenwick)*, Cecil Parker *(Stanley Millington)*, Linden Travers *(Laura Millington)*, Milton Rosmer *(Harry Nugent)*, George Carney *(Slogger Gowan)*

p, Isadore Goldsmith; d, Carol Reed; w, J.B. Williams (based on the novel by A.J. Cronin); ph, Ernest Palmer (uncredited), Henry Harris (uncredited), Mutz Greenbaum; ed, Reginald Beck; m, Hans May; art d, James Carter

Made in 1939, but released in the U.S. at around the same time as HOW GREEN WAS MY VALLEY, this superb view of the plight of British miners was unfortunately overlooked at the box office. Though related in subject, THE STARS LOOK DOWN is much grimmer than John Ford's classic.

Based on a novel by A.J. Cronin, Carol Reed's first major film is set in a bleak coal mining town in northern England, where Rigby and Price have struggled to give their son (Redgrave) an opportunity for a better life and a university education. Rigby works in the mine with his younger son (Desmond Tester) and attempts to organize his fellow miners, who are working under dangerous conditions. While away at school, Redgrave meets Lockwood. A vain young woman, Lockwood has been rejected by Williams, and now traps

Redgrave into marriage. When Williams, an unctuous type, renews his affair with Lockwood, Redgrave leaves her and turns his attention to helping the miners back home, who have been forced to return to work after an aborted strike. Redgrave, who has ambitions of becoming an MP, tries to rally support for the union, but to no avail. After a cave-in at the mine in which many—including Rigby and Tester—are killed, he decides to stay in the small town and devote his life to improving the lot of the miners.

At once topical and enduring, this powerful drama influenced by the social realism of the British documentary greatly enhanced the growing reputation of Reed, then a young director. Shot partially at a colliery in Cumberland, THE STARS LOOK DOWN was also an important film for the young Michael Redgrave, who was still fresh from the British stage (and from THE LADY VANISHES). He gives a strong performance, as do Lockwood and Williams, with Rigby and Price lending fine support.

STARSHIP TROOPERS   DVD
1997 129m c   Science Fiction/Action   ★★★
Touchstone/Columbia TriStar   (U.S.)   R

Casper Van Dien *(Johnny Rico)*, Dina Meyer *(Dizzy Flores)*, Denise Richards *(Carmen Ibanez)*, Jake Busey *(Ace Levy)*, Neil Patrick Harris *(Carl Jenkins)*, Clancy Brown *(Sergeant Zim)*, Seth Gilliam *(Sugar Watkins)*, Patrick Muldoon *(Zander Barcalow)*, Michael Ironside *(Jean Rasczak)*, Marshall Bell *(General Owen)*

p, Alan Marshall, Jon Davison; d, Paul Verhoeven; w, Ed Neumeier (based on the novel by Robert A. Heinlein); ph, Jost Vacano; ed, Mark Goldblatt, Caroline Ross; m, Basil Poledouris; prod d, Allan Cameron; fx, John Richardson, John McLeod, Laura Buff, Phil Tippett, Scott E. Anderson, Alec Gillis; cos, Ellen Mirojnick

---

AAN Best Visual Effects: Phil Tippett, Scott E. Anderson, Alec Gillis, John Richardson

---

Looking for a rip-roaring, heartlessly violent, no-holds-barred war movie? How about a full-throttle soap opera featuring yards of fresh, nubile flesh? Well, look no farther. Here's a movie nasty enough to kill off most of the major characters and still manage a happy ending.

The ever-unsubtle Paul Verhoeven returns to the satiric excesses of ROBOCOP, starting with those campy FED NET propaganda commercials that suck the viewer right into the problem at hand: humanity is threatened by a race of smart, vicious, and practically unstoppable mutant bugs from space. Our hero is high school grad Johnny Rico (Casper Van Dien), who's head over heels over Carmen Ibanez (Denise Richards). But she's smarter than he is and headed for the Fleet Academy, where she plans to become a starship pilot. Rich-boy Johnny's wounded manhood leads him to the Mobile Infantry, trailed by lovelorn Dizzy Flores (Dina Meyer), who's willing to brave Sgt. Zim's (Clancy Brown) brutal training program for a shot at Johnny. Carmen throws Johnny over for flyboy Zander Barcalow (Patrick Muldoon) and the big bugs annihilate Johnny's hometown with a well-aimed asteroid.

Intricate plots aren't what draw people to movies about giant space bugs: they go for the sheer exhilaration of hearing the volume cranked up and seeing absolutely amazing bugs getting their innards blown all over space. The consummately self-conscious Verhoeven gives the audience all the unbridled, unexpurgated violence he thinks they crave, serves it up complete with Fascist imagery and a Neanderthal, kill 'em all mentality, and then dares anyone to enjoy it. You've been warned.

STARSKY & HUTCH

2004 97m c   Action/Comedy/Crime   ★★½

Riche-Ludwig Productions/Weed Road   PG-13
Pictures/Red Hour Productions/
Dimension/Warner Bros.   (U.S.)

Ben Stiller *(Detective David Starsky)*, Owen Wilson *(Detective Ken "Hutch" Hutchinson)*, Snoop Dogg *(Huggy Bear)*, Will Ferrell *(Big Earl—uncredited)*, Fred Williamson *(Captain Doby)*, Vince Vaughn *(Reese Feldman)*, Juliette Lewis *(Kitty)*, Jason Bateman *(Kevin)*, Amy Smart *(Holly)*, Carmen Electra *(Staci)*

p, William Blinn, Stuart Cornfield, Akiva Goldsman, Tony Ludwig, Alan Riche; d, Todd Phillips; w, Scot Armstrong (based on a story by Stevie Long and John O'Brien, based on characters created by William Blinn); ph, Barry Peterson; ed, Leslie Jones; m, Theodore Shapiro; prod d, Edward Verreaux; art d, Greg Papalia; fx, David D. Johnson, Mike Meinardus; cos, Louise Mingenbach

"Starsky and Hutch" helped refine the mix of action, wise-cracking, and intense male bonding between mismatched partners that made buddy-cop pictures what they are today. This feature ups the comedy, tones down the violence, and makes hay with the homoerotic subtext that prompted some to dub the original series the gayest thing in prime time.

By the book, second-generation Bay City detective David Starsky (Ben Stiller) is so irritating that he's run through 12 partners in four years. Malibu Ken Hutchinson (Owen Wilson)—"Hutch" to his friends—is so laid-back about rules that he supplements his income robbing bookies in Chinatown. Their antics have landed both on the personal blacklist of exasperated Captain Doby (Fred Williamson), so he makes them partners. A body in the bay and a tip from Hutch's flamboyant snitch, Huggy Bear (Snoop Dog), puts them on the trail of big-time cocaine dealer Reese Feldman (Vince Vaughn). Feldman and partner Kevin (Jason Bateman) are about to flood Bay City with a genetically altered form of coke. Starsky and Hutch's unorthodox attempts to get the goods on the drug lords, whom everyone believes are respectable businessmen, get them into further hot water.

Director/cowriter Todd Phillips's relatively clever conceit involves playing the dated material straight while subtly undermining it; the sappy '70s love songs that underscore the detectives' scenes together are a pretty good running gag. But Stiller's performance throws the whole enterprise out of whack—he's a grotesque mass of tics, twitches, and swaggering macho shoulder action—and too much of the script relies on smug, lazy strip-mining of second-rate pop-culture sources for no better reason that to give hipsters an opportunity to snicker at disco fashions.

STARTING OVER

1979 106m c   Romance/Comedy   ★★★½

Paramount   (U.S.)   R

Burt Reynolds *(Phil Potter)*, Jill Clayburgh *(Marilyn Hornberg)*, Candice Bergen *(Jessica Potter)*, Charles Durning *(Michael "Mickey" Potter)*, Frances Sternhagen *(Marva Potter)*, Austin Pendleton *(Paul)*, Mary Kay Place *(Marie)*, MacIntyre Dixon *(Dan Ryan)*, Jay O. Sanders *(Larry)*, Charles Kimbrough *(Salesman)*

p, Alan J. Pakula, James L. Brooks; d, Alan J. Pakula; w, James L. Brooks (based on the novel by Dan Wakefield); ph, Sven Nykvist (Movielab Color); ed, Marion Rothman; m, Marvin Hamlisch; prod d, George Jenkins; cos, John Boxer

AAN Best Actress: Jill Clayburgh; AAN Best Supporting Actress: Candice Bergen

In perhaps his best performance, Burt Reynolds, cast here against type, stars as a lonely man whose wife leaves him to spread her wings and try to build a career as a singer-songwriter (although she exhibits a striking lack of talent). Stunned when she announces her desire for freedom, he goes to Boston where he is consoled by Durning and Sternhagen, a duo of relatives who also happen to be psychiatrists. At first Reynolds has no idea that in addition to yearning for freedom Bergen is having an affair with her boss. Struck by this new situation, Reynolds soon meets Clayburgh, a schoolteacher who shies away from any commitment. He also joins a divorced men's group, which provides some touching and funny moments. Reynolds shaved off his moustache for the film and with it went his hirsute, macho image; he presents instead a feeling and vulnerable man. Bergen's character is gently made fun of. In a very funny sequence, she sings her dreadful autobiographical songs in a caterwauling screech. While all of the acting is top-notch, Reynolds steals the show with his underplaying and understanding of the role. He has been quoted as saying, "It was very close to the story of my life," and his grasp of the character's emotions is evident from the start. Audiences like to see their heroes in familiar roles, however, and the film was not the great success its producers hoped for, although it grossed over $20 million on initial release. Brooks, the producer-screenwriter who came from the "Mary Tyler Moore Show," later went on to make a name for himself as a director-writer-producer with TERMS OF ENDEARMENT.

STARTUP.COM

2001 103m c   Documentary   ★★★

Noujaim Films/Pennebaker Hegedus Films   (U.S.)   R

Kaleil Isaza Tuzman, Tom Herman, Kenneth Austin, Tricia Burke, Roy Burston, David Camp, Jose Feliciano, Dora Glottman, Julian Herbstein, Christina Ortez

d, Chris Hegedus, Jehane Noujaim; ph, Jehane Noujaim; ed, Chris Hegedus, Jehane Noujaim, Erez Laufer

Ostensibly the rise-and-fall story of a fledgling Internet company, this timely documentary winds up being a sad illustration of the old adage that mixing business and friendship is an invitation to trouble.

Kaleil Isaza Tuzman and Tom Herman went to high school together and remained friends long after graduation; in 1999, they joined the ranks of online entrepreneurs with govWorks.com. The site sprang from a simple but enticing idea that quickly mushroomed into something more ambitious: a one-stop site where people would have easy access to a wide range of government services. Isaza Tuzman left a lucrative job at investment firm Goldman Sachs to seek his fortune online, providing the business acumen for the project, with Herman overseeing the technical side. Made by Isaza Tuzman's former roommate, Jehane Noujaim, and veteran documentary filmmaker Chris Hegedus, the film covers the period between May 1999 and December 2000, during which the company grew from a handful of employees to more than 200, blew through millions of dollars, and was beset by troubles: a mysterious break-in, competition from a rival site, technological failure, and a rift between Isaza Tuzman and Herman that led to the latter's ignominious ouster from the company he co-founded.

The intricacies of the business are duly chronicled, but they're eclipsed by the complicated relationship between Herman and Isaza Tuzman. And that's what elevates the film above TV news magazine level: the story of the business is historically interesting, but the story of a friendship tested to the breaking point is timeless. An ironic postscript: despite their bitter and public break, Isaza Tuzman and Herman subsequently went back into business together. They formed a company to help failing Internet-based companies negotiate the complicated legal and emotional terrain of bankruptcy.

STATE FAIR

1945 100m c Musical
Fox (U.S.)

Jeanne Crain *(Margy Frake)*, Dana Andrews *(Pat Gilbert)*, Dick Haymes *(Wayne Frake)*, Vivian Blaine *(Emily Joyce)*, Charles Winninger *(Abel Frake)*, Fay Bainter *(Melissa Frake)*, Donald Meek *(Hippenstahl)*, Frank McHugh *(McGee)*, Percy Kilbride *(Miller)*, Harry Morgan, billed as Henry Morgan *(Barker)*

p, William Perlberg; d, Walter Lang; w, Oscar Hammerstein II, Sonya Levien, Paul Green (based on the novel by Phil Stong); ph, Leon Shamroy (Technicolor); ed, J. Watson Webb; art d, Lyle Wheeler, Lewis Creber; fx, Fred Sersen

AAN Best Score (Musical): Charles Henderson, Alfred Newman; *AA Best Song:* "It Might as Well Be Spring"; Richard Rodgers (Music), Oscar Hammerstein II (Lyrics)

This second version of STATE FAIR improves on its predecessor of 1933. Oscar Hammerstein based his screenplay on the 1933 adaptation of Phil Stong's bucolic novel, and, with Richard Rodgers, contributed the score. The story is virtually the same, but the addition of the marvelous songs made the musical remake a smash. It's still pleasant mid-summer in Iowa, where Abel and Melissa Frake (Charles Winninger and Fay Bainter) are the parents of the teenage Margy (Jeanne Crain) and Wayne (Dick Haymes). Abel wants to enter his pig at the state fair and treats the porker like a king, lavishing more attention on the beast than his wife. Melissa is preparing her locally famous pickles and mincemeat, hoping to win a blue ribbon herself. At the fair, Wayne falls for Emily (Vivian Blaine), a dance-band singer, and Margy meets Pat (Dana Andrews), a newspaper reporter. After the obligatory romantic complications, Abel's pig hogs the show, Melissa's mincemeat is spiked with brandy and gets the judges tipsy enough to award her the prize, and the couples wind up happy. The story is as light as cotton candy, but everyone has such a good time and rural life seems so sweetly appealing that urbanites flocked to real state fairs after this movie was released.

STATE OF SIEGE

(ETAT DE SIEGE)
1972 120m c Political/Thriller ★★★½
Reggana/Cinema 10/Unidis/Euro Intl./Dieter Geissler PG
(France/U.S./Italy/West Germany)

Yves Montand *(Philip Michael Santore)*, Renato Salvatori *(Capt. Lopez)*, O.E. Hasse *(Carlos Ducas)*, Jacques Weber *(Hugo)*, Jean-Luc Bideau *(Este)*, Evangeline Peterson *(Mrs. Santore)*, Maurice Teynac *(Minister of Internal Security)*, Yvette Etievant *(Woman Senator)*, Harald Wolff *(Minister of Foreign Affairs)*, Nemesio Antunes *(President of the Republic)*

p, Jacques Perrin; d, Constantin Costa-Gavras; w, Franco Solinas, Constantin Costa-Gavras; ph, Pierre-William Glenn (Eastmancolor); ed, Francoise Bonnot; m, Mikis Theodorakis; prod d, Jacques D'Ovidio; art d, Jacques d'Ovidio

Taking aim at the repressive right-wing government of a Latin American country (a thinly veiled Uruguay) and the support it received from at least one employee of the U.S. Agency for International Development (AID), Costa-Gavras offers here another tightly knit political thriller along the lines of his Z, MISSING and THE CONFESSION. Set in the 1970s, STATE OF SEIGE chronicles the kidnaping of AID "traffic expert" Philip Santore (Yves Montand) by Tupamaro-like left-wing guerrillas who are determined to prove he is behind the introduction of sophisticated torture methods in their country and in others as well—an international criminal. As the guerrillas try to extract a confession from the wounded but cool Santore, the government's search begins to zero in on

their location, with tension mounting as the demand for a prisoner exchange is rejected by the government. When Santore confesses, his captors are left with the difficult decision of whether or not to execute him. Told mostly in flashback and allegedly based on the case of real-life AID officer Daniel Mitrione, STATE OF SIEGE was banned from the American Film Institute theater in Washington upon its release, its opponents arguing that it glorified assassination and was violently anti-American. Never one to pull political punches, Costa-Gavras delivers yet another impassioned, intensely dramatic indictment of the abuse of power.

STATE OF THE UNION

1948 124m bw Political ★★★★
Liberty (U.S.)

Spencer Tracy *(Grant Matthews)*, Katharine Hepburn *(Mary Matthews)*, Van Johnson *(Spike McManus)*, Angela Lansbury *(Kay Thorndyke)*, Adolphe Menjou *(Jim Conover)*, Lewis Stone *(Sam Thorndyke)*, Howard Smith *(Sam Parrish)*, Maidel Turner *(Lulubelle Alexander)*, Raymond Walburn *(Judge Alexander)*, Charles Dingle *(Bill Hardy)*

p, Frank Capra; d, Frank Capra; w, Anthony Veiller, Myles Connolly (based on the play by Howard Lindsay, Russel Crouse); ph, George Folsey; ed, William Hornbeck; m, Victor Young; art d, Cedric Gibbons, Urie McCleary; fx, A. Arnold Gillespie; cos, Irene

Spencer Tracy stars in this political drama as a millionaire aircraft manufacturer who is seeking the Republican presidential nomination. A party outsider, Tracy isn't given much of a chance to capture the nomination. Further, his personal life is not the kind most voters would find endearing. He has been separated from his wife, Hepburn, for some years, and is having an affair with Lansbury, a wealthy newspaper publisher. With Lansbury's newspapers supporting Tracy's candidacy, he could become a much more legitimate contender for the nomination. Still, his personal life needs to be set straight, so he asks Hepburn to return to him and pose as his loving wife during the campaign. Hepburn agrees but makes it clear that it will be on a temporary basis and that she won't stay beyond his election, if he ever gets the nomination. Tracy's campaign picks up steam and Menjou, a powerful political boss, gives Tracy his substantial support. Also joining the campaign is Johnson, a successful newspaperman who takes a leave from his job to serve as Tracy's publicist. Tracy had begun the campaign with strong convictions, but as the campaign grind continues and as the nomination becomes a very real possibility, he is soon making accommodations and compromises, most suggested to him by Lansbury and Menjou. Hepburn watches her husband alter his values to suit others, and she becomes upset by these developments. Her love for Tracy has started to return and she can't bear to see him sell out. At a dinner party, she tells him that she thinks his advisers are morally bankrupt and urges him to distance himself from them and to retain his own sense of values. Tracy is moved by Hepburn's words and then on a radio broadcast, announces to the listening audience that he is taking his name off the nominating slate because he feels he is not worthy of consideration on the voters' part. He then returns to Hepburn's open arms.

One of the joys of the Broadway hit upon which this film is based was that the authors changed the dialogue almost weekly to reflect what was happening in the news. In making the movie, the dialogue obviously was frozen, but many of the jokes and barbs were clearly aimed at events surrounding the 1948 presidential election pitting President Harry S. Truman against Republican challenger Thomas E. Dewey. The film was originally set to star Gary Cooper and Claudette Colbert, and when that casting fell through, Tracy was immediately picked for the male lead. Despite the fact that Hepburn had turned down the same role in the play, she was anxious to do it opposite Tracy in the film and a deal was struck. There was much tension on the set between Hepburn and Menjou. During this time the government had begun to investigate the Hollywood community, searching for communists, a practice Hepburn deplored and Menjou supported. This may have helped the picture, since the characters played by Hepburn and Menjou are adversaries throughout the film. The acting is first-rate as are the script, direction, and technical credits. Though it may seem somewhat dated to younger audiences, it remains an entertaining and uplifting movie experience.

STATE OF THINGS, THE
(DER STAND DER DINGE)
1982 121m bw Drama ★★★½
Gray City/VO Filmes/Road Movies
(U.S./Portugal/West Germany)

CAST OF "The Survivors:" Isabelle Weingarten *(Anna)*, Rebecca Pauly *(Joan)*, Jeffrey Kime *(Mark)*, Geoffrey Carey *(Robert)*, Camilla Mora *(Julia)*, Alexandra Auder *(Jane)*, CREW OF "The Survivors:" Patrick Bauchau *(Friedrich "Fritz" Munro—the Director)*, Paul Getty III *(Dennis—the Writer)*, Viva Auder *(Kate—the Scriptgirl)*, Samuel Fuller *(Joe Corby—the Cameraman)*

p, Chris Sievernich; d, Wim Wenders; w, Wim Wenders, Robert Kramer; ph, Henri Alekan, Fred Murphy; ed, Barbara von Weitershausen; m, Jurgen Knieper; prod d, Ze Branco; cos, Maria Gonzaga

Wim Wenders's THE STATE OF THINGS is a comically bleak look at the clash between the auteurist European filmmaking sensibility and the commercial Hollywood style, that mirrors its subject by being more of a private diary than a traditional narrative film.

German director Friedrich "Fritz" Munro (Patrick Bauchau) is in Portugal shooting his first American film, a low-budget science-fiction movie, when he learns that the company has run out of film. Fritz assures everyone that Gordon (Allen Garfield, billed here as Allen Goorwitz), the film's producer, will come through with more money, but in the meantime the production shuts down. Fritz soon travels to L.A. to look for Gordon. He eventually finds him hiding out in a huge mobile home, and goes inside to talk to him. As they drive through the night, Gordon explains that he's on the run from the loan sharks, who demanded their money back after they screened the film's rushes and saw that they were in black-and-white and that the film had no story.

THE STATE OF THINGS is a deeply personal work that came about as a result of the numerous interruptions of Wenders's trouble-plagued American debut HAMMETT (1982). While visiting friends in Lisbon who were working on Raul Ruiz's THE TERRITORY (1983), Wenders borrowed most of that film's cast and crew and decided to quickly improvise and shoot a film that would be a comment on his difficulties in Hollywood. The film's poetic black-and-white photography is starkly beautiful, and Wenders's use of sound and music is as impressive as ever, but the conditions under which the film was made accounts for its often self-indulgent, desultory quality, and the improvisations of the cast quickly become tiresome, apart from Samuel Fuller's robust performance as Fritz s grizzled Hollywood cameraman, and the mobile-home finale where Fritz rambles on about "life, death, images, and art," while Gordon completely ignores him and sings a morose little ditty about Hollywood (written by Goorwitz/Garfield himself). The film is an existential study of the nature of creativity (Fritz echoes Wenders's preference for atmosphere and mood over plot and structure), and what it feels like to be a stranger in a strange land (the L.A. scenes are shot like a sci-fi film, with alienated overhead shots of traffic, parking lots, fast-food restaurants and monolithic office buildings).

STATION AGENT, THE
2003 90m c Drama/Comedy ★★★½
SenArt Films/Next Wednesday (U.S.) R

Peter Dinklage *(Finbar McBride)*, Patricia Clarkson *(Olivia Harris)*, Bobby Cannavale *(Joe Oramas)*, Paul Benjamin *(Henry Styles)*, Raven Goodwin *(Cleo)*, John Slattery *(David)*, Michelle Williams *(Emily)*, Jase Blankfort *(Store Customer)*, Paula Garces *(Cashier)*, Josh Pais *(Carl)*

p, Robert May, Mary Jane Skalski, Kathryn Tucker; d, Tom McCarthy; w, Tom McCarthy; ph, Oliver Bokelberg; ed, Tom McArdle; m, Stephen Trask; prod d, John Paino; art d, Len X. Clayton; cos, Jeanne Dupont

Often the only thing worse than an actor who wants to direct is an actor who goes ahead and does it, but the first feature from actor turned writer/director Tom McCarthy is a sweet and genuinely quirky delight.

Dressed in a sharp black suit and standing only four feet five inches tall, Finbar McBride (Peter Dinklage) is bound to attract notice on Hoboken streets, but doesn't seem to care. The only thing Fin does care about is trains; he likes nothing more than poring over schedules and hanging around train yards. Fin's life takes an unexpected detour when a friend bequeaths him a decommissioned train depot in rural New Jersey. Fin packs a small bag and "walks the rails" to his new home where, without a phone or electricity, he intends to indulge his passion in peaceful isolation. But his first morning there, Fin finds the gregarious Joe (Bobby Cannavale) manning a snack truck in his parking lot; that afternoon, Fin is nearly run down—twice—by Olivia Harris (Patricia Clarkson), a painter who's retreated to her getaway house to escape her marriage and the pain of a terrible tragedy. Olivia nearly breaks through Fin's defensive shell but retreats into her own when her husband (John Slattery) suddenly reappears. Only Joe, a needy extrovert engaged in an unconditional love affair with life, can draw them together again.

This charmingly unassuming comedy won the Audience Award for Best Drama at the 2003 Sundance Film Festival, and there's an awful lot here for audiences to love; Cannavale in particular is a crowd-pleaser. With its quiet pacing and dry-as-a-bone wit, the film strongly recalls the deadpan comedies of Jim Jarmusch or early Hal Hartley, but McCarthy gradually reveals a welcome new sensibility that's all his own.

STAVISKY
1974 115m c Political/Biography ★★★½
Ariane/Cerita/Euro Intl. (France) PG

Jean-Paul Belmondo *(Serge Alexandre Stavisky)*, Charles Boyer *(Raoul)*, Francois Perier *(Borelli)*, Anny Duperey *(Arlette)*, Michel Lonsdale *(Mezy)*, Claude Rich *(Bonny)*, Marcel Cuvilier *(Bosseaud)*, Jacques Spiesser *(Granville)*, Gigi Balista *(Henriet)*, Roberto Bisacco *(Montalvo)*

d, Alain Resnais; w, Jorge Semprun; ph, Sacha Vierny *(Eastmancolor)*; ed, Albert Jurgenson; m, Stephen Sondheim

A fascinating true story of the man who almost brought down the French government. Serge Stavisky committed suicide on January 3, 1934. The Russian-born promoter had been involved with the issuance of phony bonds and several other crimes, but he had evidently been protected by officials in high places (he supposedly distributed millions of francs in bribes). When one of the officials was murdered, there were accusations that this man in the public prosecutor's office was silenced to keep from spilling the beans. Factions from all of the parties began stirring up trouble and claiming that it was due to the basic corruption in the elected government. Riots began on February 6-8, and a general strike was called. The government teetered and fell, then a new coalition was formed by people who had been outside of the Stavisky influence, and France went on. That's how it ended. How it all happened is the subject of the movie by Resnais, a different kind of film from the director who helmed LAST YEAR AT MARIENBAD and HIROSHIMA, MON AMOUR. The screenplay is by the man who wrote Z, so it is literate and has more than a bit of politics attached. Belmondo plays the title role, a small-time hustler who migrates to France, becomes an embezzler, and uses his personal charm and diabolical tactics to rise quickly to a place of economic importance with a rash of bold moves. Belmondo's wife is Duperey, who goes along with his machinations, and Boyer is a poor Spanish nobleman who dreams of stirring up a civil war in Spain and taking over after the current regime has been destroyed. The picture belongs to Belmondo, who oozes confidence as he makes his way up through the whirlpools of politics and emerges as the most powerful man in the country. Then, when it seems as though he's gone too far, all of his associates desert him and he is left with only one recourse, the taking of his own life. With that, he duplicates what his father did upon hearing that his son had been clapped in jail. The picture is technically brilliant, visually stunning, and ceaselessly interesting. But the hero is a villain without much to like, and audiences want someone to root for; thus, this movie did not make a great deal at the box office. Sondheim's music is a bit too intellectual for the emotions seen on-screen.

STEALING BEAUTY 📀
(LO BALLO DA SOLA)
1996 119m c   Romance/Drama   ★★½
Fiction Cinematografica/Recorded Picture   R
Company/UGC Images   (Italy/U.K./France)

Liv Tyler (Lucy Harmon), Jeremy Irons (Alex Parrish), Sinead Cusack (Diana Grayson), Carlo Cecchi (Carlo Lisca), Jean Marais (M. Guillaume), Donal McCann (Ian Grayson), D.W. Moffett (Richard Reed), Stefania Sandrelli (Noemi), Rachel Weisz (Miranda Fox), Joseph Fiennes (Christopher Fox)

p, Jeremy Thomas; d, Bernardo Bertolucci; w, Susan Minot (from a story by Bernardo Bertolucci); ph, Darius Khondji; ed, Pietro Scalia; m, Richard Hartley; prod d, Gianni Silvestri; art d, Domenico Sica; cos, Louise Stjernsward, Giorgio Armani

It's refreshing to see director Bernardo Bertolucci return to smaller-scale film making, but STEALING BEAUTY, the tale of a young girl's sexual awakening, lacks the artistic and political passion of his early work.

Following her mother's suicide, young American Lucy Harmon (Liv Tyler) travels to Tuscany for the summer, staying with her mother's friends Ian and Diana Grayson (Donal McCann and Sinead Cusack). She reads her mother's diaries, trying to figure out the identity of her biological father. Lucy spends her time posing for Ian and getting to know the other houseguests: Alex (Jeremy Irons), a terminally-ill playwright; Guillaume (Jean Marais), an elderly French art dealer; Miranda (Rachel Weisz), Diana's daughter from a previous marriage; Richard (D.W. Moffett), Diana's boyfriend; and Noemi (Stefania Sandrelli), an advice columnist. The assorted expatriates take an interest in Lucy's many dilemmas, particularly the teenager's desire to lose her virginity. By the end of the summer, Lucy has succeeded in both her aims.

STEALING BEAUTY's main problem is its screenplay, written by Bertolucci and novelist Susan Minot. The setting and structure of the drama invoke Chekhov, but the dialogue sounds pretentious, forcing the talented cast to struggle with poorly-written roles. Bertolucci keeps the images looking sumptuous throughout, although the endless parade of life, love, food, and beauty dulls the palate. The best-known actors, Irons and Marais, tend to overplay the

two potentially most moving parts. Tyler makes her Henry James-style heroine more appealing than she might have been; Cusack is given little to work with as Diana but hints at a great untold story behind her character; and McCann lends solidity to the role of Ian.

STEEL HELMET, THE
1951 84m bw War   ★★★★
Deputy   (U.S.)

Gene Evans (Sgt. Zack), Robert Hutton (Pvt. "Conchie" Bronte), Richard Loo (Sgt. "Buddahhead" Tanaka), Steve Brodie (Lt. Driscoll), James Edwards (Cpl."Medic" Thompson), Sid Melton (Joe, 2nd GI), Richard Monahan (Pvt. Baldy), William Chun ("Short Round"), Harold Fong (The Red), Neyle Morrow (1st GI)

p, Samuel Fuller; d, Samuel Fuller; w, Samuel Fuller; ph, Ernest Miller; ed, Philip Cahn; m, Paul Dunlap; art d, Theobold Holsopple; fx, Ben Southland, Ray Mercer; cos, Alfred Berke

Scripted in a week, shot in 10 days, and released only six months after the start of the Korean War, Sam Fuller's THE STEEL HELMET stands as one of the best films about that war or any war. Dark, violent, and disturbing, this film doesn't celebrate duty, honor, and heroism; it shows men simply trying to survive the madness. Evans, a wounded sergeant whose platoon has been wiped out, is saved from sniper fire by Chun, a South Korean orphan nicknamed "Short Round" (a name adopted by Steven Spielberg for his cute Asian kid in INDIANA JONES AND THE TEMPLE OF DOOM). With the kid tagging along, Evans meets up with a group of raw recruits, and agrees to lead them in exchange for a box of cigars. The tiny group then proceeds to an ancient Buddhist temple which is to be used as an army observation post. Before long, the Americans find themselves furiously besieged by the enemy.

THE STEEL HELMET is a film made for an audience tired of war. The world had welcomed home its battle-weary soldiers from WWII only five years before, and many were less than enthusiastic when another war—one neither so popular nor so ideologically clearcut—dragged men away again. This time the public wondered whether the bloodshed was necessary. THE STEEL HELMET reflects these doubts. Those soldiers who are not confused and scared are cold and cynical. The rules of this war are different from the last. The enemy looks exactly like the people the soldiers are supposed to be defending. A confused soldier asks Evans, "How do you tell a North Korean from a South Korean?" Evans replies, "If he's running with you he's a South Korean. If he's running after you he's a North Korean." Director Fuller emphasizes this confusion visually. The film is very claustrophobic (most of the action takes place on a single set) and the characters nearly always seem to be immersed in smoke and fog. Things are never what they seem. GI Monahan's snoring is mistaken for the whistle of incoming shells, Buddhist priests turn out to be North Korean soldiers in disguise, and Loo, the intelligent and brave South Korean soldier, isn't trusted by the American lieutenant. By the end of the film, the American soldiers who have survived are on the brink of madness. Fuller's final comment on the situation comes with the closing credit, which reads, "There is no end to this story." He spoke the truth: his movie became the model for nearly every Vietnam war film.

STEEL MAGNOLIAS 📀
1989 118m c   Comedy/Drama   ★★★
Rastar   (U.S.)   PG

Sally Field (M'Lynn Eatenton), Dolly Parton (Truvy Jones), Shirley MacLaine (Ouiser Boudreaux), Daryl Hannah (Annelle Dupuy Desoto), Olympia Dukakis (Clairee Belcher), Julia Roberts

(Shelby Eatenton Latcherie), Tom Skerritt *(Drum Eatenton),* Dylan McDermott *(Jackson Latcherie),* Kevin J. O'Connor *(Sammy Desoto),* Sam Shepard *(Spud Jones)*

p, Ray Stark; d, Herbert Ross; w, Robert Harling (based on his play); ph, John A. Alonzo; ed, Paul Hirsch; m, Georges Delerue; prod d, Gene Callahan, Edward Pisoni; art d, Hub Braden, Michael Okowita; chor, Spencer Henderson; cos, Julie Weiss

AAN Best Supporting Actress: Julia Roberts

Based on screenwriter Robert Harling's award-winning off-Broadway play, STEEL MAGNOLIAS tells the story of six southern women whose lives interconnect in a beauty parlor in their small Louisiana town. M'Lynn Eatenton (Sally Field), mother of headstrong Shelby (Julia Roberts), is worried about her daughter's upcoming marriage, fearing for the children that the diabetic, seizure-prone Shelby wants to have. Their friends at the beauty parlor—Truvy (Dolly Parton), who runs the parlor; Annelle (Daryl Hannah), her assistant; Clairee (Olympia Dukakis), an aristocratic widow; and Ouiser (Shirley MacLaine), the town scold—gossip and cope with a variety of problems, among them a failing marriage for Truvy, and some chameleonlike changes for Annelle. Shelby marries and has her baby, but just when things look rosy, tragedy rears its head. STEEL MAGNOLIAS is an old-fashioned "klatsch" film, a prefeminist relic in which a group of women eschew the public world of men in favor of the community of the coffee table. Their world is shown as inferior to men's in terms of power but superior to it in emotion and insight into the things that "really matter." Not surprisingly, the "klatscher" myth has been concocted largely by men (most notably by George Cukor). Here director Herbert Ross (TURNING POINT) gets generally strong performances from his ensemble, and an especially good one from Field in a role that really doesn't suit her. The film was shot on location in Natchitoches, Louisiana, hometown of actor-turned-writer Harling, who based his play on the experiences of his own mother and sister.

STELLA DALLAS   📀
1937 104m bw Drama   ★★★★
UA   (U.S.)

Barbara Stanwyck *(Stella Martin Dallas),* John Boles *(Stephen Dallas),* Anne Shirley *(Laurel Dallas),* Barbara O'Neil *(Helen Morrison),* Alan Hale *(Ed Munn),* Marjorie Main *(Mrs. Martin),* Edmund Elton *(Mr. Martin),* George Walcott *(Charlie Martin),* Gertrude Short *(Carrie Jenkins),* Tim Holt *(Richard)*

p, Samuel Goldwyn; d, King Vidor; w, Sarah Y. Mason, Victor Heerman (based on the novel by Olive Higgins Prouty and the play by Harry Wagstaff Gribble, Gertrude Purcell); ph, Rudolph Mate; ed, Sherman Todd; art d, Richard Day; cos, Omar Kiam

AAN Best Actress: Barbara Stanwyck; *AAN Best Supporting Actress:* Anne Shirley

Grand Vidor soap opera, boasting a brilliant Stanwyck performance. She's a tough cookie, a bit of a shrew and a grasping woman who snares Boles, a well-born young man whose family lost its old money when his father committed suicide. Boles has moved to a tiny New England town where he meets Stanwyck. He had been engaged to O'Neil, a woman of the same social level as himself, but when his fortune was lost he left, and she took up with another. Stanwyck is aware of his background from reading the tabloids. They have a daughter, but the difference in their classes continues to keep them distanced from one another. When Boles is offered a job in New York and asks Stanwyck to come with him, she fears being laughed at by his society friends, so he goes south and she stays in the mill town.

Stanwyck begins running around with the rough-hewn, hard-drinking friends of her youth but she remains a good mother, almost too good, as she lavishes love and affection on the child (played as an adult by Shirley). Hale would like to marry Stanwyck, but her life is devoted to her daughter. One day, while riding a train, Hale gets abusive and offends many of the townspeople, who associate him with Stanwyck and Shirley. When Shirley invites her friends to a birthday party, she and Stanwyck are snubbed in a particularly touching scene. Boles would like a divorce so he can wed O'Neil, a widow with two sons, but Stanwyck will not give her consent. Shirley and Stanwyck visit a posh resort on the strength of Boles's cash, and on this trip Stanwyck learns that her coarse behavior and garish clothing stand in the way of Shirley's happiness.

Despite unforgettable work in a slew of other films, Stanwyck was quoted as saying that this was the best acting she'd ever done and it remained her favorite role. Only 30 years old at the time of STELLA, she had to be aged considerably to look right as the mother of an adult daughter. The role demanded a vast range of emotion, and Stanwyck wrung every last smile and tear out of every speech. Even when she was simply reacting, Stanwyck emanated frustration channeled into maternal martyrdom, but without an ounce of self-pity. She is well-supported by Shirley and Hale, with John Boles his typical handsome if rather stolid self and Barbara O'Neill fine as the noble rich woman. The film was remade in 1990 as STELLA, with Bette Midler having some effective moments, with no help from anyone else.

STEPFATHER, THE
1987 90m c   Horror/Thriller   ★★★½
ITC   (U.S.)   R

Terry O'Quinn *(Jerry Blake, the Stepfather/Henry Morrison/Bill Hodgkins),* Jill Schoelen *(Stephanie Maine),* Shelley Hack *(Susan Blake),* Charles Lanyer *(Dr. Bondurant),* Stephen Shellen *(Jim Ogilvie),* Stephen Miller *(Al Brennan),* Robyn Stevan *(Karen),* Jeff Schultz *(Paul Baker),* Lindsay Bourne *(Art Teacher),* Anna Hagan *(Mrs. Leitner)*

p, Jay Benson; d, Joseph Ruben; w, Donald E. Westlake (based on a story by Carolyn Lefcourt, Brian Garfield, Westlake); ph, John Lindley; ed, George Bowers; m, Patrick Moraz; prod d, James William Newport; art d, David Willson; cos, Mina Mittleman

Just when it looked like slasher movies were wholly irredeemable, director Joseph Ruben came along to prove there is some intelligent life in this otherwise bereft subgenre. Featuring a fascinating script by novelist Donald Westlake, some taut direction, and an absolutely absorbing performance by Terry O'Quinn, THE STEPFATHER is not just another slice-and-dice thriller. Loosely based on a real-life case, the film begins in a picturesque suburb, where a rugged-looking, bearded man (O'Quinn) washes blood from his hands, cuts his hair, shaves, and changes clothes to emerge a completely different person. As he walks downstairs, we see that the man's entire family has been massacred. One year later, the man resurfaces as Jerry Blake—in a new suburb, with a new job, a new wife (Shelley Hack), and a teenage stepdaughter (Jill Schoelen). Gradually the secret madness and alternate lives of Jerry Blake begin to surface. THE STEPFATHER fits in nicely among such examinations of the seedy underbelly of "perfect" family life as Alfred Hitchcock's SHADOW OF A DOUBT and David Lynch's BLUE VELVET. Although the last part of the picture disintegrates into some typical slasher-movie conventions and a plethora of clumsy Hitchcock homages, the majority of the film is *definitely* not typical. Fueled by an intense and intricate performance by O'Quinn, the movie is a fascinating examination of America's predilection for appearances over substance. Jerry Blake is the consummate actor, masking his crazed state with an air of friendliness and easy charm, whose false veneer of bliss has been spoon-fed to his diseased mind via television. He wants the perfect TV family; but when reality rears its ugly head and day-to-day problems cannot be dealt with in a matter of minutes, his repressed rage erupts.

STEPFORD WIVES, THE

1975   114m   c   Science Fiction/Comedy   ★★½
Palomar/Fadsin   (U.S.)   PG

Katharine Ross *(Joanna)*, Paula Prentiss *(Bobby)*, Peter Masterson *(Walter)*, Nanette Newman *(Carol)*, Patrick O'Neal *(Dale Coba)*, Tina Louise *(Charmaine)*, Carol Rossen *(Dr. Fancher)*, William Prince *(Artist)*, Paula Trueman *(Welcome Wagon Lady)*, Remak Ramsay *(Atkinson)*

p, Edgar J. Scherick; d, Bryan Forbes; w, William Goldman (based on the novel by Ira Levin); ph, Owen Roizman (TVC Color); ed, Timothy Gee; m, Michael Small; prod d, Gene Callahan; fx, Dick Smith

Ira Levin is an eclectic writer who has done comedy-drama *(Sleuth)*, adventure *(The Boys from Brazil)*, thrillers *(Rosemary's Baby)*, and science fiction such as *The Stepford Wives*. But Goldman's screenplay and Forbes's ponderous direction slow his exciting novel to a laborious pace. Goldman, an often excellent writer, scripted BUTCH CASSIDY AND THE SUNDANCE KID, and Forbes proved himself with SEANCE ON A WET AFTERNOON, as well as many other films. So what happened here? The first hour takes what feels like two, and the last 44 minutes goes like an Indy car, so the pace is alternately a snail's and a Lamborghini's. Ross and her husband, Masterson, leave the hectic world of Manhattan and settle in the small, tranquil town of Stepford, Connecticut (actually shot in Westport). She meets the local wives, who seem weird to her, talking about dumb things and sounding like Procter & Gamble commercials. The two women who perplex her most are Louise and Newman (Forbes's wife in real life). They are perfect—they're devoted to their husbands, to keeping their homes squeaky clean, to having every hair in place, etc. This odd contentment gnaws at Ross. Her only normal friend is also a newcomer, Prentiss. O'Neal is the important man in the town and runs a men's club that Ross and Prentiss would like to know more about. After much palaver, the truth comes out. These women are not women at all, just flawlessly executed robot replicas of the real wives who came to Stepford, and who knows what's happened to the originals? The only difference is that these women never argue with their husbands, do everything that's asked of them, and fulfill every male chauvinist fantasy ever imagined. Ross would like to expose the truth once she learns it, but by that time it's too late. She and Prentiss are seen at the conclusion as two of a gaggle of Stepford Wives, happily exchanging recipes in the supermarket as they shop for their hubbies' favorite dishes. The film has more than a passing similarity to THE INVASION OF THE BODY SNATCHERS, although that was played totally serious and this has more than a few laughs, particularly when the wives are acting in their "whatever you want, darling" mode. With 15 minutes cut out of the opening 60, this would have been a whizzer.

STEPFORD WIVES, THE

2004   93m   c   Comedy/Thriller   ★½
Scott Rudin Productions/De Line Pictures/   PG-13
DreamWorks/Paramount   (U.S.)

Nicole Kidman *(Joanna Eberhart)*, Matthew Broderick *(Walter Kresby)*, Bette Midler *(Bobbie Markowitz)*, Glenn Close *(Claire Wellington)*, Christopher Walken *(Mike Wellington)*, Roger Bart *(Roger Bannister)*, David Marshall Grant *(Jerry Harmon)*, Jon Lovitz *(Dave Markowitz)*, Faith Hill *(Sarah Sunderson)*, Dylan Hartigan *(Peter Kresby)*

p, Donald De Line, Gabriel Grunfeld, Scott Rudin, Edgar Scherick; d, Frank Oz; w, Paul Rudnick (based on the novel by Ira Levin); ph, Rob Hahn; ed, Jay Rabinowitz; m, David Arnold; prod d, Jackson De Govia; art d, Peter Rogness; fx, Steve Kirshoff, Frank Petzold, Scott Souter, Phil Tippett; cos, Ann Roth

This sumptuous remake of THE STEPFORD WIVES replaces feminist paranoia with mild satirical jabs at Martha Stewart-inflected conformity, but shoots itself in the perfectly manicured foot by pretending that the novel's disturbing implications don't matter.

High-powered Manhattan TV exec Joanna Eberhart (Nicole Kidman) is fired after a humiliated contestant on one of her salacious reality shows goes murderously insane. While Joanna undergoes electroshock therapy for her subsequent nervous breakdown, her supportive, milquetoast husband, Walter Kresby (Matthew Broderick), buys a palatial home in gated Stepford, CT. Though self-appointed local social director Claire Wellington (Glenn Close) does her best to sell Joanna on the Stepford way of life, Joanna has trouble warming up to her vacuous, perfectly coiffed neighbors, whose days are a pastel flurry of shopping, cooking, cleaning, and even exercising in figure-hugging sun dresses, heels, and broad-brimmed hats. Joanna instead befriends kindred malcontents Bobbie Markowitz (Bette Midler), a frumpy, highly successful writer, and fabulously bitchy architect Roger Bannister (Roger Bart). After Roger changes overnight into a Log Cabin Republican like his politically ambitious partner (David Marshall Grant), Bobbie and Joanna get serious about figuring out what's going on in Stepford.

Repositioning Ira Levin's feminist-backlash thriller as a black comedy isn't a bad idea, just a difficult one. If you can't find a way to soften the story's bedrock conceit—the Stepford husbands are so threatened by independent women that they're willing to trade in their flesh-and-blood spouses for flawless fembots programmed to please—without thoroughly defanging it, you're sunk. Not surprisingly, the movie takes a desperately wrong turn about 45 minutes in, and you can almost hear the great sucking sound as the whole thing churns down the drain in a swirl of narrative contradictions.

STEPMOM

1998   124m   c   Drama   ★★
Wendy Finerman Production/1492 Production/   PG-13
Chris Columbus Production   (U.S.)

Susan Sarandon *(Jackie Harrison)*, Julia Roberts *(Isabel Kelly)*, Ed Harris *(Luke Harrison)*, Jena Malone *(Anna Harrison)*, Liam Aiken *(Ben Harrison)*, Lynn Whitfield *(Dr. Sweikert)*, Darrell Larson *(Duncan Samuels)*, Mary Louise Wilson *(School Counselor)*, Andre Blake *(Cooper)*, Russel Harper *(Photo Assistant)*

p, Wendy Finerman, Chris Columbus, Mark Radcliffe, Michael Barnathan; d, Chris Columbus; w, Gigi Levangie, Jessie Nelson, Steven Rogers, Karen Leigh Hopkins, Ron Bass; ph, Donald M. McAlpine; ed, Neil Travis; m, John Williams; prod d, Stuart Wurtzel; art d, Raymond Kluga; fx, Todd R. Wolfeil, Robert J. Scupp; cos, Joseph G. Aulisi

Don't expect any surprises from this lightweight drama with a heavyweight cast: the most impressive thing about it is that the actors manage to sound earnest while mouthing the most shameless cliches imaginable.

Workaholic lawyer Luke Harrison (Ed Harris) has just moved his glamorous photographer girlfriend Isabel (Julia Roberts) into his fabulous loft. The only problem: ex-wife Jackie, an earthy and devoted mom who takes issue with Isabel's parenting chops. Jackie and the kids—bratty preteen Anna (Jena Malone) and cute-as-a-button Ben (Liam Aiken)—resent Isabel's bumbling intrusion into their lives, but as weekend stepmothers go, pretty Isabel is no wicked witch: the worst that can be said is that she has punctuality issues.

This humdrum film virtually begs the audience to equate the stars with their characters, because there's really no other reason to care: these people don't even have trouble finding curbside parking in New York City. While trying to reinvent the melodramatic wheel, a slew of Hollywood screenwriters only succeed in making the flat premise even more trite and sentimental by giving Jackie a terminal illness. The not very enlightening insight beneath it all is that really nice people will be there for each other in times of trouble, and just in case you miss the point, they play "Ain't No Mountain High Enough," throw pillows, and tickle one another at significant junctures. That's Hollywood shorthand for bonding.

STERILE CUCKOO, THE

1969 108m c Romance/Comedy ★★★½
Boardwalk (U.S.) PG

Liza Minnelli *(Pookie)*, Wendell Burton *(Jerry)*, Tim McIntire *(Charlie Schumacher)*, Elizabeth Harrower *(Landlady)*, Austin Green *(Pookie's Father)*, Sandra Faison *(Nancy Putnam)*, Chris Bugbee *(Roe)*, Jawn McKinley *(Helen Upshaw)*, Fred Lerner, A. Frederick Gooseen

p, Alan J. Pakula; d, Alan J. Pakula; w, Alvin Sargent; ph, Milton Krasner (Technicolor); ed, Sam O'Steen, John W. Wheeler; m, Fred Karlin; art d, Roland Anderson; fx, Charles Spurgeon; cos, Jennifer Parsons, John A. Anderson

AAN Best Actress: Liza Minnelli; *AAN Best Original Song:* "Come Saturday Morning"; Fred Karlin (Music), Dory Previn (Lyrics)

Pakula's directorial debut, after he had produced pictures directed by his partner, Robert Mulligan, is thoroughly crafted. Unlike many first-timers (especially during the indulgent late '60s), Pakula uses understatement, avoids cinematic tricks, and carefully guides young stars Minnelli (who was nominated for an Oscar) and Burton, who was making his screen debut after starring on Broadway for three years in the title role of "You're a Good Man, Charlie Brown." Shot primarily at the Hamilton College campus in upstate New York, the film is a youth-oriented tearjerker that is just perceptive enough to transcend the genre.

Minnelli and Burton meet on a bus going up to school; her quirky behavior during the ride embarrasses him and he's relieved to discover that they're attending different colleges. He's a quiet young man studying etymology; she's a motherless waif with a neglectful father. Burton settles into his dorm room with slob McIntire, a beer-drinking boor and bore who talks endlessly of his sexual conquests, and is stunned when Minelli arrives and announces that she intends to spend the weekend. The strained relationship develops into romance, but the two have different expectations for the future.

Minnelli's boilerplate "lovable kook" is a matter of taste— Liza worshippers should swoon; others may wince. Burton, who seemed to disappear after his next picture, FORTUNE AND MEN'S EYES, is excellent. The syrupy theme song, "Come Saturday Morning" (Fred Karlin, Dory Previn), was a big hit for The Sandpipers.

STING, THE

1973 129m c Crime/Comedy ★★½
Richard D. Zanuck/David Brown (U.S.) PG

Paul Newman *(Henry Gondorff/Mr. Shaw)*, Robert Redford *(Johnny Hooker/Kelly)*, Robert Shaw *(Doyle Lonnegan)*, Charles Durning *(Lt. William Snyder)*, Ray Walston *(J.J. Singleton)*, Eileen Brennan *(Billie)*, Harold Gould *(Kid Twist)*, John Heffernan *(Eddie Niles)*, Dana Elcar *(FBI Agent Polk)*, Jack Kehoe *("Erie Kid")*

p, Tony Bill, Julia Phillips, Michael Phillips; d, George Roy Hill; w, David S. Ward; ph, Robert Surtees (Technicolor); ed, William Reynolds; m, Scott Joplin, John Philip Sousa; art d, Henry Bumstead; fx, Bob Warner, Albert Whitlock; cos, Edith Head

AA Best Picture; AAN Best Actor: Robert Redford; *AA Best Director:* George Roy Hill; *AA Best Original Story and Screenplay:* David S. Ward; *AAN Best Cinematography:* Robert Surtees; *AA Best Film Editing:* William Reynolds; *AA Best Song Score:* Marvin Hamlisch; *AA Best Art Direction-Set Decoration:* Henry Bumstead, James Payne; *AA Best Costume Design:* Edith Head; *AAN Best Sound:* Ronald K. Pierce, Robert Bertrand

Vastly overrated Crooks-R-Us—this time *you* wear the moustache, enhanced by fine period trappings and flavor. Ultimately empty stuff, but preferable to BUTCH CASSIDY.

By reuniting director George Roy Hill and actors Robert Redford and Paul Newman (BUTCH CASSIDY AND THE SUNDANCE KID), THE STING emerged an equally successful entertainment, outgrossing every other picture of the year. Frightening. The story begins in September, 1936, in Joliet, Illinois. The city is run by corrupt officials, and the numbers racket runs rampant. When two-bit drifter Redford and his partner, Robert Earl Jones, the veteran bunco artist of the area, con one of the racketeers out of a $5,000 delivery, they find themselves mixed up with the big boys in Chicago and their head man, Shaw, a sleazy gangster who would gladly kill a drifter like Redford to retain control of his operation. Police lieutenant Durning shakes down Redford, who has already gambled away most of the money, threatening to kill him if he doesn't pay it back. Jones, who has decided to retire from the con game and get into a legitimate business is killed by two of Shaw's thugs. On the run from Joliet police and Shaw's goons, Redford heads for Chicago to meet a friend of Jones, a man described as "the greatest con artist of them all," Newman. Determined to avenge the murder of Jones, Redford makes plans to "sting" Shaw out of a fortune. Newman, a drunk who lives in backroom squalor in a joint run by Brennan, is wary of hooking up with the still inexperienced Redford. Newman is, however, finally convinced, and they set the gears into motion.

Much of the film's success is a result of its visual brilliance: the aged look of Surtees' photography evokes a feeling of nostalgia, and the art direction, set decoration, and costuming are equally effective. Marvin Hamlisch did a fine job of adapting Scott Joplin's classic rags, especially "The Entertainer," which was soon a radio commonplace and sparked a renewed interest in the composer.

STIR OF ECHOES, A

1999 110m c Horror/Thriller/Drama ★★★½
Hofflund/Polone (U.S.) R

Kevin Bacon *(Tom)*, Illeana Douglas *(Lisa)*, Kevin Dunn *(Frank)*, Zachary David Cope *(Jake)*, Kathryn Erbe *(Maggie)*, Conor O'Farrell *(Harry)*, Lusia Strus *(Sheila)*, Stephen Eugene Walker *(Bobby)*, Mary Kay Cook *(Vanessa)*, Larry Neumann Jr. *(Lenny)*

p, Gavin Polone, Judy Hofflund; d, David Koepp; w, David Koepp (based on the novel by Richard Matheson); ph, Fred Murphy; ed, Jill Savitt; m, James Newton Howard; prod d, Nelson Coates; art d, David Krummel; fx, John Milinac, Casey Cannon, Van Ling; cos, Leesa Evans

Ignore the inevitable, unflattering comparisons to THE SIXTH SENSE, even though both films revolve around a youngster who sees dead people. THE SIXTH SENSE may have the boffo twist ending, but on a sustained level, this is by far the better film and features what has to be one of the creepiest first half-hours in recent film history.

Tom Witzkey (Kevin Bacon), his devoted wife, Maggie (Kathryn Erbe), and their precocious son, Jake (Zachary

David Cope), have recently moved into a house in a solid, working-class Chicago neighborhood, and Maggie is pregnant again. The trouble begins innocuously enough; there's a party, drinking, and an argument about hypnosis between Maggie's college-educated sister (Illeana Douglas) and the down-to-earth Tom. On a dare, he allows her to hypnotize him, and she leaves behind a post-hypnotic suggestion that he be more open-minded. Unfortunately, his mind is suddenly an open door, and all manner of spooky things step through, whispering and afflicting Tom with terrifying visions. More unsettlingly, Tom realizes that little Jake hears them too, and always has. Tom's awakening ends with a truly chilling apparition; it's almost a relief when the story shifts into lower gear as Tom realizes that he's getting a message about some long-buried wrong and swears to find out what it is.

Bacon gives a fine, affecting performance, and Cope is a genuinely likable child actor; you'd love to protect Jake from the dead and their oppressive needs. Working from a novel by sci-fi legend Richard Matheson, writer-turned-director David Koepp has fashioned a scary, intelligent thriller that remains haunting long after it's over.

STOLEN CHILDREN, THE
(IL LADRO DI BAMBINI)
1992 108m c Drama   ★★★★
Erre Produzioni/Alia Film/Arena Films/Vega Film
(Italy/France/Switzerland)

Enrico Lo Verso (Antonio), Valentina Scalici (Rosetta), Giuseppe Ieracitano (Luciano), Florence Darel (Martine), Marina Golovine (Nathalie), Fabio Alessandrini (Grignani), Agnostino Zumbo (Priest At Children's Home), Vincenzo Peluso (Neopolitan Carabiniere), Maria Pia Di Giovanni (Mother), Vitalba Andrea (Antonio's Sister)

p, Angelo Rizzoli, Stefano Munafo; d, Gianni Amelio; w, Gianni Amelio, Sandro Petraglia, Stefano Rulli (from a story by Rulli, Petraglia and Amelio); ph, Tonino Nardi, Renato Tafuri; ed, Simona Paggi; m, Franco Piersanti; art d, Andrea Crisanti, Giuseppe M. Gaudino

Inspired by a newspaper article about a woman who prostituted her eight-year-old daughter, this rigorous, immensely affecting portrait of a pair of emotionally damaged children marks an entirely successful revival of Italian neorealist filmmaking.

In a Milan slum, a woman (Maria Pia Di Giovanni) is arrested for prostituting her eleven-year-old daughter Rosetta (Valentina Scalici). Emotionally stunted Antonio (Enrico Lo Verso), a shy, 25-year-old *carabiniere*, and his partner Grigani (Fabio Alessandrini) are ordered to deliver the sullen, rebellious Rosetta and her brother Luciano (Giuseppe Ieracitano) to a Catholic orphanage in northern Italy. Grigani abandons the group to visit his girlfriend in Bologna and Antonio and the children are turned away from the orphanage. The trio head south on a three-day trip, mostly by train, to a home for troubled children in Sicily. En route, the children begin to shed their defenses and Antonio becomes increasingly attached to them, even though he knows he must soon turn them over to the authorities.

With a background in socially conscious Italian TV movies, director Gianni Amelio made STOLEN CHILDREN in what he terms a "naked" style, improvising on the script, shooting in unadorned, unpicturesque locations and casting several non-professional performers, including the two extraordinary children. The straightforward, linear narrative takes its time in getting beneath the skin of the characters, in a manner that recalls the documentary-like 1940s classics of Roberto Rossellini and, perhaps most closely, de Sica's 1949 THE BICYCLE THIEF. Though the film has a deep, cumulative emotional pull, it offers no solutions to the problems

encountered: the power of STOLEN CHILDREN lies in its unsettled, unfinished quality.

STOLEN KISSES   📀
(BAISERS VOLES)
1968 90m c Romance/Comedy   ★★★★
Carrosse/Artistes (France)   R

Jean-Pierre Leaud (Antoine Doinel), Delphine Seyrig (Fabienne Tabard), Michel Lonsdale (M. Tabard), Claude Jade (Christine Darbon), Harry-Max (M. Henri Tabard), Daniel Ceccaldi (M. Darbon), Claire Duhamel (Mme. Darbon), Catherine Lutz (Mme. Catherine), Andre Falcon (M. Blady), Paul Pavel (Julien)

p, Marcel Berbert; d, Francois Truffaut; w, Francois Truffaut, Bernard Revon, Claude de Givray; ph, Denys Clerval (Eastmancolor); ed, Agnes Guillemot; m, Antoine Duhamel; art d, Claude Pignot

AAN Best Foreign Language Film

Sadly complacent comedy of French charm, and Paris was never so beguiling. STOLEN KISSES covers the installment in the life of Antoine Doinel (Jean-Pierre Leaud), which began in THE 400 BLOWS and continued through the LOVE AT TWENTY episode entitled "Antoine and Colette." The film picks up as Doinel is discharged from the army at age 20. Unable to make Christine (Claude Jade) love him, he continues his search for the perfect woman. In the process Doinel lands a job with a detective agency, where the rookie Sherlock Holmes bungles every case he investigates. He finally gets a simple assignment in a shoe store after demonstrating his "technical proficiency" by wrapping a shoe box. Doinel is supposed to discover why the store's owner, M. Tabard (Michel Lonsdale), feels hated and whether there is a conspiracy against him; but while working late one night, he begins an affair with Tabard's wife, Fabienne (Delphine Seyrig). Dismissed, as Truffaut's work often is, as overly charming and simplistic, STOLEN KISSES was oddly enough made during a time of extremely intense political crisis in Paris, with a sidebar of artistic controversy. Dedicated to Henri Langlois and his Cinematheque Francaise, STOLEN KISSES was made while Truffaut worked with a defense committee that fought for the reinstatement of the Cinematheque director. Langlois, who in his lifetime was probably responsible for the film education of every aspiring director in France, was ordered removed by Minister of Culture Andre Malraux—a move met with opposition by the entire international film community. Truffaut stated, "If STOLEN KISSES is good, it will be thanks to Langlois." As violence erupted in the streets of Paris, Truffaut continued his filming, but, instead of making the political film one might expect to emerge from a period of revolt, the director chose to reaffirm his belief in cinema.

STORMY MONDAY   📀
1988 93m c Crime/Romance   ★★★½
British Screen/Film Four/Moving Picture (U.K.) R

Melanie Griffith (Kate), Tommy Lee Jones (Cosmo), Sting (Finney), Sean Bean (Brendan), James Cosmo, Mark Long, Brian Lewis, Derek Hoxby, Heathcote Williams, Prunella Gee

p, Nigel Stafford-Clark; d, Mike Figgis; w, Mike Figgis; ph, Roger Deakins (Rank/Agfa Color); ed, David Martin; m, Mike Figgis; prod d, Andrew McAlpine; cos, Sandy Powell

This feature debut from British writer-director-composer Mike Figgis is a tautly constructed, deftly executed crime thriller. The action is set in Newcastle, England, an economically depressed city desperate for jobs. American business magnate-gangster, Cosmo (Tommy Lee Jones), is launching an ambitious money-laundering scheme by buying up lots of real estate.

One man refuses all of Jones's lucrative offers: Finney (Sting), the owner of a successful jazz club. Caught up in the conflict are Kate (Melanie Griffith), an American who has worked for Cosmo as a call girl, and Brendan (Sean Bean), a young jazz enthusiast. When two thugs from London are hired to "persuade" Finney to sell his club, he turns the tables and sends the head assassin back to London with a broken arm. But Cosmo escalates the violence. STORMY MONDAY draws its strength from subtle shadings of character and a vivid evocation of its setting, Newcastle. The little violent action there is takes place either very quickly or offscreen. Figgis's moody realization of the screenplay is quietly effective and brimming with visual nuance and irony—particularly in its perceptive take on the contradictions of the global economy.

STORMY WEATHER

1943 77m bw Musical ★★★½
Fox (U.S.)

Lena Horne *(Selina Rogers)*, Bill Robinson *(Corky)*, Cab Calloway and His Band, Fats Waller, The Nicholas Brothers *(Themselves)*, Ada Brown *(Ada)*, Dooley Wilson *(Gabe)*, Ned Stanfield, Johnny Horace *(The Shadracks)*, Emmett "Babe" Wallace *(Chick Bailey)*

p, William LeBaron; d, Andrew L. Stone; w, Frederick Jackson, Ted Koehler, H.S. Kraft (based on a story by Jerry Horwin, Seymour B. Robinson); ph, Leon Shamroy; ed, James B. Clark; art d, James Basevi, Joseph C. Wright; fx, Fred Sersen; chor, Clarence Robinson; cos, Helen Rose

Because it contains performances by many of the great black musical stars of its day, STORMY WEATHER will be studied for years to come. The slim story into which the acts are incorporated concerns veteran entertainer Corky (Bill Robinson), who, as he reflects on his career, flashes back to a number of scenes that are all neat musical bits in themselves. (A few were later released as short subjects in black theaters.) Corky's struggles and rise in show business, as well as his split and eventual reconciliation with his wife (Lena Horne), are thinly sketched, with a cavalcade of musical numbers in between. Cab Calloway, Fats Waller, Robinson, Horne, Mae Johnson, The Nicholas Brothers, Babe Wallace, Ada Brown, and many others are featured; about the only cast member who doesn't perform is Dooley Wilson, whose singing was so important in CASABLANCA. Horne, who had just completed CABIN IN THE SKY, was 26, making the 65-year-old Robinson old enough to be her grandfather, not her husband, but the discrepancy is overlooked. Jazz fans will recognize Zutty Singleton at the drums, Coleman Hawkins playing sax, and Taps Miller on trumpet, among several others.

STORY OF A CHEAT, THE

(LE ROMAN D'UN TRICHEUR)
1936 83m bw Drama ★★★★½
Cineas (France)

Sacha Guitry *(The Cheat)*, Jacqueline Delubac *(Young Woman)*, Rosine Derean *(The Jewel Thief)*, Marguerite Moreno *(The Countess)*, Pauline Carton *(Mme. Morlot)*, Gaston Dupray *(Waiter)*, Serge Grave *(The Cheat)*, Pierre Assy *(The Cheat)*, Frehel *(Singer)*, Henri Pfeifer *(M. Charbonnier)*

d, Sacha Guitry; w, Sacha Guitry (based on his novel *Memoires D'un Tricheur*); ph, Marcel Lucien; ed, Myriam; m, Adolphe Borchard

An exciting, funny, innovative, and brilliant effort from one of France's most prolific playwrights and filmmakers, Sacha Guitry. Considered to be Guitry's masterpiece, THE STORY OF A CHEAT is told to the audience by the cheat (Guitry, as usual, playing the role) himself, as he writes his memoirs in a Parisian cafe, while on the screen we see the events he is speaking of, acted out without dialogue. All we get to hear is Guitry's witty commentary. His life story begins with the first time he is caught being a cheat, an act which gets him sent to his room without supper. In a stroke of luck, however, his entire family eat poison mushrooms that evening and die. Thus begins a long string of events in which Guitry benefits from his cheating instead of paying for it. Not only is the film itself unique, with its cutting back and forth between past and present and its use of reverse motion and wipes, but its title sequence is also exceptional. Like Francois Truffaut's FAHRENHEIT 451, the credits are spoken by the director, but here we see the characters and filmmakers involved. Not surprisingly, his experimentation and humor have gone on to influence greatly those who've seen the picture, especially the filmmakers of the New Wave. It was chiefly the favorable criticism of filmmakers such as Truffaut, Jean-Luc Godard, and Alain Resnais (who cited THE STORY OF A CHEAT as one of the primary influences of HIROSHIMA MON AMOUR) that have brought about the reassessment of Guitry. An outstanding contribution to cinematic and narrative technique which Guitry never quite equaled again.

STORY OF A THREE DAY PASS, THE

(LA PERMISSION)
1967 87m bw Drama ★★★½
OPERA (France)

Harry Baird *(Turner)*, Nicole Berger *(Miriam)*, Christian Marin *(Hotelman)*, Pierre Doris *(Peasant)*, Hal Brav, Tria French

p, Guy Belfond; d, Melvin Van Peebles; w, Melvin Van Peebles; ph, Michel Kelber; ed, Liliane Korb; m, Mickey Baker, Melvin Van Peebles

An impressive first feature from Melvin Van Peebles has a black American soldier, Baird, stationed in France and visiting Paris on a three-day pass. He meets and falls for a French girl, Berger, and together they spend his last two days living a poetically romantic existence. Upon his return, he is demoted by his captain for having dated a white girl. The film is a moving and brutally honest achievement from Van Peebles, who moved to Paris after living in San Francisco, Mexico, and Holland. He started in Paris (without knowing the language) as an author, eventually writing in French and becoming eligible for admission to the French Cinema Center as a director. He then applied for a grant and received $70,000 after expecting no more than $10,000. With a completed film, Van Peebles went back to the U.S. as a French filmmaker, confusing and surprising everyone when they learned he was actually a black American. Actress Berger, who also appeared in Francois Truffaut's SHOOT THE PIANO PLAYER, was killed just a short time after completing this picture.

STORY OF ADELE H., THE

(L'HISTOIRE D'ADELE H.)
1975 97m c Biography ★★★★
Carrosse/Artistes (France) PG

Isabelle Adjani *(Adele Hugo)*, Bruce Robinson *(Lt. Albert Pinson)*, Sylvia Marriott *(Mrs. Saunders)*, Reubin Dorey *(Mr. Saunders)*, Joseph Blatchley *(Mr. Whistler)*, M. White *(Col. White)*, Carl Hathwell *(Lt. Pinson's Batman)*, Ivry Gitlis *(Hypnotist)*, Cecil De Sausmarez *(Mr. Lenoir)*, Raymond Falla *(Judge Johnstone)*

p, Marcel Berbert; d, Francois Truffaut; w, Francois Truffaut, Jean Gruault, Suzanne Schiffman, Jan Dawson (based on the book *Le Journal d'Adele Hugo* by Frances V. Guille); ph, Nestor Almendros

(Eastmancolor); ed, Yann Dedet; m, Maurice Jaubert; art d, Jean-Pierre Kohut-Svelko; cos, Jacqueline Guyot

AAN Best Actress: Isabelle Adjani

Truffaut's hauntingly poetic tale of obsession stars the beautiful Isabelle Adjani as Adele Hugo, daughter of France's most beloved author, Victor Hugo. The picture opens in Halifax, Nova Scotia, in 1863, after Adele has left her father's Guernsey home to seek out Albert Pinson (Bruce Robinson), a young English lieutenant who wants nothing to do with the determined young woman. Although her obsession with Pinson grows to the point that she announces to her father a pending engagement, Adele's only real contact with him is from a distance—spying on him while he makes love to another woman, or following him (or those she believes to be him) in the streets. Adele is obsessed not only with the lieutenant, but also with her own writing, paying frequent visits to a local bookstore to buy reams of paper and then retreating to her room to scrawl indecipherable coded messages in her journal.

One of Truffaut's most complex films, a love story that shows only one half of an affair, this film combines the fascination with obsessive women that fills his films (Catherine from JULES AND JIM, Julie Kohler from THE BRIDE WORE BLACK, Camille Bliss from SUCH A GORGEOUS KID LIKE ME) with his love of books, diaries and the process of writing (FAHRENHEIT 451 and THE WILD CHILD). The true story of Adele Hugo is already engrossing; unable to live up to her father's expectations, she thought she could not fill the void in his heart after his favorite daughter, Leopoldine, drowned. Truffaut's disturbing film on the subject is as difficult to walk away from as it is to watch.

STORY OF ALEXANDER GRAHAM BELL, THE
1939 97m   bw   Biography   ★★★½
Fox   (U.S.)

Don Ameche *(Alexander Graham Bell)*, Loretta Young *(Mrs. Bell)*, Henry Fonda *(Tom Watson)*, Charles Coburn *(Gardner Hubbard)*, Spring Byington *(Mrs. Hubbard)*, Gene Lockhart *(Thomas Sanders)*, Sally Blane *(Gertrude Hubbard)*, Polly Ann Young *(Grace Hubbard)*, Georgiana Young *(Berta Hubbard)*, Bobs Watson *(George Sanders)*

p, Kenneth MacGowan; d, Irving Cummings; w, Lamar Trotti (based on a story by Ray Harris); ph, Leon Shamroy; ed, Walter Thompson; cos, Royer

THE STORY OF ALEXANDER GRAHAM BELL is the film for which Don Ameche will be best remembered, despite his Oscar-winning performance in COCOON more than 40 years later. The film opens in 1873 with Alexander Graham Bell (Ameche) trying to earn his living by working with deaf-mutes while spending his off-hours inventing. Bell is soon enamored of a pretty young Scot (Loretta Young) whom he has been asked to teach. They fall in love, and she asks her father to unbuckle his copious money belt to back one of Bell's inventions. Bell hopes to perfect a process whereby he can use the same kind of wires Western Union uses for sending dots and dashes to transmit the sound of a human voice. After much trial and error, he succeeds and, in doing so, becomes one of the most famous inventors in history. Not even remotely factual, this Hollywood-invented story is an enjoyable feature nonetheless, especially when the boyish and earnest Ameche is onscreen.

STORY OF ESTHER COSTELLO, THE
1957 103m   bw   Drama   ★★★★
Romulus/Valiant   (U.K.)

Joan Crawford *(Margaret Landi)*, Rossano Brazzi *(Carlo Landi)*, Heather Sears *(Esther Costello)*, Lee Patterson *(Harry Grant)*,

Ron Randell *(Frank Wenzel)*, Fay Compton *(Mother Superior)*, John Loder *(Paul Marchant)*, Denis O'Dea *(Father Devlin)*, Sidney James *(Ryan)*, Bessie Love *(Matron in Art Gallery)*

p, Jack Clayton, David Miller; d, David Miller; w, Charles Kaufman (based on the novel by Nicholas Monsarrat); ph, Robert Krasker; ed, Ralph Kemplen; m, Georges Auric; art d, George Provis, Tony Masters; cos, Jean Louis

A powerful if sometimes seamy look at a problem more famously dealt with in THE MIRACLE WORKER. Crawford is a wealthy American, estranged from her husband, who is visiting her birthplace in Ireland when she meets Sears, a young girl who is deaf, blind, and mute as a result of psychological trauma. Since there is no specialized medical service in her small town, Sears' condition has remained untreated. At the urging of a local priest, the childless Crawford decides to take Sears into her life as a surrogate daughter. After much struggle and many years, the girl begins to respond to treatment. Then Brazzi, Crawford's ex, reappears. From Crawford, he wants money; from Sears—now grown to young womanhood—he wants something else.

It's more melodramatic than THE MIRACLE WORKER, and the focus is as much on the people around the girl as the girl herself. Crawford showed off her acting range in familiar melo territory, and the result was a Best Actress Award from the British Film Academy. A strong story, good acting, and a most literate script from Charles Kaufman, who also wrote the screenplay for FREUD.

STORY OF G.I. JOE, THE   📀
1945 109m   bw   Biography/War   ★★★★
UA   (U.S.)

Burgess Meredith *(Ernie Pyle)*, Robert Mitchum *(Lt. Walker)*, Freddie Steele *(Sgt. Warnicki)*, Wally Cassell *(Pvt. Dondaro)*, Jimmy Lloyd *(Pvt. Spencer)*, Jack Reilly *(Pvt. Murphy)*, William Murphy *(Pvt. Mew)*, William Self *(Cookie Henderson)*, Dick Rich *(Sergeant at Showers)*, Billy Benedict *(Whitey)*

p, Lester Cowan; d, William A. Wellman; w, Leopold Atlas, Guy Endore, Philip Stevenson (based on the book by Ernie Pyle); ph, Russell Metty; ed, Otho Lovering, Al Joseph; m, Ann Ronell, Louis Applebaum; art d, James Sullivan, David Hall

AAN Best Supporting Actor: Robert Mitchum; *AAN Best Screenplay:* Leopold Atlas, Guy Endore, Philip Stevenson; *AAN Best Song:* "Linda"; Ann Ronell; *AAN Best Score (Drama or Comedy):* Louis Applebaum, Ann Ronell

This story of the greatest of America's WWII combat correspondents, Ernie Pyle, immortalizes the man who celebrated the common soldier in his dispatches and books *(Brave Men* and *Here Is Your War)*. As the film begins, Pyle (Burgess Meredith) catches up with a tired platoon of infantrymen in Italy, observing and comforting them as they fight through town after town, enduring death, misery, boredom, and fear. Leading the platoon is Lt. Walker (Robert Mitchum), a tough but likable officer who is respected and admired by his men. The film has no real story, only the consistent wearing down of the men through combat and fatigue. Meredith is superb, conveying the humanity and caring of Pyle, but it is Mitchum, in a star-making performance, who steals the show. This great picture had the full cooperation of Pyle, who was killed in the South Pacific before seeing THE STORY OF G.I. JOE.

STORY OF LOUIS PASTEUR, THE
1936 85m   bw   Biography   ★★★★
Warner Bros.   (U.S.)

Paul Muni *(Louis Pasteur)*, Josephine Hutchinson *(Mme. Pasteur)*, Anita Louise *(Annette Pasteur)*, Donald Woods *(Jean Martel)*, Fritz Leiber *(Dr. Charbonnet)*, Henry O'Neill *(Roux)*,

Porter Hall *(Dr. Rosignol)*, Raymond Brown *(Dr. Radisse)*, Akim Tamiroff *(Dr. Zaranoff)*, Walter Kingsford *(Napoleon III)*

p, Henry Blanke; d, William Dieterle; w, Sheridan Gibney, Pierre Collings (based on the story by Gibney, Collings); ph, Tony Gaudio; ed, Ralph Dawson; art d, Robert Haas; cos, Milo Anderson

AAN Best Picture; AA Best Actor: Paul Muni; *AA Best Original Story:* Pierre Collings, Sheridan Gibney; *AA Best Screenplay:* Pierre Collings, Sheridan Gibney

This film biography stars Paul Muni as Louis Pasteur, the French scientist who worked to find a cure for anthrax and hydrophobia. His colleagues at the Medical Academy are convinced his experiments are a waste of time and ridicule his research, so he and his family move to the French countryside, where he can conduct his experiments in peace. Authorities soon learn that the sheep in Pasteur's area are disease-free as a result of his efforts, a finding which causes some stir in the Medical Academy, as Pasteur is now praised for his groundbreaking work by his former critics. THE STORY OF LOUIS PASTEUR is well told, with an intelligent script, excellent performances, and careful attention to scientific accuracy. Muni offers a fine characterization that shows the famed scientist as a man faced with extraordinary obstacles.

STORY OF QIU JU, THE
(QIU JU DA GUANSI)
1992 114m c Comedy/Drama/Political ★★★★
Sil-Metropole Organization/Beijing Film PG
Academy-Youth Film Studio (China/Hong Kong)

Gong Li *(Wan Qiu Ju)*, Lei Laosheng *(Wan Shantung—Village Head)*, Liu Peiqi *(Wan Qing Lai—Husband)*, Yang Liuchun *(Meizi)*, Ge Zhijun *(Officer Li)*, Zhu Qanqing, Cui Luowen, Yang Huiqin, Wang Jianfa, Lin Zi

p, Ma Fung-kwok; d, Zhang Yimou; w, Liu Heng (from the novel *The Wan Family's Lawsuit* by Chen Yuanbin); ph, Chi Xiaoling, Yu Xiaoqun; ed, Du Yuan; m, Zhao Jiping; art d, Cao Jiuping

Preeminent Chinese director Zhang Yimou ventures onto contemporary terrain for the first time with this lovingly detailed, gently satirical tale of a country woman's campaign to seek redress for a minor grievance. Star Gong Li delivers a meticulously scaled performance in a daringly unglamorous role.

Qiu Ju (Gong Li) is a pregnant farm laborer driven to seek justice when the village elder, Shantung (Lei Laosheng), kicks her husband (Liu Peiqi) in the groin after the husband has mocked the elder over his inability to sire a son. After being assured by the village apothecary that her husband is not permanently damaged, Qiu Ju demands an apology from the culprit. Shantung dismisses her semi-articulate request, moving Qiu Ju to visit the local magistrate, Officer Li (Ge Zhijun). Li acts as a mediator between the two parties, suggesting that Shantung pay 200 yuan for lost labor and medical expenses. Shantung agrees, but refuses to apologize; he further insults Qiu Ju by throwing the money on the ground so she will have to bow to him to pick it up. Qiu Ju's crusade then leads her far from her village, through increasingly labyrinthine bureaucracies, developing a momentum of its own that eventually proves disastrous for one of the characters.

Using real settings and, in some cases, real people interacting spontaneously with Gong Li as a hidden camera records the action, Zhang gives his film a distinctly documentary feel. Yet much of QIU JU plays almost like a Preston Sturges farce in which an ordinary person's quest for justice is taken to comical extremes. Along the way, Zhang provides a rich, lively tapestry of modern Chinese daily life and a powerful warning about what can happen when the traditional process of saving face is neglected.

STORY OF THE WEEPING CAMEL, THE *DVD*
(DIE GESCHICHTE VOM WEINENDEN KAMEL)
2004 90m c Drama/Documentary ★★★
Hochschule für Fernsehen und Film München/ PG
FilmFernsehFonds Bayern (Mongolia/Germany)

Odgerel Ayusch *(Odgoo)*, Ikhbayar Amgaabazar *(Ikchee)*, Uuganbaatar Ikhbayar *(Ugna)*, Enkhbulgan Ikhbayar *(Dude)*, Guntbaatar Ikhbayar *(Guntee)*, Zeveljamz Nyam *(Grandmother Zevel)*, Amgaabazar Gonson *(Grandfather Amgaa)*, Chimed Ohin *(Great-Grandmother Chimed)*, Janchiv Ayurzana *(Great-Grandfather Janchiv)*, Munkhbayar Lhagvaa *(Violin Teacher)*

p, Natalie Lambsdorff, Evi Stangassinger; d, Byambasuren Davaa, Luigi Falorni; w, Luigi Falorni, Byambasuren Davaa (based on an idea by Davaa and Batbayar Davgador); ph, Luigi Falorni; ed, Anja Pohl

AAN Best Documentary Feature

A newborn camel is rejected by its mother and a Mongolian herding family scrambles to rectify the situation in Byambasuren Davaa and Luigi Falorni's debut feature that's part ethnographic study, part fable.

Odgoo and Ikchee share three yurts (traditional animal-skin tents) with their parents, grandparents, and children—sons Dude, Ugna, and Guntee, a toddler. Their camp is some 30 miles from the nearest settlement, and they live in close proximity to the animals whose milk and wool sustain them. During calving season, everything goes well until one young camel undergoes an unusually arduous labor and wants nothing to do with the gangly, mewling creature she delivers. Family members try to bottle feed the white calf while searching for a solution to the fractured bond between the animals.

Inspired by the films of Robert Flaherty, who combined pure documentary footage with staged sequences, the filmmakers recruited a real multigenerational family of nomadic herders and recorded their daily lives in the harsh Gobi desert while improvising a preconceived story. While not as aggressively anthropomorphized as such vintage Disney family fare as CHARLIE, THE LONESOME COUGAR, Davaa and Falorni's film does suggest that camels have inner lives as rich and complicated as the human beings with whom they live in such intimate proximity. But they're also wholly camels, matted, goopy-eyed, gritty with sand, and quick to knee an adorable calf in the snout when its demands become annoying.

STORY OF VERNON AND IRENE CASTLE, THE
1939 90m bw Musical/Biography ★★★½
RKO (U.S.)

Fred Astaire *(Vernon Castle)*, Ginger Rogers *(Irene Castle)*, Edna May Oliver *(Maggie Sutton)*, Walter Brennan *(Walter Ash)*, Lew Fields *(Himself)*, Etienne Girardot *(Papa Aubel)*, Janet Beecher *(Mrs. Foote)*, Rolfe Sedan *(Emile Aubel)*, Leonid Kinskey *(Artist)*, Robert Strange *(Dr. Foote)*

p, George Haight, Pandro S. Berman; d, H.C. Potter; w, Richard Sherman, Oscar Hammerstein II, Dorothy Yost (based on the books *My Husband* and *My Memories of Vernon Castle* by Irene Castle); ph, Robert de Grasse; ed, William Hamilton; art d, Van Nest Polglase, Perry Ferguson; fx, Vernon L. Walker, Douglas Travers; chor, Hermes Pan; cos, Walter Plunkett, Edward Stevenson, Irene Castle

This fine film biography of the title beloved dance team was Ginger Rogers and Fred Astaire's final film together for RKO. (Astaire and Rogers teamed once again a decade later, in MGM's THE BARKLEYS OF BROADWAY, but the magic of their pairing had largely fled.) After Irene Foote (Rogers), the daughter of a well-known New Rochelle physician, meets vaudeville performer Vernon Castle (Astaire), they fall in love, marry, go to Paris, and become a famous ballroom dancing duo. Soon all the world wants to be like the Castles: not only do they invent several dance steps, but her hair is duplicated in wigs, cigars are named after him, and they have their own line of cosmetics. During WWI, Vernon becomes a pilot with the Canadian Royal Flying Corps, while Irene works on the silent film PATRIA by herself. He sends for her to join him in Texas, where he has a huge romantic reunion planned, including an orchestra to play for them alone. All does not go as planned, however, and sudden tragedy strikes the Castles.

The fact that the real Vernon Castle was British didn't enter into matters; Astaire was not required to mimic an English accent because hardly anyone had ever heard the famed dancer speak. The details of the team's meteoric rise to stardom are sketchily intertwined among the many songs in the score, with Edna May Oliver providing supporting highlights as the agent who had faith in the happy-couple and pushed hard to make them stars. The real Irene Castle (upon whose books the film is based) served as technical advisor, and the dancing re-creates the Castles' original steps with little in the way of alteration by Astaire and choreographer Hermes Pan. The score contains a tremendous number of songs, and it's a tribute to the talents of musical director Victor Baravalle, who died before the film was released, that they feel right and never seem crammed in for their own sake. Astaire and Rogers are both in very fine form, and if the final image of their ghosts dancing down a path comes across as exceptionally moving, it's because this film is as much a farewell to this amazing duo as it is to the characters they play onscreen.

STORY OF WOMEN

1988 110m c Drama ★★★
MK2/Camelia/La Sept/La Sofica Sofinergie/A2
(France)

Isabelle Huppert *(Marie)*, Francois Cluzet *(Paul)*, Niels Tavernier *(Lucien)*, Marie Trintignant *(Lulu/Lucie)*, Louis Ducreux, Michel Beaune, Dominique Blanc, Marie Bunel

p, Marin Karmitz; d, Claude Chabrol; w, Colo Tavernier O'Hagan, Claude Chabrol (based on *Une Affaire de Femmes* by Francis Szpiner); ph, Jean Rabier; ed, Monique Fardoulis; m, Matthieu Chabrol

In a German-occupied French village in 1941, Marie (Isabelle Huppert) struggles to eke out an existence for herself and two children, then begins supporting her family in style by performing amateur abortions. Her husband, Paul (Francois Cluzet), whom Marie grows to despise, returns from the war a broken man, but when her affair with a young collaborator (Nils Tavernier) becomes increasingly overt, Paul turns informer, and Marie finds herself standing trial in Paris for her "crime against the state."

Loosely based on the life of Marie-Louise Giraud, an actual abortionist who was executed by the Vichy government, this absorbing account of a dark period in French history is technically impressive on every level. Chabrol's economical control of cinematic narrative, as usual, stands him in good stead, lending his depiction of the nightmare of the Occupation the kind of melodramatic tension that is his specialty. STORY OF WOMEN unfolds with inexorable logic, though it is too schematic in conception to achieve real tragic power. Huppert (who took the best actress award at the 1988 Venice Film Festival for her performance here) remains stoically in character throughout, daring viewers to sympathize with her cool demeanor, but even her fine work is not enough to overcome the problems in the script.

STORYTELLING

2001 87m c Comedy ★★★
Good Machine/Killer Films (U.S.) R

"Fiction": Selma Blair *(Vi)*, Leo Fitzpatrick *(Marcus)*, Robert Wisdom *(Mr. Gary Scott)*, "Nonfiction": Paul Giamatti *(Toby Oxman)*, Mark Webber *(Scooby Livingston)*, John Goodman *(Marty Livingston)*, Julie Hagerty *(Fern Livingston)*, Franka Potente *(Toby's Editor)*, Noah Fleiss *(Brady Livingston)*, Lupe Ontiveros *(Consuelo)*

p, Ted Hope, Christine Vachon; d, Todd Solondz; w, Todd Solondz; ph, Frederick Elmes; ed, Alan Oxman; m, Belle & Sebastian, Nathan Larson; prod d, James Chinlund; art d, Judy Rhee; fx, Drew Jiritano; cos, John Dunn

In what often feels like a self-consciously reactive diatribe, writer-director Todd Solondz furthers his contentious relationship with audiences and insensitive critics with this typically provocative two-part picture. As the title suggests, the subject is storytelling; specifically, the problems the teller faces once the cord is cut and the story becomes audience property.

In "Fiction," white college student Vi (Selma Blair) learns about intentional fallacy the hard way when she turns a scary sexual encounter with her black writing professor (Robert Wisdom) into a short story. Her professor points out that regardless of the "truth" of the matter, it's now fiction, and subject to the ruthless criticism of her deeply offended classmates. In "Nonfiction," aspiring documentarian Toby Oxman (Paul Giamatti, looking quite a bit like Solondz himself) attempts to capture the reality of contemporary teenage life by following sweet-natured slacker Scooby Livingston (Mark Webber) with a video camera. To the horror of his upwardly mobile, upper-middle-class parents (John Goodman, Julie Hagerty), Scooby has few ambitions beyond getting high, and his on-camera observations are often unintentionally hilarious. Toby's producer (Franka Potente) thinks Toby's making fun of his subject; Toby, hardly a man of personal conviction, suggests leaving it up to a test audience to decide.

How this far less focused story ties into "Fiction" isn't entirely clear until the very end, when the snarky laughter of Toby's test audience turns his bad sociological documentary into a cruel comedy. Neither Toby nor Vi nor Solondz, for that matter, has much control over how their art is received. The film is all a little Lit Crit 101 and full of hurt finger pointing, but it's well played and often very funny. But beware: Solondz uses humor as a booby trap, so be careful what you laugh at.

STRAIGHT STORY, THE

1999 111m c Drama ★★★★
Straight Story, Inc. (U.S.) G

Richard Farnsworth *(Alvin Straight)*, Sissy Spacek *(Rose Straight)*, Harry Dean Stanton *(Lyle Straight)*, Everett McGill *(Tom, the John Deere Dealer)*, John Farley *(Thorvald)*, Kevin Farley *(Harald)*, Jane Galloway Heitz *(Dorothy)*, Joseph A. Carpenter *(Bud)*, Donald Wiegert *(Sig)*, Jennifer Edwards-Hughes *(Brenda)*

p, Mary Sweeney, Neal Edelstein; d, David Lynch; w, John Roach, Mary Sweeney; ph, Freddie Francis; ed, Mary Sweeney; m, Angelo Badalamenti; prod d, Jack Fisk; fx, Gary D'Amico; cos, Patricia Norris

AAN Best Actor: Richard Farnsworth

Could this heartfelt, unabashedly sentimental family drama really have been directed by David Lynch, the man who introduced sadomasochism to the cineplex with BLUE VELVET and brought incest and teenage prostitution rings to TV with *Twin Peaks*? Oddly, this uncharacteristic offering from a director whose name evokes a very particular kind of film—call it postmodern American gothic—is also one of his best.

It's based on the true story of Alvin Straight, a 73-year-old widower who, in 1994, traveled 240 miles from his home in Larens, Iowa, to reconcile with his ailing brother in Blue River, Wisconsin. On a lawnmower. Denied a driver's license because of poor eyesight, Straight rigged up his 1966 lawn tractor with a homemade trailer and hit the road for a six-week, five-mph odyssey. Lynch turns Straight's odd trek into a warm meditation on aging, embracing both the wisdom life experience brings and the sadness of remembering that your failing body was once young.

Central to the film's gentle strength is Richard Farnsworth's Alvin—stubborn, but grounded in a quiet, salt-of-the-Earth dignity—and Sissy Spacek's performance as his daughter Rose, who builds birdhouses and harbors a deep sadness of her own. So much of the film resembles Lynch's earlier work (the opening scene could have been an alternate take from BLUE VELVET) that it's hard not to marvel at the complete lack of menacing irony. People are still pretty strange, but there's no pestilence festering under the green lawns of Larens, and foreboding grain elevators only hum with an unearthly, low-end frequency because it's harvest time. Here, the highway's double-yellow lines no longer lead into darkness and an uncertain future, but to family and a reconciliation with the past.

STRAIGHT TIME
1978 114m c   Crime   ★★★★
First Artists/Sweetwall   (U.S.)   R

Dustin Hoffman (*Max Dembo*), Theresa Russell (*Jenny Mercer*), Harry Dean Stanton (*Jerry Schue*), Gary Busey (*Willy Darin*), M. Emmet Walsh (*Earl Frank*), Sandy Baron (*Manny*), Kathy Bates (*Selma Darin*), Edward Bunker (*Mickey*), Fran Ryan (*Cafe Owner*), Rita Taggart (*Carol Schue*)

p, Stanley Beck, Tim Zinnemann; d, Ulu Grosbard; w, Alvin Sargent, Edward Bunker, Jeffrey Boam (based on the novel *No Beast So Fierce* by Bunker); ph, Owen Roizman (Technicolor); ed, Sam O'Steen, Randy Roberts; m, David Shire; prod d, Stephen Grimes; art d, Richard Lawrence; cos, Bernie Pollack

A gripping, disturbing, and unglamorized portrait of a professional thief who thrives on the thrill and danger of his actions. Hoffman, in one of the best performances of his career, plays a thief who is released from prison after a six-year sentence for armed robbery. Hoffman tries to go straight but is continually thwarted by slimy parole officer Walsh, as well as his old friends, a motley assortment of junkies and small-time hoods.

Based on ex-convict Edward Bunker's novel *No Beast So Fierce*, STRAIGHT TIME was an obsessive labor of love for its star, who had purchased the rights to the novel in 1972. Hoffman struck a deal with First Artists that would give him the right to direct the film and supervise the final cut. To research his role Hoffman had himself booked at Los Angeles County Jail and went through the procedure all inmates go through (this was later re-created for the film in documentary-like fashion). Hoffman also sneaked into San Quentin prison and mingled with the prisoners for several hours incognito to get the feel of prison life. The actor also interviewed ex-cons and visited their homes. During production, however, Hoffman found that acting and directing were too much for him, so he hired his old friend Grosbard to take over the helm. When the filming was completed, First Artists president Phil Feldman took control of the film and refused Hoffman his right to final cut (Feldman was the same man who tampered with Sam Peckinpah's THE WILD BUNCH, cutting over 20 minutes of character development behind the director's back). Hoffman sued for damages. The studio, which thought the film was a disaster, dumped the movie into release, where it received bad reviews and little box office attention. Hoffman's case was thrown out, and to this day the actor speaks little of it. But Hoffman has nothing to be ashamed of. STRAIGHT

TIME is a powerful film that shows a criminal as he is. The film has no tired explanations for Hoffman's behavior, no fingers are pointed, no apologies or excuses are offered. Hoffman is a habitual criminal and that is the way he is. Though the parole system is taken to task for the "Catch 22"-type restrictions given to ex-cons, this is not presented as an excuse for Hoffman's return to crime—only a match that ignites the fuse already inside the man. The performances in STRAIGHT TIME are nothing less than superb. Walsh is perfect as the slimy parole officer who couldn't care less about his charges. Busey once again proves his versatility and is unforgettable as the pathetic addict. Russell is fine as the naive girl willing to let Hoffman drift through her life, and Stanton practically steals the film as the ex-thief yearning to escape from the boredom of his suburban lifestyle. Grosbard's direction is straightforward and professional. A highlight is the electrifying scene of a jewelry store robbery.

STRANGE DAYS   DVD
1995 145m c   Science Fiction/Thriller/Drama ★★½
First Light/Lightstorm Entertainment   (U.S.)   R

Ralph Fiennes (*Lenny Nero*), Angela Bassett (*Lornette "Mace" Mason*), Juliette Lewis (*Faith Justin*), Tom Sizemore (*Max Peltier*), Michael Wincott (*Philo Gant*), Vincent D'Onofrio (*Burton Steckler*), Glenn Plummer (*Jeriko One*), Brigitte Bako (*Iris*), Richard Edson (*Tick*), William Fichtner (*Dwayne Engelman*)

p, James Cameron, Steven-Charles Jaffe; d, Kathryn Bigelow; w, James Cameron, Jay Cocks (from a story by James Cameron); ph, Matthew F. Leonetti; ed, Howard Smith; m, Graeme Revell; prod d, Lilly Kilvert; art d, John Warnke; fx, Terry Frazee, James Lima, Digital Domain, Michael "Tony" Meagher; cos, Ellen Mirojnick

Despite its high-tech trappings, slick surfaces and relentless self-reflexivity, Kathryn Bigelow's STRANGE DAYS is shopworn pulp. Though executed with superior style and showy performances, it fails to realize the potential of its premise.

In the last days of 1999, former vice cop Lenny Nero (Ralph Fiennes) prowls a chaotic Los Angeles dealing illegal "clips." These are contraband recordings of sensory experiences made directly from the brains of individuals equipped with the Superconducting Quantum Interference Device (SQUID), a device easily secreted under a hat or hairpiece. A principled pusher, Lenny refuses to deal in "snuff" clips. He uses the forbidden technology himself to relive his own happier days with Faith Justin (Juliette Lewis) who has since become a rising pop star under the control of menacing promoter Philo Gant (Michael Wincott). Lenny keeps tabs on Faith through his friend Max Peltier (Tom Sizemore), a former cop turned bodyguard. In turn, Lenny's friend Lornette "Mace" Mason (Angela Bassett), a formidable security specialist, keeps a protective eye on him. He'll need it: before long, Lenny and Mace are swept up in a murder conspiracy that threatens to bring about a racial apocalypse.

A cultural by-product of the videotaped beating of black motorist Rodney King by L.A. police, the film seems a calculated attempt to restore the audience's faith in (white) police authority. Bigelow's decision to let authority off the hook eliminated any possibility that STRANGE DAYS could make a meaningful statement about the racial, social, and economic meaning of the Rodney King beating and the subsequent L.A. riots. There's nothing here about how American society actually *works* as the end of the 20th century approaches. What's left is pure sensation and visually stylish pyrotechnics. There's very little at stake; the generic elements function as a template for empty virtuosity.

STRANGE LOVE OF MARTHA IVERS, THE

1946 116m bw Crime ★★★★
Paramount (U.S.)

Barbara Stanwyck *(Martha Ivers)*, Van Heflin *(Sam Masterson)*, Lizabeth Scott *(Toni Marachek)*, Kirk Douglas *(Walter O'Neil)*, Judith Anderson *(Mrs. Ivers)*, Roman Bohnen *(Mr. O'Neil)*, Darryl Hickman *(Sam Masterson as a Boy)*, Janis Wilson *(Martha Ivers as a Girl)*, Ann Doran *(Secretary)*, Frank Orth *(Hotel Clerk)*

p, Hal B. Wallis; d, Lewis Milestone; w, Robert Rossen (based on the story "Love Lies Bleeding" by Jack Patrick); ph, Victor Milner; ed, Archie Marshek; m, Miklos Rozsa; art d, Hans Dreier, John Meehan; fx, Farciot Edouart; cos, Edith Head

AAN Best Original Story: Jack Patrick

A dark and perverse melodrama which stars Stanwyck as the wicked Martha Ivers, a wealthy and powerful woman who has gained control of the small town of Iverstown, Pennsylvania, after inheriting a large family fortune. She lives with her weakling husband Walter (Douglas, in his first film), a district attorney who is preparing to make a bid for mayor. What no one in the town knows, however, is that Martha and Walter share a deep secret—as a young girl, Martha murdered her aunt while planning to elope with then-sweetheart Sam Masterson. In order to protect the family name, an innocent man was executed for the crime. After a long absence, Sam (Heflin) returns to Iverstown. The couple fear that he is preparing to blackmail them, but their paranoia only makes him more curious about Martha's childhood secret. A cruel *film noir* which, although it starts somewhat slowly, builds to a frenzied state of suspense in which the characters, all of them vile, have a perverse hold over one another. The result is an often gripping film which shows the collaborative efforts of such talents as Wallis, Milestone, Rossen, Rozsa, art director Hans Dreier, and costumer Edith Head. This film also includes among its credits four future directors: screenwriter Rossen, Kirk Douglas, assistant director Robert Aldrich, and, as a bit player, Blake Edwards.

STRANGER, THE

1946 95m bw Thriller/War ★★★★
International Pictures (U.S.)

Edward G. Robinson *(Wilson)*, Loretta Young *(Mary Longstreet)*, Orson Welles *(Prof. Charles Rankin/Franz Kindler)*, Philip Merivale *(Judge Longstreet)*, Richard Long *(Noah Longstreet)*, Byron Keith *(Dr. Jeff Lawrence)*, Billy House *(Potter)*, Konstantin Shayne *(Konrad Meinike)*, Martha Wentworth *(Sara)*, Isabel O'Madigan *(Mrs. Lawrence)*

p, Sam Spiegel; d, Orson Welles; w, Anthony Veiller, John Huston (uncredited), Orson Welles (based on the story by Victor Trivas, Decla Dunning); ph, Russell Metty; ed, Ernest Nims; m, Bronislau Kaper; art d, Perry Ferguson; cos, Michael Woulfe

AAN Best Original Story: Victor Trivas

After having made three commercial disasters in a row (THE MAGNIFICENT AMBERSONS; JOURNEY INTO FEAR; and IT'S ALL TRUE), Orson Welles was badly in need of a hit that would right him in the eyes of Hollywood. The result was THE STRANGER, the most restrained and conventional of Welles's films, but still a thrilling entertainment. Set shortly after WWII, the film casts Edward G. Robinson as Wilson, a Nazi hunter assigned the task of finding the infamous Franz Kindler, one of the architects of the genocide of the Jews. Wilson traces Kindler to the sleepy college town of Hartford, Connecticut, where he comes to suspect that Prof. Charles Rankin (Welles) is actually Kindler hiding behind a new identity. Although Rankin does a fine job of casting doubt on Wilson's suspicions, the latter's dogged pursuit of the truth wins out and Kindler is exposed. In THE STRANGER, Welles gives us one of the cinema's most realistic and chilling portrayals of a Nazi. His Franz Kindler is not a cartoon character in uniform spouting propaganda and clicking his heels, but an arrogant, cynical, amoral, and wholly self-confident creature who believes that he is superior to anyone he meets—evil incarnate. Robinson is also quite good as the hunter determined to catch his prey. Technically, as one expects with Welles, the film is superb. THE STRANGER is not as wildly creative as his other films, but all the Welles trademarks are present, including superior lighting, inventive camera angles, strong transitions, and characters silhouetted in darkness.

STRANGER ON THE THIRD FLOOR

1940 64m bw Crime ★★★★
RKO (U.S.)

Peter Lorre *(Stranger)*, John McGuire *(Michael Ward)*, Margaret Tallichet *(Jane)*, Charles Waldron *(District Attorney)*, Elisha Cook Jr. *(Joe Briggs)*, Charles Halton *(Meng)*, Ethel Griffies *(Mrs. Kane)*, Cliff Clark *(Martin)*, Oscar O'Shea *(Judge)*, Alec Craig *(Defense Attorney)*

p, Lee Marcus; d, Boris Ingster; w, Frank Partos; ph, Nicholas Musuraca; ed, Harry Marker; m, Roy Webb; art d, Van Nest Polglase; fx, Vernon L. Walker

This extremely weird B movie has been hailed as the first true *film noir*, and it certainly has all the *noir* elements, both visual and thematic. Feeling guilty because his eyewitness testimony has sent a man who could be innocent to the electric chair, reporter Michael Ward (McGuire) returns to his apartment in a state of depression. On the stairs he notices an odd-looking little man wearing a white scarf (Lorre) loitering in the building and chases him off. In his room, the reporter realizes that his nosy next door neighbor, Mr. Meng (Halton), isn't doing his usual loud snoring. Tired and upset, Michael wonders if Meng is dead and recalls the several nasty, and public, run-ins he has had with the man. Falling asleep, Michael has a nightmare where he is wrongly accused of his neighbor's murder and is sentenced to die in the electric chair. Upon awakening, Michael checks on Meng and to his horror, finds the man murdered. Arrested for the crime, Michael must rely on his fiance, Jane (Tallichet), to track down the mysterious man in the white scarf.

First-time director Boris Ingster, cinematographer Nicholas Musuraca, and art director Van Nest Polglase created a frightening, claustrophobic, and nightmarish urban environment ruled by indifference, injustice, and moral corruption. The forces of order (the police, district attorney, juries, judges, and institutions) are the true villains here as they quickly and carelessly dispense judgement on citizens. Lorre's killer is obviously mad (an escaped mental patient), but in his brief screen time he is seen to be a sympathetic victim of harsh and thoughtless treatment (he describes being held in a straight-jacket and doused with ice-water). Ingster's direction shows the heavy influence of the Germanic expressionist films of the 1920s and the film is a visual delight. He never again directed anything nearly as interesting or influential as this nearly forgotten B picture.

STRANGER THAN PARADISE

1984 95m bw Drama ★★★★
Grokenberger/ZDF/Cinesthesia (U.S./West Germany) R

John Lurie *(Willie)*, Eszter Balint *(Eva)*, Richard Edson *(Eddie)*, Cecilia Stark *(Aunt Lottie)*, Danny Rosen *(Billy)*, Rammellzee *(Man with Money)*, Tom Docillo *(Airline Agent)*, Richard Boes *(Factory Worker)*, Rockets Redglare, Harvey Perr p, Sara Driver; d, Jim Jarmusch; w, Jim Jarmusch; ph, Tom DiCillo; ed, Jim Jarmusch, Melody London; m, John Lurie, Aaron Picht

A bleak but mordantly funny portrait of three aimless characters who discover that "paradise" isn't such an easy place to find. Displaying a hip formalism, Jim Jarmusch's second feature (his first, 1980's PERMANENT VACATION, received scant exposure) is divided into three distinct sections; individual sequences within each section are presented in one sustained take, and are separated by blackouts. The first finds Willie (John Lurie, of Lounge Lizard renown), a Hungarian emigre and self-styled hipster, living in a stark, dreary section of New York City. Willie's day-to-day existence is interrupted when his relatives ask him to house his young female cousin, Eva (Eszter Balint), upon her arrival from the old country. Willie dutifully, but reluctantly, obliges. Eva, however, is anything but a helpless foreigner and promptly goes about her own business. Still, when she departs 10 days later, a strange affection has developed between them.

In the second section, Willie and his buddy Eddie (Richard Edson) decide to head for Cleveland in the dead of winter to visit Eva, who now lives there with her irritable Aunt Lotte (Cecilia Stark). Once again, the characters do little of import together, spending their time staring at TV and visiting Lake Erie. In the third and final section, the trio abandons the frozen north for Florida, where they check into an empty seaside motel and the boys squander most of their money at the dog races. Then Eva suddenly comes into a huge stash of loot.

Although STRANGER THAN PARADISE's premise is inarguably slight, Jarmusch compensates for it with the sheer stylishness of the film. Fortunately, he also transcends the obvious theme of alienation, fashioning instead an ironic comedy about communication and the lack thereof. The film received the Camera d'Or at the 1984 Cannes Film Festival and was cited as best picture of the year by the National Society of Film Critics. Jarmusch went on direct such films as MYSTERY TRAIN, NIGHT ON EARTH and DEAD MAN.

STRANGERS KISS

1984 93m c/bw Romance ★★★★
Kill (U.S.) R

Peter Coyote *(Stanley, the Director)*, Victoria Tennant *(Carol Redding/Betty)*, Blaine Novak *(Stevie Blake/Billy)*, Dan Shor *(Farris, the Producer)*, Richard Romanus *(Frank Silva)*, Linda Kerridge *(Shirley)*, Carlos Palomino *(Estoban)*, Vincent Palmieri *(Scandelli)*, Jay Rasumny *(Jimmy)*, Jon Sloan *(Mikey)*

p, Douglas Dilge; d, Matthew Chapman; w, Blaine Novak, Matthew Chapman (based on a story by Novak); ph, Mikhail Suslov; ed, William Carruth; m, Gato Barbieri; art d, Virginia Randolph; cos, Tracy Tynan

A stylish, charming, honest, romantic, and obsessive look at filmmaking during the B-movie days of the 1950s that transcends its period setting and speaks to filmmakers and viewers of all times. Stanley (Peter Coyote) is a crazed, manipulative director who is driven to make his picture "Strange and Dangerous" at all costs. With his sheepish, boy-wonder producer, Farris (Dan Shor), at his side, Stanley meets with gangster Frank Silva (Richard Romanus) about funding the film. The likable but dangerous Silva agrees, with one condition—that his girl friend Carol (Victoria Tennant) get the lead role. Distressed at the lack of chemistry between Carol and her dopey, insecure costar, Stevie Blake (Blaine Novak), Stanley plots to have his stars fall in love, a scheme that will permanently sever his financial tie with Silva. Photographed in cool, vibrant color reminiscent of the 1950s and scored with a jazzy saxophone melody, STRANGERS KISS stuns with one fresh scene after another. The film shines on all levels, from technique to acting performances, from the direction to the script. What is most apparent in

STRANGERS KISS is the director's and screenwriter's love for filmmaking. For anyone who is enthralled by that strange species known as "filmmakers" or for those who just love well-made entertainment reminiscent of a bygone era, STRANGERS KISS is highly recommended.

STRANGERS ON A TRAIN   DVD

1951 101m bw Thriller ★★★★★
Warner Bros. (U.S.)

Farley Granger *(Guy Haines)*, Ruth Roman *(Anne Morton)*, Robert Walker *(Bruno Antony)*, Leo G. Carroll *(Sen. Morton)*, Patricia Hitchcock *(Barbara Morton)*, Laura Elliot *(Miriam)*, Marion Lorne *(Mrs. Antony)*, Jonathan Hale *(Mr. Antony)*, Howard St. John *(Capt. Turley)*, John Brown *(Prof. Collins)*

p, Alfred Hitchcock; d, Alfred Hitchcock; w, Raymond Chandler, Czenzi Ormonde, Whitfield Cook (based on the novel by Patricia Highsmith); ph, Robert Burks; ed, William Ziegler; m, Dimitri Tiomkin; art d, Ted Haworth; fx, H.F. Koenekamp; cos, Leah Rhodes

AAN Best B/W Cinematography: Robert Burks

Gripping all the way, this is a Hitchcock thriller in which, through happenstance, two men, completely different, are drawn inexorably together and toward an uncommon goal—murder. Hitchcock opens this electrifying film by showing two sets of male feet, those of Guy Haines (Granger) and Bruno Antony (Walker), hurrying towards a train. Guy wears conservative-looking shoes, Bruno black and white spectator shoes, and from their very movements, the sure gait of Guy, the anxious steps of Bruno, the viewer can easily tell, once the two are shown fully on camera, their distinctive personalities. After some club car chit-chat in which both men discuss some personal problems, Bruno proposes, *in theory,* of course, that they each murder the person vexing the other person's life—Bruno would murder Guy's wife in exchange for Guy murdering Bruno's father. Guy is appalled at the idea, but is even more appalled when Bruno carries out his half of the deal and then expects Guy to do the same.

STRANGERS ON A TRAIN ranks at the top of Hitchcock's most accomplished works, a masterpiece that is so carefully constructed and its characters so well developed that the viewer is quickly intimate and comfortable with the story long before Bruno turns killer. After reading Patricia Highsmith's novel, Hitchcock paid $7,500 for the rights to adapt the book and then went about having a rough draft written for the screen, later bringing in Raymond Chandler to do the finished script—a collaboration which was thoroughly frustrating for both parties. At first Hitchcock insisted that he work at Chandler's side, working out every detail of the film as he, Hitchcock, envisioned it, a routine that soon had the brilliant, booze-sipping Chandler nervous and often upset. Chandler's script nevertheless was the basic one employed by Hitchcock, although the director later asked his favorite writer, Ben Hecht, to come in and "spruce it up." Since Hecht was engaged on several other projects, he assigned Czenzi Ormonde, who worked for him, to clean up some of the dialogue and tighten some scenes before Hecht himself gave final approval. Granger is excellent as the innocent victim of the evil plot, and Walker (who would make only one more film before his death) is, like Joseph Cotten's "Uncle Charlie" in SHADOW OF A DOUBT, one of Hitchcock's most diabolical and charismatic villains—a frightening alter ego to the film's hero. Remade in 1969 as ONCE YOU KISS A STRANGER, and the basis for the 1987 comedy THROW MOMMA FROM THE TRAIN.

STRAPLESS
DVD

1989 97m c Drama ★★★½
Granada/Film Four (U.K.) R

Blair Brown (Dr. Lillian Hempel), Bruno Ganz (Raymond Forbes), Bridget Fonda (Amy Hempel), Alan Howard (Mr. Cooper), Michael Gough (Douglas Brodie), Hugh Laurie (Colin), Suzanne Burden (Romaine Salmon), Camille Coduri (Mrs. Clark), Gary O'Brien (Mr. Clark), Julian Bunster (Carlos)

p, Rick McCallum; d, David Hare; w, David Hare; ph, Andrew Dunn (Technicolor); ed, Edward Marnier; m, Nick Bicat; prod d, Roger Hall

From the writer of PLENTY and writer-director of WETHERBY, British playwright David Hare, comes yet another decidedly odd but utterly irresistible study of isolation, loneliness, and strength. Blair Brown stars as a cancer specialist and expatriate American, Dr. Lillian Hempel, who meets shady, romantic Raymond Forbes (Bruno Ganz) while touring the continent. Enchanted but cautious, Lillian lunches with him but balks at a later rendezvous at his hotel and returns to England without giving him her address. Soon Raymond abruptly shows up on Lillian's doorstep, having obtained her home address from a hotel where she stayed, and resumes his courtship. When he proposes marriage, Lillian again balks, though she agrees to move in with him. Raymond's idea of playing house turns out to be an extended stay at a casino-hotel that ends on an ominous note when he bounces a check in attempting to cover his betting losses. Lillian makes good on Raymond's bad check and returns home. In the face of the mounting chaos in her life, Lillian suffers a minor breakdown but impulsively agrees to marry Raymond, who carries over his romantic excesses into their domestic life.

STRAPLESS is an ode to both independence and interdependence. While Lillian's repression and forced isolation lead her to be seduced by Raymond's romanticism, her independent strength allows her to take the experience on its own terms and use it to enrich her own life. That strength leads her to break out of her shell and become a participant in the lives of those around her. At the same time, her sister learns from Lillian the need to pull back and tend to her inner needs to make a proper environment for her new baby.

In spite of its dreamy allegorical tone and terse political overtones, STRAPLESS is anything but dour and preachy. Instead it is alive with feeling for its characters and their world. Though beautifully controlled under Hare's direction, STRAPLESS is full of poignant, human moments of precise observation, gentle comedy, and penetrating drama. It's also full of exquisite performances, especially from Brown, Ganz, and Fonda, who make the most of the rich roles Hare has written for them.

STRAW DOGS
DVD

1971 118m c Crime ★★★★
ABC/Amerbroco/Talent Associates (U.K.) R

Dustin Hoffman (David Sumner), Susan George (Amy Sumner), Peter Vaughan (Tom Hedden), T.P. McKenna (Maj. Scott), Del Henney (Charlie Venner), Ken Hutchison (Scutt), Colin Welland (Rev. Hood), Jim Norton (Cawsey), Sally Thomsett (Janice), Donald Webster (Riddaway)

p, Daniel Melnick; d, Sam Peckinpah; w, David Zelag Goodman, Sam Peckinpah (based on the novel The Siege of Trencher's Farm by Gordon M. Williams); ph, John Coquillon (Eastmancolor); ed, Paul Davies, Roger Spottiswoode, Tony Lawson; m, Jerry Fielding; prod d, Ray Simm; art d, Ken Bridgeman; cos, Tiny Nicholls

AAN Best Original Dramatic Score: Jerry Fielding

STRAW DOGS is one of Sam Peckinpah's finest films, a relentless study in violence and machismo that is shocking, not only for its explicit gore, but for the degree to which it manipulates "civilized" audiences. Even the most passive viewer may find himself silently cheering on the carnage at the film's climax—an act that, in retrospect, gives much cause for discomfort.

David Sumner (Dustin Hoffman), a quiet mathematician, and his wife Amy (Susan George) seek to escape urban violence by moving to her birthplace, a small Cornish village. They hire four locals to build a garage and it isn't long before they start making life unpleasant for David. Led by Charlie (Del Henney), an ex-boyfriend of Amy's, the four workers ridicule David and ogle Amy, who seems to encourage their attentions. David, trying to win their acceptance, accepts an invitation to accompany them on a hunting trip; they desert him, and two of the men return to the cottage and rape Amy, who is ambivalent about the experience and doesn't tell her husband.

Some time later, the couple attend a local church function where Amy, haunted by memories of the rape, has a breakdown. Driving home in a dense fog, they knock down Henry (David Warner), the town simpleton. Unbeknownst to the couple, Henry has just strangled a young girl who taunted him. They take the injured man back to their home and, when an angry mob (including David's tormentors) learn of Henry's whereabouts and lay siege to the house, David resolves to fight them. What follows is a brilliantly edited, spectacularly violent climax.

STRAW DOGS generated tremendous controversy upon its release in 1971. Many found the violence too graphic and gratuitous, as well as taking offence at the film's neolithic sexual politics: by resorting to brutal, deadly violence, the man proves himself true master of his "property"—his house and his wife. The film is played as a power struggle between husband and wife (David and Amy play several symbolic games of chess during the proceedings), with Amy pushing her partner's tolerance to breaking point. Her strategies include teasing the workers and disrupting David's work, while he counters by abusing her cat and accepting the hunting invitation. But David's checkmate comes when—after he's killed a few men and become shockingly abusive—he compells Amy to shoot one of the assailants. David has thus "won" the game, losing everything that he stood for in the process. This cynical premise, combined with the fact that David has actually enjoyed the violence, is difficult to swallow.

STRAW DOGS contains one of Hoffman's most layered performances, with the final explosion of violence all the more believable thanks to his initial, mild-mannered quietude. George combines suggestive sexuality with spitefulness to create an equally unforgettable character. Peckinpah handles everything with consummate skill, exerting complete control over his audience's responses. STRAW DOGS is full of arresting images (the mesmerizing opening dissolve was borrowed by David Cronenberg for the beginning of THE FLY), perfectly complemented by Jerry Fielding's eerie, Oscar-nominated score. Whatever your reservations about its content and philosophy, STRAW DOGS remains one of the strongest and most memorable statements about violence ever put on screen.

STRAY DOG
DVD

(NORA INU)
1949 122m bw Crime/Drama ★★★★
Shin Toho (Japan)

Toshiro Mifune (Murakami), Takashi Shimura (Sato), Ko Kimura (Yusa), Keiko Awaji (Harumi), Reisaburo Yamamoto (Honda), Noriko Sengoku (Girl)

p, Sojiro Motoki; d, Akira Kurosawa; w, Ryuzo Kikushima, Akira Kurosawa; ph, Asakazu Nakai; ed, Yoshi Sugihara; m, Fumio Hayasaka; art d, So Matsuyama

STRAY DOG, about a rookie homicide detective named Murakami (Toshiro Mifune) searching for his stolen gun in 1949 Tokyo, is the first great film directed by Akira Kurosawa and is equally superb as a riveting detective thriller, a painstaking police procedural, and a sociological study of the moral and economic conditions of postwar Japan. Kurosawa consciously follows the model of Hollywood films noirs, with lots of moody low-key lighting and the depiction of a morally ambiguous "hero's" descent into the underbelly of society, and as Murakami becomes immersed in his obsessive quest (a favorite Kurosawa theme), the homeless and unemployed, the defeated soldiers, and the black marketers and prostitutes all become a microcosm of Japanese society in the wake of WWII. Stylistically, the film is one of Kurosawa's best and he infuses it with numerous innovative visual ideas, including optical wipes, a mobile, hand-held camera, and most notably, authentic, documentary-like street-scenes, particularly the extraordinary eight-minute dialogue-free sequence where Murakami poses as a returned soldier and wanders through the slums looking for a gun dealer. Probably the longest montage in film history, it consists entirely of close-ups of eyes dissolving into feet and faces as the sun beats down on the sweltering crowds, and was actually shot by Ishiro Honda, the film's second-unit director, who would later gain fame as the director of Toho's classic monster movies, including the original GODZILLA (1956) and most of the sequels. Another excellent example of this quasi-documentary style is the tension-filled baseball game sequence which presents a real game in progress, intercut with Murakami frantically searching for a criminial in the crowd. It's a brilliantly filmed and edited scene that's quite possibly the first time a sporting event was used in the context of a manhunt, something that would later become a staple of crime movies.

STREAMERS

1983 118m c Drama/War ★★★½
UA Classics (U.S.) R

Matthew Modine (Billy), Michael Wright (Carlyle), Mitchell Lichtenstein (Richie), David Alan Grier (Roger), Guy Boyd (Rooney), George Dzundza (Cokes), Albert Macklin (Martin), B.J. Cleveland (Pfc. Bush), Bill Allen (Lt. Townsend), Paul Lazar (MP Lieutenant)

p, Robert Altman, Nick J. Mileti; d, Robert Altman; w, David Rabe (based on the play by Rabe); ph, Pierre Mignot (Movielab Color); ed, Norman Smith; prod d, Wolf Kroeger; art d, Steve Altman; cos, Scott Bushnell

In the 1980s, Robert Altman (NASHVILLE, THE PLAYER) seemed more interested in the stage than the screen, directing movie versions of critically acclaimed plays such as Secret Honor, Come Back to the 5 and Dime, Jimmy Dean, Jimmy Dean, and Fool for Love. STREAMERS, based on a play by David Rabe, is set in an Army barracks circa 1965, where a group of young soldiers awaits assignment to Vietnam. The draftees come from a variety of backgrounds and include two blacks, a country boy, and a Yale-educated homosexual. They are confronted by two brutal sergeants, veterans of the Korean War. Sexual and racial tensions build as the men await their transfer orders in the claustrophobic barracks, and eventually shocking violence erupts. Rabe uses the microcosmic barracks as a site for exploring the explosive emotions and issues that preoccupied Americans during the Vietnam War, and on stage, the play was an excruciatingly intense experience. Altman, working in a cooler medium, wisely opts for a somewhat distanced approach. This very low-budget film feels more stagebound than the director's other stage-to-screen

projects, but Altman elicits marvelous performances from his cast—especially Matthew Modine, Michael Wright and George Dzundza. The title is Army slang for paratroopers whose chutes have failed to open.

STREET SCENE
DVD
1931 80m bw Drama ★★★★
UA (U.S.)

Sylvia Sidney (Rose Maurrant), William Collier Jr. (Sam Kaplan), Estelle Taylor (Anna Maurrant), Beulah Bondi (Emma Jones), Max Montor (Abe Kaplan), David Landau (Frank Maurrant), Matt McHugh (Vincent Jones), Russell Hopton (Steve Sankey), Greta Granstedt (Mae Jones), Tom Manning (George Jones)

p, Samuel Goldwyn; d, King Vidor; w, Elmer Rice (based on his play); ph, George Barnes; ed, Hugh Bennett; m, Alfred Newman; art d, Richard Day

Elmer Rice's Pulitzer Prize-winning play about the lives and loves of the people who live on a West Side Manhattan street proved to have national appeal under the sure hand of director King Vidor. To insure quality, eight of the original Broadway cast were hired to reprise their roles, including Beulah Bondi, who made her screen debut here and went on to have a long film career. Practically all of the shooting was done on a huge street set. It's summer and the windows are open. The neighborhood people can't bear to stay in their stifling apartments, so the action takes place outside. As the film opens, the big topic of conversation is the love affair between mature woman Estelle Taylor and Russell Hopton, a man who collects for the milk company. Taylor's husband, David Landau, suspicious of Hopton and his wife, is just waiting to catch them. As the sun rises, Taylor's daughter, Sylvia Sidney, goes off to work, while Landau mentions that he has to travel to Connecticut for the day. After Landau leaves, Sidney's beau, Max Montor, sees Hopton surreptitiously make his way to Taylor's flat. The shades come down—every other shade on the block is up to let in fresh air—and within a few seconds Landau is back in the apartment. Screams are heard, noises of a fight, then a single shot rings out. The people on the street turn their eyes to the sound, the shade comes up, and Hopton stands at the window. Then there's another shot, and Hopton disappears. An instant later, Landau, looking crazed, comes running out of the brownstone with the gun in his hand; the people on the street shrink back when he tells them to scatter. Landau turns the corner and disappears down an alley as police cars and ambulances rush into the street. A crowd gathers, eager to watch but not to help, waiting to see what will happen next.

Featuring excellent acting all around, STREET SCENE moves very quickly, with hardly a wasted word. Although somewhat dated by today's standards, it must be judged by those of the 1930s, when it was a stunning achievement. The play ran for more than two years and is still revived often. An added dimension was composer Alfred Newman's main theme (since used in many films), which ranks, to this day, among the most evocative pieces of music ever written, immediately conjuring up the crowded streets, the hustle, and the oppressive claustrophobia of the Big Apple.

STREET SMART
DVD
1987 95m c Crime ★★★
Golan-Globus (U.S.) R

Christopher Reeve (Jonathan Fisher), Morgan Freeman (Fast Black), Kathy Baker (Punchy), Mimi Rogers (Alison Parker), Jay Patterson (Leonard Pike), Andre Gregory (Ted Avery), Anna

Maria Horsford *(Harriet)*, Frederick Rolf *(Joel Davis)*, Erik King *(Reggie)*, Michael J. Reynolds *(Art Sheffield)*

p, Menahem Golan, Yoram Globus; d, Jerry Schatzberg; w, David Freeman; ph, Adam Holender (TVC Color); ed, Priscilla Nedd; m, Robert Irving III, Miles Davis; prod d, Dan Leigh; art d, Serge Jacques; cos, Jo Ynocencio

AAN Best Supporting Actor: Morgan Freeman

Jonathan Fisher (Reeve) is a magazine journalist who gets an assignment to write about the lifestyle of a pimp. When he can't get any real pimps to talk to him, Fisher creates a fictional portrait that is chosen as a cover story and turns him into a celebrity with his own TV news show. Fisher then gets to know "Fast Black" (Freeman), a vicious, high-powered pimp who is being charged with murder. Meanwhile, an assistant D.A. comes to believe that Fast Black is the real-life subject of Fisher's article, and subpoenas the writer's (non-existent) notes as evidence in the trial. Fast Black exerts pressure on Fisher to create false notes that will provide him with an alibi; Fisher resists, until he realizes how far the pimp will go to get what he wants.

Thanks to a terrific performance by Freeman and slick direction by Jerry Schatzberg, this is a fast-moving, intermittently riveting crime drama. Reeve is good as the naive writer who gets in over his head, and Kathy Baker is outstanding as one of Fast Black's "girls."

STREETCAR NAMED DESIRE, A

1951 125m bw Drama
Warner Bros. (U.S.)

DVD
★★★★

Vivien Leigh *(Blanche DuBois)*, Marlon Brando *(Stanley Kowalski)*, Kim Hunter *(Stella Kowalski)*, Karl Malden *(Mitch)*, Rudy Bond *(Steve Hubbell)*, Nick Dennis *(Pablo Gonzales)*, Peg Hillias *(Eunice Hubbell)*, Wright King *(Young Collector)*, Richard Garrick *(Doctor)*, Ann Dere *(The Matron)*

p, Charles K. Feldman; d, Elia Kazan; w, Tennessee Williams, Oscar Saul (adapted from the play by Williams); ph, Harry Stradling; ed, David Weisbart; m, Alex North; art d, Richard Day; cos, Lucinda Ballard

AAN Best Picture; AAN Best Actor: Marlon Brando; AA Best Actress: Vivien Leigh; AA Best Supporting Actor: Karl Malden; AA Best Supporting Actress: Kim Hunter; AAN Best Director: Elia Kazan; AAN Best Screenplay: Tennessee Williams; AAN Best B/W Cinematography: Harry Stradling; AAN Best Score (Drama or Comedy): Alex North; AA Best Art Direction-Set Decoration (B/W): Richard Day, George James Hopkins; AAN Best Costume Design (B/W): Lucinda Ballard; AAN Best Sound Recording: Colonel Nathan Levinson

In this consensual screen classic, Marlon Brando is electrifying as working-class hunk Stanley Kowalski, reprising his Broadway role in Tennessee Williams's most famous play. Elia Kazan, who directed the play in New York, made the trek west for the film, joined by Brando, Kim Hunter, Karl Malden, Rudy Bond, Nick Dennis, Peg Hillias, and Edna Thomas from the stage version. Only Jessica Tandy, who had been a smash as Blanche DuBois on Broadway, was replaced—studio chiefs felt that she wasn't well-known enough for the movie. The role went to Vivien Leigh, who had been starring in a London presentation of the play directed by her husband, Laurence Olivier. The resulting film is an actors' showcase and a flamboyant, sometimes uneasy admixture of Manhattan and Hollywood sensibilitites.

The film opens with Blanche (Leigh) arriving in New Orleans, where she intends to stay with her pregnant sister Stella Kowalski (Hunter) and her brutish husband Stanley (Brando). (To get to their seedy apartment, Blanche has to take a streetcar named Desire—named for a New Orleans street.)

Stella, an earthy, pragmatic woman, seems happy in her marriage to the trashy but overtly sexual Stanley, but Blanche is delicate, morose, and deeply neurotic. Stanley immediately sees through Blanche's southern-belle facade and the two are quickly at odds. As sexual and financial tensions escalate, Stanley sets out to reveal the truth about Blanche.

A STREETCAR NAMED DESIRE features some of the finest ensemble acting ever offered on the screen, speaking some Williams's most vivid dialogue. Kazan's direction, however, sometimes verges on the pedestrian, as though he's struggling to recreate his Broadway staging in a much more visually demanding medium. Leigh, in the final great triumph of her screen career, is the very picture of tattered magnificence. She's like a cracked figurine from *The Glass Menagerie* come to life; her emotional choices are tragic and horrifying at the same time. Brando's character is strictly scratch, mumble, flex, and roar, but it's telegraphed a through force-of-nature persona. As countless subsequent productions have shown, Brando has no peer when it comes to conveying the physical threat and sexual potency that make the character work. Kim Hunter is more than adequate in the most sketchily written role. Three minutes of footage censored from the original were restored in a 1994 video re-release.

STRICTLY BALLROOM

1992 92m c Comedy/Dance/Romance
M&A Film Corporation (Australia)

DVD
★★½
PG

Paul Mercurio *(Scott Hastings)*, Tara Morice *(Fran)*, Bill Hunter *(Barry Fife)*, Barry Otto *(Doug Hastings)*, Pat Thompson *(Shirley Hastings)*, Gia Carides *(Liz Holt)*, Peter Whitford *(Les Kendall)*, John Hannan *(Ken Railings)*, Sonia Kruger-Taylor *(Tina Sparkle)*, Pip Mushin *(Wayne Burns)*

p, Tristam Miall; Ted Albert; d, Baz Luhrmann; w, Baz Luhrmann, Craig Pearce; ph, Steve Mason; ed, Jill Bilcock; m, David Hirshfelder; prod d, Catherine Martin; cos, Trathie Angus

Australian director Baz Luhrman's first film takes satirical potshots at an easy target, the world of competitive ballroom dancing, adding a dash of John Waters-style camp into the mix for extra effect. Welcome to STRICTLY BALLROOM, a world of deeply regimented dancing competition (hence the title, implying no deviations from set form) that mirrors the rigid social order of the Warataw (southern Australia) districts.

Competition is keen, especially between Kim Rallings (John Hannan), a drunken, platinumed lothario, and Scott Hastings (Paul Mercurio), the earnest, handsome, self-absorbed, rising-star son of dance school owners. When Scott departs from the time-honored formula during a samba competition, he causes a furor among the powers-that-be of the Dance Federation: Scott's coach, Les Kendall (Peter Whitford); corrupt Federation president, Barry Fife (Bill Hunter); and Scott's own parents, Shirley and Doug Hastings (Pat Thomson, Barry Otto). Scott's ambitious partner Liz (Gia Carrides) deserts him, and Scott joins forces with ugly duckling newcomer Fran (Tara Morice). Is it a surprise that she blossoms into a impassioned and seductive dancer, or that Scott ignores every obstacle and succeeds in doing things his own way?

One would have to be heartless not to be engaged by STRICTLY BALLROOM's romantic, dewy sentiment, but the predictable plot is difficult to bear, as are the broad characterizations. Some spirited performances breathe life into the limp central idea, and BALLROOM's cast demonstrates genuine dance talent; costume designer Angus Strathie and choreographer John "Cha Cha" O'Connell appear to have enjoyed their work, and Luhrman has given the entire enterprise his loving, detailed attention—it looks terrific.

STRIKE UP THE BAND

1940 120m bw · Musical/Comedy ★★★½
MGM (U.S.)

Mickey Rooney (Jimmy Connors), Judy Garland (Mary Holden), Paul Whiteman and His Orchestra (Themselves), June Preisser (Barbara Frances Morgan), William Tracy (Phillip Turner), Ann Shoemaker (Mrs. Connors), Larry Nunn (Willie Brewster), George Lessey (Mr. Morgan), Francis Pierlot (Mr. Judd), Harry McCrillis (Booper Barton)

p, Arthur Freed; d, Busby Berkeley; w, Herbert Fields (uncredited), Kay Van Riper (uncredited), John Monks Jr., Fred Finklehoffe; ph, Ray June; ed, Ben Lewis; art d, Cedric Gibbons, John S. Detlie; cos, Dolly Tree, Gile Steele

AAN Best Score: George Stoll, Roger Edens; *AAN Best Song:* "Our Love Affair"; Roger Edens (Music & Lyrics), Georgie Stoll (Music & Lyrics); *AA Best Sound Recording:* Douglas Shearer

Mickey Rooney and Judy Garland, two of the great young stars of their day, team up in this musical comedy as a pair of high school students. Mary (Garland) works in the library after school, and Jimmy (Rooney) spends his free time practicing the drums. He wants to smack the skins in a dance band, but his widowed mother yearns for him to become a doctor. Jimmy and a bunch of his pals form an orchestra with the intention of entering a contest sponsored by big band "King of Jazz" Paul Whiteman. The kids manage to scrape together the money for their trip to the coast, but when one of them needs an emergency operation, Jimmy decides to pay for it and sacrifice his big chance. Luckily, Paul Whiteman is in town and Jimmy and his boys get a chance to play for him anyway. Rooney and Garland deliver their usual energy-packed performances, but one unexpected scene is a standout: as Jimmy uses a bowl of fruit to illustrate an idea he has for a musical number, the fruit turns into little animated puppet models (masterminded by George Pal) that perform "Do the Conga." Also included is the big band classic "Sing, Sing, Sing."

STRIPES

1981 106m c Comedy ★★★
Columbia (U.S.) R

Bill Murray (John Winger), Harold Ramis (Russell Zitsky), Warren Oates (Sgt. Hulka), P.J. Soles (Stella), Sean Young (Louise), John Candy (Ox), John Larroquette (Capt. Stillman), Judge Reinhold (Elmo), John Voldstad (Aide), John Diehl (Cruiser)

p, Ivan Reitman, Dan Goldberg; d, Ivan Reitman; w, Len Blum, Dan Goldberg; ph, Bill Butler (Metrocolor); ed, Eva Ruggiero, Michael Luciano, Harry Keller; m, Elmer Bernstein; prod d, James H. Spencer; chor, Ronn Forella, Arthur Goldweit; cos, Richard Bruno

Though it's occasionally tasteless and eventually crumbles, STRIPES is an often hilarious film that provided Bill Murray with a perfect opportunity in which to display his comedic skills. Murray stars as John Winger, an irresponsible goof-off who, as the film opens, has just lost his job, his girl, his apartment and his car. As he ponders his fate with his equally unsuccessful best friend, Russell Zitsky (Harold Ramis), a man who teaches English to recent immigrants, it occurs to him that enlisting in the Army seems to be a sensible career move. He persuades Zitsky to go along on the adventure and soon they find themselves in boot camp surrounded by a group of misfits that includes the overweight Ox (John Candy), the temperamental Psycho (Conrad Dunn), the dopey Cruiser (John Diehl), and druggie Elmo (Judge Reinhold in his film debut). Given the unenviable task of pre-siding over this collection of dolts is tough Army veteran Sgt. Hulka (Warren Oates), and it isn't long before Winger finds his way to the sergeant's bad side. While STRIPES was ideally suited to Murray's wise-ass, rebel-who-has-no-use-for-a-cause character, what really makes the film work is his relationship with Ramis. The two make a delightful comedy team, with the somewhat more sensible Ramis serving as the perfect foil to Murray. His expressive face and low-key manner provide a comic perspective that serves to enhance Murray's clowning. The rest of the cast is also first-rate, especially Oates who imbues his weary sergeant with an unexpected wit and intelligence. While basic training has been the subject of countless screen comedies, the subject is one which offers great comic potential, and this film exploits that potential. Unfortunately, it flags considerably once basic ends and the characters set off on their inane adventure behind enemy lines.

STUART LITTLE

1999 92m c Children's/Fantasy ★★★
Red Wagon Productons/Columbia (U.S.) PG

Michael J. Fox (Voice of Stuart Little), Geena Davis (Mrs. Little), Hugh Laurie (Mr. Little), Jonathan Lipnicki (George Little), Julia Sweeney (Mrs. Keeper), Nathan Lane (Voice of Snowbell), Jennifer Tilly (Voice of Camille Stout), Bruno Kirby (Voice of Reginald Stout), Chazz Palminteri (Voice of Smokey), Steve Zahn (Voice of Monty)

p, Douglas Wick; d, Rob Minkoff; w, M. Night Shyamalan, Greg Brooker (based on the book Stuart Little by E.B. White); ph, Guillermo Navarro; ed, Tom Finan; m, Alan Silvestri; prod d, Bill Brzeski; art d, Philip Toolin; fx, Eric Allard (mechanical Effects), Jerome Chen, John Dykstra, Henry F. Anderson III, Sony Pictures Imageworks (visual Effects), Joseph Conti (digital Effects), Phil Notaro, Thunderstone Model Shop, Bill Westenhofer; cos, Joseph Porro; anim, Henry Anderson

AAN Best Visual Effects: John Dykstra, Jerome Chen, Henry F. Anderson III, Eric Allard

A charming, technically sensational version of E.B. White's children's classic, though purists may find it a wee bit sappier than the master intended.

All-around swell parents Mr. and Mrs. Little (Hugh Laurie and Geena Davis) decide to adopt a younger brother for nine-year-old George (Jonathan Lipnicki). At the orphanage, however, they meet and immediately fall in love with the titular, computer-generated mouse (voiced, a tad cloyingly, by Michael J. Fox). George is, of course, nonplussed by the whole idea of a mouse brother, and Stuart's assimilation isn't made easier by family cat Snowbell (voice of Nathan Lane). Humiliated at having Stuart for a master instead of lunch, Snowbell arranges a rodent hit with the help of some local alley cats, including boss Smokey (voice of Chazz Palminteri, in what amounts to a feline reprise of his small-time wiseguy character in A BRONX TALE). Various plot machinations later, Snowbell is redeemed, the bad kitties get their comeuppance, George comes to love his diminutive brother, and the family learns that there's a little Stuart Little in all of us.

All that uplift, of course, is not terribly surprising, though it's sure to make kids happy. Fortunately for adults, there's also plenty to admire: the gorgeous, stylized soundstage re-creation of Manhattan and Brooklyn; a gloriously kinetic toy-ship race around the Central Park boat basin; amazing "how'd they do that" cat effects; and Rob Minkoff's direction, which actually makes a virtue of shooting from a mouse's-eye level.

STUCK ON YOU

2003   118m   c   Comedy   **DVD**
Conundrum Entertainment/20th Century Fox   ★★½
(U.S.)   PG-13

Matt Damon (Bob), Greg Kinnear (Walt), Eva Mendes (April),
Wen Yann Shih (May), Seymour Cassel (Morty O'Reilly), Cher
(Herself), Pat Crawford Brown (Mimmy), Ray Valliere, billed as
Ray "Rocket" Valliere (Rocket), Tommy Songin (Tommy), Terence
Bernie Hines (Moe)

p, Bobby Farrelly, Peter Farrelly, Bradley Thomas, Charles B.
Wessler; d, Bobby Farrelly, Peter Farrelly; w, Peter Farrelly, Bobby
Farrelly (based on a story by Charles B. Wessler, Bennet Yellin,
Peter Farrelly, and Bobby Farrelly); ph, Dan Mindel; ed,
Christopher Greenbury; m, Michael Andrews; prod d, Sidney J.
Bartholomew; art d, Richard Fojo, Arlan Jay Vetter; fx, Frank
Ceglia, Kevin Harris; cos, Deena Appel

Two heads aren't necessarily better than one, as sibling directors Peter and Bobby Farrelly's tag-team effort to make a sentimental comedy about conjoined twins proves.

Brothers Walt (Greg Kinnear) and Bob Tenor (Matt
Damon) couldn't be more different, but circumstances dictate
that they must spend every second of their lives together:
they're joined at the waist. Well-spoken Walt is a sharp-
dressed Casanova, while athletic but retiring Bob is prone to
panic attacks. They work at their own greasy spoon in
Martha's Vineyard, but Walt has dreams of becoming a movie
star. Bob agrees to move to L.A., where he'll finally meet his
Internet girlfriend, May (Wen Yann Shih). Casting directors
can't see past the conjoined thing, so in desperation, Walt hires
a sleazy former agent, Morty (Seymour Cassel). Morty can
only get Walt a part in an adult film, and the dejected duo is
just about to throw in the towel when the brothers run into
Cher, who wants to cast them in a TV series. Meanwhile,
Bob's attachment to his brother threatens his budding relationship with May. Their conflicting desires force the siblings
to consider separation, but the operation could cost Walt his
life.

The Farrellys have taken up the banner of representing
disabled people in a positive light, which mostly means that
they become the butt of the same gross-out and slapstick gags
as everyone else. Here the message—it's not nice to ridicule
people just because they're different—is obvious and verges
on the oppressive; more of the Farrellys' trademark over-the-
top comedy would have lightened the load. Nevertheless,
Kinnear and Damon's good-natured performances are charmingly light, despite the fact that they're practically on top of
each other.

STUNT MAN, THE

1980   129m   c   Comedy/Drama   **DVD**
Fox   (U.S.)   ★★★★
                                                 R

Peter O'Toole (Eli Cross), Steve Railsback (Cameron), Barbara
Hershey (Nina Franklin), Allen Garfield, billed as Allen Goorwitz
(Sam), Alex Rocco (Jake), Sharon Farrell (Denise), Adam Roarke
(Raymond Bailey), Philip Bruns (Ace), Chuck Bail (Chuck
Barton), John Garwood (Gabe)

p, Richard Rush; d, Richard Rush; w, Larry Marcus, Richard Rush
(based on the novel by Paul Brodeur); ph, Mario Tosi (Metrocolor);
ed, Jack Hofstra, Caroline Ferriol; m, Dominic Frontiere; art d,
James Schoppe; cos, Rosanna Norton

AAN Best Actor: Peter O'Toole; AAN Best Director: Richard Rush;
AAN Best Adapted Screenplay: Lawrence B. Marcus Richard Rush

Peter O'Toole, a megalomaniacal film director, tyrannizes
his writer and plays games with his actors, manipulating
their actions in reality, just as he does in the story he is film-

ing. Steve Railsback is on the run from the law, and he
stumbles upon the movie company as they shoot a scene on
the beach. After his top stuntman is killed, O'Toole, who
has shielded Railsback from the law, persuades the young
man to take the dead man's place. Railsback is then thrust
into the not-so-glamorous world of moviemaking and gets
involved with Barbara Hershey, O'Toole's beautiful star
and lover. Lawrence B. Marcus's script, which pits real life
against reel life, offers plenty of wit, with most of the bons
mots handed to O'Toole.

SUBJECT WAS ROSES, THE

1968   107m   c   Drama   ★★★★
MGM   (U.S.)

Patricia Neal (Nettie Cleary), Jack Albertson (John Cleary),
Martin Sheen (Timmy Cleary), Don Saxon (Nightclub Master
of Ceremonies), Elaine Williams (Woman), Grant Gordon
(Man in Restaurant)

p, Edgar Lansbury; d, Ulu Grosbard; w, Frank D. Gilroy (based on
his play); ph, Jack Priestley (Metrocolor); ed, Jerry Greenberg; m,
Lee Pockriss; art d, George Jenkins; cos, Anna Hill Johnstone

AAN Best Actress: Patricia Neal; AA Best Supporting Actor:
Jack Albertson

Frank Gilroy's Pulitzer Prize-winning drama was beautifully
realized in this film adaptation. WWII has just ended, and
Sheen returns home from the battle to live with parents Neal
and Albertson. In the years since he's been away, his parents'
marriage has disintegrated into rancor, disagreements and
highly charged hostility. Before he left, Sheen was the apple
of Neal's eye and only had a passing relationship with
Albertson. Now that he's matured, however, he has a closer tie
to Albertson, finding that they are two of a kind. Sheen can't
bear to see his parents at such loggerheads and attempts to
mediate their differences without standing in either's corner.

Neal begins a subtle campaign of sabotage against
Albertson but Sheen sees through this and confronts his mother by saying that he will not side with her or Albertson in any
dispute, preferring to remain completely neutral. Neal can't
handle Sheen's attitude but she later discovers Sheen drunk
and arguing with Albertson in much the same way he had
argued with her. Sheen, despite the booze he's ingested, makes
some sense. This situation will never get better as long as
things remain the same. He thinks that his parents must work
out their marital differences without using him as a referee, so
he tells them that he is going to leave and strike out on his own.

The movie was not a hit, despite the terrific acting, sharp
writing, and outstanding direction from Grosbard, who also
staged the play. Never does the emotion explode into oratory,
so almost every scene has an underlying tension that continues to bubble.

SUCH A GORGEOUS KID LIKE ME

(UNE BELLE FILLE COMME MOI)
1973   100m   c   Comedy/Drama   ★★★
Carrosse   (France)   R

Bernadette Lafont (Camille Bliss), Claude Brasseur (Monsieur
Murene), Charles Denner (Arthur), Guy Marchand (Sam Golden),
Andre Dussollier (Stanislas Previne), Philippe Leotard (Clovis Bliss),
Anne Kreis (Helene), Gilberte Geniat (Isobel Bliss), Daniele Girard
(Florence Golden), Martine Ferriere (Prison Secretary)

p, Marcel Berbert; d, Francois Truffaut; w, Francois Truffaut, Jean-
Loup Dabadie (based on the novel by Henry Farrell); ph, Pierre-
William Glenn (Eastmancolor); ed, Yann Dedet; m, Georges
Delerue; art d, Jean-Pierre Kohut-Svelko; cos, Monique Dury

An often ignored film by Truffaut, this black comedy is about women and their seemingly magical hold over men. Lafont, who first appeared in his 1957 short, LES MISTONS, takes up where she left off some 15 years earlier. In LES MISTONS she was tormented by a quintet of young boys who were very much in love with her. Here Lafont is able to take revenge on her tormentors.

The picture starts with a sociologist, Dussollier, preparing to write a book called *Criminal Women* (which he never gets to publish). He visits a women's prison and decides to interview convicted murderess Lafont, passing up offers to interview a woman who dismembered her victims and another who strangles them using only one hand. Dussollier discovers that Lafont is indirectly responsible for the deaths of her father and her mother-in-law, and was unsuccessful in her attempts to kill attorney Brasseur and husband Leotard with rat poison. She is eventually acquitted of her crime and rises to become a famed singer, not because of her voice (which is wretched) but because of the publicity that surrounds her case. Backstage at one of her performances, she is confronted by Leotard and Dussollier kills Leotard. But Lafont still has her own unique resources at hand.

SUCH A GORGEOUS KID LIKE ME, though it may not initially seem Truffautesque, has roots in a number of his previous films. He compares this film to THE WILD CHILD. Lafont's murderous female character is also seen in JULES AND JIM and THE BRIDE WORE BLACK (and to a lesser, non-violent extent in THE STORY OF ADELE H.). While it may not be an audience pleaser, SUCH A GORGEOUS KID LIKE ME is a definite must for those who are interested in learning about the "total" Truffaut.

SUGAR CANE ALLEY 📀
(RUE CASES NEGRES)
1983 103m c Drama ★★★½
Su Ma Fa/Orca/NEF Diffusion (France) PG

Garry Cadenat (*Jose*), Darling Legitimus (*M'Man Tine*), Douta Seck (*Medouze*), Joby Bernabe (*M. Saint-Louis*), Francisco Charles (*Le Gereur*), Marie-Jo Descas (*La Mere de Leopold*), Marie-Ange Farot (*Mme. Saint-Louis*), Henri Melon (*M. Roc*), Eugene Mona (*Douze Orteils*), Joel Palcy (*Carmen*)

p, Michel Loulergue, Alix Regis; d, Euzhan Palcy; w, Euzhan Palcy (based on the novel *La Rue Cases Negres* by Joseph Zobel); ph, Dominique Chapius (Fujicolor); ed, Marie-Josephe Yoyotte; m, Groupe Malavoi; art d, Hoang Thanh At; cos, Isabelle Filleul

Set in the French colony of Martinique in the 1930s, this stark, charming film takes a look at life in "Rue Cases Negres," a wooden-shack community isolated in the middle of a sugar plantation. While the adults toil in the fields, the children romp the "alley," but for many of the youngsters this will be their last summer on the plantation. The brightest among them will find better jobs or go on to school, while the less fortunate will remain to assist their parents in the fields. Most prominently featured is Jose (Garry Cadenat), a frolicsome 11-year-old who earns a prestigious scholarship to a school in Fort-de-France. This well-acted film is an unexpected delight, showing that a ray of hope can materialize amid the despondency of a shantytown. SUGAR CANE ALLEY was a double prizewinner at the Venice Film Festival, taking a Silver Lion and Darling Legitimus garnering a Best Actress award.

SUGARBABY
(ZUCKERBABY)
1985 86m c Drama/Comedy ★★★½
Pelemele (West Germany)

Marianne Sagebrecht (*Marianne*), Eisi Gulp (*Huber 133*), Toni Berger (*Old Subway Driver*), Manuela Denz (*Huber's Wife*), Will

Spindler (*Funeral Director*), The Paul Wurges Combo (*Dance Hall Band*), Hans Stadlbauer

d, Percy Adlon; w, Percy Adlon; ph, Johanna Heer; ed, Jean-Claude Piroue; m, Dreieier; cos, Regina Batz, Silvia Risa

The first installment of Percy Adlon's delightful "Marianne" trilogy, SUGARBABY stars the utterly winning Marianne Sagebrecht in a sweetly romantic story which also bears the rare distinction of being a Teutonic comedy.

Marianne (Sagebrecht) is a hugely overweight mortuary attendant who, while commuting to work one morning on the subway, becomes infatuated with the conductor (Eisi Gulp), a handsome, blond hunk in a tight-fitting uniform. She quickly determines to win him over and, failing to locate him the following day, goes to great lengths to procure his name and route number: Huber 133. Next, under the guise of finding work for her nephew, she gets her hands on the complex work schedule for subway drivers. After an obsessive search, she finally figures out Huber's schedule. In the meantime, Marianne has been preparing herself for her future lover, buying sexy lingerie (which must be specially ordered in her size), flashy high heels and pink satin sheets. Although it seems likely that all this preparation will backfire, Huber, nicknamed "Sugarbaby" by Marianne, accepts her invitation to dinner and romance quickly blossoms.

Adlon combines the free-spirited energy of his characters with technique to match, fashioning a magnificent lighting scheme that relies heavily on color effects, a minimalist set reduced to the barest essentials and a frantic camera style that allows the camera to wander, sway, and zig-zag through the set. Rather than creating a feeling of pretension or intrusive stylization, however, Adlon's film is lighthearted and energetic. He lets no barriers stand in his way and, as a result, the entire picture is an engaging, intelligent entertainment. And in Marianne, marvelously incarnated by Sagebrecht, viewers will find a lovable heroine with whom most would gladly spend time in the real world.

SUGARLAND EXPRESS, THE 📀
1974 109m c Adventure ★★★★
Universal (U.S.) PG

Goldie Hawn (*Lou Jean Poplin*), Ben Johnson (*Capt. Tanner*), Michael Sacks (*Officer Slide*), William Atherton (*Clovis Poplin*), Gregory Walcott (*Officer Mashburn*), Steve Kanaly (*Jessup*), Louise Latham (*Mrs. Looby*), Harrison Zanuck (*Baby Langston*), A.L. Camp (*Mr. Nocker*), Jessie Lee Fulton (*Mrs. Nocker*)

p, Richard D. Zanuck, David Brown; d, Steven Spielberg; w, Hal Barwood, Matthew Robbins (based on a story by Spielberg, Barwood, Robbins); ph, Vilmos Zsigmond (Panavision, Technicolor); ed, Edward Abroms, Verna Fields; m, John Williams; art d, Joe Alves; fx, Frank Brendel

This is Steven Spielberg's first effort at the helm in feature filmmaking (the earlier DUEL being a made-for-TV movie), and it contains much of the raw sense of adventure (though without the technical gadgetry) that would make his later films so popular and such good clean fun. After his success with THE SUGARLAND EXPRESS, he went on to direct the highly profitable, beloved, and much-imitated JAWS in 1975. Based on a true story, this film features Hawn playing a woman who helps her husband, Atherton, escape from prison. She needs him to join her in the fight against forces who want to put her child up for adoption. What ensues is one long chase across America's highways. Throughout the film, more and more police, and the media, want in on the action. Spielberg exhibits that he still had a bit to learn in the world of filmmaking. The film moves well and never loses its gripping tension, but the lighthearted tone of the beginning takes a dive into an abyss that shocks many viewers. With this role, Hawn further proves she was an actress of some talent and not just an attractive woman to be taken lightly.

SULLIVAN'S TRAVELS   DVD
1941 91m   bw   Comedy/Drama   ★★★★★
Paramount   (U.S.)

Joel McCrea *(John L. Sullivan)*, Veronica Lake *(The Girl)*, Robert Warwick *(Mr. Lebrand)*, William Demarest *(Mr. Jones)*, Franklin Pangborn *(Mr. Casalais)*, Porter Hall *(Mr. Hadrian)*, Byron Foulger *(Mr. Valdelle)*, Margaret Hayes *(Secretary)*, Robert Greig *(Sullivan's Butler)*, Eric Blore *(Sullivan's Valet)*

p, Paul Jones; d, Preston Sturges; w, Preston Sturges; ph, John Seitz; ed, Stuart Gilmore; m, Leo Shuken, Charles Bradshaw; art d, Hans Dreier, Earl Hedrick; fx, Farciot Edouart; cos, Edith Head

A Hollywood variation on *Gulliver's Travels* and just as successful as satire. This brilliant, often devastating look at Hollywood and the real world behind its tinsel is arguably Preston Sturges's greatest film. McCrea, in one of his best roles, plays a successful Hollywood film director who has made nothing but lightweight films with titles like "So Long, Sarong." When he is suddenly struck with the desire to make a searing drama about human suffering, his studio bosses (Warwick and Hall) laugh and tell him that the proposal is ridiculous, since McCrea has no personal experience of such difficulty. Accordingly, McCrea sets out to suffer. He will don hobo clothes and, with only 10 cents in his pocket, go forth into poverty and experience adversity for himself. Knowing they can't change his mind, Warwick and Hall humor the eccentric director's whim, but decide to turn McCrea's nomadic adventure into a publicity stunt that will benefit the studio. To this end they provide him with a publicity entourage and a luxury van that follows McCrea as he travels on foot, and that carries McCrea's butler, Greig, and valet, Blore, who both urge their employer to give up this mad idea, telling him that the poor insist upon their privacy and don't want him intruding upon it.

Though the plot may sound a bit contrived, everything in this wonderful film works. And it presents a spectacular array of emotions and situations that allow for Sturges's magical direction and script to quickly turn all the film's sharp corners with his characters. SULLIVAN'S TRAVELS is a wonderful comedy-drama, the type of a one-of-a-kind film for which Sturges—basically a writer with a good sense of camera use and visuals, who as a director was always trying out new techniques—was noted. Unlike many of his other films, which were made for sheer entertainment value, SULLIVAN'S TRAVELS contains a message, which Sturges himself later explained: "SULLIVAN'S TRAVELS is the result of an urge, an urge to tell some of my fellow filmwrights that they were getting a little too deep-dish and to leave the preaching to the preachers."

SUM OF ALL FEARS, THE   DVD
2002 124m   c   Thriller   ★★
Mace Neufeld Productions/Paramount   (U.S.)   PG-13

Ben Affleck *(Jack Ryan)*, Morgan Freeman *(DCI William Cabot)*, James Cromwell *(President Fowler)*, Liev Schreiber *(John Clark)*, Bridget Moynahan *(Dr. Cathy Muller)*, Alan Bates *(Dressler)*, Ciaran Hinds *(President Nemerov)*, Philip Baker Hall *(Defense Secretary Becker)*, Ron Rifkin *(Secretary of State Owens)*, Bruce McGill *(National Security Advisor Revell)*

p, Mace Neufeld; d, Phil Alden Robinson; w, Paul Attanasio, Daniel Pyne (based on the novel by Tom Clancy); ph, John Lindley; ed, Nicolas De Toth; m, Jerry Goldsmith; prod d, Jeannine Oppewall; art d, Andrew Neskoromny, Claude Pare; fx, Louis Craig, Al DiSarro, Glenn Neufeld; cos, Marie-Sylvie Deveau

Based on the 1991 Tom Clancy technothriller, this big-budget spectacle treads an uneasy path between globe-trotting espionage movies and nuclear scare pictures like FAIL SAFE. The two don't really go together; one is meant to be fun and the other is meant to induce nightmares.

Chronologically, the events come after those in THE HUNT FOR RED OCTOBER, PATRIOT GAMES, and CLEAR AND PRESENT DANGER, all of which feature veteran CIA agent Jack Ryan. But it's actually a kind of prequel—Ryan (Ben Affleck) is just starting his career at the Agency—incongruously set in the present. CIA director William Cabot (Morgan Freeman) plucks the rumpled Ryan from deskbound obscurity when longtime Russian President Zorkin (Richard Marner) drops dead and political upstart Nemerov (Ciaran Hinds) steps into his shoes. Ryan is an expert on Nemerov, but while all the president's men are obsessing about Russia's vast stockpile of nuclear weapons, a threat is building elsewhere. An unexploded nuclear bomb has wound up in the hands of billionaire Austrian Dressler (Alan Bates), a neo-Nazi whose master plans involves sparking a nuclear confrontation between Russia and the U.S. so a new Reich can rise from the radioactive ashes. Ryan's knowledge of Nemerov's habits and character wind up being all that stands between the world and nuclear annihilation, a weighty responsibility for an untried pup.

Clancy purists will question the degree to which the novel has been altered, but the film's real sticky wicket is that the bad guys not only threaten to nuke a major American city, they go ahead and do it—a conceit that might have been more amusing before terrorists destroyed the World Trade Center. Witnesses said the WTC attack looked like a movie; they didn't say it was a movie they wanted to see.

SUMMER HOLIDAY
1948 92m   c   Musical/Comedy   ★★★★
MGM   (U.S.)

Mickey Rooney *(Richard Miller)*, Gloria DeHaven *(Muriel McComber)*, Walter Huston *(Nat Miller)*, Frank Morgan *(Uncle Sid)*, Jackie "Butch" Jenkins *(Tommy Miller)*, Marilyn Maxwell *(Belle)*, Agnes Moorehead *(Cousin Lily)*, Selena Royle *(Mrs. Miller)*, Michael Kirby *(Arthur Miller)*, Shirley Johns *(Mildred Miller)*

p, Arthur Freed; d, Rouben Mamoulian; w, Frances Goodrich, Albert Hackett, Irving Brecher, Jean Holloway (based on the play "Ah, Wilderness!" by Eugene O'Neill); ph, Charles Schoenbaum (Technicolor); ed, Albert Akst; m, Harry Warren; art d, Cedric Gibbons, Jack Martin Smith; chor, Charles Walters; cos, Irene, Walter Plunkett

This fine musical version of Eugene O'Neill's "Ah, Wilderness!" stars Mickey Rooney as a boy struggling with the pitfalls of adolescence. In early 1900s New England we meet the Miller clan: Nat (Walter Huston), a newspaper editor and staunch upholder of Yankee tradition; his wife (Selena Royle), ever the doting mother; Richard (Rooney), their oldest son; and Tommy ("Butch") Jenkins), their youngest. Also living in their comfortable household are an old maid cousin (Agnes Moorehead) and a bachelor uncle (Frank Morgan). Richard is extraordinarily bright and has big ideas about changing the world. He adores neighbor Muriel McComber (Gloria DeHaven), but has been forbidden to see her by her conservative father. Peeved at his inability to see the girl he loves, Richard goes off on a drunk, meets a dance-hall girl, spends every cent he has, and gets kicked out of the bar. Naturally, he catches hell from his dad, but by the end he and Muriel are finally allowed to be together.

A sweet movie with good work by all the actors, SUMMER HOLIDAY benefits immeasurably from director Mamoulian's inventiveness and the handsome cinematography and production values. Even if "The Stanley Steamer" is an obvious attempt to cash in on the appeal of "The Trolley Song" from the very similar MEET ME IN ST.

LOUIS, the songs are quite appealing and eminently suitable. An earlier version of the O'Neill play appeared in 1935 as AH, WILDERNESS, with Rooney playing the role of the younger brother.

SUMMER OF '42

1971 102m c Drama
Warner Bros. (U.S.)

DVD
★★★
PG

Jennifer O'Neill *(Dorothy)*, Gary Grimes *(Hermie)*, Jerry Houser *(Oscy)*, Oliver Conant *(Benjie)*, Katherine Allentuck *(Aggie)*, Christopher Norris *(Miriam)*, Lou Frizzell *(Druggist)*, Walter Scott *(Dorothy's Husband)*, Robert Mulligan *(Narrator)*, Maureen Stapleton *(Voice of Hermie's Mother)*

p, Richard A. Roth; d, Robert Mulligan; w, Herman Raucher; ph, Robert Surtees (Technicolor); ed, Folmar Blangsted; m, Michel Legrand; prod d, Albert Brenner

AAN Best Original Story and Screenplay: Herman Raucher; *AAN Best Cinematography:* Robert Surtees; *AAN Best Film Editing:* Folmar Blangstad; *AA Best Original Dramatic Score:* Michel Legrand

People who actually recall 1942 will more greatly appreciate the waves of nostalgia that bathe this affectionate coming-of-age drama, set on a tiny island off New England. Director Mulligan (as the adult Hermie) narrates his recollections, and all of the names used in the story were the real names of the people involved (or so claimed screenwriter Raucher, who wrote the screenplay in less than two weeks). Grimes is the 15-year-old whose life we observe on the tranquil island, where the horrors of war seem a million miles away. Grimes and his friends, Houser and Conant, pal around together, get into minor scrapes, go see movies like NOW, VOYAGER, and spend a great deal of time poring over an educational sex manual. Houser reads the manual as though it were the Bible and he a seminary student; Grimes is more interested in the practical aspects of sex and yearns for O'Neill, an "older woman" in her twenties who is married to absent soldier Scott.

SUMMER OF SAM

1999 145m c Crime/Drama
40 Acres and a Mule Filmworks/Touchstone
(U.S.)

DVD
★★★½
R

John Leguizamo *(Vinny)*, Adrien Brody *(Ritchie)*, Jennifer Esposito *(Ruby)*, Mira Sorvino *(Dionna)*, Michael Rispoli *(Joey T.)*, Saverio Guerra *(Woodstock)*, Brian Tarantino *(Bobby Del Fiore)*, Al Palagonia *(Anthony)*, Ken Garito *(Brian)*, Bebe Neuwirth *(Gloria)*

p, Spike Lee, Jon Kilik; d, Spike Lee; w, Victor Colicchio, Michael Imperioli, Spike Lee; ph, Ellen Kuras; ed, Barry Alexander Brown; m, Terence Blanchard; prod d, Therese DePrez; art d, Nicholas Lundy; fx, Todd Shifflett; chor, Otis Sallid; cos, Ruth E. Carter

A tabloid slice of tabloid life, ragged, vivid, awkward, and punchy all at once.

Writer-producer-director Spike Lee's hopped-up, sexed-up reimagining of the long hot summer of 1977, when dirty, un-tourist-friendly New York City sweltered in the shadow of the .44 caliber killer, is an unexpected companion piece to DO THE RIGHT THING. They're both kinetic swirls of insular New York neighborhood life, laced with mob mentality, heat waves, fast girls and macho guys, street dynamics, intergenerational strife, and childhood loyalties shredded on the teeth of adult life's endless conflict and compromise. What it's not really about is lumbering psycho "Son of Sam" (Michael Badalucco), the bogeyman who stalks spooning couples and rants his way into every character's consciousness. The story turns on Vinny (John Leguizamo), a newlywed hairdresser who's cheating with every girl in the neighborhood while keeping starry-eyed bride Dionna (Mira Sorvino) perched unhappily on a pedestal at home. Meanwhile Vinny's long-absent buddy Richie (Adrien Brody) comes home sporting punk duds and attitude, at the same time a self-appointed neighborhood protection squad take it upon themselves to hunt down Son of Sam. For their money, anyone with hair as freaky as Richie's is a likely candidate.

Lee isn't a subtle filmmaker: "Why just let a group of local lowlifes hang around shooting the breeze when you can cluster them in front of a 'Dead End' sign?' seems to be his motto. And he's sometimes astonishingly clumsy: almost every sex scene—there are many—goes on long enough for its emotional grip to dissolve into clinical detachment. But Lee also taps into some powerful energy: the lifestyle chasm between disco flash and punk sleaze, the hellbound hedonism of Plato's Retreat, the blind fury unleashed by the great blackout of July 13.

SUMMERTIME

1955 100m c Romance
Lopert/London Films (U.S.)

DVD
★★★★

Katharine Hepburn *(Jane Hudson)*, Rossano Brazzi *(Renato Di Rossi)*, Isa Miranda *(Signora Fiorina)*, Darren McGavin *(Eddie Jaeger)*, Mari Aldon *(Phyl Jaeger)*, Jane Rose *(Mrs. McIlhenny)*, MacDonald Parke *(Mr. McIlhenny)*, Gaitano Audiero *(Mauro)*, Andre Morell *(Englishman)*, Jeremy Spenser *(Vito)*

p, Ilya Lopert; d, David Lean; w, David Lean, H.E. Bates (based on the play *The Time of the Cuckoo* by Arthur Laurents); ph, Jack Hildyard (Eastmancolor); ed, Peter Taylor; m, Alessandro Cicognini; art d, Vincent Korda

AAN Best Actress: Katharine Hepburn; *AAN Best Director:* David Lean

Based loosely on Arthur Laurents's play *The Time Of The Cuckoo*, SUMMERTIME is a romance set in Venice. Hepburn is an Ohio old maid who works as a secretary and has saved her money for a trip to Venice. She's traveling alone, and, on her first night there, she wanders around the city and sees lovers walking hand in hand. She meets Audiero, a charming child who hustles tourists, and he becomes her guide to the wonders of the city.

The next day, they go sightseeing and meet Brazzi who owns an antique shop. They fall in love, and there's a whirlwind montage as they walk, hand in hand, through the twisting streets of the main island. While waiting for Brazzi in the Piazza San Marco, she's approached by Spenser, a young man who tells her that Brazzi will be late. She soon learns that he is Brazzi's son and that her lover has a wife and family he's never mentioned. Although hurt by this revelation, Hepburn realizes that this is the most romantic interlude of her spinsterish existence; she's not about to end it now.

Touching, warm, often funny and lushly photographed. SUMMERTIME comes as close to capturing the essence of Venice as you will ever see. Lean had earlier directed BRIEF ENCOUNTER, so the story was familiar to him, although the terrain was vastly altered. There are places where the picture could have used some pruning, especially in the travelogue portions, but Hepburn and Brazzi emerge as the best middle-aged couple (short of Hepburn and Tracy) of the 1950s.

SUN ALSO RISES, THE

1957 129m c Drama
Fox (U.S.)

★★★★

Tyrone Power *(Jake Barnes)*, Ava Gardner *(Lady Brett Ashley)*, Mel Ferrer *(Robert Cohn)*, Errol Flynn *(Mike Campbell)*, Eddie Albert *(Bill Gorton)*, Gregory Ratoff *(Count Mippipopolous)*,

Juliette Greco *(Georgette)*, Marcel Dalio *(Zizi)*, Henry Daniell *(Doctor)*, Bob Cunningham *(Harris)*

p, Darryl F. Zanuck; d, Henry King; w, Peter Viertel (based on the novel by Ernest Hemingway); ph, Leo Tover (CinemaScope, DeLuxe Color); ed, William Mace; m, Hugo Friedhofer, Alexander Courage; art d, Lyle Wheeler, Mark-Lee Kirk; cos, Charles LeMaire, Fontana Sisters

Author Hemingway's paean to the Lost Generation in the wake of WWI has been adapted to the screen more faithfully than have any of his other works. Power is the aimless postwar expatriate drifting around Europe, seeking thrills to compensate for his impotence, the result of a war wound. In the company of sultry prostitute Greco, he threads his way through the bistros of Paris. He's still in love with beautiful aristocrat Gardner, who helped him recover from his wounds during the war. She is being pursued by amorous Greek tycoon Ratoff, and also by young would-be writer Ferrer. Power sets off for Pamplona with his trusted friend, fellow expatriate Albert, arriving only to find that Gardner, Ferrer, and Ratoff have preceded him there to witness the annual running of the bulls. The group is joined by carefree Scottish playboy Flynn, Gardner's former fiance. Behind the hilarity and fun, tensions mount, as all the men lust after Gardner while she wants only Power.

Producer Zanuck greatly admired Hemingway, whom he had met in Paris, introduced by screenwriter Viertel, years before. Zanuck and Hemingway both wintered in Sun Valley for a number of years and were great friends, but their friendship had been flawed by Hemingway's reaction to Zanuck's production of THE SNOWS OF KILIMANJARO. At 43, Power was old for the role. This was to be the actor's second-to-last film, and his last for Fox; he died of a heart attack the following year. This was one of Flynn's last pictures, and his self-parody is a joy, the best thing in the film. The fourth-billed Flynn had, for the first time in years and over his weak protests, accepted less than the top spot in the credits, an honor he had been accorded ever since his success in CAPTAIN BLOOD. Power's habitually petulant facial expression is wrong for this film; a contrapuntal masculinity would have served the story better. Ferrer is fine in his part as the resentful introvert. His wife Audrey Hepburn, who joined him on location in both Pamplona and in Morelia, Mexico (which doubled for the Spain location), was the one who suggested Greco to Zanuck for the role of the sympathetic prostitute. Greco was then singing at the Waldorf-Astoria in New York City, but she had a substantial cult following in Europe, where she had appeared in movies. This was her U.S. film debut. She and producer Zanuck had an on-location romance which was to continue long past the picture's release. Touted as a Zanuck "find," Evans had been a clothing manufacturer. He had actually been "found" by Norma Shearer, whose late husband, Irving Thalberg, he had portrayed in THE MAN WITH A THOUSAND FACES (not yet released at the time). Evans later became production chief at Paramount. Zanuck, goaded by the mischievous Flynn, actually ran with the bulls himself at Pamplona, but only after carefully timing himself to make certain he could stay ahead of them. The picture was reported to have cost $5 million, but it made money for the studio.

SUNDAY IN THE COUNTRY, A 📀
(UN DIMANCHE A LA CAMPAGNE)
1984 94m   c   Drama   ★★★★½
Sara/A2   (France)   G

Louis Ducreux *(M. Ladmiral)*, Sabine Azema *(Irene)*, Michel Aumont *(Gonzague/(Edouard))*, Genevieve Mnich *(Marie-Therese)*, Monique Chaumette *(Mercedes)*, Claude Winter *(Mme. Ladmiral)*, Thomas Duval *(Emile)*, Quentin Ogier *(Lucien)*, Katia Wostrikoff *(Mireille)*, Valentine Suard

p, Alain Sarde; d, Bertrand Tavernier; w, Bertrand Tavernier, Colo Tavernier (based on the novella *Monsieur Ladmiral Va Bientot Mourir* by Pierre Bost); ph, Bruno de Keyzer (Eastmancolor); ed, Armand Psenny; m, Gabriel Faure, Louis Ducreux, Marc Perrone; prod d, Patrice Mercier; cos, Yvonne Sassinot de Nesle

This beautiful film details a day in the life of an elderly painter, Ladmiral (Louis Ducreux), a holdover from the days of the French Impressionists. On one average Sunday in 1912, Ladmiral entertains his son (Michel Aumont) and the latter's family. They walk through the picturesque grounds of Ladmiral's country estate, prepare dinner, and tell wonderful stories about life and art. Unexpectedly, Ladmiral's daughter, Irene (Sabine Azema), pays a rare visit. Although Irene is the troubled outcast of the family, she is still her father's favorite, making this otherwise average Sunday exciting and worthwhile.

The story line may appear simple and undramatic, but the movie's beauty lies in this simplicity. The old painter's Sunday is serene. He is an old man who has lived a quiet life and enjoys reminiscing, his surroundings are bathed in a peaceful light, his canvas quietly awaits his artistic touch. The sum of these simple parts is a rich view of life. Betrand Tavernier, named Best Director at the Cannes Film Festival for this film, successfully evokes the essence of French life in the early 20th century. Tavernier and cinematographer Bruno de Keyzer have made a conscious effort to attain the appearance of French Impressionist painting. In fact, A SUNDAY IN THE COUNTRY is nothing short of a painting come to life.

SUNDAY, BLOODY SUNDAY 📀
1971 110m   c   Drama   ★★★½
Vectia   (U.K.)   R

Glenda Jackson *(Alex Greville)*, Peter Finch *(Dr. Daniel Hirsh)*, Murray Head *(Bob Elkin)*, Peggy Ashcroft *(Mrs. Greville)*, Tony Britton *(George Harding)*, Maurice Denham *(Mr. Greville)*, Bessie Love *(Answering Service Lady)*, Vivian Pickles *(Alva Hodson)*, Frank Windsor *(Bill Hodson)*, Thomas Baptiste *(Prof. Johns)*

p, Joseph Janni; d, John Schlesinger; w, Penelope Gilliatt; ph, Billy Williams (DeLuxe Color); ed, Richard Marden; m, Ron Geesin, Wolfgang Amadeus Mozart; prod d, Luciana Arrighi; art d, Norman Dorme; cos, Jocelyn Richards

AAN Best Actor: Peter Finch; *AAN Best Actress:* Glenda Jackson; *AAN Best Director:* John Schlesinger; *AAN Best Original Story and Screenplay:* Penelope Gilliatt

Too deliberate, but among Schlesinger's best; a strong drama about a *menage a trois* among homosexual Finch, heterosexual Jackson, and bisexual Head, who alternates between the other two. Time may decree the film a classic.

Written by *New Yorker* magazine movie critic Gilliatt, the plot presents Finch as a middle-aged bachelor doctor in London who shares his answering service with Jackson, a divorced woman who works at an employment agency. Both of them know Windsor and Pickles, a happy couple in the area, and both of them sleep with Head, a younger designer of modern sculpture. Both Jackson and Finch are aware of each other because Head is an honest sort, almost to the point of naivete. Windsor and Pickles have five children and need some time away from home, so Jackson and Head offer to stay at their home and tend the quintet while the parents go off to attend an educational seminar. On Saturday morning Head excuses himself from Jackson and only says he's "going out." She knows that he's on his way to see Finch, and the thought of it knocks her off her strict diet and into an orgy of fudge consumption. At Finch's the two men discuss an upcoming vacation to Italy, then Head returns to an annoyed Jackson, who resents having to share her lover with a man.

The characters are terribly civilized about the whole thing—too civilized, in fact, with only Jackson betraying any real emotion. The major problem with this film is that it is not easy to see what an intelligent man like Finch and an equally intelligent woman like Jackson see in Head—his character is not realized nearly so well as those of the other two. Schlesinger said that he conceived the idea of the film on the basis of some people he knew, then hired Gilliatt. She, on the other hand, claims total responsibility for the idea because she'd written a novel with a similar plot. Perhaps their differences explain the movie's unresolved undercurrent.

SUNDOWNERS, THE
1960 133m c Drama ★★★★½
Warner Bros. (U.S.)

Deborah Kerr (Ida Carmody), Robert Mitchum (Paddy Carmody), Peter Ustinov (Venneker), Glynis Johns (Mrs. Firth), Dina Merrill (Jean Halstead), Chips Rafferty (Quinlan), Michael Anderson Jr. (Sean), Lola Brooks (Liz), Wylie Watson (Herb Johnson), John Meillon (Bluey)

p, Fred Zinnemann, Gerry Blattner; d, Fred Zinnemann; w, Isobel Lennart (based on the novel by Jon Cleary); ph, Jack Hildyard (Technicolor); ed, Jack Harris; m, Dimitri Tiomkin; art d, Michael Stringer; cos, Elizabeth Haffenden

AAN Best Picture; AAN Best Actress: Deborah Kerr; AAN Best Supporting Actress: Glynis Johns; AAN Best Director: Fred Zinnemann; AAN Best Adapted Screenplay: Isobel Lennart

A splendid, sprawling saga of Australia. Set in the 1920s, it's the story of a single family, how they interact with the pioneers around them, how they extract a living from the land, how they live and love and cope. Lennart's adaptation of the Cleary novel is full of wit, sly philosophy and solid, motivated action. The title refers to those people who roam the land and live wherever they stop when the sun sets.

Mitchum is married to Kerr, and the two travel the land with their son, Anderson. They have no money, just a great love and a continuing hope that things will get better. Still, tiring of this nomadic existence, Kerr and Anderson yearn for a place where they can hang their hats. But instead of settling down, Mitchum takes a job leading more than a thousand sheep on a long trek to Cawndilla in western Australia. Since there are so many sheep to look after, Mitchum has to ask Ustinov, a onetime ship's captain, to help.

The journey is arduous and filled with excitement. Along the way, the four stop and visit with another group of Sundowners who have given up the road for a sedentary existence. Kerr and Anderson envy the life led by this family, but Mitchum pays it no mind. Mitchum and company continue on, finally delivering their sheep and collecting their fee. Then the four take jobs on a large station, with Kerr hoping they will be able to save enough money to buy their own spread.

Mitchum is splendid and Kerr was nominated for an Academy Award, as were Johns, Zinnemann, Lennart, and the picture itself. Kerr plays with little makeup and her natural beauty shines through all the dust. Johns is also a delight in her small but telling role, and Ustinov does his usual excellent job. Indeed, every aspect of the movie is first-rate, and even the smallest roles are wonderfully cast, including Australia's favorite actor, Chips Rafferty, as the sheep-shearing foreman. (Rafferty was in just about every Australian movie made in the 1940s, 1950s and 1960s, with his most famous appearance being in THE OVERLANDERS.) Big, funny, tender and humane all at the same time, THE SUN-DOWNERS is a true "family" film, without any of the cloying connotations of that term.

SUNRISE AT CAMPOBELLO
1960 144m c Biography ★★★★
Warner Bros. (U.S.)

Ralph Bellamy (Franklin D. Roosevelt), Greer Garson (Eleanor Roosevelt), Hume Cronyn (Louis Howe), Jean Hagen (Missy Le Hand), Ann Shoemaker (Sara Roosevelt), Alan Bunce (Al Smith), Tim Considine (James Roosevelt), Zina Bethune (Anna Roosevelt), Pat Close (Elliot Roosevelt), Robin Warga (Franklin D. Roosevelt)

p, Dore Schary; d, Vincent J. Donehue; w, Dore Schary (based on his play); ph, Russell Harlan (Technicolor); ed, George Boemler; m, Franz Waxman; art d, Edward Carrere; cos, Marjorie Best

AAN Best Actress: Greer Garson; AAN Best Art Direction-Set Decoration (Color): Edward Carrere, George James Hopkins; AAN Best Costume Design (Color): Marjorie Best; AAN Best Sound: George R. Groves

A heartwarming look at the early years of Franklin D. Roosevelt, adapted by legendary MGM producer Dore Schary from his award-winning stage play. Ralph Bellamy is superb as Roosevelt, capturing every nuance of a man who was the most photographed and listened-to politician of his generation. Surpassing Bellamy, though, is Garson, who doesn't play Eleanor Roosevelt, she becomes her.

It's 1921 and the Roosevelt family is vacationing on the small island of Campobello, off New Brunswick. The Roosevelts are a patrician group, with plenty of money and no worries at all. Bellamy has an eye toward public service and is the assistant secretary of the Navy, over the wishes of his mother, Shoemaker, who would prefer that he spend his time leisurely alternating between Campobello and the family's estate at Hyde Park. Returning from sailing one day, Bellamy takes to bed to recover from a "chill." When his legs suddenly become paralyzed, he's whisked to the hospital where he soon learns from doctor Ferguson that he's the victim of polio and will never again walk. Shoemaker insists that Bellamy give up his political aspirations, but Cronyn, a behind-the-scenes politico, believes his friend will be better off if he stops feeling sorry for himself and gets on with his life.

Garson's excels in an atypical role; she used some prosthetic teeth to better simulate Eleanor Roosevelt's looks, but she needn't have because her acting comes from within. She's able to emulate Eleanor's unique, often quavery voice, and she submerges her own inimitable persona into that of the president's wife to such a degree that one forgets Garson ever was Mrs. Miniver. The movie was released in September 1960, just as the Kennedy-Nixon race was going strong. Kennedy's Catholicism was still an issue with many voters, and by incorporating the anti-Catholic sentiment Al Smith had faced into his screenplay, Schary helped to minimize the religious issue in the 1960 race. Since Schary was a staunch Democrat, it seems likely that the timing of the movie's release was calculated for maximum power at the polls, as well as at the box office.

SUNSET BLVD.
DVD
1950 110m bw Drama ★★★★★
Paramount (U.S.)

William Holden (Joe Gillis), Gloria Swanson (Norma Desmond), Erich von Stroheim (Max von Mayerling), Nancy Olson (Betty Schaefer), Fred Clark (Sheldrake), Lloyd Gough (Morino), Jack Webb (Artie Green), Cecil B. DeMille, Hedda Hopper, Buster Keaton

p, Charles Brackett; d, Billy Wilder; w, Billy Wilder, Charles Brackett, D.M. Marshman Jr. (based on the story "A Can of

Beans" by Brackett, Wilder); ph, John Seitz; ed, Doane Harrison, Arthur Schmidt; m, Franz Waxman, Richard Strauss; art d, Hans Dreier, John Meehan; fx, Gordon Jennings, Farciot Edouart; cos, Edith Head

AAN Best Picture; AAN Best Actor: William Holden; *AAN Best Actress:* Gloria Swanson; *AAN Best Supporting Actor:* Erich Von Stroheim; *AAN Best Supporting Actress:* Nancy Olson; *AAN Best Director:* Billy Wilder; *AA Best Story and Screenplay:* Charles Brackett, Billy Wilder, D.M. Marshman Jr.; *AAN Best B/W Cinematography:* John F. Seitz; *AAN Best Film Editing:* Arthur Schmidt, Doane Harrison; *AA Best Score (Drama or Comedy):* Franz Waxman; *AA Best Art Direction-Set Decoration (B/W):* Hans Dreier, John Meehan, Sam Comer, Ray Moyer

No other motion picture about Hollywood comes near Billy Wilder's searing, uncompromising and utterly fascinating portrait of the film community. Beneath it all is vanity, madness, murder, and a twisted obsession with filmdom's past. Wilder's work is a sardonic portrait of an aging silent film star and a cynical young man who is engulfed by the demented siren's delusions.

The movie opens with a jolt: the bullet-riddled body of a young man is seen floating face down in the pool next to a mansion. The ghostly voice of Joe Gillis (William Holden) recounts the events leading up to his death, which are shown in flashback. A hack screenwriter, Joe is hounded by creditors and desperate for cash. After failing to sell a script—his last hope—he's driving aimlessly when he spots a couple of repo men who are after his car. He speeds off, gets a flat, and pulls into the driveway of a dilapidated mansion, where he hears an arresting female voice calling down to him, ordering him into the house. Max (Erich von Stroheim), a severe-looking, bald-headed butler, waves Joe inside, where he is shown into the august presence of silent screen star Norma Desmond (Gloria Swanson). After lamenting the current state of the film industry, she offers Joe a job writing a reworking of *Salome*, which she plans to use as a comeback vehicle. Joe knows it's a pipe dream, but he needs the work. The creepily seductive Norma insists that he stay with her while working on the script. Observed by Norma and the somber, silent Max, Joe becomes a virtual prisoner of the actress and her strange past.

SUNSET BOULEVARD is Billy Wilder's sour, insightful critique of showbiz nostalgia—the myths by which a tawdry, profit-driven industry has managed to define itself as a dream machine of unfailing glamour. Essentially satirical, the film works equally well for those fans who read it as straightforward melodrama, largely because of Swanson's remarkable performance. This was a comeback for Swanson, who achieved what her tragic character in SUNSET BOULEVARD could not. Yet the attention she received upon her return to Hollywood still couldn't match the adulation lavished on Swanson in the 1920s, when tens of thousands turned out to cheer her in mammoth parades. Swanson was thus in a singular position to empathize with her character's longing for Hollywood's past glories. As Norma says: "We didn't need dialogue. We had faces then." There is much of Norma Desmond that *is* Swanson. Not only did she allow Wilder to exploit her hard-earned image, but she let him incorporate her silent career, including footage of her work in von Stroheim's QUEEN KELLY, into the film. Swanson, however, was never the neurotic, mentally disturbed creature that Norma is off-screen. Before Swanson was chosen, Wilder and producer-coscenarist Charles Brackett talked about the possibility of using Mary Pickford, Mae Murray, Pola Negri, or even Mae West as Norma. It is unlikely that any of them could have come close to the magnificent performance given by Swanson, whose penetrating, courageous grasp of the character astounded critics, public, and peers. In 1989, SUNSET BOULEVARD was selected by the National Film Registry of the Library of Congress as one of 25 landmark films, leading examples of American cinematic art.

SUNSHINE BOYS, THE

1975 111m c   Comedy   ★★★½
UA (U.S.)   PG

Walter Matthau *(Willy Clark)*, George Burns *(Al Lewis)*, Richard Benjamin *(Ben Clark)*, Lee Meredith *(Nurse in Sketch)*, Carol Arthur *(Doris)*, Rosetta LeNoire *(Nurse)*, F. Murray Abraham *(Mechanic)*, Howard Hesseman *(Commercial Director)*, James Cranna *(TV Director)*, Ron Rifkin *(TV Floor Manager)*

p, Ray Stark; d, Herbert Ross; w, Neil Simon; ph, David M. Walsh; ed, John F. Burnett; prod d, Albert Brenner; cos, Patricia Norris

AAN Best Actor: Walter Matthau; *AA Best Supporting Actor:* George Burns; *AAN Best Adapted Screenplay:* Neil Simon; *AAN Best Art Direction-Set Decoration:* Albert Brenner, Marvin March

One of the best films ever made from a Neil Simon play, an engaging homage to the tradition of vaudeville in which the two halves of a once-famous double act (they now hate each other) re-team for a TV special.

The film opens in the 1970s with Matthau as a semi-retired comic scraping by doing commercials that his agent/nephew Benjamin has secured for him. He's auditioning for a silly potato chip TV spot for advertising director Hesseman when he blows his lines and decides that this isn't show business and he no longer wants to be a part of it. A nostalgic TV special is coming up, and Benjamin books Matthau on it, hoping that he will put aside his rancor toward his former partner, Burns, and unite this last time for the benefit of all those people who never saw them together in the flesh. Burns and Matthau haven't spoken in decades, and the mere mention of Burns is enough to send Matthau's blood pressure soaring. But he buries his enmity and agrees to see his erstwhile friend. The two men meet and began rehearsing the sketch that made them household names way back when they were known as the Sunshine Boys, but battles begin immediately as they argue over the first words of the sketch.

THE SUNSHINE BOYS is a solid movie with stellar performances from all—seldom have Simon's lines been delivered with as much bite and wit as they are here. This was Burns' first film in 35 years and he was perfect, earning a Best Supporting Actor Oscar at the age of 79. Matthau earned a nomination for Best Actor (he lost to Jack Nicholson for ONE FLEW OVER THE CUCKOO'S NEST, which collected most of the statuettes in 1975), and nominations also went to the screenplay and the art direction. Simon's inspiration for the story came from real-life vaudevillians Smith and Dale. In their very advanced years, the comics teamed to do their "Dr. Kronkheit" sketch on the Ed Sullivan show, reviving a classic piece of comedy for a whole new generation of viewers.

SUNSHINE STATE

2002 141m c   Drama   ★★★½
Anarchists' Convention   (U.S.)   PG-13

Angela Bassett *(Desiree Perry)*, Edie Falco *(Marly Temple)*, James McDaniel *(Reggie Perry)*, Ralph Waite *(Furman Temple)*, Richard Edson *(Steve Tregaskis)*, Timothy Hutton *(Jack Meadows)*, Mary Steenburgen *(Francine Pinkney)*, Jane Alexander *(Delia Temple)*, Marc Blucas *(Scotty Duval)*, Mary Alice *(Eunice Stokes)*

p, Maggie Renzi; d, John Sayles; w, John Sayles; ph, Patrick Cady; ed, John Sayles; m, Mason Daring; prod d, Mark Ricker; art d, Shawn Carroll; fx, Dan Schmit; cos, Mayes Rubeo

Ramshackle, leisurely, and crammed with fine actors allowed to do what they do best, this portrait of a divided Florida community recalls writer-director John Sayles's earlier LONE STAR and, to a lesser degree, LIMBO.

Island communities Delrona Beach and Lincoln Beach lie side by side but are worlds apart. Delrona Beach is an anonymous tourist town, while Lincoln Beach, a dwindling African-American enclave, is a holdover from the pre-civil rights era when the black community's best and brightest flocked there to escape Southern racism. Both are coveted by unscrupulous developers ready to do whatever it takes to get property owners to sell so that the developers can build pricey vacation condos, golf courses, and hotels. Caught in this larger conflict are ordinary Floridians entangled in their own problems. Marly Temple (Edie Falco) runs Delrona Beach's Sea Vue motel and loathes every minute of it; she doesn't care for her pathetic ex-husband (Richard Edson) either and much prefers her younger boyfriend (Marc Blucas). While drowning her sorrows in tequila shots, Marly meets landscaper Jack Meadows (Timothy Hutton), who briefly holds out hope for a better future. Meanwhile, in Lincoln Beach, small-time actress Desiree Perry (Angela Bassett) is making her first visit in years to see her disapproving mother, Eunice (Mary Alice). Desiree, who left town as an unmarried, pregnant teenager, is accompanied by her new husband, successful anesthesiologist Reggie (James McDaniel), but the minute she returns to her mother's house, old feelings of inadequacy rush back in.

Like LONE STAR, this group portrait mourns a rapidly vanishing American landscape while acknowledging that the past, free of corporate homogeneity though it may have been, is never the unspoiled paradise it appears in retrospect.

SUPER SIZE ME
2004 96m c Documentary ★★★½
Roadside Attractions (U.S.) PG

Morgan Spurlock, Dr. Daryl Isaacs, Dr. Lisa Ganjhu, Dr. Stephen Siegel, Bridget Bennett, Eric Rowley, Alexandra Jamieson, Dr. David Satcher, John Banzhaf III, John Robbins

p, The Con, Morgan Spurlock; d, Morgan Spurlock; ph, Scott Ambrozy; ed, Stela Gueorguieva, Julie "Bob" Lombardi; m, Steve Horowitz, Michael Parrish; art d, Joe the Artist

AAN Best Documentary Feature

Morgan Spurlock's entertaining documentary delivers a blinding glimpse of the obvious: fast food is bad for you and fast-food companies spend millions so you'll eat it anyway. His stroke of genius was to prove it by personally undertaking a 30-day, all-McDonald's diet and recording the results.

A genial New Yorker from West Virginia, the six-foot two-inch Spurlock started out weighing a healthy 185 pounds, with 11 percent body fat and exemplary blood pressure, cholesterol levels, and liver function. Three doctors and a nutritionist monitored his progress as he replaced a vegetable- and whole-grain-heavy diet with three squares a day worth of Big Macs, french fries, and bottomless cups of soda. Spurlock sampled every item on the McDonald's menu at least once and supersized his order when asked; he also curtailed his physical activity to a level commensurate with that of an office worker who drives everywhere. By the third week of the regimen, Spurlock was nearly 25 pounds heavier, plagued by headaches, lethargy, and mood swings, and looking at elevated cholesterol levels and a liver that one doctor vividly compared to foie gras.

Though gussied-up with eye-catching charts, goofy graphics, and animated illustrations, the film is held together by Spurlock's good-natured sense of humor; he's like a less belligerent and better-groomed Michael Moore. Spurlock lacks the killer instinct that would have led Moore to storm McDonald's corporate headquarters after his polite interview requests were blown off over the phone. Spurlock's feature-length call to arms is as compulsively watchable as one of the old classroom-scare pictures it often resembles, and perhaps as useless. But by co-opting the same visual language as commercial advertising's seductive come-ons, Spurlock gives his message a fighting chance.

SUPERCOP   *DVD*
(JINGCHA GUSHI III: CHAOJI JINGCHA)
1992 96m c Action/Crime/Martial Arts ★★★½
Golden Way (Hong Kong)

Jackie Chan *(Detective Kevin Chan aka Fu Sheng)*, Michelle Yeoh, billed as Michelle Khan *(Director Yang aka Hana)*, Maggie Cheung *(May)*, Bill Tung *(Uncle Bill)*, Kenneth Tsang, billed as Ken Tsang *(Chaibat aka Big Brother Wei)*, Yuen Wah *(Panther)*, Josephine Koo *(Madame Chaibat)*, Lo Lieh, billed as Law Lit *(Thai General)*, Shum Wai *(Drug Dealer)*

p, Willie Chan, Edward Tang; d, Stanley Tong; w, Edward Tang, Fibe Ma, Lee Wei-yee; ph, Ardy Lam; ed, Peter Cheung, Cheung Kar-fei; m, Joel McNeely; prod d, Wong Yue Man; art d, But Yiu Kwong; cos, Hung Wei-chuk

With this second sequel to his enormously popular POLICE STORY, Jackie Chan edges ever closer to matching American action films in scope, even if his budgets are lower. This one cost $10 million, paltry by U.S. standards but huge for a Hong Kong film; one can only wish that the care lavished on the stunt sequences had been applied to the screenplay as well.

Chan is Kevin Chan, who is drafted by his Hong Kong superiors to be the "supercop" requested by the police force in mainland China. They need someone to help them bring down an international drug ring run by Big Brother Wei (Kenneth Tsang), and Chan seems to fit the bill. But first, he must prove himself to Chinese police director Yang (Michelle Yeoh), and does so in a martial arts duel with the best fighter on her squad. He then goes undercover in a prison camp, where he helps Wei's younger brother, known as "The Panther" (Yuen Wah) "escape" from the place. After some initial doubt, Wei's gang accepts Chan into their midst, but soon it looks like his cover might be blown.

SUPERCOP: POLICE STORY III shares many of the strengths and weaknesses of Chan's latter-day films. After he moved away from the pure martial arts films that made his name (including the amazing PROJECT A, which remains one of the best kung-fu films ever made), his movies became more dependent on plot and large-scale stunts than his incredible hand-to-hand combat choreography. Like ARMOR OF GOD (another Chan title to get U.S. exposure recently), POLICE STORY III is overly dependent on plot for the first two-thirds, and the action doesn't come as enjoyably thick and fast as in his all-martial-arts fests. But, as in most Asian genre films, the final half-hour makes it all worthwhile, and what makes Chan's work continually astonishing is that the actor does all his own stunts.

The movie also benefits from Chan's considerable comic skills—he's always incorporated humor into his films, and isn't afraid to be the butt of the jokes—and from costar Yeoh (billed here as Michelle Khan), who proves to be every bit the martial artist he is. In fact, she may be the best of all the female sidekicks that have populated recent action films, treated with neither overt sensitivity nor sentimentality; she gets knocked down and jumps up again as much as Chan, and rarely gets into situations where she's dependent on him to save her. The scene in which Chan takes on Yang's best fighter, surprisingly and disappointingly, is done with sped-up visuals, but the action gets better as it goes along, culminating in the astonishing, extended final sequence that ends atop a speeding train. As usual, the film ends with outtakes of Chan and Yeoh getting into alternately funny- and painful-looking accidents in the course of shooting the action scenes.

SUPERFLY

1972 96m c Action/Crime ★★★★ DVD
Warner Bros. (U.S.) R

Ron O'Neal *(Youngblood Priest)*, Carl Lee *(Eddie)*, Sheila Frazier *(Georgia)*, Julius Harris *(Scatter)*, Charles MacGregor *(Fat Freddie)*, Nate Adams *(Dealer)*, Polly Niles *(Cynthia)*, Yvonne Delaine *(Mrs. Freddie)*, Henry Shapiro *(Robbery Victim)*, K.C. *(Pimp)*

p, Sig Shore; d, Gordon Parks Jr.; w, Phillip Fenty; ph, James Signorelli (Technicolor); ed, Bob Brady; m, Curtis Mayfield; cos, Nate Adams

This interesting feature is one of the few Hollywood films that takes an honest look at the lives of African-Americans in the ghetto. O'Neal plays a Harlem cocaine pusher whose success (via connections with corrupt police officials) has gained him the respect and envy of the neighborhood. He wants to retire from the business and enjoy the comforts this life has brought him, but first he must make one last million-dollar dope deal.

The moral ambiguity of the film may disturb some viewers, but the film smacks of realistic grit throughout. Parks, one of the few blacks to direct in Hollywood, had a real feeling for the Harlem locations and the language of its residents. The action sequences are good, and a fine score by Mayfield helps out as well. SUPERFLY was financially backed by a group of Harlem businessmen, marking one of the first times a Black-oriented film was actually financed by Blacks. It was also one of the first to use a nonwhite cast and crew. Director Parks was the son of Gordon Parks, Sr., the director of the "Shaft" movies. A sequel, SUPERFLY T.N.T., followed.

SUPERMAN

1978 143m c Science Fiction ★★★ DVD
Warner Bros. (U.S.) PG

Marlon Brando *(Jor-El)*, Gene Hackman *(Lex Luthor)*, Christopher Reeve *(Superman/Clark Kent)*, Ned Beatty *(Otis)*, Jackie Cooper *(Perry White)*, Glenn Ford *(Pa Kent)*, Trevor Howard *(1st Elder)*, Margot Kidder *(Lois Lane)*, Jack O'Halloran *(Non)*, Valerie Perrine *(Eve Teschmacher)*

p, Pierre Spengler; d, Richard Donner; w, Mario Puzo, David Newman, Leslie Newman, Robert Benton (based on the story by Puzo, from the comic strip created by Jerry Siegel, Joe Shuster); ph, Geoffrey Unsworth (Panavision, Technicolor); ed, Stuart Baird; m, John Williams; prod d, John Barry; fx, Colin Chilvers, Roy Field, Derek Meddings, Zoran Perisic, Denys Coop, Les Bowie; cos, Yvonne Blake

AAN Best Film Editing: Stuart Baird; *AAN Best Original Score:* John Williams; *AAN Best Sound:* Gordon K. McCallum, Graham Hartstone, Nicolas LeMessurier, Roy Charman; *AA Special Achievement Award—Visual Effects:* Les Bowie, Colin Chilvers, Denys Coop, Roy Field, Derek Meddings, Zoran Perisic

"You'll believe a man can fly," the ads said, and by SUPERMAN's end that's just about true. Christopher Reeve essays the title role and makes it his own, combining correctly chiseled features with a likable comic humanity, while the film itself nicely balances special effects with the romance of Superman and Lois Lane (Margot Kidder). The story opens on the planet Krypton, where Superman's father (Marlon Brando) sends his son off to Earth, where he grows up to be "mild-mannered reporter" Clark Kent. Flying around in tights and cape, Superman-alias-Clark saves the day—and Lois—a number of times. Eventually he rescues all mankind from the evil Lex Luthor (Gene Hackman) and his assistants (Ned Beatty and Valerie Perrine, in an excellent bit of comic caricature) as they plot to take over the world. Lois is killed in the course of events, but Superman circles the globe at such ter-

rific speed that its rotation is reversed, bringing his beloved back to life. The film burdens itself with too many story lines and an overlong (though beautifully photographed) prologue, but things really get moving when Reeve takes the screen. A worldwide hunt was conducted to find the right man for the role, with Robert Redford, Burt Reynolds, Nick Nolte, Kris Kristofferson, Sylvester Stallone, Ryan O'Neal, Clint Eastwood, and Charles Bronson among the candidates. So excellent is Reeve, however, that it is nearly impossible to think of anyone else as the Man of Steel.

SUPERMAN II

1980 127m c Science Fiction ★★★½ DVD
Warner Bros. (U.S./U.K.) PG

Gene Hackman *(Lex Luthor)*, Christopher Reeve *(Clark Kent/Superman)*, Ned Beatty *(Otis)*, Jackie Cooper *(Perry White)*, Sarah Douglas *(Ursa)*, Margot Kidder *(Lois Lane)*, Jack O'Halloran *(Non)*, Valerie Perrine *(Eve Teschmacher)*, Susannah York *(Lara)*, Clifton James *(Sheriff)*

p, Pierre Spengler; d, Richard Lester; w, Mario Puzo, David Newman, Leslie Newman (based on a story by Puzo, from characters created by Jerry Siegel, Joe Shuster); ph, Geoffrey Unsworth, Robert Paynter (Panavision, Technicolor); ed, John Victor-Smith; m, Ken Thorne; prod d, John Barry, Peter Murton; art d, Maurice Fowler; fx, Colin Chilvers, Roy Field, Zoran Perisic; cos, Yvonne Blake, Sue Yelland

Poking fun at its American mythos, but never descending into camp comedy, this sequel makes for a wonderful time. Christopher Reeve reprises his role as the bumbling reporter/Man of Steel with marvelous success. The film opens with a fury as terrorists who have taken over the Eiffel Tower threaten to blow it up with a nuclear bomb. Lois Lane (Margot Kidder), ever the inquisitive reporter, tries to interview the terrorists and finds herself in more trouble than she bargained for. Fortunately, Superman comes to save the day, rescuing Lois and flinging the bomb into outer space. But this sets off a nuclear explosion that frees some bad guys (Terence Stamp, Sarah Douglas, and Jack O'Halloran) from the cosmic prison they were sentenced to in SUPERMAN. The movie hits its full stride as the villains come to take over Earth, not knowing their fellow Kryptonian is that planet's hero. The result is an especially fun movie and a rare instance of a sequel that not only equals, but even betters, its original. The same cannot be said for SUPERMAN III or SUPERMAN IV: THE QUEST FOR PEACE, despite Reeve's continued command of the role.

SURE THING, THE

1985 94m c Comedy ★★★ DVD
Monument (U.S.) PG-13

John Cusack *(Walter "Gib" Gibson)*, Daphne Zuniga *(Alison Bradbury)*, Anthony Edwards *(Lance)*, Boyd Gaines *(Jason)*, Lisa Jane Persky *(Mary Ann Webster)*, Viveca Lindfors *(Prof. Taub)*, Nicollette Sheridan *(The Sure Thing)*, Tim Robbins *(Gary Cooper)*, Fran Ryan *(Louise)*, George Memmoli *(Al)*

p, Roger Birnbaum, Andrew Scheinman; d, Rob Reiner; w, Steven L. Bloom, Jonathan Roberts; ph, Robert Elswit (DeLuxe Color); ed, Robert Leighton; m, Tom Scott; prod d, Lilly Kilvert; fx, John Frazier, Jeff Wischnack; cos, Durinda Wood

A charming surprise, THE SURE THING is IT HAPPENED ONE NIGHT with acne. It's life in the Ivy League. Walter "Gib" Gibson (John Cusack) is a junk food junkie, a beer-swilling freshman who lives for women but strikes out more often than a pitcher. Alison Bradbury (Daphne Zuniga) is an all-American lass who has planned her life down to where she'll retire. They meet in a writing class and sparks fly, but the wrong kind of sparks. They hate each other on sight, or so it seems. Gib's pal, Lance (Anthony Edwards), invites him to spend Christmas in the West and says that he can arrange a date in California with a girl who is "a sure thing." Gib plans to drive out with a California-bound couple. At the same time, Alison arranges to go with the same couple to visit her own boy friend in California. Lots of good music, good humor, affection, and more than some passing philosophy as writers Steven L. Bloom and Jonathan Roberts poke fun at the effete East and the laidback West.

SUSPICION   DVD
1941   99m   bw   Thriller   ★★★★
RKO   (U.S.)

Cary Grant *(Johnnie Aysgarth)*, Joan Fontaine *(Lina McLaidlaw)*, Cedric Hardwicke *(Gen. McLaidlaw)*, Nigel Bruce *(Beaky Thwaite)*, Dame May Whitty *(Mrs. McLaidlaw)*, Isabel Jeans *(Mrs. Newsham)*, Heather Angel *(Ethel, Maid)*, Auriol Lee *(Isobel Sedbusk)*, Reginald Sheffield *(Reggie Wetherby)*, Leo G. Carroll *(Capt. Melbeck)*

d, Alfred Hitchcock; w, Samson Raphaelson, Joan Harrison, Alma Reville (based on the novel *Before the Fact* by Frances Iles); ph, Harry Stradling; ed, William Hamilton; m, Franz Waxman; art d, Van Nest Polglase, Carroll Clark; fx, Vernon L. Walker; cos, Edward Stevenson

AAN Best Picture; AA Best Actress: Joan Fontaine; *AAN Best Score (Drama):* Franz Waxman

SUSPICION is so grimly powerful that its Hollywood-style happy ending has infuriated audiences for years. Cary Grant plays penniless society wastrel Johnnie Aysgarth, who cynically romances Lina McLaidlaw (Joan Fontaine), the sheltered daughter of wealthy parents. Rapidly approaching old maidenhood, Lina escapes her oppressive home by marrying Johnnie, even though she's been warned that he's a fortune hunter and an incorrigible playboy. Apparently true to form, Johnnie becomes involved in an embezzlement scheme, which is complicated when his friend Beaky (Nigel Bruce, playing his usual lovable bumbler) dies in Paris under curious circumstances; Lina begins to suspect that Johnnie murdered him. Now Lina imagines that she's to be Johnnie's next victim and seems to find her suspicions confirmed in his every action. The tension mounts (and the humor of the film's first half subsides) as Lina becomes increasingly fearful, especially since she can find no convincing evidence that her charming husband is a killer. Soon, she's afraid to drink her nightly glass of milk, brought to her in bed by Johnnie in one of the director's most famous sequences (the milk glows ominously—Hitchcock had a light bulb placed in the glass). But the milk isn't poisoned, and the climax occurs later, when the couple are driving along a rocky cliff high above the ocean.

Based on Frances Iles' novel *Before the Fact*, in which the husband really is a murderer, SUSPICION's ending disappointed many, especially considering the slow, delicious building of Hitchcockian suspense that preceded it. With REAR WINDOW and VERTIGO, the film is one of Hitchcock's most trenchant critiques of spectatorship, as the frustrating passivity displayed by bookish fantasist Lina seems driven by a perverse desire to watch the narrative unfold. Joan Fontaine's Oscar was widely considered a compensation for the Oscar she *didn't* receive for the previous year's REBECCA.

SUSPIRIA   DVD
1976   97m   c   Horror   ★★★★
Seda Spettacoli   (Italy)   R

Jessica Harper *(Susy Banyon)*, Joan Bennett *(Madame Blank, the School Head)*, Alida Valli *(Miss Tanner, the Ballet Mistress)*, Udo Kier *(Frank)*, Flavio Bucci *(Daniel)*, Stefania Casini *(Sara)*,

Miguel Bose *(Mark)*, Barbara Magnolfi *(Olga)*, Susanna Javicoli *(Sonia)*, Eva Axen *(Pat)*

p, Claudio Argento; d, Dario Argento; w, Dario Argento, Daria Nicolodi; ph, Luciano Tovoli (Technicolor); ed, Franco Fraticelli; m, The Goblins, Dario Argento; art d, Giuseppe Bassan; cos, Piero Cicoletti

The original ad campaign boasted that the only thing more terrifying than the last five minutes of SUSPIRIA were the first 90. Actually, it's the first 15 minutes that contain some of the most frightening footage ever committed to celluloid, but why quibble.

American dance student Susy Banyon (Jessica Harper) arrives too late at night to gain admittance to her new school, Tanz Academy, but before returning to town, Susy witnesses a hysterical student, Pat (Eva Axen), fleeing the grounds in terror. By the time Susy begins classes the next day, Pat has been brutally murdered, although the academy, under the watchful eyes of administrator Madame Blank (Joan Bennett), fearsome dance instructor Miss Tanner (Alida Valli), and the school's directress, who never appears in public, insists she was expelled. Pat's death is just the first in a string of bizarre occurrences at the school that include a mysterious maggot infestation, phantom breathing, and several more gruesome murders.

Unlike many of the films it has inspired, Dario Argento's SUSPIRIA has lost little of its hallucinatory power over the years. Although anyone with an ounce of common sense would have checked out of Tanz Academy *tout de suite*, the film floats by on its own eerie logic, unfolding like a nightmare into which the viewer is dragged kicking and screaming. Not since James Whale's expressionist masterworks (1932's THE OLD DARK HOUSE and 1935's THE BRIDE OF FRANKENSTEIN) has a fright film boasted such impressive art direction and scenic design: the Tanz Academy might have been created by Erte for balletomane descendants of the Marquis de Sade. Throughout this nerve-wracking journey, Argento's sly gift is to strike when you least expect it, often when the soundtrack grows silent, and always after you've expected the knife blade to plunge in earlier.

S.W.A.T.   DVD
2003   117m   c   Crime/Action   ★★½
Original Film/Camelot Pictures/   PG-13
Chris Lee Productions   (U.S.)

Samuel L. Jackson *(Sgt. Dan "Hondo" Harrelson)*, Colin Farrell *(Jim Street)*, Michelle Rodriguez *(Chris Sanchez)*, LL Cool J, billed as James Todd Smith *(Deacon "Deke" Kaye)*, Josh Charles *(T.J. McCabe)*, Jeremy Renner *(Brian Gamble)*, Brian Van Holt *(Michael Boxer)*, Olivier Martinez *(Alex Montel)*, Reg E. Cathey *(Lt. Greg Velasquez)*, Larry Poindexter *(Capt. Thomas Fuller)*

p, Dan Halsted, Neal H. Moritz; d, Clark Johnson; w, David Ayer, Jim McClain, Ron Mita, David McKenna (from a story by Ron Mita and Jim McClain, based on characters created by Robert Hamner); ph, Gabriel Beristain; ed, Michael Tronick; m, Elliot Goldenthal; prod d, Mayne Berke; art d, Gershon Ginsburg; fx, Jon G. Belyeu; cos, Christopher Lawrence

A touch of retro grit distinguishes this formulaic cop film, inspired by the short-lived but fondly remembered 1970s television series, from the current crop of CGI-bloated action pictures.

Elite training and heavy ordnance equip LAPD's Special Weapons and Tactics team to handle domestic terrorism, snipers, and hostage situations like the one that lands officers Street (Colin Farrell) and Gamble (Jeremy Renner) in the hot seat with their boss, Captain Fuller (Larry Poindexter), when they accidentally wound a hostage. Gamble prefers quitting to demotion, while Street swallows his pride and hopes for a second chance. Six months later, he gets one. With the S.W.A.T. division under fire for their hot-dogging tactics, seasoned Sergeant "Hondo" Harrelson (Samuel L. Jackson) is called in to assemble a new and improved team, but he recruits a misfit brigade guaranteed to enrage Fuller: Deke Kaye (LL Cool J), Chris Sanchez (Michelle Rodriguez) and Street. Hondo rounds out the team with S.W.A.T. veterans Michael Boxer (Brian Van Holt) and T.J. McCabe (Josh Charles). The newly minted team is put to the test when they're charged with escorting international crime lord Alex Montel (Olivier Martinez) to a federal facility. Montel uses the presence of clamoring TV crews to offer $100,000,000 to whomever breaks him out of custody.

Actor-turned-director Clark Johnson uses all the flashy, up-to-the-minute editing and camera stunts action fans expect, but keeps the mayhem on a recognizably human scale; it's big, but not insanely overblown. Fans of the series will welcome cameos by Steve Forrest and Rod Perry, the original Hondo and Deke, and composer Elliot Goldenthal's liberal reprises of the distinctive theme music.

SWEET AND LOWDOWN   DVD

1999   95m   c   Drama   ★★★
Magnolia Productions/Sweetland Films   (U.S.)   PG-13

Sean Penn (Emmet Ray), Anthony LaPaglia (Al Torrio), Brian Markinson (Bill Shields), Gretchen Mol (Ellie), Samantha Morton (Hattie), Uma Thurman (Blanche), James Urbaniak (Harry), John Waters (Mr. Haynes), Woody Allen (Himself), Marc Damon Johnson (Omer)

p, Jean Doumanian; d, Woody Allen; w, Woody Allen; ph, Zhao Fei; ed, Alisa Lepselter; prod d, Santo Loquasto; art d, Tom Warren; fx, John Ottesen, Ron Ottesen, Tom Rosseter; cos, Linda Cunningham Bauer

AAN Best Actor: Sean Penn; *AAN Best Supporting Actress:* Samantha Morton

Woody Allen's least perfunctory film in years is also the first since BULLETS OVER BROADWAY to escape contemporary New York and Allen's usual neurotic, Upper-East-Side navel gazers.

Affectionate, melancholy, and anchored by a well thought-out performance from Sean Penn, SWEET AND LOWDOWN purports to look at the life and legend of an obscure jazz musician named Emmet Ray (Penn). Allen himself, jazz historian Nat Hentoff, and other experts appear periodically, speaking to an unseen interviewer about this fictitious guitarist whom they rate second only to authentic jazz idol Django Reinhardt. But Allen doesn't force the mockumentary issue; the talking heads mostly serve as a kind of Greek chorus, commenting on the less-than-certain facts of Ray's life. His fanciful story begins in a mobbed-up nightclub and ends in a railway yard; in between there are gangsters, swanky soirees, love affairs, opium dens, chorus girls, after-hours jam sessions, and even a trip to Hollywood—the kind of tantalizing, glittering snippets that swirl around all legendary artists. At the heart of the Ray legend are two loves: Django Reinhardt, whose music moved Ray to tears, and Hattie (Samantha Morton), the mute laundress he abandoned at the height of his success.

Working with Allen seems to awe many actors to such a degree that they forget to actually act. Not so Penn, who imagines Ray as a selfish, insecure, childish popinjay whose only redeeming quality is his undeniable talent. With his mingy moustache and shifty eyes, scuttling down the street as though his flashy shoes were a little too tight, Penn's Ray is simultaneously pathetic and despicable. But when he plays, some unsuspected inner goodness seems to trickle out through his fingers.

SWEET BIRD OF YOUTH

1962   120m   c   Drama   ★★½
Roxbury/MGM   (U.S.)

Paul Newman (Chance Wayne), Geraldine Page (Alexandra Del Lago), Shirley Knight (Heavenly Finley), Ed Begley ("Boss" Finley), Rip Torn (Thomas J. Finley), Mildred Dunnock (Aunt Nonnie), Madeleine Sherwood (Miss Lucy), Philip Abbott (Dr. George Scudder), Corey Allen (Scotty), Barry Cahill (Bud)

p, Pandro S. Berman; d, Richard Brooks; w, Richard Brooks (based on the play by Tennessee Williams); ph, Milton Krasner (CinemaScope, Metrocolor); ed, Henry Berman; art d, George W. Davis, Urie McCleary; fx, Lee LeBlanc; cos, Orry-Kelly

AAN Best Actress: Geraldine Page; *AA Best Supporting Actor:* Ed Begley; *AAN Best Supporting Actress:* Shirley Knight

Williams's steamy play gets the Richard Brooks whitewash—as with CAT ON A HOT TIN ROOF. Instead of Newman's hustler getting castrated, it's the original stage piece that gets emasculated here. Newman, Page, Sherwood, and Torn repeat their Broadway roles, and Hollywood replaced Sidney Blackmer, Diana Hyland, and Martine Bartlett with Begley, Knight, and Dunnock—all in good form. Admittedly, Brooks was under orders to make changes to the play in order to secure approval from the Production Code. But he doesn't allow the expert cast to go to the mat like they need to.

Newman is a gigolo who thinks he can make it in film; all he needs is a break. In Florida, he meets Page, a fading movie star who is at the end of her tether. Her last movie is, she is certain, a dismal flop. When she meets Newman and he gives her a ride to his home town, she begs him for more gin. Later, when they stay in a motel together, she demands an oxygen inhalator. Then she asks Newman if he can find her some hashish to smoke. In order to keep the virile Newman at her side, she tells him that she can help him get his start in Hollywood by introducing him to the right people. They travel to Newman's hometown before going back to California. Newman wants to see his one-time girlfriend, Knight, who is the apple of her father's (Begley's) eye. Begley, a corrupt politician who runs the area, hates Newman with a passion because the last time Newman came through town he left Knight pregnant and she had to get an abortion. (In the play, she was liberally infected with syphilis by her lover and had to have her ovaries removed.) Begley wants to get even with Newman for what he did to Knight, so he plots revenge with his lackey son, Torn.

All of Williams's Southern Gothic themes are intermingled here: violence, familial conflict, sexual neurosis, the mentality of the mob. Most of it comes across as overheated nonsense, but Page's egomaniacal telephone soliloquy at the film's climax is reason enough to tune in. (For devotees of camp, BIRD was filmed for TV in 1989 in an almost total misfire directed by Nicholas Roeg, with Mark Harmon more flaccid than Newman, Rip Torn moving up a generation to Begley's role, the underrated Valerie Perrine in for Sherwood, and Elizabeth Taylor playing Alexandra Del Lago like a pretty Marie Dressler.)

SWEET CHARITY   DVD

1969   157m   c   Musical/Comedy   ★★★½
Universal   (U.S.)   G

Shirley MacLaine (Charity Hope Valentine), Sammy Davis Jr. (Big Daddy), Ricardo Montalban (Vittorio Vitale), John McMartin (Oscar Lindquist), Chita Rivera (Nickie), Paula Kelly (Helene), Stubby Kaye (Herman), Barbara Bouchet (Ursula), Alan Hewitt (Nicholsby), Dante D'Paulo (Charlie)

p, Robert Arthur; d, Bob Fosse; w, Peter Stone (based on the play by Neil Simon, Cy Coleman, Dorothy Fields, adapted from the screenplay "Notti Di Cabiria" by Federico Fellini, Tullio Ponelli, Ennio Flaiano); ph, Robert Surtees (Panavision, Technicolor); ed, Stuart Gilmore; m, Cy Coleman; art d, Alexander Golitzen, George Webb; chor, Bob Fosse; cos, Edith Head

AAN Best Score (Musical): Cy Coleman; *AAN Best Art Direction-Set Decoration:* Alexander Golitzen, George C. Webb, Jack D. Moore; *AAN Best Costume Design:* Edith Head

SWEET CHARITY is a very good musical that should have been a great musical. Bob Fosse, making his film directorial debut, couldn't convey the verve he injected into the play to the movie version, which starred Shirley MacLaine as Charity, a dime-a-dance hostess in a tacky New York ballroom whose boyfriend takes all of her hard-earned savings, pushes her off a low bridge in Central Park, and absconds with the cash. Charity, however, is a die-hard optimist, down but not out. Walking along the street one evening, she comes across Italian movie star Vittorio (Ricardo Montalban) in a furious argument with his lover, Ursula (Barbara Bouchet). Vittorio takes the gamine Charity out for a night on the town in Ursula's stead—but just when sparks seem about to strike, a contrite Ursula shows up at his apartment, leaving Charity stuck hiding in a closet while Vittorio and Ursula make up. Later, Charity is trapped in a stalled elevator with Oscar (John McMartin), a mild-mannered and terribly claustrophobic insurance clerk. The two hit it off, but the romance is complicated because Oscar doesn't know Charity works in a dance hall. Eventually he does find out what she does for a living but still wants to marry her. After meeting her friends (Paula Kelly and Chita Rivera), seeing her place of employment, and discovering she wears a tattoo, however, he backs out. The film ends, as a depressed Charity is handed a flower by a band of hippies in Central Park, after which she takes new heart. Cy Coleman and Dorothy Fields wrote the fine score for the play and two new numbers for the movie, and their songs, along with Fosse's choreography and some fine supporting performances, provide the film's high points. MacLaine works very hard at not seeming to work hard but gives a somewhat studied portrayal nonetheless.

SWEET HEREAFTER, THE ★★★★
1997 110m c Drama
Ego Film Arts/Alliance Communications (Canada) R

Ian Holm *(Mitchell Stephens)*, Sarah Polley *(Nicole Burnell)*, Bruce Greenwood *(Billy Ansell)*, Tom McCamus *(Sam Burnell)*, Gabrielle Rose *(Dolores Driscoll)*, Arsinee Khanjian *(Wanda Otto)*, Alberta Watson *(Risa Walker)*, Maury Chaykin *(Wendell Walker)*, Brooke Johnson *(Mary Burnell)*, Earl Pastko *(Hartley Otto)*

p, Camelia Frieberg, Atom Egoyan; d, Atom Egoyan; w, Atom Egoyan (based on the novel by Russell Banks); ph, Paul Sarossy; ed, Susan Shipton; m, Mychael Danna; prod d, Phillip Barker; art d, Kathleen Climie; fx, Dawn Rivard; cos, Beth Pasternak

AAN Best Director: Atom Egoyan; *AAN Best Adapted Screenplay:* Atom Egoyan

Atom Egoyan's THE SWEET HEREAFTER is a beautifully crafted and quietly devastating adaptation of Russell Banks' novel about the cataclysmic effect of a tragic school bus accident on a small Canadian community.

Following a school bus accident that killed 14 children in a town in British Columbia, lawyer Mitchell Stephens (Ian Holm) tries to enlist the bereaved parents into a filing a lawsuit against the bus company. Stephens convinces a number of parents to join the lawsuit, including Sam Burnell (Tom McCamus) and his wife, Mary (Brooke Johnson), whose daughter Nicole (Sarah Polley) was one of the few survivors of the crash, but is now wheelchair bound. However, Stephens meets resistance from widower Billy Ansell (Bruce Greenwood) who lost two children in the accident and actually witnessed it while following the bus in his truck, which was part of his daily routine. While Stephens carefully chooses those parents to represent the community which he believes to have the highest moral characters, he's unaware of various secrets which could jeopardize his case, including the fact that Nicole was involved in an incestuous relationship with her father.

The preceding synopsis doesn't adequately convey THE SWEET HEREAFTER's most impressive attribute, which is its complex time-jumping structure. Egoyan creates a multi-layered texture by intercutting disparate images and incidents in his customarily elliptical and enigmatic manner. While somewhat disconcerting at first, the complicated design starts to kick in about halfway through, building powerfully to the sequence where Billy watches the bus slide off the icy road as he's waving to his kids, followed by a stunning cut to the film's signature image—an overhead shot of a sleeping, cuddling family—presumably Stephens, his wife, and his daughter as a baby. The film does contain some heavy-handed symbolism—still, with all of its flaws, Egoyan has created a work that is often psychologically dense and visually transcendent.

SWEET HOME ALABAMA ★★½
2002 109m c Romance/Comedy
Touchstone (U.S.) PG-13

Reese Witherspoon *(Melanie Carmichael)*, Josh Lucas *(Jake Perry)*, Patrick Dempsey *(Andrew Hennings)*, Candice Bergen *(Kate)*, Mary Kay Place *(Pearl Smooter)*, Fred Ward *(Earl Smooter)*, Jean Smart *(Stella Kay)*, Ethan Embry *(Bobby Ray)*, Melanie Lynskey *(Lurlynn)*, Courtney Gains *(Wade)*

p, Stokely Chaffin, Neal H. Moritz; d, Andy Tennant; w, C. Jay Cox (based on a story by Douglas J. Eboch); ph, Andrew Dunn; ed, Tory Takaki, Tracy Wadmore-Smith; m, George Fenton; prod d, Clay A. Griffith; art d, Jay Pelisser; fx, Mat Beck, David Fletcher; chor, Karen Beyer; cos, Sophie de Rakoff Carbonell

Diverting fluff in the tradition of Hollywood's screwball comedies of remarriage, SWEET HOME ALABAMA may lack the wit or grace of, say, THE AWFUL TRUTH, but it's rescued from mediocrity by the charming Reese Witherspoon.

Steel magnolia Melanie Carmichael (Witherspoon) has taken New York City by storm, establishing herself as a hot young fashion designer and winning the heart of the town's most eligible bachelor. Andrew (Patrick Dempsey), who also happens to be the son of New York City's formidable mayor (Candice Bergen), orchestrates the perfect marriage proposal (he keeps Tiffany's open after hours), but Melanie hesitates. Contrary to what she's led people to believe, she was really raised in scruffy Pigeon Creek, AL, and her only connection to the wealthy Carmichael family was hanging out with their closeted gay son, Bobby Ray (Ethan Embry), back when she was better known as Melanie Smooter. Her parents, Earl and Pearl (Fred Ward, Mary Kay Place), live in a trailer, and there's the vexing matter of high-school sweetheart Jake (Josh Lucas), who wouldn't be a big deal if Melanie hadn't married him. So she hightails it back to Pigeon Creek to sort things out, starting with the divorce papers Jake's refused to sign for six years. And just when she thinks she's out, Melanie gets dragged back into the down-home life.

The good news is that for all its clumsiness, the movie manages some tidy twists on the tried-and-true formula. But for every small pleasure there's a coarse, obvious joke, and the movie would fall flat were it not for Witherspoon. She may not have Katharine Hepburn's aristocratic looks, but she's mastered her trademark mix of snippy resolve and evident intelligence.

SWEET SMELL OF SUCCESS
1957 96m   bw   Drama   DVD
Hecht-Hill-Lancaster   (U.S.)   ★★★★★

Burt Lancaster (*J.J. Hunsecker*), Tony Curtis (*Sidney Falco*), Susan Harrison (*Susan Hunsecker*), Martin Milner (*Steve Dallas*), Sam Levene (*Frank D'Angelo*), Barbara Nichols (*Rita*), Jeff Donnell (*Sally*), Joseph Leon (*Robard*), Edith Atwater (*Mary*), Emile Meyer (*Harry Kello*)

p, James Hill; d, Alexander Mackendrick; w, Clifford Odets, Ernest Lehman (based on the short story "Tell Me About It Tomorrow" by Lehman); ph, James Wong Howe; ed, Alan Crosland Jr.; m, Elmer Bernstein; art d, Edward Carrere

Emerging from a posh nightclub into the rain-slicked streets of midtown Manhattan, where a couple of hoodlums can be seen rolling a drunk, ruthless showbiz journalist J.J. Hunsecker experiences a pre-dawn epiphany. "I love this dirty town," he exclaims.

The moment is typical of SWEET SMELL OF SUCCESS, Alexander Mackendrick's perverse, masterly romance of urban menace and moral decay. Best known as the director of lovably quirky Ealing comedies (e.g., THE MAN IN THE WHITE SUIT), Mackendrick turns to film noir with a vengeance, evincing a very British fascination with (and simultaneous distaste for) naked American ambition. With the assistance of legendary cinematographer James Wong Howe, he fashions a stark, neon-lit urban landscape that seems to comprehend and surpass all of its predecessors in the genre.

Sidney Falco (Tony Curtis) is a Broadway flack whose income depends on getting media exposure for his showbiz clients. The most coveted form of publicity is a mention in the syndicated newspaper column written by Hunsecker (Burt Lancaster), a Walter Winchell type with a nationwide audience and sufficient clout to intimidate the President. Desperate to plant items for his clients, Falco panders shamelessly to the columnist. Hunsecker, who spends his evenings sipping coffee in a trendy nightspot, is a sternly forbidding, collossally repressed bachelor with no apparent interest in women apart from his younger sister Susan (Susan Harrison). Neurotically overprotective of Susan, who lives with him in an implicitly incestuous arrangement, Hunsecker feels threatened by her blossoming romance with jazz musician Steve Dallas (Martin Milner). Hunsecker pressures Falco to break up the relationship; should he fail, he'll lose all access to the column.

After fabricating a blind item implying that the young musician is a pot-smoking Communist, Falco inveigles a cigarette girl (Barbara Nichols) into sleeping with an entertainment reporter; in exchange for her favors, the reporter runs the item. Dallas loses his gig and is forced to appeal to Hunsecker, who offers to get him his job back if he agrees to stay away from Susan. Dallas furiously refuses. Hunsecker then extracts a promise from his sister that she will not see Dallas again. She soon breaks her word, however, meeting the musician at a secluded spot by the river, where he persuades her that she is being manipulated by her older brother. When Hunsecker discovers the couple's surreptitious reunion, he again turns to Falco to scotch the romance. This time Falco is guaranteed a period of carte blanche access to the column should his machinations succeed. Unable to resist the lucrative offer, Falco plants a reefer in Dallas's topcoat pocket and tips police detective Harry Kello (Emile Meyer). Kello finds the marijuana and viciously beats Dallas with pair of shot-loaded gloves.

As Falco celebrates, he receives a call from Susan, who sounds suicidal. He races to the Hunseckers' apartment and tries to comfort the half-dressed girl while sitting on her bed. Hunsecker arrives and, assuming the worst, tosses Falco out and interrogates Susan. Knowing that Falco is mixed up in her boyfriend's persecution, she refuses to defend him. In a jealous rage, Hunsecker calls Kello and informs the sadistic detective that he's been hoodwinked by Falco. Kello tracks Falco

down near a highway overpass and, as the younger man shouts his defiance, again pulls on his sinister gloves. Meanwhile, Susan packs a suitcase and walks out of her brother's apartment forever.

SWEET SMELL OF SUCCESS captures the sleazy allure of Manhattan like no other film; Howe's atmospheric night-for-night location shooting turns a Broadway juice bar into a cross between a Weegee photo and an Edward Hopper canvas. The charmingly venal Sidney Falco was a breakthrough role for Tony Curtis, whose frequent miscasting, particularly in costume adventures, had become something of a Hollywood joke. Here, comfortable for once in an urban milieu, Curtis does a remarkable job, managing to elicit sympathy without compromising his character's essential tawdriness. His brash '50s hepcat—a kid who's risen a little above his station and masks his insecurities with manufactured bravado—is a reminder that Cool wasn't invented by James Dean (who never even played a city boy). Lancaster, vividly sinister, seems ready to implode from surplus repression. Co-screenwriter Clifford Odets ("Golden Boy") contributes passages of lyrical slang to a Freudian scenario based on a novella by Ernest Lehman (NORTH BY NORTHWEST). The brisk jazzy score was contributed by Elmer Bernstein, who makes canny use of the Chico Hamilton Quintet.

SWEET SWEETBACK'S BAADASSSSS SONG   DVD
1971 97m   c   Action/Drama   ★★★★
Cinemation Industries   (U.S.)   X

Melvin Van Peebles (*Sweetback*), Simon Chuckster (*Beetle*), Hubert Scales (*Mu-Mu*), John Dullaghan (*Commissioner*), Rhetta Hughes (*Old Girl Friend*), West Gale, Niva Rochelle, Nick Ferrari, Ed Rue, Mario Van Peebles

d, Melvin Van Peebles; w, Melvin Van Peebles; ph, Bob Maxwell; ed, Melvin Van Peebles; m, Melvin Van Peebles

A landmark in black filmmaking in the U.S., this angry, extravagant, loud, belligerent movie reaches a high pitch early on and stays there. It's written, directed, photographed, scored by, and stars Melvin Van Peebles, who'd always wanted to be a filmmaker, went to France to do a conventional film (STORY OF A THREE DAY PASS), came back to try his hand in Hollywood (WATERMELON MAN), and finally wound up here, an independent in full control of his product.

The narrative is linear and relatively unimaginative. Sweetback (Van Peebles), who's working in a brothel when the film begins, is finally moved to action, stomps a couple of cops unconscious, then begins running. He runs for the rest of the film, finally escaping to Mexico.

SWEET SWEETBACK is not an easy film to admire: it's violent, even sadistic, obscene, frenzied, painful. Some critics condemned it for trading on a classic Black stereotype, the "buck." On the surface, the film has all the extreme elements of the most cynical "Blaxploitation" movies, but Van Peebles actually uses these elements in order to comment upon them. The pain with which he washes the screen is meant to be transmuted into anger by audiences, and then into political action. Obviously, this didn't happen, and probably never could. But the film succeeds as a *cri de coeur*, an announcement that black militancy has reached your neighborhood theater and that things will never be the same.

SWEET SWEETBACK caused considerable controversy among black commentators and critics, but it remains one of very few black films from the 1970s to spring entirely from a black artistic sensibility. Although this independent release didn't appear on *Variety* charts, it grossed more than $10 million, thus becoming one of the most financially rewarding independent productions of all time.

SWEETIE
1989 97m c Comedy ★★★★
Arenafilm (Australia)

Genevieve Lemon *(Dawn)*, Karen Colston *(Kay)*, Tom Lycos *(Louis)*, Jon Darling *(Gordon)*, Dorothy Barry *(Flo)*, Michael Lake *(Bob)*, Andre Pataczek *(Clayton)*, Jean Hadgraft *(Mrs. Schneller)*, Paul Livingston *(Teddy Schneller)*, Louise Fox *(Cheryl)*

p, John Maynard; d, Jane Campion; w, Jane Campion, Gerard Lee (based on an idea by Jane Campion); ph, Sally Bongers; ed, Veronika Heussler; m, Martin Armiger; prod d, Peter Harris; cos, Amanda Lovejoy

To appreciate the complexity and uniqueness of SWEETIE, Jane Campion's remarkably assured first feature, try to imagine Roman Polanski's REPULSION reworked as a romantic comedy or Brian De Palma's SISTERS refashioned as a farce.

Kay (Karen Colston) is a gaunt, withdrawn young woman whose life is ruled by superstition. A control freak, she fervidly accepts a fortune teller's prediction that she'll meet a man with a question mark on his forehead and promptly steals a coworker's fiance (Tom Lycos) who fits the bill: he sports a wayward curl of hair over a beauty mark. For a while, the uptight woman relaxes, but her phobic behavior is never completely overcome. When her obese sister Dawn (Genevieve Lemon) appears on the scene, unannounced and uninvited, we begin to understand just why Kay's a paranoid bundle of repression. Manipulative and alternately petulant or hysterical, the eponymous "Sweetie" gobbles life voraciously, sampling food and men with the same relish; she's a female Peter Pan straitjacketed in a little girl's frilly party dress. Not surprisingly, her wildly inappropriate behavior has brought her family to the end of its rope.

In this darkly stylish debut, New Zealander Campion has fashioned a slapstick domestic tragedy. In addition to being a remarkable visual stylist (brilliantly aided by cinematographer and former classmate Sally Bongers), Campion elicits miracles of acting from her cast. In this comically heightened version of reality, the actors might all too easily have overplayed the laughs and forced the tears; instead they are effectively disquieting and colorful. Cruelly honest and pitilessly funny, SWEETIE is one of the nakedest explorations of familial love and desperation ever filmed.

SWEPT AWAY **DVD**
2002 89m c Romance/Comedy ★★
SKA Films/CODI SpA (U.K./Italy) R

Madonna *(Amber Leighton)*, Adriano Giannini *(Giuseppe)*, Jeanne Tripplehorn *(Marina)*, Michael Beattie *(Todd)*, Elizabeth Banks *(Debi)*, Bruce Greenwood *(Tony Leighton)*, David Thornton *(Michael)*, Yorgo Voyagis *(Captain)*, Lorenzo Ciompi *(Rich Man)*, Francis Pardeilhan *(Tony's Assistant)*

p, Matthew Vaughn; d, Guy Ritchie; w, Guy Ritchie (based on the screenplay *Swept Away ... by an Unusual Destiny in the Blue Sea of August*, by Lina Wertmüller); ph, Alex Barber; ed, Eddie Hamilton; m, Michel Colombier; prod d, Russell De Rozario; art d, Damon Earnshaw; cos, Arianne Phillips

What happens when a brittle, overbearing socialite is stranded on an uninhabited island with the macho sailor she humiliated for kicks? In Guy Ritchie's ill-advised remake of Lina Wertmüller's controversial 1974 fable, love conquers all—once the brawny he-man has taught his peroxide harpy some lessons in humility.

Filthy-rich Tony Leighton (Bruce Greenwood) surprises his wife, Amber (Madonna), and friends (Michael Beattie, Elizabeth Banks, David Thornton, Jeanne Tripplehorn) with a Mediterranean vacation aboard a chartered yacht. Amber, who's demanding, fickle, and just plain mean, focuses her spiteful wrath on deckhand Giuseppe (Adriano Giannini, whose father starred in the original), demeaning him at every

opportunity. The tables are turned when Amber and Giuseppe find themselves washed ashore on a deserted, Darwinian paradise. Giuseppe adapts quickly, while hunger forces the helpless Amber to play by Giuseppe's rules; if she wants to eat, she must debase herself by doing menial tasks, calling him master, and literally kissing his feet.

Both versions of SWEPT AWAY are driven by the shifting balance of power between the characters, who are really just broad-stroke embodiments of principles: effete, wealthy parasitism vs. working-class self-reliance. The effectiveness of this kind of give-and-take relies heavily on casting, and Ritchie puts himself at a disadvantage: Madonna looks terrific in a bikini but she can't act, and the younger Giannini is simply stunt casting. He's not bad, but he lacks the chops to compensate for a blank-slate costar. More importantly, Ritchie and Madonna misunderstand the story's fundamental dynamics. If you de-emphasize the brutal sexual interplay and highlight the comic spectacle of a snooty rich lady getting taken down a few pegs, you're remaking OVERBOARD, not SWEPT AWAY.

SWEPT AWAY ... BY AN UNUSUAL DESTINY IN **DVD** THE BLUE SEA OF AUGUST
1974 116m c Drama/Comedy ★★★½
Medusa (Italy) R

Giancarlo Giannini *(Gennarino)*, Mariangela Melato *(Raffaella)*

p, Romano Cardarelli; d, Lina Wertmuller; w, Lina Wertmuller; ph, Giulio Battiferri, Giuseppe Fornari, Stefano Ricciotti; m, Piero Piccioni; cos, Enrico Job

Aboard a chartered yacht a group of wealthy northern Italians discuss a variety of topics while basking in the sun. The snobbish Melato takes particular delight in taunting Giannini, a Sicilian deckhand, ridiculing his smelly shirt and communist ideology. Surely, Giannini is the last man on earth Melato would ever want to be shipwrecked with on a desert isle. SWEPT AWAY is a wild romp and certainly lives up to its elongated title. When destiny does indeed shipwreck the two, none of Melato's arrogance can keep this two-person war between the sexes and classes from taking some passionately amorous turns. Director-screenwriter Lina Wertmuller's 11th film (the fourth to gain a U.S. release) provoked much controversy for what many perceived as a reactionary, sexist treatment of Melato's role by Wertmuller, a self-described feminist. (One beating scene goes on for a *long* time.) The argument has merit, although it ignores the broadness of Wertmuller's treatment here of some of her favorite themes. Gender and class politics are ever-present throughout the story, but laced with a delightfully satiric bite that provokes laughter as well as thought. Giannini and Melato are perfectly matched as the combatants/lovers, providing a chemistry that lends Wertmuller's parable some degree of naturalism and honesty. With lesser actors the story might never have worked, and it certainly wouldn't have made such a splash at the box office.

SWIMMER, THE **DVD**
1968 94m c Drama ★★½
Horizon/Dover (U.S.) PG

Burt Lancaster *(Ned Merrill)*, Janet Landgard *(Julie Hooper)*, Janice Rule *(Shirley Abbott)*, Tony Bickley *(Donald Westerhazy)*, Marge Champion *(Peggy Forsburgh)*, Nancy Cushman *(Mrs. Halloran)*, Bill Fiore *(Howie Hunsacker)*, John Garfield Jr. *(Ticket Seller)*, Kim Hunter *(Betty Graham)*, Rose Gregorio *(Sylvia Finney)*

p, Frank Perry, Roger Lewis; d, Frank Perry, Sydney Pollack (uncredited); w, Eleanor Perry (based on the short story by John Cheever); ph, David Quaid, Michael Nebbia (Technicolor); ed,

Sidney Katz, Carl Lerner, Pat Somerset; m, Marvin Hamlisch; art d, Peter Dohanos; cos, Anna Hill Johnstone, Elizabeth Stewart

Frequently silly but oddly memorable and unsettling, THE SWIMMER is an underrated blend of existential fable and social satire. Based on a *New Yorker* short story by John Cheever, it's buoyed by the music of a 22-year-old Marvin Hamlisch making his film scoring debut.

It's a summer day in suburban Connecticut, and successful advertising executive Ned Merrill (Burt Lancaster), clad only in swim trunks, finds himself several miles from home. Rather than walk straight back to his house, he decides to "swim" home, touring the pools of all his friends and neighbors. These include Betty Graham (Kim Hunter), on whom he once harbored a crush; Julie Hooper (Janet Landgard, in her film debut), who used to baby-sit his daughters and lust after him, but meets his latterday advances with bewilderment; and his former mistress, Shirley Abbott (Janice Rule), who shatters Ned with her assertion that she never loved him. Many of those Ned encounters are openly critical, commenting on his failed marriage or the children who have turned their backs on him. Each of these revelations seems to come as a shock, as though he's been unaware of them until now. As the journey continues, Ned's life is seen to be progressively disintegrating, until he reaches his own home, a dilapidated place which has clearly been empty for years, and breaks down in tears.

A collaboration between director Frank Perry (DAVID AND LISA) and his then-wife and screenwriter, Eleanor Perry, THE SWIMMER was deemed too confusing by its producers, who brought in Sydney Pollack to turn the Lancaster/Rule scene into a neater ending. Much of the film is still confusing, not to mention portentous and credibility-straining, but it remains genuinely affecting. Shot on location in Westport, Connecticut.

SWIMMING POOL 📀

2003 102m c   Mystery/Drama   ★★★½
Canal Plus/Fidelite Productions/France 2   R
Cinema/Gimages/Headforce   (U.K./France)

Charlotte Rampling *(Sarah Morton)*, Ludivine Sagnier *(Julie)*, Charles Dance *(John Bosload)*, Marc Fayolle *(Marcel)*, Jean-Marie Lamour *(Franck)*, Mireille Mosse *(Marcel's Daughter)*, Michel Fau *(First Man)*, Jean-Claude Lecas *(Second Man)*, Emilie Gavois Kahn *(Waitress at Cafe)*, Erarde Forestali *(Old Man)*

p, Olivier Delbosc, Marc Missonnier; d, Francois Ozon; w, Emmanuele Bernheim, Francois Ozon; ph, Yorick Le Saux; ed, Monica Coleman; m, Philippe Rombi; art d, Wouter Zoon; cos, Pascaline Chavanne

Francois Ozon's tricky thriller relies on its smoothly unrippled surface, leisurely pacing, and slightly awkward performances to create a false sense of security that sets up viewers for a shock when it takes an abrupt turn into Patricia Highsmith territory.

Successful, middle-aged English novelist Sarah Morton (Charlotte Rampling) is crippled by writer's block and suspicious that her longtime publisher, John Bosload (Charles Dance), is more interested in newer writers than old stalwarts like herself. Sarah accepts John's offer of his summer house in the South of France, thinking a change of scenery could be inspiring. Sarah eases into the gentle rhythms of nearby Luberon, where she eats lunch at the town's small cafe, flirting diffidently with waiter Franck (Jean-Marie Lamour). This idyllic quiet is shattered when Julie (Ludivine Sagnier), John's neglected teenage daughter, suddenly arrives. Loud and recklessly promiscuous, Julie is openly contemptuous of the tightly wound Sarah, but the women eventually reach a rapprochement. In fact, Sarah becomes so intrigued by Julie that she begins drawing heavily on Julie's confidences for her new novel. But when Julie brings home Franck for a one night

stand, she creates an uncomfortable situation from which Sarah decorously withdraws. When Franck fails to show up at work the next day, Sarah begins entertaining dark suspicions about what transpired after she went to bed.

Ozon's cool sensibilities are a perfect match for French novelist Emmanuele Bernheim's elliptical screenplay; her elegantly untrustworthy narrative knits together clever psychological parrying and cliched mystery elements, then delivers an unsettling ending that casts the entire story in a different light. Rampling and Sagnier's prickly rapport is most ambiguous when it seems a bit obvious—there's always a revelation waiting around the bend.

SWIMMING TO CAMBODIA 📀

1987 87m   c   Drama/Comedy   ★★★½
Screenliner Productions/Cinecom International
Films/Swimming Company   (U.S.)

Spalding Gray, Sam Waterston, Ira Wheeler

p, Renne A. Shafransky; d, Jonathan Demme; w, Spalding Gray (from his performance piece); ph, John Bailey; ed, Carol Littleton; m, Laurie Anderson; prod d, Sandy McLeod

A surprisingly compelling film adaptation of Spalding Gray's one-man, two-evening stage performance about his experiences in Cambodia while filming a small role in Roland Joffe's THE KILLING FIELDS. Director Jonathan Demme has boiled the original monologue down to 87 minutes that still manage to encompass everything from Gray's search for his "perfect" moment, to his adventures in Hollywood (where, among other things, he auditions for a TV show opposite Farrah Fawcett), to his grisly evocation of the reign of the Khmer Rouge, whom he at one point compares to upstate New York hicks. Gray is a spellbinding monologist, and Demme constructs a perfect, uncluttered showcase for his subject's powers. All we get is Gray, a table, a glass of water, a couple of maps, and some "sound images" courtesy of Laurie Anderson; but that's enough to create a mesmerizing odyssey through the mind of a uniquely talented performer, as well as through one of the gorier chapters of modern history.

SWINDLE, THE 📀

(IL BIDONE)
1955 92m   bw   Drama   ★★★½
Titanus/SGC (France/Italy)

Broderick Crawford *(Augusto)*, Richard Basehart *(Picasso)*, Franco Fabrizi *(Roberto)*, Giulietta Masina *(Iris)*, Lorella De Luca *(Patrizia)*, Giacomo Gabrielli *(Vargas)*, Sue Ellen Blake *(Anna)*, Alberto De Amicis *(Rinaldo)*, Irene Cefaro *(Marisa)*, Xenia Valderi *(Luciana)*

p, Mario Derecchi; d, Federico Fellini; w, Federico Fellini, Ennio Flaiano, Tullio Pinelli (based on a story by Fellini, Flaiano); ph, Otello Martelli; ed, Mario Serandrei, Giuseppe Vari; m, Nino Rota

To many people the films of Fellini are an obnoxious blend of tiresome episodes filled with ugly characters and extreme symbolism. Others find these same elements to be a magical universe filled with the forces influencing an individual's fate. They appreciate the revealing caricatures, lively costumes and sets, and extenuating sounds that create a poetic vision. The latter camp will find much to entertain themselves with in THE SWINDLE, a film similar to its predecessor, LA STRADA, in its depiction of a man who goes through life almost blind to its wonders and with little pity for other humans. Crawford plays a petty thief who teams up with Basehart and Fabrizi to swindle poor people. Fabrizi is the first to back out of these schemes—not to redeem himself but to go on to "better" things. Of the three, his character is the least sympathetic because his acts of thievery are done so casually. In a moment of enlightenment, Basehart forsakes this lifestyle to return to his wife Masina who, as in LA STRADA, looks on the events with her large round eyes. She is the direct opposite of the soulless Fabrizi. This leads Crawford to assemble another bunch to assist in his operations. In the touching final scenes, Crawford is dressed in a bishop's robes in order to execute a scheme when he is approached by an invalid, Blake, who takes him for the real thing, bending down to kiss his hand. Crawford finally feels remorse for his deeds, realizing that he has been taking advantage of people who are driven by pure faith. But by this time it's too late for him to repent. A very dark vision that isn't always pleasant to look at but is nonetheless fascinating. The film did not get a U.S. release until 1962.

SWING SHIFT

DVD

1984 113m c Drama/War ★★★½
Warner Bros. (U.S.) PG

Goldie Hawn (Kay Walsh), Kurt Russell (Lucky Lockhart), Christine Lahti (Hazel Zanussi), Fred Ward (Biscuits Toohey), Ed Harris (Jack Walsh), Sudie Bond (Annie), Holly Hunter (Jeannie Sherman), Patty Maloney (Laverne), Lisa Pelikan (Violet Mulligan), Susan Peretz (Edith Castle)

p, Jerry Bick; d, Jonathan Demme; w, Nancy Dowd, Bo Goldman, Ron Nyswaner; ph, Tak Fujimoto (Technicolor); ed, Craig McKay; m, Patrick Williams; prod d, Peter Jamison; art d, Bo Welch; cos, Joe I. Tompkins

AAN Best Supporting Actress: Christine Lahti

This latter-day look at "Rosie the Riveter" stars Goldie Hawn as Kay Walsh, whose husband, Jack (Ed Harris), is sent off to fight in WWII. Kay goes to work at an aircraft factory where she meets Lucky (Kurt Russell), whose heart problem has kept him out of uniform. They begin an affair, and Kay also develops a close friendship with her "loose" (i.e., emancipated) neighbor, Hazel (Christine Lahti). When Jack comes home on furlough, he discovers Kay's infidelity and goes back to war with a broken heart. In turn, Lucky, feeling rejected, sleeps with the lonely Hazel, upsetting relations among the three civilians. SWING SHIFT's view of adultery isn't very palatable—since Jack is at least as likable, if not more, than Lucky and seems to have a "good" marriage with Kay. Many castigated the film for using wartime hardships to justify Kay's affair and tarnish the patriotic image of the homefront Rosies. A fairer assessment suggests that director Jonathan Demme's characteristic generosity toward his characters and refusal to make absolute moral judgments are strong points, while the feminist subtext adds freshness to the story. The dullness of Kay and Lucky's romance, however, does damage the film, and may be the result of friction between Demme and Hawn, who reportedly had another director brought in to shoot new scenes that conventionalized the love triangle and downplayed Lahti's Hazel. Supporting Actress Oscar. Released at 113, 100, and 99 minutes, the movie is on videocassette at 100 minutes.

SWING TIME

1936 105m bw Musical/Romance ★★★★★
RKO (U.S.)

Fred Astaire (John "Lucky" Garnett), Ginger Rogers (Penelope "Penny" Carrol), Victor Moore (Dr. Cardetti), Helen Broderick (Mabel Anderson), Eric Blore (Mr. Gordon), Betty Furness (Margaret Watson), George Metaxa (Ricardo Romero), Landers Stevens (Judge Watson), John Harrington (Dice Raymond), Pierre Watkin (Al Simpson)

p, Pandro S. Berman; d, George Stevens; w, Howard Lindsay, Allan Scott (based on a story by Erwin Gelsey); ph, David Abel; ed, Henry Berman; m, Jerome Kern; art d, Van Nest Polglase,

Carroll Clark; fx, Vernon L. Walker; chor, Hermes Pan; cos, Bernard Newman, John Harkrider

AA Best Song: "The Way You Look Tonight"; Jerome Kern (Music), Dorothy Fields (Music); AAN Best Dance Direction: Hermes Pan

TOP HAT may be more energetic and glossy, but SWING TIME is arguably the most magical of the ten films Fred Astaire and Ginger Rogers made together. Their dancing and acting rapport are at a peak and director George Stevens shows more finesse than Mark Sandrich in lending the couple's rocky romance a genuinely heartfelt quality. This film seems to be more about the Astaire-Rogers mystique than any of the others, so it's especially poignant when Fred sings that he's "Never Gonna Dance" if he can't have Ginger.

The story tells of "Lucky" Garnett (Astaire), a gambler and and dancer engaged to Margaret Watson (Furness, in her pre-consumer advocacy days). When Lucky shows up late for his wedding, Margaret's father (Landers Stevens, the director's real-life father) tells him not to return until he earns $25,000 to prove that he's not just a layabout. Once Lucky meets dance teacher Penny Carrol (Rogers), however, his main problem is to keep from earning the 25 grand, since, of course, he falls in love with Penny. Highlights include a complex and delightful routine to "Pick Yourself Up," one of the greatest of the Astaire-Rogers light courtship duets, just as their luminous turn to "Waltz in Swing Time" stands today as one of their finest romantic turns. Their last duet, to the aforementioned "Never Gonna Dance," really signals the end of the Astaire-Rogers golden years; this number, with the scene preceding it, constitutes the team's most touching five minutes together on film.

SWING TIME also features Astaire's incredible solo dance to "Bojangles of Harlem," perhaps the only blackface number on film which doesn't make one squirm today. His skin made up as an African-American rather than a minstrel-show caricature of one, Astaire dances an obvious tribute to the great Bill Robinson, even if the black dancer he more closely approximates is John Bubbles of PORGY AND BESS fame. The marvelous score, with music by Jerome Kern and lyrics by Dorothy Fields, consists of one classic song after another, and they are all stunningly staged. Astaire's rendition of "The Way You Look Tonight" comes while Rogers washes her hair. Her final appearance gently mocks the tender lyric, but her rubbing of Astaire's shoulder confirms the sentiment of the moment. "A Fine Romance," meanwhile, that famous sardonic love duet, appears while the couple walks around a gorgeous set of a snowy inn, the final swishing of the car's wiper blades perfectly rounding out the tune. The supporting cast, led by the acerbic Broderick, the sweetly bumbling Moore and the unctuous Blore, adds plenty of laughs, and, at the center of it all, Hollywood's ideal couple shines at their brightest. A film to cherish.

SWISS FAMILY ROBINSON

DVD

1960 126m c Children's ★★★½
Walt Disney Productions (U.K.) G

John Mills (Father), Dorothy McGuire (Mother), James MacArthur (Fritz), Janet Munro (Roberta), Sessue Hayakawa (Pirate Chief), Tommy Kirk (Ernst), Kevin Corcoran (Francis), Cecil Parker (Capt. Moreland), Andy Ho (Auban), Milton Reid (Big Pirate)

p, Bill Anderson; d, Ken Annakin; w, Lowell S. Hawley (based on the novel by Johann Wyss); ph, Harry Waxman (Panavision, Technicolor); ed, Peter Boita; m, William Alwyn; prod d, John Howell; art d, John Howell; fx, Danny Lee, Walter Stones; cos, Julie Harris

Disney's version of the famous novel is a superior adventure following the exploits of the title family. Father and Mother Robinson (John Mills and Dorothy McGuire) and their three sons, Fritz, Francis, and Ernst (James MacArthur, Kevin

Corcoran, and Tommy Kirk), flee Napoleon and look for someplace to live in the South Seas, but in the course of the search they are chased by pirates and their ship is pounded by an angry sea. After the ship's crew deserts the sinking vessel with only the family on board, the Robinsons crash along a rocky shore and emerge to find a tropical island Eden. Since the ship, which is only half-submerged, is filled with food and gear, they prepare to settle in. Numerous adventures follow in this exciting and humorous picture filled with classic Disney touches. It's a tongue-in-cheek movie that avoids the sappy sentiment of so many "family" films and concentrates on sheer entertainment instead. The scenery is lush and colorful; the film's success made Tobago a tourist haven for many years afterward.

SWITCHBLADE SISTERS

1975 91m c Action/Crime **DVD**
Centaur (U.S.) ★★½
R

Robbie Lee *(Lace)*, Joanne Nail *(Maggie)*, Monica Gayle *(Patch)*, Kitty Bruce *(Donut)*, Janice Karman *(Bunny)*, Marlene Clark *(Muff)*, Michael Miller *(Hammer)*, Asher Brauner *(Dominic)*, Chase Newhart *(Crabs)*, Don Stark *(Hook)*

p, John Prizer; d, Jack Hill; w, F.X. Maier (based on a story by F.X. Maier, John Prizer and Jack Hill); ph, Stephen Katz; ed, Mort Tubor; m, Les Baxter; prod d, Robinson Royce, B.B. Neel; cos, Jodie Tillen

Kinetic, colorful, and cartoony, this girl-gang actioner developed a cult following after its disastrous first run when it reappeared on the midnight-movie circuit in 1988. In all its solarized, wah-wah-pedal glory, it's as emblematic as any film of its era.

In a scenario that borrows freely from *Othello*, Lace (chipmunk-voiced chippie Robbie Lee) leads the Silver Dagger gang's auxiliary, the Dagger Debs. Her Iago is a one-eyed cutie named Patch (Monica Gayle). Lace loves Dominic (Asher Brauner), the Daggers' leader. In steps new girl Maggie (Joanne Nail), a cool blonde who whips a mean chain. A rival gang, headed by politically savvy hustler Crabs (Chase Newhart), operates a power-to-the-people community center that serves free lunches, gets government funding, and fronts for his drug dealing. When Crabs's high school closes down and his gang transfers to Dom's, trouble is inevitable.

Except for Chase Newhart, the acting here is so uniformly godawful that it almost suggests a stylistic choice. And with the exception of Donut (Kitty Bruce, daughter of comedian Lenny), the "teens" all look a mite long in the tooth. Fortunately, smart direction, tightly choreographed action sequences, and decent camerawork (albeit on cheap-looking stock) make SWITCHBLADE SISTERS seem better than it is.

SYLVIA

2003 110m c Biography/Drama **DVD**
Ariel Films/BBC Films/British Film Council/ ★★★
Capitol Films/Ruby Films (U.K.) R

Gwyneth Paltrow *(Sylvia Plath)*, Daniel Craig *(Ted Hughes)*, Jared Harris *(Al Alvarez)*, Blythe Danner *(Aurelia Plath)*, Michael Gambon *(Professor Thomas)*, Amira Casar *(Assia Wevill)*, Andrew Havill *(David Wevill)*, Lucy Davenport *(Doreen)*, Liddy Holloway *(Martha Bergstrom)*, David Birkin *(Morecambe)*

p, Alison Owen; d, Christine Jeffs; w, John Brownlow; ph, John Toon; ed, Tariq Anwar; m, Gabriel Yared; prod d, Maria Djurkovic; art d, Jane Cecchi, John Hill; fx, Ken Durey; cos, Sandy Powell

Gwyneth Paltrow's powerful interpretation of doomed poet Sylvia Plath is a welcome return to form after such forgettable junk as a VIEW FROM THE TOP. Skipping Plath's early years entirely, New Zealand director Christine Jeffs focuses exclusively on Plath's seven-year marriage to English poet Ted Hughes.

Three years after surviving a suicide attempt, Sylvia (Paltrow) meets the rakishly handsome Ted (Daniel Craig) in 1956 at a Cambridge University soiree. Sexual sparks fly, and within months Sylvia and Ted are married and living in a Boston suburb near Sylvia's widowed mother, Aurelia (Paltrow's real-life mother, Blythe Danner). Sylvia teaches poetry at Smith College while Ted lectures adoring coeds at the University of Massachusetts—an arrangement that stirs Sylvia's deep-seated distrust. She finds it increasingly hard to write in the shadow of Ted's growing fame, and once the couple moves back to England, where Sylvia gives birth to the first of their two children, the indifference that greets her first book of poems aggravates her depression. Sylvia and Ted retreat to the picturesque gloom of the Devon countryside, where Ted finally admits to having an affair with the wife of a fellow poet. Sylvia once again slips into a suicidal despair while producing her greatest work.

The Plath-Hughes marriage has long been the subject of intense controversy between those who hold that Plath was driven to self-destruction by a cruel, philandering husband and those who argue that she was the victim of her own personal demons. Jeffs doesn't bring much to the public debate—the film is soft on Hughes and navigates a safe middle ground—but it's a first-rate showcase for Paltrow. With her beautiful, haunted eyes, Paltrow carefully underplays what a lesser actor would have rendered luridly histrionic.

T

T-MEN

1947 91m bw Crime **DVD**
Eagle-Lion (U.S.) ★★★★

Dennis O'Keefe *(Dennis O'Brien)*, Alfred Ryder *(Tony Genaro)*, Mary Meade *(Evangeline)*, Wallace Ford *(Schemer)*, June Lockhart *(Tony's Wife)*, Charles McGraw *(Moxie)*, Jane Randolph *(Diana)*, Art Smith *(Gregg)*, Herbert Heyes *(Chief Carson)*, Jack Overman *(Brownie)*

p, Aubrey Schenck; d, Anthony Mann; w, John C. Higgins (based on a story by Virginia Kellogg); ph, John Alton; ed, Fred Allen; m, Paul Sawtell; art d, Edward C. Jewell; fx, George J. Teague; cos, Frances Ehren

AAN Best Sound Recording: Sound Services Inc.

One of Anthony Mann's finest forays into film noir, T-MEN was also one of the director's first financial triumphs. O'Keefe and Ryder are two treasury agents determined to crack a successful counterfeiting ring after a fellow agent is killed during the investigation. In order to obtain first-class information, the agents pose as underworld hoods and infiltrate a powerful Detroit mob family headed by Kosta. They discover that Ford, a sleazy L.A.-based hood with a penchant for steam baths, may hold the key to the counterfeiting ring, so the agents ingratiate themselves with him. Ford is afraid he'll soon be knocked off by the boys in Detroit, and his fears are justified; they have sent McGraw to kill him. Suspecting that Ryder is a T-Man, Ford informs McGraw of his suspicions, hoping that he'll be allowed to live. McGraw accepts the news and then locks Ford in a steam bath and turns the steam on full blast. The sadistic killer stands and watches as the hysterical Ford tries to smash the glass in the tiny window, to no avail. Meanwhile, Ryder finally cracks the secret of the counterfeiting operation, just as McGraw and the gang, O'Keefe among them, arrive intending to kill him.

When PRC studios and Britain's J. Arthur Rank organization merged to form Eagle-Lion, the new owners encouraged better scripts and more artistic creativity while providing bigger budgets to achieve their goals. Director Mann rose to the occasion and began a series of fascinating film noir crime dramas (T-MEN, RAW DEAL, and THE BLACK BOOK) with superb cinematographer John Alton. Presented in a documentary-like style with narration by Reed Hadley, T-MEN shifts from the bureaucratic staunchness of a voiceover to the shadowy, out-of-control world of film noir. In what would become a major theme in Mann's later work (especially in his westerns with Jimmy Stewart), the film examines the thin line between the law and the lawless, the hunters and the hunted. Though lawmen O'Keefe and Ryder plunge themselves into the criminal element with fervor, they are party to acts only sanctioned by society if one wears a badge. These themes are illustrated beautifully by Alton's visuals, which put the agents in the same shadowy light as the criminals. The film is at its most shocking during the steam bath murder and the scene is intense and horrifying enough to disturb most sensitive viewers. Mann and Alton's work for Eagle-Lion was so distinguished that MGM took note and signed both of them.

TAILOR OF PANAMA, THE
2001 110m c Spy   ★★★½
Merlin Films/Columbia   (U.S./Ireland)   R

Pierce Brosnan (Osnard), Geoffrey Rush (Harry), Jamie Lee Curtis (Louisa), Leonor Varela (Marta), Brendan Gleeson (Mickie Abraxas), Harold Pinter (Uncle Benny), Catherine McCormack (Francesca), Daniel Radcliffe (Mark), Lola Boorman (Sarah), David Hayman (Luxmore)

p, John Boorman; d, John Boorman; w, Andrew Davies, John Le Carre, John Boorman (based on the novel The Tailor of Panama by John Le Carre); ph, Philippe Rousselot; ed, Ron Davis; m, Shaun Davey; prod d, Derek Wallace; art d, Irene O'Brien, Lucinda Thompson; fx, Clive Beard, Peter Chiang; cos, Maeve Paterson

A cut above the preposterous action spectacles that now pass for espionage films, John Le Carre's sly tale of intrigue and mendacity above and beyond the call of duty is enlivened by the complementary performances of Geoffrey Rush and Pierce Brosnan.

The year is 1999, and the Panama canal has recently been returned to the Panamanian government. Meanwhile, back in England, smug MI-6 operative Andy Osnard (Brosnan) is in disgrace after yet another sexual indiscretion. Osnard's career expectations were clearly formed by Ian Fleming novels, and when the reality is disappointing, he simply reworks it until it's more to his liking. A sympathetic superior (David Hayman) ships him off to sleepy Panama, figuring he can't get into much trouble down there. Osnard quickly "recruits" Harry Pendel (Rush), a purveyor of bespoke suits, reasoning that men tell their haberdashers everything—and well aware that Pendel is a one-time arsonist who later "tailored" his own past into something more respectable. Possessed of no covert knowledge worth having, Pendel fabricates tales out of whole cloth; he concocts for Osnard a "Silent Opposition" to the government out of nothing more than his acquaintance with two weary former student radicals (Brendan Gleeson and Leonor Varela).

The story begins in the blackly comic tradition of Graham Greene's OUR MAN IN HAVANA, then spirals into something very near to tragedy. Director John Boorman's storytelling conceits don't always work, but this slippery tale is

solid enough to wriggle through the rough patches, which include the appearance of Pendel's late Uncle Benny (playwright Harold Pinter) whenever Pendel has a moral decision to make. Uncle Benny invariably advises lying or denying, which is amusing enough, but feels jarring in this otherwise realistic—if utterly absurd—milieu.

TAKE ME OUT TO THE BALL GAME
1949 93m c Sports/Musical   [DVD] ★★★★
MGM (U.S.)

Frank Sinatra (Dennis Ryan), Esther Williams (K.C. Higgins), Gene Kelly (Eddie O'Brien), Betty Garrett (Shirley Delwyn), Edward Arnold (Joe Lorgan), Jules Munshin (Nat Goldberg), Richard Lane (Michael Gilhuly), Tom Dugan (Slappy Burke), Murray Alper (Zalinka), Wilton Graff (Nick Donford)

p, Arthur Freed; d, Busby Berkeley; w, Harry Tugend, Harry Crane (uncredited), George Wells (based on a story by Gene Kelly and Stanley Donen); ph, George Folsey (Technicolor); ed, Blanche Sewell; m, Roger Edens; art d, Cedric Gibbons, Daniel B. Cathcart; fx, Warren Newcombe, Peter Ballbusch; chor, Gene Kelly, Stanley Donen; cos, Helen Rose, Valles

Dennis Ryan (Frank Sinatra) and Eddie O'Brien (Gene Kelly) are a popular song-and-dance team on the vaudeville circuit who spend their summers playing baseball in a semiprofessional league. Ready to begin a new season, the pair are surprised and delighted to find that a woman, K.C. Higgins (Esther Williams), is the new team owner as well as their manager. Both men find her attractive, but K.C. is only interested in fielding a good team. When Eddie is benched for moonlighting as a dance director for a nightclub chorus line, he falls under the spell of Joe Lorgan (Edward Arnold), a seemingly benevolent man who in reality is a big-time gambler, and trouble brews for Eddie and his team.

While there's not much baseball played here, this is an amiable film, marked by the enjoyable cast and some lively, if not memorable, music. TAKE ME OUT TO THE BALL GAME was Sinatra and Kelly's follow-up to ANCHORS AWEIGH, and the two are again well-matched partners. The film was based on an original idea of Kelly and Stanley Donen's that closely resembled a minor 1930 film, THEY LEARNED ABOUT WOMEN. After concocting the story, Kelly and Donen asked for the chance to direct, but it was decided to bring in the legendary Busby Berkeley—who had fallen on hard times—and the film turned out to be his last directorial effort. Kelly and Donen, however, were allowed to direct TAKE ME OUT TO THE BALL GAME's musical sequences and producer Arthur Freed was impressed enough to allow them to direct the next Kelly-Sinatra film, the classic ON THE TOWN, later that year.

TAKE THE MONEY AND RUN
1969 85m c Crime/Prison/Comedy   [DVD] ★★★½
Heywood/Hillary/Palomar (U.S.)   M

Woody Allen (Virgil Starkwell), Janet Margolin (Louise), Marcel Hillaire (Fritz), Jacquelyn Hyde (Miss Blaire), Lonny Chapman (Jake), Jan Merlin (Al), James Anderson (Chain Gang Warden), Howard Storm (Fred), Mark Gordon (Vince), Micil Murphy (Frank)

p, Charles H. Joffe; d, Woody Allen; w, Woody Allen, Mickey Rose; ph, Lester Shorr, Fouad Said (Eastmancolor); ed, Ralph Rosenblum, James T. Heckert, Ron Kalish, Paul Jordan; m, Marvin Hamlisch; art d, Fred Harpman; fx, A.D. Flowers

Woody Allen's first directorial achievement is a frequently hilarious, sometimes misfiring satire of crime movies. Allen plays the typical shlemiel, a put-upon wimp who becomes a compulsive criminal. Told in semidocumentary fashion, with a rambling narration by Jackson Beck (who was heard as the narrator on radio's "Superman" for years), it prefigures Allen's work years later in ZELIG.

One-liners galore, lots of episodic scenes and some good satire, with the intercutting of actual news footage to establish the era (President Richard Nixon and Dwight Eisenhower figure prominently). A bit of homage to Claude Lelouch in the love scenes between Allen and Margolin, then into the jail sequences that can best be appreciated by those familiar with I AM A FUGITIVE FROM A CHAIN GANG, THE LAST MILE, or any of several jail movies. A spotty picture with many delicious moments, including a sequence where Allen hires an over-the-hill movie director (Hillaire) to pretend he is shooting a film about a bank robbery so that Allen and his men can use that as a cover for their actual robbery of the institution. Everything is going well until a rival gang arrives with the same intention. Several inside jokes are unfathomable to viewers from the hinterlands.

TAKING LIVES

2004 103m c Thriller **★★½** DVD
Village Roadshow Pictures/Mark Canton Productions/ R
Warner Bros. (U.S.)

Angelina Jolie *(Special Agent Illeana Scott)*, Ethan Hawke *(Costa)*, Kiefer Sutherland *(Hart)*, Gena Rowlands *(Mrs. Asher)*, Olivier Martinez *(Paquette)*, Tcheky Karyo *(Leclair)*, Jean-Hugues Anglade *(Duval)*, Paul Dano *(Young Asher)*, Justin Chatwin *(Matt Soulsby)*, Andre Lacoste *(Cashier)*

p, Mark Canton, Bernie Goldmann; d, D.J. Caruso; w, Jon Bokenkamp (based on the novel by Michael Pye); ph, Amir Mokri; ed, Anne V. Coates; m, Philip Glass; prod d, Tom Southwell; art d, Serge Bureau; fx, Louis Craig, Stephen Gilbert, Pierre Rivard; cos, Marie-Sylvie Deveau

Very loosely adapted from Michael Pye's novel, this multiple-twist thriller gets off to a fine, creepy start but eventually becomes too preposterous for its own good.

A handsome woman of a certain age (Gena Rowlands) gets off a Montreal ferry and tells the nearest policeman that she has just seen her son, who had supposedly been killed by a truck nearly 20 years earlier. Martin, the formidable Mrs. Asher continues, was a disturbed teenager and is no doubt now a very dangerous man. Simultaneously, a mangled corpse is unearthed at a construction site, and art dealer John Costa (Ethan Hawke) interrupts a deadly assault. Although the victim dies, Costa produces a sketch of the assailant. Inspector Leclair (Tcheky Karyo), who's supervising the investigation, requests the assistance of American FBI agent Illeana Scott (Angelina Jolie), a cum laude graduate of the spooky intuition school of criminal profiling. She confirms their suspicion that the two crimes are linked, and further deduces that they're only the most recent in a decades-long string of murders by a killer who slips into the lives of his victims. The investigation swiftly comes to focus on Martin Asher, and Scott believes that their best chance of catching him is to use Costa as bait.

It goes without saying that the words "it's over" are spoken far too early in the proceedings to mean any such thing. Where Pye's novel was a literary meditation on identity, Jon Bokenkamp's adaptation is a conventional serial-killer picture in which the twists are consistently surprising because they don't make much sense. And Agent Scott is a men's magazine fantasy of a tough, smart woman; the drape of her T-shirts is far more carefully imagined than the workings of her mind.

TAKING OF PELHAM ONE TWO THREE, THE

1974 104m c Crime **★★★½** DVD
Palomar/Palladium (U.S.) R

Walter Matthau *(Lt. Garber)*, Robert Shaw *(Blue)*, Martin Balsam *(Green)*, Hector Elizondo *(Grey)*, Earl Hindman *(Brown)*, James Broderick *(Denny Doyle)*, Dick O'Neill *(Correll)*, Lee Wallace *(The Mayor)*, Tom Pedi *(Caz Dolowicz)*, Beatrice Winde *(Mrs. Jenkins)*

p, Gabriel Katzka, Edgar J. Scherick; d, Joseph Sargent; w, Peter Stone (based on the novel by John Godey); ph, Owen Roizman (Panavision, Technicolor); ed, Jerry Greenberg, Robert Q. Lovett; m, David Shire; art d, Gene Rudolf; cos, Anna Hill Johnstone

This exciting, suspenseful drama of a subway car held for ransom begins with Matthau, a New York transit cop, giving some visiting Japanese a guided tour of the subway control center. Matthau mocks and insults the party, not realizing that his guests speak English. Meanwhile, in the subway tunnels of New York, a train pulls out of the Pelham station at 1:23 p.m. Aboard are four men wearing identical hats, glasses, mustaches, and raincoats. The group, led by Shaw, separates one car from the train, taking the conductor (Broderick) and the passengers on board hostage. Their demands are chillingly simple: the city must pay $1 million ransom in exactly one hour or else they will begin killing hostages. A dialogue begins over the radio between Matthau and Shaw as the detective tries to negotiate a safe release for the hostages. One of the kidnappers, Balsam, is suffering from a bad cold, and Matthau blesses him with each sneeze. Shaw eventually has Broderick killed when the demands have not been met. The ransom money is finally delivered, and the gang make their plan to escape.

Though Matthau and Shaw spend most of the film communicating through a microphone, the tension between the two is well developed. The editing back and forth is sharp, accentuating the two strong performances and adding to the suspense. Shaw is excellent as the cold-blooded killer, with a steely performance that fascinates as well as frightens. The one low point is the slice-of-life group of passengers aboard the subway. Each hostage is a stereotype, ranging from a mother with two bratty children to a streetwise pimp, to Gorrin's know-it-all old man. The direction is sharp, using the small, darkened world of the subway to its fullest, and backed by Shire's exciting jazz score that complements the suspense. The film was advertised in many large cities with posters displayed in subway stations, but this ad campaign emphasizing every commuter's nightmare was dumped when subway riders across the country complained.

TAKING OFF

1971 92m c Comedy/Drama **★★★½**
Forman/Crown/Hausman (U.S.) R

Lynn Carlin *(Lynn Tyne)*, Buck Henry *(Larry Tyne)*, Linnea Heacock *(Jeannie Tyne)*, Georgia Engel *(Margot)*, Tony Harvey *(Tony)*, Audra Lindley *(Ann Lockston)*, Paul Benedict *(Ben Lockston)*, Vincent Schiavelli *(Schiavelli)*, David Gittler *(Jamie)*, Ike Turner

p, Alfred W. Crown; d, Milos Forman; w, Milos Forman, John Guare, Jean-Claude Carriere, John Klein; ph, Miroslav Ondricek (Movielab Color); ed, John Carter; art d, Robert Wightman; cos, Peggy Farrell

Milos Forman's first U.S. movie is a rather dated look at the mores of the country he had just adopted. At the time of its release, critics welcomed the Czech-born Forman's skewed perspective on a transitional period of American culture, but today the film, like so much else from the late '60s and early '70s, can best be appreciated as a historical curio.

Heacock is a a teenager who has run away from her affluent Long Island home and settled in New York's East Village, where she hopes to make a career as a singer. Parents Carlin and Henry team up with Lindley, who also has a runaway child, to search for their daughter amidst the countercultural milieu that they fear and despise. At first, they're repelled, but it isn't long before they begin to respond to the allure of marijuana and sexual freedom.

The movie is more satire than farce, and satire "is what closes on Saturday nights," said George S. Kaufman.

Kaufman was right, and this movie did nowhere near the business it deserved, although it did serve to introduce Forman to the U.S. audience after his European successes with LOVES OF A BLONDE and THE FIREMAN'S BALL. Henry had done cameo appearances in THE GRADUATE and CATCH-22 and here has a full-fledged leading role. His work is exemplary, and he more than holds his own with the other, more experienced actors. Carlin first came to prominence in FACES, although her career never went as far as her talent could have taken her. Heacock was an amateur whom Forman spotted in Central Park. Forman enjoys using nonprofessionals and always seems to evoke excellent results from them. The promise of this first U.S. movie was realized when Forman distinguished himself with ONE FLEW OVER THE CUCKOO'S NEST and AMADEUS. The script was written by a formidable quartet composed of Forman, playwright Guare (whose "The House of Blue Leaves" won several Tony Awards in June, 1986), French author Carriere (who co-wrote BELLE DU JOUR and THE MILKY WAY), and Klein.

TALE OF TWO CITIES, A   DVD
1935 120m bw Historical   ★★★★★
MGM (U.S.)

Ronald Colman (Sydney Carton), Elizabeth Allan (Lucie Manette), Edna May Oliver (Miss Pross), Blanche Yurka (Mme. DeFarge), Reginald Owen (Stryver), Basil Rathbone (Marquis St. Evremonde), Henry B. Walthall (Dr. Manette), Donald Woods (Charles Darnay), Walter Catlett (Barsad), Fritz Leiber (Gaspard)

p, David O. Selznick; d, Jack Conway; w, W.P. Lipscomb, S.N. Behrman (based on the novel by Charles Dickens); ph, Oliver T. Marsh; ed, Conrad A. Nervig; m, Herbert Stothart; art d, Cedric Gibbons, Frederic Hope; cos, Dolly Tree

AAN Best Picture; AAN Best Film Editing: Conrad A. Nervig

Easily the best film version of Charles Dickens's classic novel (out of at least seven), A TALE OF TWO CITIES follows the turmoil and aftermath of the French Revolution. Sydney Carton (Colman) is a world-weary London barrister in love with Lucie Manette (Allan). She thinks of him only as a friend, however, and marries Charles Darnay (Woods), a descendant of a noble Frenchman who is also Carton's lookalike. Darnay's uncle, the Marquis St. Evremonde (Rathbone), is a heartless tyrant who is killed at the Revolution's onset. As the nephew of the hated Marquis, Darnay is arrested in Paris and sentenced to death. Lucie is frantic with worry over her husband, and Carton, devoted to Lucie but seeing no hope of happiness, goes to Paris, where he frees Darnay and takes his place in prison. His last words as he ascends the scaffold have become so identified with Colman that they are almost impossible to say without slipping into his distinctive accent: "It is a far, far better thing that I do than I have ever done; it is a far, far better rest that I go to than I have ever known."

This superb, lavish production features an MGM stock company playing every small role to perfection, and Colman gives one of the best performances of his life in a role he had long wanted to play. He captures Carton's intellectualism, cynicism, self-pity and nobility in equal measure, achieving a richness of characterization that would have pleased Dickens himself. Equally memorable is Blanche Yurka as the sinister Mme. DeFarge. This is nastiness to rival Mercedes McCambridge's ripe, blistering work in JOHNNY GUITAR. And, as in that Nicholas Ray film, Yurka has her own Joan Crawford to confront: the inimitable Edna May Oliver, representing the forces of virtue. Their final struggle is one of the highlights of the film. The film has, in fact, many great moments, among the most beautiful of which is Carton's walk through the snow as the holiday carolers go by. The finale, as Carton awaits death, is equally powerful and touching. In a small role as a seamstress also being executed, Isabel Jewell gets to pull off yet another marvelous dramatic vignette.

One of director Jack Conway's finest efforts, the film never suffers from a sense that the novel has been compressed or rushed. Moving, fresh and aware of its effects, this film stands as one of Hollywood's finest adaptations of a novel. Its huge and deserved success gave producer David O. Selznick the freedom to walk away from MGM (and his father-in-law, Louis B. Mayer) and set up Selznick International Pictures. "Tis a far, far better thing" indeed.

TALENTED MR. RIPLEY, THE   DVD
1999 139m c Thriller   ★★★½
Timnick Films/Mirage Enterprises   (U.S.)   R

Matt Damon (Tom Ripley), Gwyneth Paltrow (Marge Sherwood), Jude Law (Dickie Greenleaf), Cate Blanchett (Meredith Logue), Philip Seymour Hoffman (Freddie Miles), Jack Davenport (Peter Smith-Kingsley), James Rebhorn (Herbert Greenleaf), Sergio Rubini (Inspector Roverini), Philip Baker Hall (Alvin MacCarron), Celia Weston (Aunt Joan)

p, William Horberg, Tom Sternberg; d, Anthony Minghella; w, Anthony Minghella (based on the novel The Talented Mr. Ripley by Patricia Highsmith); ph, John Seale; ed, Walter Murch; m, Gabriel Yared; prod d, Roy Walker; art d, John Fenner; fx, Richard Conway; cos, Ann Roth, Gary Jones

AAN Best Supporting Actor: Jude Law; AAN Best Art Direction: Roy Walker, Bruno Cesari; AAN Best Costume Design: Ann Roth, Gary Jones; AAN Best Original Score: Gabriel Yard; AAN Best Adapted Screenplay: Anthony Minghella

Based on Patricia Highsmith's 1955 literary crime novel, this coolly beautiful film is both a superior thriller and an engrossing study of a sociopath's progress.

Life hasn't been especially generous to Tom Ripley (Matt Damon): he's handsome and charming, to be sure, but he's also penniless, badly educated, and has none of the connections that open doors. Then coincidence throws wealthy Herbert Greenleaf (James Rebhorn) Ripley's way. Greenleaf's shiftless son, Dickie (Jude Law) is knocking around southern Italy, squandering his allowance on jazz, women, and liquor. Greenleaf hopes that Ripley, whom he thinks knew Dickie at college, might be willing to go abroad and talk some sense into the boy. Ripley needs no persuasion, but he's not interested in getting Dickie to come home. Once in Italy, Ripley befriends Dickie's well-bred girlfriend (Gwyneth Paltrow), immerses himself in Dickie's favorite music, and takes to Dickie's hedonistic lifestyle as though to the manner born. Having tasted la dolce vita, Ripley must now figure out how to hang on to it.

For movie buffs, Anthony Minghella's film labors in the shadow of Rene Clement's 1961 PURPLE NOON, but it's a fine thriller in its own right and actually truer to the novel; among other things, neither Damon nor Minghella shies away from its homoerotic undertones. Minghella aspires to the look of glossy, late-'50s Hitchcock films (Hitchcock, of course, adapted Highsmith's perverse STRANGERS ON A TRAIN), all tainted glamour and swank corruption. He also embraces the cynical sympathies that make Highsmith's books feel so unnervingly timeless, notably her clear-eyed understanding that not only does wickedness often go unpunished, but if it's packaged attractively enough, it's often actively rewarded.

TALES OF MANHATTAN
1942 118m bw Comedy   ★★★½
Fox (U.S.)

Charles Boyer (Paul Orman), Henry Fonda (George), Ginger Rogers (Diane), Rita Hayworth (Ethel Halloway), Charles Laughton (Charles Smith), Paul Robeson (Luke), Ethel Waters

(Esther), Edward G. Robinson *(Larry Browne),* Cesar Romero *(Harry Wilson),* J. Carrol Naish *(Costello)*

p, Boris Morros, Sam Spiegel; d, Julien Duvivier; w, Ben Hecht, Ferenc Molnar, Donald Ogden Stewart, Samuel Hoffenstein, Alan Campbell, Ladislas Fodor, Laslo Vadnay, Laszlo Gorog, Lamar Trotti, Henry Blankfort, Buster Keaton (uncredited); Edmund Beloin, William Morrow; ph, Joseph Walker; ed, Robert Bischoff; m, Sol Kaplan; art d, Richard Day, Boris Leven; cos, Irene, Dolly Tree, Bernard Newman, Gwen Wakeling, Oleg Cassini

TALES OF MANHATTAN follows the adventures of a fancy tail coat as it goes from riches to rags. A famous actor (Charles Boyer) initially buys the coat, only to be told the garment carries a curse. Later, it winds up with a man (Cesar Romero) whose fiancee (Ginger Rogers) finds a love letter in one of the pockets. He insists the coat belongs to his pal (Henry Fonda), but his strategy backfires when, impressed by the letter's passion, she runs off with the friend. The cursed jacket then passes from a composer (Charles Laughton) to an impoverished lawyer (Edward G. Robinson), who wears it to a college reunion, where three former classmates decide to help him get back on his feet. Next to own the garment is a crook (J. Carrol Naish) who wears it while he pulls off a job. Pocketing the loot, he boards a plane, but during the flight he throws the coat out the window, forgetting it's stuffed with $40,000. The money flutters to the ground and is picked up by two sharecroppers (Paul Robeson and Ethel Waters) who take it to the local preacher, while the coat ends up on a scarecrow. TALES OF MANHATTAN unfolds with charm. Under the fine direction of Julien Duvivier (who directed the similarly episodic UN CARNET DU BAL, 1938), the episodes flow smoothly. It has, however, been criticized for its simplistic presentation of blacks in the final episode, and Robeson later denounced the film. Also unfortunate is that what might have been the best sequence, featuring W.C. Fields, didn't make the final cut.

TALES OF TERROR

1962   90m   c   Horror   **DVD** ★★★½
Alta Vista   (U.S.)

Vincent Price *(Locke/Fortunato/Valdemar),* MORELLA: Maggie Pierce *(Lenora),* Leona Gage *(Morella),* Edmund Cobb *(Driver),* THE BLACK CAT: Peter Lorre *(Montresor),* Joyce Jameson *(Annabel),* Lennie Weinrib, John Hackett *(Policemen),* THE CASE OF MR. VALDEMAR: Basil Rathbone *(Carmichael),* Debra Paget *(Helene)*

p, Roger Corman; d, Roger Corman; w, Richard Matheson (based on the short stories "Morella," "The Black Cat," and "The Strange Facts in the Case of M. Valdemar" by Edgar Allan Poe); ph, Floyd Crosby (Panavision, Pathe Color); ed, Anthony Carras; m, Les Baxter; art d, Daniel Haller; fx, Pat Dinga

The fourth entry in Roger Corman's Edgar Allan Poe series, this film is an anthology of three short pieces based on tales by Poe, and all three—"Morella," "The Black Cat," and "The Case of Mr. Valdemar"—feature Vincent Price in the starring role. In "Morella," Price is an embittered widower who has lived alone in his gloomy mansion since the death of his wife, Gage, after giving birth some 26 years ago. His daughter, Pierce, arrives and finds that her father loathes her because he blames her for his wife's death. Prowling around the house, Pierce finds Gage's mummified body lying on a bed. Price explains he couldn't bear to have her beauty buried beneath the ground, so he had her corpse moved into the house. Pierce reveals to her father that she is dying and only has a few months left. Father and daughter are reconciled, but that night Pierce dies and her body becomes possessed by Gage, who has been waiting all these years to return and wreak her vengeance on Price—the father of the baby that killed her. In "The Black Cat," Lorre is superb as a drunken loser whose

behavior forces his wife to seek comfort in the arms of wine-taster Price. To get even, Lorre captures his wife and her lover and walls them up in the cellar. Unbeknownst to him, however, the family cat is also entombed, and its wails give the scheme away. The final story, "The Case of Mr. Valdemar," features Price as a dying man who has fallen under the spell of an evil mesmerist, Rathbone. Price agrees to be the subject of an experiment wherein Rathbone will put him in a state of hypnosis at the moment of death, which will, perhaps, prevent him from dying. The trick works, but when the evil Rathbone attempts to steal Price's wife and estate, Price snaps out of the spell and attacks the mesmerist, his dead flesh melting around him. "Morella," the scariest of the tales, is an interesting precursor to THE TOMB OF LIGEIA (1965). "The Black Cat" combines the title Poe tale with Poe's "The Cask of Amontillado." It is a wonderfully funny prototype of THE RAVEN (1963), with both Lorre and Price having a grand time poking fun at the material and themselves. The final story has several memorable moments—especially when Price's disembodied voice can be heard pleading for release from his undead state—but the ending is marred by some unnecessary optical effects that obscure his melted visage (indeed, the production stills from this tale are more frightening than what appears in the movie).

TALK OF THE TOWN, THE

DVD
1942   118m   bw   Comedy   ★★★★
Columbia   (U.S.)

Cary Grant *(Leopold Dilg),* Jean Arthur *(Nora Shelley),* Ronald Colman *(Michael Lightcap),* Edgar Buchanan *(Sam Yates),* Glenda Farrell *(Regina Bush),* Charles Dingle *(Andrew Holmes),* Emma Dunn *(Mrs. Shelley),* Rex Ingram *(Tilney),* Leonid Kinskey *(Jan Pulaski),* Tom Tyler *(Clyde Bracken)*

p, George Stevens; d, George Stevens; w, Irwin Shaw, Sidney Buchman (based on a story by Sidney Harmon, adapted by Dale Van Every); ph, Ted Tetzlaff; ed, Otto Meyer; m, Frederick Hollander; art d, Lionel Banks, Rudolph Sternad; fx, Donald Starling; cos, Irene

AAN Best Picture; AAN Best Original Story: Sidney Harmon; *AAN Best Screenplay:* Sidney Buchman, Irwin Shaw; *AAN Best B/W Cinematography:* Ted Tetzlaff; *AAN Best Film Editing:* Otto Meyer; *AAN Best Score (Drama or Comedy):* Frederick Hollander, Morris Stoloff; *AAN Best Interior Decoration (B/W):* Lionel Banks, Rudolph Sternad, Fay Babcock

The contrivance of plot is compensated by one of the most genial casts in history. Full of wonderful *bon mots,* TOWN is acted with comic fervor by Grant, Arthur, and Colman.

Colman plays a renowned law professor who wants to spend a quiet summer writing while he awaits an appointment to the Supreme Court. He takes lodgings in the home of Arthur, a schoolteacher, but Colman's summer proves to be anything but quiet. Grant, who has escaped from jail after being labeled as the man behind a deadly factory fire, has taken refuge in the house as well. Arthur tells the bearded professor that Grant is the gardener, taking great care to protect Grant's secret. Colman is set in his ways when it comes to legalities, but what's more, he soon learns the real reason for Grant's stay at the house. It turns out that Grant was framed by a corrupt local government. The foreman who supposedly died in the blaze is very much alive, and both Colman and Grant develop an active interest in Arthur.

Grant, Arthur, and Colman are a terrific threesome, playing well off one another in a finely constructed love triangle. Both men want Arthur, yet Colman never lets his desire for her take precedence over the justice that must be done. Stevens directs his cast well, handling the double-edged story with grace and style. He originally shot two endings, one with Colman getting Arthur, and the other having Arthur pair with

Grant. Both endings were shown in preview screenings, and audience polls decided how the film would end. This was Colman's first film at Columbia since 1937's LOST HORIZON. Much to his delight, he learned that Stevens had arranged it so the actor would not have to deal with studio chief Harry Cohn during TALK OF THE TOWN's production. At the time Colman had been experiencing some popularity problems at the box office, and this hit film gave his career the desired boost.

TALK TO HER   *DVD*
(HABLE CON ELLA)
2002 113m c Drama   ★★★★
El Deseo (Spain)   R

Javier Camara *(Benigno)*, Dario Grandinetti *(Marco Zuloaga)*, Leonor Watling *(Alicia)*, Rosario Flores *(Lydia)*, Geraldine Chaplin *(Katarina Bilova, the Dance Teacher)*, Mariola Fuentes *(Rosa)*, Lola Duenas *(Matilde)*, Roberto Alvarez *(Doctor)*, Paz Vega *(Amparo)*, Adolfo Fernandez *(Nino de Valencia)*

p, Agustin Almodóvar; d, Pedro Almodóvar; w, Pedro Almodóvar; ph, Javier Aguirresarobe; ed, Jose Salcedo; m, Alberto Inglesias; prod d, Esther Garcia; art d, Antxon Gomez; fx, David Martin , Montse Ribe; chor, Pina Bausch; cos, Sonia Grande

AA Best Original Screenplay: Pedro Almodóvar; *AAN Best Director:* Pedro Almódovar

Pedro Almodóvar's transformation from rude boy into sophisticated interpreter of modern melodramas is remarkable, all the more so because he retained his gleeful willingness to affront conventional mores. This ode to romantic and platonic love is simultaneously perverse and truly moving, a high-wire act that finds humor in the grotesque and hope in emotional malformation.

Benigno (Javier Camara) and Marco (Dario Grandinetti) meet while watching German choreographer Pina Bausch's nerve-wracking pas de trois *Cafe Muller*. Plump, slightly effeminate Benigno is a private nurse devoted to Alicia (Leonor Watling), an aspiring dancer whom he once adored from afar but who now languishes in a coma after being struck by a car. Journalist Marco, meanwhile, spots fiery matador Lydia (Rosario Flores) on a talk show and is besotted. Lydia usually shuns reporters—they want her to tell all about her recent breakup with fellow matador Nino de Valencia (Adolfo Fernandez)—but Marco lends a sympathetic ear, and they become a couple. Then Lydia is gored in the ring; comatose, she's moved to the same facility where Alicia lies. Benigno and Marco strike up a wary friendship rooted in circumstance. Neither is actually what the other wants, but a connection takes root anyway.

Almodóvar's depiction of life with the comatose is simultaneously intimate and dispassionate, and he displaces the story's most disturbing turn into a silent film-within-the-film called "The Shrinking Lover," in which a Buster Keaton-esque man quaffs his brainy girlfriend's revolutionary weight-loss potion, only to shrink to the size of a Ken doll. His transformation of adversity into bizarrely liberating fantasy mirrors the dazzling achievement of Almodóvar's slyly compassionate film.

TALL BLOND MAN WITH ONE BLACK SHOE, THE
(LE GRAND BLOND AVEC UNE CHAUSSURE NOIRE)
1972 90m c Mystery/Comedy   ★★½
Gueville/Madeline/Gaumont (France)   PG

Pierre Richard *(Francois)*, Bernard Blier *(Milan)*, Jean Rochefort *(Toulouse)*, Mireille Darc *(Christine)*, Jean Carmet *(Maurice)*, Colette Castel *(Paulette)*, Paul Le Person *(Perrache)*, Jean Obe *(Botrel)*, Robert Castel *(Georghiu)*, Roger Caccia *(M. Boudart)*

p, Alain Poire, Yves Robert; d, Yves Robert; w, Yves Robert, Francis Veber; ph, Rene Mathelin (Eastmancolor); ed, Ghislaine Desjonqueres; m, Vladimir Kosma

Filled with dry humor and featuring an understated comic performance by the expressionless Pierre Richard, this French farce concentrates on the silly aspects of the espionage world. Because of infighting in the French Secret Service, chief Louis Toulouse (Jean Rochefort) sets a trap for an ambitious underling, Bernard Milan (Bernard Blier), who is after his job. As a result, the innocent Francois Perrin (Richard), a tall blond with one black shoe, is randomly chosen as a decoy to trap Milan, who immediately puts his men to work on Francois's past, his contacts, his mission, and his real identity, convinced that he is a "superagent." In the tradition of the silent comics, Francois walks through this danger zone of espionage completely oblivious to the gangs of assassins out to kill him.

What is especially funny about the film is its send-up of the genre. Milan and his top agents assume that every one of Francois's actions has a double meaning: if he goes to the dentist, they think it is to meet a contact; when he plays the violin, they think it is a secret signal. They even try to decode an innocent message inscribed on a photo from his mistress. A sequel followed in 1974 titled, appropriately enough, RETURN OF THE TALL BLOND MAN WITH ONE BLACK SHOE. The original was remade in 1985 as THE MAN WITH ONE RED SHOE, starring Tom Hanks.

TALL MEN, THE
1955 122m c Western   ★★★½
Fox (U.S.)

Clark Gable *(Ben Allison)*, Jane Russell *(Nella Turner)*, Robert Ryan *(Nathan Stark)*, Cameron Mitchell *(Clint Allison)*, Juan Garcia *(Luis)*, Harry Shannon *(Sam)*, Emile Meyer *(Chickasaw)*, Steve Darrell *(Colonel)*, Will Wright *(Gus, the Bartender)*, Robert Adler *(Wrangler)*

p, William A. Bacher, William B. Hawks; d, Raoul Walsh; w, Sydney Boehm, Frank S. Nugent (based on the novel by Clay Fisher); ph, Leo Tover (CinemaScope, DeLuxe Color); ed, Louis Loeffler; m, Victor Young; art d, Lyle Wheeler, Mark-Lee Kirk; fx, Ray Kellogg; cos, Travilla

Texas brothers Gable and Mitchell, who had ridden with Quantrill's Raiders during the Civil War, head North to Montana in search of gold. Desperate for cash, the men waylay Ryan, a wealthy businessman transporting $20,000. The fast-thinking Ryan turns the robbery to his advantage, however, by offering Gable and Mitchell a chance to be his partners in what is to be an arduous and fateful cattle drive from Texas to Montana.

Shot in CinemaScope and color by cinematographer Leo Tover, THE TALL MEN is a beautiful film to look at and also boasts a good script, solid performances, and typically fine direction from veteran director Walsh. Though the action is supposed to take place in Texas and Montana, Walsh learned that there were not enough longhorn cattle in the area to make a decent herd for the film. The cast and crew were sent to Durango, Mexico, where large herds of longhorn roamed the countryside. Walsh was assisted by a man named Carlos, the governor's son-in-law. Carlos spoke English, was a fan of American movies, and had good connections with the local cattle ranchers. According to Walsh's autobiography, after one week of shooting, a pistol-packing representative of the beef-growers' association, Diaz, showed up on the set and demanded more money for the cattle. The governor's son-in-law reminded the man that they had signed a contract which stated a specific price for the cattle. According to Walsh, when this did not faze the cattleman, "my self-appointed protector jumped in his car and raised more dust between us and the town. When he came back, he was driving a truck with 10 soldiers in it. That was the end of the holdup. The soldiers prodded Diaz into the truck after taking his gun away. 'You can roll your cameras now,' Carlos grinned, 'but I would advise you to get out of town the day you finish the picture.'"

The rest of the shooting proceeded smoothly, though director Walsh and his cast enjoyed playing tricks and teasing each other. Walsh roomed with Gable, Ryan roomed with Mitchell, and Russell had a house to herself. One night the director borrowed a tame skunk that had been "deodorized" by two young Mexican boys and tossed it into Gable's bedroom. When Gable spotted the creature, he yelled for help, and Walsh calmly advised the actor to slowly get out of bed and whistle to the skunk because skunks are afraid of whistling. So Gable stood in the corner whistling "Ol' Man River" and "If I Loved You," while Walsh came over and picked up the little beast. The next day Gable told the entire company how brave Walsh was for removing the animal. Somehow, Walsh managed to keep a straight face through the entire affair.

TALL T, THE

1957 78m c Western ★★★★
Columbia (U.S.)

Randolph Scott (*Pat Brennan*), Richard Boone (*Usher*), Maureen O'Sullivan (*Doretta Mims*), Arthur Hunnicutt (*Ed Rintoon*), Skip Homeier (*Billy Jack*), Henry Silva (*Chink*), John Hubbard (*Willard Mims*), Robert Burton (*Tenvoorde*), Robert Anderson (*Jace*), Fred Sherman (*Hank Parker*)

p, Harry Joe Brown; d, Budd Boetticher; w, Burt Kennedy (based on the story "The Captive" by Elmore Leonard); ph, Charles Lawton Jr. (Technicolor); ed, Al Clark; m, Heinz Roemheld; art d, George Brooks

Veteran cowboy actor Scott is on the trail again, but this is not the standard shoot-'em-up. The story has more suspense than most, and the whole film moves along at a brisk pace with elements of both comedy and drama. Scott is captured by Boone and his thugs, who have also kidnapped newlyweds O'Sullivan and Hubbard. Boone and his boys want to rob a stagecoach, but the slimy Hubbard, in an attempt to save himself, tells them that O'Sullivan comes from a wealthy family, and it would be easier to get money by holding her for ransom. From there, the tension builds as Scott plans to outwit their captors.

This film has received a fair amount of critical analysis in recent years, particularly in light of the interest paid to genre films. Burt Kennedy's script and Budd Boetticher's direction have been applauded as solid in this psychological western which makes use of modern adult themes and depicts the struggle between good and evil as a complicated one—too complicated, in fact, for a black-and-white presentation. Rather, the viewer is shown how elements outside humans' control can influence the struggle and make clear-cut conclusions impossible. Scott is the strong-willed, laconic representation of the (pre-Eastwood) Western man pitted against an equally strong-minded, laconic villain. The struggle between Scott and Boone is depicted as a delicate balance of power in which Scott, the force of good, is not necessarily stronger—or even better in all aspects of his life, he is merely more wily in the end. THE TALL T, like the Leone westerns to follow, used the American West as the perfect setting for an eternal struggle, the outcome of which is always a crap shoot.

TAMING OF THE SHREW, THE

(LA BISBETICA DOMATA) *DVD*
1967 122m c Comedy ★★★½
Royal/FAI (U.S./Italy)

Elizabeth Taylor (*Katharina*), Richard Burton (*Petruchio*), Cyril Cusack (*Grumio*), Michael Hordern (*Baptista*), Alfred Lynch (*Tranio*), Alan Webb (*Gremio*), Victor Spinetti (*Hortensio*), Roy Holder (*Biondello*), Mark Dignam (*Vincentio*), Bice Valori (*The Widow*)

p, Richard Burton, Elizabeth Taylor, Franco Zeffirelli; d, Franco Zeffirelli; w, Paul Dehn, Suso Cecchi D'Amico, Franco Zeffirelli (based on the play by William Shakespeare); ph, Oswald Morris, Luciano Trasatti (Panavision, Technicolor); ed, Peter Taylor, Carlo Fabianelli; m, Nino Rota; prod d, John De Cuir; art d, Giuseppe Mariani, Elven Webb; fx, Augie Lohman; cos, Irene Sharaff, Danilo Donati

AAN Best Art Direction-Set Decoration: Renzo Mongiardino (Art Direction), John DeCuir (Art Direction), Elven Webb (Art Direction), Giuseppe Mariani (Art Direction), Dario Simoni (Set Decoration), Luigi Gervasi (Set Decoration); *AAN Best Costume Design:* Irene Sharaff, Danilo Donati

The Liz and Dick Show, Part II. The Battling Burtons go at it again onscreen in this follow-up to their joint triumph in WHO'S AFRAID OF VIRGINIA WOOLF? And, although it may initially be hard to picture La Liz reciting blank verse, both she and the film are fine. Zeffirelli is famous (or infamous) for his sometimes unsubtle editing of Shakespeare's plays when he turns them into films that "ordinary folk" can understand (a piece of advice, Franco: we're not that stupid). Purists will doubtless be upset by this flick, but the bawdy humor is engaging, the photography and musical score work just fine, and the most famous married couple in the world at that time are really having a ball here. Not really an actress noted for playing feminists, La Liz manages the transition from spoiled filly—typecasting here, folks—to submissive wife—which is all the eight-times-around Mrs. Hilton Fisher Burton Warner Fortensky whoever really wants after all, right?

TAMPOPO

1986 114m c Comedy *DVD* ★★★½
Itami (Japan)

Ken Watanabe, Tsutomu Yamazaki, Nobuko Miyamoto, Koji Yakusho, Rikiya Yasuoka, Kinzo Sakura, Shuji Otaki

p, Yasushi Tamaoki, Seigo Hosogoe; d, Juzo Itami; w, Juzo Itami; ph, Masaki Tamura; ed, Akira Suzuki; m, Kunihiko Murai; art d, Takeo Kimura

A hilarious comedy from Japan concerned exclusively with food, TAMPOPO begins in a movie theater as we (the viewing audience) sit watching the audience in the film. In walks a suave yakuza attended by his girlfriend and an entourage of goons. Gangster and moll sit down in the front row, while the henchmen set up a table filled with delectable food. As the gangster eats, he suddenly notices us watching him, leans forward into the camera, and asks, "What are you eating?" He then informs us that he hates noise in movie theaters—especially people who crinkle wrappers and eat loudly. Of course, a man behind him is eating too noisily, and the gangster angrily threatens to kill the confused moviegoer if he continues. He then sits down to enjoy the show, urging us to do the same. Now TAMPOPO proper begins, a string of rollicking comic vignettes concerning food that—more or less—tell the story of a heroic truck driver and his sidekick's attempts to help a young widow improve her noodle-shop business.

The second feature by director Juzo Itami (preceded by THE FUNERAL, 1984), TAMPOPO is a wonderfully funny and creative film with a cornucopia of comical characters in absurd situations. These loony elements combine to offer some perceptive observations about human joy, fear, and passion for food. TAMPOPO also satirizes filmmaking (with references to THE SEVEN SAMURAI, American westerns, Steven Spielberg, and Japanese yakuza films), though Itami's film is itself heavily indebted to Luis Bunuel. With his first two films (his "Taxing Woman" entries, unfortunately, have less bite), Itami moved to the forefront of the irreverent young Japanese directors who have recently put a comedic spotlight on Japanese society, finding some very funny and disturbing truths about life there.

TARGETS   *DVD*
1968 90m   c   Horror/Crime   ★★★★½
Saticoy   (U.S.)

Boris Karloff *(Byron Orlok)*, Tim O'Kelly *(Bobby Thompson)*, Nancy Hsueh *(Jenny)*, James Brown *(Robert Thompson)*, Sandy Baron *(Kip Larkin)*, Arthur Peterson *(Ed Loughlin)*, Mary Jackson *(Charlotte Thompson)*, Tanya Morgan *(Ilene Thompson)*, Monty Landis *(Marshall Smith)*, Peter Bogdanovich *(Sammy Michaels)*

p, Peter Bogdanovich; d, Peter Bogdanovich; w, Peter Bogdanovich (based on a story by Polly Platt and Peter Bogdanovich); ph, Laszlo Kovacs (Pathe Color); ed, Peter Bogdanovich; m, Charles Greene, Brian Stone; prod d, Polly Platt

On target. An unconventional horror picture that draws a comparison between the real-life horror of the 1966 Charles Whitman murder spree and the fictional horrors of movie legend Boris Karloff, TARGETS opens with a film clip (the flood scene) from Roger Corman's 1963 film, THE TERROR. The clip then ends, revealing a screening room occupied by aging horror star Byron Orlok (Karloff, extremely moving here), filmmaker Sammy Michaels (played by director Bogdanovich), and some film executives. Orlok informs them that he's had enough of horror films and plans to return to his home in England. He is aware that his films no longer frighten people and that the public is only affected by the horrors in the headlines, stating, "The world belongs to the young. Make way for them. Let them have it. I am an anachronism." Meanwhile, in a gun house across the street, a clean-cut young man, Bobby Thompson (Tim O'Kelly), adds a high-powered rifle to the already huge arsenal of weapons stashed in his car trunk. Thompson begins a bloody rampage, first murdering his wife, then sniping at innocent drivers from a tower near a highway. TARGETS' brilliant finale, set at a drive-in premiere of the latest Orlok opus, puts both of these horrors—the movieland fiction of Orlok and the real-life danger of Thompson—up on the screen together. Down below, the audience screams in fright, not at Orlok but at Thompson, whose rifle shots are picking them off one by one. TARGETS is an insightful comment on the changing state of the horror film: Whereas Karloff's films concerned gruesome monsters with frightening physical attributes, TARGETS is about—to use Bogdanovich's phrase—"the ghouls next door," the all-American killers who are all the more frightening because the deformities exist *inside* their heads.

TARNISHED ANGELS, THE
1957 91m   bw   Drama   ★★★★
Universal   (U.S.)

Rock Hudson *(Burke Devlin)*, Robert Stack *(Roger Shumann)*, Dorothy Malone *(LaVerne Shumann)*, Jack Carson *(Jiggs)*, Robert Middleton *(Matt Ord)*, Alan Reed *(Col. Fineman)*, Alexander Lockwood *(Sam Hagood)*, Christopher Olsen *(Jack Shumann)*, Bob Wilke *(Hank)*, Troy Donahue *(Frank Burnham)*

p, Albert Zugsmith; d, Douglas Sirk; w, George Zuckerman (based on the novel *Pylon* by William Faulkner); ph, Irving Glassberg (Cinemascope); ed, Russell Schoengarth; m, Frank Skinner; art d, Alexander Golitzen, Alfred Sweeney; fx, Clifford Stine; cos, Bill Thomas

The best-ever adaptation of a Faulkner novel for the screen, directed with passion and perception by Sirk. The once underrated director, now recognized as a master of implicitly subversive melodrama, draws excellent portrayals from Hudson

(who had come a long way as an actor by this point), Stack, Malone, and Carson in an authentic and stimulating Depression-era drama of racing pilots and daredevil exploits.

Stack arrives in New Orleans in 1932 with his barnstorming troupe, his wife Malone, his son, Olsen, and his loyal-unto-death mechanic, Carson. They have arrived to participate in an air show and race, with Stack hoping to win the big prize money with a dilapidated plane. Hudson, an idealistic reporter for one of the local newspapers, is assigned to write some features about the air show, so he interviews Stack and his family, intrigued by their gypsyish lifestyle. As he comes to know these people, his initial sarcastic attitude toward them changes to one of respect. Middleton, a wealthy old man who lusts after Malone, gives Stack a plane to fly in the air show, but wants Malone in return. Stack, meanwhile, proves himself master of the air until his plane develops a problem while turning the last pylon to win the race.

The acting is first-rate here, and the script is outstanding, full of wit, black humor, and occasional fine poetic monologues, especially the lines delivered by Stack when he wistfully looks back upon WWI and those of Hudson when he returns drunk to his newspaper and describes the lives of the nomads of the air. Sirk does a marvelous job with his action scenes, all of which appear realistic. Faulkner saw this film and considered it the best picture ever made of his work. The author based much of his story on the exploits of his own brother, Dean Faulkner, who was a barnstorming pilot in the early 1930s.

TARZAN   *DVD*
1999 88m   c   Animated/Children's/Adventure   ★★½
Walt Disney Pictures   (U.S.)   G

VOICES OF: Tony Goldwyn *(Tarzan)*, Minnie Driver *(Jane)*, Glenn Close *(Kala)*, Rosie O'Donnell *(Terk)*, Wayne Knight *(Tantor)*, Nigel Hawthorne *(Professor Porter)*, Brian Blessed *(Clayton)*, Alex D. Linz *(Young Tarzan)*, Lance Henriksen *(Kerchak)*

p, Bonnie Arnold; d, Kevin Lima, Chris Buck; w, (based on the novel *Tarzan of the Apes* by Edgar R. Burroughs); m, Mark Mancina; anim, Glen Keane

AA Best Original Song: "You'll Be in My Heart"; Phil Collins

One opposable thumb down. Disney breaks with its own traditions with this lushly animated retelling of Edgar Rice Burroughs's famous tale of an Englishman raised by apes: it's wildly kinetic, overtly violent, and hardly a musical at all. In fact, the most "Disney" thing about it is the blockheaded choice of source material.

There are no Africans in this Africa, but there's a colony of anthropomorphic apes who speak English, live in social groups, and love their children. Soon after losing her baby, gentle gorilla Kala (voiced by Glenn Close) happens upon the blood-smeared treehouse of a shipwrecked English couple and saves their orphaned son from becoming leopard lunch-meat. Kala takes the hairless creature home and, deaf to the gorilla clan's intolerance, names him Tarzan and raises him as her own. Tarzan grows up happy but sensing that something's not quite right: Mom's awfully dark and hairy, and her thumb's in the wrong place. Worse, he can't win the acceptance of gorilla patriarch Kerchak (Lance Henriksen) and courts disaster by trying to integrate "his own kind"—a team of English explorers, including fortune-hunting Clayton (Brian Blessed), a primatologist (Nigel Hawthorne), and his dotty daughter Jane (Minnie Driver)—into the ape clan.

Disney is faced with retrofitting a reactionary and essentially racist source material to suit its far more liberal agenda, and on the surface Burroughs's story has been reconfigured into a heart-tugging paean to mother/child love. But enough of his central concerns, notably the idea that a white, European aristocrat will inevitably become Lord of the Jungle by virtue of superior breeding, remains to monkey-wrench the whole thing. It's hard *not* to read the film in racial terms—Tarzan smearing his pink skin with mud makes the subtext pretty clear—and its refusal to confront the issue directly results in a tangle of mixed signals and a climax that substitutes brutal action for satisfactory thematic resolution. Parents should be warned about the frequent gunfire and a grisly death by hanging.

TARZAN AND HIS MATE

1934 105m bw Adventure/Romance **DVD**
MGM (U.S.) ★★★½

Johnny Weissmuller *(Tarzan)*, Maureen O'Sullivan *(Jane Parker)*, Neil Hamilton *(Harry Holt)*, Paul Cavanagh *(Martin Arlington)*, Forrester Harvey *(Beamish)*, William Stack *(Pierce)*, Desmond Roberts *(Van Ness)*, Nathan Curry *(Saidi)*, Paul Porcasi *(Mons. Gironde)*

p, Bernard H. Hyman; d, Jack Conway (uncredited), Cedric Gibbons; w, Howard Emmett Rogers, Leon Gordon (based on the story by James Kevin McGuinness and the characters created by Edgar Rice Burroughs); ph, Charles Clarke, Clyde De Vinna; ed, Tom Held

The second MGM "Tarzan" film, a sequel to TARZAN THE APE MAN, features Johnny Weissmuller and Maureen O'Sullivan as its eponymous pair. The story is as scant as O'Sullivan's costume: the jungle couple are living together atop the trees when O'Sullivan's civilized beau, Neil Hamilton, arrives on the scene with greedy ivory hunter Paul Cavanagh. The outsiders are still searching for Mutia Escarpment, the elephant burial grounds, and Cavanagh wounds one pachyderm in the hope that it will lead them to the grounds. When he objects to the merciless treatment of his animal friends, Weissmuller is shot and left to die. His ape companions rescue him and he regains his health, but Hamilton and Cavanagh are not so fortunate; after making it to the burial grounds, they and their bearers are devoured by lions. Stampeding elephants rescue O'Sullivan before she too becomes lunch, and the jungle lovers are reunited.

The most interesting aspect of this "Tarzan" installment is its adult appeal: Weissmuller and O'Sullivan's Tarzan and Jane are obviously living in sexual freedom as they swing through the trees. O'Sullivan's character, a formerly civilized Londoner, has thrown away all inhibitions here; she wears her revealing animal-skin outfit only so others "won't think [her] immodest," but sleeps in the nude, and one scene—clipped from the film after Legion of Decency protests—reveals her bare breasts as Weissmuller and a stand-in for O'Sullivan go skinny-dipping. Not surprisingly, the Hays Code brought about changes in later "Tarzan" films. To appease those who wanted double beds for the pair (a rather unfeasible arrangement in the treetops), a jungle house was built for them, complete with four walls and ceiling. So began the downfall of the series. Although the first talkie TARZAN was directed by W.S. Van Dyke, with Cedric Gibbons as art director, MGM finally gave in to Gibbons' wishes and let him direct here. The move proved less than successful, however, and Gibbons was relieved of his duties after a few weeks (MGM made its "Tarzan" films slowly and carefully, with large budgets and generous shooting schedules). Gibbons was replaced by the more experienced Jack Conway, who directed most of the film, but did not receive screen credit.

TARZAN, THE APE MAN

1932 99m bw Adventure/Romance **DVD**
MGM (U.S.) ★★★★

Johnny Weissmuller *(Tarzan)*, Neil Hamilton *(Harry Holt)*, Maureen O'Sullivan *(Jane Parker)*, C. Aubrey Smith *(James Parker)*, Doris Lloyd *(Mrs. Cutten)*, Forrester Harvey *(Beamish)*, Ivory Williams *(Riano)*, Cheta the Chimp

p, Irving Thalberg; d, W.S. Van Dyke II; w, Cyril Hume, Ivor Novello (based on the characters created by Edgar Rice Burroughs); ph, Harold Rosson, Clyde De Vinna; ed, Ben Lewis, Tom Held; art d, Cedric Gibbons

The original swinger, with the original call of the wild. A legend was born when MGM cast Johnny Weissmuller, a 28-year-old Olympic swimming champion, as Tarzan in this film. The Edgar Rice Burroughs character had been popular in silent films, but this was the first sound version. Jane Parker (Maureen O'Sullivan), her father (C. Aubrey Smith), and her boyfriend (Neil Hamilton) venture into the African wilds in search of the ivory-laden Elephant's Graveyard and experience great danger in the process. Fears are heightened when Tarzan's jungle yell is heard, and before long, Jane is screaming and kicking as Tarzan carries her into the treetops. Her father and suitor threaten to shoot Tarzan, but after she is released, Jane defends the ape-man with whom she is falling in love. She is soon swinging through the trees under his arm, clowning around with the captivating chimp Cheta, and taking swims with Tarzan. Their happiness is threatened, however, when they are captured by pygmies and lowered into a pit with a giant ape.

The first of six MGM Weissmuller-O'Sullivan "Tarzan" adventures, TARZAN, THE APE MAN suffers in technological comparison with today's Steven Spielbergian jungle adventures, but still has enough thrills to put most modern films to shame. The near-nonstop excitement holds up wonderfully, making this one of Hollywood's most memorable adventure films. And the two leads, through countless casting calls, have never been beaten. Okay, Bo Derek, you can clean the cage now.

TASTE OF CHERRY

(TA'M E GUILASS) **DVD**
1997 98m c Drama
Abbas Kiarostami Productions (Iran) ★★★½

Homayoun Ershadi *(Mr. Badii)*, Abdolhossein Bagheri *(Taxidermist)*, Afshin Khorshidbakhtair *(Worker)*, Safar Ali Moradi *(Soldier)*, Mir Hossein Noori *(Seminarian)*, Ahman Ansari *(Factory Guard)*, Hamid Massomi *(Man in Phone Booth)*, Elham Imani *(Woman in Front of Museum)*

p, Abbas Kiarostami; d, Abbas Kiarostami; w, Abbas Kiarostami; ph, Homayon Payvar; ed, Abbas Kiarostami

Another small-scale fable from Iranian director Abbas Kiarostami, TASTE OF CHERRY tells the tale of a suicidal man's last days. The film is refreshingly without sentiment, but it's almost too subdued artistically to stay with viewers.

A wealthy Iranian named Badii (Homayoun Ershadi) drives around in circles, picking up several men and offering to pay them well for an easy job, but he refuses to specify what he needs done. He naturally arouses suspicion, but what he's looking for isn't sex—he's searching for someone to bury him after he commits suicide. When the men discover what it is he needs done, rejection follows—cruel, baffled, or tolerant, depending on the man.

TASTE OF CHERRY seems to tell a rather simple story with a plain moral message of carpe diem (espoused in the title), but like his other films, including THROUGH THE OLIVE TREES, writer-director-producer-editor Kiarostami adds a reflexive element and some wistful nuance. But as with the film-within-the-film framework of THROUGH THE OLIVE TREES, Kiarostami uses self-reflexivity in an innocuous way that indeed creates a distancing effect to the story and characters, but adds little more than another layer of playful whimsy. Likewise, TASTE OF CHERRY makes a tentative socio-political statement about modern Iran—the differences of secular and religious beliefs, the influx of different cultures, the uncertainty of the country's future—but these issues are not addressed in a satisfyingly clear way. Though adeptly made, TASTE OF CHERRY is a little *too* open-ended.

TASTE OF HONEY, A
1961 100m bw Drama ★★★★½
Woodfall (U.K.)

Dora Bryan *(Helen)*, Rita Tushingham *(Jo)*, Robert Stephens *(Peter)*, Murray Melvin *(Geoffrey)*, Paul Danquah *(Jimmy)*, David Boliver *(Bert)*, Moira Kaye *(Doris)*, Herbert Smith *(Shoe Shop Proprietor)*, Valerie Scarden *(Woman in Shoe Shop)*, Rosalie Scase *(Nurse)*

p, Tony Richardson; d, Tony Richardson; w, Shelagh Delaney, Tony Richardson (based on the play by Delaney); ph, Walter Lassally; ed, Anthony Gibbs; m, John Addison; art d, Ralph Brinton; cos, Sophie Harris

A taste of the British "Kitchen Sink" school at its best. Honest depiction of life in the British working class with an offbeat treatment, superb acting, realistic direction, and a complex script.

Tushingham plays a 17-year-old who lives with her promiscuous, alcoholic mother, Bryan, in various furnished rooms Tushingham is gawky, not terribly attractive, and desperate to be held. On holiday in Blackpool, she wanders around the docks and meets Danquah, a black sailor on a brief shore leave. She sleeps with him. On returning home, she discovers that her mother has impulsively married current boyfriend Stephens; the girl is to be left on her own. She secures employment in a shoe store and meets Melvin, a gentle and kind homosexual who needs a place to stay. They move in together. Then Tushingham realizes that she's carrying Danquah's child.

The movie was shot for a pittance on location in Blackpool and on the Salford docks. Delaney was only 19 when she wrote the play, which had a long run in the West End as well as on Broadway after first trying out at Stratford-upon-Avon in May 1958. Tushingham had been a backstage worker and did a bit in Arnold Wesker's play "The Kitchen" at Liverpool Rep before she answered an ad, walked in, auditioned, and won this plum role. Bryan had spent most of her career as a comedienne in movies since she began in ODD MAN OUT. Casting her here was an inspired choice as she showed her scope. If you have a sharp ear, you may be able to recognize Johnny Dankworth's theme from SATURDAY NIGHT AND SUNDAY MORNING, which was uncredited. Richardson coproduced that film with Harry Saltzman, so it can be assumed he had permission for the tune's use. The hit song "A Taste of Honey" had nothing to do with this film. It was written by Ric Marlow and Bobby Scott and traded on the success of the movie, which won Cannes Film Festival awards for Melvin and Tushingham as well as British Film Academy Awards for Best Picture, Best Actress (Bryan), Best Screenplay (Delaney and Richardson), and Most Promising Actress (Tushingham).

TAXI BLUES
1990 110m c Drama ★★★½
Marin Karmitz Productions/Lenfilm Studios/
Ask Eurofilm/La Sept (France/U.S.S.R.)

Pyotr Nikolajevitch Mamonov *(Liocha)*, Piotr Zaitchenko *(Schlikov)*, Vladimir Kachpour *(Old Netchiporenko)*, Natalia Koliakanova *(Christina)*, Hal Singer *(Himself)*, Elena Saphonva *(Nina—Liocha's Wife)*, Serguei Gazarov *(Administrator)*, Evgueni

Gortchakov *(Bald Musician in the Taxi)*, Dimitri Prigov *(Writer Typing in the Train)*, Igor Zolotovitsky *(Petiountchik)*

p, Marin Karmitz; d, Pavel Lounguine; w, Pavel Lounguine; ph, Denis Evstigneef; ed, Elizabeth Guido; m, Vladimir Chekassine; art d, Valery Yourkevitch; cos, Natalia Dianova

The precedent-shattering TAXI BLUES, helmed by screenwriter-turned-director Pavel Lounguine, is a wrenching, prolonged study in impotence and frustration.

Schlikov (Pyotr Zaitchenko) is a solidly working-class Russian taxi driver, racist and largely friendless, with the burly build of a bully. Liocha (Piotr Nikolajevitch Mamonov) is a flamboyant, self-destructive Jewish jazz musician. When Liocha stiffs Schlikov for a 70-ruble fare one drunken evening, Schlikov tracks him down, beats him up and takes his saxophone. However, Schlikov is sufficiently intrigued by Liocha to offer him vodka and a bed in his flat—much to the anger of Schlikov's neighbor, the rabidly anti-Semitic Netchiporenko (Vladimir Kachpour).

Shot in Moscow over a four-month period in 1989, with the flowering of *perestroika* already showing signs of blight and the crumbling of the Soviet Union soon to come, TAXI BLUES proved a rude shock to the struggling Russian film establishment.

Lounguine, who also wrote the screenplay, has described his style here as "extremist" and the story as autobiographical. The film has some of the narrative looseness of the French New Wave, as well as plenty of that movement's characteristic handheld camerawork. Although Lounguine has termed it a comedy, Westerners will find it only occasionally amusing. To its credit, the film, styled mostly as a two-character study, never falters into an "Odd Couple"-style formula. Both characters, as superbly played by Zaitchenko and Mamonov (whom Lounguine calls "the oldest Russian rock star, mythical in Moscow for his excesses") are equally disagreeable, making audience identification nearly impossible. The excesses of both are delineated in long, boisterous, often ugly scenes (including a rape) that seem to verge on escaping directorial control.

TAXI DRIVER

1976 112m c Drama ★★★★★
Bill-Phillips (U.S.) R

Robert De Niro *(Travis Bickle)*, Cybill Shepherd *(Betsy)*, Jodie Foster *(Iris Steensman)*, Peter Boyle *(Wizard)*, Harvey Keitel *(Sport)*, Albert Brooks *(Tom)*, Leonard Harris *(Charles Palantine)*, Martin Scorsese *(Passenger)*, Diahnne Abbott *(Concession Girl)*, Frank Adu *(Angry Black Man)*

p, Michael Phillips, Julia Phillips; d, Martin Scorsese; w, Paul Schrader; ph, Michael Chapman (Panavision, Metrocolor); ed, Marcia Lucas, Tom Rolf, Melvin Shapiro; m, Bernard Herrmann; art d, Charles Rosen; fx, Tony Parmelee; cos, Ruth Morley

AAN Best Picture; AAN Best Actor: Robert De Niro; AAN Best Supporting Actress: Jodie Foster; AAN Best Original Score: Bernard Herrmann

A landmark of '70s American cinema that announced to the world the arrival of director Martin Scorsese, screenwriter Paul Schrader and star Robert De Niro. Though critics remain divided over the ultimate merits of TAXI DRIVER, it is an undeniably brilliant, nightmarish portrait of one man's personal hell.

TAXI DRIVER is an alarmingly plausible character study of Vietnam vet Travis Bickle (De Niro), an alienated insomniac who spends his nights driving a New York cab. Much of what we see of the city is viewed through his windshield. After long night shifts, he still can't sleep and spends hours in porno theatres or alone in his squalid room. He has nothing but contempt for the "scum" he sees all around him and prophesies that someday a big rain will come and clean all the filth from the streets. Travis' world brightens a little when he sees a beautiful blonde woman, Betsy (Cybill Shepherd), in the campaign offices of presidential candidate Charles Palantine (Leonard Harris). He quickly develops a crush on her, and she finds him intriguing enough to agree to go out with him. When he takes her, though, to a porn film (the only type of movie he knows) she walks out in disgust. An even more frustrated Travis then meets Iris (Jodie Foster), a 12-year-old runaway turned prostitute who is managed by a long-haired pimp known as Sport (Harvey Keitel). Travis becomes obsessed with "rescuing" Iris from her situation, turning himself into a one-man killing machine as he prepares for a bloody crusade which he believes will put the world to rights.

TAXI DRIVER is a fevered, paranoid take on the perils of contemporary urban life. Scorsese paints a picture of New York City with stark, unforgettable images—steaming sewers, rainslicked streets, glaring neon lights—that together constitute a vision of hell on earth. All this is helped immensely by Bernard Herrmann's visceral score (his last; he passed away a day after its completion), and Michael Chapman's grainy cinematography. The climactic killing sequence is a sustained, hallucinatory triumph of shot composition and editing—as stomach-churning as it is technically astonishing. (Much of the negative critical reaction to the film focused on Scorsese's moral stance toward this bloodbath, claiming—short-sightedly—that it is portrayed as a positive, cleansing ritual that redeems Travis' character. TAXI DRIVER is far more ironic and multi-layered than such an interpretation suggests.)

De Niro's mesmerizing performance is central to the film's success. He appears in nearly every scene and we see nearly everything through his skewed vision. He commands the screen and evokes such power and authority—even during Travis's meekest moments—that we are inexorably drawn into his life. Shepherd is highly effective as the Hitchcockian icy blonde, and the young Jodie Foster effortlessly conveys both youthful innocence and a street-smart, wise-beyond-her-years quality. Her breakfast scene with De Niro is riveting. In smaller roles, Boyle is great fun as an eccentric cabbie; comedian/filmmaker Albert Brooks plays Shepherd's somewhat nerdy co-worker; and Harvey Keitel makes a memorably sleazy Sport.

TAXI DRIVER won the Golden Palm at the Cannes Film Festival, and Scorsese and De Niro were honored as Best Director and Best Actor by the New York Film Critics.

TAXING WOMAN, A

(MARUSA NO ONNA)   DVD
1987 127m c   Comedy
Itami/New Century   (Japan)   ★★★½

Nobuko Miyamoto (Ryoko Itakura, Tax Inspector), Tsutomu Yamazaki (Hideki Gondo), Masahiko Tsugawa (Assistant Chief Inspector Hanamura), Hideo Murota (Ishii, Motel President), Shuji Otaki (Tsuyuguchi, Tax Office Manager), Daisuke Yamashita (Taro Gondo), Shinsuke Ashida, Keiju Kobayashi, Mariko Okada, Kiriko Shimizu

p, Yasushi Tamaoki, Seigo Hosogoe; d, Juzo Itami; w, Juzo Itami; ph, Yonezo Maeda; ed, Akira Suzuki; m, Toshiyuki Honda

Continuing his series of hilariously incisive examinations of modern Japanese culture (burial rites in THE FUNERAL, food in TAMPOPO), director Juzo Itami here turns his gaze on that most sacred of contemporary obsessions—money. Part social satire, part procedural drama, A TAXING WOMAN takes its title from spunky, dedicated tax agent Ryoko Itakura (wonderfully acted by Nobuko Miyamoto, Itami's wife), who uses her demure looks to lull tax cheats into false confidence before she lowers the boom. Most of the film details her deter-

mined attempt to get the goods on suave "adult motel" tycoon Hideki Gondo (Tsutomu Yamazaki), who launders his money through the yakuza (gangsters), phony corporations, real estate, and his mistress. He's sharp, but Ryoko's sharper; and by the end, not only are the interests of the Japanese Tax Office served, but love (though unrequited) makes an appearance. Although not as out-and-out loopy as TAMPOPO, Itami's portrait of money-mad Japanese society has a biting satiric edge. The boundless energy of the Japanese seems to be what really fascinates the director, who is well on his way to becoming the leading chronicler of life in modern-day Japan. His 1988 sequel to this film, A TAXING WOMAN'S RETURN, is less satisfying than the original.

TEA AND SYMPATHY

1956 122m c   Drama   ★★★½
MGM (U.S.)

Deborah Kerr (Laura Reynolds), John Kerr (Tom Robinson Lee), Leif Erickson (Bill Reynolds), Edward Andrews (Herb Lee), Darryl Hickman (Al), Norma Crane (Ellie Martin), Dean Jones (Ollie), Jacqueline de Wit (Lilly Sears), Tom Laughlin (Ralph), Ralph Votrian (Steve)

p, Pandro S. Berman; d, Vincente Minnelli; w, Robert Anderson (based on the play by Anderson); ph, John Alton (CinemaScope, Metrocolor); ed, Ferris Webster; m, Adolph Deutsch; art d, William A. Horning, Edward Carfagno; cos, Helen Rose

Watered-down version of a landmark Broadway play that dealt with alleged homosexuality and an older woman's desire to prove the machismo of the suspect young man.

John Kerr is a married writer with three children who returns to his exclusive prep school in New England for a reunion. In a flashback to his troubled years at the school, we see that he is inept at every school except tennis (which is regarded as a sissy pastime), which sets him apart from the other boys. He wears his hair long and spends his off-hours in romantic pastimes which the other students scorn. His room-mate is Hickman, who is slightly embarrassed by Kerr's behavior but defends him to the others. Kerr's housemaster is big, hearty Erickson, a smiling boor who emphasizes masculine games for his charges. Erickson is in league with Andrews, Kerr's father, who shares the housemaster's belief that the boy should have his hair cut and make an attempt to get into the mainstream of the school's activities. Kerr is shunned by almost everyone at the school except Hickman and Erickson's wife, played by Deborah Kerr. She is a sensitive woman who realizes that this lad is in trouble. (He reminds her of her late first husband, a boy who volunteered for the Army during WWII in order to show everyone that he was fearless and left her widowed.) Gradually, her feelings for the boy deepen into something more than maternal concern.

The two Kerrs and Erickson all effectively reprised the roles they had played in the stage version, which opened in September, 1953, and ran for more than 700 performances. Since Anderson himself wrote the screenplay (with the censors looking over his shoulder), any bowdlerization must be attributed to him. Minnelli's direction is true to the material.

TEA WITH MUSSOLINI

1999 116m c   Drama   DVD
Cattleya Film/Medusa Film/Cineritmo/Film   ★★★
and General Productions   (Italy)   PG

Cher (Elsa), Judi Dench (Arabella), Joan Plowright (Mary), Maggie Smith (Lady Hester), Lily Tomlin (Georgie), Baird Wallace (Luca), Charlie Lucas (Luca—Child), Massimo Ghini (Paolo), Paolo Seganti (Vittorio), Claudio Spadaro (Mussolini)

p, Ricardo Tozzi, Giovannella Zannoni, Clive Parsons; d, Franco Zeffirelli; w, John Mortimer, Franco Zeffirelli (based on the autobiography of Zeffirelli); ph, David Watkin; ed, Tariq Anwar; m, Alessio Vlad, Stefano Arnaldi; prod d, Carlo Centolavigna; art d, Carlo Centolavigna, Gioia Fiorella Mariani; cos, Jenny Beavan, Alberto Spiazzi, Anna Anni, Ermanno Daelli (Cher's costumes)

A gauzy look at the formative years of an Italian boy who's raised by a gaggle of expatriate women against the backdrop of WWII.

1935. Luca (played as a child by Charlie Lucas, and as a teenager by Baird Wallace), the illegitimate son of a local businessman who wants little to do with him, is taken in by Mary Wallace (Joan Plowright), an older English woman living in a local *pensione*. Mary's friends pitch in and help care for the child, taking him to school and to museums, teaching him to love literature, and firmly inculcating him with steadfast notions of right and wrong. His mentors include artistic Arabella (Judi Dench); Elsa (Cher), a flighty, fabulously wealthy American who knew Luca's late mother; and lesbian archeologist Georgie (Lily Tomlin). The self-deluded queen bee of the expatriate community, Lady Hester Random (Maggie Smith), refuses to believe that rapidly changing European politics will affect their lives and even wangles assurance from Il Duce Mussolini (Claudio Spadara) himself that no harm will befall them. Needless to say, history catches up with them, and their lives change dramatically before the war ends.

The culmination of director Franco Zeffirelli's lifelong desire to explore his own childhood, this semi-autobiographical film falls prey to a misconception that afflicts many reality-based projects. It proceeds from the notion that if a story is true, it doesn't have to be worked out as rigorously as fiction; after all, that's the way it was. And while the divas make their characters hugely entertaining, they're also such high profile actresses in such a soft-edged film that it's hard to actually worry about what's to become of them. Elsa may be a Jew in Fascist Italy, but she's also Cher: her worst tribulation is that she has to go out without proper make-up.

TEAHOUSE OF THE AUGUST MOON, THE   DVD
1956 123m   c   Comedy   ★★★★
MGM   (U.S.)

Marlon Brando (Sakini), Glenn Ford (Capt. Fisby), Machiko Kyo (Lotus Blossom), Eddie Albert (Capt. McLean), Paul Ford (Col. Purdy), Jun Negami (Mr. Seiko), Nijiko Kiyokawa (Miss Higa Jiga), Mitsuko Sawamura (Little Girl), Harry Morgan, billed as Henry Morgan (Sgt. Gregovich), Shizicho Takeda (Ancient Man)

p, Jack Cummings; d, Daniel Mann; w, John Patrick (based on the novel by Vern J. Sneider and the play by Patrick); ph, John Alton (CinemaScope, Metrocolor); ed, Harold F. Kress; m, Saul Chaplin; art d, William A. Horning, Eddie Imazu; chor, Masaya Fujima

---

This charming adaptation of the novel and play shows that Brando has a flair for comedy. In a prologue, Okinawan Brando introduces himself and the other players and asserts with pride that Okinawa has the honor of being the most subjugated place in history. It has been overrun by the Chinese and the Japanese and, now, the U.S. Glenn Ford, an American officer, is charged with bringing "civilization" to a small village. With Brando as his official interpreter, Glenn Ford is supposed to start a women's club, build a schoolhouse, and establish democracy according to the plan sent out from Washington. The villagers, however, have other plans: what they desire most is a teahouse with plenty of geisha girls.

Paul Ford, a befuddled colonel, had played the same role on Broadway more than 1,000 times and yet managed to bring a freshness to it for the screen. He was later to do the same kind of role on TV's "You'll Never Get Rich" when he played Sgt. Bilko's (Phil Silvers) commanding officer. Kyo

spoke no English when she accepted the role. She had previously been seen in GATE OF HELL and RASHOMON. The music was mostly Okinawan and Japanese, and that lent authenticity to the affair. Although David Wayne was a marvel in the play (which won the Tony as Best Play that year), he was not a movie star, so when Brando indicated he wanted the part, he got it. Brando does one of his best roles here, submerging his own powerful personality. He spent months learning the proper way to move like an Asian. Some of the humor is labored, and Glenn Ford overplays a bit, but the ultimate result is a charming, though somewhat talky, movie that elevates whimsy to a new high.

TEAM AMERICA: WORLD POLICE   DVD
2004 98m   c   Animated/Comedy/Adventure   ★★★
Scott Rudin Productions/Paramount   (U.S.)   R

VOICES OF: Trey Parker (Gary/Joe/Kim/Blix/Carson/Drunk/Damon/Robbins), Matt Stone (Chris/Matt Damon), Kristen Miller (Lisa), Masasa (Sarah), Daran Norris (Spottiswoode), Phil Hendrie (I.N.T.E.L.L.I.G.E.N.C.E./Chechnyan Terrorist), Maurice LaMarche (Alec Baldwin), Chelsea Magritte (French Mother), Jeremy Shada (Jean Francois), Fred Tatasciore (Samuel L. Jackson)

p, Pam Brady, Trey Parker, Scott Rudin, Matt Stone; d, Trey Parker; w, Pam Brady, Trey Parker, Matt Stone; ph, Bill Pope; ed, Thomas M. Vogt; m, Harry Gregson-Williams; prod d, Jim Dultz; art d, Ramsey Avery, John Berger, Tom Valentine; fx, Eric Pascarelli, Joseph Viskocil; cos, Karen Patch; anim, Edward Chiodo (puppet producer), Stephen Chiodo (puppet supervisor), Charles Chiodo (puppet art director), Norman Tempia (puppet designer)

Ever on the lookout for new ways to offend, "South Park" creators Trey Parker and Matt Stone turned their scabrous talents to crafting a mind-bogglingly vulgar action-picture parody, cast entirely with two-foot-tall marionettes designed to recall the "Thunderbirds" TV series and feature films. The result is undeniably offensive and occasionally very funny.

Based in their headquarters deep within Mount Rushmore, Team America is always at the ready to fight terrorism and protect truth, justice and the American way. Joe (voice of Parker), Chris (Stone), Sarah (Masasa), and Lisa (Kristen Miller) lose teammate Carson while battling terrorists in Paris, so their fearless leader, Mr. Spottswoode (Daran Norris), recruits Broadway actor Gary Johnston (also Parker) to take his place. Unfortunately, Gary's presence disrupts the team's delicate chemistry and his first mission, infiltrating the terrorist underground in Egypt, is an unqualified disaster that sparks a devastating attack on the Panama Canal. Gary leaves the team and sinks into a morass of despair, while Spottswoode dispatches the others on an ill-fated mission to stop North Korean president Kim Jong Il (Parker again) from launching a worldwide assault on civilization. Can Gary get his act together and make things right, or is the world as we know it doomed?

Parker and Stone never pass up an opportunity to get a horrified laugh, whether they're voicing Kim Jong Il as a cross between a stereotypical Chinese waiter and "South Park"'s Cartman or staging a marionette kama sutra sequence that nearly earned the film an NC-17 rating. Some of their satirical conceits are right on target, including the rousing theme song "America, F--- Yeah!" while others too numerous to list are just juvenile in the grossest possible way.

TEMPTRESS MOON   DVD
(FENGYUE)
1996 116m   c   Historical/Drama/Romance   ★★★★
Tomson Films/Shanghai Film Studios   R
(Hong Kong/China)

Leslie Cheung (Yu Zhongliang), Gong Li (Pang Ruyi), Kevin Lin, billed as Lin Jianhua (Pang Duanwu), He Saifei (Yu Xiuyi—Zhongliang's

Sister), Xie Tian (Shanghai Boss), Zhang Shi (Li Niangjiu—His Lieutenant), Zhou Yemang (Pang Zhengda), Lin Lianqun (Pang An), Ge Xiangting (Elder Qi), David Wu, billed as Wu Dawei (Mr. Jing—Ruyi's Fiance)

p, Tong Cunlin, Hsu Feng; d, Chen Kaige; w, Shu Kei (based on an original story by Chen Kaige and Wang Anyi); ph, Christopher Doyle; ed, Pei Xiaonan; m, Zhao Jiping; art d, Huang Qiagui; cos, William Chang, Chen Changmin

In this, his sixth feature, director Chen Kaige lures the viewer into a mysterious web of family intrigue in 1920s Shanghai.

Old and new China clash when westernized Zhongliang (Leslie Cheung), a Shanghai gigolo who seduces and blackmails wealthy women, returns to the traditional rural plantation where he once briefly lived with his older sister, Xiuyi (He Saifei). For the first time in family history, the Pang family holdings are being administered by a woman, beautiful opium addict Ruyi (Gong Li), with the face-saving assistance of country cousin Duanwu (Kevin Lin), who secretly loves her. The dark story behind this sad state of affairs: rightful male heir Zhengda (Zhou Yemang) is brain-damaged, the legacy of a mysterious incident years earlier—the same incident that sent Zhongliang fleeing under cover of darkness. Lust, betrayal, dark family secrets, and opium addiction all conspire bring the situation to a tragic conclusion.

Viewers may disagree on the film's measure of success, but TEMPTRESS MOON, with its complicated and psychologically sophisticated story, certainly registers as a serious work of cinematic art. Chen exploits every formal element available, while the mesmerizing camerawork of Christopher Doyle sets the haunted tone of the film. The performances of Cheung and Gong are excellent, as usual, and He Saifei (RAISE THE RED LANTERN) stands out from the supporting cast. Some critics perceived the film as an allegory of contemporary China, with Duanwu, a country bumpkin who eventually inherits control of the Pang estate, representing President Jiang Zemin. Even if the parallel was unintentional, it caused the film to be banned in China.

10
1979 122m c Comedy **DVD**
Orion (U.S.) ★★★
R

Dudley Moore (George), Julie Andrews (Sam), Bo Derek (Jenny), Robert Webber (Hugh), Dee Wallace Stone, billed as Dee Wallace (Mary Lewis), Sam Jones (David), Brian Dennehy (Bartender), Max Showalter (Reverend), Rad Daly (Josh), Nedra Volz (Mrs. Kissel)

p, Blake Edwards, Tony Adams; d, Blake Edwards; w, Blake Edwards; ph, Frank Stanley (Panavision, Metrocolor); ed, Ralph E. Winters; m, Henry Mancini; prod d, Rodger Maus; fx, Fred Cramer; cos, Patricia Edwards

AAN Best Original Score: Henry Mancini; AAN Best Original Song: "Song from 10 (It's Easy to Say)"; Henry Mancini (Music), Robert Wells (Lyrics)

A funny if somewhat retrograde film that sent Dudley Moore's career soaring briefly, while making some telling points about the problems of middle age. Moore is a successful songwriter with four Oscars to his name. Suffering from a combination of ennui and self-doubt, Moore sees a limousine go past in his ritzy neighborhood. In it is Derek, on her way to get married to Jones at a Beverly Hills church. This is the woman of Moore's dreams, whom he rates "11" on a scale of one to 10. Moore learns Derek's identity, and impulsively follows the newlywed couple to Mexico, where he commences a blundering pursuit of Derek.

Derek enjoyed brief stardom on the basis of her part in this film but has failed to achieve any further success. Several standout comedy bits include Moore getting drunk, being stung on the nose by a bee, and burning his feet on the hot

beach sand. Moore also played the piano (which he does well) in the band that provided the background music. Mancini and Robert Wells's song "It's Easy to Say" was nominated for an Oscar. The movie made about $40 million, thus qualifying it as the "sleeper" of 1979.

TEN COMMANDMENTS, THE
1956 219m c Religious **DVD**
Paramount (U.S.) ★★★½

Charlton Heston (Moses), Yul Brynner (Rameses), Anne Baxter (Nefretiri), Edward G. Robinson (Dathan), Yvonne De Carlo (Sephora), Debra Paget (Lilia), John Derek (Joshua), Cedric Hardwicke (Sethi), Nina Foch (Bithiah), Martha Scott (Yochabel)

p, Cecil B. DeMille; d, Cecil B. DeMille; w, Aeneas MacKenzie, Jesse Lasky Jr., Jack Gariss, Fredric M. Frank (based on the novels The Prince of Egypt by Dorothy Clarke Wilson, Pillar of Fire by the Rev. J.H. Ingraham, and On Eagle's Wings by the Rev. G.E. Southon, and in accordance with the Bible, the ancient texts of Josephus, Eusebius, Philo, and The Midrash); ph, Loyal Griggs, John F. Warren, W. Wallace Kelley, Peverell Marley (VistaVision, Technicolor); ed, Anne Bauchens; m, Elmer Bernstein; art d, Hal Pereira, Walter Tyler, Albert Nozala; fx, John P. Fulton; chor, LeRoy Prinz, Ruth Godfrey; cos, Edith Head, Ralph Jester, John Jensen, Dorothy Jeakins, Arnold Friberg

AAN Best Picture; AAN Best Color Cinematography: Loyal Griggs; AAN Best Film Editing: Anne Bauchens; AAN Best Art Direction-Set Decoration (Color): Hal Pereira, Walter H. Tyler, Albert Nozaki, Sam M. Comer, Ray Moyer; AAN Best Costume Design (Color): Edith Head, Ralph Jester, John Jensen, Dorothy Jeakins, Arnold Friberg; AAN Best Sound Recording: Loren L. Ryder; AA Best Special Effects: John Fulton

A great big wallow, sublime hootchy-kootchy hokum, peppered with lightning that does automatic writing and an unsurpassed homage to the joys of jello. Director-producer Cecil B. DeMille ended his great career with this gigantic production, packed with enormous crowd scenes, lavish spectacles, and wide-screen special effects orchestrated with dazzling brilliance.

DeMille's Exodus (a tale he had also filmed in 1923) opens as the Egyptian pharaoh is told that the deliverer of the enslaved Hebrews will soon be born. He orders the slaughter of all newborn Jewish males, but one is placed on a basket in the Nile, found by the pharaoh's sister, and brought up as her own. Years pass and the now-adult Moses (Charlton Heston) has become a beloved prince, much to the chagrin of Rameses (Yul Brynner), the pharaoh's son. When Moses's lineage is revealed, he is banished into the desert, but after several peaceful years, he learns of his destiny in his encounter with the burning bush. The film then depicts his return and his confrontation with Rameses II, the mass exodus of the Hebrews, Moses's parting of the Red Sea, his receipt of the Ten Commandments, the Jews' worship of the idolatrous Golden Calf, and their 40 years of wandering as punishment. Finally, the aged Moses watches Joshua lead his people into the Promised Land.

DeMille tells the biblical story on a scale no other filmmaker ever attempted, yet the star cast cannot be overwhelmed by the epic production, even if the orgy did take three weeks to film. The exodus itself is truly moving, and Hardwicke lends a convincing old Pharaoh. Heston's stalwart prophet really does look like Michelangelo's Moses—how can he miss? Brynner and Baxter supply velvet and villainy, Robinson and Vincent Price are accomplished camps, and Paget and DeCarlo contribute beautous support. THE TEN COMMANDMENTS eventually grossed over $80 million, enjoying several re-releases, and DeMille's vision remains a powerful one, a testament to his inestimable talent as the master of epic vulgarity and self-justified righteousness.

10 RILLINGTON PLACE

1970 111m c Crime ★★★½
Genesis/Filmways/Columbia (U.K.) GP

Richard Attenborough (John Reginald Christie), Judy Geeson (Beryl Evans), John Hurt (Timothy John Evans), Pat Heywood (Mrs. Ethel Christie), Isobel Black (Alice), Miss Riley (Baby Geraldine), Phyllis McMahon (Muriel Eady), Ray Barron (Workman Willis), Douglas Blackwell (Workman Jones), Gabrielle Daye (Mrs. Lynch)

p, Martin Ransohoff, Leslie Linder; d, Richard Fleischer; w, Clive Exton (based on the book by Ludovic Kennedy); ph, Denys Coop (Eastmancolor); ed, Ernest Walter; m, John Dankworth; art d, Maurice Carter

Richard Attenborough portrays murderer John Reginald Christie, whose actions led to the hanging of an innocent man and the eventual abolition of capital punishment in Britain. The film picks up in 1944 as Christie coaxes a young lady into his flat, then rapes and strangles her, burying the body in his back yard. Several years later, Timothy John Evans (Hurt) and wife Beryl (Geeson), along with their baby daughter, move into the building and are charmed by Christie, who claims all sorts of medical and legal knowledge. When Beryl learns she is pregnant, the young couple allows Christie to perform an abortion. Instead of performing an abortion Christie rapes and murders Beryl, then tells Timothy his wife died during the operation and suggests he go away and leave their daughter in his care. The none-too-bright Timothy does as he is told, and that same night Christie kills his daughter. Eventually Timothy goes to the police and confesses to murdering Beryl. At his trial he relates the facts but is condemned by perjured testimony from Christie and hanged. Christie goes on to take the lives of several other victims, including his own wife, before justice is served.

Based on the historical Christie-Evans case, this painstakingly accurate film was shot in the building next door to the one where the actual killings took place. After filming was completed, the entire block, now renamed Ruston Close, was razed and council houses were built on the location. Attenborough is excellent as the banal, middle-class killer, and John Hurt is effective as usual as the man too dim to keep himself from being executed for a crime he didn't commit. 10 RILLINGTON PLACE is somber and frightening and omits the stylistic flourishes that marred director Richard Fleischer's previous excursion into the world of true crime, THE BOSTON STRANGLER. Fleischer directed two other suspense-filled films that same year, THE LAST RUN and SEE NO EVIL.

TENANT, THE 📀
(LE LOCATAIRE)
1976 124m c Horror ★★★½
Paramount (France) R

Roman Polanski (Trelkovsky), Isabelle Adjani (Stella), Shelley Winters (Concierge), Melvyn Douglas (Mr. Zy), Jo Van Fleet (Mme. Dioz), Bernard Fresson (Scope), Lila Kedrova (Mme. Gaderian), Claude Dauphin (Husband), Claude Pieplu (Neighbor), Rufus (Badar)

p, Andrew Braunsberg; d, Roman Polanski; w, Roman Polanski, Gerard Brach (based on the novel Le Locataire Chimerique by Roland Topor); ph, Sven Nykvist (Panavision, Eastmancolor); ed, Francoise Bonnot; m, Philippe Sarde; prod d, Pierre Guffroy; art d, Claude Moesching, Albert Rajau; cos, Jacques Schmidt

Roman Polanski's psychological horror film stars Polanski himself as Trelkovsky, a Polish office clerk in Paris. He rents an apartment in a quiet building whose elderly residents seem to feel malevolence toward the new tenant from the start. After he learns that the previous occupant jumped from the apartment window, he visits the dying woman—who is covered head to toe in wrappings—in the hospital, and meets her friend Stella (Isabelle Adjani). The woman suddenly lets out a bloodcurdling scream and dies, an event that forms a bond between Trelkovsky and Stella, who nearly become lovers but drift apart. Meanwhile, Trelkovsky, while experiencing increasing difficulty with his fellow tenants—they complain that he makes noise (though we don't see or hear anything) and threaten to "take steps"—grows steadily more obsessed with uncovering the mystery of the deceased woman and her fate and becomes positive his neighbors are trying to kill him. As the film progresses, however, his paranoia seems less and less justified, and his actions more and more insane.

In many ways, THE TENANT is Polanski's REPULSION (1965) with the director in the Catherine Deneuve role. In both films, a character's vision of the world clashes with "reality" to the point that no sense can be made of either, and in both the conflict leads to violence. We are never really sure that there isn't a plot against Polanski, even though logic suggests he is imagining everything, and this uneasy sense that maybe Polanski's character is right makes the film extremely, scarily effective (it is also surprisingly funny). Technically, THE TENANT is superb, with stunning camerawork by Sven Nykvist, an eerie score by Philippe Sarde, and thoroughly convincing performances from the entire cast.

TENDER MERCIES 📀

1983 89m c Drama ★★★½
EMI (U.S.) PG

Robert Duvall (Mac Sledge), Tess Harper (Rosa Lee), Betty Buckley (Dixie), Wilford Brimley (Harry), Ellen Barkin (Sue Anne), Allan Hubbard (Sonny), Lenny Von Dohlen (Robert), Paul Gleason (Reporter), Michael Crabtree (Lewis Menefee), Norman Bennett (Rev. Hotchkiss)

p, Philip S. Hobel, Mary-Ann Hobel, Horton Foote, Robert Duvall; d, Bruce Beresford; w, Horton Foote; ph, Russell Boyd (Movielab Color); ed, William Anderson; m, George Dreyfus; art d, Jeannine Oppewall; chor, Nick Felix; cos, Elizabeth McBride

AAN Best Picture; AA Best Actor: Robert Duvall; AAN Best Director: Bruce Beresford; AA Best Original Screenplay: Horton Foote; AAN Best Song: "Over You"; Austin Roberts (Music & Lyrics), Bobby Hart (Music & Lyrics)

This low-key drama set in Texas is one of the continuing stories of screenwriter Horton Foote's life in the hinterlands. Robert Duvall, who won an Oscar for his performance, is Mac Sledge, a down-and-out singer who has recently broken up with his wife, Dixie (Betty Buckley), also a country singer. Mac gets rip-roaring drunk and wakes up in a motel-gas-station owned by a religious widow, Rosa Lee (Tess Harper), with a young son (Allan Hubbard). Rosa offers Mac a job, so he stays on, and the two fall in love. Meanwhile, Dixie and her manager (Wilford Brimley) are lurking in the background, and Mac attempts to patch matters up with her and their daughter (Ellen Barkin). He also tries to make a comeback.

TENDER MERCIES is an episodic gem that offers little in the way of action or melodrama but gets by on fine performances (particularly from Barkin and from Duvall, who does his own singing), atmospheric cinematography, and spare, unglamorous writing. Australian director Bruce Beresford's first American assignment, the film bears interesting comparison with Englishman Michael Apted's COAL MINER'S DAUGHTER (another outsider's vision of the world of country), and with Foote's later, probably superior, THE TRIP TO BOUNTIFUL.

10TH VICTIM, THE 📀
(LA DECIMA VITTIMA)
1965 92m c Science Fiction/Comedy ★★★
Champion/Concordia/Les Films (France/Italy)

Marcello Mastroianni *(Marcello Polletti)*, Ursula Andress *(Caroline Meredith)*, Elsa Martinelli *(Olga)*, Salvo Randone *(Professor)*, Massimo Serato *(Lawyer)*, Evi Rigano *(Victim)*, Milo Quesada *(Rudi)*, Luce Bonifassy *(Lidia)*, Anita Sanders *(Relaxatorium Girl)*, Mickey Knox *(Chet)*

p, Carlo Ponti; d, Elio Petri; w, Elio Petri, Ennio Flaiano, Tonino Guerra, Giorgio Salvioni (based on the short story "The Seventh Victim" by Robert Sheckley); ph, Gianni Di Venanzo (Technicolor); ed, Ruggero Mastroianni; m, Piero Piccioni; art d, Piero Poletto; chor, Gino Landi; cos, Giulio Coltellacci

A bizarre, pop look at life in the future which stars Mastroianni and Andress as participants in a game of legalized murder known as "Man Hunt," a replacement for violence and war. Andress must kill her tenth victim to achieve the pinnacle of success, and Mastroianni happens to be the chosen one. He also is plotting to kill her, which confuses the situation, especially when they fall in love. Petri creates an eccentric and flamboyant world, with some of his wackier invention including Andress's deadly, double-barreled bra and a trendy nightery called Club Masoch.

TEOREMA
1968 93m c Drama ★★★★
Aetos (Italy)

Terence Stamp *(Visitor)*, Silvana Mangano *(Mother)*, Massimo Girotti *(Father)*, Anne Wiazemsky *(Daughter)*, Laura Betti *(Maid)*, Andres Jose Cruz Soublette *(Son)*, Alfonso Gatto *(Doctor)*, Ninetto Davoli *(Messenger)*, Susanna Pasolini *(Old Peasant)*, Adele Cambria

p, Franco Rossellini, Manolo Bolognini; d, Pier Paolo Pasolini; w, Pier Paolo Pasolini (based on his novel); ph, Giuseppe Ruzzolini (Movielab); ed, Nino; m, Ennio Morricone, Wolfgang Amadeus Mozart; art d, Luciano Puccini; fx, Goffredo Rocchetti; cos, Marcella De Marchis, Roberto Capucci

A heavily symbolic and highly intellectual look at the bourgeois milieu and the effect that a mysterious visitor, Stamp, has on one specific family. Into the life of a prominent Milanese family walks Stamp, an angelic-looking stranger (although Pasolini acknowledges that he may also represent the devil), whose spiritual sexuality touches each member of the household in a different way, elevating each to a certain level of grace. He becomes involved with Mangano, the wife; Girotti, the husband; Wiazemsky, their daughter; Cruz, their son; and Betti, the housemaid. Then one day Stamp leaves as mysteriously as he arrived. The family feels the void, can no longer attain the level of spirituality that Stamp provided, and falls back into the worldliness of the bourgeoisie. Mangano tries to recapture that state by wandering the streets and picking up lovers at random; Wiazemsky enters a catatonic trance and completely withdraws from her society; Cruz becomes an artist whose dissatisfaction with his paintings prompts him to urinate on them; and Girotti relinquishes control of his factory to the workers and wanders naked through a vast wasteland. Only Betti, the maid, can survive without Stamp. This is because she, unlike the family that employs her, is from the peasant class and has a naive faith to sustain her—not only in Stamp's divinity but in what he has taught her faith can do. Instead of deteriorating, Betti returns to her village, performs miracles for the peasants, and even levitates. For her brilliant performance (the rest of the cast is equally admirable), Betti was awarded the Best Actress prize at the 1968 Venice Film Festival. The film's release, like so many of Pasolini's films,

was shrouded in controversy. The left wing of the Italian Catholics gave the film an award for its "mysticism" while the Catholic right unleashed a scathing attack on the picture. According to Pasolini (whose self-analysis is usually more confusing than clarifying): "The point of the film is roughly this: a member of the bourgeoisie, whatever he does, is always wrong ... anything done by the bourgeoisie, however sincere, profound, and noble it is, is always on the wrong side of the track." Pasolini had hoped to include Orson Welles in the cast, although he didn't make clear whether he would have had Stamp's or Girotti's role. In either case, the mind boggles.

TERMINAL, THE 📀
2004 128m c Comedy/Drama ★★½
Amblin Entertainment/Parkes/ PG-13
MacDonald Productions/DreamWorks (U.S.)

Tom Hanks *(Viktor Navorski)*, Catherine Zeta-Jones *(Amelia Warren)*, Stanley Tucci *(Frank Dixon)*, Chi McBride *(Mulroy)*, Diego Luna *(Enrique Cruz)*, Barry Shabaka Henley *(Thurman)*, Kumar Pallana *(Gupta Rajan)*, Zoe Saldana *(Torres)*, Eddie Jones *(Salchak)*, Michael Nouri *(Max)*

p, Laurie MacDonald, Walter F. Parkes, Steven Spielberg; d, Steven Spielberg; w, Sacha Gervasi, Jeff Nathanson (based on a story by Andrew Niccol and Sacha Gervasi); ph, Janusz Kaminski; ed, Michael Kahn; m, John Williams; prod d, Alex McDowell; art d, Christopher Burian-Mohr; fx, Charles Gibson, Heather Ignarro, Steven Kirshoff, Michael Lantieri; cos, Mary Zophres

Inspired by the case of a displaced, undocumented Iranian trapped in a French airport for more than a decade, Steven Spielberg downplays the absurd ambiguities inherent in this Kafka-esque premise and crafts a squishy fairy tale about the pluck and fundamental decency of the common man.

While Viktor Navorski (Tom Hanks) is in transit between his native Krakozhia—a generic Slavic country somewhere in Russia's general vicinity—and New York, a military coup takes place. He debarks at JFK airport and steps into a bureaucratic quagmire; his passport and U.S. entry visa are now invalid, but he can't be sent home until Krakozhia's new government is officially recognized. Viktor's only legal option, explains brusque security official Frank Dixon (Stanley Tucci), is to remain in the international terminal until the situation resolves itself. Isolated and destitute, Viktor gamely makes the best of things, building a makeshift shelter near an unused gate, figuring out how to earn money, learning English from travel guides, and making friends among the airport's employees, including Mexican food-service worker Enrique (Diego Luna), Indian janitor Gupta (Kumar Pallana), and African-American maintenance worker Mulroy (Chi McBride). Viktor even romances a comely flight attendant (Catherine Zeta-Jones).

Hanks' beleaguered Viktor is heir to the tradition of Charlie Chaplin's hapless Tramp, but Spielberg can't leave well enough alone. Viktor must not only prevail in the face of bad luck and bureaucratic indifference, he must also be on a sentimental journey to honor his father and become an inspiration to the downtrodden. There's a thin line between fable and twaddle, and this feel-good trifle veers dangerously close to the latter.

TERMINATOR, THE 📀
1984 108m c Science Fiction/Thriller ★★★★
Hemdale/Pacific Western (U.S.) R

Arnold Schwarzenegger *(Terminator)*, Michael Biehn *(Kyle Reese)*, Linda Hamilton *(Sarah Connor)*, Paul Winfield *(Traxler)*, Lance Henriksen *(Vukovich)*, Rick Rossovich *(Matt)*, Bess Motta *(Ginger)*, Earl Boen *(Silberman)*, Dick Miller *(Pawn Shop Clerk)*, Shawn Schepps *(Nancy)*

p, Gale Anne Hurd; d, James Cameron; w, James Cameron, Gale Anne Hurd, William Wisher Jr.; ph, Adam Greenberg (CFI Color); ed, Mark Goldblatt; m, Brad Fiedel; art d, George Costello; fx, Stan Winston, Gene Warren Jr., Peter Kleinow; cos, Hillary Wright

Back before Arnold Schwarzenegger's ascendence to his current status as Hollywood's designated Action Hero of choice, husband to Kennedys, and buddy of presidents, he was still willing to play villains. As such he made an indelible impression as the titular character of THE TERMINATOR. This was the film that demonstrated to the dubious everyone that the musclebound fellow with that outrageous accent might be more than just another passing blip on our pop culture radar screens. The sleeper hit of fall 1984, THE TERMINATOR is an intelligent, smoothly crafted, and stylish low-budget science fiction action movie that astounded fans of the genre. This was an enormous career booster for writer-director James Cameron (ALIENS, THE ABYSS, TERMINATOR 2) as well as stars Schwarzenegger and Linda Hamilton (TV's cult favorite "Beauty and the Beast" and TERMINATOR 2).

The movie opens in the hellish Los Angeles of the year 2029. We see a world destroyed by nuclear war and run by sophisticated machines that have decided to obliterate the weak humans who created them. The action then shifts back to Los Angeles in 1984. In two separate locations, two men—the Terminator (Arnold Schwarzenegger) and Kyle Reese (Michael Biehn)—materialize out of what appear to be small electrical storms and wander off into the night. The next day, after having stolen several deadly weapons and a car, the Terminator looks up the name "Sarah Connor" in the phone book. There are three Sarah Connors listed. The stoical mystery man sets off to kill each of them. Two of the women are killed, but the third (Linda Hamilton) has gone out for the evening. Noticing she is being followed by Reese, the nervous Sarah ducks into a nightclub aptly named Tech Noir and tries to disappear into the crowd. But the Terminator has traced her to the nightclub. Fortunately for her so has Reese. From him Sarah will learn about her destiny and that of the human race.

THE TERMINATOR is an amazingly effective picture that becomes doubly impressive when one considers its small budget. Looking better than most big-budget efforts, it contains dozens of impressive visual effects, including some very good stop-motion animation. For our money, this film is far superior to its mega-grossing mega-budgeted sequel. This is fresh, exciting, and surprisingly witty viewing. Like most genre films made post-STAR WARS, it alludes to many other works. However, this film went a bit further than most. The producers were successfully sued by cult fantasy author Harlan Ellison who claimed that significant chunks of plot and imagery were lifted from two of his celebrated teleplays for "The Outer Limits," a beloved science fiction series from the early 1960s. The two episodes in question are "Soldier" and "Demon with a Glass Hand." Anyone who has seen those episodes will readily agree that THE TERMINATOR took its homage a bit too far.

TERMINATOR 2: JUDGMENT DAY 📀

1991 135m c Science Fiction/Thriller ★★★½
Pacific Western/Canal Plus/Lightstorm R
Entertainment/Carolco (U.S.)

Arnold Schwarzenegger (The Terminator), Linda Hamilton (Sarah Connor), Robert Patrick (T-1000), Edward Furlong (John Connor), Earl Boen (Dr. Silberman), Joe Morton (Miles Dyson), S. Epatha Merkerson (Tarissa Dyson), Castulo Guerra (Enrique Salceda), Danny Cooksey (Tim), Jenette Goldstein (Janelle Voight)

p, James Cameron; d, James Cameron; w, James Cameron, William Wisher; ph, Adam Greenberg; ed, Conrad Buff, Mark Goldblatt, Richard A. Harris; m, Brad Fiedel; prod d, Joseph Nemec III; art d, Joseph P. Lucky; fx, Stan Winston, Dennis Muren; cos, Marlene Stewart

AAN Best Cinematography: Adam Greenberg; AAN Best Film Editing: Conrad Buff, Mark Goldblatt, Richard A. Harris; AA Best Sound: Tom Johnson, Gary Rydstrom, Gary Summers, Lee Orloff; AA Best Visual Effects: Dennis Muren, Stan Winston, Gene Warren, Jr., Robert Skotak; AA Best Makeup: Stan Winston, Jeff Dawn; AA Best Sound Effects Editing: Gary Rydstrom, Gloria S. Borders

TERMINATOR 2: JUDGMENT DAY dazzled its global audience with astonishing special effects and re-confirmed Arnold Schwarzenegger's mega-star status. Trend-setting visuals compensate for a plot that lacks the imagination and edge of the 1984 original.

In a future, war-ravaged L.A., where human rebels led by an adult John Connor (Michael Edwards) do battle with silvery, skeletal robots. Two "intelligent machines" have been dispatched to the past, one to protect the young Connor, the other to kill him. On late 20th-century Earth, young John Connor (Edward Furlong) finds himself pursued by two androids. The one who would be his guardian (Arnold Schwarzenegger) is a replica of the Terminator model T-800 which dominated the original film; the other is a newer model, the T-1000 (Robert Patrick), which takes on the appearance of a young policeman—the first human it dispatches after arriving on Earth. The "bad" Terminator is able to assume the exact shape and appearance of anything with which it comes into contact. Now convinced that androids from the future really do exist, John realizes that his mother, Sarah Connor (Linda Hamilton), is far from crazy. (Sarah s belief in killer robots has had her detained in Pescadero State Hospital.) Now the boy and his Terminator must somehow free Sarah, destroy the T-1000, and prevent an impending nuclear apocalypse.

Though Arnold Schwarzenegger is the nominal star of TERMINATOR 2: JUDGMENT DAY, the show is stolen by extraordinary special effects, particularly the "morphing" in which the liquid metal T-1000 transforms itself into a multitude of organic and inorganic forms. On a dramatic level, the film is less satisfactory. Like an increasing number of big-budget extravaganzas, it bears all the hallmarks of having been created by a demography-minded committee. Thus the violence is offset by a more user-friendly Schwarzenegger, who is forbidden to kill anyone. Meanwhile, Linda Hamilton is given a lot of New Age, motherly things to say; nevertheless, her muscle-bound, gun-toting persona is refreshing. Flaws aside, TERMINATOR 2 is an enjoyable, often exhilarating piece of filmmaking, with a wry sense of humor to boot.

TERMINATOR 3: RISE OF THE MACHINES 📀

2003 109m c Science Fiction/Thriller ★★★
Intermedia/IMF/C2 Pictures/Mostow/ R
Lieberman Productions (U.S.)

Arnold Schwarzenegger (Terminator), Nick Stahl (John Connor), Claire Danes (Kate Brewster), Kristanna Loken (T-X), David Andrews (Robert Brewster), Mark Famiglietti (Scott Petersen), Earl Boen (Dr. Peter Silberman), Moira Harris (Betsy), Chopper Bernet (Chief Engineer), Chris Lawford (Brewster's Aide)

p, Mario F. Kassar, Hal Lieberman, Joel B. Michaels, Andrew G. Vajna, Colin Wilson; d, Jonathan Mostow; w, John Brancato, Michael Ferris (based on a story by Michael Ferris, John Brancato and Tedi Sarafian); ph, Don Burgess; ed, Nicolas de Toth, Neil Travis; m, Marco Beltrami; prod d, Jeff Mann; fx, Allen Hall, Don Lee, Gabor Marinov, John P. Nugent, Pablo Helman, Stan Winston; cos, April Ferry

Picking up some 10 years after T2 left off, this intelligently conceived follow-up is a respectable conclusion to the TERMINATOR trilogy.

The hellish future envisioned in THE TERMINATOR, in which the human survivors of a nuclear war battle ever-more sophisticated killer robots, was apparently averted in TERMINATOR 2. But John Connor (Nick Stahl) has grown into a gloomy young man, so traumatized by his late mother's life-long exhortations that he's destined to lead the anti-machine resistance that he's haunted by constant nightmares. He lives "off the grid," without ties to anyone or anything that might allow machine assassins to pinpoint his whereabouts and return through time to kill him. John's fears turn out to be well founded: Two naked robo-killers soon arrive simultane-ously in the Los Angeles area. The first, a liquid-metal T-X ter-minator (Kristanna Loken), sets about killing John's future lieutenants with alarming efficiency. The second terminator is a rather battered T-101 (the suitably weathered Arnold Schwarzenegger) sent to protect John. Meanwhile, archetypal girl-next-door Kate Brewster (Claire Danes) and her thor-oughly expendable fiance (Mark Famiglietti) are setting up their wedding registry. Necessary plot contrivances unite Kate and John at a veterinary clinic where, amidst escalating termi-nator mayhem, they discover that they were junior-high class-mates. Coincidence? Not in the third installment of a series driven by issues of destiny and the immutable weight of future responsibility.

Director Jonathan Mostow packs the film with muscular action sequences, but the human factor provided by Linda Hamilton's Sarah Connor is sorely missed. Her transforma-tion from hash-house waitress to half-mad "mother of the future" swung the first two films' balance from mechanical explosions, vehicular pandemonium and gunfights to poignantly human concerns. Game though they are, Stahl and Danes can't fill her combat boots.

TERMS OF ENDEARMENT

1983 130m c   Comedy/Drama   ★★★½
Paramount   (U.S.)   PG

Debra Winger (Emma Horton), Shirley MacLaine (Aurora Greenway), Jack Nicholson (Garrett Breedlove), Danny DeVito (Vernon Dahlart), Jeff Daniels (Flap Horton), John Lithgow (Sam Burns), Betty King (Rosie), Lisa Hart Carroll (Patsy Clark), Huckleberry Fox (Toddy), Megan Morris (Melanie)

p, James L. Brooks, Penney Finkelman Cox, Martin Jurow; d, James L. Brooks; w, James L. Brooks (based on the novel by Larry McMurtry); ph, Andrzej Bartkowiak (Metrocolor); ed, Richard Marks, Sidney Wolinsky; m, Michael Gore; prod d, Polly Platt; art d, Harold Michelson; cos, Kristi Zea, Anthony J. Faso

AA Best Picture, AA Best Actress: Shirley MacLaine; AAN Best Actress: Debra Winger; AA Best Supporting Actor: Jack Nicholson; AAN Best Supporting Actor: John Lithgow; AA Best Director: James L. Brooks; AA Best Adapted Screenplay: James L. Brooks; AAN Best Film Editing: Richard Marks; AAN Best Original Score: Michael Gore; AAN Best Art Direction-Set Decoration: Polly Platt, Harold Michelson, Tom Pedigo, Anthony Mondello; AAN Best Sound: Donald O. Mitchell, Rick Kline, Kevin O'Connell, Jim Alexander

Lopsided comedy turned tearjerker, saved by excellent per-formances. TV veteran James Brooks ("Mary Tyler Moore Show") wrote, directed, and co-produced the film which examines a 30-year period in the lives of Aurora Greenway (Shirley MacLaine) and her daughter, Emma (as a child, Jennifer Josey; as an adult, Debra Winger). Aurora is guilty of "smother" love, and, as Emma grows up, she can't wait to escape her mother's suffocating hold. In the face of her moth-er's anger, Emma marries Flap (Jeff Daniels), has three chil-dren, and moves away. All the while, Aurora is wooed by ex-astronaut Garrett Breedlove (Jack Nicholson), an uncouth bachelor whose persistence and unfailing good humor begin to wear her down.

Winger is absolutely winning all the way, with a deathbed scene that may not have been equalled since Bette Davis lay down in DARK VICTORY. MacLaine works like a slow-cooker. The early scenes are her usual stabs at caricature (almost every choice in a dining room scene is wrong), but she

is freed by Nicholson; their scenes have a great element of play to them. About the time she demands better hospital treatment for her daughter, she begins to take chances and ven-tures into virtuoso territory. Nicholson, while certainly not worth the $1 million pricetag for his services, delivers an amusing variation on himself. Brooks writes some of the best dialogue around, but the film is directed in a perfunctory fash-ion, and many scenes go on far too long. Needless to say, it was a huge commercial success; it's one of those movies that manipulates you into thinking it touched you while it's bal-ancing its bank account. And the box-office profited by gossip that the leading ladies despised each other—making it one of those detective watches for more hardened viewers. Something for everyone, indeed.

TERROR IN A TEXAS TOWN

1958 80m   bw   Western   ★★★½
UA   (U.S.)·

Sterling Hayden (George Hansen), Sebastian Cabot (Ed McNeil), Carol Kelly (Molly), Eugene Martin (Pepe Mirada), Ned Young (Johnny Crale), Victor Millan (Jose Mirada), Ann Varela (Rosa Mirada), Sheb Wooley (Baxter), Fred Kohler Jr. (Weed), Steve Mitchell (Keeno)

p, Frank N. Seltzer; d, Joseph H. Lewis; w, Ben L. Perry; ph, Ray Rennahan; ed, Frank Sullivan, Stefan Arnsten; m, Gerald Fried; art d, William Ferrari

A minor cult classic, the last film directed by a major cult tal-ent, Joseph H. Lewis (GUN CRAZY, MY NAME IS JULIA ROSS). This offbeat, low-budget western casts Sterling Hayden as George Hansen, a Swede who returns home from the sea to find that his father, a farmer, has gunned down by the greedy Johnny Crale (Young), who wants to buy up everyone's land in order to drill for oil. At the final showdown, it's six-shooter vs. harpoon.

A leisurely paced, almost hypnotic western, TERROR IN A TEXAS TOWN relies more on characterization and form than on plot. Although the film's title and the final con-frontation sound campy, this flick is lean, mean, and grip-pingly serious. Sharp-eyed viewers will recognize Sheb Wooley, who made the charts in 1958 with his immortal hit, "Purple People Eater."

TESS

1979 170m   c   Drama   ★★★
Renn/Burrill   (France/U.K.)   PG

Nastassja Kinski (Tess Durbeyfield), Leigh Lawson (Alec d'Urberville), Peter Firth (Angel Clare), John Collin (John Durbeyfield), David Markham (Rev. Mr. Clare), Rosemary Martin (Mrs. Durbeyfield), Richard Pearson (Vicar of Marlott), Carolyn Pickles (Marian), Pascale de Boysson (Mrs. Clare), Tony Church (Parson Tringham)

p, Claude Berri; d, Roman Polanski; w, Roman Polanski, Gerard Brach, John Brownjohn (based on the novel Tess of the d'Urbervilles by Thomas Hardy); ph, Geoffrey Unsworth, Ghislain Cloquet (Eastmancolor); ed, Alastair McIntyre, Tom Priestley; m, Philippe Sarde; prod d, Pierre Guffroy; art d, Jack Stephens; chor, Sue Lefton; cos, Anthony Powell

AAN Best Picture; AAN Best Director: Roman Polanski; AA Best Cinematography: Geoffrey Unsworth, Ghislain Cloquet; AAN Best Original Score: Philippe Sarde; AA Best Art Direction-Set Decoration: Pierre Guffroy Jack Stephens; AA Best Costume Design: Anthony Powell

Roman Polanski's delicate, visually rich adaptation of Thomas Hardy's classic novel places the supremely photo-genic Nastassja Kinski in the title role. Peasant girl Tess

Durbeyfield is sent to the estate of the wealthy d'Urbervilles by her desperate father after he learns that the two families are distantly related. It turns out, however, that the d'Urbervilles are not the d'Urbervilles after all, but a family that bought the noble line's name. Alec d'Urberville (Leigh Lawson), the cocky young master of the household, takes Tess as his lover, but later she returns home, disillusioned and pregnant. After the death of her baby, Tess is left to work on a dairy farm, where she falls in love with Angel Clare (Peter Firth). Their romance leads to a marriage that ends abruptly on their wedding night when her outraged husband refuses to accept her past. With nowhere else to go, Tess returns to Alec, a decision that leads to a violent end.

Visually, TESS is a masterpiece, capturing in amazing detail the scenery and atmosphere of the England of yore. The film's chief drawback, however, is its lack of vitality. Instead of Hardy's passionate tale of ruin and disenchantment, TESS is cautious and reserved.

TEST PILOT

1938 118m bw Drama   ★★★★
MGM   (U.S.)

Clark Gable (Jim Lane), Myrna Loy (Ann Barton), Spencer Tracy (Gunner Sloane), Lionel Barrymore (Howard B. Drake), Samuel S. Hinds (Gen. Ross), Arthur Aylesworth (Frank Barton), Claudia Coleman (Mrs. Barton), Gloria Holden (Mrs. Benson), Louis Jean Heydt (Benson), Ted Pearson (Joe)

p, Louis D. Lighton; d, Victor Fleming; w, Vincent Lawrence, Waldemar Young, Howard Hawks (based on a story by Frank Wead); ph, Ray June; ed, Tom Held; m, Franz Waxman; cos, Dolly Tree

AAN Best Picture; AAN Best Original Story: Frank Wead; AAN Best Film Editing: Tom Held

One of the best Hollywood aviation dramas, TEST PILOT sparkles with a great cast and sprightly direction by Fleming, a "man's director" who had the good sense to feature a great female performer, Loy, in this action film. Gable plays a world-renowned test pilot who meets and marries farm girl Loy. She wants him to settle down, but Gable—who calls the sky "that lady all dressed in blue"—deeply enjoys putting his life on the line. When Army general Hinds requests that Gable test the Army's new B-17 bomber, Gable accepts the challenge. Loy is on the verge of a crackup by the time Gable and his copilot-buddy Tracy climb into the bomber. Gable pushes the plane beyond its presumed limit and keeps going, trying to reach 30,000 feet. The bomber cannot take the pressure and gives out, plummeting earthward in a screaming nosedive…

According to some sources (though not Lynn Tornabee, author of the Gable biography Long Live the King), it was actually Tracy who, during the production of this film, gave Gable the sobriquet for which he would be forever known. Reportedly, as Tracy attempted to drive into the MGM lot one morning, his car was blocked by scores of screaming female fans who were besieging Gable, demanding that the star sign their pictures of him. Tracy beeped his horn, but the fans ignored him. Finally, the frustrated Tracy stood up in his convertible and shouted at Gable, "Long live the king! And now, for Christ's sake, let's get inside and go to work!" The prop department subsequently made Gable a cardboard crown lined with rabbit's fur, after which Ed Sullivan heard about the incident and conducted a nationwide poll to find out who the king and queen of Hollywood really were. Fans overwhelmingly elected Gable and Loy. Tracy was frequently frustrated at having to perform in support of screen idol Gable and is said to have stretched out some of his own scenes to insure that he would make a good impression. Regardless, the rapport of the three leads is the film's greatest strength.

Buoyed as well by its stunning aerial photography, TEST PILOT was a box-office smash.

TESTAMENT   DVD

1983 90m   c   Science Fiction/Drama/War   ★★★
Entertainment Events/American Playhouse (U.S.)   PG

Jane Alexander (Carol Wetherly), William Devane (Tom Wetherly), Ross Harris (Brad Wetherly), Roxana Zal (Mary Liz Wetherly), Lukas Haas (Scottie Wetherly), Philip Anglim (Hollis), Lilia Skala (Fania), Leon Ames (Henry Abhart), Lurene Tuttle (Rosemary Abhart), Rebecca De Mornay (Cathy Pitkin)

p, Jonathan Bernstein, Lynne Littman; d, Lynne Littman; w, John Sacret Young (based on the story "The Last Testament" by Carol Amen); ph, Steven Poster (CFI Color); ed, Suzanne Pettit; m, James Horner; prod d, David Nichols; art d, Linda Pearl; cos, Julie Weiss

AAN Best Actress: Jane Alexander

Set in a small town in northern California, this flawed but moving film begins by establishing the pattern of everyday life for an average American family, then rips it apart by introducing the nightmare of nuclear apocalypse. Tom and Carol Wetherly (William Devane and Jane Alexander), the loving parents of three children (Lukas Haas, Ross Harris, and Roxana Zal), joke, bicker, and make love until one day Tom doesn't come home from work because war has broken out. Thereafter, the film shows the effects of fallout, both physical and psychological, on the little town and particularly the Wetherlys. As living conditions deteriorate, looting begins, and people start dying, including two of the Wetherly children; Carol and her surviving son search for solace in the past, stirring their memories with home movies of happier times. Ultimately, they find the will to go on into the bleak future.

While TESTAMENT is less sensational than the similar TV movie, "The Day After," first-time director Lynne Littman lays on the sentiment and symbolism a little thickly, and some may find the pre-disaster sequences slow going. The acting is undeniably strong, particularly Alexander's heartfelt performance.

TESTAMENT OF DR. MABUSE, THE   DVD

(DAS TESTAMENT DES DR. MABUSE)
1933 122m bw   Science Fiction/Crime   ★★★★★
Nero/Constantine/Deutsche Universal   (Germany)

Rudolf Klein-Rogge (Dr. Mabuse), Oscar Beregi Sr. (Prof. Dr. Baum), Karl Meixner (Hofmeister), Theodor Loos (Dr. Kramm), Otto Wernicke (Commissioner Karl Lohmann), Klaus Pohl (Muller), Wera Liessem (Lilli), Gustav Diesel (Kent), Camilla Spira (Juwelen-Anna), Rudolph Schundler (Hardy)

p, Fritz Lang; d, Fritz Lang; w, Fritz Lang (based on the characters from the novel by Norbert Jacques); ph, Fritz Arno Wagner, Karl Vash; m, Hans Erdmann; prod d, Karl Vollbrecht, Emile Hasler; art d, Karl Vollbrecht, Emil Hasler

A haunting, suspenseful sequel to the great Fritz Lang's 1922 silent DR. MABUSE, THE GAMBLER picks up where the original left off—with Rudolf Klein-Rogge, reprising his role as the mad Dr. Mabuse, in a cell in an insane asylum. When Mabuse dies, Prof. Baum (Oskar Beregi), the director of the asylum, becomes possessed by the dead doctor's spirit and is compelled to carry out the madman's master plan to destroy the state through theft, violence, murder, and destruction. Although Baum engineers these chaotic acts, he manages to lead a double life, retaining his position at the asylum. Interwoven into this story is the tale of two lovers—Lilli (Wera Liessem) and Kent (Gustav Diesel), a member of Baum's gang who wants out and manages to prove the connection between Mabuse's plans and the chaos that is rocking Berlin.

Filmed in 1932 and coscripted by Lang's wife, Thea von Harbou, THE TESTAMENT OF DR. MABUSE was made during the Nazi party's rise to power, and completed just before Lang fled, without von Harbou (who would become a top Nazi screenwriter), to the U.S. Whether or not it was Lang's intention, there are distinct parallels between THE TESTAMENT OF DR. MABUSE and the real-life events of the day—Prof. Baum symbolizing all those whose minds had become controlled by the thought of carrying out the "master plan." It should come as no surprise, then, that this remarkable testament to Lang's artistry was banned, and nearly destroyed, by the Nazis.

TESTAMENT OF ORPHEUS, THE
(LE TESTAMENT D'ORPHEE)
1959   79m   c/bw   Drama   ★★★★★
Editions Cinegraphiques   (France)

Jean Cocteau *(Himself, the Poet)*, Edouard Dermit *(Cegeste)*, Jean-Pierre Leaud *(The Schoolboy)*, Henri Cremieux *(The Professor)*, Francoise Christophe *(The Nurse)*, Maria Casares *(The Princess)*, Francois Perier *(Heurtebise)*, Yul Brynner *(The Court Usher)*, Daniel Gelin *(The Intern)*, Nicole Courcel *(The Young Mother)*

p, Jean Thuillier; d, Jean Cocteau; w, Jean Cocteau; ph, Roland Pontoiseau; ed, Marie-Josephe Yoyotte; m, Georges Auric, Martial Solal, Johann Sebastian Bach, George Frederick Handel, Christophe Gluck; art d, Pierre Guffroy

Poet-filmmaker-sculptor-painter Jean Cocteau bade a fond farewell to cinema with this free-flowing, spirited collection of images and scenes that includes characters from his past films and personal friends. What there is of a story retreads the ground of Cocteau's THE BLOOD OF A POET (1930) and ORPHEUS (1949), bringing his cinematic career (which is difficult to separate from his other pursuits) full circle. For fans of Cocteau, everything in this picture will strike a familiar chord—a poet lives, must die, is resurrected, and must die again to qualify for immortality. Cocteau again employs some of the most inventive and beautiful photographic manipulations ever done in films, including the reverse motion techniques that never fail to bring a smile to his devotees. The cast reads like a cultural who's who—Pablo Picasso, Charles Aznavour, Francoise Sagan, Brigitte Bardot, Roger Vadim, Jean-Pierre Leaud, and, yes, Yul Brynner. Also making appearances are familiar faces from ORPHEUS, including Jean Marais, Maria Casares, Edouard Dermit, Francois Perier, and Henri Cremieux. Francois Truffaut, in honor of one of his masters, assisted with the production and financing of the picture. A pure, personal poem from one of the greats, THE TESTAMENT OF ORPHEUS allows Cocteau to live on forever.

TETSUO: THE IRON MAN   DVD
1989   67m   bw   Science Fiction/Horror/Erotic   ★★★
Kaiju Theatre   (Japan)

Tomoro Taguchi, billed as Tomoroh Taguchi *(The Salaryman)*, Kei Fujiwara *(The Salaryman's Girlfriend)*, Nobu Kanaoka *(Woman in Glasses)*, Shinya Tsukamoto *(Young Metals Fetishist)*, Naomasa Musaka *(Doctor)*, Renji Ishibashi *(Tramp)*

p, Shinya Tsukamoto; d, Shinya Tsukamoto; w, Shinya Tsukamoto; ph, Kei Fujiwara, Shinya Tsukamoto; ed, Shinya Tsukamoto; m, Chu Ishikawa; art d, Shinya Tsukamoto; fx, Shinya Tsukamoto; cos, Kei Fujiwara

Shinya Tsukamoto has infused TETSUO: THE IRON MAN with a satirical sensibility—as well as a graphic blend of vio-

lence and sexuality—that makes this featurette a wildly original departure from standard sci-fi.

In a disturbingly realistic scene prior to the opening credits, viewers see a young man (Tsukamoto) wandering through an abandoned factory. In between close-ups of discarded machinery and cables, the youth, a metals fetishist, carves open his upper thigh and implants a piece of metal tubing. The next character viewers encounter is a bespectacled young man in a business suit, a typical "salaryman" (Tomoroh Taguchi), against a background of steel mill processes. While shaving, he notices a small metal thorn growing out of his face, and he seems to have flashbacks of a hit-and-run accident involving the metals fetishist.

While commuting to work, the salaryman has to fight off a young woman (Nobu Kanaoka) who is suddenly controlled by a mutant substance that converts her arm into a fungoid claw. Even the salaryman's dreams seem contaminated, since he has a nightmare in which a mutated woman sodomizes him with an enormous metallic phallus. Later, while making love to his girlfriend (Kei Fujiwara), the salaryman finds that he is changing into a collection of machinery and runs to hide. Undaunted, the woman tries to console him, until she realizes the extent of his mutation—his penis now boasts a power-driven screw head!

The frankly erotic element alone would distinguish this production, but it also features a fractured continuity that demands attention, if only to figure out what is going on. The contortion of the narrative line, like the graphic emphasis on sex and blood, emphasizes the alien nature of mutation; Tsukamoto's creatures are not just plain folks with odd body parts, but original monsters. Although not for the priggish or squeamish, Tsukamoto's film is both outstanding sci-fi and a smart, gleefully perverse satire of urban dehumanization in an age increasingly dominated by commodity fetishism and robotics.

TEX   DVD
1982   103m   c   Drama   ★★★
Walt Disney Productions   (U.S.)   PG

Matt Dillon *(Tex McCormick)*, Jim Metzler *(Mason McCormick)*, Meg Tilly *(Jamie Collins)*, Bill McKinney *(Pop McCormick)*, Frances Lee McCain *(Mrs. Johnson)*, Ben Johnson *(Cole Collins)*, Emilio Estevez *(Johnny Collins)*, Phil Brock *(Lem Peters)*, Jack Thibeau *(Coach Jackson)*, Zeljko Ivanek *(Hitchhiker)*

p, Tim Zinnemann; d, Tim Hunter; w, Tim Hunter, Charlie Haas (based on the novel by S.E. Hinton); ph, Ric Waite (Technicolor); ed, Howard Smith; m, Pino Donaggio; prod d, Jack T. Collis; art d, John B. Mansbridge

Matt Dillon takes his urban toughness to Oklahoma as Tex, a young farmboy raised by his elder brother when their mother dies and their father wanders away. The film probes the pitfalls of growing up, tackling such subjects as sex, boozing, and fighting—three areas the Disney folks have stayed clear of in the past. Dillon, though occasionally annoying, turns in a decent performance, as do Jim Metzler as his brother and Meg Tilly (THE BIG CHILL, PSYCHO II, AGNES OF GOD) as his girlfriend. The screenplay is based on a teen novel by S.E. Hinton (who also appears in the film).

TEXAS CHAINSAW MASSACRE, THE   DVD
1974   83m   c   Horror   ★★★★
Vortex/Henkel/Hooper   (U.S.)   R

Marilyn Burns *(Sally)*, Allen Danziger *(Jerry)*, Paul A. Partain *(Franklin)*, William Vail *(Kirk)*, Teri McMinn *(Pam)*, Edwin Neal *(Hitchhiker)*, Jim Siedow *(Old Man)*, Gunnar Hansen *(Leatherface)*, John Dugan *(Grandfather)*, Jerry Lorenz *(Pickup Driver)*

p, Tobe Hooper; d, Tobe Hooper; w, Kim Henkel, Tobe Hooper; ph, Daniel Pearl (CFI Color); ed, Sallye Richardson, Larry Carroll; m, Tobe Hooper, Wayne Bell; art d, Robert Burns

Though its exploitation title would suggest that THE TEXAS CHAIN SAW MASSACRE is just another mindless gore-fest, it is in fact an intelligent, absorbing, and deeply disturbing horror film that is nearly bloodless in its depiction of violence. Using the age-old technique of suggestion, combined with a gritty, well-executed (no pun intended) visual style, the film seems much bloodier than it actually is. Disturbed by news reports that vandals have been desecrating the remote Texas cemetery where her grandfather is buried, Burns and her wheelchair-bound brother, Partain, gather some of their friends and take the family van to see if their grandfather's grave is still intact. While in the area they decide to visit the old farmhouse where Grandpa lived. Nearby is another farmhouse—one decorated with grisly items made from human and animal skin and bones—in which resides a family of unemployed slaughterhouse workers, the most frightening of whom is "Leatherface" (Hansen), who wears a mask of human flesh and has a way with a chainsaw.

Obviously based on real-life Wisconsin farmer Ed Gein (whose grotesque exploits also inspired Hitchcock's PSYCHO), THE TEXAS CHAIN SAW MASSACRE is one of the best examples of the "horror of the family" subgenre, which takes as its subject the American family—traditionally a wholesome, positive force—and examines its dark side, the side that is claustrophobic, stifling, and incestuous. Tobe Hooper's film is deeply disturbing and is meant to be. The best films in the horror genre don't exist just to "scare" people but to examine the darker impulses, fears, taboos, and repressed desires found in human beings and to purge them from our collective subconscious.

THAT HAMILTON WOMAN
1941 128m bw Biography/War ★★★
UA (U.S.)

Vivien Leigh (Emma Hart Hamilton), Laurence Olivier (Lord Horatio Nelson), Alan Mowbray (Sir William Hamilton), Sara Allgood (Mrs. Cadogan-Lyon), Gladys Cooper (Lady Nelson), Henry Wilcoxon (Capt. Hardy), Heather Angel (Street Girl), Halliwell Hobbes (Rev. Nelson), Gilbert Emery (Lord Spencer), Miles Mander (Lord Keith)

p, Alexander Korda; d, Alexander Korda; w, Walter Reisch, R.C. Sherriff; ph, Rudolph Mate; ed, William Hornbeck; m, Miklos Rozsa; prod d, Vincent Korda; fx, Lawrence Butler; cos, Rene Hubert

AAN Best B/W Cinematography: Rudolph Mate; AAN Best Interior Decoration (B/W): Vincent Korda, Julia Heron; AA Best Sound Recording: Jack Whitney; AAN Best Special Effects: Lawrence Butler (Photographic), William H. Wilmarth (Sound)

A drunken crone (played by Vivien Leigh), jailed on charges of theft and assault, begins to tell the story of her life to a cellmate, and the tale of THAT HAMILTON WOMAN unfolds in flashback. In 1786, young Emma Hart (Leigh) arrives at the court of Naples, expecting to wed the British ambassador's nephew. He proves a rascal, but Emma's joie de vivre soon attracts the ambassador himself, Sir William Hamilton (Alan Mowbray), and she eventually becomes his bride. Seven years later, British naval hero Lord Nelson (Laurence Olivier) arrives in Naples, seeking the king's aid in the war against Napoleon, and the rest, as they say, is history—or at least producer-director Alexander Korda's version of such. The film traces the growth in Naples of Emma and Nelson's love (to which her husband turns a blind eye, though tongues wag back home) and their return to England, where the lovers set up house, although Nelson's wife refuses to divorce him. The war goes badly, and Emma persuades Nelson to return to his

command, leading to his mortal wounding in the victory at Trafalgar, which in turn begins her slide into despair. Despite the marquee pull of newlyweds Olivier and Leigh (she fresh from GONE WITH THE WIND), THAT HAMILTON WOMAN was not the hit its makers hoped it would be—though it reportedly was Winston Churchill's favorite movie. Korda, shooting in the U.S. with little money, was forced to film quickly, without the lavish sets that were his specialty, and the script's "tastefulness"—which downplays Nelson's sensuality and alters facts in making Emma pay for her sins later in the classic Hollywood style—while pleasing to 1941 censors and strengthening its propaganda value for then-embattled Britain, also lowers the level of excitement. For a more accurate account, see Glenda Jackson and Peter Finch in THE NELSON AFFAIR (1973).

THAT MAN FROM RIO
(L'HOMME DE RIO)
1964 114m c Comedy/Adventure ★★★
Ariane/Artistes/Dear (France/Italy)

Jean-Paul Belmondo (Adrien Dufourquet), Francoise Dorleac (Agnes), Jean Servais (Prof. Catalan), Simone Renant (Lola), Milton Ribeiro (Tupac), Ubiracy de Oliveira (Sir Winston), Adolfo Celi (Senor De Castro), Daniel Ceccaldi, Roger Dumas, Sabu do Brasil

p, Alexandre Mnouchkine, Georges Dancigers; d, Philippe de Broca; w, Jean-Paul Rappeneau, Ariane Mnouchkine, Daniel Boulanger, Philippe de Broca; ph, Edmond Sechan (Eastmancolor); ed, Laurence Mery-Clark, Francoise Javet; m, Georges Delerue; fx, Gil Delamare

AAN Best Original Story and Screenplay: Jean-Paul Rappeneau, Ariane Mnouchkine, Daniel Boulanger, Philippe DeBroca

A wacky adventure yarn that begins with French air force pilot Belmondo on an eight-day pass to visit girlfriend Dorleac in Paris. Unfortunately Belmondo arrives just in time to see Dorleac kidnaped by South American Indians who are trying to get a hold of a set of valuable statues that, when assembled, will point the way to an Amazon treasure. Dorleac is taken because her late father led an expedition in the area, so the Indians suspect she knows where the statues are. After a lengthy series of misadventures in the jungle, Belmondo and Dorleac eventually escape and return to Paris just in time for Belmondo to return to his unit. Belmondo, as always, is a delight. The film received an Oscar nomination for Best Screenplay.

THAT OBSCURE OBJECT OF DESIRE 📀
(CET OBSCUR OBJECT DU DESIR)
1977 100m c Drama ★★★★½
Greenwich/Galaxie/Inine (France/Spain) R

Fernando Rey (Mathieu), Carole Bouquet (Conchita), Angela Molina (Conchita), Julien Bertheau (Judge), Milena Vukotic (Traveler), Andre Weber (Valet), Pierre Pieral (Psychologist), Maria Asquerino, Ellen Bahl, Valerie Blanco

p, Serge Silberman; d, Luis Bunuel; w, Luis Bunuel, Jean-Claude Carriere (based on the novel La Femme et la Pantin by Pierre Louys); ph, Edmond Richard (Eastmancolor); ed, Helene Plemiannikov; art d, Pierre Guffroy

AAN Best Foreign Language Film; AAN Best Adapted Screenplay: Luis Bunuel, Jean-Claude Carriere

The final film from the 77-year-old Luis Bunuel shows the playful director in as outrageous form as ever, casting two women—the graceful Carole Bouquet and the saucy Angela Molina—in the role of Conchita, a beautiful but elusive Spanish girl who becomes the object of obsession for Mathieu

(Fernando Rey, his voice dubbed into French by Michel Piccoli), an upstanding French businessman. Widowed seven years ago, Mathieu regards love and sex moralistically, priding himself on his ability to count on one hand the number of times he had sex with a woman he didn't love. When he sees Conchita, however, his mind overflows with thoughts of her. Although Conchita professes her love to Mathieu, she leaves him and flees to Switzerland, only to return later as his maid. When Mathieu finally manages to bed her, she is dressed in such an impenetrable outfit (a chastity belt of sorts) that he is unable to satisfy his uncontrollable sexual urge.

This straightforward tale of obsessive love is colored with the always amazing Bunuelian touches. Mathieu's story is framed by a train trip in which he speaks of Conchita to his fellow passengers: a French official, a woman and her teenage daughter, and a dwarf psychologist. Also prevalent throughout the picture is a rash of bombings by a terrorist group that calls itself the Revolutionary Army of the Infant Jesus. The most fascinating aspect of THAT OBSCURE OBJECT OF DESIRE, however, is the character of Conchita, who is exactly what the title promises—so obscure that Bunuel chose to cast two actresses in her role. LAST TANGO IN PARIS star Maria Schneider was originally cast to play Conchita by herself, but she was replaced early in the shooting. In a stroke of genius, Bunuel then cast two women in the same role—a completely logical dualism, since Conchita seems to vary greatly in her feelings for Mathieu, loving him one day and leaving him the next.

THAT SINKING FEELING

1979 82m   c   Crime/Comedy   ★★★
Minor Miracle Film Cooperative   (U.K.)   PG

Robert Buchanan *(Ronnie)*, John Hughes *(Vic)*, Billy Greenlees *(Wal)*, Douglas Sannachan *(Simmy)*, Alan Love *(Alec)*, Danny Benson *(Policeman)*, Eddie Burt *(Van Driver)*, Tom Mannion *(Doctor)*, Eric Joseph *(The Wee Man)*, Janette Rankin *(Mary)*

p, Bill Forsyth; d, Bill Forsyth; w, Bill Forsyth; ph, Michael Coulter (Fujicolor Negative); ed, John Gow; m, Colin Tully; prod d, Adrienne Atkinson; cos, Adrienne Atkinson

Early comedy by Scottish director Bill Forsyth (GREGORY'S GIRL, LOCAL HERO) which follows the goofy exploits of a gang of unemployed youths who steal and try to sell a shipment of stainless steel sinks. Of course the boys have a bit of trouble unloading their loot, and the film details their increasingly frustrated efforts to turn a sticky situation into a profitable one. Great performances from nonprofessionals are directed with Forsyth's usual insightful wit. Some viewers may have trouble deciphering the Scottish accents.

THAT TOUCH OF MINK   DVD

1962 99m   c   Romance/Comedy   ★★★
Granley/Arwin/Nob Hill   (U.S.)

Cary Grant *(Philip Shayne)*, Doris Day *(Cathy Timberlake)*, Gig Young *(Roger)*, Audrey Meadows *(Connie)*, Alan Hewitt *(Dr. Gruber)*, John Astin *(Beasley)*, Richard Sargent *(Young Man)*, Joey Faye *(Short Man)*, John Fiedler *(Mr. Smith)*, Willard Sage *(Hodges)*

p, Martin Melcher, Stanley Shapiro; d, Delbert Mann; w, Stanley Shapiro, Nate Monaster; ph, Russell Metty (Panavision, Eastmancolor); ed, Ted J. Kent; m, George Duning; art d, Alexander Golitzen, Robert Clatworthy; cos, Norman Norell, Rosemary Odell

AAN Best Original Story and Screenplay: Stanley Shapiro, Nate Monaster; *AAN Best Art Direction-Set Decoration (Color):* Alexander Golitzen, Robert Clatworthy, George Milo; *AAN Best Sound:* Walden O. Watson

A bouncy if rather smarmy comedy from the mind of Stanley Shapiro, who also contributed to PILLOW TALK and

LOVER COME BACK. Shapiro and coauthor Monaster have come up with a thin plot but scads of funny dialogue enhanced by Grant, Day, and Young in enjoyable performances. Day is out of work in New York and about to cash her unemployment check when Grant's passing limousine splashes her with mud. Grant is a corporate raider who has spent his life gobbling up companies and neglecting his personal life. (Humphrey Bogart did the same role in SABRINA.) Day walks into the local automat. Grant sends Young, his tippling financial advisor, into the restaurant to offer Day money for her muddied dress. Meadows, Day's roommate (in a wisecracking, Eve Arden-like role), and Young tell Day to give Grant what-for if she is so indignant at him. Day marches into Grant's fabulous office, where her wrath is soon assuaged by Grant's incomparable suavity. When Grant has to make a business trip to Maryland, he invites her to join him and she agrees. Thus begins a whirlwind journey as he takes her to Philadelphia for drinks, to the UN where he gives a speech, then down to Baltimore for dinner and a game between the Yankees and the Orioles. (Seen briefly are Mickey Mantle, Roger Maris, and Yogi Berra as themselves.) This cat-and-mouse game has to end eventually, and it does when Grant asks Day if she'd like to go to Bermuda with him. The lady doth protest at first, but when Grant plies her with lavish clothing (designed by Rosemary Odell) and a full-length mink coat, Day changes her mind. As nighttime approaches in their vacation spot, Day realizes that this is nothing out of Plato; Grant wants to take Richmond here, and there is no getting away from it. Day conveniently breaks out in a rash, leaving Grant to spend the night playing cards. The romantic trip becomes a disaster. Day feels awful about what's happened and wants another chance. Prior to their next date, Day begins to drink to relax herself and falls off a terrace. Grant feels that the whole affair is a waste of time and won't call her anymore. Day is frustrated and wants to make Grant jealous, so she asks Young for his help. Young arranges a motel tryst with Astin, an unemployment clerk with a lecherous gleam in his eye. Then Young notifies Grant so he can rescue Day from this fate. Once Day is out of Astin's clutches, Grant realizes that she is the woman for him. Skin problems, though, once again enter the picture.

Most of the jokes are verbal rather than slapstick in this script, which, rather surprisingly, copped an Oscar nomination. The film whips along like a Formula One car under Mann's capable direction. The main problem is that 58-year-old Grant and 38-year-old Day were getting slightly long in the tooth for this kind of "will she or won't she?" story. Astin is excellent, appearing in his second movie after WEST SIDE STORY. Right after this, he teamed with Marty Ingels in his first TV series, "I'm Dickens, He's Fenster."

THEATRE OF BLOOD   DVD

1973 104m   c   Horror   ★★★★
UA   (U.K.)   R

Vincent Price *(Edward Lionheart)*, Diana Rigg *(Edwina Lionheart)*, Ian Hendry *(Peregrine Devlin)*, Harry Andrews *(Trevor Dickman)*, Coral Browne *(Miss Chloe Moon)*, Robert Coote *(Oliver Larding)*, Jack Hawkins *(Solomon Psaltery)*, Michael Hordern *(George Maxwell)*, Arthur Lowe *(Horace Sprout)*, Robert Morley *(Meredith Merridew)*

p, John Kohn, Stanley Mann; d, Douglas Hickox; w, Anthony Greville-Bell; ph, Wolfgang Suschitzky (DeLuxe Color); ed, Malcolm Cooke; m, Michael J. Lewis; prod d, Michael Seymour; fx, John Stears; chor, Tutte Lemkow; cos, Michael Baldwin

After the horrible deaths of three of his colleagues in the prestigious London Theatre Critics Circle, Peregrine Devlin (Ian Hendry) approaches the baffled police with a bizarre theory: perhaps the murders are being committed by Edward Lionheart (Vincent Price), an aging Shakespearean actor who was outraged when the Critic's Circle award went to another actor. So incensed was Lionheart, that he pushed his way onto the stage, stole the award, and jumped into the Thames, supposedly killing himself. Since the three murders closely parallel deaths detailed in the plays of Shakespeare, the cops think that Devlin may be right. The now-insane Lionheart, aided by his lovely though equally mad daughter, Edwina (Diana Rigg), and a group of derelicts who rescued him from the Thames, is indeed killing the critics.

Clearly inspired by the success of the "Dr. Phibes" series, THEATRE OF BLOOD goes one better by allowing Price to glory in his peculiarly Gothic acting style. He is wonderful here, delighting in every grotesque killing and relishing the excerpts from Shakespeare while outfitted in a variety of outlandish costumes. While Price dominates the film with his superb performance, he is ably supported by a top-notch cast—all of whom agreed to do the film in homage to Price. Director Douglas Hickox wisely chooses a very fluid cinematic style to provide a contrast to the distinctly theatrical script. He skillfully intertwines hilarious black humor with some surprisingly intense Grand Guignol effects. Wholly entertaining and memorable, THEATRE OF BLOOD is ripe camp, an excellent film, and a lasting tribute to the career of one of the most important actors in the genre.

THELMA & LOUISE
1991 128m c   Drama/Adventure/Comedy ★★★★
Percy Main Productions   (U.S.)   R

Geena Davis (*Thelma*), Susan Sarandon (*Louise*), Harvey Keitel (*Hal*), Michael Madsen (*Jimmy*), Christopher McDonald (*Darryl*), Stephen Tobolowsky (*Max*), Brad Pitt (*J.D.*), Timothy Carhart (*Harlan*), Lucinda Jenney (*Lena the Waitress*), Jason Beghe (*State Trooper*)

p, Ridley Scott, Mimi Polk; d, Ridley Scott; w, Callie Khouri; ph, Adrian Biddle; ed, Thom Noble; m, Hans Zimmer; prod d, Norris Spencer; art d, Lisa Dean; cos, Elizabeth McBride

AAN Best Actress: Geena Davis; *AAN Best Actress:* Susan Sarandon; *AAN Best Director:* Ridley Scott; *AA Best Original Screenplay:* Callie Khouri; *AAN Best Cinematography:* Adrian Biddle; *AAN Best Film Editing:* Thom Noble

THELMA & LOUISE is a rowdy, feminist road movie in which a pair of gutsy, independent women discover the strength of sisterhood during a hell-raising, joy-riding escape from the laws of men. One of the most hotly debated films of 1991, it features outstanding performances from stars Geena Davis and Susan Sarandon.

Louise (Sarandon) is a strong-willed waitress who convinces her friend Thelma (Davis), a timid housewife, to join her on a weekend camping trip. Against the wishes of Darryl (Christopher McDonald), her possessive, sexist husband, Thelma sneaks away for the outing. Along the way the pair let loose at a country bar, drinking and dancing; Thelma flirts mildly with a handsome but abusive man, Harlan (Timothy Carhart). Harlan attempts to rape Thelma in the parking lot and is discovered by Louise, who shoots and kills him. The women decide that the police are not likely to believe their version of events, so they flee in a panic.

From Arkansas they head through Oklahoma, where they pick up J.D. (Brad Pitt), a young cowboy stud who has a one-night stand with Thelma. He also steals the money Louise had convinced Jimmy (Michael Madsen), her sometime boyfriend, to withdraw from her savings account. Again victimized by men, they turn desperado, robbing stores to finance their attempted escape to Mexico. Because Louise refuses to take the direct route through Texas (where, it turns out, she herself was once raped), their getaway turns into an extended driving tour of the Southwest. Along the way they feel oddly empowered by their ability to assert themselves against authority, and develop a penchant for improvised holdups. But all the while, the FBI is closing in.

Critical reaction to THELMA & LOUISE indicated that many male viewers felt threatened by these pistol-packing female outlaws, but complaints about the movie's chauvinist treatment of men are largely unjustified. Gender warfare aside, THELMA & LOUISE is a fun, breezy roadtrip across the Western landscape. In the natural grandeur of this setting, director Scott abandons his trademark high-tech atmospherics in favor of a bright, glossy, photographic style that makes picture postcards of the Route 66 backdrop. Yet actresses Davis and Sarandon manage to upstage even Monument Valley. Together they forge a believable and appealing bond that carries the film through some of its improbable plot twists. Even the daring finish—a freeze-frame apotheosis of the duo's leap into the Grand Canyon—works, thanks to the vividness of Davis's and Sarandon's portrayals. It all adds up to a highly enjoyable ride.

THEM!
1954 93m   bw   Science Fiction   ★★★½
Warner Bros. (U.S.)

James Whitmore (*Sgt. Ben Peterson*), Edmund Gwenn (*Dr. Harold Medford*), Joan Weldon (*Dr. Patricia Medford*), James Arness (*Robert Graham*), Onslow Stevens (*Brig. Gen. O'Brien*), Sean McClory (*Maj. Kibbee*), Chris Drake (*Officer Ed Blackburn*), Sandy Descher (*Little Girl*), Mary Alan Hokanson (*Mrs. Lodge*), Don Shelton (*Captain of Troopers*)

p, David Weisbart; d, Gordon Douglas; w, Ted Sherdeman, Russell Hughes (based on a story by George Worthing Yates); ph, Sid Hickox; ed, Thomas Reilly; m, Bronislau Kaper; art d, Stanley Fleischer; fx, Ralph Ayres, William Mueller, Francis J. Scheid; cos, Edith Head

AAN Best Special Effects

THEM! is one of the best of a 1950s spate of monster movies rooted in nuclear paranoia. Whitmore and Drake, two New Mexico state troopers patrolling the desert, happen across a trailer home that has been peeled open like a sardine can and gutted. Hiding nearby is a little girl who is nearly catatonic from fear. All she can utter is the word "Them." As the mystery deepens, FBI man Arness, scientist Gwenn, and his daughter Weldon (a scientist in her own right), are called in to help in the investigation. Eventually they learn that secret atomic testing in the area has spawned a colony of 20-foot-long ants. Realizing that if the queen is able to mate, the world may be overrun by the giant creatures, Whitmore and company hurriedly work to locate the nest and destroy it. They trace the creatures to the Los Angeles drainage system (in perhaps the best use of that overly photographed location). Armed with large flame throwers, they confront the monstrous critters.

THEM! pulls all this off quite convincingly. The giant ants do look a bit phony, but they are never on screen long enough to become bothersome. In fact, the image of dozens of giant ants in their underground nest is unforgettable. There was no stop-motion animation used in the film. Instead, two actual-sized models were constructed by prop man Dick Smith (one entire ant, and another front section for closeups). Special effects supervisor Ayres was nominated for an Academy Award for his work on the film. The film is produced and performed with such seriousness that one becomes engrossed in the logistics of dealing with such creatures and forgets about plausibility. THEM! was Warner Brothers' highest grossing film of 1954 and inspired countless imitations, all of which were inferior to the original.

THEODORA GOES WILD
1936 94m   bw   Comedy   ★★★½
Columbia   (U.S.)

Irene Dunne (*Theodora Lynn*), Melvyn Douglas (*Michael Grant*), Thomas Mitchell (*Jed Waterbury*), Thurston Hall (*Arthur Stevenson*), Rosalind Keith (*Adelaide Perry*), Spring Byington

(Rebecca Perry), Elisabeth Risdon *(Aunt Mary)*, Margaret McWade *(Aunt Elsie)*, Nana Bryant *(Ethel Stevenson)*, Henry Kolker *(Jonathan Grant)*

p, Everett Riskin; d, Richard Boleslawski; w, Sidney Buchman (based on a story by Mary E. McCarthy); ph, Joseph Walker; ed, Otto Meyer; m, M.W. Stoloff; art d, Stephen Goosson; cos, Bernard Newman

AAN Best Actress: Irene Dunne; *AAN Best Film Editing:* Otto Meyer

Dunne's first starring comedy role after several weepers was good enough to secure her an Oscar nomination, her second after the 1931 CIMARRON. Dunne plays the title role, a New England woman who writes a steamy best-seller about the morals of a sleepy little town located north of New York City. The book takes off and she decides to see the big city for herself. Once she arrives in Manhattan she meets the ultrasophisticated artist (Douglas) who did the illustrations for her book, and her escapades begin, arising from her situation as a fish out of water in New York. The quaint and hard-bitten Yankees from her village are examined vis-a-vis the sharp Big Apple types and the film draws the conclusion that there are nuts in both places.

The idea was to produce a screwball comedy on the style of some of Capra's Columbia pictures, but this movie had the wrong Riskin (producer Everett, rather than Capra's longtime associate and screenwriter, Robert) and it just wasn't wacky enough, despite a valiant try by Dunne to breathe life into Buchman's modest if clever script. Her efforts did earn her a Best Actress Oscar nomination, but she lost to Luise Rainer for THE GREAT ZIEGFELD.

Director Boleslawski, the Polish stage director who cut his teeth with the Moscow Arts Theatre, made a number of fine films, most notably CLIVE OF INDIA, THE PAINTED VEIL, and LES MISERABLES, which he directed in succession in 1934-35.

THERE'S NO BUSINESS LIKE SHOW BUSINESS 📀
1954 117m c Musical ★★★½
Fox (U.S.)

Ethel Merman *(Molly Donahue)*, Donald O'Connor *(Tim Donahue)*, Marilyn Monroe *(Vicky)*, Dan Dailey *(Terrance Donahue)*, Johnny Ray *(Steve Donahue)*, Mitzi Gaynor *(Katy Donahue)*, Richard Eastham *(Lew Harris)*, Hugh O'Brian *(Charles Gibbs)*, Frank McHugh *(Eddie Duggan)*, Rhys Williams *(Father Dineen)*

p, Sol C. Siegel; d, Walter Lang; w, Phoebe Ephron, Henry Ephron (based on a story by Lamar Trotti); ph, Leon Shamroy (CinemaScope, DeLuxe Color); ed, Robert Simpson; m, Irving Berlin; art d, Lyle Wheeler, John De Cuir; fx, Ray Kellogg; chor, Robert Alton

AAN Best Motion Picture Story: Lamar Trotti; *AAN Best Score (Musical):* Alfred Newman, Lionel Newman; *AAN Best Costume Design (Color):* Charles LeMaire, Travilla, Miles White

Packed with tunes by the incomparable Irving Berlin, this entertaining musical concerns the plight of the Five Donahues, a vaudeville act comprised of Molly and Terrence Donahue (Ethel Merman and Dan Dailey) and their children. Steve (Johnny Ray), the oldest child, who goes off to become a priest, is the first of the brood to leave. Next brother Tim (Donald O'Connor) and sister Katy (Mitzi Gaynor) get antsy and decide to carry on the family tradition in New York. Katy's romance with songwriter Charles Gibbs (Hugh O'Brian) is no problem, but Tim's involvement with nightclub hatcheck girl and aspiring singer Vicky (Marilyn Monroe) is another story. When he believes that Vicky is cheating on him, Tim gets drunk and ends up in an automobile accident. Ultimately, though, things work out for the best, as they have a way of

doing in musicals, and all of the Donahues come together for one more big number, the rousing title tune.

THERE'S NO BUSINESS LIKE SHOW BUSINESS is packed with every vaudeville cliché the movies have ever conjured up, yet it is presented in a fresh, colorful, heart-warming manner. Merman is a standout, but the lively cast never allows the singer to dominate, and Monroe, in particular, adds much-needed buoyancy to the somewhat flat story, turning up the temperature with her sexy rendition of "Heat Wave."

THERE'S SOMETHING ABOUT MARY 📀
1998 120m c Romance/Comedy ★★★
20th Century Fox (U.S.) R

Ben Stiller *(Ted Stroehmann)*, Cameron Diaz *(Mary Jenson)*, Matt Dillon *(Pat Healy)*, Chris Elliott *(Dom)*, Lin Shaye *(Magda)*, Lee Evans *(Tucker/Norm)*, Jeffrey Tambor *(Sully)*, W. Earl Brown *(Warren)*, Markie Post *(Mary's Mom)*, Keith David *(Mary's Stepfather)*

p, Charles Wessler, Bradley Thomas, Frank Beddor, Michael Steinberg; d, Peter Farrelly, Bobby Farrelly; w, Peter Farrelly, Bobby Farrelly, Ed Decter, John J. Strauss (from a story by Ed Decter and John J. Strauss); ph, Mark Irwin; ed, Christopher Greenbury; m, Jonathan Richman; art d, Arlen Jay Vetter; fx, Kevin Harris; cos, Mary Zophres

A romantic gross-out comedy: what a concept!

Ted (Ben Stiller) and high-school hottie Mary (Cameron Diaz) once went on a bad prom date of epic proportions: while using Mary's bathroom, Ted inadvertently got a glimpse of the undressed beauty and got so flustered he caught his privates in his zipper. Ted was carted off in an ambulance after having been humiliated in front of Mary, her parents, and half the neighborhood. Twenty years later, he wonders what might have been and hires seedy PI Pat Healy (Matt Dillon) to find out. Healy locates Mary down in Florida where she's now a highly successful orthopedic surgeon, a devoted sister who cares for her retarded brother (W. Earl Brown), an avid golfer who loves corn dogs ("there aren't enough meats on sticks," she declares), and an all-around perfect human being who spends her days committing random acts of kindness. Smitten, Healy discourages Ted by reporting that Mary's a fat slag in a wheelchair and hightails it to Florida, planning to use the tricks of the surveillance trade to win her for himself.

Fairly standard romantic comedy hijinks, right? Wrong: we're talking about a movie by the Farrelly brothers, of DUMB & DUMBER and KINGPIN infamy, so be warned that the lovey-dovey comedy of errors is liberally studded with gags about serial murder, semen, the physically and mentally challenged, hives, fellatio, and masturbation. The laughs are low—*very* low—and the comedy often flags. But two elaborate sequences involving a bad-tempered little ankle-biter are standouts, as is the zipper calamity. And the scene in which a certain bodily fluid is mistaken for a hair-care product will be the movie's calling card.

THESE THREE
1936 93m bw Drama ★★★★½
UA (U.S.)

Miriam Hopkins *(Martha Dobie)*, Merle Oberon *(Karen Wright)*, Joel McCrea *(Dr. Joseph Cardin)*, Catharine Doucet *(Mrs. Lily Mortar)*, Alma Kruger *(Mrs. Tilford)*, Bonita Granville *(Mary Tilford)*, Marcia Mae Jones *(Rosalie Wells)*, Carmencita Johnson *(Evelyn)*, Mary Anne Durkin *(Joyce Walton)*, Margaret Hamilton *(Agatha)*

p, Samuel Goldwyn; d, William Wyler; w, Lillian Hellman (based on her play "The Children's Hour"); ph, Gregg Toland; ed, Daniel Mandell; m, Alfred Newman; art d, Richard Day; cos, Omar Kiam

AAN Best Supporting Actress: Bonita Granville

One of Wyler's finest films, and the occasion for one of the finest Goldwynisms. When warned that the play he'd just bought, Lillian Hellman's *The Children's Hour*, was about lesbians, Goldwyn supposedly replied, "That's okay: we'll turn them into Americans." Although Hellman's screenplay jettisons explicit lesbianism in conformance with the Hays Code, the resulting movie abounds with repressed eroticism and is far superior to Wyler's post-Code remake THE CHILDREN'S HOUR.

Bonita Granville, in an Oscar-nominated role, plays Mary Tilford, a mean, vicious girl who is censured by her teachers at a posh private school run by college friends Martha and Karen (Miriam Hopkins and Merle Oberon). Martha is an austere Yankee type, while Karen is a warm woman who is in love with local doctor Joseph Cardin (Joel McCrea). He reciprocates her passion but maintains a close friendship with Martha. Mary retaliates by telling her grandmother (Alma Kruger) that Martha and Joe had been "carrying on" in a bedroom near the student's quarters. The grandmother believes her, especially after the lie is corroborated by nine-year-old Rosalie (Marcia Mae Jones, every bit as good as Granville). Mary is ruthlessly blackmailing the other girl with the knowledge that Rosalie has stolen another girl's gold bracelet. Martha, Karen, and Joe file a libel suit against Mary's grandmother after she advises parents to remove their children from the iniquitous school, but it's dismissed in court. The truth eventually comes out, but the damage is done.

Samuel Goldwyn took advantage of the notoriety of Hellman's scandalous stage effort by releasing the movie while the play was still running, but the Production Code people insisted he remove much of what made it such a sensation. Goldwyn hired Hellman to make the alterations, and her script changes, there are many moments when it seems that Hopkins is more interested in Oberon than McCrea. However one reads it, THESE THREE is gripping, adult cinema. Oberon gives one of her best dramatic performances and McCrea is also quite fine. The two child actresses have the showiest parts, but the real performances to watch are those of Alma Kruger and Miriam Hopkins. Hopkins, in particular, has rarely been better, her intense, high-strung quality perfectly suited to the role of a woman unable to stop her world from falling apart around her.

THEY DRIVE BY NIGHT   📀
1940   93m   bw   Drama   ★★★★½
Warner Bros.   (U.S.)

George Raft *(Joe Fabrini)*, Ann Sheridan *(Cassie Hartley)*, Ida Lupino *(Lana Carlsen)*, Humphrey Bogart *(Paul Fabrini)*, Gale Page *(Pearl Fabrini)*, Alan Hale *(Ed J. Carlsen)*, Roscoe Karns *(Irish McGurn)*, John Litel *(Harry McNamara)*, Henry O'Neill *(District Attorney)*, George Tobias *(George Rondolos)*

p, Mark Hellinger; d, Raoul Walsh; w, Jerry Wald, Richard Macaulay (based on the novel *The Long Haul* by A.I. Bezzerides); ph, Arthur Edeson; ed, Oliver S. Garretson, Thomas Richards; m, Adolph Deutsch; art d, John Hughes; fx, Byron Haskin, H.F. Koenekamp, James Gibbons, John Holden, Edwin DuPar; cos, Milo Anderson

Amid tough competition, Ida Lupino steals it. This cult classic is one of the best road movies to emerge from a major studio in the 1940s. Raft and Bogart are truck-driving brothers who have left the large company run by Hale and bought their own truck to work as independents. The first half of the film details their rise as they drive all night, skimp on needed repairs, and struggle to keep their fledgling business afloat. Bogart is married to Page, who resents his neglect of her in favor of the business. One night, when Bogart and Raft are pulled over at a roadside diner, they meet waitress Sheridan.

She has a sharp tongue and a mane of red hair, and Raft is almost instantly attracted to her. Later, the hitchhiker the two men pick up turns out to be Sheridan, who has quit her job in the face of her boss's continued advances. Raft sets her up with a room in a boardinghouse. Shyly, he makes some romantic comments, which Sheridan turns away without being discouraging. Bogart falls asleep at the wheel one night and loses his arm in the subsequent accident, forcing Raft to take a job with Hale as traffic manager. Lupino, Hale's venomous wife, sets her sights on Raft, but he refuses to fool around with the boss's wife. Lupino then decides to get rid of her husband, leaving him drunk and unconscious in the car while she closes the door and leaves the engine running. She offers to share with Raft the company she has inherited, but when he refuses, Lupino goes to the police and tells them that Raft forced her to kill her husband. In no time Raft is arrested and charged. Sheridan comes to jail and pleads with Lupino to tell the truth, but Lupino tells her that she will take Raft with her wherever she goes. Things go badly for Raft in court, with circumstantial evidence implicating him and the testimony of his friends doing nothing to clear him. But several people have yet to be heard from, and help comes from the strangest of places.

A loose remake of BORDERTOWN (in which Bette Davis asphyxiates husband Eugene Pallette in order to win Paul Muni), THEY DRIVE BY NIGHT could have been another routine film but for Lupino's incredibly forceful performance and Raft's smooth depiction of the tough trucker. Bogart—still wallowing in the lull in his career between the time THE PETRIFIED FOREST established him as a serious actor and the time HIGH SIERRA finally made him a star—is very good, especially when he is embittered by the loss of his arm. Walsh's direction is as forceful and vigorous as always and this film is among his very best.

THEY LIVE BY NIGHT
1949   95m   bw   Crime   ★★★★★
RKO   (U.S.)

Cathy O'Donnell *(Keechie)*, Farley Granger *(Bowie)*, Howard da Silva *(Chickamaw)*, Jay C. Flippen *(T-Dub)*, Helen Craig *(Mattie)*, Will Wright *(Mobley)*, Marie Bryant *(Singer)*, Ian Wolfe *(Hawkins)*, William Phipps *(Young Farmer)*, Harry Harvey *(Hagenheimer)*

p, John Houseman; d, Nicholas Ray; w, Charles Schnee, Nicholas Ray (based on the novel *Thieves Like Us* by Edward Anderson); ph, George E. Diskant; ed, Sherman Todd; m, Woody Guthrie (uncredited), Leigh Harline; art d, Albert S. D'Agostino, Al Herman; fx, Russell A. Cully

Nicholas Ray's energetic first feature, THEY LIVE BY NIGHT tells the tragic story of two doomed lovers and of their short, fast life together before they are torn apart by the criminal world.

As the film opens, Granger and O'Donnell are shown kissing. A title is superimposed: "This boy and this girl were never properly introduced to the world we live in." In this manner, the young lovers' saga hits the screen. Granger, a decent enough fellow whose greatest fault is his naivete, joins a prison break engineered by da Silva and Flippen, two callous criminals who spare no sentimental thought for Granger's innocence, but simply take him along because they need a third hand for a bank job. An auto accident caused by da Silva injures Granger, who recovers in a dark hideout. He is nursed to health by O'Donnell, a young woman who quickly falls in love with Granger, sensing that he is not like his two partners. Granger returns O'Donnell's affections and the two are soon involved in passionate romance. Soon they make it legal, marrying in the dilapidated office of a justice of the peace. When da Silva asks him to join another bank job, Granger is not strong enough to say no, but it's not long before Flippen is killed and da Silva has angrily gone off on his own. Soon da

Silva, too, is killed, leaving Granger the last of the gang and still sought by the police. The young fugitive wants nothing more than a quiet home for himself and his wife, but his fate has been sealed.

More than a standard cops-and-robbers tale, THEY LIVE BY NIGHT is a Depression-era saga about lovers on the run. Entangled in a fate they cannot escape, and over which they have absolutely no control, they love to the fullest before they are inevitably, tragically separated. Though based on the novel *Thieves Like Us* by Edward Anderson (later filmed by Robert Altman under Anderson's title), THEY LIVE BY NIGHT owes an equal debt to the Bonnie and Clyde myth, which, while it bears no resemblance to this film in plot, has permeated the cinema's image of lovers on the run. (It's an image that can also be seen in 1949's GUN CRAZY and the 1937 Fritz Lang picture YOU ONLY LIVE ONCE.) Ray undertook the project enthusiastically, bringing to his film a personal style and vision evident from its beginning. After Granger and O'Donnell's kiss at the opening, a getaway car carrying the three criminals is seen traveling down a dusty road, pursued by police. Rather than shoot with a standard camera setup, Ray demanded that the scene be photographed from a helicopter, a highly unorthodox idea that has now become a standard element of the cinematic lexicon. Not only did this sequence open the film with a burst of unharnessed energy, it also conveyed a sense of godlike fate, looking down on Granger and relentlessly pursuing him. Beautifully acted, THEY LIVE BY NIGHT stands today as one of the most poignant and unforgettable noirs ever made.

THEY MADE ME A FUGITIVE

1947 78m bw Crime — DVD ★★★★
Shipman/Gloria/Alliance (U.K.)

Sally Gray *(Sally)*, Trevor Howard *(Clem Morgan)*, Griffith Jones *(Narcey)*, Rene Ray *(Cora)*, Mary Merrall *(Aggie)*, Vida Hope *(Mrs. Fenshawe)*, Ballard Berkeley *(Inspector Rockliffe)*, Phyllis Robins *(Olga)*, Eve Ashley *(Ellen)*, Charles Farrell *(Curley)*

p, Nat A. Bronsten, James Carter; d, Alberto Cavalcanti; w, Noel Langley (based on the novel *Convict Has Escaped* by Jackson Budd); ph, Otto Heller; ed, Marjorie Saunders; m, Marius-Francois Gaillard; art d, Andrew Mazzei

Although film noir in the United States has received the attention it deserves, the same cannot be said for British noir, a movement equally downbeat and striking but more indebted to French poetic realism than to German Expressionism. THEY MADE ME A FUGITIVE, though more Teutonic than some other British noirs, is nonetheless one of the finest representations of the postwar malaise which also infected Great Britain. Trevor Howard is Clem, an RAF officer who falls from grace, winds up a crook, gets framed by Narcey (Jones), and is thrown in the pen. Getting out, Clem heads for London's Soho district, seeking revenge on Narcey and his dope-dealing gang. It's up to Sally (Gray) to try to save him from sinking too low.

Artfully sculpted and suspenseful, THEY MADE ME A FUGITIVE makes for gripping, adult cinema. Few stars began their film careers with more outstanding films made back to back than did Howard, who plumbs the depths of Clem's decline without ever sinking into bathos. He is well supported by Gray as a sympathetic noir blonde, and by a seasoned cast of British veterans, with Jones especially good as the chilling Narcey. With its striking compositions and starkly dramatic lighting, the film shows the mastery of director Alberto Cavalcanti, an eclectic talent who began making short avant-garde silent films in France, made several outstanding features (DEAD OF NIGHT, WENT THE DAY WELL?) in Great Britain and later attempted to imitate Hollywood's industrial success when he headed up the short-lived Vera Cruz studios in Brazil.

THEY SHOOT HORSES, DON'T THEY?

1969 129m c Drama — DVD ★★★★
Palomar (U.S.) M

Jane Fonda *(Gloria Beatty)*, Michael Sarrazin *(Robert Syverton)*, Susannah York *(Alice)*, Gig Young *(Rocky)*, Red Buttons *(Sailor)*, Bonnie Bedelia *(Ruby)*, Bruce Dern *(James)*, Michael Conrad *(Rollo)*, Al Lewis *(Turkey)*, Robert Fields *(Joel)*

p, Irwin Winkler, Robert Chartoff, Sydney Pollack; d, Sydney Pollack; w, James Poe, Robert E. Thompson (based on the novel by Horace McCoy); ph, Philip Lathrop (Panavision, DeLuxe Color); ed, Fredric Steinkamp; m, Johnny Green; prod d, Harry Horner; fx, Blondie Anderson; chor, Tom Panko; cos, Donfeld

AAN Best Actress: Jane Fonda; *AA Best Supporting Actor:* Gig Young; *AAN Best Supporting Actress:* Susannah York; *AAN Best Director:* Sydney Pollack; *AAN Best Adapted Screenplay:* James Poe, Robert E. Thompson; *AAN Best Film Editing:* Fredric Steinkamp; *AAN Best Score (Musical):* John Green, Albert Woodbury; *AAN Best Art Direction-Set Decoration:* Harry Horner, Frank McKelvy; *AAN Best Costume Design:* Donfeld

An allegorical, socially conscious response to the injustices of the Depression era, THEY SHOOT HORSES, DON'T THEY? has managed to survive the late 1960s, unlike so many other films of that period, without appearing the least bit dated. Preparing the audience for the inevitable, the film begins with Robert Syverton (Sarrazin) standing trial for murder, the details of which are purposely vague. The scene then switches to Chicago's famous Aragon Ballroom, where a dance marathon is about to get underway. Among the contestants is Gloria Beatty (Fonda), an independent, disagreeable loner who seems to enjoy lashing out at those around her. She replaces her original partner with Robert, a drifter with no real desire to participate. Also wearing numbers on their backs are a pregnant farm woman (Bedelia), her husband (Dern), a sailor and veteran marathoner with heart trouble (Buttons), and a Jean Harlow clone (York) who hopes to be discovered while dancing in the spotlight. As the master of ceremonies, whose job it is to keep the audience content and the dancers dancing, is the sleazy, unshaven Rocky (Young). Everyone's reason for participating is simple—three meals a day and a chance at winning the $1,500 prize, a bonanza in the days of record unemployment and bread lines. The tension builds as the emcee goads the dancers to self-destruction and the driven contestants fight among themselves. Several deaths result, and when Robert is asked why he has committed murder, responds, "They shoot horses, don't they?"

Although it is at times heavy-handed, THEY SHOOT HORSES, DON'T THEY? is a *tour de force* of acting. Fonda, best known at the time as Roger Vadim's wife and the sex toy of BARBARELLA, here got her first chance to prove herself as a serious, dramatic actress. For bringing such gritty, sweaty, hopeless self-degradation to the screen, Fonda received universal praise, as well as an Oscar nomination for Best Actress. Young is superb in his role, a sharp switch from his usual *bon vivant* parts. The rest of the acting is similarly fine, even though Sarrazin, in what is admittedly one of the film's less interesting parts, doesn't really bring enough presence or imagination to his performance. Pollack does one of his best jobs of directing, even if his primary strength lies in his rapport with actors. The look of the film is just right and Pollack skillfully evokes the ratty atmosphere amid which explosive emotions come to a boil. At one point camerawork was even done on roller skates to achieve just the right effect for the bedraggled characters on the dance floor. The film uses much Depression-era music for period flavor and contains many references to the Hollywood of that era. This kind of reflexivity helps highlight the dance floor as an arena of action, a microcosm of America, and the parallels with the situation in Vietnam are pretty obvious. Based on a 1935 novel feted by

French existentialists and first purchased by Charlie Chaplin, THEY SHOOT HORSES, DON'T THEY? remains a suitably glum yet cathartic film experience.

THEY WERE EXPENDABLE 📀
1945 135m bw War ★★★★★
MGM (U.S.)

Robert Montgomery (*Lt. John Brickley*), John Wayne (*Lt. J.G. "Rusty" Ryan*), Donna Reed (*2nd Lt. Sandy Davyss*), Jack Holt (*Gen. Martin*), Ward Bond (*"Boots" Mulcahey*), Marshall Thompson (*Ens. Snake Gardner*), Paul Langton (*Ens. Andy Andrews*), Leon Ames (*Maj. James Morton*), Arthur Walsh (*Seaman Jones*), Donald Curtis (*Lt. J.G. "Shorty" Long*)

p, John Ford; d, John Ford, Robert Montgomery (uncredited); w, Frank Wead (based on the book by William L. White); ph, Joseph August; ed, Frank E. Hull, Douglas Biggs; m, Herbert Stothart; art d, Cedric Gibbons, Malcolm Brown; fx, A. Arnold Gillespie

AAN Best Sound Recording: Douglas Shearer; *AAN Best Special Effects:* A. Arnold Gillespie, Donald Jahraus, R. A. MacDonald, Michael Steinore

In direct contrast to the flag-waving, jingoistic propaganda films typical of Hollywood during WWII, John Ford's THEY WERE EXPENDABLE is a somber and moving account of America's defeat in the Philippines early in the war. Filming this grim failure, Ford beautifully and poetically captures the heroism and bravery of the men and women who fought there—and, does so without impassioned speechifying or gushing patriotism. Instead, Ford commemorates the quiet and uncomplaining devotion to duty, the will to serve, and the nobility of sacrifice of those left in an untenable situation. Based on the exploits of Lt. John Bulkeley, commander of Motor Torpedo Boat Squadron No. 3 (the predecessor of the Navy PT boat force), the film follows the coolly professional lieutenant (Robert Montgomery, in one of his best performances), renamed "Brickley" for the film, and his hot-headed executive officer, Lt. J.G. "Rusty" Ryan (John Wayne), as they struggle to get the Navy to accept the PT boats as a valuable new tool in the war effort. The top commanders, however, see no use for the unit and relegate Brickley and crew to running messages and ferrying supplies. As Bataan and Corregidor fall to the Japanese, however, the PT unit proves itself valuable by sinking many enemy ships, although the effort proves too little too late. Japan emerges triumphant and the American brass is forced to leave their troops stranded before the enemy and to flee to Australia, where they will regroup and plan their return.

From the time Ford shot THEY WERE EXPENDABLE to the day he died, the director was ambivalent about the film, his opinion of the work alternating between disapproval and satisfaction. This may have been largely due to the fact that he was pressured into making THEY WERE EXPENDABLE soon after having seen action himself in the South Pacific as a documentary filmmaker for the Navy. Capt. Ford had lost 13 men in his unit and the making of this film no doubt stirred painful memories for the director, memories he may have preferred to ignore when asked to discuss his films later in life. Despite Ford's ambivalence, THEY WERE EXPENDABLE is one of the greatest films to come out of WWII, a lasting and poignant tribute to those who go in harm's way.

THIEF 📀
1981 122m c Crime ★★★½
UA (U.S.) R

James Caan (*Frank*), Tuesday Weld (*Jessie*), Willie Nelson (*Okla*), James Belushi (*Barry*), Robert Prosky (*Leo*), Tom Signorelli

(*Attaglia*), Dennis Farina (*Carl*), Nick Nickeas (*Nick*), W.R. Brown (*Mitch*), Norm Tobin (*Guido*)

p, Jerry Bruckheimer, Ronnie Caan; d, Michael Mann; w, Michael Mann (based on the book *The Home Invaders* by Frank Hohimer); ph, Donald Thorin (Technicolor); ed, Dov Hoenig; m, Tangerine Dream; prod d, Mel Bourne; art d, Mary Dodson

Frank (James Caan) is a professional thief, one of the best in the business, who wants to make one last big score so he can settle down with his girlfriend Jessie (Tuesday Weld). That desire gets him involved with vicious big-time mobster Leo (Robert Prosky) and the robbery of a high-security vault in Los Angeles, aided by his friend Barry (Jim Belushi). This was the first feature film for director Michael Mann (MANHUNTER, TV's "Miami Vice"), and it was a stunner. Mann demonstrates an understanding of the casting, location, costumes, music (a superior score by Tangerine Dream), and visuals. The performances by Caan, Prosky, Belushi, and Weld are nothing less than terrific. Caan has his best role since THE GODFATHER, but Prosky (TV's "Hill Street Blues") nearly steals the film by underplaying the role of the powerful mob chieftain. This film is brutally realistic in its street language and violence, so sensitive viewers should be warned.

THIEF OF BAGDAD, THE 📀
1940 106m c Fantasy ★★★★★
London Films (U.K.)

Conrad Veidt (*Jaffar*), Sabu (*Abu*), June Duprez (*Princess*), John Justin (*Ahmad*), Rex Ingram (*Djinni*), Miles Malleson (*Sultan*), Morton Selten (*King*), Mary Morris (*Halima*), Bruce Winston (*Merchant*), Hay Petrie (*Astrologer*)

p, Alexander Korda; d, Ludwig Berger, Michael Powell, Tim Whelan, Zoltan Korda, William Cameron Menzies, Alexander Korda; w, Lajos Biro, Miles Malleson; ph, Georges Perinal, Osmond Borradaile (Technicolor); ed, William Hornbeck, Charles Crichton; m, Miklos Rozsa; prod d, Vincent Korda; fx, Lawrence Butler, Tom Howard, John Mills; cos, Oliver Messel, John Armstrong, Marcel Vertes

AA Best Color Cinematography: George Perinal; *AAN Best Original Score:* Miklos Rozsa; *AA Best Interior Decoration (Color):* Vincent Korda; *AA Best Special Effects:* Lawrence Butler (Photographic), Jack Whitney (Sound)

Perhaps the most splendid fantasy film ever made. Alexander Korda produced, Michael Powell and five others directed this breathtaking attempt to capture *The Arabian Nights* on film. An early example of outstanding Technicolor work, this became a cult favorite among young Hollywood directors of the 1970s such as Francis Coppola and George Lucas. The special effects, though quaint by today's standards, still deliver the goods. This lively collection of incidents from the Arabian Nights fables makes most modern fantasy blockbusters look anemic in comparison.

Abu (Sabu), a charming street urchin, is thrown into a Bagdad dungeon for thievery. Before long, Prince Ahmad (John Justin), the deposed ruler of the realm, joins him there. Ahmad has been overthrown by his righthand man, the evil grand vizier, Jaffar (Conrad Veidt). The unlikely duo manage to escape and flee to exotic Basra, where Ahmad is smitten by Basra's princess (June Duprez). Learning that Jaffar is about to abduct the beauty, Ahmad and Abu try to thwart the plan, but the wicked magician turns them into a blind beggar and a dog respectively. When the princess promises to wed Jaffar, he revokes his curse, though against her own will. All seems lost until Abu—after a series of adventures involving a genie, an "All-Seeing Eye," and a magic carpet—finds a way to save the day.

Although six directors worked on the film, it remains surprisingly seamless as it maintains such a consistent grandeur and even pace. The marvelous set designs by Vincent Korda seem *truly* out of this world, and Miklos Rozsa has created a dynamic and memorable score. Conrad Veidt, looking cool and cruel in his dashing black outfits, is one of the screen's great villains. Sabu is simply adorable as the little thief of Bagdad. Duprez's unusual but stunning beauty is only enhanced by the rich Technicolor and the handsome Justin looks just right as the wan prince. African-American actor Rex Ingram is outstanding in the small but unforgettable role of the genie.

THIEVES LIKE US

1974 123m c Crime ★★★½
UA (U.S.) R

Keith Carradine *(Bowie)*, Shelley Duvall *(Keechie)*, John Schuck *(Chicamaw)*, Bert Remsen *(T-Dub)*, Louise Fletcher *(Mattie)*, Ann Latham *(Lula)*, Tom Skerritt *(Dee Mobley)*, Al Scott *(Capt. Stammers)*, John Roper *(Jasbo)*, Mary Waits *(Noel)*

p, Jerry Bick; d, Robert Altman; w, Calder Willingham, Joan Tewkesbury, Robert Altman (based on the novel by Edward Anderson); ph, Jean Boffety; ed, Lou Lombardo

A well-done remake of THEY LIVE BY NIGHT that's slightly long but unusually free of Altman's customary indulgences. A 1930s crime story with humor and humanity, THIEVES LIKE US owes more than a passing nod to BONNIE AND CLYDE and BADLANDS in theme and treatment. Young killer-crook Carradine escapes from a Mississippi jail with older, hard-bitten criminals Remsen and Schuck. After a brief respite, they return to the only way they know how to make a living: robbing banks.

Unlike BONNIE AND CLYDE, there is a real love story between Carradine and Duvall that comes across. The music and background sounds were supplied by John Dunning, who is credited for "radio research." He provided radio shows like "Gangbusters," "The Heart of Gold," remote band broadcasts, and an actual "Romeo and Juliet" dramatization that is heard while Duvall and Carradine are making love. Most of the killings are referred to rather than seen, so this is a character study more than a violence film. The executive producer was George Litto, who used to be Altman's agent and was making his bow in production. Litto was later responsible for a few of De Palma's debacles. Fletcher, wife of producer Bick, makes her film debut in this picture. Remsen, who is one of Altman's stock company, has another career as one of the most respected casting directors in Hollywood. Coscreenwriter Tewkesbury makes a cameo.

THIN ICE

1937 78m bw Musical/Comedy/Romance ★★★
Fox (U.S.)

Sonja Henie *(Lili Heiser)*, Tyrone Power *(Prince Rudolph)*, Arthur Treacher *(Nottingham)*, Raymond Walburn *(Uncle Dornic)*, Joan Davis *(Orchestra Leader)*, Alan Hale *(Baron)*, Sig Rumann *(Prime Minister)*, Melville Cooper *(Krantz)*, Maurice Cass *(Count)*, George Givot *(Alex)*

p, Raymond Griffith; d, Sidney Lanfield; w, Boris Ingster, Milton Sperling (based on the play "Der Komet" by Attila Obok); ph, Robert Planck, Edward Cronjager; ed, Robert Simpson; art d, Mark-Lee Kirk; chor, Harry Losee; cos, Royer

AAN Best Dance Direction: Harry Losee

Smile, Sonja. Skate, Sonja. Just don't try to act. One of the most popular and best-remembered of the dozen ice musicals the three-time Olympic skater made in Hollywood in the late 1930s and early '40s, THIN ICE casts her as a skating instructor (surprise, surprise) who is romanced by a prince (Power) masquerading as a reporter. Having won the gold medal in ice skating in 1928, 1932 *and* 1936, the Norwegian Henie drove a hard bargain with 20th Century Fox, who carefully built a series of bland but genial light entertainments around her. She does have a certain placid charm, her dimples are adorable (if you like that sort of thing) and, though her skating may seem less dazzling to an age used to triple toe loops and double axles, she's still pretty impressive on those blades. Her numbers are lavishly mounted and showcase her admirably, though she's got more competition on dry land opposite the impossibly gorgeous looks of a very young Power. Henie is also surrounded with plenty of contract second bananas, especially rubber-limbed, rubbed-faced Joan Davis. Thin ice, maybe, but reasonably sturdy entertainment, if you keep your expectations modest.

THIN MAN, THE `DVD`

1934 93m bw Mystery/Comedy ★★★★½
MGM (U.S.)

William Powell *(Nick Charles)*, Myrna Loy *(Nora Charles)*, Maureen O'Sullivan *(Dorothy Wynant)*, Nat Pendleton *(Lt. John Guild)*, Minna Gombell *(Mimi Wynant)*, Porter Hall *(MacCauley)*, Henry Wadsworth *(Tommy)*, William Henry *(Gilbert Wynant)*, Harold Huber *(Nunheim)*, Cesar Romero *(Chris Jorgenson)*

p, Hunt Stromberg; d, W.S. Van Dyke II; w, Albert Hackett, Frances Goodrich (based on the novel by Dashiell Hammett); ph, James Wong Howe; m, Robert J. Kern; art d, Cedric Gibbons, David Townsend, Edwin B. Willis; cos, Dolly Tree

AAN Best Picture; AAN Best Actor: William Powell; *AAN Best Director:* W.S. Van Dyke; *AAN Best Writing (Adaptation):* Frances Goodrich, Albert Heckett

Nick Charles (Powell) is a retired detective who has married the wealthy Nora (Loy) and now intends to devote himself to looking after her money and doing some serious drinking. (You can tell this film was made just after the repeal of Prohibition.) They travel to New York for the holidays, and there meet Dorothy (O'Sullivan), who asks Nick to help her find her missing father (Ellis). He's an inventor who months before went into seclusion to work on a project but hasn't been heard from since. Nick, whose reputation precedes him, isn't anxious to end his happy retirement, but Nora, eager for thrills, prods him into it. Together with their wire-haired terrier Asta, the newlyweds solve the case.

Praise should go to the writers of the film's delightful dialogue and to the underrated Van Dyke, a director of craft who knows how to make a film move. The story, meanwhile, faithfully taken from Hammett's novel, proves eminently serviceable if not quite the stuff of genius. What really makes THE THIN MAN an enduring classic, though, is the interplay between Powell and Loy, one of the greatest *happily* married couples ever to flicker on a screen. The repartee they shoot back and forth is priceless, as in one scene the morning after a gunman has broken into their suite and superficially wounded Nick before being subdued and hauled away. As they read the morning papers about the event, Powell says, "I'm a hero, I was shot twice in the *Tribune*." Loy: "I read you were shot five times in the tabloids." "It's not true. He didn't come anywhere near my tabloids," Powell parries. Loy has a terrific comic bit entering a scene loaded down with packages and dragged by their feisty pooch, and Powell has great fun shooting the balls off a Christmas tree with his favorite present, a gun. Loy and Powell proved so popular that they were teamed twelve more times during their careers (thirteen if you count her cameo in THE SENATOR WAS INDISCREET), six of the pairings coming in the THIN MAN series. These sleuthfests would continue with lessening success for 13 years, but at their peak (the first three films), Nick and Nora were one of the best movie buys around. Loy and Powell set a style for connubial comic banter which many performers still attempt in vain to duplicate today.

THIN RED LINE, THE

1998   166m   c   War/Action   **DVD**
Fox 2000 Pictures/Phoenix Pictures   (U.S.)   ★★★★ R

Sean Penn *(First Sergeant Welsh)*, Adrien Brody *(Corporal Fife)*, James Caviezel, billed as Jim Caviezel *(Pvt. Witt)*, Ben Chaplin *(Bell)*, George Clooney *(Bosche)*, Nick Nolte *(Colonel Tall)*, John Cusack *(Gaff)*, Woody Harrelson *(Keck)*, Elias Koteas *(Captain "Bugger" Staros)*, John Travolta *(Qintard)*

p, Robert Michael Geisler, John Roberdeau, Grant Hill; d, Terrence Malick; w, Terrence Malick (based on the novel by James Jones); ph, John Toll; ed, Billy Weber, Leslie Jones, Saar Klein; m, Hans Zimmer; prod d, Jack Fisk; art d, Ian Gracy; fx, Brian Cox; cos, Margot Wilson

AAN Best Picture; AAN Best Director: Terrence Malick; *AAN Best Adapted Screenplay:* Terrence Malick; *AAN Best Cinematography:* John Toll; *AAN Best Film Editing:* Billy Weber, Leslie Jones, Saar Klein; *AAN Best Original Dramatic Score:* Hans Zimmer; *AAN Best Sound:* Andy Nelson, Anna Behlmer, Paul Brincat

Call it the anti-SAVING PRIVATE RYAN. Terrence Malick's graceful, chaotic adaptation of James Jones' 1962 novel about the bloody campaign to take Guadalcanal Island in 1942-43 is an intensely internalized portrait of external pandemonium.

THE THIN RED LINE most closely resembles APOC-ALYPSE NOW, both in its vaguely hallucinatory ambiance and its Pacific front setting: Malick's soldiers are as out of place in the jungle as Coppola's, and the scenery's riotous beauty makes the sudden bursts of bloody violence just that little bit more grotesque. The protagonists are the officers and enlisted men of Charlie Company, whose orders are to take the island, starting with a nameless hill topped by enemy machine gunners entrenched in a fortified bunker. With the exception of a deceptively lyrical opening involving two AWOL GIs hiding out in a Melenesian village, the movie is as chaotic as the campaign. Individuals emerge from the ensemble and then disappear into the crowd, their stories woven together in blood and mud. The ranking officer in the fray is Lt. Colonel Tall (Nick Nolte), an aspiring Patton who's finally found his war. Under him are Captains Staros (Elias Koteas) and Gaff (John Cusack), Sgts. Keck (Woody Harrelson) and Welsh (Sean Penn)—each determined in his own way to protect the men he commands—and hundreds of grunts with little more on their minds than trying not to lose them in the muck and gore. Conflicts arise and get lost in the fray, soldiers have their moments in the spotlight, then vanish into the sea of green uniforms.

It's a slippery, insidiously haunting work of poetry rather than brilliantly realized pulp. By aiming for the head rather than the gut, Malick has pretty much guaranteed that his film won't capture the audiences Spielberg's has. But it's a power-ful, memorable vision of war well worth experiencing.

THING, THE

1982   108m   c   Science Fiction   **DVD**
Universal   (U.S.)   ★★ R

Kurt Russell *(MacReady)*, Wilford Brimley *(Blair)*, T.K. Carter *(Nauls)*, David Clennon *(Palmer)*, Keith David *(Childs)*, Richard Dysart *(Dr. Copper)*, Charles Hallahan *(Norris)*, Peter Maloney *(Bennings)*, Richard Masur *(Clark)*, Donald Moffat *(Garry)*

p, David Foster, Lawrence Turman; d, John Carpenter; w, Bill Lancaster (based on the story "Who Goes There?" by John W. Campbell Jr.); ph, Dean Cundey (Panavision, Technicolor); ed, Todd Ramsay; m, Ennio Morricone; prod d, John J. Lloyd; art d, Henry Larrecq; fx, Roy Arbogast, Albert Whitlock, Leroy Routly, Rob Bottin, Michael Clifford

A major disappointment. Horror director John Carpenter let the special effects run amok in this remake of the 1951 sci-ence-fiction classic THE THING, and they ooze over every-thing in the film. The plot is pared down to the essentials: a group of American scientists in the Antarctic find the frozen remains of an alien, which they soon thaw out. The only prob-lem is that the alien is not dead, and it springs back to life, tak-ing on whatever form suits its purpose (dogs, men, etc.). The cast is superb, but unfortunately the actors are not allowed to show their stuff because their characters are nothing more than fodder for the effects, and their performances are limited to standing around grimacing at the gore. Kurt Russell once again sleepwalks through his role (as he did in ESCAPE FROM NEW YORK), and the ending of the film is unsatis-fying and ambiguous. The effects are absolutely fantastic, complicated, and grotesque, but this remake ultimately fails because it is more an exercise in technique than an essay in human terror.

THING FROM ANOTHER WORLD, THE

1951   87m   bw   Science Fiction   **DVD**
Winchester   (U.S.)   ★★★★

Kenneth Tobey *(Capt. Pat Hendry)*, James Arness *(The Thing)*, Margaret Sheridan *(Nikki Nicholson)*, Robert Cornthwaite *(Dr. Arthur Carrington)*, Douglas Spencer *(Ned "Scotty" Scott)*, James Young *(Lt. Ed Dykes)*, Dewey Martin *(Bob)*, Robert Nichols *(Lt. Ken Erickson)*, William Self *(Sgt. Barnes)*, Eduard Franz *(Dr. Stern)*

p, Howard Hawks; d, Christian Nyby, Howard Hawks (uncredited); w, Ben Hecht (uncredited), Charles Lederer (based on the story "Who Goes There" by Don A. Stuart, aka John W. Campbell Jr.); ph, Russell Harlan; ed, Roland Gross; m, Dimitri Tiomkin; art d, Albert S. D'Agostino, John Hughes; fx, Don Steward, Linwood Dunn

Classic sci-fi chiller about a slimy alien presence (James Arness, who would later be Marshall Dillon on TV's "Gunsmoke") that invades an arctic station. THE THING FROM ANOTHER WORLD is very much a film of its pro-ducer, Howard Hawks, although Christian Nyby, Hawks's editor on RED RIVER, was credited as director. Hawks's style, themes, and handling of actors arguably dominate the film.

Set in the subzero environment of the North Pole, the film follows an Air Force captain, Tobey, as he and his crew fly to Polar Expedition Six—a group of scientists led by Cornthwaite who are studying arctic conditions—to investi-gate reports that a flying craft of some sort has crashed into the ice. At the base camp Tobey finds an old flame, Sheridan, who is working as Cornthwaite's secretary. Sheridan is a tough woman in the Hawksian mold, and the romantic banter between her and Tobey is a joy to watch. When Tobey meets with Cornthwaite, he is shown pictures of the strange object as it streaked across the sky. A party is organized to investigate the crash site, and when they arrive they discover that the object has sunk into the ice and has been frozen. The soldiers, scientists, and Spencer, a journalist, fan out to determine the shape of the object. When they all take their places at the edge of the object, they have formed a perfect circle.

The men decide to melt the ship out of the ice by deto-nating thermite bombs around it, but the plan goes awry and the ship is destroyed. Gravely disappointed, the men head back for their plane only to discover something else frozen in the ice—an alien. Using axes, they cut out a block of ice encasing the extraterrestrial corpse and bring it back to the base camp. While the soldiers and scientists debate over what to do with the creature, the ice melts and the eight-foot tall thing breaks free of its prison, very much alive—and not at all friendly.

THE THING FROM ANOTHER WORLD was based rather loosely on a science-fiction story by John W. Campbell, Jr. (it was first published under his pseudonym, Don A. Stuart), in which the alien had the ability to change its shape at will, causing havoc among the soldiers who begin to suspect *each other* of harboring the monster. Lederer's screenplay (rumor has it that frequent Lederer-Hawks collaborator Ben Hecht had a hand in it as well) streamlines the narrative and allows Hawks to concentrate on the human interaction in the face of crisis. Whereas the original story (and Carpenter's remake) is a study of paranoia among comrades, Hawks's film revels in the interworkings of a tough group of professionals capable of handling any crisis if they stick together. The characters operate as an ensemble with no one being given much solo screen time. Their unity is what the film is about, a familiar Hawksian theme.

In a genre often dependent upon elaborate special effects, THE THING is relatively stark and restrained. The monster is only glimpsed in shadows and darkness, thus allowing the imagination of the audience fill in the terrifying details. Harlan's cinematography and Tiomkin's eerie early electronic score (he used a theremin) provide enough chills to satisfy any horror fan. No ray-guns, strange costumes, or futuristic inventions are needed here; even the spaceship is only suggested, never seen. The fact that the alien closely resembles a man heightens the sense of personal, human struggle that is the cornerstone of all good drama.

THINGS TO COME

1936 113m bw Science Fiction DVD ★★★★
London Films (U.K.)

Raymond Massey *(John Cabal/Oswald Cabal)*, Edward Chapman *(Pippa Passworthy/Raymond Passworthy)*, Ralph Richardson *(The Boss)*, Margaretta Scott *(Roxana/Rowena)*, Cedric Hardwicke *(Theotocopulos)*, Maurice Braddell *(Dr. Harding)*, Sophie Stewart *(Mrs. Cabal)*, Derrick de Marney *(Richard Gordon)*, Ann Todd *(Mary Gordon)*, Pearl Argyle *(Catherine Cabal)*

p, Alexander Korda; d, William Cameron Menzies; w, H.G. Wells, Lajos Biro (based on the book *The Shape of Things to Come* by H.G. Wells); ph, Georges Perinal; ed, Charles Crichton, Francis D. Lyon; m, Arthur Bliss; prod d, Vincent Korda; fx, Ned Mann, Lawrence Butler, Edward Cohen, Harry Zech, Wally Vaevers, Ross Jacklin; cos, John Armstrong, Rene Hubert, Marchioness of Queensbury

Not since Fritz Lang's METROPOLIS had there been a science fiction film of such epic scope and vision as Alexander Korda's production of H.G. Wells's 1933 treatise on the future, *The Shape of Things to Come*. Set in an urban metropolis known as Everytown, the film charts the course of a chilling future in which war, disease, and totalitarianism nearly destroy mankind.

THINGS TO COME is best remembered for its prescient depiction of massive aerial bombing, which was to change the face of war (and urban England) within three years of its release. Eager to have Wells's participation in the project, producer Korda approached the great author and offered him the chance to write the screenplay. Two years and four drafts later, with considerable help from Korda, writer Lajos Biro, and director William Menzies, the script was completed. Wells was allowed to wander around the set during production influencing every detail of the film from the costumes and set design to the blocking of the actors. Everything about THINGS TO COME, its strengths and its considerable weaknesses, may be directly attributed to Wells. While the epic

scope of the film and its vision of the future are impressive, the human element is sorely lacking. The dialogue is very stilted and uninteresting: there is little interaction among characters and everyone makes speeches. It is a tribute to Massey's skill as an actor that the speeches play as well as they do.

Though the film fails as a human drama, it succeeds impressively in the scenes of devastation and reconstruction—a purely visual experience. Korda's brother Vincent was in charge of the production design and he plundered every new concept in architecture, industry, and design for the Everytown of 2036. Famed Hungarian futurist Laszlo Moholy-Nagy was hired to contribute his vision, but his designs were scrapped as too impractical. Wells, of course, had final approval on everything, but eventually he grew frustrated with the filmmaking process and admitted he knew little about making movies. Menzies, one of the most influential art directors in the history of motion pictures, was the perfect choice to direct the film (though Lewis Milestone was signed on at one time). Though his skill in directing actors was negligible, Menzies possessed a true feel for design and knew how to photograph it. At Wells' insistence, Arthur Bliss was brought in before production started to compose the score based on the script and Wells' suggestions. (The author felt that the music should be incorporated into the filmmaking process from the beginning, instead of after the filming was completed.) The resulting music was thus wholly integrated with the visuals. Bliss's work on the film proved so popular with the critics and the public that his music for THINGS TO COME was the first movie score to be recorded commercially and sold in record stores. When it was all over, Korda had spent over $1.5 million on THINGS TO COME, an incredible sum for the time. The film failed to ignite the box office, but it eventually made money. The original release in Britain ran 130 minutes, but the running time was cut for the U.S. (There are several different versions of the film now in distribution, running the gamut from 96 min. to 130 min.) Despite its flaws, THINGS TO COME is a truly epic work which continues to fascinate.

THIRD MAN, THE

1949 104m bw Thriller DVD ★★★★★
London Films (U.K.)

Joseph Cotten *(Holly Martins)*, Orson Welles *(Harry Lime)*, Alida Valli *(Anna Schmidt)*, Trevor Howard *(Maj. Calloway)*, Paul Hoerbiger *(Porter)*, Ernst Deutsch *(Baron Kurtz)*, Erich Ponto *(Dr. Winkel)*, Siegfried Breuer *(Popescu)*, Bernard Lee *(Sgt. Paine)*, Geoffrey Keen *(British Policeman)*

p, David O. Selznick, Alexander Korda, Carol Reed; d, Carol Reed; w, Graham Greene; ph, Robert Krasker; ed, Oswald Hafenrichter; m, Anton Karas; prod d, Vincent Korda, Joseph Bato, John Hawkesworth

AAN Best Director: Carol Reed; *AA Best B/W Cinematography:* Robert Krasker; *AAN Best Film Editing:* Oswald Hafenrichter

A gripping, beautifully structured picture and a *tour de force* from British director Carol Reed. American pulp novelist Holly Martins (Cotten) arrives in bleak postwar Vienna, having been promised a job by old friend Harry Lime (Welles). Holly soon is informed that his dear friend Harry is dead, killed in an accident and, in fact, his body is about to be lowered into a grave. He attends the funeral, where he meets the beautiful Anna (Valli), Lime's one-time lover. Inquiring of British officer Calloway (Howard) about Lime, Holly learns that his friend was a racketeer. Holly vows to carry out his own investigation into Lime's background and clear him of the crimes Calloway insists he committed. What results makes for a powerful examination of friendship and loyalty in the face of social obligations.

There's so much to recommend THE THIRD MAN that one can only scratch the surface in mentioning its strengths. It

gives the incredibly intoxicating feel of being a happy accident, and yet the ingredients are all there. Anton Karas's amazing zither music will haunt you for the rest of your life, and yet
you will never mind. The camerawork of genius Krasker
(Britain's greatest at that time) makes marvelous use of realistic city locales, darkly menacing alleys and inventively canted
framings. The dozens of references to Harry Lime really
prime us for his delayed appearance, and Orson Welles's enigmatic performance is so electric that one is not disappointed.
(That entrance, in fact, remains one of cinema's greatest.)
Cotten, meanwhile, gives a tangy yet subtle spin to the concept of the Ugly American abroad, and Howard lends both
sympathy and edge to the determined police inspector. Valli,
an intense and gifted Italian star, gives a poignant performance
as well. Reed's direction has perhaps never been better, from
the thrilling chase through the sewers to the accusations of the
little boy to the quieter romantic moments, and Graham
Greene's script is both adult and suspenseful. It's hard to
choose just one scene to sum up this poetic thriller, but the legendary scene on the ferris wheel may best represent its perfect
blend of great writing, acting, and directing. The fadeout, too,
is unforgettable.

THIRTEEN

2003 95m c Drama ★★★½
Michael London Productions/ R
Antidote Films/Working Title Films (U.S.)

Evan Rachel Wood (Tracy), Nikki Reed (Evie Zamora), Holly
Hunter (Melanie), Jeremy Sisto (Brady), Brady Corbet (Mason),
Deborah Unger (Brooke), Kip Pardue (Luke), Sarah Clarke
(Birdie), Vanessa Anne Hudgens (Noel), Ulysses Estrada (Rafa)

p, Jeffrey Levy-Hinte, Michael London; d, Catherine Hardwicke; w,
Catherine Hardwicke, Nikki Reed; ph, Elliot Davis; ed, Nancy
Richardson; m, Mark Mothersbaugh; prod d, Carol Strober; art d,
Johnny Jos; cos, Cindy Evans

AAN Best Supporting Actress: Holly Hunter

It starts with a punch in the face as two giggling tween-age
girls huff nitrous oxide from a whipped-cream can and smack
each other around for kicks. "Harder," they scream, laughing.
"I can't feel anything!" It's a shock effect worthy of Larry
Clark, but what first-time director Catherine Hardwicke's first
feature lacks in subtlety it more than makes up for in impact.
The film is one of the most honest and harrowing looks at
female adolescence ever to reach the screen.

Thirteen-year-old Tracy (Evan Rachel Wood) and her
older brother, Mason (Brady Corbet), live in suburban L.A.
with their hardworking divorced mom, Melanie (Holly
Hunter). A good student who writes poetry when she's not
studying, Tracy nevertheless falls under the beguiling spell of
Evie Zamora (Nikki Reed), the "hottest chick" in Portola
Middle School and the leader of an elite, cell-phone-wielding
posse of girls in low-slung jeans, barely-there T-shirts, thongs,
and body jewelry. Tracy is thrilled when Evie invites her to go
"shopping" on Melrose, and when Tracy realizes that shopping really means shop*lifting*, she proves herself by stealing
an unsuspecting woman's wallet. Within days, Tracy's transformed. She's dumped her old friends and completely co-
opted Evie's sexpot look; she's also dropping acid, hanging
out with much-older boys, getting her tongue pierced, and
blowing off school.

Both Wood and Reed are frighteningly good, and the film
wields a raw edge that feels entirely real. Credit Reed, who
cowrote the script with Hardwicke and served as the film's
chief inspiration. The film is not without its share of awkward
moments, but as an insightful critique of "girl culture" and the
mounting war over the hearts and minds of adolescent girls
that's currently being waged in the media, it's mandatory
viewing.

THIRTEEN DAYS

2000 135m c Historical/Thriller ★★★½
Beacon Pictures/New Line (U.S.) PG-13

Kevin Costner (Kenny O'Donnell), Bruce Greenwood (John F.
Kennedy), Steven Culp (Robert F. Kennedy), Dylan Baker (Robert
McNamara), Henry Strozier (Dean Rusk), Frank Wood
(McGeorge Bundy), Michael Fairman (Adlai Stevenson), Len
Cariou (Dean Acheson), Janet Coleman (Evelyn Lincoln),
Stephanie Romanov (Jacqueline Kennedy)

p, Armyan Bernstein, Peter O. Almond, Kevin Costner; d, Roger
Donaldson; w, David Self (based on the book *The Kennedy
Tapes: Inside the White House During the Cuban Missile Crisis* by
Ernest R. May and Philip D. Zelikow); ph, Andrzej Bartikowiak; ed,
Conrad Buff; m, Trevor Jones; prod d, Dennis Washington; art d,
Thomas T. Taylor, Ann Harris; fx, Louis Lantieri, Michael J.
McAlister, Allen Maris; cos, Isis Mussenden

The trouble with history is we all know how it ends. The fact
that the Cuban Missile Crisis of 1962 was defused pretty
much goes without saying, given that we're all still here. But
Roger Donaldson's account of the tense two weeks when it
looked as though America and the USSR were going to start
a global nuclear war is thoroughly gripping.

The crisis begins on October 16, when U.S. surveillance
photos detect Russian-built missiles in Cuba, a worrying 90
miles off the Florida coast. That this is no minor matter
becomes quickly apparent, and the government is on alert in a
matter of hours. The daunting list of key players includes
President Kennedy (Bruce Greenwood); his brother, Attorney
General Robert Kennedy (Steven Culp); Special Assistant to
the President Kenny O'Donnell (Kevin Costner); Secretary of
Defense Robert McNamara (Dylan Baker); Secretary of State
Dean Rusk (Henry Strozier); Special Assistant for National
Security Affairs McGeorge Bundy (Frank Wood); and
Ambassador to the United Nations Adlai Stevenson (Michael
Fairman). While the military brass argue that the Soviets only
understand force, the president is reluctant to start on a path
that will inevitably lead to nuclear annihilation, a position
secretly perceived by some of his own advisers as weak.

Shots of planes, missiles, warships, and ominous nuclear
clouds notwithstanding, the real action unfolds in a series of
smoky rooms whose claustrophobia is suffocating. This is a
work of fact-based fiction, not a documentary; the script no
doubt takes liberties with the details. But it effectively evokes
the terror of the time for viewers too young to remember a
near disaster far more frightening than any imaginary apocalypse involving rogue meteors or hostile extraterrestrials.

13 GOING ON 30

2004 97m c Comedy ★★★
Revolution Studios/Thirteen Productions (U.S.) PG-13

Jennifer Garner (Jenna Rink), Mark Ruffalo (Matt Flamhaff), Judy
Greer (Lucy), Christa B. Allen (Young Jenna Rink), Andy Serkis
(Richard), Kathy Baker (Beverly Rink), Phil Reeves (Wayne Rink),
Alex Black (Young Christopher Grandy), Alexandra Kyle (Young
Tom-Tom), Renee Olstead (Becky)

p, Susan Arnold, Gina Matthews, Donna Roth; d, Gary Winick; w,
Josh Goldsmith, Cathy Yuspa, Niels Mueller (from a story by
Cathy Yuspa and Josh Goldsmith); ph, Don Burgess; ed, Susan
Littenberg; m, Theodore Shapiro; prod d, Garreth Stover; art d,
Ray Kluga

Although it's basically BIG with a girly twist, this sprightly
coming-of-age-too-soon comedy rises above its derivative
concept by virtue of a well-cast ensemble and a quick-witted
screenplay.

It's 1987, and Jenna Rink's (Christa B. Allen) 13th birthday brings an unwelcome revelation: being a teenager isn't all

it's cracked up to be. With the exception of her goofy best friend, Matt (Jack Salvatore Jr.), boys don't seem to notice her, and she has to bribe the cool girls to come to her party. Jenna's heart's desire is to skip the tortures of adolescence and proceed straight to becoming one of these put-together women, and lo and behold, with the help of some magical powder, Jenna gets her wish: she wakes up in 2004 a successful, 30-year-old executive editor (Jennifer Garner) at *Poise* magazine who's dating a hockey star and whose best friend (Judy Greer) is one of the popular girls who used to torment her. But inside, Jenna's still a confused teenager, and she quickly makes a fool of herself in front of her boss (Andy Serkis). When she turns to a now-adult Matt (Mark Ruffalo) for help, she realizes that even though she's living her dream life, she hasn't grown up to be a very nice person.

Best known as the tough and sexy crime-fighter of TV's "Alias," Garner gamely embraces her frilly side, complete with girlish giggles and some sharply executed physical comedy; the low-key Ruffalo is the perfect foil for Garner's high-energy antics. The soundtrack is heavy on the fizzy hits of the '80s and, overall, director Gary Winick serves up enough giddy fun that it's easy to turn a blind eye to the film's minor anachronisms.

39 STEPS, THE   DVD
1935 85m   bw Spy   ★★★★★
Gaumont   (U.K.)

Madeleine Carroll *(Pamela)*, Robert Donat *(Richard Hannay)*, Lucie Mannheim *(Miss Smith/Annabella)*, Godfrey Tearle *(Prof. Jordan)*, Peggy Ashcroft *(Margaret)*, John Laurie *(John)*, Helen Haye *(Mrs. Jordan)*, Wylie Watson *(Mr. Memory)*, Frank Cellier *(Sheriff Watson)*, Peggy Simpson *(Young Maid)*

p, Michael Balcon, Ivor Montagu; d, Alfred Hitchcock; w, Charles Bennett, Alma Reville, Ian Hay (based on the novel by John Buchan); ph, Bernard Knowles; ed, Derek Twist; m, Louis Levy; prod d, Otto Wendroff, Albert Jullion; fx, Jack Whitehead; cos, Joe Strassner

Along with THE LADY VANISHES, one of Hitchcock's best British films, and a prototype for so much of what would follow in his American career. For those who love a grand spy mystery, a wild chase, and a harrowing portrait of an innocent man struggling to prove his innocence while the world turns inexplicably against him, THE 39 STEPS is ideal. Richard Hannay (Donat) is on vacation in London when he meets a mysterious woman (Mannheim) who tells him of a spy ring which she is trying to crack. She doesn't know the identity of the masterspy, but does know that he is missing a portion of the little finger on his right hand. She also cryptically mentions something about "The 39 Steps." Later she is murdered—before Hannay can learn anything more. His own life now in danger, Hannay flees to a town in Scotland which she has circled on a map, and sets out to find the man with the disfigured finger. Along the way he meets Pamela (Carroll), who decides to assist him after the crooks handcuff her to him. An encounter with a memory expert proves to be the key to uncracking this corker.

This is one of the best films of its genre and it richly displays Hitchcock's complete and playful mastery of the language of filmmaking. The handcuffing sequence (which still influences films today, e.g., the remake of D.O.A.) is one of the cinema's greatest. Hitch also has great fun with the sound bridge linking a screaming woman with a train whistle, and the final assassination attempt recalls THE BIRTH OF A NATION. Carroll makes for an appealing heroine and Donat brings his oddly wispy quality to the man on the run. He looks curiously androgynous in this film; the oh-so-trim mustache and his lilting voice add a vulnerability to his character which distinguishes it from the run-of-the-mill hero. Tearle is splendid, as is Watson in his most famous role, but who we really

like are Peggy Ashcroft and John Laurie. This gifted stage actress and this striking, reliable actor of many films lend something intense to the married couple Hannay encounters while on the run. Ashcroft is extremely moving as a woman strangled in her marriage and home life, desperately grateful for whatever the strange Hannay may bring into it. Scenes such as this linger in the memory as long as the more typically Hitchcockian setpieces, and it does credit to the master director's versatility. (It somehow seems more his style that he actually handcuffed Carroll and Donat on the set one day to get them used to their scenes together… he of course then vanished from the set!)

THIRTY SECONDS OVER TOKYO
1944 138m bw War   ★★★★
MGM   (U.S.)

Spencer Tracy *(Lt. Col. James H. Doolittle)*, Van Johnson *(Capt. Ted W. Lawson)*, Robert Walker *(David Thatcher)*, Phyllis Thaxter *(Ellen Jones Lawson)*, Tim Murdock *(Dean Davenport)*, Scott McKay *(Davey Jones)*, Gordon McDonald *(Bob Clever)*, Don DeFore *(Charles McClure)*, Robert Mitchum *(Bob Gray)*, John R. Reilly *(Shorty Manch)*

p, Sam Zimbalist; d, Mervyn LeRoy; w, Dalton Trumbo (based on the book by Capt. Ted W. Lawson, Robert Considine); ph, Harold Rosson, Robert Surtees; ed, Frank Sullivan; m, Herbert Stothart; art d, Cedric Gibbons, Paul Groesse; fx, A. Arnold Gillespie, Warren Newcombe, Donald Jahraus

AAN Best B/W Cinematography: Robert Surtees, Harold Rosson; *AA Best Special Effects:* A. Arnold Gillespie (Photographic), Donald Jahraus (Photographic), Warren Newcombe (Photographic), Douglas Shearer (Sound)

In 1942, 131 days after the Japanese bombing of Pearl Harbor, an American force retaliated, bombing the major Japanese cities of Tokyo and Yokohama. This picture, a quasi-documentary re-creation of that event, was authored by one of the survivors of the raid, Ted Lawson (played here by Van Johnson). Since land bases near the target are unavailable—and in-flight refueling techniques undeveloped—a dangerous, untried tactic must be employed for the top-secret mission: for the first time in history, twin-engine bombers are to take off from the deck of an aircraft carrier. Because the planes are too large to land on a carrier deck, after the attack they must continue on to mainland China—occupied by the Japanese—and then make their way to Allied-held territory as best they can. Weeks of preparation and training take place before the aircraft and their crews are finally loaded aboard the USS *Hornet*. Following a final shipboard briefing by mission leader Lt. Col. Jimmy Doolittle (Spencer Tracy), the fliers man their twin-engine Mitchell bombers and are catapulted from the flight deck. The remainder of the film follows the adventures of Lawson's crew only. A well-made war film, THIRTY SECONDS OVER TOKYO was sufficiently accurate to prompt all the real-life principals to approve the use of their names in the picture. Screenwriter Dalton Trumbo wisely elected not to attempt to alter the limited perspective of Lawson's memoir by including more of the details of the famous raid. In the actual event, all 16 participating bombers made it to China, although three men died in crashes and eleven others were captured by the Japanese, who executed three of them. Although top-billed, Tracy's appearance here is basically a cameo, with Johnson the real star of the film.

THIRTY-TWO SHORT FILMS ABOUT GLENN GOULD DVD
1993 94m c Biography   ★★★
Max Film (Canada)

Colm Feore *(Glenn Gould)*, Derek Keurvorst *(Gould's Father)*, Katya Lada *(Gould's Mother)*, Devon Anderson *(Glenn Age—Three)*,

Joshua Greenblatt *(Glenn Age—Eight)*, Sean Ryan *(Glenn Age—13)*, Kate Hennig *(Chambermaid)*, Sean Doyle *(Porter)*, Sharon Bernbaum *(Female Guide)*, Don McKellar *(Concert Promoter)*

p, Niv Fichman; d, Francois Girard; w, Francois Girard, Don McKellar; ph, Alain Dostie; ed, Gaetan Huot; m, Johann Sebastian Bach, Richard Wagner, Ludwig Von Beethoven, Glenn Gould, Richard Strauss, Tony Hatch, Jean Sibelius, Sergei Prokofiev, Alexander Scriabin, Paul Hindemith, Arnold Schoenberg; art d, John Rubino; cos, Linda Muir

The title of this offbeat Canadian feature, which echoes Beethoven's "Thirty Two Variations in C Minor" (one of which is heard in the film), reflects the style and structure employed by director Francois Girard in his treatment of the reclusive concert pianist and recording artist Glenn Gould (Colm Feore). Between intertitles borrowed from the lexicon of classical music (the Prelude, the Fugue, the Theme and Variations), Girard weaves together a series of impressions, interviews, and dramatizations in an attempt to find cinematic correlatives for musical forms. The result is less a biopic than a meditation on creativity, isolation, and the nature of communication in a technological age.

After his retirement from the concert stage, Gould became a cult figure in classical music, with all that that implies; his work is still subjected to probing critical analysis, revisionist interpretations, and not a few vitriolic attacks. It is probably impossible to separate Gould's personal history from the continuing reassessment of his performing career, and Girard and co-writer Don McKellar nimbly sidestep the pitfalls of critical debate by narrowing their focus to specific moments and impressions. Without attempting a sweeping, comprehensive summation of Gould-the-man or Gould-the-performer, Girard and McKellar still manage to suggest greater depths of artistry and personality than the conventions of traditional film biography might allow.

THIS BOY'S LIFE   *DVD*
1993 115m c   Drama   ★★★½
Knickerbocker Films   (U.S.)   R

Robert De Niro *(Dwight)*, Ellen Barkin *(Caroline)*, Leonardo DiCaprio *(Toby)*, Jonah Blechman *(Arthur Gayle)*, Eliza Dushku *(Pearl)*, Chris Cooper *(Roy)*, Carla Gugino *(Norma)*, Zack Ansley *(Skipper)*, Tracey Ellis *(Kathy)*, Kathy Kinney *(Marian)*

p, Art Linson; d, Michael Caton-Jones; w, Robert Getchell (from the autobiography by Tobias Wolff); ph, David Watkin; m, Carter Burwell; prod d, Stephen J. Lineweaver; art d, Sandy Cochrane; fx, Nick Lawson, Mike Vezina; cos, Richard Hornung

Based on Tobias Wolff's brilliant memoir of the same title, THIS BOY'S LIFE is a well-acted film about an extremely painful adolescence. In capturing the compelling battle between a boy and his abusive stepfather, director Michael Caton-Jones cannily avoids obvious sentimentality, opting to let a rather brutal story tell itself.

1957. Angel-faced but troubled Toby "Jack" Wolff (Leonardo DiCaprio) and his brassy blonde mom, Caroline (Ellen Barkin), hit the road in search of a better life. Caroline is wooed by Dwight (Robert De Niro), an auto mechanic who lives far away in Concrete, Washington with his three kids, and marries him to give Toby a stable family life. Neither is happy: Dwight is a sadistic disciplinarian whose abuse Toby suffers for the sake of his mother, while Caroline endures a loveless marriage for the sake of her son. The conflict between Dwight and Toby escalates frighteningly, and the two are soon locked in a brutal battle of wills.

Screenwriter Robert Getchell's adaptation often simplifies its source, but for the most part he and Caton-Jones remain faithful to Wolff's remarkable story. Young DiCaprio makes a very strong impression in his first leading role, delineating the many moods of adolescence with ease. Robert De Niro often

seems forced in comparison; in fact, his savage portrayal stands as the movie's main blemish. Still, this is powerful and moving stuff.

THIS GUN FOR HIRE   *DVD*
1942 80m   bw   Crime/Spy   ★★★★½
Paramount   (U.S.)

Veronica Lake *(Ellen Graham)*, Robert Preston *(Michael Crane)*, Laird Cregar *(Willard Gates)*, Alan Ladd *(Philip Raven)*, Tully Marshall *(Alvin Brewster)*, Mikhail Rasumny *(Slukey)*, Marc Lawrence *(Tommy)*, Pamela Blake *(Annie)*, Harry Shannon *(Steve Finnerty)*, Frank Ferguson *(Albert Baker)*

p, Richard Blumenthal; d, Frank Tuttle; w, Albert Maltz, W.R. Burnett (based on the novel *A Gun for Sale* by Graham Greene); ph, John Seitz; ed, Archie Marshek; m, David Buttolph; art d, Hans Dreier

Outstanding *film noir*, based on Graham Greene's novel *A Gun For Sale*, which presents one of the most disturbed (and disturbing) killers ever to cross the screen. Ladd is scary because he doesn't care; he is simply a killing machine hired out by whoever will pay. Only when Lake takes the time to break through the emotional fortress that he has built around himself does Ladd show any signs of humanity.

This is the film that made Alan Ladd a star. Although director Tuttle had originally intended to cast Preston in the lead role, he later decided to hunt for an unknown. When Tuttle was introduced to Ladd, the director was convinced that the 28-year-old blonde could make the cold-blooded killer Phillip Raven a sympathetic character. Contracted at $300 per week, Ladd underwent screen tests, and even had his hair dyed black in keeping with his character's name. Though the film was conceived as a Lake-Preston vehicle, it soon became quite apparent that the studio had something in Ladd, and the script was reworked during production to favor the actor. The film became, in more ways than one, the Alan Ladd story—with all the attention being paid to him and his role. As a result, the film's romantic angle was soon tossed away and Preston reduced to a plot device. But even though Ladd and Lake did not so much as exchange a kiss, they still became one of Hollywood's hottest and most bankable love teams, with three more pictures following—THE GLASS KEY; THE BLUE DAHLIA; and SAIGON.

THIS GUN FOR HIRE was originally to have begun with a dream in which a young Raven (played by Dickie Jones) is seen murdering his aunt and guardian (Hermine Sterler) after she attacks him and injures his wrist. This rather morbid beginning was omitted, however, and the film begins, instead, with Ladd awaking from the dream. THIS GUN FOR HIRE was remade in 1957 as the James Cagney-directed SHORT CUT TO HELL.

THIS HAPPY BREED   *DVD*
1944 110m c   Drama   ★★★★
Two Cities   (U.K.)

Robert Newton *(Frank Gibbons)*, Celia Johnson *(Ethel Gibbons)*, John Mills *(Billy Mitchell)*, Kay Walsh *(Queenie Gibbons)*, Stanley Holloway *(Bob Mitchell)*, Amy Veness *(Mrs. Flint)*, Alison Leggatt *(Aunt Sylvia)*, Eileen Erskine *(Vi)*, John Blythe *(Reg)*, Guy Verney *(Sam Ledbetter)*

p, Noel Coward, Anthony Havelock-Allan; d, David Lean; w, David Lean, Ronald Neame, Anthony Havelock-Allan (based on the play by Noel Coward); ph, Ronald Neame (Technicolor); ed, Jack Harris; m, Noel Coward, Muir Mathieson; art d, C.P. Norman

Based on Noel Coward's hit play (in which he also starred), this cavalcade of British life between wars was one of the top moneymakers in the UK in 1944, but it took three more years to reach U.S. screens. Laurence Olivier narrates the episodic story of a family that lives in a small row house, totally indistinguishable from all the other houses surrounding it. This average working-class family includes father Newton, mother Johnson, and their two children, Walsh (who just happened to be married to director Lean at the time) and Blythe. WWI is ending and Newton, who has served four years in the army, is coming home to take Johnson and the children away from the home they've occupied with Johnson's mother, Veness, and her sister, Leggart. The whole group moves into a larger residence in Clapham and looks forward to a happy life. But life isn't always pleasant for Leggart and Veness, who battle constantly. To get out of the house and away from Veness' sharp tongue, Leggart, a spinster, volunteers for just about every committee and charity group around. Meanwhile, the children continue to grow and become increasingly independent, watched over by Newton (in an understated performance that is a departure from his usual scene-stealing tactics). When a general strike occurs, Blythe is right in the middle of it, coming home one evening with bruises and cuts sustained in a riot. Hoping to better her lot, Walsh takes a job in a fashionable beauty salon in London's posh West End. She's been dating Mills, the sailor son of Holloway, who lives next door, and it is just assumed that they will eventually wed. At the same time, Blythe is engaged to Betty Fleetwood. The applecart is overturned when Walsh runs off with a married man, and the family is crushed. Blythe and Fleetwood are married, but tragedy strikes when both are killed in an auto crash and the news is given to the family in one of the most memorable scenes in British cinema.

Coward and Lean codirected IN WHICH WE SERVE, and the great actor-playwright was impressed enough by Lean's work to hand the director the film rights for this film as well as for "Brief Encounter" and "Blithe Spirit." Here Lean is partnered with cinematographer Neame (who later became a producer and director) and writer Havelock-Allan. In 1944, there were almost no color cameras in England, but somehow they managed to find one of them for this film, although the color is muted and not nearly as stark as the process used in the U.S. at the time. Still, this is an immensely charming movie, with many tears and many moments of warmth. Newton is excellent, and Johnson, who could look glamorous when the part called for it, is deliberately dressed dowdily and de-glamorized for her role here, she which performs with great aplomb.

THIS IS SPINAL TAP   *DVD*
1984   82m   c   Comedy   ★★★½
Spinal Tap   (U.S.)   R

Rob Reiner *(Marty DiBergi)*, Michael McKean *(David St. Hubbins)*, Christopher Guest *(Nigel Tufnel)*, Harry Shearer *(Derek Smalls)*, R.J. Parnell *(Mick Shrimpton)*, David Kaff *(Viv Savage)*, Tony Hendra *(Ian Faith)*, Bruno Kirby *(Tommy Pischedda)*, Kimberly Stringer, Chazz Dominguez

p, Karen Murphy; d, Rob Reiner; w, Christopher Guest, Michael McKean, Harry Shearer, Rob Reiner; ph, Peter Smokler (CFI Color); ed, Kent Beyda, Kim Secrist, Robert Leighton; m, Christopher Guest, Michael McKean, Harry Shearer, Rob Reiner; prod d, Bryan Jones; cos, Renee Johnston

Hilarious pseudo-documentary spoof of a British rock group that was so on-target in its satire, many viewers took it for the real thing.

Spinal Tap is an aging British heavy metal band who are limping their way across the U.S. while Marty DiBergi (Reiner) makes a "rockumentary" film about them. (Reiner is a Yank who has been following the group since they burst onto the scene 17 years before. Now that they're fading, he decides to tell their story rather than make some commercials for Wheat Thins.) Every disaster that can befall a rock group

happens to Nigel Tufnel (Guest), David St. Hubbins (McKean), and Derek Smalls (Shearer). Management woes, promotional difficulties, nonexistent hotel accommodations, phony business people, props that don't work, and an album that hasn't yet been distributed in the stores, all add up to major problems.

The American cast make pretty convincing English rockers, and the album-of-the-film, "The Best of Spinal Tap," became a hit in Japan. In 1992, the group became the stuff of pop-culture legend, releasing a follow-up album, "Break Like the Wind," completing a national tour of the U.S., and even appearing in animated form on hit Fox TV show "The Simpsons."

THIS IS THE ARMY   *DVD*
1943   120m   c   Musical/War   ★★★
Warner Bros.   (U.S.)

Irving Berlin *(Himself)*, George Murphy *(Jerry Jones)*, Joan Leslie *(Eileen Dibble)*, George Tobias *(Maxie Stoloff)*, Alan Hale *(Sgt. McGee)*, Charles Butterworth *(Eddie Dibble)*, Rosemary DeCamp *(Ethel)*, Dolores Costello *(Mrs. Davidson)*, Una Merkel *(Rose Dibble)*, Stanley Ridges *(Maj. Davidson)*

p, Jack L. Warner, Hal B. Wallis; d, Michael Curtiz; w, Casey Robinson, Claude Binyon (based on the play by Irving Berlin); ph, Bert Glennon, Sol Polito (Technicolor); ed, George Amy; art d, John Keonig, John Hughes; fx, Jack Cosgrove; chor, LeRoy Prinz, Robert Sidney; cos, Orry-Kelly

AA Best Score (Musical): Ray Heindorf; *AAN Best Interior Decoration (Color):* John Hughes, Lieutenant John Koenig, George James Hopkins; *AAN Best Sound Recording:* Nathan Levinson

This star-studded musical salute to the American soldier is filled with Irving Berlin's songs and morale-boosting patriotism. Taken from Berlin's stage play, which opened July 4, 1942, THIS IS THE ARMY also adapts portions of Berlin's earlier musical "Yip Yip Yaphank." Jerry Jones (George Murphy) is a big-time

Broadway star who, at the beginning of WWI, is drafted into the service and given the job of putting on a big show. He does his bit and, when the show ends, cast and crew go off to fight in Europe. Years pass and Jerry is now a producer with a son, Johnny (Ronald Reagan, who joined Murphy in rising through California politics), who is drafted in WWII and given the same job as his father. Johnny writes a terrific show *and* marries sweetheart Eileen Dibble (Joan Leslie). The show tours the country and at the final performance, before the boys go to war, Irving Berlin (as himself) comes onstage in Washington to sing. The plot is just barely enough to hang the musical numbers on, but it's the tunes that count. Berlin used his clout to get the Army to lend him more than 300 soldiers for the stage show, promising to donate more than a million dollars from the show's receipts to a relief fund for the families the boys left behind.

THIS LAND IS MINE
1943   103m   bw   War   ★★★½
RKO   (U.S.)

Charles Laughton *(Arthur Lory)*, Maureen O'Hara *(Louise Martin)*, George Sanders *(George Lambert)*, Walter Slezak *(Maj. Erich von Keller)*, Kent Smith *(Paul Martin)*, Una O'Connor *(Mrs. Emma Lory)*, Philip Merivale *(Prof. Sorel)*, Thurston Hall *(Mayor Henry Manville)*, George Coulouris *(Prosecuting Attorney)*, Nancy Gates *(Julie Grant)*

p, Jean Renoir, Dudley Nichols; d, Jean Renoir; w, Dudley Nichols; ph, Frank Redman; ed, Frederic Knudtson; m, Lothar Perl; prod d, Eugene Lourie; art d, Albert S. D'Agostino, Walter E. Keller; fx, Vernon L. Walker; cos, Renie

AA Best Sound Recording: Stephen Dunn

Set "somewhere in Europe" (clearly Jean Renoir's French homeland), THIS LAND IS MINE stars Charles Laughton as a cowardly schoolteacher, Arthur Lory, who whimpers during air raids and can only be comforted by his overly possessive mother (Una O'Connor). Arthur chooses to keep a low profile and go about his business unnoticed until his mentor, Prof. Sorel (Philip Merivale), lights a patriotic spark in him. Aware of his cowardice, he turns to fellow schoolteacher Louise Martin (Maureen O'Hara), who is sympathetic both to his fears and to the cause of the Resistance, of which her brother Paul (Kent Smith) is an active member who throws bombs at German officers. As much as he tries to remain neutral, Arthur finds himself increasingly sympathetic to the Resistance movement.

Although some consider THIS LAND IS MINE preachy and overly talky, it must be praised for its understanding of humanity. Instead of painting the Germans as mighty evildoers and the French as innocent victims, Renoir took a more daring and honest approach, implicating the French as being partly responsible for the Occupation, when many citizens collaborated with the Nazis to ensure that they would remain immune from punishment and that their orderly lives would not be shattered by the invaders. Renoir avoided propagandistic cliches and took into consideration human nature; human nature, however, is not what people look for in war heroes and patriotic messages. Although long considered a propaganda film, THIS LAND IS MINE is more correctly seen as anti-propagandistic. There is no black and white, no good or evil. There is only grey, and, in that grey area, an understanding of the frailty of human nature.

THIS MAN MUST DIE

(QUE LA BETE MEURE)
1970 115m c Thriller ★★★★
Boetie/Rizzoli(France/Italy) GP

Michel Duchaussoy *(Charles Thenier)*, Caroline Cellier *(Helene Lanson)*, Jean Yanne *(Paul Decourt)*, Anouk Ferjac *(Jeanne)*, Marc Di Napoli *(Philippe Decourt)*, Maurice Pialat *(Police Inspector)*, Guy Marly *(Jacques Ferrand)*, Lorraine Rainer *(Anna Ferrand)*, Stephane Di Napoli *(Michel Thenier)*, Louise Chevalier *(Mme. Levenes)*

p, Andre Genoves; d, Claude Chabrol; w, Claude Chabrol, Paul Gegauff (based on the novel *The Beast Must Die* by Nicholas Blake); ph, Jean Rabier (Eastmancolor); ed, Jacques Gaillard; m, Pierre Jansen; art d, Guy Littaye

One of Chabrol's best films. When Duchaussoy's son is killed by a hit-and-run driver, the quiet author of children's books can think only of revenge. He begins a search for the killer, recording each step he takes in a diary. First, he meets a farmer who tells him that on the day of the accident he saw a damaged sports car in which TV personality Cellier was a passenger. Duchaussoy travels to Paris and meets Cellier. Soon the two are having an affair, and the writer learns that Cellier's brother-in-law (Yanne) runs an auto repair shop. Immediately, Yanne becomes Duchaussoy's prime suspect. Eventually Duchaussoy grows close to Yanne's son (Marc Di Napoli), who tells the writer that he plans to kill his father. Duchaussoy then takes Yanne out on a sailboat to drown him. However, Yanne pulls a pistol on the vengeful writer, saying that he's read Duchaussoy's diary. Duchaussoy leaves Paris with Cellier, but the plot twists don't end there. Another of the quietly handled but solidly engrossing melodramas Chabrol was making at the time, and well worth the effort.

THIS SPORTING LIFE

DVD

1963 129m bw Sports ★★★★
Independent Artists (U.K.)

Richard Harris *(Frank Machin)*, Rachel Roberts *(Mrs. Hammond)*, Alan Badel *(Weaver)*, William Hartnell *(Johnson)*, Colin Blakely *(Maurice Braithwaite)*, Vanda Godsell *(Mrs. Weaver)*, Arthur Lowe *(Slomer)*, Anne Cunningham *(Judith)*, Jack Watson *(Len Miller)*, Harry Markham *(Wade)*

p, Karel Reisz; d, Lindsay Anderson; w, David Storey (based on the novel by Storey); ph, Denys Coop; ed, Peter Taylor; m, Roberto Gerhard; art d, Alan Withy; cos, Sophie Devine

AAN Best Actor: Richard Harris; *AAN Best Actress:* Rachel Roberts

From its virtuoso opening shot of a rugby scrum—from the bottom, looking up—to its final emotionally draining moments, THIS SPORTING LIFE is a captivating, visceral film experience. Not only is Lindsay Anderson's (IF..., O LUCKY MAN!) first feature film one of the most poignant sports-centered movies ever made, it is also a landmark in the history of British cinema, an "Angry Young Man" classic. Adapted by David Storey (who played professional rugby at one time) from his own novel, the film follows the fortunes of Frank Machin (Richard Harris), a loutish former Yorkshire coal miner who bashes his way to local celebrity as a professional rugby player. Although pursued by a number of women, Frank starves for the love of his landlady, Mrs. Hammond (Rachel Roberts), a bitter, passionless widow, who eventually has a physical relationship with Frank but refuses to give herself to him emotionally. Meanwhile, Frank remains the darling of the rugby club's management and supporters, and as long as he performs on the field, his sullen rebelliousness is tolerated. In time, Mrs. Hammond grows tired of Frank's callousness, they fight terribly, and he moves out. Realizing how much he needs her love, Frank tries to patch things up, but tragedy awaits his attempt at reconciliation. Finally, Frank is left only with the violent world of rugby, in which he is only as good as his last game. THIS SPORTING LIFE is both a biting indictment of class-based exploitation (the club owners treat the players as mindless beasts) and a tragic story of love that founders on suppressed feelings and unconscious macho insensitivity. Harris gives an extraordinary, gut-wrenching performance reminiscent of young Marlon Brando, and Roberts brings considerable complexity to her exceptional portrayal of a woman whose emotional life is as dormant as Frank's is frustrated. The game action is hard-hitting and well captured, and cinematographer Denys Coop's gritty, detailed black and white is in the best tradition of British kitchen-sink realism.

THOMAS CROWN AFFAIR, THE

DVD

1968 102m c Crime ★★★
Mirisch/Simkoe/Solar (U.S.) R

Steve McQueen *(Thomas Crown)*, Faye Dunaway *(Vicky Anderson)*, Paul Burke *(Eddy Malone)*, Jack Weston *(Erwin Weaver)*, Biff McGuire *(Sandy)*, Yaphet Kotto *(Carl)*, Todd Martin *(Benjy)*, Sam Melville *(Dave)*, Addison Powell *(Abe)*, Sidney Armus *(Arnie)*

p, Norman Jewison; d, Norman Jewison; w, Alan R. Trustman; ph, Haskell Wexler (DeLuxe Color); ed, Hal Ashby, Ralph E. Winters, Byron Brandt; m, Michel Legrand; art d, Robert Boyle; fx, Pablo Ferro Films; cos, Ron Postal, Theadora Van Runkle, Alan Levine

AAN Best Original Score (Not a Musical): Michel Legrand; *AA Best Original Song:* "The Windmills of Your Mind"; Michel Legrand (Music), Alan Bergman (Lyrics), Marilyn Bergman (Lyrics)

A very expensive caper picture that drowns in its own artiness, using multi-images, cinematic tricks, and other pretentious film gimmicks—all of which detract from the story. Set and partially filmed in Boston, it's the tale of a self-made millionaire, McQueen, who decides that he has been a member of the Establishment long enough. With the help of aides who never actually meet him, McQueen arranges a brilliant bank robbery that nets millions. McQueen pays off his assistants (most notable is Weston) and banks the remainder, almost $3 million, in Switzerland. The bank's insurance company pays off the loss, then assigns its number one investigator, Dunaway, to the case. She is working in league with police officer Burke, and, through a totally unbelievable gut instinct, she picks McQueen as the most likely suspect (audiences groaned at this jump of logic). Dunaway moves in on McQueen, and the two recognize each other as the enemy. In an artsy sequence, Jewison sends his camera around the two (the way it was done in A MAN AND A WOMAN) as they fall in love after a chess game that parodies the eating sequence in TOM JONES. Dunaway is completely ga-ga over McQueen and thinks she can get him off without a prison sentence if he gives back the money. The chances of that are slim to none, and McQueen wants to see if she really loves him or is using her body as part of her investigation. McQueen says he's about to pull off another caper and wants her to meet him in a local cemetery after the job's done. She shows up there with Burke, and the money is in a garbage can. McQueen's Rolls-Royce arrives, and she thinks it's him. But no—further double-cross ensues.

Split-screen techniques, which were all the rage after having been seen to great advantage at the 1964 World's Fair, are used time and again. The Bergman song "The Windmills of Your Mind," written with Legrand, won an Oscar, and Legrand was nominated for his music. The supervising film editor was Hal Ashby, who also was associate producer. Walter Hill (who later became a writer-director) was one of the assistant directors and, thankfully, picked up none of Jewison's bad ideas. Trustman was a practicing attorney when he wrote the script; he has since written several more films. McQueen is charming, reads his lines well, and shows that he isn't just another short actor with an interesting face. Watching the film today, one can sense the era in which it was filmed, as many other movies of that period made the mistake of placing technique over characterization.

THOMAS CROWN AFFAIR, THE   DVD
1999 113m c   Crime/Romance/Drama   ★★★
Irish DreamTime/United Artists   (Ireland/U.S.)   R

Pierce Brosnan (Thomas Crown), Rene Russo (Catherine Banning), Denis Leary (Michael McCann), Ben Gazzara (Andrew Wallace), Faye Dunaway (Psychiatrist), Frankie Faison (Paretti), Fritz Weaver (John Reynolds), Charles Keating (Golchan), Mark Margolis (Knutzhorn), Michael Lombard (Proctor McKinley)

p, Pierce Brosnan, Beau St. Clair; d, John McTiernan; w, Leslie Dixon, Kurt Wimmer (based on a story by Alan R. Trustman); ph, Tom Priestly; ed, John Wright; m, Bill Conti; prod d, Bruno Rubeo; art d, Dennis Bradford; fx, Connrad F. Brink; chor, John Carrafa; cos, Kate Harrington

This swank, self-consciously erotic caper flick gets off to a dreadfully ordinary start but finds its footing when the head games begin.

Life for billionaire Thomas Crown (Pierce Brosnan) isn't worth living without a challenge, so he orchestrates a daredevil, daylight theft of a priceless Monet from the Metropolitan Museum of Art. It looks as though he's home free, until Catherine Banning (Rene Russo) sashays into the investigation, ostensibly on behalf of the museum's insurance company. She immediately figures Crown for the mastermind and is sure she can retrieve the painting, enriching her bank account in the process. Her plan, however, involves getting dangerously close to the charismatic burglar, and the two consummate game players are immediately drawn to each other.

Or are they? The apparently incendiary romance might be part of a game whose stakes grow higher with each kiss.

This remake of the fondly remembered 1968 Faye Dunaway-Steve McQueen picture is surprisingly faithful. Screenwriters Leslie Dixon and Kurt Wimmer tweak Alan Trustman's original script without resolving its fundamental structural imbalance: the attenuated opening heist delays the far more interesting cat-and-mouse romance. New scenes involving Crown and his psychiatrist (Dunaway) serve no purpose except to accommodate Dunaway's diva-ish presence, but while the first film was distinguished by annoyingly gimmicky camera tricks, this one glides along on sheer, luxurious gloss. It's enjoyable poppycock, obsessed with the trappings of wealth (the camera lingers as lovingly on expensive clothes, lavish dwellings, and rich-boy toys as on Russo and Brosnan's often bare flesh) and in love with its own chic affectations.

THOSE MAGNIFICENT MEN IN THEIR FLYING   DVD
MACHINES; OR HOW I FLEW FROM LONDON
TO PARIS IN 25 HOURS AND 11 MINUTES
1965 133m c   Comedy   ★★★½
Fox   (U.K.)   G

Stuart Whitman (Orvil Newton), Sarah Miles (Patricia Rawnsley), James Fox (Richard Mays), Alberto Sordi (Count Emilio Ponticelli), Robert Morley (Lord Rawnsley), Gert Frobe (Col. Manfred von Holstein), Jean-Pierre Cassel (Pierre Dubois), Eric Sykes (Courtney), Terry-Thomas (Sir Percival Ware-Armitage), Irina Demick (Brigitte/Ingrid/Marlene/Francoise/Yvette/Betty)

p, Stan Margulies; d, Ken Annakin; w, Jack Davies, Ken Annakin; ph, Christopher Challis (Todd-AO, DeLuxe Color); ed, Gordon Stone, Anne V. Coates; m, Ron Goodwin; prod d, Tom Morahan; art d, Jim Morahan; fx, Richard Parker, Ron Ballanger; cos, Osbert Lancaster, Dinah Greet; anim, Ralph Ayres

AAN Best Original Story and Screenplay: Jack Davies, Ken Annakin

This rip-roaring comedy takes place in 1910, when English press bigwig Lord Rawnsley (Robert Morley) sets out to prove that Great Britain is No. 1 in the air. Putting up 10,000 pounds as a prize, he invites the world's best pilots to compete in an air race from London to Paris. All sorts of dandy planes arrive, but Rawnsley roots for his daughter's (Sarah Miles's) fiance, Richard Mays (James Fox), a Royal Navy lieutenant. Other contenders include an Italian count (Alberto Sordi); a fanatical Prussian who will die before he lets anyone else win (Gert Frobe); a Frenchman (Jean-Pierre Cassel) followed by a sextet of women (all played by Irina Demick); a villainous Brit (Terry-Thomas); an inscrutable Japanese (Yujiro Ishihara); and American barnstormer Orvil Newton (Stuart Whitman), who decides that Rawnsley's daughter is the woman for him. After a series of slapstick mishaps, the competitors are winnowed until only the Italian and the two romantic rivals remain. Heroism and fair play are the order of the day in the big finish, but it's up to Rawnsley's daughter to decide which of the competitors has won her heart. Good, clean fun, with fast and furious action, good cinematography, crisp dialogue, wonderful planes, and a host of some of the funniest people in movies in the cast.

THOUSAND CLOWNS, A
1965 117m bw   Comedy/Drama   ★★★★
UA   (U.S.)

Jason Robards Jr. (Murray Burns), Barbara Harris (Sandra), Martin Balsam (Arnold Burns), Barry Gordon (Nick), Gene Saks (Leo), William Daniels (Albert)

p, Fred Coe; d, Fred Coe; w, Herb Gardner (based on his play); ph, Arthur J. Ornitz; ed, Ralph Rosenblum; m, Don Walker; cos, Ruth Morley

AAN Best Picture; AA Best Supporting Actor: Martin Balsam; *AAN Best Adapted Screenplay:* Herb Gardner; *AAN Best Adapted Score:* Don Walker

This warm and wonderful comedy-drama is a paean to non-conformity. Robards is an out-of-work writer who quit his last job writing a kiddie TV show called "Chuckles the Chipmunk" when he could no longer stand the stupidity. Unemployed for five months, he needs cash to help support his nephew, Gordon, a bright 12-year-old whom his sister dropped off one afternoon seven years ago, then vanished. Gordon is illegitimate and, after living with Robards this long, more like a son than a nephew. The relationship between them is warm, loving, and respectful. Robards has never legally adopted Gordon, so a social worker, Harris, comes by to see if she can straighten out the situation. With her is Daniels, a prissy man who is a by-the-book social worker. Unless Robards can prove that he has a real job, they are going to have to take Gordon out of the ratty apartment and give him a foster home. Of course, Harris and Robards become romantically involved. Harris now has a personal stake in keeping the family together but can she and Gordon persuade Robards to return to the daily grind of a regular job? Will he willingly become one of the "thousand clowns" one sees running for the morning bus?

Touching and often funny, A THOUSAND CLOWNS offers superb performances by everyone, especially the young Gordon who read lines like a seasoned pro. Saks, who is also a well-known stage and film director, is sensational as the grotesque "Chuckles," a portrayal that is actually more memorable than Balsam's as Robard's brother, the agent, who won the Best Supporting Actor Oscar for his role.

THOUSAND EYES OF DR. MABUSE, THE 📀
(DIE TAUSEND AUGEN DES DR. MABUSE)
1960 103m bw Crime/Science Fiction ★★★½
CCC/CEI Incom Criterion (France/Italy/West Germany)

Dawn Addams *(Marion Menil)*, Peter Van Eyck *(Henry B. Travers)*, Gert Frobe *(Comm. Krauss)*, Wolfgang Preiss *(Jordan/Cornelius)*, Werner Peters *(Hieronymous P. Mistelzweig)*, Andrea Checchi *(Insp. Berg)*, Rene Kolldehoff *(The Clubfoot)*, Howard Vernon *("No. 12")*, Jean-Jacques Delbo *(Deiner the Servant)*, Christiane Maybach *(Pretty Blonde)*

p, Fritz Lang; d, Fritz Lang; w, Fritz Lang, Heinz Oskar Wuttig (based on an idea by Jan Fethke, from a character created by Norbert Jacques); ph, Karl Lob; ed, Walter Wischniewsky; m, Bert Grund, Gerhard Becker; art d, Erich Kettelhut, Johannes Ott; cos, Ina Stein

Noted German director Lang returned to his native land to make his last film, a fine, low-budget sequel to his prewar films dealing with the notorious Dr. Mabuse, DR. MABUSE DER SPIELER (1922) and THE TESTAMENT OF DR. MABUSE (made in 1932, but not released in the U.S. until 1943). Lang had fled Germany after Hitler, impressed with Lang's METROPOLIS, offered him a position as the official Nazi filmmaker. (Lang expected the offer to be a trap and feared the Nazis would learn of his mother's Jewish background.) Lang went to France, where he directed one film. In 1934, in London, he was signed by producer David O. Selznick to a one-picture deal with MGM. He sailed to the U.S. and became a citizen in 1935. Taking his inspiration from an actual Nazi blueprint on how to bug a hotel, Lang fashioned this story about a series of strange murders in Berlin's fictional Hotel Luxor. Authorities come to believe the man behind the crimes may be someone who believes he is a reincarnation

of the evil Dr. Mabuse. Van Eyck is an American millionaire who saves Addams from killing herself at the Luxor, and the two become involved in the investigation. Frobe (later of GOLDFINGER) is the police commissioner who thinks that either Preiss or Peters is the killer. Preiss is a supposedly blind clairvoyant, and Peters is an insurance salesman. Lang fills his eerie tale with a tightly controlled *mise-en-scene*, a world of hidden cameras, two-way mirrors, and mistaken impressions. This film, which was dubbed into English for American release, is pure cinema, using camera angle, shot composition, and lighting to achieve an overwhelming power that stays long after the final reel goes through the projector. Five sequels followed in the wake of this film's enormous popularity: THE RETURN OF DR. MABUSE (1961); SCOTLAND YARD HUNTS DR. MABUSE (1963); DR. MABUSE'S RAYS OF DEATH (1964); THE INVISIBLE DR. MABUSE (1965) and THE TERROR OF DR. MABUSE (1965).

THREAT, THE
1949 66m bw Crime ★★★★
RKO (U.S.)

Michael O'Shea *(Williams)*, Virginia Grey *(Carol)*, Charles McGraw *(Kluger)*, Julie Bishop *(Ann)*, Frank Conroy *(Mac)*, Robert Shayne *(Murphy)*, Anthony Caruso *(Nick)*, Don McGuire *(Joe Turner)*, Frank Richards *(Lefty)*, Michael McHale *(Jensen)*

p, Hugh King; d, Felix Feist; w, Hugh King, Dick Irving Hyland (based on a story by King); ph, Harry Wild; ed, Samuel E. Beetley; m, Paul Sawtell; art d, Albert S. D'Agostino, Charles F. Pyke

Despite its B-movie budget, THE THREAT is an exciting, tightly controlled film that never lets its audience down. McGraw is a vicious killer who breaks out of prison and is determined to get even with everyone responsible for putting him there. He kidnaps O'Shea, the cop who arrested him; Conroy, the district attorney who convicted him; and Grey, the nightclub singer McGraw is convinced ratted on him in the first place. Shayne is the cop who must stop McGraw and rescue the hostages. The film becomes a violent cat-and-mouse game among the principals, with tension that doesn't let up. The performances are also excellent. McGraw is the quintessential psychotic, drawing his character well and making him terrifyingly believable. The direction pays close attention to all details, from police investigations to tense confrontations. It's films like this that the writers and directors of the French New Wave rightfully recognized as true cinema.

THREE CABALLEROS, THE 📀
1945 70m c Animated/Musical/Children's ★★★★
Walt Disney Productions (U.S.) G

VOICES OF: Clarence Nash *(Donald Duck)*, Jose Olivera *(Joe Carioca)*, Joaquin Garay *(Panchito)*, Fred Shields, Sterling Holloway, Frank Graham, Aurora Miranda, Carmen Molina, Dora Luz, Nestor Amarale

p, Norman Ferguson; d, Norman Ferguson, Clyde Geronimi, Jack Kinney, Bill Roberts, Harold Young; w, Homer Brightman, Ernest Terrazzas, Ted Sears, Bill Peet, Ralph Wright, Elmer Plummer, Roy Williams, William Cottrell, Del Connell, James Bodrero; ph, Ray Rennahan (Technicolor); ed, John Haliday; art d, Richard Irvine; chor, Billy Daniels, Aloysio Oliveira, Carmelita Maracci; anim, Ward Kimball, Eric Larson, Fred Moore, John Lounsbery, Les Clark, Milt Kahl, Hal King, Franklin Thomas, Harvey Toombs, Bob Carlson, John Sibley, Bill Justice, Oliver M. Johnston Jr., Milt Neil, Marvin Woodward, John Patterson

AAN Best Score (Musical): Edward Plumb, Paul J. Smith, Charles Wolcott; *AAN Best Sound Recording:* C.O. Slyfield

A smashing follow-up to SALUDOS AMIGOS, this is one of the most dazzling achievements of the cartoon genre. Donald Duck opens presents on his birthday, the first of which is a movie projector. He puts film on the projector and we are plunged into the tale of Pablo the Penguin, who is sick and tired of the Antarctic cold and wants to live in the tropics, and a story about a little Mexican boy who finds a donkey with wings. Donald's next present is a large book. The moment he opens it, up pops Joe Carioca (from SALUDOS AMIGOS), then we're off on one of the fastest-moving cartoon sequences ever devised, as the two travel to Brazil, where Donald meets and falls in love with Aurora Miranda (in a huge production number that's as elaborate as anything Busby Berkeley ever choreographed). A breakneck trip around Mexico follows, during which Donald, Joe, and Panchito the rooster cavort with beautiful women and dance with animated plants (as well as with Carmen Molina, who does her trademark "Jesusita" number). THREE CABALLEROS also includes the famous sequence in which Donald gets into the soundtrack, represented by a moving line. So much more happens on-screen that no synopsis of this fast and funny picture will begin to do it justice. A must for all ages.

THREE CAME HOME   DVD
1950 106m bw War   ★★★★
Fox   (U.S.)

Claudette Colbert *(Agnes Keith)*, Patric Knowles *(Harry Keith)*, Florence Desmond *(Betty Sommers)*, Sessue Hayakawa *(Col. Suga)*, Sylvia Andrew *(Henrietta)*, Mark Keuning *(George)*, Phyllis Morris *(Sister Rose)*, Howard Chuman *(Lt. Nekata)*, Drue Mallory, Virginia Keiley

p, Nunnally Johnson; d, Jean Negulesco; w, Nunnally Johnson (based on a book by Agnes Newton Keith); ph, Milton Krasner; ed, Dorothy Spencer; m, Hugo Friedhofer; art d, Lyle Wheeler, Leland Fuller

A powerful and moving picture that examines life in a Japanese POW camp from a woman's point of view. Colbert plays American writer Agnes Newton Keith, who is married to British administrator Knowles. They live in the East Indian islands and, shortly after the outbreak of WWII, are arrested along with other noncombatants, then imprisoned in a concentration camp. They are given paltry food rations, as well as beatings and other humiliations. Colbert refuses to lose her spirit and, at one point, risks punishment to spend a few minutes with her husband. Hayakawa is the U.S.-educated Japanese colonel who runs the camp, a man torn between obedience to orders and the dictates of his conscience. The prisoners, including children, fight to maintain a semblance of dignity, hoping to survive until the GIs arrive. Based on Keith's autobiography, this film ably develops the intricate relationships among its characters. Colbert is stunning in the lead; Hayakawa, a former silent-film actor, creates a character of high intensity and internal struggle. A fine film in all departments.

THREE COINS IN THE FOUNTAIN   DVD
1954 101m c   Romance   ★★★
Fox   (U.S.)

Clifton Webb *(Shadwell)*, Dorothy McGuire *(Miss Francis)*, Jean Peters *(Anita)*, Louis Jourdan *(Prince Dino Di Cessi)*, Maggie McNamara *(Maria)*, Rossano Brazzi *(Georgio)*, Howard St. John *(Burgoyne)*, Kathryn Givney *(Mrs. Burgoyne)*, Cathleen Nesbitt *(Principessa)*, Vincent Padula *(Dr. Martinelli)*

p, Sol C. Siegel; d, Jean Negulesco; w, John Patrick (based on the novel by John H. Secondari); ph, Milton Krasner (CinemaScope, DeLuxe Color); ed, William Reynolds; m, Victor Young; art d, Lyle Wheeler, John De Cuir; cos, Dorothy Jeakins

AAN Best Picture; AA Best Color Cinematography: Milton Krasner; *AA Best Song:* "Three Coins in a Fountain"; Jule Styne (Music), Sammy Cahn (Lyrics)

This pleasant boy-meets-girl story (times three) is more distinguished for its photography and title song than for its predictable plot. This was the first CinemaScope picture ever made on location, and Rome and Venice never looked better. Peters, McGuire, and McNamara are a trio of American women living in Rome in a posh apartment. A legend states that if you throw a coin into the Fountain of Trevi and you want to come back to the Eternal City, your wish will be granted. McNamara had come to work as a secretary and meets Italian prince Jourdan, whose mother, Nesbitt, is watching out that some gold digger doesn't snap him up. McNamara is naive but also sharp in some ways and eventually captures Jourdan as her own. McGuire is a quiet older woman who works as the secretary to Webb, an American writer who prefers living in Rome. She finally convinces Webb that she should be his life's companion and the final scene between the two, as she goes wading in the Trevi Fountain, is a lovely moment. Peters is a high-powered executive who has had it with the board rooms and now wants to find a simpler existence. She falls for Brazzi—a wolf who haunts the Via Veneto—and by the time the movie is over, he's donned sheep's clothing, for real. That's about it for the story. There are the customary romantic complications, but the conclusion is as easy to spot as an elephant at a mouse picnic. There are a few sexy (for the time) lines of dialogue but a general feeling of traditional romance sweetens the tales. The same director, Negulesco, handled another movie about a trio of women on the make, HOW TO MARRY A MILLIONAIRE. It was later remade, sort of, as THE PLEASURE SEEKERS with Negulesco again directing.

THREE COMRADES
1938 100m bw Drama   ★★★★
MGM   (U.S.)

Robert Taylor *(Erich Lohkamp)*, Margaret Sullavan *(Pat Hollmann)*, Franchot Tone *(Otto Koster)*, Robert Young *(Gottfried Lenz)*, Guy Kibbee *(Alfons)*, Lionel Atwill *(Franz Breuer)*, Henry Hull *(Dr. Heinrich Becker)*, George Zucco *(Dr. Plauten)*, Charley Grapewin *(Local Doctor)*, Monty Woolley *(Dr. Jaffe)*

p, Joseph L. Mankiewicz; d, Frank Borzage; w, F. Scott Fitzgerald, Edward E. Paramore (based on the novel by Erich Maria Remarque); ph, Joseph Ruttenberg; ed, Frank Sullivan; m, Franz Waxman; art d, Cedric Gibbons, Paul Groesse

AAN Best Actress: Margaret Sullavan

Erich Maria Remarque's international best-seller was brought to the screen here with a stellar cast and a script cowritten by F. Scott Fitzgerald. The scene is post-WWI Germany, a time and place of want and astronomical inflation, where Deutschmarks are borne to the marketplace in wheelbarrows to be exchanged for a beefsteak. Three returning German soldiers—Taylor, Tone, and Young—are among the many war-weary, now homeless, hopeless young men who travel from the trenches of France to their war-ravaged homeland. Prewar friends, the three reunite and decide to try their luck in the republic-to-be's emerging automobile market, pooling their meager resources to set up a repair shop. Working with bits and pieces of salvaged wrecks, they put together a car of their own—which they affectionately dub "Heinrich"—and scramble for business in the intensely competitive field. Motoring on a highway, the three engage in an informal race with the owner of a shiny new automobile, Atwill. Victorious, they stop to eat at an inn and are joined by the vanquished Atwill. Saying, "You wiped me off the map!" Atwill admires their scrap-heap amalgam and introduces them to his driving companion, the lovely Sullavan. The travelers dine together, and Taylor persuades Sullavan to give him her telephone number. He renews the acquaintance the following day, visiting her in the elegant apartment in which Atwill has established the beauty, a child of wealth now reduced to poverty. Sullavan ultimately joins the trio of comrades, but is reluctant to marry Taylor because she suffers from tuberculosis. Eventually, she is persuaded by Taylor's two friends to live what remains of her life to the fullest, and she and Taylor wed amidst the ominous setting of an unstable, pre-Hitler Germany. Young is killed in a street riot; Sullavan, refusing further treatment for her malady, hastens her own demise. As the film ends, Tone and Taylor—joined by the spirits of their late companions (in double exposure)—face a most uncertain future.

Sullavan is superb in this bleak drama, her throaty voice and striking looks at their very best. (She was to gain an Oscar nomination for her role and was named the year's best actress by the New York Film Critics Association.) The actress was a bit difficult during filming, however. According to a long-standing superstition, she refused to work until a rainfall occurred, and she also protested that some of coscripter Fitzgerald's dialogue was unspeakable. Producer Mankiewicz agreed with his star and, with the help of other studio writers, rewrote and excised much of the script, to Fitzgerald's great disgruntlement and later vilification of Mankiewicz. In fact, Mankiewicz was himself a talented screenwriter and understood far better than the proud novelist the basic elements of a good visual presentation. (Other scenes were edited out for less obvious reasons, among them several that concerned the rise of Naziism. Objections were raised by the Breen Office—the industry's self-censorship group—and the film was also cut as a result of studio chief Louis B. Mayer's reluctance to offend the Germans and lose the export market.) Although he continued to write screenplays, and was even signed by the studio at the enormously high salary (for the time) of $1,250 weekly, this was to be Fitzgerald's only *credited* screenwriting assignment. Sullavan's leading man, Taylor, is unconvincing in his role, which he had not wanted to play. Cinemogul Mayer had to persuade the actor that the part would lend him prestige and help to erase the pretty-boy image he had developed over the course of his career. The picture is well directed by romance-drama specialist Borzage, but overlong, and only partly redeemed by Sullavan's splendid performance.

THREE CROWNS OF THE SAILOR
(LES TROIS COURONNES DU MATELOT)
1983 117m c/bw Fantasy   ★★★
L'Institut de l'Audiovisuel/Antenne 2   (France)

Jean-Bernard Guillard *(The Sailor)*, Philippe Deplanche *(The Student)*, Jean Badin *(The Officer)*, Nadege Clair *(Maria)*, Lisa Lyon *(Mathilde)*, Claude Derepp *(The Captain)*, Frank Oger *(The Blindman)*, Raoul Guillet, Hugo Santiago *(Voices)*, Jose De Carvalho

p, Jean Lefaux, Maya Feuiette, Jose-Luis Vasconselos; d, Raul Ruiz; w, Raul Ruiz, Emilio de Solar, Francois Ede; ph, Sacha Vierny; ed, Janine Verneau, Valeria Sarmiento, Jacqueline Simoni-Adamus, Pascale Sueur; m, Jorge Arriagada

A strongly praised work of surrealism from expatriate Chilean director Ruiz—living and working in France since 1973—about a story-telling sailor, Guillard, who catches a student murdering his tutor. He proceeds to regale the lad with tales of his bizarre adventures in South American ports visiting the seedy opium dens and frequenting the brothels. It's not what happens in THREE CROWNS OF THE SAILOR but how it happens. Following the tradition of surrealism set in the 1920s, Ruiz directs this film with no basis in logic or reality—

dreamy locations are filled with macabre individuals speaking mystical nonsense. As difficult as it is to pin down, THREE CROWNS OF THE SAILOR is thoroughly enjoyable just as long as you don't try to understand it.

THREE DAYS OF THE CONDOR   DVD
1975 117m c   Thriller   ★★★½
Wildwood/Paramount   (U.S.)   R

Robert Redford *(Joe Turner)*, Faye Dunaway *(Kathy Hale)*, Cliff Robertson *(Higgins)*, Max von Sydow *(Joubert)*, John Houseman *(Mr. Wabash)*, Addison Powell *(Atwood)*, Walter McGinn *(Sam Barber)*, Tina Chen *(Janice)*, Michael Kane *(Wicks)*, Don McHenry *(Dr. Lappe)*

p, Stanley Schneider; d, Sydney Pollack; w, Lorenzo Semple Jr., David Rayfiel (based on the novel *Six Days of the Condor* by James Grady); ph, Owen Roizman (Panavision, Technicolor); ed, Fredric Steinkamp, Don Guidice; m, Dave Grusin; prod d, Stephen Grimes; art d, Gene Rudolf; fx, Augie Lohman; cos, Joseph G. Aulisi

AAN Best Film Editing: Fredric Steinkamp, Don Guidice

Redford is the bookish and bespectacled reader for the Literary Historical Society, but the organization actually serves as a CIA front located in a brownstone in Manhattan. One day he goes out to get lunch for the others (it's his turn), and while he's picking up the food, killers armed with automatic weapons enter the building and massacre everyone there. Redford returns with lunch and finds all his coworkers murdered. Fearing that he may be next, he goes to a phone booth and calls headquarters, identifying himself by his code name, "Condor." He is told to meet an agent at a nearby hotel, but when the fellow CIA man tries to kill him, Redford realizes his own organization is responsible for the slaughter. Determined to survive and to blow the whistle on the CIA, Redford kidnaps woman photographer Dunaway and forces her to help him. Based on James Grady's novel *Six Days of the Condor* (the film compresses the time frame of the novel), this taut espionage thriller gained greater plausibility during its shooting when a sudden raft of sensational post-Watergate news items began coming out of Washington regarding illegal wiretaps, surveillance, and killings motivated by political expediency. What was once merely a fanciful exploitation of antigovernment paranoia, became a thrilling pseudo-expose on the corrupt inner workings of covert organizations. The public ate it up and the film was a hit at the box office.

THREE FACES OF EVE, THE   DVD
1957 91m bw Drama   ★★★
Fox   (U.S.)

Joanne Woodward *(Eve)*, David Wayne *(Ralph White)*, Lee J. Cobb *(Dr. Luther)*, Edwin Jerome *(Dr. Day)*, Alena Murray *(Secretary)*, Nancy Kulp *(Mrs. Black)*, Douglas Spencer *(Mr. Black)*, Terry Ann Ross *(Bonnie)*, Ken Scott *(Earl)*, Mimi Gibson *(Eve)*

p, Nunnally Johnson; d, Nunnally Johnson; w, Nunnally Johnson (based on a book by Corbett H. Thigpen, M.D., and Hervey M. Cleckley, M.D.); ph, Stanley Cortez; ed, Marjorie Fowler; m, Robert Emmett Dolan; art d, Lyle Wheeler, Herman A. Blumenthal; cos, Renie

AA Best Actress: Joanne Woodward

Joanne Woodward's showy but nonetheless highly impressive performance in the tile role required her to play three roles with enough separation in the characterizations to make the audience believe she was a woman with a trio of personalities bubbling inside her. Woodward is married to Wayne, an insensitive clod. She is emotionally disturbed, has headaches, and forgets things, so she decides she needs the professional help of a psychiatrist, although Wayne thinks she's faking it. At first, Cobb, the doctor, gives her the usual advice: get more rest, try to calm down, etc. Woodward goes home to Wayne and her daughter, Ross, but her mental woes continue. She returns to Cobb's office later, but instead of being an unsure housewife, she is suddenly a loose woman with an attitude of total irresponsibility. She denies being the mother of Ross and lives for hedonistic pleasure. Wayne is rapidly getting disgusted with Woodward, but Cobb is intrigued when one of Woodward's personality switches occurs while she's in his presence. Eventually, a third person emerges. This one is a well-balanced woman who speaks in a different pattern. Whereas the first two talk in southern dialect, this one sounds as though she went to Cornell and graduated *summa cum laude*. Cobb uses hypnotic techniques on Woodward and is able to conjure up each "face" by merely suggesting that she step forward. The next step is to try to merge the three faces of Eve.

It's an interesting psychological tale that is not without humor, much of which is supplied by the witty narration of Alistair Cooke. The movie is based on a true story, documented by the psychiatrists who treated the woman in real life, but the ultimate solution as represented is both too simplistic and underexplained. The film is basically a two-character piece featuring Woodward and Cobb and probably would have made a very good play. Cinematically, it's lacking on several levels. Wayne, a marvelous actor, was apparently directed to play his role for laughs in order to take the edge off Woodward's dramatics. The mixture of styles works against the ultimate outcome.

THREE GODFATHERS, THE
1948 106m c Western ★★★★
Argosy (U.S.)

John Wayne *(Robert Marmaduke Hightower)*, Pedro Armendariz *(Pedro "Pete" Roca Fuerte)*, Harry Carey Jr. *(William Kearney, "The Abilene Kid")*, Ward Bond *(Perley "Buck" Sweet)*, Mildred Natwick *(The Mother)*, Charles Halton *(Mr. Latham)*, Jane Darwell *(Miss Florie)*, Mae Marsh *(Mrs. Perley Sweet)*, Guy Kibbee *(Judge)*, Dorothy Ford *(Ruby Latham)*

p, John Ford, Merian C. Cooper; d, John Ford; w, Laurence Stallings, Frank S. Nugent (based on the story by Peter B. Kyne); ph, Winton C. Hoch (Technicolor); ed, Jack Murray; m, Richard Hageman; art d, James Basevi

John Ford's THE THREE GODFATHERS is a wonderful, sentimental western about a bad man who redeems himself. It is also a tribute to Ford's mentor and friend, actor Harry Carey, who died in 1947. The film follows a trio of outlaws—Robert Marmaduke Hightower (John Wayne), "Pete" Roca Fuerte (Pedro Armendariz), and "The Abilene Kid" (Harry Carey, Jr.)—who flee a posse after robbing the bank at Welcome. After losing their horses in a desert sandstorm, they arrive at Terrapin Tanks, where they find an abandoned woman in labor. After giving birth, the dying woman (Mildred Natwick) begs the men to save her baby, and they agree, deciding to bring it to the nearby town of New Jerusalem—a hazardous journey with a biblical analogy not lost on the outlaws. Only Hightower makes it, however, stumbling into New Jerusalem with the baby on Christmas Eve. Later, the sheriff of Welcome (Ward Bond) offers to drop the charges if the outlaw will give up custody of the baby, but Hightower's response shouldn't surprise anyone. Ford first filmed this story in 1919 as MARKED MEN with Harry Carey, who also appeared in the first version of the story, THREE GODFATHERS, in 1916. This version, Ford's first color film, begins as a silhouetted cowboy astride Carey's favorite horse rides to the top of a hill,

pushing his hat back on his head as the words "Dedicated to Harry Carey, a bright star in the early western sky" appear.

THREE KINGS
1999 115m c War/Comedy/Drama *DVD*
Coast Ridge/Atlas Entertainment (U.S.) ★★★★ R

George Clooney *(Archie Gates)*, Mark Wahlberg *(Troy Barlow)*, Ice Cube *(Chief Elgin)*, Nora Dunn *(Adrianna Cruz)*, Jamie Kennedy *(Walter Wogaman)*, Mykelti Williamson *(Colonel Horn)*, Cliff Curtis *(Amir Abdullah)*, Said Taghmaoui *(Captain Said)*, Spike Jonze *(Conrad Vig)*, Holt McCallany *(Captain Van Meter)*

p, Charles Roven, Paul Junger Witt, Edward L. McDonnell; d, David O. Russell; w, David O. Russell (based on a story by John Ridley); ph, Thomas Newton Sigel; ed, Robert K. Lambert; m, Carter Burwell; prod d, Catherine Hardwicke; art d, Jann K. Engel, Derek R. Hill; fx, Martin Bresin; cos, Kym Barrett

An astonishing movie that keeps you off-balance from the very first scene. It starts out a wisecracking, cynical action lark about four Gulf War GIs and ends up a sad, resigned indictment of American foreign policy wrapped in a moving story of personal sacrifice and small, compromised victories. And the whole thing is mordantly funny to boot.

Sgt. Troy Barlow (Mark Wahlberg) and enlisted men Chief (Ice Cube) and Vig (Spike Jonze) come into possession of a map that shows the location of a bunker full of gold. With the help of thoroughly disaffected special-forces operative Major Archie Gates (George Clooney), they decide to make it their own going-away present. "Saddam stole it from the sheiks. I have no problem stealing it from him," says Gates by way of clearing up the heist's ethical dimension, pointing out that amid the post-cease-fire pandemonium, no one will notice or care what they're doing.

Naturally, it doesn't go as easily as they anticipate. Surprisingly, they get sucked into helping a group of anti-Saddam Iraqi refugees who know their only hope of post-war survival lies in fleeing the country before the American military pulls out. The GIs are fairly decent guys, in a lazy kind of way, capable of pretending that wrong is right until somehow utter bloody chaos marches them, one baby step at a time, into doing the right thing at the moment when it stands to cost them the most. This is an amazing leap for writer-director David O. Russell, who graduates from sharply observed, small-scale stories about screwed-up families (FLIRTING WITH DISASTER) to a thought-provoking dispatch from a profoundly screwed-up world.

THREE LITTLE WORDS
1950 102m c Biography/Musical ★★★★
MGM (U.S.)

Fred Astaire *(Bert Kalmar)*, Red Skelton *(Harry Ruby)*, Vera-Ellen *(Jessie Brown Kalmar)*, Arlene Dahl *(Eileen Percy)*, Keenan Wynn *(Charlie Kope)*, Gale Robbins *(Terry Lordel)*, Gloria DeHaven *(Mrs. Carter DeHaven)*, Phil Regan *(Himself)*, Harry Shannon *(Clanahan)*, Debbie Reynolds *(Helen Kane)*

p, Jack Cummings; d, Richard Thorpe; w, George Wells (based on the lives and songs of Bert Kalmar and Harry Ruby); ph, Harry Jackson (Technicolor); ed, Ben Lewis; art d, Cedric Gibbons, Urie McCleary; chor, Hermes Pan

AAN Best Score (Musical): Andre Previn

An utter delight, this musical biography portrays the lives of composers Bert Kalmar (Fred Astaire) and Harry Ruby (Red Skelton). Kalmar is a vaudeville song-and-dance man and would-be magician who turns to writing lyrics after a knee injury puts an end to his dancing. Ruby plays the piano at a Coney Island honky-tonk and also writes lyrics, though he dreams of playing baseball. Eventually, the two meet, and a great songwriting team is born; they go on to write numerous hits for Broadway and the movies. A misunderstanding ends the partnership, but Kalmar's wife, Jessie (Vera-Ellen), and Ruby's wife, Eileen (Arlene Dahl), finally bring the two men back together for a happy, if somewhat fictionalized, conclusion. For the most part, though, this movie sticks to the facts, and it never fails to entertain. Astaire is as suave as usual and dances a couple numbers with Vera-Ellen, while Skelton gives one of the best performances of his career. The film is sparked by wonderful supporting work by Vera-Ellen and Dahl. Appearing as themselves in cameo roles are Phil Regan and Harry Mendoza. Ruby himself served as technical advisor.

3 MEN AND A BABY

1987 99m c Comedy ★★½
Touchstone/Silver Screen Partners III/Jean PG
Francois Lepetit/Interscope (U.S.)

Tom Selleck (Peter Mitchell), Steve Guttenberg (Michael Kellam), Ted Danson (Jack Holden), Nancy Travis (Sylvia), Margaret Colin (Rebecca), Lisa Blair, Michelle Blair (Mary, the Baby), Celeste Holm (Mrs. Holden), Philip Bosco (Detective Melkowitz), Derek De Lint (Jan Clopatz)

p, Ted Field, Robert W. Cort, Edward Teets; d, Leonard Nimoy; w, James Orr, Jim Cruickshank (based on the French film TROIS HOMMES ET UN COUFFIN by Coline Serreau); ph, Adam Greenberg (Deluxe Color); ed, Michael A. Stevenson; m, Marvin Hamlisch; prod d, Peter Larkin; art d, Dan Yarhi; fx, Michael Kavanagh; cos, Larry Wells

Peter Mitchell (Tom Selleck), Jack Holden (Ted Danson), and Michael Kellam (Steve Guttenberg) are three swinging bachelors who share an opulent penthouse apartment in Manhattan. Their unfettered existence is quickly thrown into turmoil, however, when they're forced to care for a baby girl who unexpectedly turns up on their doorstep. Relentless in its pursuit of "cute," this comedy (a remake of the French film TROIS HOMMES ET UN COUFFIN) proved enormously popular at the box office. The leads acquit themselves fairly well, but the biggest winner is Selleck, whose low-key charm and gift for light comedy are put to good use here.

THREE MEN AND A CRADLE

(TROIS HOMMES ET UN COUFFIN)
1985 100m c Comedy ★★★
Flach/TF1/Soprofilm (France) PG-13

Roland Giraud (Pierre), Michel Boujenah (Michel), Andre Dussollier (Jacques), Philippine Leroy Beaulieu (Sylvia), Dominique Lavanant (Madame Rapons), Marthe Villalonga (Antoinette), Annick Alane (Pharmacist)

p, Jean-Francois Lepetit; d, Coline Serreau; w, Coline Serreau; ph, Jean-Yves Escoffier; ed, Catherine Renault; m, Franz Schubert; art d, Ivan Maussion

AAN Best Foreign Language Film

An engaging French comedy about three bachelors who find an abandoned baby at their door (a plot line direct from John Ford's THREE GODFATHERS). Though many of jokes are familiar and the outcome easily predictable, the picture scored an Oscar nomination as Best Foreign-Language Film (it lost to THE OFFICIAL STORY) and French Cesars for Best Picture, Best Screenplay, and Best Supporting Actor (Michel Boujenah). The film begins with the arrival of a baby in a basket before the closed door of goofy roommates Jacques (Andre Dussollier), Pierre (Roland Giraud), and Michel (Boujenah), one of whom, it turns out, is the unwitting father. The men become increasingly attached to the

cute little bundle and soon become jealous of one another's paternalism. Things take a more complex turn when Jacques hides a smuggled cache of heroin in the baby's diapers, and the trio gets drawn into a drug-dealing subplot. The most popular picture in France during the 1985-86 film year (handily beating out such contenders as RAMBO II; OUT OF AFRICA; ROCKY IV; and BACK TO THE FUTURE), THREE MEN AND A CRADLE was also, of course, the movie that inspired the 1987 Hollywood remake THREE MEN AND A BABY, which performed similar magic at the box office.

THREE MUSKETEERS, THE

1948 126m c Adventure/Comedy ★★★★
MGM (U.S.)

Lana Turner (Countess Charlotte de Winter), Gene Kelly (D'Artagnan), June Allyson (Constance Bonacieux), Van Heflin (Robert Athos), Angela Lansbury (Queen Anne), Frank Morgan (King Louis XIII), Vincent Price (Richelieu the Prime Minister), Keenan Wynn (Planchet), John Sutton (George), Gig Young (Porthos)

p, Pandro S. Berman; d, George Sidney; w, Robert Ardrey (based on the novel by Alexandre Dumas); ph, Robert Planck (Technicolor); ed, Robert J. Kern, George Boemler; m, Herbert Stothart; art d, Cedric Gibbons, Malcolm Brown; fx, Warren Newcombe; cos, Walter Plunkett

AAN Best Color Cinematography: Robert Planck

THE THREE MUSKETEERS is a rollicking version of the oft-filmed Dumas classic, with Gene Kelly playing the role of D'Artagnan with great panache. The film opens as D'Artagnan leaves his country home for Paris, to join the famed Musketeers. He proves his ability in a duel with Athos (Van Heflin) and adopts the "one for all and all for one" motto, joining the Musketeers in serving King Louis XIII (Frank Morgan). Prime Minister Richelieu (Vincent Price) plots to end the king's reign, enlisting Louis's mistress, Lady de Winter (Lana Turner), in his evil scheme. The Musketeers, however, are not about to let that happen.

Kelly is a sheer delight, attacking the swashbuckling story with enormous zest. His acrobatics are a sight to behold, a marvelous extension of his much loved dancing skills. This was Kelly's favorite role in his nonmusical films, and he had hoped his performance here would convince MGM to let him do a musical version of "Cyrano de Bergerac." Alas, it didn't. The supporting cast is marvelous, especially Morgan in a wonderful portrayal of King Louis XIII.

THREE MUSKETEERS, THE

1973 105m c Adventure/Comedy ★★★★
Fox (U.K.) PG

Oliver Reed (Athos), Raquel Welch (Constance), Richard Chamberlain (Aramis), Michael York (D'Artagnan), Frank Finlay (Porthos), Christopher Lee (Rochefort), Jean-Pierre Cassel (Louis XIII), Geraldine Chaplin (Anne of Austria), Simon Ward (Duke of Buckingham), Faye Dunaway (Milady)

p, Michael Alexander, Ilya Salkind; d, Richard Lester; w, George MacDonald Fraser (based on the novel by Alexander Dumas); ph, David Watkin; ed, John Victor Smith; m, Michel Legrand; cos, Yvonne Blake, Ron Talsky

The oft-told tale by Dumas gets a terrific rendering here. York is a happy rustic youth, a bit of a bumbler, but with such high spirits that he is instantly lovable. He would like to become part of the Musketeers, the leaders of whom are Reed, Chamberlain, and Finlay, a trio more intrigued by cleavage and cash than by any sort of loyalty to their king, Cassel, who is, at best, an idiot. Cassel's wife is Chaplin, a duplicitous queen who is having a royal fling with Ward, a peer of England. Evil cardinal Charlton Heston learns of the affair and plans to use it to destroy the queen, opening the door for him to assume a more influential role with the king. He enlists the aid of the adventurous and ambitious Dunaway in his scheme. Meanwhile, the Musketeers have taken a liking to York, and he has fallen in love with Welch, Chaplin's best friend and lady-in-waiting. She is on to Heston's plot and tells York about it, and the four swordsmen set out to foil Heston's scheme. In the past, the story had been so trifled with by filmmakers that it seldom resembled what Dumas had written. Here, writer Fraser and director Lester went back to the original and hewed closely to the source material, but adding a lot of fun. Some good slapstick combines with moments of real drama and menace to make this movie a winner. The producer, Salkind, paid the cast for one picture but shot two at the same time without telling them. In 1975, Salkind brought out a sequel, THE FOUR MUSKETEERS, and the cast banded together to sue the producer for more wages. They were awarded a considerable sum, though not nearly as much as if they'd been hired to make two movies. Despite glowing reviews, the movie did not knock audiences over at the box office, although it turned a tidy profit after all the receipts were counted.

THREE SMART GIRLS *DVD*
1936 86m   bw   Musical/Comedy   ★★★★
Universal   (U.S.)

Deanna Durbin *(Penny Craig)*, Binnie Barnes *(Donna Lyons)*, Alice Brady *(Mrs. Lyons)*, Ray Milland *(Lord Michael Stuart)*, Charles Winninger *(Judson Craig)*, Mischa Auer *(Count Arisztid)*, Nan Grey *(Joan Craig)*, Barbara Read *(Kay Craig)*, Ernest Cossart *(Binns the Butler)*, Hobart Cavanaugh *(Wilbur Lamb)*

p, Joe Pasternak; d, Henry Koster; w, Adele Comandini, Austin Parker (based on the story by Adele Comandini); ph, Joseph Valentine; ed, Ted J. Kent; art d, John Harkrider; cos, John Harkrider

AAN Best Picture; AAN Best Original Story: Adele Commandini; *AAN Best Sound Recording:* Homer G. Tasker

In her film debut, 14-year-old singing sensation Deanna Durbin is cast as Penny Craig, one of three sisters who try to keep their father from marrying a gold digger. Penny is the devoted matchmaker who tries everything to bring about their parents' reconciliation before her father exchanges vows with his new love. By the picture's finale, Penny's efforts have been all too successful—her sisters have found prospective husbands, and her mother and father have rekindled their romance. Penny is still single, however, though thoroughly content with everyone's newfound happiness.

A highly pleasing first cousin to the screwball comedies of the day, THREE SMART GIRLS wisely centers on Durbin, a wonderful singer and a genuinely charming screen personality. The film earned Academy Award nominations for Best Picture (losing to THE GREAT ZIEGFELD), Best Original Story, and Best Sound. It spawned two sequels, THREE SMART GIRLS GROW UP, and HERS TO HOLD, both starring Durbin. There was also a remake, THREE DARING DAUGHTERS, which put Jane Powell in the Durbin role.

3:10 TO YUMA *DVD*
1957 92m   bw   Western   ★★★½
Columbia   (U.S.)

Van Heflin *(Dan Evans)*, Glenn Ford *(Ben Wade)*, Felicia Farr *(Emmy)*, Leora Dana *(Alice Evans)*, Henry Jones *(Alex Potter)*, Richard Jaeckel *(Charlie Prince)*, Robert Emhardt *(Mr. Butterfield)*, Sheridan Comerate *(Bob Moons)*, George Mitchell *(Bartender)*, Robert Ellenstein *(Ernie Collins)*

p, David Heilweil; d, Delmer Daves; w, Halsted Welles (based on the story by Elmore Leonard); ph, Charles Lawton Jr.; ed, Al Clark; m, George Duning; art d, Frank Hotaling; cos, Jean Louis

This fine western opens with Heflin as a rancher whose family is suffering from the devastating effects of a long drought. Heflin needs $200 to build a well, then learns he can obtain the money as a reward for delivering Ford, a notorious outlaw now in the hands of the law, to the state prison in Yuma, Arizona. Though this will put Heflin in great personal danger, the peaceful man accepts the assignment, knowing what the money will mean to his family. Heflin and Ford hole up in a small hotel in another town while waiting for the train to Yuma. The outlaw begins toying with Heflin's mind, talking in a friendly manner about Heflin's job and financial situation. Playing psychological games, Ford tries to convince Heflin to take $10,000 to look the other way while he escapes. Heflin finds himself in a quandary, desperately needing the money yet being bound by his word to carry out the job. Ford's gang, led by Jaeckel, discovers where their leader is hidden and sets out to rescue him. The town officials abandon Heflin rather than put themselves in danger, leaving the troubled rancher alone to face off with the outlaws. Ford ends up assisting Heflin, helping his captor on to the 3:10 to Yuma, explaining: "I owed you that." Heflin has come through the ordeal, body and integrity intact, and, as if in answer to this baptism by fire, the skies burst forth with rain, putting an end to the drought.

Much like HIGH NOON, this film deals with a man alone after town officials have passed on their duties, leaving him to face both his adversaries and his conscience. Daves's direction is gritty, confining much of the story to the small hotel room, with a hard-hitting use of close-ups. His outdoor sequences are equally good, particularly the portrait of a land desperate for water. Heflin is superior in the role with his intense portrait of a man caught between personal needs and social duties. Ford is equally good, mixing amiable feelings with monstrous qualities. This is a landmark western, redefining what the genre was capable of doing, and is one of Daves's best works.

3 WOMEN *DVD*
1977 122m   c   Drama   ★★★★
Lion's Gate   (U.S.)   PG

Shelley Duvall *(Millie Lammoreaux)*, Sissy Spacek *(Pinky Rose)*, Janice Rule *(Willie Hart)*, Robert Fortier *(Edgar Hart)*, Ruth Nelson *(Mrs. Rose)*, John Cromwell *(Mr. Rose)*, Sierra Pecheur *(Mr. Bunweill)*, Craig Richard Nelson *(Dr. Maas)*, Maysie Hoy *(Doris)*, Belita Moreno *(Alcira)*

p, Robert Altman; d, Robert Altman; w, Robert Altman; ph, Charles Rosher Jr.; ed, Dennis M. Hill; m, Gerald Busby; art d, James Vance; fx, Modern Film Effects

3 WOMEN is one of Robert Altman's best and most personal films as well as one of his strangest from the 1970s, his most productive period. Shelley Duvall, Sissy Spacek, and Janice Rule star as a trio whose divergent personalities first clash, then intertwine and finally merge in a complex psychological story of transference and dependence.

Newly arrived in a Southern California desert community from Texas, timid Pinky Rose (Sissy Spacek) gets a job at a rehabilitation center for the elderly. She's trained by another Texan, Millie Lammoreaux (Shelley Duvall), whom she eventually moves in with and comes to idolize, despite the fact that Millie s supposed popularity and image as a swinger is an obvious charade. Millie introduces Pinky to her friends Edgar (Robert Fortier) a former TV stuntman, and his silent, pregnant wife Willie (Janice Rule), who spends all of her time painting giant, erotically-charged tableaux. One night, after a dinner party planned by Millie is scuttled, the two roommates argue. Pinky jumps into the swimming pool and is taken to the hospital, where she lapses into a coma. When Pinky awakens from her coma, she doesn't recognize her parents and when she moves back in with Millie, she becomes the dominant one, callously ordering Millie around, sleeping with Edgar, and calling herself by her real first name, Mildred.

Numerous films are described as being "dreamlike," but 3 WOMEN, which Altman based on a dream he had about two women who meet in the desert, is one of the very few that truly is. Its mysterious story and abstract imagery possess the crystalline clarity as well as the incoherence of a dream, and it is open to myriad interpretations. Altman's films are all about layers: visual, aural, and thematic, and 3 WOMEN is one of the richest examples of that. Visually, Altman superbly employs his patented exploratory use of combination zooms and tracking shots, packing the widescreen frame with dense images in which water symbolizing the life cycle of fertility, birth, and death is prominently featured. A film such as this, which relies on mood, atmosphere, and ideas, rather than plot, depends on its acting to be effective, and the entire cast is extraordinary, with Shelley Duvall and Sissy Spacek both giving their finest performance ever. Duvall is marvelous as the self-deluded Millie, who's ignored by everyone except Pinky as she babbles on endlessly about TV commercials, recipes she s gotten from magazines and her (non-existent) social life. The actress brilliantly makes Millie a pathetic yet gallant creature, making the film itself, and her transformation into a matriarchal figure, profoundly moving.

THREEPENNY OPERA, THE
(DIE DREIGROSCHENOPER)
1931   113m   bw   Opera   ★★★
Nero/Tobis Klangfilm/Warner Bros.   (U.S./Germany)

Rudolf Forster (Mackie Messer), Carola Neher (Polly), Reinhold Schunzel (Tiger Brown), Fritz Rasp (Peachum), Valeska Gert (Mrs. Peachum), Lotte Lenya (Jenny), Herman Thimig (Vicar), Ernst Busch (Street-Singer), Vladimir Sokoloff (Smith), Paul Kemp

p, Seymour Nebenzal; d, G.W. Pabst; w, Leo Lania, Bela Balasz, Ladislas Vajda, Solange Bussi, Andre Mauprey, Ninon Steinhoff (based on the play by Bertolt Brecht, adapted from The Beggar's Opera by John Gay); ph, Fritz Arno Wagner; ed, Hans Oser, Henri Rust; m, Kurt Weill; prod d, Andre Andrejew

Less revered today than the Bertolt Brecht play or the Kurt Weill songs, G.W. Pabst's film version of "The Threepenny Opera" is still a fine example of pre-Hitler German filmmaking. In the German version available on videocassette (a French version exists with a different cast, while the planned English version was never completed), Rudolf Forster plays the infamous Mackie Messer, or Mack the Knife, an underworld gangster of the 1890s whose territory is London. A dashing and respected criminal, Mackie is best of friends with the corrupt police chief, Tiger Brown (Reinhold Schunzel). After meeting Polly (Carola Neher), Mackie decides to marry her. In a dusty underground warehouse—the room lavishly prepared with goods stolen from London's top shops—the wedding is attended by a crowd of beggars and thieves, as well as Tiger Brown. Polly, however, is the daughter of Peachum (Fritz Rasp), the king of the beggars, who strongly opposes the marriage. He puts pressure on Tiger Brown to send Mackie to the gallows, threatening to organize a beggars' revolt to disrupt the queen's upcoming coronation if the police chief does not accede to his wishes.

Based on the John Gay satire of 1728, "The Beggar's Opera," Pabst's film lacks the punch that made the Brecht-Weill collaboration so potent when it hit the stage in 1928. The sting of social criticism is lessened here, with greater emphasis placed on dramatics; in fact, Brecht was so disappointed with the director's interpretation that he ended his own work on the screenplay. What the film lacks in Brechtian qualities,

however, it makes up for in the aesthetics of Pabst. Having previously exposed the seedier side of London in the silent PANDORA'S BOX, Pabst once again brings it to the screen here in a unique mixture of realism and expressionism, taking great care to evoke the textures of London's underworld—populated by the lowest of lowlifes—in both his visuals and his soundtrack. Although there is a noticeable absence of some of Weill's tunes—"Ballad of Sexual Dependency," "The Ballad for the Hangman," and "The Tango Ballad"—the film does open and close with the Ernst Busch rendition of "Moritat," a song which became the 1957 pop music hit "Mack the Knife." Also prominently featured is "Pirate Jenny" (Brecht-Weill), delivered by the inimitable Lenya.

THRONE OF BLOOD   💿
(KUMONOSUJO)
1957   110m   bw   Drama/War   ★★★★½
Brandon   (Japan)

Toshiro Mifune (Taketoki Washizu), Isuzu Yamada (Asaji), Takashi Shimura (Noriyasu Odagura), Minoru Chiaki (Yoshaki Miki), Akira Kubo (Yoshiteru), Takamaru Sasaki (Kuniharu Tsuzuki), Yoichi Tachikawa (Kunimaru), Chieko Naniwa (Witch)

p, Akira Kurosawa, Sojiro Motoki; d, Akira Kurosawa; w, Hideo Oguni, Shinobu Hashimoto, Ryuzo Kikushima, Akira Kurosawa (based on the play "Macbeth" by William Shakespeare); ph, Asaichi Nakai (Tohoscope); ed, Akira Kurosawa; m, Masaru Sato; art d, Yoshiro Muraki, Kohei Ezaki

Kabuki Macbeth, and like nothing you've ever seen. A truly remarkable film combining beauty and terror to produce a mood of haunting power, THRONE OF BLOOD was the brilliant fulfillment of Japanese master Akira Kurosawa's longtime ambition to bring Shakespeare to Japanese audiences. Kurosawa set the story in feudal Japan, and the transposition of cultures is surprisingly successful, with all the plot elements intact. After putting down a mutinous rebellion for their lord, warriors Taketoki Washizu (Toshiro Mifune) and Yoshaki Miki (Minoru Chiaki) are called to the main castle for an audience. Riding through the dense and foggy forest that protects the warlord's castle, they encounter a mysterious old woman bathed in white light and mist. When questioned, the woman prophesies that Washizu will be given command of a castle and soon become warlord, but his reign will be brief and his throne will be occupied by his friend's son thereafter. When it appears her predictions are coming true, Washizu grows increasingly corrupted by his own ambitions. THRONE OF BLOOD is filled with unforgettable, haunting imagery. Departing from his usual (very Western) fluid camera style and fast-paced editing, Kurosawa borrowed here from the conventions of Noh theater. While the visuals are gorgeous, the compositions are static and stagy, concentrating on the emotional moment as it seems to hang in the air, unaltered by editing or camera movement. The visual and acting styles work marvelously with the material, although the film is somewhat cold and detached, containing little of the exhilarating passion found in Kurosawa's other work. Kurosawa has a lot of fun with the advance of Birnam Wood, Yamanda's Lady Macbeth is a virtuoso fright and Mifune's demise is in the most grand, outrageous Kabuki fashion. This is filmmaking with risk and greatness in its blood.

THROW MOMMA FROM THE TRAIN   💿
1987   88m   c   Comedy   ★★½
Orion   (U.S.)   PG-13

Danny DeVito (Owen Lift), Billy Crystal (Larry Donner), Anne Ramsey (Momma), Kim Greist (Beth), Kate Mulgrew (Margaret), Branford Marsalis (Lester), Rob Reiner (Joel), Bruce Kirby, Oprah Winfrey, Joey DePinto p, Larry Brezner; d, Danny DeVito; w, Stu Silver; ph, Barry Sonnenfeld (CFI Color); ed, Michael Jablow; m, David Newman; prod d, Ida Random; art d, William Elliott; cos, Marilyn Vance

AAN Best Supporting Actress: Anne Ramsey

Making a surprisingly assured directorial debut that is hampered only by a weak script, Danny DeVito stars as Owen Lift, a childlike 40-year-old bachelor whose life is totally dominated by his mean-spirited mother (Anne Ramsey). Owen meets Larry Donner (Billy Crystal), a hapless would-be writer whose ex-wife (Kate Mulgrew) ran off with his only completed manuscript, sold it as her own, and is now a millionaire. Owen gets it into his head that Larry wants to "swap" murders with him, with each committing an unmotivated crime that cannot be traced—Owen's momma for Larry's ex-wife. After beginning as a promising black comedy, THROW MOMMA FROM THE TRAIN deteriorates into a repetitive affair that betrays the brazen nastiness with which it began. DeVito does a nice job modulating his own performance, managing to evoke sympathy for his loony character. Crystal, sadly, is hampered by a script that limits him to spells of griping, whining, and full-blown hysteria.

THUNDERBALL

1965 130m c Spy ★★★
Eon (U.K.) GP

Sean Connery *(James Bond),* Claudine Auger *(Domino Derval),* Adolfo Celi *(Emilio Largo),* Luciana Paluzzi *(Fiona Volpe),* Rik Van Nutter *(Felix Leiter),* Bernard Lee *("M"),* Martine Beswicke, billed as Martine Beswick *(Paula Caplan),* Guy Doleman *(Count Lippe),* Molly Peters *(Patricia Fearing),* Desmond Llewelyn *("Q")*

p, Kevin McClory; d, Terence Young; w, Richard Maibaum, John Hopkins (based on the characters created by Ian Fleming and the story by McClory, Jack Whittingham, Fleming); ph, Ted Moore, Lamar Boren (Panavision, Technicolor); ed, Peter Hunt; m, John Barry; prod d, Ken Adam; art d, Peter Murton; fx, John Stears; cos, Anthony Mendleson

AA Best Special Visual Effects: John Stears

This relatively disappointing fourth entry in the James Bond series centers on the hijacking of a NATO bomber carrying a nuclear payload. After sweating out the effects of his louche lifestyle at a health spa, James Bond (Sean Connery) is dispatched to the sunny Bahamas, where the aircraft is hidden underwater. SPECTRE's No. 2 man, Emilio Largo (Adolfo Celi), is behind the scheme, and Bond, well-equipped with state-of-the art spy gadgetry, catches up with the villain and his equally well-equipped mistress, Domino (Auger), who eventually embraces both Bond and his cause. Bond locates the downed plane and calls in American aquaparatroops, who do underwater battle with SPECTRE scuba divers while 007 chases Largo, who flees in his yacht-turned-hydrofoil.

　　With THUNDERBALL, the wildly popular Bond series started to slip, substituting gadgets and gimmicks for story and character development. The action is reasonably well-staged, but the film is overlong and occasionally draggy. THUNDERBALL was meant to be the first in the series, but Bond creator Ian Fleming engaged in a long legal battle over the rights to his novel, eventually losing in court to Kevin McClory. However, McClory was unable to put together a workable package to turn the novel into a movie, largely because Sean Connery was by now under contract to regular Bond producers Cubby Broccoli and Harry Saltzman. Eventually, Saltzman, Broccoli, and McClory struck a deal that gave McClory the producer credit and a percentage of the profits (McClory also retained the right to

produce a remake after a 10 years had elapsed; the result was 1983's NEVER SAY NEVER AGAIN). Despite its shortcomings, the film was the top moneymaker of 1966, grossing more than any other picture in the series. Julie Christie, Raquel Welch, and Faye Dunaway—then relatively unknown players—were all considered for the role of Domino before Claudine Auger was chosen. Welch was actually signed to play the part, but Broccoli reluctantly released her as a favor to 20th Century Fox production head Richard Zanuck, who wanted her for FANTASTIC VOYAGE. Tom Jones sings the title song, written by John Barry and Don Black.

THUNDERBOLT AND LIGHTFOOT

1974 114m c Crime ★★★½
Malpaso (U.S.) R

Clint Eastwood *(John "Thunderbolt" Doherty),* Jeff Bridges *(Lightfoot),* Geoffrey Lewis *(Goody),* Catherine Bach *(Melody),* Gary Busey *(Curly),* George Kennedy *(Red Leary),* Jack Dodson *(Vault Manager),* Gene Elman, Lila Teigh *(Tourists),* Burton Gilliam *(Welder)*

p, Robert Daley; d, Michael Cimino; w, Michael Cimino; ph, Frank Stanley (Panavision, DeLuxe Color); ed, Ferris Webster; m, Dee Barton; art d, Tambi Larsen; fx, Sass Bedig

AAN Best Supporting Actor: Jeff Bridges

Before the disastrous HEAVEN'S GATE and YEAR OF THE DRAGON, and before the success of THE DEER HUNTER, intermittently brilliant director Michael Cimino directed his marvelous first film, THUNDERBOLT AND LIGHTFOOT. Eastwood, whose production company produced the film, had become impressed with Cimino after Cimino coauthored the screenplay for another Eastwood vehicle, MAGNUM FORCE (1973). The film is a crisp, well-written cast caper movie sporting some stunning landscapes and a fine core of performances (Bridges earned an Academy Award nomination as Best Supporting Actor). Young drifter Bridges hooks up with ex-thief Eastwood, who has been on the lam from his former partners for several years because they believe he set them up and took off with the loot from a government vault they robbed in Montana. The two remaining members of his gang, Kennedy, a sadistic war buddy of Eastwood, and Lewis, a likable dimwit, are in pursuit of revenge and hot on Eastwood's tail. The thief, therefore, reluctantly strikes up a friendship with Bridges to escape. Bridges admires Eastwood and wants to prove himself worthy of his friendship, so the crazy kid takes part in the dangerous maneuvering. Eventually Kennedy and Lewis corner the pair and prepare to kill them. Eastwood convinces Kennedy he has no idea where the money is (it was hidden behind the blackboard of an old schoolhouse that no longer exists) and their lives are spared. With nothing better to do, Bridges convinces the group it should rob the same vault, the same way, all these years later because no one would suspect another attempt (they shot their way into the vault with a Howitzer cannon). After some elaborate planning, the four men successfully execute the robbery, but their getaway goes awry.

　　THUNDERBOLT AND LIGHTFOOT is a multifaceted caper film told in fine detail with richly developed characters. Eastwood is nearly overshadowed by Bridges, Kennedy, and Lewis, who brings great depth to his weak-willed, somewhat stupid, character without resorting to cliches. Here, as well as in THE DEER HUNTER, Cimino's main characters—Eastwood and De Niro—seem detached from their peers and unmoved by their environment, until events beyond their control force them to realize what it was they had. It is only then that they experience a melancholy sense of loss. Cimino's first two films succeed because he allows well-drawn characters to affect the audience, not the epic scale of the production. The power of THUNDERBOLT AND LIGHTFOOT and THE DEER HUNTER stems from their eloquent, complex, honest characters.

THUNDERHEAD—SON OF FLICKA
1945   78m   bw   Drama
Fox   (U.S.)

Roddy McDowall *(Ken McLaughlin)*, Preston Foster *(Rob McLaughlin)*, Rita Johnson *(Nelle)*, James Bell *(Gus)*, Diana Hale *(Hildy)*, Carleton Young *(Maj. Harris)*, Ralph Sanford *(Mr. Sargent)*, Robert Filmer *(Tim)*, Alan Bridge *(Dr. Hicks)*

p, Robert Bassler; d, Louis King; w, Dwight Cummins, Dorothy Yost (based on a novel by Mary O'Hara); ph, Charles Clarke (Technicolor); ed, Nick De Maggio; m, Cyril J. Mockridge; art d, Lyle Little, Fred J. Rode

An enjoyable and engaging tale, this follow-up to MY FRIEND FLICKA is every bit as entertaining as the original. Ken McLaughlin (Roddy McDowall, returning from the original film) is trying to break in Thunderhead, the title horse. The all-white colt is trained for racing, and Ken enters him in competition. At a county race it appears Thunderhead is going to win when the horse suddenly pulls a tendon. Ken is content to restrict his use of Thunderhead to his father's ranch, but trouble brews when the albino horse who sired Thunderhead goes wild. That horse causes trouble for all the ranchers in the valley by stealing mares, but eventually it is challenged by Thunderhead. The brave colt saves Ken, then takes on the albino. The two horses engage in a terrific fight, with Thunderhead defeating his renegade father. Ken's horse returns to his master, but shows a desire to live free on the range. Though heartbroken, Ken understands what is best for his friend and allows the horse to go free. The film is well acted, though the players are really secondary to the real stars of the film: the horses and the beautiful Utah locations. Perfect family viewing.

THUNDERHEART
1992   118m   c   Thriller
TriBeCa Productions/Waterhorse Productions/TriStar   R
(U.S.)

Val Kilmer *(Ray Levoi)*, Sam Shepard *(Frank Coutelle)*, Graham Greene *(Walter Crow Horse)*, Fred Dalton Thompson *(William Dawes)*, Fred Ward *(Jack Milton)*, Sheila Tousey *(Maggie Eagle Bear)*, Chief Ted Thin Elk *(Grandpa Sam Reaches)*, John Trudell *(Jimmy Looks Twice)*, Julius Drum *(Richard Yellow Hawk)*, Sarah Brave *(Maisy Blue Legs)*

p, Robert De Niro, Jane Rosenthal, John Fusco; d, Michael Apted; w, John Fusco; ph, Roger Deakins; ed, Ian Crafford; m, James Horner; prod d, Dan Bishop; art d, Bill Ballou; cos, Susan Lyall

THUNDERHEART is a thoughtful, atmospheric thriller set on a North Dakota Native American reservation in the 1970s. Loosely based on a real-life incident, the film involves a series of murders, a deadly, government-backed uranium mining operation, and the attempts of a group of American Indian activists to protect their land and culture.

Val Kilmer stars as Ray Levoi, a one-quarter Sioux F.B.I. agent who is assigned to the murder investigation as a token Indian (the natives mockingly refer to him as the "Washington Redskin"). His partner, tough old-timer Frank "Cooch" Coutelle (Sam Shepard), is more interested in making a quick arrest than in getting to the root of the situation. Levoi, though, suspects the case is more complex than it seems. Influenced and impressed by some of the Indians (particularly savvy native cop Walter Crow Horse, winningly played by Graham

Greene), he overcomes his initial embarrassment about his Indian blood and discovers the meaning of his heritage. As he uncovers a trail of conspiracy and corruption, Levoi is forced to decide where his true sympathies lie.

THX 1138
1971   88m   c   Science Fiction
American Zoetrope   (U.S.)   PG

Robert Duvall *(THX 1138)*, Donald Pleasence *(SEN 5241)*, Don Pedro Colley *(SRT)*, Maggie McOmie *(LUH 3417)*, Ian Wolfe *(PTO)*, Sid Haig *(NCH)*, Marshall Efron *(TWA)*, John Pearce *(DWY)*, Johnny Weissmuller Jr., Robert Feero *(Chrome Robots)*

p, Lawrence Sturhahn; d, George Lucas; w, George Lucas, Walter Murch (based on a story by Lucas); ph, David Myers, Albert Kihn (Techniscope, Technicolor); ed, George Lucas; m, Lalo Schifrin; art d, Michael Haller; cos, Donald Longhurst

George Lucas's feature debut is muted, brooding sci-fi, expanded (under the auspices of Francis Ford Coppola) from the short film with which Lucas won the 1967 National Student Film Festival. A young Robert Duvall plays THX (pronounced "Thix"), who attempts to escape from a futuristic society located beneath the Earth's surface. Reminiscent of the repressive societies described in George Orwell's *1984*, Aldous Huxley's *Brave New World*, and especially E.M. Forster's "The Machine Stops," Duvall's society has outlawed love and sex, with drugs as mandatory dietary supplements. McOmie plays Duvall's love interest, who awakens him to the pleasures of love after she and Duvall stop taking the libido-stifling drugs. They're arrested, and in prison she discovers she's pregnant. They hook up with Pleasence, who persuades the two to escape with him. Ponderous and largely static, this film shows little of the movie-making flair Lucas would later exhibit—except for a tense, stylishly edited car chase, in which the director makes impressive use of a relatively low budget, and a few flashes of wit, like the computerized confession boxes. Sharp-eyed Lucas fans may have noticed that in AMERICAN GRAFFITI, Paul Le Mat's Deuce Coupe sports license plates that read "THX 138."

TIE ME UP! TIE ME DOWN!
(ATAME)
1990   101m   c   Comedy/Romance/Erotic
El Deseo   (Spain)   ★★½

Victoria Abril *(Marina)*, Antonio Banderas *(Ricky)*, Francisco Rabal *(Maximo Espejo)*, Loles Leon *(Lola)*, Julieta Serrano *(Alma)*, Maria Barranco, Rossy de Palma

p, Agustin Almodovar; d, Pedro Almodovar; w, Pedro Almodovar; ph, Jose Luis Alcaine; ed, Jose Salcedo; m, Ennio Morricone; prod d, Esther Garcia

This outrageous title is a little deceiving, especially for a film from Spain's most controversial export, Pedro Almodovar. The director's usual campy, boisterous hilarity has been replaced in TIE ME UP! TIE ME DOWN! by anguished—albeit offbeat—romantic heterosexual yearning.

Ricky (Antonio Banderas) is released from a mental institution with one burning ambition. On a previous escape from the hospital, he met and made love to Marina (Victoria Abril), a junkie and former porn star. Obsessed by the memory of her, he determines to seek her out again and win her love. He finds her on the set of a legitimate film, working under the direction of the aged Maximo Espejo (Francisco Rabal), who is also obsessed with her. Marina has no recollection of Ricky when she sees him, but he trails her home and kidnaps her. Tying her up in her own apartment, he makes her a captive audience for his desperate romantic overtures. She is at first fiercely resistant to him, but gradually succumbs, especially when he returns to her bruised and bloodied after an attempt to score drugs for her. Eventually, Marina's sister, Lola (Loles Leon), comes to the rescue, but by that time, Marina's fate is (happily) sealed.

The shock effects of Almodovar's earlier work were considerably diluted in his Lubitschian crazy-love roundelay, WOMEN ON THE VERGE OF A NERVOUS BREAKDOWN, and TIE ME UP!, despite its bondage theme and lightly sadomasochistic overtones, makes a similar attempt to enter the mainstream. The film recalls Hitchcock's THE 39 STEPS, with its bickering handcuffed lovers, as well as the sweeping romantic intensity of Douglas Sirk's 1950s trash-fests. Ennio Morricone's ubiquitous music contributes to this attempt to explore the traditions of classic cinema, but it lacks the savvy, finger-popping verve of the more street-smart scores of other Almodovar films. The screenplay lacks the frantic multitude of characters that have typified Almodovar's work, and the non-sequiturs and comic asides we have come to expect are also kept to a minimum. Staying with TIE ME UP! demands some patience, but the director's timing never fails him, and he brings things to a close on an upbeat note.

TIM BURTON'S THE NIGHTMARE BEFORE CHRISTMAS   📀 DVD

1993 75m c Fantasy/Musical/Animated ★★★½
Skellington Productions/Touchstone (U.S.) PG

VOICES OF: Danny Elfman (Jack Skellington (songs)/Barrel/Clown with the Tear Away Face), Chris Sarandon (Jack Skellington), Catherine O'Hara (Sally/Shock), William Hickey (Evil Scientist), Glenn Shadix (Mayor), Paul Reubens (Lock), Ken Page (Oogie Boogie), Ed Ivory (Santa), Susan McBride (Big Witch W W D), Debi Durst (Corpse Kid/Corpse Mom/Small Witch)

p, Denise DiNovi, Tim Burton; d, Henry Selick; w, Caroline Thompson (from the story and characters by Tim Burton); ph, Pete Kozachik; ed, Stan Webb; m, Danny Elfman; art d, Deane Taylor; fx, Ariel Velasco Shaw, Pete Kozachik; anim, Eric Leighton

AAN Best Visual Effects: Gordon Baker, Pete Kozachik, Eric Leighton, Ariel Velasco Shaw

There's a new Santa Claus in town, and if you're lucky your Christmas gifts could include a hungry snake or a severed, shrunken head.

Welcome to THE NIGHTMARE BEFORE CHRISTMAS, producer Tim Burton's animated, musical vision of a world where skeletons are considered handsome and spiders tasty. Working within the relatively obscure techniques of stop-motion animation (by which puppets are manipulated, one frame at a time, to create the illusion of movement), Burton and director Henry Selick have pulled off a spectacular visual coup, revolving around a character known as Jack the Pumpkin King. Frustrated with the limitations of his native Halloweentown, which is peopled by assorted macabre types and presided over by a (literally) two-faced mayor, Jack tries to conquer neighboring Christmastown, where the nice people live.

NIGHTMARE betrays almost demonic powers of invention, every frame crammed with eye-catching (and frequently eyebrow-raising) detail. It's also appealing to the ears, courtesy of Danny Elfman's infectious, amusing songs. Yet the richness of the canvas only draws our attention to the weakness of the narrative. Burton seems to waver between rooting for the scary guys and the cuddly ones, and his indecision makes it hard for us to respond on an emotional level. The result, though refreshingly different from mainstream animated fare, is ultimately more trick than treat.

TIME AFTER TIME   📀 DVD

1979 112m c Science Fiction/Thriller ★★★
Orion/Warner Bros. (U.K.) PG

Malcolm McDowell (Herbert G. Wells), David Warner (Dr. John Lesley Stevenson), Mary Steenburgen (Amy Robbins), Charles Cioffi (Lt. Mitchell), Laurie Main (Inspector Gregson), Andonia Katsaros (Mrs. Turner), Patti D'Arbanville (Shirley), Keith McConnell (Harding), Geraldine Baron (Carol), James Garrett (Edwards)

p, Herb Jaffe; d, Nicholas Meyer; w, Nicholas Meyer (based on a story by Karl Alexander and Steven Hayes); ph, Paul Lohmann (Panavision, Metrocolor); ed, Donn Cambern; m, Miklos Rozsa; prod d, Edward Carfagno; fx, Larry Fuentes, Jim Blount; cos, Sal Anthony, Yvonne Kubis

What if Jack the Ripper (David Warner) were really an old friend of H.G. Wells (Malcolm McDowell) and what if H.G. Wells actually invented a time machine and what if Jack the Ripper used it to escape to San Francisco circa 1979 and what if H.G. Wells figured out a way to follow him? What if H.G. fell in love with a kooky bank officer (Mary Steenburgen) and what if Jack tried to kill her? It's convoluted and the plot device that allows Wells to follow Jack is laughable, but this is such a conscientious undertaking you might as well take a look.

Meyer had tried this historical twist before with his screenplay for THE SEVEN-PERCENT SOLUTION, in which Sherlock Holmes meets Sigmund Freud, but TIME AFTER TIME actually works better. It's a well-crafted blend of fiction and history boosted by some excellent special effects. McDowell is marvelous as the free-thinking Victorian who is suddenly confronted with the future—a spectacle he finds both wonderful and horrifying. Steenburgen, in her first major role, does an engaging turn as the daffy bank worker, and the chemistry between the two is good. (They fell in love while making TIME AFTER TIME and were later married.) Meyer makes a fine directorial debut, pacing the film for optimal suspense despite some obvious holes in the script. For some more sophisticated treatments of time travel, see Alain Resnais's JE T'AIME, JE T'AIME, or Chris Marker's LA JETEE, a haunting parable composed almost entirely of still images.

TIME BANDITS   📀 DVD

1981 110m c Science Fiction/Fantasy/Comedy ★★★★
HandMade (U.K.) PG

John Cleese (Robin Hood), Sean Connery (King Agamemnon), Shelley Duvall (Pansy), Katherine Helmond (Mrs. Ogre), Ian Holm (Napoleon), Michael Palin (Vincent), Ralph Richardson (Supreme Being), Peter Vaughan (Ogre), David Warner (Evil Genius), David Rappaport (Randall)

p, Terry Gilliam; d, Terry Gilliam; w, Michael Palin, Terry Gilliam; ph, Peter Biziou (Technicolor); ed, Julian Doyle; m, Mike Moran; prod d, Millie Burns; art d, Norman Garwood

Gilliam and Palin, from Monty Python's Flying Circus, masterminded this madcap journey through history. A curious boy, Kevin (David Warnock) is whisked out of his dreary English home by six mischievous dwarfs who possess a map stolen from the Supreme Being (Sir Ralph Richardson) that reveals gaps in the universe. Utilizing these "time holes," they travel through history encountering the likes of Robin Hood (Cleese), Greek warrior King Agamemnon (Connery), and Napoleon (Holm)—and robbing them of their treasures. God wants his map back and he keeps popping up at the most inopportune times for Kevin and the time bandits. The Evil Genius (David Warner) also wants to get his hands on this great treasure. Who will win?

This wild and sometimes woolly fantasy is delivered in the customary chaotic Python style, resulting in an onslaught of witticisms and slapstick. We can also see definite signs of the major filmmaker Gilliam (director of BRAZIL, THE ADVENTURES OF BARON MUNCHHAUSEN, THE FISHER KING) would later become. In many ways, this remains his most satisfying film. However, be warned; this film is unusually dark for a modern children's film. At times a grimly comic fairy tale, TIME BANDITS offers little reassurance. It's a tough world out there—even in our imaginative life. Perhaps that is why we need heroes so badly.

Connery, in particular, stands out in a sterling cast. His portrayal of Agamemnon emerges as an idealized surrogate father that any boy would love to have. Cleese is priceless as a primly officious Robin Hood. The band of little people is also splendid, especially the late David Rappaport as their leader, Randall. Chances are good that this eccentric film will gain in stature in the years to come.

TIME CODE
2000 93m c Crime/Drama ★★★½
Red Mullet (U.S.) R

Stellan Skarsgard (Alex Green), Saffron Burrows (Emma), Salma Hayek (Rose), Jeanne Tripplehorn (Lauren Hathaway), Julian Sands (Quentin), Holly Hunter (Executive), Kyle MacLachlan (Bunny Drysdale), Steven Weber (Darren Fetzer), Mia Maestro (Ana Pauls), Alessandro Nivola (Joey Z)

p, Annie Stewart, Mike Figgis; d, Mike Figgis; w, Mike Figgis; ph, Patrick Alexander Stewart, James Wharton O'Keefe, Tony Cucchiai; m, Mike Figgis, Anthony Marinelli; prod d, Charlotte Malmlof; fx, Ron Bolanowski; cos, Donna Casey

Ladies and gentlemen, synchronize your watches. Mike Figgis's new film is driven by the striking visual conceit—a gimmick, you might say—of four interrelated stories unfolding on screen simultaneously and in real time. It's demanding, but the stories are genuinely gripping, and Figgis makes it all surprisingly easy to follow.

Lauren (Jeanne Tripplehorn) suspects her lover, Rose (Salma Hayek), of infidelity; on the way to an audition for hip producer Alex Green (Stellan Skarsgard), Lauren bugs Rose's purse and spends the next hour and a half listening in on Rose's activities. Alex is coming apart at the seams; he's drinking so much his partners are considering an intervention, his estranged wife Emma (Saffron Burroughs) has decided to leave him, and Rose—who is indeed having an affair with him—is unhappy with the way he's treating her. Hotshot young director Lester Moore (Richard Edson) is having trouble casting his new film, which Alex is producing. Alex's partners are worried about getting him to their upcoming meeting with hot young multimedia artist Ana (Mia Maestro) and her boyfriend Joey Z (Alessandro Nivola), who are on their way to pitch a project.

Figgis shot the film (or is it films?) on professional-quality digital video, and shot each segment in one continuous 93-minute take, a mind-boggling feat of coordination. It's even more amazing given that he encouraged the actors—who include Julian Sands, Holly Hunter, Steven Weber and Kyle MacLachlan—to improvise within a set of fixed guidelines. Figgis's bold narrative strategy turns what could have been a standard-issue chronicle of shallow Hollywood lives into a fluid and enthralling experience.

TIME MACHINE, THE
1960 103m c Science Fiction ★★★★
Galaxy (U.K./U.S.) G

Rod Taylor (George), Alan Young (David Filby/James Filby), Yvette Mimieux (Weena), Sebastian Cabot (Dr. Philip Hillyer), Tom

Helmore (Anthony Bridewell), Whit Bissell (Walter Kemp), Doris Lloyd (Mrs. Watchell), Bob Barran (Eloi Man), Paul Frees (Voice of the History Machine)

p, George Pal; d, George Pal; w, David Duncan (based on the novel by H.G. Wells); ph, Paul C. Vogel (Metrocolor); ed, George Tomasini; m, Russell Garcia; art d, George W. Davis, William Ferrari; fx, Gene Warren, Tim Baer, Wah Chang

AA Best Special Effects: Gene Warren, Tim Baar

This smashing science-fiction adaptation of H.G. Wells's famous novel has more creativity in every frame than most latter-day rip-offs have in their entirety. Rod Taylor plays George, an inventor who confounds his contemporaries in Victorian England by unveiling his new time machine. His friends think he's lost his mind, but after they leave, George takes off in his machine, whizzing through time but not through space. Therefore, all of his adventures take place in the same general area of England but at various points in history. He makes brief stops at both World Wars, the atomic confrontations of the future (1966 according to this film), and even as far ahead as the year 802,701. In this futuristic era, he finds humanity divided into two groups—the Eloi, normal-looking humans who live above ground, and the Morlocks, horrifying mutants who live beneath the ground. The Eloi are a vapid, incredibly passive lot, and George is stunned to learn that they are nothing more than cattle for the cannibalistic Morlocks. He falls in love with Weena (Yvette Mimieux), one of the Eloi, and sets out to help her people overcome their oppressors. Producer-director George Pal had already made quite a name for himself with his "Puppetoon" stop-motion animation techniques, and here he again delivers some amazing special effects.

TIME OF THE GYPSIES
1989 142m c Drama ★★★★
Forum Film/Sarajevo (Yugoslavia) R

Davor Dujmovic (Perhan), Bora Todorovic (Ahmed), Ljubica Adzovic (Grandmother), Elvira Sali (Danira), Sinolicka Trpkova (Azra), Husnija Hasimovic (Merdzan), Zabit Memedov

p, Mirza Pasic; d, Emir Kusturica; w, Emir Kusturica, Gordan Mihic; ph, Vilko Filac; m, Goran Bregovic

The third film from the Yugoslavian director of the acclaimed WHEN FATHER WAS AWAY ON BUSINESS was inspired by a newspaper article on the inter-European trade in young Gypsy children. The result is an extraordinary epic that employs an elliptical, fantastic style influenced by Latin American magic realism and features nonprofessional, gypsy actors delivering most of their dialogue in Romanian (a language the director barely understands). It's a remarkable achievement.

A kindhearted Gypsy teenager, Perhan (Dujmovic, who costarred in WHEN FATHER WAS AWAY), is forced to leave his ramshackle home in the Skopje ghetto to accompany his young sister Danira (Sali) on a journey to a hospital where she is to undergo an operation on her bad leg, courtesy of Ahmed (Todorovic), the richest man in the ghetto. Danira and Perhan become separated, and he spends the rest of the film trying to find her so that he can return home and marry Azra (Trpkova), the girl of his dreams. During his odyssey Perhan loses his innocence and learns the brutal ways of the world.

Kusturica has said that his style in this film is a mixture of Ford and Bunuel, and GYPSIES has telling echoes of both, bringing its characters vividly and vitally to life. But there are also echoes of Coppola's GODFATHER films here—in GYPSIES' operatic tone and tragic vision, as well as the parallels between both films' treatment of a criminal ethnic subculture. Kusturica also conveys a genuine sense of wonder at the Gypsies' ability to live, love, and dream amid the squalor by which they are surrounded. This is a major work that augurs well for the director's future.

TIME OUT DVD
(L'EMPLOI DU TEMPS)
2001　132m　c　Drama　★★★★
Haut et Court/Havas Images/Rhone-Alpes Cinema/　PG-13
arte France Cinema　(France)

Aurelien Recoing (Vincent), Karin Viard (Muriel), Serge Livrozet (Jean-Michel), Jean-Pierre Mangeot (Father), Monique Mangeot (Mother), Nicolas Kalsch (Julien), Marie Cantet (Alice), Felix Cantet (Felix), Maxime Sassier (Nono), Elisabeth Joinet (Jeanne)

p, Caroline Benjo; d, Laurent Cantet; w, Robin Campillo, Laurent Cantet; ph, Pierre Milon; ed, Robin Campillo; m, Jocelyn Pook; prod d, Romain Denis; cos, Elisabeth Mehu

With only two feature films to his credit, writer-director Laurent Cantet has established himself as a great cinematic dramatist of the workplace. His superb HUMAN RESOURCES explored class conflict and family strife at an embattled French factory. Here, Cantet explores the way in which personal identity is defined by what we do, and the result is something of a thriller.

To all appearances, Vincent (Aurelien Recoing) is a highly motivated financial consultant. He leaves his house early, works late, and often spends days at a time away from his family on business trips. But the truth of the matter is that Vincent was fired from his job three months ago. While his wife, Muriel (Karin Viard), thinks he's at work, Vincent is aimlessly roaming the highways, hanging out at rest stops, and sleeping in his car. In order to support his family while maintaining the deception, Vincent concocts a plan to defraud some old friends out of their savings by letting them in on a bogus foreign investment scheme. Vincent conducts his "business" out of a hotel lounge, where he happens to catch the eye of Jean-Michel (Serge Livrozet), a real operator who knows a con when he sees one. Jean-Michel offers Vincent a job in his "organization" and, ironically, a chance at redemption.

Beautifully shot against the frozen winter landscapes of Grenoble and Geneva, the film unfolds with all the mounting tension of an expert thriller, until the tragedy reveals itself. Thanks to a perfectly modulated performance by Recoing, Vincent is revealed to be an idealist who simply wants the power to redefine himself as a better person, regardless of what he does—or doesn't do—for a living.

TIME REGAINED DVD
(LE TEMPS RETROUVE)
1999　155m　c　Drama　★★★★
Gemini/CNC/France 2 Cinema/Blu Cinematografica/Les Films du Lendemain/Madragoa Filmes/Studio Canal Plus (France/Italy)

Catherine Deneuve (Odette de Crecy), Emmanuelle Beart (Gilberte), Vincent Perez (Morel), John Malkovich (Charlus), Pascal Greggory (Saint-Loup), Marie-France Pisier (Madame Verdurin), Arielle Dombasle (Madame Verdurin), Marcello Mazzarella (The Narrator, Marcel Proust), Edith Scob (Oriane, the Duchess of Guermantes), Chiara Mastroianni (Albertine)

p, Paulo Branco; d, Raul Ruiz; w, Gilles Taurand, Raul Ruiz (based on the book Time Regained by Marcel Proust); ph, Ricardo Aronovich; ed, Denise DeCasabianca; m, Jorge Arriagada; prod d, Bruno Beauge; cos, Gabriella Pescucci, Caroline DeVivaise

If you've never read Remembrance of Things Past, there's a good chance you won't have the slightest idea what this hauntingly beautiful film is all about. The good news is that it doesn't really matter. Raul Ruiz's splendid adaptation of the final volume of Marcel Proust's sprawling, autobiographical novel is such an enthralling visual experience, the plot details are really secondary.

The film opens with the novelist on his death bed, hurrying to finish his magnum opus. As he dictates, the light changes, the furniture shifts and with all the abruptness of automatic recall the viewer is suddenly a guest at a grand, WWI-era soiree. There the novel's unnamed narrator (Marcello Mazzarella) encounters his great, unrequited loves: the aristocratic and empty Duchess of Guermantes (Edith Scob); the scandalous Odette (Catherine Deneuve), an upwardly mobile courtesan; and Odette's daughter, Gilberte (Emmanuelle Beart), wife of the narrator's bisexual best friend, Saint-Loup (Pascal Greggory). Triggered by the sound of a musical phrase, the sight of an old advertisement or the flavor of a cookie, the action leaps back and forth in time in a delirious collision of magic-lantern fantasies, sudden memories, and specters from the past that include Saint-Loup's uncle, the Baron de Charlus (John Malkovich), a masochist who shared his nephew's passion for an opportunistic young violinist (Vincent Perez), and the ever-elusive Albertine (Chiara Mastroianni), the narrator's great romantic obsession.

Rather than reduce the monumental scale of the novel to a simple narrative, Ruiz has chosen instead to capture its spirit, often at the expense of comprehensibility. It's a worthwhile sacrifice. With its huge cast of sumptuously costumed characters and stunning decor, the film resembles an Impressionist masterpiece come to life, and ends with a tremendously moving acceptance of art and mortality.

TIN DRUM, THE DVD
(DIE BLECHTROMMEL)
1979　142m　c　Drama/War　★★★½
Artemis/Hallelujah Argos　R
(France/Yugoslavia/Poland/West Germany)

David Bennent (Oskar Matzerath), Mario Adorf (Alfred Matzerath), Angela Winkler (Agnes Matzerath), Daniel Olbrychski (Jan Bronski), Katharina Thalbach (Maria), Charles Aznavour (Sigismund Markus), Heinz Bennent (Greff), Andrea Ferreol (Lina Greff), Fritz Hakl (Bebra), Mariella Oliveri (Raswitha Raguna)

p, Franz Seitz, Anatole Dauman; d, Volker Schlondorff; w, Franz Seitz, Volker Schlondorff, Jean-Claude Carriere, Gunter Grass (based on the novel The Tin Drum by Grass); ph, Igor Luther (Eastmancolor); ed, Suzanne Baron; m, Friedrich Meyer, Maurice Jarre; prod d, Nicos Perakis; art d, Nicos Perakis; fx, Georges Jaconelli

AA Best Foreign Language Film

Winner of the Academy Award for Best Foreign-Language Film and cowinner (along with APOCALYPSE NOW) of the top prize at the Cannes Film Festival, THE TIN DRUM is a startlingly successful realization of an "unfilmable" novel by Gunter Grass, the leading German practitioner of magical realism.

Oskar (David Bennent), born to a German rural family in the 1920s, becomes disgusted with the behavior of adults and decides, on his third birthday, not to grow any more, preferring instead to beat his tin drum (a birthday present) and shatter glass with his shrill scream. As he "ages," little Oskar continues to observe the hypocritical behavior of adults, beating out a constant tattoo on his tin drum to control the world around him. His small stature also makes for a very peculiar relationship with a teenage girl, Maria (Katharina Thalbach), who is also mistress to a much older, and bigger, man. THE TIN DRUM is a disturbing film, rich with black humor, that takes a decidedly bitter and horrific look at the German people. Director Volker Schlondorff brilliantly translates Grass' allegorical treatment of the rise of Nazism and manages to suggest much of the novelist's complex critique of German notions of history. Only Oskar, in his singularly demented way, is the voice of reason, proclaiming, "Once there was a credulous people who believed in Santa Claus, but Santa Claus turned out to be the gas man." The film is often difficult to watch and downright frightening, especially due to the haunting face of 12-year-old actor Bennent.

TIN MEN
DVD
1987 112m c Comedy ★★★
Touchstone/Silver Screen Partners II (U.S.) R

Richard Dreyfuss (Bill "BB" Babowsky), Danny DeVito (Ernest Tilley), Barbara Hershey (Nora Tilley), John Mahoney (Moe, Partner to "BB"), Jackie Gayle (Sam, Tilley's Partner), Stanley Brock (Gil), Seymour Cassel (Cheese), Bruno Kirby (Mouse), J.T. Walsh (Wing), Richard Portnow (Carly)

p, Mark Johnson; d, Barry Levinson; w, Barry Levinson; ph, Peter Sova; ed, Stu Linder; m, David Steele, Andy Cox; prod d, Peter Jamison; cos, Gloria Gresham

Director Barry Levinson (RAINMAN; GOOD MORNING, VIETNAM) returns to his hometown of Baltimore for this story of a battle between two aluminum siding salesmen in 1963. The trouble begins when Bill "BB" Babowsky (Richard Dreyfuss) backs his new Cadillac into the car owned by Ernest Tilley (Danny DeVito), who is busy arguing with his wife Nora (Barbara Hershey) at the time. Soon the two men are locked in a comical struggle for revenge. Though much of the plot action is downright silly, Dreyfuss, DeVito, and Hershey offer wonderful performances, and director Levinson keeps things moving with some nice comic touches. As he did in his first film, DINER, Levinson again effectively uses a diner setting in which his characters are allowed to engage in some rambling but very funny dialogue. Comedian Jackie Gayle provides some hilarious observations.

TITANIC
DVD
1953 98m bw Historical ★★★½
Fox (U.S.)

Clifton Webb (Richard Sturges), Barbara Stanwyck (Julia Sturges), Robert Wagner (Giff Rogers), Audrey Dalton (Annette Sturges), Thelma Ritter (Mrs. Maude Young), Brian Aherne (Capt. E.J. Smith), Richard Basehart (George Healey), Allyn Joslyn (Earl Meeker), James Todd (Sandy Cornstock), William Johnstone (John Jacob Astor)

p, Charles Brackett; d, Jean Negulesco; w, Charles Brackett, Walter Reisch, Richard Breen; ph, Joseph MacDonald; ed, Louis Loeffler; m, Sol Kaplan; art d, Lyle Wheeler, Maurice Ransford; fx, Ray Kellogg; chor, Robert Alton; cos, Dorothy Jeakins

AA Best Story and Screenplay: Charles Brackett, Walter Reisch, Richard Breen; AAN Best Art Direction-Set Decoration (B/W): Lyle Wheeler, Maurice Ransford, Stuart Reiss

The Titanic disaster of April 15, 1912, has been filmed several times, and this time the tragedy gets the full Hollywood melodrama treatment. Stanwyck is the mother of two children and the wife of Webb, whom she is leaving, because he is a snobbish socialite. She is taking her children back to America with her to keep them from their father's corrupting influence. Webb manages to get passage on the ship by buying the third-class tickets of a Basque family whom he has persuaded to catch another ship. He and Stanwyck have

a number of confrontations on board before she drives him away once and for all by telling him that her son, Harper Carter, is not his child. Wagner is a young college student who falls in love with Dalton, Stanwyck's daughter. Basehart is a priest defrocked for alcoholism. The ship's captain, Aherne, is pushing for a record crossing-time, and is ignoring warnings of icebergs in the area. Finally the inevitable disaster strikes the "unsinkable" ship, and an underwater spur on a berg tears a long hole in the side of the ship. Before long, the ship begins to list, and the passengers start for the lifeboats, only to discover that there are entirely too few to hold all of them.

Despite an overly melodramatic main story line, the film is quite effective in conveying the panic and the calm of the sinking. A 20-foot-long model of the ship is featured in scenes of the sinking which are a tour de force of special effects. Even the actors were affected by the magnitude of the tragedy they were re-creating. Stanwyck later said: "The night we were filming the scene of the dying ship in the outdoor tank at 20th Century Fox, it was bitter cold. I was 47 feet up in a lifeboat swinging on the davits. The water below was agitated into a heaving, rolling mass and it was thick with other lifeboats full of women and children. I looked down and thought: if one of these ropes snaps now, it's good-bye for you. Then I looked up at the faces lining the rail, those left behind to die with the ship. I thought of the men and women who had been through this thing. We were re-creating an actual tragedy and I burst into tears. I shook with great racking sobs and couldn't stop."

TITANIC
DVD
1997 194m c Historical/Drama/Disaster ★★★★½
Lightstorm Entertainment/20th Century Fox/ PG-13
Paramount (U.S.)

Leonardo DiCaprio (Jack Dawson), Kate Winslet (Rose DeWitt Bukater), Bill Paxton (Brock Lovett), Kathy Bates (Molly Brown), Suzy Amis (Lizzy Calvert), Gloria Stuart (Rose Calvert), David Warner (Spicer Lovejoy), Danny Nucci (Fabrizio De Rossi), Billy Zane (Cal Hockley), Frances Fisher (Ruth DeWitt Bukater)

p, James Cameron, Jon Landau; d, James Cameron; w, James Cameron; ph, Russell Carpenter; ed, Conrad Buff, James Cameron, Richard A. Harris; m, James Horner; prod d, Peter Lamont; art d, Charles Lee; fx, Thomas L. Fisher, Robert Legato, Mark Lasoff, Michael Kanfer, Digital Domain, VIFX, Industrial Light & Magic; cos, Deborah L. Scott

AA Best Picture; AA Best Director: James Cameron; AA Best Art Direction: Peter Lamont, Michael Ford; AA Best Cinematography: Russell Carpenter; AA Best Sound: Gary Rydstrom, Tom Johnson, Gary Summers, Mark Ulano; AA Best Sound Effects Editing: Tom Bellfort, Christopher Boyes; AA Best Original Dramatic Score: James Horner; AA Best Original Song: "My Heart Will Go On"; James Horner, Will Jennings; AA Best Costume Design: Deborah L. Scott; AA Best Film Editing: Conrad Buff, James Cameron, Richard A. Harris; AA Best Visual Effects: Robert Legato, Mark Lasoff, Thomas L. Fisher, Michael Kanfer; AAN Best Actress: Kate Winslet; AAN Best Supporting Actress: Gloria Stuart; AAN Best Makeup: Tina Earnshaw, Greg Cannom, Simon Thompson

Sumptuously filmed and meticulously designed, TITANIC is a glorious epic that garnered 11 Academy Awards, including Best Picture, tying BEN HUR (1959) for the record. The film's combination of romance and astounding visual effects easily sets it apart from past films about the doomed ship, as well as other 1990s big-budget extravaganzas.

Rose DeWitt Bukater (Kate Winslet), one of the passengers on Titanic's fateful maiden voyage, is a young debutante engaged to Cal Hockley (Billy Zane), the pompous heir to a Pittsburgh steel fortune. Rose finds Hockley's world suffocating—so much so that, one night, she rushes to *Titanic*'s stern and considers throwing herself off. She is dissuaded by Jack Dawson (Leonardo DiCaprio), a young pauper who won his passage aboard the ship in a poker game. Rose begins an affair with Jack. Persuaded by her mother (Frances Fisher), who fears that without Hockley's money she and Rose will lose their social standing, Rose reluctantly agrees to stop seeing Jack. She cannot deny her heart, though, and soon Rose returns to him. Meanwhile, *Titanic* meets its destiny: an iceberg, detected too late to avoid. The huge ship skims the side of the iceberg, tearing long holes in her hull. The passengers panic and struggle to survive as the giant ship begins to sink.

At the time of its release, TITANIC was the most expensive production in film history, easily topping $200 million, cementing writer-director James Cameron's reputation for delivering films that are behind schedule, over budget… and often amazing. What makes the film entertaining, though, is not the effects but the love story. DiCaprio and Winslet are both terrific in their roles as the Romeo-and-Juliet-style star-crossed lovers, displaying a passion that is as furtive and all-consuming as it is doomed.

Gaining steam as the weeks went on, TITANIC earned more money faster than any film before it, docking at the top of the box office for months and surpassing 1977's STAR WARS as the biggest moneymaker in history—even before it won Best Picture. Though admittedly somewhat maudlin, TITANIC proves that old-time moviemaking still has its place in modern theaters.

TO BE OR NOT TO BE

1942 99m bw War/Drama/Comedy ★★★★★
UA (U.S.)

Carole Lombard *(Maria Tura)*, Jack Benny *(Joseph Tura)*, Robert Stack *(Lt. Stanislav Sobinski)*, Felix Bressart *(Greenberg)*, Lionel Atwill *(Rawitch)*, Stanley Ridges *(Prof. Alexander Siletsky)*, Sig Rumann *(Col. Ehrhardt)*, Tom Dugan *(Bronski)*, Charles Halton *(Dobosh)*, Peter Caldwell *(Wilhelm Kunze)*

p, Ernst Lubitsch; d, Ernst Lubitsch; w, Edwin Justus Mayer (based on a story by Lubitsch, Melchior Lengyel); ph, Rudolph Maté; ed, Dorothy Spencer; m, Miklos Rozsa; prod d, Vincent Korda; fx, Lawrence Butler; cos, Irene

AAN Best Score (Drama or Comedy): Werner R. Heymann

A masterpiece of satire and one of the more controversial films of its day, TO BE OR NOT TO BE is a brilliant example of how comedy can be as effective in raising social and political awareness as a serious propaganda film, while still providing hilarious entertainment.

The film begins in Poland, 1939, where Joseph Tura (Jack Benny), a tremendously vain Polish actor, and his wife, Maria (Carole Lombard), a conceited national institution in Warsaw, are starring in an anti-Nazi stage play that subsequently is censored and replaced with a production of "Hamlet." Maria has taken a fancy to a young Polish fighter pilot, Sobinski (Robert Stack), who is called to duty when Germany invades Poland. In England, he and his fellow pilots in the Polish squadron of the RAF bid farewell to their much-loved mentor, Prof. Siletsky (Stanley Ridges), who confides to them that he is on a secret mission to Warsaw. Sobinski, however, begins to suspect that Siletsky is a spy and flies to Warsaw to stop him from keeping an appointment with Nazi colonel Ehrhardt (Sig Rumann)—an appointment that will destroy the Warsaw underground. There, Sobinski enlists the aid and special talents of the Tura's theater group to save and protect the Resistance.

A satire built around a rather complex spy plot and directed with genius by Ernst Lubitsch, TO BE OR NOT TO BE lampoons the Nazis and paints the Poles as brave patriots fighting for their land, for whom Hamlet's question "To be or

not to be" takes on national implications. Released in 1942, in the midst of America's involvement in WWII, the film drew a great deal of criticism from people who felt that Lubitsch, a German (though he left long before Hitler's rise), was somehow making fun of the Poles. TO BE OR NOT TO BE is also remembered as the last screen appearance for the dazzling Lombard, who, just after the film's completion, was killed in a plane crash while on her way to Hollywood for a war bonds spot on Benny's radio show. TO BE was a perfect and brash finale to Lombard's great comic genius, especially because of it's examination of play-acting. Was there ever as playful a spirit on a movie set as Lombard? The film came from an idea by Melchior Lengyel—as did NINOTCHKA. Mel Brooks's remake of the story was released in 1983, with Brooks and Anne Bancroft playing the leads. While not as good, it's a perfectly watchable, if unnecessary, tribute to the original, with Bancroft faring better than Brooks.

TO CATCH A THIEF

1955 103m c Crime/Romance/Comedy ★★★
Paramount (U.S.)

Cary Grant *(John Robie)*, Grace Kelly *(Frances Stevens)*, Jessie Royce Landis *(Mrs. Jessie Stevens)*, John Williams *(H.H. Hughson)*, Charles Vanel *(Bertani)*, Brigitte Auber *(Danielle Foussard)*, Jean Martinelli *(Foussard)*, Georgette Anys *(Germaine)*, Roland Lessaffre *(Jean Hebey)*, Rene Blancard *(Commissioner Lepic)*

p, Alfred Hitchcock; d, Alfred Hitchcock; w, John Michael Hayes (based on the novel by David Dodge); ph, Robert Burks (VistaVision, Technicolor); ed, George Tomasini; m, Lyn Murray; art d, Hal Pereira, Joseph MacMillan Johnson; fx, John P. Fulton; cos, Edith Head

AA Best Color Cinematography: Robert Burks; *AAN Best Art Direction-Set Decoration (Color):* Hal Pereira, Joseph McMillan Johnson, Sam Comer, Arthur Krams; *AAN Best Costume Design (Color):* Edith Head

Cary Grant is at his most suave and Grace Kelly is stunningly beautiful in TO CATCH A THIEF, a bubbly and effervescent Alfred Hitchcock romantic-suspenser that finds the Master in a relaxed and purely entertaining mood. Grant stars as a former high-class American thief known as "The Cat," who has retired on the French Riviera. When the area is hit by a wave of jewel robberies, he becomes the prime suspect and gets mixed up with a seductive American socialite (Kelly) while trying to prove his innocence.

Hitchcock himself conceded that the film was "a lightweight," but even minor Hitchcock is more entertaining than the best efforts of his imitators and the film offers plenty to enjoy, not the least of which is its sleek and elegant look, courtesy of the dazzling Technicolor photography of the French Riviera that won an Oscar. Kelly is incredibly sensuous as the quintessential Hitchcockian ice-princess. In the beginning, Hitchcock keeps cutting to her cold, distant profile, but when Cary walks her back to her hotel room, she suddenly grabs him and thrusts her lips right up to his mouth. Hitch also delights in inserting as much sexual innuendo and suggestive imagery as possible, lingering on provocative necklace-cleavage shots and wry double-entendres. During a picnic, Kelly teasingly asks Cary if he wants a breast or a leg while she nibbles on cold chicken, and she fondles a long umbrella after being frustrated that she can't seduce him. The film's most famous scene is the classic fireworks-kissing sequence, where exploding fireworks are orgasmically intercut with Kelly trying to seduce Cary. The suspense takes a back seat to the romance and travelogue aspects of the film, but there is the usual amount of sly Hitchcock humor, provided by the dryly comical John Williams and the wonderfully boisterous Jesse Royce Landis as Kelly's vulgar mother.

TO DIE FOR
1995 100m c Crime/Comedy/Drama
LH Productions/Laura Ziskin Productions/
Columbia (U.S.)

DVD
★★★
R

Nicole Kidman *(Suzanne Stone)*, Matt Dillon *(Larry Maretto)*, Joaquin Phoenix *(Jimmy Emmett)*, Casey Affleck *(Russell Hines)*, Illeana Douglas *(Jancie Maretto)*, Alison Folland *(Lydia Mertz)*, Dan Hedaya *(Joe Maretto)*, Wayne Knight *(Ed Grant)*, Kurtwood Smith *(Earl Stone)*, Holland Taylor *(Carol Stone)*

p, Laura Ziskin; d, Gus Van Sant; w, Buck Henry (based on the novel by Joyce Maynard); ph, Eric Alan Edwards; ed, Curtiss Clayton; m, Danny Elfman; prod d, Missy Stewart; art d, Vlasta Svoboda; fx, Laird McMurray Film Services; cos, Beatrix Aruna Pasztor

Not *just* another facile attempt to blame societal ills on TV, TO DIE FOR leavens its heavy-handed satire of mainstream American values with genuine empathy for its marginal characters. Adapted from Joyce Maynard's fact-based novel about a New Hampshire teacher who bullied her teenaged lover into murdering her husband, TO DIE FOR was a comeback of sorts for both director Gus Van Sant—whose EVEN COWGIRLS GET THE BLUES (1994) was a genuine debacle—and screenwriter Buck Henry, who hadn't written a critical or commercial hit since 1978's HEAVEN CAN WAIT.

Little Hope, New Hampshire, is the center of a media whirlwind involving lovely local weathergirl Suzanne Stone (Nicole Kidman) and murder most foul. Suzanne is the brightly chatty narrator of her own bizarre story. Hell-bent on conquering the world of television—"You're nobody in America unless you're on TV," Suzanne coos, "because what's the point of doing something worthwhile if nobody's watching?"—she's prepared to bump off anyone who stands in her way. Which is too bad for hubby Larry (Matt Dillon), a small-town tavern-keeper who saw his best days in high school.

A solid narrative with a disappointing and obvious subtext, TO DIE FOR opts to finger the usual suspects: TV, unseemly ambition, and some generalized flaw in the American character. Kidman's wildly overrated performance shows some comic flair, but the part is woefully underwritten. Dillon fares better in a role that could easily have descended into caricature: his death scene has a tragic humanity that the film rarely achieves with the other "straight" characters. Van Sant and Henry's contempt for Middle America rivals Robert Altman's; they can't even be bothered to get the details right. None of the film's TV recreations have the ring of truth, a substantial liability in this media-mad context.

TO EACH HIS OWN
1946 122m bw Drama
Paramount (U.S.)

★★★★

Olivia de Havilland *(Miss Josephine Norris)*, John Lund *(Capt. Bart Cosgrove/Gregory Piersen)*, Mary Anderson *(Corinna Piersen)*, Roland Culver *(Lord Desham)*, Phillip Terry *(Alex Piersen)*, Bill Goodwin *(Mac Tilton)*, Virginia Welles *(Liz Lorimer)*, Victoria Horne *(Daisy Gingras)*, Griff Barnett *(Mr. Norris)*, Alma Macrorie *(Belle Ingham)*

p, Charles Brackett; d, Mitchell Leisen; w, Charles Brackett, Jacques Thery (based on a story by Brackett); ph, Daniel Fapp; ed, Alma Macrorie; m, Victor Young; art d, Hans Dreier, Roland Anderson; fx, Gordon Jennings, Farciot Edouart; cos, Edith Head

AA Best Actress: Olivia de Havilland; *AAN Best Original Story:* Charles Brackett

What might have been a trite soap opera is elevated to the status of superior emotional drama by a wise script, sensitive direction, and an Oscar-winning performance by de

Havilland, her first and the first for an actress at Paramount. Covering 27 years in the life and times of a woman who loved neither wisely nor well, it begins during the blitz on London. Middle-aged de Havilland is an air raid warden and marches her beat with confidante Culver, a peer of the realm and another warden. When she learns that a handsome U.S. pilot, Lund, is in town, her thoughts flash back to an earlier time in her life, when her love affair with a dashing pilot (also played by Lund) resulted in a disastrous pregnancy.

Lund, who had already established himself on Broadway, made his film debut here. An interesting sidelight is that de Havilland hadn't worked for two years. She'd been on suspension from Warner Bros. and was trying to break a contract which they claimed included all of her suspension time. She sued the studio successfully and the result was a law that limited studios to a seven-year agreement with an actor, with no clause regarding suspensions. That became known as the "de Havilland Decision," and actors have thanked her ever since. Leisen and de Havilland had worked together in HOLD BACK THE DAWN, and when she asked for him to direct, he passed on it at first, then was convinced when the studio gave him script approval as well as several other concessions. It was sentimental but never bathetic. Leisen knew that de Havilland had given a star performance and on the wrap day gifted her with a bracelet that featured a mini-Oscar. His prophecy was on the money, and she took the Oscar home at the next awards ceremony. Brackett's story was nominated for a statuette, but that was it from the Academy. Audiences loved it, and credit must be given to the studio for attempting a "soft" picture at the time. No one expected it to do as well as it did. Good editing by Macrorie and Victor Young's music kept the mood swings right on target. Miss de Havilland's winning of the Oscar was a surprise to many who had placed their bets on the formidable quartet of losers in 1946. They were Celia Johnson for BRIEF ENCOUNTER, Jane Wyman in THE YEARLING, Jennifer Jones for DUEL IN THE SUN, and Rosalind Russell as SISTER KENNY.

TO HAVE AND HAVE NOT
1944 100m bw Drama
Warner Bros. (U.S.)

DVD
★★★★

Humphrey Bogart *(Harry Morgan)*, Walter Brennan *(Eddie)*, Lauren Bacall *(Marie Browning)*, Dolores Moran *(Helene De Bursac)*, Hoagy Carmichael *(Cricket)*, Walter Molnar *(Paul De Bursac)*, Sheldon Leonard *(Lt. Coyo)*, Marcel Dalio *(Gerard)*, Walter Sande *(Johnson)*, Dan Seymour *(Capt. M. Renard)*

p, Howard Hawks; d, Howard Hawks; w, Jules Furthman, William Faulkner (based on the novel by Ernest Hemingway); ph, Sid Hickox; ed, Christian Nyby; m, Franz Waxman (uncredited); art d, Charles Novi; fx, Roy Davidson; cos, Milo Anderson

The dialogue is sharp, the direction first-rate, and the acting superb, but TO HAVE AND HAVE NOT is undoubtedly best remembered for the on- and offscreen romance between Bogart and Bacall. Warner Bros. wanted another CASABLANCA, and in many ways Bogart's character here resembles his classic portrait of Rick Blaine.

It is WWII and France has just fallen to the Nazi occupation. Bogart, living on the island of Martinique, is the owner of a cabin cruiser, the *Queen Conch*, on which he takes wealthy customers on fishing trips. Working with him is Brennan, a not-too-bright alcoholic with an amiable demeanor. Bogart is approached by Dalio, a member of the French resistance, who asks Bogart to help smuggle one of the underground movement's top leaders (Molnar) into Martinique. Bogart, who cares little for politics, turns him down. Bacall appears, asking Bogart for help in getting off the island. Now Bogart agrees to make the dangerous run for Dalio.

Stylish and loaded with humor, this immensely entertaining film was the result of an argument between director Hawks and novelist Ernest Hemingway. On a fishing trip in Florida with the author, Hawks tried to convince Hemingway that he should come to Hollywood to work on a screenplay. When Hemingway indicated no interest in Hawks's proposal, the filmmaker reportedly responded by boasting that he could make a film out of Hemingway's worst book, which Hawks felt was *To Have and Have Not*. Hemingway's novel is set in Cuba and the Florida Keys in the 1930s. In it, the character Bogart plays is less heroic, a married man with children, who is forced to run booze and men on his boat when his financial situation becomes desperate. Hawks kept the title and the character, then threw out the Hemingway story. The next task for Hawks was casting. Bogart seemed perfect for the part of Harry Morgan, but who was fiery enough to play opposite him? Hawks took a chance on an unknown talent named Betty Bacall, a beautiful 18-year-old New York model who was virtually unknown in Hollywood. Hawks had become interested in Bacall after his wife spotted her on the cover of *Vogue*. The electricity between the two stars was always intended to be the heart of the film, but Bogart and Bacall's onscreen romance had a steamy verisimilitude that went way beyond anybody's expectations. As it became obvious the two were becoming involved, Hawks reportedly warned Bacall that the 45-year-old Bogart was just using his young costar to escape from a bad marriage and that when the filming was over, Bogart would forget about her. Worried that Bacall's infatuation with Bogart would cause the young actress to blow her big chance, Hawks is said to have threatened to sell her contract to Monogram. Of course, this was an empty threat, and some have even suggested that Hawks used the offscreen affair to heighten the on-screen romance. (Tellingly, in the film Bogart and Bacall refer to each other as "Steve" and "Slim," the pet names Hawks and his wife had for each other.)

TO KILL A MOCKINGBIRD   *DVD*

1962 129m bw Drama   ★★★★
Universal   (U.S.)

Gregory Peck (*Atticus Finch*), Mary Badham (*Jean Louise "Scout" Finch*), Phillip Alford (*Jem Finch*), John Megna (*Dill Harris*), Frank Overton (*Sheriff Heck Tate*), Robert Duvall (*Arthur "Boo" Radley*), Rosemary Murphy (*Miss Maudie Atkinson*), Ruth White (*Mrs. Dubose*), Brock Peters (*Tom Robinson*), Estelle Evans (*Calpurnia*)

p, Alan J. Pakula; d, Robert Mulligan; w, Horton Foote (based on the novel by Harper Lee); ph, Russell Harlan; ed, Aaron Stell; m, Elmer Bernstein; art d, Alexander Golitzen, Henry Bumstead; cos, Rosemary Odell, Viola Thompson

AAN Best Picture; AA Best Actor: Gregory Peck; *AAN Best Supporting Actress:* Mary Badham; *AAN Best Director:* Robert Mulligan; *AAN Best Adapted Screenplay:* Horton Foote; *AAN Best B/W Cinematography:* Russell Harlan; *AAN Best Original Score:* Elmer Bernstein; *AA Best Art Direction-Set Decoration (B/W):* Alexander Golitzen, Henry Bumstead, Oliver Emert

Peck's peak. Based on Harper Lee's semiautobiographical, Pulitzer Prize-winning novel of 1960, TO KILL A MOCKINGBIRD is a hauntingly nostalgic portrayal of childhood mischief set in a racially divided Alabama town in the 1930s. If the film's tone sometimes seems overly righteous, it's offset by a poetic lyricism that is difficult to resist embracing.

Gregory Peck plays incorruptible lawyer Atticus Finch, a widower with two children, 10-year-old Alford and tomboyish six-year-old Badham. During the summer, Alford and Badham amuse themselves by rolling each other down the street in a tire or playing in a treehouse. What occupies them most, however, is the creaky wooden house where Robert Duvall lives. According to neighborhood legend, Duvall is crazy and chained to his bed by his father, though he has never

been seen, at least by the children. While the kids play, Peck agrees to represent a black man who is accused of raping a young white woman. A number of people try to pressure him into stepping down from the case, but his pursuit of justice is unwavering. As the trial proceeds, Peck, Alford, and especially Badham learn as much about each other as they do about their own fears and prejudices.

Since its release, this intelligent, atmospheric film has been warmly received by audiences responding not only to their own childhood, but also to the heroic image portrayed by Peck, a shining example of citizenship and affectionate fatherhood.

There is also a superb score by Elmer Bernstein. The language, emotions, and general subject matter of the trial scenes may be a bit rough for some children, but in Peck's solid, idealistic hands, all good things triumph. This was Robert Duvall's film debut.

TO LIVE   *DVD*

(HUOZHE)
1994 125m c   Historical/Political/Drama   ★★★★
ERA International Ltd./Shanghai Film Studios
(China/Taiwan)

Ge You (*Fugui*), Gong Li (*Jiazhen*), Niu Ben (*Town Chief Niu*), Guo Tao (*Chunsheng*), Jiang Wu (*Wan Erxi*), Ni Dahong (*Long'er*), Liu Tianchi (*Adult Fengxia*), Zhang Lu (*Teenage Fengxia*), Xiao Cong (*Fengxia—as a child*), Dong Fei (*Youqing*)

p, Chiu Fu-Sheng; d, Zhang Yimou; w, Yu Hua, Lu Wei (based on the novel by Yu Hua); ph, Lu Yue; ed, Du Yuan; m, Zhao Jiping; prod d, Cao Jiuping; cos, Dong Huamiao

Boasting superb central performances from Ge You and the astonishing Gong Li, Zhang Yimou's TO LIVE is truly epic in its historical scope while retaining the emotional intimacy of such earlier masterworks as RED SORGHUM, JU DOU, and RAISE THE RED LANTERN.

The eldest son of a prominent local family, Fugui (Ge You) is indolent by nature but passionate about gambling. Although his wife, Jiazhen (Gong Li), threatens to leave him, Fugui soon loses his family's fortune and is reduced to selling thread on the street. With the long-suffering Jiazhen, Fugui struggles to hold his family together through years of social turmoil, coping with a harrowing stint in the Nationalist Army and the brutal upheavals of Mao's Great Leap Forward and the Cultural Revolution.

Visually, TO LIVE is surprisingly straightforward, even static, lacking the cinematic sweep of Chen Kaige's FAREWELL, MY CONCUBINE. Instead, Zhang has created a domestic drama on an epic scale, choosing to view historic events through the lens of a nuclear family. He's also chosen to focus on performances, and his two stars don't disappoint. Known for her breathtaking beauty and spitfire intensity, Gong Li once again confirms her status as one of the screen's most affecting actresses. Ge You is a revelation: he delivers a subtle, beautifully nuanced, and deeply humane performance for which he was honored as Best Actor at the 1994 Cannes Film Festival.

Although TO LIVE raised the hackles of the Chinese government during its production (Zhang was subsequently banned from participating in any foreign co-productions), it is not by any means an attack on the PRC; still, it doesn't flinch from depicting the fearful consequences of Mao's utopianism. The film's greatest achievement transcends partisan politics: TO LIVE breathes new and persuasive life into what has a become a humanist cliché, depicting the triumph of the human spirit as the ability to persevere, if not exactly flourish, under the most difficult conditions.

TO LIVE AND DIE IN L.A.
1985 116m c Crime
New Century/SLM (U.S.) 📀 ★★★½
R

William Petersen, billed as William L. Petersen *(Richard Chance)*, Willem Dafoe *(Rick Masters)*, John Pankow *(John Vukovich)*, Debra Feuer *(Bianca Torres)*, John Turturro *(Carl Cody)*, Darlanne Fluegel *(Ruth Lanier)*, Dean Stockwell *(Bob Grimes)*, Steve James *(Jeff Rice)*, Robert Downey Jr. *(Thomas Bateman)*, Michael Greene *(Jim Hart)*

p, Irving H. Levin; d, William Friedkin; w, William Friedkin, Gerald Petievich (based on the novel by Petievich); ph, Robby Muller (Technicolor); ed, Scott Smith, Bud Smith; m, Wang Chung; prod d, Lilly Kilvert; art d, Buddy Cone; fx, Phil Corey; cos, Linda Bass

An astonishing, brilliantly edited car chase—with pursuer and pursued speeding the wrong way along the L.A. Freeway—is one of many pleasures in this darkly stylish crime film, director William Friedkin's best effort since THE EXORCIST. Richard Chance (William L. Petersen) is a Secret Service agent whose partner (Michael Greene) is brutally slain by a counterfeiting gang led by Rick Masters (Willem Dafoe). Chance is now teamed with tyro John Vukovich (John Pankow) and is determined to bring his partner's killer to justice. His quest leads him into the world of Masters, a talented artist who has given up painting and turned to making superb reproductions of $20 bills. Extremely violent, subversively homoerotic, and visually remarkable, with an electric soundtrack by Wang Chung.

TO SIR, WITH LOVE
1967 105m c Drama
James Clavell (U.K.) 📀 ★★★

Sidney Poitier *(Mark Thackeray)*, Christian Roberts *(Denham)*, Judy Geeson *(Pamela Dare)*, Suzy Kendall *(Gillian Blanchard)*, Lulu *(Barbara Pegg)*, Faith Brook *(Mrs. Evans)*, Geoffrey Bayldon *(Weston)*, Edward Burnham *(Florian)*, Gareth Robinson *(Tich)*, Grahame Charles *(Fernman)*

p, James Clavell; d, James Clavell; w, James Clavell (based on the novel by E.R. Braithwaite); ph, Paul Beeson (Technicolor); ed, Peter Thornton; m, Ron Grainer; art d, Tony Woollard

A sentimental picture starring Poitier as an engineer from British Guiana who, because he is black, cannot find work in his field. He accepts a teaching position in a slummy high school in London's East End. He quickly learns that he signed on for more than he bargained for—the students are poorly educated, viciously rebellious, and downright crude to authority figures. Rather than end up like the previous string of instructors—who gave up on the students—Poitier tries an unorthodox method. Instead of relying on textbooks, Poitier teaches from experience. His belief is that the students must be treated like adults in order for them to behave as such. Gradually Poitier gains the students' trust and respect. What makes TO SIR, WITH LOVE such an enjoyable film is the mythic nature of Poitier's character. He manages to come across as a real person, while simultaneously embodying everything there is to know about morality, respect, and integrity. The film's success baffled Columbia executives who just didn't know how to market it. In an attempt to learn why people liked the film so much, they even handed out questionnaires—a method that proved fruitless. One factor in the picture's popularity and its sustaining charm is the tuneful title song, which was a top hit for Lulu and is heard throughout the film. TO SIR, WITH LOVE went on to become the eighth largest grosser of the year, raking in $7.2 million.

TO SLEEP WITH ANGER
1990 95m c Drama
Edward R. Pressman/SVS (U.S.) ★★★★
PG

Danny Glover *(Harry Mention)*, Richard Brooks *(Babe Brother)*, Paul Butler *(Gideon)*, Mary Alice *(Suzie)*, Carl Lumbly *(Junior)*, Sheryl Lee Ralph *(Linda)*, Vonetta McGee *(Pat)*, Wonderful Smith *(Preacher)*, Ethel Ayler *(Hattie)*

p, Caldecot Chubb, Thomas S. Byrnes, Darin Scott; d, Charles Burnett; w, Charles Burnett; ph, Walt Lloyd; ed, Nancy Richardson; m, Stephen James Taylor; prod d, Penny Barrett; art d, Troy Myers; cos, Gaye Shannon-Burnett

Although with this movie writer-director Charles Burnett received considerable attention as one of a "new wave" of black filmmakers, he had already been making films for more than a decade. An atypical look at suburban middle-class black life, TO SLEEP WITH ANGER boasts a rich and resonant screenplay, strong performances, and expressive direction.

Danny Glover, who used some of his post-LETHAL WEAPON clout to finance the film, won for himself a rare opportunity to show his dramatic range. Harry Mention (Glover), a hard-bitten drifter, shows up one day at the suburban Los Angeles home of Gideon (Paul Butler) and his wife Suzie (Mary Alice). He is an old friend who grew up with the couple in the South. The household is filled with tension, much of it created by son Samuel (Richard Brooks), who resents hard-working, successful older brother Junior (Carl Lumbly). Junior, meanwhile, resents the way his parents dote on Samuel, despite the fact that Junior does all the heavy work around the house while supporting his pregnant wife, Pat (Vonetta McGee). Harry's arrival initially adds some excitement to the family life, but his behavior develops an insidious edge. He starts bringing his old friends into the house: blues singers, gamblers, and other shady characters who drink heavily and have vaguely violent pasts. We learn that Harry himself may have been involved in a couple of murders. When Gideon is disabled by a stroke, Harry assumes control of the household with bleak results, exploiting the family's weaknesses and tensions.

What really sticks out in TO SLEEP WITH ANGER is its richness of imagery. The opening credits play over an image of Gideon sitting placidly in a chair as flames burn first on his feet and eventually over his entire body as the hymn "Precious Memories" plays on the soundtrack. Other memorable scenes include shots of the kid next door struggling to play a trumpet, undercutting the stereotypes about blacks and music; Harry cutting his toenails in Gideon's favorite chair as Gideon lies stricken upstairs; and the poignant montage showing the deterioration of Gideon's beloved garden in the wake of his illness.

TOBACCO ROAD
1941 84m bw Comedy/Drama
Fox (U.S.) ★★★★

Charley Grapewin *(Jeeter Lester)*, Marjorie Rambeau *(Sister Bessie)*, Gene Tierney *(Ellie May Lester)*, William Tracy *(Duke Lester)*, Elizabeth Patterson *(Ada Lester)*, Dana Andrews *(Dr. Tim)*, Slim Summerville *(Henry Peabody)*, Ward Bond *(Lov Bensey)*, Grant Mitchell *(George Payne)*, Zeffie Tilbury *(Grandma Lester)*

p, Darryl F. Zanuck; d, John Ford; w, Nunnally Johnson (based on the play by Jack Kirkland and the novel by Erskine Caldwell); ph, Arthur Miller; ed, Barbara McLean; m, David Buttolph; art d, Richard Day, James Basevi

A twisty, humorous antithesis to the usual Fordian style of family bonding, TOBACCO ROAD is a beautifully photographed examination of life among the "poor white trash" of Georgia's Tobacco Road area during the Depression. One of three

Nunnally Johnson-scripted Ford films—following the PRISON-ER OF SHARK ISLAND and THE GRAPES OF WRATH—TOBACCO ROAD takes the long-running Kirkland play, which opened in 1933 and was based on the popular Caldwell novel, and turns it into a strangely distorted story of individualism and integrity. The film opens with the apocalyptic statement, "All that they were, and all that they had, is gone with the wind and the dust," establishing a somber tone for this character study of man battered by the elements. But Ford, not to be easily pigeon-holed, plays much of the film for laughs. Cast as husband and wife, Grapewin and Patterson do their best to hold their family together while struggling to pay the bills. Grandmother Tilbury just gets up and leaves one day, walking into the forest, presumably to die, and is never seen again. Tracy, the rambunctious son, is more concerned with buying a car, blowing its horn, and making a wreck of it after one day than he is with helping his father in daily affairs. It is this car, however, that brings the family together in admiration of its design. The unity, however, is short-lived.

A masterful combination of Ford's pictorial skills and Johnson's character sketches (which also can be seen in the classic Jean Renoir portrait of the South, THE SOUTHERN-ER, to which Johnson and William Faulkner contributed), TOBACCO ROAD is an oddity in Ford's filmography, which is full of movies that celebrate family values, the love of the land, the work ethic, and honesty. In this film, however, these qualities are parodied, and the result, while unorthodox, is highly enjoyable, making TOBACCO ROAD perhaps Ford's most underrated achievement. Photographed by Arthur C. Miller, the man responsible for the breathtaking visuals of HOW GREEN WAS MY VALLEY (for which he won an Oscar), TOBACCO ROAD is, if nothing else, a marvel to look at.

TOGETHER   *DVD*
(TILLSAMMANS)
2000 106m c   Comedy/Drama   ★★★★
Film i Vast/Keyfilms Roma/Memfis Film & Television/   R
SVT Drama, Goteborg/TV1000 AB/Zentropa
Entertainments/Nordisk Film & TV Fond
(Italy/Denmark/Sweden)

Lisa Lindgren *(Elisabeth)*, Michael Nyqvist *(Rolf)*, Gustav Hammarsten *(Goran)*, Anja Lundkvist *(Lena)*, Jessica Liedberg *(Anna)*, Ola Norell *(Lasse)*, Shanti Roney *(Klas)*, Sam Kessel *(Stefan)*, Emma Samuelsson *(Eva)*, Olle Sarri *(Erik)*

p, Lars Jonsson; d, Lukas Moodysson; w, Lukas Moodysson; ph, Ulf Brantas; ed, Fredrik Abrahamsen, Michal Leszczylowski; art d, Carl Johan de Geer; cos, Mette Moller

Swedish director Lukas Moodysson gives the revolutionary fervor of the 1960s gentle ribbing in this warm and genuinely funny follow-up to his 1998 debut, SHOW ME LOVE.

Though it's 1975, the Age of Aquarius is still in full swing for the residents of "Tillsammans" ("Together"), a communal home in the heart of a residential Stockholm neighborhood. But their dedication to the Marxist ideals they hold sacred and the lifestyle rules they strictly observe is about to change. The catalyst for this mini-revolution-within-the-revolution is Elisabeth (Lisa Lindgren), the sister of the house's mild-mannered leader, Goran (Gustav Hammarsten). Unlike the other women of Tillsammans, Elisabeth is a completely ordinary, entirely bourgeois housewife who leaves her abusive husband, Rolf (Michael Nyqvist), and moves into what little space is left in the crowded house with her two adolescent children, Stefan and Eva (Sam Kessel, Emma Samuelsson). As Goran's girlfriend, Lena (Anja Lundqvist), tests the limits of their open relationship with Communist firebrand Erik (Olle Sarri), Elisabeth falls under the spell of Anna (Jessica Liedberg), a divorcee who now claims to be a lesbian. Faced for the first time in her life with the forces of change, Elisabeth begins to rethink her complacency, her politics (or lack thereof), and her shaved armpits.

Ultimately, this affectionate film boils down to a celebration of human companionship, above and beyond the realm of politics; "Loneliness is the most awful thing in the world," as one character says to another. It's easy to scoff at such sentiment in the abstract, but Moodysson puts it across with a sincerity that's genuinely heartwarming, and he sets it all to a surprisingly good soundtrack culled from the Swedish rock (who knew?) of the era.

TOKYO STORY   *DVD*
(TOKYO MONOGATARI)
1953 134m   bw   Drama   ★★★★★
Shochiku/Ofuna   (Japan)

Chishu Ryu *(Shukishi Hirayama)*, Chieko Higashiyama *(Tomi Hirayama)*, So Yamamura *(Koichi)*, Kuniko Miyake *(Fumiko)*, Haruko Sugimura *(Shige Kaneko)*, Nobuo Nakamura *(Kurazo Kaneko)*, Kyoko Kagawa *(Kyoko)*, Setsuko Hara *(Noriko)*, Shiro Osaka *(Keiso)*, Eijiro Tono *(Sanpei Numata)*

p, Takeshi Yamamoto; d, Yasujiro Ozu; w, Yasujiro Ozu, Kogo Noda; ph, Yuharu Atsuta; ed, Yoshiyasu Hamamura; m, Takanobu Saito; art d, Tatsuo Hamada, Itsuo Takahashi; cos, Taizo Saito

TOKYO STORY, Ozu's masterpiece and a landmark in Japanese cinema, didn't make it to the U.S. until 19 years after its initial release, but American critics were immediately taken with this stately, powerful critique of the family and its discontents.

An elderly couple (Ryu and Higashiyama) journey with their youngest daughter (Kagawa) to Tokyo to visit their doctor son (Yamamura) and a daughter (Sugimura) who runs a beauty salon. The children are too busy to meet with their parents, so they send them to a resort. After a sleepless night in the noisy resort the parents return to Tokyo. Before leaving, however, the mother spends a night with the widow (Hara) of another son, and the father visits some old drinking buddies. As it turns out, only this daughter-in-law gives the elderly couple the attention and love they need. The couple's own children soon have cause to regret their neglect, but their emotional ties to their parents have been all but severed by then. It comes as no surprise that they can so easily return to their own self-absorbed lives.

The film may not sound like much in a bald summary, but Ozu's cinema is remarkably powerful for those willing to give it a chance. Ryu is a familiar face in the films of many fine directors, and his marvelous low-key performance is but one of many in the film. Delicately constructed and deliberately leisurely, TOKYO STORY allows its dramatic content and thematic concerns to envelop an audience the way social mores envelop the films' characters. Ozu seems at once critical of certain aspects of Japanese tradition and reconciled to their status and use value. His trademark stylistics are equally intriguing, from his casually non-mainstream editing patterns to his limited camera movement. Most famous of all, though, are Ozu's trademark *tatami*-level shots. Using a special camera dolly to simulate the three-foot height of the average person kneeling or sitting on a *tatami* pad, Ozu creates a way of seeing the world that is specifically Japanese. Although one should resist seeing this great filmmaker as simply the most traditional of Japanese directors, his films do mirror the basics of contemporary Japan in a manner fascinating for those interested in this complex culture.

Of Yasujiro Ozu's 53 films only a few have been released in the U.S., and 34 were silents directed before 1936, many of which have been destroyed.

TOM JONES   *DVD*
1963 131m   c   Comedy   ★★★★★
Woodfall   (U.K.)

Albert Finney *(Tom Jones)*, Susannah York *(Sophie Western)*, Hugh Griffith *(Squire Western)*, Edith Evans *(Miss Western)*, Joan Greenwood *(Lady Bellaston)*, Diane Cilento *(Molly Seagrim)*,

George Devine (*Squire Allworthy*), David Tomlinson (*Lord Fellamar*), Joyce Redman (*Mrs. Waters/Jenny Jones*), George A. Cooper (*Fitzpatrick*)

p, Tony Richardson; d, Tony Richardson; w, John Osborne (based on the novel by Henry Fielding); ph, Walter Lassally (Eastmancolor); ed, Anthony Gibbs; m, John Addison; prod d, Ralph Brinton; art d, Ted Marshall; cos, John McCorry

---

AA Best Picture; AAN Best Actor: Albert Finney; AAN Best Supporting Actor: Hugh Griffith; AAN Best Supporting Actress: Diane Cilento; AAN Best Supporting Actress: Edith Evans; AAN Best Supporting Actress: Joyce Redman; AA Best Director: Tony Richardson; AA Best Adapted Screenplay: John Osborne; AA Best Original Score: John Addison; AAN Best Art Direction-Set Decoration (Color): Ralph Brinton, Ted Marshall, Jocelyn Herbert, Josie MacAvin

---

A rollicking comedic condensation of Fielding's sprawling novel about a lusty young man's adventures in 18th-century England, TOM JONES was an enormous box office success that won four Oscars for Best Picture, Best Screenplay, Best Direction, and Best Score.

Featuring superb performances from Albert Finney and Susannah York and marking the film debut of Lynn Redgrave, TOM JONES is a brilliant melding of naturalistic 18th-century backgrounds with frantic, Keystone Kops-style slapstick and silent film devices like undercranking, titles, wipes, stop-motion photography, etc. Cutting down and molding Fielding's huge 1749 episodic novel was a gargantuan task. Screenwriter Osborne, best known for social realist works like LOOK BACK IN ANGER, may have seemed an odd choice (Richardson and Osborne were both from the "Angry Young Man" school), but he succeeded beyond all expectations.

Several set pieces stand out in memory: the huge stag hunt at the estate of Griffith; the Georges Feydeau-style bedroom farce at the inn; but, most of all, the famous Redman-Finney scene which, while it shows nothing sexual—just two people staring into each others' eyes as they rip food apart and stuff it in their faces—remains among the most cheekily erotic few minutes in cinema. The other achievement of TOM JONES was that it put Fielding's novel back onto the best-seller lists, more than two centuries after it was published.

TOMMY

1975 111m c Musical   **DVD**
Columbia (U.K.)   ★½ PG

Ann-Margret (*Nora Walker Hobbs*), Oliver Reed (*Frank Hobbs*), Roger Daltrey (*Tommy Walker*), Elton John (*Pinball Wizard*), Eric Clapton (*Preacher*), Jack Nicholson (*Specialist*), Robert Powell (*Capt. Walker*), Paul Nicholas (*Cousin Kevin*), Tina Turner (*Acid Queen*), Barry Winch (*Young Tommy*)

p, Robert Stigwood, Ken Russell; d, Ken Russell; w, Ken Russell (based on the musical drama by Pete Townshend, John Entwistle, and Keith Moon); ph, Dick Bush, Ronnie Taylor, Robin Lehman (Metrocolor); ed, Stuart Baird; m, Pete Townshend, Roger Daltrey, John Entwistle, Keith Moon; art d, John Clark; chor, Gillian Gregory; cos, Shirley Russell

---

AAN Best Actress: Ann-Margret; AAN Best Song Score: Peter Townshend

---

Fans of the Who beware. Ken Russell applies his rococo outpourings to Pete Townshend's rock opera and botches not only the visuals but the fine score. With its beginnings as a 1969 album by the Who, one of rock music's most beloved and respected bands, TOMMY went on to become a stage smash in England. Then Russell, with his taste for the flamboyant and meaningless, added Ann-Margret and Oliver Reed, cast lead singer Roger Daltrey in the title role, and wasted a number of talents in useless cameos. The story, told entirely in song, centers on Tommy, a "deaf, dumb, and blind kid" who shuns the rest of the world after the death of his father. His mother, Ann-Margret, and stepfather, Reed, bring him to a doctor, Jack Nicholson, for treatment, but nothing seems to help—that is, until Tommy discovers pinball. "Playing by sense of smell," he beats even the Pinball Wizard (Elton John) and eventually breaks free and starts life anew. Drummer Keith Moon is a highlight as perverted Holiday Camp counsellor Uncle Ernie, Eric Clapton transfers his real-life role as rock guitar god to the screen, and Tina Turner is explosive as the Acid Queen but comes and goes with little explanation. Regrettably, Townshend's extraordinary songs are mauled by Ann-Margret, Reed, and Nicholson. Daltrey, however, proves himself an engaging screen presence and would continue to find work as an actor.

TOMORROW NEVER DIES

1997 119m c Action/Thriller/Spy   **DVD**
Danjaq Productions/EON Productions/United   ★★½
Artists Pictures (U.S./U.K.)   PG-13

Pierce Brosnan (*James Bond—Agent 007*), Jonathan Pryce (*Elliot Carver*), Michelle Yeoh (*Wai Lin*), Teri Hatcher (*Paris Carver*), Judi Dench (*M*), Desmond Llewelyn (*Q*), Samantha Bond (*Miss Moneypenny*), Gotz Otto (*Stamper*), Joe Don Baker (*Jack Wade*), Ricky Jay (*Henry Gupta*)

p, Michael G. Wilson, Barbara Broccoli; d, Roger Spottiswoode; w, Bruce Feirstein; ph, Robert Elswit; ed, Dominique Fortin, Michel Arcand; m, David Arnold; prod d, Allan Cameron; art d, Jonathan Lee, Giles Masters, Tony Reading, Stephen Scott, Ken Court; fx, Chris Corbould, Bill Neil, Mara Bryan, Sharon Lark; cos, Lindy Hemming

---

Agent 007 may take chances, but the producers of the James Bond films rarely do. The 18th Bond film, and the second with Pierce Brosnan as the globe-trotting British superspy, is watchable, but entirely predictable.

Worldwide media mogul Elliot Carver (Jonathan Pryce) isn't content just to cover the news: he wants to manufacture it. To this end, he foments war between Britain and China by using his private "stealth boat" to sink a British frigate and shoot down a Chinese MiG. He then sits back as the two nations blame each other for the incident. Lest sanity break out between the two belligerents and rob Carver of his exclusive story, he plans to escalate the crisis by stealing a cruise missile from the sunken British ship and using it against the Chinese. British intelligence suspects Carver's involvement, and sends in James Bond.

Director Roger Spottiswoode and producers Michael G. Wilson and Barbara Broccoli seem content to deliver the gold-plated but vacuous product their customers expect. But to counter the possible charge that the series itself is anachronistic, recent Bond films have added painfully topical plot elements: here, the script by Bruce Feirstein vilifies the media. Perhaps this movie's best stunt is to suggest that national heroes like Bond can defeat the multinationals. Brosnan and Hong Kong action superstar Michelle Yeoh, who plays Bond's unlikely partner, do make for good comic chemistry, but their relationship is never allowed to rival the stunts and explosions they are forced to race through. Of the film's several good casting choices, only Jonathan Pryce is afforded the opportunity to develop his character—an absurd amalgam of William Randolph Hearst and Rupert Murdoch.

TONI

(LES AMOURS DE TONI)
1935 90m bw Drama   ★★★½
d'Aujourd'hui (France)

Charles Blavette (*Antonio "Toni" Canova*), Celia Montalvan (*Josepha*), Jenny Helia (*Marie*), Edouard Delmont (*Fernand*),

Andrex *(Gaby)*, Andre Kovachevitch *(Sebastian)*, Max Dalban *(Albert)*, Paul Bozzi *(Jacques Bozzi the Guitarist)*, Jacques Mortier

p, Pierre Gault; d, Jean Renoir; w, Jean Renoir, Carl Einstein (based on material gathered by Jacques Levert); ph, Claude Renoir; ed, Marguerite Renoir, Suzanne de Troeye; m, Paul Bozzi

TONI has often been called the first "neorealist" film, preceding Luchino Visconti's OSSESSIONE by seven years; since the Italian director was one of Jean Renoir's assistants on the project, his influence on his work seems clear. Basing his film on police files dealing with an incident that occurred in the small town of Les Martigues, Renoir, seeking authenticity, brought his crew to that town and used its citizens as characters. The story centers on Toni (Charles Blavette), an Italian laborer who falls in love with his landlady (Jenny Helia) and then with a Spanish woman, Josepha (Celia Montalvan). After receiving permission from Josepha's father to marry her, Toni discovers that she has been raped by a sleazy foreman, whom Josepha ends up marrying, eventually deserts and accidentally kills. Not surprisingly, Toni takes the blame. An insightful portrayal of male-female relationships and a skillful rendering of its near-pulp novel plot (again predating Visconti's adaptation of James M. Cain), TONI is nonetheless far from perfect, riddled with numerous technical weaknesses and some seemingly improvised direction. Still, it is clearly one of Renoir's important technical experiments.

TOOTSIE
1982 116m c Comedy/Romance ★★½
Columbia (U.S.) PG

Dustin Hoffman *(Michael Dorsey/Dorothy Michaels)*, Jessica Lange *(Julie)*, Teri Garr *(Sandy)*, Dabney Coleman *(Ron)*, Charles Durning *(Les)*, Bill Murray *(Jeff)*, Sydney Pollack *(George Fields)*, George Gaynes *(John Van Horn)*, Geena Davis *(April)*, Doris Belack *(Rita)*

p, Sydney Pollack, Dick Richards; d, Sydney Pollack; w, Larry Gelbart, Elaine May (uncredited), Murray Schisgal (based on a story by Don McGuire, Gelbart); ph, Owen Roizman (Technicolor); ed, Fredric Steinkamp, William Steinkamp; m, Dave Grusin; prod d, Peter Larkin; cos, Ruth Morley

AAN Best Picture; AAN Best Actor: Dustin Hoffman; *AA Best Supporting Actress:* Jessica Lange; *AAN Best Supporting Actress:* Teri Garr; *AAN Best Director:* Sydney Pollack; *AAN Best Original Screenplay:* Larry Gelbart, Murray Schisgal, Don McGuire; *AAN Best Cinematography:* Owen Roizman; *AAN Best Film Editing:* Fredric Steinkamp, William Steinkamp; *AAN Best Original Song:* "It Might Be You"; Dave Grusin (Music), Alan Bergman (Lyrics), Marilyn Bergman (Lyrics); *AAN Best Sound:* Arthur Piantadosi, Les Fresholtz, Dick Alexander, Les Lazarowitz

A sitcom ode to the Hoffman ego. Like Hoffman in drag, it doesn't look at itself very closely; it might crack the mirror. Rather than confront what it sets up, it takes the one joke and runs—till it runs out of steam. Paging Billy Wilder.

TOOTSIE is about a man who pretends to be a woman in order to secure employment as an actor-actress. Michael Dorsey (Dustin Hoffman), a stage actor trying to make ends meet, dresses in drag and auditions for a part as a mature woman at a New York soap opera. Everyone is fooled, and he gets the part. His rise to fame as "Dorothy Michaels" is almost instant, but his personal relationships become a minefield.

The film's problem is its sitcom style, which doesn't really allow for the suspension of disbelief achieved in SOME LIKE IT HOT. It leaves one no choice but to try and accept Hoffman at, well, face value. As Dorothy, Hoffman's Dorsey is hardly believable as a woman, much less an actress or someone playing an actress. Except for Lange (at the peak of her beauty, playing a stereotype with such effortless ease that

she almost steals the film) and Murray (who *does* steal the film), the rest of the cast lacks comic energy—they're not sprightly enough.

The screenplay is credited to Larry Gelbart and Murray Schisgal, but many writers contributed to it, including Elaine May; meanwhile, Hoffman's tantrums escalated set conditions to a hellish state, with Pollack, playing Hoffman's agent, and Bill Murray, Geena Davis, and Dabney Coleman around to take sides. The make-up artists worked as best they could to transform the raw material at hand—hiding Hoffman's burro ears and temporarily capping his large teeth.

TOP GUN
1986 110m c Drama/War ★★
Paramount (U.S.) PG

Tom Cruise *(Lt. Pete Mitchell)*, Anthony Edwards *(Lt. Nick Bradshaw)*, Kelly McGillis *(Charlotte Blackwood)*, Tom Skerritt *(Cmdr. Mike Metcalf)*, Val Kilmer *(Tom Kasanzky)*, Michael Ironside *(Dick Wetherly)*, Rick Rossovich *(Ron Kerner)*, Barry Tubb *(Henry Ruth)*, Whip Hubley *(Rick Neven)*, Clarence Gilyard Jr. *(Evan Gough)*

p, Don Simpson, Jerry Bruckheimer; d, Tony Scott; w, Jim Cash, Jack Epps Jr.; ph, Jeffrey L. Kimball (Metrocolor); ed, Billy Weber, Chris Lebenzon; m, Harold Faltermeyer; prod d, John De Cuir; fx, Gary Gutierrez

AAN Best Film Editing: Billy Weber, Chris Lebenzon; *AA Best Original Song:* "Take My Breath Away"; Giorgio Moroder (Music), Tom Whitlock (Lyrics); *AAN Best Sound:* Donald O. Mitchell, Kevin O'Connell, Rick Kline, William B. Kaplan; *AAN Best Sound Effects Editing:* Cecelia Hall, George Watters, II

This paean to hotshot Navy fighter pilots and high technology attracted mass audiences despite its familiar plot and characters so vapid they vanish from memory as soon as the house lights come up. Brash young pilot Lt. Pete Mitchell (Tom Cruise), nicknamed "Maverick" for his individualistic flying style, is sent to Miramar Naval Air Station, where he trains with the country's best fighter pilots. The best student from each class wins the prized "Top Gun" award, and the privilege of remaining at Miramar as an instructor. Maverick's chief competition is Tom Kasanzky (Val Kilmer), nicknamed "Ice Man," and eventually an international incident arises that allows the pilots to prove themselves. In an unlikely subplot, Maverick has an affair with Charlotte Blackwood (Kelly McGillis), a civilian expert on the physics of high-speed jet performance.

What TOP GUN contributes to the genre is an increased emphasis on military hardware and an almost homoerotic attraction for male bodies, mostly sweaty ones. In the final analysis, though, everything that happens on the ground is irrelevant to the real heart of the film, the flying sequences. Much praised, the airborne footage seamlessly intercuts live action shots of planes with special effects models. But for all the skill of their execution, the flying scenes are often confusing, rarely giving any idea of where the planes are in relation to one another. Jets streak by and pilots spin their heads around yelling, "Where'd he go? Where'd he go?" until the beepers aboard their planes tell them they've been shot down. Ultimately, TOP GUN is a facile movie in which Americans kill Russians with aplomb—proving their inherent superiority—and Tom Cruise gets the girl.

TOP HAT
1935 101m bw Comedy/Musical/Romance ★★★★★
RKO (U.S.)

Fred Astaire *(Jerry Travers)*, Ginger Rogers *(Dale Tremont)*, Edward Everett Horton *(Horace Hardwick)*, Helen Broderick *(Madge*

Hardwick), Erik Rhodes *(Alberto Beddini)*, Eric Blore *(Bates)*, Lucille Ball *(Flower Clerk)*, Leonard Mudie *(Flower Salesman)*, Edgar Norton *(Hotel Manager)*, Gino Corrado *(Hotel Manager)*

p, Pandro S. Berman; d, Mark Sandrich; w, Dwight Taylor, Allan Scott (based on the musical *The Gay Divorcee* by Dwight Taylor, Cole Porter and the play *The Girl Who Dared* by Alexander Farago, Aladar Laszlo); ph, David Abel; ed, William Hamilton; art d, Van Nest Polglase, Carroll Clark; fx, Vernon L. Walker; chor, Fred Astaire, Hermes Pan; cos, Bernard Newman

AAN Best Picture; AAN Best Interior Decoration: Carroll Clark, Van Nest Polglase (Art Direction); *AAN Best Song:* "Cheek To Cheek"; Irving Berlin; *AAN Best Dance Direction:* Hermes Pan

The fourth pairing of Fred Astaire and Ginger Rogers and the first with a screenplay written specifically for them, TOP HAT is the quintessential Astaire-Rogers musical, complete with a silly plot, romance, dapper outfits, art deco sets, and plenty of wonderful songs and dance numbers. Set in London (though the story really unfolds in Hollywood's mythical Fred-and-Ginger-Land), TOP HAT's tale of mistaken identity concerns American song-and-dance man Jerry Travers (Astaire), who becomes so enamored of lovely Dale Tremont (Rogers) as she is of him. Problems arise, however, when Dale comes to believe that Jerry is the husband (whom she's never met) of her good friend Madge (Broderick) and rebuffs his advances, finally fleeing to Venice with Madge. Jerry and Horace Hardwick (Horton), Madge's real husband and the producer of the show in which Jerry stars, follow them to Venice, and the confusion grows as Dale tells Madge that Horace has been unfaithful. Dale then marries her dress designer, Albert (Rhodes), before Jerry gets a chance to straighten things out. Not to worry: Horace's faithful butler (Eric Blore) to the rescue.

An effervescent musical that was the perfect panacea for Depression-era audiences, this wonderfully whimsical reworking of 1934's THE GAY DIVORCEE (whose leading players are reunited here) offers perhaps the most famous Astaire-Rogers duet, "Cheek to Cheek," wherein the dancers shift from effortless gliding to moves of dazzling exuberance. Despite the problems it caused in filming, La Ginger was absolutely right about not changing the famous feathered dress—it does move beautifully, and she looks as light as a feather dancing in it. Built around Irving Berlin's hit-laden score, TOP HAT also boasts Astaire's brilliant, signature solo number, "Top Hat, White Tie and Tails." Fred and Ginger once again display their incredible rapport as actors as well as dancers, and the supporting cast is uniformly perfect, even though Rhodes's Italian caricature so offended Italian officials (and even the top guy, Mussolini himself), that TOP HAT, like THE GAY DIVORCEE (in which Rhodes played a similar character), was banned in Italy. With over $3 million in receipts, TOP HAT was RKO's biggest moneymaker of the decade. Tip top.

TOP SECRET! 🟥*DVD*
1984 90m c Comedy/Spy/Musical ★★★
Paramount (U.S.) PG

Omar Sharif *(Cedric)*, Jeremy Kemp *(Gen. Streck)*, Warren Clarke *(Col. Von Horst)*, Tristram Jellinek *(Maj. Crumpler)*, Val Kilmer *(Nick Rivers)*, Billy J. Mitchell *(Martin)*, Major Wiley *(Porter)*, Gertan Klauber *(Mayor)*, Richard Mayes *(Biletnikov)*, Peter Cushing *(Bookstore Proprietor)*

p, Jon Davison, Hunt Lowry; d, Jim Abrahams, David Zucker, Jerry Zucker; w, Jim Abrahams, David Zucker, Jerry Zucker, Martyn Burke; ph, Christopher Challis (Metrocolor); ed, Bernard Gribble; m, Maurice Jarre; prod d, Peter Lamont; art d, John Fenner, Michael Lamont; fx, Nick Allder; chor, Gillian Gregory; cos, Emma Porteous

A strange mix that might have been titled "Beach Blanket Espionage," this overlooked comedy by Zucker, Abrahams, and Zucker doesn't always work, nor does it measure up to their hilarious AIRPLANE! It is, nevertheless, very funny as it lampoons two genres: the spy movie and the teenage musical. While in East Germany to perform at big cultural festival, rock star Nick Rivers (Val Kilmer) finds himself embroiled in international intrigue involving an East German plot to take over West Germany, an imprisoned scientist (Michael Gough), and his beautiful daughter, Hillary (Lucy Gutteridge), who, naturally, becomes Nick's love interest. While helping Hillary thwart the takeover scheme, Nick, in the tradition of countless Elvis films, bursts into song on the slightest provocation. Equally without rhyme or reason is the movie's plot. In parodying pictures like THE SPY WHO CAME IN FROM THE COLD, Zucker, Abrahams, and Zucker present a narrative that is hopelessly convoluted, but that, of course, is exactly their intention as they pile joke upon joke, filling their film with inventive sight gags. Omar Sharif appears as a spy and is uproarious in what amounts to a cameo appearance, even though he gets top billing. This film hits more than it misses.

TOPAZ 🟥*DVD*
1969 126m c Spy ★★★
Universal (U.S.) PG

John Forsythe *(Michael Nordstrom)*, Frederick Stafford *(Andre Devereaux)*, Dany Robin *(Nicole Devereaux)*, John Vernon *(Rico Parra)*, Karin Dor *(Juanita de Cordoba)*, Michel Piccoli *(Jacques Granville)*, Philippe Noiret *(Henri Jarre)*, Claude Jade *(Michele Picard)*, Michel Subor *(Francois Picard)*, Roscoe Lee Browne *(Philippe Dubois)*

p, Alfred Hitchcock; d, Alfred Hitchcock; w, Samuel Taylor (based on the novel by Leon Uris); ph, Jack Hildyard (Technicolor); ed, William Ziegler; m, Maurice Jarre; prod d, Henry Bumstead; fx, Albert Whitlock; cos, Edith Head

An espionage story that takes the cameras to Copenhagen, Paris, New York City, Harlem, Virginia, and a California hacienda that doubles as Cuba. Loosely based on the true-life exploits of French spy Philippe de Vosjoli and the 1962 "Sapphire" scandals in which top French officials were uncovered as Soviet agents, the film has a sense of authenticity but fails to fire up as much suspense as most of Hitchcock's intrigues. With an international cast of semirecognizable names (Michel Piccoli, Philippe Noiret, and just one American, John Forsythe), TOPAZ gleaned most of its attention from the star status of its director. Hitchcock considered the film a disaster because it went into production without a finished script (in complete antithesis to his normal working methods of full preparedness), without full casting, and without an ending.

TOPKAPI 🟥*DVD*
1964 120m c Comedy/Crime ★★★★
Filmways (U.S.)

Melina Mercouri *(Elizabeth Lipp)*, Peter Ustinov *(Arthur Simpson)*, Maximilian Schell *(William Walter)*, Robert Morley *(Cedric Page)*, Akim Tamiroff *(Geven)*, Gilles Segal *(Giulio)*, Jess Hahn *(Fischer)*, Titos Vandis *(Harback)*, Ege Ernart *(Maj. Tufan)*, Senih Orkan

p, Jules Dassin; d, Jules Dassin; w, Monja Danischewsky (based on the novel *The Light of Day* by Eric Ambler); ph, Henri Alekan (Technicolor); ed, Roger Dwyre; m, Manos Hadjidakis; art d, Max Douy; cos, Denny Vachlioti

AA Best Supporting Actor: Peter Ustinov

Dassin went back to his hit RIFIFI and spoofed it with this enjoyable, fast-moving tale of a caper pulled by some of the most delightful characters ever assembled on one screen. Filmed on location in Istanbul and Greece, TOPKAPI cleverly employs every cinematic trick in the book—to an accompaniment of clever dialogue. As long as you realize TOPKAPI failed to accomplish what it set out to do—top RIFIFI—and if you don't care—this is glamorous, hambone stew.

Sexpot Mercouri (Dassin's real-life wife) and her lover want to steal a priceless dagger from the heavily secured museum in Istanbul known as Topkapi. To pull off the job, they enlist aid: Morley is an addled but brilliant British inventor and expert in electronics and burglar alarms, Segal is a mute acrobat who could climb a sheer wall with his fingernails and Hahn is a muscular, remarkably strong lout. While in Kavala, Greece, the gang hires Ustinov, a low-life con artist, to drive an expensive car across the border into Turkey. Ustinov doesn't know that the car carries weapons and gear for the robbery; when he is stopped at the border, one of the Turkish police (Emart) thinks that some terrorists are using him as a dupe. Rather than arrest Ustinov, Emart asks him to infiltrate the group that his hired him and to report back. Ustinov delivers the goods (some bombs, a high-powered rifle) to the gang's villa in Turkey. The daring robbery is carefully calculated. The floor of the museum is wired so that a single step will set off the alarm, so Hahn will hold a rope and lower Segal through a window. Then Segal will hang from the rope, reach down, and take the dagger without ever touching the floor. Meanwhile, at the gang's sumptuous mansion, the alcoholic cook, Tamiroff, is convinced that Mercouri and the others are Soviet agents. He passes this intelligence on to Ustinov, who still doesn't know about the robbery, and Ustinov informs Emart. The robbery is about to take place when Tamiroff accidentally crushes Hahn's powerful hand with a door. With the strong man immobilized, Ustinov is pressed into service as the one to hold the rope, a job for which the paunchy Brit is obviously ill-equipped.

The film was based on a little-known book by Ambler and was adapted beautifully by screenwriter Danischewsky. Mercouri is the only woman of consequence in the movie, and she has a field day surrounded by the men—indeed, her touch is lighter than usual. A Supporting Oscar went to Ustinov (who keeps his numerous awards in a glass case in his bathroom. When a producer was scandalized by his placing kudos in such a room, Ustinov explained that it was the only location in his residence where he could ponder his achievements without seeming egotistical.). A great movie—with lots of laughs, a bit of the aforementioned RIFIFI, a smidgeon of BEAT THE DEVIL, and some of its own originality.

TOPPER 📀

1937 98m bw Science Fiction/Comedy ★★★★
MGM (U.S.)

Constance Bennett (Marion Kerby), Cary Grant (George Kerby), Roland Young (Cosmo Topper), Billie Burke (Henrietta Topper), Alan Mowbray (Wilkins), Eugene Pallette (Casey), Arthur Lake (Elevator Boy), Hedda Hopper (Mrs. Stuyvesant), Virginia Sale (Miss Johnson), Theodore von Eltz (Hotel Manager)

p, Hal Roach; d, Norman Z. McLeod; w, Jack Jevne, Eric Hatch, Eddie Moran (based on the novel The Jovial Ghosts by Thorne Smith); ph, Norbert Brodine; ed, William Terhune; m, Edward B. Powell, Hugo Friedhofer; art d, Arthur Rouce; fx, Roy Seawright; cos, Samuel Lange, Irene, Howard Schraps

AAN Best Supporting Actor: Roland Young; AAN Best Sound Recording: Elmer Raguse

Sophisticated, but a touch too mild, saved by an ebullient cast. Low-budget comedy producer Hal Roach, who had made a fortune on his Laurel and Hardy shorts, finally decided to risk a big-budget, feature-length comedy, and he came up with a

winner that spawned two sequels, a television series, and a made-for-television remake.

George and Marion Kerby (Cary Grant and Constance Bennett) are a young, wealthy, happy-go-lucky married couple whose main pursuit in life is having a good time. Though they are the chief stockholders in a bank, their minds are on anything but business. One night, while driving recklessly in their big car, they hit a tree and are killed. Their spirits walk out of the wreck, but are dismayed to learn that they have not ascended to the heavens but are still on Earth, albeit in a rather astral form (they can turn invisible at will). George and Marion then decide that they will probably be trapped on Earth forever unless they make amends for their frivolous lifestyle by doing something of value.

The original casting for the film—Harlow for Bennett, W.C. Fields for Young—might have made for a screwier, more frenetic mix. Harlow's comedic touch had a more child-like sense of mischief. When she died a month before filming, Bennett, whose box-office was languishing due to too many formulaic weepies, landed the risk of TOPPER. She's a teasing minx, rather than a playful kitten. But audiences responded enthusiastically to her portrayal. Additional laughs result from TOPPER's special effects—the invisible duo makes objects appear to move by themselves. Avoid the the computer-colored version, which recently appeared on the market.

TOPSY-TURVY 📀

1999 161m c Drama/Musical ★★★½
Thin Man Films/Film Four (U.K.) R

Jim Broadbent (William Schwenck Gilbert), Allan Corduner (Arthur Sullivan), Lesley Manville (Lucy Gilbert—'Kitty'), Ron Cook (Richard D'Oyly Carte), Shirley Henderson (Leonora Braham), Wendy Nottingham (Helen Lenoir), Timothy Spall (Richard Temple), Dorothy Atkinson (Jessie Bond), Dexter Fletcher (Louis), Sukie Smith (Clothilde)

p, Simon Channing-Williams; d, Mike Leigh; w, Mike Leigh; ph, Dick Pope; ed, Robin Sales; prod d, Eve Stewart; art d, Helen Scott; chor, Francesca James; cos, Lindy Hemming

AA Best Costume Design: Lindy Hemming; AA Best Makeup: Christine Blundell, Trefor Proud; AAN Best Art Direction: Eve Stewart, John Bush; AAN Best Original Screenplay: Mike Leigh

Director Mike Leigh is best known for gritty films about contemporary British life, and for collaborative improvisations with his actors. It's hard to imagine what drew him to the story of W.S. Gilbert (Jim Broadbent) and Arthur Sullivan (Allan Corduner)—England's masters of light opera—and the creation of one of their best works, The Mikado. But how marvelous that he was; this slice of ruthlessly genteel Victorian life is charming, witty, and offers its ensemble cast a wealth of dramatic opportunities. Although their names are inevitably linked, Gilbert and Sullivan were profoundly unalike. The robust Gilbert was a blustering family man, English to the core, while Sullivan was often ill, inclined to hedonism, and widely admired for his continental sophistication. In the wake of the relative failure of Princess Ida, the two men clash over their next project for theatrical impresario Richard D'Oyly Carte (Ron Cook). Sullivan wants time off to devote himself to serious music, while Gilbert is insulted that his partner doesn't like his new libretto, a variation on the "topsy-turvy" fantasies that have served them well in the past. After a visit to an exhibition on Japanese life and arts, Gilbert is inspired to spin a tale set in Japan, an idea that also intrigues and energizes Sullivan. All that remains is to pull the thing together, despite temperamental actors (whose off-stage troubles include alcoholism, drug addiction, and illegitimate children), vulgar choreography, costume crises, and financial worries.

It's a loving, gently funny, and slightly claustrophobic tribute to theatrical life. Leigh's meticulously researched film requires neither knowledge of nor devotion to Gilbert and Sullivan, though a little of both certainly helps.

TORCH SONG TRILOGY
DVD
1988 120m c Drama ★★★
Howard Gottfried-Ronald K. Fierstein (U.S.) R

Anne Bancroft (Ma), Matthew Broderick (Alan), Harvey Fierstein (Arnold Beckoff), Brian Kerwin (Ed), Karen Young (Laurel), Eddie Castrodad (David), Ken Page (Murray), Charles Pierce (Bertha Venation), Axel Vera (Marina Del Rey), Benji Schulman (Young Arnold)

p, Howard Gottfried; d, Paul Bogart; w, Harvey Fierstein (based on his play); ph, Mikael Salomon (Metrocolor); ed, Nicholas C. Smith; m, Peter Matz; prod d, Richard Hoover; chor, Scott Salmon; cos, Colleen Atwood

When Harvey Fierstein's "Torch Song Trilogy" premiered Off-Broadway in the early 1980s, it became a word-of-mouth sensation for its caustically humorous homosexual script and performances. The film stays close to the stage production, with a story set in New York City between 1971 and 1980 that follows the roller-coaster love life of a gravel-voiced female impersonator (Fierstein). Fierstein falls for both a handsome and tender young hunk (Brian Kerwin) and a 21-year-old fashion model (Matthew Broderick), tries to act as a father to a teenage boy (Eddie Castrodad), and all the way battles his domineering mother (Anne Bancroft). Fierstein gives a strong and winning performance, and much of his story is funny and heartfelt. Kerwin and Broderick are merely perfunctory in their roles, but Bancroft nearly single-handedly destroys the picture with her scenery chewing. She's Harvey's mother because she's a star and because the script says so, not because the audience believes her.

TORN CURTAIN
DVD
1966 126m c Spy ★★½
Universal (U.S.)

Paul Newman (Prof. Michael Armstrong), Julie Andrews (Sarah Sherman), Lila Kedrova (Countess Kuchinska), Hansjorg Felmy (Heinrich Gerhard), Tamara Toumanova (Ballerina), Ludwig Donath (Prof. Gustav Lindt), Wolfgang Kieling (Hermann Gromek), Gunter Strack (Prof. Karl Manfred), David Opatoshu (Mr. Jacobi), Gisela Fischer (Dr. Koska)

p, Alfred Hitchcock; d, Alfred Hitchcock; w, Brian Moore (based on a story by Moore); ph, John F. Warren (Technicolor); ed, Bud Hoffman; m, John Addison; prod d, Hein Heckroth; art d, Frank Arrigo; cos, Edith Head

This was Alfred Hitchcock's fiftieth film and one of his least successful, despite the box-office names of Paul Newman and Julie Andrews. Michael Armstrong (Newman) is a top U.S. nuclear physicist who defects to East Germany in order to get a secret formula in the possession of enemy scientist Gustav Lindt (Donath). Having Newman play a physicist at the peak of his sly but only semi-articulate animal sexiness (HUD, COOL HAND LUKE) is like having Elizabeth Taylor play Golda Meir. Putting Julie Andrews in a Hitchcock film at all, meanwhile, proves that a spoonful of sugar doesn't help the medicine go down... in the most de-light-ful way. Dull and way too long, TORN CURTAIN is only memorable for one very shocking and brutal scene in which Armstrong and a farmer's wife (played by Carolyn Conwell) have to murder a Soviet soldier. They stab the man, choke him, and finally gas him in the kitchen stove, graphically showing just how difficult can be to kill a human being.

TORTILLA FLAT
DVD
1942 105m bw Drama ★★★★
MGM (U.S.)

Spencer Tracy (Pilon), Hedy Lamarr (Dolores "Sweets" Ramirez), John Garfield (Danny), Frank Morgan (The Pirate), Akim Tamiroff (Pablo), Sheldon Leonard (Tito Ralph), John Qualen (Jose Maria Corcoran), Donald Meek (Paul D. Cummings), Connie Gilchrist (Mrs. Torrelli), Allen Jenkins (Portagee Joe)

p, Sam Zimbalist; d, Victor Fleming; w, John Lee Mahin, Benjamin Glazer (based on the novel by John Steinbeck); ph, Karl Freund; ed, James E. Newcom; m, Franz Waxman; art d, Cedric Gibbons, Paul Groesse; fx, Warren Newcombe; cos, Robert Kalloch, Gile Steele

AAN Best Supporting Actor: Frank Morgan

This excellent adaptation of Steinbeck's novel features Tracy and Tamiroff as two ne'er-do-wells constantly in search of a free meal in their home of Monterey, California. Garfield is an eager young man who considers himself to be wealthy after inheriting two houses located on Tortilla Flat. Proud of his new status, Garfield allows Tracy and his friends to move into one of the homes, keeping the other for himself. But Garfield's newfound wealth—not to mention his attraction to local cannery worker Lamarr—soon threatens come between the pals.

TORTILLA FLAT is an affectionate tale, told with sensitivity and a wonderfully offbeat sense of humor. Steinbeck's engaging characters are well treated by the talents of this ensemble and by Fleming's caring direction. Lamar is excellent (she considered this the best of all her roles) as the levelheaded, spunky woman who refuses to settle for anything she doesn't want. Her relationship with Garfield, a mixture of attraction and suspicion, is realistic and honest, a rarity for a screen romance. Garfield puts his heart into his portrayal of the earnest Danny, contributing a memorable characterization that complements Lamarr's wonderful work. Tracy's lovable rogue and Morgan's holy roller add to the film's cast of colorful characters. Indeed, Morgan received a well-deserved Oscar nomination as Best Supporting Actor, though he lost that year to Van Heflin in JOHNNY EAGER.

Fleming captures the nuances and ambience of life in this small town, a sincere effort that guides the performers with care through the material. MGM built an entire village over three acres of land for the film that Garfield dearly wanted to do, though he had to wait some time before Warner Bros. agreed to loan him to MGM. Louis B. Mayer, MGM's head, also liked the idea of Garfield in the role, and, reportedly, the powerful mogul was not above some unorthodox pressuring to get his man. Mayer is said to have threatened to expose Warner Bros. for not making good on their pledges to certain charitable groups unless Garfield was allowed to make the film.

TOTAL RECALL
DVD
1990 109m c Action/Science Fiction ★★
Mario Kassar-Andrew Vajna-Carolco-Ronald Shusett R (U.S.)

Arnold Schwarzenegger (Doug Quaid), Rachel Ticotin (Melina), Sharon Stone (Lori Quaid), Ronny Cox (Cohaagen), Michael Ironside (Richter), Marshall Bell (George/Kuato), Mel Johnson Jr. (Benny), Michael Champion (Helm), Roy Brocksmith (Dr. Edgemar), Ray Baker (McClane)

p, Buzz Feitshans, Ronald Shusett; d, Paul Verhoeven; w, Ronald Shusett, Dan O'Bannon, Gary Goldman (based on a story by Ronald Shusett, Dan O'Bannon, Jon Povill, from the short story "We Can Remember It for You Wholesale" by Phillip K. Dick); ph, Jost Vacano (Technicolor); ed, Frank J. Urioste; m, Jerry Goldsmith; prod d, William Sandell; art d, James Tocci, Jose Rodriguez Granada; fx, Rob Bottin, Thomas L. Fisher, Eric Brevig; cos, Erica Edell Phillips; anim, Jeff Burks

AAN Best Sound: Nelson Stoll, Michael J. Kohut, Carlos DeLarios, Aaron Rochin; AA Best Visual Effects: Eric Brevig, Rob Bottin, Tim McGovern, Alex Funke; AAN Best Sound Effects Editing: Stephen H. Flick

Ugly, stupid, loud, offensive, and pointlessly violent—let's not mince words—this film should be called TOTAL REJECT. This is prime example of an unfortunate tendency in modern blockbuster moviemaking. Runningly mindlessly amok drunk on money and contempt, TOTAL RECALL is overloaded with inelegant special effects, bone-crunching "action," hideously cheesy make up effects, and gaping plot holes. That's entertainment? Any intelligent science fiction fan would be well advised to steer clear of this turkey and read a book instead. The late great Philip K. Dick must be retching in his grave at this "adaptation" of his short story, "We Can Remember It for You Wholesale." One would never know from watching this headache-inducing movie that Dick was one of the most cerebral writers in science fiction. Part of what makes this film so infuriating is that the premise is pure gold but the execution is insulting to the audience. Still it does have its passionate admirers. It takes all kinds....

Set in the year 2084, TOTAL RECALL tells the story of Doug Quaid (Schwarzenegger), a construction worker with a beautiful wife (Sharon Stone) and a nice home. This society of the future has provided a fairly good life for Quaid. Mars has become a colony of Earth but Quaid has never had time to vacation there though he dreams of it every night (and of a mysterious woman he has never met). Quaid decides to pay a visit to Rekall Inc., a "travel" service that specializes in implanting artificial memories of vacations into its customers' brains. One can recline in a high-tech chair and enjoy all the pleasures of a vacation at an accelerated rate with none of the fuss. Quaid purchases a memory of a trip to Mars. Included in the package is Rekall's special "Ego Trip" which allows the customer to take his "trip" as another person. Quaid chooses to travel as a fictional secret agent. When the doctors begin the implant, something goes terribly wrong. Even before the memory is implanted, Quaid becomes crazed, claiming that he *is* a secret agent from Mars. Is this a previous implant or is it a real memory that had been obscured? The doctors subdue and tranquilize Quaid and release him. Later, Quaid is attacked by coworkers and nearly killed by his wife. She confirms that he really is an agent posing as a construction worker. She also explains that she is not really his wife but actually another agent assigned to watch him. After fighting off would-be killers and learning more about his past (with the help of a pre-recorded message from himself), Quaid escapes to Mars to unlock the rest of the mystery.

Up to this point TOTAL RECALL is fascinating as it deals with some recurring themes from Dick's fiction such as the search for identity, the slippery nature of reality, and the effect of drugs on perception. Rumor has it that Matthew Broderick was originally slated to star. If he had been the protagonist, this would have been a radically different film, probably a much better one. Broderick would have been credible as a regular Walter Mitty who discovers that he may have had, unbeknownst to himself, a secret life of high adventure. In contrast, who could be less convincing as a regular guy than Schwarzenegger? The Arnold can be just fine in the right vehicle (e.g. THE TERMINATOR and PREDATOR) but here his presence, and the obligatory tone that goes with it, turns an interesting science fiction premise into just another noisy dumb shoot-em-up. Pity.

TOTO LE HEROS

1991 90m c Drama/Comedy/Fantasy ★★★★
Iblis Films/Les Productions Philippe Dussart/   PG-13
Metropolis Filmproduktion/RTBF Telefilms/FR3
Films Production/Zweites Deutsches Fernsehen/
Jacqueline Pierreux (Belgium/France/Germany)

Michel Bouquet (Thomas—As an Old Man/Voice of Adult Thomas), Mireille Perrier (Voice of Evelyne As an Old Woman/Adult Evelyne), Jo De Backer (Thomas—As an Adult), Thomas Godet (Thomas—As a Child), Sandrine Blancke (Alice),

Fabienne Loriaux (Thomas's Mother), Klaus Schindler (Thomas's Father), Patrick Waleffe (Voice of Thomas's Father), Didier DeNeck (Mr. Kant), Peter Bohlke (Alfred—As an Old Man)

p, Pierre Drouot, Dany Geys; d, Jaco Van Dormael; w, Jaco Van Dormael; ph, Walther Vanden Ende; ed, Susana Rossberg; m, Pierre Van Dormael; art d, Hubert Pouille; cos, Suzanne Van Well

A remarkable, visually enchanting first feature from former professional clown Jaco Van Dormael. TOTO skips back and forth through time, unraveling the obsessed thoughts of the bitter, retired Thomas Van Hosebroeck (Michel Bouquet). Thomas is convinced that, as a baby, he was accidentally switched with neighbor Alfred Kant, who grew up in the lap of luxury while Thomas had to endure the hardships and indignities of a tough working-class upbringing. Thomas's troubled childhood includes falling in love with his sister Alice (in his eyes they aren't really related), who is killed when, at Thomas's urging, she sets a retaliatory fire on Alfred's property. As an adult, Thomas begins an affair with Alfred's wife, Evelyne, who agrees to run away with Thomas but is late for their train-station rendezvous. (Certain he's been abandoned again, Thomas leaves the station, failing to see Evelyne arrive an instant later.) At sixty, Thomas at last perceives an opportunity to get even with his lifelong secret nemesis, now a prominent industrialist, via a plot involving political terrorists. Recurring throughout Thomas's daydreams is Toto, an archetypal fantasy figure who looks like a stockier version of Inspector Clouseau and is perpetually doing battle with the forces of evil (gangster stand-ins for Alfred).

One can hardly imagine any other way for the intricate, metaphysical premise of TOTO to unfold, other than through this controlled explosion of impressions. The multi-flashback structure uses recurrent motifs and coincident images, notably of family, fire and flight, to vividly evoke the wonders and horrors of childhood.

TOUCH OF CLASS, A

1973 105m c Comedy/Romance   DVD
Brut (U.K.)   ★★★★
                                            PG

George Segal (Steve Blackburn), Glenda Jackson (Vicki Allessio), Paul Sorvino (Walter Menkes), Hildegard Neil (Gloria Blackburn), Cec Linder (Wendell Thompson), K. Callan (Patty Menkes), Mary Barclay (Martha Thompson), Michael Elwyn (Cecil), Nadim Sawalha (Night Hotel Manager), Ian Thompson (Derek)

p, Melvin Frank; d, Melvin Frank; w, Melvin Frank, Jack Rose; ph, Austin Dempster (Panavision, Technicolor); ed, Bill Butler; m, John Cameron; prod d, Terrence Marsh; art d, Alan Tomkins; cos, Ruth Myers

AAN Best Picture; AA Best Actress: Glenda Jackson; AAN Best Original Story and Screenplay: Melvin Frank, Jack Rose; AAN Best Original Dramatic Score: John Cameron; AAN Best Song: "All That Love Went to Waste"; Georgie Barrie (Music), Sammy Cahn (Lyrics)

Joseph E. Levine (THE GRADUATE, THE LION IN WINTER, CARNAL KNOWLEDGE) picked a winner when he elected to present this very funny film about infidelity in London. Segal is an American insurance executive living in London with wife (Neil) and children. He's playing softball in the regular Sunday game near the Albert Memorial in Hyde Park one Sunday when he meets Jackson, a divorcee with two children of her own. Segal suggests that they have a tryst in Spain and is very surprised when she agrees. Making excuses to his wife, Segal takes Jackson to Malaga for what he hopes will be a sexual idyll. But Segal's friend Sorvino is on the same plane. Farcical complications, and romance, ensue.

The company behind the film was Brut Productions, part of the Brut cosmetics firm headed by George Barrie.

Barrie always fancied himself a composer and cowrote the film's Oscar-nominated song (lyrics by Sammy Cahn), "All That Love Went to Waste," as well as two other tunes. Shot on location in Spain and London, and interiors were done at Lee Studios in London. The picture did quite well at the box office. Segal is charming, but everyone knew he could play comedy. The big surprise was Jackson's impeccable comic timing, which some likened to that of Katharine Hepburn. The softball scene at the start of the film features many of the expatriate Americans who lived in London at the time and played regularly. Frank was not nominated for his direction, but he should have been. The film is in excellent taste and is a tribute to Frank and his cowriter, Jack Rose. Later, George Barrie would team up with Frank's former partner, Norman Panama, and produce I WILL, I WILL... FOR NOW with less than spectacular results.

TOUCH OF EVIL
1958 108m bw Crime ★★★★★
Universal   (U.S.)

Charlton Heston (Ramon Miguel "Mike" Vargas), Janet Leigh (Susan Vargas), Orson Welles (Hank Quinlan), Joseph Calleia (Pete Menzies), Akim Tamiroff ("Uncle Joe" Grandi), Val DeVargas (Pancho), Ray Collins (District Attorney Adair), Dennis Weaver (Motel Clerk), Joanna Moore (Marcia Linnekar), Mort Mills (Schwartz)

p, Albert Zugsmith; d, Orson Welles, Harry Keller (uncredited); w, Orson Welles (based on the novel Badge of Evil by Whit Masterson); ph, Russell Metty; ed, Virgil Vogel, Aaron Stell; m, Henry Mancini; art d, Alexander Golitzen, Robert Clatworthy; cos, Bill Thomas

Wild Welles rides again—adapting a shelved script written by Paul Manash for Albert Zugsmith, King of the Bs, from Whit Masterson's novel Badge of Evil (which Welles never bothered to read). The result? A film about love of film even more than the stinking, perverse little thriller it presents itself as. Already famous for directing perhaps the greatest film ever made, CITIZEN KANE, Welles opens TOUCH OF EVIL with what may be the greatest single shot ever put on film. It is a spectacular tracking crane shot which crosses the Mexican/U.S. border, thereby visually foreshadowing the thematic elements to come—the differences that exist between two peoples, the Mexican and the Americans; the line Charlton Heston's character crosses from being a law-abiding husband to a vengeful madman; and the line Orson Welles's character crosses from good cop to evil cop. When a car explodes after crossing the border, both U.S. cop Hank Quinlan (Welles) and Mexican narcotics agent Mike Vargas (Heston) begin their investigations. Almost immediately Quinlan has a suspect, Sanchez (Victor Millan), a young Mexican who is involved with the dead man's daughter Marcia (Moore). In order to secure a conviction, Quinlan plants some dynamite in Sanchez's flat, but Vargas is wise to Quinlan's game. With help from Pete Menzies (Calleia), a long-time friend of Quinlan's, Vargas investigates Quinlan's past, all the while trying to solve the murder and protect his wife (Leigh) from a number of dangerous locals. Directing his first film in America since 1948's MACBETH, Welles was originally just supposed to act in TOUCH OF EVIL. The misunderstanding that led to this bizarre and twisted masterpiece began when Heston read a script based on the novel Badge of Evil. Hearing that Welles was involved, and assuming that his involvement meant as actor and director, Heston told producer Zugsmith that he would love to do the project. Rather than lose Heston, Zugsmith managed to get Universal to agree to let Welles direct, on the condition that he could also rewrite. Although much of the mystery element is revealed to the audience, it is Vargas who cannot unravel all the threads and make his clues add up to anything.

This nightmarish descent into dark entertainment has so much weirdness going on it's amazing. Marlene Dietrich, reprising her GOLDEN EARRINGS drag, smoking cigars and scraping pots, almost steals it. Complete with German accent and huge, light eyes at half mast, she's the most surreal excuse for a Mexican gypsy you've ever seen. When she sees Welles, big as a house with a false nose, it's the film's best line and a prophecy of Wellesian doom: "You're a mess, honey. You've been eating too much candy." Like Dietrich, Heston skips the Mexican accent as well. He looks like a muscular, surly version of an El Greco. Janet Leigh is at her most perversely innocent, and besides lots of grisly scenes (a murder by Welles the worst), there are a slew of outrageous cameos by Welles crony Joseph Cotten, Zsa Zsa Gabor (totally unaware what kind of film she's making), Dennis Weaver (unbelievably loopy), Ray Collins and the wildest, Mercedes McCambridge as a butch biker chick. The blonde in the exploding car is Joi Lansing, the poor man's Mamie Van Doren. EVIL was filmed at Universal, with some locations at Venice Beach. It's greatly enhanced by Mancini's dangerous, Latin Rock score. Go for the rediscovered (1976) 108 minute version. Baroque, maddening, and totally inspired.

TOUCHING THE VOID
2004 106m c/bw Documentary/Docudrama ★★★★
FilmFour/Darlow Smithson Productions/
Film Council/PBS   (U.K./U.S.)

Joe Simpson (Himself), Simon Yates (Himself), Richard Hawking (Himself), Brendan Mackey (Joe Simpson), Nicholas Aaron (Simon Yates), Ollie Ryall (Richard Hawking)

p, John Smithson (based on the book by Joe Simpson); d, Kevin MacDonald; ph, Mike Eley; ed, Justine Wright; m, Alex Heffes; art d, Patrick Bill; fx, Red Vision; cos, Patrick Bill

Combining recent interviews with real-life mountain climbers Joe Simpson and Simon Yates with re-creations stunningly shot on location, Kevin Macdonald's gripping docudrama tells the unbelievable true story of a dangerous expedition gone horribly awry.

In 1985, the young but experienced British climbers set out to scale the west face of Siula Grande, a previously unconquered 21,000-foot ascent in the Peruvian Andes. Yates, 21, and Simpson, 25, were climbing Alpine style, tied together with ropes and carrying their belongings instead of establishing a series of camps. The technique leaves little room for error, and the simplest of accidents could spell catastrophe. Simpson and Yates reached the summit with little incident, but misfortune struck on the way down: Simpson slid down a steep slope and broke his leg; with his tibia forced up through his knee, he was in extreme pain and unable to walk. Yates attempted to lower his partner down from the mountaintop using their available rope, but another disaster soon followed: Inching along in the dark, Yates accidentally lowered Simpson over a ledge. Unbeknownst to Yates, Simpson now dangled over an 80-foot drop, and fierce winds made communication impossible. Faced with a terrible choice—cutting the rope and almost certainly killing his partner, or sliding over the edge himself—Yates cut the rope. The next morning, Yates climbed down to their original campsite at the mountain's base, presuming Simpson was dead. He wasn't, and his 150-foot fall into a deep crevasse proved to be only the beginning of a nightmare.

The fact that Simpson appears onscreen to narrate his own story means the outcome is a foregone conclusion, but it hardly matters. You'll watch the entire harrowing ordeal with your heart firmly lodged in your mouth.

TOUS LES MATINS DU MONDE

1991 114m c   Drama/Biography/Musical   ★★★½
Film par film/Divali Films/DD Productions/Sedif/
FR3 Films Production/Paravision International
(France)

Jean-Pierre Marielle *(Monsieur de Saint Colombe)*, Gerard
Depardieu *(Marin Marias)*, Anne Brochet *(Madeleine)*, Guillaume
Depardieu *(Young Marin Marais)*, Caroline Sihol *(Madame de
Sainte Colombe)*, Carole Richert *(Toinette)*, Violaine Lacroix
(Young Madeleine), Nadege Teron *(Young Toinette)*, Myriam
Boyer *(Guignotte)*, Jean-Claude Dreyfus *(Abbe Mathieu)*

p, Jean-Louis Livi; d, Alain Corneau; w, Alain Corneau, Pascal
Quignard (from his novel); ph, Yves Angelo; ed, Marie-Josephe
Berroyer; m, Jordi Savall; prod d, Yves Angelo; cos, Corrine Jorry

TOUS LES MATINS DU MONDE recounts the real-life
story of master 17th-century French musician M. de Saint
Colombe (Jean-Pierre Marielle) and his brilliant protege,
Marin Marais. A grandly sentimental, eccentric romance, the
film also tackles some hefty philosophical and aesthetic questions. It's a heady, intoxicating mix. The film's framing narrative introduces us to the mature Marais (a periwigged Gerard
Depardieu at his bloated, foppish best), surrounded by his
adoring students in the royal musical chambers. Despite having found fame and fortune as musical director at the court of
Louis XIV, Marais is unfulfilled. Compared to his former
mentor, the legendary Saint Colombe, Marais feels like an
impostor. In flashback, he ruefully recalls his salad days as a
student of Saint Colombe and lover of his mentor's elder
daughter, Madeleine (Anne Brochet).

Though he's not on screen for very long, Gerard
Depardieu gives a marvelously fussy performance as the
older Marais. In an impressive film debut, his 21-year-old
son Guillaume portrays the aspiring artist as a young man
with real charm and conviction. Anne Brochet exudes a win-
ning blend of naivete and sophistication and Jean-Pierre
Marielle's deadpan portrayal of Saint Colombe is wonder-
fully offbeat, filled with either long silences or aphorisms.
("Urinating is a chromatic descent; music exists to say things
words cannot say.") The driving force of TOUS LES
MATINS, though, is the music—original compositions of
Saint Colombe and Marais, with additional works by Lully,
Couperin and Savall, conducted and performed by Jordi
Savall and the Concert of Nations.

TOUT VA BIEN

1972 95m   c   Drama   **DVD** ★★★½
Lido/Empire (France)

Jane Fonda *(She)*, Yves Montand *(He)*, Vittorio Caprioli *(Factory
Manager)*, Jean Pignol *(Delegate)*, Pierre Ondry *(Frederic)*,
Ilizabeth Chauvin *(Genevieve)*, Eric Chartier *(Lucien)*, Yves
Gabrielli *(Leon)*

p, Jean-Pierre Rassam; d, Jean-Luc Godard, Jean-Pierre Gorin;
w, Jean-Luc Godard, Jean-Pierre Gorin; ph, Armand Marco; ed,
Kernout Peitier

Jean-Luc Godard's most commercial film since WEEKEND
and his strongest attempt to bring political thought into popular film. In order to deliver his message of class struggle
Godard signed two famous actors—Jane Fonda and Yves
Montand. The plot of TOUT VA BIEN exists only, as
Godard says in the film, to provide "a story for those who
shouldn't still need one." Fonda is an American news reporter
living in Paris with her husband, Montand, a former "New
Wave" film director, who has turned to directing commercials. They pay a visit to a sausage factory and find themselves in the middle of a work stoppage. The workers spout
Maoist slogans and read political speeches into the cameras

while taking over the factory's corporate offices. The plant
manager is locked in his office and not even allowed to go to
the bathroom. TOUT VA BIEN ends without neatly tying up
the narrative, letting "each individual create his own history."
It is different from Godard's other political films (WIND
FROM THE EAST, SEE YOU AT MAO, and VLADIMIR
ET ROSA to name a few). It received a commercial release
(many of his other political films were shown only to workers and students), had two "movie stars" and even received
financial backing from Paramount (which opted not to distribute). The most impressive visuals are a multileveled cutaway of an office building which allows a view of all the
offices at the same time, and a bravura tracking shot through
an ultra-modern supermarket. TOUT VA BIEN was a noble
effort to bring anti-bourgeois cinema to the masses; needless
to say, the masses stayed home.

TOWERING INFERNO, THE

1974 165m   c   Disaster   **DVD** ★★
Fox/Warner Bros.   (U.S.)   PG

Steve McQueen *(Fire Chief Michael O'Hallorhan)*, Paul Newman
(Doug Roberts), William Holden *(Jim Duncan)*, Faye Dunaway
(Susan Franklin), Fred Astaire *(Harlee Claiborne)*, Susan Blakely
(Patty Simmons), Richard Chamberlain *(Roger Simmons)*,
Jennifer Jones *(Lisolette Mueller)*, O.J. Simpson *(Security Chief
Jernigan)*, Robert Vaughn *(Sen. Gary Parker)*

p, Irwin Allen; d, John Guillermin, Irwin Allen; w, Stirling Silliphant
(based on the novels *The Tower* by Richard Martin Stern and *The
Glass Inferno* by Thomas M. Scortia, Frank M. Robinson); ph,
Fred Koenekamp, Joseph Biroc, Jim Freeman (Panavision,
DeLuxe Color); ed, Harold F. Kress, Carl Kress; m, John Williams;
prod d, William J. Creber; art d, Ward Preston; fx, A.D. Flowers,
Logan Frazee, L.B. Abbott; cos, Paul Zastupnevich

AAN Best Picture; AAN Best Supporting Actor: Fred Astaire; *AA
Best Cinematography:* Fred J. Koenekamp, Joseph Biroc; *AA Best
Film Editing:* Harold F. Kress, Carl Kress; *AAN Best Original
Dramatic Score:* John Williams; *AA Best Song:* "We May Never
Love Like This Again"; Al Kasha (Music & Lyrics), Joel Hirschhorn
(Music & Lyrics); *AAN Best Art Direction-Set Decoration:* William
Creber, Ward Preston, Raphael Bretton; *AAN Best Sound:*
Theodore Soderberg, Herman Lewis

Burn, baby, burn—and it's not a disco inferno, either. The disaster film which mercifully signaled the end of a cycle, THE
TOWERING INFERNO places an all-star cast consisting
mostly of has-beens and never-weres in a spangly glass tower,
only to torch the sucker. Faye Dunaway looks stoned, Paul
Newman and Steve ("When are you architects going to
learn?") McQueen look bored, William Holden looks sick,
O.J. Simpson gets to rescue a cat, Richard Chamberlain is
unpleasant, and Fred Astaire and Jennifer Jones act as if the
film is entitled THE COWERING INFERNO. No wonder
everybody's so afraid of burning to death here—their characters are cardboard!

TOY STORY

1995 80m   c   Animated/Fantasy/Children's   **DVD** ★★★½
Walt Disney Pictures/PIXAR Productions   (U.S.)   G

VOICES OF: Tom Hanks *(Woody)*, Tim Allen *(Buzz Lightyear)*,
Don Rickles *(Mr. Potato Head)*, Jim Varney *(Slinky Dog)*, Wallace
Shawn *(Rex)*, John Ratzenberger *(Hamm)*, Annie Potts *(Bo
Peep)*, John Morris *(Andy)*, Erik Von Detten *(Sid)*, Laurie Metcalf
(Mrs. Davis)

p, Ralph Guggenheim, Bonnie Arnold; d, John Lasseter; w, Joss
Whedon, Andrew Stanton, Joel Cohen, Alec Sokolow (from an
original story by John Lasseter, Pete Docter, Andrew Stanton,

and Joe Ranft); ed, Robert Gordon, Lee Unkrich; m, Randy Newman; art d, Ralph Eggleston; anim, Pete Docter, Rich Quade, Ash Brannon, Pixar Animation Studios

AAN Best Original Screenplay: Joss Whedon, Andrew Stanton, Joel Cohen, Alec Sokolow; story by John Lasseter, Pete Docter, Andrew Stanton, Joe Ranft; *AAN Best Musical or Comedy Score:* Randy Newman; *AAN Best Original Song:* "You've Got a Friend"; Randy Newman

Kids are mad about it; it's far from painful for parents; the voice of Mr. Potato Head is Don Rickles. What more could you ask?

Clever, fast-moving, and unobtrusively self-conscious, Disney's marketing triumph describes a struggle for status between two toys—old favorite Woody, a low-tech talking cowboy voiced by Tom Hanks, and newcomer Buzz Lightyear (voice of Tim Allen), an arrogant space ranger who threatens to upset the toy box. The mismatched heroes must team up against a vicious brat who's fond of mutilating his playthings and turning them into scary mutants. Needless to say, Woody and Buzz learn to set aside their differences and respect each other along the way, imparting a valuable lesson to viewers too young to have seen the LETHAL WEAPON films.

Billed as the first feature film constructed entirely of computer animation, TOY STORY is a visual masterpiece that must truly be seen to be believed. The brainchild of director John Lasseter and his team of computer animators at Pixar, TOY STORY genuinely makes viewers forget they're watching an animated film. For its considerable techincal achievements—which took four years and an army of computer animators to complete—TOY STORY was given a special Academy Award. Its bravura set pieces—notably the astonishing toy's-eye-view flying sequence—mark new milestones in animation. That such astonishing amounts of money, technology, and highly-skilled labor were put to use in constructing a kiddie matinee presumably says something disturbing about American capitalism and culture, but we'd rather not think about it.

TOY STORY 2
1999 92m c Animated/Drama ★★★
PIXAR Animation Studios/Walt Disney Pictures G
(U.S.)

VOICES OF: Tom Hanks *(Woody)*, Tim Allen *(Buzz Lightyear)*, Joan Cusack *(Jessie)*, Kelsey Grammer *(Prospector)*, Don Rickles *(Mr. Potato Head)*, Jim Varney *(Slinky Dog)*, Wallace Shawn *(Rex)*, John Ratzenberger *(Hamm)*, Annie Potts *(Bo Peep)*, Wayne Knight *(Al McWhiggin)*

p, Helene Plotkin, Karen Robert Jackson; d, John Lasseter, Lee Unkrich, Ash Brannon; w, Andrew Stanton, Rita Hsiao, Doug Chamberlin, Chris Webb (from an original story by John Lasseter, Pete Docter, Ash Brannon and Andrew Stanton); ph, Sharon Calahan; ed, Edie Bleiman, David Ian Salter, Lee Unkrich; m, Randy Newman; prod d, William Cone, Jim Pearson; art d, Matt White; fx, Kelly T. Peters; anim, Glenn McQueen, Kyle Balda, Dylan Brown

AAN Best Original Song: "When She Loved Me"; Randy Newman

Contrary to what the title might suggest, this sequel to Pixar's 1995 milestone in computer animation is neither an unimaginative retread nor a second-rate follow up, but rather a fresh, touching, and very clever comedy in its own right. Unbeknownst to everyone including himself, Woody (voice of Tom Hanks), the lovable pull-string cowboy, isn't just any old toy: he was once the star of "Woody's Roundup," a vintage TV puppet show. Sweaty nostalgia merchant Al McWhiggin (Wayne Knight) has already assembled the rest of the highly collectible "Roundup" gang—rootin' tootin' cowgirl Jessie (Joan Cusack), lovable horse Bullseye, cranky prospector Stinky Pete (Kelsey Grammer)—and with Woody in place, McWhiggin can sell his whole collection to a museum in Japan for a pretty penny. With so much at stake, toynapping seems a small risk to run. And so it falls to Buzz Lightyear (Tim Allen), Mr. Potato Head (Don Rickles), piggy bank Hamm (John Ratzenberger), plastic dinosaur "Nervous" Rex (Wallace Shawn), and Slinky Dog (Jim Varney) to retrieve Woody from McWhiggin's lair before the youngster who owns and loves them all gets home from cowboy camp.

The story is simple enough for young children to follow, and the computer-animated images are both bright and surprisingly complex. Adults won't find the action heart-stopping (it would take a four-year-old to believe there's actually a chance that Mr. Potato Head might be crushed by oncoming traffic), but they'll find plenty to smile at in the film's clever homages to films ranging from STAR WARS to JURASSIC PARK. And the pain of toys abandoned by growing children is enough to tug at the tightest heartstrings.

TRADING PLACES
DVD
1983 106m c Comedy ★★★
Paramount (U.S.) R

Dan Aykroyd *(Louis Winthorpe III)*, Eddie Murphy *(Billy Ray Valentine)*, Ralph Bellamy *(Randolph Duke)*, Don Ameche *(Mortimer Duke)*, Denholm Elliott *(Coleman)*, Kristin Holby *(Penelope Witherspoon)*, Paul Gleason *(Clarence Beeks)*, Jamie Lee Curtis *(Ophelia)*, James Belushi *(Harvey)*, Al Franken

p, Aaron Russo; d, John Landis; w, Timothy Harris, Herschel Weingrod; ph, Robert Paynter (Metrocolor); ed, Malcolm Campbell; m, Elmer Bernstein; prod d, Gene Rudolf; cos, Deborah Nadoolman

AAN Best Song Score: Elmer Bernstein

The plot of this fine comedy owes more than a passing nod to Mark Twain's *The Prince and the Pauper:* street hustler Billy Ray Valentine (Eddie Murphy) and upscale yuppie Louis Winthorpe III (Dan Aykroyd) are forced to switch positions in life to resolve a bet between two rich brothers, Mortimer and Randolph Duke (Don Ameche and Ralph Bellamy), who frame Winthorpe and welcome Valentine into their business in his place. The rise of Valentine and the fall of Winthorpe are a source of great fun. The street hustler proves that his years in back alleys have stood him in good stead, providing him with all sorts of fresh business ideas. In Winthorpe's case, however, it is only when he meets and falls for hooker Ophelia (Jamie Lee Curtis) that he begins to appear in a sympathetic light. Although it tends to rely heavily on slapstick in the second half, the movie provides plenty of laughs and is one of director Landis's best efforts—despite overtones of racism that were perhaps intended ironically but have no business in the story.

TRAFFIC
(TRAFIC)
1972 89m c Comedy ★★★★
Corona (France) G

Jacques Tati *(Mons. Hulot)*, Maria Kimberly *(Maria, the Public Relations Girl)*, Marcel Fraval *(Truck Driver)*, Honore Bostel *(Managing Director of ALTRA)*, Tony Kneppers *(Dutch Garage Proprietor)*, Francois Maisongrosse *(Francois)*, Franco Ressel, Mario Zanuelli

p, Robert Dorfmann; d, Jacques Tati; w, Jacques Tati, Jacques Lagrange; ph, Marcel Weiss, Edward Van Der Enden

(Eastmancolor); ed, Maurice Laumain, Sophie Tatischeff, Jacques Tati; m, Charles Dumont; art d, Adrien de Rooy

Jacques Tati's fifth picture in 25 years (his fourth, PLAY-TIME, was not released until 1973), TRAFFIC is a collection of sight gags concerning the modern problem of automobile overpopulation. Tati again plays himself in this English-dubbed outing—the rain-coated, pipe-smoking eccentric—though now he has invented an ultramodern camping vehicle. With Kimberly, the public relations girl of his firm, he plans to take his new car from Paris to an Amsterdam auto show. A long series of misadventures befalls them.

Any plot synopsis of a Tati picture proves to be fruitless since what is most important are the visual gags. So vital are the visuals that Tati rarely uses dialogue, thereby negating the need for subtitles. One of the picture's funniest moments is Tati's attempt to climb the vines that cling to a house, pulling them down in the process. Instead of stopping there, however, he yanks them back up and winds up hanging upside down by his foot, refusing to give in and yell for help. Many of the film's brightest moments do not even include Tati (it was his wish that he would eventually be only a minor character in his films). One gag has Kimberly thinking that her dog has been crushed by the back wheel of her sports car. She is unaware that a group of mischievous passersby simply put one of their coats (which is made from the same fur as the dog) under the wheel. Various other brilliant bits are created through montage. Various people are seen picking their noses while waiting for traffic to advance; or a connection is made between the car a person drives and that person's physical appearance; or a con-nection between the person and the movement of their wind-shield wipers. Tati, who's brilliant at commenting on modernization, here again provides insights into modern life that make for one of the freshest and funniest pictures to hit the screen in years.

TRAFFIC

2000 140m c   Crime/Thriller   ★★★½
Beford Falls/Fifty Cannon/Gramercy Pictures/   R
USA Films   (U.S.)

Michael Douglas (Robert Wakefield), Benicio Del Toro (Javier Rodriguez), Catherine Zeta-Jones (Helena Ayala), Don Cheadle (Montel Gordon), Erika Christensen (Caroline Wakefield), Luis Guzman (Ray Castro), Miguel Ferrer (Eduardo Ruiz), Dennis Quaid (Arnie Metzger), Topher Grace (Seth Abrahams), Steven Bauer (Carlos Ayala)

p, Edward Zwick, Marshall Herskovitz, Laura Bickford; d, Steven Soderbergh; w, Stephen Gaghan (based on Traffik by Simon Moore); ph, Peter Andrews; ed, Stephen Mirrione; m, Cliff Martinez; prod d, Philip Messina; art d, Keith P. Cunningham; fx, Kevin Hannigan; cos, Louise Frogley

AA Best Actor: Benicio Del Toro; AA Best Director: Steven Soderbergh; AA Best Film Editing: Stephen Mirrione; AA Best Adapted Screenplay: Stephen Gaghan; AAN Best Picture

Inspired by a six-hour UK miniseries, this examination of the cocaine trade and its effects on families from both sides of the U.S.-Mexican border is intelligently scripted by Stephen Gaghan and deftly directed by Steven Soderbergh.

Three main narrative threads branch off as the film unfolds. In Mexico, straight-arrow cop Javier (Benicio Del Toro) and his partner (Jacob Vargas), join forces with General Arturo Salazar (Tomas Milian), who claims he wants to smash the big-time Obregon drug cartel. Javier suspects Salazar's motives but can't easily extricate himself from the general's circle. In San Diego, CA, two DEA agents (Luis Guzman and Don Cheadle) pressure a busted mid-level deal-er (Miguel Ferrer) to roll over on bigwig Carlos Ayala (Steven Bauer), whose prosperous, suburban life is paid for by drugs.

Ayala's pregnant wife (Catherine Zeta-Jones) must make hard decisions about her future in the wake of her husband's arrest. And in Ohio, State Supreme Court Justice Robert Wakefield (Michael Douglas), newly appointed as the country's drug czar, is blissfully unaware that his daughter, Caroline (Erika Christensen), has begun freebasing crack cocaine with her boyfriend (Topher Grace).

Together, these stories paint a portrait of the drug trade from virtually every point of view: from street-level dealers and cops on the beat to international traffickers and policy makers. Soderbergh gives the film a harsh but stylized look, manipulating color (scraped-looking sepia for the Southwestern sequences, icy blue for Ohio and Washington, DC), and using available light and handheld camera. Though meticulously researched and filled with striking moments, the movie ultimately feels oddly disconnected. Ironically, the problem may be the subject itself. Decades of media coverage of America's drug war may have exhausted interest in even as astute a treatment as this.

TRAIL OF THE LONESOME PINE, THE

1936 102m c   Drama   ★★★½
Paramount   (U.S.)

Sylvia Sidney (June Tolliver), Fred MacMurray (Jack Hale), Henry Fonda (Dave Tolliver), Fred Stone (Judd Tolliver), Nigel Bruce (Mr. Thurber), Beulah Bondi (Melissa), Robert Barrat (Buck Falin), Spanky McFarland (Buddy), Fuzzy Knight (Tater), Otto Fries (Corsey)

p, Walter Wanger; d, Henry Hathaway; w, Grover Jones, Harvey Thew, Horace McCoy (based on the novel by John Fox Jr.); ph, W. Howard Greene, Robert C. Bruce (Technicolor); ed, Robert Bischoff; art d, Hans Dreier

AAN Best Song: "A Melody From The Sky"; Louis Alter (Music), Sidney Mitchell (Lyrics)

This was the first outdoor Technicolor three-strip film and Henry Fonda's first movie in color. Set in the backwoods of Kentucky in the early years of the 20th century, it's the story of feudin' and fussin' mountain people. Two clans have been battling for years, and, as the movie begins, Robert Barrat's family is firing at the cabin of Fred Stone's family, just as Beulah Bondi is giving birth to a daughter. Time passes and Sylvia Sidney grows up under the watchful eye of her broth-er, Fonda. He is almost killed in a fight with the rival clan, but Fred MacMurray, an engineer who has come to the locale with the railroad, saves his life. Fonda wants to keep his sister away from city slickers like MacMurray, believing she would be better off in love with a local boy. The advent of the railroad has brought new prosperity. MacMurray arranges for Sidney to be accepted by a school in Louisville, but Fonda is angered and lets MacMurray know it. The two men get into a fist fight, but then stop to fend off the Barrat clan, who have launched an onslaught on the railroad camp. The workers are frightened for their lives and leave the area in a shambles. Younger broth-er Spanky McFarland is killed in the battle, so, when Sidney returns from school in Louisville, she calls for a blood bath. MacMurray angers her when he attempts to inject a modicum of sanity into the proceedings. Fonda realizes that the feud must cease and offers to meet the rival clan leader. Barrat accepts and the time is set for the ritual handshake. In the meantime, however, Fonda is shot by one of Barrat's clan. Barrat can't believe what's happened and pays a visit to the Stone house to express his sorrow as Fonda lies moments from death. Fonda bids Stone and Barrat to shake hands, then watches as Sidney and MacMurray move close to each other.

Often poignant, filled with action, well-photographed, and even scored with four songs, this is a slice of Americana that proved successful at the box office. Cecil B. DeMille's version (1916) starred Charlotte Walker in the Sidney role, while Mary Miles Minter played the part in the 1923 version, directed by Charles Maigne. McFarland, who was only eight years old and already a veteran of several "Our Gang" shorts; shows his versatility in this film. Years later, Al Capp admitted that he'd based his famed "Li'l Abner" character on Fonda's role, and collectors of comic book lore will recognize some of Capp's early drawings as looking quite a bit like Fonda. Fuzzy Knight does a fine job acting and warbling the tunes. The song "Melody from the Sky" earned an Oscar nomination for Best Song. Other songs were: "Stack O' Lee Blues" (which may have been "Stagger Lee"), and "When It's Twilight on the Trail" (all by Sidney Mitchell and Lou Alter), plus Harry Carroll's "Trail of the Lonesome Pine."

TRAIN, THE 📀
(LE TRAIN)
1965 140m bw Thriller/War ★★★★
Artistes/Ariane/Dear (France/Italy/U.S.)

Burt Lancaster (*Labiche*), Paul Scofield (*Col. von Waldheim*), Jeanne Moreau (*Christine*), Michel Simon (*Papa Boule*), Suzanne Flon (*Miss Villard*), Wolfgang Preiss (*Herren*), Richard Munch (*Von Lubitz*), Albert Remy (*Didont*), Charles Millot (*Pesquet*), Jacques Marin (*Jacques*)

p, Jules Bricken; d, John Frankenheimer; w, Franklin Coen, Frank Davis, Walter Bernstein, Albert Husson (based on the novel *Le Front de l'Art* by Rose Valland); ph, Jean Tournier, Walter Wottitz; ed, David Bretherton, Gabriel Rongier; m, Maurice Jarre; prod d, Willy Holt; fx, Lee Zavitz; cos, Jean Zay

AAN Best Original Story and Screenplay: Franklin Coen, Frank Davis

A superior WWII film that provides plenty of edge-of-the-seat thrills, THE TRAIN also poses a rather serious philosophical question: is the preservation of art worth a human life? Set in France in the summer of 1944, with the Germans in retreat, the film begins as a German colonel, von Waldheim (Paul Scofield), is ordered to transport the collection of the Jeu de Paume Museum—including numerous masterpieces—by train to the Fatherland. The curator of the museum gets word of the plan to the Resistance, and they persuade Labiche (Burt Lancaster), a railway inspector, to try to save the priceless works of art. THE TRAIN was originally to have been helmed by Arthur Penn, but during the first two weeks of shooting the director had some severe disagreements with Lancaster and producer Jules Bricken and left the production. Lancaster then called in John Frankenheimer, whom he had just worked with on SEVEN DAYS IN MAY (they had also collaborated on THE YOUNG SAVAGES and THE BIRDMAN OF ALCA-TRAZ). The film was shot entirely on location in France, and Frankenheimer employed a number of cameras shooting simultaneously so that the action with the trains would be captured from several different angles with as few takes as possible. His camera placement perfectly captures the massive trains (no models or miniatures were used) from every conceivable perspective, and their movement is directly contrasted with the chess game played by Labiche and von Waldheim. The acting in the film is superb, with Scofield taking top honors as the obsessed German colonel, though veteran French character actor Michel Simon nearly steals the film as a determined old engineer.

TRAINING DAY 📀
2001 115m c Crime/Thriller ★★★½
Village Roadshow Pictures/NPV Entertainment/ R
Outlaw Productions/Warner Bros. (U.S.)

Denzel Washington (*Alonzo Harris*), Ethan Hawke (*Jake Hoyt*), Scott Glenn (*Roger*), Tom Berenger (*Stan Gursky*), Harris Yulin (*Doug Rosselli*), Raymond J. Barry (*Lou Jacobs*), Dr. Dre (*Paul*), Snoop Dogg (*Blue*), Macy Gray (*Sandman's Wife*), Cliff Curtis (*Smiley*)

p, Bobby Newmyer, Jeffrey Silver; d, Antoine Fuqua; w, David Ayer; ph, Mauro Fiore; ed, Conrad Buff; m, Mark Mancina; prod d, Naomi Shohan; art d, David Lazan; fx, Martin Bresin; cos, Michele Michel

AA Best Actor: Denzel Washington; *AAN Best Supporting Actor:* Ethan Hawke

The first day on a new job is never easy, but how many new hires are expected to smoke PCP-laced marijuana at gunpoint shortly after breakfast or have cocktails with a high-level drug dealer before lunch? Such is training day for LAPD rookie Jack Hoyt (Ethan Hawke), the closest thing to a hero in Antoine Fuqua's dark and extremely violent police thriller.

Hoyt figures the quick way to make detective is through the aggressive narcotics unit headed by Detective Sergeant Alonzo Harris (Denzel Washington). Clad in head-to-toe black, with heavy gold chains and a tattoo that reads "Death is certain. Life is not," Harris is a seasoned veteran of South Central L.A.'s mean streets, where he's learned not only how to stay alive, but how to turn a profit as well. Harris sets about upping Hoyt's street IQ by forcing him to smoke the doctored weed they pilfer from a bust and paying a visit to a dealer (Scott Glenn) who seems more like Harris's drinking buddy than a serious felon. But Harris has other things on his mind: he recently spent a very expensive weekend in Vegas during which he sank himself deep into debt with the Russian mob, who'd now like to have a word with him. As the day progresses, Hoyt's bright-eyed eagerness turns first to dismay, then terror, as his big career break fast becomes his biggest nightmare.

This is an uncharacteristically brutal performance from Academy Award winner Washington, who, after a string of upright but less interesting roles, is quite consciously playing against type. He's never seemed so menacing, nor has the City of Angels: Fuqua presents his hometown as a simmering cauldron of crime, though seeing such larger-than-life pop stars as Macy Gray and Snoop Dogg in bit parts undercuts the otherwise carefully constructed realism.

TRAINSPOTTING 📀
1995 93m c Drama ★★★½
Figment Films/Noel Gay Motion Picture Company/ R
Channel Four Films (U.K.)

Ewan McGregor (*Mark Renton*), Ewen Bremner (*Spud*), Jonny Lee Miller (*Sick Boy*), Kevin McKidd (*Tommy*), Robert Carlyle (*Begbie*), Kelly Macdonald (*Diane*), Peter Mullan (*Swanney*), James Cosmo (*Mr. Renton*), Eileen Nicholas (*Mrs. Renton*), Susan Vidler (*Allison*)

p, Andrew Macdonald; d, Danny Boyle; w, John Hodge (based on the novel by Irvine Welsh); ph, Brian Tufano; ed, Masahiro Hirakubo; prod d, Kave Quinn; art d, Tracey Gallacher; fx, Grant Mason, Tony Steers; cos, Rachael Fleming

AAN Best Adapted Screenplay: John Hodge

Perhaps the most influential, certainly the most hotly debated, UK film of the '90s. Brought to you by the writer-producer-director team that made their debut with SHALLOW GRAVE, TRAINSPOTTING is a rambling chronicle of high times in low company—DRUGSTORE COWBOY goes to Edinburgh. By turns cheeky, surreal, exhilarating, and stomach-churning, it follows assorted days in the lives of mangy Mark Renton (Ewan McGregor) and the scabby crew of junkies, deadbeats, thieves, liars, and nut jobs he calls friends.

TRAINSPOTTING proves that no novel—not even one as loosely structured and reliant on interior monologue as Welsh's—is unfilmable. Renton may be a degenerate boil on society's backside, but he also makes a clever, witty screen hero. Though the film softens the edges of Welsh's book, it doesn't back off from its most controversial theme; these characters are not duped by evil drug pushers, but consciously choose drugs over the banality of… well, pretty much everything else. While getting the squalor and degradation of the junkie lifestyle down to the last grotesque detail, TRAINSPOTTING also captures the way drug addiction gives structure and purpose to aimless lives, and evokes the breathtaking rapture of a fix. All this and a happy ending, too.

TRAPEZE

1956 105m c Drama ★★★½
Susan (U.S.)

Burt Lancaster *(Mike Ribble)*, Tony Curtis *(Tino Orsini)*, Gina Lollobrigida *(Lola)*, Katy Jurado *(Rosa)*, Thomas Gomez *(Bouglione)*, Johnny Puleo *(Max the Dwarf)*, Minor Watson *(John Ringling North)*, Gerard Landry *(Chikki)*, Jean-Pierre Kerien *(Otto)*, Sidney James *(Snake Charmer)*

p, James Hill; d, Carol Reed; w, James R. Webb, Liam O'Brien (based on the novel *The Killing Frost* by Max Catto); ph, Robert Krasker (CinemaScope, DeLuxe Color); ed, Bert Bates; m, Malcolm Arnold; art d, Rino Mondellini; fx, Jack Lannan

Despite some stiff acting and a ponderous script, this was a smash at the box office, if only because audiences got to see Lancaster, himself a former circus performer, playing against the attractive Lollobrigida and the handsome Curtis. Lancaster is a lame acrobat who is famed for having done the impossible, a "triple" off the trapeze before having the accident that caused his limp. Two somersaults in mid-air are a commonplace, but a triple is the stuff of which high flyer's dreams are made. He's working as a rigger for a Parisian circus when Curtis arrives, eager to meet Lancaster and learn from him. Curtis is the son of a former circus friend of Lancaster and wants to learn to do a triple. Lancaster does everything he can to discourage Curtis, but circus-owner Gomez would love to have some enormous starring act to help business. After a while, Curtis wears Lancaster down and the older man decides that he might recapture his own glory by helping Curtis achieve the feat. The two men become very close. Lollobrigida is a scheming member of a tumbling act who would like to have the fame and fortune that trapeze artists merit. She begins using her wiles on Lancaster, but he has no interest, so she turns to the more naive Curtis. The high-wire work is very exciting and Reed's direction of the triple is breathtaking. These assets more than compensate for the shortcomings of the remainder of the movie. Seen briefly is Johnny Puleo, the little person who served for so many years as one of the Harmonica Rascals with Borah Minevitch. The ambience of circus life is quite well conveyed.

TREASURE ISLAND

1934 109m bw Adventure ★★★½
MGM (U.S.)

Wallace Beery *(Long John Silver)*, Jackie Cooper *(Jim Hawkins)*, Lionel Barrymore *(Billy Bones)*, Otto Kruger *(Dr. Livesey)*, Lewis Stone *(Capt. Alexander Smollett)*, Nigel Bruce *(Squire Trelawney)*, Charles "Chic" Sale *(Ben Gunn)*, William V. Mong *(Pew)*, Charles McNaughton *(Black Dog)*, Dorothy Peterson *(Mrs. Hawkins)*

p, Hunt Stromberg; d, Victor Fleming; w, John Lee Mahin, Leonard Praskins, John Howard Lawson (based on the novel by Robert Louis Stevenson); ph, Ray June, Harold Rosson, Clyde De Vinna; ed, Blanche Sewell; m, Herbert Stothart; art d, Cedric Gibbons, Merrill Pye, Edwin B. Willis; cos, Dwight Franklin

Robert Louis Stevenson's *Treasure Island* transfers easily from the page to the screen in this first sound version of the classic adventure tale. Wallace Beery plays the famous Long John Silver and Jackie Cooper takes the role of the doughty Jim Hawkins. The film opens at a rough-and-tumble coastal pub where young Jim meets the drunken Billy Bones (Lionel Barrymore) and learns that the old rummy has a secret map of

an island in the Caribbean where a trove was left by a well-known pirate. When Billy Bones dies, Jim and two friends book passage on a ship run by Capt. Smollett (Lewis Stone). What they don't know, at first, is that practically all of the ship's men are one-time associates of the late pirate and one step from being cutthroats. What's more, all of them want their share of the booty. A beautiful production, a fine score, and a strong script all contribute to making this a respectable version of Stevenson's work.

TREASURE ISLAND

1950 96m c Adventure
Walt Disney Productions (U.K.)
DVD ★★★★ G

Bobby Driscoll *(Jim Hawkins)*, Robert Newton *(Long John Silver)*, Basil Sydney *(Capt. Smollett)*, Walter Fitzgerald *(Squire Trelawney)*, Denis O'Dea *(Dr. Livesey)*, Ralph Truman *(George Merry)*, Finlay Currie *(Capt. Bones)*, John Laurie *(Pew)*, Francis de Wolff *(Black Dog)*, Geoffrey Wilkinson *(Ben Gunn)*

p, Perce Pearce; d, Byron Haskin; w, Lawrence E. Watkin (based on the novel by Robert Louis Stevenson); ph, Freddie Young; ed, Alan Jaggs; m, Clifton Parker; prod d, Tom Morahan

This was Disney's first totally live-action movie, and it is, by far, the best film version of the familiar Stevenson story. Disney regular Bobby Driscoll takes on the coveted role of Jim Hawkins, and a number of reliable British actors round out the cast. This version has a marvelous full-bodied visual style that never appears to be studio-bound. When Disney wanted to rerelease the film in the 1970s, the MPAA rating system had arrived, and because of some rather graphic violence, the movie was given the dreaded (by Disney) "PG" rating. The offending scenes had to be snipped to acquire the desired "G" rating, depriving audiences of some excitement, but this remains an extremely satisfying film.

TREASURE OF THE SIERRA MADRE, THE

1948 126m bw Adventure
Warner Bros. (U.S.)
DVD ★★★★★

Humphrey Bogart *(Fred C. Dobbs)*, Walter Huston *(Howard)*, Tim Holt *(Curtin)*, Bruce Bennett *(Cody)*, Barton MacLane *(McCormick)*, Alfonso Bedoya *(Gold Hat)*, Arturo Soto Rangel *(Presidente)*, Manuel Donde *(El Jefe)*, Jose Torvay *(Pablo)*, Margarito Luna *(Pancho)*

p, Henry Blanke; d, John Huston; w, John Huston (based on the novel by Berwick Traven Torsvan); ph, Ted McCord; ed, Owen Marks; m, Max Steiner; art d, John Hughes; fx, William McGann, H.F. Koenekamp

AAN Best Picture; AA Best Supporting Actor: Walter Huston; AA Best Director: John Huston; AA Best Screenplay: John Huston

Arguably John Huston's greatest film, this powerful study of masculinity under pressure retains its power. There's gold in them thar hills and Humphrey Bogart, Walter Huston, and Tim Holt are hell-bent to find it. The rather preachy B. Traven novel about greed and its tragic consequences is made more lively and much more human by the father-and-son team of actor Walter Huston and director/writer John, with the invaluable assistance of Bogart. What a nice present to give your father at the end of his career. Bogart gives one of his most memorable performances as Fred C. Dobbs, an ordinary guy who gets transformed and finally consumed by greed.

On the bum in Tampico, Mexico, Bogart is reduced to panhandling. He meets and befriends another struggling American, Holt, and the two of them go to work for a shady contractor, MacLane, who takes them to a remote site where they slave away, their pay withheld until the job is done. When the work is finished and they return to Tampico, MacLane says he must go and pick up the payroll. Bogart and Holt complain that they don't have a cent, even to buy a beer, and he gives them a few dollars. They go to a cantina and drink, then check in at a flophouse where they take bunks next to a colorful, garrulous old man (Huston). Huston is regaling the other tramps about prospecting for gold, explaining that he has been at it since the Klondike days, having dug up fortunes and spent them. As Huston spins his tales, he adds that greed is usually the undoing of all prospectors. Bogart goes to sleep and the next day he and Holt look for MacLane and learn that he has a reputation for not paying his workers. They run into him on the street and have to beat him nearly senseless to get him to come up with their pay. Now that they have a little money, they decide prospecting might be a good idea, so they find Huston and ask if he wants to join them. He agrees, and says he's got a little money he can put into the venture. Just then, a young Mexican boy (Robert "Bobby" Blake, veteran of OUR GANG comedies and later famous as TV's "Baretta") who had earlier sold Bogart a lottery ticket, shows up and tells Bogart that his ticket is a winner. Bogart then adds his winnings to the stake and the three men set out to get the gear and equipment they'll need. The three start out as good buddies but wind up in a murderous tangle.

Both director John Huston and his distinguished father, Walter, won Oscars for this film, the only time father and son won the coveted gold statuettes. (In 1985, a third generation of the family won an Oscar when Anjelica Huston, John's daughter and Walter's granddaughter, was named Best Supporting Actress for her role in PRIZZI'S HONOR—also directed by John Huston.)

TREE GROWS IN BROOKLYN, A

1945 128m bw Drama ★★★★
Fox (U.S.)

Dorothy McGuire (Katie), Joan Blondell (Aunt Sissy), James Dunn (Johnny Nolan), Lloyd Nolan (McShane), Peggy Ann Garner (Francie Nolan), Ted Donaldson (Neeley Nolan), James Gleason (McGarrity), Ruth Nelson (Miss McDonough), John Alexander (Steve Edwards), B.S. Pully (Christmas Tree Vendor)

p, Louis D. Lighton; d, Elia Kazan; w, Tess Slesinger, Frank Davis (based on the novel by Betty Smith); ph, Leon Shamroy; ed, Dorothy Spencer; m, Alfred Newman; art d, Lyle Wheeler; fx, Fred Sersen; cos, Bonnie Cashin

AA Best Supporting Actor: James Dunn; AAN Best Screenplay: Frank Davis, Tess Slesinger

Elia Kazan's first directorial assignment in films proved to be one of the most endearing, honest family dramas of the era and is still timeless enough to be watched and savored decades later. Set in the Williamsburg area of Brooklyn in the first years of the 20th century, this film memorably captures the local ambiance, and the struggle of the urban poor, as it focuses on the drama of one Irish family. Matriarch McGuire worries about every penny because her husband, amiable loser Dunn, can't ever seem to earn enough to support her and their children (Donaldson and Garner). Protagonist Garner wants to write and dreams of a better life elsewhere. In the tenement there is a small tree that heroically withstands the harsh winter and the humid summer; for Garner, it becomes a symbol of survival, particularly when death strikes the family.

This episodic, charmingly sentimental movie is a trifle lengthy but never tedious. McGuire had only made one movie before, the charming CLAUDIA, and was only about 13 years older than Garner and 13 years younger than Dunn at the time of shooting. Kazan did not fall into the trap to which so many first-time directors are prey, i.e., impressing the eye with cinematic tricks. Instead, he wisely concentrated on evoking memorable performances from all concerned, and none was more rewarding than that of Dunn, who had starred in many

B movies for years before getting the opportunity to show his stuff here. Dunn, for many years, had been a notorious heavy drinker, and when he was first proposed for the role of the Irish singing waiter, Fox executives said no, that he was unreliable and a drunk. But studio boss Zanuck was persuaded that that was exactly what Dunn would be playing and, against all advice, cast the easygoing tippler in the role.

TREE OF WOODEN CLOGS, THE DVD

(L'ALBERO DEGLI ZOCCOLI)
1978 185m c Drama ★★★★½
G.P.C. Gruppo/Gaumont (Italy)

Luigi Ornaghi (Batisti), Francesca Moriggi (Batistina), Omar Brignoli (Minek), Antonio Ferrari (Tuni), Teresa Brescianini (Widow Runk), Giuseppe Brignoli (Grandpa Anselmo), Carlo Rota (Peppino), Pasqualina Brolis (Teresina), Massimo Fratus (Pierino), Francesca Villa (Annetta)

d, Ermanno Olmi; w, Ermanno Olmi; ph, Ermanno Olmi; ed, Ermanno Olmi; m, Johann Sebastian Bach

Approaching verite in style, and heavily influenced by American documentarist Robert Flaherty's ethnological classics, this naturalistic portrayal of Italian peasants neither glorifies their lives nor looks down on them. Olmi, who directed, scripted, photographed, and edited the film, concentrates on three peasant families (all finely acted by nonprofessionals) and their daily existence for the period of about one year. They live on an estate governed by a practically nonexistent landlord and work his land with the greatest of care and devotion. Interestingly, however, the least important facet of THE TREE OF WOODEN CLOGS is its plot. Instead, the focus is on the bond between people, as well as their relationship to the land. Olmi resists the urge to overly moralize the lives of these people as he considers what is beautiful as well as what is stagnant about their lives. At times he seems to suggest that here may reside a model for human existence, but he is generally content to present the film as an extended vignette. (It is interesting, though, how Olmi largely fails to consider the class relations structuring certain aspects of these people's lives.) A memorable picture which takes a sensitive, poetic look at a remarkable group of human beings without getting too romanticized about it, THE TREE OF WOODEN CLOGS was winner of the Golden Palm at the 1978 Cannes Film Festival, making it the second Italian film in a row to take top honors (the 1977 winner was the Taviani Brother's PADRE PADRONE).

TREES LOUNGE DVD

1996 94m c Comedy/Drama ★★★½
LIVE Entertainment/Addis/Wechsler/Hanley- R
Wyman/Seneca Falls Productions (U.S.)

Steve Buscemi (Tommy Basilio), Mark Boone Jr. (Mike), Chloe Sevigny (Debbie), Michael Buscemi (Raymond); Anthony LaPaglia (Rob), Elizabeth Bracco (Theresa), Daniel Baldwin (Jerry), Carol Kane (Connie), Debi Mazar (Crystal), Seymour Cassel (Uncle Al)

p, Brad Wyman, Chris Hanley; d, Steve Buscemi; w, Steve Buscemi; ph, Lisa Rinzler; ed, Kate Williams; m, Evan Lurie; prod d, Steve Rosenzweig; art d, Jennifer Alex; cos, Mari-An Ceo

Steve Buscemi—leading character actor of countless independent American films and a particular favorite of the Coen brothers and Quentin Tarantino—takes his turn behind the camera, and it's a winner.

Thirty-one-year-old Tommy Basilio (Buscemi) is what is commonly known as a loser. He's been fired from his job at the garage, has lost his girlfriend (Elizabeth Bracco) to his ex-best friend/ex-boss (Anthony LaPaglia), has been getting a little too comfy with his ex-girlfriend's underage niece (Chloe Sevigny), and he can't even cut it driving his late uncle's (Seymour Cassel) ice cream truck, because he gives kids the creeps. Tommy is also an alcoholic, and the greater part of his day is spent in a stupor on a bar stool at the Trees Lounge, chumming it up the with other not so beautiful losers.

It's clear from the outset that writer-director Buscemi has seen his share of John Cassavetes films. With his own fine ensemble cast, he's quite capable of capturing a similar sense of improvisatory spontaneity—Carol Kane's worn-out bartender and Debi Mazar's lacquered cookie in stiletto heels are superb creations. But where Cassavetes often uncovered the grotesquerie underlying such desperate lives (usually after one round too many), Buscemi's vison is rooted in compassion and a quirky humor that's entirely his own. Set in the Long Island, NY town of Valley Stream (Buscemi's home town), the film perfectly captures the suburban malaise that can waylay those New Yorkers who left the big city with dreams of a better life amid the green grass, picket fences, and corner bars.

TREMBLING BEFORE G-D   DVD

2001   84m   c   Documentary   ★★★★

Simcha Leib Productions/Turbulent Arts/Keshet Broadcasting Ltd./Pretty Pictures/Cinephil Ltd. (U.S./France/Israel)

Rabbi Steven Greenberg, Schlomo Ashkinazy, "Malka," "Leah," Mark, David, Michelle, "Devorah," Israel, "Chaim"

p, Sandi Simcha DuBowski, Marc Smolowitz; d, Sandi Simcha DuBowski; ph, Sandi Simcha DuBowski; ed, Susan Korda; m, John Zorn

---

This thought-provoking documentary about gay Orthodox Jews opens with two rather brutal quotations. The first is the infamous line from Leviticus that prescribes death for any "man who lies with a man." The second is a lesser-known passage from the Shulchan Aruch, a compendium of Jewish religious law, forbidding "women to rub against each other." Filmmaker Sandi Simcha DuBowski uses these quotes to underscore persistent attitudes that bring great suffering to those gay Orthodox men and women who are unable to deny their sexuality but wish to remain religious.

DuBowski profiles a number of Jews, both in the United States and Israel, who face just that moral dilemma. After years of counseling, 35-year-old David knows there's no "cure" for homosexuality, but can't reconcile himself to either celibacy or life apart from his faith. Brooklynites "Malka" and "Leah" lead relatively open lives as Orthodox lesbians, but coming out effectively destroyed Malka's relationship with her very conservative parents. Mark stepped out of the closet when he was 15. Though he's been tossed out of several yeshivas for his "activities," David remains determined to practice his faith. And even though Israel says that he turned his back on the Orthodox Brooklyn community into which he was born, insisting that queerness and Orthodoxy don't mix, he returns to the old neighborhood leading tourists on his "Big Knish" tours.

Their voices are full of courage, strength, and inspiration, but, sadly, not one remains untouched by regret or doubt. Nevertheless, this is a brave, groundbreaking film. We learn at the end that the silhouettes of men and women seen participating in traditional shabat celebrations throughout the film are actually members of gay Orthodox organizations—underground groups one hopes won't have to remain underground for very long.

TREMORS   DVD

1990   96m   c   Comedy/Horror   ★★★
No Frills/Wilson-Maddock   (U.S.)   PG-13

Kevin Bacon (*Valentine McKee*), Fred Ward (*Earl Basset*), Finn Carter (*Rhonda LeBeck*), Michael Gross (*Burt Gummer*), Reba McEntire (*Heather Gummer*), Bobby Jacoby (*Melvin Plug*), Charlotte Stewart (*Nancy*), Tony Genaro (*Miguel*), Ariana Richards (*Minday*), Richard Marcus (*Nestor*)

p, Brent Maddock, S.S. Wilson; d, Ron Underwood; w, S.S. Wilson, Brent Maddock (based on a story by S.S. Wilson, Brent Maddock, and Ron Underwood); ph, Alexander Gruszynski (Deluxe Color); ed, O. Nicholas Brown; m, Ernest Troost; prod d, Ivo Cristante; art d, Donald Maskovich; fx, Gene Warren Jr.

TREMORS fondly recalls monster movies of the '50s, and wisely treads a middle path between knowing sendup and cannily crafted chiller.

Trying to escape their dead-end life in the desert town of Perfection (population 14), handymen Val (Kevin Bacon) and Earl (Fred Ward) find themselves sidetracked when corpses mysteriously begin piling up around them, the causes of death ranging from the strange (an old drunk is found halfway up an electrical tower dead from dehydration) to the unknown. When the handymen have a run-in with some creepy tentacled creatures that have apparently made lunch out of a road crew, they realize they are in deep trouble and retreat to the town to spread some hysteria and prepare for Mankind's last stand against a really disgusting menace: giant, foul-smelling, flesh-eating, mutant maggots.

TREMORS bends its movie cliches just enough to keep the action interesting and entertaining. One of the most fondly held conventions of '50s horror films was to withhold a straight-on view of the monsters until late in the picture; in TREMORS the beasts emerge early in the action, which, in another departure from convention, takes place almost entirely in broad daylight. The special effects are first-rate, with the maggots easily withstanding extended camera scrutiny. Another upended convention places a female scientist (Finn Carter) in the thick of the action, although she contributes little to our knowledge of the beasts and, before long, becomes irritated by the questions of the excited townsfolk. It turns out that the dumbest guys in the movie, Val and Earl, contribute the most towards eradicating the big bugs, with their prime motivation being to get the job done so they can continue their rudely interrupted journey out of Perfection.

You don't have to be a perennial late-night movie vidiot to get a kick out of TREMORS. It's fast-moving fun for kids of all ages who harbor a secret delight in movies starring gooey, smelly monsters. It's also very well cast, with Ward and Bacon proving affable and enjoyable comedy leads. Carter also has an offbeat appeal as the irritable woman of science, while Michael Gross and country star Reba McEntire, in a most unlikely film debut (she also wrote and sings the end-credit song, "Why Not Tonight?"), provide solid support as a survivalist couple who dispatch one of the creatures in a hail of bullets. It may not top anyone's 10-best list, but TREMORS is nevertheless solid entertainment.

TRIAL, THE   DVD

(LE PROCES)
1963   118m   bw   Drama   ★★★½
Paris Europa/Hisa   (France/Italy/West Germany)

Anthony Perkins (*Josef K*), Orson Welles (*Hastler*), Jeanne Moreau (*Miss Burstner*), Romy Schneider (*Leni*), Elsa Martinelli (*Hilda*), Akim Tamiroff (*Bloch*), Arnoldo Foa (*Inspector A*), William Kearns (*1st Assistant Inspector*), Jess Hahn (*2nd Assistant Inspector*), Suzanne Flon (*Miss Pittl*) p, Yves Laplanche, Miguel Salkind, Alexander Salkind; d, Orson Welles; w, Orson Welles (based on the novel by Franz Kafka); ph, Edmond Richard; ed, Yvonne Martin; m, Jean Ledrut, Tomaso Albinoni; art d, Jean Mandaroux; cos, Helen Thibault

Welles applied his bravura directorial style to Kafka's landmark 1925 novel about Joseph K (Perkins), an office clerk who gets arrested without being told why.

The film opens over a series of pin-screen pictures (a technique using pins, cloth, light, and shadows created by A. Alexeieff) of a guard in front of a huge door, preventing a man from entering. For years the man awaits entrance through the door which leads to the Law, but he never gains admittance. The narrator (Welles) then explains, "It has been said that the logic of this story is the logic of a dream. Do you feel lost in a labyrinth? Do not look for a way out. You will not be able to find one … There is no way out."

Kafka's novel doesn't translate well into film, being too dependent on the internal thoughts and frustrations of Joseph K during his quest. Aware of this problem, Welles has chosen to concentrate on the atmosphere of K's world, accompanied by the dreamy musical leitmotif of Albinoni's "Adagio." The sets are typical Welles baroque—massive structures which engulf K in the same way Xanadu swallowed Charles Foster Kane in CITIZEN KANE. These sets alone—with their haunting shadows and claustrophobic walls and ceilings—make THE TRIAL essential viewing. Welles's enthusiasm for the film is remarkable: "Say what you like, but THE TRIAL is the best film I ever made."

The film's genesis goes back to Miguel and Alexander Salkind, the father-and-son producing team, who offered Welles a list of 15 classic novels which were in public domain. Welles was to choose one that he wanted to film and, without much enthusiasm (Welles admits he had a "lack of profound sympathy for Kafka"), he agreed to The Trial. Production began in Zagreb, Yugoslavia, but was soon shut down for lack of funds. Skipping out on bills owed there, Welles and his entourage returned to Paris to complete the film at the abandoned Gare d'Orsay train station, an overwhelming structure which seems to have been built with Welles in mind. Although the film has its admirers, its opening was less than favorable. Originally scheduled to play the 1962 Venice Film Fest, it did not open until December 21 of that year in Paris. Not only did Welles have to overcome financial and scheduling restrictions, but he had problems with the casting. He had first cast himself as a priest, but when no suitable actor could be found for the advocate, Welles took over the role, scrapping the footage he had already shot. Shot in English, THE TRIAL was dubbed for its foreign-language releases, which had a variety of running times. Two players were cut from the U.S. release: Katina Paxinou, as a scientist, and Van Doude, who played an archivist.

The chief difference between Welles's Joseph K and Kafka's is in the extent of their guilt. While Kafka stresses ambiguity, Welles is clear in his feelings: "He is a little bureaucrat. I consider him guilty … He belongs to a guilty society; he collaborates with it." Welles further points to his differences with Kafka: "I do not share Kafka's point of view in The Trial. I believe that he is a good writer, but Kafka is not the extraordinary genius that people today see in him." Nonetheless, Kafka's story is far more successful as a novel than a film.

TRIAL OF JOAN OF ARC
(PROCES DE JEANNE D'ARC)
1962 65m bw Historical   ★★★
Pathe   (France)

Florence Carrez (Jeanne D'Arc), Jean-Claude Fourneau (Bishop Cauchon), Marc Jacquier (Jean Lemaitre), Roger Honorat (Jean Beaupere), Jean Gillibert (Jean de Chatillon), Andre Regnier (D'Estivet), Michel Herubel (Frere Isambart de la Pierre), Philippe Dreux (Frere Martin Ladvenu), Jean Darbaud (Nicolas de Houppeville), E.R. Pratt (Warwick)

p, Agnes Delahaie; d, Robert Bresson; w, Robert Bresson (based on "Proces de Condamnation et de Rehabilitation de Jeanne D'Arc"); ph, L.H. Burel; ed, Germaine Artus; m, Francis Seyrig; art d, Pierre Charbonnier; cos, Lucilla Mussini

The most commonly known film rendition of the famous French legend of Joan of Arc is the 1920s version by Dreyer in which Falconetti gave a stunning performance of the girl burned as a witch. From the outset of this newer project, Bresson chose an entirely different angle from that of Dreyer, for he was concerned with creating a more objective rendition, unprejudiced by the filmmaker's camera technique and personal manipulations. His efforts were fairly successful. He based the script solely on the notes from the trial, with Carrez playing Joan in a manner that makes her appear brighter and more scheming than she has usually been represented. Joan was a French peasant girl brought to trial as an enemy of the government, and after enduring a long court case and torture she was burned as a witch. Unlike the earlier version, Bresson concentrates quite heavily on the psychological and physical torture, showing how Joan broke down during the trial and recanted her faith. The purpose of Bresson was not to destroy the myth of Joan of Arc; what he did was reveal the processes that helped to create a legend.

TRIP TO BOUNTIFUL, THE   DVD
1985 105m c Drama   ★★★★
Bountiful/Film Dallas   (U.S.)   PG

Geraldine Page (Mrs. Watts), John Heard (Ludie Watts), Carlin Glynn (Jessie Mae), Richard Bradford (Sheriff), Rebecca De Mornay (Thelma), Kevin Cooney (Roy), Norman Bennett, Harvey Lewis (Bus Ticket Men), Kirk Sisco (Ticket Agent), David Tanner (Billy Davis)

p, Sterling Van Wagenen, Horton Foote; d, Peter Masterson; w, Horton Foote (based on his play); ph, Fred Murphy; ed, Jay Freund; m, J.A.C. Redford; prod d, Neil Spisak; art d, Philip Lamb; cos, Gary Jones

AA Best Actress: Geraldine Page; AAN Best Adapted Screenplay: Horton Foote

A luminous performance by Geraldine Page and one of the most touching pictures of the decade. The year is 1947; the place, Houston, Texas. Mrs. Watts (Page) is an elderly woman given to humming hymns and living the remaining years of her life with her wimp son, Ludie (John Heard), and his shrewish wife, Jessie Mae (Carlin Glynn), in a cramped apartment. Mrs. Watts's heart is weak, she has spells, and she can't get along with Jessie Mae at all. She has but one fervent desire left in her life: she wants to return to Bountiful, the small Texas town where she was born and grew up. The memories of the tranquility of Bountiful haunt her constantly as a reminder of a better time and life. When the stress gets too much for her, Mrs. Watts hides her pension check from Ludie and Jessie Mae and plans her escape. The movie is wonderfully made, and the first-time direction by stage director Peter Masterson is extraordinary. No guns, no violence, no nudity—just a caring story that will wet the driest eye and warm the coldest heart. Every single role is perfectly cast and perfectly played, and Horton Foote's script is a marvel of economy.

TRIPLETS OF BELLEVILLE, THE   DVD
(LES TRIPLETTES DE BELLEVILLE)
2003 80m c Animated/Comedy/Adventure   ★★★
Canal +/Cofimage 12/France 3 Cinema/   PG-13
Gimages 3/Les Armateurs/Production Champion/
RGP France/Telefilm Canada/Vivi Film   (France)

VOICES OF: Jean-Claude Donda, Michel Robin, Monica Viegas, SINGING VOICES: Betty Bonifassi, Marie-Lou Gauthier, Line Boudreault, Mathieu Chedid, billed as M p, Didier Brunner, Paul Cadieux; d, Sylvain Chomet; w, Sylvain Chomet; ed, Chantal Colibert Brunner; m, Benoit Charest; prod d, Evgeni Tomov; art d, Thierry Million; anim, Sylvain Chomet, Pieter Van Houte (3D)

AAN Best Animated Feature: ; AAN Best Original Song: "The Triplets of Belleville"; Benoit Charest (music), Sylvain Chomet (lyric)

French animator Sylvain Chomet's surreal and nearly wordless film may be off-putting to viewers accustomed to Disney's bright, fast-paced cartoon features, but it should appeal to adventurous types looking for something a little more challenging.

Sweet Madame Souza attempts to cheer up her sad and lonely young grandson, Champion, with piano lessons and a dog, Bruno, but to no avail. She finally stumbles upon a solution when she presents the boy with a new bicycle; under her demanding training regimen, Champion grows up to compete in the famed *Tour de France*. But in the heat of the road race, Champion is kidnapped and loaded onto a large ship. The enterprising and determined Madame Souza bundles Bruno and herself into a small dinghy and follows the kidnappers to the bustling metropolis of Belleville. There they find assistance in the form of the titular triplets, three aging music-hall stars who offer the new arrivals food, shelter, and invaluable help in rescuing Champion from the clutches of local gangsters.

Chomet offers plenty of laugh-out-loud moments, many courtesy of the affable Bruno, but for each amusing gag there's a corresponding darkly humorous conceit, like the triplets' obsession with frogs or Madame Souza's unorthodox training methods. The film occasionally drags, despite the 80-minute running time and Chomet's clever homages to animation pioneers ranging from Tex Avery to Dave Fleischer, who created Betty Boop. The manic energy of the outrageous opening sequence and the springy score set a tone and pace the film can't maintain.

TRISTANA

1970 98m c Drama ★★★★
Epoca/Talia/Selenia/Corona (Spain/Italy/France) PG

Catherine Deneuve *(Tristana)*, Fernando Rey *(Don Lope)*, Franco Nero *(Horacio)*, Lola Gaos *(Saturna)*, Antonio Casas *(Don Cosme)*, Jesus Fernandez *(Saturno)*, Vicente Soler *(Don Ambrosio)*, Jose Calvo *(Bellringer)*, Fernando Cebrian *(Dr. Miquis)*, Candida Losada *(Senora Burguesa)*

d, Luis Bunuel; w, Luis Bunuel, Julio Alejandro (based on the novel by Benito Perez Galdos); ph, Jose F. Aguayo (Eastmancolor); ed, Pedro del Rey; art d, Enrique Alarcon; fx, Julian Ruiz; cos, Rosa Garcia

AAN Best Foreign Language Film

A tauting black comedy with Surrealist touches. Bunuel's reworking of Benito Perez Galdos' novel, like all the works of this prolific filmmaker, has much beneath its surface. In a role that capitalizes on her placid beauty, Deneuve is a young woman who becomes the ward of hypocritical aristocrat Rey, who makes much of the fact that he hasn't taken advantage of her beauty. The truth is—he has. Prior to receiving an inheritance from his sister, the more-or-less-impoverished Rey refuses to take a job because he believes a man of his social standing is above menial labor. Instead, he sells all his belongings. At the same time he sees himself as a leader of the common man and makes great speeches to his cronies about improving the lot of the masses. Deneuve leaves the protection of Rey's home when she falls in love with artist Nero, but she is unwilling to make a commitment to him, so she returns to Rey, who asks for her hand. After losing a leg because of a

tumor, she accepts Rey's proposal and begins a passionless marriage despite her continued love for Nero.

Perhaps what makes this work so powerful is Bunuel's subtle use of key situations to represent much larger ideas. In comparison with such Bunuel masterpieces as VIRIDIANA and LOS OLVIDADOS, TRISTANA's assault on religion and politics is tame. Nevertheless, Bunuel's subtle presentation here (he uses, very little camera movement and little music), effectively conveys a world in desperate need of change.

TROUBLE IN MIND

1985 111m c Crime/Romance ★★
Raincity (U.S.) R

Kris Kristofferson *(Hawk)*, Keith Carradine *(Coop)*, Lori Singer *(Georgia)*, Genevieve Bujold *(Wanda)*, Joe Morton *(Solo)*, Divine *(Hilly Blue)*, George Kirby *(Lt. Gunther)*, John Considine *(Nate Nathanson)*, Dirk Blocker *(Rambo)*, Albert Hall *(Leo)*

p, Carolyn Pfeiffer, David Blocker; d, Alan Rudolph; w, Alan Rudolph; ph, Toyomichi Kurita (CFI Color); ed, Sally Allen, Tom Walls; m, Mark Isham; prod d, Steven Legler; fx, Bob Burns; cos, Tracy Tynan

An ambitious but ultimately pretentious film that attempts to mix film noir, Theater of the Absurd, romance, and science fiction but falls flat on almost all counts. It's set in the near future in the mythical town of Rain City. The place is ruled by martial law but populated with 1940s gangsters and 1950s diners. Hawk (Kris Kristofferson) is an ex-cop who has just come back from jail for having killed a man in self-defense. He looks up his old flame, Wanda (Genevieve Bujold), who is now running a cafe. He would like to put his life together, mind his own business, and have a pleasant few years. Coop (Keith Carradine) and Georgia (Lori Singer) are a newlywed couple who have come to Rain City to try to find jobs. When work doesn't materialize, Coop gets involved with crook Solo (Joe Morton), soon dealing in stolen goods. When Hawk learns what's transpiring, he takes it upon himself to save Coop and protect Georgia. TROUBLE IN MIND is offbeat, unique, and interesting, and for that alone it should be noted. It is a shame that none of the elements ever come together, so this film winds up being a beautiful, atmospheric mess.

TROUBLE IN PARADISE

1932 83m bw Comedy DVD
Paramount (U.S.) ★★★★★

Miriam Hopkins *(Lily Vautier)*, Kay Francis *(Mariette Colet)*, Herbert Marshall *(Gaston Monescu/La Valle)*, Charlie Ruggles *(the Major)*, Edward Everett Horton *(Francois Filiba)*, C. Aubrey Smith *(Adolph Giron)*, Robert Greig *(Jacques the Butler)*, George Humbert *(Waiter)*, Rolfe Sedan *(Purse Salesman)*, Luis Alberni *(Annoyed Opera Fan)*

p, Ernst Lubitsch; d, Ernst Lubitsch; w, Grover Jones, Samson Raphaelson (based on the play "The Honest Finder" by Laszlo Aladar); ph, Victor Milner; m, W. Franke Harling; art d, Hans Dreier; cos, Travis Banton

For six decades this film has been unmatched in the realm of sophisticated farce. Films from THE AWFUL TRUTH to THE LADY EVE to SOME LIKE IT HOT are sublime on their more modest social scale and in their basic Americanness. By contrast, TROUBLE IN PARADISE has all the class and Continental elegance one associates with the Paramout of the 1930s. Made before the Production Code clampdown of 1934, this Lubitsch masterpiece shows his talent for sly sexual innuendo at its most witty and polished. The result is pure caviar, only tastier.

The story tells of two jewel thieves, Gaston (Marshall) and Lily (Hopkins), who together work at bilking a merry widow, Mariette Colet (Francis), out of a small fortune. They secure jobs as her secretary and maid, but trouble begins in paradise when Gaston starts falling for his lovely prey and when one of her many suitors (Horton), a former victim of Gaston's, begins to recognize Mme. Colet's new secretary.

The many laughs in this consistently delightful souffle come not only from Raphaelson's marvelous screenplay but also from Lubitsch's supple visual wit. On one hand there's delightful repartee about a former secretary who enjoyed an antique bed a bit too much, and on the other we have the sexy silhouette of Gaston and Mariette cast over a chaise lounge. From the opening shot of an operatic gondolier who turns out to be a garbageman to a police report about theft and tonsils translated for Italian officials, this film is full of unforgettable moments of merriment.

The cast, too, is peerless. In one of his earliest Hollywood efforts, Herbert Marshall does the greatest work of his career. Too often maligned for playing stodgy consorts to dynamic star actresses such as Garbo, Davis, and Shearer, Marshall here gets to display his impeccable timing and supple grace. Frequently hilarious, his quiet approach and crushed velvet voice still let him remain suave throughout. Even Cary Grant would be hard pressed to match this portrayal. (He'd be too frantic.) Kay Francis, too, that popular sufferer of countless "women's films" with her "twoublesome" r's, gives of her very best. With her sleek, glamorous style and elegantly wry line readings, she is light, sexy, and totally captivating. Her doorway caresses and her finger-snapping seduction of Gaston are priceless. Miriam Hopkins was luckier in that she had many more chances to display her comic flair in film. Today one of the most underrated and unfairly maligned stars of the 1930s, the brittle, feisty Hopkins can rattle off witty banter at a breakneck pace or she can be deliciously languorous and coy. Her enjoyment of her own sexuality is heady even today and the thieving competition between Gaston and Lily, in which escalating crimes turn into escalating passion, remains one of the greatest scenes of foreplay ever caught on film. Ruggles and Horton prove yet again that they are two of the greatest farceurs in Hollywood, and the rest of the cast is equally choice. (One standout is Leonid Kinskey, whose bit as a leftist radical only foregrounds the satiric anarchy of the entire film.) Beautifully handled from start to finish, gleamingly shot and full of Dreier's incredible Art Deco designs, TROUBLE IN PARADISE is Lubitsch's greatest film and one of the indisputable highlights of comic cinema.

TROUBLE WITH HARRY, THE
1955 99m c Comedy 🄳🅅🄳
Paramount (U.S.) ★★★½

Edmund Gwenn (*Capt. Albert Wiles*), John Forsythe (*Sam Marlowe, the Painter*), Shirley MacLaine (*Jennifer Rogers, Harry's Wife*); Mildred Natwick (*Miss Graveley*), Mildred Dunnock (*Mrs. Wiggs*), Jerry Mathers (*Arnie Rogers, Harry's Son*), Royal Dano (*Calvin Wiggs*), Parker Fennelly (*Millionaire*), Barry Macollum (*Tramp*), Dwight Marfield (*Dr. Greenbow*)

p, Alfred Hitchcock; d, Alfred Hitchcock; w, John Michael Hayes (based on the novel by Jack Trevor Story); ph, Robert Burks (VistaVision, Technicolor); ed, Alma Macrorie; m, Bernard Herrmann; art d, Hal Pereira, John B. Goodman; fx, John P. Fulton; cos, Edith Head

A quiet, picturesque Vermont autumn, its leaves in full color, provides the setting for this splendid Hitchcock black comedy in which Harry Worp just won't stay dead. Shirley MacLaine, in her film debut, is Jennifer Rogers, a young mother who recognizes Harry's corpse as that of her dead husband. She is certain that she accidentally killed him. Retired sea captain Albert Wiles (Gwenn), and the dotty old Miss Graveley (Natwick)

also believe they are the murderers. Enter eccentric painter Sam Marlowe (Forsythe), a tongue-in-cheek nod to gumshoes Sam Spade and Philip Marlowe, who tries to get to the bottom of Harry's death. Two love stories are interspersed as Jennifer and Sam fall for each other, and the captain and Miss Graveley do the same. Jerry Mathers, of "Leave It to Beaver" fame, is MacLaine's often-hysterical young son.

TROY
2004 163m c War/Historical 🄳🅅🄳
Radiant Productions/Plan B/Warner Bros. (U.S.) ★★½
R

Brad Pitt (*Achilles*), Eric Bana (*Hector*), Orlando Bloom (*Prince Paris of Troy*), Diane Kruger (*Queen Helen of Sparta*), Brian Cox (*Agamemnon*), Sean Bean (*Odysseus*), Brendan Gleeson (*King Menelaus of Sparta*), Peter O'Toole (*King Priam*), Julie Christie (*Thetis*), Tyler Mane (*Ajax*)

p, Wolfgang Petersen, Diana Rathbun, Colin Wilson; d, Wolfgang Petersen; w, David Benioff (inspired by *The Iliad* by Homer); ph, Roger Pratt; ed, Peter Honess; m, James Horner; prod d, Nigel Phelps; art d, John King, Kevin Phipps, Les Tomkins; fx, Laya Armian, Nick Davis, Paul Ladd, Joss Williams, Andrea Williams, Gina Willis; cos, Bob Ringwood

AAN Best Costume Design: Bob Ringwood

A vigorous spin on the glorious excesses of classic sword-and-sandal epics, Wolfgang Petersen's stripped-down chronicle of the 10-year Trojan War is fatally undermined by golden boy Brad Pitt's reduction of legendary warrior Achilles to a sullen fame whore with to-die-for cheekbones.

Trojan princes Hector (Eric Bana) and Paris (Orlando Bloom) are sent by their father, King Priam (Peter O'Toole), to seal a peace treaty with King Menelaus of Sparta (Brendan Gleeson). But callow Paris seduces Menelaus' wife, Helen (Diana Kruger), and spirits her back to Troy, too besotted to care that his actions will condemn his country to war. The cuckolded Menelaus appeals to his power-hungry older brother, Agamemnon (Brian Cox), who sees an excuse to add Troy to his empire of conquered nations. Agamemnon recruits the volatile, self-interested Achilles and raises an army with a single purpose: the destruction of Troy.

Petersen orchestrates a handsome battle sequence, but this attenuated stew of stagy posturing and unconvincing domestic drama runs aground on Pitt's preening deportment and drama-class line readings, even with Achilles reconceived as a celebrity-craving bad boy with authority issues. Bloom took the lion's share of criticism for being too shallow and pretty to play a Bronze Age brawler, but Paris isn't supposed to be a warrior; he was always a pampered lothario predestined to do the wrong thing. Sean Bean makes the most of the cruelly truncated role of Odysseus, who conceives the treacherous wooden horse that seals Troy's fate, and Bana negotiates the transitions between family melodrama and armored smack-downs with surprising grace.

TRUE CONFESSIONS
1981 108m c Crime ★★★★
UA (U.S.) R

Robert De Niro (*Des Spellacy*), Robert Duvall (*Tom Spellacy*), Charles Durning (*Jack Amsterdam*), Ed Flanders (*Dan T. Champion*), Burgess Meredith (*Seamus Fargo*), Rose Gregorio (*Brenda Samuels*), Cyril Cusack (*Cardinal Danaher*), Kenneth McMillan (*Frank Crotty*), Dan Hedaya (*Howard Terkel*), Gwen Van Dam (*Mrs. Fazenda*)

p, Irwin Winkler, Robert Chartoff; d, Ulu Grosbard; w, John Gregory Dunne, Joan Didion (based on the novel by Dunne); ph, Owen Roizman (Technicolor); ed, Lynzee Klingman; m, Georges

Delerue; prod d, Stephen Grimes; art d, Stewart Campbell; chor, Alfonse L. Palermo; cos, Joe I. Tompkins

Underrated at the time of release, TRUE CONFESSIONS is a fascinating film that exposes the dark underside of the Catholic Church and fixes it firmly in the seedy, corrupt world of film noir. The first on-screen teaming of De Niro and Duvall (they appeared in GODFATHER II but never in the same scene), the film is largely set in Los Angeles in the 1940s. Tom Spellacy (Duvall) is a hard-boiled homicide detective whose investigation of the grisly murder of a porno starlet leads him to believe that his brother Des (De Niro), an ambitious Catholic monsignor, is involved with corrupt local businessman Jack Amsterdam (Durning)—Spellacy's chief suspect. Adapted by the husband-and-wife team of Dunne and Didion from Dunne's fine novel, all of the characters in TRUE CONFESSIONS are corrupt to the core. The period detail is letter-perfect, the cast is uniformly excellent, and Delerue's score is haunting and evocative. TRUE CONFESSIONS is a thoughtful but deeply disturbing film, and its frank portrayal of corruption and murder makes it for adults only.

TRUE GRIT

1969 128m c Western   DVD

Paramount (U.S.)   ★★★★

                                             G

John Wayne *(Reuben J. "Rooster" Cogburn)*, Glen Campbell *(La Boeuf)*, Kim Darby *(Mattie Ross)*, Jeremy Slate *(Emmett Quincy)*, Robert Duvall *(Ned Pepper)*, Dennis Hopper *(Moon)*, Alfred Ryder *(Goudy)*, Strother Martin *(Col. G. Stonehill)*, Jeff Corey *(Tom Chaney)*, Ron Soble *(Capt. Boots Finch)*

p, Hal B. Wallis; d, Henry Hathaway; w, Marguerite Roberts (based on the novel by Charles Portis); ph, Lucien Ballard (Technicolor); ed, Warren Low; m, Elmer Bernstein; prod d, Walter Tyler; fx, Dick Johnson; cos, Dorothy Jeakins

AA Best Actor: John Wayne; *AAN Best Original Song:* "True Grit"; Elmer Bernstein (Music), Don Black (Lyrics)

An enormously entertaining adventure that is as much about John Wayne's image as it is about a girl seeking revenge for her father's murder. Mattie Ross (Kim Darby) is a level-headed 14-year-old who goes to Rooster Cogburn (Wayne) after her father is killed. The murderer, Tom Chaney (Jeff Corey), has since fled into Indian territory, and Mattie wants a man of "true grit" to help bring him to justice. Cogburn, a paunchy U.S. marshal with a patch over one eye, admires Mattie's spunk and agrees to take on the job. Joining them is La Boeuf (Glen Campbell), a Texas Ranger whom Mattie despises. He, too, is searching for Chaney, hoping to collect a reward offered by the family of a murdered Texas politician. Much of the film's entertainment comes from the obvious contrasts and subtle similarities between Cogburn and Mattie. Cogburn is fat, drunken, and not entirely honest, but he has an underlying sense of honor, the "true grit" that Mattie demands. Although Wayne's characterizations in STAGECOACH and THE SEARCHERS are more complex, TRUE GRIT provides him with some of his most memorable screen moments. He reprised the role in ROOSTER COGBURN, costarring with Katharine Hepburn. TRUE GRIT was redone for television in 1978, with Warren Oates in the lead role, but neither project approached this film in either quality or spirit.

TRUE LIES

1994 141m c Action/Adventure   DVD

Lightstorm Entertainment (U.S.)   ★★★½

                                             R

Arnold Schwarzenegger *(Harry Tasker)*, Jamie Lee Curtis *(Helen Tasker)*, Tom Arnold *(Gib)*, Bill Paxton *(Simon)*, Tia Carrere *(Juno Skinner)*, Charlton Heston *(Spencer Trilby)*, Art

Malik *(Aziz)*, Eliza Dushku *(Dana Tasker)*, Grant Heslov *(Faisil)*, Marshall Manesh *(Khaled)*

p, James Cameron, Stephanie Austin; d, James Cameron; w, James Cameron (based on the screenplay "La Totale!" by Claude Zidi, Simon Michael, and Didier Kaminka); ph, Russell Carpenter; ed, Conrad Buff, Mark Goldblatt, Richard A. Harris, Shawn Broes, Scott Michael Keppler; m, Brad Fiedel; prod d, Peter Lamont; art d, Robert Laing, Michael Novotny; fx, Thomas L. Fisher, John Bruno, Jacques Stroweis, Patrick McClung; chor, Lynn Hockney; cos, Marlene Stewart

AAN Best Visual Effects: John Bruno, Thomas L. Fisher, Jacques Stroweis, Patrick McClung

A James Bond pastiche for the 1990s, TRUE LIES is hugely elaborate and ultimately disturbing, a big empty gloss on action formulas with an ugly edge that belies its all-in-good-fun surface.

Special agent Harry Tasker (Arnold Schwarzenegger) emerges from the water outside a heavily guarded mansion, peels off his wetsuit to reveal the dinner jacket underneath, and strolls into a swanky party. He tangos with a treacherous woman (Tia Carrere), steals some computer files, and escapes in a spectacular flurry of gunfire and masked pursuers on skis. Now for the joke: Harry goes home to mousy wife Helen (Jamie Lee Curtis) and the sham of his domestic life, in which he pretends to be a computer salesman. Helen is so bored by household routine that she's on the verge of giving in to smarmy used-car salesman Simon (Bill Paxton), who woos her by claiming to be a spy. For the rest of the film, Harry must serve two masters: while pursuing Arab terrorists led by charismatic Aziz (Art Malik), he attempts to save his marriage, which involves using the Agency's considerable resources to terrorize Simon and Helen.

It's so hard to separate TRUE LIES the movie from TRUE LIES the $120 million phenomenon that perhaps it's not worth trying. Interestingly enough, the film is based on a much-lower-budgeted French comedy called "La Totale!" (1981), directed by Claude Zidi (MY NEW PARTNER). James Cameron's reworking of that film, however, is a smirking monument to self-referential excess: everything is big, bigger, biggest, from the action sequences to the star, and when something doesn't work on the level of spectacle, it's played as a joke. On the surface, TRUE LIES is an affectionate homage to James Bond movies, ratcheted up to meet the action/adventure expectations of today's audiences.

But TRUE LIES also picks up a lot of nasty subtext from the Bond films and expands upon it (deliberately or not), and the larky atmosphere is ultimately poisoned by racism, homophobia, and misogyny. In the wake of the film's release, many noted that no other racial stereotype is so widely tolerated as that of Arabs as wild-eyed terrorists in kaffiyehs, and TRUE LIES panders to that image shamelessly. It also puts forth, without a trace of irony, the idea that exotic women are two-faced temptresses, as well as the notion that all women are whores at heart, and stupid ones at that. True lies, indeed.

TRUE LOVE

1989 104m c Comedy   DVD

Forward Films (U.S.)   ★★★

                                             R

Annabella Sciorra *(Donna)*, Ron Eldard *(Michael)*, Star Jasper *(J.C.)*, Aida Turturro *(Grace)*, Roger Rignack *(Dom)*, Michael J. Wolfe *(Brian)*, Kelly Cinnante *(Yvonne)*, Rick Shapiro *(Kevin)*, Suzanne Costallos *(Fran)*, Vinny Pastore *(Angelo)*

p, Richard Guay, Shelley Houis; d, Nancy Savoca; w, Nancy Savoca, Richard Guay; ph, Lisa Rinzler (Duart Color); ed, John Tintori; prod d, Lester Cohen; art d, Pamela Woodbridge; cos, Deborah Anderko

The top prize-winner at the 1989 U.S. Film Festival, TRUE LOVE is a low-budget feature debut which, while no landmark, is an entertaining comedy filled with likable characters. Like fellow NYU alum Martin Scorsese, first-time director Nancy Savoca turned for inspiration to her own working-class Italian-American roots to create this story. The film centers on the strong but somewhat empty-headed Donna (Annabella Sciorra) who is determined to get her man Michael (Ron Eldard) to the altar. Michael doesn't mind getting engaged and exchanging an occasional "I love you," but who would rather hang around with his neighborhood buddies than actually exchange marriage vows. The story is as old as the movies themselves, but the uncanny resemblance its people and situations bear to real life makes TRUE LOVE enjoyable. The characters are created with care and a feeling for individuality, and each scene comes to life with humor and poignancy. Among the cast, the most pleasant surprise is Sciorra, in her first feature.

TRUE ROMANCE
DVD

1993 119m c Action/Thriller ★★★½

True Romance Productions/Morgan Creek/ R
Davis Films (U.S.)

Christian Slater (*Clarence Worley*), Patricia Arquette (*Alabama Whitman*), Dennis Hopper (*Clifford Worley*), Val Kilmer (*Elvis (uncredited)*), Gary Oldman (*Drexl Spivey*), Brad Pitt (*Floyd - Dick's Roommate*), Christopher Walken (*Vincenzo Coccotti*), Bronson Pinchot (*Elliot Blitzer*), Samuel L. Jackson (*Big Don*), Michael Rapaport (*Dick Ritchie*)

p, Samuel Hadida, Steve Perry, Bill Unger; d, Tony Scott; w, Quentin Tarantino; ph, Jeffrey L. Kimball; ed, Michael Tronick, Christian Wagner; m, Hans Zimmer; prod d, Benjamin Fernandez; art d, James J. Murakami; fx, Robert Henderson, Mike Meinardus, Larry Shorts; cos, Susan Becker

TRUE ROMANCE is about as good as contemporary Hollywood movies get. It boasts an engaging pair of leads (Christian Slater and Patricia Arquette); a snappy plot; dialogue that bristles with great one-liners; a gallery of accurately, hilariously observed minor characters; and a happy ending complete with a slew of corpses. What more could you ask?

The story begins in Detroit, where Alabama Whitman (Arquette), a call-girl with three days' experience, bumps into—or, more exactly, tips a carton of popcorn over—lowly store clerk Clarence Worley (Slater) during a kung fu triple bill at Clarence's local theater. Within a matter of hours, Alabama has renounced her nascent career and found true love; Clarence, meanwhile, has got himself into a bloody shootout with Alabama's former "manager" and found himself in possession of a suitcase full of cocaine—not to mention a really cheesy pair of sunglasses. The couple head off to L.A. in an attempt to sell their loot that involves them with a supremely bad actor (Dick Ritchie), whom we first see auditioning for "T.J. Hooker"; an unctuous movie producer (Saul Rubinek); his fawning, preppy assistant (Bronson Pinchot); a band of pursuing mafia hit men; and a bunch of wisecracking L.A. cops.

TRUE ROMANCE blends and recycles elements of scores of crime and road movies, from BONNIE AND CLYDE to BADLANDS, but it does so with enough energy and verve to create something entirely fresh and infectiously entertaining. The filmmakers demonstrate a passion for pop culture that gives everything an air of comic-book unreality, while also making for some genuinely haunting moments. Highlights: the gloriously un-PC scene in which Clarence's dad (Dennis Hopper) faces off against a mob lieutenant (Christopher Walken); and the bloody, protracted motel-room battle (trimmed for theatrical release, restored for video) between Alabama and a goon who—like the audience—gets more than he bargained for.

TRUE STORIES
DVD

1986 89m c Comedy ★★★½

True Stories Ventures (U.S.) PG

David Byrne (*Narrator*), John Goodman (*Louis Fyne*), Swoosie Kurtz (*Miss Rollings*), Spalding Gray (*Earl Culver*), Alix Elias (*The Cute Woman*), Annie McEnroe (*Kay Culver*), Roebuck "Pops" Staples (*Mr. Tucker*), Humberto Larriva (*Ramon*), John Ingle (*The Preacher*), Matthew Posey (*The Computer Guy*)

p, Gary Kurfirst; d, David Byrne; w, David Byrne, Beth Henley, Stephen Tobolowsky; ph, Edward Lachman (Technicolor); ed, Caroline Biggerstaff; m, David Byrne, The Talking Heads; prod d, Barbara Ling; chor, Meredith Monk, Dee McCandless, Gene Menger; cos, Elizabeth McBride

David Byrne, then the front man for the Talking Heads, makes his feature film directorial debut with a deliciously offbeat and affectionate look at American madness. Byrne himself plays the narrator, a friendly outsider every bit as strange as the oddball characters he observes. Wearing a large cowboy hat, he talks to the camera as he drives along in a big red convertible. Virtually plotless, the film follows Byrne as he takes us on a tour of Virgil, Texas, and its inhabitants. We meet the "Laziest Woman in the World" (Swoozie Kurtz); the "Lying Woman" (Jo Harvey Allen), who spices up her mundane workday with incredible stories; a civic leader (Spalding Gray) and his wife (Annie McEnroe), who haven't spoken directly to each other in 15 years; a paranoid preacher (John Ingle) who sees conspiracy around every corner; and the man who comes closest to being the film's main character, Louis Fyne (John Goodman), a lovable panda-bear of a man who is looking for matrimony with a capital "M." Supposedly inspired by bizarre clippings found in the slezoid tabloids that adorn grocery checkout line, TRUE STORIES attempts to provide a fond, kindly glimpse of the heartland of America. Some were offended by what they perceived to be the film's smug hipness and sense of superiority. We could not disagree more. It's a lovely loving film that also has some terrific Talking Heads tunes. The actors all do amazingly well with their rather sketchy characterizations. All in all, this is a commendable first effort from neophyte director Byrne. We hope to hear—and see—more from him.

TRULY, MADLY, DEEPLY
DVD

1991 105m c Romance/Fantasy ★★★½

BBC Films (U.K.) PG

Juliet Stevenson (*Nina*), Alan Rickman (*Jamie*), Bill Paterson (*Sandy*), Michael Maloney (*Mark*), Jenny Howe (*Burge*), Carolyn Choa (*Translator*), Christopher Rozycki (*Titus*), Keith Bartlett (*Plumber*), David Ryall (*George*), Stella Maris (*Maura*)

p, Robert Cooper; d, Anthony Minghella; w, Anthony Minghella; ph, Remi Adefarasin; ed, John Stothart; m, Barrington Pheloung; prod d, Barbara Gasnold; cos, James Keast

The first feature film from writer-director Anthony Minghella, TRULY, MADLY, DEEPLY is a funny, touching story about dealing with bereavement and learning to love again.

Nina (Juliet Stevenson) is having a hard time getting over the sudden death of her lover Jamie (Alan Rickman). London is a lonely place, she finds, as she returns home from work every day to an empty flat—empty, that is, save for a recent infestation of rats. The memory of her relationship with Jamie is always on her mind, the music he played on his cello echoing her thoughts at every turn. Sandy (Bill Paterson), who runs the translation agency where she works, tries to shake Nina out of the doldrums, but without success. Titus (Christopher Rozycki), another colleague who wants to fix up her rundown flat, is smitten with her, but she good-humoredly ignores his advances. Nina admits to her bereavement therapist that she feels as though Jamie is somehow still around. Lost in her memories, Nina begins to slip away from reality and, in the process, literally wills her dead lover back in the form of a ghost.

Labelled by many critics as a "thinking person's GHOST," TRULY, MADLY, DEEPLY is sensitively written and charmingly acted. Juliet Stevenson brings tremendous depth to a role that was created specifically for her, and Alan Rickman proves himself capable of something quite different from the bad-guy roles (DIE HARD, ROBIN HOOD: PRINCE OF THIEVES) for which he's best known. Minghella's background in TV, though (he worked with the late Jim Henson on a series of European folk tales for NBC and created the BBC drama series, "What If It's Raining") is evident in the limited scope of the piece, particularly its rather uninspired visuals. Special mention should go to Barrington Pheloung for his lilting, poignant musical score.

TRUMAN SHOW, THE

1998 102m c   Drama/Fantasy/Comedy   ★★★½
Scott Rudin Productions   (U.S.)   PG

Jim Carrey (*Truman Burbank*), Laura Linney (*Meryl*), Noah Emmerich (*Marlon*), Natascha McElhone (*Lauren/Sylvia*), Holland Taylor (*Truman's Mother*), Ed Harris (*Christof*), Brian Delate (*Kirk—Truman's Father*), Paul Giamatti (*Simeon—Control Room Director*), Harry Shearer (*Mike Michaelson—Interviewer*), Blair Slater (*Young Truman*)

p, Scott Rudin, Andrew Niccol, Edward S. Feldman, Adam Schroeder; d, Peter Weir; w, Andrew Niccol; ph, Peter Biziou; ed, William Anderson, Lee Smith; m, Burkhard Dallwitz, Philip Glass; prod d, Dennis Gassner; art d, Richard L. Johnson; fx, Michael J. McAlister, Larz Anderson, Craig Barron, Cinesite; cos, Marilyn Matthews

AAN Best Supporting Actor: Ed Harris; *AAN Best Director:* Peter Weir; *AAN Best Original Screenplay:* Andrew Niccol

A cool indictment of television's near-irresistible pandering to the inner peeping tom.

Truman Burbank (Jim Carrey) lives in preternaturally picturesque Seahaven, an oasis of friendly neighbors and natural beauty, but finds himself increasingly troubled by the vague feeling that something's going on behind his back. He's more right than he can imagine. Beneath the picket-fence facade of his life lies an almost incomprehensible secret to which everyone but Truman is privy: it's all a carefully calculated, commodified spectacle. Seahaven is a massive set studded with hidden cameras; the friends and neighbors are actors; and the whole thing is on the air 24 hours a day, the world over. Truman has literally grown up on television, the unwitting star of a twisted, epic episode of "Candid Camera."

That's pretty much it for both premise and plot, and as premise it's brilliant, in a "Twilight Zone"-ish way and with all due respect to THE BUBBLE, a 30-year-old sci-fi trifle which pioneered the image of a human habitrail, and Paul Bartel's short film "The Secret Cinema." TV has, after all, already brought us prefab-reality programming like "An American Family," "The Real World," and "Cops," and spawned a nation of voyeuristic slugs addicted to entertaining themselves to death. As plot, it's a little thin, especially when you already know the premise—a bind as hard to wiggle out of in a review as in an ad campaign. The performances are uniformly pitch-perfect, though fans of Carrey's manic antics will probably find him perplexingly humorless, and director Peter Weir courageously resists at every turn the temptation to make it big. The laughs are modest and uncomfortable, and Truman's emancipation prefigures only an uncertain future.

TRUST

1991 90m c   Romance/Comedy/Drama   ★★★
Zenith Productions/Last Moment Films/   R
True Fiction Pictures   (U.S.)

Adrienne Shelly (*Maria Coughlin*), Martin Donovan (*Matthew Slaughter*), Merritt Nelson (*Jean Coughlin*), John A. MacKay, billed as John MacKay (*Jim Slaughter*), Edie Falco (*Peg Coughlin*), Marko Hunt (*John Coughlin*)

p, Bruce Weiss; d, Hal Hartley; w, Hal Hartley; ph, Michael Spiller; ed, Nick Gomez; m, Phil Reed; prod d, Daniel Ouellette; art d, Julie Fabian; cos, Claudia Brown

The second full-length film from director-screenwriter Hal Hartley, TRUST displays all the characteristics which made his first feature, THE UNBELIEVABLE TRUTH, a cult hit—suburban Long Island settings, deadpan dialogue mixing metaphysical ponderings with *non sequiturs*, understated black humor. TRUST, though, fails to break any new ground, and lacks some of the spontaneous charm of the previous work.

The film begins with seventeen-year-old Maria Coughlin (Adrienne Shelly) confronting her father John (Marko Hunt) with the news that she's pregnant and plans to drop out of high school. He insults her; she slaps him and leaves home; he falls down dead of a heart attack. Maria wanders the town and meets Rachel, a despondent housewife who confides all her woes in Maria and gives her money for food. Maria fights off a would-be-rapist shopkeeper while trying to buy beer, and emerges from the store to find that a baby has been kidnapped; she suspects Rachel of the crime. Maria hides out in an old abandoned house where she meets Matthew Slaughter (Martin Donovan), a troubled young man who carries around a hand grenade his father brought back from Korea just in case he decides to kill himself. With Matthew, Maria faces—*inter alia*—angry parents, a search for the missing baby, an abortion, and some twisted sexual intrigue.

TRUST is stylishly photographed and crammed with quirky, offbeat incidents and dialogue. As in THE UNBELIEVABLE TRUTH, Adrienne Shelley gives an engaging performance as a confused, alienated suburban girl who meets up with an enigmatic, potentially violent stranger. Hartley has an appealing and distinctive world-view; those who enjoyed THE UNBELIEVABLE TRUTH, however, may feel as though they've seen it all before, and that it was better structured and more convincingly performed the first time around.

TRUTH ABOUT CHARLIE, THE

2002 104m c   Mystery/Romance
MediaStream Film/Clinica Estetico Productions/   ★★
Universal   (U.S.)   PG-13

Mark Wahlberg (*Joshua Peters*), Thandie Newton (*Regina Lambert*), Tim Robbins (*Mr. Bartholomew*), Joong-Hoon Park (*Il-Sang Lee*), Ted Levine (*Emil Zadapec*), Lisa Gay Hamilton (*Lola Jansco*), Charles Aznavour (*Himself*), Anna Karina (*Karina*), Agnes Varda (*The Widow Hyppolite*), Stephen Dillane (*Charles Lambert*)

p, Jonathan Demme, Peter Saraf, Edward Saxon; d, Jonathan Demme; w, Steve Schmidt, Peter Stone, Jessica Bendinger, Jonathan Demme (based on the screenplay for the motion picture CHARADE by Peter Stone); ph, Tak Fujimoto; ed, Carol Littleton; m, Rachel Portman; prod d, Hugo Luczyc-Wyhowski; art d, Bertrand Clercq-Roques, Delphine Mabed, Ford Wheeler; fx, Peter Donen; cos, Catherine Leterrier

For film students in search of paper topics, Jonathan Demme's remake of CHARADE is a godsend. Unfortunately, it's also the kind of spectacularly misconceived lark that only a sophisticated cinephile could have perpetrated.

While vacationing in the Caribbean, unhappily married Regina "Reggie" Lambert (Thandie Newton) decides to divorce Charles (Stephen Dillane), whom she impulsively wed after a whirlwind courtship. But when she returns home, she finds their Paris apartment ransacked and police officers waiting with the news that Charles is dead. Among his effects are a handful of passports in different names, Reggie's first inkling that her murdered husband had a secret life. Reggie is contacted by an American embassy official (Tim Robbins), stalked by three mercenaries (Ted Levine, Joong-Hoon Park, Lisa Gay Hamilton), and helped by enigmatic good samaritan Joshua Peters (Mark Wahlberg), who may be in cahoots with the bad guys. Her good-faith efforts to uncover the truth about her mysterious husband's doings only lead Reggie deeper into a web of lies and deception and may be endangering her life.

Inspired by the realization that CHARADE, the quintessential star-driven Hollywood entertainment, was shooting in Paris at the same time *Nouvelle Vague* wunderkinder were reinventing French cinema, Demme undertook to pull the original apart and reassemble it with all the seams showing. Using multiple film stocks, jump cuts, disorienting angles, slow motion, and nostril-magnifying close-ups, Demme shifts focus away from the tale and onto the telling. Demme even stages a pair of Brechtian cameos for SHOOT THE PIANO PLAYER star Charles Aznavour, casts filmmaker Agnes Varda as a deranged harridan, and builds a surreal tango bar sequence around French New Wave poster girl Anna Karina, all of which is very clever without actually being enjoyable.

TRUTH OR DARE
1991 118m   c/bw Documentary/Musical
Propaganda Films   (U.S.)

DVD ★★★

R

Madonna, Donna Delory, Niki Harris, Luis Camacho, Oliver Crumes, Salim Gauwloos, Jose Guitierez, Kevin Stea, Gabriel Trupin, Carlton Wilborn *(Dancers)*

p, Tim Clawson, Jay Roewe, Steve Golin, Sigurjon Sighvatsson; d, Alek Keshishian; ph, Robert Leacock, Doug Nichol, Christophe Lanzenberg, Marc Reshovsky, Daniel Pearl, Toby Phillips; ed, Barry Alexander Brown, John Murray; chor, Vincent Paterson

Shot during 1989's "Blonde Ambition" world tour, TRUTH OR DARE is a documentary look at Madonna Louise Ciccone, arguably the most famous woman in the world today.

Director Alek Keshishian, who cut his teeth on music video, follows the pop diva from stage to hotel room to parties, press conferences, rehearsals and shopping expeditions. He photographs her talking to her family, eating, getting her hair done and horsing around with her dancers, back-up singers and other tour personnel, then intercuts the footage—shot in self-conscious B&W—with color footage of her elaborate stage show. The result is a surprisingly engaging portrait of a media phenomenon for whom the distinction between "onstage" and "offstage" is almost irrelevant.

Keshishian is ruthless, showing Madonna as she bitches at the tech crew, strips in her dressing room, prays at her mother's grave (there's a wireless mike concealed in the dirt) and fellates a bottle during a parlor game—the "Truth or Dare" of the title. About the only thing Keshishian doesn't show is Madonna at home cleaning the toilet, but that's because she's on the road, wrapped in the cocoon of touring ritual and intense, superficial camaraderie. But you get the sense that this is her real life; when then-boyfriend Warren Beatty passes through and suggests she isn't interested in living off-camera, the remark sounds unexpectedly profound.

Madonna is a star for the voyeuristic age, an age when wars start on television and confession is only good for the soul if it's picked up by the wires. When the camera captures Madonna observing two of her male dancers kiss, she's absorbed by the same contradictory spectacle audiences experience when they look at TRUTH OR DARE: intimacy designed to be watched.

TUCK EVERLASTING
2002 88m   c   Fantasy/Drama
Beacon Communications/Jane Startz Productions/
Scholastic Productions/Walt Disney Pictures

DVD ★★★½

PG
(U.S.)

Alexis Bledel *(Winnie Foster)*, William Hurt *(Angus Tuck)*, Sissy Spacek *(Mae Tuck)*, Jonathan Jackson *(Jesse Tuck)*, Scott Bairstow *(Miles Tuck)*, Ben Kingsley *(Man in the Yellow Suit)*, Amy Irving *(Mother Foster)*, Victor Garber *(Robert Foster)*, Kosha Engler *(Miles's Wife)*, Elisabeth Shue *(Narrator)*

p, Marc Abraham, Jane Startz; d, Jay Russell; w, Jeffrey Lieber, James V. Hart (based on the book by Natalie Babbitt); ph, James L. Carter; ed, Jay Cassidy; m, William Ross; prod d, Tony Burrough; art d, Ray Kluga; fx, Mat Beck, Mark Bero, Mark Freund; cos, Carol Ramsey

Grand performances by its grown-up stars and a surprisingly complex turn from young Alexis Bledel lift this adaptation of Natalie Babbitt's classic children's novel beyond its plot holes and into a state of lightheaded grace.

Summer, 1914: Stifled under corsets and her parents' expectations, headstrong 14-year-old Winnie Foster (Bledel) bolts from home. Deep in her family's woods, she stumbles upon 17-year-old Jesse Tuck (Jonathan Jackson). At least he looks 17; he's actually 104. Nearly a century earlier, his settler family drank from a spring which, to their astonishment, proved to be the fountain of youth, and they haven't aged since. But eternal life isn't paradise; other lives come and go while they remain, as one Tuck puts it, like rocks. Winnie is spirited away to the Tuck family's remote cabin, where patriarch Angus (William Hurt) and earth mother Mae (Sissy Spacek) take her in. While her parents (a fine Victor Garber and a stilted Amy Irving) search the countryside, Winnie falls in love with Jesse. Meanwhile, the Tucks are being stalked by the single-minded Man in the Yellow Suit (Ben Kingsley), an enigmatic, seemingly supernatural presence.

The film is heavy with meaning—the message "You don't have to live forever. You just have to live," is delivered in exactly those words—and occasionally marred by purple narration. Yet its mythical characters come across as genuine, vulnerable human beings. Spacek and Hurt vividly convey the sense of Angus and Mae's isolation through voice and expression. In keeping with the excellence of the older actors around her, the surprisingly accomplished Bledel is similarly able to project the quicksilver contradictions of Winnie's character without words.

TUCKER: THE MAN AND HIS DREAM
1988 111m   c   Biography
Lucasfilm   (U.S.)

DVD ★★★★

PG

Jeff Bridges *(Preston Tucker)*, Joan Allen *(Vera Tucker)*, Martin Landau *(Abe Karatz)*, Frederic Forrest *(Eddie Dean)*, Mako *(Jimmy Sakuyama)*, Lloyd Bridges *(Sen. Homer Ferguson)*, Elias Koteas *(Alex Tremulis)*, Christian Slater *(Junior)*, Nina Siemaszko *(Marilyn Lee Tucker)*, Anders Johnson *(Johnny Tucker)*

p, Fred Roos, Fred Fuchs; d, Francis Ford Coppola; w, Arnold Schulman, David Seidler; ph, Vittorio Storaro (Technovision, Technicolor); ed, Priscilla Nedd; m, Joe Jackson, Carmine Coppola; prod d, Dean Tavoularis; fx, David Pier; chor, Paula Smuin; cos, Milena Canonero

AAN Best Supporting Actor: Martin Landau; *AAN Best Art Direction-Set Decoration:* Dean Tavoularis, Armin Ganz; *AAN Best Costume Design:* Milena Canonero

A long-delayed dream project for director Francis Ford Coppola, TUCKER: THE MAN AND HIS DREAM was one of the most visually sumptuous American films of the 1980s. In a style that hearkens back to the boundless optimism of 1940s American advertising art, the film tells the story of Preston Tucker—part inventor, part con man—who in the late 1940s attempted to produce his own car, which he dubbed the Tucker Torpedo, "The Car of Tomorrow—Today!" Tucker (Jeff Bridges) has worked his way up in the auto industry and starts up a company to build his dream car. Meanwhile, the big three auto manufacturers in Detroit get wind of Tucker's scheme and set out to squash the tiny interloper.

A glorious celebration of the creative process, TUCKER is Coppola's most overtly autobiographical film, even though it is about someone else's life. Coppola's treatment of the material is remarkably upbeat and joyous. Even when things get extremely dark for our hero, the film's style remains perversely buoyant. Tucker's increasingly frenzied upbeat renditions of "Hold That Tiger" begin to take on the quality of madness. As with Frank Capra heroes, there is a strong suggestion of dark undercurrents beneath the surface optimism. While a darker film would have been more honest, TUCKER: THE MAN AND HIS DREAM is a gorgeous, fluid, wonderfully exhilarating movie. Continuing and expanding upon the visual experiments he began in the notorious commercial flop ONE FROM THE HEART, Coppola fills TUCKER with some flawlessly executed scene transitions that will startle even the most jaded audience.

TUPAC: RESURRECTION

DVD

2004 90m   c/bw Documentary
Amaru Entertainment/MTV Films   (U.S.)   ★★½
R

Tupac Shakur, Afeni Shakur, Sean Combs, Marion "Suge" Knight, Tabitha Soren, Snoop Dogg

p, Karolyn Ali, Preston Holmes, Lauren Lazin; d, Lauren Lazin; ph, Jon Else; ed, Richard Calderon

AAN Best Documentary Feature

Using material culled from the many TV and radio interviews rapper Tupac Shakur gave before his murder in 1996 at age 25, Lauren Lazin's documentary attempts to tell Shakur's story in his own voice.

Born in New York City and raised in Harlem, Baltimore, and Oakland, Shakur grew up financially impoverished but culturally rich; his education included an interval at the Baltimore School of the Arts. By the time he was in his early 20s, Shakur was a rap superstar whose consistently controversial lyrics dealt with black-on-black racism, institutionalized poverty, and ghetto violence. He was arrested repeatedly and embraced the materialism of hip-hop culture, but his intelligence, political awareness (his mother, Afeni, was a member of the Black Panther Party), and personal charisma offset the "Thug Life" image he cultivated.

Lazin's film gets off to a bad start with a miscalculated opening sequence presented in a way that implies we're listening to Shakur speak about his own murder, an impossibility that undermines the film's documentary credibility. It takes a while to get over the beatific images of clouds accompanied by Shakur's voice saying, "I got shot. I'm surprised but I'm happy," and trust that the film is playing straight, not using recreations or taking poetic license with the facts. (Shakur was shot multiple times in an apparent robbery attempt two years before his death, and that's the real incident to which he's alluding). The irony is that Shakur's speaking voice is the film's greatest asset: His transformation from eager-to-please teenager to gangsta icon is vividly apparent in the sound bites.

TURNING POINT, THE

DVD

1977 119m   c   Dance   ★★★
Hera   (U.S.)   PG

Anne Bancroft *(Emma Jacklin)*, Shirley MacLaine *(Deedee Rodgers)*, Mikhail Baryshnikov *(Kopeikine)*, Leslie Browne *(Emilia Rodgers)*, Tom Skerritt *(Wayne Rodgers)*, Martha Scott *(Adelaide)*, Antoinette Sibley *(Sevilla)*, Alexandra Danilova *(Dahkarova)*, Starr Danias *(Carolyn)*, Marshall Thompson *(Carter)*

p, Herbert Ross, Arthur Laurents; d, Herbert Ross; w, Arthur Laurents; ph, Robert Surtees (Panavision, DeLuxe Color); ed, William Reynolds; prod d, Albert Brenner; chor, John Cranko, Alvin Ailey, Marius Petipa, George Balanchine, Dennis Nahat, Alexander Minz, Jean Coralli, Jules Perrot, Harald Lander, Kenneth MacMillan, Frederick Ashton, Michel Fokine, Lev Ivanov; cos, Albert Wolsky

AAN Best Picture; AAN Best Actress: Anne Bancroft; *AAN Best Actress:* Shirley MacLaine; *AAN Best Supporting Actor:* Mikhail Baryshnikov; *AAN Best Supporting Actress:* Leslie Browne; *AAN Best Director:* Herbert Ross; *AAN Best Original Screenplay:* Arthur Laurents; *AAN Best Cinematography:* Robert Surtees; *AAN Best Film Editing:* William Reynolds; *AAN Best Art Direction-Set Decoration:* Albert Brenner, Marvin March; *AAN Best Sound:* Theodore Soderberg, Paul Wells, Douglas O. Williams, Jerry Jost

Only the second ballet-based picture (the first was THE RED SHOES) to ever make a dent with popular audiences, THE TURNING POINT is a well-made soap opera with a story that right out of a 1930s backstage musical.

The American Ballet Theatre is touring the U.S. and makes a stop in Oklahoma City. The company's star is Bancroft, painfully thin, dedicated to dance, and having very little life away from her work. Living in DC is her former associate, MacLaine, who opted for love and marriage 20 years before when they were rivals for the prima ballerina role in the company. MacLaine is married to Skerritt; they have three children and a successful ballet school. MacLaine goes to the performance and is bothered by her choice in life. Had she stayed with the ABT and continued, would that prima ballerina on the stage be her and not Bancroft? MacLaine introduces 19-year-old daughter Browne to Bancroft, who recognizes herself and MacLaine in the ambitious girl. Bancroft arranges an audition for Browne, and she is accepted. As the new season approaches, Browne bids farewell to her parents and goes to New York to prepare for her work in the ABT. Bancroft has been a star for many years, and the time has come for her to hang up her tutu. The leading roles are being given to younger ballerinas, and Bancroft realizes that the moment is near when she will begin to teach more than dance. This is depressing for Bancroft, and she wonders if MacLaine didn't make the right decision by marrying Skerritt way back then. Browne is comfortably ensconced in New York by now and has been joined by MacLaine, apparently as a chaperone. But the truth is that MacLaine wants to see if she did right by leaving the ballet. Browne is the lever between the women as they both coach her in various regimens while keeping an eye on each other.

THE TURNING POINT features a few laughs, lots of maudlin moments, superior dancing from a host of real ballerinas, and an occasionally perceptive script. Executive producer Nora Kaye (wife of the director) is herself a former famed ballerina, and producer-director Ross is a one-time choreographer. Ross does his best to convince us that Bancroft can dance, but his fiddling with fast cuts and closeups won't fool anyone who knows anything about ballet.

12 ANGRY MEN

DVD

1957 95m   bw   Drama   ★★★★
Orion/Nova   (U.S.)

Henry Fonda *(Juror No. 8)*, Lee J. Cobb *(Juror No. 3)*, Ed Begley *(Juror No. 10)*, E.G. Marshall *(Juror No. 4)*, Jack Warden *(Juror*

No. 7), Martin Balsam (Juror No. 1), John Fiedler (Juror No. 2), Jack Klugman (Juror No. 5), Edward Binns (Juror No. 6), Joseph Sweeney (Juror No. 9)

p, Henry Fonda, Reginald Rose; d, Sidney Lumet; w, Reginald Rose (based on his television play); ph, Boris Kaufman; ed, Carl Lerner; m, Kenyon Hopkins; art d, Robert Markell

AAN Best Picture; AAN Best Director: Sidney Lumet; AAN Best Adapted Screenplay: Reginald Rose

Lumet's debut, Rose's adaptation of his television play: verbose, stage-bound, predictable and acted to within an inch of its life. This classic courtroom drama begins in the final hours of a trial for murder in a hot, muggy New York City courtroom. The tired trial judge gives 12 weary jurors their instructions, exhorting them to adhere to the basic rule that weights the scales of justice: the defendant must be seen to be innocent unless proven guilty beyond a reasonable doubt. The jurors shuffle slowly to their chamber and consider the case of a teenage Puerto Rican boy accused of knifing his father to death. Expecting a rapid verdict in what appears a conclusive case, the jury foreman invites an immediate vote. When the ballots are tallied, 11 prove to be for conviction. Fonda is the lone holdout. They deliberate, and the character of each emerges.

Though the film now appears anachronistic, MEN was a landmark film in its day, one which brought a new style to cinema. The teleplay-turned-movie made use of a single static set—an actual New York City jury room—and had a total of 365 separate takes, nearly all of them from different angles. The result was cinema heresy that *worked*. Director Lumet, making his film debut (though he was accomplished in stage and television productions), was teaching lessons to the old-timers. With cameraman Kaufman (the brother of famed Soviet director Dziga Vertov), Lumet carefully plotted and sketched every visual nuance. As had been his habit with theatrical productions, he also rehearsed his cast for a full two weeks before the actual 20-day shoot. The resulting real-time drama made film history.

This was Fonda's one experience as a movie producer. He had admired the television play authored by co-producer Rose and had attempted to get Hollywood's established studios interested in it, with little success. Released as a conventional booking in large theaters, the film failed to make a profit, and Fonda never received his deferred salary. Despite his financial loss, Fonda remembered it fondly as one of his three best efforts (along with THE GRAPES OF WRATH and THE OX-BOW INCIDENT). Fonda is fine in the picture, and the others in the cast (whom he hand-picked) were the leading stage and TV actors of Gotham, whose wonderful work was rewarded in many cases by eventual cinematic stardom. The film is an unsettling one in many ways, as much an indictment as an affirmation of America's jury system. One wonders what might have happened had Fonda's voice-of-reason character not been present. The technique of the film has been repeated since, but this is the one that set the precedent.

TWELVE CHAIRS, THE
DVD
1970 94m   c   Comedy ★★★½
Crossbow/UMC   (U.S.) PG

Ron Moody (Ippolit Vorobyaninov), Frank Langella (Ostap Bender), Dom DeLuise (Father Fyodor), Mel Brooks (Tikon), Bridget Brice (Young Woman), Robert Bernal (Curator), David Lander (Engineer Bruns), Andreas Voutsinas (Nikolai Sestrin), Vlada Petric (Sevitsky), Diana Coupland (Mme. Bruns)

p, Michael Hertzberg; d, Mel Brooks; w, Mel Brooks (based on a novel by Ilya Arnoldovich Ilf, Yevgeniy Petrov, translated by Elizabeth Hill, Doris Mudie as Diamonds to Sit On); ph, Djordje

Nikolic (Movielab Color); ed, Alan Heim; m, John Morris; art d, Mile Nokolic; cos, Ruth Myers

One of Mel Brooks's best films, THE TWELVE CHAIRS was made before he discovered that nothing succeeds like excess. Based on a Russian novel from the 1920s that was translated into English by Doris Mudie and Elizabeth Hill and retitled *Diamonds to Sit On*, this fast-paced period piece is well-made, funny, and a pleasure to watch from start to finish. Shot on location in Yugoslavia, it begins as Moody, a onetime nobleman's son now reduced to working as a clerk for the government, is told by his dying mother that the family fortune was hidden in one of a set of a dozen chairs 10 years previously. In an attempt to claim the money, Moody returns to the family's former home and makes the mistake of telling his story to Langella, a beggar with big ideas. Now that Langella knows the secret, he is cut in as a partner when he promises to help Moody. DeLuise, a Russian Orthodox priest who heard the old woman's final confession, is now also searching for the jewels.

Brooks plays a small role as the onetime valet of Moody's father who is now acting as the janitor in the family's old house. He does a drunk routine that is a marvel of timing and understatement (which is rare for Brooks). Unfortunately, DeLuise is out of his class opposite Moody and Langella. Moody's work proves that his brilliance in OLIVER was anything but a fluke. Langella plays it straight, which is perfect in the script by Brooks. All in all, THE TWELVE CHAIRS is a charming movie about larceny in Communist Russia, with a few moments of questionable taste that make it less than approporiate for the kids.

TWELVE MONKEYS
DVD
1995 130m   c   Science Fiction/Fantasy/Drama ★★★★
Atlas Entertainment/BBC/Polygram/Classico/ R
Shochiku/Telemunchen/UGC/Universal
(U.S./U.K./Germany/Japan/France)

Bruce Willis (James Cole), Madeleine Stowe (Kathryn Railly), Brad Pitt (Jeffrey Goines), Christopher Plummer (Dr. Goines), Jon Seda (Jose), David Morse (Dr. Peters), Frank Gorshin (Dr. Fletcher), Irma St. Paule (Poet), Joey Perillo (Detective Franki), Harry O'Toole (Louie/Raspy Voice)

p, Charles Roven; d, Terry Gilliam; w, David Peoples, Janet Peoples (inspired by the film LA JETTE written by Chris Marker); ph, Roger Pratt; ed, Mick Audsley; m, Paul Buckmaster; prod d, Jeffrey Beecroft; art d, William Ladd Skinner; fx, Anthony Simonaitas, Vincent Montefusco, Kent Houston, Susi Roper, Peerless Camera Co.; cos, Julie Weiss

AAN Best Supporting Actor: Brad Pitt; AAN Best Costume Design: Julie Weiss

A glorious dystopian downer, ready-made for years of fanboy dissection. For once, the packagers didn't outsmart themselves: a creative match made in movie heaven—director Terry Gilliam (BRAZIL) plus screenwriter David Peoples (BLADE RUNNER)—yielded an instant cult classic that's everything you wanted it to be.

Perhaps more important, TWELVE MONKEYS is none of the things you hoped it *wouldn't* be: it's a time-travel movie that doesn't get bogged down in time-travel technicalities, a killer-virus movie without Dustin Hoffman or that adorable monkey (title notwithstanding, there are no monkeys at all), a Brad Pitt movie in which Hollywood's leading pretty boy looks even worse than he did in SEVEN, a Bruce Willis movie without a single smart-ass one-liner. It's BRAZIL crossed with THE TERMINATOR, and just when you think the production design is in danger of overwhelming the story, Gilliam goes for a note of pure, inevitable tragedy and hits it solidly.

In the near future, the planet's surface has been devastated by a deadly virus; the few human survivors have fled underground. James Cole (Willis), a prisoner, is ordered to participate in a bizarre experiment: he's to travel back in time and gather information about the fatal outbreak before it occurs. But nothing works out quite the way it's supposed to, and what Cole finds in the past is his own inexorable fate. It may not mean anything to anyone except die-hard movie buffs, but we're compelled to mention that the screenplay is loosely based on Chris Marker's 1962 experimental classic, LA JETEE. It was an act of sheer hubris to remake Marker's futuristic meditation on *temps perdu*—told almost entirely in still images—as a big-budget, mainstream picture starring Bruce Willis. That Terry Gilliam managed to make TWELVE MONKEYS into a clever, complex, and poignant success is as astonishing as it is satisfying.

TWELVE O'CLOCK HIGH

1949 132m bw War ★★★★½
Fox (U.S.)

Gregory Peck *(Gen. Frank Savage)*, Hugh Marlowe *(Lt. Col. Ben Gately)*, Gary Merrill *(Col. Keith Davenport)*, Dean Jagger *(Maj. Harvey Stovall)*, Millard Mitchell *(Gen. Pritchard)*, Robert Arthur *(Sgt. McIllhenny)*, Paul Stewart *(Capt. "Doc" Kaiser)*, John Kellogg *(Maj. Cobb)*, Robert Patten *(Lt. Bishop)*, Lee MacGregor *(Lt. Zimmerman)*

p, Darryl F. Zanuck; d, Henry King; w, Sy Bartlett, Beirne Lay Jr. (based on their novel); ph, Leon Shamroy; ed, Barbara McLean; m, Alfred Newman; art d, Lyle Wheeler, Maurice Ransford

AAN Best Picture; AAN Best Actor: Gregory Peck; AA Best Supporting Actor: Dean Jagger; AA Best Sound Recording: 20th Century Fox Sound Department

Firm film, peak Peck in this Henry King-directed drama about the physical and emotional stress that results from giving the "maximum effort" day after day. The film opens obscurely and hauntingly as a bald, bespectacled man, Harvey Stovall (Dean Jagger), wanders through postwar England, arriving at the edge of a former American air base, now overgrown with weeds. As the onetime major looks into the sky, his memory takes over: bomber squadrons return from the daylight missions in Germany. The 918th Bomber Group is under the command of Col. Keith Davenport (Gary Merrill), a likable leader who operates as a friend to his men. However, it is Col. Davenport's identification with his men—boys really—that leads to his downfall. Overly concerned with their health and well-being (after a seemingly endless succession of dangerous bombing missions, the squadron is a jumble of wounds and jangled nerves), the colonel is unable to meet the demands of his superiors, Gen. Pritchard (Millard Mitchell) and Gen. Frank Savage (Peck). Davenport is relieved of his duties and replaced by Gen. Savage, a callous martinet who tries to whip the men back into shape, immediately cutting back on three-day passes, closing the local bar, demanding that he be saluted and that everyone be properly uniformed. Most of the pilots put in for a transfer; however, one confused but heroic young pilot, Lt. Bishop (Bob Patten), rallies them. Moved by his men's show of unity, Savage becomes increasingly friendly, identifying with them even more than his predecessors had.

One of the first films to take a complex look at WWII heroism, TWELVE O'CLOCK HIGH is not afraid to show its fighting men as vulnerable. Four years after the war's end, audiences no longer needed the blatant propaganda that filled wartime screens. Instead, Savage's character (based on the real life and nervous breakdown of Air Corps Maj. Gen. Frank A. Armstrong) is entirely human—a man with real emotions, fears, and inadequacies. Peck gives a flawless portrayal of Gen. Savage, but the film's pivotal performance is Jagger's

Maj. Stovall. Stovall is an introspective, older military man; friend and assistant to both Davenport and Savage, he has lived through one world war and now holds together the frayed ends of the 918th Bomber Group. In addition to the fine acting, TWELVE O'CLOCK HIGH features some gorgeous camerawork by Leon Shamroy and one of the most horrifying aerial attack sequences ever put on film. Judging from this picture alone, the subsequent devaluation of King's work is a gross injustice.

TWENTIETH CENTURY

DVD

1934 91m bw Comedy ★★★½
Columbia (U.S.)

John Barrymore *(Oscar Jaffe)*, Carole Lombard *(Mildred Plotka/Lily Garland)*, Roscoe Karns *(Owen O'Malley)*, Walter Connolly *(Oliver Webb)*, Ralph Forbes *(George Smith)*, Dale Fuller *(Sadie)*, Etienne Girardot *(Matthew J. Clark)*, Herman Bing, Lee Kohlmar *(Bearded Men)*, James Burtis *(Train Conductor)*

p, Howard Hawks; d, Howard Hawks; w, Charles MacArthur, Ben Hecht (based on their play, adapted from the play "Napoleon on Broadway" by Charles Bruce Milholland); ph, Joseph August; ed, Gene Havlick

Though the film has a large cast, TWENTIETH CENTURY remains essentially a one-man show for John Barrymore, who plays one of the most preposterous and memorable characters to spring from the minds of Ben Hecht and Charles MacArthur. Directed with breakneck pace by Howard Hawks (as in his later Hecht-MacArthur adaptation, HIS GIRL FRIDAY [1940]), it's the story of a maniacal Broadway director (Barrymore) who transforms shopgirl Carole Lombard from a talented amateur to a smashing Great White Way success adored by public and press. For three years, Barrymore has been both Lombard's lover and her Svengali, shepherding her career, controlling her behavior, and directing her plays. They battle regularly, but make up passionately. Now a huge star of the New York stage, Lombard yearns for some peace and respite from the manic Barrymore. One final disagreement does the trick, and Lombard heads for the palm trees of Hollywood and a screen career. Barrymore's fortunes subsequently plummet, causing creditors to dog his heels in Chicago. To escape, he boards the Twentieth Century Limited train in the Windy City, accompanied by his manager, Walter Connolly, and press representative Roscoe Karns, heading for what they hope will be newfound success in New York. As luck would have it, Lombard and her new fiance, football player Ralph Forbes, are also on the train. Barrymore despises the ruggedly handsome Forbes and doesn't bother to hide his disdain as he moves in on Lombard (who has become as big a star on the screen as she was on the stage), trying to convince her to appear in his latest production. The remainder of the picture is a farcical series of biting verbal exchanges, opening and closing doors, hurled insults, thrown kisses, a madcap procession of several weird characters on board the train, and some of the biggest laughs Barrymore ever received. In the end, as expected, Barrymore has convinced Lombard that Broadway is the place for her, and by the time the Twentieth Century pulls into Grand Central Station, she is safely under his influence once more. Barrymore is a wonder as he does imitations of camels, tramples over his fellow actors' lines, sprinkles his dialog with foreign phrases, and generally leaves the rest of the cast looking like his stooges. The picture was not a hit when it first came out, perhaps because its satire of flamboyant theater people failed to capture the imagination of moviegoing audiences; later it became the basis for the Broadway musical "On the Twentieth Century."

20,000 LEAGUES UNDER THE SEA

1954 120m c   Science Fiction
Walt Disney Productions   (U.S.)   ★★★★

Kirk Douglas *(Ned Land)*, James Mason *(Capt. Nemo)*, Paul Lukas *(Prof. Pierre Aronnax)*, Peter Lorre *(Conseil, His Assistant)*, Bob Wilke *(1st Mate of "Nautilus")*, Carleton Young *(John Howard)*, Ted de Corsia *(Capt. Farragut)*, Percy Helton *(Diver)*, Ted Cooper *(Mate of "Abraham Lincoln")*, Eddie Marr *(Shipping Agent)*

p, Walt Disney; d, Richard Fleischer; w, Earl Felton (based on the novel *Twenty Thousand Leagues under the Sea* by Jules Verne); ph, Franz Planer, Ralph Hammeras, Till Gabbani (CinemaScope, Technicolor); m, Paul J. Smith, Johann Sebastian Bach; art d, John Meehan; fx, John Hench, Joshua Meador; cos, Norman Martien

AAN Best Film Editing: Elmo Williams; *AA Best Art Direction-Set Decoration (Color):* John Meehan, Emile Kuri; *AA Best Special Effects*

One of the best Disney live action films and a classic fantasy-adventure, 20,000 LEAGUES UNDER THE SEA is a fairly respectful adaptation of Jules Verne's prophetic tale (published in 1870) of submarines and atomic power. It's 1868 and San Francisco is agog over reports of a sea-roving "monster" that devours any ship that ventures near it. Many voyages are canceled and the government is forced to send a warship to investigate and clear the sea lanes. That ship is sunk by the heinous "creature" and only three people survive the ordeal: a professional harpoonist (Kirk Douglas), a professor from the Nautical Museum in Paris (Paul Lukas), and his aide (Peter Lorre). They are plucked from the sea by the dreaded "monster" which is actually the *Nautilus*, a fabulous submarine. The sub is commanded by Capt. Nemo (James Mason), scientist, inventor, crazed visionary, and radical peace activist. He's taken to sinking ships in a well-meaning effort to end warfare at sea. In an awesome adventure brimming over with fantastic elements, one sequence rises above the fray to become indelible: the fight with the giant squid. The marvelous sets—with their quaint blend of Victorian and futuristic elements—are worth the price of admission alone. The direction is sharp as are the special effects. All the major performances are fun but James Mason is a standout. Dare we say it? It's fun for the entire family!

20,000 YEARS IN SING SING

1933 81m   bw   Prison
Warner Bros./First National (U.S.)   ★★★★

Spencer Tracy *(Tom Connors)*, Bette Davis *(Fay)*, Lyle Talbot *(Bud)*, A.S. Byron *(Warden Long)*, Grant Mitchell *(Dr. Ames)*, Warren Hymer *(Hype)*, Louis Calhern *(Joe Finn)*, Sheila Terry *(Billie)*, Edward McNamara *(Chief of Guards)*, Spencer Charters *(Daniels)*

p, Robert Lord; d, Michael Curtiz; w, Courtney Terrett, Robert Lord, Wilson Mizner, Brown Holmes (based on the book by Lewis E. Lawes); ph, Barney McGill; ed, George Amy; m, Bernhard Kaun; art d, Anton Grot; cos, Orry-Kelly

The praises of a prison, the famous Sing Sing, are sung in this picture authored by Sing Sing's long-term reform warden, Lewis E. Lawes. Cocksure criminal Spencer Tracy is sent to the slammer on a felony rap. There he is greeted by the kindly warden, A.S. Byron, who explains that good behavior brings certain privileges. Tough-guy Tracy starts a near-riot and gets 90 days in solitary, where he resolves to escape. He joins some prisoners who are planning an escape attempt until he discovers that their plan is set for Tuesday (he has an odd superstition relating to the days of the week). Beaten at last, he determines to win parole through good behavior. Meanwhile,

Tracy's girlfriend Davis—attempting to win his parole by other means—seeks the assistance of powerful mob chief Harold Huber. In return for his help, Huber wants Davis's favors. While speeding down a street in a car, Davis repels the gangster's groping and is seriously injured in the resulting automobile crash. When warden Byron hears of her condition, he offers Tracy—now a trusty—compassionate leave to visit Davis. On the outside, however, Tracy runs into some detectives who mistake him for an escapee. A disastrous shootout follows.

Tracy's role in the film seems tailored more to James Cagney's cinematic persona than to his own—indeed, Cagney, who made the mold in a number of gangster films, was Jack Warner's first choice for the part. But Tracy handled the characterization beautifully. Davis' performance is excessively histrionic; not even domineering director Michael Curtiz could hold the actress back. This was to be the only time that two-time Oscar winners Davis and Tracy worked together. At the time the picture was made, author Lawes was the warden of Sing Sing and cooperated in every possible way for the production, allowing the film crew to enter the prison to shoot and permitting real prisoners to play in the mob scenes. The film was the first of many to be based on Lawes's accounts of prison life; others include OVER THE WALL, YOU CAN'T GET AWAY WITH MURDER, INVISIBLE STRIPES, and CASTLE ON THE HUDSON, the latter a remake of 20,000 YEARS IN SING SING, starring John Garfield, Ann Sheridan, and Pat O'Brien. Despite the grimness of its subject matter, 20,000 YEARS IN SING SING is laced with humor.

21 GRAMS

2003 125m   c   Drama/Thriller
Y Productions/This Is That Productions   (U.S.)   ★★★   R

Sean Penn *(Paul Rivers)*, Naomi Watts *(Cristina Peck)*, Benicio Del Toro *(Jack Jordan)*, Charlotte Gainsbourg *(Mary Rivers)*, Melissa Leo *(Marianne Jordan)*, Clea DuVall *(Claudia Williams)*, Danny Huston *(Michael)*, Carly Nahon *(Katie)*, Claire Pakis *(Laura)*, Nick Nichols *(Boy)*

p, Alejandro Gonzalez Inarritu, Robert Salerno; d, Alejandro Gonzalez Inarritu; w, Guillermo Arriaga; ph, Rodrigo Prieto; ed, Stephen Mirrione; m, Gustavo Santaolalla; prod d, Brigitte Broch; art d, Deborah Riley; fx, Kathleen Tonkin; cos, Marlene Stewart

AAN Best Actress: Naomi Watts; *AAN Best Supporting Actor:* Benicio Del Toro

There's not much more to Alejandro Gonzalez Inarritu's ostentatious follow-up to AMORES PERROS than what meets the eye. In fact, once the film's chronologically fractured, tripartite storyline falls into place, there's considerably less.

Inarritu's kaleidoscopic script follows three initially unrelated characters as they hurtle toward a fateful meeting in a Phoenix motel room. Paul Rivers (Sean Penn) is a college professor who will be dead within a few months if he doesn't receive a heart transplant. Cristina (Naomi Watts) is a happily married mother of two who's put her party-hearty days behind her in exchange for a life of suburban comfort with her architect husband, Michael (Danny Huston). Living in an entirely different world is Jack (Benicio Del Toro), a married ex-con who's been in and out of jail since he was 16. Jack's found Jesus, and when he's not supporting his family by caddying at the country club, Jack spends his free time down at his church helping troubled kids. Paul, Cristina, Jack: three complete strangers whose lives are irrevocably altered by a terrible accident that puts paid to Jack's belief that just as Jesus gives, he also taketh away. And often without mercy.

Del Toro and Penn are both excellent, and Watts gives another demonstration of a startling emotional range that rivals her revelatory turn in MULHOLLAND DR. But as in AMORES PERROS, the real star is once again the audacious Gonzalez Inarritu. Given just how many balls he keeps in the air at once, it's amazing that the story coheres at all; his control is absolutely masterful. But aside from a little eleventh-hour pseudo-mysticism about death and the weight of the soul, the story is really little more than an unusually gripping thriller.

28 DAYS
DVD

2000 103m c Comedy/Drama ★★★½
Tall Trees (U.S.) PG-13

Sandra Bullock (*Gwen Cummings*), Viggo Mortensen (*Eddie Boone*), Dominic West (*Jasper*), Elizabeth Perkins (*Lily*), Azura Skye (*Andrea*), Steve Buscemi (*Cornell*), Alan Tudyk (*Gerhardt*), Michael O'Malley (*Oliver*), Marianne Jean-Baptiste (*Roshanda*), Diane Ladd (*Bobbie Jean*)

p, Jenno Topping; d, Betty Thomas; w, Susannah Grant; ph, Declan Quinn; ed, Peter Teschner; m, Richard Gibbs; prod d, Marcia Hinds-Johnson; art d, Bo Johnson; fx, Connie Brink; cos, Ellen Lutter

Anyone can mock the rituals and touchie-feelie newspeak of rehab: one AA meeting and you're armed with a year's worth of gut-busters. But this dark comedy pulls off something far harder, managing the delicate balancing act of jeering at 12-step culture's absurdity without ridiculing rehab itself.

Gwen Cummings (Sandra Bullock) is an Olympic-caliber party animal; she and boyfriend Jasper (Dominic West) are triathletes of drinking, drugging, and dancing on tables. But Gwen raises the bar at her older sister Lily's (Elizabeth Perkins) wedding: She arrives late and disheveled, makes a painfully tasteless toast, falls into the wedding cake and takes the bridal limo for a joyride, crashing it into a neighbor's porch. Next stop: court-ordered rehab at an isolated rural facility full of losers, all of whom know exactly what Gwen thinks of them before she ever opens her snarky mouth. They include a 17-year-old heroin addict (Azura Skye); German go-go boy Gerhardt (the hilarious Alan Tudyk); a sour, middle-aged doctor (Reni Santoni); country-boy baseball star Eddie (Viggo Mortensen); a spoiled rich kid (Michael O'Malley); a drug-addicted single mother (Marianne Jean-Baptiste); and a downtrodden middle-aged housewife (Diane Ladd).

Gwen skewers them mercilessly, but the prickly laughs don't stop as she realizes that she's no better off than they are, her sharp tongue notwithstanding; the movie's slyest trick is shifting almost imperceptibly from Gwen's snide mockery to the shared graveyard humor of the rehabbers. Bullock is the glue that holds this film together, but she's supported by an amazing ensemble, including Steve Buscemi as the group counselor who's walked the walk and now talks the talk. Funny, thought-provoking and, yes, touching.

28 DAYS LATER...
DVD

2002 113m c Horror ★★★½
DNA Films/Film Council (U.K.) R

Cillian Murphy (*Jim*), Naomie Harris (*Selena*), Brendan Gleeson (*Frank*), Megan Burns (*Hannah*), Christopher Eccleston (*Major Henry West*), Luke Mably (*Private Clifton*), Stuart McQuarrie (*Sergeant Farrell*), Ricci Harnett (*Corporal Mitchell*), Leo Bill (*Private Jones*), Noah Huntley (*Mark*)

p, Andrew Macdonald; d, Danny Boyle; w, Alex Garland; ph, Anthony Dod Mantle; ed, Chris Gill; m, John Murphy; prod d, Mark Tildesley; art d, Mark Digby, Patrick Rolfe; fx, Richard Conway, Bob Hollow, Tony Lawrence, Clear; cos, Rachael Fleming

Every generation gets the zombies it deserves, and in an age of free-floating fury and fear of uncontainable new diseases,

the walking not-quite-dead of this particular nightmare are infected with a rapidly transmitted blood disorder that turns victims into homicidal horrors.

It begins in a primate research lab where, thanks to a band of misguided animal activists, chimps injected with "rage" erupt from their cages in a blur of slashing fangs and gore. Twenty-eight days later, bike messenger Jim (Cillian Murphy) awakes from a coma in an empty hospital. The London streets are eerily deserted, old newspaper headlines scream "Evacuation!," and everywhere the evidence of panic and desperation litters the pavements. When Jim finds life, it's a snarling nest of savage, infected humans; only the timely intervention of healthy survivors Selena (Naomie Harris) and Mark (Noah Huntley) saves him. The rules of the grim new world are simple: arm yourself, avoid the infected—even if they don't tear you to pieces, a single drop of their blood is enough to infect you—and don't think about the future because there isn't one.

Heir to a long tradition of apocalyptic scare stories, the film wears its influences proudly: Richard Matheson's "I Am Legend," John Wyndham's "Day of the Triffids," J.G. Ballard's "High-Rise," and George Romero's THE CRAZIES and DEAD trilogy. Director Danny Boyle and screenwriter Alex Garland tip their hats to these and many others without succumbing to ironic self-referentiality. The thematic underpinnings never disrupt the story's stripped-down momentum, and the ray-of-hope ending in no way undercuts the horror of the 100 minutes that precede it.

25TH HOUR
DVD

2002 135m c Drama ★★★
40 Acres and a Mule/Industry Entertainment/ R
Gamut Films/Touchstone (U.S.)

Edward Norton (*Monty Brogan*), Philip Seymour Hoffman (*Jakob Elinsky*), Barry Pepper (*Francis Xavier Slaughtery*), Rosario Dawson (*Naturelle Riviera*), Anna Paquin (*Mary D'Annuzio*), Brian Cox (*James Brogan*), Tony Siragusa (*Kostya Novotny*), Levani (*Uncle Nikolai*), Misha Kuznetsov (*Senka Valghobek*), Isiah Whitlock Jr. (*Agent Flood*)

p, Julia Chasman, Jon Kilik, Spike Lee, Tobey Maguire; d, Spike Lee; w, David Benioff (based on his novel); ph, Rodrigo Prieto; ed, Barry Alexander Brown; m, Terence Blanchard; prod d, James Chinlund; art d, Nicholas Lundy; fx, Randy Balsmeyer; cos, Sandra Hernandez

Spike Lee's compelling film is ostensibly about a convicted drug dealer's last 24 hours of freedom before he begins a seven-year prison sentence, but it's also an interesting take on post-9/11 New York City and its inhabitants.

Dealer Monty Brogan (Edward Norton) is charismatic, attractive, and compassionate, but he allows only a few people to get close to him. That select group includes his seductive younger girlfriend, Naturelle (Rosario Dawson); his obnoxious Ukrainian bodyguard, Kostya (Tony Siragusa); his father (Brian Cox); and two high-school pals, Wall Street hustler Francis Xavier Slaughtery (Barry Pepper) and teacher Jakob Elinsky (Philip Seymour Hoffman). Over the course of a single tumultuous day, Monty attempts to make amends to each and discover who turned him in to the cops. Several friends question Naturelle's motives, and Monty can't help but wonder whether they have a point, but as the day wears on, the initially urgent question of responsibility takes on a different cast. During the film's pivotal moment, Monty stares himself down in a mirror and concludes that he can't keep blaming other people for his own mistakes.

The sequence is archetypal Lee, complete with a provocative tirade and an accompanying montage, but it's also undeniably powerful. Norton convincingly portrays both the good and bad sides of this conflicted man, but a great deal of the insight into his character comes from the strong supporting cast and the network of subplots, including one involving Jakob's attraction to a 17-year-old student (Anna Paquin). Lee's decision to include footage of Manhattan's ravaged financial district—including the raw pit where the World Trade Center once stood—is generally a good one, though the images occasionally threaten to overwhelm the characters.

24-HOUR PARTY PEOPLE   *DVD*
2001   115m   c   Biography   ★★★★
Film Consortium/Film Council/FilmFour/Revolution   R
Films/Baby Cow Films/UA   (U.K.)

Steve Coogan *(Tony Wilson)*, Shirley Henderson *(Lindsay Wilson)*, Paddy Considine *(Rob Gretton)*, Sean Harris *(Ian Curtis)*, Danny Cunningham *(Shaun Ryder)*, Andy Serkis *(Martin Hannett)*, Chris Coghill *(Bez)*, Lennie James *(Alan Erasmus)*, Mani *(Sound Engineer)*, Mark E. Smith *(Punter)*

p, Andrew Eaton; d, Michael Winterbottom; w, Frank Cottrell Boyce; ph, Robby Muller; ed, Trevor Waite; prod d, Mark Tildesley; art d, Paul Cripps; fx, David Bryan; cos, Stephen Noble, Natalie Ward

"This is not a film about me," insists Tony Wilson, the Mancunian TV host and post-punk impresario portrayed so brilliantly by Steve Coogan. "This is a story about the music." And so it is. Director Michael Winterbottom's witty, audacious account of Wilson's wild ride on fortune's wheel is jam-packed with the sounds of the edgy noisemakers who erupted out of Manchester in the wake of punk rock.

Blown away by a local Sex Pistols gig, Wilson (Coogan) begins booking bands at a Manchester club he renames "The Factory." Hoping to capture the exciting new sounds of his city, Wilson forms Factory Records and records the group that would soon become the label's flagship band: Joy Division. Throughout, Wilson holds down his day job but begins indulging his penchant for grand artistic gestures and stylish profligacy that would soon prove his downfall. The first half of the film chronicles Joy Division's rise and the sudden death of lead singer Ian Curtis (Sean Harris). The second half sees Wilson through the lean early '80s, when the remnants of Joy Division regroup as New Order and Wilson risks everything on a cavernous nightclub and a scruffy band of troublemakers, the Happy Mondays.

Shot on digital video by Robby Muller and edited with a rhythm that matches the soundtrack's scratchy guitars and funky bass lines, this could very well be one of the most self-referential movies ever made; Wilson constantly pauses mid-scene to explain an interesting bit of symbolism, or jumps ahead to offer some ironic 20/20 hindsight. Also featured are countless cameos from local superstars ranging from the Fall's Mark E. Smith to Mani of the Stone Roses, making the film an absolute thrill for fans of the Manchester scene.

TWILIGHT'S LAST GLEAMING
1977   146m   c   Historical/Thriller/War   ★★★½
Geria/Lorimar/Bavaria   (U.S./West Germany)   R

Burt Lancaster *(Lawrence Dell)*, Richard Widmark *(Martin MacKenzie)*, Charles Durning *(President Stevens)*, Melvyn Douglas *(Zachariah Guthrie)*, Paul Winfield *(Willis Powell)*, Burt Young *(Augie Garvas)*, Joseph Cotten *(Arthur Renfrew)*, Roscoe Lee Browne *(James Forrest)*, Gerald S. O'Loughlin *(Brig. Gen. Michael O'Rourke)*, Richard Jaeckel *(Capt. Stanford Towne)*

p, Merv Adelson; d, Robert Aldrich; w, Ronald M. Cohen, Edward Huebsch (based on the novel *Viper Three* by Walter Wager); ph, Robert B. Hauser (Technicolor); ed, Michael Luciano, Maury Weintrobe; m, Jerry Goldsmith; prod d, Rolf Zehetbauer; art d, Werner Achmann; fx, Henry Millar, Willy Neuner; cos, Tom Dawson

A flawed but nonetheless highly exciting political thriller, TWILIGHT'S LAST GLEAMING has some deeply disturbing things to say about the powers that be in America. The action begins in 1981 (the near future for this 1977 release) and centers on former U.S. Air Force general Lawrence Dell (Burt Lancaster), a Vietnam veteran who served five years as a POW. Upon his return, Dell became a vocal advocate of disclosing the truth behind U.S. involvement in Southeast Asia in the hope that a post-Watergate America would forgive its government and have renewed faith in its leaders. Because of his radical stance, however, Dell is eventually sent to prison on trumped-up manslaughter charges. Still determined, he recruits three inmates (Paul Winfield, Burt Young, and William Smith) to help him escape and take over a nearby SAC base that he helped design. Once in control of the base, Dell demands that the president (Charles Durning) reveal the truth about the Vietnam War to the American people by reading National Security Council document 9759 on national television. If these demands are not met, Dell promises to send the nine Titan missiles to their targets in the Soviet Union. TWILIGHT'S LAST GLEAMING is a stunning indictment of the arrogance of America's decision makers and the lengths to which they will go to maintain "business as usual." At the same time it also dramatizes the danger of our unthinking faith in technology. Tellingly, it comes as a deep shock to the military that their usually reliable machines and detailed procedures seem to have gone haywire on the day of the siege, leaving them powerless to stop Dell. Though a bit slow at the outset and suffering from some occasional lapses of logic, Robert Aldrich's film—shot in Germany with no cooperation from the U.S. military—is a fascinating, tension-filled effort. Lancaster contributes a fine performance as the righteous, populist general, and Durning is superb as the president who comes to share Lancaster's high hopes. Further, Aldrich uses some remarkable split-screen techniques that add to the film's tension and speed up the complicated expository passages. Despite some flaws, TWILIGHT'S LAST GLEAMING is a gripping drama that will have you on the edge of your seat until the bitter end.

TWISTER   *DVD*
1996   117m   c   Thriller   ★★★
Amblin Entertainment/Universal/Warner Bros.   PG-13
(U.S.)

Bill Paxton *(Bill Harding)*, Helen Hunt *(Jo Harding)*, Cary Elwes *(Dr. Jonas Miller)*, Jami Gertz *(Melissa)*, Lois Smith *(Aunt Meg)*, Alan Ruck *(Dusty)*, Philip Seymour Hoffman *(Rabbit)*, Abraham Benrubi *(Bubba)*, Nicholas Sadler *(Kubrick)*, Sean Whalen *(Sanders)*

p, Kathleen Kennedy, Ian Bryce, Michael Crichton; d, Jan De Bont; w, Michael Crichton, Anne-Marie Martin; ph, Jack N. Green; ed, Michael Khan; m, Mark Mancina; prod d, Joseph Nemec III; art d, Dan Olexiewicz; fx, Stefen Fangmeier, John Frazier, Habib Zargarpour, Henry La Bounta, Industrial Light & Magic; cos, Ellen Mirojnick

AAN Best Visual Effects: Stefen Fangmeier, John Frazier, Habib Zargarpour, Henry La Bounta; *AAN Best Sound:* Steve Maslow, Gregg Landaker, Kevin O'Connell, Geoffrey Patterson

A by-the-numbers blockbuster with even less in the way of plot than JURASSIC PARK, TWISTER stormed the U.S. box office in the summer of 1996 and became one of the top 10 all-time grossers within six weeks of its release.

Bill (Bill Paxton) has abandoned the wild life of chasing tornadoes for a sedate berth as a weatherman and imminent marriage to therapist Melissa (Jami Gertz); he just needs wife Jo (Helen Hunt) to sign the divorce papers. Meanwhile, spunky Jo and her group of scrappy, pure-hearted tornado chasers are trying to beat the big, bad corporate-financed tornado chasers—you can tell them by their glossy black vans—to some Very Important Discovery about the structure of killer twisters.

That's about all. But the barebones plotting is beside the point: TWISTER stands or falls on the tornado effects, and they're stupendous, even if the lion's roar incorporated into the sound mix errs a tad on the side of overstatement (the twister is a monster—we get it). Those who recall that Bill Paxton once had an edgy, feral appeal should be forewarned that TWISTER batters him into two-dimensional blandness; anyone fooled by the synopsis into hoping for an entertaining hybrid of disaster movie brouhaha and comedy-of-remarriage high jinks will be sorely disappointed. Extreme-weather buffs, thrill-ride junkies, and anyone else in search of utterly mindless entertainment need look no further.

2 DAYS IN THE VALLEY 📀

1996 105m c   Crime/Thriller/Comedy   ★★★
Rysher Entertainment/Redemption/MGM   (U.S.)   R

Danny Aiello (Dosmo Pizzo), James Spader (Lee Woods), Greg Cruttwell (Allan Hopper), Jeff Daniels (Alvin Strayer), Teri Hatcher (Becky Foxx), Charlize Theron (Helga Svelgen), Glenne Headly (Susan Parish), Peter Horton (Roy Foxx), Marsha Mason (Audrey Hopper), Paul Mazursky (Teddy Peppers)

p, Jeff Wald, Herb Nanas; d, John Herzfeld; w, John Herzfeld; ph, Oliver Wood; ed, Jim Miller, Wayne Wahrman; m, Anthony Marinelli; prod d, Catherine Hardwicke; art d, Kevin Constant; fx, Larry Fioritto; cos, Betsy Heimann

Promoted at the time of its release as a Quentin Tarantino-style thriller, 2 DAYS IN THE VALLEY is actually more reminiscent of the complex, multi-character films of Alan Rudolph.

Has-been hitman Dosmo Pizzo (Danny Aiello) is hired by sociopath Lee Woods (James Spader) to assist in a contract killing, but Dosmo soon discovers he's meant to be the fall guy. After he murders his target and shoots Dosmo, Lee and his sexy partner Helga (Charlize Theron) try to collect their fee from the victim's widow, Becky (Teri Hatcher). The money, however, is locked in a safe back at the crime scene—Becky's house. Meanwhile, saved by his bulletproof vest, Dosmo hides out in the home of art dealer Allan Hopper (Greg Cruttwell), whom Dosmo takes hostage along with Allan's abused assistant, Susan (Glenne Headly), his half-sister, Audrey (Marsha Mason), and Teddy Peppers (Paul Mazursky), a down-and-out director. Lee's attempt to recover his money and Dosmo's thirst for revenge lead the two men back to the scene of the crime for a bloody showdown.

Despite the busy plot, writer-director John Herzfeld is really more interested in characters than story, and 2 DAYS works best as a showcase for its ensemble cast. But while the film's focus may be on sympathetic losers Dosmo and Teddy, Herzfeld's most engaging characters are the unrepentant bad guys. Spader steals the film as an ice-cool killer with a macabre sense of humor; Cruttwell is only slightly less odious here than the monstrous yuppie he played in Mike Leigh's NAKED (1993); and Theron, as Spader's dangerous, spandex-sheathed consort, makes a memorable debut. While this admirably ambitious film may ultimately fail in achieving all it hopes for, it still has enough small virtues to make for entertaining viewing.

TWO ENGLISH GIRLS 📀
(LES DEUX ANGLAISES ET LE CONTINENT)
1971 132m c   Drama   ★★★½
Carosse/Simar/Cinetel   (France)   R

Jean-Pierre Leaud (Claude Roc), Kika Markham (Anne Brown), Stacey Tendeter (Muriel Brown), Sylvia Marriott (Mrs. Brown), Marie Mansart (Madame Roc), Philippe Leotard (Diurka), Irene

Tunc (Ruta), Mark Peterson (Mr. Flint), David Markham (Palmist), Georges Delerue (Claude's Business Agent)

p, Claude Miler; d, Francois Truffaut; w, Francois Truffaut, Jean Gruault (based on the novel by Henri-Pierre Roche); ph, Nestor Almendros (Eastmancolor); ed, Yann Dedet; m, Georges Delerue; art d, Michel de Broin; cos, Gitt Magrini

Francois Truffaut's TWO ENGLISH GIRLS is a love story examining the complications of one man's romance with two women, in a reversal of JULES AND JIM (both films are based on novels by Henri-Pierre Roche). Set at the beginning of the 20th century, the film focuses on Claude (Jean-Pierre Leaud), a young art critic and aspiring author who charms his way through life. In Paris he meets Anne (Kika Markham), a liberated young woman who invites him to spend the summer at the seaside cottage she shares with her sister, Muriel (Stacey Tendeter). Though Anne shows some initial interest in Claude, she secretly intends that he fall in love with the puritanical Muriel. Her plot works, but when she herself has a tryst with Claude, the situation becomes increasingly intense. One of Truffaut's darker films, TWO ENGLISH GIRLS is compared much too often to its companion piece, JULES AND JIM. Both films shine light on the personality of Roche (Truffaut had access to his unpublished diaries), mainly through the characters of Catherine (Jeanne Moreau in JULES AND JIM) and Claude. However, TWO ENGLISH GIRLS is more interestingly viewed as a precursor to Truffaut's later film THE STORY OF ADELE H., with Muriel bearing remarkable similarities to Adele Hugo.

TWO FOR THE ROAD
1967 112m c   Comedy/Drama   ★★★½
Fox   (U.K.)

Audrey Hepburn (Joanna Wallace), Albert Finney (Mark Wallace), Eleanor Bron (Cathy Manchester), William Daniels (Howard Manchester), Claude Dauphin (Maurice Dalbret), Nadia Gray (Francoise Dalbret), Georges Descrieres (David), Gabrielle Middleton (Ruth Manchester), Jacqueline Bisset (Jackie), Judy Cornwell (Pat)

p, Stanley Donen; d, Stanley Donen; w, Frederic Raphael; ph, Christopher Challis (Panavision, DeLuxe Color); ed, Richard Marden, Madeleine Gug; m, Henry Mancini; art d, Willy Holt, Marc Frederix; fx, Gilbert Manzon; cos, Hardy Amies, Ken Scott, Michele Posier, Paco Rabanne, Mary Quant, Foale and Tuffin

AAN Best Original Story and Screenplay: Frederic Raphael

Like a cheap wine, TWO FOR THE ROAD has not stood up well to the passing of time. What seemed so chic in 1967 looks like a soap opera with jumpcuts today. Still, one must measure it by the temper of the times; in 1967, it was on the money. A small cult of aficionados feels that the film remains one of the best of the genre.

Audrey Hepburn and architect Albert Finney are a married couple taking a car trip from England to the French Riviera. They are about to visit the home of Dauphin, the Frenchman who helped the successful Finney get his first break. From the nature of the biting dialogue between the two, it's obvious that this is a marriage in jeopardy. Flash back to a dozen years before when Finney and Hepburn first met. He's a backpacking student looking at European buildings, and she's one of several female music students going to a festival. Finney is attracted to Jacqueline Bisset but winds up with Hepburn as the other women all come down with chicken pox. They travel together to the edge of the sea and decide they are in love and will get married. Flash forward to their next trip on the Continent. They are newlyweds traveling with William Daniels, Eleanor Bron, and their incorrigible daughter, Gabrielle Middleton. This little girl is enough to sour any woman from having a child, but Hepburn manages to overcome her hatred for the little brat. She and Finney make a pact never again to travel with anyone else. On yet another trip along the same road, Hepburn tells Finney that she is pregnant, and they meet Dauphin, who gives Finney his chance to go from minor jobs to major homes in the south of France. The film cuts between past, present, and future, presenting Finney having a one-night stand with Karyn Balm and Hepburn submitting to the amorous advances of Georges Descrieres, a sober intellectual who turns out to be far too dour for Hepburn's lighthearted personality. The two are reunited and realize that, through it all, they love each other and no amount of petty quarreling or even major spats will ever divide them.

Finney's character remains essentially the same throughout, a slightly boorish lout. Hepburn changes visibly from a naive waif to a mature wife and mother to a bored matron. There were some complaints that Hepburn was too old for Finney, but she is actually just about seven years his senior. Her career had been twice the length of Finney's, and people were just used to seeing her more often. The usually fastidious Hepburn was dressed by Mary Quant, Paco Rabanne, Ken Scott, and others, and, wonder of wonders, she even wore blue jeans. Location scenes were done in Paris, Nice, St. Tropez, La Colle sur le Loup, and Beauallon. Good aerial photography by Guy Tabary and an excellent score by Henry Mancini also enhance the film. Although Bron plays an American, she is actually a British actress who scored in HELP, ALFIE, WOMEN IN LOVE, and the Dudley Moore-Peter Cook production, BEDAZZLED, also directed by Stanley Donen. Donen's direction here is a trifle trendy and frantic, with sometimes jarring results.

TWO HUNDRED MOTELS
1971 98m c Musical/Experimental/Fantasy ★★★
UA (U.K.) R

The Mothers of Invention (Themselves), Theodore Bikel (Rance Muhammitz), Ringo Starr (Larry the Dwarf/Frank Zappa), Keith Moon (Hot Nun), Jimmy Carl Black (Lonesome Cowboy Burt), Martin Lickert (Jeff), Janet Ferguson (Groupies), Lucy Offerall (Groupies), Pamela Miller (Interviewer), Don Preston (Bif Debris)

p, Jerry Good, Herb Cohen; d, Frank Zappa, Tony Palmer; w, Frank Zappa, Tony Palmer (based on a story by Zappa); ph, Tony Palmer (Technicolor); ed, Richard Harrison, Barry Stephens; m, Frank Zappa; prod d, Calvin Schenkel; art d, Leo Austin; fx, Bert Luxford; chor, Gillian Lynne; cos, Sue Yelland; anim, Mara Kam

Always ahead of his time, avant-garde musician Zappa anticipates the rock video in what can best be described as the visual equivalent to any of his recordings in the late 1960s and early 1970s. TWO HUNDRED MOTELS is a hodgepodge of color and sound linked by ex-Beatle Starr playing Zappa, complete with curly-locked wig and the signature goatee. The film is a marvelous whirl of color and visual effects, with some fine animation and Zappa's delicious wit present throughout the entire production. This was the first color production to be transferred from videotape to film, and the technique works well. The special visual effects available at the time were used to create some amazing surreal images and optical illusions. This is certainly not for everyone, and sometimes the picture causes eyestrain, but, for the adventurous, TWO HUNDRED MOTELS is definitely a film to experience. Zappa codirected with Palmer, taking credit for "characterizations." Palmer was said to have directed the visuals and was also responsible for the shooting script from the "story" and screenplay by Zappa. Watch for Moon, the drummer of The Who, in a cameo as a nun!

TWO-LANE BLACKTOP
`DVD`
1971 102m c Drama ★★★★
Universal (U.S.) R

James Taylor (The Driver), Warren Oates (G.T.O.), Laurie Bird (Girl), Dennis Wilson (The Mechanic), David Brake (Needles Station Attendant), Richard Ruth (Needles Station Mechanic), Rudolph Wurlitzer (Hot Rod Driver), Jaclyn Hellman (Driver's Girl), Bill Keller (Texas Hitchhiker), Harry Dean Stanton (Oklahoma Hitchhiker)

p, Michael S. Laughlin; d, Monte Hellman; w, Rudy Wurlitzer, Will Corry (based on a story by Corry); ph, Jackson Deerson (Technicolor); ed, Monte Hellman; cos, Richard Bruno

Real-life rock stars Taylor and Wilson (the latter a member of the Beach Boys) are a pair of car freaks driving down the endless roads of the American Southwest in search of a race. They drive an old 1955 Chevy, using race winnings to keep the souped-up auto in shape. The pair have little to say to each other beyond car talk. At a small Arizona diner they meet Bird, who gets in the car with them, no questions asked. After winning another race, Taylor and Bird make love; the next evening it's Wilson's turn with her. Later the three meet up with Oates, an older drifter who travels across the U.S. in his brand new GTO. He challenges them to a cross-country race to Washington, DC, with the winner taking ownership of the loser's car. Along the way the participants' interest in the race begins to wane. Wilson suggests to Bird that they ride off together. Taylor enters a race in Memphis, and Bird, bored with the younger men, heads off to North Carolina with Oates. Later she takes off with a motorcyclist, and Oates continues his aimless driving. Eventually, Wilson and Taylor find another race to run, and the movie ends ominously as they drive away from the camera down a two-lane road and the film burns and melts in the gate, leaving only a bright white light. Certainly not an average car chase movie, TWO-LANE BLACKTOP is perhaps director Monte Hellman's finest film. Known for his small, brooding existential westerns (THE SHOOTING, RIDE IN THE WHIRLWIND), Hellman once again brings to life characters desperately searching for meaning. Oates, a close personal friend of Hellman's and lead player in nearly all his films, is magnificent in TWO-LANE BLACKTOP, bringing a perfect blend of comedy, mystery, and pathos to his role. It is a powerful and memorable screen appearance that is somewhat weakened by the amateur support from nonactors Taylor, Wilson, and Bird, whose limited abilities required delicate handling by Hellman. Expectations were high for this somber film, with the studio convinced they had another EASY RIDER on their hands. Esquire magazine ran a cover story on the film, reprinted screenwriter Wurlitzer's screenplay in its entirety, and proclaimed it "the movie of the year." The predictions fell far short; the majority of the moviegoing public failed to understand the picture and found its portrayal of youthful boredom to be just that: boring. TWO-LANE BLACKTOP is very similar to the work of popular European existential filmmakers, but the fickle American "art house" crowd stayed away in droves, obviously preferring that their serious psychological dramas be imported from abroad.

TWO OR THREE THINGS I KNOW ABOUT HER
(DEUX OU TROIS CHOSES QUE JE SAIS D'ELLE)
1966 90m c Drama ★★★★★
Anouchka/Argos/Carrosse/Parc (France)

Marina Vlady (Juliette Janson), Anny Duperey (Marianne), Roger Montsoret (Robert Janson), Jean Narboni (Roger), Christophe Bourseiller (Christophe), Marie Bourseiller (Solange), Raoul Levy (The American), Joseph Gehrard (M. Gerard), Helena Bielicic (Girl in Bath), Robert Chevassu (Meter-Reader)

p, Raoul Levy; d, Jean-Luc Godard; w, Jean-Luc Godard (based on a letter from Catherine Vimenet that appeared in *Le Nouvel Observateur*); ph, Raoul Coutard (Techniscope, Eastmancolor); ed, Francoise Collin, Chantal Delattre; m, Ludwig van Beethoven; cos, Gitt Marrini

Arguably the greatest film made by arguably the most important world director to emerge since WWII. Not recognized as one of Godard's foremost achievements at the time, TWO OR THREE THINGS I KNOW ABOUT HER now seems the richest of his films, made at the perfect halfway moment between his playful iconoclasm and his later political anger. What little "plot" there is concerns a housewife (Vlady) who works part-time on the sly as a prostitute. What Godard and crew milk from this topic is extraordinary: a sociologically oriented dissection of modern middle-class life as an act of prostitution.

The film's title alone suggests the richness of what unfolds—"her" is at once our heroine Juliette, actress Vlady, Paris, consumerism, politics, structuralism, and about a dozen other things. The use of disjunctive editing, saturated color schemes, endless quotation (from Marx to Wittgenstein), and deadpan performance style make this film deliberately "difficult" to engage. Godard is challenging us, asking us to consider how we watch films and how we live our lives. Unforgettable moments are numerous: the opening introductions of Vlady as Vlady, then Vlady as Juliette; the little boy recounting his dream of Vietnam while his mother lies covered in the red, white, and blue of her nightgown and bedding; the babysitter, paid with canned goods, attempting to comfort a squalling child while lovers tryst in adjoining rooms; two naked women wearing airline tote bags on their heads. Perhaps greatest of all is the satiric final shot of a Paris neighborhood constructed from grocery goods, and the amazing close-up wherein a cup of coffee becomes the cosmos. (As we stare in awe, the whispering voice-over of Godard himself considers the philosophical terrain underpinning contemporary French intellectual thought.) Shot at the same time as MADE IN U.S.A. (Godard filmed one in the mornings, the other in the afternoons), TWO OR THREE THINGS I KNOW ABOUT HER is a uniquely rewarding film that requires *many* viewings—a brilliant, powerful and overtly political film that's still relevant today.

to be profound by virtue of its incomprehensibility, 2001 is nevertheless an astounding visual experience—one to be enjoyed, if possible, only on the big screen.

The film opens with (as a title modestly announces) The Dawn of Man. Man dawns when a tribe of apelike hominids is visited by a huge black monolith, which instructs them in the use of tools and weapons. Cut to the year 2001, when a scientist (Sylvester) is investigating a baffling archaeological discovery on the moon—it is, of course, a huge black monolith, which later sends a signal in the direction of the planet Jupiter. Dissolve to a year later, as a spaceship makes its way to Jupiter. Dullea and Lockwood run the ship with the help of HAL 9000, the most sophisticated computer ever devised. HAL turns on its human masters, killing Lockwood, and Dullea ventures further into space, eventually confronting a huge black monolith. Later, after witnessing a truly spectacular light show, he enounters a relatively small black monolith.

The screenplay—which is often quite witty, especially in the largely satirical Sylvester sequences—probably was meant sincerely, but has the feel of something that was never thought through. Kubrick seems to have understood that, with the emergence of drug culture and middle-class spiritual yearnings during the late '60s, anything really huge and really vague stood a good chance of being received as something really deep. If so, Kubrick's strategy worked: made at a cost of $10.5 million, the film began to build slowly but eventually took in almost $15 million in North America, then about half that upon rerelease in the slightly shorter version (141 minutes) in 1972. Many hailed it as a religious experience, and underground newspapers counseled readers to time their ingestion of hash brownies so as to be optimally stoned during the psychedelic final scenes. Clarke's short story was first made into a novel, then into the screenplay that MGM financed for $6 million. The budget kept rising, and the studio execs feared a disaster. The casting of Lockwood, Dullea, and Sylvester, three undynamic actors (in these roles), must have been deliberate, as Kubrick didn't want anything in the way of his vision (whatever that was). 2001 continues to annoy and delight audiences; for sheer spectacle, it may be unsurpassed. Its relatively low-tech special effects, masterfully engineered by Douglas Trumbull, remain more astonishing and persuasive than much of today's computer-generated gimmickry.

2001: A SPACE ODYSSEY   DVD

| 1968 | 160m | c | Science Fiction | ★★★★½ |
| Hawk/MGM | (U.S./U.K.) | | | G |

Keir Dullea *(David Bowman)*, Gary Lockwood *(Frank Poole)*, William Sylvester *(Dr. Heywood Floyd)*, Daniel Richter *(Moonwatcher)*, Leonard Rossiter *(Smyslov)*, Margaret Tyzack *(Elena)*, Robert Beatty *(Halvorsen)*, Sean Sullivan *(Michaels)*, Frank Miller *(Mission Controller)*, Alan Gifford *(Poole's Father)*

p, Stanley Kubrick; d, Stanley Kubrick; w, Stanley Kubrick, Arthur C. Clarke (based on the short story "The Sentinel" by Clarke); ph, Geoffrey Unsworth, John Alcott (Super Panavision, Cinerama, Technicolor, Metrocolor); ed, Ray Lovejoy; prod d, Tony Masters, Harry Lange, Ernest Archer; art d, John Hoesli; fx, Stanley Kubrick, Wally Veevers, Douglas Trumbull, Con Pederson, Tom Howard, Colin J. Cantwell, Bryan Loftus, Frederick Martin, Bruce Logan, David Osborne, John Jack Malick; cos, Hardy Amies

AAN Best Director: Stanley Kubrick; AAN Best Original Story and Screenplay: Stanley Kubrick, Arthur C. Clarke; AAN Best Art Direction-Set Decoration: Tony Masters, Harry Lange, Ernie Archer; AA Best Special Visual Effects: Stanley Kubrick

A beautiful, confounding picture that had half the audience cheering and the other half snoring. Kubrick clearly means to say something about the dehumanizing effects of technology, but exactly *what* is hard to say. One of those works presumed

TWO WOMEN   DVD
(LA CIOCIARA)

| 1960 | 105m | bw | Drama/War | ★★★★ |
| C.C. Champion/Marceau/Cocinor/S.G.C. | | (Italy/France) | | |

Sophia Loren *(Cesira)*, Jean-Paul Belmondo *(Michele)*, Eleanora Brown *(Rosetta)*, Raf Vallone *(Giovanni)*, Renato Salvatori *(Florindo)*, Carlo Ninchi *(Michele's Father)*, Andrea Checchi *(Fascist)*, Pupella Maggio, Emma Baron, Bruna Cealti

p, Carlo Ponti; d, Vittorio De Sica; w, Cesare Zavattini, Vittorio De Sica (based on the novel by Alberto Moravia); ph, Gabor Pogany, Mario Capriotti (CinemaScope); ed, Adriana Novelli; m, Armando Trovajoli; art d, Gastone Medin; cos, Elio Costanzi

AA Best Actress: Sophia Loren

Mama Mia! Loren deservedly won a Best Actress Oscar—the first to a non-American actress in a foreign-language film—for this Vittorio De Sica film, adapted by screenwriter Cesare Zavattini from an Alberto Moravia novel. It's not a great De Sica-Zavattini collaboration; much of the movie suffers from poor pacing and listlessness, but Loren is a marvel to behold.

She plays Cesira, a young widow in 1943 Italy who leaves her grocery store in San Lorenzo in the hands of her sometime lover (Raf Vallone), fleeing Allied bombing with her teenage daughter, Rosetta (Eleanora Brown), to return to her native village. There, after an arduous journey, she meets

Michele (Jean-Paul Belmondo), the intellectual son of a local farmer with whom Rosetta falls in love, though he falls for her lovely mother. As the town grows increasingly besieged by bombing and shortages, Michele is forced to guide some fleeing Germans on an escape route, while Cesira and Rosetta go back to Rome for safety. Along the way, mother and daughter suffer a tragedy that changes both their lives forever, despite Cesira's best efforts to protect her child from the ravages of war. Loren also won the Best Actress Award at Cannes and the same honor from the British Film Academy; more important, she demonstrated in this film that she was a mature actress with talent to match her looks. And that deglamourized, she was still magnificent. But Eleanora Brown's role (originally meant for Loren, with Magnani to play the mother; the latter refused) is underwritten, Belmondo's character is a rehashed cliché, and Loren's affair with Vallone has had all the sex sucked out of it. It's almost as though everyone pinned their hopes on a big, international success for Loren, so they sidestepped her earth mother getting too carnal. But if the plot turns feel predictable, Loren rises to their occasions with the primal maternal force almost as old as time itself.

De Sica (who also won an Oscar for the film) and Zavattini's previous collaborations included SHOESHINE, THE BICYCLE THIEF, and UMBERTO D., while TWO WOMEN doesn't match the greatness or simplicity of those neo-realist masterworks, it remains a remarkably moving, humane vision of individual struggle in an inhumane world.

U

U-571
2000   116m   c   War/Drama
Dino De Laurentiis/Universal/
Canal Plus Image

DVD
★★★
PG-13
(U.S.)

Matthew McConaughey (Lt. Andrew Tyler), Bill Paxton (Lt. Commander Mike Dahlgren), Harvey Keitel (Chief Klough), Jon Bon Jovi (Lt. Pete Emmett), David Keith (Marine Major Coonan), Thomas Kretschmann (Kapitanlieutenant Wassner), Jake Weber (Lt. Hirsch), Jack Noseworthy (Wentz), Thomas Guiry (Trigger), Will Estes (Rabbit)

p, Dino De Laurentiis, Martha De Laurentiis; d, Jonathan Mostow; w, Johnathan Mostow, Sam Montgomery, David Ayer; ph, Oliver Wood; ed, Wayne Wahrman; m, Richard Marvin; prod d, W.M. Ladd Skinner, Gotz Weidner; art d, Marco Trentini, Maria Teresa Barbasso; fx, Allen Hall, Henric Nieminen (Visual), Cinesite (Visual); chor, Leontine Snell; cos, April Ferry

AA Best Sound Editing: Jon Johnson; AAN Best Sound: Steve Maslow, Gregg Landaker, Rick Kline, Ivan Sharrock

Calling a movie "claustrophobic" isn't usually praise, but in submarine pictures, claustrophobia is all. This tautly directed thriller doesn't take the submarine movie to new heights—or would that more properly be depths?—but it's well acted and consistently suspenseful, even though a remark like, "Mother of God, those Germans know how to make a submarine," is inevitably a cue for rivets to start popping.

A small crew of American sailors is conscripted for a special mission: they must board a crippled German U-boat and capture a coveted Enigma code machine. The crew is led by Lt. Andrew Tyler (Matthew McConaughey), who's smarting at having been denied his own submarine command and who

doesn't much like Lt. Hirsch (Jake Weber), the German-speaking mastermind behind the daring plan. With the exception of grizzled Navy lifer Chief Klough (Harvey Keitel), Tyler's men are young and wet behind the ears, right down to Wentz (Jack Noseworthy), the fresh-faced farm boy tapped for a pivotal role in the operation purely because he's fluent in German. The plan: convince the U-boat's crew they're a German rescue squad, overpower them while they're off guard, grab the coding device, and scuttle the ship. Naturally, the plan goes horribly awry, and Tyler must get his men and the precious machine out of a series of increasingly hopeless-looking situations.

Loosely inspired by several actual WWII missions and writer-director Jonathan Mostow's longtime interest in submarine warfare, this is a profoundly old-fashioned war film. That's an observation rather than a criticism; it's clearly intended as a celebration of courage under fire, rather than a revisionist take on the much-examined WWII. As such, it's straightforwardly entertaining and a genuine nail-biter.

UFORIA
1985   100m   c   Science Fiction/Comedy   ★★★½
Simon   (U.S.)   PG

Cindy Williams (Arlene), Harry Dean Stanton (Brother Bud), Fred Ward (Sheldon), Beverly Hope Atkinson (Naomi), Harry Carey Jr. (George Martin), Diane Diefendorf (Delores), Robert Gray (Emile), Ted Harris (Gregory), Darrell Larson (Toby), Peggy McKay (Celia Martin)

p, Gordon Wolf, Susan Spinks; d, John Binder; w, John Binder; ph, David Myers (Deluxe Color); ed, Dennis M. Hill; m, Richard Baskin; prod d, Bill Malley; cos, Thomas Ed Sunly, Betsy Heimann

Shot independently in 1981, this funny, quirky, wholly likable little film sat on the shelf until 1985 when Universal finally decided to release it. Unfortunately, the film was given little fanfare and failed to find an audience—which is a shame, for UFORIA is a wonderfully offbeat comedy that manages to capture many of the eccentricities of small-town America.

Set in the deserts of the Southwest, the film follows Sheldon (Fred Ward), a happy-go-lucky drifter whose wanderings bring him to a dusty desert town. In the grocery store he meets Arlene (Cindy Williams), a somewhat dippy cashier whose born-again Christianity combines faith in Jesus Christ with a strong belief that UFOs are the chariots of God. In a matter of days Sheldon has moved into Arlene's tiny trailer home. Also in town is Sheldon's seedy cousin (Harry Dean Stanton), whose latest con has put him on the evangelical bandwagon. Calling himself "Brother Bud," he has gathered a flock of the faithful who come to his tent meetings for a little preachin' and healin' in exchange for sizable donations. UFORIA is an engaging movie that has great affection for all its quirky characters. The cast is superb—with Ward, Williams, and Stanton taking top honors.

UGETSU
(UGETSU MONOGATARI)
1953   96m   bw   Drama   ★★★★★
Daiei   (Japan)

Machiko Kyo (Lady Wukasa), Masayuki Mori (Genjuro), Kinuyo Tanaka (Miyagi), Sakae Ozawa (Tobei), Mitsuko Mito (Ohama), Sugisaku Aoyama (Old Priest), Ryosuke Kagawa (Village Chief), Kichijiro Tsuchida (Silk Merchant), Mitsusaburo Ramon (Captain of Tamba Soldiers), Ichisaburo Sawamura (Genichi)

p, Masaichi Nagata; d, Kenji Mizoguchi; w, Matsutaro Kawaguchi, Yoshikata Yoda (based on two stories from Ugetsu Monogatari by Akinari Ueda); ph, Kazuo Miyagawa; ed, Mitsuji Miyata; m, Fumio

Hayasaka, Ichiro Saito; art d, Kisaku Ito; chor, Kinshichi Kodera; cos, Kusune Kainosho

---

AAN Best Costume Design (B/W): Tadaoto Kainoscho

Set in 16th-century Japan, this lyrical, enchanting film by Mizoguchi is one of Japanese cinema's greatest masterpieces. As civil warfare ravages the land, Genjuro and Tobei (Mori and Ozawa), peasant potters, dream of finding glory. They risk their own and their families' lives making pottery to sell at market and then head for the big city. Genjuro leaves his wife behind when he is taken in by a noblewoman (Kyo) who is not what she seems. Tobei, meanwhile, pursues his long-standing desire to become a samurai, something he achieves when, with extreme luck, he manages to kill an established warrior. What happens to the two men's wives (Tanaka and Mito), however, is another story.

Mizoguchi's background as a painter shows in the lovely and artful compositions he sets before the viewer. The image of Lady Wukasa, her servant, and Genjuro trekking through the high reeds is, among many others, unforgettable. Mizoguchi, however, does not neglect the soundtrack, and the use of offscreen sound during such moments as the opening approach of the raiders skillfully suggests the threat to village life. The aesthetic appeal of UGETSU, however, is not merely indulged for its own sake; rather, the film uses the resources of film to explore a recurrent theme in this filmmaker's work. Like a painter determined to catch one vista in canvas after canvas, Mizoguchi considers how the price of indulging men's desires is often the suffering of women. This is done in individual shots (e.g. the highway robbers in the background gorging themselves on food the victimized Miyagi was carrying) as well as in the film as a whole. On another level the film can be read as paralleling the plight of post-WWII Japan. Either way, the film's subtle mix of realism and fantasy (consider a tracking shot with a near-invisible dissolve which "impossibly" links a sensual bath with a picnic) makes for challenging viewing. Working within Japanese genre conventions which seek to validate traditional values, Mizoguchi also considers their inherent contradictions. Look carefully at the pan and tracking shot as the errant Genjuro thinks he's returning to home and hearth near the end and you will witness a great moment in the history of cinema as both art and social commentary.

ULEE'S GOLD 📀

1997 113m c   Drama   ★★★★
Clinica Estetico/Orion   (U.S.)   R

Peter Fonda *(Ulee Jackson)*, Patricia Richardson *(Connie Hope)*, Jessica Biel *(Casey Jackson)*, J. Kenneth Campbell *(Sheriff Bill Floyd)*, Christine Dunford *(Helen Jackson)*, Steven Flynn *(Eddie Flowers)*, Dewey Weber *(Ferris Dooley)*, Tom Wood *(Jimmy Jackson)*, Vanessa Zima *(Penny Jackson)*, Traber Burns *(Chance Barrow)*

p, Victor Nunez; d, Victor Nunez; w, Victor Nunez; ph, Virgil Marcus Mirano; ed, Victor Nunez; m, Charles Engstrom; prod d, Robert "Pat" Garner; art d, Debbie Devilla; cos, Marilyn Wall-Asse, Lisa Martin-Stuart (co-designer)

AAN Best Actor: Peter Fonda

A quiet character study, ULEE'S GOLD received attention for its star, Peter Fonda, who was singled out for praise by reviewers. Fonda was dubbed 1997's comeback actor of the year; he even scored an Academy Award nomination for Best Actor for his troubles.

Ulysses "Ulee" Jackson (Peter Fonda) is a widower and third-generation beekeeper, who toils in the swamps of the Florida panhandle manufacturing premium-grade tupelo honey. At home, Ulee is struggling to raise his two granddaughters. The girls' drug-addicted mother, Helen (Christine Dunford), has abandoned them, and their father, Jimmy (Tom Wood), Ulee's son, is in prison for robbing an armored truck. After learning that his former cohorts, Eddie (Steven Flynn) and Ferris (Dewey Weber), "have" Helen, Jimmy asks his father to retrieve her—a request to which Ulee agrees only grudgingly. Ferris and Eddie have learned from strung-out Helen about $100,000 of loot that Jimmy has stashed away, and they want it... or else. When Ulee agrees to deliver the money to them, they release Helen. Over the next several days, Ulee labors to harvest his honey and get Helen through home detox, with the help of a neighbor, a nurse named Connie Hope (Patricia Richardson).

ULEE'S GOLD is meditative and paced like dripping honey, but never is it dull. Chronicling his lead character's odyssey, Florida based writer-director Victor Nunez has taken on, and succeeded at, the difficult task of connecting an audience to a character who is emotionally disconnected from others. Fonda scores a triumph with his superb performance. He purportedly sought the role because Ulee's stoicism reminded him of his father Henry, and often here his resemblance to his famous father is striking and resonant. So long the rebel, Peter Fonda may have finally discovered his own place in the acting world through a reconciliation with his heritage.

ULZANA'S RAID 📀

1972 103m c   Western/War   ★★★★
Universal   (U.S.)   R

Burt Lancaster *(McIntosh)*, Bruce Davison *(Lt. Garnett DeBuin)*, Jorge Luke *(Ke-Ni-Tay)*, Richard Jaeckel *(Sergeant)*, Joaquin Martinez *(Ulzana)*, Lloyd Bochner *(Capt. Gates)*, Karl Swenson *(Rukeyser)*, Douglas Watson *(Maj. Cartwright)*, Dran Hamilton *(Mrs. Riordan)*, John Pearce *(Corporal)*

p, Carter DeHaven; d, Robert Aldrich; w, Alan Sharp; ph, Joseph Biroc (Technicolor); ed, Michael Luciano; m, Frank DeVol; art d, James Vance

---

One of the greatest films made by often overlooked director Robert Aldrich, ULZANA'S RAID isn't a true war film, but within its traditional western format, Aldrich and screenwriter Alan Sharp transform the material into an effective and damning allegory of America's involvement in Vietnam. Set in Arizona during the late 1880s, the film centers on Lancaster, a hard-riding scout who accompanies idealistic, young lieutenant Davison in his pursuit of a group of rapacious renegade Apaches led by Martinez (playing Ulzana). On the trail it becomes apparent that Lancaster and Davison hold radically different views of Martinez's actions—the scout is cold and cynical, while Davison's Christian morality is incensed by the Apache atrocities. As the film progresses it poses a complex series of questions about the nature of heroism, racism, and American imperialism. However, as an allegorical indictment of the Vietnam War, ULZANA'S RAID avoids the preachy stance of similarly themed westerns such as SOLDIER BLUE, benefiting from Aldrich's stark, violent treatment of Sharp's well-developed script. Regrettably, this challenging film was much abused by its studio, and several different versions were circulated, including a European cut containing alternative takes and slightly altered scene construction (most noticeable in the film's opening section). This was the third time Lancaster and Aldrich had worked together, after a lapse of 18 years (their previous collaborations, APACHE and VERA CRUZ), and they would soon team again on TWILIGHT'S LAST GLEAMING.

UMBERTO D. 📀

1952 89m bw Drama   ★★★★★
Amato/Rizzoli   (Italy)

Carlo Battisti *(Umberto Domenico Ferrari)*, Maria Pia Casilio *(Maria)*, Lina Gennari *(Landlady)*, Alberto Albani Barbieri

(Fiance), Elena Rea *(Sister)*, Ileana Simova *(Surprised Woman)*, Memmo Carotenuto *(Voice of Light)*

p, Vittorio De Sica; d, Vittorio De Sica; w, Cesare Zavattini, Vittorio De Sica (based on a story by Zavattini); ph, Aldo Graziati; ed, Eraldo di Roma; m, Alessandro Cicognini; prod d, Virgilio Marchi

AAN Best Motion Picture Story: Cesare Zavattini

Simple on its surface but actually multi-layered and complex, this shattering portrait of an old man is an indictment of post-war Italy and its treatment of the aged. Umberto Domenico Ferrari (non-pro Carlo Battisti, a university professor) is a retired civil servant with no friends, family, or prospects, and only his dog, Flike, to keep him company. His meager pension does not provide enough for him to both eat and afford shelter, so Umberto is far behind on his rent for the room he has lived in for three decades. When he used to work during the day, his landlady (Lina Gennari) rented his room to lovers, but since his continual presence isn't adding to her income, she is planning to evict him. Umberto is one of many elderly people who voice their opposition to the way the government is treating pensionsers. Depressed by the lack of response, he determines there is no way out but suicide. He puts those thoughts aside, however, when he realizes that his dog would be at the mercy of the streets. One of the greatest films of all time and one of the handful of masterpieces to emerge from the Italian neo-realist period, UMBERTO D. is as cerebral as it is emotional, as bleak as it is warm. There is no sentimentality or pandering for sympathy in De Sica's direction. The emotions one feels watching Umberto and Flike are cathartic. This is a remarkable collaboration by De Sica, Battista, and screenwriter Cesare Zavattini.

UMBRELLAS OF CHERBOURG, THE   *DVD*
(LES PARAPLUIES DE CHERBOURG)
1964 91m   c   Musical   ★★★½
Madeleine/Parc/Beta   (France/West Germany)

Catherine Deneuve *(Genevieve Emery)*, Nino Castelnuovo *(Guy Foucher)*, Anne Vernon *(Madame Emery)*, Ellen Farner *(Madeleine)*, Màrc Michel *(Roland Cassard)*, Mireille Perrey *(Aunt Elise)*, Jean Champion *(Aubin)*, Pierre Caden *(Bernard)*, Jean-Pierre Dorat *(Jean)*, Bernard Fradet *(Gas Station Apprentice)*

p, Mag Bodard; d, Jacques Demy; w, Jacques Demy; ph, Jean Rabier (Eastmancolor); ed, Anne-Marie Cotret, Monique Teisseire; m, Michel Legrand; art d, Bernard Evein; cos, Real, Jacqueline Moreau

AAN Best Foreign Language Film ; *AAN Best Original Story and Screenplay:* Jacques Demy; *AAN Best Original Score:* Michel Legrand, Jacques Demy; *AAN Best Adapted Score:* Michel Legrand; *AAN Best Song:* "I Will Wait for You"; Michel Legrand (Music), Jacques Demy (Lyrics), Norman Gimbel (Lyrics)

Although inspired by the Hollywood musical, Jacques Demy's vibrant, inventive film forgoes the familiar backdrop of a Broadway show or movie premiere to revel instead in the myth and magic of everyday romance, in all its sentimental and banal glory. Not quite a musical or an operetta, THE UMBRELLAS OF CHERBOURG is, as Demy has described it, "a film in color and song." What separates it from the Hollywood musical is Demy and composer Michel Legrand's decision to deliver all the dialogue—every last meaningless word—in song form. Divided into three acts—Departure, Absence, Return—and set in Cherbourg on the coast of Normandy, the film begins with the blossoming romance of two young lovers: Genevieve (the beautiful 19-year-old Catherine Deneuve), who works in her mother's umbrella store, and Guy (Nino Castelnuovo), a service station attendant. They fall in love, have an evening of romantic bliss,

and are then separated when Guy receives his draft notice. In the second act, Genevieve learns that she is pregnant and, after failing to hear from Guy, agrees to marry the accommodating Roland (Marc Michel) and move to Paris. Voila, Guy returns to Cherbourg. A feast of movement, color, and song, THE UMBRELLAS OF CHERBOURG transforms the quotidian into a celebration. By inflating the life of a common shop girl into a musical spectacle, Demy succeeds in turning a tedious existence into a fantasy, yet he and cinematographer Jean Rabier and art director Bernard Evein do so without creating a false world. Instead they discover the "poetic realism" in Genevieve's world of umbrellas, hat, chairs, and shop windows.

UN COEUR EN HIVER
1992 105m   c   Drama/Romance   ★★★★
Film Par Film/Cinea/FR3 Film Productions/DA Film/ Sedis/Roissy Films   (France)

Daniel Auteuil *(Stephane)*, Emmanuelle Beart *(Camille)*, Andre Dussollier *(Maxime)*, Elisabeth Bourgine *(Helene)*, Brigitte Catillon *(Regine)*, Maurice Garrel *(Lachaune)*, Myriam Boyer *(Madame Amet)*, Stanislas Carre DeMalberg *(Brice)*, Jean-Luc Bideau *(Ostende)*

p, Philippe Carcassonne, Jean-Louis Livi; d, Claude Sautet; w, Yves Ulmann, Claude Sautet; ph, Yves Angelo; ed, Jacqueline Thiedot; m, Maurice Ravel; cos, Corrine Jorry

Passion without eroticism, melancholia without mawkishness, a love triangle with only two active participants—UN COEUR EN HIVER breaks the rules so tenderly and assuredly that the viewer, like its main character, sees no danger until it's too late.

Passive Stephane (Daniel Auteuil) is a master repairer/restorer of violins. His partner in business and society is Maxime (Andre Dussollier), an outgoing older man. Their relationship is so intimate and comfortable that one almost suspects the men might be the screen's most contented lovers, until Maxime drops the bombshell that he's just left his unseen wife and children for their new client Camille (Emmanuelle Beart), a beautiful young violin virtuoso whom he plans to marry. Stephane responds to Camille's intrusion like a perfect gentleman, with only the faintest trace of reserve, but she falls madly, perversely in love with him, even as she moves in with Maxime. How will this repressed triangle work itself out?

UN COEUR EN HIVER unfolds in the rarefied world of concert violinists, where director Claude Sautet (once a music critic) finds apt metaphors for Stephane's soulless civility: he can tune an instrument to perfect pitch, but gave up playing because there was no personality to his technique. A cool and intelligent story of jealousy and obsession, Sautet's film leaves viewers puzzling to the last: does Stephane subtly, deliberately seduce Camille, or is he a bewildered victim of inescapable fate? Auteuil and Beart deliver fine, nuanced performances, and UN COEUR EN HIVER won Cesars (France's Oscar) for Best Director and Best Supporting Actor (Andre Dussollier).

UNBEARABLE LIGHTNESS OF BEING, THE   *DVD*
1988 171m   c   Romance/Erotic/War   ★★½
Orion   (U.S.)   R

Daniel Day-Lewis *(Tomas)*, Juliette Binoche *(Tereza)*, Lena Olin *(Sabina)*, Derek De Lint *(Franz)*, Erland Josephson *(The Ambassador)*, Pavel Landovsky *(Pavel)*, Donald Moffat *(Chief Surgeon)*, Daniel Olbrychski *(Interior Ministry Official)*, Stellan Skarsgard *(The Engineer)*, Tomek Bork *(Jiri)*

p, Saul Zaentz; d, Philip Kaufman; w, Jean-Claude Carriere, Philip Kaufman (based on the novel by Milan Kundera); ph, Sven

Nykvist (Technicolor); ed, Walter Murch; m, Mark Adler, Keith Richards, Leos Janacek; prod d, Pierre Guffroy; fx, Trielli Brothers; cos, Ann Roth

AAN Best Adapted Screenplay: Jean-Claude Carriere, Philip Kaufman; *AAN Best Cinematography:* Sven Nykvist

Phil Kaufman's film version of Milan Kundera's acclaimed novel opens in Prague shortly before the Soviet invasion of 1968, where Tomas (Daniel Day-Lewis), a brilliant playboy surgeon, lives a "light" existence free of commitment. Tomas falls in love with the shy, provincial Tereza (Juliette Binoche), eventually marrying her. He continues to womanize, though, especially with the similarly free and easy Sabina (Lena Olin), defending his adultery by insisting that sex and love are not the same thing. When the Soviet tanks roll into Prague, Sabina flees to Geneva, but Tomas and Tereza stay behind—she snapping pictures of the clampdown, riots, demonstrations, and violence. Eventually they, too, head for Geneva, and Tomas resumes his liaison with Sabina. When Tereza decides to return to Czechoslovakia, Tomas follows her home. There they sustain the weight of Soviet influence fairly easily, until authorities discover that Tomas once wrote an anti-Communist article. Though Tomas, typically, wrote the piece on a whim, he refuses to renounce it and suffers professionally. In the meantime, he continues to philander and Tereza continues to try to understand his philosophy of sex versus love. With its distinguished international cast and crew, volatile historical backdrop, and numerous erotic scenes, all filtered through the eye of American director Kaufman (THE RIGHT STUFF), THE UNBEARABLE LIGHTNESS OF BEING is the perfect European art film for American audiences who thirst for movies that are "intellectual" but not so much so that they can't understand them. Unfortunately, for all its credentials and the virtuoso performances of its three leads, this lengthy movie doesn't add up to much. It fails to explore its themes—love and hedonism, freedom and commitment (political and sexual)—in depth, floating haphazardly from scene to scene without emotional or intellectual development. Shot in Geneva and Lyon, France (the latter town standing in for Prague, where Kundera's work is banned), the film places greater stress on the actual events of the 1968 Soviet invasion than does its source, incorporating real black-and-white footage of the time with simulated shots featuring Binoche and Day-Lewis.

UNBELIEVABLE TRUTH, THE

1990 90m c Comedy/Drama   📀 ★★★½
Action Features (U.S.)   R

Adrienne Shelly *(Audry Hugo)*, Robert Burke *(Josh Hutton)*, Christopher Cooke *(Vic Hugo)*, Julia Mueller *(Pearl)*, Mark Bailey *(Mike)*, Gary Sauer *(Emmet)*, Katherine Mayfield *(Liz Hugo)*, David Healy *(Todd Whitbread)*, Matt Malloy *(Otis)*, Edie Falco *(Jane, the Waitress)*

p, Bruce Weiss; d, Hal Hartley; w, Hal Hartley; ph, Michael Spiller; ed, Hal Hartley; m, Jim Coleman, Wild Blue Yonder, The Brothers Kendall; prod d, Carla Gerona; cos, Kelly Reichardt

THE UNBELIEVABLE TRUTH proved a promising feature-film debut for writer-director Hal Hartley, who was dubbed "the Godard of Long Island" by critics with more sense of humor than of substance. In the vein of Jim Jarmusch's STRANGER THAN PARADISE and the work of David Lynch, THE UNBELIEVABLE TRUTH searches for the unexpected, bizarre, and magical essence of prosaic American locales. For director Hartley, that locale is Lindenhurst, Long Island, hometown of Josh Hutton (Robert Burke), a paroled convict who, as the film opens, returns to the area (where everyone remembers the details of his crime differently) because he has nowhere else to go. Haunted by a past

that includes the manslaughter of his sweetheart and a prison stretch for killing her grieving father in an argument about her death, Hutton is too shell-shocked to begin his life anew until he meets Audry Hugo (Adrienne Shelly), a high-school student with an obsessive fear of nuclear attack. When Audry's father, garage owner Vic (Christopher Cooke), agrees to hire Josh for his exceptional mechanical skills, Audry and Josh can no longer suppress their growing mutual attraction.

Hartley exhibits a born filmmaker's eye for composition and camera placement in this offbeat, dryly humorous film. His screenwriting skills are less solid, however, and the film is further damaged by the uneven quality of its cast, which weakens the already delicate balance in this black comedy. Although Burke makes the ideal loner hero, Shelly is saddled with a role that's more a collection of nonconformist attitudes than a true character. More damaging is the casting of Cooke, whose delineation of the harried middle-class father is amateurish.

Despite these flaws, THE UNBELIEVABLE TRUTH captivates with its committedly off-center vision of suburban angst. Long Island becomes a world of identity crises, serendipitous occurrences, and amusing non-sequiturs. It's an impressive, if not always cogent, attempt to mine humor out of tragic circumstances, and it manages to send up small-town life without being condescending—no mean feat. Unfortunately, Hartley's subsequent features, from TRUST to SIMPLE MEN to AMATEUR, seem to have mined the exact same territory, to increasingly meager dramatic and emotional effect.

UNBREAKABLE

2000 107m c Drama/Thriller   📀
Barry Mendel Productions/Touchstone (U.S.)   ★★
    R

Bruce Willis *(David Dunn)*, Samuel L. Jackson *(Elijah Price)*, Robin Wright, billed as Robin Wright Penn *(Audrey Dunn)*, Spencer Treat Clark *(Joseph Dunn)*, Charlayne Woodard *(Elijah's Mother)*, Eamonn Walker *(Dr. Mathison)*, Leslie Stefanson *(Kelly)*, Johnny Hiram Jamison *(Elijah at 13)*, Michaelia Carroll *(Babysitter)*, Bostin Christopher *(Comic Book Clerk)*

p, Barry Mendel, Sam Mercer; d, M. Night Shyamalan; w, M. Night Shyamalan; ph, Eduardo Serra; ed, Dylan Tichenor; m, James Newton Howard; prod d, Larry Fulton; art d, Steve Arnold; fx, Steve Cremin, Jodi Birdsong, Richard Hoover, Darin Hollings, The Secret Lab; cos, Joanna Johnston

A gloomy, preposterous psychological thriller which, like writer-director M. Night Shyamalan's hugely popular THE SIXTH SENSE, slowly builds up to an eleventh-hour twist.

The story revolves around the intertwined destinies of two very different Philadelphia men. Elijah Price (Samuel L. Jackson) was born with a rare brittle-bone disease. Hospitalized for long stretches, young Elijah was a voracious comic book reader; as an adult, he deals in classic comic art. David Dunn (Bruce Willis) abandoned a promising career in college football and wound up as a security guard at a local college stadium. Dunn's marriage to his college sweetheart (Robin Wright Penn) is on the rocks, and the tension at home has made their young son (Spencer Treat Clark) anxious and wary. Then something extraordinary happens. The New York-bound train Dunn is riding derails, killing everyone onboard save one. Dunn not only survives, but walks away completely unscathed. Elijah seeks him out so he can share a theory spawned by the comics he devoured as a child. If the human race can produce a man as breakable as Elijah, might it also produce the opposite? And could these "unbreakable" men be the core of truth coiled within the outlandish stories of super-heroes and caped crusaders?

Cool idea. But as much screen time goes to Dunn's drab, unhappy home life as to his slow assimilation of the notion that perhaps he really is something special. You could argue that Shyamalan's movie is a brilliant critique of superhero origin stories, but a considerable emotional investment in comic book lore is required for that to make this glum, poky picture worth watching through to the final revelation.

UNCLE BUCK DVD
1989 100m c Comedy ★★½
Universal (U.S.) PG

John Candy (Uncle Buck Russell), Jean Kelly (Tia Russell), Gaby Hoffman (Maizy Russell), Macaulay Culkin (Miles Russell), Amy Madigan (Chanice Kobolowski), Elaine Bromka (Cindy Russell), Garrett Brown, billed as Garrett M. Brown (Bob Russell), Laurie Metcalf (Marcie Dahlgren-Frost), Jay Underwood (Bug), Brian Tarantina (Rog)

p, John Hughes, Tom Jacobson; d, John Hughes; w, John Hughes; ph, Ralf D. Bode (Deluxe Color); ed, Lou Lombardo, Tony Lombardo, Peck Prior; m, Ira Newborn; prod d, John W. Corso; chor, Miranda Garrison; cos, Marilyn Vance

The late John Candy, in what may be his most celebrated role, stars as the eponymous Buck. He's a painfully inept, irredeemable slob who becomes a most unlikely baby-sitter for eight-year-old Miles (Macaulay Culkin), six-year-old Maizy (Gaby Hoffman), and teenaged Tia (Jean Kelly) when Buck's brother and sister-in-law have to leave town to visit a sick relative. Supposedly ill-equipped to take care of children, Uncle Buck keeps Maizy and Miles amused and eventually wins the reluctant respect of Tia by protecting her from her creepy boyfriend. In the process, however, he nearly ruins his own eight-year relationship with Chanice (Amy Madigan). Mostly thanks to Candy's sympathetic performance, the film has become a video perennial; like many John Hughes films, however, it has a distinctly reactionary subtext—Buck proves his worth not so much by winning the hearts of the kiddies as by exerting patriarchal authority over Tia.

UNDER SIEGE DVD
1992 100m c Action/Thriller ★★½
Canal Plus/Alcor Films/Regency Enterprises R
(U.S.)

Steven Seagal (Casey Ryback), Gary Busey (Commander Krill), Tommy Lee Jones (William Strannix), Erika Eleniak (Jordan Tate), Colm Meaney (Daumer), Patrick O'Neal (Captain Adams), Michael Des Barres (Damiani), Nick Mancuso (Tom Breaker), Bernie Casey (Commander Harris), Damian Chapa (Tackman)

p, Steven Reuther, Arnon Milchan, Steven Seagal; d, Andrew Davis; w, J.F. Lawton, John Mason, Michael Rae; ed, Frank Tidy; ed, Robert A. Ferretti, Dennis Virkler, Don Brochu, Dov Hoenig; m, Gary Chang; prod d, Bill Kenney; art d, Bill Hiney; cos, Richard Bruno

AAN Best Sound: Don Mitchell, Frank A. Montano, Rick Hart, Scott Smith; AAN Best Sound Effects Editing: John Leveque, Bruce Stambler

Despite some occasional flashes of inspiration, this is yet another B movie with bloated production values. Instantly tagged as "DIE HARD on a battleship," UNDER SIEGE gives us Steven Seagal as Casey Ryback, a former Navy SEAL who, because of his resistance to the U.S. invasion of Panama, has been demoted to the post of cook on the USS Missouri. He's called on to do more than sling hash when the ship's second-in-command, Commander Krill (Gary Busey), arranges a "surprise" party for the Captain's birthday featuring rock singer Strannix (Tommy Lee Jones), outside caterers and a topless dancer (Erika Eleniak). Strannix turns out to be a renegade CIA agent who, with his "cater-

ers," takes over the ship with an eye to removing and selling its weaponry. But he hasn't reckoned on Ryback, who teams up with the topless dancer and a few of the ship's officers to put matters to rights.

During its opening scenes, UNDER SIEGE threatens to achieve something like DIE HARD's blend of wit, ingenuity and action, with Jones and Busey making highly entertaining, creepy-funny villains. Once the stolid Seagal takes over, however, we settle into a predictable high-tech groove of explosions, gunplay and gore. Though as capable at staging explosions as anybody, director Davis still betrays no more feeling for character or suspense than he did in his earlier films, THE PACKAGE and ABOVE THE LAW.

UNDER THE ROOFS OF PARIS DVD
(SOUS LES TOITS DE PARIS)
1930 96m bw Drama ★★★
Tobis (France)

Albert Prejean (Albert), Pola Illery (Pola), Edmond T. Greville (Louis), Gaston Modot (Fred), Paul Olivier (Drunkard), Bill Bocket (Bill), Jane Pierson (Neighborhood Woman), Raymond Aimos (Thief), Thomy Bourdelle (Francois)

d, Rene Clair; w, Rene Clair; ph, Georges Perinal, Georges Raulet; ed, Rene Le Henaff; art d, Lazare Meerson

Billed upon its release as "the most beautiful film in the world," UNDER THE ROOFS OF PARIS may well have fit that description—at least at the time. In this first "100 percent French talking and singing film," Rene Clair was determined to make sound and visuals equal partners. Instead of simply employing synchronous sound techniques, he chose to use sound only when needed, refusing to toss in dialogue just for the sake of doing so.

The story itself is a simple one. Street singer Albert (Prejean) and Pola (Illery) are lovers, though she enjoys flirting with his best friend, Louis (Greville). When Albert finds himself in prison for a crime he didn't commit, the door is open for Pola and Edmond to act upon their mutual attraction. Upon his release from prison, Albert is enraged by Pola and Edmond's romance, but the final arrangement the three arrive at is unexpected indeed. In 1931, using practically the same set of technicians, Clair went on to make his two of his greatest films—LE MILLION and A NOUS LA LIBERTE, improvements which continued his experiments with sound. Much of this film's visual style, however, can be attributed to the great art director Lazare Meerson, who collaborated with Clair on the director's greatest works.

UNDER THE SAND DVD
(SOUS LE SABLE)
2000 95m c Drama ★★★★
Arte France Cinema/Euro Space/Fidelite R
Productions/Haut et Court (France)

Charlotte Rampling (Marie Drillon), Bruno Cremer (Jean Drillon), Jacques Nolot (Vincent), Alexandra Stewart (Amanda), Pierre Vernier (Gerard), Andree Tainsy (Suzanne), Maya Gaugler (German Woman), Damien Abbou (Chief Lifeguard), David Portugais (Young Lifeguard), Pierre Soubestre (Policeman)

p, Olivier Delbosc, Marc Missonnier; d, Francois Ozon; w, Emmanuelle Bernheim, Marina De Van, Francois Ozon, Marcia Romano; ph, Antoine Heberle, Jeanne Lapoirie; ed, Laurence Bawedin; m, Philippe Rombi; prod d, Sandrine Canaux; art d, Sandrine Canaux; cos, Pascaline Chavanne

A haunting tale of obsession and loss, this drama of a vanished husband and a wife's denial marks a departure from director Francois Ozon's frequent theme of lives destroyed by unspoken desires.

Professor Marie Drillon (Charlotte Rampling) and Jean (Bruno Cremer), her husband of 25 years, are spending the summer at their cottage near the beach when Jean announces he's going for a swim. He never returns. The police can't find a body or a single lead, and Marie returns to Paris stunned and alone. She dines with friends but speaks of Jean in the present tense, as if he's waiting for her at home. Indeed, when fellow dinner guest Vincent (Jacques Nolot), a successful architect, drops Marie at her flat, we find Jean, looking tired but happy to see her. Is it really him? A ghost? A memory? As Marie begins a tentative affair with Vincent, the truth is gradually revealed. Marie eventually returns to the beach, and the film ends with one of the most chilling and expertly photographed shots imaginable.

Rising to the next level as a filmmaker, Ozon fulfills the promise he showed in his early shorts but that eluded him in his subsequent features. The British-born Rampling, working in French, delivers what is perhaps her deepest, most effortlessly nuanced performance. If her iconic face has mellowed from angular to kindly, it's no less shaded by vulnerability. Ozon does tend to press a point long after it's been made, but this exploration of devastating loss and our imperfect mechanisms for dealing with it resonates with a pathos that moves well beyond mere sadness.

UNDER THE SKIN

1997   83m   c   Drama   *DVD*
                                                  ★★★½
Strange Dog Productions/Rouge Films/British Film Institute/Channel Four Television   (U.K.)

Samantha Morton (Iris Kelley), Claire Rushbrook (Rose), Rita Tushingham (Mum), Stuart Townsend (Tom), Christine Tremarco ("Vron"—Veronica), Matthew Delamere (Gary), Mark Womack (Frank), Clare Francis (Elena), Daniel O'Meara (Max), Crissy Rock (Compere)

p, Kate Ogborn; d, Carine Adler; w, Carine Adler; ph, Barry Ackroyd; ed, Ewa J. Lind; m, Ilona Sekacz; prod d, John-Paul Kelly; art d, Niall Moroney; cos, Frances Tempest

Samantha Morton gives an absolutely riveting performance as a young woman teetering on the brink of emotional collapse after the death of her mother.

Iris (Morton) and her older sister Rose (Claire Rushbrook) are different in a ways that only sisters can be: both in their 20s, Rose is a responsible married woman with a baby on the way and a steady job at a travel agency. Iris, on the other hand, is a childish, aspiring singer who lives with her boyfriend and is jealous of Rose's close relationship with their mother (Rita Tushingham). Both are equally shattered when Mum dies suddenly, but while Rose begins processing the reality of her loss, Iris loses all sense of who she is. She introduces herself to strangers as "Rose" and dons her mother's wig, fur coat, and lingerie to troll sleazy pickup bars for anonymous sex. It's a dangerous, self-destructive sort of sexual liberation, and as Iris begins drinking heavily, her choices of one-night stands grows increasingly reckless.

First-time writer-director Carine Adler's portrait of emotional disintegration is in many ways as harrowing as Roman Polanski's REPULSION, thanks in large part to Morton's terrifying performance; she forgoes the predictable twisted-sister histrionics for a seductive giddiness that barely hides a chilling vacancy. Her personal disintegration is echoed in the film's stylish chaos: dissolves, jump-cuts, and disorienting shifts of focus effectively draw the viewer into Iris's growing dislocation. Adler's inexperience is apparent only in the occasional repetitive scene and an ending whose patness would be more disturbing if you weren't so relieved by it.

UNDER THE VOLCANO

1984 112m   c   Drama   ★★★½
Ithaca/Conacine   (U.S.)   R

Albert Finney (Geoffrey Firmin), Jacqueline Bisset (Yvonne Firmin), Anthony Andrews (Hugh Firmin), Ignacio Lopez Tarso (Dr. Vigil), Katy Jurado (Senora Gregoria), James Villiers (Brit), Dawson Bray (Quincey), Carlos Riquelme (Bustamante), Jim McCarthy (Gringo), Rene Ruiz (Dwarf)

p, Moritz Borman, Wieland Schulz-Keil; d, John Huston; w, Guy Gallo (based on the novel by Malcolm Lowry); ph, Gabriel Figueroa (Technicolor); ed, Roberto Silvi; m, Alex North; prod d, Gunther Gerzso; art d, Jose Rodriguez Granada; cos, Angela Dodson

AAN Best Actor: Albert Finney; AAN Best Original Score: Alex North

A bizarre journey into the mystical Mexican underworld in 1939, UNDER THE VOLCANO is set during the morbid holiday known as the Day of the Dead—a day on which the souls of the dead spew forth from hell amid the colorful and lively festivities of the village of Cuernavaca. Geoffrey Firmin (Albert Finney), a former British consul, is there for the celebration, drinking himself to death. The spirit of celebration is alive, but Geoffrey appears lifeless, almost zombielike as he wanders the streets. His former wife, Yvonne (Jacqueline Bisset), arrives, and with the help of Geoffrey's brother, Hugh (Anthony Andrews), tries to get him away from Mexico to a farm in the U.S., hoping it will curb his drinking. After wandering about the village pathetically for hours on end, Geoffrey slips away and winds up in a sleazy bar-whorehouse, drinking himself into oblivion. Based on the 1947 novel by Malcom Lowry, who began the work in 1936 at the age of 27, UNDER THE VOLCANO has been a project kicked around Hollywood since the book's publication. Lowry, a suicidal alcoholic, wrote the novel without any clear narrative line, relying instead on marvelously visual images, thereby causing many people to label the novel "unfilmable"—until it ended up in the lap of John Huston. The result is very much worth the wait, bringing to life the mysticism of Mexico with a superb script by Guy Gallo, exquisite photography, and the unparalleled performance by Finney.

UNDERGROUND

(IL ETAIT UNE FOIS UN PAYS)   *DVD*
1995 167m   c   Historical/Comedy/Drama   ★★★★
CiBy 2000/Pandora Films/Barrandov Studios/Novo Film (France/Germany/Hungary)

Miki Manojlovic (Marko), Mirjana Jokovic (Natalija), Lazar Ristovski (Petar Popara—"Blacky"), Slavko Stimac (Ivan), Ernst Stotzner (Franz), Srdan Todorovic (Jovan), Mirjana Karanovic (Vera), Milena Pavlovic (Jelena), Bata Stojkovic (Deda), Bora Todorovic (Golub)

d, Emir Kusturica; w, Dusan Kovacevic, Emir Kusturica (based on a story by Dusan Kovacevic); ph, Vilko Filac; ed, Branka Ceperac; m, Goran Bregovic; prod d, Miljen "Kreka" Kljakovic; art d, Branimir Babic, Mladen Lisavac, Vladislav Lasic; fx, Petar Zivkovic, Roman Tudzaroff, Martin Kulhanek; cos, Nebojsa Lipanovic

Emir Kusturica's magnificent fresco rips through half a century of the tragic history of his homeland—the former Yugoslavia—with the solemnity of an amusement park ride. It won the 1995 Cannes Film Festival's *Palme d'Or*, but also stirred up vicious controversy: some critics construed this essentially nonpartisan film as pro-Serbian propaganda.

As the Germans begin their 1941 siege of Belgrade, entrepreneurs Marko (Miki Manojlovic) and Blacky (Lazar Ristovski) manufacture black market arms. Their self-serving impulses are mistaken for patriotism, and the pair become heroes of the Communist Party freedom fighters. After Blacky is arrested and tortured by the Nazis for kidnapping the actress (Mirjana Jokovic) he loves during a performance, Marko stages a bold rescue. He then hides Blacky in a cellar with the other arms makers, and there they stay for the next 15 years, believing Marko's assurances that the war rages on. Blacky emerges deluded and out of touch in 1961, stepping from one daydream into another—Tito's Yugoslavia—before slipping into a nightmare 30 years later when, during yet another Balkan crisis, he becomes the leader of a commando unit.

Like Lina Wertmuller's SEVEN BEAUTIES, which treated history and national character with similar reckless abandon, Kusturica delivers some discomforting suggestions—not the least of which is that "history" and "national identity" are lies, and you're as culpable as you are gullible—at a rollicking, almost slapstick pace. But even as Kusturica's "wasn't that a time!" treatment of the past leaves him open to doubts about his own convictions, the film comes with a built-in retort: no character is guiltier of mythmaking and the perpetuation of falsehoods than the filmmaker commissioned to tell the "true story" of Blacky and Marko's heroism. The past may be a pack of lies, Kusturica suggests, but after everything's gone to pieces, it's hard not to feel nostalgic for *something*.

UNFAITHFUL

2002 123m c Crime/Thriller/Drama ★★½
Fox 2000 Pictures/Regency Enterprises/Epsilon R
Motion Pictures (U.S.)

Richard Gere *(Edward Sumner)*, Diane Lane *(Connie Sumner)*, Olivier Martinez *(Paul Martel)*, Chad Lowe *(Bill Stone)*, Kate Burton *(Tracy)*, Margaret Colin *(Sally)*, Erik Per Sullivan *(Charlie Sumner)*, Dominic Chianese *(Frank Wilson)*, Myra Lucretia Taylor *(Gloria)*, Michelle Monaghan *(Lindsay)*

p, G. Mac Brown, Adrian Lyne; d, Adrian Lyne; w, Alvin Sargent, William Broyles Jr. (based on LA FEMME INFIDELE, written and directed by Claude Chabrol); ph, Peter Biziou; ed, Anne V. Coates; m, Jan A.P. Kaczmarek; prod d, Brian Morris; art d, John Kasarda; fx, Steve Kirshoff; cos, Ellen Mirojnick

AAN Best Actress: Diane Lane

An apparently happy marriage is shattered when the wife has an impulsive affair.

Connie (Diane Lane) and Edward Sumner (Richard Gere) seem to have an enviable life. They have a son, Charlie (Erik Per Sullivan), and a beautiful suburban home near New York City, where Edward owns his own home security business. Then Connie has a chance encounter on a SoHo street with a handsome, much younger French book dealer, Paul Martel (Olivier Martinez). She initially resists his flirtatious advances, but Connie is soon slipping off to his loft for steamy trysts. After catching his wife in small lies regarding her whereabouts, Edward hires a detective, who supplies him with Paul's address. An ill-considered confrontation ends when Edward spots a heavy glass snow globe he gave Connie in Paul's loft and, before he knows what he's doing, cracks the young man's skull with it.

Despite the extensive screen time devoted to the affair and Edward's growing realization of Connie's betrayal, the movie's real dramatic energy lies in what happens *after* the confrontation, and that's also where the film goes quietly wrong. In remaking Claude Chabrol's notoriously icy LA FEMME INFIDELE, Adrian Lyne conceives the film as being about the emotional repercussions of adultery, but the characters' actions (which speak louder than words) delineate a tale of the brutally expedient lengths to which a bourgeois couple will go to keep up appearances—not just external appearances, but their own internalized self-portraits. Lyne muffles this fundamentally cold and, yes, very French conceit in fuzzy layers of very American soul-baring, and yet the film's most devastating image is of Paul, reduced to an unsightly mess that must be swept from the manicured surface of the Sumners' life.

UNFAITHFULLY YOURS

1948 105m bw Comedy ★★★★★
Fox (U.S.)

Rex Harrison *(Sir Alfred de Carter)*, Linda Darnell *(Daphne de Carter)*, Barbara Lawrence *(Barbara Henshler)*, Rudy Vallee *(August Henshler)*, Kurt Kreuger *(Anthony)*, Lionel Stander *(Hugo Standoff)*, Edgar Kennedy *(Detective Sweeney)*, Alan Bridge *(House Detective)*, Julius Tannen *(Tailor)*, Torben Meyer *(Dr. Schultz)*

p, Preston Sturges; d, Preston Sturges; w, Preston Sturges; ph, Victor Milner; ed, Robert Fritch; m, Gioacchino Rossini, Richard Wagner, Peter Ilich Tchaikovsky; art d, Lyle Wheeler, Joseph C. Wright; fx, Fred Sersen; cos, Bonnie Cashin

The last of Sturges's Hollywood films, and one of his finest. This farce of misconceptions, infidelities, and murder is a brilliantly stylish work that imaginatively squeezes everything it can from the film medium.

Harrison, in a marvelous performance, is a famous British conductor married to Darnell. The two are much in love, but, when Harrison returns from Europe, a seed of jealousy is planted in his mind by his brother-in-law, Vallee. It seems that Vallee had a private detective, Kennedy, follow Darnell through her daily activities, and his report, which Harrison refuses to look at, suggests that Darnell indulged in some extracurricular activities with Harrison's private secretary, Kreuger, when the conductor was abroad. Harrison tears up the report and throws it out of his hotel room, but eventually the pages are put back together and wind up back in Harrison's hands. This time Harrison burns the document, nearly setting his dressing room ablaze. However, Harrison slowly begins to think there just might be something to the report, so he goes to Kennedy's office. Kennedy, it turns out, is a big fan of Harrison (who loves how the conductor "handles Handel") and dredges up the original report from his files. Now Harrison's jealous imagination goes wild. That night, as he begins conducting Rossini's "Semiramide" overture at a concert, the camera zeros in on Harrison's eye. The scene flashes to Harrison and Darnell as they return to their hotel room. As part of an elaborate plan, Harrison has arranged for Darnell to spend a night on the town with Kreuger. Using his straight razor, Harrison murders his wife, then sets up the room so Kreuger will appear to be the culprit. Harrison's plan works to perfection, and the conductor laughs maniacally when Kreuger is found guilty of the crime. The music comes to a conclusion, and the camera pulls away from Harrison's eye, back to the concert. The entire scenario has taken place in his mind, as do the next two sequences. To the accompaniment of Wagner's "Tannhauser" overture, Harrison imagines writing a fat check for Darnell, enabling her to run off with her young lover. Finally, with Tchaikovsky's "Francesca da Rimini" wafting in the background, Harrison challenges Darnell and Kreuger to a game of Russian roulette. He ends up with a bullet in his temple as the concert comes to an end. Harrison, now convinced that Darnell and Kreuger are dallying behind his back, returns to his hotel room and tries to set up the murderous plan he imagined during the concert. His real-life plans are a disaster, and Harrison finally realizes that Kennedy's report was the result of many misconceptions.

UNFAITHFULLY YOURS is a near perfect combination of sound and image. Sturges orchestrates the fantasy sequences with care and precision, using editing and performance rhythms that are in perfect synch with the underscoring music. Harrison is a sheer delight, turning in a devilish performance brimming with wit and style. Darnell, Kreuger, Vallee, and Lawrence fill out the lead roles with elegance and wit, while consummate character player Kennedy adds a nice touch of buffoonery. Sturges had gotten the idea of music affecting the conductor's thoughts while writing the screenplay for THE POWER AND THE GLORY. "I had a scene all written and had only to put it down on paper. To my surprise, it came out quite unlike what I had planned," Sturges said later. "I sat back wondering what the hell had happened, then noticed that someone had left the radio on in the next room and realized that I had been listening to a symphony broadcast from New York and that this, added to my thoughts, had changed the total." (Quoted in James Curtis, *Between Flops*.)

Despite many critical plaudits, UNFAITHFULLY YOURS never caught on with the public—an undeserved fate for a film of such brilliance. It was remade in 1984 by Howard Zieff with Dudley Moore and Nastassja Kinski as leads.

UNFORGIVEN   **DVD**

1992 130m c Western   ★★★★½
Malpaso Productions/Warner Bros.   (U.S.)   R

Clint Eastwood *(William Munny)*, Gene Hackman *(Sheriff "Little Bill" Daggett)*, Morgan Freeman *(Ned Logan)*, Richard Harris *(English Bob)*, Jaimz Woolvett *(The "Schofield Kid")*, Saul Rubinek *(W.W. Beauchamp)*, Frances Fisher *(Strawberry Alice)*, Anna Thomson *(Delilah Fitzgerald)*, David Mucci *(Quick Mike)*, Rob Campbell *(Davey Bunting)*

p, Clint Eastwood; d, Clint Eastwood; w, David Peoples; ph, Jack N. Green; ed, Joel Cox; m, Lennie Niehaus; prod d, Henry Bumstead; art d, Rick Roberts, Adrian Gorton

---

AA Best Picture; AAN Best Actor: Clint Eastwood; *AA Best Supporting Actor:* Gene Hackman; *AA Best Director:* Clint Eastwood; *AAN Best Original Screenplay:* David Webb Peoples; *AAN Best Cinematography:* Jack N. Green; *AA Best Film Editing:* Joel Cox; *AAN Best Art Direction-Set Decoration:* Henry Bumstead, Janice Blackie-Goodine; *AAN Best Sound:* Les Fresholtz, Vern Poore, Dick Alexander, Rob Young

---

One of Eastwood's finest outings to date, an elegiac western that ironically undermines the conventions of the genre, only to deliver a finale as legendary as the shootout at the O.K. Corral.

Wyoming, the 1880s. William Munny (Clint Eastwood) is a former murderer who, transformed by the love of a good woman, gave up a life of indiscriminate killing to raise a family and try his hand at pig farming. With his wife now dead and his farm a failure, Munny is lured back into his old ways by the "Schofield Kid" (Jaimz Woolvett), an aspiring young gunfighter who brings the older man word of a bounty being offered in the frontier town of Big Whiskey. (After a cowboy slashed the face of a prostitute there, the woman's co-workers have offered a reward for the death of the attacker and his accomplice.) Munny refuses the young man's offer of partnership but later reconsiders, teaming up with his old sidekick Ned Logan (Morgan Freeman) and setting off to join Schofield. The journey will bring him up against "Little Bill" Daggett (Gene Hackman), the autocratic sheriff of Big Whiskey, as well as forcing him to acknowledge that killing is, in fact, what he does best.

It's easy to see why Eastwood was drawn by this script, written by David Webb Peoples (BLADE RUNNER) in the 1970s. Munny is descended in a direct line from Eastwood's two most famous characters: the Man with No Name, from his '60s Westerns with Sergio Leone; and Dirty Harry, the anti-hero of Don Siegel's cop thrillers. Leone's presence is most strongly felt in the revisionist content of UNFORGIVEN, while Siegel's influence is manifest in the film's lean, moody, no-nonsense style. Both of Eastwood's directorial

mentors are acknowledged in the film's on-screen dedication, "to Sergio and Don."

The West of UNFORGIVEN is a place of few illusions, despite a mythology of heroism symbolized by Beauchamp (Saul Rubinek), a pulp biographer who has written heavily embellished accounts of the life of notorious gunslinger "English Bob" (marvelously played by Richard Harris). At one point, Little Bill ruptures this mythology by telling Beauchamp the inglorious real story behind one of the scenes described in his books—a pattern that is reprised throughout the film, as awe-struck tales of earlier heroes and exploits are undercut by cynical, down-to-earth dismissals. Eastwood as director finally turns this strategy on its head at the film's climax, when Munny pulls off a gunslinging feat of genuinely mythic proportions.

As with Leone's masterworks, UNFORGIVEN depicts a West driven solely by forces of commerce, not ideals of freedom or manifest destiny, with killing being Munny's sole marketable skill. Yet, just as Eastwood's occasional efforts to abandon his nihilist screen persona have been inconclusive, so is Munny haunted by his inability to escape the role society has decreed for him. Though he's the only protagonist left standing when the smoke clears, his story is the only one with the status of tragedy, his flaw being his very invincibility.

The cast is universally strong. Hackman, Freeman and Harris don't do anything they haven't done before, but the roles suit their personae to a degree where they approach archetypal status. The same applies to Eastwood, who casts himself as part of an ensemble rather than as the conscious star. And that's as it should be. With UNFORGIVEN, Eastwood achieves a new level of authority as a filmmaker and actor who has nothing to prove.

UNINVITED, THE

1944 98m bw Horror   ★★★★
Paramount   (U.S.)

Ray Milland *(Roderick Fitzgerald)*, Ruth Hussey *(Pamela Fitzgerald)*, Donald Crisp *(Cmdr. Bench)*, Cornelia Otis Skinner *(Miss Holloway)*, Dorothy Stickney *(Miss Hird)*, Barbara Everest *(Lizzie Flynn)*, Alan Napier *(Dr. Scott)*, Gail Russell *(Stella Meredith)*, Jessica Newcombe *(Miss Ellis)*, John Kieran *(Foreword Narrator)*

p, Charles Brackett; d, Lewis Allen; w, Dodie Smith, Frank Partos (based on the novel by Dorothy Macardle); ph, Charles Lang; ed, Doane Harrison; m, Victor Young; art d, Hans Dreier, Ernst Fegte; fx, Farciot Edouart

---

AAN Best B/W Cinematography: Charles Lang

An unusual and fascinating item, a ghost story that takes itself seriously. Milland and his sister, Hussey, buy a house on the Cornish cliffs and are soon bedeviled by phenomena such as cold spots in rooms, the smell of mimosas permeating the air, and the dog refusing to go upstairs. They are often visited by a local girl, Russell, whose grandfather, Crisp, forbids her to go into the house. It's suspected that the place is haunted by the spirit of Russell's mother, who fell from the cliffs to her death. More strange things happen, such as flowers wilting immediately in a room, and eventually the phantom itself is seen at the top of the stairs (one of the most convincing and scary ghosts to appear on the screen). Russell is confined by her grandfather to an asylum, but Milland and Hussey figure out that it is not one but two ghosts that haunt their home, carrying their rivalry from life beyond the grave. They eventually solve the mystery surrounding the death of Russell's mother, and when they do the spirits depart.

This film was greatly influenced by Val Lewton's productions for RKO in which the horror is only suggested, and almost never shown—for the monster in one's mind is much more frightening than the one on the screen. Some of the film doesn't work so well; it drags in spots and much of it seems a direct cop from REBECCA (house on the cliffs, scary folks coming in and out talking about the dead woman who lived there before, etc., and the advertising for the film went out of its way to compare itself to the Hitchcock film). Milland is as good as ever, and the rest of the cast does an admirable job, particularly Crisp and Skinner. Although the film garnered favorable reviews and decent returns at the box office, it would be many years before Hollywood would get serious about the spirit world again (THE HAUNTING).

UNION PACIFIC

1939	135m	bw	Western	★★★★
Paramount	(U.S.)			

Barbara Stanwyck (Mollie Monahan), Joel McCrea (Jeff Butler), Akim Tamiroff (Fiesta), Robert Preston (Dick Allen), Lynne Overman (Leach Overmile), Brian Donlevy (Sid Campeau), Robert Barrat (Duke Ring), Anthony Quinn (Jack Cordray), Stanley Ridges (Gen. Casement), Henry Kolker (Asa M. Barrows)

p, Cecil B. DeMille; d, Cecil B. DeMille; w, Walter DeLeon, C. Gardner Sullivan, Jesse Lasky Jr., Jack Cunningham (based on the novel Trouble Shooters by Ernest Haycox); ph, Victor Milner, Dewey Wrigley; ed, Anne Bauchens; m, George Antheil, Sigmund Krumgold, John Leipold; art d, Hans Dreier, Roland Anderson; fx, Gordon Jennings, Loren L. Ryder, Farciot Edouart; cos, Natalie Visart

AAN Best Special Effects: Farciot Edouart (Photographic), Gordon Jennings (Photographic), Loren Ryder (Sound)

After finishing his pirate epic THE BUCCANEER, Cecil B. DeMille was caught in a quandary regarding his next picture. Should it concern planes, ships, or trains? Deciding on trains, he faced another choice: the Union Pacific or the Sante Fe? The producer-director of spectacles reportedly flipped a coin, and UNION PACIFIC landed face up.

McCrea stars in this lavishly produced western, playing the supervisor of the construction of the Union Pacific Railroad. While on the job, he meets Stanwyck, a tough but feminine postmistress for the railroad. McCrea falls for her; meanwhile, Kolker, a seedy politician with a financial interest in the rival Central Pacific line, hires crooked gambler Donlevy to delay construction of the line. Aided by Preston, a comrade of McCrea's from the Civil War, Donlevy sets up a gambling den and begins distracting the Union Pacific workers with the prospect of gambling, liquor, and fast women. The lure of a good time causes havoc at the railroad—as does the robbery of the payroll, performed by Preston. Stanwyck, who has been seeing Preston as well as McCrea, learns that Preston is responsible for the theft and talks him into returning the money. Soon after, the train is attacked by Indians. Stanwyck holds her ground to fight alongside McCrea and Preston, and it looks as though they will all be slaughtered. Will the cavalry arrive in time?

UNION PACIFIC is a big, sprawling western epic produced with the usual DeMille extravagance and eye for detail. DeMille gained the cooperation of the Union Pacific Railroad, which made available heaps of old records and papers pertaining to the line's construction. In addition to the research material, the Union Pacific supplied DeMille with vintage trains and experienced crews to run them. The film was shot on locations in Utah and Oklahoma, and at the Canoga Park lot in Hollywood, where the reenactment of the golden spike ceremony was staged. Moreover, the actual golden spike (driven on May 10, 1869) that was used at that ceremony was loaned to the production by Stanford University and brought to Hollywood in great secrecy. The director had to undergo an operation during the production, and much of the location shooting was directed by Arthur Rosson and James Hogan

during his absence. When DeMille returned to the production, he directed from a stretcher and was carried from set to set by crew members.

UNMARRIED WOMAN, AN

1978	124m	c	Drama/Comedy	★★★
Fox	(U.S.)			R

Jill Clayburgh (Erica), Alan Bates (Saul), Michael Murphy (Martin), Cliff Gorman (Charlie), Pat Quinn (Sue), Kelly Bishop (Elaine), Lisa Lucas (Patti), Linda G. Miller (Jeannette), Andrew Duncan (Bob), Daniel Seltzer (Dr. Jacobs)

p, Paul Mazursky, Tony Ray; d, Paul Mazursky; w, Paul Mazursky; ph, Arthur J. Ornitz (Movielab Color); ed, Stuart Pappe; m, Bill Conti; prod d, Pato Guzman; cos, Albert Wolsky

AAN Best Picture; AAN Best Actress: Jill Clayburgh; AAN Best Original Screenplay: Paul Mazursky

AN UNMARRIED WOMAN became a beacon of the women's movement in the 1970s, though its tentative feminism seems tame by today's standards. Jill Clayburgh, in the title role, learns to take control of her own life after her schlump of a husband (beautifully played by Michael Murphy) leaves her for a girl he met in Bloomingdale's.

Set in the New York milieus Mazursky knows so well, AN UNMARRIED WOMAN has some great insights and is superbly acted by all involved. The director populates the film with his usual, very real and attractive modern characters, but you may think it cops out in the end, when Clayburgh falls into the arms of romantic SoHo painter Alan Bates. Nonetheless, Mazursky spares nobody and nothing with his comic darts. Some of the most hysterically funny scenes occur when Clayburgh and her three pals (Quinn, Bishop, and Miller) have regular luncheons in which they let down their hair and frankly talk about their sex lives.

UNTIL THE END OF THE WORLD

1991	178m	c	Science Fiction	★★½
Trans Pacific Films/Road Movies Film/Argos Films/Village Roadshow	(France/Germany/Australia)			R

William Hurt (Trevor McPhee/Sam Farber), Solveig Dommartin (Claire Tourneur), Sam Neill (Eugene Fitzpatrick), Max von Sydow (Henry Farber), Rudiger Vogler (Philip Winter), Ernie Dingo (Burt), Jeanne Moreau (Edith Farber), Lois Chiles (Elsa), Chick Ortega (Chico), Elena Smirnowa (Krasikova)

p, Jonathan Taplin; d, Wim Wenders; w, Wim Wenders, Peter Carey (from the story by Wenders and Solveig Dommartin); ph, Robby Muller; ed, Peter Przygodda; m, Graeme Revell; prod d, Thierry Flamand, Sally Campbell; art d, Ian Gracie; cos, Montserrat Casanova

Wim Wenders's UNTIL THE END OF THE WORLD is really two movies, joined rather awkwardly at the hip. The first half of this three-hour marathon is an enjoyable, off-the-cuff road movie with a post-modernist, technological spin; the second is a half-baked, indulgent meditation on the nature of the recorded image.

The year is 1999, and the world is on the brink of a nuclear confrontation. Claire Tourneur (Solveig Dommartin), a disenchanted young bohemian, is involved in a lackluster relationship with novelist Eugene Fitzpatrick (Sam Neill). Driving across Europe on her way home from a decadent party, she has a car accident that involves her with two bank robbers, Chico and Raymond (Chick Ortega and Eddy Mitchell). Claire ends up agreeing to transport their heist to Paris in exchange for a cut of the proceeds. Then she meets Sam Farber (William Hurt), an enigmatic traveler who steals some of the loot from her car before going on his mysterious way. Enraged and intrigued, Claire sets off to track him down. Her quest takes her around the world in a cosmopolitan blur of languages, cultures and high-tech computer images, ending in the Australian outback, where Sam's father (Max von Sydow) has a laboratory.

Sam, it develops, has been using a special camera to collect images from his global trek. His father is working on a process that will enable Sam's mother (Jeanne Moreau) to "see" these images, even though she is blind. Convinced by an absence of radio signals that a nuclear holocaust has taken place, everyone devotes themselves to helping with Mr. Farber's experiments. Their work bears fruit; the machine not only gives sight to the blind but also allows users to view their dreams on screen. These beautiful images, however, prove dangerously addictive.

One of the most highly respected directors of the New German Cinema, Wim Wenders completed a remarkable trilogy of road movies—ALICE IN THE CITIES, WRONG MOVE and KINGS OF THE ROAD—early in his career, and made a partial return to the genre with PARIS, TEXAS. (His production company is even called Road Movies.) The themes which illuminated those earlier movies, though—the difficulty of communication, the nature of wanderlust, urban alienation—get skimpy treatment here. The first half of the film is a flip, engaging romp which offers us some stylish visuals and a knowing, *fin de siecle* attitude. Once the film gets bogged down in the outback, however, it comes to a virtual stop. Wenders seems to be saying something pretty banal about the emotional emptiness of the recorded image as opposed to the "real thing." If that's the point, why make a film at all? Worth seeing nevertheless, if only for the outstanding soundtrack and the nicely realized dream images.

UNTOUCHABLES, THE   **DVD**
1987 119m c   Crime/Drama   ★★★★
Paramount   (U.S.)   R

Kevin Costner *(Eliot Ness)*, Sean Connery *(James Malone)*, Charles Martin Smith *(Oscar Wallace)*, Andy Garcia *(George Stone)*, Robert De Niro *(Al Capone)*, Richard Bradford *(Mike)*, Jack Kehoe *(Walter Payne)*, Brad Sullivan *(George)*, Billy Drago *(Frank Nitti)*, Patricia Clarkson *(Catherine Ness)*

p, Art Linson; d, Brian De Palma; w, David Mamet; ph, Stephen H. Burum (Technicolor); ed, Jerry Greenberg, Bill Pankow; m, Ennio Morricone; art d, William Elliott; cos, Marilyn Vance

AA Best Supporting Actor: Sean Connery; *AAN Best Original Score:* Ennio Morricone; *AAN Best Art Direction-Set Decoration:* Patrizia Von Brandenstein, Hal Gausman; *AAN Best Costume Design:* Marilyn Vance-Straker

Kevin Costner became a star as the legendary "G-Man" Eliot Ness in THE UNTOUCHABLES, a slam-bang gangster saga with bravura direction by Brian De Palma, a witty David Mamet script and superb acting, including Robert De Niro as Al Capone and Sean Connery's Oscar-winning turn as a wily veteran cop. The film has virtually nothing in common with the famous 1950s TV series, and even less to do with real history, but it's a terrifically entertaining and exciting movie nonetheless. The story is almost totally fictionalized (Ness never killed Frank Nitti and had nothing to do with Capone's income-tax rap), but this becomes completely irrelevant in light of the beautifully crafted film's accomplishments. De Palma, who has often been accused of emphasizing style over content, here has a strong and substantial script to work with, and his flashy direction meshes perfectly with the film's flamboyantly operatic design. Mamet's script may not be true to history, but it's true to human emotion and very moving, personalizing the battle between good and evil by concentrating on the impact that violence and corruption has on families. The concept of fam-

ily and children as being representative of all that's good and pure becomes the film's central motif, as virtually every act of violence is followed by a tender scene between Ness and his wife and kids. Thus, it makes perfect sense that the film's most famous set-piece involves a mother and her child—the 10-minute long train-station sequence that pays homage to BATTLESHIP POTEMKIN (1925)—with a baby carriage bouncing down the steps in slow-motion as Ness and Capone's gang shoot it out. The film's other set-pieces are all technical tours de force, including a rooftop chase with Ness and Nitti, and a Canadian border ambush, which is shot like a Sergio Leone western, replete with Mounties on horseback and Ennio Morricone's jangling harmonica music.

UNZIPPED   **DVD**
1995 80m   c   Documentary   ★★★½
Hachette Filipacchi Productions/Elle Magazine   R
(U.S.)

Isaac Mizrahi, Nina Santisi, Eartha Kitt, Sandra Bernhard, Naomi Campbell, Mark Morris, Madonna, Roseanne

p, Michael Alden; d, Douglas Keeve; ph, Ellen Kuras; ed, Paula Heredia

Burned by Robert Altman's READY TO WEAR? Don't let that scare you away from UNZIPPED, a flossy, crowd-pleasing documentary about *haute couture*. The subject is designer Isaac Mizrahi, who's about to start a new collection and is desperately casting about for inspiration. It comes in the form of Loretta Young, radiant in a snowdrift, in 1935's CALL OF THE WILD. "Think Eskimos!" squeals the irrepressible Mizrahi, and the race against time is on. Supermodels, celebrity friends, opinionated magazine editors: Mizrahi eclipses them all with his bitchy wit and camp-inflected dedication to the ephemeral world of fashion. The only person who steals his spotlight is his kvelling mom, who knew her son was a genius when at age five he noticed the daisies on her shoes. And oh, that climactic fashion show: it's a genuine thrill.

UP IN ARMS
1944 106m c   Musical/Comedy/War   ★★★★
Goldwyn   (U.S.)

Danny Kaye *(Danny Weems)*, Constance Dowling *(Mary Morgan)*, Dinah Shore *(Virginia Merrill)*, Dana Andrews *(Joe Nelson)*, Louis Calhern *(Col. Ashley)*, George Mathews *(Blackie)*, Benny Baker *(Butterball)*, Elisha Cook Jr. *(Info Jones)*, Lyle Talbot *(Sgt. Gelsey)*, Walter Catlett *(Maj. Brock)*

p, Don Hartman; d, Elliott Nugent; w, Don Hartman, Allen Boretz, Robert Pirosh (based on the play *The Nervous Wreck* by Owen Davis, Sr.); ph, Ray Rennahan (Technicolor); ed, Daniel Mandell, James E. Newcom; m, Ray Heindorf; art d, Perry Ferguson, Stewart Chaney, McClure Capps; fx, Clarence Slifer, Ray Binger; chor, Danny Dare

AAN Best Score (Musical): Louis Forbes, Ray Heindorf; *AAN Best Song:* "Now I Know"; Harold Arlen (Music), Ted Koehler (Lyrics)

This is the lavish musical comedy that introduced 31-year-old vaudeville and stage star Danny Kaye to the movie audience. He plays confirmed hypochondriac Danny Weems, who is so fearful of illness that he works as a medical building's elevator operator—if disease strikes, help is no more than a scream away. When Danny and his best pal, Joe (Dana Andrews), are drafted into the Army, he must tell the woman he loves, Mary (Constance Dowling), that they are going off to war. Accordingly, Mary—who really likes Joe—joins the WACs with her friend Virginia (Dinah

Shore), who signs on as a nurse because, of course, she's in love with Danny. The boys are shipped out to the Far East, but fate and the screenwriters intervene when Mary and Virginia, who came to bid them goodbye, are trapped on the ship. Not being a nurse like Virginia, Mary must stow away to avoid court-martial, and is shunted around the ship to escape the eagle eye of the martinet captain (Louis Calhern). Soon enough, Mary is discovered, Danny takes the blame, and things look bleak as Danny is placed in an Army jail after the ship docks. Then the Japanese attack and take Danny prisoner, but in a series of wonderfully funny escapades our neurotic hero escapes and even manages to nab some of the enemy. Kaye's superb comic timing is already in full evidence, allowing him to dominate every scene. Excellent choreography, superb sets, fine costumes, and a host of songs (several by Harold Arlen and Ted Koehler) round out the enjoyment.

UP IN SMOKE
DVD
1978   86m   c   Comedy   ★★★
Paramount   (U.S.)   R

Cheech Marin, billed as Richard "Cheech" Marin (*Pedro De Pacas*), Tommy Chong (*Man Stoner*), Stacy Keach (*Sgt. Stedenko*), Tom Skerritt (*Strawberry*), Edie Adams (*Tempest Stoner*), Strother Martin (*Mr. Stoner*), Louisa Moritz (*Officer Gloria*), Zane Buzby (*Jade East*), Anne Wharton (*Debbie*), Mills Watson (*Harry*)

p, Lou Adler, Lou Lombardo; d, Lou Adler; w, Thomas Chong, Richard "Cheech" Marin; ph, Gene Polito, Jack Willoughby (Panavision, Metrocolor); ed, Lou Lombardo; art d, Leon Ericksen; fx, Knott Limited

"Up in smoke, that's where my money's gone." So goes the opening song of this weedfest/comedy, despised by most critics, parents and lovers of cinema but cherished by anyone who's ever had a bad case of the munchies. The story opens with Man Stoner (Tommy Chong) being tossed out of his parents' plush Hollywood Hills house only to stumble upon Pedro de Pacos ("Cheech" Marin), leader of a rock band and lover of "canabus." What ensues is an 86-minute ride from L.A. to Mexico and back, with our smoking heroes driving a van made entirely of "Fibreweed" (pure marijuana) across the border, outwitting the cops and the van's owners, and still managing to win a climactic "Battle of the Bands" contest.

The funniest of all the Cheech and Chong movies, UP IN SMOKE provides a feast of gags for the sympathetically minded. Best exchange, on the subject of Pedros's cousin: "He went to Vietnam and came back weirded out." "'Nam grass can do weird things to you."

UPTOWN SATURDAY NIGHT
DVD
1974   104m   c   Comedy   ★★★
First Artists   (U.S.)   PG

Sidney Poitier (*Steve Jackson*), Bill Cosby (*Wardell Franklin*), Harry Belafonte (*Geechie Dan Beauford*), Flip Wilson (*The Reverend*), Richard Pryor (*Sharp Eye Washington*), Rosalind Cash (*Sarah Jackson*), Paula Kelly (*Leggy Peggy*), Lee Chamberlin (*Mme. Zenobia*), Johnny Sekka (*Geechie's Henchman*)

p, Melville Tucker; d, Sidney Poitier; w, Richard Wesley; ph, Fred Koenekamp (Technicolor); ed, Pembroke J. Herring; m, Tom Scott; prod d, Alfred Sweeney; fx, Charles Spurgeon

A fine comedy starring and directed by Sidney Poitier, who plays a bored factory worker. He, along with his taxi-driving friend, Cosby, decides to live it up one night, and they venture into a seedy, illegal, underground gambling den for some fun. While they are at the club, gangsters hold up the guests, making off with jewelry, cash, and wallets. When Poitier and Cosby learn that the lottery ticket in Poitier's stolen wallet happens to be worth $50,000, the desperate friends plunge headfirst into the criminal underworld to retrieve it. Pryor turns up as an incompetent private eye, Wilson is a preacher, Browne plays a shady black congressman, and Belafonte steals the movie with a hilarious parody of Marlon Brando's "Godfather" as the mobster who owns the town. The film spawned two sequels: LET'S DO IT AGAIN and A PIECE OF THE ACTION.

URBAN COWBOY
DVD
1980   135m   c   Drama   ★★
Paramount   (U.S.)   PG

John Travolta (*Bud*), Debra Winger (*Sissy*), Scott Glenn (*Wes*), Madolyn Smith (*Pam*), Barry Corbin (*Uncle Bob*), Brooke Alderson (*Aunt Corene*), Cooper Huckabee (*Marshall*), James Gammon (*Steve Strange*), Betty Murphy (*Bud's Mom*), Ed Geldart (*Bud's Dad*)

p, Robert Evans, Irving Azoff; d, James Bridges; w, James Bridges, Aaron Latham (based on a story by Latham); ph, Reynaldo Villalobos (Panavision, Movielab Color); ed, David Rawlins; m, Ralph Burns; prod d, Stephen Grimes; art d, Stewart Campbell; chor, Patsy Swayze

If you can accept John Travolta as a Texan, half the problems of URBAN COWBOY have been surmounted. Here he plays a country boy who ventures to the big city to work at an oil refinery. Soon he's immersed in the nightlife that revolves around Gilley's, a cavernous honky-tonk with a famous mechanical bull. He meets sexy Debra Winger and, after a brief, intense courtship, the two are married. Problems, however, soon plague the relationship. Aside from Winger's winning performance, not much else here is interesting, save for Scott Glenn's solid portrayal of a heavy. Director James Bridges fails to instill much life into a narrative peopled with vapid characters.

USED CARS
DVD
1980   113m   c   Comedy   ★★★½
Columbia   (U.S.)   R

Kurt Russell (*Rudy Russo*), Jack Warden (*Roy L. Fuchs/Luke Fuchs*), Gerrit Graham (*Jeff*), Frank McRae (*Jim, the Mechanic*), Deborah Harmon (*Barbara Fuchs*), Joe Flaherty (*Sam Slaton*), David L. Lander (*Freddie Paris*), Michael McKean (*Eddie Winslow*), Michael Talbott (*Mickey*), Harry Northrup (*Carmine*)

p, Bob Gale; d, Robert Zemeckis; w, Robert Zemeckis, Bob Gale; ph, Donald Morgan (Metrocolor); ed, Michael Kahn; m, Patrick Williams; prod d, Peter Jamison

Before director-writer Bob Zemeckis found success with blockbuster hits BACK TO THE FUTURE and FORREST GUMP, he directed this raunchy, hysterically funny comedy. Kurt Russell turns in a brilliant performance as Rudy Russo, the unscrupulous but likable head salesman of a dying used car lot owned by Roy L. Fuchs (Jack Warden). Roy's brother, Luke (also played by Warden), owns a successful car lot across the street and is conspiring to get Roy's property. When Roy dies Rudy and his colleague Jeff (Gerrit Graham) try to conceal the death from Roy's daughter (Deborah Harmon) and Luke. Filled with riotous plot twists and effective black humor, this is a truly inventive and memorable comedy, which was virtually ignored at the box office. Fans of television's "Hill Street Blues" may want to look for Betty Thomas as a topless dancer (a role she would no doubt like to forget) bumping and grinding in one of the R-rated commercials with which Rudy jams a Presidential address.

USUAL SUSPECTS, THE

1995 96m c Crime/Thriller

Rosco Film GmbH/Blue Parrott Productions/
Bad Hat Harry Productions/PolyGram/Spellings
Films International (U.S.)

DVD
★★★
R

Kevin Spacey *(Roger "Verbal" Kint)*, Chazz Palminteri *(Kujan)*, Stephen Baldwin *(McManus)*, Gabriel Byrne *(Dean Keaton)*, Benicio Del Toro *(Fenster)*, Kevin Pollak *(Hockney)*, Pete Postlethwaite *(Kobayashi)*, Suzy Amis *(Edie)*, Giancarlo Esposito *(Jack Baer)*, Dan Hedaya *(Sgt. Rabin)*

p, Bryan Singer, Michael McDonnell; d, Bryan Singer; w, Christopher McQuarrie; ph, Newton Thomas Sigel; ed, John Ottman; m, John Ottman; prod d, Howard Cummings; art d, David Lazan; fx, Roy Downey; cos, Louise Mingenbach

AA Best Supporting Actor: Kevin Spacey; *AA Best Original Screenplay:* Christopher McQuarrie

This twisty and twisted yarn, one of the more successful entries in the post-Tarantino cycle of hip, violent crime flicks, marks a promising major-league debut for director Bryan Singer.

Special investigator Kujan (Chazz Palminteri) grills "Verbal" Kint (Kevin Spacey), a crippled con-man who is the lone survivor of an L.A. boat explosion that claimed more than 20 victims. Kujan wants to confirm that his nemesis, the rogue cop Keaton (Gabriel Byrne), is actually dead. Kint relates the majority of the film in flashback, beginning with the fateful day when five shifty guys meet in a police-station lineup in New York City. Along with dour Keaton, Kint encounters cheerfully sociopathic McManus (Stephen Baldwin), mordantly sarcastic Hockney (Kevin Pollak), and Fenster (Benicio Del Toro), whose speech is virtually incomprehensible. Together their plot to steal a small fortune in gems from "New York's Finest Taxi Service"—crooked cops who provide escort service for visiting drug kingpins. What follows is a shell-game of violence and betrayal, all hinging on the identity of a mysterious villain called Keyser Soze.

THE USUAL SUSPECTS is an intricately plotted, densely layered story, and although the resolution of Soze's identity is dramatically fulfilling—and not all that surprising—it has the effect of undermining the entire narrative. But fans of taut, self-consciously clever puzzles will find this film a delightful excursion, full of talented actors having great fun with their quirky, nasty characters. Pollak shines early, though his good lines diminish as the film progresses, and Baldwin is surprisingly chilling. Byrne holds the center with his patented brooding intensity, and Del Toro is simply hysterical as a jumble of visual and verbal tics. But it's Spacey who carries the weight of the film, and he rises admirably to the challenge of epitomizing pure evil with a blandly human face.

V

VAGABOND

(SANS TOIT NI LOI)

1985 105m c Drama

Cine Tamaris/Ministere de la Culture/A2 (France)

DVD
★★★½

Sandrine Bonnaire *(Mona)*, Macha Meril *(Madame Landier)*, Stephane Freiss *(Jean-Pierre)*, Laurence Cortadellas *(Elaine)*, Marthe Jarnias *(Tante Lydie)*, Yolande Moreau

(Yolande), Joel Fosse *(Paulo)*, Patrick Lepcynski, Yahiaoui Assouna, Setti Ramdane

p, Oury Milshtein; d, Agnes Varda; w, Agnes Varda; ph, Patrick Blossier; ed, Agnes Varda, Patricia Mazuy; m, Joanna Bruzdowicz

Atmospheric, cold, and distancing, yet somehow engaging, VAGABOND combines a stylized documentary technique with the fictional vision of writer-director Agnes Varda. The picture opens in the dead of winter, as a farmhand discovers a woman's frozen corpse in a ditch—her long hair a tangle of knots, her skin hidden beneath a well-worn leather jacket and filthy blue jeans. This was Mona (Bonnaire), a fiercely independent "vagabond" whose last weeks are reconstructed in flashback and in "interviews" (both with actors and nonprofessionals Varda found during shooting) with people who met Mona. It soon becomes clear, however, that no one really knew her. Mona is not a character many will entirely like or identify with, nor is one expected to. Varda presents her story without any sentiment, and in the process she tells the stories of a number of different people whose lives were altered, perhaps permanently, by their contact with the vagabond.

After working in the shadow of the more popular French New Wave directors for years, the then 57-year-old Varda broke new ground in narrative film with her methods in VAGABOND. Her visual prowess is on ample display as well, potently rendering a rich portrait of Mona and her world. Equal credit for the movie's success, however, must go to Bonnaire, who perfectly transforms herself into the filthy, aimless, and enigmatic wanderer that the role calls for. Bonnaire justly won a French Cesar for her remarkable performance, and the film itself took the Golden Lion for Best Picture at the Venice Film Festival.

VALLEY GIRL

1983 95m c Romance

Atlantic (U.S.)

DVD
★★★½
R

Nicolas Cage *(Randy)*, Deborah Foreman *(Julie Richman)*, Elizabeth Daily *(Loryn)*, Michael Bowen *(Tommy)*, Cameron Dye *(Fred)*, Heidi Holicker *(Stacey)*, Michelle Meyrink *(Suzie)*, Tina Theberge *(Samantha)*, Lee Purcell *(Beth Brent)*, Colleen Camp *(Sarah Richman)*

p, Wayne Crawford, Andrew Lane; d, Martha Coolidge; w, Wayne Crawford, Andrew Lane; ph, Frederick Elmes; ed, Eva Gordos; m, Scott Wilk, Marc Levinthal; prod d, Mary Delia Javier

Insightful and genuine, VALLEY GIRL tells the unlikely tale of Julie (Deborah Foreman), a deb from the Valley, and Randy (Nicholas Cage), a punk rocker from Hollywood, falling in love. As prom time approaches, Julie bows to pressure from her friends to stop dating the "creep" from "Hollyweird." She dumps Randy for her old boyfriend, Tommy (Michael Bowen), a mindless jock. Randy tries a number of unsuccessful stunts to win her back, then reluctantly decides to go to the prom and force a confrontation. This simplified Romeo and Juliet tale was written and performed with such heart and care that it is impossible to dislike. The cast is wonderful, headed by the engaging couple of Cage and Foreman and wittily directed by Coolidge. VALLEY GIRL also boasts an eclectic pop score that features songs by Modern English, Josie Cotton, Men at Work, The Plimsouls, Sparks, Psychedelic Furs, and Eddie Grant, among others.

VALLEY OF THE DOLLS

1967 123m c Drama

Red Lion (U.S.)

★★
PG

Barbara Parkins *(Anne Welles)*, Patty Duke *(Neely O'Hara)*, Paul Burke *(Lyon Burke)*, Sharon Tate *(Jennifer North)*, Tony Scotti *(Tony Polar)*, Martin Milner *(Mel Anderson)*, Charles Drake *(Kevin*

Gilmore), Alexander Davion *(Ted Casablanca)*, Lee Grant *(Miriam)*, Naomi Stevens *(Miss Steinberg)*

p, David Weisbart; d, Mark Robson; w, Helen Deutsch, Dorothy Kingsley (based on the novel by Jacqueline Susann); ph, William Daniels (Panavision, DeLuxe Color); ed, Dorothy Spencer; m, John Williams; art d, Jack Martin Smith, Richard Day; fx, L.B. Abbott, Art Cruickshank, Emil Kosa Jr.; chor, Robert Sidney; cos, Travilla

AAN Best Adapted Score: John Williams

Pure trash, based on a trashy book, filled to the brim with trashy performances, now becoming a trashy cult film. Based on Jacqueline Susann's novel detailing the horrors of stardom (the author has a bit part as a journalist, which she has trouble pulling off), the film stars Tate, Parkins, and Duke as three aspiring actresses who each attain a degree of success followed by a dependence on pills (nicknamed "dolls"). Tate, who is told by everyone she meets that she has no talent but a great body, meets and marries a young singer, Scotti, who soon is stricken with a fatal illness requiring expensive hospitalization. To pay the bills, Tate appears in European porno films and becomes quite a sensation. Unfortunately, she soon discovers she has breast cancer and needs to have her "talent" removed. Realizing there is no future in porno after such surgery, Tate kills herself by taking an overdose of sleeping pills.

Duke, meanwhile, (who turns in the worst performance of the three, only because she is capable of so much more) lands a minor part in a new Broadway show opposite aging superstar Hayward (who replaced the originally cast Judy Garland, a dropout despite the perquisites proffered by the studio, including the dressing-room pool table she had demanded). The ambitious newcomer makes herself such a nuisance that she soon finds herself out of a job. As luck would have it, Duke winds up doing a quick singing spot on a national television fundraiser and becomes a superstar overnight (oh, sure). Of course, her sudden success leads to a horrible drug addiction that eventually turns her into a pathetic, whining has-been who *should* commit suicide to end the audience's suffering. Unfortunately, she doesn't.

Not all success stories are grim, however, as we follow the likable Parkins from her small East Coast town to New York where she hits it big as a model. This, once again, leads to a bout with the ever-present pills and an unstable love life, but Parkins eventually finds the inner strength to abandon her success and hightail it back to her hometown before she winds up as just another tragic statistic. Banal, ignorant, crass and just plain lousy, this film went on to gross over $20 million, becoming one of 20th Century Fox's biggest hits ever and reaffirming the belief that the public deserves what it gets.

VAMPYR **DVD**
(VAMPYR, OU L'ETRANGE AVENTURE DE DAVID GRAY)
1932 83m bw Horror ★★★★★
Dreyer/Tobis/Klangfilm (France/Germany)

Julian West *(David Gray)*, Henriette Gerard *(Marguerite Chopin)*, Jan Hieronimko *(Doctor)*, Maurice Schutz *(Lord of the Manor)*, Rena Mandel *(His Daughter Gisele)*, Sybille Schmitz *(His Daughter Leone)*, Albert Bras *(Servant)*, N. Babanini *(The Girl)*, Jane Mora *(The Religious Woman)*

p, Baron Nicolas de Gunzberg, Carl-Theodor Dreyer; d, Carl-Theodor Dreyer; w, Carl-Theodor Dreyer, Christen Jul (based on stories from In a Glass Darkly by Joseph Sheridan Le Fanu); ph, Rudolph Mate, Louis Nee; m, Wolfgang Zeller; art d, Hermann Warm, Hans Bittmann, Cesare Silvagni

Much to the dismay of his admirers, Danish filmmaker Dreyer followed his silent masterpiece THE PASSION OF JOAN OF ARC with a horror film. The result, his first foray into sound, was the greatest vampire film ever made and one of the few undisputed masterpieces of the horror genre.

Thrillseekers, beware, though, because it's not that kind of film. VAMPYR, rather, is subtly unsettling rather than gory or shocking; it is such stuff as nightmares are made of.

Loosely based on the Le Fanu collection of stories, *In a Glass Darkly*, the film begins as young David Gray (West) arrives in a dark, mysterious European village and takes a room at the inn. That night a strange old man (Schutz) gives him a package to be opened in the event of his death. David later witnesses many strange events, among which is the murder of the old man. David meets the dead man's daughters (Schmitz and Mandel) and opens the package, which contains a copy of *Strange Tales of Vampires*. Realizing that the town is at the mercy of one of the undead (Gerard), David struggles to save himself and the two young women.

Such are the bare bones of the plot, but its unfolding, leisurely and fragmented, is not of tantamount importance. What really matters are features like the muffled offscreen sounds and the lack of dialogue explaining them; the misty shooting style (achieved via filters and by working at dawn); and Zeller's spare but sinister music (a highlight is his "Shadow Polka"). The sequence using this music subtly suggests the vampire's power. Angry at the villagers' revels she cannot join, she stands alone, framed in silhouette by a doorway and with large wheels around her. She shrieks for quiet and, without a cutaway, Dreyer tells us her command has been obeyed. Another sequence, in which the one-legged gamekeeper's shadow leaves his body behind to do the vampire's bidding, is also left unexplained. Throughout VAMPYR, a deep, muffling sense of terror slowly envelops both village and viewer, reinforced by Dreyer's brilliantly disjunctive construction of space. Mate's cinematography creates many memorable images, from the scythe-bearer by the water to the tainted elder sister awakening to the call of bloodlust as she eyes her innocent sibling. The marvelous Schmitz (remembered in the title role of Frank Wysbar's classic FERRYMAN MARIA), in the difficult role of the semi-vampire daughter, makes this moment one of the most horrific in the entire film. Best of all, though, are two more famous sequences. The doctor, one of the vampire's accomplices, meets his doom in a flour mill, smothered by the cascading (and purifying) white dust as the agonizingly slow workings of fate and the machinery take their toll. Earlier, David, after donating blood to help a victim, dreams of his own burial. Handled largely from David's view, with the sealing of the coffin lid, the ride to the cemetery and the icy glimpse of the elderly vampiress through the coffin window, this imitated but never duplicated sequence must rank among the greatest uses of point-of-view camera ever filmed. Sensual but remote and vague, gripping and yet somehow unsatisfying, VAMPYR is yet another of Dreyer's brilliant meditations on faith, love and salvation. For him, the vampire's curse haunts the soul foremost, and this unique film experience is likely to haunt your memory long after the film runs out.

VAN HELSING **DVD**
2004 125m c Horror/Action ★★
Sommers Company/Universal/Carpathian Pictures/ PG-13
Stillking Films (U.S.)

Hugh Jackman *(Gabriel Van Helsing)*, Kate Beckinsale *(Anna Valerious)*, Richard Roxburgh *(Count Vladislaus Dracula)*, David Wenham *(Carl)*, Shuler Hensley *(Frankenstein's Monster)*, Will Kemp *(Velkan Valerious)*, Kevin J. O'Connor *(Igor)*, Elena Anaya *(Dracula's Bride Aleera)*, Silvia Colloca *(Dracula's Bride Verona)*, Josie Maran *(Dracula's Bride Marishka)*

p, Bob Ducsay, Stephen Sommers; d, Stephen Sommers; w, Stephen Sommers; ph, Allan Aviau; ed, Bob Ducsay, Kelly Matsumoto; m, Alan Silvestri; prod d, Allan Cameron; art d, Steve Arnold, Keith P. Cunningham, Giles Masters, Tony Reading; fx,

Steve Cremin, Mark Freund, Jill E. Hughes, Industrial Light & Magic; cos, Gabriella Pescucci, Carlo Poggioli

Although promoted as a bold reimagining of classic horror characters, writer-director Stephen Sommers' frenetic action spectacle is a hokey monster mish-mash.

It starts promisingly, with a glistening B&W sequence recapping FRANKENSTEIN's familiar conclusion, with a twist. The doomed doctor (Samuel West) once again animates his sad creature (Shuler Hensley) as angry, torch-bearing villagers storm his castle, but now Count Dracula (Richard Roxburgh), Frankenstein's secret financial backer, lurks in the shadows. The action shifts to Paris where a mysterious figure confronts the simian Dr. Hyde (Robbie Coltrane) in Notre Dame Cathedral. Hyde's nemesis is Gabriel Van Helsing (Hugh Jackman), a 19th-century Indiana Jones by way of James Bond, answering to a cabal located deep within the Vatican and armed with a license to kill fiends, madmen, and man-made monsters. Van Helsing has no memory of his past and faces an uncertain future: as the 20th century approaches and popular belief in monsters wanes, his crusade looks an awful lot like a murder spree. Assured by his holy handlers that these tribulations are penance for past transgressions, Van Helsing is shipped off to Transylvania to assist the Valerious family. A rash ancestor swore no Valerious would enter Heaven until Dracula was dead, and with the noble gypsy clan reduced to siblings Anna and Velkan (Kate Beckinsale, Will Kemp), generations of immortal souls are imperiled. Worse, Velkan has been bitten by a werewolf and is fast succumbing to the beast within.

Nonstop action can't quite cover the story's thinness and most of the actors affect hyperbolic foreign accents that make everything they say sound camp. Reconceiving Van Helsing as a haunted mercenary is a perfectly good idea, but this extravagant exercise in kick-ass nonsense smacks of the same desperation that prompted Universal to combine its exhausted horror properties in the 1940s. That's no way to start a megabucks franchise.

VANILLA SKY   DVD
2001   115m   c   Thriller/Science Fiction   ★★
Cruise-Wagner Productions/Vinyl Films   (U.S.)   R

Tom Cruise *(David Aames)*, Penelope Cruz *(Sofia Serrano)*, Cameron Diaz *(Julie Gianni)*, Kurt Russell *(Dr. Curtis McCabe)*, Jason Lee *(Brian Shelby)*, Noah Taylor *(Edmund Ventura)*, Timothy Spall *(Thomas Tipp)*, Tilda Swinton *(Rebecca Dearborn)*, Michael Shannon *(Aaron)*, Delaina Mitchell *(David's Assistant)*

p, Cameron Crowe, Tom Cruise, Paula Wagner; d, Cameron Crowe; w, Cameron Crowe (based on the film ABRE LOS OJOS/OPEN YOUR EYES written by Alejandro Amenabar and Mateo Gil); ph, John Toll; ed, Joe Hutshing, Mark Livolsi; m, Nancy Wilson; prod d, Catherine Hardwicke; art d, John Chichester, Beat Frutiger, Michael Rizzo, James T. Truesdale; fx, Gary D'Amico, Alison O'Brien, Rochelle Gross, CFX, Cinesite, DigiScope, Digital Domain; cos, Betsy Heimann

AAN Best Original Song: "Vanilla Sky"; Paul McCartney

An overblown "Twilight Zone" episode, this nearly scene-for-scene remake of 1998's creepy OPEN YOUR EYES feels enervated and logy, its energy sucked into the vacuum of Tom Cruise's star power.

David Aames (Cruise) is on top of the world. He's rich, handsome, and runs his late father's magazine empire with all the haughty, hedonistic disdain of a prince. At David's 33rd birthday party, his less handsome, considerably less wealthy best friend Brian (Jason Lee) shows up with a personable beauty named Sofia (Penelope Cruz, who also starred in the original film) on his arm. Friendship doesn't stop David from turning on the high-voltage charm. Brian isn't the only party-

goer miffed by David's shameless flirting. The following morning, David finds leggy beauty Julie Gianni (Cameron Diaz), with whom he's been enjoying what he thought of as a meaningless fling, waiting for him outside Sofia's apartment. She entices David into her car, then, bitterly decrying his faithlessness, drives headlong off a bridge. When David eventually emerges from his coma, he learns that Julie is dead and he's been horribly disfigured. David tells this tale to a psychiatrist (Kurt Russell) who's been appointed by the court; it seems David has been arrested for murdering someone—maybe Julie, maybe Sofia—but he can't be certain of anything. His life has become a nightmare.

Writer-director Cameron Crowe preserves the original film's plot twists and turns, but his version lumbers when it should be whipping along, daring you to keep up. The wall-to-wall pop music soundtrack eventually becomes oppressive, and Cruise's oily smile doesn't really constitute a characterization. Tilda Swinton blows him out of the water in her all-too-few minutes of 11th-hour screen time.

VANISHING, THE   DVD
(SPOORLOOS)
1986   120m   c   Mystery/Drama   ★★★★
Golden Egg Films/MGS Film/Ingrid Productions
(Netherlands)

Gene Bervoets *(Rex Hofman)*, Johanna Ter Steege *(Saskia Wagter)*, Bernard-Pierre Donnadieu *(Raymond Lemorne)*, Gwen Eckhaus *(Lienexe)*, Bernadette LeSache *(Simone Lemorne)*, Tania Latarjet *(Denise)*, Lucille Glenn *(Gabrielle)*, Roger Souza *(Manager)*, Caroline Apperre *(Cashier)*, Pierre Forget *(Farmer Laurent)*

p, Anne Lordon, George Sluizer; d, George Sluizer; w, George Sluizer, Tim Krabbe (adapted from his novel *The Golden Egg*); ph, Toni Kuhn; ed, George Sluizer, Lin Friedman; m, Henry Vrienten; art d, Santiago Isidro Pin, Cor Spijk; cos, Sophie Dussaud

Through some fiendish alchemy, THE VANISHING manages to scare people out of their wits more effectively than a legion of better-known horror films. This Dutch production has a pleasantly efficient veneer to it that hides a truly awesome undercurrent.

Two young Dutch lovers are motoring through France. They are flushed with optimism and affection for each other. While arguing playfully, Saskia Wagter (Johanna Ter Steege), the young woman, tells Rex Hofman (Gene Bervoets), the young man, her recurring dream. She is trapped in a golden egg in the midst of darkness with no hope of escaping. Recently, she tells Rex, she has dreamt of another egg traveling beside her. When their car stalls in the middle of a dark tunnel, Saskia has an emotional explosion of claustrophobia and abandonment. Her lover cruelly neglects her, going off to get some gas. Returning, the two make up quickly. They stop at a nearby gas station. Saskia goes to make a purchase in the store. Rex waits for her outside. She never comes back. Three years later Rex is still searching for Saskia. As Rex searches, the audience is introduced to Raymond Lemorne (Bernard-Pierre Donnadieu) who, through different time frames, slowly reveals Saskia's fate. It is only in the last few moments of the film that the mystery is fully revealed to us. And those moments are deeply horrific.

The choice of actors in this film is uncanny. Johanna Ter Steege's vanished Saskia is luminous in her opening scenes. Her presence continues to haunt the film after her disappearance. And Bernard-Pierre Donnadieu as Raymond Lemorne does a remarkable job. Lemorne is a sociopath and, unlike the scores of other movie villains, Donnadieu's Lemorne's humanity is not a conceit. His beneficence makes his monstrousness even more hard to take. The director, George Sluizer, lets the whole film play out in a contemporary world of freeways, efficiency lighting and sports commentary spilling over from the radio. Into this banal universe he plays out themes that haven't been so effectively conjured up since the early '60s. Sluizer himself directed a predictably inferior American remake released in 1993.

VANITY FAIR

2004 137m c Historical/Comedy/Drama ★★½ DVD
Inside Track Films 2 LLP/Focus Features/Granada PG-13
Film Productions/Tempesta Films/USA Films (U.S./U.K.)

Reese Witherspoon *(Becky Sharp)*, James Purefoy *(Rawdon Crawley)*, Rhys Ifans *(William Dobbin)*, Romola Garai *(Amelia Sedley)*, Jonathan Rhys Meyers *(George Osborne)*, Eileen Atkins *(Miss Matilda Crawley)*, Jim Broadbent *(Mr. Osborne)*, Bob Hoskins *(Sir Pitt Crawley)*, Roger Lloyd Pack *(Francis Sharp)*, Gabriel Byrne *(The Marquess of Steyne)*

p, Janette Day, Donna Gigliotti, Lydia Dean Pilcher; d, Mira Nair; w, Matthew Faulk, Mark Skeet, Julian Fellowes (based on the novel by Wiliam Makepeace Thackeray); ph, Declan Quinn; ed, Allyson C. Johnson; m, Mychael Danna; prod d, Maria Djurkovic; art d, Nick Palmer; fx, Mark Holt; chor, Farah Khan, Jack Murphy; cos, Beatrix Aruna Pasztor

Having perfectly cast Reese Witherspoon as Becky Sharp, the thoroughly amoral antiheroine of Thackeray's 1848 satirical masterpiece, it comes as a huge disappointment that director Mira Nair couldn't resist that impulse to find 21st-century prototypes in 19th-century literary characters. Instead of Thackeray's scheming adventuress who claws her way into high 19th-century English society, we get Becky the plucky protofeminist.

Born to a starving artist and a French opera singer, Becky secures a position as governess to the children of slovenly aristocrat Sir Pitt Crawley (Bob Hoskins) at his miserable country estate. As awful as her new surroundings may be, Becky finds herself in the perfect position to woo not only the lord's son, dashing Capt. Rawdon Crawley (James Purefoy), but also Sir Pitt's spinster sister, Miss Matilda Crawley (Eileen Atkins), who controls the purse strings of the family fortune. As Becky's star rises, the fortunes of her dear friend Amelia Sedley (Romola Garai), an innocent lamb engaged to despicable wolf Capt. George Osborne (Jonathan Rhys Meyers), take a tumble. Amelia's father (John Franklyn-Robbins) faces financial ruin, and her loathsome future father-in-law (Jim Broadbent) forbids his son to marry the newly impoverished girl. And there are even darker clouds looming on the horizon: Napoleon is cutting a swath toward Waterloo, where his army is due for a fateful encounter with captains Crawley and Osborne, as well as the one person who truly loves Amelia, awkward Lt. Dobbin (Rhys Ifans).

At a certain point, Nair's kinder, gentler Becky no longer makes sense; Thackeray's plot eventually requires her to act in ways that are entirely at odds with this more heroic conception of her. Witherspoon and the rest of the cast are fine, however, and the production design is stunning. Sumptuous visions of India are never far from Nair's British Empire.

VANYA ON 42ND STREET

1994 119m c Drama ★★★ DVD
The Vanya Company/Laura Pels Productions/ PG
New Media Finance (U.S.)

Wallace Shawn *(Vanya Voynitsky)*, Julianne Moore *(Yelena)*, Brooke Smith *(Sonya)*, Larry Pine *(Dr. Michael Astrov)*, George Gaynes *(Alexander Serybryakov)*, Lynn Cohen *(Maman)*, Phoebe Brand *(Marina)*, Jerry Mayer *(Waffles)*, Madhur Jaffrey *(Mrs. Chao)*, Andre Gregory *(Himself)*

p, Fred Berner; d, Louis Malle; w, David Mamet (based on the play *Uncle Vanya* by Anton Chekhov); ph, Declan Quinn; ed, Nancy Baker; m, Joshua Redman; prod d, Eugene Lee; cos, Gary Jones

Wallace Shawn, Andre Gregory, and director Louis Malle, the brain trust behind MY DINNER WITH ANDRE, concoct a staged reading of *Uncle Vanya* in Broadway's condemned New Amsterdam Theater, amid the incongruous dilapidation of Times Square.

As the camera roves the abandoned grandeur of the opera-house interior, and the actors prattle and nosh, Andre Gregory, as the play's director, bids us take our seats and we slip effortlessly into a walkthrough of the play. Vanya Voynitsky—Uncle Vanya (Wallace Shawn)—is a dreamer in his late 40s, living with his mother (Lynn Cohen) on the estate of Alexander Serybryakov (George Gaynes), a great man and revered thinker in the autumn of his life, whose first wife was Vanya's sister. The marriage produced a daughter, the plain and pure Sonya (Brooke Smith), whose hopes rest on Michael Astrov, the local doctor (Larry Pine). Meanwhile, everyone else's attentions reside with Yelena (vivid Julianne Moore), the 27-year-old beauty who is the professor's second wife.

Louis Malle's direction is elegant and unobtrusive, but this movie (based on an invitation-only workshop production that was celebrated as much for its trendy exclusivity as for its quality) is essentially a filmed record of a work by Gregory and Shawn. Briefly the thinking person's Abbott and Costello after the surprise success of MY DINNER WITH ANDRE, Shawn and Gregory never appear together here, but their mildly arty, anachronistic sensibility—closer to the WWI-era bohemianism of the Provincetown Players than any contemporary avant-garde—pervades the piece. While they want us to admire their boldness in staging *Vanya* as an ironically distanced, modern-dress sitcom, in fact they chose the safest possible approach to the material. While there are moments of considerable power here—due in particular to standout performances by Moore and Smith—this stripped-down rendering gives us something more like a latterday dysfunctional family than Chekhov's doomed bourgeosie.

VELVET GOLDMINE

1998 120m c Musical/Fantasy/Drama ★★★★ DVD
Killer Films/Zenith Productions/Single Cell Pictures R
(U.K./U.S.)

Ewan McGregor *(Curt Wild)*, Christian Bale *(Arthur Stuart)*, Jonathan Rhys Meyers *(Brian Slade)*, Toni Collette *(Mandy Slade)*, Eddie Izzard *(Jerry Divine)*, Emily Woof *(Shannon)*, Michael Feast *(Cecil)*, Mariad McKinley *(Wilde Housemaid)*, Janet McTeer *(Female Narrator)*, Luke Morgan Oliver *(Oscar Wilde—Eight)*

p, Christine Vachon; d, Todd Haynes; w, Todd Haynes; ph, Maryse Alberti; ed, James Lyons; m, Carter Burwell; prod d, Christopher Hobbs; art d, Andrew Munro; fx, Evolution FX; chor, Lea Anderson; cos, Sandy Powell

AAN Best Costume Design: Sandy Powell

A luscious, richly textured dream of the glam-rock era, reimagined by writer-director Todd Haynes as a short-lived utopia of erotic possibility.

The year is 1984: not some '80s-nostalgia 1984, but a proper Orwellian 1984 of oppressive architecture and totalitarian gloom. Reporter Arthur Stuart (Christian Bale) is assigned to a 10th-anniversary investigation into the disappearance of English glam rocker Brian Slade (Jonathan Rhys Myers), who engineered the fake murder of his stage persona, Maxwell Demon, only to see his career take a real nosedive. Arthur hunts down Slade's ex-wife Mandy (Toni Collette), now a second-rate cabaret performer, and his wheelchair-bound first manager, Cecil (Michael Feast), trying unsuccessfully to contact American proto-punk Curt Wild (Ewan McGregor), whose career was briefly but spectacularly intertwined with Slade's. Haynes isn't just fashioning a cheeky homage to CITIZEN KANE. He's mounted a full-scale, slinky deconstruction of the flash-in-the-glam era of mutable identity and sexual ambiguity. Every time you're about to surrender to the divine decadence of his lustrous images, Haynes pulls some high-brow mirror trick, having a spaceship deliver the baby Oscar Wilde—the changeling dandy who gloried in razor-edged camp before there was a word for such things—to the doorstep of unsuspecting Victorians. Or inventing the mercurial figure of Jack Fairy (Micko Westmoreland), who adopts and sheds a series of flamboyant personas like some exotic insect (eventually settling for Quentin Crisp by way of Sally Bowles) and links several generations of sartorial revolutionaries. Ignore the temptation to play roman a clef: of course Brian Slade bears an unmistakable resemblance to David Bowie; Curt Wild is an Iggy Pop-Lou Reed hybrid (with a startling dash of Kurt Cobain); and Mandy Slade echoes Angie Bowie. But this densely textured extravaganza is more than thinly veiled pop biography. It's a shimmering, thorny, and consummately self-aware valentine to a paradise, however illusory, lost.

VERA CRUZ

1954 94m c Western   DVD
Hecht/Hill/Lancaster   (U.S.)   ★★★

Gary Cooper *(Benjamin Trane)*, Burt Lancaster *(Joe Erin)*, Denise Darcel *(Countess Marie Duvarre)*, Cesar Romero *(Marquis de Labordere)*, Sarita Montiel *(Nina)*, George Macready *(Emperor Maximilian)*, Ernest Borgnine *(Donnegan)*, Morris Ankrum *(Gen. Aguilar)*, Henry Brandon *(Danette)*, Charles Bronson, billed as Charles Buchinsky *(Pittsburgh)*

p, James Hill; d, Robert Aldrich; w, Roland Kibbee, James R. Webb (based on the story by Borden Chase); ph, Ernest Laszlo (SuperScope, Technicolor); ed, Alan Crosland Jr.; m, Hugo Friedhofer

This broadly played, action-packed western teams Cooper and Lancaster as two American soldiers of fortune on a foray into Mexico during the revolution of 1866. Cooper, a former Confederate major, and Lancaster, a constantly grinning outlaw, leave the U.S. in search of mercenary work. It doesn't matter to them which side they fight for, as long as it pays better than the other. In Mexico they meet a beautiful young girl, Montiel, who falls for Cooper and begs him and his partner to fight for Juarez and the revolutionaries. The American gunslingers are tugged in the opposite direction by Romero, a supporter of Maximilian, who offers them huge sums of cash. While mulling the offers over, Cooper and Lancaster encounter Darcel, a seductive and extremely rich countess who asks them to escort her while she transports a gold shipment from Mexico City to Maximilian's forces in Vera Cruz. The men agree and quickly assemble a motley crew of gunfighters and government regulars to accompany them through the rough territory. On the trail, the wily Darcel suggests that they steal the gold and split it three ways. The Americans agree to the plan, with each suspecting the other of planning double crosses. Maximilian loyalist Romero discovers the plot and takes off with the gold to make sure it gets delivered. The Americans chase Romero to the fort in Vera Cruz, and after a bloody battle, Lancaster manages to get his hands on the gold. Cooper, however, has had a change of heart due to Montiel's revolutionary fervor, and demands Lancaster hand over the gold to Juarez's forces. Lancaster doesn't buy Cooper's commitment to the revolution and refuses to release the gold. Cooper is forced to kill Lancaster in a showdown and then gives the gold to Montiel.

The film is directed with an emphasis on action by Aldrich (who had just guided Lancaster through APACHE the year before), and most of the actors in VERA CRUZ are allowed to ham it up quite a bit. For contrast there is Cooper, forever the tight-lipped, serious professional wary of those around him, especially Lancaster's grinning gunman. The film was produced by Lancaster's own company on a budget of $1.7 million and became quite a hit, grossing more than $11 million worldwide, though critical opinion at the time was extremely negative. Lancaster gladly gave top billing to Cooper, well aware of the older actor's box-office pull. As is typical with director Aldrich's work, the violence is well staged and frequent, going a bit overboard at times specifically with regard to Darcel, who is shown being slapped and knocked about by Lancaster more than once. Aldrich and Lancaster would collaborate again in the 1970s with ULZANA'S RAID and TWILIGHT'S LAST GLEAMING.

VERA DRAKE   DVD

2004 125m c Drama   ★★★½
UK Film Council/Thin Man Films/Les Films Alain   R
Sarde/Inside Track/StudioCanal/Untitled 03
(U.K./France/New Zealand)

Imelda Staunton *(Vera Drake)*, Phil Davis *(Stan Drake)*, Peter Wight *(Detective Inspector Webster)*, Adrian Scarborough *(Frank)*, Heather Craney *(Joyce)*, Daniel Mays *(Sid)*, Alex Kelly *(Ethel)*, Sally Hawkins *(Susan)*, Eddie Marsan *(Reg)*, Ruth Sheen *(Lily)*

p, Alain Sarde, Simon Channing Williams; d, Mike Leigh; w, Mike Leigh; ph, Dick Pope; ed, Jim Clark; m, Andrew Dickson; prod d, Eve Stewart; art d, Andrew Grant, Ed Walsh; cos, Jacqueline Durran

AAN Best Actress: Imelda Staunton; *AAN Best Director:* Mike Leigh; *AAN Best Original Screenplay:* Mike Leigh

Heartrending even by the standards of director Mike Leigh's most sentimental films, his somewhat reductive treatment of a complex subject is saved by yet another typically brilliant cast.

London, 1950: Chipper Vera Drake (Imelda Staunton) is a hardworking wife and mother who supplements the income her husband, Stan (Phil Davis), brings home from his brother's (Adrian Scarborough) auto-repair shop by cleaning the homes of upper-class families. When she's not polishing brass andirons in some tony drawing room, she's home in her own cramped flat preparing supper for Stan and their children, socially awkward Ethel (Alex Kelly) and outgoing haberdasher Sid (Daniel Mays). Unbeknownst to her family, however, Vera secretly performs another service for "girls who need help": she's an abortionist. Vera doesn't do it for the money; she does it because, in her view, life is hard enough for working-class women without the added burden of unplanned pregnancy or the stigma of bearing an illegitimate child. Vera's method has so far proved safe, but abortion is a crime in England, and with each new client she takes on, Vera runs a very serious risk.

Leigh works in rather obvious juxtapositions, particularly when it comes to class. We know the warmth of the Drake household because we first see the cold sterility of the upper-class homes Vera uncomplainingly cleans. We realize the terrible double standard that punishes poor pregnant women because we first see how rich girls are able to secure technically illegal abortions. None of this is terribly subtle, but it's undeniably effective, and this is one of Leigh's most powerful films, thanks to its nakedly emotional subject matter and an extraordinary performance by Staunton.

VERDICT, THE   DVD

1982 129m c Drama   ★★★★
Fox   (U.S.)   R

Paul Newman *(Frank Galvin)*, Charlotte Rampling *(Laura Fischer)*, Jack Warden *(Mickey Morrissey)*, James Mason *(Ed*

Concannon), Milo O'Shea (Judge Hoyle), Lindsay Crouse (Kaitlin Costello Price), Edward Binns (Bishop Brophy), Julie Bovasso (Maureen Rooney), Roxanne Hart (Sally Doneghy), James Handy (Kevin Doneghy)

p, Richard D. Zanuck, David Brown; d, Sidney Lumet; w, David Mamet (based on the novel by Barry Reed); ph, Andrzej Bartkowiak (Panavision, DeLuxe Color); ed, Peter C. Frank; m, Johnny Mandel; prod d, Edward Pisoni; art d, John Kasarda; cos, Anna Hill Johnstone

AAN Best Picture; AAN Best Actor: Paul Newman; AAN Best Supporting Actor: James Mason; AAN Best Director: Sidney Lumet; AAN Best Adapted Screenplay: David Mamet

This powerful study of a man's fight to regain his dignity features a fine performance from Paul Newman as failed attorney Frank Galvin. He takes on a seemingly open-and-shut case of malpractice, in which a woman lapsed into a coma while having a baby, the apparent victim of a mistake by an anesthesiologist at a prominent Catholic hospital in Boston. At first willing to take a settlement for the victim's family, Galvin realizes after visiting the comatose woman that he should put up a fight on her behalf. Up against the powerful Catholic establishment of Boston, he works to build a case, and, with it, renewed self-respect. He is also battling his dependence on alcohol, another reason behind his downfall. Newman's portrayal of his character is a sympathetic and totally candid performance. Every wart shows, from his alcoholism to the ill-prepared opening statement he delivers in a nervous stammer to the packed courtroom. Small moments come across as something special, and the actor received a well-deserved Oscar nomination for his performance. Sidney Lumet directs effectively, keeping the tension strong, and unfolding David Mamet's intelligent screenplay slowly but with maximum impact.

VERONIKA VOSS 📀
(DIE SEHNS UCHT DER VERONIKA VOSS)
1982   105m   bw   Drama   ★★★★
Rialto/Maran/Larua/Tango   (West Germany)   R

Rosel Zech (Veronika Voss), Hilmar Thate (Robert Krohn), Cornelia Froboess (Henriette), Annemarie Duringer (Dr. Katz), Doris Schade (Josefa), Erik Schumann (Dr. Edel), Peter Berling (Fat Film Producer), Gunther Kaufmann (G.I. Dealer), Sonja Neudorfer (Saleswoman), Lilo Pempeit (Her Boss)

p, Thomas Schuhly; d, Rainer Werner Fassbinder; w, Peter Marthesheimer, Pia Frohlich, Rainer Werner Fassbinder; ph, Xaver Schwarzenberger; ed, Juliane Lorenz; m, Peer Raben; prod d, Rolf Zehetbauer

At the very end of his amazing yet tragically short career, Fassbinder still gives us his Douglas Sirk-influenced view of the world, except this time colored with Billy Wilder's SUNSET BOULEVARD and Robert Aldrich's THE LEGEND OF LYLAH CLARE for good measure. The result, in typical Fassbinder fashion, is a visually incredible portrait of German corruption as well as the UFA star system and the loneliness of once-famous screen star Veronika Voss (Zech). The fading star is drawn into an affair with sportswriter Robert Krohn (Thate), who soon discovers the actress's dependency on drugs. Her doctor (Duringer) fuels her addiction, forcing Voss to turn over all of her personal property in exchange for more morphine. Krohn and his girlfriend bring the doctor to the attention of the authorities, unaware that they, too, are involved in the doctor's scheme. On Easter Sunday, Voss is locked in her room by the doctor. Suffering from withdrawal symptoms after being refused morphine, she is given enough sleeping pills to kill herself. Zech is quite remarkable at the film's close.

One of the most stylish of Fassbinder's many films, VERONIKA VOSS features dizzying camerawork and stark black-and-white photography. Not among Fassbinder's greatest achievements, this striking film is nonetheless a worthy companion piece to his earlier two films about postwar Germany, THE MARRIAGE OF MARIA BRAUN and LOLA. The actual story is loosely based on the life of Sybille Schmitz (VAMPYR, FERRYMAN MARIA) a gifted German film star who committed suicide in the mid-1950s, unable to cope with the loss of her celebrity.

VERTIGO 📀
1958   127m   c   Thriller   ★★★★★
Paramount   (U.S.)

James Stewart (John "Scottie" Ferguson), Kim Novak (Madeleine Elster/Judy Barton), Barbara Bel Geddes (Midge), Tom Helmore (Gavin Elster), Henry Jones (Coroner), Raymond Bailey (Doctor), Ellen Corby (Manageress), Konstantin Shayne (Pop Leibel), Lee Patrick (Older Mistaken Identity), Paul Bryar (Capt. Hansen)

p, Alfred Hitchcock; d, Alfred Hitchcock; w, Alec Coppel, Samuel Taylor (based on the novel D'Entre les Morts by Pierre Boileau and Thomas Narcejac); ph, Robert Burks (VistaVision, Technicolor); ed, George Tomasini; m, Bernard Herrmann; art d, Hal Pereira, Henry Bumstead; fx, John P. Fulton, Farciot Edouart, Wallace Kelly; cos, Edith Head

AAN Best Art Direction-Set Decoration: Hal Pereira, Henry Bumstead, Sam Comer, Frank McKelvy; AAN Best Sound: George Dutton

The most-discussed work of the master; despairingly sardonic and demanding of multiple viewings. Hitchcock's intensely personal and frighteningly self-revealing picture, VERTIGO is the story of a man (Stewart as Hitch) who is possessed by the image of a former love (Novak as Vera Miles) and becomes increasingly compulsive in his attempts to make another woman (Novak as Novak) over in that image. We'll explain.

Stewart is a former San Francisco policeman who suffers from vertigo—a dizzying sensation brought on by his acrophobia. When he gets a call from a former classmate, shipping magnate Gavin Elster (Helmore), he agrees to play detective and shadow the millionaire's wife Madeleine (Novak) whom Elster fears is going to wind up dead. Elster ominously asks him "Do you believe that someone dead, someone out of the past, can take possession of a living being?" After following Madeleine for a short while Stewart becomes obsessed with her—lost deep in a labyrinthine plot from which he cannot escape.

Based on a novel by Pierre Boileau and Thomas Narcejac (who previously supplied the source material for DIABOLIQUE), VERTIGO appealed to Hitchcock for reasons which become clearer the more one knows about the director's personality. VERTIGO is, in fact, nothing less than Hitchcock revealing himself to his audience—his obsessions and desire to make over women are embodied in Stewart's character and the perfect Hitchcock woman is embodied in Madeleine. VERTIGO is also a masterpiece of filmmaking which includes one of the most important technical discoveries since the dawn of cinema—the dolly-out, zoom-in shot, which visually represents the dizzying sensation of vertigo. The result is a shot unique to Hitchcock, unlike any other before in film, one which will always bear his stamp.

But more than that, the behind-the-scenes preparation of VERTIGO resembles the story itself. Hitchcock had directed Vera Miles in THE WRONG MAN, and stood poised to make her a star in VERTIGO. This would be, of course, according to Hitchcock tradition: the cool blonde, whose whorish carnality is hidden beneath sleekly understated clothes and simple hair. But his plan went awry when Miles married after filming was over and soon became pregnant ("I lost interest. I couldn't get the rhythm going with her again," said Hitchcock in an interview, but later he threw her a bone in PSYCHO). He convinced Novak to take the role; her somnambulistic quality made her very effective in the role, but he and Edith Head had hell convincing her to tone down.

Yet perhaps Novak is the unsung quintessential Hitchheroine. Hitchcock himself described Stewart's character's obsession with Novak's as a "form of necrophilia"; it's chilling when you think of the director re-creating his dreamgirl again and again. Novak's heroine is degraded by suffusing her own identity to become what men want her to be. Did she feel degraded when Hitchcock and Head tried to bury the established Novak? Did it make her feel like a cheap pawn, forced to impersonate a lady, that is in itself an impersonation, within the confines of an acting job (an impersonation anyway)? And how much of her real self—Marilyn Novik—had fused with the manufactured Kim Novak? The latter was a star persona placed in an impossible-to-please situation in the first place. Groomed as a successor to Hayworth and a threat to Monroe, it's small wonder Novak fled the film industry to hide in Big Sur. To examine her within the context of VERTIGO is another dizzying vortex—a virtual vertigo in itself.

VERY LONG ENGAGEMENT, A   DVD
(UN LONG DIMANCHE DE FIANCAILLES)
2004 133m c   Romance/War   ★★★½
2003 Productions/Warner Bros. France/Tapioca Films/   R
TF1 Films/Canal+

Audrey Tautou (Mathilde), Gaspard Ulliel (Manech), Ticky Holgado (Germain Prie), Jean-Pierre Becker (Lieutenant Esperanza), Dominique Bettenfeld (Ange Bassignano), Clovis Cornillac (Benoit Notre Dame), Marion Cotillard (Tina Lombardi), Jean-Pierre Darroussin (Benjamin Gordes), Chantal Neuwirth (Benedicte), Dominque Pinon (Sylvain)

d, Jean-Pierre Jeunet; w, Jean-Pierre Jeunet, Guillaume Laurant (from a story by Jean-Pierre Jeunet and Guillaume Laurant, based on the novel by Sebastien Japrisot); ph, Bruno Delbonnel; ed, Herve Schneid; m, Angelo Badalamenti; prod d, Aline Bonetto; fx, Yves Domenjoud, Olivier Gleyze; cos, Madeline Fontaine

AAN Best Art Direction: Aline Bonetto (art direction); AAN Best Cinematography: Bruno Delbonnel

French director Jean-Pierre Jeunet, who's best known for the dark-hued but dazzling images of films like DELICATESSEN and CITY OF LOST CHILDREN, finally balances style and substance with this visually stunning and emotionally resonant parable of love lost in the aftermath of a devastating war.

The Western Front, 1917: Five French soldiers, condemned to death for mutilating themselves in hopes of being sent home, are escorted to a front-line trench nicknamed the "Bingo Crepuscule" and, as dawn breaks, cruelly tossed into the no-man's-land separating the French and German troops. Three years later, Mathilde (Audrey Tautou), a young woman whom childhood polio left with a limp, still has trouble believing her lover, Manech (Gaspard Ulliel), was killed that terrible morning. Raised on the Breton coast by her aunt and uncle (Chantal Neuwirth, Dominique Pinon) close to the lighthouse where Manech once helped his father guide boats to safety, Mathilde feels the deep emotional tie she always shared with Manech remains unbroken. Certain that he's alive somewhere, Mathilde sets about searching for the veterans of the "Bingo Crepuscule" to learn exactly what happened that morning. With just a box of the convicts' mementos, some highly confidential documents, and the help of a notorious private detective (Ticky Holgado) at her disposal, Mathilde goes looking for her lost lover.

Not since James Cameron's TITANIC have digital effects been used so convincingly to reconstruct a long-gone time and place, but there's nothing quaint about any of it. The war scenes are appropriately grisly, and a number of startling sequences reflect Jeunet's predilection for the bizarre. The film is a trifle too long for its rather slim mystery, but in the face of so much beauty and invention that's a small quibble.

VICTIM   DVD
1961   100m   bw   Crime   ★★★★
Parkway/Allied   (U.K.)

Dirk Bogarde (Melville Farr), Sylvia Syms (Laura Farr), Dennis Price (Calloway), Anthony Nicholls (Lord Fullbrook), Peter Copley (Paul Mandrake), Norman Bird (Harold Doe), Peter McEnery (Jack Barrett), Donald Churchill (Eddy Stone), Derren Nesbitt (Sandy Youth), John Barrie (Detective Inspector Harris)

p, Michael Relph; d, Basil Dearden; w, Janet Green, John McCormick; ph, Otto Heller; ed, John D. Guthridge; m, Philip Green; art d, Alex Vetchinsky

A powerful film that deals with homosexuality in England and the fact that most of the blackmail cases in that country were aimed against men trying to stay in the closet. In 1961, any homosexual acts were illegal and, while this film was hardly an overt plea to change the laws, it did have some impact; a few years later homosexuality was no longer punishable by time in jail. Bogarde, in one of the best roles of his career to date, plays Melville Farr, a closeted lawyer aware of his own homosexual desires. He is married now to Laura (Syms), who knows about his past affairs but accepts him nonetheless. Some years before, Farr had an affair with construction worker Jack Barrett (McEnery) but denies it. Barrett is now a wanted man, having stolen money from his building company. When he's caught by the police, the truth emerges that Barrett doesn't have a brass farthing to his name. Since a great deal of money had been purloined, this sets the law to wondering where it all went. Barrett needs a lawyer and tries to contact Farr, but the eminent queen's counsel avoids him. When Barrett hangs himself rather than answer any police questions, Farr realizes that his former lover was being blackmailed and that Barrett was trying to protect Farr's good name. The blackmailers are extracting money from several people, including a barber, an actor, a used car salesman and a photographer. (The film earnestly tries to avoid stereotyping, though to some extent these "victims" do represent a variety of "types.") Although it may damage both his career and his marriage, Farr decides to go after the blackmailers and prosecute them himself.

Immensely significant in its plea for tolerance for gay men (interestingly, lesbianism is not discussed here), VICTIM works hard arguing that gays are part of the typical, healthy fabric of society. For that alone, it was highly controversial and was refused the Seal of the Motion Picture Association of America. On its own terms, the film works quite well. The drama is exciting, the writing cogent, the acting often superb and the production and direction by the team of Dearden and Relph quite fine. Every role, no matter how small, is very intelligently cast and even the blackmailers were given some depth and character contradictions. In acting terms, the film quite properly belongs to the dynamic yet sensitive Bogarde, but McEnery, as his former lover, and Price, as a blackmailed actor, also stand out. The film does, of course, shy away from certain aspects of its provocative subject matter, and a great deal of emphasis is laid on Farr's heterosexual relations with his wife. (It probably takes up more footage than is actually necessary, but this subplot broadens the role of Farr and is fairly well handled.) A liberal film on the subject of homosexuality rather than the radical film some considered it at the time, VICTIM still stands as an intelligent film attempting to address an important social issue.

VICTOR/VICTORIA

DVD

1982   133m   c   Musical/Comedy   ★★★½

Peerford/Arista/Ladbroke/Blake Edwards   PG

Entertainment   (U.K.)

Julie Andrews *(Victoria Grant/Count Victor Grazinski)*, James Garner *(King Marchan)*, Robert Preston *(Carroll "Toddy" Todd)*, Lesley Ann Warren *(Norma)*, Alex Karras *(Squash)*, John Rhys-Davies *(Andre Cassell)*, Graham Stark *(Waiter)*, Peter Arne *(Labisse)*, Sherloque Tanney *(Bovin—the Detective)*, Michael Robbins *(Hotel Manager)*

p, Blake Edwards, Tony Adams; d, Blake Edwards; w, Blake Edwards (based on the film VICTOR UND VIKTORIA by Rheinhold Schuenzel, Hans Hoemburg); ph, Dick Bush (Panavision); ed, Ralph E. Winters; m, Henry Mancini; prod d, Rodger Maus; art d, Tim Hutchinson, William Craig Smith; chor, Paddy Stone; cos, Patricia Norris

AAN Best Actress: Julie Andrews; *AAN Best Supporting Actor:* Robert Preston; *AAN Best Supporting Actress:* Lesley Ann Warren; *AAN Best Adapted Screenplay:* Blake Edwards; *AA Best Song Score:* Henry Mancini, Leslie Bricusse; *AAN Best Art Direction-Set Decoration:* Rodger Maus, Tim Hutchinson, William Craig Smith, Harry Cordwell; *AAN Best Costume Design:* Patricia Norris

A musical boudoir farce, captivating at times, infuriating at others. A British singer (Julie Andrews) and an aging homosexual (Robert Preston) are down-and-out nightclub performers in Paris. Hungry and broke, they're desperate for employment until Toddy (Preston) recasts his friend as the female impersonator singer-dancer Victor/Victoria—putting the chanteuse in the unusual position of being a woman who pretends to be a man who performs as a woman onstage. She is an immediate hit at a local nightclub, where King (James Garner), a gangster from Chicago traveling with his blowsy girlfriend (a Jean Harlowesque Lesley Ann Warren) and his bodyguard, Squash (Alex Karras), sees her perform. King is attracted to Victor/Victoria, but thinks, like everyone else, that she is a transvestite. The burly Squash, meanwhile, watches in amazement as his macho boss apparently loses his yen for beautiful women and becomes attracted to his own kind.

Edwards' film forces audiences to examine their own ideas about gender and sexuality, and that's great. But Andrews, despite looking very Berlin Bowie in her tux, is so safe and sane, she brings no madness of her own to the farce. Everything therefore swirls around a still center—in the film's one good number, "Le Jazz Hot," she climbs a staircase like she has weights on her feet. Nor can she summon any of the impersonator's hauteur or joy to her masquerade. Robert Preston is wonderful—he plays a cliché with such malice and relish, he revitalizes it, and Garner is successful kidding his own past macho image. A platinumed Warren is also quite good, but Edwards makes her dopey sweetness go sour—he humiliates her, especially in a chorus line number that could make a feminist a raging virago. Will someone please give Warren a role worthy of her undeniable talent? The film's best moments are early on: Andrews warbling for disinterested cabaret owners, or the preparation of Victoria to become Victor. After that, this becomes increasingly coarse and overstated. Edwards directs like a grizzly bear whipping up a souffle. The screenplay was based on VIKTOR UND VIKTORIA, a 1933 German film, first refashioned in 1935 into a star vehicle for the ever-delightful Jessie Mathews, FIRST A GIRL.

VICTORIA THE GREAT

1937   110m   c/bw Biography/Historical   ★★★★

Imperator   (U.K.)

Anna Neagle *(Queen Victoria)*, Anton Walbrook *(Prince Albert)*, Walter Rilla *(Prince Ernest)*, Mary Morris *(Duchess of Kent)*, H.B.
Warner *(Lord Melbourne)*, Grete Wegener *(Baroness Lehzen)*, C.V. France *(Archbishop of Canterbury)*, James Dale *(Duke of Wellington)*, Charles Carson *(Sir Robert Peel)*, Hubert Harben *(Lord Conyngham)*

p, Herbert Wilcox; d, Herbert Wilcox; w, Miles Malleson, Charles de Grandcourt (based on the play "Victoria Regina" by Laurence Housman); ph, Freddie Young; m, Anthony Collins

This beautiful and elaborate film gives an intimate portrait of England's long-reigning monarch, following her from the first years of her reign to the celebration of her Diamond Jubilee. Neagle is excellent as Victoria, who assumes the throne at the age of 18. The film details her courtship and marriage to Prince Albert (Walbrook), and a foiled attempt on the queen's life, thwarted when Albert risks death himself to shield Victoria from the would-be assassin. The story then concentrates on the royal couple's domestic life, with such figures as Disraeli, Wellington, and Lincoln introduced peripherally. Closing with the Jubilee, the film switches from black and white to a brilliant Technicolor.

Fictionalizing the lives of the royal family has long been a touchy issue in England, but producer-director Wilcox treats his subject respectfully, avoiding treacly sentiment. Neagle (who would later marry Wilcox) is completely believable as she takes her character from young girl to octogenarian, and is a marvel to watch as she transcends her craft and becomes the character. Released 100 years after Victoria began her reign, the film was enormously popular in England, prompting Wilcox, Neagle, and Walbrook to make a sequel, SIXTY GLORIOUS YEARS (1938), an all-color production that concentrated more on the political events of Victoria's rule. In 1942, Wilcox cut the first portion of VICTORIA THE GREAT into the latter half of SIXTY GLORIOUS YEARS to create a single feature, simply titled QUEEN VICTORIA.

Wilcox began production on VICTORIA THE GREAT after Edward VIII (who later abdicated to marry American divorcee Wallis Warfield Simpson) personally requested that the filmmaker produce a feature about the queen. It took an amazingly short five weeks to film. Attention to period detail was immaculate; Neagle's costumes were copied from Victoria's actual dresses, which were kept at the British Museum. Released in America through RKO, VICTORIA THE GREAT was popular in its initial run at Radio City Music Hall, where it turned a handsome profit, but it did not fare as well in smaller cities. Both Neagle and Wilcox toured the U.S. to promote the film, though this too was not as successful as its backers hoped. However, Wilcox's association with RKO did result in a lucrative agreement with the studio, under which the independent producer was to turn out a number of features under the American company's banner, an arrangement that helped reduce the burden of the United Kingdom's restrictive quotas on domestic screenings of imported films. VICTORIA THE GREAT also features Paul Henreid in his first British film, appearing in a small role under his real name.

VIDEODROME

DVD

1983   88m   c   Horror   ★★★½

Filmplan   (Canada)   R

James Woods *(Max Renn)*, Sonja Smits *(Bianca O'Blivion)*, Deborah Harry *(Nicki Brand)*, Peter Dvorsky *(Harlan)*, Les Carlson *(Barry Convex)*, Jack Creley *(Prof. Brian O'Blivion)*, Lynne Gorman *(Masha)*, Julie Khaner *(Briley)*, Reiner Schwarz *(Moses)*, David Bolt *(Rafe)*

p, Claude Heroux; d, David Cronenberg; w, David Cronenberg; ph, Mark Irwin; ed, Ronald Sanders; m, Howard Shore; prod d, Carol Spier; art d, Nick Kosonic; fx, Frank Carere, Rick Baker, Michael Lennick; chor, Kirsteen Etherington; cos, Delphine White

Director David Cronenberg's most visionary and audacious film up to the time of its making, VIDEODROME is a fascinating rumination on humanity, technology, entertainment, sex, and politics that is virtually incomprehensible on first viewing and needs to be seen several times before one can even begin to unlock its mysteries. James Woods, in one of the best performances of his career, stars as Max Renn, an ambitious cable television programmer who, in his off hours, is a closet voyeur of sex and violence. Looking for something new, something "sensational" for his cable station, Renn stumbles across a show called "Videodrome" while pirating signals from satellite dishes. The show seems to depict the actual torture and murder of a different victim every night. Fascinated and excited by the program, Renn tries to find out where the show originates. During the investigation, he becomes deeply embroiled in a bizarre, intriguing, and sometimes incomprehensible fusion of television, politics, and mind-control that seems to herald some sort of "new order" for society.

VIDEODROME very well may be the most incomprehensible mainstream film ever made. As Cronenberg's narrative veers from hallucination to reality and back again—the line between them more blurred each time—he unleashes his bizarre visual imagination, bombarding viewers with such sights as an open stomach cavity that becomes a repository for videocassettes and guns, throbbing television sets, a literal hand-gun, and humans who crack open and spew forth all manner of flesh, blood, and multicolored goo. While these images are undeniably powerful (the throbbing, living television set is amazing) and the film is compulsively watchable, it does tend to become wholly impenetrable toward the end and may leave the uninitiated frustrated or even angry. Nevertheless, this is a remarkable film that will continue to be debated and analyzed for decades to come.

VILLAGE, THE   𝐃𝐕𝐃
2004   107m   c   Horror   ★★
Touchstone Pictures/Blinding Edge Pictures   (U.S.)   PG-13

Joaquin Phoenix *(Lucius Hunt)*, Bryce Dallas Howard *(Ivy Walker)*, Adrien Brody *(Noah Percy)*, William Hurt *(Edward Walker)*, Sigourney Weaver *(Alice Hunt)*, Brendan Gleeson *(August Nicholson)*, Cherry Jones *(Mrs. Clack)*, Celia Weston *(Vivian Percy)*, Judy Greer *(Kitty Walker)*, John Christopher Jones *(Robert Percy)*

p, Sam Mercer, Scott Rudin, M. Night Shyamalan; d, M. Night Shyamalan; w, M. Night Shyamalan; ph, Roger Deakins; ed, Christopher Tellefsen; m, James Newton Howard; prod d, Tom Foden; art d, Michael Manson; fx, Steve Cremin, Syd Dutton, Crash McCreery (creature designer), Bill Taylor; chor, Lynne Hockney; cos, Ann Roth

AAN Best Original Score: James Newton Howard

M. Night Shyamalan's portentous period thriller wrings some efficient thrills from clichéd elements but collapses under the weight of a labored and unsatisfying ending.

The close-knit farming settlement of Covington Woods, Pennsylvania, embraces a simple way of life. Having rejected the corruption of "The Towns," they take their meals together, abide by the decisions of the village elders, and support each other in times of sorrow and loss. But a shadow hangs over their apparently idyllic existence: The deep, dark woods are alive with mysterious creatures so terrible they're called only "those we don't speak of" in hushed, frightened tones. For years now, the creatures have stayed in the woods and left the villagers to their business. Flighty Kitty Walker (Judy Greer) falls in and out of love with every handsome boy in town, including quiet Lucius Hunt (Joaquin Phoenix). Lucius favors Kitty's blind, tomboyish sister, Ivy (Bryce Dallas Howard), but is too shy to say so. Lucius's mother, Alice (Sigourney

Weaver), and Ivy and Kitty's father, Edward (William Hurt), guide the committee of elders; August Nicholson (Brendan Gleeson) mourns his young son's death; village idiot Noah Percy (Adrien Brody) cuts capers. Then something upsets the delicately balanced truce between the villagers and the inhabitants of the woods, and the horror begins.

If THE SIXTH SENSE was 90 minutes of gloom with a nifty parlor trick at the end, this film dispenses with the parlor trick. There's a twist, but it's dumb and a cheat as well. A crucial scrap of information in the film's first scene is a lie. Shyamalan is great at justifying—there are explanations for all the film's oddities—but having an answer for everything isn't the same as constructing a fundamentally satisfying narrative.

VILLAGE OF THE DAMNED   𝐃𝐕𝐃
1960   77m   bw   Horror/Science Fiction   ★★★
MGM   (U.K.)

George Sanders *(Gordon Zellaby)*, Barbara Shelley *(Anthea Zellaby)*, Michael Gwynn *(Maj. Alan Bernard)*, Laurence Naismith *(Dr. Willers)*, John Phillips *(Gen. Leighton)*, Richard Vernon *(Sir Edgar Hargraves)*, Jenny Laird *(Mrs. Harrington)*, Richard Warner *(Mr. Harrington)*, Thomas Heathcote *(James Pawle)*, Alexander Archdale *(Coroner)*

p, Ronald Kinnoch; d, Wolf Rilla; w, Wolf Rilla, Stirling Silliphant, George Barclay (based on the novel *The Midwich Cuckoos* by John Wyndham); ph, Geoffrey Faithfull (Metroscope); ed, Gordon Hales; m, Ron Goodwin; art d, Ivan King; fx, Tom Howard

A very frightening adaptation of the John Wyndham novel about a small English village that becomes the victim of unfriendly aliens. During a 24-hour period all the inhabitants of Midwich are put to sleep, waking to find a dozen of the women pregnant. When these babies are born, their mothers love them as if they were conceived under normal circumstances. However, all of these children look the same, with bright blond hair. The are also possessed of superior intelligence and telekinetic powers. Sanders, a physicist and the husband of Shelley, who has given birth to the leader of the children, undertakes the job of educating these youngsters and soon discovers that their mission is not a friendly one: they plan to take control of the entire planet. Sanders then sees that the children are destroyed, killing himself in the process. Sanders' role required more outward emotion than he had in his repertoire, but this casting mistake is more than compensated for by the weird atmosphere provided by the children. Made in England for less than $300,000, the picture grossed more than $1.5 million in initial release in the U.S. and Canada alone. It spawned a host of possessed-children-as-villains films, including THE OMEN and THE BOYS FROM BRAZIL. This intriguing story also gave rise to a sequel, CHILDREN OF THE DAMNED, which proved every bit as good as the original.

VINCENT AND THEO   𝐃𝐕𝐃
1990   138m   c   Biography   ★★★★
Belbo/Central/La Sept/Telepool/RAI Uno/   R
Vara/Sofica Valor   (U.K./France/U.S.)

Tim Roth *(Vincent van Gogh)*, Paul Rhys *(Theodore van Gogh)*, Jip Wijngaarden *(Sien Hoornik)*, Johanna Ter Steege *(Jo Bonger)*, Wladimir Yordanoff *(Paul Gauguin)*, Jean-Pierre Cassel *(Dr. Paul Gachet)*, Bernadette Giraud *(Marguerite Gachet)*, Adrian Brine *(Uncle Cent)*, Jean-Francois Perrier *(Leon Bouscod)*, Vincent Vallier *(Rene Valadon)*

p, Ludi Boeken; d, Robert Altman; w, Julian Mitchell; ph, Jean Lepine (Eastmancolor); ed, Francois Coispeau, Geraldine Peroni; m, Gabriel Yared; prod d, Stephen Altman; art d, Dominique Douret, Ben Van, Jan Roelfs; cos, Scott Bushnell

Altman tackles the monumental story of Vincent van Gogh and his brother Theo and, for the most part, comes up a winner. Working from a minimalist script by Julian Mitchell, the director offers us a stripped-to-the-bones drama that leaves most screen takes on the artistic life—from the Hollywood bombast of LUST FOR LIFE to the self-conscious quirkiness of Derek Jarman's CARAVAGGIO—way behind.

The film's beginning is the director's most audacious conceit. We see actual footage of the painting "Sunflowers" as it is being auctioned off at Christie's, and Altman, one of the keenest users of sound in all cinema, sustains the soundtrack of the bidding during his opening scene between Vincent and Theo. As the brothers argue over the money their rich uncle sends each month to Vincent to sustain his creative, if uncommercial, journey, the point is clearly made about the often arbitrary elusiveness of artistic success. Familiar ground is subsequently covered, including Vincent's fascination with prostitutes and Theo's syphilitic torment. The story continues through Vincent's uneasy friendship with Gauguin, his encroaching mental instability, Theo's personal financial struggles as a gallery owner, and his troubled courtship and marriage to Jo Bonger (Ter Steege). The fate of the two troubled brothers resolves the action.

As photographed by Jean Lepine, the film is visually stunning. VINCENT AND THEO is brimful of the pictorial splendors of nature and the human form, but they are captured fleetingly, in an off-the-cuff kind of way that suggests the finely attuned peripheral vision, the febrile antennae, of an artist. The early scene of Vincent observing and rapidly sketching the whore as she takes a break from posing, stretches, looks through the window at the moon, and even relieves herself, comes as close to depicting the actual creative process of painting as anything ever filmed. The creation of the sunflower paintings is aptly expressed in the silent, sketchy takes of him out in the fields, experiencing quick frustration more than anything else, with the end result a terse, panning shot of his room in Arles, filled with his finished efforts glowing from the walls.

VIRGIN SPRING, THE

(JUNGFRUKALLAN)
1959 88m bw Drama ★★★½
Svensk (Sweden)

Max von Sydow (Herr Tore), Brigitta Pettersson (Karin Tore), Birgitta Valberg (Mareta Tore), Gunnel Lindblom (Ingeri), Axel Duberg (Thin Herdsman), Tor Isedal (Mute Herdsman), Ove Porath (Boy), Allan Edwall (Beggar), Gudrun Brost (Frida), Oscar Ljung (Simon)

p, Ingmar Bergman, Allan Ekelund; d, Ingmar Bergman; w, Ulla Isaksson (based on the 14th-century ballad "Tores Dotter I Vange"); ph, Sven Nykvist, Rolf Halmquist; ed, Oscar Rosander; m, Erik Nordgren; art d, P.A. Lundgren; cos, Marik Vos

AA Best Foreign Language Film ; AAN Best Costume Design (B/W): Marik Vos

The Best Foreign-Language Film Oscar awarded to THE VIRGIN SPRING was director Ingmar Bergman's first Academy Award, and the film still numbers among the director's classics. The story takes place in 13th-century Sweden, as Christianity and folklore vie for dominance in the popular belief. Karin (Birgitta Pettersson), the spoiled young virgin daughter of wealthy landowner Tore (Max von Sydow), is to go to church to light candles for the Virgin, and is allowed to wear a special gown, handmade by 15 virgins, on the occasion. Riding in the woods, Karin is raped, and then killed, by shepherds. The men take her gown, hoping to sell it, and move on, arriving at Tore's house, where they receive food and shelter. Their crime is discovered, however, moving Tore to enact

bloody revenge and testing the bereaved father's faith. THE VIRGIN SPRING is based on a medieval ballad, and is full of the folk-tale oppositions (a good sister and a bad one) and motifs (the tell-tale gown, the trio of shepherds) so beloved by Bergman (the film is also true to its origins in its extreme violence). As always, those with little affinity for Bergman's preoccupations will find the film overlong and overdone. Most, however, will be rewarded by the depth of the director's moral and religious questioning, the emotional power of the story and acting, the haunting and symbolic imagery, and the excellent black-and-white photography of Sven Nykvist. Nominated by the Academy for Best Costume Design.

VIRGIN SUICIDES, THE

2000 97m c Drama ★★★½
American Zoetrope/Muse/Eternity/Illusion (U.S.) R

James Woods (Mr. Lisbon), Kathleen Turner (Mrs. Lisbon), Kirsten Dunst (Lux Lisbon), Josh Hartnett (Trip Fontaine), Hanna Hall (Cecilia Lisbon), Chelse Swain (Bonnie Lisbon), A.J. Cooke (Mary Lisbon), Leslie Hayman (Therese Lisbon), Danny DeVito (Dr. Horniker), Michael Pare (Trip Fontaine '97)

p, Francis Ford Coppola, Julie Costanzo, Dan Halsted, Chris Hanley; d, Sofia Coppola; w, Sofia Coppola (based on the novel The Virgin Suicides by Jeffrey Eugenides); ph, Edward Lachman; ed, James Lyons, Melissa Kent; m, Nicholas Godin, Jean Benoit Dunkel; prod d, Jasna Stefanovic; art d, Jon P. Goulding; cos, Nancy Steiner

Sofia Coppola's visually expressive directorial debut does not quite nail the leering, voyeuristic quality that made Jeffrey Eugenides' novel such an unsettling read, but she has transformed the material into something intriguingly eerie: a morbid teen movie for melancholy adults.

It's the mid-1970s, and over the course of a single year in tony Grosse Point, Michigan, all five teenage daughters of the Lisbons (James Woods and Kathleen Turner) will meet a tragic end. Smiling, golden-blond, and entirely inaccessible, the Lisbon girls are the stuff of which teenage dreams—and, sometimes, lifelong obsessions—are made. The first to die is the youngest (Hanna Hall), who throws herself out of an upper-story window during a party. The girls are then put under house arrest by their desperate parents—a move prompted in large part by the aggressive sexuality of Lux (Kirsten Dunst)—and it all ends in an utterly baffling tragedy.

Contrary to the expectations of cynics who still blame Coppola for ruining THE GODFATHER, PART III, this film is quite an achievement, and it didn't direct itself. Coppola wisely treats the sad fate of the Lisbon girls as more than a conventional mystery; her film is *about* mystery, specifically the mystery of adolescent girls in the eyes of adolescent boys. And if she mistakenly reads the creepy tone of the book's first-person-plural narrator as wistful nostalgia, other details are close to perfect. Heart, ELO, and Todd Rundgren feature prominently on the soundtrack, the costume design is hideously accurate, and the production design—guided by Bill Owens's celebrated photos of suburbia—offers a frightening vision of domestic hell: flocked wallpaper, sectional sofas, and brown paneled rec rooms.

VIRGINIAN, THE

1929 92m bw Western ★★★½
Famous Players/Paramount (U.S.)

Gary Cooper (The Virginian), Walter Huston (Trampas), Mary Brian (Molly Stark Wood), Richard Arlen (Steve), Helen Ware ("Ma" Taylor), Chester Conklin (Uncle Hughey), Eugene Pallette ("Honey" Wiggin), Victor Potel (Nebraskey), E.H. Calvert (Judge Henry), Tex Young (Shorty)

p, Louis D. Lighton; d, Victor Fleming; w, Howard Estabrook, Edward E. Paramore, Grover Jones, Keene Thompson (based on the play by Owen Wister, Kirk La Shelle, and the novel by Owen Wister); ph, J. Roy Hunt, Edward Cronjager; ed, William Shea

Gary Cooper's first all-talkie, this film adaptation of Owen Wister's popular novel established Cooper's heroic image in the public eye. As the title character, Cooper is foreman of a Wyoming ranch. He gives a job to an old friend, Richard Arlen, with whom he is vying for the affections of school-marm Mary Brian. Cooper wins out and Arlen goes bad, taking up with local villain Walter Huston to rustle cattle from Cooper's herd. Cooper catches his friend changing brands and warns him, but when Arlen is later caught stealing cattle again, along with two other rustlers, Cooper oversees the lynching of all three. Plagued by guilt, Cooper swears to get Huston, whom he knows to be the leader of the gang. When Brian finds out what Cooper has done, she rejects him. Later, though, in a skirmish with Huston, Cooper is wounded and Brian takes care of him, eventually agreeing to marry him. On their wedding day, Huston brings matters to a head, and the two men square off in the street for a showdown. Cooper is faster on the draw and Huston dies in the dust. The bit for which this film is most remembered occurs during a card game, when Huston calls Cooper an insulting name. Cooper pulls his gun out, lays it on the table and says, "If you want to call me that, smile." The phrase caught on immediately and was used extensively in advertising for the film. Cooper played his role well, and his performance helped him escape the typecasting he had been saddled with. Now he could play rugged male leads instead of juvenile lovers. Huston is even better, his Trampas the essence of western villainy and the standard to be imitated for years to come. This was the third film of the novel, which had previously been done in 1921 starring Dustin Farnum, and in 1923 starring Kenneth Harlan. A major box-office success, it was remade in 1946 with Joel McCrea, and became a television series in 1962 starring James Drury in the title role.

VIRIDIANA

1961 90m bw Drama ★★★★★
Uninci/Films 59/Gustavo Alatriste (Mexico/Spain)

Silvia Pinal (Viridiana), Francisco Rabal (Jorge), Fernando Rey (Don Jaime), Margarita Lozano (Ramona), Victoria Zinny (Lucia), Teresa Rabal (Rita), Jose Calvo, Joaquin Roa, Luis Heredia, Jose Manuel Martin

p, Ricardo Munoz Suay; d, Luis Bunuel; w, Luis Bunuel, Julio Alejandro (based on a story by Bunuel); ed, Pedro del Rey; m, Wolfgang Amadeus Mozart, George Frederick Handel; art d, Francisco Canet

Luis Bunuel had been absent from his native land for 25 years when he was invited by the Franco government to produce a film in Spain. The result was VIRIDIANA. Ironically, it was never shown in Spanish theaters, having been banned by the Franco government immediately after its debut at the Cannes Film Festival, where it won the Golden Palm. Pinal plays the title role, a religious novitiate who visits her last remaining relative, the wealthy Don Jaime (Rey), before she takes her vows. Viridiana, firmly intent on resisting the corruption of her uncle's estate, is surprised to find him most gracious, kind, and gentle. He, however, is secretly obsessed with her resemblance to his wife, who died 30 years earlier on their wedding night. After Don Jaime attempts to ravish the nun-to-be, who has obliged the lonely man by putting on his wife's wedding gown, he feels such remorse that he commits suicide. Viridiana inherits the estate, along with Don Jaime's son Jorge (Rabal) and she intends to use her new position to benefit the local poor. Once again her virtuous intentions backfire. Oh, that final card game!

VIRIDIANA is filled with allegories concerning the general state of the world and Spain in particular, conveyed with the master surrealist's usual mix of black humor and stunning images. Foremost among them is the famous "Last Supper," in which a group of thoroughly degenerate beggars carouse drunkenly, in a visual parody of Da Vinci's painting, to the strains of Handel's "Messiah." You will *never* forget this moment. Viridiana, who wishes to redeem these miscreants through her idealism, is mocked in the process—as is the Catholicism that Bunuel believed had to be overthrown if Spain was to avoid becoming a decaying mess like Don Jaime's estate. Viridiana's ineffectual faith is contrasted with Jorge's more beneficial pragmatism. The changes he attempts to realize can perhaps do but minimal good, as indicated in one of Bunuel's most famous jokes: just after Jorge has rescued a dog that was being dragged mercilessly from a cart by buying it from its owner, the director shows another cur in the same predicament, attached to another cart coming from the opposite direction. Still, Jorge does represent a practical approach to achieving modest changes for the better. Immediately after the film was shot, it was shipped to Paris, where it was quickly edited in time for Cannes. Spanish authorities, who had not seen the final print before the festival screening, were shocked when it won the Golden Palm. Further scandal followed the film to Italy, where Bunuel was threatened with a prison sentence if he entered the country. Despite all this controversy, VIRIDIANA has a deceptively artless quality, stemming from the poetic formality with which Bunuel allows the picture to unfold. He steered away from complex and confusing images or camera movement, and created, along with THE EXTERMINATING ANGEL, one of the most magnificent films of his incredible career.

VITELLONI ⏵DVD

(I VITELLONI)
1953 103m bw Drama ★★★★
PEG/Cite (Italy/France)

Franco Interlenghi (Moraldo), Franco Fabrizi (Fausto), Alberto Sordi (Alberto), Leopoldo Trieste (Leopoldo), Riccardo Fellini (Riccardo), Leonora Ruffo (Sandra), Lida Baarova (Giulia), Arlette Sauvage (Woman in the Cinema), Maja Nipora (Actress), Jean Brochard (Father of Fausto)

p, Mario de Vecchi; d, Federico Fellini; w, Federico Fellini, Ennio Flaiano (based on the story by Fellini, Flaiano and Tullio Pinelli); ph, Otello Martelli, Luciano Trasatti, Carlo Carlini; ed, Rolando Benedetti; m, Nino Rota; art d, Mario Chiari

AAN Best Original Story and Screenplay: Federico Fellini, Ennio Flaiano, Tullio Pinelli

This semiautobiographical work by Federico Fellini was the first film to bring him a measure of world attention. As in AMARCORD (his film of nearly two decades later), the setting is the seaside town of Rimini, Fellini's birthplace. The plot follows the adventures of five youths who refuse to grow up and accept responsibility. Only one of the gang, Moraldo (Franco Interlenghi, the young boy from SHOESHINE) comes to understand that life in the small town is a relatively empty existence, while his friends are content to play meaningless games that lend momentary security but ultimately make them puppets to forces beyond their control. VITELLONI is filled with the cinematic excesses that were to clutter Fellini's later films, though here they seem much more insightful in describing the tribulations of adolescent rites of passage.

VIVA LAS VEGAS ⏵DVD

1964 85m c Musical ★★★½
MGM (U.S.)

Elvis Presley (Lucky Jackson), Ann-Margret (Rusty Martin), Cesare Danova (Count Elmo Mancini), William Demarest (Mr. Martin), Nicky Blair (Shorty Farnsworth), Jack Carter (Himself),

Robert B. Williams *(Swanson)*, Bob Nash *(Big Gus Olson)*, Roy Engel *(Baker)*, Barnaby Hale *(Mechanic)*

p, Jack Cummings, George Sidney; d, George Sidney; w, Sally Benson; ph, Joseph Biroc (Panavision, Metrocolor); ed, John McSweeney Jr.; m, George Stoll; art d, George W. Davis, Edward Carfagno; chor, David Winters; cos, Don Feld

Presley's one really good musical, mainly because it features a female costar, Ann-Margret, who can match the coiffed one in the charisma stakes. Elvis plays Lucky Jackson, a race-car driver who comes to Las Vegas to compete in the upcoming Grand Prix against his arch-rival, Count Elmo Cancini (Cesare Danova). To earn money for a new engine, Presley takes a job as a waiter at a casino, romancing swimming teacher Rusty Martin (Ann-Margret) and singing songs in his spare time before the race. They include: "The Lady Loves Me" (Sid Tepper, Roy C. Bennett); "Viva Las Vegas," "I Need Somebody to Lean On," (Doc Pomus); "What'd I Say" (Ray Charles); "Come On, Everybody" (Stanley Chinese); "Today, Tomorrow and Forever" (Bill Giant, Bernie Baum, Florence Kaye); "If You Think I Don't Need You" (Bob "Red" West); "Appreciation," "My Rival" (Marvin More, Bernie Wayne); "The Climb," "The Yellow Rose of Texas" (Don George); and "The Eyes of Texas Are upon You."

VIVA VILLA!

1934   115m   bw   Biography   ★★★★
MGM   (U.S.)

Wallace Beery *(Pancho Villa)*, Fay Wray *(Teresa)*, Stuart Erwin *(Johnny Sykes)*, Leo Carrillo *(Sierra)*, Donald Cook *(Don Felipe)*, George E. Stone *(Chavito)*, Joseph Schildkraut *(Gen. Pascal)*, Henry B. Walthall *(Madero)*, Katherine DeMille *(Rosita)*, David Durand *(Bugle Boy)*

p, David O. Selznick; d, Howard Hawks (uncredited), Jack Conway; w, Ben Hecht (based on the book by Edgecumb Pinchon, O.B. Stade); ph, James Wong Howe; ed, Robert J. Kern; m, Herbert Stothart; art d, Harry Oliver; cos, Dolly Tree

AA Best Assistant Director: John Waters; *AAN Best Picture; AAN Best Writing (Adaptation):* Ben Hecht; *AAN Best Sound Recording:* Douglas Shearer

The life of the famous Mexican bandit and revolutionary is told in this exciting action drama. The film opens as young Pancho Villa (Phillip Cooper) watches his father whipped to death by a soldier for some minor offense. Soon afterward, the boy murders the soldier and takes to the hills where he grows into adulthood and gathers a band of followers who join him in pillaging the homes of the rich and giving part of the proceeds to the poor. On one of these raids, Villa (played as an adult by Wallace Beery) meets an American reporter (Stuart Erwin), and the two become close friends. Later he meets a wealthy landowner (Donald Cook) and his sister (Fay Wray), who are sympathetic to Beery and his goals. They introduce the bandit to the intellectual head (Henry Walthall) of the peasant revolt which is starting to gather strength. Walthall persuades Beery to add his forces to the peasant army as its fighting core. Soon a renegade general (Joseph Schildkraut) joins the rebels with his men, and the resulting body soon sweeps through Mexico to victory. The president resigns and Walthall is named in his place. Beery's army is disbanded and he is sent home to his ranch. When Beery takes up bank robbery and kills a teller in the process, Schildkraut seizes the opportunity to eliminate his closest rival and orders him executed for murder. Walthall pardons Beery on the condition that he leave the country. Schildkraut then murders Walthall and seizes power for himself. Beery returns and reactivates his army, but without the guiding intelligence of Walthall, Beery and his men run wild, robbing and killing almost at random. Cook and Wray refuse to support Beery. He attacks Wray, and when she shoots him in the arm, he orders

her flogged. Later a stray bullet fired by one of Beery's men kills her. Beery's forces triumph over Schildkraut's, and, when the general is captured, Beery has him covered in honey and left out for the ants to eat. Beery takes over as president, but with his limited education the job is too much for him. He retires to his ranch once again. Some time later, he visits Mexico City and runs into his old friend Erwin. As they talk, they are spotted by Cook, who shoots the bandit to avenge his sister's death. The mortally wounded Beery feels that momentous last words are in order, so Erwin composes them for him.

Beery's performance as Villa is one of the highlights of his long and diverse career, and his portrayal of the man as equal parts child, crusader, peasant, and murderous bandito is near perfect. When finally completed, the film proved a huge success, earning stacks of money for MGM.

VIVA ZAPATA!

1952   113m   bw   Biography   ★★★★
Fox   (U.S.)

Marlon Brando *(Emiliano Zapata)*, Jean Peters *(Josefa Espejo)*, Anthony Quinn *(Eufemio Zapata)*, Joseph Wiseman *(Fernando Aguirre)*, Arnold Moss *(Don Nacio)*, Alan Reed *(Pancho Villa)*, Margo *(La Soldadera)*, Harold Gordon *(Don Francisco Madero)*, Lou Gilbert *(Pablo)*, Mildred Dunnock *(Senora Espejo)*

p, Darryl F. Zanuck; d, Elia Kazan; w, John Steinbeck (based on the novel *Zapata the Unconquered* by Edgcumb Pichon); ph, Joseph MacDonald; ed, Barbara McLean; m, Alex North; art d, Lyle Wheeler, Leland Fuller

AAN Best Actor: Marlon Brando; *AA Best Supporting Actor:* Anthony Quinn; *AAN Best Story and Screenplay:* John Steinbeck; *AAN Best Score (Drama or Comedy):* Alex North; *AAN Best Art Direction-Set Decoration (B/W):* Lyle Wheeler Leland Fuller, Thomas Little, Claude Carpenter

Great acting exercise, Tabascoed with Brando, peppered with Quinn, but otherwise Kazan/Steinbeck refried beans.

Kazan directs this exciting biography of the peasant who rose to be a revolutionary leader and President of his country with great relish, graphically capturing a bloody era of Mexican history, and Brando gives an electrifying performance. But the adventure lags, marred by pretentious brooding as the script strains to moralize about the corruptive influence of power.

Nor can Brando's acting justify the liberties taken. The real Emiliano Zapata was a small man with large, dark eyes and delicate hands—a tenant-farmer who finally rose up against the tyrannical rule of Porfirio Diaz, as did Pancho Villa in the north, and led an army to victory over Diaz. He waged his civil wars, 1911-19, not to conquer Mexico but to free the land for the peasants of Morelos and other southern provinces. Kazan presents a whitewashed version of the great leader; the historical Zapata was in reality barbaric and did not hesitate to execute his enemies en masse. Quinn is marvelous as the hard-riding, hard-drinking brother willing to die for passion. Frank Silvera as Huerta, Roope as Diaz, and Wiseman as the intense war-mongering journalist are startling villains, not far from their real-life counterparts in posture and character. Gilbert, who acts as Brando's intellectual conscience, is a bit too dramatic and unbelievable in some scenes. Gordon as Madero gives a realistic profile, but Peters and Margo are given little to do. Though he is on camera for only a few scenes, Reed, playing Pancho Villa, captures the brooding charisma of the revolutionary leader.

VON RYAN'S EXPRESS

1965   117m   c   War   ★★★½
P-R   (U.S.)

Frank Sinatra *(Col. Joseph L. Ryan)*, Trevor Howard *(Maj. Eric Fincham)*, Raffaella Carra *(Gabriella)*, Brad Dexter *(Sgt. Bostick)*,

Sergio Fantoni *(Capt. Oriani)*, John Leyton *(Orde)*, Edward Mulhare *(Constanzo)*, Wolfgang Preiss *(Maj. von Klemment)*, James Brolin *(Pvt. Ames)*, John Van Dreelen *(Col. Gortz)*

p, Saul David; d, Mark Robson; w, Wendell Mayes, Joseph Landon (based on the novel by David Westheimer); ph, William Daniels (CinemaScope, Deluxe Color); ed, Dorothy Spencer; m, Jerry Goldsmith; art d, Jack Martin Smith

AAN Best Sound Effects: Walter A. Rossi

Frank Sinatra stars in this implausible but relatively engaging WWII POW escape film, playing Col. Joseph Ryan, a downed U.S. Army Air Corps pilot who leads 600 British and American prisoners in a dramatic escape through Italy aboard a commandeered train. Aided by some of their Italian jailers, who are anxious to jump sides as the 1943 Allied invasion gets under way, the POWs take over a train and, with some of their number masquerading as Germans guards, set off for neutral Switzerland. Initially called "von Ryan" by the other prisoners, who thought him too accommodating to the enemy, the American colonel proves his courage over and over again as the train makes its way to freedom, fending off attacking Messerschmitts and narrowly escaping a pursuing German troop train. Sinatra is convincing as the gutsy American officer who engineers the escape, and Trevor Howard gives a strong performance as the British major Sinatra replaces as ranking prisoner, but there isn't much else that's believable in VON RYAN'S EXPRESS. Nonetheless, Mark Robson's film is packed with action and occasionally technically impressive, especially in the duel between the train and the German planes that attack it in the mountains of northern Italy. If it's realism you're after, look elsewhere; but if you enjoy straightforward wartime thrills (or films with particularly stupid German soldiers), VON RYAN'S EXPRESS is just the ticket.

W

WAG THE DOG

1997 105m c Comedy ★★½
Tribeca Productions/Punch Productions/ R
Baltimore Pictures/New Line (U.S.)

Dustin Hoffman *(Stanley Motss)*, Robert De Niro *(Conrad Brean)*, Anne Heche *(Winifred Ames)*, Denis Leary *(Fad King)*, Willie Nelson *(Johnny Green)*, Andrea Martin *(Liz Butsky)*, Kirsten Dunst *(Tracy Lime)*, William H. Macy *(Mr. Young)*, Craig T. Nelson *(Senator Neal)*, Suzie Plakson *(Suzie Plakson)*

p, Jane Rosenthal, Robert De Niro, Barry Levinson; d, Barry Levinson; w, Hilary Henkin, David Mamet (based on the novel *American Hero* by Larry Beinhart); ph, Robert Richardson; ed, Stu Linder; m, Mark Knopfler; prod d, Wynn Thomas; art d, Mark Worthington; fx, Dennis King; cos, Rita Ryack

AAN Best Actor: Dustin Hoffman; *AAN Best Adapted Screenplay:* Hilary Henkin, David Mamet

This dark political satire from director Barry Levinson is an effective, if somewhat uneven, statement on the easy manipulation of public opinion.

Less than two weeks before the presidential election, the president of the United States is caught in a sex scandal with an underage girl, and political "Mr. Fix-It" Conrad Brean (Robert De Niro) is called in by the president's aide (Anne

Heche) to repair the damage. Brean decides to manufacture a war with Albania—no real battles, just enough fake television coverage to divert the public's attention away from the president's indiscretions. He enlists the aid of Hollywood film producer Stanley Motss (Dustin Hoffman), who accepts the challenge. Motss assembles a crack creative team, including a songwriter (Willie Nelson) to come up with a suitably jingoistic theme song, and the "fad king" (Denis Leary) to arrange the merchandise tie-ins. Instantly, the war becomes front-page news, with the sex scandal all but forgotten.

Filmed "commando-style" by Levinson while production of his sci-fi flick SPHERE was in a stall, WAG THE DOG is a biting satire of modern politics that became embarrassingly topical. (The film was released while President Bill Clinton was mired in dual controversies over alleged sexual liaisons with Paula Jones and White House intern Monica Lewinsky.) Thanks to a canny script by Hilary Henkin and David Mamet, and the wonderful onscreen chemistry between De Niro and Hoffman, the film is at its best when it's just Brean and Motss discussing just how similar the jobs of Washington spin doctor and Hollywood producer really are. However, about two-thirds into the film, WAG THE DOG begins to lose steam, and by the end, it all but coasts to a stop.

WAGES OF FEAR, THE 〔DVD〕

(LE SALAIRE DE LA PEUR)
1952 140m bw Adventure ★★★★½
Filmsonor/CICC/Vera/Fono Roma (France/Italy)

Yves Montand *(Mario)*, Charles Vanel *(Jo)*, Vera Clouzot *(Linda)*, Folco Lulli *(Luigi)*, Peter Van Eyck *(Bimba)*, William Tubbs *(Bill O'Brien)*, Dario Moreno *(Hernandez)*, Jo Dest *(Smerloff)*, Antonio Centa *(Camp Chief)*, Luis de Lima *(Bernardo)*

p, Henri-Georges Clouzot; d, Henri-Georges Clouzot; w, Henri-Georges Clouzot, Jerome Geronimi (based on the novel by Georges Arnaud); ph, Armand Thirard; ed, Henri Rust, Madeleine Gug, Etiennette Muse; m, Georges Auric; prod d, Rene Renoux

Excellent, but nasty stuff. When the powerful oil company that controls the poverty-stricken Central American village of Las Piedras is faced with a well-fire disaster 300 miles away, they call for drivers to haul a load of highly volatile nitroglycerine across the dangerous terrain to the disaster site. After the driving skills of the applicants are tested, four men are chosen—Mario (Yves Montand), a French-raised Corsican; Luigi (Folco Lulli), his husky Italian roommate; Bimba (Peter Van Eyck), a cold and egotistical German; and Jo (Charles Vanel), a fifth choice who has gotten rid of the man before him. Driving two trucks at a snail's pace, they must overcome numerous obstacles to reach their destination, including a rickety wooden platform suspended over a deep ravine, a giant boulder that blocks the road and must be destroyed with a nitro charge, a swamp of oil and their greatest natural danger—fear. A superb suspense film that eats at one's nerves for its entire last half, THE WAGES OF FEAR can almost be thought of as two movies. While director Henri-Georges Clouzot, relying on visuals, devotes the latter portion of the film to the passage of the trucks, he spends the first half building characters and atmosphere—the sweaty, dusty, hellish existence in Las Piedras, which is little better than death. From the opening shot—of four frantic beetles that have been strung together by a mischievous child—it is clear that the four characters are prisoners of the place. Remade in 1977 by William Friedkin as the crummy SORCERER.

WAGONMASTER

1950 86m bw Western ★★★★
Argosy (U.S.)

Ward Bond *(Elder Wiggs)*, Ben Johnson *(Travis Blue)*, Harry Carey Jr. *(Sandy Owens)*, Joanne Dru *(Denver)*, Charles Kemper *(Uncle*

Shiloh Clegg), Jane Darwell (Sister Ledeyard), Alan Mowbray (Dr. A. Locksley Hall), Ruth Clifford (Fleuretty Phyffe), Russell Simpson (Adam Perkins), Kathleen O'Malley (Prudence Perkins)

p, John Ford, Merian C. Cooper; d, John Ford; w, Frank S. Nugent, Patrick Ford (based on a story by John Ford); ph, Bert Glennon; ed, Jack Murray; m, Richard Hageman; art d, James Basevi; fx, Jack Caffee; cos, Wesley V. Jefferies, Adele Parmenter

When asked by Peter Bogdanovich to comment on WAGONMASTER during their famous interview in 1966, director Ford replied that he thought the film, "along with THE FUGITIVE and THE SUN SHINES BRIGHT … came closest to being what I had wanted to achieve." Written by the director's son Patrick together with Frank Nugent, and based on a story by Ford himself, WAGONMASTER is a deceptively simple tale about a Mormon wagon train headed for the promised land. Along the way the group, led by Bond, forges alliances with two young horse traders (Johnson and Carey), four members of a traveling medicine show (Mowbray, Clifford, Francis Ford, and Dru) and a tribe of nomadic Navajo Indians. Bad guys materialize in the form of a sleazy band of varmints known as the Clegg family (Kemper, Arness, Libby, Worden, and Mickey Simpson), who we have seen rob an express office and murder a clerk during the pre-credit sequence.

WAGONMASTER is a first-rate film about solidarity, sacrifice, and tolerance, with Ford displaying consummate skill in everything from the brilliant visual compositions to the casting of the bit players. The relaxed, natural feel of the film is helped by the absence of stars; by putting his supporting players in lead roles, Ford was able to develop their characters in fresh and unexpected ways. Bond, Johnson, and Dru are nothing short of brilliant, turning in performances which, together with breathtaking scenery and an engaging sense of humor, make this well worth repeated watching.

WAIT UNTIL DARK

1967 107m c Thriller DVD
★★★½
Warner Bros. (U.S.)

Audrey Hepburn (Susy Hendrix), Alan Arkin (Roat), Richard Crenna (Mike Talman), Efrem Zimbalist Jr. (Sam Hendrix), Jack Weston (Carlino), Samantha Jones (Lisa), Julie Herrod (Gloria), Frank O'Brien (Shatner), Gary Morgan (Boy), Jean Del Val (The Old Man)

p, Mel Ferrer; d, Terence Young; w, Robert Carrington, Jane Howard Carrington (based on the play by Frederick Knott); ph, Charles Lang (Technicolor); ed, Gene Milford; m, Henry Mancini; art d, George Jenkins

AAN Best Actress: Audrey Hepburn

A real edge-of-your-seat thriller adapted from a Broadway stage hit written by Frederick Knott, author of DIAL M FOR MURDER. Hepburn, a blind Manhattan housewife, is terrorized by a trio of vicious killers (Crenna, Arkin, and Weston) who are after a fortune in heroin that has been hidden in a toy doll her husband, Zimbalist, gave to her. What follows is an excruciatingly suspenseful battle of wits between the blind Hepburn and her sadistic tormentors. Expertly directed by veteran British helmsman Young (Arthur Penn had directed the stage version), WAIT UNTIL DARK is an exciting, original chiller. Hepburn turns in a strong, realistic performance as the terrorized blind woman—a role she researched diligently with the help of two young blind women from the Lighthouse for the Blind school. For weeks the actress (and director Young) wore a special shade over her eyes and learned how to use a cane properly, feel the texture of different objects, and listen carefully to distinguish the quality and distance of sounds. The film was a tremendous success at the box office, and for added

effect, some theater owners turned the house lights off completely during the final 15 minutes.

WAITING TO EXHALE

1995 121m c Drama DVD
★★½
Schindler-Swerdlow Productions (U.S.) R

Whitney Houston (Savannah), Angela Bassett (Bernadine), Loretta Devine (Gloria), Lela Rochon (Robin), Gregory Hines (Marvin), Dennis Haysbert (Kenneth), Mykelti Williamson (Troy), Michael Beach (John, Sr.), Leon Robinson, billed as Leon (Russell), Wendell Pierce (Michael)

p, Ezra Swerdlow, Deborah Schindler; d, Forest Whitaker; w, Terry McMillan, Ronald Bass (based upon the novel by Terry McMillan); ph, Toyomichi Kurita; ed, Richard Chew; m, Kenneth "Babyface" Edmonds; prod d, David Gropman; art d, Marc Fisichella; fx, Thomas C. Ford; cos, Judy Ruskin

Had there been no Million Man March, this movie alone might have prompted one. If there's an African-American male here who isn't a sneaky, two-timing, narcissistic, wallet-stealing, white-woman-dating, dope-taking, bad-in-bed, sorry son of a bitch, we missed him: he must have been hiding in some closet, behind all those fabulous clothes. Forest Whitaker's adaptation of Terry McMillan's best-selling novel is more about gender than race, and it comes uncomfortably close to pinning the blame for all the troubles of black women on black men. Four genuinely charismatic actresses (Whitney Houston, Angela Bassett, Lela Rochon, and Loretta Devine) play close friends whose relationship appears to be entirely founded on complaining about their boyfriends. With its diva-heavy cast, this feels like THE WOMEN for the '90s—which may mean that its superficial feminism is just an excuse for a wallow in self-hatred.

WALK IN THE SUN, A

1945 117m bw War DVD
★★★★½
Fox (U.S.)

Dana Andrews (Sgt. Tyne), Richard Conte (Rivera), John Ireland (Windy), George Tyne (Friedman), Lloyd Bridges (Sgt. Ward), Sterling Holloway (McWilliams), Herbert Rudley (Sgt. Porter), Norman Lloyd (Archimbeau), Steve Brodie (Judson), Huntz Hall (Carraway)

p, Lewis Milestone; d, Lewis Milestone; w, Robert Rossen (based on a story by Harry Brown); ph, Russell Harlan; ed, Duncan Mansfield; m, Freddie Rich; art d, Max Bertisch

One of the better films to emerge from the final days of WWII, A WALK IN THE SUN is the story of one infantry platoon, covering one morning, from the time they hit the beach at Salerno until they reach and capture their objective, a farmhouse six miles inland. Before they even get ashore things begin to go badly, and the green lieutenant in command is killed. A sergeant takes over for a time, but the stress proves too great and he cracks. The men encounter a German armored car for which they set up an ambush, raining it with grenades, then continue on their mission with natural leader Sgt. Tyne (Dana Andrews) now in command. Eventually, the soldiers reach their objective, but the situation appears suicidal and Sgt. Tyne must devise some way to complete the mission with a minimum loss of life. Throughout the film, as it follows the men in battle, the soundtrack picks up their chatty conversations and private thoughts. They think about their place in the great scheme of the war, about their fear of being killed, and about the hard, dirty, tedious, and dangerous job of being a front-line foot soldier. A languorous sense of resignation holds sway over all: weary, hard-bitten, and somewhat cynical, they are there to do a job, and although they don't even understand what part they play in the big picture, they do it anyway, even at the cost of their lives.

Although director Lewis Milestone seemed to have put the pacifism of his earlier ALL QUIET ON THE WESTERN FRONT on hold for the duration of WWII, A WALK IN THE SUN mostly avoids the patriotic posing and outright racism (indeed, the enemy is never given a face here) of his THE PURPLE HEART from the year before and instead concentrates on the rugged day-to-day existence of the common foot soldier. While the film is consistently engaging, some of the narrative devices Milestone employs, such as the voice-over narration and the occasional off-screen singing of a somewhat sappy folk song dedicated to foot soldiers, now seem more of an intrusion on the visuals than a complement.

WALKABOUT   DVD
1971 95m c Adventure/Drama ★★★★½
20th Century Fox (Australia/U.S.) PG

Jenny Agutter *(Girl)*, Lucien John *(Brother)*, David Gulpilil *(Aborigine)*, John Meillon *(Father)*, Peter Carver *(No Hoper)*, John Illingsworth *(Husband)*, Barry Donnelly *(Australian Scientist)*, Noelene Brown *(German Scientist)*, Carlo Manchini *(Italian Scientist)*

p, Si Litvinoff; d, Nicolas Roeg; w, Edward Bond (based on the novel by James Vance Marshall); ph, Nicolas Roeg (Eastmancolor); ed, Anthony Gibbs, Alan Pattillo; m, John Barry; prod d, Brian Eatwell; art d, Terry Gough

One of the most original, visually stunning, and provocative films of the 1970s, WALKABOUT is timeless in its beauty and unique approach to a classic coming-of-age story. The film is arguably director Nicolas Roeg's finest achievement.

While on a picnic with his two children in the Australian outback, a man goes insane and kills himself. His 14-year-old daughter (Jenny Agutter), who had witnessed the suicide, tries to prevent her six-year-old brother (Lucien John) from discovering their father's dead body by taking him away into the desert. Lost and hungry, they meet up with a teenage aborigine (David Gulpilil) who is on a "walkabout," a ritual during which adolescent aborigine boys must survive several weeks alone in the desert. He is able to kill animals for food and find water underneath the ground, thereby providing sustenance for himself, the boy, and girl. He speaks no English, and the girl has little patience for his native language. The young boy, however, learns to communicate with him via signals and gestures. As the trio continue their journey, the girl slowly becomes comfortable around the aborigine, although she refuses to acknowledge the mating dance he does in her honor.

WALKABOUT is set in terrain stranger and more awe-inspiring than that of any science-fiction film. It is filled with hissing lizards, ominous bugs, blinding red sand, and short, misshapen trees. The film has a straightforward story, little dialogue, and few characters. Nevertheless, it is a remarkably rich and complex narrative. On a basic level, the film is about the way traditional roles and "civilized" upbringings affect people so deeply that the roles cannot be overcome. By placing the children in a setting that's as scary as it is awe-inspiring, WALKABOUT presents one of cinema's deepest and most convincing studies of the mysteries and wonders of growing up. A restored version of the film was released in the United States in 1997, containing a scene that had been lost from American prints for years. The aborigine, momentarily separated from the boy and girl, is approached by a white woman. He rebuffs her advances, and she returns to her nearby home, where she lies in bed alone as her husband teaches aborigine children to paint. The scene adds a new dimension to the aborigine, proof that he knew all along that civilization was near, but chose not to bring the boy and girl there.

WALKING TALL   DVD
1973 125m c Biography/Crime ★★½
BCP (U.S.) R

Joe Don Baker *(Buford Pusser)*, Elizabeth Hartman *(Pauline Pusser)*, Gene Evans *(Sheriff Al Thurman)*, Noah Beery Jr. *(Grandpa Carl Pusser)*, Brenda Benet *(Luan Paxton)*, John Brascia *(Prentiss Parley)*, Bruce Glover *(Grady Coker)*, Arch Johnson *(Buel Jaggers)*, Felton Perry *(Obra Eaker)*, Richard X. Slattery *(Arno Purdy)*

p, Mort Briskin; d, Phil Karlson; w, Mort Briskin; ph, Jack Marta (DeLuxe Color); ed, Harry Gerstad; m, Walter Scharf; prod d, Stan Jolley; fx, Sass Bedig; cos, Oscar Rodriguez, Phyllis Garr

Baker stars as real-life Tennessee sheriff Buford Pusser, whose one-man battle against gambling, moonshine whiskey, and prostitution in his county elevated him to folk-hero stature in three movies (WALKING TALL, PART 2 and FINAL CHAPTER—WALKING TALL followed this one) and a shortlived TV series. In this story of an angry redneck with a big stick, Baker smashes all illegal activities in his jurisdiction, much to the dismay of the criminal kingpins in Tennessee. The crooks band together in an effort to eliminate the troublesome sheriff. After several life-threatening beatings and the murder of his wife, Hartman, Baker finally gets *really mad*, grabs his stick, and cleans out the whole town, killing several people. Incredibly, the film grossed over $17 million at the box office, and the sequels were already in the works.

WALL, THE
(LE MUR)
1983 117m c Prison ★★★½
MK2/Guney/TF1/Ministere de la Culture (France)

Tuncel Kurtiz, Ayse Emel Mesci, Nicolas Hossein, Isabelle Tissandier, Malik Berrichi, Ahmet Ziyrek, Ali Berktay, Selahattin Kuzuoglu, Jean-Pierre Colin, Jacques Dimanche

p, Marin Karmitz; d, Yilmaz Guney; w, Yilmaz Guney; ph, Izzet Akay (Fujicolor); ed, Sabine Mamou; m, Ozan Garip Sahin, Setrak Bakrirel, Ali Dede Altuntas, Robert Kempler

THE WALL is an unceasingly brutal film about life in a Turkish prison. Director Yilmaz Guney, who died in 1984, served three separate jail sentences (one for murder) before finally escaping in 1981. Working from this firsthand experience in France (in an abbey converted to a jail for the production), Guney brings to the screen a film that stands up defiantly and violently for the rights of the imprisoned. The prison depicted here is a re-creation of the one in Ankara, Turkey, that was the sight of an inmate rebellion in 1976. It segregates men, women, and children but has no policy of separating violent offenders from political dissidents. In an indictment of the barbaric Turkish penal system, Guney presents an overcrowded prison with no windows, heat, hot water, or decent food, and with inhumane visiting conditions. The inmates (mostly children in the film) are treated savagely: one is kicked in the eye, another is forced to swallow a louse found on his body, and yet another is savagely battered on the soles of his feet while his blood-chilling screams are transmitted through the prison's public address system. These children pray to God not to be released but simply to be sent to another prison. Although the subject has been brought to the screen before and certain elements of THE WALL have become cliches, the power of the film's message is not lessened. THE WALL is perhaps not the most artful or poetic picture (although it does contain one of the most amazingly photographed birth scenes in cinema); it is nonetheless one of the most necessary.

WALL STREET

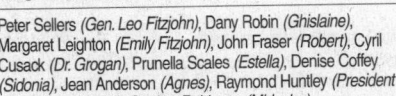

1987 124m c Drama ★★★
American Entertainment (U.S.) R

Charlie Sheen *(Bud Fox)*, Michael Douglas *(Gordon Gekko)*, Martin Sheen *(Carl Fox)*, Terence Stamp *(Sir Larry Wildman)*, Sean Young *(Kate Gekko)*, Daryl Hannah *(Darien Taylor)*, Sylvia Miles *(Realtor)*, James Spader *(Roger Barnes)*, Hal Holbrook *(Lou Mannheim)*, Saul Rubinek *(Harold Salt)*

p, Edward R. Pressman, A. Kitman Ho; d, Oliver Stone; w, Oliver Stone, Stanley Weiser; ph, Robert Richardson (Deluxe Color); ed, Claire Simpson; m, Stewart Copeland; prod d, Stephen Hendrickson; art d, John J. Moore, Hilda Stark; cos, Ellen Mirojnick

AA Best Actor: Michael Douglas

Writer-director Oliver Stone, who shows an uncanny knack for anticipating public interest in the subjects he chooses, explores the much-publicized inside trading scandals of the mid-1980s. Set in 1985, the film follows the career of young Wall Street broker Bud Fox (Charlie Sheen) as he scrambles to make his first million. His idol is ruthless big-time corporate raider Gordon Gekko (Michael Douglas). Fox insinuates himself into Gekko's good graces by giving Gekko inside information about an airline, information he has learned from his father (Martin Sheen), an airline mechanic and local representative of his union. With the promise of big financial rewards negating his momentary apprehension about breaking the law, Fox willingly goes to work for Gekko. With WALL STREET, Stone intentionally set out to make a good old-fashioned liberal drama about the evils of unchecked capitalism. This approach results in a film with few shades of gray and lots of moralizing speeches, but Stone nearly pulls it off through his usual visual verve and keen casting instincts. Charlie Sheen is fine as the young, inexperienced kid whose soul is battled for by the forces of good and evil. Better yet is Douglas, whose Gordon Gekko is a predatory animal seducing the weak into his lair.

WALTZ OF THE TOREADORS

1962 104m c Comedy ★★★½
Independent Artists (U.K.)

Peter Sellers *(Gen. Leo Fitzjohn)*, Dany Robin *(Ghislaine)*, Margaret Leighton *(Emily Fitzjohn)*, John Fraser *(Robert)*, Cyril Cusack *(Dr. Grogan)*, Prunella Scales *(Estella)*, Denise Coffey *(Sidonia)*, Jean Anderson *(Agnes)*, Raymond Huntley *(President of the Court Martial)*, Cardew Robinson *(Midgeley)*

p, Peter de Sarigny; d, John Guillermin; w, Wolf Mankowitz (based on the play by Jean Anouilh); ph, John Wilcox (Eastmancolor); ed, Peter Taylor; m, Richard Addinsell; prod d, Wilfred Shingleton; art d, Harry Pottle; cos, Beatrice Dawson

Sellers is outstanding as a Leo Fitzjohn, a retired general looking to escape a bleak existence in this fine adaptation of Jean Anouilh's bittersweet stage comedy. The film opens just before the outbreak of WWI. Fitzjohn has retired from the army and now lives on his manor with his shrewish wife, Emily (Leighton), whom he can't stand. Tortured by loneliness, Fitzjohn pines for the days when he had a platonic affair 17 years before with Ghislaine (Robin), a beautiful young Frenchwoman. Surprisingly, Ghislaine arrives at the manor claiming fidelity to the general and demanding that they consummate the relationship. Fitzjohn jumps at the chance, but circumstances force a postponement of their rendezvous and he leaves his former love under the care of his aide, Robert (Fraser). In two days, the aide succeeds where Fitzjohn has failed, and the angry general puts the young soldier in for a court-martial. Fitzjohn learns during the trial that Robert is actually his illegitimate son, so he stops the proceedings and allows the young couple to marry. Unhinged by the reality that he is stuck with Emily for the rest of his life, Fitzjohn considers doing something desperate, but a new arrival on the scene changes his mind.

WANDERERS, THE

1979 113m c Drama ★★★★
Orion (U.S.) R

Ken Wahl *(Richie)*, John Friedrich *(Joey)*, Karen Allen *(Nina)*, Toni Kalem *(Despie Galasso)*, Alan Rosenberg *(Turkey)*, Jim Youngs *(Buddy)*, Tony Ganios *(Perry)*, Linda Manz *(Peewee)*, William Andrews *(Emilio)*, Erland Van Lidth *(Terror)*

p, Martin Ransohoff; d, Philip Kaufman; w, Rose Kaufman, Philip Kaufman (based on the novel by Richard Price); ph, Michael Chapman (Technicolor); ed, Ronald Roose, Stuart Pappe; art d, John J. Moore; cos, Robert de Mora

The best of the gang films to be released in 1979 (the list includes THE WARRIORS, WALK PROUD, and BOULE-VARD NIGHTS), THE WANDERERS is a strangely compelling film directed with flair by Philip Kaufman (INVASION OF THE BODY SNATCHERS, THE RIGHT STUFF). While basically just a string of vignettes about a gang of Italian-American teenagers living in the Bronx circa 1963, the film has an air of authenticity, as if it episodes were based on adolescent recollections. The performances in the film are uniformly strong, with Wahl, the protagonist, showing a great screen promise he has never fulfilled (FORT APACHE, THE BRONX; and THE SOLDIER being dismal wastes of his talent). Little Linda Manz (DAYS OF HEAVEN and OUT OF THE BLUE) nearly steals the film as a pint-sized tough gal who is the girlfriend of Van Lidth, the giant leader of a rival street gang known as "The Fordham Baldies." Kaufman infuses the film with a wistful sadness for an era about to end with the assassination of JFK. Many incidents will stick with the viewer, including the very funny sequence where all the members of the Fordham Baldies get drunk and join the Marines, and the haunting, almost surrealistic battle with the mysterious and violent rival gang known as "The Ducky Boys." All in all a fascinating film with an outstanding musical score consisting of jukebox hits from the period.

WAR AND PEACE

1956 208m c Drama/War ★★★★
Ponti/DEG (Italy/U.S.)

Audrey Hepburn *(Natasha Rostov)*, Henry Fonda *(Pierre Bezukhov)*, Mel Ferrer *(Prince Andrei Bolkonsky)*, Vittorio Gassman *(Anatole Kuragin)*, John Mills *(Platon Karatayev)*, Herbert Lom *(Napoleon)*, Oscar Homolka *(Gen. Mikhail Kutuzov)*, Anita Ekberg *(Helene Kuragin)*, Helmut Dantine *(Dolokhov)*, Barry Jones *(Count Ilya Rostov)*

p, Dino De Laurentiis; d, King Vidor; w, Bridget Boland, Robert Westerby, King Vidor, Mario Camerini, Ennio De Concini, Ivo Perilli, Irwin Shaw (based on the novel by Leo Tolstoy); ph, Jack Cardiff, Aldo Tonti (VistaVision, Technicolor); ed, Stuart Gilmore, Leo Catozzo; m, Nino Rota; art d, Mario Chiari, Franz Bachelin, Gianni Polidori; cos, Maria De Matteis

AAN Best Director: King Vidor; *AAN Best Color Cinematography:* Jack Cardiff; *AAN Best Costume Design (Color):* Maria De Matteis

King Vidor's version of Tolstoy's great novel seems insufficient at more than three hours and fared ill both with the critics and at the box office, but it does deliver the spectacular visuals expected of historical epics. As Napoleon (Herbert Lom) prepares to invade Russia, the gentle, awkward, intellectual Pierre Bezukhov (Henry Fonda) falls in undeclared love with young Natasha Rostov (Audrey Hepburn). Soon afterward, his father dies—making Pierre the wealthy new

Count Bezukhov and a desirable marriage prospect—and Bezukhov marries the luscious, adulterous Helene (Anita Ekberg). Meanwhile, his dear friend Prince Andrei (Mel Ferrer), a haughty, gloomy aide to General Kutuzov (Oscar Homolka), returns home from battle after being wounded. Depressed after his wife's death in childbirth, Andrei rediscovers the joy of life when he, too, falls in love with Natasha, and she with him—the two having been introduced by Pierre, who battles his own spiritual malaise after the failure of his loveless marriage. Andrei returns to the front and is wounded critically in the disastrous Russian defeat at Borodino. Pierre observes the carnage in horror and vows to assassinate Napoleon, but he is captured and held prisoner when the French occupy Moscow. When all looks darkest, however, the Russian winter sets in, the French are routed, Pierre is reunited with Natasha, and the love that was hinted at in the opening scenes finally comes to fruition.

Lovers of Tolstoy's work are likely to be frustrated by this somewhat static film, which, inevitably, omits a great deal of Tolstoy's characterization, plots, philosophy, and historical analysis, while on the other hand plays up the Pierre-Natasha romance. The performances are similarly limited, though Hepburn charmingly captures the gamine radiance of the young Natasha and Fonda (who felt he was miscast) effectively communicates Pierre's integrity. Cinematographers Jack Cardiff and Aldo Tonti contribute the film's most stunning work, as does Mario Soldati, who directed the battle scenes.

WAR AND PEACE
(VOYNA I MIR)   *DVD*
1967   434m   c   Drama/War/Historical   ★★★★
Mosfilm   (U.S.S.R.)

Lyudmila Savelyeva *(Natasha Rostova)*, Sergei Bondarchuk *(Pierre Bezuhov)*, Vyacheslav Tikhonov *(Prince Andrey Bolkonsky)*, Viktor Stanitsyn *(Ilya Andreevich Rostov)*, Kira Golovko *(Countess Rostova)*, Oleg Tabakov *(Nikolay Rostov)*, Nikolay Kodin *(Teen Petya Rostov)*, Seryozha Yermilov *(Boy Petya Rostov)*, Irina Gubanova *(Sonya)*, Anatoly Ktorov *(Prince Nikolai Andreyevich Bolkonsky)*

p, Sergei Bondarchuk; d, Sergei Bondarchuk; w, Sergei Bondarchuk, Vasiliy Solovyov (based on the novel *Voyna i Mir* by Leo Tolstoy); ph, Anatoliy Petritskiy (Sovscope 70, Sovcolor); ed, Tatyana Likhachyova; m, Vyacheslav Ovchinnikov; art d, Mikhail Bogdanov, Gennadiy Myasnikov; cos, Mikhail Chikovani, Vladimir Burmeyster

AAN Best Art Direction-Set Decoration: Mikhail Bogdanov, Gennady Myasnikov, G. Koshelev, V. Uvarov; *AA Best Foreign Language Film*

If King Vidor's version of *War and Peace* suffered from its Hollywood-style simplification of Tolstoy's tale, Soviet director Sergei Bondarchuk's WAR AND PEACE may be *too* painstakingly faithful to the novel. Originally released in the USSR in four parts totaling almost nine hours, the film was cut to 380 minutes for its U.S. and video release. Russian sources estimated its production to cost over $100 million. The picture is most successful in its epic battle scenes (the battle of Borodino runs nearly an hour), which stunningly portray the scope and inhumanity of war, and in its equally staggering, lavishly re-created visions of the Russian aristocracy's glamor and wealth, most notably the ball at which Andrei (Vyacheslav Tikhonov) meets Natasha (Ludmilla Savelyeva). (Bondarchuk himself plays Pierre.) In between the spectacles, however, are some failures of dramatic finesse and pacing—particularly Bondarchuk's overreliance on narration and interior monolog to convey the complexity of Tolstoy's characters—flaws compounded for English-speaking viewers by the affectless quality of the dubbing. Nonetheless, Bondarchuk's film, which won a Best Foreign Film Oscar and

was also serialized for British television, is certainly the definitive movie version of *War and Peace*, memorably impressive in its scope and ambition. The film was also nominated for the Best Art Direction Oscar.

WAR OF THE ROSES, THE   *DVD*
1989   116m   c   Comedy   ★★★★
Gracie   (U.S.)   R

Michael Douglas *(Oliver Rose)*, Kathleen Turner *(Barbara Rose)*, Danny DeVito *(Gavin D'Amato)*, Marianne Sagebrecht *(Susan)*, Sean Astin *(Josh, Age 17)*, Heather Fairfield *(Carolyn, Age 17)*, G.D. Spradlin *(Harry Thurmont)*, Trenton Teigen *(Josh, Age 10)*, Bethany McKinney *(Carolyn, Age 10)*, Peter Donat *(Larrabee)*

p, James L. Brooks, Arnon Milchan; d, Danny DeVito; w, Michael Leeson (based on the novel by Warren Adler); ph, Stephen H. Burum (Deluxe Color); ed, Lynzee Klingman, Nicholas C. Smith; m, David Newman; prod d, Ida Random; art d, Mark Mansbridge; cos, Gloria Gresham

Few things are sadder, sillier, or scarier than the break-up of a long-married pair, and in THE WAR OF THE ROSES, director Danny DeVito captures this fiasco in its full, blackly comic ingloriousness. After 17 years of wedlock, Barbara Rose (Kathleen Turner) can't stand her husband, Oliver (Michael Douglas). He still loves her—but he loves their big, beautiful, antique-filled house more, and therein lies the cautionary tale, told by Gavin D'Amato (director DeVito), a divorce lawyer who recounts the progressively crazier story to a prospective client. Stuck (for legal reasons) in the house together as they begin divorce proceedings, the Roses escalate tensions until the hostilities erupt into full-scale, no-prisoners war.

DeVito films this tale with a fiendish gusto, yet with psychological realism and meticulous attention to an inexorable logic in the plotting, even as the Roses' war moves from the outlandish to the surreal. At once horrific and hilarious, THE WAR OF THE ROSES is made with a high level of cinematic craft: Turner and Douglas (ROMANCING THE STONE, JEWEL OF THE NILE) again prove to be the quintessential antiromantic screen couple for the antiromantic 1980s, and DeVito exerts a control behind the camera that is otherwise almost nonexistent in contemporary American film comedy.

WAR OF THE WORLDS, THE   *DVD*
1953   85m   c   Science Fiction   ★★★½
Paramount   (U.S.)

Gene Barry *(Dr. Clayton Forrester)*, Ann Robinson *(Sylvia Van Buren)*, Les Tremayne *(Gen. Mann)*, Lewis Martin *(Pastor Matthew Collins)*, Robert Cornthwaite *(Dr. Pryor)*, Sandro Giglio *(Dr. Bilderbeck)*, William Phipps *(Wash Perry)*, Paul Birch *(Alonzo Hogue)*, Jack Kruschen *(Salvatore)*, Vernon Rich *(Col. Heffner)*

p, George Pal; d, Byron Haskin; w, Barre Lyndon (based on the novel by H.G. Wells); ph, George Barnes (Technicolor); ed, Everett Douglas; m, Leith Stevens; art d, Hal Pereira, Albert Nozaki; fx, Gordon Jennings, Paul K. Lerpae, Wallace Kelly, Ivyl Burks, Jan Domela, Irmin Roberts, Walter Hoffman, Chesley Bonestell; cos, Edith Head

AAN Best Film Editing: Everett Douglas; *AAN Best Sound Recording:* Loren L. Ryder; *AA Best Special Effects*

A key sci-fi film of the 1950s, George Pal's THE WAR OF THE WORLDS is a vividly realized adaptation of the classic H.G. Wells novel, updated from 19th-century London to 20th-century California. Though it's bogged down by a stiff cast, a yawn-inspiring conventional romance, and a sappy religiosity, it remains a landmark in the history of special effects. The lumbersome triopods of the Wells novel are jettisoned in favor of cool, green, slickly contoured flying saucers that fire death rays accompanied by one of the most fondly remembered sound effects in screen history. Filmed on a relatively modest budget of $2 million ($1.3 million went to special effects), THE WAR OF THE WORLDS was a solid box office hit.

WAR REQUIEM
1989 93m c Experimental ★★★★
Anglo International Films/Liberty Films/BBC Enterprises (U.K.)

Nathaniel Parker *(Wilfrid Owen)*, Tilda Swinton *(Nurse)*, Laurence Olivier *(Old Soldier)*, Patricia Hayes *(Mother)*, Rohan McCullough *(Enemy Mother)*, Nigel Terry *(Abraham)*, Owen Teale *(Unknown Soldier)*, Sean Bean *(German Soldier)*

p, Don Boyd; d, Derek Jarman; w, Derek Jarman (from the poetry of Wilfred Owen); ph, Richard Greatrex; ed, Rick Elgood; m, Benjamin Britten; prod d, Lucy Morahan; cos, Linda Alderson

Marshalling an astonishing parade of images—brutal, exquisite, erotic, and painterly by turns—avant-garde director Derek Jarman supplies visual counterpoint to Benjamin Britten's masterwork, the 1961 oratorio *War Requiem*. Jarman's hallucinatory vision of war draws on the life and verse of WWI poet Wilfred Owen, who was killed on a French battlefield two weeks before the Armistice. Owen's preoccupations—e.g., the Christ-like martyrdom of soldiers, the interplay of sexuality and death, the pity and horror evoked by the mutilation of young bodies—mesh perfectly with those of the director. An anti-war film of surpassing power, WAR REQUIEM can also be read as a metaphorical treatment of the devastation of youth by AIDS. The soundtrack recording of Britten's music, by the London Symphony Orchestra with soloists including Peter Pears and Dietrich Fischer-Dieskau, is first-class. Laurence Olivier's cameo is his last screen appearance.

WAR ZONE, THE   DVD
1998 99m c Drama ★★★★
Film Four/Sarah Radclyffe Productions/Portobello R
Productions (U.K.)

Ray Winstone *(Dad)*, Lara Belmont *(Jessie)*, Freddie Cunliffe *(Tom)*, Tilda Swinton *(Mum)*, Annabelle Apsion *(Nurse)*, Kate Ashfield *(Lucy)*, Colin Farrell, billed as Colin J. Farrell *(Nick)*, Aisling O'Sullivan *(Carol)*, Megan Thorp *(Baby Alice)*, Kim Wall *(Barman)*

d, Tim Roth; w, Alexander Stuart (based on his novel); art d, Karen Wakefield; fx, Dave Beavis, Alex Hope; cos, Mary Jane Reyner

Brace yourself: Actor Tim Roth's austere directing debut is one of the most difficult, emotionally wrenching experiences you're likely to have in a movie theater anytime soon. But if you can stand it, you'll find this unflinching portrayal of one English family undone by incest impeccably acted; it reveals a careful, assured director who never lets the explosive material get the better of his good judgement. Soon after his father (Ray Winstone) relocates his London-based family to a cramped farmhouse in the damp and remote Devonshire countryside, 15-year-old Tom (Freddie Cunliffe) stumbles upon an awful secret. Arriving home from shopping one afternoon with his mother (Tilda Swinton), Tom spies his father and 17-year-old sister, Jessie (Lara Belmont), alone together in the bath. When he confronts Jessie with what he's seen, she denies anything happened; it is, after all, a small house, and no one else in the family seems to have a problem with casual nudity. But the closer Tom looks, the more he sees, until the evidence against his father becomes irrefutable, and the dam-

age done to his sister becomes impossible to ignore. It's all so brutally matter-of-fact that it's often hard not to turn away. Adapted by screenwriter Alexander Stuart from his own novel, the film first astutely maps the treacherous psychological terrain of the family romance—alone in the middle-of-nowhere, Tom himself shows an unwholesome sexual curiosity towards his mother and sister—then journeys straight into hell. And there's no going back: Roth is merciless in detailing the horrors of sexual abuse and the pain and corruption it leaves behind. At the center of this powerful, modern-day Greek tragedy is newcomer Belmont's shattering performance; she burns like a raw nerve and leaves you with a picture of suffering that's impossible to shake.

WARLOCK   DVD
1959 121m c Western ★★★★
Fox (U.S.)

Richard Widmark *(Johnny Gannon)*, Henry Fonda *(Clay Blaisdell)*, Anthony Quinn *(Tom Morgan)*, Dorothy Malone *(Lilly Dollar)*, Dolores Michaels *(Jessie Marlow)*, Wallace Ford *(Judge Holloway)*, Tom Drake *(Abe McQuown)*, Richard Arlen *(Bacon)*, DeForest Kelley *(Curley Burne)*, Regis Toomey *(Skinner)*

p, Edward Dmytryk; d, Edward Dmytryk; w, Robert Alan Aurthur (based on the novel by Oakley Hall); ph, Joseph MacDonald (CinemaScope, Technicolor); ed, Jack W. Holmes; m, Leigh Harline; art d, Lyle Wheeler, Herman A. Blumenthal; fx, L.B. Abbott; cos, Charles LeMaire

A unique and often overlooked adult western that goes much deeper than most movies in this genre, WARLOCK would seem on the surface to be a fairly standard story. The citizens of the small town of Warlock are a kind, God-fearing lot who live in dread because a group of brawling cowboys, led by Drake, likes to come into town from time to time and shoot up the place. They hire Fonda, a well-known gunslinger, to be local marshal. It's 1881, and men of Fonda's type are either dying of old age or being shot down by younger, faster cowboys, so he's something of an anachronism. He accepts the job on the provision that he also can run the local gambling and dance parlor. Fonda soon meets Michaels, and an attraction between the two grows. Drake and his cohorts mosey back into Warlock accompanied by Widmark, who becomes disenchanted with Drake and his group so he quits the gang and decides to remain in Warlock as Fonda's deputy. Fonda manages to get Drake and the other troublemakers out of town, and for a while law and order reign. The townsfolk decide that they don't need a professional gunslinger anymore, now that Drake and the others have been cowed. Inevitably, however, the bad guys return.
    WARLOCK was shot partly in Utah, although not much of the glorious scenery there was utilized. The filmmakers preferred instead to concentrate on the scene within the confines of the small town and the multilayered stories going on among the principals. There's a sense of brooding and Greek tragedy here not usually presented in a cowboy movie. Yet under Dmytryk's strong direction of the Aurthur adaptation, the tone and story lines all work to great advantage. Fonda had bombed in two previous films and had to get back into mainstream movies. While this was hardly a typical western, it did reestablish him in the eyes of the movie-going public as more than the effete Easterner he had portrayed in STAGE STRUCK and 12 ANGRY MEN. Lots of action punctuates the excellent dialogue, enhanced by a strong supporting cast.

WARRIORS, THE   DVD
1979 90m c Action ★★★½
Paramount (U.S.) R

Michael Beck *(Swan)*, James Remar *(Ajax)*, Thomas Waites *(Fox)*, Dorsey Wrights *(Cleon)*, Brian Taylor *(Snow)*, David

Harris *(Cochise)*, Tom McKitterick *(Cowboy)*, Marcelino Sanchez *(Rembrandt)*, Terry Michos *(Vermin)*, Deborah Van Valkenburgh *(Mercy)*

p, Lawrence Gordon; d, Walter Hill; w, David Shaber, Walter Hill (based on the novel by Sol Yurick); ph, Andrew Laszlo (Panavision, Movielab Color); ed, David Holden; m, Barry DeVorzon; art d, Don Swanagan, Robert Wightman; cos, Bobbie Mannix, Mary Ellen Winston

Kinetic is the word for the films of director Walter Hill. While some of them may lack complex characterizations (particularly true of THE DRIVER and THE WARRIORS), Hill makes up for these deficiencies with stunning visual panache. THE WARRIORS advertised its subject matter in somewhat belligerent terms: "These are the Armies of the Night. They are 100,000 strong. They outnumber the cops five to one. They could run New York City," and as a result the film was widely criticized as an incitement to gang violence. While the film depicts gangs, however, it does so in a highly stylized manner, and the criticism seems therefore to reflect a naive confusion of art with life. Indeed, without moralizing, the film achieves insight into the blighted lives and emotions of the young gang members. Loosely based on Sol Yurick's 1965 novel about a reprehensible New York street gang, THE WARRIORS opens (after a marvelous credits sequence that sets the mood for the movie) at a rally held by Roger Hill, playing the ambitious leader of a gang known as the Riffs, who seeks to unite all the street gangs into one army. Each gang has sent a handful of representatives to the meeting, all of whom have agreed to come unarmed. The leader of a gang called the Rogues, however, pulls a gun, kills Hill, and frames the Warriors for the crime. The film then turns into a battle in which the Warriors try to make it home through enemy territory with every rival gang in the city out to get them. The Warriors finally straggle back to Coney Island, where the truth is revealed, leaving Kelly and his gang in the hands of a very angry group of Riffs.

THE WARRIORS is a visual feast. Director Hill fills the frame with vibrant colors, bright lights, and nonstop motion. The uniforms of the various gangs are unique, funny, fearsome, and more than a bit theatrical. The exciting fight scenes are brilliantly choreographed, and instead of focusing on the violence, Hill concentrates on pure movement (most of the cast were actually dancers). Alongside all the glitz are a few moments of insight into the characters. In a simple but effective scene, the Warriors are sprawled exhausted in a subway car. Two teenage couples fresh from a prom enter and sit opposite gang-leader Beck and his girl, Valkenburgh. The street kids stare at the tuxedos, prom dresses, and flowers of the "wholesome" kids. The visual contrast is enough to suggest the ways in which the street kids have missed out and been denied a normal adolescence.

WASHINGTON SQUARE

1997   117m   c   Romance/Drama   ★★★
Hollywood Pictures/Caravan Pictures/Ann Dubinet   PG
(U.S.)

Jennifer Jason Leigh *(Catherine Sloper)*, Albert Finney *(Dr. Austin Sloper)*, Ben Chaplin *(Morris Townsend)*, Maggie Smith *(Aunt Lavinia Penniman)*, Judith Ivey *(Aunt Elizabeth Almond)*, Betsy Brantley *(Mrs. Montgomery)*, Jennifer Garner *(Marian Almond)*, Peter Maloney *(Jacob Webber/Notary)*, Robert Stanton *(Arthur Townsend)*, Arthur Laupus *(Mr. Almond)*

p, Roger Birnbaum, Julie Bergman Sender; d, Agnieszka Holland; w, Carol Doyle (based on the novel by Henry James); ph, Jerzy Zielinski; ed, David Siegel; m, Jan A.P. Kaczmarek; prod d, Allan Starski; art d, Alan E. Muraoka; fx, Douglas Retzler; cos, Anna Sheppard

A faithful, nuanced adaptation of Henry James' classic novel, WASHINGTON SQUARE is not as dramatically compelling as William Wyler's earlier big-screen rendition of the tale, THE HEIRESS. However, the film does rise above the level of the average period piece, thanks to the sensitive direction of Agnieszka Holland and strong performances by Jennifer Jason Leigh and Albert Finney.

New York in the 19th century. Catherine Sloper (Leigh) lives under the sway of her domineering father, Dr. Austin Sloper (Finney). At a formal party held at the home of her Aunt Elizabeth (Judith Ivey), Catherine is thoroughly captivated by Morris Townsend (Ben Chaplin). Morris begins to visit Catherine regularly; her father condemns the young man as a shiftless fortune hunter. Catherine's Aunt Lavinia (Maggie Smith) believes otherwise and encourages Morris to court Catherine. After Morris formally asks Dr. Sloper for Catherine's hand in marriage, Dr. Sloper informs Catherine that he will disinherit her if she marries Morris. His adamant stand compels the disappointed Morris to break off with Catherine. Time passes. After Dr. Sloper dies, Catherine is revisited by Morris. Transformed into an independent soul by his rejection years before, she turns him away.

In WASHINGTON SQUARE, Holland and scripter Carol Doyle eschew the melodramatic tactics used in THE HEIRESS, opting instead to explore the ambiguities of character suggested by James's novel. What results is a delicately conceived character study which elicits a more limited amount of emotional involvement from the viewer. That said, the film does have its virtues. The film's centerpiece is a brilliantly understated turn by Leigh. Affecting a childlike gait and letting her character's vulnerability and romantic longing rule her expressions, Leigh does a masterful job of conveying Catherine's dilemma. Offering top-notch support is Finney, who exhibits a snobbish menace as the verbally abusive Dr. Sloper. Smith impresses as Aunt Lavinia, who at points seems more infatuated with Morris than Catherine is.

WATCH ON THE RHINE   📀

1943   114m   bw   Drama/War   ★★½
Warner Bros. (U.S.)

Bette Davis *(Sara Muller)*, Paul Lukas *(Kurt Muller)*, Geraldine Fitzgerald *(Marthe de Brancovis)*, Lucile Watson *(Fanny Farrelly)*, Beulah Bondi *(Anise)*, George Coulouris *(Teck de Brancovis)*, Donald Woods *(David Farrelly)*, Henry Daniell *(Phili von Ramme)*, Donald Buka *(Joshua Muller)*, Eric Roberts *(Bodo Muller)*

p, Hal B. Wallis; d, Herman Shumlin; w, Dashiell Hammett, Lillian Hellman (based on the play by Hellman); ph, Merritt Gerstad, Hal Mohr; ed, Rudi Fehr; m, Max Steiner; art d, Carl Jules Weyl; fx, Jack Holden, Edwin DuPar; cos, Orry-Kelly

AAN Best Picture; AA Best Actor: Paul Lukas; AAN Best Supporting Actress: Lucile Watson; AAN Best Screenplay: Dashiell Hammett, Lillian Hellman

Yawn. Lillian Hellman's respected play was adapted for film by Hellman and Dashiell Hammett, her longtime companion, and helmed by Herman Shumlin, who directed the stage original and cast some of its players here. The resulting drama, intermittently powerful stuff, was nominated for Best Picture, Script, and Supporting Actress (Lucile Watson) Oscars, with Paul Lukas, repeating his stage role, won as Best Actor. Kurt and Sara Muller (Lukas and Bette Davis), refugees from Nazi Germany, arrive with their children after a long absence to visit Sara's mother (Watson) in her Washington, DC, home. Already there are Teck de Brancovis (George Coulouris), a Rumanian count, and his American wife (Geraldine Fitzgerald). The Mullers plan to stay in the U.S. only until Kurt's health improves; then he will return to his "business" abroad, the exact nature of which is unclear. When the count, who socializes at the German embassy, hears of the Gestapo's unsuccessful attempts to crack an underground resistance group, he suspects that Kurt may be one of them and offers to spy on him, then in turn tries to blackmail Kurt, who must take desperate measures to protect himself and his family.

One of the first American films to present the philosophy—rather than just the warmongering—of fascism as a danger, WATCH ON THE RHINE is rather dully helmed by stage director Shumlin, who too often fails to avoid the static pitfalls of so many play adaptations. Lukas and most of the cast (especially Coulouris) are in fine form, though, partially redeeming a film that has not worn particularly well. Davis, too, (in a fairly small role, though top-billed) tones down her usual fireworks here to fairly good effect. She's better in spit-fire mode, though.

WATERBOY, THE

1998 86m c Comedy/Sports ★★★
The Robert Simonds Company/Touchstone PG-13
(U.S.)

Adam Sandler (*Bobby Boucher*), Henry Winkler (*Coach Klein*), Kathy Bates (*Mama Boucher*), Fairuza Balk (*Vicki Vallencourt*), Jerry Reed (*Red Beaulieu*), Larry Gilliard Jr. (*Derek Wallace*), Blake Clark (*Farmer Fran*), Peter Dante (*Gee Grenouille*), Jonathan Loughran (*Lyle Robideaux*), Al Whiting (*Casey Bugge*)

p, Robert Simonds, Jack Giarraputo; d, Frank Coraci; w, Adam Sandler, Tim Herlihy; ph, Steven Bernstein; ed, Tom Lewis; m, Alan Pasqua; prod d, Perry Andelin Blake; art d, Alan Au; cos, Tom Bronson

Good and dumb, in equal measure. Adam Sandler and co-writer Tim Herlihy recycle the best bits from their hit-and-miss successes (HAPPY GILMORE, BILLY MADISON), rehire the director of Sandler's best movie to date (THE WEDDING SINGER), and wind up with something that actually works in its own sweet, knuckleheaded way.

Simple of mind but pure of heart, 31-year-old Bobby Boucher (Adam Sandler) has faithfully served as Water Distribution Engineer (read: waterboy) for the University of Louisiana's football team since he was a kid, enduring the abuse of his teammates while bravely waging a personal war against dehydration. When he's suddenly fired, Bobby finds himself pouring for the considerably less prestigious SCLSU Mud Dogs, a piss-poor losing team with a neurotic coach (Henry Winkler), a mush-mouthed Cajun assistant coach (Blake Clark), and a bevy of drunken cheerleaders. But in Bobby, the Mud Dogs discover a secret weapon. When riled—a crack about the quality of his water or his crazed, overbearing mama (Kathy Bates) will usually do the trick—the mild-mannered waterboy is transformed into an unstoppable tackling machine, and the team has a chance of breaking a 40-game losing streak and going all the way to the Bourbon Bowl.

Herlihy and Sandler, a veteran of TV's long-running Saturday Night Live, have basically taken the "Cajun Man" character he developed on the show (imagine the comic's usual half-wit shtick garnished with a thick bayou drawl) and written him into a gentler version of HAPPY GILMORE. Much of the film's humor is of the hit-in-the-head-with-a-football variety, but it's dopey, harmless fun (unless, perhaps, you're Cajun), packed with silly sentiment and an entertaining supporting cast. No one does deranged quite like Kathy Bates, and the running gag involving Bates and the delicacies of Cajun cuisine is hilarious. And Fairuza Balk, as Bobby's knife-wielding, juvenile delinquent love interest, is a refreshing change from what usually passes for cool.

WATERDANCE, THE

1992 106m c Comedy/Drama ★★★½
No Frills Films/JBW (U.S.) R

Eric Stoltz (*Joel Garcia*), Wesley Snipes (*Raymond Hill*), William Forsythe (*Bloss*), Helen Hunt (*Anna*), Elizabeth Pena (*Rosa*), William Allen Young (*Les*), James Roach (*Guy in the Electronic Wheelchair*), Henry Harris (*Mr. Gibson*), Tony Genaro (*Victor*), Eva Rodriguez (*Victor's Wife*)

p, Gale Anne Hurd, Marie Cantin; d, Neal Jimenez, Michael Steinberg; w, Neal Jimenez; ph, Mark Plummer; ed, Jeff Freeman; m, Michael Convertino; prod d, Bob Ziembicki; cos, Isis Mussenden

Screenwriter and first-time director Neal Jimenez drew on personal experience for THE WATERDANCE, a tough-minded comedy-drama about three paraplegics adapting to life in a wheelchair. Joel Garcia (Eric Stolz) is a promising young novelist who has broken his neck in a hiking accident. Garcia was having an affair with his married editor, Anna (Helen Hunt), who was about to leave her husband for him when Garcia's accident occurred. With his world turned upside down, Garcia begins having second thoughts about their relationship and questions whether Anna will stay with him in his new, physically dependent condition. He has little regard or use for his wardmates at first, but gradually he gets to know them. A member of a biker gang, Bloss (William Forsythe) was broadsided by a car while riding drunk. Though an unapologetic redneck bigot, Bloss strikes up a bickering friendship with Black wardmate Raymond Hill (Wesley Snipes). Hill continually brags about his sexual conquests, but his only visible partner is his wife, who is divorcing him and taking their daughter with her.

Co-directed with Michael Steinberg, Jimenez populates his episodic tale with characters who are believable rather than heroic, sympathetic if not always likable, and avoids the sentimental or the moralistic by undercutting the tragedy with some barbed humor. The cast is generally good, with Hunt (MR. SATURDAY NIGHT, PEGGY SUE GOT MARRIED) taking top honors for giving substance to a relatively sketchy part. Stolz and Forsythe are solid and Snipes is extraordinary. He disappears so thoroughly into Raymond that it's hard to imagine the same actor as the slick, successful architect in Spike Lee's JUNGLE FEVER. Elizabeth Pena (JACOB'S LADDER) contributes an effective turn as the ward's head nurse. The real star here, though, is Jimenez, a talented filmmaker who clearly has a lot more still to offer.

WATERLOO BRIDGE

1940 103m bw Romance ★★★★
MGM (U.S.)

Vivien Leigh (*Myra Lester*), Robert Taylor (*Capt. Roy Cronin*), Lucile Watson (*Lady Margaret Cronin*), C. Aubrey Smith (*Duke*), Maria Ouspenskaya (*Mme. Olga*), Virginia Field (*Kitty*), Leo G. Carroll (*Policeman*), Clara Reid (*Mrs. Bassett*), Steffi Duna (*Lydia*), Leonard Mudie (*Parker*)

p, Sidney Franklin; d, Mervyn LeRoy; w, S.N. Behrman, Hans Rameau, George Froeschel (based on the play by Robert E. Sherwood); ph, Joseph Ruttenberg; ed, George Boemler; m, Herbert Stothart; art d, Cedric Gibbons, Urie McCleary; chor, Ernst Matray; cos, Adrian, Gile Steele

AAN Best B/W Cinematography: Joseph Ruttenberg; AAN Best Original Score: Herbert Stothart

In London during WWII, a British colonel, Taylor, is caught in a blackout in his chauffeured army sedan. He steps from the vehicle to tread the pavement of the famed Waterloo Bridge and begins to reminisce. In flashback, Taylor is a handsome young captain on the eve of WWI. He meets and falls in love with ballerina Leigh; they make plans to wed, but before they can do so Taylor's regiment is called into battle. Leigh abandons her performance to bid her lover farewell at Waterloo Station and is fired from the ballet company. Impoverished, she resorts to prostitution. She plies her trade on the Waterloo Bridge where, months later, she meets the returning Taylor—who has spent the intervening time as a POW—and, thinking fast, conceals her profession during the shocking reunion. Their romance continues; it appears that her degradation was no more than a nightmare, best forgotten. But inevitably, her indiscretions come to light.

Leigh is stunning in this second cinematic version of author Sherwood's hit play. (A fine first version was made in 1931 by James Whale and starred Mae Clarke and Douglass Montgomery.) WATERLOO BRIDGE was Leigh's first movie following the record-breaking David Selznick production of GONE WITH THE WIND, which had made her the most visible, most desirable actress in the world. Selznick had loaned Leigh to MGM for the picture in repayment for help that studio's head had given him for the previous picture. Leigh was in the midst of a divorce from her husband Leigh Holman at the time, her romance with Laurence Olivier—also wed at the time—a continuing scandal. She and Olivier had both invested every farthing they had in their planned theatrical production of William Shakespeare's "Romeo and Juliet," and both were desperately in need of money. Olivier accepted the male lead in PRIDE AND PREJUDICE, and the lovers were forced to separate temporarily. Leigh was irate about the parting, believing that Olivier should have gotten the role assigned to Taylor. Taylor drew kudos for his mature, restrained performance, which revitalized his then-fading career by demonstrating that he was more than just another pretty face, although critics were none too tolerant of his "Nebraska accent." Of all his seventy-plus screen performances, this was Taylor's personal favorite. The story was filmed again in 1956 as GABY, a disappointing version starring Leslie Caron and John Kerr.

WATERSHIP DOWN
1978 92m c Animated ★★★
Nepenthe (U.K.) PG

VOICES OF: John Hurt *(Hazel)*, Richard Briers *(Fiver)*, Michael Graham-Cox *(Bigwig)*, John Bennett *(Capt. Holly)*, Simon Cadell *(Blackberry)*, Roy Kinnear *(Pipkin)*, Richard O'Callaghan *(Dandelion)*, Terence Rigby *(Silver)*, Ralph Richardson *(Chief Rabbit)*, Denholm Elliott *(Cowslip)*

p, Martin Rosen; d, Martin Rosen; w, Martin Rosen (based on the novel by Richard Adams); ed, Terry Rawlings; m, Angela Morley, Malcolm Williamson

Expertly and realistically animated, this version of the popular novel didn't seem to have an audience. It was much too violent for kids, and wasn't the type of picture that an adult would go out and see, in part because it is animated. The spirit of the book is captured here as the rabbits, faced with problems of ecology, are forced to find a new home. Their trek is filled with surprises and adventures, as well as bloodshed. The job of personifying the rabbits is nicely achieved due to expert readings by the cast.

WATERWORLD
1995 134m c Adventure/Action/Science Fiction ★★½
King Kona Productions/The Gordon Company/ PG-13
TIG Productions/Davis Entertainment/Licht/
Mueller Film Corp./Universal (U.S.)

Kevin Costner *(Mariner)*, Dennis Hopper *(Deacon)*, Jeanne Tripplehorn *(Helen)*, Tina Majorino *(Enola)*, Michael Jeter *(Gregor)*, Gerard Murphy *(Nord)*, R.D. Call *(Enforcer)*, Chaim Jeraffi *(Drifter #1)*, Kim Coates *(Drifter #2)*, John Fleck *(Doctor)*

p, Charles Gordon, John A. Davis, Kevin Costner; d, Kevin Reynolds; w, David Twohy, Peter Rader, Joss Whedon (uncredited); ph, Dean Semler; ed, Peter Boyle; m, James Newton Howard; prod d, Dennis Gassner; art d, David Klassen; fx, Marty Bresin, Michael McAlister, Sean Phillips, Boss Film Studios, Brad Kuehn, Jamie Price, Cinesite; cos, John Bloomfield

AAN Best Sound: Steve Maslow, Gregg Landaker, Keith A. Wester

This is the way the WATERWORLD fiasco ends: not with a bang but a whimper. After all the thud and blunder of its production, the most expensive movie ever made emerged as a marginally better-than-average, entirely forgettable summer action picture. Those who were hoping for a debacle of HEAVEN'S GATE proportions were disappointed: this huge, rather awkward ROAD WARRIOR ripoff managed to turn a slight profit worldwide, partly because star Kevin Costner surrendered his upfront fee.

In a postapocalyptic future world where all land is submerged beneath the surface of the ocean, an amphibious loner called the Mariner (Costner) roams the sea in search of fresh water and dry land, tangling with a gang of punked-out losers led by one-eyed evildoer Deacon (Dennis Hopper, in a nod to his biker-pic background). Tepid love interest is supplied by Jeanne Tripplehorn, but the film's really all about Costner—his image, his ego, and his revamped build—who throws himself around the floating sets with commendable energy.

Of course, any Hollywood spectacle that opens with its superstar protagonist drinking his own urine—distilled, granted, but pee nonetheless—has something going for it. WATERWORLD aspires to laud ecological values—the villains burn oil, smoke cigarettes and eat a processed meat product called "Smeat," while the hero lives at peace with the sea—but in the end, its sheer profligacy undermines the message.

WAY AHEAD, THE
1944 115m bw War ★★★½
Two Cities (U.K.)

David Niven *(Lt. Jim Perry)*, Raymond Huntley *(Davenport)*, William Hartnell *(Sgt. Fletcher)*, Stanley Holloway *(Brewer)*, James Donald *(Lloyd)*, John Laurie *(Luke)*, Leslie Dwyer *(Beck)*, Hugh Burden *(Parsons)*, Jimmy Hanley *(Stainer)*, Renee Asherson *(Marjorie Gillingham)*

p, John Sutro, Norman Walker; d, Carol Reed; w, Eric Ambler, Peter Ustinov (based on a story by Eric Ambler); ph, Guy Green; ed, Fergus McDonell; m, William Alwyn; art d, David Rawnsley

Bracing, spirited and lovely. Carol Reed had already developed a reputation in Britain as an accomplished director by the time WWII broke out, so when he joined the Army it was no surprise that he was assigned to the film unit. His 1942 short instructional documentary THE NEW LOT and an idea by Lt. Col. David Niven provided the inspiration for THE WAY AHEAD (a.k.a. THE IMMORTAL BATTALION). Set in the aftermath of the Dunkirk evacuation, the story focuses on Lt. Jim Perry (Niven) as he whips a group of ordinary conscripts into soldiers and then leads them against Rommel's Afrika Korps at El Alamein. This pseudo-documentary was a big success in Britain, earning Reed even greater respect and leading to ODD MAN OUT, THE FALLEN IDOL and THE THIRD MAN, and serving as a patriotic contribution to the war effort.

WAY OUT WEST
1937 65m bw Comedy/Western ★★★★½
Hal Roach (U.S.)

Stan Laurel, Oliver Hardy *(Themselves)*, James Finlayson *(Mickey Finn)*, Sharon Lynne *(Lola Marcel)*, Stanley Fields *(Sheriff)*, Rosina Lawrence *(Mary Roberts)*, James Mason *(Anxious Patron)*, James C. Morton, Frank Mills, David Pepper *(Bartenders)*

p, Stan Laurel; d, James W. Horne; w, Charles Rogers, Felix Adler, James Parrott (based on a story by Jack Jevne, Charles Rogers); ph, Art Lloyd, Walter Lundin; ed, Bert Jordan; m, Marvin Hatley, LeRoy Shield, Egbert Van Alstyne, J.L. Hill, Nathaniel Shilkret, Irving Berlin, Franz von Suppe; art d, Arthur I. Royce; fx, Roy Seawright

AAN Best Score: Hal Roach Studio Music Department, Marvin Hatley (Dept. Head)

Laurel and Hardy's only western spoof, WAY OUT WEST, ranks among the best of their films, with more exuberant laughs crammed into its scant 65 minutes than can be found in a dozen modern comedies. With their faithful mule, the boys head into Brushwood Gulch to deliver a gold mine deed to their departed partner's daughter. But they get hopelessly lost, and make the mistake of asking bartender Mickey Finn (James Finlayson) for advice. Finn's scullery maid, Mary Roberts (Rosina Lawrence), is actually the woman they seek, but he deliberately steers them toward his wife, Lola Marcel (Sharon Lynn)—a brassy blonde who is so obviously not the right person that everyone can see she cries crocodile tears upon learning of her "father's" death. Everyone, that is, except Laurel and Hardy. Included is the song "Trail of the Lonesome Pine."

WAY WE WERE, THE [DVD]
1973 118m c Romance ★★★
Rastar (U.S.) PG

Barbra Streisand (*Katie Morosky*), Robert Redford (*Hubbell Gardiner*), Bradford Dillman (*J.J.*), Lois Chiles (*Carol Ann*), Patrick O'Neal (*George Bissinger*), Viveca Lindfors (*Paula Reisner*), Allyn Ann McLerie (*Rhea Edwards*), Murray Hamilton (*Brooks Carpenter*), Herb Edelman (*Bill Verso*), Diana Ewing (*Vicki Bissinger*)

p, Ray Stark; d, Sydney Pollack; w, Arthur Laurents, Alvin Sargent (uncredited), David Rayfiel (based on the novel by Laurents); ph, Harry Stradling Jr. (Panavision, Eastmancolor); ed, Margaret Booth; m, Marvin Hamlisch; prod d, Stephen Grimes; chor, Grover Dale; cos, Dorothy Jeakins, Moss Mabry

AAN Best Actress: Barbra Streisand; *AAN Best Cinematography:* Harry Stradling, Jr.; *AA Best Original Dramatic Score:* Marvin Hamlisch; *AA Best Song:* "The Way We Were"; Marvin Hamlisch (Music), Alan Bergman (Lyrics), Marilyn Bergman (Lyrics); *AAN Best Art Direction-Set Decoration:* Stephen Grimes, William Kiernan; *AAN Best Costume Design:* Dorothy Jeakins, Moss Mabry

La Babs with a blondish Afro spouting leftist rhetoric? Just call her Harpo Marxist. Here we have an engrossing, if occasionally ludicrous, hit tearjerker with Pollack, Streisand, and Redford doing a good job of bringing Arthur Laurents's script to the screen. It's a great campy romance and it does tell us something about the way we were from the '30s through the '50s, but a lot of the politics of the Blacklist period are missing from the film, apparently cut just before release.

Redford is a handsome WASP college student in the late 1930s. He yearns to be a writer, spends his spare time in mindless social activities, and is politically neutral. Streisand, in her big bid for old-fashioned romantic movie star status, is a radical Jewish student who joins every political organization. She is the butt of many jokes at the college (what a surprise!), and the sharpest barbs come from Redford's pals, though he doesn't feel the same way. They meet briefly at a dance and there is an attraction, but that's put on the back burner. Years pass, and WWII begins. Streisand is on the radio talking politics, and Redford is now a member of the armed forces. They meet again, but he is drunk, so she takes him back to her apartment where he passes out in her bed. Still later, he's a published author, and, while discussing his book, it's evident to both that the attraction they felt in college

is still there. Redford's snobbish friends again try to wreck the relationship. She won't put up with their attitude, and Redford decides this might be the time to end their romance. They are reconciled, however, marry and move to California where Redford has received a screenplay assignment. She goes off to Washington to fight against the House Un-American Activities Committee. Streisand fears that Redford is selling out his talent. He begins to agree with her and is soon in trouble with the studio executives. Dillman, an old buddy of Redford, is the wishy-washy producer assigned to the project, and he wants certain changes in the script that Redford is loath to make. While Streisand is away, Redford seeks solace in the arms of an ex-girlfriend. Pregnant, Streisand is distraught and wants to end their marriage. They will wait until after their child is born, then part amicably. Years later, though, they meet again in New York. Redford has now sold out totally and makes his living writing for TV. Streisand has remarried. They meet in Central Park, and in a rather predictable ending, bid each other farewell. She walks away handing out "Ban the Bomb" leaflets as he shakes his head and calls out after her, "You never give up, do you?" Whether the screenwriter was referring to the character or the actress is *anybody's* guess. Give it up, girl.

WAYNE'S WORLD [DVD]
1992 95m c Comedy ★★★½
Paramount (U.S.) PG-13

Mike Myers (*Wayne Campbell*), Dana Carvey (*Garth Algar*), Rob Lowe (*Benjamin Oliver*), Tia Carrere (*Cassandra*), Brian Doyle-Murray (*Noah Vanderhoff*), Lara Flynn Boyle (*Stacy*), Colleen Camp (*Mrs. Vanderhoff*), Donna Dixon (*Dreamwoman*), Meat Loaf (*Tiny*), Ione Skye (*Elyse*)

p, Lorne Michaels; d, Penelope Spheeris; w, Mike Myers, Bonnie Turner, Terry Turner (from the characters created by Mike Myers); ph, Theo Van de Sande; ed, Malcolm Campbell; m, J. Peter Robinson; prod d, Gregg Fonseca; art d, Bruce Miller

Given the huge cultural significance of this film, based on the "Saturday Night Live" sketch starring Mike Myers and Dana Carvey, we felt the situation called for more than just a review. So we asked Dr. Stephen Stratocaster, Professor of Popular Culture at the University of Illinois-Aurora, to interview Wayne and Garth in an attempt to pin down the reason for the film's massive appeal.

S.S.: "I'd like to begin by talking about the plot of your film, which involves an ultra-smooth video producer, played by Rob Lowe. He tries to turn your public-access cable show, which you've been producing from a basement in suburban Illinois, into a mainstream network success. But he also dupes you into giving the show's new sponsor—a video arcade owner—his own spot on the program. Then he tries to iron out the show's rough edges, turning it into a cheesy, plastic version of the real thing. Did you intend this as a satire on the crass, commercial nature of network TV?"

WAYNE: "No way, Professor; we just needed a story so we could string a lot of gags together without it getting too boring."

GARTH: "Yeah, like NAKED GUN!"

S.S.: "I see. Well, let's talk about the other storyline, which involves Wayne falling in love with Cassandra (Tia Carrere), a beautiful Asian woman who sings in a rock band. I was deeply moved, Wayne, by one scene in which you're sitting on the roof of a nightclub with Cassandra, and you launch into fluent Cantonese, a language you've learned specifically so you can get to know her better. I feel the scene says a lot about our current need for a global understanding—an understanding that can best be achieved by studying the languages and customs of other cultures. Is that what you were trying to express?"

WAYNE: "Oui, exactement."

S.S.: "My next question concerns the satirical references to modern pop culture, from TV shows like 'Mission Impossible' to sports personalities like Stan Mikita, which saturate your movie. I'm particularly interested in the way you got pop-culture icons to turn in cameo performances. Ed O'Neill, for instance, from TV's 'Married With Children,' plays a donut-shop manager with a psychopathic conversational style; and rock performer Alice Cooper delivers a speech on the socio-political history of Milwaukee. In addition, you both address the camera directly, as though you *know* you're in a movie. All this makes for a very post-modern, self-referential tone which seems to reflect the media-saturated nature of contemporary society. Was this an effect you were actively seeking?"

WAYNE: "Absolutely, Professor. Our film confronts the cultural emptiness of late 20th-century life head-on, revealing a profound hollowness in the heart of modern man (and babe). But we manage to find humor in the midst of this despair."

S.S.: "Well, thank you, gentlemen, that was most enlightening."

WAYNE: "No, thank *you*, Professor. You've helped us understand our work in a new light … NOT!"

WAYS OF LOVE

1950 119m bw Drama ★★★★★
Joseph Burstyn (Italy/France)

A DAY IN THE COUNTRY: Sylvia Bataille *(Henriette)*, Gabriel *(Mons. Doufour)*, Jeanne Marken *(Mme. Doufour)*, Georges St. Saens *(Henry)*, Bordan *(Anatole)*, Jacques Borel *(Rudolph)*, Jean Renoir *(Innkeeper)*, THE MIRACLE: Anna Magnant *(Nanni)*, Federico Fellini *(The Stranger)*, JOFROI: Vincent Scotto *(Jofroi)*

p, Pierre Braunberger; d, Jean Renoir, Roberto Rossellini, Marcel Pagnol; w, Jean Renoir, Roberto Rossellini, Tullio Pinelli (based on stories by Guy de Maupassant, Federico Fellini and Jean Giono); ph, Claude Renoir, Jean Bourgoin; ed, Marguerite Renoir; m, Joseph Kosma, Renzo Rossellini

A peculiar masterpiece since it is actually a compilation of three brilliant short films—Jean Renoir's A DAY IN THE COUNTRY (1946), Roberto Rossellini's THE MIRACLE (1948), and Marcel Pagnol's JOFROI (1933) brought together by foreign film importer Joseph Burstyn for the benefit of American audiences, who would not otherwise get a chance to see them. Renoir's film is one of his most perfect, adapting a Guy de Maupassant story about a bourgeois mother and daughter who get involved with two oarsmen. Rossellini's picture was originally released in Italy in a diptych entitled L'AMORE and was meant as a vehicle for Magnani. Besides being Fellini's only acting credit, THE MIRACLE was also the film that increased the odds for free speech in motion pictures. When New York's Cardinal Spellman saw the picture, he was morally outraged and attempted to have it banned. For once, the U.S. Justice Department had enough good sense to let it play. The final episode, JOFROI, is a tale of a peasant who sells his land and then tries to prevent the owner from cutting down the olive trees that grow on it. All three episodes have been released as short films and are masterpieces in their own right.

WEATHER UNDERGROUND, THE

DVD
2003 92m c/bw Documentary ★★★½
Free History Project/Upstate Films (U.S.)

Bernardine Dohrn, Mark Rudd, Brian Flanagan, David Gilbert, Bill Ayers, Naomi Jaffe, Todd Gitlin, Laura Whitehorn, Don Strickland, Kathleen Cleaver

p, Sam Green, Carrie Lozano, Bill Siegel, Marc Smolowitz; d, Sam Green, Bill Siegel; ph, Andrew Black, Federico Salsano; ed, Sam Green, Dawn Logsdon; m, Dave Cerf, Amy Dominques

AAN Best Documentary Feature

Without the proper context, it's easy to snicker at the Weather Underground, a group of middle- and upper-middle-class white kids who adopted the poses and rhetoric of the Black Panthers and Ho Chi Minh and vowed to smash racist/imperialist America through a people's revolution. Context is everything when it comes to the antiwar movement of the 1960s and '70s, and while Sam Green and Bill Siegel's informative documentary is far from sympathetic to the WU's terrorist tactics, the background the film provides helps make the group's motivations somewhat comprehensible.

Inspired by "Third World revolutionary struggles" and frustrated by the escalating body count in Vietnam, racism at home, and the apparent ineffectiveness of the protest movement, the WU broke ranks with Students for a Democratic Society (SDS), which, by the end of the 1960s, was splintered by ideological infighting. Renouncing SDS's commitment to nonviolence, WU members presented themselves as a fighting force that would bring the war home to the streets of American cities through armed struggle. Conflicts with police and a series of bombings across the country—including one at the Capitol in Washington—followed, and many Weathermen spent much of the 1970s underground.

Through archival news footage and interviews with such WU figures as Bernardine Dohrn and Bill Ayers, the film traces key moments in the WU's short history and the numerous bombings that, if nothing else, landed the WU members on the FBI's wanted list and isolated them from much of the Left. Green and Siegel are more interested in the personalities involved than the group's politics, but the film does an excellent job of capturing the pervasive violence that rocked the era, from Vietnam to Altamont.

WE THE LIVING

1942 174m bw Drama ★★★★
Scalera/Duncan Scott (Italy)

Alida Valli *(Kira Argounova)*, Rossano Brazzi *(Leo Kovalensky)*, Fosco Giachetti *(Andrei Taganov)*, Giovanni Grasso *(Tishenko)*, Emilio Cigoli *(Pavel Syerov)*, Cesarina Gherardi *(Comrade Sonia)*, Mario Pisu *(Victor Dunaev)*, Guglielmo Sinaz *(Morozov)*, Gero Zambuto *(Alexei Argounov)*, Annibale Betrone *(Vassili Dunaev)*

p, Duncan Scott, Henry Mark Holzer, Erika Holzer; d, Goffredo Alessandrini; w, Anton Giulio Majano (based on the novel by Ayn Rand); ph, Giuseppe Caracciolo; ed, Eraldo Da Roma; m, Renzo Rossellini; art d, Andrea Beloborodoff, Giorgio Abkhasi, Amleto Bonetti; cos, Rosi Gori

They don't make films like this anymore. First shown in Italy in 1942, but banned by Mussolini's government and lost until it was rediscovered and re-edited (after an intensive search by the producers), WE THE LIVING has a syrupy score, misty photography, melodramatic confrontations, heroic renunciations, and suicides in the name of lost ideals. And it works. An adaptation of Ayn Rand's novel, the film mixes lots of anti-Communist politics with its passion, but there's still much passion in this tale set in Russia in the early 1920s. Opposed to the new Bolshevik regime are the lovers Kira Argounova (Alida Valli) and Leo Kovalensky (Rossano Brazzi). When Leo is arrested and subsequently contracts tuberculosis, Kira becomes the mistress of idealistic Party man and secret police member Andrei Taganov (Fosco Giachetti) as a means of paying for Leo's stay at a sanitarium. Unfortunately, Leo repays her sacrifice by becoming as corrupt as his erstwhile oppressors, while Andrei becomes disillusioned with the government and shoots himself after finding out that Kira doesn't care for him. The film ends as Kira, still incorruptibly anti-Red, prepares to leave Russia and Leo forever. Though filled with Rand's predictable dogma, WE THE LIVING is unforgettably romantic, and still stands up as a moving love story and as a declaration of female independence that was way ahead of its time. The lush sets, exquisite cinematography, impeccable black-and-white values, and exceptional casting lend the proceedings much splendor, even if the splendor is preposterous.

WE WERE SOLDIERS

2002 138m c War ★★½
Icon Entertainment International/Wheelhouse/ R
Motion Picture Production GmbH/Erste KG
(U.S./Germany)

Mel Gibson (Lt. Col. Hal Moore), Madeleine Stowe (Julie Moore), Greg Kinnear (Major Bruce Crandall), Sam Elliott (Sgt. Major Basil Plumley), Chris Klein (Lt. Jack Geoghegan), Keri Russell (Barbara Geoghegan), Barry Pepper (Joe Gallaway), Don Duong (Lt. Col. Nguyen Huu Ahn), Josh Dougherty (Spec 4 Bob Ouelette), Edwin Morrow (Private Willie Godboldt)

p, Bruce Davey, Stephen McEveety, Randall Wallace; d, Randall Wallace; w, Randall Wallace (based on the book We Were Soldiers Once... and Young, by Joe Galloway and Lt. Gen. Harold Moore); ph, Dean Semler; ed, William Hoy; m, Nick Glennie-Smith; prod d, Thomas Sanders; art d, Daniel Dorrance; fx, Stan Blackwell, David Goldberg, Paul J. Lombardi; cos, Michael T. Boyd

The savage five-day melee that erupted at two separate locations in South Vietnam's Ia Drang river valley in November 1965 was the first full-on engagement between American and North Vietnamese troops. Adapted from the acclaimed book by Lt. General Harold G. Moore and Joe Galloway, writer-director Randall Wallace's loud and grisly bloodbath tells the first half of the story: the battle surrounding the landing zone dubbed "X-Ray."

Instead of a little historical context for American involvement in Indochina, Wallace spends the first half-hour on sentimental backstory. Moore (played with twinkling bonhomie by Mel Gibson) is shown putting his kids to bed, canoodling with his wife (Madeleine Stowe), and assuring youthful Second Lieutenant Jack Geoghegan (Chris Klein) that being a good soldier makes a guy a good father. Then it's off to Vietnam with the 1st Battalion, 7th Cavalry. Their orders are simple: Find the enemy and kill them. U.S. troops are flown into X-Ray by helicopter, a military innovation that saved time but ensured that everyone knew the Yanks were coming. The 1/7 is almost immediately surrounded by thousands of North Vietnamese soldiers, and despite the expert leadership of Moore and his second-in-command, Sergeant Major Basil Plumley (a very good Sam Elliott), this small patch of ground quickly becomes a hell on Earth. Like most of BLACK HAWK DOWN and the first 20 minutes of SAVING PRIVATE RYAN, this is war movie-making as a purely sensory experience; Wallace is so determined to realistically simulate combat that the big picture is hard to see. Who these brave men were and why they fought disappears under the usual clichés, while the astounding acts of courage that occurred at Ia Drang are lost to the dust and din.

WEDDING, A

1978 125m c Comedy/Drama ★★½
Lion's Gate (U.S.) PG

Lillian Gish (Nettie Sloan), Ruth Nelson (Beatrice Sloan Cory), Ann Ryerson (Victoria Cory), Desi Arnaz Jr. (Dino Corelli), Belita Moreno (Daphene Corelli), Vittorio Gassman (Luigi Corelli), Nina Van Pallandt (Regina Corelli), Virginia Vestoff (Clarice Sloan),

Dina Merrill (Antoinette Sloan Goddard), Pat McCormick (Mackenzie Goddard)

p, Robert Altman; d, Robert Altman; w, John Considine, Patricia Resnick, Allan Nicholls, Robert Altman (based on a story by Considine and Altman); ph, Charles Rosher Jr.; ed, Tony Lombardo; m, John Hotchkis

Altman's ambitious film is sadly one of his less successful. A WEDDING is extraordinarily self-indulgent, which is really saying something in light of this great filmmaker's astonishingly uneven career.

The setting is a wedding between the daughter of a southern parvenu family and the scion of a clan that is a combination of old money and Mafia. Altman trots more than 50 characters across the screen in what must have been an attempt to prove that he could top the feat he achieved with the 24 stars he used in NASHVILLE. In this case, though, more is less. So many people appear onscreen in so many snippets of stories that not only is it difficult to care about anyone, it's hard to remember who they are. The movie has no narrative thrust, coming across as a ragged collection of occasionally amusing scenes. This is social satire delivered with a shotgun blast.

That great gray goddess of Hollywood films, Lillian Gish, makes her 100th film appearance, but gets killed off far too early. Arnaz, the groom, is set to marry Amy Stryker, the bride with conspicuous braces. Stryker's sister Mia Farrow has already had an affair with Arnaz and is pregnant by him. Stryker's mother is Carol Burnett. She is bored with husband Paul Dooley (an Altman favorite who played Wimpy in POPEYE) and has a sexual liaison with Arnaz's uncle, McCormick. Arnaz's mother is Van Pallandt, a confirmed heroin addict. The wedding coordinator is Geraldine Chaplin, a lesbian (how amusing!), and John Cromwell is the senile priest who forgets his lines and is so myopic that he speaks to a corpse and wonders why his remarks go unanswered. Perhaps the movie's best moment goes to Howard Duff, a lech and a lush of a doctor. At one point late in the film, during a major dramatic scene, we hear him far off-screen, two floors below, very quietly reply when asked if he wants his glass refilled: "Just to the brim, please!" It's the most thrown-away of all great throwaway lines in the movies.

WEDDING BANQUET, THE DVD

(XIYAN)
1993 107m c Comedy ★★★
Central Motion Picture Corporation/Good Machine Inc.
(Taiwan)

Winston Chao (Wai Tung), May Chin (Wei-Wei), Ah-Leh Gua (Mrs. Gao), Sihung Lung (Mr. Gao), Mitchell Lichtenstein (Simon), Neal Huff (Steve), Jeffrey Howard (Street Musician), Anthony "Iggy" Ingoglia (Restaurant Manager), Dion Birney (Andrew), Jeanne Kuo Chang (Wai Tung's Secretary)

p, James Schamus, Ted Hope, Ang Lee; d, Ang Lee; w, Ang Lee, Neil Peng, James Schamus; ph, Jong Lin; ed, Tim Squyres; m, Mader; prod d, Steve Rosenzweig; art d, Rachel Weinzimer; cos, Michael Clancy

AAN Best Foreign Language Film

THE WEDDING BANQUET is a farcical, freewheeling account of what happens when one half of an interracial gay couple gets married to a woman in order to satisfy his parents' dearest wish. The film has a universal appeal that crosses all racial and sexual divisions, and will be of particular delight to anyone who has ever experienced an elaborate wedding ceremony.

Manhattanites Gao Wai Tung (Winston Chao) and Simon (Mitchell Lichtenstein) are an ideal same-sex couple: young, attractive, successful. Pressured by his parents in Taiwan to marry, Wai Tung takes up Simon's suggestion that he make a marriage of convenience with Wei-Wei (May Chin), a rebellious, decidedly untraditional artist who needs a green card. Wai Tung's parents (Sihung Lung, Ah-Leh Gua) put a major kink in the proceedings when they come to Manhattan for the wedding. With all five characters in nervously close cohabitation, Wai Tung and Simon's townhouse becomes a setting for Feydeau-esque confusion: the lovers must sleep apart; undomestic Wei-Wei pretends to whip up the flawless Chinese dinners that are, in fact, secretly prepared by Simon; and so on. The wedding ceremony, ensuing banquet, and closely supervised honeymoon bring further complications.

Taiwanese director Ang Lee has pulled off one of the most congenial, richly affectionate extended party sequences ever put on film: the banquet is a creamily photographed, cartoonish modern variant of those elaborate, over-populated Chinese scrolls depicting the human comedy in all its infinite sentiment and absurdity. Lee sustains the bubbling hilarity, but also provides quieter, deeper observation of the characters' motives and moods.

WEDDING IN GALILEE 📀
(NOCE EN GALILEE)
1987   116m   c   Drama   ★★★★
Marisa/LPA/French Ministry of Culture/French Community Ministry/ZDF   (Belgium/France)

Ali Mohammed El Akili *(Abu Adel, the Mukhtar)*, Bushra Karaman *(The Mother)*, Nazih Akleh *(Adel, the Groom)*, Makhram Khouri *(Military General)*, Anna Achdian *(Samia, the Bride)*, Sonia Amar *(Sumaya, the Daughter)*, Youssef Abou Warda *(Baccum)*, Eyad Anis *(Hassan)*, Wael Barckouti *(Ziad)*, Juliano Mer Khamis

d, Michel Khleifi; w, Michel Khleifi; ph, Eddy van der Enden; ed, Marie Castro Vasquez; m, Jean-Marie Senia

WEDDING IN GALILEE is a moving and remarkable Belgian-French coproduction about Palestinian wedding customs, military and patriarchal dominance, and the quest for peace in the Middle East. Directed by the 36-year-old, Nazareth-born Michel Khleifi, who resides in Belgium, this film has not come to American shores without its share of accolades. It was awarded the 1987 Cannes Critic's Prize, named Best Film of the Year in Belgium, and took the Grand Prize at the San Sebastian Film Festival—where jury member Alain Tanner said to Khleifi, "Your film is greater than any prize we could give it."

Filmed before the escalation in Palestinian-Israeli tensions of late 1987, WEDDING IN GALILEE is set (and was photographed) in the occupied West Bank, where the village *mukhtar* (elder), played by Akili, has vowed to give his son a great wedding. The obstacle to this planned festivity is the imposed curfew that takes effect every evening at sundown. Akili appeals to the military governor, Khouri, to make an exception in this case, but to no avail. Khouri does propose that the wedding can take place on the condition that he and his Israeli aides are invited as guests of honor. Without pondering the consequences, Akili agrees and parts with the military governor on friendly terms. When he explains to his villagers that the Israelis will be in attendance, there is an immediate split, with hostilities and insults hurled about at once. Even Akili's son, groom-to-be Akleh, disagrees with his father's decision. The wedding, however, *will* take place as Akili has promised.

A rich, lyrical film of many textures, WEDDING IN GALILEE presents Western audiences with a world rarely seen onscreen, familiar only from violent television news reports. As an anthropological film, it is educational and enlightening, presenting foreign locations and nonprofessional actors. But WEDDING IN GALILEE is much more than

a film of cultural curiosity. It is a human drama, ranging in tone from comic to poignant, from tense to sensual. Director Michel Khleifi is not afraid to let his camera linger on his locations, allowing it to move through the space and stare out an open window long after the characters have left and the action has ceased. Often the haunting musical score overpowers all other sounds until it is the only thing heard.

WEDDING SINGER, THE 📀
1998   95m   c   Comedy/Romance   ★★★
The Robert Simonds Company/Brillstein-Grey   PG-13
Entertainment/New Line   (U.S.)

Adam Sandler *(Robbie Hart)*, Drew Barrymore *(Julia)*, Christine Taylor *(Holly)*, Allen Covert *(Sammy)*, Angela Featherstone *(Linda)*, Matthew Glave *(Glenn)*, Alexis Arquette *(George)*, Frank Sivero *(Andy)*, Christina Pickles *(Angie)*, Ellen Albertini Dow *(Rosie)*

p, Robert Simonds, Jack Giarraputo; d, Frank Coraci; w, Tim Herlihy; ph, Tim Suhrstedt; ed, Tom Lewis; m, Teddy Castellucci; prod d, Perry Andelin Blake; art d, Alan Au; cos, Mona May

Sweet, shamelessly sentimental, and 100-percent cynicism-free, this conversation-heart-colored celebration of the joys of true romance doesn't have a mean bone in its body.

Robbie Hart (Adam Sandler) is the wedding singer who gets stood up at his own nuptials; Julie (Drew Barrymore) is the true-blue waitress who's about to get married to Glenn (Matthew Glave), a Grade-A, gold-plated schmuck. Since Glenn's too busy making millions trading junk bonds and fooling around on the side to help plan his own wedding, Julia turns to the heartbroken Robbie for help. Who better than a wedding professional to help a girl get the best deal on flowers, photographers, bridesmaids' dresses, and catering? Afflicted by the same mysterious ailment that blinds all romantic-comedy heroines to the fact that Mr. Right is standing by her side, Julia fails to see that she and Robbie are made for one another until the last possible moment, giving him plenty of time to write self-pitying songs and stare longingly up at her bedroom window. It's all set in 1985, the better to pad out the whisper-thin story line with gags about "Miami Vice," DeLoreans, "Dynasty," Rubik's cubes, Madonna wannabes, and the greatest hits of New Wave pop. Billy Idol stops by for a surprisingly funny cameo at the eleventh hour, and Barrymore and Sandler are very sweet together; it's no stretch to believe everyone who keeps saying what an adorable couple they make. Yes, it's sappy. It's also silly, utterly unironic, a sketch stretched out to feature length, and, if you're in the right mood, pretty darned cute.

WEE WILLIE WINKIE
1937   103m   bw   Drama/Comedy   ★★★
Fox   (U.S.)

Shirley Temple *(Priscilla Williams)*, Victor McLaglen *(Sgt. MacDuff)*, C. Aubrey Smith *(Col. Williams)*, June Lang *(Joyce Williams)*, Michael Whalen *(Lt. "Coppy" Brandes)*, Cesar Romero *(Khoda Khan)*, Constance Collier *(Mrs. Allardyce)*, Douglas Scott *(Mott)*, Gavin Muir *(Capt. Bibberbeigh)*, Willie Fung *(Mohammet Dihn)*

p, Gene Markey; d, John Ford; w, Ernest Pascal, Julien Josephson (based on a story by Rudyard Kipling); ph, Arthur Miller; ed, Walter Thompson; m, Louis Silvers; art d, William Darling; cos, Gwen Wakeling

AAN Best Interior Decoration: William S. Darling, David Hall

Little Shirley Temple works her charms on India in this starring vehicle, which is very loosely based on a Rudyard Kipling story and directed by, of all people, John Ford, best known for his classic westerns. At the turn of the century, Priscilla (Shirley Temple) and her widowed mother (June

Lang) go to live with her grandfather, Col. Williams (C. Aubrey Smith), on a British army base in India. Priscilla goes through maneuvers with the troops, donning a darling pint-sized uniform and managing to win over everyone she comes in contact with, including rebel leader Khoda Khan (Cesar Romero). The entire political situation is solved when Priscilla asks why the two factions are mad at each other, thus bringing about a peaceful resolution.

WEEDS

1987 115m c Drama ★★★½
Kingsgate (U.S.) R

Nick Nolte *(Lee Umstetter)*, Lane Smith *(Claude)*, William Forsythe *(Burt the Booster)*, John Toles-Bey *(Navarro)*, Joe Mantegna *(Carmine)*, Ernie Hudson *(Bagdad)*, Mark Rolston *(Dave)*, J.J. Johnson *(Lazarus)*, Rita Taggart *(Lillian Bingington, Newspaper Critic)*, Orville Stoeber *(Lead Guitar)*

p, Bill Badalato; d, John Hancock; w, Dorothy Tristan, John Hancock; ph, Jan Weincke (Technicolor); ed, Dennis M. O'Connor; m, Angelo Badalamenti; prod d, Joseph T. Garrity; art d, Pat Tagliaferro; fx, Mike Menzel, Marvin Gardner, Rick Barefoot; chor, Jerry Evans; cos, Mary Kay Stolz

WEEDS is an offbeat look at the American penal system and the criminals who pass through it. Lee Umstetter (Nick Nolte), an inmate sentenced to life with no chance of parole, tries to distract his mind from his fate by reading. Then after watching a local theater troupe perform for the prisoners, Umstetter writes his own play, basing it on the dehumanizing prison experience. He is given permission to perform the play for the inmates, and the playwright casts his work with enthusiastic prisoners. Lillian Bingington (Rita Taggart), a San Francisco drama critic, sees the play and is so impressed with both Umstetter's writing and acting that she works to get him paroled. Based loosely on the real-life saga of inmate Rick Cluchey, WEEDS is a fascinating, touching, funny, and at times brutal look at the wreckage of the American penal system. While pulling no punches when it comes to the harsh realities of the situation, the film's message is ultimately a hopeful one. The script, authored by director John Hancock and his wife, Dorothy Tristan, falters at times, but the excellent cast pulls the movie through some rough spots. Nolte is superb with a skillful, detailed performance filled with intelligence and nuance.

WEEKEND

1967 103m c Drama ★★★★½
Comacico/Copernic/Lira/Ascot (France/Italy)

Mireille Darc *(Corinne)*, Jean Yanne *(Roland)*, Jean-Pierre Kalfon *(Leader of FLSO)*, Valerie Lagrange *(His Moll)*, Jean-Pierre Leaud *(Saint-Just/Man in Phone Booth)*, Yves Beneyton *(Member of FLSO)*, Paul Gegauff *(Pianist)*, Daniel Pommereulle *(Joseph Balsamo)*, Yves Afonso *(Gros Poncet)*, Blandine Jeanson *(Emily Bronte/Girl in Farmyard)*

d, Jean-Luc Godard; w, Jean-Luc Godard; ph, Raoul Coutard (Eastmancolor); ed, Agnes Guillemot; m, Antoine Duhamel, Wolfgang Amadeus Mozart (Piano Sonata K.576)

A brutally satirical film somewhat reminiscent of the works of Luis Bunuel, this was Jean-Luc Godard's most ambitious and vociferous "revolutionary" movie before he retired to the shelter of the Dziga-Vertov group. It's full of funny anti-bourgeois set pieces including one of the great sequences in all cinema: a full reel, ten-minute tracking shot that proceeds with a stately pace past a very, very long line of stalled automobiles on a French country highway lined with poplars.

This mind boggling film stacks analogy upon analogy and allegory upon allegory with hallucinatory fervor in an episodic odyssey of an unpleasant upper-class Parisian pair out for a weekend trip to visit the wife's mother. Opening with a psychiatric-session monologue by the delicate Darc, clad only in panties and perched first on a desk, then on a refrigerator as she hesitantly describes a sexual encounter involving an egg and an orifice, the movie quickly moves to the carnage of the roadways during a sunny weekend. A bumper-to-bumper carnival of cars ensues, honking, careening, crashing, overturning, and burning along with their grotesque occupants as Darc and Yanne proceed on their trip. Along the way social values regarding sex, consumerism, and family are explored in myriad surreal ways. The final result can be viewed as a darkly funny vision of Hell that culminates in one possible brave new world. One of the essential films of the 1960s.

WELCOME TO L.A.

1976 106m c Drama ★★½
UA (U.S.) R

Keith Carradine *(Carroll Barber)*, Sally Kellerman *(Ann Goode)*, Geraldine Chaplin *(Karen Hood)*, Harvey Keitel *(Ken Hood)*, Lauren Hutton *(Nona Bruce)*, Viveca Lindfors *(Susan Moore)*, Sissy Spacek *(Linda Murray)*, Denver Pyle *(Carl Barber)*, John Considine *(Jack Goode)*, Richard Baskin *(Eric Wood)*

p, Robert Altman; d, Alan Rudolph; w, Alan Rudolph (based on the music suite "City of the One Night Stands" by Richard Baskin); ph, David Myers (DeLuxe Color); ed, William A. Sawyer, Tom Walls; m, Richard Baskin; cos, Jules Melillo

Although heralded by some as one of the most original and innovative directorial debuts of the 1970s, Alan Rudolph's WELCOME TO L.A., like his REMEMBER MY NAME, seems specifically designed for cult status. It takes an off-beat look at a self-important group of Los Angeles bohemians and their essentially worthless lives, which revolve mainly around sex, drinking, and driving (though not necessarily at the same time). Carradine and his fellow Altman veterans just seem to wander around a lot, and the film's success or failure depends almost entirely on how much you like them.

WELCOME TO THE DOLLHOUSE

1995 87m c Comedy/Drama ★★★½
Suburban Pictures (U.S.) R

Heather Matarazzo *(Dawn Wiener)*, Brendan Sexton III, billed as Brendan Sexton Jr. *(Brandon McCarthy)*, Daria Kalinina *(Missy Wiener)*, Matthew Faber *(Mark Wiener)*, Angela Pietropinto *(Mrs. Wiener)*, Eric Mabius *(Steve Rodgers)*, Bill Buell *(Mr. Wiener)*, Victoria Davis *(Lolita)*, Christina Brucato *(Cookie)*, Christina Vidal *(Cynthia)*

p, Todd Solondz; d, Todd Solondz; w, Todd Solondz; ph, Randy Drummond; ed, Alan Oxman; m, Jill Wisoff; prod d, Susan Block; art d, Lori Solondz; cos, Melissa Toth

Nightmarishly hilarious and stunningly frank, writer-director Todd Solondz's evocation of awkward adolescence is a bracing antidote to the counterfeit nostalgia so egregiously exploited by heartwarming TV sitcoms and saccharine coming-of-age movies.

Eleven-year-old misfit Dawn Wiener (Heather Matarazzo) is the patron saint of cootie girls, complete with nerd glasses and clueless wardrobe. At home, she's a put-upon middle child—her younger sister is an adorable little ballerina; her older brother, a brainy computer geek. At school, the cool girls torment her mercilessly, calling her "wiener dog" and "lesbo" (she's too dorky even to register on the radar of cool boys). Her parents offer little in the way of sympathy or support, and even her teachers treat her with spiteful indifference.

WELCOME TO THE DOLLHOUSE adroitly renders the relentless pecking order of abuse, but it doesn't make the sentimental error of suggesting that people become noble, kind, or empathetic simply by virtue of being persecuted. Dawn (portrayed with spirited honesty by 11-year-old Matarazzo) isn't one of those sensitive, misunderstood outsiders familiar from REBEL WITHOUT A CAUSE or *The Catcher in the Rye*. She's an victim, to be sure, but Solondz refuses to romanticize her predicament: she's abrasive, unsightly, socially maladroit, and exasperatingly complicit in her own ostracism.

WELL, THE
DVD
1999 102m c Drama/Thriller ★★★½
NSW Film & TV Office/Australian Film Finance/Southern Star Xanadu (Australia)

Pamela Rabe *(Hester)*, Miranda Otto *(Katherine)*, Paul Chubb *(Harry Bird)*, Frank Wilson *(Francis Harper)*, Steve Jacobs *(Rod Borden)*, Genevieve Lemon *(Jen Borden)*, Simon Lydon *(Jock)*, Kati Edwards, Luke Harrison, Daniel Harrison

p, Sandra Levy; d, Samantha Lang; w, Laura Jones (based on the novel by Elizabeth Jolley); ph, Mandy Walker; ed, Dany Cooper; m, Stephen Rae; prod d, Michael Philips; art d, Anne Beauchamp; cos, Anna Borghesi

A grim and deliciously twisted Gothic chiller from the dark side of sunny Down Under.

Middle-aged, unmarried, and entirely devoted to the care of her ailing father and his sprawling homestead, Hester Harper (Pamela Rabe) returns from town one afternoon with something for herself: a teenage orphan named Kathy (Miranda Otto), whom Hester claims to have hired to help out with the housework. But when Kathy balks at doing any actual work, a smitten Hester begs her to stay anyway, and Kathy soon becomes Hester's pampered guest. Once Hester's father dies, all restraint and responsibility fly out the window: The two spend their time frittering away Hester's inheritance, planning fantastic trips to Europe and warbling German lieder on the dusty upright piano. Having let the farm go to seed, Hester is forced to sell the big house and retire to a cramped and decrepit cottage on the edge of the Harper property. There, an unexpected visitor intrudes on their idyll, a horrible accident occurs, and Hester's dream world comes crashing down.

First-time feature director Samantha Lang and veteran screenwriter Laura Jones stick close to Elizabeth Jolley's mordant novel while making a few wise excisions: rather than reproducing Jolley's offbeat dialogue, they rely on the extraordinary chemistry between Otto and the Canadian-born Rabe to flesh out Jolley's themes of destructive erotic obsession, deviousness, and betrayal. Jones has adapted novels for Jocelyn Moorehouse (A THOUSAND ACRES), Gillian Armstrong (OSCAR AND LUCINDA), and Jane Campion (AN ANGEL AT MY TABLE, PORTRAIT OF A LADY), whose earlier films are thematically and stylistically echoed here. Jones writes short, pungent scenes that, combined with Mandy Walker's ice-blue cinematography, create an overall mood that's as dank and chilling as the film's central image: the deep well in front of Hester's cottage, that holds something far murkier than water.

WEST SIDE STORY
DVD
1961 153m c Musical ★★★★
Mirisch/Seven Arts/Beta (U.S.)

Natalie Wood *(Maria)*, Richard Beymer *(Tony)*, Russ Tamblyn *(Riff)*, Rita Moreno *(Anita)*, George Chakiris *(Bernardo)*, Simon

Oakland *(Lt. Schrank)*, William Bramley *(Officer Krupke)*, Tucker Smith *(Ice)*, Tony Mordente *(Action)*, Eliot Feld *(Baby John)*

p, Robert Wise; d, Robert Wise, Jerome Robbins; w, Ernest Lehman (based on the stage play by Arthur Laurents, based on a conception by Robbins, inspired by a play by William Shakespeare); ph, Daniel Fapp (Panavision, Technicolor); ed, Thomas Stanford; m, Leonard Bernstein; prod d, Boris Leven; chor, Jerome Robbins; cos, Irene Sharaff

AA Best Picture; AA Best Supporting Actor: George Chakiris; *AA Best Supporting Actress:* Rita Moreno; *AA Best Director:* Jerome Robbins, Robert Wise; *AAN Best Adapted Screenplay:* Ernest Lehman; *AA Best Color Cinematography:* Daniel L. Fapp; *AA Best Film Editing:* Thomas Stanford; *AA Best Score (Musical):* Saul Chaplin, Johnny Green, Sid Ramin, Irwin Kostal; *AA Best Art Direction-Set Decoration (Color):* Boris Leven, Victor A. Gangelin; *AA Best Costume Design (Color):* Irene Sharaff; *AA Best Sound:* Fred Hynes, Gordon E. Sawyer

When it's good, very good; when it's bad, a stinker. WEST SIDE STORY is the filmed version of the hit Broadway musical inspired by "Romeo and Juliet." Jerome Robbins, who conceived the stage version, gets co-director credit here. He was originally slated to direct the entire film, but his perfectionism meant twice the budget. United Artists brought in Robert Wise after less than a month of rehearsals, assigning him direction of the non-musical sequences. Before long, Robbins was booted all together. The numbers he choreographed remain the most inventive, energetic sequences in the film: the lengthy opening sequence (including "The Jet Song"), "America," "I Feel Pretty" and "Cool." If Robbins had done the whole of it, we might be left with a more dynamic and explosive film. But there's no discounting that whenever WEST SIDE STORY proclaims the leads' love it goes predictable on us—musically, first and foremost, so no director could entirely change that. Wise saddled these moments with all the usual—soft-focus camera work, stars in the sky, Rodgers and Hammerstein ballet. Nor is this helped by Natalie Wood and Richard Beymer (dubbed by Marni Nixon and Jim Bryant). When they're not mouthing like fish in tanks, they're wrestling the awkward dialogue of these sequences. Lucky for us, everything—and everyone—else is first-rate; especially the three meaty supporting parts played by Moreno (alas, dubbed also, by Betty Wand—but Moreno acts with fire and can dance), gorgeous, pantherine Chakiris and winning Tamblyn.

Sticking closely to Arthur Laurents's original book, the film follows the escalating tensions between rival teenage gangs the Jets (who are white) and the Sharks (who are Puerto Rican) as they battle for turf in Manhattan's Upper West Side. The Sharks are led by Bernardo, boyfriend of the tempestuous Anita; the Jets follow Riff (Tamblyn). Caught in the middle are Bernardo's sister, Maria (Wood), who has just arrived from Puerto Rico, and Tony (Beymer), a member of the Jets who is Riff's best friend. Tony and Maria fall in love, despite the hatred between their friends and relatives, but the romance is destined to end tragically.

WEST SIDE STORY became one of the most popular film musicals in history, largely on the strength of its youth appeal and the aforementioned Robbins's choreography—a spectacular combination of ballet, acrobatics, and jazz excitingly adapted for the camera. The score by Leonard Bernstein (with lyrics by Stephen Sondheim) has become an acknowledged and much-beloved classic.

WESTERN UNION
1941 93m c Western ★★★★
Fox (U.S.)

Randolph Scott *(Vance Shaw)*, Robert Young *(Richard Blake)*, Dean Jagger *(Edward Creighton)*, Virginia Gilmore *(Sue*

Creighton), John Carradine *(Doc Murdoch)*, Slim Summerville *(Herman)*, Chill Wills *(Homer)*, Barton MacLane *(Jack Slade)*, Russell Hicks *(Governor)*, Victor Kilian *(Charlie)*

p, Harry Joe Brown; d, Fritz Lang; w, Robert Carson (based on a story by Zane Grey); ph, Edward Cronjager, Allen Davey (Technicolor); ed, Robert Bischoff, Gene Flowler Jr. (uncredited); m, David Buttolph; art d, Richard Day, Albert Hogsett; cos, Travis Banton

After the success of his first western, THE RETURN OF FRANK JAMES, German director Lang was assigned to do another, this one based on the construction of the Western Union telegraph line from Omaha, Nebraska, to Salt Lake City, Utah. Randolph Scott stars as an outlaw looking to reform his wicked ways.

The most epic and beautiful of Lang's westerns (it was the director's personal favorite), WESTERN UNION is an outstanding entry in the genre. Lang, who loved the American West and spent much time traveling there, researched the period thoroughly and paid painstaking attention to detail. Having studied American Indians for some time, he was delighted with the opportunity to present them in their full glory, with accurate warpaint and battle gear photographed in beautiful Technicolor. The photography by Cronjager is some of the most beautiful work of the 1940s, and the cast is filled with outstanding character actors such as Carradine, Wills, Summerville, and Kilian. There is much humor in WESTERN UNION, most of it centering around Summerville, the timid cook scared witless of the "Wild West." Lang would make only one more western, RANCHO NOTORIOUS, yet another superior entry from a German director working in a distinctly American genre.

WESTERNER, THE *DVD*
1940 100m bw Western ★★★★★
UA (U.S.)

Gary Cooper *(Cole Hardin)*, Walter Brennan *(Judge Roy Bean)*, Doris Davenport *(Jane-Ellen Mathews)*, Fred Stone *(Caliphet Mathews)*, Paul Hurst *(Chickenfoot)*, Chill Wills *(Southeast)*, Charles Halton *(Mort Borrow)*, Forrest Tucker *(Wade Harper)*, Tom Tyler *(King Evans)*, Arthur Aylesworth *(Mr. Dixon)*

p, Samuel Goldwyn; d, William Wyler; w, Jo Swerling, Niven Busch (based on a story by Stuart N. Lake); ph, Gregg Toland; ed, Daniel Mandell; m, Alfred Newman (uncredited); Dimitri Tiomkin; art d, James Basevi; fx, Archie Stout, Paul Eagler; cos, Irene Saltern

AA Best Supporting Actor: Walter Brennan; *AAN Best Original Story:* Stuart N. Lake; *AAN Best Interior Decoration (B/W):* James Basevi

A superior western that mixes fine cinematography, terrific performances, and a script of higher caliber than most to produce a film still fondly remembered today. Cooper is a drifter who runs afoul of the law when he is falsely accused of stealing a horse. He is taken in front of Brennan, who serves as a justice of the peace and *is* the "Law west of the Pecos," as a cemetery full of his victims will attest. He tries Cooper in a hasty mockery of justice and sentences him to hang, but Cooper, knowing Brennan's admiration and even love for stage star Lily Langtry (after whom Brennan has named his town), convinces the judge that he is a personal friend of Langtry and will obtain a lock of her hair for the judge if the judge lets him go. Brennan is so love-struck that he doesn't see through this obvious lie, and the two men soon become friends of a sort. That night, Cooper steals Brennan's gun and escapes, stopping at the farm of Stone and his daughter, Davenport. Brennan is conducting a campaign, through his deputies, aimed at driving the homesteaders off the range. Cooper, who has become smitten with Davenport, decides to stay in the area and be the advocate for the homesteaders with Brennan. For a time things go smoothly, and Cooper gives Brennan a lock of Davenport's hair, telling him it is from Langtry; but then Brennan's terrorizing of the farmers takes on new fervor, and Stone is murdered. Cooper sets out for a reckoning with Brennan, but learns that the judge has left Langtry to travel to Fort Davis, where he has bought every seat in the theater to see Langtry in person for the first time. The curtain rises, and it is Cooper who is standing there, guns at the ready. The two men shoot it out in the gaslit hall, and Cooper finally manages to wound Brennan mortally. Dying, Brennan is taken backstage by Cooper to meet his dream, played here by Lilian Bond, whose hand he kisses before he dies.

Cooper was initially reluctant to take the part of the drifter, thinking it too minor for an actor of his stature. Director Wyler shamed him out of that attitude, though, with a variation of the "no small parts, only small actors" bit, and he gave Cooper enough good scenes to make the actor happy. It is Brennan, however, who steals the picture, making Judge Roy Bean one of the most unforgettable characters ever seen in a western film, researching his character and adopting a neck dislocation to represent an injury the historical judge incurred when he was hanged and cut down. Cinematographer Toland's work is superb, filling his western skies with gnarled trees and amazing clouds, and underscoring the story with a strangely somber tone. The score by Tiomkin was completely scrapped at the last minute and a new one written by Alfred Newman, though he did not receive screen credit. Dana Andrews and Forrest Tucker made their debuts here.

WESTWORLD *DVD*
1973 91m c Science Fiction/Western ★★★½
MGM (U.S.) PG

Yul Brynner *(Gunslinger)*, Richard Benjamin *(Peter Martin)*, James Brolin *(John Blane)*, Norman Bartold *(Medieval Queen)*, Dick Van Patten *(Banker)*, Linda Scott *(Arlette)*, Steve Franken *(Technician)*, Michael T. Mikler *(Black Knight)*, Terry Wilson *(Sheriff)*, Majel Barrett *(Miss Carrie)*

p, Paul N. Lazarus III; d, Michael Crichton; w, Michael Crichton; ph, Gene Polito (Panavision, Metrocolor); ed, David Bretherton; m, Fred Karlin; art d, Herman A. Blumenthal; fx, Charles Schulthies

The title refers to a futuristic Disney-type fantasy land which features android Western figures. Benjamin and Brolin are two businessman who come to WESTWORLD to live out their fantasies, and Brynner is the robot Benjamin kills in a saloon fight. Suddenly everything goes haywire, and the machines stalk the visitors. Brynner guns down Brolin, and chases Benjamin. Brynner is very good, his austere presence and unflinching intent making him seem indestructible. The film grossed a healthy $3.4 million in the U.S. and Canada and was the last film from MGM before it dissolved its releasing company. Ten minutes have been deleted from the original footage to allow WESTWORLD's present PG rating. The gardens of movie comedian Harold Lloyd's estate were used for some of the amusement park sequences. The film was followed by a sequel, FUTUREWORLD.

WETHERBY *DVD*
1985 102m c Drama ★★★½
Greenpoint/Film Four/Zenith (U.K.) R

Vanessa Redgrave *(Jean Travers)*, Ian Holm *(Stanley Pilborough)*, Judi Dench *(Marcia Pilborough)*, Marjorie Yates *(Verity Braithwaite)*, Tom Wilkinson *(Roger Braithwaite)*, Tim McInnerny

(John Morgan), Suzanna Hamilton (Karen Creasy), Stuart Wilson (Mike Langdon), Mike Kelly (CID Policeman), Diane Whitley

p, Simon Relph; d, David Hare; w, David Hare; ph, Stuart Harris (Technicolor); ed, Christopher Wimble; m, Nick Bicat; prod d, Hayden Griffin; art d, Jamie Leonard; cos, Jane Greenwood, Lindy Hemming

---

A very intelligent picture that needs to be looked at closely in order to fathom some of its subtleties. David Hare, the playwright of PLENTY, wrote and directed this film, and it's a corker. Wetherby is a small, cold town in Yorkshire. Jean Travers (Vanessa Redgrave) is a local teacher who never married. Her teenage crush was killed in Malaya in the 1950s, and she has never gotten over it. When John Morgan (Tim McInnerny) shows up at Jean's for a dinner party, Jean assumes that he is with one of the couples she has invited and they assume that he is a friend of hers. He is neither. The following day, Morgan comes by Jean's home, has a pleasant chat, then, without a bit of warning and apparently no motivation, puts a gun in his mouth and blows his brains out. It is an incredibly shocking moment. The movie flits in the present, the recent past, and sometime in the early 1950s. Hare uses an intriguing technique as he keeps going back to the seemingly ordinary dinner party in memory, and we realize that what we saw before was only the tip of the iceberg. There are more questions asked than answered in this movie, but the mental gymnastics are all worth the effort. The performances are all first-rate as well, including that of Joely Richardson, Redgrave's daughter with director Tony Richardson, as the young Jean.

WHALE RIDER   *DVD*
2003 105m c   Drama   ★★★★
Pandora Film Production/Apollo Media/   PG-13
South Pacific Pictures/A the Works Ltd.
(New Zealand)

Keisha Castle-Hughes (Pai), Rawiri Paratene (Koro), Vicky Haughton (Nanny Flowers), Cliff Curtis (Porourangi), Rawinia Clarke (Miro), Tammy Davis (Willie), Grant Roa (Rawiri), Mana Taumaunu (Hemi), Rachel House (Shilo), Taungaroa Emile (Dog)

p, John Barnett, Frank Hubner, Tim Sanders; d, Niki Caro; w, Niki Caro (based on the book The Whale Rider by Witi Ihimaera); ph, Leon Narbey; ed, David Coulson; m, Lisa Gerrard; prod d, Grant Major; art d, Grace Mok; fx, Charlie McClellan; cos, Kirsty Cameron

---

AAN Best Actress: Keisha Castle-Hughes

Niki Caro's touching feminist parable, based on Witi Ihimaera's novel, recasts a thousand-year-old legend in a contemporary light and creates a beautifully framed picture window onto a virtually hidden culture.

The setting is Whangara, a remote village on the coast of New Zealand's North Island, where the indigenous Maori people lay claim to a fabulous provenance. According to legend, the Ngati Konohi tribe's founder, Paikea, arrived on the back of a tremendous whale. Ever since, each successive generation's first-born son is considered the venerable Paikea's latest incarnation and given his name. This child is expected to fulfill his destiny by becoming the tribe's new leader. But as the film opens, a terrible tragedy occurs: An eagerly awaited male baby and his mother die during childbirth and only the child's twin—a baby girl—miraculously survives. Despite the infant's sex, her bereaved father, Porourangi (Cliff Curtis), names her Paikea. This outrages Porourangi's own father, town elder Koro (Rawiri Paratene), who's entrusted with naming the new leader. Aspiring artist Porourangi soon moves to Paris and leaves his daughter in the care of her disappointed

grandfather, who will only call her "Pai," and grandmother Nanny Flowers (Vicky Haughton), who's wise to the sexist ways of the patriarchal culture in which Whangara's women are raised. When Pai (played as a young adult by the wonderful Keisha Castle-Hughes) turns 13, the village is still without a leader. Desperate, Koro begins searching for the next leader among the town's unremarkable adolescent boys, even though it's obvious that Pai is actually his "man." She's not only adept at handling the tiaha, the traditional Maori spear, but it's clear that the headstrong girl is a born rangatira—a leader endowed with all the qualities needed to pull her declining village from its slump. Who's to say that Paikea couldn't be reincarnated as a girl? Koro, for one; he refuses to even consider the matter, even when destiny begins to outweigh the decisions of mere mortal men.

This marvelous story both respects the beliefs of a traditional people and points to a middle ground where observing tradition doesn't necessarily mean clinging to outmoded sexism. But what makes Caro's film a future classic is what so many movies geared toward younger audiences lack: a cool and very courageous 'tween heroine whom boys and girls of all ages can admire.

WHALES OF AUGUST, THE   *DVD*
1987 90m   c   Drama   ★★★
Alive/Circle/Nelson   (U.S.)

Bette Davis (Libby Strong), Lillian Gish (Sarah Webber), Vincent Price (Mr. Nikolai Maranov), Ann Sothern (Tisha Doughty), Harry Carey Jr. (Joshua Brackett), Frank Grimes (Mr. Beckwith), Frank Pitkin (Old Randall), Mike Bush (Young Randall), Margaret Ladd (Young Libby), Tisha Sterling (Young Tisha)

p, Carolyn Pfeiffer, Mike Kaplan; d, Lindsay Anderson; w, David Berry (based on the play by David Berry); ph, Mike Fash (CFI Color); ed, Nicolas Gaster; m, Alan Price; prod d, Jocelyn Herbert; art d, K.C. Fox, Bob Fox; cos, Rudy Dillon, Julie Weiss

---

AAN Best Supporting Actress: Ann Sothern

It is 1954, and Libby Strong (Bette Davis) and her younger sister Sarah Webber (Lillian Gish) have gone to a small Maine island for the summer, just as they have done for the past 60 years. Libby is now blind, and Sarah has cheerfully looked after her for 15 years. As girls, they had stood on the cliffs and watched for whales. Now the whales come no more. Sarah still anticipates their appearance and wants to put in a new picture window, but Libby, who has grown bitter and cynical, thinks it would be frivolous and vetoes the idea. Tisha Doughty (Ann Sothern), their lifelong friend and the island's resident busybody, pays them a visit and tries to persuade Sarah to put Libby in her daughter's care and to move in with her.

With its extraordinary cast, THE WHALES OF AUGUST would have made cinema history even if its script had been taken from a cereal box. In fact, the screenplay, adapted by David Berry from his own largely autobiographical stage play, isn't one of the film's stronger elements. Suffering from heavy-handed symbolism and offering few real insights, it nonetheless provides the blueprint from which these exceptional actors are able to build their performances. THE WHALES OF AUGUST has more than a few problems, but anyone interested in the art of acting, the history of the cinema, or in seeing an unpatronizing portrait of elderly characters will find the film rewarding.

WHAT A WAY TO GO!   *DVD*
1964 111m   c   Comedy   ★★½
Fox   (U.S.)

Shirley MacLaine (Louisa), Paul Newman (Larry Flint), Robert Mitchum (Rod Anderson), Dean Martin (Leonard Crawley), Gene Kelly (Jerry Benson), Robert Cummings (Dr. Stephanson), Dick

Van Dyke (Edgar Hopper), Reginald Gardiner (Painter), Margaret Dumont (Mrs. Foster), Roy Gordon (Minister)

p, Arthur P. Jacobs; d, J. Lee Thompson; w, Betty Comden, Adolph Green (based on a story by Gwen Davis); ph, Leon Shamroy (CinemaScope, DeLuxe Color); ed, Marjorie Fowler; m, Nelson Riddle; art d, Jack Martin Smith, Ted Haworth; fx, L.B. Abbott, Dick Smith, Emil Kosa Jr.; chor, Gene Kelly, Richard Humphrey; cos, Edith Head, Moss Mabry

AAN Best Art Direction-Set Decoration (Color): Jack Martin Smith, Ted Haworth, Walter M. Scott, Stuart A. Reiss; *AAN Best Costume Design (Color):* Edith Head, Moss Mabry

Former press agent Jacobs always felt that "bigger was better," so for this, his first venture into film producing, he decided to do a huge comedy, filled with stars, huge sets, and colorful costumes. It all went to prove that bigger isn't better. As the film opens, MacLaine is sharing her tale of woe with psychiatrist Cummings. Seems she's worth $200 million, but she wants to give the money to the IRS because she believes it's cursed. In flashback, the story unfolds, beginning with her refusal to marry the very wealthy Martin. Instead, she weds Van Dyke, a poor shopkeeper. Upset because Martin has told her she's made a big mistake, Van Dyke works tirelessly to amass a fortune and dies from the exertion. MacLaine, now a wealthy widow, meets and marries a series of hapless men— including bohemian painter Newman, high-powered businessman Mitchum, and smalltime entertainer Kelly—each of whom is done in by the effort of keeping her happy.

The size of this production was awesome. Costumer Edith Head had half a million dollars to play with for the more than 70 MacLaine costumes, and jeweler Harry Winston lent a bauble collection of almost $4 million to the production. A musical-extravaganza number featured Kelly and MacLaine in a satire of every nautical musical ever made. Comden, Green, and Jule Styne collaborated on "Musical Extravaganza" and "I Think You and I Should Get Acquainted." Thompson employed several shooting styles. The Van Dyke episode is reminiscent of a silent movie. The Newman section is shot as a French film, right down to the English subtitles. The Mitchum section is a Doris Day-Rock Hudson Universal look-alike. And the Gene Kelly piece resembles a Busby Berkeley production. On paper this picture seemed to have everything going for it. Unfortunately, movies are made on film, and it sank. The fact was that it simply wasn't very funny. Some interesting cameos include veteran players like Dumont (in her last film after having served so long as the Marx Brothers' foil), former boxer Lou Nova, Tom Conway (in his last role; he is the former "Falcon" of the movies and brother of George Sanders), and comics Lenny Kent, Sid Gould, and Wally Vernon. A real flopperoo—which proves that excess for its own sake means little or nothing to movie audiences.

WHAT EVER HAPPENED TO BABY JANE? 📀

1962 132m bw Thriller ★★★★
Aldrich (U.S.)

Bette Davis (Jane Hudson), Joan Crawford (Blanche Hudson), Victor Buono (Edwin Flagg), Anna Lee (Mrs. Bates), Maidie Norman (Elvira Stitt), Marjorie Bennett (Mrs. Della Flagg), Dave Willock (Ray Hudson), Anne Barton (Cora Hudson), Barbara D. Merrill (Liza Bates), Julie Allred (Young Jane)

p, Robert Aldrich; d, Robert Aldrich; w, Lukas Heller (based on the novel by Henry Farrell); ph, Ernest Haller; ed, Michael Luciano; m, Frank DeVol; art d, William Glasgow; fx, Don Steward; chor, Alex Romero; cos, Norma Koch

AAN Best Actress: Bette Davis; *AAN Best Supporting Actor:* Victor Buono; *AAN Best B/W Cinematography:* Ernest Haller; *AA*

Best Costume Design (B/W): Norma Koch; *AAN Best Sound:* Joseph Kelly

Star wars, trenchantly served, with Davis as wharf rat and Crawford a frantic parakeet. If it sometimes looks like a posionous senior citizen show with over-the-top spoiled ham, just try to look away. Bringing the screen's queens of sadism and masochism together for this slice of Camp Hollywood gothic horror revitalized the careers of both.

The Hudson sisters—Davis and Crawford—are aging actresses who live in a rotting Los Angeles mansion. Davis had been a spoiled brat vaudeville headliner known as "Baby Jane," but as she grew older her career faded. Crawford lived in her shadow as a girl but had an enormously successful adult career as a screen glamour girl. But she was unable to help Davis gain a career in film, due to the latter's drinking and eccentric behavior. At the peak of her stardom, Crawford suffered a career-ending accident for which Davis was seemingly responsible. Ever since then the two have lived together in mutual enmity, tended to by their maid, Norman. When Davis learns that her wheelchair-bound sister is planning to sell the mansion and put her in a sanitarium, she begins terrorizing Crawford; at the same time, she enlists the service of Buono, a young pianist who she hopes will help her make a comeback. The film then suspensefully builds its way to a conclusion that puts a new spin on the relationship between the two sisters.

As in the best Hitchcock movies, suspense, rather than actual mayhem, drives the film. The screenplay, by Lukas Heller, was based on the novel by Henry Farrell (who also authored the novel HUSH, HUSH SWEET CHARLOTTE and scripted WHAT'S THE MATTER WITH HELEN?).

Aldrich had his hands full balancing the overblown but sensitive egos of the rival actresses. If full-scale battle never erupted, it is still correct to say that battle lines were constantly being drawn. The original choice to star with Davis was Tallulah Bankhead (a far more lethal combination than the eventual one) when the property began floating around Hollywood, but Crawford acquired rights to the property, and offered it to Davis while the latter was unhappily appearing on Broadway in *Night of the Iguana*. Davis commanded a larger salary, Crawford a larger percentage of the gross (Joan's years at Pepsi-Cola paid off). Davis's foot allegedly made contact with Crawford's head during a scene where Baby Jane punts her sister around the living room. Crawford supposedly retaliated by use of the old Veronica Lake trick (see I MARRIED A WITCH) by rigging weights under her robe for a scene where Davis had to drag her, and Davis hurt her back. Crawford shared a private joke on Davis by sending hairdresser Peggy Shannon to MGM to secure her old blonde wig from ICE FOLLIES OF 1939 for Davis to wear. Davis bitched to Aldrich about Crawford's drinking (both were alcoholics) and padded brassieres; Crawford insulted Davis's daughter (who appeared in the film—to put it kindly, she was not burdened by her mother's talent), and the incidents go on and on.

In a bucket of gooey make-up, Davis cried when she saw herself in rushes (the limited budget precluded re-shooting) but her excessive performance is riveting—capturing the malevolence Lynn Redgrave lacked in the 1991 TV remake. Crawford wisely underacts—if her performance isn't as showy as Davis's, it's not any less accomplished.

WHAT TIME IS IT THERE? 📀

(NI NEI PIEN CHI TIEN)
2001 116m c/bw Drama ★★★★
Arena Films/Homegreen Films/Arte France Cinema (Taiwan/France/Italy)

Lee Kang-sheng (Hsiao Kang), Chen Shiang-chyi (Shiang-chyi), Lu Hsiao-ling, billed as Lu Yi-ching (Mother), Miao Tien

(Father/Old Man at the Park), Cecilia Yip *(Woman in Paris)*, Chen Chao-jung *(Man in Subway Station)*, Tsai Guei *(Prostitute)*, Arthur Nauczyciel *(Man at Phone Booth)*, David Ganansia *(Man at Restaurant)*, Jean-Pierre Leaud *(Man at the Cemetery)*

p, Bruno Pesery; d, Tsai Ming-liang; w, Tsai Ming-liang, Yang Pi-ying; ph, Benoit Delhomme; ed, Chen Sheng-chang; prod d, Yip Kam Tim; fx, Du Tuu-chih; cos, Wang Chia-hui

More of the same from Taiwanese auteur Tsai Ming-liang—good news to anyone who's already fallen under this unique director's sweet, melancholy spell. Those coming to Tsai's work for the first time should prepare themselves for long takes, not much dialogue, elliptical plotting, a hilariously deadpan sense of humor, and a poet's appreciation of isolation and heartache.

Once again, Lee Kang-sheng stars as Hsiao Kang, the ever-evolving protagonist of Tsai's four previous features. Here, Hsiao Kang is peddling watches on the streets of Taipei when he's approached by a pretty young woman (Chen Shiang-chyi) who asks for a dual-time watch. She's leaving for France the next day and wants to be able to tell time in both Paris and Taipei, and eventually convinces Hsiao Kang to sell her his own watch. It's not much of an encounter, but it's enough for the emotionally isolated Hsiao Kang to grasp onto. His father (Miao Tien) has just died, and his heartbroken mother (Lu Yi-ching) is obsessed with his reincarnation. Hsiao Kang is also mourning an absence and attempts to establish a connection with the young woman who now wears his watch by setting all the clocks in Taipei to Paris time.

To say that Tsai is revisiting familiar material shouldn't be taken as a criticism; repetition is what his work is all about. He uses the same cast (Tsai uses Lee much in the same way Truffaut once used Jean-Pierre Leaud, who puts in an amusing appearance in this film) and the same locales, and similar shots echo from film to film. With each new entry into the cycle, Tsai is carefully building a rich, remarkably coherent body of work that eloquently describes urban spaces and all the loneliness they contain.

WHAT'S LOVE GOT TO DO WITH IT

1993 120m c Biography/Musical/Drama ★★★
Touchstone (U.S.) R

Angela Bassett *(Tina Turner)*, Laurence Fishburne *(Ike Turner)*, Jenifer Lewis *(Zelma Bullock)*, Phyllis Yvonne Stickney *(Alline Bullock)*, Rae'ven Kelly *(Young Anna Mae)*, Virginia Capers *(Choir Mistress)*, Emery Shaw *(Organ Player)*, Cora Lee Day *(Grandma Georgiana)*, Sherman Augustus *(Reggie)*, Chi *(Fross)*

p, Doug Chapin, Barry Krost; d, Brian Gibson; w, Kate Lanier (from the autobiography *I, Tina* by Tina Turner and Kurt Loder); ph, Jamie Anderson; ed, Lisa Day, Stuart Pappe, Dave Rawlins, Michael J. Hill, Thomas G. Finnan; m, Stanley Clarke; prod d, Stephen Altman; art d, Richard Johnson; chor, Michael Peters; cos, Ruth Carter

AAN Best Actor: Laurence Fishburne; *AAN Best Actress:* Angela Bassett

This enjoyable biopic of rock singer Tina Turner was made at more or less the height of her success, and very much under her control. Adapted from Turner's autobiography, *I, Tina*, it plays something like A STAR IS BORN, plus rhythm and blues soundtrack, minus a third-act death scene.

Shy, gawky, country-raised teenager Anna Mae Bullock (Angela Bassett) joins her mother in the big city and spends her nights at the club where her sister, Alline, works. It's here that she first spies sexy Ike Turner (Laurence Fishburne) and his Kings of Rhythm onstage. When the microphone is passed around for audience participation, it's the little girl with the great big voice who wins the biggest ovation. Recognizing

Anna Mae's talent, Ike retools the band around her, christens her Tina, and takes the show on the road. Ike and Tina marry and, while they achieve fame and fortune, their home life descends into a hell of abuse and humiliation. Finally, Tina must find the strength to leave her husband and forge a new career without him.

Two things lift WHAT'S LOVE out of the realm of showbiz boilerplate. One is the music, with knockout production numbers crystallizing major turns in the emotional life of the protagonists: a rousing "Make Me Over" at their first studio session; "Think It's Gonna Work Out Fine" over their bordertown nuptials; "A Fool in Love" at the couple's starmaking first Apollo show, where the beleaguered Tina can barely go on. The other is the two stars: Fishburne and Bassett are both extraordinary, and though the story is inevitably slanted to Tina's perspective, Fishburne makes Ike a complex and compelling presence.

WHAT'S EATING GILBERT GRAPE? DVD

1993 117m c Comedy/Drama ★★★
Gilbert Grape Partners/Meir Teper Productions/ PG-13
DM Productions (U.S.)

Johnny Depp *(Gilbert Grape)*, Juliette Lewis *(Becky)*, Leonardo DiCaprio *(Arnie Grape)*, Mary Steenburgen *(Betty Carver)*, Crispin Glover *(Bobby McBurney)*, John C. Reilly *(Tucker Van Dyke)*, Darlene Cates *(Momma)*, Laura Harrington *(Amy Grape)*, Mary Kate Schellhardt *(Ellen Grape)*, Kevin Tighe *(Mr. Carver)*

p, Meir Teper, Bertil Ohlsson, David Matalon; d, Lasse Hallstrom; w, Peter Hedges (from his novel); ph, Sven Nykvist; ed, Andrew Mondshein; m, Alan Parker, Bjorn Isfalt; prod d, Bernt Capra; cos, Renee Ehrlich Kalfus

AAN Best Supporting Actor: Leonardo DiCaprio

Whimsical to a fault, WHAT'S EATING GILBERT GRAPE? hangs together in large part because of fine performances by Johnny Depp, as the preciously named Gilbert Grape, and Leonardo DiCaprio, who received an Academy Award nomination for his performance as Gilbert's retarded teenage brother.

Gilbert is encumbered by more burdens than any young man ought to have. He lives in isolated Endora, a dying small town, and stocks shelves at a grocery whose business has decamped to the new mall supermarket. Gilbert's 500-pound mother (Darlene Cates) hasn't left the house since his father hanged himself in the basement, his sisters (Laura Harrington and Mary Kate Schellhardt) quarrel relentlessly, and his retarded brother Arnie (DiCaprio) requires constant supervision. Gilbert's best buddies are a novice undertaker (Crispin Glover) and a gung-ho loser (John C. Reilly) who sees his future in a Burger Barn franchise. And Gilbert is having a desultory affair with frustrated housewife Betty Carver (Mary Steenburgen), whose reckless sexual demands have begun to alarm him. Everyone needs the preternaturally patient Gilbert, whose future seems grimly assured until worldly Becky (Juliette Lewis) and her grandmother (Penelope Branning) coast into town in an ailing camper, opening Gilbert's eyes to the wider world outside Endora.

Based on the first novel by Peter Hedges (who also wrote the screenplay), which has a small but intense cult following, WHAT'S EATING GILBERT GRAPE? is meandering, quirky, and resolutely small in scale. The film is heavy on character and atmosphere and light on action, though what does happen is so bizarre as to verge on the ridiculous. As directed by Swedish filmmaker Lasse Hallstrom (MY LIFE AS A DOG), it's endearingly loopy without degenerating into a carnival tent show.

WHAT'S NEW, PUSSYCAT? 🆅🅳🆅🅳
(QUOI DE NEUF, PUSSYCAT?)
1965 108m c Comedy ★★★½
Famous Artists/Famartists (U.S./France)

Peter Sellers (*Dr. Fritz Fassbender*), Peter O'Toole (*Michael James*), Romy Schneider (*Carole Werner*), Capucine (*Renee Lefebvre*), Paula Prentiss (*Liz*), Woody Allen (*Victor Shakapopulis*), Ursula Andress (*Rita*), Eddra Gale (*Anna Fassbender*), Katrin Schaake (*Jacqueline*), Richard Burton (*Man in Bar*)

p, Charles K. Feldman; d, Clive Donner; w, Woody Allen; ph, Jean Badal (Technicolor); ed, Fergus McDonell; m, Burt Bacharach; art d, Jacques Saulnier; fx, M. MacDonald; chor, Jean Guelis; cos, Gladys de Segonzac, Mia Fonssagrives, Vicky Tiel

AAN Best Song: "What's New, Pussycat?"; Burt Bacharach (Music), Hal David (Lyrics)

A most significant film to buffs in that it marks the first time Woody Allen appeared on screen in a script drawn from his own typewriter. Until this time he'd been a successful nightclub and TV variety show comic, and WHAT'S NEW PUSSYCAT? gave a wider audience to his patented neuroses. It's a good example of the "swinging sixties" style under the broad direction of Clive Donner, who had begun his career in films as an assistant director. O'Toole, fresh from his triumphs in LAWRENCE OF ARABIA and BECKET, shows that he can deliver the goods comedically as well as dramatically; here he takes the role of a lover of gorgeous women who fears nothing in this world save marriage. Sellers is a freaked-out, Beatle-wigged analyst attempting to help O'Toole deal with his problems but is so lecherous himself that he is of little value to the disturbed O'Toole. Allen is an intellectual nebbish whose life is a perpetual attempt to learn why he can't attract women.

WHAT'S NEW, PUSSYCAT? is a classic comedy of its time and captures the period in sight and sound. It doesn't wear as well as a true classic, though, and many of the gags would feel dated 20 years later. Sets and costumes are superb, as are the scenes at the "Crazy Horse." Burt Bacharach's music and Hal David's lyrics helped immensely, with the title tune being reaching No. 3 in pop music polls that year. The movie was a box-office success, appealing, no doubt, to those who doubted the sexual "double standard" as well as the Teutonic psychiatrist so aptly portrayed by Sellers. Richard Burton does a cameo, as does Allen's wife at the time, Louise Lasser. By making O'Toole the editor on a Paris fashion magazine, the tale was able to move with lighting speed and also justify his coming into contact with so many gorgeous women—every man's dream, but most particularly Woody Allen's.

WHAT'S UP, DOC? 🆅🅳🆅🅳
1972 94m c Comedy ★★★
Saticoy (U.S.) G

Barbra Streisand (*Judy Maxwell*), Ryan O'Neal (*Prof. Howard Bannister*), Madeline Kahn (*Eunice Burns*), Kenneth Mars (*Hugh Simon*), Austin Pendleton (*Frederick Larrabe*), Sorrell Booke (*Harry*), Stefan Gierasch (*Fritz*), Mabel Albertson (*Mrs. Van Hoskins*), Michael Murphy (*Mr. Smith*), Graham Jarvis (*Bailiff*)

p, Peter Bogdanovich; d, Peter Bogdanovich; w, Buck Henry, David Newman, Robert Benton (based on a story by Bogdanovich); ph, Laszlo Kovacs (Technicolor); ed, Verna Fields; m, Artie Butler; prod d, Polly Platt; art d, Herman A. Blumenthal; fx, Robert MacDonald; cos, Nancy McArdle, Ray Phelps

Peter Bogdanovich's attempt to revive the screwball comedy genre is more imitation than homage, especially if you've seen the Howard Hawks classic BRINGING UP BABY. Still, the film has plenty of good 1930s slapstick and cartoon humor to hold your attention and to justify Bugs Bunny's famed opening line (which serves as the title) and Porky Pig's equally famed closing: "Th-th-that's all, folks!" Ryan O'Neal, a clumsy, shy professor from Iowa, hopes to win a $20,000 fellowship in musicology. He carries some ancient rocks in a plaid suitcase; the rocks demonstrate his theory on music's prehistoric origins. O'Neal arrives at a San Francisco hotel with his fiancee, Kahn (in her film debut), while other guests with identical suitcases, including the breezy Streisand, are also checking in. Naturally, the suitcases get hopelessly mixed up—a daffy coincidence leading to countless comic scenes. While WHAT'S UP, DOC? may not be as great as the classic screwball comedies of the 1930s and '40s, director Bogdanovich has delivered a film with energy, wit, and a madcap pace that is well worth watching.

WHAT'S UP, TIGER LILY? 🆅🅳🆅🅳
1966 80m c Comedy ★★★½
Toho/Benedict (U.S.) PG

Tatsuya Mihashi (*Phil Moscowitz*), Mie Hama (*Terri Yaki*), Akiko Wakabayashi (*Suki Yaki*), Tadao Nakamaru (*Shepherd Wong*), Susumu Kurobe (*Wing Fat*), Woody Allen (*Narrator/Host/Voice*), Frank Buxton, Len Maxwell, Louise Lasser, Mickey Rose

p, Woody Allen; d, Senkichi Taniguchi; w, Kazuo Yamada, Woody Allen, Frank Buxton, Len Maxwell, Louise Lasser, Mickey Rose, Bryna Wilson, Julie Bennett; ph, Kazuo Yamada (Tohoscope, Eastmancolor); ed, Richard Krown; m, Jack Lewis, The Lovin' Spoonful

Woody Allen took a low-grade Japanese spy film called KAGI NO KAGI (Key of Keys) and dubbed in new dialogue (improvised with Buxton, Maxwell, Lasser, Rose, Wilson, and Bennett) to create this wonderfully cockeyed movie. The story describes the adventures of Phil Moscowitz, a Japanese James Bond who is searching for the world's greatest egg salad recipe. The balance of world power hangs on whether or not Moscowitz can keep this recipe—"so delicious you could *plotz*"—from falling into the wrong hands. After many plucky escapades, Moscowitz confronts Shepherd Wong, the evil mastermind trying to get the recipe for his own nefarious doings. Moscowitz defeats Wong's henchmen and then returns to his loves, Suki and Terri Yaki. They are eager for him to arrive, "bringing with him the constant promise of joy and fulfillment in its most primitive form." But alas, Moscowitz is now under the delusion that he is a Pan Am jet!

WHAT'S UP, TIGER LILY? is cleverly devised, hinging on a well-developed sense of the absurd. Allen and his cohorts make good use of the source movie's situations, turning its obvious cliches into some wonderful parodic gems. The one-liners spew out like popcorn, an effect that wears a little thin towards the end. Footage of the pop group the Lovin' Spoonful edited into the story also detracts from the pell-mell pacing. Though Allen had limited control over the visual content, many of the themes and ideas he would later develop in such films as LOVE AND DEATH and HANNAH AND HER SISTERS are evident in the dialogue—themes of sexual frustration, psychiatry and neurosis, Judaism, and the influence of movies. Executive producer Saperstein paid only $66,000 for the rights to KEY OF KEYS and certainly got more than his money's worth when he turned it over to the rising comedian. Heard on the soundtrack are Lasser, Allen's second wife, and Rose, cowriter with Allen of TAKE THE MONEY AND RUN and BANANAS.

WHEN FATHER WAS AWAY ON BUSINESS 🖵DVD
(OTAC NA SLUZBENOH PUTU)
1985 144m c Drama/Comedy ★★★★
Centar/Forum (Yugoslavia) R

Moreno D'E Bartolli (*Malik*), Miki Manojlovic (*Mesha*), Mirjana Karanovic (*Senija*), Mustafa Nadarevic (*Zijo*), Mira Furlan (*Ankica*), Davor Dujmovic (*Mirza*), Predrag Lakovic (*Franjo*), Pavle Vujisic (*Muzamer*), Eva Ras (*Zivka*), Aleksandar Dorcev (*Dr. Ljahaov*)

d, Emir Kusturica; w, Abdulah Sidran; ph, Vilko Filac (WS Color); ed, Andrija Zafranovic; m, Zoran Simjanovic; cos, Divna Jovanovic

AAN Best Foreign Language Film

Director Emir Kusturica deservedly won the prestigious Golden Palm at Cannes with this complex, moving drama, his second feature.

It is the early 1950s in Yugoslavia, which, under the leadership of Marshal Tito, has broken with the USSR. No-one can be sure if their next-door neighbor is just shooting off his mouth, or deliberately trying to bait someone else into making an anti-government statement. If that happens, police arrive in the middle of the night and the individual is soon "away on business." Malik (Moreno D'E Bartolli) is the six-year-old child who narrates the story of his father, Mesha (Miki Manojlovic), a privileged Labor Ministry official who is sent off to a work camp. The family likes everyone to think that Mesha is in jail for unspecified political actions, but just about everyone knows the truth—that he was set up by his former lover, Ankica (Mira Furlan). Malik and his older brother (Davor Dujmovic) do their best to keep up their mother's (Mirjana Karanovic) spirits while her husband is gone, but that's a tall order when she knows that the man who arrested her husband is her own brother, the local police commissioner, who is also sexually involved with Ankica and wanted to get his competition out of the way.

WHEN FATHER WAS AWAY has its fair share of humor and whimsy; Malik's sleepwalking assumes an almost fairy-tale dimension, and the state propaganda machine is the source of some well-observed laughs. But Kusturica never allows us to entirely forget the harsh underpinnings of his tale, and doesn't flinch from depicting the charming Mesha's less savory qualities. The banished father's chauvinism threatens, on occasion, to strain our sympathy beyond breaking point, and the last scene, in which he exacts a viciously nasty revenge on his former lover, is a masterpiece of emotional manipulation; even though we abhor Micha's behavior, we clutch our seats in the hope that he will *not* be caught red-handed. Not in front of the children, anyway.

WHEN HARRY MET SALLY... 🖵DVD
1989 96m c Comedy/Romance ★★★
Castle Rock/Nelson (U.S.) R

Billy Crystal (*Harry Burns*), Meg Ryan (*Sally Albright*), Carrie Fisher (*Marie*), Bruno Kirby (*Jess*), Steven Ford (*Joe*), Lisa Jane Persky (*Alice*), Michelle Nicastro (*Amanda*), Gretchen Palmer (*Stewardess*), Robert Alan Beuth (*Man on Aisle*), David Burdick (*Nine-year-old Boy*)

p, Rob Reiner, Andrew Scheinman, Jeffrey Stott, Steve Nicolaides; d, Rob Reiner; w, Nora Ephron; ph, Barry Sonnenfeld (Duart Color, CFI Color); ed, Robert Leighton; m, Marc Shaiman, Harry Connick Jr.; prod d, Jane Musky; cos, Gloria Gresham

AAN Best Original Screenplay: Nora Ephron

Harry (Billy Crystal) meets Sally (Meg Ryan) on a post-graduation drive from the University of Chicago to New York, but when she rebuffs his flip advances, instant antipathy is born. Nonetheless, over the next 10 years in Manhattan, the two bump into each other at various emotionally crucial points in their lives and eventually manage to effect a friendship. Then sex rears its insistent head once more, and, following a period of readjustment, commitment-shy Harry learns that staying an entire night—and possibly an entire life—with one's object of lust is actually possible. The plot may seem anything but fresh (and the borrowings from Woody Allen certainly are stale), but director Rob Reiner has a killer instinct for setting up jokes and punch-lines, and is vastly aided by the performances and chemistry of Crystal and Ryan, as well as crisp supporting work from Carrie Fisher and Bruno Kirby.

WHEN THE WIND BLOWS
1986 85m c Animated ★★★★
Meltdown/British Screen/Film Four/TVC London/Penguin Books (U.K.)

VOICES OF: Peggy Ashcroft (*Hilda Bloggs*), John Mills (*Jim Bloggs*), Robin Houston (*Announcer*), James Russell, Matt Irving, David Dundas

p, John Coates; d, Jimmy T. Murakami; w, Raymond Briggs (based on his book); ed, John Cary; m, Roger Waters; fx, Stephen Weston

With its striking simplicity, WHEN THE WIND BLOWS is a moving parable of nuclear holocaust. Told through animation, the story follows a retired English couple, James Bloggs (voiced by John Mills) and his wife, Hilda (voiced by Peggy Ashcroft), as they face the postnuclear winter in a small cottage in the British countryside. World tensions have been building, according to radio reports, and war is imminent. When the bomb goes off, destroying the England James and Hilda love so dearly, they are convinced the situation is merely a temporary crisis and, like WWII, one they can stick out until things get back to normal. Gradually, radiation begin taking its toll on the couple, and small but important details of their lives start to slip out of their control. These developments are handled with a gentle, sympathetic humor that subtly brings out the hopelessness of their plight. Mills and Ashcroft are perfectly cast in their cartoon roles. The variety of animation styles frequently produces captivating visual effects. WHEN THE WIND BLOWS is an eloquent vision of the ultimate tragedy.

WHERE EAGLES DARE 🖵DVD
1969 155m c War ★★★½
Winkast (U.K.) M

Richard Burton (*John Smith*), Clint Eastwood (*Lt. Morris Schaffer*), Mary Ure (*Mary Ellison*), Patrick Wymark (*Col. Turner*), Michael Hordern (*Vice Adm. Rolland*), Donald Houston (*Christiansen*), Peter Barkworth (*Berkeley*), Robert Beatty (*Cartwright Jones*), William Squire (*Thomas*), Derren Nesbitt (*Maj. von Hapen*)

p, Elliott Kastner; d, Brian G. Hutton; w, Alistair MacLean; ph, Arthur Ibbetson (Panavision 70, Metrocolor); ed, John Jympson; m, Ron Goodwin; art d, Peter Mullins; fx, Richard Parker, Fred Hellenburgh

A high-powered, big-budget WWII espionage thriller, WHERE EAGLES DARE follows an elite group of Allied commandos, led by John Smith (Richard Burton) and assigned to rescue an American general being held captive by the Nazis in a castle high in the Bavarian Alps. Ably assisted by a young American lieutenant, Morris Schaffer (Clint Eastwood), Smith and his crew of six don German uniforms and parachute into enemy territory. One of their number is found dead after landing, and Smith begins to suspect that one of his men is a double agent. He meets up with a pair of Allied agents, Mary Ellison (Mary Ure) and Heidi (Ingrid Pitt), and they manage to infiltrate the castle, which is accessible only by a tramway. An exciting picture with much derring-do and adventure, WHERE EAGLES DARE is also a lengthy film, though there is more than enough action to keep it moving along. Of course, it's all a bit hard to credit (especially since the Germans can't seem to hit anything with their machine guns), but that's part of the fun. Burton, in a switch from the heavy dramatic roles that made him famous, is excellent as an action hero, but Eastwood is the one who makes it all worthwhile. If it's explosions, gunplay, and wartime treachery that you like, WHERE EAGLES DARE delivers.

WHERE THE BOYS ARE

DVD

1960 99m c Comedy ★★½
Euterpe (U.S.)

Dolores Hart (Merritt Andrews), George Hamilton (Ryder Smith), Yvette Mimieux (Melanie), Jim Hutton (TV Thompson), Barbara Nichols (Lola), Paula Prentiss (Tuggle Carpenter), Connie Francis (Angie), Chill Wills (Police Captain), Frank Gorshin (Basil), Rory Harrity (Franklin)

p, Joe Pasternak; d, Henry Levin; w, George Wells (based on the novel by Glendon Swarthout); ph, Robert Bronner (CinemaScope, Metrocolor); ed, Fredric Steinkamp; m, George Stoll, Pete Rugolo; art d, George W. Davis, Preston Ames; chor, Robert Sidney; cos, Kitty Mager

It's spring break, and college kids from around the country descend en masse to Fort Lauderdale, Florida. Hart, Mimieux, Prentiss, and Francis are four friends in search of sun, parties, and boys, though not necessarily in that order. The episodic plot line follows each girl in her respective success or failure with members of the opposite gender. Prentiss (in her film debut) is a scatterbrained lass who falls for Hutton, though their relationship takes a jealous turn when Hutton is briefly infatuated with Nichols, a nightclub entertainer who performs an underwater act in a glass tank. Recording star Francis also makes her first film appearance, capitalizing more on her vocal talents than acting ability. Hart meets Ivy Leaguer Hamilton, and romance blooms. Mimieux is determined to get herself an Ivy Leaguer any way she can, mistaking sexual passion for true love.

WHERE THE BOYS ARE is plenty moralistic, yet the film is not without a naive sense of charm. Hart, who doesn't give in so easily to Hamilton, is the pinnacle of everything good and proper, while poor Mimieux gets exactly what she deserves for responding so swiftly to Harrity's importunities—or so the film would have us believe. This sexual moralizing is a bit much, portraying women as either good or bad while the boys who chase them have just one thing in mind. Fortunately, the black-and-white ethics are balanced with the lighter involvements of the other couples. Prentiss and Hutton give their story a silly sweetness, going through predictable situations with fine comic flair. Considering the radical movements that would sweep college campuses in the 1960s, this film holds some interest as a relic of sexual attitudes in the 1950s. A 1984 remake showed just how much Hollywood had changed in portraying sexual antics on screen, though the later film has none of the original's appeal.

WHERE'S POPPA?

DVD

1970 83m c Comedy ★★★½
UA (U.S.) R

George Segal (Gordan Hocheiser), Ruth Gordon (Mrs. Hocheiser), Trish Van Devere (Louise Callan), Ron Leibman (Sidney Hocheiser), Rae Allen (Gladys Hocheiser), Vincent Gardenia (Coach Williams), Joe Keyes (Gang Leader), Alice Drummond (Woman in Elevator), Tom Atkins (Policeman in Apartment), Florence Tarlow (Miss Morgiani)

p, Jerry Tokofsky, Marvin Worth; d, Carl Reiner; w, Robert Klane (based on the novel by Robert Klane); ph, Jack Priestley (DeLuxe Color); ed, Bud Molin, Chic Ciccolini; m, Jack Elliott; art d, Warren Clymer; cos, Albert Wolsky

Once again, George Segal is saddled with a difficult Jewish mother, as he was in NO WAY TO TREAT A LADY and LOST AND FOUND. This time, though, she's little short of a senile psychopath. Robert Klane wrote the screenplay from his hysterical novel, and Reiner directed it, but missed many of the jokes that worked so well in the book.

A New York attorney, Segal, lives with Gordon, his aged and quite senile mother. He has never married because she has fouled up all of his relationships. She deserves to be in a home, but Segal promised his late father that he would look after her. At the beginning of the film, Segal awakens to a local radio show, showers, shaves, puts on a gorilla suit, and races into Gordon's room. We're not sure if he wants to cheer her up or cause her to have a heart attack. She responds by punching him hard in the groin and saying, "You almost scared me to death," as she laughs. Segal, doubled over in pain, mumbles, "Almost is not good enough." Gordon prepares orange slices for Segal's breakfast, then eats them herself, along with breakfast cereal smothered in Coca-Cola. Segal's brother, Leibman, is married to Allen and refuses to help in the care of Gordon, so Segal hires a succession of nurses, but none stay past noon because Gordon is impossible to deal with. Eventually Segal meets and hires Van Devere, a sweet nurse with a strange background. She's been married once, for 32 hours. After her first sexual experience with her husband, she was appalled to find that he'd defecated in bed. Van Devere is thrilled to find a man like Segal, and the two are soon in love, though Gordon does her best to scare the young woman off.

The ultimate black comedy about difficult Jewish mothers, WHERE'S POPPA? can be very funny, but suffers from the non-stop barrage of jokes. A few quieter moments would have allowed the humor more room to breathe. Reiner's son, Rob, a onetime cast member of television's "All in the Family" who would go on to be an acclaimed director in his own right (STAND BY ME, MISERY), makes a cameo appearance. Filmed on location in New York City, WHERE'S POPPA? has become a cult favorite, though it has been radically edited for television showings and must be seen in its entirety to be fully appreciated.

WHILE THE CITY SLEEPS

1956 100m bw Crime ★★★★
Thor (U.S.)

Dana Andrews (Edward Mobley), Rhonda Fleming (Dorothy Kyne), Sally Forrest (Nancy Liggett), Thomas Mitchell (John Day Griffith), Vincent Price (Walter Kyne), Howard Duff (Lt. Burt Kaufman), Ida Lupino (Mildred Donner), George Sanders (Mark Loving), James Craig (Harry Kritzer), John Drew Barrymore (Robert Manners)

p, Bert E. Friedlob; d, Fritz Lang; w, Casey Robinson (based on the novel The Bloody Spur by Charles Einstein); ph, Ernest Laszlo (SuperScope); ed, Gene Fowler Jr.; m, Herschel Burke Gilbert; art d, Carroll Clark; cos, Norma

Lang's finest film since THE BIG HEAT and his last great success, WHILE THE CITY SLEEPS is a crime drama sending its lead actors on a twisted, dog-eat-dog journey into the underworld in their quest for success. The plot revolves around the aspirations of three newsmen—Mitchell, Sanders, and Craig—each in line for the job of editor-in-chief of a New York tabloid called The Sentinel. Upon the death of newspaper owner Robert Warwick, his manipulative, dilettante son Price takes charge. The city is being terrorized by a sex murderer known as "The Lipstick Killer" (played with conventional dementia by Barrymore), a mama's boy who preys on beautiful woman at night. In a perverse power game, Price offers the newspaper's top position to the man who can crack the case. Naturally, Mitchell, Sanders, and Craig become rivals. Mitchell, a leathery, hard-drinking Irishman, is clear about his motive—he needs the money that the position pays. Sanders, the head of the wire service, is a ruthless cad interested in the societal implications of being the boss. Photoeditor Craig tries to use his romantic link with Price's wife, Fleming, as his inroad to the top job, spending more time wooing her than investigating the crime. To help achieve his goal, Mitchell bribes streetwise reporter Andrews for assistance. Each character's lack of moral values is soon made evident when they all employ the services of women to find the killer—risking the ladies' lives instead of their own. Mitchell agrees to Andrews's plan to use Andrews's fiancee, Forrest, as a decoy for Barrymore. Sanders cons gutsy columnist Lupino into helping him secure information by seducing Andrews, while Craig continues working through Fleming and her influence over Price. Forrest is nearly killed when Barrymore tries to enter her apartment. A climactic chase leads Andrews, hot on the trail of the pathetic killer, to the New York subway system. A battle ensues between him and Barrymore, eventually ending up on the subway tracks. The roar of a northbound train thunders closer, while the lights of a southbound loom larger by the second. At the very last moment, Andrews is tossed past the oncoming train and lands safely, while Barrymore escapes up the stairs only to be apprehended by the police.

Although viewed rather narrow-mindedly by some as an unsuccessful thriller because Lang reveals the killer's identity too early, WHILE THE CITY SLEEPS is clearly more than a thriller. Lang's interest is not in the killer's motivation and methods, but in the journalists' ruthless, morally guilty minds. These are men who are entrusted to uphold society's morals and protect a community, yet they readily put other people in danger for their own benefit. This superbly constructed and multilayered film was Lang's second favorite film, following his 1936 U.S. masterpiece, FURY. Produced independently, WHILE THE CITY SLEEPS was set for release by United Artists, though in the end it was distributed by RKO.

WHILE YOU WERE SLEEPING DVD
1995 100m c Comedy/Romance ★★★
SST Productions/Caravan Pictures/ PG
Hollywood Pictures (U.S.)

Sandra Bullock (Lucy Moderatz), Bill Pullman (Jack), Peter Gallagher (Peter), Peter Boyle (Ox), Jack Warden (Saul), Glynis Johns (Elsie), Michael Rispoli (Joe Jr.), Jason Bernard (Jerry), Micole Mercurio (Midge), Ally Walker (Ashley Bacon)

p, Joe Roth, Roger Birnbaum; d, Jon Turteltaub; w, Daniel G. Sullivan, Fredric Lebow; ph, Phedon Papamichael; ed, Bruce Green; m, Randy Edelman; prod d, Garreth Stover; art d, Chris Cornwell; fx, Guy Clayton Jr.; cos, Betsy Cox

Warm and sentimental, with suitably engaging stars, this romantic comedy remains winning even when it takes the occasional misstep.

Sandra Bullock plays Lucy, a Chicago subway token clerk who has a crush on one of her daily fares, handsome lawyer Peter (Peter Gallagher). When he's mugged and thrown off the platform, Lucy jumps onto the tracks and somehow manages to move his unconscious body out of the way of an oncoming train. At the emergency room, she's mistaken for Peter's fiancee by an overzealous nurse. Thus begins

a series of confusions that finds Lucy progressively enmeshed with Peter's loving, if slightly kooky, family—especially his amiable brother Jack (Bill Pullman).

Shot against a wintry Chicago backdrop, WHILE YOU WERE SLEEPING has the warm, cuddly feel of a plush toy. Bullock is appropriately charming, but Pullman, previously typecast as a perennial loser, steals the show. His slightly fuzzy good looks and wry smile have a relaxed appeal that is especially welcome in a time when Hollywood seems dominated by chiseled action heroes and troubled boy-men. Director Jon Turteltaub enhances the clear narrative flow and leisurely pacing of a workmanlike screenplay, exploiting moments of comic relief in situations that could easily collapse into mawkishness or over-the-top sentimentality.

WHISTLE DOWN THE WIND
1961 98m bw Drama ★★★½
Beaver/Allied Film Makers (U.K.)

Hayley Mills (Kathy Bostock), Bernard Lee (Mr. Bostock), Alan Bates (Arthur Blakey), Diane Holgate (Nan Bostock), Alan Barnes (Charles Bostock), Norman Bird (Eddie), Diane Clare (Miss Lodge), Patricia Heneghan (Salvation Army Girl), Elsie Wagstaffe (Auntie Dorothy), John Arnatt (Teesdale)

p, Richard Attenborough; d, Bryan Forbes; w, Keith Waterhouse, Willis Hall (based on the novel by Mary Hayley Bell); ph, Arthur Ibbetson; ed, Max Benedict; m, Malcolm Arnold; art d, Ray Simm

Bryan Forbes's directorial debut was a beauty. Not satisfied to cut his teeth on a proven commercial vehicle, he used the unique novel by Mary Hayley Bell as the basis for this unique film. In today's world, anyone proclaiming himself to be Jesus Christ would be whisked away by the authorities before many moments passed. And children today are a lot keener on life's realities than they were a quarter of a century ago, perhaps due to the influence of television. But on a grim Lancashire farm, a man claiming to be Christ wins the trust of three motherless children who have been strongly influenced by their strict religious training. Mills is the eldest of Lee's children; the others are Barnes and Holgate. The trio finds a bearded man hiding in the family barn. Beards are not common in that area, and when Mills asks the wild-eyed fellow who he is, he mutters, "Jesus Christ." They take him at his word, and do their best to shield and care for him. Only later is it revealed that Bates is a fugitive criminal.

This could have been a mawkish movie if it had gone over the edge, but Forbes kept matters realistic and still managed to enfold several bits of New Testament symbolism into the picture without hammering anyone on the head. The novel's author was Mills' mother (and wife of actor John Mills), and although there is no proof that she wrote the book with her daughter in mind, the youngster was surely the right choice for the role. It was her fourth movie; she had already completed TIGER BAY, POLLYANNA, and THE PARENT TRAP before this. Bates was wonderful in his difficult role. Prior to this, he had established himself as a stage actor and had appeared in THE ENTERTAINER the year before in his debut. Holgate and Barnes are so delicious in their naivete that they almost steal the film from Mills. It's an allegory, the second film produced by actor Richard Attenborough, who later became the Oscar-winning director of GANDHI.

WHITE DVD
(TROIS COULEURS: BLANC)
1994 92m c Drama/Comedy/Romance ★★★½
Marin Karmitz Productions (France/Poland/Switzerland) R

Zbigniew Zamachowski (Karol Karol), Julie Delpy (Dominique), Janusz Gajos (Mikolaj), Jerzy Stuhr (Jurek), Grzegorz Warchol (Elegant Man), Jerzy Nowak (Old Farmer),

Aleksander Bardini *(Lawyer)*, Cezary Harasimowicz *(Inspector)*, Jerzy Trela *(Monsieur Bronek)*, Cezary Pazura *(Bureau de Change Proprietor)*

p, Marin Karmitz; d, Krzysztof Kieslowski; w, Krzysztof Kieslowski, Krzysztof Piesiewicz, Agnieszka Holland, Edward Zebrowski; ph, Edward Klosinski; ed, Ursula Lesiak; m, Zbigniew Preisner; art d, Halina Dobrowolska, Claude Lenoir.

The second film in Krzysztof Kieslowski's THREE COLORS trilogy lacks the power of the first and third installments, BLUE and RED, but produces its own distinct pleasures. WHITE's story of obsessive love is originally told and surprisingly funny.

In a Paris courtroom, Dominique (Julie Delpy), a French woman, divorces her Polish husband, Karol (Zbigniew Zamachowski), a hairdresser, because he has been unable to consummate their marriage. After the hearing, Dominique, who is still angry at Karol, burns their hair salon and frames her ex-husband for the arson. Karol is forced to flee to the Paris subways, where he meets Mikolaj (Janusz Gajos), a businessman who convinces him to return to Poland. In Warsaw, Karol manages to strike it rich and plots a fantastic revenge against his former wife.

Compared to the previous BLUE and subsequent RED, WHITE is a curiosity. The film is distinguished by quirky humor and farcical plot developments, and it is directed in a straightforward, less stylized fashion than the other two films. Still, WHITE effectively continues Kieslowski's search for meaning amidst unusual relationships. Karol's incredible fall-and-rise produces moments ranging from pathos to hilarity, and Zbigniew Zamachowski's performance as Karol ("Charles") deliberately evokes the bittersweet charm of Charlie Chaplin's Little Tramp.

WHITE represents the "equality" section of the French tricolor in an eccentric and rather disturbing way. The national, economic, and sexual "equality" achieved here leaves the bitter aftertaste of revenge, which is at odds with the more optimistic conclusions of the other tricolor films. Indeed, Kieslowski seems to view equality as a chimerical goal—sexual relationships are innately antagonistic, the market (black or white) rewards the ruthless at the expense of the powerless. A more satisfying ending of WHITE occurs at the end of RED, the last story in the trilogy, during which Karol and Dominique reappear together in an unexpected way.

WHITE CHRISTMAS **DVD**
1954 120m c Musical/Comedy ★★★
Paramount (U.S.)

Bing Crosby *(Bob Wallace)*, Danny Kaye *(Phil Davis)*, Rosemary Clooney *(Betty)*, Vera-Ellen *(Judy)*, Dean Jagger *(Gen. Waverly)*, Mary Wickes *(Emma)*, John Brascia *(Joe)*, Anne Whitfield *(Susan)*, Richard Shannon *(Adjutant)*, Grady Sutton *(General's Guest)*

p, Robert Emmett Dolan; d, Michael Curtiz; w, Norman Krasna, Norman Panama, Melvin Frank; ph, Loyal Griggs (VistaVision, Technicolor); ed, Frank Bracht; art d, Hal Pereira, Roland Anderson; chor, Robert Alton; cos, Edith Head

AAN Best Song: "Count Your Blessings Instead of Sheep"; Irving Berlin

This eagerly awaited musical comedy had all the ingredients for success: two of its day's biggest-box office draws, a solid director, and a score by America's treasure, Irving Berlin. And though it's not as satisfying as it might have been, it still boasts great stars and catchy songs in addition to a love story, and is a perennial holiday favorite. Bob Wallace (Bing Crosby) and Phil Davis (Danny Kaye) meet during the war and team up afterward to become the hottest song-and-dance duo around. After five years of heady success, they think it's about time to

take a vacation, so they travel to a New England ski resort in the company of lovely sister entertainers Betty (Rosemary Clooney) and Judy (Vera-Ellen) for some rest and recuperation. They arrive to find the place in terrible financial condition and in desperate need of an infusion of money, because there hasn't been any snow for almost a year. The man who runs the inn is their old Army topkick, Gen. Waverly (Dean Jagger). Bob and Phil decide to aid Waverly by staging a benefit show that is, of course, a smash. Included is the title song, which Irving Berlin had written for HOLIDAY INN 12 years before. With that tune as the core, the script was fashioned, and several more Berlin tunes were added.

WHITE CLIFFS OF DOVER, THE
1944 126m bw War ★★★½
MGM (U.S.)

Irene Dunne *(Susan Dunn Ashwood)*, Alan Marshal *(Sir John Ashwood)*, Frank Morgan *(Hiram Porter Dunn)*, Roddy McDowall *(John Ashwood II as a Boy)*, Peter Lawford *(John Ashwood II at age 24)*, Dame May Whitty *(Nanny)*, C. Aubrey Smith *(Colonel)*, Gladys Cooper *(Lady Jean Ashwood)*, Van Johnson *(Sam Bennett)*, John Warburton *(Reggie)*

p, Sidney Franklin; d, Clarence Brown; w, Claudine West, Jan Lustig, George Froeschel (based on the poem "The White Cliffs of Dover" by Alice Duer Miller, with additional material by Robert Nathan); ph, George Folsey; ed, Robert J. Kern, Al Jennings; m, Herbert Stothart; art d, Cedric Gibbons, Randall Duell; fx, A. Arnold Gillespie, Warren Newcombe; cos, Irene

AAN Best B/W Cinematography: George Folsey

Alice Duer Miller's poem was the inspiration for this sentimental look at the ravages of war and at the courage of one woman who lost both her husband and son in the two world wars that dominated this century. Dunne is a Red Cross supervisor in England, awaiting casualties of WWII. At her desk, she ruminates about her past and flashes back to 1914, when she comes to England with Morgan, her father, a newspaper publisher in a medium-sized town in the U.S. In no time at all, Dunne meets, falls in love with, and marries wealthy and titled Marshal. They are ecstatic, but their happiness is brief; WWI breaks out, and Marshal must serve his country in France, where he is killed on the battlefield. By the time of his death, Dunne has given birth to a son, and though the war is over, she stays in England to raise the boy. Played first by McDowall, then by Lawford, the boy grows to be a credit to his father. WWII breaks out and Dunne becomes a worker for the Red Cross assigned to a hospital in London. The wounded servicemen are brought in for surgery and she is shocked to see that one of them is her son, Lawford, now 24. He is dying of his injuries and she is powerless to help. At the conclusion, Dunne looks out a window and observes a battalion of American soldiers as they march past, the first such warriors to reach the British shores.

At the advent of the war, MGM made several pro-English features, the most successful being MRS. MINIVER. The studio wanted the same type of success again, but couldn't find the right material until producer Franklin happened on Miller's poem (which was given some additional words by Robert Nathan). Dunne was busy on A GUY NAMED JOE, but that production had to go on hiatus while Van Johnson recovered from an auto accident. In the meantime, this one began, and when Johnson was able to get back before the cameras more quickly than anyone had anticipated, Dunne found herself working on two major features at the same time. Beside MRS. MINIVER, MGM had already made GOODBYE, MR. CHIPS and RANDOM HARVEST and was in danger of being classified as a strictly Anglophile studio. This movie didn't achieve the success of the aforementioned films, but still managed a respectable gross of more than $4 million.

Good acting, superior production values, sensitive direction, and one of Dunne's finest performances enhance the film. In order to make the settings authentic, MGM hired Major Cyril Seys Ramsey-Hill as technical advisor; he must have done his job because Britons living in the U.S. sobbed at the showings.

WHITE DOG

1982 90m c Drama ★★★½
Edgar J. Scherick (U.S.) PG

Kristy McNichol (Julie Sawyer), Paul Winfield (Keys), Burl Ives (Carruthers), Jameson Parker (Roland Gray), Lynne Moody (Molly), Marshall Thompson (Director), Bob Minor (Joe), Vernon Weddle (Vet), Christa Lang (Nurse), Tony Brubaker (Sweeper Driver)

p, Jon Davison; d, Samuel Fuller; w, Samuel Fuller, Curtis Hanson (based on the novella by Romain Gary); ph, Bruce Surtees (Metrocolor); ed, Bernard Gribble; m, Ennio Morricone; prod d, Brian Eatwell

One of the most famous "unseen" films, WHITE DOG never got a theatrical run in the U.S. even though it had a well-known cast, a legendary director, and a powerful subject—racism. Kristy McNichol plays Julie Sawyer, a young actress who adopts a beautiful white stray dog. When a rapist breaks into Julie's home, the dog, which has been playful and gentle up to this, attacks and nearly tears the man limb from limb before the police arrive. The beautiful dog, she learns, has been trained to kill blacks. A black animal-trainer, Keys (Paul Winfield), begins an attempt to recondition the dog, although Carruthers (Burl Ives), who runs the training center, maintains that it can never be completely broken of its desire to kill. In the meantime, Julie meets the person who trained the dog in the first place. The rights the award-winning novella by Romain Gary on which the film is based were bought by Paramount 10 years before production began. Once the movie was made, the studio got cold feet, fearing that the volatile subject would incite racial controversy, although Sam Fuller's film is anything but racist. When WHITE DOG finally opened in Paris and London it was hailed as a masterpiece by some critics. The film finally did show up on cable television in January of 1984, in a re-edited version from Paramount that foolishly turned the dog from a killer to one that merely bites.

WHITE HEAT

1949 114m bw Crime 📀 ★★★★★
Warner Bros. (U.S.)

James Cagney (Arthur Cody Jarrett), Virginia Mayo (Verna Jarrett), Edmond O'Brien (Hank Fallon/Vic Pardo), Margaret Wycherly (Ma Jarrett), Steve Cochran (Big Ed Somers), John Archer (Phillip Evans), Wally Cassell (Giovanni Cotton Valetti), Fred Clark (Daniel Winston, the Trader), Ford Rainey (Zuckie Hommell), Fred Coby (Happy Taylor)

p, Louis F. Edelman; d, Raoul Walsh; w, Ivan Goff, Ben Roberts (based on a story by Virginia Kellogg); ph, Sid Hickox; ed, Owen Marks; m, Max Steiner; art d, Edward Carrere; fx, Roy Davidson, H.F. Koenekamp; cos, Leah Rhodes

AAN Best Motion Picture Story: Virginia Kellogg

Ten years later, a flaming farewell to the '30s gangster picture, scripted like a Greek tragedy on speed. Raoul Walsh supplies the Freudian direction, Cagney the daring acting and sizzling star power. WHITE HEAT is primal, flamboyant stuff—close your eyes and you could be watching a '30s picture. But don't close them more than momentarily; the film's visuals make it linger in the mind's eye.

Cagney plays psychopathic gangster Cody Jarrett, Margaret Wycherly the mother who drives him to crime and

whose death makes him go literally berserk. Virginia Mayo is Jarrett's wife, who has a hankering for gang member Big Ed (Steve Cochran), Edmond O'Brien plays a police informant who shares a cell with Jarrett, and John Archer is the FBI agent on the madman's tail.

One of the toughest and most brilliant crime films ever made, WHITE HEAT marked a breakthrough in the explicitly psychological depiction of screen bad guys. Cagney's character was based on notorious real-life gangster Arthur "Doc" Barker, Wycherly's on the equally infamous "Ma" Barker, the alleged catalyst for his criminal exploits. Cagney graphically demonstrates Jarrett's mother fixation when the actor, following one of his epileptic-style seizures, allows her to sit him in her lap and soothe him. This startling scene, like many in this classic film noir, was Cagney's own idea. The prison mess hall sequence, where Jarrett hears of his mother's murder, is the most charged moment in Cagney's outstanding career. The final image, shot atop an actual oil refinery in Torrance, CA, in which Jarrett calls out his warped triumph to his dead mother before blowing himself skyward, is one of the best-known scenes in film history.

WHITE HUNTER, BLACK HEART

1990 112m c Adventure/Drama 📀 ★★½
Malpaso/Rastar (U.S.) PG

Clint Eastwood (John Wilson), Jeff Fahey (Pete Verrill), Charlotte Cornwell (Miss Wilding), Norman Lumsden (Butler George), George Dzundza (Paul Landers), Edward Tudor Pole (Reissar), Roddy Maude-Roxby (Thompson), Richard Warwick (Basil Fields), John Rapley (Gun Shop Salesman), Catherine Neilson (Irene Saunders)

p, Clint Eastwood; d, Clint Eastwood; w, Peter Viertel, James Bridges, Burt Kennedy (based on the novel Roman a Clef by Peter Viertel); ph, Jack N. Green (Technicolor); ed, Joel Cox; m, Lennie Niehaus; prod d, John Graysmark; art d, Tony Reading; fx, John Evans, Roy Field; chor, Arlene Phillips; cos, John Mollo

Based on Peter Viertel's roman a clef, WHITE HUNTER, BLACK HEART uses the making of a classic film, THE AFRICAN QUEEN, as the setting for an investigation into the creative process. It's also the story of one enigmatic film director as told by another. Star-director Clint Eastwood plays a thinly disguised John Huston, here called John Wilson.

Set in 1951, the film begins as Wilson has summoned an old friend, writer Pete Verrill (Jeff Fahey), to his Irish estate to recruit him for his latest project—the title of which he never can remember—about a salty, hard-drinking boat captain and a prissy schoolmarm who take on the German navy in Africa during WWII. All Wilson really cares about is that the film will give him a fast infusion of cash to put a dent in personal debts totalling a quarter of a million dollars. Even more important, it will provide him with an all-expenses-paid opportunity to fulfill his longtime dream of going big-game hunting. Meetings with producer Paul Landers (George Dzundza, playing a role modeled on real-life producer Sam Spiegel) and potential backers put the production on track, and Wilson and Verrill begin work on the script. But a major dispute arises over the fate of the leading characters, who, in Wilson's version, are killed, while Verrill insists they should live as the fair reward for their extraordinary heroism. Even after Wilson and Verrill's arrival in Africa, the film continues to take a back seat to the director's planned safari to kill an elephant.

WHITE HUNTER is an ambitious and intriguing project that never amounts to anything more than the sum of its parts—a trait shared by many of Eastwood's other major project as an independent filmmaker, BIRD. The personification of the post-Hemingway action hero, Eastwood looks and sounds uncomfortable filling Huston's decidedly Hemingwayesque shoes. As the action shifts to Africa, he seems inordinately laid-back as his character's obsession grows. He can't quite get a hold on the first predominantly unsympathetic character he's played since TIGHTROPE. And as a director, Eastwood has yet to pose much of a threat to Huston. WHITE HUNTER, like other Eastwood-directed films, lacks precisely the clear, lean narrative approach that characterizes Huston's best work (including THE AFRICAN QUEEN) or even that of Eastwood's mentor, director Don Siegel (DIRTY HARRY, ESCAPE FROM ALCATRAZ).

WHITE MEN CAN'T JUMP

DVD
1992 115m c Sports/Comedy ★★½
Finger Roll Inc/Fox (U.S.) R

Wesley Snipes *(Sidney Deane)*, Woody Harrelson *(Billy Hoyle)*, Rosie Perez *(Gloria Clemente)*, Tyra Ferrell *(Rhonda Deane)*, Cylk Cozart *(Robert)*, Kadeem Hardison *(Junior)*, Ernest Harden Jr. *(George)*, John Marshall Jones *(Walter)*, Marques Johnson *(Raymond)*, David Roberson *(T.J.)*

p, Don Miller, David Lester; d, Ron Shelton; w, Ron Shelton; ph, Russell Boyd; ed, Paul Seydor, Kimberly Ray; m, Bennie Wallace; prod d, Dennis Washington; art d, Roger Fortune

Ron Shelton's second outing since his breakout success with BULL DURHAM aims to be a high-energy remake of THE HUSTLER in a street-basketball setting, but succeeds only intermittently. Playground hoops phenomenon Billy Hoyle (Woody Harrelson) walks onto a tough Venice court and smokes the competition, including reigning champ Sidney Deane (Wesley Snipes), who is duly impressed. Or so it seems, until Deane conspires with some friends to con Hoyle out of the nest egg he's saved while living with his sexy, volatile girlfriend Gloria Clemente (Rosie Perez). Gloria knocks heads with Sidney's wife Rhonda (Tyra Ferrell), and together they come up with a plan for Sidney and Billy to compete in a sponsored two-on-two playground competition for a $5000 first prize. Sidney and Billy win easily, but Billy loses his half to Sidney on a foolish slam-dunking bet on the way home (thus the film's title). A disgusted Gloria walks out on Billy, but he wins her back by helping her achieve her lifetime ambition to compete on the game show "Jeopardy," which she wins easily. With her winnings, Gloria wants Billy to buy some decent clothes and get a straight job. Instead, Billy wants to take the money and bet it on one last playground match.
    WHITE MEN CAN'T JUMP is engaging if inconsistent, with its manifest plot loopholes compensated for by the colorful court scenes, rapid-fire dialogue and enthusiastic performances from all concerned.

WHITE OLEANDER

DVD
2002 110m c Drama ★★★
Pandora/Warner Bros./Gaylord Films/Oleander PG-13
Productions/John Wells Productions (U.S.)

Alison Lohman *(Astrid Magnussen)*, Michelle Pfeiffer *(Ingrid Magnussen)*, Robin Wright Penn *(Starr Thomas)*, Renèe Zellweger *(Claire Richards)*, Billy Connolly *(Barry)*, Patrick Fugit *(Paul Trout)*, Cole Hauser *(Ray)*, Noah Wyle *(Mark Richards)*, Stephen Root *(Michael)*, Svetlana Efremova *(Rena)*

p, Hunt Lowry, John Wells; d, Peter Kosminsky; w, Mary Agnes Donoghue (based on the novel by Janet Fitch); ph, Elliot Davis; ed, Chris Ridsdale; m, Thomas Newman; prod d, Donald Graham Burt; art d, Anthony Rivero Stabley; fx, Thad Beier, Jeff Denes, Jay Mark Johnson; cos, Susie DeSanto

If any film could be unfairly labeled and dismissed as a chick flick, this is it. Based on the hugely popular Oprah's Book Club selection by Janet Fitch about a trou-

bled mother-daughter relationship, it stars *three* name-brand actresses and one exceptional newcomer, Alison Lohman. But while the film may drop a few of the novel's more disturbing moments, it still travels some emotionally rocky territory.
    Fifteen-year-old Astrid Magnussen (Lohman) is tossed into the California foster-care system when her mother, the brilliant but emotionally disturbed artist Ingrid Magnussen (Michelle Pfeiffer), poisons her wayward boyfriend (Billy Connolly) with oleander blossoms, Astrid is first placed with Starr Thomas (Robin Wright Penn), a recovering alcoholic who lives with her own kids in a mobile home in the California desert, then with Claire Richards (Renee Zellweger), a lonely B-movie actress with marital troubles. Astrid forms an emotional attachment to each of her foster mothers, but both situations end badly. Throughout her ordeal, Astrid pays periodic visits to Ingrid in prison, who tries to maintain her hold over her daughter by warning her away from the rest of the world. Astrid begins to suspect that Ingrid's parenting style has more to do with her own narcissism than with genuine love for her daughter.
    Unadventurously adapted by Mary Agnes Donoghue (BEACHES) and directed with some flair by Peter Kosminsky, the film is really a showcase for a talented cast that manages to overcome the built-in liabilities of the script. Where the novel allowed itself time to develop Ingrid's complex character before the murder, the film must rely on Pfeiffer's resourcefulness as an actress to reveal Ingrid's tragic inability to separate her own needs from those of Astrid.

WHITE SHEIK, THE

DVD
(LO SCEICCO BIANCO)
1952 86m bw Comedy ★★½
Producers Distributors/OFI (France/Italy)

Alberto Sordi *(Fernando Rivoli)*, Brunella Bovo *(Wanda Cavalli)*, Leopoldo Trieste *(Ivan Cavalli)*, Giulietta Masina *(Cabiria)*, Lilia Landi *(Felga)*, Ernesto Almirante *(Director of "White Sheik" Strip)*, Fanny Marchio *(Marilena Vellardi)*, Gina Mascetti *(White Sheik's Wife)*, Enzo Maggio *(Hotel Concierge)*, Ettore Margadonna *(Ivan's Uncle)*

p, Luigi Rovere; d, Federico Fellini; w, Federico Fellini, Tullio Pinelli, Ennio Flaiano (based on a story by Federico Fellini and Tullio Pinelli from an idea by Michelangelo Antonioni); ph, Arturo Galea; ed, Rolando Bebedetti; m, Nino Rota; art d, Raffaello Tolfo

Federico Fellini's first solo directorial effort (he codirected VARIETY LIGHTS with Alberto Lattuada in 1951) is an enjoyable romp that shows the director's early promise. Newlyweds Wanda (Brunella Bovo) and Ivan Cavalli (Leopoldo Trieste) are honeymooning in Rome. The couple is mismatched: Ivan is conservative in nature, while his bride is full of spontaneity and eager to pursue her dreams. When Wanda learns that the popular photographic comic book "The White Sheik" is being shot nearby, she heads off to ogle the sheik (Alberto Sordi), sending Ivan on a frantic search for her all over Rome and jeopardizing their planned papal audience. When Wanda actually meets her idol, however, the sheik proves to be less than dashing. Already displaying his fascination with the romantic dreams of everyday people, Fellini orchestrates fantasy and reality deftly here as the newlyweds' perceptions of life and of each other change under the pressure of their unusual circumstances. The film falters in its pacing, however, which is somewhat too slow. Originally proposed as a project for Michelangelo Antonioni, THE WHITE SHEIK is not one of Fellini's masterworks (and uncharacteristically farcical), but it is a must-see for those interested in the director's oeuvre and an entertaining piece on its own.

WHO FRAMED ROGER RABBIT

DVD

1988 103m c   Animated/Comedy/Mystery   ★★★
Touchstone/Amblin/Silver Screen Partners III   PG
(U.S.)

Bob Hoskins *(Eddie Valiant)*, Christopher Lloyd *(Judge Doom)*, Joanna Cassidy *(Dolores)*, Stubby Kaye *(Marvin Acme)*, Alan Tilvern *(R.K. Maroon)*, Richard Le Parmentier *(Lt. Santino)*, Joel Silver *(Raoul Raoul, Director)*, Paul Springer *(Augie)*, Richard Ridings *(Angelo)*, Edwin Craig *(Arthritic Cowboy)*

p, Robert Watts, Frank Marshall; d, Robert Zemeckis; w, Jeffrey Price, Peter Seaman (based on the book *Who Censored Roger Rabbit?* by Gary K. Wolf); ph, Dean Cundey (Rank Color); ed, Arthur Schmidt; m, Alan Silvestri; prod d, Elliot Scott, Roger Cain; fx, Peter Biggs, Brian Morrison, Roger Nichols, David Watkins, Brian Lince, Tony Dunsterville, Brian Warner; chor, Quinny Sacks, David Toguri; cos, Joanna Johnston; anim, Richard Williams

AAN Best Cinematography: Dean Cundey; *AA Best Film Editing:* Arthur Schmidt; *AAN Best Art Direction-Set Decoration:* Elliot Scott, Peter Howitt; *AAN Best Sound:* Robert Knudson, John Boyd, Don Digirolamo, Tony Dawe; *AA Best Visual Effects:* Ken Ralston, Richard Williams, Edward Jones, George Gibbs; *AA Best Sound Effects Editing:* Charles L. Campbell, Louis L. Edemann; *AA Special Achievement Award—Animation Direction:* Richard Williams

A startling combination of live action and animation, WHO FRAMED ROGER RABBIT? was instantly catapulted into the ranks of cinema classics. While flawlessly delivered, it's overkill—so loud and excessive, it makes our head swim. And its peak comes early on, when Jessica Rabbit sings, "Why Don't You Do Right?" Adult viewers are generally used to only Disney—104 minutes of the racous rukus of Warners style cartoons is well, too much of a dumb thing. This film could only have been made during the decade when Miss Piggy became a star.

Set in Los Angeles circa 1947, the film takes place in a universe where cartoon characters really exist and work alongside human beings. Disdainfully referred to as "Toons" by humans, the cartoon characters are underpaid by human standards and are forced to live in a segregated ghetto known as Toontown. When Maroon Cartoons studio chief R.K. Maroon (Alan Tilvern) is found murdered, it appears that the studio's biggest star, Roger Rabbit, is the culprit. Desperate to clear his name, Roger hires down-on-his-luck private detective Eddie Valiant (Bob Hoskins) to crack the case. A human, Eddie is reluctant to take the case, for he hates Toons because his brother was killed by one. As the plot thickens, however, Roger begins to grow on Eddie and the pair team up to solve the mystery of Toontown, battling the sinister Judge Doom (Christopher Lloyd) in the process.

We salute the technical brilliance of this movie. A small army of animators led by Richard Williams and assisted by Industrial Light and Magic performed the meticulous task of matching animation with camera movement and film noir lighting to give the cartoon characters a 3-D effect. And admittedly Hoskins had a tough job—interacting with thin air and floating props (the Toons handle real objects) because the animation was added to the frame months after principal photography had been completed. Director Bob Zemeckis deserves a Purple Heart for taking on the monumental technical headaches involved in the production and somehow managing to deliver a film that works. A must-see for all ages, but not a work that lingers in the imagination. It's like a sumptuous banquet composed entirely of fast food; fills you up but entirely forgettable.

WHOLE TOWN'S TALKING, THE

1935 95m   bw   Comedy/Crime   ★★★★★
Columbia   (U.S.)

Edward G. Robinson *(Arthur Ferguson Jones/Killer Mannion)*, Jean Arthur *(Wilhelmina "Bill" Clark)*, Arthur Hohl *(Detective Sgt. Mike Boyle)*, Wallace Ford *(Healy)*, A.S. Byron *(District Atty. Spencer)*, Donald Meek *(Hoyt)*, Paul Harvey *(J.G. Carpenter)*, Edward Brophy *(Bugs Martin)*, Etienne Girardot *(Seaver)*, James Donlan *(Detective Sgt. Pat Howe)*

p, Lester Cowan; d, John Ford; w, Jo Swerling, Robert Riskin (based on the novel by W.R. Burnett); ph, Joseph August; ed, Viola Lawrence

One of the most underrated of John Ford's early films, THE WHOLE TOWN'S TALKING is a marvelous gangster film told in a comic vein and sporting a superb performance from Edward G. Robinson, playing a timid clerk working for a hardware company. He has a superlative work record and has been on time every morning for eight years. He is in love with one of his coworkers (Jean Arthur) from afar. While he is having lunch with her one day, the police arrive and arrest him, having mistaken him for Public Enemy No. 1, Killer Mannion, recently escaped from prison and the hardware clerk's exact double. After much confusion over his identity, the district attorney is satisfied that Robinson isn't the gangster they are looking for and issues the clerk an identity card he can show police to avoid being arrested by mistake again. Unfortunately, the news about Robinson's misadventure hits all the newspapers—partly because Robinson's boss urges his employee to write about Mannion for the papers—and the real Killer Mannion (also played by Robinson) reads the story. When the gangster shows up at the clerk's house and demands the ID card, the fun really begins.

Adapted by screenwriters Jo Swerling and Robert Riskin from a story by W.R. Burnett (who wrote the novel *Little Caesar*), THE WHOLE TOWN'S TALKING is a masterful balance of comedy and drama with a very dark subtext. Robinson the clerk and Robinson the gangster are two sides of the same coin. The clerk is a milquetoast who can't bring himself to tell the woman he loves how he feels about her, but once he dons the identity of the gangster and orders a man to be killed, he is suddenly infused with self-confidence and power which finally enable him to speak his mind and take action. Though the film is essentially a comedy and Robinson the clerk's actions are well enough motivated for his character to remain sympathetic, it is an undeniably chilling and ambiguous moment. Robinson handles the role beautifully, bringing several shadings and subtleties to a double role that could easily have disintegrated into gimmicky silliness. Because of the ambiguity and subtle handling of the darker aspects of the story, director Ford and actor Robinson turned what could have been dismissed as just another light, frivolous entertainment into an evocative work of art.

WHO'LL STOP THE RAIN?

DVD

1978 125m   c   Crime/War   ★★★½
UA   (U.S.)   R

Nick Nolte *(Ray Hicks)*, Tuesday Weld *(Marge Converse)*, Michael Moriarty *(John Converse)*, Anthony Zerbe *(Antheil)*, Richard Masur *(Danskin)*, Ray Sharkey *(Smitty)*, Gail Strickland *(Chairman)*, Charles Haid *(Eddy)*, David Opatoshu *(Bender)*

p, Herb Jaffe, Gabriel Katzka; d, Karel Reisz; w, Judith Rascoe, Robert Stone (based on the novel *Dog Soldiers* by Stone); ph, Richard H. Kline; ed, John Bloom; m, Laurence Rosenthal

An effective film adaptation of Robert Stone's excellent novel *Dog Soldiers*, WHO'LL STOP THE RAIN? begins in Vietnam and follows jaded, cynical, and bitter photojournalist

John Converse (Michael Moriarty) as he arranges to smuggle a large shipment of Asian heroin into the U.S. To assist him, Converse enlists Vietnam vet Ray Hicks (Nick Nolte). Once a Marine, now working for the Merchant Marine, Hicks can easily smuggle the heroin out of Vietnam and into the docks at Oakland, California, where he is to hook up with Converse's wife, Marge (Tuesday Weld), and await Converse's return to the U.S. Unfortunately, Antheil (Anthony Zerbe), a corrupt federal drug enforcement agent, has gotten wind of the shipment and has sent two of his men (Richard Masur and Ray Sharkey) to kill Marge and Hicks and confiscate the heroin for his own purposes. Fueled by excellent performances from the entire cast—with Nolte a definite standout—WHO'LL STOP THE RAIN? is a gripping action film that also illustrates the bitter disillusionment of Americans who witnessed the corruption, confusion, and moral chaos of the country's leadership during the Vietnam era. Smartly directed by Karel Reisz (a Czech-born Englishman), whose previous feature was the memorable THE GAMBLER with James Caan, the film boasts fine photography by Richard H. Kline and an unforgettable climax in the surreal ruins of an abandoned hippie commune.

WHOOPEE
1930 94m   c   Musical/Comedy   ★★★½
UA   (U.S.)

Eddie Cantor (Henry Williams), Eleanor Hunt (Sally Morgan), Paul Gregory (Wanenis), Jack Rutherford (Sheriff Bob Wells), Ethel Shutta (Mary Custer), Spencer Charters (Jerome Underwood), Chief Caupolican (Black Eagle), Albert Hackett (Chester Underwood), William H. Philbrick (Andy McNabb), Walter Law (Judd Morgan)

p, Samuel Goldwyn, Florenz Ziegfeld; d, Thornton Freeland; w, William Conselman (based on the Ziegfeld musical "Whoopee" by William Anthony McGuire, Walter Donaldson, Gus Kahn, the comedy "The Nervous Wreck" by Owen Davis, Sr., and the story "The Wreck" by E.J. Rath); ph, Lee Garmes, Ray Rennahan, Gregg Toland; ed, Stuart Heisler; art d, Richard Day; chor, Busby Berkeley; cos, John Harkrider

AAN Best Interior Decoration: Richard Day

After the smash hit Broadway show in 1928-29 finished its long run, Sam Goldwyn joined forces with Flo Ziegfeld to re-create "Whoopee" for one of the first Technicolor films, making Eddie Cantor a Goldwyn star and the song "Making Whoopee" a standard. Cantor plays Henry Williams, a hypochondriac whose supposedly poor health causes him to travel West with his nurse-companion Mary Custer (Ethel Shutt). They wind up in Arizona, where busybody Henry pokes his nose into the affairs of Sally Morgan (Eleanor Hunt). Sally is engaged to local sheriff Bob Wells (John Rutherford), but really loves Indian brave Wanenis (Paul Gregory). Henry manages to extricate Sally from Bob's arms into those of Wanenis, who, it later turns out, is really a paleface who had been abandoned and raised by local Native Americans. Several splendid Busby Berkeley production numbers, a bevy of "Goldwyn Girls" (among them a very young Betty Grable), and Oscar-nominated art direction by Capt. Richard Day enliven the silly plot—but the real drawing card is Cantor (just as it was Danny Kaye, when Goldwyn remade this movie as 1944's UP IN ARMS). Neither Goldwyn nor Ziegfeld enjoyed working with a partner, and the two split when Ziegfeld wanted his name first in the billing of the company. Goldwyn released the film in the nadir of the Depression and charged $5 per ticket, the equivalent of a day's pay back then.

WHO'S AFRAID OF VIRGINIA WOOLF?   DVD
1966 131m bw Drama   ★★★★
Warner Bros.   (U.S.)

Elizabeth Taylor (Martha), Richard Burton (George), George Segal (Nick), Sandy Dennis (Honey)

p, Ernest Lehman; d, Mike Nichols; w, Ernest Lehman (based on the play by Edward Albee); ph, Haskell Wexler; ed, Sam O'Steen; m, Alex North; prod d, Richard Sylbert; cos, Irene Sharaff

AAN Best Picture; AAN Best Actor: Richard Burton; AA Best Actress: Elizabeth Taylor; AAN Best Supporting Actor: George Segal; AA Best Supporting Actress: Sandy Dennis; AAN Best Director: Mike Nichols; AAN Best Adapted Screenplay: Ernest Lehman; AA Best B/W Cinematography: Haskell Wexler; AAN Best Film Editing: Sam O'Steen; AAN Best Original Score: Alex North; AA Best Art Direction-Set Decoration (B/W): Richard Sylbert, George James Hopkins; AA Best Costume Design (B/W): Irene Sharaff; AAN Best Sound: George R. Groves

The Liz and Dick Show. A vitriol Valentine to that most public of famous marriages, The Battling Burtons, in their finest work (together).

It's two in the morning in New England. Burton is a defeated history professor married to Taylor, a harridan whose father is the president of the college where Burton lectures. After two decades their union is alternately loving and vicious. Taylor likes to compare her weakling husband with her strong father (who is never seen) because she knows it rankles Burton. They have invented a son and talk about him as though he actually exists. Earlier that night, they attended a faculty party where they met Segal and Dennis, a self-proclaimed ladies' man and a sniveling mouse of a woman. The older couple have invited the younger to their comfortable home for a nightcap. Enter Segal and Dennis. She is already tipsy but has more to drink, which makes her worse. Taylor, behaving boorishly, makes advances at Segal which Burton does nothing to stop. Dennis begins to feel sick and Segal gets increasingly drunk. Segal confides to Burton that Dennis trapped him into marriage by pretending to be pregnant. As the late evening drags into early morning, Taylor takes Segal up to her bedroom. Burton stands in the yard below and watches their shadows in the window. Later, Segal mentions Burton's and Taylor's "son," and Burton explodes, vowing to destroy Taylor, who matches his threat.

Producer Lehman's screenplay left most of Albee's play intact, which shocked movie audiences not accustomed to hearing four-letter words cannonading off the screen. At first, the Production Code seal was denied to the movie, but Jack Warner used his personal clout and secured the seal. The play was bought by Warners for half a million dollars; an additional million each went to the Burtons—out of a total budget of $5 million. The movie grossed large numbers at the box office, nearly $15 million the first time around, due, in part, to the draw of the stars.

Dennis in her second role after a small part in SPLENDOR IN THE GRASS was absolutely right in a part that became the definitive Dennis role. The same cannot be said for Segal, who lacks the bulk and WASP look for Nick—where was Robert Redford when Nichols needed him? Burton and Taylor both took British Oscars for their work. Hiring Nichols (comedy partner of Elaine May) in his directorial debut was a risk because the former nightclub comic had done only lighter work. But the script is fueled by acid, sarcastic dialogue which his direction paces flawlessly, his sense of comic timing serving him well. The film was rehearsed like a play for three weeks before a camera ever turned. This also marked Lehman's debut as a producer. Strong stuff, intensely watchable, but definitely not for children.

WICKER MAN, THE

DVD

1973 102m c Horror/Mystery ★★★½
British Lion (U.K.) R

Edward Woodward (Sgt. Neil Howie), Christopher Lee (Lord Summerisle), Diane Cilento (Miss Rose), Britt Ekland (Willow MacGregor), Ingrid Pitt (Librarian-Clerk), Lindsay Kemp (Alder MacGregor), Russell Waters (Harbormaster), Aubrey Morris (Old Gardener-Gravedigger), Irene Sunters (May Morrison), Walter Carr (Schoolmaster)

p, Peter Snell; d, Robin Hardy; w, Anthony Shaffer; ph, Harry Waxman; ed, Eric Boyd-Perkins; m, Paul Giovanni; art d, Seamus Flannery; chor, Stewart Hopps; cos, Sue Yelland

Sgt. Neil Howie (Woodward) is a devoutly Christian policeman and lay minister, still an unmarried virgin though middleaged. After receiving an anonymous lead pertaining to the whereabouts of a missing girl, Neil heads out to Summerisle, a Scottish island community within his jurisdiction, in search of clues. What he finds on the island is a pagan cult led by Lord Summerisle (Lee), which offers a human sacrifice every year. Here we have the unusual case of a film about a pagan cult that has developed a cult of its very own. Drastically cut by its original distributors (from 102 minutes to 87 minutes), poorly marketed, and subsequently little seen, THE WICKER MAN developed a reputation as a lost masterpiece of mystery and the macabre. Fueled by actor Christopher Lee's comments that the film contained his best performance, a rabid group of fans went about extolling the movie's virtues. When director Robin Hardy's reconstructed original cut of the film was finally released on videocassette (seven minutes are still missing), opinion over the much-anticipated film was split: people either loved it or hated it. While no masterpiece, the film is a fascinating examination of the conflict between fundamental Christianity and paganism. The performances are uniformly excellent, and Hardy's direction is quite evocative, bizarre, witty, erotic, and downright chilling.

WILD ANGELS, THE

DVD

1966 83m c Action ★★★
AIP (U.S.)

Peter Fonda (Heavenly Blues), Nancy Sinatra (Mike), Bruce Dern (Loser/Joey Kerns), Lou Procopio (Joint), Coby Denton (Bull Puckey), Marc Cavell (Frankenstein), Buck Taylor (Dear John), Norman Alden (Medic), Michael J. Pollard (Pigmy), Diane Ladd (Gaysh)

p, Roger Corman; d, Roger Corman; w, Charles B. Griffith; ph, Richard Moore (Panavision, Pathe Color); ed, Monte Hellman; m, Mike Curb; prod d, Rick Beck-Myer; art d, Leon Ericksen

The first of a wave of biker movies that hit American screens in the late '60s, this seminal exploitation film stars soon-to-be cult hero Peter Fonda as the leader of a leather-clad biker gang. When one of the cyclists, Loser (Bruce Dern), is injured, Heavenly Blues (Fonda) and company snatch him from his hospital bed, taking time to trash the place and gang-rape a nurse. Loser dies en route to a hideout, and his comrades requisition a church and hold a funeral service that soon degenerates into a festive, drugged-out orgy. Soon after, the bikers find themselves in a pitched battle with furious local townspeople and police.

Unusually violent for its time, THE WILD ANGELS became one of AIP's most successful films, grossing some $25 million on a production budget of $350,000. Most critics hated the film, but some defenders called it an allegory of America's descent toward nihilism; today, it's of interest as a vivid piece of pop culture history and as a watershed in several careers. Peter Bogdanovich was called in to rewrite the screenplay (he also acted as Corman's assistant and played a small role); Michael J. Pollard went on to a major role in BONNIE AND CLYDE the following year; Monte Hellman, the editor, later directed TWO-LANE BLACKTOP and THE SHOOTING. WILD ANGELS was better received in Europe than in the U.S., and Corman was invited to bring the picture to the Venice Film Festival—the only U.S. picture that year to be so honored.

WILD AT HEART

DVD

1990 126m c Comedy/Drama/Romance ★★½
Polygram-Propaganda (U.S.) R

Nicolas Cage (Sailor Ripley), Laura Dern (Lula Pace Fortune), Diane Ladd (Marietta Pace), Willem Dafoe (Bobby Peru), Isabella Rossellini (Perdita Durango), Harry Dean Stanton (Johnnie Farragut), Crispin Glover (Dell), Grace Zabriskie (Juana), J.E. Freeman (Marcello Santos), W. Morgan Sheppard (Mr. Reindeer)

p, Monty Montgomery, Steve Golin, Sigurjon Sighvatsson; d, David Lynch; w, David Lynch (based on the novel by Barry Gifford); ph, Frederick Elmes; ed, Duwayne Dunham; m, Angelo Badalamenti; prod d, Patricia Norris; fx, David B. Miller, Louis Lazara, David Domeyer; cos, Patricia Norris

AAN Best Supporting Actress: Diane Ladd

Based on the novel by Barry Gifford, this winner of the Cannes Film Festival's Palme d'Or is a wacky, occasionally inventive road movie that fails to display the vision or the dark intensity of director Lynch's earlier work.

Sailor Ripley (Nicolas Cage), a rebellious, 23-year-old Elvis acolyte, has just been released from prison. Waiting for him on the outside is Lula Fortune (Laura Dern), a 20-year-old, gum-popping, sex-loving cyclone of a gal. Embarking on a journey that takes them from the Carolinas to Texas, they encounter nightmarish accidents and outrageously evil characters, all the while trying to keep one step ahead of Lula's murderous, witchlike mother, Marietta (Diane Ladd, Dern's real-life mother). Interwoven into their cross-country odyssey are numerous references to THE WIZARD OF OZ.

Besides Crispin Glover as a cousin of Lula's who likes to put cockroaches in his underwear, and Willem Dafoe as a psychotic, rotten-toothed ex-marine called Bobby Peru, Lynch's Rogues Gallery includes W. Morgan Sheppard as Mr. Reindeer, a mysterious crime lord who is constantly surrounded by topless hookers; Freddie Jones as a bar patron with a mangled voice; Isabella Rossellini as Perdita, Peru's bleached-blonde girlfriend; Jack Nance, John Lurie, and Scott Coffey as three of the many eccentrics that populate Big Tuna, Texas; and David Patrick Kelly, Calvin Lockhart, and Grace Zabriskie as a trio of psycho killers. At the center of this wild hodge-podge, Cage and Dern turn in undeniably effective performances.

There are many powerful moments in WILD AT HEART—particularly one sequence in which Sailor and Lula come upon the scene of a nighttime accident, and find Sherilyn Fenn (best known for Lynch's TV show "Twin Peaks") wandering in a bloody daze by the side of the road. But these moments never add up to very much; the film plays as a series of vignettes, each with its own visual or aural or psychological *raison d'etre*, but never really tying into anything else that's going on.

WILD BOYS OF THE ROAD

1933 77m bw Drama ★★★★★
Warner Bros./First National (U.S.)

Frankie Darro (Eddie Smith), Dorothy Coonan (Sally), Edwin Phillips (Tommy), Rochelle Hudson (Grace), Ann Hovey (Lola), Arthur Hohl (Dr. Heckel), Grant Mitchell (Mr. Smith), Claire

McDowell *(Mrs. Smith)*, Sterling Holloway *(Ollie)*, Charley Grapewin *(Mr. Cadmust)*

p, Robert Presnell; d, William A. Wellman; w, Earl Baldwin (based on the story "Desperate Youth" by Daniel Ahearn); ph, Arthur Todd; ed, Thomas Pratt; art d, Esdras Hartley

WILD BOYS OF THE ROAD is a marvelous piece of Americana, a look at the social confusion of the Depression era. The film's two chief characters, Frankie Darro and Edwin Phillips, are California youths enjoying a comfortable lifestyle with their parents. When the Depression hits and their fathers lose their jobs, the boys hop an eastbound freight train to find work. They soon learn that there are thousands just like themselves, all looking for work, all trying to fight the economic depression that is destroying the country. Darro and Phillips find not only a number of other "wild boys" but also Dorothy Coonan and Rochelle Hudson, tough girls who take to the rails with them. Along the way, this mobile group of naive vagrants become a pack of outlaws when they kill a brakeman who has raped Hudson. The kids are finally forced off the tracks in Ohio, where they assemble their own "sewer city" from sewer pipes and supplies—a city founded on new ideals and a commitment to equality. Their city, however, breeds theft in the nearby community, prompting the police and fire department to wash away the vagrants with fire hoses. The gang moves on, suffering from lack of food and money. After getting involved in a theft ring, they're arrested and hauled off to court, where they get a lesson in New Deal ideology.

Blasted by countless critics for its political stance, WILD BOYS OF THE ROAD, if sometimes naive politically, is still superb entertainment. Director William A. Wellman tackled a straightforward "road movie" structure and applied the simplest of New Deal ideas to it. WILD BOYS OF THE ROAD shows with amazing accuracy the feeling of emptiness and apparent hopelessness that ran rampant in the country. The chief problem with the film is its refusal to lay the blame for the Depression at anyone's feet. The film's finish, though technically a happy ending, is rather mindless, leaving the audience with a "don't worry, everything will be fine" promise. Despite these faults, WILD BOYS OF THE ROAD is one of the finest films about youthful idealism to hit the screen. Costing $203,000 to produce, the film had only minimal success at the box office. Besides the superb Coonan (Wellman's fourth wife), the film is peopled with numerous teens, most of whom were, before and after the film, unknowns, adding to the authenticity of the film's atmosphere. The standout among the cast, however, is the appealing, pint-sized Darro, who became one of the foremost Depression era tough kids of the screen.

WILD BUNCH, THE [DVD]

1969 143m c Western ★★★★★
Warner Bros. (U.S.) R

William Holden *(Pike Bishop)*, Ernest Borgnine *(Dutch Engstrom)*, Robert Ryan *(Deke Thornton)*, Edmond O'Brien *(Sykes)*, Warren Oates *(Lyle Gorch)*, Jaime Sanchez *(Angel)*, Ben Johnson *(Tector Gorch)*, Emilio Fernandez *(Mapache)*, Strother Martin *(Coffer)*, L.Q. Jones *(T.C.)*

p, Phil Feldman; d, Sam Peckinpah; w, Walon Green, Sam Peckinpah (based on a story by Green, Roy N. Sickner); ph, Lucien Ballard (Panavision, Technicolor); ed, Lou Lombardo; m, Jerry Fielding; art d, Edward Carrere; fx, Bud Hulburd

AAN Best Original Story and Screenplay: Walon Green, Roy N. Sickner, Sam Peckinpah; *AAN Best Original Score (Not a Musical):* Jerry Fielding

An extraordinarily well-made film about anachronistic outlaws in the early 20th century, Sam Peckinpah's THE WILD BUNCH feels like it should have been the final western. This harsh yet elegaic story proved controversial upon its release not only because, like BONNIE AND CLYDE two years before, it upped the ante on American screen violence but also, in industry circles, because of the war it started between the producer, Feldman, and the director.

As with the majority of Peckinpah's work, the studios and producers mutilated the film to suit their needs (to cut its length, to eliminate controversy, to prove their power over the ever-difficult Peckinpah) and distributed a movie vastly different from the one the director had originally envisioned. The cutting occurred while Peckinpah was vacationing in Hawaii, *after* his film had been shown uncut to reviewers on the East Coast. (*New York Times* critic Vincent Canby expressed dismay when he went to see the film again and discovered scenes missing.) Certainly it was not adverse preview reaction that spurred Feldman to make the cuts (the trimmed scenes contained important motivational information vital to the portrayals of the main characters—none of the deletions was a particularly violent scene). These revisions were simply made to bring the film's running time down to two hours, to enable theater owners to turn more of a profit from the feature. With the director's uncut version now readily available on video and laserdisc, there is no reason for anyone to subject themselves to the butchered version.

WILD CHILD, THE [DVD]

(L'ENFANT SAUVAGE) ★★★★½
1969 90m bw Drama
Carrosse/Artistes (France) G

Jean-Pierre Cargol *(Victor the Boy)*, Francois Truffaut *(Dr. Jean Itard)*, Jean Daste *(Prof. Philippe Pinel)*, Francoise Seigner *(Mme. Guerin)*, Paul Ville *(Remy)*, Claude Miler *(M. Lemeri)*, Annie Miler *(Mme. Lemeri)*, Pierre Fabre *(Orderly at Institute)*, Rene Levert *(Police Offical)*, Jean Mandaroux *(Itard's Doctor)*

p, Marcel Berbert; d, Francois Truffaut; w, Francois Truffaut, Jean Gruault (based on *Memoire et Rapport sur Victor de L'Aveyron* by Jean-Marc Gaspard Itard); ph, Nestor Almendros; ed, Agnes Guillemot; m, Antonio Vivaldi; art d, Jean Mandaroux; cos, Gitt Magrini

As in Francois Truffaut's THE 400 BLOWS and SMALL CHANGE, THE WILD CHILD is devoted to the perceptual honesty and education of children. In this case, director and star Truffaut has made a deceptively clear and simple picture on the classic subject (Romulus and Remus, Tarzan) of the socialization of a boy discovered in the forest. Based on an actual case study published in 1806, THE WILD CHILD stars Jean-Pierre Cargol as Victor, a long-haired nature boy who, apparently abandoned in the woods by his parents years earlier, is found and placed in the Institute for the Deaf and Dumb in Paris. The boy is treated as a perverse outcast and freak, but Jean Itard (Truffaut), a patient and enlightened doctor, intervenes and cares for the child in his country home rather than allow him to be sent to an asylum. Raised in an orphanage himself, Truffaut had an affinity for children that was expressed in nearly all his pictures. Probably the director's most ambitious film, THE WILD CHILD spins a modern myth with resonances for parents and children, teachers and students, and even filmmakers, actors and audiences. Its concern with language and images mirrors the longstanding French philosophical interest in linguistics, and through it all Truffaut examines the many issues at hand with warmth, concern and wisdom.

WILD ONE, THE

1953 79m bw Drama
Columbia (U.S.)

DVD
★★★½

Marlon Brando *(Johnny)*, Mary Murphy *(Kathie)*, Robert Keith *(Harry Bleeker)*, Lee Marvin *(Chino)*, Jay C. Flippen *(Sheriff Singer)*, Peggy Maley *(Mildred)*, Hugh Sanders *(Charlie Thomas)*, Ray Teal *(Frank Bleeker)*, John Brown *(Bill Hannegan)*, Will Wright *(Art Kleiner)*

p, Stanley Kramer; d, Laslo Benedek; w, John Paxton (based on a story by Frank Rooney); ph, Hal Mohr; ed, Al Clark; m, Leith Stevens; prod d, Rudolph Sternad; art d, Walter Holscher

The first and best biker movie begins as a group of 40 leather-jacketed motorcyclists roar down a lonely country road straight at the camera. The bikers, who call themselves the Black Rebels, invade a legitimate motorcycle race and try to join the competition, but they are soon thrown out by the mass of motorcycle enthusiasts. Before leaving, a gang member manages to snatch the first-prize trophy and presents it to their leader, Brando. With the trophy strapped to his handlebars, Brando leads his pack of rowdies into the small town of Wrightsville where they drag up and down the street, forcing an old man to drive his car into a light pole. Many of the bikers pile into the local bar, Bleeker's Cafe, which is owned and operated by the sheriff, Keith. Keith is overwhelmed by the disturbance and does little to calm things down as the bikers drink themselves into oblivion. Brando's minions amuse themselves by terrorizing the town, while Brando spots a good-looking girl, Murphy, and follows her into the bar. To his surprise he learns that she is Keith's daughter, and he tries to impress her by giving her the stolen trophy. Though she is intrigued by this strange, somewhat withdrawn, brutish young man, she refuses the gift. More trouble soon thunders into town in the guise of Marvin, a former member of Brando's gang who has left and formed his own pack.

THE WILD ONE was inspired by an incident in 1947 in which a gang of 4,000 motorcyclists took over the small town of Hollister, California, for the Fourth of July weekend and destroyed it. Producer Kramer put together a film that he hoped would illustrate the frustration and alienation felt by a younger generation, and the result became an anthem for disaffected American youth. Brando's performance enthralled audiences, who became fascinated with his contradictory character. He seemed powerful and brutal, but also demonstrated a caring, vulnerable side that he tried hard to repress—laying the groundwork for a whole school of moody antiheroes that would include James Dean in REBEL WITHOUT A CAUSE. Even without these virtues, the film would be immortal merely for the legendary exchange in which Murphy asks Brando, "What are you rebelling against?" and he replies, "What have you got?"

WILD PARTY, THE

1929 77m bw Comedy/Romance
Paramount (U.S.)

★★★

Clara Bow *(Stella Ames)*, Fredric March *(Gil Gilmore)*, Shirley O'Hara *(Helen Owens)*, Marceline Day *(Faith Morgan)*, Joyce Compton *(Eva Tutt)*, Adrienne Dore *(Babs)*, Virginia Thomas *(Tess)*, Kay Bryant *(Thelma)*, Alice Adair *(Mazie)*, Jean Lorraine *(Ann)*

p, E. Lloyd Sheldon; d, Dorothy Arzner; w, E. Lloyd Sheldon, John V.A. Weaver, George Marion Jr. (based on a story by Warner Fabian); ph, Victor Milner; ed, Otho Lovering; cos, Travis Banton

Though the plot practically grows mold before the viewer's eyes, and some of the production qualities are laughable, THE WILD PARTY remains fascinating to watch from first reel to last. One of the popular happy-go-lucky college-based films of the era, this has an added benefit in featuring Bow in her talkie debut. She is, naturally, a wild party girl who's enrolled in college for the good times rather than to advance her education. Bow and her girlfriends decide to take a class taught by March, not for his stunning classroom abilities, but because he's cute! March is a no-nonsense type and the course proves to be much more difficult than Bow and company had anticipated. To relieve this academic pressure, the coeds pull a few classroom pranks. Bow attends a ball but is kicked out for wearing a low-cut dress. She later goes to a roadhouse, where an inebriated Ben Hendricks tries to have his way with her. March, who inexplicably is also at the roadhouse, puts a stop to this, then gives Bow a lift. Compton, a fellow classmate of Bow's, sees the campus flirt leaving March's car, and her nimble mind immediately assumes there's funny business involved. Gossip spreads thick, so March chews out Bow in front of other students to prove they aren't an item. Bow angrily walks out of the classroom. She and roommate O'Hara go to a party (no one ever studies at this school), where O'Hara falls for Jack Luden. Hendricks, still angry with March for the earlier altercation, finds the professor and shoots him. Bow tells the wounded March of her love for him, giving Compton more fuel for her gossip mill. A letter from O'Hara to Luden turns up, and its spicy contents create a scandal.

It's silly, but so what? Arzner's direction is good and Bow gives an energetic performance, her Brooklyn accent serving the "It" girl's well-known personality with absolute perfection. The advertising campaign played up on this with glee, claiming: "You've had an eyeful of *IT*... now get an earful!" March, in only his second film, takes his part seriously, which adds to the picture's inherent campiness. Bow was terrified of making a talkie, but she handled herself well in the funfest. Reportedly, her voice was so loud it blew meters on the sound equipment when she spoke her first line. At times her voice is muddled on the soundtrack, partly the fault of the new technology and partly due to her accent. In England, THE WILD PARTY was released as a silent film. Within a few years Bow would be gone from the screen forever, while March would become one of filmdom's most respected thespians.

WILD REEDS

1994 110m c Drama
IMA Films/Les Films Alain Sarde/Canal Plus/La Sept/ARTE/IMA Productions/SFP Productions (France)

DVD
★★★★

Frederic Gorny *(Henri)*, Gael Morel *(Francois)*, Elodie Bouchez *(Maite)*, Stephane Rideau *(Serge)*, Michele Moretti *(Madame Alvarez)*, Nathalie Vigne *(Young Bride)*, Laurent Groulout *(The Photographer)*, Jacques Nolot *(Monsieur Morelli)*, Eric Kreikenmayer *(Young Bridegroom)*, Michel Ruhl *(Monsieur Cassagne)*

p, Alain Sarde, Georges Benayoun; d, Andre Techine; w, Andre Techine, Gilles Taurand, Olivier Massart; ph, Jeanne Lapoirie; ed, Martine Giordano; cos, Elisabeth Tavernier

Andre Techine's lovely coming-of-age film—set in 1962, near the end of the Algerian war for independence—evokes the vulnerability and desperation of adolescence through the stories of a group of teenagers whose lives intersect at a boarding school in southwestern France. The title derives from La Fontaine's fable "The Oak and the Reeds" and serves to place the characters within the broader context of nature: Techine often frames them within a landscape of rolling hills and pans gently across the frame, giving the film the wistful flow of reeds in the wind.

There are four youngsters: Maite (Elodie Bouchez), the feminist, Communist daughter of the school's literature instructor; timid, intelligent Francois (Gael Morel), who's discovering his homosexuality; Serge (Stephane Rideau), the passionate and physical son of emigre Italian farmers; and

Henri (Frederic Gorny), older than the rest and an Algerian refugee who supports the reactionary OAS. Moments of passion, beauty, and self-discovery result from this complicated friendship, but the turmoil surrounding the Algerian War soon spills over into the adolescent idyll.

Informed but not constrained by the conventions of 1950s melodramas, WILD REEDS does a remarkable job of exploring the volatile space in which personal affairs and international events intersect. It was produced as part of a series called *Tous les garcons et les filles de leur age* (*All the Boys and Girls of their Time*), for which nine directors were invited to make films about teenagers, set in the periods of their own youth. It won four 1994 Cesar awards (the French equivalent of the Oscar), including Best Picture, Director, and Screenplay, and was France's official entry that year for the Academy Award for Best Foreign Language Film.

WILD RIVER
1960 115m c Drama ★★★★
Fox (U.S.)

Montgomery Clift (*Chuck Glover*), Lee Remick (*Carol Baldwin*), Jo Van Fleet (*Ella Garth*), Albert Salmi (*F.J. Bailey*), Jay C. Flippen (*Hamilton Garth*), James Westerfield (*Cal Garth*), Big Jeff Bess (*Joe John Garth*), Robert Earl Jones (*Ben*), Frank Overton (*Walter Clark*), Barbara Loden (*Betty Jackson*)

p, Elia Kazan; d, Elia Kazan; w, Paul Osborn (based on the novels *Mud on the Stars* by William Bradford Huie and *Dunbar's Cove* by Borden Deal); ph, Ellsworth Fredricks (CinemaScope, DeLuxe Color); ed, William Reynolds; m, Kenyon Hopkins; art d, Lyle Wheeler, Herman A. Blumenthal; cos, Anna Hill Johnstone

Although it was not a great success at the box office (issue-oriented films were not what the public seemed to want in 1960), this dramatic tug-of-war between progress and tradition remains a memorable example of director Kazan at his best. Set in the 1930s, the story focuses on Clift, an agent for the Tennessee Valley Authority (TVA), which is in the process of clearing land to build much-needed dams. This project cannot be accomplished without the demolition of many homes and the relocation of their inhabitants. One of Clift's most unpleasant tasks is the removal of Van Fleet, an 80-year-old widow, from her home. Van Fleet, who has lived on her land for more than 50 years, refuses to leave. As if Clift's plight isn't bad enough, the locals look upon him as an interloper and make his life miserable. Local whites grow particularly hostile when Clift treats the area's blacks fairly, and it isn't long before some of the more racist townsfolk try to beat some sense into the TVA man. Nevertheless, Van Fleet's young widowed granddaughter, Remick, falls in love with Clift and they eventually marry. In time, Van Fleet finally gives up her battle, the land is flooded, and the proud old woman dies shortly after moving into her new home.

An emotionally charged movie that offers little respite for the viewer, WILD RIVER was skillfully scripted by Osborn, masterfully directed by Kazan, and features excellent acting and strong production values. Shot on location in Tennessee at Lake Chickamauga, the Hiwassee River, and in the towns of Cleveland and Charleston, this film was the end of a 25-year dream for Kazan. He had been to the area in the mid-1930s and always wanted to do a movie about the TVA, but it took more than two decades to find a studio and the right script to fulfill his desire. Many nonprofessional Tennesseans appear in the film, lending it a realism seldom seen when Hollywood extras are employed. Kazan's wife, Barbara Loden, plays a small role, and if you keep an eye out you'll see a very young Bruce Dern appearing in his first movie. However, Van Fleet's performance is the film's standout; though she was only 41 at the time the film was made, the actress is completely convincing as an 80-year-old, thanks in no small part to Ben Nye's wonderful makeup work. Clift also gives a fine per-

formance. He was never easy to work with, as he had several personal problems, not the least of which was his drinking and his difficulty in coming to grips with his homosexuality. Reportedly, he'd promised to stay off the sauce for the picture and kept his word until the final week when he went on a bender that almost submarined the movie.

WILD STRAWBERRIES
(SMULTRONSTALLET)
1957 90m bw Drama ★★★★½
Svensk (Sweden)

Victor Sjostrom (*Prof. Isak Borg*), Bibi Andersson (*Sara*), Ingrid Thulin (*Marianne Borg*), Gunnar Bjornstrand (*Evald Borg*), Jullan Kindahl (*Agda*), Folke Sundquist (*Anders*), Bjorn Bjelvenstam (*Viktor*), Naima Wifstrand (*Isak's Mother*), Gunnel Brostrom (*Mrs. Berit Almann*), Gertrud Fridh (*Isak's Wife*)

p, Allan Ekelund; d, Ingmar Bergman; w, Ingmar Bergman; ph, Gunnar Fischer, Bjorn Thermenius; ed, Oscar Rosander; m, Erik Nordgren; art d, Gittan Gustafsson; cos, Millie Strom

AAN Best Original Story and Screenplay: Ingmar Bergman

Possibly Ingmar Bergman's finest film and a landmark in film history. Victor Sjostrom stars as Isak Borg, a medical professor on his way to accept an honorary degree on the 50th anniversary of his graduation from the University at Lund. He rides with his daughter-in-law, Marianne (Ingrid Thulin), who has decided to leave her husband. They don't get along, mainly because the old man reminds her so much of her husband. En route, they stop at Isak's childhood house, where he recalls his family in the days of his youth (although he is unseen by the characters and not present in the flashback). He sees his sweetheart, Sara (Bibi Andersson), picking wild strawberries and carrying on seductively with his brother. Later he is awakened (in the present) by a teenage girl named Sara (again played by Andersson). She asks the old man for a ride, bringing along two male friends. This foray proves less than idyllic, hampered by a car crash and Isak's disturbing nightmares.

WILD STRAWBERRIES is viewed by many as Bergman's greatest achievement. Its most striking segment, which perhaps best illustrates Bergman's technique, is a dream sequence in which Isak walks through a desolate city, is approached by a faceless man, sees a clock without hands, and watches a funeral wagon crash and leave a coffin in the middle of the street. As he nears the coffin, it opens, and the corpse—again Isak—emerges and attempts to pull him into the afterlife. The visual and aural symbolism is chilling, and the entire scene is perfectly integrated into the "reality" of the rest of the picture. Sjostrom, in his final film, delivers one of the finest performances in any Bergman film—a major accomplishment considering the virtuosity that Bergman's actors consistently display.

WILD THINGS
1998 113m c Thriller ★★★
McNaughton/Jones Motion Pictures/Mandalay R
Entertainment (U.S.)

Kevin Bacon (*Ray Duquette*), Matt Dillon (*Sam Lombardo*), Neve Campbell (*Suzie Toller*), Denise Richards (*Kelly Van Ryan*), Daphne Rubin-Vega (*Gloria Perez*), Bill Murray (*Ken Bowden*), Theresa Russell (*Sandra Van Ryan*), Robert Wagner (*Tom Baxter*), Carrie Snodgress (*Ruby*), Jeff Perry (*Bryce Hunter*)

p, Rodney Liber, Steven A. Jones; d, John McNaughton; w, Stephen Peters; ph, Jeffrey L. Kimball; ed, Elena Maganini; m, George S. Clinton; prod d, Edward T. McAvoy; art d, Bill Hiney; fx, Kevin Harris; cos, Kimberly A. Tillman

A sleazy, seamy, flashy, steamy, vulgar exploitation thriller that revels in every minute of its own trashiness and delivers some pretty solid—if prurient—entertainment before strangling in a one-twist-too-many ending.

In sun-kissed Blue Bay, FL, where wealthy socialites live cheek to jowl with gator-wrestling swamp trash, hunky gold-digging high-school guidance counselor Sam Lombardo (Matt Dillon) is about to take a gut-wrenching detour into tabloid hell. A wealthy Lolita, Kelly Van Ryan (Denise Richards), accuses Lombardo of sexual assault, and a second student, wrong-side-of-the-tracks Suzie (Neve Campbell), soon adds her own tale of rape to the sordid outcry. Kelly's vindictive mom (Teresa Russell), one of many wealthy local women with whom Sam has had a fling, mounts a full scale legal campaign to destroy him. Local detectives Duquette (Kevin Bacon) and Perez (Daphne Rubin-Vega) suspect there's more to the case than meets the eye, but are told to butt out by departmental higher-ups.

Director John McNaughton, whose erratic career has lurched from the vicious indie high of HENRY: PORTRAIT OF A SERIAL KILLER to the bland, mainstream low of MAD DOG AND GLORY, gives this seedy malarky a fine, sweaty sheen, and he clearly sees the humor in the genre's excesses. You can feel it in the reaction shots of swamp wildlife, and you can almost hear McNaughton snickering over the truly bizarre casting, which includes the mummified Robert Wagner as an old-money jurist, Bill Murray as a local ambulance chaser, and Carrie Snodgress as Suzie's white-trash grandma. The tawdry ambiance and wall-to-wall shots of fresh young flesh in various enticing states of undress fairly scream "direct-to-video erotic thriller," but this vulgar romp through pulp-fiction cliches is wildly entertaining until it gets bogged down in the scummy meshes of its own plot.

WILD WILD WEST

1999 105m c Action/Western/Comedy ★★½
Sonnenfeld/Josephson Worldwide Entertainment/ PG-13
Peters Entertainment Co./Warner Bros. (U.S.)

Will Smith (James T. West), Kevin Kline (Artemus Gordon), Kevin Kline (President Ulysses S. Grant—Uncredited), Kenneth Branagh (Dr. Arliss Loveless), Salma Hayek (Rita Escobar), Musetta Vander (Munitia), Frederique Van Der Wal (Amazonia), Bai Ling (Miss East), Sofia Eng (Miss Lippenreider), Ted Levine (McGrath)

p, Jon Peters, Barry Sonnenfeld; d, Barry Sonnenfeld; w, Brent Maddock, Steve Wilson, Jeffrey Price, Peter S. Seaman, Jim Thomas (story), John Thomas (story); ph, Michael Ballhaus; ed, Jim Miller; prod d, Bo Welch; art d, Tom Duffield; cos, Deborah L. Scott

The quintessential cotton-candy movie: it's pleasant, brightly colored, and the minute it's done it's as though it were never there.

Inspired by the '60s TV show starring Robert Conrad and Ross Martin, a James Bond-ish Western with a kinky edge, this period sci-fi action comedy disguises its fundamental blandness under layers of juvenile vulgarity, furious action, and whiz-bang gadgetry. The plot, as far as it goes, pits James T. West and the eccentric Artemus Gordon (Kevin Kline) against mad genius Dr. Arliss Loveless (Kenneth Branagh). A Southern aristocrat maimed in the Civil War—he's literally half the man he used to be—Loveless, surrounded by kidnapped scientists and bodacious women in abbreviated costumes, has a diabolical plan to shatter the Union and bring the North to its knees, ha-ha-ha-ha-ha-ha-ha! It involves an 80-foot, steam-driven, mechanical spider, fully loaded with state-of-the-art weaponry, the kind of thing Jules Verne might have asked Industrial Light & Magic to whip up for him if he'd had the opportunity.

Branagh overacts wildly; Kline looks vaguely uneasy, as though he's never quite sure what he might have to do next; poor Salma Hayek flutters and looks nice in her fancy clothes; Smith just moseys along being his charming self. Casting him as a Secret Service agent in the 1869 West was a leap of faith in his ability to transcend the historical unlikeliness of the situation. Sure, there were black cowboys and homesteaders and gunslingers, but a black man who can march into the White House—late—and talk turkey with the President? That's a tribute to Hollywood's blindness to any color that isn't green, and the movie's sense of history lies so lightly over its sight gags, vulgar breast and butt jokes, and timeless buddy banter that plausibility scarcely matters anyway.

WILDE
(OSCAR WILDE) 📀
1997 116m c Biography/Drama ★★★
Samuelson Productions/Dove International/NDF R
International/Pony Canyon/Pandora Film/Capitol
Films/BBC Films (U.K.)

Stephen Fry (Oscar Wilde), Jude Law (Lord Alfred Douglas), Jennifer Ehle (Constance Wilde), Vanessa Redgrave (Lady Speranza Wilde), Gemma Jones (Lady Queensberry), Judy Parfitt (Lady Mount-Temple), Michael Sheen (Robert Ross), Zoe Wanamaker (Ada Leverson), Tom Wilkinson (Marquess of Queensberry), Ioan Gruffudd (John Gray)

p, Marc Samuelson, Peter Samuelson; d, Brian Gilbert; w, Julian Mitchell (from the biography Oscar Wilde by Richard Ellmann); ph, Martin Fuhrer; ed, Michael Bradsell; m, Debbie Wiseman; prod d, Maria Djurkovic; art d, Martyn John; fx, Bob Hollow; cos, Nic Ede

A fairly conventional biopic, but adapted from Richard Ellmann's celebrated life of Oscar Wilde with surprising emotional resonance.

We first meet Wilde (Stephen Fry) in 1882, as the famed playwright and satirist is wrapping up a tour of America before returning to England to marry Constance Lloyd (Jennifer Ehle). Wilde discovers his homosexuality soon after when acolyte Robert Ross (Michael Sheen) presses himself upon his intellectual mentor, and Wilde is off on a rampage of sexual self-discovery. Wilde's undoing lies in the dashing but petulant Lord Alfred Douglas (Jude Law), a.k.a. "Bosie," a self-styled poet who bullies and cajoles Wilde into an extravagant life involving rent boys and various London dens of iniquity. Bosie flaunts his relationship with Wilde in order to needle his brutish father, the Marquess of Queensberry (Tom Wilkinson). But the Marquess is not amused, and such behavior does not go unpunished.

Director Brian Gilbert and screenwriter Julian Mitchell manage the neat trick of seamlessly interweaving Wilde's creative endeavors, such as the writing and staging of Lady Windemere's Fan and The Importance of Being Earnest, with the playwright's own personal drama. Since Wilde's not-so-private life was virtually crawling with handsome young things, there's quite a bit of young male flesh on display. Some viewers will be shocked (others may be delighted), but the film is hardly prurient. Fry's stellar performance gets to the very depths of this fascinating and doomed artist.

WILL SUCCESS SPOIL ROCK HUNTER?
1957 94m c Comedy ★★★★
Fox (U.S.)

Jayne Mansfield (Rita Marlowe), Tony Randall (Rock Hunter), Betsy Drake (Jenny), Joan Blondell (Violet), John Williams (Le Salle), Henry Jones (Rufus), Lili Gentle (April), Mickey Hargitay (Bobo), Georgia Carr (Calypso Number), Groucho Marx (Surprise Guest)

p, Frank Tashlin; d, Frank Tashlin; w, Frank Tashlin (based on the play by George Axelrod); ph, Joseph MacDonald (CinemaScope, DeLuxe Color); ed, Hugh S. Fowler; m, Cyril J. Mockridge; art d, Lyle Wheeler, Leland Fuller; fx, L.B. Abbott; cos, Charles LeMaire

A panic. Jayne's twin peaks triumph, for which she received a Tony, gets transferred from Hollywood lampoon to advertising satire. Tashlin produced, directed and wrote the screenplay, and in true Tashlin form, it feels like a like an outrageous, gaudy cartoon. The frantic Randall performance, Blondell's usual canny job and Hargitay, Mansfield's real life muscleman husband doing a turn as a TV Tarzan, all score. But it's Jayne's last word on Hollywood Blondes that will have you howling. Her best takes: Seclusion and Catherine the Great. And wait until you see who she really carries a torch for. Jayne's broad comedic talent was only properly utilized twice by Fox. Instead of basing her persona on Marilyn Monroe, her studio should have built her along the lines of a combo of Mae West and Jane Russell, and taken advantage of her unique brand of sexual anarchy. French critics enjoyed this picture immensely, and Jean-Luc Godard had it on his 10-best list. In a small role as one of the scrubwomen appears Minta Durfee, former silent-screen comedienne who worked with Charlie Chaplin, among others, and married Roscoe "Fatty" Arbuckle.

WILLIAM SHAKESPEARE'S ROMEO + JULIET ★★
DVD
1996 113m c   Romance/Drama
Bazmark Productions   (U.S./Australia/Canada)   PG-13

Leonardo DiCaprio (Romeo), Claire Danes (Juliet), John Leguizamo (Tybalt), Harold Perrineau (Mercutio), Diane Venora (Gloria Capulet), Paul Sorvino (Fulgencio Capulet), Brian Dennehy (Ted Montague), Pete Postlethwaite (Father Laurence), Miriam Margoyles (The Nurse), Christina Pickles (Mrs. Montague)

p, Gabriella Martinelli, Baz Luhrmann; d, Baz Luhrmann; w, Baz Luhrmann, Craig Pearce (based on the play by William Shakespeare); ph, Don McAlpine; ed, Jill Bilcock; prod d, Catherine Martin; art d, Doug Hardwick; fx, Laurencio "Chov" Cordero; cos, Kym Barett

AAN Best Art Direction: Catherine Martin, Brigitte Broch

Recklessly energetic, Baz Luhrmann's bold adaptation of *Romeo and Juliet* doesn't so much pump up a classic for easily bored teens as use the play as a pretext for directorial handsprings and back flips.

In the smoggy, crime-filled metropolis of Verona, two corporate dynasties, the Montagues, headed by Mr. Montague (Brian Dennehy), and the Capulets, presided over by Mr. Capulet (Paul Sorvino), compete so viciously that succeeding generations are poisoned by their rivalry. On the eve of her betrothal, Juliet Capulet (Claire Danes) becomes smitten by Romeo Montague (Leonardo DiCaprio), and the lovers prevail upon Juliet's maid (Miriam Margolyes) and Romeo's priest, Father Laurence (Pete Postlethwaite), to facilitate their secret wedding, but happiness proves short-lived for the starcrossed pair.

To their credit, director Baz Luhrmann and co-screenwriter Craig Pearce foster a sense of urgency in their retelling of this centuries-old play by investing the characters with a state of adrenaline overdrive; everyone seems to be hurtling toward premature death. However, Luhrmann doesn't bother to support or dramatize Shakespeare's tragedy-laden text; his startling imagery pushes all the pesky dialogue into the wings where it's left to fend for itself. Unlike the magically revamped RICHARD III (1995), which positioned that upstart's treachery in a 20th-century fascist environment, this febrile adaptation is pointlessly updated with pop-culture references and a hip sensibility. Moreover, his abuse of Shakespeare runs a close second to his thrashing of a talented cast. Gloriously photogenic Leonardo DiCaprio gives a moving performance

only when he isn't required to speak; Claire Danes summons up the mournfulness of a cheerleader who's been stood up on prom night. Only Margolyes and Postlethwaite acquit themselves with any dignity.

WINCHESTER '73
DVD ★★★★
1950 92m   bw   Western
Universal   (U.S.)

James Stewart (Lin McAdam), Shelley Winters (Lola Manners), Dan Duryea (Waco Johnny Dean, the Kansas Kid), Stephen McNally (Dutch Henry Brown), Millard Mitchell (Johnny "High Spade" Williams), Charles Drake (Steve Miller), John McIntire (Joe Lamont), Will Geer (Wyatt Earp), Jay C. Flippen (Sgt. Wilkes), Rock Hudson (Young Bull)

p, Aaron Rosenberg; d, Anthony Mann; w, Robert L. Richards, Borden Chase (based on the story by Stuart N. Lake); ph, William Daniels; ed, Edward Curtiss; m, Joseph Gershenson (assisted by Jesse Hibbs); art d, Bernard Herzbrun, Nathan Juran, Russell A. Gausman, A. Roland Fields; cos, Yvonne Wood

The first collaboration between director Mann and actor Stewart, a team that would create a series of superior westerns that added a new, psychological dimension to the genre.

WINCHESTER '73 begins as Stewart, who is pursuing his father's killer, rides into Dodge City with his friend, Mitchell. The whole town is celebrating the Fourth of July under the watchful eye of the fatherly Wyatt Earp (Geer), who collects pistols from gun-toting strangers and keeps them in his office until they leave. Stewart enters the local saloon and orders a drink. Out of the corner of his eye he sees McNally, and both men spastically grope for their sidearms, only to find empty holsters. Stewart's nerves are frazzled by the event, and he leaves the saloon shaking. The two men square off again, this time in a shooting contest with a brand new "one-of-1,000" Winchester '73 rifle as the first prize. The contestants are evenly matched in an intense fight, but Stewart manages to best McNally and wins the coveted rifle. Before Stewart can leave town with his prize, however, McNally attacks him and steals the rifle. Stewart then sets off on a maniacal pursuit of McNally and his rifle which culminates in a memorable shoot-out with decidedly Oedipal overtones.

WINCHESTER '73 was the first of the so-called "psychological" westerns that became the benchmark of the genre in the 1950s. Mann and Stewart present a basically decent hero driven to the brink of madness by dark forces from his past. Played out against breathtaking landscapes that reflect the emotional turmoil of the main characters, Mann's film gives us one of Stewart's greatest performances, his manic intensity evoking both terror and pathos. The supporting cast is fine, with both Tony Curtis and Rock Hudson appearing in small roles.

WINCHESTER '73 was once a project for Fritz Lang, who worked on the script with Silvia Richards in 1948. Lang eventually walked away from the film, and Mann took over at Stewart's suggestion. Beginning a collaboration that would last through two more westerns (BEND OF THE RIVER, 1952, and THE FAR COUNTRY, 1955), Mann rewrote the script with Borden Chase. WINCHESTER '73 was a great success at the box office and reestablished Stewart (who was suffering a decline in popularity) as one of Hollywood's top actors. In addition to providing both star and director with a career boost, the film launched a whole new series of adult westerns directed by such notables as Mann, Budd Boetticher, Don Siegel, Sam Fuller, and Nicholas Ray.

WIND AND THE LION, THE

DVD

1975 119m c   Adventure/Historical/War   ★★★½
MGM (U.S.)   PG

Sean Connery *(Mulay el Raisuli)*, Candice Bergen *(Eden Pedecaris)*, Brian Keith *(Theodore Roosevelt)*, John Huston *(John Hay)*, Geoffrey Lewis *(Gummere)*, Steve Kanaly *(Capt. Jerome)*, Vladek Sheybal *(The Bashaw)*, Nadim Sawalha *(Sherif of Wazan)*, Roy Jenson *(Adm. Chadwick)*, Deborah Baxter *(Alice Roosevelt)*

p, Herb Jaffe; d, John Milius; w, John Milius; ph, Billy Williams (Panavision, Metrocolor); ed, Robert Wolfe; m, Jerry Goldsmith; prod d, Gil Parando; art d, Antonio Paton; cos, Richard LaMotte

AAN Best Original Score: Jerry Goldsmith; *AAN Best Sound:* Harry W. Tetrick, Aaron Rochin, William McCaughey, Roy Charman

A stirring, if grossly inaccurate, look at the dawn of U.S. interventionism, THE WIND AND THE LION features Brian Keith as a Teddy Roosevelt determined to establish his Presidential identity, having come to office after the death of William McKinley. When a rebellious Arab chieftain, Mulay el Raisuli (Sean Connery), seizes American woman Eden Pedecaris (Candice Bergen) and her children, Roosevelt prepares to send in the Marines. At the same time the Germans land in North Africa in force, looking for a way to turn the situation to their advantage. The chieftain and Eden talk a great deal of philosophy, and the Arab ruler begins to take on heroic stature in the eyes of her son. Eventually, under pressure from Roosevelt, Raisuli releases his hostages to the Marines and is immediately arrested and imprisoned by the Germans. The Marines are none too happy about this development—since Roosevelt had promised Raisuli his freedom if he released his prisoners—so they march into the town (in a scene almost directly stolen from THE WILD BUNCH) and shoot it out with the Germans.

THE WIND AND THE LION is certainly jingoistic to a fault, and its portrayal of the various factions is little above the cartoon level, but thanks to marvelous performances by Keith and Connery, the film works as a maker of myths. The real facts of the incident were not so grand: Raisuli, a brigand chief, kidnapped a balding, overweight businessman who bore no resemblance to the lovely Bergen, to embarrass the Sultan of Morocco, who was already having troubles with the U.S. The man was freed after only a couple of days, but before his release was made public, the Republican Party, looking for a rallying issue, announced that a telegram had been sent to the kidnapper demanding the man be freed or Raisuli would be pay with his life. No troops landed. No one was killed. But historical truth isn't what's important here; heroes and myth are the currency of this film, and it delivers two heroes in admirable fashion.

WINDTALKERS

DVD

2002 135m c   War.   ★★½
Lion Rock/MGM (U.S.)   R

Nicolas Cage *(Joe Enders)*, Adam Beach *(Ben Yahzee)*, Christian Slater *(Pete "Ox" Henderson)*, Frances O'Connor *(Rita)*, Peter Stormare *(Hjelmstad)*, Noah Emmerich *(Chick)*, Roger Willie *(Charlie Whitehorse)*, Mark Ruffalo *(Pappas)*, Brian Van Holt *(Harrigan)*, Martin Henderson *(Nellie)*

p, Terence Chang, Tracie Graham, Alison Rosenzweig, John Woo; d, John Woo; w, Joe Batteer, John Rice; ph, Jeffrey Kimball; ed, Jeff Gullo, Steven Kemper, Tom Rolf; m, James Horner; prod d, Holger Gross; art d, Kevin Ishioka; fx, Jan H. Aaris , Phil Corey, John Frazier, Kevin Lingenfelser, David Simmons

Whatever its faults—and there are a number of them—John Woo's spectacularly violent war movie sheds some light on the crucial contribution Navajo-Americans made to the WWII effort.

Camp Pendleton, CA, 1943: Native American Ben Yahzee (Adam Beach) is one of several hundred Navajo men recruited by the Marine Corps to serve as "codetalkers," radio operators trained to relay highly sensitive information in their native tongue. Since the unwritten Navajo language is virtually unknown to anyone born outside the tribe, Japanese interceptors have little chance of cracking the code—if they don't have access to a Navajo translator. Yahzee is to be accompanied onto the battlefields of Saipan—an important foothold on the road to taking Tokyo—by Marine Sergeant Joe Enders (Nicolas Cage), who is under orders to "protect the code at all costs." The meaning isn't lost on Enders: It's his job to make sure that Yahzee isn't captured by the enemy, even if it means killing the codetalker himself.

No one can choreograph mayhem quite like Woo, who fills the battlefields of Saipan with severed limbs, rolling heads, burning bodies, and bullets, bullets, bullets. But Woo isn't really the right man to tell this particular story. Fascinated by the bonds violence forges among men, Woo concentrates solely on the difficult relationship between the tormented Enders and the likeable young recruit he may one day have to kill. The movie deals superficially with Native American pride and racism in the ranks, but it's hardly about the codetalkers at all, and Woo completely misses the bitter irony inherent in a Native American soldier protecting his land by serving the very government that took it from him in the first place.

WINDOW, THE

1949 73m   bw   Thriller   ★★★★
RKO (U.S.)

Barbara Hale *(Mrs. Woodry)*, Bobby Driscoll *(Tommy Woodry)*, Arthur Kennedy *(Mr. Woodry)*, Paul Stewart *(Mr. Kellerton)*, Ruth Roman *(Mrs. Kellerton)*, Anthony Ross *(Ross)*, Richard Benedict *(Drunken Seaman)*, Jim Nolan *(Stranger on Street)*, Ken Terrell *(Man)*, Lee Phelps

p, Frederic Ullman Jr.; d, Ted Tetzlaff; w, Mel Dinelli (based on the novelette *The Boy Cried Murder* by Cornell Woolrich); ph, William Steiner; ed, Frederic Knudtson; m, Roy Webb; art d, Walter E. Keller, Sam Corso; fx, Russell A. Cully

AAN Best Film Editing: Frederic Knudtson

Set in the tenement section of New York's Lower East Side, this incredibly tense nail-biter stars Driscoll as a young boy who has a habit of crying wolf. One night, while trying to beat the heat by making his bed on the fire escape, he climbs up to the next floor and sees Stewart and Roman murder a drunken seaman, Benedict. Of course, no one, not even the boy's parents (Kennedy and Hale), believes Driscoll when he tells what he has seen, since they all assume that this is just another of the boy's tales. Danger lurks.

Based on a story by Cornell Woolrich (whose writing was also the basis for Hitchcock's similar REAR WINDOW), THE WINDOW presents a frightening vision of helplessness, vividly conveying childish frustration at being dismissed or ignored by one's parents. Director and onetime cameraman Tetzlaff adroitly injects a maximum of suspense into the film, enabling the audience to identify with Driscoll's predicament and, interestingly, to view his parents as evil, almost as evil as the murderers themselves. Having photographed Hitchcock's NOTORIOUS just three years before, Tetzlaff had, without a shadow of a doubt, learned something of his suspense-building craft from the master of that art (as did just about every working director). By casting the 12-year-old Driscoll, star of such heartwarming Disney pictures as SONG OF THE SOUTH and SO DEAR TO MY HEART, Tetzlaff was able to twist the idyllic Disney image of childhood into a nightmare world of death and violence, in which parents and neighbors are the child's worst fears come true. Adding to the film's effect is the on-location photography and the dark ambience of the tenements, where evil and death seem to lurk in every shadow, where the seaman's corpse is found, and where the pursued boy is nearly killed. (In a perverse twist of fate, it was in an abandoned, crumbling New York City tenement that actor Driscoll was found dead some 20 years later, the victim of an apparent drug overdose.) THE WINDOW, which cost only $210,000 to produce and made many times that at the box office, was voted the best mystery film of the year by the Mystery Writers of America. Editor Knudtson was nominated for an Academy Award, while Driscoll was named Outstanding Juvenile Actor and given a miniature statuette. An exceptional film.

WINGED MIGRATION   *DVD*
2001   89m   c   Documentary   ★★★★
President Films/Galatee Films/France 2 Cinema/   G
France 3 Cinema/Bac Films/Les Productions de la
Gueville/Pandora Films/Westdeutscher Rundfunk/
Filmstiftung NRW/Wanda Vision/Les Productions
JMH/Television Suisse Romande/Eyescreen/
Lucky Red   (France/Spain/Italy/Germany/Switzerland)

Jacques Perrin *(Narrator)*

p, Christophe Barratier; d, Jacques Perrin, Jacques Cluzaud (co-director), Michel Debats (co-director); w, Jean Dorst, Stephane Durand, Guy Jarry, Jacques Perrin, Francis Roux; ph, Olli Barbe, Michael Benjamin, Sylvie Carcedo-Dreujou, Laurent Charbonnier, Luc Drion, Laurent Fleutot, Philippe Garguil, Dominique Gentil, Bernard Lutic, Thierry Machado, Stephane Martin, Fabrice Moindrot, Ernst Sasse, Michael Terrasse, Thierry Thomas; ed, Marie-Josephe Yoyotte; m, Bruno Coulais; prod d, Regis Nicolino

First and foremost, this absolutely breathtaking documentary is an astonishing act of imaginative restoration, bringing the sheer wonder of everyday sights into sharp focus with shots of flying birds so intimate that the film is compelled to open with the statement they're not special effects. Second, the film represents a marshalling of personnel and resources, combined with extraordinary feats of skill, daring, and organization.

Between 1998 and 2001, director Jacques Perrin employed 450 people scattered throughout 40 countries to follow migrating birds from Europe to Greenland, the Far East to Siberia, the Gulf of Mexico to Canada, Africa to Europe and back again. Using a combination of gliders, helicopters, balloons, and cameras with long lenses, Perrin's collaborators got close enough to record the muscles working on a flying crane's back and high enough to see human and natural landmarks—the Eiffel Tower, the Great Wall of China, the Russian steppes, the World Trade Center—from a bird's eye perspective. They filmed birds both large and small, flying hundreds, even thousands of miles in orderly formations and swarming flocks. The film is a feast of amazing sights and sounds: water boiling with submerged pelicans, rockhopper penguins waddling the overland portion of their 620-mile migration, feeding gannets rocketing into the water like arrows, amorous sand grouse spreading their tail feathers, terns floating placidly on sheets of arctic ice.

Like the enthralling MICROCOSMOS, which examines the lives of insects, a certain inevitable anthropomorphization arises through the editing. But overall the film rejects CHARLIE, THE LONESOME COUGAR-style sentimentality in favor of letting the birds tell their own eternal yet infinitely varied story of eating, breeding, and dying.

WINGS OF DESIRE   *DVD*
(DER HIMMEL UBER BERLIN)
1987   130m   c/bw   Fantasy   ★★★★½
Road Movies/Argos/WDR   (France/West Germany)   PG-13

Bruno Ganz *(Damiel)*, Solveig Dommartin *(Marion)*, Otto Sander *(Cassiel)*, Curt Bois *(Homer)*, Peter Falk *(Himself)*

p, Wim Wenders, Anatole Dauman; d, Wim Wenders; w, Wim Wenders, Peter Handke; ph, Henri Alekan; ed, Peter Przygodda; m, Jurgen Knieper; prod d, Heidi Ludi; cos, Monika Jacobs

A rich, mystical near-masterpiece. With WINGS OF DESIRE, Wim Wenders creates a visual poem about the walls that exist in our world—those that separate fiction from reality, Heaven from Earth, history from the present, those who observe from those who feel. Bruno Ganz and Otto Sander play two angels who circulate in a black-and-white Berlin, where they "observe, collect, testify to, and preserve" the world around them, unseen by all but innocent children. The angels focus their attentions on three individuals—an octogenarian poet (Curt Bois); an American film and TV star (Peter Falk, playing himself); and a French trapeze artist (Solveig Dommartin). But, while helping these mortals, Ganz also struggles with his own desires to be able to feel, not just emotionally but physically as well. Although WINGS OF DESIRE draws on many sources, from Cocteau's filmic depiction of angels to the writings of Rainer Maria Rilke, the film's roots are perhaps closest to Walter Ruttmann's classic 1927 silent documentary, BERLIN: SYMPHONY OF A CITY. WINGS OF DESIRE, too, is a symphony on Berlin, though under Wenders's direction the city limits (which were then bisected by the Wall) become fantastic, extending far above to include those angels who keep a watchful eye on the world below. WINGS OF DESIRE enjoyed an overwhelmingly positive reception both at the box office—where it exceeded the success normally enjoyed by art-house offerings—and at the hands of the critics. The jury of the 1987 Cannes Film Festival named Wenders Best Director.

WINGS OF THE DOVE, THE   *DVD*
1997   102m   c   Romance/Drama/Historical   ★★★½
Renaissance Dove/Miramax   (U.S.)   R

Helena Bonham Carter *(Kate Croy)*, Linus Roache *(Merton Densher)*, Alison Elliott *(Millie Theale)*, Elizabeth McGovern *(Susan Stringham)*, Michael Gambon *(Lionel Croy)*, Charlotte Rampling *(Aunt Maude)*, Alex Jennings *(Lord Mark)*, Ben Miles *(Journalist 1)*, Philip Wright *(Journalist 2)*, Alexander John *(Butler)*

p, Stephen Evans, David Parfitt; d, Iain Softley; w, Hossein Amini (inspired by the novel by Henry James); ph, Eduardo Serra; ed, Tariq Anwar; m, Ed Shearmur; prod d, John Beard; art d, Andrew Sanders; fx, Effects Associates; cos, Sandy Powell

AAN Best Actress: Helena Bonham Carter; AAN Best Adapted Screenplay: Hossein Amini; AAN Best Cinematography: Eduardo Serra; AAN Best Costume Design: Sandy Powell

Henry James's novel of social climbing, friendship, forbidden love, and betrayal is given a lush treatment that neglects neither the elaborate period trappings nor the story's surprisingly contemporary emotional underpinnings.

Kate Croy (Helena Bonham Carter) is the daughter of a socially prominent mother who abandoned her station for the love of an opium-addicted wastrel (Michael Gambon). After her mother's death, Kate is taken under the wing of her steely aunt Maude (Charlotte Rampling) and faced with a wrenching choice: she can return to the life of money and privilege into which her mother was born, but only if she abandons her lover, journalist Merton Densher (Linus Roache). A meeting with fabulously wealthy but ailing American heiress Millie Theale (Alison Elliott) suggests an ingenious but cold-blooded way out, one that demands she betray her growing friendship with Millie and both manipulate and morally compromise the man she loves.

Undaunted by James's complicated prose, Softley and screenwriter Hossein Amini excavate a crisp and very modern story of heads and hearts at cross-purposes. They move the time period forward a few years (from 1902 to 1910) in order to heighten the sense of bold personalities—particularly Kate and Millie—chafing at the strictures of a dying code of social behavior that's not dying quite fast enough to liberate *them*. The sight of elaborately costumed Kate smoking and riding the subway—let alone making frenzied love to Merton against a Venetian wall—packs a surprising wallop, and Bonham Carter's performance as the calculating Kate should put those "Helena Bonham Corsets" jokes to rest for a while.

WINSLOW BOY, THE

1948 97m   bw   Drama   ★★★½
Anatole de Grunwald/London Films/Eagle-Lion
(U.K.)

Robert Donat (*Sir Robert Morton*), Margaret Leighton (*Catherine Winslow*), Cedric Hardwicke (*Arthur Winslow*), Basil Radford (*Esmond Curry*), Kathleen Harrison (*Violet*), Francis L. Sullivan (*Attorney General*), Marie Lohr (*Grace Winslow*), Jack Watling (*Dickie Winslow*), Frank Lawton (*John Watherstone*), Neil North (*Ronnie Winslow*)

p, Anatole de Grunwald; d, Anthony Asquith; w, Terence Rattigan, Anthony Asquith, Anatole de Grunwald (based on the play by Rattigan); ph, Freddie Young, Osmond Borradaile; ed, Gerald Turney-Smith; m, William Alwyn; prod d, Andre Andrejew; cos, William Chappell

In 1912 in London, Hardwicke is a retired bank official whose 14-year-old son, North, is expelled from naval college when he is accused of stealing a five-shilling postal order from another cadet. Hardwicke is convinced of his son's innocence but he is prevented by British law and unconcerned bureaucrats from fighting for his son's honor. Stymied at every turn, he hires the most famous attorney in Britain, Donat. Donat makes an impassioned speech in the House of Commons that results in a Petition of Right that allows Hardwicke to sue the Admiralty and make them prove in the courts that his son stole the postal order. The case is making headlines now and Hardwicke's family is facing the consequences: Hardwicke's daughter, suffragette Leighton, is left by her fiance; son Watling is forced to leave Oxford; and various legal fees are bringing Hardwicke almost to bankruptcy. In a courtroom trial, Donat finally gets North to admit the truth about what he was doing when the postal order was stolen: sneaking a cigarette in the locker room. The court finds in favor of North and Donat makes clear that he intends to see a great deal more of Leighton.

The story may seem rather dry, but the performances of Hardwicke, as the father prepared to face ruin to restore his son's honor, and of Donat, as the brilliant lawyer who finally breaks through the boy's own personal code of honor to exonerate him, keep the movie an engrossing experience. Based on the true Archer-Shee case of 1912.

WINTER KILLS   DVD

1979 97m   c   Comedy/Mystery/Political   ★★★★
Avco Embassy   (U.S.)   R

Jeff Bridges (*Nick Kegan*), John Huston (*Pa Kegan*), Anthony Perkins (*John Ceruti*), Sterling Hayden (*Z.K. Dawson*), Eli Wallach (*Joe Diamond*), Dorothy Malone (*Emma Kegan*), Tomas Milian (*Frank Mayo*), Belinda Bauer (*Yvette Malone*), Ralph Meeker (*Gameboy Baker*), Toshiro Mifune (*Keith*)

p, Fred Caruso; d, William Richert; w, William Richert (based on the novel by Richard Condon); ph, Vilmos Zsigmond; ed, David Bretherton; m, Maurice Jarre; prod d, Robert Boyle; art d, Norman Newberry

Bridges stars as Nick Kegan, the youngest son of a Kennedyesque family presided over by an eccentric tycoon (Huston). Not wanting to follow in the footsteps of his older brother, who became president and was then assassinated, Nick has drifted through life trying to avoid the influence of his father. But when a dying man claims to have been the "second rifle" at the president's assassination 19 years before, the revelation sets into motion a bizarre series of events which sees Nick dig deeper and deeper into the past to find out who is truly responsible for his brother's assassination. Director William Richert has turned Richard Condon's novel about the insanity of the American power structure into a wickedly funny black comedy spiced up by some deliciously off-the-wall performances. The fact that Richert got the project off the ground at all is a miracle. To be taken seriously by the studio, this first-time director went out and got written commitments from such acting notables as Huston, Bridges, Perkins, and Elizabeth Taylor. Filling out his cast with Mifune, Malone, Hayden, Wallach, and Richard Boone, he began production and acquired Alfred Hitchcock's favorite production designer, Robert Boyle (who also makes a humorous cameo as a hotel desk clerk) to execute the lush, detailed look of the film. About a week before the $6.5 million production was completed, the studio inexplicably pulled the financial plug. Richert finished the project on his own and struck complicated financial deals with Avco Embassy in an effort to complete and distribute it. Though it garnered little attention in theaters, it has become a cult favorite on video.

WISE BLOOD

1979 106m   c   Drama/Comedy   ★★★½
Ithaca/Anthea   (U.S./West Germany)   PG

Brad Dourif (*Hazel Motes*), Ned Beatty (*Hoover Shoates*), Harry Dean Stanton (*Asa Hawks*), Dan Shor (*Enoch Emery*), Amy Wright (*Sabbath Lily*), Mary Nell Santacroce (*Landlady*), John Huston (*Grandfather*)

p, Michael Fitzgerald, Kathy Fitzgerald; d, John Huston; w, Benedict Fitzgerald, Michael Fitzgerald (based on the novel by Flannery O'Connor); ph, Gerry Fisher; ed, Roberto Silvi; m, Alex North; cos, Sally Fitzgerald

At the age of 73, John Huston allowed his affinity for losers to attract him to the least marketable project of his career. The story of an obsessive, young, southern evangelist and several equally eccentric characters affected by him, WISE BLOOD, an unusual mixture of comedy, tragedy, satire, and horror, is an ungratiating but haunting work.

After his army discharge, young Hazel Motes (Brad Dourif) returns to his Southern hometown to find the family house boarded up. After taking a train to the city, he rents a room in a seedy boardinghouse, occupied by Asa Hawks (Harry Dean Stanton), an evangelist who claims to have blinded himself for God, and his daughter, Sabbath Lily (Amy Wright), a teenager who becomes infatuated with Hazel. Hazel becomes a street preacher for the "Church of Truth Without Christ," a secular religion of his own invention. One night, he is approached by Hoover Shoates (Ned Beatty), an opportunist who wants to become Hazel's promoter. The young man rebuffs him. Hazel discovers that Hawks is not blind, and winds up moving in with Sabbath Lily. When Shoates hires a preacher (William Hickey) to compete with Hazel, Hazel tracks down his rival and runs him over.

In the late 1970s, after being approached about adapting *Wise Blood* by the son of Flannery O'Connor s literary executor, Huston went down to Macon, GA with a crew of only 25 and shot the film in 48 days. Although the movie earned its director a standing ovation at the Cannes Film Festival and his best reviews in years, no major Hollywood studio would distribute it. Nonetheless, Huston declared himself "intensely proud of it, as proud of it as anything I've ever done."

Perfectly cast as Hazel, Dourif parlays all the eccentricity, frustration, righteousness, humorlessness, and rage of youth into one darkly comic package. Wright is splendid as trashy seductress Sabbath Lily. In addition to Huston's keenly focused direction, the film is blessed with bracing, wintry pictures by cinematographer Gerry Fisher, and a melancholy Alex North arrangement of the "Tennessee Waltz" that is so affecting and haunting that it goes a long way toward persuading the viewer that WISE BLOOD's appalling personae are indeed worth caring about and grieving for.

WITCHES, THE   *DVD*
1990   91m   c   Fantasy   ★★★½
Jim Henson/Lorimar   (U.K./U.S.)   PG

Anjelica Huston (*Mrs. Ernst/Grand High Witch*), Mai Zetterling (*Helga*), Jasen Fisher (*Luke*), Rowan Atkinson (*Mr. Stringer*), Bill Paterson (*Mr. Jenkins*), Brenda Blethyn (*Mrs. Jenkins*), Charlie Potter (*Bruno Jenkins*), Anna Lambton (*Woman in Black*), Jane Horrocks (*Miss Irvine*), Sukie Smith (*Marlene*)

p, Mark Shivas; d, Nicolas Roeg; w, Allan Scott (based on the book by Roald Dahl); ph, Harvey Harrison (Eastman Color); ed, Tony Lawson; m, Stanley Myers; prod d, Andrew Sanders; art d, Norman Dorme; fx, Jim Henson's Creature Shop, Steve Norrington, Nigel Booth, John Stephenson; cos, Marit Allen

Never known for the accessibility of his films, director Nicolas Roeg (DON'T LOOK NOW, THE MAN WHO FELL TO EARTH, INSIGNIFICANCE) here has created a wildly entertaining fairy tale.

The film begins in Germany, where a little boy named Luke (Jasen Fisher) listens to bedtime stories read by his grandmother Helga (Mai Zetterling). Helga warns Luke about witches and their insidious ways. Some time after the story-telling session, Luke's parents are killed in a car accident, leaving the boy and his grandmother alone. They travel to England and, when Helga is stricken with a mild attack of diabetes, they head for a seaside resort. Coincidentally, all the witches in England arrive at the resort, summoned there by Mrs. Ernst (Anjelica Huston) for seminars on how to capture British children. While exploring the hotel, Luke stumbles upon a meeting of the witches, who are posing as conventioneers. He is stunned to see Mrs. Ernst transform herself into the frightening Grand High Witch, who announces that she's developed a magic potion that turns children into mice. When the witches discover Luke, he is forced to drink some of the potion and becomes a mouse. It's now up to Luke the mouse, together with his grandmother, to thwart the witches' heinous plans.

Based on a story by Roald Dahl (source author of WILLY WONKA AND THE CHOCOLATE FACTORY, and screenwriter for CHITTY CHITTY BANG BANG), THE WITCHES weaves many classic childhood fears into its entertaining—and genuinely eerie—action. Roeg directs with his usual visual flair, notably excelling during the wondrous mouse point-of-view scenes. (These sequences feature mouse puppets designed by the late Jim Henson, who served as the film's executive producer, the last film in which he was involved before his death in 1990.) In addition to the lively visuals, THE WITCHES features sharp art direction and beautiful locations. The actors seem to be having a good time, particularly Huston, who gives a wonderfully over-the-top performance as the Grand High Witch. Zetterling, making her first appearance in a U.S. release since THE MAN WHO FINALLY DIED in 1967, is impressive, turning in a performance that is both rich and comic, and giving the film its emotional center.

WITCHES OF EASTWICK, THE   *DVD*
1987   118m   c   Horror/Comedy   ★★
Warner Bros.   (U.S.)   R

Jack Nicholson (*Daryl Van Horne*), Cher (*Alexandra Medford*), Susan Sarandon (*Jane Spofford*), Michelle Pfeiffer (*Sukie Ridgemont*), Veronica Cartwright (*Felicia Alden*), Richard Jenkins (*Clyde Alden*), Keith Jochim (*Walter Neff*), Carel Struycken (*Fidel*), Helen Lloyd Breed (*Mrs. Biddle*), Caroline Struzik (*Carol Medford*)

p, Neil Canton, Peter Guber, Jon Peters; d, George Miller; w, Michael Cristofer (based on the novel by John Updike); ph, Vilmos Zsigmond (Panavision, Technicolor); ed, Richard Francis-Bruce, Hubert C. de La Bouillerie; m, John Williams; prod d, Polly Platt; art d, Mark Mansbridge, Dave Howard Stein; fx, Mike Lanteri, Rob Bottin; cos, Aggie Guerard Rodgers; anim, Ellen Lichtwardt, John Armstrong, Chris Green

AAN Best Original Score: John Williams; *AAN Best Sound:* Wayne Artman, Tom Beckert, Tom Dahl, Art Rochester

A haphazard and slickly dumb adaptation of John Updike's best-selling novel, THE WITCHES OF EASTWICK is a star-studded special-effects extravaganza about the battle of the sexes. A trio of bored, sexually repressed New England women—Alex (Cher), Jane (Susan Sarandon), and Sukie (Michelle Pfeiffer), each of them left to live without their respective husbands—innocently conjures up a mysterious stranger who, they are convinced, will relieve their frustrations. This mystery man is Daryl Van Horne (Jack Nicholson), the filthy rich, wild-eyed Devil incarnate, who buys a local mansion. Within days, Alex, Jane, and Sukie have all been to bed with the Devil and discovered in themselves the almighty power of the female form. By the finale, the female trinity is pitted against the Devil, a mildly sympathetic misogynist who only wants to be loved *and* have someone to iron his shirts. While the underlying message of THE WITCHES OF EASTWICK may be of interest, the execution by George (MAD MAX) Miller is downright pathetic. The film plays like a TV sitcom, with an overdose of raunch added to the proceedings; when the Devil spews forth his profanities, one almost expects to hear a diabolical laugh track.

WITH A FRIEND LIKE HARRY   *DVD*
(HARRY, UN AMI QUI VOUS VEUT DU BIEN)
2000   117m   c   Thriller   ★★★½
Diaphana Films/M6 Films/Canal Plus/Centre   R
National de la Cinematographie/Sofinergie 5   (France)

Laurent Lucas (*Michel*), Sergi Lopez (*Harry*), Mathilde Seigner (*Claire*), Sophie Guillemin (*Plum*), Liliane Rovere (*Mother*), Dominique Rozan (*Father*), Michel Fau (*Eric*), Victoire de Koster (*Jeanne*), Laurie Caminita (*Sarah*), Lorena Caminita (*Iris*)

p, Michel Saint-Jean; d, Dominik Moll; w, Dominik Moll, Gilles Marchand; ph, Matthieu Poirot-Delpech; ed, Yannick Kergoat; m, David Sinclair Whitaker; prod d, Michel Barthelemy; cos, Virginie Montel

Patricia Highsmith—that misanthropic scribe of sociopathic male bonding—would have loved this.

After a sweltering afternoon's drive spent bickering with his wife, Claire (Mathilde Seigner), and three squabbling daughters, Michel (Laurent Lucas) pulls into a rest stop. There, in the men's room, he meets Harry (Sergi Lopez), a smiling stranger who claims to be an old high-school acquaintance. Harry invites himself and his curvaceous girlfriend, Plum (Sophie Guillemin), to Michel and Claire's ramshackle country house, where they install themselves in the guest room. Michel doesn't remember Harry at all, but Harry remembers all sorts of things about Michel, like every last, tortured word of that embarrassing poem Michel wrote for the high school literary journal. Preaching a disturbingly callous philosophy of hedonism and self-actualization, Harry is convinced that Michel could fulfill his dream of becoming a writer if it weren't for all those pesky distractions: those interfering parents, that suffocating wife, those clamoring kids. . . . What begins with a discomfiting disregard for social boundaries ends in something far more sinister, as the helpful Harry takes matters in hand.

The thematic similarities between this darkly humorous psychological thriller and Highsmith's famous *Strangers on a Train* should be noted: with each outrageous transgression, one gets the gnawing feeling that Harry, in true doppelganger fashion, might be actually fulfilling Michel's darkest desires. But director Dominik Moll takes it one cruel step further—Harry isn't just a psychopath, he's the spirit of artistic impulse in all its antisocial glory. Lopez has a smooth charm that works on both Michel and the audience, and Moll evinces a natural flair for creating atmosphere that's crucial to this kind of suspense thriller. Fans of the genre are in for a wickedly entertaining treat.

WITH A SONG IN MY HEART

1952   116m   c   Musical/Biography   ★★★½
Fox   (U.S.)

Susan Hayward *(Jane Froman)*, Rory Calhoun *(John Burns)*, David Wayne *(Don Ross)*, Thelma Ritter *(Clancy)*, Robert Wagner *(GI Paratrooper)*, Helen Westcott *(Jennifer March)*, Una Merkel *(Sister Marie)*, Richard Allan *(Dancer)*, Max Showalter *(Guild)*, Lyle Talbot *(Radio Director)*

p, Lamar Trotti; d, Walter Lang; w, Lamar Trotti; ph, Leon Shamroy (Technicolor); ed, J. Watson Webb; art d, Lyle Wheeler, Joseph C. Wright, Earle Hagen; fx, Fred Sersen, Ray Kellogg; chor, Billy Daniel; cos, Charles LeMaire

AAN Best Actress: Susan Hayward; *AAN Best Supporting Actress:* Thelma Ritter; *AA Best Score (Musical):* Alfred Newman; *AAN Best Costume Design (Color):* Charles LeMaire; *AAN Best Sound Recording:* Thomas T. Moulton

This fairly accurate film biography stars Susan Hayward as singer Jane Froman, whose story is told in flashback. In 1936 she gets her first break on a Cincinnati radio station, and from there it's on to personal appearances at Radio City Music Hall and across the country. Although she's somewhat ambivalent about the match, Jane eventually marries her mentor, Don Ross (David Wayne). Problems arise, however, as Don becomes jealous of his wife's success. When Jane goes off to entertain the troops during WWII, her plane crashes off the Portuguese coast. Rescued by pilot John Burn (Rory Calhoun), the badly injured singer undergoes a difficult recuperation in a Lisbon hospital, becoming fast friends with her nurse, Clancy (Thelma Ritter, whose character is fictional). John, meanwhile, falls in love with Jane, who stifles her own feelings because she is married. She returns to the U.S., undergoes a series of painful operations (with faithful Clancy by her side), and works with Don's help to get her career back on track. There are setbacks along the way, including a serious argument with Don, but eventually Jane makes a triumphant comeback and Don frees her to marry John.

Froman provides Hayward's singing voice, to glorious effect, in a host of standards from various writers (with uncredited background vocals provided by the Skylarks, Modernaires, Melody Men, King's Men, Starlighters, and Four Girlfriends). Five-time Oscar nominee Hayward, as always, gives her best, making WITH A SONG IN MY HEART a satisfying film on all levels.

WITHNAIL & I   *DVD*

1987   108m   c   Drama   ★★★½
HandMade   (U.K.)   R

Richard E. Grant *(Withnail)*, Paul McGann *(Marwood)*, Richard Griffiths *(Monty)*, Ralph Brown *(Danny)*, Michael Elphick *(Jake)*, Daragh O'Malley *(Irishman)*, Michael Wardle *(Issac Parkin)*, Una Brandon-Jones *(Mrs. Parkin)*, Noel Johnson *(General)*, Irene Sutcliffe *(Waitress)*

p, Paul M. Heller; d, Bruce Robinson; w, Bruce Robinson (based on his novel); ph, Peter Hannan; ed, Alan Strachan; m, David Dundas; prod d, Michael Pickwoad; art d, Henry Harris; cos, Andrea Galer

A hilarious black comedy and already something of a cult favorite, WITHNAIL & I opens in a cluttered, refuse-ridden flat in North London. This confused mess is home for two out-of-work actors: gaunt, sarcastic, vaguely aristocratic, and dissipated Withnail (Richard E. Grant); and handsome, bespectacled Marwood (Paul McGann), whose journal notations, heard in voice-over, serve as the film's narration. It is 1969, and the pair visit Withnail's wealthy eccentric uncle Monty (Richard Griffiths) in hopes of getting the use of his country cottage for a weekend away to "rejuvenate." Uncle is agreeable, and the two drive off to the cottage only to find it a rustic version of their own flat—ice cold, damp, totally without provisions. As usual, Withnail leaves the practical matters to Marwood to solve. WITHNAIL & I is a wry portrait of '60s low-life bohemia which gets plenty of comic mileage from the rapid-fire repartee, colorfully drawn characters, and occasionally Monty Pythonesque moments of director-writer Bruce Robinson's script.

WITNESS   *DVD*

1985   112m   c   Crime   ★★★★
Paramount   (U.S.)   R

Harrison Ford *(John Book)*, Kelly McGillis *(Rachel)*, Josef Sommer *(Schaeffer)*, Lukas Haas *(Samuel)*, Jan Rubes *(Eli Lapp)*, Alexander Godunov *(Daniel Hochleitner)*, Patti LuPone *(Elaine)*, Danny Glover *(McFee)*, Brent Jennings *(Carter)*, Angus MacInnes *(Fergie)*

p, Edward S. Feldman; d, Peter Weir; w, Earl W. Wallace, William Kelley (based on a story by Kelley, Wallace, Pamela Wallace); ph, John Seale (Technicolor); ed, Thom Noble; m, Maurice Jarre; prod d, Stan Jolley; fx, John R. Elliott; cos, Shari Feldman, Dallas Dornan

AAN Best Picture; AAN Best Actor: Harrison Ford; *AAN Best Director:* Peter Weir; *AA Best Original Screenplay:* Earl W. Wallace, William Kelley, Pamela Wallace; *AAN Best Cinematography:* John Seale; *AA Best Film Editing:* Thom Noble; *AAN Best Original Score:* Maurice Jarre; *AAN Best Art Direction-Set Decoration:* Stan Jolley, John Anderson

Sure-footed thriller, beautifully photographed, with Ford's best performance thus far. Australian director Peter Weir's first Hollywood film examines the tenuous survival of innocence in pockets of post-war America. The story begins as Rachel (Kelly McGillis), a young Amish widow, is traveling into the city with her young son, Samuel (Lukas Haas). While they're waiting for their train in the crowded Philadelphia station, Samuel wanders into the men's room where, undetected, he witnesses a murder. Questioned by tough, cynical cop John Book (Harrison Ford), the boy identifies a narcotics officer (Danny Glover) as the killer. Suspecting a conspiracy and fearing for the safety of his young witness, Book tries to get Samuel and Rachel back to the safe obscurity of Lancaster County, home to a peaceful, idyllic community of Amish farmers. But trouble follows, even as Rachel and Book become attracted to each other.

The cast is uniformly excellent, while John Seale's cinematography and Maurice Jarre's score are memorably atmospheric.

WITNESS FOR THE PROSECUTION
1957 114m bw Mystery   DVD
Theme (U.S.)   ★★★★½

Tyrone Power (Leonard Stephen Vole), Marlene Dietrich (Christine Helm/Vole), Charles Laughton (Sir Wilfrid Robarts), Elsa Lanchester (Miss Plimsoll), John Williams (Brogan Moore), Henry Daniell (Mayhew), Ian Wolfe (Carter), Una O'Connor (Janet MacKenzie), Torin Thatcher (Mr. Meyers), Francis Compton (Judge)

p, Arthur Hornblow Jr.; d, Billy Wilder; w, Billy Wilder, Harry Kurnitz, Larry Marcus (based on the novel and the play by Agatha Christie); ph, Russell Harlan; ed, Daniel Mandell; m, Matty Malneck; art d, Alexander Trauner; cos, Edith Head, Joe King

AAN Best Picture; AAN Best Actor: Charles Laughton; AAN Best Supporting Actress: Elsa Lanchester; AAN Best Director: Billy Wilder; AAN Best Film Editing: Daniel Mandell; AAN Best Sound: Gordon Sawyer

Dietrich steals it. WITNESS FOR THE PROSECUTION is a witty, terse adaptation of the Agatha Christie hit play brought to the screen with ingenuity and vitality by Billy Wilder. Sir Wilfrid Robarts (Laughton) is a sickly barrister who is told by his doctors and forced by his pesty nurse Miss Plimsoll (Lanchester, Laughton's real-life wife), to retire from criminal cases. When his solicitor Mayhew (Daniell) arrives at his home with murder suspect Leonard Vole (Power), Robarts cannot resist. Hearing Vole's story, Robarts becomes convinced of the man's innocence, but because his only alibi is his wife Christine (Dietrich), prospects for an acquittal look dim. Before their meeting ends, word is received that Vole has inherited a fortune from the deceased's estate. Because of the apparent clarity of Vole's motive, Scotland Yard places him under arrest. Robarts, however, is not completely convinced and continues examining the clues, uncovering more than even he imagined.

Improving on Christie's play, Wilder has rid WITNESS FOR THE PROSECUTION of much of the usual static courtroom scenes and filled the film with an active, visual excitement. Whether it be the fluidity of the camera, the use of an occasional flashback, or the diversion of Robarts's constant medical attention, Wilder succeeds in finding a way to relieve the boredom that typically accompanies the courtroom. Wilder even introduces the Miss Plimsoll character into Christie's scenario to add some life and a comic angle. At the film's halfway point Wilder flashes back to wartime Germany for the standard Dietrich-as-cabaret-singer scene, giving her a chance to show off one of her attractive legs, play the accordion, and deliver "I Never Go There Anymore" (Ralph Arthur Roberts, Jack Brooks). The part, one of her finest, was pure Dietrich, casting her as a woman who throws away everything—her homeland, her reputation, and her life—for the man she loves.

WIZARD OF OZ, THE
1939 101m c/bw Fantasy/Musical   DVD
MGM (U.S.)   ★★★★★

Judy Garland (Dorothy), Ray Bolger (Hunk/The Scarecrow), Bert Lahr (Zeke/The Cowardly Lion), Jack Haley (Hickory/The Tin Woodsman), Billie Burke (Glinda), Margaret Hamilton (Miss Gulch/The Wicked Witch), Charley Grapewin (Uncle Henry), Clara Blandick (Auntie Em), Pat Walsh (Nikko), Frank Morgan (Prof. Marvel/The Wizard/Guard/Coachman)

p, Mervyn LeRoy; d, Victor Fleming, King Vidor (uncredited); w, Noel Langley, Florence Ryerson, Edgar Allan Woolf (based on the novel by L. Frank Baum); ph, Harold Rosson (Technicolor); ed, Blanche Sewell; m, Herbert Stothart; art d, Cedric Gibbons; fx, A. Arnold Gillespie; chor, Bobby Connolly; cos, Adrian

AAN Best Picture; AA Best Original Score: Herbert Stothart; AA Best Song: "Over the Rainbow"; Harold Arlen (Music), E.Y. Harburg (Lyrics); AAN Best Color Cinematography: Harold Rosson; AAN Best Interior Decoration: Cedric Gibbons, William A. Horning; AAN Best Special Effects: A. Arnold Gillespie (Photograhic), Douglas Shearer (Sound)

There's no place like home, and there will never be another movie like THE WIZARD OF OZ. Forget that it's nearly 70 years old, that here and there it creaks a tiny bit: it stirs in all of us the feeling of wanting to belong, of having security, but wanting enchantment at the same time. OZ gives us enchantment unparalleled for a hundred different reasons, foremost among which is the ageless appeal of young Judy Garland, perhaps the most beloved of all film actresses. Watching her now, we're aware of all the sadness Garland's life would encompasses (the consummate showbiz pro, she was quick to milk her suffering), but Dorothy captures her poised on the brink of legend, before the ravages of unhappiness set in. And chances are, for most of us, we first saw her in OZ before life took any serious tolls upon us, before broken hearts, or deaths, or money troubles or career disappointments. Sometimes you watch Garland longingly sing "Over the Rainbow" and it sweeps you away to somewhere you can't even explain. THE WIZARD OF OZ is a dazzling fantasy musical, so beautifully directed and acted that it deserves its classic status.

Dorothy (Garland) is a schoolgirl living in Kansas with family and her little dog, Toto. One afternoon, a twister sucks up Dorothy's house and she and Toto are dropped beyond the rainbow into Munchkinland. With a pair of magical red slippers and some advice from Glinda the Good Witch (Billie Burke), Dorothy, Toto and three new friends—the Scarecrow (Ray Bolger), Tin Man (Jack Haley), and Cowardly Lion (Bert Lahr)—follow the yellow brick road to the Emerald City, where they must ask the all-powerful Wizard of Oz (Frank Morgan) to get Dorothy and Toto back home. The Wicked Witch (Margaret Hamilton), however, is determined to get her hands on the slippers, and sends out her flying monkeys to capture the group—as if you needed to know any of this.

Curiously, Garland, forever to be identified with the wide-eyed Dorothy, was not the first choice for the part; both Shirley Temple and Deanna Durbin were considered for the role. Had Jean Harlow not died, ending the loan-out deal to exchange her for IN OLD CHICAGO with Temple for OZ, we'd be watching Temple's forthright moppet, instead of Garland's tender waif. The mind boggles. We could regale you for hours on end with behind the scenes trivia on OZ. Books have been written on nothing but, and they're not hard to find. But we'll toss you a few: Frank Morgan spent half his time on set drunk. Clara Blandick (Auntie Em) was just as unhappy as she appears; she ended up a recluse who eventually took her own life. Harlow's third and last husband, Harold Rosson, did OZ's cinematography and King Vidor did some uncredited directorial work. L.B. Mayer's nickname for Garland was his "little humpback." The original Wizard was to have been W.C. Fields, the original Tin Man Buddy Ebsen (who fell ill from all the makeup preparation) and the original Wicked Witch was to have been played as an evil siren by Gale Sondergaard. Bolger, Haley, Lahr, and Morgan were not the kindly uncles you might think. All were grizzled showbiz vets not about to give Garland an inch of scene-stealing capacity onscreen; when she takes a scene, it's not because anyone let her. See if you can hear the female Munchkin who runs forward to Garland and shouts "Judy" instead of "Dorothy" after Hamilton's first exit. And watch for inconsistencies in Garland's hairstyles during the time she is beautified in OZ.

WOLF MAN, THE   DVD
1941 71m   bw   Horror   ★★★★
Universal   (U.S.)

Claude Rains (Sir John Talbot), Lon Chaney Jr. (Larry Talbot), Evelyn Ankers (Gwen Conliffe), Ralph Bellamy (Capt. Paul Montford), Warren William (Dr. Lloyd), Patric Knowles (Frank Andrews), Maria Ouspenskaya (Maleva), Bela Lugosi (Bela), Fay Helm (Jenny Williams), Leyland Hodgson (Kendall)

p, George Waggner; d, George Waggner; w, Curt Siodmak; ph, Joseph Valentine; ed, Ted J. Kent; art d, Jack Otterson

A feast of horror, for animals of all kinds. Bearing no resemblance to Universal's 1935 film THE WEREWOLF OF LONDON, THE WOLF MAN was given a whole new look and treatment by the studio. Lon Chaney Jr., stars as Larry Talbot, a young British heir who returns to the mansion of his father (Claude Rains) after getting a college education in America. Learning about the legend of the werewolf from antique store employee Gwen (Evelyn Ankers), gypsy fortune teller Maleva (Maria Ouspenskaya), and Maleva's son, Bela (Bela Lugosi), Larry laughs it off as superstition. When the young man hears a bone-chilling wolf's howl and a blood-curdling scream emanating from the foggy moors, however, he rushes to the source of the hideous noises and is attacked and bitten by a vicious, hairy beast. Later, Maleva tells Larry that he will transform into a savage, murderous wolf when the moon is full and that he can only be killed by silver—be it a silver bullet, knife, or cane. Larry tries to deny her superstitious forecast, but when the next full moon arises, his nose becomes a wet snout, his hands and feet turn to paws, and his body is covered with thick fur. An animal trapped in a bedroom, the wolf man crashes through the window and runs off into the night in search of his prey.

Fearing comparison with his famous father, Lon Jr. avoided appearing in horror films, but as he gained confidence in his abilities he agreed to try the genre and created the character with whom he would always be identified—the wolf man. Through the genius of Universal makeup artist Jack Pierce, Chaney underwent a complete transformation nearly as complete as his character's—gaining a rubber snout, fangs, claws, and lots of yak hair. Screenwriter Curt Siodmak patched together the legend of the werewolf by combining elements from lycanthropic folklore, witchcraft, and Bram Stoker's *Dracula*, creating a new monster for the screen. All elements combined to make a thrilling, scary, and ultimately tragic horror classic. Chaney essayed the role of the werewolf five more times, in FRANKENSTEIN MEETS THE WOLFMAN, HOUSE OF FRANKENSTEIN, HOUSE OF DRACULA, and ABBOTT AND COSTELLO MEET FRANKENSTEIN, as well as a guest appearance on the television show "Route 66."

WOLFEN   DVD
1981 115m   c   Horror   ★★★½
Orion   (U.S.)   R

Albert Finney (Dewey Wilson), Diane Venora (Rebecca Neff), Edward James Olmos (Eddie Holt), Gregory Hines (Whittington), Tom Noonan (Ferguson), Dick O'Neill (Warren), Dehl Berti (Old Indian), Peter Michael Goetz (Ross), Sam Gray (Mayor), Ralph Bell (Commissioner)

p, Rupert Hitzig; d, Michael Wadleigh; w, David Eyre, Michael Wadleigh (based on the novel by Whitley Strieber); ph, Gerry Fisher (Panavision, Technicolor); ed, Chris Lebenzon, Dennis Dolan, Martin Bram, Marshall M. Borden; m, James Horner; prod d, Paul Sylbert; art d, David Chapman; fx, Carl Fullerton, Robert Blalack, Betz Bromberg; cos, John Boxer

This straightforward, intelligent film puts a new spin on the werewolf legend, presenting the creatures as a superior species living in the slums of New York City. Police detective Dewey Wilson (Albert Finney) is assigned to investigate the savage murder of a rich industrialist. When the city coroner (Gregory Hines, in his film debut) suggests that the dead man was mutilated by a wild animal, Wilson and criminal psychologist Rebecca Neff (Diane Venora) connect the killing with several murders that have occurred in which the bodies of winos, drug addicts, and bums have been found with their throats ripped out. Further investigation by Wilson and Neff leads to a group of Native American construction workers and to a strange tale of the "Wolfen" that once roamed the land that is now New York City. Directed by Michael Wadleigh, whose only other feature is the 1970 rock documentary WOODSTOCK, WOLFEN is an intelligent, insightful, and visually creative twist on the werewolf legend. Although occasionally preachy, it is a fascinating horror tale that is as engrossing as it is horrifying. The visual effects are sensational, introducing to the screen a previously unseen "Wolfen vision" that, through a variety of optical printing techniques, conveys the wolves' heightened awareness of heat, smell, movement, and texture. The gore effects by Carl Fullerton are effective, if somewhat gratuitous.

WOMAN IN THE DUNES   DVD
(SUNA NO ONNA)
1964 123m   bw   Drama/Adventure   ★★★★
Teshigahara   (Japan)

Eiji Okada (Jumpei Niki—the Man), Kyoko Kishida (The Woman), Koji Mitsui, Hiroko Ito, Sen Yano, Ginzo Sekigushi, Kiyohiko Ichihara, Tamotsu Tamura, Hiroyuki Nishimoto (Villagers)

p, Kiichi Ichikawa, Tadashi Ohno; d, Hiroshi Teshigahara; w, Kobo Abe (based on his novel Suna no Onna); ph, Hiroshi Segawa; ed, Fusako Shyzui; m, Toru Takemitsu; art d, Toutetsu Hirakawa, Masao Yamazaki

AAN Best Foreign Language Film; AAN Best Director: Hiroshi Teshigahara

A profoundly moving parable told with beautiful simplicity, WOMAN IN THE DUNES begins as Niki Jumpei (Eiji Okada), a reserved entomologist, collects specimens along a Japanese beach. He is met by some villagers, who offer him both a place to sleep and a woman, and is led to a shack located at the bottom of a sand pit, where he climbs down a rope ladder to the woman, Kyoko (Kyoko Kishida). The next morning, he notices that the ladder has been removed. A panicky urge to climb out of the pit is followed by a futile attempt to scale the sand walls, which cascade beneath his feet. Helpless, he watches as Kyoko endlessly shovels the sand into buckets, which are then hoisted by the villagers above. In return, food and water are sent down—no shoveling, no food. Niki soon realizes the necessity of the woman's work. He becomes accustomed to his new lifestyle and takes the woman as his lover. She becomes pregnant, and he must wrestle with his urge to escape and his growing devotion to Kyoko and his new life.

Beautifully photographed and confined almost exclusively to a single set, WOMAN IN THE DUNES is a poetic affirmation of life. As frustrating and claustrophobic as the man's situation may first appear, the film becomes increasingly seductive as it lulls the audience into the woman's sandpit existence. Based on a novel by Kobo Abe.

WOMAN IN THE WINDOW, THE
1945 99m   bw   Thriller   ★★★★
Christie/International Pictures   (U.S.)

Edward G. Robinson (Prof. Richard Wanley), Joan Bennett (Alice Reed), Raymond Massey (Frank Lalor), Edmund Breon (Dr. Michael Barkstone), Dan Duryea (Heidt/Doorman),

Thomas Jackson (Inspector Jackson), Arthur Loft (Claude Mazard/Frank Howard), Dorothy Peterson (Mrs. Wanley), Frank Dawson (Collins, the Steward), Carol Cameron (Elsie Wanley)

p, Nunnally Johnson; d, Fritz Lang; w, Nunnally Johnson (based on the novel Once Off Guard by J.H. Wallis); ph, Milton Krasner; ed, Marjorie Johnson, Gene Fowler Jr.; m, Arthur Lange; art d, Duncan Cramer; fx, Vernon L. Walker; cos, Muriel King

AAN Best Score (Drama or Comedy): Hugo Friedhofer, Arthur Lange

A gripping psychological thriller which stars Robinson as a fortyish, intellectual college professor who, with his friends, discusses the dangers of becoming too adventurous at their age. Robinson has a wife and children (who are away on vacation) and sees no reason to wander from his staid, secure path. However, while admiring a portrait of a beautiful model in a gallery window, he notices the model, Bennett, standing beside him. Bennett asks if Robinson would like to come up to her apartment under honest pretenses: "I'm not married. I have no designs on you," she assures him. Once in her apartment, this fantasy girl of Robinson's brings about his downfall, though unintentionally. Her boyfriend, wealthy financier Loft, arrives unexpectedly and, thinking that the two are having an affair, begins to slap his mistress around. He then lunges at Robinson, who grabs a nearby scissors and, in self-defense, stabs his attacker in the back. Frightened both of the police and of the disgrace he will cause his family, Robinson plots, with Bennett, to dispose of the body. Battling countless obstacles and nearly getting caught a number of times, they take the corpse, sitting up in the back seat of a car with open, glazed eyes, to a secluded woody area. They manage to carry out their plan without getting caught. Robinson, however, is still subject to mental torture, especially by his friend, Massey, a district attorney who continually talks about the case, unaware that Robinson is the man he's after. Through Massey, Robinson learns all the most intricate details of the investigation and is able to follow the progress of the police. He also learns his mistakes, which mount by the day. Making matters worse is a blackmail scheme engineered by Loft's bodyguard, Duryea, who has discovered Robinson's guilt.

With its terse pacing and elegant camerawork, THE WOMAN IN THE WINDOW was a great box-office success and one of the most praised films noir of its time. Robinson, in a role different from his standard gangster part, shines and holds the film's credibility together by turning in a convincing portrayal of a good man who is caught off guard just once (to paraphrase the title of the novel, Once Off Guard, on which the film is based). Bennett, in her second Lang film after 1941's MAN HUNT, is dazzlingly alluring as the fantasy girl who comes to life for Robinson. The collaboration between Bennett and Lang was so amiable that they would work together two more times, in SCARLET STREET with Robinson again as costar, and in SECRET BEYOND THE DOOR, both produced by her and husband Walter Wanger's own Diana Productions. Although many people feel cheated by the film's ending, Lang always felt (in later interviews) that his decision was justified. Either way, it's still a fine film.

WOMAN IS A WOMAN, A 🖵DVD
(UNE FEMME EST UNE FEMME)
1960 80m c Drama ★★★★
Rome/Paris Pathe (France/Italy)

Anna Karina (Angela), Jean-Claude Brialy (Emile Recamier), Jean-Paul Belmondo (Alfred Lubitsch), Nicole Paquin (Suzanne), Marie Dubois (1st Prostitute), Marion Sarraut (2nd Prostitute), Jeanne Moreau (Woman in Bar), Catherine Demongeot

p, Carlo Ponti, Georges de Beauregard; d, Jean-Luc Godard; w, Jean-Luc Godard (based on an idea by Genevieve Cluny); ph, Raoul Coutard (FranScope, Eastmancolor); ed, Agnes Guillemot, Lila Herman; m, Michel Legrand; art d, Bernard Evein; cos, Bernard Evein

Godard's third feature film and his first in color, A WOMAN IS A WOMAN is one of the most enjoyable of all the master's works. Taking an extremely lighthearted approach, it bursts with a passion for the medium of film expressed in every shot. The plot is very simple and could almost be taken for homage to Hollywood musical comedy, but homage seems much too tacky a term to express the fascination Godard had and the playful manner in which he approached this film. Karina (Godard's wife at the time) plays a stripper living with her boyfriend (Brialy), who refuses to marry her in spite of her expressed desire to have a child. Using an old feminine ploy, she starts to turn her attentions toward another man (Belmondo), easily making him fall in love with her. Sure enough, it works, with the boyfriend breaking down when faced with the prospect of losing the girl he loves.

Every moment of this picture is filled with charm, from Brialy riding a bicycle around their apartment in a strange mating dance to the buffoonish manner in which Belmondo tries to declare his love for Karina. The loose style almost seems to suggest that Godard just placed the camera down and then told his three stars to play; they look like children who have not yet outgrown the play lot and are unwilling to accept responsibility. The way Karina announces that she wants to have a baby is totally whimsical, a thing to do because that is what couples do when they are in love. Next to Godard's non-stylish stylishness, the most outstanding feature is the mere presence of Karina; her subtle glance and loftiness coincide with little mistakes in technical performance that most directors would not tolerate, but which actually serve to make her that much more human and irresistible. In fact, the picture appears almost to be a private photograph album showcasing the charming Karina in many moods. This is the first of Godard's films to be shot largely in a studio under tightly controlled conditions. The director insisted on using sets with ceilings in the interest of naturalism. This was also Godard's first experience with direct synchronous sound; his previous films had been dubbed. Elements of some of the director's earlier short subjects—most notably the 10-minute UNE FEMME COQUETTE—can be seen in the plot and the characterizations. Raoul Coutard's superlative wide-screen camera work will be diminished on the TV screen.

WOMAN OF THE YEAR 🖵DVD
1942 112m bw Comedy/Drama ★★★★
MGM (U.S.)

Spencer Tracy (Sam Craig), Katharine Hepburn (Tess Harding), Fay Bainter (Ellen Whitcomb), Reginald Owen (Clayton), Minor Watson (William Harding), William Bendix (Pinkie Peters), Gladys Blake (Flo Peters), Dan Tobin (Gerald), Roscoe Karns (Phil Whittaker), William Tannen (Ellis)

p, Joseph L. Mankiewicz; d, George Stevens; w, Ring Lardner Jr., Michael Kanin; ph, Joseph Ruttenberg; ed, Frank Sullivan; m, Franz Waxman; art d, Cedric Gibbons, Randall Duell; cos, Adrian

AAN Best Actress: Katharine Hepburn; AA Best Original Screenplay: Michael Kanin, Ring Lardner Jr.

The first onscreen pairing of Tracy and Hepburn, a team that would last 25 years until Tracy's death in 1967. He plays a sportswriter for a New York newpaper who becomes angry after hearing Hepburn on a radio broadcast boldly state that baseball should be eliminated until WWII comes to an end. Hepburn, the daughter of diplomat Watson and an international affairs writer, works on the same paper as Tracy, and her remarks begin a battle waged in their respective columns.

Once they meet in person, they are attracted to each other, much to the surprise of their friends and colleagues. Eventually Tracy and Hepburn wed, but their marriage rests on shaky ground. Hepburn's attempts at homemaking are an outright disaster, as she feels her job must come before anything else. Tracy is angered by her lack of commitment to the marriage and ends up getting too drunk to write his column. Hepburn, whose knowledge of sports isn't much better than her abilities as a housewife, pens Tracy's column and the results are catastrophic. Hepburn is voted "Woman of the Year," ironically hearing the news while she is contemplating whether to remain with Tracy. When her father remarries, Hepburn listens closely as marriage vows are read. The words move her and she decides to go back to Tracy with renewed zeal for married life.

WOMAN OF THE YEAR is a marvelous comedy-drama, brimming with wit, style, and sophistication. Hepburn is strong and assured, a woman fueled by intense pride along with a good-sized ego. (Maybe that's why the final breakfast scene, amusing as it is, leaves a bad taste in the mouth, as it milks rather obvious laughs from Hepburn's lack of traditonally "feminine" skills.) Tracy is her male opposite, just as opinionated and just as stubborn. Their chemistry is engaging, a solid teaming that enhances the accomplished script.

WOMAN UNDER THE INFLUENCE, A 🟥 DVD
1974 155m   c   Drama   ★★★★
Faces International Films   (U.S.)   R

Peter Falk (*Nick Longhetti*), Gena Rowlands (*Mabel Longhetti*), Matthew Cassel (*Tony Longhetti*), Matthew Laborteaux (*Angelo Longhetti*), Christina Grisanti (*Maria Longhetti*), Katherine Cassavetes (*Mama Longhetti*), Lady Rowlands (*Martha Mortensen*), Fred Draper (*George Mortensen*), O.G. Dunn (*Garson Cross*), Mario Gallo (*Harold Jensen*)

p, Sam Shaw; d, John Cassavetes; w, John Cassavetes; ph, Caleb Deschanel (MGM Color); ed, Tom Cornwell, David Armstrong, Elizabeth Bergeron, Sheila Viseltear; m, Bo Harwood; art d, Phedon Papamichael; cos, Carole Smith

AAN Best Actress: Gena Rowlands; *AAN Best Director:* John Cassavetes

Tough-minded, moving study of a working-class housewife's mental breakdown, enhanced by superb performances from Rowlands, in the title role, and Falk as her husband. Laborteaux, Grisanti, and Cassel play the children. A kind of tragic duet between the two leads, A WOMAN remains an insightful essay on sexual politics. As Rowlands delicately crosses the line of sanity, it becomes apparent that imposed social roles are the cause.

Both Rowlands (who lost to Ellen Burstyn for ALICE DOESN'T LIVE HERE ANYMORE) and Cassavetes (for direction) were nominated for Oscars for this unexpected minor hit, which grossed well over $6 million the first time around. It began as a theatrical piece for Rowlands, but she balked at having to play such a demanding role nightly and the suggestion was made to transform it into a movie. Cassavetes took out a mortgage on his home, contacted friends and relatives for financing, and then began a two-year shooting schedule dictated by his own personal finances. Cassavetes's work is often mistaken for improvisational, or even as *cinema verite*. In fact, his films are thoughtful celebrations of the art of acting and, in most cases, are shot from precise scripts (even if those scripts are themselves based on extensive improvisational exercises).

WOMEN, THE 🟥 DVD
1939 132m   c/bw   Comedy   ★★★★½
MGM   (U.S.)

Norma Shearer (*Mary Haines*), Joan Crawford (*Chrystal Allen*), Rosalind Russell (*Sylvia Fowler*), Mary Boland (*Countess DeLave*), Paulette Goddard (*Miriam Aarons*), Joan Fontaine (*Peggy Day*), Lucile Watson (*Mrs. Moorehead*), Phyllis Povah (*Edith Potter*), Florence Nash (*Nancy Blake*), Virginia Weidler (*Little Mary*)

p, Hunt Stromberg; d, George Cukor; w, Anita Loos, Jane Murfin (based on the play by Clare Boothe Luce); ph, Oliver T. Marsh, Joseph Ruttenberg (Part Technicolor); ed, Robert J. Kern; m, Edward Ward, David Snell; art d, Cedric Gibbons, Wade B. Rubottom; cos, Adrian

Every feminist's nightmare? In some ways, yes; in others no. Adapted from the hit Broadway play by Clare Boothe (who was later Mrs. Luce, by dint of marriage to the founder of *Time* magazine), THE WOMEN does portray its subjects as inordinately fond of catty gossip, but also has some interesting points to make about female bonding and societal pressures.

Norma Shearer plays Mary Haines, a wealthy and loving woman married to an adoring husband and the mother of sweet Little Mary (Weidler, admirably pulling off a difficult part). Contented Mary, though, has no idea that her mate is having an affair with predatory perfume seller Crystal Allen (Joan Crawford). Mary's girlfriends know, and the bitchiest of the lot, Sylvia Fowler (Rosalind Russell), arranges for Mary to get the news herself from the gossipy manicurist (Dennie Moore) who first started circulating the story. Mary's mother, Mrs. Morehead (Lucile Watson), though, advises her to say nothing and simply let the affair play itself out. Unfortunately, Mary encounters Crystal at a fancy clothing salon and, in a blistering scene, the two women exchange words. Mary leaves New York to race to Reno for a six-week divorce and meets the Countess de Lave (Mary Boland), an aging former showgirl who has been married several times. She also encounters younger chorine Miriam Aarons (Paulette Goddard), who is having an affair with Sylvia's husband. Mary and the others check in to a ranch owned by Lucy (Marjorie Main, along with the marvelous Phyllis Povah, the only holdover from the original Broadway cast), a funny and voluble woman. Sylvia arrives, and when she realizes that it was Miriam who stole her husband, a battle ensues between the two women. Mary's surprise, though, is soon tempered as she learns that her former mate, rather than calling her to stop the divorce at the 11th hour, has married Crystal.

Later, when she gets home to New York, Mary discovers that her ex is unhappy in his new marriage, and that Crystal has taken to both spending money with a passion and having an affair with a radio singing cowboy married to the former Countess. Finally showing her mother that, she, too, has had her nails done in "Jungle Red," Mary embraces the predatory principles of her friends and artfully tries to win her husband back.

Filled with witty repartee and vicious gossip, THE WOMEN portrays a world where women seem to do nothing but obsess over men. Playwright Clare Boothe always defended her work, claiming that only empty-headed, spoilt rich women were being satirized here. Close examination of the film script, though, reveals considerable insight into female bonding. The several mother-daughter relationships are interestingly portrayed, and even the fights over men, as dramatized in this vast improvement on Boothe's original, are not without their lessons about the roles imposed on women by society.

All the performances are joys. Shearer has never been more restrained, and but for two moments (dropping to her knees to cry at her mother's feet, and the final reconciliation), her performance never falters. Her crying jag in Reno is one of the most convincing of its kind; even technically better actresses like Davis and Hepburn couldn't always pull tears off this well. Another great moment to look for is the way Shearer hits the flowers her errant husband sends her. Crawford, meanwhile, brilliantly revitalized her career with one of her finest acting achievements, a funny, spot-on portrait of the scheming, sexy Crystal. Hard as nails throughout, she uses her velvet voice to great effect, and her parting salvo at the end is a killer ("There's a word for you ladies, but it is seldom used in high society, outside of a kennel"). Russell (in a showcase part that made her a top star) and Goddard (rarely better) are equally good, though perhaps the funniest performance is contributed by the marvelous Boland. Cukor's direction is rich and confident, and the whole production fairly shimmers.

WOMEN IN LOVE

1969 130m c Drama ★★★½
Brandywine (U.K.) R

Alan Bates (*Rupert Birkin*), Oliver Reed (*Gerald Crich*), Glenda Jackson (*Gudrun Brangwen*), Jennie Linden (*Ursula Brangwen*), Eleanor Bron (*Hermione Roddice*), Alan Webb (*Thomas Crich*), Vladek Sheybal (*Loerke*), Catherine Willmer (*Mrs. Crich*), Sarah Nicholls (*Winifred Crich*), Sharon Gurney (*Laura Crich*)

p, Larry Kramer; d, Ken Russell; w, Larry Kramer (based on the novel by D.H. Lawrence); ph, Billy Williams (DeLuxe Color); ed, Michael Bradsell; m, Georges Delerue, Peter Ilich Tchaikovsky; art d, Ken Jones; chor, Terry Gilbert; cos, Shirley Russell

AA Best Actress: Glenda Jackson; *AAN Best Director:* Ken Russell; *AAN Best Adapted Screenplay:* Larry Kramer; *AAN Best Cinematography:* Billy Williams

Fine adaptation of D.H. Lawrence's classic novel with some interesting visual sequences typical of director Russell's style.

It is 1920s England. Jackson is a free-thinking artist who, along with her schoolteacher sister, Linden, watches from a graveyard as Gurney and Christopher Gable are married. Later, at an outdoor luncheon given for the couple, the two women meet Reed and Bates. Bates, a school inspector, constantly ruminates on the topic of love and begins a fledgling relationship with Linden. At a picnic at the plush home of Gurney's wealthy family, the newlyweds are lost beneath the dark waters of the estate's lake. When the water is drained from the lake, the two drowned bodies are discovered entwined together in the muddy lake bed. That night Bates and Reed, in a discussion on friendship, strip before a fireplace and engage in a nude wrestling match. After Bates and Linden marry, they go with Reed and Jackson for a honeymoon in Switzerland. Jackson meets Sheybal, a sculptor like herself, and engages in an affair with the bisexual man, when her sister and brother-in-law leave Switzerland. Reed, enraged at Sheybal's intrusion, attacks the man and tries to choke Jackson. Then Reed flees into the snow and wanders until he dies. Bates, stunned by the death, still questions the mystery of relations between men and women.

There are moments of great beauty here, such as the view of Bates and Linden running naked into each other's arms in a wheatfield. The camera is turned horizontally, and the bodies seem to defy gravity, moving up and down within the frame through the golden vegetation. In another, much-heralded piece of editing, Russell cuts from the intertwined bodies of Bates and Linden after a lovemaking session to the cold, stiff corpses of Gurney and Gable on the bottom of the emptied lake. Russell did some of his own camerawork (although Williams received credit as cinematographer) and showed an excellent eye for shot composition and editing rhythms. His ability as a storyteller is less in evidence, however. Despite the passion of the topic and the beauty of the images, the narrative tends toward the stat-

ic, particularly in the later stages. Russell incorporated many dance images into WOMEN IN LOVE, expanding on what he considered to be a central theme of the novel. He later stated that he "should have turned the whole thing into a musical; it wasn't far off in some ways."

WOMEN ON THE VERGE OF A NERVOUS BREAKDOWN

DVD
1988 98m c Drama ★★★★
Lauren Films/El Deseo (Spain)

Carmen Maura (*Pepa*), Antonio Banderas (*Carlos*), Fernando Guillen (*Ivan*), Julieta Serrano (*Lucia*), Maria Barranco (*Candela*), Rossy de Palma (*Marisa*), Kiti Manver (*Paulina*), Chus Lampreave, Yayo Calvo, Loles Leon

d, Pedro Almodovar; w, Pedro Almodovar; ph, Jose Luis Alcaine (Eastmancolor); ed, Jose Salcedo; m, Bernardo Bonezzi; cos, Jose Maria de Cossio

AAN Best Foreign Language Film

In WOMEN ON THE VERGE OF A NERVOUS BREAKDOWN, Pedro Almodovar has written and directed an incisive, fast-paced romp with the serious theme of obsessive love. The film's cascade of missed connections and riotous coincidences is triggered when Ivan (Fernando Guillen) abruptly abandons his longtime lover, Pepa (Carmen Maura). Finding herself pregnant, Pepa frantically tries to track down the elusive Ivan. In the course of her search she discovers some of his secrets, including Lucia (Julieta Serrano), by whom he has fathered a now-grown son. Pepa, distraught and contemplating suicide, prepares a batch of gazpacho laced with enough barbiturates to put a small town into coma and puts her apartment up for rent—after which people start showing up in waves. The pitcher of gazpacho becomes the key to some strange and unexpected events, culminating in a loopy car chase. Almodovar, who was an obscure telephone company employee just six years earlier, consolidates his reputation as a cult moviemaker with this one. He is great at inventing simple but stunning visual jokes and staging running gags. Further, he brings the best out of his uniformly skillful cast, in particular Carmen Maura. An Almodovar regular and consummate farceur, Maura can also play the pathos of the role with moving veracity. The film is flushed with bright light and cartoon hues, nicely accenting the fast-paced stew of incidents.

WONDER BOYS

2000 112m c Comedy/Drama ★★★★
Scott Rudin/Paramount (U.S.) R

Michael Douglas (*Grady Tripp*), Tobey Maguire (*James Leer*), Frances McDormand (*Sara Gaskell*), Robert Downey Jr. (*Terry Crabtree*), Katie Holmes (*Hannah Green*), Rip Torn (*Q*), Richard Knox (*Vernon Hardapple*), Jane Adams (*Oola*), Michael Cavadias (*Miss Sloviak*), Richard Thomas (*Walter Gaskell*)

p, Scott Rudin, Curtis Hanson; d, Curtis Hanson; w, Steve Kloves (based on the novel by Michael Chabon); ph, Dante Spinotti; ed, Dede Allen; m, Christopher Young; prod d, Jeannine Oppewall; art d, Don Woodruff; fx, John D. Milinac, Jerry Pooler (Visual), Cinesite (Visual); cos, Beatrix Aruna Pasztor

AA Best Original Song: "Things Have Changed"; Bob Dylan; *AAN Best Film Editing:* Dede Allen; *AAN Best Adapted Screenplay:* Steve Kloves

Quiet desperation, academic back-biting, and suicidal despair were made funny and utterly believable in novelist Michael Chabon's *Wonder Boys*. Screenwriter Steven Kloves and director Curtis Hanson have translated the novel to film with all its sly sense of humor and sharply telling details intact.

Grady Tripp (Michael Douglas) is terrified that he's a one-hit wonder: his first novel was a huge success, but the manuscript of his follow-up—seven years (and counting) in the making—has ballooned to *War and Peace* proportions, with no ending in sight. While working on this magnum opus, Grady has gotten married, secured a post teaching writing at a small Pittsburgh college, embarked on an affair with colleague Sara Gaskell (Frances McDormand)—inconveniently enough, her husband, Walter (Richard Thomas), chairs the English department—and smoked a lot of dope. Grady's troubles multiply during the school's "Wordfest" weekend. His wife decamps, his agent (Robert Downey Jr.) arrives to nag about the accursed book, Sara announces she's pregnant, and morbid but hugely talented student James Leer (Tobey Maguire) turns up at a faculty-student shindig swearing the gun in his pocket is a toy until the moment he shoots Walter's dog.

Grady and James embark on a road trip of sorts (they don't get far, but log a lot of time in the car), and their joint misadventures—no pun intended—are both poignant and surprisingly entertaining. It's a gleefully sardonic and fabulously acted coming-of-age story. Maguire and Douglas are both extraordinary (though Douglas feels a little old for his role, which seems to have been written for a man in his early 40s), and even Downey delivers a sharp, understated performance.

WONDER MAN   DVD

1945 98m c Comedy/Musical ★★★★
Goldwyn (U.S.)

Danny Kaye (*Buzzy Bellew/Edwin Dingle*), Virginia Mayo (*Ellen Shanley*), Vera-Ellen (*Midge Mallon*), Donald Woods (*Monte Rossen*), S.Z. Sakall (*Schmidt*), Allen Jenkins (*Chimp*), Edward Brophy (*Torso*), Steve Cochran (*Ten-Grand Jackson*), Otto Kruger (*District Attorney R.J. O'Brien*), Richard Land (*Assistant District Attorney Grosset*)

p, Samuel Goldwyn; d, H. Bruce Humberstone; w, Don Hartman, Melville Shavelson, Philip Rapp, Jack Jevne, Eddie Moran (based on a story by Arthur Sheekman); ph, Victor Milner, William Snyder (Technicolor); ed, Daniel Mandell; m, Ray Heindorf; art d, Ernst Fegte, McClure Capps; fx, John P. Fulton; chor, John Wray

AAN Best Score (Musical): Lou Forbes, Ray Heindorf; AAN Best Song: "So in Love"; David Rose (Music), Leo Robin (Lyrics); AAN Best Sound Recording: Gordon Sawyer; AA Best Visual Effects: John Fulton, A.W. Johns

In one of his most likable films, Danny Kaye takes on a dual role, playing two brothers—one an entertainer about to marry who is killed when he witnesses a mob hit, and the other an intellectual in love with a librarian. The dead brother's spirit approaches the living brother and asks that he help bring the murderous mobsters to justice. Since the egghead is afraid to get involved, the spirit of the dead brother enters the body of the living one. Not surprisingly, this causes a great deal of confusion, especially for the two women who are now in love with him, the librarian and the dead brother's fiancee. Filled with lots of laughs, WONDER MAN features a splendid performance by Kaye that is spiced with verve and zeal.

WOODEN HORSE, THE

1950 101m bw War/Prison ★★★½
Wessex (U.K.)

Leo Genn (*Peter*), David Tomlinson (*Phil*), Anthony Steel (*John*), David Greene (*Bennett*), Peter Burton (*Nigel*), Patrick Waddington (*Senior British Officer*), Michael Goodliffe (*Robbie*),

Anthony Dawson (*Pomfret*), Bryan Forbes (*Paul*), Franz Schaftheitlin (*Commandant*)

p, Ian Dalrymple; d, Jack Lee; w, Eric Williams (based on the book by Williams); ph, C. Pennington-Richards; ed, John Seabourne, Peter Seabourne; m, Clifton Parker; prod d, William Kellner

One of the cleverest escapes of WWII was pulled off by British prisoners in 1943, and this film tells their story. Pondering a method of escaping their camp, POWs Peter (Leo Gerin), John (Anthony Steel), and Phil (David Tomlinson) hit upon a brilliant scheme. They construct a boxlike vaulting horse, which is brought out to the yard daily for a few hours of exercise by their fellow internees. Inside the horse, however, are one and sometimes two men who start a tunnel from underneath the horse, then cover it up at the end of each day's vaulting. After months of digging and close calls, the tunnel is ready. Three men remain inside it until after dark, then break through the last few feet of ground to the surface beyond the fence. Peter and John travel together and are eventually spirited by the Danish underground to Sweden, where they rejoin Phil. This was the first of the British POW films and set the subgenre's style, in which Stalag life takes on the character of a British public school, a rigorous discipline and hierarchy in which the Germans function as "rather nasty prefects, who exist simply to be tricked and humiliated," as one critic put it. THE WOODEN HORSE subscribes to this trivialization of what was really a horrible, degrading experience, but as an adventure the film is very successful—suspenseful and fast-paced, with all the leads well done in suitably stiff-upper-lip style.

WOODSMAN, THE   DVD

2004 87m c Drama ★★★½
Dash Films/Lee Daniels Entertainment (U.S.) R

Kevin Bacon (*Walter*), Kyra Sedgwick (*Vickie*), Mos Def (*Sgt. Lucas*), Benjamin Bratt (*Carlos*), David Alan Grier (*Bob*), Eve (*Mary-Kay*), Kevin Rice (*Candy*), Michael Shannon (*Rosen*), Hannah Pilkes (*Robin*), Carlos Leon (*Pedro*)

p, Lee Daniels; d, Nicole Kassell; w, Steven Fechter, Nicole Kassell (based on the play by Steven Fechter); ph, Xavier Perez Grobet; ed, Lisa Fruchtman; m, Brian A. Kates; art d, Stephen Beatrice; fx, Thomas Varga (mixer); chor, Keith Yurevitz; cos, Christine Wick

First-time feature filmmaker Nicole Kassell's adaptation of Steven Fechter's play about a child molester walks a thin line. It elicits empathy for Walter (Kevin Bacon), a smoldering heap of resentment and self-pity just waiting for a spark, but without looking for sympathy.

Fresh out of jail and determined to reenter the world without reverting to his old ways, Walter is still dangerously in thrall to his desires and self-justifications: he never hurt the girls, he insists fiercely; he always made sure they were between 10 and 12 years old. But forces conspire against him. The only landlord who'll rent to Walter puts him in an apartment across the street from a grammar school. He's ostracized by his sister and can't visit his 10-year-old niece. His lumberyard co-workers know he's done time, and busybody receptionist Mary-Kay (Eve) makes it her business to find out why. His court-appointed therapist (Michael Shannon) harps on disturbing memories Walter would rather let lie, and a skeptical local cop (Mos Def) is playing head games. The only good thing in the gloomy morass of Walter's life is Vickie (Kyra Sedgwick), who sticks around even after he's told her everything.

The moment you start to question the prevalence of abusers and victims in Fechter and Kassell's gray, grainy world is the moment you realize how skillfully they've maneuvered you into seeing through Walter's eyes. Imprisoned by his utterly unacceptable desires, he never stops to consider that there might be more than two kinds of people: adults who successfully resist the impulse to molest children and those who don't. Kassell's visual influences are evident—she's clearly a fan of the down-and-dirty films of the '70s—but the consistently fine performances smooth over the rough patches.

WORKING GIRL
DVD

1988 113m c Romance ★★★½
Fox (U.S.) R

Harrison Ford (*Jack Trainer*), Melanie Griffith (*Tess McGill*), Sigourney Weaver (*Katharine Parker*), Alec Baldwin (*Mick Dugan*), Joan Cusack (*Cyn*), Philip Bosco (*Oren Trask*), Nora Dunn (*Ginny*), Oliver Platt (*Lutz*), James Lally (*Turkel*), Kevin Spacey (*Bob Speck*)

p, Douglas Wick; d, Mike Nichols; w, Kevin Wade; ph, Michael Ballhaus (Deluxe Color); ed, Sam O'Steen; m, Carly Simon; prod d, Patrizia von Brandenstein; cos, Ann Roth

AAN Best Picture; AAN Best Actress: Melanie Griffith; *AAN Best Supporting Actress:* Sigourney Weaver; *AAN Best Supporting Actress:* Joan Cusack; *AAN Best Director:* Mike Nichols; *AA Best Original Song:* "Let the River Run"; Carly Simon (Music & Lyrics)

Melanie Griffith, excellent in another strong 1988 film, STORMY MONDAY, gives an even more dazzling performance here as Tess McGill, an industrious secretary at a brokerage firm who longs to break out of the secretarial mold. After a run-in with her boss, she finds herself in a last-chance opportunity as the secretary to Katharine Parker (Sigourney Weaver). The astute secretary has an idea for putting together a deal for a client (Philip Bosco). Later, while Katharine recovers from a skiing accident, Tess learns that her boss has been moving ahead on the idea with no apparent intention of giving Tess any credit. Tess decides to engineer the big deal herself, with the help of Jack Trainer (Harrison Ford), an outside deal-maker who also happens to be Katharine's lover. Director Mike Nichols (THE GRADUATE, CATCH-22, BILOXI BLUES) demonstrates again his assured command of the film medium—coaxing outstanding performances from lead and supporting players alike, using the camera to brilliant effect, and infusing the story with tension, romance, and humor. Funny, touching, and ultimately tremendously buoyant—reflecting the optimism engendered by the short-lived 1980s economic boom—WORKING GIRL is a "feel good" movie with some intelligence. However, its Horatio Alger premise—that hard work, pluck, and intelligence are inevitably rewarded in the world of business—may be hard to swallow, particularly in an era of diminishing expectations.

WORKING GIRLS
DVD

1986 90m c Drama ★★★★
Lizzie Borden/Alternate Current (U.S.)

Louise Smith (*Molly*), Ellen McElduff (*Lucy*), Amanda Goodwin (*Dawn*), Marusia Zach (*Gina*), Janne Peters (*April*), Helen Nicholas (*Mary*)

p, Lizzie Borden, Andi Gladstone; d, Lizzie Borden; w, Lizzie Borden, Sandra Kay; ph, Judy Irola (Eastmancolor); ed, Lizzie Borden; m, David van Tieghem; prod d, Kurt Ossenfort

WORKING GIRLS concentrates on the daily routine of a modern-day Manhattan prostitute in a detached, clinical manner, breaking away from old myths to create an insightful and, in many ways, disturbing interpretation of what has been called the "world's oldest profession." Molly (Louise Smith) is a Yale graduate, nearing 30, who temporarily works in a Manhattan brothel to help make ends meet. The Manhattan brothel she works in appears as a normal office. The girls dress like secretaries, and harmlessly chat about their personal lives,

the job, and their general disdain for their boss, as they patiently wait for the day to end so they can go home.

Director Lizzie Borden's usually sharp eye for detail pervades WORKING GIRLS, and here maintains a high level of interest throughout. The down-to-earth portrayals possess none of the stereotypes popular in media representations of prostitutes, and, as a result, are frighteningly realistic. A film with an interesting and provocative feminist edge.

WORLD ACCORDING TO GARP, THE
DVD

1982 136m c Comedy/Drama ★★½
Pan Arts (U.S.) R

Robin Williams (*T.S. Garp*), Mary Beth Hurt (*Helen Holm*), Glenn Close (*Jenny Fields*), John Lithgow (*Roberta Muldoon*), Hume Cronyn (*Mr. Fields*), Jessica Tandy (*Mrs. Fields*), Swoosie Kurtz (*Hooker*), James McCall (*Young Garp*), Peter Michael Goetz (*John Wolfe*), George Ede (*Dean Bodger*)

p, George Roy Hill, Robert L. Crawford; d, George Roy Hill; w, Steve Tesich (based on the novel by John Irving); ph, Miroslav Ondricek (Technicolor); ed, Ronald Roose, Stephen A. Rotter; prod d, Henry Bumstead; art d, Woods Mackintosh; cos, Ann Roth; anim, John Canemaker

AAN Best Supporting Actor: John Lithgow; *AAN Best Supporting Actress:* Glenn Close

Empty shortening of Irving's book reaches for profundity, and comes up courageous but brainless. It's actually a bittersweet string of sketches, attempting to explain a man's growth from birth to adulthood and how he deals with the vices of lust and fanaticism that whirl around him.

Garp is born to a formidable unmarried mother, Jenny Fields, played by Glenn Close. (The various stages of Garp's childhood are played by Thomas Peter Daikos, Brendon Roth, and James McCall before Robin Williams takes over as Garp reaches young adulthood.) The story follows him through childhood at a boys' prep school, where Jenny is the school nurse, through his high school passions—wrestling, writing, and sex—to marriage with his high school sweetheart, children, marital disaffection, and a career as a writer. Jenny meanwhile has become a famous feminist, espousing an eccentric cause. The plot details an abundance of comic and tragicomic episodes, outlandish physical, emotional, and sexual adventures. Williams gives another puppy-dog performance—he has yet to land a script that takes advantage of his wildness and anarchy. Although these qualities are undoubtedly couched in the cuteness of Williams's persona, they come from anywhere but. He's like a wild bird with clipped wings. GARP is stolen by Lithgow, who imparts dignity and depth to his role of a king-sized transsexual, and Close's feminist mom. The movie was not a success—even at 136 minutes, GARP still feels like its dialogue and its action are going in opposite directions. Audiences were confused; we're not—we can't work up that much of a lather.

WORLD APART, A

1988 113m c Biography ★★★★
Working Title/British Screen (U.K.) PG

Barbara Hershey (*Diana Roth*), Jodhi May (*Molly Roth*), Jeroen Krabbe (*Gus Roth*), Carolyn Clayton-Cragg (*Miriam Roth*), Merav Gruer (*Jude Roth*), Yvonne Bryceland (*Bertha*), Albee Lesotho (*Solomon*), Linda Mvusi (*Elsie*), Rosalie Crutchley (*Mrs. Harris*), Mackay Tickey (*Milius*)

p, Sarah Radclyffe; d, Chris Menges; w, Shawn Slovo; ph, Peter Biziou (Eastmancolor); ed, Nicolas Gaster; m, Hans Zimmer; prod d, Brian Morris; cos, Nic Ede

Set in Johannesburg in 1963, A WORLD APART is an utterly convincing, impeccably constructed indictment of apartheid, based on a semiautobiographical screenplay by Shawn Slovo. (Slovo is the daughter of Joe Slovo, head of the South African Communist Party and one of two white members of the ANC executive council, and Ruth First, who was assassinated by a parcel bomb in Mozambique in 1982.) Jodhi May plays the younger Slovo as a 13-year-old whose world revolves around Spanish dancing lessons, hula-hooping, and swimming in the pool of her equally privileged best friend (Nadine Chalmers). Her world is turned upside down when her father (Jeroen Krabbe), an ANC official, departs in the middle of the night not to return, leaving her journalist mother (Barbara Hershey) both to take care of May and her two younger sisters and to continue the political struggle. Much to May's confusion, Hershey's involvement with the movement makes her, not a bad mother, but a distracted, inattentive one—distant because she fears she cannot trust her daughter with life-and-death secrets. The film is driven by the tension between May's resentment at what she perceives as her mother's neglect of the family, and her gradual acknowledgment of the importance of the political imperatives by which her mother is compelled.

The feature-film directorial debut of Academy Award-winning cinematographer Chris Menges (THE KILLING FIELDS; THE MISSION), A WORLD APART was the second major film in two years to deal with South African issues, coming soon after Richard Attenborough's 1987 effort, CRY FREEDOM. In A WORLD APART, Menges has chosen to explore apartheid primarily through the eyes of whites, though his black characters—particularly Elsie (Linda Mvusi), the family's live-in maid, and her brother Solomon (Albee Lesotho), a political activist—are considerably more developed than those in Attenborough's film. The performances in A WORLD APART are uniformly excellent, and the extraordinarily moving work of Barbara Hershey, Jodhi May, and Linda Mvusi garnered a shared Best Actress award at the Cannes Film Festival.

WORLD IS NOT ENOUGH, THE   DVD
1999 128m c   Action/Adventure/Thriller   ★★
Albert R. Broccoli's Eon Productions Ltd.   PG-13
(U.S./U.K.)

Pierce Brosnan (James Bond), Denise Richards (Dr. Christmas Jones), Sophie Marceau (Elektra King), Robert Carlyle (Renard), Robbie Coltrane (Valentin Zukovsky), Judi Dench (M), Desmond Llewelyn (Q), Samantha Bond (Moneypenny), John Cleese (R), Serena Scott Thomas (Dr. Molly Warmflash)

p, Michael G. Wilson, Brabara Broccoli; d, Michael Apted; w, Neal Purvis, Robert Wade, Bruce Feirstein (from a story by Neal Purvis and Robert Wade); ph, Adrian Biddle; ed, Jim Clark; m, David Arnold; prod d, Peter Lamont; art d, Neil Lamont; fx, Chris Corbould, Mara Bryan

The world changes and special agent James Bond soldiers on.

In this newest installment in the 007 saga (the 19th or 21st, depending on where you stand on CASINO ROYALE and NEVER SAY NEVER AGAIN), Bond is pitted against a walking dead man named Renard (Robert Carlyle), who feels no pain because of the bullet lodged his brain. Renard seems to be gunning for beautiful Elektra King (Sophie Marceau), who's inherited an oil empire from her murdered father (an old law school chum of Judi Dench's M) and is constructing a pipeline through a network of unstable former Soviet republics. But what's Elektra really up to, and what's the real story behind her kidnapping several years earlier, an ordeal that left her missing part of an ear? Bond finds himself entangled with both Elektra and Dr. Christmas Jones (Denise Richards), a scientist whose expertise comes in mighty handy

when someone needs to explain why it's imperative to disarm that thermonuclear thingamabob sometime in the next three minutes, lest Istanbul become toast.

The requisite gadgets include the usual fully loaded car and a pair of X-ray spex that briefly turn Bond into the Immoral Mr. Teas; the action set pieces owe a great deal to previous films, including the ski chase from THE SPY WHO LOVED ME and LIVE AND LET DIE's speed boat hijinks. Purists may be bothered that Bond spends an awful lot of time being rescued by supporting characters, and Richards reaches astonishing heights of ineptitude; Dr. Jones's degree appears to be in aerobics, with a minor in Valley Speak. And like all recent Bond movies, the whole thing goes on way too long.

WORLD OF APU, THE   DVD
(APUR SANSAR) •
1958 106m bw Drama   ★★★★½
Satyajit Ray   (India)

Soumitra Chatterjee (Apurba Kumar Roy—"Apu"), Sarmila Tagore (Aparna), Swapan Mukerjee (Pulu), Alok Chakravarti (Kajal), Sefalika Devi (Aparna's Mother), Dhiresh Majumdar (Sasinaryan—Aparna's Father), Dhiren Ghosh (Landlord), Abhijit Chatterjee (Aparna's Brother), Belarani (Apu's Neighbor), Shanti Bhattacharjee (Office Associate)

p, Satyajit Ray, Amiyanath Mukerjee; d, Satyajit Ray; w, Satyajit Ray (based on the novel Aparajito by Bibhutibhusan Bandopadhaya); ph, Subrata Mitra; ed, Dulal Dutta; m, Ravi Shankar; art d, Banshi Chandragupta

THE WORLD OF APU is the third and final installment of Satyajit Ray's "Apu Trilogy," the most famous group of films to come out of India. After following the young character of Apu from his early years (PATHER PANCHALI) to his schooldays (THE UNVANQUISHED), the trilogy picks up with Soumitra Chatterjee in the role of Apu as a young man. His desire is to become a writer, but a lack of finances has forced him to abandon his university studies. His life changes, however, when he again meets his old friend Pulu (Swapan Mukerjee). Together, the two travel to the wedding of Pulu's cousin, Aparna (Sarmila Tagore). When the bridegroom turns out to be insane and the wedding is canceled, Apu agrees to marry Aparna to save her from ridicule. They return to his Calcutta apartment to start a new life, but destiny does not look kindly upon the newlyweds. In this final entry, Ray rounds out the life of Apu, charting his loss of innocence and painting a detailed and textured portrait of Indian life in the process. In Apu, Ray has brought to the screen a character who lives out his story, though he is never able to finally put it on paper. A rich and insightful picture, THE WORLD OF APU, despite being rooted deep in Indian culture, strikes a universal humanistic chord. Exquisitely photographed and scored.

WORLD OF HENRY ORIENT, THE   DVD
1964 115m c   Comedy   ★★★
UA   (U.S.)

Peter Sellers (Henry Orient), Paula Prentiss (Stella), Tippy Walker (Valerie Boyd), Merrie Spaeth (Marian "Gil" Gilbert), Angela Lansbury (Isabel Boyd), Tom Bosley (Frank Boyd), Phyllis Thaxter (Mrs. Gilbert), Bibi Osterwald (Boothy), Peter Duchin (Joe Byrd), John Fiedler (Sidney)

p, Jerome Hellman; d, George Roy Hill; w, Nora Johnson, Nunnally Johnson (based on the novel by Nora Johnson); ph, Boris Kaufman, Arthur J. Ornitz (Panavision, DeLuxe Color); ed, Stuart Gilmore; m, Elmer Bernstein, Ken Lauber; prod d, James Sullivan; art d, Jan Scott; fx, Dick Smith; cos, Ann Roth

THE WORLD OF HENRY ORIENT is a charming comedy about the agony of adolescent infatuation. Walker and Spaeth are boarding school chums who keep busy pursuing egotistical concert pianist Sellers. The girls, just 14 or so, believe that they are in love with Sellers, a Casanova whose latest conquest is the married Prentiss. Prentiss is convinced that the girls have been hired by her husband to trail her, and after that the groupies' idolatry creates a number of ridiculous situations. This is one of the rare films in which someone steals scenes from Sellers. Walker and Spaeth are a joy—with none of the professional, cloying sweetness so often seen in younger performers—and the best part of the movie is the depiction of the girls, which never strays from truth, even when the teens are on wild flights of fancy. Director George Roy Hill made another, equally charming, tale of young love 15 years later: A LITTLE ROMANCE.

WRITTEN ON THE WIND
DVD

1956 99m   c   Drama   ★★★★½
Universal   (U.S.)

Rock Hudson *(Mitch Wayne)*, Lauren Bacall *(Lucy Moore Hadley)*, Robert Stack *(Kyle Hadley)*, Dorothy Malone *(Marylee Hadley)*, Robert Keith *(Jasper Hadley)*, Grant Williams *(Biff Miley)*, Bob Wilke *(Dan Willis)*, Edward Platt *(Dr. Paul Cochrane)*, Harry Shannon *(Hoak Wayne)*, John Larch *(Roy Carter)*

p, Albert Zugsmith; d, Douglas Sirk; w, George Zuckerman (based on the novel by Robert Wilder); ph, Russell Metty (Technicolor); ed, Russell Schoengarth; m, Frank Skinner; art d, Alexander Golitzen, Robert Clatworthy; fx, Clifford Stine; cos, Bill Thomas, Jay A. Morley Jr.

AAN Best Supporting Actor: Robert Stack; *AA Best Supporting Actress:* Dorothy Malone; *AAN Best Song:* "Written on the Wind"; Victor Young (Music), Sammy Cahn (Lyrics)

The ultimate in lush melodrama, WRITTEN ON THE WIND is, along with IMITATION OF LIFE, Douglas Sirk's finest directorial effort, and one of the most notable critiques of the American family ever made.

A Texas oil baron (Stack) has a whirlwind romance with a secretary (Bacall) and then marries her, but later has doubts as to whether the child she is expecting is really his. Stack's nymphomaniac sister (Malone) stokes up his suspicions that his best friend, geologist Rock Hudson, is really the father, and sets off a series of larger-than-life confrontations and crises from which no-one escapes lightly.

WRITTEN ON THE WIND successfully combines all the elements of the genre that has has become synonymous with Sirk's name. Sirk's melodrama, though, diverges from what is usually understood by that term to encompass a highly developed sense of ironic social critique. Some critics have seen his sumptuous visual style, full of parody and cliché, as a kind of Brechtian distancing that draws attention to the artificiality of the film medium, in turn commenting on the hollowness of middle-class American life. The lake in WRITTEN ON THE WIND, for example, is presented as a patently artificial studio interior, ironically pointing up the romantic self-delusion with which Malone sees her world.

WRONG MAN, THE
DVD

1956 105m bw Crime   ★★★★★
Warner Bros.   (U.S.)

Henry Fonda *(Christopher Emmanuel "Manny" Balestrero)*, Vera Miles *(Rose Balestrero)*, Anthony Quayle *(Frank O'Connor)*, Harold J. Stone *(Lt. Bowers)*, Esther Minciotti *(Mrs. Balestrero)*, Charles Cooper *(Detective Matthews)*, Nehemiah Persoff *(Gene Conforti)*, Laurinda Barrett *(Constance Willis)*, Norma Connolly *(Betty Todd)*, Doreen Lang *(Ann James)*

p, Alfred Hitchcock; d, Alfred Hitchcock; w, Maxwell Anderson, Angus Macphail (based on "The True Story of Christopher Emmanuel Balestrero" by Anderson); ph, Robert Burks; ed, George Tomasini; m, Bernard Herrmann; art d, Paul Sylbert, William L. Kuehl

The bleakest of Hitchcock's films, this stark, deliberate probing of a man wrongfully accused is almost wholly based on fact, creating its drama from a celebrated New York City case. Fonda plays Manny Balestrero, a family man who plays stand-up bass at a Queens nightspot called the Stork Club. Although he doesn't have much money, he manages to keep his life together with the help of his devoted wife, Rose (Miles). When she complains of dental pains, Manny decides to borrow on her life insurance policy (the last place they can borrow money since their debts have already piled too high) to pay for medical attention. Although he makes a practice of picking horses in the race section of the newspaper, he never dares to actually bet on them even though a win could get him out of debt. The following morning, Manny goes to the insurance office where he is identified by the office girls as the man who had robbed them previously. Later that night, he is arrested at the Stork Club. After being identified by a number of witnesses, Manny is interrogated at the police station. When he makes a nervous mistake in a handwriting test (misspelling the word "drawer" as "draw"—the same mistake made on the robber's ransom note), he is fingerprinted, photographed, and imprisoned. Finally released on bail, Manny is joyfully reunited with Rose and hires a defense attorney (Quayle). When Manny cannot find any witnesses to provide his alibi, the prospect of an acquittal looks dim. Meanwhile, Rose begins to crack under the pressure and is no longer able to deal with her husband's trial and defense. Although legal justice is ultimately served, Manny's family must nonetheless pay a considerable price for his freedom. Having become accustomed to the lighter, more commercial tone of such films as TO CATCH A THIEF, the public was taken aback when they viewed the unexpectedly bleak, hopeless, Kafka-esque style of THE WRONG MAN. Basing the film on incidents occurring to a real-life Queens bass player, Hitchcock takes us to the actual locations with the intent of representing the case in all its authenticity. Hitchcock spares us nothing in procedural terms. The questioning of the suspect, for example, is done in necessary tedium, wearing down the audience as much as Fonda's character. While the film centers chiefly on Manny's trauma, Hitchcock doesn't ignore the mental torture Rose is put through, temporarily departing from the story of Fonda's conviction to delve further into her problems. Don't look for Hitchcock's trademark cameo in this picture; he had originally intended to be seen as a customer walking into the Stork Club but edited himself out of the final print.

WUTHERING HEIGHTS
DVD

1939 103m bw Romance   ★★★★½
Goldwyn   (U.S.)

Merle Oberon *(Cathy Linton)*, Laurence Olivier *(Heathcliff)*, David Niven *(Edgar Linton)*, Donald Crisp *(Dr. Kenneth)*, Flora Robson *(Ellen Dean)*, Hugh Williams *(Hindley Earnshaw)*, Geraldine Fitzgerald *(Isabella Linton)*, Leo G. Carroll *(Joseph)*, Cecil Humphreys *(Judge Linton)*, Miles Mander *(Lockwood)*

p, Samuel Goldwyn; d, William Wyler; w, Ben Hecht, Charles MacArthur (based on the novel by Emily Bronte); ph, Gregg Toland; ed, Daniel Mandell; art d, James Vasevi; cos, Omar Kiam

AAN Best Picture; AAN Best Actor: Laurence Olivier; *AAN Best Supporting Actress:* Geraldine Fitzgerald; *AAN Best Director:* William Wyler; *AAN Best Screenplay:* Ben Hecht, Charles MacArthur; *AA Best B/W Cinematography:* Gregg Toland; *AAN*

Best Original Score: Alfred Newman; *AAN Best Interior Decoration:* James Basevi

Haunting, beautiful film version of Emily Bronte's tragic novel, with Olivier at his romance period peak, but marred slightly by Oberon's relative lack of passion.

WUTHERING HEIGHTS is a beautifully told story, displaying impeccable talent both in front of and behind the camera. Wyler had been interested in Bronte's story as a vehicle for Charles Boyer and Sylvia Sidney, who had starred in his 1937 film DEAD END. Hecht and MacArthur were assigned to write the film, and they headed for the island home of drama critic Alexander Woolcott. Here they labored to create a script faithful to the novel, though Woolcott was convinced the two writers would destroy Bronte's passionate and poetic story. Wyler eventually got Goldwyn to back the script, though Boyer was no longer being considered for the lead. The next choice was Olivier, a relative unknown to American audiences at the time. Hecht, who was an uncredited writer on QUEEN CHRISTINA, remembered Olivier from that film. The Briton had originally been hired to play opposite Garbo in that film, but was removed from the production in favor of John Gilbert. Olivier was furious, and had harbored ill feelings towards Hollywood ever since. He was interested in the part of Heathcliff however, and agreed to portray the doomed lover only if his wife, Vivien Leigh, could be his Cathy. But Oberon had already been signed for the role, and Goldwyn would not consider firing her. Leigh was offered the role of Olivier's unloved wife instead, but she turned this down, saying she felt more akin to the tragic lead character. Besides, Leigh had already been featured as the lead in several British films and was simply unwilling to step down for Hollywood. Eventually Olivier agreed to take the role, and Leigh ended up playing Scarlett O'Hara in GONE WITH THE WIND that year. Olivier and Oberon had previously appeared together in THE DIVORCE OF LADY X, a 1938 British film; many believe they made an unforgettable romantic duo.

Though the film understandably condenses Bronte's lengthy novel, Goldwyn spared no expense in creating the right atmosphere for the picture. A tract of 450 acres of land in California's Conejo Hills was transformed into authentic-looking English moors. One thousand heather plants were transplanted, and Goldwyn completed its re-creation by building a period manor on the site. However, he switched the novel's period from the original Regency to the Georgian era. His reasoning was simple: the Georgian period was marked by fancier dresses for women, and he was eager to show off Oberon in beautiful costumes. Gregg Toland won an Academy Award for his brilliant photography, a moody black-and-white perfectly suited to the material.

WUTHERING HEIGHTS
(ABISMOS DE PASION)
1953 90m bw Romance ★★★★
Tepeyac (Mexico)

Irasema Dilian *(Catalina)*, Jorge Mistral *(Alejandro)*, Lilia Prado, Ernesto Alonso, Luis Aceves Castaneda, Francisco Reiguera, Hortensia Santovena, Jaime Gonzalez

p, Oscar Dancigers; d, Luis Bunuel; w, Luis Bunuel, Julio Alejandro, Dino Maiuri (based on the novel by Emily Bronte); ph, Agustin Jiminez; ed, Carlos Savage; m, Raul Lavista, Richard Wagner

Luis Bunuel's long-planned version of Emily Bronte's novel (the screenplay was written some 20 years before the film was made, but no backer could be found), a favorite work of the Surrealists, shifts the setting from the English moors to a small Mexican estate and turns Heathcliff into Alejandro (Jorge Mistral) and Cathy into Catalina (Irasema Dilian). As the Spanish title implies, the lovers fall into an "abyss of passion"— a place where love exists above and beyond all else. Unlike

Hollywood's sanitized backlot version of Bronte, Bunuel's reworking is rooted in the darker aspects of love. The film opens with a slow-motion image of crows as they scatter from a twisted, leafless tree, frightened by an off-screen gunshot. This image of death and decay hangs over the film. The film is flawed (the acting is flatter than usual, the emphasis is overly literary), but it is one of the most passionate and expressionistic works of Bunuel's Mexican period, featuring an ending as brilliant as anything ever accomplished by a surrealist artist.

X

X-FILES, THE

1998 121m c Science Fiction/Action ★★★
Ten Thirteen Productions/20th Century Fox PG-13
(U.S.)

David Duchovny *(FBI Special Agent Fox Mulder)*, Gillian Anderson *(FBI Special Agent Dana Scully)*, Martin Landau *(Dr. Alvin Kurtzweil)*, Armin Mueller-Stahl *(Strughold)*, Mitch Pileggi *(FBI Assistant Director Walter Skinner)*, Terry O'Quinn *(Michaud)*, Blythe Danner *(Cassidy)*, William B. Davis *(The Cigarette-Smoking Man)*, John Neville *(The Well-Manicured Man)*, Jeffrey DeMunn *(Dr. Ben Brohnshweig)*

p, Chris Carter, Daniel Sackheim; d, Rob Bowman; w, Chris Carter (from a story by Chris Carter and Daniel Sackheim); ph, Ward T. Russell; ed, Stephen Mark; m, Mark Snow; prod d, Christopher Nowak; art d, Gregory Bolton, Hugo Santiago; fx, Paul Lombardi; cos, Marlene Stewart

Before there were scary basements and flashlights with which to poke around them, foolhardy cavemen were exploring spooky caverns with torches, and no good came of it. Caveat "X"-philes: that's probably the biggest revelation in the "X-Files" feature, a motion picture spin-off of the hit cult TV show.

For the benefit of those who've been in isolation wards for the last five years, agents Fox "Spooky" Mulder (David Duchovny) and Dana Scully (Gillian Anderson) are the FBI's resident ghostbusters, their provenance a set of cases that defy rational explanation known collectively as the X-Files. Mulder is driven by the childhood memory of having seen his sister abducted by aliens, while skeptical Scully, initially assigned to debunking Mulder's work, has become his partner in crime. The movie opens with some Texas tykes discovering the fossilized remains of some nosy Neanderthals, and one youngster has a close encounter of the nasty kind with an alien entity in the form of a black viscous fluid. A massive cover-up soon leads Mulder and Scully from Blackwood, TX, to the frozen Antarctic in search of the truth.

Series background is a huge asset; without it, the story and character relationships seem a bit thin. Directed by "X-Files" veteran Rob Bowman and coscripted by series creator Chris Carter, the feature is essentially a supersize episode that ignores a slew of the show's recent plot developments and adds yet another monster to the mix, one that owes a striking debt to ALIEN. Some fans will be pleased, others annoyed, and endless online discussion will be generated. "X" virgins will most likely wonder what all the fuss is about.

"X"—THE MAN WITH THE X-RAY EYES

1963 80m c Science Fiction ★★★½
Alta Vista (U.S.)

Ray Milland *(Dr. James Xavier)*, Diana Van Der Vlis *(Dr. Diane Fairfax)*, Harold J. Stone *(Dr. Sam Brant)*, John Hoyt *(Dr. Willard Benson)*, Don Rickles *(Crane)*, John Dierkes *(Preacher)*, Lorie Summers *(Party Dancer)*, Vicki Lee *(Young Girl Patient)*, Kathryn Hart *(Mrs. Mart)*, Carol Irey *(Woman Patient)*

p, Roger Corman; d, Roger Corman; w, Robert Dillon, Ray Russell (based on his story); ph, Floyd Crosby (Spectarama, Eastmancolor); ed, Anthony Carras; m, Les Baxter; art d, Daniel Haller; fx, Butler-Glouner, Inc.; cos, Marjorie Corso

Memorable, viscerally disturbing sci-fi/horror picture with Ray Milland as Dr. Xavier, a medical scientist who develops a serum that gives him X-ray vision. He's able to see through paper, clothes, and skin (a valuable asset to have around the operating room). As his powers grow stronger, he becomes increasingly demented and loses his job, signing up with a sideshow tout (Don Rickles) as a mind reader. His condition now causes him pain so severe that he needs to wear lead glasses. In agony and desperation, Xavier flees, eventually smashing his car and wandering into a revival meeting. There he hears a preacher quoting the Bible: "If thine eye offend thee, pluck it out." At wit's end, Dr. Xavier chooses to interpret the admonition literally. One of Roger Corman's finest directorial efforts, the movie took top honors at the Trieste Science Fiction Film Festival. In his book of casual horror criticism, *Danse Macabre*, Stephen King claims to have heard of an alternative ending that Corman deemed too horrifying: after tearing out his eyes, Dr. Xavier is supposed to have screamed, "I can still see!"

X-MEN

2000 97m c Science Fiction/Action ★★★
Marvel Entertainment/Donners' Company/ PG-13
Bad Hat Harry (U.S.)

Hugh Jackman *(Wolverine)*, Patrick Stewart *(Xavier)*, Ian McKellen *(Magneto)*, Famke Janssen *(Jean Grey)*, James Marsden *(Cyclops)*, Halle Berry *(Storm)*, Anna Paquin *(Rogue)*, Tyler Mane *(Sabretooth)*, Ray Park *(Toad)*, Rebecca Romijn-Stamos *(Mystique)*

p, Lauren Shuler Donner, Ralph Winter; d, Bryan Singer; w, David Hayter (from a story by Tom DeSanto and Bryan Singer); ph, Newton Thomas Sigel; ed, Steve Rosenblum, Kevin Stitt, John Wright; m, Michael Kamen; prod d, John Myhre; art d, Tamara Deverell, Paul Denham Austerberry; fx, Michael Fink, Colin Chilvers; cos, Louise Mingenbach

Stylish, exciting, and even a little poignant, this big-budget adaptation of the Marvel Comics series about misunderstood mutants counts flashes of wit and a thoughtful subtext among its unexpected bonuses.

In the not-too-distant future, mutants—humans with extraordinary powers—are as numerous as they are unpopular. Telepathic Dr. Charles Xavier (Patrick Stewart, in a role he was born to play) runs a school where mutants learn to control and direct their superpowers, while his former colleague, Holocaust survivor Magneto (played with a perfect combination of gravitas and glee by Ian McKellen), believes war between mutants and *Homo sapiens* is inevitable. Xavier's X-Men include the splendidly monikered Wolverine (Hugh Jackman), a guy with fierce mutton chops and retractable claws; Storm (Halle Berry), who has power over weather; Cyclops (James Marsden), who keeps his piercing (literally) eyes covered with wraparound sunglasses; and Dr. Jean Grey (Famke Janssen), a telekinetic telepath. Joined by Rogue (Anna Paquin), a teenaged runaway with a deadly touch, they

must do battle with Magneto's minions, including Sabretooth (Tyler Mane) and a blue-skinned shapeshifter named Mystique (Rebecca Romijn-Stamos).

The setup is a little complicated, but director Bryan Singer stages it efficiently enough and fills the film with moments of outrageous surrealist beauty; one highlight involves an evil mutant hanging from the Statue of Liberty by his 16-foot tongue. Now *there's* something you don't see everyday. Better still, one senses the presence of something even rarer in blockbusters than brains: heart. At the core of this splashy sci-fi spectacle is a simple parable about tolerance; the fact that things also blow up real good is merely icing on the cake.

X2

2003 133m c Science Fiction/Action ★★★½
Bad Hat Harry/Marvel Enterprises/Donners' PG-13
Company/20th Century Fox (U.S.)

Patrick Stewart *(Professor Charles Xavier)*, Hugh Jackman *(Logan/Wolverine)*, Ian McKellen *(Eric Lehnsherr/Magneto)*, Halle Berry *(Storm)*, Famke Janssen *(Jean Grey)*, James Marsden *(Scott Summers/Cyclops)*, Rebecca Romijn-Stamos *(Mystique)*, Brian Cox *(William Stryker)*, Alan Cumming *(Kurt Wagner/Nightcrawler)*, Cotter Smith *(President McKenna)*

p, Lauren Shuler Donner, Ralph Winter; d, Bryan Singer; w, Michael Dougherty, Dan Harris; ph, Newton Thomas Sigel; ed, John Ottman; m, John Ottman; prod d, Guy Hendrix Dyas; art d, Helen Jarvis; fx, Michael Fink, Mike Vezina; chor, Terry Notary; cos, Louise Mingenbach

For the most part, Bryan Singer's sequel to his massively successful X-MEN is an exhilarating experience—part political drama of behind-closed-doors intrigue, part sci-fi adventure punctuated by bursts of dizzyingly choreographed battles that take action sequences to the next level.

The film opens with teleporting mutant Nightcrawler (Alan Cumming) attacking the U.S. president (Cotter Smith) in the White House. The public responds to the assassination attempt by clamoring for a Mutant Registration Act, and the president gives hard-line military scientist William Stryker (Brian Cox) the go-ahead to investigate what Stryker paints as a terrorist training camp: Xavier's School for Gifted Youngsters, where Charles Xavier (Patrick Stewart), who advocates peaceful coexistence, trains young mutants to use their special powers responsibly. Stryker, who's used foul means to gather information from imprisoned mutant supremacist Erik Lehnsherr, aka Magneto (Ian McKellan), heads an assault on the peaceful prep school when the grownups, except brooding bad-ass Wolverine (Hugh Jackman), are away.

As in X-MEN, carefully written dramatic moments explore surprisingly complex social issues, but once the regrouped X-Men track the kidnapped students to Stryker's underground facility, the movie becomes attenuated, repetitive, and just a tiny bit silly. Halle Berry and James Marsden are blandly unconvincing in their roles, but McKellen, Stewart, and Cox are first rate. As thoughtful spectacle with uncommonly rich characterizations, consider this Singer's mostly X-cellent adventure.

XXX

2002 124m c Action ★★
Original Film/Revolution Studios (U.S.) R

Vin Diesel *(Xander Cage)*, Asia Argento *(Yelena)*, Samuel L. Jackson *(Agent Augustus Gibbons)*, Marton Csokas *(Yorgi)*, Michael Roof *(Toby Lee Shavers)*, Eve *(J.J.)*, Danny Trejo *(El Jefe)*, Tom Everett *(Senator Dick Hotchkiss)*, Thomas Ian Griffith *(Agent Jim McGrath)*, Richy Muller *(Milan Sova)* p, Neal H. Moritz; d, Rob Cohen; w, Rich Wilkes; ph, Dean Semler; ed, Chris Lebenzon, Joel Negron, Paul Rubell; m, Randy Edelman; prod d, Gavin Bocquet; art d, Jonathan Lee; fx, John Frazier, Joel Hynek, Stan Parks; cos, Sanja Milkovic Hays

Video-game kicks rule in this high-concept, lowbrow action picture, as cynically calculated as it is efficiently executed.

Having just lost a suave, James Bond-style agent on a mission in Prague, veteran espionage agent Augustus Gibbons (Samuel L. Jackson) is looking for an unconventional spy to take his place. Even among "the best and the brightest of the bottom of the barrel," extreme-sports outlaw Xander Cage (Vin Diesel) stands out among the other candidates. Gibbons makes his patriotic pitch, but Xander refuses. Undaunted, Gibbons switches to the DIRTY DOZEN approach: If Xander doesn't do his bit for flag and country, his tattooed ass is going to jail for a good long time. That works better, and Xander is dispatched to the Czech Republic to infiltrate a gang of leather-clad thrill freaks led by disillusioned former Soviet soldier Yorgi (Marton Csokas). Xander's cover is bolstered by his X-games credibility, and he's soon in like Flynn with Yorgi and Yorgi's lethal-looking lady (Asia Argento). Xander also learns that beneath their hard-partying exterior, Yorgi and his Gen-X comrades are masterminding a plan to plunge the world into chaos by unleashing a biological weapon code-named "Silent Night."

The movie is designed to showcase Diesel's strengths (nice tats, surly delivery, wicked abs), pretty much to the exclusion of other considerations. The movie isn't hard to watch; it zips along at a good clip, never wasting time on exposition when there's something to break. But the irony is that, for all its "not your father's spy movie" posing, it's *exactly* like the later James Bond pictures: predictable, lightweight, and 100 percent disposable.

Y

Y TU MAMA TAMBIEN

2001 105m c Comedy/Erotic ★★★★ DVD
Besame Mucho Pictures/Producciones Anhelo (Mexico)

Maribel Verdu *(Luisa Cortes)*, Gael Garcia Bernal *(Julio Zapata)*, Diego Luna *(Tenoch Iturbide)*, Marta Aura *(Enriqueta "Queta" Allende)*, Diana Bracho *(Silvia Allende de Iturbide)*, Emilio Echevarria *(Miguel Iturbide)*, Veronica Langer *(Maria Eugenia Calles de Huerta)*, Arturo Rios *(Esteban Morelos)*, Juan Carlos Remolina *(Alejandro "Jano" Montes de Oca)*, Daniel Gimenez Cacho *(Narrator)*

p, Alfonso Cuaron, Jorge Vergara; d, Alfonso Cuaron; w, Carlos Cuaron, Alfonso Cuaron; ph, Emmanuel Lubezki; ed, Alfonso Cuaron, Alex Rodriguez; prod d, Miguel Angel Alvarez; art d, Diana Quiroz; fx, Effecine Mobile, Salvadore Servin, Alejandro Vazquez; cos, Gabriela Diaque

A raunchy Mexican teen comedy with surprising depth and the nerve to confront subtexts that normally get short shrift in pictures aimed primarily at young men.

Seventeen-year-old Tenoch (Diego Luna) and Julio (Gael Garcia Bernal) are best friends who come from very different backgrounds. Tenoch is the son of a wealthy politician and lives in his parents' luxurious house; Julio lives with his single mother in a shabby housing complex. Fresh out of high

school, the teenagers are facing a long summer without their girlfriends, who'll be vacationing in Europe. Though the boys extract fervent promises of fidelity, they plan to make hay while the summer sun shines. At a family wedding, Tenoch and Julio encounter Luisa (Maribel Verdu), the sleek wife of Tenoch's pretentious older cousin, Jano (Juan Carlos Remolina Suarez), and clumsily suggest a trip to a distant strip of sand so perfect it's called *Boca del Cielo*—Heaven's Mouth. To their surprise, Luisa accepts the invitation. They don't know that Luisa has just learned that Jano is cheating on her, or that she's been to the doctor for some test results. Callow though the boys may be, they quickly recognize that their fevered fantasies are bound up with complicated reality, starting from the moment they try to spy on Luisa undressing and instead catch her sobbing uncontrollably. Competition for Luisa's sexual favors sparks revelations with far-reaching emotional consequences and eventually leads to an encounter that simultaneously fulfills the boys' wildest dreams and dredges up their most strenuously repressed anxieties.

For what could easily have been a slick but vulgar variation on AMERICAN PIE or PORKY'S, this libidinous comedy explores some unusually complicated territory, and benefits greatly from Verdu's unpredictable performance as Luisa.

YAABA

1989 90m c Drama ★★★★
Arcadia/L'Avenir/Thelma/Suisse Romande TV/ZDF/La Sept/Centre de la Cinemagraphic/Department des Affaires Etrangeres/Coe (Burkina Faso)

Fatimata Sanga *(Yaaba)*, Noufou Ouedraogo *(Bila)*, Roukietou Barry *(Nopoko)*, Adama Ouedraogo *(Kougri)*, Amade Toure *(Tibo)*, Sibidou Ouedraogo *(Poko)*, Adama Sidibe *(Razougou)*, Rasmane Ouedraogo *(Noaga)*, Kinda Moumouni *(Finse)*, Assita Ouedraogo *(Koudi)*

p, Freddy Denaes, Michel David, Pierre-Alain Meier, Idrissa Ouedraogo; d, Idrissa Ouedraogo; w, Idrissa Ouedraogo; ph, Matthias Kalin; ed, Loredana Cristelli; m, Francis Bebey

Set in a village in Burkina Faso, YAABA concerns two young cousins, Bila (Noufou Ouedraogo) and Nopoko (Roukietou Barry), whose lives are forever changed by their association with the mysterious Sana (Fatimata Sanga), an old woman who has been branded a witch and ostracized by the adults in their village. While carefully depicting the social codes of the village's quarrelsome extended family, director Idrissa Ouedraogo pits the innocence of Bila and Nopoko against the intrigue and superstition among the elders. The curious and sensitive Bila becomes something of a "problem child" when he develops a relationship with the outcast Sana—who, far from being a witch, is a contemplative sort given to dispensing small nuggets of wisdom. Bila savors these nuggets and respectfully calls her "Yaaba" (Grandmother). When Nopoko suffers an injury that leads to an infection that is misdiagnosed as malaria, Sana journeys to get a healer to help her. However, the villagers continue to persecute Sana right up to the film's touching closing.

The winner of the International Critics Prize at the 1989 Cannes Film Festival, YAABA is a visually striking, poignant film that communicates much through refreshingly economical means. Director Ouedraogo (YAM DAABO) filmed this elegant work in his own village, using a nonprofessional cast that renders uniformly convincing and natural performances. Relying on deft *mise-en-scene*, Ouedraogo captures the village's unique rhythms with precision and wrests great emotional power from the simple story.

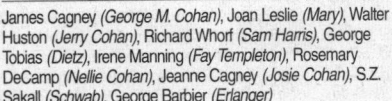

YAKUZA, THE

1975   112m   c   Crime   ★★★½
Warner Bros./Toei   (U.S./Japan)   R

Robert Mitchum *(Harry Kilmer)*, Ken Takakura *(Tanaka Ken)*, Brian Keith *(George Tanner)*, Herb Edelman *(Oliver Wheat)*, Richard Jordan *(Dusty)*, Kishi Keiko *(Tanaka Eiko)*, Okada Eiji *(Tono Toshiro)*, James Shigeta *(Goro)*, Kyosuke Mashida *(Kato Jiro)*, Christina Kokubo *(Hanako)*

p, Sydney Pollack; d, Sydney Pollack; w, Paul Schrader, Robert Towne (based on a story by Leonard Schrader); ph, Okazaki Kozo, Duke Callaghan (Panavision, Technicolor); ed, Fredric Steinkamp, Thomas Stanford, Don Guidice; m, Dave Grusin; prod d, Stephen Grimes; art d, Ishida Yoshiyuki; fx, Richard Parker, Kasai Tomoo; cos, Dorothy Jeakins

Interesting and well-acted, if clumsy, American take on the Japanese gangster genre. Robert Mitchum stars as a private detective who goes to Japan to rescue an American girl who has been kidnapped by a yakuza, with Japanese screen idol Ken Takakura as a former gangster who helps him in his quest. Kishi Keiko plays a woman with whom Mitchum had had a love affair while stationed in Japan at the end of WWII, and whom he now re-encounters.

   Written by Paul Schrader from a story by his brother Leonard (the screenplay was then rewritten by famed script doctor Robert Towne), THE YAKUZA was a commendable attempt to expose American audiences to some of the conventions of Japanese genre films. By making the Ken character an anachronistic yakuza who still lives by the codes of the past (he's described as a "lone wolf" by his brother) while trying to exist in present-day capitalist Japan, the filmmakers were able to interestingly compare ancient rituals and values with more contemporary practices. Director Pollack does a workmanlike job, neither giving added resonance to the material, nor ruining a good idea with overbearing direction. His camera is just there to record the performances and really does little else. This film belongs to the actors, and they succeed in making it fascinating viewing. Co-screenwriter Paul Schrader is a student of Japanese culture and cinema, and his obsession with their notion of honor and sacrifice climaxed in 1985 with MISHIMA.

YANKEE DOODLE DANDY

1942   126m   bw   Musical   ★★★★★
Warner Bros.   (U.S.)

James Cagney *(George M. Cohan)*, Joan Leslie *(Mary)*, Walter Huston *(Jerry Cohan)*, Richard Whorf *(Sam Harris)*, George Tobias *(Dietz)*, Irene Manning *(Fay Templeton)*, Rosemary DeCamp *(Nellie Cohan)*, Jeanne Cagney *(Josie Cohan)*, S.Z. Sakall *(Schwab)*, George Barbier *(Erlanger)*

p, William Cagney; d, Michael Curtiz; w, Robert Buckner, Edmund Joseph (based on a story by Robert Buckner); ph, James Wong Howe; ed, George Amy; art d, Carl Jules Weyl; chor, LeRoy Prinz, Seymour Felix, John Boyle; cos, Milo Anderson

AAN Best Picture; AA Best Actor: James Cagney; *AAN Best Supporting Actor:* Walter Huston; *AAN Best Director:* Michael Curtiz; *AAN Best Original Story:* Robert Buckner; *AAN Best Film Editing:* George Amy; *AA Best Score (Musical):* Ray Heindorf, Heinz Roemheld; *AA Best Sound Recording:* Nathan Levinson

The real George M. Cohan had just had a serious operation and was recuperating at his upstate New York home when he was shown, in a private screening, this film of his life starring the indefatigable James Cagney. The great showman watched the movie without a word. When it was finished he was asked how he liked it. Cohan grinned, shook his head, and paid the great Cagney his highest compliment: "My God, what an act

to follow!" This beguiling film, which deservedly won Cagney a Best Actor Oscar, presents an irresistible portrait of song-and-dance man Cohan and of early 20th-century America. It's heartfelt entertainment and anyone who ever whistled a tune, tapped a toe or hummed a bar of music will love it. This was Cagney's favorite film and his favorite number was, in his own words, "when I did the 'wings' coming down the stairs at the White House. Didn't think of it until five minutes before I went on. I didn't consult with the director or anything, I just did it."

YEAR OF LIVING DANGEROUSLY, THE

1983   115m   c   Adventure/Romance   ★★★½
MGM   (Australia)   PG

Mel Gibson *(Guy Hamilton)*, Sigourney Weaver *(Jill Bryant)*, Linda Hunt *(Billy Kwan)*, Michael Murphy *(Pete Curtis)*, Bembol Roco *(Kumar)*, Domingo Landicho *(Hortono)*, Hermono De Guzman *(Immigration Officer)*, Noel Ferrier *(Wally O'Sullivan)*, Paul Sonkkila *(Kevin Condon)*, Ali Nur *(Ali)*

p, James McElroy; d, Peter Weir; w, David Williamson, Peter Weir, C.J. Koch (based on the novel by Koch); ph, Russell Boyd (Panavision, Metrocolor); ed, Bill Anderson; m, Maurice Jarre; art d, Herbert Pinter; cos, Terry Ryan

AA Best Supporting Actress: Linda Hunt

Ambitious, stylish, and ideologically confused, THE YEAR OF LIVING DANGEROUSLY falters in its attempts to succeed simultaneously as thriller, romance, and political tract, while also encompassing director Peter Weir's penchant for half-baked mysticism. Still, it's a gripping film, set in 1965 as Australian reporter Guy Hamilton (Gibson) arrives in Jakarta, Indonesia. His photographer, Billy Kwan (Hunt), a Chinese-Australian, shows him the ropes, introducing him to the city's poverty and corruption and to various contacts, including Jill Bryant (Weaver), an embassy attache with whom Guy begins a romance. When Jill secures information on a planned Communist coup against President Sukarno and urges Guy to leave, he betrays her confidence and files a major story—for which she is the obvious source. Billy, previously a fence-sitter, now comes out against Sukarno, feeling that he has betrayed Indonesia in much the same way as Guy betrayed Jill (whom Billy also loves). Revolt and reaction explode on all sides.

   Weir is only partly successful in attempting to link his various themes symbolically with reflexive images of Indonesian shadow puppetry and Billy's advice to "look at the shadows, not at the puppets," but the director indisputably made the right move in his risky casting of the tiny, gravel-voiced Hunt to play Billy Kwan. Physically convincing in the role, Hunt's achievement is not merely cosmetic; her Billy negotiates among a compelling range of motivations and emotions. Gibson and Weaver, too, enjoy two of their few interesting roles to date, and respond to the challenges put them with intensity and intelligence. The film's hot, humid, seedy ambience is nearly palpable, enhancing this fascinating story of Sukarno's downfall.

   Unfortunately, the film's politics are puerile—Weir appears to endorse Kwan's smug rejection of social reform in favor of individual charity—and its historical material is sketchy and misleading. Viewers not already familiar with the events of 1965 in Indonesia will come away no wiser; in particular, they will not learn that the "Communist coup" was an invented cover story for a CIA-engineered military coup against Sukarno that led to one of the bloodiest massacres of the post-war era (according to most estimates, some 500,000 alleged Communists and Sukarno supporters were slaughtered in the space of a few weeks). Considered purely as a romantic adventure, the film mightn't need come to grips with such unpleasant realities, but it desperately wants to be taken seriously. Taken seriously, it largely fails.

YEARLING, THE   DVD
1946 134m c   Drama   ★★★★
MGM   (U.S.)

Gregory Peck (Pa Baxter), Jane Wyman (Ma Baxter), Claude Jarman Jr. (Jody Baxter), Chill Wills (Buck Forrester), Clem Bevans (Pa Forrester), Margaret Wycherly (Ma Forrester), Henry Travers (Mr. Boyles), Forrest Tucker (Lem Forrester), Donn Gift (Fodderwing), Dan White (Millwheel)

p, Sidney Franklin; d, Clarence Brown; w, Paul Osborn (based on the novel by Marjorie Kinnan Rawlings); ph, Charles Rosher, Leonard Smith, Arthur E. Arling (Technicolor); ed, Harold F. Kress; m, Herbert Stothart; art d, Cedric Gibbons, Paul Groesse; fx, Warren Newcombe, Chester M. Franklin

AAN Best Picture; AAN Best Actor: Gregory Peck; AAN Best Actress: Jane Wyman; AAN Best Director: Clarence Brown; AA Best Color Cinematography: Charles Rosher, Leonard Smith, Arthur Arling; AAN Best Film Editing: Harold Kress; AA Best Interior Decoration (Color): Cedric Gibbons, Paul Groesse, Edwin B. Willis

THE YEARLING is a splendid family film set just after the Civil War in the wilds of southern Florida, where the Baxters—Ma, Pa, and their one surviving child, Jody (Gregory Peck, Jane Wyman, and Claude Jarman)—are having a tough time eking out a living on their small farm. Pa's ambition is to earn enough from his next crop to be able to sink a well nearer the house, so that Ma won't have to tote water. As an only child in the wilderness, Jody needs some company and asks his parents if he might have a pet. When Pa is bitten by a rattlesnake and in danger of dying, Ma and Jody must kill a deer and make an elixir out of its innards. The doe has a fawn, and when Jody begs his parents to allow him to raise the baby, they do. Time passes and the bond between boy and animal deepens, but as the deer grows it begins eating some of the crops so vital to the family's existence. Pa is left with no choice but to tell Jody that the youth must kill his beloved companion. Similar to OLD YELLER in its lessons, THE YEARLING was a huge success and one of MGM's top moneymakers. A remarkable film that is truly for the entire family.

YELLOW EARTH
(HUANG TUDI)
1984 89m c   Drama   ★★★½
World Entertainment Release   (China)

Xue Bai (Ciu Qiao), Wang Xueqi (Gu Qing), Tan Tuo (The Father), Liu Qiang (Hanhan)

d, Chen Kaige; w, Zhang Ziliang (based on the essay "Sanwen" by Ke Lan); ph, Zhang Yimou; m, Zhao Jiping; art d, He Qun

One of a handful of films by the group of young Chinese directors labeled "the Fifth Generation," YELLOW EARTH is set during the skirmishes between China and Japan prior to WWII. Xueqi plays a communist soldier studying the local folk songs of the Shaanxi province. He settles in the house of Tuo, a farmer who continues to plough his barren land in the hope the gods will reward him with a good crop. Along with Tuo are his 10-year-old son, and 14-year-old daughter, Bai, rumored to have the most beautiful voice in the province. The taciturn family slowly begins to open up to Xueqi as he helps them with their daily work, but the tension between his "progressive" ideals and the time-honored protocols of village life leads to tragedy.

    YELLOW EARTH was one of the first "Fifth Generation" films to reach Western eyes and was justifiably celebrated for its daring, colorful visuals and innovative, eye-opening rhythms.

YELLOW SKY
1948 98m   bw   Western   ★★★★
Fox   (U.S.)

Gregory Peck (Stretch), Anne Baxter (Mike), Richard Widmark (Dude), Robert Arthur (Bull Run), John Russell (Lengthy), Harry Morgan, billed as Henry Morgan (Half Pint), James Barton (Grandpa), Charles Kemper (Walrus), Robert Adler (Jed), Victor Kilian (Bartender)

p, Lamar Trotti; d, William A. Wellman; w, Lamar Trotti (based on the novel by W.R. Burnett); ph, Joseph MacDonald; ed, Harmon Jones; m, Alfred Newman; art d, Lyle Wheeler, Albert Hogsett; fx, Fred Sersen

Set in the post-Civil War Old West, the film begins as Peck leads a band of seven masked desperadoes in a bank robbery. Loading the bullion into their saddlebags, the robbers gallop off, the U.S. Cavalry in hot pursuit. An enormous salt flat is the outlaws' only conceivable avenue of escape, so Peck leads his men into the arid, sun-blistered area. Their water gone, the dehydrated desperadoes chance upon a ghost town, heralded by a sign that reads "Yellow Sky—fastest growing town in the territory." The town is completely deserted, save for dotty old prospector Barton and his tomboy granddaughter Baxter. Greed for both the gold and the girl causes dissension among the men, a situation further exacerbated when Barton hides the outlaws' loot. Villain Widmark makes a try at wresting the role of leader from Peck and poses a threat to both beautiful Baxter and her grandfather. A showdown follows.

    The unlikely ending doesn't injure this brilliantly filmed and directed Western, which qualifies as one of the best of the genre. The high-contrast black-and-white photography by MacDonald is stunning; the salt-flat scenes made audiences run to the theater lobby water fountain. Dialogue is all the more telling for being sparse; the story is carried visually. The music by Newman is fine, beginning the action of each scene, then fading as stark realism takes hold and only natural sounds are heard. Peck is thoroughly believable in a part which contrasts so greatly with many of his others. Tanned and lined, etched with fatigue and thirst, his usually pallid countenance completely altered by makeup artist Nye's fine simulation of the ravages of weather, the leadership qualities of Peck's strong, short-of-speech badman are never in doubt. Basically a formula Western, the film was transmuted into a movie of major impact by the talents of its production staff and its cast. In his first film in this genre, Widmark plays the sort of smiling psychopath that brought him fame in his screen debut, KISS OF DEATH. The supporting cast members all do a fine job. Screenwriter Trotti and author Burnett received an award from the Writers Guild of America for Best Written American Western of the year.

YELLOW SUBMARINE   DVD
1968 85m   c   Animated/Musical   ★★★½
King Features/Subafilms   (U.K.)   G

Paul McCartney, John Lennon, Ringo Starr, George Harrison (The Beatles), VOICES OF: John Clive (John), Geoffrey Hughes (Paul), Peter Batten (George), Paul Angelis (Ringo/Chief Blue Meanie), Dick Emery (Lord Mayor/Nowhere Man/Max), Lance Percival (Old Fred)

p, Al Brodax; d, George Dunning; w, Lee Minoff, Al Brodax, Erich Segal, Jack Mendelsohn (based on a story by Minoff, from the song by John Lennon and Paul McCartney); ph, John Williams (DeLuxe Color); ed, Brian J. Bishop; art d, Heinz Edelmann; fx, Charles Jenkins; anim, Jack Stokes, Robert Balser

A zesty, satisfying celebration of animation, fantasy, love, and the Beatles that pleases the eyes as much as the ears. YELLOW SUBMARINE tells the glorious tale of a make-believe world inhabited by Blue Meanies, a wicked little bunch who suck the color out of people and bop them on the heads with apples. The Beatles and Old Fred are called in to stop the Blue Meanies' rage. The singing heroes hop in their yellow submarine and sail the seas—of green, of science, of time, of monsters, and, best of all, of holes—until they finally reach Pepperland and straighten out the villains by overpowering them with love, love, love. The animation is superb, filled with exciting and unexpected transformations that are thoughtfully complemented by the music. The Fab Four themselves appear in the live-action coda. This was the first animated feature made in Britain in 14 years; no wonder everyone got a hand in it. Director Dunning contributed the memorable "Lucy" section himself. Erich Segal, who wrote the fast-food romance *Love Story*, had a hand in the script.

YENTL

1983 134m c Musical ★★★
Ladbroke/Barwood (U.S.) PG

Barbra Streisand (*Yentl*), Mandy Patinkin (*Avigdor*), Amy Irving (*Hadass*), Nehemiah Persoff (*Papa*), Steven Hill (*Reb Alter Vishkower*), Allan Corduner (*Shimmele*), Ruth Goring (*Esther Rachel*), David De Keyser (*Rabbi Zalman*), Bernard Spear (*Tailor*), Doreen Mantle (*Mrs. Shaemen*)

p, Barbra Streisand, Rusty Lemorande; d, Barbra Streisand; w, Barbra Streisand, Jack Rosenthal (based on the short story "Yentl, the Yeshiva Boy" by Isaac Bashevis Singer); ph, David Watkin (Technicolor); ed, Terry Rawlings; m, Michel Legrand; prod d, Roy Walker; art d, Leslie Tomkins; fx, Alan Whibley; chor, Gillian Lynne; cos, Judy Moorcroft

AAN Best Supporting Actress: Amy Irving; AA Best Song Score: Michel Legrand, Alan Bergman, Marilyn Bergman; AAN Best Song: "Papa, Can You Hear Me?"; Michel Legrand (Music), Alan Bergman (Lyrics), Marilyn Bergman (Lyrics); AAN Best Song: "The Way He Makes Me Feel"; Michel Legrand, Alan Bergman (Lyrics), Marilyn Bergman (Lyrics); AAN Best Art Direction-Set Decoration: Roy Walker, Leslie Tomkins, Tessa Davies

Isaac Bashevis Singer's beautiful short story "Yentl, the Yeshiva Boy" is turned into a musical ego trip in Barbra Streisand's directorial debut. Set in Eastern Europe in 1904, the story concerns the fortunes of Yentl (Streisand), a girl who wants to study the Torah. Strict Jewish law prohibits such knowledge for women, but Yentl won't give in to community pressure, so, after the death of her father, she disguises herself as a young man and leaves home, hoping to be accepted into a yeshiva. In this guise, she falls in love with fellow student Avigdor (Mandy Patinkin), who takes a liking to young Yentl, but never realizes that his friend is really a woman. When Avigdor's engagement to Hadass (Amy Irving) breaks off because her parents disapprove of him, Avigdor asks Yentl to marry Hadass in his stead. Can the deception continue?

Streisand has undertaken an extremely ambitious project to mark her directorial debut and, while far from perfect, the superstar performer shows undeniable promise. The production values are topflight but Streisand lacks visual skill and relies on the musical numbers to link episodes and detail character motivation. In the opening sequences these songs, all sung by Streisand and structured as musical soliloquies, work quite well but they later become repetitious and intrusive—important characters are tossed aside to make room for her to belt out another tune. In all fairness, however, Streisand is actually quite credible in her role and she elicits beautifully shaded performances from a large cast, particularly Patinkin and Irving. Streisand owned the movie rights to Singer's story for 14 years and finally acquired the clout to bring the project

to life after many years of trying. Singer, however, was appalled by the film.

YESTERDAY, TODAY, AND TOMORROW DVD
(IERI, OGGI E DOMANI)
1963 119m c Comedy/Drama ★★★
C.C. Champion/Concordia (Italy/France)

Sophia Loren (*Adelina/Anna/Mara*), Marcello Mastroianni (*Carmine/Renzo/Augusto Rusconi*), Aldo Giuffre (*Pasquale Nardella*), Agostino Salvietti (*Lawyer Verace*), Lino Mattera (*Amadeo Scapece*), Tecla Scarano (*Bianchina Verace*), Silvia Monelli (*Elvira Nardella*), Carlo Croccolo (*Auctioneer*), Pasquale Cennamo (*Police Captian*), Armando Trovajoli (*Other Man*)

p, Carlo Ponti; d, Vittorio De Sica; w, Eduardo De Filippo, Isabella Quarantotti, Cesare Zavattini, Billa Billa Zanuso (based on the story "Troppo Ricca" by Alberto Moravia); ph, Giuseppe Rotunno (Techniscope, Technicolor); ed, Adriana Novelli; m, Armando Trovajoli; art d, Ezio Frigerio; chor, Jacques Ruet; cos, Piero Tosi, Christian Dior, Annamode, Jean Barthet

AA Best Foreign Language Film

This Italian sex trilogy teams up two of that country's biggest stars, Sophia Loren and Marcello Mastroianni, with director Vittorio De Sica. The first and most interesting episode, "Adelina," features Loren as the title Neopolitan who is in trouble with the law and Mastroianni as her husband who discovers a legal loophole: pregnant women cannot be jailed until six months after the child's birth. Adelina duly gets pregnant, and pregnant again, and so on until her mate can no longer take it. "Anna" casts Loren as the Milanese wife of an industrialist who drops her lover (Mastroianni) after he nearly wrecks her beloved sports car. Lastly, in "Mara," the eponymous Roman prostitute (Loren) resists the temptation to seduce a young seminarian (Giovanni Ridolfi) who has fallen in love with her and even takes a one-week vow of chastity herself, much to the frustration of her most devoted client (Mastroianni). Although YESTERDAY, TODAY AND TOMORROW won a Best Foreign-Language Film Academy Award, it's hardly representative of the best work of its stars, director (UMBERTO D, THE BICYCLE THIEF, SHOESHINE), or screenwriters (Cesare Zavattini, De Sica's frequent collaborator, contributes "Anna" and "Mara"). It is, however, an enjoyable romp, buoyed by the professionalism of all concerned.

YI YI DVD
2000 173m c Drama ★★★★
Pony Canyon/Atom Films and Theater/1+2 Seisaku Iinkai (Taiwan/Japan/Hong Kong)

Wu Nienjen (*NJ Jian*), Issey Ogata (*Mr. Ota*), Elaine Jin (*Min-Min*), Kelly Lee (*Ting-Ting*), Jonathan Chang (*Yang-Yang*), Chen Xisheng (*A-Di*), Ke Suyun (*Sherry Chang-Breitner*), Michael Tao (*Da-Da*), Tang Ruyun (*Grandma*), Xiao Sushen (*Xiao Yan*)

p, Kawai Shinya, Tsukeda Naoko; d, Edward Yang; ph, Yang Weihan; ed, Chen Bowen; m, Peng Kaili; prod d, Peng Kaili

Taiwanese director Edward Yang's portrait of a modern-day Taipei family builds so gradually you probably won't realize it's a near-masterpiece until that last, heart-tugging fade-out.

A chance encounter with an old flame precipitates a crisis of faith in an emotionally remote middle-aged businessman: faith in his marriage, his job, and the conviction that he's made the right choices. While attending his brother-in-law's wedding banquet, NJ Jian (Wu Nienjen) runs into Sherry (Ke Suyun), a girl he once loved but abandoned, and the source of his deepest regret. What if he *hadn't* stood her up that night? Through a series of circumstances, NJ gets a chance to find out. When his mother-in-law (Tang Ruyun) suffers a stroke and slips into a coma, NJ's wife Min-Min (Elaine Jin) confesses her own deep unhappiness and decamps to a temple retreat. Meanwhile, NJ's boss sends him to Japan to woo a computer-game developer (Issey Ogata) while engaging a Chinese company to knock off his software. NJ has serious reservations about such dishonorable treatment of an honorable man but agrees to go and arranges to meet Sherry in Tokyo.

From the doubled title and character names to the way cinematographer Yang Weihan captures the actors during their most introspective moments, Yang's film is structured around reflections, and it's fascinating to watch how the lives of NJ's children echo their father's. Teenage daughter Ting-Ting (Kelly Lee) is having her first lessons in love, guilt, and heartache, while eight-year-old Yang-Yang (Jonathan Chang) is starting to realize that nothing about life really makes much sense. At nearly three hours, this exquisitely crafted film moves slowly but is never dull, and while elegant medium and long shots predominate, it's both warm and intimate. The camera's distance from the action allows Yang to take it all in—life, death, and the whole confusing mess in between.

YOJIMBO

DVD

1961　110m　bw　Action　★★★★½
Toho/Kurosawa　(Japan)

Toshiro Mifune (Sanjuro Kuwabatake), Eijiro Tono (Gonji the Sake Seller), Seizaburo Kawazu (Seibei), Isuzu Yamada (Orin), Hiroshi Tachikawa (Yoichiro), Kyu Sazanka (Ushitora), Daisuke Kato (Inokichi), Tatsuya Nakadai (Unosuke), Kamatari Fujiwara (Tazaemon), Takashi Shimura (Tokuemon)

d, Akira Kurosawa; w, Akira Kurosawa, Ryuzo Kikushima, Hideo Oguni; ph, Kazuo Miyagawa (Tohoscope); m, Masaru Sato; art d, Yoshiro Muraki; cos, Yoshiro Muraki

AAN Best Costume Design (B/W): Yoshiro Muraki

Akira Kurosawa's masterly black comedy/samurai film YOJIMBO stars Toshiro Mifune in a career-defining role (which he would reprise in Kurosawa's SANJURO) as a mercenary *ronin* (a masterless samurai) caught between two rival gangs vying for control of a small town in 1860 Japan. With Mifune's tongue-in-cheek performance and the wildly stylized battle scenes featuring mallet and pistol-wielding samurai, YOJIMBO may just be the first post-modern samurai film. Kurosawa draws on the traditions of American Westerns (such as SHANE and HIGH NOON), showing a lone stranger coming to the rescue as dust blows across the village's empty main street and the frightened citizens peer out from behind shutters; only in this town, a dog calmly trots through the street carrying a severed hand in its mouth, and the stranger is a cynical killer. This mocking attitude and subversive style would, in turn, beget the Spaghetti Western, with its indestructible antiheroes and outrageous violence, when Sergio Leone remade YOJIMBO as A FISTFUL OF DOLLARS (1964) (it was also remade-uncredited-by Walter Hill as LAST MAN STANDING in 1996).

The explosive outbursts of violence in YOJIMBO are superbly choreographed, with Kurosawa's customary use of a telephoto lens creating a hallucinatory feeling as an unending stream of swordsmen come pouring out of every corner of the widescreen frame and the tiny solitary figure of Sanjuro is invariably trapped between them. Hitching his shoulders, fingering his beard stubble, chewing on a toothpick, and scratching his head, Mifune brilliantly communicates his character's personality through purely physical means. The few times he does speak, he delivers lines such as "Get two coffins... no,

maybe three" with consummate cool, culminating with the final scene when he calmly surveys the carnage, puts his sword back in his belt, and blithely remarks "Now it will be quiet in this town," then struts out of the village.

YOU CAN COUNT ON ME

DVD

2000　110m　c　Drama　★★★½
Hart Sharp Entertainment/Shooting Gallery/　　R
Cappa Productions　(U.S.)

Laura Linney (Sammy), Mark Ruffalo (Terry), Matthew Broderick (Brian), Rory Culkin (Rudy), Jon Tenney (Bob), J. Smith-Cameron (Mabel), Gaby Hoffmann (Sheila), Amy Ryan (Mrs. Prescott), Michael Countryman (Mr. Prescott), Adam LeFevre (Sheriff Darryl)

p, John N. Hart, Jeffrey Sharp, Larry Meistrich, Barbara De Fina; d, Kenneth Lonergan; w, Kenneth Lonergan; ph, Stephen Kazmierski; ed, Anne McCabe; m, Lesley Barber; prod d, Michael Shaw; art d, Shawn Carroll; cos, Melissa Toth

AAN Best Actress: Laura Linney; *AAN Best Original Screenplay:* Kenneth Lonergan

This beautifully acted, minutely observed story about a brother and sister whose lives have taken very different paths was a *succes d'estime* at Sundance 2000 before garnering Laura Linney an Academy Award nomination for Best Actress.

Sammy Prescott (Linney) and her brother, Terry (Mark Ruffalo), were children when they were orphaned by a car accident. As adults, they've drifted into diametrically different lives but remain linked by a powerful emotional bond. Sammy, the single mother of eight-year-old Rudy (Rory Culkin), has stayed in the tiny, upstate New York town where she and Terry were born. She's had the same job for seven years, attends church regularly, and lives in her late parents' house. Terry, by contrast, has spent years drifting across the country, scraping by on odd jobs and even doing some jail time. When Terry comes to visit after a two-year absence, it's to borrow money; apparently he's left behind a pregnant, emotionally fragile girlfriend (Gaby Hoffmann). Yet Terry prolongs his stay and befriends the sheltered, cautious Rudy, and while Terry and Sammy inevitably get on each other's nerves, in the end there's more holding them together than driving them apart.

Unlike many successful mainstream screenwriters who claim they really want to make more personal films, Lonergan—whose credits include the off-Broadway play *This Is Our Youth* and the sceenplays for ANALYZE THIS and THE ADVENTURES OF ROCKY & BULLWINKLE—actually did it, and his script offers leads Linney and Ruffalo the kind of dramatic opportunities for which most actors would kill. Matthew Broderick also stands out in a supporting role as Sammy's new boss, a petty martinet with whom she has a brief affair.

YOU CAN'T TAKE IT WITH YOU

DVD

1938　126m　bw　Comedy　★★★½
Columbia　(U.S.)

Jean Arthur (Alice Sycamore), Lionel Barrymore (Martin Vanderhof), James Stewart (Tony Kirby), Edward Arnold (Anthony P. Kirby), Mischa Auer (Kolenkhov), Ann Miller (Essie Carmichael), Spring Byington (Penny Sycamore), Samuel S. Hinds (Paul Sycamore), Donald Meek (Poppins), H.B. Warner (Ramsey)

p, Frank Capra; d, Frank Capra; w, Robert Riskin (based on the play by George S. Kaufman and Moss Hart); ph, Joseph Walker; ed, Gene Havlick; m, Dimitri Tiomkin; art d, Stephen Goosson; cos, Bernard Newman, Irene

AA Best Picture; AAN Best Supporting Actress: Spring Byington; *AA Best Director:* Frank Capra; *AAN Best Screenplay:* Robert Riskin; *AAN Best Cinematography:* Joseph Walker; *AAN Best Film Editing:* Gene Havlick; *AAN Best Sound Recording:* John Livadary

Frank Capra took the phenomenally successful (if somewhat overrated) Kaufman-Hart stage play "You Can't Take It with You" and turned it into this well-received (if somewhat overrated) film. Amazingly, it garnered Capra his third Oscar for Best Director, as well as winning the Best Picture Oscar (it was also nominated for Best Supporting Actress [Byington], screenplay, cinematography, editing, and sound recording).

Barrymore is the eccentric patriarch of a clan of frustrated artists who decided 30 years earlier to retire from the rat-race and use his fortune to encourage friends and family to pursue vocations that really interest them. He has taken up painting, which he does badly, but at least he enjoys himself. His daughter, Byington, has taken up writing mystery novels; her husband, Hinds, tinkers with explosives in the basement. Their daughter Miller desires to be a ballet dancer, and her cynical Russian teacher, Auer, follows her around barking instructions. Miller's husband, Dub Taylor, practices playing the xylophone, while Barrymore's friend Meek invents new toys and party masks. The huge house is a frenzy of bizarre activities and in the center of it all is Barrymore's other granddaughter, Arthur, who is pursuing a relatively normal life by working as a receptionist in the offices of Arnold, a powerful businessman who wants to have Barrymore's mansion torn down so he can build on the property. Arthur is in love with Arnold's son Stewart, who fears that his father will never approve of a girl from such a family. The couple decides to arrange a dinner for the families to be held at Arthur's house, and Barrymore commands the clan to tone down their normal antics in order to make a good impression on Arnold and his stuffy wife, Mary Forbes. Unfortunately, there is confusion over the date of the dinner, and Stewart shows up with his parents a day early. The ensuing madness is unrestrained and hilarious.

YOU CAN'T TAKE IT WITH YOU is an entertaining, if saccharine film, packed with enough loony activity to keep the laughs coming from start to finish. Capra assembled a superb cast of players, and all score solidly in their roles, even if their behavior doesn't today seem as anarchic as it must have then. Capra himself, however, doesn't do as well, turning out a stagey product that represents one of his lesser directorial efforts. Perhaps the most amusing character in the film is Meek, a milquetoast of a man who enjoys sneaking up on family members and scaring them with his latest Halloween mask. YOU CAN'T TAKE IT WITH YOU was the first film for veteran actor Barrymore in which the crippling arthritis which would soon put him in a wheelchair became evident. To remedy the situation, Capra had a fake leg cast put on the actor and explained it by having him state that he broke his leg while sliding down a bannister—just the kind of reckless, carefree act one would expect from his character. Character actor Dub Taylor, who has appeared in hundreds of films and television shows, made his acting debut in this film.

YOU ONLY LIVE ONCE
1937 86m bw Crime ★★★★
UA (U.S.)

Sylvia Sidney (*Joan Graham*), Henry Fonda (*Eddie Taylor*), Barton MacLane (*Stephen Whitney*), Jean Dixon (*Bonnie Graham*), William Gargan (*Father Dolan*), Warren Hymer (*Muggsy*), Charles "Chic" Sale (*Ethan*), Margaret Hamilton (*Hester*), Guinn "Big Boy" Williams (*Rogers*), Jerome Cowan (*Dr. Hill*)

p, Walter Wanger; d, Fritz Lang; w, Gene Towne, Graham Baker (based on a story by Towne); ph, Leon Shamroy; ed, Daniel Mandell; m, Alfred Newman; art d, Alexander Toluboff

This brooding and powerful tale, which suggests the story of Bonnie and Clyde, is one of Lang's best efforts in Hollywood. Fonda and Sidney are excellent as the average Depression-era couple made into criminals through circumstances and just plain bad luck. Fonda is not the average law-abiding citizen, however; he has committed many robberies in the past and has served three prison terms. He vows, however, that he is going straight. He gets a job and marries his patient, long-time sweetheart, Sidney. But his past catches up with him when his landlord turns him and his wife out of their room after finding out he has a record. Soon after, his employer at the trucking firm fires him. Then Fonda's hat is found at the scene of a bank holdup where a guard has been killed. He is quickly tried and sentenced to death. Once in prison, Fonda resolves to fight back against a system that offers him no way of surviving. He pretends to be ill and is sent to the prison hospital. There he obtains a gun and uses the prison doctor as a shield to get to the prison yard. The prison chaplain runs to him to say that he has been pardoned but by then Fonda will believe nothing any authority figure tells him. He thinks the chaplain is trying to hoodwink him into surrendering and, when the priest makes the wrong move, Fonda fires, killing the chaplain. He manages to escape the prison and rejoin wife Sidney. Together they drive toward the Canadian border, trying to get out of a country that has persecuted and hounded them. They do manage to reach the border but their joy is only momentary. A sharp-shooting member of the New York State Police raises his rifle and spots the fugitives through his telescopic sights. He fires several rounds which mortally wound both Fonda and Sidney. Sidney is first hit and Fonda takes her in his arms, carrying her the last few steps into Canada, freedom, and death for both of them.

This tragedy is distinguished by Lang's meticulous direction and carefully constructed scenes. Fonda gives a terrific performance as the social pariah fighting for his very existence. Sidney's performance is poignant and beautiful. It was once stated that this superb actress had the face of the Great Depression, and this film is undoubtedly the reason for the sobriquet. There is little mirth in this film loaded with permanent steel-gray skies, and the director's murky, diffused shots suggest a kind of unbearable futility to life. His figures, especially in the prison escape scenes, are hazy, almost transparent, as mist covers the yard and searchlights reach out for Fonda who moves like a ghost before them. Fonda held Lang in high regard as a director but felt that Lang pushed his actors too hard in his quest to attain perfection, causing, in the 46-day shooting schedule of this film, his cast and crew to go without sleep and to physically exhaust themselves to achieve the effect he desired. There is a grimness to this film that is often overwhelming, and though it is technically flawless, it offers little hope to the viewer for satisfaction. Justice is not served here, only irony.

YOU ONLY LIVE TWICE
1967 117m c Adventure/Spy ★★★
Eon (U.K.)

Sean Connery (*James Bond*), Akiko Wakabayashi (*Aki*), Donald Pleasence (*Ernst Stavro Blofeld*), Tetsuro Tamba (*Tiger Tanaka*), Mie Hama (*Kissy Suzuki*), Teru Shimada (*Osato*), Karin Dor (*Helga Brandt*), Lois Maxwell (*Miss Moneypenny*), Desmond Llewelyn ("*Q*"), Charles Gray (*Henderson*)

p, Albert R. Broccoli, Harry Saltzman; d, Lewis Gilbert; w, Roald Dahl, Harold Jack Bloom (based on the novel by Ian Fleming); ph, Freddie Young (Panavision, Technicolor); ed, Peter Hunt; m, John Barry; prod d, Ken Adam; art d, Harry Pottle; fx, John Stears; cos, Eileen Sullivan

Sean Connery's disenchantment with his starring role is unmistakable in this, the fifth Bond spectacular. After turning in an enervated performance here, Connery refused to renew his contract with the profitable 007 franchise, although he was lured back for 1971's DIAMONDS ARE FOREVER and 1983's NEVER SAY NEVER AGAIN.

When both Russian and American spaceships start disappearing, each country suspects the other is responsible, bringing the planet to the brink of WWIII—exactly what SPECTRE agent Ernst Blofeld (Donald Pleasence), the architect of this international crisis, had in mind. Connery is sent to Japan to investigate. Hoping to give himself a little breathing room, he fakes his own death before exploring the volcano that houses Blofeld's own extraordinary spacecraft.

Limited by a Bond formula that demanded, among other things, that 007 be involved with at least three women, screenwriter Roald Dahl produced a contrived scenario that prevents YOU ONLY LIVE TWICE from ever really taking off. The film was also hampered by the last-minute casting of Pleasence to replace Jan Werich. Pleasence experimented with a variety of disfigurements and disabilities—finally settling on a facial scar—but nothing made him look quite sinister enough. Despite its obvious shortcomings and $10 million budget (staggering by mid-1960s standards), YOU ONLY LIVE TWICE was a tremendous commercial success. Nancy Sinatra sings the wistful title song, and the action scenes are enhanced by some of composer John Barry's best work for the Bond series.

YOU WERE NEVER LOVELIER
1942 97m bw Musical   ★★★½
Columbia (U.S.)

Fred Astaire *(Robert Davis)*, Rita Hayworth *(Maria Acuna)*, Adolphe Menjou *(Edwardo Acuna)*, Leslie Brooks *(Cecy Acuna)*, Adele Mara *(Lita Acuna)*, Isobel Elsom *(Mrs. Maria Castro)*, Gus Schilling *(Fernando)*, Barbara Brown *(Mrs. Delfina Acuna)*, Douglas Leavitt *(Juan Castro)*, Catherine Craig *(Julia Acuna)*

p, Louis F. Edelman; d, William A. Seiter; w, Michael Fessier, Ernest Pagano, Delmer Daves (based on the story and screenplay "The Gay Senorita" by Carlos Olivari, Sixto Pondal Rios); ph, Ted Tetzlaff; ed, William Lyon; m, Jerome Kern; art d, Lionel Banks, Rudolph Sternad; chor, Val Raset; cos, Irene

AAN Best Score (Musical): Leigh Harline; *AAN Best Song:* "Dearly Beloved"; Jerome Kern (Music), Johnny Mercer (Lyrics); *AAN Best Sound Recording:* John Livadary

The second and last screen pairing of Fred Astaire and Rita Hayworth features the former as Robert Davis, an American dancer stranded in Buenos Aires. Desperate for funds (he lost his money gambling), he seeks work at the hotel owned by Edwardo Acuna (Adolphe Menjou), where Xavier Cugat and His Orchestra are currently playing. Edwardo, however, has more pressing matters to deal with: his eldest daughter is about to wed and his two youngest want to, but his second child, Maria (Hayworth), is ruining everyone's plans. Edwardo has a strict rule for his children: they must marry in order of their age, and Maria's romantic ideals are so lofty no man can measure up to them. Edwardo has been secretly sending her flowers and love notes, hoping to put a dent in her fantasies. Robert is mistaken for a messenger and sent to deliver the latest bouquet, and Maria thinks he's her mystery man. Edwardo now hires Robert to play Maria's secret admirer, but idealistic Maria has a counter to every argument for marriage. More complications arise when Mrs. Acuna starts wondering who her spouse has been sending *billets-doux*, but all works out happily in the end, of course. Hayworth is a wonderful complement to Astaire in the dance numbers, gliding about the floor with natural ease and looking ravishing. Her singing is dubbed for the film by Nan Wynn.

YOUNG AND INNOCENT
1937 84m bw Crime   ★★★½
G.B./Gaumont (U.K.)

Nova Pilbeam *(Erica Burgoyne)*, Derrick de Marney *(Robert Tisdall)*, Percy Marmont *(Col. Burgoyne)*, Edward Rigby *(Old Will)*, Mary Clare *(Aunt Margaret)*, John Longden *(Inspector Kent)*, George Curzon *(Guy)*, Basil Radford *(Uncle Basil)*, Pamela Carme *(Christine Clay)*, George Merritt *(Sgt. Miller)*

p, Edward Black; d, Alfred Hitchcock; w, Charles Bennett, Alma Reville, Anthony Armstrong, Edwin Greenwood, Gerald Savory (based on the novel *A Schilling for Candles* by Josephine Tey); ph, Bernard Knowles; ed, Charles Frend; m, Louis Levy; art d, Alfred Junge

One of Hitchcock's more charming efforts, this thriller stars the endearing 18-year-old Pilbeam as Erica Burgoyne, the daughter of police constable Col. Burgoyne (Marmount), who is heading an investigation into the strangulation death of an actress whose body has washed ashore, along with the murder weapon—the belt of a raincoat. The prime, and in fact only, suspect is Robert Tisdall (de Marney) who maintains his innocence, despite the fact that everything is against him—he was friendly with the dead woman, he was included in her will, and his raincoat is missing. After giving the suspect a ride to a desolate farmhouse, Erica is faced with the choice of helping Tisdall prove his innocence, despite her fear of the repercussions of her father and his office. Naturally she finds herself falling in love with him, and he with her, and together the young and innocent fugitives must steer clear of the authorities and find the real murderer. While not generally considered one of Hitchcock's finer films, YOUNG AND INNOCENT, because of its simplicity (or innocence, in keeping with the title), is often overlooked, especially in light of the director's other British successes, THE MAN WHO KNEW TOO MUCH, THE 39 STEPS, and THE LADY VANISHES. Although its plot is simply a reworking of THE 39 STEPS without the spy angle, YOUNG AND INNOCENT has a certain delightful charm to it, due entirely to the young Pilbeam, with her glowing Sylvia Sidney-type face. The film also boasts some of Hitchcock's most memorable visual effects, namely a remarkable crane and dolly shot which travels across a grand ballroom and into the face of the murderer with his twitching eye.

YOUNG FRANKENSTEIN
1974 108m bw Comedy/Horror   ★★★★½
Fox (U.S.)   PG

Gene Wilder *(Dr. Frederick Frankenstein)*, Peter Boyle *(Monster)*, Marty Feldman *(Igor)*, Madeline Kahn *(Elizabeth)*, Cloris Leachman *(Frau Blucher)*, Teri Garr *(Inga)*, Kenneth Mars *(Inspector Kemp)*, Gene Hackman *(Blind Hermit)*, Richard Haydn *(Herr Falkstein)*, Liam Dunn *(Mr. Hilltop)*

p, Michael Gruskoff; d, Mel Brooks; w, Gene Wilder, Mel Brooks (based on the characters from the novel *Frankenstein* by Mary Wollstonecraft Shelley); ph, Gerald Hirschfeld; ed, John C. Howard; m, John Morris; art d, Dale Hennesy; fx, Hal Millar, Henry Miller Jr.; cos, Dorothy Jeakins

AAN Best Adapted Screenplay: Gene Wilder, Mel Brooks; *AAN Best Sound:* Richard Portman, Gene Cantamessa

Mel Brooks's follow-up to his enormously successful western spoof, BLAZING SADDLES, tackles the horror genre—specifically, FRANKENSTEIN and THE BRIDE OF FRANKENSTEIN. This time Brooks tones down his broad humor a bit to create a work that is both an affectionate parody and a knowledgeable homage to its cinematic forebears. Gene Wilder plays Dr. Frederick Frankenstein (now defiantly pronounced "FRONK-en-steen"), a med school lecturer who thinks his infamous grandfather's work is "doo-doo." The younger Frankenstein must finally face his destiny when he inherits his grandfather's Transylvanian estate. Once there, he meets Igor (pronounced "eye-gore" and played by the eye-popping Marty Feldman), whose hunchback inexplicably changes from the left side to the right throughout the movie; Inga (Teri Garr), a young woman who will assist the doctor; and Frau Blucher (Cloris Leachman), a hideous old woman who causes horses to whinny in fright at the mere mention of her name. Eventually, Frederick finds his grandfather's private library and a copy of his book, *How I Did It*. Of course, Frederick cannot keep himself from righting his grandfather's wrongs and creating a new monster (Peter Boyle), a big, dumb corpse with a zipper round his neck and an abnormal brain in his head. The laughs come along at a fast and furious rate. One of the film's highlights is the "Puttin' on the Ritz" duet performed by Frederick and the Monster.

YOUNG FRANKENSTEIN is Brooks's most accomplished work, combining his well-known brand of comedy with stylish direction and a uniformly excellent cast. The handsome black-and-white cinematography really captures the look of an early 1930s film. The direction achieves a seemingly impossible task, balancing Brooks's off-the-wall humor within the framework of the style of a classic Universal Frankenstein film. The Frankenstein castle, with its cobwebs, dust, skulls, original lab equipment, and strange goings-on, could easily have been inhabited by Boris Karloff or Bela Lugosi. Wilder, wildly funny here, later attempted his own genre spoof, HAUNTED HONEYMOON, which came nowhere near YOUNG FRANKENSTEIN.

YOUNG LIONS, THE
1958 167m bw War **DVD** ★★★★
Fox (U.S.)

Marlon Brando *(Christian Diestl)*, Montgomery Clift *(Noah Ackerman)*, Dean Martin *(Michael Whiteacre)*, Hope Lange *(Hope Plowman)*, Barbara Rush *(Margaret Freemantle)*, May Britt *(Gretchen Hardenberg)*, Maximilian Schell *(Capt. Hardenberg)*, Dora Doll *(Simone)*, Lee Van Cleef *(Sgt. Rickett)*, Liliane Montevecchi *(Francoise)*

p, Al Lichtman; d, Edward Dmytryk; w, Edward Anhalt (based on the novel by Irwin Shaw); ph, Joseph MacDonald (CinemaScope); ed, Dorothy Spencer; m, Hugo Friedhofer; art d, Lyle Wheeler, Addison Hehr; fx, L.B. Abbott; cos, Adele Balkan, Charles LeMaire

AAN Best B/W Cinematography: Joe MacDonald; *AAN Best Score (Drama or Comedy):* Hugo Friedhofer; *AAN Best Sound:* Carl Faulkner

A somewhat bloated adaptation of Irwin Shaw's sprawling WWII novel, THE YOUNG LIONS follows three soldiers—one German, two American—from the time of their enlistment until the end of the war. Christian Diestl (Marlon Brando) is an idealistic young German who believes in Hitler and becomes a lieutenant in the Wehrmacht. As he makes his way from the occupation of Paris to duty in Rommel's Afrika Korps and then back into Europe, Diestl becomes disillusioned and embittered over Nazi brutality and comes to hate his uniform and everything it represents. Meanwhile, in the U.S., a young Jew, Noah Ackerman (Montgomery Clift), and a popular singer, Michael Whiteacre (Dean Martin), meet as draftees and become fast friends. Although patriotic and dedicated, Ackerman becomes the victim of the Army's anti-Semitism, and is forced to fight his fellow Americans before ever facing the Germans. As the years go by, the fates of Ackerman, Whiteacre, and Diestl grow closer, until they eventually intersect outside a concentration camp. Great departures were made in the script from Shaw's original

story, mostly in the character of the German, Diestl. In the book, he is an unredeemed Nazi to the last, and in the final confrontation kills the Jewish soldier, then is killed by the other American. It was largely Brando who made the German a sympathetic character, arguing that Shaw had written his book in the immediate, angry aftermath of the war, although Shaw later told the actor that he wouldn't have changed his opinions even if he had written the book 10 years later. Although Edward Dmytryk's direction was never more than workmanlike and the film is bit overlong and draggy at times, it does contain a pair of worthwhile performances from Brando and Clift.

YOUNG MAN WITH A HORN
1950 111m bw Musical **DVD** ★★★★
Warner Bros. (U.S.)

Kirk Douglas *(Rick Martin)*, Lauren Bacall *(Amy North)*, Doris Day *(Jo Jordan)*, Hoagy Carmichael *(Smoke Willoughby)*, Juano Hernandez *(Art Hazzard)*, Jerome Cowan *(Phil Morrison)*, Mary Beth Hughes *(Margo Martin)*, Nestor Paiva *(Louis Galba)*, Orley Lindgren *(Rick as a Boy)*, Walter Reed *(Jack Chandler)*

p, Jerry Wald; d, Michael Curtiz; w, Carl Foreman, Edmund H. North (based on the novel by Dorothy Baker); ph, Ted McCord; ed, Alan Crosland Jr.; art d, Edward Carrere; cos, Milo Anderson

Inspired by the tragic life of jazz cornet player Bix Beiderbecke, who died at age 28 in 1931 after a long battle with alcoholism, YOUNG MAN WITH A HORN stars Kirk Douglas as the great musician's fictional counterpart, Rick Martin. While pianist Smoke Willoughby (Hoagy Carmichael) reminisces about the talented trumpeter, Rick's life is shown in flashback, beginning with his youthful fascination with music and Art Hazzard (Juano Hernandez), a black jazz musician. Rick saves up to buy a trumpet and learns to play under Art's tutelage, and by age 20 Rick is performing with a dance band that includes Smoke and torch singer Jo Jordon (Doris Day). He's quickly frustrated by the band's dull sound, however, and gets himself and Smoke fired. The two continue to play in cheap dives, broke but having fun, after which Rick ends up in New York City, where he finds Jo singing with a new band. Rick's brilliant playing soon makes him a sensation, but stardom brings trouble in the form of a rich, neurotic, beautiful, and controlling Amy North (Lauren Bacall), who both marries Rick and ruins him—although the film's ending suggest that he may be on his way back, with the help of the loyal Smoke and Jo. YOUNG MAN WITH A HORN suffers from excessive melodrama, but boasts several fine performances and plenty of enjoyable jazz. Douglas studied under trumpeter Larry Sullivan and learned how to "play" convincingly, although all his trumpeting is dubbed by Harry James, the film's musical adviser (some of Carmichael's piano was dubbed by Buddy Cole, and Jimmy Zito handled Hernandez's playing).

YOUNG MR. LINCOLN
1939 100m bw Biography/Political ★★★★
Fox (U.S.)

Henry Fonda *(Abraham Lincoln)*, Alice Brady *(Abigail Clay)*, Marjorie Weaver *(Mary Todd)*, Arleen Whelan *(Hannah Clay)*, Eddie Collins *(Efe Turner)*, Pauline Moore *(Ann Rutledge)*, Richard Cromwell *(Matt Clay)*, Ward Bond *(John Palmer Cass)*, Donald Meek *(John Felder)*, Spencer Charters *(Judge Herbert A. Bell)*

p, Kenneth MacGowan; d, John Ford; w, Lamar Trotti; ph, Bert Glennon, Arthur Miller; ed, Walter Thompson; m, Alfred Newman; art d, Richard Day, Mark-Lee Kirk; cos, Royer

AAN Best Original Story: Lamar Trotti

The early days of Abraham Lincoln get the full treatment in this film by Ford, who simultaneously makes Lincoln both a man and a myth. The film opens with a poem familiar to most: "If Nancy Hanks/came back as a ghost/seeking news/of what she loved most/She'd ask first/"Where's my son?/What's happened to Abe?/What's he done?"" This sets the tone for the rest of the film, in which these questions are answered, but only in the context of what Lincoln (played by Fonda) had done by 1837. The film's first scene has Fonda making a speech to a convention of the Whig party in 1832, in which the first words from his mouth are "You all know me." In that same year he talks with his girlfriend, Moore, by a riverside, which dissolves to the same riverside five years later, covered with ice. Moore is dead, and her grave is on the same spot where they had spoken. Fonda speaks to it and asks her to help him decide his future. He stands a stick up on the grave, holding it with his finger at the top, and tells her that if it falls on her grave, he'll go into the legal profession. It falls for the law, and soon we see Fonda practicing his first case, a dispute between two men. Fonda listens to both of them, then proposes a compromise. They both refuse that solution, so he threatens them: "Did you fellas ever hear 'bout the time I butted two heads together?'" They acquiesce, and it is with great satisfaction that Fonda collects his fee. Following a fair in which Fonda serves as the pie judge, there is a murder during a fight involving the two sons of an old friend, Brady, and two local roughnecks, of whom the survivor is Bond. Fonda takes on the boys' defense, first by stopping a lynch mob from killing the pair on the spot. He tries to learn from Brady which of her sons killed the victim, but she can't say. Bond indicates that it was the bigger of the two, though neither is especially larger than the other. The judge tries to convince Fonda that he is too inexperienced for a case of this importance and suggests that he let an established lawyer take on the defense, namely Milburn Stone, a noted trial lawyer and Fonda's rival for the hand of socialite Weaver. Fonda refuses, and in court he manages to uses the *Farmer's Almanac* to trap Bond into confessing to the crime himself. Fonda is triumphant, and Stone comes up to him and says he'll never underestimate him again. Fonda walks away in a rainstorm that just happened to come up that day of shooting, and as he is lost in the rain, the film dissolves to a picture of the statue in the Lincoln Memorial.

Ford was originally reluctant to take on the film. He had just made STAGECOACH and was in a position to pick and choose his work. Two plays had recently been on Broadway on the subject of Lincoln's early years, and Ford felt that the subject had been "worked to death." But when he read the Lamar Trotti script he changed his mind. Executive Producer Darryl F. Zanuck wanted rising actor Fonda to take on the title role, but Fonda was too much in awe of the character and he turned it down at first. But after talking to Ford, Fonda changed his mind and took the part, turning in a marvelous performance that simultaneously captures both the awkwardness of the young man and his promise. Unlike most of Ford's films after STAGECOACH, this was very much a studio project, and Ford knew he was going to move on to his next film almost immediately after finishing work on this, leaving control of the editing to others. Since Ford had already argued with Zanuck over the slow, elegiac pace Ford was taking with the material, the director ensured that the film would be cut the way he wanted by editing in the camera, setting up slow dissolves, and destroying the negatives of all the takes except the ones he wanted. Throughout the film Zanuck gave Ford a lot of input about how he thought the film should go, mostly suggesting it move faster. The story of the murder in the film is taken from Trotti's own experiences as a reporter in the South. There he had reported on a murder case in which one of two brothers was accused of killing a man. Their mother refused to tell which of them did it, so both were hanged. A superb motion picture, and one in which Ford's obsession with Americana and the forces and emotions that made this country what it is are plainly in view.

Z

Z
1969 127m c   Political
Reggane   (France/Algeria)
★★★★
M

Yves Montand *(The Deputy)*, Jean-Louis Trintignant *(The Examining Magistrate)*, Irene Papas *(Helene, the Deputy's Wife)*, Jacques Perrin *(Photojournalist)*, Charles Denner *(Manuel)*, Francois Perier *(Public Prosecutor)*, Pierre Dux *(The General)*, Julien Guiomar *(The Colonel)*, Bernard Fresson *(Matt)*, Renato Salvatori *(Yago)*

p, Jacques Perrin, Hamed Rachedi; d, Constantin Costa-Gavras; w, Constantin Costa-Gavras, Jorge Semprun (based on the novel by Vassili Vassilikos); ph, Raoul Coutard (Technicolor); ed, Francoise Bonnot; m, Mikis Theodorakis; art d, Jacques d'Ovidio

AAN Best Picture; AAN Best Director: Constantin Costa-Gavras; AAN Best Adapted Screenplay: Constantin Costa-Gavras, Jorge Semprun; AA Best Film Editing: Francoise Bonnot; AA Best Foreign Language Film

A chilling, manipulative rollercoaster ride. Originally subtitled "The Anatomy of a Political Assassination," this intense political thriller is based on the real-life 1963 killing of Gregorios Lambrakis, a Greek liberal whose extreme popularity and advocacy of peace shook the stability of the government in power. Starring is Yves Montand, who, although referred to only as "the Deputy," is clearly Lambrakis. After his liberal organization, the Friends of Peace, loses a large meeting hall at the last moment, the Deputy is forced to find another venue. He appeals and is given a permit to hold the meeting in a small, 200-seat auditorium, although it is expected to draw over 4,000. During the meeting, the Deputy's supporters are taunted by a violent right-wing faction, while the police "protection" stands by passively. Later, the police do little to protect the Deputy from a truck that speeds by, from which one of the passengers ferociously clubs the Deputy in the head, killing him. In order to give the appearance of an investigation, the general in charge appoints an Examining Magistrate (Jean-Louis Trintignant) who is believed to be a pawn of the government, but soon surprises all by probing deep into a government conspiracy and cover-up.

Rather than appealing only to a politically minded audience, Z found a great deal of enthusiastic support from almost everyone who saw it. At the Cannes Film Festival it received a unanimous vote for the Jury Prize, with Trintignant receiving Best Actor honors. The Academy Awards also responded, with Oscars for Best Foreign Film and Best Editing (it was nominated for Best Picture as well). Z succeeds where so many political pictures have failed because of its concentration on the thriller aspects of the story. Borrowing heavily from American gangster/prison/anti-Facist melodrama conventions, Costa-Gavras' film contains many breathtaking, pressure-filled scenes that help pummel home the sometimes confusing politics. Rather than worrying about which right-wing general did what, the audience becomes wrapped up in whether or not a character will survive a beating, or be run down by a speeding car. Detractors complained that the film commercialized and simplified the Lambrakis incident and politics in general. Costa-Gavras responded: "That's the way it is in Greece. Black and white. No nuances." The glorious Irene Papas plays Montand's wife—she's an actress whose eyes speak volumes even when she's standing stock-still. The score is by Mikis Theodorakis—who was under arrest in Greece at the time. Z was filmed in Algeria, in French.

ZABRISKIE POINT
1970 112m c Drama ★★
MGM/Trianon (U.S.) R

Mark Frechette (Mark), Daria Halprin (Daria), Rod Taylor (Lee Allen), Paul Fix (Cafe Owner), G.D. Spradlin (Lee's Associate), Bill Garaway (Morty), Kathleen Cleaver (Kathleen)

p, Carlo Ponti; d, Michelangelo Antonioni; w, Michelangelo Antonioni, Fred Gardner, Sam Shepard, Tonino Guerra, Clare Peploe (based on a story by Michelangelo Antonioni); ph, Alfio Contini (Panavision, Metrocolor); ed, Franco Arcalli; prod d, Dean Tavoularis; fx, Earl McCoy; cos, Ray Summers

In his super-successful BLOW-UP, Antonioni made an attempt to understand the English youth movement of the 1960s. Here, in his first American film, Antonioni took his search for answers to the States. Unfortunately, with this picture the director falls into two traps: employing endless "anti-Establishment" cliches and saddling himself with the underwhelming talents of Mark Frechette. The picture opens in documentary style, with a meeting of college radicals discussing the meaning of revolution. Mark (Frechette), disgusted with the students' stagnant ideals, declares that he is ready to die—but not of boredom—and walks out. Identified as a cop killer during a campus riot, Mark flees to a nearby airfield, steals a small private plane, flies through Death Valley, and meets Daria (Daria Halprin), a pretty, pot-smoking, meditative secretary. It's not long before they are holding hands at Zabriskie Point, a tourist spot marked by a small plaque explaining that a man named Zabriskie discovered mineral matter there. The psychedelic happenings plod along until the explosive, apocalyptic finale. On the basis of Antonioni's "art-house" following in the U.S., MGM decided to jump on the bandwagon and give the director carte blanche for this film. The result is a critical but relatively accurate portrait of America in the late 1960s, which, however, now seems horribly dated. Antonioni concentrates chiefly on the gaps between student radicals and the establishment, naturalism and plasticity, free-spirited individualism and the restraints of modern life. While Antonioni's visual sense is once again in top form, his "mind-expanding" hippie dialogue, as delivered by his amateur leads, is painful to experience. MGM hoped that a combination of art-house and hippie audiences would help return their $7 million investment. Instead the film was a box-office and critical bomb, surviving today as a nugget of the hippie culture.

ZANDY'S BRIDE
1974 116m c Western ★★½
Warner Bros. (U.S.) PG

Gene Hackman (Zandy Allan), Liv Ullmann (Hannah Lund), Eileen Heckart (Ma Allan), Harry Dean Stanton (Songer), Joe Santos (Frank Gallo), Frank Cady (Pa Allan), Sam Bottoms (Mel Allan), Susan Tyrrell (Maria Cordova), Bob Simpson (Bill Pincus), Fabian Gregory Cordova (Paco)

p, Harvey Matofsky; d, Jan Troell; w, Marc Norman (based on the novel The Stranger by Lillian Bos Ross); ph, Jordan Cronenweth (Panavision, Technicolor); ed, Gordon Scott; m, Michael Franks; prod d, Albert Brenner; cos, Patricia Norris

A beautifully photographed, intimate little western shot in the Big Sur area of California that boasts some fine acting but really nothing more. Hackman stars as an ill-tempered rancher who decides to end his loneliness by sending off for a mail-order bride (Ullmann). When the woman arrives, she is shocked by Hackman's apparent cruelty and heartlessness toward her as he treats her like a slave. She decides to fight back against his tyranny, and the shock of someone standing up to him begins to arouse long-repressed feelings of tenderness and compassion in Hackman. By the end of the film, Hackman accepts Ullmann as an equal and demonstates his ability to be a loving father when she bears his child. Despite the gorgeous scenery and strong performances, ZANDY'S BRIDE is a rather hollow film that suffers from lackadaisical scripting. There is not much plot here (and there is nothing wrong with that if the characters are interesting), and the people and their actions are cliched and predictable. There is no spontaneity; it all seems very cold and mannered. Hackman and Ullmann (with able support from Heckart, Stanton, and Bottoms) struggle to wring some life and meaning out of the material, and it is through their efforts that ZANDY'S BRIDE works at all. Directed by celebrated Swedish director Troell, whose films THE EMIGRANTS and THE NEW LAND were magnificent period pieces about Swedes settling in America during the 19th century, ZANDY'S BRIDE suffered because of his inability to adjust to American production methods. In Sweden, Troell worked with a close-knit crew of 15 and had complete access to the camera—even shooting scenes himself if he chose to. Warner Bros. gave the director a union crew of 100. The sheer number of these strangers intimidated the director and made him extremely nervous and self-conscious. He was also not allowed anywhere near the camera—union rules. In her book Changing, Ullmann relates how Troell and his actors sneaked a camera into the cabin and "rehearsed" while the director photographed the whole scene hand-holding the camera—finally able to feel as if he controlled the set. Problems aside, ZANDY'S BRIDE is beautiful to watch and at times an interesting look into frontier life.

ZAZIE
(ZAZIE DANS LE METRO)
1960 86m c Comedy ★★★½
Nouvelle Editions de Films (France)

Catherine Demongeot (Zazie), Philippe Noiret (Uncle Gabriel), Hubert Deschamps (Turnadot), Antoine Roblot (Charles), Annie Fratellini (Mado), Carla Marlier (Albertine), Vittorio Caprioli (Trouscaillon), Yvonne Clech (Mme. Mouaque), Nicolas Bataille (Fedor), Jacques Dufilho (Gridoux)

p, Louis Malle; d, Louis Malle; w, Louis Malle, Jean-Paul Rappeneau (based on the book Zazie dans le Metro by Raymond Queneau); ph, Henri Raichi (Eastmancolor); ed, Kenout Peltier; m, Andre Pontin, Fiorenzo Carpi; art d, Bernard Evein; fx, Locafilms; cos, Marc Doelnitz

Demongeot is an 11-year-old nuisance who must spend a few days with her uncle, Noiret, in Paris when her mother goes off with a new lover. She wants nothing more than to ride the subway, but a strike by the Paris Metro workers prevents this. The foul-mouthed girl blames it on grownups but decides to have fun in spite of this setback. She takes Noiret on a mad chase through the town, and at one point he's forced to leap from the Eiffel Tower using a balloon as a parachute. Finally she is granted her wish when the strike ends, but Demongeot is tuckered out from all the loony goings on and ends up falling asleep on the way home. This is a great romp with some wonderfully wild moments. A fine early effort from the director of ATLANTIC CITY and MURMUR OF THE HEART.

ZELIG

DVD

1983 79m c/bw Comedy ★★★½
Orion (U.S.) PG

Woody Allen (Leonard Zelig), Mia Farrow (Dr. Eudora Fletcher), John Buckwalter (Dr. Sindell), Marvin Chatinover (Glandular Diagnosis Doctor), Stanley Swerdlow (Mexican Food Doctor), Paul Nevens (Dr. Birsky), Howard Erskine (Hypodermic Doctor), George Hamlin (Experimental Drugs Doctor), Ralph Bell, Richard Whiting

p, Robert Greenhut; d, Woody Allen; w, Woody Allen; ph, Gordon Willis; ed, Susan E. Morse; m, Dick Hyman; prod d, Mel Bourne; art d, Speed Hopkins; fx, Joel Hynek, Stuart Robinson, Richard Greenberg; chor, Danny Daniels; cos, Santo Loquasto; anim, Steven Plastrik

AAN Best Cinematography: Gordon Willis; AAN Best Costume Design: Santo Loquasto

ZELIG employs technical wizardry to create a memorable fable of cultural assimilation. Leonard Zelig (Woody Allen) is a minor celebrity of the Depression era whose abilities as a "human chameleon" astound the world. Desperate to be accepted by others, he goes to extraordinary lengths to become one of the crowd. This desire is realized, formally speaking, through a number of astonishing lab effects by which Allen's character is seamlessly blended with archival footage from the 1930s: he appears waiting in the on-deck circle as Babe Ruth is batting, among a crowd of Nazis cheering Hitler, and growing a beard to become a Hassidic rabbi. His case captures the imagination of America, as well as the attentions of a psychiatrist (Mia Farrow) who falls in love with him.

ZELIG's loving recreation of Depression-era pop culture is accomplished with amazing verisimilitude; the *faux*-documentary sequences are among the best since CITIZEN KANE. Allen's ongoing struggles with psychoanalysis and his Jewish identity—stridently literal preoccupations in most of his work—are for once rendered allegorically. The result is deeply satisfying.

ZERO FOR CONDUCT

(ZERO DE CONDUITE)
1933 44m bw Drama ★★★★★
Gaumont/Franco Film/Aubert (France)

Jean Daste, le nain Delfin, Robert Le Flem, Louis de Gonzague-Frick, Louis Lefebvre, Gilbert Pluchon, Gerard de Bedarieux, Constantin Goldstein-Kehler

p, Jean Vigo; d, Jean Vigo; w, Jean Vigo; ph, Boris Kaufman; ed, Jean Vigo; m, Maurice Jaubert

One of the greatest films about children ever made and a haunting celebration of anarchic rebellion. The first fictional work from writer/director/scenarist/editor Jean Vigo, ZERO FOR CONDUCT was closely based on his own miserable experiences as a boarding-school pupil and influenced other screen classics of disaffected youth including Truffaut's THE 400 BLOWS and Lindsay Anderson's IF....

The plot follows the misadventures of a group of young students as they endure the absurdities and deprivations forced upon them by their petty, authoritarian teachers. After a confrontation in which one of the students repeats before the entire faculty the phrase with which he has rebuffed the sexual advances of a teacher (literally, "shit on you"), matters escalate into a full-scale dormitory rebellion. Beds are overturned and pillows ripped open, resulting in a rain of feathers which falls over everything—one of the most beautiful images in this, or any, film. Finally, locked in an attic for the duration of the school fete, the young rebels

escape onto the roof and rain down a barrage of books, stones, and shoes onto a group of visiting dignitaries, inspiring the rest of the boys to revolt and take over the school.

Vigo, whose promising career was cut short by his death from septicemia at the age of 29, demonstrates a complete mastery of his art in ZERO, only the third film he had made. Despite occasionally poor acting (the cast was largely nonprofessional), several sequences stand out as near-perfect fusions of shot composition, editing, lighting, and dialogue. The "rain of feathers" sequence is justly celebrated; so is the scene in which three of the boys, after being ordered to stand still for two hours at the bedside of a supervisor, plead with him to allow one of them, who has developed a stomach ache, to visit the bathroom. Their repeated pleas become a kind of incantation which takes on a haunting, other-worldly quality.

ZERO was made for a mere 200,000 francs and shot by Vigo's friend Boris Kaufman, younger brother of Soviet "Kino-Eye" pioneer Dziga Vertov. It received a mixed reception on its initial 1933 release and was soon banned for fear it would instigate civil unrest. Rereleased in 1945, it has since been accepted as a landmark of world cinema.

ZIEGFELD FOLLIES

1945 110m c Musical ★★★★
MGM (U.S.)

William Powell (The Great Ziegfeld), Fred Astaire, Lucille Ball, Judy Garland, Lena Horne, Esther Williams, Red Skelton, Gene Kelly, Fanny Brice, Edward Arnold

p, Arthur Freed; d, Vincente Minnelli, George Sidney, Charles Walters, Roy Del Ruth, Lemuel Ayers; w, E.Y. Harburg, Jack McGowan, Guy Bolton, Frank Sullivan, John Murray Anderson, Lemuel Ayers, Don Loper, Kay Thompson, Roger Edens, Hugh Martin, Ralph Blane, William Noble, Wilkie Mahoney, Cal Howard, Erik Charell, Max Liebman, Bill Schorr, Harry Crane, Lou Holtz, Eddie Cantor, Allen Boretz, Edgar Allan Woolf, Philip Rapp, Al Lewis, Joseph Schrank, Robert Alton, Eugene Loring, Robert Lewis, Charles Walters, James O'Hanlon, David Freedman, Joseph Erons, Irving Brecher, Samson Raphaelson, Everett Freeman, Devery Freeman; ph, George Folsey, Charles Rosher, William Ferrari (Technicolor); ed, Albert Akst; art d, Cedric Gibbons, Jack Martin Smith, Merrill Pye, Lemuel Ayers; chor, Robert Alton; cos, Florence Bunin, Irene, Helen Rose

On his deathbed, a delirious Florenz Ziegfeld reportedly cried out stage directions ("Ready for the last finale! Great! The show looks good! The show looks good!") continually. ZIEGFELD FOLLIES takes its cue from there, and the film opens up with Ziegfeld (William Powell, reprising his role in THE GREAT ZIEGFELD) up in heaven, dreaming about a new show. A group of puppets (caricatures of some of his original Follies stars) entertain him, followed by Fred Astaire, Lucille Ball, and Cyd Charisse in the first of a whopping 13 musical and comic sequences featuring MGM's top stars (Astaire and Gene Kelly among them, dancing together for the first time in "The Babbitt and the Bromide"). The film was shot by several directors, starting with George Sidney, who was replaced by Vincente Minnelli, while Robert Lewis, Norman Taurog, Charles Walters, Roy Del Ruth, and Lemuel Ayres also lent uncredited hands. With so many big names in the cast, it had to be shot bit by bit, with the actors called off other productions and many writers paged from other projects. The film premiered with 19 sequences, clocking in at 273 minutes, too long for any sensible release, so several segments were cut, including a duet between Mickey Rooney and Judy Garland (who parodies Greer Garson in "A Great Lady Has an Interview") and some comic bits. The film eventually made over $5 million in theaters—deservedly, since ZIEGFELD FOLLIES is a marvel of music and dance as only MGM could do it.

ZIEGFELD GIRL
1941 131m bw Musical
MGM (U.S.)

DVD
★★★½

James Stewart *(Gilbert Young)*, Judy Garland *(Susan Gallagher)*, Hedy Lamarr *(Sandra Kolter)*, Lana Turner *(Sheila Regan)*, Tony Martin *(Frank Merton)*, Jackie Cooper *(Jerry Regan)*, Ian Hunter *(Geoffrey Collis)*, Charles Winninger *(Pop Gallagher)*, Edward Everett Horton *(Noble Sage)*, Paul Kelly *(John Slayton)*

p, Pandro S. Berman; d, Robert Z. Leonard; w, Marguerite Roberts, Sonya Levien (based on a story by William Anthony McGuire); ph, Ray June; ed, Blanche Sewell; m, Herbert Stothart; art d, Cedric Gibbons, Daniel B. Cathcart; chor, Busby Berkeley; cos, Adrian

This MGM extravaganza details the fortunes of Ziegfeld girls Susan Gallagher (Judy Garland), Sandra Kolter (Hedy Lamarr), and Sheila Regan (Lana Turner). Show business trouper Susan quits the vaudeville act run by her father (Charles Winninger) to further her Follies career, and soon falls in love with the brother (Jackie Cooper) of former elevator operator Sheila, another new Ziegfeld girl. Meanwhile, Sheila's head is turned by the glamor of it all, and she begins to hobnob with high society, especially Park Avenue socialite Geoffrey Collis (Ian Hunter). Left behind is truck driver Gilbert Young (James Stewart), who, in the hopes of winning back his wayward love, tries to make extra money as a bootlegger and winds up in prison. Sandra, the third Ziegfeld girl, finds life on the stage more eventful than life with her penniless violinist husband (Philip Dorn)—until she finally comes to her senses and realizes that love means more to her than show business. Eventually, Susan uses her success to renew interest in her father's career, while Sheila botches her life and career, becoming an alcoholic. For all the melodramatic goings on among the principals, the true stars of this entertaining film are, quite fittingly, the lavish, spectacular dance numbers, employing hundreds of Ziegfeld girls in glittering costumes in the best style of both Florenz Ziegfeld and Busby Berkeley.

ZOOLANDER
2001 89m c Comedy
Red Hour Productions/Paramount/Scott Rudin
Productions/Village Roadshow Productions/
VH1/NPV Productions (U.S.)

DVD
★★½
PG-13

Ben Stiller *(Derek Zoolander)*, Owen Wilson *(Hansel)*, Christine Taylor *(Matilda Jeffries)*, Will Ferrell *(Mugatu)*, Milla Jovovich *(Katinka)*, Jerry Stiller *(Maury Ballstein)*, David Duchovny *(J.P. Prewitt)*, Jon Voight *(Larry Zoolander)*, Judah Friedlander *(Scrappy Zoolander)*, Nathan Lee Graham *(Todd)*

p, Stuart Cornfeld, Scott Rudin, Ben Stiller; d, Ben Stiller; w, John Hamburg, Drake Sather, Ben Stiller (from a story by Drake Sather and Ben Stiller); ph, Barry Peterson; ed, Greg Hayden; m, David Arnold; prod d, Robin Standefer; art d, Stephen Alesch; fx, Steve Kirshoff, Alison O'Brien; chor, Joey McKneely; cos, David C. Robinson

THE MANCHURIAN CANDIDATE meets UNZIPPED in Ben Stiller's loopy spoof of New York fashionistas.

The new prime minister of Malaysia (Woodrow Asai) has declared war on sweatshops, so a shadowy cabal of designers whose businesses rely on cheap third-world labor has put a price on his head. Meanwhile, spectacularly stupid male model Zoolander (Stiller) is in the midst of a personal crisis: He's been ridiculed in a *Time* magazine cover story by investigative reporter Matilda Jeffries (Christine Taylor, Stiller's

wife) and has just seen the VH1 Male Model of the Year award given to arch-rival Hansel (Owen Wilson). The shaken Zoolander announces his intention to retire and devote himself to more meaningful pursuits—maybe he'll teach kids to read good. But flamboyant designer Jacopo Mugatu (Will Ferrell), who's been recruited by the evil conspirators of cut-rate chic, has other ideas. The Malaysian prime minister will be in New York City for Fashion Week, so Mugatu entices Zoolander out of retirement to do his runway show. With the help of sinister but gorgeous sidekick Katinka (Milla Jovovich), he kidnaps and brainwashes the brainless himbo into serving as a ruthless killing machine. Can this nefarious plot be foiled before Zoolander's fame becomes infamy?

The movie's attention to detail is unimpeachable, and it's suitably chock-a-block with celebrity cameos, from designer Tommy Hilfiger to sleazy socialite Paris Hilton. But the conceit, originally developed for the 1996 VH1/Vogue Fashion Awards show, isn't really rich enough to fill out a feature-length running time; the film often feels slack and attenuated. How funny you find it will probably depend on whether or not the mere sight of Stiller sucking in his cheeks, widening his eyes, and striking preposterous poses makes you laugh uproariously.

ZORBA THE GREEK
(ZORBA)
1964 142m bw Drama
Fox/Cacoyannis-Rochley (U.S./Greece)

DVD
★★★½

Anthony Quinn *(Alexis Zorba)*, Alan Bates *(Basil)*, Irene Papas *(The Widow)*, Lila Kedrova *(Mme. Hortense)*, George Foundas *(Mavrandoni)*, Eleni Anousaki *(Lola)*, Sotiris Moustakas *(Mimithos)*, Takis Emmanuel *(Manolakas)*, Yorgo Voyagis *(Pavlo)*, Anna Kyriakou *(Soul)*

p, Michael Cacoyannis; d, Michael Cacoyannis; w, Michael Cacoyannis (based on the novel by Nikos Kazantzakis); ph, Walter Lassally; ed, Michael Cacoyannis; m, Mikis Theodorakis; art d, Vassele Fotopoulos; cos, Anna Stavropoulou

AAN Best Picture; AAN Best Actor: Anthony Quinn; AA Best Supporting Actress: Lila Kedrova; AAN Best Director: Michael Cacoyannis; AAN Best Adapted Screenplay: Michael Cacoyannis; AA Best B/W Cinematography: Walter Lassally; AA Best Art Direction-Set Decoration (B/W): Vassilis Fotopoulos

As spritely and exuberant as a tank, but worth a watch. Although Quinn has often played earthy, force-of-nature characters, his title role in ZORBA THE GREEK was a career performance loved by both critics and audiences—so much, in fact, that he's been doing it ever since.

The film opens with Bates, a young English writer, arriving in Greece to collect his thoughts and discover his own identity. When he goes to Crete to work at a lignite mine, an inheritance from his native-Greek father, he is joined by Quinn, a lusty Greek peasant who also wants to work at the mine. The unusual duo move into a hotel run by Kedrova, a tattered French prostitute, former lover to four different admirals, and ex-cabaret dancer. Quinn begins wooing her and encourages Bates to show some attention to Papas, a beautiful widow much desired by the local male population. The mine is in need of some repairs, so the irrepressible Quinn cons a group of monks into letting him remove some lumber from a forest on a nearby mountain. Quinn devises a scheme to transport the lumber to the mine but must first obtain the necessary equipment. When Quinn ventures into the city, Kedrova helps Bates overcome his bashfulness, and the Englishman gathers up the courage to visit Papas. They make love, and rumors begin spreading about the island after Bates is seen leaving the house.

Through several upheavals, ZORBA boils down to the joyful dance that expresses Quinn's surpassingly positive philosophy—life may be painful, but it is beautiful nonetheless.

Quinn brings all his larger-than-life magic to his part—that of a character who is happy, devil-may-care, and zestfully mad. (When ZORBA THE GREEK was adapted into a spirited Broadway musical, "Zorba," for the 1968-1969 season, Quinn was chosen for the title role.) Bates, as the inhibited Englishman, is a fine contrast, never overshadowed by the enormity of Quinn's character as he learns about the forces of life. And both Kedrova and Papas are wonderful.

Despite its loose structure and excessive length, ZORBA THE GREEK has some marvelous moments. The film itself was somewhat revolutionary in its language and irreverent sense of humor, although these elements, controversial in 1964, have since become commonplace.

ZULU

DVD

| 1964 | 135m | c | Historical/War | ★★★★★ |
| Diamond | (U.K.) | | | |

Stanley Baker *(Lt. John Chard)*, Jack Hawkins *(Rev. Otto Witt)*, Ulla Jacobsson *(Margareta Witt)*, James Booth *(Pvt. Henry Hook)*, Michael Caine *(Lt. Gonville Bromhead)*, Nigel Green *(Color Sgt. Bourne)*, Ivor Emmanuel *(Pvt. Owen)*, Paul Daneman *(Sgt. Maxfield)*, Glynn Edwards *(Cpl. Allen)*, Neil McCarthy *(Pvt. Thomas)*

p, Stanley Baker, Cy Endfield; d, Cy Endfield; w, John Prebble, Cy Endfield (based on a story by Prebble); ph, Stephen Dade

(Technirama, Technicolor); ed, John Jympson; m, John Barry; art d, Ernest Archer; cos, Arthur Newman

Set in 1879 in Natal, this magnificently staged, brilliantly acted film tells the story of the heroic defense by overwhelmingly outnumbered British troops of the tiny outpost Rorke's Drift. Having been warned by a pacifist missionary (Jack Hawkins) that a British army contingent has been massacred by Zulu warriors, Lt. John Chard (Stanley Baker, the film's producer) orders his troops to dig in, despite the pleas of Lt. Gonville Bromhead (Michael Caine), the blueblood second-in-command who wants to abandon the post and who feels that he, rather than Chard (an engineer), should be in charge. Rather than fleeing, however, the courageous Brits withstand attack after attack, night and day, from 4,000 Zulus, and eventually triumph through a combination of ingenuity, determination, and luck. This amazing film is devastatingly accurate in its depiction of the Rorke's Drift action, and is superbly directed by Cy Endfield, whose battle scenes are some of the most terrifying ever committed to film. Producer Baker, however, had a difficult time getting his Zulu extras to cooperate on the location shoot in Natal. None had ever seen a motion picture, and he couldn't make the chiefs understand what he wanted to do. Finally, Baker had an old western starring Gene Autry flown in and showed it to the Zulus, who, grasping the fictional game at hand, later cooperated and lent the battle scenes tremendous power. ZULU is dramatically narrated by Richard Burton, who points out that of the 1,344 Victoria Crosses awarded since 1856, 11 were given to the defenders at Rorke's Drift, an all-time record for one engagement.

INDEX OF ACTORS

The index includes the names of all actors and actresses listed in the cast sections of the film reviews. Immediately following each entry are the tiles of all films in which they appeared that are reviewed in this book.

Adzovic, Ljubica
Time of the Gypsies (89)

Aernouts, Kenny
Innocence (00)

Affleck, Ben
Good Will Hunting (97); Armageddon (98);
Shakespeare in Love (98); Dogma (99); Pearl
Harbor (01); Sum of All Fears, The (02); Changing
Lanes (02); Daredevil (03); Gigli (03)

Affleck, Casey
To Die For (95); Good Will Hunting (97); Ocean's
Eleven (01); Ocean's Twelve (04)

Afonso, Yves
Clockmaker, The (73)

Agar, John
Fort Apache (48); Sands of Iwo Jima (49); She
Wore a Yellow Ribbon (49)

Agarwal, Anirudh
Bandit Queen (95)

Agashe, Mohan
Mississippi Masala (92)

Agee, Arthur
Hoop Dreams (94)

Agee, Arthur "Bo"
Hoop Dreams (94)

Agee, Sheila
Hoop Dreams (94)

Aghdashloo, Shohreh
House of Sand and Fog (03)

Agnew, Robert
Gold Diggers of 1933 (33)

Agterberg, Toon
Spetters (80)

Agudelo, Wilmar
Our Lady of the Assassins (00)

Aguglia, Mimi
Outlaw, The (43); Rose Tattoo, The (55)

Aguilar, Rich
Last Movie, The (71)

Agutter, Jenny
Railway Children, The (70); Walkabout (71);
Equus (77); American Werewolf in London,
An (81); Darkman (90)

Ah-Leh Gua
Wedding Banquet, The (93); Eat Drink Man
Woman (94)

Ahdout, Jonathan
House of Sand and Fog (03)

Aherne, Brian
Juarez (39); Titanic (53)

Aherne, Michael
Commitments, The (91)

Ahlstedt, Boerje
Fanny and Alexander (82)

Ahmed, Lalita
Bhaji on the Beach (94)

Ahn, Philip
Back to Bataan (45); Shock Corridor (63)

Ahrens, Thekla
Eternal Mask, The (37)

Aiello, Danny
Once Upon a Time in America (84); Purple Rose of
Cairo, The (85); Moonstruck (87); Do the Right
Thing (89); Jacob's Ladder (90); Hudson
Hawk (91); 2 Days in the Valley (96)

Aikawa, Sho
Eel, The (97)

Aiken, Liam
Henry Fool (98); Stepmom (98); Road to
Perdition (02); Lemony Snicket's A Series of
Unfortunate Events (04)

Aimee, Anouk
La Dolce Vita (60); Lola (61); 8 1/2 (63); Man and
a Woman, A (66)

Aimos, Raymond
Under the Roofs of Paris (30); Port of
Shadows (38)

Aird, Holly
Possession (02)

Aitken, Maria
Fish Called Wanda, A (88)

Ajaye, Franklyn
Car Wash (76)

Ajdini, Florijan
Black Cat, White Cat (98)

Ajibade, Ade-Yemi
Dirty Pretty Things (02)

Akers, Andra
Desert Hearts (85)

Akhtar, Fatemeh Cheragh
Day I Became a Woman, The (00)

Aki, Takejo
Ballad of Narayama, The (83)

Akili, Ali Mohammed El
Wedding in Galilee (87)

Akinnuoye-Agbaje, Adewale
Bourne Identity, The (02)

Akins, Claude
Defiant Ones, The (58); Rio Bravo (59); Inherit the
Wind (60); Comanche Station (60); Killers,
The (64)

Akleh, Nazih
Wedding in Galilee (87)

Al-Amir, Hudhail
Boyz N the Hood (91)

Alaimo, Marc
Hardcore (79)

Alameda, Richard
Old Man and the Sea, The (58)

Alan-Williams, Gregory
In the Line of Fire (93)

Alvin, John
Objective, Burma! (45)

Alzate, Jairo
Our Lady of the Assassins (00)

Amador, Andrew
L.A. Story (91)

Amagula, Nanjiwarra
Last Wave, The (77)

Amagula, Walter
Last Wave, The (77)

Amar, Sonia
Wedding in Galilee (87)

Amarale, Nestor
Three Caballeros, The (45)

Ameche, Don
In Old Chicago (38); Alexander's Ragtime
Band (38); Midnight (39); Story of Alexander
Graham Bell, The (39); Heaven Can Wait (43);
Trading Places (83); Cocoon (85)

Amedee
Forbidden Games (52)

Amedori, John Patrick
Butterfly Effect, The (04)

Amelio, Lucio
Seven Beauties (76)

Amendola, Tony
Mask of Zorro, The (98)

Amer, Nicholas
Draughtsman's Contract, The (82)

Ames, Elsie
Minnie and Moskowitz (71)

Ames, Jean
Male Animal, The (42)

Ames, Joyce
Hello, Dolly! (69)

Ames, Leon
Meet Me in St. Louis (44); Anchors Aweigh (45);
They Were Expendable (45); Postman Always
Rings Twice, The (46); Lady in the Lake (47);
Absent-Minded Professor, The (61);
Testament (83); Peggy Sue Got Married (86)

Amgaabazar, Ikhbayar
Story of the Weeping Camel, The (04)

Amidou
Hideous Kinky (98)

Amidou, Souad
Man and a Woman, A (66)

Amiot, Paul
J'Accuse (38)

Amis, Suzy
Usual Suspects, The (95); Titanic (97)

Amos, John
Coming to America (88)

Amplas, John
Martin (78); Day of the Dead (85)

Amstutz, Roland
Every Man for Himself (80)

Anampio, Munto
King Solomon's Mines (50)

Anaya, Elena
Van Helsing (04)

Anaya, Yano
Christmas Story, A (83)

Anconina, Richard
Police (84)

Andar, David
House of Usher (60)

Andelin, James
Field of Dreams (89)

Anden, Matthew
David and Lisa (62)

Anderberg, Bertil
Hour of the Wolf, The (68)

Andere, Jacqueline
Exterminating Angel, The (62)

Anders, Glenn
Laughter (30); Lady from Shanghai, The (48)

Anders, Luana
Pit and the Pendulum, The (61); Dementia 13 (63);
Easy Rider (69); Last Detail, The (73)

Andersen, Bibi
Law of Desire (87); Kika (93)

Anderson, Anthony
Life (99); Barbershop (02)

Anderson, Beaudine
No Greater Glory (34)

Anderson, Daphne
Beggar's Opera, The (52); Hobson's Choice (54)

Anderson, Dave
Orphans (99)

Anderson, Devon
Thirty-Two Short Films about Glenn Gould (93)

Anderson, Donna
On the Beach (59); Inherit the Wind (60)

Anderson, Eddie "Rochester"
Cabin in the Sky (43); Brewster's Millions (45)

Anderson, Gillian
Princess Mononoke (97); X-Files, The (98); House
of Mirth, The (00)

Anderson, Herbert
Male Animal, The (42)

Anderson, James
Connection, The (62); Take the Money and
Run (69)

Anderson, Jean
Barretts of Wimpole Street, The (56); Waltz of the
Toreadors (62)

Anderson, Jeff
Clerks (94)

Arias, Imanol
Labyrinth of Passion (82); Flower of My Secret, The (95)

Aries, Dominick
In the Cut (03)

Arishima, Ichiro
Chushingura (62)

Ariza, Virgina
Maria Full of Grace (04)

Arizmendi, Yareli
Like Water for Chocolate (92)

Arizono, Yoshiki
Ichi the Killer (01)

Arkell, Marie-Monique
Diary of a Country Priest (50)

Arkin, Adam
Halloween H2O: Twenty Years Later (98); Hitch (05)

Arkin, Alan
Wait Until Dark (67); Catch-22 (70); Hearts of the West (75); Seven-Per-Cent Solution, The (76); Glengarry Glen Ross (92); Grosse Pointe Blank (97)

Arkin, David
I Love You, Alice B. Toklas! (68); M*A*S*H (70); Long Goodbye, The (73); Nashville (75)

Arkins, Robert
Commitments, The (91)

Arledge, John
Daddy Long Legs (31)

Arlen, Richard
Virginian, The (29); Island of Lost Souls (33); Warlock (59)

Arletty
Daybreak (39); Children of Paradise (45)

Arlin, Georg
Cries and Whispers (72)

Arliss, Florence
Disraeli (29); House of Rothschild, The (34)

Arliss, George
Disraeli (29); House of Rothschild, The (34)

Armand, Gisken
Insomnia (98)

Armas, Guillermo
Balseros (04)

Armendariz, Pedro
Fugitive, The (47); Three Godfathers, The (48); Fort Apache (48); From Russia with Love (63); Mask of Zorro, The (98)

Armetta, Henry
Farewell to Arms, A (32); Merry Widow, The (34); Black Cat, The (34)

Armisen, Fred
Anchorman: The Legend of Rob Burgundy (04)

Armstrong, Alun
Duellists, The (77); Millions (04)

Armstrong, Curtis
Risky Business (83); Revenge of the Nerds (84); Ray (04)

Armstrong, Louis
Cabin in the Sky (43); High Society (56); Hello, Dolly! (69)

Armstrong, Peter
Cars That Ate Paris, The (74)

Armstrong, R.G.
Ride the High Country (62); El Dorado (67); Ballad of Cable Hogue, The (70); Great White Hope, The (70); Great Northfield, Minnesota Raid, The (72); Hammett (82); Predator (87)

Armstrong, Robert
Most Dangerous Game, The (32); King Kong (33); Remember Last Night? (35); G-Men (35); Fugitive, The (47); Mighty Joe Young (49)

Armstrong, Todd
Jason and the Argonauts (63)

Armstrong, Xander
Birthday Girl (02)

Armus, Sidney
Thomas Crown Affair, The (68)

Arnatsiaq, Peter Henry
Fast Runner (Atanarjuat), The (01)

Arnatt, John
Whistle Down the Wind (61)

Arnaud, Yvonne
My Uncle (58)

Arnaz, Desi
Bataan (43)

Arnaz Jr., Desi
Wedding, A (78)

Arndt, Denis
Basic Instinct (92)

Arne, Peter
Return of the Pink Panther, The (75); Victor/Victoria (82)

Arness, James
Thing from Another World, The (51); Them! (54)

Arnette, Jeannetta
Boys Don't Cry (99)

Arno, Sig
Palm Beach Story, The (42); Song to Remember, A (45)

Arnold, Edward
Rasputin and the Empress (32); I'm No Angel (33); Remember Last Night? (35); Easy Living (37); You Can't Take It with You (38); Mr. Smith Goes to Washington (39); Meet John Doe (41); Devil and Daniel Webster, The (41); Johnny Eager (42); Ziegfeld Follies (45); Hucksters, The (47); Take Me Out to the Ball Game (49); Annie Get Your Gun (50)

Arnold, Monroe
Alice's Restaurant (69)

Ashmore, Jonathan
Kid for Two Farthings, A (55)

Ashton, John
Beverly Hills Cop (84); Midnight Run (88)

Ashton-Griffiths, Roger
Gangs of New York (02)

Askam, Earl
Flash Gordon (36)

Askew, Desmond
Go (99)

Askew, Luke
Cool Hand Luke (67); Easy Rider (69); Great
Northfield, Minnesota Raid, The (72); Rolling
Thunder (77)

Askin, Leon
Knock on Wood (54); One, Two, Three (61)

Aslan, Gregoire
Our Man in Havana (59); Golden Voyage of
Sinbad, The (73); Return of the Pink Panther,
The (75)

Aslanian, Jacques
Shoot the Piano Player (60)

Asmussen, Troels
Pelle the Conqueror (87)

Asnar, Nathalie
Celine and Julie Go Boating (74)

Asner, Edward
El Dorado (67); Elf (03)

Aspegren, Chuck
Deer Hunter, The (78)

Asquerino, Maria
That Obscure Object of Desire (77)

Assan, Ratna
Papillon (73)

Assante, Armand
Private Benjamin (80); Q&A (90)

Asselin, Philippe
Au Hasard, Balthazar (66)

Assouna, Yahiaoui
Vagabond (85)

Assy, Pierre
Story of a Cheat, The (36)

Astaire, Fred
Flying Down to Rio (33); Gay Divorcee, The (34);
Roberta (35); Top Hat (35); Follow the Fleet (36);
Swing Time (36); Shall We Dance (37); Story of
Vernon and Irene Castle, The (39); Holiday
Inn (42); You Were Never Lovelier (42); Ziegfeld
Follies (45); Easter Parade (48); Barkleys of
Broadway, The (49); Three Little Words (50);
Royal Wedding (51); Band Wagon, The (53); Silk
Stockings (57); Funny Face (57); On the
Beach (59); Towering Inferno, The (74)

Astar, Ben
Five Fingers (52)

Asti, Adriana
Accattone! (61); Before the Revolution (64);
Phantom of Liberty, The (74)

Astin, John
That Touch of Mink (62)

Astin, MacKenzie
Last Days of Disco, The (98)

Astin, Sean
War of the Roses, The (89); Lord of the Rings: The
Fellowship of the Ring, The (01); Lord of the
Rings: The Two Towers, The (02); Lord of the
Rings: The Return of the King, The (03); 50 First
Dates (04)

Astor, Mary
Kennel Murder Case, The (33); Dodsworth (36);
Hurricane, The (37); Prisoner of Zenda, The (37);
Midnight (39); Maltese Falcon, The (41); Across
the Pacific (42); Palm Beach Story, The (42); Meet
Me in St. Louis (44); Kiss before Dying, A (56);
Hush ... Hush, Sweet Charlotte (64)

Astrologo, Pacifico
Shoeshine (46)

Ates, Roscoe
Champ, The (31); Cimarron (31); Freaks (32)

Atherton, Ray
Henry: Portrait of a Serial Killer (89)

Atherton, William
Sugarland Express, The (74); Day of the Locust,
The (75); Looking for Mr. Goodbar (77);
Ghostbusters (84); Die Hard (88); Pelican Brief,
The (93)

Atiko, Robert
Sexy Beast (00)

Atkine, Feodor
Love and Death (75); Le Beau Mariage (82);
Pauline at the Beach (83); Henry & June (90)

Atkins, Dave
Prick Up Your Ears (87)

Atkins, Eileen
Equus (77); Dresser, The (83); Cold Comfort
Farm (95); Gosford Park (01); Vanity Fair (04)

Atkins, Jeffrey
Assault on Precinct 13 (05)

Atkins, Tom
Where's Poppa? (70); Escape from New York (81);
Lethal Weapon (87)

Atkinson, Beverly Hope
UFOria (85)

Atkinson, Dorothy
Topsy-Turvy (99)

Atkinson, Jayne
Free Willy (93)

Atkinson, Rosalind
Pumpkin Eater, The (64)

Atkinson, Rowan
Witches, The (90); Lion King, The (94);
Scooby-Doo (02)

Babu, Mohanraj
Salaam Bombay! (88)

Baca, Patrick
Stand and Deliver (88)

Bacall, Lauren
To Have and Have Not (44); Big Sleep, The (46); Dark Passage (47); Key Largo (48); Young Man with a Horn (50); Written on the Wind (56); Harper (66); Murder on the Orient Express (74); Shootist, The (76); Misery (90); Dogville (03); Birth (04)

Bacall, Michael
Free Willy (93)

Bacarin, Morena
Roger Dodger (02)

Baccala, Donna
Last Movie, The (71)

Bach, Barbara
Spy Who Loved Me, The (77)

Bach, Catherine
Thunderbolt and Lightfoot (74); Hustle (75)

Backer, Brian
Fast Times at Ridgemont High (82)

Backlinie, Susan
Jaws (75)

Backus, Georgia
Force of Evil (48)

Backus, Jim
Bright Victory (51); Rebel without a Cause (55); Man of a Thousand Faces (57)

Baclanova, Olga
Freaks (32)

Bacon, Edmund
My Architect (03)

Bacon, Irving
Meet John Doe (41); Holiday Inn (42); Shadow of a Doubt (43); Glenn Miller Story, The (53); Star Is Born, A (54)

Bacon, Kevin
Diner (82); Planes, Trains, and Automobiles (87); Tremors (90); Few Good Men, A (92); Apollo 13 (95); Wild Things (98); Stir of Echoes, A (99); Mystic River (03); In the Cut (03); Woodsman, The (04)

Bacon, Shelby
Holiday Inn (42)

Bacquier, Gabriel
Manon of the Spring (86)

Bacri, Jean-Pierre
Entre Nous (83); C'est la Vie (90)

Badalucco, Michael
O Brother, Where Art Thou? (00); Man Who Wasn't There, The (01)

Baddeley, Angela
Quartet (49)

Baddeley, Hermione
Brighton Rock (47); Passport to Pimlico (49); Belles of St. Trinian's, The (54); Mary Poppins (64); Secret of Nimh, The (82)

Badel, Alan
This Sporting Life (63); Day of the Jackal, The (73)

Badel, Sarah
Mrs. Dalloway (97)

Bader, Diedrich
Ice Age (02); Napoleon Dynamite (04)

Badham, Mary
To Kill a Mockingbird (62)

Badia, Nuria
Barcelona (94)

Badie, Laurence
Forbidden Games (52); Muriel (63); Soft Skin, The (64)

Badie, Mina
Roger Dodger (02)

Badin, Jean
Three Crowns of the Sailor (83)

Badland, Annette
Angels and Insects (95)

Badu, Erykah
Cider House Rules, The (99)

Baena, Carlos Martinez
El (52)

Baer, Buddy
Quo Vadis (51); Big Sky, The (52)

Baer, Max
Harder They Fall, The (56)

Baer, Parley
Gypsy (62)

Baff, Regina
Paper Chase, The (73)

Baffico, James A.
Dawn of the Dead (79)

Bagdasarian, Ross
Rear Window (54)

Bagdonas, Vladas
Come and See (85)

Baggett, Lynne
D.O.A. (50)

Bagheri, Abdolhossein
Taste of Cherry (97)

Bagley, Tim
Mask, The (94)

Bagneris, Vernel
Pennies from Heaven (81); Down by Law (86)

Bahl, Ellen
Milky Way, The (69); That Obscure Object of Desire (77)

Bai, Akhtari
Music Room, The (58)

Bai Ling
Crow, The (94)

Baier, Richmond
Groove Tube, The (74)

Baier, Sybille
Alice in the Cities (74)

Baigneres, Claude
In Praise of Love (01)

Bail, Chuck
Stunt Man, The (80)

Bailey, Mark
Unbelievable Truth, The (90)

Bailey, Pearl
Carmen Jones (54); Porgy and Bess (59)

Bailey, Raymond
Incredible Shrinking Man, The (57); Vertigo (58)

Bailly, Mireille
Rosetta (99)

Bain, Conrad
I Never Sang for My Father (70); Postcards from the Edge (90)

Bainter, Fay
Make Way for Tomorrow (37); Jezebel (38); Our Town (40); Babes on Broadway (41); Woman of the Year (42); State Fair (45); Secret Life of Walter Mitty, The (47)

Baio, Scott
Bugsy Malone (76); Foxes (80)

Baird, Anthony
Dead of Night (45)

Baird, Harry
Story of a Three Day Pass, The (67)

Bairstow, Scott
Tuck Everlasting (02)

Baisho, Mitsuko
Dreams (90); Eel, The (97)

Bajpai, Manjoj
Bandit Queen (95)

Baka, Miroslaw
Short Film about Killing, A (87)

Bakalyan, Richard
Chinatown (74)

Baker, Becky Ann
Simple Plan, A (98)

Baker, Benny
Up in Arms (44)

Baker, Betsy
Evil Dead, The (83)

Baker, Blanche
Seduction of Joe Tynan, The (79); Sixteen Candles (84)

Baker, Bubba
Monster (03)

Baker, Carroll
Baby Doll (56); Giant (56); How the West Was Won (63); Cheyenne Autumn (64); Star 80 (83)

Baker, Diane
Journey to the Center of the Earth (59); Diary of Anne Frank, The (59); Marnie (64); Silence of the Lambs, The (91); Cable Guy, The (96)

Baker, Don
In the Name of the Father (93)

Baker, Dottie Bee
Rainmaker, The (56)

Baker, Dylan
Planes, Trains, and Automobiles (87); Disclosure (94); Happiness (98); Cell, The (00); Thirteen Days (00); Road to Perdition (02); Changing Lanes (02); Spider-Man 2 (04); Kinsey (04)

Baker, Frank
Hellraiser (87); Secret Garden, The (93)

Baker, George
On Her Majesty's Secret Service (69)

Baker, Hylda
Saturday Night and Sunday Morning (60)

Baker, Jack Thorpe
Life Is Sweet (91)

Baker, Joby
Gidget (59)

Baker, Joe
Dumb & Dumber (94); Pocahontas (95)

Baker, Joe Don
Junior Bonner (72); Walking Tall (73); Charley Varrick (73); Natural, The (84); Living Daylights, The (87); Cape Fear (91); Goldeneye (95); Tomorrow Never Dies (97)

Baker, Kathy
Street Smart (87); Jacknife (89); Edward Scissorhands (90); Jennifer Eight (92); Mad Dog and Glory (93); Cold Mountain (04); 13 Going on 30 (04)

Baker, Kenny
Star Wars (77); Dressed to Kill (80); Empire Strikes Back, The (80); Amadeus (84)

Baker, Lenny
Next Stop, Greenwich Village (76)

Baker, Phil
Gang's All Here, The (43)

Baker, Ray
Silverado (85); Total Recall (90)

Baker, Robert
Out of Time (03)

Baker, Simon
Ring Two, The (05)

Baker, Stanley
Cruel Sea, The (53); Richard III (55); Guns of Navarone, The (61); Zulu (64); Accident (67)

Baker, Tom
Last Movie, The (71); Nicholas and Alexandra (71); Golden Voyage of Sinbad, The (73)

Baker, Tungia
Piano, The (93)

Bakewell, Gary
Backbeat (94)

Bakewell, Joan
Iris (01)

Bakewell, William
All Quiet on the Western Front (30)

Bako, Brigitte
Strange Days (95)

Bakula, Scott
American Beauty (99)

Balaban, Bob
Close Encounters of the Third Kind (77); Girlfriends (78); Absence of Malice (81); Prince of the City (81); Deconstructing Harry (97); Ghost World (01); Majestic, The (01); Mighty Wind, A (03)

Balachov, Vladimir
Ivan the Terrible, Part I (45); Ivan the Terrible, Part II: The Revolt of the Boyars (58)

Balaski, Belinda
Howling, The (81)

Baldaccini, Anna
Every Man for Himself (80)

Balducci, Armenia
Sacco and Vanzetti (71)

Baldwin, Adam
My Bodyguard (80); Full Metal Jacket (87); Cohen and Tate (89)

Baldwin, Alec
Working Girl (88); Beetlejuice (88); Married to the Mob (88); Miami Blues (90); Hunt for Red October, The (90); Glengarry Glen Ross (92); Pearl Harbor (01); Cooler, The (03); Dr. Seuss' The Cat in the Hat (03); Aviator, The (04); SpongeBob Squarepants Movie, The (04)

Baldwin, Bill
Rocky (76)

Baldwin, Daniel
Trees Lounge (96)

Baldwin, Janit
Prime Cut (72)

Baldwin, Judith
Pretty Woman (90)

Baldwin, Stephen
Last Exit to Brooklyn (89); Usual Suspects, The (95)

Baldwin, Walter
Murder, He Says (45)

Baldwin, William
Backdraft (91)

Bale, Christian
Empire of the Sun (87); Little Women (94); Pocahontas (95); Portrait of a Lady, The (96); Velvet Goldmine (98); American Psycho (00); Machinist, The (04)

Balfour, Katharine
Love Story (70)

Balin, Ina
Projectionist, The (70)

Balin, Mireille
Pepe le Moko (37)

Balint, Andras
Colonel Redl (84)

Balint, Eszter
Stranger than Paradise (84)

Balista, Gigi
Stavisky (74)

Balk, Fairuza
Gas Food Lodging (92); American History X (98); Waterboy, The (98); Personal Velocity (02)

Ball, Angeline
Commitments, The (91); General, The (98)

Ball, Lucille
Top Hat (35); Follow the Fleet (36); Stage Door (37); Ziegfeld Follies (45)

Ball, Nicholas
Croupier (99)

Ball, Vincent
Breaker Morant (80); Phar Lap (83)

Ballesteros, Anderson
Our Lady of the Assassins (00)

Ballew, Smith
Red Badge of Courage, The (51)

Ballot, Nadine
Six in Paris (65)

Balpetre, Antoine
Diary of a Country Priest (50)

Balsam, Martin
12 Angry Men (57); Psycho (60); Breakfast at Tiffany's (61); Cape Fear (62); Seven Days in May (64); Thousand Clowns, A (65); Little Big Man (70); Catch-22 (70); Anderson Tapes, The (71); Taking of Pelham One Two Three, The (74); Murder on the Orient Express (74); All the President's Men (76); Cuba (79); Cape Fear (91)

Balsan, Humbert
Lancelot of the Lake (74)

Baltz, Kirk
Reservoir Dogs (92)

Bamattre, Martha
American in Paris, An (51)

Bamber, David
High Hopes (88)

Bambushek, Vyacheslav
Freeze—Die—Come to Life (90)

Bamford, Freda
Ipcress File, The (65)

Bamman, Gerry
Home Alone (90); Lorenzo's Oil (92)

Bana, Eric
Black Hawk Down (01); Hulk (03); Troy (04)

Bancroft, Anne
Miracle Worker, The (62); Pumpkin Eater, The (64); Graduate, The (67); Turning Point, The (77); Elephant Man, The (80); Agnes of God (85); 'Night, Mother (86); 84 Charing Cross Road (87); Torch Song Trilogy (88); Honeymoon in Vegas (92); Great Expectations (98); Antz (98)

Bancroft, George
Mr. Deeds Goes to Town (36); Angels with Dirty Faces (38); Stagecoach (39)

Banderas, Antonio
Labyrinth of Passion (82); Law of Desire (87); Women on the Verge of a Nervous Breakdown (88); Tie Me Up! Tie Me Down! (90); Philadelphia (93); Interview with the Vampire (94); Evita (96); Mask of Zorro, The (98); Spy Kids (01); Frida (02); Spy Kids 2: The Island of Lost Dreams (02); Once Upon a Time in Mexico (03); Shrek 2 (04)

Bando, Kotaro
Gate of Hell (53)

Banerjee, Kanu
Pather Panchali (55); Aparajito (56)

Banerjee, Karuna
Pather Panchali (55); Aparajito (56)

Banerjee, Runki
Pather Panchali (55)

Banerjee, Subir
Pather Panchali (55)

Banerjee, Victor
Home and the World, The (84); Passage to India, A (84)

Banes, Lisa
Marie (85)

Bang, Joy
Play It Again, Sam (72)

Bang-Hansen, Arne
Autumn Sonata (78)

Banionis, Donatas
Solaris (72)

Bankhead, Tallulah
Lifeboat (44)

Banks, Elizabeth
Swept Away (02); Seabiscuit (03)

Banks, Geoffrey
Kes (69)

Banks, Joan
Bright Victory (51)

Banks, Jonathan
48 Hrs. (82); Beverly Hills Cop (84); Dark Blue (03)

Banks, Lenore
Passion Fish (92)

Banks, Leslie
Most Dangerous Game, The (32); Man Who Knew Too Much, The (34); Fire Over England (37); Henry V (44)

Banks, Tyra
Adam Sandler's Eight Crazy Nights (02)

Bannen, Ian
Flight of the Phoenix, The (65); Gorky Park (83); Defence of the Realm (85); Hope and Glory (87); Damage (92); Braveheart (95)

Banner, Jill
President's Analyst, The (67)

Banner, John
Fallen Sparrow, The (43); Juggler, The (53)

Bannister, Monica
Mystery of the Wax Museum, The (33)

Banquells, Rafael
El (52)

Bansagi, Ildiko
Mephisto (81)

Banzhaf III, John
Super Size Me (04)

Baptiste, Thomas
Ipcress File, The (65); Sunday, Bloody Sunday (71)

Baquet, Maurice
Crime of Monsieur Lange, The (36)

Bar, Dietmar
Men... (85)

Bara, Roy
Last Wave, The (77)

Baran, Jack
David Holzman's Diary (68)

Baranski, Christine
Reversal of Fortune (90); Birdcage, The (96); Bulworth (98); Cruel Intentions (99); Dr. Suess' How the Grinch Stole Christmas (00); Chicago (02)

Barash, Olivia
Repo Man (84)

Barbacini, Maurizio
La Traviata (82)

Barbaud, Pierre
Hiroshima Mon Amour (59); Last Year at Marienbad (61)

Barbeau, Adrienne
Escape from New York (81); Creepshow (82); Back to School (86)

Barber, Amanda
Crossover Dreams (85)

Barber, Frances
Sammy and Rosie Get Laid (87)

Barber, Paul
Full Monty, The (97)

Barbi, Vincent
Blob, The (58)

Barbier, George
Smiling Lieutenant, The (31); Merry Widow, The (34); Yankee Doodle Dandy (42); Man Who Came to Dinner, The (42)

Barbieri, Alberto Albani
Umberto D. (52)

Baron, Geraldine
Time After Time (79); Cutter's Way (81)

Baron, Sandy
Targets (68); Out-of-Towners, The (70); Straight
Time (78); Birdy (84); Broadway Danny Rose (84)

Baroni, Paolo
Dark Eyes (87)

Barouh, Pierre
Man and a Woman, A (66)

Barr, Jean-Marc
Hope and Glory (87); Breaking the Waves (96);
Dancer in the Dark (00)

Barr, Jeanne
Long Day's Journey into Night (62)

Barra, Peppe
Pinocchio (02)

Barran, Bob
Time Machine, The (60)

Barranco, Maria
Women on the Verge of a Nervous Breakdown (88);
Tie Me Up! Tie Me Down! (90)

Barrat, Pierre
Rise of Louis XIV, The (66)

Barrat, Robert
Kennel Murder Case, The (33); Fog Over
Frisco (34); Last of the Mohicans, The (36); Trail
of the Lonesome Pine, The (36); Union
Pacific (39); Northwest Passage (40); Adventures of
Mark Twain, The (44); Road to Utopia (45); Road
to Rio (47)

Barrault, Jean-Louis
Children of Paradise (45); La Ronde (50); La Nuit
de Varennes (82)

Barrault, Marie-Christine
My Night at Maud's (69); Cousin, Cousine (75);
Stardust Memories (80)

Barre, Chantal
Human Resources (00)

Barrett, Edith
I Walked with a Zombie (43)

Barrett, Jacinda
Human Stain, The (03); Ladder 49 (04); Bridget
Jones: The Edge of Reason (04)

Barrett, John
Far from the Madding Crowd (67)

Barrett, Laurinda
Wrong Man, The (56)

Barrett, Majel
Westworld (73); Star Trek IV: The Voyage
Home (86)

Barrett, Ray
Don's Party (76)

Barrie, Barbara
Breaking Away (79); Private Benjamin (80); Judy
Berlin (00)

Barrie, Christopher
Lara Croft: Tomb Raider (01)

Barrie, Elaine
Midnight (39)

Barrie, John
Victim (61)

Barrie, Wendy
Private Life of Henry VIII, The (33); Dead
End (37); Hound of the Baskervilles, The (39)

Barrier, Edgar
Journey into Fear (42); Phantom of the Opera (43);
Cornered (45); Cyrano de Bergerac (50)

Barrier, Maurice
Black and White in Color (76); Return of Martin
Guerre, The (82); Life and Nothing But (89)

Barrile, Anthony
Hamburger Hill (87)

Barron, Ray
10 Rillington Place (70)

Barron, Robert V.
Bill & Ted's Excellent Adventure (89)

Barrow, Bernard
Rachel, Rachel (68)

Barrows, Dan
Eating Raoul (82)

Barry, B. Constance
Orphans (87)

Barry, Don "Red"
Only Angels Have Wings (39); I'll Cry
Tomorrow (55); Junior Bonner (72)

Barry, Dorothy
Sweetie (89)

Barry, Gene
War of the Worlds, The (53)

Barry, Michael
Dawn of the Dead (04)

Barry, Raymond J.
Cop (88); Born on the Fourth of July (89); Dead
Man Walking (95); Flubber (97); Deep End,
The (01); Training Day (01)

Barry, Roukietou
Yaaba (89)

Barry, Tony
Coca-Cola Kid, The (85)

Barry, Yane
Man and a Woman, A (66)

Barrymore, Drew
E.T. The Extra-Terrestrial (82); Batman
Forever (95); Everyone Says I Love You (96);
Scream (96); Wedding Singer, The (98); Ever
After (98); Charlie's Angels (00); Donnie
Darko (01); Confessions of a Dangerous Mind (02);
Charlie's Angels: Full Throttle (03); 50 First
Dates (04); Fever Pitch (05)

Barrymore, Ethel
Rasputin and the Empress (32); None but the
Lonely Heart (44); Spiral Staircase, The (46);
Farmer's Daughter, The (47); Portrait of
Jennie (48); Pinky (49)

Beatty, Robert
Odd Man Out (47); Magic Box, The (51); Captain
Horatio Hornblower (51); 2001: A Space
Odyssey (68); Where Eagles Dare (69)

Beatty, Warren
Roman Spring of Mrs. Stone, The (61); Splendor in
the Grass (61); Bonnie and Clyde (67); McCabe
and Mrs. Miller (71); $ (Dollars) (71); Parallax
View, The (74); Shampoo (75); Fortune, The (75);
Heaven Can Wait (78); Reds (81); Ishtar (87); Dick
Tracy (90); Bugsy (91); Bulworth (98)

Beauchamp, Edmond
Le Beau Serge (58)

Beaulieu, Philippine Leroy
Three Men and a Cradle (85)

Beaumont, Hugh
Fallen Sparrow, The (43); Seventh Victim, The (43);
Blue Dahlia, The (46)

Beaumont, Kathryn
Alice in Wonderland (51); Peter Pan (53)

Beaumont, Lucy
Devil-Doll, The (36)

Beaune, Michel
Get Out Your Handkerchiefs (78); Coup de
Torchon (81); Story of Women (88)

Beauvais
Jour de Fete (49)

Beauvais, Robert
Four Hundred Blows, The (59)

Beavers, Louise
Imitation of Life (34); Holiday Inn (42); Mr.
Blandings Builds His Dream House (48)

Beavers, Richard
Easter Parade (48)

Beccaria, Mario
Le Boucher (69)

Beck, John
Pat Garrett and Billy the Kid (73); Sleeper (73);
Rollerball (75)

Beck, Michael
Warriors, The (79)

Beck, Stanley
Lenny (74)

Beck, Thomas
Charlie Chan at the Opera (36)

Beckel, Graham
Paper Chase, The (73); Marie (85); Jennifer
Eight (92); Leaving Las Vegas (95)

Becker, Gerry
Donnie Brasco (97); Spider-Man (02)

Becker, Jacques
Boudu Saved from Drowning (32)

Becker, Jean-Pierre
Very Long Engagement, A (04)

Becker, Marie
My Night at Maud's (69)

Becker, Rolf
Lost Honor of Katharina Blum, The (75)

Beckett, James
Poor Cow (67)

Beckett, Scotty
Love Affair (39); My Favorite Wife (40); Jolson
Story, The (46)

Beckett, Stephen
Enchanted April (91)

Beckinsale, Kate
Cold Comfort Farm (95); Last Days of Disco,
The (98); Pearl Harbor (01); Van Helsing (04);
Aviator, The (04)

Beckley, Tony
Chimes at Midnight (66); Get Carter (71)

Beckman, Henry
Marnie (64); Brood, The (79)

Beckwith, Reginald
Genevieve (53); Horse's Mouth, The (58)

Becourt, Alain
My Uncle (58)

Bedall, Rod
Mona Lisa (86)

Bedard, Irene
Pocahontas (95)

Beddoe, Don
Golden Boy (39); Bachelor and the Bobby-Soxer,
The (47); Enforcer, The (51); Narrow Margin,
The (52); Night of the Hunter, The (55)

Bedelia, Bonnie
They Shoot Horses, Don't They? (69); Lovers and
Other Strangers (70); Heart Like a Wheel (83); Die
Hard (88); Presumed Innocent (90)

Bedella, David
Alexander (04)

Bednarz, Aleksander
Short Film about Killing, A (87)

Bedos, Guy
Pardon Mon Affaire (77)

Bedoya, Alfonso
Treasure of the Sierra Madre, The (48); Black
Rose, The (50)

Bedoya, Jose Luis
Our Lady of the Assassins (00)

Beecher, Janet
Story of Vernon and Irene Castle, The (39); Mark
of Zorro, The (40); Lady Eve, The (41)

Beer, Erica
Deep End (70)

Beerblock, Maurice
Man Escaped, A (56)

Beery Jr., Noah
Of Mice and Men (39); Sergeant York (41); Red
River (48); Jubal (56); 7 Faces of Dr. Lao (64);
Walking Tall (73)

Beery Sr., Noah
Kid from Spain, The (32); She Done Him
Wrong (33)

Beery, Wallace
Min and Bill (30); Big House, The (30); Champ,
The (31); Grand Hotel (32); Dinner at Eight (33);
Treasure Island (34); Viva Villa! (34); Ah,
Wilderness! (35)

Beghe, Jason
Thelma & Louise (91)

Begley, Ed
Boomerang (47); Sorry, Wrong Number (48); Great
Gatsby, The (49); Patterns (56); 12 Angry
Men (57); Odds Against Tomorrow (59); Sweet
Bird of Youth (62)

Begley Jr., Ed
Citizens Band (77); Blue Collar (78); Eating
Raoul (82); Accidental Tourist, The (88); Batman
Forever (95); Mighty Wind, A (03)

Begnez, Michel
Human Resources (00)

Behar, Joy
Manhattan Murder Mystery (93)

Behn, Peter
Bambi (42)

Behr, Jason
Shipping News, The (01); Grudge, The (04)

Bejo, Berenice
Knight's Tale, A (01)

Bekassy, Stephen
Song to Remember, A (45)

Bekir, Adnan
Black Cat, White Cat (98)

Beks, Jakob
Antonia's Line (95)

Bel Geddes, Barbara
I Remember Mama (48); Vertigo (58)

Belack, Doris
Tootsie (82)

Belafonte, Harry
Carmen Jones (54); Odds Against Tomorrow (59);
Uptown Saturday Night (74); Kansas City (96)

Belarani
World of Apu, The (58)

Belasco, Leon
Road to Morocco (42)

Belaubre, Anik
Confidentially Yours (83)

Belbin, George
Eye of the Needle (81)

Beldam, Lia
Shining, The (80)

Belgrave, Richard
Riff-Raff (91)

Belita
Man of the Eiffel Tower, The (49); Silk
Stockings (57)

Belkhadra, Karim
Hate (95)

Bell, Frankie and His Bellboys
Rock Around the Clock (56)

Bell, Ann
Fahrenheit 451 (66)

Bell, Catherine
Bruce Almighty (03)

Bell, Gene
Days of Heaven (78)

Bell, James
Holiday Inn (42); I Walked with a Zombie (43); My
Friend Flicka (43); Thunderhead—Son of
Flicka (45); Spiral Staircase, The (46)

Bell, Jamie
Billy Elliot (00); Nicholas Nickleby (02)

Bell, Jeannie
Mean Streets (73)

Bell, Marshall
Total Recall (90); Starship Troopers (97)

Bell, Nicholas
Shine (96)

Bell, Ralph
Wolfen (81); Zelig (83)

Bell, Rini
Bring It On (00)

Bell, Tom
L-Shaped Room, The (62); Prospero's Books (91)

Bella, Rachael
Ring, The (02)

Bellamy, Bill
Love Jones (97)

Bellamy, Ned
Being John Malkovich (99)

Bellamy, Ralph
Hands Across the Table (35); Awful Truth,
The (37); His Girl Friday (40); Wolf Man,
The (41); Sunrise at Campobello (60); Rosemary's
Baby (68); Trading Places (83); Pretty Woman (90)

Bellaver, Harry
House on 92nd Street, The (45); From Here to
Eternity (53); Love Me or Leave Me (55); Old Man
and the Sea, The (58); Blue Collar (78)

Bellei, Mino
Pinocchio (02)

Bellew, Cosmo Kyrle
Disraeli (29)

Belli, Agostina
Seduction of Mimi, The (72); Seduction of Mimi,
The (72)

Belli, Melvin
Gimme Shelter (70)

Bello, Maria
Auto Focus (02); Cooler, The (03); Assault on
Precinct 13 (05)

Bennett, Constance
Topper (37)

Bennett, Enid
Intermezzo: A Love Story (39)

Bennett, Frank
It Happened Here (63)

Bennett, Jeff Glen
Powerpuff Girls Movie, The (02)

Bennett, Jill
Lust for Life (56); Charge of the Light Brigade,
The (68); For Your Eyes Only (81)

Bennett, Jimmy
Polar Express, The (04)

Bennett, Joan
Disraeli (29); Little Women (33); Man in the Iron
Mask, The (39); Man Hunt (41); Woman in the
Window, The (45); Scarlet Street (45); Macomber
Affair, the (47); Father of the Bride (50);
Suspiria (76)

Bennett, John
Watership Down (78)

Bennett, Jonathan
Mean Girls (04)

Bennett, Joseph
Howards End (92)

Bennett, Leila
Doctor X (32)

Bennett, Marjorie
Monsieur Verdoux (47); Autumn Leaves (56); What
Ever Happened to Baby Jane? (62)

Bennett, Norman
Tender Mercies (83); Trip to Bountiful, The (85)

Bennett, Richard
Arrowsmith (31); Magnificent Ambersons, The (42)

Benny, Jack
Charley's Aunt (41); To Be or Not to Be (42)

Benrubi, Abraham
Twister (96); Open Range (03)

Benson, Anthony
1984 (84)

Benson, Danny
That Sinking Feeling (79)

Benson, George
Private Life of Sherlock Holmes, The (70)

Benson, Jodi
Little Mermaid, The (89); Flubber (97)

Benson, John
Blob, The (58)

Benson, Martin
King and I, The (56); Goldfinger (64); Omen,
The (76)

Benson, Perry
Sid and Nancy (86); Last Resort (00)

Benson, Robby
Beauty and the Beast (91)

Bentahar, Meaachou
Police (84)

Bentley, James
Others, The (01)

Bentley, Wes
American Beauty (99)

Bento, Serge
Les Biches (68); La Femme Infidele (69)

Benton, Mark
Career Girls (97)

Bentt, Michael
Ali (01)

Benureau, Didier
C'est la Vie (90)

Benzali, Daniel
Grey Zone, The (02)

Beradino, John
Seven Thieves (60)

Beran, Ladislav
Hellboy (04)

Beranger, George Andre
Road House (48)

Berard, Jack
Love and Death (75)

Berbert, Marcel
Mississippi Mermaid (69); Green Room, The (78);
Last Metro, The (80)

Beregi Sr., Oscar
Testament of Dr. Mabuse, The (33)

Berenger, Tom
Looking for Mr. Goodbar (77); Big Chill, The (83);
Platoon (86); Someone to Watch Over Me (87);
Training Day (01)

Berens, Harold
Hear My Song (91)

Berenson, Marisa
Death in Venice (71); Cabaret (72); Barry
Lyndon (75)

Beresford, Harry
Doctor X (32); Follow the Fleet (36)

Berezowska, Teresa
Kanal (57)

Berg, Erik J.
Saddest Music in the World, The (04)

Berg, Peter
Midnight Clear, A (92); Last Seduction, The (94);
Cop Land (97); Collateral (04)

Bergen, Candice
Sand Pebbles, The (66); Getting Straight (70);
Carnal Knowledge (71); Wind and the Lion,
The (75); Starting Over (79); Gandhi (82); Sweet
Home Alabama (02)

Bergen, Edgar
I Remember Mama (48)

Bergen, Polly
Cape Fear (62); Cry-Baby (90)

Billeray, Raoul
Betty Blue (86)

Billett, Don
Prince of the City (81)

Billings, Earl
Stakeout (87); One False Move (92); Antwone Fisher (02); American Splendor (03)

Billingsley, Barbara
Airplane! (80)

Billingsley, John
Out of Time (03)

Billingsley, Peter
Christmas Story, A (83)

Bilotta, Bruno
Double Team (97)

Binder, Mike
Minority Report (02)

Bindi, Clara
Black Sunday (60)

Bindon, John
Poor Cow (67); Performance (70)

Bing, Herman
Guardsman, The (31); Black Cat, The (34); Twentieth Century (34); Maytime (37); Dumbo (41)

Bingenheimer, Rodney
End of the Century: The Story of the Ramones (04)

Bingham, David
Pink Floyd—The Wall (82)

Bini, Rene-Marc
Savage Nights (93)

Biniak, Bob
Dogtown and Z-Boys (02)

Binney, Claire
Don's Party (76)

Binns, Col. Percy
It Happened Here (63)

Binns, Edward
12 Angry Men (57); Compulsion (59); Judgment at Nuremberg (61); Fail Safe (64); Patton (70); Night Moves (75); Verdict, The (82)

Binoche, Juliette
Hail, Mary (85); Bad Blood (86); Unbearable Lightness of Being, The (88); Damage (92); Blue (93); English Patient, The (96); Chocolat (00)

Birch, Paul
War of the Worlds, The (53)

Birch, Thora
Patriot Games (92); American Beauty (99); Ghost World (01)

Bird, Brad
Incredibles, The (04)

Bird, Laurie
Two-Lane Blacktop (71)

Bird, Norman
Victim (61); Whistle Down the Wind (61)

Birkett, Janine
Billy Elliot (00)

Birkin, David
Sylvia (03)

Birkin, Jane
Blowup (66)

Birman, Serafima
Ivan the Terrible, Part I (45); Ivan the Terrible, Part II: The Revolt of the Boyars (58)

Birney, Dion
Wedding Banquet, The (93)

Birt, Christopher
Bodyguard, The (92)

Bisacco, Roberto
Stavisky (74)

Bishop, Debbie
Sid and Nancy (86)

Bishop, Julie
Black Cat, The (34); Rhapsody in Blue (45); Sands of Iwo Jima (49); Threat, The (49)

Bishop, Kelly
Unmarried Woman, An (78); Dirty Dancing (87)

Bishop, Pat
Don's Party (76)

Bisley, Steve
Mad Max (79)

Bissell, Whit
Double Life, A (47); He Walked by Night (48); Raw Deal (48); It Should Happen to You (54); Defiant Ones, The (58); Time Machine, The (60); Hud (63); Seven Days in May (64)

Bisset, Jacqueline
Two for the Road (67); Detective, The (68); Bullitt (68); Airport (70); Day for Night (73); Murder on the Orient Express (74); Under the Volcano (84)

Bisso, Patricio
Kiss of the Spider Woman (85)

Bissonnette, Genevieve
Afterglow (97)

Biswas, Chhabi
Music Room, The (58)

Biswas, Seema
Bandit Queen (95)

Bitorajac, Rene
No Man's Land (01)

Bixler, Denise
Evil Dead 2: Dead by Dawn (87)

Bjelvenstam, Bjorn
Secrets of Women (52); Smiles of a Summer Night (55); Wild Strawberries (57)

Bjerrum, Anne Lise Hirsch
Pelle the Conqueror (87)

Bjork
Dancer in the Dark (00)

Bond, Rudy
Streetcar Named Desire, A (51); Run Silent, Run Deep (58); Rose, The (79)

Bond, Samantha
Tomorrow Never Dies (97); World Is Not Enough, The (99); Die Another Day (02)

Bond, Sheila
Spirit of St. Louis, The (57)

Bond, Sudie
Come Back to the 5 & Dime, Jimmy Dean, Jimmy Dean (82); Silkwood (83); Swing Shift (84)

Bond, Ward
Young Mr. Lincoln (39); Long Voyage Home, The (40); Maltese Falcon, The (41); Sergeant York (41); Tobacco Road (41); Gentleman Jim (42); Guy Named Joe, A (44); They Were Expendable (45); It's a Wonderful Life (46); My Darling Clementine (46); Fugitive, The (47); Three Godfathers, The (48); Fort Apache (48); Wagonmaster (50); Quiet Man, The (52); Johnny Guitar (54); Mister Roberts (55); Searchers, The (56); Rio Bravo (59)

Bondarchuk, Nathalie
Solaris (72)

Bondarchuk, Sergei
War and Peace (67)

Bondi, Beulah
Street Scene (31); Arrowsmith (31); Trail of the Lonesome Pine, The (36); Make Way for Tomorrow (37); Mr. Smith Goes to Washington (39); Our Town (40); Remember the Night (40); Watch on the Rhine (43); Back to Bataan (45); Southerner, The (45); It's a Wonderful Life (46); Snake Pit, The (48)

Bonds, De'Aundre
Get on the Bus (96)

Bondy, Luc
Marianne and Juliane (81)

Bonerz, Peter
Medium Cool (69)

Bonet, Lisa
Enemy of the State (98); High Fidelity (00)

Bonetti, Massimo
Night of the Shooting Stars, The (81)

Bonham Carter, Helena
Room with a View, A (85); Howards End (92); Mighty Aphrodite (95); Wings of the Dove, The (97); Merry War, A (97); Fight Club (99); Planet of the Apes (01); Big Fish (03)

Bonheur, Stella
Roman Spring of Mrs. Stone, The (61)

Bonifas, Paul
Charade (63)

Bonifassi, Betty
Triplets of Belleville, The (03)

Bonifassy, Luce
10th Victim, The (65)

Bonilla, Jesus
Kika (93)

Bonnaffe, Jacques
First Name: Carmen (83)

Bonnaire, Jean-Paul
Chorus, The (04)

Bonnaire, Sandrine
A Nos Amours (84); Police (84); Vagabond (85); Monsieur Hire (89)

Bonnard, Arlette
Peppermint Soda (77)

Bonnell, Vivian
Leadbelly (76)

Bonner, Beverly
Basket Case (82)

Bonner, Tony
Man from Snowy River, The (82)

Bonnet, Frank Olivier
Quest for Fire (81)

Bonnevie, Maria
Insomnia (98)

Bonneville, Hugh
Notting Hill (99); Iris (01)

Bonnier, Valerie
Man Who Loved Women, The (77)

Bono, Sonny
Hairspray (88)

Bonora, Cristiano
Italian Job, The (03)

Booke, Sorrell
What's Up, Doc? (72)

Boone Junior, Mark
Trees Lounge (96)

Boone, Mark
Memento (01)

Boone, Pat
Journey to the Center of the Earth (59)

Boone, Richard
Desert Fox, The (51); Robe, The (53); Tall T, The (57); Shootist, The (76)

Boorman, Charley
Emerald Forest, The (85)

Boorman, Katrine
Camille Claudel (88)

Boorman, Lola
Tailor of Panama, The (01)

Booth, Anthony
L-Shaped Room, The (62)

Booth, Connie
And Now for Something Completely Different (71); Monty Python and the Holy Grail (75)

Booth, James
Zulu (64)

Boujenah, Michel
Three Men and a Cradle (85)

Boulane, Ahmed
Hideous Kinky (98)

Boulanger, Daniel
Breathless (59); Shoot the Piano Player (60)

Bould, Samuel
End of the Affair, The (99)

Bouloc, Rene
Lacombe, Lucien (74)

Boulton, Matthew
Sabotage (36); Night Must Fall (37)

Bouquet, Carole
That Obscure Object of Desire (77); For Your Eyes
Only (81)

Bouquet, Michel
La Femme Infidele (69); Mississippi Mermaid (69);
Toto le Heros (91)

Bourdelle, Thomy
Under the Roofs of Paris (30)

Bourgine, Elisabeth
Un Coeur en Hiver (92)

Bourne, Lindsay
Stepfather, The (87)

Bourne, Whitney
Crime without Passion (34)

Bourseiller, Antoine
Cleo from 5 to 7 (62)

Bourseiller, Christophe
Two or Three Things I Know about Her (66)

Bourseiller, Marie
Two or Three Things I Know about Her (66)

Boushel, Joy
Fly, The (86)

Boutefeu, Nathalie
Irma Vep (96)

Boutleroff, Serge
Read My Lips (01)

Bouton, Jim
Long Goodbye, The (73)

Bouy, Stephane
Lacombe, Lucien (74)

Bova, Joe
Pretty Poison (68)

Bova, Raoul
Alien vs. Predator (04)

Bovasso, Julie
Saturday Night Fever (77); Verdict, The (82);
Moonstruck (87)

Bovo, Brunella
Miracle in Milan (51); White Sheik, The (52)

Bow, Clara
Wild Party, The (29)

Bowdon, Dorris
Drums Along the Mohawk (39); Grapes of Wrath,
The (40)

Bowen, Cameron
Mystic River (03)

Bowen, Michael
Valley Girl (83); Less Than Zero (87); Jackie
Brown (97); Magnolia (99)

Bowen, Roger
Petulia (68); M*A*S*H (70)

Bowens, Malick
Out of Africa (85)

Bower, David
Four Weddings and a Funeral (94)

Bower, Tom
River's Edge (87); Georgia (95); Pollock (00)

Bowers, Wendy
Misery (90)

Bowes, Bob
Kes (69)

Bowie, David
Man Who Fell to Earth, The (76); Just a
Gigolo (78); Merry Christmas, Mr. Lawrence (83);
Absolute Beginners (86); Labyrinth (86); Last
Temptation of Christ, The (88)

Bowlegged Lou
House Party (90)

Bowles, Peter
Blowup (66); Charge of the Light Brigade, The (68)

Bowman, Alan
Kurt and Courtney (98)

Bowman, Lee
Love Affair (39); Bataan (43); Cover Girl (44)

Boxer, John
Bridge on the River Kwai, The (57)

Boyar, Sully
King of Marvin Gardens, The (72); Dog Day
Afternoon (75); Car Wash (76)

Boyd, Alexandra
Mr. Holland's Opus (95)

Boyd, Billy
Lord of the Rings: The Fellowship of the Ring,
The (01); Lord of the Rings: The Two Towers,
The (02)

Boyd, Bob
Slacker (91)

Boyd, Guy
Streamers (83); Jagged Edge (85); Lucas (86)

Boyd, Karin
Mephisto (81)

Boyd, Stephen
Ben-Hur (59); Fantastic Voyage (66)

Boyd, William
Hopalong Cassidy (35)

Boyden, Peter
Blow Out (81)

Braga, Sonia
Dona Flor and Her Two Husbands (76); Kiss of the Spider Woman (85)

Brake, David
Two-Lane Blacktop (71)

Brambell, Wilfrid
Hard Day's Night, A (64)

Bramley, William
West Side Story (61); Getting Straight (70)

Branagh, Kenneth
Henry V (89); Dead Again (91); Hamlet (96); Wild Wild West (99); Harry Potter and the Chamber of Secrets (02); Rabbit-Proof Fence (02)

Brancato, Lillo
Bronx Tale, A (93); Crimson Tide (95)

Branch, Pamela
Lilies of the Field (63)

Branche, Derrick
My Beautiful Laundrette (85)

Brancia, Armando
Amarcord (73)

Brand, Neville
D.O.A. (50); Stalag 17 (53); Birdman of Alcatraz (62)

Brand, Phoebe
Vanya on 42nd Street (94)

Brandauer, Klaus Maria
Mephisto (81); Never Say Never Again (83); Colonel Redl (84); Out of Africa (85); Russia House, The (90)

Brandenburg, Larry
Shawshank Redemption, The (94); Santa Clause, The (94)

Brandenburg, Otto
Kingdom, The (94)

Brando, Jocelyn
Big Heat, The (53); Movie Movie (78); Mommie Dearest (81)

Brando, Marlon
Men, The (50); Streetcar Named Desire, A (51); Viva Zapata! (52); Julius Caesar (53); Wild One, The (53); On the Waterfront (54); Teahouse of the August Moon, The (56); Sayonara (57); Young Lions, The (58); One-Eyed Jacks (61); Godfather, The (72); Last Tango in Paris (72); Missouri Breaks, The (76); Superman (78); Apocalypse Now (79); Dry White Season, A (89); Freshman, The (90); Apocalypse Now Redux (01)

Brandon, Henry
Babes in Toyland (34); Vera Cruz (54); Searchers, The (56)

Brandon, Michael
Lovers and Other Strangers (70)

Brandon-Jones, Una
Withnail & I (87)

Brandt, Carlo
Ridicule (96)

Brandt, Hank
Dumb & Dumber (94)

Brannen, Ralph
Eating Raoul (82)

Brantley, Betsy
Washington Square (97)

Bras, Albert
Vampyr (32)

Braschi, Nicoletta
Down by Law (86); Mystery Train (89); Life Is Beautiful (97); Pinocchio (02)

Brascia, John
White Christmas (54); Walking Tall (73)

Brasfield, Rod
Face in the Crowd, A (57)

Brasil, Sabu do
That Man from Rio (64)

Brasselle, Keefe
Place in the Sun, A (51)

Brasseur, Claude
Band of Outsiders (64); Such a Gorgeous Kid Like Me (73); Pardon Mon Affaire (77)

Brasseur, Pierre
Port of Shadows (38); Children of Paradise (45); King of Hearts (66)

Bratt, Benjamin
Demolition Man (93); Clear and Present Danger (94); Catwoman (04); Woodsman, The (04)

Braugher, Andre
Glory (89); Get on the Bus (96); City of Angels (98); Standing in the Sahdows of Motown (02)

Brauner, Asher
Swithcblade Sisters (75)

Brauss, Arthur
$ (Dollars) (71); Goalie's Anxiety at the Penalty Kick, The (71)

Brav, Hal
Story of a Three Day Pass, The (67)

Brave, Sarah
Thuderheart (92)

Bravo, Antonio
Exterminating Angel, The (62)

Bray, Dawson
Under the Volcano (84)

Bray, Robert
Bus Stop (56)

Brazeau, Jay
Double Jeopardy (99)

Brazzi, Rossano
We the Living (42); Three Coins in the Fountain (54); Summertime (55); Story of Esther Costello, The (57); South Pacific (58)

Breakston, George
No Greater Glory (34); Life Begins for Andy Hardy (41)

Suspicion (41); Lassie Come Home (43); Limelight (52)

Bruce, Sally Jane
Night of the Hunter, The (55)

Bruce, Shelbie
Spanglish (04)

Bruce, Virginia
Great Ziegfeld, The (36)

Bruchon, Pascale
Small Change (76)

Brucker, Jane
Dirty Dancing (87)

Bruckschwaiger, Karl
Before Sunrise (95)

Bruhl, Daniel
Good Bye, Lenin! (03)

Bruhn, Erik
Hans Christian Andersen (52)

Brunelle, Thomas
Misery (90); Your Friends & Neighbors (98)

Brunet, Genevieve
French, They Are a Funny Race, The (55); City of Lost Children, The (95)

Brunetti, Argentina
King of the Khyber Rifles (53)

Bruni, Peter
Assault on Precinct 13 (76)

Bruni-Tedeschi, Valeria
C'est la Vie (90)

Brunius, Jacques
L'Age d'Or (30)

Brunjes, David
Lord of the Flies (63)

Bruno, Frank
Driver, The (78)

Bruno, Nando
Open City (45)

Brunoy, Blanchette
La Bete Humaine (38)

Bruns, Philip
Out-of-Towners, The (70); Harry and Tonto (74); Stunt Man, The (80)

Bryan, Dora
Green Man, The (56); Taste of Honey, A (61)

Bryan, Jane
Kid Galahad (37)

Bryans, Kenneth
Shallow Grave (94)

Bryant, Adam
Fisher King, The (91)

Bryant, Joy
Antwone Fisher (02)

Bryant, Kay
Wild Party, The (29)

Bryant, Marie
They Live by Night (49)

Bryant, Michael
Ruling Class, The (72)

Bryant, Nana
Theodora Goes Wild (36); Adventures of Tom Sawyer, The (38); Corsican Brothers, The (41); Hangmen Also Die (43); Brewster's Millions (45); Harvey (50); Bright Victory (51)

Bryant, Sally
Boy Friend, The (71)

Bryar, Paul
Vertigo (58)

Bryceland, Yvonne
World Apart, A (88)

Bryniarski, Andrew
Hudson Hawk (91)

Bryning, John
Rembrandt (36)

Brynner, Yul
King and I, The (56); Anastasia (56); Ten Commandments, The (56); Brothers Karamazov, The (58); Testament of Orpheus, The (59); Magnificent Seven, The (60); Westworld (73)

Brynolfsson, Reine
Les Miserables (98)

Bucatinsky, Dan
Opposite of Sex, The (98)

Bucci, Flavio
Suspiria (76)

Buccola, Gino
Chuck & Buck (00)

Buchanan, Edgar
Talk of the Town, The (42); Cheaper by the Dozen (50); Shane (53); Ride the High Country (62); Benji (74)

Buchanan, Ian
Panic Room (02)

Buchanan, Jack
Monte Carlo (30); Band Wagon, The (53); French, They Are a Funny Race, The (55)

Buchanan, John
Black Stallion, The (79)

Buchanan, Nigel
Quartet (49)

Buchanan, Robert
That Sinking Feeling (79); Gregory's Girl (81)

Buchanan, Stuart
Snow White and the Seven Dwarfs (37)

Bucher, Anita
Ali, Fear Eats the Soul (74)

Buchholz, Horst
Magnificent Seven, The (60); One, Two, Three (61); Life Is Beautiful (97)

Buchma, Amvrosy
Ivan the Terrible, Part I (45); Ivan the Terrible, Part II: The Revolt of the Boyars (58)

Burton, Frederick
Big Trail, The (30)

Burton, John
Black Stallion, The (79)

Burton, Julian
Masque of the Red Death, The (64)

Burton, Kate
Unfaithful (02)

Burton, LeVar
Star Trek: First Contact (96); Star Trek: Insurrection (98); Star Trek: Nemesis (02)

Burton, Norman
Diamonds Are Forever (71); Save the Tiger (73)

Burton, Peter
Wooden Horse, The (50)

Burton, Richard
Robe, The (53); Look Back in Anger (59); Cleopatra (63); Becket (64); Night of the Iguana, The (64); Spy Who Came in from the Cold, The (65); What's New, Pussycat? (65); Who's Afraid of Virginia Woolf? (66); Taming of the Shrew, The (67); Anne of the Thousand Days (69); Where Eagles Dare (69); Equus (77); 1984 (84)

Burton, Robert
Big Heat, The (53); Jubal (56); Tall T, The (57); Compulsion (59)

Burton, Tony
Assault on Precinct 13 (76); Rocky II (79); Shining, The (80)

Burton, Wendell
Sterile Cuckoo, The (69)

Busby, Linda
Love and Death on Long Island (98)

Buscemi, Michael
Trees Lounge (96)

Buscemi, Steve
Parting Glances (86); King of New York (90); Barton Fink (91); Reservoir Dogs (92); Fargo (96); Kansas City (96); Trees Lounge (96); Con Air (97); Big Lebowski, The (98); Armageddon (98); 28 Days (00); Monsters, Inc. (01); Ghost World (01); Grey Zone, The (02); Spy Kids 2: The Island of Lost Dreams (02)

Busch, Ernst
Threepenny Opera, The (31); Kameradschaft (31)

Busey, Gary
Thunderbolt and Lightfoot (74); Star Is Born, A (76); Straight Time (78); Buddy Holly Story, The (78); Lethal Weapon (87); Under Siege (92); Firm, The (93); Lost Highway (97); Fear and Loathing in Las Vegas (98)

Busey, Jake
Contact (97); Starship Troopers (97)

Busfield, Timothy
Revenge of the Nerds (84); Field of Dreams (89)

Bush, Billy "Green"
Five Easy Pieces (70); Alice Doesn't Live Here Anymore (74)

Bush, Grand L.
Colors (88); Demolition Man (93)

Bush, Mike
Whales of August, The (87)

Bushell, Anthony
Disraeli (29); Scarlet Pimpernel, The (35); Night to Remember, A (58)

Busia, Akosua
Color Purple, The (85)

Busquets, Manuel
Our Lady of the Assassins (00)

Bussieres, Pascale
Set Me Free (99)

Bussieres, Raymond
Jonah Who Will Be 25 in the Year 2000 (76)

Busto, Humberto
Amores Perros (00)

Bustric, Sergio
Life Is Beautiful (97)

Butel, Mitchell
Dark City (98)

Butler, Daws
Phantom Tollbooth, The (70)

Butler, Dean
Desert Hearts (85)

Butler, Gerard
Mrs. Brown (97); Andrew Lloyd Webber's The Phantom of the Opera (04)

Butler, Jimmy
No Greater Glory (34)

Butler, Paul
To Sleep with Anger (90); Homicide (91); Glengarry Glen Ross (92)

Butler, Roy
My Dinner with Andre (81)

Butrick, Merritt
Star Trek II: The Wrath of Khan (82); Shy People (88)

Butters, Mike
Saw (04)

Butterworth, Charles
Love Me Tonight (32); Bulldog Drummond Strikes Back (34); This Is the Army (43)

Butterworth, Tyler
Darling (65)

Buttinger, Haymon Maria
Before Sunrise (95)

Buttons, Red
Sayonara (57); They Shoot Horses, Don't They? (69); Movie Movie (78)

Buttram, Pat
Rescuers, The (77)

Buxton, Frank
What's Up, Tiger Lily? (66)

Buxton, Sarah
Less Than Zero (87)

Carol, Martine
Lola Montes (55); French, They Are a Funny Race, The (55); Around the World in 80 Days (56)

Caron, Leslie
American in Paris, An (51); Lili (53); Gigi (58); L-Shaped Room, The (62); Father Goose (64); Is Paris Burning? (66); Man Who Loved Women, The (77); Contract (80); Dangerous Moves (84); Damage (92); Funny Bones (94); Chocolat (00)

Carotenuto, Bruno
Fistful of Dollars, A (64)

Carotenuto, Memmo
Umberto D. (52); Big Deal on Madonna Street (58)

Carpenter, John
Network (76)

Carpenter, Joseph A.
Straight Story, The (99)

Carpentieri, Renato
Caro Diario (94)

Carr, Alexander
Christmas in July (40)

Carr, Charmian
Sound of Music, The (65)

Carr, Cynthia
Last House on the Left, The (72)

Carr, Georgia
Will Success Spoil Rock Hunter? (57); Phar Lap (83)

Carr, Jane
Prime of Miss Jean Brodie, The (69)

Carr, Marian
Kiss Me Deadly (55)

Carr, Patti
American Gigolo (80)

Carr, Walter
Wicker Man, The (73)

Carra, Raffaella
Von Ryan's Express (65)

Carradine, David
Death Race 2000 (75); Bound for Glory (76); Long Riders, The (80); Q (82); Kill Bill: Vol. 1 (03); Kill Bill: Vol. 2 (04)

Carradine, John
Prisoner of Shark Island, The (36); Hurricane, The (37); Captains Courageous (37); Alexander's Ragtime Band (38); Hound of the Baskervilles, The (39); Jesse James (39); Drums Along the Mohawk (39); Stagecoach (39); Grapes of Wrath, The (40); Man Hunt (41); Blood and Sand (41); Western Union (41); Adventures of Mark Twain, The (44); Fallen Angel (45); Johnny Guitar (54); Around the World in 80 Days (56); Man Who Shot Liberty Valance, The (62); Shootist, The (76); Howling, The (81); Secret of Nimh, The (82)

Carradine, Keith
McCabe and Mrs. Miller (71); Thieves Like Us (74); Nashville (75); Welcome to L.A. (76); Duellists, The (77); Pretty Baby (78); Long Riders, The (80); Southern Comfort (81); Choose Me (84); Trouble in Mind (85); Moderns, The (88)

Carradine, Robert
Coming Home (78); Long Riders, The (80); Big Red One, The (80); Revenge of the Nerds (84)

Carrasco, Ada
Like Water for Chocolate (92)

Carrell, Lianella
Gold of Naples (54)

Carrera, Barbara
Never Say Never Again (83)

Carrere, Tia
Wayne's World (92); True Lies (94); Lilo & Stitch (02)

Carrey, Jim
Ace Ventura: Pet Detective (94); Mask, The (94); Dumb & Dumber (94); Batman Forever (95); Cable Guy, The (96); Liar Liar (97); Truman Show, The (98); Man on the Moon (99); Dr. Suess' How the Grinch Stole Christmas (00); Majestic, The (01); Bruce Almighty (03); Eternal Sunshine of the Spotless Mind (04); Lemony Snicket's A Series of Unfortunate Events (04)

Carrey, Leah
Radio Days (87)

Carrez, Florence
Trial of Joan of Arc (62)

Carrier, Corey
After Dark, My Sweet (90)

Carriere, Jean-Claude
Diary of a Chambermaid (64)

Carrillo, Elpidia
Salvador (86); Predator (87)

Carrillo, Leo
Manhattan Melodrama (34); Viva Villa! (34); Phantom of the Opera (43); Fugitive, The (47)

Carroll, Diahann
Carmen Jones (54); Porgy and Bess (59)

Carroll, Helena
Friends of Eddie Coyle, The (73); Dead, The (87)

Carroll, Janet
Risky Business (83)

Carroll, Joan
Bells of St. Mary's, The (45)

Carroll, John
Only Angels Have Wings (39)

Carroll, Leo G.
Wuthering Heights (39); Waterloo Bridge (40); Suspicion (41); House on 92nd Street, The (45); Spellbound (45); Father of the Bride (50); Desert Fox, The (51); Strangers on a Train (51); Bad and the Beautiful, The (52); Snows of Kilimanjaro, The (52); North by Northwest (59)

Carroll, Lisa Hart
Terms of Endearment (83)

Chapman, Kevin
Mystic River (03); Ladder 49 (04)

Chapman, Lonny
Baby Doll (56); Take the Money and Run (69)

Chapman, Marguerite
Seven Year Itch, The (55)

Chapman, Sean
Hellraiser (87)

Chappelle, Dave
Nutty Professor, The (96); Con Air (97); You've
Got Mail (98)

Chappey, Jean-Francois
Six in Paris (65)

Chapuis, Pierre-Alain
First Name: Carmen (83)

Charbonneau, Patricia
Desert Hearts (85)

Charieras, Paul
Chorus, The (04)

Charisse, Cyd
Singin' in the Rain (52); Band Wagon, The (53);
Brigadoon (54); It's Always Fair Weather (55); Silk
Stockings (57)

Charles, Francisco
Sugar Cane Alley (83)

Charles, Grahame
To Sir, with Love (67)

Charles, Jeannette
Naked Gun: From the Files of Police Squad!,
The (88)

Charles, John
Open Water (04)

Charles, Josh
Dead Poets Society (89); S.W.A.T. (03)

Charles, Ray
Blues Brothers, The (80)

Charleson, Ian
Chariots of Fire (81); Gandhi (82); Greystoke: The
Legend of Tarzan, Lord of the Apes (84)

Charlesworth, John
Magic Box, The (51)

Charlia, Georges
Kameradschaft (31)

Charlton, Bob
Harder They Come, The (73)

Charney, Jordan
Network (76)

Charnley, Hetta
Midwinter's Tale, A (95)

Charpin, Fernand
Marius (31); Fanny (32); Cesar (36); Pepe le
Moko (37); Baker's Wife, The (38)

Charters, Spencer
Whoopee (30); 20,000 Years in Sing Sing (33);
Young Mr. Lincoln (39)

Chartier, Eric
Tout Va Bien (72)

Chase, Barrie
Cape Fear (62)

Chase, Chevy
Groove Tube, The (74)

Chase, Daveigh
Donnie Darko (01); Spirited Away (01); Ring,
The (02); Lilo & Stitch (02); Ring Two, The (05)

Chase, Duane
Sound of Music, The (65)

Chase, Ilka
Now, Voyager (42); Big Knife, The (55)

Chase, James
Leather Boys, The (63)

Chase, Stephen
Blob, The (58); Macbeth (71)

Chassing, Martine
Man Who Loved Women, The (77)

Chatinover, Marvin
Zelig (83)

Chatterjee, Abhijit
World of Apu, The (58)

Chatterjee, Bimala
Home and the World, The (84)

Chatterjee, Soumitra
World of Apu, The (58); Charulata (64); Home and
the World, The (84)

Chatterjee, Swatilekha
Home and the World, The (84)

Chatterton, Ruth
Dodsworth (36)

Chatto, Daniel
Little Dorrit (88)

Chatwin, Justin
Taking Lives (04)

Chaumette, Monique
Sunday in the Country, A (84)

Chautard, Emile
Shanghai Express (32)

Chauvin, Ilizabeth
Tout Va Bien (72)

Chaves, Richard
Predator (87)

Chavez, Jose
Adventures of Robinson Crusoe, The (52)

Chaykin, Maury
Dances with Wolves (90); My Cousin Vinny (92);
Devil in a Blue Dress (95); Sweet Hereafter,
The (97); Love and Death on Long Island (98);
Mask of Zorro, The (98); Entrapment (99); Being
Julia (04)

Cheadle, Don
Hamburger Hill (87); Colors (88); Devil in a Blue
Dress (95); Boogie Nights (97); Bulworth (98); Out
of Sight (98); Family Man, The (00); Traffic (00);

Ocean's Eleven (01); Hotel Rwanda (04); Ocean's Twelve (04)

Checchi, Andrea
Thousand Eyes of Dr. Mabuse, The (60); Two Women (60)

Chedid, Mathieu
Triplets of Belleville, The (03)

Cheena, Parvesh
Barbershop (02)

Cheirel, Micheline
Cornered (45)

Chelimsky, Thomas
Charade (63)

Chemin, Henri
Man and a Woman, A (66)

Chen Chao-jung
What Time Is It There? (01)

Chen Dao Ming
Hero (02)

Chen, Joan
Last Emperor, The (87)

Chen Kaige
Emperor and the Assassin, The (99)

Chen, Lester
Eat Drink Man Woman (94)

Chen Man Lei
Fallen Angels (95)

Chen Shiang-chyi
What Time Is It There? (01)

Chen Shu
Shanghai Triad (95)

Chen, Tina
Alice's Restaurant (69); Three Days of the Condor (75)

Chen Xisheng
Yi Yi (00)

Cheng, Kent
Once Upon a Time in China (91)

Cheng, Mark
Peking Opera Blues (86)

Cheng Pei Pei
Crouching Tiger, Hidden Dragon (00)

Cher
Come Back to the 5 & Dime, Jimmy Dean, Jimmy Dean (82); Silkwood (83); Moonstruck (87); Witches of Eastwick, The (87); Tea with Mussolini (99); Stuck on You (03)

Chereau, Patrice
Danton (82); Last of the Mohicans, The (92)

Cherkassov, Nikolai
Alexander Nevsky (38); Ivan the Terrible, Part I (45); Ivan the Terrible, Part II: The Revolt of the Boyars (58)

Cherry, Eugene
Killer of Sheep (78)

Cheshire, Elizabeth
Melvin and Howard (80)

Chesney, Diana
Great Mouse Detective, The (86)

Chester, Colby
Salvador (86)

Chester, Vanessa Lee
Little Princess, A (95); Lost World: Jurassic Park, The (97)

Chestnut, Morris
Boyz N the Hood (91); Ladder 49 (04)

Cheta the Chimp
Tarzan, the Ape Man (32)

Cheung, Jacky
Once Upon a Time in China (91)

Cheung, Leslie
Farewell, My Concubine (93); Temptress Moon (96)

Cheung, Maggie
Supercop (92); Irma Vep (96); In the Mood for Love (00); Hero (02)

Chevalier, Louise
La Femme Infidele (69); This Man Must Die (70)

Chevalier, Maurice
Love Parade, The (29); Smiling Lieutenant, The (31); Love Me Tonight (32); Merry Widow, The (34); Gigi (58)

Chevassu, Robert
Two or Three Things I Know about Her (66)

Chevit, Maurice
Hairdresser's Husband, The (92)

Chevolleau, Richard
Narc (02)

Chew, Helen
Dim Sum: A Little Bit of Heart (85)

Chew, Kim
Dim Sum: A Little Bit of Heart (85)

Chew, Laureen
Chan Is Missing (81); Dim Sum: A Little Bit of Heart (85)

Chey, Katherine Krapum
Killing Fields, The (84)

Chi Dae-han
Oldboy (04)

Chiaki, Minoru
Rashomon (50); Seven Samurai, The (54); Throne of Blood (57); Hidden Fortress, The (58)

Chianese, Dominic
Unfaithful (02)

Chiao, Roy
Indiana Jones and the Temple of Doom (84)

Chiari, Giulio
Bicycle Thief, The (48)

Chiba, Sonny
Kill Bill: Vol. 1 (03)

Coote, Robert
Gunga Din (39); Stairway to Heaven (46); Ghost and Mrs. Muir, The (47); Othello (52); Horse's Mouth, The (58); Theatre of Blood (73)

Cope, Zachary David
Stir of Echoes, A (99)

Copeland, Maurice
Blow Out (81)

Copeman, Michael
Fly, The (86)

Coplen Jr., Elbert
Bachelor Mother (39)

Copleston, Geoffrey
Belly of an Architect, The (87)

Copley, Peter
Victim (61); King and Country (64)

Coppola, Sam
Saturday Night Fever (77)

Coppola, Sofia
Godfather, Part III, The (90)

Corbeil, Yves
Afterglow (97)

Corbella, Vincenzo
La Notte (61)

Corbellini, Vanni
Belly of an Architect, The (87)

Corbet, Brady
Thirteen (03)

Corbett, Ed
Near Dark (87)

Corbett, Glenn
Shenandoah (65); Dead Pigeon on Beethoven Street (72)

Corbett, John
My Big Fat Greek Wedding (02)

Corbin, Barry
Urban Cowboy (80)

Corby, Ellen
Spiral Staircase, The (46); Gunfighter, The (50); Angels in the Outfield (51); Vertigo (58)

Corcoran, Donna
Angels in the Outfield (51)

Corcoran, Kevin
Old Yeller (57); Pollyanna (60); Swiss Family Robinson (60)

Cordell, Cathleen
Gaslight (40)

Cordova, Fabian Gregory
Zandy's Bride (74)

Corduner, Allan
Yentl (83); Topsy-Turvy (99); Grey Zone, The (02); Moonlight Mile (02); De-Lovely (04)

Cordy, Annie
Rider on the Rain (70)

Cordy, Raymond
A Nous la Liberte (31); Million, The (31)

Corey, Irwin
Car Wash (76)

Corey, Isabelle
Bob le Flambeur (55); And God Created Woman (56)

Corey, Jeff
My Friend Flicka (43); Cincinnati Kid, The (65); Seconds (66); In Cold Blood (67); True Grit (69); Butch Cassidy and the Sundance Kid (69); Little Big Man (70); Getting Straight (70)

Corey, Wendell
Search, The (48); Sorry, Wrong Number (48); Rear Window (54); Big Knife, The (55); Rainmaker, The (56)

Cork, Charles
Long Good Friday, The (80)

Corley, Annie
Bridges of Madison County, The (95); Monster (03)

Cormack, Lynn
Dead Ringers (88)

Corman, Roger
Silence of the Lambs, The (91)

Cornelius, Billy
Long Good Friday, The (80)

Cornillac, Clovis
Very Long Engagement, A (04)

Cornthwaite, Robert
Thing from Another World, The (51); War of the Worlds, The (53); Spirit of St. Louis, The (57)

Cornu, Aurora
Claire's Knee (70)

Cornwell, Charlotte
White Hunter, Black Heart (90)

Cornwell, Judy
Two for the Road (67)

Corone, Antoni
Out of Time (03)

Corot, Jacqueline
Rise of Louis XIV, The (66)

Corr, Rachel
Palindromes (05)

Corrado, Gino
Top Hat (35)

Corraface, Georges
Impromptu (90)

Correa, Rubens W.
Man Facing Southeast (86)

Correll, Mady
Monsieur Verdoux (47)

Corri, Adrienne
River, The (51); Doctor Zhivago (65); Clockwork Orange, A (71)

Corri, Nick
Nightmare on Elm Street, A (84)

Corrigan, Kevin
Buffalo '66 (98); Henry Fool (98)

Crampton, Barbara
Re-Animator (85)

Crane, Norma
Tea and Sympathy (56); Fiddler on the Roof (71)

Craney, Heather
Vera Drake (04)

Cranham, Kenneth
Prospero's Books (91)

Cranna, James
Sunshine Boys, The (75)

Cranshaw, Patrick
Best in Show (00)

Cravat, Nick
Run Silent, Run Deep (58)

Cravat, Noel
5,000 Fingers of Dr. T., The (53)

Craven, Frank
Our Town (40); City for Conquest (40)

Craven, Matt
Jacob's Ladder (90); Crimson Tide (95); Paulie (98); Assault on Precinct 13 (05)

Craviotto, Darlene
I Never Promised You a Rose Garden (77)

Crawford, Broderick
Beau Geste (39); All the King's Men (49); Born Yesterday (50); Swindle, The (55); Little Romance, A (79)

Crawford Brown, Pat
Stuck on You (03)

Crawford, David
Dawn of the Dead (79)

Crawford, Joan
Grand Hotel (32); Women, The (39); Mildred Pierce (45); Johnny Guitar (54); Autumn Leaves (56); Story of Esther Costello, The (57); What Ever Happened to Baby Jane? (62)

Crawford, John
Night Moves (75)

Crawford, Michael
Knack ... and How to Get It, The (65); Funny Thing Happened on the Way to the Forum, A (66); How I Won the War (67); Hello, Dolly! (69)

Crawford, Perry
Breakfast Club, The (85)

Creamer, William
Blood Simple (84)

Cregar, Laird
Blood and Sand (41); Charley's Aunt (41); Black Swan, The (42); This Gun for Hire (42); Heaven Can Wait (43); Lodger, The (44)

Crehan, Joseph
Phantom Lady (44)

Creighton, Francis
Barcelona (94)

Creley, Jack
Dr. Strangelove or: How I Learned to Stop Worrying and Love the Bomb (63); Videodrome (83)

Cremer, Bruno
Under the Sand (00)

Cremieux, Henri
Orpheus (49); Testament of Orpheus, The (59)

Crenna, Richard
Sand Pebbles, The (66); Wait Until Dark (67); Star! (68); Body Heat (81); Flamingo Kid, The (84)

Crenshaw, Marshall
La Bamba (87)

Crewes, Laurie
Rain People, The (69)

Crews, Laura Hope
Camille (37)

Crewson, Wendy
Santa Clause, The (94); Santa Clause 2, The (02)

Cribbins, Bernard
Railway Children, The (70); Frenzy (72)

Crider, Missy
Gigli (03)

Crino, Isa
Lilies of the Field (63)

Crisham, Walter
Moulin Rouge (52); Captain's Paradise, The (53)

Crisp, Donald
Mutiny on the Bounty (35); Charge of the Light Brigade, The (36); Life of Emile Zola, The (37); Jezebel (38); Dawn Patrol, The (38); Juarez (39); Wuthering Heights (39); Knute Rockne—All American (40); City for Conquest (40); Dr. Ehrlich's Magic Bullet (40); Sea Hawk, The (40); How Green Was My Valley (41); Lassie Come Home (43); National Velvet (44); Adventures of Mark Twain, The (44); Uninvited, The (44); Man from Laramie, The (55); Pollyanna (60)

Crisp, Quentin
Orlando (93)

Cristal, Linda
Alamo, The (60)

Cristani, Dhia
Ossessione (42)

Cristiano, Giuseppe
I'm Not Scared (03)

Crkalova, Jana
Loves of a Blonde (65)

Croccolo, Carlo
Yesterday, Today, and Tomorrow (63)

Croghan, Declan
My Left Foot (89)

Crohem, Daniel
Paris Belongs to Us (60)

Crombie, Peter
Safe (95); Seven (95)

Cruttwell, Greg
Naked (93); 2 Days in the Valley (96)

Cruz, Alexis
Stargate (94)

Cruz, Brandon
Bad News Bears, The (76)

Cruz, Ernesto Gomez
El Norte (83); Crime of Father Amaro, The (02)

Cruz, Penelope
Belle Epoque (92); Live Flesh (97); All about My
Mother (99); All the Pretty Horses (00); Blow (01);
Vanilla Sky (01); Gothika (03)

Cruz, Raymond
Dead Again (91); Alien Resurrection (97)

Cryer, David
American Gigolo (80)

Cryer, Jon
Pretty in Pink (86); Hot Shots! (91)

Crystal, Billy
Throw Momma from the Train (87); When Harry
Met Sally... (89); City Slickers (91); Hamlet (96);
Deconstructing Harry (97); Analyze This (99);
Monsters, Inc. (01); Analyze That (02)

Cserhalmi, Gyorgy
Mephisto (81); Damnation (88)

Csokas, Marton
xXx (02); Bourne Supremacy, The (04)

Cucciolla, Riccardo
Sacco and Vanzetti (71)

Cucinotta, Maria Grazia
Postman, The (94)

Cuervo, Fernando G.
Law of Desire (87)

Cui Cun-hua
Red Sorghum (87)

Cui Luowen
Story of Qiu Ju, The (92)

Cui Zhigang
Raise the Red Lantern (91)

Cuka, Frances
Scrooge (70)

Culkin, Kieran
She's All That (99); Cider House Rules, The (99);
Dangerous Lives of Altar Boys, The (02); Igby
Goes Down (02)

Culkin, Macaulay
Uncle Buck (89); Home Alone (90)

Culkin, Rory
You Can Count on Me (00); Signs (02); Igby Goes
Down (02)

Cullen, Lorraine
Diary of a Mad Housewife (70)

Cullen, Max
My Brilliant Career (79)

Culley, Frederick
Four Feathers, The (39)

Cullum, John David
Glory (89)

Culp, Robert
Bob & Carol & Ted & Alice (69); Pelican Brief,
The (93)

Culp, Steven
Thirteen Days (00); Emperor's Club, The (02)

Culver, Michael
Passage to India, A (84)

Culver, Roland
Night Train to Munich (40); Life and Death of
Colonel Blimp, The (43); Dead of Night (45); To
Each his Own (46); Magic Box, The (51)

Cumbuka, Ji-Tu
Bound for Glory (76)

Cumbuka, Mwako
One Flew Over the Cuckoo's Nest (75)

Cumming, Alan
Goldeneye (95); Emma (96); Eyes Wide Shut (99);
Spy Kids (01); X2 (03)

Cumming, Dorothy
Applause (29)

Cummings, Constance
American Madness (32); Remember Last
Night? (35); Blithe Spirit (45)

Cummings, Jim
Shrek (01)

Cummings, Quinn
Goodbye Girl, The (77)

Cummings, Robert
Devil and Miss Jones, The (41); Kings Row (42);
Saboteur (42); Dial M for Murder (54); What a
Way to Go! (64)

Cummins, Gregory Scott
Cliffhanger (93)

Cummins, Peggy
Late George Apley, The (47); Gun Crazy (49)

Cunliffe, Freddie
War Zone, The (98)

Cunningham, Anne
This Sporting Life (63)

Cunningham, Bob
I, the Jury (53); Sun Also Rises, The (57)

Cunningham, Cecil
Awful Truth, The (37)

Cunningham, Danny
24-Hour Party People (01)

Cunningham, Jocelyn
Hanging Garden, The (98)

Cunningham, Joe
Kid Galahad (37)

Cunningham, Liam
Little Princess, A (95); Jude (96)

Cunningham, Neil
Draughtsman's Contract, The (82)

Daniels, Anthony
Star Wars (77); Empire Strikes Back, The (80); Return of the Jedi (83); Star Wars Episode III: Revenge of the Sith (05)

Daniels, Bebe
Counsellor-at-Law (33); 42nd Street (33)

Daniels, Ben
Madeline (98)

Daniels, Erin
One Hour Photo (02)

Daniels, Hank
Meet Me in St. Louis (44)

Daniels, Jeff
Terms of Endearment (83); Marie (85); Purple Rose of Cairo, The (85); Something Wild (86); Speed (94); Dumb & Dumber (94); Fly Away Home (96); 101 Dalmatians (96); 2 Days in the Valley (96); Pleasantville (98); Hours, The (02)

Daniels, LeRoy
Band Wagon, The (53)

Daniels, Mark
Candyman (92)

Daniels, Phil
Quadrophenia (79); Chicken Run (00)

Daniels, Walker
Love Story (70)

Daniels, William
Thousand Clowns, A (65); Two for the Road (67); Graduate, The (67); Parallax View, The (74); Black Sunday (77)

Danilova, A.S.
Alexander Nevsky (38)

Danilova, Alexandra
Turning Point, The (77)

Danko, Rich
Last Waltz, The (78)

Danner, Blythe
Hearts of the West (75); Great Santini, The (79); Another Woman (88); Prince of Tides, The (91); X-Files, The (98); Meet the Parents (00); Sylvia (03); Meet the Fockers (04)

Dannio
Don Quixote (33)

Dano, Paul
Emperor's Club, The (02); Taking Lives (04)

Dano, Royal
Red Badge of Courage, The (51); Johnny Guitar (54); Far Country, The (55); Trouble with Harry, The (55); Man of the West (58)

Danova, Cesare
Cleopatra (63); Viva Las Vegas (64); Mean Streets (73); National Lampoon's Animal House (78)

Danquah, Paul
Taste of Honey, A (61)

Danson, Ted
Onion Field, The (79); Body Heat (81); Creepshow (82); 3 Men and a Baby (87); Saving Private Ryan (98)

Dante
Golden Coach, The (52)

Dante, Michael
Seven Thieves (60)

Dante, Peter
Waterboy, The (98)

Dantine, Helmut
Edge of Darkness (43); Passage to Marseille (44); War and Peace (56); Bring Me the Head of Alfredo Garcia (74)

Danton, Ray
I'll Cry Tomorrow (55)

Danziger, Allen
Texas Chainsaw Massacre, The (74)

Danziger, Maia
Last Exit to Brooklyn (89)

Dapkunaite, Ingeborga
Shadow of the Vampire (00)

Dapporto, Carlo
Family, The (87)

Dapporto, Massimo
Family, The (87)

Darbaud, Jean
Trial of Joan of Arc (62)

Darby, Kim
True Grit (69)

Darc, Mireille
Weekend (67); Tall Blond Man with One Black Shoe, The (72)

Darcel, Denise
Vera Cruz (54)

Darcey, Janine
Rififi (54)

Darcy, Georgine
Rear Window (54)

Darden, Severn
President's Analyst, The (67)

Dare, Dorothy
Gold Diggers of 1935 (35)

Darel, Dominique
Andy Warhol's Dracula (74)

Darel, Florence
Stolen Children, The (92)

Darfler, Gene
Faces (68)

Darget, Chantal
Band of Outsiders (64); Masculine Feminine (66)

Dargin, Alan
Adventures of Priscilla, Queen of the Desert, The (94)

Darien, Frank
Cimarron (31); Outlaw, The (43)

Backdraft (91); Hand That Rocks the Cradle, The (92)

de Nicola, Francesco
Shoeshine (46)

De Niro, Robert
Greetings (68); Bang the Drum Slowly (73); Mean Streets (73); Godfather, Part II, The (74); Taxi Driver (76); 1900 (76); New York, New York (77); Deer Hunter, The (78); Raging Bull (80); True Confessions (81); King of Comedy, The (83); Once Upon a Time in America (84); Brazil (85); Mission, The (86); Untouchables, The (87); Midnight Run (88); Jacknife (89); Goodfellas (90); Awakenings (90); Cape Fear (91); Backdraft (91); Bronx Tale, A (93); This Boy's Life (93); Mad Dog and Glory (93); Casino (95); Heat (95); Cop Land (97); Jackie Brown (97); Wag the Dog (97); Great Expectations (98); Ronin (98); Analyze This (99); Meet the Parents (00); Analyze That (02); Shark Tale (04); Meet the Fockers (04)

de Oliveira, Lourdes
Black Orpheus (59)

de Oliveira, Ubiracy
That Man from Rio (64)

de Oliveira, Vinicius
Central Station (98)

de Palma, Rossy
Women on the Verge of a Nervous Breakdown (88); Tie Me Up! Tie Me Down! (90); Kika (93); Flower of My Secret, The (95)

de Pandelaere, Veronique
Human Resources (00)

de Pasquale, Frederic
French Connection, The (71)

De Penguern, Arthus
Amelie (01)

De Poliolo, Dorothy
L'Avventura (60)

De Ravenel, Ariel
Love Is the Devil: Study for a Portrait of Francis Bacon (98)

De Rolf, Paul
Seven Little Foys, The (55)

de Santelices, Gaspar
Death of a Bureaucrat (66)

De Sausmarez, Cecil
Story of Adele H., The (75)

De Sica, Vittorio
Earrings of Madame de ... , The (53); Gold of Naples (54); General della Rovere (59); Andy Warhol's Dracula (74)

de Silva, Enrico
Shoeshine (46)

De Souza, Edward
Phantom of the Opera, The (62)

de Souza, Waldetar
Black Orpheus (59)

de Vilallonga, Jose-Luis
Lovers, The (59); Breakfast at Tiffany's (61); Cleo from 5 to 7 (62); Darling (65)

de Wilde, Brandon
Member of the Wedding, The (52); Shane (53); Hud (63)

de Wit, Jacqueline
All That Heaven Allows (55); Tea and Sympathy (56)

de Wolff, Francis
Treasure Island (50); Ivanhoe (52); From Russia with Love (63)

De Young, Cliff
Blue Collar (78); F/X (86)

Dea, Marie
Orpheus (49)

Deacon, Richard
Solid Gold Cadillac, The (56)

Dean, Allison
Coming to America (88)

Dean, Billy
Gumshoe (71)

Dean, E. Brian
Nighthawks (81)

Dean, Erin J.
Lolita (97)

Dean, James
East of Eden (55); Rebel without a Cause (55); Giant (56)

Dean, Jimmy
Diamonds Are Forever (71)

Dean, Julia
Nightmare Alley (47)

Dean, Laura
Fame (80)

Dean, Loren
Say Anything (89); Enemy of the State (98)

Dean, Quentin
In the Heat of the Night (67)

Dean, Ron
Breakfast Club, The (85)

Debaar, Andre
Lumumba (00)

Debelka, Frantisek
Fireman's Ball, The (67)

DeBenning, Jeff
How to Succeed in Business without Really Trying (67)

Deborb, Michel
Masculine Feminine (66)

Debucourt, Jean
Mayerling (36); Devil in the Flesh, The (46); Earrings of Madame de ... , The (53)

DeCamp, Rosemary
Hold Back the Dawn (41); Jungle Book, The (42); Yankee Doodle Dandy (42); This Is the Army (43); Pride of the Marines (45); Rhapsody in Blue (45)

Decazes, Pierre
Lacombe, Lucien (74)

Decker, Diana
Lolita (62)

Decleir, Jan
Antonia's Line (95); Character (97)

DeClercq, Kuulei
Hurricane, The (37)

Decomble, Guy
Jour de Fete (49); Bob le Flambeur (55); Cousins, The (59); Four Hundred Blows, The (59)

Decou, Patricia
Blair Witch Project, The (99)

Decroux, Etienne
Children of Paradise (45)

Dedet, Yann
Confidentially Yours (83)

Dee, Blanche
Hallelujah the Hills (63)

Dee, Frances
If I Had a Million (32); Little Women (33); Of Human Bondage (34); Becky Sharp (35); I Walked with a Zombie (43)

Dee, Ruby
Raisin in the Sun, A (61); Do the Right Thing (89)

Dee, Sandra
Imitation of Life (59); Gidget (59)

Deel, Sandra
Junior Bonner (72)

Deem, Lola
Pirate, The (48)

Deering, Elizabeth
Minnie and Moskowitz (71)

Deering, Olive
Samson and Delilah (49)

Dees, Rick
La Bamba (87)

Deezen, Eddie
Polar Express, The (04)

Def, Mos
Monster's Ball (01)

DeFore, Don
Male Animal, The (42); Guy Named Joe, A (44); Thirty Seconds Over Tokyo (44)

DeGeneres, Ellen
EdTV (99); Finding Nemo (03)

Degermark, Pia
Elvira Madigan (67)

Degideo, April
Spellbound (03)

Deguy, Nicolas
Devil, Probably, The (77)

DeHaven, Carter
Great Dictator, The (40)

DeHaven, Gloria
Summer Holiday (48); Three Little Words (50)

Dehner, John
Apache (54); Left-Handed Gun, The (58); Man of the West (58); Boys from Brazil, The (78); Jagged Edge (85)

DeHoyos, Jaime
El Mariachi (93)

Dehuff, Nicole
Meet the Parents (00)

Dekker, Albert
Beau Geste (39); Killers, The (46); Gentleman's Agreement (47); Kiss Me Deadly (55); East of Eden (55)

DeKnight, Fannie Belle
Hallelujah (29)

del Amo Oruet, Nieves
Sexy Beast (00)

Del Lago, Alicia
El Norte (83)

Del Rio, Dolores
Flying Down to Rio (33); Journey into Fear (42); Fugitive, The (47); Cheyenne Autumn (64)

Del Rio, Evelyn
Bank Dick, The (40)

del Sol, Laura
Carmen (83); Hit, The (84)

Del Toro, Benicio
Fearless (93); Usual Suspects, The (95); Fear and Loathing in Las Vegas (98); Traffic (00); Pledge, The (01); 21 Grams (03); Frank Miller's Sin City (05)

Del Toro, Guadalupe
Dona Herlinda and Her Son (86)

Del Val, Jean
Fantastic Voyage (66); Wait Until Dark (67)

Del Valle, Oscar
Balseros (04)

Delahalle, France
Playtime (67)

Delahaye, Michel
Alphaville (65)

Delain, Florian
Rosetta (99)

Delaine, Yvonne
Superfly (72)

Delair, Suzy
Rocco and His Brothers (60)

Delaitre
J'Accuse (38)

Delalande, Anatole
Cyrano de Bergerac (90)

Delamare, Jean-Philippe
Man Escaped, A (56)

Delamare, Lise
La Marseillaise (38); Lola Montes (55)

Delamere, Matthew
Under the Skin (97)

Delaney, Joan
President's Analyst, The (67)

Delaney, Trevor
Cul-de-Sac (66)

Delannoy, Laurence
Devil, Probably, The (77)

Delany, Cathleen
Dead, The (87)

Delany, Dana
Fly Away Home (96)

Delate, Brian
Truman Show, The (98)

Delbo, Jean-Jacques
Thousand Eyes of Dr. Mabuse, The (60)

Delcassan
Jour de Fete (49)

Delcevski, Boris
Before the Rain (94)

Delerue, Georges
Two English Girls (71)

Delevanti, Cyril
Night of the Iguana, The (64)

Delfin, le nain
Zero for Conduct (33)

Delhumeau, Jean-Paul
Man Escaped, A (56)

DeLisle, Grey
Powerpuff Girls Movie, The (02)

Dell, Claudia
Algiers (38)

Dell, Gabriel
Angels with Dirty Faces (38)

Della Noce, Luisa
Juliet of the Spirits (65)

Della Seta, Claudia
Son's Room, The (01)

Delmar, Delores
Husbands (70)

Delmont, Edouard
Marius (31); Fanny (32); Toni (35); Port of Shadows (38)

DeLoach, Heather
Little Princess, A (95)

Delon, Alain
Rocco and His Brothers (60); Leopard, The (63); Is Paris Burning? (66); Le Samourai (67)

Delon, Nathalie
Le Samourai (67); Romantic Englishwoman, The (75)

Delora, Jennifer
Frankenhooker (90)

Delorme, Daniele
Pardon Mon Affaire (77)

Delory, Donna
Truth of Dare (91)

Delpy, Albert
Hairdresser's Husband, The (92); Ridicule (96); Before Sunset (04)

Delpy, Julie
Bad Blood (86); Europa, Europa (91); White (94); Before Sunrise (95); Before Sunset (04)

Delrich, Hal
Evil Dead, The (83)

Delubac, Jacqueline
Story of a Cheat, The (36)

Deluca, Claudio
Small Change (76)

Deluca, Franck
Small Change (76)

DeLuise, Dom
Twelve Chairs, The (70); Secret of Nimh, The (82)

Deman, Robert
Papillon (73)

DeMarco, Tony
Gang's All Here, The (43)

Demarest, William
Hands Across the Table (35); Easy Living (37); Christmas in July (40); Great McGinty, The (40); Lady Eve, The (41); Devil and Miss Jones, The (41); Sullivan's Travels (41); Miracle of Morgan's Creek, The (44); Hail the Conquering Hero (44); Jolson Story, The (46); Viva Las Vegas (64)

Demas, Mary
Henry: Portrait of a Serial Killer (89)

Demazis, Orane
Marius (31); Fanny (32); Cesar (36)

Demick, Irina
Those Magnificent Men in Their Flying Machines; or How I Flew from London to Paris in 25 Hours and 11 Minutes (65)

DeMille, Cecil B.
Sunset Blvd. (50)

DeMille, Katherine
Viva Villa! (34); Call of the Wild (35)

DeMita, John
Princess Mononoke (97)

Demongeot, Catherine
Zazie (60); Woman Is a Woman, A (60)

Dempsey, Jack
Requiem for a Heavyweight (62)

Dempsey, Patrick
Emperor's Club, The (02); Sweet Home Alabama (02)

Dempsey, Patrick O'Brien
Miracle (04)

Dempster, Hugh
Anna Karenina (47)

DeMunn, Jeffrey
Shawshank Redemption, The (94); X-Files, The (98); Majestic, The (01)

Dench, Judi
Room with a View, A (85); Wetherby (85); 84 Charing Cross Road (87); Goldeneye (95); Mrs. Brown (97); Tomorrow Never Dies (97); Shakespeare in Love (98); Tea with Mussolini (99); World Is Not Enough, The (99); Chocolat (00); Iris (01); Shipping News, The (01); Die Another Day (02)

DeNeck, Didier
Toto le Heros (91)

Deneuve, Catherine
Umbrellas of Cherbourg, The (64); Repulsion (65); Belle de Jour (67); Mississippi Mermaid (69); Tristana (70); Hustle (75); Last Metro, The (80); Time Regained (99); Dancer in the Dark (00); 8 Women (01)

Denham, Maurice
Sink the Bismarck! (60); Sunday, Bloody Sunday (71); Day of the Jackal, The (73); 84 Charing Cross Road (87)

Denis, Jacques
Clockmaker, The (73); Jonah Who Will Be 25 in the Year 2000 (76)

Denison, Leslie
Five Graves to Cairo (43)

Denison, Michael
Magic Box, The (51); Importance of Being Earnest, The (52)

Denman, Tony
Fargo (96)

Dennehy, Brian
Semi-Tough (77); 10 (79); Gorky Park (83); Cocoon (85); Silverado (85); F/X (86); Belly of an Architect, The (87); Presumed Innocent (90); William Shakespeare's Romeo + Juliet (96); Assault on Precinct 13 (05)

Dennek, Barbara
Playtime (67)

Dennen, Barry
Kentucky Fried Movie, The (77); Dark Crystal, The (82)

Denner, Charles
Sleeping Car Murder, The (65); Z (69); Such a Gorgeous Kid Like Me (73); Man Who Loved Women, The (77)

Dennett, Peter
Piano, The (93)

Denning, Richard
Glass Key, The (42)

Dennis, Nick
Streetcar Named Desire, A (51); Kiss Me Deadly (55)

Dennis, Peter
Shrek (01)

Dennis, Sandy
Who's Afraid of Virginia Woolf? (66); Out-of-Towners, The (70); Come Back to the 5 & Dime, Jimmy Dean, Jimmy Dean (82); Another Woman (88)

Dennis, Winston
Adventures of Baron Munchausen, The (89)

Dennison, Jo-Carroll
Jolson Story, The (46)

Dennison, Sabrina
Santa Sangre (89)

Denny, Reginald
Private Lives (31); Lost Patrol, The (34); Of Human Bondage (34); Anna Karenina (35); Remember Last Night? (35); Rebecca (40); Macomber Affair, the (47); My Favorite Brunette (47); Secret Life of Walter Mitty, The (47); Mr. Blandings Builds His Dream House (48); Cat Ballou (65)

Denton, Coby
Wild Angels, The (66)

Denton, Crahan
Birdman of Alcatraz (62); Hud (63)

Denton, Will
Palindromes (05)

Denz, Manuela
Sugarbaby (85)

Depardieu, Elisabeth
Jean de Florette (86); Manon of the Spring (86)

Depardieu, Gerard
Going Places (74); 1900 (76); Get Out Your Handkerchiefs (78); Last Metro, The (80); Mon Oncle d'Amerique (80); Danton (82); Return of Martin Guerre, The (82); Moon in the Gutter, The (83); Police (84); Jean de Florette (86); Camille Claudel (88); Cyrano de Bergerac (90); Tous les Matins du Monde (91)

Depardieu, Guillaume
Tous les Matins du Monde (91)

DePinto, Joey
Throw Momma from the Train (87)

Deplanche, Philippe
Three Crowns of the Sailor (83)

Depp, Johnny
Nightmare on Elm Street, A (84); Cry-Baby (90); Edward Scissorhands (90); Arizona Dream (91); What's Eating Gilbert Grape? (93); Benny & Joon (93); Ed Wood (94); Dead Man (96); Donnie Brasco (97); Fear and Loathing in Las Vegas (98); Sleepy Hollow (99); Chocolat (00); Before Night Falls (00); Blow (01); From Hell (01); Pirates of the Caribbean: The Curse of the Black Pearl (03); Once Upon a Time in Mexico (03); Finding Neverland (04)

Dequenne, Emilie
Rosetta (99); Brotherhood of the Wolf (01)

Deragon, Lynne
Rabid (77)

Doherty, James
Backbeat (94)

Doherty, Shannen
Secret of Nimh, The (82); Heathers (89)

Dohrn, Bernardine
Weather Underground, The (03)

Dolan, Michael
Captain Horatio Hornblower (51); Hamburger
Hill (87); Blioxi Blues (88)

Dole, Emily
Personal Best (82)

Doleman, Guy
On the Beach (59); Ipcress File, The (65);
Thunderball (65); Funeral in Berlin (66)

Dolenz, George
Last Time I Saw Paris, The (54)

Dolenz, Micky
Head (68)

Doll, Dora
Young Lions, The (58); Black and White in
Color (76); Julia (77)

Dolleris, Helle
Celebration, The (98)

Dombasle, Arielle
Le Beau Mariage (82); Pauline at the Beach (83);
L'Ennui (98); Time Regained (99)

Domburh, Andrea
Soldier of Orange (77)

Domeier, Richard
Evil Dead 2: Dead by Dawn (87)

Domingo, Placido
La Traviata (82)

Dominguez, Chano
Calle 54 (00)

Dominguez, Chazz
This Is Spinal Tap (84)

Dominguez, Frances
Ace in the Hole (51)

Dominici, Arturo
Black Sunday (60); Investigation of a Citizen
Above Suspicion (70)

Dominici, Germana
Black Sunday (60)

Dommartin, Solveig
Wings of Desire (87); Until the End of the
World (91)

Donahue, Don
Crumb (95)

Donahue, Elinor
Pretty Woman (90)

Donahue, Heather
Blair Witch Project, The (99)

Donahue, Patricia
Cutter's Way (81)

Donahue, Troy
Tarnished Angels, The (57)

Donald, James
Way Ahead, The (44); Lust for Life (56); Bridge on
the River Kwai, The (57); Great Escape, The (63)

Donaldson, Norma
Across 110th Street (72)

Donaldson, Ted
Tree Grows in Brooklyn, A (45)

Donat, Peter
China Syndrome, The (79); War of the Roses,
The (89); Deep End, The (01)

Donat, Robert
Private Life of Henry VIII, The (33); Count of
Monte Cristo, The (34); 39 Steps, The (35); Ghost
Goes West, The (36); Knight without Armor (37);
Citadel, The (38); Goodbye Mr. Chips (39);
Winslow Boy, The (48)

Donath, Ludwig
Jolson Story, The (46); Gilda (46); Torn
Curtain (66)

Donda, Jean-Claude
Triplets of Belleville, The (03)

Donde, Manuel
Treasure of the Sierra Madre, The (48); El (52)

Donella, Chad
Shattered Glass (03)

Dong Fei
To Live (94)

Dong Zhi Hua
Kung Fu Hustle (04)

Donlan, James
Whole Town's Talking, The (35)

Donlevy, Brian
In Old Chicago (38); Beau Geste (39); Jesse
James (39); Destry Rides Again (39); Union
Pacific (39); Great McGinty, The (40); Glass Key,
The (42); Hangmen Also Die (43); Miracle of
Morgan's Creek, The (44); Kiss of Death (47)

Donnadieu, Bernard-Pierre
Return of Martin Guerre, The (82); Vanishing,
The (86)

Donnell, Jeff
In a Lonely Place (50); Sweet Smell of
Success (57)

Donnelly, Barry
Walkabout (71)

Donnelly, Donal
Knack ... and How to Get It, The (65); Dead,
The (87)

Donnelly, Jamie
Grease (78)

Donnelly, Patrice
Personal Best (82)

Donnelly, Ruth
Footlight Parade (33); Hands Across the Table (35);
Bells of St. Mary's, The (45); Autumn Leaves (56)

Donner, Judith
Seance on a Wet Afternoon (64)

Duffy, Ciara
Snapper, The (93)

Duffy, Karen
Dumb & Dumber (94)

Duffy, Sean
Smash Palace (81)

Dufilho, Jacques
Zazie (60); Black and White in Color (76)

Dugan, Dennis
Howling, The (81)

Dugan, John
Texas Chainsaw Massacre, The (74)

Dugan, Tom
To Be or Not to Be (42); Take Me Out to the Ball Game (49)

Duggan, Andrew
It's Alive (74)

Dugger, Aaron
She's Gotta Have It (86)

Dugger, Florrie
Bugsy Malone (76)

Duhamel, Claire
Stolen Kisses (68)

Duhamel, Herve
Le Beau Mariage (82)

Duhamel, Marcel
Crime of Monsieur Lange, The (36)

DuJanerand, Philippe
La Femme Nikita (90)

Dujmovic, Davor
When Father Was Away on Business (85); Time of the Gypsies (89)

Dukakis, Olympia
Idolmaker, The (80); Moonstruck (87); Steel Magnolias (89); Look Who's Talking (89); Mighty Aphrodite (95); Mr. Holland's Opus (95)

Duke, Bill
Car Wash (76); American Gigolo (80); Predator (87); Menace II Society (93)

Duke, Desmond
Hotel Rwanda (04)

Duke, Patty
Miracle Worker, The (62); Valley of the Dolls (67)

Duke, Robin
Groundhog Day (93)

Dukes, David
Little Romance, A (79); Gods and Monsters (98)

Dullac, Paul
Marius (31); Cesar (36)

Dullaghan, John
Sweet Sweetback's Baadasssss Song (71)

Dullea, Keir
David and Lisa (62); 2001: A Space Odyssey (68)

Dumas, Roger
That Man from Rio (64)

Dumas, Sandrine
Double Life of Veronique, The (91)

Dumat, Philippe
Soft Skin, The (64)

Dumbrille, Douglas
Fog Over Frisco (34); Lives of a Bengal Lancer, The (35); Naughty Marietta (35); Mr. Deeds Goes to Town (36); Day at the Races, A (37); Road to Utopia (45); Son of Paleface (52)

Dumin Kitei, Lynne
Raising Arizona (87)

Dumke, Ralph
All the King's Men (49); Lili (53); Invasion of the Body Snatchers (56); Solid Gold Cadillac, The (56)

Dummar, Melvin E.
Melvin and Howard (80)

Dumont, Margaret
Cocoanuts, The (29); Animal Crackers (30); Duck Soup (33); Night at the Opera, A (35); Day at the Races, A (37); What a Way to Go! (64)

Dumont, Sky
Eyes Wide Shut (99)

Dun, Dennis
Last Emperor, The (87)

Duna, Steffi
Anthony Adverse (36); Waterloo Bridge (40)

Dunagan, Donnie
Son of Frankenstein (39); Bambi (42)

Dunaway, Faye
Bonnie and Clyde (67); Thomas Crown Affair, The (68); Little Big Man (70); Three Musketeers, The (73); Chinatown (74); Towering Inferno, The (74); Four Musketeers, The (74); Three Days of the Condor (75); Network (76); Mommie Dearest (81); Barfly (87); Arizona Dream (91); Thomas Crown Affair, The (99)

Dunbar, Adrian
Hear My Song (91); Crying Game, The (92); General, The (98)

Duncan, Andrew
Rain People, The (69); Hospital, The (71); Slap Shot (77); Unmarried Woman, An (78); Little Romance, A (79)

Duncan, Anna
Black Cat, The (34)

Duncan, Cerall
Love Jones (97)

Duncan, Kenne
My Pal Trigger (46)

Duncan, Lindsay
Prick Up Your Ears (87); Ideal Husband, An (99); Mansfield Park (99)

Duncan, Mary
Morning Glory (33)

Duncan, Michael Clarke
Green Mile, The (99); Planet of the Apes (01); Daredevil (03)

Tootsie (82); Cop (88); Dick Tracy (90); Hudsucker Proxy, The (94); O Brother, Where Art Thou? (00)

Durst, Debi
Tim Burton's The Nightmare before Christmas (93)

Dury, Monique
Green Room, The (78)

Duryea, Dan
Little Foxes, The (41); Pride of the Yankees, The (42); Sahara (43); None but the Lonely Heart (44); Ministry of Fear (45); Woman in the Window, The (45); Scarlet Street (45); Criss Cross (49); Winchester '73 (50); Flight of the Phoenix, The (65)

Duse, Vittorio
Ossessione (42)

Dusenberry, Ann
Cutter's Way (81)

Dushku, Eliza
This Boy's Life (93); True Lies (94); Bring It On (00)

Dusseldorp, Marta
Innocence (00)

Dussollier, Andre
Such a Gorgeous Kid Like Me (73); Le Beau Mariage (82); Three Men and a Cradle (85); Melo (86); Un Coeur en Hiver (92)

Dutoit, Roger
Pierrot le Fou (65)

Dutronc, Jacques
Every Man for Himself (80)

Dutt, Nargis
Mother India (57)

Dutt, Sunil
Mother India (57)

Dutt, Utpal
Shakespeare Wallah (65)

Dutton, Charles S.
Jacknife (89); Q&A (90); Alien³ (92); Mississippi Masala (92); Menace II Society (93); Gothika (03)

Duval, James
Donnie Darko (01)

Duval, Thomas
Sunday in the Country, A (84)

Duval, Veronique
Married Woman, The (64)

DuVall, Clea
Faculty, The (98); Girl, Interrupted (99); 21 Grams (03); Grudge, The (04)

Duvall, Robert
To Kill a Mockingbird (62); Bullitt (68); Rain People, The (69); True Grit (69); M*A*S*H (70); THX 1138 (71); Godfather, The (72); Great Northfield, Minnesota Raid, The (72); Godfather, Part II, The (74); Network (76); Seven-Per-Cent Solution, The (76); Apocalypse Now (79); Great Santini, The (79); True Confessions (81); Tender Mercies (83); Natural, The (84); Colors (88); Rambling Rose (91); Falling Down (93); Sling

Blade (96); Apostle, The (97); Deep Impact (98); Civil Action, A (98); Apocalypse Now Redux (01); Open Range (03)

Duvall, Shelley
McCabe and Mrs. Miller (71); Thieves Like Us (74); Annie Hall (77); 3 Women (77); Shining, The (80); Time Bandits (81); Roxanne (87); Portrait of a Lady, The (96)

Dux, Pierre
Z (69)

Dvorak, Ann
Guardsman, The (31); Scarface (32); G-Men (35)

Dvorjetzki, Vladislav
Solaris (72)

Dvorsky, Peter
Videodrome (83)

Dwarves, The
Kurt and Courtney (98)

Dwyer, Leslie
Way Ahead, The (44)

Dwyer, William
Charly (68)

Dyall, Franklin
Private Life of Henry VIII, The (33)

Dyall, Valentine
Brief Encounter (45); Haunting, The (63)

Dye, Cameron
Valley Girl (83)

Dye, Dale
Blue Sky (94); Mission: Impossible (96)

Dyer, Charles
Knack ... and How to Get It, The (65)

Dyer, Raymond
Loneliness of the Long Distance Runner, The (62)

Dylan, Bob
Pat Garrett and Billy the Kid (73); Last Waltz, The (78)

Dynam, Jacques
Le Petit Theatre de Jean Renoir (69); French Connection II (75)

Dyne, Aminta
Ministry of Fear (45)

Dyneley, Peter
Roman Spring of Mrs. Stone, The (61)

Dyrenforth, James
Night to Remember, A (58)

Dyrholm, Trine
Celebration, The (98)

Dysart, Richard
Petulia (68); Hospital, The (71); Day of the Locust, The (75); Being There (79); Thing, The (82); Pale Rider (85); Falcon and the Snowman, The (85)

Dysart, Tommy
Man from Snowy River, The (82)

Dziekan-Vajda, Barbara
Short Film about Killing, A (87)

Eden, Barbara
7 Faces of Dr. Lao (64)

Eden, Mark
Seance on a Wet Afternoon (64)

Edery, David
Man Facing Southeast (86)

Edgerton, Joel
King Arthur (04)

Edgington, Lyn
Dirty Harry (71)

Edmett, Verity
L-Shaped Room, The (62)

Edmond, Elsie
Royal Family of Broadway, The (30)

Edmonds, Dale
Paisan (46)

Edmunds, William
Anna and the King of Siam (46)

Edney, Beatie
In the Name of the Father (93)

Edson, Richard
Stranger than Paradise (84); Platoon (86); Good
Morning, Vietnam (87); Do the Right Thing (89);
Strange Days (95); Sunshine State (02)

Edwall, Allan
Virgin Spring, The (59); Emigrants, The (71);
Fanny and Alexander (82); Sacrifice, The (86)

Edward-Stevens, Michael
Babe (95)

Edwards, Anthony
Heart Like a Wheel (83); Revenge of the
Nerds (84); Sure Thing, The (85); Top Gun (86);
Client, The (94); Forgotten, The (04)

Edwards, Bill
Hail the Conquering Hero (44)

Edwards, Bruce
Fallen Sparrow, The (43); Cool World, The (63)

Edwards, Cliff
Sin of Madelon Claudet, The (31); His Girl
Friday (40); Pinocchio (40); Dumbo (41)

Edwards, Daryl
Brother from Another Planet, The (84)

Edwards, Don
Horse Whisperer, The (98)

Edwards, Eric
Blade (98)

Edwards, Glynn
Zulu (64)

Edwards, Henry
Green for Danger (46); Oliver Twist (48)

Edwards, Hilton
Othello (52)

Edwards, Hugh
Lord of the Flies (63)

Edwards, James
Set-Up, The (49); Steel Helmet, The (51); Bright
Victory (51); Member of the Wedding, The (52);
Pork Chop Hill (59); Manchurian Candidate,
The (62); Coogan's Bluff (68); Patton (70)

Edwards, Jason
Drowning by Numbers (87)

Edwards, Kati
Well, The (99)

Edwards, Michael
Mommie Dearest (81)

Edwards, Paddi
Little Mermaid, The (89)

Edwards, Percy
Dark Crystal, The (82)

Edwards, Sam
Bambi (42)

Edwards, Snitz
Phantom of the Opera, The (25)

Edwards, Stacy
In the Company of Men (97)

Edwards, Tony
Starman (84)

Edwards, Vince
Killing, The (56)

Edwards-Hughes, Jennifer
Straight Story, The (99)

Efremova, Svetlana
White Oleander (02)

Efron, Marshall
THX 1138 (71)

Egan, Michael
Next Stop, Greenwich Village (76)

Egan, Richard
Pollyanna (60)

Egan, Susan
Hercules (97); Spirited Away (01)

Egerer, Carla
Knife in the Head (78)

Eggar, Samantha
Doctor Dolittle (67); Seven-Per-Cent Solution,
The (76); Brood, The (79); Hercules (97)

Egger, Josef
For a Few Dollars More (65)

Eggerth, Marta
For Me and My Gal (42)

Eginton, Margaret
Scent of a Woman (92)

Eglevsky, Andre
Limelight (52)

Ehle, Jennifer
Backbeat (94); Wilde (97); Possession (02)

Eichhorn, Lisa
Cutter's Way (81)

Fluellen, Joel
Raisin in the Sun, A (61); Learning Tree, The (69); Great White Hope, The (70)

Flying Burrito Brothers
Gimme Shelter (70)

Flynn, Errol
Captain Blood (35); Charge of the Light Brigade, The (36); Prince and the Pauper, The (37); Adventures of Robin Hood, The (38); Dawn Patrol, The (38); Dodge City (39); Santa Fe Trail (40); Sea Hawk, The (40); Gentleman Jim (42); Edge of Darkness (43); Objective, Burma! (45); Sun Also Rises, The (57)

Flynn, Joe
Rescuers, The (77)

Flynn, Marie
Intermezzo: A Love Story (39)

Flynn, Miriam
Babe (95)

Flynn, Steven
Ulee's Gold (97)

Foa, Arnoldo
Trial, The (63)

Focas, Spiros
Rocco and His Brothers (60); Jewel of the Nile, The (85)

Foch, Nina
Song to Remember, A (45); American in Paris, An (51); Executive Suite (54); Ten Commandments, The (56); Spartacus (60)

Fofanah, Abu Bakaar
Amistad (97)

Foil, David
sex, lies, and videotape (89)

Foldi, Erzebet
All That Jazz (79)

Foley, Dave
Bug's Life, A (98)

Foley, Ellen
Fatal Attraction (87)

Foley, Joan
Love Streams (84)

Folland, Alison
To Die For (95); Boys Don't Cry (99)

Fonda, Bridget
Scandal (89); Strapless (89); Godfather, Part III, The (90); Single White Female (92); Singles (92); Jackie Brown (97); Simple Plan, A (98)

Fonda, Henry
Trail of the Lonesome Pine, The (36); You Only Live Once (37); Jezebel (38); Jesse James (39); Young Mr. Lincoln (39); Drums Along the Mohawk (39); Story of Alexander Graham Bell, The (39); Grapes of Wrath, The (40); Lady Eve, The (41); Male Animal, The (42); Tales of Manhattan (42); Ox-Bow Incident, The (43); My Darling Clementine (46); Fugitive, The (47); Fort Apache (48); Mister Roberts (55); War and

Peace (56); Wrong Man, The (56); 12 Angry Men (57); Warlock (59); Longest Day, The (62); Advise and Consent (62); How the West Was Won (63); Fail Safe (64); Madigan (68); Once Upon a Time in the West (69); On Golden Pond (81)

Fonda, Jane
Cat Ballou (65); Barefoot in the Park (67); They Shoot Horses, Don't They? (69); Klute (71); Tout Va Bien (72); Julia (77); Coming Home (78); California Suite (78); China Syndrome, The (79); 9 to 5 (80); On Golden Pond (81); Agnes of God (85)

Fonda, Peter
Wild Angels, The (66); Easy Rider (69); Ulee's Gold (97); Limey, The (99)

Fondacaro, Phil
Polar Express, The (04)

Fong, Benson
Our Man Flint (66); Charley Varrick (73)

Fong, Harold
Steel Helmet, The (51)

Fontaine, Frank
Confessions of a Dangerous Mind (02)

Fontaine, Jacqueline
Country Girl, The (54)

Fontaine, Joan
Women, The (39); Gunga Din (39); Rebecca (40); Suspicion (41); Jane Eyre (44); Letter from an Unknown Woman (48); Ivanhoe (52)

Fontaine, Lilian
Lost Weekend, The (45)

Fontaine, William E.
Hallelujah (29)

Fontanel, Genevieve
Madame Rosa (77); Man Who Loved Women, The (77)

Fontani, Amerigo
Life Is Beautful (97)

Fontanne, Lynn
Guardsman, The (31)

Fonzi, Dolores
Burnt Money (00)

Foote, Hallie
1918 (85)

Foote Jr., Horton
1918 (85)

Foran, Dick
Petrified Forest, The (36); Dangerous (36); Four Daughters (38); My Little Chickadee (40); Fighting 69th, The (40)

Foray, June
Phantom Tollbooth, The (70)

Forbes, Bryan
Wooden Horse, The (50)

Forbes, Charles
Lock, Stock and Two Smoking Barrels (98)

Forbes, Chris
Sleeper (73)

Forbes, Mary
Farewell to Arms, A (32); Bombshell (33)

Forbes, Meriel
Oh! What a Lovely War (69)

Forbes, Ralph
Smilin' Through (32); Barretts of Wimpole Street, The (34); Twentieth Century (34); Romeo and Juliet (36); Hound of the Baskervilles, The (39)

Ford, Alan
Exorcist: The Beginning (04)

Ford, Carole Ann
Day of the Triffids, The (62)

Ford, David
Comfort of Strangers, The (91)

Ford Davies, Oliver
Mrs. Dalloway (97)

Ford, Dorothy
Three Godfathers, The (48)

Ford, Faith
Pacifier, The (05)

Ford, Francis
She Wore a Yellow Ribbon (49); Quiet Man, The (52)

Ford, Glenn
Gilda (46); Big Heat, The (53); Blackboard Jungle (55); Jubal (56); Teahouse of the August Moon, The (56); 3:10 to Yuma (57); Pocketful of Miralces (61); Is Paris Burning? (66); Superman (78)

Ford, Grace
Devil-Doll, The (36)

Ford, Harrison
American Graffiti (73); Conversation, The (74); Star Wars (77); Apocalypse Now (79); Empire Strikes Back, The (80); Raiders of the Lost Ark (81); Blade Runner (82); Return of the Jedi (83); Indiana Jones and the Temple of Doom (84); Witness (85); Mosquito Coast, The (86); Working Girl (88); Frantic (88); Indiana Jones and the Last Crusade (89); Presumed Innocent (90); Patriot Games (92); Fugitive, The (93); Clear and Present Danger (94); Devil's Own, The (97); Apocalypse Now Redux (01); K-19: The Widowmaker (02)

Ford, Mick
How to Get Ahead in Advertising (89)

Ford, Paul
Teahouse of the August Moon, The (56); Music Man, The (62)

Ford, Steven
When Harry Met Sally... (89)

Ford, Wallace
Freaks (32); Lost Patrol, The (34); Informer, The (35); Whole Town's Talking, The (35); Shadow of a Doubt (43); T-Men (47); Set-Up, The (49);

Harvey (50); Man from Laramie, The (55); Rainmaker, The (56); Warlock (59)

Foree, Ken
Dawn of the Dead (79)

Foreman, Deborah
Valley Girl (83)

Foreman, Jamie
Elizabeth (98)

Forest, Denis
Cliffhanger (93)

Forestali, Erarde
Swimming Pool (03)

Forget, Pierre
Vanishing, The (86)

Forlani, Claire
Meet Joe Black (98)

Forlani, Remo
In Praise of Love (01)

Forneiro, Raul Garcia
Bad Education (04)

Fornicola, Nino
Le Petit Theatre de Jean Renoir (69)

Foronjy, Richard
Prince of the City (81); Midnight Run (88); Carlito's Way (93)

Forque, Veronica
Kika (93)

Forrest, Christine
Martin (78)

Forrest, Frederic
Conversation, The (74); Missouri Breaks, The (76); Rose, The (79); Apocalypse Now (79); Hammett (82); Tucker: The Man and His Dream (88); Music Box (89); Falling Down (93); Apocalypse Now Redux (01)

Forrest, Sally
While the City Sleeps (56)

Forrest, Steve
North Dallas Forty (79); Mommie Dearest (81)

Forristal, Susan
L.A. Story (91)

Forster, Robert
Medium Cool (69); Jackie Brown (97); Psycho (98); Mulholland Dr. (01)

Forster, Rudolf
Threepenny Opera, The (31)

Forsyth, Bruce
Star! (68); Bedknobs and Broomsticks (71)

Forsyth, Rosemary
Shenandoah (65); Disclosure (94)

Forsythe, Henderson
Interiors (78)

Forsythe, John
Trouble with Harry, The (55); In Cold Blood (67); Topaz (69); Charlie's Angels (00); Charlie's Angels: Full Throttle (03)

Gambon, Michael
Cook, the Thief, His Wife & Her Lover, The (89); Wings of the Dove, The (97); Sleepy Hollow (99); Gosford Park (01); Sylvia (03); Open Range (03); Harry Potter and the Prisoner of Azkaban (04); Being Julia (04); Sky Captain and the World of Tomorrow (04)

Gamlin, Lionel
Seance on a Wet Afternoon (64)

Gammon, James
Urban Cowboy (80); Iron Giant, The (99); Cell, The (00); Cold Mountain (04)

Gampel, Chris
Desperate Characters (71)

Gampu, Ken
Naked Prey, The (66); Gods Must Be Crazy, The (81)

Ganansia, David
What Time Is It There? (01)

Gandolfini, James
Get Shorty (95); Crimson Tide (95); 8mm (99); Man Who Wasn't There, The (01)

Gang Hye-jung
Oldboy (04)

Gangopadhaya, Rama
Pather Panchali (55)

Ganguly, Subodh
Aparajito (56)

Ganios, Tony
Wanderers, The (79)

Ganjhu, Dr. Lisa
Super Size Me (04)

Ganoung, Richard
Parting Glances (86)

Gans, Danny
Bull Durham (88)

Gant, David
Draughtsman's Contract, The (82)

Gant, Richard
Freshman, The (90)

Ganz, Bruno
American Friend, The (77); Nosferatu, the Vampire (78); Knife in the Head (78); Circle of Deceit (81); Wings of Desire (87); Strapless (89); Last Days of Chez Nous, The (93); Downfall (04); Manchurian Candidate, The (04)

Gao Xian
Crouching Tiger, Hidden Dragon (00)

Gaos, Lola
Tristana (70)

Garai, Romola
Nicholas Nickleby (02); Vanity Fair (04)

Garaway, Bill
Zabriskie Point (70)

Garay, Joaquin
Three Caballeros, The (45)

Garber, Matthew
Mary Poppins (64)

Garber, Victor
Sleepless in Seattle (93); Exotica (95); Legally Blonde (01); Tuck Everlasting (02)

Garbo, Greta
Anna Christie (30); Mata Hari (31); Grand Hotel (32); Queen Christina (33); Anna Karenina (35); Camille (37); Ninotchka (39)

Garces, Delia
El (52)

Garces, Paula
Station Agent, The (03)

Garcia, Allan
Modern Times (36)

Garcia, Andy
Untouchables, The (87); Stand and Deliver (88); Godfather, Part III, The (90); Dead Again (91); Jennifer Eight (92); Ocean's Eleven (01); Ocean's Twelve (04)

Garcia, Antonio Lopez
Dream of Light (93)

Garcia Bernal, Gael
Amores Perros (00); Y Tu Mama Tambien (01); Crime of Father Amaro, The (02); Motorcycle Diaries, The (04); Bad Education (04)

Garcia, Juan
Tall Men, The (55)

Garcia, Lea
Black Orpheus (59)

Garcia, Nicole
Mon Oncle d'Amerique (80)

Garcia, Violetta
Hunt, The (66)

Garcia-Ville, Luce
Last Year at Marienbad (61)

Garcin, Ginette
Cousin, Cousine (75)

Garcin, Patricia
Lovers, The (59)

Garde, Betty
Call Northside 777 (48)

Garden, Helen
Monte Carlo (30)

Gardenia, Vincent
Where's Poppa? (70); Bang the Drum Slowly (73); Front Page, The (74); Heaven Can Wait (78); Little Shop of Horrors (86); Moonstruck (87)

Gardiner, Reginald
Marie Antoinette (38); Great Dictator, The (40); Man Who Came to Dinner, The (42); Christmas in Connecticut (45); What a Way to Go! (64)

Gardner, Ava
Killers, The (46); Hucksters, The (47); Show Boat (51); Snows of Kilimanjaro, The (52); Band Wagon, The (53); Mogambo (53); Sun Also Rises,

Gish, Annabeth
Double Jeopardy (99)

Gish, Lillian
Duel in the Sun (46); Portrait of Jennie (48); Night of the Hunter, The (55); Wedding, A (78); Whales of August, The (87)

Gisladottir, Gudrun
Sacrifice, The (86)

Gist, Robert
Band Wagon, The (53); Operation Petticoat (59)

Gitai, Amos
Kadosh (99)

Gitlin, Todd
Weather Underground, The (03)

Gitlis, Ivry
Story of Adele H., The (75)

Gittler, David
Taking Off (71)

Giuffre, Aldo
Yesterday, Today, and Tomorrow (63); Good, the Bad and the Ugly, The (66)

Giuffre, Carlo
Pinocchio (02)

Givney, Kathryn
Three Coins in the Fountain (54)

Givot, George
Thin Ice (37); Road to Morocco (42); Lady and the Tramp (55)

Gladis, Michael J.X.
K-19: The Widowmaker (02)

Glahn, Therese
Celebration, The (98)

Glanzelius, Anton
My Life As a Dog (85)

Glaser, Paul Michael
Fiddler on the Roof (71); Something's Gotta Give (03)

Glaser, Sabine
Man Who Loved Women, The (77)

Glaser, Vaughan
Saboteur (42)

Glass, Everett
Elmer Gantry (60)

Glass, Ned
Charade (63)

Glass, Seamon
Deliverance (72)

Glasser, David
Pee-wee's Big Adventure (85)

Glassner, Barry
Bowling for Columbine (02)

Glaudini, Lola
Your Friends & Neighbors (98)

Glave, Matthew
Wedding Singer, The (98)

Gleason, Jackie
Hustler, The (61); Requiem for a Heavyweight (62); Smokey and the Bandit (77)

Gleason, James
Here Comes Mr. Jordan (41); Babes on Broadway (41); Meet John Doe (41); Arsenic and Old Lace (44); Guy Named Joe, A (44); Clock, The (45); Tree Grows in Brooklyn, A (45); Bishop's Wife, The (47); Night of the Hunter, The (55)

Gleason, Joanna
Crimes and Misdemeanors (89)

Gleason, Lucille
Clock, The (45)

Gleason, Pat
Detour (45)

Gleason, Paul
Tender Mercies (83); Trading Places (83); Breakfast Club, The (85); Die Hard (88); Miami Blues (90)

Gleason, Russell
All Quiet on the Western Front (30)

Gleeson, Brendan
Braveheart (95); Butcher Boy, The (97); General, The (98); Mission: Impossible II (00); Tailor of Panama, The (01); A.I.: Artificial Intelligence (01); Gangs of New York (02); 28 Days Later... (02); Dark Blue (03); Troy (04); Cold Mountain (04); Village, The (04); Kingdom of Heaven (05)

Gleizer, Michele
Europa, Europa (91)

Glen, Georgie
Mrs. Brown (97)

Glen, Iain
Gorillas in the Mist (88); Lara Croft: Tomb Raider (01); Kingdom of Heaven (05)

Glendenning, Candace
Nicholas and Alexandra (71)

Glenn, Jacquelyn
Projectionist, The (70)

Glenn, Lucille
Vanishing, The (86)

Glenn, Scott
Apocalypse Now (79); Urban Cowboy (80); Personal Best (82); Right Stuff, The (83); Silverado (85); Hunt for Red October, The (90); Backdraft (91); Silence of the Lambs, The (91); Carla's Song (96); Shipping News, The (01); Training Day (01); Apocalypse Now Redux (01)

Glenn Sr., Roy E.
Carmen Jones (54); Raisin in the Sun, A (61); Guess Who's Coming to Dinner (67)

Glezer, Marina
Motorcycle Diaries, The (04)

Glicken, Laura
Groove Tube, The (74)

Gligorijevic, Bratoljub
Innocence Unprotected (68)

Graff, Jerry
Spanish Prisoner, The (98)

Graff, Wilton
Take Me Out to the Ball Game (49); Lili (53)

Graham, Frank
Three Caballeros, The (45)

Graham, Gary
Hardcore (79)

Graham, Gerrit
Greetings (68); Pretty Baby (78); Used Cars (80);
One True Thing (98)

Graham, Heather
Drugstore Cowboy (89); Six Degrees of
Separation (93); Boogie Nights (97); Austin
Powers: The Spy Who Shagged Me (99); From
Hell (01); Anger Management (03)

Graham, Holter
Fly Away Home (96)

Graham, John Michael
Halloween (78)

Graham, Lauren
One True Thing (98); Bad Santa (03); Pacifier,
The (05)

Graham, Nathan Lee
Hitch (05)

Graham, Richard
My Beautiful Laundrette (85)

Graham, Ronnie
Gallipoli (81)

Graham, Stuart
Butcher Boy, The (97)

Graham, Winston
My Beautiful Laundrette (85)

Graham-Cox, Michael
Watership Down (78)

Grahame, Gloria
It's a Wonderful Life (46); Crossfire (47); In a
Lonely Place (50); Bad and the Beautiful, The (52);
Greatest Show on Earth, The (52); Big Heat,
The (53); Oklahoma! (55); Odds Against
Tomorrow (59); Chilly Scenes of Winter (79);
Melvin and Howard (80)

Grahame, Margot
Informer, The (35); Beggar's Opera, The (52)

Grainger, Gawn
Love and Death on Long Island (98)

Graley, Barbara
Eye of the Needle (81)

Gramatica, Emma
Miracle in Milan (51)

Grammer, Kelsey
Anastasia (97); Toy Story 2 (99)

Gran, Enrique
Dream of Light (93)

Granach, Alexander
Kameradschaft (31); Ninotchka (39); Hangmen
Also Die (43)

Granath, Bjorn
Pelle the Conqueror (87)

Grandinetti, Dario
Talk to Her (02)

Grandjacquet, Francesco
Open City (45)

Grandsart, Herve
Full Moon in Paris (84)

Grandval, Berthe
Mother and the Whore, The (73)

Granger, Farley
Rope (48); They Live by Night (49); Strangers on a
Train (51); O. Henry's Full House (52); Hans
Christian Andersen (52)

Granger, Seth
Accidental Tourist, The (88)

Granger, Stewart
Caesar and Cleopatra (45); King Solomon's
Mines (50)

Granstedt, Greta
Street Scene (31); Crime without Passion (34)

Grant, A. Cameron
Postman Always Rings Twice, The (46)

Grant, Beth
Speed (94); Matchstick Men (03)

Grant, Campbell
Adventures of Ichabod and Mr. Toad, The (49)

Grant, Cary
Blonde Venus (32); I'm No Angel (33); She Done
Him Wrong (33); Awful Truth, The (37);
Topper (37); Bringing Up Baby (38); Only Angels
Have Wings (39); Gunga Din (39); His Girl
Friday (40); My Favorite Wife (40); Philadelphia
Story, The (40); Suspicion (41); Talk of the Town,
The (42); None but the Lonely Heart (44); Arsenic
and Old Lace (44); Notorious (46); Bachelor and
the Bobby-Soxer, The (47); Bishop's Wife,
The (47); Mr. Blandings Builds His Dream
House (48); People Will Talk (51); To Catch a
Thief (55); Indiscreet (58); North by
Northwest (59); Operation Petticoat (59); That
Touch of Mink (62); Charade (63); Father
Goose (64)

Grant, David Marshall
Stepford Wives, The (04)

Grant, Hugh
Maurice (87); Impromptu (90); Remains of the
Day, The (93); Four Weddings and a Funeral (94);
Sense and Sensibility (95); Notting Hill (99);
Bridget Jones's Diary (01); About a Boy (02); Love
Actually (03); Bridget Jones: The Edge of
Reason (04)

Grant, James
Prick Up Your Ears (87)

Grant, Kathryn
7th Voyage of Sinbad, The (58); Anatomy of a
Murder (59)

Grant, Lawrence
Shanghai Express (32); Count of Monte Cristo, The (34); Son of Frankenstein (39)

Grant, Lee
Detective Story (51); In the Heat of the Night (67); Valley of the Dolls (67); Plaza Suite (71); Shampoo (75); Mulholland Dr. (01)

Grant, Richard E.
Withnail & I (87); How to Get Ahead in Advertising (89); Henry & June (90); Hudson Hawk (91); L.A. Story (91); Player, The (92); Bram Stoker's Dracula (92); Age of Innocence, The (93); Portrait of a Lady, The (96); Merry War, A (97); Spice World (98); Gosford Park (01)

Grant, Rodney A.
Dances with Wolves (90)

Grant, Shelby
Our Man Flint (66)

Grant, Tom
Kurt and Courtney (98)

Grantham, Lucy
Last House on the Left, The (72)

Granval, Charles
Boudu Saved from Drowning (32)

Granville, Bonita
These Three (36); Now, Voyager (42); Glass Key, The (42)

Grapewin, Charley
Wild Boys of the Road (33); Alice Adams (35); Ah, Wilderness! (35); Libeled Lady (36); Petrified Forest, The (36); Captains Courageous (37); Good Earth, The (37); Three Comrades (38); Wizard of Oz, The (39); Grapes of Wrath, The (40); Tobacco Road (41)

Graskoff, Christiane
Mephisto (81)

Grasset, Pierre
Rififi (54)

Grasso, Giovanni
We the Living (42)

Gravage, Vann
River Runs through It, A (92)

Grave, Alexis
Sorrow and the Pity, The (70)

Grave, Louis
Sorrow and the Pity, The (70)

Grave, Serge
Story of a Cheat, The (36)

Graves, Karron
Crucible, The (96)

Graves, Peter
Stalag 17 (53); Night of the Hunter, The (55); Airplane! (80)

Graves, Rupert
Room with a View, A (85); Maurice (87); Damage (92); Madness of King George, The (94); Mrs. Dalloway (97)

Gravety, Fernand
La Ronde (50)

Gravina, Carla
Big Deal on Madonna Street (58)

Gray, Billy
Day the Earth Stood Still, The (51); Seven Little Foys, The (55); Some Like It Hot (59)

Gray, Carsen
Peter Pan (03)

Gray, Charles
You Only Live Twice (67); Diamonds Are Forever (71); Rocky Horror Picture Show, The (75); Seven-Per-Cent Solution, The (76)

Gray, Coleen
Kiss of Death (47); Nightmare Alley (47); Red River (48); Killing, The (56)

Gray, Dolores
It's Always Fair Weather (55)

Gray, Donald
Four Feathers, The (39)

Gray, Dorian
Nights of Cabiria (57)

Gray, Dorothy
Rose Marie (36)

Gray, Harry
Hallelujah (29)

Gray, Janine
Pumpkin Eater, The (64)

Gray, Macy
Training Day (01)

Gray, Marc
Flirting (90)

Gray, Nadia
La Dolce Vita (60); Two for the Road (67)

Gray, Robert
UFOria (85)

Gray, Sally
Green for Danger (46); They Made Me a Fugitive (47)

Gray, Sam
Wolfen (81)

Gray, Spalding
Killing Fields, The (84); True Stories (86); Swimming to Cambodia (87); Beaches (88)

Gray, Vernon
Barretts of Wimpole Street, The (56)

Gray, Vivean
Picnic at Hanging Rock (75); Last Wave, The (77)

Gray-Stanford, Jason
Beautiful Mind, A (01)

Grayson, Diane
Prime of Miss Jean Brodie, The (69)

Grayson, Jessie
Little Foxes, The (41)

Hale, Alan
Sin of Madelon Claudet, The (31); It Happened One Night (34); Lost Patrol, The (34); Of Human Bondage (34); Our Relations (36); Prince and the Pauper, The (37); Stella Dallas (37); Thin Ice (37); Adventures of Robin Hood, The (38); Algiers (38); Man in the Iron Mask, The (39); Dodge City (39); Fighting 69th, The (40); Santa Fe Trail (40); Sea Hawk, The (40); They Drive by Night (40); Gentleman Jim (42); This Is the Army (43); Adventures of Mark Twain, The (44); Pursued (47)

Hale, Barbara
Window, The (49)

Hale, Barnaby
Viva Las Vegas (64)

Hale, Diana
My Friend Flicka (43); Thunderhead—Son of Flicka (45)

Hale, Georgina
Boy Friend, The (71)

Hale, Jennifer
Powerpuff Girls Movie, The (02)

Hale, John
Inside Daisy Clover (65)

Hale, Jonathan
Alice Adams (35); Boys Town (38); Strangers on a Train (51)

Hale, Louise Closser
Daddy Long Legs (31); Shanghai Express (32)

Hale, Richard
Julius Caesar (53); Friendly Persuasion (56)

Haley and the Comets, Bill
Rock Around the Clock (56)

Haley, Jack
Alexander's Ragtime Band (38); Wizard of Oz, The (39)

Haley, Jackie Earle
Bad News Bears, The (76); Breaking Away (79)

Hall, Albert
Leadbelly (76); Apocalypse Now (79); Trouble in Mind (85); Fabulous Baker Boys, The (89); Malcolm X (92); Devil in a Blue Dress (95); Get on the Bus (96); Beloved (98); Apocalypse Now Redux (01)

Hall, Anthony Michael
Sixteen Candles (84); Breakfast Club, The (85); Edward Scissorhands (90); Six Degrees of Separation (93)

Hall, Arsenio
Coming to America (88)

Hall, Bradley
Spider (02)

Hall, Evelyn
Hell's Angels (30)

Hall, Grayson
Night of the Iguana, The (64)

Hall, Hanna
Virgin Suicides, The (00)

Hall, Huntz
Dead End (37); Walk in the Sun, A (45)

Hall, Irma P.
Midnight in the Garden of Good and Evil (97); Beloved (98); Collateral (04)

Hall, James
Hell's Angels (30)

Hall, Jerry
Batman (89)

Hall, Jon
Hurricane, The (37); Lady in the Dark (44)

Hall Jr., William
Driving Miss Daisy (89)

Hall, Juanita
South Pacific (58)

Hall, Kevin Peter
Predator (87)

Hall, Lois
Dead Again (91)

Hall, Ollie
Dead-End Drive-In (86)

Hall, Peter
Pedestrian, The (74)

Hall, Philip Baker
Kiss of Death (95); Psycho (98); Cradle Will Rock (99); Magnolia (99); Insider, The (99); Talented Mr. Ripley, The (99); Sum of All Fears, The (02); Bruce Almighty (03); In Good Company (04)

Hall, Porter
Thin Man, The (34); Petrified Forest, The (36); Story of Louis Pasteur, The (36); Make Way for Tomorrow (37); His Girl Friday (40); Sullivan's Travels (41); Miracle of Morgan's Creek, The (44); Double Indemnity (44); Going My Way (44); Murder, He Says (45); Miracle on 34th Street (47); Intruder in the Dust (49); Ace in the Hole (51)

Hall, Russell
My Little Chickadee (40)

Hall, Ruth
Monkey Business (31); Kid from Spain, The (32)

Hall, Thurston
Theodora Goes Wild (36); Great McGinty, The (40); This Land Is Mine (43); Secret Life of Walter Mitty, The (47); Band Wagon, The (53)

Hallahan, Charles
Going in Style (79); Thing, The (82); Silkwood (83); Pale Rider (85)

Hallam, John
Dragonslayer (81)

Hallaren, Jane
Modern Romance (81); Body Heat (81); Lianna (83)

Hallatt, May
Black Narcissus (46)

Handzlik, Jan
Auntie Mame (58)

Haney, Anne
Mrs. Doubtfire (93); Liar Liar (97); Midnight in the Garden of Good and Evil (97); Psycho (98)

Haney, Carol
Pajama Game, The (57)

Haney-Jardine, Perla
Kill Bill: Vol. 2 (04)

Hanft, Helen
Stardust Memories (80)

Hanin, Roger
Rocco and His Brothers (60)

Hankin, Larry
Escape from Alcatraz (79)

Hanks, Tom
Splash (84); Big (88); Philadelphia (93); Sleepless in Seattle (93); Forrest Gump (94); Apollo 13 (95); Toy Story (95); Saving Private Ryan (98); You've Got Mail (98); Green Mile, The (99); Toy Story 2 (99); Cast Away (00); Road to Perdition (02); Catch Me if You Can (02); Polar Express, The (04); Terminal, The (04)

Hanley, Jimmy
Gaslight (40); Way Ahead, The (44)

Hanly, Peter
Braveheart (95)

Hann-Byrd, Adam
Ice Storm, The (97); Halloween H2O: Twenty Years Later (98)

Hannah, Daryl
Blade Runner (82); Splash (84); Roxanne (87); Wall Street (87); Steel Magnolias (89); Kill Bill: Vol. 1 (03); Kill Bill: Vol. 2 (04)

Hannah, John
Four Weddings and a Funeral (94); Sliding Doors (98); Mummy, The (99)

Hannah, Scott
My Name Is Joe (98)

Hannan, John
Strictly Ballroom (92)

Hannigan, Alyson
American Pie (99)

Hanover, Donna
People vs. Larry Flynt, The (96)

Hanrion, Regis
Devil, Probably, The (77)

Hansard, Glen
Commitments, The (91)

Hansen, Ann Elisabeth
Ordet (55)

Hansen, Gale
Dead Poets Society (89)

Hansen, Gunnar
Texas Chainsaw Massacre, The (74)

Hansen, Holger Juul
Kingdom, The (94)

Hansen, Lars Arentz
Beach, The (00)

Hansen, William
Member of the Wedding, The (52); Fail Safe (64); Save the Tiger (73)

Hanson, David
Slap Shot (77)

Hansson, Maud
Seventh Seal, The (57)

Hara, Doug
Mad Dog and Glory (93)

Hara, Setsuko
Tokyo Story (53); Late Autumn (60); Chushingura (62)

Harada, Mieko
Ran (85); Dreams (90)

Harareet, Haya
Ben-Hur (59)

Harasimowicz, Cezary
White (94)

Harben, Hubert
Victoria the Great (37)

Harbord, Carl
Sahara (43); Macomber Affair, the (47)

Harbort, Christine
Mephisto (81)

Harcourt, James
Night Train to Munich (40); Adventuress, The (46)

Harden, Jacques
Lola (61)

Harden Jr., Ernest
White Men Can't Jump (92)

Harden, Marcia Gay
Miller's Crossing (90); Flubber (97); Meet Joe Black (98); Pollock (00); Mystic River (03); Mona Lisa Smile (03)

Hardie, Kate
Mona Lisa (86); Croupier (99)

Hardie, Russell
Camille (37); Fail Safe (64)

Hardin, Jerry
Chilly Scenes of Winter (79); Missing (82)

Harding, Ann
Man in the Gray Flannel Suit, The (56)

Harding, Jan Leslie
Amateur (94)

Harding, Lyn
Fire Over England (37); Goodbye Mr. Chips (39)

Harding, Mike
Dangerous Lives of Altar Boys, The (02)

Hardison, Kadeem
White Men Can't Jump (92)

Hardman, Karl
Night of the Living Dead (68)

Hashemian, Amir Farrokh
Children of Heaven (97)

Hashiguchi, Erina
Twilight Samurai, The (03)

Hasimovic, Husnija
Time of the Gypsies (89)

Hasketh, Trevor
Kes (69)

Hassan, Maryam
School of Rock (03)

Hasse, O.E.
Decision Before Dawn (51); State of Siege (72)

Hassell, George
Captain Blood (35)

Hassing, Louise
Idiots, The (98)

Hasso, Signe
Heaven Can Wait (43); House on 92nd Street, The (45); Double Life, A (47); I Never Promised You a Rose Garden (77)

Hastrup, Vibeke
Babette's Feast (87)

Hatcher, Teri
2 Days in the Valley (96); Tomorrow Never Dies (97); Spy Kids (01)

Hatfield, Hurd
Picture of Dorian Gray, The (45); Left-Handed Gun, The (58); King of Kings (61)

Hathaway, Anne
Nicholas Nickleby (02)

Hathaway, Noah
NeverEnding Story, The (84)

Hathwell, Carl
Story of Adele H., The (75)

Hatosy, Shawn
In & Out (97); Faculty, The (98); Cooler, The (03)

Hattab, Yoram
Kadosh (99)

Hattan, Tom
Secret of Nimh, The (82)

Hattangady, Rohini
Gandhi (82)

Hatten, Yankton
Places in the Heart (84)

Haudepin, Sabine
Jules and Jim (62); Last Metro, The (80)

Hauer, Rutger
Soldier of Orange (77); Spetters (80); Nighthawks (81); Blade Runner (82); Ladyhawke (85); Confessions of a Dangerous Mind (02); Frank Miller's Sin City (05)

Haughton, Vicky
Whale Rider (03)

Haupt, Ullrich
Morocco (30)

Hauser, Cole
Good Will Hunting (97); White Oleander (02)

Hausman, Willo
House of Games (87)

Hausmeister, Ruth
Pedestrian, The (74)

Havelkova, Libuse
Closely Watched Trains (66)

Havers, Nigel
Chariots of Fire (81); Passage to India, A (84); Empire of the Sun (87)

Havier, J. Alex
Back to Bataan (45)

Havill, Andew
Nicholas Nickleby (02)

Havill, Andrew
Sylvia (03)

Havoc, June
Brewster's Millions (45); Gentleman's Agreement (47)

Havrilla, Joann
Driving Miss Daisy (89)

Haw, Alex
Following (98)

Hawke, Ethan
Dead Poets Society (89); Midnight Clear, A (92); Before Sunrise (95); Great Expectations (98); Hamlet (00); Training Day (01); Taking Lives (04); Before Sunset (04); Assault on Precinct 13 (05)

Hawkes, John
Perfect Storm, The (00)

Hawking, Richard
Touching the Void (04)

Hawkins, Cole
Changing Lanes (02)

Hawkins, Frank
Indiscreet (58)

Hawkins, Jack
Black Rose, The (50); Cruel Sea, The (53); Bridge on the River Kwai, The (57); Ben-Hur (59); Lawrence of Arabia (62); Zulu (64); Lord Jim (65); Kidnapped (71); Theatre of Blood (73)

Hawkins, Ronnie
Last Waltz, The (78); Heaven's Gate (80)

Hawkins, Sally
Vera Drake (04)

Hawkins, Screamin' Jay
Mystery Train (89)

Hawn, Goldie
$ (Dollars) (71); Sugarland Express, The (74); Shampoo (75); Private Benjamin (80); Swing Shift (84); Death Becomes Her (92); First Wives Club, The (96); Everyone Says I Love You (96)

Hawthorne, Nigel
Black Cauldron, The (85); Demolition Man (93); Madness of King George, The (94); Richard

III (95); Amistad (97); Object of My Affection, The (98); Madeline (98); Tarzan (99)

Hawtrey, Charles
Carry on Nurse (59)

Hay, Alexandra
Guess Who's Coming to Dinner (67)

Hayakawa, Sessue
Three Came Home (50); Bridge on the River Kwai, The (57); Swiss Family Robinson (60)

Hayashi, Joichi
Kwaidan (64)

Hayashi, Marc
Chan Is Missing (81)

Haycraft, John
Remains of the Day, The (93)

Hayden, Harry
Christmas in July (40)

Hayden, James
Once Upon a Time in America (84)

Hayden, Melissa
Limelight (52)

Hayden, Sterling
Asphalt Jungle, The (50); Johnny Guitar (54); Killing, The (56); Terror in a Texas Town (58); Dr. Strangelove or: How I Learned to Stop Worrying and Love the Bomb (63); Godfather, The (72); Long Goodbye, The (73); 1900 (76); Winter Kills (79); 9 to 5 (80)

Haydn, Richard
Ball of Fire (41); Charley's Aunt (41); And Then There Were None (45); Late George Apley, The (47); Alice in Wonderland (51); Sound of Music, The (65); Young Frankenstein (74)

Haydon, Julie
Bill of Divorcement, A (32); Scoundrel, The (35)

Haye, Helen
39 Steps, The (35); Hobson's Choice (54)

Hayek, Salma
From Dusk till Dawn (96); Faculty, The (98); Wild Wild West (99); Dogma (99); Time Code (00); Frida (02); Once Upon a Time in Mexico (03)

Hayes, Chris
In the Company of Men (97)

Hayes, George "Gabby"
Hopalong Cassidy (35); My Pal Trigger (46)

Hayes, Grace
Babes in Arms (39)

Hayes, Helen
Sin of Madelon Claudet, The (31); Arrowsmith (31); Farewell to Arms, A (32); Anastasia (56); Airport (70)

Hayes, Isaac
Escape from New York (81); I'm Gonna Git You Sucka (88); South Park: Bigger, Longer & Uncut (99)

Hayes, Margaret
Sullivan's Travels (41); Glass Key, The (42); Blackboard Jungle (55)

Hayes, Patricia
Fish Called Wanda, A (88); War Requiem (89)

Hayes, Peter Lind
5,000 Fingers of Dr. T., The (53)

Hayes, Reggie
Being John Malkovich (99)

Hayes, Sean
Pieces of April (03); Dr. Seuss' The Cat in the Hat (03)

Hayes, Sioban
Iris (01)

Haygarth, Tony
Chicken Run (00)

Hayle, Grace
Great Dictator, The (40)

Hayman, David
Sid and Nancy (86); Hope and Glory (87); My Name Is Joe (98); Tailor of Panama, The (01)

Hayman, Leslie
Virgin Suicides, The (00)

Haymes, Dick
State Fair (45)

Haynes, Daniel
Hallelujah (29)

Haynes, Dick
Real Life (79)

Haynes, Linda
Rolling Thunder (77)

Haynes, Tiger
Mosquito Coast, The (86)

Haynie, Jim
Pretty in Pink (86); Bridges of Madison County, The (95)

Hays, Robert
Airplane! (80)

Haysbert, Dennis
Waiting to Exhale (95); Far from Heaven (02)

Hayward, Louis
Anthony Adverse (36); Man in the Iron Mask, The (39); And Then There Were None (45)

Hayward, Susan
Beau Geste (39); I Married a Witch (42); David and Bathsheba (51); Lusty Men, The (52); Snows of Kilimanjaro, The (52); With a Song in My Heart (52); I'll Cry Tomorrow (55); I Want to Live! (58)

Haywood, Chris
Man of Flowers (84); Coca-Cola Kid, The (85); Navigator, The (88); Innocence (00)

Haywood, Clair
Last Days of Chez Nous, The (93)

Hayworth, Rita
Only Angels Have Wings (39); Angels Over Broadway (40); Blood and Sand (41); You Were

Never Lovelier (42); Tales of Manhattan (42); Cover Girl (44); Gilda (46); Lady from Shanghai, The (48); Pal Joey (57); Separate Tables (58)

Haze, Jonathan
Little Shop of Horrors, The (61)

He Saifei
Raise the Red Lantern (91); Temptress Moon (96)

Heacock, Linnea
Taking Off (71)

Head, Murray
Romeo and Juliet (68); Sunday, Bloody Sunday (71)

Headey, Lena
Mrs. Dalloway (97); Possession (02)

Headley, Shari
Coming to America (88)

Headly, Glenne
Dick Tracy (90); Mortal Thoughts (91); Mr. Holland's Opus (95); 2 Days in the Valley (96)

Heald, Anthony
Orphans (87); Silence of the Lambs, The (91); Client, The (94); Kiss of Death (95); 8mm (99); Red Dragon (02)

Healy, Betty
Our Relations (36)

Healy, David
Unbelievable Truth, The (90)

Healy, Mary
5,000 Fingers of Dr. T., The (53)

Healy, Michael
Career Girls (97)

Healy, Ted
Bombshell (33); Mad Love (35); San Francisco (36)

Heard, John
Chilly Scenes of Winter (79); Cutter's Way (81); Trip to Bountiful, The (85); After Hours (85); Big (88); Beaches (88); Awakenings (90); Home Alone (90); Rambling Rose (91); Pelican Brief, The (93); Pollock (00)

Hearn, Ann
Accused, The (88); Lorenzo's Oil (92)

Hearn, George
Devil's Own, The (97)

Hearne, Richard
Captain Horatio Hornblower (51)

Heasley, John
5,000 Fingers of Dr. T., The (53)

Heasley, Robert
5,000 Fingers of Dr. T., The (53)

Heath, Dody
Diary of Anne Frank, The (59)

Heath, Geoffrey
Heavenly Creatures (94)

Heathcote, Thomas
Village of the Damned (60)

Heather, Jean
Double Indemnity (44); Going My Way (44); Murder, He Says (45)

Heatter, Gabriel
Champagne for Caesar (50)

Heavy D
Cider House Rules, The (99)

Hebert, Chris
Last Starfighter, The (84)

Heche, Anne
Donnie Brasco (97); I Know What You Did Last Summer (97); Wag the Dog (97); Psycho (98); Birth (04)

Hecht, Jessica
Sideways (04)

Hecht, Lawrence
Scream (96)

Hecht, Ted
So Proudly We Hail (43)

Heckart, Eileen
Somebody Up There Likes Me (56); Bus Stop (56); Zandy's Bride (74); First Wives Club, The (96)

Hector, Louis
Northwest Passage (40)

Hedaya, Dan
True Confessions (81); Blood Simple (84); Addams Family, The (91); Searching for Bobby Fischer (93); Benny & Joon (93); To Die For (95); Clueless (95); Usual Suspects, The (95); First Wives Club, The (96); Alien Resurrection (97); Mulholland Dr. (01)

Heder, Jon
Napoleon Dynamite (04)

Hedley, Jack
How I Won the War (67); For Your Eyes Only (81)

Hedlund, Garrett
Friday Night Lights (04)

Hedren, Tippi
Birds, The (63); Marnie (64)

Heffernan, John
Sting, The (73)

Heffner, Kyle T.
Runaway Train (85)

Heflin, Marta
Star Is Born, A (76); Come Back to the 5 & Dime, Jimmy Dean, Jimmy Dean (82); King of Comedy, The (83)

Heflin, Nora
Chilly Scenes of Winter (79)

Heflin, Van
Santa Fe Trail (40); Johnny Eager (42); Strange Love of Martha Ivers, The (46); Green Dolphin Street (47); Three Musketeers, The (48); Shane (53); Patterns (56); 3:10 to Yuma (57); Airport (70)

Hefner, Keith
Star 80 (83)

Hegarty, Susan
Lilo & Stitch (02)

Heggie, O.P.
Mysterious Dr. Fu Manchu, The (29); Smilin'
Through (32); Count of Monte Cristo, The (34)

Heigl, Katherine
Bride of Chucky (98)

Heilbron, Vivien
Kidnapped (71)

Heimel, Otto
My Little Chickadee (40)

Heineman, Laurie
Save the Tiger (73)

Heinle, Amelia
Limey, The (99)

Heinz, Gerd
Nowhere in Africa (01)

Heinzman, Bill
Night of the Living Dead (68)

Heitz, Jane Galloway
Straight Story, The (99)

Helgenberger, Marg
Erin Brockovich (00); In Good Company (04)

Helhoski, Maria
Driller Killer (79)

Helia, Jenny
Toni (35); La Bete Humaine (38)

Hell, Erik
Passion of Anna, The (69)

Heller, Randee
Karate Kid, The (84)

Hellman, Irving
Pee-wee's Big Adventure (85)

Hellman, Jaclyn
Two-Lane Blacktop (71)

Helm, Fay
Light That Failed, The (39); Wolf Man, The (41);
Phantom Lady (44)

Helm, Levon
Last Waltz, The (78); Coal Miner's Daughter (80)

Helmkamp, Charlotte
Frankenhooker (90)

Helmond, Katherine
Family Plot (76); Time Bandits (81); Brazil (85);
Lady in White (88); Fear and Loathing in Las
Vegas (98)

Helmore, Tom
Vertigo (58); Time Machine, The (60)

Helpmann, Robert
Red Shoes, The (48)

Helton, Percy
Criss Cross (49); Set-Up, The (49); 20,000 Leagues
under the Sea (54)

Hemblen, David
Exotica (95); Fly Away Home (96)

Hemingway, Mariel
Manhattan (79); Personal Best (82); Star 80 (83)

Hemmings, David
Blowup (66); Charge of the Light Brigade,
The (68); Juggernaut (74); Just a Gigolo (78); Last
Orders (01); League of Extraordinary Gentlemen,
The (03)

Hemmings, Nolan
Last Orders (01)

Henare, George
Once Were Warriors (94)

Henderson, Jo
Lianna (83)

Henderson, Lorna
Belles of St. Trinian's, The (54)

Henderson, Martin
Ring, The (02); Windtalkers (02)

Henderson, Sarah
Kids (95)

Henderson, Shirley
Topsy-Turvy (99); Bridget Jones's Diary (01);
24-Hour Party People (01); Bridget Jones: The
Edge of Reason (04)

Hendra, Tony
This Is Spinal Tap (84)

Hendricks, Sebie
Imitation of Life (34)

Hendrickson, Benjamin
Manhunter (86)

Hendrie, Phil
Team America: World Police (04)

Hendrix, Elaine
Parent Trap, The (98)

Hendrix, Wanda
Prince of Foxes (49)

Hendry, Ian
Repulsion (65); Get Carter (71); Theatre of
Blood (73); Passenger, The (75)

Heneghan, Patricia
Whistle Down the Wind (61)

Henie, Sonja
Thin Ice (37)

Henley, Barry "Shabaka"
Life (99)

Henley, Barry Shabaka
Collateral (04); Terminal, The (04)

Henn, Carrie
Aliens (86)

Henner, Marilu
Hammett (82); L.A. Story (91)

Henney, Del
Straw Dogs (71)

Hennig, Kate
Thirty-Two Short Films about Glenn Gould (93)

Henning, Pat
On the Waterfront (54)

Hoechlin, Tyler
Road to Perdition (02)

Hoerbiger, Paul
Third Man, The (49)

Hoey, Dennis
Anna and the King of Siam (46); David and Bathsheba (51)

Hoffman, Basil
Ordinary People (80); My Favorite Year (82)

Hoffman, Bern
On the Town (49)

Hoffman, Dustin
Graduate, The (67); Midnight Cowboy (69); Little Big Man (70); Straw Dogs (71); Papillon (73); Lenny (74); Marathon Man (76); All the President's Men (76); Straight Time (78); Kramer vs. Kramer (79); Tootsie (82); Ishtar (87); Rain Man (88); Dick Tracy (90); Hook (91); Wag the Dog (97); Moonlight Mile (02); Runaway Jury (03); Finding Neverland (04); Meet the Fockers (04); I Heart Huckabees (04)

Hoffman, Gerard
My Life to Live (62)

Hoffman, Guy
Agnes of God (85)

Hoffman, Kara
Lemony Snicket's A Series of Unfortunate Events (04)

Hoffman, Margaret
Monsieur Verdoux (47)

Hoffman, Philip Seymour
Scent of a Woman (92); Nobody's Fool (94); Twister (96); Boogie Nights (97); Happiness (98); Magnolia (99); Talented Mr. Ripley, The (99); Punch-Drunk Love (02); Red Dragon (02); 25th Hour (02); Cold Mountain (04)

Hoffman, Shelby
Lemony Snicket's A Series of Unfortunate Events (04)

Hoffman, Thom
Orlando (93)

Hoffmann, Gaby
Uncle Buck (89); Field of Dreams (89); Sleepless in Seattle (93); You Can Count on Me (00)

Hoffmeister, John
Ganja and Hess (73)

Hofschneider, Marco
Europa, Europa (91)

Hofschneider, Rene
Europa, Europa (91)

Hogan, Dick
Rope (48)

Hogan, Fiona
I, Robot (04)

Hogan, Paul
"Crocodile" Dundee (86)

Hogan, Susan
Brood, The (79)

Hogarth, Jane
Millions (04)

Hoger, Hannelore
Lost Honor of Katharina Blum, The (75)

Hogue, Eades
Baby Doll (56)

Hohl, Arthur
Island of Lost Souls (33); Kennel Murder Case, The (33); Wild Boys of the Road (33); Footlight Parade (33); Cleopatra (34); Bulldog Drummond Strikes Back (34); Whole Town's Talking, The (35); Devil-Doll, The (36); Show Boat (36); Adventures of Sherlock Holmes, The (39)

Hojfeldt, Solbjorg
Kingdom, The (94)

Hokanson, Mary Alan
Them! (54); Desperate Characters (71)

Holbrook, Hal
Great White Hope, The (70); All the President's Men (76); Julia (77); Creepshow (82); Wall Street (87); Firm, The (93); Majestic, The (01)

Holby, Kristin
Trading Places (83)

Holcomb, Sarah
Caddyshack (80)

Holcombe, Harry
Fortune Cookie, The (66)

Holden, Fay
Life Begins for Andy Hardy (41); Samson and Delilah (49)

Holden, Frankie J.
Proof (92)

Holden, Gloria
Life of Emile Zola, The (37); Test Pilot (38); Corsican Brothers, The (41)

Holden, James
Sands of Iwo Jima (49)

Holden, Jennifer
Jailhouse Rock (57)

Holden, Larry
Memento (01)

Holden, Laurie
Majestic, The (01)

Holden, William
Golden Boy (39); Our Town (40); Born Yesterday (50); Sunset Blvd. (50); Moon Is Blue, The (53); Stalag 17 (53); Country Girl, The (54); Executive Suite (54); Sabrina (54); Bridges at Toko-Ri, The (54); Picnic (55); Bridge on the River Kwai, The (57); Horse Soldiers, The (59); Casino Royale (67); Wild Bunch, The (69); Towering Inferno, The (74); Network (76)

Holder, Geoffrey
Doctor Dolittle (67)

Holder, Roy
Taming of the Shrew, The (67)

Holderread Jr., Noble Lee
Bob & Carol & Ted & Alice (69)

Holekamp, Mike
Dreamcatcher (03)

Holgado, Ticky
Delicatessen (91); Hairdresser's Husband, The (92);
Very Long Engagement, A (04)

Holgate, Diane
Whistle Down the Wind (61)

Holicker, Heidi
Valley Girl (83)

Holiday, Hope
Apartment, The (60); Irma la Douce (63)

Holland, Hilary
Man Who Fell to Earth, The (76)

Hollander, Jack
Miracle Worker, The (62)

Hollar, Steve
Hoosiers (86)

Holliday, Judy
Adam's Rib (49); Born Yesterday (50); It Should
Happen to You (54); Solid Gold Cadillac, The (56);
Bells Are Ringing (60)

Holliday, Polly
Mrs. Doubtfire (93); Parent Trap, The (98)

Holliman, Earl
Bridges at Toko-Ri, The (54); Rainmaker, The (56);
Forbidden Planet (56); Gunfight at the O.K.
Corral (57)

Hollis, Tommy
Malcolm X (92)

Holloway, Liddy
Sylvia (03)

Holloway, Stanley
Way Ahead, The (44); This Happy Breed (44);
Brief Encounter (45); Hamlet (48); Passport to
Pimlico (49); Lavender Hill Mob, The (51);
Beggar's Opera, The (52); My Fair Lady (64);
Private Life of Sherlock Holmes, The (70)

Holloway, Sterling
Wild Boys of the Road (33); Merry Widow,
The (34); Remember the Night (40); Dumbo (41);
Three Caballeros, The (45); Walk in the Sun,
A (45); Alice in Wonderland (51); Jungle Book,
The (67)

Holly, Lauren
Dragon: The Bruce Lee Story (93); Dumb &
Dumber (94); Any Given Sunday (99); Spirited
Away (01)

Holly, Martin
Shop on Main Street, The (64)

Holm, Celeste
Gentleman's Agreement (47); Road House (48);
Snake Pit, The (48); Champagne for Caesar (50);
All About Eve (50); High Society (56); 3 Men and
a Baby (87)

Holm, Claus
Berlin Alexanderplatz (79)

Holm, Ian
Oh! What a Lovely War (69); Homecoming,
The (73); Juggernaut (74); Robin and Marian (76);
Alien (79); Time Bandits (81); Chariots of
Fire (81); Greystoke: The Legend of Tarzan, Lord
of the Apes (84); Dance with a Stranger (85);
Brazil (85); Wetherby (85); Another Woman (88);
Naked Lunch (91); Madness of King George,
The (94); Fifth Element, The (97); Sweet Hereafter,
The (97); eXistenZ (99); Lord of the Rings: The
Fellowship of the Ring, The (01); From Hell (01);
Aviator, The (04); Garden State (04)

Holmes, Denis
Moonlighting (82)

Holmes, Katie
Ice Storm, The (97); Go (99); Wonder Boys (00);
Gift, The (00); Phone Booth (03); Pieces of
April (03)

Holmes, Mark
Adventures of Priscilla, Queen of the Desert,
The (94)

Holmes, Philip
Children of a Lesser God (86)

Holmes, Taylor
Kiss of Death (47); Boomerang (47); Nightmare
Alley (47); Father of the Bride (50); Gentlemen
Prefer Blondes (53); Sleeping Beauty (59)

Holmsten, Karl-Arne
Secrets of Women (52)

Holst, Svea
Passion of Anna, The (69)

Holt, Charlene
Man's Favorite Sport? (64); El Dorado (67)

Holt, David
Adventures of Tom Sawyer, The (38)

Holt, Jack
San Francisco (36); Cat People (42); They Were
Expendable (45); My Pal Trigger (46)

Holt, Sandrine
Black Robe (91)

Holt, Tim
Stella Dallas (37); Stagecoach (39); Back
Street (41); Magnificent Ambersons, The (42); My
Darling Clementine (46); Treasure of the Sierra
Madre, The (48)

Holton, Mark
Pee-wee's Big Adventure (85)

Holtzmann, Thomas
Funeral in Berlin (66)

Holzman, Daniel
It's Alive (74)

Homar, Lluis
Bad Education (04)

Homeier, Skip
Gunfighter, The (50); Tall T, The (57); Comanche
Station (60)

Hormel, Smokey
Georgia (95)

Horne, David
Seventh Veil, The (45)

Horne, Geoffrey
Bridge on the River Kwai, The (57)

Horne, Lena
Stormy Weather (43); Cabin in the Sky (43);
Ziegfeld Follies (45)

Horne, Victoria
To Each his Own (46); Ghost and Mrs. Muir,
The (47); Harvey (50)

Horrocks, Jane
Witches, The (90); Life Is Sweet (91); Chicken
Run (00)

Horsfall, Bernard
On Her Majesty's Secret Service (69)

Horsford, Anna Maria
Street Smart (87); Presumed Innocent (90)

Horton, Edward Everett
Front Page, The (31); Trouble in Paradise (32);
Merry Widow, The (34); Gay Divorcee, The (34);
Top Hat (35); Lost Horizon (37); Shall We
Dance (37); Here Comes Mr. Jordan (41); Ziegfeld
Girl (41); Gang's All Here, The (43); Arsenic and
Old Lace (44); Pocketful of Miralces (61)

Horton, Louisa
All My Sons (48)

Horton, Peter
2 Days in the Valley (96)

Horwarth, Maritta
Nowhere in Africa (01)

Hoskins, Bob
Long Good Friday, The (80); Pink Floyd—The
Wall (82); Cotton Club, The (84); Brazil (85);
Mona Lisa (86); Who Framed Roger Rabbit (88);
Hook (91); Nixon (95); Michael (96); Felicia's
Journey (99); Last Orders (01); Maid in
Manhattan (02); Vanity Fair (04)

Hossein, Nicolas
Wall, The (83)

Hossein, Robert
Rififi (54)

Hosseinian, Moahammad-Hasan
Children of Heaven (97)

Hou De Jian
Most Terrible Time in My Life, The (93)

Hough, Julian
Shout, The (78)

Houghton, Katharine
Guess Who's Coming to Dinner (67)

Hoult, Nicholas
About a Boy (02)

Hounsou, Djimon
Stargate (94); Amistad (97); Gladiator (00); In
America (03)

House, Billy
Stranger, The (46); Egg and I, The (47)

House, Rachel
Whale Rider (03)

Houseman, John
Paper Chase, The (73); Rollerball (75); Three Days
of the Condor (75); Another Woman (88); Naked
Gun: From the Files of Police Squad!, The (88)

Houser, Jerry
Summer of '42 (71); Bad Company (72); Slap
Shot (77)

Housman, Arthur
Our Relations (36)

Houston, Candice
Land before Time, The (88)

Houston, Donald
Doctor in the House (54); Room at the Top (59);
Where Eagles Dare (69)

Houston, Renee
Belles of St. Trinian's, The (54); Horse's Mouth,
The (58); Repulsion (65); Cul-de-Sac (66)

Houston, Robert
Hills Have Eyes, The (78)

Houston, Robin
When the Wind Blows (86)

Houston, Whitney
Bodyguard, The (92); Waiting to Exhale (95)

Hovey, Ann
Wild Boys of the Road (33)

Howard, Alan
Strapless (89); Cook, the Thief, His Wife & Her
Lover, The (89)

Howard, Arliss
Full Metal Jacket (87); Lost World: Jurassic Park,
The (97)

Howard, Bryce Dallas
Village, The (04)

Howard, Clint
Jungle Book, The (67); Rock 'n' Roll High
School (79)

Howard, David S.
Meet Joe Black (98)

Howard, Dennis
Go Tell the Spartans (78)

Howard, Esther
Detour (45); Murder, My Sweet (45)

Howard, Jeffrey
Wedding Banquet, The (93)

Howard, Jeremy
Dr. Suess' How the Grinch Stole Christmas (00)

Howard, John
Lost Horizon (37); Philadelphia Story, The (40)

Howard, Kathleen
It's a Gift (34); Death Takes a Holiday (34); Man
on the Flying Trapeze, The (35)

Huckabee, Cooper
Urban Cowboy (80); Cohen and Tate (89)

Hudak, Coni
David and Lisa (62)

Hudd, Walter
Rembrandt (36); I Know Where I'm Going! (45);
Importance of Being Earnest, The (52)

Huddleston, David
Rio Lobo (70); Bad Company (72); Blazing
Saddles (74); Frantic (88); Big Lebowski, The (98)

Hudgens, Vanessa Anne
Thirteen (03)

Hudson, Ernie
Ghostbusters (84); Weeds (87); Hand That Rocks
the Cradle, The (92); Crow, The (94)

Hudson, Garth
Last Waltz, The (78)

Hudson, Haley
Freaky Friday (03)

Hudson, Kate
Almost Famous (00)

Hudson, Rochelle
Wild Boys of the Road (33); She Done Him
Wrong (33); Imitation of Life (34); Les
Miserables (35); Curly Top (35); Rebel without a
Cause (55)

Hudson, Rock
Winchester '73 (50); Magnificent Obsession (54);
All That Heaven Allows (55); Written on the
Wind (56); Giant (56); Tarnished Angels, The (57);
Pillow Talk (59); Man's Favorite Sport? (64);
Seconds (66); Darling Lili (70)

Huertes, Luisa
Crime of Father Amaro, The (02)

Huet, Henri-Jacques
Breathless (59)

Huff, Neal
Wedding Banquet, The (93)

Huffman, David
Onion Field, The (79)

Huffman, Felicity
Reversal of Fortune (90); Spanish Prisoner,
The (98)

Hughes, Barnard
Midnight Cowboy (69); Hospital, The (71)

Hughes, Frank John
Catch Me if You Can (02)

Hughes, Geoffrey
Yellow Submarine (68)

Hughes, John
That Sinking Feeling (79)

Hughes, Kathleen
It Came from Outer Space (53)

Hughes, Mary Beth
Orchestra Wives (42); Ox-Bow Incident, The (43);
Young Man with a Horn (50)

Hughes, Miko
Apollo 13 (95)

Hughes, Rhetta
Sweet Sweetback's Baadasssss Song (71)

Hughes, Robert
Crumb (95)

Hughes, Robin
Dial M for Murder (54)

Hughes, Sally
In the Line of Fire (93)

Hughes, Tresa
Hospital, The (71); Coming Home (78)

Hughes, Wendy
My Brilliant Career (79); My First Wife (84)

Huguel, Sylvie
Henry & June (90)

Huison, Steve
Full Monty, The (97)

Hulce, Tom
National Lampoon's Animal House (78);
Amadeus (84); Parenthood (89); Fearless (93);
Hunchback of Notre Dame, The (96)

Hull, Arthur Stuart
Palm Beach Story, The (42)

Hull, Diane
Onion Field, The (79)

Hull, Henry
Boys Town (38); Three Comrades (38); Jesse
James (39); Stanley and Livingstone (39); High
Sierra (41); Lifeboat (44); Objective, Burma! (45);
Portrait of Jennie (48); Great Gatsby, The (49)

Hull, Josephine
Arsenic and Old Lace (44); Harvey (50)

Humbert, George
Farewell to Arms, A (32); Trouble in Paradise (32)

Hume-Kendall, Simon
Go-Between, The (71)

Humphreys, Cecil
Wuthering Heights (39)

Humphreys, Michael Conner
Forrest Gump (94)

Humphries, Barry
Bedazzled (67)

Hundley, Dylan
Metropolitan (90)

Hunnam, Charlie
Nicholas Nickleby (02)

Hunnicutt, Arthur
Red Badge of Courage, The (51); Lusty Men,
The (52); Big Sky, The (52); Tall T, The (57); Cat
Ballou (65); El Dorado (67); Harry and Tonto (74)

Hunt, Barbara Leigh
Merry War, A (97)

Hunt, Bonnie
Rain Man (88); Dave (93); Jerry Maguire (96);
Green Mile, The (99); Cheaper by the Dozen (03)

Irons, Jeremy
French Lieutenant's Woman, The (81); Betrayal (82); Moonlighting (82); Mission, The (86); Dead Ringers (88); Reversal of Fortune (90); Damage (92); Lion King, The (94); Stealing Beauty (96); Lolita (97); Being Julia (04); Kingdom of Heaven (05)

Ironside, Michael
Scanners (81); Top Gun (86); Total Recall (90); Free Willy (93); Starship Troopers (97); Machinist, The (04)

Irvine, Joanna
In the Name of the Father (93)

Irving, Amy
Carrie (76); Yentl (83); Tuck Everlasting (02)

Irving, Charles
Face in the Crowd, A (57)

Irving, George
Dangerous (36); Bringing Up Baby (38)

Irving, Margaret
Animal Crackers (30); San Francisco (36); Charlie Chan at the Opera (36)

Irving, Matt
When the Wind Blows (86)

Irwin, Bill
Eight Men Out (88); Hot Shots! (91); Dr. Suess' How the Grinch Stole Christmas (00)

Isaac, Estelle
Baise-Moi (00)

Isaacs, Dr. Daryl
Super Size Me (04)

Isaacs, Jason
Armageddon (98); End of the Affair, The (99); Patriot, The (00); Peter Pan (03)

Isabelle, Katherine
Insomnia (02)

Isaki, Mitsunori
Dreams (90)

Isaza Tuzman, Kaleil
Startup.com (01)

Isbell, Tom
Jacknife (89)

Isedal, Tor
Virgin Spring, The (59)

Isham, Gyles
Anna Karenina (35)

Ishibashi, Renji
Tetsuo: The Iron Man (89); Audition (99)

Ishibashi, Ryo
Audition (99); Grudge, The (04)

Ishida, Keisuke
Black Rain (89)

Ishida, Taro
Akira (88)

Ishiguro, Tatsuya
Gate of Hell (53)

Ishikura, Saburo
Blind Swordsman: Zatoichi, The (03)

Ishiyama, Kenjiro
High and Low (63)

Ismare, Sigifredo
Mission, The (86)

Israel
Trembling before G-D (01)

Isunza, Agustin
El Topo (71)

Isyanov, Ravil
K-19: The Widowmaker (02)

Itami, Ichizo
Lord Jim (65)

Itkine, Sylvain
Grand Illusion (37)

Ito, Hiroko
Woman in the Dunes (64)

Ito, Miki
Twilight Samurai, The (03)

Ito, Robert
Adventures of Buckaroo Banzai: Across the 8th Dimension, The (84)

Itsumi, Taro
Fireworks (97)

Iturbi, Jose
Anchors Aweigh (45)

Itzin, Gregory
Fabulous Baker Boys, The (89); Small Soldiers (98)

Ivalu, Madeline
Fast Runner (Atanarjuat), The (01)

Ivalu, Sylvia
Fast Runner (Atanarjuat), The (01)

Ivan, Rosalind
Scarlet Street (45); Johnny Belinda (48)

Ivanek, Zeljko
Tex (82); Donnie Brasco (97); Civil Action, A (98); Hannibal (01)

Ivasbeva, V.S.
Alexander Nevsky (38)

Ivashov, Vladimir
Ballad of a Soldier (59)

Ivatts, Peter
Long Day Closes, The (92)

Ivernel, Daniel
Diary of a Chambermaid (64)

Ives, Burl
East of Eden (55); Cat on a Hot Tin Roof (58); Our Man in Havana (59); Our Man in Havana (59); White Dog (82)

Ivey, Dana
Color Purple, The (85); Addams Family, The (91)

Ivey, Judith
Washington Square (97)

Jaffa, Melissa
Cars That Ate Paris, The (74)

Jaffe, Carl
Roman Spring of Mrs. Stone, The (61)

Jaffe, Naomi
Weather Underground, The (03)

Jaffe, Sam
Scarlet Empress, The (34); Lost Horizon (37);
Gunga Din (39); Gentleman's Agreement (47);
Asphalt Jungle, The (50); Day the Earth Stood Still,
The (51); Ben-Hur (59); Bedknobs and
Broomsticks (71)

Jaffrey, Madhur
Shakespeare Wallah (65); Vanya on 42nd
Street (94)

Jaffrey, Saeed
Man Who Would Be King, The (75); My Beautiful
Laundrette (85)

Jaffrey, Sakina
Indian in the Cupboard, The (95)

Jagger, Dean
Western Union (41); Pursued (47); Twelve O'Clock
High (49); Robe, The (53); Executive Suite (54);
White Christmas (54); Bad Day at Black
Rock (55); Nun's Story, The (59); Elmer
Gantry (60)

Jagger, Mick
Performance (70); Gimme Shelter (70)

Jago, June
Man from Snowy River, The (82)

Jakub, Lisa
Rambling Rose (91); Mrs. Doubtfire (93);
Matinee (93)

Jam, Kia
House of Sand and Fog (03)

Jambrino, Francisco
Los Olvidados (50)

James, Anthony
Hearts of the West (75)

James, Brion
Southern Comfort (81); Blade Runner (82); 48
Hrs. (82); Player, The (92); Fifth Element, The (97)

James, Clifton
David and Lisa (62); Cool Hand Luke (67); Last
Detail, The (73); Juggernaut (74); Rancho
Deluxe (75); Superman II (80); Lone Star (96)

James, Don
Hamburger Hill (87)

James, Emrys
Dragonslayer (81)

James, Gennie
Places in the Heart (84)

James, Hawthorne
Speed (94)

James, Jesse
As Good As It Gets (97); Blow (01); Butterfly
Effect, The (04)

James, Jessica
Diner (82)

James, Jonathan
Raining Stones (93)

James, Ken
Equus (77); Fly Away Home (96)

James, Kevin
Hitch (05)

James, Lennie
24-Hour Party People (01)

James, Mark
Slacker (91)

James, Olga
Carmen Jones (54)

James, Sidney
Lavender Hill Mob, The (51); Detective, The (54);
Kid for Two Farthings, A (55); Trapeze (56); Story
of Esther Costello, The (57)

James, Steve
Brother from Another Planet, The (84); To Live and
Die in L.A. (85); I'm Gonna Git You Sucka (88)

Jameson, House
Naked City, The (48)

Jameson, Joyce
Tales of Terror (62); Outlaw Josey Wales, The (76)

Jamieson, Alexandra
Super Size Me (04)

Jamison, Johnny Hiram
Unbreakable (00)

Jamison, Richard
Over the Edge (79)

Janczar, Krzysztof
Man of Iron (80)

Janczar, Tadeusz
Kanal (57)

Janda, Krystyna
Man of Marble (77); Man of Iron (80);
Mephisto (81); Short Film about Killing, A (87)

Jandl, Ivan
Search, The (48)

Jane, Thomas
Dreamcatcher (03)

Jane, Topsy
Loneliness of the Long Distance Runner, The (62)

Janevski, Boban
Delicatessen (91)

Janis, Conrad
Buddy Holly Story, The (78)

Jankowski, Oleg
My 20th Century (89); Mute Witness (95)

Janney, Allison
American Beauty (99); Finding Nemo (03)

Janney, Leon
Charly (68)

Kirk, Tommy
Old Yeller (57); Swiss Family Robinson (60);
Absent-Minded Professor, The (61)

Kirkland, Sally
Star Is Born, A (76); EdTV (99)

Kirkpatrick, Jess
D.O.A. (50)

Kirshner, Mia
Exotica (95)

Kiser, Terry
Rachel, Rachel (68)

Kishibe, Ittoku
Blind Swordsman: Zatoichi, The (03)

Kishida, Kyoko
Woman in the Dunes (64)

Kishimoto, Kayoko
Fireworks (97)

Kishonti, Ildiko
Mephisto (81)

Kissner, Jeremy James
Great Expectations (98)

Kitamura, Kazuo
Black Rain (89)

Kitano, Takeshi
Merry Christmas, Mr. Lawrence (83);
Sonatine (94); Gonin (95); Fireworks (97); Blind
Swordsman: Zatoichi, The (03)

Kitchen, Michael
Out of Africa (85); Russia House, The (90);
Enchanted April (91); Mrs. Dalloway (97)

Kitt, Eartha
Unzipped (95); Emperor's New Groove, The (00)

Kitzmiller, John
Dr. No (62)

Kivel, Barry
Bound (96)

Kiyokawa, Nijiko
Teahouse of the August Moon, The (56); Ballad of
Narayama, The (83)

Kjellin, Alf
Juggler, The (53)

Kjellqvist, Tommy
Sacrifice, The (86)

Kjellson, Ingvar
Shame (68)

Kjer, Bodil
Babette's Feast (87)

Klar, Gary Howard
Day of the Dead (85)

Klarwein, Eleonore
Peppermint Soda (77)

Klauber, Gertan
Top Secret! (84)

Klausner, Uri Ran
Kadosh (99)

Klaussner, Burghart
Good Bye, Lenin! (03)

Klebaner, Audrey
In Praise of Love (01)

Kleiber, Erich
Knife in the Head (78)

Klein, Adelaide
Naked City, The (48); Enforcer, The (51)

Klein, Chris
Election (99); American Pie (99); We Were
Soldiers (02)

Klein, Gerard
Frantic (88)

Klein, Nita
Muriel (63)

Klein-Lork, Robert
Blue Angel, The (30)

Klein-Rogge, Rudolf
Testament of Dr. Mabuse, The (33)

Klek, George Robert
Abyss, The (89)

Klemena, Vladimir
Dersu Uzala (75)

Kleyla, Brandon
Gods and Monsters (98)

Kline, Kevin
Sophie's Choice (82); Big Chill, The (83);
Silverado (85); Fish Called Wanda, A (88); Grand
Canyon (91); Chaplin (92); Dave (93); Hunchback
of Notre Dame, The (96); Ice Storm, The (97); In &
Out (97); Wild Wild West (99); Emperor's Club,
The (02); De-Lovely (04)

Kline, Marvin
Counsellor-at-Law (33)

Klossowski, Pierre
Au Hasard, Balthazar (66)

Klugman, Jack
12 Angry Men (57); Days of Wine and Roses (62);
Detective, The (68)

Knaiz, Judy
Hello, Dolly! (69)

Knapp, Stanley
Liquid Sky (82)

Knaup, Herbert
Run Lola Run (98)

Knepper, Robert
Gas Food Lodging (92)

Kneppers, Tony
Traffic (72)

Knesich, Tony
Gloria (80)

Knight, Davidson
Bugsy Malone (76)

Knight, Esmond
Contraband (40); Henry V (44); Black
Narcissus (46); Red Shoes, The (48); River,

Laudenbach, Philippe
Muriel (63); Mon Oncle d'Amerique (80);
Confidentially Yours (83); Betty Blue (86)

Laughlin, Tom
Tea and Sympathy (56); Gidget (59)

Laughton, Charles
If I Had a Million (32); Old Dark House, The (32);
Island of Lost Souls (33); Private Life of Henry
VIII, The (33); Barretts of Wimpole Street,
The (34); Les Miserables (35); Mutiny on the
Bounty (35); Ruggles of Red Gap (35);
Rembrandt (36); Hunchback of Notre Dame,
The (39); Tales of Manhattan (42); This Land Is
Mine (43); Big Clock, The (48); Man of the Eiffel
Tower, The (49); O. Henry's Full House (52);
Hobson's Choice (54); Witness for the
Prosecution (57); Spartacus (60); Advise and
Consent (62)

Laupus, Arthur
Washington Square (97)

Laurance, Mitchell
Hand That Rocks the Cradle, The (92)

Laure, Carole
Get Out Your Handkerchiefs (78)

Laurel, Stan
Babes in Toyland (34); Our Relations (36); Way
Out West (37)

Laurence, Andrew
Macbeth (71)

Laurence, Ashley
Hellraiser (87)

Laurence, Michael
Othello (52)

Laurenson, James
Pink Floyd—The Wall (82)

Laurent, Jacqueline
Daybreak (39)

Laurent, Remi
La Cage aux Folles (78)

Lauria, Dan
Stakeout (87)

Laurie, Hugh
Strapless (89); 101 Dalmatians (96); Stuart
Little (99)

Laurie, John
39 Steps, The (35); Life and Death of Colonel
Blimp, The (43); Way Ahead, The (44); I Know
Where I'm Going! (45); Hamlet (48); Treasure
Island (50)

Laurie, Piper
Hustler, The (61); Carrie (76); Children of a Lesser
God (86); Faculty, The (98)

Lauter, Ed
Longest Yard, The (74); Family Plot (76);
Seabiscuit (03)

Lauterbach, Heiner
Men... (85)

Lautsiavitchus, Lyubomiras
Come and See (85)

Laval, Jean-Daniel
La Balance (82)

Lavanant, Dominique
Three Men and a Cradle (85)

Lavant, Denis
Bad Blood (86)

LaVecchia, Antoinette
Jesus' Son (00)

Lavi, Daliah
Lord Jim (65); Casino Royale (67)

Lavine, Charles
King of Marvin Gardens, The (72)

Law, John Phillip
Golden Voyage of Sinbad, The (73)

Law, Jude
Midnight in the Garden of Good and Evil (97);
Wilde (97); eXistenZ (99); Talented Mr. Ripley,
The (99); A.I.: Artificial Intelligence (01); Road to
Perdition (02); Cold Mountain (04); Aviator,
The (04); Closer (04); Lemony Snicket's A Series
of Unfortunate Events (04); Sky Captain and the
World of Tomorrow (04); Alfie (04); I Heart
Huckabees (04)

Law, Phyllida
Before the Rain (94)

Law, Walter
Whoopee (30)

Lawford, Chris
Terminator 3: Rise of the Machines (03)

Lawford, Myarn
Rabbit-Proof Fence (02)

Lawford, Ningali
Rabbit-Proof Fence (02)

Lawford, Peter
White Cliffs of Dover, The (44); Picture of Dorian
Gray, The (45); Easter Parade (48); Royal
Wedding (51); It Should Happen to You (54);
Exodus (60); Advise and Consent (62)

Lawless, Doc
King of Comedy, The (83)

Lawrence, Barbara
Captain from Castile (47); Unfaithfully Yours (48);
Letter to Three Wives, A (49); Oklahoma! (55)

Lawrence, Bruno
Smash Palace (81)

Lawrence, Carolyn
SpongeBob Squarepants Movie, The (04)

Lawrence, Douglas
SpongeBob Squarepants Movie, The (04)

Lawrence, Elizabeth
Sleeping with the Enemy (91)

Lawrence, Gertrude
Rembrandt (36)

Lawrence, Josie
Enchanted April (91)

Lowe, Rob
Outsiders, The (83); Bad Influence (90); Wayne's World (92); Contact (97); Austin Powers: The Spy Who Shagged Me (99)

Lowell, Carey
Sleepless in Seattle (93)

Lowenadler, Holger
Lacombe, Lucien (74)

Lowens, Curt
Midnight Clear, A (92)

Lowensohn, Elina
Schindler's List (93); Amateur (94)

Lowery, Robert
Drums Along the Mohawk (39); Mark of Zorro, The (40)

Lowitsch, Klaus
Cross of Iron (77); Marriage of Maria Braun, The (78)

Lowry, Judith
Effect of Gamma Rays on Man-in-the-Moon Marigolds, The (72)

Lowry, Morton
Dawn Patrol, The (38); Hound of the Baskervilles, The (39); How Green Was My Valley (41); None but the Lonely Heart (44); Picture of Dorian Gray, The (45)

Lowther, T.J.
Perfect World, A (93)

Loy, Myrna
Connecticut Yankee, A (31); Arrowsmith (31); Love Me Tonight (32); Manhattan Melodrama (34); Thin Man, The (34); Libeled Lady (36); After the Thin Man (36); Great Ziegfeld, The (36); Test Pilot (38); Love Crazy (41); Best Years of Our Lives, The (46); Bachelor and the Bobby-Soxer, The (47); Mr. Blandings Builds His Dream House (48); Cheaper by the Dozen (50)

Loya, Javier
Exterminating Angel, The (62)

Loza, Richard
Carla's Song (96)

Lozano, Carlos
All about My Mother (99)

Lozano, Margarita
Viridiana (61); Fistful of Dollars, A (64); Night of the Shooting Stars, The (81)

Lu Hsiao-ling
What Time Is It There? (01)

Lu Lei
Big Parade, The (85)

Lu, Lisa
Joy Luck Club, The (93)

Lu Qi
Farewell, My Concubine (93)

Lu Xiahoe
Emperor and the Assassin, The (99)

Lubaszenko, Edward
Contract (80)

Lucas, Charlie
Tea with Mussolini (99)

Lucas, Josh
American Psycho (00); Beautiful Mind, A (01); Deep End, The (01); Sweet Home Alabama (02); Hulk (03)

Lucas, Laurent
With a Friend Like Harry (00)

Lucas, Lisa
Unmarried Woman, An (78)

Lucas, William
Sons and Lovers (60)

Lucena, Carlos
Hit, The (84)

Luchini, Fabrice
Claire's Knee (70); Full Moon in Paris (84)

Lucien, Joseph
City of Lost Children, The (95)

Luckey, Susan
Carousel (56)

Luckham, Cyril
Providence (77)

Lucking, William
Limey, The (99)

Lucy, Arnold
Dr. Jekyll and Mr. Hyde (32)

Luddy, Barbara
Lady and the Tramp (55); Sleeping Beauty (59)

Ludlam, Charles
Big Easy, The (87)

Ludwig, Adam
Scanners (81)

Ludwig, Karen
Manhattan (79)

Ludwig, Pamela
Over the Edge (79)

Ludwig, Salem
I Love You, Alice B. Toklas! (68)

Luez, Laurette
D.O.A. (50)

Lugagne, Francoise
Diary of a Chambermaid (64)

Lugosi, Bela
Dracula (31); Island of Lost Souls (33); Black Cat, The (34); Son of Frankenstein (39); Ninotchka (39); Wolf Man, The (41); Abbott and Costello Meet Frankenstein (48); Plan 9 from Outer Space (59)

Luguet, Andre
French, They Are a Funny Race, The (55)

Lui Chun
In the Mood for Love (00)

Luis, Jacqueline
El Topo (71)

Lukas, Florian
Good Bye, Lenin! (03)

Lukas, Paul
Little Women (33); Dodsworth (36); Lady Vanishes, The (38); Confessions of a Nazi Spy (39); Watch on the Rhine (43); 20,000 Leagues under the Sea (54); Lord Jim (65)

Luke, Benny
La Cage aux Folles (78)

Luke, Derek
Antwone Fisher (02); Pieces of April (03); Friday Night Lights (04)

Luke, Jorge
Ulzana's Raid (72)

Luke, Keye
Mad Love (35); Charlie Chan at the Opera (36); Good Earth, The (37)

Lukschy, Wolfgang
Fistful of Dollars, A (64)

Lulli, Folco
Wages of Fear, The (52)

Lulu
To Sir, with Love (67)

Lum, Harry
Liquid Sky (82)

Lumbly, Carl
To Sleep with Anger (90)

Lumet, Baruch
Pawnbroker, The (65)

Lumet, Jenny
Q&A (90)

Lumley, Joanna
Cold Comfort Farm (95)

Lumsden, Norman
White Hunter, Black Heart (90)

Luna, Diego
Y Tu Mama Tambien (01); Frida (02); Open Range (03); Terminal, The (04)

Luna, Margarito
Treasure of the Sierra Madre, The (48)

Luna, Victoria
Spanglish (04)

Lunardi, Iole
Before the Revolution (64)

Lund, John
To Each his Own (46); High Society (56)

Lund, Jordan
Jacknife (89)

Lund, Lucille
Black Cat, The (34)

Lund, Zoe
Bad Lieutenant (92)

Lundberg, Raymond
Shame (68)

Lundigan, William
Fighting 69th, The (40); Santa Fe Trail (40); Sea Hawk, The (40); Pinky (49)

Lundkvist, Anja
Together (00)

Lundy, Jessica
Single White Female (92)

Lung Sihung
Crouching Tiger, Hidden Dragon (00)

Lunghi, Cherie
Excalibur (81); Mission, The (86)

Lunt, Alfred
Guardsman, The (31)

Luoyong Wang
Dragon: The Bruce Lee Story (93)

Lupersio, Leticia
Dona Herlinda and Her Son (86)

Lupino, Ida
Light That Failed, The (39); Adventures of Sherlock Holmes, The (39); They Drive by Night (40); High Sierra (41); Sea Wolf, The (41); Road House (48); Big Knife, The (55); While the City Sleeps (56); Junior Bonner (72)

LuPone, Patti
Witness (85); Driving Miss Daisy (89)

Lupovici, Marcel
Rififi (54)

Lurie, John
Paris, Texas (84); Stranger than Paradise (84); Down by Law (86)

Luske, Tommy
Peter Pan (53)

Luttazzi, Lelio
L'Avventura (60)

Lutter, Alfred
Alice Doesn't Live Here Anymore (74); Bad News Bears, The (76)

Lutz, Catherine
Lola (61); Stolen Kisses (68)

Lutz, Regine
Lost Honor of Katharina Blum, The (75)

Luu, Thuy An
Diva (81)

Luz, Dora
Three Caballeros, The (45)

Luzi, Maria Pia
La Notte (61)

Lyby, Troels
Idiots, The (98)

Lycos, Tom
Sweetie (89)

Lydiard, Bob
Paper Chase, The (73)

Lydon, James
Life with Father (47)

Lydon, John
Filth and the Fury, The (00)

Lydon, Simon
Well, The (99)

Lynch, Alfred
Taming of the Shrew, The (67)

Lynch, John
In the Name of the Father (93); Secret Garden, The (93); Secret of Roan Inish, The (95); Sliding Doors (98)

Lynch, John Carroll
Fargo (96); Face/Off (97); Good Girl, The (02); Gothika (03)

Lynch, Kelly
Drugstore Cowboy (89); Charlie's Angels (00)

Lynch, Richard
Scarecrow (73)

Lynch, Susan
Secret of Roan Inish, The (95); From Hell (01)

Lynde, Paul
Charlotte's Web (73)

Lynn, Betty
Cheaper by the Dozen (50)

Lynn, Diana
Major and the Minor, The (42); Miracle of Morgan's Creek, The (44); Bedtime for Bonzo (51)

Lynn, George
Magnificent Obsession (54)

Lynn, Jeffrey
Four Daughters (38); Roaring Twenties, The (39); All This and Heaven Too (40); Fighting 69th, The (40); Letter to Three Wives, A (49); Butterfield 8 (60)

Lynn, Leni
Babes in Arms (39)

Lynn, William
Harvey (50)

Lynne, Sharon
Way Out West (37)

Lynskey, Melanie
Heavenly Creatures (94); Ever After (98); Sweet Home Alabama (02); Shattered Glass (03)

Lyon, Ben
Hell's Angels (30)

Lyon, Lisa
Three Crowns of the Sailor (83)

Lyon, Richard
Anna and the King of Siam (46)

Lyon, Sue
Lolita (62); Night of the Iguana, The (64)

Lyonne, Natasha
Everyone Says I Love You (96); American Pie (99); Grey Zone, The (02)

Lyonnet, Louis
Life and Nothing But (89)

Lyons, Bruce
Navigator, The (88)

Lyons, Phyllis
Bridges of Madison County, The (95)

Lyons, Robert F.
Getting Straight (70)

Lys, Lya
L'Age d'Or (30); Confessions of a Nazi Spy (39)

Lysell, Allan
Accused, The (88)

M'Baye, Seyba
Brightness (87)

M'Doulabia, Christophe
Mandabi (68)

Ma Jingwu
Raise the Red Lantern (91)

Ma Ling
Life on a String (92)

Ma Mingwei
Farewell, My Concubine (93)

Maas, Sybil
Cousin, Cousine (75)

Maazel, Lincoln
Martin (78)

Maberly, Kate
Secret Garden, The (93)

Mabius, Eric
Welcome to the Dollhouse (95); Cruel Intentions (99)

Mably, Luke
28 Days Later... (02)

Mac, Bernie
Life (99); Ocean's Eleven (01); Bad Santa (03); Charlie's Angels: Full Throttle (03); Ocean's Twelve (04)

MacArthur, James
Swiss Family Robinson (60)

MacArthur, Roy
Liquid Sky (82)

Macartney, Carol
Gregory's Girl (81)

Macaulay, Charles
Head (68); Big Red One, The (80)

Macaulay, Marc
Monster (03)

MacBride, Donald
My Favorite Wife (40); Northwest Passage (40); Here Comes Mr. Jordan (41); Love Crazy (41); Glass Key, The (42); Killers, The (46); Egg and I, The (47); Seven Year Itch, The (55)

Maccanti, Roberto
1900 (76)

Macchio, Ralph
Outsiders, The (83); Karate Kid, The (84); My Cousin Vinny (92)

MacDonald, Bruce
Return of the Secaucus Seven (80)

MacDonald, Edmund
Detour (45)

MacDonald, Ian
Road House (48); High Noon (52); Apache (54)

MacDonald, J. Farrell
Show Boat (36)

MacDonald, James
Cinderella (50)

MacDonald, Jeanette
Love Parade, The (29); Monte Carlo (30); Love Me Tonight (32); Merry Widow, The (34); Naughty Marietta (35); Rose Marie (36); San Francisco (36); Maytime (37)

MacDonald, Jessica
Lianna (83)

Macdonald, Kelly
Trainspotting (95); Elizabeth (98)

MacDowell, Andie
Greystoke: The Legend of Tarzan, Lord of the Apes (84); sex, lies, and videotape (89); Hudson Hawk (91); Short Cuts (93); Groundhog Day (93); Four Weddings and a Funeral (94); Michael (96)

Mace, Paul
Lords of Flatbush, The (74)

Macer, Sterling
Dragon: The Bruce Lee Story (93)

Macey, Elizabeth
Bound for Glory (76)

MacFadyen, Angus
Braveheart (95); Cradle Will Rock (99)

MacGill, Moyna
Green Dolphin Street (47)

MacGinnis, Niall
49th Parallel (41); Anna Karenina (47); Lust for Life (56); Jason and the Argonauts (63)

MacGowran, Jack
Darby O'Gill and the Little People (59); Cul-de-Sac (66); How I Won the War (67); Exorcist, The (73)

MacGrath, Leueen
Pygmalion (38)

MacGraw, Ali
Love Story (70); Getaway, The (72)

MacGreevy, Oliver
Ipcress File, The (65)

MacGregor, Charles
Superfly (72)

MacGregor, Hector
Stage Fright (50)

MacGregor, Lee
Twelve O'Clock High (49)

MacGuire, Marlena
Five Easy Pieces (70)

Machado, Mario
RoboCop (87)

Machowski, Ignacy
Ashes and Diamonds (58)

Macht, Gabriel
Recruit, The (03)

MacInnes, Angus
Atlantic City (81); Witness (85)

MacIvor, Daniel
Beefcake (99)

Mack, Helen
His Girl Friday (40)

Mack, James T.
Anna Christie (30)

Mackay, Fulton
Gumshoe (71); Local Hero (83); Defence of the Realm (85)

MacKay, John A.
Trust (91)

MacKay, Michael Reid
Apt Pupil (98)

MacKenna, Kenneth
Judgment at Nuremberg (61)

MacKenna, Stephen
Eye of the Needle (81)

MacKenzie, Joyce
Racket, The (51)

Mackey, Brendan
Touching the Void (04)

Mackey, Kathleen
Gothika (03)

Mackie, Anthony
Million Dollar Baby (04)

Mackintosh, Steven
Lock, Stock and Two Smoking Barrels (98)

Macklin, Albert
Streamers (83)

Macko, Denny
Driver, The (78)

MacLachlan, Andrew
Monty Python's The Meaning of Life (83)

MacLachlan, Janet
Sounder (72)

MacLachlan, Kyle
Blue Velvet (86); Hidden, The (87); Doors, The (91); Flintstones, The (94); Showgirls (95); Time Code (00)

MacLaine, Shirley
Trouble with Harry, The (55); Around the World in 80 Days (56); Some Came Running (58); Apartment, The (60); Irma la Douce (63); What a Way to Go! (64); Sweet Charity (69); Desperate Characters (71); Turning Point, The (77); Being There (79); Terms of Endearment (83); Madame Sousatzka (88); Steel Magnolias (89); Postcards from the Edge (90)

MacLane, Barton
G-Men (35); Prince and the Pauper, The (37); You Only Live Once (37); High Sierra (41); Maltese Falcon, The (41); Western Union (41); Treasure of the Sierra Madre, The (48); Glenn Miller Story, The (53)

MacLaren, Deborah
Naked (93)

MacLaren, Ian
Cleopatra (34)

MacLaren, John
Double Jeopardy (99)

MacLean, Peter
Friends of Eddie Coyle, The (73)

MacLiam, Eanna
My Left Foot (89); Snapper, The (93); Angela's Ashes (99)

MacLiammoir, Michael
Othello (52)

MacMahon, Aline
Gold Diggers of 1933 (33); Ah, Wilderness! (35); Search, The (48); Man from Laramie, The (55)

MacMahon, Horace
Detective Story (51); Detective, The (68)

MacMillian, Will
Salvador (86)

MacMurray, Fred
Alice Adams (35); Hands Across the Table (35); Trail of the Lonesome Pine, The (36); Remember the Night (40); Double Indemnity (44); Murder, He Says (45); Egg and I, The (47); Caine Mutiny, The (54); Apartment, The (60); Absent-Minded Professor, The (61)

MacNaughton, Robert
E.T. The Extra-Terrestrial (82)

Macnee, Patrick
Les Girls (57); Howling, The (81)

MacNeil, Cornell
La Traviata (82)

MacNeil, Jennie
Fist in His Pocket (66)

MacNeil, Legs
End of the Century: The Story of the Ramones (04)

MacNeil, Rita
Candy Mountain (87)

MacNeill, Peter
Crash (96); Hanging Garden, The (98)

MacNicol, Peter
Dragonslayer (81); Sophie's Choice (82)

Macollum, Barry
Trouble with Harry, The (55)

Macrae, Arthur
Horse's Mouth, The (58)

MacRae, Elizabeth
Conversation, The (74)

MacRae, Gordon
Oklahoma! (55); Carousel (56)

MacRae, Heather
Bang the Drum Slowly (73)

Macready, George
Song to Remember, A (45); Gilda (46); Big Clock, The (48); Knock on Any Door (49); Desert Fox, The (51); Detective Story (51); Julius Caesar (53); Vera Cruz (54); Kiss before Dying, A (56); Paths of Glory (57); Seven Days in May (64)

Macrorie, Alma
To Each his Own (46)

MacSunday, Lon
Smiling Lieutenant, The (31)

Macy, Bill
Late Show, The (77); My Favorite Year (82); Analyze This (99)

Macy, William H.
Homicide (91); Searching for Bobby Fischer (93); Benny & Joon (93); Mr. Holland's Opus (95); Fargo (96); Boogie Nights (97); Wag the Dog (97); Civil Action, A (98); Pleasantville (98); Psycho (98); Magnolia (99); Cooler, The (03); Seabiscuit (03)

Madden, Dave
Charlotte's Web (73)

Madden, Peter
Loneliness of the Long Distance Runner, The (62)

Madigan, Amy
Places in the Heart (84); Uncle Buck (89); Field of Dreams (89); Pollock (00)

Madison, Guy
Since You Went Away (44)

Madison, Julian
It's a Gift (34)

Madison, Noel
G-Men (35)

Madonna
Desperately Seeking Susan (85); Dick Tracy (90); Truth of Dare (91); Unzipped (95); Evita (96); Swept Away (02)

Madsen, Michael
Doors, The (91); Thelma & Louise (91); Reservoir Dogs (92); Free Willy (93); Donnie Brasco (97); Die Another Day (02); Kill Bill: Vol. 1 (03); Kill Bill: Vol. 2 (04)

Madsen, Virginia
Candyman (92); John Grisham's The Rainmaker (97); Haunting, The (99); Sideways (04)

Maenpaa, Outi
Match Factory Girl, The (90); Man without a Past, The (02)

Maestre, Francisco
Bad Education (04)

Maestro, Mia
Time Code (00); Frida (02); Motorcycle Diaries, The (04)

Maffia, Roma
Disclosure (94)

Mage, Francis
Disenchanted, The (90)

Magee, Patrick
Dementia 13 (63); Servant, The (63); Masque of
the Red Death, The (64); Seance on a Wet
Afternoon (64); Clockwork Orange, A (71); Barry
Lyndon (75)

Magerman, William
Radio Days (87)

Maggart, Brandon
Dressed to Kill (80)

Maggio, Dante
Boccaccio '70 (62)

Maggio, Enzo
White Sheik, The (52)

Maggio, Pupella
Two Women (60); Amarcord (73); Cinema
Paradiso (88)

Maggio, Tony
Bad Influence (90)

Maggiorani, Lamberto
Bicycle Thief, The (48)

Maghenzani, Giuseppe
Before the Revolution (64)

Magid, Paul David
Jewel of the Nile, The (85)

Magnani, Anna
Open City (45); Ways of Love (50); Golden Coach,
The (52); Rose Tattoo, The (55); Mamma
Roma (62)

Magnier, Pierre
Rules of the Game (39)

Magnolfi, Barbara
Suspiria (76)

Magnuson, Ann
Small Soldiers (98); Panic Room (02)

Magre, Judith
Lovers, The (59)

Magrini, Gitt
La Notte (61); Last Tango in Paris (72)

Magritte, Chelsea
Team America: World Police (04)

Maguelon, Pierre
Cyrano de Bergerac (90)

Maguire, Barry
President's Analyst, The (67)

Maguire, Leonard
Dry White Season, A (89)

Maguire, Tobey
Ice Storm, The (97); Fear and Loathing in Las
Vegas (98); Pleasantville (98); Cider House Rules,
The (99); Wonder Boys (00); Spider-Man (02);
Seabiscuit (03); Spider-Man 2 (04)

MaGuire, Vincent
Distant Voices, Still Lives (88)

Mahaffey, Valerie
Seabiscuit (03)

Mahal, Taj
Sounder (72)

Mahan, Wayne
Fat City (72)

Maher, Joseph
Heaven Can Wait (78)

Mahiguiran, Nourieh
Day I Became a Woman, The (00)

Mahlowe, David
Kind of Loving, A (62)

Mahoney, John
Moonstruck (87); Tin Men (87); Eight Men
Out (88); Frantic (88); Say Anything (89); Russia
House, The (90); Barton Fink (91); In the Line of
Fire (93); Hudsucker Proxy, The (94); Iron Giant,
The (99)

Mahoney, William
Passion Fish (92)

Maia, Nuno Leal
Kiss of the Spider Woman (85)

Maiden, Rita
Married Woman, The (64)

Mailer, Kate
King Lear (87)

Mailer, Norman
King Lear (87)

Mailer, Stephen
Cry-Baby (90)

Maille, Anne-Sophie
A Nos Amours (84)

Maille, Claudette
Like Water for Chocolate (92)

Maille, Maite
A Nos Amours (84)

Mailloux, Hazel
Punch-Drunk Love (02)

Mailman, Deborah
Rabbit-Proof Fence (02)

Main, Laurie
Time After Time (79); Great Mouse Detective,
The (86)

Main, Marjorie
Dead End (37); Stella Dallas (37); Heaven Can
Wait (43); Meet Me in St. Louis (44); Murder, He
Says (45); Egg and I, The (47); Friendly
Persuasion (56)

Mairesse, Valerie
Sacrifice, The (86)

Maisongrosse, Francois
Traffic (72)

Maistre, Francois
Paris Belongs to Us (60); Milky Way, The (69)

Manners, David
Miracle Woman, The (31); Dracula (31); Mummy,
The (32); Bill of Divorcement, A (32); Black Cat,
The (34)

Mannheim, Lucie
39 Steps, The (35)

Manni, Ettore
City of Women (80)

Manning, Irene
Yankee Doodle Dandy (42)

Manning, Ned
Dead-End Drive-In (86)

Manning, Taryn
Eight Mile (02)

Manning, Tom
Street Scene (31)

Mannion, Tom
That Sinking Feeling (79); Croupier (99)

Manno, Dana
Leadbelly (76)

Manoff, Dinah
Grease (78); Ordinary People (80)

Manojlovic, Miki
When Father Was Away on Business (85);
Underground (95); Set Me Free (99)

Mans, Lorenzo
David Holzman's Diary (68)

Mansard, Claude
Lovers, The (59); Breathless (59); Four Hundred
Blows, The (59); Shoot the Piano Player (60)

Mansart, Marie
Two English Girls (71)

Mansfield, Jayne
Will Success Spoil Rock Hunter? (57)

Manson, Alan
Leadbelly (76)

Manson, Helena
Lola Montes (55)

Manson, Marilyn
Bowling for Columbine (02)

Mantee, Paul
Great Santini, The (79)

Mantegna, Joe
House of Games (87); Weeds (87); Godfather, Part
III, The (90); Bugsy (91); Homicide (91);
Searching for Bobby Fischer (93)

Mantel, Bronwen
Gothika (03)

Mantell, Joe
Marty (55); Birds, The (63)

Mantell, Michael
Passion Fish (92)

Mantenuto, Michael
Miracle (04)

Mantle, Doreen
Yentl (83)

Manuel, Richard
Last Waltz, The (78)

Manuel, Robert
Rififi (54)

Manver, Kiti
Women on the Verge of a Nervous Breakdown (88);
Flower of My Secret, The (95)

Manville, Lesley
High Hopes (88); Secrets & Lies (95);
Topsy-Turvy (99)

Manz, Linda
Days of Heaven (78); Wanderers, The (79)

Mapother, William
Mission: Impossible II (00); In the Bedroom (01);
Grudge, The (04)

Mara, Adele
You Were Never Lovelier (42); Sands of Iwo
Jima (49)

Mara, Mary
Blue Steel (90); Bound (96); Civil Action, A (98)

Marais, Jean
Beauty and the Beast (46); Les Parents
Terribles (48); Orpheus (49); Stealing Beauty (96)

Maran, Josie
Van Helsing (04)

Marangosoff, Janna
Men... (85)

Maranne, Andre
Shot in the Dark, A (64); Darling Lili (70); Return
of the Pink Panther, The (75); Pink Panther Strikes
Again, The (76)

Marbaix, Bernard
Rosetta (99)

Marc, Sebastien
Small Change (76)

Marceau, Sophie
Police (84); Braveheart (95); World Is Not Enough,
The (99)

March, Eve
Adam's Rib (49)

March, Fredric
Wild Party, The (29); Laughter (30); Royal Family
of Broadway, The (30); Dr. Jekyll and Mr.
Hyde (32); Smilin' Through (32); Barretts of
Wimpole Street, The (34); Death Takes a
Holiday (34); Les Miserables (35); Anna
Karenina (35); Anthony Adverse (36); Nothing
Sacred (37); Star Is Born, A (37); I Married a
Witch (42); Adventures of Mark Twain, The (44);
Best Years of Our Lives, The (46); Death of a
Salesman (51); Executive Suite (54); Bridges at
Toko-Ri, The (54); Desperate Hours, The (55); Man
in the Gray Flannel Suit, The (56); Inherit the
Wind (60); Seven Days in May (64)

March, Hal
It's Always Fair Weather (55)

Marchal, Georges
Belle de Jour (67)

Mark, Michael
Frankenstein (31)

Markam, Agesh
Bandit Queen (95)

Marken, Jeanne
Ways of Love (50); And God Created Woman (56)

Markham, David
Two English Girls (71); Tess (79)

Markham, Harry
This Sporting Life (63)

Markham, Kika
Two English Girls (71)

Markham, Petra
Get Carter (71)

Markinson, Brian
Sweet and Lowdown (99); Curse of the Jade Scorpion, The (01)

Marley, John
Cat Ballou (65); Faces (68); Love Story (70); Godfather, The (72)

Marley, Ziggy
Shark Tale (04)

Marlier, Carla
Zazie (60)

Marlow, Elgin
Out of Sight (98)

Marlow, Lucy
Star Is Born, A (54)

Marlowe, Hugh
Twelve O'Clock High (49); Night and the City (50); All About Eve (50); Day the Earth Stood Still, The (51); Birdman of Alcatraz (62); Seven Days in May (64)

Marlowe, Jo Ann
Mildred Pierce (45)

Marlowe, Kathryn
Dodsworth (36)

Marly, Guy
La Femme Infidele (69); This Man Must Die (70)

Marmont, Percy
Secret Agent (36); Young and Innocent (37)

Marner, Richard
African Queen, The (51); Sum of All Fears, The (02)

Maro, Akaji
Most Terrible Time in My Life, The (93)

Maropis, Adoni
Hidalgo (04)

Maross, Joe
Run Silent, Run Deep (58); Elmer Gantry (60)

Marq, Nick
Lock, Stock and Two Smoking Barrels (98)

Marquand, Christian
And God Created Woman (56); Flight of the Phoenix, The (65)

Marquand, Serge
Big Red One, The (80)

Marquardt, Peter
El Mariachi (93)

Marquez, Vanessa
Stand and Deliver (88)

Marquez, William
Mask of Zorro, The (98)

Marr, Eddie
20,000 Leagues under the Sea (54)

Marrero, Ralph
Day of the Dead (85)

Marriott, John
Little Foxes, The (41)

Marriott, Moore
Green for Danger (46)

Marriott, Sylvia
Two English Girls (71); Story of Adele H., The (75)

Mars, Kenneth
Producers, The (68); Butch Cassidy and the Sundance Kid (69); Desperate Characters (71); What's Up, Doc? (72); Young Frankenstein (74); Night Moves (75); Little Mermaid, The (89)

Mars, Marjorie
Brief Encounter (45)

Marsalis, Branford
Throw Momma from the Train (87)

Marsan, Eddie
Vera Drake (04)

Marsan, Guido A.
La Notte (61)

Marsden, Betty
Leather Boys, The (63); Dresser, The (83)

Marsden, James
X-Men (00); X2 (03); Notebook, The (04)

Marsden, Jason
Spirited Away (01)

Marsh, Carol
Brighton Rock (47); Horror of Dracula (58)

Marsh, Garry
Dreyfus Case, The (31)

Marsh, Mae
Three Godfathers, The (48)

Marsh, Michele
Fiddler on the Roof (71)

Marsh, Reginald
It Happened Here (63)

Marshal, Alan
After the Thin Man (36); Night Must Fall (37); Hunchback of Notre Dame, The (39); Adventures of Sherlock Holmes, The (39); White Cliffs of Dover, The (44)

Marshall, Brenda
Sea Hawk, The (40)

Marshall, Bryan
Spy Who Loved Me, The (77); Long Good Friday, The (80)

Marshall, Connie
Mr. Blandings Builds His Dream House (48)

Marshall, E.G.
Caine Mutiny, The (54); 12 Angry Men (57); Compulsion (59); Interiors (78); Creepshow (82); Nixon (95)

Marshall, Ellye
Champagne for Caesar (50)

Marshall, Gary K.
Lost in America (85)

Marshall, Helene
Incredible Shrinking Man, The (57)

Marshall, Herbert
Murder (30); Blonde Venus (32); Trouble in Paradise (32); Letter, The (40); Foreign Correspondent (40); Little Foxes, The (41); Moon and Sixpence, The (42); Enchanted Cottage, The (45); Duel in the Sun (46); Razor's Edge, The (46); List of Adrian Messenger, The (63)

Marshall, James
Few Good Men, A (92)

Marshall, Joshua
Flirting (90)

Marshall, Lisa
Baise-Moi (00)

Marshall, Paula
New Age, The (94)

Marshall, Sarah
Long, Hot Summer, The (58); Lord Love a Duck (66)

Marshall, Tully
Big Trail, The (30); Ball of Fire (41); This Gun for Hire (42)

Marshall, William
Blacula (72)

Marshall, Zena
Dr. No (62)

Marsili, Marco
Down and Dirty (76)

Marson, Ania
Nicholas and Alexandra (71)

Marteau, Henri
La Femme Infidele (69)

Martel, K.C.
Amityville Horror, The (79); E.T. The Extra-Terrestrial (82)

Martelli, Norma
Night of the Shooting Stars, The (81)

Marti, Virgilio
Crossover Dreams (85)

Martial, J.F.
My Uncle (58)

Martin, Andrea
Wag the Dog (97); Hedwig and the Angry Inch (01); My Big Fat Greek Wedding (02)

Martin, Barney
Charly (68); Arthur (81)

Martin, Chris-Pin
Mark of Zorro, The (40); Fugitive, The (47)

Martin, Christopher
House Party (90)

Martin, Damon
Pee-wee's Big Adventure (85)

Martin, Dan
Casualties of War (89)

Martin, Daniel
Fistful of Dollars, A (64)

Martin, Dave
Beefcake (99)

Martin, Dean
Young Lions, The (58); Some Came Running (58); Rio Bravo (59); Bells Are Ringing (60); What a Way to Go! (64); Airport (70)

Martin, Dean Paul
Heart Like a Wheel (83)

Martin, Dewey
Thing from Another World, The (51); Big Sky, The (52); Desperate Hours, The (55)

Martin, Edie
Lavender Hill Mob, The (51)

Martin, Eugene
Terror in a Texas Town (58)

Martin, George
Awakenings (90)

Martin, Jean
Battle of Algiers, The (65)

Martin, Jennifer
Powerpuff Girls Movie, The (02)

Martin, Jose Manuel
Viridiana (61)

Martin, Kellie
Matinee (93)

Martin, Kiel
Panic in Needle Park, The (71)

Martin, Lewis
Ace in the Hole (51); War of the Worlds, The (53)

Martin, Lock
Day the Earth Stood Still, The (51)

Martin, Lori
Cape Fear (62)

Martin, Marion
Man in the Iron Mask, The (39)

Martin, Melvyn
Les Enfants Terribles (50)

Martin, Michael
In the Company of Men (97)

Mazar, Debi
Batman Forever (95); Trees Lounge (96); Insider, The (99); Collateral (04)

Mazeika, Jack Griffin
Beefcake (99)

Mazurki, Mike
Murder, My Sweet (45); Nightmare Alley (47); Night and the City (50)

Mazurowna, Ernestine
Jean de Florette (86)

Mazursky, Paul
Fear and Desire (53); Blume in Love (73); Down and Out in Beverly Hills (86); 2 Days in the Valley (96)

Mazza, Marc
Rider on the Rain (70)

Mazzacurati, Carlo
Caro Diario (94)

Mazzacurati, Rosy
La Notte (61)

Mazzarella, Marcello
Time Regained (99)

Mazzello, Joseph
Jurassic Park (93)

McAdams, Rachel
Mean Girls (04); Notebook, The (04)

McAnally, Ray
Mission, The (86); My Left Foot (89)

McAndrew, Marianne
Hello, Dolly! (69)

McAndrew, Robert
Medium Cool (69)

McArdle, Kip
Honeymoon Killers, The (69)

McArthur, Alex
Desert Hearts (85)

McAuley, Nichole
Nutty Professor, The (96)

McAvoy, Alex
Pink Floyd—The Wall (82)

McBride, Chi
What's Love Got to Do with It (93); Narc (02); I, Robot (04); Terminal, The (04)

McBride, Fern
David Holzman's Diary (68)

McBride, Melissa Suzanne
Dangerous Lives of Altar Boys, The (02)

McBride, Susan
Tim Burton's The Nightmare before Christmas (93)

McBroom, Marcia
Beyond the Valley of the Dolls (70)

McCabe, Richard
Notting Hill (99)

McCabe, Ruth
My Left Foot (89); Snapper, The (93)

McCabe, Sandra
Rose, The (79)

McCafferty, Frankie
Secret of Roan Inish, The (95)

McCain, Frances Lee
Real Life (79); Tex (82)

McCain, Teddy
Cool World, The (63)

McCairbe, Roman
Michael Collins (96)

McCall, James
World According to Garp, The (82)

McCallany, Holt
Alien³ (92); Three Kings (99)

McCallister, Lon
Stage Door Canteen (43)

McCallum, David
Great Escape, The (63); Hear My Song (91)

McCalman, Macon
Smokey and the Bandit (77)

McCambridge, Mercedes
All the King's Men (49); Johnny Guitar (54); Giant (56)

McCamus, Tom
Sweet Hereafter, The (97)

McCann, Chuck
Projectionist, The (70)

McCann, Donal
Dead, The (87); Stealing Beauty (96)

McCann, Sean
Affliction (98); Miracle (04)

McCart, Mollie
Kiss before Dying, A (56)

McCarthy, Andrew
Pretty in Pink (86); Less Than Zero (87)

McCarthy, Frank
Dead Men Don't Wear Plaid (82)

McCarthy, Jeanne
1918 (85)

McCarthy, Jim
Under the Volcano (84)

McCarthy, Kevin
Death of a Salesman (51); Invasion of the Body Snatchers (56); Misfits, The (61); Invasion of the Body Snatchers (78); Howling, The (81)

McCarthy, Molly
Flamingo Kid, The (84)

McCarthy, Neil
Zulu (64)

McCarthy, Nyla
Mala Noche (85)

McCarthy, Tom
Meet the Parents (00)

McDaniel, Hattie
Gone with the Wind (39); Male Animal, The (42);
Since You Went Away (44); Song of the South (46)

McDaniel, James
Sunshine State (02)

McDermott, Dean
Open Range (03)

McDermott, Dylan
Hamburger Hill (87); Steel Magnolias (89); In the
Line of Fire (93); Runaway Jury (03)

McDermott, Hugh
Pimpernel Smith (41); Seventh Veil, The (45)

McDermott, John
Capturing the Friedmans (03)

McDermott, Kathleen
Morvern Callar (02)

McDevitt, Ruth
Birds, The (63)

McDiarmid, Ian
Return of the Jedi (83); Star Wars Episode I: The
Phantom Menace (99); Star Wars Episode II: Attack
of the Clones (02); Star Wars Episode III: Revenge
of the Sith (05)

McDonald, Chris
Faculty, The (98)

McDonald, Christopher
Thelma & Louise (91); Quiz Show (94);
Flubber (97); Iron Giant, The (99); Perfect Storm,
The (00); Requiem for a Dream (00)

McDonald, Francis
Morocco (30); Prisoner of Shark Island, The (36);
Sea Wolf, The (41); My Pal Trigger (46)

McDonald, Garry
Moulin Rouge (01); Rabbit-Proof Fence (02)

McDonald, Gordon
Thirty Seconds Over Tokyo (44)

McDonald, Kevin
Lilo & Stitch (02)

McDonald, Peter
Felicia's Journey (99)

McDonald, Ray
Babes on Broadway (41); Life Begins for Andy
Hardy (41)

McDonnell, Col. G.L.
Dr. Jekyll and Mr. Hyde (32)

McDonnell, Mary
Matewan (87); Dances with Wolves (90); Grand
Canyon (91); Passion Fish (92); Independence
Day (96); Donnie Darko (01)

McDormand, Frances
Blood Simple (84); Raising Arizona (87);
Mississippi Burning (88); Darkman (90);
Fargo (96); Lone Star (96); Madeline (98); Wonder
Boys (00); Almost Famous (00); Man Who Wasn't
There, The (01); Something's Gotta Give (03)

McDowall, Roddy
How Green Was My Valley (41); Man Hunt (41);
Lassie Come Home (43); My Friend Flicka (43);
White Cliffs of Dover, The (44); Thunderhead—
Son of Flicka (45); Inside Daisy Clover (65); Lord
Love a Duck (66); Planet of the Apes (68);
Bedknobs and Broomsticks (71); Fright Night (85)

McDowell, Claire
Wild Boys of the Road (33); It Happened One
Night (34)

McDowell, Malcolm
If... (68); Clockwork Orange, A (71); O Lucky
Man! (73); Time After Time (79); Company,
The (03)

McEachin, James
Play Misty for Me (71)

McElduff, Ellen
Working Girls (86)

McElheron, Fergal
Secret of Roan Inish, The (95)

McElhone, Natascha
Devil's Own, The (97); Mrs. Dalloway (97);
Truman Show, The (98); Ronin (98); Solaris (02)

McElroy, Brian
Bad Lieutenant (92)

McEnery, John
Romeo and Juliet (68); Duellists, The (77)

McEnery, Peter
Victim (61); Entertaining Mr. Sloane (69)

McEnroe, Annie
True Stories (86)

McEntire, Reba
Tremors (90)

McEwan, Geraldine
Robin Hood: Prince of Thieves (91)

McFadden, Bobby Joe
Red Rock West (93)

McFadden, Gates
Star Trek: First Contact (96); Star Trek:
Insurrection (98); Star Trek: Nemesis (02)

McFarland, Spanky
Trail of the Lonesome Pine, The (36)

McFarlane, Hamish
Navigator, The (88)

McFerran, Douglas
Sliding Doors (98)

McGann, Paul
Withnail & I (87); Alien³ (92)

McGarrity, Everett
Hallelujah (29)

McGarry, Parnell
Bedazzled (67)

McGavin, Darren
Man with the Golden Arm, The (55);
Summertime (55); Christmas Story, A (83)

McGee, Vonetta
Blacula (72); To Sleep with Anger (90)

McGhee, Bill
1918 (85)

McGhee, Michael
Brood, The (79)

McGibbon, Lewis
Millions (04)

McGill, Bruce
Citizens Band (77); National Lampoon's Animal House (78); My Cousin Vinny (92); Perfect World, A (93); Insider, The (99); Matchstick Men (03); Runaway Jury (03); Collateral (04)

McGill, Everett
Quest for Fire (81); Straight Story, The (99)

McGill, Heather
Pleasantville (98)

McGill, Jan
Cop (88)

McGillis, Kelly
Witness (85); Top Gun (86); Accused, The (88)

McGinley, John C.
Platoon (86); Midnight Clear, A (92); Seven (95)

McGinley, Sean
General, The (98)

McGinley, Ted
Revenge of the Nerds (84)

McGinn, Walter
Three Days of the Condor (75)

McGiver, John
Breakfast at Tiffany's (61); Manchurian Candidate, The (62); Man's Favorite Sport? (64); Midnight Cowboy (69)

McGlynn Jr., Frank
Hopalong Cassidy (35)

McGlynn Sr., Frank
Min and Bill (30); Captain Blood (35); Last of the Mohicans, The (36)

McGoohan, Patrick
Escape from Alcatraz (79); Scanners (81); Braveheart (95)

McGovern, Elizabeth
Ordinary People (80); Ragtime (81); Once Upon a Time in America (84); Shock to the System, A (90); Wings of the Dove, The (97); House of Mirth, The (00)

McGowan, Mickie
Spirited Away (01)

McGowan, Rose
Scream (96)

McGowan, Tom
Birdcage, The (96); Ghost World (01)

McGrath, Doug
Pale Rider (85)

McGrath, Matt
Boys Don't Cry (99)

McGrath, Paul
Face in the Crowd, A (57)

McGraw, Charles
T-Men (47); Threat, The (49); Narrow Margin, The (52); Bridges at Toko-Ri, The (54); Defiant Ones, The (58); Birds, The (63); In Cold Blood (67)

McGraw, Tim
Friday Night Lights (04)

McGregor, Ewan
Shallow Grave (94); Trainspotting (95); Emma (96); Pillow Book, The (96); Velvet Goldmine (98); Star Wars Episode I: The Phantom Menace (99); Moulin Rouge (01); Black Hawk Down (01); Star Wars Episode II: Attack of the Clones (02); Big Fish (03); Robots (05); Star Wars Episode III: Revenge of the Sith (05)

McGrory, Matthew
Big Fish (03)

McGuire, Biff
Thomas Crown Affair, The (68); Serpico (73)

McGuire, Don
Pride of the Marines (45); Threat, The (49)

McGuire, Dorothy
Enchanted Cottage, The (45); Tree Grows in Brooklyn, A (45); Spiral Staircase, The (46); Gentleman's Agreement (47); Three Coins in the Fountain (54); Friendly Persuasion (56); Old Yeller (57); Swiss Family Robinson (60)

McGuire, John
Stranger on the Third Floor (40); He Walked by Night (48)

McGuire, Kim
Cry-Baby (90)

McGuire, Linda
Morvern Callar (02)

McGuire, Michael
Bird (88)

McGuire, Victor
Andrew Lloyd Webber's The Phantom of the Opera (04)

McHale, Michael
Threat, The (49)

McHallem, Chris
Girl with a Pearl Earring (03)

McHattie, Stephen
Secretary (02)

McHenry, Don
Three Days of the Condor (75)

McHugh, Frank
Front Page, The (31); Mystery of the Wax Museum, The (33); Footlight Parade (33); Midsummer Night's Dream, A (35); Gold Diggers of 1935 (35); Four Daughters (38); Dodge City (39); Roaring Twenties, The (39); City for Conquest (40); Fighting 69th, The (40); Back Street (41); Going My Way (44); State Fair (45); Mighty Joe Young (49); There's No Business like Show Business (54)

Mejia, Al
Jim Thorpe—All American (51)

Mejia, Alfonso
Los Olvidados (50)

Mejia, Gerardo
Colors (88)

Melador, Danielle
Human Resources (00)

Melato, Mariangela
Seduction of Mimi, The (72); Swept Away ... by an Unusual Destiny in the Blue Sea of August (74)

Mele, Anielo
Shoeshine (46)

Melelaus, Jane
Quills (00)

Melford, Jill
Servant, The (63)

Melki, Claude
Six in Paris (65)

Melki, Lucien
Danton (82)

Mell, Randle
Grand Canyon (91)

Mellish, Fuller
Crime without Passion (34)

Mellish Jr., Fuller
Applause (29)

Mello, Breno
Black Orpheus (59)

Melo, Gaston
Crime of Father Amaro, The (02)

Melon, Henri
Sugar Cane Alley (83)

Meloni, Christopher
Bound (96)

Melton, Sid
Steel Helmet, The (51); Lady Sings the Blues (72)

Melville, Jean-Pierre
Breathless (59)

Melville, Pauline
How to Get Ahead in Advertising (89)

Melville, Sam
Thomas Crown Affair, The (68)

Melvin, Murray
Taste of Honey, A (61); Boy Friend, The (71)

Memarzia, Nasser
Millions (04)

Memedov, Zabit
Time of the Gypsies (89)

Memmoli, George
Mean Streets (73); New York, New York (77); Blue Collar (78); Sure Thing, The (85)

Mendes, Eva
Once Upon a Time in Mexico (03); Out of Time (03); Stuck on You (03); Hitch (05)

Mendes, Helen
High Art (98)

Mendes-France, Pierre
Sorrow and the Pity, The (70)

Mendez, Ray
Fast, Cheap & Out of Control (97)

Mendillo, Stephen
Lianna (83)

Mendl, Michael
Downfall (04)

Mendonca, George
Fast, Cheap & Out of Control (97)

Mendonca, Mauro
Dona Flor and Her Two Husbands (76)

Mendoza, Antonio
Easy Rider (69)

Mendoza, Victor Manuel
Los Olvidados (50)

Menez, Bernard
Day for Night (73)

Menjou, Adolphe
Morocco (30); Front Page, The (31); Farewell to Arms, A (32); Morning Glory (33); Gold Diggers of 1935 (35); One Hundred Men and a Girl (37); Star Is Born, A (37); Stage Door (37); Golden Boy (39); You Were Never Lovelier (42); Hucksters, The (47); State of the Union (48); Paths of Glory (57); Pollyanna (60)

Menken, Shepard
Phantom Tollbooth, The (70)

Mensaros, Laszlo
Colonel Redl (84)

Mensik, Vladimir
Loves of a Blonde (65)

Menzel, Jiri
Closely Watched Trains (66)

Menzer, Ernest
Band of Outsiders (64)

Menzies, Heather
Sound of Music, The (65)

Menzies, Mary
Pit and the Pendulum, The (61)

Menzies, Robert
Innocence (00)

Mer Khamis, Juliano
Wedding in Galilee (87)

Merad, Kad
Chorus, The (04)

Merande, Doro
Our Town (40); Man with the Golden Arm, The (55)

Mercado, Patrick
Dreamlife of Angels, The (98)

Millan, Victor
Terror in a Texas Town (58)

Milland, Ray
Three Smart Girls (36); Easy Living (37); Beau Geste (39); Major and the Minor, The (42); Lady in the Dark (44); Uninvited, The (44); Ministry of Fear (45); Lost Weekend, The (45); Big Clock, The (48); Dial M for Murder (54); "X"—The Man with the X-Ray Eyes (63); Love Story (70)

Millard, Helene
Divorcee, The (30)

Miller, Allan
Bound for Glory (76)

Miller, Ann
You Can't Take It with You (38); Easter Parade (48); On the Town (49); Kiss Me Kate (53); Mulholland Dr. (01)

Miller, Barry
Saturday Night Fever (77); Fame (80); Peggy Sue Got Married (86)

Miller, Ben
Birthday Girl (02)

Miller, Chris
Shrek (01)

Miller, David
Attack of the Killer Tomatoes (78)

Miller, Dean R.
My Bodyguard (80)

Miller, Dennis
Disclosure (94)

Miller, Dick
Little Shop of Horrors, The (61); Hollywood Boulevard (76); New York, New York (77); Rock 'n' Roll High School (79); Terminator, The (84); After Hours (85); Gremlins 2: The New Batch (90); Small Soldiers (98)

Miller, Frank
2001: A Space Odyssey (68)

Miller, Geri
Flesh (68)

Miller, Glenn
Orchestra Wives (42)

Miller, Harold
Love Affair (39)

Miller, Jason
Exorcist, The (73)

Miller, John
Ratcatcher (99)

Miller, Jonny Lee
Trainspotting (95); Afterglow (97); Mansfield Park (99); Melinda and Melinda (05)

Miller, Joshua
Near Dark (87); River's Edge (87)

Miller, Kathleen
Last Detail, The (73)

Miller, Kristen
Team America: World Police (04)

Miller, Larry
Nutty Professor, The (96)

Miller, Linda G.
Unmarried Woman, An (78)

Miller, Martin
Peeping Tom (60); Phantom of the Opera, The (62)

Miller, Michael
Swithcblade Sisters (75)

Miller, Mirta
Cria! (76)

Miller, Omar Benson
Eight Mile (02); Shall We Dance? (04)

Miller, Pamela
Two Hundred Motels (71)

Miller, Penelope Ann
Blioxi Blues (88); Freshman, The (90); Awakenings (90); Chaplin (92); Carlito's Way (93)

Miller, Ruth
Come Back to the 5 & Dime, Jimmy Dean, Jimmy Dean (82)

Miller, Sidney
Star 80 (83)

Miller, Sienna
Alfie (04)

Miller, Stephen
Stepfather, The (87)

Miller, Wentworth
Human Stain, The (03)

Millhollin, James
No Time for Sergeants (58)

Millican, James
Man from Laramie, The (55)

Milligan, Spencer
Sleeper (73)

Milligan, Spike
Bed Sitting Room, The (69)

Millot, Charles
Train, The (65); French Connection II (75)

Mills, Danny
Pink Flamingos (72)

Mills, Donna
Play Misty for Me (71)

Mills, Frank
Way Out West (37)

Mills, Hayley
Pollyanna (60); Whistle Down the Wind (61)

Mills, John
Goodbye Mr. Chips (39); In Which We Serve (42); This Happy Breed (44); Great Expectations (46); Hobson's Choice (54); War and Peace (56); Swiss Family Robinson (60); Ryan's Daughter (70); Gandhi (82); When the Wind Blows (86)

Mills, Mort
Touch of Evil (58)

Mills, Rob
Labyrinth (86)

Milly
Conformist, The (70)

Milner, Martin
Sweet Smell of Success (57); Compulsion (59);
Valley of the Dolls (67)

Milo, Sandra
General della Rovere (59); 8 1/2 (63)

Milosavljevic, Ana
Innocence Unprotected (68)

Milosavljevic, Pera
Innocence Unprotected (68)

Milski, Stanislaw
Ashes and Diamonds (58)

Milton, Ruby
Morvern Callar (02)

Miluwi, John Omirah
Gorillas in the Mist (88)

Milyutenko, D.
My Name Is Ivan (62)

Mimieux, Yvette
Time Machine, The (60); Where the Boys Are (60)

Mims, William
Ballad of Cable Hogue, The (70)

Minakata, Eiji
Sonatine (94)

Minami, Yoshie
Ikiru (52)

Minamimagoe, Kazuyoshi
Lost in Translation (03)

Minato, Aoi
Last Samurai, The (03)

Minciotti, Esther
Marty (55); Wrong Man, The (56)

Minciotti, Silvio
Clash by Night (52)

Mineo, Sal
Rebel without a Cause (55); Somebody Up There
Likes Me (56); Giant (56); Exodus (60); Cheyenne
Autumn (64)

Miner, Jan
Lenny (74)

Ming, Lau Siu
Eat a Bowl of Tea (90)

Minnelli, Liza
Sterile Cuckoo, The (69); Cabaret (72); New York,
New York (77); Arthur (81)

Minor, Bob
White Dog (82)

Minot, Dominique
Charade (63)

Minotis, Alexis
Notorious (46)

Minty, Emil
Road Warrior, The (81)

Miou-Miou
Going Places (74); Jonah Who Will Be 25 in the
Year 2000 (76); Entre Nous (83)

Mira, Brigitte
Ali, Fear Eats the Soul (74); Enigma of Kaspar
Hauser, The (75); Berlin Alexanderplatz (79)

Mirabal, Manuel "Guajiro"
Buena Vista Social Club, The (99)

Miracle, Irene
Midnight Express (78)

Miranda, Aurora
Phantom Lady (44); Three Caballeros, The (45)

Miranda, Carmen
Gang's All Here, The (43)

Miranda, Isa
La Ronde (50); Summertime (55)

Miranda, Robert
Midnight Run (88); Sister Act (92)

Mironova, Olga
Come and See (85)

Mirren, Helen
O Lucky Man! (73); Long Good Friday, The (80);
Excalibur (81); Mosquito Coast, The (86); Cook,
the Thief, His Wife & Her Lover, The (89);
Comfort of Strangers, The (91); Madness of King
George, The (94); Prince of Egypt, The (98);
Pledge, The (01); Gosford Park (01); Last
Orders (01); Hitchhiker's Guide to the Galaxy,
The (05)

Misclaida
Balseros (04)

Missirini, Giuliano
Red Desert (64)

Mistral, Jorge
Wuthering Heights (53)

Mitchell, Billy J.
Top Secret! (84)

Mitchell, Cameron
Death of a Salesman (51); Love Me or Leave
Me (55); Tall Men, The (55); Carousel (56)

Mitchell, Charlotte
French Lieutenant's Woman, The (81)

Mitchell, Daryl
Galaxy Quest (99)

Mitchell, Delaina
Vanilla Sky (01)

Mitchell, Donna
Less Than Zero (87)

Mitchell, Eddy
Coup de Torchon (81)

Mitchell, Elizabeth
Santa Clause 2, The (02)

Mitchell, Geneva
Morning Glory (33)

Mitchell, George
3:10 to Yuma (57)

Mullaney, Jack
South Pacific (58)

Mullard, Arthur
Ring-a-Ding Rhythm (62); Morgan! (66)

Mullen, Leanne
Ratcatcher (99)

Mullen, Patty
Frankenhooker (90)

Muller, Christiane
Going Places (74)

Muller, Martin
Crumb (95)

Muller, Richy
xXx (02)

Muller, Rolf
Blue Angel, The (30)

Mulligan, Richard
Little Big Man (70)

Mulligan, Robert
Summer of '42 (71)

Mulligan, Terry David
Accused, The (88)

Mullinar, Rod
Breaker Morant (80); Dead Calm (89)

Mullins, Bartlett
Peeping Tom (60)

Mulroney, Dermot
Kansas City (96); My Best Friend's Wedding (97);
About Schmidt (02)

Mummert, Danny
Member of the Wedding, The (52)

Mumy, Bill
Papillon (73)

Mumy, Liliana
Santa Clause 2, The (02); Cheaper by the
Dozen (03)

Munch, Richard
Train, The (65); Patton (70)

Mundin, Herbert
Cavalcade (33); Mutiny on the Bounty (35)

Mundy, Meg
Fatal Attraction (87)

Mune, Ian
Piano, The (93)

Muni
Diary of a Chambermaid (64); Milky Way,
The (69); Discreet Charm of the Bourgeoisie,
The (72)

Muni, Paul
I Am a Fugitive from a Chain Gang (32);
Scarface (32); Story of Louis Pasteur, The (36);
Life of Emile Zola, The (37); Good Earth,
The (37); Juarez (39); Song to Remember, A (45)

Munier, Ferdinand
Babes in Toyland (34); Roberta (35); Hands Across
the Table (35)

Munne, Pep
Barcelona (94)

Munoz, Gloria
Flower of My Secret, The (95)

Munoz, Lucio
Dream of Light (93)

Munro, Caroline
Golden Voyage of Sinbad, The (73); Spy Who
Loved Me, The (77)

Munro, Janet
Darby O'Gill and the Little People (59); Swiss
Family Robinson (60)

Munro, John
Circle of Deceit (81)

Munro, Nan
Morgan! (66)

Munroe, Jan
Grifters, The (90)

Munshin, Jules
Easter Parade (48); On the Town (49); Take Me Out
to the Ball Game (49); Silk Stockings (57)

Munzuk, Maxim
Dersu Uzala (75)

Murakami, Fuyuki
Godzilla, King of the Monsters (54)

Muramatsu, Katsumi
Ring (97)

Murata, Hideo
Kagemusha (80)

Murdock, Jack
Rain Man (88)

Murdock, Tim
Thirty Seconds Over Tokyo (44)

Murgia, Tiberio
Big Deal on Madonna Street (58)

Murota, Hideo
Taxing Woman, A (87)

Murphy, Audie
Red Badge of Courage, The (51)

Murphy, Betty
Urban Cowboy (80)

Murphy, Brittany
Clueless (95); Girl, Interrupted (99); Eight
Mile (02)

Murphy, Christopher
Abyss, The (89)

Murphy, Cillian
28 Days Later... (02); Girl with a Pearl Earring (03)

Murphy, Donald
Lord Love a Duck (66)

Murphy, Donna
Star Trek: Insurrection (98); Spider-Man 2 (04)

Murphy, Eddie
48 Hrs. (82); Trading Places (83); Beverly Hills
Cop (84); Coming to America (88); Nutty
Professor, The (96); Dr. Dolittle (98); Mulan (98);

N'Zonzi, Pascal
Lumumba (00)

Nabor, Principe
Bye-Bye Brazil (80)

Nachtergaele, Matheus
Central Station (98); City of God (02)

Nadajan
House of Usher (60)

Nadarevic, Mustafa
When Father Was Away on Business (85)

Nadeau, Elayne
Martin (78)

Nader, Khwaja
Osama (03)

Nag, Harimoran
Pather Panchali (55)

Nagahara, Yuki
Mishima (85)

Nagase, Masatoshi
Mystery Train (89); Most Terrible Time in My Life,
The (93)

Nagashima, Toshiyuki
Gonin (95)

Nagel, Conrad
Divorcee, The (30); All That Heaven Allows (55)

Naghavi, Fatemeh
Circle, The (00)

Nagler, Morgan
Bird (88)

Nagra, Parminder
Bend It Like Beckham (02)

Nahon, Carly
21 Grams (03)

Nahon, Philippe
I Stand Alone (98); Irreversible (02)

Naidu, Ajay
Bad Santa (03)

Naidu, Chandrashekhar
Salaam Bombay! (88)

Nail, Jimmy
Evita (96)

Nail, Joanne
Swithcblade Sisters (75)

Naim, Fouad
Circle of Deceit (81)

Naish, J. Carrol
Kid from Spain, The (32); Beau Geste (39);
Corsican Brothers, The (41); Blood and Sand (41);
Tales of Manhattan (42); Sahara (43); Southerner,
The (45); Fugitive, The (47); Annie Get Your
Gun (50); Rio Grande (50); Clash by Night (52)

Naismith, Laurence
Mogambo (53); Barretts of Wimpole Street,
The (56); Sink the Bismarck! (60); Village of the
Damned (60); Jason and the Argonauts (63);
Scrooge (70)

Naji, Amir
Children of Heaven (97)

Najimy, Kathy
Sister Act (92)

Nakadai, Tatsuya
Yojimbo (61); High and Low (63);
Kagemusha (80); Ran (85)

Nakagawa, Anna
Cure (97)

Nakajima, Aoi
In the Realm of the Senses (76)

Nakajima, Shu
Dreams (90)

Nakakita, Chieko
Drunken Angel (48)

Nakamaru, Tadao
What's Up, Tiger Lily? (66)

Nakamura, Ganemon
Kwaidan (64)

Nakamura, Ganjiro
Kwaidan (64)

Nakamura, Katsuo
Kwaidan (64)

Nakamura, Nobuo
Ikiru (52); Tokyo Story (53)

Nakamura, Shichinosuke
Last Samurai, The (03)

Nakano, Toshihiko
Dreams (90)

Nakatani, Miki
Ring (97)

Nakaya, Noboru
Kwaidan (64)

Namdeo, Govind
Bandit Queen (95)

Nanbara, Kiyotaka
Most Terrible Time in My Life, The (93)

Nance, Jack
Eraserhead (76); Barfly (87)

Naniwa, Chieko
Sansho the Bailff (54); Throne of Blood (57)

Nanty, Isabelle
Amelie (01)

Napier, Alan
Cat People (42); Uninvited, The (44); Ministry of
Fear (45); Connecticut Yankee in King Arthur's
Court, A (49); Criss Cross (49); Julius Caesar (53);
Journey to the Center of the Earth (59); Marnie (64)

Napier, Charles
Citizens Band (77); Miami Blues (90); Grifters,
The (90); Silence of the Lambs, The (91); Austin
Powers: International Man of Mystery (97)

Napier, Marshall
Navigator, The (88)

Narboni, Jean
Two or Three Things I Know about Her (66)

Nardini, Tom
Cat Ballou (65)

Nardone, Sebastiano
Caro Diario (94)

Narducci, Kathrine
Bronx Tale, A (93)

Narelle, Brian
Dark Star (75)

Nascarella, Arthur J.
Cooler, The (03)

Nascimento, Milton
Fitzcarraldo (82)

Nash, Bob
Viva Las Vegas (64)

Nash, Clarence
Three Caballeros, The (45)

Nash, Florence
Women, The (39)

Nash, Mary
Easy Living (37); Philadelphia Story, The (40)

Nash, Russell Lee
Salome's Last Dance (88)

Nathan, Adam
Parting Glances (86)

Nathan, Vivian
Klute (71)

Natheaux, Louis
Modern Times (36)

Nathenson, Zoe
Mona Lisa (86)

Natrop, Gull
Smiles of a Summer Night (55)

Natsukawa, Yui
Blind Swordsman: Zatoichi, The (03)

Natsuki, Yosuke
Chushingura (62)

Natwick, Mildred
Long Voyage Home, The (40); Enchanted Cottage,
The (45); Late George Apley, The (47); Three
Godfathers, The (48); She Wore a Yellow
Ribbon (49); Cheaper by the Dozen (50); Quiet
Man, The (52); Trouble with Harry, The (55);
Barefoot in the Park (67); Dangerous Liaisons (88)

Nauczyciel, Arthur
What Time Is It There? (01)

Naughton, David
American Werewolf in London, An (81)

Naughton, James
Paper Chase, The (73); Glass Menagerie, The (87)

Navarro, Jesus
Los Olvidados (50)

Nayar, Nisha
Bhaji on the Beach (94)

Nayyar, Harsh
Hidalgo (04)

Nazarov, Pavel
Freeze—Die—Come to Life (90)

Nazimova, Alla
Blood and Sand (41)

Nazvanov, Mikhail
Ivan the Terrible, Part I (45); Ivan the Terrible, Part
II: The Revolt of the Boyars (58)

Nazzari, Amedeo
Nights of Cabiria (57)

Ndiaye, Thierno
Guelwaar (93)

Neagle, Anna
Victoria the Great (37)

Neal, Billie
Down by Law (86); Mortal Thoughts (91)

Neal, Edwin
Texas Chainsaw Massacre, The (74)

Neal, Patricia
Hasty Heart, The (49); Day the Earth Stood Still,
The (51); Face in the Crowd, A (57); Breakfast at
Tiffany's (61); Hud (63); Subject Was Roses,
The (68)

Neal, Tom
Detour (45)

Nealon, Kevin
Adam Sandler's Eight Crazy Nights (02); Daddy
Day Care (03)

Near, Holly
Minnie and Moskowitz (71)

Near, Laurel
Eraserhead (76)

Nebhan, Hassan
Day I Became a Woman, The (00)

Neckar, Vaclav
Closely Watched Trains (66)

Neeson, Liam
Excalibur (81); Mission, The (86); Darkman (90);
Husbands and Wives (92); Schindler's List (93);
Michael Collins (96); Les Miserables (98);
Haunting, The (99); Star Wars Episode I: The
Phantom Menace (99); Gangs of New York (02);
K-19: The Widowmaker (02); Love Actually (03);
Kinsey (04); Kingdom of Heaven (05)

Neff, Hildegarde
Decision Before Dawn (51); Snows of Kilimanjaro,
The (52)

Nega, Alison
In the Cut (03)

Negami, Jun
Teahouse of the August Moon, The (56)

Negishi, Tohsie
Audition (99)

Negley, Howard
Abbott and Costello Meet Frankenstein (48)

Negret, Francois
Au Revoir, les Enfants (87)

Negro, Del
Aguirre, the Wrath of God (72)

Negro, Giorgio
La Notte (61)

Neher, Carola
Threepenny Opera, The (31)

Neidorf, David
Hoosiers (86); Bull Durham (88)

Neiiendam, Sigrid
Day of Wrath (43)

Neil, Hildegard
Touch of Class, A (73)

Neill, Sam
My Brilliant Career (79); Cry in the Dark, A (88);
Dead Calm (89); Hunt for Red October, The (90);
Until the End of the World (91); Piano, The (93);
Jurassic Park (93); Horse Whisperer, The (98)

Neilsen, Inga
Funny Thing Happened on the Way to the Forum,
A (66)

Neilson, Catherine
White Hunter, Black Heart (90)

Neilson, David
Life Is Sweet (91)

Neilson-Terry, Phyllis
Look Back in Anger (59)

Neiman, Christopher
Auto Focus (02)

Nejad, Badr Irouni
Day I Became a Woman, The (00)

Nejad, Cyrus Kahouri
Day I Became a Woman, The (00)

Nell, Krista
Pierrot le Fou (65)

Nelligan, Kate
Romantic Englishwoman, The (75); Eye of the
Needle (81); Prince of Tides, The (91); Cider
House Rules, The (99)

Nelsen, Anny
Jules and Jim (62)

Nelson, Adam
Abyss, The (89); Mystic River (03)

Nelson, Barry
Johnny Eager (42); Bataan (43); Guy Named Joe,
A (44); Airport (70); Shining, The (80)

Nelson, Chris
Kill Bill: Vol. 2 (04)

Nelson, Craig Richard
Paper Chase, The (73); 3 Women (77)

Nelson, Craig T.
Poltergeist (82); Silkwood (83); Killing Fields,
The (84); Wag the Dog (97); Incredibles, The (04)

Nelson, David
Peyton Place (57)

Nelson, Gene
Oklahoma! (55)

Nelson, Gwen
Kind of Loving, A (62)

Nelson, Jerry
Muppet Movie, The (79); Great Muppet Caper,
The (81); Dark Crystal, The (82)

Nelson, Judd
Breakfast Club, The (85)

Nelson, Kenneth
Hellraiser (87)

Nelson, Merritt
Trust (91)

Nelson, Novella
Orphans (87); Judy Berlin (00); Antwone
Fisher (02)

Nelson, Portia
Doctor Dolittle (67)

Nelson, Ralph
Lilies of the Field (63)

Nelson, Ricky
Rio Bravo (59)

Nelson, Ruth
Tree Grows in Brooklyn, A (45); Late Show,
The (77); 3 Women (77); Wedding, A (78);
Awakenings (90)

Nelson, Sandra
De-Lovely (04)

Nelson, Sean
Fresh (94)

Nelson, Tim Blake
O Brother, Where Art Thou? (00); Minority
Report (02); Good Girl, The (02)

Nelson, Tracy
Down and Out in Beverly Hills (86)

Nelson, Willie
Thief (81); Wag the Dog (97)

Neri, Francesca
Live Flesh (97); Hannibal (01)

Neri, Tommaso
Battle of Algiers, The (65)

Nero, Franco
Tristana (70)

Nesbitt, Cathleen
Three Coins in the Fountain (54); Separate
Tables (58); French Connection II (75); Family
Plot (76)

Nesbitt, Derren
Victim (61); Where Eagles Dare (69)

Nesbitt, James
Millions (04)

Nesmith, Michael
Head (68)

Nesmith, Ottola
Inside Daisy Clover (65)

Nesnow, Joe
Romancing the Stone (84)

Noonan, Tom
Gloria (80); Wolfen (81); Manhunter (86); Mystery Train (89); Last Action Hero (93)

Noonan, Tommy
Gentlemen Prefer Blondes (53); Star Is Born, A (54)

Noori, Mir Hossein
Taste of Cherry (97)

Norby, Ghita
Babette's Feast (87); Kingdom, The (94)

Nordstrom, Clarence
Gold Diggers of 1933 (33)

Norell, Ola
Together (00)

Norgaard, Carsten
Alien vs. Predator (04)

Noriega, Eduardo
Burnt Money (00)

Norman, Lucille
For Me and My Gal (42)

Norman, Maidie
What Ever Happened to Baby Jane? (62)

Norman, Susan
Safe (95)

Norman, Zack
Romancing the Stone (84)

Noro, Line
Pepe le Moko (37); J'Accuse (38)

Norring, Ava
Snows of Kilimanjaro, The (52)

Norris, Bruce
Civil Action, A (98); Sixth Sense, The (99)

Norris, Christopher
Summer of '42 (71)

Norris, Daran
Team America: World Police (04)

Norris, Edward
Boys Town (38)

Norris, Jan
Splendor in the Grass (61)

Norris, Terry
Innocence (00)

North, Alan
Glory (89)

North, Neil
Winslow Boy, The (48)

North, Sheree
Madigan (68); Charley Varrick (73); Shootist, The (76)

North, Virginia
Abominable Dr. Phibes, The (71)

Northam, Jeremy
Carrington (95); Emma (96); Ideal Husband, An (99); Possession (02)

Northrup, Harry
Over the Edge (79); Used Cars (80)

Norton, Alex
Local Hero (83); Orphans (99)

Norton, Cliff
Phantom Tollbooth, The (70)

Norton, Edgar
Love Parade, The (29); Dr. Jekyll and Mr. Hyde (32); Top Hat (35); Son of Frankenstein (39)

Norton, Edward
People vs. Larry Flynt, The (96); Everyone Says I Love You (96); American History X (98); Fight Club (99); Frida (02); Red Dragon (02); 25th Hour (02); Italian Job, The (03); Kingdom of Heaven (05)

Norton, Jim
Straw Dogs (71)

Noseworthy, Jack
U-571 (00)

Noth, Chris
Cast Away (00)

Nottingham, Wendy
Topsy-Turvy (99)

Nougaro, Pierre
Jean de Florette (86); Manon of the Spring (86)

Nouri, Michael
Hidden, The (87); Terminal, The (04)

Novak, Blaine
Strangers Kiss (84)

Novak, Kim
Man with the Golden Arm, The (55); Picnic (55); Pal Joey (57); Vertigo (58); Just a Gigolo (78)

Novakova, Jana
Loves of a Blonde (65)

Novarro, Ramon
Mata Hari (31)

Novas, Tamar
Sea Inside, The (04)

Novikoff, Rashel
Lenny (74)

Novikov, V.
Alexander Nevsky (38)

Novis, Donald
Monte Carlo (30)

Novotna, Jarmila
Search, The (48)

Novy, Pavel
Little Otik (00)

Nowak, Jerzy
White (94)

Nox, Andre
J'Accuse (38)

Ntshinga, Thoko
Dry White Season, A (89)

Ntshona, Winston
Dry White Season, A (89)

O'Shea, Daniel
Hamburger Hill (87)

O'Shea, Michael
Threat, The (49); It Should Happen to You (54)

O'Shea, Milo
Romeo and Juliet (68); Sacco and Vanzetti (71);
Verdict, The (82); Purple Rose of Cairo, The (85)

O'Shea, Oscar
Captains Courageous (37); Of Mice and Men (39);
Stranger on the Third Floor (40)

O'Shea, Tessie
Bedknobs and Broomsticks (71)

O'Sullivan, Aisling
War Zone, The (98)

O'Sullivan, Archie
Ryan's Daughter (70)

O'Sullivan, Arthur
Girl with Green Eyes (64); Barry Lyndon (75)

O'Sullivan, Jerry
Pickup on South Street (53)

O'Sullivan, Maureen
Connecticut Yankee, A (31); Tarzan, the Ape
Man (32); Barretts of Wimpole Street, The (34);
Tarzan and His Mate (34); Thin Man, The (34);
David Copperfield (35); Anna Karenina (35);
Devil-Doll, The (36); Day at the Races, A (37);
Pride and Prejudice (40); Big Clock, The (48); Tall
T, The (57); Peggy Sue Got Married (86); Hannah
and Her Sisters (86)

O'Sullivan, Michael
You're a Big Boy Now (66)

O'Toole, Annette
Smile (75); 48 Hrs. (82)

O'Toole, Harry
Twelve Monkeys (95)

O'Toole, Peter
Lawrence of Arabia (62); Becket (64); Lord
Jim (65); What's New, Pussycat? (65); Lion in
Winter, The (68); Ruling Class, The (72); Stunt
Man, The (80); My Favorite Year (82); Last
Emperor, The (87); Troy (04)

Oakie, Jack
If I Had a Million (32); Call of the Wild (35); Great
Dictator, The (40)

Oakland, Simon
I Want to Live! (58); Psycho (60); West Side
Story (61); Sand Pebbles, The (66); Bullitt (68)

Oaks, Brittany
Dr. Seuss' The Cat in the Hat (03)

Oates, Cicely
Man Who Knew Too Much, The (34)

Oates, Warren
Ride the High Country (62); In the Heat of the
Night (67); Wild Bunch, The (69); Shooting,
The (71); Two-Lane Blacktop (71); Badlands (73);
Bring Me the Head of Alfredo Garcia (74);
Stripes (81)

Obanhein, William
Alice's Restaurant (69)

Obe, Jean
Tall Blond Man with One Black Shoe, The (72)

Ober, Philip
Come Back, Little Sheba (52); From Here to
Eternity (53); North by Northwest (59)

Oberon, Merle
Private Life of Henry VIII, The (33); Scarlet
Pimpernel, The (35); These Three (36); Wuthering
Heights (39); Lodger, The (44); Song to
Remember, A (45)

Ocasio, Jose
Plaza Suite (71)

Occhipinti, Andrea
Family, The (87)

Ochoa, Eliades
Buena Vista Social Club, The (99)

Ochoa, Jesus
Man on Fire (04)

Ochsen, U.A.
Das Boot (81)

Ochsenknecht, Uwe
Men... (85)

Odagiri, Miki
Ikiru (52)

Odent, Christophe
First Name: Carmen (83); A Nos Amours (84)

Oerlemans, Jacques
Man Escaped, A (56)

Offerall, Lucy
Two Hundred Motels (71)

Ogata, Issey
Yi Yi (00)

Ogata, Ken
Ballad of Narayama, The (83); Mishima (85);
Pillow Book, The (96)

Ogen, Tom
Blob, The (58)

Oger, Frank
Three Crowns of the Sailor (83)

Ogier, Bulle
Discreet Charm of the Bourgeoisie, The (72);
Celine and Julie Go Boating (74); Candy
Mountain (87); Irma Vep (96)

Ogier, Pascale
Full Moon in Paris (84)

Ogier, Quentin
Sunday in the Country, A (84)

Ogilvy, Ian
Death Becomes Her (92)

Ogwawa, Toranosuke
Godzilla, King of the Monsters (54)

Oh Dal-su
Oldboy (04)

Persons, Mark
Silent Running (72)

Pesci, Joe
Raging Bull (80); Once Upon a Time in America (84); Lethal Weapon 2 (89); Goodfellas (90); Home Alone (90); JFK (91); Lethal Weapon 3 (92); My Cousin Vinny (92); Bronx Tale, A (93); Casino (95); Lethal Weapon 4 (98)

Pescow, Donna
Saturday Night Fever (77)

Pessin, Leo B.
Letter from an Unknown Woman (48)

Peter
Ran (85)

Peters, Bernadette
Longest Yard, The (74); Pennies from Heaven (81); Impromptu (90); Anastasia (97)

Peters, Brock
Carmen Jones (54); Porgy and Bess (59); To Kill a Mockingbird (62); Pawnbroker, The (65)

Peters, Clarke
Mona Lisa (86)

Peters, Janne
Working Girls (86)

Peters, Jean
Captain from Castile (47); O. Henry's Full House (52); Viva Zapata! (52); Niagara (53); Pickup on South Street (53); Three Coins in the Fountain (54); Apache (54)

Peters, Kelly Jean
Little Big Man (70)

Peters, Molly
Thunderball (65)

Peters, Robert
Go (99)

Peters, Susan
Random Harvest (42)

Peters, Werner
Thousand Eyes of Dr. Mabuse, The (60)

Peters, Willy
Shame (68)

Petersen, Peter
Eternal Mask, The (37)

Petersen, William
To Live and Die in L.A. (85); Manhunter (86)

Peterson, Arthur
Targets (68)

Peterson, Dorothy
I'm No Angel (33); Treasure Island (34); Dark Victory (39); Saboteur (42); Woman in the Window, The (45)

Peterson, Evangeline
State of Siege (72)

Peterson, Mark
Two English Girls (71)

Petit, Roland
Hans Christian Andersen (52)

Petito, Enzo
Good, the Bad and the Ugly, The (66)

Petraglia, Jorge
Official Story, The (85)

Petrella, Ian
Christmas Story, A (83)

Petri, Nina
Run Lola Run (98)

Petric, Vlada
Twelve Chairs, The (70)

Petrie, Hay
Knight without Armor (37); Contraband (40); Thief of Bagdad, The (40); One of Our Aircraft Is Missing (41)

Petrie, Howard
Seven Brides for Seven Brothers (54); Kiss before Dying, A (56)

Petrikat, Didi
Alice in the Cities (74)

Petrocelli, Antonio
Caro Diario (94)

Petronelli, Stefano
Italian Job, The (03)

Petrucci, Giovanni
L'Avventura (60)

Pettersson, Brigitta
Virgin Spring, The (59)

Pettersson, Hjordis
Passion of Anna, The (69)

Pettet, Joanna
Casino Royale (67)

Pettingell, Frank
Gaslight (40)

Pettitt, Frank
Saturday Night and Sunday Morning (60)

Petty, Lori
Free Willy (93)

Pevney, Joseph
Body and Soul (47)

Peyrelon, Michel
Going Places (74)

Pfeifer, Henri
Story of a Cheat, The (36)

Pfeiffer, Michelle
Scarface (83); Ladyhawke (85); Witches of Eastwick, The (87); Dangerous Liaisons (88); Married to the Mob (88); Fabulous Baker Boys, The (89); Russia House, The (90); Age of Innocence, The (93); Prince of Egypt, The (98); White Oleander (02)

Pflug, Jo Ann
M*A*S*H (70)

Pfohl, Frederic
I Stand Alone (98)

Placido, Michele
Lamerica (94)

Plakson, Suzie
Wag the Dog (97)

Plana, Tony
Officer and a Gentleman, An (82); Salvador (86)

Planas, Silvia
Death of a Bureaucrat (66)

Planchon, Roger
Danton (82); Return of Martin Guerre, The (82)

Plasteig, Mariane
Before Sunset (04)

Platt, Edward
Written on the Wind (56); North by
Northwest (59); Cape Fear (62)

Platt, Howard
Prime Cut (72)

Platt, Louise
Stagecoach (39)

Platt, Marc
Seven Brides for Seven Brothers (54)

Platt, Oliver
Working Girl (88); Married to the Mob (88);
Indecent Proposal (93); Benny & Joon (93); Funny
Bones (94); Dr. Dolittle (98); Bulworth (98); Pieces
of April (03); Kinsey (04)

Platt, Ruth
Pianist, The (02)

Platters, The
Rock Around the Clock (56)

Pleasence, Donald
Look Back in Anger (59); Sons and Lovers (60);
Great Escape, The (63); Cul-de-Sac (66); Fantastic
Voyage (66); You Only Live Twice (67);
Kidnapped (71); THX 1138 (71); Hearts of the
West (75); Halloween (78); Escape from New
York (81)

Pleshette, Suzanne
Birds, The (63); Spirited Away (01)

Plessis, Pierre
Cousin, Cousine (75)

Plimpton, Martha
Another Woman (88); Running on Empty (88); Shy
People (88); Parenthood (89); I Shot Andy
Warhol (96)

Plotnick, Jack
Gods and Monsters (98)

Plowden, Roger
Five Fingers (52)

Plowright, Joan
Entertainer, The (60); Equus (77); Brimstone and
Treacle (82); Drowning by Numbers (87);
Avalon (90); Enchanted April (91); 101
Dalmatians (96); Tea with Mussolini (99); Bringing
Down the House (03)

Pluchon, Gilbert
Zero for Conduct (33)

Pluhar, Erika
Goalie's Anxiety at the Penalty Kick, The (71); Just
a Gigolo (78)

Plummer, Amanda
Fisher King, The (91); Pulp Fiction (94)

Plummer, Christopher
Inside Daisy Clover (65); Sound of Music,
The (65); Battle of Britain (69); Man Who Would
Be King, The (75); Return of the Pink Panther,
The (75); Twelve Monkeys (95); Insider, The (99);
Beautiful Mind, A (01); Nicholas Nickleby (02);
National Treasure (04); Alexander (04)

Plummer, Glenn
Colors (88); Menace II Society (93); Speed (94);
Showgirls (95); Strange Days (95)

Pochet, Alex
Beat the Devil (53)

Pogson, Kathryn
Company of Wolves, The (84)

Pohl, Klaus
Testament of Dr. Mabuse, The (33)

Pohlkotte, Tanya
New Age, The (94)

Pohlmann, Eric
Mogambo (53); Belles of St. Trinian's, The (54)

Poindexter, Larry
S.W.A.T. (03)

Pointer, Priscilla
Looking for Mr. Goodbar (77); Onion Field,
The (79); Mommie Dearest (81); Falcon and the
Snowman, The (85); Blue Velvet (86)

Poiret, Jean
Last Metro, The (80)

Poirier, Henri
Murmur of the Heart (71)

Poitier, Earl C.
Drumline (02)

Poitier, Sidney
Blackboard Jungle (55); Band of Angels (57);
Defiant Ones, The (58); Porgy and Bess (59);
Raisin in the Sun, A (61); Lilies of the
Field (63); In the Heat of the Night (67); To Sir,
with Love (67); Guess Who's Coming to
Dinner (67); Uptown Saturday Night (74)

Pokitillow, David
Shadows (60)

Polack, Fernando Sanchez
Hunt, The (66)

Polanha, Armando
Aguirre, the Wrath of God (72)

Polanski, Roman
Andy Warhol's Dracula (74); Chinatown (74);
Tenant, The (76)

Pole, Edward Tudor
White Hunter, Black Heart (90)

Poletti, Victor
And the Ship Sails On (83)

Portnow, Richard
Tin Men (87); Barton Fink (91); Sister Act (92); Seven (95); Ghost Dog: The Way of the Samurai (99)

Portugais, David
Under the Sand (00)

Portuondo, Omara
Buena Vista Social Club, The (99)

Poschl, Hanno
Before Sunrise (95)

Posey, Matthew
True Stories (86)

Posey, Parker
Dazed and Confused (93); Henry Fool (98); You've Got Mail (98); Best in Show (00); Personal Velocity (02)

Posey, Tyler Garcia
Maid in Manhattan (02)

Posier, Jean-Pierre
Le Samourai (67)

Post Jr., William
House on 92nd Street, The (45)

Post, Markie
There's Something about Mary (98)

Post, Saskia
Proof (92)

Postlethwaite, Pete
Distant Voices, Still Lives (88); In the Name of the Father (93); Usual Suspects, The (95); William Shakespeare's Romeo + Juliet (96); Lost World: Jurassic Park, The (97); Amistad (97); Shipping News, The (01)

Potel, Victor
Virginian, The (29); Palm Beach Story, The (42)

Potente, Franka
Run Lola Run (98); Blow (01); Storytelling (01); Bourne Identity, The (02); Bourne Supremacy, The (04)

Potter, Charlie
Witches, The (90)

Potter, Chris
Pacifier, The (05)

Potter, Jerry
Misery (90)

Potter, Martin
Fellini Satyricon (69)

Potter, Monica
Con Air (97)

Potters, Tim
Entrapment (99)

Pottinger, Alan
Blioxi Blues (88); Reversal of Fortune (90)

Potts, Annie
Ghostbusters (84); Pretty in Pink (86); Toy Story (95); Toy Story 2 (99)

Potts, Cliff
Silent Running (72)

Potts, Nell
Rachel, Rachel (68); Effect of Gamma Rays on Man-in-the-Moon Marigolds, The (72)

Potts, Sarah Jane
My Son the Fanatic (98)

Poujouly, Georges
Forbidden Games (52); And God Created Woman (56)

Pounder, CCH
Bagdad Cafe (87); Benny & Joon (93)

Povah, Phyllis
Women, The (39); Pat and Mike (52)

Powell, Addison
Thomas Crown Affair, The (68); Three Days of the Condor (75)

Powell, Clifton
Ray (04)

Powell, Dick
Footlight Parade (33); 42nd Street (33); Gold Diggers of 1933 (33); Midsummer Night's Dream, A (35); Gold Diggers of 1935 (35); Christmas in July (40); Cornered (45); Murder, My Sweet (45); Bad and the Beautiful, The (52)

Powell, Don
Funny Face (57)

Powell, Jane
Royal Wedding (51); Seven Brides for Seven Brothers (54)

Powell, Jenny
8mm (99)

Powell, Lovelady
I Never Sang for My Father (70)

Powell, Robert
Tommy (75)

Powell, Russ
Big Trail, The (30)

Powell, William
Kennel Murder Case, The (33); Manhattan Melodrama (34); Thin Man, The (34); Libeled Lady (36); My Man Godfrey (36); After the Thin Man (36); Great Ziegfeld, The (36); Love Crazy (41); Ziegfeld Follies (45); Life with Father (47); Mister Roberts (55)

Power, Camilla
Alice (88)

Power, Hartley
Roman Holiday (53)

Power Sr., Tyrone
Big Trail, The (30)

Power, Tyrone
Thin Ice (37); In Old Chicago (38); Marie Antoinette (38); Alexander's Ragtime Band (38); Jesse James (39); Mark of Zorro, The (40); Blood and Sand (41); Black Swan, The (42); Razor's Edge, The (46); Captain from Castile (47); Nightmare Alley (47); Prince of Foxes (49); Black Rose, The (50); King of the Khyber Rifles (53);

Rafalowicz, Alex
Shine (96)

Rafferty, Chips
Sundowners, The (60)

Rafferty, Frances
Girl Crazy (43)

Rafferty, Tom
Big Sleep, The (46)

Rafiee, Behzad
Children of Heaven (97)

Raft, George
If I Had a Million (32); Scarface (32); They Drive by Night (40); Some Like It Hot (59)

Ragas, Roef
Breaking the Waves (96)

Ragland, Rags
Girl Crazy (43); Anchors Aweigh (45)

Ragon, Laurence
Green Room, The (78)

Ragsdale, William
Fright Night (85)

Raho, Umberto
Bird with the Crystal Plumage, The (69)

Railsback, Steve
Stunt Man, The (80)

Raimi, Ted
Evil Dead 2: Dead by Dawn (87); Darkman (90); Candyman (92); Spider-Man (02); Grudge, The (04)

Raimu
Marius (31); Fanny (32); Cesar (36); Baker's Wife, The (38)

Rain, Jeramie
Last House on the Left, The (72)

Raine, Jack
Quartet (49)

Rainer, Lorraine
This Man Must Die (70)

Rainer, Luise
Great Ziegfeld, The (36); Good Earth, The (37)

Raines, Cristina
Duellists, The (77)

Raines, Ella
Phantom Lady (44); Hail the Conquering Hero (44); Brute Force (47)

Rainey, Ford
White Heat (49); Sand Pebbles, The (66)

Rains, Claude
Invisible Man, The (33); Crime without Passion (34); Anthony Adverse (36); Prince and the Pauper, The (37); Adventures of Robin Hood, The (38); Four Daughters (38); Mr. Smith Goes to Washington (39); Juarez (39); Sea Hawk, The (40); Here Comes Mr. Jordan (41); Wolf Man, The (41); Kings Row (42); Now, Voyager (42); Casablanca (42); Phantom of the Opera (43); Passage to Marseille (44); Caesar and

Cleopatra (45); Notorious (46); Lawrence of Arabia (62)

Raisch, Bill
Lonely Are the Brave (62)

Raitt, John
Pajama Game, The (57)

Rajot, Pierre-Loup
A Nos Amours (84)

Rajskub, Mary Lynn
Punch-Drunk Love (02)

Rall, Tommy
Kiss Me Kate (53); Seven Brides for Seven Brothers (54); Pennies from Heaven (81)

Ralli, Giovanna
General della Rovere (59)

Ralph, Jessie
Les Miserables (35); San Francisco (36); After the Thin Man (36); Camille (37); Good Earth, The (37); Drums Along the Mohawk (39); Bank Dick, The (40)

Ralph, Sheryl Lee
To Sleep with Anger (90)

Ramage, Cecil
Kind Hearts and Coronets (49)

Ramage, Jack
Kramer vs. Kramer (79)

Rambeau, Marjorie
Min and Bill (30); Tobacco Road (41); Man of a Thousand Faces (57)

Ramdane, Setti
Vagabond (85)

Rameau, Emil
Gaslight (44)

Ramer, Henry
Apprenticeship of Duddy Kravitz, The (74)

Ramey, Ed
Deliverance (72)

Ramirez, Carlos
Anchors Aweigh (45)

Ramirez, Efren
Napoleon Dynamite (04)

Ramirez, Mary Carmen
Belle Epoque (92)

Ramis, Harold
Stripes (81); Ghostbusters (84)

Rammellzee
Stranger than Paradise (84)

Ramon, Mitsusaburo
Ugetsu (53)

Ramon, Poncho
El Mariachi (93)

Ramone, Dee Dee
End of the Century: The Story of the Ramones (04)

Ramone, Joey
End of the Century: The Story of the Ramones (04)

Reiner, Alysia
Sideways (04)

Reiner, Carl
Dead Men Don't Wear Plaid (82)

Reiner, Rob
This Is Spinal Tap (84); Throw Momma from the Train (87); Postcards from the Edge (90); Sleepless in Seattle (93); Bullets over Broadway (94); EdTV (99)

Reinhold, Judge
Stripes (81); Fast Times at Ridgemont High (82); Beverly Hills Cop (84); Ruthless People (86); Santa Clause, The (94); Santa Clause 2, The (02)

Reininger, Scott
Dawn of the Dead (79)

Reinking, Ann
Movie Movie (78); All That Jazz (79)

Reis, Jose Marcio
Bye-Bye Brazil (80)

Reis, Michelle
Fallen Angels (95)

Reiser, Paul
Diner (82); Aliens (86)

Reitherman, Bruce
Jungle Book, The (67)

Reitinger, Richard
Match Factory Girl, The (90)

Rekert, Winston
Agnes of God (85)

Relli, Santa
Jour de Fete (49)

Remar, James
Warriors, The (79); 48 Hrs. (82); Cotton Club, The (84); Drugstore Cowboy (89)

Remi, Jean-Francois
La Guerre est Finie (66)

Remick, Lee
Face in the Crowd, A (57); Long, Hot Summer, The (58); Anatomy of a Murder (59); Wild River (60); Days of Wine and Roses (62); Detective, The (68); Omen, The (76)

Remignard, Jean
Au Hasard, Balthazar (66)

Remini, Leah
Old School (03)

Remolina, Juan Carlos
Y Tu Mama Tambien (01)

Remsen, Bert
McCabe and Mrs. Miller (71); Thieves Like Us (74)

Remy, Albert
Four Hundred Blows, The (59); Shoot the Piano Player (60); Train, The (65)

Rena, Alexia
Arizona Dream (91)

Renaldo, Tito
Anna and the King of Siam (46)

Renant, Simone
That Man from Rio (64)

Renard, Jacques
Mother and the Whore, The (73)

Renavent, Georges
Queen Christina (33)

Rendi, R.
Stalker (79)

Rendine, Aldo
Investigation of a Citizen Above Suspicion (70)

Renfro, Brad
Client, The (94); Apt Pupil (98); Ghost World (01)

Renier, Jeremie
Brotherhood of the Wolf (01)

Renn, Katherina
Rise of Louis XIV, The (66)

Renner, Jeremy
S.W.A.T. (03)

Rennie, Callum Keith
eXistenZ (99); Memento (01)

Rennie, Guy
Lenny (74)

Rennie, James
Now, Voyager (42)

Rennie, Michael
Black Rose, The (50); Day the Earth Stood Still, The (51); Five Fingers (52); King of the Khyber Rifles (53); Robe, The (53)

Reno, Jean
La Femme Nikita (90); Mission: Impossible (96); Ronin (98); Godzilla (98)

Reno, Kelly
Black Stallion, The (79)

Renoir, Jean
La Bete Humaine (38); Rules of the Game (39); Ways of Love (50)

Renoir, Pierre
La Marseillaise (38); Children of Paradise (45)

Renoir, Rita
Red Desert (64)

Renoir, Sophie
Le Beau Mariage (82)

Renucci, Robin
Entre Nous (83); Dreamers, The (03)

Renzi, Eva
Funeral in Berlin (66); Bird with the Crystal Plumage, The (69)

Renzi, Maggie
Return of the Secaucus Seven (80); Brother from Another Planet, The (84)

Repulles, Alejandro
Aguirre, the Wrath of God (72)

Requeraz, Jean Pierre
Man Facing Southeast (86)

Resin, Dan
Caddyshack (80)

The (97); Sleepy Hollow (99); Chicken Run (00); Hours, The (02); Spider (02); Andrew Lloyd Webber's The Phantom of the Opera (04)

Richardson, Natasha
Comfort of Strangers, The (91); Parent Trap, The (98); Maid in Manhattan (02)

Richardson, Patricia
Ulee's Gold (97)

Richardson, Ralph
Things to Come (36); Citadel, The (38); Four Feathers, The (39); Anna Karenina (47); Fallen Idol, The (48); Heiress, The (49); Richard III (55); Our Man in Havana (59); Exodus (60); Long Day's Journey into Night (62); Doctor Zhivago (65); Khartoum (66); Bed Sitting Room, The (69); Oh! What a Lovely War (69); O Lucky Man! (73); Rollerball (75); Watership Down (78); Dragonslayer (81); Time Bandits (81); Greystoke: The Legend of Tarzan, Lord of the Apes (84)

Richardson, Salli
Antwone Fisher (02)

Richardson, Sy
Repo Man (84); Colors (88); Mystery Train (89)

Richert, Carole
Tous les Matins du Monde (91)

Richert, William
My Own Private Idaho (91)

Richman, Charles
Dark Victory (39)

Richman, Josh
River's Edge (87)

Richman, Mark
Friendly Persuasion (56)

Richter, Daniel
2001: A Space Odyssey (68)

Richter, Jason James
Free Willy (93)

Richter, Jorg
Heimat (84)

Richwine, Maria
Buddy Holly Story, The (78)

Rickles, Don
Run Silent, Run Deep (58); "X"—The Man with the X-Ray Eyes (63); Casino (95); Toy Story (95); Toy Story 2 (99)

Rickman, Alan
Die Hard (88); Robin Hood: Prince of Thieves (91); Truly, Madly, Deeply (91); Bob Roberts (92); Sense and Sensibility (95); Michael Collins (96); Galaxy Quest (99); Dogma (99); Love Actually (03); Hitchhiker's Guide to the Galaxy, The (05)

Rideau, Stephane
Wild Reeds (94)

Ridgely, John
Air Force (43); Pride of the Marines (45); Big Sleep, The (46)

Ridgely, Robert
Philadelphia (93)

Ridges, Stanley
Crime without Passion (34); Scoundrel, The (35); Union Pacific (39); Sea Wolf, The (41); Sergeant York (41); To Be or Not to Be (42); This Is the Army (43)

Ridings, Richard
Who Framed Roger Rabbit (88)

Ridley, Judith
Night of the Living Dead (68)

Riegert, Peter
National Lampoon's Animal House (78); Chilly Scenes of Winter (79); Local Hero (83); Man in Love, A (87); Shock to the System, A (90); Mask, The (94)

Riehle, Richard
Free Willy (93)

Riento, Virgilio
Miracle in Milan (51)

Riesco, Armando
Garden State (04)

Rietty, Robert
Madame Sousatzka (88)

Rifkin, Ron
Silent Running (72); Sunshine Boys, The (75); Manhattan Murder Mystery (93); L.A. Confidential (97); Negotiator, The (98); Sum of All Fears, The (02)

Rigano, Evi
10th Victim, The (65)

Rigby, Edward
Young and Innocent (37); Stars Look Down, The (39)

Rigby, Terence
Accident (67); Homecoming, The (73); Watership Down (78)

Rigg, Diana
On Her Majesty's Secret Service (69); Hospital, The (71); Theatre of Blood (73); Great Muppet Caper, The (81)

Rigillo, Mariana
Postman, The (94)

Rignack, Roger
True Love (89)

Rignault, Alexandre
Number Two (75); Mon Oncle d'Amerique (80)

Riis, Anne-Grethe Bjarup
Idiots, The (98)

Rijker, Lucia
Million Dollar Baby (04)

Riju, Go
Mishima (85); Eureka (00)

Riley, Gary
Stand by Me (86)

Riley, Jack
High Anxiety (77); Attack of the Killer Tomatoes (78)

Riley, Larry
Soldier's Story, A (84)

Riley, Miss
10 Rillington Place (70)

Rilla, Walter
Scarlet Pimpernel, The (35); Victoria the Great (37)

Rimmer, Shane
Rollerball (75); Spy Who Loved Me, The (77)

Ring, Cyril
Cocoanuts, The (29)

Ringwald, Molly
Sixteen Candles (84); Breakfast Club, The (85); Pretty in Pink (86); King Lear (87)

Riordan, Marjorie
Stage Door Canteen (43)

Rios, Arturo
Y Tu Mama Tambien (01)

Rios, Orlando
Calle 54 (00)

Rioton, Louise
La Femme Infidele (69)

Rioufol, Marc
Baise-Moi (00)

Rioux, Genevieve
Decline of the American Empire, The (86)

Ripley, Fay
Mute Witness (95)

Rippy, Leon
Stargate (94); Alamo, The (04)

Riquelme, Carlos
Under the Volcano (84)

Risch, Maurice
Last Metro, The (80)

Risch, Pierre
Soft Skin, The (64)

Risdon, Elisabeth
Theodora Goes Wild (36); Make Way for Tomorrow (37); Roaring Twenties, The (39); High Sierra (41); Life with Father (47)

Rispoli, Michael
While You Were Sleeping (95); Summer of Sam (99)

Rissi, Claudio
Burnt Money (00)

Risterucci, Vincent
L'Argent (83)

Ristovski, Lazar
Underground (95)

Ritchard, Cyril
Blackmail (29)

Ritchie, June
Kind of Loving, A (62)

Riton
Get Out Your Handkerchiefs (78)

Ritter, Huntley
Bring It On (00)

Ritter, John
Sling Blade (96); Bride of Chucky (98); Bad Santa (03)

Ritter, Thelma
All About Eve (50); With a Song in My Heart (52); Pickup on South Street (53); Titanic (53); Rear Window (54); Pillow Talk (59); Misfits, The (61); Birdman of Alcatraz (62)

Ritz, James
Real Life (79)

Riva, Emmanuelle
Hiroshima Mon Amour (59); Blue (93)

Rivas, Carlos
King and I, The (56)

Rivera, Carlos
Old Man and the Sea, The (58)

Rivera, Cecilia
Aguirre, the Wrath of God (72)

Rivera, Chita
Sweet Charity (69)

Rivera, Mabel
Sea Inside, The (04)

Rivera, Marcelino
Mixed Blood (84)

Rivero, Jorge
Rio Lobo (70)

Rivet, Gilberte
Lacombe, Lucien (74)

Rivet, Pascal
Au Revoir, les Enfants (87)

Riveyre, Jean
Diary of a Country Priest (50)

Rix, Colin
Eye of the Needle (81)

Riza, Bella
Hideous Kinky (98)

Rizzi, Gene
Outlaw, The (43)

Roa, Grant
Whale Rider (03)

Roa, Joaquin
Viridiana (61)

Roach, Bert
Man in the Iron Mask, The (39)

Roach, James
Waterdance, The (92)

Roache, Linus
Wings of the Dove, The (97); Forgotten, The (04)

Roache, Viola
Royal Wedding (51)

Roarke, Adam
Stunt Man, The (80)

Rocca, Daniela
Divorce, Italian Style (62)

Roccardi, Albert
Love Parade, The (29)

Rocco, Alex
Slither (73); Friends of Eddie Coyle, The (73);
Hearts of the West (75); Stunt Man, The (80); Lady
in White (88)

Rocha, Kali
Object of My Affection, The (98)

Roche, Eugene
Late Show, The (77)

Roche, John
Monte Carlo (30)

Rochefort, Jean
Tall Blond Man with One Black Shoe, The (72);
Clockmaker, The (73); Pardon Mon Affaire (77);
Hairdresser's Husband, The (92); Ridicule (96)

Rochelle, Niva
Sweet Sweetback's Baadasssss Song (71)

Rochon, Lela
Waiting to Exhale (95)

Rock, Bob
Metallica: Some Kind of Monster (04)

Rock, Chris
Lethal Weapon 4 (98); Dogma (99)

Rock, Crissy
Under the Skin (97)

Rocket, Charles
Dances with Wolves (90); Dumb & Dumber (94)

Rockwell, Alexandre
Caro Diario (94)

Rockwell, Sam
Galaxy Quest (99); Green Mile, The (99); Charlie's
Angels (00); Confessions of a Dangerous
Mind (02); Matchstick Men (03); Hitchhiker's
Guide to the Galaxy, The (05)

Roco, Bembol
Year of Living Dangerously, The (83)

Rodas, Rodolfo
Man Facing Southeast (86)

Rodd, Marcia
Citizens Band (77)

Roddan, Allison
Monsieur Verdoux (47)

Rode, Thierry
Hail, Mary (85)

Roden, Karel
Hellboy (04); Bourne Supremacy, The (04)

Rodgers, Anton
Scrooge (70); Impromptu (90)

Rodgers, Gaby
Kiss Me Deadly (55)

Rodgers, Michael
Auto Focus (02)

Rodine, Alex
Colossus: The Forbin Project (70)

Rodman, Dennis
Double Team (97)

Rodney, John
Pursued (47); Key Largo (48)

Rodrigues, Alexandre
City of God (02)

Rodriguez, Estelita
Rio Bravo (59)

Rodriguez, Eva
Waterdance, The (92)

Rodriguez, Michelle
Girlfight (00); S.W.A.T. (03)

Rodriguez, Nicolas
Man's Hope (47)

Rodriguez, Sixto
Fat City (72)

Rodriguez, Spain
Crumb (95)

Rodriguez, Yolanda
Cool World, The (63)

Rodriquez, William
Emerald Forest, The (85)

Rodway, Norman
Chimes at Midnight (66)

Roe, Raymond
Major and the Minor, The (42)

Roebling, Paul
Prince of the City (81)

Roebuck, Daniel
River's Edge (87); Fugitive, The (93)

Roeves, Maurice
Last of the Mohicans, The (92)

Roffe, Carlos
Burnt Money (00)

Rogak, Gina
Girlfriends (78)

Rogan, John
Drowning by Numbers (87)

Rogers, Ginger
Flying Down to Rio (33); 42nd Street (33); Gold
Diggers of 1933 (33); Gay Divorcee, The (34);
Roberta (35); Top Hat (35); Follow the Fleet (36);
Swing Time (36); Shall We Dance (37); Stage
Door (37); Bachelor Mother (39); Story of Vernon
and Irene Castle, The (39); Kitty Foyle (40); Major
and the Minor, The (42); Tales of Manhattan (42);
Lady in the Dark (44); Barkleys of Broadway,
The (49)

Rogers, Ingrid
Carlito's Way (93)

Rogers, Jean
Flash Gordon (36)

Velvet (44); Summer Holiday (48); Bridges at Toko-Ri, The (54); Breakfast at Tiffany's (61); Requiem for a Heavyweight (62); It's a Mad, Mad, Mad, Mad World (63); Black Stallion, The (79)

Rooney, Wallace
Exorcist, The (73)

Roope, Fay
Day the Earth Stood Still, The (51)

Roos, Joanna
Patterns (56); Splendor in the Grass (61)

Roose, Thirkild
Day of Wrath (43)

Roosendahl, Jennifer
'Night, Mother (86)

Root, Alexandra
sex, lies, and videotape (89)

Root, Stephen
Ice Age (02); White Oleander (02); Finding Nemo (03); Dodgeball: A True Underdog Story (04)

Roper, Jack
Angels Over Broadway (40)

Roper, John
Thieves Like Us (74)

Roquevert, Noel
Diabolique (55)

Rory, Rossana
Big Deal on Madonna Street (58)

Rosa, Tony
Old Man and the Sea, The (58)

Rose, Bartholomew
Flirting (90)

Rose, Gabrielle
Sweet Hereafter, The (97)

Rose, George
New Leaf, A (71)

Rose, Jane
Summertime (55)

Rose, Mickey
What's Up, Tiger Lily? (66)

Roseanne
Unzipped (95)

Roselius, John
Lost Highway (97)

Roseman, Ralph
Blob, The (58)

Rosen, Danny
Stranger than Paradise (84)

Rosenbaum, Michael
Bringing Down the House (03)

Rosenberg, Alan
Wanderers, The (79)

Rosenberg, Arthur
Cutter's Way (81)

Rosenblatt, Marcell
Sophie's Choice (82)

Rosenbloom, Maxie
Nothing Sacred (37)

Rosener, George
Doctor X (32)

Rosenfeld, Dr. Isadore
Man on the Moon (99)

Rosenfeld, Moishe
Sophie's Choice (82)

Rosenfield, Maurice
Bang the Drum Slowly (73)

Rosenmeyer, Grant
Royal Tenenbaums, The (01)

Rosenthal, Clara
Projectionist, The (70)

Rosenthal, Harry
Great McGinty, The (40)

Rosenthal, Rachel
New Age, The (94)

Rosette
Pauline at the Beach (83)

Rosier, Cathy
Le Samourai (67)

Rosmer, Milton
Stars Look Down, The (39); Goodbye Mr. Chips (39)

Ross, Adam
Seduction of Joe Tynan, The (79)

Ross, Annie
Blue Sky (94)

Ross, Anthony
Kiss of Death (47); Window, The (49); Gunfighter, The (50); Country Girl, The (54)

Ross, Chelcie
Basic Instinct (92); Simple Plan, A (98)

Ross, Diana
Lady Sings the Blues (72)

Ross, Ellen
Lady in the Lake (47); Pirate, The (48)

Ross, Gaylen
Dawn of the Dead (79)

Ross, Katharine
Shenandoah (65); Graduate, The (67); Butch Cassidy and the Sundance Kid (69); Stepford Wives, The (75); Donnie Darko (01)

Ross, Lee
Secrets & Lies (95)

Ross, Marion
Glenn Miller Story, The (53); Colossus: The Forbin Project (70)

Ross, Matt
Last Days of Disco, The (98); American Psycho (00)

Ross, Stanley Ralph
Sleeper (73)

Sand, Paul
Chuck & Buck (00)

Sanda, Dominique
Gentle Creature, A (69); Conformist, The (70);
Garden of the Finzi-Continis, The (71); 1900 (76)

Sandars, Clare
Mrs. Miniver (42)

Sande, Walter
To Have and Have Not (44); Racket, The (51);
Apache (54); Bad Day at Black Rock (55)

Sander, Otto
Wings of Desire (87)

Sanders, Anita
10th Victim, The (65)

Sanders, C.J.
Ray (04)

Sanders, Chris
Lilo & Stitch (02)

Sanders, Dirk
Pierrot le Fou (65)

Sanders, George
Confessions of a Nazi Spy (39); Foreign
Correspondent (40); Rebecca (40); Man Hunt (41);
Moon and Sixpence, The (42); Black Swan,
The (42); This Land Is Mine (43); Lodger,
The (44); Picture of Dorian Gray, The (45); Ghost
and Mrs. Muir, The (47); Samson and Delilah (49);
All About Eve (50); Ivanhoe (52); While the City
Sleeps (56); Village of the Damned (60); Shot in
the Dark, A (64); Jungle Book, The (67)

Sanders, Henry Gayle
Killer of Sheep (78)

Sanders, Hugh
Wild One, The (53); Jailhouse Rock (57)

Sanders, Jay O.
Starting Over (79); JFK (91); Day After Tomorrow,
The (04)

Sanders, Joe
Dark Star (75)

Sanderson, William
Coal Miner's Daughter (80); Blade Runner (82)

Sandford, Christopher
Deep End (70)

Sandford, Tiny
Modern Times (36)

Sandler, Adam
Wedding Singer, The (98); Waterboy, The (98);
Adam Sandler's Eight Crazy Nights (02);
Punch-Drunk Love (02); Anger
Management (03); 50 First Dates (04);
Spanglish (04)

Sandman, Lee
Lenny (74)

Sandoval, Miguel
Clear and Present Danger (94)

Sandrelli, Stefania
Divorce, Italian Style (62); Conformist, The (70);
Family, The (87); Stealing Beauty (96)

Sandrowicz, Marta
Europa, Europa (91)

Sands, Diana
Raisin in the Sun, A (61)

Sands, Johnny
Bachelor and the Bobby-Soxer, The (47)

Sands, Julian
Killing Fields, The (84); Room with a View, A (85);
Impromptu (90); Naked Lunch (91); Leaving Las
Vegas (95); Time Code (00)

Sands, Tommy
Longest Day, The (62)

Sandweiss, Ellen
Evil Dead, The (83)

Sane, Joseph
Guelwaar (93)

Sanfelice, Giuseppe
Son's Room, The (01)

Sanford, Erskine
Citizen Kane (41); Magnificent Ambersons,
The (42); Ministry of Fear (45); Lady from
Shanghai, The (48); Letter from an Unknown
Woman (48)

Sanford, Isabel
Guess Who's Coming to Dinner (67)

Sanford, Ralph
Thunderhead—Son of Flicka (45); My Pal
Trigger (46)

Sanga, Fatimata
Yaaba (89)

Sangare, Aoua
Brightness (87)

Sangare, Koke
Brightness (87)

Sangweni, Kombisile
Kirikou and the Sorceress (98)

Sannachan, Douglas
That Sinking Feeling (79); Gregory's Girl (81)

Sano, Shiro
Most Terrible Time in My Life, The (93)

Sanogo, Niamanto
Brightness (87)

Sansbury, Tianna
Rabbit-Proof Fence (02)

Sanson, Yvonne
Conformist, The (70)

Santacroce, Mary Nell
Wise Blood (79)

Santaya, Frederic
Le Petit Theatre de Jean Renoir (69)

Santesso, Walter
La Dolce Vita (60)

Sauer, Gary
Unbelievable Truth, The (90)

Sauli, Anneli
Man without a Past, The (02)

Saunders, Cliff
Spider (02)

Saunders, Jennifer
Midwinter's Tale, A (95); Spice World (98);
Shrek 2 (04)

Saunders, Lanna
Body Heat (81)

Saunders, Terry
King and I, The (56)

Sauvage, Arlette
Vitelloni (53)

Savage, Ann
Detour (45)

Savage, Fred
Princess Bride, The (87); Rules of Attraction,
The (02); Austin Powers in Goldmember (02)

Savage, John
Bad Company (72); Deer Hunter, The (78); Onion
Field, The (79); Hair (79); Salvador (86)

Savage, Nick
Fright Night (85)

Savalas, Telly
Birdman of Alcatraz (62); Cape Fear (62); On Her
Majesty's Secret Service (69)

Savant, Doug
Godzilla (98)

Savelyeva, Lyudmila
War and Peace (67)

Saviange, Sonia
Salo, or the 120 Days of Sodom (75)

Savini, Tom
Martin (78); Dawn of the Dead (04)

Savino, Joe
Crying Game, The (92)

Savkin, Ivan
My Name Is Ivan (62)

Savoy, Suzanne
Cohen and Tate (89)

Sawaki, Tetsu
Audition (99)

Sawalha, Julia
Midwinter's Tale, A (95); Chicken Run (00)

Sawalha, Nadim
Touch of Class, A (73); Wind and the Lion,
The (75)

Sawamura, Ichisaburo
Ugestu (53)

Sawamura, Mitsuko
Teahouse of the August Moon, The (56)

Sawaya, George
Dead Men Don't Wear Plaid (82)

Sawyer, Joe
Informer, The (35); Petrified Forest, The (36);
Roaring Twenties, The (39); Long Voyage Home,
The (40); Outlaw, The (43); Brewster's
Millions (45); Gilda (46); Double Life, A (47); It
Came from Outer Space (53); Killing, The (56)

Saxon, Don
Subject Was Roses, The (68)

Saxon, John
Enter the Dragon (73); Nightmare on Elm Street,
A (84)

Sayle, Alexei
Gorky Park (83)

Sayles, Francis
Blonde Venus (32)

Sayles, John
Return of the Secaucus Seven (80); Lianna (83);
Something Wild (86)

Sazanka, Kyu
Bad Sleep Well, The (60); Yojimbo (61)

Sazio, Carmela
Paisan (46)

Sbaraglia, Leonardo
Burnt Money (00)

Sbarge, Raphael
Risky Business (83)

Sbarra, Galliano
Fellini's Roma (72)

Sbragia, Mattia
Passion of the Christ, The (04)

Scacchi, Greta
Coca-Cola Kid, The (85); Defence of the
Realm (85); Man in Love, A (87); Presumed
Innocent (90); Player, The (92); Emma (96)

Scal, Dolly
Pickpocket (59)

Scala, Gia
Guns of Navarone, The (61)

Scales, Hubert
Sweet Sweetback's Baadasssss Song (71)

Scales, Prunella
Hobson's Choice (54); Waltz of the Toreadors (62);
Howards End (92)

Scaletta, Lenny
Mean Streets (73)

Scalici, Valentina
Stolen Children, The (92)

Scandiuzzi, Giancarlo
Bugsy (91)

Scanlan, Joanna
Girl with a Pearl Earring (03)

Scannell, Frank
Country Girl, The (54); Incredible Shrinking Man,
The (57)

Scaramuzza, Cristina
Man Facing Southeast (86)

Seven, Johnny
Apartment, The (60)

Severance, Scott H.
Feyer Pitch (05)

Severdzan, Bajram
Black Cat, White Cat (98)

Severin, Gaston
Diary of a Country Priest (50)

Severn, Ernest
Pursued (47)

Sevigny, Chloe
Kids (95); Trees Lounge (96); Last Days of Disco,
The (98); Boys Don't Cry (99); American
Psycho (00); Dogville (03); Shattered Glass (03);
Melinda and Melinda (05)

Sevilla, Carmen
King of Kings (61)

Sewell, George
Get Carter (71)

Sewell, Rufus
Carrington (95); Cold Comfort Farm (95); Dark
City (98); Knight's Tale, A (01)

Seweryn, Andrzej
Man of Iron (80); Schindler's List (93)

Sexton III, Brendan
Welcome to the Dollhouse (95); Boys Don't
Cry (99)

Seyferth, Wilfried
Decision Before Dawn (51)

Seyfried, Amanda
Mean Girls (04)

Seyler, Athene
Beggar's Opera, The (52)

Seymour, Anne
All the King's Men (49)

Seymour, Cara
American Psycho (00); Dancer in the Dark (00);
Adaptation. (02); Hotel Rwanda (04); Birth (04)

Seymour, Carolyn
Gumshoe (71); Ruling Class, The (72)

Seymour, Dan
To Have and Have Not (44); Johnny Belinda (48);
Key Largo (48)

Seymour, Ralph
Rain Man (88)

Seymour, Stephanie
Pollock (00)

Seyrig, Delphine
Last Year at Marienbad (61); Muriel (63);
Accident (67); Stolen Kisses (68); Discreet Charm
of the Bourgeoisie, The (72)

Shada, Jeremy
Team America: World Police (04)

Shadix, Glenn
Beetlejuice (88); Heathers (89); Demolition
Man (93); Tim Burton's The Nightmare before
Christmas (93)

Shafer, Robert
Damn Yankees (58)

Shah, Naseeruddin
Monsoon Wedding (01); League of Extraordinary
Gentlemen, The (03)

Shail, Gary
Quadrophenia (79)

Shakar, Martin
Saturday Night Fever (77)

Shakur, Afeni
Tupac Resurrection (04)

Shakur, Tupac
Tupac Resurrection (04)

Shalhoub, Tony
Barton Fink (91); Men in Black (97); Paulie (98);
Civil Action, A (98); Siege, The (98); Galaxy
Quest (99); Spy Kids (01); Man Who Wasn't There,
The (01); Men in Black II (02)

Shallo, Karen
Mortal Thoughts (91)

Shamata, Charles
Scanners (81)

Shamsi, Mohammed
Man Who Would Be King, The (75)

Shane, Sara
Magnificent Obsession (54)

Shannon, Frank
Flash Gordon (36)

Shannon, Harry
This Gun for Hire (42); Mr. Blandings Builds His
Dream House (48); Champion (49); Three Little
Words (50); Tall Men, The (55); Written on the
Wind (56); Gypsy (62)

Shannon, Johnny
Performance (70)

Shannon, Michael
Vanilla Sky (01); Woodsman, The (04)

Shannon, Molly
Analyze This (99); Dr. Suess' How the Grinch Stole
Christmas (00)

Shannon, Richard
Bridges at Toko-Ri, The (54); White
Christmas (54); Seven Little Foys, The (55)

Shanti
Born into Brothels (04)

Shapiro, George
Man on the Moon (99)

Shapiro, Helen
Ring-a-Ding Rhythm (62)

Shapiro, Henry
Superfly (72)

Shapiro, Ken
Groove Tube, The (74)

Shapiro, Rick
True Love (89)

Sheen, Charlie
Lucas (86); Platoon (86); Wall Street (87); Eight Men Out (88); Hot Shots! (91)

Sheen, Martin
Subject Was Roses, The (68); Catch-22 (70); Badlands (73); Little Girl Who Lives Down the Lane, The (76); Apocalypse Now (79); Gandhi (82); Dead Zone, The (83); Wall Street (87); Apocalypse Now Redux (01); Catch Me if You Can (02)

Sheen, Michael
Wilde (97)

Sheen, Ruth
High Hopes (88); Vera Drake (04)

Sheffer, Craig
River Runs through It, A (92)

Sheffield, Reginald
Of Human Bondage (34); Suspicion (41)

Sheffler, Marc
Last House on the Left, The (72)

Sheiner, David
Odd Couple, The (68)

Shellen, Stephen
Stepfather, The (87); River Runs through It, A (92)

Shelley, Barbara
Village of the Damned (60)

Shelley, Carole
Odd Couple, The (68)

Shelley, Norman
Adventuress, The (46)

Shelley, Paul
Macbeth (71)

Shelley, Rachel
Lagaan: Once Upon a Time in India (01)

Shelly, Adrienne
Unbelievable Truth, The (90); Trust (91)

Shelly, Jacques
A Nous la Liberte (31)

Shelton, Don
Them! (54)

Shelton, Sloane
Jacknife (89)

Shenar, Paul
Secret of Nimh, The (82); Scarface (83)

Shenkman, Ben
Roger Dodger (02)

Shepard, Sam
Days of Heaven (78); Right Stuff, The (83); Steel Magnolias (89); Thuderheart (92); Pelican Brief, The (93); Hamlet (00); All the Pretty Horses (00); Pledge, The (01); Black Hawk Down (01); Notebook, The (04)

Shepherd, Cybill
Last Picture Show, The (71); Taxi Driver (76)

Shepherd, Simon
Henry V (89)

Shepherd, Suzanne
Lolita (97)

Shepodd, Jon
Attack! (56)

Sheppard, Paula
Liquid Sky (82)

Sheppard, W. Morgan
Wild at Heart (90)

Sher, Antony
Mrs. Brown (97)

Sherbedgia, Rade
Before the Rain (94); Mission: Impossible II (00); Quiet American, The (02)

Sheridan, Ann
Angels with Dirty Faces (38); Dodge City (39); City for Conquest (40); They Drive by Night (40); Kings Row (42); Man Who Came to Dinner, The (42); Edge of Darkness (43)

Sheridan, Dan
Lonely Are the Brave (62)

Sheridan, Dave
Ghost World (01)

Sheridan, Dinah
Genevieve (53); Railway Children, The (70)

Sheridan, Jamey
Ice Storm, The (97)

Sheridan, Joe
Dangerous Liaisons (88)

Sheridan, Margaret
Thing from Another World, The (51); I, the Jury (53)

Sheridan, Nicollette
Sure Thing, The (85)

Sheridan, Richard
Secret of Roan Inish, The (95)

Sheridan, Susan
Black Cauldron, The (85)

Sherman, Fred
Tall T, The (57)

Sherman, Geraldine
Poor Cow (67)

Sherman, Hiram
Solid Gold Cadillac, The (56)

Sherman, Howard
Day of the Dead (85)

Sherman, John
Hasty Heart, The (49)

Sherman, Kerry
48 Hrs. (82)

Shermet, Hazel
Star Is Born, A (54)

Sherwood, Bobby
Pal Joey (57)

Sherwood, Madeleine
Cat on a Hot Tin Roof (58); Sweet Bird of Youth (62)

Sorvino, Mira
Barcelona (94); Mighty Aphrodite (95); Summer of
Sam (99); Grey Zone, The (02)

Sorvino, Paul
Touch of Class, A (73); Reds (81); Dick Tracy (90);
Goodfellas (90); Nixon (95); William
Shakespeare's Romeo + Juliet (96); Bulworth (98);
Cooler, The (03)

Sossamon, Shannyn
Knight's Tale, A (01); Rules of Attraction, The (02)

Sothern, Ann
Letter to Three Wives, A (49); Whales of August,
The (87)

Sotirov, Stojan
Black Cat, White Cat (98)

Soto, Hugo
Man Facing Southeast (86)

Soubestre, Pierre
Under the Sand (00)

Soublette, Andres Jose Cruz
Teorema (68)

Soutendijk, Renee
Spetters (80)

Southern, Eve
Morocco (30)

Souza, Roger
Vanishing, The (86)

Sovagovic, Filip
No Man's Land (01)

Sow, Serigne
Mandabi (68)

Sowie, Theophile Moussa
Lumumba (00)

Space, Arthur
Spirit of St. Louis, The (57)

Spacek, Sissy
Prime Cut (72); Badlands (73); Carrie (76);
Welcome to L.A. (76); 3 Women (77); Coal
Miner's Daughter (80); Missing (82); Marie (85);
'Night, Mother (86); JFK (91); Affliction (98);
Straight Story, The (99); In the Bedroom (01); Tuck
Everlasting (02); Ring Two, The (05)

Spacey, Kevin
Working Girl (88); Henry & June (90); Glengarry
Glen Ross (92); Usual Suspects, The (95);
Seven (95); L.A. Confidential (97); Midnight in the
Garden of Good and Evil (97); Negotiator,
The (98); Bug's Life, A (98); American
Beauty (99); Shipping News, The (01)

Spadaro, Claudio
Tea with Mussolini (99)

Spadaro, Odoardo
Golden Coach, The (52); Divorce, Italian Style (62)

Spade, David
Emperor's New Groove, The (00)

Spader, James
Pretty in Pink (86); Less Than Zero (87); Wall
Street (87); sex, lies, and videotape (89); Bad
Influence (90); Bob Roberts (92); Stargate (94);
Crash (96); 2 Days in the Valley (96);
Secretary (02)

Spaeth, Merrie
World of Henry Orient, The (64)

Spagnuolo, Filomena
Gloria (80)

Spall, Timothy
Life Is Sweet (91); Secrets & Lies (95);
Topsy-Turvy (99); Chicken Run (00); Vanilla
Sky (01); Last Samurai, The (03); Harry Potter and
the Prisoner of Azkaban (04); Lemony Snicket's A
Series of Unfortunate Events (04)

Spalla, Ignazio
Mixed Blood (84)

Spalova, Petra
Kolya (96)

Spanjer, Maarten
Spetters (80)

Spano, Vincent
Over the Edge (79); Rumble Fish (83)

Sparke, Pip
Father Goose (64)

Sparks, Cheryl
Silent Running (72)

Sparks, Ned
Gold Diggers of 1933 (33); Imitation of Life (34)

Sparrow, Walter
Secret Garden, The (93)

Sparv, Camilla
Downhill Racer (69)

Spear, Bernard
Yentl (83)

Spector, Lisa
Punch-Drunk Love (02)

Spector, Phil
Easy Rider (69)

Speechley, Joseph
About a Boy (02)

Speechley, Ryan
About a Boy (02)

Speedman, Scott
Dark Blue (03)

Speer, Hugo
Full Monty, The (97); Interpreter, The (05)

Speer, Martin
Hills Have Eyes, The (78)

Spellos, Peter
Bound (96)

Spence, Bruce
Cars That Ate Paris, The (74); Road Warrior,
The (81); Dark City (98)

Spence, Sebastian
Boys of St. Vincent, The (93)

Spencer, Douglas
Thing from Another World, The (51); Shane (53);
Three Faces of Eve, The (57); Diary of Anne Frank,
The (59)

Spencer, John
Sea of Love (89); Presumed Innocent (90);
Negotiator, The (98)

Spencer, Kenneth
Cabin in the Sky (43)

Spenser, Jeremy
Summertime (55); Prince and the Showgirl,
The (57); Roman Spring of Mrs. Stone, The (61);
King and Country (64); Fahrenheit 451 (66)

Sperber, Milo
Providence (77)

Sperber, Wendie Jo
Back to the Future (85)

Spevack, Jason
Fever Pitch (05)

Spielberg, David
Effect of Gamma Rays on Man-in-the-Moon
Marigolds, The (72)

Spies, Manfred
Passenger, The (75)

Spiesser, Jacques
Stavisky (74); Black and White in Color (76)

Spike the Dog
Old Yeller (57)

Spill, Luke
Finding Neverland (04)

Spindler, Will
Sugarbaby (85)

Spinell, Joe
Rocky (76); Rocky II (79); Nighthawks (81)

Spinelli, Italo
Caro Diario (94)

Spiner, Brent
Star Trek: First Contact (96); Star Trek:
Insurrection (98); Star Trek: Nemesis (02)

Spinetti, Victor
Hard Day's Night, A (64); Help! (65); Taming of
the Shrew, The (67)

Spira, Camilla
Testament of Dr. Mabuse, The (33)

Spira, Francois
Last Year at Marienbad (61)

Spivey, Victoria
Hallelujah (29)

Spivy, Madame
Requiem for a Heavyweight (62)

Spoonauer, Lisa
Clerks (94)

Spradlin, G.D.
Zabriskie Point (70); Godfather, Part II, The (74);
North Dallas Forty (79); War of the Roses,
The (89); Ed Wood (94)

Spriggs, Elizabeth
Sense and Sensibility (95)

Springer, Paul
Who Framed Roger Rabbit (88)

Springsteen, Bruce
High Fidelity (00)

Sprouse, Cole
Adam Sandler's Eight Crazy Nights (02)

Sprouse, Dylan
Adam Sandler's Eight Crazy Nights (02)

Spurlock, Morgan
Super Size Me (04)

Squibb, June
About Schmidt (02)

Squire, Katherine
Days of Wine and Roses (62)

Squire, William
Anne of the Thousand Days (69); Where Eagles
Dare (69)

Squires, Jacey
Music Man, The (62)

Srivastava, Aditya
Bandit Queen (95)

Ssenjovu, Patrick
Interpreter, The (05)

St. Clair, Lydia
House on 92nd Street, The (45)

St. Clair, Michael
Our Man Flint (66)

St. Cyr, Vince
Comanche Station (60)

St. Gerard, Michael
Hairspray (88)

St. Helier, Ivy
Henry V (44)

St. Jacques, Raymond
Cotton Comes to Harlem (70)

St. James, Gaylord
Last House on the Left, The (72)

St. John, Betta
Robe, The (53)

St. John, Christopher
Shaft (71)

St. John, Howard
Men, The (50); Born Yesterday (50); Strangers on a
Train (51); Three Coins in the Fountain (54); One,
Two, Three (61)

St. John, Jahnni
Meet Joe Black (98)

St. John, Jill
Roman Spring of Mrs. Stone, The (61); Diamonds
Are Forever (71)

Stanton, Robert
Washington Square (97); Quiet American, The (02)

Stanwyck, Barbara
Miracle Woman, The (31); Stella Dallas (37);
Union Pacific (39); Golden Boy (39); Remember
the Night (40); Ball of Fire (41); Lady Eve,
The (41); Meet John Doe (41); Double
Indemnity (44); Christmas in Connecticut (45);
Strange Love of Martha Ivers, The (46); Sorry,
Wrong Number (48); Clash by Night (52);
Titanic (53); Executive Suite (54)

Staples, Roebuck "Pops"
True Stories (86)

Staples, The
Last Waltz, The (78)

Stapleton, Jean
Damn Yankees (58); Bells Are Ringing (60);
Klute (71); Michael (96); You've Got Mail (98)

Stapleton, Maureen
Airport (70); Plaza Suite (71); Summer of '42 (71);
Interiors (78); Reds (81); Cocoon (85); Nuts (87)

Stapley, Richard
King of the Khyber Rifles (53)

Staquet, Georges
Band of Outsiders (64)

Starenios, Dimos
Never on Sunday (60)

Stark, Cecillia
Stranger than Paradise (84)

Stark, Don
Switchblade Sisters (75)

Stark, Graham
Shot in the Dark, A (64); Victor/Victoria (82)

Stark, Jonathan
Fright Night (85)

Starke, Michael
Distant Voices, Still Lives (88)

Starr, Mike
Goodfellas (90); Miller's Crossing (90);
Bodyguard, The (92); Mad Dog and Glory (93); Ed
Wood (94); Dumb & Dumber (94)

Starr, Ringo
Hard Day's Night, A (64); Help! (65); Yellow
Submarine (68); Two Hundred Motels (71)

Starr, Ronald
Ride the High Country (62)

Starrett, Charles
Royal Family of Broadway, The (30)

Statham, Jason
Lock, Stock and Two Smoking Barrels (98); Italian
Job, The (03)

Staunton, Imelda
Chicken Run (00); Vera Drake (04)

Staunton, Kim
Changing Lanes (02)

Stea, Kevin
Truth of Dare (91)

Steadman, Alison
Life Is Sweet (91)

Steadman, John
Longest Yard, The (74)

Steadman, Lynda
Career Girls (97)

Steady, Maduka
Lorenzo's Oil (92)

Stechschulte, Tom
Manchurian Candidate, The (04)

Steedman, Shirley
Prime of Miss Jean Brodie, The (69)

Steedman, Tony
Bill & Ted's Excellent Adventure (89)

Steel, Anthony
Wooden Horse, The (50)

Steele, Anna
Romantic Englishwoman, The (75)

Steele, Barbara
Black Sunday (60); Pit and the Pendulum,
The (61); 8 1/2 (63); Pretty Baby (78)

Steele, Bob
Of Mice and Men (39); Big Sleep, The (46);
Enforcer, The (51); Pork Chop Hill (59)

Steele, Don
Death Race 2000 (75); Rock 'n' Roll High
School (79)

Steele, Freddie
Hail the Conquering Hero (44); Story of G.I. Joe,
The (45)

Steele, Jadrien
Mosquito Coast, The (86)

Steele, James
Phar Lap (83)

Steele, Karen
Marty (55)

Steele, Sarah
Spanglish (04)

Steen, Paprika
Celebration, The (98)

Steenburgen, Mary
Time After Time (79); Melvin and Howard (80);
Parenthood (89); What's Eating Gilbert
Grape? (93); Nixon (95); Sunshine State (02);
Elf (03)

Steers, Burr
Last Days of Disco, The (98)

Stefani, Gwen
Aviator, The (04)

Stefanopoli, Rachel
Number Two (75)

Stefanson, Leslie
Unbreakable (00)

Steffans, Peggy
Hallelujah the Hills (63)

Strickland, Don
Weather Underground, The (03)

Strickland, Gail
Bound for Glory (76); Who'll Stop the Rain? (78); Norma Rae (79)

Strickland, Helen
Scoundrel, The (35)

Strickland, Kadee
Something's Gotta Give (03); Anything Else (03)

Strickland, KaDee
Grudge, The (04); Fever Pitch (05)

Strickland, Robert
Girl Crazy (43)

Stride, John
Macbeth (71)

Strimpell, Stephen
Hester Street (75)

Stringer, Kimberly
This Is Spinal Tap (84)

Stringer, Nick
Shout, The (78)

Stritch, Elaine
Providence (77)

Strobye, Axel
Pelle the Conqueror (87)

Strode, Woody
Pork Chop Hill (59)

Stroesco, Constantin
Million, The (31)

Stroh, Kandice
Foxes (80)

Strohmeier, Tara
Hollywood Boulevard (76); Kentucky Fried Movie, The (77)

Strong, Leonard
Back to Bataan (45)

Strong, Michael
Point Blank (67)

Strong, Tara
Spirited Away (01); Ice Age (02); Powerpuff Girls Movie, The (02)

Strongin, Dorothy
Basket Case (82)

Stroud, Claude
Love Me or Leave Me (55)

Stroud, Don
Madigan (68); Coogan's Bluff (68); Buddy Holly Story, The (78); Amityville Horror, The (79)

Strozier, Henry
Thirteen Days (00)

Strudwick, Shepperd
All the King's Men (49); Place in the Sun, A (51); Autumn Leaves (56)

Strummer, Joe
Candy Mountain (87); End of the Century: The Story of the Ramones (04)

Strus, Lusia
Stir of Echoes, A (99); 50 First Dates (04)

Struthers, Sally
Five Easy Pieces (70); Getaway, The (72)

Struycken, Carel
Witches of Eastwick, The (87); Addams Family, The (91); Addams Family Values (93)

Struzik, Caroline
Witches of Eastwick, The (87)

Stuart, Freddie
Hit, The (84)

Stuart, Gloria
Old Dark House, The (32); Invisible Man, The (33); Gold Diggers of 1935 (35); Prisoner of Shark Island, The (36); Titanic (97)

Stuart, John
Mummy, The (59)

Stuart, Josephine
Oliver Twist (48)

Stuart, Maxine
Days of Wine and Roses (62)

Stuart, Randy
Incredible Shrinking Man, The (57)

Stubbs, Harry
Invisible Man, The (33)

Stucker, Stephen
Airplane! (80)

Studi, Wes
Last of the Mohicans, The (92); Heat (95)

Stuhr, Jerzy
White (94)

Sturridge, Tom
Being Julia (04)

Stuthman, Fred
Escape from Alcatraz (79)

Suard, Valentine
Sunday in the Country, A (84)

Suarez, Cecilia
Spanglish (04)

Suarez, Miguel
Bananas (71)

Suarez, Ricardo
Death of a Bureaucrat (66)

Subkoff, Tara
Last Days of Disco, The (98); Cell, The (00)

Sublett, John "Bubbles"
Cabin in the Sky (43)

Subor, Michel
Topaz (69)

Suchet, David
Falcon and the Snowman, The (85); Pinocchio (02)

Suchitra
Born into Brothels (04)

Sudarikov, Semion
Cast Away (00)

Toure, Amade
Yaaba (89)

Toure, Moustapha
Mandabi (68)

Tousey, Sheila
Thuderheart (92)

Toutain, Roland
Rules of the Game (39)

Towers, Constance
Horse Soldiers, The (59); Shock Corridor (63)

Towle, Phil
Metallica: Some Kind of Monster (04)

Towles, Tom
Henry: Portrait of a Serial Killer (89); Mad Dog
and Glory (93)

Towne, Katharine
Mulholland Dr. (01)

Townes, Harry
Brothers Karamazov, The (58)

Townsend, Robert
Soldier's Story, A (84)

Townsend, Stuart
Under the Skin (97); League of Extraordinary
Gentlemen, The (03)

Townsley, Samantha
Angel at My Table, An (90)

Tozer, Joseph R.
Hands Across the Table (35)

Tozere, Frederic
Confessions of a Nazi Spy (39)

Trabaud, Pierre
Round Midnight (86)

Tracey, Ian
Stakeout (87)

Tracy, Lee
Doctor X (32); Dinner at Eight (33);
Bombshell (33)

Tracy, Spencer
20,000 Years in Sing Sing (33); Libeled Lady (36);
San Francisco (36); Fury (36); Captains
Courageous (37); Test Pilot (38); Boys Town (38);
Stanley and Livingstone (39); Northwest
Passage (40); Edison, the Man (40); Woman of the
Year (42); Tortilla Flat (42); Guy Named Joe,
A (44); Thirty Seconds Over Tokyo (44); State of
the Union (48); Adam's Rib (49); Father of the
Bride (50); Pat and Mike (52); Bad Day at Black
Rock (55); Old Man and the Sea, The (58); Inherit
the Wind (60); Judgment at Nuremberg (61); How
the West Was Won (63); It's a Mad, Mad, Mad,
Mad World (63); Guess Who's Coming to
Dinner (67)

Tracy, William
Shop Around the Corner, The (40); Strike Up the
Band (40); Tobacco Road (41)

Trainor, Kevin
Hellboy (04)

Trainor, Mary Ellen
Romancing the Stone (84); Moonlight Mile (02)

Tramonti, Sergio
Investigation of a Citizen Above Suspicion (70)

Tran Nu Yen-Khe
Cyclo (95)

Tran, Tung Thanh
Good Morning, Vietnam (87)

Traore, Soumba
Brightness (87)

Trapp, Roger
Le Petit Theatre de Jean Renoir (69)

Trask, Stephen
Hedwig and the Angry Inch (01)

Travers, Bill
Browning Version, The (51); Barretts of Wimpole
Street, The (56)

Travers, Henry
Invisible Man, The (33); Death Takes a
Holiday (34); Stanley and Livingstone (39); Dark
Victory (39); Dodge City (39); Edison, the
Man (40); High Sierra (41); Ball of Fire (41); Mrs.
Miniver (42); Random Harvest (42); Madame
Curie (43); Shadow of a Doubt (43); Bells of St.
Mary's, The (45); It's a Wonderful Life (46);
Yearling, The (46)

Travers, Linden
Lady Vanishes, The (38); Stars Look Down,
The (39)

Travers, Susan
Abominable Dr. Phibes, The (71)

Travers, Sy
Mikey and Nicky (76)

Travis, Daniel
Open Water (04)

Travis, Greg
Showgirls (95)

Travis, Nancy
3 Men and a Baby (87)

Travis, Richard
Man Who Came to Dinner, The (42)

Travis, Stacey
Ghost World (01)

Travolta, John
Carrie (76); Saturday Night Fever (77);
Grease (78); Urban Cowboy (80); Blow Out (81);
Look Who's Talking (89); Pulp Fiction (94); Get
Shorty (95); Broken Arrow (96); Michael (96);
Face/Off (97); Thin Red Line, The (98); Primary
Colors (98); Civil Action, A (98); Ladder 49 (04)

Traylor, Susan
New Age, The (94)

Treacher, Arthur
Curly Top (35); Thin Ice (37); Mary Poppins (64)

Treacy, Emerson
Adam's Rib (49)

Truffaut, Francois
Wild Child, The (69); Day for Night (73); Close Encounters of the Third Kind (77); Green Room, The (78)

Trujillo, Robert
Metallica: Some Kind of Monster (04)

Truman, Ralph
Henry V (44); Oliver Twist (48); Treasure Island (50); Golden Coach, The (52); Man Who Knew Too Much, The (56)

Trupin, Gabriel
Truth of Dare (91)

Truro, Victor
Manhattan (79)

Trzeciak, Frantiszek
Man of Iron (80)

Ts'ui Fu-sheng
Daughter of the Nile (87)

Tsai Chin
Joy Luck Club, The (93)

Tsai Guei
What Time Is It There? (01)

Tsai, Robert
School of Rock (03)

Tsang, Kenneth
Peking Opera Blues (86); Killer, The (89); Supercop (92); Die Another Day (02)

Tsarong, Tenzin Thuthob
Kundun (97)

Tschechowa, Olga
Eternal Mask, The (37)

Tselikovskaya, Ludmila
Ivan the Terrible, Part I (45)

Tsiang Chi Wai, Eric
Eat a Bowl of Tea (90)

Tsuchida, Kichijiro
Ugestu (53)

Tsuchiya, Yoshio
Seven Samurai, The (54)

Tsugawa, Masahiko
Taxing Woman, A (87)

Tsukamoto, Shinya
Tetsuo: The Iron Man (89); Most Terrible Time in My Life, The (93); Ichi the Killer (01)

Tsukasa, Yoko
Late Autumn (60); Chushingura (62)

Tsuneta, Fujio
Eel, The (97)

Tsurumi, Shingo
Gonin (95)

Tubb, Barry
Top Gun (86)

Tubbs, William
Paisan (46); Wages of Fear, The (52)

Tucci, Lin
Showgirls (95)

Tucci, Stanley
Pelican Brief, The (93); Kiss of Death (95); Road to Perdition (02); Maid in Manhattan (02); Terminal, The (04); Shall We Dance? (04); Robots (05)

Tuck, Jessica
Secretary (02)

Tucker, Chris
Fifth Element, The (97); Rush Hour (98)

Tucker, Forrest
Westerner, The (40); Yearling, The (46); Sands of Iwo Jima (49); Auntie Mame (58)

Tucker, Joe
Career Girls (97)

Tucker, Jonathan
Deep End, The (01)

Tucker, Larry
Shock Corridor (63)

Tucker, Michael
Diner (82); Radio Days (87)

Tudyk, Alan
28 Days (00); Knight's Tale, A (01); Ice Age (02); Dodgeball: A True Underdog Story (04); I, Robot (04)

Tufts, Sonny
So Proudly We Hail (43); Seven Year Itch, The (55)

Tuinman, Peter
Spetters (80)

Tukur, Ulrich
Solaris (02)

Tull, Patrick
Parting Glances (86)

Tulli, Marco
Beat the Devil (53)

Tully, Tom
Lady in the Lake (47); Moon Is Blue, The (53); Caine Mutiny, The (54); Love Me or Leave Me (55); Coogan's Bluff (68)

Tulugarjuk, Lucy
Fast Runner (Atanarjuat), The (01)

Tunc, Irene
Two English Girls (71)

Tune, Tommy
Hello, Dolly! (69)

Tung, Bill
Supercop (92)

Tung Wai
Hard-Boiled (92)

Tung-Foo, Lee
Across the Pacific (42)

Turkel, Joseph
Paths of Glory (57); Shining, The (80); Blade Runner (82)

Turken, Greta
Sophie's Choice (82)

Van Dyke, Dick
Mary Poppins (64); What a Way to Go! (64)

Van Dyke, Marcia
In the Good Old Summertime (49)

Van Eyck, Peter
Five Graves to Cairo (43); Wages of Fear, The (52);
Thousand Eyes of Dr. Mabuse, The (60); Spy Who
Came in from the Cold, The (65)

Van Eyssen, John
Horror of Dracula (58)

Van Fleet, Jo
I'll Cry Tomorrow (55); East of Eden (55); Rose
Tattoo, The (55); Gunfight at the O.K. Corral (57);
Wild River (60); Cool Hand Luke (67); I Love You,
Alice B. Toklas! (68); Tenant, The (76)

Van Hentenryck, Kevin
Basket Case (82)

Van Holt, Brian
Windtalkers (02); S.W.A.T. (03)

van Huet, Fedja
Character (97)

van Hulzen, Joop
Prince of Foxes (49)

Van Husen, Dan
Nosferatu, the Vampire (78)

Van Lidth, Erland
Wanderers, The (79)

Van Loon, Robert
Paisan (46)

van Lyck, Henry
Enigma of Kaspar Hauser, The (75)

Van Norden, Peter
Gigli (03)

Van Nutter, Rik
Thunderball (65)

van Overloop, Veerle
Antonia's Line (95)

Van Pallandt, Nina
Long Goodbye, The (73); Wedding, A (78);
American Gigolo (80); Cutter's Way (81)

Van Patten, Dick
Charly (68); Westworld (73); High Anxiety (77)

Van Patten, Joyce
I Love You, Alice B. Toklas! (68); Bad News Bears,
The (76); Mikey and Nicky (76)

Van Patten, Vincent
Rock 'n' Roll High School (79)

Van Peebles, Mario
Sweet Sweetback's Baadasssss Song (71)

Van Peebles, Melvin
Sweet Sweetback's Baadasssss Song (71)

Van Pellicom, Kristien
Innocence (00)

Van Rooten, Luis
Champion (49); Cinderella (50)

Van Sloan, Edward
Dracula (31); Frankenstein (31); Mummy, The (32)

Van Sprang, Alan
Narc (02)

Van Tongeren, Hans
Spetters (80)

van Uchelen, Marc
Assault, The (86)

Van Valkenburgh, Deborah
Warriors, The (79)

Van Vooren, Monique
Gigi (58)

Vanasse, Karine
Set Me Free (99)

Vanbrugh, Irene
Knight without Armor (37)

Vancamp, Emily
Ring Two, The (05)

Vance, Courtney B.
Hunt for Red October, The (90)

Vander, Musetta
Wild Wild West (99)

Vandis, Titos
Never on Sunday (60); Topkapi (64); Exorcist,
The (73)

Vaneau, Yara
Emerald Forest, The (85)

Vanel, Charles
Wages of Fear, The (52); Diabolique (55); To Catch
a Thief (55)

Vanni, Renata
Lady in White (88)

Vannucchi, Sabina
Night of the Shooting Stars, The (81)

Varady, Brien
Last Seduction, The (94)

Varas, Jean
Devil in the Flesh, The (46)

Varconi, Victor
Roberta (35); My Favorite Blonde (42); For Whom
the Bell Tolls (43)

Varda, Agnes
Truth about Charlie, The (02)

Vardalos, Nia
My Big Fat Greek Wedding (02)

Varden, Evelyn
Pinky (49); Night of the Hunter, The (55)

Varden, Norma
Gentlemen Prefer Blondes (53); Doctor
Dolittle (67)

Varela, Ann
Terror in a Texas Town (58)

Varela, Leonor
Tailor of Panama, The (01)

Varelli, Alfredo
Belly of an Architect, The (87)

Varennes, Jacques
Orpheus (49)

Vargas, Jacob
Gas Food Lodging (92)

Vargas, Manuela
Flower of My Secret, The (95)

Varley, Sarah Jane
And the Ship Sails On (83)

Varney, Jim
Toy Story (95); Toy Story 2 (99)

Varsi, Diane
Peyton Place (57); Compulsion (59)

Vartan, Michael
One Hour Photo (02)

Varte, Rosy
Love on the Run (79)

Vasquez, Yul
Fresh (94)

Vassort, Cecile
Clockmaker, The (73)

Vatel, Martine
Muriel (63)

Vattier, Robert
Marius (31); Fanny (32); Cesar (36); Baker's Wife, The (38)

Vaughan, David
Killer's Kiss (55)

Vaughan, Martin
Phar Lap (83)

Vaughan, Peter
Straw Dogs (71); Time Bandits (81); French Lieutenant's Woman, The (81); Brazil (85); Remains of the Day, The (93); Crucible, The (96); Les Miserables (98); Ideal Husband, An (99)

Vaughn, Robert
Magnificent Seven, The (60); Bullitt (68); Towering Inferno, The (74)

Vaughn, Vince
Lost World: Jurassic Park, The (97); Psycho (98); Cell, The (00); Old School (03); Starsky & Hutch (04); Dodgeball: A True Underdog Story (04); Anchorman: The Legend of Rob Burgundy (04)

Vaverka, Anton
Phantom of the Opera, The (25)

Vawter, Ron
sex, lies, and videotape (89); Philadelphia (93)

Veazie, Carol
Catered Affair, The (56)

Veena
Pakeezah (71)

Vega, Alexa
Spy Kids (01); Spy Kids 2: The Island of Lost Dreams (02)

Vega, Isela
Bring Me the Head of Alfredo Garcia (74)

Vega, Makenzie
Family Man, The (00)

Vega, Paz
Talk to Her (02); Spanglish (04)

Vega, Yenny Paola
Maria Full of Grace (04)

Veidt, Conrad
Contraband (40); Thief of Bagdad, The (40); Casablanca (42)

Veinotte, Troy
Hanging Garden, The (98)

Vela, Roseanne
Heaven's Gate (80)

Velasco, Manuela
Law of Desire (87)

Velasquez, Ernest
Salt of the Earth (54)

Velasquez, Fernando
Maria Full of Grace (04)

Velez, Eddie
Repo Man (84)

Veljohnson, Reginald
Die Hard (88)

Velkov, Dejan
Before the Rain (94)

Velletti, Aldo
Salo, or the 120 Days of Sodom (75)

Venable, Evelyn
Death Takes a Holiday (34); Alice Adams (35); Pinocchio (40)

Venable, Sarah
Martin (78)

Venegas, Arturo
Madeline (98)

Veness, Amy
This Happy Breed (44)

Venhuizen, Mark
About Schmidt (02)

Venito, Lenny
Gigli (03)

Venora, Diane
Wolfen (81); F/X (86); Bird (88); Heat (95); William Shakespeare's Romeo + Juliet (96); Insider, The (99); Hamlet (00)

Ventimiglia, John
Personal Velocity (02)

Venton, Harley
Sleeping with the Enemy (91)

Ventura, Jesse
Predator (87)

Venture, Richard
Effect of Gamma Rays on Man-in-the-Moon Marigolds, The (72); Missing (82); Scent of a Woman (92)

Wallace, Paul
Gypsy (62)

Wallace, Roy
Groove Tube, The (74)

Wallace Stone, Dee
Hills Have Eyes, The (78); 10 (79); Howling, The (81); E.T. The Extra-Terrestrial (82)

Wallach, Eli
Baby Doll (56); Magnificent Seven, The (60); Seven Thieves (60); Misfits, The (61); Lord Jim (65); Good, the Bad and the Ugly, The (66); Movie Movie (78); Girlfriends (78); Winter Kills (79); Nuts (87); Godfather, Part III, The (90)

Wallach, Katherine
King of Comedy, The (83)

Wallach, Roberta
Effect of Gamma Rays on Man-in-the-Moon Marigolds, The (72)

Waller, Fats
Stormy Weather (43)

Wallet, Jacques
La Guerre est Finie (66)

Walley, Deborah
Beach Blanket Bingo (65)

Wallgren, Gunn
Fanny and Alexander (82)

Wallgren, Pernilla
Fanny and Alexander (82)

Wallis, Shani
Oliver! (68)

Walls, Kevin Patrick
Blade (98)

Walls, Nancy
Anger Management (03)

Walsh, Angela
Distant Voices, Still Lives (88)

Walsh, Arthur
They Were Expendable (45)

Walsh, Dylan
Nobody's Fool (94)

Walsh, J.T.
House of Games (87); Tin Men (87); Good Morning, Vietnam (87); Grifters, The (90); Russia House, The (90); Backdraft (91); Few Good Men, A (92); Red Rock West (93); Last Seduction, The (94); Client, The (94); Sling Blade (96); Negotiator, The (98); Pleasantville (98)

Walsh, Jack
Simple Plan, A (98)

Walsh, Joseph
Hans Christian Andersen (52); Juggler, The (53); Driver, The (78)

Walsh, Kay
In Which We Serve (42); This Happy Breed (44); Oliver Twist (48); Stage Fright (50); Horse's Mouth, The (58)

Walsh, Kenneth
Day After Tomorrow, The (04)

Walsh, M. Emmet
Mikey and Nicky (76); Straight Time (78); Ordinary People (80); Reds (81); Blade Runner (82); Blood Simple (84); Back to School (86); My Best Friend's Wedding (97); Wild Wild West (99); Iron Giant, The (99)

Walsh, Nathan
Distant Voices, Still Lives (88)

Walsh, Pat
Wizard of Oz, The (39)

Walsh, Susan
Pink Flamingos (72)

Walston, Ray
Damn Yankees (58); South Pacific (58); Apartment, The (60); Sting, The (73); Fast Times at Ridgemont High (82)

Walter, Harriet
Sense and Sensibility (95); Merry War, A (97)

Walter, Jessica
Play Misty for Me (71); Flamingo Kid, The (84)

Walter, Lisa Ann
Parent Trap, The (98); Shall We Dance? (04)

Walter, Tracey
Repo Man (84); Something Wild (86); At Close Range (86); City Slickers (91); Philadelphia (93)

Walters, Julie
Educating Rita (83); Prick Up Your Ears (87); Billy Elliot (00)

Walters, Melora
Magnolia (99); Butterfly Effect, The (04)

Walters, Patricia
River, The (51)

Walters, Thorley
Phantom of the Opera, The (62)

Walthall, Henry B.
Viva Villa! (34); Tale of Two Cities, A (35); Devil-Doll, The (36)

Walther, Leon
Earrings of Madame de ... , The (53)

Walton, Douglas
Lost Patrol, The (34); Bride of Frankenstein (35); Murder, My Sweet (45)

Wanamaker, Sam
Spy Who Came in from the Cold, The (65); Private Benjamin (80)

Wanamaker, Zoe
Wilde (97); Harry Potter and the Sorcerer's Stone (01)

Wane, Samba
Guelwaar (93)

Wang Deming
Crouching Tiger, Hidden Dragon (00)

Wang Jianfa
Story of Qiu Ju, The (92)

White, Ashley
Spellbound (03)

White, Betty
Bringing Down the House (03)

White, Carol
Poor Cow (67)

White, Dan
Yearling, The (46); Rainmaker, The (56)

White, De'voreaux
Die Hard (88)

White, Dorothy
Get Carter (71)

White, Harriet
Paisan (46)

White, Jacqueline
Crossfire (47); Narrow Margin, The (52)

White, Jesse
Harvey (50); Bedtime for Bonzo (51); Death of a
Salesman (51)

White, Julianne
Sexy Beast (00)

White, Lari
Cast Away (00)

White, Lillias
Pieces of April (03)

White, M.
Story of Adele H., The (75)

White, Mike
Chuck & Buck (00); Good Girl, The (02); School
of Rock (03)

White, Richard
Beauty and the Beast (91)

White, Ruth
Nun's Story, The (59); To Kill a Mockingbird (62);
Charly (68); Midnight Cowboy (69)

White, Sammy
Show Boat (36); Pat and Mike (52); Somebody Up
There Likes Me (56)

White, Ted
Starman (84)

Whitehead, O.Z.
Grapes of Wrath, The (40); Road House (48); Lion
in Winter, The (68)

Whitehead, Paxton
Back to School (86)

Whitehorn, Laura
Weather Underground, The (03)

Whitehouse, Paul
Harry Potter and the Prisoner of Azkaban (04)

Whitelaw, Billie
Gumshoe (71); Frenzy (72); Omen, The (76); Dark
Crystal, The (82); Maurice (87); Quills (00)

Whitelaw, Sandy
American Friend, The (77)

Whiteman, Paul and His Orchestra
Strike Up the Band (40)

Whitfield, Anne
White Christmas (54)

Whitfield, June
Jude (96)

Whitfield, Lynn
Stepmom (98)

Whitfield, Mitchell
My Cousin Vinny (92)

Whitfield, Smoki
Born Yesterday (50)

Whitford, Bradley
Scent of a Woman (92); Philadelphia (93); Perfect
World, A (93)

Whitford, Peter
My Brilliant Career (79); Dead-End Drive-In (86);
Strictly Ballroom (92)

Whiting, Al
Waterboy, The (98)

Whiting, Gordon
Railway Children, The (70)

Whiting, Leonard
Romeo and Juliet (68)

Whiting, Richard
Zelig (83)

Whitley, Crane
My Favorite Blonde (42)

Whitley, Diane
Wetherby (85)

Whitlock Jr., Isiah
25th Hour (02); Pieces of April (03)

Whitman, Ernest
Road to Zaznibar (41)

Whitman, Stuart
Those Magnificent Men in Their Flying
Machines; or How I Flew from London to Paris in
25 Hours and 11 Minutes (65)

Whitmire, Steve
Dark Crystal, The (82)

Whitmore, James
Battleground (49); Asphalt Jungle, The (50);
Kiss Me Kate (53); Them! (54); Oklahoma! (55);
Madigan (68); Planet of the Apes (68); Hills Have
Eyes, The (78); Nuts (87); Shawshank Redemption,
The (94)

Whitney, Dorothy
Breakfast at Tiffany's (61)

Whitney, Grace Lee
Irma la Douce (63)

Whitney, Peter
Murder, He Says (45); Big Heat, The (53); Ballad
of Cable Hogue, The (70)

Whitrow, Benjamin
Brimstone and Treacle (82); Chicken Run (00)

Whittell, Josephine
It's a Gift (34); Enchanted Cottage, The (45)

Winfield, Paul
Sounder (72); Hustle (75); Twilight's Last
Gleaming (77); White Dog (82); Terminator,
The (84); Presumed Innocent (90)

Winfrey, Oprah
Color Purple, The (85); Throw Momma from the
Train (87); Beloved (98)

Wing, Anna
Providence (77)

Winger, Debra
Urban Cowboy (80); Officer and a Gentleman,
An (82); Terms of Endearment (83)

Wingett, Mark
Quadrophenia (79)

Winkler, Angela
Lost Honor of Katharina Blum, The (75); Knife in
the Head (78); Tin Drum, The (79); Danton (82)

Winkler, Henry
Lords of Flatbush, The (74); Scream (96);
Waterboy, The (98)

Winkler, Mel
Devil in a Blue Dress (95)

Winn, Kitty
Panic in Needle Park, The (71); Exorcist, The (73)

Winninger, Charles
Sin of Madelon Claudet, The (31); Show Boat (36);
Three Smart Girls (36); Nothing Sacred (37); Babes
in Arms (39); Destry Rides Again (39); Ziegfeld
Girl (41); State Fair (45)

Winningham, Mare
Shy People (88); Georgia (95)

Winocourt, Marc
Murmur of the Heart (71)

Winslet, Kate
Heavenly Creatures (94); Sense and
Sensibility (95); Jude (96); Hamlet (96);
Titanic (97); Hideous Kinky (98); Holy
Smoke (99); Quills (00); Iris (01); Eternal Sunshine
of the Spotless Mind (04); Finding Neverland (04)

Winslow, George "Foghorn"
Gentlemen Prefer Blondes (53)

Winslowe, Paula
Bambi (42)

Winston, Bruce
Thief of Bagdad, The (40)

Winston, Hattie
Jackie Brown (97)

Winstone, Ray
War Zone, The (98); Sexy Beast (00); Last
Orders (01); Cold Mountain (04); King Arthur (04)

Winter, Alex
Bill & Ted's Excellent Adventure (89)

Winter, Claude
Sunday in the Country, A (84); Savage Nights (93)

Winter, Philip
Rebecca (40)

Winters, Jonathan
It's a Mad, Mad, Mad, Mad World (63); Loved
One, The (65)

Winters, Shelley
Double Life, A (47); Great Gatsby, The (49);
Winchester '73 (50); Place in the Sun, A (51);
Executive Suite (54); I Am a Camera (55); Night of
the Hunter, The (55); Big Knife, The (55); Odds
Against Tomorrow (59); Diary of Anne Frank,
The (59); Lolita (62); Alfie (66); Harper (66);
Blume in Love (73); Next Stop, Greenwich
Village (76); Tenant, The (76); Portrait of a Lady,
The (96)

Winton, Jane
Hell's Angels (30)

Winwood, Estelle
Darby O'Gill and the Little People (59); Misfits,
The (61); Producers, The (68)

Wisdom, Robert
Storytelling (01)

Wise, Alfie
Smokey and the Bandit (77)

Wise, Greg
Sense and Sensibility (95)

Wise, Ray
RoboCop (87); Bob Roberts (92)

Wise, William
In the Bedroom (01)

Wiseman, Joseph
Detective Story (51); Viva Zapata! (52); Dr.
No (62); Apprenticeship of Duddy Kravitz,
The (74)

Wisniewski, Andreas
Living Daylights, The (87)

Witcher, Gabrielle
Monster's Ball (01)

Witford, Bradley
Client, The (94)

Withers, Googie
One of Our Aircraft Is Missing (41); Night and the
City (50); Shine (96)

Withers, Grant
Rio Grande (50)

Withers, Jane
Giant (56)

Witherspoon, Cora
Libeled Lady (36); Dark Victory (39); Bank Dick,
The (40)

Witherspoon, Jimmy
Georgia (95)

Witherspoon, Reese
Pleasantville (98); Election (99); Cruel
Intentions (99); American Psycho (00); Legally
Blonde (01); Sweet Home Alabama (02); Vanity
Fair (04)

Withrow, Glenn
Outsiders, The (83)

Witney, Michael
Darling Lili (70)

Witt, Alicia
Mr. Holland's Opus (95)

Wittig, John
Pelle the Conqueror (87)

Wivesson, Gudmar
Babette's Feast (87)

Wixted, Kevin Gerard
Lucas (86)

Wojcik, Wieslaw
Man of Marble (77)

Wolf, Hillary
Home Alone (90)

Wolf, Rita
My Beautiful Laundrette (85)

Wolf, Scott
Go (99)

Wolfe, David
Salt of the Earth (54)

Wolfe, Ian
Barretts of Wimpole Street, The (34);
Saboteur (42); Mr. Blandings Builds His Dream
House (48); They Live by Night (49); Seven Brides
for Seven Brothers (54); Witness for the
Prosecution (57); THX 1138 (71); Fortune,
The (75); Reds (81)

Wolfe, Michael J.
True Love (89)

Wolfe, Traci
Lethal Weapon (87); Lethal Weapon 2 (89); Lethal
Weapon 3 (92); Lethal Weapon 4 (98)

Wolff, Frank
Salvatore Giuliano (61); Once Upon a Time in the
West (69)

Wolff, Harald
State of Siege (72)

Wolfit, Donald
Room at the Top (59); Lawrence of Arabia (62);
Becket (64)

Wolfman Jack
American Graffiti (73)

Wolheim, Louis
All Quiet on the Western Front (30)

Wollter, Sven
Sacrifice, The (86)

Womack, Mark
Under the Skin (97)

Wonacott, Edna May
Shadow of a Doubt (43)

Wong, Anna May
Shanghai Express (32)

Wong, Anthony
Hard-Boiled (92)

Wong, B.D.
Jurassic Park (93); Mulan (98)

Wong, Benedict
Dirty Pretty Things (02)

Wong, Fann
Shanghai Knights (03)

Wong, Faye
Chungking Express (94)

Wong, Russell
Eat a Bowl of Tea (90)

Wong, Victor
King Kong (33); Dim Sum: A Little Bit of
Heart (85); Last Emperor, The (87); Eat a Bowl of
Tea (90)

Wontner, Arthur
Life and Death of Colonel Blimp, The (43);
Genevieve (53)

Woo, George
Chan Is Missing (81)

Wood, David
If... (68)

Wood, Douglas
Prisoner of Shark Island, The (36)

Wood, Elijah
Avalon (90); Ice Storm, The (97); Deep
Impact (98); Lord of the Rings: The Fellowship of
the Ring, The (01); Lord of the Rings: The Two
Towers, The (02); Lord of the Rings: The Return of
the King, The (03); Eternal Sunshine of the
Spotless Mind (04); Frank Miller's Sin City (05)

Wood, Evan Rachel
Thirteen (03)

Wood, Frank
Thirteen Days (00)

Wood, G.
Harold and Maude (71)

Wood, John
Ladyhawke (85); Purple Rose of Cairo, The (85);
Orlando (93); Madness of King George, The (94);
Richard III (95); Ideal Husband, An (99);
Chocolat (00)

Wood, Lana
Diamonds Are Forever (71)

Wood, Natalie
Miracle on 34th Street (47); Ghost and Mrs. Muir,
The (47); Rebel without a Cause (55); Searchers,
The (56); Splendor in the Grass (61); West Side
Story (61); Gypsy (62); Love with the Proper
Stranger (63); Inside Daisy Clover (65); Bob &
Carol & Ted & Alice (69)

Wood, Peggy
Sound of Music, The (65)

Wood, Philip
Our Town (40)

Wood, Salvador
Death of a Bureaucrat (66)

Wood, Tom
Fugitive, The (93); Ulee's Gold (97)

Wood, Ward
Air Force (43)

INDEX OF DIRECTORS

The following index includes filmographies for notable directors whose films appear in this book. Titles reviewed in this guide are indicated by a bullet. In the case of directors whose careers date back to the silent era, listings include sound films only.

ANDERSON, BRAD
Darien Gap, The (96); Next Stop,
Wonderland (98); Happy Accidents (00); Session
9 (01); •Machinist, The (04)

ANDERSON, LINDSAY
Meet the Pioneers (48); Idlers That Work (49);
Three Installations (52); Wakefield Express (52); O
Dreamland (53); Thursday's Children (53); Foot
and Mouth (55); Every Day Except
Christmas (57); •This Sporting Life (63); White
Bus, The (67); Singing Lesson, The (67);
•If. . . (68); •O Lucky Man! (73); In
Celebration (74); Britannia Hospital (82); Wish
You Were There (85); •Whales of August,
The (87); Glory! Glory! (89); Is That All There
Is? (92)

ANDERSON, PAUL THOMAS
Hard Eight (96); •Boogie Nights (97);
•Magnolia (99); •Punch-Drunk Love (02)

ANDERSON, WES
Bottle Rocket (96); •Rushmore (98); •Royal
Tenenbaums, The (01); •Life Aquatic with Steve
Zissou, The (04)

ANNAUD, JEAN-JACQUES
•Black and White in Color (76); Coup de
Tete (79); •Quest For Fire (81); •Name of the
Rose, The (86); •Bear, The (89); Lover, The (92);
Wings of Courage (95); Seven Years in Tibet (97);
Enemy at the Gates (01); Two Brothers (04)

ANTONIONI, MICHELANGELO
Story of a Love Affair (50); Vanquished, The (53);
Lady Without Camellias, The (53); Love in the
City (53); Le Amiche (55); Cry, The (57); Questo
Nostro Mondo (57); •L'Avventura (60); •La
Notte (61); Eclipse (62); Il Fiore e la
Violenza (63); •Red Desert (64); Three Faces of a
Woman (65); •Blowup (66); •Zabriskie Point (70);
Chung Kuo (72); •Passenger, The (75); Oberwald
Mystery, The (80); •Identification of A
Woman (82); Beyond the Clouds (95); Just to Be
Together (01)

APTED, MICHAEL
Triple Echo, The (73); Stardust (74); Squeeze,
The (77); Stronger Than the Sun (78); Agatha (79);
•Coal Miner's Daughter (80); Continental
Divide (81); Kipperbang (82); •Gorky Park (83);
Firstborn (84); 28 Up (85); Bring on the
Night (85); Critical Condition (87); •Gorillas in the
Mist (88); Long Way Home, The (89); Class
Action (91); 35 Up (91); Incident at Oglala (92);
•Thunderheart (92); Blink (94); Nell (94); Moving
the Mountain (95); Extreme Measures (96);
Inspirations (97); 42 Up (98); Always
Outnumbered (98); •World Is Not Enough,
The (99); Me & Isaac Newton (01); Enigma (01);
Enough (02)

ARAU, ALFONSO
Calzonzin Inspector (74); Mojado Power (80);
Chido Guan (84); •Like Water for Chocolate (92);
Walk in the Clouds, A (95); Picking Up the
Pieces (00); Magnificent Ambersons, The (02);
Painted House, A (03); Zapata (04)

ARCAND, DENYS
Seul ou avec d'Autres (62); On Est au Coton (70);
Quebec: Duplessis et Apres. . . (72); La Maudite
Galette (72); Rejeanne Padovani (73);
Gina (74); Le Confort et l'Indifference (81); Le
Crime d'Ovide Plouffe (84); •Decline of the
American Empire, The (86); •Jesus of
Montreal (89); Montreal Vu Par. . . (91); Love and
Human Remains (93); Joyeux Calvaire (96);
Stardom (00); •Barbarian Invasions, The (03)

ARGENTO, DARIO
•Bird with the Crystal Plumage, The (69); Cat
O'Nine Tails (71); Four Flies on Grey Velvet (72);
Deep Red (75); •Suspiria (76); Inferno (80);
Unsane (82); Creepers (84); Terror at the
Opera (87); Two Evil Eyes (90); Trauma (94);
Stendhal Syndrome, The (96); Phantom of the
Opera, The (98); Sleepless (01); Card Player,
The (04)

ARMITAGE, GEORGE
Hit Man (72); Private Duty Nurses (72); Vigilante
Force (76); •Miami Blues (90); •Grosse Point
Blank (97); Big Bounce, The (04)

ARMSTRONG, GILLIAN
Singer and the Dancer, The (76); •My Brilliant
Career (79); Starstruck (82); Mrs. Soffel (84); High
Tide (87); Fires Within (91); •Last Days of Chez
Nous, The (93); •Little Women (94); •Oscar and
Lucinda (97); Charlotte Gray (01)

ARNOLD, JACK
Girls in the Night (53); Glass Web, The (53); •It
Came from Outer Space (53); Creature from the
Black Lagoon (54); Man from Bitter Ridge,
The (55); Revenge of the Creature (55);
Tarantula (55); This Island Earth (55); Outside the
Law (56); Red Sundown (56); •Incredible
Shrinking Man, The (57); Man in the Shadow (57);
Tattered Dress, The (57); High School
Confidential! (58); Lady Takes a Flyer, The (58);
Monster on the Campus (58); Space Children,
The (58); •Mouse That Roared, The (59); No
Name on the Bullet (59); Bachelor in
Paradise (61); Global Affair, A (64); Lively Set,
The (64); Hello Down There (69); Black Eye (74);
Boss Nigger (74); Swiss Conspiracy, The (76)

ARONOFSKY, DARREN
Pi (98); •Requiem for A Dream (00)

ARTETA, MIGUEL
Star Maps (97); •Chuck & Buck (00); •Good Girl,
The (02)

ARZNER, DOROTHY
Fashions for Women (27); Ten Modern
Commandments (27); Get Your Man (27);
Manhattan Cocktail (28); •Wild Party, The (29);
Anybody's Woman (30); Sarah and Son (30);
Honor Among Lovers (31); Working Girls (31);
Merrily We Go to Hell (32); Christopher
Strong (33); Nana (34); •Craig's Wife (36); Bride
Wore Red, The (37); Dance, Girl, Dance (40); First
Comes Courage (43)

ASHBY, HAL
•Landlord, The (70); •Harold and Maude (71);
•Last Detail, The (73); •Shampoo (75); •Bound for
Glory (76); •Coming Home (78); •Being
There (79); Second-Hand Hearts (81); Lookin' to

Get Out (82); Let's Spend the Night Together (82); Slugger's Wife, The (85); 8 Million Ways to Die (86)

ASQUITH, ANTHONY
Runaway Princess, The (29); Escaped from Dartmoor (30); Battle of Gallipoli (31); Dance Pretty Lady (32); Lucky Number, The (33); Unfinished Symphony, The (34); I Stand Condemned (36); •Pygmalion (38); French Without Tears (39); Quiet Wedding (40); Bombsight Stolen (41); Voice in the Night, A (41); Uncensored (42); Adventure for Two (43); We Dive at Dawn (43); Welcome to Britain (43); Man of Evil (44); Johnny in the Clouds (45); While the Sun Shines (46); •Winslow Boy, The (48); Woman in Question, The (50); •Browning Version, The (51); •Importance of Being Earnest, The (52); Final Test, The (53); Project M7 (53); Chance Meeting (54); Court Martial (54); Doctor's Dilemma, The (58); Orders to Kill (58); Libel (59); Millionairess, The (60); Two Living, One Dead (61); Guns of Darkness (62); V.I.P.s, The (63); Evening with the Royal Ballet, An (64); Yellow Rolls-Royce, The (64)

ASSAYAS, OLIVIER
L' Unique (85); Disorder (86); Winter's Child (89); Paris at Dawn (91); Zone (91); New Life, A (93); Cold Water (94); •Irma Vep; HHH: Portrait de Hou Hsiao-Hsien (97); Late August, Early September (98); Les Destinees Sentimentales (00); Demonlover (02); Clean (2004)

ATTENBOROUGH, RICHARD
•Oh! What a Lovely War (69); Young Winston (72); •Bridge Too Far, A (77); Magic (78); •Gandhi (82); Chorus Line, A (85); Cry Freedom (87); •Chaplin (92); Shadowlands (93); In Love and War (96); Grey Owl (99)

AUDIARD, JACQUES
See How They Fall (94); Self-Made Hero, A (96); •Read My Lips (01); Beat that My Heart Skipped, The (05)

AUGUST, BILLE
In My Life (78); Zappa (83); Twist and Shout (84); •Pelle the Conqueror (87); Best Intentions, The (92); House of the Spirits, The (94); Jerusalem (96); Smilla's Sense of Snow (97); •Les Miserables (98); Song for Martin, A (00); Detaljer (03); Return to Sender (04)

AVARY, ROGER
Killing Zoe (94); Mr. Stitch (96); •Rules of Attraction, The (02)

AVILDSEN, JOHN G.
Turn on to Love (69); Guess What We Learned in School Today? (70); Joe (70); Okay Bill (71); Stoolie, The (72); •Save the Tiger (73); Foreplay (75); W.W. and the Dixie Dancekings (75); •Rocky (76); Slow Dancing in the Big City (78); Formula, The (80); Neighbors (81); Traveling Hopefully (82); Night in Heaven, A (83); •Karate Kid, The (84); Karate Kid Part II, The (86); Happy New Year (87); For Keeps (88); Karate Kid Part III, The (89); Lean on Me (89); Rocky V (90); Power of One, The (92); 8 Seconds (94); Fine and Private Place, A (98); Coyote Moon (99)

AVNET, JON
•Fried Green Tomatoes (91); War, The (94); Up Close and Personal (96); Red Corner (97); Uprising (01)

BABENCO, HECTOR
King of the Night (75); Lucio Flavio—Passaqeioro da Agonia (79); •Pixote (81); •Kiss of the Spider Woman (85); Ironweed (87); At Play in the Fields of the Lord (91); Foolish Heart (98); Carandiru (03)

BADHAM, JOHN
Bingo Long Traveling All-Stars and Motor Kings, The (76); •Saturday Night Fever (77); Dracula (79); Whose Life Is It Anyway? (81); Blue Thunder (83); Wargames (83); American Flyers (85); Short Circuit (86); •Stakeout (87); Bird on a Wire (90); Hard Way, The (91); Another Stakeout (93); Point of No Return (93); Drop Zone (94); Nick of Time (95); Incognito (97); Floating Away (98); Jack Bull (99); Last Debate, The (00); Brother's Keeper (02); Obsessed (02); Footsteps (03); Evel Knievel (04)

BALLARD, CARROLL
•Black Stallion, The (79); Never Cry Wolf (83); Nutcracker: The Motion Picture (86); Wind (92); •Fly Away Home (96); Duma (05)

BARKER, CLIVE
•Hellraiser (87); Nightbreed (90); Lord of Illusions (95)

BARTEL, PAUL
Private Parts (72); •Death Race 2000 (75); Cannonball (76); •Eating Raoul (82); Not for Publication (84); Lust in the Dust (85); Longshot, The (86); Scenes from the Class Struggle in Beverly Hills (89); Shelf Life (93)

BAVA, MARIO
L'Orrechio (46); Santa Notte (47); Legenda Sinfonica (47); Anfiteatro Flavio (47); Variazioni Sinfoniche (49); I Vampiri (56); Caltiki, The Immortal Monster (59); Giant of Marathon (59); •Black Sunday (60); Esther and the King (60); Hercules at the Center of the Earth (61); Erik the Conqueror (61); Black Sabbath (63); Evil Eye (63); What! (63); Road to Fort Alamo, The (64); Blood and Black Lace (64); Planet of the Vampires (65); Knives of the Avenger (65); Dr. Goldfoot and the Girl Bombs (66); Savage Gringo (66); Kill Baby Kill (66); Danger: Diabolik (67); Hatchet for a Honeymoon (69); Roy Colt and Winchester Jack (70); Five Dolls for an August Moon (70); Baron Blood (72); Twitch of the Death Nerve (72); Four Times That Night (72); Lisa and the Devil (74); Rabid Dogs (74); Shock/Beyond the Door II (77); Venus of Ille (78)

BAY, MICHAEL
Bad Boys (95); Rock, The (96); •Armageddon (98); •Pearl Harbor (01); Bad Boys II (03)

BEATTY, WARREN
•Heaven Can Wait (78); •Reds (81); •Dick Tracy (90); •Bulworth (98)

BECKER, HAROLD
Ragman's Daughter, The (72); •Onion Field, The (79); Black Marble, The (80); Taps (81); Vision Quest (85); Boost, The (88); •Sea of Love (89); Malice (93); City Hall (96); Mercury Rising (98); Domestic Disturbance (01)

BENIGNI, ROBERTO
You Disturb Me (83); There's Nothing Left to Do But Cry (84); Little Devil, The (88); Johnny Stecchino (91); Monster, The (94); •Life Is Beautiful (97); •Pinocchio (02)

BEINEIX, JEAN-JACQUES
Le Chien de Monsieur Michel (77); •Diva (81); •Moon in the Gutter, The (83); •Betty Blue (86); Roselyne et les Lions (89); Ip5 (92); Otaku (94); Mortal Transfer (00); Loft Paradoxe (02)

BELLOCCHIO, MARCO
•Fist in His Pocket (66); China Is Near (67); Vangelo '70 (69); In the Name of the Father (71); Strike the Monster on Page One (72); Victory March (75); Fit to Be Untied (75); Seagull, The (77); Leap into the Void (79); Vacation in Val Trebbia (80); Eyes, the Mouth, The (82); Henry IV (84); Devil in the Flesh (86); Witches' Sabbath, The (88); Conviction, The (91) Butterfly's Dream, The (94); Broken Dreams (95); Prince of Homburg, The (97); Nanny, The (99); My Mother's Smile (02); Good Morning, Night (03)

BENEDEK, LASLO
Kissing Bandit, The (48); Port of New York (49); •Death of a Salesman (52); •Wild One, The (53); Bengal Brigade (54); Kinder Mutter und ein General (55); Affair in Havana (57); Moment of Danger (59); Recourse in Grace (60); Namu, the Killer Whale (66); Daring Game (68); Night Visitor, The (70); Assault on Agathon (75)

BENNETT, COMPTON
•Seventh Veil, The (45); Daybreak (46); Years Between, The (46); My Own True Love (48); That Forsyte Woman (49); •King Solomon's Mines (50); Glory at Sea (52); It Started in Paradise (52); So Little Time (52); Desperate Moment (53); After the Ball (57); City After Midnight (57); Mailbag Robbery (57); Beyond the Curtain (60)

BENTON, ROBERT
•Bad Company (72); •Late Show, The (77); •Kramer vs. Kramer (79); Still of the Night (82); •Places in the Heart (84); Nadine (87); Billy Bathgate (91); •Nobody's Fool (94); Twilight (98); Human Stain, The (03)

BERESFORD, BRUCE
Adventures of Barry Mckenzie, The (72); Barry Mckenzie Holds His Own (74); Side by Side (75); •Don's Party (76); Getting of Wisdom, The (77); Money Movers (78); •Breaker Morant (80); Club, The (80); Fortress (81); Puberty Blues (81); •Tender Mercies (83); Fringe Dwellers, The (84); King David (85); Crimes of the Heart (86); Aria (87); •Driving Miss Daisy (89); Her Alibi (89); •Black Robe (91); Mister Johnson (91); Rich in Love (93); Good Man in Africa, A (94); Silent Fall (94); Last Dance (96); Paradise Road (97); •Double Jeopardy (99); Bride of the Wind (01); Evelyn (02); And Starring Pancho Villa as Himself (03)

BERG, PETER
Very Bad Things (98); Rundown, The (03); •Friday Night Lights (04)

BERGMAN, INGMAR
Crisis (45); It Rains on Our Love (46); Night Is My Future (48); Ship to India, A (47); Port of Call (48); Devil's Wanton, The (49); Thirst (49); To Joy (50); This Can't Happen Here (50); Illicit Interlude (51); •Secrets of Women (52); Monika (53); Sawdust and Tinsel (53); Naked Night, The (53); Lesson in Love, A (54); Dreams (55); •Smiles of a Summer Night (55); •Seventh Seal, The (57); •Wild Strawberries (57); Brink of Life (58); •Magician, The (58); •Virgin Spring, The (59); Devil's Eye, The (60); Through a Glass Darkly (61); Winter Light (62); Silence, The (63); All These Women (64); •Persona (66); Stimulantia (67); •Hour of the Wolf, The (68); •Shame (68); •Passion of Anna, The (69); Ritual, The (69); Faro Documentary, The (70); Touch, The (71); •Cries and Whispers (72); •Scenes from a Marriage (73); Magic Flute, The (74); •Face to Face (76); Serpent's Egg, The (77); •Autumn Sonata (78); Faro 1979 (79); From the Life of the Marionettes (80); •Fanny and Alexander (82); After the Rehearsal (84); Making of Fanny and Alexander, The (86); De Tva Saliga (86); Karin's Face (86); Markisinnan de Sade (92); Last Gasp, The (95); In the Presence of a Clown (97); Bildmakarna (00); Saraband (03)

BERKELEY, BUSBY
She Had to Say Yes (33); •Footlight Parade (33); Bright Lights (35); •Gold Diggers of 1935 (35); I Live for Love (35); Stage Struck (36); Go-Getter, The (37); Hollywood Hotel (37); Comet Over Broadway (38); Garden of the Moon (38); Men Are Such Fools (38); •Babes in Arms (39); Fast and Furious (39); They Made Me A Criminal (39); Forty Little Mothers (40); •Strike Up the Band (40); •Babes on Broadway (41); Blonde Inspiration (41); •For Me and My Gal (42); •Gang's All Here, The (43); Cinderella Jones (46); •Take Me Out to the Ball Game (49)

BERRI, CLAUDE
Les Baisers (64); La Chance et l'Amour (64); •Two of Us, The (67); Marry Me! Marry Me! (69); Man with Connections, The (70); Le Cinema De Papa (70); Le Sex Shop (72); Le Male du Siecle (75); First Time, The (76); Un Moment d'Egarement (77); I Love You (80); Le Maitre d'Ecole (82); Tchao Pantin (83); •Jean De Florette (86); •Manon of the Spring (86); Uranus (91); Germinal (93); Lucie Aubrac (97); Hard Off (99); Housekeeper, A (02); L'un Rest, l'autre Part (05)

BERTOLUCCI, BERNARDO
Grim Reaper, The (62); •Before the Revolution (64); Vangelo '70 (67); Partner (68); Spider's Stratagem, The (70); •Conformist, The (70); •Last Tango in Paris (73); •1900 (76); Luna (79); Tragedy of a Ridiculous Man, The (81); •Last Emperor, The (87); Sheltering Sky, The (90); Little Buddha (94); •Stealing Beauty (96); Besieged (98); •Dreamers, The (03)

Charenton Under the Direction of the Marquis de Sade, The) (66); Tell Me Lies (68); King Lear (70); Meetings with Remarkable Men (79); Tragedy of Carmen, The (83); Mahabharata, The (90); Tragedy of Hamlet, The (02)

BROOKS, ALBERT
•Real Life (79); •Modern Romance (81); •Lost in America (85); Defending Your Life (91); Mother (96); Muse, The (99)

BROOKS, JAMES L.
•Terms of Endearment (83); •Broadcast News (87); I'll Do Anything (94); •As Good As It Gets (97); •Spanglish (04)

BROOKS, MEL
•Producers, The (67); •Twelve Chairs, The (70); •Blazing Saddles (74); •Young Frankenstein (74); Silent Movie (76); •High Anxiety (77); History of the World, Part 1 (81); Spaceballs (87); Life Stinks (91); Robin Hood: Men in Tights (93); Dracula: Dead and Loving It (95)

BROOKS, RICHARD
Crisis (50); Light Touch, The (51); Deadline—U.S.A. (52); Battle Circus (53); Take the High Ground (53); Flame and the Flesh (54); •Last Time I Saw Paris, The (54); •Blackboard Jungle (55); •Catered Affair, The (56); Last Hunt, The (56); Something of Value (57); •Brothers Karamazov, The (58); •Cat on a Hot Tin Roof (58); •Elmer Gantry (60); •Sweet Bird of Youth (62); •Lord Jim (65); Professionals, The (66); •In Cold Blood (67); Happy Ending, The (69); •$ (Dollars) (71); Bite the Bullet (75); •Looking for Mr. Goodbar (77); Wrong Is Right (82); Fever Pitch (85)

BROOMFIELD, NICK
Juvenile Liaison (75); Proud to Be British (78); Tattooed Tears (78); Who Cares (78); Behind the Rent Strike (79); Whittingham (80); Fort Augustus (81); Marriage Guidance (81); Soldier Girls (81); Chicken Ranch (83); Lily Tomlin (86); Driving Me Crazy (88); Dark Obsession (89); Juvenile Liaison 2 (90); Leader, His Driver and the Driver's Wife, The (91); Monster in a Box (91); Too White for Me (91); Aileen Wuornos: The Selling of a Serial Killer (92); Tracking Down Maggie (94); Heidi Fleiss: Hollywood Madam (95); Fetishes (96); •Kurt and Courtney (98); Biggie and Tupac (02); Aileen: Life and Death of a Serial Killer (03)

BROWN, CLARENCE
Wonder of Women (29); •Anna Christie (30); Navy Blues (30); Romance (30); •Free Soul, A (31); Inspiration (31); Possessed (31); Emma (32); Letty Lynton (32); Son-Daughter, The (32); Looking Forward (33); Night Flight (33); Chained (34); Sadie Mckee (34); •Ah, Wilderness! (35); •Anna Karenina (35); Gorgeous Hussy, T∫he (36); Wife vs. Secretary (36); Conquest (37); Of Human Hearts (38); Idiot's Delight (39); Rains Came, The (39); •Edison, the Man (40); Come Live with Me (41); They Met in Bombay (41); Human Comedy, The (43); •National Velvet (44); •White Cliffs of Dover, The (44); •Yearling, The (46); Song of Love (47); •Intruder in the Dust (49); To Please a Lady (50);

•Angels in the Outfield (51); It's a Big Country (51); Plymouth Adventure (52); When in Rome (52)

BROWNING, TOD
Outside the Law (30); Thirteenth Chair, The (30); •Dracula (31); Iron Man, The (31); •Freaks (32); Fast Workers (33); Mark of the Vampire (35); •Devil Doll, The (36); Miracles for Sale (39)

BUNUEL, LUIS
•L'Age D'Or (30); •Los Olvidados (50); Daughter of Deceit (51); Mexican Bus Ride (51); Woman Without Love, A (51); •Adventures of Robinson Crusoe, The (52); Brute, The (52); •El (52); •Wuthering Heights (53); Illusion Travels by Streetcar, The (54); Criminal Life of Archibaldo de la Cruz, The (55); Death in the Garden (56); Nazarin (58); Young One, The (60); •Viridiana (61); •Exterminating Angel, The (62); •Diary of a Chambermaid (64); •Belle de Jour (67); •Milky Way, The (69); •Tristana (70); •Discreet Charm of the Bourgeoisie, The (72); •Phantom of Liberty, The (74); •That Obscure Object of Desire (77)

BURNETT, CHARLES
•Killer of Sheep (77); My Brother's Wedding (83); •To Sleep with Anger (90); America Becoming (91); Glass Shield, The (95); When it Rains (95); Nightjohn (96); Selma, Lord, Selma (99); Annihilation of Fish, The (99); Finding Buck McHenry (00); Nat Turner: A Troublesome Property (03)

BURTON, TIM
•Pee-wee's Big Adventure (85); •Beetlejuice (88); •Batman (89); •Edward Scissorhands (90); Batman Returns (92); •Ed Wood (94); •Mars Attacks! (96); •Sleepy Hollow (99); •Planet of the Apes (00); •Big Fish (03); Charlie and the Chocolate Factory (05)

CACOYANNIS, MICHAEL
Windfall in Athens (54); Stella (55); Girl in Black, A (56); Final Lie, The (58); Our Last Spring (60); Electra (60); Wastrel, The (61); •Zorba the Greek (64); Day the Fish Came Out, The (67); Trojan Women, The (71); Story of Jacob and Joseph, The (74); Attila '74 (74); Iphigenia (77); Sweet Country (87); Zoe (89); Pano Kato Ke Plagios (93); Up, Down and Sideways (94); Cherry Orchard, The (99)

CAMERON, JAMES
Piranha II: The Spawning (81); •Terminator, The (84); •Aliens (86); •Abyss, The (89); •Terminator 2: Judgment Day (91); •True Lies (94); •Titanic (97); Ghosts of the Abyss (03)

CAMMELL, DONALD
•Performance (70); Demon Seed (77); White of the Eye (87); Wild Side (96)

CAMPION, JANE
Two Friends (86); •Sweetie (89); •Angel at My Table, An (90); •Piano, The (93); •Portrait of a Lady, The (96); •Holy Smoke (99); In the Cut (03)

CAMUS, MARCEL
Fugitive in Saigon (57); •Black Orpheus (59); Os Bandeirantes (60); Dragon Sky (62); Le Chant du Monde (65); L'Homme de New York (67); Vivre la Nuit (68); Le Mur de l'Atlantique (70); Un Ete Sauvage (70); Os Pastoris da Noite (77)

CANTET, LAURENT
Les Sanguinaires (98); •Human Resources (00); •Time Out (01)

CAPRA, FRANK
Tramp Tramp Tramp (26); Strong Man, The (26); Long Pants (27); For the Love of Mike (27); That Certain Thing (28); Say It with Sables (28); Submarine (28); Power of the Press, The (28); Donovan Affair, The (29); Flight (29); Younger Generation, The (29); Ladies of Leisure (30); Rain or Shine (30); Dirigible (31); •Miracle Woman, The (31); Platinum Blonde (31); •American Madness (32); Forbidden (32); Bitter Tea of General Yen, The (33); Lady for a Day (33); Broadway Bill (34); •It Happened One Night (34); •Mr. Deeds Goes to Town (36); •Lost Horizon (37); •You Can't Take It with You (38); •Mr. Smith Goes to Washington (39); •Meet John Doe (41); •Arsenic and Old Lace (44); •It's a Wonderful Life (46); •State of the Union (48); Riding High (50); •Here Comes the Groom (51); Hole in the Head, A (59); •Pocketful of Miracles (61)

CARAX, LEOS
•Boy Meets Girl (85); •Bad Blood (87); Les Amants du Pont Neuf (91); Pola X (99)

CARDIFF, JACK
Intent to Kill (58); Web of Evidence (59); Scent of Mystery (60); •Sons and Lovers (60); Lion, The (62); My Geisha (62); Long Ships, The (64); Young Cassidy (65); Liquidator, The (66); Dark of the Sun (68); Girl on a Motorcycle, The (68); Mutations, The (72)

CARNAHAN, JOE
Blood, Guts, Bullets and Octane (98); •Narc (02)

CARNE, MARCEL
Jenny (36); Bizarre Bizarre (36); •Port of Shadows (38); Hotel du Nord (38); •Daybreak (39); Devil's Envoys, The (42); •Children of Paradise (45); Gates of the Night (46); La Marie du Port (50); Juliette ou la Cle des Songes (51); Therese Raquin (53); L'Air de Paris (54); Le Pays d'Ou Je Viens (56); Cheaters, The (58); Terrain Vague (60); Du Mouron Pour Les Petits Oiseaux (63); Trois Chambres a Manhattan (65); Young Wolves, The (68); Les Assassins de l'Ordre (71); La Merveilleuse Visite (74); La Bible (76)

CARO, MARC
•Delicatessen (91); •City of Lost Children, The (95)

CARPENTER, JOHN
•Dark Star (75); •Assault on Precinct 13 (76); •Halloween (78); Fog, The (80); •Escape from New York (81); •Thing, The (82); Christine (83); •Starman (84); Big Trouble in Little China (86); Prince of Darkness (87); •They Live (88); Memoirs of an Invisible Man (92); In the Mouth of Madness (95); Village of the Damned (95); John Carpenter's Escape from L.A. (96); John Carpenter's Vampires (98); John Carpenter's Ghosts of Mars (01)

CASSAVETES, JOHN
•Shadows (60); Too Late Blues (62); Child Is Waiting, A (63); •Faces (68); •Husbands (70); •Minnie and Moskowitz (71); •Woman Under the Influence, A (74); Killing of a Chinese Bookie, The (76); Opening Night (77); •Gloria (80); •Love Streams (84); Big Trouble (86)

CATON-JONES, MICHAEL
•Scandal (89); Memphis Belle (90); Doc Hollywood (91); •This Boy's Life (93); Rob Roy (95); Jackal, The (97), City by the Sea (02); Shooting Dogs (05)

CAVALCANTI, ALBERTO
48 Hours (42); Champagne Charlie (44); •Dead of Night (45); Nicholas Nickleby (47); •They Made Me a Fugitive (47); For Them That Trespass (48); Affairs of a Rogue, The (49); Monster of Highgate Ponds, The (60)

CHABROL, CLAUDE
•Le Beau Serge (58); •Cousins, The (59); Web of Passion (59); Les Bonnes Femmes (60); Les Godelureaux (60); Seven Capital Sins (61); Third Lover, The (62); Ophelia (62); Landru (63); Beautiful Swindlers, The (64); Tiger Likes Fresh Blood, The (64); •Six in Paris (65); Marie-Chantal Contre le Docteur Kha (65); Orchid for the Tiger, An (65); La Ligne de Demarcation (66); Champagne Murders, The (67); Who's Got the Black Box? (67); •Les Biches (68); •La Femme Infidele (69); •Le Boucher (69); •This Man Must Die (70); La Rupture (70); Just Before Nightfall (71); Docteur Popaul (72); Ten Days' Wonder (72); Wedding in Blood (73); De Grey—Le Banc De Desolation (73); Nada Gang, The (74); Histoires Insolites (74); Piece of Pleasure, A (75); Les Magiciens (75); Dirty Hands (75); Twist, The (76); Alice, or the Last Escapade (77); Blood Relatives (78); Violette (78); Horse of Pride (80); Hatter's Ghost, The (82); Blood of Others, The (84); Poulet au Vinaigre (85); Inspector Lavardin (86); Cry of the Owl, The (87); Masques (87); •Story of Women (88); Alouette, Je Te Plumerai (88); Docteur M (89); Quiet Days in Clichy (90); Club Extinction (90); Madame Bovary (91); Betty (92); Eye of Vichy, The (93); L'Enfer (94); La Ceremonie (95); Swindle, The (97); Color of Lies, The (99); Merci Pour le Chocolat (00); Flower of Evil, The (03); La Demoiselle d'Honneur (04)

CHAPLIN, CHARLES
•Modern Times (36); •Great Dictator, The (40); •Monsieur Verdoux (47); •Limelight (52); King in New York, A (57); Countess from Hong Kong, A (67)

CHAPMAN, MATTHEW
Hussy (79); •Strangers Kiss (84); Slow Burn (86); Heart of Midnight (89)

CHELSOM, PETER
Treacle (88); •Hear My Song (91); •Funny Bones (95); Mighty, The (98); Town & Country (01); Serendipity (01); •Shall We Dance? (04)

CHEN KAIGE
•Yellow Earth (86); •Big Parade, The (87); King of Children (86); •Life on a String (92); •Farewell, My Concubine (93); •Temptress Moon (96); •Emperor and the Assassin, The (99); Killing Me Softly (02); Together (02)

CHOW, STEPHEN
King of Destruction (94); From Beijing with Love (94); God of Cookery (94); Forbidden City Cop (96); King of Comedy, The (99); Shaolin Soccer (01); •Kung Fu Hustle (04)

CHEREAU, PATRICE
La Chair de l'Orchidee (74); Judith Therpauve (78); L'Homme Blesse (83); Hotel de France (87); Contre l'Oubli (92); Le Temps et la Chambre (92); •Queen Margot (94); Those Who Love Me Can Take the Train (98); Intimacy (01); Son Frere (03)

CIMINO, MICHAEL
•Thunderbolt and Lightfoot (74); •Deer Hunter, The (78); •Heaven's Gate (80); Year of the Dragon (85); Sicilian, The (87); Desperate Hours (90); Sunchaser (96)

CISSE, SOULEYMANE
Five Days in a Life (73); Girl, The (75); Baara (78); Finye (83); •Brightness (87); Waati (95)

CLAIR, RENE
•Under the Roofs of Paris (30); •A Nous la Liberte (31); •Million, The (31); July 14th (33); Le Dernier Milliardaire (34); •Ghost Goes West, The (36); Break the News (38); Flame of New Orleans, The (41); •I Married a Witch (42); Forever and a Day (43); It Happened Tomorrow (44); •And Then There Were None (45); Man About Town (47); Beauty and the Devil (49); Les Belles-de-Nuit (52); Grand Maneuver, The (55); Gates of Paris (57); Love and the Frenchwoman (61); Tout l'Or du Monde (61); Three Fables of Love (62); Les Fetes Galantes (65)

CLARK, BOB
She Man, The (67); Children Shouldn't Play with Dead Things (72); Deathdream (72); Black Christmas (74); Breaking Point (76); Murder by Decree (79); Tribute (80); Porky's (82); •Christmas Story, A (83); Porky's II: The Next Day (83); Rhinestone (84); Turk 182! (85); From the Hip (87); Loose Cannons (90); It Runs in the Family (94); Baby Geniuses (99); I'll Remember April (99); Now & Forever (02); Unleashed (02); Maniac Magee (03); Karate Dog, The (04); Baby Geniuses 2: Return of the Super Babies (04)

CLARK, LARRY
•Kids (95); •Another Day in Paradise (98); Bully (01); Teenage Caveman (02); Ken Park (03)

CLARKE, ALAN
Hallelujah Handshake (70); Everybody Say Cheese (71); Follower for Emily, A (71); Funny Farm (75); Diane (75); Scum (79); Psy-Warriors (81); Beloved Enemy (81); Made in Britain (82); Contact (85); Billy the Kid and the Green Baize Vampire (85); •Rita, Sue and Bob Too! (86); Road (87); Firm, The (88); Elephant (89)

CLARKE, SHIRLEY
Dance in the Sun (53); In Paris Parks (54); Bullfight (55); Moment in Love, A (57); Loops (58); Bridges-Go-Round (59); Scary Time, A (60); Skyscraper, The (59); •Connection, The (62); Robert Frost: a Lover's Quarrel with the World (63); •Cool World, The (63); Man in the

Polar Regions (67); Portrait of Jason (67); 24 Frames per Second (77); Initiation (78); Mysterum (79); Four Journeys into Mystic Time (80); Savage/Love (81); Tongues (83); Ornette: Made in America (85)

CLAYTON, JACK
•Room at the Top (59); •Innocents, The (61); •Pumpkin Eater, The (64); Our Mother's House (67); Great Gatsby, The (74); Something Wicked this Way Comes (83); Lonely Passion of Judith Hearne, The (87)

CLEMENT, RENE
Battle of the Rails (46); Mr. Orchid (46); Damned, The (47); Walls of Malapaga, The (49); Le Chateau de Verre (50); •Forbidden Games (52); Lovers Happy Lovers (54); Gervaise (56); This Angry Age (58); Purple Noon (60); Quelle Joie de Vivre (61); Day and the Hour, The (63); Joy House (64); •Is Paris Burning? (66); •Rider on the Rain (70); And Hope to Die (72); Deadly Trap, The (72); La Baby Sitter (75)

CLOUZOT, HENRI-GEORGES
Murderer Lives at Number 21, The (42); Raven, The (43); Jenny Lamour (47); Manon (49); Retour a la Vie (49); Miquette (50); •Wages of Fear, The (52); •Diabolique (55); Mystery of Picasso, The (56); Les Espions (57); Truth, The (60); La Prisonniere (69)

COCTEAU, JEAN
Blood of a Poet, The (30); •Beauty and the Beast (46); Eagle with Two Heads (48); •Les Parents Terribles (48); •Orpheus (49); •Testament of Orpheus, The (59)

COEN, JOEL
•Blood Simple (84); •Raising Arizona (87); •Miller's Crossing (90); •Barton Fink (91); •Hudsucker Proxy, The (94); •Fargo (96); •Big Lebowski, The (98); •O, Brother Where Art Thou? (00); •Man Who Wasn't There, The (01); Intolerable Cruelty (03); Ladykillers, The (04)

COHEN, LARRY
Bone (72); Black Caesar (73); Hell Up in Harlem (73); •It's Alive (74); God Told Me To (76); It Lives Again (78); Private Files of J. Edgar Hoover, The (78); Full Moon High (82); •Q (82); Perfect Strangers (84); Special Effects (84); Stuff, The (85); Deadly Illusion (87); It's Alive III: Island of the Alive (88); Return to Salem's Lot, A (88); Wicked Stepmother (89); Ambulance, The (93); Original Gangstas (96)

COHEN, ROB
Small Circle of Friends, A (80); Scandalous (84); •Dragon: The Bruce Lee Story (93); Dragonheart (96); Daylight (96); Rat Pack, The (98); Skulls, The (00); Fast and the Furious, The (01); •xXx (02); Stealth (05)

COLUMBUS, CHRIS
Adventures in Babysitting (87); Heartbreak Hotel (88); •Home Alone (90); Only the Lonely (91); Home Alone 2: Lost in New York (92); •Mrs. Doubtfire (93); Nine Months (95); •Stepmom (98); Bicentennial Man (99); •Harry Potter and the Sorcerer's Stone (01); •Harry Potter and the Chamber of Secrets (02)

CONDON, BILL
Sister, Sister (88); Murder 101 (91); White Lie (91); Dead in the Water (91); Deadly Relations (93); Candyman: Farewell to the Flesh (95); Man Who Wouldn't Die, The (95); •Gods and Monsters (98); •Kinsey (04)

CONWAY, JACK
Alias Jimmy Valentine (28); Our Modern Maidens (29); Untamed (29); New Moon (30); They Learned About Women (30); Unholy Three, The (30); Easiest Way, The (31); Just a Gigolo (31); Arsene Lupin (32); But the Flesh Is Weak (32); Red Headed Woman (32); Hell Below (33); Nuisance, The (33); Solitaire Man, The (33); Gay Bride, The (34); Girl from Missouri, The (34); •Tarzan and his Mate (34); •Viva Villa! (34); One New York Night (35); •Tale of Two Cities, A (35); •Libeled Lady (36); •Saratoga (37); Too Hot to Handle (38); Yank at Oxford, A (38); Lady of the Tropics (39); Let Freedom Ring (39); Boom Town (40); •Northwest Passage (40); Honky Tonk (41); •Love Crazy (41); Crossroads (42); Assignment in Brittany (43); Dragon Seed (44); High Barbaree (47); •Hucksters, The (47); Julia Misbehaves (48)

COOLIDGE, MARTHA
Not a Pretty Picture (76); •Valley Girl (83); City Girl (84); Joy of Sex (84); Real Genius (85); Plain Clothes (88); Trenchcoat in Paradise (88); Bare Essentials (91); •Rambling Rose (91); Crazy in Love (92); Neil Simon's Lost in Yonkers (93); Angie (94); Three Wishes (95); Out to Sea (97); Introducing Dorothy Dandridge (99); If These Walls Could Talk (00); Flamingo Rising (01); Ponder Heart, The (01); Prince & Me, The (04); Twelve Days of Christmas Eve, The (04)

COPPOLA, FRANCIS FORD
Tonight for Sure! (62); Playgirls and the Bellboy, The (62); Terror, The (63); •Dementia 13 (63); •You're a Big Boy Now (66); Finian's Rainbow (68); •Rain People, The (69); •Godfather, The (72); •Conversation, The (74); •Godfather, Part II, The (74); •Apocalypse Now (79); One from the Heart (82); •Outsiders, The (83); •Rumble Fish (83); •Cotton Club, The (84); •Peggy Sue Got Married (86); •Gardens of Stone (87); •Tucker: The Man and His Dream (88); New York Stories (89); •Godfather, Part III, The (90); •Bram Stoker's Dracula (92); Jack (96); •John Grisham's The Rainmaker (97); •Apocalypse Now Redux (01)

CORMAN, ROGER
Apache Woman (55); Five Guns West (55); Day the World Ended, The (56); Gunslinger (56); It Conquered the World (56); Oklahoma Woman, The (56); Swamp Women (56); Attack of the Crab Monsters (57); Carnival Rock (57); Naked Paradise (57); Not of this Earth (57); Rock All Night (57); Saga of the Viking Women and Their Voyage to the Waters of the Great Sea Serpent, The (57); Sorority Girl (57); Teenage Doll (57); Undead, The (57); Machine Gun Kelly (58); She Gods of Shark Reef (58); Teenage Caveman (58); War of the Satellites (58); Bucket of Blood, A (59); I, Mobster (59); Wasp Woman, The (59); Atlas (60); •House of Usher (60); Last Woman on Earth, The (60); Ski Troop Attack (60); Creature from the Haunted Sea (61); •Little Shop of Horrors, The (61); •Pit and the Pendulum, The (61); Intruder, The (62); Premature Burial, The (62); •Tales of Terror (62); Tower of London (62); Haunted Palace, The (63); Raven, The (63); Terror, The (63); •"X"—The Man with the X-Ray Eyes (63); Young Racers, The (63); •Masque of the Red Death, The (64); Secret Invasion, The (64); Tomb of Ligeia, The (64); •Wild Angels, The (66); St. Valentine's Day Massacre, The (67); Trip, The (67); Target: Harry (69); Bloody Mama (70); Gas-s-s-s! (70); Von Richthofen and Brown (70); Frankenstein Unbound (90)

CORNEAU, ALAIN
France Societe Anonyme (74); Police Python 357 (76); La Menace (77); Serie Noire (79); Case Against Ferro, The (80); Choice of Arms (81); Fort Saganne (84); Le Mome (86); Nocturne Indien (89); •Tous Les Matins du Monde (91); Contre l'Oubli (92); New World, The (95); Le Cousin (97); Prince of the Pacific, The (00); Fear and Trembling (03); Some Kind of Blue (05)

CORNELIUS, HENRY
•Passport to Pimlico (49); Galloping Major, The (51); •Genevieve (53); •I Am a Camera (55); Next to No Time (58)

COSTA-GAVRAS, CONSTANTIN
•Sleeping Car Murder, The (65); Shock Troops (67); •Z (69); •Confession, The (70); •State of Siege (72); Special Section (75); Womanlight (79); •Missing (82); Hannah K. (83); Family Business (86); Betrayed (88); •Music Box (89); Contre l'Oubli (92); Minor Apocalypse, The (93); Mad City (97); Amen. (02); Le Couperet (05)

COX, ALEX
•Repo Man (84); •Sid and Nancy (86); Straight to Hell (87); Walker (87); Highway Patrolman (93); Death and the Compass (96); Winner, The (96); Three Businessmen (98); Kurosawa: The Last Emperor (99); Hard Look, A (00); Revenger's Tragedy, A (02)

COX, PAUL
Illuminations (76); Inside Looking Out (77); Kostas (79); Lonely Hearts (81); •Man of Flowers (84); •My First Wife (84); Death and Destiny (85); Cactus (86); Vincent: The Life and Death of Vincent Van Gogh (87); Gift, The (88); Island (89); Golden Braid, The (90); Woman's Tale, A (91); Nun and the Bandit, The (92); Touch Me (93); Exile (94); Lust and Revenge (96); Four Million Houseguests/The Hidden Dimension (97); Molokai: The Story of Father Damien (99); •Innocence (00); Diaries of Vaslav Nijinski, The (01); Human Touch (04)

CRAVEN, WES
•Last House on the Left (72); •Hills Have Eyes, The (78); Deadly Blessing (81); Swamp Thing (82); •Nightmare on Elm Street, A (84); Hills Have Eyes II, The (85); Deadly Friend (86); Serpent and the Rainbow, The (88); Shocker (89); People Under the Stairs, The (91); Wes Craven's

New Nightmare (94); Vampire in Brooklyn (95); •Scream (96); Scream 2 (97); Music of the Heart (99); Scream 3 (00); Cursed (05)

CRICHTON, CHARLES
For Those in Peril (43); •Dead of Night (45); Girl on the Canal, The (45); Hue and Cry (46); Against the Wind (47); Another Shore (48); Train of Events (49); Dance Hall (50); •Lavender Hill Mob, The (51); Stranger in Between, The (52); Titfield Thunderbolt, The (52); Love Lottery, The (53); Divided Heart, The (54); Decision Against Time (56); Floods of Fear (58); Law and Disorder (58); Battle of the Sexes, The (60); Boy Who Stole a Million, The (60); Third Secret, The (64); He Who Rides a Tiger (65); Tomorrow's Island (68); •Fish Called Wanda, A (88)

CROMWELL, JOHN
Close Harmony (29); Dance of Life, The (29); Mighty, The (29); For the Defense (30); Street of Chance (30); Texan, The (30); Tom Sawyer (30); Rich Man's Folly (31); Scandal Sheet (31); Unfaithful (31); Vice Squad, The (31); World and the Flesh, The (32); Ann Vickers (33); Double Harness (33); Silver Cord, The (33); Sweepings (33); Fountain, The (34); •Of Human Bondage (34); Spitfire (34); This Man Is Mine (34); I Dream Too Much (35); Jalna (35); Village Tale (35); Banjo on My Knee (36); Little Lord Fauntleroy (36); To Mary—With Love (36); •Prisoner of Zenda, The (37); •Algiers (38); In Name Only (39); Made for Each Other (39); •Abe Lincoln in Illinois (40); Victory (40); So Ends Our Night (41); Son of Fury (42); •Since You Went Away (44); •Enchanted Cottage, The (45); •Anna and the King of Siam (46); Dead Reckoning (47); Night Song (47); Caged (50); Company She Keeps, The (50); •Racket, The (51); Goddess, The (58); Scavengers, The (59); Matter of Morals, A (61)

CRONENBERG, DAVID
Stereo (69); Crimes of the Future (70); They Came from Within (75); •Rabid (77); Fast Company (79); •Brood, The (79); •Scanners (81); •Videodrome (83); •Dead Zone, The (83); •Fly, The (86); •Dead Ringers (88); •Naked Lunch (91); M. Butterfly (93); •Crash (96); •eXistenZ (99); Spider (02); History of Violence, A (05)

CROWE, CAMERON
•Say Anything (89); •Singles (92); •Jerry Maguire (96); •Almost Famous (00); •Vanilla Sky (01)

CUARON, ALFONSO
Love in the Time of Hysteria (91); •Little Princess, A (95); •Great Expectations (98); •Y Tu Mama Tambien (01); •Harry Potter and the Prisoner of Azkaban (04)

CUKOR, GEORGE
Grumpy (30); •Royal Family of Broadway, The (30); Virtuous Sin, The (30); Girls About Town (31); Tarnished Lady (31); •Bill of Divorcement, A (32); One Hour with You (32); Rockabye (32); What Price Hollywood? (32); •Dinner at Eight (33); •Little Women (33); Our Betters (33); •David Copperfield (35); No More Ladies (35); •Romeo and Juliet (36); Sylvia

Scarlett (36); •Camille (37); •Prisoner of Zenda, The (37); Holiday (38); I Met My Love Again (38); •Gone with the Wind (39); •Women, The (39); Zaza (39); •Philadelphia Story, The (40); Susan and God (40); Two-Faced Woman (41); Woman's Face, A (41); Her Cardboard Lover (42); Keeper of the Flame (42); •Gaslight (44); Winged Victory (44); Desire Me (47); •Double Life, A (47); •Adam's Rib (49); Edward, My Son (49); Life of Her Own, A (50); •Born Yesterday (51); Model and the Marriage Broker, The (51); Marrying Kind, The (52); •Pat and Mike (52); Actress, The (53); •It Should Happen to You (54); •Star Is Born, A (54); Bhowani Junction (56); •Les Girls (57); Wild Is the Wind (57); Heller in Pink Tights (60); Let's Make Love (60); Song Without End (60); Chapman Report, The (62); •My Fair Lady (64); Justine (69); Travels with My Aunt (72); Blue Bird, The (76); Rich and Famous (81)

CURTIZ, MICHAEL
Noah's Ark (28); Tenderloin (28); Gamblers, The (29); Glad Rag Doll, The (29); Hearts in Exile (29); Madonna of Avenue A, The (29); Mammy (30); Matrimonial Bed, The (30); Under A Texas Moon (30); Bright Lights (31); God's Gift to Women (31); Mad Genius, The (31); River's End (31); Soldier's Plaything, A (31); Cabin in the Cotton, The (32); •Doctor X (32); Strange Love of Molly Louvain, The (32); Woman from Monte Carlo, The (32); Female (33); Goodbye Again (33); •Kennel Murder Case, The (33); Keyhole, The (33); •Mystery of the Wax Museum, The (33); Private Detective 62 (33); •20,000 Years in Sing Sing (33); British Agent (34); Jimmy the Gent (34); Key, The (34); Mandalay (34); Black Fury (35); •Captain Blood (35); Case of the Curious Bride, The (35); Front Page Woman (35); Little Big Shot (35); •Charge of the Light Brigade, The (36); Walking Dead, The (36); •Kid Galahad (37); Mountain Justice (37); Perfect Specimen, The (37); Stolen Holiday (37); •Adventures of Robin Hood, The (38); •Angels with Dirty Faces (38); •Four Daughters (38); Four's A Crowd (38); Gold Is Where You Find It (38); Daughters Courageous (39); •Dodge City (39); Four Wives (39); Private Lives of Elizabeth and Essex, The (39); •Santa Fe Trail (40); •Sea Hawk, The (40); Virginia City (40); Dive Bomber (41); •Sea Wolf, The (41); Captains of the Clouds (42); •Casablanca (42); •Yankee Doodle Dandy (42); Mission to Moscow (43); •This Is the Army (43); Janie (44); •Passage to Marseille (44); •Mildred Pierce (45); Roughly Speaking (45); Night and Day (46); •Life with Father (47); Unsuspected, The (47); Romance on the High Seas (48); Flamingo Road (49); Lady Takes a Sailor, The (49); My Dream Is Yours (49); Breaking Point, The (50); Bright Leaf (50); •Young Man with a Horn (50); Force of Arms (51); I'll See You in My Dreams (51); •Jim Thorpe—All American (51); Story of Will Rogers, The (52); Jazz Singer, The (53); Trouble Along the Way (53); Boy from Oklahoma, The (54); Egyptian, The (54); •White Christmas (54); We're No Angels (55); Best Things in Life Are Free, The (56); Scarlet Hour, The (56); Vagabond King,

The (56); Helen Morgan Story, The (57); King Creole (58); Proud Rebel, The (58); Hangman, The (59); Man in the Net, The (59); Adventures of Huckleberry Finn, The (60); Breath of Scandal, A (60); Comancheros, The (61); Francis of Assisi (61)

DA COSTA, MORTON
•Auntie Mame (58); •Music Man, The (62); Island of Love (63)

DAHL, JOHN
Kill Me Again (90); •Last Seduction, The (94); •Red Rock West (94); Unforgettable (96); Rounders (98); Joy Ride (01); Great Raid, The (05)

DALDRY, STEPHEN
•Billy Elliot (00); •Hours, The (02)

DANTE, JOE
•Hollywood Boulevard (76); Piranha (78); •Howling, The (81); Twilight Zone—The Movie (83); Gremlins (84); Explorers (85); Amazon Women on the Moon (87); Innerspace (87); 'burbs, The (89); •Gremlins 2: The New Batch(90); •Matinee (93); Runaway Daughters (94); Second Civil War, The (97); Warlord: The Battle for the Galaxy (98); •Small Soldiers (98); Looney Tunes: Back in Action (03)

DARABONT, FRANK
•Shawshank Redemption, The (94); •Green Mile, The (99); •Majestic, The (01)

DASSIN, JULES
Affairs of Martha, The (42); Nazi Agent (42); Reunion in France (42); Young Ideas (43); Canterville Ghost, The (44); Letter for Evie, A (45); Two Smart People (46); •Brute Force (47); •Naked City, The (48); Thieves' Highway (49); •Night and the City (50); •Rififi (54); Where the Hot Wind Blows (58); •Never on Sunday (60); Phaedra (62); •Topkapi (64); 10:30 P.M. Summer (66); Uptight (68); Promise at Dawn (70); Dream of Passion, A (78); Circle of Two (80)

DAVES, DELMER
Destination Tokyo (44); •Hollywood Canteen (44); Very Thought of You, The (44); •Pride of the Marines (45); •Dark Passage (47); Red House, The (47); To the Victor (48); Kiss in the Dark, A (49); Task Force (49); Broken Arrow (50); Bird of Paradise (51); Return of the Texan (52); Never Let Me Go (53); Treasure of the Golden Condor (53); Demetrius and the Gladiators (54); Drum Beat (54); •Jubal (56); Last Wagon, The (56); •3:10 to Yuma (57); Badlanders, The (58); Cowboy (58); Kings Go Forth (58); Hanging Tree, The (59); Summer Place, A (59); Parrish (61); Susan Slade (61); Rome Adventure (62); Spencer's Mountain (63); Battle of the Villa Fiorita, The (64); Youngblood Hawke (64)

DAVIES, TERENCE
Madonna and Child (80); Death and Transfiguration (83); •Distant Voices, Still Lives (88); •Long Day Closes, The (92); Neon Bible, The (95); •House of Mirth, The (00)

DAVIS, ANDREW
Stony Island (78); Final Terror, The (83); Code of Silence (85); Above the Law (88); Package, The (89); •Under Siege (92); •Fugitive, The (93);

Steal Big, Steal Little (95); Chain Reaction (96); Perfect Murder, A (98); Collateral Damage (02); Holes (03)

DAVIS, OSSIE
•Cotton Comes to Harlem (70); Kongi's Harvest (71); Black Girl (72); Gordon's War (73); Countdown at Kusini (76)

DE BONT, JAN
•Speed (94); •Twister (96); Speed 2: Cruise Control (97); •Haunting, The (99); Lara Croft Tomb Raider: The Cradle of Life (03)

DE BROCA, PHILIPPE
Love Game, The (60); Joker, The (61); Five Day Lovers, The (61); Seven Capital Sins (61); Les Veinards (62); Cartouche (62); Male Companion (64); •That Man from Rio (64); Up to His Ears (65); •King Of Hearts (66); Oldest Profession, The (67); Devil by the Tail, The (69); Give Her the Moon (70); Touch and Go (71); Chere Louise (72); Magnificent One, The (73); Incorrigible (75); Julie Pot de Colle (77); Dear Detective (77); Jupiter's Thigh (79); Le Cavaleur (79); Psy (81); African, The (83); Louisiane (84); Gypsy, The (86); Chouans! (88); Scheherazade (90); Les Cles du Paradis (91); Green House, The (95); Le Veilleur de Nuit (96); Le Bossu (97); Amazon (00); Madame Sans-Gene (02); Y Aura pas Ecole Demain (03); Viper in the Fist (04)

DE PALMA, BRIAN
•Greetings (68); Murder a la Mod (68); Wedding Party, The (69); •Hi, Mom! (70); Get to Know Your Rabbit (72); Sisters (73); Phantom of the Paradise (74); •Carrie (76); Obsession (76); Fury, The (78); Home Movies (79); •Dressed to Kill (80); •Blow Out (81); •Scarface (83); Body Double (84); Wise Guys (86); •Untouchables, The (87); •Casualties of War (89); Bonfire of the Vanities, The (90); Raising Cain (92); •Carlito's Way (93); •Mission: Impossible (96); Snake Eyes (98); Mission to Mars (00); Femme Fatale (02)

DE SICA, VITTORIO
Rose Scarlatte (40); Maddalena Zero in Condotta (41); Doctor Beware (41); Un Garibaldino al Convento (42); Little Martyr, The (43); •Shoeshine (46); La Porta del Cielo (46); •Bicycle Thief, The (48); •Miracle in Milan (51); •Umberto D. (52); Indiscretion of an American Wife (53); •Gold of Naples (54); Roof, The (56); •Two Women (60); Il Giudizio Universale (61); •Boccaccio '70 (62); Condemned of Altona, The (62); •Yesterday, Today, and Tomorrow (63); Marriage—Italian Style (64); After the Fox (66); Young World, A (66); Witches, The (67); Woman Times Seven (67); Place for Lovers, A (69); Sunflower (70); •Garden of the Finzi-Continis, The (71); Lo Chiameremo Andrea (72); Brief Vacation, A (73); Voyage, The (73)

DE TOTH, ANDRE
Passport to Suez (43); Dark Waters (44); None Shall Escape (44); Other Love, The (47); Ramrod (47); Pitfall (48); Slattery's Hurricane (49); Man in the Saddle (51); Carson City (52); Last of the Comanches (52); Springfield

Rifle (52); •House of Wax (53); Stranger Wore a Gun, The (53); Thunder Over the Plains (53); Bounty Hunter, The (54); Crime Wave (54); Riding Shotgun (54); Tanganyika (54); Indian Fighter, The (55); Hidden Fear (57); Monkey on My Back (57); Two-Headed Spy, The (58); Day of the Outlaw (59); Man on a String (60); Morgan the Pirate (60); Mongols, The (61); Gold for the Caesars (63); Play Dirty (69)

DEARDEN, BASIL
Black Sheep of Whitehall, The (41); Goose Steps Out, The (42); Bells Go Down, The (43); My Learned Friend (43); Half-Way House, The (44); They Came to a City (44); •Dead of Night (45); Captive Heart, The (46); Frieda (47); Saraband (48); Blue Lamp, The (49); Train of Events (49); Cage of Gold (50); Pool of London (50); Gentle Gunman, The (52); I Believe in You (52); Square Ring, The (53); Out of the Clouds (54); Rainbow Jacket, The (54); Ship That Died of Shame, The (55); Who Done It? (56); Smallest Show on Earth, The (57); Violent Playground (58); •Sapphire (59); League of Gentlemen, The (60); All Night Long (61); Man in the Moon (61); Secret Partner, The (61); •Victim (61); Walk in the Shadow (62); Mind Benders, The (63); Place to Go, A (63); Woman of Straw (64); Masquerade (65); •Khartoum (66); Assassination Bureau, The (68); Only When I Larf (68); Man Who Haunted Himself, The (70)

DEMILLE, CECIL B.
Godless Girl, The (29); Dynamite (30); Madame Satan (30); Squaw Man, The (31); Sign of the Cross (32); This Day and Age (33); •Cleopatra (34); Four Frightened People (34); Crusades, The (35); Plainsman, The (37); Buccaneer, The (38); •Union Pacific (39); Northwest Mounted Police (40); Reap the Wild Wind (42); Story of Dr. Wassell, The (44); Unconquered (47); •Samson and Delilah (49); •Greatest Show on Earth, The (52); •Ten Commandments, The (56)

DEMME, JONATHAN
Caged Heat (74); Crazy Mama (75); Fighting Mad (76); •Citizens Band (77); Last Embrace (79); •Melvin and Howard (80); Who Am I This Time? (82); •Swing Shift (84); •Something Wild (86); •Swimming to Cambodia (87); •Married to the Mob (88); •Silence of the Lambs, The (91); Cousin Bobby (92); •Philadelphia (93); •Beloved (98); Storefront Hitchcock (98); Truth About Charlie, The (02); Agronomist, The (04); •Manchurian Candidate, The (04)

DEMME, TED
Who's the Man? (93); Ref, The (94); Beautiful Girls (96); Monument Ave. (98); •Life (99); •Blow (01); Decade Under the Influence, A (03)

DEMY, JACQUES
•Lola (61); Seven Capital Sins (61); Bay of Angels (62); •Umbrellas of Cherbourg, The (64); Young Girls of Rochefort, The (67); Model Shop, The (69); Donkey Skin (71); Pied Piper, The (72); Lady Oscar (78); Parking (85)

DEUTCH, HOWARD
•Pretty in Pink (86); Some Kind of Wonderful (87); Great Outdoors, The (88); Article 99 (92); Getting Even with Dad (94); Grumpier Old Men (95); Neil Simon's The Odd Couple II (98); Replacements, The (00); Gleason (02); Whole Ten Yards, The (04)

DIEGUES, CARLOS
Domingo (61); Ganga Zumba (64); Big City, The (66); Inheritors, The (69); Un Sejour (70); Receita de Futebol (71); When the Carnival Comes (72); Joana a Francesca (73); Xica (76); Anibal Machado (74); Summer Rain, A (77); •Bye-Bye Brazil (80); •Quilombo (84); Subway to the Stars (88); Better Days Ahead (89); Rio's Love Songs (94); Tieta (96); Orfeu (99); God Is Brazilian (03)

DIETERLE, WILLIAM
Her Majesty Love (31); Last Flight, The (31); Crash, The (32); Jewel Robbery (32); Man Wanted (32); Scarlet Dawn (32); Six Hours to Live (32); Adorable (33); Devil's in Love, The (33); Female (33); From Headquarters (33); Grand Slam (33); Lawyer Man (33); Fashions of 1934 (34); Firebird, The (34); •Fog Over Frisco (34); Madame du Barry (34); Dr. Socrates (35); •Midsummer Night's Dream, A (35); Secret Bride, The (35); Satan Met a Lady (36); •Story of Louis Pasteur, The (36); White Angel, The (36); Another Dawn (37); Great O'Malley, The (37); •Life of Emile Zola, The (37); Blockade (38); •Hunchback of Notre Dame, The (39); •Juarez (39); Dispatch from Reuters, A (40); •Dr. Ehrlich's Magic Bullet (40); •Devil and Daniel Webster, The (41); Syncopation (42); Tennessee Johnson (42); I'll Be Seeing You (44); Kismet (44); Love Letters (45); This Love of Ours (45); Searching Wind, The (46); •Portrait of Jennie (48); Accused, The (49); Rope of Sand (49); Dark City (50); Paid in Full (50); September Affair (50); Peking Express (51); Red Mountain (51); Boots Malone (52); Turning Point, The (52); Salome (53); Volcano (53); Elephant Walk (54); Magic Fire (56); Life, Loves and Adventures of Omar Khayyam, The (57); Mistress of the World (59); Die Fastnachtsbeichte (60); Quick, Let's Get Married (65)

DMYTRYK, EDWARD
Million Dollar Legs (39); Television Spy (39); Emergency Squad (40); Golden Gloves (40); Her First Romance (40); Mystery Sea Raider (40); Blonde from Singapore, The (41); Confessions of Boston Blackie (41); Devil Commands, The (41); Secrets of the Lone Wolf (41); Sweetheart of the Campus (41); Under Age (41); Counter-Espionage (42); Hitler's Children (42); Seven Miles from Alcatraz (42); Behind the Rising Sun (43); Captive Wild Woman (43); Falcon Strikes Back, The (43); Tender Comrade (43); •Back to Bataan (45); •Cornered (45); •Murder, My Sweet (45); Till the End of Time (46); •Crossfire (47); So Well Remembered (47); Hidden Room, The (49); Salt to the Devil (49); Eight Iron Men (52); Mutiny (52); Sniper, The (52); •Juggler, The (53); Broken Lance (54); •Caine Mutiny, The (54); End of the Affair, The (54); Left Hand of God, The (55); Soldier of Fortune (55); Mountain,

The (56); Raintree County (57); •Young Lions,
The (58); Blue Angel, The (59); •Warlock (59);
Reluctant Saint, The (62); Walk on the Wild
Side (62); Carpetbaggers, The (64); Where Love
Has Gone (64); Mirage (65); Alvarez Kelly (66);
Anzio (68); Shalako (68); Bluebeard (72); Human
Factor, The (75)

DONALDSON, ROGER
Sleeping Dogs (77); •Smash Palace (81); Bounty,
The (84); •Marie (85); •No Way Out (87);
Cocktail (88); Cadillac Man (90); White
Sands (92); Getaway, The (94); Species (95);
Dante's Peak (97); •Thirteen Days (00); •Recruit,
The (03)

DONEN, STANLEY
•On the Town (49); •Royal Wedding (51); Fearless
Fagan (52); Love Is Better than Ever (52); •Singin'
in the Rain (52); Give a Girl a Break (53); Deep in
My Heart (54); •Seven Brides for Seven
Brothers (54); •It's Always Fair Weather (55);
•Funny Face (57); Kiss Them for Me (57); •Pajama
Game, The (57); •Damn Yankees (58);
•Indiscreet (58); Grass Is Greener, The (60); Once
More, with Feeling (60); Surprise Package (60);
•Charade (63); Arabesque (66); •Bedazzled (67);
•Two for the Road (67); Staircase (69); Little
Prince, The (74); Lucky Lady (75); •Movie
Movie (78); Saturn 3 (80); Blame It on Rio (84);
Love Letters (99)

DONNER, RICHARD
X-15 (61); Salt and Pepper (68); Lola (69); •Omen,
The (76); •Superman (78); Inside Moves (80); Toy,
The (82); Goonies, The (85); •Ladyhawke (85);
•Lethal Weapon (87); Scrooged (88); •Lethal
Weapon 2 (89); •Lethal Weapon 3 (92); Radio
Flyer (92); Maverick (94); Assassins (95);
Conspiracy Theory (97); •Lethal Weapon 4 (98);
Timeline (03)

DORRIE, DORIS
First Waltz, The (77); Straight Through the
Heart (83); In the Belly of the Whale (84);
•Men. . . (85); Paradise (86); Me and Him (89);
Money (89); Happy Birthday, Turke! (92); Nobody
Loves Me (94); Am I Beautiful? (98);
Enlightenment Guaranteed (00); Naked (02); Ein
Seltsames Paar (04)

DREYER, CARL-THEODOR
•Vampyr (32); •Day of Wrath (43); Two
People (45); •Ordet (55); Gertrud (64)

DUIGAN, JOHN
Firm Man, The (75); Trespassers, The (76); Mouth
to Mouth (78); Dimboola (79); Winter of Our
Dreams (81); Far East (83); One Night Stand (83);
Year My Voice Broke, The (87); Romero (89);
•Flirting (90); Wide Sargasso Sea (93);
Sirens (94); Journey of August King, The (95);
Leading Man, The (96); Lawn Dogs (97);
Molly (99); Paranoid (00); Parole Officer,
The (01); Head in the Clouds (04)

DUVIVIER, JULIEN
David Golder (30); Les Cinq Gentlemen
Maudits (32); Allo Berlin? Ici Paris! (32); Poil de
Carotte (32); La Venus du College (32); La Tete
d'un Homme (33); La Machine a Refaire la
Vie (33); Le Petit Roi (33); La Paquebot

"Tenacity" (34); Naked Heart, The (34); Escape
from Yesterday (35); Golgotha (35); Golem,
The (36); Man of the Hour, The (36); They Were
Five (36); •Pepe le Moko (37); Un Carnet de
Bal (37); Great Waltz, The (38); •Marie
Antoinette (38); End of a Day, The (39); La
Charrette Fantome (39); Lydia (41); •Tales of
Manhattan (42); Heart of a Nation, The (43); Flesh
and Fantasy (43); Destiny (44); Imposter, The (44);
Panique (46); •Anna Karenina (47); Sinners,
The (49); Captain Black Jack (50); Little World of
Don Camillo, The (51); Under the Paris Sky (51);
Holiday for Henrietta (52); Return of Don Camillo,
The (53); On Trial (54); Marianne of My
Youth (55); Deadlier than the Male (56); Man in
the Raincoat, The (57); Pot-Bouille (57); Female,
The (59); Marie Octobre (59); La Grande Vie (60);
Boulevard (60); Burning Court, The (62); Devil
and the Ten Commandments, The (62); Highway
Pickup (63); Diabolically Yours (67)

DWAN, ALLAN
Frozen Justice (29); Iron Mask, The (29); South
Sea Rose (29); What a Widow! (30); Chances (31);
Man to Man (31); Wicked (31); Her First
Affaire (32); While Paris Sleeps (32); Counsel's
Opinion (33); I Spy (33); Hollywood Party (34);
Black Sheep (35); 15 Maiden Lane (36); High
Tension (36); Human Cargo (36); Navy Wife (36);
Song and Dance Man, The (36); Heidi (37); One
Mile from Heaven (37); That I May Live (37);
Woman-Wise (37); Josette (38); Rebecca of
Sunnybrook Farm (38); Suez (38); Frontier
Marshal (39); Gorilla, The (39); Three Musketeers,
The (39); Sailor's Lady (40); Trail of the
Vigilantes (40); Young People (40); Look Who's
Laughing (41); Rise and Shine (41); Friendly
Enemies (42); Here We Go Again (42); Around the
World (43); Abroad with Two Yanks (44); Up in
Mabel's Room (44); •Brewster's Millions (45);
Getting Gertie's Garter (45); Rendezvous with
Annie (46); Calendar Girl (47); Driftwood (47);
Northwest Outpost (47); Angel in Exile (48);
Inside Story, The (48); •Sands of Iwo Jima (49);
Surrender (50); Belle le Grand (51); I Dream of
Jeanie (52); Montana Belle (52); Wild Blue
Yonder, The (52); Flight Nurse (53); Sweethearts
on Parade (53); Woman They Almost Lynched,
The (53); Cattle Queen of Montana (54);
Passion (54); Silver Lode (54); Escape to
Burma (55); Pearl of the South Pacific (55);
Tennessee's Partner (55); Hold Back the
Night (56); Slightly Scarlet (56); Restless Breed,
The (57); River's Edge, The (57); Enchanted
Island (58); Most Dangerous Man Alive (61)

EASTWOOD, CLINT
•Play Misty for Me (71); Breezy (73); •High Plains
Drifter (73); Eiger Sanction, The (75); •Outlaw
Josey Wales, The (76); Gauntlet, The (77);
Bronco Billy (80); Firefox (82); Honkytonk
Man (82); Sudden Impact (83); •Pale Rider (85);
•Heartbreak Ridge (86); •Bird (88); Rookie,
The (90); •White Hunter, Black Heart (90);
•Unforgiven (92); •Perfect World, A (93); •Bridges
of Madison County, The (95); Absolute
Power (97); •Midnight in the Garden of Good and

Evil (97); True Crime (99); Space Cowboys (00);
Blood Work (02); •Mystic River (03); •Million
Dollar Baby (04)

EDEL, ULI
Christiane F. (81); Eine Art von Zorn (84); •Last
Exit to Brooklyn (89); Body of Evidence (93);
Confessions of a Sorority Girl (94); Tyson (95);
Rasputin (96); Purgatory (99); Little Vampire,
The (00); King of Texas (02); Julius Caesar (02);
Evil Never Dies (03); Ring of the Nibelungs (04)

EDWARDS, BLAKE
Bring Your Smile Along (55); He Laughed
Last (56); Mister Cory (57); Perfect Furlough,
The (58); This Happy Feeling (58); •Operation
Petticoat (59); High Time (60); •Breakfast at
Tiffany's (61); •Days of Wine and Roses (62);
Experiment in Terror (62); •Pink Panther, The (64);
•Shot in the Dark, A (64); Great Race, The (65);
What Did You Do in the War, Daddy? (66);
Gunn (67); Party, The (68); •Darling Lili (70);
Wild Rovers (71); Carey Treatment, The (72);
Tamarind Seed, The (74); •Return of the Pink
Panther, The (75); •Pink Panther Strikes Again,
The (76); Revenge of the Pink Panther (78);
•10 (79); S.O.B. (81); Trail of the Pink Panther,
The (82); •Victor/Victoria (82); Curse of the Pink
Panther (83); Man Who Loved Women, The (83);
Micki & Maude (84); Fine Mess, A (86); That's
Life! (86); Blind Date (87); Sunset (88); Skin
Deep (89); Switch (91); Blake Edwards' Son of the
Pink Panther (93)

EDZARD, CHRISTINE
Stories from a Flying Trunk (79); Biddy (83);
•Little Dorrit (88); Fool, The (90); As You Like
It (92); Imax Nutcracker, The (97); Children's
Midsummer Night's Dream, The (01)

EGOYAN, ATOM
Howard in Particular (79); After Grad with
Dad (80); Peep Show (81); Open House (82); Next
of Kin (84); In this Corner (85); Men: A Passion
Playground (85); Family Viewing (87); Final
Twist, The (87); La Boite a Soleil (88); Looking
for Nothing (88); Speaking Parts (89); Montreal Vu
Par. . . (91); Adjuster, The (91); Gross
Misconduct (92); Calendar (93); •Exotica (94);
•Sweet Hereafter, The (97); Bach Cello Suite #4:
Sarabande (97); •Felicia's Journey (99);
Ararat (02); Where the Truth Lies (05)

EISENSTEIN, SERGEI
•Alexander Nevsky (38); •Ivan the Terrible, Parts I
& II (58)

ELLIOTT, STEPHAN
Frauds (93); •Adventures of Priscilla, Queen of
The Desert, The (94); Welcome to Woop
Woop (97); Eye of The Beholder (99)

EMMERICH, ROLAND
Noah's Ark Principle, The (84); Making
Contact/Joey (85); Ghost Chase (88); Moon
44 (91); Universal Soldier (92); •Stargate (94);
•Independence Day (96); •Godzilla (98); •Patriot,
The (00); •Day After Tomorrow, The (04)

ENYEDI, ILDIKO
Flirt (81); Rosenkavalier (81); New Books (82);
Viewer, The (85); Invasion (85); Mole, The (86);
•My 20th Century (89); Winter War (91); Magic
Hunter (94); Tamas et Juli (97); Simon Magus (99)

EPHRON, NORA
This Is My Life (92); •Sleepless in Seattle (93);
Mixed Nuts (94); •Michael (96); •You've Got
Mail (98); Lucky Numbers (00)

ERICE, VICTOR
•Spirit of the Beehive, The (73); El Sur (83);
•Dream oOf Light (93)

EUSTACHE, JEAN
Bad Company (67); •Mother and the Whore,
The (73); My Little Loves (75); Dirty Story, A (77)

EYRE, RICHARD
Imitation Game, The (80); Country (81); Loose
Connections (83); •Ploughman's Lunch, The (83);
Laughterhouse (84); Past Caring (85); Insurance
Man, The (85); Tumbledown (85); Suddenly, Last
Summer (93); King Lear (97); Rockaby (00);
•Iris (01); Stage Beauty (04)

FARRELLY, PETER and BOBBY
•Dumb & Dumber (94); Kingpin (96); •There's
Something About Mary; Me, Myself & Irene (00);
Osmosis Jones (01); Shallow Hal (01); •Stuck on
You (03); •Fever Pitch (04)

FARROW, JOHN
Men in Exile (37); She Loved a Fireman (37);
West of Shanghai (37); Broadway
Musketeers (38); Invisible Menace, The (38); Little
Miss Thoroughbred (38); My Bill (38); Five Came
Back (39); Full Confession (39); Reno (39); •Saint
Strikes Back, The (39); Sorority House (39);
Women in the Wind (39); Bill of Divorcement,
A (40); Married And in Love (40); Commandos
Strike at Dawn, The (42); •Wake Island (42);
China (43); Hitler Gang, The (44); You Came
Along (45); California (46); Two Years before the
Mast (46); Blaze of Noon (47); Calcutta (47); Easy
Come, Easy Go (47); Beyond Glory (48); •Big
Clock, The (48); Night Has a Thousand Eyes (48);
Alias Nick Beal (49); Red, Hot and Blue (49);
Copper Canyon (50); Where Danger Lives (50);
His Kind of Woman (51); Submarine
Command (51); Botany Bay (53); Hondo (53);
Plunder of the Sun (53); Ride, Vaquero! (53);
Bullet Is Waiting, A (54); Sea Chase, The (55);
Back from Eternity (56); Unholy Wife, The (57);
Alias Jesse James (59); John Paul Jones (59)

FASSBINDER, RAINER WERNER
Love Is Colder than Death (69);
Katzelmacher (69); American Soldier, The (70);
Gods of the Plague (70); Why Does Herr R. Run
Amok? (70); The Niklashausen Journey (70); Rio
Das Mortes (71); Recruits in Ingolstadt(71); The
Coffeehouse (71); Whity (71); Beware the Holy
Whore (71); Merchant of Four Seasons, The (72);
Bitter Tears of Petra Von Kant, The (72);
Bremen Freedom (72); Jail Bait (72); •Effi
Briest (74); •Ali, Fear Eats The Soul (74); World
on a Wire (74); Fox and His Friends (75); Mother
Kusters Goes to Heaven (75); Fear of Fear (76);
Chinese Roulette (76); I Only Want You to Love
Me (76); Satan's Brew (76); Stationmaster's Wife,

The (77); Women in New York (77); Despair (78);
Germany in Autumn (78); In a Year Of Thirteen
Moons (78); •Marriage of Maria Braun, The (78);
Third Generation, The (79); •Berlin
Alexanderplatz (79); •Lili Marleen (81); Theater in
Trance (81); Lola (82); •Veronika Voss (82);
Querelle (82)

FELLINI, FEDERICO
Variety Lights (50); •White Sheik, The (52);
•Vitelloni (53); •La Strada (54); •Swindle,
The (55); •Nights of Cabiria (57); •La Dolce
Vita (60); •Boccaccio '70 (62); •8 1/2 (63); •Juliet
of the Spirits (65); Spirits of the Dead (68); •Fellini
Satyricon (69); •Fellini's Roma (72);
•Amarcord (74); Casanova (76); •City of
Women (80); •And the Ship Sails On (83); Ginger
and Fred (86); Intervista (87)

FERRARA, ABEL
•Driller Killer (79); Ms. 45 (81); Fear City (84);
China Girl (87); •King of New York (90); Cat
Chaser (91); •Bad Lieutenant (92); Dangerous
Game (93); Body Snatchers (94); Addiction,
The (95); Funeral, The (96); Blackout, The (97);
New Rose Hotel (98); R-Xmas (01)

FIGGIS, MIKE
House, The (84); •Stormy Monday (88); Internal
Affairs (90); Liebestraum (91); Mr. Jones (93);
Browning Version, The (94); •Leaving Las
Vegas (95); One Night Stand (97); Loss of Sexual
Innocence, The (99); Miss Julie (99); •Time
Code (00); Hotel (02); Battle of Orgreave,
The (2001); Cold Creek Manor (03)

FINCHER, DAVID
•Alien³ (92); •Seven (95); Game, The (97); •Fight
Club (99); •Panic Room (02)

FISHER, TERENCE
Colonel Bogey (48); Girl in the Painting, The (48);
Song for Tomorrow, A (48); Astonished Heart,
The (49); Marry Me! (49); So Long at the
Fair (50); Home to Danger (51); Dead on
Course (52); Distant Trumpet (52); Four-Sided
Triangle (52); Man Bait (52); Stolen Face (52);
Blood Orange (53); Spaceways (53); Three's
Company (53); Unholy Four, The (53); Woman in
Hiding (53); Black Glove (54); Blackout (54);
Children Galore (54); Final Appointment (54);
Race for Life, A (54); Flaw, The (55); Stolen
Assignment (55); Dynamiters, The (56); Last Man
to Hang, The (56); Curse of Frankenstein,
The (57); Kill Me Tomorrow (57); •Horror of
Dracula (58); Revenge of Frankenstein, The (58);
Hound of the Baskervilles, The (59); Man Who
Could Cheat Death, The (59); •Mummy, The (59);
Brides of Dracula, The (60); House of Fright (60);
Stranglers of Bombay, The (60); Sword of
Sherwood Forest (60); Curse of the Werewolf,
The (61); •Phantom of the Opera, The (62);
Sherlock Holmes and the Deadly Necklace (62);
Earth Dies Screaming, The (64); Gorgon, The (64);
Horror of It All, The (64); Dracula—Prince of
Darkness (66); Frankenstein Created Woman (66);
Island of Terror (66); Island of the Burning
Damned (67); Devil's Bride, The (68);
Frankenstein Must Be Destroyed! (69);
Frankenstein and the Monster from Hell (73)

FITZGERALD, THOM
•Hanging Garden, The (98); •Beefcake (99); Wild
Dogs, The (02); Event, The (03)

FLEISCHER, RICHARD
Child of Divorce (46); Banjo (47);
Bodyguard (48); So This Is New York (48); Clay
Pigeon, The (49); Follow Me Quietly (49);
Trapped (49); Armored Car Robbery (50); Happy
Time, The (52); •Narrow Margin, The (52);
Arena (53); •20,000 Leagues Under The Sea (54);
Girl in the Red Velvet Swing, The (55); Violent
Saturday (55); Bandido (56); Between Heaven and
Hell (56); Vikings, The (58); •Compulsion (59);
These Thousand Hills (59); Crack in the
Mirror (60); Big Gamble, The (61); Barabbas (62);
•Fantastic Voyage (66); •Doctor Dolittle (67);
Boston Strangler, The (68); Che! (69); •10
Rillington Place (70); Tora! Tora! Tora! (70); Last
Run, The (71); See No Evil (71); New Centurions,
The (72); Don Is Dead, The (73); Soylent
Green (73); Mr. Majestyk (74); Spikes Gang,
The (74); Mandingo (75); Incredible Sarah,
The (76); Crossed Swords (78); Ashanti (79); Jazz
Singer, The (80); Amityville 3-D (83); Tough
Enough (83); Conan the Destroyer (84); Red
Sonja (85); Million Dollar Mystery (87)

FLEMING, VICTOR
Abie's Irish Rose (28); •Virginian, The (29); Wolf
Song (29); Common Clay (30); Renegades (30);
Red Dust (32); Wet Parade, The (32);
•Bombshell (33); White Sister, The (33); •Treasure
Island (34); Farmer Takes a Wife, The (35);
Reckless (35); •Captains Courageous (37); •Test
Pilot (38); •Gone with the Wind (39); •Wizard of
Oz, The (39); Dr. Jekyll and Mr. Hyde (41);
•Tortilla Flat (42); •Guy Named Joe, A (44);
Adventure (45); Joan of Arc (48)

FOLEY, JAMES
Reckless (84); •At Close Range (86); Who's That
Girl (87); •After Dark, My Sweet (90); •Glengarry
Glen Ross (92); Two Bits (95); Fear (96);
Chamber, The (96); Corruptor, The (99);
Confidence (03)

FORBES, BRYAN
•Whistle Down the Wind (61); •L-Shaped Room,
The (62); Of Human Bondage (64); •Seance on a
Wet Afternoon (64); King Rat (65); Whisperers,
The (66); Wrong Box, The (66); Deadfall (68);
Madwoman of Chaillot, The (69); Long Ago,
Tomorrow (70); I Am a Dancer (72); •Stepford
Wives, The (75); Slipper and the Rose, The (76);
International Velvet (78); Sunday Lovers (80);
Jessie (80); Better Late than Never (83); Naked
Face, The (84); Endless Game, The (90)

FORD, JOHN
Black Watch, The (29); Salute (29); Born
Reckless (30); Men Without Women (30); Up the
River (30); •Arrowsmith (31); Brat, The (31); Seas
Beneath (31); Air Mail (32); Flesh (32); Dr.
Bull (33); Pilgrimage (33); Judge Priest (34);
•Lost Patrol, The (34); World Moves On, The (34);
•Informer, The (35); Steamboat 'Round the
Bend (35); •Whole Town's Talking, The (35);
Mary of Scotland (36); Plough and the Stars,
The (36); •Prisoner of Shark Island, The (36);
•Hurricane, The (37); •Wee Willie Winkie (37);

Four Men and a Prayer (38); •Drums Along the Mohawk (39); •Stagecoach (39); •Young Mr. Lincoln (39); •Grapes of Wrath, The (40); •Long Voyage Home, The (40); •How Green Was My Valley (41); •Tobacco Road (41); •They Were Expendable (45); •My Darling Clementine (46); •Fugitive, The (47); •Fort Apache (48); •Three Godfathers, The (48); •She Wore a Yellow Ribbon (49); •Rio Grande (50); •Wagonmaster (50); When Willie Comes Marching Home (50); •Quiet Man, The (52); What Price Glory? (52); •Mogambo (53); Sun Shines Bright, The (53); Long Gray Line, The (55); •Mister Roberts (55); •Searchers, The (56); Rising of the Moon, The (57); Wings of Eagles, The (57); Gideon of Scotland Yard (58); Last Hurrah, The (58); •Horse Soldiers, The (59); Sergeant Rutledge (60); Two Rode Together (61); •Man Who Shot Liberty Valance, The (62); Donovan's Reef (63); •How the West Was Won (63); •Cheyenne Autumn (64); Young Cassidy (65); Seven Women (66)

FORMAN, MILOS
Black Peter (64); •Loves of a Blonde (65); •Fireman's Ball, The (67); •Taking Off (71); Visions of Eight (73); •One Flew Over the Cuckoo's Nest (75); •Hair (79); •Ragtime (81); •Amadeus (84); Valmont (89); •People vs. Larry Flynt, The (96); •Man on the Moon (99)

FORSTER, MARC
Everything Put Together (00); •Monster's Ball (01); •Finding Neverland (04)

FORSYTH, BILL
•That Sinking Feeling (79); •Gregory's Girl (81); •Local Hero (83); Comfort and Joy (84); •Housekeeping (87); Breaking In (89); Being Human (94); Gregory's 2 Girls (98)

FOSSE, BOB
•Sweet Charity (69); •Cabaret (72); •Lenny (74); •All That Jazz (79); •Star 80 (83)

FRANCIS, FREDDIE
Two and Two Make Six (61); Brain, The (62); •Day of the Triffids, The (63); Nightmare (63); Paranoiac (63); Evil of Frankenstein, The (64); Dr. Terror's House of Horrors (65); Hysteria (65); Skull, The (65); Traitor's Gate (65); Psychopath, The (66); Deadly Bees, The (67); They Came from Beyond Space (67); Torture Garden (67); Dracula Has Risen from the Grave (69); Mumsy, Nanny, Sonny, and Girly (70); Trog (70); Creeping Flesh, The (72); Tales from the Crypt (72); Craze (73); Tales That Witness Madness (73); Son of Dracula (74); Ghoul, The (75); Doctor and the Devils, The (85); Dark Tower (89)

FRANK, MELVIN
Reformer and the Redhead, The (50); Callaway Went Thataway (51); Strictly Dishonorable (51); Above and Beyond (53); •Knock on Wood (54); •Court Jester, The (56); That Certain Feeling (56); Jayhawkers, The (59); Li'L Abner (59); Facts of Life, The (60); Strange Bedfellows (65); Buona Sera, Mrs. Campbell (68); •Touch of Class, A (73); Prisoner of Second Avenue, The (75); Duchess and the Dirtwater Fox, The (76); Lost and Found (79); Walk Like a Man (87)

FRANKENHEIMER, JOHN
Young Stranger, The (57); Young Savages, The (61); All Fall Down (62); •Birdman of Alcatraz (62); •Manchurian Candidate, The (62); •Seven Days in May (64); •Train, The (65); •Grand Prix (66); •Seconds (66); Fixer, The (68); Extraordinary Seaman, The (69); Gypsy Moths, The (69); •I Walk the Line (70); Horsemen, The (71); •Iceman Cometh, The (73); Impossible Object (73); 99 And 44/100% Dead (74); •French Connection II (75); •Black Sunday (77); Prophecy (79); Challenge, The (82); Rainmaker, The (82); Holcroft Covenant, The (85); 52 Pick-Up (86); Riviera (87); Dead-Bang (89); Fourth War, The (90); Year of the Gun (91); Against the Wall (94); Burning Season, The (94); Andersonville (96); Island oOf Dr. Moreau, The (96); George Wallace (97); •Ronin (98); Reindeer Games (00); Path to War (02)

FRANKLIN, CARL
Nowhere to Run (89); Eye of the Eagle II: Inside the Enemy (89); Full Fathom Five (90); •One False Move (92); •Devil in a Blue Dress (95); •One True Thing (98); High Crimes (02); •Out of Time (03)

FRANKLIN, SIDNEY
Devil May Care (29); Last of Mrs. Cheyney, The (29); Lady of Scandal, The (30); Lady's Morals, A (30); •Guardsman, The (31); •Private Lives (31); •Smilin' Through (32); Reunion in Vienna (33); •Barretts of Wimpole Street, The (34); Dark Angel, The (35); •Good Earth, The (37); •Barretts of Wimpole Street, The (56)

FREARS, STEPHEN
•Gumshoe (71); Three Men in a Boat (75); Bloody Kids (83); Loving Walter (83); Saigon—Year of the Cat (83); •Hit, The (84); •My Beautiful Laundrette (85); Song of Experience (86); Mr. Jolly Lives Next Door (87); •Prick Up Your Ears (87); •Sammy and Rosie Get Laid (87); •Dangerous Liaisons (88); •Grifters, The (90); Hero (92); •Snapper, The (93); Typically British (95); Mary Reilly (96); Van, The (96); Hi-Lo Country, The (98); •High Fidelity (00); Fail Safe (00); Liam (00); •Dirty Pretty Things (02); Deal, The (03)

FREUND, KARL
•Mummy, The (32); Moonlight and Pretzels (33); Countess of Monte Cristo, The (34); Gift of Gab (34); I Give My Love (34); Madame Spy (34); Uncertain Lady (34); •Mad Love (35)

FRIEDKIN, WILLIAM
Good Times (67); Birthday Party, The (68); Night They Raided Minsky's, The (68); Boys in the Band, The (70); •French Connection, The (71); •Exorcist, The (73); Sorcerer (77); Brink's Job, The (78); Cruising (80); Deal of the Century (83); •To Live and Die in L.A. (85); Guardian, The (90); Rampage (92); Blue Chips (94); Jade (95); 12 Angry Men (97); Rules of Engagement (00); Hunted, The (03)

FULLER, SAMUEL
•I Shot Jesse James (49); Baron of Arizona, The (50); Fixed Bayonets (51); •Steel Helmet, The (51); Park Row (52); •Pickup on South Street (53); Hell and High Water (54); House of

GUTIERREZ ALEA, TOMAS
Little Red Riding Hood (47); Fakir, The (47); Everyday Mix-Up, An (50); Il Sogno di Giovanni Basain (53); El Megano (55); This Land Is Ours (59); Stories of the Revolution (60); General Assembly (60); Death to the Invader (61); Twelve Chairs, The (62); Cumbite (66); •Death of a Bureaucrat (66); Memories of Underdevelopment (68); Cuban Fight against the Demons, A (71); Art of Tobacco, The (74); Last Supper, The (76); Survivors, The (78); Up to a Certain Point (84); Letters from the Park (88); With You in the Distance (91); Strawberry and Chocolate (93); Guantanamera (95)

HACKFORD, TAYLOR
•Idolmaker, The (80); •Officer and a Gentleman, An (82); Against All Odds (84); White Nights (85); Chuck Berry: Hail! Hail! Rock 'N' Roll (87); Everybody's All-American (88); Bound by Honor (93); Dolores Claiborne (95); Devil's Advocate, The (97); Proof of Life (00); •Ray (04)

HAINES, RANDA
Jilting of Granny Weatherall, The (80); Something About Amelia (84); •Children of a Lesser God (86); Doctor, The (91); Wrestling Ernest Hemingway (93); Dance with Me (98); Outsider, The (01)

HALLSTROM, LASSE
Lover and His Lass, A (75); Abba—The Movie (77); Father to Be (79); Rooster, The (81); •My Life As a Dog (85); Children of Bullerby Village, The (86); More About the Children of Bullerby Village (87); Once Around (91); •What's Eating Gilbert Grape? (93); Something to Talk About (95); Children of Noisy Village, The (96); •Cider House Rules, The (99); •Chocolat (00); •Shipping News, The (01)

HAMER, ROBERT
•Dead of Night (45); Pink String and Sealing Wax (45); It Always Rains on Sunday (47); •Kind Hearts and Coronets (49); Spider and the Fly, The (49); His Excellency (51); Long Memory, The (52); •Detective, The (54); To Paris with Love (55); Scapegoat, The (59); •School for Scoundrels (60)

HAMILTON, GUY
Ringer, The (52); Intruder, The (53); Colditz Story, The (54); Inspector Calls, An (54); Charley Moon (56); Stowaway Girl (57); Devil's Disciple, The (59); Touch of Larceny, A (59); Best of Enemies, The (61); •Goldfinger (64); Man in the Middle (64); Party's Over, The (65); •Funeral in Berlin (66); •Battle of Britain (69); •Diamonds Are Forever (71); Live and Let Die (73); Man with the Golden Gun, The (74); Force 10 from Navarone (78); Mirror Crack'd, The (80); Evil Under the Sun (82); Remo Williams: The Adventure Begins . . . (85); Try This One for Size (89)

HAMPTON, CHRISTOPHER
•Carrington (95); Joseph Conrad's The Secret Agent (96); Imagining Argentina (03)

HANSON, CURTIS
Arousers, The (70); Little Dragons, The (80); Losin' It (83); Bedroom Window, The (87); •Bad Influence (90); •Hand That Rocks the Cradle, The (92); River Wild, The (94); •L.A. Confidential; •Wonder Boys (00); •8 Mile (02)

HARE, DAVID
•Wetherby (85); Paris by Night (88); •Strapless (89); Heading Home (91); Designated Mourner, The (97)

HARLIN, RENNY
Born American (86); Nightmare on Elm Street 4: The Dream Master, A (88); Prison (88); Adventures of Ford Fairlane, The (90); Die Hard 2: Die Harder (90); •Cliffhanger (93); Cutthroat Island (95); Long Kiss Goodnight, The (96); Deep Blue Sea (99); Driven (01); Mindhunters (04); •Exorcist: The Beginning (04)

HARRON, MARY
•I Shot Andy Warhol (96); •American Psycho (00)

HARTLEY, HAL
•Unbelievable Truth, The (90); •Trust (91); Simple Men (92); •Amateur (95); Flirt (96); •Henry Fool (98); Book of Life, The (98); No Such Thing (01); Girl from Monday, The (05)

HASKIN, BYRON
I Walk Alone (48); Man-Eater of Kumaon (48); Too Late for Tears (49); •Treasure Island (50); Silver City (51); Tarzan's Peril (51); Warpath (51); Denver and Rio Grande, The (52); Naked Jungle, The (53); •War of the Worlds, The (53); His Majesty O'Keefe (54); Long John Silver (54); Conquest of Space (55); Boss, The (56); First Texan, The (56); From the Earth to the Moon (58); Little Savage, The (59); Jet Over the Atlantic (60); September Storm (60); Armored Command (61); Captain Sindbad (63); Robinson Crusoe on Mars (64); Power, The (68)

HATHAWAY, HENRY
Wild Horse Mesa (32); Heritage of the Desert (33); Man of the Forest (33); Sunset Pass (33); To the Last Man (33); Under the Tonto Rim (33); Come On, Marines (34); Last Round-Up, The (34); Now and Forever (34); Thundering Herd, The (34); Witching Hour, The (34); •Lives of a Bengal Lancer, The (35); Peter Ibbetson (35); Go West, Young Man (36); •Trail of the Lonesome Pine, The (36); Souls at Sea (37); Spawn of the North (38); Real Glory, The (39); Brigham Young—Frontiersman (40); Johnny Apollo (40); Shepherd of the Hills, The (41); Sundown (41); China Girl (42); Ten Gentlemen from West Point (42); Home in Indiana (44); Wing and a Prayer (44); •House on 92nd Street, The (45); Nob Hill (45); Dark Corner, The (46); 13 Rue Madeleine (46); •Kiss of Death (47); •Call Northside 777 (48); Down to the Sea in Ships (49); •Black Rose, The (50); •Desert Fox, The (51); Fourteen Hours (51); Rawhide (51); You're in the Navy Now (51); Diplomatic Courier (52); O. Henry's Full House (52); •Niagara (53); White Witch Doctor (53); Garden of Evil (54); Prince Valiant (54); Racers, The (55); Bottom of the Bottle, The (56); 23 Paces to Baker Street (56); Legend of the Lost (57); From Hell to Texas (58);

Woman Obsessed (59); North to Alaska (60); •Seven Thieves (60); •How the West Was Won (63); Circus World (64); Of Human Bondage (64); Sons of Katie Elder, The (65); Nevada Smith (66); Last Safari, The (67); Five Card Stud (68); •True Grit (69); •Airport (70); Raid on Rommel (71); Shoot Out (71); Hangup (74)

HAUFF, REINHARD
Revolt, The (69); Matthias Kneissl (70); Haus am Meer (72); Desaster (73); Brutalization of Franz Blum, The (74); Paule Paulander (76); Main Actor, The (77); Fuses (77); •Knife in the Head (78); Endstation Freiheit (80); Slow Attack (81); Man on the Wall, The (82); 10 Days in Calcutta (84); Stammheim (86); Line 1 (87); Blue-Eyed (89)

HAWKS, HOWARD
Air Circus, The (28); •Dawn Patrol, The (30); Criminal Code, The (31); Crowd Roars, The (32); •Scarface (32); Tiger Shark (32); Today We Live (33); •Twentieth Century (34); •Viva Villa! (34); Barbary Coast (35); Ceiling Zero (35); Come and Get It (36); Road to Glory, The (36); •Bringing Up Baby (38); •Only Angels Have Wings (39); •His Girl Friday (40); •Ball of Fire (41); •Sergeant York (41); •Air Force (43); •Outlaw, The (43); •To Have and Have Not (44); •Big Sleep, The (46); •Red River (48); Song Is Born, A (48); I Was a Male War Bride (49); •Thing, The (51); •Big Sky, The (52); Monkey Business (52); O. Henry's Full House (52); •Gentlemen Prefer Blondes (53); Land of the Pharaohs (55); •Rio Bravo (59); Hatari! (62); •Man's Favorite Sport? (64); Red Line 7000 (65); •El Dorado (67); •Rio Lobo (70)

HAYNES, TODD
Superstar: The Karen Carpenter Story (88); Poison (91); •Safe (95); •Velvet Goldmine (98); •Far from Heaven (02)

HECHT, BEN
•Crime Without Passion (34); •Scoundrel, The (35); Once in a Blue Moon (36); Soak the Rich (36); •Angels Over Broadway (40); Specter of the Rose (46); Actors and Sin (52)

HECKERLING, AMY
•Fast Times at Ridgemont High (82); Johnny Dangerously (84); National Lampoon's European Vacation (85); •Look Who's Talking (89); Look Who's Talking Too (90); •Clueless (95); Loser (00)

HEISLER, STUART
Straight from the Shoulder (36); •Hurricane, The (37); Biscuit Eater, The (40); Among the Living (41); Monster and the Girl, The (41); •Glass Key, The (42); Remarkable Andrew, The (42); Along Came Jones (45); •Blue Skies (46); Smash-Up, The Story of a Woman (47); Tokyo Joe (49); Tulsa (49); Chain Lightning (50); Dallas (50); Storm Warning (50); Vendetta (50); Journey into Light (51); Island of Desire (52); Star, The (53); Beachhead (54); This Is My Love (54); I Died a Thousand Times (55); Lone Ranger, The (55); Burning Hills, The (56); Hitler (62)

HELLMAN, MONTE
Beast from the Haunted Cave (60); Terror, The (63); Back Door to Hell (64); Flight to Fury (66); Ride in the Whirlwind (66); •Shooting, The (71); •Two-Lane Blacktop (71); Born to Kill (75); Shatter (75); China 9, Liberty 37 (78); Iguana (88); Silent Night, Deadly Night 3: Better Watch Out! (89)

HENENLOTTER, FRANK
•Basket Case (82); Brain Damage (88); Basket Case 2 (90); •Frankenhooker (90); Basket Case 3: The Progeny (92)

HENSON, JIM
•Great Muppet Caper, The (81); •Dark Crystal, The (82); •Labyrinth (86)

HERMAN, MARK
Unusual Ground Floor Conversation (87); Blame It on the Bellboy (92); •Brassed Off (96); Little Voice (98); Purely Belter (00); Hope Springs (03)

HERZOG, WERNER
Signs of Life (68); Flying Doctors of East Africa, The (69); Even Dwarves Started Small (70); Fata Morgana (71); Handicapped Future (71); Land of Silence and Darkness (71); •Aguirre, The Wrath Of God (72); The Great Ecstasy of Woodcarver Steiner (74); •Every Man for Himself and God Against All (74); Heart of Glass (76); Stroszek (76); How Much Wood Would a Woodchuck Chuck (76); La Soufriere (77); •Nosferatu, The Vampire (78); Woyzeck (79); God's Angry Man (80); Huie's Sermon (80); •Fitzcarraldo (82); Ballad of The Little Soldier, The (84); Dark Glow of the Mountains, The (84); Where the Green Ants Dream (84); Cobra Verde (88); Woodaabe—Herdsmen of the Sun (89); Echoes from a Somber Empire (90); Jag Mandir (91); Scream of Stone (91); Lessons of Darkness (92); Bells from the Deep (93); Transformation of the World into Music, The (94); Death for Five Voices (95); Little Dieter Needs to Fly (97); Wings of Hope (98); My Best Fiend: Klaus Kinski (99); Invincible (01); Wheel of Time (03); White Diamond, The (04); Grizzly Man (05)

HICKOX, DOUGLAS
Giant Behemoth, The (59); It's All Over Town (63); •Entertaining Mr. Sloane (69); Sitting Target (72); •Theatre of Blood (73); Brannigan (75); Sky Riders (76); Zulu Dawn (79); Pheonix, The (81); Hound of the Baskervilles, The (83); Master of Ballantrae, The (84); Blackout (85)

HICKS, SCOTT
Freedom! (81); Sebastian and the Sparrow (88); •Shine (96); Snow Falling on Cedars (99); Hearts in Atlantis (01)

HILL, GEORGE ROY
Period of Adjustment (62); Toys in the Attic (63); •World of Henry Orient, The (64); Hawaii (66); Thoroughly Modern Millie (67); •Butch Cassidy and the Sundance Kid (69); Slaughterhouse-Five (72); •Sting, The (73); Great Waldo Pepper, The (75); •Slap Shot (77); Little

Romance, A (79); •World According to Garp, The (82); Little Drummer Girl, The (84); Funny Farm (88)

HILL, WALTER
Hard Times (75); •Driver, The (78); •Warriors, The (79); •Long Riders, The (80); •Southern Comfort (81); •48 Hrs. (82); Streets of Fire (84); Brewster's Millions (85); Crossroads (86); Extreme Prejudice (87); Red Heat (88); Johnny Handsome (89); Another 48 Hrs. (90); Trespass (92); Geronimo: An American Legend (93); Wild Bill (95); Last Man Standing (96); Supernova (00); Undisputed (02)

HILLER, ARTHUR
Careless Years, The (57); Miracle of the White Stallions (63); Wheeler Dealers, The (63); Americanization of Emily, The (64); Penelope (66); Promise Her Anything (66); Tobruk (66); Tiger Makes Out, The (67); Popi (69); •Love Story (70); •Out-of-Towners, The (70); •Hospital, The (71); •Plaza Suite (71); Man of La Mancha (72); Crazy World of Julius Vrooder, The (74); Man in the Glass Booth, The (75); Silver Streak (76); W.C. Fields and Me (76); In-Laws, The (79); Nightwing (79); Author! Author! (82); Making Love (82); Romantic Comedy (83); Lonely Guy, The (84); Teachers (84); Outrageous Fortune (87); See No Evil, Hear No Evil (89); Taking Care of Business (90); Babe, The (92); Married to It (93); Carpool (96); Burn Hollywood Burn (98)

HITCHCOCK, ALFRED
•Blackmail (29); Juno and the Paycock (30); •Murder (30); Skin Game, The (31); Number Seventeen (32); Rich and Strange (32); Strauss's Great Waltz (33); •Man Who Knew Too Much, The (34); •39 Steps, The (35); •Sabotage (36); •Secret Agent (36); •Young and Innocent (37); •Lady Vanishes, The (38); Jamaica Inn (39); •Foreign Correspondent (40); •Rebecca (40); Mr. and Mrs. Smith (41); •Suspicion (41); •Saboteur (42); •Shadow of a Doubt (43); •Lifeboat (44); •Spellbound (45); •Notorious (46); Paradine Case, The (47); •Rope (48); Under Capricorn (49); •Stage Fright (50); •Strangers on a Train (51); I Confess (53); •Dial M for Murder (54); •Rear Window (54); •To Catch a Thief (55); •Trouble with Harry, The (55); •Man Who Knew Too Much, The (56); •Wrong Man, The (56); •Vertigo (58); •North by Northwest (59); •Psycho (60); •Birds, The (63); •Marnie (64); •Torn Curtain (66); •Topaz (69); •Frenzy (72); •Family Plot (76)

HODGES, MIKE
•Get Carter (71); Pulp (72); Terminal Man, The (74); Flash Gordon (80); Missing Pieces (83); Squaring the Circle (84); Morons from Outer Space (85); Florida Straits (86); Prayer for the Dying, A (87); Healer, The (92); Black Rainbow (91); •Croupier (98); I'll Sleep When I'm Dead (03)

HOFFMAN, MICHAEL
Privileged (82); Restless Natives (85); Promised Land (87); Some Girls (88); Soapdish (91); Restoration (95); One Fine Day (96); William Shakespeare's A Midsummer Night's Dream (99); •Emperor's Club, The (02); Game 6 (05)

HOGAN, P.J.
Humpty Dumpty Man, The (86); Muriel's Wedding (94); •My Best Friend's Wedding (97); Unconditional Love (02); •Peter Pan (03)

HOLLAND, AGNIESZKA
Evening at Abdon's (74); Sunday Children (76); Something for Something (77); Screen Test (77); Provincial Actors (79); Fever (80); Woman Alone, A (82); Angry Harvest (84); To Kill a Priest (88); •Europa, Europa (91); Olivier, Olivier (92); •Secret Garden, The (93); Total Eclipse (95); •Washington Square (97); Third Miracle, The (99); Shot in the Heart (01); Golden Dreams (01); Julie Walking Home (02)

HOOPER, TOBE
•Texas Chainsaw Massacre, The (74); Eaten Alive (76); Salem's Lot (79); Funhouse, The (81); •Poltergeist (82); Lifeforce (85); Invaders from Mars (86); Texas Chainsaw Massacre Part 2, The (86); Spontaneous Combustion (90); I'm Dangerous Tonight (90); Tobe Hooper's Night Terrors (94); Mangler, The (95); Apartment Complex, The (99); Crocodile (00); Toolbox Murders, The (03);

HOPPER, DENNIS
•Easy Rider (69); •Last Movie, The (71); Out of the Blue (82); •Colors (88); Hot Spot, The (90); Backtrack (92); Chasers (94)

HOU HSIAO-HSIEN
Cute Girls (80); Cheerful Wind (81); Growing Up (82); Sandwich Man, The (83); Boys from Fengkuei, The (83); Summer At Grandpa's, A (84); Time to Live and A Time to Die, A (85); Dust in the Wind (86); •Daughter of the Nile (87); City of Sadness, A (89); Puppetmaster, The (93); Good Men, Good Women (95); Flowers of Shanghai, The (98); Millennium Mambo (01); Cafe Lumiere (03)

HOWARD, LESLIE
•Pygmalion (38); •Pimpernel Smith (41); •Spitfire (42); Gentle Sex, The (43)

HOWARD, RON
Grand Theft Auto (77); Night Shift (82); •Splash (84); •Cocoon (85); Gung Ho (86); Willow (88); •Parenthood (89); •Backdraft (91); Far and Away (92); Paper, The (94); •Apollo 13 (95); Ransom (96); •EdTV(99); •Dr. Seuss' How the Grinch Stole Christmas (00); •Beautiful Mind, A (01); Missing, The (03)

HUDLIN, REGINALD
•House Party (90); Boomerang (92); Cosmic Slop (94); Great White Hype, The (96); Ladies Man, The (00); Serving Sara (02)

HUDSON, HUGH
•Chariots of Fire (81); •Greystoke: The Legend of Tarzan, Lord of the Apes (84); Revolution (85); Lost Angels (89); My Life So Far (99); I Dreamed of Africa (00)

HUGHES, ALBERT and ALLEN
•Menace II Society (93); Dead Presidents (95); American Pimp (00); •From Hell (01)

HUGHES, JOHN
•Sixteen Candles (84); •Breakfast Club, The (85); Weird Science (85); Ferris Bueller's Day Off (86); •Planes, Trains, and Automobiles (87); She's Having a Baby (88); •Uncle Buck (89); Curly Sue (91)

HUNTER, TIM
•Tex (82); Sylvester (85); •River's Edge (87); Paint It Black (90); Saint of Fort Washington, The (93); People Next Door, The (96); Rescuers: Stories of Courage—Two Couples (98); Maker, The (97); Mean Streak (99); Anatomy of a Hate Crime (00); Video Voyeur: The Susan Wilson Story (01); Failures, The (03); Control (05)

HUSTON, JOHN
•Maltese Falcon, The (41); •Across the Pacific (42); In This Our Life (42); •Key Largo (48); •Treasure of the Sierra Madre, The (48); We Were Strangers (49); •Asphalt Jungle, The (50); •African Queen, The (51); •Red Badge of Courage, The (51); •Moulin Rouge (52); •Beat the Devil (53); •Moby Dick (56); Heaven Knows, Mr. Allison (57); Barbarian and the Geisha, The (58); Roots of Heaven, The (58); Unforgiven, The (60); •Misfits, The (61); Freud (62); •List of Adrian Messenger, The (63); •Night of the Iguana, The (64); Bible. . . In the Beginning, The (66); •Casino Royale (67); Reflections in a Golden Eye (67); Sinful Davey (68); Walk with Love and Death, A (69); Kremlin Letter, The (70); •Fat City (72); Life and Times of Judge Roy Bean, The (72); Mackintosh Man, The (73); •Man Who Would Be King, The (75); •Wise Blood (79); Phobia (80); Victory (81); Annie (82); •Under the Volcano (84); •Prizzi's Honor (85); •Dead, The (87)

HYTNER, NICHOLAS
•Madness of King George, The (94); •Crucible, The (96); •Object of My Affection, The (98); Center Stage (00)

ICHASO, LEON
El Super (79); •Crossover Dreams (85); Table at Ciro's, A (87); Power, Passion and Murder (87); Take, The (90); Fear Inside, The (92); Sugar Hill (94); Kiss to Die For, A (93); Zooman (95); Bitter Sugar (96); Free of Eden (99); Execution of Justice (99); Ali: An American Hero (00); Hendrix (00); Pinero (01)

IMAMURA, SHOHEI
Stolen Desire (58); Lights of Night (58); Endless Desire (58); My Second Brother (59); Pigs and Battleships (61); Insect Woman, The (64); Unholy Desire (64); Pornographers, The (66); Man Vanishes, A (67); Profound Desire of the Gods, The (68); History of Postwar Japan as Told by a Bar Hostess (70); Still in Search of Unreturned Soldiers (71); Report on Two People Named Yoshinobu (75); Karayuki-San, The Making of a Prostitute (75); Vengeance Is Mine (79); Why Not? (81); •Ballad of Narayama, The (83); Lord of

the Brothels, The (87); •Black Rain (89); •Eel, The (97); Dr. Akagi (98); Warm Water Under a Red Bridge (01)

IRVIN, JOHN
Possessions (74); •Dogs of War, The (80); Ghost Story (81); Champions (83); •Turtle Diary (85); Raw Deal (86); •Hamburger Hill (87); Next of Kin (89); Eminent Domain (91); Robin Hood (91); Freefall (94); Widows' Peak (94); Month by the Lake, A (94); Crazy Horse (96); City of Industry (97); When Trumpets Fade (98); Noah's Ark (99); Shiner (00); Fourth Angel, The (01); Boys from County Clare, The (03); Dot.Kill (04)

ITAMI, JUZO
•Funeral, The (84); •Tampopo (86); •Taxing Woman, A (87); Taxing Woman's Return, A (88); A-ge-man (90); Minbo—or the Gentle Art of Japanese Extortion (94); Daibyonin (95); Supermarket Woman (96); Marutai No Onna (97)

IVORY, JAMES
Householder, The (63); •Shakespeare Wallah (65); Guru, The (69); Bombay Talkie (70); Savages (72); Wild Party, The (75); Roseland (77); Hullabaloo Over Georgie and Bonnie's Pictures (78); Europeans, The (79); Jane Austen in Manhattan (80); Quartet (81); Heat and Dust (83); Bostonians, The (84); •Room with a View, A (85); •Maurice (87); Slaves of New York (89); Mr. and Mrs. Bridge (90); •Howards End (92); •Remains of the Day, The (93); Jefferson in Paris (95); Surviving Picasso (96); Soldier's Daughter Never Cries, A (98); Golden Bowl, The (00); Le Divorce (03)

JACKSON, MICK
How to Pick Up Girls (78); Threads (84); Yuri Nosenko: KGB (86); Race for the Double Helix, The (87); Very British Coup, A (88); Chattahoochee (89); •L.A. Story (91); •Bodyguard, The (92); Clean Slate (94); Indictment: The McMartin Trial (95); Volcano (97); Tuesdays with Morrie (99); First $20 Million Is Always the Hardest, The (02); Live from Baghdad (02)

JACKSON, PETER
Bad Taste (88); Meet the Feebles (89); Dead Alive (92); •Heavenly Creatures (94); Frighteners, The (96); Forgotten Silver (96); •Lord of the Rings: The Fellowship of the Ring, The (01); •Lord of the Rings: The Two Towers, The (02); •Lord of the Rings: The Return of the King, The (03)

JACQUOT, BENOIT
L'Assassin Musicien (75); Les Enfants du Placard (77); Les Ailes de la Colombe (81); Corps et Biens (86); Les Mendiants (87); •Disenchanted, The (90); Marianne (94); Single Girl, A (95); Seventh Heaven (97); School of Flesh, The (98); Par Coeur (98); Keep It Quiet/Pas de Scandale (99); False Servant (00); Sade (00); Tosca (01); Adolphe (02); Princesse Marie (04); A Tout de Suite (04)

JARMAN, DEREK
Sebastiane (76); Jubilee (78); Tempest, The (79); In the Shadow of the Sun (80); Angelic Conversation, The (85); •Caravaggio (86);

Aria (87); Last of England, The (87); •War Requiem (89); Garden, The (90); Edward II (91); Wittgenstein (93); •Blue (94)

JARMUSCH, JIM
Permanent Vacation (82); •Stranger Than Paradise (84); •Down by Law (86); •Mystery Train (89); •Night on Earth (92); •Dead Man (96); Year of the Horse (97); •Ghost Dog: The Way of the Samurai (99); Coffee and Cigarettes (04); Broken Flowers (05)

JEUNET, JEAN-PIERRE
•Delicatessen (91); •City of Lost Children, The (95); •Alien Resurrection (97); •Amelie (01); •Very Long Engagement, A (04)

JEWISON, NORMAN
Forty Pounds of Trouble (62); Thrill of It All, The (63); Send Me No Flowers (64); Art of Love, The (65); •Cincinnati Kid, The (65); Russians Are Coming, the Russians Are Coming, The (66); •In the Heat of the Night (67); •Thomas Crown Affair, The (68); Gaily, Gaily (69); •Fiddler on the Roof (71); Jesus Christ, Superstar (73); •Rollerball (75); F.I.S.T. (78); . . . And Justice for All (79); Best Friends (82); •Soldier's Story, A (84); •Agnes of God (85); •Moonstruck (87); In Country (89); Other People's Money (91); Only You (94); Bogus (96); Hurricane, The (99); Dinner with Friends (01); Statement, The (03)

JODOROWSKY, ALEXANDRO
Fando and Lis (67); •El Topo (71); Holy Mountain, The (75); Tusk (78); •Santa Sangre (89); Rainbow Thief, The (90)

JOFFE, ROLAND
•Killing Fields, The (84); •Mission, The (86); Fat Man and Little Boy (89); City of Joy (92); Scarlet Letter, The (95); Goodbye Lover (99); Vatel (00)

JOHNSON, NUNNALLY
Black Widow (54); Night People (54); How to Be Very, Very Popular (55); •Man in the Gray Flannel Suit, The (56); Oh, Men! Oh, Women! (57); •Three Faces of Eve, The (57); Man Who Understood Women, The (59); Angel Wore Red, The (60)

JONES, DAVID HUGH
Barbara of the House of Grebe (73); Langrishe, Go Down (78); Look Back in Anger (80); Merry Wives of Windsor, The (82); •Betrayal (82); Pericles, Prince of Tyre (84); •84 Charing Cross Road (87); Christmas Wife, The (88); •Jacknife (89); Sensibility and Sense (90); Fire in the Dark (91); Trial, The (93); Requiem Apache (94); And Then There Was One (94); Is There Life Out There? (94); Sophie and the Moonhanger (95); Time to Say Goodbye? (97); Unexpected Life, An (98); Confession, The (99); Christmas Carol, A (99); Custody of the Heart (00)

JONES, TERRY
•Monty Python and the Holy Grail (75); •Monty Python's Life of Brian (79); •Monty Python's the Meaning of Life (83); Personal Services (87); Erik the Viking (89); Wind in the Willows, The (96)

JONZE, SPIKE
•Being John Malkovich (99); •Adaptation. (02)

JORDAN, NEIL
•Angel (82); •Company of Wolves, The (84); •Mona Lisa (86); High Spirits (88); We're No Angels (89); Miracle, The (91); •Crying Game, The (92); •Interview with the Vampire (94); •Michael Collins (96); •Butcher Boy, The (97); In Dreams (99); •End of the Affair, The (99); Good Thief, The (03)

KADAR, JAN
Katya (50); Hijack (52); Music from Mars (54); House at the Terminus (57); Three Wishes (58); Magic Lantern II (60); Youth (60); Spartakiade (60); Death Is Called Engelchen (63); Accused, The (64); •Shop on Main Street, The (65); Angel Levine, The (70); Adrift (71); Blue Hotel, The (73); Case against Milligan, The (75); Lies My Father Told Me (75); Other Side of Hell, The (78); Freedom Road (79)

KAPUR, SHEKHAR
Masoom (83); Mr. India (87); •Bandit Queen (94); •Elizabeth (98); Four Feathers, The (02)

KALATOZOV, MIKHAIL
Blind (30); Salt for Svanetia (30); Nail in the Boot, A (32); Manhood (39); Wings of Victory (41); Invicible (43); Moscow Music-Hall (45); Conspiracy of the Doomed (50); True Friends (54); First Echelon, The (56); Hostile Wind, The (56); Woman from Warsaw, The (56); •Cranes Are Flying, The (57); Letter That Was Never Sent, The (60); I Am Cuba (66); Red Tent, The (71)

KANIN, GARSON
Man to Remember, A (38); Next Time I Marry (38); •Bachelor Mother (39); Great Man Votes, The (39); •My Favorite Wife (40); They Knew What They Wanted (40); Tom, Dick and Harry (41); Some Kind of a Nut (69); Where It's At (69)

KAPLAN, JONATHAN
Slams, The (73); Student Teachers, The (73); Night Call Nurses (74); Truck Turner (74); White Line Fever (75); Mr. Billion (77); •Over the Edge (79); •Heart Like a Wheel (83); Project X (87); •Accused, The (88); Immediate Family (89); Love Field (92); •Unlawful Entry (92); Bad Girls (94); In Cold Blood (96); Brokedown Palace (99)

KARLSON, PHIL
Scandal Sheet (31); Wave, a Wac and a Marine, A (44); G.I. Honeymoon (45); Shanghai Cobra, The (45); There Goes Kelly (45); Behind the Mask (46); Bowery Bombshell (46); Dark Alibi (46); Live Wires (46); Missing Lady, The (46); Swing Parade of 1946 (46); Wife Wanted (46); Black Gold (47); Kilroy Was Here (47); Louisiana (47); Adventures In Silverado (48); Ladies of the Chorus (48); Thunderhoof (48); Big Cat, The (49); Down Memory Lane (49); Iroquois Trail, The (50); Lorna Doone (51); Mask of the Avenger (51); Texas Rangers, The (51); Brigand, The (52); Kansas City Confidential (52); 99 River Street (53); They Rode West (54); 5 Against the House (55); Hell's Island (55); Phenix City Story, The (55); Tight Spot (55); Brothers Rico, The (57); Gunman's Walk (58); Hell to Eternity (60); Key Witness (60);

Secret Ways, The (61); Young Doctors, The (61);
Kid Galahad (62); Scarface Mob, The (62);
Rampage (63); Silencers, The (66); Time for
Killing, A (67); Wrecking Crew, The (68);
Hornet's Nest (70); Ben (72); •Walking Tall (73);
Framed (75)

KASDAN, LAWRENCE
•Body Heat (81); •Big Chill, The (83);
•Silverado (85); •Accidental Tourist, The (88); I
Love You to Death (90); •Grand Canyon (91);
Wyatt Earp (94); French Kiss (95); Mumford (99);
•Dreamcatcher (03)

KASSOVITZ, MATHIEU
Fierrot le Pou (90); White Nightmare (91);
Assassins (92); Cafe au Lait/Metisse (93);
•Hate (95); Assassins (97); Deja Vu (99); Crimson
Rivers, The (00); •Gothika (03)

KAUFMAN, PHILIP
Goldstein (64); Fearless Frank (67); •Great
Northfield, Minnesota Raid, The (72); White
Dawn, The (74); •Invasion of the Body
Snatchers (78); •Wanderers, The (79); •Right Stuff,
The (83); •Unbearable Lightness of Being,
The (88); •Henry and June (90); Rising Sun (93);
•Quills (00); Twisted (04)

KAURISMAKI, AKI
Saimaa Gesture, The (81); Crime and
Punishment (83); Calamari Union (85); Rocky
VI (86); Shadows in Paradise (86); Hamlet Gets
Business (87); Thru the Wire (87); Ariel (89);
Leningrad Cowboys Go America, The (90);
•Match Factory Girl, The (90); I Hired a Contract
Killer (90); La Vie de Boheme (92); Those Were
the Days (92); Total Balalaika Show, The (93);
These Boots (93); Leningrad Cowboys Meet
Moses (94); Take Care of Your Scarf, Tatiana (94);
Drifting Clouds (96); Juha (99); •Man Without a
Past, The (02)

KAZAN, ELIA
•Tree Grows in Brooklyn, A (45);
•Boomerang (47); •Gentleman's Agreement (47);
Sea of Grass, The (47); •Pinky (49); Panic in the
Streets (50); •Streetcar Named Desire, A (51);
•Viva Zapata! (52); Man on a Tightrope (53); •On
the Waterfront (54); •East of Eden (55); •Baby
Doll (56); •Face in the Crowd, A (57); •Wild
River (60); •Splendor in the Grass (61); America,
America (63); Arrangement, The (69); Visitors,
The (72); Last Tycoon, The (76)

KEIGHLEY, WILLIAM
Match King, The (32); •Footlight Parade (33);
Ladies They Talk About (33); Babbitt (34); Big
Hearted Herbert (34); Doctor Monica (34); Easy to
Love (34); Journal of a Crime (34); Kansas City
Princess (34); •G-Men (35); Mary Jane's Pa (35);
Right to Live, The (35); Special Agent (35); Stars
Over Broadway (35); Bullets or Ballots (36);
•Green Pastures (36); Singing Kid, The (36); God's
Country and the Woman (37); •Prince and the
Pauper, The (37); Varsity Show (37); •Adventures
of Robin Hood, The (38); Brother Rat (38); Secrets
of an Actress (38); Valley of the Giants (38); Each
Dawn I Die (39); Yes, My Darling Daughter (39);
•Fighting 69th, The (40); No Time for
Comedy (40); Torrid Zone (40); Bride Came

C.O.D., The (41); Four Mothers (41); George
Washington Slept Here (42); •Man Who Came to
Dinner, The (42); Honeymoon (47); Street with No
Name, The (48); Rocky Mountain (50); Close to
My Heart (51); Master of Ballantrae, The (53)

KELLY, GENE
•On the Town (49); •Singin' in the Rain (52); •It's
Always Fair Weather (55); •Invitation to the
Dance (56); Happy Road, The (57); Tunnel of
Love, The (58); Gigot (62); Guide for The Married
Man, A (67); •Hello, Dolly! (69); Cheyenne Social
Club, The (70)

KERSHNER, IRVIN
Stakeout on Dope Street (58); Young Captives,
The (59); Hoodlum Priest, The (61); Face in the
Rain, A (63); Luck of Ginger Coffey, The (64);
Fine Madness, A (66); Flim-Flam Man, The (67);
Loving (70); Up the Sandbox (72); S*P*Y*S (74);
Return of a Man Called Horse, The (76); Eyes of
Laura Mars (78); •Empire Strikes Back, The (80);
•Never Say Never Again (83); Robocop 2 (90)

KIAROSTAMI, ABBAS
Traveller, The (74); Wedding Suit, The (76);
Report, The (77); First Case, Second Case (79);
Fellow Citizen (83); First Graders (84); Where Is
the Friend's House? (87); Homework (89);
Close-Up (90); And Life Goes On. . . (92);
Through the Olive Trees (94); •Taste Of
Cherry (97); Wind Will Carry Us, The (99); ABC
Africa (01); Ten (02); Five Dedicated to
Ozu (03); 10 on Ten (04)

KIESLOWSKI, KRZYSZTOF
Picture (69); Workers (72); First Love (74);
Personnel (75); Biography (75); Scar (76);
Politics (76); Hospital (77); Calm (77); Seen by the
Night Porter (78); Station (78); Camera Buff (79);
Talking Heads (80); Short Day's Work, A (82); No
End (84); Blind Chance (82); Dekalog (88);
•Short Film About Killing, A (88); Short Film
About Love, A (88); City Life (90); •Double Life
of Veronique, The (91); •Blue (93); •Red (94);
•White (94)

KING, HENRY
She Goes to War (29); Eyes of the World,
The (30); Hell Harbor (30); Lightnin' (30); Merely
Mary Ann (31); Over the Hill (31); Woman in
Room 13, The (32); I Loved You Wednesday (33);
State Fair (33); Carolina (34); Marie Galante (34);
One More Spring (35); Way Down East (35);
Country Doctor, The (36); Lloyds of London (36);
Ramona (36); Seventh Heaven (37); •Alexander's
Ragtime Band (38); •In Old Chicago (38); •Jesse
James (39); •Stanley and Livingstone (39); Chad
Hanna (40); Little Old New York (40);
Maryland (40); Remember the Day (41); Yank in
the R.A.F., A (41); •Black Swan, The (42); •Song
of Bernadette, The (43); Wilson (44); Bell For
Adano, A (45); Margie (46); •Captain from
Castile (47); Deep Waters (48); •Prince of
Foxes (49); •Twelve O'Clock High (49);
•Gunfighter, The (50); •David and Bathsheba (51);
I'd Climb the Highest Mountain (51); O. Henry's
Full House (52); •Snows of Kilimanjaro, The (52);
Wait Till the Sun Shines, Nellie (52); •King of the
Khyber Rifles (53); Love Is a Many-Splendored
Thing (55); Untamed (55); •Carousel (56);

•Sun Also Rises, The (57); Bravados, The (58); Beloved Infidel (59); This Earth Is Mine (59); Tender Is the Night (61)

KITANO, TAKESHI
Violent Cop (89); Boiling Point (90); Scene at the Sea, A (89); •Sonatine (93); Getting Any? (94); Kids Return (96); •Fireworks (Hana-Bi) (97); Kikujiro (99); Brother (00); Dolls (02); The Blind Swordsman: Zatoichi (03)

KLEISER, RANDAL
•Grease (78); Blue Lagoon, The (80); Summer Lovers (82); Grandview, U.S.A. (84); Flight of The Navigator (86); Big Top Pee-wee (88); Getting It Right (89); White Fang (91); Honey, I Blew Up the Kid (92); It's My Party (96); Shadow of Doubt (98); Royal Standard (99); Lovewrecked (05)

KLOS, ELMAR
Hijack (52); Music from Mars (54); House at the Terminus (57); Three Wishes (58); Magic Lantern II (60); Youth (60); Spartakiade (60); Death Is Called Engelchen (63); Accused, The (64); •Shop on Main Street, The (65); Adrift (69)

KLOVES, STEVE
•Fabulous Baker Boys, The (89); Flesh and Bone (93)

KONCHALOVSKY, ANDREI
First Teacher, The (65); Asya's Happiness (67); Nest of Gentlefolk, A (69); Uncle Vanya (71); Romance for Lovers (74); Siberiade (78); Maria's Lovers (85); •Runaway Train (85); Duet for One (86); •Shy People (88); Tango and Cash (89); Homer & Eddie (90); Inner Circle, The (91); Ryaba My Chicken (94); Odyssey, The (97); House of Fools (02); Lion in Winter, The (03)

KORDA, ALEXANDER
Stolen Bride, The (27); Private Life of Helen of Troy, The (27); Yellow Lily, The (28); Night Watch, The (28); Love and the Devil (29); Her Private Life (29); Squall, The (29); Lilies of the Field (30); Princess and the Plumber, The (30); Women Everywhere (30); Die Manner um Lucie (31); •Marius (31); Reserved for Ladies (32); Wedding Rehearsal (32); Girl from Maxim's, The (33); •Private Life of Henry Viii, The (33); Private Life of Don Juan, The (34); •Scarlet Pimpernel, The (35); •Rembrandt (36); •Thief of Baghdad, The (40); •That Hamilton Woman (41); Vacation from Marriage (45); Ideal Husband, An (47)

KORDA, ZOLTAN
Men of Tomorrow (32); For Love or Money (33); Sanders of the River (35); Forever Yours (36); Elephant Boy (37); •Drums (38); •Four Feathers, The (39); Conquest of the Air (40); •Thief of Baghdad, The (40); •Jungle Book, The (42); •Sahara (43); Counter-Attack (45); •Macomber Affair, The (47); Woman's Vengeance, A (47); Cry, The Beloved Country (51); Storm Over the Nile (55)

KOSTER, HENRY
•One Hundred Men and a Girl (37); •Three Smart Girls (37); Affairs of Maupassant (38); Rage of Paris, The (38); First Love (39); Three Smart Girls Grow Up (39); Spring Parade (40); It Started with Eve (41); Between Us Girls (42); Music for Millions (44); Two Sisters from Boston (46); •Bishop's Wife, The (47); Unfinished Dance, The (47); Luck of the Irish, The (48); Come to the Stable (49); Inspector General, The (49); •Harvey (50); My Blue Heaven (50); Wabash Avenue (50); Elopement (51); Mr. Belvedere Rings the Bell (51); No Highway in the Sky (51); My Cousin Rachel (52); O. Henry's Full House (52); Stars and Stripes Forever (52); •Robe, The (53); Desiree (54); Good Morning, Miss Dove (55); Man Called Peter, A (55); Virgin Queen, The (55); D-Day the Sixth of June (56); Power and the Prize, The (56); My Man Godfrey (57); Fraulein (58); Naked Maja, The (59); Story of Ruth, The (60); Flower Drum Song (61); Mr. Hobbs Takes a Vacation (62); Take Her, She's Mine (63); Dear Brigitte (65); Singing Nun, The (66)

KOZINTSEV, GREGORY
Alone (31); Youth of Maxim (35); Return of Maxim (37); New Horizons (39); Belinski (53); Plain People (56); •Don Quixote (57); Hamlet (64); King Lear (72)

KRAMER, STANLEY
Not As a Stranger (55); Pride and the Passion, The (57); •Defiant Ones, The (58); •On the Beach (59); •Inherit the Wind (60); •Judgment at Nuremberg (61); •It's a Mad, Mad, Mad, Mad World (63); •Ship of Fools (65); •Guess Who's Coming to Dinner (67); Secret of Santa Vittoria, The (69); R.P.M. (70); Bless the Beasts and Children (71); Oklahoma Crude (73); Domino Principle, The (77); Runner Stumbles, The (79)

KUBRICK, STANLEY
•Fear and Desire (53); •Killer's Kiss (55); •Killing, The (56); •Paths of Glory (57); •Spartacus (60); •Lolita (62); •Dr. Strangelove: Or How I Learned to Stop Worrying and Love the Bomb (63); •2001: A Space Odyssey (68); •Clockwork Orange, A (71); •Barry Lyndon (75); •Shining, The (80); •Full Metal Jacket (87); •Eyes Wide Shut (99)

KUROSAWA, AKIRA
•Drunken Angel (48); •Stray Dog (49); •Rashomon (50); Scandal (50); Idiot, The (51); •Ikiru (52); •Seven Samurai, The (54); I Live in Fear (55); Lower Depths, The (57); •Throne of Blood (57); •Hidden Fortress, The (58); •Bad Sleep Well, The (60); •Yojimbo (61); Sanjuro (62); •High and Low (63); Red Beard (65); Dodes 'Ka-Den (70); •Dersu Uzala (75); •Kagemusha (80); •Ran (85); •Dreams (90); Rhapsody in August (91); Madadayo (93)

KUROSAWA, KIYOSHI
Kandagawa Wars (83); Excitement of the Do-Re-Mi-Fa Girl, The (85); Sweet Home (89); Guard from Underground, The (92); Whirlpool of Joy (92); Yakuza Taxi (94); Men of Rage (94); Suit Yourself or Shoot Yourself 1—The Heist (95); Suit Yourself or Shoot Yourself 2—The Escape (95); Suit Yourself or Shoot Yourself 3—The Loot (95); Suit Yourself or Shoot Yourself 4—The Reversal (95); Door III (96); Suit Yourself or Shoot Yourself 5—The Nouveau Riche (96); Suit Yourself or Shoot Yourself 6—The Hero (96); The Revenge—A Visit from Fate (97); The Revenge—The Scar That Never Fades (97); •Cure (97);

Serpent's Path (97); Eyes of the Spider (98); License to Live (99); Charisma (99); Barren Illusion (99); Seance (00); Pulse (01); Bright Future (03); Doppelganger (03)

KURYS, DIANE
•Peppermint Soda (77); Cocktail Molotov (80); •Entre Nous (83); •Man in Love, A (87); •C'est la Vie (90); Love after Love (94); Six Days, Six Nights (94); Les Enfants du Siecle (99); Je Reste! (03)

KUSTURICA, EMIR
Guernica (76); Do You Remember Dolly Bell? (81); •When Father Was Away on Business (85); •Time of the Gypsies (89); •Arizona Dream (93); •Underground (95); •Black Cat, White Cat (98); Super 8 Stories (01); La Vie Est une Miracle! (03)

LABUTE, NEIL
•In the Company of Men (97); •Your Friends & Neighbors (98); Nurse Betty (00); Bash: Latterday Plays (00); •Possession (02); Shape of Things, The

LANDIS, JOHN
Schlock (73); •Kentucky Fried Movie, The (77); •National Lampoon's Animal House (78); •Blues Brothers, The (80); •American Werewolf in London, An (81); •Trading Places (83); Twilight Zone—The Movie (83); Into the Night (85); Spies Like Us (85); Three Amigos (86); Amazon Women on the Moon (87); •Coming to America (88); Oscar (91); Innocent Blood (92); Beverly Hills Cop III (94); Stupids, The (96); Susan's Plan (98); Blues Brothers 2000 (98); Dying to Get Rich/Susan's Plan (98); Slasher (04)

LANG, FRITZ
•M (31); •Testament of Dr. Mabuse, The (33); Liliom (34); •Fury (36); •You Only Live Once (37); You and Me (38); Return of Frank James, The (40); •Man Hunt (41); •Western Union (41); Moontide (42); •Hangmen Also Die (43); •Ministry of Fear (45); •Scarlet Street (45); •Woman in the Window, The (45); Cloak and Dagger (46); Secret beyond the Door, The (48); American Guerilla in the Philippines, An (50); House by the River (50); •Clash by Night (52); •Rancho Notorious (52); •Big Heat, The (53); Blue Gardenia, The (53); Human Desire (54); Moonfleet (55); Beyond a Reasonable Doubt (56); •While the City Sleeps (56); Journey to the Lost City/Tiger of Bengal (59); •Thousand Eyes of Dr. Mabuse, The (60)

LANG, WALTER
Brothers (30); Cock O' the Walk (30); Costello Case, The (30); Hello Sister (30); Command Performance, The (31); Hell Bound (31); Women Go on Forever (31); Meet the Baron (33); No More Orchids (33); Warrior's Husband, The (33); Mighty Barnum, The (34); Party's Over, The (34); Whom the Gods Destroy (34); Carnival (35); Hooray For Love (35); Love Before Breakfast (36); Second Honeymoon (37); Wife, Doctor and Nurse (37); Baroness and the Butler, The (37); I'll Give a Million (38); Little Princess, The (39); Blue Bird, The (40); Great Profile, The (40); Star Dust (40); •Tin Pan Alley (40); Moon Over Miami (41); Weekend in Havana (41);

Magnificent Dope, The (42); Song of the Islands (42); Coney Island (43); Greenwich Village (44); •State Fair (45); Claudia and David (46); Sentimental Journey (46); Mother Wore Tights (47); •Sitting Pretty (48); When My Baby Smiles at Me (48); You're My Everything (49); •Cheaper by the Dozen (50); Jackpot, The (50); On the Riviera (51); •With a Song in My Heart (52); Call Me Madam (53); •There's No Business Like Show Business (54); •King and I, The (56); Desk Set (57); But Not for Me (59); Can-Can (60); Marriage-Go-Round, The (60); Snow White and the Three Stooges (61)

LEAN, DAVID
•Major Barbara (41); •In Which We Serve (42); •This Happy Breed (44); •Blithe Spirit (45); •Brief Encounter (45); •Great Expectations (46); •Oliver Twist (48); One Woman's Story (48); Madeleine (49); Breaking the Sound Barrier (52); •Hobson's Choice (54); •Summertime (55); •Bridge on the River Kwai, The (57); •Lawrence of Arabia (62); •Doctor Zhivago (65); •Ryan's Daughter (70); •Passage to India, A (84)

LECONTE, PATRICE
Les Veces Etaient Fermes de l'Interieur (75); Les Bronzes (78); Les Bronzes Font du Ski (79); Viens Chez Moi J'Habite Chez une Copine (80); Ma Femme S'Appelle Reviens (82); Circulez y'a Rien a Voir (83); Les Specialistes (85); Tandem (87); •Monsieur Hire (89); •Hairdresser's Husband, The (92); Contre l'Oubli (92); Le Batteur du Bolero (92); Tango (93); Yvonne's Perfume (94); Grand Dukes, The (95); •Ridicule (96); Une Chance sur Deux (98); Girl on the Bridge, The (99); Widow of St. Pierre, The (00); Felix and Lola (00); Rue des Plaisirs (02); Man on the Train, The (02); Intimate Strangers (04); Dogora: Ouvrons les Yeux (04)

LEE, ANG
Pushing Hands (91); •Wedding Banquet, The (93); •Eat Drink Man Woman (94); •Sense and Sensibility (95); •Ice Storm, The (97); Ride with the Devil (99); •Crouching Tiger, Hidden Dragon (00); •Hulk (03); Brokeback Mountain (05)

LEE, ROWLAND V.
Dangerous Woman, A (29); •Mysterious Dr. Fu Manchu, The (29); Wolf of Wall Street, The (29); Derelict (30); Ladies Love Brutes (30); Man from Wyoming, A (30); Return of Dr. Fu Manchu, The (30); Guilty Generation, The (31); Ruling Voice, The (31); Overnight (33); Zoo in Budapest (33); •Count of Monte Cristo, The (34); Gambling (34); I Am Suzanne (34); Cardinal Richelieu (35); Three Musketeers, The (35); One Rainy Afternoon (36); •Love from a Stranger (37); Toast of New York, The (37); Mother Carey's Chickens (38); Service De Luxe (38); •Son of Frankenstein (39); Sun Never Sets, The (39); Tower of London (39); Son of Monte Cristo, The (41); Powder Town (42); Bridge of San Luis Rey, The (44); Captain Kidd (45)

LEE, SPIKE
•She's Gotta Have It (86); School Daze (88); •Do the Right Thing (89); •Mo' Better Blues (90); Jungle Fever (91); •Malcolm X (92);

•Crooklyn (94); Clockers (95); Girl 6 (96); •Get on the Bus (96); Four Little Girls (97); Freak (98); He Got Game (98); •Summer of Sam (99); Original Kings of Comedy, The (00); Bamboozled (00); Huey P. Newton Story, A (01); Jim Brown: All American (02); •25th Hour (02); She Hate Me (04); Sucker Free City (04)

LEHMANN, MICHAEL
•Heathers (89); •Hudson Hawk (91); Meet the Applegates (91); Airheads (94); Truth About Cats and Dogs, The (96); My Giant (98); 40 Days and 40 Nights (02)

LEIGH, MIKE
Bleak Moments (71); Hard Labour (73); Nuts in May (75); Kiss of Death, The (77); Abigail's Party (77); Who's Who (78); Grown-Ups (80); Home Sweet Home (82); Meantime (83); Four Days in July (84); •High Hopes (88); •Life Is Sweet (91); •Naked (93); •Secrets & Lies (95); •Career Girls (97); •Topsy-Turvy (99); All or Nothing (02); •Vera Drake (04)

LEISEN, MITCHELL
Cradle Song (33); •Death Takes a Holiday (34); Murder at the Vanities (34); Behold My Wife (35); Four Hours to Kill (35); •Hands Across the Table (35); Big Broadcast of 1937, The (36); 13 Hours by Air (36); Big Broadcast of 1938, The (37); •Easy Living (37); Swing High, Swing Low (37); Artists and Models Abroad (38); •Midnight (39); Arise, My Love (40); •Remember the Night (40); •Hold Back the Dawn (41); I Wanted Wings (41); Lady Is Willing, The (42); Take a Letter, Darling (42); No Time for Love (43); Frenchman's Creek (44); •Lady in the Dark (44); Practically Yours (44); Kitty (45); Masquerade in Mexico (45); •To Each His Own (46); Dream Girl (47); Golden Earrings (47); Suddenly It's Spring (47); Bride of Vengeance (49); Song of Surrender (49); Captain Carey, U.S.A. (50); No Man of Her Own (50); Darling, How Could You! (51); Mating Season, The (51); Young Man with Ideas (52); Tonight We Sing (53); Bedevilled (55); Girl Most Likely, The (57)

LELOUCH, CLAUDE
Right of Man, The (60); L'Amour avec des Si (63); To Be a Crook (65); Les Grands Moments (65); •Man and A Woman, A (66); Live For Life (67); Les Gauloises Bleu (68); Life Love Death (69); Love Is a Funny Thing (69); Crook, The (71); Smic Smac Smoc (71); Money Money Money (72); Happy New Year (73); And Now My Love (75); Cat and Mouse (75); Good and the Bad, The (76); Second Chance (76); Another Man, Another Chance (77); Robert et Robert (78); Adventure for Two, An (79); Bolero (81); Edith and Marcel (83); Vie la Vie (84); Going and Coming Back (85); Bandits (86); •Man and a Woman: 20 Years Later, A (86); Itinerary of a Spoiled Child (88); There Were Days and Moons (90); La Belle Histoire (92); Tout Ca. . . Pour Ca! (93); Les Miserables (95); Hommes, Femmes: Mode d'Emploi (96); Chances and Coincidences (98); One 4 All (99); And Now... Ladies and Gentleman (02); Le Genre Humain—1ere Partie: Les Parisiens (04)

LEONARD, ROBERT Z.
Lady of Chance, A (28); Marianne (29); •Divorcee, The (30); In Gay Madrid (30); Let Us Be Gay (30); Bachelor Father, The (31); Five and Ten (31); It's a Wise Child (31); Susan Lenox: Her Fall and Rise (31); Lovers Courageous (32); Strange Interlude (32); Dancing Lady (33); Peg O' My Heart (33); Outcast Lady (34); After Office Hours (35); Escapade (35); •Great Ziegfeld, The (36); Piccadilly Jim (36); Firefly, The (37); •Maytime (37); Girl of the Golden West, The (38); Broadway Serenade (39); New Moon (40); •Pride and Prejudice (40); Third Finger, Left Hand (40); When Ladies Meet (41); •Ziegfeld Girl (41); Stand by for Action (42); We Were Dancing (42); Man from Down Under, The (43); Marriage Is a Private Affair (44); Weekend at the Waldorf (45); Secret Heart, The (46); Cynthia (47); B.F.'s Daughter (48); Bribe, The (49); In the Good Old Summertime (49); Duchess of Idaho (50); Grounds for Marriage (50); Nancy Goes to Rio (50); Too Young to Kiss (51); Everything I Have Is Yours (52); Clown, The (53); Great Diamond Robbery, The (53); Her Twelve Men (54); King's Thief, The (55); Kelly and Me (57)

LEONE, SERGIO
Colossus of Rhodes, The (60); Sodom and Gomorrah (62); •Fistful of Dollars, A (64); •For a Few Dollars More (65); •Good, the Bad, and the Ugly, The (66); •Once Upon a Time in the West (69); Duck, You Sucker (72); •Once Upon a Time in America (84)

LEROY, MERVYN
Broadway Babies (29); Hot Stuff (29); Little Johnny Jones (30); Numbered Men (30); Playing Around (30); Showgirl in Hollywood (30); Top Speed (30); Broadminded (31); Five Star Final (31); Gentleman's Fate (31); •Little Caesar (31); Local Boy Makes Good (31); Tonight or Never (31); Too Young to Marry (31); Big City Blues (32); Heart of New York, The (32); High Pressure (32); •I Am a Fugitive from a Chain Gang (32); Three on a Match (32); Two Seconds (32); Elmer the Great (33); •Gold Diggers of 1933 (33); Hard to Handle (33); Tugboat Annie (33); World Changes, The (33); Happiness Ahead (34); Heat Lightning (34); Hi, Nellie! (34); I Found Stella Parish (35); Oil for the Lamps of China (35); Page Miss Glory (35); Sweet Adeline (35); •Anthony Adverse (36); Three Men on a Horse (36); King and the Chorus Girl, The (37); •They Won't Forget (37); Fools for Scandal (38); Escape (40); •Waterloo Bridge (40); Blossoms in the Dust (41); Unholy Partners (41); •Johnny Eager (42); •Random Harvest (42); •Madame Curie (43); •Thirty Seconds Over Tokyo (44); Without Reservations (46); Desire Me (47); Homecoming (48); Any Number Can Play (49); East Side, West Side (49); Little Women (49); •Quo Vadis (51); Lovely to Look At (52); Million Dollar Mermaid (52); Latin Lovers (53); Rose Marie (54); •Mister Roberts (55); Strange Lady in Town (55); Bad Seed, The (56); Toward the Unknown (56); Home Before Dark (58); •No Time for Sergeants (58); FBI Story, The (59); Wake Me When It's

Over (60); Devil at 4 O'Clock, The (61); Majority of One, A (61); •Gypsy (62); Mary, Mary (63); Moment to Moment (66)

LESTER, RICHARD
•Ring-a-Ding Rhythm (62); Mouse on the Moon, The (63); •Hard Day's Night, A (64); •Help! (65); •Knack. . . and How to Get It, The (65); •Funny Thing Happened on the Way to the Forum, A (66); •How I Won the War (67); •Petulia (68); •Bed Sitting Room, The (69); •Juggernaut (74); •Three Musketeers, The (74); •Four Musketeers, The (75); •Royal Flash (75); Ritz, The (76); •Robin and Marian (76); Butch and Sundance: The Early Days (79); •Cuba (79); •Superman II (80); Superman III (83); Finders Keepers (84); Get Back (91)

LEVINSON, BARRY
•Diner (82); •Natural, The (84); Young Sherlock Holmes (85); •Good Morning, Vietnam (87); •Tin Men (87); •Rain Man (88); •Avalon (90); •Bugsy (91); Toys (92); •Disclosure (94); Jimmy Hollywood (94); Sleepers (96); •Wag the Dog (97); Sphere (98); Liberty Heights (99); Everlasting Piece, An (00); Bandits (01); Envy (04)

LEWIS, JERRY
Bellboy, The (60); Errand Boy, The (61); Ladies' Man, The (61); •Nutty Professor, The (63); Patsy, The (64); Family Jewels, The (65); Three on a Couch (66); Big Mouth, The (67); One More Time (70); Which Way to the Front? (70); Hardly Working (81); Smorgasbord (83)

LEWIS, JOSEPH H.
Courage of the West (37); Singing Outlaw (37); Border Wolves (38); Last Stand, The (38); Spy Ring, The (38); Blazing Six Shooters (40); Boys of the City (40); Man from Tumbleweeds, The (40); Return of Wild Bill, The (40); Texas Stagecoach (40); That Gang of Mine (40); Two-Fisted Rangers (40); Arizona Cyclone (41); Criminals Within (41); Invisible Ghost, The (41); Pride of the Bowery (41); Bombs Over Burma (42); Boss of Hangtown Mesa (42); Mad Doctor of Market Street, The (42); Secrets of a Co-Ed (42); Silver Bullet, The (42); Minstrel Man (44); Falcon in San Francisco, The (45); My Name Is Julia Ross (45); So Dark the Night (46); Swordsman, The (47); Return of October, The (48); •Gun Crazy (49); Undercover Man, The (49); Lady Without Passport, A (50); Desperate Search (52); Retreat, Hell! (52); Cry of the Hunted (53); Big Combo, The (55); Lawless Street, A (55); Seventh Cavalry (56); Halliday Brand, The (57); •Terror in a Texas Town (58)

LIMAN, DOUG
Getting In (94); Swingers (96); •Go (99); •Bourne Identity, The (02); Mr. and Mrs. Smith (05)

LINK, CAROLINE
Beyond Silence (96); Annaluise & Anton (99); •Nowhere in Africa (01)

LINKLATER, RICHARD
•Slacker (91); •Dazed and Confused (93); •Before Sunrise (95); Suburbia (97); Newton Boys, The (98); Waking Life (02); Tape (02); •School of Rock (03); •Before Sunset (04)

LITVAK, ANATOLE
Dolly Gets Ahead (30); Be Mine Tonight (33); Sleeping Car (33); •Mayerling (36); Tovarich (37); Woman I Love, The (37); Amazing Doctor Clitterhouse, The (38); Sisters, The (38); •Confessions of a Nazi Spy (39); •Roaring Twenties, The (39); •All This and Heaven Too (40); Castle on the Hudson (40); •City for Conquest (40); Blues in the Night (41); Out of the Fog (41); This Above All (42); Long Night, The (47); •Snake Pit, The (48); •Sorry, Wrong Number (48); •Decision Before Dawn (51); Act of Love (53); Deep Blue Sea, The (55); •Anastasia (56); Journey, The (59); Goodbye Again (61); Five Miles to Midnight (63); Night of the Generals, The (67); Lady in the Car with Glasses and a Gun, The (70)

LLOYD, FRANK
Dark Streets (29); Drag (29); Weary River (29); Young Nowheres (29); Lash, The (30); Son of the Gods (30); Way of All Men, The (30); Age for Love, The (31); East Lynne (31); Right of Way, The (31); Passport to Hell (32); Berkeley Square (33); •Cavalcade (33); Hoop-La (33); Servants' Entrance (34); •Mutiny on the Bounty (35); Big Noise, The (36); Under Two Flags (36); Maid of Salem (37); Wells Fargo (37); If I Were King (38); Rulers of the Sea (39); Howards of Virginia, The (40); Lady from Cheyenne, The (41); This Woman Is Mine (41); Forever and a Day (43); Blood on the Sun (45); Shanghai Story, The (54); Last Command, The (55)

LOACH, KEN
•Poor Cow (67); •Kes (69); Family Life (71); Gamekeeper, The (78); Black Jack (79); •Looks and Smiles (82); Fatherland (86); Hidden Agenda (90); •Riff-Raff (91); •Raining Stones (93); Ladybird, Ladybird (94); Land and Freedom (95); •Carla's Song (96); Flickering Flame, The (97); •My Name Is Joe (98); Bread and Roses (00); Navigators, The (01); Sweet Sixteen (02); Fond Kiss . . . , A (04)

LOGAN, JOSHUA
I Met My Love Again (38); •Picnic (55); •Bus Stop (56); •Sayonara (57); •South Pacific (58); Tall Story (60); Fanny (61); Ensign Pulver (64); Camelot (67); Paint Your Wagon (69)

LONCRAINE, RICHARD
Radio Wonderful (72); Flame (74); Haunting of Julia, The (76); •Brimstone and Treacle (82); Missionary, The (82); Bellman and True (88); Wedding Gift, The (94); •Richard III (95); Gathering Storm, The (02); My House in Umbria (03); Wimbledon (04)

LOSEY, JOSEPH
Boy with Green Hair, The (48); Lawless, The (50); Big Night, The (51); M (51); Prowler, The (51); Sleeping Tiger, The (54); Finger of Guilt (56); Gypsy and the Gentleman, The (57); Time Without Pity (57); Chance Meeting (59); Concrete Jungle, The (60); Eva (62); •Servant, The (63); These Are the Damned (63); •King and Country (64); Modesty Blaise (66); •Accident (67); Boom! (68); Secret Ceremony (68); Figures in a Landscape (70); •Go-Between, The (71);

Assassination of Trotsky, The (72); Doll's House, A (73); Galileo (75); •Romantic Englishwoman, The (75); Mr. Klein (76); Don Giovanni (79); Trout, The (82); Steaming (85)

LUBITSCH, ERNST
Patriot, The (28); •Love Parade, The (29); •Monte Carlo (30); •Smiling Lieutenant, The (31); Broken Lullaby (32); •If I Had a Million (32); One Hour with You (32); •Trouble in Paradise (32); Design for Living (33); •Merry Widow, The (34); Angel (37); Bluebeard's Eighth Wife (38); •Ninotchka (39); •Shop Around the Corner, The (40); That Uncertain Feeling (41); •To Be or Not to Be (42); •Heaven Can Wait (43); Cluny Brown (46); That Lady in Ermine (48)

LUCAS, GEORGE
•Thx 1138 (71); •American Graffiti (73); •Star Wars (77); •Star Wars Episode I: The Phantom Menace (99); •Star Wars Episode II: The Attack of the Clones (02); •Star Wars Episode III: Revenge of the Sith (05).

LUHRMANN, BAZ
•Strictly Ballroom (92); •William Shakespeare's Romeo + Juliet (96); •Moulin Rouge (01)

LUMET, SIDNEY
•12 Angry Men (57); Stage Struck (58); That Kind of Woman (59); Fugitive Kind, The (60); •Long Day's Journey into Night (62); View from the Bridge, A (62); •Fail Safe (64); Hill, The (65); •Pawnbroker, The (65); •Deadly Affair, The (66); Group, The (66); Bye Bye Braverman (68); Sea Gull, The (68); Appointment, The (69); •Anderson Tapes, The (71); Child's Play (72); Offense, The (72); •Serpico (73); Lovin' Molly (74); •Murder on the Orient Express (74); •Dog Day Afternoon (75); •Network (76); •Equus (77); Wiz, The (78); •Just Tell Me What You Want (80); •Prince of the City (81); Deathtrap (82); •Verdict, The (82); Daniel (83); Garbo Talks (84); Morning After, The (86); Power (86); •Running on Empty (88); Family Business (89); •Q&A (90); Stranger among Us, A (92); Guilty As Sin (93); Night Falls on Manhattan (97); Critical Care (97); Gloria (99); Strip Search (04)

LYNCH, DAVID
•Eraserhead (78); •Elephant Man, The (80); Dune (84); •Blue Velvet (86); •Wild at Heart (90); Twin Peaks: Fire Walk with Me (92); •Lost Highway (97); •Straight Story, The (99); •Mulholland Dr. (01)

LYNE, ADRIAN
•Foxes (80); Flashdance (83); 9 1/2 Weeks (86); •Fatal Attraction (87); •Jacob's Ladder (90); •Indecent Proposal (93); •Lolita (97); •Unfaithful (02)

MACARTHUR, CHARLES
•Crime Without Passion (34); •Scoundrel, The (35); Once in a Blue Moon (36); Soak the Rich (36)

MACKENDRICK, ALEXANDER
Tight Little Island (49); •Man in the White Suit, The (51); Crash of Silence (52); High and Dry (54); •Ladykillers, The (55); •Sweet Smell of Success (57); Boy Ten Feet Tall, A (63); High Wind

in Jamaica, A (65); Don't Make Waves (67); Oh Dad, Poor Dad, Mama's Hung You in the Closet and I'm Feelin' So Sad (67)

MACKINNON, GILLIES
Grass Arena, The (91); Playboys, The (92); Simple Twist of Fate, A (94); Trojan Eddie (96); Small Faces (96); Regeneration (97); •Hideous Kinky (98); Last of the Blond Bombshells, The (00); Escapist, The (01); Pure (02); Gunpowder, Treason and Plot (04)

MADDEN, JOHN
Wings (83); Grown Ups (85); Wreath of Roses, A (87); Widowmaker, The (90); Ethan Frome (93); Golden Gate (94); Meat (94); Truth or Dare (96); •Mrs. Brown (97); •Shakespeare in Love (98); Captain Corelli's Mandolin (01); Proof (05)

MAKAVEJEV, DUSAN
Man Is Not a Bird (66); •Love Affair; or the Case of the Missing Switchboard Operator (67); •Innocence Unprotected (68); WR: Mysteries of the Organism (71); I Miss Sonia Henie (72); Sweet Movie (74); Wet Dreams (74); Montenegro (81); •Coca-Cola Kid, The (85); Manifesto (88); Gorilla Bathes at Noon (93); Hole in the Soul, A (95); Danish Girls Show Everything (96)

MAKHMALBAF, MOHSEN
Nasooh Repentance (82); Two Blind Eyes (83); Seeking Sanctuary (84); Boycott (85); Peddlar, The (87); Cylcist, The (87); Marriage of the Blessed (89); Time of Love (90); Nights of Zyandeh-Rood, The (91); Once Upon a Time, Cinema (92); Images from the Ghajar Dynasty (93); Actor, The (93); Salaam Cinema (95); Gabbeh (96); Moment of Innocence, A (96); Silence, The (98); •Kandahar (01); Afghan Alphabet (02)

MALICK, TERRENCE
•Badlands (74); •Days of Heaven (78); •Thin Red Line, The (98)

MALLE, LOUIS
Frantic (58); •Lovers, The (59); •Zazie (60); Very Private Affair, A (62); Fire Within, The (63); Viva Maria! (65); Thief of Paris, The (67); Spirits of the Dead (68); •Murmur of the Heart (71); •Lacombe, Lucien (74); Black Moon (75); •Pretty Baby (78); •Atlantic City (81); •My Dinner with Andre (81); Crackers (84); Alamo Bay (85); •Au Revoir, les Enfants (87); May Fools (90); •Damage (92); •Vanya on 42nd Street (94)

MAMET, DAVID
•House of Games (87); Things Change (88); •Homicide (91); Oleanna (94); •Spanish Prisoner, The (98); Winslow Boy, The (99); State and Main (00); Heist (01); Spartan (04)

MAMOULIAN, ROUBEN
•Applause (29); City Streets (31); •Dr. Jekyll and Mr. Hyde (32); •Love Me Tonight (32); •Queen Christina (33); Song of Songs (33); •We Live Again (34); •Becky Sharp (35); Gay Desperado, The (36); High, Wide and Handsome (37); •Golden Boy (39); •Mark of Zorro, The (40); •Blood and Sand (41); Rings on Her Fingers (42); •Summer Holiday (48); •Silk Stockings (57)

MANGOLD, JAMES
Heavy (96); •Cop Land (97); •Girl,
Interrupted (99); Kate & Leopold (01);
Identity (03)

MANKIEWICZ, JOSEPH L.
Dragonwyck (46); Somewhere in the Night (46);
•Ghost and Mrs. Muir, The (47); Late George
Apley, The (47); Escape (48); •Letter to Three
Wives, A (48); House of Strangers (49); •All About
Eve (50); No Way Out (50); •People Will
Talk (51); •Five Fingers (52); •Julius Caesar (53);
Barefoot Contessa, The (54); Guys and Dolls (55);
Quiet American, The (58); Suddenly, Last
Summer (59); •Cleopatra (63); Honey Pot,
The (67); There Was a Crooked Man (70);
•Sleuth (72)

MANN, ANTHONY
Dr. Broadway (42); Moonlight in Havana (42);
Nobody's Darling (43); My Best Gal (44);
Strangers in the Night (44); Great Flamarion,
The (45); Sing Your Way Home (45); Two
O'Clock Courage (45); Bamboo Blonde, The (46);
Strange Impersonation (46); Desperate (47);
Railroaded (47); •T-Men (47); •He Walked by
Night (48); •Raw Deal (48); Black Book, The (49);
Border Incident (49); Devil's Doorway (50);
Furies, The (50); Side Street (50); •Winchester
'73 (50); Tall Target, The (51); Bend of the
River (52); •Glenn Miller Story, The (53); •Naked
Spur, The (53); Thunder Bay (53); •Far Country,
The (55); Last Frontier, The (55); •Man from
Laramie, The (55); Strategic Air Command (55);
Serenade (56); Men in War (57); Tin Star,
The (57); God's Little Acre (58); •Man of the
West (58); Cimarron (60); •Spartacus (60); •El
Cid (61); Fall of the Roman Empire, The (64);
Heroes of Telemark, The (65); Dandy in Aspic,
A (68)

MANN, DANIEL
•Come Back, Little Sheba (52); About Mrs.
Leslie (54); •I'll Cry Tomorrow (55); •Rose
Tattoo, The (55); •Teahouse of the August
Moon, The (56); Hot Spell (58); Last Angry Man,
The (59); •Butterfield 8 (60); Mountain Road,
The (60); Ada (61); Five Finger Exercise (62);
Who's Got the Action? (62); Who's Been Sleeping
in My Bed? (63); Judith (65); •Our Man Flint (66);
For Love of Ivy (68); Dream of Kings, A (69);
Willard (71); Revengers, The (72); Interval (73);
Maurie (73); Journey into Fear (74); Lost in the
Stars (74); Matilda (78)

MANN, DELBERT
•Marty (55); Bachelor Party, The (57); Desire
under the Elms (58); •Separate Tables (58); Middle
of the Night (59); Dark at the Top of the Stairs,
The (60); Lover Come Back (61); Outsider,
The (62); •That Touch of Mink (62); Gathering of
Eagles, A (63); Dear Heart (64); Quick, Before It
Melts (64); Mister Buddwing (66); Fitzwilly (67);
Pink Jungle, The (68); David Copperfield (70);
Jane Eyre (71); •Kidnapped (71); Birch
Interval (76); Night Crossing (82)

MANN, MICHAEL
•Thief (81); Keep, The (83); •Manhunter (86);
•Last of the Mohicans, The (92); •Heat; •Insider,
The (99); •Ali (01); •Collateral (04)

MARQUAND, RICHARD
Legacy, The (78); •Eye of the Needle (81); •Return
of the Jedi (83); Until September (84); •Jagged
Edge (85); Hearts of Fire (87)

MARSHALL, GARRY
Young Doctors in Love (82); •Flamingo Kid,
The (84); Nothing in Common (86);
Overboard (87); •Beaches (88); •Pretty
Woman (90); Frankie and Johnny (91); Exit to
Eden (94); Dear God (96); Other Sister, The (99);
Runaway Bride (99); Princess Diaries, The (01);
Raising Helen (04); Princess Diaries 2: Royal
Engagement, The (04)

MARSHALL, PENNY
Jumpin' Jack Flash (86); •Big (88);
•Awakenings (90); •League of Their Own, A (92);
Renaissance Man (94); Preacher's Wife, The (96);
Riding in Cars with Boys (01)

MARSHALL, ROB
Annie (99); •Chicago (02)

MATE, RUDOLPH
It Had to Be You (47); Dark Past, The (48);
•D.O.A. (50); No Sad Songs for Me (50); Union
Station (50); Branded (51); Prince Who Was a
Thief, The (51); When Worlds Collide (51); Green
Glove, The (52); Paula (52); Sally and Saint
Anne (52); Forbidden (53); Mississippi Gambler,
The (53); Second Chance (53); Black Shield of
Falworth, The (54); Siege at Red River, The (54);
Far Horizons, The (55); Violent Men, The (55);
Miracle in the Rain (56); Port Afrique (56);
Rawhide Years, The (56); Three Violent
People (56); Deep Six, The (58); For the First
Time (59); Seven Seas to Calais (62); 300
Spartans, The (62)

MAY, ELAINE
•New Leaf, A (71); Heartbreak Kid, The (72);
•Mikey and Nicky (76); •Ishtar (87)

MAYSLES, ALBERT AND DAVID
Showman (62); What's Happening! The Beatles in
the U.S.A. (64); Visit with Truman Capote, A (65);
Meet Marlon Brando (66); Salesman (68); •Gimme
Shelter (70); Chirsto's Valley Curtain (73); Grey
Gardens (74); Running Fence (78); Muhammad
and Larry (80); Vladimir Horowitz, the Last
Romantic (85); Islands (86); Christo in Paris (90)

MAYSLES, ALBERT
Primary (60); Umbrellas (94); Concert of Wills:
Making the Getty Center (98); Lalee's Kin: The
Legacy of Cotton (01)

MAZURSKY, PAUL
•Bob & Carol & Ted & Alice (69); Alex in
Wonderland (70); •Blume in Love (73); •Harry and
Tonto (74); •Next Stop, Greenwich Village (76);
•Unmarried Woman, An (78); Willie and Phil (80);
Tempest (82); •Moscow on the Hudson (84);
•Down and Out in Beverly Hills (86); Moon Over
Parador (88); Enemies, a Love Story (89); Scenes
from a Mall (91); Pickle, The (93); Faithful (96);
Winchell (98); Coast to Coast (04)

MCBRIDE, JIM
•David Holzman's Diary (68); My Girlfriend's
Wedding (69); Glen and Randa (71); Hot
Times (74); Breathless (83); •Big Easy, The (87);

Great Balls of Fire (89); Blood Ties (91); Wrong Man, The (93); Uncovered (94); Pronto, The (97); Informant, The (97); Dead by Midnight (97); Meat Loaf: To Hell and Back (00)

MCCAREY, LEO
Sophomore, The (29); Let's Go Native (30); Part Time Wife (30); Red Hot Rhythm (30); Wild Company (30); Indiscreet (31); •Kid from Spain, The (32); •Duck Soup (33); Belle of the Nineties (34); Six of a Kind (34); •Ruggles of Red Gap (35); Milky Way, The (36); •Awful Truth, The (37); •Make Way for Tomorrow (37); •Love Affair (39); Once Upon a Honeymoon (42); •Going My Way (44); •Bells of St. Mary's, The (45); Good Sam (48); My Son John (52); Affair to Remember, An (57); Rally 'Round the Flag, Boys! (58); Satan Never Sleeps (62)

MCGRATH, DOUGLAS
•Emma (96); Company Man (00); •Nicholas Nickleby (02)

MCLEOD, NORMAN Z.
Along Came Youth (31); •Monkey Business (31); Touchdown (31); •Horse Feathers (32); Miracle Man, The (32); Alice in Wonderland (33); Lady's Profession, A (33); Mama Loves Papa (33); •It's a Gift (34); Many Happy Returns (34); Melody in Spring (34); Coronado (35); Here Comes Cookie (35); Redheads on Parade (35); Early to Bed (36); Pennies from Heaven (36); Mind Your Own Business (37); •Topper (37); Merrily We Live (38); There Goes My Heart (38); Remember? (39); Topper Takes a Trip (39); Little Men (40); Lady Be Good (41); Trial of Mary Dugan, The (41); Jackass Mail (42); Panama Hattie (42); Powers Girl, The (42); Swing Shift Maisie (43); Kid from Brooklyn, The (46); •Road to Rio (47); •Secret Life of Walter Mitty, The (47); Isn't It Romantic? (48); Paleface, The (48); Let's Dance (50); My Favorite Spy (51); Never Wave at a WAC (52); Casanova's Big Night (54); Public Pigeon No. 1 (57)

MCNAUGHTON, JOHN
•Henry: Portrait of a Serial Killer (89); Borrower, The (91); Sex, Drugs, Rock & Roll (91); •Mad Dog and Glory (93); Girls in Prison (94); Normal Life (96); •Wild Things (98); Lansky (99); Condo Painting (00); Speaking of Sex (01)

MCTIERNAN, JOHN
Nomads (85); •Predator (87); •Die Hard (88); •Hunt for Red October, The (90); Medicine Man (92); •Last Action Hero (93); Die Hard with a Vengeance (95); •Thomas Crown Affair, The (99); Rollerball (02); Basic (03)

MEDAK, PETER
Negatives (68); Day in the Death of Joe Egg, A (72); •Ruling Class, The (72); Third Girl from the Left, The (73); Ghost in the Noonday Sun (73); Sporting Chance (1976); Cosmic Princess (76); Odd Job, The (78); Changeling, The (79); Babysitter, The (80); Mistress of Paradise (81); Zorro, the Gay Blade (81); Cry for the Strangers (82); Breakin' Through (84); Men's Club, The (86); Krays, The (90); Let Him Have It (91);

Pontiac Moon (94); Romeo Is Bleeding (94); Hunchback, The (97); Species II (98); David Copperfield (00); Feast of All Saints (01)

MELVILLE, JEAN-PIERRE
Le Silence de la Mer (49); •Les Enfants Terribles (50); Quand Tu Lira Cette Lettre (53); •Bob le Flambeur (55); Deux Hommes dans Manhattan (59); Leon Morin Pretre (61); Fingerman, The (62); Magnet of Doom (62); Second Breath (66); •Le Samurai (67); Godson, The (67); L'Armee des Ombres (69); Le Cercle Rouge (70); Cop, A (72)

MENDES, SAM
Company (96); •American Beauty (99); •Road to Perdition (02)

MENZEL, JIRI
Pearls on the Ground (65); Crime at the Girls' School (65); •Closely Watched Trains (66); Capricious Summer (68); Larks on a String (69); Who Seeks a Handful of Gold (75); Seclusion Near a Forest (76); Magicians of the Silver Screen (78); Short Cut (80); Snowdrop Festival, The (82); Prague (85); My Sweet Little Village (85); End of the Good Old Days, The (89); Beggar's Opera, The (91); Life and Extraordinary Adventures of Private Ivan Chonkin (95)

MENZIES, WILLIAM CAMERON
Always Goodbye (31); Spider, The (31); Almost Married (32); Chandu The Magician (32); I Loved You Wednesday (33); Wharf Angel, The (34); •Things to Come (36); Green Cockatoo, The (37); •Thief of Baghdad, The (40); Address Unknown (44); Drums in the Deep South (51); Whip Hand, The (51); Invaders from Mars (53); Maze, The (53)

MEYER, RUSS
Immoral Mr. Teas, The (59); This Is My Body (59); Eve and the Handyman (60); Naked Camera (60); Erotica (61); Immoral West, The (62); Europe in the Raw (63); Heavenly Bodies (63); Lorna (64); Fanny Hill: Memoirs of a Woman of Pleasure (65); Mudhoney (65); Motorpsycho (65); Rope of Flesh (65); •Faster, Pussycat, Kill! Kill! (66); Mondo Topless (66); Good Morning. . . and Goodbye (67); Common-Law-Cabin (67); Finders Keepers, Lovers Weepers (68); Vixen (68); •Beyond the Valley of the Dolls (70); Seven Minutes, The (71); Sweet Suzy (73); Supervixens (75); Up! (76); Beneath the Valley of the Ultravixens (79)

MICHELL, ROGER
Buddha of Suburbia, The (93); Persuasion (95); Titanic Town (98); •Notting Hill (99); •Changing Lanes (02); Mother, The (03); Enduring Love (04)

MIKHALKOV, NIKITA
Quiet Day at the End of the War, A (70); At Home among Strangers (74); Slave of Love, A (77); Unfinished Piece for a Mechanical Piano, An (77); Five Evenings (79); Oblomov (80); Family Relations (82); Without Witnesses (83); •Dark Eyes (87); Avtostop (90); Close to Eden (91); Remembering Chekhov (93); Anna (94); Burnt by the Sun (94); Barber of Siberia, The (98)

MILESTONE, LEWIS

New York Nights (29); •All Quiet on the Western Front (30); •Front Page, The (31); Rain (32); Hallelujah, I'm a Bum (33); Captain Hates the Sea, The (34); Paris in Spring (35); Anything Goes (36); General Died at Dawn, The (36); Night of Nights, The (39); •Of Mice and Men (39); Lucky Partners (40); My Life with Caroline (41); •Edge of Darkness (43); North Star, The (43); Purple Heart, The (44); •Walk in the Sun, A (45); •Strange Love of Martha Ivers, The (46); Arch of Triumph (48); No Minor Vices (48); Red Pony, The (49); Halls of Montezuma (51); Kangaroo (52); Les Miserables (52); Melba (53); They Who Dare (53); •Pork Chop Hill (59); Ocean's Eleven (60); Mutiny on the Bounty (62)

MILIUS, JOHN

Dillinger (73); •Wind and the Lion, The (75); Big Wednesday (78); Conan the Barbarian (82); Red Dawn (84); Farewell to the King (89); Flight of the Intruder (91); Motorcycle Gang (94); Rough Riders (97)

MILLER, GEORGE

•Mad Max (79); •Road Warrior, The (81); Twilight Zone—The Movie (83); Mad Max beyond Thunderdome (85); •Witches of Eastwick, The (87); •Lorenzo's Oil (92); Babe: Pig in the City (98)

MILLER, GEORGE

Last Outlaw, The (80); •Man from Snowy River, The (82); Aviator, The (85); Cool Change (86); Far Country, The (86); Les Patterson Saves the World (87); Miracle Down Under (87); Goodbye Miss 4th of July (88); Spooner (89); Neverending Story II: The Next Chapter, The (91); Mom for Christmas, A (90); In the Nick of Time (91); Frozen Assets (92); Over the Hill (92); Gross Misconduct (94); Andre (94); Great Elephant Escape, The (95); Robinson Crusoe (96); Zeus and Roxanne (97); Tidal Wave: No Escape (97); In the Doghouse (98); Journey to the Center of the Earth (99); Cybermutt (02); Night of the Saber Tooth (05)

MINGHELLA, ANTHONY

•Truly, Madly, Deeply (91); Mr. Wonderful (93); •English Patient, The (96); •Talented Mr. Ripley, The (99); •Cold Mountain (03)

MINNELLI, VINCENTE

•Cabin in the Sky (43); I Dood It (43); •Meet Me in St. Louis (44); •Clock, The (45); Yolanda and the Thief (45); •Ziegfeld Follies (45); Undercurrent (46); •Pirate, The (48); Madame Bovary (49); •Father of the Bride (50); •American in Paris, An (51); Father's Little Dividend (51); •Bad and the Beautiful, The (52); •Band Wagon, The (53); Story of Three Loves, The (53); •Brigadoon (54); Long, Long Trailer, The (54); Cobweb, The (55); Kismet (55); •Lust for Life (56); •Tea and Sympathy (56); Designing Woman (57); •Gigi (58); Reluctant Debutante, The (58); •Some Came Running (59); •Bells Are Ringing (60); Home from the Hill (60); Four Horsemen of the Apocalypse, The (62); Two Weeks in Another Town (62); Courtship of Eddie's Father, The (63); Goodbye Charlie (64); Sandpiper, The (65); On a Clear Day You Can See Forever (70); Matter of Time, A (76)

MIYAZAKI, HAYAO

Lupin III: Castle of Cagliostro (79); Sherlock Hound, the Detective (84); Nausicaa of the Valley of Wind (84); Laputa: Castle in the Sky (86); My Neighbor Totoro (88); Kiki's Delivery Service (89); Crimson Pig (92); •Princess Mononoke (97); •Spirited Away (01); Howl's Moving Castle (04)

MIZOGUCHI, KENJI

Home Town (30); Mistress of a Foreigner (30); And Yet They Go (31); Man of the Moment, The (32); Dawn of Manchuria and Mongolia, The (32); Water Magician, The (33); Gion Festival (33); Jimpu Group, The (33); Mountain Pass of Love and Hate, The (34); Downfall of Osen (34); Oyuki the Virgin (35); Poppy (35); Osaka Elegy (36); •Sisters of the Gion (36); Straits of Love and Hate, The (37); Ah, My Home Town (38); Song of the Camp, The (38); Story of the Last Chrysanthemum, The (39); Woman of Osaka, The (40); Life of an Actor, The (41); 47 Ronin, The (Parts I & II) (41); Three Generations of Danjuro (44); Swordsman, The (44); Noted Sword, The (45); Victory Song (45); Victory of Women, The (46); Utamarro and His Five Women (46); Love of Sumako the Actress, The (47); Women of the Night (48); My Love Has Been Burning (49); Picture of Madame Yuki, A (50); Miss Oyu (51); Lady Musashino (51); •Life of Oharu, The (52); Geisha, A (53); •Ugetsu Monogatari (53); •Sansho the Bailiff (54); Woman in the Rumor, The (54); Crucified Lovers, The (54); Empress Yang Kwi-Fei, The (55); Taira Clan, The (55); Street of Shame (56)

MOODYSSON, LUKAS

Show Me Love (98); •Together (00); Lilya 4-Ever (02); Terrorists: The Kids They Sentenced (03); Hole in My Heart, A (04)

MOORE, MICHAEL

Roger and Me (89); Pets or Meat: The Return to Flint (92); Canadian Bacon (95); Big One, The (97); •Bowling for Columbine (02); •Fahrenheit 9/11 (04)

MOORHOUSE, JOCELYN

Pavane (83); Siege of Barton's Bathroom, The (86); •Proof (91); How to Make an American Quilt (95); Thousand Acres, A (97)

MORETTI, NANNI

Come Parli, Frate? (74); I Am Self Sufficient (76); Ecce Bombo (78); Sweet Dreams (81); Sweet Body of Bianca (83); Mass Is Ended, The (85); Red Wood Pigeon (90); Thing, The (90); •Caro Diario (94); Opening Day of Close-Up, The (96); April (98); •Son's Room, The (01)

MORRIS, ERROL

Gates of Heaven (78); Vernon, Florida (81); Thin Blue Line, The (88); Dark Wind, The (91); Brief History of Time, A (92); •Fast, Cheap & Out of Control (97); Mr. Death: The Rise and Fall of Fred A. Leuchter, Jr. (99); •Fog of War: Eleven Lessons from the Life of Robert S. McNamara, The (03)

MORRISSEY, PAUL
Civilization and Its Discontents (62); Sleep Walk (64); My Hustler (65); Chelsea Girls, The (66); **** (67); Loves of Ondine, The (67); I, a Man (67); Bike Boy (67); Lonesome Cowboys (67); •Flesh (68); Trash (70); Women in Revolt (71); Heat (72); L'Amour (73); Andy Warhol's Frankenstein (74); •Andy Warhol's Dracula (74); Hound of the Baskervilles, The (77); Madame Wang's (81); Forty Deuce (82); •Mixed Blood (84); Beethoven's Nephew (85); Spike of Bensonhurst (88)

MULLIGAN, ROBERT
•Fear Strikes Out (57); Great Impostor, The (60); Rat Race, The (60); Come September (61); Spiral Road, The (62); •To Kill a Mockingbird (62); •Love with the Proper Stranger (63); Baby, the Rain Must Fall (65); •Inside Daisy Clover (65); Up the Down Staircase (67); Stalking Moon, The (69); Pursuit of Happiness, The (71); •Summer of '42 (71); Other, The (72); Nickel Ride, The (74); Bloodbrothers (78); Same Time, Next Year (78); Kiss Me Goodbye (82); Clara's Heart (88); Man in the Moon, The (91)

NAIR, MIRA
•Salaam Bombay! (88); •Mississippi Masala (92); Perez Family, The (95); Kama Sutra: A Tale of Love (96); My Own Country (98); •Monsoon Wedding (01); Hysterical Blindness (02); •Vanity Fair (04)

NAKATA, HIDEO
Ghost Actress (96); •Ringu (98); Chaos (99); Ringu 2 (99); Sadistic and Masochistic (00); Sleeping Bride (00); Dark Water (02); Last Scene (02); •Ring Two, The (05)

NAVA, GREGORY
Confessions of Amans, The (77); •El Norte (83); Time of Destiny, A (88); My Family: Mi Familia (95); Selena (97); Why Do Fools Fall in Love (98)

NEAME, RONALD
Take My Life (47); Golden Salamander (49); Promoter, The (52); Man with a Million (54); Man Who Never Was, The (56); Seventh Sin, The (57); Windom's Way (57); •Horse's Mouth, The (58); •Tunes of Glory (60); Escape from Zahrain (62); I Could Go on Singing (63); Chalk Garden, The (64); Mister Moses (65); Gambit (66); Man Could Get Killed, A (66); Prudence and the Pill (68); •Prime of Miss Jean Brodie, The (69); •Scrooge (70); Poseidon Adventure, The (72); Odessa File, The (74); Meteor (79); •Hopscotch (80); First Monday in October (81); Foreign Body (86); Magic Balloon, The (90)

NEEDHAM, HAL
•Smokey and the Bandit (77); Hooper (78); Villain, The (79); Death Car on the Freeway (79); Stunts Unlimited (80); Smokey and the Bandit II (80); Cannonball Run, The (81); Megaforce (82); Stroker Ace (83); Cannonball Run II (84); Rad (86); Body Slam (87); Hard Time: Hostage Hotel (99)

NEGULESCO, JEAN
Singapore Woman (41); Conspirators, The (44); •Mask of Dimitrios, The (44); Humoresque (46) Nobody Lives Forever (46); Three Strangers (46); Deep Valley (47); •Johnny Belinda (48); •Road House (48); Affairs of Adelaide (49); Mudlark, The (50); •Three Came Home (50); Under My Skin (50); Take Care of My Little Girl (51); Lure of the Wilderness (52); Lydia Bailey (52); O. Henry's Full House (52); Phone Call from a Stranger (52); How to Marry a Millionaire (53); Scandal at Scourie (53); •Titanic (53); •Three Coins in the Fountain (54); Woman's World (54); •Daddy Long Legs (55); Rains of Ranchipur, The (55); Boy on a Dolphin (57); Certain Smile, A (58); Gift of Love, The (58); Best of Everything, The (59); Count Your Blessings (59); Jessica (62); Pleasure Seekers, The (64); Hello—Goodbye (70); Invincible Six, The (70)

NELSON, RALPH
•Requiem for a Heavyweight (62); •Lilies of the Field (63); Soldier in the Rain (63); Fate Is the Hunter (64); •Father Goose (64); Once a Thief (65); Duel at Diablo (66); Counterpoint (67); •Charly (68); Soldier Blue (70); . . . Tick. . . Tick. . . Tick. . . (70); Flight of the Doves (71); Wrath of God, The (72); Wilby Conspiracy, The (75); Embryo (76); Hero Ain't Nothin' but a Sandwich, A (77)

NELSON, TIM BLAKE
Eye of God (97); O (01); •Grey Zone, The (02)

NEWELL, MIKE
Awakening, The (80); Bad Blood (82); •Dance with a Stranger (85); Good Father, The (86); Amazing Grace and Chuck (87); Soursweet (88); •Enchanted April (91); Into the West (93); •Four Weddings and a Funeral (94); Awfully Big Adventure, An (95); •Donnie Brasco (97); Pushing Tin (99); •Mona Lisa Smile (03)

NEWMAN, PAUL
•Rachel, Rachel (68); Sometimes a Great Notion (71); •Effect of Gamma Rays on Man-in-the-Moon Marigolds, The (72); Harry and Son (84); •Glass Menagerie, The (87)

NICHOLS, MIKE
•Who's Afraid of Virginia Woolf? (66); •Graduate, The (67); •Catch-22 (70); •Carnal Knowledge (71); Day of the Dolphin, The (73); •Fortune, The (75); •Silkwood (83); Heartburn (86); •Biloxi Blues (88); •Working Girl (88); •Postcards from the Edge (90); Regarding Henry (91); Wolf (94); •Birdcage, The (96); •Primary Colors (98); What Planet Are You From? (00); Wit (01); Angels in America (03); •Closer (04)

NOLAN, CHRISTOPHER
•Following (98); •Memento (01); •Insomnia (02); Batman Begins (05)

NOYCE, PHILLIP
Backroads (77); Newsfront (78); Heatwave (83); Echoes of Paradise (87); •Dead Calm (89); Blind Fury (90); •Patriot Games (92); Sliver (93); •Clear and Present Danger (94); Saint, The (97); Bone Collector, The (99); •Rabbit-Proof Fence (02); •Quiet American, The (02)

NUNEZ, VICTOR
Gal Young 'Un (79); •Flash of Green, A (84); Ruby in Paradise (93); •Ulee's Gold (97); Coastlines (02)

O'CONNOR, PAT
Cal (84); Month in the Country, A (87); Stars and Bars (88); January Man, The (89); Fools of Fortune (90); Circle of Friends (95); Inventing the Abbotts (97); •Dancing at Lughnasa (98); Sweet November (01)

ODETS, CLIFFORD
•None but the Lonely Heart (44); Story on Page One, The (59)

OLIVIER, LAURENCE
•Henry V (44); •Hamlet (48); •Richard III (55); •Prince and the Showgirl, The (57); Three Sisters (70)

OPHULS, MARCEL
•Love at Twenty (62); Banana Peel (64); Feu a Volante (65); •Sorrow and the Pity, The (71); Sense of Loss, A (72); Memory of Justice, The (76); Hotel Terminus: Klaus Barbie—His Life and Times (88); November Days (91); Troubles We've Seen, The (94)

OPHULS, MAX
Bartered Bride, The (32); Une Histoire d'Amour (33); Man Stolen (34); Divine (35); Tender Enemy, The (36); Werther (38); Mayerling to Sarajevo (40); Exile, The (47); •Letter from an Unknown Woman (48); Caught (49); Reckless Moment, The (49); •La Ronde (50); Vendetta (50); Le Plaisir (52); •Earrings of Madame de . . . , The (53); •Lola Montes (55)

OSHIMA, NAGISA
Town of Love and Hope, A (59); Naked Youth (60); Sun's Burial, The (60); Night and Fog in Japan (60); Catch, The (61); Revolutionary, The (62); Child's First Adventure, A (64); I'm Here Bellet (64); Pleasures of the Flesh, The (66); Violence at Noon (66); Band of Ninja (67); Sing a Song of Sex (67); Japanese Summer: Double Suicide (67); Death by Hanging (68); Sinner in Paradise, A (68); Diary of a Shinjuku Burglar (69); Boy (69); He Died After the War (70); Ceremony, The (71); Dear Summer Sister (72); •In the Realm of The Senses (76); Empire of the Passions (78); •Merry Christmas, Mr. Lawrence (83); Max, Mon Amour (86); Yunbogi No Nikki (86); Kyoto, My Mother's Place (91); 100 Years of Japanese Cinema (95); Gohatto (00)

OUEDRAOGO, IDRISSA
Poko (81); Les Ecuelles (83); Les Funerailles du Larle Naaba (84); Issa le Tisserand (85); Ouagadougou, Ouag Deux Roues (85); Yam Daabo (87); •Yaaba (89); Tilai (90); Karim Na Sala (91); Obi (91); Samba Traore (92); Heart's City, The (94); Africa, My Africa (95); Kini & Adams (97); Anger of the Gods (03)

OZ, FRANK
•Dark Crystal, The (82); •Muppets Take Manhattan, The (84); •Little Shop of Horrors (86); Dirty Rotten Scoundrels (88); What About Bob? (91); Housesitter (92); •Indian in the Cupboard, The (95); •In & Out (97); Bowfinger (99); Score, The (01); •Stepford Wives, The (04)

OZON, FRANCOIS
Sitcom (98); Criminal Lovers (99); Water Drops on Burning Rocks (99); •Under The Sand (00); •8 Women (02); •Swimming Pool (03); 5x2 (04)

OZU, YASUJIRO
Introduction to Marriage (30); Walk Cheerfully (30); I Flunked But. . . (30); That Night's Wife (30); Revengeful Spirit of Eros, The (30); Lost Luck (30); Young Miss (30); Lady and the Beard, The (31); Beauty's Sorrows (31); Tokyo Chorus (31); Spring Comes with the Ladies (32); I Was Born but. . . (32); Where Are the Dreams of Youth? (32); Until the Day We Meet Again (32); Woman of Tokyo (33); Women on the Firing Line (33); Passing Fancy (33); Mother Should Be Loved, A (34); Story of Floating Weeds, A (34); Innocent Maid, An (35); Inn in Tokyo, An (35; College Is a Nice Place (36); Only Son, The (36); What Did the Lady Forget? (37); Toda Brothers and Sisters, The (41); There Was a Father (42); Record of a Tenement Gentleman, The (47); Hen in the Wind, A (48); Late Spring (49); Munekata Sisters, The (50); Early Summer (51); Tea and Rice (52); •Tokyo Story (53); Early Spring (56); Tokyo Twilight (57); Equinox Flower (58); Floating Weeds (59); Ohayo (59); •Late Autumn (60); Early Autumn (61); An Autumn Afternoon (62)

PABST, G.W.
•Kameradschaft (31); •Threepenny Opera, The (31); Mistress of Atlantis, The (32); •Don Quixote (33); From Top to Bottom (33); Modern Hero, A (34); Street of Shadows (37); Shanghai Drama, The (38); Jeunes Filles en Detresse (39); Komodianten (41); Paracelsus (43); Der Fall Molander (45); Trial, The (48); Geheimnisvolle Tiefen (49); Voice of Silence, The (52); Cose da Pazzi (53); Confession of Ina Kahr, The (54); Last Ten Days, The (55); Jackboot Mutiny, The (55); Ballerina (56); Durch eie Walder Durch eie Auen (56)

PAGNOL, MARCEL
Direct au Coeur (33); Le Gendre de Monsieur Poirier (33); Leopold le Bien-Aime (33); Ways of Love (34); Le Voyage de Monsieur Perrichon (34); L'Article 330 (34); Angele (34); Merlusse (35); Cigalon (35); •Cesar (36); Topaze (36); Harvest (37); Heartbeat (38); •Baker's Wife, The (38); Well-Digger's Daughter, The (41); La Belle Meuniere (48); Ways of Love (50); Topaze (51); Manon des Sources (52); Letters from My Windmill (54); Le Cure de Cucugnan (67)

PAKULA, ALAN J.
•Sterile Cuckoo, The (69); •Klute (71); Love and Pain and the Whole Damn Thing (73); •Parallax View, The (74); •All the President's Men (76); Comes a Horseman (78); •Starting Over (79); Rollover (81); •Sophie's Choice (82); Dream Lover (86); •Orphans (87); See You in the Morning (89); •Presumed Innocent (90); Consenting Adults (92); •Pelican Brief, The (93); •Devil's Own, The (97)

PAL, GEORGE
Tom Thumb (58); •Time Machine, The (60); Atlantis, The Lost Continent (61); Wonderful World of the Brothers Grimm, The (62); •7 Faces of Dr. Lao (64)

PALCY, EUZHAN
•Sugar Cane Alley (83); •Dry White Season, A (89); Simeon (92); Amie Cesaire: A Voice for History (94); Ruby Bridges (98); Wings against the Wind (99); Killing Yard, The (01)

PARK CHAN-WOOK
Joint Security Area (00); Sympathy for Mr. Vengeance (02); •Oldboy (03)

PARKER, ALAN
•Bugsy Malone (76); •Midnight Express (78); •Fame (80); Shoot the Moon (82); •Pink Floyd—The Wall (82); •Birdy (84); Angel Heart (87); •Mississippi Burning (88); Come See the Paradise (90); •Commitments, The (91); Road to Wellville, The (94); •Evita (96); •Angela's Ashes (99); Life of David Gale, The (03)

PARKER, TREY
Cannibal: The Musical! (96); Orgazmo (97); •South Park: Bigger, Longer & Uncut (99); •Team America: World Police (04)

PARKS, GORDON
•Learning Tree, The (69); •Shaft (71); Shaft's Big Score! (72); Super Cops, The (74); •Leadbelly (76); Solomon Northrup's Odyssey (84)

PARKS, JR., GORDON
•Superfly (72); Thomasine and Bushrod (74); Three the Hard Way (74); Aaron Loves Angela (79)

PASOLINI, PIER PAOLO
•Accattone! (61); •Mamma Roma (62); Love Meetings (64); •Gospel According to St. Matthew, The (64); Hawks and the Sparrows, The (66); Oedipus Rex (67); Witches, The (67); •Teorema (68); (69); Porcile (69); Decameron, The (70); Medea (70); Canterbury Tales, The (71); Arabian Nights (74); •Salo, or the 120 Days of Sodom (75)

PASSER, IVAN
Intimate Lighting (66); Born to Win (71); Law and Disorder (74); Crime and Passion (76); Silver Bears (78); •Cutter's Way (81); Creator (85); Haunted Summer (88); Fourth Story (91); Colors of Love, The (92); Stalin (92); While Justice Sleeps (94); Kidnapped (95); Wishing Tree, The (99); Picnic (00)

PAYNE, ALEXANDER
Citizen Ruth (96); •Election (99); •About Schmidt (02); •Sideways (04)

PECK, RAOUL
Haitian Corner (87); Lumumba: Death of a Prophet (92); Man by the Shore, The (93); Haiti—Le Silence des Chiens (94); Desounen: Dialogue with Death (94); It's Not About Love (98); •Lumumba (00); Profit & Nothing But! (01); Sometimes in April (05)

PECKINPAH, SAM
Deadly Companions, The (61); •Ride the High Country (62); Major Dundee (65); •Wild Bunch, The (69); •Ballad of Cable Hogue, The (70); •Straw Dogs (71); •Getaway, The (72); •Junior Bonner (72); •Pat Garrett and Billy the Kid (73); •Bring Me the Head of Alfredo Garcia (74); Killer Elite, The (75); •Cross of Iron (77); Convoy (78); Osterman Weekend, The (83)

PENN, ARTHUR
•Left-Handed Gun, The (58); •Miracle Worker, The (62); Mickey One (65); Chase, The (66); •Bonnie and Clyde (67); •Alice's Restaurant (69); •Little Big Man (70); •Night Moves (75); •Missouri Breaks, The (76); •Four Friends (81); Target (85); Dead of Winter (87); Penn & Teller Get Killed (89); Inside (96)

PENN, SEAN
Indian Runner, The (91); Crossing Guard, The (95); •Pledge, The (01)

PERRY, FRANK
•David and Lisa (62); Ladybug, Ladybug (63); •Swimmer, The (68); Last Summer (69); Truman Capote's Trilogy (69); •Diary of a Mad Housewife (70); Doc (71); Play It As It Lays (72); Man on a Swing (74); •Rancho Deluxe (75); •Mommie Dearest (81); Monsignor (82); Compromising Positions (85); Hello Again (87); On the Bridge (92)

PETERSEN, WOLFGANG
I Will Kill You, Wolf (71); Tatort—Blechschaden (71); Tatort—Strandgut (72); Anna und Toto (72); Smog (73); Tartot—Jagdrevier (73); Van der Valk und die Reichin (73); One or the Other (73); Tatort—Nachtfrost (74); Aufs Kreuz gelegt (74); Stellenweise Glatteis (75); Kurzschluss (75); Vier gegen eie Blank (76); Hans im Gluck (76); Tartort—Reifezeugnis (76); Planubung (77); Consequence, The (77); Black and White Like Day and Night (78); •Das Boot (81); •Neverending Story, The (84); Enemy Mine (85); Shattered (91); •In the Line of Fire (93); Outbreak (95); Air Force One (97); •Perfect Storm, The (00); •Troy (04)

PETRI, ELIO
Assassin, The (61); High Infidelity (64); •Tenth Victim, The (65); We Still Kill the Old Way (67); Quiet Place in the Country, A (68); •Investigation of a Citizen Above Suspicion (70)

PIALAT, MAURICE
L'Enfance nue (68); We Won't Grow Old Together (72); Mouth Agape (74); Loulou (79); Graduate First (79); Loulou (80); •A Nos Amours (84); •Police (84); Under the Sun of Satan (87); Van Gogh (91); Le Garcu (95); Les Auto-Stoppeuses (97)

PITOF
Vidocq (01); •Catwoman (04)

POITIER, SIDNEY
Buck and the Preacher (72); Warm December, A (73); •Uptown Saturday Night (74); Let's Do It Again (75); Piece of the Action, A (77); Stir Crazy (80); Hanky-Panky (82); Fast Forward (85); Ghost Dad (90)

POLANSKI, ROMAN
•Knife in the Water (62); Beautiful Swindlers, The (64); •Repulsion (65); •Cul-de-Sac (66); Fearless Vampire Killers, or Pardon Me but Your Teeth Are in My Neck, The (67); •Rosemary's Baby (68); •Macbeth (71); Diary of Forbidden Dreams (73); •Chinatown (74); •Tenant, The (76); •Tess (79); Pirates (86); •Frantic (88); Bitter Moon (92); •Death and the Maiden (94); Ninth Gate, The (99); •Pianist, The (02)

POLLACK, SYDNEY
Slender Thread, The (65); This Property Is Condemned (66); Scalphunters, The (68); •Swimmer, The (68); Castle Keep (69); •They Shoot Horses, Don't They? (69); Jeremiah Johnson (72); •Way We Were, The (73); •Three Days of the Condor (75); •Yakuza, The (75); Bobby Deerfield (77); Electric Horseman, The (79); •Absence of Malice (81); •Tootsie (82); •Out of Africa (85); Havana (90); Firm, The (93); Sabrina (95); Random Hearts (99); •Interpreter, The (05)

POLONSKY, ABRAHAM
•Force of Evil (48); Tell Them Willie Boy Is Here (69); Romance of a Horse Thief (71)

PONTECORVO, GILLO
Wide Blue Road, The (57); Kapo (60); •Battle of Algiers, The (65); Burn! (69); Orgo (79)

POTTER, H.C.
Beloved Enemy (36); Wings Over Honolulu (37); Cowboy and the Lady, The (38); Romance in the Dark (38); Shopworn Angel, The (38); Blackmail (39); •Story of Vernon and Irene Castle, The (39); Congo Maisie (40); •Hellzapoppin' (41); Mr. Lucky (43); •Farmer's Daughter, The (47); Likely Story, A (47); •Mr. Blandings Builds His Dream House (48); •Time of Your Life, The (48); You Gotta Stay Happy (48); Miniver Story, The (50); Three for the Show (55); Top Secret Affair (57)

POTTER, SALLY
Thriller (79); Gold Diggers, The (84); Tears, Laughter, Fear and Rage (86); London Story, The (87); I Am An Ox, I Am a Horse, I Am a Woman (88); •Orlando (93); Tango Lesson, The (97); Man Who Cried, The (00); Yes (05)

POWELL, MICHAEL
My Friend the King (31); Born Lucky (32); C.O.D. (32); His Lordship (32); Hotel Splendide (32); Fire Raisers, The (33); Girl in the Crowd, The (34); Night of the Party, The (34); Phantom Light, The (34); Something Always Happens (34); Strike! (34); Her Last Affaire (35); Lazybones (35); Love Test, The (35); Price of a Song, The (35); Some Day (35); Brown Wallet, The (36); Crown vs. Stevens (36); Man Behind the Mask, The (36); Edge of the World, The (37); Lion Has Wings, The (39); Spy in Black, The (39); Blackout (40); •Thief of Baghdad, The (40); •49th Parallel (41); •One of Our Aircraft Is Missing (41); •Life and Death of Colonel Blimp, The (43); Canterbury Tale, A (44); •I Know Where I'm Going! (45); •Black Narcissus (46); •Stairway to Heaven (46); •Red Shoes, The (48); Hour of Glory (49); Fighting Pimpernel, The (50);

Wild Heart, The (50); Tales of Hoffman, The (51); Oh, Rosalinda!! (55); Pursuit of the Graf Spee (56); Night Ambush (57); •Peeping Tom (60); Queen's Guards, The (60); They're A Weird Mob (66); Age of Consent (69); Boy Who Turned Yellow, The (72)

PRASAD, UDAYAN
They Never Slept (90); 102 Boulevard Haussmann (91); Running Late (92); Femme Fatale (93); Brothers in Trouble (96); •My Son The Fanatic (98); Gabriel & Me (01)

PREMINGER, OTTO
Under Your Spell (36); Danger—Love at Work (37); Margin for Error (43); In the Meantime, Darling (44); •Laura (44); •Fallen Angel (45); Royal Scandal, A (45); Centennial Summer (46); Daisy Kenyon (47); Forever Amber (47); That Lady in Ermine (48); Fan, The (49); Whirlpool (49); Where the Sidewalk Ends (50); 13th Letter, The (51); Angel Face (53); •Moon Is Blue, The (53); •Carmen Jones (54); River of No Return (54); Court-Martial of Billy Mitchell, The (55); •Man with the Golden Arm, The (55); Saint Joan (57); Bonjour Tristesse (58); •Anatomy of a Murder (59); •Porgy and Bess (59); •Exodus (60); •Advise and Consent (62); Cardinal, The (63); Bunny Lake Is Missing (65); In Harm's Way (65); Hurry Sundown (67); Skidoo (68); Tell Me That You Love Me, Junie Moon (70); Such Good Friends (71); Rosebud (75); Human Factor, The (79)

PRESSBURGER, EMERIC
•One of Our Aircraft Is Missing (41); Canterbury Tale, A (44); •I Know Where I'm Going (45); •Black Narcissus (46); •Stairway to Heaven (46); •Red Shoes, The (48); Hour of Glory (49); Fighting Pimpernel, The (50); Wild Heart, The (50); Tales of Hoffman, The (51); Twice Upon a Time (53); Oh, Rosalinda!! (55); Pursuit of the Graf Spee (56); Night Ambush (57)

PROYAS, ALEX
Spirits of the Air, Gremlins of the Clouds (89); •Crow, The (94); •Dark City (98); Garage Days (02); •I, Robot (04)

RADEMAKERS, FONS
Village on the River (58); Joyous Eve, The (60); Knife, The (61); Spitting Image, The (63); Dance of the Heron, The (66); Mira (71); Because of the Cats (73); Max Havelaar (76); Mysteries (78); My Friend (79); •Assault, The (86); Diary of an Old Man (87); Rose Garden, The (89)

RADFORD, MICHAEL
White Bird Passes (80); Another Time, Another Place (84); •1984 (84); White Mischief (88); •Postman (Il Postino), The (94); B. Monkey (98); Dancing at the Blue Iguana (00); Dancing at the Blue Iguana (00); Merchant of Venice (04)

RAFELSON, BOB
•Head (68); •Five Easy Pieces (70); •King of Marvin Gardens, The (72); Stay Hungry (76); Postman Always Rings Twice, The (81); Black Widow (87); Mountains of the Moon (90); Man Trouble (92); Tales of Erotica (93); Blood & Wine (97); Poodle Springs (98); House on Turk Street, The (02)

RAIMI, SAM
•Evil Dead, The (83); Crimewave (85); •Evil Dead 2: Dead by Dawn (87); •Darkman (90); Army of Darkness (93); Quick and the Dead, The (95); •Simple Plan, A (98); For Love of the Game (99); •Gift, The (01); •Spider-Man (02); •Spider-Man 2 (04)

RAMIS, HAROLD
•Caddyshack (80); National Lampoon's Vacation (83); Club Paradise (86); •Groundhog Day (93); Stuart Saves His Family (95); Multiplicity (96); •Analyze This (99); Bedazzled (00); Analyze That (02)

RAMSAY, LYNNE
•Ratchatcher (99); •Morvern Callar (02)

RAPPENEAU, JEAN-PAUL
Matter of Resistance, A (66); Swashbuckler, The (70); Savage, The (75); All Fired Up (82); •Cyrano de Bergerac (90); Horseman on the Roof, The (95); Bon Voyage (03)

RAPPER, IRVING
One Foot in Heaven (41); Shining Victory (41); Gay Sisters, The (42); •Now, Voyager (42); •Adventures of Mark Twain, The (44); Corn Is Green, The (45); •Rhapsody in Blue (45); Deception (46); Voice of the Turtle, The (47); Anna Lucasta (49); Glass Menagerie, The (50); Another Man's Poison (51); Forever Female (53); Bad for Each Other (54); Brave One, The (56); Strange Intruder (56); Marjorie Morningstar (58); Miracle, The (59); Story of Joseph and His Brethren, The (60); Pontius Pilate (64); Christine Jorgensen Story, The (70); Born Again (78)

RATNER, BRETT
Money Talks (97); •Rush Hour (98); •Family Man, The (00); Rush Hour 2 (01); •Red Dragon (02); After the Sunset (04)

RAY, NICHOLAS
•They Live by Night (49); •Knock on Any Door (49); Woman's Secret, A (49); Born to Be Bad (50); •In a Lonely Place (50); Flying Leathernecks (51); On Dangerous Ground (51); •Racket, The (51); •Lusty Men, The (52); Macao (52); •Johnny Guitar (54); •Rebel Without a Cause (55); Run for Cover (55); Bigger Than Life (56); Hot Blood (56); True Story of Jesse James, The (57); Bitter Victory (58); Party Girl (58); Wind Across the Everglades (58); Savage Innocents, The (59); •King of Kings (61); 55 Days at Peking (63)

RAY, SATYAJIT
•Pather Panchali (55); •Aparajito (56); Philosopher's Stone, The (57); •Music Room, The (58); •World of Apu, The (59); Goddess, The (60); Two Daughters (61); Kanchenjungha (62); Expedition, The (62); Big City, The (63); •Charulata (64); Coward and the Holy Man, The (65); Nayak (66); Chiriakhana (67); Adventures of Goopy and Bagha, The (69); Days and Nights in the Forest (70); Adversary, The (71); Simbaddha (72); Distant Thunder (73); Golden Fortress, The (74); Middleman, The (75); Chess Players, The (77); Elephant God, The (78); Kingdom of Diamonds, The (80); Sadghati (81); •Home and the World, The (84); Ganashatru (89); Branches of the Tree (90); Agantuk (92)

REDFORD, ROBERT
•Ordinary People (80); Milagro Beanfield War, The (88); •River Runs Through It, A (92); •Quiz Show (94); •Horse Whisperer, The; Legend of Bagger Vance, The (00)

REED, CAROL
It Happened in Paris (35); Men of the Sea (35); Laburnum Grove (36); Talk of the Devil (37); Who's Your Lady Friend? (37); Bank Holiday (38); Climbing High (38); Penny Paradise (38); Girl Must Live, A (39); •Stars Look Down, The (39); Girl in the News, The (40); •Night Train to Munich (40); Remarkable Mr. Kipps (41); Young Mr. Pitt, The (42); •Way Ahead, The (44); •Odd Man Out (47); •Fallen Idol, The (48); •Third Man, The (49); Outcast of the Islands (51); Man Between, The (53); •Kid for Two Farthings, A (55); •Trapeze (56); Key, The (58); •Our Man in Havana (59); Running Man, The (63); Agony and the Ecstasy, The (65); •Oliver! (68); Flap (70); Public Eye, The (72)

REINER, CARL
•Enter Laughing (67); Comic, The (69); •Where's Poppa? (70); Oh, God! (77); One and Only, The (78); Jerk, The (79); •Dead Men Don't Wear Plaid (82); •Man with Two Brains, The (83); •All of Me (84); Summer Rental (85); Summer School (87); Bert Rigby, You're a Fool (89); Sibling Rivalry (90); Fatal Instinct (93); That Old Feeling (97)

REINER, ROB
•This Is Spinal Tap (84); •Sure Thing, The (85); •Stand by Me (86); •Princess Bride, The (87); •When Harry Met Sally. . . (89); •Misery (90); •Few Good Men, A (92); North (94); American President, The (95); Ghosts of Mississippi (96); Story of Us, The (99); Alex and Emma (03)

REISZ, KAREL
•Saturday Night and Sunday Morning (60); Night Must Fall (64); •Morgan! (66); Isadora (68); Gambler, The (74); •Who'll Stop the Rain? (78); •French Lieutenant's Woman, The (81); Sweet Dreams (85); Everybody Wins (90)

REITMAN, IVAN
Foxy Lady (71); Cannibal Girls (72); Meatballs (79); •Stripes (81); •Ghostbusters (84); Legal Eagles (86); Twins (88); Ghostbusters II (89); Kindergarten Cop (90); •Dave (93); Junior (94); Fathers' Day (97); Six Days, Seven Nights (98); Evolution (01)

REITZ, EDGAR
Lust for Love (67); Fussnoten (67); Cadillac (69); Geschichten Vom Kubelkind (70); Kino II (71); Golden Fleece, The (71); Die Reise Nach Wien (73); Middle of the Road Is a Very Dead End, The (74); Zero Hour (76); Germany in Autumn (78); Tailor from Ulm, The (78); •Heimat (84); Das Schweigen des Dichters (86); Die Zweite Heimat: Leaving Home (92); Night of the Filmmakers, The (95)

Dolls (67); Daddy's Gone A-Hunting (69); Happy
Birthday, Wanda June (71); Limbo (72);
Earthquake (74); Avalanche Express (79)

ROCHA, GLAUBER
Storm, The (62); Black God White Devil (64);
Earth Entranced (67); O Cancer (68); •Antonio das
Mortes (69); Lion Has Seven Heads, The (70);
Severed Heads (71); Claro! (75); Age of the Earth,
The (80)

RODRIGUEZ, ROBERT
•El Mariachi (93); Roadracers (94); Four
Rooms (95); Desperado (95); •From Dusk till
Dawn (96); •Faculty, The (98); •Spy Kids (01);
•Spy Kids 2: The Island of Lost Dreams (02); Spy
Kids 3-D: Game Over (03); •Once Upon a Time in
Mexico (03); •Frank Miller's Sin City (05)

ROEG, NICOLAS
•Performance (70); •Walkabout (71); •Don't Look
Now (73); •Man Who Fell to Earth, The (76); Bad
Timing: A Sensual Obsession (80); Eureka (82);
Insignificance (85); Castaway (86); Aria (87);
Track 29 (88); •Witches, The (90); Sweet Bird of
Youth (90); Cold Heaven (92); Heart of
Darkness (94); Hotel Paradise (95); Full Body
Massage (96); Two Deaths (95); Samson and
Delilah (96)

ROHMER, ERIC
Sign of Leo, The (59); •Six in Paris (65); La
Boulangere de Monceauf (62); La Carriere de
Suzanne (63); •La Collectionneuse (67); •My
Night at Maud's (69); •Claire's Knee (70); •Chloe
in the Afternoon (72); Marquise of O. . . ,
The (76); Perceval (78); Aviator's Wife, The (81);
•Le Beau Mariage (82); •Pauline at the Beach (83);
•Full Moon in Paris (84); Summer (86); Four
Adventures of Reinette and Mirabelle (87);
Boyfriends and Girlfriends (87); Tale of
Springtime, A (90); Tale of Winter, A (91);
L'Arbre, le Maire et la Mediatheque (92);
Rendezvous in Paris (96); Tale of Summer, A (96);
Autumn Tale (98); Lady and the Duke, The (01);
Triple Agent (04)

ROMERO, GEORGE
•Night of the Living Dead (68); There's Always
Vanilla (72); Crazies, The (73); Hungry
Wives (73); •Martin (78); •Dawn of the Dead (79);
Knightriders (81); •Creepshow (82); •Day of the
Dead (85); Monkey Shines: An Experiment in
Fear (88); Two Evil Eyes (90); Dark Half,
The (93); Bruiser (00); Land of the Dead (05)

ROSE, BERNARD
Paperhouse (88); Chicago Joe and the
Showgirl (90); •Candyman (92); Immortal
Beloved (94); Anna Karenina (97); Ivans xtc. (00)

ROSI, FRANCESCO
Anita Garibaldi (52); Challenge, The (58); I
Magliari (59); •Salvatore Giuliano (61); Over the
City (63); Moment of Truth, The (65); More Than
a Miracle (67); Uomini Contro (70); Mattei Affair,
The (72); Re: Lucky Luciano (74); Il
Contesto (75); Illustrious Corpses (76); Christ
Stopped at Eboli (79); •Three Brothers (80);
Bizet's Carmen (84); Chronicle of a Death
Foretold (87); Palermo Connection, The (90);
Truce, The (97)

ROSS, HERBERT
Goodbye Mr. Chips (69); Owl and the Pussycat,
The (70); T.R. Baskin (71); •Play It Again,
Sam (72); •Last of Sheila, The (73); Funny
Lady (75); •Sunshine Boys, The (75);
•Seven-Per-Cent Solution, The (76); •Goodbye
Girl, The (77); •Turning Point, The (77);
•California Suite (78); Nijinsky (80); •Pennies
from Heaven (81); I Ought to Be in Pictures (82);
Max Dugan Returns (83); Footloose (84);
Protocol (84); Dancers (87); Secret of My Success,
The (87); •Steel Magnolias (89); My Blue
Heaven (90); True Colors (91); Undercover
Blues (93); Boys On The Side (95)

ROSSELLINI, ROBERTO
La Nava Bianca (41); Una Pilota Ritorna (42);
L'Uomo della Croce (43); Desiderio (43); •Open
City (45); •Paisan (46); Germany, Year
Zero (47); La Macchina Ammazzacattivi (48);
Stromboli (49); •Flowers of St. Francis, The (50);
Ways of Love (50); Greatest Love, The (51); Seven
Deadly Sins, The (52); Dov'e la Liberte? (53);
Strangers, The (53); Fear (54); Joan at the
Stake (54); India (58); •General Della Rovere (59);
Era Notte a Roma (59); Viva l'Italia (60); Betrayer,
The (61); Anima Nera (62); Rogopag (62); •Rise
of Louis XIV, The (66); Socrates (68); Augustine
of Hippo (72); Blaise Pascal (75); Year One (75);
Messiah, The (78); Age of the Medici, The (79)

ROSSEN, ROBERT
•Body and Soul (47); Johnny O'Clock (47); •All
the King's Men (49); Brave Bulls, The (51);
Mambo (54); Alexander the Great (56); Island in
the Sun (57); They Came to Cordura (59);
•Hustler, The (61); Lilith (64)

ROZEMA, PATRICIA
Passion: A Letter in 16mm (85); I've Heard the
Mermaids Singing (87); White Room (90); When
Night Is Falling (95); •Mansfield Park (99)

RUBEN, JOSEPH
Sister-in-Law, The (75); Pom-Pom Girls, The (76);
Joyride (77); Our Winning Season (78); Gorp (80);
Dreamscape (84); •Stepfather, The (87); True
Believer (89); •Sleeping with the Enemy (91);
Good Son, The (93); Money Train (95); Return to
Paradise (98); •Forgotten, The (04)

RUDOLPH, ALAN
Barn of the Naked Dead (76); •Welcome to
L.A. (76); Remember My Name (78); Roadie (80);
Endangered Species (82); •Choose Me (84);
Songwriter (84); •Trouble in Mind (85); Made in
Heaven (87); •Moderns, The (88); Love at
Large (90); •Mortal Thoughts (91); Equinox (93);
Mrs. Parker and the Vicious Circle (94);
•Afterglow (97); Breakfast of Champions (99);
Trixie (00); Investigating Sex (01); Secret Lives of
Dentists, The (02)

RUIZ, RAOUL
Three Sad Tigers (68); Que Hacer? (70); La
Colonia Penal (71); Nadje Dijo Nada (71); La
Exproprioacion (72); El Realismo Socialista (73);
Palomilla Blanca (73); Palomilla Brava (73);
Dialogo de Exilados (74); Mensch Verstreut und
Verkehrt (75); La Vocation Suspendue (76);
Hypothesis of the Stolen Painting, The (78);

De Grands Evenements et des Gens
Ordinaires (78); Le Jeu de l'Oie (80); Territory,
The (81); On Top of the Whale (82); •Three
Crowns of the Sailor (83); Berenice (84); La Ville
des Pirates (84); Voyage Autour d'Une Main (84);
l'Eveille du Pont de l'Alma (85); Les Destins de
Mancel (85); Regime Sans Pain (86);
Mamamme (86); Treasure Island (86); Richard
III (86); Life Is a Dream (87); La Chouette
Aveugle (87); Le Professeur Taranne (87); Tous les
Nuages Sont des Horloges (88); Derriere le
Mur (88); Palla y Talla (89); Golden Boat,
The (90); La Telenovella Errante (90);
L'Exode (90); Dark at Noon (92); Fado Majeur et
Mineur (94); Three Lives and Only One
Death (96); Genealogies of a Crime (97); Shattered
Image (98); •Time Regained (99); Love Torn in a
Dream (00); Comedy of Innocence (00); Savage
Souls (01); Chilean Rhapsody (02); Medee (03);
That Day (03); Une Place Parmi les Vivants (03);
Dias de Campo (04)

RUSH, RICHARD
Too Soon to Love (60); Of Love and Desire (63);
Fickle Finger of Fate, The (67); Hell's Angels on
Wheels (67); Man Called Dagger, A (67); Thunder
Alley (67); Psych-Out (68); Savage Seven,
The (68); •Getting Straight (70); Freebie and the
Bean (74); •Stunt Man, The (80); Color of
Night (94)

RUSSELL, CHUCK
Nightmare on Elm Street 3: Dreams Warriors,
A (87); Blob, The (88); •Mask, The (94);
Eraser (96); Bless the Child (00); Scorpion King,
The (02)

RUSSELL, DAVID O.
Spanking the Monkey (94); Flirting with
Disaster (96); •Three Kings (99); •I Heart
Huckabees (04)

RUSSELL, JAY
End of the Line (88); My Dog Skip (00); •Tuck
Everlasting (02); •Ladder 49 (04)

RUSSELL, KEN
Amelia and the Angel (58); French Dressing (63);
Billion Dollar Brain (67) •Women in Love (69);
Devils, The (70); Music Lovers, The (70); •Boy
Friend, The (71); Savage Messiah (72);
Mahler (74); Lisztomania (75); •Tommy (75);
Valentino (77); Altered States (80); Crimes of
Passion (84); Aria (87); Gothic (87); Lair of the
White Worm, The (88); •Salome's Last
Dance (88); Rainbow, The (89); Whore (91); Lady
Chatterley (93); Mindbender (95); Dogboys (98);
Fall of the House of Usher, The (02);

RYDELL, MARK
Fox, The (67); Reivers, The (69); Cowboys,
The (72); Cinderella Liberty (73); Harry and
Walter Go to New York (76); •Rose, The (79); •On
Golden Pond (81); River, The (84); For the
Boys (91); Intersection (94); Crime of the
Century (96); James Dean (01)

SAKS, GENE
•Barefoot in the Park (67); •Odd Couple, The (68);
Cactus Flower (69); Last of the Red Hot
Lovers (72); Mame (74); Brighton Beach
Memoirs (86); Fine Romance, A (92); Bye Bye
Birdie (95)

SALLES, WALTER
High Art (91); Foreign Land (95); •Central
Station (98); Midnight (98); Behind the Sun (01);
•Motorcycle Diaries, The (04); Dark Water (05)

SANDRICH, MARK
Talk of Hollywood, The (29); Aggie Appleby,
Maker of Men (33); Melody Cruise (33);
Cockeyed Cavaliers (34); •Gay Divorcee, The (34);
Hips, Hips, Hooray (34); •Top Hat (35); •Follow
the Fleet (36); Woman Rebels, A (36); •Shall We
Dance (37); Carefree (38); Man About Town (39);
Buck Benny Rides Again (40); Love Thy
Neighbor (40); Skylark (41); •Holiday Inn (42);
•So Proudly We Hail (43); •Here Come the
Waves (44); I Love a Soldier (44)

SAURA, CARLOS
La Cuenca (58); Urchins, The (60); Lament for a
Bandit (64); •Hunt, The (66); Peppermint
Frappe (67); Stress es Tres Tres (68); Honeycomb,
The (69); Garden of Delights, The (70); Anna and
the Wolves (73); Cousin Angelica (74); •Cria! (76);
Elisa My Life (77); Blindfold (78); Mama Turns
100 (79); Hurry Hurry (80); Sweet Hours (81);
Blood Wedding (81); Antonieta (82);
•Carmen (83); Stilts, The (84); •El Amor
Brujo (86); El Dorado (88); Dark Night, The (89);
Ay, Carmela! (90); Sevillanas (92); Barcelona (92);
Dispara! (93); Marathon (93); Flamenco (95);
Taxi (96); Pajarico (97); Tango (98); Goya (99);
Bunuel and King Solomon's Table (01);
Salome (02); Seventh Day, The (04)

SAUTET, CLAUDE
Bonjour Sourire (55); Big Risk, The (60);
Backfire (64); Guns for the Dictator (65);
L'Amante (70); Things of Life, The (70); Max et
tes Ferrailleurs (70); Cesar and Rosalie (72);
Vincent, Francois, Paul. . . Et les Autres (74);
Mado (76); Un Histoire Simple (78); Un Mauvais
Fils (80); Garcon! (83); Few Days with Me,
A (88); •Un Coeur en Hiver (92); Nelly and M.
Arnaud (95)

SAVOCA, NANCY
•True Love (89); Dogfight (91); Household
Saints (93); If These Wall Could Talk (97); 24
Hour Woman, The (99); Reno: Rebel without a
Pause (03); Dirt (03)

SAYLES, JOHN
•Return of the Secaucus Seven (80); Baby, It's
You (83); •Lianna (83); •Brother from Another
Planet, The (84); •Matewan (87); •Eight Men
Out (88); City of Hope (91); •Passion Fish (92);
•Secret of Roan Inish, The (95); •Lone Star (96);
Men With Guns (98); Limbo (99); •Sunshine
State (02); Casa de los Babys (03); Silver City (04)

SCHAFFNER, FRANKLIN J.
Stripper, The (63); •Best Man, The (64); War Lord,
The (65); Double Man, The (67); •Planet of the
Apes (68); •Patton (70); •Nicholas and
Alexandra (71); •Papillon (73); Islands in the
Stream (77); •Boys from Brazil, The (78);
Sphinx (81); Yes, Giorgio (82); Lionheart (87);
Welcome Home (89)

SCHATZBERG, JERRY
Puzzle of a Downfall Child (70); •Panic in Needle
Park, The (71); •Scarecrow (73); Dandy, the All
American Girl (76); •Seduction of Joe Tynan,

The (79); Honeysuckle Rose (80);
Misunderstood (84); No Small Affair (84); •Street
Smart (87); Reunion (89); Day the Ponies Come
Back, The (00)

SCHELL, MAXIMILIAN
First Love (70); •Pedestrian, The (74); End of the
Game (75); Geschichten aus dem
Wienerwald (78); Marlene (86); Candles in the
Dark (93); My Sister Maria (02)

SCHEPISI, FRED
Libido (73); Devil's Playground, The (76); Chant
of Jimmie Blacksmith, The (78); Barbarosa (82);
Iceman (84); Plenty (85); •Roxanne (87); •Cry in
the Dark, A (88); •Russia House, The (90); Mr.
Baseball (92); •Six Degrees of Separation (93);
I.Q. (94); Fierce Creatures (97); •Last
Orders (02); It Runs in the Family (03)

SCHLESINGER, JOHN
•Kind of Loving, A (62); •Billy Liar (63);
•Darling (65); •Far from the Madding Crowd (67);
•Midnight Cowboy (69); •Sunday, Bloody
Sunday (71); Visions of Eight (73); •Day of the
Locust, The (75); •Marathon Man (76); Yanks (79);
Honky Tonk Freeway (81); Englishman Abroad,
An (83); •Falcon and the Snowman, The (85);
Believers, The (87); •Madame Sousatzka (88);
Pacific Heights (90); Innocent, The (93); •Cold
Comfort Farm (95); Eye for an Eye (96); Tale of
Sweeney Todd, The (98); Next Best Thing (00)

SCHLONDORFF, VOLKER
Young Torless (66); Degree of Murder, A (67);
Michael Kolhass—Der Rebell (69); Sudden Wealth
of the Poor People of Halbfass,The (71); Die
Moral der Ruth Halbfass (71); Summer
Lightning (72); Uberachtung in Tirol (72);
Georginas Grunde (74); •Lost Honor of Katharina
Blum, The (75); Coup de Grace (76); Nur Rum
Spass Nur Um Spiel: Kaleidoskop Valeska
Gert (77); Germany in Autumn (78); •Tin Drum,
The (79); Der Kandidat (80); •Circle of
Deceit (81); War and Peace (83); •Swann in
Love (84); Death of a Salesman (85); Odds and
Ends (87); Handmaid's Tale, The (90);
Voyager (91); Ogre, The (96); Palmetto (98);
Legend of Rita, The (99); Ninth Day, The (04)

SCHOEDSACK, ERNEST B.
Rango (31); •Most Dangerous Game, The (32);
Blind Adventure (33); •King Kong (33); Monkey's
Paw, The (33); Son of Kong (33); Long Lost
Father (34); Last Days of Pompeii, The (35);
Outlaws of the Orient (37); Trouble in
Morocco (37); Dr. Cyclops (40); Mighty Joe
Young (49)

SCHRADER, PAUL
•Blue Collar (78); •Hardcore (79); •American
Gigolo (80); Cat People (82); •Mishima (85); Light
of Day (87); Patty Hearst (88); •Comfort of
Strangers, The (91); •Light Sleeper (92);
Witch Hunt (94); Touch (97); •Affliction (98);
Forever Mine (99); •Auto Focus (02); Exorcist:
The Original Prequel (05)

SCHROEDER, BARBET
More (69); Valley, The (72); Idi Amin Dada (74);
Maitresse (76); Koko Le Gorille Qui Parle (78);
Les Tricheurs (84); Charles Bukowski Tapes,
The (85); •Barfly (87); •Reversal of Fortune (90);

•Single White Female (92); •Kiss of Death (95);
Before and After (96); Desperate Measures (98);
•Our Lady of the Assassins (00); Murder by
Numbers (02)

SCHUMACHER, JOEL
Incredible Shrinking Woman, The (81); D.C.
Cab (83); St. Elmo's Fire (85); Lost Boys,
The (87); Cousins (89); Flatliners (90); Dying
Young (91); •Falling Down (93); •Client, The (94);
•Batman Forever (95); Time to Kill, A (96);
Batman & Robin (97); •8mm (99); Flawless (99);
Tigerland (00); Bad Company (02); •Phone
Booth (03); Veronica Guerin (03); •Andrew Lloyd
Webber's The Phantom of the Opera (04)

SCOLA, ETTORE
•Let's Talk About Women (64); One Million
Dollars (65); Thrilling (66); Devil in Love,
The (68); Will Our Heroes Be Able to Find Their
Friend Who Has Mysteriously Disappeared in
Africa? (68); Police Chief Pepe (69); Motive Was
Jealousy, The (70); My Name Is Rocco
Papaleo (71); Most Wonderful Evening of My
Life, The (72); Trevico-Torino: Viaqqio Nel
Fiat-Nam (73); We All Loved Each Other So
Much (75); Confronto Partecipazione Unita (75);
•Down and Dirty (76); Silenzio e Complicita (76);
Goodnight, Ladies and Gentlemen (76); Special
Day, A (77); Viva Italia! (77); Passione
d'Amore (81); •La Nuit de Varennes (82); Le
Bal (82); Macaroni (85); •Family, The (87);
Splendor (88); What Time Is It? (89); Captain
Fracassa's Journey (90); Mario, Maria and
Mario (93); Romanzo di un Giovane
Povero (95); La Cena (98); Unfair
Competition (01); Another World Is Possible (01);
Gente di Roma (03)

SCORSESE, MARTIN
Who's That Knocking at My Door? (68); Boxcar
Bertha (72); •Mean Streets (73); •Alice Doesn't
Live Here Anymore (75); •Taxi Driver (76); •New
York, New York (77); •Last Waltz, The; •Raging
Bull (80); •King of Comedy, The (83); •After
Hours (85); •Color of Money, The (86); •Last
Temptation of Christ, The (88); New York
Stories (89); •Goodfellas (90); •Cape Fear (91);
•Age of Innocence, The (93); •Casino; Personal
Journey with Martin Scorsese Through American
Movies, A (95); •Kundun (97); •Bringing Out the
Dead (99); My Voyage to Italy (99); •Gangs of
New York (02); •Aviator, The (04)

SCOTT, RIDLEY
•Duellists, The (77); •Alien (79); •Blade
Runner (82); Legend (85); •Someone to Watch
Over Me (87); Black Rain (89); •Thelma &
Louise (91); 1492: The Conquest of Paradise (92);
White Squall (96); G.I. Jane (97); •Gladiator (00);
•Hannibal (01); •Black Hawk Down (01);
•Matchstick Men (03); Kingdom of Heaven (05)

SCOTT, TONY
Loving Memory (70); Hunger, The (83); •Top
Gun (86); Beverly Hills Cop II (87); Revenge (90);
Days of Thunder (90); Last Boy Scout, The (91);
•True Romance (93); •Crimson Tide (95); Fan,
The (96); •Enemy of the State (98); Spy
Game (01); •Man on Fire (04)

SEIDELMAN, SUSAN
Smithereens (82); •Desperately Seeking Susan (85); Making Mr. Right (87); Cookie (89); She-Devil (89); Tales of Erotica (93); Barefoot Executive, The (95); Cooler Climate, A (99); Gaudi Afternoon (00); Power and Beauty (02); Ranch, The (04)

SEMBENE, OUSMANE
Black Girl (66); •Mandabi (68); Emitai (71); Xala (74); Ceddo (78); Camp du Thiaroye (88); •Guelwaar (93); Faat Kine (00); Moolaade (04)

SHADYAC, TOM
•Ace Ventura: Pet Detective (94); •Nutty Professor, The (96); •Liar Liar (97); Patch Adams (98); Dragonfly (02); •Bruce Almighty (03)

SHELTON, RON
•Bull Durham (88); Blaze (89); •White Men Can't Jump (92); Cobb (94); Tin Cup (96); Play It to the Bone (99); •Dark Blue (02); Hollywood Homicide (03)

SHERIDAN, JIM
•My Left Foot (89); Field, The (90); •In the Name of the Father (93); Boxer, The (97); In America (02)

SHYAMALAN, M. NIGHT
Praying with Anger (92); Wide Awake (98); •Sixth Sense, The (99); •Unbreakable (00); •Signs (02); •Village, The (04)

SIDNEY, GEORGE
Free and Easy (41); Pacific Rendezvous (42); Pilot No. 5 (43); •Thousands Cheer (43); Bathing Beauty (44); •Anchors Aweigh (45); •Ziegfeld Follies (45); Harvey Girls, The (46); Holiday in Mexico (46); Cass Timberlane (47); •Three Musketeers, The (48); Red Danube, The (49); •Annie Get Your Gun (50); Key to the City (50); •Show Boat (51); Scaramouche (52); •Kiss Me Kate (53); Young Bess (53); Jupiter's Darling (55); Eddy Duchin Story, The (56); Jeanne Eagels (57); •Pal Joey (57); Pepe (60); Who Was That Lady? (60); Bye Bye Birdie (63); Ticklish Affair, A (63); •Viva Las Vegas (64); Swinger, The (66); Half a Sixpence (67)

SIEGEL, DON
Verdict, The (46); Big Steal, The (49); Night unto Night (49); Duel at Silver Creek, The (52); No Time for Flowers (52); China Venture (53); Count the Hours (53); Private Hell 36 (54); Riot in Cell Block 11 (54); Annapolis Story, An (55); Crime in the Streets (56); •Invasion of the Body Snatchers (56); Baby Face Nelson (57); Gun Runners, The (58); Lineup, The (58); Spanish Affair (58); Edge of Eternity (59); Hound-Dog Man (59); Flaming Star (60); Hell Is for Heroes (62); •Killers, The (64); •Coogan's Bluff (68); •Madigan (68); Death of a Gunfighter (69); Two Mules for Sister Sara (70); Beguiled, The (71); •Dirty Harry (71); •Charley Varrick (73); Black Windmill, The (74); •Shootist, The (76); Telefon (77); •Escape from Alcatraz (79); Rough Cut (80); Jinxed! (82)

SILBERLING, BRAD
Casper (95); •City of Angels (98); •Moonlight Mile (02); •Lemony Snicket's A Series of Unfortunate Events (04)

SILVER, JOAN MICKLIN
•Hester Street (75); Between the Lines (77); •Chilly Scenes of Winter (79); Crossing Delancey (88); Loverboy (89); Big Girls Don't Cry . . . They Get Even (92); Private Matter, A (92); in the Presence of Mine Enemies (96); Fish in the Bathtub, A (99); Charms for the Easy Life (02); Hunger Point (03)

SINGER, BRYAN
•Usual Suspects, The (95); •Apt Pupil (98); •X-Men (00); X2: X-Men United (03)

SINGLETON, JOHN
•Boyz N the Hood (91); Poetic Justice (93); Higher Learning (95); Rosewood (97); Shaft (99); Baby Boy (01); 2 Fast 2 Furious (03)

SIODMAK, ROBERT
Tempest (31); Compliments of Mr. Flow (36); Hatred (38); Personal Column (39); West Point Widow (41); Fly by Night (42); My Heart Belongs to Daddy (42); Night Before the Divorce, The (42); Someone to Remember (43); Son of Dracula (43); Christmas Holiday (44); Cobra Woman (44); •Phantom Lady (44); Suspect, The (44); Uncle Harry (45); •Dark Mirror, The (46); •Killers, The (46); •Spiral Staircase, The (46); Time Out of Mind (47); Cry of the City (48); •Criss Cross (49); Great Sinner, The (49); Deported (50); File on Thelma Jordon, The (50); Whistle at Eaton Falls (51); Crimson Pirate, The (52); Flesh and the Woman (54); Rats, The (55); Devil Strikes at Night, The (57); Magnificent Sinner (59); Portrait of a Sinner (59); Escape from East Berlin (62); Custer of the West (68); Fight for Rome (69)

SIRK, DOUGLAS
Girl from the Marsh Croft, The (35); Pillars of Society (35); Court Concert, The (36); Final Chord, The (36); La Habanera (37); Life Begins Anew (38); Boefje (39); Hitler's Madman (43); Summer Storm (44); Scandal in Paris, A (46); Lured (47); Sleep, My Love (48); Shockproof (49); Slightly French (49); Mystery Submarine (50); First Legion, The (51); Lady Pays Off, The (51); Thunder on the Hill (51); Weekend with Father (51); Has Anybody Seen My Gal? (52); Meet Me at the Fair (52); No Room for the Groom (52); All I Desire (53); Take Me to Town (53); •Magnificent Obsession (54); Sign of the Pagan (54); Taza, Son of Cochise (54); •All that Heaven Allows (55); Captain Lightfoot (55); Never Say Goodbye (56); There's Always Tomorrow (56); •Written on the Wind (56); Battle Hymn (57); Interlude (57); •Tarnished Angels, The (57); Time to Love and a Time to Die, A (58); •Imitation Of Life (59)

SKOLIMOWSKI, JERZY
Identification Marks: None (64); Walkover (65); Barrier (66); Le Depart (67); Hands Up! (67); Adventures of Gerard, The (70); •Deep End (70); King, Queen, Knave (72); •Shout, The (78); •Moonlighting (82); Success Is the Best Revenge (84); Lightship, The (86); Torrents of Spring (90); Ferdydurke (91)

SLUIZER, GEORGE
Love and Music (71); Joao (72); Twice a
Woman (79); Red Desert Penitentiary (85);
•Vanishing, The (86); Utz (92); Vanishing,
The (93); Dying to Go Home (96);
Crimetime (96); Commissioner, The (98); Stone
Raft, The (00)

SMITH, JOHN N.
Gala (82); Masculine Mystique, The (84); First
Stop, China (84); Sitting in Limbo (86); Train of
Dreams (87); Welcome to Canada (89);
Dieppe (93); •Boys of St. Vincent, The (93);
Dangerous Minds (95); Sugartime (95); Cool Dry
Place, A (98); Revenge of the Land (99); Random
Passage (01); Geraldine's Fortune (04)

SMITH, KEVIN
•Clerks (94); Mallrats (95); Chasing Amy (97);
Dogma (99); Jay and Silent Bob Strike Back (01);
Jersey Girl (04)

SODERBERGH, STEVEN
•sex, lies, and videotape (89); Kafka (91); King of
the Hill (93); Underneath, The (95); Gray's
Anatomy (97); Schizopolis (97); •Out of
Sight (98); •Limey, The (99); •Erin
Brockovich (00); •Traffic (00); •Ocean's
Eleven (01); Full Frontal (02); •Solaris (03);
•Ocean's Twelve (04)

SOFTLEY, IAIN
•Backbeat (94); Hackers (95); •Wings of the Dove,
The (98); K-PAX (01); Skeleton Key, The (05)

SOLONDZ, TODD
Fear, Anxiety and Depression (89); •Welcome to
the Dollhouse (96); •Happiness (98);
•Storytelling (01); •Palindromes (05)

SONNENFELD, BARRY
•Addams Family, The (91); •Addams Family
Values (93); For Love or Money (93); Get
Shorty (95); •Men in Black (97); •Wild Wild
West (99); Big Trouble (02); •Men in Black II (02)

SPHEERIS, PENELOPE
Decline of Western Civilization, The (81);
Suburbia (84); Boys Next Door, The (85);
Hollywood Vice Squad (86); Dudes (88); Decline
of Western Civilization II: The Metal Years,
The (88); Thunder and Mud (90); •Wayne's
World (92); Beverly Hillbillies, The (93); Little
Rascals, The (94); Black Sheep (96);
Senseless (98); Decline of Western Civilization
Part III, The (98); Crooked E: The Unshredded
Truth About Enron (03)

SPIELBERG, STEVEN
Duel (73); •Sugarland Express, The (74);
•Jaws (75); •Close Encounters of the Third
Kind (77); 1941 (79); •Raiders of the Lost
Ark (81); •E.T. The Extra-Terrestrial (82); Twilight
Zone—The Movie (83); •Indiana Jones and the
Temple of Doom (84); •Color Purple, The (85);
•Empire of the Sun (87); Always (89); •Indiana
Jones and the Last Crusade (89); •Hook (91);
•Jurassic Park (93); •Schindler's List (93);
•Lost World: Jurassic Park, The (97);
•Amistad (97); •Saving Private Ryan (98); •A.I.:
Artificial Intelligence (01); •Minority Report (02);
•Catch Me if You Can (02); •Terminal, The (04);
War of the Worlds (05)

SPOTTISWOODE, ROGER
Terror Train (80); Pursuit of D.B. Cooper,
The (81); Under Fire (83); Best of Times,
The (86); Shoot to Kill (88); Turner & Hooch (89);
Air America (90); Stop! or My Mom Will
Shoot (92); Hiroshima (95); •Tommorow Never
Dies (97); Noriega: God's Favorite (00); 6th Day,
The (00); Matthew Shepard Story, The (02); Ice
Bound (03); Spinning Boris (03); Ripley Under
Ground (05)

STAHL, JOHN M.
Lady Surrenders, A (30); Seed (31); •Strictly
Dishonorable (31); Back Street (32); Only
Yesterday (33); •Imitation of Life (34);
Magnificent Obsession (35); Parnell (37); Letter of
Introduction (38); When Tomorrow Comes (39);
Our Wife (41); Holy Matrimony (43); Immortal
Sergeant, The (43); Eve of St. Mark, The (44);
Keys of the Kingdom, The (44); Leave Her to
Heaven (46); Foxes of Harrow, The (47); Walls of
Jericho, The (48); Father Was a Fullback (49); Oh,
You Beautiful Doll (49)

STEVENS, GEORGE
Cohens and Kellys in Trouble, The (33); Bachelor
Bait (34); •Alice Adams (35); Annie Oakley (35);
Kentucky Kernels (35); Laddie (35); Nitwits,
The (35); •Swing Time (36); Damsel in Distress,
A (37); Quality Street (37); Vivacious Lady (38);
•Gunga Din (39); Vigil in the Night (40); Penny
Serenade (41); •Talk of the Town, The (42);
•Woman of The Year (42); More the Merrier,
The (43); •I Remember Mama (48); •Place in the
Sun, A (51); Something to Live For (52);
•Shane (53); •Giant (56); •Diary of Anne Frank,
The (59); Greatest Story Ever Told, The (65); Only
Game in Town, The (70)

STEVENSON, ROBERT
Happy Ever After (32); Falling for You (33); Lady
Jane Grey (36); Man Who Lived Again, The (36);
Two of Us, The (36); •King Solomon's Mines (37);
Non-Stop New York (37); To the Victor (38); Ware
Case, The (38); Young Man's Fancy (39); Return
to Yesterday (40); Tom Brown's School Days (40);
•Back Street (41); Joan of Paris (42); Forever and a
Day (43); •Jane Eyre (44); Dishonored
Lady (47); To the Ends of the Earth (48); Walk
Softly, Stranger (50); Woman On Pier 13,
The (50); My Forbidden Past (51); Las Vegas
Story, The (52); Johnny Tremain (57); •Old
Yeller (57); •Darby O'Gill and the Little
People (59); Kidnapped (60); •Absent-Minded
Professor, The (61); In Search of the
Castaways (62); Son of Flubber (63); •Mary
Poppins (64); Misadventures of Merlin Jones,
The (64); Monkey's Uncle, The (65); That Darn
Cat (65); Gnome-Mobile, The (67); Blackbeard's
Ghost (68); Love Bug, The (68); •Bedknobs and
Broomsticks (71); Herbie Rides Again (74); Island
at the Top of the World, The (74); One of Our
Dinosaurs Is Missing (75); Shaggy D.A., The (76)

STILLER, BEN
Reality Bites (94); •Cable Guy, The (96);
•Zoolander (01)

STILLMAN, WHIT
•Metropolitan (90); •Barcelona (94); •Last Days of
Disco, The (98)

STONE, OLIVER
Seizure (74); Hand, The (81); •Platoon (86); •Salvador (86); •Wall Street (87); Talk Radio (88); •Born on the Fourth of July (89); •Doors, The (91); •JFK (91); Heaven and Earth (93); •Natural Born Killers (94); •Nixon (95); U Turn (97); Any Given Sunday (99); Comandante (03); Looking for Fidel (04); •Alexander (04)

STREISAND, BARBRA
•Yentl (83); •Prince of Tides, The (91); Mirror Has Two Faces, The (96)

STURGES, JOHN
Man Who Dared, The (46); Shadowed (46); For the Love of Rusty (47); Keeper of the Bees (47); Best Man Wins, The (48); Sign of the Ram, The (48); Walking Hills, The (49); Capture, The (50); Magnificent Yankee, The (50); Mystery Street (50); Right Cross (50); It's a Big Country (51); Kind Lady (51); People Against O'Hara, The (51); Girl in White, The (52); Escape from Fort Bravo (53); Fast Company (53); Jeopardy (53); •Bad Day at Black Rock (55); Scarlet Coat, The (55); Underwater! (55); Backlash (56); •Gunfight at the O.K. Corral (57); Law and Jake Wade, The (58); •Old Man and the Sea, The (58); Last Train from Gun Hill (59); Never So Few (59); •Magnificent Seven, The (60); By Love Possessed (61); Girl Named Tamiko, A (62); Sergeants 3 (62); •Great Escape, The (63); Hallelujah Trail, The (65); Satan Bug, The (65); Hour of the Gun (67); Ice Station Zebra (68); Marooned (69); Joe Kidd (72); Chino (73); Mc Q (74); Eagle Has Landed, The (76)

STURGES, PRESTON
•Christmas in July (40); •Great Mcginty, The (40); •Lady Eve, The (41); •Sullivan's Travels (41); •Palm Beach Story, The (42); Great Moment, The (44); •Hail the Conquering Hero (44); •Miracle of Morgan's Creek, The (44); •Unfaithfully Yours (48); Beautiful Blonde from Bashful Bend, The (49); •Mad Wednesday (50); Vendetta (50); •French, They Are a Funny Race, The (55)

SVANKMAJER, JAN
Kostnice (70); Jabberwocky (71); Moznosti Dialogu (82); Do Pivnice (83); Kyvaldo, Jama A Nadeje (83); •Alice (88); Leonarduv Denik (880; Animated Self-Portraits (89); Muzne Hry (89); Darkness, Light, Darkness (90); Death of Stalinism in Bohemia, The (90); Food (93); Faust (94); Conspirators of Pleasure (96); •Little Otik (00)

SVERAK, JAN
Elementary School, The (91); Akumulator 1 (94); Ride, The (94); •Kolya (96); Dark Blue World (01)

SWAIM, BOB
La Nuit de Saint-Germain des Pres (77); •La Balance (82); Half Moon Street (86); Masquerade (88); Atlantide (92); Climb, The (97); Nos Amis les Flics (04)

SWIFT, DAVID
•Pollyanna (60); Parent Trap, The (61); Interns, The (62); Love Is a Ball (63); Under the Yum Yum Tree (63); •Good Neighbor Sam (64); •How to Succeed in Business Without Really Trying (67)

SZABO, ISTVAN
Age of Illusions (64); Father (66) Film About Love, A (70); 25 Firemen's Street (74); Premiere (76); Tales of Budapest (77); Hungarians, The (78); Confidence (79); •Mephisto (81); •Colonel Redl (84); Hanussen (88); Opera Europa (90); Meeting Venus (91); Sweet Emma, Dear Bobe (92); Offenbach Titkai (96); Sunshine (99); Taking Sides (01); •Being Julia (04)

TAMAHORI, LEE
•Once Were Warriors (94); Mulholland Falls (96); Edge, The (97); Along Came a Spider (01); Die Another Day (02); xXx: State of the Union (05)

TANNER, ALAIN
Charles, Dead or Alive (69); Salamander, The (71); Return from Africa (72); Middle of the World (74); •Jonah Who Will Be 25 in the Year 2000 (76); Messidor (79); Light Years Away (81); In the White City (83); No Man's Land (85); Flame in My Heart, A (87); La Vallee Fantome (87); La Femme de Rose Hill (89); L'Homme Qui a Perdu Som Ombre (92); Diary of Lady M (93); Fourbi (96); Les Hommes du Port (96); Requiem (98); Jonas et Lila, a Demain (99); Fleurs de Sang (02); Paul s'en Va (04)

TARANTINO, QUENTIN
•Reservoir Dogs (92); •Pulp Fiction (94); •Jackie Brown (97)

TARKOVSKY, ANDREI
Violin and Roller (60); •My Name Is Ivan (62); Andrei Roublev (66); •Solaris (72); Mirror, The (75); •Stalker (79); •Nostalghia (83); •Sacrifice, The (86)

TASHLIN, FRANK
First Time, The (52); •Son of Paleface (52); Marry Me Again (53); Susan Slept Here (54); Artists and Models (55); Girl Can't Help It, The (56); Hollywood or Bust (56); Lieutenant Wore Skirts, The (56); •Will Success Spoil Rock Hunter? (57); Geisha Boy, The (58); Rock-a-Bye Baby (58); Say One for Me (59); Cinderfella (60); Bachelor Flat (62); It's Only Money (62); Man from the Diners' Club, The (63); Who's Minding the Store? (63); Disorderly Orderly, The (64); Alphabet Murders, The (65); Glass Bottom Boat, The (66); Caprice (67); Private Navy of Sgt. O'Farrell, The (68)

TATI, JACQUES
•Jour de Fete (49); •Mr. Hulot's Holiday (53); •My Uncle (58); •Playtime (67); •Traffic (72); Parade (74)

TAVERNIER, BERTRAND
La Chance et l'Amour (64); Les Baisers (65); •Clockmaker, The (73); Let Joy Reign Supreme (75); Judge and the Assassin, The (76); Spoiled Children, The (77); •Death Watch (80); Week's Vacation, A (80); •Coup de Torchon (81); Philippe Soupault (82); Mississippi Blues (83); •Sunday in the Country, A (84); •Round Midnight (86); Beatrice (88); Daddy Nostalgia (90); •Life and Nothing But (90); 50 Ans de Cinema Americaine (91); Undeclared War, The (91); L.627 (92); Contre l'Oubli (92); D'Artagnan's Daughter (94); Live Bait (95); Capitaine Conan (96); It All Starts Today (99);

Histoires des Vies Brisees: Le "Double Peine" de Lyon (01); Les Enfants de Thies (01); Safe Conduct (02)

TAVIANI, PAOLO and VITTORIO
Subversives, The (68); Under the Sign of Scorpio (69); San Michele Aveva un Gallo (72); Allonsanfan (74); •Padre Padrone (77); Meadow, The (79); •Night of the Shooting Stars, The (81); Kaos (84); Good Morning, Babylon (87); Sun Also Shines at Night, The (90); Fiorile (93); Elective Affinities (96); You Laugh (98)

TAYMOR, JULIE
Titus (99); •Frida (02)

TECHINE, ANDRE
Paulina s'en Va (69); French Provincial (75); Barocco (77); Bronte Sisters, The (79); Hotel des Ameriques (81); La Matiouette ou l'Arriere-Pays (83); Rendez-Vous (85); Scene of the Crime (86); Les Innocents (87); J'Embrasse Pas (91); Ma Saison Preferee (93); •Wild Reeds (94); Les Voleurs (96); Alice et Martin (98); Far Away (01)

TEMPLE, JULIEN
Great Rock 'n' Roll Swindle, The (79); Secret Policeman's Other Ball, The (81); Mantrap (84); •Absolute Beginners (86); Running Out of Luck (86); Aria (87); Earth Girls Are Easy (89); Rolling Stones "At the Max" (91); Bullet (95); Vigo: A Passion for Life (99); Pandaemonium (00); •Filth and the Fury, The (00)

TENNANT, ANDY
Keep the Change (92); Solomon's Choice (92); Amy Fisher Story, The (93); It Takes Two (95); Fools Rush In (97); •Ever After (98); Anna and the King (99); •Sweet Home Alabama (02); •Hitch (05)

TESHIGAHARA, HIROSHI
Pitfall, The (61); •Woman in the Dunes (64); That Tender Age (64); Face of Another, The (66); Man Without a Map, The (68); Summer Soldiers (72); Antonio Gaudi (85); Rikyu (89); Basara: Princess Goh (92)

THOMAS, BETTY
Only You (92); My Breast (94); Brady Bunch, The (95); Late Shift, The (96); Private Parts (97); •Doctor Dolittle (98); •28 Days (00); I-Spy (02)

THORNTON, BILLY BOB
•Sling Blade (96); •All the Pretty Horses (00); Daddy and Them (02)

TOLKIN, MICHAEL
Rapture, The (91); •New Age, The (94)

TORNATORE, GIUSEPPE
Professor, The (86); •Cinema Paradiso (88); Everybody's Fine (90); Especially on Sunday (91); Pure Formality, A (94); Star Maker, The (95); Lo Schermo a Tre Punte (96); Legend of 1900, The (98); Malena (00)

TOURNEUR, JACQUES
Nick Carter, Master Detective (39); They All Come Out (39); Phantom Raiders (40); Doctors Don't Tell (41); •Cat People (42); •I Walked with a Zombie (43); Leopard Man, The (43); Days of Glory (44); Experiment Perilous (44); Canyon Passage (46); •Out of the Past (47); Berlin Express (48); Easy Living (49); Flame and the Arrow, The (50); Stars in My Crown (50); Anne of The Indies (51); Circle of Danger (51); Way of a Gaucho (52); Appointment in Honduras (53); Stranger on Horseback (55); Wichita (55); Great Day in the Morning (56); Nightfall (56); Curse of the Demon (58); Fearmakers, The (58); Giant of Marathon, The (59); Timbuktu (59); Comedy of Horrors, The (64); City under the Sea (65)

TOWNE, ROBERT
•Personal Best (82); Tequila Sunrise (88); Without Limits (98)

TRAN ANH HUNG
Scent of Green Papaya, The (93); •Cyclo (95); Vertical Ray of the Sun, The (00)

TROELL, JAN
Here's Your Life (66); Who Saw Him Die? (68); •Emigrants, The (71); •New Land, The (72); •Zandy's Bride (74); Bang! (77); Flight of the Eagle, The (78); Hurricane (79); Ingenjor Andrees Luftfard (82); Sagolandet (86); Swedish Requiem, A (91); Hamsum (96); Frozen Dream, A (97); As White as Snow (01)

TRUEBA, FERNANDO
Opera Prima (80); Mientras el Cuerpo Aguante (82); Sal Gorda (83); Be Wanton and Tread No Shame (85); Year of Awakening, The (86); Twisted Obsession (90); •Belle Epoque (92); Two Much (95); Girl of My Drams, The (98); •Calle 54 (00); Shanghai Spell, The (02)

TRUFFAUT, FRANCOIS
•Four Hundred Blows, The (59); •Shoot the Piano Player (60); •Jules and Jim (62); •Love at Twenty (62); •Soft Skin, The (64); •Fahrenheit 451 (66); Bride Wore Black, The (67); •Stolen Kisses (68); •Mississippi Mermaid (69); •Wild Child, The (69); •Bed and Board (70); •Two English Girls (71); •Day for Night (73); •Such a Gorgeous Kid Like Me (73); •Story of Adele H., The (75); •Small Change (76); •Man Who Loved Women, The (77); •Green Room, The (78); •Love on the Run (79); •Last Metro, The (80); •Woman Next Door, The (81); •Confidentially Yours (83)

TSAI MING-LIANG
Rebels of the Neon God (92); Vive l'Amour (96); My New Friends (95); River, The (97); Hole, The (98); •What Time Is It There? (01)

TSUI HARK
Butterfly Murders (79); We're Going to Eat You (80); Dangerous Encounters of the First Kind (80); All the Wrong Clues (81); Zu Warriors (83); Aces Go Places III (84); Shanghai Blues (84); Working Class (85); •Peking Opera Blues (86); Chinese Ghost Story (87); Better Tomorrow III, A (89); Master, The (89); Swordsman (90); Chinese Ghost Story III, A (90); Raid, The (91); •Once Upon A Time In China (91); Banquet, The (91); Swordsman II (92); Once Upon A Time In China II (92); Dragon Inn (92); King of Chess (92); Twin Dragons (92); Swordsman III (93); Wicked City, The (93); Green Snake (94); Butterfly Lovers (94); Once Upon A Time In China III (94); Once Upon A Time In China

IV (94); Love in the Time of Twilight (94); Once Upon A Time In China V (94); Chinese Feast, The (95); Blade, The (95); Tristar (96); •Double Team (97); Knock Off (98); Time and Tide (00); Legend of Zu, The (01); Black Mask 2: City of Masks (01)

TURTELTAUB, JON
Driving Me Crazy (91); 3 Ninjas (92); Cool Runnings (93); •While You Were Sleeping (95); Phenomenon (96); Instinct (99); Disney's The Kid (00); •National Treasure (04)

ULMER, EDGAR G.
Damaged Lives (33); Mr. Broadway (33); •Black Cat, The (34); Thunder Over Texas (34); Damaged Lives (37); Girl from Poltava (37); Green Fields (37); Singing Blacksmith (38); Cossacks in Exile (39); Tomorrow We Live (42); Girls in Chains (43); Isle of Forgotten Sins (43); My Son, The Hero (43); Bluebeard (44); Jive Junction (44); •Detour (45); Strange Illusion (45); Club Havana (46); Her Sister's Secret (46); Strange Woman, The (46); Carnegie Hall (47); Ruthless (48); Pirates of Capri, The (49); Man from Planet X, The (51); St. Benny the Dip (51); Babes in Bagdad (52); Loves of Three Queens, The (54); Murder Is My Beat (55); Naked Dawn, The (55); Daughter of Dr. Jekyll (57); Amazing Transparent Man, The (60); Beyond the Time Barrier (60); Hannibal (60); Journey Beneath the Desert (61); Cavern, The (66)

UNDERWOOD, RON
•Tremors (90); •City Slickers (91); Heart and Souls (93); Speechless (94); Mighty Joe Young (98); Adventures of Pluto Nash, The (02)

VADIM, ROGER
•And God Created Woman (56); No Sun in Venice (57); Night Heaven Fell, The (58); Les Liaisons Dangereuses (59); Blood and Roses (60); Please, Not Now! (61); Seven Capital Sins (61); Love on a Pillow (62); Nutty, Naughty Chateau (63); Vice and Virtue (63); Circle of Love (64); Game Is Over, The (66); Barbarella (68); Spirits of the Dead (68); Pretty Maids All in a Row (71); Helle (72); Ms. Don Juan (73); Charlotte (74); Un Femme Fidele (76); Night Games (80); Surprise Party (83); Come Back (83); And God Created Woman (88); Safari (91); Amour Fou (93); Mon Pere Avait Raison (96); Un Coup de Baguette Magique (97)

VAN DORMAEL, JACO
•Toto le Heros (91); Eighth Day, The (96)

VAN DYKE II, W.S.
White Shadows in The South Seas (28); Pagan, The (29); Cuban Love Song, The (31); Guilty Hands (31); Never the Twain Shall Meet (31); Trader Horn (31); Night Court (32); •Tarzan, the Ape Man (32); Penthouse (33); Prizefighter and the Lady, The (33); Hide-Out (34); Laughing Boy (34); •Manhattan Melodrama (34); •Thin Man, The (34); Forsaking All Others (35); I Live My Life (35); •Naughty Marietta (35); •After the Thin Man (36); Devil Is a Sissy, The (36); His Brother's Wife (36); Love on the Run (36); •Rose Marie (36); •San Francisco (36); Personal Property (37); •Prisoner of Zenda, The (37);

Rosalie (37); They Gave Him a Gun (37); •Marie Antoinette (38); Sweethearts (38); Andy Hardy Gets Spring Fever (39); Another Thin Man (39); It's a Wonderful World (39); Stand Up and Fight (39); Bitter Sweet (40); I Love You Again (40); I Take This Woman (40); Dr. Kildare's Victory (41); Feminine Touch, The (41); Rage in Heaven (41); Shadow of the Thin Man (41); Cairo (42); I Married an Angel (42); •Journey for Margaret (42)

VAN PEEBLES, MELVIN
Sunlight (58); Three Pickup Men for Herrick (58); •Story of a Three Day Pass, The (67); Watermelon Man (70); •Sweet Sweetback's Baadasssss Song (71); Don't Play Us Cheap (72); Identity Crisis (91); Tales of Erotica (94); Gang in Blue (96); Bellyful (00)

VAN SANT, GUS
•Mala Noche (85); •Drugstore Cowboy (89); •My Own Private Idaho (91); Even Cowgirls Get The Blues (94); •To Die For (95); •Good Will Hunting (97); •Psycho (98); Finding Forrester (00); Gerry (02)

VARDA, AGNES
La Pointe Courte (54); Riviera: Today's Eden, The (58); Les Fiances du Pont Macdonald (61); •Cleo from 5 to 7 (62); Le Bonheur (65); Les Creatures (66); Lions Love (69); One Sings, the Other Doesn't (77); •Vagabond (85); Kung Fu Master (87); Jacquot (91); A Hundred and One Nights (95); Universe of Jacques Demy, The (95); Gleaners & I, The (00); Gleaners & I: Two Years Later, The (02)

VERBINSKI, GORE
Mouse Hunt (97); Mexican, The (01); •Ring, The (02); Pirates of the Caribbean: The Curse of the Black Pearl (03)

VERHOEVEN, PAUL
Business Is Business (71); Turkish Delight (73); Cathy Tippel (75); •Soldier of Orange (77); Fourth Man, The (79); •Spetters (80); Flesh and Blood (85); •Robocop (87); •Total Recall (90); •Basic Instinct (92); •Showgirls (95); •Starship Troopers (97); Hollow Man (00)

VIDOR, CHARLES
Double Door (34); Sensation Hunters (34); Arizonian, The (35); Strangers All (35); His Family Tree (36); Muss 'Em Up (36); Doctor's Diary, A (37); Great Gambini, The (37); She's No Lady (37); Blind Alley (39); Romance of the Redwoods (39); Those High Grey Walls (39); Lady in Question, The (40); My Son, My Son! (40); Ladies in Retirement (41); New York Town (41); Tuttles of Tahiti, The (42); Desperadoes, The (43); •Cover Girl (44); Together Again (44); Over 21 (45); •Song to Remember, A (45); •Gilda (46); Loves of Carmen, The (48); Edge of Doom (50); It's a Big Country (51); •Hans Christian Andersen (52); Thunder in the East (53); Rhapsody (54); •Love Me or Leave Me (55); Swan, The (56); Farewell to Arms, A (57); Joker Is Wild, The (57); Song Without End (60)

WANG, WAYNE
Man, a Woman and a Killer, A (75); •Chan Is Missing (81); •Dim Sum: A Little Bit of Heart (85); Slamdance (87); •Eat a Bowl of Tea (90); Life Is Cheap. . . But Toilet Paper Is Expensive (90); •Joy Luck Club, The (93); Smoke (95); Blue in the Face (95); Chinese Box (97); Anywhere but Here (99); Center of the World, The (01); •Maid in Manhattan (02)

WARD, VINCENT
Vigil (84); •Navigator, The (88); Map of the Human Heart (93); What Dreams May Come (98)

WARHOL, ANDY
Blow Job (63); Eat (63); Kiss (63); Haircut (63); Sleep (63); Couch (63); Empire (64); Beauty #4 (65); Poor Little Rich Girl (65); Harlot (65); Screen Test (65); My Hustler (65); Vinyl (65); Horse (65); •Chelsea Girls, The (66); I, a Man (67); Bike Boy (67); Nude Restaurant, The (67); Lonesome Cowboys (68); Fuck (69); L'Amour (73)

WATERS, JOHN
Mondo Trasho (70); Multiple Maniacs (71); •Pink Flamingos (73); Female Trouble (75); Desperate Living (77); Polyester (81); •Hairspray (88); •Cry-Baby (90); Serial Mom (94); Pecker (98); Cecil B. Demented (00)

WEIR, PETER
Three to Go (70); •Cars That Ate Paris, The (74); •Picnic at Hanging Rock (75); •Last Wave, The (77); Plumber, The (80); •Gallipoli (81); •Year of Living Dangerously, The (83); •Witness (85); •Mosquito Coast, The (86); •Dead Poets Society (89); Green Card (90); •Fearless (93); •Truman Show, The (98)

WEITZ, CHRIS and PAUL
•American Pie (99); Down to Earth (01); •About a Boy (02); •In Good Company (04)

WELLES, ORSON
•Citizen Kane (41); •Magnificent Ambersons, The (42); It's All True (42); •Stranger, The (46); •Lady from Shanghai, The (48); Macbeth (48); •Othello (52); Mr. Arkadin (55); •Touch of Evil (58); •Trial, The (63); •Chimes at Midnight (66); Immortal Story, The (68); F for Fake (75)

WELLMAN, WILLIAM A.
Beggars of Life (28); Chinatown Nights (29); Man I Love, The (29); Woman Trap (29); Dangerous Paradise (30); Maybe It's Love (30); Young Eagles (30); Night Nurse (31); Other Men's Women (31); •Public Enemy, The (31); Safe in Hell (31); Star Witness (31); Conquerors, The (32); Hatchet Man, The (32); Love Is a Racket (32); Purchase Price, The (32); So Big (32); Central Airport (33); College Coach (33); Frisco Jenny (33); Heroes for Sale (33); Lilly Turner (33); Midnight Mary (33); •Wild Boys of the Road (33); Looking for Trouble (34); President Vanishes, The (34); Stingaree (34); •Call of the Wild (35); Robin Hood of El Dorado, The (36); Small Town Girl (36); •Nothing Sacred (37); •Star Is Born, A (37); Men with Wings (38); •Beau Geste (39); •Light that Failed, The (39); Reaching for the Sun (41); Great Man's Lady, The (42); Roxie Hart (42); Thunder Birds (42); Lady of Burlesque (43); •Ox-Bow Incident, The (43); Buffalo Bill (44); •Story of G.I. Joe, The (45); This Man's Navy (45); Gallant Journey (46); Magic Town (47); Iron Curtain, The (48); •Yellow Sky (48); •Battleground (49); Happy Years, The (50); Next Voice You Hear, The (50); Across the Wide Missouri (51); It's a Big Country (51); Westward The Women (51); My Man and I (52); Island in the Sky (53); •High and the Mighty, The (54); Ring of Fear (54); Track of the Cat (54); Blood Alley (55); Goodbye, My Lady (56); Darby's Rangers (58); Lafayette Escadrille (58)

WENDERS, WIM
Summer In The City (Dedicated to the Kinks) (70); •Goalie's Anxiety at the Penalty Kick, The (71); Scarlet Letter, The (73); •Alice in the Cities (74); Wrong Movement, The (75); •Kings of the Road (76); •American Friend, The (77); Lightning Over Water (80); •Hammett (82); •State of Things, The (82); Chambre 666 (84); •Paris, Texas (84); Tokyo-Ga (85); •Wings of Desire (87); Notebook on Cities and Clothes (89); •Until the End of the World (91); Faraway, So Close (93); Lisbon Story (95); Trick of the Light, A (95); End of Violence, The (96); •Buena Vista Social Club (99); Million Dollar Hotel, The (00); Ode to Cologne: A Rock 'n' Roll Film (02)

WERTMULLER, LINA
Lizards, The (63); Let's Talk About Men (65); Don't Sting the Mosquito (67); •Seduction of Mimi, The (72); All Screwed Up (73); Love and Anarchy (73); •Swept Away. . . By an Unusual Destiny in the Blue Sea of August (74); •Seven Beauties (76); End of the World (In Our Usual Bed in a Night Full of Rain), The (78); Shimmy Lagano Tarantelle e Vino (78); Blood Feud (79); Joke of Destiny Lying in Wait Around the Corner Like a Street Bandit, A (83); A Complex Plot About Women, Alleys, and Crimes (85); Sotto, Sotto (84); Summer Night with a Greek Profile, Almond Eyes, and Scent of Basil (86); Tenth One Hiding, The (84); Of Crystal or Cinders, Fire or Wind, As Long As It's Love (89); Saturday, Sunday, and Monday (90); Ciao, Professore! (94); Blue Collar Worker and the Hairdresser in a Whirl of Sex and Politics, The (96); Nymph, The (96); Interesting State, An (99); Ferdinando e Carolina (99); Francesca and Nunziata (01)

WEXLER, HASKELL
Bus, The (65); •Medium Cool (69); Brazil: A Report on Torture (71); Introduction to the Enemy (74); Underground (76); Bus II (83); Latino (85); Bus Rider's Union (99)

WHALE, JAMES
•Hell's Angels (30); Journey's End (30); •Frankenstein (31); Waterloo Bridge (31); Impatient Maiden, The (32); •Old Dark House, The (32); •Invisible Man, The (33); Kiss Before the Mirror, The (33); By Candlelight (34); One More River (34); •Bride of Frankenstein, The (35); •Remember Last Night? (35); •Show Boat (36); Great Garrick, The (37); Road Back, The (37); Port of Seven Seas (38); Sinners in Paradise (38);

Wives Under Suspicion (38); •Man in the Iron Mask, The (39); Green Hell (40); They Dare Not Love (41)

WHITAKER, FOREST
Strapped (93); •Waiting to Exhale (95); Black Jaq (98); Hope Floats (98)

WIDERBERG, BO
Pram, The (63); Raven's End (64); Love 65 (65); Thirty Times Your Money (66); •Elvira Madigan (67); Adalen 31 (69); Joe Hill (71); Stubby (74); Man on the Roof (77); Victoria (79); Man from Majorca, The (84); Serpent's Way, The (86); Up the Naked Rock (88); All Things Fair (95)

WILDER, BILLY
Mauvaise Graine (33); •Major and the Minor, The (42); •Five Graves to Cairo (43); •Double Indemnity (44); •Lost Weekend, The (45); Emperor Waltz, The (48); Foreign Affair, A (48); •Sunset Boulevard (50); •Ace in the Hole (51); •Stalag 17 (53); •Sabrina (54); •Seven Year Itch, The (55); Love in the Afternoon (57); •Spirit of St. Louis, The (57); •Witness for the Prosecution (57); •Some Like It Hot (59); •Apartment, The (60); •One, Two, Three (61); •Irma La Douce (63); Kiss Me, Stupid (64); •Fortune Cookie, The (66); •Private Life of Sherlock Holmes, The (70); Avanti! (72); •Front Page, The (74); Fedora (78); Buddy Buddy (81)

WILLIAMS, PAUL
Out of It (69); Revolutionary, The (70); •Dealing: Or the Berkeley-to-Boston Forty-Brick Lost-Bag Blues (71); Nunzio (78); November Men (94); Mirage (95)

WINTERBOTTOM, MICHAEL
Forget About Me (90); Under the Sun (92); Cracker: The Madwoman in the Attic (93); Family, The (94); Butterfly Kiss (94); •Go Now (95); •Jude (96); Welcome to Sarajevo (97); I Want You (98); Wonderland (99); With or Without You (99); Claim, The (00); •24-Hour Party People (02); In this World (02)

WISE, ROBERT
•Magnificent Ambersons, The (42); Curse of the Cat People, The (44); Mademoiselle Fifi (44); Body Snatcher, The (45); Game of Death, A (45); Criminal Court (46); Born to Kill (47); Blood on the Moon (48); Mystery in Mexico (48); •Set-Up, The (49); Three Secrets (50); Two Flags West (50); •Day the Earth Stood Still, The (51); House on Telegraph Hill, The (51); Captive City, The (52); Something for the Birds (52); Desert Rats, The (53); Destination Gobi (53); So Big (53); •Executive Suite (54); Helen of Troy (55); •Somebody Up There Likes Me (56); Tribute to a Bad Man (56); This Could Be the Night (57); Until They Sail (57); •I Want to Live! (58); •Run Silent, Run Deep (58); •Odds Against Tomorrow (59); •West Side Story (61); Two for the Seesaw (62); •Haunting, The (63); •Sound of Music, The (65); •Sand Pebbles, The (66); •Star! (68); Andromeda Strain, The (71); Two People (73); Hindenburg, The (75); Audrey Rose (77); •Star Trek—The Motion Picture (79); Rooftops (89); Stolen Summer, A (00)

WONG KAR-WAI
As Tears Go By (88); Days of Being Wild (90); Ashes of Time (94); •Chungking Express (94); •Fallen Angels (95); Happy Together (97); •In the Mood for Love (00)

WOO, JOHN
Young Dragons, The (73); Dragon Tamers, The (74); Princess Chang Ping (75); Countdown in Kung Fu/Hand of Death (76); Money Crazy (77); Follow the Star (77); Last Hurrah for Chivalry (78); Hello, Late Homecomers (78); From Rags to Riches (79); To Hell with the Devil (81); Laughing Times (81); Plain Jane to the Rescue (82); Heroes Shed No Tears (83); Time You Need a Friend, The (84); Run Tiger Run (85); Better Tomorrow, A (86); Better Tomorrow II, A (87); Just Heroes (89); •Killer, The (89); Bullet in the Head (90); Once a Thief (91); •Hard-Boiled (92); Hard Target (93); •Broken Arrow (96); •Face/Off (97); Blackjack (98); •Mission: Impossible II (00); •Windtalkers (02)

WOOD JR., EDWARD D.
Glen or Glenda (53); Jail Bait (54); Bride of the Monster (55); Night of the Ghouls (59); •Plan 9 from Outer Space (59); Sinister Urge, The (61); Take it Out in Trade (70)

WOOD, SAM
So This Is College (29); Girl Said No, The (30); It's a Great Life (30); Paid (30); Sins of the Children (30); They Learned About Women (30); Way for a Sailor (30); Man in Possession, The (31); New Adventures of Get-Rich-Quick Wallingford, The (31); Tailor Made Man, A (31); Huddle (32); Prosperity (32); Barbarian, The (33); Christopher Bean (33); Hold Your Man (33); Stamboul Quest (34); Let 'Em Have It (35); •Night at the Opera, A (35); Unguarded Hour, The (36); Whipsaw (36); •Day at the Races, A (37); Madame X (37); Navy Blue and Gold (37); Lord Jeff (38); Stablemates (38); •Gone with The Wind (39); •Goodbye Mr. Chips (39); Raffles (39); •Kitty Foyle (40); •Our Town (40); Rangers of Fortune (40); •Devil and Miss Jones, The (41); •Kings Row (42); •Pride of the Yankees, The (42); •For Whom the Bell Tolls (43); Casanova Brown (44); Guest Wife (45); Saratoga Trunk (45); Heartbeat (46); Ivy (47); Command Decision (48); Stratton Story, The (49); Ambush (50)

WYLER, WILLIAM
Love Trap, The (29); Shakedown, The (29); Hell's Heroes (30); Storm, The (30); House Divided, A (32); Tom Brown of Culver (32); •Counsellor-at-Law (33); Her First Mate (33); Glamour (34); Gay Deception, The (35); Good Fairy, The (35); Come and Get It (36); •Dodsworth (36); •These Three (36); •Dead End (37); •Jezebel (38); Raffles (39); •Wuthering Heights (39); •Letter, The (40); •Westerner, The (40); •Little Foxes, The (41); •Mrs. Miniver (42); •Best Years of Our Lives, The (46); •Heiress, The (49); •Detective Story (51); Carrie (52); •Roman Holiday (53); •Desperate Hours, The (55); •Friendly Persuasion (56); Big Country, The (58); •Ben-Hur (59); Children's

FILMS BY STAR RATING

All films in this volume are listed below by their star rating.
★★★★★ = Masterpiece; ★★★★ = Excellent; ★★★ = Good; ★★ = Fair; ★ = Poor

★★★★★

A Nous la Liberte
Adventures of Robin Hood,
  The
African Queen, The
Aguirre, the Wrath of God
All About Eve
All Quiet on the Western
  Front
All the King's Men
Amadeus
American in Paris, An
Apartment, The
Applause
Au Hasard, Balthazar
Awful Truth, The
Bad and the Beautiful, The
Badlands
Ball of Fire
Ballad of a Soldier
Bambi
Beauty and the Beast
Belle de Jour
Best Years of Our Lives, The
Bicycle Thief, The
Big Sleep, The
Black Narcissus
Blue Angel, The
Breathless
Bride of Frankenstein
Brief Encounter
Bringing Up Baby
Camille
Captains Courageous
Casablanca
Cat People
Charulata
Children of Paradise
Chinatown
Citizen Kane
Close Encounters of the Third
  Kind
Contempt
Conversation, The
Counsellor-at-Law
Day for Night
Day of Wrath
Dinner at Eight
Dr. Strangelove or: How I
  Learned to Stop Worrying
  and Love the Bomb

Dodsworth
Dog Day Afternoon
Double Indemnity
Duck Soup
Earrings of Madame de ... ,
  The
8 1/2
Flowers of St. Francis, The
Footlight Parade
Forbidden Games
Foreign Correspondent
42nd Street
Four Feathers, The
Four Hundred Blows, The
Frankenstein
From Here to Eternity
Gaslight
Godfather, The
Godfather, Part II, The
Gold Diggers of 1933
Gone with the Wind
Good Earth, The
Grand Hotel
Grand Illusion
Grapes of Wrath, The
Great Expectations
Green for Danger
Gunga Din
Heiress, The
Henry V
High Noon
Hiroshima Mon Amour
His Girl Friday
How Green Was My Valley
I Am a Fugitive from a Chain
  Gang
I Walked with a Zombie
In a Lonely Place
It Happened One Night
It's a Gift
It's a Wonderful Life
Jules and Jim
Killer of Sheep
Killers, The
Kind Hearts and Coronets
Kings of the Road
Kiss Me Deadly
La Ronde
La Strada
La Terra Trema
Lady Eve, The
Lady Vanishes, The

L'Age d'Or
L'Argent
Last Year at Marienbad
L'Atalante
Laura
Lawrence of Arabia
Letter from an Unknown
  Woman
Lola Montes
Long Day's Journey into
  Night
Long Voyage Home, The
Los Olvidados
Love Me Tonight
M
Maedchen in Uniform
Magnificent Ambersons, The
Maltese Falcon, The
Man Escaped, A
Man in the White Suit, The
Man of the West
Married Woman, The
Mask of Dimitrios, The
Mayerling
Meet Me in St. Louis
Melo
Merry Widow, The
Midnight
Mildred Pierce
Million, The
Miracle of Morgan's Creek,
  The
Mr. Deeds Goes to Town
Mr. Smith Goes to
  Washington
Modern Times
Mummy, The
Muriel
Mutiny on the Bounty
My Darling Clementine
My Life to Live
Nashville
Night of the Hunter, The
Ninotchka
Northwest Passage
Nothing Sacred
Notorious
Odd Man Out
Once Upon a Time in the
  West
Out of the Past
Ox-Bow Incident, The

Paisan
Pather Panchali
Paths of Glory
Peeping Tom
Persona
Pinocchio
Prisoner of Zenda, The
Psycho
Pygmalion
Queen Christina
Quiet Man, The
Raging Bull
Raise the Red Lantern
Ran
Rashomon
Rear Window
Red Badge of Courage, The
Red Desert
Red River
Red Shoes, The
Repulsion
Ride the High Country
Rififi
River, The
Rules of the Game
Sansho the Bailff
Scarface
Scarlet Empress, The
Scarlet Street
Schindler's List
Sea Hawk, The
Searchers, The
Seven Samurai, The
Seventh Seal, The
Shoot the Piano Player
Shop Around the Corner, The
Shop on Main Street, The
Singin' in the Rain
Snow White and the Seven
　　Dwarfs
Some Like It Hot
Spiral Staircase, The
Stage Door
Stagecoach
Star Is Born, A
Strangers on a Train
Sullivan's Travels
Sunset Blvd.
Sweet Smell of Success
Swing Time
Tale of Two Cities, A
Taxi Driver
Testament of Dr. Mabuse, The
Testament of Orpheus, The
They Live by Night
They Were Expendable
Thief of Bagdad, The
Third Man, The
39 Steps, The

To Be or Not to Be
Tokyo Story
Tom Jones
Top Hat
Touch of Evil
Treasure of the Sierra Madre,
　　The
Trouble in Paradise
Two or Three Things I Know
　　about Her
Ugestu
Umberto D.
Unfaithfully Yours
Vampyr
Vertigo
Viridiana
Ways of Love
Westerner, The
White Heat
Whole Town's Talking, The
Wild Boys of the Road
Wild Bunch, The
Wizard of Oz, The
Wrong Man, The
Yankee Doodle Dandy
Zero for Conduct
Zulu

★★★★½

Alphaville
Amarcord
American Graffiti
Anatomy of a Murder
Asphalt Jungle, The
Au Revoir, les Enfants
Bachelor Mother
Ballad of Narayama, The
Band Wagon, The
Bank Dick, The
Beauty and the Beast
Ben-Hur
Big House, The
Birdy
Black Cat, The
Black Sunday
Black Swan, The
Body and Soul
Bonnie and Clyde
Boys of St. Vincent, The
Breakfast at Tiffany's
Bridge on the River Kwai,
　　The
Browning Version, The
Cabaret
Champion
Chungking Express

Citadel, The
Company of Wolves, The
Conformist, The
Cries and Whispers
Darby O'Gill and the Little
　　People
David Copperfield
Dead, The
Dead of Night
Dead Ringers
Death in Venice
Deer Hunter, The
Diabolique
Diary of a Country Priest
Discreet Charm of the
　　Bourgeoisie, The
Diva
Do the Right Thing
D.O.A.
Dr. Jekyll and Mr. Hyde
Dona Herlinda and Her Son
Don't Look Now
Drugstore Cowboy
Dumbo
East of Eden
Effi Briest
El
Entre Nous
Executive Suite
Exterminating Angel, The
Fanny and Alexander
Five Graves to Cairo
5,000 Fingers of Dr. T., The
Fly, The
Fog Over Frisco
Follow the Fleet
Force of Evil
Fort Apache
49th Parallel
French Connection, The
Front Page, The
Funny Face
Fury
Ganja and Hess
Genevieve
Goldfinger
Goodbye Mr. Chips
Gospel According to St.
　　Matthew, The
Graduate, The
Great Dictator, The
Gun Crazy
Hard Day's Night, A
Hoop Dreams
Hope and Glory
Hustler, The
I Know Where I'm Going!
I Married a Witch
I Want to Live!

If...
Ikiru
Importance of Being Earnest, The
Invisible Man, The
Irma Vep
Island of Lost Souls
Johnny Belinda
Julius Caesar
Kennel Murder Case, The
Killing, The
King and Country
King Kong
King of Comedy, The
Kings Row
Kiss of Death
Knife in the Water
Lady from Shanghai, The
Ladykillers, The
Last Emperor, The
Last Picture Show, The
Leopard, The
Life and Death of Colonel Blimp, The
Life of Emile Zola, The
Lifeboat
Little Big Man
Little Women
Local Hero
Lost Weekend, The
Lust for Life
Mad Love
Magician, The
Major and the Minor, The
Major Barbara
Man Facing Southeast
Man Hunt
Manchurian Candidate, The
Manhattan
M*A*S*H
Maytime
McCabe and Mrs. Miller
Mean Streets
Memento
Miracle Worker, The
Mr. Hulot's Holiday
Mon Oncle d'Amerique
Murder, My Sweet
Music Room, The
My Left Foot
My Man Godfrey
Oliver Twist
On the Waterfront
Orpheus
Pakeezah
Pat and Mike
Patton
Pepe le Moko
Playtime

Point Blank
Pride and Prejudice
Pride of the Yankees, The
Private Lives
Public Enemy, The
Raiders of the Lost Ark
Room at the Top
Rose Marie
Rumble Fish
Secrets & Lies
Separate Tables
Seven Brides for Seven Brothers
Shadow of a Doubt
Shame
She Done Him Wrong
Show Boat
Silence of the Lambs, The
Smiling Lieutenant, The
Sorrow and the Pity, The
Southerner, The
Spartacus
Stairway to Heaven
Stalag 17
Star Is Born, A
Star Wars
Story of a Cheat, The
Sunday in the Country, A
Sundowners, The
Targets
Taste of Honey, A
That Obscure Object of Desire
These Three
They Drive by Night
Thin Man, The
This Gun for Hire
Throne of Blood
Titanic
Tree of Wooden Clogs, The
Twelve O'Clock High
2001: A Space Odyssey
Unforgiven
Wages of Fear, The
Walk in the Sun, A
Walkabout
Way Out West
Weekend
Wild Child, The
Wild Strawberries
Wings of Desire
Witness for the Prosecution
Women, The
World of Apu, The
Written on the Wind
Wuthering Heights
Yojimbo
Young Frankenstein

★★★★

Abbott and Costello Meet Frankenstein
Accident
Accidental Tourist, The
Adaptation.
Adventures of Ichabod and Mr. Toad, The
Adventures of Sherlock Holmes, The
Adventuress, The
After Hours
Afterglow
Age of Innocence, The
Ah, Wilderness!
Aladdin
Alexander Nevsky
Algiers
Ali, Fear Eats the Soul
Alice Adams
Alien
All That Heaven Allows
All the President's Men
All This and Heaven Too
Almost Famous
American Beauty
American Friend, The
Anastasia
And Then There Were None
Angel at My Table, An
Angels Over Broadway
Angels with Dirty Faces
Anna and the King of Siam
Anna Karenina
Anne of the Thousand Days
Annie Hall
Aparajito
Apocalypse Now
Apocalypse Now Redux
Apprenticeship of Duddy Kravitz, The
Around the World in 80 Days
Ace in the Hole
Assault, The
Audition
Auntie Mame
Baby Doll
Back Street
Bad Company
Bad Day at Black Rock
Bad Education
Baker's Wife, The
Balseros
Band of Angels
Barfly
Barretts of Wimpole Street, The
Barry Lyndon

Basket Case
Bataan
Battle of Algiers, The
Battleground
Beat the Devil
Becket
Before Night Falls
Before the Rain
Being There
Bells of St. Mary's, The
Berlin Alexanderplatz
Best in Show
Big Heat, The
Big Red One, The
Bill of Divorcement, A
Billy Elliot
Billy Liar
Bird
Bird with the Crystal
  Plumage, The
Birds, The
Black Rose, The
Black Stallion, The
Black Sunday
Blackmail
Blade Runner
Blair Witch Project, The
Blithe Spirit
Blonde Venus
Blood and Sand
Blood Simple
Blow Out
Bob le Flambeur
Bombshell
Boogie Nights
Boomerang
Born into Brothels
Born Yesterday
Bound for Glory
Boyz N the Hood
Breaking Away
Brewster's Millions
Bridges at Toko-Ri, The
Bright Victory
Brightness
Bring Me the Head of Alfredo
  Garcia
Brute Force
Bulldog Drummond Strikes
  Back
Bullitt
Bulworth
Bus 174
Cabin in the Sky
Caesar and Cleopatra
Caine Mutiny, The
Call Northside 777
Calle 54
Cape Fear

Captain Blood
Captain from Castile
Carousel
Cat on a Hot Tin Roof
Catered Affair, The
Cavalcade
Celebration, The
Central Station
Champagne for Caesar
Chan Is Missing
Character
Charade
Charlotte's Web
Chelsea Girls, The
Cheyenne Autumn
Chicken Run
Children of a Lesser God
Children of Heaven
Chocolat
Choose Me
Christmas in July
Christmas Story, A
Chunhyang
Chushingura
Cincinnati Kid, The
Cinderella
Circle of Deceit
Circle, The
City of God
Clash by Night
Cleopatra
Clock, The
Clockwork Orange, A
Closely Watched Trains
Clueless
Coal Miner's Daughter
Comanche Station
Come Back, Little Sheba
Compulsion
Confessions of a Nazi Spy
Cool Hand Luke
Cornered
Count of Monte Cristo, The
Cousins, The
Cover Girl
Cradle Will Rock
Craig's Wife
Cranes Are Flying, The
Cria!
Crime of Monsieur Lange,
  The
Crime without Passion
Crossfire
Crouching Tiger, Hidden
  Dragon
Cruel Sea, The
Crumb
Cry in the Dark, A
Crying Game, The

Cure
Curly Top
Cyclo
Cyrano de Bergerac
Daddy Long Legs
Damn Yankees
Damnation
Damned, The
Dance with a Stranger
Dangerous Liaisons
Dark Mirror, The
Dark Victory
Das Boot
David Holzman's Diary
Dawn of the Dead
Dawn Patrol, The
Day I Became a Woman, The
Day of the Jackal, The
Day of the Locust, The
Day the Earth Stood Still, The
Daybreak
Days of Heaven
Days of Wine and Roses
Dead End
Dead Man
Dead Men Don't Wear Plaid
Death of a Salesman
Death Takes a Holiday
Decision Before Dawn
Deep End
Defiant Ones, The
Delicatessen
Deliverance
Desire
Desperate Hours, The
Destry Rides Again
Detective, The
Detective Story
Detour
Devil and Daniel Webster,
  The
Devil-Doll, The
Devil in a Blue Dress
Devil in the Flesh, The
Devil, Probably, The
Diary of a Chambermaid
Diary of Anne Frank, The
Diner
Dirty Dozen, The
Divorce, Italian Style
Dr. Ehrlich's Magic Bullet
Doctor in the House
Doctor X
Doctor Zhivago
Dodge City
Don Quixote
Don's Party
Double Life, A
Downfall

Downhill Racer
Draughtsman's Contract, The
Dream of Light
Dreamlife of Angels, The
Dresser, The
Dreyfus Case, The
Driver, The
Drums
Drums Along the Mohawk
Drunken Angel
E.T. The Extra-Terrestrial
Easy Rider
Edge of Darkness
El Norte
Elephant Man, The
Elmer Gantry
Emerald Forest, The
Emigrants, The
Emperor and the Assassin,
  The
Emperor Jones, The
Emperor's New Groove, The
Empire Strikes Back, The
Enigma of Kaspar Hauser,
  The
Entertainer, The
Entertaining Mr. Sloane
Eraserhead
Eternal Mask, The
Eternal Sunshine of the
  Spotless Mind
Eureka
Europa, Europa
Every Man for Himself
Exodus
Eyes Wide Shut
Face in the Crowd, A
Face to Face
Faces
Fahrenheit 451
Fallen Angels
Fallen Idol, The
Family Plot
Fantasia
Far Country, The
Far from Heaven
Farewell to Arms, A
Fast Runner (Atanarjuat), The
Fat City
Father of the Bride
Fear Strikes Out
Felicia's Journey
Fellini Satyricon
Fight Club
Fighting 69th, The
Filth and the Fury, The
Fire Over England
Fireworks
Fitzcarraldo

Five Easy Pieces
Five Fingers
Flash Gordon
Flight of the Phoenix, The
Flying Down to Rio
Following
For a Few Dollars More
Forbidden Planet
Fortune, The
Four Daughters
Four Nights of a Dreamer
Frantic
Freaks
French Cancan
Frenzy
Fresh
Friendly Persuasion
From Russia with Love
Fugitive, The
Full Metal Jacket
Full Monty, The
Funny Bones
Funny Girl
G-Men
Gallipoli
Garden of the Finzi-Continis,
  The
Gas Food Lodging
Gaslight
Gay Divorcee, The
General della Rovere
Gentle Creature, A
Gentleman Jim
Gentleman's Agreement
Gentlemen Prefer Blondes
Georgy Girl
Ghost and Mrs. Muir, The
Ghost Goes West, The
Ghost World
Giant
Gilda
Gimme Shelter
Girl Crazy
Glass Key, The
Glass Menagerie, The
Glengarry Glen Ross
Glenn Miller Story, The
Glory
Go
Go-Between, The
Gods and Monsters
Gods Must Be Crazy, The
Going in Style
Going My Way
Golden Boy
Golden Coach, The
Good Bye, Lenin!
Good, the Bad and the Ugly,
  The

Goodbye Girl, The
Goodfellas
Great Escape, The
Great McGinty, The
Greatest Show on Earth, The
Green Man, The
Gremlins 2: The New Batch
Grey Zone, The
Grifters, The
Guadalcanal Diary
Guardsman, The
Gunfight at the O.K. Corral
Gunfighter, The
Hail, Mary
Hail the Conquering Hero
Hair
Hairdresser's Husband, The
Hallelujah
Halloween
Hamlet
Hammett
Hands Across the Table
Hanging Garden, The
Hannah and Her Sisters
Happiness
Harder They Fall, The
Harvey
Hasty Heart, The
He Walked by Night
Heat
Heavenly Creatures
Hedwig and the Angry Inch
Henry: Portrait of a Serial
  Killer
Henry V
Here Comes Mr. Jordan
Hero
Hidden Fortress, The
High and Low
High Hopes
High Sierra
Hilary and Jackie
Hobson's Choice
Hold Back the Dawn
Homecoming, The
Horror of Dracula
Horse Feathers
Hound of the Baskervilles,
  The
House of Games
House of Mirth, The
House of Rothschild, The
House on 92nd Street, The
How to Succeed in Business
  without Really Trying
Human Resources
Hunt, The
Hurricane, The
Husbands and Wives

I Remember Mama
If I Had a Million
I'll Cry Tomorrow
I'm All Right, Jack
Imitation of Life
In the Bedroom
In the Heat of the Night
In the Mood for Love
Incredible Shrinking Man, The
Incredibles, The
Informer, The
Inherit the Wind
Innocence
Innocence Unprotected
Innocents, The
Intruder in the Dust
Invasion of the Body Snatchers
Investigation of a Citizen Above Suspicion
Iron Giant, The
It Happened Here
It Should Happen to You
It's Always Fair Weather
Ivan the Terrible, Part I
Ivan the Terrible, Part II: The Revolt of the Boyars
Jaws
Jesse James
Jezebel
Johnny Eager
Johnny Guitar
Jolson Story, The
Jour de Fete
Journey into Fear
Ju Dou
Judgment at Nuremberg
Jungle Book, The
Kadosh
Kagemusha
Kameradschaft
Kes
Key Largo
Kid for Two Farthings, A
Kid from Spain, The
Kill Bill: Vol. 2
Killer, The
Kind of Loving, A
King and I, The
King Solomon's Mines
Kingdom, The
Kirikou and the Sorceress
Kiss Me Kate
Kiss of the Spider Woman
Kitty Foyle
Klute
Knack ... and How to Get It, The

Knife in the Head
Knight without Armor
Kolya
Kramer vs. Kramer
Kwaidan
L-Shaped Room, The
L.A. Confidential
La Femme Infidele
La Guerre est Finie
La Nuit de Varennes
La Traviata
Labyrinth of Passion
Lacombe, Lucien
Lady and the Tramp
Lady in White
Lagaan: Once Upon a Time in India
Lamerica
Lancelot of the Lake
Lassie Come Home
Last Detail, The
Last of the Mohicans, The
Last Orders
Last Resort
Last Tango in Paris
Last Temptation of Christ, The
Last Waltz, The
Last Wave, The
Late George Apley, The
Lavender Hill Mob, The
L'Avventura
Le Beau Mariage
Le Boucher
Le Gai Savoir
Le Petit Theatre de Jean Renoir
Le Samourai
Les Miserables
Les Parents Terribles
Letter, The
Letter to Three Wives, A
Libeled Lady
Life with Father
Light That Failed, The
Limelight
Lion in Winter, The
Little Caesar
Little Dorrit
Little Romance, A
Lives of a Bengal Lancer, The
Lock, Stock and Two Smoking Barrels
Lodger, The
Lolita
Lone Star
Loneliness of the Long Distance Runner, The
Lonely Are the Brave

Long Day Closes, The
Long Goodbye, The
Long, Hot Summer, The
Long Riders, The
Longest Day, The
Lord Jim
Lord of the Rings: The Fellowship of the Ring, The
Lord of the Rings: The Return of the King, The
Lost Honor of Katharina Blum, The
Lost Horizon
Love Affair
Love and Death
Love Crazy
Love Me or Leave Me
Love Streams
Love with the Proper Stranger
Loved One, The
Lumumba
Lusty Men, The
Macbeth
Madame Curie
Magic Box, The
Magnificent Seven, The
Magnolia
Make Way for Tomorrow
Mala Noche
Malcolm X
Male Animal, The
Mamma Roma
Man for All Seasons, A
Man from Laramie, The
Man in the Iron Mask, The
Man of Iron
Man of the Eiffel Tower, The
Man on the Flying Trapeze, The
Man Who Came to Dinner, The
Man Who Knew Too Much, The
Man Who Knew Too Much, The
Man Who Would Be King, The
Man without a Past, The
Manchurian Candidate, The
Manhattan Melodrama
Man's Hope
Marathon Man
Marie Antoinette
Marius
Mark of Zorro, The
Marnie
Marriage of Maria Braun, The
Martin

Marty
Mary Poppins
Masculine Feminine
Masque of the Red Death,
  The
Matewan
Meet John Doe
Men, The
Mephisto
Merry Christmas, Mr.
  Lawrence
Metropolitan
Midnight Cowboy
Midnight Express
Million Dollar Baby
Min and Bill
Ministry of Fear
Minority Report
Miracle in Milan
Missing
Modern Romance
Moderns, The
Mogambo
Monkey Business
Monsieur Hire
Monsieur Verdoux
Monte Carlo
Monty Python and the Holy
  Grail
Monty Python's Life of Brian
Moon and Sixpence, The
Moonlighting
Moonstruck
Morocco
Morvern Callar
Most Terrible Time in My
  Life, The
Mother and the Whore, The
Moulin Rouge
Mouse That Roared, The
Movie Movie
Mulan
Mulholland Dr.
Murder
Murder, He Says
Murmur of the Heart
Music Box
Music Man, The
My Architect
My Beautiful Laundrette
My Bodyguard
My Brilliant Career
My Favorite Brunette
My Favorite Wife
My Favorite Year
My First Wife
My Friend Flicka
My Name Is Ivan
My Night at Maud's

My Own Private Idaho
My 20th Century
My Uncle
Mystery of the Wax Museum,
  The
Naked
Naked City, The
Naked Spur, The
National Velvet
Naughty Marietta
Network
New Age, The
Next Stop, Greenwich Village
Niagara
Night and the City
Night at the Opera, A
Night Must Fall
Night of the Living Dead
Night to Remember, A
Night Train to Munich
Nightmare Alley
Nights of Cabiria
No Greater Glory
No Man's Land
None but the Lonely Heart
Norma Rae
North by Northwest
Nostalghia
Now, Voyager
Number Two
Nun's Story, The
O Lucky Man!
Objective, Burma!
Odds Against Tomorrow
Of Human Bondage
Of Mice and Men
Old Dark House, The
Oldboy
Oliver!
On the Town
Once Upon a Time in
  America
Once Upon a Time in China
One False Move
One Flew Over the Cuckoo's
  Nest
One Hundred Men and a Girl
Only Angels Have Wings
Open City
Opposite of Sex, The
Orchestra Wives
Ordet
Orphans
Osama
Our Man in Havana
Our Relations
Our Town
Our Vines Have Tender
  Grapes

Outlaw Josey Wales, The
Pajama Game, The
Pal Joey
Palm Beach Story, The
Papillon
Paris, Texas
Passenger, The
Patterns
Pawnbroker, The
Peking Opera Blues
Pennies from Heaven
People Will Talk
Peter Pan
Petrified Forest, The
Phantom Lady
Phantom of Liberty, The
Phantom of the Opera, The
Philadelphia Story, The
Pianist, The
Piano, The
Pickpocket
Pickup on South Street
Picnic
Pierrot le Fou
Pinky
Pixote
Place in the Sun, A
Planet of the Apes
Platoon
Player, The
Plaza Suite
Ploughman's Lunch, The
Pollyanna
Pork Chop Hill
Port of Shadows
Portrait of Jennie
Postman Always Rings Twice,
  The
Pride of the Marines
Prime of Miss Jean Brodie,
  The
Prince of Foxes
Princess Bride, The
Prisoner of Shark Island, The
Private Life of Henry VIII,
  The
Prizzi's Honor
Producers, The
Providence
Pulp Fiction
Pumpkin Eater, The
Quadrophenia
Quartet
Quiet American, The
Quilombo
Rabbit-Proof Fence
Racket, The
Raisin in the Sun, A
Rambling Rose

Rancho Notorious
Rasputin and the Empress
Razor's Edge, The
Rebecca
Rebel without a Cause
Red
Red Sorghum
Rembrandt
Remember Last Night?
Reservoir Dogs
Reversal of Fortune
Right Stuff, The
Ring
Rio Bravo
Rio Grande
Road to Morocco
Road to Perdition
Road Warrior, The
Roaring Twenties, The
Roberta
Rocco and His Brothers
Rock 'n' Roll High School
Rocky
Roger Dodger
Roman Holiday
Romeo and Juliet
Romeo and Juliet
Room with a View, A
Rose Tattoo, The
Rosemary's Baby
Round Midnight
Royal Family of Broadway,
The
Royal Wedding
Ruggles of Red Gap
Run Lola Run
Rushmore
Russian Ark
Saboteur
Sacrifice, The
Safe
Sahara
Salaam Bombay!
Salt of the Earth
Salvador
San Francisco
Sand Pebbles, The
Sands of Iwo Jima
Saturday Night and Sunday
Morning
Saturday Night Fever
Saving Private Ryan
Say Anything
Sayonara
Scarface
Scarlet Pimpernel, The
School for Scoundrels
Scoundrel, The
Sea Wolf, The

Seance on a Wet Afternoon
Search, The
Seconds
Secret Life of Walter Mitty,
The
Sergeant York
Serpico
Set-Up, The
Seven Days in May
Seven Thieves
Seventh Veil, The
Seventh Victim, The
Shadows
Shakespeare in Love
Shall We Dance
Shane
Shanghai Express
Shanghai Triad
She Wore a Yellow Ribbon
Shining, The
Ship of Fools
Shooting, The
Shootist, The
Short Film about Killing, A
Shot in the Dark, A
Shrek
Sid and Nancy
Sideways
Silk Stockings
Silkwood
Sin of Madelon Claudet, The
Since You Went Away
Sink the Bismarck!
Sisters of the Gion
Sky Captain and the World of
Tomorrow
Sleuth
Small Change
Smile
Smiles of a Summer Night
Smilin' Through
So Proudly We Hail
Sobibor, Oct. 14, 1943, 4 pm
Solaris
Solid Gold Cadillac, The
Some Came Running
Son of Frankenstein
Song of Bernadette, The
Song of the South
Sorry, Wrong Number
Sounder
Spellbound
Spellbound
Spider-Man
Spider-Man 2
Spirit of the Beehive, The
Spirited Away
Spy Who Came in from the
Cold, The

Stage Door Canteen
Stage Fright
Stanley and Livingstone
Star 80
Stars Look Down, The
State Fair
State of the Union
Steel Helmet, The
Stella Dallas
Stolen Children, The
Stolen Kisses
Story of Adele H., The
Story of Esther Costello, The
Story of G.I. Joe, The
Story of Louis Pasteur, The
Story of Qiu Ju, The
Straight Story, The
Straight Time
Strange Love of Martha Ivers,
The
Stranger, The
Stranger on the Third Floor
Stranger than Paradise
Strangers Kiss
Straw Dogs
Stray Dog
Street Scene
Streetcar Named Desire, A
Stunt Man, The
Subject Was Roses, The
Sugarland Express, The
Summer Holiday
Summertime
Sun Also Rises, The
Sunrise at Campobello
Superfly
Suspicion
Suspiria
Sweet Hereafter, The
Sweet Sweetback's
Baadasssss Song
Sweetie
T-Men
Take Me Out to the Ball
Game
Talk of the Town, The
Talk to Her
Tall T, The
Tarnished Angels, The
Tarzan, the Ape Man
Teahouse of the August
Moon, The
Temptress Moon
Teorema
Terminator, The
Test Pilot
Texas Chainsaw Massacre,
The
Theatre of Blood

Thelma & Louise
They Made Me a Fugitive
They Shoot Horses, Don't They?
Thin Red Line, The
Thing from Another World, The
Things to Come
Thirty Seconds Over Tokyo
This Happy Breed
This Man Must Die
This Sporting Life
Thousand Clowns, A
Threat, The
Three Caballeros, The
Three Came Home
Three Comrades
Three Godfathers, The
Three Kings
Three Little Words
Three Musketeers, The
Three Musketeers, The
Three Smart Girls
3 Women
Thunderhead—Son of Flicka
Time Bandits
Time Machine, The
Time of the Gypsies
Time Out
Time Regained
To Each his Own
To Have and Have Not
To Kill a Mockingbird
To Live
To Sleep with Anger
Tobacco Road
Together
Topkapi
Topper
Tortilla Flat
Toto le Heros
Touch of Class, A
Touching the Void
Traffic
Train, The
Treasure Island
Tree Grows in Brooklyn, A
Trembling before G-D
Trip to Bountiful, The
Tristana
True Confessions
True Grit
Tucker: The Man and His Dream
12 Angry Men
Twelve Monkeys
20,000 Leagues under the Sea
20,000 Years in Sing Sing
24-Hour Party People

Twilight Samurai, The
Two-Lane Blacktop
Two Women
Ulee's Gold
Ulzana's Raid
Un Coeur en Hiver
Under the Sand
Underground
Uninvited, The
Union Pacific
Untouchables, The
Up in Arms
Vanishing, The
Velvet Goldmine
Verdict, The
Veronika Voss
Victim
Victoria the Great
Vincent and Theo
Vitelloni
Viva Villa!
Viva Zapata!
Wagonmaster
Wanderers, The
War and Peace
War and Peace
War of the Roses, The
War Requiem
War Zone, The
Warlock
Waterloo Bridge
We the Living
Wedding in Galilee
West Side Story
Western Union
Whale Rider
What Ever Happened to Baby Jane?
What Time Is It There?
When Father Was Away on Business
When the Wind Blows
While the City Sleeps
Who's Afraid of Virginia Woolf?
Wild Reeds
Wild River
Will Success Spoil Rock Hunter?
Winchester '73
Window, The
Winged Migration
Winter Kills
Witness
Wolf Man, The
Woman in the Dunes
Woman in the Window, The
Woman Is a Woman, A
Woman of the Year

Woman under the Influence, A
Women on the Verge of a Nervous Breakdown
Wonder Boys
Working Girls
World Apart, A
Wuthering Heights
Y Tu Mama Tambien
Yaaba
Yearling, The
Yellow Sky
Yi Yi
You Only Live Once
Young Lions, The
Young Man with a Horn
Young Mr. Lincoln
Your Friends & Neighbors
Z
Ziegfeld Follies

★★★½

About Schmidt
Across 110th Street
Across the Pacific
Adam's Rib
Adventures of Robinson Crusoe, The
Adventures of Tom Sawyer, The
Advise and Consent
After Dark, My Sweet
After the Thin Man
Air Force
Alexander's Ragtime Band
Alfie
Alice
Alice in Wonderland
All about My Mother
All My Sons
American Gigolo
American History X
American Pie
American Splendor
Angels and Insects
Angels in the Outfield
Animal Crackers
Anna Karenina
Annie Get Your Gun
Another Day in Paradise
Another Woman
Antonio das Mortes
Any Given Sunday
Apollo 13
Arizona Dream
Armageddon

Arsenic and Old Lace
Assault on Precinct 13
At Close Range
Atlantic City
Auto Focus
Babe
Babes on Broadway
Babette's Feast
Back to Bataan
Bad Lieutenant
Bagdad Cafe
Ballad of Cable Hogue, The
Bandit Queen
Bang the Drum Slowly
Barefoot in the Park
Barkleys of Broadway, The
Barretts of Wimpole Street, The
Barton Fink
Battle of Britain
Bear, The
Beau Geste
Bedazzled
Beefcake
Beetlejuice
Before Sunrise
Before Sunset
Being John Malkovich
Being Julia
Bells Are Ringing
Betrayal
Big
Big Clock, The
Big Deal on Madonna Street
Big Fish
Big Knife, The
Big Sky, The
Blioxi Blues
Birdman of Alcatraz
Black Cat, White Cat
Black Cauldron, The
Black Orpheus
Black Rain
Black Robe
Blackboard Jungle
Blind Swordsman: Zatoichi, The
Blow
Blowup
Blue Collar
Blue Dahlia, The
Body Heat
Boudu Saved from Drowning
Bound
Bowling for Columbine
Boy Friend, The
Boys Don't Cry
Boys from Brazil, The
Bram Stoker's Dracula

Brazil
Brighton Rock
Bring It On
Broadcast News
Broadway Danny Rose
Brood, The
Brother from Another Planet, The
Brotherhood of the Wolf
Buddy Holly Story, The
Buena Vista Social Club, The
Bugsy
Bull Durham
Bullets over Broadway
Burnt Money
Bus Stop
Butch Cassidy and the Sundance Kid
Butcher Boy, The
California Suite
Candidate, The
Candy Mountain
Candyman
Cape Fear
Captain Horatio Hornblower
Captain's Paradise, The
Capturing the Friedmans
Caravaggio
Career Girls
Carmen
Carnal Knowledge
Carrie
Cast Away
Cat Ballou
Celine and Julie Go Boating
Cesar
Champ, The
Charge of the Light Brigade, The
Charley Varrick
Charlie Chan at the Opera
Chicago
Chilly Scenes of Winter
Chimes at Midnight
China Syndrome, The
Christmas in Connecticut
Chuck & Buck
Cimarron
City for Conquest
City of Lost Children, The
City Slickers
Claire's Knee
Clear and Present Danger
Closer
Cocoanuts, The
Cohen and Tate
Cold Comfort Farm
Color of Money, The
Color Purple, The

Come and See
Coming Home
Company, The
Confidentially Yours
Connecticut Yankee, A
Contract
Coogan's Bluff
Cook, the Thief, His Wife & Her Lover, The
Cool World, The
Cop
Corsican Brothers, The
Cotton Club, The
Country Girl, The
Coup de Torchon
Crime of Father Amaro, The
Crimes and Misdemeanors
Crimson Tide
Criss Cross
Crow, The
Crucible, The
Cry-Baby
Cuba
Cul-de-Sac
Cutter's Way
Cyrano de Bergerac
Dangerous Moves
Dark Eyes
Dark Passage
Darkman
Darling Lili
Daughter of the Nile
Dave
David and Bathsheba
David and Lisa
Day at the Races, A
Day of the Dead
Dead Calm
Dead-End Drive-In
Dead Zone, The
Deadly Affair, The
Death and the Maiden
Death Watch
Decline of the American Empire, The
Deconstructing Harry
Defence of the Realm
Dersu Uzala
Desert Fox, The
Desert Hearts
Desperate Characters
Desperately Seeking Susan
Detective, The
Devil and Miss Jones, The
Dial M for Murder
Diary of a Mad Housewife
Dick Tracy
Dim Sum: A Little Bit of Heart

Dirty Harry
Disenchanted, The
Disraeli
Distant Voices, Still Lives
Divorcee, The
Dr. No
Dogtown and Z-Boys
Dogville
$ (Dollars)
Donnie Brasco
Donnie Darko
Down and Dirty
Down and Out in Beverly
  Hills
Dragon: The Bruce Lee Story
Dragonslayer
Dreams
Dressed to Kill
Driving Miss Daisy
Drumline
Duel in the Sun
East Palace, West Palace
Easter Parade
Easy Living
Eat a Bowl of Tea
Eat Drink Man Woman
Ed Wood
Edison, the Man
Edward Scissorhands
Eel, The
Effect of Gamma Rays on
  Man-in-the-Moon
  Marigolds, The
Egg and I, The
84 Charlie Mopic
El Dorado
El Mariachi
Election
Elephant
Elf
Emma
Empire of the Sun
Enchanted Cottage, The
End of the Affair, The
End of the Century: The Story
  of the Ramones
Enforcer, The
Entrapment
Escape from Alcatraz
Evil Dead, The
Evil Dead 2: Dead by Dawn
Exorcist, The
Eye of the Needle
Face/Off
Fail Safe
Fallen Angel
Family, The
Family Man, The
Fanny

Fantasia 2000
Fantastic Voyage
Farewell, My Concubine
Fargo
Farmer's Daughter, The
Fast, Cheap & Out of Control
Fearless
Female Convict "Scorpion"—
  Jailhouse 41
Fiddler on the Roof
Finding Nemo
Finding Neverland
Fireman's Ball, The
First Name: Carmen
Fist in His Pocket
Flamingo Kid, The
Flash of Green, A
Flirting
Flower of My Secret, The
Fly Away Home
For Me and My Gal
For Your Eyes Only
Fortune Cookie, The
48 Hrs.
Four Musketeers, The
Four Weddings and a Funeral
Frank Miller's Sin City
Freeze—Die—Come to Life
French Connection II
French Lieutenant's Woman,
  The
Friday Night Lights
Fried Green Tomatoes
Friends of Eddie Coyle, The
Fright Night
Fugitive, The
Full Moon in Paris
Funeral in Berlin
Galaxy Quest
General, The
Georgia
Get Carter
Get Out Your Handkerchiefs
Getaway, The
Getting Straight
Ghostbusters
Gift, The
Gigi
Girl with Green Eyes
Girlfight
Gladiator
Gloria
Go Tell the Spartans
Goalie's Anxiety at the
  Penalty Kick, The
Godzilla, King of the
  Monsters
Gold Diggers of 1935

Golden Voyage of Sinbad,
  The
Gonin
Good Morning, Vietnam
Good Will Hunting
Grand Canyon
Great Expectations
Great Gatsby, The
Great Mouse Detective, The
Great Muppet Caper, The
Great Santini, The
Great White Hope, The
Green Room, The
Greetings
Gregory's Girl
Greystoke: The Legend of
  Tarzan, Lord of the Apes
Grosse Pointe Blank
Groundhog Day
Guelwaar
Gumshoe
Guns of Navarone, The
Gypsy
Hairspray
Hallelujah the Hills
Hamburger Hill
Hand That Rocks the Cradle,
  The
Hangmen Also Die
Hard-Boiled
Harder They Come, The
Harold and Maude
Harry Potter and the Chamber
  of Secrets
Harry Potter and the Prisoner
  of Azkaban
Harry Potter and the
  Sorcerer's Stone
Haunting, The
Hearts of the West
Heathers
Heaven Can Wait
Heimat
Hell's Angels
Help!
Here Comes the Groom
Hester Street
High and the Mighty, The
High Art
High Fidelity
High Plains Drifter
Hills Have Eyes, The
Hit, The
Homicide
Honeymoon in Vegas
Honeymoon Killers, The
Hoosiers
Horse's Mouth, The
Hospital, The

Hotel Rwanda
House of Flying Daggers
House of Usher
Housekeeping
How the West Was Won
How to Get Ahead in
    Advertising
Howards End
Howling, The
Hucksters, The
Hud
Hunchback of Notre Dame,
    The
Husbands
Hush ... Hush, Sweet
    Charlotte
Hustle
I Never Promised You a Rose
    Garden
I Never Sang for My Father
I Stand Alone
Ice Age
Ideal Husband, An
Idolmaker, The
I'm No Angel
I'm Not Scared
Imitation of Life
Impromptu
In Cold Blood
In Praise of Love
In the Company of Men
In the Line of Fire
In the Name of the Father
In Which We Serve
Indian in the Cupboard, The
Indiscreet
Insider, The
Insomnia
Interiors
Intermezzo: A Love Story
Ipcress File, The
Iris
It Came from Outer Space
Ivanhoe
J'Accuse
Jackie Brown
Jacob's Ladder
Jailhouse Rock
Jane Eyre
Jason and the Argonauts
Jean de Florette
Jerry Maguire
Jesus of Montreal
Jesus' Son
JFK
Jonah Who Will Be 25 in the
    Year 2000
Journey to the Center of the
    Earth

Juarez
Jubal
Judy Berlin
Juggernaut
Juggler, The
Juliet of the Spirits
Jungle Book, The
Junior Bonner
Jurassic Park
Kandahar
Kansas City
Kid Galahad
Kill Bill: Vol. 1
Killer's Kiss
Killing Fields, The
King Lear
King of Hearts
King of Kings
King of the Khyber Rifles
King Solomon's Mines
Kiss of Death
Knock on Any Door
Kundun
La Bete Humaine
La Cage aux Folles
La Dolce Vita
La Marseillaise
Labyrinth
Lady in the Lake
Ladyhawke
Land before Time, The
Last Exit to Brooklyn
Last House on the Left, The
Last Metro, The
Last of Sheila, The
Last Seduction, The
Last Starfighter, The
Last Time I Saw Paris, The
Late Show, The
Laughter
Law of Desire
Laws of Gravity
Le Beau Serge
Leadbelly
Left-Handed Gun, The
Legally Blonde
Lemony Snicket's A Series of
    Unfortunate Events
L'Ennui
Les Biches
Lethal Weapon
Life and Nothing But
Life Begins for Andy Hardy
Life Is Sweet
Like Water for Chocolate
Lili
Lilies of the Field
Limey, The
Liquid Sky

List of Adrian Messenger,
    The
Little Foxes, The
Little Girl Who Lives Down
    the Lane, The
Little Otik
Little Women
Live Flesh
Living Daylights, The
Long Good Friday, The
Longest Yard, The
Lord of the Rings: The Two
    Towers, The
Lorenzo's Oil
Lost Highway
Lost in Translation
Lost Patrol, The
Lost World: Jurassic Park,
    The
Love Actually
Love Is the Devil: Study for a
    Portrait of Francis Bacon
Love on the Run
Love Parade, The
Lovers and Other Strangers
Loves of a Blonde
Macomber Affair, the
Mad Max
Mad Wednesday
Madame Rosa
Madigan
Madness of King George, The
Magnificent Obsession
Man and a Woman, A
Man in Love, A
Man of a Thousand Faces
Man of Flowers
Man of Marble
Man Who Fell to Earth, The
Man Who Shot Liberty
    Valance, The
Man with the Golden Arm,
    The
Man with Two Brains, The
Mandabi
Manon of the Spring
Maria Full of Grace
Marianne and Juliane
Marie
Married to the Mob
Mask of Zorro, The
Master and Commander: The
    Far Side of the World
Mata Hari
Match Factory Girl, The
Matchstick Men
Matrix, The
Medium Cool
Melvin and Howard

Men...
Men in Black
Metallica: Some Kind of
  Monster
Midnight Clear, A
Midnight Run
Mighty Wind, A
Milky Way, The
Miller's Crossing
Millions
Minnie and Moskowitz
Miracle
Miracle on 34th Street
Miracle Woman, The
Misfits, The
Mishima
Mississippi Masala
Mississippi Mermaid
Mr. Blandings Builds His
  Dream House
Mixed Blood
Mo' Better Blues
Moby Dick
Mona Lisa
Monsoon Wedding
Monster
Moscow on the Hudson
Mosquito Coast, The
Most Dangerous Game, The
Mother India
Motorcycle Diaries, The
Mrs. Dalloway
Murder on the Orient Express
My Big Fat Greek Wedding
My Favorite Blonde
My Life As a Dog
My Pal Trigger
Mystery Train
Mystic River
Naked Gun: From the Files of
  Police Squad!, The
Naked Prey, The
Napoleon Dynamite
Narc
National Lampoon's Animal
  House
Near Dark
Negotiator, The
NeverEnding Story, The
New York, New York
Nicholas and Alexandra
'Night, Mother
Night Moves
Nighthawks
Nightmare on Elm Street, A
1918
No Time for Sergeants
Nobody's Fool
North Dallas Forty

Notting Hill
Nowhere in Africa
O. Henry's Full House
Object of My Affection, The
Ocean's Eleven
Odd Couple, The
Officer and a Gentleman, An
Official Story, The
Oh! What a Lovely War
Old Yeller
On Golden Pond
On Her Majesty's Secret
  Service
One-Eyed Jacks
One Hour Photo
One Hundred and One
  Dalmatians
One of Our Aircraft Is
  Missing
One True Thing
One, Two, Three
Open Water
Operation Petticoat
Ordinary People
Orphans
Oscar and Lucinda
Ossessione
Othello
Our Lady of the Assassins
Out of Sight
Out-of-Towners, The
Over the Edge
Padre Padrone
Pale Rider
Paper Moon
Parallax View, The
Pardon Mon Affaire
Parenthood
Passage to India, A
Passage to Marseille
Passion Fish
Pat Garrett and Billy the Kid
Paulie
Pauline at the Beach
Pedestrian, The
Pee-wee's Big Adventure
People vs. Larry Flynt, The
Peppermint Soda
Performance
Personal Velocity
Petulia
Phantom Tollbooth, The
Phar Lap
Picnic at Hanging Rock
Picture of Dorian Gray, The
Pillow Talk
Pimpernel Smith
Pink Flamingos
Pink Narcissus

Pink Panther, The
Pirate, The
Pit and the Pendulum, The
Places in the Heart
Play It Again, Sam
Play Misty for Me
Pledge, The
Pocketful of Miralces
Porgy and Bess
Portrait of a Lady, The
Postman, The
Prancer
Predator
President's Analyst, The
Presumed Innocent
Pretty Baby
Pretty Poison
Prick Up Your Ears
Primary Colors
Prince and the Pauper, The
Prince and the Showgirl, The
Prince of Egypt, The
Prince of the City
Princess Mononoke
Private Life of Sherlock
  Holmes, The
Projectionist, The
Proof
Punch-Drunk Love
Purple Rose of Cairo, The
Pursued
Q
Quiz Show
Quo Vadis
Rachel, Rachel
Radio Days
Rain Man
Raining Stones
Rancho Deluxe
Random Harvest
Ratcatcher
Read My Lips
Real Life
Red Rock West
Reds
Remains of the Day, The
Remember the Night
Repo Man
Requiem for a Heavyweight
Return of Martin Guerre, The
Return of the Jedi
Return of the Pink Panther,
  The
Return of the Secaucus Seven
Revenge of the Nerds
Rhapsody in Blue
Richard III
Richard III
Rider on the Rain

Ridicule
Ring, The
Risky Business
River's Edge
Road to Rio
Road to Utopia
Road to Zaznibar
RoboCop
Rocky II
Roman Spring of Mrs. Stone, The
Romancing the Stone
Romantic Englishwoman, The
Rosetta
Roxanne
Ruling Class, The
Runaway Train
Russia House, The
Ruthless People
Sabotage
Sabrina
Saddest Music in the World, The
Salome's Last Dance
Sammy and Rosie Get Laid
Samson and Delilah
Santa Clause, The
Santa Fe Trail
Scream
Scrooge
Sea Inside, The
Sea of Love
Seabiscuit
Searching for Bobby Fischer
Secret Agent
Secret of Roan Inish, The
Secrets of Women
Seduction of Joe Tynan, The
Seduction of Mimi, The
Sense and Sensibility
Servant, The
Set Me Free
Se7en
7 Faces of Dr. Lao
Seven Little Foys, The
7th Voyage of Sinbad, The
sex, lies, and videotape
Sexy Beast
Shadow of the Vampire
Shampoo
Shattered Glass
Shaun of the Dead
Shawshank Redemption, The
Shenandoah
Shine
Shock Corridor
Shock to the System, A
Shoeshine
Short Cuts

Show Boat
Shrek 2
Shy People
Silent Running
Simple Plan, A
Singles
Slacker
Sleeper
Sleeping Beauty
Sleeping Car Murder, The
Sleepy Hollow
Sling Blade
Smash Palace
Smoke
Snake Pit, The
Snapper, The
Snows of Kilimanjaro, The
Soldier of Orange
Soldier's Story, A
Somebody Up There Likes Me
Something Wild
Son of Paleface
Sonatine
Song to Remember, A
Sons and Lovers
Son's Room, The
South Pacific
Southern Comfort
Speed
Spider
Spirit of St. Louis, The
Splash
Spy Kids
Stakeout
Stalker
Stand by Me
Standing in the Sahdows of Motown
Star!
Star Trek II: The Wrath of Khan
Star Trek: Insurrection
Starting Over
State of Siege
State of Things, The
Station Agent, The
Stavisky
Stepfather, The
Sterile Cuckoo, The
Stir of Echoes, A
Stormy Monday
Stormy Weather
Story of a Three Day Pass, The
Story of Alexander Graham Bell, The
Story of Vernon and Irene Castle, The

Strapless
Streamers
Strike Up the Band
Sugar Cane Alley
Sugarbaby
Summer of Sam
Sunday, Bloody Sunday
Sunshine Boys, The
Sunshine State
Super Size Me
Supercop
Superman II
Sweet Charity
Swept Away ... by an Unusual Destiny in the Blue Sea of August
Swimming Pool
Swimming to Cambodia
Swindle, The
Swing Shift
Swiss Family Robinson
Tailor of Panama, The
Take the Money and Run
Taking of Pelham One Two Three, The
Taking Off
Talented Mr. Ripley, The
Tales of Manhattan
Tales of Terror
Tall Men, The
Taming of the Shrew, The
Tampopo
Tarzan and His Mate
Taste of Cherry
Taxi Blues
Taxing Woman, A
Tea and Sympathy
Ten Commandments, The
10 Rillington Place
Tenant, The
Tender Mercies
Terminator 2: Judgment Day
Terms of Endearment
Terror in a Texas Town
Them!
Theodora Goes Wild
There's No Business like Show Business
Thief
Thieves Like Us
Thirteen
Thirteen Days
This Boy's Life
This Is Spinal Tap
This Land Is Mine

Those Magnificent Men in
  Their Flying Machines; or
  How I Flew from London
  to Paris in 25 Hours and 11
  Minutes
Thousand Eyes of Dr.
  Mabuse, The
Three Days of the Condor
3:10 to Yuma
Thunderbolt and Lightfoot
Tim Burton's The Nightmare
  before Christmas
Time Code
Tin Drum, The
Titanic
To Live and Die in L.A.
Toni
Topsy-Turvy
Tous les Matins du Monde
Tout Va Bien
Toy Story
Traffic
Trail of the Lonesome Pine,
  The
Training Day
Trainspotting
Trapeze
Treasure Island
Trees Lounge
Trial, The
Trouble with Harry, The
True Lies
True Romance
True Stories
Truly, Madly, Deeply
Truman Show, The
Tuck Everlasting
Twelve Chairs, The
Twentieth Century
28 Days
28 Days Later...
Twilight's Last Gleaming
Two English Girls
Two for the Road
UFOria
Umbrellas of Cherbourg, The
Unbelievable Truth, The
Under the Skin
Under the Volcano
Unzipped
Used Cars
Vagabond
Valley Girl
Vera Drake
Very Long Engagement, A
Victor/Victoria
Videodrome
Virgin Spring, The
Virgin Suicides, The

Virginian, The
Viva Las Vegas
Von Ryan's Express
Wait Until Dark
Wall, The
Waltz of the Toreadors
War of the Worlds, The
Warriors, The
Waterdance, The
Way Ahead, The
Wayne's World
Weather Underground, The
Weeds
Welcome to the Dollhouse
Well, The
Westworld
Wetherby
What's New, Pussycat?
What's Up, Tiger Lily?
Where Eagles Dare
Where's Poppa?
Whistle Down the Wind
White
White Cliffs of Dover, The
White Dog
Who'll Stop the Rain?
Whoopee
Wicker Man, The
Wild One, The
Wind and the Lion, The
Wings of the Dove, The
Winslow Boy, The
Wise Blood
Witches, The
With a Friend Like Harry
With a Song in My Heart
Withnail & I
Wolfen
Women in Love
Wooden Horse, The
Woodsman, The
Working Girl
"X"—The Man with the X-
  Ray Eyes
X2
Yakuza, The
Year of Living Dangerously,
  The
Yellow Earth
Yellow Submarine
You Can Count on Me
You Can't Take It with You
You Were Never Lovelier
Young and Innocent
Zazie
Zelig
Ziegfeld Girl
Zorba the Greek

★★★

Abe Lincoln in Illinois
Abominable Dr. Phibes, The
About a Boy
Absent-Minded Professor,
  The
Absolute Beginners
Accattone!
Ace Ventura: Pet Detective
Adam Sandler's Eight Crazy
  Nights
Addams Family Values
Adventures of Baron
  Munchausen, The
Adventures of Mark Twain,
  The
Adventures of Milo and Otis,
  The
Adventures of Priscilla,
  Queen of the Desert, The
Affliction
Agnes of God
A.I.: Artificial Intelligence
Alamo, The
Alfie
Ali
Alice Doesn't Live Here
  Anymore
Alice in the Cities
Alice's Restaurant
Aliens
All That Jazz
All the Pretty Horses
Amateur
Amelie
American Madness
American Psycho
American Werewolf in
  London, An
Amistad
Amores Perros
Analyze This
Anchorman: The Legend of
  Ron Burgundy
And Now for Something
  Completely Different
And the Ship Sails On
Anderson Tapes, The
Andy Warhol's Dracula
Angela's Ashes
Anna Christie
Antwone Fisher
Antz
Apache
Apostle, The
Apt Pupil
Arthur
Ashes and Diamonds

Assault on Precinct 13
Attack!
Austin Powers: International Man of Mystery
Autumn Leaves
Avalon
Aviator, The
Babes in Arms
Babes in Toyland
Bachelor and the Bobby-Soxer, The
Back to School
Back to the Future
Backbeat
Backdraft
Bad Blood
Bad Influence
Bad News Bears, The
Bad Sleep Well, The
Baise-Moi
Bananas
Band of Outsiders
Barbarian Invasions, The
Barbershop
Barcelona
Batman
Beautiful Mind, A
Bed Sitting Room, The
Bedknobs and Broomsticks
Before the Revolution
Beggar's Opera, The
Belle Epoque
Belles of St. Trinian's, The
Belly of an Architect, The
Beloved
Bend It Like Beckham
Benji
Betty Blue
Beverly Hills Cop
Beyond the Valley of the Dolls
Bhaji on the Beach
Big Easy, The
Big Parade, The
Big Trail, The
Birth
Birthday Girl
Bishop's Wife, The
Black and White in Color
Black Hawk Down
Blacula
Blue
Blue Sky
Blue Steel
Blue Velvet
Blume in Love
Bob & Carol & Ted & Alice
Born on the Fourth of July
Bourne Identity, The

Bourne Supremacy, The
Boys Town
Brainstorm
Braveheart
Breaker Morant
Breakfast Club, The
Breaking the Waves
Bridges of Madison County, The
Brimstone and Treacle
Broken Arrow
Bronx Tale, A
Bug's Life, A
Bugsy Malone
Butterfield 8
Bye-Bye Brazil
Call of the Wild
Car Wash
Carla's Song
Carlito's Way
Carmen Jones
Caro Diario
Carrington
Casino
Casualties of War
Cat and the Canary, The
Catch Me if You Can
Cell, The
Changing Lanes
Chariots of Fire
Charley's Aunt
Cheaper by the Dozen
Chloe in the Afternoon
Chorus, The
Citizens Band
City of Angels
City of Women
Cleo from 5 to 7
Clerks
Client, The
Cliffhanger
Clockmaker, The
Coca-Cola Kid, The
Cocoon
Cold Mountain
Collateral
Colonel Redl
Colossus: The Forbin Project
Comfort of Strangers, The
Commitments, The
Con Air
Connecticut Yankee in King Arthur's Court, A
Cooler, The
Cotton Comes to Harlem
Cousin, Cousine
Crash
"Crocodile" Dundee
Crooklyn

Cross of Iron
Crossover Dreams
Cruel Intentions
Damage
Dancer in the Dark
Dances with Wolves
Dangerous
Dangerous Lives of Altar Boys, The
Danton
Daredevil
Dark Blue
Dark City
Dark Crystal, The
Darling
Dazed and Confused
Dead Again
Dead Pigeon on Beethoven Street
Death of a Bureaucrat
Death Race 2000
Dementia 13
Demolition Man
Diamonds Are Forever
Die Hard
Dirty Dancing
Dirty Pretty Things
Disclosure
Dr. Suess' How the Grinch Stole Christmas
Dogma
Dona Flor and Her Two Husbands
Double Life of Veronique, The
Down by Law
Dracula
Dreamers, The
Dry White Season, A
Duellists, The
Dumb & Dumber
Eating Raoul
Ecstasy
Educating Rita
Eight Men Out
8 Women
84 Charing Cross Road
Elizabeth
Elvira Madigan
Emperor's Club, The
Enemy of the State
English Patient, The
Enter the Dragon
Equus
Erin Brockovich
Escape from New York
Ever After
Evita
Excalibur

eXistenZ
Fahrenheit 9/11
Falcon and the Snowman, The
Fallen Sparrow, The
Falling Down
Fame
Farewell, My Lovely
Fast Times at Ridgemont
   High
Faster, Pussycat! Kill! Kill!
Fatal Attraction
Father Goose
Fear and Desire
Fever Pitch
Few Good Men, A
Field of Dreams
Firm, The
Fish Called Wanda, A
Fistful of Dollars, A
Flesh
Fog of War: Eleven Lessons
   from the Life of Robert S.
   McNamara, The
For Whom the Bell Tolls
Forrest Gump
Frankenhooker
Freaky Friday
French, They Are a Funny
   Race, The
Freshman, The
From Hell
Funeral, The
Funny Thing Happened on
   the Way to the Forum, A
F/X
Gandhi
Gang's All Here, The
Garden State
Gardens of Stone
Gate of Hell
Get on the Bus
Get Shorty
Ghost
Girl, Interrupted
Girl with a Pearl Earring
Girlfriends
Going Places
Gold of Naples
Goldeneye
Good Girl, The
Gorillas in the Mist
Gorky Park
Gosford Park
Grease
Great Northfield, Minnesota
   Raid, The
Great Ziegfeld, The
Green Mile, The
Groove Tube, The

Grudge, The
Guy Named Joe, A
Halloween H2O: Twenty
   Years Later
Hamlet
Hannibal
Hans Christian Andersen
Hardcore
Harper
Harry and Tonto
Head
Hear My Song
Heart Like a Wheel
Hello, Dolly!
Hellzapoppin'
Hidalgo
Hidden, The
Hideous Kinky
High Anxiety
High Society
Hitch
Hitchhiker's Guide to the
   Galaxy, The
Holiday Inn
Hollywood Boulevard
Holy Smoke
Home Alone
Home and the World, The
Honey, I Shrunk the Kids
Hook
Hopalong Cassidy
Horse Soldiers, The
Horse Whisperer, The
Hot Shots!
Hour of the Wolf, The
Hours, The
House of Wax
House Party
How I Won the War
Hudsucker Proxy, The
I Know What You Did Last
   Summer
I, Robot
I Shot Andy Warhol
I, the Jury
Ice Storm, The
Ichi the Killer
Igby Goes Down
I'm Gonna Git You Sucka
In America
In & Out
In Old Chicago
In the Cut
In the Realm of the Senses
Indecent Proposal
Indiana Jones and the Last
   Crusade
Indiana Jones and the Temple
   of Doom

Insomnia
Interview with the Vampire
Irma la Douce
Irreversible
It's a Mad, Mad, Mad, Mad
   World
It's Alive
Jacknife
Jagged Edge
Jewel of the Nile, The
Jim Thorpe—All American
John Grisham's The
   Rainmaker
Joy Luck Club, The
Jude
Julia
Just a Gigolo
Kanal
Karate Kid, The
Kentucky Fried Movie, The
Khartoum
Kidnapped
Kids
Killers, The
King of New York
Kingdom of Heaven
Kinsey
Kiss before Dying, A
Knock on Wood
Kung Fu Hustle
Kurt and Courtney
La Balance
La Collectionneuse
La Femme Nikita
La Notte
Lady in the Dark
Lady Sings the Blues
Last Days of Chez Nous, The
Last of the Mohicans, The
Last Samurai, The
Late Autumn
Learning Tree, The
Leather Boys, The
Leaving Las Vegas
Lenny
Les Enfants Terribles
Les Girls
Lethal Weapon 2
Lianna
Liar Liar
Life
Life on a String
Lilo & Stitch
Lion King, The
Little Mermaid, The
Little Princess, A
Little Shop of Horrors
Little Shop of Horrors, The
Lola

Lolita
Look Back in Anger
Look Who's Talking
Lord Love a Duck
Lords of Flatbush, The
Love and Death on Long
  Island
Love Jones
Lovers, The
Lucas
Machinist, The
Mad Dog and Glory
Madame Sousatzka
Madeline
Man from Snowy River, The
Man in the Gray Flannel Suit,
  The
Man Who Loved Women, The
Manhunter
Mansfield Park
Mars Attacks!
Matinee
Matrix Reloaded, The
Matrix Revolutions, The
Mean Girls
Meet the Parents
Member of the Wedding, The
Menace II Society
Merry War, A
Miami Blues
Michael
Midsummer Night's Dream,
  A
Midwinter's Tale, A
Mighty Aphrodite
Misery
Mission, The
Mission: Impossible
Mission: Impossible II
Missouri Breaks, The
Monster's Ball
Monsters, Inc.
Monty Python's The Meaning
  of Life
Moon in the Gutter, The
Moonlight Mile
Morgan!
Morning Glory
Mortal Thoughts
Moulin Rouge
Mrs. Doubtfire
Mrs. Miniver
Mummy, The
Mummy, The
Muppet Movie, The
Murder by Death
Mute Witness
My Best Friend's Wedding
My Cousin Vinny

My Dinner with Andre
My Name Is Joe
My Son the Fanatic
Mysterious Dr. Fu Manchu,
  The
Naked Lunch
Name of the Rose, The
Narrow Margin, The
Natural, The
Natural Born Killers
Never on Sunday
New Leaf, A
Nicholas Nickleby
Night of the Shooting Stars,
  The
Night on Earth
9 to 5
1984
No Way Out
Nosferatu, the Vampire
Nothing but a Man
Nutty Professor, The
O Brother, Where Art Thou?
Oklahoma!
Old Man and the Sea, The
Omen, The
Once Upon a Time in Mexico
Once Were Warriors
101 Dalmatians
Onion Field, The
Open Range
Our Man Flint
Outsiders, The
Panic Room
Parent Trap, The
Paris Belongs to Us
Parting Glances
Passion of Anna, The
Passion of the Christ, The
Passport to Pimlico
Peggy Sue Got Married
Pelle the Conqueror
Perfect Storm, The
Personal Best
Peter Pan
Phantom of the Opera
Phantom of the Opera, The
Philadelphia
Phone Booth
Pieces of April
Pink Panther Strikes Again,
  The
Pirates of the Caribbean: The
  Curse of the Black Pearl
Planes, Trains, and
  Automobiles
Pleasantville
Pocahontas
Police

Postcards from the Edge
Powerpuff Girls Movie, The
Pretty in Pink
Prime Cut
Prospero's Books
Queen Margot
Quest for Fire
Quills
Ragtime
Railway Children, The
Rain People, The
Rainmaker, The
Raising Arizona
Raw Deal
Ray
Re-Animator
Recruit, The
Requiem for a Dream
Rescuers, The
Riff-Raff
Rise of Louis XIV, The
Road House
Robin and Marian
Robots
Rock Around the Clock
Rocky Horror Picture Show,
  The
Rollerball
Rolling Thunder
Ronin
Rope
Rose, The
Royal Tenenbaums, The
Rules of Attraction, The
Run Silent, Run Deep
Runaway Jury
Running on Empty
Rush
Sacco and Vanzetti
Salvatore Giuliano
Santa Sangre
Savage Nights
Save the Tiger
Saw
Scandal
Scanners
Scarecrow
Scenes from a Marriage
Scent of a Woman
School of Rock
Secret Garden, The
Secret of Nimh, The
Semi-Tough
Seven Beauties
Seven-Per-Cent Solution, The
Seven Year Itch, The
Shaft
Shakespeare Wallah
Shall We Dance?

She's All That
She's Gotta Have It
Shout, The
Signs
Six Degrees of Separation
Six in Paris
Sixteen Candles
Slap Shot
Sleeping with the Enemy
Sleepless in Seattle
Slither
Small Soldiers
Someone to Watch Over Me
Sommersby
Sophie's Choice
Sound of Music, The
South Park: Bigger, Longer &
    Uncut
Spanglish
Spetters
Spice World
Splendor in the Grass
Stand and Deliver
Star Is Born, A
Star Trek IV: The Voyage
    Home
Star Trek: First Contact
Star Wars Episode I: The
    Phantom Menace
Stargate
Starman
Starship Troopers
Startup.com
Steel Magnolias
Story of the Weeping Camel,
    The
Story of Women
Storytelling
Street Smart
Stripes
Stuart Little
Such a Gorgeous Kid Like
    Me
Summer of '42
Superman
Sure Thing, The
Sweet and Lowdown
Sylvia
Tea with Mussolini
Team America: World Police
10
10th Victim, The
Terminator 3: Rise of the
    Machines
Tess
Testament
Tetsuo: The Iron Man
Tex
That Hamilton Woman

That Man from Rio
That Sinking Feeling
That Touch of Mink
There's Something about
    Mary
Thin Ice
13 Going on 30
Thirty-Two Short Films about
    Glenn Gould
This Is the Army
Thomas Crown Affair, The
Thomas Crown Affair, The
Three Coins in the Fountain
Three Crowns of the Sailor
Three Faces of Eve, The
Three Men and a Cradle
Threepenny Opera, The
Thunderball
Thuderheart
Time After Time
Tin Men
To Catch a Thief
To Die For
To Sir, with Love
Top Secret!
Topaz
Torch Song Trilogy
Toy Story 2
Trading Places
Tremors
Trial of Joan of Arc
Triplets of Belleville, The
True Love
Trust
Truth of Dare
Turning Point, The
25th Hour
21 Grams
Twister
2 Days in the Valley
Two Hundred Motels
U-571
Under the Roofs of Paris
Unmarried Woman, An
Up in Smoke
Uptown Saturday Night
Usual Suspects, The
Vanya on 42nd Street
Vera Cruz
Village of the Damned
Wall Street
Washington Square
Waterboy, The
Watership Down
Way We Were, The
Wedding Banquet, The
Wedding Singer, The
Wee Willie Winkle
Whales of August, The

What's Love Got to Do with
    It
What's Eating Gilbert Grape?
What's Up, Doc?
When Harry Met Sally...
While You Were Sleeping
White Christmas
White Oleander
Who Framed Roger Rabbit
Wild Angels, The
Wild Party, The
Wild Things
Wilde
World of Henry Orient, The
X-Files, The
X-Men
Yentl
Yesterday, Today, and
    Tomorrow
You Only Live Twice
You're a Big Boy Now

★★½

A Nos Amours
Absence of Malice
Abyss, The
Accused, The
Addams Family, The
Adventures of Buckaroo
    Banzai: Across the 8th
    Dimension, The
Airplane!
Akira
Alamo, The
Alien³
Alien Resurrection
All of Me
Anastasia
Anchors Aweigh
Andrew Lloyd Webber's The
    Phantom of the Opera
Anything Else
Arrowsmith
Austin Powers in
    Goldmember
Autumn Sonata
Awakenings
Basic Instinct
Batman Forever
Beach, The
Beach Blanket Bingo
Becky Sharp
Bedtime for Bonzo
Benny & Joon
Big Chill, The

Bill & Ted's Excellent Adventure
Blazing Saddles
Blues Brothers, The
Bob Roberts
Boccaccio '70
Bride of Chucky
Bridge Too Far, A
Bridget Jones's Diary
Bringing Down the House
Brothers Karamazov, The
Butterfly Effect, The
Cable Guy, The
Caddyshack
Camille Claudel
Carry on Nurse
Catch-22
C'est la Vie
Chaplin
Charge of the Light Brigade, The
Charly
Cider House Rules, The
Cinema Paradiso
Civil Action, A
Cleopatra
Colors
Coma
Come Back to the 5 & Dime, Jimmy Dean, Jimmy Dean
Coming to America
Confessions of a Dangerous Mind
Connection, The
Contact
Contraband
Cop Land
Croupier
Curse of the Jade Scorpion, The
Dark Star
Dawn of the Dead
Day of the Triffids, The
Dead Man Walking
Dead Poets Society
Death Becomes Her
Deep End, The
Devil's Own, The
Die Another Day
Divine Secrets of the Ya-Ya Sisterhood
Dr. Dolittle
Double Team
Driller Killer
Drowning by Numbers
EdTV
Eight Mile
Emmanuelle
Enchanted April

Everyone Says I Love You
Exotica
Fabulous Baker Boys, The
Faculty, The
Far from the Madding Crowd
Fear and Loathing in Las Vegas
Fellini's Roma
Fifth Element, The
50 First Dates
Fisher King, The
Flintstones, The
Foxes
Free Willy
Frida
Front Page, The
Gangs of New York
Ghost Dog: The Way of the Samurai
Gidget
Godfather, Part III, The
Green Dolphin Street
Guess Who's Coming to Dinner
Hamlet
Hate
Heaven Can Wait
Heaven's Gate
Hellboy
Hellraiser
Henry & June
Henry Fool
Hunchback of Notre Dame, The
Hunt for Red October, The
I Am a Camera
I Heart Huckabees
Idiots, The
In Good Company
In the Good Old Summertime
Independence Day
Interpreter, The
Invasion of the Body Snatchers
Is Paris Burning?
Italian Job, The
Jennifer Eight
K-19: The Widowmaker
King of Marvin Gardens, The
Knight's Tale, A
Knute Rockne—All American
La Bamba
L.A. Story
Ladder 49
Lara Croft: Tomb Raider
Last Days of Disco, The
Last Movie, The
Legends of the Fall
Les Miserables

Life Is Beautful
Looking for Mr. Goodbar
Lord of the Flies
Lost in America
Man on Fire
Man on the Moon
Man Who Wasn't There, The
Manhattan Murder Mystery
Man's Favorite Sport?
Mask, The
Maurice
Meet Joe Black
Melinda and Melinda
Michael Collins
Midnight in the Garden of Good and Evil
Mikey and Nicky
Mister Roberts
Mommie Dearest
Mona Lisa Smile
Moonraker
Mrs. Brown
My Little Chickadee
Navigator, The
Never Say Never Again
Night of the Iguana, The
1900
Nixon
Notebook, The
Nuts
Nutty Professor, The
Old School
On the Beach
Orlando
Others, The
Out of Africa
Paper Chase, The
Patriot Games
Patriot, The
Pearl Harbor
Perfect World, A
Pillow Book, The
Plan 9 from Outer Space
Planet of the Apes
Polar Express, The
Pollock
Poor Cow
Pretty Woman
Prince of Tides, The
Private Benjamin
Psycho
Q&A
Red Dragon
Ring Two, The
Ring-a-Ding Rhythm
River Runs through It, A
Robe, The
Robin Hood: Prince of Thieves

Rush Hour
Ryan's Daughter
Salo, or the 120 Days of
    Sodom
Santa Clause 2, The
Scooby-Doo
Secretary
Shallow Grave
Siege, The
Silverado
Single White Female
Sister Act
Sliding Doors
Soft Skin, The
Solaris
Something's Gotta Give
Spanish Prisoner, The
SpongeBob Squarepants
    Movie, The
Spy Kids 2: The Island of
    Lost Dreams
Star Wars Episode II: Attack
    of the Clones
Stardust Memories
Starsky & Hutch
Stealing Beauty
Stepford Wives, The
Sting, The
Strange Days
Strictly Ballroom
Stuck on You
S.W.A.T.
Sweet Bird of Youth
Sweet Home Alabama
Swimmer, The
Swithcblade Sisters
Taking Lives
Tall Blond Man with One
    Black Shoe, The
Tarzan
Terminal, The
3 Men and a Baby
Throw Momma from the
    Train
THX 1138
Tie Me Up! Tie Me Down!
Tomorrow Never Dies
Tootsie
Torn Curtain
Troy
Tupac Resurrection
Unbearable Lightness of
    Being, The
Uncle Buck
Under Siege
Unfaithful
Until the End of the World
Vanity Fair
Wag the Dog

Waiting to Exhale
Walking Tall
Watch on the Rhine
Waterworld
We Were Soldiers
Wedding, A
Welcome to L.A.
What a Way to Go!
Where the Boys Are
White Hunter, Black Heart
White Men Can't Jump
White Sheik, The
Wild at Heart
Wild Wild West
Windtalkers
World According to Garp,
    The
Zandy's Bride
Zoolander

★★

Airport
Alexander
Alien vs. Predator
And God Created Woman
Anthony Adverse
Antonia's Line
As Good As It Gets
Austin Powers: The Spy Who
    Shagged Me
Beaches
Birdcage, The
Blade
Bodyguard, The
Bridget Jones: The Edge of
    Reason
Brigadoon
Bringing Out the Dead
Buffalo '66
Cars That Ate Paris, The
Casino Royale
Catwoman
Charlie's Angels
Charlie's Angels: Full
    Throttle
Cheaper by the Dozen
Creepshow
Day After Tomorrow, The
Deep Impact
De-Lovely
Dodgeball: A True Underdog
    Story
Doors, The
Double Jeopardy
Dreamcatcher
8mm

El Topo
First Wives Club, The
Flubber
Forgotten, The
From Dusk till Dawn
Godzilla
Gothika
Haunting, The
Hercules
House of Sand and Fog
Hudson Hawk
Hulk
Human Stain, The
I Love You, Alice B. Toklas!
Inside Daisy Clover
Ishtar
Jackass: The Movie
Kika
King Arthur
Last Action Hero
Lethal Weapon 3
Life Aquatic with Steve
    Zissou, The
Lili Marleen
Love Story
Majestic, The
Meet the Fockers
Men in Black II
Mighty Joe Young
Mississippi Burning
Mr. Holland's Opus
Moon Is Blue, The
My Fair Lady
National Treasure
Ocean's Twelve
Out of Time
Pacifier, The
Palindromes
Panic in Needle Park, The
Pelican Brief, The
Peyton Place
Pink Floyd—The Wall
Pinocchio
Poltergeist
Possession
Rabid
Shanghai Knights
Shark Tale
Shipping News, The
Sixth Sense, The
Spy Who Loved Me, The
Star Trek: Nemesis
Stepmom
Sum of All Fears, The
Swept Away
Thing, The
Top Gun
Total Recall
Towering Inferno, The

Trouble in Mind
Truth about Charlie, The
Unbreakable
Urban Cowboy
Valley of the Dolls
Van Helsing
Vanilla Sky
Village, The
William Shakespeare's
   Romeo + Juliet
Witches of Eastwick, The
World Is Not Enough, The
xXx
You've Got Mail
Zabriskie Point

★½

Amityville Horror, The
Anger Management
Bad Santa
Big Lebowski, The
Blob, The
Bruce Almighty
Daddy Day Care
Doctor Dolittle
Less Than Zero
Maid in Manhattan
Rio Lobo
Showgirls
Smokey and the Bandit

Stepford Wives, The
Tommy

★

Analyze That
Attack of the Killer Tomatoes
Dr. Seuss' The Cat in the Hat
Exorcist: The Beginning
Gigli
League of Extraordinary
   Gentlemen, The
Lethal Weapon 4
Outlaw, The